2021
Harris
Virginia
Industrial Directory

Exclusive Provider of
Dun & Bradstreet Library Solutions

Published March 2021 next update March 2022

Publisher

Mergent Inc.
444 Madison Ave
New York, NY 10022

©Mergent Inc All Rights Reserved
2021 Mergent Business Press
ISSN 1080-2614
ISBN 9781649720849

MERGENT
BUSINESS PRESS
by FTSE Russell

2020 HARRIS ADVERTISING

The **_2020 Harris Directories_** provides you with the most up-to-date information on the region's most prominent companies. Through offering you multiple ways to look up any specific business within the area, important data can easily be located.
. For reliability and assurance, Harris directories are the source for all pertinent information for all companies in there state.

To **_Highlight_** your company and get the most exposure necessary you can now get full page color advertisements inserted in the front of the book. This gives your company a step up showing all your company's information while remaining competitive with the larger companies. These ad pages are supplied by you and can showcase your company logo's, shareholder letters or any other information you would like the thousands of readers who use the Harris Directories to see.

You also get **_complimentary_** books highlighting your company's information and you can also purchase extra books at a 40% discount.

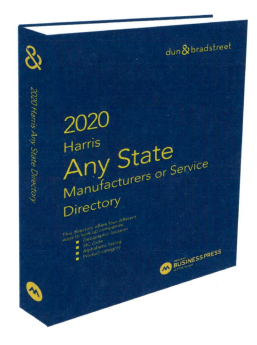

Plan 1

$1,500

1 full page 4 color ad. (Supplied by you)

3 free books (Additional books can be purchased at a 40% discount of regular price)

Plan 2

$2,100

2 full page 4 color ads. (Supplied by you)

5 free books (Additional books can be purchased at a 40% discount of regular price)

Plan 3

$4,000

4 full page color ads. (Supplied by you)

10 Free Book (Additional books can be purchased at 40% discount off original costs)

For additional information or to order please contact

Thomas Wecera at 212-413-7726 thomas.wecera@mergent.com

 Exclusive Provider of these D&B Library Solutions  First Research

TABLE OF CONTENTS

Summary of Contents & Explanatory Notes 4
User's Guide to Listings 6

Geographic Section
County/City Cross-Reference Index 9
Firms Listed by Location 13

Standard Industrial Classification (SIC) Section
SIC Alphabetical Index 533
SIC Numerical Index 535
Firms Listed by SIC 537

Alphabetic Section
Firms Listed by Firm Name 677

Product Section
Product Index 873
Firms Listed by Product Category 891

SUMMARY OF CONTENTS

Number of Companies 16,011
Number of Decision Makers 23,565
Minimum Number of Employees 1

EXPLANATORY NOTES

How to Cross-Reference in This Directory

Sequential Entry Numbers. Each establishment in the Geographic Section is numbered sequentially (G-0000). The number assigned to each establishment is referred to as its "entry number." To make cross-referencing easier, each listing in the Geographic, SIC, Alphabetic and Product Sections includes the establishment's entry number. To facilitate locating an entry in the Geographic Section, the entry numbers for the first listing on the left page and the last listing on the right page are printed at the top of the page next to the city name.

Source Suggestions Welcome

Although all known sources were used to compile this directory, it is possible that companies were inadvertently omitted. Your assistance in calling attention to such omissions would be greatly appreciated. A special form on the facing page will help you in the reporting process.

Analysis

Every effort has been made to contact all firms to verify their information. The one exception to this rule is the annual sales figure, which is considered by many companies to be confidential information. Therefore, estimated sales have been calculated by multiplying the nationwide average sales per employee for the firm's major SIC/NAICS code by the firm's number of employees. Nationwide averages for sales per employee by SIC/NAICS codes are provided by the U.S. Department of Commerce and are updated annually. All sales—sales (est)—have been estimated by this method. The exceptions are parent companies (PA), division headquarters (DH) and headquarter locations (HQ) which may include an actual corporate sales figure—sales (corporate-wide) if available.

Types of Companies

Descriptive and statistical data are included for companies in the entire state. These comprise manufacturers, machine shops, fabricators, assemblers and printers. Also identified are corporate offices in the state.

Employment Data

The employment figure shown in the Geographic Section includes male and female employees and embraces all levels of the company: administrative, clerical, sales and maintenance. This figure is for the facility listed and does not include other plants or offices. It should be recognized that these figures represent an approximate year-round average. These employment figures are broken into codes A through G and used in the Product and SIC Sections to further help you in qualifying a company. Be sure to check the footnotes on the bottom of pages for the code breakdowns.

Standard Industrial Classification (SIC)

The Standard Industrial Classification (SIC) system used in this directory was developed by the federal government for use in classifying establishments by the type of activity they are engaged in. The SIC classifications used in this directory are from the 1987 edition published by the U.S. Government's Office of Management and Budget. The SIC system separates all activities into broad industrial divisions (e.g., manufacturing, mining, retail trade). It further subdivides each division. The range of manufacturing industry classes extends from two-digit codes (major industry group) to four-digit codes (product).

For example:

Industry Breakdown	Code	Industry, Product, etc.
*Major industry group	20	Food and kindred products
Industry group	203	Canned and frozen foods
*Industry	2033	Fruits and vegetables, etc.

*Classifications used in this directory

Only two-digit and four-digit codes are used in this directory.

Arrangement

1. The **Geographic Section** contains complete in-depth corporate data. This section is sorted by cities listed in alphabetical order and companies listed alphabetically within each city. A County/City Index for referencing cities within counties precedes this section.

IMPORTANT NOTICE: It is a violation of both federal and state law to transmit an unsolicited advertisement to a facsimile machine. Any user of this product that violates such laws may be subject to civil and criminal penalties, which may exceed $500 for each transmission of an unsolicited facsimile. Harris InfoSource provides fax numbers for lawful purposes only and expressly forbids the use of these numbers in any unlawful manner.

2. The **Standard Industrial Classification (SIC) Section** lists companies under approximately 500 four-digit SIC codes. An alphabetical and a numerical index precedes this section. A company can be listed under several codes. The codes are in numerical order with companies listed alphabetically under each code.

3. The **Alphabetic Section** lists all companies with their full physical or mailing addresses and telephone number.

4. The **Product Section** lists companies under unique Harris categories. An index preceding this section lists all product categories in alphabetical order. Companies can be listed under several categories.

USER'S GUIDE TO LISTINGS

GEOGRAPHIC SECTION

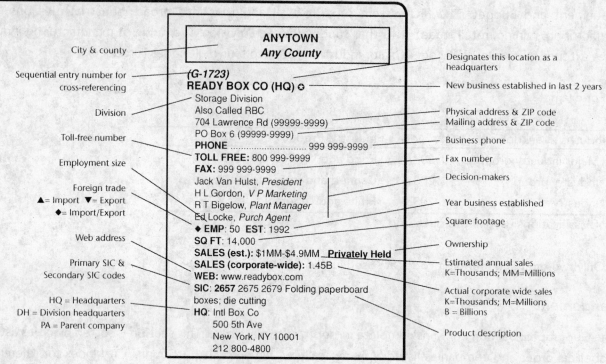

City & county

Sequential entry number for cross-referencing

Division

Toll-free number

Employment size

Foreign trade
▲= Import ▼= Export
◆= Import/Export

Web address

Primary SIC &
Secondary SIC codes

HQ = Headquarters
DH = Division headquarters
PA = Parent company

ANYTOWN
Any County

(G-1723)
READY BOX CO (HQ) ✪
Storage Division
Also Called RBC
704 Lawrence Rd (99999-9999)
PO Box 6 (99999-9999)
PHONE 999 999-9999
TOLL FREE: 800 999-9999
FAX: 999 999-9999
Jack Van Hulst, *President*
H L Gordon, *V P Marketing*
R T Bigelow, *Plant Manager*
Ed Locke, *Purch Agent*
◆ **EMP:** 50 **EST:** 1992
SQ FT: 14,000
SALES (est.): $1MM-$4.9MM __Privately Held__
SALES (corporate-wide): 1.45B
WEB: www.readybox.com
SIC: 2657 2675 2679 Folding paperboard
boxes; die cutting
HQ: Intl Box Co
500 5th Ave
New York, NY 10001
212 800-4800

Designates this location as a headquarters

New business established in last 2 years

Physical address & ZIP code
Mailing address & ZIP code

Business phone

Fax number

Decision-makers

Year business established

Square footage

Ownership

Estimated annual sales
K=Thousands; MM=Millions

Actual corporate wide sales
K=Thousands; M=Millions
B = Billions

Product description

SIC SECTION

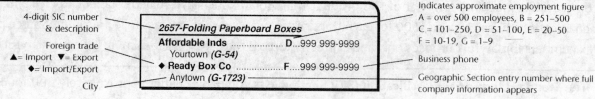

4-digit SIC number
& description

Foreign trade
▲= Import ▼= Export
◆= Import/Export

City

2657-Folding Paperboard Boxes
Affordable Inds .... D...999 999-9999
Yourtown *(G-54)*
◆ **Ready Box Co** .... F....999 999-9999
Anytown *(G-1723)*

Indicates approximate employment figure
A = over 500 employees, B = 251–500
C = 101–250, D = 51–100, E = 20–50
F = 10-19, G = 1–9

Business phone

Geographic Section entry number where full company information appears

ALPHABETIC SECTION

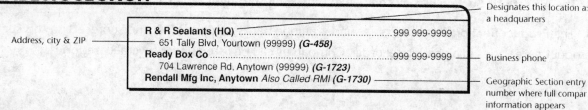

Address, city & ZIP

R & R Sealants (HQ) 999 999-9999
651 Tally Blvd, Yourtown (99999) *(G-458)*
Ready Box Co 999 999-9999
704 Lawrence Rd, Anytown (99999) *(G-1723)*
Rendall Mfg Inc, Anytown *Also Called RMI (G-1730)*

Designates this location as a headquarters

Business phone

Geographic Section entry number where full company information appears

PRODUCT SECTION

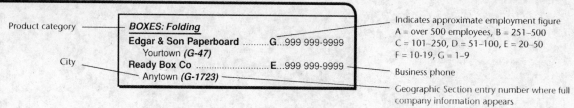

Product category

City

BOXES: Folding
Edgar & Son Paperboard ....G...999 999-9999
Yourtown *(G-47)*
Ready Box Co ....E...999 999-9999
Anytown *(G-1723)*

Indicates approximate employment figure
A = over 500 employees, B = 251–500
C = 101–250, D = 51–100, E = 20–50
F = 10-19, G = 1–9

Business phone

Geographic Section entry number where full company information appears

GEOGRAPHIC SECTION
Companies sorted by city in alphabetical order
In-depth company data listed

STANDARD INDUSTRIAL CLASSIFICATIONS
Alphabetical index of classifcation descriptions
Numerical index of classifcation descriptions
Companies sorted by SIC product groupings

ALPHABETIC SECTION
Company listings in alphabetical order

PRODUCT INDEX
Product categories listed in alphabetical order

PRODUCT SECTION
Companies sorted by product and manufacturing service classifications

GEOGRAPHIC

SIC

ALPHABETIC

PRDT INDEX

PRODUCT

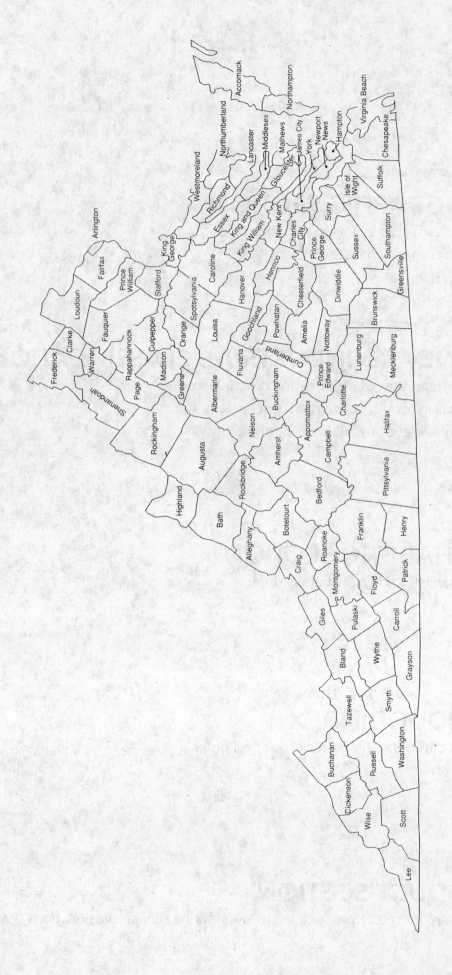

Virginia County Map

COUNTY/CITY CROSS-REFERENCE INDEX

ENTRY #   **ENTRY #**   **ENTRY #**   **ENTRY #**   **ENTRY #**

Accomack
Accomac	(G-71)
Atlantic	(G-1525)
Bloxom	(G-1839)
Chincoteague	(G-3561)
Greenbackville	(G-5992)
Greenbush	(G-5996)
Hallwood	(G-6055)
Mappsville	(G-8218)
Mears	(G-8597)
Melfa	(G-8708)
New Church	(G-9125)
Onancock	(G-10188)
Onley	(G-10200)
Painter	(G-10240)
Parksley	(G-10261)
Pungoteague	(G-10650)
Tangier	(G-13809)
Temperanceville	(G-13840)
Wallops Island	(G-14972)

Albemarle
Charlottesville	(G-2585)
Covesville	(G-3775)
Crozet	(G-3828)
Earlysville	(G-4284)
Free Union	(G-5506)
Greenwood	(G-6000)
Keswick	(G-7041)
North Garden	(G-10074)
Scottsville	(G-12657)

Alexandria City
Alexandria	(G-114)

Alleghany
Clifton Forge	(G-3678)
Iron Gate	(G-6999)
Lowmoor	(G-7598)

Amelia
Amelia Court House	(G-648)
Jetersville	(G-7015)
Mannboro	(G-8214)

Amherst
Amherst	(G-680)
Madison Heights	(G-7866)
Monroe	(G-8986)

Appomattox
Appomattox	(G-801)
Spout Spring	(G-12925)

Arlington
Arlington	(G-833)

Augusta
Churchville	(G-3619)
Craigsville	(G-3806)
Crimora	(G-3821)
Fishersville	(G-5000)
Greenville	(G-5997)
Lyndhurst	(G-7841)
Middlebrook	(G-8714)
Mount Sidney	(G-9084)
Mount Solon	(G-9086)
Steeles Tavern	(G-13310)
Stuarts Draft	(G-13642)
Verona	(G-13982)

Weyers Cave	(G-15165)

Bath
Hot Springs	(G-6945)
Millboro	(G-8934)
Warm Springs	(G-14973)
Williamsville	(G-15351)

Bedford
Bedford	(G-1617)
Big Island	(G-1701)
Coleman Falls	(G-3706)
Forest	(G-5049)
Goode	(G-5888)
Goodview	(G-5894)
Huddleston	(G-6952)
Moneta	(G-8955)
Montvale	(G-9029)
Thaxton	(G-13841)

Bland
Bastian	(G-1592)
Bland	(G-1834)
Rocky Gap	(G-12304)

Botetourt
Blue Ridge	(G-1845)
Buchanan	(G-2117)
Cloverdale	(G-3693)
Daleville	(G-3938)
Eagle Rock	(G-4278)
Fincastle	(G-4992)
Troutville	(G-13902)

Bristol City
Bristol	(G-1963)

Brunswick
Alberta	(G-98)
Brodnax	(G-2099)
Dolphin	(G-4116)
Ebony	(G-4298)
Freeman	(G-5511)
Gasburg	(G-5657)
Lawrenceville	(G-7176)
Valentines	(G-13974)
White Plains	(G-15179)

Buchanan
Big Rock	(G-1705)
Conaway	(G-3754)
Grundy	(G-6027)
Hurley	(G-6968)
Maxie	(G-8372)
Oakwood	(G-10165)
Raven	(G-10756)
Rowe	(G-12396)
Vansant	(G-13975)
Whitewood	(G-15191)
Wolford	(G-15638)

Buckingham
Andersonville	(G-726)
Arvonia	(G-1232)
Buckingham	(G-2131)
Dillwyn	(G-4094)
Howardsville	(G-6951)
New Canton	(G-9117)

Buena Vista City
Buena Vista	(G-2137)

Campbell
Altavista	(G-622)
Brookneal	(G-2107)
Concord	(G-3755)
Evington	(G-4374)
Gladys	(G-5690)
Lynch Station	(G-7627)
Rustburg	(G-12434)

Caroline
Bowling Green	(G-1906)
Ladysmith	(G-7154)
Milford	(G-8928)
Port Royal	(G-10385)
Ruther Glen	(G-12448)
Woodford	(G-15839)

Carroll
Cana	(G-2226)
Dugspur	(G-4188)
Fancy Gap	(G-4933)
Hillsville	(G-6882)
Laurel Fork	(G-7175)
Woodlawn	(G-15843)

Charles City
Charles City	(G-2568)

Charlotte
Charlotte C H	(G-2582)
Drakes Branch	(G-4130)
Keysville	(G-7054)
Phenix	(G-10354)
Randolph	(G-10747)
Red Oak	(G-10759)
Saxe	(G-12648)
Wylliesburg	(G-15871)

Charlottesville City
Charlottesville	(G-2719)

Chesapeake City
Chesapeake	(G-2948)

Chesterfield
Chester	(G-3382)
Chesterfield	(G-3471)
Midlothian	(G-8766)
Moseley	(G-9032)
North Chesterfield	(G-9804)
Richmond	(G-11023)

Clarke
Berryville	(G-1669)
Bluemont	(G-1885)
Boyce	(G-1908)
White Post	(G-15180)

Colonial Heights City
Colonial Heights	(G-3731)
South Chesterfield	(G-12793)

Covington City
Covington	(G-3776)

Craig
New Castle	(G-9120)

Culpeper
Amissville	(G-716)
Boston	(G-1902)
Brandy Station	(G-1937)

Culpeper	(G-3861)
Elkwood	(G-4340)
Jeffersonton	(G-7012)
Lignum	(G-7425)
Mitchells	(G-8954)
Rapidan	(G-10753)
Richardsville	(G-11009)
Rixeyville	(G-11877)
Viewtown	(G-14164)

Cumberland
Cumberland	(G-3934)

Danville City
Danville	(G-3951)

Dickenson
Clinchco	(G-3684)
Clintwood	(G-3685)
Haysi	(G-6457)
Mc Clure	(G-8373)
Nora	(G-9407)

Dinwiddie
Church Road	(G-3618)
Dewitt	(G-4092)
Ford	(G-5047)
Mc Kenney	(G-8379)
Sutherland	(G-13803)
Wilsons	(G-15367)

Essex
Caret	(G-2238)
Champlain	(G-2356)
Dunnsville	(G-4267)
Millers Tavern	(G-8939)
Tappahannock	(G-13810)

Fairfax
Alexandria	(G-393)
Annandale	(G-727)
Burke	(G-2179)
Centreville	(G-2287)
Chantilly	(G-2359)
Clifton	(G-3657)
Dunn Loring	(G-4263)
Fairfax	(G-4393)
Fairfax Station	(G-4700)
Falls Church	(G-4741)
Fort Belvoir	(G-5114)
Great Falls	(G-5934)
Herndon	(G-6598)
Lorton	(G-7456)
Mc Lean	(G-8383)
Mclean	(G-8586)
Newington	(G-9152)
Oak Hill	(G-10135)
Oakton	(G-10140)
Reston	(G-10777)
Springfield	(G-12933)
Tysons	(G-13940)
Tysons Corner	(G-13951)
Vienna	(G-14001)

Fairfax City
Fairfax	(G-4587)

Falls Church City
Falls Church	(G-4899)

Fauquier
Bealeton	(G-1596)
Broad Run	(G-2066)
Calverton	(G-2224)
Catlett	(G-2262)
Delaplane	(G-4072)
Goldvein	(G-5877)
Hume	(G-6960)
Markham	(G-8247)
Marshall	(G-8249)
Midland	(G-8749)
Remington	(G-10767)
Sumerduck	(G-13789)
The Plains	(G-13842)
Upperville	(G-13966)
Warrenton	(G-14976)

Floyd
Check	(G-2943)
Copper Hill	(G-3764)
Floyd	(G-5016)
Indian Valley	(G-6998)
Willis	(G-15352)

Fluvanna
Bremo Bluff	(G-1943)
Fork Union	(G-5107)
Kents Store	(G-7038)
Palmyra	(G-10243)
Troy	(G-13920)

Franklin
Boones Mill	(G-1893)
Callaway	(G-2219)
Ferrum	(G-4966)
Glade Hill	(G-5669)
Hardy	(G-6285)
Henry	(G-6594)
Penhook	(G-10285)
Rocky Mount	(G-12309)
Union Hall	(G-13957)
Wirtz	(G-15609)

Franklin City
Franklin	(G-5138)

Frederick
Clear Brook	(G-3643)
Cross Junction	(G-3827)
Gore	(G-5920)
Middletown	(G-8736)
Star Tannery	(G-13235)
Stephens City	(G-13311)
Stephenson	(G-13331)
Winchester	(G-15368)

Fredericksburg City
Fredericksburg	(G-5166)

Galax City
Galax	(G-5626)

Giles
Glen Lyn	(G-5832)
Narrows	(G-9096)
Pearisburg	(G-10271)
Pembroke	(G-10280)
Rich Creek	(G-11007)
Ripplemead	(G-11876)
Staffordsville	(G-13214)

| ENTRY # | | ENTRY # | | ENTRY # | | ENTRY # | | ENTRY # |

Gloucester

Dutton	(G-4269)
Gloucester	(G-5834)
Gloucester Point	(G-5871)
Hayes	(G-6393)
Ordinary	(G-10236)

Goochland

Columbia	(G-3752)
Crozier	(G-3857)
Goochland	(G-5880)
Gum Spring	(G-6043)
Maidens	(G-7887)
Manakin Sabot	(G-7894)
Oilville	(G-10176)
Sandy Hook	(G-12643)

Grayson

Elk Creek	(G-4320)
Fries	(G-5514)
Independence	(G-6979)
Mouth of Wilson	(G-9091)
Troutdale	(G-13901)

Greene

Dyke	(G-4276)
Ruckersville	(G-12398)
Stanardsville	(G-13215)

Greensville

Emporia	(G-4351)
Jarratt	(G-7009)
Skippers	(G-12700)

Halifax

Alton	(G-646)
Clover	(G-3691)
Crystal Hill	(G-3859)
Halifax	(G-6048)
Nathalie	(G-9102)
Scottsburg	(G-12654)
South Boston	(G-12745)
Vernon Hill	(G-13981)
Virgilina	(G-14192)

Hampton City

| Fort Monroe | (G-5133) |
| Hampton | (G-6065) |

Hanover

Ashland	(G-1359)
Beaverdam	(G-1608)
Doswell	(G-4118)
Hanover	(G-6280)
Mechanicsville	(G-8598)
Montpelier	(G-9015)
Rockville	(G-12284)

Harrisonburg City

| Harrisonburg | (G-6290) |
| Rockingham | (G-12238) |

Henrico

Glen Allen	(G-5703)
Henrico	(G-6468)
Highland Springs	(G-6850)
Richmond	(G-11069)
Sandston	(G-12608)

Henry

Axton	(G-1531)
Bassett	(G-1577)
Collinsville	(G-3708)
Fieldale	(G-4984)
Ridgeway	(G-11838)

| Spencer | (G-12872) |

Highland

Blue Grass	(G-1842)
DOE Hill	(G-4115)
Mc Dowell	(G-8374)
Monterey	(G-9000)

Hopewell City

| Hopewell | (G-6916) |
| North Prince George | (G-10086) |

Isle Of Wight

Battery Park	(G-1595)
Carrollton	(G-2239)
Carrsville	(G-2248)
Smithfield	(G-12702)
Windsor	(G-15603)
Zuni	(G-16011)

James City

| Toano | (G-13855) |
| Williamsburg | (G-15198) |

King And Queen

King Queen Ch	(G-7125)
Mattaponi	(G-8357)
Shacklefords	(G-12682)
Walkerton	(G-14971)

King George

| King George | (G-7080) |
| Ninde | (G-9387) |

King William

Aylett	(G-1544)
Cologne	(G-3719)
King William	(G-7128)
Manquin	(G-8215)
West Point	(G-15152)

Lancaster

Irvington	(G-7000)
Kilmarnock	(G-7068)
Lancaster	(G-7158)
Lively	(G-7439)
Weems	(G-15150)
White Stone	(G-15185)

Lee

Dryden	(G-4144)
Ewing	(G-4385)
Jonesville	(G-7018)
Keokee	(G-7040)
Pennington Gap	(G-10291)
Rose Hill	(G-12361)

Lexington City

| Lexington | (G-7385) |

Loudoun

Aldie	(G-100)
Ashburn	(G-1235)
Brambleton	(G-1925)
Broadlands	(G-2072)
Chantilly	(G-2524)
Dulles	(G-4191)
Fairfax	(G-4699)
Hamilton	(G-6056)
Hillsboro	(G-6859)
Lansdowne	(G-7170)
Leesburg	(G-7212)
Lovettsville	(G-7577)
Middleburg	(G-8715)
Paeonian Springs	(G-10238)
Potomac Falls	(G-10508)

Purcellville	(G-10651)
Round Hill	(G-12373)
South Riding	(G-12867)
Sterling	(G-13336)
Waterford	(G-15080)

Louisa

Bumpass	(G-2160)
Louisa	(G-7545)
Mineral	(G-8942)

Lunenburg

| Kenbridge | (G-7032) |
| Victoria | (G-14000) |

Lynchburg City

| Lynchburg | (G-7630) |

Madison

Aroda	(G-1224)
Brightwood	(G-1961)
Etlan	(G-4372)
Locust Dale	(G-7440)
Madison	(G-7849)
Reva	(G-10999)
Rochelle	(G-12232)

Manassas City

| Manassas | (G-7908) |

Martinsville City

| Martinsville | (G-8262) |

Mathews

Cobbs Creek	(G-3694)
Diggs	(G-4093)
Foster	(G-5137)
Gwynn	(G-6045)
Mathews	(G-8355)
Moon	(G-9031)
North	(G-9802)
Port Haywood	(G-10381)
Susan	(G-13802)

Mecklenburg

Boydton	(G-1913)
Bracey	(G-1921)
Buffalo Junction	(G-2158)
Chase City	(G-2909)
Clarksville	(G-3626)
La Crosse	(G-7139)
Nelson	(G-9116)
South Hill	(G-12841)

Middlesex

Deltaville	(G-4078)
Hartfield	(G-6390)
Jamaica	(G-7008)
Locust Hill	(G-7453)
Saluda	(G-12600)
Topping	(G-13885)
Urbanna	(G-13970)
Wake	(G-14963)

Montgomery

Blacksburg	(G-1720)
Christiansburg	(G-3567)
Elliston	(G-4343)
Pilot	(G-10356)
Riner	(G-11860)
Shawsville	(G-12686)

Nelson

Afton	(G-73)
Arrington	(G-1227)
Faber	(G-4388)

Gladstone	(G-5681)
Lovingston	(G-7588)
Lowesville	(G-7595)
Nellysford	(G-9113)
Piney River	(G-10360)
Roseland	(G-12368)
Schuyler	(G-12649)
Shipman	(G-12698)
Tyro	(G-13939)

New Kent

Barhamsville	(G-1570)
Lanexa	(G-7164)
New Kent	(G-9128)
Providence Forge	(G-10617)
Quinton	(G-10694)

Newport News City

Fort Eustis	(G-5126)
Hampton	(G-6275)
Newport News	(G-9154)

Norfolk City

| Norfolk | (G-9409) |

Northampton

Birdsnest	(G-1719)
Cape Charles	(G-2229)
Cheriton	(G-2946)
Eastville	(G-4296)
Exmore	(G-4387)
Franktown	(G-5164)
Machipongo	(G-7845)
Nassawadox	(G-9100)

Northumberland

Burgess	(G-2174)
Callao	(G-2215)
Heathsville	(G-6459)
Lewisetta	(G-7384)
Lottsburg	(G-7543)
Reedville	(G-10761)
Wicomico Church	(G-15194)

Norton City

| Norton | (G-10112) |

Nottoway

Blackstone	(G-1809)
Burkeville	(G-2207)
Crewe	(G-3807)

Orange

Barboursville	(G-1559)
Gordonsville	(G-5898)
Locust Grove	(G-7441)
Mine Run	(G-8941)
Orange	(G-10202)
Unionville	(G-13962)
Zion Crossroads	(G-16005)

Page

Luray	(G-7600)
Shenandoah	(G-12688)
Stanley	(G-13231)

Patrick

Ararat	(G-829)
Claudville	(G-3637)
Critz	(G-3823)
Meadows of Dan	(G-8590)
Patrick Springs	(G-10269)
Stuart	(G-13603)
Woolwine	(G-15863)

Petersburg City

North Dinwiddie	(G-10047)
Petersburg	(G-10301)
South Chesterfield	(G-12831)
South Prince George	(G-12865)

Pittsylvania

Blairs	(G-1830)
Callands	(G-2213)
Cascade	(G-2249)
Chatham	(G-2918)
Dry Fork	(G-4140)
Gretna	(G-6001)
Hurt	(G-6970)
Java	(G-7011)
Keeling	(G-7025)
Pittsville	(G-10362)
Ringgold	(G-11867)
Sandy Level	(G-12646)
Sutherlin	(G-13806)

Poquoson City

| Hampton | (G-6276) |
| Poquoson | (G-10363) |

Portsmouth City

| Portsmouth | (G-10386) |

Powhatan

| Powhatan | (G-10527) |

Prince Edward

Farmville	(G-4936)
Green Bay	(G-5987)
Meherrin	(G-8704)
Prospect	(G-10612)
Rice	(G-11004)

Prince George

Disputanta	(G-4102)
Fort Lee	(G-5128)
Prince George	(G-10586)

Prince William

Bristow	(G-2045)
Catharpin	(G-2261)
Dumfries	(G-4233)
Gainesville	(G-5567)
Haymarket	(G-6411)
Lake Ridge	(G-7156)
Manassas	(G-8016)
Manassas Park	(G-8185)
Montclair	(G-8997)
Nokesville	(G-9388)
Occoquan	(G-10172)
Quantico	(G-10688)
Triangle	(G-13888)
Woodbridge	(G-15639)

Pulaski

Allisonia	(G-618)
Draper	(G-4137)
Dublin	(G-4147)
Hiwassee	(G-6908)
New River	(G-9151)
Pulaski	(G-10630)

Radford City

| Fairlawn | (G-4736) |
| Radford | (G-10702) |

Rappahannock

Chester Gap	(G-3470)
Flint Hill	(G-5014)
Huntly	(G-6964)

ENTRY #	ENTRY #	ENTRY #	ENTRY #	ENTRY #
Sperryville .... (G-12876)	Fulks Run .... (G-5565)	New Market .... (G-9140)	**Surry**	Glade Spring .... (G-5673)
Washington............... (G-15074)	Grottoes .... (G-6011)	Quicksburg .... (G-10692)	Claremont .... (G-3624)	Meadowview............ (G-8594)
Woodville .... (G-15862)	Hinton .... (G-6905)	Strasburg .... (G-13571)	Dendron.................... (G-4091)	**Waynes City**
Richmond	Keezletown .... (G-7026)	Toms Brook............... (G-13882)	Elberon .... (G-4318)	Waynesboro .... (G-15091)
Farnham .... (G-4962)	Linville .... (G-7434)	Woodstock................ (G-15847)	Spring Grove .... (G-12929)	**Westmoreland**
Sharps .... (G-12685)	Mc Gaheysville .... (G-8377)	**Smyth**	Surry .... (G-13795)	Colonial Beach .... (G-3720)
Warsaw .... (G-15060)	McGaheysville .... (G-8583)	Atkins....................... (G-1515)	**Sussex**	Hague .... (G-6046)
Richmond City	Mount Crawford .... (G-9051)	Chilhowie .... (G-3544)	Stony Creek.............. (G-13567)	Kinsale...................... (G-7133)
North Chesterfield..... (G-10016)	Penn Laird .... (G-10287)	Marion .... (G-8219)	Wakefield................. (G-14964)	Montross.................. (G-9023)
Richmond .... (G-11465)	Port Republic............ (G-10383)	Saltville .... (G-12584)	Waverly..................... (G-15085)	**Winchester City**
Roanoke	Singers Glen............. (G-12699)	Sugar Grove .... (G-13787)	Yale.......................... (G-15929)	Winchester............... (G-15523)
Bent Mountain .... (G-1666)	Timberville .... (G-13845)	**Southampton**	**Tazewell**	**Wise**
Catawba .... (G-2260)	**Russell**	Boykins .... (G-1918)	Amonate .... (G-725)	Appalachia................ (G-796)
Roanoke .... (G-11881)	Castlewood............... (G-2254)	Capron...................... (G-2237)	Bandy....................... (G-1557)	Big Stone Gap .... (G-1706)
Vinton .... (G-14165)	Cleveland .... (G-3655)	Courtland.................. (G-3766)	Bluefield................... (G-1857)	Coeburn................... (G-3695)
Roanoke City	Honaker.................... (G-6914)	Drewryville .... (G-4138)	Cedar Bluff............... (G-2270)	Pound .... (G-10511)
Roanoke .... (G-12026)	Lebanon .... (G-7188)	Ivor.......................... (G-7007)	Doran....................... (G-4117)	Saint Paul .... (G-12465)
Rockbridge	Rosedale .... (G-12365)	Sedley .... (G-12679)	Falls Mills .... (G-4931)	Wise........................ (G-15620)
Fairfield.................... (G-4729)	Swords Creek........... (G-13807)	**Spotsylvania**	North Tazewell .... (G-10093)	**Wythe**
Glasgow .... (G-5699)	**Salem City**	Fredericksburg.......... (G-5239)	Pounding Mill .... (G-10515)	Austinville .... (G-1527)
Goshen .... (G-5924)	Salem .... (G-12471)	Partlow .... (G-10263)	Richlands................. (G-11012)	Barren Springs......... (G-1575)
Natural Bridge.......... (G-9105)	**Scott**	Spotsylvania .... (G-12880)	Tazewell................... (G-13828)	Crockett .... (G-3825)
Natural Bridge Stati .. (G-9108)	Duffield .... (G-4175)	**Stafford**	**Virginia Beach City**	Ivanhoe.................... (G-7003)
Naturl BR STA .... (G-9110)	Fort Blackmore .... (G-5120)	Falmouth .... (G-4932)	Virginia Beach .... (G-14194)	Max Meadows .... (G-8365)
Raphine .... (G-10749)	Gate City .... (G-5661)	Fredericksburg.......... (G-5395)	**Warren**	Rural Retreat .... (G-12417)
Rockbridge Baths ..... (G-12235)	Hiltons .... (G-6904)	Garrisonville............. (G-5656)	Front Royal .... (G-5519)	Wytheville .... (G-15873)
Vesuvius .... (G-13998)	Nickelsville............... (G-9384)	Hartwood .... (G-6392)	Lake Frederick.......... (G-7155)	**York**
Rockingham	Weber City............... (G-15149)	Stafford .... (G-13111)	Linden...................... (G-7427)	Grafton .... (G-5931)
Bridgewater .... (G-1947)	**Shenandoah**	**Staunton City**	**Washington**	Hampton................... (G-6277)
Broadway .... (G-2085)	Edinburg .... (G-4299)	Staunton .... (G-13238)	Abingdon .... (G-1)	Seaford.................... (G-12671)
Dayton .... (G-4052)	Fort Valley .... (G-5134)	**Suffolk City**	Bristol .... (G-2003)	Yorktown.................. (G-15930)
Elkton .... (G-4323)	Maurertown.............. (G-8360)	Suffolk...................... (G-13662)	Damascus................ (G-3946)	
	Mount Jackson .... (G-9064)			

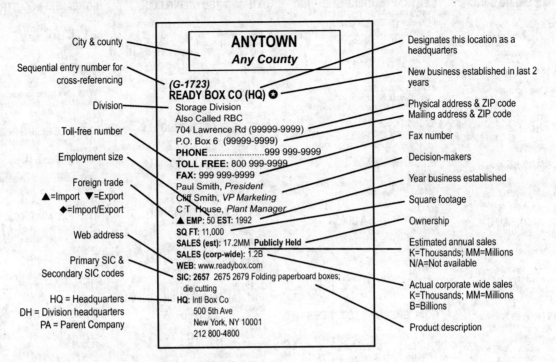

City & county

Sequential entry number for cross-referencing

Division

Toll-free number

Employment size

Foreign trade
▲=Import ▼=Export
◆=Import/Export

Web address

Primary SIC & Secondary SIC codes

HQ = Headquarters
DH = Division headquarters
PA = Parent Company

ANYTOWN
Any County

(G-1723)
READY BOX CO (HQ) ✪
Storage Division
Also Called RBC
704 Lawrence Rd (99999-9999)
P.O. Box 6 (99999-9999)
PHONE 999 999-9999
TOLL FREE: 800 999-9999
FAX: 999 999-9999
Paul Smith, *President*
Cliff Smith, *VP Marketing*
C T House, *Plant Manager*
▲ **EMP:** 50 **EST:** 1992
SQ FT: 11,000
SALES (est): 17.2MM **Publicly Held**
SALES (corp-wide): 1.2B
WEB: www.readybox.com
SIC: 2657 2675 2679 Folding paperboard boxes; die cutting
HQ: Intl Box Co
500 5th Ave
New York, NY 10001
212 800-4800

Designates this location as a headquarters

New business established in last 2 years

Physical address & ZIP code
Mailing address & ZIP code

Fax number

Decision-makers

Year business established

Square footage

Ownership

Estimated annual sales
K=Thousands; MM=Millions
N/A=Not available

Actual corporate wide sales
K=Thousands; MM=Millions
B=Billions

Product description

See footnotes for symbols and codes identification.
• This section is in alphabetical order by city.
• Companies are sorted alphabetically under their respective cities.
• To locate cities within a county refer to the County/City Cross Reference Index.

IMPORTANT NOTICE: It is a violation of both federal and state law to transmit an unsolicited advertisement to a facsimile machine. Any user of this product that violates such laws may be subject to civil and criminal penalties which may exceed $500 for each transmission of an unsolicited facsimile. Harris InfoSource provides fax numbers for lawful purposes only and expressly forbids the use of these numbers in any unlawful manner.

Abingdon
Washington County

(G-1)
ABINGDON MILLWORK
550 Lowry Dr Sw (24210-3060)
PHONE 276 676-2951
Gary Fuller, *Principal*
EMP: 2 EST: 2008
SALES (est): 187.9K **Privately Held**
WEB:
www.abingdonmillwork.snappages.com
SIC: 2431 Millwork

(G-2)
ABINGDON PRE-CAST PRODUCTS
15455 Steinman Rd (24210-1627)
PHONE 276 628-2472
Bobby Gentry, *President*
Carl Gentry, *Corp Secy*
EMP: 4 EST: 1998
SALES (est): 890K **Privately Held**
WEB: www.abingdonprecast.com
SIC: 3272 5191 Tanks, concrete; farm supplies

(G-3)
ABINGDON PRINTING INC
1272 Hill St (24210-4708)
PHONE 276 628-4221
Fax: 540 628-8504
EMP: 5
SQ FT: 2,000
SALES (est): 290K **Privately Held**
SIC: 2752 Commercial Offset Printing

(G-4)
ABINGDON SIGN CO INC
17156 Lee Hwy (24210-7878)
PHONE 276 628-2594
Robert Hockett, *President*
EMP: 1
SQ FT: 1,500
SALES (est): 132K **Privately Held**
WEB: www.abingdon-va.gov
SIC: 3993 Signs & advertising specialties

(G-5)
ABINGDON STEEL INC
25479 Hillman Hwy (24210-7609)
P.O. Box 1243 (24212-1243)
PHONE 276 628-9269
Jeffrey A Stroup, *President*
Gloria Stroup, *Vice Pres*
EMP: 20
SQ FT: 10,000
SALES (est): 5MM **Privately Held**
WEB: www.hapco.com
SIC: 3441 Fabricated structural metal

(G-6)
ACP LLC
Also Called: Appalachian Cast Products
26372 Hillman Hwy (24210-7618)
PHONE 276 619-5080
Michael Ferracci, *President*
Stephen Canonico, *Vice Pres*
Richard Cocilova, *Vice Pres*
Duffie Cox, *CFO*
EMP: 2
SQ FT: 15,000
SALES (est): 9MM **Privately Held**
WEB: www.appalachiancast.com
SIC: 3559 3365 Foundry, smelting, refining & similar machinery; aluminum & aluminum-based alloy castings

(G-7)
ACTIVE SENSE TECHNOLOGIES LLC
165 Park St Se (24210-3322)
P.O. Box 1134 (24212-1134)
PHONE 352 226-1479
Charles Perry, *President*
EMP: 1 EST: 2017
SALES (est): 64.6K **Privately Held**
SIC: 3663 8711 8748 7389 Light communications equipment; ; electrical or electronic engineering; systems engineering consultant, ex. computer or professional;

(G-8)
AFG INDUSTRIES - VA
18370 Oak Park Dr (24210-8091)
PHONE 276 619-6000
Teresa Carter, *Manager*
▲ **EMP:** 2
SALES (est): 160.9K **Privately Held**
WEB: www.agcglass.com
SIC: 3999 Manufacturing industries

(G-9)
AGGREGATES USA LLC
21339 Gravel Lake Rd (24211)
PHONE 276 628-9337
Jim McGill, *Branch Mgr*
EMP: 6 Publicly Held
WEB: www.aggregatesusa.com
SIC: 3273 Ready-mixed concrete
HQ: Aggregates Usa, Llc
3300 Cahaba Rd Ste 302
Birmingham AL 35223

(G-10)
AMERICAN MOUNTAIN TECH LLC
19182 Sterling Dr (24211-6742)
PHONE 423 646-1864
William Arnold,
William Michael Arnold,
EMP: 1
SALES (est): 140.5K **Privately Held**
SIC: 2655 Fiber shipping & mailing containers

(G-11)
ANDIS PALLET CO INC
25058 Regal Dr (24211-7442)
P.O. Box 2172 (24212-2172)
PHONE 276 628-9044
Fred Andis, *President*
EMP: 13 EST: 1974
SQ FT: 17,000
SALES (est): 1.8MM **Privately Held**
WEB: www.andispallet.com
SIC: 2448 Pallets, wood

(G-12)
APPALACHIAN CAST PRODUCTS INC (PA)
26372 Hillman Hwy (24210-7618)
PHONE 276 619-5080
Michael Ferracci, *Principal*
Steve Canonico, *Vice Pres*
▲ **EMP:** 138
SQ FT: 40,000
SALES (est): 30.6MM **Privately Held**
WEB: www.appalachiancast.com
SIC: 3363 Aluminum die-castings

(G-13)
APPALACHIAN ENERGY INC (PA)
230 Charwood Dr (24210-2566)
P.O. Box 2406 (24212-2406)
PHONE..............................276 619-4880
Frank D Henderson, *President*
EMP: 12
SALES (est): 1.9MM **Privately Held**
WEB: www.shalepro.com
SIC: **1382** Oil & gas exploration services

(G-14)
AWNING & SIGN COMPANY INC
17311 Lee Hwy (24210-7831)
PHONE..............................276 628-8069
James A Stepp, *President*
EMP: 1
SALES (est): 50.6K **Privately Held**
WEB:
www.theawningandsigncompany.com
SIC: **3993** Signs & advertising specialties

(G-15)
BLUE RIDGE STONE MFG
26053 Harrison Rd (24210)
PHONE..............................276 676-0040
Gary McField, *President*
EMP: 1
SALES (est): 114.4K **Privately Held**
WEB: www.blueridgestonemfg.com
SIC: **3272** Cast stone, concrete

(G-16)
BRISTOL ORTHOTIC & PROSTHETIC
445 Prtrfeld Hwy Sw Ste C (24210)
PHONE..............................276 963-1186
Jerry Graybeal, *Manager*
EMP: 1
SALES (corp-wide): 722.9K **Privately Held**
WEB: www.bristoloandp.com
SIC: **3842** Limbs, artificial
PA: Bristol Orthotic & Prosthetic
553 Highway 126
Bristol TN 37620
423 968-4442

(G-17)
BROWNS WELDING & TRAILER REPR
24487 Regal Dr (24211-7439)
PHONE..............................276 628-4461
Albert P Brown, *Owner*
EMP: 3
SALES (est): 280K **Privately Held**
SIC: **7692 3441** Welding repair; fabricated structural metal

(G-18)
BULLET EQUIPMENT SALES INC
15696 Porterfield Hwy (24210-8464)
PHONE..............................276 623-5150
Jerry D Farmer, *President*
EMP: 6
SALES (est): 769.9K **Privately Held**
SIC: **3743** Freight cars & equipment

(G-19)
BURKE PRINT SHOP
370 Trigg St (24210-3473)
P.O. Box 1266 (24212-1266)
PHONE..............................276 628-3033
Joe W Burke Sr, *Owner*
EMP: 2 EST: 1946
SQ FT: 1,000
SALES (est): 173.6K **Privately Held**
SIC: **2752** Commercial printing, offset

(G-20)
CAPITAL COAL CORPORATION
23377 Harbor Light Cir (24211-5517)
P.O. Box 1426, Grundy (24614-1426)
PHONE..............................276 935-7562
Hank Matney, *President*
Carter Brown, *Vice Pres*
Eddie Looney, *Vice Pres*
Rick Matney, *Vice Pres*
Fred Matney, *Admin Sec*
EMP: 10
SALES (est): 1.1MM **Privately Held**
SIC: **1222** Underground mining, subbituminous

(G-21)
CENTRAL MACHINE SHOP INC
14773 Wallace Pike (24210-8193)
P.O. Box 1785, Bristol (24203-1785)
PHONE..............................276 669-2816
William G Hyatt, *President*
William T Hyatt, *Vice Pres*
Sharon Hyatt, *Admin Sec*
EMP: 16
SQ FT: 16,500
SALES (est): 1.5MM **Privately Held**
WEB: www.centralmachineshop.com
SIC: **3599** Machine shop, jobbing & repair

(G-22)
CHARLIE ECO PUBLISHING INC
19410 Rich Valley Rd (24210-1746)
PHONE..............................800 357-0121
Everett Robinson, *CEO*
EMP: 1
SALES (est): 43.9K **Privately Held**
SIC: **2711** Newspapers

(G-23)
CHRISTOPHER A DIXON
Also Called: Highland Sign
25218 Lee Hwy (24211-7460)
PHONE..............................276 644-4222
Christopher A Dixon, *Owner*
EMP: 2
SALES (est): 6.5K **Privately Held**
SIC: **3993** Signs & advertising specialties

(G-24)
COAL ENERGY RESOURCES INC
966 W Main St Ste C (24210-2483)
P.O. Box 2043 (24212-2043)
PHONE..............................276 676-3101
Jim Gott, *President*
Martin Gott, *Vice Pres*
Greg Jordon, *Vice Pres*
EMP: 5
SQ FT: 2,000
SALES (est): 404.6K **Privately Held**
WEB: www.conturaenergy.com
SIC: **1221** Bituminous coal & lignite-surface mining

(G-25)
CONTECH ENGNERED SOLUTIONS LLC
25581 Hillman Hwy (24210-7611)
PHONE..............................513 645-7000
EMP: 2 **Privately Held**
WEB: www.conteches.com
SIC: **3444** Sheet metalwork; culverts, sheet metal
HQ: Contech Engineered Solutions Llc
9025 Centre Pointe Dr # 400
West Chester OH 45069
513 645-7000

(G-26)
CORPORATE DESIGNS
25177 Watauga Rd (24211-7117)
PHONE..............................276 676-9048
Tim Webb, *Principal*
EMP: 1
SALES (est): 81.8K **Privately Held**
SIC: **2395** Embroidery products, except schiffli machine

(G-27)
DAMASCUS EQUIPMENT LLC
26161 Old Trail Rd 2 (24210-7631)
PHONE..............................276 676-2376
Eric Miller, *President*
Richard Mullins, *Vice Pres*
Leno Rainero, *Vice Pres*
EMP: 30
SQ FT: 25,000
SALES (est): 8MM **Privately Held**
WEB: www.damascuscorp.com
SIC: **3532** Mining machinery

(G-28)
DAWSON ENTERPRISES INC
21306 Crosswinds Dr (24211-4200)
PHONE..............................276 964-7245
EMP: 3 EST: 2019
SALES (est): 247.4K **Privately Held**
SIC: **3317** Steel pipe & tubes

(G-29)
DYNAMIC RECYCLING LLC
26319 Old Trail Rd (24210-7635)
PHONE..............................276 628-6636
EMP: 1
SALES (corp-wide): 10K **Privately Held**
SIC: **2869** Mfg Industrial Organic Chemicals
PA: Dynamic Recycling Llc
220 N Industrial Dr
Bristol TN 37620
276 628-6636

(G-30)
ENERVEST OPERATING LLC
408 W Main St (24210-2608)
PHONE..............................276 628-1569
EMP: 5
SALES (est): 656K **Privately Held**
WEB: www.enervest.net
SIC: **1382** Oil & gas exploration services

(G-31)
FULL TILT PERFORMANCE
1099 Cummings St (24211-3645)
PHONE..............................276 628-0036
Wes Keller, *Principal*
EMP: 1
SALES (est): 56.4K **Privately Held**
SIC: **3462** Iron & steel forgings

(G-32)
GENERAL ENGINEERING CO VA
26485 Hillman Hwy (24210-7681)
P.O. Box 549 (24212-0549)
PHONE..............................276 628-6068
Donald W Tuckwiller, *Ch of Bd*
John E Owens, *President*
Michael Sanders, *CFO*
Greg Sluss, *Sales Mgr*
EMP: 91 EST: 1948
SQ FT: 60,000
SALES (est): 20.6MM **Privately Held**
WEB: www.generalengr.com
SIC: **3593 3599** Fluid power cylinders, hydraulic or pneumatic; custom machinery

(G-33)
GIGIS
8436 Hidden Valley Rd (24210-4856)
PHONE..............................276 608-5737
Carey Gilbert, *Partner*
Lori Gilbert, *Partner*
EMP: 2
SALES (est): 10K **Privately Held**
SIC: **2099** Food preparations

(G-34)
GOOD TYMES ENTERPRISES INC
228 Preston St Sw (24210-3022)
P.O. Box 2073 (24212-2073)
PHONE..............................276 628-2335
Michael Gonzalez, *CEO*
EMP: 2
SALES (est): 50K **Privately Held**
WEB: www.goodtymesent.com
SIC: **3949** Sporting & athletic goods

(G-35)
GRAHAM GRHAM CNVAS SIGN SHOPPE
1002 W Main St (24210-4744)
P.O. Box 1805 (24212-1805)
PHONE..............................276 628-8069
Howard Graham Jr, *President*
Bobbie Jo Graham, *Treasurer*
Sharon Graham, *Admin Sec*
Tabatha Graham, *Exec Sec*
EMP: 8
SALES (est): 491.1K **Privately Held**
SIC: **2394** Awnings, fabric: made from purchased materials

(G-36)
HIGHLANDS GLASS COMPANY LLC
918 E Main St (24210-4416)
PHONE..............................276 623-0021
Leann Dale, *Principal*
EMP: 5
SALES (est): 325K **Privately Held**
WEB: www.highlands-glass-company.business.site
SIC: **3231** Products of purchased glass

(G-37)
HIGHLANDS LOG STRUCTURES INC
26289 Harrison Rd (24210)
P.O. Box 1747 (24212-1747)
PHONE..............................276 623-1580
Winston Johnson, *President*
Pamela Johnson, *Vice Pres*
EMP: 4
SALES (est): 416.3K **Privately Held**
WEB: www.highlandslog.com
SIC: **2452** Log cabins, prefabricated, wood

(G-38)
HOBBS LOGGING INC
22505 Breezy Point Rd (24211-5085)
PHONE..............................276 628-4952
Kimberly K Hobbs, *Manager*
EMP: 3
SALES (est): 26.7K **Privately Held**
SIC: **2411** Logging

(G-39)
HOSS EXCAVATING & LOGGING CO L
15402 Providence Rd (24210-9038)
PHONE..............................276 628-4068
Shelby Hoss, *Principal*
EMP: 3
SALES (est): 218.7K **Privately Held**
SIC: **2411** Logging camps & contractors

(G-40)
HOUSE OF STITCHES & PRINTS INC
1271 W Main St (24210-4705)
PHONE..............................276 525-1796
T Colstone, *General Mgr*
Theresa Colstone, *General Mgr*
EMP: 2
SALES (est): 189K **Privately Held**
SIC: **2752** Commercial printing, lithographic

(G-41)
HUCKS & HUCKS LLC
Also Called: Mountaintop Custom Kennels
26669 Newbanks Rd (24210-7592)
PHONE..............................276 525-1100
John Hucks,
Lydia Hucks,
EMP: 9
SALES (est): 1.2MM **Privately Held**
WEB: www.mtck.com
SIC: **3441 4212** Fabricated structural metal; animal transport

(G-42)
J M H DIAGNOSTIC CENTER
605 Campus Dr (24210-9700)
PHONE..............................276 628-1439
Margaret Stroup, *Principal*
EMP: 3
SALES (est): 165.7K **Privately Held**
SIC: **3841** Diagnostic apparatus, medical

(G-43)
J W CREATIONS
22530 Aven Ln (24211-5072)
PHONE..............................276 676-3770
Joe L Norton, *Owner*
Wanda Norton, *Co-Owner*
EMP: 2
SQ FT: 4,400
SALES (est): 70K **Privately Held**
WEB: www.jwcinc.com
SIC: **2431 2434 2511 2391** Moldings, wood: unfinished & prefinished; wood kitchen cabinets; wood household furniture; curtains & draperies

(G-44)
JERRYS SIGNS INC
Also Called: Jerry's Signs & Awnings
15775 Porterfield Hwy (24210-8467)
PHONE..............................276 676-2304
Jerry Lee Adkins Jr, *President*
Jerry Lee Adkins Sr, *Vice Pres*
EMP: 15
SQ FT: 3,000
SALES (est): 2MM **Privately Held**
WEB: www.jerryssignsinc.com
SIC: **3993** Electric signs

▲ = Import ▼=Export
◆ =Import/Export

(G-45)
JOY GLOBAL UNDERGROUND MIN LLC
26161 Old Trail Rd Ste 1 (24210-7631)
PHONE...................................276 623-2000
Mitzi Hill, *Engineer*
Ron Thorn, *Branch Mgr*
EMP: 131 **Privately Held**
SIC: 3532 3535 3441 Drills, bits & similar equipment; mine cars, plows, loaders, feeders & similar equipment; conveyors & conveying equipment; bucket type conveyor systems; bulk handling conveyor systems; fabricated structural metal
HQ: Joy Global Underground Mining Llc
   40 Pennwood Pl
   Warrendale PA 15086
   724 779-4500

(G-46)
KCSL
22619 Montego Bay Rd (24211-5061)
PHONE...................................276 206-5977
Brian Cole, *Bd of Directors*
Brock Blankenship, *Bd of Directors*
EMP: 3 **EST:** 2017
SALES (est): 139.9K **Privately Held**
SIC: 3356 7389 Welding rods;

(G-47)
KEARNEY-NATIONAL INC
Also Called: Hapco Division
26252 Hillman Hwy (24210-7616)
PHONE...................................276 628-7171
David Oakley, *Division Mgr*
Bobby Bennett, *Engineer*
Rebekah Casey, *Sales Staff*
Austin Clifton, *Sales Staff*
Chad Huffman, *Research Analys*
EMP: 145
SALES (corp-wide): 468.4MM **Privately Held**
WEB: www.hapco.com
SIC: 3444 3354 3446 Sheet metalwork; aluminum extruded products; flagpoles, metal
HQ: Kearney-National Inc.
   565 5th Ave Fl 4
   New York NY 10017
   212 661-4600

(G-48)
KOMATSU MINING CORP
26161 Old Trail Rd (24210-7631)
PHONE...................................276 623-2000
EMP: 8 **Privately Held**
WEB: www.mining.komatsu
SIC: 3532 Mining machinery
HQ: Komatsu Mining Corp.
   100 E Wscnsin Ave Ste 278
   Milwaukee WI 53202
   414 319-8500

(G-49)
MARTIN LEE ENTERPRISES INC
20308 Alvarado Rd (24211-6337)
PHONE...................................276 623-0125
Robert Carlson, *President*
EMP: 1
SALES (est): 4.8K **Privately Held**
WEB: www.abingdonwinery.com
SIC: 2084 Wines, brandy & brandy spirits

(G-50)
MISTY MTN SPRING WTR CO LLC
26331 Hillman Hwy (24210)
P.O. Box 129 (24212-0129)
PHONE...................................276 623-5000
Steven Miller, *President*
Gene Belcher, *Principal*
EMP: 25
SALES (est): 3.7MM **Privately Held**
WEB: www.mistymountainwater.com
SIC: 2086 Mineral water, carbonated: packaged in cans, bottles, etc.

(G-51)
MONKS WELDING LLC
18373 Eden Ln (24211-7157)
PHONE...................................276 206-8051
Jeremy Allen Monk, *Principal*
EMP: 1
SALES (est): 35.9K **Privately Held**
SIC: 7692 Welding repair

(G-52)
OLIVE OILS ABINGDON ASSOC LLC (PA)
Also Called: Abingdon Olive Oil Company
152 E Main St Ste 2w (24210-2849)
PHONE...................................276 525-1524
K C St Louis, *Owner*
▲ **EMP:** 7
SALES (est): 13.7MM **Privately Held**
WEB: www.abingdonoliveoilco.com
SIC: 2079 Olive oil

(G-53)
PITTSTON COAL COMPANY (DH)
16016 Porterfield Hwy (24210-8470)
P.O. Box 1268 (24212-1268)
PHONE...................................276 739-3420
J B Hartough, *President*
David Fields, *President*
W B Perkins, *Principal*
Austin Reed, *Admin Sec*
EMP: 10
SQ FT: 12,000
SALES (est): 30.3MM
SALES (corp-wide): 3.6B **Publicly Held**
WEB: www.us.brinks.com
SIC: 1222 Bituminous coal-underground mining
HQ: Pittston Minerals Group Inc.
   1801 Bayberry Ct Fl 4
   Richmond VA 23226
   804 289-9600

(G-54)
POWER FUELS LLC
21360 Crosswinds Dr (24211-4200)
P.O. Box 1884 (24212-1884)
PHONE...................................276 676-2945
Walter Crickmer, *Administration*
EMP: 4
SALES (est): 599.6K **Privately Held**
WEB: www.power-fuels.com
SIC: 2869 Fuels

(G-55)
R & R DEVELOPERS INC
19444 Spoon Gap Rd (24211-6712)
PHONE...................................276 628-3846
Tony Roark, *President*
Nancy Roark, *Vice Pres*
EMP: 5
SALES (est): 434.8K **Privately Held**
SIC: 3241 Masonry cement

(G-56)
RANGE RESOURCES
408 W Main St (24210-2608)
PHONE...................................276 628-1568
Jerry Grantham, *President*
EMP: 2 **EST:** 2015
SALES (est): 164.3K **Privately Held**
SIC: 1382 Oil & gas exploration services

(G-57)
RAYMOND DAWSON
21306 Crosswinds Dr (24211-4200)
PHONE...................................276 676-9068
Raymond Dawson, *Principal*
EMP: 4
SALES (est): 390.8K **Privately Held**
SIC: 3317 Steel pipe & tubes

(G-58)
RINKER MATERIALS S CENTL INC
21339 Gravel Lake Rd (24210)
P.O. Box 1325 (24212-1325)
PHONE...................................276 628-9337
Gary Roark, *Superintendent*
EMP: 13 **Privately Held**
SIC: 3273 Ready-mixed concrete
HQ: Rinker Materials South Central, Inc.
   2209 W Blount Ave
   Knoxville TN 37920
   865 573-4501

(G-59)
SAM HURT
402 E Main St (24210-3408)
P.O. Box 1927 (24212-1927)
PHONE...................................276 623-1926
Sam Hurt, *Owner*
EMP: 1
SALES (est): 97K **Privately Held**
SIC: 1382 Oil & gas exploration services

(G-60)
SHELL
15785 Porterfield Hwy (24210-8467)
PHONE...................................276 676-0699
EMP: 2
SALES (est): 81.9K **Privately Held**
SIC: 1311 Crude petroleum & natural gas

(G-61)
SOUTHERN MACHINING INC
16331 Mountain Spring Rd (24210-8747)
PHONE...................................276 628-1072
Jeffrey S Ingle, *President*
Connie Ingle, *Treasurer*
EMP: 4
SALES (est): 449.7K **Privately Held**
SIC: 3599 Machine shop, jobbing & repair

(G-62)
STRONGWELL CORPORATION
26770 Newbanks Rd (24210-7501)
PHONE...................................276 623-0935
Spike Tsckle, *Manager*
James Taylor, *Supervisor*
EMP: 45
SALES (corp-wide): 81.5MM **Privately Held**
WEB: www.strongwell.com
SIC: 3089 Awnings, fiberglass & plastic combination
PA: Strongwell Corporation
   400 Commonwealth Ave
   Bristol VA 24201
   276 645-8000

(G-63)
SUNSHINE SEWING
793 W Main St Ste 5 (24210-2482)
PHONE...................................276 628-2478
Wayne Twiddy, *Owner*
Soni Twiddy, *Owner*
EMP: 2
SALES (est): 81K **Privately Held**
WEB: www.sunshinesewingva.com
SIC: 2395 7219 7389 Embroidery & art needlework; garment making, alteration & repair; embroidering of advertising on shirts, etc.

(G-64)
VIRGINIA GAS EXPLORATION CO
1096 Olleberry Dr Se Va (24210)
PHONE...................................276 676-2380
William Clear, *President*
Hill G Scott, *Vice Pres*
EMP: 25
SQ FT: 2,000
SALES (est): 1.2MM
SALES (corp-wide): 53.6MM **Privately Held**
WEB: www.unitedwayswva.org
SIC: 1382 4925 Oil & gas exploration services; gas production and/or distribution
HQ: Appalachian Production Services, Inc.
   2487 Rose Rdg
   Clintwood VA 24228

(G-65)
VIRGINIA HIGHLANDS MACHINING
24431 Regal Dr (24211-7439)
P.O. Box 695 (24212-0695)
PHONE...................................276 628-8555
Robert Lester, *President*
EMP: 10
SQ FT: 5,000
SALES (est): 1.1MM **Privately Held**
SIC: 3599 Machine shop, jobbing & repair

(G-66)
VIRGINIA LASER CORPORATION
18533 Pond Dr (24211-7609)
PHONE...................................276 628-9284
Thomas C Deskins, *President*
EMP: 6
SQ FT: 8,000
SALES (est): 961.1K **Privately Held**
SIC: 3599 Machine shop, jobbing & repair

(G-67)
VIRGINIA METALS INC
26336 Hillman Hwy (24210-7618)
P.O. Box 1217 (24212-1217)
PHONE...................................276 628-8151
Joe D Andis, *President*
Nanabee G Andis, *Vice Pres*
EMP: 15 **EST:** 1978
SQ FT: 18,000
SALES (est): 2.9MM **Privately Held**
SIC: 3443 3469 Fabricated plate work (boiler shop); machine parts, stamped or pressed metal

(G-68)
WHITE PINES ALPACAS LLC
27331 Denton Valley Rd (24211-6237)
PHONE...................................276 475-5831
EMP: 2
SALES (est): 110.4K **Privately Held**
SIC: 2231 Wool Broadwoven Fabric Mill

(G-69)
WOLF HILLS ENTERPRISES
21086 Green Spring Rd (24211-5952)
PHONE...................................276 628-8635
Edward Hibbitts, *President*
EMP: 3
SALES (est): 306.9K **Privately Held**
SIC: 2992 Lubricating oils & greases

(G-70)
WOLF HILLS FABRICATORS LLC
26161 Old Trail Rd Ste 2 (24210-7631)
PHONE...................................276 466-2743
Steve Thorogood, *President*
Scott Booth, *Sales Staff*
EMP: 12
SALES (est): 910.9K **Privately Held**
WEB: www.wolfhillsfab.com
SIC: 3536 3532 3441 Hoists, cranes & monorails; cranes, overhead traveling; mine cars, plows, loaders, feeders & similar equipment; building components, structural steel

Accomac
Accomack County

(G-71)
EASTERN SHORE VA MSTR GRDNERS
23203 Front St (23301-2178)
P.O. Box 60 (23301-0060)
PHONE...................................757 678-7688
Julie Rogers, *President*
EMP: 2 **EST:** 2018
SALES (est): 93.1K **Privately Held**
WEB: www.esvmg.com
SIC: 7372 Prepackaged software

(G-72)
K E MARINE
24263 Baylys Neck Rd (23301-1417)
P.O. Box 455 (23301-0455)
PHONE...................................757 787-1313
EMP: 4
SALES (est): 111.9K **Privately Held**
WEB: www.k-emarine.com
SIC: 7694 5551 Armature rewinding shops; marine supplies

Afton
Nelson County

(G-73)
AFTON MOUNTAIN VINEYARDS CORP
234 Vineyard Ln (22920-3702)
PHONE...................................540 456-8667
Thomas Corpora, *President*
Shinko Corpora, *Vice Pres*
EMP: 3
SALES (est): 270.9K **Privately Held**
WEB: www.aftonmountainvineyards.com
SIC: 2084 Wines

(G-74)
AGAINST GRAIN WOODWORKING INC
101 Woodpecker Way (22920-2655)
PHONE..................434 760-2055
Chad Widdifield, *Administration*
EMP: 2
SALES (est): 166.1K **Privately Held**
SIC: 2431 Millwork

(G-75)
BLUE MOUNTAIN BREWERY INC
9519 Critzers Shop Rd (22920-2415)
PHONE..................540 456-8020
Taylor S Smack, *President*
Josh Sprouse, *General Mgr*
Tambra Miller, *Business Mgr*
Mandi L Smack, *Vice Pres*
Peter Ramsey, *Manager*
EMP: 33
SALES (est): 5.9MM **Privately Held**
WEB: www.bluemountainbrewery.com
SIC: 2082 Beer (alcoholic beverage)

(G-76)
CARDINAL POINT VINEYARD WINERY
9423 Batesville Rd (22920-2661)
PHONE..................540 456-8400
Sarah Gorman, *Director*
EMP: 4
SALES (est): 357.3K **Privately Held**
WEB: www.cardinalpointwinery.com
SIC: 2084 5921 Wines; wine

(G-77)
COLE SOFTWARE LLC
736 Fox Hollow Rd (22920-7500)
PHONE..................540 456-8210
David B Cole, *Mng Member*
EMP: 6
SALES (est): 483.3K **Privately Held**
WEB: www.colesoft.com
SIC: 7372 7371 Prepackaged software; custom computer programming services

(G-78)
CONSCIOUS CULTURES LLC
Also Called: Barefoot Bucha
615 Pauls Creek Rd (22920-3078)
PHONE..................434 227-9297
Kate Zuckerman,
Ethan Zuckerman,
EMP: 11
SALES (est): 962.2K **Privately Held**
WEB: www.blueridgebucha.com
SIC: 2086 Carbonated beverages, nonalcoholic: bottled & canned

(G-79)
ENNIS MOUNTAIN WOODS INC
292 Woodpecker Way (22920-2645)
PHONE..................540 471-9171
Donald Bailey, *President*
EMP: 1
SALES (est): 78K **Privately Held**
WEB: www.ennismountain.com
SIC: 2499 5712 Decorative wood & woodwork; furniture stores

(G-80)
EQUUS THERAPEUTICS INC
1874 Castle Rock Rd (22920-1915)
PHONE..................540 456-6767
Susanne C Merrill, *President*
EMP: 1
SALES (est): 119.4K **Privately Held**
WEB: www.equustherapeutics.com
SIC: 3199 Boots, horse

(G-81)
FLYING FOX VINEYARD LC
845 Elk Mountain Rd (22920-2518)
PHONE..................434 361-1692
C Hinnant, *Principal*
EMP: 3
SALES (est): 218.3K **Privately Held**
WEB: www.flyingfoxvineyard.com
SIC: 2084 Wines

(G-82)
GOODWIN CREEK FARM & BAKERY
151 Goodwin Creek Trl (22920-2851)
PHONE..................434 260-1135
John Hellerman, *Principal*
Nancy Hellerman, *Principal*
EMP: 2
SALES (est): 140K **Privately Held**
WEB: www.aftonvirginia.com
SIC: 2051 Bakery: wholesale or wholesale/retail combined

(G-83)
GOTHAM GRAPHIX LLC
8125 Batesville Rd (22920-1739)
PHONE..................540 456-6600
EMP: 2
SALES (est): 90.3K **Privately Held**
WEB: www.gothamgraphix.com
SIC: 2759 Screen printing

(G-84)
HAMBSCH FAMILY VINEYARD LLC
2559 Craigs Store Rd (22920-2015)
PHONE..................434 996-1987
Karl Hambsch, *Principal*
EMP: 1
SALES (est): 56K **Privately Held**
SIC: 2084 Wines

(G-85)
JB PINKER INC
179 Azalea Dr (22920-2516)
PHONE..................540 943-2760
Jonathan Eccard, *President*
EMP: 3
SALES (est): 263.4K **Privately Held**
SIC: 2721 Magazines: publishing & printing

(G-86)
R DAVID ROSSON
Also Called: R David Rosson Logging
8720 Rockfish Gap Tpke (22920-1606)
PHONE..................540 456-8108
R David Rosson, *Owner*
EMP: 2 EST: 1968
SALES (est): 170.5K **Privately Held**
SIC: 2411 2421 Timber, cut at logging camp; sawmills & planing mills, general

(G-87)
ROBERT DAVID ROSSON
8720 Rockfish Gap Tpke (22920-1606)
PHONE..................540 456-6173
Robert Rosson, *Owner*
EMP: 3
SALES (est): 258.5K **Privately Held**
SIC: 2411 Logging

(G-88)
ROCKFISH BAKING COMPANY LLC
887 Rockfish Orchard Dr (22920-3194)
PHONE..................703 314-7944
Coral Allen Kemp, *Administration*
EMP: 4
SALES (est): 255.2K **Privately Held**
SIC: 2051 Bread, cake & related products

(G-89)
SILVERBACK SPIRITS LLC
Also Called: Silverback Distillery
9520 Rockfish Valley Hwy (22920-3113)
PHONE..................540 456-7070
Christine Riggleman, *CEO*
Denver Riggleman, *Principal*
▲ EMP: 5
SALES (est): 650.1K **Privately Held**
WEB: www.sbdistillery.com
SIC: 2085 Neutral spirits, except fruit

(G-90)
STELLING BANJO WORKS LTD
7258 Banjo Ln (22920-2153)
PHONE..................434 295-1917
Geoff Stelling, *President*
Sherry Stelling, *Treasurer*
EMP: 6
SQ FT: 2,000

SALES (est): 367K **Privately Held**
WEB: www.stellingbanjo.com
SIC: 3931 5736 5099 Banjos & parts; musical instrument stores; musical instruments

(G-91)
TRAILER BUFF INC
732 Rockfish School Ln (22920-3003)
P.O. Box 697, Nellysford (22958-0697)
PHONE..................434 361-2500
David Makel, *President*
EMP: 5
SALES (est): 513.7K **Privately Held**
SIC: 3715 Truck trailers

(G-92)
TRANSFOAM LLC
8200 Dick Woods Rd (22920-1638)
PHONE..................631 747-0255
Alec Brewer, *CEO*
EMP: 5
SALES (est): 229.7K **Privately Held**
SIC: 2821 Thermosetting materials

(G-93)
TURK MOUNTAIN VINEYARDS
8982 Dick Woods Rd (22920-1541)
PHONE..................540 456-8252
EMP: 2
SALES (est): 118.3K **Privately Held**
WEB: www.turkmountainvineyards.com
SIC: 2084 Wines

(G-94)
VERITAS WORKS LLC
151 Veritas Ln (22920-2342)
PHONE..................540 456-8000
George Hodson, *General Mgr*
Andrew Hodson, *Principal*
Molly O'Halloran, *Business Mgr*
Bill Tonkins, *Manager*
EMP: 14 EST: 2012
SALES (est): 1.5MM **Privately Held**
WEB: www.veritaswines.com
SIC: 2084 Wines

(G-95)
WALLACE PRECISION TOOLING
9734 Batesville Rd (22920-2623)
PHONE..................540 456-6437
Darrell Wallace, *Owner*
Blenda Wallace, *Co-Owner*
EMP: 5
SQ FT: 4,500
SALES (est): 500K **Privately Held**
SIC: 3544 Forms (molds), for foundry & plastics working machinery; special dies & tools

(G-96)
WOOD PROVISION
2488 Blackberry Rd (22920-1931)
PHONE..................540 456-8522
Tim Wright, *Principal*
EMP: 2
SALES (est): 100K **Privately Held**
SIC: 2434 Wood kitchen cabinets

(G-97)
ZENITH AEROTECH INC
10517 Critzers Shop Rd (22920-2432)
PHONE..................434 202-7790
Kutlay Kaya, *CEO*
EMP: 5
SALES (est): 500K **Privately Held**
SIC: 3721 Research & development on aircraft by the manufacturer

Alberta
Brunswick County

(G-98)
GENERAL IRON AND STEEL CO INC
400 Virginia Ave (23821)
P.O. Box 26 (23821-0026)
PHONE..................434 676-3975
William C Bennett, *President*
Joyce Bennett, *Treasurer*
EMP: 10 EST: 1968

SALES (est): 1.2MM **Privately Held**
WEB: www.playitagainrecords.com
SIC: 3312 Blast furnaces & steel mills

(G-99)
TREESCAPES INC
597 Second Ave (23821-2052)
P.O. Box 10, Blackstone (23824-0010)
PHONE..................434 294-0865
Bernadette Gunn,
EMP: 2
SALES (est): 199.4K **Privately Held**
WEB: www.treescapesva.com
SIC: 3531 7389 Plows: construction, excavating & grading; business services

Aldie
Loudoun County

(G-100)
ALPINE METHOD TECHNOLOGIES LLC
Also Called: Alpine Mthod Tchnlges/ Alpine
41144 Hickory Hedge Pl (20105-3147)
PHONE..................716 310-4935
Michael Szalkowski, *Mng Member*
EMP: 3
SALES (est): 200K **Privately Held**
SIC: 7372 Operating systems computer software

(G-101)
BEE SYSTEMS LLC
39367 Saddleridge Ln (20105-2853)
PHONE..................760 484-6194
Adam McBride, *Principal*
EMP: 12
SALES (est): 487.7K **Privately Held**
SIC: 3721 Aircraft

(G-102)
BOREDACIOUS INC
24660 James Monroe Hwy (20105-2740)
PHONE..................703 327-5490
EMP: 3
SALES (est): 260K **Privately Held**
SIC: 1381 Oil/Gas Well Drilling

(G-103)
C CS LINEN PLUS
41568 Tring Ln (20105-3088)
PHONE..................703 665-0059
Stella Timioh, *Owner*
EMP: 1
SALES (est): 80.2K **Privately Held**
WEB: www.cclinenplus.com
SIC: 2392 Chair covers & pads: made from purchased materials

(G-104)
COGNITION POINT INC
25492 Tomey Ct (20105-3047)
PHONE..................703 402-8945
Jason Nuhfer, *President*
EMP: 2
SALES (est): 73.9K **Privately Held**
SIC: 7372 7373 7371 8748 Application computer software; systems software development services; computer software development; systems engineering consultant, ex. computer or professional

(G-105)
CUSTOMTAYLOR33
26077 Blackberry Knoll Ct (20105-5721)
PHONE..................703 785-7919
EMP: 2
SALES (est): 162.2K **Privately Held**
WEB: www.customtaylor33.com
SIC: 3993 Signs & advertising specialties

(G-106)
GRAYMAN USA LLC
40487 Aspen Highlands Ct (20105-2282)
PHONE..................703 598-6934
Aimee Vinyard,
EMP: 2
SALES (est): 97.7K **Privately Held**
WEB: www.graymanusa.com
SIC: 3484 Guns (firearms) or gun parts, 30 mm. & below

(G-107)
HERALD SCHLRLY OPEN ACCESS LLC
41891 Fraser Downs Ter (20105-5875)
PHONE..............................202 412-2272
Brahma Chirra, *Administration*
EMP: 4
SALES (est): 143.5K **Privately Held**
WEB: www.heraldopenaccess.us
SIC: 2711 Newspapers, publishing & printing

(G-108)
KM DATA STRATEGISTS LLC
24310 Wrens Landing Ct (20105-5939)
PHONE..............................703 689-1087
Anand Thiagarajan, *Principal*
EMP: 1
SALES (est): 41.9K **Privately Held**
WEB: www.kmdatastrategists.com
SIC: 7372 7371 8243 Application computer software; computer software development; software training, computer

(G-109)
NEXT SCREEN MEDIA
42053 Porch Light Dr (20105-2660)
PHONE..............................571 295-6398
Sandeep Mittal, *CEO*
EMP: 1 EST: 2013
SALES (est): 92.9K **Privately Held**
WEB: www.nextscreenmedia.com
SIC: 7372 7371 Application computer software; business oriented computer software; publishers' computer software; custom computer programming services

(G-110)
QUATTRO GOOMBAS WINERY
22860 James Monroe Hwy (20105-1916)
PHONE..............................703 327-6052
David Gaetani, *Owner*
EMP: 2
SALES (est): 203.4K **Privately Held**
WEB: www.quattrogoombas.com
SIC: 2084 Wines

(G-111)
SEA PUBLISHING LLC
41663 Mcmonagle Sq (20105-6011)
PHONE..............................832 744-7049
Eric Hoeny,
EMP: 1 EST: 2017
SALES (est): 37.5K **Privately Held**
SIC: 2741 Miscellaneous publishing

(G-112)
SIGNATURE SERIES - USA LLC
22077 Oatlands Rd (20105-1713)
PHONE..............................703 201-2543
Gib Godwin, *Mng Member*
EMP: 2
SALES (est): 87.2K **Privately Held**
SIC: 3711 Automobile assembly, including specialty automobiles

(G-113)
THESIA INC
42195 Highbank Pl (20105-5726)
PHONE..............................703 726-8845
Piyush Thesia, *President*
EMP: 3
SALES (est): 500K **Privately Held**
SIC: 3911 7631 Jewelry, precious metal; diamond setter

Alexandria
Alexandria City County

(G-114)
A K METAL FABRICATORS INC
4401 Wheeler Ave (22304-6434)
PHONE..............................703 823-1661
Gary Lancaster, *President*
Andrew Lancaster, *VP Opers*
EMP: 16
SALES (est): 4.1MM **Privately Held**
WEB: www.akmetalfab.com
SIC: 3469 Stamping metal for the trade

(G-115)
A Z PRINTING AND DUP CORP (PA)
421 Clifford Ave (22305-2710)
PHONE..............................703 549-0949
Azfar Aziz, *President*
EMP: 2
SQ FT: 1,500
SALES (est): 500K **Privately Held**
WEB: www.azprintingandduplicating.com
SIC: 2759 7338 Commercial printing; secretarial & court reporting

(G-116)
A Z PRINTING AND DUP CORP
2000a Jffrson Davis Hwy F (22301)
PHONE..............................703 549-0949
Azfar Aziz, *Branch Mgr*
EMP: 1
SALES (corp-wide): 500K **Privately Held**
WEB: www.azprintingandduplicating.com
SIC: 2752 Commercial printing, offset
PA: A Z Printing And Duplicating Corporation
421 Clifford Ave
Alexandria VA 22305
703 549-0949

(G-117)
ACCURACY PRESS INSTITUTE
5270 Duke St Apt 328 (22304-2957)
PHONE..............................804 869-8577
Mohamad Zaid Mastou, *Principal*
EMP: 1
SALES (est): 41.3K **Privately Held**
SIC: 2741 Miscellaneous publishing

(G-118)
ADANI SYSTEMS INC (PA)
901 N Pitt St Ste 325 (22314-1549)
P.O. Box 2565, Seabrook NH (03874-2565)
PHONE..............................703 528-0035
Vladimir Linev, *CEO*
Lineva Elena, *President*
Elena Linev, *President*
Vladimir Klokov, *Vice Pres*
Mahesh Mistry, *Manager*
EMP: 2
SALES (est): 639.1K **Privately Held**
WEB: www.adanisystems.us
SIC: 3844 5047 X-ray apparatus & tubes; X-ray film & supplies

(G-119)
ADVANTAGE SYSTEMS
3917 Wheeler Ave (22304-6410)
PHONE..............................703 370-4500
EMP: 2 EST: 2019
SALES (est): 79.9K **Privately Held**
WEB: www.americleansouthflorida.com
SIC: 3589 Service industry machinery

(G-120)
ADVANTECH INC
3213 Duke St (22314-4533)
PHONE..............................703 402-0590
EMP: 2
SALES (est): 105.5K **Privately Held**
SIC: 3663 Radio & TV communications equipment

(G-121)
AERO INTERNATIONAL LLC (HQ)
641 S Washington St (22314-4109)
PHONE..............................571 203-8360
Timothy Gale, *CEO*
Timothy A Delany, *President*
EMP: 2
SQ FT: 490
SALES (est): 8.6MM **Privately Held**
WEB: www.aerointl.com
SIC: 3728 5065 5088 Aircraft parts & equipment; electronic parts; aircraft & space vehicle supplies & parts

(G-122)
AETHER PRESS LLC
3201 Landover St Apt 803 (22305-1919)
PHONE..............................703 409-5684
Joseph D'Urso, *Principal*
EMP: 2
SALES (est): 50K **Privately Held**
SIC: 2741 Miscellaneous publishing

(G-123)
AH LOVE OIL AND VINEGAR LLC
601 S View Ter (22314-4921)
PHONE..............................703 966-0668
Cary Kelly, *Branch Mgr*
EMP: 1
SALES (corp-wide): 446K **Privately Held**
WEB: www.cookeryshops.com
SIC: 2099 Vinegar
PA: Ah Love Oil And Vinegar, Llc
4017b Campbell Ave
Arlington VA 22206
703 820-2210

(G-124)
ALCHEMICAL HYDROGEN LLC
1776 Potomac Greens Dr (22314-6231)
PHONE..............................703 399-9235
Michael Antario, *Mng Member*
Anthony G Fabrizio,
EMP: 2
SALES (est): 74.4K **Privately Held**
SIC: 2865 Chemical indicators

(G-125)
ALEXANDRIA FUSION
1900 Duke St (22314-3447)
PHONE..............................703 566-3055
EMP: 3
SALES (est): 99K **Privately Held**
WEB: www.alexandriagazette.com
SIC: 2711 Newspapers, publishing & printing

(G-126)
ALEXANDRIA GAZETTE PACKET
1606 King St (22314-2719)
PHONE..............................703 821-5050
Jerry Vernon, *Publisher*
EMP: 4
SALES (est): 138.1K **Privately Held**
WEB: www.alexandriagazette.com
SIC: 2711 Newspapers, publishing & printing

(G-127)
ALEXANDRIA TIMES
300 S Washington St (22314-5403)
PHONE..............................703 739-0001
EMP: 3
SALES (est): 118.6K **Privately Held**
WEB: www.alextimes.com
SIC: 2711 Newspapers, publishing & printing

(G-128)
ALLERGOPHARMA USA INC
1940 Duke St Ste 200 (22314-3452)
PHONE..............................919 749-6213
David McCullough, *President*
EMP: 1
SALES (corp-wide): 17.8B **Privately Held**
SIC: 2834 Pharmaceutical preparations
PA: Merck Kg Auf Aktien
Frankfurter Str. 250
Darmstadt 64293
615 172-0

(G-129)
ALLIANCE OFFICE FURNITURE CO
307 Yoakum Pkwy Apt 922 (22304-4025)
EMP: 2
SALES (est): 294.6K **Privately Held**
SIC: 2521 Office Furniture Deal

(G-130)
ALS USED TIRES & RIMS
1108 Queen St (22314-2451)
PHONE..............................703 548-3000
Jules Mahi, *Principal*
EMP: 2
SALES (est): 150K **Privately Held**
WEB: www.alstires.com
SIC: 3011 5531 Tire & inner tube materials & related products; automotive tires

(G-131)
AMERICAN LIGHT WORKS LLC
907 W Glebe Rd (22305-1461)
PHONE..............................804 332-3229
EMP: 3

SALES (est): 175.6K **Privately Held**
SIC: 3993 Signs & advertising specialties

(G-132)
AMERICAN SOC FOR HORT SCIENCE
Also Called: Ashs
1018 Duke St (22314-3512)
PHONE..............................703 836-4606
Neal De Vos, *Editor*
Michael Neff, *Director*
EMP: 12 EST: 1903
SALES: 1.8MM **Privately Held**
WEB: www.ashs.org
SIC: 2731 8621 Books: publishing only; professional membership organizations

(G-133)
AMERICAN SPECTATOR
122 S Royal St (22314-3328)
PHONE..............................703 807-2011
Alfred S Regnery, *President*
Amy Mitchell, *Managing Dir*
EMP: 9
SQ FT: 1,400
SALES: 1.5MM **Privately Held**
WEB: www.spectator.org
SIC: 2721 Magazines: publishing only, not printed on site

(G-134)
ANALYSTSOFT INC
901 N Pitt St Ste 325 (22314-1549)
PHONE..............................844 782-8758
Oleksii Simachov, *CEO*
EMP: 3
SALES (est): 163.4K **Privately Held**
SIC: 7372 Publishers' computer software

(G-135)
ANLAC LLC
Also Called: Alexandria Armature Works
3025 Colvin St (22314-4501)
PHONE..............................703 370-3500
Quan Hoang, *CEO*
Yvonne Boysen, *Opers Mgr*
Van-Anh Pham, *Mng Member*
EMP: 6
SQ FT: 20,000
SALES (est): 822K **Privately Held**
WEB: www.aawva.com
SIC: 7694 Electric motor repair

(G-136)
ANNEKER CORP
514 E Glendale Ave (22301-1602)
PHONE..............................202 630-3007
Alexander L Anneker, *President*
Alexander Anneker, *President*
Larry Chipps, *Vice Pres*
EMP: 12
SALES (est): 857.3K **Privately Held**
SIC: 2721 Magazines: publishing & printing

(G-137)
ANTENSAN USA INC
637 S Washington St (22314-4109)
PHONE..............................703 836-0300
Tim Gale, *CEO*
Doug Henry, *President*
EMP: 2
SALES (est): 295K **Privately Held**
SIC: 3663 Radio & TV communications equipment
PA: Ams Group, Inc.
659 S Washington St
Alexandria VA 22314

(G-138)
APOTHECARY SPICES
1200 N Quaker Ln (22302-3004)
PHONE..............................703 868-2333
Edward Gonzalez, *Owner*
EMP: 1
SALES (est): 50K **Privately Held**
WEB: www.apothecaryspices.com
SIC: 2099 Seasonings & spices

(G-139)
ARC DOCUMENT SOLUTIONS INC
300 N Henry St (22314-2439)
PHONE..............................703 518-8890
Eric Fisher, *Branch Mgr*
EMP: 7

SALES (corp-wide): 382.4MM **Publicly Held**
WEB: www.e-arc.com
SIC: 2759 Commercial printing
PA: Arc Document Solutions, Inc.
　　12657 Alcosta Blvd # 200
　　San Ramon CA 94583
　　925 949-5100

(G-140)
ARGENT LINE LLC
211 N Union St (22314-2657)
PHONE.................................703 519-1209
George Zoulias,
EMP: 2 EST: 2014
SALES (est): 62K **Privately Held**
SIC: 7372 Business oriented computer software

(G-141)
ARTISAN II INC
4311 Wheeler Ave (22304-6416)
PHONE.................................703 823-4636
Kathy Harkey, *Principal*
James Harkey, *Principal*
Bo Davis, *Plant Mgr*
Meghan Harkey, *Marketing Staff*
Adriana Macgregor, *Software Dev*
EMP: 8
SALES (est): 1MM **Privately Held**
WEB: www.artisan2inc.com
SIC: 2759 Invitation & stationery printing & engraving

(G-142)
ASAP PRINTING & MAILING CO
Also Called: ASAP Printing & Graphics
2805 Mount Vernon Ave (22301-1172)
PHONE.................................703 836-2288
Dean Grande, *CEO*
Joe Brocato, *President*
Curtis Stephanie, *Department Mgr*
EMP: 8 EST: 1980
SQ FT: 3,000
SALES (est): 950K **Privately Held**
WEB: www.asapfast.com
SIC: 2752 7331 Commercial printing, offset; mailing service

(G-143)
AUDIO-VISUALS ACTIONS INC
3919 Wheeler Ave (22304-6410)
PHONE.................................703 751-1010
Mohamed Elhajjam, *President*
Amine Lounes, *Vice Pres*
EMP: 4
SQ FT: 3,700
SALES (est): 768.7K **Privately Held**
WEB: www.avactions.com
SIC: 3663 7812 7359 3648 Television broadcasting & communications equipment; video production; audio-visual equipment & supply rental; sound & lighting equipment rental; stage lighting equipment; computer rental & leasing

(G-144)
BANANA BANNER INC
Also Called: Banana Banner Signs
3148 Duke St (22314-4532)
PHONE.................................703 823-5933
Brian R Treece, *President*
Brian Treece, *General Mgr*
Randy Brown, *Opers Staff*
Stacy Howard, *Office Mgr*
Dan M Treece, *Admin Sec*
EMP: 12
SALES (est): 1.6MM **Privately Held**
WEB: www.bananabanner.com
SIC: 3993 2399 Signs & advertising specialties; banners, made from fabric

(G-145)
BARRINGTON WORLDWIDE LLC
526 King St Ste 211 (22314-3143)
P.O. Box 320123 (22320-4123)
PHONE.................................202 255-4611
EMP: 3
SALES (est): 98.1K **Privately Held**
WEB: www.mullings.com
SIC: 2711 Newspapers, publishing & printing

(G-146)
BEAUTYMANIA
5801 Duke St (22304-3208)
PHONE.................................703 300-9042
Abdulaye Sene, *Bd of Directors*
EMP: 2
SALES (est): 110.8K **Privately Held**
SIC: 2844 Perfumes & colognes

(G-147)
BINDERY PLUS
3221 Colvin St (22314-4504)
PHONE.................................703 357-5002
EMP: 1
SALES (est): 53.1K **Privately Held**
SIC: 2789 Bookbinding & related work

(G-148)
BLINKCLOUD LLC
65 N Wash St Ste 425 (22314)
PHONE.................................484 429-3340
Jonathan Luzader, *Mng Member*
EMP: 1
SALES (est): 200K **Privately Held**
WEB: www.blink.cloud
SIC: 2741 7379 ; computer related consulting services

(G-149)
BLUE SKYS WOODSHOP
1502 Mount Vernon Ave (22301-1718)
PHONE.................................703 567-6220
EMP: 1
SALES (est): 41.5K **Privately Held**
SIC: 2499 Laundry products, wood

(G-150)
BLUF MILITARY BENEFITS
3023 King St (22302-3514)
PHONE.................................402 315-7831
Jefferson D Mitchell, *CEO*
Morgan Mitchell, *Admin Sec*
EMP: 1
SALES (est): 37.5K **Privately Held**
SIC: 2741 Miscellaneous publishing

(G-151)
BON VIVANT COMPANY LLC
107 S West St (22314-2824)
PHONE.................................703 862-5038
Jawad Laouaouda, *Principal*
EMP: 3 EST: 2011
SALES (est): 137.3K **Privately Held**
SIC: 2099 Food preparations

(G-152)
BRINKMANN PUBLISHING LLC
5233 Bessley Pl (22304-8647)
PHONE.................................703 461-6991
Bruce Greenberg, *Principal*
EMP: 2
SALES (est): 112.7K **Privately Held**
WEB: www.sykesvillehistory.us
SIC: 2741 Miscellaneous publishing

(G-153)
BROKEN COLUMN PRESS LLC
244 S Reynolds St Apt 409 (22304-4467)
PHONE.................................703 338-0267
Carl Weaver,
EMP: 1
SALES (est): 35.9K **Privately Held**
WEB: www.brokencolumnpress.com
SIC: 2731 Book publishing

(G-154)
BROOK VANCE PUBLISHING LLC
127 S Fairfax St Ste 326 (22314-3301)
PHONE.................................703 660-1214
James Green, *Mng Member*
EMP: 2
SALES (est): 25K **Privately Held**
SIC: 2741 Technical manuals: publishing only, not printed on site

(G-155)
BUCKEYES MEADOW LLC
424 N West St (22314-2123)
PHONE.................................703 535-6868
EMP: 2
SALES: 50K **Privately Held**
SIC: 3695 Consulting It Video Productions

(G-156)
BUSINESS CHECKS OF AMERICA
3221 Colvin St (22314-4504)
PHONE.................................703 823-1008
Sandy Horner, *CEO*
EMP: 1
SALES (est): 70.5K **Privately Held**
WEB: www.bcachecks.com
SIC: 2782 Checkbooks

(G-157)
C L TOWING
624 Notabene Dr (22305-1541)
PHONE.................................703 625-7126
Bruce Blum, *Principal*
EMP: 2
SALES (est): 137K **Privately Held**
SIC: 3499 Ironing boards, metal

(G-158)
C2C SMART COMPLIANCE LLC
110 N Royal St Ste 525 (22314-3279)
P.O. Box 2537, Vienna (22183-2537)
PHONE.................................703 872-7340
Steve Crutchley, *CEO*
Edward Alexander,
EMP: 11
SALES (est): 767.1K **Privately Held**
WEB: www.c2csmartcompliance.com
SIC: 7372 8748 Business oriented computer software; business consulting

(G-159)
CAPITOL NET
4 Herbert St (22305-2628)
P.O. Box 25706 (22313-5706)
PHONE.................................703 739-3790
Judy Schneider, *Vice Pres*
EMP: 1
SALES (est): 37.5K **Privately Held**
WEB: www.thecapitol.net
SIC: 2741 Miscellaneous publishing

(G-160)
CARLA BEDARD
5273 Colonel Johnson Ln (22304-8672)
PHONE.................................212 773-1851
Carla Bedard, *Executive*
EMP: 2
SALES (est): 62.1K **Privately Held**
SIC: 7372 Prepackaged software

(G-161)
CAROTANK ROAD LLC
1800 Diagonal Rd Ste 600 (22314-2840)
PHONE.................................703 951-7790
James Curtin, *Principal*
EMP: 2
SALES (est): 106.8K **Privately Held**
WEB: www.carotankroad.com
SIC: 3484 7389 8711 Guns (firearms) or gun parts, 30 mm. & below; ; mechanical engineering

(G-162)
CENTENNIAL BOOKS
1591 Chapel Hill Dr (22304-1615)
PHONE.................................703 751-6162
EMP: 1
SALES (est): 46K **Privately Held**
SIC: 2731 Books-Publishing/Printing

(G-163)
CENTURY LIGHTING SOLUTIONS LLC
311 N Washington St 3l (22314-2523)
PHONE.................................202 281-8393
William Roulidis,
EMP: 3
SALES (est): 192.6K **Privately Held**
WEB: www.centurylightingsolutions.com
SIC: 3646 Commercial indusl & institutional electric lighting fixtures

(G-164)
CFS-KBR MRNAS SUPPORT SVCS LLC
1725 Duke St Ste 400 (22314-3470)
PHONE.................................202 261-1900
EMP: 50

SALES (est): 2.3MM **Privately Held**
SIC: 3731 4492 7538 8744 Shipbuilding/Repairing Towing/Tugboat Service General Auto Repair Facilities Support Svcs

(G-165)
CIRCLE OF HOPE - ASCA FNDATION
1101 King St Ste 625 (22314-2957)
PHONE.................................800 306-4722
Kwok Sze Wong, *Principal*
EMP: 3
SALES (est): 137.6K **Privately Held**
SIC: 2741 Miscellaneous publishing

(G-166)
COCA COLA ENTERPRISES
Also Called: Coca-Cola
5401 Seminary Rd (22311-1213)
PHONE.................................703 578-6447
Fax: 703 575-4800
EMP: 11
SALES (est): 1MM **Privately Held**
SIC: 2086 Carb Sft Drnkbtlcn

(G-167)
COCA-COLA BOTTLING
5349 Seminary Rd (22311)
PHONE.................................800 241-2653
EMP: 2
SALES (est): 62.3K **Privately Held**
SIC: 2086 Bottled & canned soft drinks

(G-168)
COCA-COLA CONSOLIDATED INC
5401 Seminary Rd (22311-1213)
PHONE.................................703 578-6759
Johnny Palmer, *Branch Mgr*
EMP: 45
SQ FT: 150,000
SALES (corp-wide): 4.8B **Publicly Held**
WEB: www.cokeconsolidated.com
SIC: 2086 Bottled & canned soft drinks
PA: Coca-Cola Consolidated, Inc.
　　4100 Coca Cola Plz # 100
　　Charlotte NC 28211
　　704 557-4400

(G-169)
CODEWORX LC
2256 N Beauregard St # 1 (22311-2256)
PHONE.................................571 306-3859
Rachel Moore,
EMP: 1
SALES (est): 59.1K **Privately Held**
SIC: 7372 7389 Educational computer software;

(G-170)
COMMSCOPE TECHNOLOGIES LLC
422 N Alfred St (22314-2225)
PHONE.................................703 548-6777
Ron Campbell, *Branch Mgr*
EMP: 119 **Publicly Held**
SIC: 3663 Radio & TV communications equipment
HQ: Commscope Technologies Llc
　　4 Westbrook Corporate Ctr
　　Westchester IL 60154
　　708 236-6600

(G-171)
COMPOSITION SYSTEMS INC
Also Called: Csi
840 S Pickett St (22304-4606)
PHONE.................................703 205-0000
Phillip James Banks, *President*
Shawn Haley, *Exec VP*
Rafael Ley, *Vice Pres*
Joshua Davis, *Marketing Staff*
Phil Banks, *Technology*
▲ EMP: 62 EST: 1976
SQ FT: 6,000
SALES (est): 10.5MM **Privately Held**
WEB: www.csi2.com
SIC: 2752 Commercial printing, offset

▲ = Import ▼=Export
◆ =Import/Export

(G-172)
CONNECTION NEWSPAPERS LLC
1606 King St (22314-2719)
P.O. Box 221374, Chantilly (20153-1374)
PHONE.....................................703 821-5050
EMP: 14
SALES (est): 818.1K **Privately Held**
SIC: 2711 Newspapers-Publishing/Printing

(G-173)
CONNECTION PUBLISHING INC
Also Called: Connection Newspapers
1606 King St (22314-2719)
P.O. Box 221374, Chantilly (20153-1374)
PHONE.....................................703 821-5050
Peter C Labovitz, *President*
Mary Kimm, *Publisher*
Jerry Vernon, *Exec VP*
Debbie Funk, *Sales Staff*
Julie Ferrill, *Advt Staff*
EMP: 60
SALES (est): 2.9MM **Privately Held**
WEB: www.connectionnewspapers.com
SIC: 2711 Newspapers, publishing & printing

(G-174)
COOL COMFORT BY CARSON LLC
5006 Barbour Dr Ste B (22304-7709)
PHONE.....................................330 348-3149
Alison Bibb-Carson, *Principal*
EMP: 3
SQ FT: 2,000
SALES (est): 113.3K **Privately Held**
WEB: www.coolactionsuit.com
SIC: 2326 2311 Work uniforms; tailored suits & formal jackets; firemen's uniforms: made from purchased materials; military uniforms, men's & youths': purchased materials; policemen's uniforms: made from purchased materials

(G-175)
CPA GLOBAL NORTH AMERICA LLC (DH)
2318 Mill Rd Fl 12 (22314-6834)
PHONE.....................................703 739-2234
Jeffrey Maddox, *CEO*
Peter Sewell, *CEO*
McKenna Burns, *Business Mgr*
Matthew Coyle, *Business Mgr*
Aimee Gleyo, *Business Mgr*
EMP: 61
SALES (est): 16.6MM **Publicly Held**
SIC: 7372 Prepackaged software
HQ: Computer Patent Annuities International Limited
Suite 100
London EC4Y
207 549-0679

(G-176)
CPA GLOBAL SERVICES US INC
2318 Mill Rd Fl 12 (22314-6834)
PHONE.....................................703 739-2234
Timothy Philip Griffiths, *President*
Matthew Joyce, *Sales Staff*
Norman Peterson, *Sr Project Mgr*
EMP: 17 EST: 2008
SALES (est): 2MM **Publicly Held**
WEB: www.cpaglobal.com
SIC: 7372 Prepackaged software
HQ: Cpa Global Limited
Liberation House
Jersey JE1 1
153 488-8711

(G-177)
CROSSBOW STRATEGIES INC
1 W Alexandria Ave (22301-2014)
PHONE.....................................703 864-7576
Mark Frieden, *Principal*
EMP: 1
SALES (est): 51.7K **Privately Held**
WEB: www.crossbowstrategies.com
SIC: 3949 Crossbows

(G-178)
CUSTOM INK
419 King St (22314-3101)
PHONE.....................................571 364-7944
EMP: 2

SALES (est): 67K **Privately Held**
SIC: 2321 Men's & boys' furnishings

(G-179)
CYNOSURE SERVICES INC
1615 Duke St (22314-3406)
PHONE.....................................410 209-0796
Rovaida J Saleh, *Ch of Bd*
EMP: 7
SQ FT: 1,500
SALES (est): 280.7K **Privately Held**
SIC: 7372 Business oriented computer software

(G-180)
CYNTHIA CORIOPOLI DESIGN
Also Called: Corio-Poli, Cynthia
105 N Union St (22314-3217)
PHONE.....................................703 548-2086
Cynthia Coriopoli, *Owner*
EMP: 1
SALES (est): 61.5K **Privately Held**
SIC: 3911 Jewelry, precious metal

(G-181)
DANAHER FAMILY LLC
503 N Quaker Ln (22304-1826)
PHONE.....................................703 751-9712
Thomas P Danaher, *Administration*
EMP: 3
SALES (est): 172.5K **Privately Held**
SIC: 3823 Industrial instrmnts msrmnt display/control process variable

(G-182)
DARK3 INC (PA)
Also Called: Dark Cubed
202 Birch St (22305-1837)
PHONE.....................................703 398-1101
Vince Crisler, *CEO*
Peter Clay, *COO*
Theresa Payton,
EMP: 4 EST: 2015
SALES (est): 849.3K **Privately Held**
SIC: 3571 Electronic computers

(G-183)
DARKLORE PUBLISHING LLC
5375 Duke St (22304-3075)
PHONE.....................................703 566-8021
Michael Holder, *Principal*
EMP: 2
SALES (est): 102.6K **Privately Held**
WEB:
www.darklorepublishing.jimdofree.com
SIC: 2711 Newspapers

(G-184)
DATRON WRLD COMMUNICATIONS INC
Also Called: DATRON WORLD COMMUNICATIONS, INC.
500 Montgomery St Ste 400 (22314-1560)
PHONE.....................................703 647-6235
Geoff Geo, *Manager*
EMP: 62
SALES (corp-wide): 53.5MM **Privately Held**
WEB: www.dtwc.com
SIC: 3663 Receiver-transmitter units (transceiver)
PA: Datron World Communications Inc.
3055 Enterprise Ct
Vista CA 92081
760 597-1500

(G-185)
DAVIS COMMUNICATIONS GROUP
Also Called: Metro Herald, The
901 N Washington St # 603 (22314-5509)
P.O. Box 150033 (22315-0033)
PHONE.....................................703 548-8892
Paris Davis, *President*
Stephanie Davis, *Vice Pres*
Regan Kathleen Davis, *Admin Sec*
EMP: 6
SQ FT: 3,600
SALES (est): 477.2K **Privately Held**
WEB: www.metroherald.com
SIC: 2759 7336 2752 7311 Newspapers: printing; graphic arts & related design; commercial printing, offset; advertising agencies

(G-186)
DECA SOFTWARE LLC
211 N Union St (22314-2657)
PHONE.....................................202 607-5707
EMP: 2
SALES (est): 152.8K **Privately Held**
SIC: 7372 Prepackaged software

(G-187)
DIGI QUICK PRINT INC
5100 Leesburg Pike Ste B (22302-1000)
PHONE.....................................703 671-9600
Brian Bryant, *Principal*
EMP: 6
SALES (est): 599.8K **Privately Held**
WEB: www.digiqp.com
SIC: 2752 2741 Commercial printing, offset; business form & card printing, lithographic; photo-offset printing; business service newsletters: publishing & printing

(G-188)
DIGILINK INC
840 S Pickett St (22304-4606)
PHONE.....................................703 340-1800
Michael G Wight, *President*
Ed Hartman, *Senior VP*
Hank Russo, *Senior VP*
John E Hartman, *Vice Pres*
Rachel Welch, *Vice Pres*
EMP: 50
SQ FT: 36,192
SALES (est): 7.4MM **Privately Held**
WEB: www.digilink-inc.com
SIC: 2796 2759 Platemaking services; commercial printing

(G-189)
DIGITAL BEANS INC
104 Stewart Ave Apt 1 (22301-1173)
PHONE.....................................703 775-2225
James Wallace, *President*
EMP: 1
SALES (est): 82.9K **Privately Held**
WEB: www.digitalbeans.com
SIC: 7372 8721 Business oriented computer software; accounting services, except auditing

(G-190)
DISCOVERY MAP
3110 Mount Vernon Ave # 220 (22305-2664)
PHONE.....................................703 346-7166
Cindy McCartney, *Principal*
EMP: 1
SALES (est): 37.5K **Privately Held**
WEB: www.discoverymap.com
SIC: 2741 Maps: publishing & printing

(G-191)
DJS ENTERPRISES
515 Prince St (22314-3115)
PHONE.....................................703 973-0977
Joan Goehler, *Partner*
David Goehler, *Partner*
EMP: 2
SALES (est): 10K **Privately Held**
SIC: 2032 Canned specialties

(G-192)
DOLAN CONTRACTING
5508 Bradley Blvd (22311-1004)
PHONE.....................................703 768-9496
Terence Dolan, *Owner*
EMP: 4
SALES (est): 486.4K **Privately Held**
SIC: 2295 1799 Waterproofing fabrics, except rubberizing; special trade contractors

(G-193)
DONALD N JENSEN
3301 Coryell Ln (22302-2114)
PHONE.....................................202 577-9892
Donald Jensen, *Owner*
EMP: 1
SALES (est): 36.1K **Privately Held**
SIC: 2741 Miscellaneous publishing

(G-194)
DREAM GREEN INTERNATIONAL LLC
2800 Eisenhower Ave # 220 (22314-5204)
PHONE.....................................814 616-7800
EMP: 1 **Privately Held**

WEB: www.gdicwins.com
SIC: 1411 8712 1422 Trap rock, dimension-quarrying; architectural engineering; crushed & broken limestone
PA: Dream Green International Llc
32 W 8th St Ste No607
Erie PA 16501

(G-195)
DRIVE SQUARE INC (PA)
3213 Duke St Ste 656 (22314-4533)
PHONE.....................................617 762-4013
Konstantin Sizov, *CEO*
Eric Hilman, *Vice Pres*
Karen Angelini, *VP Mktg*
EMP: 4
SALES (est): 133.1K **Privately Held**
WEB: www.drivesquare.com
SIC: 3699 8732 Automotive driving simulators (training aids), electronic; research services, except laboratory

(G-196)
DUTCH LADY
1003 King St (22314-2922)
PHONE.....................................202 669-0317
Namka Menkovic, *Principal*
EMP: 2 EST: 2007
SALES (est): 121.2K **Privately Held**
SIC: 2299 5719 Linen fabrics; fireplaces & wood burning stoves

(G-197)
DX COMPANY LLC
5445 Richenbacher Ave (22304-2041)
PHONE.....................................703 919-8677
Claude D Davis Sr,
EMP: 1
SQ FT: 2,500
SALES (est): 81.2K **Privately Held**
SIC: 3069 Life jackets, inflatable: rubberized fabric

(G-198)
EFFTEX DEVELOPMENT INC
901 N Pitt St Ste 325 (22314-1549)
PHONE.....................................800 708-8894
Sergey Varnavsky, *CEO*
Yuri Bakay, *President*
EMP: 1
SALES (est): 52.1K **Privately Held**
SIC: 7372 Publishers' computer software

(G-199)
ELECTRIC ELDERS INC
701 Seaton Ave Unit 520 (22305-3083)
PHONE.....................................703 213-9327
Moe Roddick, *CEO*
EMP: 1
SALES (est): 32.7K **Privately Held**
SIC: 7372 Educational computer software

(G-200)
ELEPHANT PRINTS LLC
5400 Bradford Ct Apt 32 (22311-5414)
PHONE.....................................703 820-2631
EMP: 2
SALES (est): 83.9K **Privately Held**
SIC: 2752 Commercial printing, lithographic

(G-201)
ERIC MARGRY
Also Called: Eric Margry Engraving
105 N Union St Ste 229 (22314-3217)
PHONE.....................................703 548-7808
Eric Margry, *Owner*
EMP: 1
SALES (est): 77.1K **Privately Held**
WEB: www.ericmargryhandengraving.com
SIC: 3479 Engraving jewelry silverware, or metal

(G-202)
ERICKSON & RIPPER FRAMING
Also Called: Erickson & Ripper Gallery
628 N Washington St (22314-1914)
PHONE.....................................703 549-1616
Jeff Erickson, *Partner*
Don Ripper, *Partner*
EMP: 2
SALES (est): 194.1K **Privately Held**
WEB: www.ericksonandripper.com
SIC: 2499 8412 Picture & mirror frames, wood; art gallery

(G-203)
FALCON DEFENSE SERVICE LLC
5813 Colfax Ave (22311-1013)
PHONE.................................703 395-2007
Eric Eliades, *President*
EMP: 4
SALES (est): 205.8K **Privately Held**
SIC: 3812 Defense systems & equipment

(G-204)
FARMKART FOODS LLC
2500 N Van Dorn St Apt 12 (22302-1626)
PHONE.................................706 461-6395
Justine Avoudikpon, *Exec Dir*
EMP: 2
SALES (est): 62.3K **Privately Held**
SIC: 2099 Food preparations

(G-205)
FJORD DEFENSE INC
1725 Duke St (22314-3456)
PHONE.................................571 214-2183
Knut Saeter, *Principal*
EMP: 2
SALES (est): 73.4K **Privately Held**
SIC: 3484 Machine guns or machine gun parts, 30 mm. & below

(G-206)
FOREST CARBON OFFSETS LLC
2121 Eisenhower Ave (22314-4698)
PHONE.................................703 795-4512
Keister Evans, *President*
Jeff Waldon, *Officer*
EMP: 4
SALES (est): 204.1K **Privately Held**
WEB: www.forestcarbonoffsets.square-space.com
SIC: 2499 Wood products

(G-207)
FOUNDRY FOUNDRY-A PRINT
1420 Prince St Ste 200 (22314-2868)
PHONE.................................703 329-3300
Adriana Fanganiello, *Vice Pres*
EMP: 2
SALES (est): 83.9K **Privately Held**
SIC: 2752 Commercial printing, lithographic

(G-208)
FULLY PROMOTED OF ALEXANDRIA
108 S Early St (22304-6311)
PHONE.................................703 575-9003
EMP: 1
SALES (est): 52.5K **Privately Held**
WEB: www.fullypromoted.com
SIC: 2395 Embroidery & art needlework

(G-209)
G-HOLDINGS LLC
2121 Eisenhower Ave # 600 (22314-4698)
PHONE.................................202 255-9698
Michael Gaffney, *President*
EMP: 1
SALES (est): 55K **Privately Held**
SIC: 3841 Surgical & medical instruments

(G-210)
GAIA COMMUNICATIONS LLC
Also Called: Kwikpoint
35 E Linden St Ste 3a (22301-2219)
PHONE.................................703 370-5527
Alan Stillman, *CEO*
Laura Madonna, *Business Mgr*
EMP: 3
SALES (est): 1.2MM **Privately Held**
WEB: www.kwikpoint.com
SIC: 2741 2759 2752 Patterns, paper; publishing & printing; publication printing; commercial printing, lithographic

(G-211)
GAINSAFE INC
427 S Fairfax St (22314-3809)
PHONE.................................703 598-2583
Matthew McDonald, *CEO*
EMP: 1
SALES (est): 250K **Privately Held**
SIC: 7372 Prepackaged software

(G-212)
GAMAY FLAVORS
4717 Eisenhower Ave Ste B (22304-4805)
PHONE.................................703 751-7430
Aly Gamay, *Owner*
EMP: 6
SALES (est): 453.7K **Privately Held**
SIC: 2087 Extracts, flavoring

(G-213)
GARMONTE LLC
Also Called: Embroid ME Alexandria
4656 King St Ste A (22302-1215)
PHONE.................................703 575-9003
Gary Montante, *Owner*
EMP: 2
SALES (est): 148.9K **Privately Held**
WEB: www.fullypromoted.com
SIC: 2759 5699 Screen printing; T-shirts, custom printed

(G-214)
GERMAINE CLARK LLC
124 Dale St (22305-2413)
PHONE.................................571 309-1724
Germaine Clark, *CEO*
EMP: 1
SALES (est): 75.1K **Privately Held**
SIC: 3549 7389 Cutting-up lines;

(G-215)
GET IT LLC
1620 Fitzgerald Ln (22302-2004)
PHONE.................................703 625-6844
Eric Maier, *Exec VP*
Jacob Peebles, *Branch Mgr*
Robyn H Cain, *Director*
EMP: 17
SALES (corp-wide): 443.4K **Privately Held**
WEB: www.get.it
SIC: 2741 Miscellaneous publishing
PA: Get It, Llc
     1201 Conn Ave Nw Ste 652
     Washington DC 20036
     703 880-6630

(G-216)
GINGHAM & GROSGRAIN LLC
206 Adams Ave (22301-2110)
PHONE.................................202 674-2024
EMP: 1
SALES (est): 46.5K **Privately Held**
SIC: 2211 Ginghams

(G-217)
GLOBAL DAILY
5 Cameron St Ste 5 # 5 (22314-3235)
PHONE.................................703 518-3030
Yesemwerk Vurouk, *Principal*
EMP: 35
SALES (est): 1MM **Privately Held**
SIC: 2711 Newspapers, publishing & printing

(G-218)
GLOBAL METRO NETWORKS INC
201 N Union St Ste 300 (22314-2650)
PHONE.................................703 837-6030
Matthew Phillips, *CEO*
EMP: 1
SALES (est): 420K **Privately Held**
SIC: 3229 Fiber optics strands

(G-219)
GLONET INCORPORATED
277 S Washington St # 300 (22314-3646)
PHONE.................................571 499-5000
Krystle Okoye, *President*
EMP: 3
SALES (est): 168.1K **Privately Held**
WEB: www.glonetinc.com
SIC: 7372 Application computer software

(G-220)
GLORIA BARBRE
105 N Union St (22314-3217)
PHONE.................................703 548-2210
Gloria Barbre, *Owner*
EMP: 1

SALES (est): 50.4K **Privately Held**
WEB: www.theartleague.org
SIC: 2385 5699 Raincoats, except vulcanized rubber: purchased materials; raincoats

(G-221)
GO HAPPY PRINTING
2350 Duke St Ste D (22314-4605)
PHONE.................................315 436-1151
Thanh Do, *Principal*
EMP: 2
SALES (est): 91.2K **Privately Held**
SIC: 2752 Commercial printing, lithographic

(G-222)
GOMSPACE NORTH AMERICA LLC
Also Called: Gomspace NA
211 N Union St Ste 100 (22314-2643)
PHONE.................................703 866-8742
Frank Tobin, *Chairman*
Troels Normolle, *Bd of Directors*
Niels Buus, *Bd of Directors*
EMP: 5
SQ FT: 300
SALES (est): 286.9K **Privately Held**
WEB: www.gomspace.com
SIC: 3761 3663 Guided missiles & space vehicles, research & development; rockets, space & military, complete; receivers, radio communications; space satellite communications equipment

(G-223)
GOVHAWK LLC
3201 Landover St Apt 1706 (22305-1938)
PHONE.................................703 439-1349
David Dorsey, *President*
Timothy Showers, *Exec VP*
Paul Zurawski,
EMP: 3
SALES (est): 104.1K **Privately Held**
SIC: 7372 Business oriented computer software

(G-224)
GOVREADY PBC
Also Called: Govready Public Benefit
4324 Raleigh Ave Apt 204 (22304-5327)
PHONE.................................917 304-3488
Gregory Elin, *CEO*
EMP: 3
SQ FT: 50
SALES (est): 172K **Privately Held**
SIC: 7372 Business oriented computer software

(G-225)
GRAPHIC IMAGES CORP
3660 Wheeler Ave (22304-6403)
PHONE.................................703 823-6794
EMP: 2
SALES (est): 83.9K **Privately Held**
SIC: 2752 Lithographic Commercial Printing

(G-226)
GWEN NAPPI
3309 Russell Rd (22305-1725)
PHONE.................................703 329-4836
Douglas Nappi, *Principal*
EMP: 2
SALES (est): 122K **Privately Held**
WEB: www.mnspublicity.com
SIC: 2741 Miscellaneous publishing

(G-227)
HAMAMELIS GENOMICS LLC
105 E Windsor Ave (22301-1315)
PHONE.................................703 939-3480
Gregory Steffensen, *Principal*
EMP: 1
SALES (est): 56.3K **Privately Held**
SIC: 2835 Microbiology & virology diagnostic products

(G-228)
HENRY SHAW
Also Called: Logo In 50 Minutes
2800 Eisenhower Ave # 220 (22314-5204)
PHONE.................................844 621-2158
Henry Shaw, *Owner*
EMP: 50

SALES (est): 787.2K **Privately Held**
SIC: 7372 Application computer software

(G-229)
HIGH HAT INC
Also Called: Signs By Tomorrow Alexandria
380 S Pickett St (22304-4704)
PHONE.................................703 212-7446
Jackie Gimbel, *President*
Dave Gimbel, *Vice Pres*
EMP: 4
SALES (est): 525K **Privately Held**
WEB: www.signsbytomorrow.com
SIC: 3993 Signs & advertising specialties

(G-230)
HP INC
1316 Mount Vernon Ave (22301-1714)
PHONE.................................703 535-3355
Sean Dyer, *Technical Staff*
EMP: 219 **Publicly Held**
WEB: www.hp.com
SIC: 3571 7372 Personal computers (microcomputers); prepackaged software
PA: Hp Inc.
     1501 Page Mill Rd
     Palo Alto CA 94304
     650 857-1501

(G-231)
I BIT-LAB
704a Little St (22301-2106)
PHONE.................................703 568-4035
EMP: 2 EST: 2017
SALES (est): 86.2K **Privately Held**
WEB: www.cutepasswordmanager.com
SIC: 7372 Prepackaged software

(G-232)
IBF GROUP
3844 Brighton Ct (22305-1574)
PHONE.................................703 549-4247
Tim Winter, *Owner*
EMP: 1
SALES (est): 57.5K **Privately Held**
SIC: 2752 2782 7336 Commercial printing, lithographic; blankbooks & looseleaf binders; graphic arts & related design

(G-233)
IDEAGIRL INDUSTRIES LLC
307 Clifford Ave (22305-2708)
PHONE.................................240 672-8333
EMP: 2
SALES (est): 77K **Privately Held**
SIC: 3999 Manufacturing industries

(G-234)
IL DOLCE WINERY
2601 Park Center Dr C1407 (22302-1429)
PHONE.................................804 647-0414
Stephen Russo, *Principal*
EMP: 2
SALES (est): 78.7K **Privately Held**
SIC: 2084 Wines

(G-235)
ILMA
651 S Washington St (22314-4109)
PHONE.................................703 684-5574
EMP: 2
SALES (est): 160K **Privately Held**
SIC: 2899 Mfg Chemical Preparations

(G-236)
IMGEN TECHNOLOGIES LC
602 Virginia Ave (22302-2900)
PHONE.................................703 549-2866
Beth Clark, *Principal*
Elizabeth Clark, *Principal*
Florian Menninger, *Vice Pres*
Robert Clark, *Mktg Dir*
EMP: 5
SALES (est): 601.2K **Privately Held**
WEB: www.imgen.com
SIC: 3674 Molecular devices, solid state

(G-237)
INFORMATICA LLC
428 Hume Ave (22301-1021)
PHONE.................................650 385-7000
EMP: 2 **Privately Held**
WEB: www.informatica.com
SIC: 7372 Prepackaged software

PA: Informatica Llc
2100 Seaport Blvd
Redwood City CA 94063

(G-238)
INTEL CORPORATION
201 N Union St (22314-2642)
PHONE...................................571 312-2320
EMP: 2
SALES (corp-wide): 71.9B **Publicly Held**
WEB: www.intel.com
SIC: 3577 Computer peripheral equipment
PA: Intel Corporation
2200 Mission College Blvd
Santa Clara CA 95054
408 765-8080

(G-239)
INTELLECT COMPUTERS INC (PA)
5100 Leesburg Pike # 100 (22302-1000)
PHONE...................................703 931-5100
Fazal Noory, *President*
EMP: 17
SQ FT: 2,000
SALES (est): 1.5MM **Privately Held**
WEB: www.intellectcomputers.com
SIC: 3571 5734 Electronic computers;
computer peripheral equipment

(G-240)
INTOR INC
901 N Pitt St Ste 325 (22314-1549)
PHONE...................................757 296-2175
Yuri Bakay, *President*
EMP: 1
SALES (est): 600K **Privately Held**
SIC: 7372 4813 Application computer software;

(G-241)
J & M PRINTING INC
Also Called: Alpha Graphics US 635
1001 N Fairfax St Ste 100 (22314-2084)
PHONE...................................703 549-2432
Cathy Thomas, *President*
Jay Thomas, *Vice Pres*
EMP: 8
SQ FT: 3,200
SALES (est): 3.1MM **Privately Held**
WEB: www.jmprint.net
SIC: 2752 7334 2791 2789 Commercial
printing, offset; photocopying & duplicating services; typesetting; bookbinding &
related work

(G-242)
JACKSON 20
480 King St (22314-3102)
PHONE...................................703 842-2790
AVI Rathnakumar, *General Mgr*
▲ EMP: 1 EST: 2012
SALES (est): 121.5K **Privately Held**
WEB: www.jackson20.com
SIC: 3421 Table & food cutlery, including
butchers'

(G-243)
JENNIFER ENOS
3311 Commwl Ave Apt F (22305)
PHONE...................................571 721-9268
Jennifer Enos, *Owner*
EMP: 1
SALES (est): 36K **Privately Held**
SIC: 2789 Binding & repair of books, magazines & pamphlets

(G-244)
JET MANAGERS INTERNATIONAL INC
211 N Union St Ste 100 (22314-2643)
PHONE...................................703 829-0679
Stuart A Peebles, *Principal*
EMP: 2
SALES (est): 196.5K **Privately Held**
WEB: www.jmi.aero
SIC: 3531 Airport construction machinery

(G-245)
JNR DEFENSE LLC
1463 N Highview Ln # 101 (22311-2309)
PHONE...................................541 220-6089
Russell Hodge, *Principal*
EMP: 2 EST: 2018

SALES (est): 81.9K **Privately Held**
SIC: 3812 Defense systems & equipment

(G-246)
JOURNAL OF ORTHPDIC SPT PHYSCL
Also Called: Journal Orthopaedic Spt Physcl
1111 N Fairfax St Ste 100 (22314-1436)
PHONE...................................877 766-3450
Mike Cibulka, *President*
Edith Holmes, *Publisher*
Mark De Carlo, *Vice Pres*
EMP: 3
SALES: 1.6MM **Privately Held**
WEB: www.secure.movementsciencemedia.org
SIC: 2721 Magazines: publishing & printing

(G-247)
JR WOODWORKS
2918 Bryan St (22302-3902)
PHONE...................................703 577-2663
EMP: 2 EST: 2010
SALES (est): 100K **Privately Held**
SIC: 2431 Mfg Millwork

(G-248)
JUANITA DESHAZIOR
Also Called: Nita's Nice Alterations
5300 Holmes Run Pkwy (22304-2834)
PHONE...................................703 901-5592
Juanita Deshazior, *Owner*
EMP: 1
SALES (est): 18K **Privately Held**
SIC: 2311 7389 Military uniforms, men's &
youths': purchased materials;

(G-249)
JUSTIN COMB
Also Called: Iastv & Magazine
5145 Duke St Ste D-107 (22304-2923)
PHONE...................................703 783-1082
Justin Comb, *Owner*
EMP: 1
SALES (est): 64.3K **Privately Held**
SIC: 2721 Periodicals

(G-250)
K S E
1800 Diagonal Rd Ste 600 (22314-2840)
PHONE...................................571 366-1715
EMP: 2
SALES (est): 110.7K **Privately Held**
SIC: 3312 Blast furnaces & steel mills

(G-251)
KEMELLE NATURALS INCORPORATED
35 W Reed Ave (22305-2427)
PHONE...................................850 528-9053
Keonna Ross, *CEO*
EMP: 2
SALES (est): 60K **Privately Held**
SIC: 2844 Hair preparations, including
shampoos

(G-252)
KHAN QAISM
678 S Pickett St (22304-4620)
PHONE...................................703 212-8670
Khan Qaism, *Owner*
EMP: 2
SALES (est): 69K **Privately Held**
SIC: 3999 Cigarette lighter flints

(G-253)
KIRINTEC INC
400 Madison St Apt 2208 (22314-1736)
PHONE...................................571 527-1437
Jerry Warner, *President*
Richard Mant, *Director*
Roy Peers-Smith, *Director*
Nick Watts, *Director*
EMP: 1 EST: 2013
SALES (est): 129.1K **Privately Held**
WEB: www.kirintec.com
SIC: 3825 8731 8742 3599 Internal combustion engine analyzers, to test electronics; commercial physical research;
marketing consulting services; electrical
discharge machining (EDM); business
consulting

(G-254)
KIRKLAND HOLDINGS CO (PA)
2000 Duke St Ste 110 (22314-6101)
PHONE...................................571 348-1005
Roger B McKeague, *Principal*
EMP: 3 EST: 2015
SALES (est): 492.2K **Privately Held**
SIC: 3571 Electronic computers

(G-255)
KONGSBERG DEFENSE SYSTEMS INC
1725 Duke St Ste 600 (22314-3457)
PHONE...................................703 838-8910
EMP: 1
SALES (est): 108.4K
SALES (corp-wide): 2.6B **Privately Held**
WEB: www.kongsberg.com
SIC: 3489 Ordnance & accessories
HQ: Kongsberg Defence & Aerospace As
Kirkegardsveien 45
Kongsberg 3616

(G-256)
KONGSBERG PRTECH SYSTEMS USA C
1725 Duke St Ste 600 (22314-3457)
PHONE...................................703 838-8910
Linsey Battan, *Branch Mgr*
Michael Zaldivar, *Manager*
EMP: 7
SALES (corp-wide): 2.6B **Privately Held**
WEB: www.kongsberg.com
SIC: 3489 Ordnance & accessories
HQ: Kongsberg Protech Systems Usa Corporation
210 Industrial Park Rd
Johnstown PA 15904

(G-257)
LEGACY VULCAN LLC
Also Called: Van Dorn Yard
701 S Van Dorn St (22304-4639)
P.O. Box 22330 (22304)
PHONE...................................703 461-0333
Dale Vaughn, *Manager*
EMP: 4 **Publicly Held**
WEB: www.vulcanmaterials.com
SIC: 3272 Concrete products
HQ: Legacy Vulcan, Llc
1200 Urban Center Dr
Vestavia AL 35242
205 298-3000

(G-258)
LEITNER-WISE MANUFACTURING LLC
108 S Early St (22304-6311)
P.O. Box 612 (22313-0612)
PHONE...................................703 209-0009
Paul A Leitner-Wise,
David Gessel,
Paul Leitner-Wise,
Marc Rogers,
EMP: 4 EST: 2012
SALES (est): 368.2K **Privately Held**
WEB: www.leitner-wise.com
SIC: 3484 3482 Guns (firearms) or gun
parts, 30 mm. & below; small arms ammunition

(G-259)
LETTERING BY LYNNE
3315 Carolina Pl (22305-1707)
PHONE...................................703 548-5427
Lynne Sandler, *Owner*
EMP: 1
SALES (est): 62K **Privately Held**
WEB: www.letteringbylynne.com
SIC: 2759 Invitation & stationery printing &
engraving

(G-260)
LILY GOLDEN FOODS CORPORATION
820 S Pickett St (22304-4606)
PHONE...................................703 823-8821
CAM Luu, *President*
EMP: 4
SALES (est): 309.8K **Privately Held**
SIC: 2038 Frozen specialties

(G-261)
LIME & LEAF LLC
311 Cameron St (22314-3219)
PHONE...................................703 299-2440
Lori Morris, *Owner*
EMP: 2
SALES (est): 153.2K **Privately Held**
WEB: www.limeandleaf.com
SIC: 2392 Household furnishings

(G-262)
LITSTONE CAPITAL LLC
2800 Eisenhower Ave (22314-5204)
PHONE...................................703 576-0788
Rodyssieus Joiner, *CEO*
EMP: 1
SALES (est): 60.3K **Privately Held**
SIC: 1389 Construction, repair & dismantling services

(G-263)
LOGAN FOOD COMPANY
Also Called: Logan Sausage Company
4300 Wheeler Ave (22304-6415)
PHONE...................................703 212-6677
Clifford Logan Jr, *President*
Clifford Logan III, *Exec VP*
Kevin Logan, *Sales Staff*
Bonnie Logan, *Admin Sec*
EMP: 18
SALES (est): 2.8MM **Privately Held**
WEB: www.logansausage.com
SIC: 2013 Sausages from purchased meat

(G-264)
LORI KATZ
105 N Union St Ste 8 (22314-3217)
PHONE...................................703 475-1640
Lori E Katz, *Owner*
Lori Katz, *General Mgr*
EMP: 1
SALES (est): 128.3K **Privately Held**
WEB: www.lorikatz.com
SIC: 3443 Vessels, process or storage
(from boiler shops): metal plate

(G-265)
LORRIE CARPENTER
Also Called: L&D Healthy Foods & Snacks
2714 Williamsburg St (22314-5845)
PHONE...................................804 720-6442
Lorrie Carpenter, *Owner*
EMP: 1
SALES (est): 10K **Privately Held**
SIC: 3581 Automatic vending machines

(G-266)
LT PRESSURE WASHER SERVICES
5341 Taney Ave Apt 202 (22304-5915)
PHONE...................................703 626-9010
EMP: 3 EST: 2008
SALES (est): 94.9K **Privately Held**
SIC: 3452 Mfg Bolts/Screws/Rivets

(G-267)
MACAR INTERNATIONAL LLC
Also Called: Customscoop
4900 Leesburg Pike # 209 (22302-1101)
PHONE...................................202 842-1818
Terry Foster, *Managing Dir*
Mazen Nahawi, *CFO*
EMP: 6
SALES (est): 239.7K **Privately Held**
WEB: www.customscoop.carma.com
SIC: 7372 Business oriented computer
software

(G-268)
MACHINERY INFORMATION SYSTEMS
Also Called: Locator Services
315 S Patrick St Fl 3 (22314-3556)
PHONE...................................703 836-9700
Terry J Pitman, *COO*
Cheryl Braxton, *Human Resources*
Jim Bowman, *Sales Staff*
EMP: 6
SQ FT: 5,356

GEOGRAPHIC

SALES (est): 274.1K
SALES (corp-wide): 779.2K **Privately Held**
WEB: www.locatoronline.com
SIC: 2721 7374 Magazines: publishing only, not printed on site; data processing & preparation
PA: Machinery Dealers National Association
315 S Patrick St Fl 2
Alexandria VA 22314
703 836-9300

(G-269)
MACKLIN CONSULTING LLC
2702 King St (22302-4009)
PHONE...................................202 423-9923
Frank Harris, *Principal*
EMP: 1
SALES (est): 59.1K **Privately Held**
SIC: 3423 5411 4119 4212 Garden & farm tools, including shovels; co-operative food stores; local passenger transportation; animal & farm product transportation services

(G-270)
MARITIME ASSOCIATES INC
148 N Early St (22304-2612)
PHONE...................................571 212-0655
Erik Lindgren, *President*
EMP: 2
SALES (est): 114.4K **Privately Held**
WEB: www.bournegroupint.com
SIC: 3429 Manufactured hardware (general)

(G-271)
MATCH POINT PRESS
909 N Overlook Dr (22305-1150)
PHONE...................................703 548-4202
EMP: 1
SALES (est): 37.5K **Privately Held**
SIC: 2741 Miscellaneous Publishing, Nsk

(G-272)
MCKEON DOOR OF DC INC
Also Called: McKeon Door of Virginia
2000 Duke St Ste 300 (22314-6101)
PHONE...................................301 807-1006
Joseph McKeon, *President*
Andrew Lambridis, *Vice Pres*
Bernie Rosser, *Manager*
EMP: 1
SALES (est): 123.9K **Privately Held**
WEB: www.mckeondoor.com
SIC: 3442 Metal doors

(G-273)
MEDITERRANEAN DELIGHT INC
101 S Whiting St Ste 305 (22304-3416)
PHONE...................................703 751-2656
EMP: 3
SALES (est): 98.8K **Privately Held**
SIC: 2079 Olive oil

(G-274)
METALLUM
Also Called: Gold Smith Designer
105 N Union St Ste 201 (22314-3217)
PHONE...................................703 549-4551
Gretchen Raber, *Owner*
EMP: 1
SQ FT: 200
SALES (est): 50K **Privately Held**
SIC: 3911 Jewelry, precious metal

(G-275)
MILDEF INC
2800 Eisenhower Ave # 220 (22314-5204)
PHONE...................................703 224-8835
Tomas Odelid, *CEO*
EMP: 1
SQ FT: 20,000
SALES (corp-wide): 6MM **Privately Held**
WEB: www.mildef.com
SIC: 3571 Electronic computers; minicomputers; personal computers (microcomputers)
PA: Mildef, Inc.
630 W Lambert Rd
Brea CA 92821
703 224-8835

(G-276)
MILL CREEK PRESS LLC
1311 Kenwood Ave (22302-2314)
PHONE...................................703 638-8395
EMP: 1
SALES (est): 41.3K **Privately Held**
SIC: 2741 Miscellaneous publishing

(G-277)
MINUTEMAN PRESS INTL
1429 Duke St (22314-3402)
PHONE...................................703 299-1150
EMP: 2
SALES (est): 83.9K **Privately Held**
WEB: www.minutemanpress.com
SIC: 2752 Commercial printing, lithographic

(G-278)
MOAZ MARWA
5741 Leverett Ct Apt 373 (22311-5949)
PHONE...................................571 225-4743
Marwa Moaz, *Owner*
EMP: 1
SALES (est): 65.2K **Privately Held**
SIC: 3661 Electronic secretary

(G-279)
MOJO FRUIT DRINKS LLC
17 E Myrtle St (22301-2205)
PHONE...................................571 278-0755
Gregory William Derogatis, *President*
EMP: 1
SALES (est): 58.3K **Privately Held**
SIC: 2086 Fruit drinks (less than 100% juice): packaged in cans, etc.

(G-280)
MOM MADE FOODS LLC
950 N Washington St (22314-1534)
PHONE...................................703 740-9241
Heather Stouffer, *CFO*
Craig Stouffer,
EMP: 10
SALES (est): 1.2MM **Privately Held**
WEB: www.mommadefoods.com
SIC: 2038 Frozen specialties

(G-281)
MONTESQUIEU INC
500 Montgomery St (22314-1565)
PHONE...................................703 518-9975
Missy Carpenter, *Principal*
Stephanie Ray, *Advisor*
EMP: 2
SALES (est): 109.5K **Privately Held**
SIC: 2084 Wines

(G-282)
MOONLIGHT BINDERY
18 W Uhler Ave (22301-1548)
PHONE...................................703 549-5261
Katharine Wagner, *Principal*
EMP: 1
SALES (est): 79K **Privately Held**
SIC: 2789 Binding only: books, pamphlets, magazines, etc.

(G-283)
MORPHOTRAK LLC
675 N Washington St # 330 (22314-1934)
PHONE...................................703 797-2600
Walt Scott, *Vice Pres*
Larry Dean, *Opers Mgr*
Peter Lo, *Research*
Tuan Duong, *Senior Engr*
Allyson Thomas, *VP Human Res*
EMP: 10
SALES (corp-wide): 8.1B **Privately Held**
WEB: www.morphotrak.com
SIC: 3999 Fingerprint equipment
HQ: Morphotrak, Llc
5515 E La Palma Ave # 100
Anaheim CA 92807
714 238-2000

(G-284)
MOTLEY FOOL LLC
Also Called: Motley Fool Company
123 N Pitt St (22314-3128)
PHONE...................................703 838-3665
David Gardner, *Director*
EMP: 7 **Privately Held**
WEB: www.fool.com
SIC: 2741 Miscellaneous publishing

PA: The Motley Fool Llc
2000 Duke St Fl 4
Alexandria VA 22314

(G-285)
MOTLEY FOOL HOLDINGS INC
2000 Duke St Fl 4 (22314-6101)
PHONE...................................703 838-3665
Dan Boyd, *Editor*
Ollen Douglass, *CFO*
Steve Gilliam, *Accountant*
Lisa Shapiro, *Payroll Mgr*
Allyson Wines, *Manager*
EMP: 6 EST: 2008
SALES (est): 60.5K **Privately Held**
WEB: www.penfed.org
SIC: 2741 Miscellaneous publishing

(G-286)
MS JOS PETITE SWEETS LLC
625 N Washington St # 425 (22314-1930)
PHONE...................................571 327-9431
Erinn Roth,
EMP: 3 EST: 2016
SALES (est): 121.6K **Privately Held**
WEB: www.petitesweetsbymsjo.com
SIC: 2024 2099 2051 5461 Dairy based frozen desserts; frosting mixes, dry: for cakes, cookies, etc.; cakes, pies & pastries; bakeries

(G-287)
MUSEUM FRAMING
109 S Fairfax St (22314-3301)
PHONE...................................703 299-0100
Richard E Badwey, *Owner*
EMP: 3
SALES (est): 206K **Privately Held**
WEB: www.museumframing.com
SIC: 2499 5999 7699 Picture & mirror frames, wood; picture frames, ready made; picture framing, custom

(G-288)
NAILS HURRICANE TOO
4535 Duke St (22304-2503)
PHONE...................................703 370-5551
MAI Tran, *Principal*
EMP: 1
SALES (est): 66.3K **Privately Held**
SIC: 3999 Fingernails, artificial

(G-289)
NATIONAL ENVELOPE CORP
1617 Preston Rd (22302-2124)
PHONE...................................703 629-3881
D Lage, *Marketing Staff*
EMP: 2
SALES (est): 90.7K **Privately Held**
SIC: 2677 Envelopes

(G-290)
NAZRET CULTURAL FOODS LLC
4316 Taney Ave Apt 103 (22304-6627)
PHONE...................................215 500-9813
EMP: 3
SALES (est): 193.2K **Privately Held**
WEB: www.nazretbooks.com
SIC: 2038 Ethnic foods, frozen

(G-291)
NHSA
1111 Belle Pre Way # 728 (22314-6411)
PHONE...................................508 420-1902
EMP: 1 EST: 2017
SALES (est): 47K **Privately Held**
SIC: 3949 Sporting & athletic goods

(G-292)
NOAHS ARK TRANSPORTATION LLC
3320 S 28th St Apt 303 (22302-1342)
PHONE...................................240 476-3381
Predrag Kragujevic,
EMP: 1
SALES (est): 56K **Privately Held**
SIC: 3669 Transportation signaling devices

(G-293)
NORTH LOCK LLC
Also Called: Port City Brewing Company
2308 Mount Vernon Ave # 714 (22301-1328)
PHONE...................................703 797-2739
G William Butcher III, *Branch Mgr*

Laura Hammond, *Manager*
EMP: 2
SALES (corp-wide): 679.5K **Privately Held**
WEB: www.portcitybrewingco.com
SIC: 2082 Brewers' grain
PA: North Lock Llc
3950 Wheeler Ave
Alexandria VA 22304
703 797-2739

(G-294)
NORTHERN DEFENSE INDS LLC
Also Called: Northern Defense Inds Inc
667 S Washington St (22314-4109)
PHONE...................................703 836-8346
Tim Gale, *CEO*
Robert Janssen, *President*
Jeremy Gale, *Admin Sec*
EMP: 5
SQ FT: 1,470
SALES (est): 48MM **Privately Held**
WEB: www.northerndefense.us
SIC: 3812 Search & navigation equipment
PA: Ams Group, Inc.
659 S Washington St
Alexandria VA 22314

(G-295)
NORTHPORT RESEARCH INC
635 First St Apt 404 (22314-1586)
PHONE...................................703 508-9773
Frederic Corle, *President*
EMP: 1
SQ FT: 1,500
SALES (est): 47.2K **Privately Held**
WEB: www.northportllc.com
SIC: 2834 Drugs acting on the respiratory system

(G-296)
NORTHROP CUSTOM METAL LLC
6060 Farrington Ave (22304-4826)
P.O. Box 10440 (22310-0440)
PHONE...................................703 751-7042
Erik Northrop, *Owner*
Diane Northrop, *Bookkeeper*
EMP: 4
SALES (est): 716.2K **Privately Held**
WEB: www.northropmetal.com
SIC: 3444 Ducts, sheet metal

(G-297)
NOVA DEFENSE & AROSPC INTL LLC
414 Pendleton St Ste 400 (22314-1902)
PHONE...................................703 864-6929
William Jacobs, *President*
EMP: 2
SALES (est): 200K **Privately Held**
SIC: 3812 Acceleration indicators & systems components, aerospace

(G-298)
NUSOURCE LLC
320 King St Ste 203 (22314-3230)
PHONE...................................571 482-7404
Alexandria Bassett, *Marketing Staff*
Mark Varno,
Yim Yun Chae, *Administration*
Robert Erda,
EMP: 6
SQ FT: 4,200
SALES (est): 2.2MM
SALES (corp-wide): 57.1MM **Privately Held**
WEB: www.nusourcellc.com
SIC: 3825 8711 Electrical energy measuring equipment; mechanical engineering; electrical or electronic engineering
PA: Mpr Associates, Inc.
320 King St Ste 400
Alexandria VA 22314
703 519-0200

(G-299)
OLD TOWN SIGN CO INC
1021 Queen St (22314-2448)
PHONE...................................703 836-7000
Robin Delaney, *President*
EMP: 2
SALES (est): 219.6K **Privately Held**
WEB: www.oldtownsign.com
SIC: 3993 Signs, not made in custom sign painting shops

▲ = Import ▼=Export
◆ =Import/Export

(G-300)
ON-SITE E DISCOVERY INC
806 N Henry St (22314-1619)
PHONE..................................703 683-9710
Mark Hawn, *President*
EMP: 2100
SQ FT: 65,000
SALES (est): 60MM **Privately Held**
SIC: 2759 Commercial printing

(G-301)
ORACLE WORLDWIDE LLC
2331 Mill Rd Ste 100 (22314-4687)
PHONE..................................703 224-8806
Christian McInerney, *Principal*
EMP: 2
SALES (est): 101.7K **Privately Held**
WEB: www.oracleworldwide.com
SIC: 7372 Prepackaged software

(G-302)
P&B SYSTEMS LLC
1716 Potomac Greens Dr (22314-6229)
PHONE..................................717 566-0608
EMP: 2
SALES (est): 33.8K **Privately Held**
WEB: www.pandbsystems.com
SIC: 7372 Prepackaged software

(G-303)
PACKET STASH INC
219 Buchanan St (22314-2103)
PHONE..................................202 649-0676
Jason Meller, *CEO*
Dustin Webber, *President*
Jen Andre, *CFO*
EMP: 3
SALES (est): 122.9K **Privately Held**
SIC: 7372 7389 Utility computer software;

(G-304)
PALLET FOUNDATION
1421 Prince St Ste 340 (22314-2805)
PHONE..................................703 519-6104
Anne Lewis, *Manager*
Brent McClendon, *Admin Sec*
EMP: 3 EST: 1996
SALES: 195K **Privately Held**
WEB: www.palletcentral.com
SIC: 2448 Pallets, wood

(G-305)
PANDAMONK PUBLISHING LLC
6000 Edsall Rd Apt 103 (22304-5800)
PHONE..................................571 528-1500
Roberto Carlos Martinez, *Administration*
EMP: 2 EST: 2014
SALES (est): 68.3K **Privately Held**
WEB: www.pandamonkpublishing.com
SIC: 2741 Miscellaneous publishing

(G-306)
PARRY LABS LLC
500 Montgomery St Ste 675 (22314-1565)
PHONE..................................585 746-8335
John Parkes, *Principal*
Gus Bontzos, *COO*
EMP: 40
SQ FT: 100
SALES (est): 7.5MM **Privately Held**
WEB: www.parrylabs.com
SIC: 3812 8731 Aircraft/aerospace flight
instruments & guidance systems; com-
mercial physical research

(G-307)
**PEEK—BOO PUBG GROUP
BRND LCEN**
113 S Columbus St Ste 400 (22314-3083)
PHONE..................................703 259-8816
Erik Muendel, *Principal*
EMP: 3
SALES (est): 72.6K **Privately Held**
WEB: www.peekaboopublishing.com
SIC: 2741 Miscellaneous publishing

(G-308)
PICKLE BUCKET FOUR LLC
522 N Alfred St (22314-2227)
PHONE..................................571 259-3726
Marc Engelking, *President*
EMP: 2 EST: 2014
SALES (est): 107.2K **Privately Held**
SIC: 2035 Pickled fruits & vegetables

(G-309)
PICKLE BUCKET THREE LLC
522 N Alfred St (22314-2227)
PHONE..................................571 259-3726
Marc Engelking, *President*
EMP: 2
SALES (est): 111.3K **Privately Held**
SIC: 2035 Pickled fruits & vegetables

(G-310)
PITNEY BOWES INC
1316 Mount Vernon Ave (22301-1714)
PHONE..................................703 658-6900
EMP: 2
SALES (est): 85.9K
SALES (corp-wide): 3.5B **Publicly Held**
SIC: 3579 Office Machines, Nec, Nsk
PA: Pitney Bowes Inc.
3001 Summer St Ste 3
Stamford CT 06905
203 356-5000

(G-311)
POOL HOT TUB ALLIA
2111 Eisenhower Ave (22314-4695)
PHONE..................................703 838-0083
EMP: 1
SALES (est): 43.6K **Privately Held**
SIC: 3999 Hot tubs

(G-312)
PORK BARREL BBQ LLC
2312 Mount Vernon Ave # 200
(22301-1375)
PHONE..........................:..202 750-7500
Brett Thompson, *CEO*
Heath Hall, *President*
EMP: 5 EST: 2008
SALES (est): 4MM **Privately Held**
WEB: www.porkbarrelbbq.com
SIC: 2033 2035 5149 Barbecue sauce:
packaged in cans, jars, etc.; seasonings
& sauces, except tomato & dry; groceries
& related products

(G-313)
**POTOMAC SOLUTIONS
INCORPORATED**
300 N Lee St (22314-2658)
PHONE..................................703 888-1762
Charles T Muhs, *President*
David Barton, *Opers Staff*
EMP: 4 EST: 2014
SALES (est): 281.5K **Privately Held**
WEB: www.potomacsolutions.com
SIC: 3728 8742 Military aircraft equipment
& armament; research & dev by manuf.,
aircraft parts & auxiliary equip; manage-
ment consulting services

(G-314)
POUCHMOUSE STUDIOS INC
40 E Taylor Run Pkwy (22314-4941)
PHONE..................................310 462-0599
Peter Hastings, *CEO*
EMP: 1
SALES (est): 60K **Privately Held**
SIC: 7372 Home entertainment computer
software

(G-315)
PPG INDUSTRIES INC
5204 Eisenhower Ave (22304-4816)
PHONE..................................703 370-5636
Richard Jhairston, *Branch Mgr*
EMP: 1
SALES (corp-wide): 15.3B **Publicly Held**
WEB: www.ppg.com
SIC: 2851 Paints & allied products
PA: Ppg Industries, Inc.
1 Ppg Pl
Pittsburgh PA 15272
412 434-3131

(G-316)
PRINT PROMOTION
Also Called: Dimensional Communications
101 N Columbus St Ste 200 (22314-3030)
PHONE..................................202 618-8822
Elisa Treadway, *Owner*
EMP: 2
SALES (est): 126.3K **Privately Held**
SIC: 2752 Commercial printing, litho-
graphic

(G-317)
PRINTING DEPT LLC
5610 Magnolia Ln (22311-3736)
PHONE..................................703 931-5450
Michael Hope, *Principal*
EMP: 2
SALES (est): 157.4K **Privately Held**
WEB: www.theprintingdept.com
SIC: 2752 Commercial printing, offset

(G-318)
PROJECT SAFE
675 S Washington St (22314-4109)
PHONE..................................703 505-0440
Stephen A Maczynski, *Principal*
EMP: 5 EST: 2010
SALES (est): 271.6K **Privately Held**
SIC: 3089 Organizers for closets, drawers,
etc.: plastic

(G-319)
PROSPECT PUBLISHING LLC
621 N Saint Asaph St # 302 (22314-1996)
PHONE..................................571 435-0241
Peter F Smith, *Principal*
EMP: 2
SALES (est): 59.2K **Privately Held**
SIC: 2741 Miscellaneous publishing

(G-320)
PRUITT PARTNERS LLC
Also Called: Julies Datery
3537 Martha Bustis Dr (22305)
PHONE..................................703 299-0114
Julie Reynes, *President*
EMP: 5
SALES (est): 90K **Privately Held**
SIC: 2099 Food preparations

(G-321)
PSA PUBLISHINGS LLC
1859 Ballenger Ave (22314-5763)
PHONE..................................703 986-3288
Hadi Saadat, *Administration*
EMP: 2
SALES (est): 101.3K **Privately Held**
SIC: 2741 Miscellaneous publishing

(G-322)
Q STAR TECHNOLOGY LLC
5601 Dawes Ave (22311-1101)
PHONE..................................703 578-1495
EMP: 2 EST: 2010
SALES (est): 160.4K **Privately Held**
SIC: 3861 Mfg Photographic
Equipment/Supplies

(G-323)
R & B IMPRESSIONS INC
Also Called: Minuteman Press
678 S Pickett St (22304-4620)
PHONE..................................703 823-9050
EMP: 12 EST: 1979
SQ FT: 1,700
SALES: 883.8K **Privately Held**
SIC: 2752 Comm Prtg Litho

(G-324)
RAILWAY STATION PRESS INC
105 E Glendale Ave (22301-2003)
PHONE..................................703 683-2335
EMP: 1
SALES (est): 37.5K **Privately Held**
WEB: www.railwaystationpress.com
SIC: 2741 Miscellaneous publishing

(G-325)
RAW GOODS LLC
300 Yoakum Pkwy Apt 1220 (22304-4061)
PHONE..................................862 812-1520
Joseph Mariano,
EMP: 1 EST: 2014
SALES (est): 71.7K **Privately Held**
SIC: 3999 Novelties, bric-a-brac & hobby
kits

(G-326)
RBT CENTER LLC
309 Yoakum Pkwy Apt 518 (22304-3930)
P.O. Box 9610 (22304-0610)
PHONE..................................703 823-8664
Raili Maultsby, *Mng Member*
Maxie Maultsby,
EMP: 2

SALES (est): 50K **Privately Held**
SIC: 2731 Books: publishing only

(G-327)
REDPRINT STRATEGY
212 S Henry St (22314-3522)
PHONE..................................202 656-1002
Brian Walsh, *Admin Sec*
EMP: 2
SALES (est): 95.8K **Privately Held**
WEB: www.redprintstrategy.com
SIC: 2752 Commercial printing, litho-
graphic

(G-328)
REFURB FACTORY LLC
Also Called: Express Cmputers Alexandria Ci
5999 Stevenson Ave # 202 (22304-3302)
P.O. Box 11205 (22312-0205)
PHONE..................................301 799-8385
Charles Pleasant, *Mng Member*
EMP: 7
SALES (est): 389.7K **Privately Held**
WEB: www.refurbfactory.net
SIC: 3577 Computer peripheral equipment

(G-329)
**ROTONDO ENVMTL SOLUTIONS
LLC**
4950 Eisenhower Ave C (22304-4809)
PHONE..................................703 212-4830
Terry Siviter, *Natl Sales Mgr*
Richard Rotondo,
John Rotondo,
EMP: 4
SQ FT: 2,500
SALES (est): 802.5K **Privately Held**
WEB: www.rotondo-es.com
SIC: 3823 Water quality monitoring & con-
trol systems

(G-330)
ROUGH INDUSTRIES LLC
317 E Custis Ave (22301-1201)
PHONE..................................215 514-4144
Travis Hester, *Administration*
EMP: 2 EST: 2015
SALES (est): 94.6K **Privately Held**
WEB: www.roughindustries.com
SIC: 3999 Manufacturing industries

(G-331)
ROUND HOUSE LLC
2701 Williamsburg St # 103 (22314-6016)
PHONE..................................757 504-3142
Cole David Morano, *Principal*
EMP: 2
SALES (est): 93.2K **Privately Held**
SIC: 3949 Targets, archery & rifle shooting

(G-332)
RURAL LIFE JOURNAL LLC
817 S Royal St (22314-4340)
PHONE..................................301 774-0305
Suzanne Browning, *Principal*
EMP: 2
SALES (est): 100.4K **Privately Held**
SIC: 2711 Newspapers, publishing & print-
ing

(G-333)
SABATINI OF LONDON
491 Cameron Station Blvd (22304-8682)
PHONE..................................202 277-8227
EMP: 2
SALES (est): 122.5K **Privately Held**
WEB: www.sabatiniofiondon.com
SIC: 2311 Men's & boys' suits & coats

(G-334)
SAFRAN USA INC (HQ)
700 S Washington St # 320 (22314-4252)
PHONE..................................703 351-9898
Peter Lengyel, *President*
Reed Vandewater, *Vice Pres*
Michelle Lyle, *Marketing Staff*
Catherine Vercaemert, *Office Mgr*
▲ EMP: 10
SQ FT: 32,000

GEOGRAPHIC

SALES (est): 1B
SALES (corp-wide): 799.9MM Privately Held
WEB: www.safran-usa.com
SIC: 3643 3621 7699 3724 Connectors & terminals for electrical devices; motors & generators; engine repair & replacement, non-automotive; aircraft engines & engine parts; automotive supplies & parts; aircraft equipment & supplies
PA: Safran
2 Bd Du General Martial Valin
Paris 75015
140 608-080

(G-335)
SAMA ARTFL INTELLIGENCE LLC
4854 Eisenhower Ave # 245 (22304-4883)
PHONE..............................347 223-2437
Michael Saleh,
EMP: 3
SALES (est): 137.2K Privately Held
SIC: 3842 Limbs, artificial

(G-336)
SANDRA WOODWARD
Also Called: Quest Limited
119 N Henry St 3a (22314-2903)
PHONE..............................703 329-7938
Sandra J Woodward, *Owner*
EMP: 2
SALES (est): 120.3K Privately Held
SIC: 2741 Technical manual & paper publishing

(G-337)
SANGAMON GROUP LLC
917 Portner Pl (22314-1313)
PHONE..............................571 969-6881
Jonathan Rinehart,
EMP: 1
SALES (est): 50K Privately Held
SIC: 2741 Miscellaneous publishing

(G-338)
SARA CAMPBELL LTD
320 Prince St (22314-3316)
PHONE..............................703 996-9074
Sara Campbell, *Principal*
EMP: 3
SALES (corp-wide): 4.2MM Privately Held
WEB: www.saracampbell.com
SIC: 2337 Women's & misses' suits & coats
PA: Sara Campbell, Ltd.
67 Kemble St Ste 4
Boston MA 02119
617 423-3134

(G-339)
SATCOM-LABS LLC
115 N Lee St Apt 502 (22314-3256)
PHONE..............................805 427-5556
Steve Jacklin, *President*
EMP: 5
SQ FT: 1,000
SALES (est): 216K Privately Held
SIC: 3663 Satellites, communications

(G-340)
SDS INDUSTRIES
350 Cameron Station Blvd (22304-8624)
PHONE..............................207 266-9448
Scott Shannon, *Principal*
EMP: 2
SALES (est): 114.9K Privately Held
SIC: 3999 Manufacturing industries

(G-341)
SECTOR 5 INC
2000 Duke St Ste 110 (22314-6101)
PHONE..............................571 348-1005
Erick Kuvshinikov, *CEO*
Joseph Leonardi, *President*
Peter Mortensen, *President*
Roger B McKeague, *CFO*
EMP: 6
SQ FT: 800 Privately Held
WEB: www.sector-five.com
SIC: 3571 5961 Electronic computers; computer equipment & electronics, mail order

(G-342)
SECTOR FIVE INC
Also Called: Sector 5
2000 Duke St Ste 110 (22314-6101)
PHONE..............................571 348-1005
Roger B McKeague, *CEO*
Peter Mortensen, *President*
EMP: 3 EST: 2015
SALES (est): 408K
SALES (corp-wide): 492.2K Privately Held
WEB: www.sector-five.com
SIC: 3571 Electronic computers
PA: Kirkland Holdings Co.
2000 Duke St Ste 110
Alexandria VA 22314
571 348-1005

(G-343)
SETANTA PUBLISHING LLC
3 E Cliff St (22301-1936)
PHONE..............................703 548-3146
EMP: 2
SALES (est): 130K Privately Held
SIC: 2741 Misc Publishing

(G-344)
SHAHZADA AFGHAN AMRCN IMPORT E
6022 Edsall Rd (22304-5840)
PHONE..............................571 245-1345
Mohammad Rafiq Barekzai,
EMP: 1
SALES (est): 20K Privately Held
SIC: 2499 Food handling & processing products, wood

(G-345)
SHERMAN INDUSTRIES LLC
1 E Bellefonte Ave (22301-1434)
PHONE..............................240 888-1134
Jennifer Silverstein, *Administration*
EMP: 2
SALES (est): 106.8K Privately Held
SIC: 3999 Manufacturing industries

(G-346)
SIGNAL VINE INC
811 N Royal St (22314-1715)
PHONE..............................703 480-0278
Brian Kathman, *CEO*
Joe Weinstein, *Opers Staff*
Jason Turim, *Engineer*
Paige Altieri, *Marketing Staff*
Rachel Franco, *Manager*
EMP: 16
SQ FT: 4,800
SALES (est): 1MM Privately Held
WEB: www.signalvine.com
SIC: 7372 Application computer software

(G-347)
SKINNY JERKY LLC
2801 Park Center Dr A505 (22302-1431)
PHONE..............................703 459-8406
Mahtabuddin Ahmed, *Principal*
EMP: 3
SALES (est): 138.2K Privately Held
SIC: 2013 Snack sticks, including jerky: from purchased meat

(G-348)
SKYDWELLER AERO INC
500 Montgomery St Ste 675 (22314-1565)
PHONE..............................585 746-8335
John Parkes, *Principal*
Robert Miller,
EMP: 3
SALES (est): 437.9K Privately Held
SIC: 3812 Aircraft/aerospace flight instruments & guidance systems

(G-349)
SNATURE LLC
650 Maskell St Apt 307 (22301-1062)
PHONE..............................571 251-1573
Marvin Williams,
EMP: 1
SALES (est): 42.5K Privately Held
SIC: 2329 Men's & boys' clothing

(G-350)
SOFTWARE INSIGHT
629 S Fairfax St (22314-3833)
PHONE..............................703 549-8554

Brian Noyes, *Principal*
EMP: 1
SALES (est): 100.5K Privately Held
SIC: 7372 Prepackaged software

(G-351)
SOLITUDE PUBLISHERS LLC
4673 Longstreet Ln # 103 (22311-4937)
PHONE..............................571 970-3918
Daniel Duggan, *Principal*
EMP: 1 EST: 2014
SALES (est): 57.3K Privately Held
SIC: 2741 Miscellaneous publishing

(G-352)
SPACENEWS INC
1414 Prince St Ste 204 (22314-2853)
P.O. Box 2763, Ferndale WA (98248-2763)
PHONE..............................571 421-2300
Greg Thomas, *CEO*
Brian Berger, *Chief*
John Dawson, *Director*
Lance Marburger, *Art Dir*
EMP: 10 EST: 2013
SALES (est): 647K Privately Held
WEB: www.hostedpayload.com
SIC: 2711 Newspapers, publishing & printing

(G-353)
ST ENGINEERING NORTH AMER INC (HQ)
Also Called: Vision Technologies Systems
99 Canal Center Plz # 220 (22314-1559)
PHONE..............................703 739-2610
John Coburn, *CEO*
John Rausch, *Vice Pres*
Milly Tay, *Vice Pres*
Dan Hays, *Opers Mgr*
Patrick Lee, *Treasurer*
◆ **EMP: 44**
SQ FT: 5,500
SALES (est): 1.8B Privately Held
WEB: www.stengg.com
SIC: 3731 3531 Shipbuilding & repairing; drags, road (construction & road maintenance equipment)

(G-354)
STAAB SIGN LANGUAGE SVCS LLC
4390 King St Apt 712 (22302-1546)
PHONE..............................301 775-2279
Elizabeth Y Staab, *President*
EMP: 2 EST: 2016
SALES (est): 55.2K Privately Held
SIC: 3993 Signs & advertising specialties

(G-355)
STEELFAB INC
1330 Braddock Pl Ste 200v (22314-1650)
PHONE..............................703 538-2320
Chris Gregory, *Vice Pres*
EMP: 3
SALES (corp-wide): 445MM Privately Held
WEB: www.steelfab-inc.com
SIC: 3441 3449 Building components, structural steel; miscellaneous metalwork
PA: Steelfab, Inc.
3025 Westport Rd
Charlotte NC 28208
704 394-5376

(G-356)
STEVENS SWITCH LLC
630 S Fairfax St (22314-3834)
PHONE..............................703 838-0686
Paul Schott Stevens Sr, *Administration*
EMP: 3
SALES (est): 180.7K Privately Held
SIC: 3679 Electronic switches

(G-357)
STEWART DAVID
1101 N Gaillard St (22304-1607)
PHONE..............................703 431-7233
David Stewart, *Principal*
EMP: 2
SALES (est): 111.8K Privately Held
SIC: 2389 Clergymen's vestments

(G-358)
STRATGIC TRNSP INITIATIVES INC
1800 Diagonal Rd (22314-2840)
PHONE..............................703 647-6564
EMP: 6
SQ FT: 2,000
SALES (est): 390.3K Privately Held
SIC: 2759 Commercial Printing

(G-359)
SVANACO INC
Also Called: Americaneagle.com
901 N Pitt St Ste 130 (22314-1562)
PHONE..............................571 312-3790
Chris Foss, *Manager*
EMP: 6
SALES (corp-wide): 54.5MM Privately Held
WEB: www.americaneagle.com
SIC: 7372 7375 Educational computer software; information retrieval services
PA: Svanaco, Inc.
2600 S River Rd
Des Plaines IL 60018
847 699-0300

(G-360)
SWEET SOUNDS MUSIC THERAPY LLC
2631 Jamestown Ln Apt 203 (22314-5883)
PHONE..............................703 965-3624
Katie Myers,
EMP: 1 EST: 2017
SALES (est): 58.6K Privately Held
SIC: 3841 Surgical & medical instruments

(G-361)
TAG 5 INDUSTRIES LLC
734 S Alfred St (22314-4004)
PHONE..............................703 647-0325
Russell Davies,
EMP: 1
SQ FT: 1,500
SALES (est): 200K Privately Held
WEB: www.tag5industries.com
SIC: 3699 Security control equipment & systems

(G-362)
TATE GLOBAL LLC
1800 Diagonal Rd Ste 520 (22314-2860)
PHONE..............................703 282-0737
EMP: 2
SALES (est): 86.6K Privately Held
WEB: www.tate-global.com
SIC: 7372 Application computer software

(G-363)
THIRD EYE DEVELOPMENT INTL INC
Also Called: Tedi
4890 Leesburg Pike 610 (22302-1102)
PHONE..............................631 682-1848
Daryl Sharpe, *CEO*
EMP: 2
SALES (est): 127.8K Privately Held
SIC: 7372 7371 Application computer software; business oriented computer software; operating systems computer software; computer software development

(G-364)
TIGHTY WHITEY SOAP CANDLE LLC
1201 Braddock Pl Apt 303 (22314-1669)
PHONE..............................202 818-9169
Harron Elloso, *Principal*
EMP: 1
SALES (est): 39.6K Privately Held
SIC: 3999 Candles

(G-365)
TIMOTHY E QUINN
Also Called: Capitol Imaging
424 S Saint Asaph St (22314-3748)
PHONE..............................301 212-9700
Timothy Quinn, *Owner*
EMP: 3
SALES (est): 301.2K Privately Held
WEB: www.capitolimaging.com
SIC: 2752 Commercial printing, offset

▲ = Import ▼=Export
◆ =Import/Export

(G-366)
TN COR INDUSTRIES INCORPORATED
2900 Eisenhower Ave (22314-5202)
PHONE..............................703 682-2001
EMP: 1 EST: 2007
SALES (est): 50K **Privately Held**
SIC: 3999 Mfg Misc Products

(G-367)
TREASURES OF AFRICAN ARTISTS
105 N Alfred St (22314-3010)
PHONE..............................571 263-2152
Gelila Mariam Selassie, *CEO*
EMP: 1
SALES (est): 41K **Privately Held**
SIC: 3915 Jewelry parts, unassembled

(G-368)
TRIO CHILD LLC
416 Cook St (22314-2359)
PHONE..............................703 299-0070
Greg Viggiano,
EMP: 6
SQ FT: 2,400
SALES (est): 390K **Privately Held**
WEB: www.triochild.com
SIC: 2043 Cereal breakfast foods

(G-369)
TROESEN ENTERPRISES LLC
4233 Raleigh Ave Apt 104 (22304-5386)
P.O. Box 6452, Arlington (22206-0452)
PHONE..............................571 405-3199
Joseph Cortez,
▼ EMP: 1
SALES (est): 95.9K **Privately Held**
SIC: 3577 7389 Computer peripheral equipment;

(G-370)
TROY PATRICK
Also Called: Redisec
107 W St 545 (22314)
PHONE..............................703 507-4914
Patrick Troy, *Owner*
EMP: 5
SQ FT: 1,200
SALES (est): 207.6K **Privately Held**
SIC: 3577 7379 3674 Input/output equipment, computer; ; solid state electronic devices

(G-371)
UNDERBITE PUBLISHING LLC
3802 Keller Ave (22302-1815)
PHONE..............................703 638-8040
EMP: 2
SALES (est): 82K **Privately Held**
SIC: 2741 Misc Publishing

(G-372)
VERISMA SYSTEMS INC (PA)
1421 Prince St Ste 250 (22314-2805)
PHONE..............................866 390-7404
Marty McKenna, *CEO*
Peter McCarthy, *VP Admin*
Tiffany Ellison, *Opers Staff*
James Matas, *CFO*
EMP: 10
SALES (est): 22.6MM **Privately Held**
WEB: www.verisma.com
SIC: 7372 Business oriented computer software

(G-373)
VETERAN FORCE INDUSTRIES LLC
300 Yoakum Pkwy Apt 1417 (22304-4063)
PHONE..............................912 492-5800
Tandrea Beasley, *Principal*
EMP: 1 EST: 2017
SALES (est): 47.3K **Privately Held**
SIC: 3999 Manufacturing industries

(G-374)
VIGILENT INC
Also Called: Vigilent Labs
5380 Eisenhower Ave (22304-4818)
PHONE..............................202 550-9515
John M Falk, *President*
Gen Klaus Schafer, *Vice Chairman*
Keith Copenhagen, *CTO*
EMP: 5

SQ FT: 2,500
SALES (est): 250K **Privately Held**
SIC: 3699 Flight simulators (training aids), electronic

(G-375)
VIRGINIA CFT BRWING SPPORT LLC
218 N Columbus St (22314-2412)
PHONE..............................703 960-3230
Charles Mason, *Principal*
EMP: 3 EST: 2015
SALES (est): 87K **Privately Held**
SIC: 2082 Malt beverages

(G-376)
VIRGINIA COFFEE COMPANY LLC
510 King St Ste 350 (22314-3146)
PHONE..............................703 566-3037
Mauricio Tamargo, *Manager*
Jason Poblete, *Manager*
EMP: 2 EST: 2017
SALES (est): 74.3K **Privately Held**
SIC: 2095 Freeze-dried coffee

(G-377)
VISION TECH LAND SYSTEMS
99 Canal Center Plz # 210 (22314-1559)
PHONE..............................703 739-2610
Cheow Teck Chang, *President*
EMP: 275
SALES (est): 17.8MM **Privately Held**
WEB: www.stengg.com
SIC: 3531 Pavers
HQ: St Engineering North America, Inc.
99 Canal Center Plz # 220
Alexandria VA 22314
703 739-2610

(G-378)
VITASECRETS USA LLC
3327 Duke St (22314-4597)
PHONE..............................919 212-1742
Hengameh Allen,
EMP: 3
SALES (est): 60K **Privately Held**
WEB: www.vitasecrets.com
SIC: 2023 Dietary supplements, dairy & non-dairy based

(G-379)
WASHINGTON AED EDUCATION FUND
121 N Henry St (22314-2903)
PHONE..............................703 739-9513
EMP: 1
SALES: 123.5K **Privately Held**
SIC: 2399 Mfg Fabricated Textile Products

(G-380)
WEB WELDING LLC
116 S Jordan St (22304-4916)
PHONE..............................703 212-4840
Joseph James, *Principal*
EMP: 1
SALES (est): 35.6K **Privately Held**
SIC: 7692 Welding repair

(G-381)
WESTERN GRAPHICS INC
1259 Dartmouth Ct (22314-4784)
PHONE..............................575 849-1209
EMP: 3
SALES (corp-wide): 1.5MM **Privately Held**
WEB: www.westerngraphicsinc.com
SIC: 2752 8412 Commercial printing, offset; museums & art galleries
PA: Western Graphics, Inc
714 W Cienega Ave Ste A
San Dimas CA 91773
909 305-9500

(G-382)
WHERE GOOD GROWS LLC
950 N Washington St # 555 (22314-1534)
PHONE..............................240 506-0011
Erin Antosh, *CEO*
EMP: 1
SALES (est): 87.2K **Privately Held**
WEB: www.northropgrumman.com
SIC: 3812 Search & navigation equipment

(G-383)
WINGSPAN PUBLICATIONS
Also Called: Wings of Our Own
308 Skyhill Rd (22314-4918)
PHONE..............................703 212-0005
Paulette K Johnson, *Owner*
EMP: 1
SALES (est): 49.8K **Privately Held**
SIC: 2759 Publication printing

(G-384)
WISE FELINE INC
2606 Ridge Road Dr (22302-2831)
PHONE..............................703 609-2686
Terri Symonds Grow, *Owner*
EMP: 2
SALES (est): 92.6K **Privately Held**
WEB: www.wisefeline.com
SIC: 3999 7389 Pet supplies;

(G-385)
WOLF ZSUZSI OF BUDAPEST
105 N Union St Ste 229 (22314-3217)
PHONE..............................703 548-3319
EMP: 1
SALES (est): 73.2K **Privately Held**
SIC: 3911 Mfg Precious Metal Jewelry

(G-386)
WOOD CREATIONS
801 S Pitt St Apt 429 (22314-4357)
PHONE..............................571 235-0717
Chuck Mills, *Principal*
EMP: 1
SALES (est): 64.2K **Privately Held**
SIC: 2431 Millwork

(G-387)
WOODLAND GROUP LLC
509 Woodland Ter (22302-3318)
PHONE..............................571 312-5951
Louis Alefantis, *Principal*
EMP: 2 EST: 2015
SALES (est): 54.3K **Privately Held**
SIC: 2499 Wood products

(G-388)
WORKERS ON WHEELS
119 S Saint Asaph St (22314-3119)
PHONE..............................703 549-6287
EMP: 2 EST: 2008
SALES (est): 130K **Privately Held**
SIC: 3312 Blast Furnace-Steel Works

(G-389)
WP COMPANY LLC
Also Called: Alexandria Arlington Bureau
526 King St Ste 515 (22314-3143)
PHONE..............................703 518-3000
Ria Manglapus, *Manager*
EMP: 10 **Privately Held**
WEB: www.washingtonpost.com
SIC: 2711 8299 Newspapers, publishing & printing; tutoring school
HQ: Wp Company Llc
1301 K St Nw
Washington DC 20071

(G-390)
YBA PUBLISHING LLC
3682 King St Unit 3535 (22302-8820)
PHONE..............................703 763-2710
Angela McDowell, *CEO*
EMP: 3
SALES (est): 216.2K **Privately Held**
SIC: 2741 Miscellaneous publishing

(G-391)
YOUR PUZZLE SOURCE LLC
802 Hall Pl (22302-3405)
PHONE..............................703 461-7788
Phil Fraas, *Principal*
EMP: 1 EST: 2016
SALES (est): 46.3K **Privately Held**
WEB: www.yourpuzzlesource.com
SIC: 3944 Puzzles

(G-392)
ZEBRA PRESS LLC
1439 Juliana Pl (22304-1516)
PHONE..............................703 370-6641
Linda Hill, *Principal*
EMP: 2 EST: 2014

SALES (est): 72.9K **Privately Held**
WEB: www.thezebra.org
SIC: 2741 Miscellaneous publishing

Alexandria
Fairfax County

(G-393)
1 A LIFESAFER INC
5712 General Wash Dr (22312-2430)
PHONE..............................800 634-3077
EMP: 1 **Privately Held**
WEB: www.lifesafer.com
SIC: 3829 Measuring & controlling devices
PA: 1 A Lifesafer, Inc.
3630 Park 42 Dr Ste 170f
Cincinnati OH 45241

(G-394)
1602 GROUP LLC
Also Called: Solid State Organ System
5600 General Wash Dr (22312-2415)
PHONE..............................703 933-0024
Duncan Crundwell, *President*
Adrian Wadey, *Chief Engr*
Alan Bragg, *Manager*
Debbie Saunders, *Manager*
Mark Gilliam, *CTO*
EMP: 20
SQ FT: 2,700
SALES (est): 2.5MM **Privately Held**
WEB: www.1602group.com
SIC: 3651 Audio electronic systems

(G-395)
30+ DENIM/LEATHER PROJECT
5800 Quantrell Ave # 716 (22312-2705)
PHONE..............................301 233-0968
Mark M Booker, *Principal*
EMP: 1
SALES (est): 46.5K **Privately Held**
SIC: 2211 Denims

(G-396)
3R BEHAVIORAL SOLUTIONS INC
4203 Kimbrelee Ct (22309-3000)
PHONE..............................571 332-6232
Doug Meeker, *CEO*
EMP: 3
SALES (est): 86K **Privately Held**
WEB: www.lifesherpapp.com
SIC: 7372 7371 Application computer software; computer software development & applications

(G-397)
6TH FLOOR CANDLE COMPANY LLC
6410 Castlefin Way (22315-5513)
PHONE..............................917 580-2251
Caroline Knaby, *Principal*
EMP: 1
SALES (est): 39.6K **Privately Held**
SIC: 3999 Candles

(G-398)
A&H WELDING INC
6236 Indian Run Pkwy (22312-6436)
PHONE..............................703 628-4817
Hugo Sorto, *Principal*
EMP: 2
SALES (est): 62.1K **Privately Held**
SIC: 7692 Welding repair

(G-399)
ABC IMAGING
5290 Shawnee Rd Lbby (22312-2377)
PHONE..............................214 231-1332
EMP: 2
SALES (est): 92.1K **Privately Held**
SIC: 2759 Commercial printing

(G-400)
ABC IMAGING OF WASHINGTON (PA)
5290 Shawnee Rd Ste 300 (22312-2377)
PHONE..............................202 429-8870
Medi Falsafi, *President*
Randall Guthmiller, *Regional Mgr*
Wilson Claudell, *District Mgr*
Reza Arvin, *Vice Pres*
Brian Cann, *Opers Mgr*

EMP: 12
SQ FT: 17,000
SALES (est): 144.4MM **Privately Held**
WEB: www.abcimaging.com
SIC: 2759 Advertising literature: printing

(G-401)
ACE TITLE & ESCROW INC
5820 Tilbury Rd (22310-1607)
PHONE..................................703 629-5768
Nishta Gupta, *Administration*
EMP: 2
SALES (est): 99.5K **Privately Held**
SIC: 3571 Personal computers (microcomputers)

(G-402)
ACRE MEDIA LLC
6214 Roudsby Ln (22315-5285)
PHONE..................................703 314-4465
Shirley Johnson-Boyd,
EMP: 1 **EST:** 2013
SALES (est): 56.3K **Privately Held**
SIC: 2731 7379 8999 Book publishing; ;
commercial & literary writings

(G-403)
ADDITIVE MFG EXCH AMEX LLC
5316 Jesmond St (22315-5563)
PHONE..................................703 971-3174
Morgan Donaldson, *Principal*
EMP: 2
SALES (est): 95.6K **Privately Held**
SIC: 3999 Manufacturing industries

(G-404)
ADVANCE DESIGN & MANUFACTURING
6460a General Green Way (22312-2413)
PHONE..................................703 256-9550
Walter Watson, *President*
EMP: 69 **EST:** 1977
SQ FT: 4,500
SALES (est): 1.8MM **Privately Held**
WEB: www.machineshopadm.com
SIC: 3599 Machine shop, jobbing & repair

(G-405)
AFRITECH LLC
7912 Morning Ride Ct (22315-5051)
PHONE..................................703 550-0392
Edward Perry, *President*
EMP: 1
SALES (est): 72.6K **Privately Held**
SIC: 3523 7389 Farm machinery & equipment;

(G-406)
AI METRIX INC (DH)
5971 Kingstowne Vlg (22315-5891)
PHONE..................................703 254-2000
Eric M Demarco, *President*
Phil Carrai, *Vice Pres*
Michael W Fink, *Vice Pres*
Deanna H Lund, *CFO*
Laura L Siegal, *Treasurer*
EMP: 20
SQ FT: 4,000
SALES (est): 2.2MM **Publicly Held**
SIC: 3661 7371 Telephone & telegraph
apparatus; computer software development
HQ: Kratos Technology & Training Solutions, Inc.
10680 Treena St Fl 6
San Diego CA 92131
858 812-7300

(G-407)
ALIENFEET SPORTS SOCKS
6510 Cottonwood Dr (22310-2813)
PHONE..................................703 864-8892
EMP: 2
SALES (est): 73.4K **Privately Held**
SIC: 2252 Socks

(G-408)
ALL ABOUT FRAMES
6641 Wakefield Dr Ste 115 (22307-6859)
PHONE..................................703 998-5868
David Laforce, *Owner*
EMP: 1
SALES (est): 68.4K **Privately Held**
WEB: www.allaboutframes.com
SIC: 2499 Picture & mirror frames, wood

(G-409)
AMADI PUBLISHING LLC
4020 Javins Dr (22310-2037)
PHONE..................................703 329-4535
EMP: 2 **EST:** 2008
SALES (est): 87K **Privately Held**
SIC: 2741 Misc Publishing

(G-410)
AMAZON MLLWK INSTALLATIONS LLC
5505 Sheldon Dr (22312-6334)
PHONE..................................703 200-9076
Dereck Delgadillo, *Principal*
EMP: 1
SALES (est): 41.5K **Privately Held**
SIC: 2499 Wood products

(G-411)
AMERICAN SIGN LNGUAGE SVCS LLC
8707 Bradgate Rd (22308-2312)
PHONE..................................571 969-2751
William R Kendrick, *Manager*
Heather Kendrick,
EMP: 2
SALES (est): 170.2K **Privately Held**
WEB: www.asls.biz
SIC: 3993 Signs & advertising specialties

(G-412)
AMG INTERNATIONAL INC
6731 Applemint Ln (22310-2650)
PHONE..................................703 988-4741
EMP: 2
SALES (est): 99.5K **Privately Held**
SIC: 3914 Mfg Silverware/Plated Ware

(G-413)
ANDRES R HENRIQUZ
8625 Village Way (22309-1615)
PHONE..................................703 629-9821
Andres Henriquez, *COO*
EMP: 2 **EST:** 2016
SALES (est): 85.9K **Privately Held**
SIC: 3577 Computer peripheral equipment

(G-414)
ANTILLIAN TRADING COMPANY LLC
7204 Spring Faire Ct C (22315-4504)
PHONE..................................703 626-6333
David S James, *Mng Member*
Bernie Bolvito,
EMP: 27
SALES (est): 100K **Privately Held**
SIC: 2311 8322 7389 Military uniforms,
men's & youths': purchased materials;
meal delivery program; business services

(G-415)
APPLIED TECHNOLLOGY
6917 Tulsa Ct (22307-1730)
PHONE..................................703 660-8422
EMP: 2
SALES (est): 122.5K **Privately Held**
SIC: 3663 Receivers, radio communications

(G-416)
APPLIED TECHNOLOGY GROUP INC
2401 Huntington Ave (22303-1531)
PHONE..................................703 960-5555
James McGuinness, *President*
EMP: 45 **EST:** 1998
SALES (est): 5.2MM **Privately Held**
WEB: www.appliedtechnologygroup.com
SIC: 3444 Sheet metalwork

(G-417)
ARC DUST LLC
6148 Old Telegraph Rd (22310-3145)
PHONE..................................571 839-0223
Joseph Peebles, *CEO*
Charles Pappas, *CFO*
Michael Knox, *CTO*
EMP: 4
SALES (est): 134.5K **Privately Held**
SIC: 3295 Minerals, ground or treated

(G-418)
ASMARS MEDITERRANEAN FOOD INC
6460 Gen Green Way Ste F (22312-2413)
PHONE..................................703 750-2960
Joseph Asmar, *President*
◆ **EMP:** 15 **EST:** 1997
SQ FT: 4,000
SALES (est): 2.3MM **Privately Held**
WEB: www.asmars.com
SIC: 2099 5141 Salads, fresh or refrigerated; dips, except cheese & sour cream based; groceries, general line

(G-419)
AVN PRINTS
4003 Javins Dr (22310-2036)
PHONE..................................703 473-7498
Anabel Villarroel, *Principal*
EMP: 2
SALES (est): 83.9K **Privately Held**
WEB: www.avn-services.com
SIC: 2752 Commercial printing, lithographic

(G-420)
B&B INDUSTRIES LLC
7923 San Leandro Pl (22309-1460)
PHONE..................................703 855-2142
Marvin Barrera, *Principal*
Michelle Burgos, *Principal*
EMP: 3
SALES (est): 161.1K **Privately Held**
SIC: 3999 Manufacturing industries

(G-421)
BEST IMPRESSIONS INC
5701t General Wash Dr (22312-2408)
PHONE..................................703 518-1375
Jeff Griffith, *President*
Dale Davis, *Principal*
William Garvey, *Principal*
Ceasar Magney, *Principal*
EMP: 13
SALES (est): 650K **Privately Held**
WEB: www.bestimpressionsinc.net
SIC: 2752 7389 7334 Commercial printing, offset; mailing & messenger services; photocopying & duplicating services

(G-422)
BETTER KARMA LLC
6018 Goldenrod Ct (22310-4402)
PHONE..................................703 971-1072
Dylan Alliata,
EMP: 1
SALES (est): 66.2K **Privately Held**
WEB: www.betterkarmallc.com
SIC: 2731 Book publishing

(G-423)
BIMBO BAKERIES
6636 Fleet Dr (22310-2407)
PHONE..................................804 475-6776
EMP: 8 **EST:** 2012
SALES (est): 470.3K **Privately Held**
SIC: 2051 Bakery: wholesale or wholesale/retail combined

(G-424)
BLAKE COLLECTION
Also Called: Blake James L
6222 Tally Ho Ln (22307-1013)
PHONE..................................703 329-1599
James L Blake, *Owner*
Betty J Blake, *Principal*
EMP: 2 **Privately Held**
WEB: www.theblakecollection.com
SIC: 3211 Antique glass

(G-425)
BLISSFUL GARDENZ INC
5119 Rosemont Ave (22309-1711)
P.O. Box 15581 (22309-0581)
PHONE..................................703 360-2191
Adeyinka Laiyemo, *Owner*
EMP: 2
SALES (est): 107.2K **Privately Held**
SIC: 2741 Miscellaneous publishing

(G-426)
BRIGHTS ANTIQUE SLOT MACHINE
3406 Burgundy Rd (22303-1230)
PHONE..................................703 906-8389

Richard E Bright, *Administration*
EMP: 1
SALES (est): 48K **Privately Held**
WEB: www.rebslots.com
SIC: 3999 Slot machines

(G-427)
C & M AUTO MACHINE SHOP INC
Also Called: C and M Auto Machine Shop Svc
8804 Badger Dr (22309-4039)
PHONE..................................703 780-0566
Larry Mc Cormick, *President*
EMP: 2
SALES (est): 140K **Privately Held**
SIC: 3599 Machine shop, jobbing & repair

(G-428)
CALDWELL INDUSTRIES INC
Also Called: AAA Iron Works
4406 Longworthe Sq (22309-1226)
PHONE..................................703 403-3272
John W Caldwell Jr, *President*
EMP: 3
SALES (est): 150K **Privately Held**
SIC: 7692 1799 3446 Welding repair;
welding on site; fences or posts, ornamental iron or steel

(G-429)
CHRISTINE SMITH
Also Called: Khazana
7509 Ashby Ln Unit D (22315-5215)
PHONE..................................703 399-1944
Christine Smith, *Owner*
EMP: 1
SALES (est): 64.2K **Privately Held**
SIC: 2273 Rugs, hand & machine made

(G-430)
CL CABINETRY CORPORATION
6531 Little River Tpke A1 (22312-1418)
PHONE..................................703 586-6766
Sun Kyung Lee, *President*
EMP: 2
SALES (est): 59.1K **Privately Held**
SIC: 2434 Wood kitchen cabinets

(G-431)
CLEAN BUILDING LLC
4104 Sunburst Ct (22303-1147)
PHONE..................................703 589-9544
William Rajo, *Mng Member*
EMP: 1 **EST:** 2016
SALES (est): 250K **Privately Held**
SIC: 2752 Commercial printing, lithographic

(G-432)
CLEANPOWERPARTNERS
6614 The Pkwy (22310-3057)
PHONE..................................301 651-0690
Alexander J Eucare, *Principal*
EMP: 3
SALES (est): 100K **Privately Held**
SIC: 2951 Asphalt paving mixtures & blocks

(G-433)
CONVERGENT DATA GROUP
6421 Willowood Ln (22310-2940)
PHONE..................................571 276-0756
Hung Nguyen, *Principal*
EMP: 3
SALES (est): 235.9K **Privately Held**
SIC: 3674 Semiconductors & related devices

(G-434)
CONVOY SKATEBOARDS LTD
3544 Huntley Manor Ln (22306-5116)
PHONE..................................571 216-2740
Eamonn Timothy Bourke, *Administration*
EMP: 2 **EST:** 2010
SALES (est): 104.4K **Privately Held**
WEB: www.convoyskateboards.com
SIC: 3949 Skateboards

(G-435)
CROSSTOWN SHIPG & SUP CO LLC
2639 Arlington Dr Apt 303 (22306-3614)
PHONE..................................513 252-5370
Papa Seye,
EMP: 1

▲ = Import ▼=Export
◆ =Import/Export

SALES (est): 86.7K **Privately Held**
SIC: 2674 Shipping bags or sacks, including multiwall & heavy duty

(G-436)
CUISINE SOLUTIONS INC
85 S Bragg St Ste 600 (22312-2793)
PHONE.....................................303 904-4771
Jean-Pierre Guillaud, *Vice Pres*
EMP: 2
SALES (est): 62.3K **Privately Held**
SIC: 2099 Food preparations

(G-437)
CUSTOM CANVAS WORKS INC
4555 Interlachen Ct G (22312-3213)
PHONE.....................................571 249-6443
Kenneth Arscott, *Principal*
EMP: 2
SALES (est): 56.3K **Privately Held**
WEB: www.customcanvasworksinc.com
SIC: 2211 Canvas

(G-438)
D & P PRINTING & GRAPHICS INC
5641i General Wash Dr (22312-2403)
PHONE.....................................703 941-2114
John P Dwyer, *President*
Kathleen Dwyer, *Treasurer*
EMP: 10
SQ FT: 1,800
SALES (est): 1.3MM **Privately Held**
WEB: www.dpprinting.com
SIC: 2752 2791 2789 Commercial printing, offset; typesetting; binding only: books, pamphlets, magazines, etc.

(G-439)
DAGNEWCOMPANY INC
Also Called: Habesha View
5934 Woodfield Estates Dr (22310-1872)
PHONE.....................................703 835-0827
Theodros Dagnew, *President*
EMP: 11
SALES (est): 2.8K **Privately Held**
SIC: 2741

(G-440)
DALITSO LLC
1602 Belle View Blvd # 321 (22307-6531)
PHONE.....................................571 385-4927
Farzana Kennedy, *President*
EMP: 2
SALES (est): 83.9K
SALES (corp-wide): 10.2MM **Privately Held**
SIC: 2833 Medicinals & botanicals
PA: Jushi Holdings Inc
300 Bellevue Centre 235-15th St
West Vancouver BC
604 562-7569

(G-441)
DARWIN MARQUINA
Also Called: Darwin Hvac
4713 Perch Pl (22309-1117)
PHONE.....................................703 220-2940
Darwin Marquina, *Owner*
EMP: 1
SALES (est): 50.7K **Privately Held**
SIC: 3585 Parts for heating, cooling & refrigerating equipment

(G-442)
DAVID GASKILL
4101 Komes Ct (22306-1252)
PHONE.....................................703 768-2172
David Gaskill, *Owner*
EMP: 1
SALES (est): 500K **Privately Held**
SIC: 3829 Measuring & controlling devices

(G-443)
DECOSTA ENTERPRISES INC
Also Called: De Costa's Silkscreening
1116 Collingwood Rd (22308-1726)
PHONE.....................................703 768-4270
Richard De Costa, *President*
Charlotte De Costa, *Corp Secy*
EMP: 3
SALES (est): 500K **Privately Held**
SIC: 2396 5941 5999 7389 Screen printing on fabric articles; sporting goods & bicycle shops; trophies & plaques; engraving service

(G-444)
DELLA JS DELECTABLES LLC
6605 Schurtz St (22310-2658)
PHONE.....................................703 922-4687
Jerry Young, *Mng Member*
Lydia Tynes-Young,
EMP: 1
SALES (est): 81.3K **Privately Held**
SIC: 2099 Food preparations

(G-445)
DELTA ELECTRONICS INC
5730 General Wash Dr (22312-2407)
P.O. Box 11268 (22312-0268)
PHONE.....................................703 354-3350
William R Fox, *President*
Jeff Fu, *General Mgr*
Joe Novak, *Vice Pres*
Joseph Novak, *Vice Pres*
Lary Marash, *Engineer*
EMP: 16
SQ FT: 38,000
SALES (est): 2.5MM **Privately Held**
WEB: www.deltaelectronics.com
SIC: 3663 3823 3677 3643 Antennas, transmitting & communications; radio broadcasting & communications equipment; industrial instrmnts msrmnt display/control process variable; electronic coils, transformers & other inductors; current-carrying wiring devices

(G-446)
DEMOISELLE VERTICAL LLC
5800 Quantrell Ave # 1620 (22312-2735)
PHONE.....................................202 431-8032
Saurav Batra, *COO*
EMP: 2
SALES (est): 135.5K **Privately Held**
SIC: 2591 Blinds vertical

(G-447)
DINO SOFTWARE CORPORATION
1912 Earldale Ct Ste 200 (22306-2715)
P.O. Box 7105 (22307-0105)
PHONE.....................................703 768-2610
Murray Kruger, *President*
Larry Crilley, *Vice Pres*
Tom Doering, *Manager*
Gary Bleemer, *CTO*
Blair Svihra, *Info Tech Mgr*
EMP: 50
SALES (est): 4.9MM **Privately Held**
WEB: www.dino-software.com
SIC: 7372 Prepackaged software

(G-448)
DOI NAY NEWSPAPER
6515 Gretna Green Way (22312-3115)
PHONE.....................................703 748-1239
Tan Tran, *Publisher*
Lee Hoang, *Principal*
EMP: 5
SALES (est): 224.8K **Privately Held**
WEB: www.doinayonline.com
SIC: 2711 Newspapers

(G-449)
DOMINION PRESS WINERY LLC
8733b Cooper Rd (22309-3906)
PHONE.....................................703 395-5109
Andrew William Rosado, *Principal*
EMP: 2
SALES (est): 41.3K **Privately Held**
SIC: 2741 Miscellaneous publishing

(G-450)
DRONE SAFETY LLC
3602 Old Vernon Ct (22309-2060)
PHONE.....................................703 589-6738
Marianne Mixon, *Administration*
EMP: 2
SALES (est): 91K **Privately Held**
SIC: 3721 Motorized aircraft

(G-451)
DYNAMITE DEMOLITION LLC
8020 Ashboro Dr (22309-1306)
PHONE.....................................571 241-4658
Ana Villatoro,
EMP: 8

SALES (est): 187.6K **Privately Held**
SIC: 1081 1795 Metal mining exploration & development services; wrecking & demolition work

(G-452)
EJN LLC
Also Called: Nature By Ejn
5509 Vine St (22310-1017)
P.O. Box 532, Arlington (22216-0532)
PHONE.....................................646 621-5647
Esinam J Nduom, *CEO*
EMP: 1
SALES (est): 47.2K **Privately Held**
SIC: 2844 Shampoos, rinses, conditioners: hair; cosmetic preparations; face creams or lotions

(G-453)
ELIAS LLC
Also Called: Elias Tile
5650 General Wash Dr (22312-2415)
PHONE.....................................703 663-1192
Fatih Guner,
▲ EMP: 1
SQ FT: 135,000
SALES (est): 89.2K **Privately Held**
SIC: 3253 5032 Ceramic wall & floor tile; tile & clay products

(G-454)
ELITE CABINET LLC
5608 General Wash Dr (22312-2415)
PHONE.....................................703 909-0404
Mendsaikhan Shinejil, *Principal*
EMP: 2
SALES (est): 178.7K **Privately Held**
WEB: www.elitecabinetllc.com
SIC: 2434 Wood kitchen cabinets

(G-455)
ELITE PRINTS
8121 Richmond Hwy (22309-3613)
PHONE.....................................703 780-3403
Binyam Gebreyohannes, *CEO*
EMP: 4
SALES (est): 268.5K **Privately Held**
WEB: www.elite-prints.com
SIC: 2759 2396 2752 Screen printing; linings, apparel: made from purchased materials; screen printing on fabric articles; promotional printing, lithographic

(G-456)
ELLINGTON MECHANICAL SVCS INC
1602 Belle View Blvd # 3170 (22307-6531)
PHONE.....................................703 220-1651
Robert Butler, *CEO*
EMP: 3
SALES (est): 700K **Privately Held**
SIC: 1389 Construction, repair & dismantling services

(G-457)
ENERGIZE YOUR SIZE LLC
8237 Chancery Ct (22308-1515)
PHONE.....................................703 360-1093
Cynthia Palmerino, *Principal*
EMP: 2 EST: 2011
SALES (est): 145.9K **Privately Held**
WEB: www.energizeyoursize.com
SIC: 2899 Sizes

(G-458)
EXCLUSIVE WINE IMPORTS LLC
7210 Marlan Dr (22307-1912)
PHONE.....................................703 765-9749
James Ungerleider, *Mng Member*
▲ EMP: 4
SALES (est): 190.8K **Privately Held**
WEB: www.exclusivewineimports.com
SIC: 2084 Wines

(G-459)
EXTRA SPACE STORAGE
5321 Shawnee Rd (22312-2312)
PHONE.....................................703 719-4354
Spencer F Kirk, *CEO*
EMP: 4
SALES (est): 171.1K **Privately Held**
SIC: 2673 Food storage & frozen food bags, plastic

(G-460)
FARBES LLC
6590 Irvin Ct (22312-2216)
PHONE.....................................240 426-9680
Weijia Yan,
William Yan,
EMP: 4
SALES (est): 273.3K **Privately Held**
SIC: 3845 Electromedical equipment

(G-461)
FERRER
3096 Madison Hill Ct (22310-2216)
PHONE.....................................703 862-4891
Angel Ferrer, *Principal*
EMP: 3
SALES (est): 214.4K **Privately Held**
SIC: 2834 Pharmaceutical preparations

(G-462)
FIREFALL-LITERARY
4905 Tunlaw St (22312-2140)
PHONE.....................................703 942-6616
Elihu Blotnick, *Director*
EMP: 1
SALES (est): 61K **Privately Held**
WEB: www.firefallmedia.com
SIC: 2731 Books: publishing only

(G-463)
FLAGSTONE
5000 Treetop Ln (22310-2800)
P.O. Box 4373 (22303-0373)
PHONE.....................................815 790-0582
Jamie A Mastandrea, *Administration*
EMP: 2
SALES (est): 67.7K **Privately Held**
SIC: 3281 Flagstones

(G-464)
FONTANA LITHOGRAPH INC
1207 Alden Rd (22308-2504)
PHONE.....................................202 296-3276
EMP: 21
SALES (corp-wide): 25.2MM **Privately Held**
WEB: www.mosaic.buzz
SIC: 2752 Commercial printing, lithographic
PA: Fontana Lithograph, Inc.
4801 Viewpoint Pl
Hyattsville MD 20781
301 927-3800

(G-465)
FURNACE MFG INC
Also Called: Funace Media
6315 Bren Mar Dr Ste 195 (22312-6349)
P.O. Box 3268, Merrifield (22116-3268)
PHONE.....................................703 205-0007
Eric Astor, *President*
Ali Miller, *Vice Pres*
Jarett Minkoff, *Opers Staff*
Thao Nguyen, *Office Mgr*
Nicholas Szumigala, *Graphic Designe*
◆ EMP: 13
SQ FT: 12,000
SALES (est): 3.3MM **Privately Held**
WEB: www.furnacemfg.com
SIC: 3652 Compact laser discs, prerecorded

(G-466)
GAP PRINTING
5413a Vine St (22310-1025)
PHONE.....................................703 585-1532
EMP: 2
SALES (est): 83.9K **Privately Held**
SIC: 2752 Commercial printing, lithographic

(G-467)
GERMFREAK INC
6310 Olmi Landrith Dr (22307-1317)
PHONE.....................................443 254-0805
Elizabeth Wilmot, *President*
Lauren Wilmot, *Vice Pres*
EMP: 2 EST: 2016
SALES (est): 80K **Privately Held**
SIC: 3999 Sterilizers, barber & beauty shop

(G-468)
GHODOUSI LLC
Also Called: G-Technology Group
5700 Gen Wshngtn Dr Ste H (22312-2406)
PHONE...................................480 544-3192
Arman Ghodousi,
EMP: 7
SALES (est): 50K **Privately Held**
WEB: www.secureopensolutions.com
SIC: 3812 8711 Search & detection systems & instruments; engineering services

(G-469)
GIBRALTAR ENERGY LLC
6524 Langleigh Way (22315-3470)
PHONE...................................202 642-2704
Imran Hussain, *President*
EMP: 1
SALES (est): 92.7K **Privately Held**
SIC: 2911 4731 5172 8742 Petroleum refining; transportation agents & brokers; petroleum brokers; management consulting services

(G-470)
GOLDBELT WOLF LLC
5500 Cherokee Ave Ste 200 (22312-2321)
PHONE...................................703 584-8889
Phillip Scheible, *President*
EMP: 78
SQ FT: 2,000
SALES (est): 11.7MM **Privately Held**
WEB: www.goldbeltwolf.com
SIC: 3711 3483 Cars, armored, assembly of; ammunition components
PA: Goldbelt, Incorporated
3025 Clinton Dr Ste 100
Juneau AK 99801
907 790-4990

(G-471)
GRAIN FREE PRODUCTS INC
7503 Calderon Ct Unit F (22306-2267)
PHONE...................................703 418-0000
Fritz Juergen Wisotzki, *President*
Charity Swift, *Corp Secy*
Stephen Swift, *Vice Pres*
Helen Wisotzki, *Director*
EMP: 4
SALES (est): 370K **Privately Held**
SIC: 2899 Metal treating compounds

(G-472)
H2 AS FUEL CORPORATION
6131 Lincolnia Rd Ste 104 (22312-2706)
PHONE...................................703 980-5262
Ervin Reeves, *CEO*
EMP: 5
SALES (est): 432.9K **Privately Held**
SIC: 2813 Industrial gases

(G-473)
HAIRBOTICS LLC
5400 Shawnee Rd Ste 110 (22312-2300)
PHONE...................................703 496-6083
Afanso Bobby Spence,
EMP: 1
SALES (est): 85.2K **Privately Held**
SIC: 3842 5047 Prosthetic appliances; medical equipment & supplies

(G-474)
HANGER PROSTHETICS ORTHOTICS
7011c Manchester Blvd (22310-3426)
PHONE...................................703 719-0143
EMP: 2 EST: 2015
SALES (est): 145.6K **Privately Held**
SIC: 3842 Prosthetic appliances

(G-475)
HANKE INDUSTRIES LLC
7221 Barry Rd (22315-3434)
PHONE...................................601 665-2147
Kevin Hanke, *Principal*
EMP: 2
SALES (est): 98.4K **Privately Held**
SIC: 3999 Manufacturing industries

(G-476)
HEAVYN & HOPES CANDLE CO
6503 Grange Ln Unit 202 (22315-5813)
PHONE...................................301 980-8299
Lorraine Carroll, *Principal*
EMP: 1

SALES (est): 39.6K **Privately Held**
SIC: 3999 Candles

(G-477)
HEMLOCK DESIGN GROUP INC
Also Called: Development News Service
2804 Boswell Ave (22306-2811)
P.O. Box 6229 (22306-0229)
PHONE...................................703 765-0379
Linda Jemison, *President*
Terry Jemison, *Admin Sec*
EMP: 2
SALES (est): 10K **Privately Held**
SIC: 2741 Newsletter publishing

(G-478)
HIRSCH COMMUNICATION
5904 Mount Eagle Dr (22303-2534)
PHONE...................................703 960-3649
Barbara Hirsch, *Owner*
EMP: 2 EST: 1997
SALES (est): 61.5K **Privately Held**
SIC: 2741 Miscellaneous publishing

(G-479)
HOL INDUSTRIES LLC
8588 Richmond Hwy (22309-8000)
PHONE...................................703 835-5476
Stephan Arthur Lee, *Principal*
EMP: 2
SALES (est): 124.9K **Privately Held**
SIC: 3999 Manufacturing industries

(G-480)
HOLLIS BOOKS LLC
5904 Mount Eagle Dr # 1009 (22303-2534)
PHONE...................................703 855-7759
Brent Kroetch, *Principal*
Brandi Kroetch-Rafferty,
Brandi Kroetch Rafferty,
EMP: 2 EST: 1999
SALES (est): 40K **Privately Held**
SIC: 2731 Books: publishing only

(G-481)
ICONICLOUD INC
6220 Quander Rd (22307-1004)
PHONE...................................703 864-1203
David McDonell, *President*
Kevin Quinn, *Vice Pres*
EMP: 4
SALES (est): 147.2K **Privately Held**
SIC: 7372 7373 Application computer software; business oriented computer software; systems software development services

(G-482)
IGNACIO C GARCIA
Also Called: Ig Flooring
6310 Windsor Ave (22315-3421)
PHONE...................................703 922-9829
Ignacio C Garcia, *Principal*
EMP: 1
SALES (est): 111.9K **Privately Held**
SIC: 2426 Flooring, hardwood

(G-483)
INAMOD GROUP LLC
6387 Strawbridge Sq Dr (22312-1917)
PHONE...................................703 626-2453
Vincent Mauro, *Principal*
EMP: 1
SALES (est): 56.4K **Privately Held**
SIC: 2741 Miscellaneous publishing

(G-484)
INDIGO PEN PUBLISHING LLC
7102 Snug Harbor Ct (22315-4238)
PHONE...................................888 670-4010
James Waggoner,
EMP: 1
SALES (est): 61.5K **Privately Held**
SIC: 2731 7389 Books: publishing & printing;

(G-485)
INDUSTRIES MASSIVE
7129 Rock Ridge Ln (22315-5102)
PHONE...................................703 347-6074
EMP: 1 EST: 2018
SALES (est): 39.6K **Privately Held**
SIC: 3999 Manufacturing industries

(G-486)
INTERBYTE
7041 Kings Manor Dr (22315-5637)
PHONE...................................703 825-8774
Nino Zahrastnik, *Owner*
▲ EMP: 3
SALES (est): 1.9MM **Privately Held**
WEB: www.interbyte.com
SIC: 3728 3571 3825 3841 Aircraft parts & equipment; computers, digital, analog or hybrid; instruments for measuring electrical quantities; medical instruments & equipment, blood & bone work; radio broadcasting & communications equipment

(G-487)
INTERBYTE CORP
7041 Kings Manor Dr (22315-5637)
PHONE...................................703 825-8774
Nino Zahrastnik, *Principal*
EMP: 3
SALES (est): 266.1K **Privately Held**
SIC: 3728 Aircraft parts & equipment

(G-488)
INTERMISSION
Also Called: Intermission Magazine
6205 Redwood Ln (22310-2934)
PHONE...................................703 971-7530
Verna Karens, *Owner*
Karen Spicka, *Principal*
EMP: 1 EST: 1985
SALES (est): 91.2K **Privately Held**
SIC: 2721 Periodicals

(G-489)
IRON HORSE CO
6209 Berlee Dr (22312-1225)
PHONE...................................703 256-2853
Carolyn Moore, *President*
Moore Carolyn Smith, *Vice Pres*
EMP: 5
SALES (est): 338.3K **Privately Held**
SIC: 3944 Toy trains, airplanes & automobiles

(G-490)
J K DRAPERY INC
5641l General Wash Dr (22312-2403)
PHONE...................................703 941-3788
Jamil Khraibani, *President*
Maria Victoria Khraibani, *Vice Pres*
EMP: 11
SQ FT: 2,800
SALES (est): 530K **Privately Held**
SIC: 2391 Curtains, window: made from purchased materials

(G-491)
JANES CYBER DEFENSE LLC
Also Called: Jcd
4220 Shannon Hill Rd (22310-2939)
PHONE...................................703 489-1872
Michael Santens, *Principal*
Jane Bernat, *Principal*
EMP: 2
SALES (est): 106.6K **Privately Held**
SIC: 3812 Defense systems & equipment

(G-492)
JANICE RESEARCH GROUP
6363 Walker Ln Ste 110 (22310-3261)
PHONE...................................703 971-8901
EMP: 2
SALES (est): 100K **Privately Held**
SIC: 3812 Mfg Search/Navigation Equipment

(G-493)
JAVAWOOD USA LLC
Also Called: R Home Furniture
5641 General Wash Dr (22312-2403)
PHONE...................................703 658-9665
Nico Lengkong, *Owner*
▲ EMP: 1
SALES (est): 135.6K **Privately Held**
WEB: www.r-homefurniture.com
SIC: 2511 2599 Wood household furniture; restaurant furniture, wood or metal

(G-494)
JEFF SHEARER
6150 Manchester Park Cir (22310-4953)
PHONE...................................703 313-7670
Jeff Shearer, *Principal*

EMP: 2
SALES (est): 121.8K **Privately Held**
WEB: www.trusteditpro.biz
SIC: 3542 Machine tools, metal forming type

(G-495)
JEFFREY O HOLDREN
9440 Mount Vernon Cir (22309-3220)
PHONE...................................703 360-9739
Jeffrey Holdren, *Owner*
EMP: 1
SALES (est): 83.1K **Privately Held**
SIC: 3829 Pulse analyzers, nuclear monitoring

(G-496)
JEMBER LLC
7421 Fordson Rd Apt A11 (22306-2243)
PHONE...................................202 631-8521
Jember Medhanye, *Principal*
EMP: 1 EST: 2015
SALES (est): 53.4K **Privately Held**
SIC: 3999 Shades, lamp or candle

(G-497)
JENNIFER OUK
3901 Fairfax Pkwy (22312-1147)
PHONE...................................571 232-0991
Jennifer Ouk, *Owner*
EMP: 1 EST: 2015
SALES (est): 38.5K **Privately Held**
SIC: 2339 Women's & misses' athletic clothing & sportswear

(G-498)
JKM INDUSTRIES LLC
2413 Culpeper Rd (22308-2132)
PHONE...................................703 599-3112
Meghan Totten, *Principal*
EMP: 2
SALES (est): 101.9K **Privately Held**
SIC: 3999 Manufacturing industries

(G-499)
JOINT MANUFACTURING FORCE LLC
6010 Good Lion Ct (22315-4623)
PHONE...................................910 364-8580
Maritza Lagares, *Principal*
EMP: 2 EST: 2018
SALES (est): 68.3K **Privately Held**
SIC: 3999 Manufacturing industries

(G-500)
JOSHI RUBITA
Also Called: P & P Collection
8654 Venoy Ct (22309-1567)
PHONE...................................571 315-9772
Rubita Joshi, *Owner*
EMP: 1
SALES (est): 49.1K **Privately Held**
SIC: 3171 5137 Handbags, women's; scarves, women's & children's

(G-501)
JOVANOVICH INC
5750 Governors Pond Cir (22310-2340)
PHONE...................................301 653-1739
Dejan Jovanovic, *Owner*
EMP: 4
SALES (est): 246.3K **Privately Held**
SIC: 3949 Fishing equipment

(G-502)
JT GRAPHICS & PRINTING INC
5409a Vine St (22310-1025)
PHONE...................................703 922-6804
Jack Tahiliani, *President*
Mahesh Tahiliani, *Corp Secy*
EMP: 4
SALES (est): 385K **Privately Held**
SIC: 2752 7336 Commercial printing, offset; graphic arts & related design

(G-503)
K COMPOSITE MAGAZINE
7011 Green Spring Ln (22306-1255)
PHONE...................................703 568-6917
Keith Johnson, *CEO*
EMP: 2
SALES (est): 73.1K **Privately Held**
SIC: 2721 Periodicals

(G-504)
KCS INC
6917 Columbia Dr (22307-1606)
PHONE..............................703 981-0523
Ralph Benjamin, *President*
Richard Kitts, *Vice Pres*
EMP: 6
SALES (est): 200K **Privately Held**
WEB: www.kcscloser.com
SIC: 7372 7371 Prepackaged software;
 custom computer programming services

(G-505)
KIM BRJ INC
6251 Little River Tpke (22312-1716)
PHONE..............................703 642-2367
Tae H Kim, *President*
EMP: 4
SALES (est): 159.6K **Privately Held**
SIC: 2051 Bread, all types (white, wheat,
 rye, etc): fresh or frozen

(G-506)
KLINE ASSOC LLC MATT
1109 Waynewood Blvd (22308-2528)
PHONE..............................703 780-6466
Matthew Kline, *Principal*
EMP: 2
SALES (est): 128.9K **Privately Held**
WEB: www.mattklineassoc.com
SIC: 2392 Household furnishings

(G-507)
KNOWWHO INC
3201 Cunningham Dr (22309-2210)
PHONE..............................703 619-1544
Ann Brownson, *Owner*
John Chamberlain, *Vice Pres*
Bill Wade, *Vice Pres*
Shawna Quezada, *Manager*
EMP: 1
SALES (est): 41.3K **Privately Held**
SIC: 2741 Miscellaneous publishing

(G-508)
**KONICA MNLTA BUS SLTONS
USA IN**
Also Called: Meridian Imaging Solutions
5775 General Wash Dr (22312-2418)
PHONE..............................703 461-8195
Trent Edwards, *Vice Pres*
Patty Graves, *Opers Staff*
Juliana McKee, *VP Bus Dvlpt*
Jenna Morris, *Sales Staff*
Scott Westfall, *Sales Staff*
EMP: 115 **Privately Held**
WEB: www.kmbs.konicaminolta.us
SIC: 3579 5044 5112 5999 Typing &
 word processing machines; copying
 equipment; stationery & office supplies;
 facsimile equipment; computer mainte-
 nance & repair; electronic equipment re-
 pair
HQ: Konica Minolta Business Solutions
 U.S.A., Inc.
 100 Williams Dr
 Ramsey NJ 07446
 201 825-4000

(G-509)
KRAIN BUILDING SERVICES LLC
6698 Fleet Dr (22310-2407)
PHONE..............................703 924-1480
John Bielski, *President*
John Markogiannakis, *Vice Pres*
William Keller, *Opers Staff*
John Beliski, *CFO*
Joni Maze, *Office Mgr*
EMP: 50
SALES (est): 7.8MM **Privately Held**
WEB: www.krainbuild.com
SIC: 3253 5032 Ceramic wall & floor tile;
 granite building stone

(G-510)
KRISTINA KATHLEEN MANN
2709 Farnsworth Dr (22303-1320)
PHONE..............................703 282-9166
Kristina Mann, *Owner*
EMP: 1
SALES (est): 36.6K **Privately Held**
SIC: 2721 2741 2731 Periodicals: pub-
 lishing only; miscellaneous publishing;
 textbooks: publishing & printing

(G-511)
KWEENS ESSENTIALS LLC
3823 Monte Vista Pl (22309-1454)
PHONE..............................703 861-6764
Mikayla Munnlyn,
EMP: 2
SALES (est): 64.6K **Privately Held**
SIC: 3911 Jewelry apparel

(G-512)
L & M ELECTRIC AND PLBG LLC
Also Called: L & M Contracting
2601 Beacon Hill Rd (22306-1611)
PHONE..............................703 768-2222
Saul Romero, *President*
EMP: 10
SQ FT: 3,000
SALES (est): 2.2MM **Privately Held**
WEB: www.lmelectricandplumbing.com
SIC: 3699 1711 8748 1542 Electrical
 equipment & supplies; plumbing, heating,
 air-conditioning contractors; business
 consulting; commercial & office buildings,
 renovation & repair

(G-513)
LAURA HOOPER CALLIGRATHY
4605 Dolphin Ln (22309-3111)
PHONE..............................213 514-4170
Laura Hooper, *Owner*
Alyssa Law, *Marketing Staff*
EMP: 3
SALES (est): 145.5K **Privately Held**
SIC: 2754 Stationery & invitation printing,
 gravure

(G-514)
LAY-N-GO LLC
8418 Stable Dr (22308-2240)
PHONE..............................703 799-0799
Amy Fazackerley, *CEO*
Tanya Stamos, *Opers Staff*
EMP: 2
SALES (est): 800K **Privately Held**
WEB: www.layngo.com
SIC: 2393 5199 5699 Bags & containers,
 except sleeping bags: textile; bags, tex-
 tile; customized clothing & apparel

(G-515)
**LEGACY WORD PUBLISHING
LLC**
5906 Westchester St (22310-1123)
PHONE..............................941 915-4730
Alfreda Jackson, *Principal*
EMP: 1
SALES (est): 37.5K **Privately Held**
SIC: 2741 Miscellaneous publishing

(G-516)
LI HING SOFTWARE LLC
2059 Huntington Ave # 912 (22303-1614)
PHONE..............................703 677-7773
Scott Hiroshige, *Principal*
EMP: 2 EST: 2012
SALES (est): 112.3K **Privately Held**
SIC: 7372 Prepackaged software

(G-517)
**LIFE SENTENCE PUBLISHING
LLC**
5706 Evergreen Knoll Ct (22303-1055)
PHONE..............................703 300-0474
Matthew J Iden, *Administration*
EMP: 4
SALES (est): 206.2K **Privately Held**
SIC: 2741 Miscellaneous publishing

(G-518)
**LIVING SOLUTIONS MID
ATLANTIC**
6402 15th St (22307-1409)
PHONE..............................202 460-9919
Kenneth Heyman, *Principal*
EMP: 2
SALES (est): 140K **Privately Held**
WEB: www.livsolutions.com
SIC: 7372 Application computer software

(G-519)
LM WOODWORKING LLC
8516 Stable Dr (22308-2243)
PHONE..............................703 927-4467
Scott P McLallen, *Administration*
EMP: 1

SALES (est): 91.3K **Privately Held**
WEB: www.lmwoodworking.com
SIC: 2431 Millwork

(G-520)
MAGNESIUM MUSIC
6609 10th St Unit B1 (22307-6609)
PHONE..............................703 798-5516
Caiden Wiley, *Principal*
EMP: 2 EST: 2017
SALES (est): 90.8K **Privately Held**
SIC: 3356 Magnesium

(G-521)
**MANUFACTURING MYSTIQUE
INC**
5713 Habersham Way (22310-1214)
PHONE..............................703 719-0943
Bruce Lemaster, *COO*
EMP: 1 EST: 2018
SALES (est): 39.6K **Privately Held**
SIC: 3999 Manufacturing industries

(G-522)
MARIBETHS BAKERY INC
6441a Gen Green Way (22312-2413)
PHONE..............................703 739-5839
Maribeth Nyerges, *President*
EMP: 25
SQ FT: 5,200
SALES (est): 3.1MM **Privately Held**
WEB: www.maribethsbakery.com
SIC: 2051 Bakery: wholesale or whole-
 sale/retail combined

(G-523)
MARLA HUGHES
6102 Bayliss Knoll Ct (22310-2273)
PHONE..............................703 309-8267
Marla Hughes, *Principal*
EMP: 1
SALES (est): 40.9K **Privately Held**
SIC: 2394 Canvas & related products

(G-524)
MB SERVICES LLC
5236 Winter View Dr (22312-3976)
PHONE..............................703 906-8625
Joel Bernstein, *Exec VP*
Elizabeth Culver,
EMP: 2
SALES (est): 35K **Privately Held**
SIC: 3955 3579 8999 Ribbons, inked:
 typewriter, adding machine, register, etc.;
 time clocks & time recording devices;
 services

(G-525)
MELAMEDIA LLC
8315 Riverside Rd (22308-1542)
PHONE..............................703 704-5665
David Szabo, *Partner*
Dennis Melamed,
EMP: 1
SALES (est): 92.7K **Privately Held**
WEB: www.melamedia.com
SIC: 2741 Newsletter publishing

(G-526)
MELTED ELEMENT LLC
6100 Lincolnia Rd Apt 302 (22312-4404)
PHONE..............................703 239-7847
Jonathan Wossene,
EMP: 3 EST: 2016
SALES (est): 92.3K **Privately Held**
WEB: www.meltedelement.com
SIC: 3999 2392 5199 5023 Candles;
 household furnishings; candles; home fur-
 nishings; miscellaneous home furnish-
 ings; candle shops

(G-527)
MENTORADVISOR INC
6588 Hickman Ter (22315-5583)
PHONE..............................571 435-7222
EMP: 2
SALES (est): 117.1K **Privately Held**
SIC: 7372 Prepackaged Software Services

(G-528)
MERITFUL INC
6272 Edsall Rd Apt 4 (22312-2619)
PHONE..............................703 651-6338
EMP: 2

SALES (est): 130K **Privately Held**
SIC: 7372 Prepackaged Software Services

(G-529)
MERRILL PRESS
5901 Bing Ct (22315-4002)
PHONE..............................571 257-6273
Andrew Press, *Principal*
EMP: 2
SALES (est): 104.2K **Privately Held**
SIC: 2741 Miscellaneous publishing

(G-530)
METAL MAGIC
6239 Shields Ave (22303-2414)
PHONE..............................703 660-9180
EMP: 2
SALES (est): 68.1K **Privately Held**
WEB: www.metalmagicrefinishing.com
SIC: 1099 Metal ores

(G-531)
MICHAEL BEACH
Also Called: Bob's Printing
8403 Richmond Hwy Ste D (22309-2424)
PHONE..............................703 360-7284
Michael Andrew Beach, *Owner*
EMP: 5
SALES (est): 350K **Privately Held**
WEB: www.michaelbeach.com
SIC: 2752 5943 2791 Commercial print-
 ing, offset; office forms & supplies; type-
 setting

(G-532)
MICHAEL S BOND
5850 Cameron Run Ter (22303-1860)
PHONE..............................740 971-9157
Michael Bond, *Owner*
EMP: 1
SALES (est): 44K **Privately Held**
SIC: 2711 Newspapers: publishing only,
 not printed on site

(G-533)
MILLCRAFT LLC
6304b Gravel Ave (22310-3218)
PHONE..............................703 775-2030
Edward Erdogan,
EMP: 6 EST: 2018
SALES (est): 85.5K **Privately Held**
SIC: 2431 Interior & ornamental woodwork
 & trim

(G-534)
**MOUNT VERNON WOODWORKS
LLC**
4516 Ferry Landing Rd (22309-3117)
PHONE..............................202 222-8387
EMP: 2
SALES (est): 93.8K **Privately Held**
SIC: 2431 Millwork

(G-535)
MSL OIL & GAS CORP (PA)
6161 Fuller Ct (22310-2541)
PHONE..............................703 971-8805
Myron Levin, *President*
Douglas Levin, *Vice Pres*
EMP: 5
SQ FT: 1,000
SALES (est): 8.4MM **Privately Held**
SIC: 1382 Oil & gas exploration services

(G-536)
MUJAHID FNU
301 N Beauregard St # 706 (22312-2943)
PHONE..............................646 693-2762
Fnu Mujahid, *Owner*
EMP: 1
SALES (est): 37.4K **Privately Held**
SIC: 2741 Miscellaneous publishing

(G-537)
MUNCHKIN MONOGRAMS LLC
5711 Glamis Dr (22315-4130)
PHONE..............................215 970-4375
Tracy McClure, *Principal*
EMP: 1
SALES (est): 47K **Privately Held**
WEB: www.munchkinmonograms.com
SIC: 2395 Embroidery & art needlework

GEOGRAPHIC

(G-538)
MY MIND ON SPORTS LLC
6932 Columbia Dr (22307-1605)
PHONE.................................703 261-9629
Wilson Tarpeh, *Principal*
EMP: 3
SALES (est): 116.1K **Privately Held**
WEB: www.mymindonsports.com
SIC: 2711 Newspapers

(G-539)
MYSTIC EMPOWERMENT
7230 Stover Dr (22306-3514)
PHONE.................................703 765-0690
Andrea Arden, *Owner*
EMP: 1
SALES (est): 60.7K **Privately Held**
SIC: 2721 Periodicals: publishing only

(G-540)
MYSTIC POST PRESS LLC
7308 Rippon Rd (22307-1943)
PHONE.................................703 867-3447
Stephen Ryan, *Administration*
EMP: 2
SALES (est): 60K **Privately Held**
WEB: www.mysticpost.com
SIC: 2741 Miscellaneous publishing

(G-541)
NATURAL LIGHTING LLC
6013 Rock Cliff Ln Apt N (22315-4626)
P.O. Box 150894 (22315-0894)
PHONE.................................703 347-7004
Gaymard Mistry, *Mng Member*
EMP: 1
SALES (est): 72K **Privately Held**
SIC: 3641 Tubes, electric light

(G-542)
NEON COMPASS MARKETING LLC
6607 Kelsey Point Cir (22315-5528)
PHONE.................................580 330-4699
EMP: 3
SALES (est): 123.2K **Privately Held**
SIC: 2813 Neon

(G-543)
NIK GRAPHIX LLC
4555 Interlachen Ct B (22312-3213)
PHONE.................................703 863-1075
Farzad Nikpanjeh, *Administration*
EMP: 2 EST: 2013
SALES (est): 85.2K **Privately Held**
WEB: www.nikgraphix.com
SIC: 3993 Signs & advertising specialties

(G-544)
NOVA EXTERIORS INC
5568 General Wash Dr (22312-2465)
PHONE.................................703 322-1500
Peter C Vlantis, *President*
Gerald Egan, *Vice Pres*
Dan Sloan, *Sales Mgr*
David McSherry, *Sales Staff*
Chuck Parker, *Marketing Staff*
EMP: 12
SQ FT: 1,000
SALES (est): 2.2MM **Privately Held**
WEB: www.novaexteriors.com
SIC: 3272 Window sills, cast stone

(G-545)
NUMBER 6 PUBLISHING LLC
1799 Rampart Dr (22308-1655)
PHONE.................................703 360-6054
EMP: 1
SALES (est): 37.5K **Privately Held**
SIC: 2741 Miscellaneous publishing

(G-546)
NYX TECHNOLOGIES LLC
5285 Navaho Dr (22312-2034)
PHONE.................................703 914-8956
Manjeet Jolly,
EMP: 4
SALES (est): 239.1K **Privately Held**
SIC: 7372 Application computer software

(G-547)
ORACLE SYSTEMS CORPORATION
6190 Manchester Park Cir (22310-4954)
PHONE.................................703 364-2221

EMP: 252
SALES (corp-wide): 37.1B **Publicly Held**
SIC: 7372 Prepackaged Software Services
HQ: Oracle Systems Corporation
　　500 Oracle Pkwy
　　Redwood City CA 94065
　　650 506-7000

(G-548)
PANADERIA LATINA
6251 Little River Tpke (22312-1716)
PHONE.................................703 642-5200
Tae Kim, *Owner*
EMP: 12
SALES (est): 1.1MM **Privately Held**
SIC: 2051 Bakery: wholesale or wholesale/retail combined

(G-549)
PAVE DMV LLC
6511 Braddock Rd Ste 201 (22312-2246)
PHONE.................................703 798-1087
Hemang Narola, *Principal*
Akshay Bhalala,
EMP: 2 EST: 2018
SALES (est): 64.6K **Privately Held**
SIC: 3996 Hard surface floor coverings

(G-550)
PIC N PRESS CUSTOM PRTG LLC
6011 Archstone Way # 302 (22310-5514)
PHONE.................................571 970-2627
Kevin Brown, *Principal*
EMP: 2 EST: 2013
SALES (est): 146.7K **Privately Held**
SIC: 2752 Commercial printing, lithographic

(G-551)
PLAN B PRESS
2714 Jefferson Dr (22303-1333)
PHONE.................................215 732-2663
Kim Roberts, *Principal*
EMP: 2 EST: 2010
SALES (est): 115.8K **Privately Held**
WEB: www.planbpress.com
SIC: 2741 Miscellaneous publishing

(G-552)
POM KBF
5702 Gen Wshngtn Dr Ste H (22312-2409)
P.O. Box 931, Sterling (20167-0931)
PHONE.................................703 992-7877
EMP: 1 EST: 2019
SALES (est): 82.3K **Privately Held**
WEB: www.pomkbf.com
SIC: 2434 Wood kitchen cabinets

(G-553)
POSITIVE SIGNS LLC
Also Called: Fastsigns
7611 Richmond Hwy Ste A (22306-2847)
PHONE.................................703 768-7446
Howard Newman, *Mng Member*
Kirby Newman, *Mng Member*
EMP: 5
SALES (est): 660K **Privately Held**
WEB: www.fastsigns.com
SIC: 3993 Signs & advertising specialties

(G-554)
POTOMAC SAILMAKERS INC
5645k General Wash Dr (22312-2479)
PHONE.................................703 750-2171
Jack Wong, *President*
EMP: 3
SQ FT: 1,800
SALES (est): 291.8K **Privately Held**
WEB: www.potomacsails.com
SIC: 2394 Sails: made from purchased materials

(G-555)
PRINT TIME INC
7901 Morning Ride Ct (22315-5051)
PHONE.................................202 232-0582
Allen Watts, *VP Sales*
Zabih Norri, *Manager*
EMP: 3
SALES (est): 260K **Privately Held**
SIC: 2752 Commercial printing, lithographic

(G-556)
PRINTING 4 KIDS
3717 Rolling Hills Ave (22309-3717)
PHONE.................................703 474-1519
Douglas Ebanks Santos, *Principal*
EMP: 2
SALES (est): 92.3K **Privately Held**
SIC: 2752 Commercial printing, lithographic

(G-557)
PRO SHEET METAL INC
8020 Ashton St (22309-1343)
PHONE.................................703 675-7724
EMP: 2 EST: 2019
SALES (est): 94.5K **Privately Held**
SIC: 3444 Sheet metalwork

(G-558)
PROBUSINESS PUBLISHING LLC
4234 Corcoran St (22309-1311)
PHONE.................................571 216-3385
Alan Prochoroff, *Principal*
EMP: 2 EST: 2008
SALES (est): 124.5K **Privately Held**
WEB: www.ins-compliance.com
SIC: 2741 Miscellaneous publishing

(G-559)
PROJECT COST GVRNMENT SVCS LLC
8101 Hinson Farm Rd # 318 (22306-3403)
PHONE.................................239 334-3371
EMP: 2
SALES (est): 88.3K **Privately Held**
SIC: 3648 Lighting equipment

(G-560)
PROMOCORP INC
5515 Cherokee Ave Ste 300 (22312-2309)
PHONE.................................703 942-7100
EMP: 15
SQ FT: 4,000
SALES (est): 1.1MM
SALES (corp-wide): 52MM **Privately Held**
SIC: 2396 5199 3993 Automotive And Apparel Trimmings
PA: Boundless Network, Inc.
　　1601 Rio Grande St # 410
　　Austin TX 78701
　　512 472-9200

(G-561)
PROPELLER CLUB OF THE U S PORT
7120 Snug Harbor Ct (22315-4238)
PHONE.................................703 922-6933
EMP: 1
SALES (est): 57.6K **Privately Held**
WEB: www.propellerclubdc.org
SIC: 3366 Propellers

(G-562)
PUSH PIN CRATIVE SOLUTIONS LLC
6904 Ellingham Cir (22315-6500)
PHONE.................................703 313-0619
Monica Jacquet, *Principal*
EMP: 3 EST: 2012
SALES (est): 161K **Privately Held**
WEB: www.azarbruner.com
SIC: 3452 Pins

(G-563)
QUEENSMITH COMMUNICATIONS CORP
Also Called: Professional Pilot Magazine
5290 Shawnee Rd Ste 201 (22312-3277)
PHONE.................................703 370-0606
Murray Q Smith, *President*
Rafael Henriquez, *Assoc Editor*
EMP: 12
SQ FT: 5,000
SALES (est): 1.8MM **Privately Held**
WEB: www.propilotmag.com
SIC: 2721 Magazines: publishing only, not printed on site

(G-564)
QUICKEST RESIDUAL PAY
6202 Sage Dr (22310-2647)
PHONE.................................703 924-2620

EMP: 2 EST: 2015
SALES (est): 90.7K **Privately Held**
SIC: 2911 Petroleum Refiner

(G-565)
QUISENBERRY STN LIVE STM LLC
3903 Quisenberry Dr (22309-2049)
PHONE.................................703 799-9643
Royce Brademan, *Mng Member*
EMP: 1
SALES (est): 71.2K **Privately Held**
SIC: 3944 7699 Toy trains, airplanes & automobiles; repair services

(G-566)
RAY GORHAM
Also Called: Ray's Welding
5919 Pratt St (22310-1838)
PHONE.................................703 971-1807
Ray Gorham, *Owner*
EMP: 3
SALES (est): 152.1K **Privately Held**
SIC: 7692 4212 Welding repair; local trucking, without storage

(G-567)
RAYTHEON COMPANY
2211 Sherwood Hall Ln (22306-2743)
PHONE.................................703 768-4172
Eric Lighty, *Manager*
EMP: 1
SALES (corp-wide): 77B **Publicly Held**
WEB: www.rtx.com
SIC: 3812 Sonar systems & equipment
HQ: Raytheon Company
　　870 Winter St
　　Waltham MA 02451
　　781 522-3000

(G-568)
RECONART INC
6462 Little River Tpke (22312-1411)
PHONE.................................855 732-6627
Hristo Marintchev, *President*
Nicolo Nisbett, *Exec VP*
Geri Davies, *Vice Pres*
Jade Gold, *Internal Med*
EMP: 4
SALES (est): 373.2K **Privately Held**
WEB: www.reconart.com
SIC: 7372 5734 6289 Business oriented computer software; software, business & non-game; financial reporting

(G-569)
REIGN PRODUCTIONS LLC
5901 Mount Eagle Dr # 502 (22303-2503)
PHONE.................................703 317-1393
Shirley Lipscomb-Teal,
EMP: 3
SALES (est): 170K **Privately Held**
SIC: 2741 Miscellaneous publishing

(G-570)
RENEGADE PUBLISHING LLC
8500 Fort Hunt Rd (22308-2518)
PHONE.................................703 780-4546
Fred Sawyer, *Principal*
EMP: 1
SALES (est): 37.5K **Privately Held**
SIC: 2741 Miscellaneous publishing

(G-571)
RETROSPECT PUBLISHING
1307 Warrington Pl (22307-2055)
PHONE.................................703 765-9405
Janet McFarland, *President*
EMP: 5
SALES (est): 243.7K **Privately Held**
WEB: www.retrospectpublishing.com
SIC: 2741 Miscellaneous publishing

(G-572)
REVIVAL LABS LLC
7057 Kings Manor Dr (22315-5637)
PHONE.................................949 351-1660
Sultan Zikria, *CEO*
Sleiman Essau, *COO*
EMP: 4
SALES (est): 214.7K **Privately Held**
SIC: 2023 7389 Dietary supplements, dairy & non-dairy based;

(G-573)
RICHLYND FEDERAL LLC
85 S Bragg St Ste 402 (22312-2797)
PHONE..703 354-1500
Donald Jodrie, *Vice Pres*
Beth Newburger, *Mng Member*
EMP: 2
SALES (est): 106.4K **Privately Held**
WEB: www.richlyndfederal.com
SIC: 7372 Prepackaged software

(G-574)
RIVERFARM WOODWORKS LLC
3909 Belle Rive Ter (22309-3002)
PHONE..571 721-0988
Jerry Sinn, *Mng Member*
Hwa Hua, *Mng Member*
EMP: 2
SALES (est): 59.5K **Privately Held**
SIC: 2431 Millwork

(G-575)
RSR INDUSTRIES LLC
8602 Woodland Heights Ct (22309-2248)
PHONE..703 408-8048
Raymond Rettig, *CEO*
Melissa Rettig, *Co-Owner*
EMP: 3 EST: 2015
SALES (est): 142.8K **Privately Held**
SIC: 3999 Manufacturing industries

(G-576)
SANTIAGO SHEET METAL LLC
6310 S Kings Hwy Apt 104 (22306-1057)
PHONE..703 870-4581
Efrain Santiago, *Principal*
EMP: 2
SALES (est): 121.8K **Privately Held**
SIC: 3444 Sheet metalwork

(G-577)
SARDANA SUSHILA
Also Called: Sheel's Pickles
5801 Quantrell Ave # 201 (22312-2715)
PHONE..703 256-5091
Sushila Sardana, *Owner*
EMP: 1 EST: 2016
SALES (est): 46.5K **Privately Held**
SIC: 2035 7389 Cucumbers, pickles &
 pickle salting;

(G-578)
SAVI TECHNOLOGY INC (PA)
5285 Shawnee Rd (22312-2328)
P.O. Box 184, Occoquan (22125-0184)
PHONE..571 227-7950
J Richard Carlson, *CEO*
Sidra Berman, *Vice Pres*
Ben Harris, *Vice Pres*
Rosemary Johnston, *Vice Pres*
Mark Keffer, *Vice Pres*
EMP: 30
SALES (est): 19.7MM **Privately Held**
WEB: www.savi.com
SIC: 7372 Business oriented computer
 software

(G-579)
SCINTILEX LLC
6100 Bayliss Knoll Ct (22310-2273)
PHONE..240 593-7906
Ian Louis Pegg, *Administration*
Ian Pegg,
EMP: 1 EST: 2016
SALES (est): 73K **Privately Held**
SIC: 3829 Scintillation detectors

(G-580)
SCOTTCRAFT MONOGRAMMING
6540 Windham Ave (22315-3419)
PHONE..703 971-0309
Dean Scott, *Owner*
EMP: 4
SALES (est): 187.4K **Privately Held**
WEB: www.scottcraft-military.com
SIC: 2395 Emblems, embroidered

(G-581)
SCRIBBLES
5904 Mount Eagle Dr # 1002 (22303-2534)
PHONE..703 930-8808
Sally Browning, *Owner*
EMP: 1
SALES (est): 4.2K **Privately Held**
SIC: 2759 Invitation & stationery printing &
 engraving

(G-582)
SELF SOLUTIONS LLC
6716 W Wkfield Dr Apt B1 (22307)
PHONE..202 725-0866
Jim Pfautz, *Ch of Bd*
EMP: 30
SALES (est): 2.2MM **Privately Held**
SIC: 7372 8249 7389 8742 Business oriented computer software; business training services; ; management consulting
 services; business consulting; safety
 training service

(G-583)
SHAKIR WALIYYUD-DEEN
Also Called: TSO Global Distributors
7009 Cold Spring Ln (22306-1312)
PHONE..706 399-8893
Waliyyud-Deen Shakir, *Partner*
EMP: 1 EST: 2012
SALES (est): 75K **Privately Held**
WEB: www.collegestationaf.com
SIC: 2842 Deodorants, nonpersonal

(G-584)
SIGN ON LINE LLC
6173 Les Dorson Ln (22315-3227)
PHONE..571 246-7776
Sheila Diane Ferguson, *Administration*
EMP: 2 EST: 2013
SALES (est): 123.3K **Privately Held**
SIC: 3993 Signs & advertising specialties

(G-585)
SIGNS UNLIMITED INC (PA)
8403 Richmond Hwy Ste J (22309-2424)
PHONE..703 799-8840
Lloyd Kaufman, *President*
Cheryl Kaufman, *Corp Secy*
Joshua Kaufman, *COO*
Denson Haynes, *Technology*
Hanna Medhin, *Executive Asst*
EMP: 16 EST: 1971
SQ FT: 4,200
SALES (est): 2MM **Privately Held**
WEB: www.suicreative.com
SIC: 3993 1799 Electric signs; sign instal-
 lation & maintenance

(G-586)
SOFTWARE QUALITY INSTITUTE
5990 Kimberly Anne Way (22310-5473)
PHONE..703 313-8404
EMP: 2
SALES (est): 106.1K **Privately Held**
SIC: 7372 Prepackaged Software Services

(G-587)
SOGA INC
7503 Wexford Pl (22315-4145)
PHONE..202 465-7158
Omar Garcia Sanchez, *Principal*
EMP: 2 EST: 2009
SALES (est): 324.5K **Privately Held**
WEB: www.sogaconstruction.com
SIC: 2421 Building & structural materials,
 wood

(G-588)
SOLGREEN SOLUTIONS LLC
6510 Brick Hearth Ct (22306-3313)
PHONE..833 765-4733
Matthew Portis, *CEO*
Christopher Terry, *Manager*
EMP: 2
SALES (est): 250.2K **Privately Held**
WEB: www.solgreensolutions.com
SIC: 3699 1711 2514 2873 Electrical
 equipment & supplies; solar energy con-
 tractor; lawn furniture: metal; fertilizers:
 natural (organic), except compost; insula-
 tion & energy conservation products;
 power & distribution transformers

(G-589)
STEPHENSON PRINTING INC
5731 General Wash Dr (22312-2490)
PHONE..703 642-9000
George W Stephenson, *President*
Sandy Stephenson, *Vice Pres*
Don Kershner, *Purch Mgr*
Greg Troup, *Sales Staff*
Janet Stephenson, *Marketing Staff*
EMP: 75
SQ FT: 60,000
SALES (est): 21.8MM **Privately Held**
WEB: www.stephensonprinting.com
SIC: 2752 2796 2789 2759 Commercial
 printing, offset; platemaking services;
 bookbinding & related work; commercial
 printing

(G-590)
SUNDIGGER INDUSTRIES LLC
8711 Standish Rd (22308-2512)
PHONE..703 360-4139
Elaine M Dodge, *Administration*
EMP: 2
SALES (est): 92.8K **Privately Held**
SIC: 3999 Manufacturing industries

(G-591)
SUNRISE CIRCUITS LLC
6205 Littlethorpe Ln (22315-3700)
PHONE..703 719-9324
EMP: 3
SALES (est): 185.8K **Privately Held**
SIC: 3679 Electronic circuits

(G-592)
SUNSHINE PRODUCTS INC
1953 Shiver Dr (22307-1631)
P.O. Box 7517 (22307-0517)
PHONE..703 768-3500
James H Howren Sr, *President*
Nancy Howren, *Vice Pres*
EMP: 2
SALES (est): 281.5K **Privately Held**
SIC: 2844 Toothpastes or powders, denti-
 frices

(G-593)
SURVIVALWARE INC
8403 Porter Ln (22308-2140)
PHONE..703 780-2044
Rusty Luhing, *Principal*
EMP: 2
SALES (est): 151.1K **Privately Held**
WEB: www.survivalware.com
SIC: 7372 Prepackaged software

(G-594)
SYSTEMS RESEARCH AND MFG
CORP
7432 Grumman Pl (22306-2226)
PHONE..703 765-5827
Johnnyson Jones, *Director*
EMP: 3
SALES (est): 166.1K **Privately Held**
SIC: 3822 Thermostats & other environ-
 mental sensors

(G-595)
TEN SISTERS WINE LLC
1128 Priscilla Ln (22308-2546)
PHONE..202 577-9774
Eleanor Bartow, *Mng Member*
▲ EMP: 2 EST: 2010
SALES (est): 395.8K **Privately Held**
WEB: www.tensisterswine.com
SIC: 2084 5182 Wines; wine

(G-596)
TENANT TEMPORARY
QUARTERS
5587 Callcott Way (22312-4009)
PHONE..703 462-8623
EMP: 1 EST: 2011
SALES (est): 56K **Privately Held**
SIC: 3131 Mfg Footwear Cut Stock

(G-597)
TG POLYMERS INC
6855 Brindle Heath Way (22315-6417)
PHONE..585 670-9427
Thomas G Seidewand, *President*
▲ EMP: 1
SALES (est): 7MM **Privately Held**
SIC: 2673 7389 Bags: plastic, laminated &
 coated;

(G-598)
TILE OPTIMA LLC
5705 General Wash Dr E (22312-2408)
PHONE..703 256-5650
Beyazit Kazanci, *President*
EMP: 19
SQ FT: 45,000 **Privately Held**
WEB: www.tileoptima.com

(G-599)
TIOME INC
Also Called: Tiome.org
2056 Blunt Ln (22303-1750)
PHONE..703 531-8963
Donald Brown, *Officer*
Sherwood Brown, *Officer*
Gary Cassis, *Officer*
Lamont Johnson, *Officer*
EMP: 4
SALES (est): 127.8K **Privately Held**
SIC: 7372 7389 Educational computer
 software;

(G-600)
TISOL
8208 Treebrooke Ln (22308-1706)
PHONE..703 739-2771
Denis Phares, *Principal*
EMP: 3
SALES (est): 162.7K **Privately Held**
SIC: 3674 Semiconductors & related de-
 vices

(G-601)
TOUCAN SOCKS
5622 Brookland Ct (22310-5312)
PHONE..757 656-9497
Joseph Mosinski, *Principal*
EMP: 2
SALES (est): 73.4K **Privately Held**
SIC: 2252 Socks

(G-602)
TRI CORP
8234 Riverside Rd (22308-1538)
PHONE..703 780-8753
Mary Lee, *Principal*
EMP: 2
SALES (est): 103.9K **Privately Held**
SIC: 7372 Prepackaged software

(G-603)
VAN DORN PAWN
6116 Franconia Rd Ste A (22310-2577)
PHONE..703 924-9800
Eric Rizer, *Principal*
EMP: 3
SALES (est): 192.3K **Privately Held**
SIC: 3411 Metal cans

(G-604)
VEGNOS CORPORATION
8690 Venoy Ct (22309-1569)
PHONE..571 721-1685
Ateeq Sharfuddin, *President*
Reshma Shahabuddin, *COO*
EMP: 2
SALES (est): 140.4K **Privately Held**
WEB: www.vegnos.com
SIC: 7372 7389 Business oriented com-
 puter software; application computer soft-
 ware; educational computer software;
 publishers' computer software;

(G-605)
VIRGINIA ACADEMIC PRESS
511 N Armistead St (22312-2834)
P.O. Box 11256 (22312-0256)
PHONE..703 256-1304
William Hranicky, *Principal*
EMP: 1
SALES (est): 61.7K **Privately Held**
WEB: www.archeology.org
SIC: 2741 Miscellaneous publishing

(G-606)
VSE AVIATION INC (HQ)
6348 Walker Ln (22310-3226)
PHONE..703 328-4600
John A Cuomo, *CEO*
EMP: 21
SQ FT: 5,000
SALES (est): 65.5MM
SALES (corp-wide): 752.6MM **Publicly
Held**
WEB: www.vsecorp.com
SIC: 3728 Aircraft parts & equipment
PA: Vse Corporation
 6348 Walker Ln
 Alexandria VA 22310
 703 960-4600

(G-607)
VT AEPCO INC
5701 General Washington D (22312-2408)
PHONE..................................703 658-7500
Charlie Wilson, *Branch Mgr*
EMP: 7
SALES (corp-wide): 1.1B **Privately Held**
WEB: www.vt-group.com
SIC: 3651 Video triggers (remote control TV devices)
HQ: Vt Aepco Inc.
　　675 Discovery Dr Nw # 305
　　Huntsville AL 35806
　　757 463-2800

(G-608)
WARRIOR LUGGAGE COMPANY
5601c General Wash Dr (22312-2403)
PHONE..................................301 523-9010
Deepak Shamdasani, *President*
Michael Sujanani, *Treasurer*
Manish Butani, *Admin Sec*
EMP: 3
SQ FT: 500
SALES (est): 125.8K **Privately Held**
SIC: 2393 2392 3161 Duffle bags, canvas: made from purchased materials; bags & containers, except sleeping bags; textile; bags, garment storage: except paper or plastic film; traveling bags; wardrobe bags (luggage)

(G-609)
WHINKS COFFEE ROASTERS
4208 Javins Dr (22310-2035)
PHONE..................................571 330-6630
Michael Hinkle, *Owner*
EMP: 1
SALES (est): 12K **Privately Held**
SIC: 2095 Coffee roasting (except by wholesale grocers)

(G-610)
WINCHENDON GROUP INC
3907 Lakota Rd (22303-1023)
PHONE..................................703 960-0978
Eric Weiss, *President*
Sheila Weiss, *Vice Pres*
EMP: 2 EST: 1980
SALES (est): 250K **Privately Held**
WEB: www.winchendon.com
SIC: 7372 7371 Educational computer software; custom computer programming services

(G-611)
WINERY INC
6110 Berlee Dr (22312-1220)
PHONE..................................703 683-1876
Jane Cahill, *Principal*
EMP: 2
SALES (est): 138.7K **Privately Held**
SIC: 2084 Wines

(G-612)
WONDER BUG WELDING
6544 Fairland St (22312-2215)
PHONE..................................703 354-9499
EMP: 1
SALES (est): 33.6K **Privately Held**
SIC: 7692 Welding repair

(G-613)
WOODARDWEB
4011 Blue Slate Dr (22306-1358)
PHONE..................................202 337-3730
Eric Woodard, *Principal*
EMP: 2 EST: 2016
SALES (est): 50.1K **Privately Held**
SIC: 2499 Wood products

(G-614)
WORD PLAY BY DEB LLC
Also Called: Hidden Treasures
8319 Brockham Dr (22309-1879)
PHONE..................................703 389-5112
Deborah Hardy,
EMP: 1
SALES (est): 57K **Privately Held**
SIC: 3499 Novelties & giftware, including trophies

(G-615)
WORLD FASHION CITY INC
Also Called: Maxgen U.S. Company
6606 Schurtz St (22310-2638)
PHONE..................................703 887-8123
Soon Chang Kwon,
EMP:
SALES (est): 128.9K **Privately Held**
SIC: 3569 8748 Filters; business consulting

(G-616)
WP COMPANY LLC
Also Called: Washington Post
8796 Sacramento Dr # 302 (22309-1678)
PHONE..................................703 799-2920
Michael Poff, *Branch Mgr*
EMP: 3 **Privately Held**
WEB: www.washingtonpost.com
SIC: 2711 Newspapers, publishing & printing
HQ: Wp Company Llc
　　1301 K St Nw
　　Washington DC 20071

(G-617)
ZONES LLC
8647 Richmond Hwy (22309-4206)
PHONE..................................571 244-8206
Kalabina Baka,
EMP: 1 EST: 2015
SALES (est): 52K **Privately Held**
SIC: 2741

Allisonia
Pulaski County

(G-618)
IRON HEART WINERY LLC
3742 Boone Furnace Rd (24347-4001)
PHONE..................................540 320-0203
EMP: 2 EST: 2016
SALES (est): 70.2K **Privately Held**
WEB: www.iheartvirginiawine.com
SIC: 2084 Wines

(G-619)
LOVELY REDS CREATIONS LLC
4169 Boone Furnace Rd (24347-4039)
PHONE..................................540 320-2859
Sheena Hasty, *Mng Member*
EMP: 1
SALES (est): 15K **Privately Held**
WEB: www.lovelyredscreations.com
SIC: 2844 Face creams or lotions

(G-620)
SMYTHERS DARIS O SAWMILL
755 Smythers Mountain Rd (24347-4064)
PHONE..................................540 980-5169
Daris O Smythers, *Owner*
EMP: 9 EST: 1999
SALES (est): 721K **Privately Held**
SIC: 2421 Sawmills & planing mills, general

(G-621)
WOODLAND ARTISANS LTD
1294 Windsong Rd (24347-4005)
PHONE..................................276 766-3421
Winthrop Schwab, *Owner*
EMP: 1 EST: 1995
SALES (est): 38.7K **Privately Held**
WEB: www.wood-product-manufacturers.a2zyp.com
SIC: 2499 Wood products

Altavista
Campbell County

(G-622)
ABBOTT LABORATORIES
Also Called: Abbott Crtcal Care Systems Div
1518 Main St (24517-1173)
P.O. Box 479 (24517-0479)
PHONE..................................434 369-3100
Michael Towler, *Maint Spvr*
Tung Kieu, *Marketing Staff*
Dennis Janiak, *Manager*
Dale Elliott, *Director*
Molly Thore, *Admin Asst*

EMP: 700
SALES (corp-wide): 31.9B **Publicly Held**
WEB: www.abbott.com
SIC: 2834 Druggists' preparations (pharmaceuticals)
PA: Abbott Laboratories
　　100 Abbott Park Rd
　　Abbott Park IL 60064
　　224 667-6100

(G-623)
ABBOTT LABORATORIES INC
Also Called: Abbott Nutrition
215 Clarion Rd (24517-1101)
PHONE..................................434 369-3100
Hubbard Timothy, *Technology*
EMP: 3
SALES (est): 141.3K **Privately Held**
SIC: 2834 Pharmaceutical preparations

(G-624)
ABBOTT NUTRITION MFG INC
1518 Main St (24517-1173)
PHONE..................................434 369-3100
Jeff Rasmussen, *General Mgr*
EMP: 10
SALES (corp-wide): 31.9B **Publicly Held**
WEB: www.abbottnutrition.com
SIC: 2834 Vitamin, nutrient & hematinic preparations for human use
HQ: Abbott Nutrition Manufacturing Inc.
　　2351 N Watney Way Ste C
　　Fairfield CA 94533
　　707 399-1100

(G-625)
ANTHONY GEORGE LTD INC
1806 Elizabeth St (24517-2006)
PHONE..................................434 369-1204
Tim George, *President*
EMP: 2 **Privately Held**
SIC: 3423 Engravers' tools, hand

(G-626)
BGF INDUSTRIES INC
1523 Main St (24517-1133)
PHONE..................................434 369-4751
Will Wilson, *Branch Mgr*
EMP: 7
SALES (corp-wide): 2.6MM **Privately Held**
WEB: www.bgf.com
SIC: 3732 Boats, fiberglass: building & repairing
HQ: Bgf Industries, Inc.
　　230 Slayton Ave 1a
　　Danville VA 24540
　　843 537-3172

(G-627)
BGF INDUSTRIES INC
401 Amherst Ave (24517-1513)
PHONE..................................434 369-4751
Greg Slominski, *Engineer*
Sheri Wilmoth, *Engineer*
John Woodford, *Manager*
Richard Hawkins, *MIS Dir*
Mark Brumfield, *Executive*
EMP: 600
SALES (corp-wide): 2.6MM **Privately Held**
WEB: www.bgf.com
SIC: 2221 2241 Fiberglass fabrics; narrow fabric mills
HQ: Bgf Industries, Inc.
　　230 Slayton Ave 1a
　　Danville VA 24540
　　843 537-3172

(G-628)
C & C PIPING & FABRICATION LLC
853 Lynch Mill Rd (24517-1113)
PHONE..................................434 369-9353
Ryan Martinez, *CFO*
Codie Cyrus,
EMP: 13
SALES (est): 65.5K **Privately Held**
WEB: www.wecanweldit.com
SIC: 7692 Welding repair

(G-629)
CHANDLER CONCRETE CO INC
1503 Main St (24517-1133)
PHONE..................................434 369-4791
EMP: 1

SALES (corp-wide): 50MM **Privately Held**
WEB: www.chandlerconcrete.com
SIC: 3273 Ready-mixed concrete
PA: Chandler Concrete Co., Inc.
　　1006 S Church St
　　Burlington NC 27215
　　336 226-1181

(G-630)
CHANDLER CONCRETE OF VIRGINIA
1503 Main St (24517-1133)
PHONE..................................434 369-4791
Dan Canada, *Principal*
Peter McDaniel, *Corp Comm Staff*
EMP: 2 EST: 2009
SALES (est): 145.9K **Privately Held**
WEB: www.chandlerconcrete.com
SIC: 3273 Ready-mixed concrete

(G-631)
CUSTOM TILES LLC
Also Called: Custom-Tiles.com
1701 Avondale Dr (24517-1009)
PHONE..................................434 660-7170
Debbie Bernard, *General Mgr*
Mitchell Bernard, *Prdtn Mgr*
EMP: 1
SALES (est): 113.2K **Privately Held**
WEB: www.custom-tiles.com
SIC: 3253 Ceramic wall & floor tile

(G-632)
J&T WLDING FBRICATION CAMPBELL
569 Riverbend Rd (24517-4009)
PHONE..................................434 369-8589
Ginger Patterson, *President*
EMP: 10
SALES (est): 1MM **Privately Held**
WEB: www.jtweldinginc.com
SIC: 3441 7692 Fabricated structural metal; welding repair

(G-633)
JONES WELDING CONSTRUCTION
4361 Bedford Hwy (24517)
P.O. Box 105 (24517-0105)
PHONE..................................434 369-1069
Kenneth Jones, *Owner*
EMP: 1
SALES (est): 57.3K **Privately Held**
SIC: 7692 Welding repair

(G-634)
LEGACY MFG LLC
110 Tracie Dr (24517-4337)
PHONE..................................434 841-5331
EMP: 2 EST: 2008
SALES (est): 74K **Privately Held**
SIC: 3999 Mfg Misc Products

(G-635)
MARSHALL CON PDTS OF DANVILLE
1503 Main St (24517-1133)
PHONE..................................434 369-4791
Ronnie Sowers, *Branch Mgr*
EMP: 4
SALES (corp-wide): 4.8MM **Privately Held**
WEB: www.chandlerconcrete.com
SIC: 3271 3273 Blocks, concrete or cinder: standard; ready-mixed concrete
PA: Marshall Concrete Products Of Danville Inc
　　1088 Industrial Ave
　　Danville VA 24541
　　434 792-1233

(G-636)
MID-ATLANTIC PRINTERS LTD (PA)
503 3rd St (24517-1462)
PHONE..................................434 369-6633
Charles R Edwards, *President*
Kathy Hoover, *Prdtn Mgr*
Tammy Shelhorse, *QC Dir*
Norford Ken, *Engineer*
Nancy T Edwards, *Treasurer*
EMP: 80 EST: 1910
SQ FT: 26,000

SALES (est): 33.7MM **Privately Held**
WEB: www.mapl.net
SIC: 2752 2741 Commercial printing, off-set; newsletter publishing

(G-637)
MYRA J RUDISILL
Also Called: Embroidery By Jan
26 Cheese Creek Rd (24517-4265)
PHONE..........................540 587-0402
Myra Jan Rudisill, *Owner*
Myra Rudisill, *Owner*
EMP: 1
SALES (est): 82.3K **Privately Held**
WEB: www.photoemb.com
SIC: 2759 Screen printing

(G-638)
RAGE PLASTICS
255 Pittsylvania Ave (24517-1749)
PHONE..........................434 309-1718
EMP: 1
SALES (est): 133.1K
SALES (corp-wide): 26.1MM **Privately Held**
SIC: 2295 Resin or plastic coated fabrics
PA: Rage Corporation
3949 Lyman Dr
Hilliard OH 43026
614 771-4771

(G-639)
ROBERTSON LUMBER INC
525 7th St (24517-1815)
PHONE..........................434 369-5603
James P Kent, *Administration*
EMP: 3
SALES (est): 145.3K **Privately Held**
SIC: 2421 Lumber: rough, sawed or planed

(G-640)
SCHRADER-ALTAVISTA
205 Frazier Rd (24517-1020)
PHONE..........................434 369-8816
EMP: 2
SALES (est): 147K **Privately Held**
WEB: www.schradertpms.com
SIC: 3714 Motor vehicle parts & accessories

(G-641)
SCHRADER-BRIDGEPORT INTL INC (DH)
Also Called: Airaware
205 Frazier Rd (24517-1020)
P.O. Box 668 (24517-0668)
PHONE..........................434 369-4741
Kersi Dordi, *CEO*
Hugh W Charvat, *President*
Kelly Boor, *General Mgr*
Thomas Nelson, *Business Mgr*
Dave Berg, *Vice Pres*
◆ **EMP:** 530
SQ FT: 125,000
SALES (est): 348.8MM
SALES (corp-wide): 3.4B **Privately Held**
WEB: www.schrader-pacific.com
SIC: 3492 3714 3491 3011 Hose & tube couplings, hydraulic/pneumatic; motor vehicle wheels & parts; tire valve cores; industrial valves; tire & inner tube materials & related products; tire sundries or tire repair materials, rubber

(G-642)
SCHRADER-BRIDGEPORT INTL INC
Schrader Bridgeport Engin Prod
205 Frazier Rd (24517-1020)
PHONE..........................434 369-4741
Rob McCorkle, *Branch Mgr*
EMP: 215
SQ FT: 125,000
SALES (corp-wide): 3.4B **Privately Held**
WEB: www.schrader-pacific.com
SIC: 3491 3492 Industrial valves; fluid power valves & hose fittings
HQ: Schrader-Bridgeport International Inc.
205 Frazier Rd
Altavista VA 24517
434 369-4741

(G-643)
SIMPSON SIGNS
174 Penuel Ln (24517-4030)
PHONE..........................434 369-7389

Ricky Simpson, *Principal*
EMP: 1
SALES (est): 102K **Privately Held**
SIC: 3993 Signs & advertising specialties

(G-644)
STAUNTON RIVER OUTDOORS LLC
508b Pittsylvania Ave B (24517-1728)
PHONE..........................434 608-2601
Jonathan Arthur, *Mng Member*
EMP: 1 **EST:** 2016
SALES (est): 90.6K **Privately Held**
WEB: www.onrivertime.org
SIC: 3949 Rods & rod parts, fishing

(G-645)
WOMACK PUBLISHING CO INC
Also Called: Altavista Journal, The
1007 Main St (24517-1530)
P.O. Box 630 (24517-0630)
PHONE..........................434 369-6688
Kathy Keesee, *General Mgr*
Martha Dawson, *Assistant*
EMP: 8
SALES (corp-wide): 33.3MM **Privately Held**
WEB: www.womackpublishing.com
SIC: 2711 Newspapers: publishing only, not printed on site
PA: Womack Publishing Co Inc
28 N Main St
Chatham VA 24531
434 432-2791

Alton
Halifax County

(G-646)
CENTRAL CAROLINA BTLG CO INC
Also Called: Grand Springs Distribution
2140 Mount Carmel Rd (24520-3570)
PHONE..........................434 753-2515
Smith Robert A, *President*
Peggy H Smith, *Corp Secy*
▲ **EMP:** 17 **EST:** 2000
SALES (est): 3.3MM **Privately Held**
WEB: www.grandsprings.com
SIC: 2086 Water, pasteurized: packaged in cans, bottles, etc.

(G-647)
RACING FOR VETERANS
1025 Raceplex Rd (24520-3619)
PHONE..........................434 822-4201
EMP: 2
SALES (est): 248.8K **Privately Held**
SIC: 3799 Transportation equipment

Amelia Court House
Amelia County

(G-648)
A B M ENTERPRISES INC
Also Called: Amelia Bulletin-Monitor
16310 Goodes Bridge Rd (23002-4837)
P.O. Box 123 (23002-0123)
PHONE..........................804 561-3655
Ann Salster, *President*
Michael D Salster, *Admin Sec*
EMP: 7
SALES (est): 489.2K **Privately Held**
SIC: 2711 Commercial printing & newspaper publishing combined

(G-649)
AMELIA LUMBER COMPANY
16951 Leidig St (23002-4855)
P.O. Box 727 (23002-0727)
PHONE..........................804 561-2155
William L Scott, *President*
Joanne S Webb, *Corp Secy*
Leander O Scott Jr, *Vice Pres*
EMP: 35 **EST:** 1955
SQ FT: 3,000
SALES (est): 7.5MM **Privately Held**
WEB: www.amelialumber.com
SIC: 2421 Lumber: rough, sawed or planed

(G-650)
AMELIA SOAP AND HERB
6840 Sparks Ln (23002-3610)
PHONE..........................804 561-5229
Janice McKinney, *Owner*
EMP: 2
SALES (est): 133K **Privately Held**
WEB:
www.ameliasoapandherbcompany.com
SIC: 2844 Cosmetic preparations

(G-651)
ANDERSON BROTHERS LUMBER CO
8700 Otterburn Rd (23002-4884)
P.O. Box 109 (23002-0109)
PHONE..........................804 561-2153
Douglas E Anderson, *President*
Charles A Anderson, *Corp Secy*
EMP: 28 **EST:** 1955
SQ FT: 1,500
SALES (est): 4.3MM **Privately Held**
SIC: 2421 2491 2426 Lumber: rough, sawed or planed; wood preserving; hardwood dimension & flooring mills

(G-652)
APPOMATTOX RIVER ENGRAVING
10050 Mattoax Ln (23002-4102)
PHONE..........................804 561-3565
EMP: 2
SALES (est): 73.2K **Privately Held**
SIC: 2759 Currency: engraved

(G-653)
CARDINAL TOOL INC
Also Called: K.O. Components
8020 S Amelia Ave (23002-2223)
PHONE..........................804 561-2560
Roy D Gunter, *President*
EMP: 2
SALES (est): 126.9K **Privately Held**
SIC: 3999 Feathers & feather products

(G-654)
DAVID C WEAVER
Also Called: Weaver Logging
14851 N Lodore Rd (23002-4549)
PHONE..........................804 561-5929
David C Weaver, *Principal*
EMP: 18
SQ FT: 400
SALES (est): 1.3MM **Privately Held**
SIC: 2411 Logging camps & contractors

(G-655)
DIMENSION STONE LLC
Also Called: Rva Granites
9860 Knobs Hill Ln (23002-5042)
PHONE..........................804 615-7750
Christopher Rodriguez,
EMP: 2
SALES (est): 105.6K **Privately Held**
WEB: www.rvagranite.com
SIC: 3231 Furniture tops, glass: cut, beveled or polished

(G-656)
ERVIN COPPRIDGE MACHINE CO
9500 S Amelia Ave (23002-5037)
PHONE..........................804 561-1246
Ervin Coppridge, *President*
EMP: 3
SALES (est): 250K **Privately Held**
SIC: 3599 Machine shop, jobbing & repair

(G-657)
F & P ENTERPRISES INC (PA)
15961 Goodes Bridge Rd (23002-4962)
P.O. Box 559 (23002-0559)
PHONE..........................804 561-2784
Christopher L Pembelton, *President*
Brian T Pembleton, *Vice Pres*
Garland Ray Pembleton, *Admin Sec*
EMP: 15
SALES (est): 1MM **Privately Held**
WEB: www.fandpgroup.com
SIC: 2411 Pulpwood contractors engaged in cutting

(G-658)
GENESIS DECOR LLC
15401 Goodes Bridge Rd (23002-4730)
P.O. Box 188 (23002-0188)
PHONE..........................804 561-4844
Sam Arrington, *Webmaster*
EMP: 20
SALES (est): 1.2MM **Privately Held**
WEB: www.genesisdecor.com
SIC: 2599 Restaurant furniture, wood or metal

(G-659)
J & D SPECIALTEES
12421 Loblolly Dr (23002-3943)
PHONE..........................804 561-0817
EMP: 3
SALES (est): 119.6K **Privately Held**
SIC: 2759 Screen printing

(G-660)
JET DESIGN GRAPHICS INC
8925 Dunnston Dr (23002-4888)
PHONE..........................804 921-4164
Mary Holt, *Director*
EMP: 3
SALES (est): 158K **Privately Held**
SIC: 2759 Commercial printing

(G-661)
KEYSTONE VINTAGE LUMBER VA LLC
12700 Coverly Rd (23002-4018)
PHONE..........................804 615-7773
EMP: 2
SALES (est): 125.5K **Privately Held**
SIC: 2431 Millwork

(G-662)
L J S STORES INC
Also Called: Chula Junction
12850 Patrick Henry Hwy (23002-3929)
PHONE..........................804 561-6999
Leo Sharon, *President*
EMP: 10 **EST:** 2001
SALES (est): 1MM **Privately Held**
SIC: 3644 Junction boxes, electric

(G-663)
LEROY CARY
Also Called: Cary's Fabricating Service
5270 Dennisville Rd (23002-2400)
PHONE..........................804 561-3526
Leroy Cary, *Owner*
EMP: 5
SALES (est): 303K **Privately Held**
SIC: 3441 Fabricated structural metal

(G-664)
LODORE TRUSS COMPANY INC
18101 Genito Rd (23002-4450)
PHONE..........................804 561-4141
Michael Cary, *President*
EMP: 8
SQ FT: 8,150
SALES (est): 1.6MM **Privately Held**
SIC: 2439 Trusses, wooden roof

(G-665)
MARTIN MARIETTA MATERIALS INC
12301 Patrick Henry Hwy (23002-3980)
P.O. Box 659 (23002-0659)
PHONE..........................804 561-0570
EMP: 3 **Publicly Held**
WEB: www.martinmarietta.com
SIC: 1422 Crushed & broken limestone
PA: Martin Marietta Materials Inc
2710 Wycliff Rd
Raleigh NC 27607

(G-666)
MOREFIELD GEM MINE INC
Also Called: Morefield Mine
13400 Butlers Rd (23002-2909)
PHONE..........................804 561-3399
Sam Dunaway, *President*
Sharon Dunaway, *Corp Secy*
EMP: 3 **Privately Held**
WEB: www.morefieldgemmine.com
SIC: 1499 Gem stones (natural) mining

(G-667)
PHILLIPS CUSTOM CABINETS LLC
11560 Chula Rd (23002-3905)
PHONE..................................804 647-1328
Reinaldo Olivo, *Principal*
EMP: 2
SALES (est): 135.3K **Privately Held**
SIC: 2434 Wood kitchen cabinets

(G-668)
PROSKIT USA LLC
13302 Chula Rd (23002-4006)
PHONE..................................804 240-9355
Barbara Scott,
Roger Scott,
EMP: 2
SALES (est): 12K **Privately Held**
WEB: www.totaleclipse4u.com
SIC: 3423 Hand & edge tools

(G-669)
R L BINDERY
16424 Court St (23002-4975)
PHONE..................................804 625-2609
Lydia Carasas, *Principal*
EMP: 2
SALES (est): 95.8K **Privately Held**
SIC: 2782 Blankbooks & looseleaf binders

(G-670)
RONNIE AND BETTY BRIDGES
Also Called: Amelia Woodworks
12600 Reed Rock Rd (23002-5809)
PHONE..................................804 561-4506
Ronnie Bridges, *Partner*
Betty Bridges, *Partner*
EMP: 2
SALES (est): 251.7K **Privately Held**
SIC: 2599 Cabinets, factory

(G-671)
ROSA DARBY WINERY LLC
10390 Thompkins Ln (23002-3115)
PHONE..................................804 561-7492
Richard Jackson, *Principal*
EMP: 2
SALES (est): 86.8K **Privately Held**
SIC: 2084 Wines

(G-672)
SCOTT PALLETS INC
8660 Crowder St (23002)
P.O. Box 657 (23002-0657)
PHONE..................................804 561-2514
Jo Anne S Webb, *President*
William Lee Scott, *Corp Secy*
L O Scott Jr, *Vice Pres*
William Scott, *Executive*
EMP: 25
SQ FT: 30,000
SALES (est): 3.3MM **Privately Held**
WEB: www.scottpalletsinc.com
SIC: 2448 2421 Pallets, wood; sawmills & planing mills, general

(G-673)
STAR CHILDRENS DRESS CO INC
Also Called: Rare Edition
9120 Pridesville Rd (23002-4862)
PHONE..................................804 561-5060
Cliff Prince, *Office Mgr*
Tracy Mollen, *Manager*
Rhonda Dunlow, *Manager*
Linda Carey, *Administration*
EMP: 50
SALES (corp-wide): 31.3MM **Privately Held**
WEB: www.rareeditionsoutlet.com
SIC: 2361 2261 Dresses: girls', children's & infants'; finishing plants, cotton
PA: Star Children's Dress Co., Inc.
1250 Broadway Fl 18
New York NY 10001
212 279-1524

(G-674)
TANNER TOOL & MACHINE INC
8121 Dennisville Rd (23002-2327)
P.O. Box 726 (23002-0726)
PHONE..................................804 561-5141
Michael E Tanner, *President*
Linda R Tanner, *Corp Secy*
Tonia Tanner, *VP Sales*

Tonia Russell, *Manager*
EMP: 2
SALES (est): 349.4K **Privately Held**
WEB: www.tannertool.com
SIC: 3599 Machine shop, jobbing & repair

(G-675)
TRI COM INC
14101 Patrick Henry Hwy (23002-4732)
PHONE..................................804 561-3582
Fax: 804 561-5020
EMP: 2 EST: 2010
SALES (est): 100K **Privately Held**
SIC: 3441 Structural Metal Fabrication

(G-676)
VIRGINIAS RSRCES RECYCLED LLC
Also Called: Mary Ann's Trucking
11601 Grub Hill Church Rd (23002-4944)
PHONE..................................804 561-2543
Robert S Watkins,
William Scott,
Robert Watkins,
Mike Wingfield,
EMP: 17
SALES (est): 193.7K **Privately Held**
SIC: 2499 Mulch, wood & bark

(G-677)
WILLIAM H SCOTT
7431 Military Rd (23002-3714)
PHONE..................................804 561-5384
William Scott, *Owner*
▲ EMP: 1 EST: 1988
SALES (est): 69.3K **Privately Held**
SIC: 2411 Pulpwood contractors engaged in cutting

(G-678)
WRIGHT INC W F
Also Called: Wright Ready Mix
15636 Elm Cottage Rd (23002-4722)
P.O. Box 401 (23002-0401)
PHONE..................................804 561-2721
Randy Tennefoss, *President*
Brent Tennefoss, *Vice Pres*
EMP: 15 EST: 1965
SALES (est): 2MM **Privately Held**
WEB: www.wrightsreadymix.com
SIC: 3273 3272 Ready-mixed concrete; septic tanks, concrete

(G-679)
YODER LOGGING
15770 Redmore Ln (23002-4414)
PHONE..................................804 561-3913
Jerry Yoder, *Owner*
EMP: 2
SALES (est): 175K **Privately Held**
SIC: 2411 Logging camps & contractors

Amherst
Amherst County

(G-680)
AMHERST MILLING CO INC
140 Union Hill Rd (24521-4053)
PHONE..................................434 946-7601
Richard M Wydner, *President*
EMP: 3 EST: 1940
SALES (est): 287.5K **Privately Held**
WEB: www.amhersthabitat.org
SIC: 2041 2048 Flour: blended, prepared or self-rising; feed premixes

(G-681)
AMHERST TECHNOLOGIES
126 Sardis Rd (24521-4867)
PHONE..................................434 946-0329
William Johnston, *Owner*
EMP: 5
SALES (est): 222.4K **Privately Held**
SIC: 3444 Machine guards, sheet metal

(G-682)
BETHELS WELDING
2347 S Amherst Hwy (24521-3348)
PHONE..................................434 946-7160
Jerome Behtel, *Owner*
EMP: 2

SALES (est): 159.2K **Privately Held**
WEB: www.bethelweldingonline.com
SIC: 7692 Welding repair

(G-683)
BEYDLER CNC LLC
Also Called: Beydler's Manibolt Driller
1328 N Amherst Hwy (24521-3938)
P.O. Box 143, Esmont (22937-0143)
PHONE..................................760 954-4397
Scott Arthur Beydler, *Mng Member*
Andrea Beydler,
EMP: 2
SALES (est): 206.8K **Privately Held**
WEB: www.beydler-cnc.com
SIC: 3541 Drilling machine tools (metal cutting)

(G-684)
BLACK BOX CORPORATION
E Commerce St (24521)
PHONE..................................781 449-1900
EMP: 2
SALES (est): 85.9K
SALES (corp-wide): 774.6MM **Publicly Held**
SIC: 3577 Computer Peripheral Equipment, Nec
PA: Black Box Corporation
1000 Park Dr
Lawrence PA 15055
724 746-5500

(G-685)
BUFFALO AIR HANDLING COMPANY
467 Zane Snead Dr (24521-4383)
PHONE..................................434 946-7455
Theodore Kruger, *President*
William R Phelps, *President*
Rose Hoover, *Corp Secy*
Thomas Kent, *Vice Pres*
James C Land, *Vice Pres*
▼ EMP: 130
SALES (est): 49.6MM **Privately Held**
WEB: www.buffaloair.com
SIC: 3564 3585 3567 Ventilating fans: industrial or commercial; refrigeration & heating equipment; industrial furnaces & ovens

(G-686)
C & B PIPING (E) INC
390 Lexington Tpke (24521-3586)
PHONE..................................434 946-7170
Kenda Carroll Mawyer, *Admin Sec*
EMP: 5
SALES (est): 638.6K **Privately Held**
WEB: www.cbpiping.com
SIC: 3498 Fabricated pipe & fittings

(G-687)
CIRCLE R CARRIER SERVICE INC
Also Called: Oneil Enterprises
915 Lexington Tpke (24521-3390)
PHONE..................................434 401-5950
Roger Oneil, *President*
Susan Oneil, *Corp Secy*
EMP: 2
SALES (est): 90K **Privately Held**
SIC: 3711 Personnel carriers (motor vehicles), assembly of

(G-688)
COBLENTZ CUSTOM CABINETS
121 Blue Ledge Loop Rd (24521-4726)
PHONE..................................231 362-2728
Marvin Copeland, *Owner*
EMP: 2
SALES (est): 167.8K **Privately Held**
WEB: www.coblentzcabinets.com
SIC: 2434 Wood kitchen cabinets

(G-689)
DAVID MAYS CABINET MAKER
1063 Lowesville Rd (24521-4255)
PHONE..................................434 277-8533
David Mays, *Owner*
EMP: 1 EST: 1990
SALES (est): 121.8K **Privately Held**
SIC: 2434 Wood kitchen cabinets

(G-690)
ELLINGTON WOOD PRODUCTS INC
145 Mill Ridge Ln (24521-3544)
PHONE..................................434 922-7545
Laura Vassar, *President*
Rachael Wilkins, *Assistant*
EMP: 13
SQ FT: 87,120
SALES (est): 2MM **Privately Held**
WEB: www.ellingtonwood.com
SIC: 2448 Pallets, wood; skids, wood

(G-691)
GLAD PRODUCTS COMPANY
317 Zane Snead Dr (24521)
P.O. Box 959 (24521-0959)
PHONE..................................434 946-3100
Ric Woerner, *Electrical Engi*
D Zirnsak, *Branch Mgr*
EMP: 200 **Publicly Held**
WEB: www.thecloroxcompany.com
SIC: 2673 3081 2671 Bags: plastic, laminated & coated; unsupported plastics film & sheet; packaging paper & plastics film, coated & laminated
HQ: The Glad Products Company
1221 Broadway Ste A
Oakland CA 94612
510 271-7000

(G-692)
GOOD GUYS PRINTING LLC
450 Maple Run Rd (24521-3872)
PHONE..................................434 942-8229
Stephen Barbour, *Principal*
EMP: 2 EST: 2014
SALES (est): 117.7K **Privately Held**
SIC: 2752 Commercial printing, lithographic

(G-693)
HERMLE UHREN GMBH & CO KG
Also Called: Hermle North America
340 Industrial Park Dr (24521-4691)
P.O. Box 670 (24521-0670)
PHONE..................................434 946-7751
Chad EBY, *Managing Prtnr*
◆ EMP: 80 EST: 1975
SQ FT: 90,000
SALES (est): 10MM **Privately Held**
WEB: www.hermleclock.com
SIC: 2511 3873 Wood household furniture; clocks, assembly of

(G-694)
HOMER HAYWOOD WHEELER II
Also Called: Hw Logging
836 Campbells Mill Rd (24521-4311)
PHONE..................................434 946-5126
Homer Haywood Wheeler II, *Owner*
Haywood Whillar, *Owner*
EMP: 2
SALES (est): 98K **Privately Held**
SIC: 2411 Logging

(G-695)
HONAKER & SON LOGGING LLC
262 Bryant Hollow Rd (24521-3026)
P.O. Box 832 (24521-0832)
PHONE..................................434 661-7935
EMP: 2
SALES (est): 81.7K **Privately Held**
SIC: 2411 Logging

(G-696)
J & A TOOLS
407 Hartless Rd (24521-3880)
PHONE..................................434 414-0871
James Loyd Jr, *Principal*
EMP: 2
SALES (est): 105.2K **Privately Held**
SIC: 3541 Machine tools, metal cutting type

(G-697)
KU FORMING INC
414 Rosecliff Farms Rd (24521-2570)
PHONE..................................434 946-5934
Keith Yule, *President*
EMP: 1 EST: 2000
SALES (est): 121.2K **Privately Held**
SIC: 3253 Ceramic wall & floor tile

(G-698)
LYNCHBURG READY-MIX CON CO INC
Hwy Ste 29n (24521)
PHONE..................434 946-5562
John Wegener, *Manager*
EMP: 5
SALES (corp-wide): 3.7MM **Privately Held**
WEB: www.lrmcc.com
SIC: 3273 Ready-mixed concrete
PA: Lynchburg Ready-Mix Concrete Co., Incorporated
100 Halsey Rd
Lynchburg VA 24501
434 846-6563

(G-699)
MARVIN COBLENTZ
121 Blue Ledge Loop Rd (24521-4726)
PHONE..................434 944-1897
Marvin Copeland, *Owner*
EMP: 4
SALES (est): 234.6K **Privately Held**
WEB: www.coblentzcabinets.com
SIC: 2434 Wood kitchen cabinets

(G-700)
MILHOUS CONTROL COMPANY
Also Called: Milhous Company
144 S Main St (24521-2642)
P.O. Box 1080 (24521-1080)
PHONE..................434 946-5302
John D Milhous, *President*
Carol Milhous, *Admin Sec*
EMP: 20
SQ FT: 6,000
SALES (est): 4.4MM **Privately Held**
WEB: www.milhous.com
SIC: 3825 3559 Test equipment for electronic & electric measurement; automotive related machinery

(G-701)
MT PLEASANT LOG & EXCVTG LLC
515 Emmanuel Church Rd (24521-3822)
PHONE..................434 922-7326
Timothy Lewis,
EMP: 2
SALES (est): 144.6K **Privately Held**
SIC: 2411 Timber, cut at logging camp

(G-702)
MWB ENTERPRISES INC
1026 Sugar Hill Tunnel Rd (24521-3579)
PHONE..................434 922-7730
Mike Bradley, *President*
Debbie Bradley, *Vice Pres*
EMP: 6
SALES (est): 427.7K **Privately Held**
SIC: 2499 Mulch or sawdust products, wood

(G-703)
PA INDUSTRIES INC
164 Almae Dr (24521-3458)
PHONE..................434 845-0813
Virginia Higuchi, *Principal*
EMP: 2
SALES (est): 92.7K **Privately Held**
SIC: 3999 Manufacturing industries

(G-704)
RAMSEY & SON LUMBER CORP
Rr 608 (24521)
P.O. Box 484 (24521-0484)
PHONE..................434 946-5429
Mike Ramsey, *President*
Barbara Ramsey, *Treasurer*
EMP: 10
SALES (est): 1.3MM **Privately Held**
SIC: 2421 Sawmills & planing mills, general

(G-705)
RAMSEY CABINETS INC
126 Sardis Rd (24521-4867)
P.O. Box 816 (24521-0816)
PHONE..................434 946-0329
Gary Ramsey, *President*
EMP: 4 EST: 1979
SALES (est): 404.9K **Privately Held**
WEB: www.ramseycabinets.com
SIC: 2434 Wood kitchen cabinets

(G-706)
RAYS CUSTOM CABINETS
288 Mansion Way (24521-8006)
PHONE..................434 528-0189
Peggy Miller, *Principal*
EMP: 2 EST: 2010
SALES (est): 139.5K **Privately Held**
SIC: 2434 Wood kitchen cabinets

(G-707)
REBEC VINEYARDS INC
2229 N Amherst Hwy (24521-4378)
PHONE..................434 946-5168
Svetlozar N Kanev, *President*
Robert L Chase, *Vice Pres*
Richard R Hanson, *Vice Pres*
EMP: 4 EST: 1999
SALES (est): 365.8K **Privately Held**
WEB: www.rebecwinery.com
SIC: 2084 5812 Wines; eating places

(G-708)
SPENCER STNLESS ALUM GUTTERING
765 Mollys Mountain Rd (24521-3769)
PHONE..................434 277-8359
Noel E Spencer, *Owner*
EMP: 1
SALES (est): 88.2K **Privately Held**
SIC: 3444 Gutters, sheet metal

(G-709)
STATON & HAULING
1467 Richmond Hwy (24521-3985)
PHONE..................434 946-7913
Grover Staton, *President*
EMP: 2
SALES (est): 40K **Privately Held**
SIC: 2411 Logging

(G-710)
SWEET BRIAR SHEET METAL SVCS
162 Higginbotham Creek Rd (24521-3653)
P.O. Box 1007 (24521-1007)
PHONE..................434 946-0403
Cecil Lloyd, *President*
Jerry Lloyd, *Vice Pres*
EMP: 8
SQ FT: 6,400
SALES (est): 981.5K **Privately Held**
SIC: 3444 Sheet metalwork

(G-711)
SWISSOMATION VIRGINIA LLC
254 Industrial Park Dr (24521-4655)
P.O. Box 1079 (24521-1079)
PHONE..................434 944-3322
Susan Schjonning, *Administration*
EMP: 8 EST: 2014
SALES (est): 987.9K **Privately Held**
WEB: www.swissomation.com
SIC: 3599 Machine shop, jobbing & repair

(G-712)
VIDEO AERIAL SYSTEMS LLC
117 Martins Ln (24521)
PHONE..................434 221-3089
Charles A Greve,
▲ EMP: 9
SALES (est): 350K **Privately Held**
WEB: www.videoaerialsystems.com
SIC: 3812 Antennas, radar or communications

(G-713)
WHEELER THURSTON E LOGGING
963 Campbells Mill Rd (24521-4312)
PHONE..................434 946-5265
Thurston Wheeler, *President*
Shirley Wheeler, *Corp Secy*
Stephen Wheeler, *Vice Pres*
EMP: 5
SALES (est): 340K **Privately Held**
SIC: 2411 Logging camps & contractors

(G-714)
WONDERS INC
164 Almae Dr (24521-3458)
PHONE..................434 845-0813
Samuel Higuchi, *President*
EMP: 3
SALES (est): 199.4K **Privately Held**
SIC: 2821 Plastics materials & resins

(G-715)
WRIGHTS TRUCKING & LOGGING
159 Poplar Grove Cir (24521-3979)
PHONE..................434 946-5387
William Wright Jr, *President*
Teresa Wright, *Treasurer*
Pearl Wright, *Admin Sec*
EMP: 15 EST: 1988
SALES (est): 1MM **Privately Held**
WEB: www.wrightstruckingandlogging.com
SIC: 2411 4212 Logging camps & contractors; lumber (log) trucking, local

Amissville
Culpeper County

(G-716)
AMISSVILLE ALTERNATIVE
7564 Tapps Ford Rd (20106-3418)
PHONE..................540 364-4436
Angela Albrecht, *Principal*
EMP: 3
SALES (est): 103.3K **Privately Held**
WEB: www.rappnews.com
SIC: 2711 Newspapers, publishing & printing

(G-717)
CARDINAL APPLICATIONS LLC
154 Battle Mountain Rd (20106-4340)
PHONE..................540 270-4369
John Weir,
Adam O'Donnell,
Alex Shafran,
EMP: 3
SALES (est): 121.8K **Privately Held**
SIC: 7372 7389 Application computer software; business services

(G-718)
EDWARD L BIRCKHEAD
82 Viewtown Rd (20106-3016)
P.O. Box 353 (20106-0353)
PHONE..................540 937-4287
EMP: 3
SALES (est): 100.3K **Privately Held**
SIC: 3271 Mfg Concrete Block/Brick

(G-719)
GRAY GHOST VINEYARDS
14706 Lee Hwy (20106-4226)
PHONE..................540 937-4869
Sheryl Kellert, *Partner*
Albert Kellert, *Partner*
EMP: 3
SALES (est): 317.4K **Privately Held**
WEB: www.grayghostvineyards.com
SIC: 2084 Wines

(G-720)
NARMADA WINERY LLC
43 Narmada Ln (20106-4170)
PHONE..................540 937-8215
Pandit G Patil,
EMP: 10
SALES (est): 1.3MM **Privately Held**
WEB: www.narmadawinery.com
SIC: 2084 Wines

(G-721)
SCW SOFTWARE INC
2714 Wildwood Cir (20106-1881)
PHONE..................540 937-5332
James Shannon, *Principal*
EMP: 2
SALES (est): 142.2K **Privately Held**
SIC: 7372 Prepackaged software

(G-722)
US ANODIZING INC
15403 Covey Cir (20106-2284)
PHONE..................540 937-2801
Pedro V Mederos, *Principal*
EMP: 3
SALES (est): 206.3K **Privately Held**
WEB: www.usanodizing.com
SIC: 3471 Electroplating of metals or formed products

(G-723)
VALLEY GREEN NATURALS LLC
81 Seven Ponds Rd (20106-4212)
PHONE..................540 937-4795
Cynthia Devore, *Owner*
EMP: 6
SALES (est): 583.5K **Privately Held**
WEB: www.valleygreennaturals.com
SIC: 2841 Soap: granulated, liquid, cake, flaked or chip

(G-724)
WP COMPANY LLC
Also Called: Washington Post
15310 Lee Hwy (20106-1848)
PHONE..................540 937-4380
Mildred Marshall, *Branch Mgr*
EMP: 1 **Privately Held**
WEB: www.washingtonpost.com
SIC: 2711 Newspapers, publishing & printing
HQ: Wp Company Llc
1301 K St Nw
Washington DC 20071

Amonate
Tazewell County

(G-725)
CONSOLIDATION COAL COMPANY
Also Called: Amonate Mine
Rr 637 (24601)
PHONE..................276 988-3010
Joseph E Berry, *Branch Mgr*
EMP: 20
SALES (corp-wide): 3.4B **Privately Held**
WEB: www.consolenergy.com
SIC: 1221 Bituminous coal surface mining
HQ: Consolidation Coal Company Inc
1000 Consol Energy Dr
Canonsburg PA 15317
740 338-3100

Andersonville
Buckingham County

(G-726)
JAMMERSON LOGGING
Rr 632 (23936)
P.O. Box 533, Dillwyn (23936-0533)
PHONE..................434 983-7505
Andrew Jamerson, *Principal*
EMP: 6
SALES (est): 490K **Privately Held**
SIC: 2411 Logging camps & contractors

Annandale
Fairfax County

(G-727)
ABBADON SKATEBOARDS LLC
4006 Winterset Dr (22003-2243)
PHONE..................703 280-4818
E John Regan Jr, *Principal*
EMP: 1
SALES (est): 47K **Privately Held**
SIC: 3949 Skateboards

(G-728)
ADTA & CO INC
7039 Columbia Pike (22003-3460)
PHONE..................703 930-9280
Joe Attyah, *CEO*
Carol Attyah, *President*
EMP: 12
SALES (est): 820.6K **Privately Held**
SIC: 2741 7379 2791 5045 Posters: publishing & printing; computer related maintenance services; typesetting; computers, peripherals & software; agents, shipping

(G-729)
ALFORAS COMPANY
7138 Little River Tpke (22003-3101)
PHONE..................703 342-6910
Said Lahrichie, *President*

▲ EMP: 1
SALES (est): 54.1K **Privately Held**
SIC: 3944 5199 Games, toys & children's vehicles; general merchandise, nondurable

(G-730)
AMERICAN SOLAR INC
8703 Chippendale Ct (22003-3807)
PHONE....................................703 346-6053
John Archibald, *President*
Kathryn Mtgeeajn, *Vice Pres*
EMP: 3 **EST:** 2001
SALES (est): 400K **Privately Held**
WEB: www.americansolar.com
SIC: 3433 8748 Solar heaters & collectors; business consulting

(G-731)
BALLYHOO
7138 Little River Tpke (22003-3101)
PHONE....................................703 294-6075
David Sklar, *Owner*
EMP: 2
SALES (est): 131.6K **Privately Held**
WEB: www.ballyhoostore.com
SIC: 2396 Screen printing on fabric articles

(G-732)
BLACK SPHERE LLC
4541 Garbo Ct (22003-5737)
PHONE....................................703 776-0494
Hao Chen, *Vice Pres*
EMP: 2 **EST:** 2017
SALES (est): 76.8K **Privately Held**
SIC: 2086 Carbonated beverages, nonalcoholic: bottled & canned

(G-733)
CALBICO LLC
3845 Whitman Rd (22003-2202)
PHONE....................................571 332-3334
David Calbi, *Owner*
EMP: 1
SALES (est): 67.1K **Privately Held**
SIC: 3423 7389 Hand & edge tools;

(G-734)
CALEIGH SYSTEMS INC
7515 Little River Tpke (22003-2928)
PHONE....................................703 539-5004
Michael B Antonelli, *CEO*
Michael Antonelli, *CEO*
EMP: 10
SQ FT: 2,100
SALES (est): 302.5K **Privately Held**
WEB: www.caleighsystems.com
SIC: 3699 7382 8748 Security devices; security systems services; telecommunications consultant

(G-735)
CHRISTIAN POWER WEEKLY NEWS
7218 Poplar St (22003-3009)
PHONE....................................703 658-5272
EMP: 4
SALES (est): 180K **Privately Held**
SIC: 2711 Newspapers-Publishing/Printing

(G-736)
COMPOST LIVIN LLC
3719 Rose Ln (22003-1937)
PHONE....................................703 362-9378
Sarah Stakes, *Principal*
EMP: 3
SALES (est): 134.1K **Privately Held**
SIC: 2875 Compost

(G-737)
CREATION SIGN LLC
7364 Mcwhorter Pl (22003-5605)
PHONE....................................703 622-5958
Heejin Chang, *Principal*
EMP: 2
SALES (est): 56.5K **Privately Held**
SIC: 3993 Signs & advertising specialties

(G-738)
DALLAS G BIENHOFF
Also Called: Cislunar Space Development
8455 Chapelwood Ct (22003-4599)
PHONE....................................571 232-4554
Dallas Bienhoff, *Owner*
EMP: 1

SALES (est): 73.4K **Privately Held**
WEB: www.csdc.space
SIC: 3761 7389 Guided missiles & space vehicles, research & development;

(G-739)
DAMAS INTERNATIONAL LLC
4327 Ravensworth Rd (22003-5644)
PHONE....................................469 740-9973
Mohamad Hourania, *CEO*
EMP: 1
SALES (est): 46.4K **Privately Held**
SIC: 2099 Sandwiches, assembled & packaged: for wholesale market

(G-740)
DAWN GROUP INC
4021 Woodland Rd (22003-2606)
PHONE....................................703 750-6767
Tahira Bhatti, *President*
EMP: 1
SALES (est): 78.2K **Privately Held**
SIC: 3635 Household vacuum cleaners

(G-741)
DECORATIVE ARTS WORKSHOP
8912 Burbank Rd (22003-3860)
PHONE....................................703 321-8373
EMP: 1
SALES (est): 51.7K **Privately Held**
SIC: 3944 Mfg Games/Toys

(G-742)
DEFENSE THREAT REDUCTIO
7444 Fountain Head Dr (22003-5713)
PHONE....................................703 767-5870
EMP: 3
SALES (est): 141.8K **Privately Held**
SIC: 3812 Defense systems & equipment

(G-743)
DIAMONDEFENSE LLC
3436 Holly Rd (22003-1266)
PHONE....................................571 321-2012
Andrew Everett,
Jared Rader,
EMP: 12
SALES (est): 884.7K **Privately Held**
WEB: www.diamondefense.com
SIC: 7372 8748 8711 8742 Application computer software; systems analysis & engineering consulting services; consulting engineer; management engineering; systems software development services

(G-744)
DISPLAY & BANNER INC
8125 Briar Creek Dr (22003-4637)
PHONE....................................703 503-4447
Brad Tavelman, *President*
EMP: 3
SALES (est): 280K **Privately Held**
WEB: www.dbicreative.com
SIC: 3993 Signs & advertising specialties

(G-745)
DNA WELDING LLC
7471 Little River Tpke (22003-2915)
PHONE....................................703 256-2976
Jorge Moran, *Principal*
EMP: 8
SALES (est): 88.7K **Privately Held**
SIC: 7692 Welding repair

(G-746)
ECO FUEL LLC
7413 Little River Tpke (22003-2901)
PHONE....................................703 256-6999
EMP: 4 **EST:** 2014
SALES (est): 439.2K **Privately Held**
SIC: 2869 Fuels

(G-747)
EURO PRINT USA LLC
3728 Hummer Rd (22003-1503)
PHONE....................................703 849-8781
Alaim C Pesce, *Principal*
EMP: 2
SALES (est): 137.5K **Privately Held**
SIC: 2752 Commercial printing, lithographic

(G-748)
FASHION SEOUL
4305 Markham St (22003-3022)
PHONE....................................571 395-8555

EMP: 1
SALES (est): 46.5K **Privately Held**
SIC: 2299 Mfg Textile Goods

(G-749)
FRANCIS & MURPHY
4305 Backlick Rd (22003-3141)
PHONE....................................703 256-8644
EMP: 1
SALES (est): 40.9K **Privately Held**
SIC: 2399 Fabricated textile products

(G-750)
FULL COLOR PRINTS
6400 Holyoke Dr (22003-2106)
PHONE....................................703 354-9231
Steve Ortiz, *Principal*
EMP: 2
SALES (est): 145.5K **Privately Held**
WEB: www.fullcolorprints.biz
SIC: 2752 Commercial printing, lithographic

(G-751)
GLORY VIOLIN CO LLC
7601 Little River Tpke (22003-2644)
PHONE....................................703 439-1700
Nancy Kim, *Principal*
EMP: 2
SALES (est): 79.6K **Privately Held**
SIC: 3931 Violins & parts

(G-752)
GO HAPPY PRINTING LLC
8422 Frost Way (22003-2221)
PHONE....................................240 423-7397
Thao Tran, *Principal*
EMP: 2
SALES (est): 101.5K **Privately Held**
SIC: 2752 Commercial printing, lithographic

(G-753)
GRAPHIC SIGN WORX LLC
5025 Linette Ln (22003-4119)
PHONE....................................703 503-3286
Eben Garner Jahnke, *President*
EMP: 1
SALES (est): 50.6K **Privately Held**
SIC: 3993 Signs & advertising specialties

(G-754)
GREG NORMAN AND ASSOCIATES INC (PA)
Also Called: Kitchen and Bath Design Studio
4115 Annandale Rd Ste 102 (22003-2500)
PHONE....................................703 205-0031
Greg Norman, *President*
Mark Easter, *Vice Pres*
EMP: 15
SALES (est): 2.1MM **Privately Held**
WEB: www.gnahome.com
SIC: 2434 Wood kitchen cabinets

(G-755)
HALTRIE LLC
4209 Americana Dr Apt 103 (22003-4704)
PHONE....................................703 598-9928
Trieana Kim, *Principal*
EMP: 1
SALES (est): 56K **Privately Held**
SIC: 2512 2521 5021 Living room furniture: upholstered on wood frames; wood office furniture; bar furniture; office furniture; chairs

(G-756)
HIGH STAKES WRITING LLC
6920 Braddock Rd B-614 (22003-6036)
PHONE....................................703 819-5490
Lawrence Goodrich,
EMP: 1
SALES (est): 97.5K **Privately Held**
WEB: www.highstakeswriting.com
SIC: 2731 7389 Book publishing; business services

(G-757)
HNH PARTNERS INC
7535 Little River Tpke (22003-2991)
PHONE....................................757 539-2353
EMP: 1
SALES (est): 54.5K **Privately Held**
SIC: 3523 Farm machinery & equipment

(G-758)
IMLAY INTERNATIONAL LLC
5023 Backlick Rd Ste A (22003-6044)
PHONE....................................703 914-0526
David Orgel, *Partner*
Shawn Paxton, *Partner*
Joseph Tierney, *Representative*
EMP: 3
SQ FT: 900
SALES (est): 566.9K **Privately Held**
WEB: www.imlayintl.com
SIC: 2752 Commercial printing, offset

(G-759)
INFINITY MG INC
7700 Little River Tpke (22003-2427)
PHONE....................................703 916-0172
EMP: 2
SALES (est): 83.3K **Privately Held**
SIC: 2834 Pharmaceutical preparations

(G-760)
INNOVATION STATION MUSIC LLC
6612 Jessamine Ln (22003-6202)
PHONE....................................703 405-6727
David Mallen, *Owner*
EMP: 1 **EST:** 2010
SALES (est): 134.1K **Privately Held**
WEB: www.innovationstationmusic.com
SIC: 3652 7389 Master records or tapes, preparation of; authors' agents & brokers; music & broadcasting services

(G-761)
JAY BLUE POS INC
5105m Backlick Rd (22003-6069)
PHONE....................................703 672-2869
Phan Ngo, *CEO*
EMP: 6
SALES (est): 392.8K **Privately Held**
WEB: www.bluejaypos.com
SIC: 7372 Business oriented computer software

(G-762)
JOONG-ANG DAILY NEWS CAL INC
Also Called: Joong-Ang Daily News Wash
7023 Little River Tpke # 101 (22003-5954)
PHONE....................................703 281-9660
Jason Lee, *Manager*
Dennis Prescott, *Manager*
EMP: 40 **Privately Held**
WEB: www.koreadaily.com
SIC: 2711 Commercial printing & newspaper publishing combined; newspapers, publishing & printing
HQ: The Joong-Ang Daily News California Inc
690 Wilshire Pl
Los Angeles CA 90005
213 368-2500

(G-763)
KARA KEEN LLC
3430 Ethel Ct (22003-1616)
PHONE....................................973 713-1049
Kara Keen,
EMP: 1
SALES (est): 42.7K **Privately Held**
SIC: 2731 Book publishing

(G-764)
KOREA DAILY
7023 Little River Tpke # 300 (22003-5939)
PHONE....................................703 281-9660
Jin Suk Kim, *Principal*
▲ **EMP:** 10
SALES (est): 654.2K **Privately Held**
WEB: www.koreadaily.com
SIC: 2711 Commercial printing & newspaper publishing combined; newspapers, publishing & printing

(G-765)
KOREA TIMES WASHINGTON DC INC
7601 Little River Tpke (22003-2644)
PHONE....................................703 941-8001
Jaemin Thang, *President*
▲ **EMP:** 30 **EST:** 1970
SQ FT: 8,000

▲ = Import ▼=Export
◆ =Import/Export

SALES (est): 137.8K **Privately Held**
WEB: www.koreatimes.com
SIC: **2711** 2741 Newspapers: publishing only, not printed on site; miscellaneous publishing

(G-766)
KOREAN WEEKLY ENTERTAINMENT
7353 Mcwhorter Pl Ste 210 (22003-5648)
PHONE...........................703 354-7962
Kyung Tak Jung, *President*
▲ EMP: 4
SALES (est): 194.9K **Privately Held**
WEB: www.memphisartscouncil.org
SIC: **2711** Newspapers, publishing & printing

(G-767)
KUNG FU TEA
7895 Heritage Dr (22003-5349)
PHONE...........................703 992-8599
Janice Liu, *Owner*
EMP: 20
SALES (est): 1.1MM **Privately Held**
WEB: www.kungfutea.com
SIC: **2099** Tea blending

(G-768)
KYUNG T JUNG DBA KREAN ENTRMT
7353 Mcwhorter Pl (22003-5670)
PHONE...........................703 658-0000
Kyung T Jung, *President*
EMP: 3
SALES (est): 74K **Privately Held**
SIC: **2711** Newspapers, publishing & printing

(G-769)
LANDMARK PRINTING CO
7535 Little River Tpke 120c (22003-2984)
PHONE...........................703 226-1000
Richard Dufek, *President*
EMP: 3
SQ FT: 2,400
SALES (est): 348.1K **Privately Held**
WEB: www.landmarkprinting.net
SIC: **2752** 7336 Commercial printing, offset; graphic arts & related design

(G-770)
MANNY EXHIBITS & WOODCRAFT
6400 Holyoke Dr (22003-2106)
PHONE...........................703 354-9231
Manny Ortiz, *Owner*
Ana Ortiz, *Principal*
EMP: 1 EST: 1997
SALES (est): 88K **Privately Held**
SIC: **3993** Displays & cutouts, window & lobby

(G-771)
MARIN
4210 John Marr Dr (22003-3203)
PHONE...........................703 354-1950
Christopher Choi, *Officer*
EMP: 1
SALES (est): 55.7K **Privately Held**
SIC: **3421** Table & food cutlery, including butchers'

(G-772)
MASPAINTSERVICE LTD LBLTY CO
4415 Forest Glen Ct (22003-4839)
PHONE...........................301 547-1996
Miguel Saneaux,
EMP: 2
SALES (est): 60K **Privately Held**
SIC: **1389** Construction, repair & dismantling services

(G-773)
METHODHEAD SOFTWARE LLC
4881 Old Well Rd (22003-4454)
PHONE...........................703 338-1588
Dan Hensgen, *Principal*
EMP: 2
SALES (est): 109.4K **Privately Held**
SIC: **7372** Prepackaged software

(G-774)
MICHAEL CHUNG MD
7535 Little River Tpke B (22003-2991)
PHONE...........................443 722-5314
SOO Chung, *Principal*
EMP: 1 EST: 2007
SALES (est): 80.1K **Privately Held**
SIC: **2741** Miscellaneous publishing

(G-775)
MONALISA BLAKENEY
Also Called: Blakeney United Disposal
4600 John Hancock Ct # 2 (22003-4915)
PHONE...........................703 863-8530
Monalisa Blakeney, *Owner*
EMP: 5
SALES (est): 100K **Privately Held**
SIC: **2673** Trash bags (plastic film): made from purchased materials

(G-776)
MONTE CARLO SOFTWARE LLC
6703 Capstan Dr (22003-1953)
PHONE...........................703 642-0289
Daniel O'Connor, *Principal*
EMP: 2
SALES (est): 99.7K **Privately Held**
SIC: **7372** Prepackaged software

(G-777)
ONE MILE UP INC
4354 Greenberry Ln (22003-3219)
PHONE...........................703 642-1177
Eugene Velasquez, *President*
Eugene Velazquez, *President*
Linda Velazquez, *Administration*
EMP: 5
SQ FT: 1,500
SALES (est): 300K **Privately Held**
WEB: www.1mileup.com
SIC: **3695** Computer software tape & disks: blank, rigid & floppy

(G-778)
PACIFIC TECHNOLOGY INC
Also Called: Ptci
4200 Daniels Ave Ste 20 (22003-3177)
PHONE...........................571 421-7861
Hye C Chang, *President*
EMP: 15
SALES (est): 1.4MM **Privately Held**
SIC: **3646** Commercial indusl & institutional electric lighting fixtures

(G-779)
QUANTUM REEFS LLC
3713 Mount Airey Ln (22003-1549)
PHONE...........................703 560-1448
EMP: 3
SALES (est): 259.5K **Privately Held**
SIC: **3572** Mfg Computer Storage Devices

(G-780)
SAEAM GRAPHICS & SIGN INC
7004 Little River Tpke G (22003-5965)
PHONE...........................703 203-3233
Kyung S Park, *Administration*
EMP: 2
SALES (est): 61.3K **Privately Held**
SIC: **3993** Signs & advertising specialties

(G-781)
SAMS MONOGRAMS
4549 Maxfield Dr (22003-3529)
PHONE...........................703 866-4400
Sam Banks, *Principal*
EMP: 1 EST: 2014
SALES (est): 36.4K **Privately Held**
SIC: **2395** Embroidery & art needlework

(G-782)
SHOPRAT METAL WORKS LLC
4137 Watkins Trl (22003-2052)
PHONE...........................571 499-1534
Abraham Wine,
EMP: 2 EST: 2017
SALES (est): 94.5K **Privately Held**
SIC: **3444** Sheet metalwork

(G-783)
SPEAKEASY
6725 Alpine Dr (22003-3503)
PHONE...........................703 333-5040
Brian Oconnor, *Owner*
EMP: 1

SALES (est): 69.7K **Privately Held**
SIC: **3663** 4813 Radio & TV communications equipment; telephone communication, except radio

(G-784)
SQLEXEC LLC
8403 Tobin Rd (22003-1103)
PHONE...........................703 600-9343
Michael Vitale, *Principal*
EMP: 2
SALES (est): 109.1K **Privately Held**
SIC: **7372** Prepackaged software

(G-785)
SUN CARE INC
3318 Woodburn Village Dr (22003-1254)
PHONE...........................703 715-7070
EMP: 2 EST: 2019
SALES (est): 90.6K **Privately Held**
WEB: www.coola.com
SIC: **2844** Toilet preparations

(G-786)
SYMMETRICAL WOOD WORKS LLC
3318 Woodburn Village Dr # 22 (22003-6858)
PHONE...........................703 499-0821
Marcelo Lopez, *Principal*
EMP: 1
SALES (est): 54.1K **Privately Held**
SIC: **2431** Millwork

(G-787)
THOMAS H RHEA MD PC
4600 John Marr Dr (22003-3315)
PHONE...........................703 658-0300
Thomas Rhea, *Principal*
EMP: 2
SALES (est): 138K **Privately Held**
SIC: **3315** 8011 Wire & fabricated wire products; physicians' office, including specialists

(G-788)
TODO BLU LLC
8121 Briar Creek Dr (22003-4637)
PHONE...........................703 944-9000
Alonso Zamora, *Mng Member*
Jaime M Delporte, *Director*
Miguel Dekantor,
Jaime Munoz,
EMP: 4 EST: 2015
SALES (est): 256.9K **Privately Held**
SIC: **2841** Soap & other detergents

(G-789)
TOM JAMES COMPANY
7611 Little River Tpke 605w (22003-2615)
PHONE...........................703 916-9300
Kurt Siys, *Manager*
EMP: 19
SALES (corp-wide): 574.6MM **Privately Held**
WEB: www.tomjames.com
SIC: **2311** Suits, men's & boys': made from purchased materials; coats, overcoats & vests
PA: Tom James Company
263 Seaboard Ln
Franklin TN 37067
615 771-1122

(G-790)
TRIQUETRA PHOENIX LLC
Also Called: Tri-Phoenix
4713 Ravensworth Rd (22003-5549)
PHONE...........................571 265-6044
Judith Pendergast,
Thomas Pendergast,
EMP: 3
SALES (est): 317.3K **Privately Held**
WEB: www.tri-phoenix.com
SIC: **3761** 8733 8742 Guided missiles & space vehicles, research & development; scientific research agency; management engineering

(G-791)
VINEYARD ENGRAVERS INC (PA)
7700 Little River Tpke (22003-2427)
PHONE...........................703 941-3700
Peter Rim, *Principal*

EMP: 3 EST: 2017
SALES (est): 559K **Privately Held**
SIC: **2084** Wines

(G-792)
WALLACE-CALIVA PUBLISHING LLC
8602 Howrey Ct (22003-4214)
PHONE...........................703 313-4813
Suzanne Wallace, *Principal*
EMP: 1 EST: 2017
SALES (est): 40K **Privately Held**
SIC: **2741** Miscellaneous publishing

(G-793)
WOOD BURN ENDOSCOPY CENTER
3301 Woodburn Rd Ste 109 (22003-6880)
PHONE...........................703 752-2557
Stafford S Goldstein, *Principal*
Shubita Fernandez, *Administration*
EMP: 3
SALES (est): 429.2K **Privately Held**
WEB: www.woodburnendoscopy.com
SIC: **3845** Endoscopic equipment, electromedical

(G-794)
WORLD & I
3811 Tall Oak Ct (22003-2012)
PHONE...........................202 636-3334
EMP: 2
SALES (est): 62.9K **Privately Held**
SIC: **2711** Newspapers

(G-795)
YOUR HEALTH MAGAZINE
7617 Little River Tpke # 400 (22003-2603)
PHONE...........................703 288-3130
Scott Hunter, *Owner*
Jamison Ciskanik, *Accounts Mgr*
EMP: 20
SALES (est): 673.6K **Privately Held**
WEB: www.yourhealthmagazine.net
SIC: **2711** Newspapers, publishing & printing

Appalachia
Wise County

(G-796)
CLARK WELDING SERVICE
369 Callahan Ave (24216-1001)
PHONE...........................276 565-3607
Randy Clark, *Owner*
EMP: 3
SALES (est): 317.5K **Privately Held**
WEB: www.clarkweldingtanks.com
SIC: **7692** Welding repair

(G-797)
HILLS COAL AND TRUCKING CO
4719 Callahan Ave (24216-3007)
PHONE...........................276 565-2560
Jeff Colan, *Manager*
EMP: 5 **Privately Held**
WEB: www.hillscoalandtrucking.com
SIC: **1241** Coal mining services
PA: Hills Coal And Trucking Co
Hwy 58
Galax VA 24333

(G-798)
MULLICAN FLOORING LP
Also Called: Mullican Lumber & Mfg Co
Hwy 23 N (24216)
P.O. Box 152 (24216-0152)
PHONE...........................276 565-0220
Terry Porter, *Manager*
EMP: 85
SALES (corp-wide): 339MM **Privately Held**
WEB: www.mullicanflooring.com
SIC: **2426** 2421 2411 Lumber, hardwood dimension; sawmills & planing mills, general; logging
HQ: Mullican Flooring, L.P.
655 Woodlyn Rd
Johnson City TN 37601
423 262-8440

(G-799)
PORTER WELDING
1480 Roda Rd (24216-2504)
PHONE..................................276 565-2694
Joe Porter, *Owner*
EMP: 1
SALES (est): 50K **Privately Held**
SIC: 7692 Welding repair

(G-800)
REGENT ALLIED CARBON ENERGY
Pine Br (24216)
P.O. Box 917, Abingdon (24212-0917)
PHONE..................................276 679-4994
EMP: 35
SALES (est): 3MM **Privately Held**
SIC: 1241 1222 Coal Mining Services Bituminous Coal-Underground Mining

Appomattox
Appomattox County

(G-801)
AMERICAN MTAL FBRCATION VA LLC
3061 Holiday Lake Rd (24522-7900)
PHONE..................................434 851-1002
Malcolm Coleman, *Principal*
EMP: 1
SALES (est): 59.8K **Privately Held**
SIC: 3499 Fabricated metal products

(G-802)
APPOMATTOX LIME CO INC (HQ)
143 Quarry Rd (24522-8459)
PHONE..................................434 933-8258
Gordon C Willis Sr, *President*
Chris Willis, *General Mgr*
James Mac Donald Jr, *Vice Pres*
Gordon C Willis Jr, *Vice Pres*
Linwood W Lucas, *Admin Sec*
EMP: 18 **EST:** 1970
SQ FT: 3,000
SALES (est): 3.5MM
SALES (corp-wide): 13.3MM **Privately Held**
WEB: www.rockydalequarries.com
SIC: 1422 Limestones, ground
PA: Rockydale Quarries Corporation
2343 Highland Farm Rd Nw
Roanoke VA 24017
540 774-1696

(G-803)
APPOMATTOX QUARRY
143 Quarry Rd (24522-8459)
PHONE..................................434 295-5700
EMP: 4
SALES (est): 197.6K **Privately Held**
WEB: www.rockydalequarries.com
SIC: 1422 Crushed & broken limestone

(G-804)
AUBREY OTIS GUNTER JR
1316 Skyline Rd (24522-8477)
PHONE..................................434 352-8136
Aubrey Otis Gunter Jr, *President*
EMP: 1
SALES (est): 200K **Privately Held**
SIC: 2452 7389 Log cabins, prefabricated, wood;

(G-805)
B H FRANKLIN LOGGING INC
462 Woodlawn Trl (24522-5319)
P.O. Box 1030 (24522-1030)
PHONE..................................434 352-5484
Beverly H Franklin, *President*
Vicky Franklin, *Corp Secy*
Kevin Franklin, *Vice Pres*
EMP: 8
SALES (est): 600K **Privately Held**
SIC: 2411 0721 Logging camps & contractors; crop planting & protection

(G-806)
BEST BLOWER SALES & SVC LLC
208 Autumn Ln (24522-8004)
P.O. Box 2557 (24522-2557)
PHONE..................................434 352-1909
Kevin Paulson, *President*
EMP: 6
SQ FT: 10,000
SALES (est): 387.9K **Privately Held**
WEB: www.bestblower.us
SIC: 3564 Turbo-blowers, industrial

(G-807)
BOBS PRINTING SERVICE LLC
Hwy 460 W (24522)
P.O. Box 493, Spout Spring (24593-0493)
PHONE..................................434 352-2680
David Thompson, *Mng Member*
Joan Thompson,
EMP: 2
SQ FT: 3,200
SALES (est): 209.6K **Privately Held**
WEB: www.bobsprintingservice.com
SIC: 2752 Commercial printing, offset

(G-808)
DAVIS PUBLISHING COMPANY
677 Eldon Rd (24522-8278)
PHONE..................................434 363-2780
Joshua Davis, *Principal*
EMP: 1 **EST:** 2016
SALES (est): 50.2K **Privately Held**
SIC: 2741 Miscellaneous publishing

(G-809)
DHT WOODWORKS LLC
388 Charles Dr (24522-4050)
P.O. Box 2003 (24522-2003)
PHONE..................................434 414-2607
EMP: 2
SALES (est): 65.4K **Privately Held**
SIC: 2431 Millwork

(G-810)
FABRIKO INC
Also Called: Bagzoo.com
1065 Confederate Blvd (24522-9241)
PHONE..................................434 352-7145
William T Pugh, *President*
Julie Staton, *Accounts Exec*
Kristen Wood, *Accounts Exec*
EMP: 45
SQ FT: 35,000
SALES (est): 3.9MM **Privately Held**
WEB: www.fabriko.com
SIC: 2393 Canvas bags

(G-811)
FERGUSON PORTABLE TOILETS LLC
2556 Hancock Rd (24522-9500)
PHONE..................................434 610-9988
Noelle Ferguson,
EMP: 2
SALES (est): 143.3K **Privately Held**
WEB: www.fergusonportabletoilets.com
SIC: 3431 7389 Portable chemical toilets, metal;

(G-812)
HATCHER LOGGING
Also Called: R A Hatcher Timber Harvesting
14547 Richmond Hwy (24522)
P.O. Box 1077 (24522-1077)
PHONE..................................434 352-7975
Ramon Hatcher, *Owner*
EMP: 3 **Privately Held**
SIC: 2411 Logging camps & contractors

(G-813)
HITEK SEALING CORPORATION
191 Police Tower Rd (24522-8688)
PHONE..................................434 944-2404
Katrina Fields, *President*
Jason Brown, *Principal*
EMP: 2
SQ FT: 10,000
SALES (est): 111.5K **Privately Held**
SIC: 3053 Gaskets, all materials

(G-814)
J V RAMSEY LOGGING LLC
220 Oak Ln (24522-3582)
PHONE..................................434 610-1844
EMP: 2
SALES (est): 89.8K **Privately Held**
SIC: 2411 Logging camps & contractors

(G-815)
JL KELLEY AMERICAN APPAREL LLC
386 Cub Creek Rd (24522-7035)
PHONE..................................434 664-5243
EMP: 2
SALES (est): 73.4K **Privately Held**
SIC: 2211 Apparel & outerwear fabrics, cotton

(G-816)
JS WELDING
Hwy 460 (24522)
P.O. Box 2337 (24522-2337)
PHONE..................................434 352-0576
Jeffery Screggs, *Owner*
EMP: 3
SALES (est): 181.4K **Privately Held**
SIC: 7692 Welding repair

(G-817)
K H FRANKLIN LOGGING LLC
812 Woodlawn Trl (24522-5324)
PHONE..................................434 352-9235
Kevin Franklin, *Administration*
EMP: 6
SALES (est): 490K **Privately Held**
SIC: 2411 Logging camps & contractors

(G-818)
L3HARRIS TECHNOLOGIES INC
5155 Old Evergreen Rd (24522-5106)
PHONE..................................434 941-5441
Ricky Harris, *Branch Mgr*
EMP: 1
SALES (corp-wide): 6.8B **Publicly Held**
WEB: www.harris.com
SIC: 3812 Search & navigation equipment
PA: L3harris Technologies, Inc.
1025 W Nasa Blvd
Melbourne FL 32919
321 727-9100

(G-819)
MARTIN PRINTWEAR INC
200 Industrial Park (24522-7807)
PHONE..................................434 352-5660
Ricky Martin, *President*
Tammy Martin, *Admin Sec*
EMP: 7
SALES (est): 220K **Privately Held**
WEB: www.foglio.com
SIC: 2261 2396 Screen printing of cotton broadwoven fabrics; automotive & apparel trimmings

(G-820)
R & S MOLDS INC
400 Cedar Ln (24522-8262)
PHONE..................................434 352-8612
Donna Small, *President*
Jerry Small, *Vice Pres*
EMP: 3
SALES (est): 277.6K **Privately Held**
SIC: 3553 Sanding machines, except portable floor sanders: woodworking

(G-821)
RED ACRES EQUIPMENT INC
208 Autumn Ln (24522-8004)
P.O. Box 2459 (24522-2459)
PHONE..................................434 352-5086
Greg Evans, *President*
EMP: 6
SQ FT: 12,000
SALES (est): 580K **Privately Held**
SIC: 3441 7699 Fabricated structural metal; industrial equipment services

(G-822)
RED EAGLE INDUSTRIES LLC
271 Soybean Dr (24522-4320)
PHONE..................................434 352-5831
Todd Jennings, *Mng Member*
EMP: 4
SALES (est): 327.9K **Privately Held**
WEB: www.redeagleindustries.com
SIC: 3731 1771 1794 1751 Shipbuilding & repairing; concrete work; foundation & footing contractor; excavation work; carpentry work;

(G-823)
SUZANNE HENRI INC
Also Called: Absolute Perfection
839 Lee Grant Ave (24522-4902)
P.O. Box 2399 (24522-2399)
PHONE..................................434 352-0233
Suzanne Kadas, *President*
EMP: 3
SQ FT: 1,250
SALES (est): 190K **Privately Held**
WEB: www.brasperfectfit.com
SIC: 2342 5632 2341 Brassieres; lingerie & corsets (underwear); women's & children's underwear

(G-824)
TRITECH SOLUTIONS VIRGINIA INC
3061 Holiday Lake Rd (24522-7900)
PHONE..................................434 664-2140
Menti Purita, *CEO*
Frankie Drewry, *President*
Joey Malcolm, *Vice Pres*
EMP: 6 **EST:** 2012
SQ FT: 5,000
SALES (est): 1.5MM **Privately Held**
WEB: www.timesvirginian.com
SIC: 3443 7692 Towers (bubble, cooling, fractionating, etc.): metal plate; welding repair

(G-825)
TWO OAKS
2206 S Fork Rd (24522-9071)
PHONE..................................434 352-8181
EMP: 2 **EST:** 2010
SALES (est): 136.1K **Privately Held**
SIC: 3589 High pressure cleaning equipment

(G-826)
WEST ROCK
6969 Richmond Hwy (24522-8674)
PHONE..................................434 352-2804
EMP: 1 **EST:** 2015
SALES (est): 79.3K **Privately Held**
SIC: 2621 Paper mills

(G-827)
WESTROCK MWV LLC
Also Called: Mwv Community Dev & Lnd Mgmt
Hwy 460 W (24522)
PHONE..................................434 352-7132
Gary Youngblood, *Manager*
EMP: 20
SALES (corp-wide): 17.5B **Publicly Held**
WEB: www.westrock.com
SIC: 2631 Linerboard
HQ: Westrock Mwv, Llc
501 S 5th St
Richmond VA 23219
804 444-1000

(G-828)
WOMACK PUBLISHING CO INC
Also Called: Times-Virginian
589 Court St (24522-8212)
P.O. Box 2097 (24522-2097)
PHONE..................................434 352-8215
Marvin Hamlett, *Branch Mgr*
EMP: 9
SALES (corp-wide): 33.3MM **Privately Held**
WEB: www.womackpublishing.com
SIC: 2711 2759 Newspapers: publishing only, not printed on site; commercial printing
PA: Womack Publishing Co Inc
28 N Main St
Chatham VA 24531
434 432-2791

Ararat
Patrick County

(G-829)
A V PUBLICATION CORP
386 Hainted Rock Ln (24053-3101)
P.O. Box 280 (24053-0280)
PHONE..................................276 251-1760
Gail Riplinger, *President*
Michael Riplinger, *Admin Sec*

EMP: 3
SALES (est): 250K **Privately Held**
WEB: www.avpublications.com
SIC: 2731 7812 Books: publishing only; video production

(G-830)
CALVIN PAYNE
4037 Ararat Hwy (24053-3407)
PHONE..................276 251-5815
Calvin Payne, *Owner*
EMP: 2
SALES (est): 90K **Privately Held**
SIC: 2411 Logging camps & contractors

(G-831)
DALE HORTON LOGGING
804 Kibler Valley Rd (24053-3048)
PHONE..................276 251-5004
Dale Horton, *Owner*
EMP: 2
SALES (est): 192.2K **Privately Held**
SIC: 2411 Logging camps & contractors

(G-832)
ROLLING THUNDER RACEWAY LLC
3532 Friends Mission Rd (24053-3155)
PHONE..................336 401-2360
Alesia Nester, *Principal*
EMP: 3
SALES (est): 151.1K **Privately Held**
WEB: www.rollingthunderspeedway.net
SIC: 3644 Raceways

Arlington
Arlington County

(G-833)
01 COMMUNIQUE LABORATORY INC
1100 N Glebe Rd Ste 1010 (22201-5786)
PHONE..................703 224-8262
EMP: 3
SALES (est): 130.4K
SALES (corp-wide): 406.8K **Privately Held**
SIC: 7372 Prepackaged Software Services
PA: 01 Communique Laboratory Inc
1450 Meyerside Dr Suite 500
Mississauga ON M3C 1
905 795-2888

(G-834)
21ST CENTURY AMP LLC
5128 25th Pl N (22207-2603)
PHONE..................571 345-8990
David Coia,
EMP: 1
SALES (est): 44.3K **Privately Held**
SIC: 2741 Miscellaneous publishing

(G-835)
300 QUBITS LLC
425 N Jackson St (22201-1719)
PHONE..................202 320-0196
John Crystal,
Seth Demsey,
EMP: 2
SALES (est): 56.5K **Privately Held**
SIC: 7372 7389 Business oriented computer software; business services

(G-836)
5 PLUS 7 BOOKBINDING
5509 5th St S (22204-1204)
PHONE..................571 499-0511
Benjamin Flores, *Owner*
EMP: 1
SALES (est): 108.7K **Privately Held**
WEB: www.5plus7bookbinding.com
SIC: 2789 Binding only: books, pamphlets, magazines, etc.

(G-837)
ACCESS INTELLIGENCE LLC
Also Called: Exchange Mntor Pblctons Forums
1911 Fort Myer Dr Ste 310 (22209-1603)
PHONE..................202 296-2814
Chris Schneidmiller, *Chief*
Kelly Mahoney, *Mktg Coord*
Nancy Berlin, *Program Mgr*

Tom Williams, *Director*
EMP: 8
SALES (corp-wide): 66.7MM **Privately Held**
WEB: www.accessintel.com
SIC: 2741 8742 Newsletter publishing; industry specialist consultants
PA: Access Intelligence Llc
9211 Corporate Blvd Fl 4
Rockville MD 20850
301 354-2000

(G-838)
ACTIVU CORPORATION
1100 Wilson Blvd (22209-2249)
PHONE..................703 527-4440
Ovi Dascalu, *Engineer*
Robert Boderman, *Branch Mgr*
Kevin Anthony, *Software Engr*
EMP: 6
SALES (corp-wide): 22.8MM **Privately Held**
WEB: www.activu.com
SIC: 3823 7373 Digital displays of process variables; computer integrated systems design
PA: Activu Corporation
301 Round Hill Dr
Rockaway NJ 07866
973 366-5550

(G-839)
ADENOSINE THERAPEUTICS LLC
1881 N Nash St Unit 301 (22209-1562)
PHONE..................434 979-1902
Jonathan Sackier, *Ch of Bd*
H Jeffrey Leighton, *Vice Ch Bd*
Joseph Truluck, *Vice Pres*
Robert Capon,
Joel M Linden,
EMP: 25
SQ FT: 4,000
SALES (est): 3.3MM **Privately Held**
WEB: www.adenrx.com
SIC: 2834 Pharmaceutical preparations

(G-840)
ADOPTEES
4631 28th Rd S (22206-1148)
PHONE..................571 483-0656
EMP: 2 EST: 2018
SALES (est): 73.2K **Privately Held**
SIC: 2759 Screen printing

(G-841)
ADVANCED RESOURCES INTL INC (PA)
4501 Fairfax Dr Ste 910 (22203-1659)
PHONE..................703 528-8421
Vello A Kuuskraa, *President*
Johnathan R Kelafant, *Senior VP*
Jonathan Kelafant, *Vice Pres*
George J Koperna, *Vice Pres*
Clark Talkington, *Vice Pres*
EMP: 25
SQ FT: 10,000 **Privately Held**
WEB: www.adv-res.com
SIC: 1382 Oil & gas exploration services

(G-842)
AEROJET
1300 Wilson Blvd Ste 1000 (22209-2321)
PHONE..................703 247-2907
Brown Lee, *Principal*
Glenn Mahone, *Vice Pres*
Kristine Tortoso, *Purch Agent*
Tim Cole, *Engineer*
Stacy Gagne, *Design Engr*
EMP: 3
SALES (est): 431.6K **Privately Held**
WEB: www.rocket.com
SIC: 3812 3721 Aircraft/aerospace flight instruments & guidance systems; aircraft

(G-843)
AEROJET ROCKETDYNE INC
1300 Wilson Blvd Ste 1000 (22209-2321)
PHONE..................703 650-0270
Michele Luis, *Business Mgr*
John Schumacher, *Vice Pres*
Trent Ward, *Chief Engr*
Aaron Poehls, *Engineer*
Adam Riffe, *Engineer*
EMP: 8

SALES (corp-wide): 1.9B **Publicly Held**
WEB: www.rocket.com
SIC: 3764 Propulsion units for guided missiles & space vehicles
HQ: Aerojet Rocketdyne, Inc.
2001 Aerojet Rd
Rancho Cordova CA 95742
916 355-4000

(G-844)
AGC INFORMATION INC
2300 Olston Blvd Ste 400 (22201)
PHONE..................703 548-3118
Steve Sandherr, *President*
G Ralph Willet, *CFO*
Jordan Howard, *Associate Dir*
EMP: 50
SQ FT: 5,000
SALES (est): 4MM
SALES (corp-wide): 19.9MM **Privately Held**
WEB: www.agc.org
SIC: 2721 Magazines: publishing only, not printed on site
PA: The Associated General Contractors Of America
2300 Wilson Blvd Ste 300
Arlington VA 22201
703 837-5415

(G-845)
AGUSTAWESTLAND NORTH AMER INC (DH)
Also Called: Agustawestland NA
2345 Crystal Dr Ste 906 (22202-4817)
PHONE..................703 373-8000
Scott Rettig, *CEO*
Melvern R Rushing, *Exec VP*
Terry Higginbotham, *Vice Pres*
Dan G Hill, *Vice Pres*
Thomas J Lyons, *Vice Pres*
EMP: 10
SQ FT: 20,000
SALES (est): 1.2MM
SALES (corp-wide): 9.9B **Privately Held**
SIC: 3721 Aircraft
HQ: Agustawestland Holdings Limited
Lysander Road
Yeovil BA20
193 547-5222

(G-846)
AHMED INDUSTRIES INC
3611 18th St S (22204-5130)
PHONE..................703 828-7180
Ahmed Rifayat, *Manager*
▼ **EMP:** 1
SALES (est): 104.7K **Privately Held**
SIC: 3999 Barber & beauty shop equipment

(G-847)
AIDA HEALTH INC
1901 N Moore St Ste 1004 (22209-1706)
P.O. Box 25127 (22202-9027)
PHONE..................202 739-1345
Michael Mok, *Principal*
EMP: 1
SALES (est): 91.9K **Privately Held**
WEB: www.aidahealth.com
SIC: 7372 Prepackaged software

(G-848)
ALAN THORNHILL
2600 S Veitch St Apt 401 (22206-3012)
PHONE..................703 892-5642
EMP: 2
SALES (est): 87.2K **Privately Held**
SIC: 3711 Mfg Motor Vehicle/Car Bodies

(G-849)
ALLIANT TCHSYSTEMS OPRTONS LLC
1300 Wilson Blvd Ste 400 (22209-2330)
PHONE..................703 412-3223
EMP: 1
SALES (est): 316.2K **Publicly Held**
SIC: 3764 Mfg Space Propulsion Units/Parts
HQ: Northrop Grumman Innovation Systems, Inc.
45101 Warp Dr
Dulles VA 20166
703 406-5000

(G-850)
ALTER MAGAZINE LLC
2659 S Walter Reed Dr (22206-1242)
PHONE..................571 970-3537
Kimberly Houston, *Principal*
EMP: 3 EST: 2014
SALES (est): 137.9K **Privately Held**
SIC: 2711 Newspapers

(G-851)
AMENTUM SERVICES INC
2341 Richmond Hwy (22202-3809)
PHONE..................703 418-3020
John Mc Cullough, *Manager*
Mark A Olsberg, *Network Enginr*
EMP: 225
SALES (corp-wide): 489.5MM **Privately Held**
WEB: www.aecom.com
SIC: 3679 8711 Electronic circuits; engineering services
HQ: Amentum Services, Inc.
20501 Senca Mdw Pkwy
Germantown MD 20876

(G-852)
AMERICAN CITY BUS JOURNALS INC
Also Called: Washington Business Journal
1100 Wilson Blvd Ste 800 (22209-2297)
PHONE..................703 258-0800
Alex Orfinger, *Branch Mgr*
Caroline Rountree, *Executive*
EMP: 15
SALES (corp-wide): 5B **Privately Held**
WEB: www.acbj.com
SIC: 2721 2711 Magazines: publishing only, not printed on site; newspapers
HQ: American City Business Journals, Inc.
120 W Morehead St Ste 400
Charlotte NC 28202
704 973-1000

(G-853)
AMERICAN MEDIA INSTITUTE
2420 S Queen St (22202-1554)
PHONE..................703 872-7840
Richard Miniter, *CEO*
Nancy Bonomo, *Vice Pres*
EMP: 9
SALES (est): 577.3K **Privately Held**
WEB: www.americanmediainstitute.com
SIC: 2741

(G-854)
AMITY SOFTWARE INC
1111 Army Navy Dr (22202-2053)
PHONE..................571 312-0880
Ankit Saxena, *Principal*
EMP: 2
SALES (est): 83.1K **Privately Held**
SIC: 7372 Prepackaged software

(G-855)
ARCTAN INC
2200 Wilson Blvd 102-150 (22201-3397)
PHONE..................202 379-4723
Michael Morefield, *President*
EMP: 2
SALES (est): 140K **Privately Held**
WEB: www.arctan-group.com
SIC: 7372 Application computer software

(G-856)
ARKTIS DETECTION SYSTEMS INC
2011 Crystal Dr Ste 400 (22202-3709)
PHONE..................610 724-9748
Mario Voegeli, *CEO*
Frederick Muntz, *Vice Pres*
EMP: 3
SALES (est): 154.9K **Privately Held**
WEB: www.arktis-detectors.com
SIC: 3829 Gas detectors

(G-857)
ARLINGTON ADRNDACK WDWORKS LLC
5010 23rd St S (22206-1009)
PHONE..................703 964-7700
Jacob Fontaine Agnew, *Principal*
EMP: 1
SALES (est): 59.2K **Privately Held**
SIC: 2431 Millwork

GEOGRAPHIC

(G-858)
ARLINGTON BOCCATO LLC
1011 Arlington Blvd # 30 (22209-3925)
PHONE..................................703 516-4075
EMP: 2
SALES (est): 67.9K Privately Held
WEB: www.arlnow.com
SIC: 2711 Newspapers, publishing & printing

(G-859)
ARLINGTON COMMUNITY NEWS LAB
149 N Abingdon St (22203-2610)
PHONE..................................703 243-7501
EMP: 4 EST: 2012
SALES (est): 188.3K Privately Held
SIC: 2711 Newspapers-Publishing/Printing

(G-860)
ARROWINE INC (PA)
4508 Lee Hwy (22207-3304)
PHONE..................................703 525-0990
Doug Rosen, CEO
Jim Cutts, Consultant
EMP: 15
SQ FT: 3,000
SALES (est): 1.1MM Privately Held
WEB: www.arrowine.com
SIC: 2084 5451 Wines; cheese

(G-861)
ARTGIFTSETCCOM
3519 13th St N (22201-4907)
PHONE..................................703 772-3587
Jennifer Wheatley-Wolf, Principal
EMP: 2
SALES (est): 120K Privately Held
WEB: www.artgiftsetc.com
SIC: 3552 Embroidery machines

(G-862)
ASSOCIATED GEN CONTRS OF AMER (PA)
Also Called: A G C
2300 Wilson Blvd Ste 300 (22201-5426)
PHONE..................................703 837-5415
Steven Sandherr, CEO
Mark Knight, President
Dave Lukens, COO
Jimmy Christianson, Counsel
Art Daniel, Senior VP
EMP: 70
SQ FT: 29,000
SALES: 19.9MM Privately Held
WEB: www.agc.org
SIC: 2721 8611 Magazines: publishing & printing; trade associations

(G-863)
ASSOCIATION FOR CMPT MCHY INC
2315 N Burlington St (22207-2520)
PHONE..................................703 528-0726
Kmute Berstis, Branch Mgr
EMP: 1
SALES (corp-wide): 70.1MM Privately Held
WEB: www.acm.org
SIC: 2721 8621 Periodicals: publishing only; scientific membership association
PA: Association For Computing Machinery, Inc.
1601 Broadway Fl 10
New York NY 10019
212 869-7440

(G-864)
AUSLNX LLC
2201 Wilson Blvd Apt 904 (22201-3390)
PHONE..................................571 265-3288
Philip Power, Administration
EMP: 2 EST: 2015
SALES (est): 78.1K Privately Held
WEB: www.auslnx.com
SIC: 3111 Leather tanning & finishing

(G-865)
AUSOME ONES LLC
5929 5th St N (22203-1052)
PHONE..................................703 637-7105
EMP: 2
SALES (est): 56.5K Privately Held
SIC: 7372 Home entertainment computer software

(G-866)
AVAYA FEDERAL SOLUTIONS INC
4250 Fairfax Dr Fl 10 (22203-1665)
PHONE..................................908 953-6000
Mike Singer, President
EMP: 15 Publicly Held
WEB: www.avaya.com
SIC: 3661 Telephone & telegraph apparatus
HQ: Avaya Federal Solutions, Inc.
12730 Fair Lakes Cir
Fairfax VA 22033

(G-867)
AVENGER COMPUTER SOLUTIONS
4729 Washington Blvd (22205-2540)
PHONE..................................240 305-7835
Donald Jones, Principal
EMP: 2 EST: 2016
SALES (est): 85.9K Privately Held
SIC: 3571 Electronic computers

(G-868)
AXELL WIRELESS INC
2121 Crystal Dr Ste 625 (22202-3797)
PHONE..................................703 414-5300
Bob Murphy, CEO
EMP: 1
SALES (est): 49.1K
SALES (corp-wide): 2MM Privately Held
WEB: www.cobham.com
SIC: 3812 Antennas, radar or communications
HQ: Cobham Holdings Inc.
10 Cobham Dr
Orchard Park NY 14127
716 662-0006

(G-869)
AXIOS MEDIA INC
3100 Clarendon Blvd # 1300 (22201-5332)
PHONE..................................703 291-3600
Jim Vandehei, CEO
Roy Schwartz, President
Justin Green, Editor
Felix Salmon, Chief
Ali Rubin, Vice Pres
EMP: 28 EST: 2016
SQ FT: 1,000
SALES (est): 3MM Privately Held
WEB: www.axios.com
SIC: 2741

(G-870)
AXON ENTERPRISE INC
1100 Wilson Blvd Ste 1210 (22209-2297)
PHONE..................................602 459-1278
Patrick W Smith, Branch Mgr
EMP: 3 Publicly Held
WEB: www.axon.com
SIC: 3489 Ordnance & accessories
PA: Axon Enterprise, Inc.
17800 N 85th St
Scottsdale AZ 85255

(G-871)
B FRANKLIN PRINTER
501 S Lexington St (22204-1228)
PHONE..................................703 845-1583
Barry Stevens, Owner
EMP: 2
SALES (est): 83.9K Privately Held
WEB: www.benfranklinprinter.com
SIC: 2752 Commercial printing, lithographic

(G-872)
BAE SYSTEMS INFO & ELEC SYS
4301 Fairfax Dr Ste 800 (22203-1635)
PHONE..................................202 223-8808
Anne Taylor, Director
Megan Mitchell, Director
EMP: 1
SALES (corp-wide): 23.6B Privately Held
WEB: www.baesystems.com
SIC: 3812 Search & navigation equipment
HQ: Bae Systems Information And Electronic Systems Integration Inc.
65 Spit Brook Rd
Nashua NH 03060
603 885-4321

(G-873)
BARCROFT ASSOCIATES LTD PARTNR
1120 S George Mason Dr (22204-3802)
PHONE..................................786 507-4649
EMP: 1 EST: 1993
SALES (est): 46.5K Privately Held
WEB: www.firstchoicehouston.com
SIC: 2269 Finishing plants

(G-874)
BARCROFT CENTER
4200 S Four Mile Run Dr (22206-1189)
PHONE..................................703 228-0701
EMP: 4 EST: 2002
SALES (est): 166.8K Privately Held
WEB: www.arlnow.com
SIC: 2711 Newspapers, publishing & printing

(G-875)
BARRY SOCK COMPANY
201 N Barton St (22201-1413)
PHONE..................................703 525-1120
EMP: 2 EST: 2017
SALES (est): 73.4K Privately Held
SIC: 2252 Socks

(G-876)
BATTLESPACE GLOBAL LLC (PA)
1215 S Clark St Ste 301 (22202-4391)
PHONE..................................703 413-0556
Jerry Norris, Mng Member
EMP: 5
SQ FT: 4,104
SALES (est): 562.9K Privately Held
WEB: www.battlespace.com
SIC: 3721 Aircraft

(G-877)
BECKE PUBLISHING INCORPORATED
5101 1st St N (22203-1207)
PHONE..................................703 225-8742
EMP: 2
SALES (est): 69.2K Privately Held
SIC: 2711 Newspapers

(G-878)
BELL TEXTRON INC
2231 Crystal Dr Ste 1010 (22202-3899)
PHONE..................................817 280-2346
EMP: 2
SALES (corp-wide): 13.6B Publicly Held
WEB: www.bellflight.com
SIC: 3728 5088 3721 Aircraft parts & equipment; transportation equipment & supplies; helicopters; motorized aircraft
HQ: Bell Textron Inc.
3255 Bell Flight Blvd
Fort Worth TX 76118
817 280-2011

(G-879)
BEST CHECKS INC
1300 Crystal Dr (22202-3234)
PHONE..................................703 416-4856
EMP: 1
SALES (est): 56.5K Privately Held
WEB: www.bestchecks.com
SIC: 2782 Checkbooks

(G-880)
BEST PRINTING & DESIGN LLC
3842 Columbia Pike # 102 (22204-4130)
PHONE..................................703 593-9874
Bolivar C Tomala,
EMP: 1
SALES (est): 37K Privately Held
WEB: www.bestprintinganddesign.com
SIC: 3993 7336 7313 7389 Signs & advertising specialties; graphic arts & related design; printed media advertising representatives;

(G-881)
BEST VALUE PETROLEUM INC
5630 Lee Hwy (22207-1445)
PHONE..................................703 303-3780
Arpit Sethi, Principal
EMP: 2
SALES (est): 116.6K Privately Held
SIC: 1381 Drilling oil & gas wells

(G-882)
BETHUNE INDUSTRIES LLC
2139 N Pierce Ct (22209-1118)
PHONE..................................407 579-1308
Ross Bethune, Principal
EMP: 2
SALES (est): 108.1K Privately Held
SIC: 3999 Manufacturing industries

(G-883)
BIO-PROSTHETIC ORTHOTIC LAB
5275 Lee Hwy Ste G3 (22207-1619)
PHONE..................................703 527-3123
Gregory A Banks, President
Sharon Banks, Vice Pres
EMP: 3
SQ FT: 700
SALES (est): 153.1K Privately Held
SIC: 3842 Braces, orthopedic

(G-884)
BLACKSKY AEROSPACE LLC
623 19th St S (22202-2715)
PHONE..................................202 500-3743
Raymond Hoheisel, CEO
EMP: 2
SALES (est): 86K Privately Held
SIC: 3721 Aircraft

(G-885)
BLESSED HANDS CNSTR & MAINT
1918 S Glebe Rd (22204-5307)
PHONE..................................703 762-6595
William Westray, Owner
EMP: 5
SALES (est): 200K Privately Held
SIC: 3442 Metal doors, sash & trim

(G-886)
BLUVECTOR INC
4501 Fairfax Dr Ste 750 (22203-1659)
PHONE..................................571 565-2100
Eric Malawer, CEO
David Banks, Principal
Aaron Levine, CFO
EMP: 5
SALES (est): 20MM Publicly Held
WEB: www.bluvector.io
SIC: 7372 Prepackaged software
PA: Comcast Corporation
1701 Jfk Blvd
Philadelphia PA 19103
215 286-1700

(G-887)
BOARDEFFECT LLC
1515 N Courthouse Rd # 210 (22201-2963)
PHONE..................................866 672-2666
Todd Gibby, CEO
Brian Alexander, CFO
EMP: 30
SALES (est): 8.2MM Privately Held
WEB: www.boardeffect.com
SIC: 7372 Application computer software

(G-888)
BOEING COMPANY
929 Long Bridge Dr (22202-4208)
PHONE..................................703 465-3500
Steve Lott, President
Birnell Bruce, Vice Pres
Jack Catton, Vice Pres
Gordon Johndroe, Vice Pres
Scott Christiansen, Project Mgr
EMP: 209
SALES (corp-wide): 76.5B Publicly Held
WEB: www.boeing.com
SIC: 3728 8741 Aircraft parts & equipment; management services
PA: The Boeing Company
100 N Riverside Plz
Chicago IL 60606
312 544-2000

(G-889)
BOEING COMPANY
1215 S Clark St Ste 100 (22202-4388)
PHONE..................................703 413-3407
William Todd, Manager
Leo Christodoulou, Director
EMP: 996

SALES (corp-wide): 76.5B **Publicly Held**
WEB: www.boeing.com
SIC: 3721 Airplanes, fixed or rotary wing
PA: The Boeing Company
100 N Riverside Plz
Chicago IL 60606
312 544-2000

(G-890)
BROADSTONE SECURITY LLC
Also Called: Nova Armory
2300 N Pershing Dr Ste 2b (22201-1484)
PHONE....................................703 566-2814
Dennis Pratte, *Co-Owner*
Lauren Pratte, *Co-Owner*
Shawn Poulin,
EMP: 8 EST: 2016
SALES (est): 486.7K **Privately Held**
WEB: www.novaarmory.com
SIC: 3484 3482 Guns (firearms) or gun
parts, 30 mm. & below; small arms am-
munition

(G-891)
BUBBA ENTERPRISES INC
Also Called: Signs By Tomorrow
3300 Fairfax Dr Ste 302 (22201-4400)
P.O. Box 4226, West McLean (22103-
4226)
PHONE....................................703 524-0019
Michael Behn, *President*
Sarah Enten, *Vice Pres*
EMP: 2
SALES (est): 142.4K **Privately Held**
WEB: www.signsbytomorrow.com
SIC: 3993 Signs & advertising specialties

(G-892)
BUOYA LLC
Also Called: Artisan Group, The
1825 N Bryan St (22201-4017)
PHONE....................................703 248-9100
Sam Ayoub,
EMP: 1
SQ FT: 1,340
SALES (est): 900K **Privately Held**
WEB: www.artisangroupservices.com
SIC: 3812 Acceleration indicators & sys-
tems components, aerospace

(G-893)
**BUREAU OF NATIONAL AFFAIRS
INC (HQ)**
Also Called: Bloomberg Industry Group
1801 S Bell St Ste Cn110 (22202-4501)
PHONE....................................703 341-3000
Gregory C McCaffery, *President*
Daniel Doctoroff, *President*
Mike Mackay, *President*
Scott Mozarsky, *President*
Shaun Terril, *Managing Prtnr*
EMP: 249 EST: 1929
SQ FT: 277,000
SALES (est): 510.1MM
SALES (corp-wide): 1.8B **Privately Held**
WEB: www.bloombergindustry.com
SIC: 2711 2721 Newspapers; periodicals:
publishing only
PA: Bloomberg L.P.
731 Lexington Ave Fl Ll2
New York NY 10022
212 318-2000

(G-894)
BURWELL GROUP LLC
1404 N Sycamore St (22205-1883)
PHONE....................................703 732-6341
Rudolph Burwell,
EMP: 1
SALES (est): 91.7K **Privately Held**
WEB: www.burwellgroupllc.com
SIC: 2741 8743 Miscellaneous publishing;
public relations & publicity

(G-895)
BZK BALLSTON LLC
933 N Quincy St (22203-1907)
PHONE....................................703 248-0990
Brad Brown,
EMP: 10
SALES (est): 514.9K **Privately Held**
SIC: 2099 Food preparations

(G-896)
C & P INC
3332 Lee Hwy (22207-3712)
PHONE....................................703 522-2229
Chan Gin, *Principal*
EMP: 4 EST: 2015
SALES (est): 286.4K **Privately Held**
SIC: 2851 Paints & allied products

(G-897)
C-3 COMM SYSTEMS LLC
3100 Clarendon Blvd # 200 (22201-5330)
PHONE....................................703 829-0588
Zhongren Cao, *President*
EMP: 3
SALES (est): 207.8K **Privately Held**
SIC: 3663 8731 4899 Radio receiver net-
works; receivers, radio communications;
antennas, transmitting & communications;
electronic research; communication signal
enhancement network system

(G-898)
CABINET ARTS LLC
1510 Clarendon Blvd (22209-2727)
PHONE....................................703 870-1456
Serhat Solmaz,
EMP: 1
SALES (est): 124.1K **Privately Held**
SIC: 2434 Wood kitchen cabinets

(G-899)
CANVAS LLC
6039 27th St N (22207-1264)
PHONE....................................703 237-6491
Mong Penella, *Principal*
EMP: 4 EST: 2010
SALES (est): 383.7K **Privately Held**
WEB: www.instructure.com
SIC: 2211 Canvas

(G-900)
CAPITOL CITY PUBLISHERS LLC
3485 S Wakefield St (22206-1719)
PHONE....................................703 671-5920
Joel M Drucker,
EMP: 2
SQ FT: 500
SALES (est): 116.9K **Privately Held**
SIC: 2731 Book publishing

(G-901)
**CAPITOL EXCELLENCE PUBG
LLC**
1050 N Taylor St Apt 607 (22201-4794)
PHONE....................................571 277-9657
Ariana Roscoe, *Principal*
EMP: 1
SALES (est): 37.5K **Privately Held**
SIC: 2741 Miscellaneous publishing

(G-902)
CARANUS LLC
1027 N Livingston St (22205-1424)
PHONE....................................703 241-1683
Steve E Stylianos, *Administration*
EMP: 2
SALES (est): 77.9K **Privately Held**
SIC: 2741 Miscellaneous publishing

(G-903)
**CATHOLIC DIOCESE OF
ARLINGTON**
Also Called: Arlington Cthlic Hrald Newsppr
200 N Glebe Rd Ste 614 (22203-3763)
PHONE....................................703 841-2590
Michael Flach, *General Mgr*
Mike Flack, *Branch Mgr*
David Garcia, *Graphic Designe*
EMP: 13
SALES (corp-wide): 147MM **Privately
Held**
WEB: www.arlingtondiocese.org
SIC: 2711 Newspapers
PA: Catholic Diocese Of Arlington
200 N Glebe Rd Ste 901
Arlington VA 22203
703 841-2500

(G-904)
CERBERUS LLC
3145 17th St N (22201-5240)
PHONE....................................703 372-9750
Kristin Nelson, *Opers Staff*
Grant A Averett,

EMP: 1
SALES (est): 25K **Privately Held**
WEB: www.cerberusftp.com
SIC: 7372 Business oriented computer
software

(G-905)
CHARLES SOUTHWELL
4401 1st Rd S (22204-1318)
PHONE....................................703 892-5469
Charles Southwell, *Owner*
EMP: 1
SALES (est): 48.1K **Privately Held**
SIC: 2711 Newspapers

(G-906)
CLARITAS CREATIVE LLC
1010 20th St S (22202-2108)
PHONE....................................240 274-5029
Kimberly Hudson,
EMP: 2
SALES (est): 143.2K **Privately Held**
WEB: www.claritascreative.com
SIC: 3669 Visual communication systems

(G-907)
CLARITY CANDLES LLC
1001 N Fillmore St (22201-2169)
P.O. Box 10554, Burke (22009-0554)
PHONE....................................703 278-3760
EMP: 2
SALES (est): 104.8K **Privately Held**
SIC: 3999 Candles

(G-908)
CLOSET AND BEYOND
2300 24th Rd S Apt 927 (22206-2627)
PHONE....................................703 962-7894
Bowatch Cetiner, *Principal*
EMP: 4
SALES (est): 409.9K **Privately Held**
WEB: www.closetandbeyond.com
SIC: 2434 Wood kitchen cabinets

(G-909)
COBALT CO
2550 S Clark St Ste 850 (22202-3980)
PHONE....................................888 426-2258
EMP: 2
SALES (est): 102.1K **Privately Held**
SIC: 7372 Business oriented computer
software

(G-910)
COBALT COMPANY
2511 Richmond Hwy Ste 850 (22202-3977)
PHONE....................................888 426-2258
Russell Inman, *CEO*
Chris Capistran, *President*
Mary Davis, *Consultant*
Liudmyla Tretter, *Consultant*
Frederik Zilmer, *Consultant*
EMP: 4
SALES (est): 766.5K **Privately Held**
WEB: www.cobalt.net
SIC: 7372 Prepackaged software

(G-911)
**COBHAM AES HOLDINGS INC
(DH)**
2121 Crystal Dr Ste 625 (22202-3797)
PHONE....................................703 414-5300
Jill Kale, *CEO*
Mark Santamaria, *CFO*
Charles P Stuff, *Admin Sec*
EMP: 19
SALES (est): 393.8MM
SALES (corp-wide): 2MM **Privately Held**
WEB: www.cobham.com
SIC: 3679 3812 Microwave components;
acceleration indicators & systems compo-
nents, aerospace
HQ: Cobham Holdings Inc.
10 Cobham Dr
Orchard Park NY 14127
716 662-0006

(G-912)
**COBHAM DEFENSE PRODUCTS
INC**
2121 Crystal Dr Ste 625 (22202-3797)
PHONE....................................703 414-5300
David V Gaggin, *CEO*
▲ EMP: 5

SALES (est): 415.4K
SALES (corp-wide): 2MM **Privately Held**
WEB: www.cobham.com
SIC: 3812 Search & navigation equipment
HQ: Cobham Holdings Inc.
10 Cobham Dr
Orchard Park NY 14127
716 662-0006

(G-913)
**COBHAM MANAGEMENT
SERVICES INC**
Also Called: Cobham Corp N Amer Arlington
2121 Crystal Dr Ste 625 (22202-3797)
PHONE....................................703 414-5300
Charlie Stuff, *President*
Roman Burtyk, *President*
Clint Licqurish, *President*
Lane Dicken, *Engineer*
Robin Smith, *Engineer*
EMP: 16
SALES (est): 2.6MM **Privately Held**
WEB: www.cobham.com
SIC: 3812 Search & navigation equipment

(G-914)
**COJAX OIL AND GAS
CORPORATION**
3033 Wilson Blvd E-605 (22201-3866)
PHONE....................................703 216-8606
EMP: 2
SALES (est): 81.9K **Privately Held**
SIC: 1311 Crude petroleum & natural gas

(G-915)
COLUMBIA BOOKS INC (PA)
Also Called: Thompson Information Services
1560 Wilson Blvd Ste 825 (22209-2477)
PHONE....................................800 677-3789
Joel Poznansky, *Ch of Bd*
Brittany E Carter, *Vice Pres*
EMP: 14
SQ FT: 2,100
SALES (est): 3.7MM **Privately Held**
WEB: www.columbiabooks.com
SIC: 2741 Directories: publishing only, not
printed on site

(G-916)
COMMONLOOK
1600 Wilson Blvd (22209-2511)
PHONE....................................202 902-0986
EMP: 2
SALES (est): 56.5K **Privately Held**
WEB: www.commonlook.com
SIC: 7372 Application computer software

(G-917)
**COMPASS PUBLICATIONS INC
(PA)**
4600 Fairfax Dr Ste 304 (22203-1553)
PHONE....................................703 524-3136
C Amos Bussman, *President*
C Amos Bussmann, *President*
Jon Regh, *Area Mgr*
Russell Conward, *Prdtn Mgr*
Jason Baretto, *Sales Staff*
EMP: 8 EST: 1963
SALES (est): 846.5K **Privately Held**
WEB: www.sea-technology.com
SIC: 2721 2741 Magazines: publishing
only, not printed on site; telephone &
other directory publishing; newsletter pub-
lishing

(G-918)
COMPUTER CORP OF AMERICA
Also Called: Computer Corp America Federal
4025 38th Pl N (22207-4661)
PHONE....................................703 241-7830
Richard Ryan, *President*
EMP: 2
SALES (est): 117.9K **Privately Held**
SIC: 7372 Prepackaged software

(G-919)
COWBOY WESTERN WEAR
1708 14th St S (22204-4723)
PHONE....................................202 298-8299
Raul Silva, *Principal*
EMP: 2
SALES (est): 120K **Privately Held**
SIC: 2326 Men's & boys' work clothing

(G-920)
CRONIN DEFENSE STRATEGIES LLC
4659 28th Rd S (22206-4128)
PHONE................................810 625-7060
EMP: 3
SALES (est): 171.5K **Privately Held**
SIC: 3812 Defense systems & equipment

(G-921)
CROSS MATCH TECHNOLOGIES INC
1550 Crystal Dr Ste 505 (22202-4145)
PHONE................................703 841-6280
Bob Bucknam, *Manager*
Christopher Gillyard, *Director*
EMP: 8
SALES (corp-wide): 9.7B **Privately Held**
WEB: www.hidglobal.com
SIC: 3999 Fingerprint equipment
HQ: Cross Match Technologies, Inc.
3950 Rca Blvd Ste 5001
Palm Beach Gardens FL 33410

(G-922)
CSM INDUSTRIES INC
850 N Randolph St Ste 170 (22203-1978)
PHONE................................410 818-3262
EMP: 2
SALES (est): 83.2K **Privately Held**
SIC: 3999 Manufacturing industries

(G-923)
CUSTOM BAKED TEES
5918 3rd St S (22204-1004)
PHONE................................703 888-8539
Jimmy Nguyen, *Principal*
EMP: 2
SALES (est): 105.3K **Privately Held**
SIC: 2759 Screen printing

(G-924)
CYVIZ LLC
900 N Glebe Rd Ste 2 (22203-1822)
PHONE................................571 858-3371
Michael Wilkis, *Engineer*
Don Garwood, *Director*
Jeff Eifenhardt,
Joar Vaage,
EMP: 2
SALES (est): 729.2K
SALES (corp-wide): 25MM **Privately Held**
WEB: www.cyviz.com
SIC: 3663 Television monitors
PA: Cyviz As
Vestre Svanholmen 6
Sandnes 4313
516 355-80

(G-925)
D-TA SYSTEMS CORPORATION
2611 Richmond Hwy Ste 600 (22202-4046)
PHONE................................571 775-8924
Amber Beason, *Administration*
EMP: 2
SALES (est): 140.8K **Privately Held**
WEB: www.d-tacorp.com
SIC: 3571 Electronic computers

(G-926)
DANZO LLC
Also Called: Fastsigns
5852 Washington Blvd # 4 (22205-2925)
PHONE................................703 532-8602
Hussain F Bharmal,
Amera Bharmal,
EMP: 6
SQ FT: 3,100
SALES (est): 648.5K **Privately Held**
WEB: www.fastsigns.com
SIC: 3993 Signs & advertising specialties

(G-927)
DARLENE GROUP INC
2775 N Quincy St (22207-5055)
PHONE................................401 728-3300
Maria Baccari, *President*
Vincent Baccari, *Vice Pres*
◆ EMP: 60
SQ FT: 60,000
SALES (est): 5.6MM **Privately Held**
WEB: www.darlenegroup.com
SIC: 3961 Costume jewelry

(G-928)
DARWINS LLC
3416 3rd St N (22201-1714)
PHONE................................610 256-3716
Todd Fernley, *CEO*
EMP: 1 EST: 2014
SALES (est): 54K **Privately Held**
WEB: www.mydarwins.com
SIC: 3851 Frames, lenses & parts, eye-
glass & spectacle

(G-929)
DATA-CLEAR LLC
513 N Frederick St (22203-1450)
PHONE................................703 499-3816
Carolyn Carlson,
EMP: 3 **Privately Held**
WEB: www.data-clear.com
SIC: 2741 7375 8742 ; information re-
trieval services; management consulting
services; marketing consulting services

(G-930)
DC CUSTOM PRINT
4213 S Four Mile Run Dr (22204-3946)
PHONE................................301 541-8172
EMP: 2
SALES (est): 83.9K **Privately Held**
WEB: www.dccustomprint.com
SIC: 2752 Commercial printing, litho-
graphic

(G-931)
DD PET PRODUCTS INC
2906 N Kensington St (22207-1563)
P.O. Box 7305 (22207-0305)
PHONE................................703 532-3983
Deborah Droke, *President*
J Michael Droke, *President*
EMP: 4
SALES (est): 276.3K **Privately Held**
WEB: www.familystore.net
SIC: 2048 Bird food, prepared

(G-932)
DECISONQ INFRMTION OPRTONS INC
1776 Wilson Blvd Fl 5 (22209-2517)
PHONE................................703 938-7153
Lester Young, *CEO*
Mike Mears, *President*
EMP: 2
SALES (est): 115.8K **Privately Held**
SIC: 7372 Prepackaged software

(G-933)
DEFENSE DAILY
1911 Fort Myer Dr Ste 310 (22209-1603)
PHONE................................703 522-2012
EMP: 2 EST: 2019
SALES (est): 79.1K **Privately Held**
SIC: 2721 Magazines: publishing only, not
printed on site

(G-934)
DEFENSE INFORMATION SYS
4601 Fairfax Dr Ste 1200 (22203-1559)
PHONE................................855 401-8554
Glen Wiggins, *Systs Engr*
EMP: 1
SALES (est): 80.9K **Privately Held**
WEB: www.defense.gov
SIC: 3812 Defense systems & equipment

(G-935)
DELPHI INC
2530 N Randolph St (22207-5218)
PHONE................................703 908-0258
Gary Audin, *Principal*
EMP: 2
SALES (est): 150.2K **Privately Held**
SIC: 3714 Motor vehicle parts & acces-
sories

(G-936)
DEMONS RUN BREWING LLC
4020 41st St N (22207-4647)
PHONE................................703 945-8100
Peyton Loftis, *Principal*
EMP: 1
SALES (est): 53.6K **Privately Held**
SIC: 2082 7389 Near beer;

(G-937)
DEMSIGN
4401 Lee Hwy Apt 77 (22207-3317)
PHONE................................202 787-1518
EMP: 1
SALES (est): 60K **Privately Held**
SIC: 3993 Signs & advertising specialties

(G-938)
DESIGNPURE NANOCRYST LLC
5990 Rchmond Hwy Apt 1104 (22203)
PHONE................................571 458-0951
Radha Narayanan, *CEO*
EMP: 1
SALES (est): 47.2K **Privately Held**
SIC: 2819 Industrial inorganic chemicals

(G-939)
DEWEY PUBLICATIONS INC
1840 Wilson Blvd Ste 203 (22201-3000)
PHONE................................703 524-1355
Peter Broida, *President*
Karen Troutman, *Business Mgr*
EMP: 4
SQ FT: 1,900
SALES (est): 315K **Privately Held**
WEB: www.deweypub.com
SIC: 2741 Miscellaneous publishing

(G-940)
DIVVY CLOUD CORPORATION
Also Called: Divvycloud
2111 Wilson Blvd Ste 450 (22201-3054)
PHONE................................571 290-5077
Brian Johnson, *CEO*
Peter Scott, *COO*
David Geevaratne, *Vice Pres*
Brandie Kalinowski, *Vice Pres*
Jeremy Snyder, *Vice Pres*
EMP: 12 EST: 2016
SALES (est): 664.2K **Privately Held**
WEB: www.divvycloud.com
SIC: 7372 7371 Application computer soft-
ware; software programming applications

(G-941)
DRAKE HEARING AID CENTERS (PA)
403 S Cleve Rd (22204)
PHONE................................703 521-1404
Timothy L Drake, *President*
EMP: 2
SQ FT: 1,500
SALES (est): 236.2K **Privately Held**
SIC: 3842 Hearing aids

(G-942)
DRS HOMELAND SEC SOLUTIONS INC
2345 Crystal Dr Ste 915 (22202-4801)
PHONE................................703 682-1801
EMP: 4
SALES (est): 1.3MM
SALES (corp-wide): 9.9B **Privately Held**
WEB: www.leonardodrs.com
SIC: 3812 Search & navigation equipment
HQ: Leonardo Drs, Inc.
2345 Crystal Dr Ste 1000
Arlington VA 22202
703 416-8000

(G-943)
DRS LEONARDO INC
1235 S Clark St Ste 700 (22202-4364)
PHONE................................703 416-7600
Steve Cortese, *Exec VP*
Michael Dippold, *Vice Pres*
Fred Klein, *Engineer*
Mike Shanahan, *Branch Mgr*
EMP: 13
SALES (corp-wide): 9.9B **Privately Held**
WEB: www.leonardodrs.com
SIC: 3812 Search & navigation equipment
HQ: Leonardo Drs, Inc.
2345 Crystal Dr Ste 1000
Arlington VA 22202
703 416-8000

(G-944)
DRS LEONARDO INC (HQ)
2345 Crystal Dr Ste 1000 (22202-4801)
PHONE................................703 416-8000
William J Lynn III, *CEO*
Sally A Wallace, *President*
Terrence J Murphy, *COO*

Steve Cortese, *Exec VP*
Mark A Dorfman, *Exec VP*
▲ EMP: 120
SQ FT: 50,800
SALES (est): 2B
SALES (corp-wide): 9.9B **Privately Held**
WEB: www.leonardodrs.com
SIC: 3812 3699 3572 3669 Navigational
systems & instruments; electronic training
devices; computer storage devices; inter-
communication systems, electric; harness
assemblies for electronic use: wire or
cable; management services
PA: Leonardo Spa
Piazza Monte Grappa 4
Roma RM 00195
033 122-9111

(G-945)
DRS LEONARDO INC
2345 Crystal Dr Ste 1000 (22202-4801)
PHONE................................703 416-8000
Jerry Hathaway, *President*
Mark Dorfman, *Exec VP*
Michael Coulter, *Vice Pres*
Daniel Crosby, *Vice Pres*
Bill Guyan, *Vice Pres*
EMP: 60
SALES (corp-wide): 9.9B **Privately Held**
WEB: www.leonardodrs.com
SIC: 3812 Search & navigation equipment
HQ: Leonardo Drs, Inc.
2345 Crystal Dr Ste 1000
Arlington VA 22202
703 416-8000

(G-946)
DUPONT CIRCLE SOLUTIONS
3100 Clarendon Blvd # 200 (22201-5330)
PHONE................................202 596-8528
Erin Burgin, *Principal*
EMP: 2
SALES (est): 74.4K **Privately Held**
WEB: www.dupontcirclesolutions.com
SIC: 2879 Agricultural chemicals

(G-947)
DUPONT THREADING LLC
2250 Clarendon Blvd (22201-3332)
PHONE................................703 522-1748
EMP: 2
SALES (est): 118.8K **Privately Held**
WEB: www.dupontthreading.com
SIC: 2879 Agricultural chemicals

(G-948)
DUPONT VENTURES LLC
6034 21st St N (22205-3406)
PHONE................................574 514-3646
EMP: 2
SALES (est): 81.8K **Privately Held**
SIC: 2879 Agricultural chemicals

(G-949)
DUTCH DUCK SOFTWARE
2606 23rd Rd N (22207-4903)
PHONE................................703 525-6564
EMP: 2 EST: 2010
SALES (est): 96K **Privately Held**
SIC: 7372 Prepackaged Software Services

(G-950)
EAGLE MOBILE SERVICES INC
3233 Columbia Pike Ste B (22204-4367)
PHONE................................703 979-1848
Thomas Benitez, *Owner*
Jose Benitez, *Co-Owner*
EMP: 2
SALES (est): 174.3K **Privately Held**
SIC: 3663 Mobile communication equip-
ment

(G-951)
EASTERN CRANIAL AFFILIATES LLC
5275 Lee Hwy Ste 102 (22207-1619)
PHONE................................703 807-5899
EMP: 1
SALES (corp-wide): 1.9MM **Privately Held**
WEB: www.infinitetech.org
SIC: 3842 Foot appliances, orthopedic
PA: Eastern Cranial Affiliates Llc
10523 Main St
Fairfax VA 22030
703 807-5899

(G-952)
ECHO HILL FARM
1320 Fort Myer Dr Apt 812 (22209-3525)
PHONE.............................802 586-2239
Randi Calderwood, *Principal*
EMP: 2 **EST:** 2008
SALES (est): 99.3K **Privately Held**
WEB: www.echohillfarm.com
SIC: 2099 Syrups

(G-953)
ECOMETRIX
1510 N George Mason Dr (22205-3619)
PHONE.............................703 525-0524
Silke Reeves, *Manager*
EMP: 2 **EST:** 2016
SALES (est): 56.5K **Privately Held**
SIC: 7372 Prepackaged software

(G-954)
EDITORIAL PRJCTS IN EDCATN INC
Also Called: Education Week
4201 Wilson Blvd (22230-0001)
PHONE.............................703 292-5111
Pamela J Smith, *Opers Staff*
Cliff Braverman, *Production*
Jessie L Crain, *Research*
Kera Tyler, *Marketing Staff*
Joseph Hennessey, *Program Mgr*
EMP: 16
SALES (corp-wide): 18.1MM **Privately Held**
WEB: www.edweek.org
SIC: 2711 2721 Newspapers: publishing only, not printed on site; magazines: publishing only, not printed on site
PA: Editorial Projects In Education, Inc.
  6935 Arlington Rd Ste 100
  Bethesda MD 20814
  301 280-3100

(G-955)
EILEEN TRAMONTE DESIGN
4504 32nd Rd N (22207-4419)
PHONE.............................703 241-1996
Eileen Tramonte, *Owner*
EMP: 1
SALES (est): 52.5K **Privately Held**
SIC: 3229 Tableware, glass or glass ceramic

(G-956)
ELIZABETH NEVILLE
5521 23rd St N (22205-3107)
PHONE.............................703 409-4217
Elizabeth Neville, *Owner*
▲ **EMP:** 1
SALES (est): 5K **Privately Held**
SIC: 2741 Miscellaneous publishing

(G-957)
EMBASSY
6 N Montague St (22203-1002)
PHONE.............................703 403-3996
Jason Lund, *Owner*
EMP: 1
SALES (est): 77.5K **Privately Held**
SIC: 3829 Physical property testing equipment

(G-958)
EMC CORPORATION
2011 Crystal Dr Ste 907 (22202-3732)
PHONE.............................703 553-2522
Steve Hartell, *President*
EMP: 10 **Publicly Held**
WEB: www.emc.com
SIC: 3572 Computer storage devices
HQ: Emc Corporation
  176 South St
  Hopkinton MA 01748
  508 435-1000

(G-959)
ESSOLUTIONS INC (HQ)
1401 S Clark St Ste 200 (22202-4150)
PHONE.............................240 215-6992
Kelly Brown, *CEO*
Robert Brown, *Vice Pres*
James Saputo, *CFO*
EMP: 17
SQ FT: 692

SALES (est): 4.2MM **Privately Held**
SIC: 3571 3572 3575 3577 Electronic computers; computers, digital, analog or hybrid; personal computers (microcomputers); computer storage devices; disk drives, computer; computer terminals; computer peripheral equipment; general warehousing & storage; custom computer programming services
PA: American Systems Corporation
  14151 Pk Madow Dr Ste 500
  Chantilly VA 20151
  703 968-6300

(G-960)
EUCLIDIAN SYSTEMS INC (PA)
1100 Wilson Blvd Ste 1008 (22209-2249)
PHONE.............................703 963-7209
Jeffrey Williams, *CEO*
EMP: 1 **EST:** 2017
SALES (est): 139.1K **Privately Held**
WEB: www.bingobongo.io
SIC: 7372 7371 7389 Business oriented computer software; software programming applications; computer software systems analysis & design, custom; computer software development & applications;

(G-961)
EYL INC
2011 Crystal Dr Ste 400 (22202-3709)
PHONE.............................703 682-7018
Junghyun Baik, *CEO*
Jongwon Park, *Vice Pres*
Daehyun Nam, *CFO*
EMP: 3
SQ FT: 120
SALES (est): 137.6K **Privately Held**
WEB: www.eylpartners.com
SIC: 3674 Semiconductors & related devices

(G-962)
FANTALIFE PUBLISHING LLC
1405 S Fern St 502 (22202-2810)
PHONE.............................703 682-2125
Damon Bragg, *Mng Member*
EMP: 1
SALES (est): 33.3K **Privately Held**
SIC: 2731 Book publishing

(G-963)
FAUN TRACKWAY (USA) INC
1655 Fort Myer Dr Ste 950 (22209-3125)
PHONE.............................202 459-0802
Mr J Alun Jones, *CEO*
Michael Holdcraft, *Principal*
EMP: 1
SALES (est): 104.6K **Privately Held**
SIC: 3448 Buildings, portable: prefabricated metal

(G-964)
FEDSAFES LLC
5130 Wilson Blvd (22205-1169)
PHONE.............................703 525-1436
Michael Groves, *Mng Member*
▼ **EMP:** 5
SQ FT: 5,000
SALES (est): 1.1MM **Privately Held**
WEB: www.fedsafes.com
SIC: 2522 3499 5044 Office furniture, except wood; safes & vaults, metal; office equipment

(G-965)
FINE ARTS FRAMERS INC
4022 18th Rd N (22207-3007)
PHONE.............................703 525-3869
William Metcalfe, *President*
Bridgid Metcalfe, *Vice Pres*
EMP: 2
SALES (est): 48K **Privately Held**
SIC: 2499 Picture & mirror frames, wood

(G-966)
FINEST PRODUCTIONS INC
901 N Pollard St Apt 2408 (22203-5801)
PHONE.............................703 989-2657
Marika Urb, *President*
EMP: 1
SALES (est): 94K **Privately Held**
WEB: www.finestproductions.com
SIC: 3663 Radio & TV communications equipment

(G-967)
FIT ME BY CRYSTAL LLC
3535 S Ball St Apt 108 (22202-4427)
PHONE.............................302 573-1235
Crystal Mitchell,
EMP: 1
SALES (est): 80K **Privately Held**
SIC: 2339 Women's & misses' athletic clothing & sportswear

(G-968)
FLIR DETECTION INC
Also Called: Flir Systems
1201 S Joyce St Ste C6 (22202-2067)
PHONE.............................877 692-2120
EMP: 3
SALES (corp): 1.8B **Publicly Held**
WEB: www.detectionsupport.com
SIC: 3826 Analytical optical instruments
HQ: Flir Detection, Inc.
  1024 S Innovation Way
  Stillwater OK 74074

(G-969)
FLIR SYSTEMS INC
900 S Walter Reed Dr (22204-2310)
PHONE.............................703 416-6666
Bill Treuting, *Business Mgr*
Linda Dahlberg, *Vice Pres*
Kristine Pirnia, *Vice Pres*
Steven Williams, *Vice Pres*
Rhonda Weaver, *Buyer*
EMP: 3
SALES (corp-wide): 1.8B **Publicly Held**
WEB: www.flir.com
SIC: 3826 Analytical instruments
PA: Flir Systems, Inc.
  27700 Sw Parkway Ave
  Wilsonville OR 97070
  503 498-3547

(G-970)
FLUOR ENTERPRISES INC
2300 Clarendon Blvd # 1110 (22201-3383)
PHONE.............................703 351-1204
Bruce Stanski, *Branch Mgr*
EMP: 25
SALES (corp-wide): 14.3B **Publicly Held**
WEB: www.fluor.com
SIC: 3674 Semiconductors & related devices
HQ: Fluor Enterprises, Inc.
  6700 Las Colinas Blvd
  Irving TX 75039
  469 398-7000

(G-971)
FLYERMONSTERSCOM
3140 Washington Blvd (22201-4418)
PHONE.............................703 582-5716
EMP: 2
SALES (est): 133.2K **Privately Held**
WEB: www.flyermonsters.com
SIC: 2752 Commercial printing, offset

(G-972)
FLZHI TECHNOLOGIES LLC
3737 27th St N (22207-5053)
PHONE.............................214 616-7756
Ralph Miller,
EMP: 1
SALES (est): 39.6K **Privately Held**
SIC: 3999 Manufacturing industries

(G-973)
FORCE PROTECTION INC
2450 Crystal Dr Ste 1060 (22202-3898)
PHONE.............................703 415-7520
EMP: 255
SALES (corp-wide): 31.5B **Publicly Held**
SIC: 3711 Mfg Motor Vehicle/Car Bodies
HQ: Force Protection, Inc.
  9801 Highway 78 Bldg 1
  Ladson SC 29456
  843 574-7000

(G-974)
GAMEPLAN PRESS INC
910 S George Mason Dr (22204-1557)
PHONE.............................703 521-1546
Judith Bailey, *Principal*
EMP: 2 **EST:** 2012
SALES (est): 79K **Privately Held**
WEB: www.gameplanpress.com
SIC: 2741 Miscellaneous publishing

(G-975)
GARY D KEYS ENTERPRISES INC
Also Called: Minuteman Press
2117 Crystal Plaza Arc (22202-4602)
PHONE.............................703 418-1700
Gary D Keys, *President*
Sharla Bachrodt, *Accounts Exec*
EMP: 5
SALES (est): 900K **Privately Held**
WEB: www.minutemanpress.com
SIC: 2752 2791 2759 Commercial printing, lithographic; typesetting; commercial printing

(G-976)
GAY G-SPOT LLC
1300 S Arlington Ridge Rd # 516 (22202-1953)
P.O. Box 2165 (22202-0165)
PHONE.............................650 429-8233
Christopher Mamaril,
EMP: 1
SALES (est): 37.5K **Privately Held**
SIC: 2741 7389 ;

(G-977)
GENENTECH INC
2435 13th Ct N (22201-5864)
PHONE.............................703 841-1076
EMP: 150
SALES (corp-wide): 53.9B **Privately Held**
SIC: 2834 Mfg Pharmaceutical Preparations
HQ: Genentech, Inc.
  1 Dna Way
  South San Francisco CA 94080
  650 225-1000

(G-978)
GEORGETOWN BUSINESS SERVICES
554 23rd St S (22202-2518)
PHONE.............................214 708-0249
EMP: 2
SALES (est): 83.9K **Privately Held**
SIC: 2752 Commercial printing, lithographic

(G-979)
GIVAL PRESS LLC
5200 1st St N (22203-1252)
P.O. Box 3812 (22203-0812)
PHONE.............................703 351-0079
Robert Giron, *Mng Member*
EMP: 1 **EST:** 1998
SALES (est): 144K **Privately Held**
WEB: www.givalpress.submittable.com
SIC: 2759 Commercial printing

(G-980)
GLOBAL WATER CHALLENGE
2900 S Quincy St Ste 375 (22206-2279)
PHONE.............................703 379-2713
Monica Ellis, *CEO*
EMP: 5 **EST:** 2008
SALES: 2.9MM **Privately Held**
WEB: www.globalwaterchallenge.org
SIC: 2842 Sanitation preparations

(G-981)
GM PRINTER EXPERTS LLC
4600 S Four Mile Run Dr A (22204-6512)
PHONE.............................202 250-0569
Gerardo Villarroel, *Principal*
Myriam Villarroel, *Principal*
EMP: 2
SALES (est): 83.9K **Privately Held**
SIC: 2752 Commercial printing, lithographic

(G-982)
GMG GHOSTWRITING
4220 Campbell Ave # 607 (22206-3427)
PHONE.............................718 578-8622
Gabriella Gafni, *Principal*
EMP: 2
SALES (est): 77.6K **Privately Held**
WEB: www.gmghostwriting.com
SIC: 2741 Miscellaneous publishing

(G-983)
GODA SOFTWARE INC
2011 Crystal Dr (22202-3709)
PHONE.............................703 373-7568

GEOGRAPHIC

EMP: 2
SALES (est): 107.4K **Privately Held**
SIC: 7372 Prepackaged Software Services

(G-984)
GOLDEN QUILL EDITORIAL SVCS
4301 Columbia Pike # 235 (22204-3054)
PHONE......................240 838-0464
Stephen Goldstein, *Principal*
EMP: 2
SALES (est): 74.8K **Privately Held**
WEB: www.goldenquilleditorial.biz
SIC: 2741 Miscellaneous publishing

(G-985)
GOODRICH CORPORATION
1000 Wilson Blvd Ste 2300 (22209-3914)
PHONE......................703 558-8230
Gerrie Bjornson, *Vice Pres*
Jim Dalberg, *Director*
Dan Leonard, *Administration*
EMP: 16
SALES (corp-wide): 77B **Publicly Held**
WEB: www.collinsaerospace.com
SIC: 3728 Aircraft parts & equipment
HQ: Goodrich Corporation
2730 W Tyvola Rd
Charlotte NC 28217
704 423-7000

(G-986)
GOVTRIBE INC
2311 Wilson Blvd Fl 3 (22201-5436)
PHONE......................202 505-4681
Nathan Nash, *President*
Jay Hariani, *Principal*
Marc Vogtman, *CFO*
EMP: 3 **EST:** 2012
SALES (est): 211.7K **Privately Held**
WEB: www.govtribe.com
SIC: 7372 Business oriented computer software

(G-987)
GREENZONE SYSTEMS INC
901 N Stuart St Ste 1200 (22203-4129)
PHONE......................703 567-6039
Darren Cummings, *President*
Damon Mauceri, *Senior VP*
Andrew Riggs, *Senior VP*
Aaron Hendricks, *Engineer*
Grant Whitley, *Manager*
EMP: 4
SALES (est): 213K **Privately Held**
SIC: 3661 3674 3663 8711 Telephones & telephone apparatus; integrated circuits, semiconductor networks, etc.; studio equipment, radio & television broadcasting; electrical or electronic engineering; electronic research

(G-988)
HARARI INVESTMENTS
Also Called: Metro Media One
4600 S Four Mile Run Dr # 503 (22204-6512)
PHONE......................703 842-7462
EMP: 2 **EST:** 2008
SALES: 500K **Privately Held**
SIC: 2759 Printing

(G-989)
HARRISON MANAGEMENT ASSOCIATES
Also Called: Sowa & Nicholas Printing
1000 N Kensington St (22205-2308)
PHONE......................703 237-0418
Jamie Nicholas, *President*
Lenora Sowa, *Vice Pres*
EMP: 5
SQ FT: 3,100
SALES (est): 600K **Privately Held**
SIC: 2759 2752 Commercial printing; commercial printing, lithographic

(G-990)
HELLTOWN INDUSTRIES LLC
1812 S Oakland St (22204-5139)
PHONE......................571 312-4073
Kathryn Zajac, *Principal*
EMP: 2
SALES (est): 84.2K **Privately Held**
SIC: 3999 Manufacturing industries

(G-991)
HEY FRASE LLC
919 N Lincoln St Apt 653 (22201-2385)
PHONE......................202 372-5453
Sarah Fraser, *CEO*
EMP: 5
SALES (est): 130.5K **Privately Held**
SIC: 2741 7389 ; business services

(G-992)
HOMELAND DEFENSE JOURNAL
4301 Wilson Blvd Ste 1003 (22203-1867)
PHONE......................703 622-1187
Don Dickson, *Principal*
EMP: 1
SALES (est): 35.7K **Privately Held**
SIC: 2731 Book publishing

(G-993)
HONEYWELL INTERNATIONAL INC
1530 Wilson Blvd Ste 1000 (22209-2421)
PHONE......................703 626-8363
Eric Ball, *Sales Mgr*
Russell E Fredrick, *Director*
Alicia Collier, *Director*
EMP: 27
SALES (corp-wide): 36.7B **Publicly Held**
WEB: www.honeywell.com
SIC: 3724 Aircraft engines & engine parts
PA: Honeywell International Inc.
300 S Tryon St
Charlotte NC 28202
704 627-6200

(G-994)
HOUGHTON MIFFLIN HARCOURT PUBG
1600 Wilson Blvd Ste 710 (22209-2505)
PHONE......................703 243-2602
Floyd Rogers, *CFO*
EMP: 151 **Publicly Held**
WEB: www.hmhco.com
SIC: 2731 Textbooks: publishing only, not printed on site
HQ: Houghton Mifflin Harcourt Publishing Company
125 High St Ste 900
Boston MA 02110
617 351-5000

(G-995)
HUESPACE INC
801 15th St S Apt 210 (22202-5013)
PHONE......................540 406-0496
Seung-Jun Lee, *CEO*
EMP: 1
SALES (est): 32.7K **Privately Held**
SIC: 7372 Application computer software

(G-996)
HYBRID AIR VEHICLES (US) INC
Also Called: Havus
2300 Wilson Blvd Ste 205a (22201-5424)
PHONE......................703 524-0026
Christopher Lehman, *President*
EMP: 1
SALES (est): 81.5K **Privately Held**
SIC: 3721 Aircraft

(G-997)
I-CE-NY ARLINGTON
4150 Campbell Ave Ste 101 (22206-4206)
PHONE......................571 207-6318
EMP: 2 **EST:** 2018
SALES (est): 62.3K **Privately Held**
WEB: www.arlnow.com
SIC: 2038 Frozen specialties

(G-998)
I3 INGENUITY INC
Also Called: Signs By Tomorrow
3300 Fairfax Dr Ste 302 (22201-4400)
P.O. Box 4226, West McLean (22103-4226)
PHONE......................703 524-0019
Bowman Kell, *President*
John Kell, *Treasurer*
EMP: 4 **EST:** 2014
SALES (est): 412K **Privately Held**
WEB: www.signsbytomorrow.com
SIC: 3993 Signs & advertising specialties

(G-999)
IHEARTRHYTHM LLC
2550 Washington Blvd (22201-1151)
PHONE......................757 810-5902
Stafford Nichols, *CFO*
EMP: 3
SALES (est): 206.9K **Privately Held**
WEB: www.iheartrhythm.com
SIC: 3845 Electrocardiographs

(G-1000)
IMPROBABLE LLC
3033 Wilson Blvd Ste 260 (22201-3874)
PHONE......................571 418-6999
Brian Hamilton, *Mng Member*
Daniel Wenk, *Mng Member*
EMP: 45
SALES (est): 535.1K **Privately Held**
SIC: 7372 3944 Operating systems computer software; video game machines, except coin-operated

(G-1001)
INDUSTRIAL SIGNAL LLC
3835 9th St N Apt 808w (22203-4085)
PHONE......................703 323-7777
David Perlmutter,
EMP: 3
SALES (est): 194.6K **Privately Held**
WEB: www.indsig.com
SIC: 3669 Communications equipment

(G-1002)
INDUSTRIES 247 LLC
4238 Wilson Blvd Ste 3136 (22203-1836)
PHONE......................703 741-0151
EMP: 2
SALES (est): 85.1K **Privately Held**
SIC: 3999 Mfg Misc Products

(G-1003)
INSIDE AIR FORCE
1919 S Eads St Ste 201 (22202-3028)
PHONE......................703 416-8528
Alan Sosenko, *Owner*
EMP: 2
SALES (est): 107.1K **Privately Held**
WEB: www.insidedefense.com
SIC: 2721 Periodicals

(G-1004)
INSIDE WASHINGTON PUBLISHER
1225 S Clark St Ste 1400 (22202-4384)
PHONE......................703 416-8500
EMP: 1 **EST:** 2018
SALES (est): 41.3K **Privately Held**
WEB: www.insidehealthpolicy.com
SIC: 2741 Miscellaneous publishing

(G-1005)
INTERNATIONAL CMMNCTNS STRTGC
1916 Wilson Blvd Ste 3 (22201-3005)
P.O. Box 6877 (22206-0877)
PHONE......................703 820-1669
Michael J Weiser, *Managing Prtnr*
Robin Laird, *Mng Member*
EMP: 3
SALES (est): 162.4K **Privately Held**
SIC: 3812 Defense systems & equipment

(G-1006)
INTERNTIONAL MARITIME SEC CORP
Also Called: Imsc
2400 Clarendon Blvd (22201-5841)
PHONE......................719 494-6501
Scott Brewer, *President*
Lawrence O'Connell, *Exec VP*
Michael Brewer, *Vice Pres*
Larry Krakover, *Vice Pres*
EMP: 4
SALES (est): 283.8K **Privately Held**
WEB: www.alcyonics.com
SIC: 3731 Shipbuilding & repairing

(G-1007)
INTERNTIONAL SCANNER CORP AMER (PA)
Also Called: Iscoa
5901 Lee Hwy (22207-1428)
PHONE......................703 533-8560
Michael Ueltzen, *President*

Barbara Gosch, *Corp Secy*
Christopher Harris, *Vice Pres*
Robert R Rissland, *Vice Pres*
EMP: 15
SQ FT: 2,200
SALES (est): 1.3MM **Privately Held**
SIC: 2796 7336 2791 Color separations for printing; commercial art & graphic design; typesetting

(G-1008)
INTERNTNAL PHRM EXCPNTS ADTING
Also Called: Ipea
3138 10th St N Ste 500 (22201-2149)
PHONE......................571 814-3449
Kimberly Beals, *Principal*
Tammy Kramer, *Office Mgr*
EMP: 1
SALES: 1.1MM
SALES (corp-wide): 1.3MM **Privately Held**
WEB: www.ipecamericas.org
SIC: 2834 Pharmaceutical preparations
PA: Ipec Americas Inc
3138 10th St N Ste 500
Arlington VA 22201
571 814-3449

(G-1009)
INTERSTATE CONT READING LLC
1800 N Kent St Ste 1200 (22209-2109)
PHONE......................703 243-3355
Antoine Frem, *CEO*
George Frem, *Ch of Bd*
Charles A Feghali, *President*
Larry Brill, *General Mgr*
Ramez Skaff, *Admin Sec*
EMP: 3
SQ FT: 100,000
SALES (est): 685.2K
SALES (corp-wide): 7.3B **Privately Held**
WEB: www.interstateresources.com
SIC: 2653 Boxes, corrugated: made from purchased materials
HQ: Interstate Resources, Inc.
600 Peachtree St Ne
Atlanta GA 30308
703 243-3355

(G-1010)
INTERSTATE RESOURCES INC
1800 N Kent St (22209-2134)
PHONE......................703 243-3355
Susan Newman, *VP Human Res*
EMP: 2
SALES (corp-wide): 7.3B **Privately Held**
WEB: www.interstateresources.com
SIC: 2631 2653 7389 Kraft linerboard; boxes, corrugated: made from purchased materials; purchasing service
HQ: Interstate Resources, Inc.
600 Peachtree St Ne
Atlanta GA 30308
703 243-3355

(G-1011)
IOWAVE INC
2100 Washington Blvd # 1001 (22204-5703)
PHONE......................703 979-9283
Peter Friedli, *Ch of Bd*
Dan Saginario, *President*
Dr Kou-Hu Tzou, *President*
David Danovitch, *CFO*
EMP: 30
SQ FT: 14,000 **Privately Held**
WEB: www.iowave.com
SIC: 3661 3577 Telephone & telegraph apparatus; computer peripheral equipment

(G-1012)
IT TAKES A STITCH CUSTOM
2700 25th St N (22207-4918)
PHONE......................703 405-6688
EMP: 1
SALES (est): 45.1K **Privately Held**
WEB: www.ittakesastitch.com
SIC: 2395 Embroidery & art needlework

(G-1013)
JACKSON ENTERPRISES INC
Also Called: The Belvedere Press
4908 Washington Blvd (22205-2545)
PHONE................................703 527-1118
Caroline Jackson, *President*
EMP: 1
SALES (est): 64K **Privately Held**
WEB: www.jackprises.com
SIC: 2731 8741 Books: publishing only;
management services

(G-1014)
JAMESGATE PRESS LLC
2312 S Pierce St (22202-1519)
PHONE................................703 892-5621
Maureen Raley, *Principal*
EMP: 2 **EST:** 2013
SALES (est): 96.3K **Privately Held**
SIC: 2741 Miscellaneous publishing

(G-1015)
JAMIE NICHOLAS
Also Called: Jamie Nicholas Prtg & Graphics
4812 20th Pl N (22207-2202)
PHONE................................703 731-7966
Jamie Nicholas, *Owner*
EMP: 1
SALES (est): 606.7K **Privately Held**
WEB: www.jamienicholas.com
SIC: 2759 Advertising literature: printing

(G-1016)
**JOINT LAB SYSTEMS SEC SVCS
LLC**
Also Called: Jls3
1515 Richmond Hwy # 1623 (22202-3314)
PHONE................................443 655-9987
Jesse Storey, *Mng Member*
EMP: 1
SALES (est): 53.2K **Privately Held**
SIC: 2752 7372 7374 7371 Commercial
printing, lithographic; prepackaged soft-
ware; data processing & preparation; cus-
tom computer programming services;
computer integrated systems design;
computer facilities management

(G-1017)
JOSE GONCALVES INC
4808 Lee Hwy (22207-2510)
PHONE................................703 528-5272
Jose Goncalves, *President*
Marie Goncalves, *Administration*
EMP: 20
SALES (est): 600K **Privately Held**
WEB: www.josegoncalves.co
SIC: 2221 7641 Draperies & drapery fab-
rics, manmade fiber & silk; upholstery
work

(G-1018)
JSC FROYO LLC
4014 Campbell Ave (22206-3424)
PHONE................................571 303-0011
Peter Rim, *Principal*
EMP: 3
SALES (est): 139.8K **Privately Held**
SIC: 2024 Yogurt desserts, frozen

(G-1019)
K & W PRINTING SERVICES INC
Also Called: Minuteman Press
4001 9th St N Ste 102 (22203-1900)
PHONE................................301 868-2141
Wolf Jelinski, *President*
Jason Barnard, *Office Mgr*
EMP: 2
SALES (est): 224.6K **Privately Held**
WEB: www.minutemanpress.com
SIC: 2752 Commercial printing, litho-
graphic

(G-1020)
KALIOPA PUBLISHING LLC
1050 N Taylor St Apt 504 (22201-4774)
PHONE................................703 522-7663
Benjamin Uy, *President*
EMP: 1
SALES (est): 50.2K **Privately Held**
SIC: 2741 Music books: publishing only,
not printed on site

(G-1021)
KAY KARE LLC
3800 Fairfax Dr (22203-1711)
PHONE................................614 309-8462
Kahkashan Neseem, *Owner*
EMP: 1
SALES (est): 105.9K **Privately Held**
WEB: www.kaykare.net
SIC: 3842 Braces, elastic

(G-1022)
KERECIS LLC
2200 Clarendon Blvd # 140 (22201-3379)
PHONE................................703 465-7945
Katharine Hoffecker, *Business Mgr*
Stephen Dibiasio, *Exec VP*
Christopher Harte, *Officer*
EMP: 13
SALES (est): 2.9MM
SALES (corp-wide): 610.9K **Privately
Held**
WEB: www.kerecis.com
SIC: 2834 Pharmaceutical preparations
PA: Kerecis Hf.
  Eyrargotu 2
  Isafirdi
  562 260-1

(G-1023)
KIMBALL CONSULTING INC
3811 Fairfax Dr Ste 400 (22203-1707)
P.O. Box 46, Tilghman MD (21671-0046)
PHONE................................703 516-6000
John Gilligan, *President*
Wes Blankinship, *Senior VP*
EMP: 8 **EST:** 1996
SALES (est): 463.1K
SALES (corp-wide): 318MM **Privately
Held**
WEB: www.schafercorp.com
SIC: 7372 Prepackaged software
HQ: Schafer Government Services, Llc
  101 Billerica Ave
  North Billerica MA 01862
  978 256-2070

(G-1024)
KRUG INDUSTRIES INC
5292 Old Dominion Dr (22207-2858)
PHONE................................714 656-5316
Brian Spross, *Admin Sec*
EMP: 1
SALES (est): 43.6K **Privately Held**
SIC: 3999 Manufacturing industries

(G-1025)
LARGO RESOURCES USA INC
4250 Fairfax Dr Ste 600 (22203-1665)
PHONE................................571 491-7827
Francescho D'Alessio, *Principal*
Bianca Estiles, *Principal*
EMP: 2
SALES (est): 66K **Privately Held**
SIC: 1081 Metal mining exploration & de-
velopment services

(G-1026)
LARISSA LECLAIR
6138 12th St N (22205-1719)
PHONE................................202 270-8039
Larissa Leclair, *Owner*
EMP: 1 **EST:** 2017
SALES (est): 44.2K **Privately Held**
WEB: www.larissaleclair.com
SIC: 2741 Miscellaneous publishing

(G-1027)
LARRY ROSENBAUM
Also Called: Net Results
5500 Columbia Pike # 422 (22204-3173)
PHONE................................703 567-4052
Larry Rosenbaum, *Owner*
EMP: 1
SALES (est): 92.6K **Privately Held**
WEB: www.netresultspromotions.com
SIC: 3993 Signs & advertising specialties

(G-1028)
LATEESHIRT
Also Called: Los Angeles Tee-Shirt
5131 Lee Hwy (22207-1603)
PHONE................................703 532-7329
Ali Zinhe, *Owner*
EMP: 1
SQ FT: 1,500

SALES (est): 150K **Privately Held**
WEB: www.lateeshirtinc.com
SIC: 2759 Screen printing

(G-1029)
**LAUREL TECHNOLOGIES
PARTNR**
2345 Crystal Dr (22202-4801)
PHONE................................814 534-2027
EMP: 2
SALES (est): 92.4K **Privately Held**
SIC: 3812 Search & navigation equipment

(G-1030)
LEGACY VULCAN LLC
2651 S Shirlington Rd (22206-2529)
PHONE................................800 732-3964
EMP: 3 **Publicly Held**
WEB: www.vulcanmaterials.com
SIC: 3273 Ready-mixed concrete
HQ: Legacy Vulcan, Llc
  1200 Urban Center Dr
  Vestavia AL 35242
  205 298-3000

(G-1031)
LEOPARD MEDIA LLC
Also Called: Defense Daily
1011 Arlington Blvd # 131 (22209-3925)
PHONE................................703 522-5655
John Robinson, *Manager*
EMP: 10
SALES (corp-wide): 10.4MM **Privately
Held**
WEB: www.defensedaily.com
SIC: 2759 Publication printing
PA: Leopard Media Llc
  9420 Key West Ave Fl 4
  Rockville MD
  301 279-4200

(G-1032)
**LESTER ENTERPRISES INTL
LLC**
4500 S Four Mile Run Dr (22204-3558)
PHONE................................703 599-3485
Lester Ricky Duane, *Administration*
EMP: 2 **EST:** 2012
SALES (est): 87.4K **Privately Held**
SIC: 2396 Linings, handbag or pocketbook

(G-1033)
LI AILIN
520 12th St S Apt 721 (22202-4242)
PHONE................................573 808-7280
Ailin LI, *Owner*
EMP: 1
SALES (est): 57K **Privately Held**
SIC: 2741 7389 ;

(G-1034)
**LIBERTY MEDIA FOR WOMEN
LLC (PA)**
Also Called: Ms Magazine
1600 Wilson Blvd Ste 801 (22209-2505)
PHONE................................703 522-4201
Peg Yorkin, *Ch of Bd*
Eleanor Smeal, *President*
Elenor Smeal, *Principal*
Katherine Spillar, *Exec VP*
Kathy Spillar, *Vice Pres*
EMP: 10
SALES (est): 827.6K **Privately Held**
WEB: www.msmagazine.com
SIC: 2721 Magazines: publishing & printing

(G-1035)
LIG NEX1 CO LTD
1101 Wilson Blvd Ste 1600 (22209-2275)
PHONE................................703 888-2501
Lee Hyo Koo, *CEO*
William Cho, *Manager*
EMP: 9
SALES (est): 811.3K **Privately Held**
SIC: 3483 Arming & fusing devices for mis-
siles
PA: Lig Nex1 Co., Ltd.
  207 Mabuk-Ro, Giheung-Gu
  Yongin-Gun 16911

(G-1036)
LINES UP INC
3033 Wilson Blvd Ste 700 (22201-3868)
PHONE................................703 842-3762
Steve Mitnick, *President*

Joseph Paparello, *Vice Pres*
EMP: 6
SALES (est): 1MM **Privately Held**
SIC: 2741 Miscellaneous publishing

(G-1037)
LION MOUNTAIN FARMS LLC
2400 S Glebe Rd Apt 603 (22206-2561)
PHONE................................916 850-9232
Michael Valdez, *Principal*
Peter Amara, *Principal*
EMP: 2
SALES (est): 62.3K **Privately Held**
SIC: 2095 Roasted coffee

(G-1038)
LITTLESHOT APPS LLC
4639 5th St S (22204-1322)
PHONE................................908 433-5727
EMP: 2
SALES (est): 120K **Privately Held**
SIC: 7372 Prepackaged Software Services

(G-1039)
LIVESAFE INC
Also Called: Livesafe.ly
1400 Key Blvd Ste 100 (22209-1518)
PHONE................................571 312-4645
Carolyn Parent, *CEO*
Len Selner, *Partner*
Alex Brandt, *Vice Pres*
Matt Hagopian, *Vice Pres*
Jeff Irby, *Vice Pres*
EMP: 38
SALES (est): 500K **Privately Held**
WEB: www.livesafemobile.com
SIC: 7372 Application computer software

(G-1040)
LIVING MAKA LLC
3100 Clarendon Blvd # 200 (22201-5330)
PHONE................................888 690-7058
Brian Hill, *Mng Member*
EMP: 2
SALES (est): 62.3K **Privately Held**
SIC: 2086 Carbonated beverages, nonal-
coholic: bottled & canned

(G-1041)
LOCAL NEWS NOW LLC
4075 Wilson Blvd Fl 8 (22203-1797)
PHONE................................703 348-0583
Scott Brodbeck, *Mng Member*
Jordan Ciminelli,
EMP: 7
SALES (est): 649.9K **Privately Held**
WEB: www.lnnllc.com
SIC: 2741

(G-1042)
LOCKER LLC (HQ)
Also Called: Rapiscan Systems
2900 Crystal Dr Ste 910 (22202-3595)
PHONE................................310 978-1457
Todd Swearingen, *Director*
J J Bare,
EMP: 9
SALES (est): 2.4MM **Publicly Held**
WEB: www.rapiscansystems.com
SIC: 3844 X-ray apparatus & tubes
PA: Osi Systems, Inc.
  12525 Chadron Ave
  Hawthorne CA 90250
  310 978-0516

(G-1043)
LOCKHEED MARTIN
850 N Randolph St (22203-1978)
PHONE................................703 588-0670
Joshua Shani, *Vice Pres*
Bert Morgan, *Transportation*
Erick Acosta, *Engineer*
Carrie Brady, *Engineer*
Frank Cordek, *Engineer*
EMP: 104 **Publicly Held**
WEB: www.lockheedmartin.com
SIC: 3812 Search & navigation equipment
HQ: Lockheed Martin Integrated Systems,
Llc
  6801 Rockledge Dr
  Bethesda MD 20817

(G-1044)
LOCKHEED MARTIN
2711 Richmond Hwy # 916 (22202-4015)
PHONE................................202 863-3297

Phil Knoll, *Manager*
EMP: 100 **Publicly Held**
WEB: www.lockheedmartin.com
SIC: 3812 Search & navigation equipment
HQ: Lockheed Martin Integrated Systems,
　Llc
　6801 Rockledge Dr
　Bethesda MD 20817

(G-1045)
LOCKHEED MARTIN
CORPORATION
1711 26th St S (22206-2926)
PHONE....................703 357-7095
Thomas Comeau, *Principal*
Amy Penchuk, *Sr Software Eng*
EMP: 435 **Publicly Held**
WEB: www.lockheedmartin.com
SIC: 3812 Search & navigation equipment
PA: Lockheed Martin Corporation
　6801 Rockledge Dr
　Bethesda MD 20817

(G-1046)
LOCKHEED MARTIN
CORPORATION
2461 S Clark St Ste 125 (22202-3884)
PHONE....................703 418-4900
Fred Moosally, *Manager*
EMP: 10 **Publicly Held**
WEB: www.lockheedmartin.com
SIC: 3812 Search & navigation equipment
PA: Lockheed Martin Corporation
　6801 Rockledge Dr
　Bethesda MD 20817

(G-1047)
LOCKHEED MARTIN
CORPORATION
2461 S Clark St Ste 720 (22202-3872)
PHONE....................703 258-2784
EMP: 2 **Publicly Held**
WEB: www.lockheedmartin.com
SIC: 3761 Space vehicles, complete;
　guided missiles, complete; ballistic mis-
　siles, complete; guided missiles & space
　vehicles, research & development
PA: Lockheed Martin Corporation
　6801 Rockledge Dr
　Bethesda MD 20817

(G-1048)
LOCKHEED MARTIN INTEGRTD
SYSTM
2001 Richmond Hwy # 900 (22202-3603)
PHONE....................866 562-2363
Cathy Mitchell, *Manager*
EMP: 99 **Publicly Held**
WEB: www.lockheedmartin.com
SIC: 3812 Aircraft/aerospace flight instru-
　ments & guidance systems
HQ: Lockheed Martin Integrated Systems,
　Llc
　6801 Rockledge Dr
　Bethesda MD 20817

(G-1049)
LUIS A MATOS
3833 9th St S (22204-1529)
PHONE....................703 486-0015
Luis A Matos, *Owner*
EMP: 1
SALES (est): 109.2K **Privately Held**
SIC: 3639 Major kitchen appliances, ex-
　cept refrigerators & stoves

(G-1050)
LUMOS LLC
3601 Fairfax Dr Apt 1006 (22201-2433)
PHONE....................571 294-4290
Tyler Kuhn, *President*
EMP: 1
SALES (est): 6K **Privately Held**
SIC: 7372 7389 Prepackaged software;
　business services

(G-1051)
LUX COSTUME JEWELRY
4238 Wilson Blvd (22203-1823)
PHONE....................703 665-0674
EMP: 2 **EST:** 2019
SALES (est): 49.6K **Privately Held**
SIC: 3961 Costume jewelry

(G-1052)
MALEYS MUSIC
2499 N Harrison St (22207-1643)
PHONE....................571 335-4289
Claude Arthur, *Principal*
EMP: 2
SALES (est): 98K **Privately Held**
SIC: 3931 Musical instruments

(G-1053)
MARJORIES COOKIE SHOP LLC
4071 S Four Mile Run Dr (22204-5617)
PHONE....................901 205-9055
Marjorie Settles,
EMP: 2
SALES (est): 25K **Privately Held**
SIC: 2051 Bakery: wholesale or whole-
　sale/retail combined

(G-1054)
MARVIN RAMIREZ-AGUILAR
2150 Patrick Henry Dr (22205-3010)
PHONE....................703 241-4092
Marvin Aguilar, *Owner*
Marvin Ramirez-Aguilar, *Owner*
EMP: 2
SALES (est): 98.5K **Privately Held**
SIC: 3713 Garbage, refuse truck bodies

(G-1055)
MATERNA
2111 Wilson Blvd (22201-3043)
PHONE....................703 875-8616
Mark Kennedy, *Principal*
EMP: 2
SALES (est): 75K **Privately Held**
WEB: www.materna.com
SIC: 7372 Prepackaged software

(G-1056)
MBDA INCORPORATED (DH)
1300 Wilson Blvd Ste 550 (22209-2324)
PHONE....................703 387-7170
John Pranzatelli, *President*
Rick Cappo, *President*
Bob Darakjy, *Corp Secy*
James Pennock, *Vice Pres*
Chuck Ungermann, *Vice Pres*
▼ **EMP:** 34
SQ FT: 58,691
SALES (est): 5.8MM **Privately Held**
WEB: www.mbdainc.com
SIC: 3812 Search & navigation equipment
HQ: Mbda Uk Limited
　Six Hills Way
　Stevenage HERTS SG1 2
　143 831-2422

(G-1057)
MBDA INCORPORATED
1300 Wilson Blvd Ste 550 (22209-2324)
PHONE....................703 351-1230
Jerry Agee, *Manager*
EMP: 5 **Privately Held**
WEB: www.mbdainc.com
SIC: 3761 Guided missiles & space vehi-
　cles
HQ: Mbda Incorporated
　1300 Wilson Blvd Ste 550
　Arlington VA 22209

(G-1058)
MEANY & OLIVER COMPANIES
INC
1110 N Glebe Rd Ste 590 (22201-5720)
PHONE....................703 851-7131
Philip Meany, *Office Mgr*
EMP: 2
SALES (est): 88.9K **Privately Held**
WEB: www.meanyoliver.com
SIC: 3446 Architectural metalwork

(G-1059)
MEDIASAT INTERNATIONAL INC
4419 7th St N (22203-2002)
PHONE....................703 558-0309
Mark Brender, *President*
EMP: 2
SALES (est): 88.3K **Privately Held**
SIC: 3663 Radio & TV communications
　equipment

(G-1060)
MEDICAL SPORTS INC
1812 N George Mason Dr (22205-3622)
P.O. Box 7187 (22207-0187)
PHONE....................703 241-9720
Robert P Nirschl, *CEO*
Susanne Brown, *Vice Pres*
EMP: 4
SQ FT: 2,300
SALES (est): 125K **Privately Held**
WEB: www.countrforce.com
SIC: 3842 5999 Braces, elastic; orthope-
　dic & prosthesis applications

(G-1061)
MERCURY SYSTEMS INC
1300 Wilson Blvd Ste 575 (22209-2335)
PHONE....................703 243-9538
EMP: 3
SALES (corp-wide): 493.1MM **Publicly**
Held
SIC: 3672 Mfg Printed Circuit Boards
PA: Mercury Systems, Inc.
　50 Minuteman Rd
　Andover MA 01810
　978 256-1300

(G-1062)
MICHAEL HOLT INC
Also Called: Belusa Chocolates
2030 N Adams St Apt 807 (22201-3756)
PHONE....................703 597-6999
Michael Holt, *President*
Marjorie Holt, *Treasurer*
Raymond Holt, *Admin Sec*
EMP: 6
SQ FT: 5,000
SALES (est): 240K **Privately Held**
SIC: 2064 5145 5149 Candy & other con-
　fectionery products; confectionery; gro-
　ceries & related products

(G-1063)
MICRO ANALYTICS OF VIRGINIA
(PA)
925 Patrick Henry Dr (22205-1438)
PHONE....................703 536-6424
J Michael Hooban, *President*
EMP: 10
SQ FT: 2,950
SALES (est): 2MM **Privately Held**
SIC: 7372 Publishers' computer software

(G-1064)
MICROSOFT CORPORATION
1100 S Hayes St Unit G04a (22202-4907)
PHONE....................703 236-9140
Aaron Margosis, *Consultant*
Karan Bhatia, *Software Engr*
Kiyosha Baird, *Analyst*
EMP: 591
SALES (corp-wide): 143B **Publicly Held**
WEB: www.microsoft.com
SIC: 7372 Application computer software
PA: Microsoft Corporation
　1 Microsoft Way
　Redmond WA 98052
　425 882-8080

(G-1065)
MINUTEMAN PRESS INTL INC
4001 9th St N Ste 102 (22203-1900)
PHONE....................703 522-1944
Ronald P George, *Owner*
EMP: 6
SALES (corp-wide): 23.4MM **Privately**
Held
WEB: www.chanhassen-mn.minuteman-
press.com
SIC: 2752 Commercial printing, litho-
　graphic
PA: Minuteman Press International, Inc.
　61 Executive Blvd
　Farmingdale NY 11735
　631 249-1370

(G-1066)
MIRACLE SYSTEMS LLC
1621 N Kent St Ste 1000 (22209-2141)
PHONE....................571 431-6397
Roy Evans Jr, *Senior VP*
Daniel Fletcher Jr, *Senior VP*
Stephen Nichols, *Vice Pres*
Robert Olsen, *Vice Pres*
Sandesh Sharda, *Mng Member*
EMP: 150

SQ FT: 6,000
SALES (est): 19.1MM **Privately Held**
WEB: www.miraclesystems.net
SIC: 7372 8741 7371 Educational com-
　puter software; financial management for
　business; custom computer programming
　services

(G-1067)
MOOKIND PRESS LLC
1600 S Eads St Apt 1034n (22202-5349)
PHONE....................703 920-1884
Mark Nadel, *Principal*
EMP: 2
SALES (est): 90.6K **Privately Held**
SIC: 2741 Miscellaneous publishing

(G-1068)
MOTHERS MACAROONS
Also Called: Mothers Macaroons Gourmet
Bky
6713 Little Falls Rd (22213-1212)
PHONE....................703 532-0104
Kay Lomedico, *Owner*
EMP: 5
SQ FT: 1,300
SALES (est): 267.2K **Privately Held**
WEB: www.mothersmacaroons.com
SIC: 2052 Cookies

(G-1069)
NAILROD PUBLICATIONS LLC
3750 N Oakland St (22207-4839)
PHONE....................703 351-8130
Martha Harris, *Principal*
EMP: 4 **EST:** 2015
SALES (est): 147K **Privately Held**
SIC: 2711 Newspapers, publishing & print-
　ing

(G-1070)
NATIONAL GEOGRAPHIC ENTPS
4534 19th St N (22207-2319)
PHONE....................703 528-7868
John Fahery, *President*
EMP: 90
SALES (est): 7.5MM
SALES (corp-wide): 428.1MM **Privately**
Held
WEB: www.nationalgeographic.org
SIC: 2721 Magazines: publishing & printing
PA: National Geographic Society
　1145 17th St Nw
　Washington DC 20036
　202 857-7000

(G-1071)
NATIONAL REVIEW INSTITUTE
2221 S Clark St Ste 1200 (22202-3745)
PHONE....................202 679-7330
Lindsay Craig, *President*
EMP: 1
SALES (est): 68.7K **Privately Held**
WEB: www.nrinstitute.org
SIC: 2741 Catalogs: publishing & printing

(G-1072)
NEATHRIDGE CONTENT
SOLUTIONS
1107 20th St S (22202-2109)
PHONE....................703 979-7170
Michele Duke, *Administration*
EMP: 2
SALES (est): 62.9K **Privately Held**
SIC: 2711 Newspapers

(G-1073)
NESTLE HOLDINGS INC (HQ)
1812 N Moore St (22209-1815)
PHONE....................703 682-4600
Brad Alford, *Ch of Bd*
John Gatlin, *Senior VP*
Don Gosline, *Treasurer*
William Shy, *Credit Mgr*
Yun Au, *Admin Sec*
◆ **EMP:** 14

SALES (est): 15.1B
SALES (corp-wide): 93.5B **Privately Held**
WEB: www.nestleusa.com
SIC: **2023** 2032 2038 2033 Dry, condensed, evaporated dairy products;
canned specialties; soups & broths:
canned, jarred, etc.; beans & bean
sprouts, canned, jarred, etc.; Italian foods:
packaged in cans, jars, etc.; frozen specialties; fruits & fruit products in cans,
jars, etc.; vegetables & vegetable products in cans, jars, etc.; jams, jellies & preserves: packaged in cans, jars, etc.;
tomato products: packaged in cans, jars,
etc.; candy & other confectionery products; fluid milk
PA: Nestle S.A.
Avenue Nestle 55
Vevey VD 1800
219 242-111

(G-1074)
NESTLE USA INC
1812 N Moore St Ste 118 (22209-1818)
PHONE.............................765 778-6000
Grant Normann, *Branch Mgr*
EMP: 139
SALES (corp-wide): 93.5B **Privately Held**
WEB: www.nestleusa.com
SIC: **2023** 2033 2064 2047 Evaporated
milk; canned milk, whole; cream substi-
tutes; fruits: packaged in cans, jars, etc.;
tomato paste: packaged in cans, jars,
etc.; tomato sauce: packaged in cans,
jars, etc.; candy & other confectionery
products; breakfast bars; dog food; cat
food
HQ: Nestle Usa, Inc.
1812 N Moore St Ste 118
Rosslyn VA 22209
440 264-7249

(G-1075)
NETCENTRIC TECHNOLOGIES INC
1600 Wilson Blvd Ste 1010 (22209-2510)
PHONE.............................202 661-2180
Monir Elrayes, *President*
Ferass Elrayes, *Vice Pres*
EMP: 2
SALES (est): 900.8K **Privately Held**
WEB: www.commonlook.com
SIC: **7372** Business oriented computer
software

(G-1076)
NEURO TENNIS INC
1000 Wilson Blvd Ste 1800 (22209-3920)
PHONE.............................240 481-7640
Marc Cohen, *CEO*
Alain Cohen, *Co-CEO*
EMP: 2 EST: 2015
SQ FT: 5,000
SALES (est): 100K **Privately Held**
SIC: **3949** Tennis equipment & supplies

(G-1077)
NEWPORT TIMBER LLC (DH)
1300 Wilson Blvd Ste 1075 (22209-2330)
PHONE.............................703 243-3355
Tom Norris, *General Mgr*
Antoine Frem, *Chairman*
Ramez G Skaff, *Admin Sec*
EMP: 12
SALES (est): 67.9MM
SALES (corp-wide): 7.3B **Privately Held**
WEB: www.interstateresources.com
SIC: **2621** Bond paper
HQ: Interstate Resources, Inc.
600 Peachtree St Ne
Atlanta GA 30308
703 243-3355

(G-1078)
NIMCO US INC
1812 N Moore St (22209-1815)
PHONE.............................314 982-3204
Robert Griesse, *Vice Pres*
EMP: 3
SALES (est): 91.3K
SALES (corp-wide): 93.5B **Privately Held**
SIC: **2023** Dry, condensed, evaporated
dairy products

PA: Nestle S.A.
Avenue Nestle 55
Vevey VD 1800
219 242-111

(G-1079)
NOAH PACI
506 N Ivy St (22201-1708)
PHONE.............................703 525-5437
Noah Paci, *Principal*
EMP: 2 EST: 2008
SALES (est): 155.5K **Privately Held**
WEB: www.noahsdad.com
SIC: **2431** Millwork

(G-1080)
NORTHROP GRMMAN INNVTION SYSTE
1300 Wilson Blvd Ste 400 (22209-2330)
PHONE.............................763 744-5219
Richard R Macheske, *Chief*
Charlie Whitmeyer, *Business Mgr*
Lee Atkinson, *Vice Pres*
James Judd, *Vice Pres*
Sally Richardson, *Vice Pres*
EMP: 7 **Publicly Held**
WEB: www.northropgrumman.com
SIC: **3812** Search & navigation equipment
HQ: Northrop Grumman Innovation Sys-
tems, Inc.
45101 Warp Dr
Dulles VA 20166

(G-1081)
NORTHROP GRUMMAN CORPORATION
1101 Wilson Blvd Ste 1600 (22209-2275)
PHONE.............................212 978-2800
Kevin Schneickert, *Engineer*
John Shworzick, *Branch Mgr*
Justin Crisler, *Programmer Anys*
EMP: 2 **Publicly Held**
WEB: www.northropgrumman.com
SIC: **3812** Search & navigation equipment
PA: Northrop Grumman Corporation
2980 Fairview Park Dr
Falls Church VA 22042

(G-1082)
NORTHROP GRUMMAN SYSTEMS CORP
Also Called: Logicon Tactical Systems Div
2100 Washington Blvd (22204-5703)
PHONE.............................703 875-8463
James F Harvey, *General Mgr*
EMP: 202 **Publicly Held**
WEB: www.northropgrumman.com
SIC: **3812** Search & navigation equipment
HQ: Northrop Grumman Systems Corpora-
tion
2980 Fairview Park Dr
Falls Church VA 22042
703 280-2900

(G-1083)
NORTONLIFELOCK INC
Also Called: Symantec
400 11th St S (22202-4700)
PHONE.............................703 414-4444
EMP: 3
SALES (corp-wide): 2.4B **Publicly Held**
WEB: www.broadcom.com
SIC: **7372** Prepackaged software
PA: Nortonlifelock Inc.
60 E Rio Salado Pkwy # 1
Tempe AZ 85281
650 527-8000

(G-1084)
NOVA SYNCHRO OF VA INC
5411 22nd St N (22205-3138)
P.O. Box 5712 (22205-0712)
PHONE.............................703 241-4136
Hildie Block, *Principal*
EMP: 6 EST: 2010
SALES (est): 276.7K **Privately Held**
WEB: www.novasynchro.net
SIC: **3621** Synchros

(G-1085)
OLIVE OIL BOOM
1276 N Wayne St Apt 1125 (22201-5890)
PHONE.............................703 276-2666
EMP: 3

SALES (est): 110.5K **Privately Held**
WEB: www.oliveoilboom.com
SIC: **2079** Olive oil

(G-1086)
OLIVE OIL BOOM LLC
2001 Clarendon Blvd # 601 (22201-2954)
PHONE.............................703 276-2666
Charles McWilliams, *Principal*
EMP: 3
SALES (est): 216.5K **Privately Held**
WEB: www.oliveoilboom.com
SIC: **2079** Olive oil

(G-1087)
OMRON SCIENTIFIC TECH INC
5801 Lee Hwy (22207-1426)
PHONE.............................703 536-6070
Michael Ueltzen, *Principal*
EMP: 1 **Privately Held**
WEB: www.sti.com
SIC: **3823** Industrial instrmnts msrmnt dis-
play/control process variable
HQ: Omron Scientific Technologies Incorpo-
rated
6550 Dumbarton Cir
Fremont CA 94555
510 608-3400

(G-1088)
ONESO INC
Also Called: Transport 3pl
4001 9th St N Apt 1821 (22203-1971)
PHONE.............................704 560-6354
Nantambu Boniswa, *COO*
Renee Boniswa, *COO*
EMP: 2
SALES (est): 73K **Privately Held**
SIC: **3999** 4731 7389 Identification
badges & insignia; freight forwarding;

(G-1089)
OPENWATER SOFTWARE INC
4401 Fairfax Dr Ste 200 (22203-1622)
PHONE.............................202 765-0247
Timothy Spell, *CEO*
EMP: 25
SALES (est): 1.2MM **Privately Held**
WEB: www.getopenwater.com
SIC: **7372** Business oriented computer
software

(G-1090)
ORACLE AMERICA INC
2311 Wilson Blvd Fl 7&8 (22201-5417)
PHONE.............................703 310-3600
EMP: 5 **Publicly Held**
WEB: www.oracle.com
SIC: **7372** Prepackaged software
HQ: Oracle America, Inc.
500 Oracle Pkwy
Redwood City CA 94065
650 506-7000

(G-1091)
OSHKOSH CORPORATION
1300 17th St N Ste 1040 (22209-3801)
PHONE.............................703 525-8400
Jay Kinmitt, *Branch Mgr*
Jennifer Thompson, *Manager*
Laura Casillas, *Executive Asst*
EMP: 5
SALES (corp-wide): 6.8B **Publicly Held**
WEB: www.oshkoshcorp.com
SIC: **3713** Military motor vehicle assembly
PA: Oshkosh Corporation
1917 Four Wheel Dr
Oshkosh WI 54902
920 502-3009

(G-1092)
OUTL T INFOMARKET LLC
4320 Old Dominion Dr (22207-3247)
PHONE.............................703 927-1346
Lucien Zeigler, *CEO*
EMP: 1
SALES (est): 37.5K **Privately Held**
WEB: www.outl.it
SIC: **2741**

(G-1093)
OXIWEAR INC
1111 Arlington Blvd # 305 (22209-3245)
PHONE.............................571 212-7526
Shavini Fernando, *President*
EMP: 4

SALES (est): 148.4K **Privately Held**
SIC: **3495** Clock springs, precision

(G-1094)
PACS INC
Also Called: Power Alarm Control Services
1215 S Clark St Ste 105 (22202-4388)
PHONE.............................703 415-4411
Clifton M Hynson, *President*
Cliff Hynson, *Accounts Mgr*
EMP: 15
SQ FT: 1,500
SALES (est): 2.7MM **Privately Held**
WEB: www.pacs-inc.us
SIC: **3669** Fire alarm apparatus, electric

(G-1095)
PAE AVIATION TECHNICAL SVCS LLC
1320 N Courthouse Rd # 800
(22201-2501)
PHONE.............................703 717-6000
Donald Smith, *Human Resources*
Clinton Bickett, *Branch Mgr*
Tara Rush, *Senior Mgr*
EMP: 99
SALES (corp-wide): 332.3MM **Publicly Held**
WEB: www.pae.com
SIC: **3721** 4581 8711 8742 Airplanes,
fixed or rotary wing; aircraft servicing &
repairing; engineering services; manage-
ment consulting services; systems analy-
sis & engineering consulting services
HQ: Pae Aviation And Technical Services
Llc
1320 N Courthouse Rd # 700
Arlington VA 22201
856 866-2200

(G-1096)
PAE AVIATION TECHNICAL SVCS LLC
1320 N Courthouse Rd # 800
(22201-2501)
PHONE.............................864 458-3272
EMP: 1 **Privately Held**
SIC: **3721** 3812 Mfg Aircraft Mfg
Search/Navigation Equipment
HQ: Pae Aviation And Technical Services
Llc
1320 N Courthouse Rd # 800
Arlington VA 22201
856 866-2200

(G-1097)
PANTHEON SOFTWARE INC
2500 Wilson Blvd Ste 200 (22201-3834)
PHONE.............................703 387-4000
Mark Tobias, *President*
EMP: 15
SQ FT: 5,000
SALES (est): 1MM **Privately Held**
WEB: www.pantheonsoftware.com
SIC: **7372** 7371 7373 Prepackaged soft-
ware; computer software systems analy-
sis & design, custom; systems software
development services

(G-1098)
PAPAY HOLDCO LLC
200 N Glebe Rd Ofc 100 (22203-3755)
PHONE.............................703 226-3544
Bharet Malhotra, *Vice Pres*
Rupali Chatterjee, *Marketing Staff*
Reggie Aggarwall, *Branch Mgr*
Eric Glidden, *Manager*
Nathan Chin, *Analyst*
EMP: 40
SALES (corp-wide): 359.8MM **Privately Held**
WEB: www.cvent.com
SIC: **7372** Business oriented computer
software
PA: Papay Holdco, Llc
1765 Grnsboro Stn Pl Fl 7
Tysons Corner VA 22102
703 226-3500

(G-1099)
PARSONS CORPORATION
1911 Fort Myer Dr # 1100 (22209-1607)
PHONE.............................703 558-0036
Robert Sepucha, *CEO*
Bob Sepucha, *Branch Mgr*
EMP: 66 **Publicly Held**

WEB: www.parsons.com
SIC: 3568 Couplings, shaft: rigid, flexible, universal joint, etc.
PA: The Parsons Corporation
5875 Trinity Pkwy Ste 300
Centreville VA 20120
703 988-8500

(G-1100)
PARTLOW ASSOCIATES INC
5018 S Chesterfield Rd (22206-1021)
PHONE................................703 863-5695
John Partlow, Vice Pres
John M Partlow Jr, Exec Dir
EMP: 2
SALES (est): 72K Privately Held
SIC: 1389 Construction, repair & dismantling services

(G-1101)
PAYCOCK PRESS LLC
3819 13th St N (22201-4922)
PHONE................................703 525-9296
Richard Peabody, Principal
EMP: 2
SALES (est): 97.5K Privately Held
SIC: 2741 Miscellaneous publishing

(G-1102)
PC SANDS LLC
6144 12th Rd N (22205-1727)
PHONE................................703 534-6107
Patricia Sands, CEO
EMP: 1
SALES (est): 148.5K Privately Held
SIC: 3089 7389 Blow molded finished plastic products; business services

(G-1103)
PELLEGRINO AEROSPACE LLC
2639 Fort Scott Dr (22202-2256)
PHONE................................571 431-7011
Pellegrino Joseph, Administration
EMP: 2
SALES (est): 114.9K Privately Held
SIC: 3721 Aircraft

(G-1104)
PEREZ ARMANDO
1860 N Scott St Apt 237 (22209-1342)
PHONE................................202 716-5044
Armando Perez, Owner
EMP: 1
SALES (est): 40K Privately Held
SIC: 2711 7812 7383 Newspapers, publishing & printing; motion picture & video production; news correspondents, independent

(G-1105)
PERFECT PINK LLC
2116 S Lincoln St (22204-5333)
PHONE................................571 969-7465
Markies Hart Jr, Principal
EMP: 2
SALES (est): 126.8K Privately Held
SIC: 2051 5963 5149 7299 Bakery products, partially cooked (except frozen); party-plan merchandising; bakery products; party planning service; party supplies rental services

(G-1106)
PERFORMYARD INC
4201 Wilson Blvd (22203-4417)
PHONE................................703 870-3710
Ben Hastings, CEO
Joseph A Ryan, Sales Dir
Patricia Ferrara, Manager
Lauren Staley, Manager
Josh Buell, Software Dev
EMP: 6 EST: 2013
SALES (est): 399.7K Privately Held
WEB: www.performyard.com
SIC: 7372 Prepackaged software

(G-1107)
PERIFLAME LLC
1600 N Oak St Apt 629 (22209-2763)
P.O. Box 9704 (22219-1704)
PHONE................................888 996-3526
David Zeltser, CEO
Iurii Kryzhanovkyi, President
Iurii Kryzhanovskyi, Engineer
EMP: 10 EST: 2012

SALES (est): 119.5K Privately Held
WEB: www.periflame.com
SIC: 3519 7389 Jet propulsion engines;

(G-1108)
PERMIT PUSHERS
3540 N Valley St (22207-4445)
PHONE................................703 237-6461
Janice Marut, Owner
EMP: 2
SALES (est): 178.5K Privately Held
SIC: 3545 Pushers

(G-1109)
PERSIMMON STREET CERAMICS THAT
2332 N Tuckahoe St (22205-1948)
PHONE................................202 256-8238
Heather Lezla, President
EMP: 1
SALES (est): 117.8K Privately Held
SIC: 3269 5945 Art & ornamental ware, pottery; ceramics supplies

(G-1110)
PHASOR INC (PA)
1655 Fort Myer Dr (22209-3113)
PHONE................................202 256-2075
David Helfgott, Principal
EMP: 2
SALES (est): 257.6K Privately Held
WEB: www.phasorsolutions.com
SIC: 3663 Space satellite communications equipment

(G-1111)
PHOENIXAIRE LLC
Also Called: Airphx
1100 N Glebe Rd Ste 600 (22201-5767)
PHONE................................703 647-6546
William Pommerening, President
EMP: 2 EST: 2016
SALES (est): 118K Privately Held
SIC: 3564 Blowers & fans

(G-1112)
PLEASY LLC
2708 1st St S (22204-1819)
PHONE................................774 234-4299
Cynthia Smith,
EMP: 2
SALES (est): 56.5K Privately Held
SIC: 7372 Application computer software

(G-1113)
POLAR TRACTION INC
1801 N Tuckahoe St (22205-1815)
PHONE................................703 241-1958
Peter Bratic, President
Henry Lewin, President
EMP: 4
SALES (est): 49.5K Privately Held
WEB: www.polatrax.com
SIC: 3462 Chains, forged steel

(G-1114)
POLITICO LLC (DH)
1000 Wilson Blvd Ste 800 (22209-3901)
PHONE................................703 647-7999
Frederick Ryan Jr, President
Terrell Mizell, Partner
Brad Bosserman, Managing Dir
Simona Lightfoot, Managing Dir
Bryan Bender, Editor
EMP: 40
SALES (est): 7.1MM
SALES (corp-wide): 4.2B Publicly Held
WEB: www.politico.com
SIC: 2711 Newspapers, publishing & printing
HQ: Sinclair Television Of Capital District, Inc.
1000 Wilson Blvd Ste 2700
Arlington VA 22209
703 647-8700

(G-1115)
POLYISCYNURATE INSUL MFRS ASSN
3330 Washington Blvd # 200 (22201-4502)
PHONE................................703 224-2289
EMP: 1
SALES: 1.7MM Privately Held
WEB: www.polyiso.org
SIC: 3999 Manufacturing industries

(G-1116)
POPLICUS INCORPORATED
Also Called: Govini
1300 17th St N Ste 300 (22209-3811)
PHONE................................866 209-9100
Chris Taylor, CEO
Tara Dougherty, President
Eric Gillespie, Chairman
Joshua Amrani, Business Mgr
Charles Blanchet, Vice Pres
EMP: 39
SALES (est): 3.4MM Privately Held
WEB: www.govini.com
SIC: 7372 7375 Prepackaged software; information retrieval services

(G-1117)
POTOMAC FINE VIOLINS LLC
4620 22nd St N (22207-3503)
PHONE................................239 961-0398
Nicholas Messinger, Principal
EMP: 2
SALES (est): 88.8K Privately Held
SIC: 3931 Violins & parts

(G-1118)
POWER ANYWHERE LLC
4449 38th St N (22207-4551)
PHONE................................703 625-4115
David J Muchow, President
EMP: 4
SALES (est): 100K Privately Held
WEB: www.muchowlaw.com
SIC: 3585 Refrigeration & heating equipment

(G-1119)
PRECISION PRINTERS
1101 Wilson Blvd Lbby 3 (22209-2248)
PHONE................................703 525-5113
Frank Starks, Owner
EMP: 2
SALES (est): 227.5K Privately Held
WEB: www.precisionprinters.biz
SIC: 2752 Commercial printing, offset

(G-1120)
PRINCE GROUP OF VIRGINIA LLC (PA)
901 N Glebe Rd Ste 901 # 901 (22203-1854)
P.O. Box 808, Middleburg (20118-0808)
PHONE................................703 953-0577
Erik Prince,
EMP: 19
SALES (est): 150.3MM Privately Held
SIC: 3479 Coating of metals & formed products

(G-1121)
PROP LLC
1600 Wilson Blvd Ste 350 (22209-2596)
PHONE................................571 970-5031
Michael Peloquin,
EMP: 5
SQ FT: 400
SALES (est): 232.8K Privately Held
SIC: 7372 Application computer software

(G-1122)
PROTOCOL MEDIA LLC
1000 Wilson Blvd Ste 2700 (22209-3921)
PHONE................................703 647-8700
Robert Allbritton,
EMP: 15
SALES (est): 273.6K Privately Held
SIC: 2711 Newspapers: publishing only, not printed on site

(G-1123)
PURE MEDIA SIGN STUDIO LLC
2904 13th St S Apt 1 (22204-4828)
PHONE................................703 822-5468
Linh Ong,
EMP: 1
SALES (est): 154.1K Privately Held
WEB: www.puremediasigns.com
SIC: 3993 Signs & advertising specialties

(G-1124)
QMULOS PRODUCTS INC
1560 Wilson Blvd Ste 900 (22209-2409)
PHONE................................202 557-5162
Matthew Coose, CEO
Carlo Viqueira, Consultant

EMP: 1 EST: 2016
SQ FT: 1,500
SALES (est): 47.9K Privately Held
WEB: www.qmulos.com
SIC: 7372 Prepackaged software

(G-1125)
QUALCOMM INC
5225 Wilson Blvd (22205-1148)
PHONE................................858 587-1121
Scott Hastings, CIO
EMP: 2
SALES (est): 97.1K Privately Held
WEB: www.qualcomm.com
SIC: 3674 Integrated circuits, semiconductor networks, etc.

(G-1126)
QUEEN OF AMANNISA
320 23rd St S (22202-3738)
PHONE................................703 414-7888
EMP: 3
SALES (est): 104.4K Privately Held
WEB: www.queenamannisa.com
SIC: 2032 Chinese foods: packaged in cans, jars, etc.

(G-1127)
RACEPACKET INC
1300 Army Navy Dr Apt 209 (22202-2000)
P.O. Box 25094 (22202-8994)
PHONE................................703 486-1466
Robert Platt, President
Christopher Leyen, Opers Mgr
EMP: 3
SALES (est): 200.2K Privately Held
WEB: www.racepacket.com
SIC: 2741 Miscellaneous publishing

(G-1128)
RAPISCAN GOVERNMENT SVCS INC
2900 Crystal Dr Ste 910 (22202-3595)
PHONE................................571 227-6767
Pak Chin, CEO
▼ EMP: 5 EST: 2011
SALES (est): 709.4K Publicly Held
WEB: www.rapiscansystems.com
SIC: 3844 X-ray apparatus & tubes
HQ: Rapiscan Systems, Inc.
2805 Columbia St
Torrance CA 90503

(G-1129)
RAPISCAN SYSTEMS - AN O
1530 Wilson Blvd Ste 170 (22209-2447)
PHONE................................703 535-7848
EMP: 2
SALES (est): 104.2K Privately Held
SIC: 3829 Measuring & controlling devices

(G-1130)
RAVEN IND
2231 Crystal Dr (22202-3711)
PHONE................................703 414-3290
EMP: 3
SALES (est): 155K Privately Held
WEB: www.ravenind.com
SIC: 3081 Unsupported plastics film & sheet

(G-1131)
RAYTHEON COMPANY
2711 Richmond Hwy (22202-4015)
PHONE..............................:703 416-5800
Vince Smith, Manager
EMP: 10
SALES (corp-wide): 77B Publicly Held
WEB: www.rtx.com
SIC: 3812 Radar systems & equipment; sonar systems & equipment; fathometers; warfare counter-measure equipment
HQ: Raytheon Company
870 Winter St
Waltham MA 02451
781 522-3000

(G-1132)
RAYTHEON COMPANY
1100 Wilson Blvd Ste 2000 (22209-2249)
PHONE................................703 841-5700
Thomas M Culligan, President
Linda Dean, Principal
Sally Sullivan, Vice Pres
John Zolper, Vice Pres
Ryan Kelly, Human Res Mgr

EMP: 250
SALES (corp-wide): 77B **Publicly Held**
WEB: www.rtx.com
SIC: 3812 8743 8748 Sonar systems & equipment; public relations & publicity; business consulting
HQ: Raytheon Company
870 Winter St
Waltham MA 02451
781 522-3000

(G-1133)
RAYTHEON COMPANY
1235 S Clark St Ste 800 (22202-4365)
PHONE..............................703 413-1220
Vince Smith, *Manager*
Orlando De Castro, *Technology*
EMP: 45
SALES (corp-wide): 77B **Publicly Held**
WEB: www.rtx.com
SIC: 3812 8731 Sonar systems & equipment; commercial physical research
HQ: Raytheon Company
870 Winter St
Waltham MA 02451
781 522-3000

(G-1134)
RAYTHEON COMPANY
2361 Richmond Hwy # 1112 (22202-3876)
PHONE..............................703 418-0275
Richard Church, *Senior Engr*
Paul Mayr, *Senior Engr*
Jim Sheffield, *Manager*
EMP: 5
SQ FT: 4,000
SALES (corp-wide): 77B **Publicly Held**
WEB: www.rtx.com
SIC: 3812 Defense systems & equipment
HQ: Raytheon Company
870 Winter St
Waltham MA 02451
781 522-3000

(G-1135)
RAYTHEON COMPANY
2361 Richmond Hwy (22202-3876)
PHONE..............................703 418-0275
EMP: 2
SALES (corp-wide): 77B **Publicly Held**
WEB: www.rtx.com
SIC: 3812 3663 3761 Defense systems & equipment; space satellite communications equipment; airborne radio communications equipment; guided missiles & space vehicles, research & development; rockets, space & military, complete
HQ: Raytheon Company
870 Winter St
Waltham MA 02451
781 522-3000

(G-1136)
RAYTHEON COMPANY
1100 Wilson Blvd Ste 1600 (22209-3900)
PHONE..............................706 569-6600
Stanley Hughes, *Manager*
EMP: 2
SALES (corp-wide): 77B **Publicly Held**
WEB: www.rtx.com
SIC: 3812 Sonar systems & equipment
HQ: Raytheon Company
870 Winter St
Waltham MA 02451
781 522-3000

(G-1137)
RAYTHEON COMPANY
2461 S Clark St Ste 1100 (22202-3879)
PHONE..............................703 412-3742
Cyril Lepecha, *Program Mgr*
Portia Clark Chitty, *Manager*
EMP: 12
SALES (corp-wide): 77B **Publicly Held**
WEB: www.rtx.com
SIC: 3812 Sonar systems & equipment
HQ: Raytheon Company
870 Winter St
Waltham MA 02451
781 522-3000

(G-1138)
RAYTHEON COMPANY
2461 S Clark St (22202-3863)
PHONE..............................703 419-1400
Donna McCullough, *Manager*

EMP: 1000
SALES (corp-wide): 77B **Publicly Held**
WEB: www.rtx.com
SIC: 3674 3761 Semiconductors & related devices; guided missiles & space vehicles
HQ: Raytheon Company
870 Winter St
Waltham MA 02451
781 522-3000

(G-1139)
RAYTHEON COMPANY
2450 Crystal Dr Ste 700 (22202-3891)
PHONE..............................703 872-3400
Thomas Harvac, *Branch Mgr*
EMP: 10
SALES (corp-wide): 77B **Publicly Held**
WEB: www.rtx.com
SIC: 3812 3663 3761 3231 Defense systems & equipment; space satellite communications equipment; airborne radio communications equipment; guided missiles & space vehicles, research & development; rockets, space & military, complete; scientific & technical glassware: from purchased glass; integrated circuits, semiconductor networks, etc.; semiconductor circuit networks
HQ: Raytheon Company
870 Winter St
Waltham MA 02451
781 522-3000

(G-1140)
RAYTHEON COMPANY
1100 Wilson Blvd Ste 1600 (22209-3900)
PHONE..............................540 658-3172
Colin Schoettlander, *Branch Mgr*
EMP: 132
SALES (corp-wide): 77B **Publicly Held**
WEB: www.rtx.com
SIC: 3812 Defense systems & equipment
HQ: Raytheon Company
870 Winter St
Waltham MA 02451
781 522-3000

(G-1141)
RD STUCCO LLC
1409 S Buchanan St (22204-3411)
PHONE..............................703 926-2322
EMP: 2
SALES (est): 139.4K **Privately Held**
SIC: 3299 Stucco

(G-1142)
READY FOR HILLARY
1611 N Kent St (22209-2128)
PHONE..............................703 405-0433
Hillary Francis, *Principal*
EMP: 3
SALES (est): 121.7K **Privately Held**
SIC: 2711 Newspapers

(G-1143)
READY SET SIGN LLC
4319 36th St S (22206-1809)
PHONE..............................703 820-0022
Martin R Noretsky,
EMP: 1
SALES (est): 82K **Privately Held**
WEB: www.readysetsign.com
SIC: 3999 5961 Education aids, devices & supplies; educational supplies & equipment, mail order

(G-1144)
RECAP LLC
2116 S Kent St (22202-2126)
PHONE..............................703 521-3406
Capetanakis John, *Administration*
EMP: 2
SALES (est): 148.2K **Privately Held**
SIC: 3599 Machine shop, jobbing & repair

(G-1145)
RED APPLE PRODUCTIONS LLC
974 Patrick Henry Dr (22205-1458)
PHONE..............................703 237-1034
Manuel Vasquez, *Principal*
EMP: 2 EST: 2016
SALES (est): 90.9K **Privately Held**
SIC: 3571 Personal computers (microcomputers)

(G-1146)
REID INDUSTRIES LLC (PA)
1405 S Fern St (22202-2810)
PHONE..............................703 920-6199
Matthew D Reid, *Administration*
EMP: 6
SALES (est): 1MM **Privately Held**
SIC: 3999 Manufacturing industries

(G-1147)
REPUBLICANPAC.COM
5155 37th St N (22207-1824)
PHONE..............................703 241-8422
EMP: 3 EST: 2010
SALES (est): 116.2K **Privately Held**
WEB: www.republicanpac.com
SIC: 2711 Newspapers, publishing & printing

(G-1148)
RIYAN INDUSTRIES
4745 Lee Hwy (22207-2529)
PHONE..............................703 525-6132
Nasseer Hakimi, *Owner*
EMP: 3
SALES (est): 950K **Privately Held**
SIC: 2911 Petroleum refining

(G-1149)
RL LOGISTICS LLC
818 N Quincy St Apt 501 (22203-2080)
PHONE..............................703 209-3100
Guilbert Villarroel,
EMP: 3
SALES (est): 138.9K **Privately Held**
SIC: 3537 Trucks, tractors, loaders, carriers & similar equipment

(G-1150)
ROD FISHINFIDDLER CO
300 N Garfield St (22201-1231)
PHONE..............................703 517-0496
EMP: 1
SALES (est): 56K **Privately Held**
SIC: 3949 Mfg Sporting/Athletic Goods

(G-1151)
ROSETTA STONE INC (PA)
1621 N Kent St Ste 1200 (22209-2131)
PHONE..............................703 387-5800
A John Hass III, *Ch of Bd*
Nicholas Gaehde, *President*
Mathew Hulett, *President*
Eric Nenon, *Engineer*
Thomas Pierno, *CFO*
EMP: 33
SQ FT: 13,000
SALES (est): 182.7MM **Privately Held**
WEB: www.rosettastone.com
SIC: 7372 4813 7371 Educational computer software; ; computer software development & applications

(G-1152)
ROUTEMARKET INC
2200 N Westmoreland St (22213-1044)
PHONE..............................703 829-7087
Caleb Royer, *CEO*
EMP: 2
SALES (est): 56.5K **Privately Held**
SIC: 7372 Application computer software

(G-1153)
ROWLEY GROUP INC
Also Called: Minuteman Press
4001 9th St N Ste 102 (22203-1900)
PHONE..............................703 522-1944
David K Rowley, *President*
EMP: 9
SALES (est): 557K **Privately Held**
WEB: www.therowleygroup.com
SIC: 2752 Commercial printing, lithographic

(G-1154)
SACYR ENVIRONMENT USA LLC
3330 Washington Blvd # 400 (22201-4502)
PHONE..............................202 361-4568
Laurenia Augustin, *Director*
EMP: 6
SALES (est): 810.1K
SALES (corp-wide): 77.1MM **Privately Held**
SIC: 3822 Auto controls regulating residntl & coml environmt & applncs

PA: Sacyr Sa.
Calle Condesa De Venadito 7
Madrid 28027
902 196-360

(G-1155)
SAGA MEADERY LLC
200 N Trenton St Apt 2 (22203-2951)
PHONE..............................914 343-0394
Kevin Poplaski, *Principal*
EMP: 3
SALES (est): 180.8K **Privately Held**
WEB: www.sagameadery.com
SIC: 2084 Wines

(G-1156)
SAILFISH LLC
851 N Glebe Rd Apt 1305 (22203-4157)
PHONE..............................203 570-3553
AVI Siegel, *Principal*
Seth Clark, *Principal*
Andrew Eiche, *Principal*
Levi Lansing, *Principal*
EMP: 4
SALES (est): 176.3K **Privately Held**
SIC: 7372 7389 Application computer software;

(G-1157)
SANDBOX FAMILY COMM INC
Also Called: Sandboxx
2231 Crystal Dr Ste 325 (22202-3968)
PHONE..............................910 381-7346
Sam Meek, *CEO*
Joe Marshall, *Manager*
EMP: 35
SQ FT: 10,000
SALES (est): 2.3MM **Privately Held**
WEB: www.sandboxx.us
SIC: 2741 Miscellaneous publishing

(G-1158)
SANDUJA STRATEGIES
2100 Lee Hwy Apt 308 (22201-3557)
PHONE..............................202 826-9804
Utsav Sanduja, *Principal*
EMP: 7 EST: 2018
SALES (est): 94.4K **Privately Held**
SIC: 2711 Newspapers, publishing & printing

(G-1159)
SAS FEDERAL LLC
1530 Wilson Blvd Ste 800 (22209-2418)
PHONE..............................571 227-7000
Karen Terrell, *President*
EMP: 5
SALES (est): 305.1K
SALES (corp-wide): 1.9B **Privately Held**
WEB: www.sas.com
SIC: 7372 Application computer software
PA: Sas Institute Inc.
100 Sas Campus Dr
Cary NC 27513
919 677-8000

(G-1160)
SAS INSTITUTE INC
1530 Wilson Blvd Ste 800 (22209-2418)
PHONE..............................571 227-7000
Gloria Rodriguez, *Owner*
EMP: 23
SALES (corp-wide): 1.9B **Privately Held**
WEB: www.sas.com
SIC: 7372 Application computer software
PA: Sas Institute Inc.
100 Sas Campus Dr
Cary NC 27513
919 677-8000

(G-1161)
SASHAY COMMUNICATIONS LLC
2200 Wilson Blvd 102-329 (22201-3397)
PHONE..............................703 304-2862
Joy Butler, *Mng Member*
EMP: 1
SALES (est): 55.8K **Privately Held**
WEB: www.sashaycommunications.com
SIC: 2731 Book publishing

(G-1162)
SCHAFER GOVERNMENT SVCS LLC
3830 9th St N Apt 708w (22203-5825)
PHONE.................................202 594-4124
John Schafer, *Principal*
EMP: 3
SALES (corp-wide): 318MM **Privately Held**
WEB: www.schafercorp.com
SIC: 7372 Prepackaged software
HQ: Schafer Government Services, Llc
101 Billerica Ave
North Billerica MA 01862
978 256-2070

(G-1163)
SERIOUS GAMES INTERACTIVE INC
2767 N Wakefield St (22207-4130)
PHONE.................................703 624-0842
Kirk Taylor, *CEO*
Greg Bryant, *CFO*
EMP: 35
SALES (est): 1.2MM **Privately Held**
SIC: 7372 Educational computer software

(G-1164)
SHAMROCK ARLINGTON LLC
3211 Washington Blvd (22201-4415)
PHONE.................................703 528-7676
EMP: 4
SALES (est): 221K **Privately Held**
WEB: www.arlnow.com
SIC: 2711 Newspapers, publishing & printing

(G-1165)
SHIFTONE
3300 Fairfax Dr Ste 201 (22201-4400)
PHONE.................................415 806-5006
Kam Desai, *CEO*
Ashish Gambhir, *Administration*
EMP: 2 EST: 2015
SQ FT: 100
SALES (est): 117.7K **Privately Held**
WEB: www.shiftone.com
SIC: 7372 Business oriented computer software

(G-1166)
SIERRA NEVADA CORPORATION
2231 Crystal Dr Ste 1113 (22202-3727)
PHONE.................................703 412-1502
Mac Dorsey, *Principal*
Anthony Jarrett, *Business Mgr*
Carla Gray, *Technical Staff*
Michael Block, *Planning*
Scott Hasken,
EMP: 257
SALES (corp-wide): 1.9B **Privately Held**
WEB: www.sncorp.com
SIC: 3812 Defense systems & equipment
PA: Sierra Nevada Corporation
444 Salomon Cir
Sparks NV 89434
775 331-0222

(G-1167)
SIGARCHI MEDIA
1530 12th St N Apt 201 (22209-3653)
PHONE.................................571 296-5021
EMP: 2
SALES: 30K **Privately Held**
SIC: 2836 Mfg Biological Products

(G-1168)
SILVER WINGS INC
6032 20th St N (22205-3404)
PHONE.................................703 533-3244
EMP: 1
SALES (est): 110K **Privately Held**
SIC: 3721 Mfg Aircraft

(G-1169)
SKELLY PUBLISHING INC
3812 27th St N (22207-5020)
PHONE.................................888 753-5591
Sheila Kelly, *Principal*
EMP: 4 EST: 2011
SALES (est): 296.5K **Privately Held**
WEB: www.skellyskills.com
SIC: 2741 Miscellaneous publishing

(G-1170)
SKM AEROSPACE LLC
1600 S Eads St (22202-2926)
PHONE.................................703 217-4221
EMP: 2 EST: 2014
SALES (est): 152.4K **Privately Held**
SIC: 3721 Aircraft

(G-1171)
SKYCITY
1850 Columbia Pike # 231 (22204-6221)
PHONE.................................240 467-6270
Ali Salman, *President*
EMP: 1
SALES (est): 50K **Privately Held**
SIC: 3089 Holders: paper towel, grocery bag, etc.: plastic

(G-1172)
SOLAR SEA WATER LLC
1021 Arlington Blvd (22209-3926)
PHONE.................................215 452-9992
Qi Wang, *CEO*
Max Wang, *Principal*
EMP: 1
SALES (corp-wide): 139.5K **Privately Held**
SIC: 3589 Water treatment equipment, industrial
PA: Solar Sea Water, Llc
28 Ponderosa Dr
Holland PA 18966
215 452-9992

(G-1173)
SPARTAN SHOWER SHOE LLC
1200 N Veitch St Apt 1421 (22201-5837)
PHONE.................................540 623-6625
Jack Bonura, *CEO*
EMP: 1
SALES (est): 45K **Privately Held**
WEB: www.spartanshowershoe.com
SIC: 2392 Slipcovers: made of fabric, plastic etc.

(G-1174)
STANDARD REGISTER INC
1110 N Glebe Rd 750 (22201-4795)
PHONE.................................703 516-4014
EMP: 14
SALES (corp-wide): 4.5B **Privately Held**
SIC: 2761 Mfg Manifold Business Forms
HQ: Standard Register, Inc.
600 Albany St
Dayton OH
937 221-1000

(G-1175)
STARDOG UNION
Also Called: Complexible
2101 Wilson Blvd Ste 800 (22201-3060)
PHONE.................................202 408-8770
Michael Sachse, *CEO*
Lauren Taylor, *Vice Pres*
William Seymour, *Manager*
Kendall Clark, *CTO*
Virginia Hewitt, *Director*
EMP: 38 EST: 2012
SALES (est): 214.7K **Privately Held**
WEB: www.stardog.com
SIC: 7372 Business oriented computer software

(G-1176)
STEPHENSON LITHOGRAPH INC
4014 38th Pl N (22207-4602)
PHONE.................................703 241-0806
Sandra Stephenson, *President*
EMP: 1
SALES (est): 79.6K **Privately Held**
SIC: 2752 Commercial printing, offset

(G-1177)
STS INTERNATIONAL INCORPORATED
1225 S Clark St Ste 1300 (22202-4383)
PHONE.................................703 575-5180
Jagjit Chahal, *Vice Pres*
Vicki Compton, *Branch Mgr*
Joseph Marzen, *Manager*
Mackenzie Kelley, *Technical Staff*
EMP: 20

SALES (corp-wide): 5.7MM **Privately Held**
WEB: www.stsint.com
SIC: 3677 Transformers power supply, electronic type
PA: Sts International, Incorporated
204 Sand Mine Rd
Berkeley Springs WV 25411
304 258-2700

(G-1178)
SUNGUARD MID ATLANTIC LLC
4252 35th S (22206-1802)
PHONE.................................703 820-8118
Leonard Funk, *Mng Member*
Marilyn G McKewon,
EMP: 2 EST: 1998
SALES (est): 500K **Privately Held**
WEB: www.sunguardma.com
SIC: 2394 Shades, canvas: made from purchased materials

(G-1179)
SWAROVSKI NORTH AMERICA LTD
1100 S Hayes St (22202-4907)
PHONE.................................703 418-6665
Janes Bowamn, *Branch Mgr*
EMP: 3
SALES (corp-wide): 4.7B **Privately Held**
WEB: www.swarovski.com
SIC: 3961 Costume jewelry
HQ: Swarovski North America Limited
1 Kenney Dr
Cranston RI 02920
401 463-6400

(G-1180)
SWEET LIME STUDIOS LLC
2035 N Taylor St (22207-3121)
PHONE.................................703 312-0034
Michelle Hayes, *Principal*
EMP: 2 EST: 2010
SALES (est): 99K **Privately Held**
SIC: 3274 Lime

(G-1181)
TAX MANAGEMENT INC
Bna Software
1801 S Bell St Ste G1 (22202-4506)
PHONE.................................703 341-3000
Michael T Smith, *General Mgr*
Holly Flater, *Manager*
Dimitri Naritsin, *Software Engr*
Michael Eisenstein, *Legal Staff*
EMP: 70
SALES (corp-wide): 1.8B **Privately Held**
WEB: www.bloombergindustry.com
SIC: 2741 Guides: publishing only, not printed on site
HQ: Tax Management Inc.
1250 23rd St Nw
Washington DC

(G-1182)
TECHNICA SOFTWARE LLC
1021 Arlington Blvd # 718 (22209-3926)
PHONE.................................703 371-7134
Jack Dailey, *Principal*
EMP: 2
SALES (est): 118.2K **Privately Held**
SIC: 7372 Prepackaged software

(G-1183)
TECHNOLOGY NEWS AND LITERATURE
4521 41st St N (22207-2936)
PHONE.................................202 380-5425
Alan Kotok, *COO*
EMP: 2
SALES (est): 76.3K **Privately Held**
WEB: www.technewslit.com
SIC: 2741 Miscellaneous publishing

(G-1184)
TEKNOSTRATA INC
4601 Fairfax Dr Ste 1200 (22203-1559)
PHONE.................................877 983-5667
Mahidhar Suguru, *President*
Anup Kumar, *Director*
EMP: 3
SALES (est): 71.1K **Privately Held**
SIC: 7372 Prepackaged software

(G-1185)
TELE CONTROLS INC
1101 Wilson Blvd Fl 6 (22209-2281)
PHONE.................................571 490-4500
Markus Kurt Stelzmann, *CEO*
Daniel Kroepfl, *Principal*
EMP: 8
SALES (est): 808.9K **Privately Held**
SIC: 3714 Motor vehicle parts & accessories

(G-1186)
TELESAT US SERVICES LLC
1100 Wilson Blvd Ste 2900 (22209-3900)
PHONE.................................571 559-1500
EMP: 4
SALES (est): 117.6K
SALES (corp-wide): 313MM **Privately Held**
SIC: 3663 Space satellite communications equipment
HQ: Telesat Canada
160 Elgin St Suite 2100
Ottawa ON K2P 2
613 748-0123

(G-1187)
TERESA C SHANKMAN
Also Called: Real Time Solutions
4721 38th Pl N (22207-2914)
PHONE.................................703 533-9322
Teresa C Shankman, *Owner*
EMP: 1
SALES (est): 71.7K **Privately Held**
WEB: www.fleetwood-assoc.com
SIC: 7372 Word processing computer software

(G-1188)
TETRA TECHNOLOGIES INC
4601 Fairfax Dr Ste 600 (22203-1546)
PHONE.................................703 387-2100
Dean White, *Principal*
EMP: 23
SALES (corp-wide): 1B **Publicly Held**
WEB: www.tetratec.com
SIC: 2819 Brine
PA: Tetra Technologies, Inc.
24955 Interstate 45
The Woodlands TX 77380
281 367-1983

(G-1189)
TETRAVISTA LLC
5847 20th St N (22205-3306)
PHONE.................................703 606-6509
EMP: 5
SALES (est): 350K **Privately Held**
SIC: 7372 Prepackaged Software Services

(G-1190)
THALES USA DEFENSE & SEC INC
2733 Crystal Dr Ste 1250 (22202-3588)
PHONE.................................571 255-4600
Robert Sprigg, *President*
Phyllis Andes, *Admin Sec*
EMP: 2
SALES (est): 27.1K
SALES (corp-wide): 279.3MM **Privately Held**
WEB: www.defense.gov
SIC: 3812 Search & navigation equipment
HQ: Thales Usa, Inc.
2733 Crystal Dr
Arlington VA 22202
703 413-6029

(G-1191)
THOMAS C ALBRO II
822 S Taylor St (22204-1462)
PHONE.................................703 892-6738
Thomas C Albro II, *Principal*
EMP: 2
SALES (est): 30K **Privately Held**
SIC: 2789 Bookbinding & related work

(G-1192)
TINCTURE DISTILLERS LLC
5521 27th St N (22207-1773)
PHONE.................................443 370-2037
EMP: 3 EST: 2018
SALES (est): 75.4K **Privately Held**
SIC: 2086 2099 Carbonated beverages, nonalcoholic: bottled & canned; vinegar

▲ = Import ▼=Export
◆ =Import/Export

(G-1193)
TOSSD SALAD GROUP LLC
1615 S Oakland St (22204-5033)
PHONE..................................703 521-0646
EMP: 3
SALES (est): 112.8K **Privately Held**
SIC: 2099 Mfg Food Preparations

(G-1194)
TRAN DU
1201 S Eads St Apt 1413 (22202-2843)
PHONE..................................512 470-1794
Du Tran, *Owner*
EMP: 1
SALES (est): 94.1K **Privately Held**
SIC: 2711 Newspapers

(G-1195)
TRANSPORT TOPICS PUBG GROUP
950 N Glebe Rd Ste 210 (22203-4181)
PHONE..................................703 838-1770
Bill Graves, *President*
Lorrie Grant, *Editor*
Gary Kicinski, *Editor*
Fran Lysiak, *Editor*
Glen Kedzie, *Vice Pres*
EMP: 1 EST: 2008
SALES (est): 94.6K **Privately Held**
WEB: www.ttnews.com
SIC: 2741 Miscellaneous publishing

(G-1196)
TREMOLO SECURITY INC
4201 Wilson Blvd 110-204 (22203-4417)
PHONE..................................703 844-2727
Marc Boorshtein, *Chief Engr*
EMP: 4
SALES (est): 204.3K **Privately Held**
WEB: www.tremolosecurity.com
SIC: 7372 7389 Business oriented computer software;

(G-1197)
TRIPLE THREAT INDUSTRIES LLC
1221 S Eads St (22202-4729)
PHONE..................................703 413-7919
EMP: 2 EST: 2009
SALES (est): 88K **Privately Held**
SIC: 3999 Mfg Misc Products

(G-1198)
TRUE RELIGION APPAREL INC
1100 S Hayes St (22202-4907)
PHONE..................................323 266-3072
EMP: 3
SALES (corp-wide): 350MM **Privately Held**
WEB: www.truereligion.com
SIC: 2369 Jeans: girls', children's & infants'
HQ: True Religion Apparel, Inc.
500 W 190th St Ste 300
Gardena CA 90248
323 266-3072

(G-1199)
TRUEWAY INC
3033 Wilson Blvd Ste 700 (22201-3868)
PHONE..................................703 527-9248
Ercan Bilen, *President*
EMP: 5
SALES (est): 340.2K **Privately Held**
WEB: www.truewayinc.com
SIC: 3949 Exercising cycles

(G-1200)
TSG CONCEPTS INC
1200 N Veitch St Apt 825 (22201-6005)
PHONE..................................877 777-5734
Shauntanu Tiwari, *President*
EMP: 6 EST: 2013
SALES (est): 1MM **Privately Held**
SIC: 3993 7336 7312 8412 Signs & advertising specialties; commercial art & graphic design; outdoor advertising services; museums & art galleries; facilities support services

(G-1201)
TTG GROUP LLC
2111 Richmond Hwy (22202-3137)
PHONE..................................540 454-7235
Terrence T Griffin,
EMP: 1

SALES (est): 53.3K **Privately Held**
SIC: 2759 Publication printing

(G-1202)
UNSHRINKIT INC
1405 S Fern St Ste 517 (22202-2810)
PHONE..................................804 519-7019
Desiree Stolar,
EMP: 1
SALES (est): 62.7K **Privately Held**
SIC: 2899 5169 Chemical preparations; chemicals & allied products

(G-1203)
UPKEEPR CORP
2776 S Arlington Mill Dr U (22206-3402)
PHONE..................................703 718-6304
Todd Girvin, *President*
EMP: 1
SALES (est): 200K **Privately Held**
SIC: 7372 Application computer software

(G-1204)
URBAN WORKS PUBLICITY
3056 S Glebe Rd (22206-2769)
PHONE..................................703 625-6981
EMP: 2
SALES (est): 84.5K **Privately Held**
SIC: 2741 Miscellaneous publishing

(G-1205)
URENCO USA INC (DH)
1560 Wilson Blvd Ste 300 (22209-2453)
P.O. Box 1789, Eunice NM (88231-1789)
PHONE..................................575 394-4646
Kirk Schnoebelen, *President*
Jay Laughlin, *Opers Staff*
Wayne Bluedorn, *Electrical Engi*
Leila Castillo, *Treasurer*
Gerry Schnell, *Manager*
EMP: 6
SALES (est): 835.3K
SALES (corp-wide): 2B **Privately Held**
WEB: www.urenco.com
SIC: 2819 Nuclear fuels, uranium slug (radioactive)
HQ: Urenco Investments Inc
2600 Virginia Ave Nw # 610
Washington DC 20037
202 337-6644

(G-1206)
USGRI/BITCOIN PRESS RELEASE
1111 Army Navy Dr # 1130 (22202-2053)
PHONE..................................202 316-3222
Jeffrey Taylor, *Managing Prtnr*
Jay Taylor, *Manager*
EMP: 2
SALES (est): 86.4K **Privately Held**
WEB: www.usgri.com
SIC: 2741 Miscellaneous publishing

(G-1207)
VAN ADDO DORN LLC
509 S Taylor St (22204-1446)
PHONE..................................703 615-4769
Colleen Baribeau, *Administration*
EMP: 5
SALES (est): 535.6K **Privately Held**
SIC: 3411 Metal cans

(G-1208)
VENTURA DEFENSE US CORP
1001 19th St N Ste 1200 (22209-1731)
PHONE..................................571 527-1360
Michael D Barbero, *Ch of Bd*
EMP: 1
SALES (est): 49.1K **Privately Held**
SIC: 3812 Defense systems & equipment

(G-1209)
VENTURE GLOBL CLCSIEU PASS LLC
1001 19th St N Ste 1500 (22209-1727)
PHONE..................................202 759-6740
Robert Pender, *CEO*
EMP: 1
SALES (est): 222.8K **Privately Held**
WEB: www.ventureglobalng.com
SIC: 1321 Natural gas liquids

(G-1210)
VICTIMOLOGY INC
2333 N Vernon St (22207-4036)
PHONE..................................703 528-3387
Emillo Viano, *President*
Sheri Icenhower, *Admin Sec*
EMP: 2
SALES (est): 85.1K **Privately Held**
SIC: 2741 Telephone & other directory publishing

(G-1211)
VILLALVA INC (PA)
Also Called: Latin Tempo Distributors
239 N Glebe Rd (22203-3705)
PHONE..................................703 527-0091
Tony Villalva, *President*
EMP: 6
SALES (est): 833.3K **Privately Held**
SIC: 3613 Panel & distribution boards & other related apparatus

(G-1212)
VIRCHOW BIOTECH INC
1655 Fort Myer Dr Ste 700 (22209-3199)
PHONE..................................615 549-5999
T Murali Krishna Reddy, *Exec Dir*
EMP: 2
SALES (est): 74.4K **Privately Held**
SIC: 2834 Pharmaceutical preparations

(G-1213)
VIRGINIA DISTILLERY CO LLC
6100 35th St N (22213-1402)
PHONE..................................703 869-0083
EMP: 2 EST: 2009
SALES (est): 86.4K **Privately Held**
SIC: 2085 Distilled & blended liquors

(G-1214)
VITASPAN CORPORATION
Also Called: Biotivia Arlington Co
2503 N Harrison St 311 (22207)
PHONE..................................866 459-2773
Courtenay Betz, *President*
Daniel Kube, *COO*
Michael Betz, *Vice Pres*
EMP: 5
SALES (est): 378.5K **Privately Held**
WEB: www.biotivia.com
SIC: 2834 Pharmaceutical preparations

(G-1215)
VOELL CUSTOM KITCHENS INC
4788 Lee Hwy (22207-2528)
PHONE..................................703 528-1776
Dennis Day, *President*
EMP: 4
SQ FT: 2,500
SALES (est): 518.8K **Privately Held**
WEB: www.voellcustomkitchens.com
SIC: 2434 Wood kitchen cabinets

(G-1216)
WASHINGTNPOST NWSWEEK INTRCTIV
1560 Wilson Blvd Ste 800 (22209-2453)
PHONE..................................703 469-2500
EMP: 2
SALES (est): 62.9K **Privately Held**
SIC: 2711 Newspapers

(G-1217)
WELCOME TO BEAULIEU VINEYARD
2345 Crystal Dr Ste 910 (22202-4817)
PHONE..................................707 967-5233
Marilee Wilson, *Human Res Mgr*
EMP: 2
SALES (est): 64.3K **Privately Held**
SIC: 2084 Wines

(G-1218)
WILDERWORK PBC
1101 Wilson Blvd Fl 6 (22209-2281)
PHONE..................................202 285-9455
Graziella Jackson, *President*
EMP: 13
SALES (est): 324.9K **Privately Held**
SIC: 2741

(G-1219)
WILLIAM KEYSER
309 N Edison St (22203-1220)
PHONE..................................703 243-8777

William Keyser, *Owner*
EMP: 1
SALES (est): 10K **Privately Held**
SIC: 2499 3548 Decorative wood & woodwork; welding wire, bare & coated

(G-1220)
WILLU LLC
251 18th St S Ste 704 (22202-3541)
PHONE..................................844 809-4558
Deepak Prakash, *Vice Pres*
Steven Castellano, *Director*
EMP: 14
SALES (est): 318K **Privately Held**
WEB: www.willu.com
SIC: 7372 Application computer software

(G-1221)
WOODYS WOODWORKING INC
3132 N Nelson St (22207-5318)
PHONE..................................703 525-2030
Edward Woody, *President*
EMP: 1
SALES (est): 112.3K **Privately Held**
SIC: 2434 Wood kitchen cabinets

(G-1222)
WORLDWIDE AGENCY LLC
4601 Fairfax Dr Ste 1200 (22203-1559)
PHONE..................................202 888-5895
Timothy Sumer,
EMP: 1
SALES (est): 37.5K **Privately Held**
SIC: 2741

(G-1223)
WRITLAB LLC
3033 Wilson Blvd E-206 (22201-3866)
PHONE..................................703 996-9162
Sarah OH,
EMP: 1 EST: 2016
SALES (est): 35K **Privately Held**
SIC: 7372 Application computer software

Aroda
Madison County

(G-1224)
COUNTRYSIDE BAKERY
Also Called: Troyer, Robert
3615 Elly Rd (22709-1026)
PHONE..................................540 948-7888
Robert Troyer, *Owner*
EMP: 1
SALES (est): 56K **Privately Held**
SIC: 2051 Bakery: wholesale or wholesale/retail combined

(G-1225)
DAVID KIPPS
2022 Repton Mill Rd (22709-0905)
PHONE..................................540 948-4024
David Kipps, *CEO*
EMP: 1
SALES (est): 46.5K **Privately Held**
SIC: 2741 Miscellaneous publishing

(G-1226)
TRIPLE D SALES CO INC
976 Beautiful Run Rd (22709-0937)
P.O. Box 269, Madison (22727-0269)
PHONE..................................540 672-5821
Richard H Davis, *CEO*
Virginia L Smith, *President*
EMP: 3
SALES (est): 330K **Privately Held**
SIC: 2842 5084 Cleaning or polishing preparations; cleaning equipment, high pressure, sand or steam

Arrington
Nelson County

(G-1227)
BLUE MTN BRREL HSE ORGNIC BRWR
495 Cooperative Way (22922-3305)
PHONE..................................434 263-4002
Chad Dean, *Principal*
Aldridge Ryan, *VP Sales*
EMP: 20

SALES (corp-wide): 1.8MM **Privately Held**
WEB: www.bluemountainbrewery.com
SIC: **2082** 5181 Beer (alcoholic beverage); beer & other fermented malt liquors
PA: Blue Mountain Barrel House And Organic Brewery, Llc
9585 Critzers Shop Rd
Afton VA 22920
540 456-8020

(G-1228)
BOXLEY MATERIALS COMPANY
Also Called: Piney River Quarry
739 Warrick Barn Rd (22922-6008)
P.O. Box 13527, Roanoke (24035-3527)
PHONE..............................540 777-7600
Abney S Boxley III, *Branch Mgr*
EMP: 12
SALES (corp-wide): 2.2B **Publicly Held**
WEB: www.boxley.com
SIC: **1422** Crushed & broken limestone
HQ: Boxley Materials Company
15418 W Lynchburg Slem Tp
Blue Ridge VA 24064
540 777-7600

(G-1229)
BOXLEY MATERIALS COMPANY
Also Called: Piney River Plant
739 Warrick Barn Rd (22922-6008)
P.O. Box 13527, Roanoke (24035-3527)
PHONE..............................540 777-7600
Jeb Burton, *President*
EMP: 5
SALES (corp-wide): 2.2B **Publicly Held**
WEB: www.boxley.com
SIC: **2951** Asphalt paving mixtures & blocks
HQ: Boxley Materials Company
15418 W Lynchburg Slem Tp
Blue Ridge VA 24064
540 777-7600

(G-1230)
LOST INDUSTRIES LLC
170 Lost Ln (22922-2493)
PHONE..............................434 221-5698
Ezra Hitzeman, *Principal*
EMP: 2
SALES (est): 138.5K **Privately Held**
WEB: www.lostindustries.net
SIC: **3999** Manufacturing industries

(G-1231)
U S SIDECARS INC
Also Called: California Sidecar
100 Motorcycle Run (22922-3301)
PHONE..............................434 263-6500
John Gresh, *President*
Arden Gresh, *Corp Secy*
Todd Wightman, *Engineer*
Franklin Cassidy, *Director*
Janet Oliver, *Executive*
▲ EMP: 72
SQ FT: 40,000
SALES (est): 14.1MM **Privately Held**
WEB: www.californiasidecar.com
SIC: **3751** Motorcycles & related parts; motorcycle accessories

Arvonia
Buckingham County

(G-1232)
BUCKINGHAM SLATE COMPANY LLC
715 Arvon Rd (23004-2000)
P.O. Box 8 (23004-0008)
PHONE..............................434 581-1131
Mark W Claud, *Mng Member*
EMP: 48
SALES (est): 4MM
SALES (corp-wide): 2.2B **Publicly Held**
WEB: www.buckinghamslate.com
SIC: **1411** Dimension stone
HQ: Boxley Materials Company
15418 W Lynchburg Slem Tp
Blue Ridge VA 24064
540 777-7600

(G-1233)
HUNTS CREEK SLATE SIGNS LLC
247 Boxwood Dr (23004-2019)
P.O. Box 176 (23004-0176)
PHONE..............................434 581-1687
Kathryn Davis, *Principal*
EMP: 2
SALES (est): 117.7K **Privately Held**
SIC: **3993** Signs & advertising specialties

(G-1234)
TOMS WELDING
11045 Bridgeport Rd (23004-2003)
PHONE..............................434 989-1553
John T Noble, *Owner*
EMP: 1
SALES (est): 40.8K **Privately Held**
SIC: **7692** Welding repair

Ashburn
Loudoun County

(G-1235)
A&F CCUSTON CABINETRY BUILT
21806 Petworth Ct (20147-6727)
PHONE..............................703 598-7686
EMP: 2
SALES (est): 102K **Privately Held**
SIC: **2434** Wood kitchen cabinets

(G-1236)
ACACIA ACQUISITIONS LLC (HQ)
21445 Beaumeade Cir (20147-6036)
PHONE..............................703 554-1600
Gavin Long, *CEO*
William King, *Admin Sec*
EMP: 5 EST: 2017
SALES (est): 230MM
SALES (corp-wide): 255.6MM **Privately Held**
SIC: **3571** 5045 Personal computers (microcomputers); computers & accessories, personal & home entertainment
PA: Acacia Investment Holdings Llc
1850 Towers Crescent Plz # 500
Tysons VA 22182
703 554-1600

(G-1237)
ACHARYA BROTHERS COMPUTING
Also Called: Incubatize
43611 Picketts Corner Ter (20148-3149)
PHONE..............................703 729-3035
Darshna Joshi, *President*
Parag Acharya, *Principal*
EMP: 2 EST: 2010
SALES (est): 126.4K **Privately Held**
SIC: **7372** Application computer software

(G-1238)
ACOUSTCAL DRYWALL SLUTIONS LLC
43730 Piedmont Hunt Ter (20148-3171)
PHONE..............................703 722-6637
Augusto Noriega,
EMP: 6
SALES (est): 750K **Privately Held**
WEB: www.adsolutionsllc.net
SIC: **1389** Construction, repair & dismantling services

(G-1239)
AGARAM TECHNOLOGIES INC
20130 Lakeview Center Plz (20147-5904)
PHONE..............................703 297-8591
Mukunth Venkatesan, *CEO*
EMP: 70
SALES (est): 2MM **Privately Held**
WEB: www.agaramtech.com
SIC: **7372** 7379 7373 Application computer software; computer related consulting services; systems software development services

(G-1240)
AIRBUS GROUP SUPPLY & SVCS INC
21780 Filigree Ct (20147-6216)
PHONE..............................703 858-2235
Sean O Keefe, *CEO*
Piere Clerc-Renaud, *President*
Samuel Adcock, *Senior VP*
Michael Cosentino, *Senior VP*
Guy Hicks, *Senior VP*
EMP: 13 EST: 2001
SQ FT: 10,000
SALES (est): 505.2K
SALES (corp-wide): 77.9B **Privately Held**
SIC: **3721** Aircraft
HQ: Airbus U.S. Space & Defense, Inc.
2550 Wasser Ter Ste 9000
Herndon VA 20171
703 466-5600

(G-1241)
ANDREW CORP
19700 Janelia Farm Blvd (20147-2405)
PHONE..............................703 726-5900
Ariful Hannan, *Senior Engr*
Dave Collier, *Manager*
Denise Finney, *Manager*
EMP: 2
SALES (est): 88.3K **Privately Held**
WEB: www.comsearch.com
SIC: **3663** Radio & TV communications equipment

(G-1242)
ARETECH LLC (PA)
21720 Red Rum Dr Ste 187 (20147-5882)
PHONE..............................571 292-8889
Brendan Gilmore, *Engineer*
Karen Miyamoto, *Marketing Staff*
Joseph M Hidler PHD, *Mng Member*
EMP: 6
SQ FT: 6,000
SALES (est): 967.2K **Privately Held**
WEB: www.aretechllc.com
SIC: **3845** Electromedical equipment

(G-1243)
ASHLEY CLARK DEFENSE LLC
43732 Clemens Ter (20147-4724)
PHONE..............................703 867-6665
EMP: 1
SALES (est): 73.9K **Privately Held**
SIC: **3812** Defense systems & equipment

(G-1244)
ASTRONAUTICS CORP OF AMERICA
44735 Audubon Sq Apt 522 (20147-6279)
PHONE..............................571 707-8705
Keith McCartney, *Manager*
EMP: 2
SALES (est): 86K **Privately Held**
SIC: **3728** Aircraft parts & equipment

(G-1245)
BARNS & VINEYARDS LLC
43257 Preston Ct (20147-5307)
PHONE..............................703 801-2719
EMP: 2 EST: 2014
SALES (est): 92.1K **Privately Held**
SIC: **2084** Wines

(G-1246)
BIOHOUSE PUBLISHING GROUP INC
42783 Macauley Pl (20148-4158)
PHONE..............................703 858-1738
Ravi Sunkara, *Principal*
EMP: 2
SALES (est): 89.7K **Privately Held**
WEB: www.biohouse.us
SIC: **2741** Miscellaneous publishing

(G-1247)
BJD TEL-COMM LLC
20610 Crescent Pointe Pl (20147-3878)
PHONE..............................703 858-2931
Joan Dunn, *CEO*
EMP: 1
SALES (est): 1.5MM **Privately Held**
WEB: www.bjd-tel.com
SIC: **3728** Aircraft parts & equipment

(G-1248)
BLACKSTONE DEFENSE SVCS CORP
20254 Northpark Dr (20147-5560)
PHONE..............................571 598-2714
Betti Harvey, *President*
EMP: 14
SALES (est): 554.9K **Privately Held**
WEB: www.blackstonedefense.com
SIC: **3812** Defense systems & equipment

(G-1249)
BLUE BEACON LLC
44214 Bristow Cir (20147-3308)
PHONE..............................202 643-9043
Bradley Nestico, *Principal*
EMP: 2
SALES (est): 75.2K **Privately Held**
SIC: **7372** Business oriented computer software

(G-1250)
BOBBLEHOUSE LLC
20341 Bowfonds St (20147-7404)
PHONE..............................703 582-6797
Brad Wheedleton, *Administration*
EMP: 2
SALES (est): 102.6K **Privately Held**
WEB: www.bobblehouse.com
SIC: **3999** Manufacturing industries

(G-1251)
BOEHRINGER INGELHEIM CORP
44521 Hastings Dr (20147-6038)
PHONE..............................800 243-0127
EMP: 6
SALES (corp-wide): 21B **Privately Held**
WEB: www.boehringer-ingelheim.com
SIC: **2834** 6221 Pharmaceutical preparations; commodity contracts brokers, dealers
HQ: Boehringer Ingelheim Corporation
900 Ridgebury Rd
Ridgefield CT 06877
203 798-9988

(G-1252)
BRIGHT SOLUTIONS INC
44260 Marchand Ln (20147-6473)
PHONE..............................703 926-7451
AMI Shah, *CEO*
Jatin Shah, *President*
EMP: 2
SALES (est): 139.1K **Privately Held**
WEB: www.brightsolutionsusa.com
SIC: **7372** Application computer software

(G-1253)
CABAIDE LLC
19775 Belmont Executive P (20147-7600)
PHONE..............................571 262-2710
Dean Daisy, *Principal*
EMP: 5 EST: 2017
SALES (est): 128.6K **Privately Held**
WEB: www.daisylaw.com
SIC: **7372** Business oriented computer software

(G-1254)
CIS SECURE COMPUTING INC
21050 Ashburn Crossing Dr (20147-2981)
PHONE..............................703 996-0500
Bill Strang, *CEO*
John Borg, *Opers Mgr*
David Sawyer, *Opers Staff*
Paul Stepantschenko, *QA Dir*
Bill Hargreaves, *Engineer*
EMP: 28
SQ FT: 40,000
SALES (est): 22.3MM **Privately Held**
WEB: www.cissecure.com
SIC: **3571** Electronic computers

(G-1255)
CLARIOS
Also Called: Johnson Controls
22001 Loudoun County Pkwy (20147-6105)
PHONE..............................703 886-3961
Dave Howard, *Branch Mgr*
EMP: 94 **Privately Held**
WEB: www.johnsoncontrols.com
SIC: **2531** Seats, automobile

HQ: Johnson Controls, Inc.
5757 N Green Bay Ave
Milwaukee WI 53209
800 382-2804

(G-1256)
CNL SOFTWARE INC
19775 Belmont Executive P # 420
(20147-7607)
PHONE..............................317 522-0313
Fredrik Arfwidsson, *Principal*
EMP: 8
SALES (est): 649.6K
SALES (corp-wide): 4.7MM **Privately Held**
WEB: www.cnlsoftware.com
SIC: 7372 Prepackaged software
PA: Cnl Software Limited
Building 11
Camberley GU15
127 658-7400

(G-1257)
COMMSCOPE TECHNOLOGIES LLC
19700 Janelia Farm Blvd (20147-2405)
PHONE..............................703 726-5500
Andrew Beck, *Research*
Tom Sheehe, *Engineer*
Tammy Toma, *Human Resources*
Kathleen Mulhern, *Sales Staff*
Iris Inbar, *Manager*
EMP: 200 **Publicly Held**
WEB: www.commscope.com
SIC: 3663 Radio & TV communications equipment
HQ: Commscope Technologies Llc
4 Westbrook Corporate Ctr
Westchester IL 60154
708 236-6600

(G-1258)
CORRAVOO WOODWORKS LLC
20273 Rosedale Ct (20147-3317)
PHONE..............................703 966-0929
Chris Campbell, *Principal*
EMP: 2
SALES (est): 85.2K **Privately Held**
SIC: 2431 Millwork

(G-1259)
CRAFT OF BREWING
21140 Ashburn Crossing Dr (20147-6191)
PHONE..............................703 687-3932
EMP: 2
SALES (est): 62.3K **Privately Held**
SIC: 2082 Malt beverages

(G-1260)
CRIDERS FINISHING INC
21641 Beaumeade Cir # 317 (20147-6027)
PHONE..............................703 661-6520
Timothy Pearson, *General Mgr*
Judy Crider, *Mng Member*
EMP: 8
SALES (est): 950K **Privately Held**
WEB: www.cridersfinishing.com
SIC: 2499 2431 Decorative wood & woodwork; woodwork, interior & ornamental

(G-1261)
CRITICAL POWER GROUP INC
21760 Beaumeade Cir # 190 (20147-6220)
PHONE..............................703 443-1717
Shelly Illig, *CEO*
John Younts, *President*
Mahdiyar Akhavan, *Engineer*
EMP: 5
SALES (est): 1.2MM **Privately Held**
WEB: www.criticalpowergroup.com
SIC: 3612 3613 3621 Transformers, except electric; switchgear & switchboard apparatus; motors & generators

(G-1262)
CROSS CLOUD SOLUTIONS INC
21769 Oakville Ter (20147-6961)
PHONE..............................703 724-7526
EMP: 2 **EST:** 2019
SALES (est): 118.6K **Privately Held**
SIC: 7372 Prepackaged software

(G-1263)
CROWN SUPREME INDUSTRIES LLC
43240 Baltusrol Ter (20147-5244)
PHONE..............................703 729-1482
Shirley Steele, *Principal*
EMP: 2
SALES (est): 111K **Privately Held**
SIC: 3999 Manufacturing industries

(G-1264)
CRYPTO INDUSTRIES LLC
23507 Bentley Grove Pl (20148-1729)
PHONE..............................703 729-5059
Matthew Devost, *Owner*
EMP: 1
SALES (est): 39.6K **Privately Held**
SIC: 3999 Manufacturing industries

(G-1265)
CURTISS-WRIGHT CONTROLS INC
20130 Lakeview Center Plz # 200 (20147-5905)
PHONE..............................703 779-7800
Kristen Walsh, *Human Resources*
Lynn Patterson, *Manager*
EMP: 25 **Publicly Held**
WEB: www.cwcontrols.com
SIC: 3728 Aircraft assemblies, subassemblies & parts
HQ: Curtiss-Wright Controls, Inc.
15801 Brixham Hill Ave # 200
Charlotte NC 28277
704 869-4600

(G-1266)
CURTISS-WRIGHT CORPORATION
Also Called: Curtiss Wright Control
20130 Lakeview Center Plz # 200 (20147-5904)
PHONE..............................703 779-7800
Ginger McClellan, *Mfg Mgr*
Jeffrey Peiffer, *Technical Mgr*
Ted Droppa, *Engineer*
Jean Kim, *Senior Engr*
Elias Fahel, *Design Engr*
EMP: 12 **Publicly Held**
WEB: www.curtisswright.com
SIC: 3491 Industrial valves
PA: Curtiss-Wright Corporation
130 Harbour Place Dr # 300
Davidson NC 28036
704 869-4600

(G-1267)
D-STAR ENGINEERING CORPORATION (PA)
Also Called: D-Star Aerospace
22805 Watson Heights Cir (20148-7307)
PHONE..............................203 925-7630
S Paul Dev, *President*
EMP: 20
SQ FT: 12,000
SALES (est): 2.5MM **Privately Held**
WEB: www.dstarengineering.com
SIC: 3728 8711 Research & dev by manuf., aircraft parts & auxiliary equip; engineering services

(G-1268)
DAILY SPLAT LLC
20310 Mustoe Pl (20147-3304)
PHONE..............................703 729-0842
EMP: 3
SALES (est): 109K **Privately Held**
SIC: 2711 Newspapers-Publishing/Printing

(G-1269)
DARK WARRIOR GROUP LLC
21888 Brickshire Cir (20148-8024)
PHONE..............................757 289-6451
EMP: 1
SALES (est): 66.7K **Privately Held**
SIC: 3952 Boards, drawing, artists'

(G-1270)
DAVID BENNETT
43730 Partlow Rd (20147-4717)
PHONE..............................703 858-4669
David Bennett, *Owner*
EMP: 2

SALES (est): 111.7K **Privately Held**
SIC: 3931 Guitars & parts, electric & non-electric

(G-1271)
DIGITIZED RISK LLC
21786 Findon Ct (20147-6708)
PHONE..............................703 662-3510
David Puangmaly, *CEO*
EMP: 1
SALES (est): 58.1K **Privately Held**
SIC: 7372 7373 7375 7378 Prepackaged software; computer integrated systems design; information retrieval services; computer maintenance & repair; national security

(G-1272)
DP FACILITIES INC
Also Called: Mineral Gap
19775 Belmont Executive P (20147-7604)
P.O. Box 3268, Wise (24293-3268)
PHONE..............................866 589-6125
Mark Gerard, *President*
EMP: 20
SALES (est): 33.4K **Privately Held**
WEB: www.dpfacilities.com
SIC: 7372 Prepackaged software

(G-1273)
DULCET INDUSTRIES LLC
43367 Chokeberry Sq (20147-4000)
P.O. Box 386 (20146-0386)
PHONE..............................571 758-3191
Mahadi De Jesus, *Principal*
EMP: 2 **EST:** 2015
SALES (est): 87.2K **Privately Held**
SIC: 3999 Manufacturing industries

(G-1274)
DUPONT THREADING LLC
43149 Laughing Quail Ct (20148-7125)
PHONE..............................703 734-1425
EMP: 2 **EST:** 2018
SALES (est): 74.4K **Privately Held**
SIC: 2879 Agricultural chemicals

(G-1275)
EARTHEN CANDLE WORKS LLC
23490 Bluemont Chapel Ter (20148-6300)
PHONE..............................540 270-5938
Max McLaughlin, *Principal*
EMP: 1
SALES (est): 39.6K **Privately Held**
SIC: 3999 Candles

(G-1276)
ENVIRNMNTAL SOLUTIONS INTL INC
Also Called: Esi Total Fuel Management
20099 Ashbrook Pl Ste 170 (20147-3369)
PHONE..............................703 263-7600
Alexander C Marcus, *President*
Andrew Holmberg, *Engineer*
Charlotte M Marcus, *Treasurer*
Charlotte Marcus, *Treasurer*
EMP: 12
SQ FT: 5,000
SALES (est): 3.3MM **Privately Held**
WEB: www.fuelmanagement.com
SIC: 3823 8748 8711 3561 Industrial instrmnts msrmnt display/control process variable; environmental consultant; consulting engineer; pumps & pumping equipment; centrifugal purifiers; refinery, chemical processing & similar machinery

(G-1277)
EVENFLOW TECHNOLOGIES INC
43895 Camellia St (20147-5662)
PHONE..............................703 625-2628
Madhu Iyengar, *President*
EMP: 1
SALES (est): 72K **Privately Held**
WEB: www.evenflow.us
SIC: 2099 Packaged combination products: pasta, rice & potato

(G-1278)
FAIRFAX METALS LLC
22795 Milltown Farm Ct (20148-6754)
PHONE..............................571 594-1937
Meena Roopdaska,
EMP: 1

SALES (est): 127K **Privately Held**
SIC: 3444 Sheet metalwork

(G-1279)
FEBROCOM LLC
22457 Terra Rosa Pl (20148-7351)
PHONE..............................703 349-6316
Edward Fenley, *Principal*
EMP: 2 **EST:** 2011
SALES (est): 103.7K **Privately Held**
SIC: 3999 7389 Manufacturing industries;

(G-1280)
FLAGS OF VALOR LLC
44200 Waxpool Rd Ste 137 (20147-5950)
PHONE..............................703 729-8640
Julie Graham, *Pub Rel Staff*
Brian Steorts, *Mng Member*
EMP: 25 **EST:** 2015
SALES (est): 2.7MM **Privately Held**
WEB: www.flagsofvalor.com
SIC: 2499 Signboards, wood

(G-1281)
FLIP SWITCH EVENTS LLC
23294 Virginia Rae Ct (20148-8063)
PHONE..............................703 677-0119
EMP: 3
SALES (est): 189.5K **Privately Held**
SIC: 3679 Electronic switches

(G-1282)
FREEMAN AEROTECH LLC
43975 Lords Valley Ter (20147-3201)
PHONE..............................703 303-0102
Dennis Freeman,
EMP: 1
SALES (est): 100K **Privately Held**
SIC: 3812 Search & navigation equipment

(G-1283)
FUTURE TENSE LLC
Also Called: Calypso Labs
42582 Glass Ln (20148-4484)
PHONE..............................703 994-7814
Tyler Jon Sweatt, *Managing Dir*
EMP: 2
SALES (est): 45.4K
SALES (corp-wide): 974.2K **Privately Held**
SIC: 7372 Prepackaged software
PA: Calypso Ai Corp
2955 Campus Dr Ste 110
San Mateo CA 94403
818 624-3214

(G-1284)
GATR TECHNOLOGIES INC
21580 Beaumeade Cir # 220 (20147-6007)
PHONE..............................571 258-5020
Mike Barthlow, *Branch Mgr*
EMP: 75
SALES (corp-wide): 1.4B **Publicly Held**
WEB: www.gatr.com
SIC: 3663 Radio & TV communications equipment
HQ: Gatr Technologies, Inc.
330 Bob Heath Dr Nw
Huntsville AL 35806
256 382-1334

(G-1285)
GENERAL DYNAMICS CORPORATION
20766 Silverthistle Ct (20147-4426)
PHONE..............................703 729-3106
John Gilmore, *Principal*
EMP: 4
SALES (corp-wide): 39.3B **Publicly Held**
WEB: www.generaldynamics.com
SIC: 7372 Prepackaged software
PA: General Dynamics Corporation
11011 Sunset Hills Rd
Reston VA 20190
703 876-3000

(G-1286)
GIANT PHARMACY
43330 Junction Plz (20147-3406)
PHONE..............................703 723-2161
EMP: 2
SALES (est): 74.4K **Privately Held**
SIC: 2834 Pharmaceutical preparations

(G-1287)
GLOVESTIX LLC
21861 Parsells Ridge Ct (20148-4114)
PHONE..............................703 909-5146
Krista Koons Woods, *Administration*
EMP: 4
SALES (est): 260K **Privately Held**
WEB: www.glovestix.com
SIC: 3949 Sporting & athletic goods

(G-1288)
HADRIAN INC
43849 Tattinger Ter (20148-3126)
PHONE..............................703 724-7760
Harry Martin III, *Principal*
Gregory P Walker, *Director*
EMP: 1
SALES (est): 73K **Privately Held**
SIC: 3571 Electronic computers

(G-1289)
HERITAGE TREASURES LLC
44710 Cape Ct Ste 120 (20147-6231)
PHONE..............................571 442-8027
Audrey Seabrooks,
EMP: 4
SALES (est): 383.5K **Privately Held**
WEB: www.htprintables.com
SIC: 2759 Screen printing

(G-1290)
HERNLEY WOODWORKS
42649 Cochrans Lock Dr (20148-4103)
PHONE..............................571 419-4889
Bryan Hernley, *Principal*
EMP: 1
SALES (est): 54.1K **Privately Held**
SIC: 2431 Millwork

(G-1291)
HIS SIGN LLC
44050 Ashbrn Shpg Plz (20147-7915)
PHONE..............................877 886-8879
EMP: 1
SALES (est): 50.6K **Privately Held**
WEB: www.hissign.com
SIC: 3993 Signs & advertising specialties

(G-1292)
HORIZON GLOBAL PARTNERS LLC
20097 Old Line Ter (20147-7491)
PHONE..............................703 597-2351
William Brucato, *Vice Pres*
Noth Epta, *Mng Member*
Dan Cospantini, *Mng Member*
EMP: 15
SALES (est): 500K **Privately Held**
WEB: www.hglobalpartners.com
SIC: 3571 Computers, digital, analog or hybrid

(G-1293)
HOW HIGH PUBLISHING LLC
44383 Oakmont Manor Sq (20147-3877)
PHONE..............................703 729-9589
Linda Hiserman, *Principal*
EMP: 2
SALES (est): 90.2K **Privately Held**
SIC: 2741 Miscellaneous publishing

(G-1294)
ILANTECH INC
43413 Wheatlands Chase Ct (20148-6738)
PHONE..............................571 226-7042
Mytheenkunju Irshad, *Principal*
EMP: 3
SALES (est): 87.7K **Privately Held**
SIC: 3565 Packaging machinery

(G-1295)
IMPROVEBUILD LLC
20672 Meadowthrash Ct (20147-4444)
P.O. Box 887 (20146-0887)
PHONE..............................703 372-2646
Ricardo Reyes, *Mng Member*
Irene Reyes,
EMP: 2
SALES (est): 139.2K **Privately Held**
WEB: www.improvebuild.net
SIC: 7372 Business oriented computer software

(G-1296)
INSIGNIA TECHNOLOGY SVCS LLC
45150 Russell Branch Pkwy # 300 (20147-2902)
PHONE..............................757 591-2111
Steve Ikirt, *CEO*
Michael Nickerson, *COO*
Willer Williams, *COO*
Heather Grochowski, *Controller*
Jennifer Bryant, *Office Mgr*
EMP: 100
SQ FT: 2,374
SALES (est): 23.5MM **Privately Held**
WEB: www.insigniatechnology.com
SIC: 3669 7371 8741 7373 Intercommunication systems, electric; computer software development; management services; systems engineering, computer related

(G-1297)
INTENSE CLEANING INC
Also Called: Looney's Clean Tile and Grout
43264 Gatwick Sq (20147-4436)
PHONE..............................703 999-1933
Michael Looney, *President*
EMP: 2
SALES (est): 300K **Privately Held**
WEB: www.looneystileandgrout.com
SIC: 2842 Specialty cleaning, polishes & sanitation goods

(G-1298)
ITECHNOLOGIES INC
44037 Lords Valley Ter (20147-3202)
PHONE..............................703 723-5141
Reza Hedayati, *Owner*
EMP: 2
SALES (est): 92.6K **Privately Held**
SIC: 7372 Prepackaged software

(G-1299)
JMD JMD LLC
Also Called: Jmd Fairfax Co
44697 Malden Pl (20147-6509)
PHONE..............................703 945-0099
Nitin Chopra, *Mng Member*
Danny Kelly, *Manager*
EMP: 2 EST: 2007
SALES (est): 371.8K **Privately Held**
SIC: 3442 Moldings & trim, except automobile: metal

(G-1300)
KACE SQUARE LLC
43352 Old Ryan Rd (20148-6773)
PHONE..............................703 723-3679
Kiran Chinivar, *Principal*
EMP: 2
SALES (est): 125K **Privately Held**
SIC: 3993 Signs & advertising specialties

(G-1301)
KATAM GROUP LLC
41783 Prairie Aster Ct (20148-1743)
PHONE..............................703 927-6268
Matthew Wakabayashi, *CEO*
Susan Wakabayashi, *COO*
EMP: 1 EST: 2015
SALES (est): 96.9K **Privately Held**
WEB: www.katamgroup.com
SIC: 3691 Batteries, rechargeable

(G-1302)
KEEVA LLC
20258 Ordinary Pl (20147-3313)
PHONE..............................240 766-5382
Krishna Murthy,
EMP: 2
SALES (est): 91K **Privately Held**
SIC: 7372 Prepackaged software

(G-1303)
KIND CUPCAKES
22070 Auction Barn Dr (20148-4110)
PHONE..............................703 723-6167
EMP: 2
SALES (est): 84.2K **Privately Held**
SIC: 2051 Mfg Bread/Related Products

(G-1304)
L-3 UNMANNED SYSTEMS INC
44611 Guilford Dr Ste 125 (20147-6069)
PHONE..............................703 889-8640
Douglas Boone, *Vice Pres*
Roxy Felio, *Human Res Mgr*
EMP: 70
SALES (corp-wide): 6.8B **Publicly Held**
WEB: www.l3t.com
SIC: 3812 Search & navigation equipment
HQ: L-3 Unmanned Systems, Inc.
6900 K Ave
Plano TX 75074
469 568-2376

(G-1305)
L3 TECHNOLOGIES INC
Also Called: L-3 Mustang Technology
44611 Guilford Dr Ste 125 (20147-6069)
PHONE..............................703 889-8640
Julie Cohen, *HR Admin*
Lewis Showers, *Contract Mgr*
EMP: 220
SALES (corp-wide): 6.8B **Publicly Held**
WEB: www.l3t.com
SIC: 3663 Telemetering equipment, electronic
HQ: L3 Technologies, Inc.
600 3rd Ave Fl 34
New York NY 10016
212 697-1111

(G-1306)
LENNAH PRESS LLC
20103 Prairie Dunes Ter (20147-3190)
PHONE..............................571 235-4809
EMP: 2
SALES (est): 106.3K **Privately Held**
WEB: www.lennahpress.com
SIC: 2741 Miscellaneous publishing

(G-1307)
LINLEY PRESS LLC
43799 Michener Dr (20147-5806)
PHONE..............................561 245-1511
EMP: 1
SALES (est): 41.3K **Privately Held**
SIC: 2741 Miscellaneous publishing

(G-1308)
LITTLE GREEN MEN INC
Also Called: Aggressive Audio
20675 Exchange St (20147-3235)
PHONE..............................301 203-8702
Jonathan Bailey, *Owner*
Andrea Bailey, *Opers Mgr*
EMP: 3
SALES (est): 157.4K **Privately Held**
SIC: 3663 Radio & TV communications equipment

(G-1309)
LOCKHEED MARTIN CORPORATION
43881 Devin Shafron Dr # 150 (20147-7346)
PHONE..............................703 724-7552
Micheal Chambers, *Branch Mgr*
Robert Estelow, *Network Enginr*
EMP: 435 **Publicly Held**
WEB: www.lockheedmartin.com
SIC: 3812 Search & navigation equipment
PA: Lockheed Martin Corporation
6801 Rockledge Dr
Bethesda MD 20817

(G-1310)
LOCO CRAZY GOOD INC
21108 Stonecrop Pl (20147-5456)
PHONE..............................703 401-4058
Nathaniel Grant, *President*
EMP: 2
SALES (est): 73.4K **Privately Held**
SIC: 3411 Food & beverage containers

(G-1311)
LOONY MOOSE PUBLISHING LLC
42993 Nashua St (20147-7451)
PHONE..............................703 727-3309
John L Hickman, *Administration*
EMP: 2 EST: 2010
SALES (est): 90.1K **Privately Held**
WEB: www.loonymoosepublishing.com
SIC: 2741 Miscellaneous publishing

(G-1312)
LULUVERSE
Also Called: Luluverse Media
43353 Greyswallow Ter (20147-3758)
PHONE..............................202 821-9726
Leigh Boone, *Co-Owner*
EMP: 1
SALES (est): 32.7K **Privately Held**
WEB: www.hibiscus1.org
SIC: 7372 Educational computer software

(G-1313)
MACH278 LLC
44715 Prentice Dr # 792 (20146-8001)
PHONE..............................716 860-2889
Lawrence Colby,
EMP: 1
SALES (est): 72.2K **Privately Held**
WEB: www.mach278.com
SIC: 2211 8062 3842 Bandages, gauzes & surgical fabrics, cotton; general medical & surgical hospitals; dressings, surgical; gauze, surgical; drapes, surgical (cotton)

(G-1314)
MAGNUS AIRCRAFT INCORPORATED
20130 Lkview Ctr Plz Ste (20147)
PHONE..............................830 998-7270
EMP: 2
SALES (est): 165.1K **Privately Held**
SIC: 3721 Aircraft

(G-1315)
MARBLE MAX
21760 Beaumeade Cir # 135 (20147-6219)
PHONE..............................703 723-0071
Max Marble, *Principal*
EMP: 2
SALES (est): 172.8K **Privately Held**
WEB: www.marblemax.biz
SIC: 2541 Counter & sink tops

(G-1316)
MARDEN PRESS PRINTVERTISE INC
21662 Steatite Ct (20147-6787)
PHONE..............................571 295-5322
EMP: 1
SALES (est): 41.3K **Privately Held**
SIC: 2741 Miscellaneous publishing

(G-1317)
MICROTUDE LLC
21673 Liverpool St (20147-4537)
PHONE..............................703 581-7991
Jaskaran Jamwal, *President*
EMP: 1
SALES (est): 90.5K **Privately Held**
SIC: 3571 7389 Electronic computers;

(G-1318)
MONTAUK SYSTEMS CORPORATION
21113 Crocus Ter (20147-5466)
PHONE..............................954 695-6819
John J Dimattei, *President*
EMP: 1 **Privately Held**
WEB: www.montauksystems.com
SIC: 3571 Personal computers (microcomputers)

(G-1319)
NCH HOME SOLUTIONS LLC
42949 Heatherton Ct (20147-4014)
PHONE..............................703 723-4077
EMP: 2 EST: 2007
SALES (est): 211.6K **Privately Held**
SIC: 2842 Mfg Polish/Sanitation Goods

(G-1320)
NEDIA ENTERPRISES INC
Also Called: Nedia Home
44675 Cape Ct Ste 120 (20147-6230)
PHONE..............................571 223-0200
Siby Pothen, *CEO*
Susha Pothen, *President*
Christina Ridings, *Opers Staff*
Lovely Benny, *Business Anlyst*
◆ EMP: 25
SQ FT: 2,000

▲ = Import ▼=Export
◆ =Import/Export

SALES (est): 4.9MM **Privately Held**
WEB: www.nedia.com
SIC: 2273 5039 0181 2299 Door mats: paper, grass, reed, coir, sisal, jute, rags, etc.; carpets: twisted paper, grass, reed, coir, sisal, jute, etc.; floor coverings, textile fiber; soil erosion control fabrics; mats, preseeded: soil erosion, growing of; fabrics: linen, jute, hemp, ramie

(G-1321)
NEXT GENERATION MGT CORP (PA)
44715 Prentice Dr # 973 (20146-8001)
P.O. Box 1575, Annandale (22003-9550)
PHONE....................................703 372-1282
Darryl Reed, *Ch of Bd*
EMP: 3
SALES (est): 1.3K **Publicly Held**
WEB: www.nextgenmanagementcorp.com
SIC: 1382 2833 Oil & gas exploration services; medicinals & botanicals

(G-1322)
NORTH MEDIA LLC
44800 Milestone Sq # 303 (20147-4238)
PHONE....................................202 277-4933
Lorenzo North,
EMP: 2
SALES (est): 74.4K **Privately Held**
SIC: 2836 Culture media

(G-1323)
NUGEN MOBILITY INC
44645 Guilford Dr Ste 201 (20147-6020)
PHONE....................................703 858-0036
EMP: 2
SALES (est): 127.4K **Privately Held**
SIC: 3625 Relays & industrial controls

(G-1324)
OCTOLEAF LLC
20941 Lohengrin Ct (20147-4737)
PHONE....................................202 579-7279
Anju Debnath,
EMP: 2
SALES (est): 120K **Privately Held**
WEB: www.octoleaf.com
SIC: 7372 Application computer software

(G-1325)
PEP LABS LLC
20634 Duxbury Ter (20147-3250)
PHONE....................................202 669-2562
Dahyu Patel, *CEO*
EMP: 2
SALES (est): 5K **Privately Held**
SIC: 7372 7389 Application computer software;

(G-1326)
PERSPECTA SVCS & SOLUTIONS INC
19980 Highland Vista Dr (20147-5997)
PHONE....................................781 684-4000
EMP: 5 **Privately Held**
WEB: www.qinetiq-na.com
SIC: 3812 8731 Defense systems & equipment; engineering laboratory, except testing
HQ: Perspecta Services & Solutions Inc.
350 2nd Ave Bldg 1
Waltham MA 02451
781 684-4000

(G-1327)
POINTERRA US INC
42905 Secretariat Ct (20147-4472)
PHONE....................................571 528-8799
Randal Rhoads, *President*
Ian Olson, *Director*
EMP: 30
SALES (est): 330.9K **Privately Held**
SIC: 7372 Prepackaged software

(G-1328)
POTOMAC INTL ADVISORS LLC (PA)
44319 Ladiesburg Pl (20147-2864)
PHONE....................................202 460-9001
Athar Shaikh, *CEO*
Tariq Dilawar, *Director*
Amer Farooq, *Director*
Arshad Kazmi, *Director*
Mahomed Khan, *Director*

EMP: 2
SALES (est): 348.7K **Privately Held**
SIC: 1389 8742 6082 9411 Oil consultants; management consulting services; foreign trade & international banking institutions; administration of educational programs

(G-1329)
RABBIT SOFTWARE LLC
21414 Fairhunt Dr (20148-4328)
PHONE....................................703 939-1708
Jason Babbitt, *Principal*
EMP: 2 **EST:** 2016
SALES (est): 56.5K **Privately Held**
SIC: 7372 Prepackaged software

(G-1330)
REFIBOT INC
43401 Barnstead Dr (20148-6891)
PHONE....................................703 989-2232
Peter Bishay, *CEO*
EMP: 6
SALES (est): 251.5K **Privately Held**
SIC: 3699 Security control equipment & systems

(G-1331)
SANSKEY LLC
43087 Weatherwood Dr (20147-4450)
P.O. Box 188 (20146-0188)
PHONE....................................703 454-0703
Andrew Reisteter, *Mng Member*
EMP: 1
SALES (est): 10K **Privately Held**
WEB: www.sanskey.com
SIC: 3694 Automotive electrical equipment

(G-1332)
SCAN INDUSTRIES LLC
44017 Lords Valley Ter (20147-3202)
PHONE....................................360 320-8244
Scott Hussar, *Principal*
Ann Marie Hussar, *Principal*
EMP: 2
SALES (est): 118K **Privately Held**
SIC: 2441 2452 2431 2521 Boxes, wood; prefabricated buildings, wood; interior & ornamental woodwork & trim; stools, office: wood; industrial tools; chemical bulk station & terminal

(G-1333)
SEMANTICSOLUTIONS LLC
42897 Nashua St (20147-3638)
PHONE....................................703 980-7395
Jt Taylor, *Principal*
EMP: 4
SALES (est): 160.2K **Privately Held**
SIC: 7372 Prepackaged software

(G-1334)
SOFTWARE ENGINEERING SOLUTIONS
43141 Tall Pines Ct (20147-6601)
PHONE....................................703 842-1823
Alvaro Ruiz, *Principal*
Mary Martinez, *Principal*
EMP: 3
SALES (est): 225.6K **Privately Held**
WEB: www.soft-eng-sol.com
SIC: 7372 Prepackaged software

(G-1335)
SONAWANE WEBDYNAMICS INC
44031 Ppeline Plz Ste 305 (20147)
PHONE....................................703 629-7254
Shailendra Sonawane, *CEO*
EMP: 5
SQ FT: 200 **Privately Held**
WEB: www.sonawane.com
SIC: 7372 Application computer software

(G-1336)
STATION 6 BREWING LLC
Also Called: Station 6 Brewing Company
44427 Atwater Dr (20147-3424)
PHONE....................................571 510-3532
Rolando Negron,
EMP: 1 **EST:** 2015
SALES (est): 66.7K **Privately Held**
SIC: 2082 Malt beverages

(G-1337)
STELLOSPHERE INC
43645 Meadow Overlook Pl (20147-7488)
PHONE....................................631 897-4678
Rakhesh Govada, *CEO*
EMP: 1 **EST:** 2017
SALES (est): 32.7K **Privately Held**
SIC: 7372 Prepackaged software

(G-1338)
T&M METAL FABRICATION LLC
20859 Apollo Ter (20147-2827)
PHONE....................................703 726-6949
Tyler Smith, *Principal*
EMP: 2
SALES (est): 118.9K **Privately Held**
SIC: 3499 Fabricated metal products

(G-1339)
TELOS IDNTITY MGT SLUTIONS LLC
19886 Ashburn Rd (20147-2358)
PHONE....................................703 724-3800
Dawn E Lucini, *Vice Pres*
Mark Griffin,
EMP: 53
SALES (est): 4.3MM
SALES (corp-wide): 159.2MM **Publicly Held**
SIC: 7372 Prepackaged software
PA: Telos Corporation
19886 Ashburn Rd
Ashburn VA 20147
703 724-3800

(G-1340)
TEXACAN BEEF & PORK CO LLC
21750 Red Rum Dr Ste 142 (20147-5865)
PHONE....................................703 858-5565
EMP: 2 **EST:** 2010
SALES (est): 110K **Privately Held**
SIC: 3556 Mfg Food Products Machinery

(G-1341)
TLC PUBLISHING LLC
20898 Gardengate Cir (20147-4025)
PHONE....................................571 439-0564
Catherine M Tulloch, *Principal*
EMP: 1
SALES (est): 37.5K **Privately Held**
SIC: 2741 Miscellaneous publishing

(G-1342)
TLPUBLISHING LLC
43244 Preston Ct (20147-5307)
PHONE....................................571 992-7972
EMP: 1
SALES (est): 37.5K **Privately Held**
SIC: 2741 Miscellaneous publishing

(G-1343)
TYMPIC SOFTWARE INC
43761 Parkhurst Plz # 108 (20147-5470)
PHONE....................................703 858-0996
EMP: 3
SQ FT: 2,500
SALES (est): 133.8K **Privately Held**
SIC: 7372 Prepackaged Software Services

(G-1344)
UBIQUITYWAVE LLC
44761 Malden Pl (20147-6509)
PHONE....................................571 262-1406
Carol Corneby, *Owner*
EMP: 1
SALES (est): 71.3K **Privately Held**
WEB: www.ubiquitywave.com
SIC: 2741 4226 4813 7299 ; document & office records storage; ; personal document & information services; on-line data base information retrieval

(G-1345)
UNITED LITHO INC
21800 Beaumeade Cir (20147-6201)
PHONE....................................703 858-4213
EMP: 2
SALES (est): 83.9K **Privately Held**
SIC: 2752 Commercial printing, lithographic

(G-1346)
VANTAGE POINT DRONE LLC
20827 Grainery Ct (20147-4626)
PHONE....................................703 723-4586
Melissa Ellis, *Principal*
EMP: 2
SALES (est): 174.6K **Privately Held**
SIC: 3721 Motorized aircraft

(G-1347)
VELOCITY SOFTWARE INC
44261 Shehawken Ter (20147-6452)
PHONE....................................703 338-0909
Brian Mackey, *Principal*
EMP: 2
SALES (est): 95.8K **Privately Held**
SIC: 7372 Prepackaged software

(G-1348)
VENA PORTAE INC
44927 Grge Wash Blvd Ste (20147)
PHONE....................................703 899-9500
Ravi Papineni, *President*
EMP: 5 **EST:** 2005
SALES (est): 600K **Privately Held**
WEB: www.venaportae.com
SIC: 3695 Computer software tape & disks: blank, rigid & floppy

(G-1349)
VERTIV CORPORATION
44611 Guilford Dr Ste 180 (20147-6068)
PHONE....................................703 726-4100
Robert Filkowitz, *Manager*
EMP: 20
SALES (corp-wide): 4.4B **Publicly Held**
WEB: www.vertiv.com
SIC: 3585 Air conditioning units, complete: domestic or industrial
HQ: Vertiv Corporation
1050 Dearborn Dr
Columbus OH 43085
614 888-0246

(G-1350)
VIRGINIA NEWS GROUP LLC
21720 Red Rum Dr Ste 142 (20147-5883)
PHONE....................................703 777-1111
Peter Arundel, *President*
EMP: 2
SALES (corp-wide): 14.9MM **Privately Held**
WEB: www.loudountimes.com
SIC: 2711 Newspapers, publishing & printing
PA: Virginia News Group, Llc
1602 Village Market Blvd
Leesburg VA 20175
703 777-1111

(G-1351)
VITALCODE INC
21299 Southolme Way (20147-6087)
PHONE....................................703 622-1154
Ghafran Abbas, *CEO*
EMP: 2
SALES (est): 100K **Privately Held**
SIC: 7372 7389 Application computer software;

(G-1352)
VPS SERVICES INC
43918 Camellia St (20147-5657)
PHONE....................................202 538-1990
Verinder Singh, *Owner*
EMP: 2 **EST:** 2014
SALES (est): 164.8K **Privately Held**
WEB: www.host4fun.com
SIC: 3571 Electronic computers

(G-1353)
WRIGHT MEDICAL TECHNOLOGY INC
43288 Amanda Kay Ct (20147-3132)
PHONE....................................703 729-0643
Karen Carrico, *Manager*
Donna Melton, *Manager*
Sherry Sanders, *Media Spec*
EMP: 4
SALES (corp-wide): 298MM **Privately Held**
WEB: www.wright.com
SIC: 3841 Surgical & medical instruments

GEOGRAPHIC

HQ: Wright Medical Technology, Inc.
1023 Cherry Rd
Memphis TN 38117

(G-1354)
XACT SOLUTIONS INC
21386 Ashburn Run Pl (20147-5348)
PHONE..........................703 398-2680
Rooplin Lamba, *President*
Gagandeep Kohli, *Vice Pres*
EMP: 2
SALES (est): 136K **Privately Held**
WEB: www.xactsolutions.com
SIC: 2522 Office furniture, except wood

(G-1355)
ZACHARY SYSTEMS INC
44330 Premier Plz (20147-5070)
PHONE..........................703 286-7267
Randy Nixon, *Principal*
EMP: 1
SALES (est): 58.7K **Privately Held**
WEB: www.zacharysystems.com
SIC: 7372 Prepackaged software

(G-1356)
ZINGA
43330 Junction Plz # 100 (20147-3407)
PHONE..........................571 291-2475
EMP: 3
SALES (est): 195.3K **Privately Held**
WEB: www.zingafroyo.com
SIC: 2024 Ice cream, bulk

(G-1357)
ZIVA PRINTS LLC
43858 Sandburg Sq (20147-5851)
PHONE..........................571 265-9030
Rhoderick Delarosa, *Principal*
EMP: 2 EST: 2016
SALES (est): 108K **Privately Held**
SIC: 2752 Commercial printing, lithographic

(G-1358)
ZYNGA INC
44521 Hastings Dr (20147-6038)
PHONE..........................901 683-8310
EMP: 4
SALES (corp-wide): 1.3B **Publicly Held**
WEB: www.zynga.com
SIC: 7372 Prepackaged software
PA: Zynga Inc.
699 8th St
San Francisco CA 94103
855 449-9642

Ashland
Hanover County

(G-1359)
804 SIGNS LLC
10978 Richardson Rd (23005-3421)
PHONE..........................804 277-4272
Jose Joaquin, *Principal*
EMP: 2
SALES (est): 198.7K **Privately Held**
WEB: www.804signs.com
SIC: 3993 Signs & advertising specialties

(G-1360)
A G S HANOVER INCORPORATED
Also Called: AGS
11234 Air Park Rd (23005-3435)
P.O. Box 6444 (23005-6444)
PHONE..........................804 798-1891
A Cecil Jacobs, *President*
Andrew F Jacobs, *Corp Secy*
Stephen J Jacobs, *Vice Pres*
▲ EMP: 12
SQ FT: 30,000
SALES: 4.1MM **Privately Held**
WEB: www.agsfootweargroup.com
SIC: 3149 5139 Athletic shoes, except rubber or plastic; footwear

(G-1361)
ABC GRAPHICS
11435 Mount Hermon Rd (23005-7801)
PHONE..........................804 368-0276
Thomas Matherly, *Owner*
EMP: 3

SALES (est): 209K **Privately Held**
SIC: 2741 Posters: publishing & printing

(G-1362)
ACE REBUILDERS INC
517 S Washington Hwy (23005-2314)
P.O. Box A (23005-4025)
PHONE..........................804 798-3838
Edward Frye, *President*
Tony A Hurt, *Vice Pres*
Tommy P Baer, *Admin Sec*
EMP: 10
SALES (est): 939.6K **Privately Held**
SIC: 7694 Rebuilding motors, except automotive

(G-1363)
ADVANTAGE SIGN SUPPLY INC
303 Ashcake Rd Ste J (23005-2320)
PHONE..........................804 798-5784
James Stanley, *Manager*
EMP: 35 **Privately Held**
WEB: www.advantagesgs.com
SIC: 3993 Signs & advertising specialties
PA: Advantage Sign Supply, Inc.
4182 Royal Ct
Hudsonville MI 49426

(G-1364)
AFTON CHEMICAL CORPORATION
11289 Central Dr C (23005-8032)
PHONE..........................804 752-8420
Michael Bakken, *Branch Mgr*
EMP: 10
SALES (est): 2.1B **Publicly Held**
WEB: www.aftonchemical.com
SIC: 2899 Chemical preparations
HQ: Afton Chemical Corporation
500 Spring St
Richmond VA 23219
804 788-5800

(G-1365)
ALGONQUIN INDUSTRIES INC
Also Called: Hanover Manufacturing Plant
10117 Leadbetter Pl (23005-3411)
PHONE..........................804 550-5401
Scott Harrison, *Branch Mgr*
EMP: 21
SALES (corp-wide): 400MM **Privately Held**
WEB: www.algonquin-industries.com
SIC: 3357 Magnet wire, nonferrous
HQ: Algonquin Industries, Inc.
129 Soundview Rd
Guilford CT 06437
203 453-4348

(G-1366)
ALLIANCE MACHINE AND ENGRV LLC
10190 Maple Leaf Ct (23005-8136)
P.O. Box 1375 (23005-4375)
PHONE..........................804 798-1199
Debbie Greenberg, *Office Mgr*
Thomas Greenberg, *Mng Member*
Carl Graham, *Manager*
Deborah Greenberg, *Manager*
▲ EMP: 11 EST: 2011
SALES (est): 3.5MM **Privately Held**
WEB: www.alliancemachineandengraving.com
SIC: 3599 Machine shop, jobbing & repair

(G-1367)
AMERICAN SPIN-A-BATCH CO INTL
14523 Augusta Ln (23005-3171)
P.O. Box 1474 (23005-4474)
PHONE..........................804 798-1349
Stewart Von Herbulis, *President*
William H Garrison, *Director*
Hazel N Garrison, *Admin Sec*
EMP: 5
SQ FT: 150
SALES (est): 699.7K **Privately Held**
WEB: www.americanspinabatch.com
SIC: 3569 Liquid automation machinery & equipment

(G-1368)
AMERICAN TRACK CARRIER LLC
Also Called: Morooka USA-East
11191 Air Park Rd (23005-3428)
P.O. Box 6400 (23005-6400)
PHONE..........................804 752-7533
Kenneth M Byrd, *President*
◆ EMP: 12
SQ FT: 11,500
SALES (est): 10MM **Privately Held**
WEB: www.morookacarriers.com
SIC: 3537 Trucks, tractors, loaders, carriers & similar equipment

(G-1369)
AMERICAST INC
11352 Virginia Precast Rd (23005-7920)
PHONE..........................804 798-6068
David Brindser, *Branch Mgr*
EMP: 100
SALES (corp-wide): 200.4MM **Privately Held**
SIC: 3272 Concrete products, precast
HQ: Americast, Inc.
210 Stone Spring Rd
Harrisonburg VA 22801

(G-1370)
APEX CAPITAL LLC
11129 Air Park Rd (23005-3503)
P.O. Box 6631 (23005-6631)
PHONE..........................904 495-6422
Dante Diorio, *Manager*
EMP: 1
SALES (est): 60.5K **Privately Held**
SIC: 2421 Lumber: rough, sawed or planed

(G-1371)
ARGOS USA LLC
9680 Old Ridge Rd (23005-7308)
PHONE..........................804 227-9402
EMP: 2 **Privately Held**
SIC: 3272 Mfg Concrete Products
HQ: Argos Usa Llc
3015 Windward Plz
Alpharetta GA 30005
678 368-4300

(G-1372)
ASHLAND ROLLER MILLS INC
Also Called: Ashland Milling Co
14471 Washington Hwy (23005-7240)
P.O. Box 1775 (23005-4775)
PHONE..........................804 798-8329
Linwood P Attkisson, *President*
EMP: 20 EST: 1807
SQ FT: 1,200
SALES (est): 3.5MM **Privately Held**
WEB: www.byrdmill.com
SIC: 2041 Flour; flour mills, cereal (except rice)

(G-1373)
ASHLAND WOODWORK INC
101 Henry Clay Rd (23005-1503)
PHONE..........................804 798-4088
J Clay Stiles III, *President*
B Finley Swingle, *Vice Pres*
EMP: 17
SALES (est): 2.2MM **Privately Held**
WEB: www.pmcabinetsinc.com
SIC: 2431 Millwork

(G-1374)
AUTHENTIC BAKING COMPANY LLC
203 N Washington Hwy (23005-1623)
PHONE..........................803 422-9282
William Clelland SEC, *Principal*
EMP: 4
SALES (est): 125.3K **Privately Held**
SIC: 2051 Bread, cake & related products

(G-1375)
AWSI INC
Also Called: Ashland Woodwork & Supply
101 Henry Clay Rd (23005-1503)
P.O. Box 1625 (23005-4625)
PHONE..........................804 798-4088
Benjamin F Swingle, *President*
EMP: 12 EST: 1998
SALES (est): 1.2MM **Privately Held**
WEB: www.ashlandwood.com
SIC: 2431 Millwork

(G-1376)
B&B CONSULTING SERVICES INC
9317 Totopotomoy Trl (23005-3367)
P.O. Box 6081 (23005-6081)
PHONE..........................804 550-1517
Elliot B Meredith, *President*
EMP: 2
SALES (est): 181.3K **Privately Held**
WEB: www.bnbconsulting.net
SIC: 7372 Prepackaged software

(G-1377)
BAKER & HAZLEWOOD
11242 Hopson Rd (23005-3474)
PHONE..........................804 798-5199
Robert Shaver, *Principal*
EMP: 2
SALES (est): 145.7K **Privately Held**
SIC: 3444 Sheet metal specialties, not stamped

(G-1378)
BALLOU ENTERPRISES LLC
11034 Air Park Rd Ste 1 (23005-3449)
PHONE..........................804 496-6620
EMP: 1 EST: 2015
SALES (est): 59.3K **Privately Held**
SIC: 3482 Small arms ammunition

(G-1379)
BEAR ISLAND PAPER WB LLC
Also Called: White Birch Paper
10026 Old Ridge Rd (23005-7312)
PHONE..........................804 227-4000
Peter M Brant, *CEO*
Christopher M Brant, *President*
Edward D Sherrick, *Senior VP*
Tim Butler, *Treasurer*
EMP: 190
SALES (est): 67.6MM **Privately Held**
WEB: www.whitebirchpaper.com
SIC: 2621 Paper mills

(G-1380)
BEST IMPRESSIONS PRINTING
11034 Air Park Rd Ste 17 (23005-3449)
PHONE..........................804 740-9006
EMP: 2
SALES (est): 126.8K **Privately Held**
SIC: 2752 Commercial printing, offset

(G-1381)
BILL KELLEY METALSMITH
10423 Dow Gil Rd (23005-7639)
PHONE..........................804 798-4286
William Kelley, *Owner*
EMP: 5
SALES (est): 338.4K **Privately Held**
SIC: 3446 Railings, bannisters, guards, etc.: made from metal pipe

(G-1382)
BLACKWATER MANUFACTURING LLC
116 Sylvia Rd (23005-1320)
PHONE..........................804 299-3975
Randy Greenwood, *General Mgr*
Karen Greenwood, *Administration*
EMP: 2
SALES (est): 163.1K **Privately Held**
SIC: 3999 Barber & beauty shop equipment

(G-1383)
BOB SANSONE DBA PEGGS CO
100 Haley Rd (23005-2448)
PHONE..........................951 360-9170
Larry Pike, *Sales Staff*
▼ EMP: 9 EST: 2011
SALES (est): 1.3MM **Privately Held**
SIC: 2674 Shipping & shopping bags or sacks

(G-1384)
BRACT RTINING WALLS EXCVTG LLC
Also Called: Brw
10423 Dow Gil Rd (23005-7639)
P.O. Box 2099 (23005-5099)
PHONE..........................804 798-5097
Lisa S Nash, *President*
Chris Tyson, *Office Mgr*
Brayden Nash,
EMP: 16

SALES: 3.5MM **Privately Held**
WEB: www.bractwalls.com
SIC: 3271 1741 Blocks, concrete: land-scape or retaining wall; foundation & re-taining wall construction

(G-1385)
BRANT INDUSTRIES INC
10026 Old Ridge Rd (23005-7312)
PHONE..............................804 227-3394
Jacpus Duetchane, *Manager*
EMP: 220
SALES (corp-wide): 194.5MM **Privately Held**
WEB: www.whitebirchpaper.com
SIC: 2621 Newsprint paper
PA: Brant Industries, Inc.
80 Field Point Rd Fl 3
Greenwich CT 06830
203 661-3344

(G-1386)
CASE-POLYTECH INC
Also Called: Mechanical Technologies
11100 Air Park Rd (23005-3428)
P.O. Box 6188 (23005-6188)
PHONE..............................804 752-3500
Gary L Case, *President*
Gary R Carter, *Vice Pres*
Gary Carter, *Vice Pres*
EMP: 6
SQ FT: 5,000
SALES (est): 1.1MM **Privately Held**
WEB: www.idc-store.com
SIC: 3541 5063 5999 8742 Machine tool replacement & repair parts, metal cutting types; motors, electric; motors, electric; industrial consultant

(G-1387)
CAUTHORNE INDUSTRIES INC
12124 Washington Hwy (23005-7640)
PHONE..............................804 798-6999
EMP: 2
SALES (est): 119.2K **Privately Held**
SIC: 2679 Converted paper products

(G-1388)
CAUTHORNE PAPER COMPANY INC
12124 Washington Hwy (23005-7640)
PHONE..............................804 798-6999
John H Lewis, *President*
Dick Doak, *Manager*
EMP: 20 **EST:** 1912
SQ FT: 90,000
SALES (est): 4.2MM **Privately Held**
WEB: www.cauthornepaper.com
SIC: 2679 4111 5113 2675 Paper prod-ucts, converted; cable cars, except aerial, amusement & scenic; paper & products, wrapping or coarse; die-cut paper & board; folding paperboard boxes

(G-1389)
CHANDERS
13223 Cedar Ln (23005-7552)
P.O. Box 5467, Richmond (23220-0467)
PHONE..............................804 752-7678
John Chander, *Owner*
EMP: 4
SALES (est): 243K **Privately Held**
SIC: 2752 Commercial printing, litho-graphic

(G-1390)
CHEMTREAT INC
10040 Lickinghole Rd (23005-3224)
PHONE..............................804 513-0756
Ken Bowie, *Principal*
Jeffrey M Dowd, *Principal*
James H Hastings, *Principal*
Steve Leavell, *Vice Pres*
Jason Gunter, *Maint Spvr*
EMP: 75
SALES (corp-wide): 17.9B **Publicly Held**
WEB: www.chemtreat.com
SIC: 2899 Water treating compounds
HQ: Chemtreat, Inc.
5640 Cox Rd Ste 300
Glen Allen VA 23060
804 935-2000

(G-1391)
CLASSIC MACHINE INC
Also Called: Classic Machine & Engineering
10989 Richardson Rd (23005-3419)
P.O. Box 6038 (23005-6038)
PHONE..............................804 798-1111
Paul A Terry, *Principal*
Wanda Winston, *Info Tech Mgr*
EMP: 10 **EST:** 1977
SALES (est): 1.4MM **Privately Held**
WEB: www.classicmachine.com
SIC: 3599 Machine shop, jobbing & repair; special dies, tools, jigs & fixtures

(G-1392)
COMMONWEALTH GALVANIZING LLC
10988 Leadbetter Rd (23005-3416)
PHONE..............................804 368-0025
Steve Cavna,
EMP: 12
SALES (est): 1.5MM **Privately Held**
WEB: www.commonwealthgalv.com
SIC: 3479 Galvanizing of iron, steel or end-formed products

(G-1393)
COMMONWEALTH SPECIALTY PACKG
Also Called: Commonwealth Dimensional
12124 Washington Hwy (23005-7640)
PHONE..............................804 271-0157
David Green, *President*
Steve Casso, *Treasurer*
EMP: 12
SQ FT: 12,000
SALES (est): 800K **Privately Held**
WEB: www.commonwealthspecialtypack-aging.com
SIC: 2653 2675 2657 2652 Boxes, corru-gated: made from purchased materials; die-cut paper & board; folding paperboard boxes; setup paperboard boxes; advertis-ing specialties

(G-1394)
CONCRETE PIPE & PRECAST LLC (PA)
11352 Virginia Precast Rd (23005-7920)
PHONE..............................804 798-6068
Bill Tichacek, *President*
Stephen Hammond, *Plant Supt*
Mike Moshier, *Project Mgr*
Nancy Llinet, *Human Res Mgr*
John Kelley, *Cust Mgr*
EMP: 176 **EST:** 2012
SALES (est): 276.3MM **Privately Held**
WEB: www.concretepandp.com
SIC: 3272 Sewer pipe, concrete; concrete products used to facilitate drainage

(G-1395)
CONCRETE PIPE & PRECAST LLC
10364 Design Rd (23005-8012)
PHONE..............................804 752-1311
EMP: 41
SALES (corp-wide): 276.3MM **Privately Held**
WEB: www.concretepandp.com
SIC: 3272 Sewer pipe, concrete
PA: Concrete Pipe & Precast, Llc
11352 Virginia Precast Rd
Ashland VA 23005
804 798-6068

(G-1396)
COUNTRY WOOD CLASSICS
12625 Mount Hermon Rd (23005-7813)
PHONE..............................804 798-1587
Alan Van Dusen, *Owner*
EMP: 2
SALES (est): 103.3K **Privately Held**
SIC: 2499 Decorative wood & woodwork

(G-1397)
COUNTY OF HANOVER
Also Called: Logomotion
10417 Dow Gil Rd (23005-7639)
P.O. Box 2182 (23005-5182)
PHONE..............................804 798-9402
Florence Watts, *Manager*
EMP: 25

SALES (corp-wide): 280.1MM **Privately Held**
WEB: www.hanovercounty.gov
SIC: 3953 Screens, textile printing
PA: County Of Hanover
7497 County Complex Rd
Hanover VA 23069
804 365-6336

(G-1398)
CRAFTSMEN PRINTING INC
Also Called: We Think In Ink
305 England St (23005-2109)
PHONE..............................804 798-7885
Raymond S Tompkins III, *President*
EMP: 5
SQ FT: 2,500
SALES (est): 500K **Privately Held**
WEB: www.wethinkinink.com
SIC: 2752 Commercial printing, offset

(G-1399)
CRESSET CORPORATION
11232 Hopson Rd Ste 1 (23005-3473)
P.O. Box 2183 (23005-5183)
PHONE..............................804 798-2691
Karl Smith, *President*
EMP: 10
SQ FT: 12,000
SALES (est): 1.1MM **Privately Held**
WEB: www.awardsmith.com
SIC: 3999 3914 3479 Plaques, picture, laminated; trophies; engraving jewelry sil-verware, or metal

(G-1400)
DALLAS ELECTRICAL COMPANY INC
11038 Air Park Rd Ste 1 (23005-3479)
PHONE..............................804 798-0002
Donald Gill, *President*
▲ **EMP:** 6
SQ FT: 10,000
SALES (est): 1.1MM **Privately Held**
SIC: 3613 Control panels, electric

(G-1401)
DALTONS AUTOMOTIVE
11006 Air Park Rd (23005-3430)
PHONE..............................804 798-7909
Thomas Dalton Pearson, *Owner*
EMP: 2
SQ FT: 3,000
SALES (est): 187.2K **Privately Held**
SIC: 3599 Machine shop, jobbing & repair

(G-1402)
DISPERSION SPECIALTIES INC
Also Called: D S I
11237 Leadbetter Rd (23005-3403)
P.O. Box 2077 (23005-5077)
PHONE..............................804 798-9137
William S Webster, *President*
EMP: 14
SQ FT: 28,000
SALES (est): 255.9K **Privately Held**
WEB: www.dsiink.com
SIC: 2893 2851 Printing ink; paints & al-lied products

(G-1403)
DOBBS & ASSOC
9988 Lickinghole Rd Ste 2 (23005-3447)
PHONE..............................804 314-8871
Chris Dobbs, *Owner*
EMP: 1
SALES (est): 39.6K **Privately Held**
SIC: 2434 Wood kitchen cabinets

(G-1404)
DUCT SHOP LLC
105 Sylvia Rd (23005-1321)
PHONE..............................804 368-8543
Nathan Roady,
EMP: 4
SALES (est): 170K **Privately Held**
SIC: 3444 Sheet metalwork

(G-1405)
E I DU PONT DE NEMOURS
10431 Old Telegraph Rd (23005-8102)
PHONE..............................804 550-7560
EMP: 2
SALES (est): 74.4K **Privately Held**
WEB: www.usa.dupont.com
SIC: 2879 Agricultural chemicals

(G-1406)
EAST COAST GRAPHICS INC
11046 Air Park Rd Ste 1 (23005-3450)
PHONE..............................804 798-7100
Bruce Johansen, *President*
EMP: 5
SALES (est): 497.2K **Privately Held**
SIC: 2759 Screen printing

(G-1407)
EAST PENN MANUFACTURING CO
Also Called: Deka Batteries & Cables
10001 Whitesel Rd (23005-3406)
PHONE..............................804 798-1771
Micah Ross, *Manager*
Jason Brumbach, *Executive*
EMP: 20
SALES (corp-wide): 2.8B **Privately Held**
WEB: www.eastpennmanufacturing.com
SIC: 3691 5531 5063 Storage batteries; batteries, automotive & truck; storage bat-teries, industrial
PA: East Penn Manufacturing Co.
102 Deka Rd
Lyon Station PA 19536
610 682-6361

(G-1408)
ELECTROMATICS INCORPORATED
11080 Leadbetter Rd (23005-3443)
P.O. Box 6097 (23005-6097)
PHONE..............................804 798-8318
R J Klotz Jr, *President*
Doug L Glasscock, *Vice Pres*
EMP: 8
SQ FT: 6,000
SALES (est): 1.2MM **Privately Held**
WEB: www.electromatics.com
SIC: 3625 Electric controls & control ac-cessories, industrial

(G-1409)
EMSCO LLC
10181 Cedar Ridge Dr (23005-8133)
PHONE..............................804 752-1640
David Hancock, *Engineer*
Jay Kim, *Engineer*
Ann Hall, *Executive*
L Parker Garrett,
EMP: 10
SALES (est): 1.7MM **Privately Held**
WEB: www.emsco-inc.com
SIC: 3679 Electronic circuits

(G-1410)
ESSROC CEMENT CORPORATION
9680 Old Ridge Rd (23005-7308)
PHONE..............................804 227-4156
David Mabry, *Manager*
EMP: 2 **EST:** 2010
SALES (est): 113.1K **Privately Held**
SIC: 3273 Ready-mixed concrete

(G-1411)
EVERYDAY EDUCATION LLC
13041 Hill Club Ln (23005-3150)
PHONE..............................804 752-2517
Janice Campbell, *Principal*
EMP: 3
SALES (est): 213.6K **Privately Held**
WEB: www.everydayeducation.com
SIC: 2731 Book publishing

(G-1412)
EXTERIOR SYSTEMS INC
11505 N Lakeridge Pkwy (23005-8047)
PHONE..............................804 752-2324
EMP: 2
SALES (est): 127.4K **Privately Held**
SIC: 3089 Plastic hardware & building products

(G-1413)
FALLING CREEK LOG YARD INC
14281 Washington Hwy (23005-7238)
P.O. Box 644 (23005-0644)
PHONE..............................804 798-6121
William H Gilman, *President*
EMP: 35

SALES (est): 4.3MM **Privately Held**
WEB: www.fallingcreeklogandlumber.com
SIC: 2421 Sawmills & planing mills, general

(G-1414)
FARMER MACHINE COMPANY INC
10395 Sliding Ridge Rd (23005-3412)
PHONE......................................804 550-7310
Wilton T Farmer Jr, *President*
W T Farmer Sr, *Corp Secy*
Ryan Farmer, *Vice Pres*
Joe Talley, *Prdtn Mgr*
Zane Powell, *Manager*
EMP: 30
SQ FT: 5,000
SALES (est): 584.6K **Privately Held**
WEB: www.farmermachine.com
SIC: 3599 Machine shop, jobbing & repair

(G-1415)
FAT CAT PUBLISHINGS LLC
406 Carter Forest Dr (23005-1266)
PHONE......................................804 368-0378
Linwood Carlton Henson, *Principal*
EMP: 2
SALES (est): 59.2K **Privately Held**
SIC: 2741 Miscellaneous publishing

(G-1416)
FIELDS INC OSCAR S
Also Called: Ofi Custom Metal Fabrication
10412 Design Rd (23005-8013)
P.O. Box 851 (23005-0851)
PHONE......................................804 798-3900
Kenneth B Graves, *CEO*
James W Clifford, *President*
Mark Ogle, *Production*
Spence Glasgow, *VP Sales*
EMP: 33 **EST:** 1982
SQ FT: 30,000
SALES (est): 6.7MM **Privately Held**
WEB: www.osfi.com
SIC: 3599 3446 3444 3443 Custom machinery; architectural metalwork; sheet metalwork; fabricated plate work (boiler shop); fabricated structural metal

(G-1417)
FLOW-TECH INC
10993 Richardson Rd (23005-3419)
PHONE......................................804 752-3450
Chris Eastham, *Principal*
EMP: 1
SALES (corp-wide): 4.2MM **Privately Held**
WEB: www.crossco.com
SIC: 3829 Measuring & controlling devices
PA: Flow-Tech Inc.
   10940 Beaver Dam Rd
   Hunt Valley MD 21030
   410 666-3200

(G-1418)
FLOWERS BKG CO LYNCHBURG LLC
9474 Totopotomoy Trl (23005-3309)
PHONE......................................434 528-0441
Allen Branscome, *Principal*
Matias Lambert, *Principal*
EMP: 2
SALES (est): 62.3K **Privately Held**
SIC: 2051 Bread, cake & related products

(G-1419)
FOLEY MATERIAL HANDLING CO INC
Also Called: Virginia Crane Co
11327 Virginia Crane Dr (23005-7921)
P.O. Box 289 (23005-0289)
PHONE......................................804 798-1343
Dale R Foley, *CEO*
Richard A Foley, *President*
Schuchart Keith, *Business Mgr*
John Kain, *Vice Pres*
John King, *Vice Pres*
EMP: 100 **EST:** 1975
SQ FT: 36,000

SALES (est): 38.9MM **Privately Held**
WEB: www.virginiacrane.com
SIC: 3536 1796 5084 3441 Cranes, industrial plant; cranes, overhead traveling; machinery installation; materials handling machinery; conveyor systems; fabricated structural metal

(G-1420)
GEORGE LEICA SYSTEMS
9415 Atlee Commerce Blvd A (23005-7987)
PHONE......................................804 299-3911
EMP: 1
SALES (est): 61.7K **Privately Held**
WEB: www.newhorizonssupport.com
SIC: 3861 Photographic equipment & supplies

(G-1421)
GOGO BAND INC
201 Duncan St (23005-1903)
PHONE......................................804 869-8253
Jon A Coble, *CEO*
Timothy Baker, *President*
Steven Zyglowicz, *CTO*
EMP: 3 **EST:** 2016
SQ FT: 1,500
SALES (est): 400K **Privately Held**
WEB: www.mygogoband.com
SIC: 3841 Surgical & medical instruments

(G-1422)
GOODPASTURE KNIVES
13432 Farrington Rd (23005-7115)
PHONE......................................804 752-8363
Tom Goodpasture, *Principal*
EMP: 1
SALES (est): 67.8K **Privately Held**
WEB: www.goodpastureknives.com
SIC: 3949 Hunting equipment

(G-1423)
GRABBER CONSTRUCTION PDTS INC
Also Called: Impact East
9424 Atlee Commerce Blvd C (23005-7993)
PHONE......................................804 550-9331
Chris Layton, *Manager*
EMP: 3
SALES (corp-wide): 1.2B **Privately Held**
WEB: www.grabberman.com
SIC: 2754 Post cards, picture: gravure printing
HQ: Grabber Construction Products, Inc.
   5255 W 11000 N Ste 100
   Highland UT 84003
   801 492-3880

(G-1424)
H & R EMBROIDERY LLC
12390 Goddins Hill Rd (23005-7834)
PHONE......................................804 513-8829
Robert J Kaye, *Administration*
EMP: 2
SALES (est): 134.4K **Privately Held**
WEB: www.hrembroidery.com
SIC: 2395 Embroidery products, except schiffli machine

(G-1425)
HANNEMAN LAND CLEARING LOG LLC
12314 Wildwood Blvd (23005-3027)
PHONE......................................804 909-2349
EMP: 2 **EST:** 2018
SALES (est): 93.7K **Privately Held**
SIC: 2411 Logging

(G-1426)
HANOVER FOILS LLC
301 Hill Carter Pkwy (23005-2315)
PHONE......................................804 496-5835
Howard Hager III, *President*
Robert Snyder, *Opers Mgr*
David Worner, *Manager*
Sarah Lambert, *Office Admin*
Carol Graves,
▲ **EMP:** 25
SQ FT: 80,000
SALES (est): 5.4MM **Privately Held**
WEB: www.hanoverfoils.com
SIC: 3354 Aluminum extruded products

(G-1427)
HANOVER HERALD-PROGRESS
Also Called: Herald-Progress-Hano
112 Thompson St Ste B (23005-1527)
PHONE......................................804 798-9031
Bill Trimble, *President*
Cathy Collins, *Principal*
Pace Stephen T, *Vice Pres*
Karen Evans, *Sales Staff*
EMP: 12
SQ FT: 12,000
SALES (est): 737.3K **Privately Held**
WEB: www.hanoverva.com
SIC: 2711 Newspapers, publishing & printing

(G-1428)
HANOVER IRON & STEEL INC
11149 Leadbetter Rd (23005-3405)
PHONE......................................804 798-5604
Harold K Webb Sr, *President*
Harold Webb, *President*
Jane Webb, *Corp Secy*
Brody Webb, *Vice Pres*
Christopher N Webb, *Vice Pres*
EMP: 10
SQ FT: 13,500
SALES (est): 1.7MM **Privately Held**
WEB: www.hanoveriron.com
SIC: 3312 Structural shapes & pilings, steel

(G-1429)
HANOVER POWDER COATING LL
11535 Fox Cross Rd (23005-8055)
PHONE......................................804 798-5988
EMP: 2
SALES (est): 97.2K **Privately Held**
WEB: www.hanoverpowdercoating.com
SIC: 3479 Coating of metals & formed products

(G-1430)
HANOVER PRECAST INC
12351 Maple St (23005-7650)
P.O. Box 28 (23005-0028)
PHONE......................................804 798-2336
Buddy Cox, *President*
Ernie Nichols, *Vice Pres*
EMP: 14
SALES (est): 2.4MM **Privately Held**
WEB: www.hanoverprecast.com
SIC: 3272 Concrete products, precast

(G-1431)
HANOVER WLDG & MET FABRICATION
10998 Leadbetter Rd (23005-3454)
PHONE......................................804 550-2272
Robert Fig, *Owner*
EMP: 2
SALES (est): 86K **Privately Held**
WEB: www.orlandomagicalvillas.com
SIC: 7692 1799 Welding repair; welding on site

(G-1432)
HI CALIBER MANUFACTURING LLC
11263 Air Park Rd Ste B-4 (23005-3506)
PHONE......................................804 955-8300
EMP: 1
SALES (est): 101.6K **Privately Held**
WEB: www.hicalibermfg.com
SIC: 2851 Coating, air curing

(G-1433)
HICKORY HILL CONSULTING LLC
9174 Hickory Hill Rd (23005-7332)
PHONE......................................804 363-2719
Michael Spence,
EMP: 1
SALES (est): 70.4K **Privately Held**
SIC: 1389 Oil consultants

(G-1434)
HOLMES ENTERPRISES INC
11114 Leadbetter Rd (23005-3401)
P.O. Box 6728 (23005-6728)
PHONE......................................804 798-9201
James E Holmes, *President*
Marian Holmes, *Exec VP*
EMP: 15

SQ FT: 42,000
SALES (est): 3.2MM **Privately Held**
WEB: www.holmestrailers.com
SIC: 3715 Trailer bodies

(G-1435)
HOLMES ENTERPRISES INTL INC
11114 Leadbetter Rd (23005-3401)
P.O. Box 6728 (23005-6728)
PHONE......................................804 798-9201
James E Holmes Jr, *President*
Marian Holmes, *Exec VP*
▲ **EMP:** 25
SQ FT: 30,000
SALES (est): 2.7MM **Privately Held**
WEB: www.holmestrailers.com
SIC: 3799 Trailers & trailer equipment

(G-1436)
HOUSER SIGN WORKS
11242 Hopson Rd Ste 13 (23005-3474)
PHONE......................................804 539-1315
EMP: 1 **EST:** 2014
SALES (est): 50.6K **Privately Held**
WEB: www.housersignworks.com
SIC: 3993 Signs & advertising specialties

(G-1437)
ICE RELEASE MATERIALS LLC
10338 Stony Run Ln (23005-8129)
PHONE......................................540 239-2438
WEI Zhang, *Principal*
EMP: 2 **EST:** 2016
SALES (est): 74.4K **Privately Held**
WEB: www.icerelease.com
SIC: 2899 Chemical preparations

(G-1438)
IMAGE WORKS INC
11046 Leadbetter Rd (23005-3293)
PHONE......................................804 798-5533
J Emory Clotfelter, *Chairman*
Mark Hudson, *Vice Pres*
Karl Ustring, *Vice Pres*
Richard Baker, *CFO*
EMP: 30 **EST:** 1947
SQ FT: 30,000
SALES (est): 5.6MM **Privately Held**
WEB: www.imageworks4signs.com
SIC: 3993 Electric signs; neon signs

(G-1439)
INDUSTRIAL REPORTING INC
Also Called: Pallet Enterprises
10244 Timber Ridge Dr (23005-8135)
PHONE......................................804 550-0323
Ed Brindley, *President*
Carolyn Brindley, *Corp Secy*
Christopher Edwards, *COO*
Gary Stergar, *Representative*
EMP: 12
SQ FT: 1,250
SALES (est): 1.6MM **Privately Held**
WEB: www.ireporting.com
SIC: 2721 Magazines: publishing only, not printed on site; magazines: publishing & printing

(G-1440)
INSTRUMENTATION AND CONTROL
Also Called: I C S E
10991 Leadbetter Rd (23005-3497)
PHONE......................................804 550-5770
Richard Tinsley, *President*
Mitch Bays, *Superintendent*
Ashby E Tinsley, *Principal*
Tinsley Ashby E, *Vice Pres*
David Woodall, *Plant Mgr*
EMP: 54
SQ FT: 36,000
SALES: 15.7MM **Privately Held**
WEB: www.icseinc.com
SIC: 3613 1731 Switchgear & switchboard apparatus; electronic controls installation

(G-1441)
ITL (VIRGINIA) INC
305 Ashcake Rd Ste L (23005-2301)
PHONE......................................804 381-0905
Thomas H Cole, *Principal*
Jull Thomas Edward, *Vice Pres*
EMP: 4

SALES (est): 295.9K **Privately Held**
WEB: www.itlmedical.com
SIC: 3841 Medical instruments & equipment, blood & bone work

(G-1442)
JONES SIGN CO INC
11046 Leadbetter Rd (23005-3425)
PHONE..............................804 798-5533
Michael Baldwin, *Project Mgr*
EMP: 30
SALES (corp-wide): 88.1MM **Privately Held**
WEB: www.jonessign.com
SIC: 3993 Electric signs; neon signs
PA: Jones Sign Co., Inc.
1711 Scheuring Rd
De Pere WI 54115
920 983-6700

(G-1443)
JOSEPH RANDOLPH PIKE
Also Called: Dixie Sign Company
646 N Washington Hwy (23005-1312)
PHONE..............................804 798-7188
Joseph Pike, *Owner*
EMP: 1
SQ FT: 1,000
SALES (est): 76.7K **Privately Held**
SIC: 3993 Signs & advertising specialties

(G-1444)
JULIAN INDUSTRIES LLC
Also Called: Parkstone
10984 Leadbetter Rd (23005-3416)
PHONE..............................804 755-6888
Gregory Lancaster,
EMP: 2
SALES (est): 290.8K **Privately Held**
SIC: 2541 Counter & sink tops

(G-1445)
JUNOVENTURE LLC
14140 Washington Hwy (23005-7237)
P.O. Box 1810 (23005-4810)
PHONE..............................410 247-1908
Yancey Jones,
EMP: 5
SALES (est): 1.1MM **Privately Held**
SIC: 3571 7379 Electronic computers; computer related maintenance services

(G-1446)
JVH COMPANY INC (PA)
Also Called: Specialty's Our Name
11206 Hopson Rd (23005-3433)
P.O. Box 6534 (23005-6534)
PHONE..............................804 798-0888
James U Harrison, *President*
Donna Miles, *Purchasing*
EMP: 39
SQ FT: 35,000
SALES (est): 4.5MM **Privately Held**
WEB: www.sonmetalfab.com
SIC: 3444 3599 Sheet metal specialties, not stamped; machine shop, jobbing & repair

(G-1447)
K & T MACHINE AND WELDING INC
15100 Washington Hwy (23005-7245)
P.O. Box 1615 (23005-4615)
PHONE..............................804 296-8625
Thomas Hix, *President*
EMP: 10
SALES (est): 400K **Privately Held**
WEB: www.kandtmachine.net
SIC: 7692 Welding repair

(G-1448)
KBM POWDER COATING LLC
11042 Air Park Rd Ste 7 (23005-3478)
PHONE..............................804 496-6860
Jennifer Watts,
EMP: 2
SQ FT: 6,000
SALES (est): 112.7K **Privately Held**
WEB: www.kbmpowdercoating.com
SIC: 3479 Coating of metals & formed products

(G-1449)
KIN ART STUDIOS LLC
Also Called: Kin Art Wraps
11028 Leadbetter Rd (23005-3457)
PHONE..............................804 368-7298
EMP: 1
SALES (est): 69.8K **Privately Held**
SIC: 3993 7389 7336 7312 Signs & advertising specialties; ; art design services; outdoor advertising services

(G-1450)
KOENIG INC
Also Called: King Kong Kases
11040 Patterson Park Rd (23005)
PHONE..............................804 798-8282
Fax: 804 798-7323
▲ EMP: 3
SQ FT: 3,000
SALES (est): 200K **Privately Held**
SIC: 3161 Mfg Luggage

(G-1451)
LAWRENCE TRLR & TRCK EQP INC
11362 Washington Hwy (23005-8005)
PHONE..............................800 296-6009
Richard B Murray, *President*
Scott D Lambert, *Vice Pres*
Lawrence Harris, *CFO*
Peer A Segellee, *Admin Sec*
EMP: 16
SALES (est): 3.2MM
SALES (corp-wide): 83.2MM **Privately Held**
WEB: www.lawrencette.com
SIC: 3715 Truck trailers
PA: Lawrence Transportation Systems, Inc.
872 Lee Hwy Ste 203
Roanoke VA 24019
540 966-4000

(G-1452)
LINDE GAS NORTH AMERICA LLC
Also Called: Lifegas
11132 Progress Rd (23005-3437)
PHONE..............................804 752-2744
Joseph Klein, *Branch Mgr*
EMP: 7 **Privately Held**
WEB: www.praxair.com
SIC: 2813 Nitrogen; oxygen, compressed or liquefied
HQ: Linde Gas North America Llc
10 Riverview Dr
Danbury CT 06810

(G-1453)
LINEAR DEVICES CORPORATION
Also Called: Lectrotab
11126 Air Park Rd Ste G (23005-3519)
PHONE..............................804 368-8428
Dan Roberts, *President*
Roberts Courtney L, *Vice Pres*
Claibourne Jackson, *Manager*
▲ EMP: 6
SQ FT: 1,200
SALES (est): 981K **Privately Held**
WEB: www.lectrotab.com
SIC: 3699 3732 3429 Linear accelerators; boat building & repairing; manufactured hardware (general)

(G-1454)
LTCPCMS INC
9555 Kings Charter Dr G (23005-7994)
PHONE..............................888 513-5444
Rodney L Burton, *Principal*
EMP: 12
SALES (est): 2.3MM **Privately Held**
WEB: www.ltcpcms.com
SIC: 2834 Pharmaceutical preparations

(G-1455)
LUTRON ELECTRONICS CO INC
11520 Sunshade Ln (23005-8048)
PHONE..............................804 752-3300
Andrew Stott, *COO*
David Phelps, *Buyer*
Chris Dimberg, *Engineer*
EMP: 150

SALES (corp-wide): 554.9MM **Privately Held**
WEB: www.lutron.com
SIC: 2591 5023 3823 3442 Drapery hardware & blinds & shades; window furnishings; industrial instrmnts msrmnt display/control process variable; metal doors, sash & trim
PA: Lutron Electronics Co., Inc.
7200 Suter Rd
Coopersburg PA 18036
610 282-3800

(G-1456)
LUTRON SHADING SOLUTIONS
11520 Sunshade Ln (23005-8048)
PHONE..............................804 752-3300
Joel S Spira, *President*
Ruth R Spira, *Vice Pres*
◆ EMP: 4
SALES (est): 390K **Privately Held**
SIC: 3625 Switches, electronic applications

(G-1457)
MACHINE SPECIALTIES INC
9989 Lickinghole Rd (23005-3423)
PHONE..............................804 798-8920
C Hunter Freed Jr, *President*
Bobby Wyatt, *Vice Pres*
EMP: 11
SQ FT: 8,840
SALES (est): 1.8MM **Privately Held**
WEB: www.machinespec.com
SIC: 3599 Machine shop, jobbing & repair

(G-1458)
MAGNOLIA GRAPHICS
10421 Rapidan Way (23005-3313)
PHONE..............................804 550-0012
James Greenstreet, *Owner*
EMP: 1
SALES (est): 103.3K **Privately Held**
WEB: www.magnoliagraphics.com
SIC: 2754 Business forms: gravure printing

(G-1459)
MARTIN MARIETTA MATERIALS INC
Also Called: Doswell Quarry
12068 Stone Quarry Dr (23005)
PHONE..............................804 798-5096
Ben Steele, *Sales Staff*
George Cinnan, *Branch Mgr*
Rob Teague, *Info Tech Mgr*
EMP: 40 **Publicly Held**
WEB: www.martinmarietta.com
SIC: 1422 Crushed & broken limestone
PA: Martin Marietta Materials Inc
2710 Wycliff Rd
Raleigh NC 27607

(G-1460)
MAXWELL INCORPORATED
Also Called: Maxwell Welding
10997 Richardson Rd # 10 (23005-3444)
P.O. Box 1231, Glen Allen (23060-1231)
PHONE..............................804 370-3697
Karen Maxwell, *President*
EMP: 2 EST: 1992
SALES (est): 175K **Privately Held**
WEB: www.maxwellwelding.com
SIC: 3548 Welding apparatus

(G-1461)
MCGILL AIRFLOW LLC
700 Duncan St (23005-1948)
PHONE..............................804 965-5367
Trey Fitzgerald, *Manager*
EMP: 2
SALES (corp-wide): 72.8MM **Privately Held**
WEB: www.mcgillairflow.com
SIC: 3444 Ducts, sheet metal
HQ: Mcgill Airflow Llc
1 Mission Park
Groveport OH 43125
614 829-1200

(G-1462)
MCS DESIGN & PRODUCTION INC
10980 Richardson Rd (23005-3421)
PHONE..............................804 550-1000
Allen Jessee, *President*
Vicki Jessee, *Corp Secy*
EMP: 5

SQ FT: 3,500
SALES (est): 225K **Privately Held**
WEB: www.mcsdesignandproduction.com
SIC: 3993 8412 7922 7319 Displays & cutouts, window & lobby; signs, not made in custom sign painting shops; museums & art galleries; equipment rental, theatrical; display advertising service

(G-1463)
MODEK INC
10463 Wilden Dr (23005-8134)
PHONE..............................804 550-7300
Hans De Koning, *President*
Margaret Shaia, *General Mgr*
Debbie Curry, *Vice Pres*
Thomas Halish, *Vice Pres*
Jack Mouris, *Vice Pres*
EMP: 3
SQ FT: 70,000
SALES (est): 13.1MM **Privately Held**
WEB: www.flexicell.com
SIC: 3565 3523 3496 Packaging machinery; elevators, farm; conveyor belts

(G-1464)
MOROOKA AMERICA LLC (HQ)
Also Called: Morooka USA
11191 Air Park Rd (23005-3428)
P.O. Box 6220 (23005-6220)
PHONE..............................877 667-6652
Ken Byrd, *President*
Lisa Williams, *Controller*
◆ EMP: 17
SALES (est): 7.1MM **Privately Held**
WEB: www.morookacarriers.com
SIC: 3061 Automotive rubber goods (mechanical)

(G-1465)
MOROOKA AMERICA LLC
11096 Leadbetter Rd (23005-3407)
PHONE..............................804 368-0948
EMP: 10 **Privately Held**
WEB: www.morookacarriers.com
SIC: 3061 Automotive rubber goods (mechanical)
HQ: Morooka America, Llc
11191 Air Park Rd
Ashland VA 23005
877 667-6652

(G-1466)
MOSS SUPPLY COMPANY
Also Called: Old Dominion Window and Door
11253 Leadbetter Rd (23005-3403)
PHONE..............................804 798-8332
Ann Page, *Cust Mgr*
Tammy Chitwood, *Branch Mgr*
EMP: 70
SALES (corp-wide): 72.1MM **Privately Held**
WEB: www.mosssupply.com
SIC: 2431 Windows, wood
PA: Moss Supply Company
5001 N Graham St
Charlotte NC 28269
704 596-8717

(G-1467)
MURDOCK ACQUISITION LLC
Also Called: B C Wood Products
11364 Air Park Rd (23005-3438)
PHONE..............................804 798-9154
Leslie Anne Murdock, *Vice Pres*
Monica Byrom, *Human Res Mgr*
Alex Murdock, *Sales Executive*
Alexander Murdock, *Mng Member*
EMP: 105
SALES (est): 14.9MM **Privately Held**
WEB: www.bcwoodproducts.com
SIC: 2449 2448 Boxes, wood: wirebound; pallets, wood

(G-1468)
NAITO AMERICA
10450 Lakeridge Pkwy (23005-8124)
PHONE..............................804 550-3305
Yasunori Suzuki, *Vice Pres*
EMP: 40
SQ FT: 25,000
SALES (est): 4.3MM **Privately Held**
SIC: 3555 3444 3354 Printing plates; sheet metalwork; aluminum extruded products

PA: Naito Manufacturing Co.,Ltd.
2006-1, Endo
Fujisawa KNG 252-0

(G-1469)
NEAGLES FLEXO CORPORATION
Also Called: Neagle Flexo
11041 Richardson Rd (23005-3418)
PHONE..............................804 798-1501
Joseph O Neagle, *President*
Madeline W Neagle, *Corp Secy*
Paul Lowery, *Vice Pres*
EMP: 35
SALES (est): 4.8MM **Privately Held**
WEB: www.neaglesflexo.com
SIC: 2796 Etching on copper, steel, wood or rubber: printing plates

(G-1470)
NIBLICK INC
Also Called: Minuteman Press
9527 Kings Charter Dr (23005-7939)
PHONE..............................804 550-1607
Dana Preble, *President*
Tom Preble, *Vice Pres*
EMP: 3
SALES (est): 100K **Privately Held**
WEB: www.minutemanpress.com
SIC: 2752 Commercial printing, lithographic

(G-1471)
OLD DOMINION INNOVATIONS INC
9424 Atlee Commerce Blvd D (23005-7993)
PHONE..............................804 477-8712
Steven Fitchett, *President*
Dawn Fitchett, *Office Mgr*
EMP: 12
SALES (est): 1.8MM **Privately Held**
WEB: www.olddominioninnovations.com
SIC: 3674 Solar cells

(G-1472)
OMNI FILTER AND MFG INC
10190 Maple Leaf Ct (23005-8136)
PHONE..............................804 550-1600
Joseph H Gerschick Sr, *President*
Edna M Gerschick, *Corp Secy*
Chris Amey, *Engineer*
Trevor Waghorn, *Marketing Staff*
Kurt Myers, *Manager*
EMP: 20
SQ FT: 14,000
SALES (est): 1.5MM **Privately Held**
WEB: www.porvairfiltration.com
SIC: 3569 Filters

(G-1473)
OPTIKINETICS LTD
11211 Air Park Rd Apt A (23005-3516)
PHONE..............................800 575-6784
Andrew Silver, *Branch Mgr*
Jeanne Lemmonds, *Manager*
EMP: 8 **Privately Held**
WEB: www.optikinetics.co.uk
SIC: 3354 7319 Aluminum extruded products; display advertising service
HQ: Optikinetics Limited
38 Cromwell Road
Luton BEDS LU3 1
148 045-3663

(G-1474)
PAULETTE FABRICATORS INC
9996 Lickinghole Rd (23005-3423)
P.O. Box 1080, Powhatan (23139-1080)
PHONE..............................804 798-3700
James L Paulette II, *President*
Mary Kay Paulette, *Vice Pres*
EMP: 3
SQ FT: 6,500
SALES (est): 1.5MM **Privately Held**
SIC: 3444 Sheet metal specialties, not stamped

(G-1475)
PETERSON IDEA CONSORTIUM INC
Also Called: Interview Angel
12047 Fox Mill Run Ln (23005-3054)
PHONE..............................804 651-8242
Brent Peterson, *Director*

Michelle Chapin, *Associate*
EMP: 2
SALES (est): 100K **Privately Held**
WEB: www.gracefulresources.com
SIC: 2741 Miscellaneous publishing

(G-1476)
PITNEY BOWES INC
305 Ashcake Rd (23005-2301)
PHONE..............................804 798-3210
Peter Doyle, *Sales Staff*
Jerry Harvey, *Business Anlyst*
Jay Mankd, *Branch Mgr*
EMP: 35
SALES (corp-wide): 3.2B **Publicly Held**
WEB: www.pitneybowes.com
SIC: 3579 7359 Postage meters; business machine & electronic equipment rental services
PA: Pitney Bowes Inc.
3001 Summer St
Stamford CT 06905
203 356-5000

(G-1477)
POLY PROCESSING COMPANY LLC
106 S Railroad Ave (23005-1529)
PHONE..............................804 368-7199
EMP: 2
SALES (est): 154.5K **Privately Held**
SIC: 3559 Chemical machinery & equipment

(G-1478)
PORVAIR FILTRATION GROUP INC (HQ)
301 Business Ln (23005-2321)
PHONE..............................804 550-1600
Kevin Nelson, *President*
Tom Liddell, *Managing Dir*
Chris Amey, *Vice Pres*
Lori Losi, *Vice Pres*
Trevor Waghorn, *Vice Pres*
▲ **EMP:** 85 **EST:** 2007
SALES (est): 16.8MM
SALES (corp-wide): 186.3MM **Privately Held**
WEB: www.porvairfiltration.com
SIC: 3569 Filters

(G-1479)
PRATT INDUSTRIES INC
Also Called: Converting Division
309 Quarles Rd (23005-2447)
PHONE..............................804 412-0245
Roger Powers, *General Mgr*
Dimitris Saratsiotis, *Opers Staff*
Barbara Garlow, *Accounts Mgr*
Tony Dilbeck, *Branch Mgr*
Mike Pugh, *Manager*
EMP: 25 **Privately Held**
WEB: www.prattindustries.com
SIC: 2653 Boxes, corrugated: made from purchased materials
PA: Pratt Industries, Inc.
1800 Sarasot Bus Pkwy Ne S
Conyers GA 30013

(G-1480)
PRINTPROS LLC
Also Called: Minuteman Press
9825 Atlee Comns Dr 124 (23005)
PHONE..............................804 550-1607
Michael Berg, *Co-Owner*
Patricia Berg, *Co-Owner*
EMP: 6
SALES (est): 757.6K **Privately Held**
WEB: www.minutemanpress.com
SIC: 2752 Commercial printing, lithographic

(G-1481)
PSI GROUP
11720 N Lakeridge Pkwy (23005-8152)
PHONE..............................804 798-3210
EMP: 2
SALES (est): 199.4K **Privately Held**
SIC: 3444 Mail (post office) collection or storage boxes, sheet metal

(G-1482)
R A PEARSON COMPANY
Also Called: Flexicell, Div of
10463 Wilden Dr (23005-8134)
PHONE..............................804 550-7300

Hans De Koning, *Branch Mgr*
EMP: 51
SALES (corp-wide): 53MM **Privately Held**
WEB: www.pearsonpkg.com
SIC: 3565 3523 3496 Packaging machinery; farm machinery & equipment; miscellaneous fabricated wire products
PA: R. A. Pearson Company
8120 W Sunset Hwy
Spokane WA 99224
509 838-6226

(G-1483)
RANDOLPH-MACON COLLEGE
Also Called: Dept of Economics
204 Henry St (23005-1634)
P.O. Box 5005 (23005-5505)
PHONE..............................804 752-7200
Catherine Staples, *Manager*
EMP: 1
SALES (corp-wide): 83MM **Privately Held**
WEB: www.rmc.edu
SIC: 2711 8221 Newspapers, publishing & printing; college, except junior
PA: Randolph-Macon College
204 Henry St
Ashland VA 23005
804 752-7200

(G-1484)
REFRIGERATION SOLUTIONS INC
10984 Richardson Rd (23005-3421)
PHONE..............................804 752-3188
EMP: 2
SQ FT: 500
SALES (est): 140K **Privately Held**
SIC: 3829 Mfg Temperature Sensors

(G-1485)
REGAL PRODUCTS CO
11232 Hopson Rd Ste 1 (23005-3473)
P.O. Box 2161 (23005-5161)
PHONE..............................804 798-2691
James R Smith, *President*
Linda C Smith, *Corp Secy*
EMP: 4
SQ FT: 15,000
SALES (est): 190K **Privately Held**
WEB: www.gotoregal.com
SIC: 3914 Trophies, plated (all metals)

(G-1486)
RICHMOND STEEL INC
11104 Air Park Rd (23005-3428)
PHONE..............................804 798-4766
EMP: 1
SALES (est): 25K **Privately Held**
SIC: 7692 Welding Repair

(G-1487)
RITEMADE PAPER CONVERTERS INC
11760 N Lakeridge Pkwy (23005-8152)
PHONE..............................800 821-5484
Ned Wood, *Plant Mgr*
▲ **EMP:** 3
SALES (est): 354.1K **Privately Held**
WEB: www.iconex.com
SIC: 2621 Paper mills

(G-1488)
RIVERSIDE HYDRAULICS LLC
11027 Leadbetter Rd (23005-3408)
PHONE..............................804 545-6700
Mark Romer,
John Barbee,
EMP: 6
SALES (est): 995.6K **Privately Held**
WEB: www.riversidehydraulics.com
SIC: 3492 Hose & tube fittings & assemblies, hydraulic/pneumatic

(G-1489)
RODDERS JOURNAL
9415 Atlee Commerce Blvd E (23005-7987)
PHONE..............................804 496-6906
EMP: 4
SALES (est): 162.4K **Privately Held**
WEB: www.roddersjournal.com
SIC: 2741 Miscellaneous publishing

(G-1490)
SERVICE MACHINE & WLDG CO INC
12421 Maple St (23005-7651)
P.O. Box 2083 (23005-5083)
PHONE..............................804 798-1381
Jeffrey D Layne, *President*
Mark Conner, *Vice Pres*
John Roumillat, *Vice Pres*
Douglas Shortridge, *Vice Pres*
Crystal French, *Purch Agent*
EMP: 55 **EST:** 1928
SQ FT: 41,000
SALES (est): 14.6MM **Privately Held**
WEB: www.service-machine.com
SIC: 3443 3599 Tanks, standard or custom fabricated: metal plate; machine shop, jobbing & repair

(G-1491)
SIGN INK LLC
9830 Atlee Commons Dr # 200 (23005-8203)
PHONE..............................804 250-3700
EMP: 12
SALES (est): 61.3K **Privately Held**
SIC: 3993 Signs & advertising specialties

(G-1492)
SMARTECH INC
12195 Harley Club Dr (23005-8097)
PHONE..............................804 798-8588
Hanzhen Zheng, *Chairman*
EMP: 1
SALES (est): 46.6K **Privately Held**
SIC: 3423 Hand & edge tools

(G-1493)
SONIC TOOLS LP
10455 Dow Gil Rd (23005-7639)
PHONE..............................804 798-0538
Scott Staylor, *President*
Ludwig Preinesberger, *Partner*
◆ **EMP:** 13
SQ FT: 6,000
SALES (est): 2.1MM **Privately Held**
WEB: www.soniclp.com
SIC: 3541 Machine tools, metal cutting type

(G-1494)
SOUTH ATLANTIC LLC
11022 Lewistown Rd (23005-8031)
PHONE..............................804 798-3257
Mark Grubb, *Branch Mgr*
EMP: 40
SALES (corp-wide): 237.4MM **Privately Held**
WEB: www.southatlanticllc.com
SIC: 3479 Galvanizing of iron, steel or end-formed products
HQ: South Atlantic, Llc
1907 S 17th St Ste 2
Wilmington NC 28401
910 332-1900

(G-1495)
SPEC OPS INC
Also Called: Soi C4isr Platforms Hanover Co
319 Business Ln Ste 100 (23005-2322)
P.O. Box 697, Midlothian (23113-0697)
PHONE..............................804 752-4790
Kimberly A Spicer, *President*
Robert W Corey, *COO*
Brad O Stobb, *Vice Pres*
EMP: 16
SALES (est): 2.7MM **Privately Held**
WEB: www.hdtglobal.com
SIC: 3699 Security control equipment & systems
PA: Hunter Defense Technologies, Inc.
30500 Aurora Rd Ste 100
Solon OH 44139

(G-1496)
STAINED GLASS CREATIONS INC
10049 Lickinghole Rd F (23005-3464)
PHONE..............................804 798-8806
Diane Nahan Fairburn, *President*
EMP: 5
SQ FT: 1,500

▲ = Import ▼=Export
◆ =Import/Export

SALES (est): 526.7K **Privately Held**
WEB: www.decorativeglasssolutions.com
SIC: **3231** 5231 Leaded glass; glass, leaded or stained

(G-1497)
SUEZ TREATMENT SOLUTIONS INC
10989 Leadbetter Rd B (23005-3409)
PHONE..................................804 550-4971
Eric Fowlkes, *President*
EMP: 13
SALES (corp-wide): 100.8MM **Privately Held**
WEB: www.suez-na.com
SIC: **3589** Water treatment equipment, industrial
HQ: Suez Treatment Solutions Inc.
461 From Rd Ste 400
Paramus NJ 07652
201 767-9300

(G-1498)
SUSANNAH WAGNER JEWELERS INC
107 Hanover Ave (23005-1813)
PHONE..................................804 798-5864
Susannah Wagner, *President*
Elizabeth Spahr, *Vice Pres*
John Merrit, *Treasurer*
EMP: 5
SQ FT: 600
SALES (est): 300K **Privately Held**
WEB: www.wagnerjewellers.com
SIC: **3911** 7631 5944 Jewelry, precious metal; jewelry repair services; jewelry stores

(G-1499)
TEEN INK
12449 W Patrick Henry Rd (23005-3152)
PHONE..................................804 365-8000
Alfelia Winston, *Manager*
Cheryl Haverstein, *IT Executive*
Terry Stone, *Director*
Kathleen Berry, *Executive*
Laura Pomfrey, *Admin Sec*
EMP: 2
SALES (est): 77.9K **Privately Held**
WEB: www.teenink.com
SIC: **2741** Miscellaneous publishing

(G-1500)
TIMELESS STITCHES INC
Also Called: T S I Embroidery
123 Junction Dr (23005-2253)
PHONE..................................804 798-7677
Vebys Mills, *CEO*
Kenneth Mills, *CFO*
EMP: 4
SALES (est): 350K **Privately Held**
WEB: www.tsipromotionals.com
SIC: **2395** Embroidery products, except schiffli machine

(G-1501)
TMAC SERVICES INC
Also Called: Custom Screens Shds & Shutters
10032 Whitesel Rd (23005-3426)
PHONE..................................804 368-0936
Todd N McGregor, *President*
EMP: 10
SQ FT: 2,200
SALES (est): 1.2MM **Privately Held**
WEB: www.tmacservices.com
SIC: **3442** Screens, window, metal

(G-1502)
TRANE COMPANY
10408 Lakeridge Pkwy # 100 (23005-8139)
PHONE..................................304 348-2800
Lewis Griffith, *Accounts Mgr*
Brandon Hunt, *Accounts Mgr*
Alison Doswell, *Manager*
EMP: 6 **Privately Held**
WEB: www.trane.com
SIC: **3585** Refrigeration & heating equipment
HQ: The Trane Company
3600 Pammel Creek Rd
La Crosse WI 54601
608 787-2000

(G-1503)
TRANE US INC
10408 Lkrdge Pkwy Ste 100 (23005)
PHONE..................................804 747-4774
Scott Collins, *Controller*
EMP: 100 **Privately Held**
WEB: www.trane.com
SIC: **3585** Refrigeration & heating equipment
HQ: Trane U.S. Inc.
3600 Pammel Creek Rd
La Crosse WI 54601
608 787-2000

(G-1504)
TURNER BRAGG
504 England St (23005-2105)
PHONE..................................804 752-2244
EMP: 1 EST: 2010
SALES (est): 86K **Privately Held**
SIC: **3421** Mfg Cutlery

(G-1505)
VALVE AUTOMATION CENTER
Also Called: William W Hoitt
310 Hill Carter Pkwy (23005-2300)
PHONE..................................804 752-2700
William W Hoitt Sr, *Owner*
EMP: 6
SQ FT: 30,000
SALES (est): 548.3K **Privately Held**
WEB: www.acva.com
SIC: **3491** 5085 Industrial valves; valves & fittings

(G-1506)
VIRGINIA RAILING & GATES LLC
11042 Air Park Rd Ste 1 (23005-3478)
PHONE..................................804 798-8777
William A Mayers, *Owner*
EMP: 11
SQ FT: 3,000
SALES (est): 1.8MM **Privately Held**
WEB: www.virginiarailingandgates.com
SIC: **3446** 2431 1799 Stairs, fire escapes, balconies, railings & ladders; stair railings, wood; fence construction

(G-1507)
WATTS FABRICATION & WELDING
11535 Fox Cross Rd (23005-8055)
PHONE..................................804 798-5988
Karen Watts, *Principal*
EMP: 2
SALES (est): 364.7K **Privately Held**
SIC: **7692** Welding repair

(G-1508)
WEST ENGINEERING COMPANY INC
10106 Lewistown Rd (23005-7952)
P.O. Box 15480, Richmond (23227-5480)
PHONE..................................804 798-3966
Stephen N West, *President*
Steve West, *General Mgr*
Maynard G Totty, *Vice Pres*
Kenneth N West, *Vice Pres*
Wayne Talley, *Safety Mgr*
EMP: 40 EST: 1919
SQ FT: 50,000
SALES (est): 5MM **Privately Held**
WEB: www.west-engineering.net
SIC: **3554** 3559 7692 3549 Paper industries machinery; plastics working machinery; welding repair; metalworking machinery

(G-1509)
WHOS UP GAMES LLC
11305 Cloverhill Dr (23005-1116)
PHONE..................................804 248-2270
Sarah Chapman, *Principal*
EMP: 1 EST: 2013
SALES (est): 52.2K **Privately Held**
SIC: **7372** Application computer software

(G-1510)
WILLIAM B GILMAN (PA)
Also Called: Gilman Trucking
13423 Farrington Rd (23005-7115)
PHONE..................................804 798-7812
William B Gilman, *Owner*
EMP: 16

SALES (est): 1.6MM **Privately Held**
SIC: **2411** Logging camps & contractors

(G-1511)
WILLKAT ENVELOPES & GRAPHICS
12640 Farrington Rd (23005-7169)
PHONE..................................804 798-0243
William Crone, *President*
EMP: 1
SALES (est): 72.1K **Privately Held**
SIC: **2759** Envelopes: printing

(G-1512)
WINEBOW GROUP LLC
Also Called: Country Vintner, The
12305 N Lakeridge Pkwy (23005-8181)
PHONE..................................804 752-3670
EMP: 1
SALES (corp-wide): 558.8MM **Privately Held**
WEB: www.winebowgroup.com
SIC: **2084** Wines
PA: The Winebow Group Llc
4800 Cox Rd Ste 300
Glen Allen VA 23060
804 752-3670

(G-1513)
WOODWORTH VIRGINIA LLC
301 Business Ln (23005-2321)
PHONE..................................804 412-0206
Robert Woodworth, *Manager*
EMP: 2
SALES (est): 95.5K **Privately Held**
SIC: **3699** Electrical equipment & supplies

(G-1514)
YORK SPORTSCARS INC
11020 Leadbetter Rd Ste 6 (23005-3456)
PHONE..................................804 798-5268
John A York, *President*
EMP: 2
SALES (est): 268.2K **Privately Held**
WEB: www.yorksportscars.com
SIC: **3711** 7538 3714 Automobile assembly, including specialty automobiles; general automotive repair shops; motor vehicle parts & accessories

---

Atkins
Smyth County

(G-1515)
A STITCH IN TIME
6620 Lee Hwy (24311-3025)
PHONE..................................276 781-2014
Jimmy Osborne, *Principal*
EMP: 1
SALES (est): 69.8K **Privately Held**
SIC: **2395** Embroidery & art needlework

(G-1516)
EAST TENNESSEE NATURAL GAS CO
Also Called: Spectra Energy Partners
127 Shortly Stone Rd (24311-3266)
PHONE..................................276 429-5411
John Harris, *Manager*
EMP: 10
SALES (est): 494.7K **Privately Held**
SIC: **1321** Natural gas liquids production

(G-1517)
GENERAL SHALE BRICK INC
7164 Lee Hwy (24311-3033)
P.O. Box 306, Blue Ridge (24064-0306)
PHONE..................................276 783-3156
Jack Bolus, *Manager*
EMP: 100
SALES (corp-wide): 3.8B **Privately Held**
WEB: www.generalshale.com
SIC: **3251** Brick clay: common face, glazed, vitrified or hollow
HQ: General Shale Brick, Inc.
3015 Bristol Hwy
Johnson City TN 37601
423 282-4661

(G-1518)
INDUSTRIAL WELDING & MCH CORP
5723 Atkins Tank Rd (24311-3297)
P.O. Box 137 (24311-0137)
PHONE..................................276 783-7105
Don H Kegley, *President*
Ronald Carrico, *Corp Secy*
James Stuart Buchanan, *Vice Pres*
▲ EMP: 18 EST: 1941
SQ FT: 40,000
SALES (est): 2.3MM **Privately Held**
SIC: **3272** 3449 Concrete products; miscellaneous metalwork

(G-1519)
JACO MANUFACTURING INC
263 Nicks Creek Rd (24311-3206)
P.O. Box 550 (24311-0550)
PHONE..................................276 783-2688
Rodney Young, *President*
Bennie Carter Young, *Corp Secy*
Shane Pierce, *Sales Mgr*
EMP: 10
SQ FT: 10,000
SALES (est): 960K **Privately Held**
WEB: www.jacomanufacturing.com
SIC: **3423** 8711 Caulking tools, hand; engineering services

(G-1520)
SEXTONS INCORPORATED
538 Kelly Hill Rd (24311-3119)
PHONE..................................276 783-4212
Star Sexton, *President*
Thornton D Sexton, *Vice Pres*
EMP: 2
SALES (est): 100K **Privately Held**
SIC: **3449** Bars, concrete reinforcing; fabricated steel

(G-1521)
SMYTH CNTY MCH FABRICATION LLC
260 Gordondale Rd (24311-3157)
PHONE..................................276 783-4582
Rebecca Crouse,
Gregory Sanders,
EMP: 25
SALES (est): 4.4MM **Privately Held**
WEB: www.smythcountymachine.com
SIC: **3599** Machine shop, jobbing & repair

(G-1522)
UTILITY TRAILER MFG CO
Also Called: United Trailers Intl
124 Mountain Empire Rd (24311-3296)
PHONE..................................276 783-8800
Kevin Atwell, *Purch Mgr*
Rick Taylor, *Purch Mgr*
David McAllister, *Purch Agent*
Philip Hendren, *Engineer*
Brad Starkei, *Manager*
EMP: 600
SALES (corp-wide): 845.3MM **Privately Held**
WEB: www.utm.com
SIC: **3585** 3537 3715 Refrigeration & heating equipment; industrial trucks & tractors; semitrailers for truck tractors
PA: Utility Trailer Manufacturing Company
17295 Railroad St Ste A
City Of Industry CA 91748
626 964-7319

(G-1523)
ZF ACTIVE SAFETY & ELEC US LLC
193 Mountain Empire Rd (24311-3231)
PHONE..................................276 783-1157
EMP: 331
SALES (corp-wide): 216.2K **Privately Held**
WEB: www.zf.com
SIC: **3714** Motor vehicle parts & accessories
HQ: Zf Active Safety & Electronics Us Llc
12001 Tech Center Dr
Livonia MI 48150
734 855-2600

(G-1524)
ZF ACTIVE SAFETY & ELEC US LLC
Also Called: TRW
222 Mountain Empire Rd (24311-3162)
PHONE..................................276 783-1990
Charlie Vipperman, *Safety Dir*
Susan Shelton, *Materials Mgr*
Patrick Messer, *Engineer*
Benita McRae, *Human Res Mgr*
Kieth Lenville, *Branch Mgr*
EMP: 200
SALES (corp-wide): 216.2K **Privately Held**
WEB: www.zf.com
SIC: 3714 Motor vehicle parts & accessories
HQ: Zf Active Safety & Electronics Us Llc
12001 Tech Center Dr
Livonia MI 48150
734 855-2600

Atlantic
Accomack County

(G-1525)
MARSHALL MANUFACTURING CO
32489 Nocks Landing Rd (23303-2625)
P.O. Box 293 (23303-0293)
PHONE..................................757 824-4061
Richard J Marshall, *President*
Kim Marshall, *Corp Secy*
EMP: 12
SQ FT: 20,000
SALES (est): 2.2MM **Privately Held**
WEB: www.mmczincs.com
SIC: 3496 2298 Traps, animal & fish; rope, except asbestos & wire

(G-1526)
WOOD SHOP
702 Rr 679 (23303)
P.O. Box 147 (23303-0147)
PHONE..................................757 824-4055
Kevin Greenly, *Owner*
EMP: 1
SQ FT: 1,200
SALES (est): 112.3K **Privately Held**
SIC: 2521 Cabinets, office: wood

Austinville
Wythe County

(G-1527)
AUSTINVILLE LIMESTONE CO INC
223 Newtown Church Rd (24312-3160)
P.O. Box 569 (24312-0569)
PHONE..................................276 699-6262
Kevin Mann, *President*
John Michener, *Corp Secy*
Jerry Mc Arthur, *Vice Pres*
David McArthur, *Vice Pres*
Jerry McArthur, *Vice Pres*
EMP: 28
SALES (est): 4.1MM **Privately Held**
WEB: www.avlime.com
SIC: 3281 Cut stone & stone products

(G-1528)
BOBBYS MEAT PROCESSING
1247 Ridge Rd (24312-3281)
PHONE..................................276 728-4547
Barbara Rosenbaum, *Principal*
EMP: 3
SALES (est): 229.8K **Privately Held**
SIC: 2011 Meat packing plants

(G-1529)
KIRK BURKETT MANUFACTURING
107 C St (24312-3089)
PHONE..................................276 699-6856
Kirk Burkett, *Owner*
EMP: 1
SALES (est): 100K **Privately Held**
SIC: 3911 5094 7631 Jewelry apparel; jewelry & precious stones; jewelry repair services

(G-1530)
PIONEER MACHINE CO INC
1453 Pauley Flatwoods Rd (24312-3602)
PHONE..................................276 699-1500
Randall Shimault, *President*
EMP: 12
SALES (est): 130K **Privately Held**
WEB: www.pioneermachineva.com
SIC: 3599 Machine shop, jobbing & repair

Axton
Henry County

(G-1531)
A C FURNITURE COMPANY INC (PA)
Also Called: Acf
3872 Martin Dr (24054-4093)
P.O. Box 40013, Roanoke (24022-0013)
PHONE..................................276 650-3356
Kennon G Robertson, *President*
Anderson James, *Managing Dir*
Kathryn L Robertson, *Corp Secy*
Van Whitlow, *Vice Pres*
Chris Robertson, *VP Business*
◆ EMP: 150
SQ FT: 65,000
SALES (est): 100.2MM **Privately Held**
WEB: www.acfurniture.com
SIC: 2521 Chairs, office: padded, upholstered or plain: wood

(G-1532)
A C FURNITURE COMPANY INC
Also Called: A C Furniture
3872 Martin Dr (24054-4093)
P.O. Box 40013, Roanoke (24022-0013)
PHONE..................................276 650-1802
Ken Robertson, *Branch Mgr*
EMP: 275
SALES (corp-wide): 100.2MM **Privately Held**
WEB: www.acfurniture.com
SIC: 2599 Hotel furniture; restaurant furniture, wood or metal
PA: A. C. Furniture Company, Inc.
3872 Martin Dr
Axton VA 24054
276 650-3356

(G-1533)
C & M HEATING & AC LLC
5087 Irisburg Rd (24054-3423)
PHONE..................................276 618-0955
Jimmy D Clark,
EMP: 2
SALES (est): 87.9K **Privately Held**
SIC: 3585 Heating & air conditioning combination units

(G-1534)
DUSKITS LLC
514 Country Place Rd (24054-2566)
PHONE..................................276 732-3121
Edward M Gravely,
▼ EMP: 3
SALES (est): 283.9K **Privately Held**
SIC: 2522 Tables, office: except wood

(G-1535)
EAST COAST WALK IN TUBS
1855 Irisburg Rd (24054-2204)
PHONE..................................804 365-8703
EMP: 3 EST: 2009
SALES (est): 130K **Privately Held**
SIC: 3088 Mfg Plastic Plumbing Fixtures

(G-1536)
EASTMAN PERFORMANCE FILMS LLC
Also Called: Cpfilms
47 Brenda Dr (24054-2520)
PHONE..................................276 650-3354
Mary Lambert, *Branch Mgr*
EMP: 50 **Publicly Held**
SIC: 2821 Plastics materials & resins
HQ: Eastman Performance Films, Llc
4210 The Great Rd
Fieldale VA 24089
276 627-3000

(G-1537)
G N H & ASSOCIATES INC
1219 Irisburg Rd (24054-2391)
PHONE..................................276 632-7867
Barbara Helmick, *President*
EMP: 1
SALES (est): 9.2K **Privately Held**
SIC: 3365 Aluminum & aluminum-based alloy castings

(G-1538)
JANNIE J JONES
Also Called: Janie Draperies Shop
994 Birchwood Rd (24054-2596)
PHONE..................................276 650-3174
Jannie J Jones, *Owner*
EMP: 1
SALES (est): 62.7K **Privately Held**
SIC: 2391 Curtains & draperies

(G-1539)
LAESTRELLITA
140 Axton Rd (24054-1844)
PHONE..................................276 650-7099
Josefina Tejeda, *Owner*
EMP: 2
SALES (est): 80K **Privately Held**
SIC: 2032 Ethnic foods: canned, jarred, etc.

(G-1540)
MADA VEMI ALPACAS
125 Tommy Carter Rd (24054-2949)
PHONE..................................434 770-1972
Dawn Dolpp, *Principal*
EMP: 2
SALES (est): 112.3K **Privately Held**
SIC: 3999 Pet supplies

(G-1541)
TAKE-A-BREAK HOME IMPRV LLC
548 Maple Springs Dr (24054-2308)
PHONE..................................434 251-4557
Sunshine D Puckett,
EMP: 4
SALES (est): 240K **Privately Held**
SIC: 1389 Construction, repair & dismantling services

(G-1542)
TRIAD DIGITAL MEDIA INC
839 Kaye Trail Ln (24054-3800)
PHONE..................................336 908-5884
Robert Brown, *Principal*
Greg Robbins, *Producer*
Steven Rosati, *Account Dir*
EMP: 1
SALES (est): 53.5K **Privately Held**
WEB: www.triadinteractivemedia.com
SIC: 2741 Miscellaneous publishing

(G-1543)
WOOD HARVESTERS
16880 Martinsville Hwy (24054-1928)
PHONE..................................276 650-2603
EMP: 2
SALES (est): 116.9K **Privately Held**
SIC: 2411 Logging

Aylett
King William County

(G-1544)
AGGREGATE INDUSTRIES MGT INC
1566 Mckendree Ln (23009-2121)
PHONE..................................804 994-5533
Dan Hughes, *Branch Mgr*
EMP: 3
SALES (corp-wide): 1.7B **Privately Held**
WEB: www.lafargeholcim.us
SIC: 3273 Ready-mixed concrete
HQ: Aggregate Industries Management, Inc.
8700 W Bryn Mawr Ave # 300
Chicago IL 60631
773 372-1000

(G-1545)
B AND B WELDING SERVICE LLC
552 Hazelwood Rd (23009-2217)
PHONE..................................804 994-2797
Charles Burton, *Mng Member*
EMP: 1
SALES (est): 24K **Privately Held**
SIC: 7692 7389 Welding repair; business services

(G-1546)
BILLY BILL LOGGING
95 Mitchells Mill Rd (23009-2600)
PHONE..................................804 512-9669
EMP: 3 EST: 2015
SALES (est): 98.8K **Privately Held**
SIC: 2411 Logging

(G-1547)
COUNTRY COURIER
8127 Richmnd Tapahnock Hw (23009-3024)
P.O. Box 160, St Stephns Ch (23148-0160)
PHONE..................................804 769-0259
Danny Clark, *Owner*
EMP: 5
SALES (est): 241.2K **Privately Held**
WEB: www.countrycouriernews.com
SIC: 2711 Newspapers, publishing & printing

(G-1548)
DUAL DYNAMICS INDUSTRAIL PAINT
3156 Smokey Rd (23009-2616)
PHONE..................................804 543-3216
Shannon Throckmorton, *Owner*
EMP: 1
SALES (est): 10K **Privately Held**
SIC: 2851 Paints & allied products

(G-1549)
JEFF HOSKINS
11414 W River Rd (23009-3002)
PHONE..................................804 769-1295
Jeff Hoskins, *Principal*
EMP: 2
SALES (est): 225.2K **Privately Held**
SIC: 2431 Millwork

(G-1550)
MID ATLNTIC TREE HRVESTORS INC
100 Globe Rd (23009-3557)
PHONE..................................804 769-8826
Robert Fauteux, *President*
EMP: 25
SALES (est): 3.9MM **Privately Held**
WEB: www.midatlantictreeharvestors.com
SIC: 2411 Logging camps & contractors

(G-1551)
OSBURN COATINGS INC
7421 Richmond Tapp Hwy (23009-3018)
P.O. Box 297 (23009-0297)
PHONE..................................804 769-3030
Herbert B Osburn, *President*
Elaine F Osburn, *Corp Secy*
Lee Trible, *Office Mgr*
Elaine Osburn, *Executive*
EMP: 2
SALES (est): 140K **Privately Held**
SIC: 2952 2851 Coating compounds, tar; paints & allied products

(G-1552)
RICE S STAKE & WOOD PRODUCTS
6858 King William Rd (23009-3514)
PHONE..................................804 769-3272
Grantland C Rice, *President*
Charles William Reed, *Admin Sec*
EMP: 6
SQ FT: 1,800
SALES (est): 250K **Privately Held**
SIC: 2499 Surveyors' stakes, wood

(G-1553)
ROMANCING STONE
4917 R Tappahannock Hwy (23009)
PHONE..................................804 769-7888
Paula Kindley, *Owner*
EMP: 1

SALES (est): 79K **Privately Held**
SIC: 3911 Jewelry, precious metal

(G-1554)
SEAL R L & SONS LOGGING
401 Midway Ln (23009-3163)
PHONE..........................804 769-3696
EMP: 3
SALES (est): 180K **Privately Held**
SIC: 2411 Logging

(G-1555)
TOP SHELF COATINGS LLC
2022 Locust Hill Rd (23009-2337)
PHONE..........................804 241-8644
William Prince, *Principal*
EMP: 2 EST: 2016
SALES (est): 117.9K **Privately Held**
SIC: 3479 Metal coating & allied service

(G-1556)
VIRGINIA CUSTOM BLEND LLC
304 Dorrell Rd (23009-2311)
PHONE..........................804 994-5099
Ray Vokaty, *Principal*
EMP: 2
SALES (est): 136.5K **Privately Held**
WEB: www.vacustomblend.com
SIC: 2131 Chewing & smoking tobacco

Bandy
Tazewell County

(G-1557)
C L E LOGGING INC
380 Reynolds Ridge Rd (24602-4034)
PHONE..........................276 881-8617
Gregory Meadows, *Principal*
EMP: 3
SALES (est): 190.2K **Privately Held**
SIC: 2411 Logging camps & contractors

(G-1558)
CONSOLIDATION COAL CO
700 Dry Fork Rd (24602-9129)
P.O. Box L, Oakwood (24631-1024)
PHONE..........................276 988-3010
J Harvey, *Principal*
EMP: 2
SALES (est): 125.6K **Privately Held**
SIC: 1221 Bituminous coal & lignite-surface mining

Barboursville
Orange County

(G-1559)
CHESTNUT OAK VINEYARD LLC
5050 Stony Point Rd (22923-2125)
PHONE..........................434 964-9104
Michael Shaps,
EMP: 3
SALES (est): 254.9K **Privately Held**
WEB: www.chestnutoakvineyard.com
SIC: 2084 0762 Wines; vineyard management & maintenance services

(G-1560)
COMPRHNSIVE ENRGY SLUTIONS INC
6243 Flintstone Dr (22923-2857)
PHONE..........................434 989-2547
Brian Burgess, *Director*
EMP: 2
SALES (est): 116.6K **Privately Held**
SIC: 3629 Electrical industrial apparatus

(G-1561)
H H ELEMENTS INC
4005 Gilbert Station Rd (22923-2008)
PHONE..........................434 249-8630
Harris Haynie, *President*
▲ EMP: 3
SALES (est): 75K **Privately Held**
WEB: www.hhelementsinc.com
SIC: 2675 Die-cut paper & board

(G-1562)
JAEGER & ERNST INC
Also Called: Jaeger & Ernst Cabinetmakers
4785 Burnley Station Rd (22923-1820)
PHONE..........................434 973-7018
Walter O Jaeger III, *President*
R Craig Ernst III, *Treasurer*
EMP: 11 EST: 1973
SQ FT: 5,000
SALES (est): 1.3MM **Privately Held**
WEB: www.jaegerandernst.com
SIC: 2434 2511 2431 Wood kitchen cabinets; wood household furniture; millwork

(G-1563)
LAMS LUMBER CO
Rr 20 (22923)
P.O. Box 138 (22923-0138)
PHONE..........................540 832-5173
Tony B Lam, *Owner*
EMP: 20 EST: 1977
SALES (est): 2.1MM **Privately Held**
SIC: 2421 2426 Sawmills & planing mills, general; hardwood dimension & flooring mills

(G-1564)
LIMITLESS GEAR LLC
63 White Cedar Rd (22923-2752)
PHONE..........................575 921-7475
Patrick McCrone,
Mickey Colombo,
Darrell Stevens,
EMP: 4
SALES (est): 334.3K **Privately Held**
WEB: www.limitlessgear.com
SIC: 3089 7389 Injection molding of plastics;

(G-1565)
OHG SCIENCE & TECHNOLOGY LLC
5916 Seminole Trl (22923-2831)
P.O. Box 800, Ruckersville (22968-0800)
PHONE..........................434 990-0500
REA Everitt, *Mng Member*
EMP: 5
SALES (est): 100K **Privately Held**
SIC: 3669 Emergency alarms

(G-1566)
SHIRLEYS UNF & ALTERATIONS LLC
6420 Seminole Trl (22923-2836)
PHONE..........................434 985-2042
Janice Lamm, *Mng Member*
EMP: 1 EST: 2010
SALES (est): 44.3K **Privately Held**
SIC: 2395 Embroidery products, except schiffli machine

(G-1567)
STEVES GENERATOR SERVICE LLC
15620 Burnley Rd (22923-8412)
PHONE..........................540 661-8675
Steve Yelton,
EMP: 1
SALES (est): 99.8K **Privately Held**
SIC: 3621 Motors & generators

(G-1568)
VIRGINIA STAIR COMPANY
6420 Seminole Trl Ste 6 (22923-2836)
PHONE..........................434 823-2587
EMP: 2 EST: 2009
SALES (est): 94.1K **Privately Held**
SIC: 3446 Stairs, staircases, stair treads: prefabricated metal

(G-1569)
W A MARKS FINE WOODWORKING
5026 Burnley Ln (22923-1838)
PHONE..........................434 973-9785
William A Marks, *Administration*
EMP: 2
SALES (est): 65.4K **Privately Held**
WEB: www.marksfinewoodwork.com
SIC: 2431 Millwork

Barhamsville
New Kent County

(G-1570)
EARLYRISERS INC
18423 Heath Industrial Rd (23011-2051)
P.O. Box 1593, Newport News (23601-0593)
PHONE..........................757 566-4199
Thomas Franklin, *Principal*
EMP: 2 EST: 2007
SALES (est): 208.7K **Privately Held**
SIC: 2431 1799 Staircases, stairs & railings; special trade contractors

(G-1571)
GAUTHIER VINEYARD LLC
19665 High Bluff Ln (23011-2355)
PHONE..........................703 622-1107
B Elliott Bondurant, *Administration*
EMP: 4 EST: 2010
SALES (est): 290K **Privately Held**
WEB: www.gauthiervineyard.com
SIC: 2084 Wines

(G-1572)
JC PALLET COMPANY INC (PA)
18427 New Kent Hwy (23011-2040)
P.O. Box 277 (23011-0277)
PHONE..........................800 754-5050
Holly Miller-Bopp, *President*
Larry Bopp, *Sales Dir*
EMP: 41
SQ FT: 10,000
SALES (est): 7.7MM **Privately Held**
WEB: www.jcpallet.com
SIC: 2448 Pallets, wood

(G-1573)
SELLARS LOGGING
19601 Tabernacle Rd (23011-2108)
PHONE..........................757 566-0613
Donald T Sellars, *Owner*
EMP: 1
SALES (est): 136.6K **Privately Held**
SIC: 2411 Pole cutting contractors

(G-1574)
SICKAL LOGGING
6725 Farmers Dr (23011-2313)
PHONE..........................804 366-1965
Ray B Sickal, *Principal*
EMP: 2
SALES (est): 205.1K **Privately Held**
SIC: 2411 Logging camps & contractors

Barren Springs
Wythe County

(G-1575)
RT 100 WELDING FAB MACHIN
121 Lone Ash Rd (24313-3558)
PHONE..........................276 766-0100
Roger Erwin, *Owner*
William Erwin, *Principal*
EMP: 1
SALES (est): 72K **Privately Held**
SIC: 7692 Welding repair

(G-1576)
VALLEY WELDING
3202 Foster Falls Rd (24313-3509)
P.O. Box 182 (24313-0182)
PHONE..........................276 733-7942
Ben Chrisley, *Principal*
EMP: 1
SALES (est): 54.9K **Privately Held**
SIC: 7692 Welding repair

Bassett
Henry County

(G-1577)
BASSETT DIRECT SC LLC
3525 Fairystone Park Hwy (24055-4444)
PHONE..........................276 629-6000
EMP: 1

SALES (est): 63K
SALES (corp-wide): 452MM **Publicly Held**
SIC: 2511 Wood household furniture
PA: Bassett Furniture Industries Incorporated
3525 Fairystone Park Hwy
Bassett VA 24055
276 629-6000

(G-1578)
BASSETT FURNITURE INDS INC (PA)
3525 Fairystone Park Hwy (24055-4444)
P.O. Box 626 (24055-0626)
PHONE..........................276 629-6000
Robert H Spilman Jr, *Ch of Bd*
Kevin Bassett, *Principal*
Dean Davidson, *Regional Mgr*
John E Bassett III, *Senior VP*
Bruce R Cohenour, *Senior VP*
◆ EMP: 1189 EST: 1902
SALES: 452MM **Publicly Held**
WEB: www.bassettfurniture.com
SIC: 2511 2512 5021 5712 Wood household furniture; upholstered household furniture; furniture; furniture stores

(G-1579)
BASSETT FURNITURE INDS NC LLC (HQ)
Also Called: Weiman Company Division
3525 Fairystone Park Hwy (24055-4444)
P.O. Box 626 (24055-0626)
PHONE..........................276 629-6000
Paul Fulton,
R H Spilman Jr,
◆ EMP: 14 EST: 1946
SQ FT: 20,000
SALES (est): 110.2MM
SALES (corp-wide): 452MM **Publicly Held**
WEB: www.bassettfurniture.com
SIC: 2512 2511 Upholstered household furniture; tables, household; household: wood
PA: Bassett Furniture Industries Incorporated
3525 Fairystone Park Hwy
Bassett VA 24055
276 629-6000

(G-1580)
BASSETT MIRROR COMPANY INC
Also Called: BMC
1290 Philpott Dr (24055-4095)
P.O. Box 627 (24055-0627)
PHONE..........................276 629-3341
Lewis A Canter II, *President*
Brad Russel, *President*
Jerry Dodson, *Exec VP*
Ron Cepulo, *Vice Pres*
Brad Russell, *Vice Pres*
◆ EMP: 200 EST: 1947
SQ FT: 300,000
SALES (est): 25.7MM **Privately Held**
WEB: www.bassettmirror.com
SIC: 2512 2514 3231 2511 Wood upholstered chairs & couches; metal household furniture; furniture tops, glass: cut, beveled or polished; mirrored glass; wood household furniture

(G-1581)
DAGNAT WOODWORKS LLC
1089 Flamingo Rd (24055-3580)
PHONE..........................276 627-1039
David Helms, *Principal*
EMP: 1
SALES (est): 54.1K **Privately Held**
SIC: 2431 Millwork

(G-1582)
ECO-SIGNS AND GRAPHICS
6520 Virginia Ave (24055-5391)
PHONE..........................336 891-1334
Crystal Lusk, *Principal*
Casey Lusk, *Principal*
EMP: 2
SALES (est): 72.6K **Privately Held**
SIC: 3993 Signs & advertising specialties

(G-1583)
GAMMONS WELDING &
FABRICATION
151 Northview Cir (24055-6020)
PHONE..............................276 627-0664
Michael Ralph Gammons, *Principal*
EMP: 1 **Privately Held**
SIC: 7692 Welding repair

(G-1584)
GS INDUSTRIES BASSETT LTD
85 Rosemont Rd (24055-5557)
PHONE..............................276 629-5317
Terry Cundiff, *President*
Jeff Roberts, *Manager*
Samuel Williams, *Technology*
▲ **EMP:** 54
SQ FT: 148,000
SALES (est): 5.6MM **Privately Held**
WEB: www.gsib.com
SIC: 3089 Injection molded finished plastic
　products; injection molding of plastics

(G-1585)
LESTER GROUP
1230 Oak Level Rd (24055-4241)
PHONE..............................276 627-0346
EMP: 2
SALES (est): 92K **Privately Held**
SIC: 2411 Logging

(G-1586)
LEWIS LUMBER MILL
63 Healms Rd (24055-3077)
PHONE..............................276 629-1600
EMP: 8
SALES (est): 370K **Privately Held**
SIC: 2421 Sawmill/Planing Mill

(G-1587)
NAFF WELDING INC
4724 Philpott Dr (24055-4775)
PHONE..............................276 629-1129
David Naff, *President*
Bobby Naff, *Exec VP*
Angela Naff, *Admin Sec*
EMP: 14
SQ FT: 12,000
SALES (est): 2.3MM **Privately Held**
SIC: 3441 3599 Fabricated structural
　metal; machine shop, jobbing & repair

(G-1588)
PACKAGING PRODUCTS INC
200 Little Creek Dr (24055-5931)
PHONE..............................276 629-3481
Donald C Boaz, *President*
EMP: 20
SQ FT: 60,000
SALES (est): 3.9MM **Privately Held**
WEB: www.packagingproductsinc.com
SIC: 2653 2671 4225 Boxes, corrugated:
　made from purchased materials; packag-
　ing paper & plastics film, coated & lami-
　nated; general warehousing & storage

(G-1589)
RELIABLE WELDING &
FABRICATORS
1850 Fairystone Park Hwy (24055-4008)
PHONE..............................276 629-2593
C D Stapleton, *President*
Tracy King, *Admin Sec*
Terri Stapleton, *Administration*
EMP: 10
SQ FT: 6,600
SALES (est): 2.1MM **Privately Held**
SIC: 3535 1711 Conveyors & conveying
　equipment; sprinkler contractors

(G-1590)
RESCUE SYSTEMS INC
6520 Virginia Ave (24055-5391)
P.O. Box 596, Collinsville (24078-0596)
PHONE..............................276 629-2900
EMP: 7
SALES (est): 829.6K **Privately Held**
SIC: 3842 5099 Surgical Appliances And
　Supplies, Nsk

(G-1591)
ROBERT L PENN
112 Stoneyridge Rd (24055-4062)
PHONE..............................276 629-2211
Robert L Penn, *Principal*

EMP: 3
SALES (est): 214.3K **Privately Held**
SIC: 2411 Logging

Bastian
Bland County

(G-1592)
A A J WELDING INC
3531 Grapefield Rd (24314-5061)
PHONE..............................276 688-0191
Jimmy Page, *President*
Anna Page, *Vice Pres*
EMP: 2
SALES (est): 100K **Privately Held**
SIC: 7692 Welding repair

(G-1593)
SKYWAY OUTDOOR INC
65 Progress Dr (24314-5311)
PHONE..............................276 688-0248
Paula J Goforth, *President*
Steve Nolley, *CFO*
EMP: 14 EST: 1994
SQ FT: 15,000
SALES (est): 356.7K **Privately Held**
WEB: www.skywayoutdoor.com
SIC: 3993 Signs & advertising specialties

(G-1594)
VIRGINIA STEEL &
FABRICATION
36 Progress Dr (24314-5312)
P.O. Box 1009, Bluefield (24605-4009)
PHONE..............................276 688-2125
Arnold Maynard, *President*
David Stinson, *Vice Pres*
Teresa Lovell, *Purch Mgr*
EMP: 22 EST: 1994
SQ FT: 30,000
SALES (est): 6MM **Privately Held**
WEB: www.va-steel.weebly.com
SIC: 3441 3444 3443 Fabricated struc-
　tural metal; sheet metalwork; fabricated
　plate work (boiler shop)

Battery Park
Isle Of Wight County

(G-1595)
DOCKSIDE SEAFOOD
1002 Newport St (23304)
P.O. Box 67 (23304-0067)
PHONE..............................757 357-9298
Joseph Melzer Jr, *Owner*
EMP: 2
SALES (est): 88.8K **Privately Held**
SIC: 2091 Oysters, preserved & cured

Bealeton
Fauquier County

(G-1596)
AWESOME WELLNESS
12602 Lake Coventry Dr (22712-7337)
PHONE..............................540 439-0808
Ron Tiemens, *Principal*
EMP: 2
SALES (est): 105.1K **Privately Held**
SIC: 2023 Dietary supplements, dairy &
　non-dairy based

(G-1597)
DECALS BY ZEBRA RACING
11672 Marsh Rd (22712-7111)
PHONE..............................540 439-8883
Geoff Godfrey, *Owner*
EMP: 2
SALES (est): 95K **Privately Held**
SIC: 2759 Commercial printing

(G-1598)
DOGWOOD MONTESSORI &C
10741 James Madison Hwy (22712-7928)
PHONE..............................540 439-3572
Brenda Mooney, *Principal*
EMP: 1 EST: 2014
SALES (est): 43.9K **Privately Held**
SIC: 2499 Wood products

(G-1599)
FULL AWN FAB LLC
10251 Fayettesville Rd (22712-6918)
PHONE..............................540 439-5173
Brandon Turner, *Principal*
EMP: 3
SALES (est): 283.9K **Privately Held**
WEB: www.fullawnfab.com
SIC: 3441 Fabricated structural metal

(G-1600)
LANE ENTERPRISES INC
Also Called: Lane Metal Products
6369 Schoolhouse Rd (22712-9351)
P.O. Box 67 (22712-0067)
PHONE..............................540 439-3201
Bill Wingardner, *Manager*
EMP: 15
SQ FT: 28,049
SALES (corp-wide): 68.7MM **Privately
Held**
WEB: www.lane-enterprises.com
SIC: 3498 3444 3084 Fabricated pipe &
　fittings; sheet metalwork; plastics pipe
PA: Lane Enterprises, Inc.
　3905 Hartzdale Dr Ste 514
　Camp Hill PA 17011
　717 761-8175

(G-1601)
MORAIS VINEYARDS AND
WINERY
11409 Marsh Rd (22712-7040)
PHONE..............................540 439-9520
Jos Morais, *Principal*
Aroma Tasting, *Manager*
EMP: 4
SALES (est): 300.7K **Privately Held**
WEB: www.moraisvineyards.com
SIC: 2084 Wines

(G-1602)
NORTHERN VIRGINIA
WOODWORK INC
12948 Elk Run Rd (22712-7319)
P.O. Box 252, Hartwood (22471-0252)
PHONE..............................540 752-6128
Bill Sheffield, *Principal*
EMP: 2
SALES (est): 241.2K **Privately Held**
SIC: 2431 Millwork

(G-1603)
NOVA CONCRETE PRODUCTS
INC
5303 Ritchie Rd (22712-7142)
PHONE..............................540 439-2978
Steve Payne, *President*
Michelle Payne, *President*
EMP: 5
SQ FT: 26,398
SALES (est): 309.8K **Privately Held**
WEB: www.outputtransformer.net
SIC: 3272 2899 Concrete products; con-
　crete curing & hardening compounds

(G-1604)
PRE CAST OF VIRGINIA
5303 Ritchie Rd (22712-7142)
PHONE..............................540 439-2978
Anthony Barnhill, *Manager*
EMP: 2
SALES (est): 167.3K **Privately Held**
SIC: 3272 Concrete products, precast

(G-1605)
RAPPAHANNOCK BOAT WORKS
INC
Also Called: Tiny Power
4403 Dyes Ln (22712-9641)
PHONE..............................540 439-4045
Ronald Baird, *President*
Deanna Baird, *Admin Sec*
EMP: 2
SALES (est): 100K **Privately Held**
WEB: www.tinypower.com
SIC: 3732 Boat building & repairing

(G-1606)
ROCKIN RACK LLC
11274 Falling Creek Dr (22712-9452)
PHONE..............................540 359-2264
Dane Frasier,
EMP: 4

SALES (est): 131.1K **Privately Held**
SIC: 3999 Manufacturing industries

(G-1607)
UNIQUE FLEXIQUE LLC
11335 Whipkey Dr (22712-7738)
PHONE..............................540 439-4465
Joseph Bawol,
Marilyn Bawol,
EMP: 1
SALES (est): 51.9K **Privately Held**
SIC: 2064 7389 Cake ornaments, confec-
　tionery;

Beaverdam
Hanover County

(G-1608)
DIVERSFIED WLDG FBRICATION
LLC
19212 Woodsons Mill Rd (23015-1221)
PHONE..............................804 449-6699
Debra S Lloyd, *Administration*
EMP: 1
SALES (est): 45.3K **Privately Held**
SIC: 7692 Welding repair

(G-1609)
H L CORKER & SON INC
18310 Teman Rd (23015-1420)
PHONE..............................804 449-6686
T Edward Corker, *President*
Anita Corker, *Admin Sec*
EMP: 2 EST: 1967
SALES (est): 189.5K **Privately Held**
SIC: 2411 Logging camps & contractors

(G-1610)
M GAUTREAUX HORSESHOE
15444 Beaver Den Ln (23015-2000)
PHONE..............................540 840-3153
EMP: 2
SALES (est): 127.4K **Privately Held**
SIC: 3462 Horseshoes

(G-1611)
SIM NET INC
12664 Old Ridge Rd (23015-1741)
PHONE..............................804 752-2776
Edward F Stone Jr, *President*
EMP: 4
SQ FT: 20,000
SALES (est): 869.2K **Privately Held**
SIC: 3844 8071 Irradiation equipment; X-
　ray laboratory, including dental

(G-1612)
STEELWRIGHT PRODUCTS
20254 Shockey Ln (23015-2042)
PHONE..............................951 870-6670
Robert L Santala Jr, *Owner*
EMP: 1
SALES (est): 30K **Privately Held**
WEB: www.steelwright.com
SIC: 3599 Machine shop, jobbing & repair

(G-1613)
SURGICAL INSTR SHARPENING
INC
16205 Trainham Rd (23015-1302)
PHONE..............................804 883-6010
Elizabeth P Gassman, *President*
EMP: 2
SALES (est): 100K **Privately Held**
SIC: 3841 Surgical knife blades & handles

(G-1614)
TIGERSEAL PRODUCTS LLC
13093 Old Ridge Rd (23015-1744)
PHONE..............................800 899-9389
John Durose, *Mng Member*
Brenda Durose,
EMP: 5
SQ FT: 1,500
SALES (est): 1.2MM **Privately Held**
WEB: www.tigersealproducts.com
SIC: 2672 3565 3579 2671 Adhesive pa-
　pers, labels or tapes: from purchased ma-
　terial; packing & wrapping machinery;
　mailing, letter handling & addressing ma-
　chines; packaging paper & plastics film,
　coated & laminated

▲ = Import ▼=Export
◆ =Import/Export

(G-1615)
TIMBERLAKE CONTRACTING LLC
16370 Pine Springs Ln (23015-1627)
PHONE.............................804 449-1517
Donald Timberlake,
Lee Timberlake,
EMP: 2
SALES (est): 150K **Privately Held**
WEB: www.timberlakecontracting.com
SIC: 3272 Concrete products

(G-1616)
WINDBORNE PRESS LLC
17252 Tulip Poplar Rd (23015-1755)
PHONE.............................804 227-3431
Raymond Leffler, *Principal*
EMP: 2
SALES (est): 75.9K **Privately Held**
SIC: 2741 Miscellaneous publishing

Bedford
Bedford County

(G-1617)
ACE SCREEN PRINTING INC
1379 Pecks Rd (24523-4903)
PHONE.............................540 297-2200
Melissa Wade, *President*
EMP: 1
SALES (est): 20K **Privately Held**
SIC: 2759 Screen printing

(G-1618)
ALLEN INDUSTRIES INTL LLC
414 Jackson St (24523-3414)
PHONE.............................540 797-5230
Hunter Allen Jr, *Principal*
EMP: 2
SALES (est): 101K **Privately Held**
SIC: 3999 Manufacturing industries

(G-1619)
AMP SALES & SERVICE LLC
740 Industrial Ave (24523-3208)
PHONE.............................540 586-1021
Daniel McClain,
EMP: 8
SALES (est): 311.1K **Privately Held**
WEB: www.ampservicesllc.com
SIC: 3713 Truck & bus bodies

(G-1620)
ATX TECHNOLOGIES LLC
Also Called: Odorkill
414 Jackson St (24523-3414)
P.O. Box 469 (24523-0469)
PHONE.............................540 586-4100
Harry Hunter Allen Jr,
EMP: 1
SALES (est): 116.1K **Privately Held**
WEB: www.odorkill.com
SIC: 2842 Specialty cleaning, polishes & sanitation goods

(G-1621)
AXIOM ARMOR LLC
115 S Bridge St (24523-2701)
PHONE.............................540 583-6184
EMP: 2
SALES (est): 88.3K **Privately Held**
SIC: 3634 Electric household cooking appliances

(G-1622)
B & B PRINTING
402 E Main St (24523-2017)
PHONE.............................540 586-1020
EMP: 2
SALES (est): 83.9K **Privately Held**
SIC: 2752 Lithographic Commercial Printing

(G-1623)
BEDFORD BULLETIN LLC
402 E Main St (24523-2017)
P.O. Box 331 (24523-0331)
PHONE.............................540 586-8612
EMP: 1
SALES (est): 177.1K **Privately Held**
WEB: www.bedfordbulletin.com
SIC: 2711 Commercial printing & newspaper publishing combined

HQ: Landmark Community Newspapers, Llc
601 Taylorsville Rd
Shelbyville KY 40065
502 633-4334

(G-1624)
BEDFORD READY-MIX CON CO INC
805 Railroad Ave (24523-2153)
PHONE.............................540 586-8380
O'Brian Rebecca Holt, *Vice Pres*
Sidney Burns, *Manager*
EMP: 8
SQ FT: 4,200
SALES (est): 846.1K
SALES (corp-wide): 3.7MM **Privately Held**
WEB: www.lrmcc.com
SIC: 3273 Ready-mixed concrete
PA: Lynchburg Ready-Mix Concrete Co., Incorporated
100 Halsey Rd
Lynchburg VA 24501
434 846-6563

(G-1625)
BEDFORD STORAGE INVESTMENT LLC
Also Called: Fostek
1001 Broad St (24523-2231)
PHONE.............................574 284-1000
Staci Paul, *Accounting Mgr*
Philip R Foster, *Mng Member*
EMP: 62
SALES (est): 12MM **Privately Held**
WEB: www.fostek.com
SIC: 3086 Plastics foam products

(G-1626)
BEDFORD WEAVING INC
Also Called: GMAC
1211 Monroe St (24523-2298)
P.O. Box 449 (24523-0449)
PHONE.............................540 586-8235
Mark Garbarini, *President*
Philip J Garbarini, *President*
Betty L White, *Treasurer*
Nancy G Vest, *Admin Sec*
◆ EMP: 150 EST: 1947
SQ FT: 181,000
SALES (est): 24.2MM **Privately Held**
WEB: www.bedfordweaving.com
SIC: 2221 2241 2396 Fiberglass fabrics; fabric tapes; automotive & apparel trimmings

(G-1627)
BISON PRINTING INC
1342 On Time Rd (24523-6427)
PHONE.............................540 586-3955
Franz X Beisser IV, *President*
Jeff Bryant, *President*
Alfons J Beisser, *Vice Pres*
Christopher M Beisser, *Vice Pres*
Sharon Orange, *Accountant*
EMP: 45 EST: 1978
SQ FT: 42,000
SALES (est): 9.7MM **Privately Held**
WEB: www.bisonprinting.com
SIC: 2752 7331 2731 2759 Commercial printing, offset; lithographing on metal; direct mail advertising services; pamphlets; publishing & printing; commercial printing

(G-1628)
BLUE RIDGE OPTICS LLC
1617 Longwood Ave (24523-1705)
PHONE.............................540 586-8526
Eric Schrock, *QC Mgr*
Kish Thakurwani, *Manager*
Siehien Walter,
▲ EMP: 30
SQ FT: 45,000
SALES (est): 6MM **Privately Held**
WEB: www.blueridgeoptics.com
SIC: 3827 Optical instruments & apparatus

(G-1629)
BURNETTE CABINET SHOP INC
5106 Falling Creek Rd (24523-5053)
PHONE.............................540 586-0147
Jesse Roy Burnette, *President*
Joanne Anderson, *Corp Secy*
EMP: 5

WEB: www.burnettecabinetshop.com
SIC: 2434 2431 5211 Wood kitchen cabinets; millwork; lumber products

(G-1630)
CARDINAL MFG
940 Orange St (24523-3303)
PHONE.............................540 779-7790
Shannon Jurkus, *Principal*
EMP: 2
SALES (est): 55.9K **Privately Held**
SIC: 3999 Manufacturing industries

(G-1631)
CLAUDE COFER
Also Called: Triple-F-Farm
2488 Teass Ter (24523-5072)
PHONE.............................540 330-9921
Claude Cofer, *Owner*
EMP: 1 EST: 2013
SALES (est): 69.5K **Privately Held**
SIC: 3715 4212 Trailers or vans for transporting horses; animal & farm product transportation services

(G-1632)
CORNERSTONE ARCHTECTURAL STONE
705 Industrial Ave (24523-3209)
PHONE.............................540 297-3686
Louis Richard Witt, *President*
EMP: 7
SALES (est): 490K **Privately Held**
WEB: www.cornerstoneprecast.com
SIC: 3272 Stone, cast concrete

(G-1633)
EAST COAST FABRICATORS INC
1635 Venture Blvd (24523-3441)
PHONE.............................540 587-7170
Howard McGrath, *CEO*
Cynthia McGrath, *Vice Pres*
Joe McGrath, *Prdtn Mgr*
EMP: 6
SQ FT: 12,000
SALES (est): 1.2MM **Privately Held**
WEB: www.eastcoastfabricators.com
SIC: 3549 Metalworking machinery

(G-1634)
ELEVATING EQP INSPTN SVC LLC
Also Called: Eeis
208 W Depot St (24523-1936)
PHONE.............................800 346-0287
Carl A McDilda, *Mng Member*
EMP: 10
SALES (est): 1.3MM **Privately Held**
WEB: www.eeisonline.com
SIC: 3534 7389 Elevators & equipment; industrial & commercial equipment inspection service

(G-1635)
EMERSON CREEK POTTERY INC
1068 Pottery Ln (24523-6081)
PHONE.............................540 297-7524
Jim Leavitt, *President*
Lucy Porter, *Manager*
EMP: 20
SQ FT: 30,000
SALES (est): 1.9MM **Privately Held**
WEB: www.emersoncreekpottery.com
SIC: 3269 5719 Figures: pottery, china, earthenware & stoneware; pottery

(G-1636)
F & D MANUFACTURING & SUPPLY
1023 Pearsall Dr (24523-5735)
P.O. Box 1203 (24523-8003)
PHONE.............................540 586-6111
Mary Young, *President*
Michael David Young, *Vice Pres*
David L Young, *Manager*
EMP: 2
SALES (est): 271.7K **Privately Held**
SIC: 2899 3086 Insulating compounds; plastics foam products

(G-1637)
FOSTEK INC
Also Called: Bedford Storage
1001 Broad St (24523-2231)
PHONE.............................540 587-5870
Phil Foster, *President*
Josh Grohs, *General Mgr*
EMP: 70 EST: 2012
SALES (est): 1.9MM **Privately Held**
WEB: www.fostek.com
SIC: 3086 Plastics foam products

(G-1638)
FRANK CHERVAN
1576 Dawn Dr (24523-2217)
P.O. Box 1147 (24523-1147)
PHONE.............................540 586-5600
EMP: 2
SALES (est): 212K **Privately Held**
WEB: www.chervan.com
SIC: 2511 Wood household furniture

(G-1639)
GILLESPIE INC
3117 Glenwood Dr (24523-6192)
PHONE.............................540 297-4432
George Martin, *President*
Lou Martin, *Corp Secy*
Mark Martin, *Vice Pres*
Fuller Martin, *Treasurer*
EMP: 3
SQ FT: 500
SALES (est): 500K **Privately Held**
SIC: 2411 Logging

(G-1640)
HARRIS PRINTING COMPANY INC
401 W Franklin St (24523-2719)
PHONE.............................540 586-8326
Robert E Harris, *Branch Mgr*
EMP: 3
SALES (corp-wide): 6.7MM **Privately Held**
WEB: www.harrisprintingcompany.com
SIC: 2752 Commercial printing, offset
PA: Harris Printing Company, Inc.
201 S Trade St
West End NC
910 673-5641

(G-1641)
K & K SIGNS
Also Called: Victory Lane Karting Parts
5337 E Lynchburg Salem (24523-6929)
PHONE.............................540 586-0542
Vicki Krantz, *Owner*
EMP: 2
SALES (est): 175.2K **Privately Held**
SIC: 3993 5599 7513 Electric signs; go-carts; truck rental & leasing, no drivers

(G-1642)
KIDWELL CONSTRUCTION LLC
Also Called: Robert Allen
507 South St (24523-2840)
PHONE.............................540 296-4173
Joshua Kidwell,
EMP: 1
SALES (est): 25K **Privately Held**
SIC: 1389 Construction, repair & dismantling services

(G-1643)
LIGHTSPEED INFRARED LLC
302 W Washington St (24523-2733)
PHONE.............................540 875-6796
Jeff Tyler, *Mng Member*
EMP: 5 EST: 2013
SALES (est): 536.7K **Privately Held**
WEB: www.lightspeedir.com
SIC: 3674 3695 Thin film circuits; magnetic & optical recording media

(G-1644)
MICHAEL W TUCK
1554 Headens Bridge Rd (24523-4847)
PHONE.............................540 297-1231
Michael W Tuck, *Principal*
EMP: 2
SALES (est): 155K **Privately Held**
SIC: 2411 Logging

GEOGRAPHIC

(G-1645)
MOOG USA INC
1265 Emerald Crest Dr (24523-3215)
PHONE..................................540 586-6700
Rita Moog, *President*
Cindy Watson, *Comptroller*
▲ EMP: 1
SALES (est): 224.9K
SALES (corp-wide): 82.6K **Privately Held**
WEB: www.moog-online.com
SIC: 3829 Physical property testing equipment
HQ: Moog Gmbh Bruckenzugangstechnik
Im Gewerbegebiet 8
Deggenhausertal 88693
755 593-30

(G-1646)
NZO LLC
Also Called: Central Virginia Manufacturing
596 Blue Ridge Ave Ste 1a (24523-2604)
PHONE..................................434 660-7338
David Hanowitz, *President*
EMP: 19
SALES (est): 2.5MM **Privately Held**
WEB: www.cvmanufacturing.net
SIC: 3444 Pipe, sheet metal

(G-1647)
OG PRESSMORE LLC
2092 Wilson Church Rd (24523-4802)
PHONE..................................434 218-0304
Jacob McGlauflin, *Administration*
EMP: 2 EST: 2011
SALES (est): 123.5K **Privately Held**
WEB: www.ogpressmore.com
SIC: 2759 Screen printing

(G-1648)
PARKWAY STL RULE CTNG DIES INC
1912 Woodside Ave (24523-2318)
PHONE..................................540 586-4948
Mark Venhorst, *President*
James Bowyer, *Vice Pres*
Jean V Enhorst, *Vice Pres*
Jean V Venhorst, *Treasurer*
Jim Bowyer, *Manager*
EMP: 25
SQ FT: 15,000
SALES (est): 3.3MM **Privately Held**
WEB: www.parkwaydies.com
SIC: 3544 Dies, steel rule; special dies & tools

(G-1649)
PIEDMONT METAL PRODUCTS INC
915 Orange St (24523-5885)
P.O. Box 546 (24523-0546)
PHONE..................................540 586-0674
Frank E Williams III, *Ch of Bd*
Harvey R Johnson, *President*
EMP: 20 EST: 1974
SQ FT: 1,700
SALES (est): 4.6MM
SALES (corp-wide): 77.4MM **Privately Held**
WEB: www.wmsi.com
SIC: 3441 Fabricated structural metal
PA: Williams Industries Incorporated
1128 Tyler Farms Dr
Raleigh NC 27603
919 604-1746

(G-1650)
PINNACLE QUALITY ASRN SVCS
1106 Park St (24523-2138)
PHONE..................................540 425-4123
Merritt A Grissinger, *Principal*
EMP: 2
SALES (est): 200K **Privately Held**
SIC: 2834 Pharmaceutical preparations

(G-1651)
POLYTHANE OF VIRGINIA INC
Also Called: 5654 VI Byway
5654 Virginia Byway (24523-4743)
PHONE..................................540 586-3511
Thomas Lentesch, *President*
R K Lazorchack, *Vice Pres*
Roger K Lazorchack, *Vice Pres*
EMP: 5
SQ FT: 7,500

SALES (est): 1MM **Privately Held**
SIC: 3089 3299 2821 Molding primary plastic; ceramic fiber; plastics materials & resins

(G-1652)
**PRECISNCNTAINERTECHNOLO
GIES LL**
720 Industrial Ave (24523-3208)
PHONE..................................540 425-4756
EMP: 3
SALES (est): 198.7K **Privately Held**
WEB: www.pctllc.com
SIC: 3535 Conveyors & conveying equipment

(G-1653)
PRO TECH FABRICATIONS INC
1587 Dawn Dr (24523-2216)
P.O. Box 1166 (24523-1166)
PHONE..................................540 587-5590
Chris Bass, *President*
EMP: 5
SALES (est): 681.9K **Privately Held**
WEB: www.protechfabrications.com
SIC: 3069 Hard rubber products

(G-1654)
RAPID PRINTING INC
Also Called: Rapid Printing & Office Sups
113 N Bridge St (24523-1923)
PHONE..................................540 586-1243
Elizabeth Brown, *President*
James R Melton, *President*
Marsha Melton, *Treasurer*
EMP: 5
SQ FT: 3,400
SALES (est): 858.5K **Privately Held**
WEB: www.rapidprt.com
SIC: 2752 5943 5947 5112 Commercial printing, offset; office forms & supplies; gift shop; greeting cards

(G-1655)
REDCO MACHINE INC
3032 Forest Rd (24523-4101)
P.O. Box 866 (24523-0866)
PHONE..................................540 586-3545
Troy R Deeter, *President*
Roger E Deeter, *President*
Troy Deeter, *President*
Steve Lee, *Sales Mgr*
Carolyn Deeter, *Admin Sec*
EMP: 40
SQ FT: 24,000
SALES (est): 7.2MM **Privately Held**
WEB: www.redcomachine.com
SIC: 3599 3544 Machine shop, jobbing & repair; special dies, tools, jigs & fixtures

(G-1656)
SAM MOORE FURNITURE LLC
1556 Dawn Dr (24523-2217)
P.O. Box 339 (24523-0339)
PHONE..................................540 586-8253
Suzy Fulton, *President*
Alan Cole,
▲ EMP: 300 EST: 1940
SQ FT: 320,000
SALES (est): 46MM
SALES (corp-wide): 610.8MM **Publicly Held**
WEB: www.sammoore.com
SIC: 2512 5712 Chairs: upholstered on wood frames; furniture stores
PA: Hooker Furniture Corporation
440 Commonwealth Blvd E
Martinsville VA 24112
276 632-2133

(G-1657)
SHINY STUFF
630 Mountain Ave (24523-1945)
PHONE..................................540 586-4446
Nancy Ftrachan, *Owner*
EMP: 2
SALES (est): 176.6K **Privately Held**
WEB: www.teapotjewelry.com
SIC: 3479 Engraving jewelry silverware, or metal

(G-1658)
SMYTH COMPANIES LLC
311 W Depot St (24523-1937)
P.O. Box 609 (24523-0609)
PHONE..................................540 586-2311

Allen Cheek, *Division Mgr*
EMP: 105 **Privately Held**
WEB: www.smythco.com
SIC: 2752 Commercial printing, offset
HQ: Smyth Companies, Llc
1085 Snelling Ave N
Saint Paul MN 55108
651 646-4544

(G-1659)
**SOUTHERN FLAVORING
COMPANY INC**
1330 Norfolk Ave (24523-2223)
P.O. Box 341 (24523-0341)
PHONE..................................540 586-8565
E Thomas Messier, *Ch of Bd*
John Messier, *President*
Constance L Messier, *Admin Sec*
EMP: 17 EST: 1929
SQ FT: 33,000
SALES (est): 2.4MM **Privately Held**
WEB: www.southernflavoring.com
SIC: 2087 Extracts, flavoring

(G-1660)
TCG TECHNOLOGIES INC
502 Plunkett St (24523-2003)
P.O. Box 95, Goode (24556-0095)
PHONE..................................540 587-8624
James Kent, *President*
EMP: 4
SQ FT: 2,500
SALES (est): 1.1MM **Privately Held**
SIC: 3565 Packaging machinery

(G-1661)
TRIDENT SEAFOODS CORP
940 Orange St (24523-3303)
PHONE..................................540 707-0112
EMP: 12
SALES (est): 1.5MM **Privately Held**
SIC: 2026 Mfg Fluid Milk

(G-1662)
**UNIQUE ENGINEERING
CONCEPTS**
5700 Forest Rd (24523-4126)
PHONE..................................540 586-6761
Jonathan Fuller, *CEO*
EMP: 3
SALES (est): 280K **Privately Held**
WEB: www.ueconcepts.us
SIC: 3556 Food products machinery

(G-1663)
WIKOFF COLOR CORP
311 W Depot St (24523-1937)
PHONE..................................540 586-8111
Fax: 540 586-7008
EMP: 2 EST: 2010
SALES (est): 100K **Privately Held**
SIC: 2893 Mfg Printing Ink

(G-1664)
WINOA USA INC (DH)
Also Called: Wabrasives
1 Abrasive Ave (24523-1802)
P.O. Box 804 (24523-0804)
PHONE..................................540 586-0856
Brian Andrew, *Regional Mgr*
John Moore, *Plant Mgr*
Michael Peters, *Purchasing*
Shane Murphy, *Engineer*
Michael Cagnoli, *Manager*
◆ EMP: 49
SALES (est): 15.6MM
SALES (corp-wide): 2.6B **Privately Held**
WEB: www.wabrasives.com
SIC: 3291 Abrasive products
HQ: Winoa
528 Avenue De Savoie
Le Cheylas 38570
476 929-260

(G-1665)
X PRESS ENTERPRISES LLC
842 Sword Beach Ln (24523-2440)
PHONE..................................540 587-0100
EMP: 2 EST: 2010
SALES (est): 148.2K **Privately Held**
SIC: 2741 Miscellaneous publishing

Bent Mountain
Roanoke County

(G-1666)
AMRHEIN LTD
9243 Patterson Dr (24059-2215)
PHONE..................................540 929-4632
Russell Amrhein, *President*
EMP: 5
SALES (est): 265.6K **Privately Held**
WEB: www.amrheinwine.com
SIC: 2084 Wines

(G-1667)
BENT MT SALSA
671 Glendale Rd (24059-2001)
PHONE..................................803 427-3170
Chris Graham, *Principal*
EMP: 3
SALES (est): 112.6K **Privately Held**
SIC: 2099 Dips, except cheese & sour cream based

(G-1668)
DEN HERTOG FRITS
10063 Fortune Ridge Rd (24059-2145)
PHONE..................................540 929-4650
EMP: 2 EST: 2005
SALES (est): 130K **Privately Held**
SIC: 2899 Mfg Chemical Preparations

Berryville
Clarke County

(G-1669)
ACC CABINETRY LLC
409 Jack Enders Blvd # 4 (22611-1537)
PHONE..................................540 333-0189
EMP: 4
SALES (est): 234.2K **Privately Held**
WEB: www.acccabinetry.com
SIC: 2434 Wood kitchen cabinets

(G-1670)
**BATTLETOWN CSTM
WOODWORKS LLC**
10 Farmers Ln (22611-1122)
PHONE..................................703 618-1548
Kevin Boxx, *Principal*
EMP: 4
SALES (est): 225K **Privately Held**
WEB:
www.battletowncustomwoodworks.com
SIC: 2431 Millwork

(G-1671)
**BERRYVILLE GRAPHICS INC
(DH)**
25 Jack Enders Blvd (22611-1501)
P.O. Box N, Dallas PA (18612-0289)
PHONE..................................540 955-2750
David Liess, *CEO*
Bertram Stausberg, *Chairman*
Mitchel Weiss, *Exec VP*
Barry Hockenberry, *Prdtn Mgr*
Becky Dawson, *Transportation*
▲ EMP: 749
SQ FT: 326,000
SALES (est): 118.1MM
SALES (corp-wide): 147.7MM **Privately Held**
WEB: www.bpg-usa.com
SIC: 2732 2752 2789 Book printing; commercial printing, offset; bookbinding & related work
HQ: Bertelsmann, Inc.
1745 Broadway Fl 20
New York NY 10019
212 782-1000

(G-1672)
CALVINS ENTERPRISES
213 Josephine St (22611-1333)
PHONE..................................540 955-3948
Calvin Page, *Owner*
EMP: 1
SALES (est): 60K **Privately Held**
WEB: www.whitakerimages.com
SIC: 2541 Cabinets, lockers & shelving

(G-1673)
CHAMPION IRON WORKS INC
509 Jack Enders Blvd (22611-1534)
PHONE...................................540 955-3633
Todd Saunders, *President*
Skip Jackson, *Vice Pres*
Saunders Todd, *Vice Pres*
Jim Beach, *Technology*
Sherri Branham, *Executive*
EMP: 35
SALES (est): 5.8MM **Privately Held**
WEB: www.championironworks.com
SIC: 3441 Fabricated structural metal

(G-1674)
CLARKE COUNTY SPEED SHOP
607 E Main St (22611-1528)
PHONE...................................540 955-0479
O J Higgins, *Owner*
EMP: 2
SALES (est): 184.2K **Privately Held**
SIC: 3743 5531 Streetcars & car equipment; speed shops, including race car supplies

(G-1675)
COCHRANS LUMBER & MILLWORK INC
523 Jack Enders Blvd (22611-1534)
PHONE...................................540 955-4142
Larry Cochran, *President*
Mark Cochran, *Vice Pres*
EMP: 32
SQ FT: 35,000
SALES (est): 4.9MM **Privately Held**
WEB: www.cochranslumber.com
SIC: 2434 2426 2431 Wood kitchen cabinets; hardwood dimension & flooring mills; doors, wood

(G-1676)
CORAL GRAPHIC SERVICES INC
25 Jack Enders Blvd (22611-1501)
PHONE...................................540 869-0500
Michael Borden, *Manager*
Jessica Robertson, *Manager*
EMP: 102
SALES (corp-wide): 147.7MM **Privately Held**
WEB: www.bpg-usa.com
SIC: 2752 Commercial printing, offset
HQ: Coral Graphic Services, Inc.
840 S Broadway
Hicksville NY 11801
516 576-2100

(G-1677)
DEVEREUX BARNS LLC
1671 Lockes Mill Rd (22611-3929)
PHONE...................................540 664-1432
Joan Fine, *President*
EMP: 2 **EST:** 2017
SALES (est): 195.1K **Privately Held**
WEB: www.devereuxbarns.com
SIC: 2452 Prefabricated wood buildings

(G-1678)
DEWEY L SAMS
212 1st St (22611-1601)
PHONE...................................540 664-4034
Dewey L Sams, *Principal*
EMP: 1
SALES (est): 99.2K **Privately Held**
SIC: 3531 Automobile wrecker hoists

(G-1679)
DG2 TELER SALES
11 W Main St (22611-1284)
PHONE...................................540 955-1996
EMP: 1 **EST:** 2012
SALES (est): 67.7K **Privately Held**
SIC: 3949 Sporting & athletic goods

(G-1680)
EILEEN C JOHNSON
Also Called: Tempi Design Studio
340 Elmington Ln (22611-2657)
PHONE...................................855 533-7753
Eileen C Johnson, *Owner*
EMP: 1
SALES (est): 41K **Privately Held**
SIC: 3961 Costume jewelry

(G-1681)
HESS PUBLICATIONS
1983 Lockes Mill Rd (22611-3938)
PHONE...................................540 771-7515
EMP: 1
SALES (est): 37.5K **Privately Held**
SIC: 2741 Miscellaneous publishing

(G-1682)
HONEY GUNTERS
100 Bee Line Ln (22611-5228)
P.O. Box 657 (22611-0657)
PHONE...................................540 955-1734
Gregory C Gunter, *Owner*
EMP: 3 **EST:** 1953
SQ FT: 30,000
SALES (est): 8.5MM **Privately Held**
SIC: 2099 Honey, strained & bottled

(G-1683)
KNIGHT OWL GRAPHICS
900 Swimley Rd (22611-1710)
PHONE...................................540 955-1744
Rosalie Knight, *Owner*
Tim Knight, *Principal*
EMP: 3
SALES (est): 140K **Privately Held**
SIC: 2754 Business form & card printing, gravure

(G-1684)
LOCAL WOOD
40 Kimble Rd (22611-5249)
PHONE...................................540 955-9522
Charlie Beach, *Partner*
Scott Carpenter, *Principal*
EMP: 8
SALES (est): 750K **Privately Held**
WEB: www.localwoodva.com
SIC: 2431 Millwork

(G-1685)
NORTON EMBROIDERY INC
Also Called: Norton's Embroidery
11 S Church St (22611-1315)
P.O. Box 687, Crimora (24431-0687)
PHONE...................................540 550-7331
Cheryl Norton, *President*
Lee Norton, *Vice Pres*
Jenifer Norton, *Admin Sec*
EMP: 3
SQ FT: 4,400 **Privately Held**
WEB: www.nortonemb.com
SIC: 2395 Embroidery products, except schiffli machine

(G-1686)
PRECISION GRINDING CO
3690 Old Charles Town Rd (22611-1811)
PHONE...................................540 955-3200
Lynn Miller, *Principal*
EMP: 12 **EST:** 2001
SALES (est): 1.1MM **Privately Held**
SIC: 3599 Machine shop, jobbing & repair

(G-1687)
ROGUE CLTIVATION SOLUTIONS LLC
3 Cattlemans Ln (22611-6004)
PHONE...................................540 955-8641
Glen Franklin Koontz, *Principal*
EMP: 2
SALES (est): 85.2K **Privately Held**
WEB: www.roguecultivationsolutions.com
SIC: 3999 Manufacturing industries

(G-1688)
SAUDI TRADE LINKS
Also Called: PMG Refining
351 Station Rd (22611-1198)
PHONE...................................703 992-3220
Naji Khalek, *CEO*
Adel Tahir, *Accountant*
EMP: 2
SALES (est): 90.8K **Privately Held**
SIC: 3341 Gold smelting & refining (secondary)

(G-1689)
SB WELDING AND FAB LLC
141 Kinsky Ln (22611-4057)
PHONE...................................540 955-0797
Sean Mason, *Principal*
EMP: 1

SALES (est): 31.5K **Privately Held**
SIC: 7692 Welding repair

(G-1690)
SIGN AND SEAL
327 N Buckmarsh St (22611-1026)
PHONE...................................540 955-2422
Jennifer Poe, *Principal*
EMP: 2
SALES (est): 72.6K **Privately Held**
SIC: 3993 Signs & advertising specialties

(G-1691)
SMALLEY PACKAGE COMPANY INC
210 1st St (22611-1601)
P.O. Box 231 (22611-0231)
PHONE...................................540 955-2550
Robert W Smalley Jr, *President*
James R Livengood, *Vice Pres*
Susan Sponseller, *Treasurer*
Glassell Smalley, *Shareholder*
E Scott Smalley, *Admin Sec*
EMP: 80 **EST:** 1954
SQ FT: 1,300
SALES (est): 9.6MM **Privately Held**
WEB: www.smalley.com
SIC: 2449 2448 2441 Fruit crates, wood: wirebound; pallets, wood; boxes, wood

(G-1692)
SPIGNER STRUCTURAL & MISCELLAN
214 1st St (22611-1601)
P.O. Box 324 (22611-0324)
PHONE...................................703 625-7572
Robert Spigner, *CEO*
Jared Spigner, *Vice Pres*
EMP: 20
SQ FT: 25,000
SALES (est): 1.8MM **Privately Held**
WEB: www.spignerstructural.com
SIC: 3441 1791 1799 8741 Building components, structural steel; structural steel erection; iron work, structural; ornamental metal work; construction management

(G-1693)
STUART M PERRY INCORPORATED
426 Quarry Rd (22611-4204)
PHONE...................................540 955-1359
Joseph Renner, *Manager*
EMP: 38
SALES (corp-wide): 25.4MM **Privately Held**
WEB: www.stuartmperry.com
SIC: 1422 Limestones, ground
PA: Stuart M. Perry, Incorporated
117 Limestone Ln
Winchester VA 22602
540 662-3431

(G-1694)
TIMBERLAKE CABINET COMPANY
430 Jack Enders Blvd (22611-1536)
PHONE...................................540 955-4985
Mark Barnhart, *Manager*
Cara Jones, *Executive*
EMP: 1
SALES (est): 143.9K **Privately Held**
WEB: www.americanwoodmark.com
SIC: 2434 Wood kitchen cabinets

(G-1695)
TRELLEBORG MARINE SYSTEMS (PA)
532 Jack Enders Blvd (22611-1538)
PHONE...................................540 667-5191
Paul Welling, *President*
W Allan Potts, *Vice Pres*
Tracie Dupuy, *Controller*
Sara Boulais, *Sales Staff*
◆ **EMP:** 29
SQ FT: 5,600
SALES (est): 5.1MM **Privately Held**
SIC: 3069 Air-supported rubber structures

(G-1696)
TRELLEBORG MARINE SYSTEMS USA
532 Jack Enders Blvd (22611-1538)
PHONE...................................540 667-5191

EMP: 29 **Privately Held**
SIC: 3069 Mfg Fabricated Rubber Products
HQ: Trelleborg Marine Systems Usa, Inc.
200 Veterans Blvd Ste 3
South Haven MI 22611

(G-1697)
TTEC LLC
Also Called: Ttec Thermoelectric Tech
2342 Wickliffe Rd (22611-2972)
PHONE...................................540 336-2693
Richard Thuss, *President*
EMP: 1
SALES (est): 96.4K **Privately Held**
SIC: 3674 7389 Thermoelectric devices, solid state;

(G-1698)
VA HARDSCAPES INC
12 Cattlemans Ln (22611-6002)
PHONE...................................540 955-6245
Don Riesgraf, *Principal*
EMP: 4
SALES (est): 360.1K **Privately Held**
WEB: www.virginiahardscapes.com
SIC: 3271 Blocks, concrete or cinder: standard

(G-1699)
VERAMAR VINEYARD LLC
905 Quarry Rd (22611-4222)
PHONE...................................540 955-5510
Justin Bogaty, *Vice Pres*
James Bogaty, *Mng Member*
EMP: 9
SQ FT: 2,400
SALES (est): 173.9K **Privately Held**
WEB: www.veramar.com
SIC: 2084 Wines

(G-1700)
WOODWORKING WRKSHPS OF THE SHN
5594 Senseny Rd (22611-3342)
PHONE...................................540 955-2376
Jeff Headley, *Mng Member*
EMP: 1
SALES (est): 89.9K **Privately Held**
WEB: www.wwotsv.com
SIC: 2431 Millwork

Big Island
Bedford County

(G-1701)
ALEXANDER M ROBERTSON
Also Called: S R Firearm & Engraving Co
10327 Big Island Hwy (24526-3010)
PHONE...................................434 299-5221
Alexander M Robertson, *Owner*
EMP: 1
SALES (est): 65K **Privately Held**
SIC: 3483 Artillery shells over 30 mm.

(G-1702)
GEORGIA-PACIFIC LLC
9363 Lee Jackson Hwy (24526)
P.O. Box 40 (24526-0040)
PHONE...................................434 299-5911
Morgan Thomas, *President*
Collin Trepanitis, *Engineer*
Mark Delahunt, *Project Engr*
Ralph Sisk, *Sr Project Mgr*
Harmon Beauchamp, *Manager*
EMP: 340
SALES (corp-wide): 38.9B **Privately Held**
WEB: www.gp.com
SIC: 2621 Paper mills
HQ: Georgia-Pacific Llc
133 Peachtree St Nw
Atlanta GA 30303
404 652-4000

(G-1703)
HATCHER LOGGING CORP VIRGINIA
14437 Big Island Hwy (24526-2944)
PHONE...................................434 299-5293
Elmer E Hatcher, *President*
Jenine Hatcher, *Corp Secy*
Curtis Glen Hatcher, *Vice Pres*
EMP: 4

SALES (est): 306.5K **Privately Held**
SIC: 2411 0212 Logging camps & contractors; beef cattle except feedlots

(G-1704)
JERRY K WILSON INC
1810 Hunting Creek Rd (24526-2915)
PHONE..................................434 299-5175
Jerry K Wilson, *President*
Pansy Wilson, *Corp Secy*
EMP: 5
SALES (est): 350K **Privately Held**
SIC: 2411 Logging camps & contractors

Big Rock
Buchanan County

(G-1705)
WELLMORE ENERGY COMPANY LLC
Norton Coal Company
Hwy 700 (24603)
P.O. Box 2860, Grundy (24614-2860)
PHONE..................................276 530-7411
Gary Horn, *General Mgr*
EMP: 66 **Privately Held**
SIC: 1221 1241 Bituminous coal & lignite-surface mining; coal mining services
HQ: Wellmore Energy Company, Llc
110 Agero Dr
Blountville TN 37617
276 530-7411

Big Stone Gap
Wise County

(G-1706)
BIG STONE GAP CORPORATION
1942 Neeley Rd (24219)
P.O. Box 236 (24219-0236)
PHONE..................................276 523-7337
EMP: 4
SALES (est): 480.5K **Privately Held**
SIC: 3944 Mfg Games/Toys

(G-1707)
CARL G GILLIAM JR
Also Called: Fitcon Graphics
618 Wood Ave W Ste 100 (24219-2160)
P.O. Box 886 (24219-0886)
PHONE..................................276 523-0619
Carl G Gilliam Jr, *Owner*
EMP: 10
SQ FT: 16,000
SALES (est): 909.8K **Privately Held**
SIC: 2759 7991 2396 2395 Screen printing; health club; automotive & apparel trimmings; pleating & stitching

(G-1708)
DALE STIDHAM
Also Called: Big Stone Machine Shop
219 E 5th St S (24219-3045)
PHONE..................................276 523-1428
Dale Stidham, *Owner*
EMP: 1
SQ FT: 600
SALES (est): 147.1K **Privately Held**
WEB: www.bigstonegap.org
SIC: 3599 7692 Machine shop, jobbing & repair; welding repair

(G-1709)
DANIEL ROLLINS
Also Called: Southwest Sign Maintenance
4210 Powell Valley Rd (24219-4012)
PHONE..................................276 219-3988
Daniel Rollins, *Owner*
EMP: 1
SALES (est): 93.5K **Privately Held**
SIC: 3993 Signs & advertising specialties

(G-1710)
GETINTOFOREX LLC
106 Wood Ave W (24219-2552)
PHONE..................................251 591-2181
Tom Flora, *President*
EMP: 4

SALES (est): 460K **Privately Held**
SIC: 2844 5961 5999 7389 Cosmetic preparations; cosmetics & perfumes, mail order; cosmetics; business services

(G-1711)
LEGACY VULCAN LLC
Also Called: Norton Quarry
6420 Powell Valley Rd (24219-4110)
PHONE..................................276 679-0880
Darrell Gilbert, *Manager*
EMP: 14 **Publicly Held**
WEB: www.vulcanmaterials.com
SIC: 1422 Crushed & broken limestone
HQ: Legacy Vulcan, Llc
1200 Urban Center Dr
Vestavia AL 35242
205 298-3000

(G-1712)
MABE TACTICAL LLC
4820 Back Valley Rd (24219-4066)
PHONE..................................276 524-4912
Alex Mabe, *Administration*
EMP: 2
SALES (est): 79.5K **Privately Held**
SIC: 3489 Ordnance & accessories

(G-1713)
MINES MINERALS & ENRGY VA DEPT
Also Called: Mined Land Reclamation Div
3405 Mountain Empire Rd (24219-4634)
P.O. Box 900 (24219-0900)
PHONE..................................276 523-8100
Benny Wampler, *Deputy Dir*
EMP: 80
SALES (corp-wide): 40.9B **Privately Held**
WEB: www.virginia.gov
SIC: 1481 9512 Mine exploration, non-metallic minerals;
HQ: Virginia Department Of Mines, Minerals And Energy
1100 Bank St
Richmond VA 23219

(G-1714)
RIGGS OIL COMPANY
Also Called: Aab Coal Mining Company
1505 1st Ave E (24219-3189)
P.O. Box Aa (24219-0630)
PHONE..................................276 523-2662
Arnold Riggs, *Branch Mgr*
EMP: 27
SALES (corp-wide): 87.2MM **Privately Held**
WEB: www.riggsoil.com
SIC: 1221 Bituminous coal & lignite-surface mining
PA: Riggs Oil Company
1505 1st Ave E
Big Stone Gap VA 24219
276 523-2662

(G-1715)
STONEGA MINING & PROCESSING CO
1695 Dawson Ave W (24219-4357)
PHONE..................................276 523-5690
Harry Meador, *Principal*
EMP: 9
SALES (est): 437.1K **Privately Held**
SIC: 1221 Bituminous coal & lignite-surface mining

(G-1716)
TIMBERLINE LOGGING INC
1523 Mountain View Ave E (24219-3331)
P.O. Box 560, Duffield (24244-0560)
PHONE..................................276 393-7239
John Wade, *President*
EMP: 6
SALES (est): 863.5K **Privately Held**
SIC: 2411 Logging camps & contractors

(G-1717)
VALLEY UTILITY BUILDINGS INC
5661 Powell Valley Rd (24219-4127)
PHONE..................................276 679-6736
David Fawbush, *President*
EMP: 4

SALES (est): 406.9K **Privately Held**
WEB: www.valleyutilitybuildingsinc.com
SIC: 2452 2426 Prefabricated buildings, wood; furniture stock & parts, hardwood

(G-1718)
WISE PRINTING CO INC
Also Called: Post, The
215 Wood Ave (24219)
P.O. Box 250 (24219-0250)
PHONE..................................276 523-1141
Ada Holyfield, *Manager*
EMP: 4
SQ FT: 5,000
SALES (est): 297.8K
SALES (corp-wide): 4.7MM **Privately Held**
WEB: www.thecoalfieldprogress.com
SIC: 2711 2791 2789 2759 Job printing & newspaper publishing combined; typesetting; bookbinding & related work; commercial printing; commercial printing, lithographic
PA: Coalfield Progress
725 Park Ave Sw
Norton VA 24273
276 679-1101

Birdsnest
Northampton County

(G-1719)
GORDOS TACOS AND MORE LLC
11363 Seaside Rd (23307-1219)
PHONE..................................757 710-3317
Silvia Vera, *Principal*
Cindy Rodriguez,
EMP: 4
SALES (est): 155.8K **Privately Held**
SIC: 2599 Food wagons, restaurant

Blacksburg
Montgomery County

(G-1720)
ACS DIVISION POLYMER CHEMISTRY
Virginia Tech 410 Dvidson (24061-0001)
PHONE..................................540 231-3029
Tim Long, *Chairman*
Rigoverto Adzincula, *Treasurer*
Neta Byerly, *Manager*
EMP: 4
SQ FT: 400
SALES (est): 237.2K **Privately Held**
WEB: www.polyacs.net
SIC: 2741 Miscellaneous publishing

(G-1721)
AGILENT TECHNOLOGIES INC
2000 Kraft Dr Ste 1103 (24060-6373)
PHONE..................................540 443-9272
EMP: 1
SALES (est): 39.7K **Privately Held**
SIC: 3231 Products of purchased glass

(G-1722)
ANDERSON AUDIOLOGY HEARING AID
3607 S Main St (24060-7014)
PHONE..................................540 616-7990
EMP: 2
SALES (est): 86.6K **Privately Held**
SIC: 3842 Hearing aids

(G-1723)
ANYTHING VERTICAL LLC
1410 Ashford Ct (24060-1841)
P.O. Box 17, Sinks Grove WV (24976-0017)
PHONE..................................540 871-6519
EMP: 2
SALES (est): 140K **Privately Held**
SIC: 2591 Mfg Drapery Hardware/Blinds

(G-1724)
BAKER HUGHES A GE COMPANY LLC
2851 Commerce St (24060-6657)
PHONE..................................540 961-9532
Gloria Smith, *Mfg Staff*
Derek Carpenter, *Research*
Brian Lucas, *Engineer*
Paul Wysocki, *Engineer*
Douglas Murray, *Manager*
EMP: 25
SALES (corp-wide): 23.8B **Publicly Held**
WEB: www.bhge.com
SIC: 1389 Oil field services
HQ: Baker Hughes Holdings Llc
17021 Aldine Westfield Rd
Houston TX 77073
713 439-8600

(G-1725)
BELIVEAU DEVELOPMENT CORP
104 Roanoke St W (24060-7418)
PHONE..................................540 961-0505
EMP: 7
SALES (corp-wide): 406.7K **Privately Held**
WEB: www.beliveaufarm.com
SIC: 2084 Wines
PA: Beliveau Development Corp
3879 Eakin Farm Rd
Blacksburg VA 24060
540 961-2102

(G-1726)
BELIVEAU ESTATE VNYRD WNERY LL
3899 Eakin Farm Rd (24060-1406)
PHONE..................................540 961-2102
Yvan Beliveau,
Joyce Beliveau,
EMP: 8
SALES (est): 782.5K **Privately Held**
WEB: www.beliveaufarm.com
SIC: 2084 Wines

(G-1727)
BULL RIDGE CORPORATION
2628 Mount Tabor Rd (24060-8920)
P.O. Box 10698 (24062-0698)
PHONE..................................540 953-1171
Robert Millard Jones, *Principal*
EMP: 2
SALES (est): 103.7K **Privately Held**
SIC: 2741 Miscellaneous publishing

(G-1728)
CARDINAL MECHATRONICS LLC
207 Wharton St Se Apt 12 (24060-4877)
PHONE..................................540 922-2392
John Bird,
EMP: 1
SALES (est): 97.4K **Privately Held**
WEB: www.cardinalmechatronics.com
SIC: 3672 Printed circuit boards

(G-1729)
CAYAMBIS MUSIC PRESS LLC
1718 Honeysuckle Dr (24060-0392)
PHONE..................................540 951-3504
Keith Finch, *Administration*
EMP: 2
SALES (est): 110.7K **Privately Held**
WEB: www.cayambismusicpress.com
SIC: 2741 Miscellaneous publishing

(G-1730)
CHESAPEAKE CARTRIDGE CORP INC
2020 Kraft Dr Ste 2100 (24060-6314)
PHONE..................................703 989-0903
EMP: 2 **EST:** 2018
SALES (est): 88.3K **Privately Held**
WEB: www.chescart.com
SIC: 3482 Small arms ammunition

(G-1731)
CONSTRUCTION MATERIALS COMPANY
801 Industrial Park Rd (24060)
PHONE..................................540 552-5022
Eddie Harris, *Manager*
EMP: 1 **Privately Held**
WEB: www.rockinghamredimix.com

▲ = Import ▼=Export
◆ =Import/Export

SIC: 3273 Ready-mixed concrete
PA: Construction Materials Company
9 Memorial Ln
Lexington VA 24450

(G-1732)
DIGITAL SYNERGY LLC
2020 Kraft Dr Ste 2300 (24060-6568)
PHONE..................................540 951-5900
Pranav Mandloi, *Project Mgr*
Michael Bame, *CFO*
EMP: 2
SALES (est): 68.4K **Privately Held**
WEB: www.harmonia.com
SIC: 7372 7379 Application computer software; computer related consulting services

(G-1733)
DOGWOOD LOGIC INC
203 Roanoke St W (24060-7419)
PHONE..................................540 557-7689
Evan Lally, *CEO*
Sandra Klute, *Vice Pres*
EMP: 3
SALES (est): 93.3K **Privately Held**
SIC: 2741 7374 Miscellaneous publishing; data processing & preparation

(G-1734)
DUE NORTH VENTURES LLC
3809 S Main St (24060-7704)
PHONE..................................540 443-3990
John Bachorik, *Principal*
EMP: 4
SALES (est): 399.3K **Privately Held**
SIC: 2992 Lubricating oils

(G-1735)
ENABLED MANUFACTURING LLC
Also Called: Enabled Engineering
1412 Honeysuckle Dr (24060-0391)
PHONE..................................704 491-9414
Kumar Kandasamy, *Manager*
Senthil Marimuthu,
EMP: 2
SALES (est): 62.5K **Privately Held**
SIC: 3999 Manufacturing industries

(G-1736)
ESS TECHNOLOGIES INC
3160 State St (24060-6603)
PHONE..................................540 961-5716
Kevin Robert Browne, *President*
Linda Browne, *Exec VP*
Linda Sue Browne, *Vice Pres*
Peter Botton, *Project Mgr*
◆ **EMP:** 29
SQ FT: 17,000
SALES (est): 7.5MM **Privately Held**
WEB: www.esstechnologies.com
SIC: 3565 Packaging machinery

(G-1737)
FEDERAL-MOGUL POWERTRAIN LLC
300 Industrial Park Rd Se (24060-6608)
PHONE..................................540 557-3300
Margie Deck, *QC Dir*
EMP: 348
SALES (corp-wide): 17.4B **Publicly Held**
WEB: www.federalmogul.com
SIC: 3714 5085 5568 Motor vehicle engines & parts; bearings; power transmission equipment
HQ: Federal-Mogul Powertrain Llc
27300 W 11 Mile Rd # 100
Southfield MI 48034

(G-1738)
FEDERAL-MOGUL POWERTRAIN LLC
2901 Prosperity Rd (24060-6841)
PHONE..................................540 953-4676
EMP: 3
SALES (corp-wide): 17.4B **Publicly Held**
WEB: www.federalmogul.com
SIC: 3559 Automotive related machinery
HQ: Federal-Mogul Powertrain Llc
27300 W 11 Mile Rd # 100
Southfield MI 48034

(G-1739)
FLUXTEQ LLC
1800 Kraft Dr Ste 109 (24060-6421)
PHONE..................................540 951-0933
Chris Cirenza, *Chief Engr*
Thomas Diller,
EMP: 2 **EST:** 2015
SALES (est): 180.6K **Privately Held**
WEB: www.fluxteq.com
SIC: 3823 7389 Temperature instruments: industrial process type;

(G-1740)
FLYING FUR
301 Cork Dr (24060-3603)
PHONE..................................540 552-1351
Sharon Harrell, *Principal*
EMP: 3 **EST:** 2010
SALES (est): 182.9K **Privately Held**
WEB: www.flyingfurdogs.com
SIC: 3999 Furs

(G-1741)
GERMINAL DIMENSIONS INC
915 Allendale Ct (24060-5111)
PHONE..................................540 552-8938
Kathleen June Mullins, *Principal*
EMP: 1 **EST:** 2009
SALES (est): 74.4K **Privately Held**
SIC: 2672 Book paper, coated: made from purchased materials

(G-1742)
GOLDEN SECTION LLC
1810 New London Ct (24060-2067)
PHONE..................................540 315-4756
Robert Arthur Canfield, *President*
Robert Canfield, *President*
EMP: 1
SALES (est): 106.1K **Privately Held**
WEB: www.aoe.vt.edu
SIC: 3721 Aircraft

(G-1743)
HIGH PEAK SPORTSWEAR INC
Also Called: High Peak Teeshirt Factory
209 College Ave (24060-7415)
PHONE..................................540 953-1293
Emily Alderman, *Manager*
EMP: 5 **Privately Held**
WEB: www.hipeak.com
SIC: 2759 5199 Screen printing; advertising specialties
PA: High Peak Sportswear, Inc.
2323 Memorial Ave Ste 17
Lynchburg VA

(G-1744)
IDENTIFICATION INTL INC
Also Called: I3
3120 Commerce St (24060-6672)
PHONE..................................540 953-3343
Richard K Fenrich, *President*
Williams Hickman, *Engineer*
Matthew Valeri, *Sales Staff*
Chrissy Ganoe, *Office Mgr*
Richard Fenrich, *Bd of Directors*
◆ **EMP:** 18
SQ FT: 3,000
SALES (est): 2MM **Privately Held**
WEB: www.idintl.com
SIC: 3999 Fingerprint equipment

(G-1745)
IN MOTION US LLC
3157 State St (24060-6604)
PHONE..................................540 605-9622
Jorge Lopez, *Treasurer*
Ashley Coble, *Human Res Mgr*
▲ **EMP:** 101
SALES (est): 16.2MM **Privately Held**
WEB: www.en.evs-inmotion.com
SIC: 3625 Motor controls & accessories

(G-1746)
INTEGRITY SHIRTS LLC
3130 Commerce St (24060-6672)
PHONE..................................540 577-5544
Elijah Bailey, *Mng Member*
EMP: 1
SALES (est): 114.1K **Privately Held**
WEB: www.integrityshirts.com
SIC: 2211 Print cloths, cotton

(G-1747)
JOHNSON & ELICH ROASTERS LTD
Also Called: Mill Mountain Coffee & Tea
700 N Main St Ste C (24060-3312)
PHONE..................................540 552-7442
David Johnson, *President*
Scott Elich, *Corp Secy*
EMP: 15
SQ FT: 1,700
SALES (est): 1.3MM **Privately Held**
WEB: www.millmountaincoffee.com
SIC: 2095 5499 5719 5149 Coffee roasting (except by wholesale grocers); coffee; tea; housewares; coffee, green or roasted; chocolate; coffee brewing equipment & supplies; commercial cooking & food service equipment; cafe

(G-1748)
JUST WOODSTUFF
3829 Catawba Rd (24060-0533)
PHONE..................................540 951-2323
Richard Absher, *Owner*
EMP: 1
SALES (est): 82K **Privately Held**
SIC: 2499 Decorative wood & woodwork

(G-1749)
KALWOOD INC
Also Called: Kopy Korner
101 Mcdonald St (24060-3420)
PHONE..................................540 951-8600
Calvin R Dove, *President*
Darlene Dove, *Treasurer*
EMP: 3
SQ FT: 2,000
SALES (est): 289.2K **Privately Held**
SIC: 2759 5943 Commercial printing; office forms & supplies

(G-1750)
LANA JUAREZ
Also Called: Matrix Gallery
115 N Main St (24060-3946)
PHONE..................................540 951-3566
Lana Juarez, *Owner*
EMP: 3
SALES (est): 100K **Privately Held**
WEB: www.matrixgallery.com
SIC: 3944 Craft & hobby kits & sets

(G-1751)
LANDOS BIOPHARMA INC
1800 Kraft Dr Ste 216 (24060-6370)
PHONE..................................540 218-2262
Josep Bassaganya- Riera, *President*
Josep Bassaganya-Riera, *President*
Andrew Leber, *Director*
EMP: 8
SQ FT: 1,455
SALES (est): 452.5K **Privately Held**
WEB: www.landosbiopharma.com
SIC: 2834 Pills, pharmaceutical

(G-1752)
LEGIT BATH SALTS ONLINE
1338 S Main St (24060-5526)
PHONE..................................540 200-8618
EMP: 2
SALES (est): 74.4K **Privately Held**
WEB: www.legitbathsaltsonline.com
SIC: 2844 Bath salts

(G-1753)
LEONARD ALUM UTLITY BLDNGS INC
Also Called: Leonard Buildings & Truck ACC
3930 S Main St (24060-7706)
PHONE..................................540 951-0236
Chase Utt, *Manager*
EMP: 2
SALES (corp-wide): 88.2MM **Privately Held**
WEB: www.leonardusa.com
SIC: 3448 5599 5531 Prefabricated metal buildings; utility trailers; trailer hitches, automotive
PA: Leonard Aluminum Utility Buildings, Inc.
566 Holly Springs Rd
Mount Airy NC 27030
888 590-4769

(G-1754)
LINTRONICS SOFTWARE PUBLISHING
Also Called: Lintronics Publishing Group
1991 Mountainside Dr (24060-9283)
PHONE..................................540 552-7204
Linda Fleming, *President*
Paul Fleming, *President*
Brett Fleming, *Shareholder*
Todd Fleming, *Shareholder*
EMP: 4
SALES (est): 301.6K **Privately Held**
SIC: 7372 Educational computer software; publishers' computer software

(G-1755)
LUNA ENERGY LLC (DH)
2851 Commerce St (24060-6657)
PHONE..................................540 553-0500
Phil Vogel, *President*
▼ **EMP:** 5
SQ FT: 18,000
SALES (est): 2.3MM
SALES (corp-wide): 23.8B **Publicly Held**
SIC: 3674 Infrared sensors, solid state
HQ: Baker Hughes Holdings Llc
17021 Aldine Westfield Rd
Houston TX 77073
713 439-8600

(G-1756)
LUNA INNOVATIONS INCORPORATED
3155 State St (24060-6604)
PHONE..................................540 961-5190
Zachary Bear, *Research*
Susan Beck, *Research*
Dan Kominsky, *Research*
Fiorella Mazzini, *Research*
Sean Offenberger, *Research*
EMP: 41 **Publicly Held**
WEB: www.lunainc.com
SIC: 3661 Fiber optics communications equipment
PA: Luna Innovations Incorporated
301 1st St Sw Ste 200
Roanoke VA 24011

(G-1757)
MAGGIES RAGS
507 Rose Ave (24060-5739)
PHONE..................................540 961-1755
Margaret Radcliffe, *Owner*
EMP: 1
SALES (est): 61.6K **Privately Held**
WEB: www.maggiesrags.com
SIC: 2741 Patterns, paper: publishing only, not printed on site

(G-1758)
MAR-BAL INC
2020 Kraft Dr Ste 3003 (24060-6569)
PHONE..................................440 539-6595
Ron Poff, *Branch Mgr*
EMP: 2
SALES (corp-wide): 72.9MM **Privately Held**
WEB: www.mar-bal.com
SIC: 3089 Molding primary plastic
PA: Mar-Bal, Inc.
10095 Queens Way
Chagrin Falls OH 44023
440 543-7526

(G-1759)
MARK DEBUSK CUSTOM CABINETS
1001 Palmer Dr (24060-5330)
PHONE..................................540 552-3228
Charles Debusk, *Principal*
EMP: 2
SALES (est): 135.6K **Privately Held**
SIC: 2434 Wood kitchen cabinets

(G-1760)
MAROON ASSISTIVE TECH LLC
214 Woods Edge Ct (24060-4001)
PHONE..................................703 239-3113
Timothy Pote, *Principal*
Taylor Pesek, *Principal*
EMP: 2
SALES (est): 118.1K **Privately Held**
SIC: 3841 Surgical & medical instruments

(G-1761)
MEDIAS LLC
4543 Pearman Rd (24060-8649)
P.O. Box 10452 (24062-0452)
PHONE..............................540 230-7023
Camden McLaughlin, *Owner*
EMP: 3
SALES (est): 280K **Privately Held**
SIC: 3829 Medical diagnostic systems, nuclear

(G-1762)
MILLWORK SUPPLY INC (PA)
3120 Commerce St (24060-6672)
PHONE..............................540 552-0201
Robert Perdue, *President*
Jean D Perdue, *Vice Pres*
EMP: 14
SQ FT: 13,000
SALES (est): 1.1MM **Privately Held**
SIC: 2431 Doors, wood

(G-1763)
MOOG COMPONENTS GROUP
1501 N Main St (24060-2523)
PHONE..............................540 443-4699
EMP: 5 EST: 2012
SALES (est): 440K **Privately Held**
SIC: 3679 3841 3621 Mfg Electronic Components Mfg Surgical/Medical Instruments Mfg Motors/Generators

(G-1764)
MOOG INC
1213 N Main St (24060-3127)
PHONE..............................716 652-2000
Richard Aubrecht, *Vice Chairman*
Morris Heckman, *Maint Spvr*
Lance Johnson, *Mfg Staff*
Jeff Roberts, *Production*
Stephen Smith, *Buyer*
EMP: 9
SALES (corp-wide): 2.8B **Publicly Held**
WEB: www.moog.com
SIC: 3812 3492 3625 3769 Search & navigation equipment; fluid power valves & hose fittings; relays & industrial controls; guided missile & space vehicle parts & auxiliary equipment; aircraft parts & equipment; surgical & medical instruments
PA: Moog Inc.
　　400 Jamison Rd
　　Elma NY 14059
　　716 652-2000

(G-1765)
MOOG INC
Also Called: Moog Components Group
2200 S Main St (24060-6620)
PHONE..............................540 552-3011
Larry Ball, *Branch Mgr*
Tina Bower, *Manager*
Jeff Flippin, *Executive*
EMP: 11
SALES (corp-wide): 2.8B **Publicly Held**
WEB: www.moog.com
SIC: 3674 Semiconductors & related devices
PA: Moog Inc.
　　400 Jamison Rd
　　Elma NY 14059
　　716 652-2000

(G-1766)
MOOG INC
Moog Components Group
1213 N Main St (24060-3127)
PHONE..............................828 837-5115
Lawrence Ball, *Vice Pres*
Dennis Wade, *Purch Dir*
Debbie Hamilton, *Buyer*
Bill Ekhaml, *Engineer*
David Botos, *Design Engr*
EMP: 700
SALES (corp-wide): 2.8B **Publicly Held**
WEB: www.moog.com
SIC: 3812 Search & navigation equipment
PA: Moog Inc.
　　400 Jamison Rd
　　Elma NY 14059
　　716 652-2000

(G-1767)
MOOG INC
1501 N Main St (24060-2523)
PHONE..............................540 552-3011
Perry Moretz, *Branch Mgr*
EMP: 300
SALES (corp-wide): 2.8B **Publicly Held**
WEB: www.moog.com
SIC: 3812 Navigational systems & instruments
PA: Moog Inc.
　　400 Jamison Rd
　　Elma NY 14059
　　716 652-2000

(G-1768)
MOOG INC
2200 S Main St (24060-6620)
PHONE..............................540 552-3011
Heath N Kouns, *Engineer*
Michael Callahan, *Security Mgr*
Lori McCoy, *Admin Asst*
EMP: 200
SALES (corp-wide): 2.8B **Publicly Held**
WEB: www.moog.com
SIC: 3674 3699 Infrared sensors, solid state; electrical equipment & supplies
PA: Moog Inc.
　　400 Jamison Rd
　　Elma NY 14059
　　716 652-2000

(G-1769)
MOUNTAIN PRECISION TOOL CO INC
451 Industrial Park Rd Se (24060-6609)
PHONE..............................540 552-0178
Steven Drumheller, *President*
Russell Drumheller, *Engineer*
▼ EMP: 15
SQ FT: 10,000
SALES (est): 2MM **Privately Held**
WEB: www.mountainprecision.com
SIC: 3599 Machine shop, jobbing & repair

(G-1770)
NANOMED INC
304 Vinyard Ave (24060-1336)
PHONE..............................540 553-4070
Chenming Zhang, *Owner*
EMP: 1
SALES (est): 61.7K **Privately Held**
SIC: 2836 Vaccines & other immunizing products

(G-1771)
NATIONAL BANKSHARES INC
2280 Kraft Dr (24060-0010)
PHONE..............................540 552-0890
EMP: 2
SALES (corp-wide): 53.9MM **Publicly Held**
WEB: www.nationalbankshares.com
SIC: 2022 Processed cheese
PA: National Bankshares, Inc.
　　101 Hubbard St
　　Blacksburg VA 24060
　　540 951-6300

(G-1772)
NBE TECHNOLOGIES LLC
3710 Evergreen Trl (24060-5369)
PHONE..............................540 443-9100
Lu Guo-Quan, *Principal*
EMP: 4
SALES (est): 160.8K **Privately Held**
WEB: www.nbetech.com
SIC: 2891 Adhesives & sealants

(G-1773)
NEW RIVER CONCRETE SUPPLY INC
801 Park Dr (24060)
P.O. Box 520 (24063-0520)
PHONE..............................540 552-1721
Barry Brubaker, *President*
EMP: 14
SQ FT: 912
SALES (est): 782K **Privately Held**
SIC: 3273 3272 Ready-mixed concrete; concrete products, precast

(G-1774)
NEW RIVER ORDNANCE WORKS INC
2200 Kraft Dr Ste 2150 (24060-6326)
P.O. Box 3324, Radford (24143-3324)
PHONE..............................907 888-9615
Graham Reynolds, *President*
EMP: 5 EST: 2015
SALES (est): 407K **Privately Held**
SIC: 2892 Amatols (explosive)

(G-1775)
NEW RIVER SIGN AND VINYL LLC
2280 Kraft Dr Ste 1100 (24060-6779)
PHONE..............................703 793-0730
Bryan Katz, *CEO*
EMP: 2
SALES (est): 139K **Privately Held**
WEB: www.newriversign.com
SIC: 3993 Signs & advertising specialties

(G-1776)
OLD DOMIMION FLAGSTONE INC
3500 Prices Fork Rd (24060-3736)
PHONE..............................540 553-0511
Brad Roberts, *Principal*
EMP: 2
SALES (est): 85.8K **Privately Held**
SIC: 3281 Flagstones

(G-1777)
OPEN TECH INC
2000 Kraft Dr Ste 1101 (24060-6301)
PHONE..............................703 738-6662
Daniel Lariner, *Principal*
EMP: 1
SALES (est): 47.2K **Privately Held**
SIC: 2741 Miscellaneous publishing

(G-1778)
PAPERLESS PUBLISHING CORP
1700 Kraft Dr Ste 1000 (24060-6468)
PHONE..............................540 552-5882
Bhairyi Trivedi, *Exec Dir*
EMP: 2
SALES (est): 84.8K **Privately Held**
WEB: www.trivedichemistry.com
SIC: 2741 Miscellaneous publishing

(G-1779)
PHYTOSNITATION VAC SYSTEMS LLC
629 Shawnee Trl (24060-8859)
PHONE..............................540 641-4170
Zhangjing Chen,
EMP: 3
SALES (est): 891K **Privately Held**
SIC: 2491 Structural lumber & timber, treated wood

(G-1780)
POWER HUB VENTURES LLC
Also Called: Powerhub Systems
1700 Kraft Dr Ste 1325 (24060-6468)
PHONE..............................540 443-9214
John Lesko, *General Mgr*
Joan Elmore, *Office Mgr*
Jonathan Hodock, *Mng Member*
Jay Kidd, *Software Dev*
Glenn Skutt,
EMP: 9
SALES (est): 1.5MM **Privately Held**
WEB: www.fermataenergy.com
SIC: 3612 Autotransformers for switchboards (exc. tele. switchboards)

(G-1781)
PROFESSIONAL SERVICES
210 Prices Fork Rd Ste B (24060-3300)
PHONE..............................540 953-2223
Bruce Schleicher, *Owner*
EMP: 2
SQ FT: 916
SALES (est): 90K **Privately Held**
SIC: 2752 7338 7334 Commercial printing, offset; secretarial & typing service; word processing service; photocopying & duplicating services

(G-1782)
REAL FOOD FOR FUEL LLC
3452 Spur St (24060-8750)
PHONE..............................757 416-4458
Kristen Chang, *Principal*
EMP: 3
SALES (est): 202.8K **Privately Held**
WEB: www.realfoodforfuel.com
SIC: 2869 Fuels

(G-1783)
RGOLF INC
2000 Kraft Dr Ste 2180 (24060-6319)
P.O. Box 3065, Roanoke (24015-1065)
PHONE..............................540 443-9296
Michael O'Brien, *CEO*
Davis Wildman, *Treasurer*
Frank O'Brien, *Director*
EMP: 3
SQ FT: 650
SALES (est): 134.7K **Privately Held**
SIC: 7372 Home entertainment computer software

(G-1784)
RIEGGER MARIN
Also Called: Blue Ridge Flutes
1700 Masada Way (24060-9180)
PHONE..............................646 896-4739
Marin Riegger, *Owner*
EMP: 1
SALES (est): 41K **Privately Held**
WEB: www.blueridgeoptical.com
SIC: 3931 7389 Reeds for musical instruments; business services

(G-1785)
ROBERT H GILES JR
509 Fairview Ave (24060-5719)
PHONE..............................540 808-6334
Robert Giles, *Principal*
EMP: 2
SALES (est): 86K **Privately Held**
WEB: www.ruralsystem.com
SIC: 3728 Aircraft parts & equipment

(G-1786)
SALEM STONE CORPORATION
Also Called: Acco Stone
677 Jennelle Rd (24060-0129)
P.O. Box 174, Christiansburg (24068-0174)
PHONE..............................540 552-9292
James Moran, *Branch Mgr*
Dennis Tawney, *Manager*
Tommy Miller, *Manager*
EMP: 25
SALES (corp-wide): 34MM **Privately Held**
WEB: www.salemstonecorp.com
SIC: 1423 5032 1429 Crushed & broken granite; stone, crushed or broken; igneous rock, crushed & broken-quarrying
PA: Salem Stone Corporation
　　5764 Wilderness Rd
　　Dublin VA 24084
　　540 674-5556

(G-1787)
SCHMIDT JAYME
Also Called: Exper T'S
1419 N Main St (24060-2563)
PHONE..............................540 961-1792
Jayme Schmidt, *Owner*
EMP: 7
SQ FT: 1,500
SALES (est): 350K **Privately Held**
WEB: www.exper-ts.com
SIC: 2396 2395 2231 Screen printing on fabric articles; embroidery & art needlework; apparel & outerwear broadwoven fabrics

(G-1788)
SENTEK INSTRUMENT LLC
208 Spickard St (24060-1330)
PHONE..............................540 831-9693
Anbo Wang, *Principal*
LI Huo, *Info Tech Mgr*
EMP: 4 EST: 2012
SALES (est): 451.6K **Privately Held**
WEB: www.sentekinstrument.com
SIC: 3829 Measuring & controlling devices

(G-1789)
SENTEK INSTRUMENT LLC
1750 Kraft Dr Ste 1125 (24060-6392)
PHONE..................................540 250-2116
EMP: 2
SALES (est): 183.7K **Privately Held**
WEB: www.sentekinstrument.com
SIC: 3829 Measuring & controlling devices

(G-1790)
SEVEN BENDS LLC
4025 Mount Zion Rd (24060-0745)
PHONE..................................540 392-0553
Jeffrey Uhl,
Michael Artz,
EMP: 5
SALES (est): 269.7K **Privately Held**
SIC: 3999 Hosiery kits, sewing & mending

(G-1791)
SIGNSPOT LLC
3956 S Main St Ste 1 (24060-7724)
PHONE..................................540 961-7768
Justin Hurt,
Chantry Hurt,
EMP: 2
SALES (est): 242.2K **Privately Held**
WEB: www.signbug.com
SIC: 3993 Signs & advertising specialties

(G-1792)
SOFTWARE SPECIALISTS INC
306 Cherokee Dr Ste 500 (24060-1822)
PHONE..................................540 449-2805
Gregory Robert Lee, *Principal*
EMP: 2
SALES (est): 139.4K **Privately Held**
WEB: www.swspec.com
SIC: 7372 Prepackaged software

(G-1793)
SOUTHERN PRINTING CO INC
501 Industrial Park Rd Se (24060-6653)
PHONE..................................540 552-8352
Leo K Southern, *President*
Patricia Hughes, *Vice Pres*
Debby Starner, *Cust Mgr*
EMP: 20
SQ FT: 20,000
SALES (est): 2MM **Privately Held**
WEB: www.printatsouthern.com
SIC: 2752 Commercial printing, offset

(G-1794)
SPECTRUM BRANDS PET LLC
Also Called: Marineland
3001 Commerce St (24060-6671)
PHONE..................................540 951-5481
Randy Lewis, *General Mgr*
Dewayne Martin, *Plant Mgr*
Donal Robb, *Plant Mgr*
Rich Versprille, *Plant Mgr*
Brian McFadden, *Purch Mgr*
EMP: 10
SALES (corp-wide): 3.9B **Publicly Held**
WEB: www.dreambone.com
SIC: 2047 5149 Dog food; dog food
HQ: Spectrum Brands Pet Llc
3001 Deming Way
Middleton WI 53562
608 275-3340

(G-1795)
SUE DILLE
Also Called: Sue Dille Designs
2195 Woodland Hills Dr (24060-9267)
PHONE..................................540 951-4100
Sue Dille, *Owner*
EMP: 1
SALES (est): 65.1K **Privately Held**
SIC: 3911 5944 Jewelry apparel; jewelry
stores

(G-1796)
SWEET AND SIMPLE PRINTS
3120 Mount Tabor Rd (24060-8930)
PHONE..................................757 710-1116
EMP: 2
SALES (est): 94.6K **Privately Held**
SIC: 2752 Commercial printing, litho-
graphic

(G-1797)
TECHULON
2200 Kraft Dr Ste 2475 (24060-6726)
PHONE..................................540 443-9254

Leo Harris, *Principal*
EMP: 6
SALES (est): 749K **Privately Held**
WEB: www.techulon.com
SIC: 2822 Ethylene-propylene rubbers,
EPDM polymers

(G-1798)
TENNECO INC
300 Industrial Park Rd Se (24060-6608)
PHONE..................................540 557-3312
EMP: 2
SALES (corp-wide): 17.4B **Publicly Held**
WEB: www.tenneco.com
SIC: 3714 Motor vehicle engines & parts
PA: Tenneco Inc.
500 N Field Dr
Lake Forest IL 60045
847 482-5000

(G-1799)
TOBACCO QUITTER LLC
1905 Meadowview Cir (24060-2630)
PHONE..................................540 818-3396
Jon E Fritsch, *Administration*
EMP: 2
SALES (est): 108.2K **Privately Held**
SIC: 7372 Application computer software

(G-1800)
TRANSECURITY LLC
2000 Kraft Dr Ste 2195 (24060-6765)
PHONE..................................540 443-9231
Michael Mollenhauer,
Thomas Dingus,
Andrew Petersen,
EMP: 3
SQ FT: 200
SALES (est): 250K **Privately Held**
SIC: 3674 Semiconductors & related de-
vices

(G-1801)
TRESER FAMILY FOODS INC
1002 Auburn Dr (24060-8123)
PHONE..................................540 250-5667
Steven Treser, *President*
Miles Atchison, *Vice Pres*
EMP: 2 EST: 2008
SQ FT: 200
SALES (est): 46.9K **Privately Held**
SIC: 2033 Barbecue sauce: packaged in
cans, jars, etc.

(G-1802)
**VALLEY CONSTRUCTION SVCS
LLC**
125 N Main St Ste 128 (24060-3997)
PHONE..................................540 320-8545
Joe Jasper, *Mng Member*
Dean Frantz, *Manager*
EMP: 7
SQ FT: 6,000
SALES (est): 483K **Privately Held**
SIC: 3699 Welding machines & equipment,
ultrasonic

(G-1803)
VALLEY OUTSOURCING
2100 Keisters Branch Rd (24060-0722)
PHONE..................................540 320-0892
Harold J Smith, *Owner*
Jackie Smith, *General Mgr*
EMP: 15 EST: 1992
SQ FT: 30,000
SALES (est): 750K **Privately Held**
SIC: 3599 Amusement park equipment

(G-1804)
VIRGINIA OIL COMPANY
1710 Prices Fork Rd (24060-3836)
PHONE..................................540 552-2365
EMP: 2 EST: 2010
SALES (est): 112.2K **Privately Held**
WEB: www.vt.edu
SIC: 1389 Oil & gas field services

(G-1805)
VOLTMED INC
2000 Kraft Dr Ste 1108 (24060-6703)
PHONE..................................443 799-3072
Michael Sano, *Co-Owner*
Christopher Arena, *Co-Owner*
Rafael Davalos, *Co-Owner*
Paulo Garcia, *Co-Owner*
EMP: 1

SALES (est): 105.9K **Privately Held**
WEB: www.voltmed.com
SIC: 3841 3845 8731 Surgical & medical
instruments; electromedical equipment;
biological research; biotechnical research,
commercial; medical research, commercial

(G-1806)
**WOLVERINE ADVANCED MTLS
LLC**
Also Called: Wolverine Gasket
201 Industrial Park Rd Se (24060-6605)
PHONE..................................540 552-7674
Doug Smock, *Production*
Dick Newark, *Manager*
Terry Epperly, *Manager*
Mark Oblinsky, *Manager*
EMP: 40 **Publicly Held**
WEB: www.wamglobal.com
SIC: 3089 3053 3714 Injection molded
finished plastic products; injection mold-
ing of plastics; molding primary plastic;
gaskets, packing & sealing devices; motor
vehicle parts & accessories
HQ: Wolverine Advanced Materials, Llc
5850 Mercury Dr Ste 250
Dearborn MI 48126

(G-1807)
WORDSPRINT INC
2200 Kraft Dr Ste 2050 (24060-6704)
PHONE..................................540 382-9111
Michael Abraham, *Branch Mgr*
EMP: 5
SALES (corp-wide): 3.8MM **Privately
Held**
WEB: www.wordsprint.com
SIC: 2752 Commercial printing, offset
PA: Wordsprint, Inc.
190 W Spring St
Wytheville VA 24382
276 228-6608

(G-1808)
XP POWER
1700 Kraft Dr (24060-0012)
PHONE..................................540 552-0432
Michael Johnson, *Director*
EMP: 1
SALES (est): 96.9K **Privately Held**
SIC: 3679 Electronic loads & power sup-
plies

Blackstone
Nottoway County

(G-1809)
AAI CORPORATION
Also Called: Textron Systems
277 Dominy Corner Rd (23824-3041)
PHONE..................................410 666-1400
Maria Tam, *Principal*
John Fields, *Principal*
EMP: 2
SALES (est): 274.6K **Privately Held**
WEB: www.textron.com
SIC: 3728 Aircraft parts & equipment

(G-1810)
AAI TEXTRON
1279 W 10th St Ste B (23824-3071)
PHONE..................................434 292-5805
Sharon Gail Stumps, *Manager*
EMP: 4
SALES (est): 390.1K **Privately Held**
SIC: 3559 Electronic component making
machinery

(G-1811)
BETHANY WARTHAN
Also Called: Warthan Ammunition Solutions
957 N Main St (23824-9583)
PHONE..................................434 294-2937
Bethany Warthan, *Owner*
EMP: 1
SALES (est): 50K **Privately Held**
SIC: 3483 Ammunition loading & assem-
bling plant

(G-1812)
BLACKSTONE HERB COTTAGE
101 S Main St (23824-1841)
PHONE..................................434 292-1135

Candy Early, *Principal*
EMP: 4
SALES (est): 220K **Privately Held**
WEB: www.blackstoneherbcottage.com
SIC: 3556 Mixers, commercial, food

(G-1813)
CAROUSEL
104 N Main St (23824-1424)
PHONE..................................434 292-7721
Candy Earley, *Owner*
EMP: 1
SALES (est): 70.7K **Privately Held**
SIC: 2339 Women's & misses' athletic
clothing & sportswear

(G-1814)
**CENTRAL VIRGINIA HORSE
LOGGING**
400 7th St (23824-2408)
PHONE..................................434 390-7252
EMP: 2 EST: 2019
SALES (est): 81.7K **Privately Held**
SIC: 2411 Logging

(G-1815)
DEMPSEY & CORCORAN
926 Church St (23824-2825)
PHONE..................................434 294-3942
EMP: 2
SALES (est): 128.8K **Privately Held**
WEB: www.dempseyandco.com
SIC: 3599 Machine shop, jobbing & repair

(G-1816)
DOGGED STATE DISTILLING CO
3181 Hungarytown Rd (23824-3949)
PHONE..................................434 480-0575
Lance Alan Dorin, *Principal*
EMP: 4
SALES (est): 116.1K **Privately Held**
SIC: 2085 Distilled & blended liquors

(G-1817)
GRANDESIGN
606 S Main St (23824-2220)
PHONE..................................434 294-0665
James Hargrave, *Owner*
EMP: 1
SALES (est): 10K **Privately Held**
SIC: 3993 Signs & advertising specialties

(G-1818)
**KOPPERS UTILITY INDUS PDTS
INC**
2960 Cox Rd (23824-3078)
PHONE..................................434 292-4375
R Michael Johnson, *CEO*
EMP: 2 **Publicly Held**
WEB: www.koppersuip.com
SIC: 2411 2491 Wooden bolts, hewn;
structural lumber & timber, treated wood
HQ: Koppers Utility And Industrial Products
Inc.
860 Cannon Bridge Rd
Orangeburg SC 29115
803 534-7467

(G-1819)
**LAWSON & SONS LOGGING
LLC**
3543 Rocky Hill Rd (23824-4127)
PHONE..................................434 292-7904
Barbara Lawson,
Donald Lawson,
EMP: 2 EST: 2013
SALES (est): 186.1K **Privately Held**
SIC: 2411 Logging

(G-1820)
MCMJ ENTERPRISES LLC
Also Called: Sign Solutions
300 Church St (23824-1602)
PHONE..................................434 298-0117
Major Jones,
EMP: 1
SALES (est): 77K **Privately Held**
SIC: 3993 Electric signs

(G-1821)
NOTTOWAY PUBLISHING CO INC
Also Called: Courier Record
111 W Maple St (23824-1707)
P.O. Box 460 (23824-0460)
PHONE................................434 292-3019
James D Coleburn, *President*
EMP: 10 EST: 1890
SQ FT: 4,500
SALES (est): 671K **Privately Held**
WEB: www.courier-record.com
SIC: 2711 Commercial printing & newspaper publishing combined

(G-1822)
PEMBELTON FOREST PRODUCTS INC (PA)
402 Davis Mill Rd (23824-4236)
PHONE................................434 292-7511
J W Davis, *President*
H R Davis, *Corp Secy*
EMP: 25 EST: 1941
SQ FT: 10,000
SALES (est): 4.1MM **Privately Held**
SIC: 2421 2426 Sawmills & planing mills, general; hardwood dimension & flooring mills

(G-1823)
PENNELLS LOGGING
337 Hawthorne Dr (23824-3527)
PHONE................................434 292-5482
Mac Pennell, *Owner*
EMP: 1
SALES (est): 112.7K **Privately Held**
SIC: 2411 Logging camps & contractors

(G-1824)
PREMIER OFFICE SYSTEMS LLC
213 Forrest Dr (23824-9207)
P.O. Box 401 (23824-0401)
PHONE................................804 414-4198
Teresa J Keller,
EMP: 10
SALES (est): 100K **Privately Held**
WEB: www.premierofficesystems.com
SIC: 2531 Public building & related furniture

(G-1825)
REISS MANUFACTURING INC
1 Polymer Pl (23824)
P.O. Box 60 (23824-0060)
PHONE................................434 292-1600
Carl Reiss, *President*
Clay Beauchamp, *General Mgr*
Jack Wienuski, *COO*
Rose Carr, *QC Mgr*
Rose Ross-Carr, *QC Mgr*
EMP: 125
SALES (corp-wide): 11.3MM **Privately Held**
WEB: www.reissmfg.com
SIC: 3089 3061 Molding primary plastic; mechanical rubber goods
HQ: Reiss Manufacturing, Inc.
36 Bingham Ave
Rumson NJ 07760
732 446-6100

(G-1826)
ROBERT LEWIS
Also Called: Greentree Toner
1279 W 10th St Ste 114 (23824-3071)
PHONE................................917 640-0709
Robert Lewis, *Owner*
EMP: 1
SALES (est): 85.3K **Privately Held**
WEB: www.greentreetonerva.com
SIC: 2893 Printing ink

(G-1827)
SB COX READY MIX INC
Also Called: Nottoway Plant
800 Dearing Ave (23824-3076)
PHONE................................434 292-7300
Sue Orton, *Branch Mgr*
EMP: 10
SALES (corp-wide): 6.3MM **Privately Held**
WEB: www.coxreadymix.com
SIC: 3273 Ready-mixed concrete

PA: Sb Cox Ready Mix Inc
2160 Lanier Ln
Rockville VA

(G-1828)
SHOWBEST FIXTURE CORP
1033 Church St (23824-2837)
PHONE................................434 298-3925
Lizzy Hamlet, *Branch Mgr*
EMP: 35
SALES (corp-wide): 23.9MM **Privately Held**
WEB: www.showbest.com
SIC: 2542 Fixtures, store: except wood
PA: Showbest Fixture Corp.
4112 Sarellen Rd
Richmond VA 23231
804 222-5535

(G-1829)
SIGNS DESIGNS & MORE LLC
200 W 10th St (23824-3063)
PHONE................................434 292-4555
Sharon Fassold,
EMP: 2
SALES (est): 130K **Privately Held**
SIC: 3993 Signs & advertising specialties

Blairs
Pittsylvania County

(G-1830)
JONES & SONS INC
7521 U S Highway 29 (24527-2811)
PHONE................................434 836-3851
Carolyn T Jones, *Administration*
EMP: 2
SALES (est): 187.4K **Privately Held**
SIC: 3548 Resistance welders, electric

(G-1831)
LANDRUM HORSE SHOEING INC
324 Landrum Rd (24527-2300)
PHONE................................434 836-0847
Coy Landrum, *CEO*
EMP: 1
SALES (est): 72.4K **Privately Held**
SIC: 3462 Horseshoes

(G-1832)
MOUNTAIN TECH INC
700 David Giles Ln (24527-3764)
PHONE................................434 710-4896
John Sherman, *Owner*
Bobby Oaks, *Principal*
EMP: 5
SALES (est): 430.7K **Privately Held**
SIC: 3599 Machine & other job shop work

(G-1833)
UNIQUE INDUSTRIES INC
225 Toy Ln (24527-3110)
PHONE................................434 835-0068
Mario Sampson, *VP Opers*
Terrence Murry, *Warehouse Mgr*
Alexander Dunn, *Human Resources*
Bill Davis, *Manager*
Chuck Schamerhorn, *Manager*
EMP: 25
SALES (corp-wide): 240.4MM **Privately Held**
WEB: www.favors.com
SIC: 2679 Gift wrap & novelties, paper; crepe paper or crepe paper products: purchased material
PA: Unique Industries, Inc.
4750 League Island Blvd
Philadelphia PA 19112
215 336-4300

Bland
Bland County

(G-1834)
3300 ARTESIAN BOT WTR CO LLC
1593 Wilderness Rd (24315-4964)
PHONE................................276 928-9903
Delbert R White, *Principal*
EMP: 15

SALES (est): 1.6MM **Privately Held**
SIC: 2086 Bottled & canned soft drinks

(G-1835)
ABB ENTERPRISE SOFTWARE INC
Also Called: A B B Electric Systems
171 Industry Dr (24315-4894)
P.O. Box 38 (24315-0038)
PHONE................................276 688-3325
Herb Grant, *General Mgr*
EMP: 300 **Privately Held**
WEB: www.new.abb.com
SIC: 3612 Transformers, except electric
HQ: Abb Enterprise Software Inc.
305 Gregson Dr
Cary NC 27511
919 856-2360

(G-1836)
PASCOR ATLANTIC CORPORATION (PA)
254 Industry Dr (24315-4511)
PHONE................................276 688-2220
Travis W Garske, *CEO*
Travis Garske, *President*
Bill Hail, *President*
William D Hail, *President*
Paul J Catron, *Vice Pres*
EMP: 30 EST: 2000
SALES (est): 5.1MM **Privately Held**
WEB: www.pascoratlantic.com
SIC: 3613 3643 Switches, electric power except snap, push button, etc.; current-carrying wiring devices

(G-1837)
TNT BRADSHAW LOGGING LLC
9908 Wilderness Rd (24315-5062)
PHONE................................276 928-1579
EMP: 2
SALES (est): 81.7K **Privately Held**
SIC: 2411 Logging

(G-1838)
WRIGHT MACHINE & MANUFACTURING
Also Called: Wrightside
573 Main St (24315-5480)
P.O. Box 37 (24315-0037)
PHONE................................276 688-2391
EMP: 5
SALES (est): 502.3K **Privately Held**
SIC: 3999 3532 Mfg Misc Products Mfg Mining Machinery

Bloxom
Accomack County

(G-1839)
CANVAS TO CURTAINS
14609 Bethel Church Rd (23308-2931)
PHONE................................757 665-5406
Patsy English, *Owner*
EMP: 1
SALES (est): 15K **Privately Held**
SIC: 2394 Canvas & related products

(G-1840)
GERALDINE BROWNS CHILD CAR
15132 Bethel Church Rd (23308-2939)
PHONE................................757 665-1466
Geraldine Brown, *Principal*
EMP: 2
SALES (est): 104.1K **Privately Held**
SIC: 3944 Cars, play (children's vehicles)

(G-1841)
HAILEY BUG VENDING
16501 Kegotank Rd (23308-1121)
PHONE................................757 665-4402
Edward Matthews, *Partner*
Tiffany Gladding, *Partner*
EMP: 3
SALES (est): 231.9K **Privately Held**
SIC: 3581 7389 Automatic vending machines;

Blue Grass
Highland County

(G-1842)
HAL WARNER LOGGING
1118 Blue Grass Valley Rd (24413-2368)
PHONE................................540 474-5533
Hal Warner, *Owner*
EMP: 3
SALES (est): 31.6K **Privately Held**
SIC: 2411 Logging camps & contractors

(G-1843)
J & W LOGGING INC
1353 Wimer Mountain Rd (24413-2306)
PHONE................................540 474-3531
Jimmie J Will, *President*
Jamie T Will, *Vice Pres*
Linda H Will, *Admin Sec*
EMP: 6
SALES (est): 222K **Privately Held**
SIC: 2411 Logging camps & contractors

(G-1844)
PRIDE AND JOY LOGGING INC
1118 Blue Grass Valley Rd (24413-2368)
PHONE................................540 474-5533
Barbara Warner, *Principal*
EMP: 3
SALES (est): 165.7K **Privately Held**
SIC: 2411 Logging camps & contractors

Blue Ridge
Botetourt County

(G-1845)
BOXLEY MATERIALS COMPANY (HQ)
15418 W Lynchburg Slem Tp (24064-3033)
P.O. Box 13527, Roanoke (24035-3527)
PHONE................................540 777-7600
Jeffrey N Perkins, *President*
Brent Gleason, *Vice Pres*
Bill Hamlin, *Vice Pres*
Charles Craddock, *Plant Mgr*
Stacy Barbour, *Foreman/Supr*
EMP: 32 EST: 1923
SQ FT: 10,000
SALES (est): 148.7MM
SALES (corp-wide): 2.2B **Publicly Held**
WEB: www.boxley.com
SIC: 1422 1423 Crushed & broken limestone; crushed & broken granite
PA: Summit Materials, Inc.
1550 Wynkoop St Ste 300
Denver CO 80202
303 893-0012

(G-1846)
BOXLEY MATERIALS COMPANY
Also Called: Blue Ridge Quarry
15415 W Lynchburg Salem T (24064-3033)
P.O. Box 13527, Roanoke (24035-3527)
PHONE................................540 777-7600
Donna Cotter, *Administration*
EMP: 20
SALES (corp-wide): 2.2B **Publicly Held**
WEB: www.boxley.com
SIC: 1422 Crushed & broken limestone
HQ: Boxley Materials Company
15418 W Lynchburg Slem Tp
Blue Ridge VA 24064
540 777-7600

(G-1847)
BOXLEY MATERIALS COMPANY
Also Called: Concrete Sales Office
15418 W Lynchburg (24064)
P.O. Box 13527, Roanoke (24035-3527)
PHONE................................540 777-7600
EMP: 3
SALES (corp-wide): 2.2B **Publicly Held**
WEB: www.boxley.com
SIC: 3273 Ready-mixed concrete
HQ: Boxley Materials Company
15418 W Lynchburg Slem Tp
Blue Ridge VA 24064
540 777-7600

(G-1848)
BOXLEY MATERIALS COMPANY
Also Called: Blue Ridge Plant
139 Healing Springs Rd (24064-1825)
P.O. Box 13527, Roanoke (24035-3527)
PHONE.................................540 777-7600
Abney S Boxley III, *Branch Mgr*
EMP: 9
SALES (corp-wide): 2.2B **Publicly Held**
WEB: www.boxley.com
SIC: 3273 Ready-mixed concrete
HQ: Boxley Materials Company
15418 W Lynchburg Slem Tp
Blue Ridge VA 24064
540 777-7600

(G-1849)
GENERAL SHALE BRICK INC
770 Webster Rd (24064)
P.O. Box 306 (24064-0306)
PHONE.................................540 977-5505
Don Ballard, *Manager*
EMP: 150
SALES (corp-wide): 3.8B **Privately Held**
WEB: www.generalshale.com
SIC: 3251 3271 Brick clay: common face, glazed, vitrified or hollow; concrete block & brick
HQ: General Shale Brick, Inc.
3015 Bristol Hwy
Johnson City TN 37601
423 282-4661

(G-1850)
HOWARDS PRECISION MCH SP INC
2035 Blue Ridge Sprng Rd (24064-1360)
PHONE.................................540 890-2342
Howard L Altis, *President*
EMP: 4
SALES (est): 36.6K **Privately Held**
WEB: www.hpm-usa.com
SIC: 3599 Machine shop, jobbing & repair

(G-1851)
MAHOY ELECTRIC SERVICE CO INC
175 Macgregor Dr (24064-1527)
PHONE.................................540 977-0035
Jim Mahoy, *President*
Alda L Mahoy, *Corp Secy*
EMP: 7
SQ FT: 6,200
SALES (est): 600K **Privately Held**
SIC: 7694 5999 Electric motor repair; motors, electric

(G-1852)
MOFAT PUBLISHING LLC
336 Stratford Dr (24064-1334)
PHONE.................................540 915-5847
Joshua Egan, *Principal*
EMP: 2
SALES (est): 108.1K **Privately Held**
WEB: www.mofatpublishing.com
SIC: 2741 Miscellaneous publishing

(G-1853)
MYDRONE4HIRE LLC
2507 Blue Ridge Sprng Rd (24064-1237)
PHONE.................................540 491-4860
Tim Cooney, *Principal*
EMP: 2
SALES (est): 119.6K **Privately Held**
SIC: 3721 Motorized aircraft

(G-1854)
PERFECT PEACE ALPACAS LLC
224 Shade Hollow Rd (24064-1689)
PHONE.................................540 797-1985
EMP: 2
SALES (est): 142.9K **Privately Held**
SIC: 2231 Alpacas, mohair: woven

(G-1855)
RIDGE TOP WELDING
1396 Otter Mountain Dr (24064)
P.O. Box 496 (24064-0496)
PHONE.................................540 947-5118
EMP: 1
SALES (est): 77.1K **Privately Held**
WEB: www.ridgetopenterprisesllc.com
SIC: 7692 Welding repair

(G-1856)
VICKIE D BLANKENSHIP
1155 Colonial Rd (24064-1717)
PHONE.................................540 977-6377
EMP: 3
SALES (est): 188.2K **Privately Held**
SIC: 2411 Logging

Bluefield
Tazewell County

(G-1857)
APPALACHIAN AGGREGATES LLC
171 Saint Clair Xing (24605-9332)
PHONE.................................276 326-1145
John Wilkinson, *Branch Mgr*
EMP: 50
SALES (corp-wide): 30.6B **Privately Held**
WEB: www.appalachianaggregates.com
SIC: 1422 Crushed & broken limestone
HQ: Appalachian Aggregates, Llc
2950 Charles Ave
Dunbar WV 25064

(G-1858)
BAYSTAR COAL COMPANY INC
356 S College Ave (24605-1709)
PHONE.................................276 322-4900
Edward A Asbury, *President*
Dic Johnson, *Treasurer*
EMP: 11
SQ FT: 20,000
SALES (est): 1.3MM **Privately Held**
SIC: 1241 Coal mining services

(G-1859)
BLUEFIELD MANUFACTURING INC
215 Suppliers Rd (24605)
P.O. Box 1010 (24605-4010)
PHONE.................................276 322-3441
Ivan D Jones, *CEO*
Rita C Peery, *President*
Cindy Noel, *Corp Secy*
Walter D Hartzell, *Vice Pres*
Anne Miller, *Purchasing*
▲ EMP: 33 EST: 1981
SQ FT: 30,000
SALES (est): 8.9MM **Privately Held**
WEB: www.bluefieldmfg.com
SIC: 3532 Mining machinery

(G-1860)
COAL FILLERS INC (PA)
Hc 640 (24605)
P.O. Box 1063 (24605-4063)
PHONE.................................276 322-4675
Charles Bibbee, *President*
Brian Higginbotham, *Safety Mgr*
Dave Hofstetter, *Treasurer*
Ben Birkmeier, *Director*
◆ EMP: 6
SQ FT: 1,200
SALES (est): 5.5MM **Privately Held**
WEB: www.coalfillers.com
SIC: 3312 1221 Coal gas derived from chemical recovery coke ovens; bituminous coal & lignite loading & preparation

(G-1861)
D L WILLIAMS COMPANY
412 Ridgeway Dr (24605-1630)
PHONE.................................276 326-3338
Donald L Williams Jr, *President*
Mary K Williams, *Vice Pres*
▼ EMP: 2
SALES (est): 450K **Privately Held**
WEB: www.dlwilliamscompany.com
SIC: 3532 Crushing, pulverizing & screening equipment

(G-1862)
DFA DAIRY BRANDS FLUID LLC
37306 Gov G C Peery Hwy (24605-9037)
PHONE.................................336 714-9032
Michael Hardcastle, *Branch Mgr*
EMP: 2
SALES (corp-wide): 15.8B **Privately Held**
SIC: 2026 Fluid milk

HQ: Dfa Dairy Brands Fluid, Llc
1405 N 98th St
Kansas City KS 66111
816 801-6455

(G-1863)
DOSS FORK COAL CO INC
111 1/2 S College Ave (24605-1704)
P.O. Box 1084 (24605-4084)
PHONE.................................540 322-4066
Edward Asbury, *President*
Richard Taylor, *Corp Secy*
Herbert Asbury, *Vice Pres*
EMP: 40
SALES (est): 4.5MM **Privately Held**
SIC: 1222 Bituminous coal-underground mining

(G-1864)
IDENTITY AMERICA INC
112 Spruce St Ste 4 (24605-1755)
P.O. Box 1047 (24605-4047)
PHONE.................................276 322-2616
Rhonda Neal, *Exec VP*
Rhonda Neale, *Vice Pres*
EMP: 2 EST: 1999
SALES (est): 185.6K **Privately Held**
WEB: www.identityamerica.com
SIC: 3993 Electric signs

(G-1865)
J AND R MANUFACTURING INC
351 Industrial Park Rd (24605-9363)
PHONE.................................276 210-1647
Roy Riley, *President*
Theresa Barringer, *Exec VP*
Teresa Barringer, *Executive*
EMP: 26 EST: 1976
SQ FT: 9,500
SALES (est): 5.2MM **Privately Held**
WEB: www.jandrmanufacturinginc.com
SIC: 3643 3678 3532 Electric connectors; electronic connectors; mining machinery

(G-1866)
JOY GLOBAL UNDERGROUND MIN LLC
1081 Hockman Pike (24605-9350)
PHONE.................................276 322-5454
Ron Comer, *Manager*
EMP: 150 **Privately Held**
SIC: 3535 Bucket type conveyor systems
HQ: Joy Global Underground Mining Llc
40 Pennwood Pl
Warrendale PA 15086
724 779-4500

(G-1867)
JOY GLOBAL UNDERGROUND MIN LLC
1081 Hockman Pike (24605-9350)
PHONE.................................276 322-5421
Ron Comer, *Branch Mgr*
EMP: 10 **Privately Held**
WEB: www.mining.komatsu
SIC: 3532 Mining machinery
HQ: Joy Global Underground Mining Llc
40 Pennwood Pl
Warrendale PA 15086
724 779-4500

(G-1868)
LAWRENCE BROTHERS INC
203 Lawrence Rd (24605-9069)
P.O. Box 737 (24605-0737)
PHONE.................................276 322-4988
James Mark Lawrence, *President*
Fernando Protti, *COO*
Melanie Protti Lawrence, *Vice Pres*
Melanie Protti-Lawrence, *Vice Pres*
Frank McDonald, *Opers Mgr*
EMP: 25 EST: 1974
SQ FT: 33,000
SALES (est): 7.4MM **Privately Held**
WEB: www.lbimanufacturing.com
SIC: 3532 3443 Mining machinery; fabricated plate work (boiler shop)

(G-1869)
LIMESTONE DUST CORPORATION
230 Saint Clair Xing (24605)
PHONE.................................276 326-1103
Michael W McGlothlin, *President*
Jeanne McGlothlin, *Admin Sec*

EMP: 60
SQ FT: 50,000
SALES (est): 8MM **Privately Held**
SIC: 3281 2048 1422 Limestone, cut & shaped; prepared feeds; crushed & broken limestone

(G-1870)
MITCHELL LOCK OUT
133 Hicks St (24605-1924)
PHONE.................................276 322-4087
Russel Mitchell, *Owner*
EMP: 1
SALES (est): 100.2K **Privately Held**
SIC: 3499 7699 Locks, safe & vault: metal; lock & key services

(G-1871)
NON STOP ENTERPRISE LTD
401 Rosenbaum Rd (24605-8720)
PHONE.................................276 945-2028
Ron Joyce, *President*
Charles E Joyce, *President*
Ronald Joyce, *President*
EMP: 2
SQ FT: 2,070
SALES (est): 247.8K **Privately Held**
SIC: 3599 Machine shop, jobbing & repair

(G-1872)
PEMCO CORPORATION
1960 Valleydale St (24605-9454)
PHONE.................................276 326-2611
Robert Graf, *CEO*
David Graf, *President*
Mark Johnson, *Vice Pres*
James Johnson, *Export Mgr*
Renea Christian, *Purchasing*
▲ EMP: 80
SQ FT: 94,000
SALES (est): 31.1MM **Privately Held**
WEB: www.amrpemco.com
SIC: 3699 3612 3532 3643 Electrical equipment & supplies; power & distribution transformers; mining machinery; current-carrying wiring devices; electronic loads & power supplies
PA: American Mine Research, Inc.
12187 N Scenic Hwy
Rocky Gap VA 24366
276 928-1712

(G-1873)
PERFORMANCE DRIVES INC
145 Bunny Dr (24605-9254)
P.O. Box 1682, Richlands (24641-1682)
PHONE.................................304 327-7725
Ronnie E Hager, *President*
Avery A Richardson, *Admin Sec*
EMP: 2
SALES (est): 455.2K **Privately Held**
WEB: www.perdrives.com
SIC: 3535 Conveyors & conveying equipment

(G-1874)
PLATNICK CRANE AND STEEL LLC
269 St Clairs Xing (24605)
PHONE.................................276 322-5477
Eric Miller, *CEO*
EMP: 15
SALES (est): 3.8MM
SALES (corp-wide): 3.4MM **Privately Held**
WEB: www.platnickcrane.com
SIC: 3531 Cranes
PA: Dema, Llc
269 St Clairs Xing
Bluefield VA 24605
276 322-5477

(G-1875)
POUNDING MILL QUARRY CORP (PA)
171 Saint Clair Xing (24605-9332)
PHONE.................................276 326-1145
Toll Free:.................................888 -
William C Hunter MD, *President*
Robert Hunter, *President*
Kevin Fuller, *COO*
Nancy Hunter, *Exec VP*
Charles M Hunter Jr, *Senior VP*
◆ EMP: 40 EST: 1913

SALES (est): 49.1MM **Privately Held**
WEB: www.pmqc.com
SIC: 1422 1442 Limestones, ground; construction sand & gravel

(G-1876)
PRINT PLUS
208 Bluestone Dr (24605-9401)
P.O. Box 630 (24605-0630)
PHONE..................276 322-2043
EMP: 2
SALES (est): 83.9K **Privately Held**
SIC: 2752 Commercial printing, lithographic

(G-1877)
RABBIT CREEK PARTNERS LLC
Also Called: Acken Signs
334 Industrial Park Rd (24605-9363)
PHONE..................877 779-9977
Doren Spinner,
EMP: 60
SQ FT: 70,000
SALES (est): 5.6MM **Privately Held**
WEB: www.themcgroup.com
SIC: 3993 Electric signs; neon signs; signs, not made in custom sign painting shops

(G-1878)
RALEIGH MINE AND INDUS SUP INC
517 Bluefield Indus Park (24605)
P.O. Box 72 (24605-0072)
PHONE..................276 322-3119
Becky Sander, *General Mgr*
Becky Sanders, *Manager*
EMP: 30
SALES (corp-wide): 152.2MM **Privately Held**
WEB: www.raleighmine.com
SIC: 3713 Truck bodies & parts
PA: Raleigh Mine And Industrial Supply, Inc.
1500 Mill Creek Rd
Mount Hope WV 25880
304 877-5503

(G-1879)
STICH N PRINT
103 Thistle St (24605-1117)
P.O. Box 844 (24605-0844)
PHONE..................276 326-2005
Ray Maupin, *Principal*
EMP: 2
SALES (est): 161.9K **Privately Held**
SIC: 2752 Commercial printing, lithographic

(G-1880)
T & P SERVICING LLC
231 Wren Dr (24605)
P.O. Box 280, Boissevain (24606-0280)
PHONE..................276 945-2040
Paula Rider, *Principal*
EMP: 2 EST: 2010
SALES (est): 99.1K **Privately Held**
SIC: 1389 Roustabout service

(G-1881)
THISTLE FOUNDRY & MCH CO INC
101 Thistle St (24605-1117)
PHONE..................276 326-1196
Dewayne Johnson, *Vice Pres*
EMP: 13 EST: 1898
SQ FT: 24,000
SALES (est): 847K **Privately Held**
WEB: www.thistlefoundry.com
SIC: 3325 3599 Steel foundries; machine shop, jobbing & repair

(G-1882)
TIMCO ENERGY INC
356 S College Ave (24605-1709)
P.O. Box 1084 (24605-4084)
PHONE..................276 322-4900
Edward Asbury, *President*
EMP: 40
SALES (est): 1.2MM **Privately Held**
SIC: 1241 Coal mining services

(G-1883)
TRAMLINE INC (PA)
Also Called: Tramline Shop
356 S College Ave (24605-1709)
P.O. Box 1030 (24605-4030)
PHONE..................276 322-3183
Edward A Asbury, *President*
Herbert B Asbury Sr, *Vice Pres*
Richard L Taylor, *Admin Sec*
EMP: 8
SALES (est): 1MM **Privately Held**
SIC: 3532 5082 Mining machinery; mining machinery & equipment, except petroleum

(G-1884)
TWIN CITY MOTOR EXCHANGE INC
1225 Hockman Pike (24605-9351)
P.O. Box 1083 (24605-4083)
PHONE..................276 326-3606
Eddie Asbury, *President*
Asbury Herbert, *Vice Pres*
Dick Johnson, *Vice Pres*
Rita Money, *Admin Sec*
EMP: 5
SALES (est): 561.1K **Privately Held**
SIC: 7694 Electric motor repair

Bluemont
Clarke County

(G-1885)
BEAR CHASE BREWING COMPANY LLC
18288 Blueridge Mtn Rd (20135-1800)
PHONE..................703 930-7949
Mark Tatum,
EMP: 4
SALES (est): 100.5K **Privately Held**
SIC: 2082 Beer (alcoholic beverage)

(G-1886)
BLUEMONT
18035 Raven Rocks Rd (20135-1712)
PHONE..................202 422-6500
EMP: 2
SALES (est): 84.5K **Privately Held**
WEB: www.bluemontvineyard.com
SIC: 2084 Wines

(G-1887)
BLUMONT VINEYARDS
18755 Foggy Bottom Rd (20135-1858)
PHONE..................540 554-8439
Robert Rupy, *Principal*
EMP: 3
SALES (est): 253.4K **Privately Held**
WEB: www.bluemontvineyard.com
SIC: 2084 Wines

(G-1888)
GIBSON LOGGING LLC RUSH J
4447 River Rd (20135-5045)
PHONE..................540 539-8145
EMP: 3
SALES (est): 260.7K **Privately Held**
SIC: 2411 Logging camps & contractors

(G-1889)
IMPROVEMENTS BY BILL LLC
732 Beechwood Ln (20135-4453)
PHONE..................571 246-7257
EMP: 2 EST: 2015
SALES (est): 127.9K **Privately Held**
SIC: 3993 Signs & advertising specialties

(G-1890)
PAMELA J LUTTRELL CO
2269 Mount Carmel Rd (20135-5201)
PHONE..................540 837-1525
Pamela J Luttrell, *Owner*
EMP: 1
SALES (est): 41K **Privately Held**
SIC: 3999 Lawn ornaments

(G-1891)
SIGN DESIGN INC
1669 Feltner Rd (20135-5229)
PHONE..................239 478-8315
Patricia House, *Owner*
EMP: 1 EST: 2015

SALES (est): 47.5K **Privately Held**
SIC: 3993 Signs & advertising specialties

(G-1892)
TWIN OAKS TAVERN WINERY
18035 Raven Rocks Rd (20135-1712)
PHONE..................540 554-4547
EMP: 2
SALES (est): 97.4K **Privately Held**
WEB: www.twinoakstavernwinery.com
SIC: 2084 Wines

Boones Mill
Franklin County

(G-1893)
BOOTH LOGGING COMPANY
664 Cascade Ln (24065-4575)
PHONE..................540 334-1075
Richard Lyn Booth, *Owner*
Connie Booth, *Co-Owner*
EMP: 3
SALES (est): 150K **Privately Held**
SIC: 2411 Logging

(G-1894)
H&W WELDING CO INC
592 Harmony Rd (24065-4292)
PHONE..................540 334-1431
EMP: 1 EST: 2001
SALES (est): 55K **Privately Held**
SIC: 7692 Welding Repair

(G-1895)
JRS REPCO INC
125 Autumn Chase Ln (24065-4808)
P.O. Box 73 (24065-0073)
PHONE..................540 334-3051
Jay R Simmons, *CEO*
Teresa Simmons, *Principal*
EMP: 2
SALES (est): 193.2K **Privately Held**
SIC: 3585 Refrigeration & heating equipment

(G-1896)
KENS LEATHERCRAFT
6760 S Indian Grave Rd (24065-2040)
PHONE..................540 774-6225
Kathy Guilliams, *Owner*
EMP: 1
SALES (est): 71.3K **Privately Held**
WEB: www.kensleathercraft.com
SIC: 3199 Equestrian related leather articles

(G-1897)
METWOOD INC (PA)
819 Naff Rd (24065-4010)
PHONE..................540 334-4294
Keith M Thomas, *CEO*
Shawn Phillips, *President*
EMP: 13
SALES: 1.9MM **Publicly Held**
WEB: www.metwood.com
SIC: 3441 8711 Fabricated structural metal; engineering services

(G-1898)
NEXT LEVEL BUILDING SOLUTIONS (PA)
5170 Alean Rd (24065-4752)
PHONE..................540 400-9169
Jeffrey Moses, *President*
Ashley Rogers, *General Mgr*
EMP: 5
SALES (est): 330K **Privately Held**
SIC: 3589 Commercial cleaning equipment

(G-1899)
VISUAL COMMUNICATION CO INC
231 Red Valley Rd (24065-4641)
PHONE..................540 427-1060
Tony Hamlin, *President*
EMP: 2
SALES (corp-wide): 200K **Privately Held**
WEB: www.visualsigns.net
SIC: 2796 Engraving platemaking services
PA: Visual Communication Co Inc
229 Red Valley Rd
Boones Mill VA 24065
540 427-1060

(G-1900)
VISUAL COMMUNICATION CO INC (PA)
Also Called: Industrial Engraving Co
229 Red Valley Rd (24065-4641)
PHONE..................540 427-1060
Tony Hamlin, *President*
Kimberly Hamlin, *Vice Pres*
EMP: 2
SALES (est): 200K **Privately Held**
WEB: www.visualsigns.net
SIC: 2796 Engraving platemaking services

(G-1901)
WEB TRANSITIONS INC
109 Main St (24065)
P.O. Box 514 (24065-0514)
PHONE..................540 334-1707
Beth Garst, *CEO*
EMP: 6
SALES (est): 508.2K **Privately Held**
WEB: www.webtransitions.com
SIC: 7372 7374 Business oriented computer software; computer graphics service

Boston
Culpeper County

(G-1902)
BOSTON SPICE & TEA CO INC
12207 Obannons Mill Rd (22713-4161)
P.O. Box 38 (22713-0038)
PHONE..................540 547-3907
Joann M Neal, *President*
Joan M Neal, *President*
EMP: 9
SALES (est): 500K **Privately Held**
WEB: www.bostonspice.com
SIC: 2099 Seasonings & spices; tea blending

(G-1903)
GOODLIFE THEATRE
3753 Slate Mills Rd (22713-1703)
PHONE..................540 547-9873
Joeseph Pipik, *CEO*
Jean Wall, *Vice Pres*
EMP: 2
SALES (est): 82K **Privately Held**
WEB: www.goodlifetheater.com
SIC: 3999 7929 Puppets & marionettes; entertainment service

(G-1904)
HEAVENLY SENT CUPCAKES LLC
6401 Griffinsburg Rd (22713-4519)
PHONE..................540 219-2162
Frederick J Getty, *Administration*
EMP: 4
SALES (est): 158.3K **Privately Held**
WEB: www.heavenlyscentcupcakesandcakes.com
SIC: 2051 Bread, cake & related products

(G-1905)
WOODARD LLC
6104 Sperryville Pike (22713-4128)
P.O. Box 53 (22713-0053)
PHONE..................540 812-5016
Travis Woodard, *Principal*
EMP: 1 EST: 2016
SALES (est): 45.5K **Privately Held**
SIC: 2499 Wood products

Bowling Green
Caroline County

(G-1906)
ATLAS SCNTFIC TCHNCAL SVCS LLC
18149 Harding Dr (22427-2215)
PHONE..................540 492-5051
Gayle Lake, *Principal*
EMP: 3 EST: 2018
SALES (est): 220.9K **Privately Held**
SIC: 3663 Radio & TV communications equipment

▲ = Import ▼=Export
◆ =Import/Export

(G-1907)
SCIENCE OF SPIRITUALITY
Also Called: Sawan Kirpal Publication Ctr
19384 Smoots Rd (22427-2402)
PHONE..............................804 633-9987
Catherine Cataldo, *Director*
EMP: 1
SALES (est): 74.7K **Privately Held**
SIC: 2731 7999 Books: publishing only; instruction schools, camps & services

Boyce
Clarke County

(G-1908)
CHARLES H SNEAD CO
118 E Main St (22620-9638)
PHONE..............................540 539-5890
Charles H Snead, *Owner*
EMP: 4
SQ FT: 4,000
SALES (est): 500K **Privately Held**
SIC: 2431 Doors, combination screenstorm, wood

(G-1909)
EYE OF NEEDLE EMBROIDERY
146 Morning Star Ln (22620-2058)
PHONE..............................540 837-2089
EMP: 1
SALES (est): 33.1K **Privately Held**
SIC: 2395 Embroidery & art needlework

(G-1910)
MOBILE SHEET METAL LLC
435 Wildcat Hollow Rd (22620-2752)
PHONE..............................540 450-6324
EMP: 2
SALES (est): 184.3K **Privately Held**
SIC: 3444 Sheet metalwork

(G-1911)
RONALD LIGHT
Also Called: Lighthouse Woodworking
146 Morning Star Ln (22620-2058)
PHONE..............................540 837-2089
Ronald Light, *Owner*
EMP: 1
SALES (est): 133.1K **Privately Held**
WEB: www.lighthousewoodworking.com
SIC: 2431 Millwork

(G-1912)
SHENANDOAH CONTROL SYSTEMS
224 Mount Prospect Ln (22620-2915)
P.O. Box 157 (22620-0157)
PHONE..............................540 837-1627
Jerry L Boyles, *President*
Jane L Boyles, *Admin Sec*
EMP: 2
SALES (est): 258.8K **Privately Held**
WEB: www.shencontrols.com
SIC: 3613 Control panels, electric

Boydton
Mecklenburg County

(G-1913)
AGRIUM US INC
449 A Washington St (23917)
PHONE..............................434 738-0515
William Coleman, *Branch Mgr*
EMP: 3
SALES (corp-wide): 20B **Privately Held**
WEB: www.nutrien.com
SIC: 2873 Nitrogenous fertilizers
HQ: Agrium U.S. Inc.
5296 Harvest Lake Dr
Loveland CO 80538

(G-1914)
D AND L SIGNS AND SERVICES LLC
3482 Antlers Rd (23917-3516)
PHONE..............................434 265-4115
Charles Dunn II, *CEO*
EMP: 2
SQ FT: 1,200
SALES (est): 180K **Privately Held**
SIC: 3993 Signs & advertising specialties

(G-1915)
FELTON BROTHERS TRNST MIX INC
703 Puryear Rd (23917)
P.O. Box 37 (23917-0037)
PHONE..............................434 374-5373
Scott Spencer, *Opers-Prdtn-Mfg*
EMP: 5
SALES (corp-wide): 3.3MM **Privately Held**
WEB: www.feltonbrothers.com
SIC: 3273 Ready-mixed concrete
PA: Felton Brothers Transit Mix, Incorporated
1 Edmunds St
South Boston VA 24592
434 572-2665

(G-1916)
MICROSOFT CORPORATION
101 Herbert Dr (23917-3742)
PHONE..............................434 738-0103
Richard Tilghman, *Manager*
EMP: 34
SALES (corp-wide): 143B **Publicly Held**
WEB: www.microsoft.com
SIC: 7372 Application computer software
PA: Microsoft Corporation
1 Microsoft Way
Redmond WA 98052
425 882-8080

(G-1917)
YORK FABRICATION LLC
297 Alexander Ferry Rd (23917-4533)
PHONE..............................804 241-0136
EMP: 3 **EST:** 2016
SALES (est): 178.2K **Privately Held**
SIC: 3441 Fabricated structural metal

Boykins
Southampton County

(G-1918)
AEC VIRGINIA LLC
3205 6th E Cir (23827)
PHONE..............................757 654-6131
Kaed Hull, *Manager*
EMP: 120
SQ FT: 225,000
SALES (corp-wide): 152.7MM **Privately Held**
WEB: www.aecnarrowfabrics.com
SIC: 2241 Ribbons
HQ: Aec Virginia, Llc
32056 E Cir
Boykins VA 23827

(G-1919)
PHENIX ENGINEERED TEXTILES INC
32056 East Cir (23827)
PHONE..............................757 654-6131
Morris Cooke, *Plant Mgr*
EMP: 103
SALES (corp-wide): 14MM **Privately Held**
SIC: 2241 Narrow fabric mills
PA: Phenix Engineered Textiles, Inc.
33 Market Point Dr
Greenville SC 29607
864 616-9937

(G-1920)
PORTERS WOOD PRODUCTS INC
Rr 186 (23827)
P.O. Box 511 (23827-0511)
PHONE..............................757 654-6430
Max B Porter, *President*
Clay D Porter, *Vice Pres*
EMP: 25
SQ FT: 35,000
SALES (est): 3.3MM **Privately Held**
SIC: 2448 2421 2426 Pallets, wood; sawmills & planing mills, general; hardwood dimension & flooring mills

Bracey
Mecklenburg County

(G-1921)
BALLPARK PUBLICATIONS INC
169 Happy Trl (23919-1768)
PHONE..............................757 271-6197
Michael Hall, *Administration*
EMP: 1
SALES (est): 85.9K **Privately Held**
SIC: 2741 Miscellaneous publishing

(G-1922)
BRASS COPPER METAL REFINISHING
803 Holly Grove Ln (23919-1853)
PHONE..............................434 636-5531
Renate Morbitver, *Owner*
EMP: 1
SALES (est): 50.9K **Privately Held**
SIC: 3471 Finishing, metals or formed products

(G-1923)
CITY PUBLICATIONS CHARLOTTE
2883 Highway Nine O Three (23919-1600)
PHONE..............................434 917-5890
EMP: 1 **EST:** 2015
SALES (est): 37.5K **Privately Held**
SIC: 2741 Misc Publishing

(G-1924)
WOODWORKS
10283 Hwy Nine O Three (23919-1992)
PHONE..............................434 636-4111
EMP: 1
SALES (est): 59.5K **Privately Held**
SIC: 2431 Millwork

Brambleton
Loudoun County

(G-1925)
ALTA INDUSTRIES LLC
23394 Virginia Rose Pl (20148-6867)
PHONE..............................703 969-0999
EMP: 2 **EST:** 2017
SALES (est): 122.3K **Privately Held**
SIC: 3999 Manufacturing industries

(G-1926)
AMBERVISION TECHNOLOGIES
42771 Chatelain Cir (20148-7273)
PHONE..............................571 594-1664
Bryant Morris, *Owner*
EMP: 1
SALES (est): 90.3K **Privately Held**
SIC: 3663 Radio & TV communications equipment

(G-1927)
ENTERPRIZE SOFTWARE LLC
23082 Sullivans Cove Sq (20148-4930)
PHONE..............................571 271-5862
Peter Smith, *CEO*
Peter A Smith, *Principal*
EMP: 1
SALES (est): 98K **Privately Held**
SIC: 7372 7373 7371 Prepackaged software; computer integrated systems design; systems engineering, computer related; computer software development & applications; software programming applications

(G-1928)
FORM III DEFENSE SOLUTIONS LLC
42878 Chatelain Cir (20148-7271)
PHONE..............................703 542-7372
John Reidy,
EMP: 1
SALES (est): 87.5K **Privately Held**
WEB: www.form3defense.com
SIC: 3812 Defense systems & equipment

(G-1929)
LOOK UP PUBLICATIONS LLC
42533 Magellan Sq (20148-5610)
PHONE..............................703 542-2736
Denise Hartzler, *Principal*
EMP: 1
SALES (est): 37.5K **Privately Held**
SIC: 2741 Miscellaneous publishing

(G-1930)
MISSION IT LLC
23554 Epperson Sq (20148-7425)
PHONE..............................443 534-0130
Shawn Wells, *Principal*
EMP: 1
SALES (est): 35.4K **Privately Held**
SIC: 7372 9711 8748 7371 Prepackaged software; ; systems analysis & engineering consulting services; computer software development & applications

(G-1931)
MONTUNO SOFTWARE INC
23056 Minerva Dr (20148-7003)
PHONE..............................703 554-7505
Prab Goriparthi, *CEO*
EMP: 5
SALES (est): 169.8K **Privately Held**
WEB: www.montunosoftware.com
SIC: 7372 Application computer software

(G-1932)
ORBYSOL INC
23562 Prosperity Ridge Pl (20148-7660)
PHONE..............................703 398-1092
Sathija Pavuluri, *President*
EMP: 2
SALES (est): 120K **Privately Held**
SIC: 7372 Application computer software

(G-1933)
STEELGATE LLC
42386 Willow Creek Way (20148-4882)
PHONE..............................337 263-2490
John Patrick Curran, *Principal*
EMP: 1
SALES (est): 64.9K **Privately Held**
SIC: 2741 Miscellaneous publishing

(G-1934)
TECHNOLOGY DESTINY LLC
42593 Olmsted Dr (20148-5621)
PHONE..............................703 400-8929
Irick Burris,
EMP: 3
SALES (est): 156.7K **Privately Held**
SIC: 7372 Prepackaged software

(G-1935)
UVSITY CORPORATION
23684 Richland Grove Dr (20148-7656)
PHONE..............................571 308-3241
Heli Desai, *CEO*
EMP: 1
SALES (est): 32.7K **Privately Held**
SIC: 7372 7371 Educational computer software; computer software development & applications

(G-1936)
WOMENS MEDIA WATCH AZERBAIJAN
42492 Mayflower Ter # 30 (20148-4851)
PHONE..............................253 381-9667
Sevinj Mirzayeva, *Principal*
EMP: 2
SALES (est): 83.7K **Privately Held**
SIC: 2711 Newspapers, publishing & printing

Brandy Station
Culpeper County

(G-1937)
BRANDY PRINTING & EMB INC
19638 Church Rd (22714-2236)
PHONE..............................540 825-5583
Allan M Heyward Jr, *Administration*
EMP: 4
SALES (est): 163.5K **Privately Held**
WEB: www.brandyprinting.com
SIC: 2752 Commercial printing, offset

GEOGRAPHIC

(G-1938)
CRYOSCIENCE TECHNOLOGIES
13487 Landons Ln (22714-2050)
PHONE..................................516 338-6723
Todd A Walrich, *Principal*
EMP: 1
SALES (est): 132.2K **Privately Held**
SIC: 3369 Aerospace castings, nonferrous: except aluminum

(G-1939)
FYNE-WIRE SPECIALTIES INC
19633 Church Rd (22714)
P.O. Box 151 (22714-0151)
PHONE..................................540 825-2701
Gregory T Nedell, *President*
◆ EMP: 20
SQ FT: 26,000
SALES (est): 4.8MM **Privately Held**
WEB: www.fynewire.com
SIC: 3496 Miscellaneous fabricated wire products

(G-1940)
K C SUPPLY CORP
11453 Verga Ln (22714-1855)
PHONE..................................540 222-2932
Stephanie Kuhn, *President*
Joseph Kuhn Sr, *Vice Pres*
Tony P Carroll, *Treasurer*
EMP: 3
SALES (est): 200K **Privately Held**
SIC: 3699 Electrical equipment & supplies

(G-1941)
KKS PRINTING & STATIONERY
15051 Jats Dr (22714-2261)
PHONE..................................540 317-5440
Caitlin Troilo, *Owner*
EMP: 1
SALES (est): 347.3K **Privately Held**
WEB: www.kay-kays.com
SIC: 2759 Stationery: printing

(G-1942)
WARDS WLDG & FABRICATION LLC
15251 Wrecker Ct (22714)
PHONE..................................540 219-1460
Sabrina Ward,
EMP: 3
SALES (est): 55.3K **Privately Held**
SIC: 7692 1799 7699 Welding repair; welding on site; tank repair

Bremo Bluff
Fluvanna County

(G-1943)
ALL KINDS OF SIGNS
2878 James Madison Hwy (23022-2116)
PHONE..................................434 842-1877
Amy Gentry, *Owner*
EMP: 1
SALES (est): 67.7K **Privately Held**
SIC: 3993 Signs & advertising specialties

(G-1944)
BEARD LLC RANDALL
2614 Cloverdale Rd (23022-2319)
PHONE..................................434 602-1224
EMP: 2
SALES (est): 129K **Privately Held**
SIC: 2992 Mfg Lubricating Oils/Greases

(G-1945)
CAIN INC
765 Bremo Bluff Rd (23022-2104)
PHONE..................................434 842-3984
Wayne T Cain, *President*
EMP: 2
SALES (est): 185.2K **Privately Held**
WEB: www.waynecain.com
SIC: 3231 Art glass: made from purchased glass

(G-1946)
SAMUEL ROSS
224 Spring Rd (23022-2232)
PHONE..................................434 531-9219
Samuel Ross, *Owner*
EMP: 1

SALES (est): 63.8K **Privately Held**
SIC: 3799 Snowmobiles

Bridgewater
Rockingham County

(G-1947)
AGRI VENTILATION SYSTEMS LLC
Also Called: Shenandoah AG Supply
221 Old River Rd (22812-1217)
P.O. Box 40, Dayton (22821-0040)
PHONE..................................540 879-9864
Neil Beery, *Mng Member*
Francis Pileski, *Manager*
EMP: 20 EST: 1976
SALES (est): 4.2MM **Privately Held**
WEB: www.agrivent.com
SIC: 3564 Ventilating fans: industrial or commercial

(G-1948)
BEATIN PATH PUBLICATIONS LTD
302 E College St (22812-1509)
PHONE..................................540 828-6903
Brent Holl, *Partner*
Rob Amchin, *Admin Sec*
Michael Nichols, *Admin Sec*
EMP: 3
SALES (est): 30K **Privately Held**
WEB: www.beatinpathpublications.com
SIC: 2731 Book music: publishing only, not printed on site

(G-1949)
BLUESTONE VINEYARD INC
4702 Spring Creek Rd (22812-3630)
PHONE..................................540 828-0099
Curt Hartman, *President*
Jackie Hartman, *Vice Pres*
Richard Hartman, *Opers Mgr*
Terry Tucker, *Office Mgr*
Lee Hartman, *Manager*
EMP: 35
SALES (est): 3.6MM **Privately Held**
WEB: www.bluestonevineyard.com
SIC: 2084 Wines

(G-1950)
BRIDGEWATER DRAPERY SHOP
203 N Main St (22812-1339)
PHONE..................................540 828-3312
Carolyn Randolph, *Owner*
EMP: 3
SALES (est): 202.3K **Privately Held**
SIC: 2391 5714 Curtains & draperies; drapery & upholstery stores; draperies

(G-1951)
FRED KINKEAD
Also Called: Valley Seamless Alum Gutters
2727 N River Rd (22812-2519)
PHONE..................................540 828-2955
Fred Kinkead, *Owner*
EMP: 1
SALES (est): 85K **Privately Held**
SIC: 3444 1761 Gutters, sheet metal; roofing contractor

(G-1952)
GENERAL FINANCIAL SUPPLY INC
213b Dry River Rd (22812-1206)
P.O. Box 105 (22812-0105)
PHONE..................................540 828-3892
Vickie Andrick, *Plant Mgr*
April Ruopp, *Sales Staff*
Vicky Andrick, *Branch Mgr*
Ben Moyer, *Analyst*
Kimberly Burrows,
EMP: 40 **Publicly Held**
WEB: www.generalfinancialsupply.com
SIC: 2752 2759 Business forms, lithographed; commercial printing
HQ: General Financial Supply, Inc.
1235 N Ave
Nevada IA 50201
515 382-3549

(G-1953)
GOOD PRINTERS INC
213 Dry River Rd (22812-1242)
PHONE..................................540 828-4663
Michael A Fornadel, *President*
Cindy Hall, *President*
Tim Meredith, *General Mgr*
Dave Proctor, *General Mgr*
Jared Thompson, *COO*
EMP: 53
SQ FT: 88,000
SALES: 6.1MM **Privately Held**
WEB: www.goodprinters.com
SIC: 2752 2791 2789 Promotional printing, lithographic; typesetting; bookbinding & related work

(G-1954)
MILL CABINET SHOP INC
3889 Dry River Rd (22812-3406)
PHONE..................................540 828-6763
H Lee Stover Jr, *CEO*
Randall Stover, *President*
Patrick Shiflet, *Corp Secy*
EMP: 20 EST: 1959
SQ FT: 20,000
SALES (est): 2.4MM **Privately Held**
WEB: www.millcabinetshop.com
SIC: 2434 5712 2541 2511 Wood kitchen cabinets; cabinet work, custom; wood partitions & fixtures; wood household furniture

(G-1955)
MILNESVILLE ENTERPRISES LLC
1654 Ridge Rd (22812-2716)
PHONE..................................540 487-4073
Gary Shull,
EMP: 1
SALES (est): 101.7K **Privately Held**
SIC: 3523 7389 7699 Farm machinery & equipment; design services; farm machinery repair

(G-1956)
PERDUE FARMS INC
100 Quality St (22812-1618)
P.O. Box 238 (22812-0238)
PHONE..................................540 828-7700
Bob Rieman, *COO*
Fazio Jake, *Vice Pres*
Mitchell Hurdle, *Maint Spvr*
Tim Rice, *Maint Spvr*
Weaver Heather, *Accounting Mgr*
EMP: 102
SALES (corp-wide): 5.2B **Privately Held**
WEB: www.perdue.com
SIC: 2015 Poultry, processed
PA: Perdue Farms Inc.
31149 Old Ocean City Rd
Salisbury MD 21804
410 543-3000

(G-1957)
RIVER ROCK WOOD WORKING
8057 George Wine Rd (22812-3360)
PHONE..................................540 828-2358
John Wilfong, *Owner*
EMP: 2
SALES (est): 122.4K **Privately Held**
SIC: 2431 Woodwork, interior & ornamental

(G-1958)
SCOUTCO LLC (PA)
9201 Centerville Rd (22812-3709)
PHONE..................................540 828-0928
Michael Moore, *Principal*
EMP: 3
SALES (est): 314.2K **Privately Held**
WEB: www.scoutcoproducts.com
SIC: 3993 Signs & advertising specialties

(G-1959)
SHICKEL CORPORATION
115 Dry River Rd (22812-1202)
PHONE..................................540 828-2536
Mark A Shickel, *President*
Gary W Shickell, *Vice Pres*
Nick Hilbert, *Project Mgr*
Steve Lonas, *Production*
Terry Pennington, *Purch Agent*
EMP: 85
SQ FT: 30,242

SALES (est): 28MM **Privately Held**
WEB: www.shickel.com
SIC: 3499 3441 3599 3446 Machine bases, metal; fabricated structural metal; machine shop, jobbing & repair; architectural metalwork; sheet metalwork; fabricated plate work (boiler shop)

(G-1960)
WHITE WAVE
166 Dinkel Ave (22812-1316)
PHONE..................................540 434-5945
David Henkel, *Principal*
EMP: 4
SALES (est): 247.6K **Privately Held**
SIC: 2099 Food preparations

Brightwood
Madison County

(G-1961)
FIELD INNER PRIZES LLC
Also Called: Fip Cabinet
116 Dodson Ln (22715-1521)
PHONE..................................540 738-2060
Steven Feild, *Mng Member*
EMP: 2
SALES (est): 225K **Privately Held**
WEB: www.fieldinnerprises.weebly.com
SIC: 2434 Wood kitchen cabinets

(G-1962)
ROBERT DELUCA
Also Called: R & R Printing & Mailing
74 Foothills Ln (22715-1604)
PHONE..................................540 948-5864
Robert Deluca, *Owner*
EMP: 1
SALES (est): 66K **Privately Held**
SIC: 2759 Commercial printing

Bristol
Bristol City County

(G-1963)
A 1 SMART START INC
108 Vance St (24201-3650)
PHONE..................................276 644-3045
EMP: 2 EST: 2014
SALES (est): 130.5K **Privately Held**
SIC: 3694 Engine electrical equipment

(G-1964)
ALPHA APPALACHIA HOLDINGS INC (DH)
1 Alpha Pl (24209)
PHONE..................................276 619-4410
Vaughn R Groves, *Exec VP*
◆ EMP: 100 EST: 1920
SALES (est): 667.3MM
SALES (corp-wide): 2.2B **Publicly Held**
WEB: www.conturaenergy.com
SIC: 1222 1221 Bituminous coal-underground mining; bituminous coal & lignite loading & preparation
HQ: Alpha Natural Resources, Inc.
636 Shelby St Ste 1c
Bristol TN 37620
423 574-5100

(G-1965)
AMERICAN MEDICAL DEVICES INC
Also Called: AMD
1788 Island Rd (24201-7508)
P.O. Box 36 TN (37621-0036)
PHONE..................................276 642-0463
Robert McIlwain, *President*
Maria McIlwain, *Admin Sec*
EMP: 10
SALES (est): 1.1MM **Privately Held**
WEB: www.ammedicaldevices.com
SIC: 3841 8041 7352 Surgical & medical instruments; offices & clinics of chiropractors; medical equipment rental

(G-1966)
AMERICAN MERCHANT INC
750 Old Abingdon Hwy (24201-1847)
PHONE..................................407 446-9872
Robert Burton, *President*

EMP: 6
SALES (est): 562.3K **Privately Held**
WEB: www.ammv.us
SIC: 2211 Towels & toweling, cotton

(G-1967)
BREATHE BRISTOL
39 Piedmont Ave (24201-4160)
PHONE.............................423 254-0323
Jonya Kennedy, *Principal*
EMP: 1 EST: 2017
SALES (est): 90.9K **Privately Held**
SIC: 2621 Paper mills

(G-1968)
CAKEBATTERS LLC
1110 Glenway Ave (24201-3416)
PHONE.............................276 685-6731
Kimberly Epps,
EMP: 1
SALES (est): 39.5K **Privately Held**
SIC: 2051 Cakes, bakery: except frozen

(G-1969)
CATHERINE ELLIOTT
Also Called: Catering By Catherine
921 Lawrence Ave (24201-3421)
PHONE.............................276 274-7022
Catherine Elliott, *Owner*
EMP: 1
SALES (est): 39.5K **Privately Held**
SIC: 2032 Canned specialties

(G-1970)
CHRISTIAN NEWS & COMMENTS
44 New York St (24201-2254)
PHONE.............................276 669-6972
Ted Meeves, *President*
EMP: 4
SALES (est): 3.1K **Privately Held**
SIC: 2711 Newspapers, publishing & printing

(G-1971)
COAL EXTRACTION HOLDINGS LLC (HQ)
1005 Glenway Ave (24201-3473)
PHONE.............................276 466-3322
Kenneth Stacy,
EMP: 5
SALES (est): 629.2K
SALES (corp-wide): 224.2MM **Privately Held**
SIC: 1241 Coal mining services
PA: The United Company
    1005 Glenway Ave
    Bristol VA 24201
    276 466-3322

(G-1972)
CODY STERLING HAWKINS
110 Terrance Cir (24201-3038)
PHONE.............................276 477-0238
Cody Hawkins, *Principal*
EMP: 1
SALES (est): 60K **Privately Held**
SIC: 3531 Backhoes

(G-1973)
CUSTOM DESIGN GRAPHICS
130 Marshall Rd (24201-3156)
PHONE.............................276 466-6778
Rick Stevens, *Owner*
EMP: 1
SALES (est): 80.1K **Privately Held**
SIC: 3993 Signs & advertising specialties

(G-1974)
CUSTOMER 1 ONE INC
138 Bob Morrison Blvd (24201-3808)
PHONE.............................276 645-9003
Bill Gatton, *Principal*
EMP: 15
SALES (corp-wide): 31.8MM **Privately Held**
WEB: www.billgatton.com
SIC: 3479 Painting of metal products
PA: Customer 1 One, Inc.
    1000 W State St
    Bristol TN 37620
    423 764-5121

(G-1975)
ELECTRO-MECHANICAL CORPORATION (PA)
Also Called: Electric Motor Repair & Sls Co
1 Goodson St (24201-4510)
PHONE.............................276 669-4084
Russell Leonard, *CEO*
Howard Broadfoot, *Vice Pres*
Tom Davenport, *Vice Pres*
Thomas Eskew, *Plant Mgr*
Mike Stollings, *Plant Mgr*
◆ EMP: 277 EST: 1958
SQ FT: 128,000
SALES (est): 106.2MM **Privately Held**
WEB: www.electro-mechanical.com
SIC: 3612 5063 3829 3822 Transformers, except electric; electrical apparatus & equipment; measuring & controlling devices; auto controls regulating resldntl & coml environmt & applncs; switchgear & switchboard apparatus; aluminum extruded products

(G-1976)
ELECTRO-MECHANICAL CORPORATION
100 Goodson St (24201-4513)
PHONE.............................276 645-8232
James Miller, *Branch Mgr*
EMP: 2
SALES (corp-wide): 106.2MM **Privately Held**
WEB: www.electro-mechanical.com
SIC: 3612 Transformers, except electric
PA: Electro-Mechanical Corporation
    1 Goodson St
    Bristol VA 24201
    276 669-4084

(G-1977)
ELECTRO-MECHANICAL CORPORATION
Federal Pacific Transformer Co
601 Old Airport Rd (24201-2004)
P.O. Box 8200 (24203-8200)
PHONE.............................276 669-4084
Lee North, *Regional Mgr*
Laura Boardwine, *Vice Pres*
Kenneth Hagerman, *Production*
Shannon Barney, *Senior Buyer*
Steven Mueller, *Engineer*
EMP: 300
SALES (corp-wide): 106.2MM **Privately Held**
WEB: www.electro-mechanical.com
SIC: 3612 3677 Transformers, except electric; electronic coils, transformers & other inductors
PA: Electro-Mechanical Corporation
    1 Goodson St
    Bristol VA 24201
    276 669-4084

(G-1978)
FIBER SIGN
314 Goodson St (24201-4515)
P.O. Box 246 TN (37621-0246)
PHONE.............................276 669-9115
Klenneth Blenkenbedkler, *Owner*
EMP: 1
SALES (est): 57.8K **Privately Held**
WEB: www.fiber-sign.com
SIC: 3993 Signs, not made in custom sign painting shops

(G-1979)
FICTION-ATLAS PRESS LLC
348 Magnolia Dr (24201-2518)
PHONE.............................423 845-0243
Courtney Cannon, *Principal*
EMP: 1 EST: 2017
SALES (est): 37.5K **Privately Held**
SIC: 2741 Miscellaneous publishing

(G-1980)
JOES SMOKED MEAT SHACK
1609 Euclid Ave (24201-3733)
PHONE.............................276 644-4001
EMP: 2
SALES (est): 70.4K **Privately Held**
SIC: 2013 Smoked meats from purchased meat

(G-1981)
KED PLASMA
1315 Euclid Ave (24201-3834)
PHONE.............................276 645-6035
EMP: 3
SALES (est): 99K **Privately Held**
WEB: www.kedplasma.us
SIC: 2836 Plasmas

(G-1982)
LUCAS-MILHAUPT INC
23 Colony Cir (24201-1929)
PHONE.............................276 591-3351
Thomas Harrison, *Principal*
EMP: 5
SALES (corp-wide): 1.5B **Publicly Held**
WEB: www.lucasmilhaupt.com
SIC: 3356 Nonferrous rolling & drawing
HQ: Lucas-Milhaupt, Inc.
    5656 S Pennsylvania Ave
    Cudahy WI 53110
    414 769-6000

(G-1983)
MAGIC WAND INC
1100 Page St (24201-2401)
PHONE.............................276 466-3921
William Daugherty, *President*
William Ducherty, *President*
Jackie Brown, *Corp Secy*
EMP: 44 EST: 1966
SQ FT: 10,000
SALES (est): 5.8MM **Privately Held**
WEB: www.magicwandcarwash.com
SIC: 3589 Car washing machinery

(G-1984)
NATIONAL JUNIOR TENNIS LEAGUE
1003 Chester St (24201-3509)
P.O. Box 56 (24203-0056)
PHONE.............................276 669-7540
EMP: 1
SALES (est): 102.3K **Privately Held**
SIC: 2621 Paper Mill

(G-1985)
OTSAN TECHNICAL SERVICE LLC
311 Gate City Hwy Ste C (24201-3202)
P.O. Box 16361 (24209-6361)
PHONE.............................276 696-7163
Orlando Sanders,
EMP: 1
SALES (est): 79.9K **Privately Held**
WEB: www.otsan.net
SIC: 3575 7378 Computer terminals; computer maintenance & repair; computer & data processing equipment repair/maintenance

(G-1986)
SHEARERS FOODS LLC
110 Thomas Rd (24201-2062)
PHONE.............................276 669-6194
Christine Collins, *Business Mgr*
Mike Alonso, *Opers Mgr*
Brittani Putt, *Transportation*
Rudy Castillo, *Production*
Suzanne Weidle, *Human Res Mgr*
EMP: 1
SALES (corp-wide): 562.1MM **Privately Held**
WEB: www.shearers.com
SIC: 2096 Potato chips & other potato-based snacks
PA: Shearer's Foods, Llc
    100 Lincoln Way E
    Massillon OH 44646
    330 834-4030

(G-1987)
SNACK ALLIANCE INC (PA)
Also Called: Shearer's Foods
225 Commonwealth Ave (24201-7509)
PHONE.............................276 669-6194
John P Frostad, *President*
Pat Lindenbach, *Chairman*
Jim O Brien, *Vice Pres*
Robert D Armstrong, *CFO*
◆ EMP: 200
SALES (est): 30.8MM **Privately Held**
WEB: www.shearers.com
SIC: 2096 Potato chips & similar snacks

(G-1988)
SOUTH STAR DISTRIBUTERS
324 Montrose Dr (24201-2524)
P.O. Box 6 (24203-0006)
PHONE.............................276 466-4038
John Boyd, *Owner*
EMP: 10
SALES (est): 921.9K **Privately Held**
WEB: www.southstarfloors.com
SIC: 2879 Insecticides & pesticides

(G-1989)
SQUABBLE STATE DISTLG CO LLC
529 State St Apt 2 (24201-4314)
PHONE.............................804 393-8380
William Haden Payne II,
EMP: 2
SALES (est): 25K **Privately Held**
SIC: 2085 Distilled & blended liquors

(G-1990)
STATELY DOGS
28 Commonwealth Ave (24201-3802)
PHONE.............................276 644-4098
EMP: 2
SALES (est): 111.4K **Privately Held**
SIC: 3999 Pet supplies

(G-1991)
STRONGWELL CORPORATION (PA)
400 Commonwealth Ave (24201-3800)
P.O. Box 580 (24203-0580)
PHONE.............................276 645-8000
G David Oakley Jr, *President*
Spike Tickle, *Managing Dir*
Billy Phillips, *Superintendent*
David Gibbs, *Vice Pres*
Steve Belcher, *Project Mgr*
◆ EMP: 300
SQ FT: 400,000
SALES (est): 81.5MM **Privately Held**
WEB: www.strongwell.com
SIC: 3089 Awnings, fiberglass & plastic combination

(G-1992)
TWIN CITY WELDING COMPANY
312 Bob Morrison Blvd (24201-3812)
PHONE.............................276 669-9322
Lloyd E Sproles, *President*
EMP: 10
SQ FT: 12,800
SALES (est): 780.9K **Privately Held**
WEB: www.twincitywelding.com
SIC: 7692 Automotive welding; brazing; cracked casting repair

(G-1993)
UNITED CO
1005 Glenway Ave (24201-3473)
PHONE.............................276 466-0769
Jeffrey Keenan, *President*
Wayne L Bell, *Vice Pres*
Kenneth Dockery, *Asst Treas*
Anita W Gilliam, *Asst Sec*
EMP: 80
SQ FT: 30,000
SALES (est): 4.5MM **Privately Held**
WEB: www.unitedco.net
SIC: 1382 6552 Oil & gas exploration services; subdividers & developers

(G-1994)
UNITED COMPANY (PA)
1005 Glenway Ave (24201-3473)
PHONE.............................276 466-3322
James W.Mc Glothlin, *Ch of Bd*
Jeffrey Keenan, *President*
Steve Layfield, *COO*
Lois Clark, *Exec VP*
Al Gayle, *Vice Pres*
EMP: 100 EST: 1980
SQ FT: 30,000
SALES (est): 224.2MM **Privately Held**
WEB: www.unitedco.net
SIC: 1382 7992 Oil & gas exploration services; public golf courses

(G-1995)
UNITED SCREEN DESIGN
Also Called: Xanadu Enterprises
1305 W State St (24201-3757)
PHONE.............................276 669-4669

GEOGRAPHIC

Marlene Tester, *Owner*
EMP: 7
SALES (est): 250K **Privately Held**
WEB: www.unitedscreendesign.com
SIC: 2759 Screen printing

(G-1996)
UNIVERSAL PRINTING
1101 W State St (24201-3715)
PHONE..................................276 466-9311
Sam Morenings, *Owner*
EMP: 10
SQ FT: 15,000
SALES (est): 1.2MM **Privately Held**
WEB: www.universalprintinginc.com
SIC: 2752 Commercial printing, offset

(G-1997)
VIRGINIA WOODWORKING CO INC
190 Williams St (24201-4555)
P.O. Box 157 (24203-0157)
PHONE..................................276 669-3133
David Reeve, *President*
Donald G Costello, *Vice Pres*
▲ EMP: 20 EST: 1946
SQ FT: 10,000
SALES (est): 2.5MM **Privately Held**
WEB: www.vawood.com
SIC: 2431 Staircases & stairs, wood

(G-1998)
VOLLARA LLC
300 E Valley Dr (24201-2802)
PHONE..................................800 704-2378
Cindy Click, *Branch Mgr*
Amelia Spolec, *Officer*
EMP: 95 **Privately Held**
WEB: www.vollara.com
SIC: 3634 2833 Electric housewares & fans; medicinals & botanicals
HQ: Vollara, Llc
4100 Alpha Rd Ste 1100
Dallas TX 75244

(G-1999)
VULCAN CONSTRUCTION MTLS LLC
10 Spurgeon Ln (24201-3351)
P.O. Box 1865 (24203-1865)
PHONE..................................276 466-5436
Gary Griffitts, *Branch Mgr*
EMP: 2 **Publicly Held**
WEB: www.vulcanmaterials.com
SIC: 1422 3273 3272 Crushed & broken limestone; ready-mixed concrete; concrete products
HQ: Vulcan Construction Materials, Llc
1200 Urban Center Dr
Vestavia AL 35242
205 298-3000

(G-2000)
WILLIAMS COMPANY INCORPORATED
101 Vance St (24201-3649)
P.O. Box 189 (24203-0189)
PHONE..................................276 466-3342
Harry Williams, *President*
Craig Kistner, *Purch Agent*
EMP: 14 EST: 1937
SQ FT: 24,868
SALES: 1.4MM **Privately Held**
WEB: www.williamsusa.com
SIC: 3599 Machine shop, jobbing & repair

(G-2001)
WOLF HILLS PRESS LLC
2568 King Mill Pike (24201-3152)
PHONE..................................276 644-3119
Misty Martin, *Principal*
EMP: 1
SALES (est): 41.3K **Privately Held**
SIC: 2741 Miscellaneous publishing

(G-2002)
WOOD TELEVISION LLC
Also Called: Bristol Herald Courier
320 Morrison Blvd (24201-3812)
P.O. Box 609 (24203-0609)
PHONE..................................276 669-2181
Susan Cameron, *Editor*
Jan Patrick, *Editor*
Larry Wheeler, *Sales Mgr*
Meloney Howell, *Sales Staff*

Carl Esposito, *Branch Mgr*
EMP: 135
SALES (corp-wide): 3B **Publicly Held**
WEB: www.woodtv.com
SIC: 2711 Newspapers, publishing & printing
HQ: Wood Television Llc
120 College Ave Se
Grand Rapids MI 49503
616 456-8888

Bristol
Washington County

(G-2003)
AGILITY INC
7761 Cunningham Rd (24202-1859)
PHONE..................................423 383-0962
Dewey Allison, *President*
▲ EMP: 25
SALES (est): 500K **Privately Held**
WEB: www.agilityservices.net
SIC: 3999 Manufacturing industries

(G-2004)
AMERICAN CONCRETE GROUP LLC
618 Lime State Rd (24202)
P.O. Box 708, Pennington Gap (24277-0708)
PHONE..................................423 323-7566
EMP: 3 **Privately Held**
SIC: 2899 Mfg Concrete
PA: American Concrete Group, Llc
R-2 Woodway
Pennington Gap VA 24277

(G-2005)
ANDIS WOOD PRODUCTS INC
13455 Smith Creek Rd (24202-0723)
PHONE..................................276 628-7764
Bobby Andis, *President*
EMP: 8
SALES (est): 686.6K **Privately Held**
SIC: 2448 Pallets, wood

(G-2006)
APPALACHIA HOLDING COMPANY (DH)
Also Called: Massey Coal Export Company
1 Alpha Pl (24202)
PHONE..................................276 619-4410
J Christopher Adkins, *Senior VP*
Richard H Verheij, *Vice Pres*
Baxter F Phillips, *Vice Pres*
H Drexel Short, *Vice Pres*
Jeffrey M Jarosinski, *Ch Credit Ofcr*
▼ EMP: 12 EST: 1916
SQ FT: 50,000
SALES (est): 554.3MM
SALES (corp-wide): 2.2B **Publicly Held**
SIC: 1221 Bituminous coal surface mining; coal preparation plant, bituminous or lignite
HQ: Alpha Appalachia Holdings, Inc.
1 Alpha Pl
Bristol VA 24209
276 619-4410

(G-2007)
AZZ INC
Also Called: Azz Glvnizing Services-Bristol
14781 Industrial Park Rd (24202-3771)
PHONE..................................276 466-5558
Jason Scarboro, *Branch Mgr*
EMP: 33 **Publicly Held**
WEB: www.azz.com
SIC: 3699 3498 3613 3494 Electrical equipment & supplies; pipe sections fabricated from purchased pipe; switchgear & switchboard apparatus; valves & pipe fittings; blast furnaces & steel mills; chemicals & other products derived from coking
PA: Azz Inc.
3100 W 7th St Ste 500
Fort Worth TX 76107
817 810-0095

(G-2008)
BOBS SPORTS EQUIPMENT SALES
11192 Goose Creek Rd (24202-3132)
PHONE..................................276 669-8066

Robert Johnson Jr, *Owner*
Sharyn Johnson, *Co-Owner*
EMP: 1
SALES (est): 103.2K **Privately Held**
WEB: www.danceworkstudio.com
SIC: 2261 7299 5661 Screen printing of cotton broadwoven fabrics; stitching, custom; men's shoes

(G-2009)
BREATHE-3DP LLC
14401 Industrial Park Rd (24202-3705)
PHONE..................................276 645-6556
EMP: 3
SALES (est): 206.2K **Privately Held**
WEB: www.breathe-3dp.com
SIC: 2821 Plastics materials & resins

(G-2010)
BRISTOL SIGN CO WALDEN LLC
6870 Gate City Hwy (24202-1724)
PHONE..................................276 669-0811
Lisa Walden, *Principal*
Joseph Walden, *Principal*
EMP: 3
SALES (est): 100.5K **Privately Held**
WEB: www.bristolsign.com
SIC: 3993 Signs & advertising specialties

(G-2011)
BRISTOL WOODWORKER
24396 Briscoe Dr (24202-4520)
PHONE..................................423 557-4158
James Bardinelli, *Principal*
EMP: 1 EST: 2017
SALES (est): 54.1K **Privately Held**
SIC: 2431 Millwork

(G-2012)
CAMPBELL PRINTING BRISTOL INC
22220 Stevens Private Dr (24202)
P.O. Box 16817 (24209-6817)
PHONE..................................276 466-2311
Rhonda G Jones, *President*
Fletcher Michael C, *Vice Pres*
EMP: 2
SALES (est): 261.2K **Privately Held**
WEB: www.campbellprintingofbristol.com
SIC: 2752 7334 Commercial printing, offset; photocopying & duplicating services

(G-2013)
COMPU MANAGEMENT CORP
3127 Lee Hwy Ste B (24202-5944)
PHONE..................................276 669-3822
Jack Dennison, *President*
Jeffery Musser, *Vice Pres*
EMP: 7 EST: 1982
SALES (est): 600K **Privately Held**
SIC: 7372 5045 Business oriented computer software; accounting machines using machine readable programs

(G-2014)
CROSS RESTORATIONS
11136 Goose Creek Rd (24202-3132)
PHONE..................................276 466-8436
Howell Cross, *Owner*
EMP: 1
SALES (est): 44K **Privately Held**
SIC: 3999 7641 Buttons: Red Cross, union, identification; antique furniture repair & restoration

(G-2015)
CSC FAMILY HOLDINGS INC
Also Called: Carolina Steel Fabrication
15083 Industrial Park Rd (24202-3709)
PHONE..................................276 669-6649
Phil Aiello, *Manager*
EMP: 90
SALES (corp-wide): 17.6MM **Privately Held**
WEB: www.hirschfeld.com
SIC: 3441 3443 1622 Fabricated structural metal; fabricated plate work (boiler shop); bridge, tunnel & elevated highway
PA: Csc Family Holdings, Inc.
101 Centreport Dr Ste 400
Greensboro NC 27409
336 275-9711

(G-2016)
DIE CAST CONNECTIONS INC
14660 Industrial Park Rd (24202-3741)
PHONE..................................276 669-5991
EMP: 5
SALES (est): 489.1K **Privately Held**
SIC: 3544 Mfg Dies/Tools/Jigs/Fixtures

(G-2017)
DOUGH PAY ME OF BRISTOL LLC
15290 Turnberry Ct (24202-4985)
PHONE..................................276 644-8091
Ryan Mathesius, *Administration*
EMP: 1
SALES (est): 65.7K **Privately Held**
SIC: 2621 Paper mills

(G-2018)
FULLER ASPHALT MATERIAL
828 Tri State Lime Rd (24202-6511)
PHONE..................................423 676-4449
William Rodinette, *Owner*
EMP: 5
SALES (est): 1.5MM **Privately Held**
SIC: 2951 Asphalt & asphaltic paving mixtures (not from refineries)

(G-2019)
HELMS CANDY CO INC
3001 Lee Hwy (24202-5939)
P.O. Box 607 (24203-0607)
PHONE..................................276 669-2612
George F Helms III, *CEO*
Debbie L Smith, *President*
George F Helms IV, *Vice Pres*
Mark R Helms, *Vice Pres*
EMP: 20 EST: 1909
SQ FT: 45,000
SALES (est): 1MM **Privately Held**
WEB: www.helmscandy.com
SIC: 2834 2064 Lozenges, pharmaceutical; cough drops, except pharmaceutical preparations

(G-2020)
HOME PRIDE INC
21528 Travalite Dr Ste 2 (24202-5854)
PHONE..................................276 642-0271
Charles Hughes, *Branch Mgr*
EMP: 12 **Privately Held**
WEB: www.hpanchors.com
SIC: 2451 Mobile homes, personal or private use
PA: Home Pride, Inc.
15100 Indl Pk Rd
Bristol VA 24202

(G-2021)
HOME PRIDE INC (PA)
15100 Indl Pk Rd (24202)
P.O. Box 160387, Nashville TN (37216-0387)
PHONE..................................276 466-0502
J William Blevins, *President*
Melba Blevins, *Corp Secy*
Claude Hammonds, *Plant Mgr*
EMP: 37
SQ FT: 50,000
SALES (est): 9.1MM **Privately Held**
WEB: www.hpanchors.com
SIC: 2451 Mobile homes, personal or private use

(G-2022)
JIM CHAMPION
23531 Young Dr (24202-1443)
PHONE..................................276 466-9112
Tim Champion, *Principal*
EMP: 1
SALES (est): 54.1K **Privately Held**
SIC: 2431 Millwork

(G-2023)
KENNEDYS EXCAVATING LLC
18455 Lavender Ln (24202-3379)
PHONE..................................423 383-0143
Gary Kennedy, *President*
Travis Kennedy, *Principal*
EMP: 2
SALES (est): 98.8K **Privately Held**
SIC: 3531 Construction machinery

(G-2024)
LAUREL FORK LOGGING INC
7139 Pembroke Cir (24202-1925)
PHONE.....................................276 285-3761
EMP: 2
SALES (est): 81.7K **Privately Held**
SIC: 2411 Logging

(G-2025)
MATE CREEK ENERGY OF WEST VA (PA)
148 Bristol East Rd (24202-5500)
PHONE.....................................276 669-8599
F D Robertson, *President*
J O Bunn, *Corp Secy*
Don Nicewonder, *Vice Pres*
EMP: 3
SQ FT: 17,000
SALES (est): 1.2MM **Privately Held**
SIC: 1221 Coal preparation plant, bituminous or lignite

(G-2026)
MORETZ CANDY CO INC
3001 Lee Hwy (24202-5939)
PHONE.....................................276 669-2533
Richard Gibian, *Ch of Bd*
Kathy Gibian, *Admin Sec*
EMP: 22 EST: 1933
SQ FT: 27,000
SALES (est): 1.2MM **Privately Held**
WEB: www.helmscandy.com
SIC: 2064 Candy & other confectionery products

(G-2027)
MUMPOWER LUMBER COMPANY
21450 Gale Ave (24202-1226)
PHONE.....................................276 669-7491
Elmer L Mumpower, *Owner*
Barbara Mumpower, *Co-Owner*
EMP: 2
SALES (est): 93K **Privately Held**
SIC: 2421 5211 Furniture dimension stock, softwood; planing mill products & lumber

(G-2028)
NICE WOUNDERS GROUP
148 Bristol East Rd (24202-5500)
PHONE.....................................276 669-6476
Don Nicewonder, *President*
K R Nicewonder, *Admin Sec*
EMP: 10
SQ FT: 4,000
SALES (est): 650.6K **Privately Held**
SIC: 1221 Coal preparation plant, bituminous or lignite

(G-2029)
PIONEER GROUP INC VA
2700 Lee Hwy (24202-5873)
PHONE.....................................276 669-3400
John Matney, *President*
Clyde Stacy, *Admin Sec*
EMP: 2
SALES (est): 191.3K **Privately Held**
SIC: 1221 5052 Bituminous coal & lignite-surface mining; coal & other minerals & ores

(G-2030)
POWER DISTRIBUTION PDTS INC
14660 Industrial Park Rd (24202-3741)
P.O. Box 1688, Abingdon (24212-1688)
PHONE.....................................276 646-3296
David Whitt, *CEO*
Andy Barrett, *COO*
Brad Blake, *CFO*
◆ EMP: 31
SALES (est): 6.4MM **Privately Held**
SIC: 3612 3613 3625 Power & distribution transformers; switchgear & switchboard apparatus; relays & industrial controls

(G-2031)
RALPH MATNEY
21573 Old Dominion Rd (24202-4161)
PHONE.....................................276 644-9259
Ralph Matney, *Principal*
EMP: 1 **Privately Held**
SIC: 3531 Backhoes

(G-2032)
RAPOCA ENERGY CO
2700 Lee Hwy Ste B (24202-5873)
PHONE.....................................423 269-6900
EMP: 2
SALES (est): 66K **Privately Held**
SIC: 1221 Bituminous coal & lignite-surface mining

(G-2033)
SMC ELECTRICAL PRODUCTS INC (DH)
Also Called: Becker SMC
14660 Industrial Park Rd (24202-3741)
P.O. Box 1688, Abingdon (24212-1688)
PHONE.....................................276 285-3841
Greg Sanders, *President*
Ronald Thorne, *Corp Secy*
David Whitt, *CTO*
Justin Tidd, *Info Tech Mgr*
▲ EMP: 40 EST: 1971
SQ FT: 160,000
SALES (est): 18.2MM
SALES (corp-wide): 163.5MM **Privately Held**
WEB: www.becker-mining.com
SIC: 3643 3613 3677 3644 Current-carrying wiring devices; control panels, electric; electronic coils, transformers & other inductors; noncurrent-carrying wiring services; relays & industrial controls; transformers, except electric
HQ: Becker Mining Systems Ag
Walter-Becker-Str. 1
Friedrichsthal 66299
689 785-70

(G-2034)
SPIG INDUSTRY LLC
14675 Industrial Park Rd (24202-3777)
P.O. Box 2617, Abingdon (24212-2617)
PHONE.....................................276 644-9510
Jack Harding, *President*
Michael Breeding, *Sales Staff*
EMP: 15
SQ FT: 10,000
SALES (est): 3.3MM **Privately Held**
WEB: www.spigindustry.com
SIC: 3444 Guard rails, highway: sheet metal

(G-2035)
TENNESSEE CONSOLIDATED COAL CO
Also Called: T C C
1 Alpha Pl (24202)
PHONE.....................................423 658-5115
Don Blackenship, *CEO*
Richard H Verheij, *Vice Pres*
EMP: 2 EST: 1905
SALES (est): 280.3K
SALES (corp-wide): 2.2B **Publicly Held**
SIC: 1222 Bituminous coal-underground mining
HQ: Appalachia Holding Company
1 Alpha Pl
Bristol VA 24202
276 619-4410

(G-2036)
TRI-CITY INDUSTRIAL BUILDERS (PA)
13189 Wallace Pike (24202-3603)
PHONE.....................................276 669-4621
Joe Watson, *CEO*
EMP: 1
SQ FT: 5,000
SALES (est): 511.6K **Privately Held**
SIC: 3531 Asphalt plant, including gravel-mix type

(G-2037)
TSHIRTPOD
15427 Monticello Dr (24202-4107)
PHONE.....................................423 341-8655
EMP: 2 EST: 2016
SALES (est): 94.6K **Privately Held**
WEB: www.tshirtpod.com
SIC: 2752 Commercial printing, lithographic

(G-2038)
UNIVERSAL FIBER SYSTEMS LLC (PA)
14401 Industrial Park Rd (24202-3705)
P.O. Box 8930 (24203-8930)
PHONE.....................................276 669-1161
Marc Ammen, *CEO*
Bill Goodman, *Vice Pres*
Brendan McSheehy, *Vice Pres*
Teddy Smith, *Plant Supt*
Howard Bartholomay, *Plant Mgr*
EMP: 32 EST: 1998
SALES (est): 175.8MM **Privately Held**
WEB: www.universalfibersystems.net
SIC: 3559 Synthetic filament extruding machines

(G-2039)
UNIVERSAL FIBERS INC (HQ)
14401 Industrial Park Rd (24202-3705)
P.O. Box 8930 (24203-8930)
PHONE.....................................276 669-1161
Phil Harmon, *President*
Greg Smith, *Vice Pres*
Mike Barnes, *Engineer*
Joe Woosley, *Engineer*
Meg Collins, *Sales Staff*
◆ EMP: 380
SQ FT: 100,000
SALES (est): 138.2MM
SALES (corp-wide): 175.8MM **Privately Held**
WEB: www.universalfibers.com
SIC: 2824 2281 Organic fibers, noncellulosic; yarn spinning mills
PA: Universal Fiber Systems, Llc
14401 Industrial Park Rd
Bristol VA 24202
276 669-1161

(G-2040)
W&W-AFCO STEEL LLC
Also Called: Hirschfeld Steel
15083 Industrial Park Rd (24202-3709)
PHONE.....................................276 669-6649
William Reeves, *President*
EMP: 49
SALES (corp-wide): 9B **Publicly Held**
WEB: www.wwafcosteel.com
SIC: 3441 Fabricated structural metal
HQ: W&W-Afco Steel Llc
1730 W Reno Ave
Oklahoma City OK 73106
405 235-3621

(G-2041)
WASHINGTON COUNTY MEAT PACKING
20505 Campground Rd (24202-2019)
PHONE.....................................276 466-3000
Robert M Couch, *President*
EMP: 6
SALES (est): 519.8K **Privately Held**
SIC: 2011 Meat packing plants

(G-2042)
WIRETOUGH CYLINDERS LLC
14570 Industrial Park Rd (24202-3778)
PHONE.....................................276 644-9120
Amit Prakash, *President*
▲ EMP: 2
SALES (est): 395.1K **Privately Held**
WEB: www.wiretough.com
SIC: 3699 High-energy particle physics equipment

(G-2043)
WOODLAND LOGGING INC
4393 Saxon Dr (24202-1223)
PHONE.....................................276 669-7795
Adam Mumpower, *President*
EMP: 9
SALES (est): 943.5K **Privately Held**
WEB: www.woodlandlogging.com
SIC: 2411 Logging camps & contractors

(G-2044)
ZENITH FUEL SYSTEMS LLC
14570 Industrial Park Rd (24202-3778)
PHONE.....................................276 669-5555
William R Monkman,
▲ EMP: 95
SALES (est): 14.3MM **Privately Held**
WEB: www.zenithfuelsystems.com
SIC: 3592 Carburetors

Bristow
Prince William County

(G-2045)
APOSTOLOS PUBLISHING LLC
9648 Laurencekirk Pl (20136-2712)
PHONE.....................................703 656-8036
John F Edwards, *Principal*
EMP: 1
SALES (est): 37.5K **Privately Held**
SIC: 2741 Miscellaneous publishing

(G-2046)
ATC INC
8962 Edmonston Dr (20136-1299)
PHONE.....................................703 267-6898
Hua Xu, *President*
Wendong Wang, *Vice Pres*
▲ EMP: 5
SALES (est): 352.9K **Privately Held**
WEB: www.atcin.com
SIC: 3841 Surgical & medical instruments

(G-2047)
AUDIO - VIDEO SOLUTIONS
8802 Grantham Ct (20136-2036)
PHONE.....................................240 565-4381
Demarquise Dortch,
EMP: 1
SALES (est): 131.8K **Privately Held**
SIC: 3577 Decoders, computer peripheral equipment

(G-2048)
BRIDGEWAY PROFESSIONALS INC
9979 Broadsword Dr (20136-2610)
PHONE.....................................561 791-1005
EMP: 1
SALES (est): 37.5K **Privately Held**
WEB: www.bridgewaypro.org
SIC: 2741 Miscellaneous publishing

(G-2049)
C4 EXPLOSIVE SPT TRAINING LLC
7981 Sequoia Park Way (20136-1286)
PHONE.....................................703 881-1481
Charlie Chandler, *Principal*
EMP: 2
SALES (est): 125.8K **Privately Held**
WEB: www.c4strong.com
SIC: 2892 Explosives

(G-2050)
EASTON WELDING LLC
12615 Izaak Walton Dr (20136-1606)
PHONE.....................................703 368-9727
Robert Easton, *Principal*
EMP: 1
SALES (est): 54.9K **Privately Held**
SIC: 7692 Welding repair

(G-2051)
EXCALIBUR TECHNOLOGY SVCS LLC
8854 Stable Forest Pl (20136-5747)
PHONE.....................................703 853-8307
James M Gault, *Administration*
EMP: 2
SALES (est): 184.9K **Privately Held**
SIC: 3556 Roasting machinery: coffee, peanut, etc.

(G-2052)
EXEYE LLC
10224 Broadsword Dr (20136-5609)
PHONE.....................................703 319-0976
Mehdi Bakhtiari,
EMP: 2
SALES (est): 251.3K **Privately Held**
SIC: 3825 Instruments to measure electricity

(G-2053)
FALCON SCREENS LLC
9518 Merrimont Trace Cir (20136-2904)
PHONE.....................................703 789-3274
Richard Antonuccio, *Principal*
EMP: 2
SALES (est): 100K **Privately Held**
WEB: www.falconscreens.com
SIC: 3861 Screens, projection

GEOGRAPHIC

(G-2054)
H&G DECORATIVE PAVERS INC
8721 Linton Hall Rd (20136-1013)
PHONE...................................571 338-4949
Genny L Martinez, *President*
EMP: 4
SALES (est): 394.2K **Privately Held**
WEB: www.hgdecorativepavers.com
SIC: 2951 Asphalt paving mixtures &
blocks

(G-2055)
HP METAL FABRICATION
10302 Bristow Center Dr (20136-2201)
PHONE...................................703 466-5551
EMP: 1 EST: 2014
SALES (est): 83K **Privately Held**
SIC: 3499 Mfg Misc Fabricated Metal
Products

(G-2056)
HUGO MIRANDA
Also Called: Prime Services PC and Printers
8730 Diamond Hill Dr (20136-2302)
PHONE...................................703 898-3956
Hugo Miranda, *Owner*
EMP: 2
SALES (est): 45.1K **Privately Held**
WEB: www.primeservicespcprinters.com
SIC: 3955 Print cartridges for laser & other
computer printers

(G-2057)
JONES FAMILY OFFICE
Also Called: Paul and Sonia Jones
8000 Gainsford Ct (20136-1132)
PHONE...................................305 304-3603
Louis Giguere, *Manager*
EMP: 1
SALES (corp-wide): 5.7MM **Privately
Held**
SIC: 3429 Manufactured hardware (gen-
eral)
PA: Jones Family Office
1275 King St
Greenwich CT 06831
203 302-7412

(G-2058)
KOOL LOOKS INC
12620 Crabtree Falls Dr (20136-2160)
PHONE...................................808 224-1887
Perry Jeter II, *CEO*
Robert Unczur, *Vice Pres*
Matt Worrick, *CFO*
◆ EMP: 10
SQ FT: 5,000
SALES (est): 750K **Privately Held**
SIC: 3499 5199 Novelties & giftware, in-
cluding trophies; gifts & novelties

(G-2059)
LARSEN SWEN
9244 Bowers Brook Pl (20136-5753)
PHONE...................................703 754-2592
Swen Larsen, *Principal*
EMP: 3
SALES (est): 127.5K **Privately Held**
SIC: 3699 High-energy particle physics
equipment

(G-2060)
MICROSOFT CORPORATION
8217 Linton Hall Rd (20136-1023)
PHONE...................................571 222-8110
Greg Matthews, *Manager*
EMP: 99
SALES (corp-wide): 143B **Publicly Held**
WEB: www.microsoft.com
SIC: 7372 Application computer software
PA: Microsoft Corporation
1 Microsoft Way
Redmond WA 98052
425 882-8080

(G-2061)
**SHREWS WELDING AND
FABRICA**
9220 Ashleys Park Ln (20136-1130)
PHONE...................................703 785-8035
EMP: 1
SALES (est): 88.9K **Privately Held**
SIC: 7692 Welding repair

(G-2062)
**SOUTH EAST ASIAN LANGUAGE
PUBL**
8811 Howland Pl (20136-5708)
PHONE...................................703 754-6693
Clark Sheakley, *Principal*
EMP: 2 EST: 2008
SALES (est): 88.7K **Privately Held**
SIC: 2741 Miscellaneous publishing

(G-2063)
**TANNHAUSER ENTERPRISES
LLC**
9141 Dartford Pl (20136-1758)
PHONE...................................703 850-1927
Michael Mort, *Principal*
EMP: 1
SALES (est): 37.5K **Privately Held**
WEB: www.tannhauserpress.com
SIC: 2741 Miscellaneous publishing

(G-2064)
TERTAL PUBLISHING LLC
12320 Indigo Springs Ct (20136-2165)
PHONE...................................571 229-9699
Asa Coleman, *Principal*
EMP: 1
SALES (est): 37.5K **Privately Held**
SIC: 2741 Miscellaneous publishing

(G-2065)
**TUMMY-YMYUM GRMET CANDY
APPLES**
12184 Drum Salute Pl (20136-1936)
PHONE...................................703 368-4756
Sharita Montez-Rouse, *Principal*
EMP: 2
SALES (est): 84.3K **Privately Held**
SIC: 2064 Candy & other confectionery
products

Broad Run
Fauquier County

(G-2066)
**CULPEPER MDEL
BARNSTORMERS INC**
6061 Captains Walk (20137-1959)
PHONE...................................540 349-2733
Nicholas Pegau Burhans, *Principal*
EMP: 2 EST: 2010
SALES (est): 157.5K **Privately Held**
WEB: www.cmbclubrc.com
SIC: 3543 Industrial patterns

(G-2067)
EFFINGHAM MANOR LLC
6190 Georgetown Rd (20137-2044)
PHONE...................................703 594-2300
Chris Pearmund,
EMP: 4
SALES (est): 215.5K **Privately Held**
WEB: www.effinghammanor.com
SIC: 2084 Wines

(G-2068)
M & R STRIPING LLC
6040 Fieldcrest Ln (20137-1909)
PHONE...................................703 201-7162
Robert Wilson, *Partner*
Mary Wilson, *Partner*
EMP: 2
SALES (est): 165.8K **Privately Held**
SIC: 2851 1721 3953 Paints, asphalt or
bituminous; pavement marking contractor;
stencils, painting & marking

(G-2069)
PEARMUND CELLARS
6190 Georgetown Rd (20137-2044)
PHONE...................................540 347-3475
Chris Pearmund, *Owner*
▲ EMP: 10
SALES (est): 873.3K **Privately Held**
WEB: www.pearmundcellars.com
SIC: 2084 Wines

(G-2070)
STAIRCRAFT
6402 Old Bust Head Rd (20137-1922)
PHONE...................................540 347-7023
Donald Brellenthin, *Owner*

EMP: 4
SALES (est): 401.6K **Privately Held**
SIC: 2431 Staircases & stairs, wood

(G-2071)
**VINT HILL CRAFT WINERY LLC
(PA)**
6190 Georgetown Rd (20137-2044)
PHONE...................................540 341-1862
EMP: 6
SALES (est): 654K **Privately Held**
WEB: www.vinthillcraftwinery.com
SIC: 2084 Wines

Broadlands
Loudoun County

(G-2072)
ARCOLA INDUSTRIES LLC
21364 Chickacoan Trail Dr (20148-4035)
PHONE...................................703 723-0092
Nils Warga, *Principal*
EMP: 2
SALES (est): 145.6K **Privately Held**
SIC: 3599 Industrial machinery

(G-2073)
BETTER CABLES LLC
43300 Southern Walk Plz (20148-4463)
PHONE...................................872 222-5371
Bradley Marcus,
EMP: 1
SALES (corp-wide): 188.1K **Privately
Held**
WEB: www.bettercables.com
SIC: 3651 Household audio & video equip-
ment
PA: Better Cables Llc
43150 Arundell Ct
Broadlands VA 20148
703 724-0906

(G-2074)
BETTER CABLES LLC (PA)
43150 Arundell Ct (20148-5021)
PHONE...................................703 724-0906
Margaret Marcus, *Opers Mgr*
Brad Marcus,
EMP: 1
SALES (est): 188.1K **Privately Held**
WEB: www.bettercables.com
SIC: 3651 Household audio & video equip-
ment

(G-2075)
CHIRU SOFTWARE INC
21525 Glebe View Dr (20148-3625)
PHONE...................................703 201-1914
Qing Yu, *Principal*
EMP: 2
SALES (est): 115.3K **Privately Held**
SIC: 7372 Prepackaged software

(G-2076)
DOITE MEDIA LLC
43135 Dry Ridge Ter (20148-4438)
P.O. Box 4873, Ashburn (20148-0035)
PHONE...................................703 594-1322
EMP: 3
SALES (est): 91.5K **Privately Held**
WEB: www.doitemedia.com
SIC: 2741 7819 7389 8748 Miscella-
neous publishing; sound (effects & music
production), motion picture; recording stu-
dio, noncommercial records; publishing
consultant

(G-2077)
DP TECHNOLOGY
21411 Deepwood Ter (20148-4094)
PHONE...................................703 835-6157
EMP: 2
SALES (est): 82.5K **Privately Held**
WEB: www.espritcam.com
SIC: 7372 Prepackaged software

(G-2078)
HALO ACOUSTIC WEAR LLC
42770 Hollowind Ct (20148-3615)
PHONE...................................703 474-6081
Paul Miller, *CEO*
EMP: 12

SALES (est): 560.9K **Privately Held**
WEB: www.cozyphones.com
SIC: 3679 Headphones, radio

(G-2079)
INNOCOLL INC
42662 Kitchen Prim Ct (20148-3600)
PHONE...................................703 980-4182
Michael Myers, *President*
▼ EMP: 1
SALES (est): 7.2MM **Privately Held**
SIC: 2834 Pharmaceutical preparations

(G-2080)
PRESTO EMBROIDERY LLC
21356 Marsh Creek Dr (20148-4023)
PHONE...................................571 223-0160
Lisa Preston, *Principal*
EMP: 1
SALES (est): 50K **Privately Held**
SIC: 2395 Embroidery & art needlework

(G-2081)
SIGNS BY CLAY DOWNING
43114 Autumnwood Sq (20148-5099)
PHONE...................................703 371-6828
EMP: 2
SALES (est): 72.6K **Privately Held**
WEB: www.signsbyclaydowning.com
SIC: 3993 Signs & advertising specialties

(G-2082)
**SYNERGY ORTHTICS
PRSTHTICS LLC**
42695 Laurier Dr (20148-4117)
PHONE...................................410 788-8901
EMP: 2
SALES (est): 86.6K **Privately Held**
SIC: 3842 Limbs, artificial

(G-2083)
YOUR NEWSY NOTES LLC
43191 Thistledown Ter (20148-4080)
P.O. Box 101, Ashburn (20146-0101)
PHONE...................................703 729-3155
Beverly Schrab, *Principal*
EMP: 2
SALES (est): 118.7K **Privately Held**
WEB: www.yournewsynotes.blogspot.com
SIC: 2741 Newsletter publishing

(G-2084)
**ZACHARY SYSTEMS
INCORPORATED**
42767 Summerhouse Pl (20148-5511)
PHONE...................................703 723-8965
Randolph W Nixon, *Administration*
Randolph Nixon, *Administration*
EMP: 2
SALES (est): 122.4K **Privately Held**
WEB: www.zacharysystems.com
SIC: 7372 Prepackaged software

Broadway
Rockingham County

(G-2085)
**BRANNER PRINTING SERVICE
INC**
13963 Timber Way (22815)
P.O. Box 307 (22815-0307)
PHONE...................................540 896-8947
L B Branner, *President*
Ronald Branner, *Corp Secy*
EMP: 24 EST: 1935
SQ FT: 7,300
SALES (est): 3.9MM **Privately Held**
WEB: www.brannerprinting.com
SIC: 2752 5943 2759 2789 Commercial
printing, offset; office forms & supplies;
commercial printing; bookbinding & re-
lated work

(G-2086)
BROADWAY METAL WORKS INC
621 S Main St (22815-9579)
P.O. Box 125 (22815-0125)
PHONE...................................540 896-7027
Mark C Showalter Jr, *President*
Robert Rhodes, *Business Mgr*
Duane Sholwater, *Vice Pres*
Henry E Showalter, *Vice Pres*
Jim Hoover, *Project Mgr*

▲ = Import ▼=Export

◆ =Import/Export

EMP: 44
SQ FT: 44,000
SALES (est): 12MM **Privately Held**
WEB: www.broadwaymetal.com
SIC: 3441 7692 1761 Fabricated structural metal; welding repair; sheet metalwork

(G-2087)
BRYAN TOOL & MACHINING INC
2970 Mayland Rd (22815-3103)
PHONE..................540 896-6758
John R Bryan, *President*
Timothy R Bryan, *Vice Pres*
Scott Clatterbuck, *Project Mgr*
Joey Dean, *Opers Mgr*
Chip Wittig, *Engineer*
EMP: 17
SALES (est): 3.6MM **Privately Held**
WEB: www.bryantool.com
SIC: 3599 Machine shop, jobbing & repair

(G-2088)
E N S GRAPHICS LLC
230 Eisenhower Dr (22815-9740)
PHONE..................540 830-1776
EMP: 2
SALES (est): 132.8K **Privately Held**
WEB: www.ensgraphics.com
SIC: 3993 Signs & advertising specialties

(G-2089)
MOLDING & TRAFFIC ACC LLC
304 N Timber Way (22815-3200)
PHONE..................540 896-2459
Carl Whetzel, *Principal*
EMP: 3
SALES (est): 226.6K **Privately Held**
SIC: 3089 Molding primary plastic

(G-2090)
MUNDY QUARRIES INC C S
11261 Turleytown Rd (22815)
P.O. Box 126 (22815-0126)
PHONE..................540 833-2061
David W Harrison, *President*
EMP: 26
SQ FT: 2,500
SALES (est): 3.5MM
SALES (corp-wide): 200.4MM **Privately Held**
WEB: www.rockydalequarries.com
SIC: 1422 Limestones, ground
HQ: Valley Building Supply, Inc.
210 Stone Spring Rd
Harrisonburg VA 22801
540 434-6725

(G-2091)
NEFF LUMBER MILLS INC
12110 Turleytown Rd (22815-2619)
P.O. Box 457 (22815-0457)
PHONE..................540 896-7031
Michael Hoover, *President*
Christopher Hoover, *Vice Pres*
Eric D Hoover, *Vice Pres*
Mary Joe Wood, *Admin Sec*
EMP: 40
SQ FT: 5,000
SALES (est): 5.7MM **Privately Held**
SIC: 2421 Lumber: rough, sawed or planed

(G-2092)
ONE CUT BINDERY LLC
559 S Main St (22815-9546)
PHONE..................540 896-7290
EMP: 5
SALES (est): 402.7K **Privately Held**
SIC: 2789 Bookbinding & related work

(G-2093)
PROPST LETTERING AND ENGRAVING
12875 Mountain Valley Rd (22815-3782)
PHONE..................540 896-5368
Mary Propst, *Owner*
EMP: 2
SALES (est): 100K **Privately Held**
SIC: 3993 Signs & advertising specialties

(G-2094)
PURSUIT PACKAGING LLC
8522 Daphna Rd (22815-2905)
PHONE..................540 246-4629
Shanna Porter Allen, *Principal*
EMP: 2

SALES (est): 128.6K **Privately Held**
SIC: 2752 7389 Offset & photolithographic printing; commercial printing, offset; wrapper & seal printing, lithographic;

(G-2095)
SARANDI MANUFACTURING LLC
3707 Industrial Dr (22815-2745)
PHONE..................540 705-0205
Stan Sarandi, *Managing Dir*
Konstanine Sarandi,
Nickolay Sarandi,
EMP: 16
SALES (est): 1.6MM **Privately Held**
WEB: www.sarandimfg.com
SIC: 2434 Wood kitchen cabinets

(G-2096)
SKYLINE POST & POLE LLC
3881 Industrial Dr (22815-2751)
P.O. Box 366, Schaefferstown PA (17088-0366)
PHONE..................717 949-8170
Terrence W Butcher, *Mng Member*
Mark Musser,
EMP: 17
SQ FT: 5,000
SALES (est): 2MM **Privately Held**
SIC: 2499 Fencing, wood

(G-2097)
SPRINGBROOK CRAFT WORKS
256 W Springbrook Rd (22815-9529)
PHONE..................540 896-3404
James Junkins, *Owner*
EMP: 1
SALES (est): 51.7K **Privately Held**
SIC: 2395 Pleating & stitching

(G-2098)
TOP BEAD WELDING SERVICE INC
190 5th St (22815-9571)
PHONE..................540 901-8730
Lanny V Beach Jr, *President*
Lanny Beach, *President*
Tara Beach, *Corp Secy*
EMP: 21 EST: 1999
SALES (est): 5.6MM **Privately Held**
WEB: www.topbeadwelding.com
SIC: 7692 Welding repair

Brodnax
Brunswick County

(G-2099)
BRODNAX LUMBER COMPANY
2661 Gvrnor Harrison Pkwy (23920-2650)
P.O. Box C (23920-0129)
PHONE..................434 729-2852
Walter H Moseley, *President*
Moseley E M, *Vice Pres*
Mitchell Moseley, *Vice Pres*
Walter B Moseley Jr, *Shareholder*
EMP: 25
SQ FT: 2,100
SALES (est): 3.3MM **Privately Held**
SIC: 2421 Lumber: rough, sawed or planed

(G-2100)
CLARY LOGGING INC RANDY J
1192 Gasburg Rd (23920-3004)
PHONE..................434 636-5268
Randy J Clary, *Principal*
EMP: 6
SALES (est): 326.1K **Privately Held**
SIC: 2411 Logging

(G-2101)
CONNELL LOG THNNING LLC KNNETH
3401 Gvrnor Harrison Pkwy (23920-2646)
PHONE..................434 729-3712
Kathryn McAden, *Principal*
EMP: 6
SALES (est): 635.3K **Privately Held**
SIC: 2411 Logging camps & contractors

(G-2102)
HAWKINS LOGGING
1394 Connell Rd (23920-3103)
PHONE..................434 577-2114

Robert Hawkins, *Owner*
EMP: 2
SALES (est): 86.8K **Privately Held**
SIC: 2411 Logging camps & contractors

(G-2103)
R S BOTTOMS LOGGING
148 Weaver Rd (23920-3042)
PHONE..................434 577-3044
Ron Bottoms, *Owner*
Loretta Bottoms, *Co-Owner*
EMP: 4
SALES (est): 322.2K **Privately Held**
SIC: 2411 Logging camps & contractors

(G-2104)
REGITEX USA LLC
2 Kerr Dr (23920)
PHONE..................514 730-1110
Sylvain Fecteau, *Mng Member*
EMP: 105
SALES (est): 9.3MM
SALES (corp-wide): 18.3MM **Privately Held**
SIC: 2273 Art squares, textile fiber
PA: Regitex Inc
745 Av Guy-Poulin
Saint-Joseph-De-Beauce QC G0S 2
418 397-5775

(G-2105)
STANFORD ELECTRONICS MFG & SLS
Also Called: Sems
915 Berry Rd (23920-2015)
PHONE..................434 676-6630
Ann Klieves, *Owner*
EMP: 7
SQ FT: 2,500
SALES (est): 756.3K **Privately Held**
SIC: 3575 3672 Keyboards, computer, office machine; printed circuit boards

(G-2106)
XTREME SIGNS
3715 Country Club Rd (23920-3460)
PHONE..................434 447-5738
Henry Edmonds, *Owner*
EMP: 2
SALES (est): 154.9K **Privately Held**
SIC: 3993 Signs & advertising specialties

Brookneal
Campbell County

(G-2107)
AMERICAN PLSTIC FBRICATORS INC
536 Cook Ave (24528-3110)
P.O. Box 576 (24528-0576)
PHONE..................434 376-3404
Michael Morris, *President*
Regan Morris, *Office Mgr*
EMP: 13
SQ FT: 4,000
SALES (est): 1.5MM **Privately Held**
WEB: www.americanplasticfab.com
SIC: 3089 Injection molding of plastics

(G-2108)
BROOKNEAL MACHINE SHOP INC
102 Todd St (24528-3022)
P.O. Box 221 (24528-0221)
PHONE..................434 376-2413
Bill Dawson, *Owner*
Debra Dawson, *Treasurer*
Margaret Dawson, *Treasurer*
EMP: 3
SQ FT: 4,200
SALES (est): 335.6K **Privately Held**
WEB: www.townofbrookneal.com
SIC: 3599 3441 Machine shop, jobbing & repair; fabricated structural metal

(G-2109)
CHIPS BROOKNEAL INC
Also Called: Price Co
24 Price Ave Hwy 501 N (24528)
P.O. Box 1004 (24528-1004)
PHONE..................434 376-6202
Williams Fpioker, *Manager*
EMP: 20

SALES (corp-wide): 97.9MM **Privately Held**
SIC: 2421 2435 Planing mill, independent: except millwork; hardwood veneer & plywood
HQ: Chips Brookneal Inc
218 Midway Rte
Monticello AR 71655

(G-2110)
FELTON BROTHERS TRNST MIX INC
813b Lynchburg Ave (24528-2631)
PHONE..................434 376-2415
Chester Cook, *Principal*
EMP: 3
SALES (corp-wide): 3.3MM **Privately Held**
WEB: www.feltonbrothers.com
SIC: 3273 Ready-mixed concrete
PA: Felton Brothers Transit Mix, Incorporated
1 Edmunds St
South Boston VA 24592
434 572-2665

(G-2111)
PRINTING PLUS
403 Rush St (24528)
PHONE..................434 376-3379
Barbara Laprade, *Owner*
EMP: 1
SALES (est): 112.8K **Privately Held**
WEB: www.printplusbknl.com
SIC: 2752 Commercial printing, offset

(G-2112)
SANFACON VIRGINIA INC
933 Sanfacon Rd 18097 Us 933 Sanfacon Road (24528)
PHONE..................434 376-2301
Sanfacon Helene, *President*
Sanfacon Claude, *Treasurer*
Carrie Walker, *Manager*
▲ **EMP:** 30
SQ FT: 1,000
SALES (est): 8.7MM
SALES (corp-wide): 27.3MM **Privately Held**
WEB: www.sanfaconva.com
SIC: 2679 2676 Filter paper: made from purchased material; napkins, paper: made from purchased paper
PA: Groupe Sanfacon Inc, Le
1980 5e Rue
Levis QC
418 839-1370

(G-2113)
SHANTARAS SOAPS
5485 Staunton Hill Rd (24528-3312)
PHONE..................434 221-2382
Anita Martin, *Owner*
EMP: 1
SALES (est): 8K **Privately Held**
SIC: 2841 Soap & other detergents

(G-2114)
THREE P LOGGING
3073 Mount Carmel Rd (24528-3500)
PHONE..................434 376-9812
EMP: 2 **Privately Held**
SIC: 2411 Logging

(G-2115)
TRENT SAWMILL INC
82 Oak St (24528-2544)
PHONE..................434 376-2714
Herbert D Trent, *President*
Shirley B Trent, *Corp Secy*
Ricky D Trent, *Vice Pres*
EMP: 9
SALES (est): 1.3MM **Privately Held**
SIC: 2421 Sawmills & planing mills, general

(G-2116)
WILLIAMS LUMBER SUPPLY INC
17466 Brookneal Hwy (24528-2593)
P.O. Box 248 (24528-0248)
PHONE..................434 376-3368
Joseph S Lunsford, *President*
EMP: 20
SQ FT: 14,600

GEOGRAPHIC

SALES (est): 2.2MM **Privately Held**
WEB: www.williamslumbersupply.com
SIC: 2421 5211 Lumber: rough, sawed or
    planed; lumber & other building materials

Buchanan
Botetourt County

(G-2117)
BRINKLEYS CUSTOM CABINETS
1462 Bobletts Gap Rd (24066-5334)
PHONE..................................540 525-1780
Grant P Brinkley Jr,
EMP: 1
SALES (est): 25K **Privately Held**
WEB: www.brinkleyscabinets.com
SIC: 2434 Wood kitchen cabinets

(G-2118)
CASTELLO 1935 INC
18145 Main St (24066-5555)
PHONE..................................540 464-5275
Richard W Campbell, *President*
▲ **EMP:** 7
SALES (est): 756K **Privately Held**
WEB: www.castello1935.com
SIC: 3714 Pickup truck bed liners

(G-2119)
CRUDEWELL INC
Also Called: Crudewell Drilling
60 Drill Rig Dr (24066-5399)
PHONE..................................540 254-2289
Richard A Simmons, *President*
EMP: 25
SALES (est): 1.2MM **Privately Held**
SIC: 1381 Directional drilling oil & gas
    wells

(G-2120)
**CRYOPAK VERIFICATION TECH
INC**
Also Called: Tcp Reliable
120 Parkway Dr (24066-5574)
P.O. Box 309 (24066-0309)
PHONE..................................888 827-3393
Maurice Barakat, *CEO*
Charles Whiting, *Principal*
Chenshu Lu, *Manager*
▲ **EMP:** 10
SQ FT: 18,000
SALES (est): 2.8MM
SALES (corp-wide): 31.5MM **Privately
Held**
WEB: www.cryopak.com
SIC: 3823 Temperature measurement in-
    struments, industrial; humidity instru-
    ments, industrial process type
PA: Integreon Global, Inc.
    551 Raritan Center Pkwy
    Edison NJ 08837
    848 229-2466

(G-2121)
DENNIS W WILEY
43 Wheatland Rd (24066-4891)
PHONE..................................540 992-6631
Dennis W Wiley, *Owner*
Dennis Wiley, *Owner*
Kathy Wiley, *Co-Owner*
EMP: 2
SALES (est): 119.3K **Privately Held**
SIC: 3552 2396 Embroidery machines;
    screen printing on fabric articles

(G-2122)
MTI SPECIALTY SILICONES INC
19505 Main St (24066-5102)
PHONE..................................540 254-2020
EMP: 3
SALES (est): 247.6K **Privately Held**
SIC: 2869 Mfg Industrial Organic Chemi-
    cals

(G-2123)
**O-N MINERALS CHEMSTONE
COMPANY**
Also Called: Carmeuse Lime & Stone
684 Parkway Dr (24066-5566)
PHONE..................................540 254-1241
Rodney Sandidge, *Opers Staff*
Dillon Clark, *Production*
Laura Shifflett, *Sales Staff*

Clay Coleman, *Manager*
William Orde, *Manager*
EMP: 172
SALES (corp-wide): 177.9K **Privately
Held**
WEB: www.carmeuse.com
SIC: 1422 Crushed & broken limestone
HQ: O-N Minerals (Chemstone) Company
    11 Stanwix St Fl 21
    Pittsburgh PA 15222
    412 995-5500

(G-2124)
PLS INSTALLATION
500 Black Forest Ln (24066-4474)
PHONE..................................540 521-1261
Sean Whitson, *Owner*
EMP: 2
SALES (est): 86.7K **Privately Held**
SIC: 2452 Prefabricated wood buildings

(G-2125)
PROKNOWS
Also Called: Fantasy Factory
1193 Buttons Blf (24066-8500)
P.O. Box 12 (24066-0012)
PHONE..................................540 473-2271
Leon McBride, *Owner*
Linda McBride, *Co-Owner*
EMP: 4
SALES (est): 271K **Privately Held**
WEB: www.proknows.com
SIC: 2389 Costumes

(G-2126)
**S&H MOBILE CLEANING
SERVICE**
386 Spangler Dr (24066-5458)
PHONE..................................540 254-1135
Greg Spangler, *Owner*
EMP: 1
SALES (est): 55K **Privately Held**
SIC: 3589 High pressure cleaning equip-
    ment

(G-2127)
SDC PUBLISHING LLC
221 Berry Ridge Rd (24066-5367)
PHONE..................................540 676-3279
Allen Mahon, *Principal*
EMP: 1
SALES (est): 37.5K **Privately Held**
SIC: 2741 Miscellaneous publishing

(G-2128)
SPRINGWOOD AIRSTRIP
331 Intermont Farm Ln (24066-5002)
PHONE..................................540 473-2079
William Stewart, *Manager*
EMP: 2 **EST:** 2010
SALES (est): 131.7K **Privately Held**
SIC: 3721 Hang gliders

(G-2129)
STEVEN D THOMAS
343 17th St (24066-5486)
P.O. Box 28 (24066-0028)
PHONE..................................540 254-2964
Steven Thomas, *Principal*
EMP: 2
SALES (est): 138.2K **Privately Held**
SIC: 2411 Logging

(G-2130)
**VIRGINIA FORGE COMPANY LLC
(DH)**
17921 Main St (24066)
P.O. Box 1170, Meadville PA (16335-7170)
PHONE..................................540 254-2236
John Keller,
Wayne McKaben,
▲ **EMP:** 1
SQ FT: 51,840
SALES (est): 7.5MM
SALES (corp-wide): 98.2MM **Privately
Held**
WEB: www.meadforge.com
SIC: 3462 Iron & steel forgings
HQ: Meadville Forging Company, L.P.
    15309 Baldwin Street Ext
    Meadville PA 16335
    814 332-8200

Buckingham
Buckingham County

(G-2131)
BRADY JONES LOGGING
Rr 1 (23921)
P.O. Box 300 (23921-0300)
PHONE..................................434 969-4688
Brady Jones, *Owner*
EMP: 7
SALES (est): 930K **Privately Held**
SIC: 2411 Logging camps & contractors

(G-2132)
D K BACKHOE LOADER SERV
26 Manteo Rd (23921-2052)
PHONE..................................434 969-1685
David Turner, *Principal*
EMP: 1
SALES (est): 163.7K **Privately Held**
SIC: 3531 Backhoes

(G-2133)
GREEN PRANA INDUSTRIES INC
76 The Way Apt A (23921-2237)
PHONE..................................410 790-3011
Larry Freeland, *Principal*
EMP: 1
SALES (est): 39.6K **Privately Held**
SIC: 3999 Manufacturing industries

(G-2134)
PRINTING & DESIGN SERVICES
1700 Woodland Church Rd (23921)
PHONE..................................434 969-1133
Richard Friedel, *Owner*
EMP: 1
SALES (est): 62.7K **Privately Held**
SIC: 2759 Commercial printing

(G-2135)
ROCKRIDGE CABINETRY LLC
3237 Dixie Hill Rd (23921-3015)
PHONE..................................434 969-2665
EMP: 4
SALES (est): 320K **Privately Held**
SIC: 2521 Mfg Wood Office Furniture

(G-2136)
**ROCKRIDGE GRANITE
COMPANY LLC**
3143 Dixie Hill Rd (23921-3016)
PHONE..................................434 969-2665
Adam K Morgan, *Mng Member*
Henry Jamerson,
EMP: 5
SQ FT: 3,000
SALES (est): 500K **Privately Held**
SIC: 2434 2541 Wood kitchen cabinets;
    table or counter tops, plastic laminated

Buena Vista
Buena Vista City County

(G-2137)
**ADVANCED DRAINAGE
SYSTEMS INC**
510 Factory St (24416-1528)
PHONE..................................540 261-6131
Jj Massey, *Manager*
Dave Garrett, *Manager*
EMP: 50 **Publicly Held**
WEB: www.ads-pipe.com
SIC: 3084 3083 Plastics pipe; laminated
    plastics plate & sheet
PA: Advanced Drainage Systems, Inc.
    4640 Trueman Blvd
    Hilliard OH 43026
    800 821-6710

(G-2138)
ALLEN ENTERPRISES LLC
Also Called: O'S Ark Custom Apparel
2271 Sycamore Ave Ste A (24416-3150)
PHONE..................................540 261-2622
Jamie Allen,
EMP: 6
SALES (est): 220.7K **Privately Held**
WEB: www.osarkprinting.com
SIC: 2396 Screen printing on fabric articles

(G-2139)
**BARGERS CUSTOM CABINETS
LLC**
982 Linden Ave (24416-3729)
PHONE..................................540 261-7230
Ronald Barger, *Principal*
EMP: 4 **EST:** 2007
SALES (est): 463.9K **Privately Held**
WEB: www.bargerscustomcabinets.com
SIC: 3553 3423 Cabinet makers' machin-
    ery; carpenters' hand tools, except saws:
    levels, chisels, etc.

(G-2140)
CJ9 LTD
101 Hillside Dr (24416-9649)
PHONE..................................817 946-7421
Charles Jolley, *Partner*
EMP: 4
SALES (est): 158.8K **Privately Held**
SIC: 3949 Sporting & athletic goods

(G-2141)
**DES CHAMPS TECHNOLOGIES
INC**
Also Called: Munters Des Champs Products
225 S Magnolia Ave (24416-4707)
PHONE..................................540 291-1111
EMP: 235 **Privately Held**
SIC: 3443 3564 3433 Mfg Fabricated
    Plate Wrk Mfg Blowers/Fans Mfg Heat
    Equip-Nonelec

(G-2142)
**ENVIRONMENTAL DYNAMICS
INC**
2455 Hawthorne Ave (24416-1821)
PHONE..................................540 261-2008
Steven L Bartlett, *President*
Stephen L Bartlett, *President*
EMP: 5
SQ FT: 5,000
SALES (est): 816.9K **Privately Held**
SIC: 2836 Biological products, except diag-
    nostic

(G-2143)
EVERBRITE LLC
627 E 30th St (24416-3914)
PHONE..................................540 261-2121
Paul Ramsey, *Engineer*
Jimmy Flint, *Branch Mgr*
Middleton Justin, *Technology*
EMP: 125
SQ FT: 100,000
SALES (corp-wide): 296.3MM **Privately
Held**
WEB: www.everbrite.com
SIC: 3993 Electric signs
PA: Everbrite, Llc
    4949 S 110th St
    Greenfield WI 53228
    414 529-3500

(G-2144)
**FITZGERALD LUMBER & LOG
CO INC (PA)**
403 E 29th St (24416-1253)
P.O. Box 188 (24416-0188)
PHONE..................................540 261-3430
Calvert S Fitzgerald, *President*
Ronald O Mays, *Corp Secy*
C Wayne Fitzgerald, *Vice Pres*
▼ **EMP:** 43 **EST:** 1973
SQ FT: 20,000
SALES: 19MM **Privately Held**
WEB: www.fitzgeraldlumber.com
SIC: 2426 2421 Hardwood dimension &
    flooring mills; sawmills & planing mills,
    general

(G-2145)
**FLOWERS BAKING CO
NORFOLK LLC**
527 E 29th St (24416-1270)
PHONE..................................540 261-1559
Dean Newcomb, *Branch Mgr*
EMP: 4
SALES (corp-wide): 4.1B **Publicly Held**
SIC: 2051 Breads, rolls & buns
HQ: Flowers Baking Co. Of Norfolk, Llc
    1209 Corprew Ave
    Norfolk VA 23504
    757 622-6317

▲ = Import ▼=Export
◆ =Import/Export

(G-2146)
MARINER MEDIA INC
Also Called: Mariner Co
131 W 21st St (24416-3145)
PHONE.................................540 264-0021
Andrew Wolfe, *President*
Judy Rogers, *Editor*
Woodson Sadler, *Vice Pres*
▲ EMP: 10
SQ FT: 2,200
SALES (est): 292.7K **Privately Held**
WEB: www.marinermedia.com
SIC: 2731 8611 7373 Book publishing; growers' marketing advisory service; systems software development services

(G-2147)
MICRON BIO-SYSTEMS INC
2329 Old Buena Vista Rd (24416-4627)
P.O. Box 868 (24416-0868)
PHONE.................................540 261-2468
David Parfitt, *President*
Robert J Rhoades, *Corp Secy*
Beatrice Hostetter, *Treasurer*
John Gulya, *Technical Staff*
▼ EMP: 10
SALES (est): 1.5MM **Privately Held**
WEB: www.micronbio-systems.com
SIC: 2048 Cereal-, grain-, & seed-based feeds

(G-2148)
MODINE MANUFACTURING COMPANY
1221 Magnolia Ave (24416-3399)
PHONE.................................540 261-9821
Charles E Carr, *Plant Mgr*
Doug Penney, *Engineer*
Alison Schlobohm, *Engineer*
EMP: 40
SALES (corp-wide): 1.9B **Publicly Held**
WEB: www.modine.com
SIC: 3433 3567 Heating equipment, except electric; industrial furnaces & ovens
PA: Modine Manufacturing Company Inc
1500 Dekoven Ave
Racine WI 53403
262 636-1200

(G-2149)
NIBCO INC
Stuarts Draft Division
3200 Green Forest Ave (24416-3907)
PHONE.................................540 324-0242
Mark Frazer, *Branch Mgr*
EMP: 306
SALES (corp-wide): 704.3MM **Privately Held**
WEB: www.nibco.com
SIC: 3432 Plumbing fixture fittings & trim
PA: Nibco Inc.
1516 Middlebury St
Elkhart IN 46516
574 295-3000

(G-2150)
NORTHWEST HARDWOODS INC
302 Piedmont Ave (24416-3717)
PHONE.................................540 261-2171
EMP: 9
SALES (corp-wide): 791.1MM **Privately Held**
WEB: www.northwesthardwoods.com
SIC: 2421 Lumber: rough, sawed or planed
HQ: Northwest Hardwoods, Inc.
1313 Broadway Ste 300
Tacoma WA 98402

(G-2151)
NORTHWEST HARDWOODS INC
403 E 29th St (24416-1253)
PHONE.................................540 261-2171
EMP: 2
SALES (est): 95.4K **Privately Held**
SIC: 2421 Sawmills & planing mills, general

(G-2152)
OS ARK GROUP LLC
2271 Sycamore Ave (24416-3127)
PHONE.................................540 261-2622
Rob Rice, *Principal*
EMP: 2
SALES (est): 112.5K **Privately Held**
WEB: www.osarkprinting.com
SIC: 2759 Screen printing

(G-2153)
SAYRE ENTERPRISES INC
324 E 32nd St (24416-1275)
P.O. Box 52, Naturl BR STA (24579-0052)
PHONE.................................540 291-3800
EMP: 5
SALES (corp-wide): 15.3MM **Privately Held**
WEB: www.sayreinc.com
SIC: 3999 Embroidery kits
PA: Sayre Enterprises, Inc
45 Natural Bridge Schl Rd
Naturl Br Sta VA 24579
540 291-3808

(G-2154)
STATON & SON LOGGING
381 E 29th St (24416-1203)
PHONE.................................540 570-3614
Dennis Staton, *Principal*
EMP: 2
SALES (est): 81.7K **Privately Held**
SIC: 2411 Logging

(G-2155)
STRESSA INCORPORATED
2213 Pine Ave (24416-1929)
P.O. Box 1367, Lexington (24450-1367)
PHONE.................................540 460-9495
Emilie Davis, *President*
John Feinauer, *President*
Andrew Wolfe, *Shareholder*
Etta Feinauer, *Admin Sec*
EMP: 2 EST: 2012
SALES (est): 176.9K **Privately Held**
WEB: www.stressainc.com
SIC: 2834 Proprietary drug products

(G-2156)
VENTURE PUBLISHING LLC
2202 Holly Ave (24416-1704)
PHONE.................................540 570-1908
Hugh Bouchelle, *Principal*
EMP: 2
SALES (est): 76.8K **Privately Held**
SIC: 2741 Miscellaneous publishing

(G-2157)
Z & T SALES LLC
85 Foxey Ln (24416-2648)
PHONE.................................540 570-9500
Sharon Fox,
EMP: 1
SALES (est): 125K **Privately Held**
SIC: 3131 Footwear cut stock

Buffalo Junction
Mecklenburg County

(G-2158)
BUFFALO REPAIR SHOP
1406 Cow Rd (24529-3614)
PHONE.................................434 374-5915
Kirk Somerville, *Owner*
EMP: 2
SALES (est): 223.5K **Privately Held**
SIC: 3711 Truck & tractor truck assembly

(G-2159)
EGAP ENTERPRISES
678 Cherry Hill Church Rd (24529-3412)
P.O. Box 648 (24529-0648)
PHONE.................................434 374-9089
William Page, *Owner*
EMP: 1
SALES (est): 16.5K **Privately Held**
SIC: 2731 Book publishing

Bumpass
Louisa County

(G-2160)
BUM PASS WATER SKI CLUB INC
3654 Buckner Rd (23024-3810)
PHONE.................................240 498-7033
Corey Vaughn-Humburg, *Principal*
EMP: 2
SALES (est): 115.9K **Privately Held**
WEB: www.peaceloveandwaterskiing.com
SIC: 3949 Water skis

(G-2161)
CW HOUCHENS AND SONS LOG LLC
3022 Holly Grove Dr (23024-2514)
PHONE.................................804 615-2002
EMP: 2
SALES (est): 81.7K **Privately Held**
SIC: 2411 Logging

(G-2162)
FREON DOCTOR INC
4021 Lewiston Rd (23024-8803)
PHONE.................................877 825-2401
Machotka Veronika, *President*
EMP: 7
SALES (est): 459.7K **Privately Held**
WEB: www.freondoctor.com
SIC: 2869 Freon

(G-2163)
LA STITCHERY
115 Old Burruss Mill Rd (23024-4907)
PHONE.................................540 894-9371
Barbara Kempf, *Owner*
EMP: 1
SALES (est): 30K **Privately Held**
WEB: www.lastitchery.com
SIC: 2395 5131 Embroidery & art needlework; sewing supplies & notions

(G-2164)
LAKESIDE LOGGING INC
2165 Bumpass Rd (23024-4217)
PHONE.................................540 872-2585
Kevin E Hall, *President*
EMP: 9
SALES (est): 24.8K **Privately Held**
SIC: 2411 Logging camps & contractors

(G-2165)
MARDEN THINNING COMPANY INC
610 Diggstown Rd (23024-3713)
PHONE.................................540 872-5196
Brice Marden, *President*
Jackie Marden, *Treasurer*
EMP: 2
SALES (est): 155.6K **Privately Held**
SIC: 2411 Logging camps & contractors

(G-2166)
MEALERS WELDING REPAIRS
2314 Wickham Rd (23024-3832)
PHONE.................................251 363-4640
Jonathan Mealer, *President*
EMP: 1
SALES (est): 25K **Privately Held**
SIC: 7692 Welding repair

(G-2167)
R D KNIGHTON SAWMILL
13660 Jefferson Hwy (23024-3418)
PHONE.................................540 872-3636
R D Knighton, *Owner*
EMP: 1
SALES (est): 99.5K **Privately Held**
SIC: 2421 Sawmills & planing mills, general

(G-2168)
STITCHED MMRIES BY SHANNON LLC
324 Eagle View Ln (23024-4204)
PHONE.................................540 872-9779
EMP: 1
SALES (est): 37.3K **Privately Held**
SIC: 2395 Embroidery & art needlework

(G-2169)
TRUE AMERICAN WOODWORKERS
1508 Bumpass Rd (23024-4221)
PHONE.................................540 748-5805
David Gramling, *Principal*
EMP: 1
SALES (est): 54.1K **Privately Held**
SIC: 2431 Millwork

(G-2170)
TUMALOW INC
200 Anderson Mill Dr (23024-2251)
PHONE.................................847 644-9009
William Gathright, *President*
John Gathright, *Exec VP*

Charles Brody, *Director*
▲ EMP: 6
SALES (est): 105.1K **Privately Held**
SIC: 7372 7389 Business oriented computer software;

(G-2171)
WOODS & WATERS PUBLISHING LC
Also Called: Woods & Waters Magazine
114 Old Quarry Ln (23024-4519)
PHONE.................................540 894-9144
Christophe C McCotter, *Principal*
Christine McCotter, *Opers Staff*
EMP: 2
SQ FT: 1,000
SALES (est): 185K **Privately Held**
WEB: www.woodsandwatersmagazine.com
SIC: 2721 5941 Magazines: publishing only, not printed on site; sporting goods & bicycle shops

(G-2172)
WOODS & WATERS PUBLISHING LC
494 Kentucky Springs Rd (23024-4303)
PHONE.................................540 894-5960
EMP: 1
SALES (est): 50K **Privately Held**
SIC: 2741 Misc Publishing

(G-2173)
WOOTON CONSULTING
140 Wolftrap Ct (23024-4970)
PHONE.................................804 227-3418
David Wooton, *Owner*
EMP: 2
SALES (est): 140.3K **Privately Held**
WEB: www.wooton-consulting.com
SIC: 1311 8999 Crude petroleum & natural gas; scientific consulting

Burgess
Northumberland County

(G-2174)
HAMMOCKS PRINT SHOP
14537 N Cumberland Hwy (22432)
PHONE.................................804 453-3265
Herbert Hammock, *Partner*
Phyllis Hammock, *Partner*
EMP: 2
SALES (est): 50K **Privately Held**
SIC: 2752 Commercial printing, offset

(G-2175)
PROOFMARK CORP
2490 Hacks Neck Rd (22432)
P.O. Box 357 (22432-0357)
PHONE.................................804 453-4337
Jim Wilson, *President*
EMP: 2
SALES (est): 93K **Privately Held**
WEB: www.proofmarkbullets.com
SIC: 3482 Shotgun ammunition: empty, blank or loaded

(G-2176)
R W P JOHNSON PRODUCTS LTD
601 Old Glebe Point Rd (22432-2040)
P.O. Box 490 (22432-0490)
PHONE.................................804 453-7705
Roy W P Johnson, *President*
Marjorie Johnson, *Corp Secy*
EMP: 10
SALES (est): 630K **Privately Held**
WEB: www.johnsonproductsltd.com
SIC: 3441 Expansion joints (structural shapes), iron or steel

(G-2177)
TIDEWELL MARINE INC
15912 Northumberland Hwy (22432-2034)
P.O. Box 767 (22432-0767)
PHONE.................................804 453-6115
EMP: 5
SALES (est): 347.5K **Privately Held**
SIC: 3089 Plastic boats & other marine equipment

(G-2178)
TIFFANY YACHTS INC
2355 Jssie Dupont Mem Hwy
(22432-2107)
PHONE...........................804 453-3464
Tiffany R Cockrell, *President*
Laura Shackleford, *Treasurer*
Taylor Cockrell, *Technology*
Rebecca C Jones, *Admin Sec*
Becky Jones, *Training Super*
EMP: 15
SALES (est): 2.7MM **Privately Held**
WEB: www.tiffanyyachtsinc.com
SIC: 3732 3731 Yachts, building & repair-
ing; shipbuilding & repairing

Burke
Fairfax County

(G-2179)
A AND H OFFICE INC
5804 Wood Poppy Ct (22015-2715)
PHONE...........................703 250-0963
Allan Harrington, *Vice Pres*
EMP: 2
SALES (est): 240K **Privately Held**
WEB: www.ahoffice.com
SIC: 2521 Wood office furniture

(G-2180)
ACEL LLC
9518 Claychin Ct (22015-4187)
PHONE...........................888 801-2507
Marc Barry, *Managing Prtnr*
EMP: 5 EST: 2008
SQ FT: 12,000
SALES (est): 4MM **Privately Held**
WEB: www.soltecproducts.com
SIC: 3089 Automotive parts, plastic

(G-2181)
B & B BOUTIQUE
10700 Dundas Oak Ct (22015-2428)
PHONE...........................703 425-8256
EMP: 1
SALES (est): 47.2K **Privately Held**
SIC: 2841 Mfg Soap/Other Detergents

(G-2182)
BARRY MCVAY
Also Called: Panoptic Enterprises
6055 Ridge Ford Dr (22015-3653)
P.O. Box 11220 (22009-1220)
PHONE...........................703 451-5953
Barry McVay, *Owner*
Vivina McVay, *General Mgr*
Ivina McVay, *Co-Owner*
EMP: 2
SALES (est): 100K **Privately Held**
WEB: www.fedgovcontracts.com
SIC: 2731 2752 2721 Books: publishing
only; commercial printing, lithographic;
periodicals

(G-2183)
BATTLEFIELD INDUSTRIES LLC
6371 Birch Leaf Ct (22015-3528)
PHONE...........................703 995-4822
Andrei D Calciu, *Administration*
EMP: 2
SALES (est): 97.4K **Privately Held**
SIC: 3999 Manufacturing industries

(G-2184)
BELTWAY BAT COMPANY LLC
5942 Heritage Square Dr (22015-3325)
PHONE...........................609 760-7243
EMP: 2
SALES (est): 93.7K **Privately Held**
WEB: www.beltwaybats.com
SIC: 3949 Sporting & athletic goods

(G-2185)
BIOTRACES INC (PA)
5660 Oak Tanager Ct (22015-2206)
PHONE...........................703 793-1550
Andrzej K Drukier PHD, *Ch of Bd*
Rich Wadiak, *Treasurer*
EMP: 11
SQ FT: 9,664
SALES (est): 917.2K **Privately Held**
WEB: www.biotraces.com
SIC: 3841 Surgical & medical instruments

(G-2186)
CIRCUIT SOLUTIONS INTL LLC
6111 Wilmington Dr (22015-3825)
PHONE...........................703 994-6788
John Vaughan,
EMP: 2
SALES (est): 1,000K **Privately Held**
WEB:
www.circuitsolutionsinternational.com
SIC: 3672 Printed circuit boards

(G-2187)
CRC PUBLIC RELATIONS
6307 Buffie Ct (22015-3402)
PHONE...........................703 395-9614
Jay Hopkins, *Manager*
EMP: 1
SALES (est): 54.1K **Privately Held**
WEB: www.wright.edu
SIC: 2431 Millwork

(G-2188)
DOROTHY EDWARDS
6040 Heathwick Ct (22015-3236)
PHONE...........................859 608-3539
Dorothy Edwards, *Principal*
EMP: 3
SALES (est): 98.1K **Privately Held**
SIC: 2711 Newspapers, publishing & print-
ing

(G-2189)
ENSONS INC
9508 Ironmaster Dr (22015-4117)
PHONE...........................703 644-6694
Ram Nagrani, *President*
Meena Nagrani, *Vice Pres*
EMP: 2
SALES (est): 200K **Privately Held**
WEB: www.ensonsrealestate.com
SIC: 3585 5075 Refrigeration & heating
equipment; warm air heating & air condi-
tioning

(G-2190)
**HAMBY-STERN PUBLISHING
LLC**
5200 Dalby Ln (22015-1743)
PHONE...........................703 425-3719
Robin Hamby, *Principal*
EMP: 2
SALES (est): 97.8K **Privately Held**
WEB: www.hambymediagroup.com
SIC: 2741

(G-2191)
KNIGHTS PRESS LLC
9005 Brook Ford Rd (22015-3613)
PHONE...........................703 913-5336
Mary Hamilton, *Principal*
EMP: 1
SALES (est): 40.6K **Privately Held**
SIC: 2741 Miscellaneous publishing

(G-2192)
**MADELINE CANDLE COMPANY
LLC**
6440 Lake Meadow Dr (22015-3927)
PHONE...........................703 503-9181
George Sarantis, *Principal*
EMP: 1 EST: 2016
SALES (est): 48K **Privately Held**
SIC: 3999 Candles

(G-2193)
**METROPOLITAN ACCOUNTING
& BOOK**
10201 Scrbrugh Commons Ct
(22015-2815)
PHONE...........................703 250-5014
Faro Nabavi, *Principal*
EMP: 1
SALES (est): 64.3K **Privately Held**
SIC: 2782 Account books

(G-2194)
MIGHTY MEALS LLC
5795 Burke Centre Pkwy (22015-2262)
PHONE...........................703 303-1438
Daniel Graziano, *CEO*
EMP: 8
SALES (est): 259.3K **Privately Held**
WEB: www.eatmightymeals.com
SIC: 2099 Food preparations

(G-2195)
NEUROPRO SPINAL JAXX INC
6337 Falling Brook Dr (22015-4031)
PHONE...........................571 334-7424
Terry Carlone, *President*
Benjamin Remington, *Chairman*
John Green, *COO*
EMP: 4
SALES (est): 149.2K **Privately Held**
WEB: www.spinaljaxx.com
SIC: 3842 7389 Implants, surgical;

(G-2196)
**NUEVO MILENIO NEWSPAPER
LLC**
5643 Mount Burnside Way (22015-2145)
PHONE...........................703 501-7180
EMP: 2
SALES (est): 62.9K **Privately Held**
SIC: 2711 Newspapers

(G-2197)
OREGON WOODCRAFT INC
5731 Wters Edge Lnding Ct (22015-2611)
PHONE...........................703 477-4793
EMP: 2 EST: 2008
SALES (est): 128K **Privately Held**
SIC: 2511 Wood household furniture

(G-2198)
POSSIBILITIES PUBLISHING
6320 Buffie Ct (22015-3401)
P.O. Box 10671 (22009-0671)
PHONE...........................703 585-0934
Meredith Louise Maslich, *Administration*
EMP: 2 EST: 2012
SALES (est): 45.4K **Privately Held**
WEB: www.possibilitiespublishingcom-
pany.com
SIC: 2741 Miscellaneous publishing

(G-2199)
POSTKITE LLC
9919 Marquand Dr (22015-3808)
PHONE...........................202 230-1472
Jade Johnson,
Andrew Johnson,
EMP: 2
SALES (est): 83.1K **Privately Held**
SIC: 2741 Miscellaneous publishing

(G-2200)
PRIMROSE ESSENTIALS LLC
5484 Lighthouse Ln (22015-1917)
PHONE...........................703 503-7210
Lynn Meyer, *Principal*
EMP: 2
SALES (est): 92.4K **Privately Held**
WEB: www.primroseessentials.com
SIC: 3999 Candles

(G-2201)
RADAVERT INDUSTRIES INC
5729 Edgewater Oak Ct (22015-2230)
PHONE...........................703 425-6777
John Naegele, *Principal*
EMP: 2
SALES (est): 83.2K **Privately Held**
SIC: 3999 Manufacturing industries

(G-2202)
RONALD CARTER
Also Called: CB Suppliers
5571 Peppercorn Dr (22015-1860)
PHONE...........................571 278-6659
Ronald Carter, *Owner*
EMP: 1
SALES (est): 54.5K **Privately Held**
SIC: 3571 3663 Personal computers (mi-
crocomputers); mobile communication
equipment

(G-2203)
SPINNING IN CONTROL LLC
Also Called: Travel Host of Washington DC
9607 Little Cobbler Ct (22015-4133)
P.O. Box 2356, Springfield (22152-0356)
PHONE...........................703 455-9223
John Perisi, *Mng Member*
EMP: 8
SALES (est): 400K **Privately Held**
SIC: 2721 Magazines: publishing only, not
printed on site

(G-2204)
SYMBOLICS - DAVID K SCHMIDT
6342 Fenestra Ct (22015-3539)
P.O. Box 10862 (22009-0862)
PHONE...........................703 455-0430
David K Schmidt, *Owner*
EMP: 1
SALES (est): 60K **Privately Held**
WEB: www.symbolics-dks.com
SIC: 3571 Minicomputers

(G-2205)
TUTTI FRUTTI FROZEN
9538 Old Keene Mill Rd (22015-4208)
PHONE...........................703 440-0010
Valeria Yang, *Office Mgr*
EMP: 6
SALES (est): 303.5K **Privately Held**
SIC: 2026 Yogurt

(G-2206)
VIA SERVICES LLC
5600 Light Infantry Dr (22015-2138)
PHONE...........................703 978-2629
Javaid Jamal, *Administration*
EMP: 1 EST: 2010
SALES (est): 112.8K **Privately Held**
WEB: www.via-services.net
SIC: 2752 Commercial printing, offset

Burkeville
Nottoway County

(G-2207)
**COLONY CONSTRUCTION ASP
LLC**
920 Dutchtown Rd (23922-3200)
PHONE...........................434 767-9930
Catherine Claud, *Branch Mgr*
EMP: 6 **Privately Held**
WEB: www.colonypaving.com
SIC: 2951 Asphalt paving mixtures &
blocks
PA: Colony Construction Asphalt, Llc
2333 Anderson Hwy
Powhatan VA 23139

(G-2208)
**CREATIVE MONOGRAMMING
LLC**
629 Harper Rd (23922-2325)
PHONE...........................434 767-4880
Wendy Ellett, *Principal*
EMP: 2
SALES (est): 102K **Privately Held**
SIC: 2395 Embroidery & art needlework

(G-2209)
LUCK STONE CORPORATION
Also Called: Luck Stone-Burkeville Plant
Off Hwy 360 460 Byp (23922)
P.O. Box 117 (23922-0117)
PHONE...........................434 767-4043
Keith W Black, *Manager*
EMP: 20
SALES (corp-wide): 824.7MM **Privately
Held**
WEB: www.luckstone.com
SIC: 1423 Diorite, crushed & broken-quar-
rying; gneiss, crushed & broken-quarry-
ing; syenite, crushed & broken-quarrying
PA: Luck Stone Corporation
515 Stone Mill Dr
Manakin Sabot VA 23103
804 784-6300

(G-2210)
SOUTHSIDE YOUTH FESTIVAL
1736 S Genito Rd (23922-3407)
PHONE...........................434 767-2584
Janice Ragan, *Principal*
EMP: 3
SALES (est): 163.6K **Privately Held**
SIC: 3842 Welders' hoods

(G-2211)
TAMARA INGRAM
Also Called: Ingram's Concrete Finishing
428 Deerfield Acres Dr (23922-3366)
PHONE...........................434 392-4933
Tamara Ingram, *Owner*
EMP: 2

SALES (est): 190K Privately Held
WEB:
www.ingramsconcretefinishing.blogspot.com
SIC: 3273 Ready-mixed concrete

(G-2212)
YAKATTACK LLC
609 2nd St Nw (23922)
P.O. Box 852, Farmville (23901-0852)
PHONE...................................804 561-4274
Luther Cifers III, *President*
Christopher Demarchi, *Finance Mgr*
John Hipsher, *Sales Staff*
Dan Smullen, *Technical Staff*
EMP: 3
SALES (est): 736.5K Privately Held
WEB: www.yakattack.us
SIC: 3462 Gear & chain forgings

Callands
Pittsylvania County

(G-2213)
DANNY A WALKER
657 Mountain Dr (24530-3311)
PHONE....................................434 724-4454
Danny A Walker, *Principal*
EMP: 3
SALES (est): 194.2K Privately Held
SIC: 2411 Logging

(G-2214)
NICKS WLDG & FABRICATION LLC
645 Barn Rd (24530-2925)
PHONE....................................434 251-2696
Nicholas Reynolds, *Principal*
EMP: 1
SALES (est): 35.3K Privately Held
SIC: 7692 Welding repair

Callao
Northumberland County

(G-2215)
CABIN CREATIONS
14921 Richmond Rd (22435-2530)
PHONE....................................804 529-7245
Chuck Wilkins, *Principal*
EMP: 1 **EST:** 2001
SALES (est): 58.1K Privately Held
SIC: 2395 Embroidery products, except schiffli machine

(G-2216)
LONG METALWORK & MACHINE INC
16686 Richmond Rd (22435-2403)
P.O. Box 604 (22435-0604)
PHONE....................................804 529-6233
Lawrence Long, *CEO*
EMP: 2
SALES (est): 73K Privately Held
SIC: 7692 Welding repair

(G-2217)
R R BEASLEY INC (PA)
16944 Richmond Rd (22435-2473)
P.O. Box 719 (22435-0719)
PHONE....................................804 529-6470
Robert Beasley, *President*
Jane Crowther, *Admin Sec*
EMP: 15 **EST:** 1937
SALES (est): 5MM Privately Held
WEB: www.beasleyconcrete.com
SIC: 3273 3272 Ready-mixed concrete; septic tanks, concrete; pipe, concrete or lined with concrete; liquid catch basins, tanks & covers: concrete

(G-2218)
RAPPATOMAC INDUSTRIES INC
73 Factory Ln (22435)
PHONE....................................804 529-6440
Anthony J Mangano, *President*
EMP: 6
SQ FT: 30,000

SALES (est): 514.7K Privately Held
WEB: www.rappatomac.com
SIC: 2431 1521 5251 1542 Moldings, wood: unfinished & prefinished; new construction, single-family houses; general remodeling, single-family houses; hardware; commercial & office buildings, renovation & repair

Callaway
Franklin County

(G-2219)
BCLF CORPORATION
266 Sunflower Ln (24067-3204)
PHONE....................................540 929-1701
Charles D Bowman, *President*
EMP: 4
SALES (est): 156.7K Privately Held
SIC: 2861 Charcoal, except activated

(G-2220)
CT JAMSOS PRECAST SEPTIC TANKS
865 Algoma Rd (24067-3407)
PHONE....................................540 483-5944
Christopher Jamison, *President*
Lynette Jamison, *Treasurer*
Susan Jamison, *Admin Sec*
EMP: 9
SQ FT: 4,000
SALES (est): 1.3MM Privately Held
WEB: www.ctjamison.com
SIC: 3272 Septic tanks, concrete

(G-2221)
DAN MCPHERSON & SONS LOGGING
705 Pine Spur Rd (24067-4049)
PHONE....................................540 483-4385
Danny McPherson, *Principal*
EMP: 3
SALES (est): 295K Privately Held
SIC: 2411 Logging camps & contractors

(G-2222)
T W MCPHERSON & SONS
171 Mcpherson Ln (24067-4033)
PHONE....................................540 483-0105
Tex W McPherson, *Owner*
Randy McPherson, *Partner*
Stoney McPherson, *Partner*
EMP: 3
SALES (est): 241.3K Privately Held
SIC: 2411 Timber, cut at logging camp

(G-2223)
WINGMAN INDUSTRIES LLC
597 Five Mile Mountain Rd (24067-6041)
PHONE....................................540 489-3119
Anthony J Cesternino,
EMP: 3
SALES (est): 261.3K Privately Held
WEB: www.wingmansuperbeams.com
SIC: 3624 Fibers, carbon & graphite

Calverton
Fauquier County

(G-2224)
FIRST COLONY HOMES INC
4163 Old Calverton Rd (20138)
P.O. Box 224 (20138-0224)
PHONE....................................540 788-4222
John M Rohrbaugh Jr, *President*
John M Rohrbaugh Sr, *Chairman*
EMP: 7 **EST:** 1965
SQ FT: 14,000
SALES (est): 2MM Privately Held
WEB: www.wholesalewoodproducts.net
SIC: 2439 5031 2452 2435 Trusses, wooden roof; siding, wood; modular homes, prefabricated, wood; hardwood veneer & plywood

(G-2225)
LOUISE J WALKER
Also Called: Calverton Press
4007 Old Calverton Rd (20138)
P.O. Box 231 (20138-0231)
PHONE....................................540 788-4826

Louise J Walker, *Owner*
Kathleen Stewart, *Med Doctor*
Edwin Newland, *Agent*
Steve Wetzel, *Info Tech Mgr*
EMP: 1 **EST:** 1967
SALES (est): 30K Privately Held
WEB: www.shentel.com
SIC: 2752 Commercial printing, offset

Cana
Carroll County

(G-2226)
BLUE RIDGE CONCRETE PRODUCT
14950 Fancy Gap Hwy (24317-3709)
P.O. Box 99 (24317-0099)
PHONE....................................276 755-2000
David Williams, *President*
EMP: 20
SQ FT: 3,000
SALES (est): 2.7MM Privately Held
SIC: 3273 Ready-mixed concrete

(G-2227)
MAYES WHOLESALE TACK
86 Lacys Ln (24317-4742)
PHONE....................................276 755-3715
Lacy E Mayes, *Owner*
EMP: 3
SQ FT: 3,075
SALES (est): 96K Privately Held
WEB: www.mayeswholesaletack.com
SIC: 3199 5137 5136 Harness or harness parts; women's & children's clothing; men's & boys' clothing

(G-2228)
WINDOWS DIRECT
Also Called: E&E Home Inprovements
13762 Fancy Gap Hwy (24317-3567)
PHONE....................................276 755-5187
Cheryl D Easter, *Owner*
Robert C Easter, *Owner*
Kathy M Easter, *Partner*
EMP: 4
SALES (est): 405.8K Privately Held
SIC: 2431 5211 1761 Millwork; door & window products; siding contractor

Cape Charles
Northampton County

(G-2229)
BAYVIEW ENGRV ART GL STUDIO
309 Mason Ave (23310-3203)
PHONE....................................757 331-1595
EMP: 2 **EST:** 2016
SALES (est): 73.2K Privately Held
SIC: 2759 Commercial Printing

(G-2230)
CAPE CHARLES BREWING COMPANY
2198 Stone Rd (23310-2706)
P.O. Box 660, Eastville (23347-0660)
PHONE....................................757 678-5699
Mark Marshall, *President*
Christopher Marshall, *Vice Pres*
Deborah Marshall, *Treasurer*
EMP: 3
SQ FT: 7,000
SALES (est): 91.3K Privately Held
WEB: www.capecharlesmirror.com
SIC: 2082 Beer (alcoholic beverage)

(G-2231)
CAPE CHARLES DISTILLERY LLC
240 Monroe Ave (23310-3218)
PHONE....................................757 291-8016
William Duncan, *Principal*
EMP: 10
SALES (est): 490.4K Privately Held
WEB: www.ccdesva.com
SIC: 2085 Distilled & blended liquors

(G-2232)
CONCRETE PRECAST SYSTEMS INC
1134 Bayshore Rd (23310-3246)
PHONE....................................757 545-5215
EMP: 2 **Privately Held**
WEB: www.cpsprecast.com
SIC: 3272 Concrete products
PA: Concrete Precast Systems, Inc.
1316 Yacht Dr
Chesapeake VA 23320

(G-2233)
EASTERN SHORE CSTL RSTING ESCR
Also Called: Escr Coffee
17366 Lankford Hwy (23310-4418)
P.O. Box 131, Eastville (23347-0131)
PHONE....................................757 414-0105
Krisitin N Willis, *President*
James Willis, *Co-Owner*
Kristin Ealy Willis, *Co-Owner*
EMP: 2 **EST:** 2006
SQ FT: 1,000
SALES (est): 130K Privately Held
WEB: www.coastalroast.com
SIC: 2095 Roasted coffee

(G-2234)
EASTERN SHORE SIGNS LLC
22156 S Bayside Rd (23310-2536)
PHONE....................................757 331-4432
Andrew Buchholz,
EMP: 2
SALES (est): 201.4K Privately Held
WEB: www.easternshoresigns.com
SIC: 3993 Signs & advertising specialties

(G-2235)
PARISIAN SWEETS LLC
26223 Lankford Hwy (23310-2021)
PHONE....................................770 722-8106
Lauren Gardner, *Principal*
EMP: 1
SALES (est): 43.5K Privately Held
SIC: 2051 Cakes, pies & pastries

(G-2236)
RUBY SALTS OYSTER COMPANY LLC
2345 Cherrystone Rd (23310-4037)
PHONE....................................757 331-1495
Jennifer Lee Buck, *Administration*
EMP: 4 **EST:** 2011
SALES (est): 385.5K Privately Held
WEB: www.rubysalts.com
SIC: 2899 Salt

Capron
Southampton County

(G-2237)
AUSTINS CYCLE COMPANY
22419 Barrow Rd (23829-2046)
PHONE....................................757 653-0182
Mark A Hubbert, *President*
EMP: 2 **EST:** 1994
SALES (est): 140K Privately Held
WEB: www.austincycle.com
SIC: 3599 5941 5571 Machine shop, jobbing & repair; sporting goods & bicycle shops; motorcycles

Caret
Essex County

(G-2238)
CARET CELLARS AND VINEYARD LLC
495 Meadow Landing Ln (22436-2072)
P.O. Box 3 (22436-0003)
PHONE....................................540 413-6454
Richard Thompson, *Principal*
Junghee Thompson,
EMP: 2 **EST:** 2014
SALES (est): 100K Privately Held
WEB: www.caretcellars.com
SIC: 2084 Wines

Carrollton
Isle Of Wight County

(G-2239)
10 TIMES BETTER LLC
13249 Woodlake Dr (23314-3316)
PHONE..............................850 258-8880
EMP: 2
SALES (est): 92.3K Privately Held
SIC: 2752 Commercial printing, lithographic

(G-2240)
BLUE SKY DISTILLERY LLC
15104 S Brading Ct (23314-2819)
PHONE..............................757 234-3260
Mark Rangos, Principal
EMP: 3
SALES (est): 182.1K Privately Held
WEB: www.blueskydistillery.com
SIC: 2085 Distilled & blended liquors

(G-2241)
CATERING MACHINE COMPANY
10068 Rainbow Rd (23314-4140)
PHONE..............................757 332-0024
Charles Laboon, CEO
EMP: 1
SALES (est): 50K Privately Held
SIC: 3578 Calculating & accounting equipment

(G-2242)
GARY GRAY
Also Called: G & L Printing
15205 Carrollton Blvd (23314-2303)
PHONE..............................757 238-2135
Gary Gray, Owner
Louise Gray, Co-Owner
EMP: 4
SQ FT: 1,700
SALES (est): 200K Privately Held
WEB: www.gandlpromos.com
SIC: 2752 2791 2789 Business form & card printing, lithographic; typesetting; bookbinding & related work

(G-2243)
GLANVILLE INDUSTRIES LLC
12210 Waterview Trl (23314-4418)
PHONE..............................757 513-2700
Charles Glanville, Principal
EMP: 2
SALES (est): 81.6K Privately Held
SIC: 3999 Manufacturing industries

(G-2244)
LADY PRESS CREATIONS LLC
13408 Southwind Ct (23314-3348)
PHONE..............................757 745-7473
Tammy Johnson, Principal
EMP: 1 EST: 2016
SALES (est): 39.4K Privately Held
SIC: 2741 Miscellaneous publishing

(G-2245)
PALLET INDUSTRIES LLC
14445 Bayview Dr (23314-2425)
PHONE..............................757 238-2912
Charles Jett, Principal
EMP: 4
SALES (est): 234.2K Privately Held
WEB: www.pallet-industries.com
SIC: 2448 Pallets, wood

(G-2246)
VIRGINIA CANVAS PRODUCTS INC
15457 Gayle Way (23314-2712)
P.O. Box 210 (23314-0210)
PHONE..............................757 558-0327
David Driggers, President
Mary Driggers, Corp Secy
EMP: 5 EST: 1998
SALES (est): 350K Privately Held
WEB: www.virginiacanvas.com
SIC: 2394 5039 5999 Awnings, fabric: made from purchased materials; awnings; awnings

(G-2247)
WALTER WINGET
12109 Kings Creek Ct (23314-3837)
PHONE..............................757 339-0303
William Winget, Owner
EMP: 1
SALES (est): 54.6K Privately Held
SIC: 3799 Transportation equipment

Carrsville
Isle Of Wight County

(G-2248)
AMERICAN KNINE
4007 Burdette Rd (23315-5011)
PHONE..............................757 304-9600
Paul Roushia, Principal
EMP: 1 EST: 2010
SALES (est): 48.7K Privately Held
SIC: 3999 Pet supplies

Cascade
Pittsylvania County

(G-2249)
CASCADE CABINETS & MILLWORK
3464 Huntington Trl (24069-2542)
PHONE..............................434 685-4000
Leon Griffith, Owner
EMP: 1
SALES (est): 90.2K Privately Held
SIC: 2434 Vanities, bathroom: wood

(G-2250)
CEMEX CNSTR MTLS ATL LLC
Also Called: Aggregates - Eden Quarry
101 Solite Dr (24069-2151)
PHONE..............................434 685-7021
Tony Jones, Branch Mgr
EMP: 3 Privately Held
SIC: 3273 Ready-mixed concrete
HQ: Cemex Construction Materials Atlantic, Llc
1501 Belvedere Rd
West Palm Beach FL 33406
561 833-5555

(G-2251)
GIANT RESOURCE RECOVERY INC
Virginia Solite
Rr 1 (24069)
PHONE..............................434 685-7021
Pat Arnold, Manager
EMP: 43 Privately Held
SIC: 3295 3273 3271 Minerals, ground or treated; ready-mixed concrete; concrete block & brick
HQ: Giant Resource Recovery, Inc.
1504 Santa Rosa Rd Rm 200
Richmond VA

(G-2252)
OLD STONE CORP
Also Called: Antennamast Systems
6101 Cascade Mill Rd (24069-2741)
PHONE..............................813 731-7600
Charles Stone, President
EMP: 12
SQ FT: 15,000
SALES (est): 930.2K Privately Held
SIC: 3443 Fabricated plate work (boiler shop)

(G-2253)
WESTROCK MWV LLC
100 Leaksville Jct Rd (24069-2200)
P.O. Box 40 (24069-0040)
PHONE..............................434 685-1717
Duane Clemons, Production
Roy Haskins, Manager
EMP: 2
SALES (corp-wide): 17.5B Publicly Held
WEB: www.westrock.com
SIC: 2621 Paper mills
HQ: Westrock Mwv, Llc
501 S 5th St
Richmond VA 23219
804 444-1000

Castlewood
Russell County

(G-2254)
LARRY HICKS
595 Copper Ridge Rd (24224-9669)
PHONE..............................276 738-9010
Larry Hicks, Owner
EMP: 2
SALES (est): 91.3K Privately Held
SIC: 3931 2325 2369 5651 Musical instruments; men's & boys' trousers & slacks; girls' & children's outerwear; family clothing stores

(G-2255)
MOUNTAIN MATERIALS INC
Also Called: Old Castle Lawn and Garden
49 Quarry Rd (24224)
P.O. Box 610 (24224-0610)
PHONE..............................276 762-5563
Daniel L Cooperrider, President
EMP: 4
SALES (est): 563.1K Privately Held
WEB: www.oldcastlelogistics.com
SIC: 1422 Crushed & broken limestone

(G-2256)
RUSSELL MEAT PACKING INC
315 Sulphur Springs Cir (24224-6244)
P.O. Box 91 (24224-0091)
PHONE..............................276 794-7600
Charlie G Dickenson Jr, President
A B Chaffin, Vice Pres
Gaine W Dickenson, Vice Pres
William J Dorton, Treasurer
EMP: 8 EST: 1976
SQ FT: 2,500
SALES (est): 740.4K Privately Held
WEB: www.russellmeatpacking.com
SIC: 2011 5421 0751 Meat packing plants; meat markets, including freezer provisioners; livestock services, except veterinary

(G-2257)
SOUTHERN REGION MACHINE SVC
157 Industrial Dr (24224)
P.O. Box 236 (24224-0236)
PHONE..............................276 393-3472
Ricky Franks, President
EMP: 6
SALES (est): 625K Privately Held
SIC: 3599 Machine shop, jobbing & repair

(G-2258)
TRL INC
Also Called: Longs Repair & Welding
25392 Us Highway 58 (24224-6130)
PHONE..............................276 794-7196
Timothy Long, President
EMP: 1
SALES (est): 90K Privately Held
SIC: 7692 7538 Automotive welding; general truck repair

(G-2259)
WALROSE WOODWORKS
550 Red Oak Ridge Rd (24224-5525)
PHONE..............................276 762-3917
Larry Marshall, Principal
EMP: 1
SALES (est): 54.1K Privately Held
SIC: 2431 Millwork

Catawba
Roanoke County

(G-2260)
CATAWBA RENEWABLE ENERGY
7625 Miller Cove Rd (24070-2609)
PHONE..............................434 426-1390
Keith E Anderson, Owner
EMP: 1
SALES (est): 71.3K Privately Held
SIC: 1382 Oil & gas exploration services

Catharpin
Prince William County

(G-2261)
DIRT REMOVAL SERVICES LLC
11921 Bluebird Ln (20143-1302)
PHONE..............................703 499-1299
Eulises Rivera, Mng Member
EMP: 5
SALES (est): 920.7K Privately Held
WEB: www.dirtremovalservices.com
SIC: 3812 Search & navigation equipment

Catlett
Fauquier County

(G-2262)
AGP TECHNOLOGIES LLC
4368 Dumfries Rd (20119-1710)
PHONE..............................434 489-6025
Andrei Maltsev,
EMP: 3
SALES (est): 30K Privately Held
SIC: 1481 Nonmetallic minerals development & test boring

(G-2263)
AMMO COMPANY LLC
16022 Fleetwood Dr (20119-1201)
PHONE..............................703 304-4210
Kimberly Warren, Principal
EMP: 4
SALES (est): 232.9K Privately Held
SIC: 3482 Cartridge cases for ammunition, 30 mm. & below

(G-2264)
ANY JOB SOFTWARE INC
7801 Overbrook Dr (20119-1760)
PHONE..............................540 347-4347
Jobyna A Moran, Principal
EMP: 2 EST: 2009
SALES (est): 109.5K Privately Held
SIC: 7372 Prepackaged software

(G-2265)
BROWNS SERVICES
10767 Brent Town Rd (20119-2409)
PHONE..............................540 295-2047
Scott Brown, Owner
EMP: 1
SALES (est): 81.2K Privately Held
SIC: 1389 Construction, repair & dismantling services

(G-2266)
CLAYS WELDING CO INC
10541 Bristersburg Rd (20119-2200)
P.O. Box 59 (20119-0059)
PHONE..............................540 788-3992
Elaine C Pilkins, President
EMP: 7
SQ FT: 3,100
SALES (est): 700K Privately Held
WEB: www.clayswelding.com
SIC: 7692 3599 Welding repair; machine shop, jobbing & repair

(G-2267)
CUSTOM MOULDING & MILLWORK INC
3131 Gaskins Ln (20119-2031)
P.O. Box 249 (20119-0249)
PHONE..............................540 788-1823
EMP: 11
SQ FT: 20,000
SALES (est): 1.5MM Privately Held
SIC: 2499 Mfg Wood Products

(G-2268)
KENS WELDING
8534 Burwell Rd (20119-1910)
PHONE..............................540 788-3556
Ken Ferguson, Owner
EMP: 2
SALES (est): 150K Privately Held
SIC: 7692 Welding repair

(G-2269)
SWABY GROUP
9579 Bristersburg Rd (20119-2160)
P.O. Box 350, Calverton (20138-0350)
PHONE....................................540 788-6051
Totley Swaby, *Partner*
Elfrida Swaby, *Partner*
▲ EMP: 2
SALES (est): 223.3K **Privately Held**
WEB: www.swabygroup.com
SIC: 7692 Welding repair

Cedar Bluff
Tazewell County

(G-2270)
BAR-C SAND INC
3353 Mountain Rd (24609-8271)
PHONE....................................276 701-3888
Robyn A Raines, *Principal*
EMP: 4
SALES (est): 185.3K **Privately Held**
SIC: 1442 7389 Sand mining; business services

(G-2271)
C & B ENTERPRISE LLC
2677 Steelsburg Hwy Ste 1 (24609-7056)
PHONE....................................276 971-4052
Bobby Breeding, *Partner*
Walter Cooper, *Partner*
EMP: 2 EST: 2015
SQ FT: 3,000
SALES (est): 78.7K **Privately Held**
SIC: 1241 Bituminous coal mining services, contract basis

(G-2272)
CEDAR BLUFF VA OFFICE
2308 Cedar Valley Dr (24609-9302)
PHONE....................................276 964-4171
EMP: 2
SALES (est): 104.2K **Privately Held**
WEB: www.envisioneyeva.com
SIC: 3827 Optical instruments & lenses

(G-2273)
CNX GAS CORPORATION
627 Claypool Hill Mall Rd (24609-8585)
P.O. Box 570 (24609-0570)
PHONE....................................276 596-5000
Kevin Elkins, *Manager*
EMP: 100 **Publicly Held**
WEB: www.cnx.com
SIC: 1311 Natural gas production
HQ: Cnx Gas Llc
1000 Consol Energy Dr
Canonsburg PA 15317

(G-2274)
DESIGN DIGITAL PRINTING LLC
337 Laurelwood Acres Rd (24609-8727)
PHONE....................................276 964-9391
John Butcher, *Production*
Connie Butcher,
EMP: 2
SQ FT: 2,500
SALES (est): 125K **Privately Held**
SIC: 2752 Commercial printing, offset

(G-2275)
ELSWICK INC
Also Called: Elswick Machine
Hickory Dr Rr 609 (24609)
PHONE....................................276 971-3060
Terri Elswick, *President*
EMP: 3
SALES (est): 295.6K **Privately Held**
WEB: www.elswickmachine.com
SIC: 3599 3532 Machine shop, jobbing & repair; mining machinery

(G-2276)
FRANK CALANDRA INC
147 Champion St (24609-8896)
PHONE....................................412 963-9071
EMP: 2
SALES (corp-wide): 753.2MM **Privately Held**
WEB: www.jennmar.com
SIC: 3532 Mining machinery

PA: Calandra Frank Inc
258 Kappa Dr
Pittsburgh PA 15238
412 963-9071

(G-2277)
GLASCO DRILLING INC
3095 Steelsburg Hwy (24609-8870)
P.O. Box 330 (24609-0330)
PHONE....................................276 964-4117
Joseph Ratliff, *President*
EMP: 4
SALES (est): 400.3K **Privately Held**
SIC: 1381 Drilling oil & gas wells

(G-2278)
HEINTZMANN CORPORATION (DH)
147 Champion St (24609-8896)
P.O. Box 301 (24609-0301)
PHONE....................................304 284-8004
John J Breedlove, *President*
Joe Bower, *President*
Denny Barton, *Sales Engr*
Mark McGlothlin, *Admin Sec*
◆ EMP: 63
SQ FT: 20,000
SALES (est): 17.5MM
SALES (corp-wide): 153.4MM **Privately Held**
WEB: www.heintzmannaustralia.com
SIC: 3532 7699 Mining machinery; hydraulic equipment repair
HQ: Bochumer Eisenhutte Heintzmann Gmbh & Co, Bau- Und Beteiligungs-Kg.
Bessemerstr. 80
Bochum
234 964-600

(G-2279)
J & W SCREEN PRINTING INC
Rr 460 (24609)
P.O. Box 1427 (24609-1427)
PHONE....................................276 963-0862
Todd Whited, *President*
Woodie Whited, *Vice Pres*
EMP: 2
SQ FT: 1,300
SALES (est): 236.2K **Privately Held**
SIC: 2759 Screen printing

(G-2280)
JENNMAR OF PENNSYLVANIA LLC
470 Wardell Indus Pk Rd (24609-9123)
PHONE....................................276 964-2107
Frank Clander, *President*
EMP: 15
SALES (corp-wide): 753.2MM **Privately Held**
WEB: www.jennmar.com
SIC: 3532 Mining machinery
HQ: Jennmar Of Pennsylvania, Llc
258 Kappa Dr
Pittsburgh PA 15238
412 963-9071

(G-2281)
JENNMAR OF PENNSYLVANIA LLC
559 Wardell Ind Park Rd (24609)
PHONE....................................276 964-7000
Joe Nash, *Manager*
EMP: 2
SALES (corp-wide): 753.2MM **Privately Held**
WEB: www.jennmar.com
SIC: 3532 Mining machinery
HQ: Jennmar Of Pennsylvania, Llc
258 Kappa Dr
Pittsburgh PA 15238
412 963-9071

(G-2282)
MINEQUEST INC
421 Honeyrock Rd (24609-8898)
PHONE....................................276 963-6463
Larry Dye, *President*
Caroline Dye, *Corp Secy*
Carolyn Dye, *Office Mgr*
EMP: 20
SQ FT: 6,500

SALES (est): 2.7MM **Privately Held**
WEB: www.minequestinc.com
SIC: 3674 7629 Semiconductors & related devices; electronic equipment repair

(G-2283)
PEPSI COLA BTLG INC NORTON VA
Also Called: Pepsico
606 Wardell Indus Pk Rd (24609-9561)
PHONE....................................276 963-6606
Rick Weblester, *Manager*
EMP: 20
SALES (corp-wide): 21.1MM **Privately Held**
WEB: www.pepsico.com
SIC: 2086 Carbonated soft drinks, bottled & canned
PA: Pepsi Cola Bottling Company, Incorporated, Of Norton, Va.
12th St At Park Ave
Norton VA 24273
276 679-1122

(G-2284)
QUINN PUMPS INC
142 Mall Church Rd (24609-7081)
PHONE....................................276 345-9106
EMP: 4
SALES (est): 247.7K **Privately Held**
SIC: 1389 Oil/Gas Field Services

(G-2285)
SOUTHWEST CMPRSR PMPG PCKGES I
317 Clinic Rd (24609)
P.O. Box 1090 (24609-1090)
PHONE....................................276 963-6400
Brenda Matney, *Owner*
EMP: 5
SALES (est): 582.7K **Privately Held**
SIC: 3462 Pump & compressor forgings, ferrous

(G-2286)
SUMMIT APPALACHIA OPER CO LLC
2615 Steelsburg Hwy (24609-8872)
PHONE....................................276 963-2979
Michael Munsui, *Mng Member*
EMP: 25
SALES (est): 501.1K **Privately Held**
WEB: www.summitnaturalresources.com
SIC: 1382 Oil & gas exploration services

Centreville
Fairfax County

(G-2287)
ABSOLUTE EMC LLC
14126 Wood Rock Way (20121-3827)
PHONE....................................703 774-7505
Jason Smith, *Owner*
EMP: 2
SALES (est): 94.5K **Privately Held**
WEB: www.absolute-emc.com
SIC: 3572 Computer storage devices

(G-2288)
ADOPT A SALSA
14135 Asher Vw (20121-5315)
PHONE....................................703 409-9453
David Echegoyen, *Principal*
EMP: 3 EST: 2013
SALES (est): 137.5K **Privately Held**
WEB: www.adoptasalsa.com
SIC: 2099 Dips, except cheese & sour cream based

(G-2289)
ADVANCED LEADING SOLUTIONS INC
Also Called: Alsi
14641 Lee Hwy Ste D9 (20121-5819)
PHONE....................................703 447-3876
Mary T Hay, *Principal*
EMP: 1
SALES (est): 56K **Privately Held**
SIC: 3699 Flight simulators (training aids), electronic

(G-2290)
APEX PUBLISHERS
6002 Rockton Ct (20121-3080)
PHONE....................................703 966-1906
EMP: 2 EST: 2015
SALES (est): 50K **Privately Held**
WEB: www.apex-books.com
SIC: 2741 Miscellaneous publishing

(G-2291)
ARCADE SIGNS LLC
Also Called: Sign-A-Rama
14641 Lee Hwy Ste D7 (20121-5819)
PHONE....................................703 815-5440
Mark Reynolds, *Partner*
EMP: 5
SALES (est): 250K **Privately Held**
WEB: www.signaramava.com
SIC: 3993 Signs & advertising specialties

(G-2292)
AVEI
5584 Sequoia Farms Dr (20120-3302)
PHONE....................................571 278-0823
Derek Boudreau, *Principal*
EMP: 2
SALES (est): 85.2K **Privately Held**
WEB: www.avei.space
SIC: 3519 Jet propulsion engines

(G-2293)
AVIGATORS INCORPORATED
6331 Fairfax National Way (20120-1055)
PHONE....................................703 298-6319
Mark Gillespie, *Principal*
EMP: 5
SALES (est): 280K **Privately Held**
SIC: 3721 Aircraft

(G-2294)
BEST CABINETS AND CLOSETS LLC
14600 Jovet Ct (20120-3440)
PHONE....................................703 830-0542
Raffi Torossian, *Principal*
EMP: 1
SALES (est): 53.7K **Privately Held**
SIC: 2434 Wood kitchen cabinets

(G-2295)
BLAND WOODWORKING
5309 Caliper Ct (20120-4146)
PHONE....................................703 631-6567
Bill Devlin, *Principal*
EMP: 1
SALES (est): 54.1K **Privately Held**
SIC: 2431 Millwork

(G-2296)
BLOOMFORTH CORP
6419 Mccoy Rd (20121-1705)
PHONE....................................703 408-8993
Quy Vo, *CEO*
Michael Szoke, *Vice Pres*
Ngoc Anh Tran, *Vice Pres*
Holly Szoke, *Admin Sec*
EMP: 7
SQ FT: 25,000
SALES (est): 490K **Privately Held**
WEB: www.bloomforth.com
SIC: 7372 Prepackaged software; business oriented computer software

(G-2297)
CARAVELS LLC
5870 Trinity Pkwy Ste 600 (20120-1970)
PHONE....................................540 345-9892
EMP: 167
SALES (corp-wide): 44.7MM **Privately Held**
WEB: www.vatransformer.com
SIC: 3612 Autotransformers, electric (power transformers)
PA: Caravels, Llc
2789 Ga Highway 21 S
Rincon GA 31326
912 754-5300

(G-2298)
CIRCINUS SOFTWARE LLC
6552 Palisades Dr (20121-3809)
PHONE....................................571 522-1724
Raghavendra Karnam, *Principal*
EMP: 2

SALES (est): 115.6K **Privately Held**
SIC: 7372 Prepackaged software

(G-2299)
CUSTOM DESIGNERS INC
5866 Old Centreville Rd (20121-2426)
PHONE..703 830-8582
Debbie Brunner, *Founder*
EMP: 1 EST: 2016
SALES (est): 54.1K **Privately Held**
SIC: 3548 Welding apparatus

(G-2300)
DATA MANAGEMENT LLC
14704 Vrginia Infantry Rd (20121)
PHONE..703 222-4246
Azfer N Mallick,
EMP: 1
SALES (est): 122.6K **Privately Held**
WEB: www.dmllc.us
SIC: 3571 Electronic computers

(G-2301)
DEEP PROSE SOFTWARE LLC
15004 Tarleton Dr (20120-1455)
PHONE..703 815-0715
Danielle A Shedlick, *Principal*
EMP: 2
SALES (est): 93.8K **Privately Held**
WEB: www.deepprose.com
SIC: 7372 Prepackaged software

(G-2302)
DEFENSEWORX LLC
14110 Sorrel Chase Ct (20121-3802)
PHONE..703 568-3295
Yasin Rahman, *Partner*
Hoon Park, *Partner*
EMP: 2
SALES (est): 104.3K **Privately Held**
SIC: 3812 Defense systems & equipment

(G-2303)
DOUGLAS MANNING
5101 Doyle Ln (20120-1706)
PHONE..703 631-9064
Douglas Manning, *Principal*
EMP: 1
SALES (est): 41K **Privately Held**
SIC: 3944 Games, toys & children's vehi-
cles

(G-2304)
ELIENE TRUCKING LLC
14555 Lock Dr (20120-1349)
PHONE..571 721-0735
Eliene Pereira, *Principal*
EMP: 1
SALES (est): 92.1K **Privately Held**
SIC: 1442 4959 Construction sand &
gravel; snowplowing

(G-2305)
ESTATE CONCRETE LLC
15900 Lee Hwy (20120-2137)
PHONE..703 293-6363
Gilberto Mendonca, *Mng Member*
Mario Amorim,
Manuel Cruz,
EMP: 8
SQ FT: 15,000
SALES (est): 1.4MM **Privately Held**
SIC: 3272 Concrete products, precast

(G-2306)
GLOBAL SIGNS & GRAPHICS
5875 Trinity Pkwy Ste 110 (20120-2410)
PHONE..703 543-1046
EMP: 2
SALES (est): 55.7K **Privately Held**
SIC: 3993 Mfg Signs/Advertising Special-
ties

(G-2307)
GOTO UNIT USA
4707 Cochran Pl (20120-6446)
PHONE..703 598-6642
EMP: 1 EST: 2017
SALES (est): 70.5K **Privately Held**
WEB: www.goto-unit.com
SIC: 3651 Speaker systems

(G-2308)
GRAND DESIGNS LLC
14787 Green Park Way (20120-3110)
PHONE..412 295-7730

Thomas Bowser, *Principal*
EMP: 1
SALES (est): 86.7K **Privately Held**
SIC: 3993 7532 7389 Letters for signs,
metal; truck painting & lettering; sign
painting & lettering shop; lettering & sign
painting services

(G-2309)
H B CABINET REFACERS
5307 Sammie Kay Ln (20120-2006)
PHONE..571 213-5257
Haiber Bakeer, *Owner*
EMP: 1
SALES (est): 78K **Privately Held**
WEB: www.hbkitchenandbath.com
SIC: 2434 Wood kitchen cabinets

(G-2310)
HEE K YOON (PA)
Also Called: Personalized Engraving
6408 Brass Button Ct (20121-2325)
PHONE..703 322-9208
Hee K Yoon, *Owner*
EMP: 1
SALES (est): 410.9K **Privately Held**
SIC: 3479 Etching & engraving

(G-2311)
J & M SHEET METAL INC
14141 Asher Vw (20121-5315)
PHONE..571 722-2805
Gonzalez Julia N, *Director*
EMP: 2
SALES (est): 94.5K **Privately Held**
WEB: www.hiwayparts.com
SIC: 3444 Sheet metalwork

(G-2312)
JULPHIA SOAPWORKS
13718 Eastcliff Cir (20120-1761)
PHONE..703 815-8020
Megan Taylor, *Owner*
EMP: 1
SALES (est): 46.9K **Privately Held**
SIC: 2841 Soap & other detergents

(G-2313)
K2W ENTERPRISES CORPORATION
14227 Canteen Ct (20121-2329)
PHONE..540 603-0114
Chad C Koslow, *President*
Chad Koslow, *President*
EMP: 1
SALES (est): 61K **Privately Held**
SIC: 3482 8742 8748 Shotgun ammuni-
tion: empty, blank or loaded; management
consulting services; educational consult-
ant

(G-2314)
LE SPLENDOUR LLC
14060 Darkwood Cir (20121-4839)
PHONE..703 505-5362
Linh Le, *Principal*
EMP: 2
SALES (est): 149.6K **Privately Held**
WEB: www.lesplendour.com
SIC: 2844 Toilet preparations

(G-2315)
LOTUS ENGRAVING LLC
13673 Bent Tree Cir # 103 (20121-4887)
PHONE..703 206-8367
Albaer Maowad, *Principal*
EMP: 1
SALES (est): 53.5K **Privately Held**
SIC: 2796 Engraving on copper, steel,
wood or rubber: printing plates

(G-2316)
LUCK STONE CORPORATION
Also Called: Luck Stone-Fairfax Plant
15717 Lee Hwy (20121-2134)
P.O. Box 1817 (20122-8817)
PHONE..703 830-8880
Warren Paulson, *Opers-Prdtn-Mfg*
Sam Rinehart, *Executive*
EMP: 40
SALES (corp-wide): 824.7MM **Privately
Held**
WEB: www.luckstone.com
SIC: 1429 1442 Grits mining (crushed
stone); construction sand & gravel

PA: Luck Stone Corporation
515 Stone Mill Dr
Manakin Sabot VA 23103
804 784-6300

(G-2317)
MACS CONSTRUCTION
14508 Smithwood Dr (20120-1376)
PHONE..571 278-5371
Bernard J McInerney Sr, *Owner*
EMP: 2
SALES (est): 79.8K **Privately Held**
SIC: 2591 Drapery hardware & blinds &
shades

(G-2318)
MARKETSPACE SOLUTIONS INC
5210 Honeysuckle Ct (20120-1225)
PHONE..703 989-3509
Deepak Gupte, *CEO*
EMP: 2
SALES (est): 120.1K **Privately Held**
SIC: 7372 Prepackaged software

(G-2319)
MAVERICK CYBER-DEFENSE LLC
14001c Saint Germain Dr # 6
(20121-2338)
PHONE..202 725-7663
EMP: 3
SALES (est): 164K **Privately Held**
WEB: www.maverickcyberdefense.com
SIC: 3812 Defense systems & equipment

(G-2320)
MOLLOY SOFTWARE ASSOC INC
14374 N Slope St (20120-4148)
P.O. Box 1508 (20122-8508)
PHONE..703 825-7290
Kevin Molloy, *President*
EMP: 3
SALES (est): 246.8K **Privately Held**
SIC: 7372 Prepackaged software

(G-2321)
MONUMENTAL PEST CONTROL CO
14427 Manassas Gap Ct (20120-2863)
PHONE..571 245-6178
Jairzhino Gonzalez, *Principal*
EMP: 3 EST: 2016
SALES (est): 221.7K **Privately Held**
SIC: 3272 Monuments & grave markers,
except terrazo

(G-2322)
MORE TECHNOLOGY LLC
11951 Freedom Dr Ste 1300 (20121)
PHONE..571 208-9865
Ahkyeong Kim, *President*
EMP: 2
SALES (est): 111.5K **Privately Held**
SIC: 3672 Printed circuit boards

(G-2323)
MY ARCH INC
5102 Woodford Dr (20120-1388)
PHONE..703 375-9302
Alexander Ananiev, *President*
EMP: 1
SALES (est): 250K **Privately Held**
WEB: www.myarch.com
SIC: 7372 7371 Prepackaged software;
computer software writing services

(G-2324)
NORTHROP GRUMMAN SYSTEMS CORP
6186 Snowhill Ct (20120-1146)
P.O. Box 230507 (20120-0507)
PHONE..703 808-0961
Alfredo Rohweder, *Branch Mgr*
Steve Zika, *Software Engr*
EMP: 3 **Publicly Held**
WEB: www.northropgrumman.com
SIC: 3812 Search & navigation equipment
HQ: Northrop Grumman Systems Corpora-
tion
2980 Fairview Park Dr
Falls Church VA 22042
703 280-2900

(G-2325)
NORTHRUP GRUMMAN
14149 Gabrielle Way (20121-2415)
PHONE..305 466-4655
EMP: 2
SALES (est): 88.8K **Privately Held**
SIC: 3812 Search & navigation equipment

(G-2326)
OH SO GOOD ORGANICS LLC
14323 Johnny Moore Ct (20120-3214)
PHONE..703 577-9226
Jennifer Naqvi, *Administration*
EMP: 2
SALES (est): 120.1K **Privately Held**
WEB: www.ohsogoodorganics.com
SIC: 2844 Toilet preparations

(G-2327)
PARSONS CORPORATION
Also Called: Cobham Analytical Solutions
5875 Trinity Pkwy Ste 300 (20120-1971)
PHONE..703 988-8500
Doug Price, *Branch Mgr*
Robert Kinney, *Manager*
EMP: 120 **Publicly Held**
WEB: www.parsons.com
SIC: 3568 Couplings, shaft: rigid, flexible,
universal joint, etc.
PA: The Parsons Corporation
5875 Trinity Pkwy Ste 300
Centreville VA 20120
703 988-8500

(G-2328)
PEACE HARMONY AND LOVE LLC
14120 Lee Hwy Ste A609 (20120-1913)
PHONE..571 210-5853
Charlette Turner,
EMP: 1
SALES (est): 47.2K **Privately Held**
SIC: 2899 Essential oils

(G-2329)
PROTOQUICK PRINTING LLC
5524 Shipley Ct (20120-3307)
PHONE..202 417-4243
EMP: 2
SALES (est): 83.9K **Privately Held**
SIC: 2752 Commercial printing, litho-
graphic

(G-2330)
QINETIQ US HOLDINGS INC (DH)
5885 Trinity Pkwy Ste 130 (20120-1969)
PHONE..202 429-6630
Robert Evers, *CEO*
J D Crouch II, *President*
EMP: 50
SQ FT: 1,000
SALES (est): 313.4MM **Privately Held**
SIC: 3812 Defense systems & equipment
HQ: Qinetiq Holdings Limited
Cody Technology Park
Farnborough HANTS
125 239-2000

(G-2331)
QUINNS BATH BOMBS LLC
6147 Ridgemont Dr (20120-1167)
PHONE..703 853-5067
Jennifer Theut, *Principal*
EMP: 2
SALES (est): 76.5K **Privately Held**
SIC: 2844 Bath salts

(G-2332)
RED RIVER INTERIORS LLC
14118 Red River Dr (20121-2671)
PHONE..703 987-1698
G Fay Lartey,
EMP: 2
SALES (est): 97.9K **Privately Held**
WEB: www.redriverinteriors.blogspot.com
SIC: 2391 Curtains & draperies

(G-2333)
RETIREMENT WATCH LLC
15103 Stillfield Pl (20120-3909)
P.O. Box 222070, Chantilly (20153-2070)
PHONE..571 522-6505
EMP: 1

2021 Virginia
Industrial Directory

▲ = Import ▼=Export
◆ =Import/Export

SALES (est): 81K **Privately Held**
SIC: 2741 Misc Publishing

(G-2334)
SAFFRON FABS CORPORATION
6177 Stonepath Cir (20120-3420)
PHONE................................703 544-2791
Sunita Rana, *Director*
▲ **EMP:** 1
SALES (est): 120.8K **Privately Held**
WEB: www.saffronfabs.com
SIC: 2384 Bathrobes, men's & women's:
made from purchased materials

(G-2335)
SAPNA CREATIONS
14539 Picket Oaks Rd (20121-2358)
PHONE................................571 276-1480
Rakesh Grover, *Administration*
EMP: 2
SALES (est): 140K **Privately Held**
WEB: www.sapnacreations.com
SIC: 3915 Jewelers' materials & lapidary
work

(G-2336)
SCINTECK INSTRUMENTS LLC
6560 Skylemar Trl (20121-3838)
PHONE................................571 426-3598
Hasan Rizvi, *Branch Mgr*
EMP: 1
SALES (corp-wide): 525.3K **Privately
Held**
WEB: www.scinteck.com
SIC: 3826 Analytical instruments
PA: Scinteck Instruments Llc
10432 Balls Ford Rd
Manassas VA 20109
703 881-7783

(G-2337)
SECURITY EVOLUTIONS INC
5124 Brittney Elyse Cir J (20120-3040)
PHONE................................703 953-4739
David Kim, *President*
EMP: 2
SALES: 199.7K **Privately Held**
SIC: 3699 8711 Security control equip-
ment & systems; consulting engineer

(G-2338)
**SENNETT SECURITY
PRODUCTS LLC (PA)**
15623 Jillians Forest Way (20120-1255)
PHONE................................703 803-8880
Donald Woo, *Vice Pres*
Robert Lane, *VP Engrg*
Sandra Lane, *Mng Member*
Bob Lane, *Manager*
James Tolbert, *Director*
▲ **EMP:** 7
SQ FT: 2,500
SALES (est): 5.9MM **Privately Held**
WEB: www.sennett.net
SIC: 2752 Commercial printing, litho-
graphic

(G-2339)
SENSEWARE
14504 Smithwood Dr (20120-1376)
PHONE................................703 975-2919
Julien Stamatakis, *Principal*
EMP: 3
SALES (est): 207.6K **Privately Held**
SIC: 3679 Electronic components

(G-2340)
SIBASHI INC
Also Called: Ink Mart of Nova
14340 Compton Village Dr (20121-5700)
PHONE................................571 292-6233
Nandini Bhatia, *CEO*
Smriti Vanscoy, *Vice Pres*
EMP: 3
SALES (est): 260.3K **Privately Held**
SIC: 2899 Ink or writing fluids

(G-2341)
**STCUBE PHARMACEUTICALS
INC**
5233 Jule Star Dr (20120-3010)
PHONE................................703 815-1446
Stephen S Yoo, *Principal*
EMP: 4 **EST:** 2016

SALES (est): 257.7K **Privately Held**
SIC: 2834 Pharmaceutical preparations

(G-2342)
**SUPERIOR PAVING
CORPORATION**
15717 Lee Hwy (20121-2134)
PHONE................................703 631-5480
Jeff Powers, *Plant Mgr*
Moses Greenberg, *Accountant*
Martha Lujan, *Human Res Dir*
Kelly Cordle, *Marketing Staff*
Mark Painter, *Manager*
EMP: 8
SALES (corp-wide): 6.2MM **Privately
Held**
WEB: www.superiorpaving.net
SIC: 2951 1611 Asphalt paving mixtures &
blocks; surfacing & paving
PA: Superior Paving Corporation
5551 Wellington Rd
Gainesville VA 20155
703 631-0004

(G-2343)
SUPPLIES EXPRESS INC
Also Called: SEI Furniture and Design
5141 Pleasant Forest Dr (20120-1249)
PHONE................................703 631-4600
Carol D Allin, *President*
Philip W Allin, *Officer*
EMP: 7
SALES (est): 1.2MM **Privately Held**
WEB: www.seifurniture.com
SIC: 2522 Office furniture, except wood

(G-2344)
T2PNEUMA PUBLISHERS LLC
14451 N Slope St (20120-4151)
PHONE................................703 968-7592
Stephen Hiemstra, *Principal*
EMP: 2
SALES (est): 115.5K **Privately Held**
WEB: www.t2pneuma.com
SIC: 2741 Miscellaneous publishing

(G-2345)
TUTTI FRUITTI
5947 Centreville Crest Ln (20121-2344)
PHONE................................703 830-0036
Paul Choi, *Owner*
EMP: 3 **EST:** 2012
SALES (est): 211.2K **Privately Held**
SIC: 2024 Ice cream, bulk

(G-2346)
UH ROH MUH INC
5369 Wharton Park Ct (20120-2003)
PHONE................................703 725-1684
EMP: 2
SALES (est): 97.5K **Privately Held**
WEB: www.uhrohmuh.com
SIC: 2844 Toilet preparations

(G-2347)
US WRAP LLC
6007 Saint Hubert Ln (20121-3093)
PHONE................................202 441-6072
Resul Aksoy, *Principal*
EMP: 1
SALES (est): 47.3K **Privately Held**
SIC: 2282 Polypropylene filament yarn:
twisting, winding, etc.

(G-2348)
USR STEEL LLC
14771 Basingstoke Loop (20120-3102)
PHONE................................571 480-3497
Ramon Turcios, *Principal*
EMP: 4
SALES (est): 344.8K **Privately Held**
SIC: 3441 Fabricated structural metal

(G-2349)
**VENKOR SPECIALTY
PRODUCTS LLC**
5003 Westfileds Blvd (20120)
P.O. Box 232075 (20120-8075)
PHONE................................703 932-3840
Subraman RAO Cherukuri, *CEO*
John Humphrey, *Vice Pres*
EMP: 2
SQ FT: 180,000

SALES (est): 177.6K **Privately Held**
SIC: 2834 Druggists' preparations (pharmaceuticals)

(G-2350)
VENUTEC CORPORATION
5426 Crystalford Ln (20120-2083)
P.O. Box 2662, Merrifield (22116-2662)
PHONE................................888 573-8870
Silvestre Acedillo, *CEO*
Maria Aria, *Accountant*
Amy Sithibandith, *Marketing Staff*
EMP: 7
SQ FT: 12,000
SALES (est): 120K **Privately Held**
WEB: www.venutec.com
SIC: 2759 2741 2721 7336 Commercial
printing; posters: publishing & printing;
technical manuals: publishing & printing;
magazines: publishing & printing; com-
mercial art & graphic design; package de-
sign

(G-2351)
VERTICAL VENUS LLC
5409 Sour Gum Dr (20120-3414)
PHONE................................571 236-6484
Melissa Rose, *Principal*
EMP: 2
SALES (est): 169.9K **Privately Held**
SIC: 2591 Blinds vertical

(G-2352)
WEAR RED LIPSTICK LLC
6616 Smiths Trce (20120-3739)
PHONE................................703 627-2123
EMP: 2
SALES (est): 108.9K **Privately Held**
SIC: 2844 Lipsticks

(G-2353)
WINERY AT BULL RUN LLC
15950 Lee Hwy (20120-2137)
PHONE................................703 815-2233
Wayne Mills, *Opers Staff*
Sandi Fagan, *Bookkeeper*
Jennifer Vanderkleut, *Manager*
Lisa Damico, *Director*
Jon Hickox,
EMP: 4 **EST:** 2012
SALES (est): 451.7K **Privately Held**
WEB: www.wineryatbullrun.com
SIC: 2084 Wines

(G-2354)
WORD COLLEGE INC
13969 Baton Rouge Ct (20121-3556)
PHONE................................510 857-3309
Chang Kyu Kim, *President*
EMP: 2
SALES (est): 74K **Privately Held**
SIC: 2741 Miscellaneous publishing

(G-2355)
WRIGHT SOLUTIONS INC
6339 Paddington Ln (20120-1810)
P.O. Box 21078, Catonsville MD (21228-
0578)
PHONE................................703 652-7145
Mark Burney, *Owner*
EMP: 6
SALES (est): 503.9K **Privately Held**
SIC: 2879 Agricultural chemicals

Champlain
Essex County

(G-2356)
ROUND HOUSE
3079 Daingerfield Lndg (22438-2008)
PHONE................................804 443-4813
Edward Haile, *Owner*
EMP: 1
SALES (est): 32.5K **Privately Held**
SIC: 2731 Books: publishing only

(G-2357)
STEVENS BURIAL VAULT LLC
10664 Tidewater Trl (22438-2017)
PHONE................................804 443-5125
Angelo Stevens, *Principal*
EMP: 2

SALES (est): 91.3K **Privately Held**
SIC: 3272 Burial vaults, concrete or precast terrazzo

(G-2358)
SYNAGROW WWT INC
10647 Tidewater Trl (22438-2017)
PHONE................................804 443-2170
Steve Mc Man, *Principal*
EMP: 10
SALES (est): 1MM **Privately Held**
WEB: www.synagro.com
SIC: 2875 5191 Fertilizers, mixing only;
fertilizer & fertilizer materials

Chantilly
Fairfax County

(G-2359)
6304 GRAVEL AVENUE LLC
14000 Thunderbolt Pl K (20151-3225)
PHONE................................571 287-7544
Sevket Serkan Keskin, *Principal*
EMP: 2
SALES (est): 66K **Privately Held**
SIC: 1442 Construction sand & gravel

(G-2360)
A-TECH CORPORATION
Also Called: Applied Technology Associates
14800 Conference Cntr Dr (20151-3810)
PHONE................................703 955-7846
Andrew Suzuki, *Manager*
EMP: 3
SALES (corp-wide): 144.5MM **Privately
Held**
WEB: www.atacorp.com
SIC: 3823 3769 3812 3827 Pressure
measurement instruments, industrial;
guided missile & space vehicle parts &
auxiliary equipment; control receivers; op-
tical test & inspection equipment; electri-
cal or electronic engineering; product
certification, safety or performance
PA: A-Tech Llc
1300 Britt St Se
Albuquerque NM 87123
505 767-1200

(G-2361)
**AARDVARK SWIM AND SPORT
INC (PA)**
Also Called: Aardvark Screen Print
14221a Willard Rd # 1050 (20151-2941)
P.O. Box 231930, Centreville (20120-7930)
PHONE................................703 631-6045
Robert York, *President*
Kim Wiedemann, *Engineer*
Wendy Chung, *Admin Sec*
EMP: 20
SQ FT: 9,000
SALES (est): 3.2MM **Privately Held**
WEB: www.aardvarkswim.com
SIC: 2396 5137 5136 Screen printing on
fabric articles; swimsuits: women's, chil-
dren's & infants'; beachwear, men's &
boys'

(G-2362)
ABC IMAGING OF WASHINGTON
14101 Parke Long Ct (20151-1645)
PHONE................................202 429-8870
Tyler Bartlett, *Branch Mgr*
EMP: 30
SALES (corp-wide): 144.4MM **Privately
Held**
WEB: www.abcimaging.com
SIC: 2759 Commercial printing
PA: Abc Imaging Of Washington, Inc
5290 Shawnee Rd Ste 300
Alexandria VA 22312
202 429-8870

(G-2363)
AGILE ACCESS CONTROL INC
14101 Willard Rd Ste A (20151-2934)
PHONE................................408 213-9555
Edwin Smith, *CEO*
Marliese Wilder, *Corp Secy*
Matthew Wade, *Vice Pres*
Ron Wilder, *Vice Pres*
Sharon Sutton, *Marketing Staff*
EMP: 1
SQ FT: 5,000

SALES (est): 205.9K **Privately Held**
WEB: www.agilefleet.com
SIC: 3499 7363 Safe deposit boxes or chests, metal; help supply services

(G-2364)
AILSA SOFTWARE LLC
4314 General Kearny Ct (20151-1322)
PHONE..............................703 407-6470
Daniel S Craig, *Administration*
Dan Craig, *Author*
EMP: 2
SALES (est): 115.1K **Privately Held**
WEB: www.ailsasoftware.com
SIC: 7372 Prepackaged software

(G-2365)
ALLEGRA PRINT & IMAGING
14158 Willard Rd (20151-2976)
PHONE..............................703 378-4500
Karen King, *CEO*
EMP: 2
SALES (est): 80.6K **Privately Held**
SIC: 2752 Commercial printing, offset

(G-2366)
ALPHA INDUSTRIES INC (PA)
14200 Pk Madow Dr Ste 110 (20151)
PHONE..............................703 378-1420
Mike Cirker, *CEO*
Shou Shi, *Prdtn Mgr*
Josh Campognone, *Opers Staff*
Gina Kirkland, *Opers Staff*
Joshua Lebowitz, *Manager*
▲ **EMP:** 350
SQ FT: 70,000
SALES (est): 57.4MM **Privately Held**
WEB: www.alphaindustries.com
SIC: 2311 Military uniforms, men's & youths': purchased materials

(G-2367)
ALPHAGRAPHICS
4515 Daly Dr (20151-3712)
PHONE..............................703 818-2900
EMP: 2
SALES (est): 80.6K **Privately Held**
SIC: 2752 Commercial printing, lithographic

(G-2368)
ALPINE ARMORING INC (PA)
4170 Lafayette Center Dr # 100 (20151-1254)
PHONE..............................703 471-0002
Fred Khoroushi, *President*
Cameron Khoroushi, *Engineer*
◆ **EMP:** 10
SQ FT: 20,000
SALES (est): 2.3MM **Privately Held**
WEB: www.alpineco.com
SIC: 3711 5013 Cars, armored, assembly of; automotive supplies & parts

(G-2369)
AQUILIAN LLC
4800 Leighfield Valley Dr (20151-2332)
PHONE..............................703 967-8212
Joseph Kabeiseman,
EMP: 1
SALES (est): 83.1K **Privately Held**
SIC: 2392 Household furnishings

(G-2370)
ARCHNA & NAZISH INC
Also Called: Zindagi Granite Countertops
14000 Willard Rd (20151-4548)
PHONE..............................571 221-6224
Harshad Patel, *President*
Nawad Siddiqui, *Vice Pres*
Sawad Ansari, *Manager*
EMP: 12
SALES (est): 750K **Privately Held**
SIC: 3281 Granite, cut & shaped

(G-2371)
ASSOCIATE BUSINESS CO INC
4300 Chntly Shp Ctr Dr # 2 (20151-4012)
PHONE..............................703 222-4624
Amir Bakhtiari, *President*
EMP: 3
SALES (est): 308.8K **Privately Held**
SIC: 2759 Commercial printing

(G-2372)
ATS-SALES LLC
14522k Lee Rd (20151-1639)
PHONE..............................703 631-6661
Armand A Damiano, *Mng Member*
Bradly Mantz,
EMP: 9
SQ FT: 6,000
SALES (est): 720K **Privately Held**
WEB: www.ats-sales.com
SIC: 3669 3812 Traffic signals, electric; pedestrian traffic control equipment; air traffic control systems & equipment, electronic

(G-2373)
AVM INC
14630 Flint Lee Rd Unit D (20151-1517)
PHONE..............................703 802-6212
Vijay Kapur, *CEO*
Madhu Kapur, *Vice Pres*
Amit Kapur, *Director*
EMP: 6
SQ FT: 1,500
SALES (est): 762.7K **Privately Held**
WEB: www.avmplating.com
SIC: 3471 Electroplating of metals or formed products

(G-2374)
BARAKAT FOODS INC
13893j Willard Rd (20151-2947)
PHONE..............................703 222-9493
Mohammad H Popal, *President*
◆ **EMP:** 13
SALES (est): 1.2MM **Privately Held**
WEB: www.barakatfoods.com
SIC: 2099 Food preparations

(G-2375)
BAUSCH HEALTH AMERICAS INC
3701 Concorde Pkwy # 800 (20151-1126)
PHONE..............................703 995-2400
Mark Canton, *Branch Mgr*
EMP: 3
SALES (corp-wide): 8.6B **Privately Held**
WEB: www.bauschhealth.com
SIC: 2834 Pharmaceutical preparations
HQ: Bausch Health Americas, Inc.
　　400 Somerset Corp Blvd
　　Bridgewater NJ 08807
　　908 927-1400

(G-2376)
BECKER DESIGNED INC
Also Called: B D I
14954 Bogle Dr (20151-1724)
PHONE..............................703 803-6900
Bill Becker, *CEO*
Hanna Hajjar, *Vice Pres*
George Mercuro, *Vice Pres*
David Stewart, *Vice Pres*
Oscar Turcios, *QC Mgr*
▲ **EMP:** 42
SQ FT: 80,000
SALES (est): 9.1MM **Privately Held**
WEB: www.bdiusa.com
SIC: 2511 2514 Wood household furniture; metal household furniture

(G-2377)
BETTERA BRANDS LLC
14790 Flint Lee Rd (20151-1513)
PHONE..............................703 222-6340
Richard Oneil, *President*
EMP: 55
SALES (corp-wide): 6.1MM **Privately Held**
WEB: www.gimbalscandy.com
SIC: 2834 Vitamin preparations
PA: Bettera Brands, Llc
　　5345 Towne Square Dr # 240
　　Plano TX 75024
　　800 344-6225

(G-2378)
BOEING COMPANY
15059 Confrnce Ctr Dr # 500 (20151-3847)
PHONE..............................703 961-8174
Robert Tolbert, *Purchasing*
John Brzezinski, *Engineer*
Jim Wrightson, *Manager*
Barbara Torrico, *Analyst*
EMP: 350

SALES (corp-wide): 76.5B **Publicly Held**
WEB: www.boeing.com
SIC: 3721 Aircraft
PA: The Boeing Company
　　100 N Riverside Plz
　　Chicago IL 60606
　　312 544-2000

(G-2379)
BOEING COMPANY
15059 Confrnce Ctr Dr # 500 (20151-3847)
P.O. Box 221710 (20153-1710)
PHONE..............................703 808-2737
David Killmeyer, *Engineer*
EMP: 36
SALES (corp-wide): 76.5B **Publicly Held**
WEB: www.boeing.com
SIC: 3721 Aircraft
PA: The Boeing Company
　　100 N Riverside Plz
　　Chicago IL 60606
　　312 544-2000

(G-2380)
BRANCH BOTANICALS INC
14800 Conference Ctr (20151-3810)
PHONE..............................703 429-4217
Thomas Burns, *Ch of Bd*
Dan Tolley, *President*
Donald Roberts, *Vice Pres*
Aw Scott Frayser, *Treasurer*
Rhonda Johnson, *Bd of Directors*
EMP: 1
SALES (est): 57.1K **Privately Held**
WEB: www.spglobalinc.com
SIC: 2861 2865 Gum & wood chemicals; cyclic crudes & intermediates

(G-2381)
BREAKAWAY HOLDINGS LLC (HQ)
14100 Parke Long Ct Ste G (20151-1644)
PHONE..............................703 953-3866
Bryan Vaughan,
EMP: 16
SALES (est): 2.5MM **Publicly Held**
WEB: www.homevisit.com
SIC: 2759 Commercial printing
PA: Corelogic, Inc.
　　40 Pacifica Ste 900
　　Irvine CA 92618
　　949 214-1000

(G-2382)
BYRD ASSISTIVE TECH INC
13893 Willard Rd Ste A (20151-2947)
PHONE..............................571 512-6069
Duncan L Byrd, *Founder*
EMP: 8
SALES (est): 322.9K **Privately Held**
WEB: www.byrd-at.com
SIC: 3842 Wheelchairs

(G-2383)
C & R PRINTING INC
4447b Brkfld Crprt Dr (20151-1692)
PHONE..............................703 802-0800
Rene El-Hage, *President*
Chahine E El-Hage, *Vice Pres*
Elias Elhage, *Vice Pres*
EMP: 9
SALES (est): 1.4MM **Privately Held**
WEB: www.candrprinting.com
SIC: 2752 Commercial printing, offset

(G-2384)
C2-MASK INC
14100 Parke Long Ct Ste H (20151-1644)
PHONE..............................703 304-9319
Brian Culbertson, *Principal*
EMP: 3
SALES (est): 400K **Privately Held**
SIC: 2759 Commercial printing

(G-2385)
CABINET DISCOUNTERS INC
14501 Lee Jackson Memoria (20151-1512)
PHONE..............................703 803-7990
John Mikk, *Branch Mgr*
EMP: 17
SALES (corp-wide): 9MM **Privately Held**
WEB: www.cabinetdiscounters.com
SIC: 2434 Wood kitchen cabinets

PA: Cabinet Discounters, Inc.
　　9500 Berger Rd
　　Columbia MD 21046
　　410 381-8172

(G-2386)
CABINETS READY TO GO LLC
14801 Murdock St Ste 150 (20151-1040)
PHONE..............................703 665-5620
Hasan Ogun Heporen, *Principal*
EMP: 2
SALES (est): 202.5K **Privately Held**
SIC: 2434 Wood kitchen cabinets

(G-2387)
CAREER COLLEGE CENTRAL
14200 Park Meadow Dr 117s (20151-4210)
PHONE..............................571 267-3012
EMP: 2
SALES (est): 73.1K **Privately Held**
SIC: 2721 Magazines: publishing & printing

(G-2388)
CENTAURUS BIOTECH LLC
4229 Lafayette Center Dr (20151-1261)
PHONE..............................952 210-6881
Jean-Paul Gonzalez,
Venkat RAO,
Francisco Veas,
EMP: 4 EST: 2017
SQ FT: 800
SALES (est): 189.6K **Privately Held**
SIC: 2835 In vitro diagnostics

(G-2389)
CHANTIL TECHNOLOGY LLC
13528 Tabscott Dr (20151-2742)
PHONE..............................703 955-7867
Uri Bendelac,
EMP: 1
SALES (est): 92K **Privately Held**
WEB: www.chantiltech.com
SIC: 3821 Laboratory equipment: fume hoods, distillation racks, etc.

(G-2390)
CHANTILLY BIOPHARMA LLC
3701 Concorde Pkwy # 500 (20151-1126)
PHONE..............................703 932-3840
Subraman R Cherukuri,
EMP: 11
SALES (est): 2.3MM **Privately Held**
SIC: 2834 Pharmaceutical preparations

(G-2391)
CHANTILLY FLOOR WHOLESALER INC
14516 Lee Rd Unit K (20151-1638)
PHONE..............................703 263-0515
Scott Kim, *President*
EMP: 10 EST: 2013
SQ FT: 25,000
SALES (est): 6.4MM **Privately Held**
WEB: www.chantillyfloor.com
SIC: 2426 Hardwood dimension & flooring mills

(G-2392)
CHANTILLY SERVICES INC
Also Called: Walls Lithographics
14240 Sullyfield Cir A (20151-1661)
PHONE..............................703 830-7700
Sue Walls, *President*
Martin Walls, *Vice Pres*
Suzanne Walls,
EMP: 4
SALES (est): 550.2K **Privately Held**
WEB: www.wallslitho.com
SIC: 2752 Commercial printing, offset

(G-2393)
CLARKS LITHO INC
14700 Avion Pkwy Ste 300 (20151-1123)
PHONE..............................703 961-8888
Richard C Thomas, *President*
Amy L Thomas, *Vice Pres*
John Firestein, *CFO*
EMP: 10
SQ FT: 8,000
SALES (est): 1.5MM **Privately Held**
WEB: www.clarkslitho.com
SIC: 2752 7331 Commercial printing, offset; mailing service

(G-2394)
CNC PRINTING INC
14220 Sullyfild Cir J (20151-1628)
PHONE..............................703 378-5222
Og Kee, *Principal*
EMP: 2
SALES (est): 274.2K **Privately Held**
SIC: 2752 Commercial printing, lithographic

(G-2395)
CNJ BEEKEEPERS INC
4719 Lewis Woods Ct (20151-2539)
PHONE..............................703 378-1629
EMP: 2 **EST:** 2002
SALES (est): 97K **Privately Held**
SIC: 2099 Mfg Food Preparations

(G-2396)
COOLR GROUP INC
14100 Parke Long Ct Ste I (20151-1644)
PHONE..............................571 933-3762
Durlanbh Jain, *CTO*
EMP: 3
SQ FT: 1,100
SALES (est): 126.6K **Privately Held**
WEB: www.coolrgroup.com
SIC: 7372 Operating systems computer software

(G-2397)
COPYLAND PRINTING INC
14101 Sllyfeld Cir Ste 11 (20151)
PHONE..............................703 241-9188
Hansin Park, *President*
Hung Rim Park, *Admin Sec*
EMP: 10
SALES (est): 500K **Privately Held**
WEB: www.mediapressdc.com
SIC: 2752 Commercial printing, offset

(G-2398)
CRFS INC
4230 Lafayette Center Dr D (20151-1238)
PHONE..............................571 321-5470
Nick Balon, *General Mgr*
Marty Mosier, *General Mgr*
Kile Casey, *Office Mgr*
EMP: 4
SQ FT: 100
SALES (est): 266.5K
SALES (corp-wide): 12.8MM **Privately Held**
WEB: www.crfs.com
SIC: 3825 Spectrum analyzers
PA: Crfs Limited
Building 7200
Cambridge CAMBS CB25
122 385-9500

(G-2399)
CRYSTAL TECHNOLOGY INC
13558 Smallwood Ln (20151-2519)
PHONE..............................703 968-2590
Neol Shah, *President*
EMP: 10
SALES (est): 439.4K **Privately Held**
SIC: 7372 Prepackaged software

(G-2400)
CUPCAKES AND LACE LLC
4405 Cub Run Rd (20151-1428)
PHONE..............................703 378-1525
Devon O'Neal, *Principal*
EMP: 4 **EST:** 2010
SALES (est): 234K **Privately Held**
WEB: www.cupcakesandlace.com
SIC: 2051 Bread, cake & related products

(G-2401)
CUTON POWER INC
3725 Concorde Pkwy (20151-1156)
PHONE..............................703 996-9350
EMP: 2 **EST:** 2013
SALES (est): 91.9K **Privately Held**
WEB: www.cutonpower.com
SIC: 7694 Armature rewinding shops

(G-2402)
DAVIDA
3015 Virginia Dare Ct (20151-3460)
PHONE..............................571 278-4287
Javier Fonseca, *Principal*
EMP: 2

SALES (est): 78.3K **Privately Held**
WEB: www.davida-helmets.com
SIC: 3949 Sporting & athletic goods

(G-2403)
DEDICATED MICROS INC (HQ)
3855 Centerview Dr # 400 (20151-3285)
PHONE..............................703 904-7738
Mike Newton, *President*
Marie Nelson, *General Mgr*
Nigel Petrie, *Chairman*
John Bonsee, *Senior VP*
John Dolan, *Vice Pres*
▲ **EMP:** 43
SQ FT: 15,000
SALES (est): 11MM
SALES (corp-wide): 1.2MM **Privately Held**
WEB: www.dedicatedmicros.com
SIC: 3669 Intercommunication systems, electric

(G-2404)
DEFENSE GROUP
4803 Stonecroft Blvd (20151-3822)
PHONE..............................703 633-8300
Scott Whatmough, *Senior VP*
EMP: 2
SALES (est): 77.4K **Privately Held**
SIC: 3812 Defense systems & equipment

(G-2405)
DENIS BRITTO DR
Also Called: Britto Orthodontics
4080 Lafayette Center Dr # 160 (20151-1247)
PHONE..............................703 230-6784
Denis Britto, *Principal*
EMP: 2
SALES (est): 256.2K **Privately Held**
WEB: www.brittoorthodontics.com
SIC: 3843 8072 Enamels, dentists'; dental laboratories

(G-2406)
DENTCORE INC
Also Called: Ym Dental Lab
14100 Pk Madow Dr Ste 100 (20151)
PHONE..............................844 292-8023
Paul Kim, *President*
Yong Min Park, *Vice Pres*
EMP: 36
SALES (est): 1.4MM **Privately Held**
WEB: www.dentcore.com
SIC: 3843 Teeth, artificial (not made in dental laboratories)

(G-2407)
DEPARTMENT INFO TECH INC
Also Called: Doit
13551 Tabscott Dr (20151-2744)
PHONE..............................703 868-6691
Usman Aziz, *President*
EMP: 1
SALES (est): 58.5K **Privately Held**
WEB: www.reno.gov
SIC: 7372 7371 7373 7374 Word processing computer software; custom computer programming services; systems engineering, computer related; service bureau, computer

(G-2408)
DIGITAL ACCESS CONTROL INC
14163 Robert Paris Ct B (20151-4240)
PHONE..............................703 463-0113
Thomas Hunt, *President*
Kevin Summers, *Vice Pres*
▲ **EMP:** 15
SQ FT: 4,600
SALES (est): 1.2MM **Privately Held**
WEB: www.dacinc.com
SIC: 3577 Computer peripheral equipment

(G-2409)
DOF USA INC
14225 Sullyfield Cir E (20151-1688)
PHONE..............................888 635-4999
Felix Seori Chung, *Administration*
EMP: 2
SALES (est): 104.8K **Privately Held**
SIC: 3843 Dental equipment & supplies

(G-2410)
DONG-A PACKAGE USA CORP
4115 Pleasant Valley Rd (20151-1220)
PHONE..............................703 961-1686
James Lee, *President*
EMP: 1
SALES (est): 170.5K **Privately Held**
SIC: 3089 Plastics products

(G-2411)
DRILLCO NATIONAL GROUP INC
14620 Flint Lee Rd Unit E (20151-1517)
PHONE..............................703 631-3222
Bill McGarry, *Manager*
EMP: 7
SALES (corp-wide): 5.9MM **Privately Held**
WEB: www.drillcogroup.com
SIC: 3531 Construction machinery
PA: Drillco National Group, Inc.
2432 44th St
Long Island City NY 11103
718 726-9801

(G-2412)
DRS LEONARDO INC
3859 Centerview Dr # 200 (20151-3286)
PHONE..............................571 383-0152
EMP: 3
SALES (corp-wide): 9.9B **Privately Held**
WEB: www.leonardodrs.com
SIC: 3812 Search & navigation equipment
HQ: Leonardo Drs, Inc.
2345 Crystal Dr Ste 1000
Arlington VA 22202
703 416-8000

(G-2413)
DUBROOK CONCRETE INC
4215 Lafayette Center Dr # 1 (20151-1243)
PHONE..............................703 222-6969
Thomas Ogorchock, *President*
EMP: 70
SQ FT: 1,800
SALES (est): 17.8MM **Privately Held**
SIC: 3273 Ready-mixed concrete

(G-2414)
DUNLAP WOODCRAFTS
14600 Flint Lee Rd Whseg (20151-1517)
PHONE..............................703 631-5147
Wayne Dunlap, *Owner*
EMP: 2 **Privately Held**
WEB: www.dunlapwoodcrafts.com
SIC: 3482 Shotgun ammunition: empty, blank or loaded
PA: Dunlap Woodcrafts
14600f Flint Lee Rd
Chantilly VA 20151

(G-2415)
DYNEX TECHNOLOGIES INC (HQ)
14340 Sullyfield Cir (20151-1621)
PHONE..............................703 631-7800
David Sholevar, *CEO*
Matthew Barrell, *Vice Pres*
Duane Steele, *Vice Pres*
Deepak Valaparla, *Opers Staff*
Mark Brady, *Purch Mgr*
▲ **EMP:** 95
SQ FT: 45,000
SALES (est): 35MM **Privately Held**
WEB: www.dynextechnologies.com
SIC: 3826 7699 Analytical instruments; scientific equipment repair service

(G-2416)
ELECTRON TECHNOLOGIES INC
4431h Brkfld Crprt Dr (20151-1691)
PHONE..............................703 818-9400
EMP: 5
SALES (est): 285.1K **Privately Held**
SIC: 3699 8731 3844 3671 Mfg Elec Mach/Equip/Supp Coml Physical Research Mfg X-Ray Apparatus/Tube Mfg Electron Tubes

(G-2417)
EMBLEMAX LLC
14504f Lee Rd Ste F (20151-1634)
PHONE..............................703 802-0200
Kevin Cone, *Vice Pres*

Jennifer Sill, *Sales Staff*
Nissa Clavelli, *Director*
Mike Thornburg,
EMP: 25
SQ FT: 12,000 **Privately Held**
WEB: www.emblemax.com
SIC: 2261 2396 Screen printing of cotton broadwoven fabrics; screen printing on fabric articles

(G-2418)
EUROVIA ATLANTIC COAST LLC (HQ)
Also Called: Blythe
14500 Avion Pkwy Ste 310 (20151-1108)
PHONE..............................703 230-0850
Alan Cahill, *Mng Member*
EMP: 5
SALES (est): 23.3MM
SALES (corp-wide): 22.1MM **Privately Held**
WEB: www.blytheconstruction.com
SIC: 2951 Asphalt & asphaltic paving mixtures (not from refineries)
PA: Vinci
5 Cours Ferdinand De Lesseps
Rueil Malmaison 92500
147 164-477

(G-2419)
FAIRFAX WOODWORKING INC
14714 Old Lee Rd (20151-1701)
PHONE..............................703 339-9578
Eugene Y Kim, *President*
Kim Eugene Y, *President*
Steven Yang, *Manager*
EMP: 6
SALES (est): 3MM **Privately Held**
WEB: www.fairfaxwoodworking.com
SIC: 2431 Millwork

(G-2420)
FANNYPANTS LLC
4229 Lafayette Center Dr # 1150 (20151-1261)
PHONE..............................703 953-3099
Sophia Parker, *CEO*
▼ **EMP:** 3
SQ FT: 1,600
SALES (est): 500K **Privately Held**
WEB: www.fannypants.com
SIC: 2339 5621 5961 Service apparel, washable: women's; ready-to-wear apparel, women's; women's apparel, mail order

(G-2421)
FLOCKDATA LLC
4501 Lees Corner Rd (20151-2501)
PHONE..............................703 870-6916
Jeremy Snyder, *Vice Pres*
EMP: 2
SALES (est): 93.3K **Privately Held**
WEB: www.flockdata.com
SIC: 7372 Business oriented computer software

(G-2422)
FLOWERS BAKING CO OXFORD INC
4144 Pepsi Pl (20151-1501)
PHONE..............................610 932-2300
Paul Holshouser, *Manager*
EMP: 2
SALES (corp-wide): 4.1B **Publicly Held**
SIC: 2051 Bread, all types (white, wheat, rye, etc): fresh or frozen
HQ: Flowers Baking Co. Of Oxford, Inc.
700 Lincoln St
Oxford PA 19363

(G-2423)
FTA GOVERMENT SERVICES INC
5175 Parkstone Dr Ste 170 (20151-3836)
PHONE..............................571 612-0413
Richard Tallman, *President*
EMP: 3

GEOGRAPHIC

SALES (est): 204.4K **Privately Held**
WEB: www.aigovernmentservices.com
SIC: 3571 7371 7372 8243 Electronic computers; computer software systems analysis & design, custom; application computer software; operator training, computer; commercial art & graphic design; aviation &/or aeronautical engineering

(G-2424)
FULL COLOR PRINTS
4280 Henninger Ct (20151-2953)
PHONE............................571 612-8844
EMP: 2
SALES (est): 127.2K **Privately Held**
WEB: www.fullcolorprints.biz
SIC: 2752 Commercial printing, lithographic

(G-2425)
G2K LABS INC
4506 Daly Dr Ste 200 (20151-3710)
PHONE............................703 965-8367
Matthew Smith, *CEO*
John Sheridan, *Officer*
EMP: 8 **EST:** 2017
SALES (est): 117.6K **Privately Held**
WEB: www.g2klabs.com
SIC: 3661 Telephone & telegraph apparatus

(G-2426)
GIANT PRINTING INC
4116 Walney Rd Ste F (20151-2948)
PHONE............................703 645-2292
Dong Ho Park, *President*
June Park, *Vice Pres*
David Park, *Bookkeeper*
EMP: 3
SQ FT: 2,000
SALES (est): 36.6K **Privately Held**
SIC: 2752 Commercial printing, offset

(G-2427)
GLOBAL SCNNING AMERICAS VA INC
14155 Sullyfield Cir C (20151-4006)
PHONE............................703 717-5631
Peter Brown, *President*
Fred Pagani, *Technical Staff*
Elizabeth Anne Cooper, *Admin Sec*
EMP: 3
SALES (est): 157.9K
SALES (corp-wide): 14.4MM **Privately Held**
WEB: www.bycolortrac.eu
SIC: 3577 Computer peripheral equipment
PA: Global Scanning Uk Ltd
  3 5 Brunel Court Burrel Road
  St Ives

(G-2428)
GLOBAL TELECOM GROUP INC
4080 Lafayette Center Dr # 25 (20151-1247)
PHONE............................678 896-2468
Farrukh Ahmed, *Branch Mgr*
EMP: 3
SALES (corp-wide): 16.3MM **Privately Held**
WEB: www.globaltelecomgroup.com
SIC: 2079 Edible fats & oils
PA: Global Telecom Group, Inc.
  8220 Crestwood Heights Dr # 1401
  Mc Lean VA 22102
  571 291-9631

(G-2429)
GOD SPEDE PRINTING
4177 Meadowland Ct (20151-3565)
PHONE............................360 359-6458
William Mojica, *Principal*
EMP: 2
SALES (est): 83.9K **Privately Held**
SIC: 2752 Commercial printing, lithographic

(G-2430)
GRANITE COUNTERTOPS
4080 Walney Rd Ste F (20151-2969)
PHONE............................703 953-3330
EMP: 2 **EST:** 2019
SALES (est): 62.6K **Privately Held**
SIC: 3281 Cut stone & stone products

(G-2431)
GRANULES PHARMACEUTICALS INC (HQ)
3701 Concorde Pkwy # 800 (20151-1126)
PHONE............................571 325-5950
Priyanka Chigurubatia, *President*
EMP: 85
SQ FT: 50,000
SALES (est): 25MM **Privately Held**
WEB: www.granulesindia.com
SIC: 2834 Pharmaceutical preparations

(G-2432)
GRANULES PHARMACEUTICALS INC
3725 Concorde Pkwy (20151-1156)
PHONE............................571 325-5950
Priyanka Chigurubatia, *President*
EMP: 2 **Privately Held**
WEB: www.granulesindia.com
SIC: 2834 Pharmaceutical preparations
HQ: Granules Pharmaceuticals, Inc.
  3701 Concorde Pkwy # 800
  Chantilly VA 20151
  571 325-5950

(G-2433)
GTRAS INC
4229 Lafayette Center Dr # 1750 (20151-1261)
PHONE............................703 342-4282
Rashmi Gaba, *CEO*
Ramakanth Peechara, *President*
Bhanumathi Medavarapu, *Vice Pres*
Krishna Reddy, *Project Leader*
EMP: 72
SALES (est): 8.2MM **Privately Held**
WEB: www.netvisionresources.com
SIC: 7372 8748 Prepackaged software; business consulting

(G-2434)
HALF A FIVE ENTERPRISE LLC
Also Called: Franklin's Printing
4515 Daly Dr Ste J (20151-3712)
PHONE............................703 818-2900
Shawn Wilson,
EMP: 9
SALES (est): 1.2MM **Privately Held**
WEB: www.franklins.biz
SIC: 2752 Commercial printing, lithographic

(G-2435)
HEALTHSMARTVACCINES LLC
4437 Brkfld Crprt Dr 2 (20151-2142)
PHONE............................703 961-0734
Richard L Miles, *Principal*
EMP: 3
SALES (est): 217.9K **Privately Held**
WEB: www.healthsmartvaccines.com
SIC: 2836 Vaccines

(G-2436)
HOCL INC
3656 Centerview Dr Ste 6 (20151-3291)
PHONE............................877 435-4625
Jun Eun, *President*
EMP: 3
SALES (est): 300K **Privately Held**
SIC: 3999 Manufacturing industries

(G-2437)
HTDEPOT LLC
4124 Walney Rd Ste C (20151-2937)
PHONE............................703 830-2818
Mike Wang,
▲ **EMP:** 5
SALES (est): 575.9K **Privately Held**
WEB: www.htdepot.com
SIC: 3651 5731 Home entertainment equipment, electronic; consumer electronic equipment

(G-2438)
HUDSON WDWKG & RESTORATION LLC
14620 Flint Lee Rd (20151-1517)
PHONE............................703 817-7741
Hudson Rebekka, *VP Opers*
Rebekka Hudson,
EMP: 2
SALES (est): 262.2K **Privately Held**
WEB: www.hudsonwoodworking.com
SIC: 2431 Millwork

(G-2439)
I4C INNOVATIONS LLC
3800 Concorde Pkwy # 400 (20151-1141)
PHONE............................703 488-6100
Michael Stanfield, *CEO*
Jeff Noce, *President*
Ronald Barden, *CFO*
Tracy Ward, *Treasurer*
Paul Tupin, *Director*
EMP: 25 **EST:** 2013
SQ FT: 7,349
SALES (est): 4.6MM
SALES (corp-wide): 788K **Privately Held**
WEB: www.voyce.com
SIC: 3699 Electrical equipment & supplies
PA: One Health Group, Llc
  3800 Concorde Pkwy # 400
  Chantilly VA 20151
  703 995-4139

(G-2440)
ILUMI SCIENCES INC
4150 Lafayette Center Dr # 500 (20151-1258)
PHONE............................703 894-7576
John Tokizawa, *Vice Pres*
Martha Downing, *Assistant*
EMP: 9
SALES (est): 998.6K **Privately Held**
WEB: www.ilumiusa.com
SIC: 3843 Dental equipment
PA: Lumenz Technology, Inc.
  4f, No. 36, Jinzhou St.
  Taipei City TAP 10451

(G-2441)
IMAGINE MILLING TECH LLC
14220 Sullyfield Cir B (20151-1628)
PHONE............................571 313-1269
Felix Chung, *President*
Susan Jung, *Opers Staff*
EMP: 1
SALES (corp-wide): 1.9MM **Privately Held**
WEB: www.imagineusa.com
SIC: 3842 Prosthetic appliances
PA: Imagine Milling Technologies Llc
  607 S Euclid St
  Fullerton CA 92832
  571 313-1269

(G-2442)
IMPACT UNLIMITED INC
14291 Park Meadow Dr (20151-2225)
PHONE............................702 802-6800
Mike Sandler, *Branch Mgr*
EMP: 40
SALES (corp-wide): 60MM **Privately Held**
WEB: www.impact-xm.com
SIC: 2541 Store & office display cases & fixtures; drainboards, plastic laminated
PA: Impact Unlimited, Inc.
  250 Ridge Rd
  Dayton NJ 08810
  732 274-2000

(G-2443)
INTERLOCKING CON PAVEMENT INST
14801 Murdock St Ste 230 (20151-1045)
PHONE............................703 657-6900
Charles McGrath, *Publisher*
Robert Bowers, *Engineer*
Charles Mc Grath, *Exec Dir*
Aaron Paul, *Education*
EMP: 7 **EST:** 1993
SQ FT: 4,600
SALES: 3.8MM **Privately Held**
WEB: www.icpi.org
SIC: 2721 Periodicals

(G-2444)
IPAATTI INC
14074 Eagle Chase Cir (20151-2239)
PHONE............................703 901-7904
Kumar Sivalingam, *President*
EMP: 1
SALES (est): 44.5K **Privately Held**
WEB: www.ipaatti.us
SIC: 2731 Book publishing

(G-2445)
IRON BOW HOLDINGS INC
3635 Concorde Pkwy # 700 (20151-1109)
PHONE............................703 795-1790

EMP: 3 **Privately Held**
WEB: www.ironbow.com
SIC: 3571 Electronic computers
PA: Iron Bow Holdings, Inc.
  2303 Dulles Station Blvd # 400
  Herndon VA 20171

(G-2446)
ITEGRITY SYSTEMS
13990 Parkeast Cir (20151-2272)
PHONE............................703 968-6300
Stephen Yong, *President*
Sue Deyo, *President*
Yardena Slater, *Marketing Staff*
EMP: 1
SALES (est): 30.7K **Privately Held**
WEB: www.asc-net.com
SIC: 7372 Prepackaged software

(G-2447)
J C PRINTING CORP
Also Called: Sundra Printing
14508c Lee Rd (20151-1604)
PHONE............................703 378-3500
Todd Sundra, *President*
Claire L Sundra, *Vice Pres*
EMP: 6
SALES (est): 879K **Privately Held**
WEB: www.sundraprinting.com
SIC: 2752 Commercial printing, offset

(G-2448)
JAY MALANGA
14504 Lee Rd (20151-1634)
PHONE............................703 802-0201
Jay Malanga, *Principal*
EMP: 2
SALES (est): 104.2K **Privately Held**
SIC: 2759 Screen printing

(G-2449)
JHL INC
Also Called: Kornfections & Treasures Too
14516c Lee Rd (20151-1638)
PHONE............................703 378-0009
Gerald Lerner, *President*
Helen Lerner, *Vice Pres*
▲ **EMP:** 6
SALES (est): 486.4K **Privately Held**
WEB: www.ultimateartsandcraftswhole-salelist.blogspot.com
SIC: 2064 2099 2096 2066 Candy & other confectionery products; food preparations; potato chips & similar snacks; chocolate & cocoa products

(G-2450)
JK ELECTRIC COMPANY
14720 Flint Lee Rd (20151-1503)
PHONE............................703 378-7477
EMP: 2
SALES (est): 196K **Privately Held**
SIC: 3699 Mfg Electrical Equipment/Supplies

(G-2451)
JKT INC
4429 Brkfld Crprt Dr # 800 (20151-4026)
PHONE............................804 272-2862
John I Gray III, *President*
Kathyrn Gray, *Vice Pres*
EMP: 2
SALES (est): 134.1K **Privately Held**
WEB: www.jkt.go.tz
SIC: 3944 Structural toy sets

(G-2452)
KNP TRADERS LLC
4211 Pleasant Valley Rd # 230 (20151-1222)
PHONE............................703 376-1955
Pgatamaneni Efwara, *CEO*
EMP: 3 **EST:** 2014
SQ FT: 1,400
SALES (est): 500K **Privately Held**
SIC: 2393 Canvas bags

(G-2453)
KRIMM SIGNS LLC
4429 Brkfeld Corp Dr Ste (20151)
PHONE............................571 599-2199
EMP: 1
SALES (est): 46K **Privately Held**
SIC: 3993 Signs & advertising specialties

(G-2454)
L3HARRIS TECHNOLOGIES INC
15049 Confrnce Ctr Dr # 600 (20151-3818)
PHONE..................................703 344-1000
Denny Tharp, *Director*
EMP: 8
SALES (corp-wide): 6.8B **Publicly Held**
WEB: www.harris.com
SIC: 3663 Radio & TV communications
equipment
PA: L3harris Technologies, Inc.
1025 W Nasa Blvd
Melbourne FL 32919
321 727-9100

(G-2455)
L3HARRIS TECHNOLOGIES INC
Also Called: Harris Govt Comm Sys
4125 Lafayette Center Dr # 700
(20151-1240)
PHONE..................................703 828-1520
Bill Barry, *Branch Mgr*
EMP: 53
SALES (corp-wide): 6.8B **Publicly Held**
WEB: www.harris.com
SIC: 3812 Search & navigation equipment
PA: L3harris Technologies, Inc.
1025 W Nasa Blvd
Melbourne FL 32919
321 727-9100

(G-2456)
LB TELESYSTEMS INC
Also Called: Bickford Broadcast Vehicles
4001 Westfax Dr Ste 100 (20151-1515)
P.O. Box 2548, Purcellville (20134-4548)
PHONE..................................703 919-8991
Jacqueline Grant, *President*
Paul Bickford, *Vice Pres*
EMP: 21
SQ FT: 28,000
SALES (est): 3.1MM **Privately Held**
SIC: 3663 3444 7699 Radio & TV com-
munications equipment; sheet metalwork;
professional instrument repair services

(G-2457)
LEICA MICROSYSTEMS INC
Also Called: US Semiconductor Unit
14280 Pk Madow Dr Ste 100 (20151)
PHONE..................................812 333-5416
Joe Reinbold, *Branch Mgr*
Roland A Fleck, *Director*
EMP: 50
SALES (corp-wide): 17.9B **Publicly Held**
WEB: www.leica-microsystems.com
SIC: 3827 Optical instruments & apparatus
HQ: Leica Microsystems Inc.
1700 Leider Ln
Buffalo Grove IL 60089
847 405-0123

(G-2458)
LOCKHEED MARTIN
CORPORATION
4262 Entre Ct (20151-2105)
PHONE..................................703 378-1880
Remo Chami, *Branch Mgr*
Douglas Booth, *Director*
EMP: 435 **Publicly Held**
WEB: www.lockheedmartin.com
SIC: 3812 Search & navigation equipment
PA: Lockheed Martin Corporation
6801 Rockledge Dr
Bethesda MD 20817

(G-2459)
LV IRON WORKS & WLDG SVCS
INC
14004 Willard Rd Unit M (20151-2929)
PHONE..................................703 499-2270
Lam Vo, *President*
EMP: 2
SALES (est): 276.8K **Privately Held**
WEB: www.lvironworksinc.com
SIC: 7692 Welding repair

(G-2460)
M&M SIGNS AND GRAPHICS
LLC
14512 Lee Rd Ste A (20151-1636)
PHONE..................................703 803-1043
Paymahn Amorgholi,
EMP: 5

SALES (est): 553.5K **Privately Held**
WEB: www.mandmgraphix.com
SIC: 3993 Signs, not made in custom sign
painting shops

(G-2461)
MCFARLAND ENTERPRISES INC
Also Called: Franklin's Printing
4515 Daly Dr Ste J (20151-3712)
PHONE..................................703 818-2900
Robert McFarland, *President*
Eileen McFarland, *Vice Pres*
EMP: 6
SQ FT: 1,600
SALES (est): 522.9K **Privately Held**
WEB: www.franklins.biz
SIC: 2752 Commercial printing, litho-
graphic

(G-2462)
MEDIA PRESS
14101 Sullyfield Cir # 110 (20151-1625)
PHONE..................................703 241-9188
Janet Fianko, *General Mgr*
EMP: 8
SALES (est): 96.5K **Privately Held**
WEB: www.mediapressusb.com
SIC: 2741 Miscellaneous publishing

(G-2463)
MILLCRAFT LLC
14000 Thunderbolt Pl F (20151-3225)
PHONE..................................703 225-9860
Emrah Cinar, *Principal*
EMP: 1
SALES (est): 67K **Privately Held**
SIC: 2431 Interior & ornamental woodwork
& trim

(G-2464)
MODERN EXTERIORS
4070 Walney Rd (20151-2919)
PHONE..................................703 978-8602
EMP: 10
SALES (est): 510K **Privately Held**
SIC: 3281 Mfg Cut Stone/Products

(G-2465)
MOSS CAPE LLC
4501 Singer Ct Ste 300 (20151-1734)
PHONE..................................703 234-3890
Adrian Ordenes, *Sr Project Mgr*
EMP: 7
SALES (est): 436.2K **Privately Held**
SIC: 2092 Fresh or frozen packaged fish

(G-2466)
N ROLLS-RYCE AMER
HOLDINGS INC
14850 Conference Ctr (20151-3820)
PHONE..................................703 834-1700
James Wright, *General Mgr*
David Whetton, *Exec VP*
John Gill, *Vice Pres*
Phil Hopton, *Vice Pres*
Susan Forrester, *Human Res Dir*
EMP: 12
SALES (corp-wide): 21.4B **Privately Held**
WEB: www.rolls-royce.com
SIC: 3599 Propellers, ship & boat: ma-
chined
HQ: Rolls-Royce North America Holdings
Inc.
1900 Reston Metro Plz # 4
Reston VA 20190
703 834-1700

(G-2467)
NEITHER NGEX
14014 Sullyfield Cir (20151-1689)
PHONE..................................408 676-6439
EMP: 1
SALES (est): 37.5K **Privately Held**
SIC: 2741 Miscellaneous publishing

(G-2468)
NETWORK STORAGE CORP
14020 Thunderbolt Pl 50 (20151-3293)
PHONE..................................703 834-7500
EMP: 35
SQ FT: 10,000
SALES (est): 4.3MM **Privately Held**
SIC: 3572 Mfg Computer Network At-
tached Storage Products

(G-2469)
NORTHERN VA COMPOUNDERS
PLLC
Also Called: Akina Pharamacy
4080 Lafayette Center Dr # 27
(20151-1247)
PHONE..................................855 792-5462
Justin Thornton, *Pharmacist*
Bassem Girgis, *Mng Member*
EMP: 2
SALES (est): 423.7K **Privately Held**
WEB: www.akinapharmacy.com
SIC: 2834 Pharmaceutical preparations

(G-2470)
NORTHROP GRUMMAN
CORPORATION
4262 Entre Ct (20151-2105)
PHONE..................................703 556-5960
Dwayne Pfeiffer, *Manager*
EMP: 14 **Publicly Held**
WEB: www.northropgrumman.com
SIC: 3812 Search & navigation equipment
PA: Northrop Grumman Corporation
2980 Fairview Park Dr
Falls Church VA 22042

(G-2471)
NORTHROP GRUMMAN
CORPORATION
4807 Stonecroft Blvd (20151-3822)
PHONE..................................703 449-7120
Bart Bailey, *Branch Mgr*
Logan Rice, *Relations*
EMP: 310 **Publicly Held**
WEB: www.northropgrumman.com
SIC: 3812 Search & navigation equipment
PA: Northrop Grumman Corporation
2980 Fairview Park Dr
Falls Church VA 22042

(G-2472)
NORTHROP GRUMMAN
SYSTEMS CORP
4805 Stonecroft Blvd (20151-3822)
PHONE..................................703 633-8300
Jim Frey, *Branch Mgr*
EMP: 10 **Publicly Held**
WEB: www.northropgrumman.com
SIC: 3812 Search & navigation equipment
HQ: Northrop Grumman Systems Corpora-
tion
2980 Fairview Park Dr
Falls Church VA 22042
703 280-2900

(G-2473)
NOTALVISION INC
4500 Southgate Pl Ste 400 (20151-1714)
PHONE..................................888 910-2020
Quinton Oswald, *CEO*
Barbara Benedict, *Vice Pres*
Shirley Kleinman, *CFO*
Jim Long, *CFO*
Jon Johnson, *Director*
EMP: 15
SALES (est): 2.3MM **Privately Held**
WEB: www.foreseehome.com
SIC: 3841 Surgical & medical instruments

(G-2474)
NRJ INDUSTRIES LLC
13621 Birch Dr (20151-3305)
PHONE..................................703 707-0368
Mary Galvin, *Principal*
EMP: 1
SALES (est): 42.8K **Privately Held**
SIC: 3999 Manufacturing industries

(G-2475)
NSGDATACOM INC (PA)
Also Called: Netrix/Proteon
3859 Centerview Dr # 500 (20151-3286)
PHONE..................................703 464-0151
Richard Yalen, *CEO*
Graham King, *President*
Joseph Gibson, *General Mgr*
Joe Kimak, *Engineer*
Richard Deater, *Finance*
EMP: 50
SQ FT: 34,000
SALES (est): 6.8MM **Privately Held**
WEB: www.netrix.com
SIC: 3661 3577 Modems; data conversion
equipment, media-to-media: computer

(G-2476)
NUTRAVAIL HOLDING CORP
14790 Flint Lee Rd (20151-1513)
PHONE..................................703 222-6348
Richard O'Neil, *CEO*
Marianne Hurd, *CFO*
▲ EMP: 55
SQ FT: 60,000
SALES (est): 10.4MM **Privately Held**
WEB: www.nutravail.com
SIC: 2834 Pharmaceutical preparations

(G-2477)
OLD SOUTH PLANTATION
SHUTTERS
14514a Lee Rd (20151-1637)
PHONE..................................703 968-7822
Jeff Demuro, *Owner*
EMP: 1
SALES (est): 62.3K **Privately Held**
SIC: 2431 Window shutters, wood

(G-2478)
PARKSIDE WOODS LLC
4934 Edge Rock Dr (20151-4104)
PHONE..................................703 543-6446
Gary Scola, *Principal*
EMP: 2
SALES (est): 55.2K **Privately Held**
SIC: 2499 Wood products

(G-2479)
PERCONTEE INC
Loudoun Quarries
636 Rte 606 (20153)
P.O. Box 220005 (20153-0005)
PHONE..................................703 471-4411
Rick Hoffman, *Manager*
EMP: 35
SALES (corp-wide): 30.1MM **Privately
Held**
WEB: www.perconteereclamation.com
SIC: 1442 5032 Sand mining; gravel &
pebble mining; brick, stone & related ma-
terial
PA: Percontee, Inc.
11900 Tech Rd
Silver Spring MD 20904
301 622-0100

(G-2480)
PETROSTAR GLOBAL LLC
4159 Travers Ct (20151-2974)
PHONE..................................301 919-7879
Rajesh K Nedungadi, *CEO*
EMP: 4
SALES (est): 125.3K **Privately Held**
SIC: 2992 Lubricating oils & greases

(G-2481)
PORTFOLIO PUBLICATION
4602 Fillingame Dr (20151-2830)
P.O. Box 220251 (20153-0251)
PHONE..................................703 802-8676
Robin Y Sinckler, *Owner*
EMP: 1
SALES (est): 68.5K **Privately Held**
WEB: www.1holyspirit.com
SIC: 2741 8742 Miscellaneous publishing;
management consulting services

(G-2482)
PREMIER PINS
14110 Sullyfield Cir D (20151-1665)
P.O. Box 222783 (20153-2783)
PHONE..................................703 631-6660
Jeff Decenzo, *Manager*
EMP: 3
SALES (est): 1MM **Privately Held**
WEB: www.premierstore.net
SIC: 3965 Fasteners

(G-2483)
PROTOTYPE PRODUCTIONS
INC (PA)
Also Called: P P I
14558 Lee Rd Fl 2 (20151-1632)
PHONE..................................703 858-0011
Joe V Travez, *CEO*
Ted Rogers, *Partner*
Italo D Travez, *COO*
Italo Travez, *COO*
Tracy Meyer, *Vice Pres*
▲ EMP: 60
SQ FT: 30,000

SALES (est): 10.6MM **Privately Held**
WEB: www.protoprod.com
SIC: 3599 8711 3769 3499 Machine shop, jobbing & repair; industrial engineers; electrical or electronic engineering; space capsules; machine bases, metal; architectural services; mechanical springs, precision

(G-2484)
RAIMIST SOFTWARE LLC
Also Called: Ecm Universe
13623 Bare Island Dr (20151-4113)
PHONE.......................703 568-7638
Scott Raimist, *General Mgr*
Steven Schmidt, *Software Engr*
Scott A Raimist,
EMP: 9
SALES (est): 2.4MM **Privately Held**
WEB: www.ecmuniverse.com
SIC: 7372 7371 Business oriented computer software; computer software systems analysis & design, custom; computer software writing services; computer code authors; computer software development & applications

(G-2485)
RAYTHEON COMPANY
14280 Sullyfield Cir # 100 (20151-1699)
PHONE.......................703 830-4087
C J Debow, *Principal*
EMP: 15
SALES (corp-wide): 77B **Publicly Held**
WEB: www.rtx.com
SIC: 3812 Sonar systems & equipment
HQ: Raytheon Company
870 Winter St
Waltham MA 02451
781 522-3000

(G-2486)
REEM ENTERPRISES
13830 Rembrandt Way (20151-3255)
PHONE.......................703 608-2283
Shahid Paracha, *Owner*
EMP: 2
SALES (est): 90.4K **Privately Held**
SIC: 2522 Office furniture, except wood

(G-2487)
RITZ REFINISHING INC
14043 Willard Rd (20151-2928)
PHONE.......................703 378-0462
EMP: 2
SALES (est): 167.1K **Privately Held**
WEB: www.ritzrefinishing.com
SIC: 2434 Wood kitchen cabinets

(G-2488)
RYAN STUDIO INC
Also Called: Legacy A Ryan Company
14140 Parke Long Ct Ste N (20151-1649)
PHONE.......................703 830-6818
Daniel Ryan, *President*
EMP: 3
SALES (est): 276.6K **Privately Held**
WEB: www.ryanstudio.com
SIC: 2392 5719 Blankets, comforters & beddings; bedding (sheets, blankets, spreads & pillows)

(G-2489)
SAI BEAUTY LLC
Also Called: SAI Skin Care
13616 Pennsboro Dr (20151-2717)
PHONE.......................703 864-6372
Bina Patel, *Owner*
EMP: 3
SALES (est): 238.1K **Privately Held**
WEB: www.saiskincare.com
SIC: 2844 Cosmetic preparations

(G-2490)
SGX GRAPHIX
4215 Walney Rd (20151-2950)
PHONE.......................703 330-3550
EMP: 1 EST: 2018
SALES (est): 66K **Privately Held**
WEB: www.sgxwraps.com
SIC: 3993 Signs & advertising specialties

(G-2491)
SIGN BROKER LLC
13458 Stream Valley Dr (20151-2624)
PHONE.......................703 263-7227

Michael Proseus,
EMP: 3 EST: 2007
SALES (est): 250K **Privately Held**
WEB: www.thesignbroker.com
SIC: 3993 Signs, not made in custom sign painting shops

(G-2492)
SMART BUY KITCHEN & BATH PLUS
Also Called: Kitchen and Bath Design
3525 Armfield Farm Dr (20151-3351)
PHONE.......................571 643-1078
Ann Higginson, *Owner*
EMP: 1
SALES (est): 500K **Privately Held**
SIC: 2511 Wood household furniture

(G-2493)
SOFTWARE TO FIT LLC
13423 Melville Ln (20151-2465)
PHONE.......................703 378-7239
Steven Fuchs, *Principal*
EMP: 4
SALES (est): 272.1K **Privately Held**
SIC: 7372 Prepackaged software

(G-2494)
SOURCE360 LLC
4131 Pleasant Meadow Ct (20151-3539)
PHONE.......................703 232-1563
Melvin Scott, *President*
EMP: 1
SALES (est): 55.4K **Privately Held**
WEB: www.allsource360.com
SIC: 7372 8748 7373 7371 Application computer software; business oriented computer software; systems engineering consultant, ex. computer or professional; systems software development services; computer software development;

(G-2495)
SOUTHERN STATES COOP INC
Also Called: S S C 9717-5
14401 Penrose Pl (20151-1612)
PHONE.......................703 378-4865
Dennis Shirkey, *Manager*
EMP: 24
SALES (corp-wide): 2.1B **Privately Held**
WEB: www.southernstates.com
SIC: 2048 2873 0181 2874 Prepared feeds; nitrogenous fertilizers; bulbs & seeds; phosphatic fertilizers; liquefied petroleum gas dealers
PA: Southern States Cooperative, Incorporated
6606 W Broad St Ste B
Richmond VA 23230
804 281-1000

(G-2496)
SPECTRAREP LLC
14150 Prkeast Cir Ste 110 (20151)
PHONE.......................703 227-9690
Edward Czarnecki,
Richard V Ducey,
EMP: 14 EST: 2001
SALES (est): 1.2MM **Privately Held**
WEB: www.spectrarep.com
SIC: 3663 Radio & TV communications equipment

(G-2497)
SPORTS PLUS INCORPORATED
Also Called: Battlefield Screen Printing
4429 Brkfeld Corp Dr Ste (20151)
PHONE.......................703 222-8255
Paul Norris, *President*
William Bill Oehm, *Vice Pres*
EMP: 32
SQ FT: 10,000
SALES (est): 4.4MM **Privately Held**
WEB: www.sportsplusteam.com
SIC: 2759 Screen printing

(G-2498)
SRA COMPANIES INC
15036 Conference Ctr Dr (20151-3848)
PHONE.......................703 803-1500
Ernst Volgenau, *Ch of Bd*
William L Ballhaus, *President*
George Batsakis, *Exec VP*
Paul Nedzbala, *Exec VP*
Clyde T Nixon, *Exec VP*
EMP: 5600

SALES: 1.3B **Privately Held**
WEB: www.gdit.com
SIC: 7372 8742 Prepackaged software; management consulting services

(G-2499)
STERN WELDING LLC
13803 Leighfield St (20151-2504)
PHONE.......................571 283-1355
Matthew L Stern, *Principal*
EMP: 3
SALES (est): 135.9K **Privately Held**
SIC: 7692 Welding repair

(G-2500)
STONE STUDIO LLC
14805 Willard Rd Ste H (20151-3714)
PHONE.......................703 263-9755
EMP: 7 EST: 2006
SALES (est): 870.6K **Privately Held**
WEB: www.mystonestudio.com
SIC: 3281 Household articles, except furniture: cut stone

(G-2501)
STONE TERROIR USA LLC
4005b Westfax Dr (20151-1547)
PHONE.......................757 754-2434
Sesuk Soyruoglu, *Mng Member*
EMP: 7 EST: 2015
SALES (est): 621.1K **Privately Held**
SIC: 3281 Cut stone & stone products

(G-2502)
STORAGE TECHNOLOGY
14120 Parke Long Ct # 201 (20151-1646)
PHONE.......................703 817-1528
Tony Russo, *Principal*
EMP: 2
SALES (est): 85.9K **Privately Held**
SIC: 3577 Computer peripheral equipment

(G-2503)
SUDAY PROMOTIONS INC
Also Called: Femme Promo
14900 Bogle Dr Ste 201 (20151-1757)
PHONE.......................703 376-8640
Duyanh Nguyen, *President*
Sidney Anh Nguyen, *Managing Dir*
Sidney Nguyen, *Managing Dir*
EMP: 6 EST: 2006
SALES (est): 1.8MM **Privately Held**
WEB: www.sudaypromotions.com
SIC: 3993 7389 5199 2752 Signs & advertising specialties; advertising, promotional & trade show services; advertising specialties; commercial printing, lithographic; offset & photolithographic printing; promotional printing, lithographic; calendar & card printing, lithographic

(G-2504)
SUPERMEDIA LLC
3635 Concorde Pkwy # 400 (20151-1125)
PHONE.......................703 322-2900
Andy Smith, *Manager*
EMP: 254
SALES (corp-wide): 868.1MM **Privately Held**
WEB: www.thryv.com
SIC: 2741 Directories, telephone: publishing only, not printed on site
HQ: Supermedia Llc
2200 W Airfield Dr
Dfw Airport TX 75261
972 453-7000

(G-2505)
SUPERNOVA INDUSTRIES INC
13435 Point Pleasant Dr (20151-2447)
PHONE.......................703 731-2987
Basem Samahy, *CEO*
EMP: 2
SALES (est): 105.9K **Privately Held**
SIC: 3999 Manufacturing industries

(G-2506)
SYMBOL TECHNOLOGIES LLC
4124 Walney Rd (20151-2937)
PHONE.......................703 263-2533
Robert Watson, *Manager*
EMP: 4
SALES (corp-wide): 4.4B **Publicly Held**
WEB: www.zebra.com
SIC: 3577 Computer peripheral equipment

HQ: Symbol Technologies, Llc
3 Overlook Pt
Lincolnshire IL 60069
631 737-6851

(G-2507)
SYSTEMS AMERICA INC
4609 Lewis Leigh Ct (20151-2833)
PHONE.......................703 203-8421
Ramesh Subbanna, *President*
EMP: 1
SALES (est): 130K **Privately Held**
WEB: www.americansystems.com
SIC: 7372 Application computer software

(G-2508)
TECHNOLOGY HUB INC
14102 Sllyfeld Cir Ste 35 (20151)
PHONE.......................571 370-5100
EMP: 3
SALES (est): 214.4K **Privately Held**
SIC: 3316 Cold finishing of steel shapes

(G-2509)
TVWORLDWIDECOM INC
14428 Albemarle Point Pl # 1 (20151-1749)
PHONE.......................703 961-9250
David R Gardy, *President*
Matt Schrader, *Vice Pres*
Pat Cleveland, *Comms Dir*
EMP: 1
SQ FT: 6,100
SALES (est): 173.8K
SALES (corp-wide): 1.7MM **Privately Held**
WEB: www.tvworldwide.net
SIC: 2741
PA: Maritimetv, Inc.
4206f Technology Ct
Chantilly VA 20151
703 961-9250

(G-2510)
ULTRA ELECTRONICS 3PHOENIX INC
14585 Avion Pkwy Ste 200 (20151-1140)
PHONE.......................703 956-6480
James B Gallemore, *Principal*
John M Jamieson III, *Principal*
Joseph A Liverman, *Principal*
EMP: 3 EST: 2016
SALES (est): 124.7K **Privately Held**
SIC: 3812 Defense systems & equipment

(G-2511)
UNBOXED
13916 Leeton Cir (20151-2237)
PHONE.......................336 253-4085
Michael Ogden, *Owner*
EMP: 1 EST: 2016
SALES (est): 36K **Privately Held**
WEB: www.unboxed.in
SIC: 7372 Application computer software

(G-2512)
UNICOM TECHNOLOGY PARK INC
15000 Conference Ctr Dr (20151-3819)
PHONE.......................703 502-2850
Peter Ramirez, *Principal*
EMP: 5
SQ FT: 640,000
SALES (est): 207.9K **Privately Held**
WEB: www.unicomglobal.com
SIC: 3271 Concrete block & brick

(G-2513)
UNIVERSAL SPACE NETWORK INC
14399 Penrose Pl Ste 210 (20151-1792)
PHONE.......................703 488-4150
EMP: 2 EST: 2015
SALES (est): 117.2K **Privately Held**
SIC: 3663 Radio & TV communications equipment

(G-2514)
US CONCRETE INC
4215 Lafayette Center Dr (20151-1243)
PHONE.......................703 471-6969
William Sandbrook, *President*
EMP: 12 **Publicly Held**
WEB: www.us-concrete.com
SIC: 3273 Ready-mixed concrete

PA: U.S. Concrete, Inc.
331 N Main St
Euless TX 76039
817 835-4105

(G-2515)
US DEPT OF THE AIR FORCE
Also Called: National Reconnaissance Office
14675 Lee Rd (20151-1708)
PHONE.....................703 808-0492
Keith Hall, *Director*
EMP: 1 **Publicly Held**
WEB: www.af.mil
SIC: 3663 3699 9711 Satellites, commu-
nications; security devices; Air Force
HQ: United States Department Of The Air
Force
1000 Air Force Pentagon
Washington DC 20330

(G-2516)
VIRGINIA WELDING LLC
13632 Ellendale Dr (20151-2733)
PHONE.....................703 263-1964
EMP: 1
SALES (est): 25K **Privately Held**
SIC: 7692 Welding repair

(G-2517)
VIRTUAL NETCOM LLC
14801 Murdock St Ste 155 (20151-1043)
PHONE.....................571 445-0306
Mohan Tammisetti, *CEO*
EMP: 2
SALES (est): 102.9K **Privately Held**
SIC: 3663 Airborne radio communications
equipment

(G-2518)
WASHINGTON CABINETRY
4124 Walney Rd (20151-2937)
PHONE.....................703 466-5388
EMP: 3 EST: 2012
SALES (est): 148.5K **Privately Held**
WEB: www.wcabinet.com
SIC: 2434 Wood kitchen cabinets

(G-2519)
**WASHINGTON WDWRKRS
GUILD OF NA**
13893 Walney Park Dr (20151-2321)
PHONE.....................703 222-3460
Fred Grosse, *Administration*
EMP: 2
SALES (est): 131.3K **Privately Held**
SIC: 2431 Millwork

(G-2520)
WATERNEER USA INC
4451 Brkfld Crprt Dr (20151-1693)
PHONE.....................703 655-2279
Santanu Sengupta, *Office Mgr*
EMP: 2
SALES (est): 99.4K **Privately Held**
WEB: www.waterneerusa.com
SIC: 2032 Bean sprouts: packaged in
cans, jars, etc.

(G-2521)
WEATHERTITE INDUSTRIES INC
13410 Sand Rock Ct (20151-2472)
PHONE.....................703 830-8001
Jeffrey D Stewart, *President*
EMP: 3
SQ FT: 500
SALES (est): 364.6K **Privately Held**
SIC: 2899 Waterproofing compounds

(G-2522)
**WESTLAND TECHNOLOGIES
INC**
4501 Singer Ct Rm 220-47 (20151-1733)
PHONE.....................703 477-9847
John Grizzard, *President*
EMP: 61
SALES (est): 2.7MM **Privately Held**
SIC: 2822 Synthetic rubber

(G-2523)
Z & M SHEET METAL INC (PA)
Also Called: Zm Sheet Metal
3931 Avion Park Ct C102 (20151-3983)
PHONE.....................703 631-9600
Scott Zivic, *President*
Barbara Venish, *Corp Secy*

Sandy James, *Manager*
Joseph Zivic, *Shareholder*
EMP: 20
SALES (est): 9.9MM **Privately Held**
WEB: www.zmsheetmetal.com
SIC: 3444 Sheet metalwork

Chantilly
Loudoun County

(G-2524)
3 DONUTS PUBLISHING LLC
43868 Paramount Pl (20152-5710)
PHONE.....................703 542-7941
David Mack, *Principal*
EMP: 1
SALES (est): 37.5K **Privately Held**
SIC: 2741 Miscellaneous publishing

(G-2525)
ANRA TECHNOLOGIES INC
Also Called: Anra Aviation
25050 Riding Plz (20152-5925)
PHONE.....................703 239-3206
Amit Ganjoo, *CEO*
Rohini Ganjoo, *President*
EMP: 30
SALES (est): 129.1K **Privately Held**
WEB: www.anratechnologies.com
SIC: 3812 7371 Aircraft/aerospace flight
instruments & guidance systems; soft-
ware programming applications

(G-2526)
BALLY TECHNOLOGIES INC
24847 Myers Glen Pl (20152-4505)
PHONE.....................917 415-5649
Balbinder Singh, *Administration*
EMP: 2
SALES (est): 132.4K **Privately Held**
SIC: 3999 Manufacturing industries

(G-2527)
**BRAVATEK SOLUTIONS INC
(PA)**
42757 Cedar Ridge Blvd (20152-6370)
PHONE.....................866 490-8590
Thomas Cellucci, *CEO*
Ian Treleaven, *Vice Pres*
Debbie King, *CFO*
EMP: 1
SALES: 26.8K **Publicly Held**
WEB: www.bravatek.com
SIC: 7372 Prepackaged software

(G-2528)
**CAPITAL SOFTWARE
CORPORATION**
25669 Pleasant Woods Ct (20152-5734)
PHONE.....................703 404-3000
Dean Leonard, *President*
EMP: 4
SQ FT: 2,100
SALES (est): 374.7K **Privately Held**
WEB: www.capitalsoftware.com
SIC: 7372 7379 Application computer soft-
ware; computer related consulting serv-
ices

(G-2529)
**COMMUNICATIONS VEHICLE
SVC LLC**
Also Called: Allmetal Manufacturing
25395 Pleasant Valley Rd (20152-1402)
PHONE.....................703 542-7449
Sheila White, *Agent*
Michael Singhas,
Gary Stone,
EMP: 4
SALES (est): 602.9K **Privately Held**
WEB: www.allmetalman.com
SIC: 3663 Radio & TV communications
equipment

(G-2530)
**CONCRETE PRECAST SYSTEMS
INC**
44146 Wade Dr (20152-1347)
PHONE.....................703 327-4112
Paul Ogorchock, *President*
Mel Howard, *Vice Pres*
EMP: 24 **Privately Held**
WEB: www.cpsprecast.com

SIC: 3273 Ready-mixed concrete
PA: Concrete Precast Systems, Inc.
1316 Yacht Dr
Chesapeake VA 23320

(G-2531)
DELUXE KITCHEN AND BATH
42713 Latrobe St (20152-3947)
PHONE.....................571 594-6363
EMP: 2
SALES (est): 73.1K **Privately Held**
SIC: 2782 Blankbooks And Looseleaf
Binders, Nsk

(G-2532)
E L SCHNEIDER
42727 Iron Bit Pl (20152-6365)
PHONE.....................703 855-1925
E Schneider, *Owner*
EMP: 1
SALES (est): 80.2K **Privately Held**
WEB: www.se.com
SIC: 3699 Electrical equipment & supplies

(G-2533)
EPICIDENTITY INC
24941 Castleton Dr (20152-4381)
PHONE.....................833 723-3437
Michael Friedman, *Asst Director*
EMP: 10
SALES (est): 221.8K **Privately Held**
SIC: 7372 Prepackaged software

(G-2534)
ERP SOFTWARE SERVICES INC
25878 Rawley Springs Dr (20152-5767)
PHONE.....................703 957-3073
Sudarshan Gujjari, *Principal*
EMP: 3
SALES (est): 178.1K **Privately Held**
SIC: 7372 Prepackaged software

(G-2535)
HANDYMAN CONCRETE INC
25232 Willard Rd (20152-1354)
PHONE.....................703 437-7143
Mark Elliot, *President*
EMP: 25 EST: 1971
SALES (est): 3MM **Privately Held**
WEB: www.handymanconcrete.com
SIC: 3273 5211 1771 Ready-mixed con-
crete; masonry materials & supplies; con-
crete work

(G-2536)
HB WOODWORKS
25921 Kimberly Rose Dr (20152-3457)
PHONE.....................703 209-4639
Michael Hardin, *Principal*
EMP: 2
SALES (est): 72K **Privately Held**
SIC: 2431 Millwork

(G-2537)
HUMAN ELEMENTS LLC
25071 Kingscote Ct (20152-4376)
PHONE.....................703 542-7701
Christopher A Kennedy, *Principal*
EMP: 3
SALES (est): 147.1K **Privately Held**
SIC: 2819 Industrial inorganic chemicals

(G-2538)
ICONIX INDUSTRIES INC
43567 Mink Meadows St (20152-3609)
PHONE.....................703 489-0278
Alex Cho, *Principal*
EMP: 3
SALES (est): 114.3K **Privately Held**
SIC: 3999 Manufacturing industries

(G-2539)
K C G INC
Also Called: Rew Materials Spotsylvania Co
25793 Phar Lap Ct (20152-6322)
PHONE.....................703 542-7120
Glumsic Jr Fred, *President*
EMP: 1
SALES (est): 96.5K **Privately Held**
SIC: 2851 Paints & allied products

(G-2540)
KOIT SHEET METAL INC
25446 Stallion Branch Ter (20152-5809)
PHONE.....................703 625-3981
Eun Ko, *Principal*

EMP: 3
SALES (est): 416K **Privately Held**
SIC: 3444 Sheet metalwork

(G-2541)
**LANE CONSTRUCTION
CORPORATION**
Virginia Paving Company
25094 Tanner Ln (20152-1306)
PHONE.....................703 471-6883
Rob McKeever, *Branch Mgr*
EMP: 10
SALES (corp-wide): 2.8B **Privately Held**
WEB: www.laneconstruct.com
SIC: 2951 1611 Asphalt paving mixtures &
blocks; surfacing & paving
HQ: The Lane Construction Corporation
90 Fieldstone Ct
Cheshire CT 06410
203 235-3351

(G-2542)
LEGACY VULCAN LLC
25086 Tanner Ln (20152-1306)
PHONE.....................800 732-3964
EMP: 4 **Publicly Held**
WEB: www.vulcanmaterials.com
SIC: 3273 Ready-mixed concrete
HQ: Legacy Vulcan, Llc
1200 Urban Center Dr
Vestavia AL 35242
205 298-3000

(G-2543)
LIGHTHOUSE SOFTWARE INC
43643 Mink Meadows St (20152-3625)
PHONE.....................703 327-7650
Charles Galpin, *Principal*
EMP: 5
SALES (est): 343.3K **Privately Held**
WEB: www.lighthouse-software.com
SIC: 7372 Application computer software

(G-2544)
LOUDOUN COMPOSTING
44150 Wade Dr (20152-1347)
P.O. Box 221975 (20153-1975)
PHONE.....................703 327-8428
Tim Hutchinson, *Director*
EMP: 12
SALES (est): 2.5MM **Privately Held**
WEB: www.loudouncomposting.com
SIC: 2879 Soil conditioners

(G-2545)
MISSIONTEQ LLC
25834 Kirkwood Sq (20152-2085)
PHONE.....................703 563-0699
Howard Chapman,
David Bentley,
EMP: 4
SALES (est): 291.8K **Privately Held**
WEB: www.missionteq.com
SIC: 3663 7373 7372 Light communica-
tions equipment; computer systems
analysis & design; turnkey vendors, com-
puter systems; systems engineering,
computer related; application computer
software

(G-2546)
**MONKEY PUZZLE
PRODUCTIONS LLC**
43546 Mink Meadows St (20152-3611)
PHONE.....................703 919-0182
Debra Latiolais, *Principal*
▲ EMP: 2 EST: 2011
SALES (est): 90.9K **Privately Held**
SIC: 3944 Puzzles

(G-2547)
MOSAIC DISTRIBUTION LLC
43203 Maple Cross St (20152-5347)
PHONE.....................978 328-7001
Elizabeth Carter,
Liz Carter,
◆ EMP: 1
SALES (est): 76K **Privately Held**
WEB: www.mosaicdist.com
SIC: 3844 X-ray apparatus & tubes

(G-2548)
ORTHOINSIGHT LLC
25151 Fortitude Ter (20152-6051)
PHONE.....................703 722-2553

G E O G R A P H I C

Michael Felmet, *Manager*
EMP: 2
SALES (est): 50K **Privately Held**
SIC: 3482 Small arms ammunition

(G-2549)
PATRIOT SOLUTIONS GROUP LLC
24890 Castleton Dr (20152-4388)
PHONE......................571 367-4979
Kenneth Herbert,
EMP: 3 **EST:** 2012
SALES (est): 281.8K **Privately Held**
WEB: www.patriotsolutionsgroupllc.com
SIC: 3451 Screw machine products

(G-2550)
PI SQUARE TECHNOLOGIES INC
25993 Fair Ponds Ln (20152-3430)
PHONE......................571 255-6253
Anil D Paranganat, *Director*
EMP: 2
SALES (est): 121K **Privately Held**
SIC: 7372 Application computer software

(G-2551)
PIVIT
Also Called: Pivit Software Solutions
24910 Earlsford Dr (20152-4386)
PHONE......................301 395-0895
Andre Williams, *Partner*
Ricky Mason, *Partner*
EMP: 2
SALES (est): 101.3K **Privately Held**
SIC: 7372 7389 7371 Application computer software; ; custom computer programming services

(G-2552)
PRAMAAN INC
42357 Astors Beachwood Ct (20152-4377)
PHONE......................703 327-6750
Praveen Chinnam, *President*
EMP: 5 **EST:** 2014
SALES (est): 156K **Privately Held**
SIC: 7372 Prepackaged software

(G-2553)
RAMATECH LLC
26044 Pembrooke Cir (20152-3676)
PHONE......................240 449-7435
Dejan Kocic, *Principal*
EMP: 3 **EST:** 2011
SALES (est): 292.2K **Privately Held**
SIC: 3451 Screw machine products

(G-2554)
REGER RESEARCH
25532 Cunard Aly (20152-4488)
P.O. Box 225, The Plains (20198-0225)
PHONE......................703 328-6465
Alan Reger, *Owner*
EMP: 1
SALES (est): 100K **Privately Held**
WEB: www.reger-research.com
SIC: 7372 Prepackaged software

(G-2555)
SCIECOM LLC
43692 Gladehill Ct (20152-5731)
PHONE......................703 994-2635
Sung Woo, *Principal*
EMP: 3
SALES (est): 192.7K **Privately Held**
SIC: 3826 Analytical instruments

(G-2556)
SILENCE IN METROPOLIS LLC
43624 White Cap Ter (20152-5801)
PHONE......................571 213-4383
Bilal Arshad, *Mng Member*
EMP: 2 **EST:** 2012
SALES (est): 6K **Privately Held**
WEB: www.silenceinmetropolis.com
SIC: 2782 Record albums

(G-2557)
STEEL MOUSE TRAP PUBLICATIONS
43579 Mink Meadows St (20152-3609)
PHONE......................703 542-2327
Richard Tornello, *Principal*
EMP: 2 **EST:** 2009
SALES (est): 113.2K **Privately Held**
SIC: 2741 Miscellaneous publishing

(G-2558)
SUPERIOR CONCRETE MATERIALS
44146 Wade Dr (20152-1347)
PHONE......................703 327-4112
Bert Richardson, *Manager*
EMP: 3
SALES (est): 266K **Privately Held**
WEB: www.superior-concretematerials.com
SIC: 3273 Ready-mixed concrete

(G-2559)
TAGSTRINGCOM INC
25134 Deerhurst Ter (20152-6099)
PHONE......................954 557-8645
Daniel Rubens, *CEO*
Janine Rubens, *President*
EMP: 2
SALES (est): 168.5K **Privately Held**
WEB: www.tagstring.com
SIC: 2284 Thread mills

(G-2560)
TEKADVENTURE LLC (PA)
25050 Riding Plz (20152-5925)
PHONE......................646 580-2511
Laxit Gajjar,
EMP: 1 **EST:** 2014
SALES (est): 83.1K **Privately Held**
WEB: www.tekadventure.com
SIC: 7372 Business oriented computer software

(G-2561)
TRANSCEDENT INTEGRATION
43053 Pemberton Sq # 120 (20152-6306)
PHONE......................703 880-3019
EMP: 4
SALES: 75K **Privately Held**
SIC: 3651 Mfg Home Audio/Video Equipment

(G-2562)
VARTENDER LLC
43316 Cedar Pond Pl (20152-1965)
PHONE......................703 376-7751
Austin West, *Mng Member*
EMP: 2
SALES (est): 56.5K **Privately Held**
SIC: 7372 Application computer software

(G-2563)
VISION SOFTWARE TECHNOLOGIES
25958 Mccoy Ct (20152-1962)
PHONE......................703 722-4480
Eswara Gatamaneni, *Principal*
EMP: 2
SALES (est): 167.6K **Privately Held**
SIC: 7372 Prepackaged software

(G-2564)
VITARA LLC (PA)
43771 Brownburg Pl (20152-5753)
PHONE......................972 200-3680
Srinivas Parapapa,
EMP: 3
SALES (est): 300K **Privately Held**
WEB: www.vitaracharts.com
SIC: 7372 Application computer software

(G-2565)
VTECH SOLUTION INC
42730 Freedom St (20152-3941)
PHONE......................571 257-0913
EMP: 18
SALES (corp-wide): 8.5MM **Privately Held**
WEB: www.vtechsolution.com
SIC: 3825 Network analyzers
PA: Vtech Solution Inc.
     1100 H St Nw Ste 750
     Washington DC 20005
     202 644-9774

(G-2566)
WALKERS COVE PUBLISHING LLC
24890 Castleton Dr (20152-4388)
PHONE......................703 957-4052
Jean McCaw, *Principal*
EMP: 2
SALES (est): 82.2K **Privately Held**
SIC: 2741 Miscellaneous publishing

(G-2567)
WALLYE LLC
43577 Mckay Ter (20152-5790)
PHONE......................631 320-8868
Dian Zhu,
Shan Zhao,
EMP: 3
SALES (est): 50K **Privately Held**
SIC: 3663 Mobile communication equipment

Charles City
Charles City County

(G-2568)
ADVANCED CUSTOM WOODWORKI
609 Roxbury Indus Ctr (23030-2319)
PHONE......................804 310-0511
Steve Sirles, *Principal*
EMP: 3
SALES (est): 235K **Privately Held**
SIC: 2499 Decorative wood & woodwork

(G-2569)
AGGREGATE INDUSTRIES-WCR INC
7420 Two Mile Trl (23030-2648)
PHONE......................804 829-9783
Ernie West, *Branch Mgr*
EMP: 6
SALES (corp-wide): 1.7B **Privately Held**
WEB: www.lafargeholcim.us
SIC: 3273 Ready-mixed concrete
HQ: Aggregate Industries-Wcr, Inc.
     1687 Cole Blvd Ste 300
     Lakewood CO 80401
     303 985-1070

(G-2570)
BOBBY COLLINS LOGGING
9601 Little Elam Rd (23030-3183)
P.O. Box 457, Providence Forge (23140-0457)
PHONE......................804 519-0138
Bobby Collins, *Principal*
EMP: 3 **EST:** 2017
SALES (est): 140.9K **Privately Held**
SIC: 2411 Logging

(G-2571)
CAJO INDUSTRIES INC
21642 Old Neck Rd (23030-4129)
PHONE......................804 829-6854
Jon F Sauer, *Principal*
EMP: 2
SALES (est): 121.4K **Privately Held**
SIC: 3999 Manufacturing industries

(G-2572)
CHARLES CITY TIMBER AND MAT
5900 Chambers Rd (23030-2307)
PHONE......................804 829-5850
EMP: 3 **Privately Held**
WEB: www.cctimberandmat.com
SIC: 2273 Carpets & rugs
PA: Charles City Timber And Mat, Inc
     2221 Barnetts Rd
     Providence Forge VA 23140

(G-2573)
CHESAPEAKE STRL SYSTEMS INC
2401 Roxbury Rd (23030-2302)
PHONE......................804 966-8340
Russell Airington, *President*
Ricky Dyson, *Vice Pres*
EMP: 30 **EST:** 1997
SQ FT: 18,000
SALES (est): 4.5MM **Privately Held**
WEB: www.chestruc.com
SIC: 2439 5032 Trusses, wooden roof; brick, stone & related material

(G-2574)
CREWE BROTHERS LOGGING
8821 Stagg Run Rd (23030-4428)
PHONE......................804 829-2288
Calvin Crew, *Principal*
EMP: 2 **EST:** 2001

SALES (est): 140.4K **Privately Held**
SIC: 2411 Logging camps & contractors

(G-2575)
GAVIAL ENGINEERING AND MFG
7000 Westover Rd (23030-3329)
PHONE......................804 627-1437
EMP: 1
SALES (est): 39.6K **Privately Held**
SIC: 3999 Manufacturing industries

(G-2576)
GREENROCK MATERIALS LLC
2271 Roxbury Rd (23030-2320)
P.O. Box 810, Quinton (23141-0810)
PHONE......................804 966-8601
Michael Lamb, *President*
Lee Lamb, *Associate*
EMP: 60
SALES (est): 7.9MM **Privately Held**
WEB: www.greenrock.net
SIC: 3273 Ready-mixed concrete

(G-2577)
J AND E MACHINE SHOP INC
106 Rxbury Indus Ctr Ste (23030-2311)
PHONE......................804 966-7180
Elizabeth L Berry, *President*
Richard J Fortney, *Assistant VP*
James D Berry, *Vice Pres*
Angela Fortney, *Admin Sec*
EMP: 5
SQ FT: 6,000
SALES (est): 200K **Privately Held**
SIC: 3599 Machine shop, jobbing & repair

(G-2578)
JOHNSON JAMES THOMAS LOGGING
2421 C C Rd (23030-2151)
PHONE......................804 966-1552
James T Johnson, *Owner*
EMP: 6
SALES (est): 412.5K **Privately Held**
SIC: 2411 Logging camps & contractors

(G-2579)
POLYCRETEUSA LLC
10601 Shady Ln (23030-2849)
PHONE......................804 901-6893
Bruce Anderson, *President*
EMP: 2
SALES (est): 950K **Privately Held**
SIC: 3086 Plastics foam products

(G-2580)
UNIVERSAL MARINE LIFT INC
6160 North Bluffs Ct (23030-2250)
PHONE......................804 829-5838
Robert E Franklin, *President*
Phillip L Hill, *Vice Pres*
Karen Franklin, *Admin Sec*
EMP: 3
SQ FT: 4,000
SALES (est): 413.8K **Privately Held**
WEB: www.umlc.com
SIC: 3536 Boat lifts

(G-2581)
UPPER SHIRLEY VINEYARDS
600 Shirley Plantation Rd (23030-2920)
PHONE......................804 829-9463
Tayloe Dameron, *Owner*
Kaitlin Everett, *General Mgr*
Catherine Cristman, *Director*
Alyssa Evans, *Asst Director*
EMP: 35
SALES (est): 3MM **Privately Held**
WEB: www.uppershirley.com
SIC: 2084 Wines

Charlotte C H
Charlotte County

(G-2582)
BROWNS SAWMILL INC
445 Sawmill Rd (23923-3517)
PHONE......................434 542-5776
EMP: 2
SALES (est): 125K **Privately Held**
SIC: 2421 Sawmills & planing mills, general

▲ = Import ▼=Export
◆ =Import/Export

(G-2583)
CHARLOTTE COUNTY SCHOOL BOARD
Also Called: Statesman Computers
200 Evergreen Rd (23923-3711)
PHONE.....................................434 542-4933
Robyn Cristo, *Manager*
EMP: 32
SALES (corp-wide): 174.9MM **Privately Held**
WEB: www.ccpsk12.org
SIC: 3577 Computer peripheral equipment
PA: Charlotte County School Board
250 Legrande Ave Ste E
Charlotte C H VA 23923
434 542-5151

(G-2584)
THEOS SHOTGUN CORNER
8970 Thomas Jefferson Hwy (23923-3009)
PHONE.....................................434 248-6250
Theodore F Lyropoulos, *Principal*
EMP: 2
SALES (est): 128.2K **Privately Held**
SIC: 3489 Guns, howitzers, mortars & related equipment

Charlottesville
Albemarle County

(G-2585)
8020 SOFTWARE LLC
1015 Glenwood Station Ln (22901-5712)
PHONE.....................................434 466-8020
Sean M Horgan, *Administration*
EMP: 2 EST: 2012
SALES (est): 93K **Privately Held**
WEB: www.8020engineering.com
SIC: 7372 Prepackaged software

(G-2586)
ADIAL PHARMACEUTICALS INC
1001 Res Pk Blvd Ste 100 (22911)
PHONE.....................................434 422-9800
William B Stilley III, *President*
Kevin Schuyler, *Vice Chairman*
Joseph Truluck, *COO*
Bankole A Johnson, *Chief Mktg Ofcr*
Robertson Gilliland, *Bd of Directors*
EMP: 6 EST: 2010
SQ FT: 250
SALES (est): 511.9K **Privately Held**
WEB: www.adialpharma.com
SIC: 2834 Pharmaceutical preparations

(G-2587)
AIRBASE THERAPEUTICS
1167 Raintree Dr (22901-0905)
PHONE.....................................434 825-0074
John F Hunt,
EMP: 3
SALES (est): 216.8K **Privately Held**
SIC: 2834 Pharmaceutical preparations

(G-2588)
ANGEROLE MOUNTS LLC
100 Aviation Dr Ste 116 (22911-9016)
PHONE.....................................434 249-3977
Henry Ayres, *Principal*
EMP: 2
SALES (est): 161.8K **Privately Held**
WEB: www.angerole.com
SIC: 3663

(G-2589)
APPLIED VIDEO IMAGING LLC
355 Rio Road West Ste 101 (22901-1360)
PHONE.....................................434 974-6310
Patrick Asplin, *Principal*
Bruce Carriker,
EMP: 4 EST: 2012
SALES (est): 429.6K **Privately Held**
WEB: www.appliedvi.com
SIC: 3812 Search & detection systems & instruments

(G-2590)
ARCHIPELAGO PUBLISHERS INC
925 Marshall St (22901-3928)
PHONE.....................................434 979-5292
Katherine McNamara, *President*
EMP: 2

SALES (est): 105.4K **Privately Held**
SIC: 2741 Miscellaneous publishing

(G-2591)
ATLANTIC COMPUTING LLC
1155 Inglecress Dr (22901-8874)
PHONE.....................................434 293-2022
Jennifer Workman,
EMP: 4
SQ FT: 1,350
SALES (est): 338.1K **Privately Held**
SIC: 3577 Printers, computer

(G-2592)
BAGELADIES LLC
732 Merion Greene (22901-3176)
PHONE.....................................540 248-0908
Janet Dob, *Administration*
EMP: 4
SALES (est): 246.4K **Privately Held**
WEB: www.bageladies.com
SIC: 2051 Bagels, fresh or frozen

(G-2593)
BEHEALTH SOLUTIONS LLC
1165 Tennis Rd (22901-5032)
PHONE.....................................434 422-9090
Lee Ritterband, *Vice Pres*
Gail Billingsley, *Project Mgr*
Alan Lattimore, *Sr Software Eng*
Frances Thorndike, *Officer*
Joseph Jennings,
EMP: 6 EST: 2010
SALES (est): 449.8K **Privately Held**
WEB: www.behealthsolutions.com
SIC: 7372 Prepackaged software

(G-2594)
BETTER LIVING INC
2553 Proffit Rd (22911-5702)
PHONE.....................................434 978-1666
Richard Nunley, *Branch Mgr*
EMP: 70
SALES (corp-wide): 27.3MM **Privately Held**
WEB: www.betterlivingvirginia.com
SIC: 2431 Millwork
PA: Better Living, Inc.
2070 Seminole Trl
Charlottesville VA 22901
434 973-4333

(G-2595)
BETTER LIVING COMPONENTS INC
2553 Proffit Rd (22911-5702)
P.O. Box 7723 (22906-7723)
PHONE.....................................434 978-1666
John G Nunley, *President*
Richard L Nunley, *Vice Pres*
Judy Pitts, *Asst Controller*
April Northcutt, *Manager*
Jim Smith, *Manager*
EMP: 55
SQ FT: 5,000
SALES (est): 7MM **Privately Held**
WEB: www.betterlivingcomponents.com
SIC: 2439 Trusses, wooden roof

(G-2596)
BIOMIC SCIENCES LLC
4351 Seminole Trl (22911-8225)
P.O. Box 4574 (22905-4574)
PHONE.....................................434 260-8530
Zachary Bush MD,
Kristen Krop,
EMP: 8
SQ FT: 5,000
SALES (est): 5MM **Privately Held**
WEB: www.shop.restore4life.com
SIC: 2023 Condensed, concentrated & evaporated milk products

(G-2597)
BLACKWOLF SOFTWARE
4300 Sylvan Ln (22911-9067)
PHONE.....................................434 978-4903
Paul Dean, *Principal*
EMP: 2
SALES (est): 75.6K **Privately Held**
SIC: 7372 Prepackaged software

(G-2598)
BONUMOSE BIOCHEM LLC
1725 Discovery Dr 220 (22911-5846)
PHONE.....................................276 206-7337

Edwin Rogers, *CEO*
Ed Rogers, *CEO*
EMP: 2
SALES (est): 67.8K **Privately Held**
WEB: www.bonumose.com
SIC: 2099 Sugar

(G-2599)
BONUMOSE LLC
1725 Discovery Dr Ste 220 (22911-5846)
PHONE.....................................276 206-7337
Edwin Rogers, *Mng Member*
Daniel Wichelecki,
EMP: 7
SALES (est): 677K **Privately Held**
WEB: www.bonumose.com
SIC: 2099 Sugar powdered from purchased ingredients

(G-2600)
BRACELETS BY G JAFFE INC
3015 Colonial Dr (22911-9109)
PHONE.....................................434 409-3500
George Jaffe, *Principal*
EMP: 2
SALES (est): 106.8K **Privately Held**
SIC: 3961 Bracelets, except precious metal

(G-2601)
BUILDERS FIRSTSOURCE INC
4257 Seminole Trl (22911-8214)
PHONE.....................................434 964-1192
EMP: 1 **Publicly Held**
WEB: www.bldr.com
SIC: 2431 Millwork
PA: Builders Firstsource, Inc.
2001 Bryan St Ste 1600
Dallas TX 75201
214 880-3500

(G-2602)
CAMELOT
4285 Seminole Trl (22911)
PHONE.....................................434 978-1049
Ralph Bridgewater, *Manager*
EMP: 2
SALES (est): 79.9K **Privately Held**
SIC: 3589 Service industry machinery

(G-2603)
CARDEN JENNINGS PUBLISHING CO
Also Called: Charlottesville Guide
375 Greenbrier Dr Ste 100 (22901-1600)
PHONE.....................................434 817-2000
William T Carden Jr, *President*
Alison S Dickie, *Publisher*
Davidb Ern, *Publisher*
Joseph Jennings, *Exec VP*
Marcus Weathersby, *Vice Pres*
EMP: 25
SQ FT: 9,000
SALES (est): 2.9MM **Privately Held**
WEB: www.cjp.com
SIC: 2721 2741 Magazines: publishing only, not printed on site; telephone & other directory publishing

(G-2604)
CARETAKER MEDICAL LLC
941 Glenwood Station Ln # 301 (22901-5719)
PHONE.....................................434 978-7000
Jeff Pompeo, *CEO*
Todd Hochrein, *CFO*
Tim McGough, *VP Sales*
Jackson Gibbs, *Marketing Staff*
EMP: 4
SQ FT: 4,000
SALES (est): 504.3K **Privately Held**
WEB: www.caretakermedical.net
SIC: 3841 8731 Blood pressure apparatus; medical research, commercial

(G-2605)
CARLISLE INDSTRL BRKE & FRCTN
4040 Lewis And Clark Dr (22911-5840)
PHONE.....................................814 486-1119
Michale Brammer, *Principal*
▼ EMP: 12 EST: 1987
SALES (est): 1.4MM **Privately Held**
SIC: 3714 5013 Motor vehicle brake systems & parts; automotive brakes

(G-2606)
CHAMPION PUBLISHING INC
516 Brookway Dr (22901-3711)
PHONE.....................................434 817-7222
Sean Castrina, *Principal*
EMP: 4 EST: 2011
SALES (est): 251.3K **Privately Held**
SIC: 2741 Miscellaneous publishing

(G-2607)
CHARLOTTESVILLE FLIGHT CENTER
200 Aviation Dr Ste 140 (22911-9028)
PHONE.....................................434 964-1474
EMP: 2
SALES (est): 94.6K **Privately Held**
WEB: www.flycfc.net
SIC: 3728 Aircraft parts & equipment

(G-2608)
CHEMRING SENSORS AND ELECTR
Also Called: Cses Niitek Production Fcilty
4010 Hunterstand Ct (22911-5830)
PHONE.....................................434 964-4800
Leslie Hardy, *Branch Mgr*
EMP: 12
SALES (corp-wide): 414.1MM **Privately Held**
WEB: www.chemring.co.uk
SIC: 3812 Infrared object detection equipment
HQ: Chemring Sensors And Electronic Systems, Inc.
23031 Ladbrook Dr
Dulles VA 20166

(G-2609)
CLARIVATE ANALYTICS (US) LLC
375 Greenbrier Dr Ste 200 (22901-1600)
PHONE.....................................434 817-2000
Alison Visokay, *Project Mgr*
Kitty King, *Opers Staff*
Christine Romness, *Program Mgr*
Marie Otis, *Manager*
Patrick Dougherty, *Manager*
EMP: 80 **Publicly Held**
WEB: www.clarivate.com
SIC: 7372 Application computer software
HQ: Clarivate Analytics (Us) Llc
1500 Spring Garden St # 400
Philadelphia PA 19130
215 386-0100

(G-2610)
COMMONWLTH H20 SVCS INC-BLUE R
Also Called: Common Health H2o-Blue Ridge
325 Greenbrier Dr (22901-1618)
PHONE.....................................434 975-4426
Linda H Schroeder, *President*
Jon Davis, *Vice Pres*
Raymond Zedekar, *Vice Pres*
EMP: 11
SQ FT: 1,800
SALES (est): 1.2MM **Privately Held**
WEB: www.kinetico.com
SIC: 3589 Water filters & softeners, household type; water purification equipment, household type; water treatment equipment, industrial

(G-2611)
CONTRAVAC INC
1000 Research Park Blvd # 103 (22911-5842)
PHONE.....................................434 984-9723
EMP: 2
SALES (est): 74.4K **Privately Held**
SIC: 2835 In vivo diagnostics

(G-2612)
CROWN MOTORCAR COMPANY LLC
Also Called: BMW
1295 Richmond Rd (22911-3521)
PHONE.....................................434 979-7222
Jerry Davey, *Parts Mgr*
Brett Denver, *Mng Member*
Patricia Yurcaba, *Manager*
EMP: 30

GEOGRAPHIC

SALES (est): 403.3K **Publicly Held**
WEB: www.bmwcharlottesville.com
SIC: 3743 Railway motor cars
PA: Asbury Automotive Group, Inc.
2905 Premiere Pkwy # 300
Duluth GA 30097
770 418-8200

(G-2613)
CUSTOMINK LLC
1180 Seminole Trl (22901-5713)
PHONE..............................434 326-1051
Patrick Knaus, *Production*
Donald Thurns, *Manager*
EMP: 150 **Privately Held**
WEB: www.customink.com
SIC: 2759 5699 Screen printing; cus-
tomized clothing & apparel
PA: Customink, Llc
2910 District Ave
Fairfax VA 22031

(G-2614)
CYRIL EDWARD GROPEN
Also Called: Paragon Defense Industries
1020 Locust Ave (22901-4032)
PHONE..............................434 227-9039
Cyril Gropen, *Principal*
EMP: 2 EST: 2011
SALES (est): 102.2K **Privately Held**
SIC: 3999 Manufacturing industries

(G-2615)
DECADE FIVE LLC
400 Ivy Farm Dr (22901-8841)
PHONE..............................434 984-3065
Mary Welby Von Thelen, *CEO*
Steve Hobeck, *COO*
EMP: 3
SALES (est): 134.8K **Privately Held**
SIC: 7372 Application computer software

(G-2616)
**DELAWARE VALLEY
COMMUNICATIONS**
1716 Browns Gap Tpke (22901-6312)
PHONE..............................434 823-2282
Jane R Townsend, *President*
EMP: 1
SALES (est): 93.5K **Privately Held**
WEB: www.tdameritrade.com
SIC: 3441 Tower sections, radio & televi-
sion transmission

(G-2617)
DG OPTICS LLC
2330 Walnut Ridge Ln (22911-2200)
PHONE..............................434 227-1017
David Angeley, *Administration*
EMP: 3 EST: 2013
SALES (est): 208.1K **Privately Held**
WEB: www.dg-optics.com
SIC: 3827 Optical instruments & lenses

(G-2618)
**DIRECTED VAPOR TECH INTL
INC**
Also Called: Dvti
4006 Hunterstand Ct # 101 (22911-5847)
PHONE..............................434 977-1405
Harry A Burns III, *President*
Matthew Terry, *General Mgr*
Derek Hass, *Vice Pres*
EMP: 11 EST: 2000
SALES (est): 2.1MM **Privately Held**
WEB: www.directedvapor.com
SIC: 2812 8731 Alkalies & chlorine; com-
mercial physical research

(G-2619)
DOMINION MICROPROBES INC
Also Called: Dmprobes
1027 Stonewood Dr (22911-5771)
PHONE..............................434 962-8221
Nicolas Barker, *CEO*
Robert Weikle, *Principal*
Arthur Lichtenberger, *COO*
Bobby Weikle, *CIO*
EMP: 3
SALES (est): 281.8K **Privately Held**
WEB: www.dmprobes.com
SIC: 3679 Microwave components

(G-2620)
DUCARD VINEYARDS INC
1885 Kernwood Pl (22911-8320)
PHONE..............................434 409-4378
Scott Elliff, *President*
Marty Mitchell, *Director*
EMP: 1
SALES (est): 143.1K **Privately Held**
WEB: www.ducardvineyards.com
SIC: 2084 Wines

(G-2621)
**EARTH COMMUNICATIONS
CORP**
2370 Proffit Rd (22911-5753)
PHONE..............................434 973-7277
T W Graver, *President*
EMP: 3
SALES (est): 204.7K **Privately Held**
WEB: www.earthcomvideo.com
SIC: 3695 Video recording tape, blank

(G-2622)
ELAN PUBLISHING INC
3172 Autumn Woods Dr (22911-7213)
PHONE..............................434 973-1828
Matti Majorin, *Principal*
EMP: 2
SALES (est): 147.6K **Privately Held**
WEB: www.elanpublishing.com
SIC: 2741 Miscellaneous publishing

(G-2623)
ELECTRO-KINETICS INC
4942 Mahonia Dr (22911-9079)
PHONE..............................845 887-4930
Eric Andkjar, *President*
EMP: 13
SQ FT: 8,000
SALES (est): 2.6MM **Privately Held**
WEB: www.electrokinetics.design
SIC: 3625 Motor controls & accessories

(G-2624)
EMAX OIL COMPANY (PA)
1410 Incarnation Dr 205b (22901-5708)
P.O. Box 7844 (22906-7844)
PHONE..............................434 295-4111
James F Scott, *President*
EMP: 5
SQ FT: 3,000
SALES (est): 952.6K **Privately Held**
SIC: 1311 Crude petroleum production;
natural gas production

(G-2625)
ENCELL TECH
1412 Sachem Pl (22901-2499)
PHONE..............................434 202-8370
Alan Seidel, *Engineer*
Joseph Seidel, *Technician*
EMP: 2
SALES (est): 122.7K **Privately Held**
WEB: www.encell.com
SIC: 3691 Storage batteries

(G-2626)
ERIC WASHINGTON
Also Called: Washington & Washington
1416 Decatur Dr (22911-7499)
PHONE..............................434 249-3567
Eric Washington, *Owner*
EMP: 6
SALES (est): 473.5K **Privately Held**
SIC: 3523 7389 Grounds mowing equip-
ment;

(G-2627)
ERNIES BEEF JERKY
4696 Three Notch D Rd (22901-6362)
PHONE..............................540 460-4341
Ernie Almanza, *Principal*
EMP: 2
SALES (est): 62.3K **Privately Held**
SIC: 2013 Snack sticks, including jerky:
from purchased meat

(G-2628)
ESTER YILDIZ LLC
Also Called: Quickleen USA
675 Peter Jefferson Pkwy (22911-8618)
P.O. Box 96, Greenwood (22943-0096)
PHONE..............................434 202-7790
Andrew Eckert, *Manager*
Kutlay Kaya,

▲ EMP: 4
SQ FT: 1,400
SALES (est): 447.9K **Privately Held**
WEB: www.quickleenusa.com
SIC: 2842 Specialty cleaning, polishes &
sanitation goods

(G-2629)
EXIDE TECHNOLOGIES LLC
Also Called: GNB Industrial Power
4035 Hunterstand Ct (22911-5830)
PHONE..............................434 975-6001
John Upson, *Opers Staff*
Lance Asouline, *Purchasing*
Lance Joel, *Purchasing*
William Cosselman, *Engineer*
Rob Brock, *Sales Staff*
EMP: 40
SALES (corp-wide): 2.1B **Privately Held**
WEB: www.exide.com
SIC: 3694 3699 3629 Battery charging
generators, automobile & aircraft; electri-
cal equipment & supplies; battery charg-
ers, rectifying or nonrotating
PA: Exide Technologies, Llc
13000 Drfeld Pkwy Bldg 20
Milton GA 30004
678 566-9000

(G-2630)
**EXPLORATION PARTNERS LLC
(PA)**
Also Called: Explorations Partners
1414 Sachem Pl Ste 1 (22901-2560)
P.O. Box 3265, Staunton (24402-3265)
PHONE..............................434 973-8311
Thomas Dingledine, *President*
Louie Ferrari, *Vice Pres*
Brad Thomas, *Vice Pres*
Jacob Ford, *CFO*
EMP: 4
SQ FT: 800
SALES (est): 2.4MM **Privately Held**
SIC: 1381 1382 Drilling oil & gas wells; oil
& gas exploration services

(G-2631)
FAIRWAY ENTERPRISE LLP
977 Seminole Trl (22901-2824)
PHONE..............................434 973-8595
Janice Corrin, *Principal*
EMP: 2 EST: 2010
SALES (est): 140.1K **Privately Held**
WEB: www.fairwayenterprise.com
SIC: 2386 Hats & caps, leather

(G-2632)
**FLOWERS BKG CO LYNCHBURG
LLC**
Also Called: Deeds Thrift Stores
360 Greenbrier Dr (22901-1619)
PHONE..............................434 978-4104
Robert Deeds, *Branch Mgr*
EMP: 2
SALES (corp-wide): 4.1B **Publicly Held**
SIC: 2051 5932 Bread, cake & related
products; used merchandise stores
HQ: Flowers Baking Co. Of Lynchburg, Llc
1905 Hollins Mill Rd
Lynchburg VA 24503
434 528-0441

(G-2633)
FRANK M CHURILLO
Also Called: Extrema Cables
104 Lupine Ln (22911-9023)
PHONE..............................434 242-6895
Frank M Churillo, *Owner*
EMP: 1
SALES (est): 153.9K **Privately Held**
WEB: www.extremacables.com
SIC: 3357 Coaxial cable, nonferrous; air-
craft wire & cable, nonferrous; automotive
wire & cable, except ignition sets: nonfer-
rous; shipboard cable, nonferrous

(G-2634)
**FRED HEAN FURNITURE &
WDWRK**
Also Called: Hean, Fred Furniture and Wdwrk
3226 Lonesome Mountain Rd
(22911-6011)
PHONE..............................434 973-5960
Fred Hean, *Owner*
EMP: 2

SALES (est): 143K **Privately Held**
WEB: www.heancabinetry.com
SIC: 2434 3553 Wood kitchen cabinets;
furniture makers' machinery, woodworking

(G-2635)
FREE UNION RESTAURANT INC
3618 Free Union Rd (22901-5608)
PHONE..............................434 327-9559
Jeanna Raleigh, *Principal*
EMP: 2
SALES (est): 72.9K **Privately Held**
SIC: 2515 Mattresses & bedsprings

(G-2636)
FRF INC
Also Called: Hightech Signs
2165 Seminole Trl (22901-8302)
PHONE..............................434 974-7900
Benjamin Foster, *President*
Beth Robinson, *Vice Pres*
Ben Foster, *CFO*
Sheila Williams, *Accounting Mgr*
Kevin Pyles, *Sales Mgr*
EMP: 24
SQ FT: 9,000
SALES (est): 3.4MM **Privately Held**
WEB: www.htsva.com
SIC: 3993 Signs, not made in custom sign
painting shops

(G-2637)
GENERAL DYNAMICS CORP
321 Hillsdale Dr Ste 100 (22901-5736)
PHONE..............................434 964-5301
EMP: 4 EST: 2019
SALES (est): 272.7K **Privately Held**
SIC: 3728 Aircraft parts & equipment

(G-2638)
GRAPHTONE SIGNS
1803 Solomon Rd Apt 4 (22901-2401)
PHONE..............................434 989-9740
Mavlud Tashtanov, *Principal*
EMP: 1
SALES (est): 46K **Privately Held**
WEB: www.graphtonesigns.com
SIC: 3993 Signs & advertising specialties

(G-2639)
**GREENBROOK TMS
NEUROHEALTH CTR**
Also Called: Tms Neurohealth Centers
630 Peter Jefferson Pkwy (22911-8605)
PHONE..............................434 327-1660
Parish McKinney, *Director*
EMP: 1
SALES (corp-wide): 2.7MM **Privately
Held**
WEB: www.greenbrooktms.com
SIC: 3312 Blast furnaces & steel mills
PA: Greenbrook Tms Neurohealth Center
8405 Greensboro Dr # 120
Mc Lean VA 22102
703 356-1568

(G-2640)
GREENSTONE MATERIALS LLC
1949 Northside Dr (22911-5827)
PHONE..............................434 973-2113
Larry Hall Jr, *Partner*
EMP: 5
SQ FT: 33,000
SALES (est): 405.8K **Privately Held**
SIC: 2611 Pulp manufactured from waste
or recycled paper

(G-2641)
GRIFFIN TAPESTRY STUDIO
1800 Yorktown Dr (22901-3037)
PHONE..............................434 979-4402
Joan Griffin, *Owner*
EMP: 1
SALES (est): 67.2K **Privately Held**
SIC: 2211 Airplane cloth, cotton

(G-2642)
GRIFFINS PERCH IRONWORKS
2259 Stony Point Rd (22911-6054)
PHONE..............................434 977-0582
Scott Schultz, *Principal*
EMP: 3
SALES (est): 323.3K **Privately Held**
WEB: www.griffinsperch.com
SIC: 3446 Architectural metalwork

(G-2643)
HALMOR CORP (PA)
Also Called: Dr Pepper of Staunton, Va.
1650 State Farm Blvd (22911-4664)
PHONE......................434 295-3177
Preston Morris, *President*
Susan B Morris, *Owner*
Frank Halsey, *Principal*
EMP: 3
SALES (est): 1.4MM **Privately Held**
WEB: www.drpepper.com
SIC: 2086 Soft drinks: packaged in cans,
bottles, etc.

(G-2644)
HAMPTON WOODWORKS LLC
1235 Chatham Rdg (22901-3190)
PHONE......................434 989-7556
Charles H Willis Jr, *Administration*
EMP: 4
SALES (est): 285.7K **Privately Held**
SIC: 2431 Millwork

(G-2645)
HOLDERBY & BIERCE INC
180 Walnut Ln (22911-8650)
PHONE......................434 971-8571
Don Van Hook, *Principal*
EMP: 1
SALES (est): 42.1K **Privately Held**
SIC: 2731 8999 Books: publishing only;
communication services

(G-2646)
INFINITE STUDIO LLC
2174 Whispering Hollow Ln (22911-3590)
PHONE......................864 293-4522
Sean Brakefield,
EMP: 1
SALES (est): 32.7K **Privately Held**
SIC: 7372 Application computer software

(G-2647)
INTELLIGENT PLATFORMS LLC (HQ)
Also Called: Emerson
2500 Austin Dr (22911-8319)
PHONE......................434 978-5000
David N Farr, *CEO*
Michael Train, *President*
Lawrence Ambrose, *Business Mgr*
Daniel Marx, *Business Mgr*
Steve Pelch, *COO*
◆ EMP: 800
SALES (est): 747.8MM
SALES (corp-wide): 18.3B **Publicly Held**
WEB: www.ge.com
SIC: 3625 3674 7371 Numerical controls;
computer logic modules; custom com-
puter programming services
PA: Emerson Electric Co.
8000 West Florissant Ave
Saint Louis MO 63136
314 553-2000

(G-2648)
IVY CREEK MEDIA
2465 Williston Dr (22901-7739)
PHONE......................434 971-1787
John W Milligan, *Owner*
EMP: 1
SALES (est): 64.3K **Privately Held**
WEB: www.ivycreekfoundation.org
SIC: 2721 Magazines: publishing & printing

(G-2649)
IVY MANUFACTURING LLC
1615 W Pines Dr (22901-9422)
PHONE......................434 249-0134
Chris Hyde, *Principal*
EMP: 2
SALES (est): 71.4K **Privately Held**
SIC: 3999 Manufacturing industries

(G-2650)
J & L COMMUNICATIONS INC
Also Called: PIP Printing
909 Gardens Blvd (22901-1472)
PHONE......................434 973-1830
Richard L Benner, *President*
Marlene K Benner, *Vice Pres*
Lisa R Benner, *Director*
Joy Burbaker, *Graphic Designe*
EMP: 6

WEB: www.ziprint.com
SIC: 2752 2731 7334 Commercial printing, offset; book publishing; photocopying
& duplicating services

(G-2651)
JA-ZAN LLC
Also Called: Pepsicola
1150 Pepsi Pl Ste 100 (22901-2865)
P.O. Box 9035 (22906-9035)
PHONE......................434 978-2140
Jame L Jessut Jr, *President*
Bob Pflugfelder, *Vice Pres*
Suzanne Staton,
James Jessup,
EMP: 5
SALES (est): 2.2MM **Privately Held**
SIC: 2086 Soft drinks: packaged in cans,
bottles, etc.

(G-2652)
JOHN DEMASCO
1520 Garth Gate Ln (22901-8889)
PHONE......................434 977-4214
John Demasco, *Owner*
EMP: 3 EST: 2000
SALES (est): 212.1K **Privately Held**
SIC: 3531 Marine related equipment

(G-2653)
KLOCKNER PENTAPLAST AMER INC
1670 Discovery Dr (22911-5844)
PHONE......................540 832-3600
Dominique Schoech, *Engineer*
Rachel Rimeikiene, *Manager*
EMP: 2
SALES (corp-wide): 4.7MM **Privately Held**
WEB: www.kpfilms.com
SIC: 3081 Plastic film & sheet
HQ: Klockner Pentaplast Of America, Inc.
3585 Kloeckner Rd
Gordonsville VA 22942
540 832-1400

(G-2654)
KNUUDE LLC
Also Called: Knuude Organics Skin Care
770 Old Brook Rd (22901-1743)
PHONE......................571 298-1746
Kevin Crawford, *Mng Member*
EMP: 1
SALES (est): 100K **Privately Held**
SIC: 2844 5961 Bath salts; cosmetics &
perfumes, mail order

(G-2655)
LA VACHE MICROCREAMERY
2324 Glenn Ct (22901-2948)
PHONE......................434 989-6264
Stephanie Williams, *Principal*
EMP: 3 EST: 2014
SALES (est): 178.4K **Privately Held**
WEB: www.lavachemicrocreamery.com
SIC: 2021 Creamery butter

(G-2656)
LAWRITER LLC
1467 Greenbrier Pl 6 (22901-1697)
P.O. Box 2079, Chino Hills CA (91709-0070)
PHONE......................434 220-4324
Dave Harriman, *CEO*
Satish Sheth,
EMP: 38
SQ FT: 3,000
SALES (est): 2.8MM
SALES (corp-wide): 10.1B **Privately Held**
WEB: www.codes.ohio.gov
SIC: 2731 Book publishing
HQ: Science Information Solutions, Llc
360 Park Ave S
New York NY 10010

(G-2657)
LULULEMON
2050 Bond St Ste 120 (22901-1887)
PHONE......................434 964-0105
EMP: 1
SALES (est): 42.5K **Privately Held**
SIC: 2389 Apparel & accessories

(G-2658)
MICROAIRE SURGICAL INSTRS LLC
2400 Austin Dr (22911-8491)
PHONE......................434 975-8300
George Saiz, *President*
EMP: 10
SALES (corp-wide): 254.6B **Publicly Held**
WEB: www.microaire.com
SIC: 3841 Surgical & medical instruments
HQ: Microaire Surgical Instruments Llc
3590 Grand Forks Blvd
Charlottesville VA 22911
800 722-0822

(G-2659)
MICROAIRE SURGICAL INSTRS LLC (DH)
3590 Grand Forks Blvd (22911-9006)
PHONE......................800 722-0822
Robert A Pritzker, *Ch of Bd*
George Saiz, *President*
Francis I Lavin, *President*
Robert C Gluth, *Vice Pres*
Hank West, *Vice Pres*
◆ EMP: 115
SQ FT: 50,000
SALES (est): 17.1MM
SALES (corp-wide): 254.6B **Publicly Held**
WEB: www.microaire.com
SIC: 3841 3842 3546 Surgical & medical
instruments; surgical appliances & sup-
plies; power-driven handtools
HQ: Colson Associates, Inc.
225 W Washington St # 2200
Chicago IL 60606
312 980-1100

(G-2660)
MIKRO SYSTEMS INC
1180 Seminole Trl Ste 220 (22901-5739)
PHONE......................434 244-6480
Michael Appleby, *President*
Jim Atkinson, *CFO*
Kayla Johnson, *Technician*
Mark Scheurenbrand, *Technician*
EMP: 35 EST: 2000
SQ FT: 10,000
SALES (est): 7.9MM **Privately Held**
WEB: www.mikrosystems.com
SIC: 3724 5047 Turbines, aircraft type; di-
agnostic equipment, medical

(G-2661)
MILLENNIUM SFTWR CNSULTING LLC
2114 Angus Rd Ste 221 (22901-2770)
PHONE......................434 245-0741
Sharone Jones, *Principal*
Suresh Thurai, *Vice Pres*
EMP: 2
SALES (est): 180.8K **Privately Held**
WEB: www.msc-it.com
SIC: 7372 Business oriented computer
software

(G-2662)
MONOGRAM SHOP
628 Berkmar Cir (22901-1464)
PHONE......................434 973-1968
Gail Taffe, *President*
EMP: 2
SALES (est): 184.4K **Privately Held**
WEB: www.cvillemonogramshop.com
SIC: 2395 5719 5699 Embroidery prod-
ucts, except schiffli machine; towels; T-
shirts, custom printed

(G-2663)
NEW SILK ROAD MARKETING LLC
Also Called: Forbidden City Foods
3217 S Chesterfield Ct (22911-5768)
PHONE......................434 531-0141
Biao Sun, *Managing Prtnr*
Dennis Woodriff, *Managing Prtnr*
Mary Ann Parr, *Partner*
▲ EMP: 5
SQ FT: 2,000
SALES (est): 250K **Privately Held**
SIC: 2035 Pickles, sauces & salad dress-
ings

(G-2664)
NOBULL BURGER
Also Called: Ohongyum
1139a River Rd (22901-4109)
PHONE......................434 975-6628
Crissanne Raymond, *Principal*
EMP: 1
SALES (est): 105.5K **Privately Held**
WEB: www.nobullburger.com
SIC: 2033 5142 Vegetables & vegetable
products in cans, jars, etc.; frozen vegeta-
bles & fruit products

(G-2665)
NORTHROP GRUMMAN SPERRY
2300 Hydraulic Rd (22901-2707)
PHONE......................434 974-2000
EMP: 5
SALES (est): 259.5K **Privately Held**
SIC: 3669 Sirens, electric: vehicle, marine,
industrial & air raid

(G-2666)
NORTHROP GRUMMAN SYSTEMS CORP
1070 Seminole Trl (22901-2827)
PHONE......................434 974-2000
Melinda Hill, *General Mgr*
Wanda Isbister, *General Mgr*
Randi Almond, *Vice Pres*
Paul Becker, *Purchasing*
Shaun Arnold, *Engineer*
EMP: 600 **Publicly Held**
WEB: www.northropgrumman.com
SIC: 3812 Navigational systems & instru-
ments; radar systems & equipment; mis-
sile guidance systems & equipment;
compasses & accessories
HQ: Northrop Grumman Systems Corpora-
tion
2980 Fairview Park Dr
Falls Church VA 22042
703 280-2900

(G-2667)
NOVA MARIS PRESS
977 Seminole Trl (22901-2824)
PHONE......................434 975-0501
EMP: 1
SALES (est): 39.4K **Privately Held**
SIC: 2741 Miscellaneous publishing

(G-2668)
NTELOS INC
220 Twentyninth Place Ct (22901-7419)
PHONE......................434 760-0141
EMP: 3 **Publicly Held**
WEB: www.ntelos.com
SIC: 7372 Prepackaged software
HQ: Ntelos Inc.
1154 Shenandoah Vlg Dr
Waynesboro VA 22980

(G-2669)
OH MY GOSHYUM LLC
Also Called: Nobull Burger
1139a River Rd (22901-4109)
PHONE......................434 975-6628
Crissanne Raymond,
EMP: 2
SALES (est): 116.6K **Privately Held**
WEB: www.nobullburger.com
SIC: 3999 Plants, artificial & preserved

(G-2670)
ORIGIO INC (DH)
Also Called: Origio - Humagen Pipets
2400 Hunters Way (22911-7930)
PHONE......................434 979-4000
Jesper Funding Andersen, *CEO*
Susanne H Bendz, *Exec VP*
Soren Ostergaard, *Exec VP*
April Dean, *Vice Pres*
Marie-Louise Haxthausen, *Vice Pres*
EMP: 22
SQ FT: 10,000
SALES (est): 28.9MM
SALES (corp-wide): 13MM **Privately Held**
WEB: www.fertility.coopersurgical.com
SIC: 3841 Surgical & medical instruments
HQ: Origio A/S
Knardrupvej 2
MAIOv 2760
467 902-00

(G-2671)
PAGES PUBLISHING   LLC
97 Wild Flower Dr (22911-8547)
PHONE...............................434 296-0891
Hugh Delaunay, *Principal*
EMP: 1
SALES (est): 47.7K **Privately Held**
SIC: 2741 Miscellaneous publishing

(G-2672)
PBM FOODS INC
652 Peter Jefferson Pkwy (22911-8849)
PHONE...............................269 673-8451
EMP: 367
SALES (est): 20.2MM **Privately Held**
WEB: www.perrigonutritionals.com
SIC: 2834 Pharmaceutical preparations
HQ: Pbm Holdings, Inc.
     652 Peter Jefferson Pkwy
     Charlottesville VA 22911

(G-2673)
PBM INTERNATIONAL LTD
652 Peter Jefferson Pkwy (22911-8849)
PHONE...............................800 959-2066
Sean Stalfort, *Vice Pres*
EMP: 2
SALES (est): 127.6K **Privately Held**
WEB: www.perrigonutritionals.com
SIC: 2834 Pharmaceutical preparations

(G-2674)
PEPSI-COLA BTLG CO CENTL VA (PA)
1150 Pepsi Pl (22901-2865)
P.O. Box 9035 (22906-9035)
PHONE...............................434 978-2140
James L Jessup Jr, *President*
Suzanne J Brooks, *Exec VP*
Robert Pflugfelder, *Vice Pres*
EMP: 126 EST: 1908
SQ FT: 10,000
SALES: 111.1MM **Privately Held**
WEB: www.pepsicva.com
SIC: 2086 Carbonated soft drinks, bottled
     & canned

(G-2675)
PEPSI-COLA BTLG CO CENTL VA
330 Seminole Ct (22901-2851)
PHONE...............................434 978-2140
Wayne Davis, *Plant Mgr*
EMP: 100
SALES (corp-wide): 111.1MM **Privately Held**
WEB: www.pepsicva.com
SIC: 2086 Carbonated soft drinks, bottled
     & canned
PA: Pepsi-Cola Bottling Co Of Central Vir-
     ginia
     1150 Pepsi Pl
     Charlottesville VA 22901
     434 978-2140

(G-2676)
PERRIGO NUTRITIONALS
652 Peter Jefferson Pkwy # 300
(22911-8849)
PHONE...............................434 297-1070
Perrigo Nutritionals, *President*
Irena Saric, *Manager*
Samantha Smith, *Manager*
Lindley Stakem, *Manager*
EMP: 17
SALES (est): 3MM **Privately Held**
WEB: www.perrigonutritionals.com
SIC: 2834 Pharmaceutical preparations
HQ: Perrigo Company
     515 Eastern Ave
     Allegan MI 49010
     269 673-8451

(G-2677)
PITCHSTONE LLC
1909 Stillhouse Rd (22901-8837)
PHONE...............................434 296-2384
EMP: 2
SALES (est): 80K **Privately Held**
SIC: 2741 Miscellaneous publishing

(G-2678)
POLYMNIA LLC
110 Holly Ct (22901-3150)
PHONE...............................434 422-7842

Michael Ozment, *Principal*
EMP: 2
SALES (est): 77.6K **Privately Held**
SIC: 2741 Miscellaneous publishing

(G-2679)
POWER WRIST BLDRS BY TLOSE GRP
1515 Wilton Farm Rd (22911-7648)
PHONE...............................800 645-6673
Terry Taloose, *Supervisor*
EMP: 2
SALES (est): 65.6K **Privately Held**
SIC: 3931 Musical instruments

(G-2680)
RE DISCOVERY SOFTWARE INC (PA)
3040 Berkmar Dr Ste B1 (22901-1593)
PHONE...............................434 975-3256
David L Edwards, *President*
Janice V Edwards, *Corp Secy*
Anne Ochs, *Office Mgr*
EMP: 15
SQ FT: 4,600
SALES (est): 1.6MM **Privately Held**
WEB: www.rediscoverysoftware.com
SIC: 7372 7371 Prepackaged software;
     computer software systems analysis &
     design, custom

(G-2681)
REAL ESTATE WEEKLY
550 Hillsdale Dr Ste A (22901-5700)
PHONE...............................434 817-9330
Art Pearson, *Chairman*
EMP: 10
SALES (est): 766.2K **Privately Held**
WEB: www.caar.com
SIC: 2721 Magazines: publishing & printing

(G-2682)
RECTOR VISITORS OF THE UNIV VA
Also Called: Universty VA Automobile Sfty
4040 Lewis And Clark Dr (22911-5840)
PHONE...............................434 296-7288
Jeff Mosicki, *Manager*
Mark McCardell, *Info Tech Mgr*
EMP: 40
SALES (corp-wide): 3.2B **Privately Held**
WEB: www.virginia.edu
SIC: 3714 8734 Sanders, motor vehicle
     safety; testing laboratories
PA: Rector & Visitors Of The University Of
     Virginia
     1001 Emmet St N
     Charlottesville VA 22903
     434 924-0311

(G-2683)
REPHIDIM LLC
764 Tilman Rd (22901-6324)
PHONE...............................312 636-6947
EMP: 2
SALES (est): 162.2K **Privately Held**
SIC: 2023 Dietary supplements, dairy &
     non-dairy based

(G-2684)
RETIVUE LLC
2505 Hillwood Pl (22901-2922)
PHONE...............................434 260-2836
Paul Yates, *CEO*
EMP: 2
SALES (est): 216.3K **Privately Held**
WEB: www.retivue.com
SIC: 3851 Ophthalmic goods

(G-2685)
RIVANNA PUBG VENTURES LLC
1612 Inglewood Dr (22901-2649)
PHONE...............................202 549-7940
Mary Barbara Grogan, *Administration*
EMP: 2 EST: 2012
SALES (est): 45.4K **Privately Held**
WEB: www.rivannapublishing.com
SIC: 2741 Miscellaneous publishing

(G-2686)
RIVANNA SOFTWARE LLC
1075 Still Meadow Xing (22901-6201)
PHONE...............................434 806-6105
Thaddeus Lyman, *Principal*
EMP: 2

SALES (est): 72.4K **Privately Held**
WEB: www.rivannasoftware.com
SIC: 7372 Business oriented computer
     software

(G-2687)
RIVANNA WATER & OBSERVATORY
2385 Woodburn Rd (22901-8121)
PHONE...............................434 973-5709
David Golladay, *Manager*
EMP: 2
SALES (est): 181.2K **Privately Held**
SIC: 3589 Water treatment equipment, in-
     dustrial

(G-2688)
ROBERT DOUGLAS LLC
307 Westfield Rd (22901-1658)
PHONE...............................434 284-5111
EMP: 2
SALES (est): 100.1K **Privately Held**
SIC: 2752 Commercial printing, litho-
     graphic

(G-2689)
SANXIN WIRE DIE INC
2025 Woodbrook Ct (22901-1148)
PHONE...............................434 220-0435
Doug Thornton, *CEO*
Lee Thornton, *Vice Pres*
EMP: 2
SALES (est): 120K **Privately Held**
WEB: www.nano-die.com
SIC: 3544 Wire drawing & straightening
     dies

(G-2690)
SCRIPPS ENTERPRISES INC
633 Berkmar Cir (22901-1464)
P.O. Box 4588 (22905-4588)
PHONE...............................434 760-3311
EMP: 2
SALES (est): 88.3K **Privately Held**
WEB: www.scrippsenterprises.com
SIC: 2711 Newspapers, publishing & print-
     ing

(G-2691)
SCRIPPS ENTERPRISES INC
1405 Eagle Hill Farm (22901-5627)
P.O. Box 4588 (22905-4588)
PHONE...............................434 973-3345
Jack C Morgan, *President*
Gregory Robbins, *Vice Pres*
Betty Scripps Harvey, *Treasurer*
Betty Scripps-Harvey, *Treasurer*
EMP: 15
SALES (est): 1.4MM **Privately Held**
SIC: 2731 Book publishing

(G-2692)
SEPHORA INSIDE JCPENNEY
1639 Rio Road East (22901-1407)
PHONE...............................434 973-7851
EMP: 2
SALES (est): 74.4K **Privately Held**
SIC: 2844 Toilet preparations

(G-2693)
SIGNS BY RANDY
762 Woodlands Rd (22901-5505)
PHONE...............................434 328-8872
EMP: 1
SALES (est): 46K **Privately Held**
SIC: 3993 Signs & advertising specialties

(G-2694)
SOFTWRIGHT LLC
1857 Beech Grv (22911-2202)
P.O. Box 7205 (22906-7205)
PHONE...............................434 975-4310
Jason Burkholder,
EMP: 6
SALES (est): 539.2K **Privately Held**
WEB: www.softwright.com
SIC: 3661 3663 3669 4822 Telephone &
     telegraph apparatus; radio & TV commu-
     nications equipment; intercommunication
     systems, electric; telegraph & other com-
     munications; custom computer program-
     ming services

(G-2695)
SPRING HOLLOW PUBLISHING INC
Also Called: Lassosmart.com
1700 Owensville Rd (22901-8800)
PHONE...............................434 984-4718
Peter D Bethke, *President*
EMP: 2
SALES (est): 150.5K **Privately Held**
WEB: www.charlottesvillefamily.com
SIC: 2741 Miscellaneous publishing

(G-2696)
STAPLES PRINT & MARKETING
600 Twentyninth Place Ct (22901-7423)
PHONE...............................434 218-6425
EMP: 2 EST: 2016
SALES (est): 97.8K **Privately Held**
SIC: 2752 Commercial printing, litho-
     graphic

(G-2697)
STONER STEEL PRODUCTS
3009 Colonial Dr (22911-9109)
PHONE...............................434 973-4812
Ron Stoner, *Owner*
EMP: 1
SALES (est): 126.5K **Privately Held**
SIC: 3312 Structural shapes & pilings,
     steel

(G-2698)
SWEET TOOTH
630 Crumpet Ct (22901-3756)
PHONE...............................434 760-0047
Barbara Rosen, *Owner*
EMP: 1
SALES (est): 84.9K **Privately Held**
SIC: 2024 Ice cream & frozen desserts

(G-2699)
TALOOSE GROUP
1515 Wilton Farm Rd (22911-7648)
PHONE...............................408 221-3277
Terry Loose, *Owner*
EMP: 4
SALES (est): 25K **Privately Held**
SIC: 3931 Musical instruments

(G-2700)
TEE ZONE-VA
1600 Rio Road East (22901-1405)
PHONE...............................434 964-9245
EMP: 2 EST: 2017
SALES (est): 122.1K **Privately Held**
WEB: www.charlottesvillefashion.com
SIC: 2759 Screen printing

(G-2701)
TELEDYNE LECROY INC
337 Rio Road West (22901-1311)
PHONE...............................434 984-4500
Michael Lance, *Engineer*
Mike Winfield, *Technical Staff*
EMP: 6
SALES (corp-wide): 3.1B **Publicly Held**
WEB: www.teledynelecroy.com
SIC: 3825 Oscillographs & oscilloscopes
HQ: Teledyne Lecroy, Inc.
     700 Chestnut Ridge Rd
     Chestnut Ridge NY 10977
     845 425-2000

(G-2702)
TELEDYNE LECROY FRONTLINE INC
337 Rio Road West (22901-1311)
P.O. Box 7507 (22906-7507)
PHONE...............................434 984-4500
Dan Tuck, *President*
David Bean, *General Mgr*
Paul Russell, *Vice Pres*
Eddy Vanderkerken, *Vice Pres*
Todd Bradford, *Project Mgr*
EMP: 60
SQ FT: 12,000
SALES (corp-wide): 3.1B **Publicly Held**
WEB: www.fte.com
SIC: 3825 Radio apparatus analyzers
HQ: Teledyne Lecroy, Inc.
     700 Chestnut Ridge Rd
     Chestnut Ridge NY 10977
     845 425-2000

▲ = Import ▼=Export
◆ =Import/Export

(G-2703)
THE MILLWORK SPECIALIST LLC
2811 Hydraulic Rd (22901-8918)
PHONE..................804 262-9296
Michael W Karn, *Principal*
EMP: 1 **EST:** 2012
SALES (est): 88.9K **Privately Held**
SIC: 2431 Millwork

(G-2704)
THOMSON REUTERS CORPORATION
526 Eastbrook Dr (22901-1135)
PHONE..................434 973-4396
EMP: 325
SALES (corp-wide): 10.6B **Publicly Held**
WEB: www.thomsonreuters.com
SIC: 2741 Miscellaneous publishing
HQ: Thomson Reuters Corporation
333 Bay St
Toronto ON M5H 2
416 687-7500

(G-2705)
THREE FOOT SOFTWARE LLC
1015 Glendale Rd (22901-4047)
PHONE..................434 202-0217
Daniel Megginson II, *Principal*
EMP: 2
SALES (est): 64.9K **Privately Held**
SIC: 7372 Prepackaged software

(G-2706)
THRYV INC
943 Glenwood Station Ln # 201
(22901-5714)
PHONE..................434 974-4000
Diane Lynch, *Branch Mgr*
EMP: 15
SALES (corp-wide): 868.1MM **Privately Held**
WEB: www.thryv.com
SIC: 2741 Directories, telephone: publishing only, not printed on site
PA: Thryv, Inc.
2200 W Airfield Dr
Dfw Airport TX 75261
972 453-7000

(G-2707)
TLC PUBLISHING
1904 Dellwood Rd (22901-1222)
PHONE..................434 974-6411
Dolores Johnson, *Principal*
EMP: 2
SALES (est): 106K **Privately Held**
SIC: 2741 Miscellaneous publishing

(G-2708)
TMS CORP
2811 Hydraulic Rd (22901-8918)
PHONE..................804 262-9296
M Sapon, *Personnel Exec*
EMP: 1 **EST:** 2015
SALES (est): 83.1K **Privately Held**
SIC: 2431 Millwork

(G-2709)
V & P INVESTMENT LLC
3552 Seminole Trl (22911-8211)
PHONE..................202 631-8596
Parvin Ismayilov, *Manager*
EMP: 1
SALES (corp-wide): 1.2MM **Privately Held**
WEB: www.discovergranite.com
SIC: 3281 Cut stone & stone products
PA: V & P Investment Llc
9067 Jerrys Cir
Manassas VA 20110
703 365-7835

(G-2710)
VALUE AMERICA
1540 Insurance Ln (22911-7229)
PHONE..................434 951-4100
Joseph Page, *Principal*
EMP: 1
SALES (est): 96.1K **Privately Held**
WEB: www.va.com
SIC: 3639 Major kitchen appliances, except refrigerators & stoves

(G-2711)
VAMAZ INC
1180 Seminole Trl Ste 295 (22901-5713)
PHONE..................434 296-8812
Chad Wilcher, *Principal*
EMP: 2
SALES (est): 190.7K **Privately Held**
WEB: www.vamac.com
SIC: 3272 3561 5039 5074 Septic tanks, concrete; pumps & pumping equipment; septic tanks; water purification equipment

(G-2712)
VINEYARD SERVICES
2431 Huntington Rd (22901-1844)
PHONE..................434 964-8270
Shane Alan, *Principal*
EMP: 2
SALES (est): 114.2K **Privately Held**
SIC: 2084 Wines

(G-2713)
VIRGINIA SPECTRAL LLC
113 Lupine Ln (22911-9024)
PHONE..................434 987-2036
Jerome Ferrance,
EMP: 1 **EST:** 2017
SALES (est): 64.3K **Privately Held**
SIC: 3826 Analytical instruments

(G-2714)
W W W ELECTRONICS INC
3670 Dobleann Dr (22911-9088)
P.O. Box 168, Earlysville (22936-0168)
PHONE..................434 973-4702
Linda S Wright, *President*
Jeff Morris, *Vice Pres*
Benjamin Kidd, *Electrical Engi*
Estate of Donald R Wright, *Shareholder*
EMP: 14
SQ FT: 10,000
SALES (est): 2.5MM **Privately Held**
WEB: www.3welec.com
SIC: 3672 Printed circuit boards

(G-2715)
WILSON READY MIX LLC
3906 Seminole Trl (22911-8397)
PHONE..................434 977-2800
Mark Wilson, *Principal*
EMP: 6
SALES (est): 685.6K **Privately Held**
WEB: www.wilsonreadymix.com
SIC: 3273 Ready-mixed concrete

(G-2716)
WOOD TELEVISION LLC
Also Called: The Daily Progress
685 W Rio Rd (22901-1413)
PHONE..................434 978-7200
Jane D Sathe, *Editor*
William Marshall, *District Mgr*
David Massey, *Advt Staff*
Lawrence McConnell, *Manager*
Fred Greer, *Director*
EMP: 250
SALES (corp-wide): 3B **Publicly Held**
WEB: www.woodtv.com
SIC: 2711 Newspapers, publishing & printing
HQ: Wood Television Llc
120 College Ave Se
Grand Rapids MI 49503
616 456-8888

(G-2717)
WORLDGEN LLC
2030 Catlin Rd (22901-5316)
PHONE..................434 244-2849
Bryan D Wright, *Mng Member*
Bryan Wright, *Mng Member*
EMP: 1 **EST:** 2010
SALES (est): 80K **Privately Held**
WEB: www.worldgenllc.com
SIC: 3621 Motors & generators

(G-2718)
ZOJOI LLC
55 Lynnwood Ln (22901-8968)
PHONE..................804 397-5000
David Marsh, *Principal*
EMP: 2 **EST:** 2012
SALES (est): 166.2K **Privately Held**
WEB: www.zojoi.com
SIC: 3652 Pre-recorded records & tapes

Charlottesville
Charlottesville City County

(G-2719)
2 CITIES PRESS LLC
1957 Ridgetop Dr (22903-8808)
PHONE..................434 249-6043
Michael Hightower, *Principal*
EMP: 2 **EST:** 2016
SALES (est): 59.2K **Privately Held**
SIC: 2741 Miscellaneous publishing

(G-2720)
A-SYSTEMS INCORPORATED
Also Called: A- Systems
2030 Avon Ct Ste 8 (22902-8735)
P.O. Box 5716 (22905-5716)
PHONE..................434 295-7200
Maliwan V Artrip, *President*
Ron Wesner, *Corp Secy*
Eldon Budd, *Purch Mgr*
Harry Archer, *Design Engr*
Floyd M Artrip, *Admin Sec*
EMP: 18
SQ FT: 11,200
SALES (est): 3.3MM **Privately Held**
WEB: www.a-systems.com
SIC: 3629 3625 Electronic generation equipment; relays & industrial controls

(G-2721)
AFTON SCIENTIFIC LLC
2020 Avon Ct Ste 1 (22902-0005)
PHONE..................434 979-3737
Thomas Thorpe, *President*
Usman Madha, *Vice Pres*
Brian Mulhall, *Opers Staff*
Jessica Walker, *QA Dir*
Ashley Umberger, *Engineer*
▲ **EMP:** 40
SALES (est): 8.5MM **Privately Held**
WEB: www.aftonscientific.com
SIC: 2834 Pharmaceutical preparations

(G-2722)
ALBEMARLE COUNTY PUB SCHOOLS
907 Henry Ave (22903-5228)
PHONE..................434 296-3872
Paul Jones, *Teacher*
EMP: 1
SALES (corp-wide): 76.3MM **Privately Held**
WEB: www.k12albemarle.org
SIC: 2821 Plastics materials & resins
PA: Albemarle County Public Schools
401 Mcintire Rd
Charlottesville VA 22902
434 296-5820

(G-2723)
ALBEMARLE EDIBLES LLC
1738 Allied St (22903-5332)
PHONE..................434 242-5567
Robert Northington, *President*
EMP: 5
SQ FT: 1,700
SALES (est): 100K **Privately Held**
SIC: 2052 Cookies

(G-2724)
ALLIED CONCRETE COMPANY (HQ)
Also Called: Butler Virginia C R Orange Co
1000 Harris St (22903-5315)
P.O. Box 1647 (22902-1647)
PHONE..................434 296-7181
Rodger M Brill, *Vice Pres*
Thomas D Cobb, *Vice Pres*
Chris Bernier, *Manager*
Eric Shrieves, *Planning*
▲ **EMP:** 50 **EST:** 1945
SQ FT: 50,000
SALES (est): 25.9MM
SALES (corp-wide): 200.4MM **Privately Held**
WEB: www.alliedconcrete.com
SIC: 3271 3273 3272 Blocks, concrete or cinder: standard; ready-mixed concrete; concrete products

PA: Eagle Corporation
1020 Harris St
Charlottesville VA 22903
434 971-2686

(G-2725)
ALLTEK SYSTEMS LLC
1350 Villaverde Ln (22902-7909)
PHONE..................757 438-6905
David Seidman,
EMP: 1
SALES (est): 159.7K **Privately Held**
WEB: www.allteksystems.com
SIC: 3674 Integrated circuits, semiconductor networks, etc.

(G-2726)
AMERICAN ASSN NUROSURGEONS INC
Also Called: Journal of Neurosurgery DC
1224 Jefferson Park Ave (22903-3410)
PHONE..................434 924-5503
Laura Sutherland, *Manager*
Mary Beth Yeaton, *Director*
EMP: 20
SQ FT: 3,000
SALES (corp-wide): 22.9MM **Privately Held**
WEB: www.aans.org
SIC: 2721 Magazines: publishing only, not printed on site
PA: American Association Of Neurosurgeons, Inc.
5550 Meadowbrook Dr
Rolling Meadows IL 60008
847 378-0500

(G-2727)
AMERICAN MADE SIGNS LLC
407 Earhart St B (22903-5086)
PHONE..................434 971-7446
Brion Draper,
EMP: 2
SALES (est): 186.1K **Privately Held**
WEB: www.americanmadesigns.com
SIC: 3993 Electric signs

(G-2728)
AMERICAN SAFETY & HEALTH (PA)
Also Called: Ashp
513 Stewart St Ste G (22902-5473)
PHONE..................434 977-2700
Douglas Olson, *President*
EMP: 3
SALES (est): 330K **Privately Held**
WEB: www.americansafetyandsmokemaker.com
SIC: 3669 8748 Smoke detectors; safety training service

(G-2729)
APEX CLEAN ENERGY INC (PA)
310 4th St Ne Ste 300 (22902-5299)
PHONE..................434 220-7595
Reisky De Dubnic, *CEO*
Sandy Reisky, *CEO*
Mark Goodwin, *President*
Steve Vavrik, *Principal*
Kevin Bennett, *Business Mgr*
EMP: 112
SALES (est): 27.2MM **Privately Held**
WEB: www.apexcleanenergy.com
SIC: 2282 Throwing & winding mills

(G-2730)
ARQBALL LLC
1030 Linden Ave (22902-6242)
PHONE..................434 260-1890
Jason Lawrence, *Principal*
Michael Holroyd, *Officer*
Abhi Shelat, *Officer*
▲ **EMP:** 2 **EST:** 2010
SALES (est): 196.2K **Privately Held**
WEB: www.arqball.com
SIC: 7372 7371 7299 Educational computer software; computer software development; computer photography or portrait

(G-2731)
ASSOCIATED FABRICATORS LLC
1229 Harris St (22903-5342)
PHONE..................434 293-2333
Cedrick Kayser, *Mng Member*

EMP: 3
SALES (est): 295.7K **Privately Held**
WEB: www.weldingfabricatorsva.com
SIC: 3441 Fabricated structural metal

(G-2732)
AXON SCIENCES INC
200 Garrett St Ste H (22902-5662)
PHONE.................................434 987-4460
Cynthia M Barber, *President*
Joseph Shields, *Vice Pres*
EMP: 2 EST: 2008
SALES (est): 161.3K **Privately Held**
SIC: 2834 8099 Vitamin, nutrient & hematinic preparations for human use; nutrition services

(G-2733)
BACKWATER INC
633 W Main St (22903-5543)
PHONE.................................434 242-5675
Christian D Kelly, *Exec Dir*
EMP: 2 EST: 2009
SALES (est): 127.1K **Privately Held**
SIC: 3732 Boat building & repairing

(G-2734)
BAILEY PRINTING INC
914 Harris St (22903-5313)
PHONE.................................434 293-5434
Robert B Bailey LI, *President*
Robert B Bailey II, *President*
Bryce Bailey, *Business Anlyst*
Lois T Bailey, *Admin Sec*
EMP: 11 EST: 1950
SQ FT: 20,000
SALES (est): 2.5MM **Privately Held**
WEB: www.baileyprintinginc.com
SIC: 2752 7334 Lithographing on metal; commercial printing, offset; blueprinting service

(G-2735)
BALL PEEN PRODUCTIONS LLC
1304 East Market St Ste O (22902-5468)
PHONE.................................434 293-4392
Ed Brown,
William Nelson, *Graphic Designe*
EMP: 3
SALES (est): 330.5K **Privately Held**
WEB: www.frontrunnersigns.com
SIC: 3993 Signs & advertising specialties

(G-2736)
BARRONS-HUNTER INC
556 Dettor Rd Ste 101 (22903-7072)
PHONE.................................434 971-7626
Joseph Milbank, *President*
Anthony P O'Brien, *Admin Sec*
EMP: 6
SQ FT: 1,800
SALES (est): 665.7K **Privately Held**
WEB: www.barronshunter.com
SIC: 2311 5136 Men's & boys' suits & coats; men's & boys' clothing

(G-2737)
BEAUTY PUBLICATIONS INC
418 E Water St (22902-5242)
PHONE.................................434 296-2161
C Garren, *Principal*
EMP: 2 EST: 2008
SALES (est): 113.4K **Privately Held**
SIC: 2741 Miscellaneous publishing

(G-2738)
BEE MEASURE LLC
2319 Highland Ave (22903-3613)
PHONE.................................434 234-4630
Emily Patterson,
EMP: 1
SALES (est): 77.7K **Privately Held**
WEB: www.beemeasure.com
SIC: 3825 Analog-digital converters, electronic instrumentation type

(G-2739)
BELLAIR BIOMEDICAL LLC
34 Canterbury Rd (22903-4702)
PHONE.................................276 206-7337
Edwin Rogers, *CEO*
Ed Rogers, *CEO*
EMP: 1
SALES (est): 70K **Privately Held**
SIC: 3841 Suction therapy apparatus

(G-2740)
BIRCKHEAD SIGNS & GRAPHICS
823 Monticello Rd A (22902-5744)
PHONE.................................434 295-5962
Ed Birckhead, *Owner*
EMP: 4
SQ FT: 2,000
SALES (est): 160K **Privately Held**
WEB: www.birckheadsigns.com
SIC: 3993 1799 Signs & advertising specialties; sign installation & maintenance

(G-2741)
BLANC CREATIVES LLC
735b Walnut St (22902-5971)
PHONE.................................434 260-1692
William Corry Blanc,
EMP: 11 EST: 2018
SALES (est): 452.9K **Privately Held**
WEB: www.blanccreatives.com
SIC: 3469 Household cooking & kitchen utensils, metal; woodenware, kitchen & household

(G-2742)
BLUE RIDGE BOOK CONSERVATION
634 Big Oak Rd (22903-9730)
P.O. Box 4472 (22905-4472)
PHONE.................................434 295-9373
Robert Ortin, *Partner*
EMP: 2
SALES (est): 190.6K **Privately Held**
WEB: www.ortonbindery.com
SIC: 2679 Book covers, paper

(G-2743)
BLUE RIDGE BUCK SAVER INC
225 Heather Crest Pl (22903-9354)
P.O. Box 177, Crozet (22932-0177)
PHONE.................................434 996-2817
Clay Ramsay, *CEO*
Mary Ramsay, *President*
EMP: 2
SALES (est): 120K **Privately Held**
WEB: www.thebucksaver.com
SIC: 2754 7389 Newspapers: gravure printing, not published on site;

(G-2744)
BLUE RIDGE EMBROIDERY INC
550 Meade Ave (22902-5461)
PHONE.................................434 296-9746
Greg Pister, *President*
John Kulick, *Vice Pres*
Ruth Kulick, *Vice Pres*
Mary Pister, *Admin Sec*
EMP: 4
SQ FT: 700
SALES (est): 318K **Privately Held**
WEB: www.brgtshirts.com
SIC: 2759 Screen printing

(G-2745)
BLUETHERM CORPORATION
416 E Main St Ste 301e (22902-5396)
PHONE.................................917 446-8958
Doug Wallace, *CEO*
Hossein Haj-Hariri, *Principal*
Chris Hamlin, *Principal*
Reza Monazami, *Principal*
EMP: 1 EST: 2014
SALES (est): 93.2K **Privately Held**
SIC: 3674 Semiconductors & related devices

(G-2746)
BONDE INNOVATION LLC
315 Old Ivy Way Ste 301 (22903-4894)
PHONE.................................434 951-0444
Mike Theran,
EMP: 1
SALES (est): 55K **Privately Held**
SIC: 3845 5999 Electromedical equipment; medical apparatus & supplies

(G-2747)
BOOK ARTS PRESS INC
2023 Ivy Rd (22903-1713)
PHONE.................................434 924-8851
EMP: 1
SALES (est): 51.2K **Privately Held**
SIC: 2741 Miscellaneous publishing

(G-2748)
BOUTIQUE PAW PRINTS
201 E Main St (22902-5254)
PHONE.................................434 964-0133
EMP: 2
SALES (est): 83.9K **Privately Held**
SIC: 2752 Commercial printing, lithographic

(G-2749)
BRACHYFOAM LLC
722 Preston Ave Ste 108 (22903-4400)
PHONE.................................434 249-9554
Timothy Showalter, *CEO*
EMP: 1 EST: 2015
SALES (est): 90.9K **Privately Held**
SIC: 3844 Irradiation equipment

(G-2750)
BRIX 22 ANKIDA RDGE TASTING RM
209 2nd St Sw (22902-5042)
PHONE.................................434 989-7420
EMP: 2 EST: 2018
SALES (est): 101.6K **Privately Held**
WEB: www.22brix.wordpress.com
SIC: 2084 Wines

(G-2751)
BURRUSS SIGNS INC
704 Altavista Ave (22902-6110)
PHONE.................................434 296-6654
Larry Burruss, *President*
Teresa Pirkey, *Corp Secy*
EMP: 3
SQ FT: 3,400
SALES (est): 260K **Privately Held**
WEB: www.burrusssigns.com
SIC: 3993 7532 2759 Electric signs; truck painting & lettering; screen printing

(G-2752)
C & B CORP
Also Called: Sir Speedy
750 Harris St Ste 208 (22903-4500)
PHONE.................................434 977-1992
Michael Bellone, *President*
EMP: 8
SQ FT: 2,800
SALES (est): 1MM **Privately Held**
WEB: www.sirspeedy.com
SIC: 2752 2791 2789 Commercial printing, lithographic; typesetting; bookbinding & related work

(G-2753)
C-VILLE HOLDINGS LLC
Also Called: C-Ville Weekly
308 E Main St (22902-5234)
P.O. Box 119 (22902-0119)
PHONE.................................434 817-2749
William Chapman,
EMP: 30
SALES (est): 1.4MM **Privately Held**
WEB: www.c-ville.com
SIC: 2711 Newspapers: publishing only, not printed on site

(G-2754)
CALAVERA TOOL WORKS
1229 Harris St Ste 11 (22903-5342)
PHONE.................................434 964-6447
EMP: 3 EST: 2018
SALES (est): 164.7K **Privately Held**
WEB: www.calaveratoolworks.com
SIC: 3599 Machine shop, jobbing & repair

(G-2755)
CAMBRIO STUDIOS LLC
227 Monte Vista Ave (22903-4118)
PHONE.................................540 908-5129
Jason Lawrence,
EMP: 1
SALES (est): 60.5K **Privately Held**
SIC: 7372 7389 Application computer software;

(G-2756)
CAROLINAS SOLUTION GROUP INC
476 Cleveland Ave (22903-6407)
PHONE.................................301 257-6926
Daniel Clark, *President*
EMP: 1

SALES (est): 60.1K **Privately Held**
WEB: www.csgincofva.com
SIC: 1455 Kaolin & ball clay

(G-2757)
CASPARI INC
100 W Main St (22902-5032)
PHONE.................................434 817-7880
Michael Wowk, *Controller*
Sarah Lantz, *Marketing Mgr*
Christin Moran, *Office Mgr*
Lisa Fingeret, *Branch Mgr*
Wade Andrews, *Manager*
EMP: 24
SALES (corp-wide): 35.1MM **Privately Held**
WEB: www.casparionline.com
SIC: 2771 Greeting cards
PA: Caspari, Inc.
    99 Cogwheel Ln
    Seymour CT 06483
    203 888-1100

(G-2758)
CAVALIER CONCRETE INC
1000 Harris St (22903-5315)
PHONE.................................434 296-7181
Mark Wilson, *President*
EMP: 6
SQ FT: 300,000
SALES (est): 610.5K **Privately Held**
SIC: 3273 Ready-mixed concrete

(G-2759)
CAVANAUGH CABINET INC (PA)
1329 E High St (22902-4927)
PHONE.................................434 977-7100
James Cavanaugh, *President*
Diane Cavanaugh, *Corp Secy*
EMP: 9 EST: 1981 **Privately Held**
WEB: www.cavanaughcabinets.com
SIC: 2541 2431 Cabinets, except refrigerated: show, display, etc.: wood; table or counter tops, plastic laminated; moldings, wood: unfinished & prefinished; doors & door parts & trim, wood; windows & window parts & trim, wood

(G-2760)
CAVION INC
310 2nd St Se Ste B (22902-5676)
PHONE.................................434 200-8442
Andrew Krouse, *President*
Anne Heldreth, *Vice Pres*
Evan Newbold, *Research*
Kurt Woerpel, *CFO*
Mark Versavel, *Chief Mktg Ofcr*
EMP: 8
SALES (est): 1.2MM **Privately Held**
WEB: www.cavionpharma.com
SIC: 2834 8731 Pharmaceutical preparations; biotechnical research, commercial
PA: Jazz Pharmaceuticals Public Limited Company
    Fifth Floor
    Dublin

(G-2761)
CENTRAL VIRGINIA STUCCO INC
2725 Thmas Jefferson Pkwy (22902-7618)
PHONE.................................434 531-0752
Jamie Graves, *Principal*
EMP: 1
SALES (est): 20.5K **Privately Held**
WEB: www.centralvirginiastucco.com
SIC: 3299 Stucco

(G-2762)
CERILLO LLC
1516 Cherry Ave (22903-3714)
PHONE.................................434 218-3151
Kevin Seitter, *President*
EMP: 3 EST: 2016
SALES (est): 203.8K **Privately Held**
WEB: www.cerillo.net
SIC: 3826 Laser scientific & engineering instruments

(G-2763)
CERTIFIED ENVIRONMENTAL DRLG
2471 Poplar Dr (22903-7860)
P.O. Box 6538 (22906-6538)
PHONE.................................434 979-0123
Robert Tingley, *President*

Jeri Davis, *Corp Secy*
Gary Tingley, *Vice Pres*
EMP: 5
SALES (est): 600K **Privately Held**
WEB: www.certifiedenvdrilling.com
SIC: 2899 Drilling mud

(G-2764)
CHARLOTTESVILLE VINEYARD
508 Harris Rd (22903-4322)
P.O. Box 681, Keswick (22947-0681)
PHONE.....................................434 321-8463
Jim Bleakley, *Pastor*
EMP: 2
SALES (est): 126.4K **Privately Held**
WEB: www.cvillevineyard.org
SIC: 2084 Wines

(G-2765)
CITY CLAY LLC
700 Harris St Ste 104 (22903-4584)
PHONE.....................................434 293-0808
Randy Bill, *Principal*
EMP: 1
SALES (est): 90.4K **Privately Held**
WEB: www.cityclaycville.com
SIC: 1459 Clays (common) quarrying

(G-2766)
CIVILLE SMOKE SHOP (PA)
108 4th St Ne (22902-5226)
PHONE.....................................434 975-1175
Gan Jim, *Owner*
EMP: 1
SALES (est): 203.1K **Privately Held**
WEB: www.cvillesmokeshop.com
SIC: 2121 5999 Cigars; alarm & safety
equipment stores

(G-2767)
CLIMET INSTRUMENTS
1932 Arlington Blvd Ste 6 (22903-1560)
PHONE.....................................434 984-5634
Tom Moore, *Manager*
▲ **EMP:** 1 **EST:** 1999
SALES (est): 92.5K **Privately Held**
SIC: 3825 Instruments to measure electricity

(G-2768)
CLOUD CABIN ARTS
1719b Allied St (22903-5333)
PHONE.....................................434 218-3020
Michael Cantwell, *President*
EMP: 4
SALES (est): 345.2K **Privately Held**
WEB: www.cloudcabinarts.com
SIC: 2434 Wood kitchen cabinets

(G-2769)
COMMONHEALTH BOTANICALS LLC
604 Bleeker St (22903-3665)
PHONE.....................................434 906-2227
Katherine Knight, *Principal*
Dustin Groves, *Principal*
Kyle McCrory, *Principal*
EMP: 3
SALES (est): 139.1K **Privately Held**
SIC: 2833 7389 Medicinals & botanicals;

(G-2770)
CONTRALINE INC
1216 Harris St (22903-5340)
PHONE.....................................347 327-3676
Kevin Eisenfrats, *Principal*
Nikki Hastings, *COO*
EMP: 1
SALES (est): 127.5K **Privately Held**
WEB: www.contraline.com
SIC: 2834 Pharmaceutical preparations

(G-2771)
COSAIC
609 East Market St (22902-5303)
PHONE.....................................800 821-8147
Christian Hall, *COO*
Gus Matlis, *Vice Pres*
Cody Taylor, *Software Engr*
EMP: 6
SALES (est): 208.5K **Privately Held**
WEB: www.chartiq.com
SIC: 7372 Prepackaged software

(G-2772)
COVENANT THERAPEUTICS LLC
1229 Harris St Ste 11 (22903-5342)
PHONE.....................................434 296-8668
Michael Borton, *Mng Member*
EMP: 6
SALES (est): 291.6K **Privately Held**
SIC: 2834 Pharmaceutical preparations

(G-2773)
COYNE & DELANY COMPANY (PA)
Also Called: Delany Products
1565 Avon Street Ext (22902-8702)
P.O. Box 411 (22902-0411)
PHONE.....................................434 296-0166
Scott Delany, *President*
Biff Delany, *Vice Pres*
Peter G Delany, *Vice Pres*
Patricio Hernandez, *Vice Pres*
Martin Laverty, *CFO*
▲ **EMP:** 25
SQ FT: 4,000
SALES (est): 2.2MM **Privately Held**
WEB: www.delanyproducts.com
SIC: 3432 Plumbers' brass goods: drain
cocks, faucets, spigots, etc.; plastic
plumbing fixture fittings, assembly

(G-2774)
CREATIVE CABINET DESIGN
1109 Harris St (22903-5318)
PHONE.....................................434 293-4040
William Hinckley, *Owner*
EMP: 9
SQ FT: 4,000
SALES (est): 454K **Privately Held**
SIC: 2599 2434 5031 1751 Cabinets,
factory; wood kitchen cabinets; kitchen
cabinets; cabinet & finish carpentry

(G-2775)
CUSTOM INK
2118 Barracks Rd (22903-4810)
PHONE.....................................434 422-5206
EMP: 2
SALES (est): 87.9K **Privately Held**
WEB: www.customink.com
SIC: 2759 Screen printing

(G-2776)
CVILLE DREAM LIFE
901 Montrose Ave (22902-6231)
PHONE.....................................434 327-2600
Heather Towe, *Principal*
EMP: 3
SALES (est): 130.9K **Privately Held**
WEB: www.c-ville.com
SIC: 2711 Newspapers, publishing & printing

(G-2777)
CVILLE SIREN LLC
1117 Leonard St (22902-5936)
PHONE.....................................434 987-2008
Judy Berger, *Principal*
EMP: 2 **EST:** 2017
SALES (est): 61.9K **Privately Held**
WEB: www.c-ville.com
SIC: 2711 Newspapers, publishing & printing

(G-2778)
DBS PRODUCTIONS LLC
1808 Rugby Pl (22903-1625)
PHONE.....................................434 293-5502
Emily Koester, *Director*
Robert Koester,
EMP: 2
SALES (est): 148.8K **Privately Held**
WEB: www.dbs-sar.com
SIC: 2731 8742 8999 8732 Books: publishing only; training & development consultant; search & rescue service; research services, except laboratory

(G-2779)
DELFORT USA INC
Also Called: Terbakosky Specialty Paper
216 3rd St Ne Ste C (22902-5286)
PHONE.....................................434 202-7870
Josef Kofler, *President*
Charles Bumpus, *Plant Supt*
Chris Whetsel, *Maint Spvr*

Roland Faihs, *CFO*
Craig Walter, *Manager*
◆ **EMP:** 6
SALES (est): 991.6K **Privately Held**
WEB: www.delfortgroup.com
SIC: 2621 Paper mills

(G-2780)
DIAMONDBACK SPORT
1229 Harris St Ste 11 (22903-5342)
PHONE.....................................434 964-6447
EMP: 2
SALES (est): 108.1K **Privately Held**
SIC: 3949 Sporting & athletic goods

(G-2781)
DIAMONDBACK TOOL CO
1229 Harris St Ste 11 (22903-5342)
PHONE.....................................800 899-2358
Connor Crook, *CEO*
EMP: 5
SALES (est): 187.6K **Privately Held**
SIC: 3545 Tool holders

(G-2782)
DIFFUSION PHARMACEUTICALS INC (PA)
Also Called: Restorgenex
1317 Carlton Ave Ste 400 (22902-6193)
PHONE.....................................434 220-0718
David G Kalergis, *Ch of Bd*
Isaac Blech, *Vice Ch Bd*
Robert J Cobuzzi Jr, *President*
William Hornung, *CFO*
Ben L Shealy, *Treasurer*
EMP: 3
SQ FT: 5,000
SALES (est): 5.8MM **Publicly Held**
WEB: www.diffusionpharma.com
SIC: 2834 Pharmaceutical preparations

(G-2783)
DIFFUSION PHARMACEUTICALS LLC
1317 Carlton Ave Ste 400 (22902-6193)
PHONE.....................................434 220-0718
David G Kalergis, *CEO*
Matthew W Hantzmon, *Vice Pres*
David R Jones, *Officer*
EMP: 10
SALES (est): 1.5MM **Publicly Held**
WEB: www.diffusionpharma.com
SIC: 2834 Pharmaceutical preparations
PA: Diffusion Pharmaceuticals Inc.
1317 Carlton Ave Ste 400
Charlottesville VA 22902

(G-2784)
DOUBLE HORSESHOE SALOON
1522 E High St (22902-4931)
PHONE.....................................434 202-8714
Thomas Etheredge, *Principal*
EMP: 2 **EST:** 2016
SALES (est): 51.2K **Privately Held**
WEB:
www.thedoublehorseshoesaloon.com
SIC: 3462 Horseshoes

(G-2785)
DOUBLETHINK NEWS LLC
121 Washington Ave (22903-3062)
PHONE.....................................434 466-2092
Haotian Liu,
EMP: 3
SALES (est): 86.5K **Privately Held**
SIC: 2741 Newsletter publishing

(G-2786)
DOVA PHARMACEUTICALS INC
200 Garrett St Ste P (22902-5662)
PHONE.....................................844 506-3682
EMP: 5 **EST:** 2017
SALES (est): 424.3K **Privately Held**
WEB: www.dova.com
SIC: 2834 Pharmaceutical preparations

(G-2787)
E M COMMUNICATIONS INC
Also Called: Pixels
1201 East Market St (22902-5445)
PHONE.....................................434 971-4700
Kemper Roach Conwell, *President*
Brian Gibson, *Vice Pres*
EMP: 3
SQ FT: 3,000

SALES (est): 365.9K **Privately Held**
SIC: 2791 7374 Typesetting; service bureau, computer

(G-2788)
EDISON 2 LLC
108 2nd St Sw Ste 2 (22902-5078)
PHONE.....................................434 806-2435
Oliver Kuttner,
EMP: 10
SALES (est): 2MM **Privately Held**
SIC: 3711 Automobile assembly, including specialty automobiles

(G-2789)
ELECTRNIC CABLING ASSEMBLY INC
Also Called: E C L
711 Charlton Ave (22903-5203)
P.O. Box 746 (22902-0746)
PHONE.....................................434 293-2593
Maryann Nitchmann, *President*
William J Nitchmann, *Corp Secy*
Sean Nitchmann, *Vice Pres*
EMP: 25
SALES (est): 3.6MM **Privately Held**
WEB: www.eclinc.com
SIC: 3496 Cable, uninsulated wire: made from purchased wire

(G-2790)
EPIEP INC
315 Old Ivy Way Ste 301 (22903-4894)
PHONE.....................................864 423-2526
Colin M Rolph, *CFO*
EMP: 2
SALES (est): 191.6K **Privately Held**
WEB: www.epiep.com
SIC: 3841 Surgical & medical instruments

(G-2791)
ERIC TRUMP WINE MFG LLC
Also Called: Trump Winery
100 Grand Cru Dr (22902-7763)
PHONE.....................................434 977-3895
Eric Trump, *Mng Member*
Jacqueline Rullman, *Manager*
Austin Ashford, *Supervisor*
Logan Campbell, *Maintence Staff*
▲ **EMP:** 20
SALES (est): 4.4MM
SALES (corp-wide): 579.9MM **Privately Held**
WEB: www.trumpwinery.com
SIC: 2084 Wines
PA: The Trump Organization Inc
725 5th Ave Bsmt A
New York NY 10022
212 832-2000

(G-2792)
ERICS WELDING
107 Sundrops Ct (22902-8247)
PHONE.....................................434 996-6502
EMP: 1
SALES (est): 15K **Privately Held**
SIC: 7692 Welding Repair

(G-2793)
EUGENE C HOOPES
710 Park St (22902-4345)
PHONE.....................................434 293-5852
Eugene C Hoopes, *Principal*
EMP: 3 **EST:** 2011
SALES (est): 160.2K **Privately Held**
WEB: www.c-ville.com
SIC: 2711 Newspapers, publishing & printing

(G-2794)
EVALUATION TECH FOR DEV LLC
708 Montrose Ave (22902-6146)
PHONE.....................................434 851-0651
Isabelle Duston, *Owner*
EMP: 3 **EST:** 2012
SALES (est): 48K **Privately Held**
SIC: 7372 Educational computer software

(G-2795)
FIRST COLONY WINERY LTD
1650 Harris Creek Rd (22902-7820)
PHONE.....................................434 979-7105
Randolph McElroy Jr, *Owner*
Randy McElroy, *Co-Owner*

EMP: 4
SALES (est): 313.6K **Privately Held**
WEB: www.thatchwinery.com
SIC: 2084 Wines

(G-2796)
FOCUS MAGAZINE
34 University Cir (22903-1833)
PHONE.................................434 296-4261
Sylvia Sanides, *Correspondent*
EMP: 2
SALES (est): 73.1K **Privately Held**
SIC: 2721 Periodicals

(G-2797)
FOLLETT COLLEGE STORE 743
501 College Dr (22902-7589)
PHONE.................................434 961-5317
EMP: 2
SALES (est): 52.5K **Privately Held**
SIC: 2731 Books: publishing & printing

(G-2798)
FOX HILL EDITORIAL LLC
520 Rookwood Pl (22903-4734)
PHONE.................................434 971-1835
David Rubin, *Mng Member*
EMP: 1 **EST:** 2010
SALES (est): 10K **Privately Held**
WEB: www.foxhilleditorial.org
SIC: 2731 Book publishing

(G-2799)
FREEDOM HAWKS KAYAKS INC
200 Garrett St Ste H (22902-5662)
PHONE.................................978 225-1511
David B Cameron, *President*
EMP: 1
SALES (est): 82K **Privately Held**
SIC: 3732 Boat building & repairing

(G-2800)
GABRIEL D OFIESH II INC
908 E High St (22902-4840)
P.O. Box 2002 (22902-2002)
PHONE.................................434 295-9038
Ofiesh II Gabriel D, *President*
Mary E Maher Ofiesh, *Vice Pres*
EMP: 3
SALES (est): 404.4K **Privately Held**
WEB: www.gabrielofiesh.com
SIC: 3911 Jewelry, precious metal

(G-2801)
GAONA GRANOLA CO LLC
120 Yellowstone Dr # 303 (22903-8109)
PHONE.................................434 996-6653
Coco Sotelo, *Principal*
EMP: 1
SALES (est): 68K **Privately Held**
WEB: www.gaonagranola.com
SIC: 2043 Granola & muesli, except bars & clusters

(G-2802)
GASTON AND WYATT LLC
1317 Carlton Ave Ste 110 (22902-6193)
PHONE.................................434 293-7357
James Reyes, *Transportation*
Richard Wyatt,
EMP: 20 **EST:** 2013
SALES (est): 3.2MM **Privately Held**
WEB: www.gastonwyatt.com
SIC: 2431 Millwork

(G-2803)
GIANT SOFTWARE LLC
115 Roades Ct (22902-5797)
PHONE.................................540 292-6232
Arthur C Clarke, *Principal*
EMP: 5
SALES (est): 251.8K **Privately Held**
WEB: www.giantsoftware.com
SIC: 7372 Application computer software

(G-2804)
GLOBAL CELL SOLUTIONS INC
770 Harris St Ste 104 (22903-4583)
PHONE.................................434 327-3759
Uday Gupta, *President*
EMP: 2
SALES (est): 500K **Privately Held**
WEB: www.globalcellsolutions.com
SIC: 3826 2835 8999 Analytical instruments; in vitro & in vivo diagnostic substances; scientific consulting

(G-2805)
GOGO INDUSTRIES INC
318 4th St Se Apt 33 (22902-5788)
PHONE.................................925 708-7804
Tym Blanchard, *Principal*
EMP: 3
SALES (est): 191.1K **Privately Held**
SIC: 3999 Manufacturing industries

(G-2806)
GRATEFUL PRESS LLC
593 Rosemont Dr (22903-7694)
PHONE.................................434 202-1161
EMP: 1 **EST:** 2018
SALES (est): 41.3K **Privately Held**
SIC: 2741 Miscellaneous publishing

(G-2807)
HAR-TRU LLC (HQ)
2200 Old Ivy Rd Ste 100 (22903-4819)
PHONE.................................877 442-7878
Kimberly Schoeffel, *Sales Staff*
Kyle Utz, *Sales Staff*
Pat Hanssen, *Mng Member*
Paul Harris, *Manager*
◆ **EMP:** 29
SALES (est): 38.8K
SALES (corp-wide): 9.3MM **Privately Held**
WEB: www.hartru.com
SIC: 3949 Tennis equipment & supplies
PA: Tuckahoe Holdings, Llc
　　919 E Main St Ste 2200
　　Richmond VA 23219
　　804 644-6000

(G-2808)
HEALTH DATA SERVICES INC
503 Faulconer Dr Ste 1 (22903-4978)
PHONE.................................434 817-9000
Daniel Brody, *President*
John Dove, *Marketing Mgr*
Mitzi Santana, *Manager*
Jeff Moyers, *CIO*
Patrick Byrne, *Software Dev*
EMP: 15
SALES (est): 1.6MM **Privately Held**
WEB: www.healthdataservices.com
SIC: 7372 8082 Prepackaged software; home health care services

(G-2809)
HKL RESEARCH INC (PA)
310 Old Ivy Way Ste 301 (22903-4896)
PHONE.................................434 979-6382
Iwona Minor, *President*
Halszka Czarnocka, *Admin Sec*
EMP: 4
SQ FT: 900
SALES (est): 702.5K **Privately Held**
WEB: www.hkl-xray.com
SIC: 7372 Application computer software

(G-2810)
HKL RESEARCH INC
455 Rookwood Dr (22903-4733)
PHONE.................................434 979-5569
Iwona Minor, *President*
EMP: 1
SALES (corp-wide): 702.5K **Privately Held**
WEB: www.hkl-xray.com
SIC: 7372 Prepackaged software
PA: Hkl Research, Inc.
　　310 Old Ivy Way Ste 301
　　Charlottesville VA 23903
　　434 979-6382

(G-2811)
HOSKINS WOODWORKING LLC JOSE
537 2nd St Ne (22902-4637)
PHONE.................................434 825-2883
EMP: 2
SALES (est): 107.5K **Privately Held**
SIC: 2431 Millwork

(G-2812)
HUMAN DESIGN MEDICAL LLC
200 Garrett St Ste P (22902-5662)
PHONE.................................434 980-8100
Kevin Librett, *COO*
Elisee Bimenyanke, *Accountant*
Paul Manning,
Angelo Lomascolo, *Admin Sec*

Eugene Scavola,
EMP: 5
SQ FT: 1,000
SALES (est): 833.3K **Privately Held**
WEB: www.hdmusa.com
SIC: 3841 Inhalation therapy equipment

(G-2813)
ICARUS MEDICAL LLC
Also Called: Icarus Medical Innovation
105 E Main St (22902-5223)
PHONE.................................434 242-0258
David Johnson, *CEO*
Evan Eckersley, *COO*
EMP: 5
SALES (est): 410.5K **Privately Held**
SIC: 3069 7371 Medical & laboratory rubber sundries & related products; computer software development & applications

(G-2814)
IMOL RADIOPHARMACEUTICALS LLC
1200 Five Springs Rd (22902-8756)
PHONE.................................434 825-3323
Dongfeng Pan,
EMP: 2
SALES (est): 108.9K **Privately Held**
WEB: www.med.virginia.edu
SIC: 2835 In vitro & in vivo diagnostic substances

(G-2815)
ISOTEMP RESEARCH INC
1801 Broadway St (22902-5880)
P.O. Box 369, Crozet (22932-0369)
PHONE.................................434 295-3101
Renee A Pearison, *Corp Secy*
Todd S Tignor, *Vice Pres*
Renee Pearison, *Treasurer*
Shannon Newton, *Info Tech Mgr*
▼ **EMP:** 5
SQ FT: 9,000
SALES (est): 1.2MM **Privately Held**
WEB: www.isotemp.com
SIC: 3677 3825 3567 5065 Electronic transformers; instruments to measure electricity; industrial furnaces & ovens; electronic parts & equipment
HQ: Taitien Usa, Inc.
　　3720 Oceanic Way Ste 210
　　Oceanside CA 92056
　　510 252-0686

(G-2816)
IVY HOUSE PUBLISHING LLC
3738 Morgantown Rd (22903-7058)
PHONE.................................434 295-5015
Jason Jordan, *Principal*
EMP: 1 **EST:** 2016
SALES (est): 41.3K **Privately Held**
SIC: 2741 Miscellaneous publishing

(G-2817)
IVY PUBLICATION LLC
4282 Ivy Rd (22903-7009)
PHONE.................................434 984-4713
Robin Bethke, *Principal*
Jeniffer Bryson, *Co-Owner*
EMP: 13
SALES (est): 978.1K **Privately Held**
WEB: www.ivylifeandstylemedia.com
SIC: 2721 Magazines: publishing only, not printed on site

(G-2818)
JAMES RIVER LOGGING & EXCAV
3462 Scottsville Rd (22902-7411)
PHONE.................................434 295-8457
EMP: 9
SALES (est): 550K **Privately Held**
SIC: 2411 Logging And Excavation

(G-2819)
JEFFREY GILL
Also Called: Formymate
2508 Buck Island Rd (22902-7637)
PHONE.................................703 309-7061
Jeffrey Gill, *Owner*
EMP: 1 **EST:** 2014
SALES (est): 42.2K **Privately Held**
SIC: 3961 7389 Costume jewelry, ex. precious metal & semiprecious stones; business services

(G-2820)
JKM TECHNOLOGIES LLC
525 Rookwood Pl (22903-4735)
PHONE.................................434 979-8600
D Casey Kerrigan, *Ch of Bd*
Robert A Kusyk,
EMP: 1
SALES (est): 148K **Privately Held**
SIC: 3144 3149 3143 Women's footwear, except athletic; athletic shoes, except rubber or plastic; men's footwear, except athletic

(G-2821)
JUMP MOUNTAIN VINEYARD LLC
310 Hedge St (22902-4730)
PHONE.................................434 296-2226
Mary Hughes, *Principal*
EMP: 2
SALES (est): 166.1K **Privately Held**
SIC: 2084 Wines

(G-2822)
KINGMILL ENTERPRISES LLC
Also Called: Cardboard Safari
203 Camellia Dr (22903-4208)
P.O. Box 63 (22902-0063)
PHONE.................................877 895-9453
Christopher Jessee, *President*
EMP: 9
SALES (est): 876.9K **Privately Held**
WEB: www.cbsafari.com
SIC: 2599 Factory furniture & fixtures

(G-2823)
LASER THERMAL ANALYSIS LLC
1009 Cottage Green Way (22903-1655)
PHONE.................................703 300-3403
John Gaskins,
EMP: 2
SALES (est): 500K **Privately Held**
SIC: 3823 Thermal conductivity instruments, industrial process type

(G-2824)
LIGHT MUSIC LLC
1050 Druid Ave Apt 204 (22902-6381)
PHONE.................................914 316-7948
Daniel Berlin, *CEO*
Steve Dam,
Nicholas Durlacher,
EMP: 2
SALES (est): 98.6K **Privately Held**
SIC: 7372 Application computer software

(G-2825)
LIGHTHOUSE INSTRUMENTS LLC (PA)
2020 Avon Ct Ste 4 (22902-8734)
PHONE.................................434 293-3081
Michael Lally, *Vice Pres*
Paul Daugherty, *Project Mgr*
William Anderson, *VP Engrg*
Matthew Pierotti, *Research*
Mike Timmins, *Research*
▼ **EMP:** 43 **EST:** 1995
SQ FT: 30,000
SALES (est): 10MM **Privately Held**
WEB: www.lighthouseinstruments.com
SIC: 3823 5084 Industrial instrmnts msrmnt display/control process variable; industrial machinery & equipment

(G-2826)
LIGHTHOUSE LAND LLC
2020 Avon Ct (22902-8734)
PHONE.................................434 293-3081
EMP: 3
SALES (est): 161.7K **Privately Held**
SIC: 3826 Analytical instruments

(G-2827)
LLAMA LIFE II LLC
5232 Blenheim Rd (22902-7748)
PHONE.................................434 286-4494
Paige McGiath,
EMP: 1
SALES (est): 62K **Privately Held**
WEB: www.llamalife.com
SIC: 2721 7336 Magazines: publishing only, not printed on site; commercial art & graphic design

(G-2828)
LUCKYFOOTS SOFTWARE
1160 Foxchase Rdg (22902-8240)
PHONE..................................434 296-9358
Lorelei Szatkowski, *Principal*
EMP: 2
SALES (est): 86K **Privately Held**
SIC: 7372 Prepackaged software

(G-2829)
M S G CUSTOM WDWRK & PNTG LLC
1122 Daniel Morris Ln (22902-7444)
PHONE..................................434 977-4752
Michael S Gimbert,
EMP: 4
SALES (est): 200K **Privately Held**
SIC: 2431 Woodwork, interior & ornamental

(G-2830)
MAD HATTER FOODS LLC
1305 Belmont Park (22902-6388)
P.O. Box 4541 (22905-4541)
PHONE..................................434 981-9378
Nathan West, *Mng Member*
EMP: 4 EST: 2016
SALES (est): 196.8K **Privately Held**
SIC: 2033 Chili sauce, tomato: packaged in cans, jars, etc.

(G-2831)
MADIDROP PBC INC (USED IN)
1985 Snow Point Ln (22902-8739)
P.O. Box 2725 (22902-2725)
PHONE..................................434 260-3767
David Dusseau, *CEO*
James Smith, *Ch of Bd*
EMP: 6
SALES (est): 348.1K **Privately Held**
WEB: www.madidrop.com
SIC: 3295 Clay, ground or otherwise treated

(G-2832)
MARCO AND LUCA NOODLE STR INC
809 Park St (22902-4317)
PHONE..................................434 295-3855
Sun Da, *Principal*
EMP: 4
SALES (est): 281.3K **Privately Held**
SIC: 2098 Noodles (e.g. egg, plain & water), dry

(G-2833)
METIS MACHINE LLC
103 W Main St (22902-5031)
P.O. Box 901 (22902-0901)
PHONE..................................434 483-5692
Michael Prichard, *CEO*
Saul Yeaton, *COO*
EMP: 12
SQ FT: 2,300
SALES (est): 256K **Privately Held**
WEB: www.skafos.ai
SIC: 7372 Prepackaged software

(G-2834)
MICHAEL SHAPS WINERY MANAGEMEN (PA)
1781 Harris Creek Way (22902-7878)
PHONE..................................434 242-4559
Michael T Shaps, *Mng Member*
EMP: 25
SALES (est): 1.5MM **Privately Held**
WEB: www.virginiawineworks.com
SIC: 2084 Wines

(G-2835)
MIND PHARMACEUTICAL LLC
480 Ray C Hunt Dr Rm 282 (22903-2980)
PHONE..................................434 202-9617
Jiang He, *President*
EMP: 1 EST: 2014
SALES (est): 70.5K **Privately Held**
SIC: 2834 Pharmaceutical preparations

(G-2836)
MISSION SECURE INC
300 Preston Ave Ste 500 (22902-5096)
PHONE..................................434 284-8071
David Drescher, *Principal*
Barry Horowitz, *Principal*
Don Ward, *Senior VP*
Jessica Cue, *Manager*
Joanie Saunders, *Manager*
EMP: 2 EST: 2014
SALES (est): 285.1K **Privately Held**
WEB: www.missionsecure.com
SIC: 7372 Application computer software

(G-2837)
NERGYSENSE LLC
420 Park St (22902-4762)
P.O. Box 382 (22902-0382)
PHONE..................................434 282-2656
Robert Mosolgo,
James Wade,
EMP: 2 EST: 2013
SALES (est): 119.7K **Privately Held**
SIC: 3825 Electrical energy measuring equipment

(G-2838)
NPLAINVUE LLC
1650 Harris Creek Rd (22902-7820)
PHONE..................................434 979-7105
EMP: 1
SALES (corp-wide): 208.2K **Privately Held**
SIC: 2084 Wines, brandy & brandy spirits
PA: Nplainvue, Llc
3002 Rennes Ct
Northbrook IL

(G-2839)
OWL PEAK TECHNOLOGIES INC
525 Ridge St 305 (22902-5557)
PHONE..................................847 612-0609
Timothy Harvey, *CEO*
Turse Jason,
EMP: 4
SALES (est): 500K **Privately Held**
SIC: 3841 Diagnostic apparatus, medical

(G-2840)
PAPER COVER ROCK
321 E Main St Ste 100 (22902-3202)
PHONE..................................434 979-6366
EMP: 2
SALES (est): 120.7K **Privately Held**
SIC: 2759 Invitations: printing

(G-2841)
PASTA BY VALENTE INC
Also Called: Pasta Valente
1223 Harris St (22903-5319)
PHONE..................................434 971-3717
Mary F Valente, *Principal*
EMP: 5
SQ FT: 2,500
SALES (est): 535.6K **Privately Held**
WEB: www.pastavalente.com
SIC: 2099 5149 Pasta, uncooked: packaged with other ingredients; pasta & rice

(G-2842)
PBM PHARMACEUTICALS INC
200 Garrett St Ste F (22902-5662)
PHONE..................................434 980-8100
Paul Manning, *President*
Jim McGrath, *Exec VP*
Jack Schramm, *Vice Pres*
Scott F Jamison, *Admin Sec*
EMP: 10
SALES (est): 1.6MM **Privately Held**
WEB: www.pbmcap.com
SIC: 2834 Pharmaceutical preparations

(G-2843)
PEGGY HANK INDUSTRIES LLC
687 Tilman Rd (22903-7060)
PHONE..................................434 825-4802
Thomas D Henry, *Principal*
EMP: 1 EST: 2018
SALES (est): 39.6K **Privately Held**
SIC: 3999 Manufacturing industries

(G-2844)
PEOPLESPACE INC
101 E Water St (22902-5281)
PHONE..................................434 825-2168
Jack Smith, *Principal*
EMP: 2
SALES (est): 91.3K **Privately Held**
SIC: 3271 Concrete block & brick

(G-2845)
PEPPERIDGE FARM DISTRIBUTOR
1229 Harris St (22903-5342)
PHONE..................................540 395-4233
EMP: 4
SALES (est): 214.1K **Privately Held**
SIC: 2051 Mfg Bread/Related Products

(G-2846)
PHOTONVISION LLC
521 Pebble Hill Ct (22903-7873)
PHONE..................................540 808-6266
Yunjing Wang, *CEO*
EMP: 1
SALES (est): 84.3K **Privately Held**
SIC: 3661 Fiber optics communications equipment

(G-2847)
PLANK ROAD WOODWORKS
1229 Harris St Ste 7 (22903-5342)
PHONE..................................617 285-8522
Glenn Heimgartner, *Principal*
EMP: 1 EST: 2014
SALES (est): 54.1K **Privately Held**
WEB: www.plankroadwoodworks.com
SIC: 2431 Millwork

(G-2848)
PLUM TREE WIND LLC
310 4th St Ne Ste 200 (22902-5299)
PHONE..................................434 220-7595
Mark Goodwin, *CEO*
Sandy Reisky, *CEO*
Gordon Trousdale, *CFO*
EMP: 1
SALES (est): 62K **Privately Held**
SIC: 2282 Throwing & winding mills
PA: Apex Clean Energy, Inc.
310 4th St Ne Ste 300
Charlottesville VA 22902

(G-2849)
PORTICO PUBLICATIONS LTD (PA)
Also Called: C-Ville Weekly
308 E Main St (22902-5234)
P.O. Box 119 (22902-0119)
PHONE..................................434 817-2749
William Chapman, *Ch of Bd*
Frank Dubec, *Publisher*
Tami Keaveny, *Editor*
Caitlin White, *Editor*
Debbie Miller, *CFO*
EMP: 71
SALES (est): 2.8MM **Privately Held**
WEB: www.c-ville.com
SIC: 2711 Newspapers, publishing & printing

(G-2850)
PRECISION PAVERS INC
3620 Langford Dr (22903-9329)
PHONE..................................703 217-4955
Burch John W, *Admin Sec*
EMP: 3
SALES (est): 222.2K **Privately Held**
SIC: 2951 Asphalt paving mixtures & blocks

(G-2851)
PUTTY LLC
708 Cargil Ln (22902-4302)
PHONE..................................434 960-3954
Robert Michel, *Principal*
EMP: 1 EST: 2016
SALES (est): 47.2K **Privately Held**
SIC: 2851 Putty

(G-2852)
QUALITY WELDING INC
830 Harris St (22903-4555)
P.O. Box 6632 (22906-6632)
PHONE..................................434 296-1402
Lewis Dickerson, *President*
Betty Dickerson, *Vice Pres*
Rebecca Dickerson, *Vice Pres*
Jason Dickerson, *Treasurer*
▲ EMP: 21 EST: 1972
SQ FT: 5,000
SALES (est): 3.5MM **Privately Held**
WEB: www.qualityweldingcville.com
SIC: 7692 Welding repair

(G-2853)
QUEST EXPEDITION OUTFITTE
3305 Lobban Pl (22903-7069)
PHONE..................................434 244-7140
David Matthews, *Principal*
EMP: 1
SALES (est): 75.2K **Privately Held**
SIC: 3524 Lawn & garden equipment

(G-2854)
R WYATT INC
1317 Carlton Ave Ste 110 (22902-6193)
PHONE..................................434 293-7357
Richard H Wyatt Jr, *President*
Keith Cutts, *Vice Pres*
Scott Viemeister, *Vice Pres*
Andrew Gray, *Plant Mgr*
Mark Wingerd, *Sales Staff*
EMP: 40 EST: 1979
SQ FT: 14,000
SALES (est): 4.3MM **Privately Held**
WEB: www.gastonwyatt.com
SIC: 2431 Millwork

(G-2855)
RE INNOVATIVE SFTWR SOLUTIONS (PA)
1750 Allied St Ste B (22903-5359)
P.O. Box 1750 (22902-1750)
PHONE..................................434 989-8558
Charlie Rogers, *President*
SEI Kim,
EMP: 11
SALES (est): 1.2MM **Privately Held**
WEB: www.issvalue.com
SIC: 7372 Prepackaged software

(G-2856)
REASON
517 2nd St Ne (22902-4637)
PHONE..................................202 256-6197
EMP: 2 EST: 2017
SALES (est): 73.1K **Privately Held**
SIC: 2721 Periodicals

(G-2857)
RECTOR VISITORS OF THE UNIV VA
Also Called: University Press Warehouse
500 Edgemont Rd (22903)
PHONE..................................434 924-3469
EMP: 1
SALES (corp-wide): 3.2B **Privately Held**
WEB: www.virginia.edu
SIC: 2731 Book publishing
PA: Rector & Visitors Of The University Of Virginia
1001 Emmet St N
Charlottesville VA 22903
434 924-0311

(G-2858)
RECTOR VISITORS OF THE UNIV VA
Also Called: Modern Pathology
Old Medical Schl Rm 3876 (22908-0001)
P.O. Box 800214 (22908-0214)
PHONE..................................434 924-9136
Stacey E Mills, *Principal*
EMP: 2
SALES (corp-wide): 3.2B **Privately Held**
WEB: www.virginia.edu
SIC: 2721 9411 Periodicals; administration of educational programs
PA: Rector & Visitors Of The University Of Virginia
1001 Emmet St N
Charlottesville VA 22903
434 924-0311

(G-2859)
RECTOR VISITORS OF THE UNIV VA
University Press
210 Sprigg Ln (22903-2417)
P.O. Box 400318 (22904-4318)
PHONE..................................434 924-3468
Mark Mones, *Editor*
Anne Hegeman, *Prdtn Mgr*
Ellen Satrom, *Editor*
Penelope Kaiserlian, *Director*
Cecilia Sorochin, *Art Dir*
EMP: 23

SALES (corp-wide): 3.2B Privately Held
WEB: www.virginia.edu
SIC: 2731 9199 Books: publishing only; general government administration;
PA: Rector & Visitors Of The University Of Virginia
1001 Emmet St N
Charlottesville VA 22903
434 924-0311

(G-2860)
RECTOR VISITORS OF THE UNIV VA
Also Called: Virginia Quarterly Review, The
1 West Range (22903-3237)
PHONE................................434 924-3124
Ted Genoways, *Manager*
EMP: 4
SALES (corp-wide): 3.2B Privately Held
WEB: www.virginia.edu
SIC: 2721 9411 Trade journals: publishing only, not printed on site; administration of educational programs;
PA: Rector & Visitors Of The University Of Virginia
1001 Emmet St N
Charlottesville VA 22903
434 924-0311

(G-2861)
RED BROOK LUMBER CO
3846 Carters Mountain Rd (22902-7721)
PHONE................................434 293-2077
Robert Howard, *Owner*
EMP: 1
SALES (est): 118.9K Privately Held
WEB: www.redbrooklumber.com
SIC: 2431 5031 Millwork; lumber, plywood & millwork

(G-2862)
RED STAR CONSULTING LLC
Also Called: Red Star Merchandise
1218 East Market St (22902-5446)
PHONE................................434 872-0890
Alex Stultz,
▲ EMP: 4
SQ FT: 1,250
SALES (est): 631.3K Privately Held
WEB: www.redstarmerch.com
SIC: 2253 2396 T-shirts & tops, knit; fabric printing & stamping

(G-2863)
RIVANNA MEDICAL LLC
107 E Water St (22902-5218)
PHONE................................828 612-8191
John A Williams, *President*
Frank Mauldin, *Chairman*
Chetana Bayas, *Engineer*
Will Mauldin, *CTO*
Kevin Owen, *Bd of Directors*
EMP: 3
SALES (est): 351.8K Privately Held
WEB: www.rivannamedical.com
SIC: 3845 Electromedical equipment

(G-2864)
RK PUBLISHING COMPANY LLC
935 Rock Creek Rd (22903-3941)
PHONE................................434 249-9926
Craig Marshall, *Principal*
EMP: 2
SALES (est): 81.4K Privately Held
SIC: 2741 Miscellaneous publishing

(G-2865)
RODYN VIBRATION ANALYSIS INC
1501 Gordon Ave (22903-1915)
PHONE................................434 326-6797
E J Gunter, *President*
Peter Gunter, *President*
Gunter Mary Alice, *Vice Pres*
EMP: 2
SALES (est): 210.8K Privately Held
WEB: www.dyrobes.com
SIC: 7372 8748 Prepackaged software; business consulting

(G-2866)
RONALD STEVEN HAMM
Also Called: Steven Hamm Goldsmith Designs
1304 East Market St Ste T (22902-5487)
PHONE................................434 295-8878

Ronald S Hamm, *Owner*
EMP: 1
SALES (est): 78.2K Privately Held
WEB: www.stevenhammdesigns.com
SIC: 3911 Jewelry, precious metal

(G-2867)
ROOKWOOD PRESS INC
520 Rookwood Pl (22903-4734)
PHONE................................434 971-1835
David Lee Rubin, *President*
EMP: 5
SALES (est): 400K Privately Held
SIC: 2731 Book publishing

(G-2868)
RUSS FINE WOODS INC
1306 Knoll St (22902-6240)
PHONE................................434 974-6504
Russell Ryalls, *Owner*
EMP: 3
SALES (est): 278.2K Privately Held
WEB: www.russfinewoodsinc.com
SIC: 2521 Cabinets, office: wood

(G-2869)
S FUEL CO
901 East Market St (22902-5342)
PHONE................................434 220-1044
Sam Desai, *Principal*
EMP: 3
SALES (est): 242K Privately Held
SIC: 2869 Fuels

(G-2870)
SAFETY SOFTWARE INC
Also Called: Safetyoffice
801 W Main St Ste 100 (22903-4582)
P.O. Box 5225 (22905-5225)
PHONE................................434 296-8789
EMP: 15
SQ FT: 2,000
SALES (est): 1.2MM Privately Held
SIC: 7372 7371 Prepackaged Software Developer/Publisher

(G-2871)
SALESFORCE MAPS
Also Called: Terralign Group
922 Rugby Rd (22903-1606)
PHONE................................571 388-4990
EMP: 5 Publicly Held
WEB: www.mapanything.com
SIC: 7372 8742 Business oriented computer software; business consultant
HQ: Salesforce Maps
5200 77 Center Dr Ste 400
Charlotte NC 28217
866 547-8016

(G-2872)
SCENETHINK INC
116 E Main St Ste 1 (22902-5220)
PHONE................................434 987-6525
EMP: 5
SALES (est): 362.2K Privately Held
WEB: www.scenethink.com
SIC: 3652 Pre-recorded records & tapes

(G-2873)
SCIENTIFIC SOFTWARE SOLUTIONS
317 Monte Vista Ave (22903-4120)
PHONE................................434 293-7661
Jack Wilson, *President*
Mary Wilkins, *Vice Pres*
Mary Wilson, *Vice Pres*
Kavitha Kandagatla, *Manager*
John Dean, *Info Tech Mgr*
EMP: 15 EST: 1981
SALES (est): 1.4MM Privately Held
WEB: www.pedheart.com
SIC: 7372 Application computer software

(G-2874)
SCIVERA LLC
300 E Main St Fl 3 (22902-5219)
P.O. Box 142 (22902-0142)
PHONE................................434 974-1301
Joseph Rinkevich, *President*
Jamie Orchard-Hays, *President*
EMP: 5
SQ FT: 2,000

SALES (est): 366.8K Privately Held
WEB: www.scivera.com
SIC: 7372 Business oriented computer software

(G-2875)
SILIVHERE TECHNOLOGIES INC
106 W South St Ste 219 (22902-3600)
PHONE................................434 566-1207
Christopher Conti, *CEO*
Chrisopher Conti, *CEO*
Jim Smith, *Officer*
EMP: 4
SALES (est): 150K Privately Held
SIC: 2834 Chlorination tablets & kits (water purification)

(G-2876)
SILVER CITY IRON INC
134 10th St Nw Apt 2 (22903-2875)
P.O. Box 22, Esmont (22937-0022)
PHONE................................434 566-7644
Corry Blanc, *President*
EMP: 1
SALES (est): 60K Privately Held
SIC: 3446 Architectural metalwork

(G-2877)
SILVER RING SPLINT CO
1140 East Market St Ste A (22902-5486)
P.O. Box 2856 (22902-2856)
PHONE................................434 971-4052
Cynthia Garris, *President*
Ed Garris, *Vice Pres*
EMP: 7
SALES (est): 540K Privately Held
WEB: www.silverringsplint.com
SIC: 3842 Surgical appliances & supplies

(G-2878)
SILVERCHAIR SCNCE + CMMNCTONS
316 E Main St Ste 300 (22902-3203)
PHONE................................434 296-6333
Thane Kerner, *CEO*
Timothy Barton, *President*
Stuart Leitch, *COO*
Brian Fitzgerald, *CFO*
Jake Zarnegar,
EMP: 125
SQ FT: 12,000
SALES (est): 18.7MM Privately Held
WEB: www.silverchair.com
SIC: 2721 7338 2731 Periodicals: publishing only; editing service; book publishing

(G-2879)
SOUNDPIPE LLC
1110 East Market St 4q (22902-5364)
PHONE................................434 218-3394
Joseph Kilroy, *General Mgr*
EMP: 6
SALES (est): 524.8K Privately Held
WEB: www.sound-pipe.com
SIC: 3845 Ultrasonic medical equipment, except cleaning

(G-2880)
SPLENDORAS
317 E Main St (22902-5233)
PHONE................................434 296-8555
Henry Ayres, *Principal*
Patricia Ross, *Exec VP*
EMP: 15
SALES (est): 1.2MM Privately Held
WEB: www.splendoras.com
SIC: 2024 Ice cream & frozen desserts

(G-2881)
SQUARE ONE ORGANIC SPIRITS LLC
3370 Bear Den Ct (22903-9324)
P.O. Box 469, Ivy (22945-0469)
PHONE................................415 612-4151
Allison Evanow, *CEO*
Kimberly Charles,
William Evanow,
Debbie Jones,
Greg Jones,
▼ EMP: 3
SALES (est): 787.3K Privately Held
WEB: www.squareoneorganicspirits.com
SIC: 2085 Neutral spirits, except fruit

(G-2882)
SQURL LLC
496 Cleveland Ave (22903-6407)
PHONE................................443 481-9941
Micheal Ivory, *Principal*
Mark Harrison, *Principal*
Joyce Ivory, *Principal*
Tiffany Monroe, *Principal*
EMP: 1
SALES (est): 57.5K Privately Held
SIC: 2656 Sanitary food containers

(G-2883)
STARLIGHT EXPRESS LLC
Also Called: Nyc Shuttle
1117 East Market St Ste H (22902-5350)
PHONE................................434 295-0782
David New,
EMP: 3
SALES (est): 175.5K Privately Held
WEB: www.nycshuttle.com
SIC: 2741 Miscellaneous publishing

(G-2884)
STOCKTON CREEK PRESS LLC
366 Normandy Dr (22903-9208)
PHONE................................410 490-8863
Sara Ervin, *Principal*
EMP: 1
SALES (est): 37.5K Privately Held
SIC: 2741 Miscellaneous publishing

(G-2885)
SWEET CATASTROPHE LLC
317 E Main St (22902-5233)
PHONE................................434 296-8555
Donald D Long, *Administration*
EMP: 15
SALES (est): 976.4K Privately Held
SIC: 2024 Ice cream, bulk

(G-2886)
TEARSOLUTIONS INC
315 Old Ivy Way Ste 301 (22903-4894)
PHONE................................434 951-0444
Mark Logan, *CEO*
Colin M Rolph, *CFO*
Colin Rolph, *CFO*
EMP: 1 EST: 2013
SALES (est): 91K Privately Held
WEB: www.tearsolutions.com
SIC: 2833 Medicinals & botanicals

(G-2887)
TECH DYNAMISM LLC
110 5th St Ne (22902-5230)
PHONE................................434 227-5324
EMP: 2
SALES (est): 86.6K Privately Held
WEB: www.techdynamism.com
SIC: 3441 Fabricated structural metal

(G-2888)
TEGREX TECHNOLOGIES LLC
705 Dale Ave Ste D (22903-5273)
PHONE................................805 500-8479
James Landers, *Mng Member*
EMP: 6
SALES (est): 240.8K
SALES (corp-wide): 1.5MM Privately Held
WEB: www.tegrextechnologies.com
SIC: 3841 Diagnostic apparatus, medical
PA: Microgem International Plc
Venture Road The Innovation Centre
Southampton HANTS SO16

(G-2889)
THIBAUT-JANISSON LLC
Also Called: Thibaut-Janisson Winery
1413 Dairy Rd (22903-1301)
PHONE................................434 996-3307
Claude Thibaut, *Mng Member*
EMP: 2
SALES (est): 117.9K Privately Held
WEB: www.tjwinery.com
SIC: 2084 Wines

(G-2890)
THIERRY DUGUET ENGRAVER INC
2246 Ivy Rd Ste 9 (22903-4968)
PHONE................................434 979-3647
Thierry Duguet, *Owner*
EMP: 1

▲ = Import ▼=Export
◆ =Import/Export

SALES (est): 56K **Privately Held**
WEB: www.engraver.net
SIC: 3479 Engraving jewelry silverware, or metal

(G-2891)
THINTHERM LLC
1120 Elliott Ave (22926-6221)
PHONE..............................434 243-5328
Brian Foley,
John Gaskins,
Patrick Hopkins,
EMP: 4
SALES (est): 126.1K **Privately Held**
WEB: www.thintherm.com
SIC: 3823 7389 Temperature measurement instruments, industrial;

(G-2892)
TIMBER TEAM USA LLC
1 Morton Dr Ste 504 (22903-6807)
PHONE..............................434 989-1201
EMP: 3
SALES (est): 136.9K **Privately Held**
WEB: www.timberteam.com
SIC: 2421 Sawmills & planing mills, general

(G-2893)
TRANE US INC
1215 East Market St (22902-5512)
PHONE..............................434 327-1601
EMP: 62 **Privately Held**
WEB: www.trane.com
SIC: 3585 Refrigeration & heating equipment
HQ: Trane U.S. Inc.
3600 Pammel Creek Rd
La Crosse WI 54601
608 787-2000

(G-2894)
TRANLIN TRADING LLC
1 Boars Head Pl Ste 100 (22903-4628)
PHONE..............................866 215-8290
Jerry Zhiyuan Peng, CEO
John M Stacey, Senior VP
EMP: 4 EST: 2014
SALES (est): 292.9K **Privately Held**
WEB: www.vastly.com
SIC: 2621 Towels, tissues & napkins: paper & stock

(G-2895)
TRIED & TRUE PRINTING LLC
Also Called: Tried and Tru Supply Company
121 Danbury Ct (22902-9011)
PHONE..............................434 964-8202
Brian Brubaker, Mng Member
EMP: 2 EST: 2012
SALES (est): 187.4K **Privately Held**
WEB: www.triedandtruesupply.com
SIC: 2752 Commercial printing, lithographic

(G-2896)
TRUE STEEL LLC
2271 Ambrose Commons Dr (22903-8816)
PHONE..............................540 680-2906
Brandon Flasco, Vice Pres
Joshua M McConnell, Mng Member
EMP: 8
SALES (est): 1.7MM **Privately Held**
WEB: www.buildwithtrue.com
SIC: 3448 1521 1541 7389 Prefabricated metal buildings; general remodeling, single-family houses; renovation, remodeling & repairs: industrial buildings;

(G-2897)
TRUEFIT DME LLC
200 Garrett St Ste P (22902-5662)
PHONE..............................434 980-8100
Paul Manning, President
Sean Stalfort, Vice Pres
Eugene Scavola, CFO
Angelo Lomascllo, Admin Sec
EMP: 7
SQ FT: 2,000
SALES (est): 521.9K
SALES (corp-wide): 3.9MM **Privately Held**
SIC: 3841 Surgical & medical instruments

PA: Pbm Capital Group, Llc
200 Garrett St Ste S
Charlottesville VA 22902
434 980-8100

(G-2898)
VARIAN MEDICAL SYSTEMS INC
501 Locust Ave (22902-4869)
PHONE..............................434 977-8495
Hosea Mitchell, Manager
EMP: 20
SALES (corp-wide): 3.2B **Publicly Held**
WEB: www.varian.com
SIC: 3841 Surgical & medical instruments
PA: Varian Medical Systems, Inc.
3100 Hansen Way
Palo Alto CA 94304
650 493-4000

(G-2899)
VAS OF VIRGINIA INC
Also Called: Data Visible
1740 Broadway St (22902-5877)
P.O. Box 241, Free Union (22940-0241)
PHONE..............................434 296-5608
Patton A Janssen, CEO
Virginia J Ashcom, Treasurer
Alex Janssen, Sales Staff
EMP: 50
SQ FT: 51,000
SALES (est): 5.1MM **Privately Held**
WEB: www.datavisible.com
SIC: 2761 2522 Strip forms (manifold business forms); office furniture, except wood

(G-2900)
VIRGINIA EAGLE DISTRG CO LLC
669 Gold Eagle Dr (22903-7720)
PHONE..............................434 296-5531
Mark Stephens, General Mgr
Terence Y Sieg, Principal
Drew Argent, Sales Staff
Jason Testerman, Sales Staff
Ronnie Snook, Marketing Staff
EMP: 8
SALES (est): 1MM **Privately Held**
WEB: www.vaeagle.com
SIC: 3421 5181 Table & food cutlery, including butchers'; beer & ale

(G-2901)
VIRGINIA SPORTSMAN
1932 Arlington Blvd (22903-1560)
PHONE..............................434 971-1199
Hay Hardy, Publisher
EMP: 1
SALES (est): 74.9K **Privately Held**
WEB: www.thevirginiasportsman.com
SIC: 2741 Telephone & other directory publishing

(G-2902)
VIRGINIA WINEWORKS LLC
1781 Harris Creek Way (22902-7878)
PHONE..............................434 923-8314
Philip Stafford, Mng Member
▲ EMP: 5
SALES (est): 750K **Privately Held**
WEB: www.virginiawineworks.com
SIC: 2084 Wines

(G-2903)
VITAE SPIRITS DISTILLERY LLC
715 Henry Ave (22903-5225)
PHONE..............................434 242-0350
Ian Glomski, Mng Member
Donna Glomski,
Eric Glomski,
Terrence Glomski,
Zuzana Ponca,
EMP: 7
SALES (est): 357.8K **Privately Held**
WEB: www.vitaespirits.com
SIC: 2085 7389 Distilled & blended liquors;

(G-2904)
WEKSLER GLASS THERMOMETER CORP
556 Dettor Rd Ste 102 (22903-7072)
PHONE..............................434 977-4544
Kevin Marks, CEO

▲ EMP: 7
SALES (est): 776.8K **Privately Held**
WEB: www.wekslerglass.com
SIC: 3231 Products of purchased glass

(G-2905)
WELL HUNG VINEYARD
5274 Ivy Rd (22903-7127)
PHONE..............................434 245-0182
William Steers, Principal
EMP: 2 EST: 2009
SALES (est): 88.1K **Privately Held**
SIC: 2084 Wines

(G-2906)
WHISPERING WOODS SOFTWARE LLC
1105 Druid Ave Unit R (22902-6178)
PHONE..............................434 282-1275
Joseph Nasevich, Principal
EMP: 2 EST: 2012
SALES (est): 126.2K **Privately Held**
WEB: www.whisperingweb.com
SIC: 7372 Prepackaged software

(G-2907)
WIMBERLEY INC
Also Called: Wimberley Design
1750 Broadway St (22902-5877)
PHONE..............................703 242-9633
Clay Wimberley, President
David Wimberley, Vice Pres
Clark Andrew, Sales Mgr
Chuck Pistole, Cust Mgr
EMP: 7
SALES (est): 1.1MM **Privately Held**
WEB: www.tripodhead.com
SIC: 3861 5941 Tripods, camera & projector; sporting goods & bicycle shops

(G-2908)
YAMA MOUNTAIN GEAR
1304 East Market St (22902-5468)
PHONE..............................434 202-9717
EMP: 3
SALES (est): 164.1K **Privately Held**
WEB: www.yamamountaingear.com
SIC: 3069 Fabricated rubber products

Chase City
Mecklenburg County

(G-2909)
AMCOR PHRM PACKG USA LLC
Wheaton Industries
194 Duckworth Dr (23924-3722)
PHONE..............................434 372-5113
Gary Colwell, Manager
EMP: 120
SALES (corp-wide): 12.4B **Privately Held**
SIC: 3221 Vials, glass
HQ: Amcor Pharmaceutical Packaging Usa, Llc
625 Sharp St N
Millville NJ 08332
856 327-1540

(G-2910)
BONDURANT BROTHERS DIST LLC
9 E 3rd St (23924-1442)
PHONE..............................434 533-3083
Robert M Bondurant, Administration
EMP: 1
SALES (est): 52.6K **Privately Held**
WEB: www.bondurantbrothersdistillery.com
SIC: 2085 Distillers' dried grains & solubles & alcohol

(G-2911)
FRED LEACH
290 Boondock Rd (23924-3134)
PHONE..............................434 372-5225
Fred Leach, Principal
EMP: 2 EST: 2010
SALES (est): 94.7K **Privately Held**
SIC: 2499 Wood products

(G-2912)
HEAVY METAL CONSTRUCTION INC
501 Greenhouse Rd (23924-2724)
PHONE..............................434 547-8061

John Jones, President
EMP: 4
SALES (est): 270.7K **Privately Held**
SIC: 3441 Building components, structural steel

(G-2913)
NEWELL INDUSTRIES INTL
397 Jonbil Rd (23924-3737)
PHONE..............................434 372-0089
Robert Newell, President
▲ EMP: 16
SQ FT: 90,000
SALES (est): 880K **Privately Held**
SIC: 2842 Sweeping compounds, oil or water absorbent, clay or sawdust

(G-2914)
NIPRO GLASS AMERICAS CORP
194 Duckworth Dr (23924-3722)
PHONE..............................434 372-5113
Gary Colwell, Branch Mgr
EMP: 5 **Privately Held**
WEB: www.nipro-group.com
SIC: 3221 Vials, glass
HQ: Nipro Pharmapackaging Americas Corp.
1200 N 10th St
Millville NJ 08332

(G-2915)
PALLETONE OF VIRGINIA LLC
820 Boyd St (23924-1125)
P.O. Box 220 (23924-0220)
PHONE..............................434 372-2101
Tony Fogleman, General Mgr
EMP: 63
SALES (est): 1.7MM
SALES (corp-wide): 476.2MM **Privately Held**
WEB: www.palletone.com
SIC: 2448 Pallets, wood
PA: Palletone, Inc
6001 Foxtrot Ave
Bartow FL 33830
800 771-1147

(G-2916)
SAUDER MANUFACTURING CO
239 W B St (23924-1921)
P.O. Box 99 (23924-0099)
PHONE..............................434 372-4151
EMP: 1
SALES (est): 39.6K **Privately Held**
SIC: 3999 Manufacturing industries

(G-2917)
THOMPSON ELECTRIC MOTOR SVC
Also Called: Thompsons Fire Extinguisher SA
11190 Hwy Ninety Two (23924-4036)
PHONE..............................434 372-3814
Robert Thompson, Owner
EMP: 3
SQ FT: 2,240
SALES (est): 202.2K **Privately Held**
SIC: 7694 7389 5999 5099 Electric motor repair; fire extinguisher servicing; motors, electric; fire extinguishers

---

Chatham
Pittsylvania County

(G-2918)
ALLENS LOGGING INC
11400 Franklin Tpke (24531-4923)
PHONE..............................434 724-6493
Allen Hammock, President
Shirley Hammock, Corp Secy
EMP: 1
SALES (est): 128.3K **Privately Held**
SIC: 2411 Logging camps & contractors

(G-2919)
ARKEMA INC
Also Called: Sartomer - Chatham
601 Tightsqueeze Indus Rd (24531-3678)
PHONE..............................434 433-0300
Mike Jones, Branch Mgr
EMP: 123
SALES (corp-wide): 120.6MM **Privately Held**
WEB: www.arkema-americas.com
SIC: 2819 Industrial inorganic chemicals

HQ: Arkema Inc.
900 First Ave
King Of Prussia PA 19406
610 205-7000

(G-2920)
CARAVELLE INDUSTRIES INC (PA)
Also Called: Caravelle Vehicle Wshg Systems
2045 U S Hwy 29 N (24531)
P.O. Box 989 (24531-0989)
PHONE..................................434 432-2331
James W Roncaglione, Ch of Bd
Julie Reynolds, President
J M Roncaglione, Treasurer
EMP: 16
SALES (est): 1.8MM Privately Held
WEB: www.caravellewash.com
SIC: 3589 Car washing machinery

(G-2921)
CHATHAM KNITTING MILLS INC
119 S Main St (24531-4713)
P.O. Box 152 (24531-0152)
PHONE..................................434 432-4701
Matthew J Harris, President
EMP: 23 EST: 1951
SQ FT: 9,000
SALES (est): 1.9MM Privately Held
SIC: 2326 2329 2339 Men's & boys' work clothing; windbreakers: men's, youths' & boys'; women's & misses' outerwear

(G-2922)
CHERRYSTONE STRUCTURES LLC
2180 Walkers Well Rd (24531-3327)
PHONE..................................434 432-8484
Jason Miller, CEO
EMP: 13
SALES (est): 500K Privately Held
SIC: 2452 Farm buildings, prefabricated or portable: wood

(G-2923)
CLARENCE SHELTON JR
Also Called: C J Shelton Logging
2328 Fairview Rd (24531-3083)
PHONE..................................434 710-0448
Clarence Shelton Jr, Principal
EMP: 3
SALES (est): 197.9K Privately Held
SIC: 2411 Logging camps & contractors

(G-2924)
COMBUSTION TECHNOLOGIES INC
1804 Slatesville Rd (24531-3179)
PHONE..................................434 432-1428
Mark Percario, President
EMP: 6
SQ FT: 3,500
SALES (est): 800K Privately Held
WEB: www.combustech.com
SIC: 3728 Aircraft parts & equipment

(G-2925)
COOPERS R C TIRES
Also Called: Cooper's R C Racing Products
1020 Cooper Rd (24531-4137)
PHONE..................................434 724-7342
Patricia Cooper, Partner
Norris Cooper, Partner
EMP: 3
SALES (est): 275.2K Privately Held
WEB: www.coopersrc.com
SIC: 3061 Mechanical rubber goods

(G-2926)
CRABAR/GBF INC
Also Called: Major Business Systems
1 Ennis Dr (24531-1200)
PHONE..................................919 732-2101
Kevin Johnston, General Mgr
EMP: 22 Publicly Held
WEB: www.majorbusinesssystems.com
SIC: 2752 Business form & card printing, lithographic
HQ: Crabar/Gbf, Inc.
68 Vine St
Leipsic OH 45856
419 943-2141

(G-2927)
EASTERN PANEL MANUFACTURING
235 Woodlawn Hts (24531-3407)
P.O. Box 1036 (24531-1036)
PHONE..................................434 432-3055
Keith Van Asch, President
Bobby Woodall, Treasurer
EMP: 22
SQ FT: 23,000
SALES (est): 3.6MM Privately Held
WEB: www.easternpanel.com
SIC: 2435 2672 Panels, hardwood plywood; plywood, hardwood or hardwood faced; coated & laminated paper

(G-2928)
F W BAIRD GENERAL CONTRACTOR
581 Smith Rd (24531-4120)
PHONE..................................434 724-4499
EMP: 3 EST: 1999
SALES (est): 220K Privately Held
SIC: 3714 Mfg Motor Vehicle Parts/Accessories

(G-2929)
HJ SHELTON LOGGING INC
1565 Transco Rd (24531-3243)
PHONE..................................434 432-3840
Howard J Shelton, Principal
EMP: 8
SALES (est): 1MM Privately Held
SIC: 2411 Logging camps & contractors

(G-2930)
HOMEPLACE VINEYARD INC
880 Climax Rd (24531-3732)
PHONE..................................434 432-9463
Joseph H Williams, Principal
EMP: 3 EST: 2009
SALES (est): 232K Privately Held
WEB: www.thehomeplacevineyard.com
SIC: 2084 Wines

(G-2931)
NATIONAL TECHNICAL SVCS INC
32 Hargrave Blvd (24531-4619)
P.O. Box 854 (24531-0854)
PHONE..................................434 713-1528
Janet Hudson, President
EMP: 1
SALES (est): 107.9K Privately Held
SIC: 3612 Transformers, except electric

(G-2932)
NORTHERN PTTSYLVNIA CNTY FD CT
Weal Rd (24531)
P.O. Box 125, Gretna (24557-0125)
PHONE..................................434 656-6617
Wayne Chamlin, President
Frank Fuller, Vice Pres
Norma Elko, Admin Sec
Terri Lovel, Admin Sec
EMP: 3
SALES (est): 30.8K Privately Held
WEB: www.pittsylvaniacountyva.gov
SIC: 2099 Food preparations

(G-2933)
POLYNT COMPOSITES USA INC
Also Called: Cook Composites
920 Tightsqueeze Indus Rd (24531-3488)
PHONE..................................434 432-8836
Richard J Niesen, Manager
EMP: 24
SALES (corp-wide): 2.2B Privately Held
WEB: www.polynt.com
SIC: 2821 Plastics materials & resins
HQ: Polynt Composites Usa Inc.
99 E Cottage Ave
Carpentersville IL 60110

(G-2934)
PREMIER GRAPHICS
61 N Main St (24531-3113)
P.O. Box 1131 (24531-1131)
PHONE..................................434 432-4070
Laura Adcock, President
EMP: 5 EST: 1995
SALES (est): 639.8K Privately Held
WEB: www.premiergraphicsonline.com
SIC: 2621 Book, bond & printing papers

(G-2935)
PSM PUBLICATIONS INC
25 Lanier Ave (24531-3007)
PHONE..................................434 432-8600
Philip Stephen Mauger, Director
EMP: 1 EST: 2018
SALES (est): 37.5K Privately Held
SIC: 2741 Miscellaneous publishing

(G-2936)
SONOCO PRODUCTS COMPANY
Chatham Industrial Park (24531)
P.O. Box 271 (24531-0271)
PHONE..................................434 432-2310
Mike Baits, General Mgr
EMP: 15
SALES (corp-wide): 5.3B Publicly Held
WEB: www.sonoco.com
SIC: 2631 Paperboard mills
PA: Sonoco Products Company
1 N 2nd St
Hartsville SC 29550
843 383-7000

(G-2937)
TIMES FIBER COMMUNICATIONS INC
Also Called: TFC Amphenol
380 Tightsqueeze Indus Rd (24531-3677)
PHONE..................................434 432-1800
Harry Kes, Production
Larry Caroll, Branch Mgr
William Martin, Technology
EMP: 185
SALES (corp-wide): 8.2B Publicly Held
WEB: www.extreme-broadband.com
SIC: 3357 Nonferrous wiredrawing & insulating
HQ: Times Fiber Communications, Inc.
358 Hall Ave
Wallingford CT 06492
203 265-8500

(G-2938)
TIMES FIBER COMMUNICATIONS INC
380 Tightsqueeze Indus Rd (24531-3677)
PHONE..................................434 432-1800
EMP: 40
SALES (corp-wide): 5.5B Publicly Held
SIC: 3357 5051 3315 Metals Service Center Nonferrous Wiredrawing/Insulating Mfg Steel Wire/Related Products
HQ: Times Fiber Communications, Inc.
358 Hall Ave
Wallingford CT 06492
203 265-8500

(G-2939)
TOTAL PTRCHEMICALS REF USA INC
601 Tightsqueeze Indus Rd (24531-3678)
P.O. Box 1188 (24531-1188)
PHONE..................................434 432-3706
EMP: 30
SALES (corp-wide): 7B Publicly Held
WEB: www.totalpetrochemicalsrefiningusa.com
SIC: 2821 Plastics materials & resins
HQ: Total Petrochemicals & Refining Usa, Inc.
1201 La St Ste 1800
Houston TX 77002
713 483-5000

(G-2940)
VAN DER HYDE DAN
Also Called: Dan Van Der Hyde Repair Wldg
960 Davis Rd (24531-2903)
PHONE..................................434 250-7389
Dan Van Der Hyde, Owner
EMP: 1
SALES (est): 54.3K Privately Held
SIC: 7692 Welding repair

(G-2941)
WOMACK NEWSPAPER INC (PA)
Also Called: Yes Weekly
30 N Main St (24531-5557)
P.O. Box 111 (24531-0111)
PHONE..................................434 432-1654
Charles Womack, President
EMP: 9

SALES (est): 2.5MM Privately Held
WEB: www.clclt.com
SIC: 2711 Newspapers, publishing & printing

(G-2942)
WOMACK PUBLISHING CO INC (PA)
Also Called: Star Tribune
28 N Main St (24531-5557)
P.O. Box 111 (24531-0111)
PHONE..................................434 432-2791
Richard Ingram, General Mgr
Charles A Womack Jr, Principal
Chad Harrison, Opers Staff
Angela Starling, Bookkeeper
EMP: 14
SQ FT: 5,000
SALES (est): 33.3MM Privately Held
WEB: www.timesvirginian.com
SIC: 2711 Newspapers: publishing only, not printed on site

Check
Floyd County

(G-2943)
COLLINS WLDG & FABRICATION LLC
833 Hale Rd Ne (24072-3228)
PHONE..................................540 392-8171
Christopher Collins, Administration
EMP: 2
SALES (est): 127.7K Privately Held
SIC: 7692 Welding repair

(G-2944)
H D AND COMPANY
3291 Daniels Run Rd Ne (24072-3120)
PHONE..................................540 651-4354
Tim Vest, Partner
Doug Vest, Partner
EMP: 2
SALES (est): 175.5K Privately Held
WEB: www.hairdirect.com
SIC: 3531 Backhoes

(G-2945)
RON CAMPBELL ART AND FRAMING
350 Vest Tannery Rd Ne (24072-3334)
PHONE..................................540 651-2228
EMP: 2 EST: 2018
SALES (est): 87K Privately Held
SIC: 2499 Picture frame molding, finished

Cheriton
Northampton County

(G-2946)
BERNIES CONCHS
20400 Mill St (23316)
P.O. Box 225 (23316-0225)
PHONE..................................757 331-3861
F Vernon Rolley, Owner
EMP: 4
SQ FT: 7,500
SALES (est): 263.8K Privately Held
WEB: www.townofcheriton.org
SIC: 2092 Seafoods, fresh: prepared

(G-2947)
OPHELIAS HAT & HAIR SHOP
24127 Lankford Hwy (23316)
PHONE..................................757 331-1713
Ophelia Wright, Owner
John Wright, Partner
EMP: 1 EST: 1990
SALES (est): 87.2K Privately Held
WEB: www.pilgrimsgroupusa.com
SIC: 2353 5699 5199 Hats & caps; wigs, toupees & wiglets; wigs

▲ = Import ▼=Export
◆ =Import/Export

Chesapeake
Chesapeake City County

(G-2948)
23O5 PUBLISHING HOUSE
109 Gainsborough Sq (23320-1707)
PHONE......................................757 738-9309
Shamika Jackson, *Principal*
EMP: 1
SALES (est): 37.5K **Privately Held**
SIC: 2741 Miscellaneous publishing

(G-2949)
247 PUBLISHING INC
905 Poquoson Xing (23320-0711)
PHONE......................................757 639-8856
Thomas Noon, *Principal*
EMP: 2
SALES (est): 122.6K **Privately Held**
SIC: 2741 Miscellaneous publishing

(G-2950)
A & B MACHINE CO INC
633 Water Oak Ct (23322-2265)
PHONE......................................757 482-0505
EMP: 10
SQ FT: 17,500
SALES: 465.9K **Privately Held**
SIC: 3599 Machine Shop

(G-2951)
ABSOLUTE FURN SOLUTIONS LLC
3739 Holland Blvd (23323-1548)
PHONE......................................757 550-5630
Natanyah Yashaahla, *CEO*
EMP: 7
SALES (est): 346K **Privately Held**
SIC: 3634 Fans, electric: desk

(G-2952)
ACADEMICS IN A BOX INC
1508 Sams Cir (23320-4589)
PHONE......................................757 286-0673
Eric Holland, *CEO*
Elaine Hansen, *Principal*
EMP: 4
SALES (est): 288.8K **Privately Held**
WEB: www.groovylabinabox.com
SIC: 3999 Education aids, devices & supplies

(G-2953)
ACTION GRAPHICS AND SIGNS INC (PA)
Also Called: AG Wraps
112 Wayne Ave (23320-3930)
PHONE......................................757 548-5255
John M Hall Jr, *President*
EMP: 8
SQ FT: 3,600
SALES (est): 400K **Privately Held**
WEB: www.agwraps.com
SIC: 3993 Signs, not made in custom sign painting shops

(G-2954)
ADVANCED DESIGN FABRICATION
1220 Fleetway Dr Ste B (23323-1544)
P.O. Box 6096 (23323-0096)
PHONE......................................757 484-4486
James Divita Jr, *President*
Karen Divita, *Admin Sec*
EMP: 15
SQ FT: 7,000
SALES (est): 940K **Privately Held**
WEB: www.signs-nameplates.com
SIC: 3993 Signs & advertising specialties

(G-2955)
AFL NETWORK SERVICES INC
825 Greenbrier Cir Ste C (23320-2638)
PHONE......................................864 433-0333
EMP: 3 **Privately Held**
WEB: www.aflglobal.com
SIC: 3357 Nonferrous wiredrawing & insulating
HQ: Afl Network Services, Inc.
170 Ridgeview Center Dr
Duncan SC 29334
864 433-0333

(G-2956)
AGF DEFCOM INC
604 Green Tree Rd Ste C (23320-3685)
PHONE......................................757 842-4252
EMP: 12
SALES (est): 2.3MM **Privately Held**
WEB: www.agfdefcom.com
SIC: 3599 Machine shop, jobbing & repair

(G-2957)
AIR SYSTEMS INTERNATIONAL INC
829 Juniper Cres (23320-2627)
PHONE......................................757 424-3967
David F Angelico, *President*
David Angelico, *President*
Rowena L Angelico, *Corp Secy*
Ray Ellis Jr, *Vice Pres*
Dwayne King, *Vice Pres*
▲ EMP: 43
SQ FT: 22,000
SALES (est): 14.1MM **Privately Held**
WEB: www.airsystems.com
SIC: 3563 3564 Air & gas compressors; blowers & fans

(G-2958)
ALLCARE NON-MEDICAL WHEELCHAIR
405 Honey Locust Way (23320-9227)
PHONE......................................757 291-2500
Casey Turchetta, *Principal*
EMP: 2
SALES (est): 86.6K **Privately Held**
SIC: 3842 Wheelchairs

(G-2959)
ALLIED CON CO - SUFFOLK BLOCK
3900 Shannon St (23324-1054)
PHONE......................................757 494-5200
D Kirk Edens, *Principal*
EMP: 3
SALES (est): 204.7K **Privately Held**
WEB: www.alliedconcreteproductsusa.com
SIC: 3272 Concrete products

(G-2960)
ALLIED CONCRETE PRODUCTS LLC (DH)
3900 Shannon St (23324-1054)
PHONE......................................757 494-5200
Kirk Edens, *President*
Jim Strotmeyer, *VP Sales*
Jim Strotmyer, *Sales Executive*
▲ EMP: 9
SALES: 11.9MM
SALES (corp-wide): 30.6B **Privately Held**
WEB: www.alliedconcreteproductsusa.com
SIC: 3271 Blocks, concrete or cinder: standard

(G-2961)
ALSTON WELDING SVC
213 Thrasher Rd (23320-4727)
PHONE......................................757 547-7351
Clarence Alston, *Owner*
EMP: 1
SALES (est): 51.2K **Privately Held**
SIC: 7692 Welding repair

(G-2962)
AMBASSADOR RELIGIOUS SUPPLY
Also Called: A&D Distributors
3305b Taylor Ct (23321-4704)
PHONE......................................757 686-8314
Donald M Carter, *President*
Adelle Carter, *Vice Pres*
EMP: 5
SQ FT: 3,000
SALES (est): 477K **Privately Held**
WEB: www.a-dmusic.com
SIC: 3931 Musical instruments

(G-2963)
AMEE BAY LLC
540 Woodlake Cir Ste B (23320-8931)
PHONE......................................757 217-2720
Mike Quin, *Branch Mgr*
EMP: 90

SALES (corp-wide): 63.2MM **Privately Held**
WEB: www.ameebay.com
SIC: 3731 Shipbuilding & repairing
HQ: Amee Bay, Llc
2702 Denali St Ste 104
Anchorage AK 99503

(G-2964)
AMERICAN BORATE CORPORATION
4100 Buell St (23324-1004)
PHONE......................................800 486-1072
◆ EMP: 6 **Privately Held**
WEB: www.americanborate.com
SIC: 3295 Minerals, ground or treated
PA: American Borate Corporation
5701 Cleveland St Ste 350
Virginia Beach VA 23462

(G-2965)
AMERICAN CMG SERVICES INC (PA)
1521 Technology Dr (23320-5999)
PHONE......................................757 548-5656
Cynthia Smith, *President*
EMP: 6
SQ FT: 7,000
SALES (est): 1.1MM **Privately Held**
WEB: www.americanopc.com
SIC: 3842 5999 1542 Prosthetic appliances; abdominal supporters, braces & trusses; orthopedic & prosthesis applications; nonresidential construction; commercial & office building, new construction

(G-2966)
AMERICAN EGLE EMB GRAPHICS LLC
Also Called: Jumping Jacks
3108 Woodbaugh Dr (23321-4927)
P.O. Box 9375 (23321-9375)
PHONE......................................757 673-8337
Deborah Kidd,
EMP: 2
SALES (est): 35K **Privately Held**
WEB: www.americaneagleembroidery.com
SIC: 2395 Embroidery & art needlework

(G-2967)
AMERICAN GFM CORPORATION (PA)
Also Called: Agfm
1200 Cavalier Blvd (23323-1597)
PHONE......................................757 487-2442
Robert Kralowetz, *President*
Michael Kralowetz, *Exec VP*
Joe Baldwin, *Engineer*
Chris Richardson, *Engineer*
Jon Zogg, *Project Engr*
◆ EMP: 151 EST: 1977
SQ FT: 194,500
SALES (est): 30MM **Privately Held**
WEB: www.agfm.com
SIC: 3542 Machine tools, metal forming type

(G-2968)
AMERICAN MAR & INDUS SVCS LLC
Also Called: A M I S
912 Executive Ct (23320-3640)
PHONE......................................757 573-1209
Henry William Early Jr, *Mng Member*
Richard Faulkenberry,
EMP: 12
SQ FT: 11,000
SALES (est): 1.4MM **Privately Held**
SIC: 3498 Fabricated pipe & fittings

(G-2969)
AMERICAN MARITIME HOLDINGS INC
816 Industrial Ave (23324-2615)
PHONE......................................757 233-9055
EMP: 2 **Privately Held**
WEB: www.tecnicocorp.com
SIC: 3731 Military ships, building & repairing
PA: American Maritime Holdings, Inc.
813 Industrial Ave
Chesapeake VA 23324

(G-2970)
AMERICAN MARITIME HOLDINGS INC
800 Seaboard Ave (23324-2645)
PHONE......................................757 545-4013
EMP: 2 **Privately Held**
WEB: www.tecnicocorp.com
SIC: 3731 Shipbuilding & repairing
PA: American Maritime Holdings, Inc.
813 Industrial Ave
Chesapeake VA 23324

(G-2971)
AMERICAN MARITIME HOLDINGS INC (PA)
Also Called: A M H
813 Industrial Ave (23324-2614)
PHONE......................................757 961-9311
Gary R Brandt, *Ch of Bd*
Michael Torrech, *COO*
Armando Smith, *Project Mgr*
Francisco Hernandez, *Foreman/Supr*
Bobby Wall, *Foreman/Supr*
EMP: 20
SALES (est): 153.9MM **Privately Held**
WEB: www.tecnicocorp.com
SIC: 3731 7929 Military ships, building & repairing; entertainers & entertainment groups

(G-2972)
AMERICAN ORTHOTIC
Also Called: Cmg Contracting
1521 Technology Dr (23320-5999)
PHONE......................................757 548-5296
Cynthia Smith, *President*
Jessica Gilden, *Principal*
EMP: 5
SALES (est): 237.6K **Privately Held**
WEB: www.americanopc.com
SIC: 3646 1542 Commercial indusl & institutional electric lighting fixtures; commercial & office building, new construction

(G-2973)
AMERICAN TECHNOLOGY INDS LTD
Also Called: ATI
826 Professional Pl W (23320-3600)
P.O. Box 1846 (23327-1846)
PHONE......................................757 436-6465
Yoshiyuki Kawai, *President*
EMP: 35
SQ FT: 22,400
SALES (est): 3.1MM **Privately Held**
SIC: 3555 2796 Printing trade parts & attachments; platemaking services
PA: Nitto Kogyo Co., Ltd.
3-16-7, Kosuge
Katsushika-Ku TKY 124-0

(G-2974)
AMERICAST INC
3900 Shannon St (23324-1054)
PHONE......................................757 494-5200
Jim Richmond, *Branch Mgr*
EMP: 22
SALES (corp-wide): 200.4MM **Privately Held**
WEB: www.concretepandp.com
SIC: 3272 Culvert pipe, concrete
HQ: Americast, Inc.
210 Stone Spring Rd
Harrisonburg VA 22801

(G-2975)
AMFAB INC
1424 Campostella Rd (23320-6004)
PHONE......................................757 543-1485
William Proffitt, *President*
EMP: 6
SALES (est): 250MM **Privately Held**
SIC: 3499 Fire- or burglary-resistive products

(G-2976)
AOW GLOBAL LLC
814 Greenbrier Cir Ste B (23320-2643)
PHONE......................................757 228-5557
Chris Noyes, *Principal*
EMP: 4 EST: 2012
SALES (est): 287.6K **Privately Held**
SIC: 3341 Secondary nonferrous metals

GEOGRAPHIC

(G-2977)
APEX WELDING SERVICE LLC
662 Lacy Oak Dr (23320-4201)
PHONE......................................757 773-1151
Nathan Sprague, *Principal*
EMP: 7
SALES (est): 97.6K **Privately Held**
SIC: 7692 Welding repair

(G-2978)
ARC GLOBAL CORP
2119 Brennhaven Trl (23323-6413)
PHONE......................................757 470-9271
EMP: 2
SALES (est): 111.1K **Privately Held**
SIC: 3732 Boat building & repairing

(G-2979)
ARC LIGHTING LLC
2001 Dewald Rd (23322-2217)
PHONE......................................757 513-7717
Austin Cross, *Administration*
EMP: 1 EST: 2013
SALES (est): 109.8K **Privately Held**
SIC: 3648 Lighting equipment

(G-2980)
ARMSTRONG GORDAN
Also Called: Armstrong Welding & Repair
505 San Pedro Dr (23322-8022)
PHONE......................................757 547-1090
Gordan Armstrong, *Owner*
EMP: 7
SALES (est): 236.1K **Privately Held**
SIC: 7692 Welding repair

(G-2981)
ARTISTS INNVATORS
CREATORS LLC
2716 Spinners Way (23323-3546)
PHONE......................................757 359-6215
Jamaal Lassiter,
EMP: 1
SALES (est): 42.5K **Privately Held**
SIC: 2329 Men's & boys' clothing

(G-2982)
ASCWELDING
420 Forest Rd (23322-4325)
PHONE......................................757 274-4486
EMP: 1
SALES (est): 38.2K **Privately Held**
SIC: 7692 Welding Repair

(G-2983)
ASHEN WRIT LLC
2701 Derry Dr (23323-1727)
PHONE......................................757 818-8271
Karen R Carnegie, *Administration*
EMP: 2
SALES (est): 91.4K **Privately Held**
WEB: www.ashenwrit.com
SIC: 3861 Photographic equipment & supplies

(G-2984)
ASIAN PACIFIC SEAFOOD LLC
152 Greengable Way (23322-4278)
PHONE......................................251 751-5962
Zhao Xu, *President*
Don Flax, *Vice Pres*
▲ EMP: 3
SALES (est): 8MM **Privately Held**
SIC: 2091 7389 Crabmeat, preserved & cured;

(G-2985)
ASSOCIATION PUBLISHING INC
2117 Smith Ave (23320-2519)
PHONE......................................757 420-2434
EMP: 1
SALES (est): 67K **Privately Held**
SIC: 2741 Misc Publishing

(G-2986)
ATLANTIC WIND ENERGY LLC
305 Stonewood Ct (23320-3525)
PHONE......................................757 401-9604
Thomas Arrington, *COO*
EMP: 3
SALES (est): 950K **Privately Held**
WEB: www.atlanticwindenergy.net
SIC: 3612 Transformers, except electric

(G-2987)
ATLANTIC YACHT BASIN INC
2615 Basin Rd (23322-4012)
PHONE......................................757 482-2141
Jack Stumborg, *President*
William S Hull, *President*
Spencer Hull, *Treasurer*
Dean Debien, *Bookkeeper*
Faye Hannah, *Office Mgr*
EMP: 48 EST: 1933
SQ FT: 60,000
SALES (est): 7.2MM **Privately Held**
WEB: www.atlanticyachtbasin.com
SIC: 3732 4493 Yachts, building & repairing; boat yards, storage & incidental repair

(G-2988)
ATOMIZED PDTS GROUP
CHSPAKE IN
808 Curtis Saunders Ct (23321-2901)
PHONE......................................757 793-2922
Janet Puckett, *President*
EMP: 11
SQ FT: 22,500
SALES (est): 5MM **Privately Held**
WEB: www.atomizedproductsgroup.com
SIC: 3691 Storage batteries

(G-2989)
AVIATION & MARITIME
SUPPORT SE
516 Innovation Dr Ste 201 (23320-3866)
PHONE......................................757 995-2029
Donald Buzard,
Roberto Ortiz,
Jim Whitson,
EMP: 7
SALES (est): 427.9K **Privately Held**
SIC: 3731 Tenders, ships: building & repairing

(G-2990)
AVITECH CONSULTING LLC
721 River Strand (23320-2018)
PHONE......................................757 810-2716
Samip Patel, *CEO*
EMP: 1
SALES (est): 64.6K **Privately Held**
SIC: 7372 7373 7371 8748 Business oriented computer software; application computer software; computer integrated systems design; computer software systems analysis & design, custom; systems engineering consultant, ex. computer or professional;

(G-2991)
AWN CANDLE COMPANY
228 Crosswinds Dr Apt 303 (23320-5158)
PHONE......................................618 560-6355
Stacie Hopkins, *Principal*
EMP: 1
SALES (est): 39.6K **Privately Held**
SIC: 3999 Candles

(G-2992)
B3SK SOFTWARE LLC
3220 Meadowbrook Ln (23321-5440)
PHONE......................................757 484-4516
Richard Bryant Jr, *President*
Sue Clifton, *Sales Executive*
EMP: 2
SALES (est): 101.6K **Privately Held**
SIC: 7372 Prepackaged software

(G-2993)
BAINBRIDGE RECYCLING INC
5360 Bainbridge Blvd (23320-6712)
PHONE......................................757 472-4142
Mark Calcagni, *Owner*
EMP: 2 EST: 2016
SALES (est): 138.6K **Privately Held**
SIC: 3731 Shipbuilding & repairing

(G-2994)
BAUR LOGGING LLC
3036 Falmouth Dr (23321-5755)
PHONE......................................757 535-5693
EMP: 3 EST: 2016
SALES (est): 111.5K **Privately Held**
SIC: 2411 Logging

(G-2995)
BAYSIDE WOODWORKING INC
548 Winwood Dr (23323-3214)
PHONE......................................757 337-0380
Mark C Henry, *Principal*
EMP: 2
SALES (est): 170.8K **Privately Held**
WEB: www.baysidewoodworkinginc.com
SIC: 2431 Millwork

(G-2996)
BEAUTIFULLY MADE
CUPCAKES
1121 Railroad Ave (23324-2753)
PHONE......................................757 287-0024
EMP: 4
SALES (est): 205.1K **Privately Held**
WEB: www.beautifullymadecupcakes.com
SIC: 2051 Bread, cake & related products

(G-2997)
BEST AGE TODAY LLC
109 Gainsborough Sq (23320-1707)
PHONE......................................757 618-9181
Lori Hanselman, *Principal*
EMP: 2
SALES (est): 121.8K **Privately Held**
SIC: 2844 Face creams or lotions

(G-2998)
BEST DEAL ON SHIRTS LLC
3315 S Military Hwy (23323-3522)
PHONE......................................757 754-9855
EMP: 2
SALES (est): 116.4K **Privately Held**
WEB: www.bestdealonshirts.com
SIC: 2759 Screen printing

(G-2999)
BINGE LIVE INC
2329 Sanderson Rd (23322-1521)
PHONE......................................757 679-7715
Frederick Suria IV, *President*
Slade Cutrer, *Admin Sec*
EMP: 2 **Privately Held**
SIC: 3663 Mobile communication equipment

(G-3000)
BIOGEO GENETICS
228 Suth Mltary Hwy Ste B (23323)
PHONE......................................888 448-8376
Cornelius Warren, *CEO*
EMP: 8
SALES (est): 50K **Privately Held**
SIC: 2033 Fruit juices: packaged in cans, jars, etc.

(G-3001)
BIRDIES DOLLS
1904 Battlefield Blvd S B (23322-2181)
PHONE......................................757 421-7788
EMP: 1
SALES (est): 53.4K **Privately Held**
SIC: 3942 Mfg Dolls/Stuffed Toys

(G-3002)
BIRGE CROFT
Also Called: Turbo Specialties & Machine
1337 Lindale Dr Ste G (23320-5982)
PHONE......................................757 547-0838
Bruce Birge, *President*
EMP: 3
SQ FT: 4,500 **Privately Held**
SIC: 3511 Turbo-generators

(G-3003)
BL & SON ENTERPRISES LLC
1720 S Park Ct (23320-8920)
PHONE......................................757 502-7789
EMP: 3
SALES (est): 111.7K **Privately Held**
SIC: 2821 Plastics materials & resins

(G-3004)
BLACK MOLD BUSTERS
CHESAPEAKE
4416 Portsmouth Blvd E (23321-1583)
PHONE......................................757 606-9608
EMP: 2 EST: 2010
SALES (est): 110K **Privately Held**
SIC: 3544 Mfg Dies/Tools/Jigs/Fixtures

(G-3005)
BLAK TIE PUBLISHING CO LLC
1106 Lands End Dr (23322-6006)
PHONE......................................757 839-6727
EMP: 2
SALES (est): 49.7K **Privately Held**
SIC: 2741 Miscellaneous publishing

(G-3006)
BLOXOM SHEET METAL INC
813 Prfvnal Pl W Ste B101 (23320)
PHONE......................................757 436-4181
Warren Bloxom Jr, *President*
Warren Bloxom Sr, *Vice Pres*
Mary E Bloxom, *Treasurer*
EMP: 2
SQ FT: 3,000
SALES (est): 100K **Privately Held**
WEB: www. 1stopngo.com
SIC: 3444 Metal ventilating equipment; ducts, sheet metal

(G-3007)
BLUE JEANS PUBLISHING LLC
617 Stoneleigh Ct (23322-6881)
PHONE......................................757 277-9428
Carl Reddix, *Principal*
EMP: 2
SALES (est): 103.6K **Privately Held**
SIC: 2741 Miscellaneous publishing

(G-3008)
BLUE WAVE MOBILE MARINE
4108 Neptune Ct (23325-2527)
PHONE......................................757 831-4810
Theodore Simon Jr, *Owner*
EMP: 1
SALES (est): 36K **Privately Held**
SIC: 3732 Boat building & repairing

(G-3009)
BOBCAT SERVICE OF T N C
936 Mount Pleasant Rd (23322-3420)
PHONE......................................757 482-2773
Rod Nelson, *Principal*
EMP: 4
SALES (est): 523.6K **Privately Held**
WEB: www.bobcat.com
SIC: 3531 Construction machinery

(G-3010)
BODY COSMIC SKINCARE
1301 Canal Dr Apt 11d (23323-4846)
PHONE......................................757 701-8232
Katrina Renee, *Owner*
EMP: 3
SALES (est): 100K **Privately Held**
SIC: 2899 Essential oils

(G-3011)
BOOKERS TRANSPORT LLC
2728 Whitestone Ave (23323-2914)
PHONE......................................757 762-9233
Robert Booker,
EMP: 1
SALES (est): 60K **Privately Held**
SIC: 3537 Trucks: freight, baggage, etc.: industrial, except mining

(G-3012)
BOURBON
1105 Murray Dr (23322-1801)
PHONE......................................757 371-4710
EMP: 1 EST: 2017
SALES (est): 54.1K **Privately Held**
SIC: 2431 Millwork

(G-3013)
BOX PRINT & SHIP - C BERNEL
480 Kempsville Rd Ste 105 (23320-3868)
PHONE......................................757 410-7352
EMP: 2
SALES (est): 83.9K **Privately Held**
SIC: 2752 Lithographic Commercial Printing

(G-3014)
BRADLEY-MORRIS LLC
1545 Crossways Blvd # 200 (23320-0205)
PHONE......................................678 419-4171
Tim Best, *CEO*
Taylor Livesay, *Partner*
Mike Francomb, *Vice Pres*
Robert Reckner, *Manager*
Amy Kearby, *Consultant*

▲ = Import ▼=Export
◆ =Import/Export

EMP: 50
SALES (est): 10.7MM
SALES (corp-wide): 11.8MM **Privately Held**
WEB: www.bradley-morris.com
SIC: 3711 7361 7381 7299 Military motor vehicle assembly; placement agencies; guard services; babysitting bureau; human resource consulting services
PA: Bradley-Morris Holdings, Llc
 1825 Barrett Lakes Blvd N
 Kennesaw GA 30144
 678 819-4171

(G-3015)
BRANCHES TASTING ROOM
2125 Starmount Pkwy # 105 (23321-2237)
PHONE............................757 620-5393
EMP: 2 EST: 2019
SALES (est): 65.5K **Privately Held**
WEB: www.brancheswinetasting.org
SIC: 2084 Wines

(G-3016)
BROSWELL WATER SYSTEMS
824 Hidden Harbor Ct (23322-7076)
P.O. Box 13383 (23325-0383)
PHONE............................757 436-1871
Ed Browman, *Owner*
EMP: 1 EST: 1999
SALES (est): 119.6K **Privately Held**
WEB: www.braswell-water.com
SIC: 3589 Water treatment equipment, industrial

(G-3017)
BUMBLE BEE PRODUCTIONS INC
1049 Shoal Creek Trl (23320-9487)
PHONE............................757 410-9409
Scott Matheson, *Principal*
EMP: 2
SALES (est): 139.1K **Privately Held**
SIC: 2741 Miscellaneous publishing

(G-3018)
BUSY BS EMBROIDERY
712 Colony Dr (23322-8641)
PHONE............................757 819-7869
Barbara L Northcott, *Principal*
EMP: 1
SALES (est): 53.3K **Privately Held**
SIC: 2395 Embroidery & art needlework

(G-3019)
C & B TECHNOLOGY LLC
804 Industrial Ave Ste H (23324-2617)
PHONE............................757 545-3112
Belinda B Coker, *President*
Charles Coker, *Principal*
David Buck, *Vice Pres*
EMP: 3
SQ FT: 3,500
SALES (est): 609.4K **Privately Held**
WEB: www.c-b-technology.com
SIC: 3599 Machine shop, jobbing & repair

(G-3020)
C & L CONTAINERS INC
911 Live Oak Dr Ste 108 (23320-2500)
P.O. Box 7099, Portsmouth (23707-0099)
PHONE............................757 398-0447
EMP: 5
SQ FT: 10,000
SALES (est): 803.7K **Privately Held**
WEB: www.clcontainers.com
SIC: 2449 Shipping cases & drums, wood: wirebound & plywood

(G-3021)
C E C CONTROLS COMPANY INC
315 Great Bridge Blvd C (23320-7012)
PHONE............................757 392-0415
Brian Sobczak, *Principal*
EMP: 2
SALES (corp-wide): 12.7B **Privately Held**
WEB: www.ceccontrols.com
SIC: 3823 Industrial instrmnts msrmnt display/control process variable
HQ: C E C Controls Company, Inc.
 14555 Barber Ave
 Warren MI 48088
 586 779-0222

(G-3022)
CABINETS BY DESIGN INC
1220 Scholastic Way Ste B (23323-1631)
PHONE............................757 558-9558
Terry J Dixon, *President*
Neil Murphy, *General Mgr*
Nicole Norman, *Office Mgr*
EMP: 4
SALES (est): 385K **Privately Held**
WEB: www.cabinetsbydesignva.com
SIC: 2434 Wood kitchen cabinets

(G-3023)
CAMACHO ENTERPRISES LLC
Also Called: Dough-Licious
1403 Greenbrier Pkwy # 220 (23320-0614)
PHONE............................757 761-0407
Anjanette Camacho,
EMP: 5
SQ FT: 2,800
SALES (est): 188.7K **Privately Held**
SIC: 2064 Candy & other confectionery products

(G-3024)
CAMPBELL CUSTOM WOODWORKING
1040 Vanderploeg Dr (23320-2951)
PHONE............................757 724-2001
EMP: 1
SALES (est): 54.1K **Privately Held**
SIC: 2431 Millwork

(G-3025)
CANDIES & CHROME COATINGS LLC
908 Marble Arch (23322-8711)
PHONE............................757 812-1490
Richard Redford,
EMP: 2
SALES (est): 69.9K **Privately Held**
SIC: 3479 Metal coating & allied service

(G-3026)
CARDINAL PUMPS EXCHANGERS INC
1403 Greenbrier Pkwy # 12 (23320-0614)
PHONE............................757 485-2666
EMP: 5 **Publicly Held**
WEB: www.wabtec.com
SIC: 3443 Fabricated plate work (boiler shop)
HQ: Cardinal Pumps & Exchangers Inc.
 1425 Quaker Ct
 Salem OH 44460

(G-3027)
CAVALRY AEROSPACE LLC
516 Innovation Dr Ste 201 (23320-3866)
PHONE............................757 995-2029
Donald Buzard, *Principal*
EMP: 1
SALES (est): 54.6K **Privately Held**
SIC: 3721 Aircraft

(G-3028)
CF ADAMS BROKERAGE CO INC
1507 Mulligan Ct (23322-7439)
PHONE............................757 287-9717
Craig F Adams, *President*
Jean Adams, *Treasurer*
EMP: 3 **Privately Held**
SIC: 3621 Generating apparatus & parts, electrical

(G-3029)
CHAMPION PUBLICATIONS INC
1018 New Mill Dr (23322-7082)
PHONE............................757 580-4068
Edward Ruskowsky, *Principal*
EMP: 2
SALES (est): 9.4K **Privately Held**
WEB: www.thebestofchesapeake.com
SIC: 2741 Miscellaneous publishing

(G-3030)
CHESAPEAKE BAY ADIRONDACK LLC
732 Keeling Dr (23322-6208)
PHONE............................757 416-4583
Joseph Veneziano, *Principal*
EMP: 3

SALES (est): 235K **Privately Held**
WEB: www.chesapeake-bay-adirondack.com
SIC: 2511 7389 Wood lawn & garden furniture;

(G-3031)
CHESAPEAKE IND SFTWR TESTERS
1541 Shillelagh Rd (23323-6520)
PHONE............................757 547-1610
Victor Sorrell, *Principal*
EMP: 2
SALES (est): 86.4K **Privately Held**
SIC: 1389 Testing, measuring, surveying & analysis services

(G-3032)
CHESAPEAKE MACHINE WORKS INC
550 Freeman Ave (23324-1065)
PHONE............................757 543-1001
Charles Spear, *President*
Linda Spear, *Vice Pres*
Leslie Schiefer, *Admin Sec*
EMP: 10
SQ FT: 7,500
SALES: 2.3MM **Privately Held**
WEB: www.chesapeakemachineva.com
SIC: 3599 Machine shop, jobbing & repair

(G-3033)
CHESAPEAKE SIGNS
824 Sycamore Ln (23322-3429)
PHONE............................757 482-6989
John Wizieck, *Owner*
EMP: 1 EST: 1994
SALES (est): 48.6K **Privately Held**
WEB: www.cityofchesapeake.net
SIC: 3993 Signs & advertising specialties

(G-3034)
CHESAPEAKE YACHTS INC
1700 Shipyard Rd (23323-5502)
PHONE............................757 724-1717
Jack Stephens, *President*
EMP: 10
SQ FT: 21,600
SALES (est): 1.2MM **Privately Held**
WEB: www.chesapeakeyachtcenter.com
SIC: 3732 Yachts, building & repairing

(G-3035)
CHRISTOPHERS WOODWORKS LLC
1900 Ballahack Rd (23322-2855)
PHONE............................757 404-2683
Christopher Wratten, *Principal*
EMP: 2
SALES (est): 209.2K **Privately Held**
WEB: www.christopherswoodworks.com
SIC: 2431 Millwork

(G-3036)
CLASSIC CREATIONS OF TIDEWATER
1335 Lindale Dr Ste B (23320-5981)
PHONE............................757 548-1442
James Thomas Ayers Jr, *President*
Catherine Ayers, *Treasurer*
EMP: 6
SALES (est): 931.4K **Privately Held**
WEB: www.classiccreations.com
SIC: 2541 2434 Table or counter tops, plastic laminated; vanities; bathroom: wood

(G-3037)
CLEARLY-YOU INC
1700 S Park Ct Unit B (23320-8910)
PHONE............................757 351-0346
Chris M Noyes, *President*
EMP: 1
SALES (est): 81.2K **Privately Held**
WEB: www.clearly-you.com
SIC: 3952 Palettes, artists'

(G-3038)
CNV MARINE FUEL SPECIALIST LLC
1509 Taft Rd (23322-2715)
PHONE............................757 615-2666
EMP: 4
SALES (est): 225.1K **Privately Held**
SIC: 2869 Fuels

(G-3039)
COALZOOMCOM
1448 Carrolton Way (23320-3079)
PHONE............................304 920-2588
Tom Benner, *Director*
EMP: 2
SALES (est): 62.9K **Privately Held**
WEB: www.coalzoom.com
SIC: 2711 Newspapers, publishing & printing

(G-3040)
COASTAL CAULKING SEALANTS LLC
109 Duffield Pl (23320-6007)
PHONE............................757 679-8201
Christopher Ware, *Principal*
EMP: 4
SALES (est): 200K **Privately Held**
WEB: www.coastalcaulking.com
SIC: 2891 Sealants

(G-3041)
COASTAL CONSTRUCTORS LLC
Also Called: Concrete Precast Systems
1316 Yacht Dr Ste 307 (23320-6362)
PHONE............................757 545-0080
Dick Herrell,
Paul Ogorchock,
EMP: 2
SALES (est): 410.8K **Privately Held**
WEB: www.cpsprecast.com
SIC: 3272 Concrete products
PA: Concrete Precast Systems, Inc.
 1316 Yacht Dr
 Chesapeake VA 23320

(G-3042)
COASTAL PRECAST SYSTEMS LLC (PA)
Also Called: CPS
1316 Yacht Dr Ste 307 (23320-6362)
PHONE............................757 545-5215
Paul F Ogorchock, *Mng Member*
EMP: 13
SALES (est): 16.5MM **Privately Held**
WEB: www.cpsprecast.com
SIC: 3272 Concrete products, precast

(G-3043)
COASTAL PRSTTICS ORTHOTICS LLC (PA)
433 Network Sta (23320-3851)
PHONE............................757 892-5300
Steve Siverd, *Vice Pres*
EMP: 2
SALES (est): 306.4K **Privately Held**
WEB: www.coastalpando.com
SIC: 3842 5999 5047 Prosthetic appliances; medical apparatus & supplies; medical equipment & supplies

(G-3044)
COASTAL WATERS SALES & SVC LLC
801 Butler St Ste 17 (23323-3419)
PHONE............................757 893-9040
Sharon Silva, *Mng Member*
EMP: 1 EST: 2015
SALES (est): 150K **Privately Held**
SIC: 3462 Flange, valve & pipe fitting forgings, ferrous

(G-3045)
COLDENS CONCEPTS LLC
3613 Ahoy Dr (23321-3301)
PHONE............................757 644-9535
Jason A Colden, *Principal*
EMP: 3
SALES (est): 250K **Privately Held**
WEB: www.coldensconcepts.com
SIC: 2851 1721 Paints & allied products; painting & paper hanging

(G-3046)
COLONIAL BARNS INC (PA)
953 Bedford St (23322-1631)
PHONE............................757 482-2234
Merlin Miller, *President*
Linda Miller, *Corp Secy*
Richard Miller, *Vice Pres*
EMP: 20
SQ FT: 5,000

SALES (est): 3.1MM **Privately Held**
WEB: www.colonialbarns.com
SIC: **2452** Prefabricated buildings, wood

(G-3047)
COMMERCIAL READY MIX PDTS INC
1888 S Military Hwy (23320-2614)
PHONE..............................757 420-5800
Steve Johnson, *Branch Mgr*
EMP: 13
SALES (corp-wide): 38.3MM **Privately Held**
WEB: www.crmpinc.com
SIC: **3273** Ready-mixed concrete
PA: Commercial Ready Mix Products, Inc.
115 Hwy 158 W
Winton NC 27986
252 358-5461

(G-3048)
COMPASS GROUP USA INC
Also Called: Anchor Canteen
914 Cavalier Blvd (23323-1513)
PHONE..............................757 485-4401
Kenny Lindauer, *Branch Mgr*
EMP: 25
SALES (corp-wide): 31.5B **Privately Held**
WEB: www.compass-usa.com
SIC: **3581 7699** Automatic vending machines; vending machine repair
HQ: Compass Group Usa, Inc.
2400 Yorkmont Rd
Charlotte NC 28217

(G-3049)
CONCRETE PIPE & PRECAST LLC
3801 Cook Blvd (23323-1605)
PHONE..............................757 485-5228
EMP: 41
SALES (corp-wide): 276.3MM **Privately Held**
WEB: www.concretepandp.com
SIC: **3272** Sewer pipe, concrete; concrete products used to facilitate drainage
PA: Concrete Pipe & Precast, Llc
11352 Virginia Precast Rd
Ashland VA 23005
804 798-6068

(G-3050)
CONCRETE PRECAST SYSTEMS INC (PA)
Also Called: C P S
1316 Yacht Dr (23320-6362)
PHONE..............................757 545-5215
Paul F Ogorchock, *President*
Steve McOwin, *General Mgr*
Jackie Pilley, *COO*
Dick Hearrell, *Vice Pres*
Dan McGhee, *Vice Pres*
◆ EMP: 80
SALES (est): 26.6MM **Privately Held**
WEB: www.cpsprecast.com
SIC: **3272** Concrete products, precast

(G-3051)
CONGLOBAL INDUSTRIES LLC
Also Called: Container-Care Virginia
806 Meads Ct (23323-2212)
PHONE..............................757 487-5100
Taalor Moss, *Admin Mgr*
EMP: 20
SALES (corp-wide): 163.2MM **Privately Held**
WEB: www.cgicontainersales.com
SIC: **3731 7539 7519 2448** Shipbuilding & repairing; frame repair shops, automotive; trailer rental; cargo containers, wood & wood with metal
HQ: Conglobal Industries, Llc
8200 185th St Ste A
Tinley Park IL 60487

(G-3052)
CONSTRUCTION SOLUTIONS INC
1733 S Park Ct (23320-8911)
PHONE..............................757 366-5070
Chris Daily, *President*
EMP: 9

SALES (est): 1.1MM **Privately Held**
WEB: www.mncsl.com
SIC: **1389** Construction, repair & dismantling services

(G-3053)
COPPER WOODWORKS
2248 Shillelagh Rd (23323-6537)
PHONE..............................757 421-7328
Ronald Lewis, *Owner*
EMP: 1
SALES (est): 80.4K **Privately Held**
WEB: www.copperwoodwork.com
SIC: **3553** Furniture makers' machinery, woodworking

(G-3054)
CORNERSTONE WOODWORKS
2043 Lockard Ave (23320-2314)
PHONE..............................757 236-2334
EMP: 2 EST: 2008
SALES (est): 140.1K **Privately Held**
SIC: **2431** Millwork

(G-3055)
COVER UPS MARINE CANVAS
228 Hall Dr (23322-5210)
PHONE..............................757 312-9292
Rosemary K Kimbro, *Co-Owner*
EMP: 1
SALES (est): 90.9K **Privately Held**
SIC: **2394** Canvas & related products

(G-3056)
CRAFTED GLASS INC
1338 Atlantic Ave (23324-3304)
PHONE..............................757 543-5504
Thomas Connolly, *President*
Connolly Shirley A, *Vice Pres*
Shirley Connolly, *Vice Pres*
EMP: 7
SQ FT: 3,000
SALES (est): 622.3K **Privately Held**
WEB: www.craftedglass.co.uk
SIC: **3231 3211** Furniture tops, glass: cut, beveled or polished; flat glass

(G-3057)
CROSSROADS MACHINE INC
815 Bedford St (23322-1603)
PHONE..............................757 482-5414
Gary E Keffer, *President*
James Keffer, *Vice Pres*
▲ EMP: 7
SQ FT: 5,000
SALES (est): 901.6K **Privately Held**
SIC: **3599** Machine shop, jobbing & repair

(G-3058)
CUMBERLAND MILLWORK
1821 Engle Ave (23320-2203)
PHONE..............................757 233-4121
Thomas Barnes, *Owner*
EMP: 1
SALES (est): 40K **Privately Held**
SIC: **2431** Millwork

(G-3059)
CURTISS-WRIGHT CORPORATION
1101 Cavalier Blvd (23323-1505)
PHONE..............................757 494-3810
David Schurra, *Branch Mgr*
EMP: 85 **Publicly Held**
WEB: www.curtisswright.com
SIC: **3561** Pumps & pumping equipment
PA: Curtiss-Wright Corporation
130 Harbour Place Dr # 300
Davidson NC 28036
704 869-4600

(G-3060)
CYNTHIA KRIPAROS
Also Called: Custom Power Solutions
1201 Gillette Ct (23323-6656)
PHONE..............................757 818-3441
Cynthia L Kriparos, *Owner*
EMP: 2 EST: 2013
SALES (est): 30K **Privately Held**
SIC: **3671** Electron tubes

(G-3061)
DAG BLAST IT INC
Also Called: Nelson & Son Custom Monuments
315 Hanbury Rd W B (23322-4228)
PHONE..............................757 237-0735
Nelson Thompson, *President*
EMP: 2
SALES (est): 156.7K **Privately Held**
SIC: **1446** Blast sand mining

(G-3062)
DEAD RECKONING DISTILLERY INC
100 Columbus Ave (23321-4763)
PHONE..............................757 620-3182
Derek Ungerecht, *Principal*
EMP: 4 EST: 2014
SALES (est): 201.4K **Privately Held**
WEB: www.deadreckoningdistillery.com
SIC: **2085** Distilled & blended liquors

(G-3063)
DEEP CREEK DISTILLING CO LLC
801 Butler St Ste 12 (23323-3404)
PHONE..............................757 337-0209
EMP: 2
SALES (est): 66K **Privately Held**
SIC: **2085** Distilled & blended liquors

(G-3064)
DELAURI & ASSOCIATES
505 Hatteras Cres (23322-7927)
PHONE..............................757 482-9140
EMP: 2
SALES (est): 62.9K **Privately Held**
SIC: **2711** Newspapers

(G-3065)
DESIGNS INC
110 Battlefield Blvd N (23320-3950)
PHONE..............................757 547-5478
Joe Mazur, *Principal*
Joey Mazur, *Vice Pres*
Michelle Sumner, *Manager*
EMP: 3 **Privately Held**
WEB: www.designsva.com
SIC: **3993** Signs, not made in custom sign painting shops
PA: Designs, Inc.
110 Battlefield Blvd N
Chesapeake VA 23320

(G-3066)
DESIGNS INC (PA)
110 Battlefield Blvd N (23320-3950)
PHONE..............................757 410-1600
Mary Mazur, *Corp Secy*
Joey Mazur, *Vice Pres*
Michelle Sumner, *Vice Pres*
Troy Dongarra, *Manager*
EMP: 9
SALES (est): 1.2MM **Privately Held**
WEB: www.designsva.com
SIC: **3993** Signs & advertising specialties

(G-3067)
DEWS SCREEN PRINTER
Also Called: Dews Screen Printers
809 Prof Pl W Ste A104 (23320-3632)
PHONE..............................757 436-0908
Eloise W Walters, *President*
Warren Walters, *Vice Pres*
David Walters, *Treasurer*
Christi Satriano, *Manager*
Stuart Walters, *Admin Sec*
EMP: 10
SQ FT: 2,200
SALES (est): 954K **Privately Held**
WEB: www.dewsinc.com
SIC: **2261 5091** Screen printing of cotton broadwoven fabrics; sporting & recreation goods

(G-3068)
DLP ENTERPRISES INC (PA)
Also Called: Paige Decking
820 Greenbrier Cir Ste 10 (23320-2646)
PHONE..............................757 420-5886
Denise Paige, *President*
Stephanie Ritchie, *General Mgr*
Paige Scott, *Vice Pres*
EMP: 20

SALES (est): 2.1MM **Privately Held**
WEB: www.paigedecking.com
SIC: **3731** Shipbuilding & repairing

(G-3069)
DOCDIRECT PUBLISHING LLC
1017 Timber Neck Mall (23320-0676)
PHONE..............................757 237-1106
Holly Barla, *Principal*
EMP: 2 EST: 2010
SALES (est): 73.7K **Privately Held**
SIC: **2741** Miscellaneous publishing

(G-3070)
DOHERTY PLUMBNG CO
600 Oxbow Ct (23322-4715)
P.O. Box 15996 (23328-5996)
PHONE..............................757 842-4221
Paul Doherty, *Owner*
EMP: 3
SALES (est): 350K **Privately Held**
SIC: **3432** Plumbing fixture fittings & trim

(G-3071)
DOMINION QUIKRETE INC (PA)
Also Called: Quikrete of Virginia
932 Professional Pl (23320-3631)
PHONE..............................757 547-9411
James E Winchester Jr, *President*
Charles K Jett Jr, *President*
William R Magill, *CFO*
EMP: 50 EST: 1981
SQ FT: 10,000
SALES (est): 5.6MM **Privately Held**
SIC: **3241 5032** Cement, hydraulic; cement

(G-3072)
DOUBLE EAGLE GOLF WORKS INC
434 Las Gaviotas Blvd (23322-8065)
PHONE..............................757 436-4459
Rodney Herrera, *President*
Linda Herrera, *Owner*
EMP: 2
SALES (est): 130K **Privately Held**
SIC: **3949** Golf equipment

(G-3073)
DOZIER TANK & WELDING COMPANY
801 Industrial Ave (23324-2614)
P.O. Box 5265 (23324-0265)
PHONE..............................757 543-5759
David T Dozier, *President*
Elsie D Dozier, *Admin Sec*
EMP: 8
SQ FT: 3,200
SALES (est): 1.3MM **Privately Held**
WEB: www.doziertank.com
SIC: **7692** Welding repair

(G-3074)
DRAEGER SAFETY DIAGNOSTICS INC
Also Called: Draeger Ignition Interlock
215 Research Dr Ste 105 (23320-5977)
PHONE..............................757 819-7471
EMP: 1
SALES (corp-wide): 3B **Privately Held**
WEB: www.draegerinterlock.com
SIC: **3694** Automotive electrical equipment
HQ: Draeger Safety Diagnostics, Inc.
4040 W Royal Ln Ste 136
Irving TX 75063
972 929-1100

(G-3075)
DRAKE COMPANY
800 Twin Peak Ct (23320-8279)
PHONE..............................757 536-1509
Richard Drake, *Owner*
EMP: 2
SALES (est): 236.6K **Privately Held**
WEB: www.drakecontainer.com
SIC: **2653** Boxes, corrugated: made from purchased materials

(G-3076)
DREAMSCAPE PUBLISHING
805 Dunwood Ct (23322-8893)
PHONE..............................757 717-2734
James Corbin, *Owner*
EMP: 1

▲ = Import ▼=Export
◆ =Import/Export

SALES (est): 61.4K **Privately Held**
WEB:
www.dreamscapepublishing.webs.com
SIC: 2741 Miscellaneous publishing

(G-3077)
DRS LEONARDO INC
Also Called: Drs C3 Aviation Company
825 Greenbrier Cir (23320-2637)
PHONE...............................757 819-0700
Stacey Prather, *Manager*
David Peterson, *Director*
EMP: 12
SALES (corp-wide): 9.9B **Privately Held**
WEB: www.leonardodrs.com
SIC: 3812 Search & navigation equipment
HQ: Leonardo Drs, Inc.
   2345 Crystal Dr Ste 1000
   Arlington VA 22202
   703 416-8000

(G-3078)
DUKE INDUSTRIES LLC
Also Called: Skyfall Digital Media
813 Shipton Ct (23320-6870)
PHONE...............................252 404-2344
Ryan Duke, *Principal*
Jennifer Duke, *Principal*
EMP: 2
SALES (est): 81.9K **Privately Held**
SIC: 3999 Manufacturing industries

(G-3079)
DWIGGINS CORP
Also Called: Fastsigns
1424 Battlefield Blvd N (23320-4506)
PHONE...............................757 366-0066
Joseph Smith, *President*
EMP: 5
SALES (est): 622.4K **Privately Held**
WEB: www.fastsigns.com
SIC: 3993 2752 Signs & advertising specialties; commercial printing, lithographic

(G-3080)
DYER LLC
605 Treemont Ct (23323-4216)
PHONE...............................757 926-9374
Timothy Dyer, *Principal*
EMP: 2
SALES (est): 170.5K **Privately Held**
SIC: 3599 Machine shop, jobbing & repair

(G-3081)
EARTHCORE INDUSTRIES LLC
4000 Holland Blvd (23323-1522)
PHONE...............................757 966-7275
John McDowell, *Manager*
EMP: 9
SALES (corp-wide): 5.6MM **Privately Held**
WEB: www.earthcoreindustries.com
SIC: 3272 Fireplace & chimney material: concrete
PA: Earthcore Industries, Llc
   6899 Phillips Ind Blvd
   Jacksonville FL 32256
   904 363-3417

(G-3082)
EAST COAST STL FABRICATION INC
1401 Precon Dr Ste 102 (23320-6314)
PHONE...............................757 351-2601
Cynthia M Overman, *Principal*
Mary Miller, *Vice Pres*
Mark Overman, *Assoc VP*
▲ EMP: 37
SALES (est): 8.8MM **Privately Held**
WEB: www.ecsfi.com
SIC: 3441 Fabricated structural metal

(G-3083)
EASTCOM DIRECTIONAL DRLG INC
509 Giles Dr (23322-3808)
PHONE...............................757 377-3133
Kelly Wright, *President*
EMP: 1
SALES (est): 152.6K **Privately Held**
WEB: www.eastcomdrilling.com
SIC: 1381 1781 Directional drilling oil & gas wells; water well drilling

(G-3084)
ELECTRIC MOTOR AND CONTG CO (PA)
3703 Cook Blvd (23323-1603)
PHONE...............................757 487-2121
James L King, *President*
Steve Newing, *President*
Justin White, *COO*
Steven Garner, *Vice Pres*
Don Vivier, *Vice Pres*
EMP: 110
SQ FT: 90,000
SALES (est): 35MM **Privately Held**
WEB: www.emc-co.com
SIC: 3625 5063 3621 7694 Relays & industrial controls; motor controls, starters & relays: electric; electric motor & generator parts; armature rewinding shops

(G-3085)
ELECTRONIC DEVICES INC
Also Called: E D I
3140 Bunch Walnuts Rd (23322-2904)
PHONE...............................757 421-2968
Ray B Kauffman, *President*
Peggy L Kauffman, *Corp Secy*
EMP: 3
SALES (est): 348.9K **Privately Held**
WEB: www.dsts.com
SIC: 3531 7373 Marine related equipment; computer-aided design (CAD) systems service

(G-3086)
ELITE MASONRY CONTRACTOR LLC
1226 Priscilla Ln (23322-3700)
PHONE...............................757 773-9908
Jack Smith, *Principal*
EMP: 2
SALES (est): 85.9K **Privately Held**
SIC: 3572 Computer storage devices

(G-3087)
ELOHIM DESIGNS
Also Called: Ed's Apparel
1508 Prospect Dr (23322-1726)
PHONE...............................757 292-1890
Anthony Brown, *Owner*
EMP: 2
SALES (est): 21K **Privately Held**
SIC: 2389 7389 7374 Apparel & accessories; printed circuitry graphic layout; computer graphics service

(G-3088)
EMPC BIO ENERGY GROUP LLC
2036 Atlantic Ave (23324-3004)
PHONE...............................757 550-1103
Andrew Hammaker, *CEO*
Frank Redavide, *President*
EMP: 15 EST: 2014
SQ FT: 25,000
SALES (est): 1.6MM **Privately Held**
SIC: 2429 Shavings & packaging, excelsior

(G-3089)
ENGILITY LLC
Also Called: Command & Control Systems
825 Greenbrier Cir Ste M (23320-2638)
PHONE...............................757 366-4422
Kevin Obrien, *Branch Mgr*
EMP: 7
SALES (corp-wide): 6.3B **Publicly Held**
WEB: www.engility.com
SIC: 3824 Integrating meters, nonelectric
HQ: Engility Llc
   4803 Stonecroft Blvd
   Chantilly VA 20151
   703 708-1400

(G-3090)
ERIE BOATWORKS LLC
1020 Redstart Ave (23324-1842)
PHONE...............................757 204-1815
Zachary Blankenship, *Principal*
EMP: 3
SALES (est): 372.6K **Privately Held**
WEB: www.erieboatworks.com
SIC: 3732 Boat building & repairing

(G-3091)
ESKA USA BV INC
1910 Campostella Rd (23324-2929)
PHONE...............................757 494-7330

Herny Timmermans, *President*
Jonathan Edwards, *Controller*
▲ EMP: 45
SALES (est): 15.7MM **Privately Held**
SIC: 2675 Cards: die-cut & unprinted: made from purchased materials

(G-3092)
ESSROC CEMENT CORP
100 Pratt St (23324-1060)
PHONE...............................757 545-2481
EMP: 2
SALES (est): 82.2K **Privately Held**
SIC: 3273 Ready-mixed concrete

(G-3093)
ESTEEMED WOODCRAFTS
425 Butterfly Dr (23322-7272)
PHONE...............................757 876-5868
James Darlas, *Owner*
EMP: 2
SALES (est): 112.3K **Privately Held**
WEB: www.esteemedwoodcrafts.com
SIC: 2499 Wood products

(G-3094)
EURE CUSTOM SIGNS INC
1228 S Military Hwy Ste D (23320-2256)
PHONE...............................757 523-0000
Brian K Eure, *President*
EMP: 8
SQ FT: 4,500
SALES (est): 800.3K **Privately Held**
SIC: 3993 Signs & advertising specialties

(G-3095)
EWS INC
909 Hanbury Ct (23322-6618)
PHONE...............................757 482-2740
Emil Laroche, *Principal*
EMP: 2
SALES (est): 127.1K **Privately Held**
SIC: 2431 Woodwork, interior & ornamental

(G-3096)
F & M TOOLS LLC
1500 Linden Ave (23325-3945)
PHONE...............................757 361-9225
Martin Pantak, *Principal*
EMP: 2
SALES (est): 108.4K **Privately Held**
SIC: 3599 Industrial machinery

(G-3097)
FAR WEST PRINT SOLUTIONS LLC
722 Montebello Cir (23322-7257)
PHONE...............................757 549-1258
EMP: 2
SALES (est): 92.3K **Privately Held**
WEB: www.asb-farwest.com
SIC: 2752 Commercial printing, offset

(G-3098)
FATIM AND SALLYS CSTM TEES LLC
920 Green Sea Trl (23323-2645)
PHONE...............................619 884-5864
Tamsir Jobe, *Principal*
EMP: 2
SALES (est): 90.3K **Privately Held**
SIC: 2759 Screen printing

(G-3099)
FEDERAL EQUIPMENT COMPANY
650 Woodlake Dr (23320-8906)
PHONE...............................757 493-0404
Mike Korte, *Sales Staff*
Kevin Gaudet, *Manager*
EMP: 5
SALES (corp-wide): 22MM **Privately Held**
WEB: www.federalequipment.com
SIC: 3699 Electrical equipment & supplies
PA: Federal Equipment Company
   5298 River Rd
   Cincinnati OH 45233
   513 621-5260

(G-3100)
FIBREX GROUP INC
Also Called: Fibrex Environmental Products
738 Burrow Ave (23324-1010)
PHONE...............................800 346-4458
Ruben Leenders, *President*
Maria Garcia, *Corp Secy*
Martinus Leenders, *Vice Pres*
Suzanne Landers, *Marketing Staff*
EMP: 4
SQ FT: 12,000
SALES (est): 2.1MM **Privately Held**
WEB: www.fibrexgroup.com
SIC: 2655 Fiber cans, drums & containers

(G-3101)
FIRST RESPONDER SYSTEMS LLC
901 Cedarwood Trce (23322-2141)
PHONE...............................757 410-0353
David Pendergrass, *Principal*
EMP: 3
SALES (est): 203.8K **Privately Held**
WEB: www.firstrespondersystems.com
SIC: 3691 Storage batteries

(G-3102)
FITZGERALD WELDING & REPAIR
4906 Bainbridge Blvd (23320-6404)
PHONE...............................757 543-7312
James I Fitzgerald, *President*
Andrew Fitzgerald, *Senior VP*
Laurie Lee Fitzgerald, *Treasurer*
EMP: 4 EST: 1973
SQ FT: 5,000
SALES (est): 150K **Privately Held**
SIC: 7692 Welding repair

(G-3103)
FLORIDA TILE INC
Also Called: Florida Tile 89
500 Woodlake Cir Ste B (23320-8938)
PHONE...............................757 855-9330
Kristie Rymiszewski, *Branch Mgr*
EMP: 5
SALES (corp-wide): 35.5K **Privately Held**
WEB: www.floridatile.com
SIC: 3253 Wall tile, ceramic
HQ: Florida Tile, Inc.
   998 Governors Ln Ste 300
   Lexington KY 40513
   859 219-5200

(G-3104)
FLOWSERVE CORPORATION
3732 Cook Blvd Ste 101 (23323-1632)
PHONE...............................757 485-8044
EMP: 56
SALES (corp-wide): 3.9B **Publicly Held**
WEB: www.flowserve.com
SIC: 3561 Industrial pumps & parts
PA: Flowserve Corporation
   5215 N Ocnnor Blvd Ste 23 Connor
   Irving TX 75039
   972 443-6500

(G-3105)
FLOWSERVE CORPORATION
3900 Cook Blvd (23323-1626)
PHONE...............................757 485-8000
Matthw J O'Brien, *Vice Pres*
Jeffrey Jaglowicz, *Project Mgr*
Charles Avery, *Opers Mgr*
Jeffrey Odenwald, *Export Mgr*
Susanne Steffensen, *Senior Buyer*
EMP: 260
SALES (corp-wide): 3.9B **Publicly Held**
WEB: www.flowserve.com
SIC: 3561 Industrial pumps & parts
PA: Flowserve Corporation
   5215 N Ocnnor Blvd Ste 23 Connor
   Irving TX 75039
   972 443-6500

(G-3106)
FLUID ENERGY
404 Penhook Ct (23322-7233)
PHONE...............................757 549-5160
EMP: 4
SALES (est): 292.1K **Privately Held**
SIC: 3494 Mfg Valves/Pipe Fittings

GEOGRAPHIC

(G-3107)
FORMS UNLIMITED
1220 Executive Blvd # 105 (23320-2887)
PHONE...757 549-1258
Lee Williams, *Owner*
EMP: 2
SALES (est): 206.4K **Privately Held**
SIC: 2752 Commercial printing, lithographic

(G-3108)
FORTERRA PIPE & PRECAST LLC
Also Called: Concrete Pipe & Products Co
3801 Cook Blvd (23323-1605)
PHONE...757 485-5228
John Brabble, *Branch Mgr*
EMP: 19
SALES (corp-wide): 1.5B **Publicly Held**
WEB: www.forterrabp.com
SIC: 3272 Precast terrazo or concrete products
HQ: Forterra Pipe & Precast, Llc
511 E John Carpenter Fwy
Irving TX 75062
469 458-7973

(G-3109)
FOWLKES EAGLE PUBLISHING LLC
2003 Fern Mill Ct (23323-5350)
PHONE...757 673-8424
EMP: 1
SALES (est): 37.5K **Privately Held**
SIC: 2741 Miscellaneous publishing

(G-3110)
FREEDOM LODGING LLC
601 Montebello Cir (23322-7242)
PHONE...757 288-4514
Lori Lucas,
EMP: 1
SALES (est): 55.3K **Privately Held**
SIC: 3711 Wreckers (tow truck), assembly of

(G-3111)
FREEDOM TO DESTINY PUBG LLC
427 Gardenia Cir (23325-4643)
PHONE...757 617-8286
EMP: 1
SALES (est): 37.5K **Privately Held**
SIC: 2741 Miscellaneous publishing

(G-3112)
FUSION PWDR CATING FABRICATION
1220 Fleetway Dr Ste F (23323-1544)
P.O. Box 8395, Norfolk (23503-0395)
PHONE...757 319-3760
John Morrison, *President*
Merle Morrison, *Vice Pres*
EMP: 1
SALES (est): 15K **Privately Held**
WEB: www.fusioncaf.com
SIC: 3479 3443 3442 3446 Etching & engraving; weldments; metal doors; architectural metalwork; sheet metalwork

(G-3113)
G&M EMBROIDERY INC
205 Ashley Rd (23322-6704)
PHONE...757 482-1935
Gloria Cooley, *Principal*
EMP: 1 EST: 2009
SALES (est): 66K **Privately Held**
SIC: 2395 Embroidery & art needlework

(G-3114)
GANNETT MEDIA TECH INTL
1317 Executive Blvd # 300 (23320-3859)
PHONE...757 547-7274
EMP: 2
SALES (est): 62.1K **Privately Held**
SIC: 7372 Prepackaged software

(G-3115)
GARRITY CUSTOM SAWING LLC
4121 Sorrento Dr (23321-2060)
PHONE...757 488-9324
Paul Garrity,
EMP: 1

SALES (est): 106.4K **Privately Held**
WEB: www.sawyersite.org
SIC: 2421 Lumber: rough, sawed or planed

(G-3116)
GENERAL DYNAMICS CORPORATION
700 Independence Pkwy # 100
(23320-5186)
PHONE...757 523-2738
Dawn Jackson, *CEO*
Rose Ona, *Senior Buyer*
Bruce Stevenson, *Engineer*
Tim Pepper, *Manager*
EMP: 23
SALES (corp-wide): 39.3B **Publicly Held**
WEB: www.generaldynamics.com
SIC: 3812 Search & navigation equipment
PA: General Dynamics Corporation
11011 Sunset Hills Rd
Reston VA 20190
703 876-3000

(G-3117)
GENERAL DYNAMICS NASSCO
2620 Indian River Rd (23325-2655)
PHONE...757 215-2004
Fred Harris, *President*
EMP: 4
SALES (est): 490.3K **Privately Held**
SIC: 3731 Shipbuilding & repairing

(G-3118)
GEOQUIP INC
1111 Cavalier Blvd (23323-1505)
PHONE...757 485-2500
Gary Terwilliger, *President*
Walt Harrell, *Prdtn Mgr*
Bernie Alphonso, *Sales Staff*
Pam Patterson, *Office Mgr*
Matthew Williams, *Technical Staff*
▲ EMP: 55
SQ FT: 30,000
SALES (est): 8MM **Privately Held**
WEB: www.geoquipusa.com
SIC: 3599 7353 5082 Machine & other job shop work; heavy construction equipment rental; general construction machinery & equipment

(G-3119)
GEOQUIP MANUFACTURING INC
1111 Cavalier Blvd (23323-1505)
PHONE...757 485-8525
EMP: 50 EST: 2003
SALES (est): 4.5MM **Privately Held**
SIC: 3599 Mfg Industrial Machinery

(G-3120)
GJHMOTIVATE
3005 Camelot Blvd (23323-2714)
PHONE...757 487-5486
James Holman, *Owner*
EMP: 1
SALES (est): 66.2K **Privately Held**
SIC: 2741 Miscellaneous publishing

(G-3121)
GLENMARK GROUP LLC
Also Called: Lw Aerospace
1105a International Plz (23323-1530)
PHONE...757 955-6850
Mark Douglas Smith, *Mng Member*
Glenda Bacsa Smith,
EMP: 2
SALES (est): 104.1K **Privately Held**
WEB: www.theglenmarkgroup.com
SIC: 3728 Aircraft parts & equipment

(G-3122)
GLOBAL SERVICES INTL LLC
623 Sedgefield Ct (23322-8340)
PHONE...757 535-2394
Walter E White Jr, *Mng Member*
EMP: 1
SALES (est): 54.6K **Privately Held**
SIC: 3731 Shipbuilding & repairing

(G-3123)
GRAPHICS SHOP LLC
1700 Liberty St (23324-3531)
P.O. Box 5472 (23324-0472)
PHONE...757 485-7800
Charles Hackworth, *President*

EMP: 12
SALES (est): 1.3MM **Privately Held**
WEB: www.tgsva.com
SIC: 3993 Signs & advertising specialties

(G-3124)
GREEN FOREST CABINETRY
723 Fenway Ave (23323-3330)
PHONE...757 485-9200
Scotty Henderson, *QC Mgr*
EMP: 5
SALES (est): 265.9K **Privately Held**
WEB: www.greenforestcabinetry.com
SIC: 2434 Wood kitchen cabinets

(G-3125)
GREG & SON PALLETS
1500 Liberty St (23324-2405)
PHONE...757 449-3832
Gregory Butts, *Principal*
EMP: 8 EST: 2010
SALES (est): 857.1K **Privately Held**
WEB:
www.southnorfolkbusinessdirectory.com
SIC: 2448 Pallets, wood

(G-3126)
GREGG COMPANY LTD
1600 Dockyard Lndg (23321-6611)
PHONE...757 966-1367
Richard T Gregg, *Chairman*
Susan Gregg, *Vice Pres*
▼ EMP: 3 EST: 1903
SQ FT: 7,500
SALES (est): 1.8MM **Privately Held**
SIC: 3743 Freight cars & equipment

(G-3127)
HAMPTON ROADS VENDING
Also Called: Hampton Roads Services
1508 Sams Cir Ste B130 (23320-4589)
PHONE...703 927-6125
▲ EMP: 2
SALES: 15K **Privately Held**
SIC: 3581 Mfg Vending Machines

(G-3128)
HANSEN DEFENSE SYSTEMS LLC
3037 Curling Ct (23322-3100)
PHONE...757 389-1683
Brennan Hansen, *Principal*
EMP: 1
SALES (est): 81.8K **Privately Held**
SIC: 3812 Defense systems & equipment

(G-3129)
HAYDEN ENTERPRISES
Also Called: Airsource Filterless Tech
1151 Eagle Pointe Way (23322-7485)
PHONE...910 791-3132
Steve Hayden, *Partner*
Karen Hayden, *Partner*
EMP: 2
SALES (est): 263.6K **Privately Held**
SIC: 3564 Air purification equipment

(G-3130)
HEART SPEAKS PUBLISHING LLC
1912 Starling St Apt 302 (23322-4389)
PHONE...803 403-4266
Camille Sheppard-Parrish, *Principal*
EMP: 1
SALES (est): 41.3K **Privately Held**
SIC: 2741 Miscellaneous publishing

(G-3131)
HEMPCEUTICALS LLC
2150 Old Greenbrier Rd (23320-2659)
PHONE...757 384-2782
Adquena Faine, *Mng Member*
EMP: 1
SALES (est): 47.2K
SALES (corp-wide): 183K **Privately Held**
SIC: 2833 Alkaloids & other botanical based products
PA: Hers Limited Company
2150 Old Greenbrier Rd
Chesapeake VA 23320
757 741-8871

(G-3132)
HERB DODGE ENTERPRISES
1601 Rokeby Ave (23325-3933)
PHONE...757 714-4313
James H Dodge, *Owner*
EMP: 3
SALES (est): 201K **Privately Held**
SIC: 2211 Broadwoven fabric mills, cotton

(G-3133)
HERBAN HOUSE BEAUTY LLC
3612 Dock Point Arch (23321-3185)
PHONE...443 934-9041
Dadrian Watkins,
EMP: 2 EST: 2014
SALES (est): 99.6K **Privately Held**
SIC: 2844 Powder: baby, face, talcum or toilet

(G-3134)
HERMITAGE INDUSTRIES CO INC
3008 Trappers Run (23321-6153)
PHONE...757 638-4551
Nicole Booker, *Principal*
EMP: 2
SALES (est): 111.7K **Privately Held**
SIC: 3999 Manufacturing industries

(G-3135)
HIBISCUS CHESECAKE ELIXIRS LLC
4131 Williamson St (23324-2713)
PHONE...757 932-2539
Tanya Jenkins, *Principal*
EMP: 2
SALES (est): 145.4K **Privately Held**
SIC: 2591 Window blinds

(G-3136)
HICKORY EMBROIDERY LLC
1805 Sanderson Rd (23322-1573)
PHONE...757 482-0873
Becky Lyons, *Principal*
EMP: 1 EST: 2017
SALES (est): 43.6K **Privately Held**
SIC: 2395 Embroidery & art needlework

(G-3137)
HOTSPOT ENERGY INC
4021 Holland Blvd (23323-1521)
PHONE...757 410-8640
John Williams, *CEO*
◆ EMP: 11
SALES (est): 2.4MM **Privately Held**
WEB: www.hotspotenergy.com
SIC: 3531 Construction machinery

(G-3138)
HUGHES MECHANICAL SYSTEMS
2652 Indian River Rd (23325-2655)
PHONE...757 855-3238
A Hughes, *Principal*
EMP: 2
SALES (est): 125.8K **Privately Held**
SIC: 3444 Sheet metalwork

(G-3139)
I AM EXPRESS LLC
3216 Hector Ln (23323-1466)
PHONE...757 535-6944
Adrienne Everett,
EMP: 2
SALES (est): 150K **Privately Held**
SIC: 3743 Freight cars & equipment

(G-3140)
IDEATION WEB STUDIOS LLC
Also Called: ID Web Studios
660 Independence Pkwy # 310
(23320-5214)
PHONE...757 333-3021
Kevin Daisey, *CEO*
EMP: 5
SALES (est): 149.5K **Privately Held**
WEB: www.thisisarray.com
SIC: 2741 4813 7336 7371 ; ; commercial art & graphic design; custom computer programming services; marketing consulting services

(G-3141)
INDIVIDUAL PRODUCTS & SVCS INC
Also Called: Ips
4720 Elizabeth Harbor Dr (23321-2213)
P.O. Box 9612 (23321-9612)
PHONE......................................757 488-3363
Loretta Mabry, *President*
Ozzie Mabry, *Principal*
Isaac Mabry, *Vice Pres*
EMP: 2
SALES (est): 105K **Privately Held**
SIC: 2396 8711 Screen printing on fabric articles; marine engineering

(G-3142)
INFOSOFT PUBLISHING CO
521 San Pedro Dr (23322-8023)
PHONE......................................661 288-1414
EMP: 1
SALES (est): 37.5K **Privately Held**
SIC: 2741 Miscellaneous publishing

(G-3143)
INNOVEYOR INC
3712 Profit Way Ste B (23323-1550)
P.O. Box 7725, Portsmouth (23707-0725)
PHONE......................................757 485-0500
Daniel Stahura, *CEO*
▲ EMP: 3
SQ FT: 10,000
SALES (est): 564.3K **Privately Held**
WEB: www.innoveyor.com
SIC: 3535 Conveyors & conveying equipment

(G-3144)
INTEGRATED VERTICAL TECH LLC
401 S Monterey Dr (23320-9396)
PHONE......................................757 410-7253
Charles Hodge, *Owner*
EMP: 1
SALES (est): 76.3K **Privately Held**
SIC: 2591 Blinds vertical

(G-3145)
INTERNATIONAL PUBLISHING INC (PA)
1208 Centerville Tpke N (23320-3026)
PHONE......................................800 377-2838
Rodica Lambert, *CEO*
Timothy Lambert, *President*
Tom Jackson, *Publisher*
Timothy C Lambert, *Principal*
Townsend Lambert, *Sales Mgr*
EMP: 3
SALES (est): 1.5MM **Privately Held**
WEB: www.shepherdsguide.com
SIC: 2721 6794 Periodicals: publishing only; patent owners & lessors

(G-3146)
J P R ENTERPRISES
1011 Annette St (23324-3608)
PHONE......................................757 288-8795
James P Riley, *Owner*
EMP: 1
SALES (est): 59.4K **Privately Held**
SIC: 2759 Screen printing

(G-3147)
J&S MARINE CANVAS LLC
1629 Falls Brook Run (23322-2175)
PHONE......................................757 580-6883
EMP: 2 EST: 2012
SALES (est): 126.2K **Privately Held**
SIC: 2211 Canvas

(G-3148)
JAR-TAN INC
Also Called: Custom Plantation Shutters
936 Professional Pl C1 (23320-3627)
PHONE......................................757 548-6066
William T Beaty, *President*
EMP: 5
SALES (est): 634.4K **Privately Held**
WEB: www.cpshutters.com
SIC: 2431 Window shutters, wood

(G-3149)
JAY DEES WELDING SERVICES
3023 Elbyrne Dr (23325-3609)
PHONE......................................757 675-8368
EMP: 1

SALES (est): 33.6K **Privately Held**
SIC: 7692 Welding repair

(G-3150)
JENSEN PROMOTIONAL ITEMS INC (PA)
Also Called: Jensen Apparel
315 Great Bridge Blvd A (23320-7012)
PHONE......................................757 966-7608
Thomas H Jensen, *President*
▲ EMP: 21
SQ FT: 1,500
SALES (est): 6.3MM **Privately Held**
WEB: www.jensenapparel.com
SIC: 2321 Men's & boys' furnishings

(G-3151)
JOHN POTTER ENTERPRISES
764 Shell Rd (23323-3240)
PHONE......................................757 485-2922
John Potter, *Owner*
EMP: 1
SALES (est): 53K **Privately Held**
SIC: 2511 Wood household furniture

(G-3152)
JOHN S MONTGOMERY
1253 Kingsway Dr (23320-4742)
PHONE......................................757 816-8724
John Montgomery, *Owner*
EMP: 1
SALES (est): 40K **Privately Held**
SIC: 2211 Luggage fabrics, cotton

(G-3153)
JONES DIRECT LLC
931 Ventures Way (23320-2857)
PHONE......................................757 718-3468
Whitney Jones, *CEO*
EMP: 1
SALES (est): 116.3K **Privately Held**
WEB: www.jones-printing.com
SIC: 3579 2752 7336 Envelope stuffing, sealing & addressing machines; mailing, letter handling & addressing machines; commercial printing, lithographic; commercial printing, offset; commercial art & graphic design

(G-3154)
JONES PLUS LLC
931 Ventures Way (23320-2857)
PHONE......................................757 718-3468
Mark Jones,
EMP: 3
SALES (est): 171.9K **Privately Held**
WEB: www.jones-printing.com
SIC: 2752 Commercial printing, offset

(G-3155)
JONES PRINTING SERVICE INC (PA)
931 Ventures Way (23320-2857)
P.O. Box 1786 (23327-1786)
PHONE......................................757 436-3331
Harry A Jones, *President*
Bruce E Jones, *Vice Pres*
Bruce Jones, *Vice Pres*
Bryan M Jones, *Vice Pres*
Mark Jones, *Vice Pres*
EMP: 40
SQ FT: 28,000
SALES (est): 7.5MM **Privately Held**
WEB: www.jones-printing.com
SIC: 2752 2791 2789 Commercial printing, offset; typesetting; bookbinding & related work

(G-3156)
JORGENSEN WOODWORKING
1213 Vail Ct (23320-8271)
PHONE......................................757 312-9663
Erik Jorgensen, *Owner*
EMP: 1
SALES (est): 70K **Privately Held**
SIC: 2499 Decorative wood & woodwork

(G-3157)
JPG SOFTWARE
636 Broadwinsor Cres (23322-9544)
PHONE......................................757 546-8416
John Hartung, *Principal*
EMP: 2 EST: 2016
SALES (est): 56.5K **Privately Held**
SIC: 7372 Prepackaged software

(G-3158)
JUD CORPORATION
3732 Profit Way (23323-1511)
PHONE......................................757 485-4371
Michael Bohmer, *Managing Dir*
Michael Boehmer, *Vice Pres*
Maria Thomas, *Sales Mgr*
◆ EMP: 7
SALES (est): 1.4MM
SALES (corp-wide): 355.8K **Privately Held**
WEB: www.judcorp.com
SIC: 3554 Paper industries machinery
HQ: Ibs Austria Gesellschaft M.B.H.
HauptstraBe 22
Teufenbach 8833
358 285-110

(G-3159)
JUDIS HEART PRINTS LLC
501 Natchez Trce (23322-7283)
PHONE......................................757 482-9607
Judith Webb, *Principal*
EMP: 2 EST: 2015
SALES (est): 113.1K **Privately Held**
SIC: 2752 Commercial printing, lithographic

(G-3160)
JUDYS BOTTLE HOLDER
2222 Ships Xing (23323-4069)
PHONE......................................757 606-1093
EMP: 1
SALES (est): 62K **Privately Held**
SIC: 2675 Retail Of A Baby Bottle Holder

(G-3161)
K & W PROJECTS LLC
3304 Dietz Dr (23323-1941)
PHONE......................................757 618-9249
Keith Derr,
Wendy Jo Derr,
EMP: 5
SALES (est): 350K **Privately Held**
WEB: www.kandwprojects.com
SIC: 2499 3479 5999 5947 Novelties, wood fiber; etching & engraving; trophies & plaques; novelties

(G-3162)
KEMPSVILLE BUILDING MTLS INC (HQ)
3300 Business Center Dr (23323-2638)
PHONE......................................757 485-0782
Scott M Gandy, *President*
Bobby G Johnson, *Vice Pres*
Brenda C Onley, *Vice Pres*
EMP: 40 EST: 1955
SQ FT: 70,000
SALES (est): 25.8MM
SALES (corp-wide): 1.5B **Privately Held**
WEB: www.kempsvillebuilding.com
SIC: 2439 5211 2431 Trusses, wooden roof; trusses, except roof: laminated lumber; lumber & other building materials; millwork
PA: Carter-Jones Companies, Inc.
601 Tallmadge Rd
Kent OH 44240
330 673-6100

(G-3163)
KERNEOS INC
1316 Priority Ln (23324-1313)
PHONE......................................757 494-1947
Thomas W Green, *President*
Mark Fitzgerald, *Vice Pres*
Graham Reid, *Vice Pres*
Mark Stein, *Project Mgr*
Troy Sing, *Safety Mgr*
◆ EMP: 70
SQ FT: 3,500
SALES (est): 18.5MM
SALES (corp-wide): 3.1MM **Privately Held**
WEB: www.kerneosinc.com
SIC: 3241 Cement, hydraulic
HQ: Imerys Aluminates
43 Quai De Grenelle
Paris 75015
380 621-677

(G-3164)
KINGDOM WOODWORKS VIRGINIA LLC
1213 Fentress Airfield Rd (23322-1363)
PHONE......................................757 544-4821
EMP: 1
SALES (est): 54.1K **Privately Held**
SIC: 2431 Millwork

(G-3165)
KITCHEN CONCEPTS INC
1220 Executive Blvd # 102 (23320-2887)
PHONE......................................757 547-9238
Porter Williamson Jr, *President*
Donald L Reich, *Vice Pres*
EMP: 2
SALES (est): 650K **Privately Held**
WEB: www.kitchenconceptsonline.com
SIC: 2434 Wood kitchen cabinets

(G-3166)
KMARIE KRAFTS INC
3107 Kemet Rd Apt 202 (23325-3310)
PHONE......................................804 943-1239
Kelly Harper, *CEO*
EMP: 2
SALES (est): 10K **Privately Held**
SIC: 3161 Clothing & apparel carrying cases

(G-3167)
KRAZY TEESZ
820 Live Oak Dr Ste D (23320-2636)
PHONE......................................757 470-4976
Tonya Batten, *Manager*
EMP: 2
SALES (est): 82.7K **Privately Held**
SIC: 2759 Screen printing

(G-3168)
KRISS USA INC (HQ)
Also Called: Kriss Systems, SA
912 Corporate Ln (23320-3641)
PHONE......................................714 333-1988
Peter Ching, *CEO*
Christopher Guignard, *President*
Christina Ching, *CFO*
Nancy Torres, *Accountant*
Hikaru Okamura, *Natl Sales Mgr*
EMP: 37
SQ FT: 20,000
SALES (corp-wide): 177.9K **Privately Held**
WEB: www.kriss-usa.com
SIC: 3484 Small arms

(G-3169)
L B OIL COMPANY
305 Bartell Dr (23322-5509)
PHONE......................................757 723-8379
EMP: 2 EST: 2012
SALES (est): 121.4K **Privately Held**
SIC: 1389 Oil & gas field services

(G-3170)
LA PLAYA INCORPORATED VIRGINIA
Also Called: LPI Technical Services
550 Woodlake Cir (23320-8928)
PHONE......................................757 222-1865
John H McKenziem, *President*
Beatrice G McKenzie, *President*
Christina Hoeflein, *Exec VP*
Scott G Britton, *Vice Pres*
John H McKenzie Jr, *Vice Pres*
▲ EMP: 175
SQ FT: 60,000
SALES (est): 40.1MM **Privately Held**
WEB: www.lpits.com
SIC: 3731 7699 Shipbuilding & repairing; ship boiler & tank cleaning & repair, contractors

(G-3171)
LABELS EAST INC
817 Butler St (23323-3418)
P.O. Box 6180 (23323-0180)
PHONE......................................757 558-0800
M Keith Stafford, *President*
Christina Stafford, *Corp Secy*
Vince Olson, *Vice Pres*
EMP: 3
SALES (est): 276.7K **Privately Held**
WEB: www.labelseast.com
SIC: 2759 Labels & seals: printing

(G-3172)
LAFARGE CALCIUM ALUMINATES INC
1316 Priority Ln (23324-1313)
P.O. Box 5806 (23324-0937)
PHONE..............................757 543-8832
Thomas Green, *President*
EMP: 1
SALES (est): 137.4K **Privately Held**
WEB: www.kerneosinc.com
SIC: 3241 Cement, hydraulic

(G-3173)
LAFARGE NORTH AMERICA INC
100 Pratt St (23324-1060)
PHONE..............................757 545-2481
Craig Campbell, *Vice Pres*
R J Whelahan, *Sales/Mktg Mgr*
EMP: 15
SALES (corp-wide): 1.7B **Privately Held**
WEB: www.lafarge-na.com
SIC: 3241 5032 Cement, hydraulic; cement
HQ: Lafarge North America Inc.
    8700 W Bryn Mawr Ave
    Chicago IL 60631
    773 372-1000

(G-3174)
LAND ELECTRIC COMPANY
1525 Boxwood Dr (23323-5104)
PHONE..............................757 625-0444
William Land, *Owner*
EMP: 3
SQ FT: 3,000
SALES (est): 200K **Privately Held**
SIC: 7694 Electric motor repair

(G-3175)
LASAR CHEMICALS
704 Fordsmere Ct (23322-2123)
PHONE..............................757 286-9808
EMP: 2
SALES (est): 82.4K **Privately Held**
WEB: www.lasarchemicals.com
SIC: 2851 Paints & allied products

(G-3176)
LAST CALL MAGAZINE LLC
1013 Saint Andrews Way C (23320-8524)
PHONE..............................757 410-0229
EMP: 3
SALES (est): 140K **Privately Held**
SIC: 2721 Periodicals-Publishing/Printing

(G-3177)
LAUREL TECHNOLOGIES PARTNR
825 Greenbrier Cir Ste M (23320-2638)
PHONE..............................757 819-0700
David J Peterson, *Branch Mgr*
Stacey Prather, *Manager*
EMP: 50
SALES (corp-wide): 9.9B **Privately Held**
WEB: www.leonardodrs.com
SIC: 3812 Search & navigation equipment
HQ: Drs Systems Management, Llc
    246 Airport Rd
    Johnstown PA 15904
    814 534-8900

(G-3178)
LAURENCE WALTER AEROSPACE SOLU
1105a International Plz (23323-1530)
PHONE..............................757 966-9578
Chris Nichols, *Principal*
Mark Smith, *Manager*
▲ **EMP:** 4
SALES (est): 509.1K **Privately Held**
SIC: 3728 Aircraft parts & equipment

(G-3179)
LD WELDING & FABRICATION CO
801 Butler St Ste 6 (23323-3404)
PHONE..............................757 553-2471
Luis E Diaz Cartagena, *Principal*
Veronica Longoria, *Principal*
EMP: 10
SALES (est): 311.9K **Privately Held**
WEB: www.ldweldingandfabrication.com
SIC: 7692 Welding repair

(G-3180)
LE GRAND ASSOC OF PITTSBURGH
Also Called: LE GRAND ASSOCIATES OF PITTSBURGH INC
3800 Poplar Hill Rd Ste E (23321-5541)
PHONE..............................757 484-4900
David Legrand, *Branch Mgr*
EMP: 1
SALES (corp-wide): 930.7K **Privately Held**
WEB: www.legrandeyes.net
SIC: 3851 Contact lenses
PA: Legrand Associates Of Pittsburgh, Inc.
    1601 Walnut St Ste 616
    Philadelphia PA 19102
    215 496-1307

(G-3181)
LEARNING TO LEAN PRINTING
2501 Cedar Rd (23323-3913)
PHONE..............................757 718-5586
Jesse Featherston, *Principal*
EMP: 2
SALES (est): 83.9K **Privately Held**
SIC: 2752 Commercial printing, lithographic

(G-3182)
LEATHER LUSTER INC
908 Executive Ct Ste 103 (23320-3666)
P.O. Box 1645 (23327-1645)
PHONE..............................757 548-0146
Margaret Paquet, *President*
Sharon Paquet, *Vice Pres*
EMP: 3
SQ FT: 1,500
SALES (est): 460.3K **Privately Held**
WEB: www.leatherluster.com
SIC: 2842 5169 Leather dressings & finishes; polishes

(G-3183)
LIHT CANDLES & OILS LLC
1100 S Bttlfeld Blvd 15 # 15734 (23322)
P.O. Box 15734 (23328-5734)
PHONE..............................757 776-9005
Imani Hicks, *Owner*
EMP: 1
SALES (est): 29.2K **Privately Held**
SIC: 3999 Candles

(G-3184)
LOCKHEED MARTIN CORPORATION
Also Called: Information Systems Globl Svcs
1408 Stephanie Way (23320-0613)
PHONE..............................757 769-7251
Sheraman Franklin, *Branch Mgr*
EMP: 232 **Publicly Held**
WEB: www.lockheedmartin.com
SIC: 3812 Search & navigation equipment
PA: Lockheed Martin Corporation
    6801 Rockledge Dr
    Bethesda MD 20817

(G-3185)
LOCKHEED MARTIN CORPORATION
3416 Maori Dr (23321-4804)
PHONE..............................757 484-5789
EMP: 430
SALES (corp-wide): 47.1B **Publicly Held**
SIC: 3721 Mfg Aircraft
PA: Lockheed Martin Corporation
    6801 Rockledge Dr
    Bethesda MD 20817
    301 897-6000

(G-3186)
LOCKHEED MARTIN CORPORATION
1801 Sara Dr Ste L (23320-2647)
PHONE..............................757 390-7520
Marty Smith, *Principal*
EMP: 99 **Publicly Held**
WEB: www.lockheedmartin.com
SIC: 3812 Search & navigation equipment
PA: Lockheed Martin Corporation
    6801 Rockledge Dr
    Bethesda MD 20817

(G-3187)
LOCKHEED MARTIN SERVICES LLC
500 Woodlake Dr Ste 2 (23320-8923)
PHONE..............................757 366-3300
Jeff Farschman, *Vice Pres*
Hector Alvarez, *Program Mgr*
EMP: 12 **Publicly Held**
WEB: www.lmco.com
SIC: 3812 Search & navigation equipment
HQ: Lockheed Martin Services, Llc
    700 N Frederick Ave
    Gaithersburg MD 20879

(G-3188)
LOVE IN PRINT LLC
718 Sutherland Dr (23320-6640)
PHONE..............................757 739-2416
Sheena Griffin, *Administration*
EMP: 2
SALES (est): 139.2K **Privately Held**
SIC: 2752 Commercial printing, lithographic

(G-3189)
LUCK STONE CORPORATION
Also Called: Gilmerton
4606 Bainbridge Blvd (23320-6306)
PHONE..............................757 213-7750
Jim Herber, *Branch Mgr*
EMP: 12
SALES (corp-wide): 824.7MM **Privately Held**
WEB: www.luckstone.com
SIC: 1423 Crushed & broken granite
PA: Luck Stone Corporation
    515 Stone Mill Dr
    Manakin Sabot VA 23103
    804 784-6300

(G-3190)
LUX LIVING CANDLE CO LLC
812 Evelyn Way (23322-2488)
PHONE..............................757 462-6470
Charnelle Renee Cook, *Principal*
EMP: 1
SALES (est): 39.6K **Privately Held**
SIC: 3999 Candles

(G-3191)
LYNN DONNELL
Also Called: De-Tech Solutions
952 Saint Andrews Reach B (23320-8582)
PHONE..............................757 685-0263
Donnell Lynn, *Owner*
EMP: 1
SALES (est): 49K **Privately Held**
SIC: 3731 Tenders, ships: building & repairing

(G-3192)
MACHINE SERVICES INC
3825 Holland Blvd (23323-1518)
PHONE..............................757 487-5566
Donna J Duncan, *President*
Clinton E Spahn, *General Mgr*
Charles E Duncan, *Vice Pres*
John M Cloud, *Admin Sec*
EMP: 7
SQ FT: 5,000
SALES (est): 1.1MM **Privately Held**
SIC: 3599 Machine shop, jobbing & repair

(G-3193)
MAKER INDUSTRIES
635 Mile Creek Ln (23322-1279)
PHONE..............................757 560-1692
Adriana Weatherly, *Principal*
EMP: 2
SALES (est): 111.5K **Privately Held**
SIC: 3999 Manufacturing industries

(G-3194)
MALLORY CO INC
Also Called: M Co Marine
509 Downing Dr (23322-8710)
PHONE..............................757 803-5596
Lori Mallory, *President*
EMP: 1
SALES (est): 88.5K **Privately Held**
SIC: 3441 1542 Fabricated structural metal; commercial & office building, new construction

(G-3195)
MALPASS CONSTRUCTION CO INC
2650 Indian River Rd (23325-2655)
P.O. Box 13006 (23325-0006)
PHONE..............................757 543-3541
William D Malpass Sr, *CEO*
William D Malpass Jr, *President*
EMP: 7 **EST:** 1946
SQ FT: 7,600
SALES (est): 400K **Privately Held**
WEB: www.malpass.com
SIC: 3429 5088 Marine hardware; transportation equipment & supplies

(G-3196)
MANTIS GRAPHICS
613 Blackthorne Dr (23322-9028)
PHONE..............................757 482-4186
John Martinez, *President*
EMP: 1
SALES (est): 59.2K **Privately Held**
SIC: 2759 Screen printing

(G-3197)
MAPP MANUFACTURING CORPORATION
3712 Profit Way Ste F (23323-1557)
PHONE..............................757 410-0307
Kelly Mapp, *President*
EMP: 2
SALES (est): 304.3K **Privately Held**
WEB: www.mappmc.com
SIC: 3678 Electronic connectors

(G-3198)
MARIE LAWSON REPORTER
301 Esplanade Pl (23320-2005)
PHONE..............................757 549-2198
Marie Lawson, *Owner*
EMP: 1
SALES (est): 69.5K **Privately Held**
SIC: 2711 Newspapers, publishing & printing

(G-3199)
MAX PRESS PRINTING
Also Called: Maximilian Press Publishers
517 Kempsville Rd Ste I (23320-3643)
P.O. Box 72894, North Chesterfield (23235-8021)
PHONE..............................757 482-2273
Wil Hamel, *CEO*
▲ **EMP:** 5
SALES (est): 322.1K **Privately Held**
WEB: www.maximilianpressbookpublishers.com
SIC: 2759 Commercial printing

(G-3200)
MCELROY METAL MILL INC
Also Called: McElroy Metal Service Center
3052 Yadkin Rd (23323-2206)
PHONE..............................757 485-3100
Irvin Wiesner, *Branch Mgr*
EMP: 3
SALES (corp-wide): 362MM **Privately Held**
WEB: www.mcelroymetal.com
SIC: 3448 Prefabricated metal buildings
PA: Mcelroy Metal Mill, Inc.
    1500 Hamilton Rd
    Bossier City LA 71111
    318 747-8000

(G-3201)
MCRAE OF AMERICA INC
Also Called: McRae Storage Buildings
4416 Sunray Ave (23321-2628)
PHONE..............................757 488-6900
John McRae, *President*
EMP: 7
SALES (est): 826.1K **Privately Held**
SIC: 2452 Prefabricated buildings, wood

(G-3202)
MELLA WEEKLY
608 Helmsdale Way (23320-6600)
PHONE..............................757 436-2409
Stephen Weekly, *Principal*
EMP: 4
SALES (est): 233.7K **Privately Held**
SIC: 2711 Newspapers, publishing & printing

(G-3203)
METRO WOOD WORKS INC
3272 Cookes Mill Rd (23323-1301)
PHONE....................757 479-1100
Stephen E Croxton, *President*
EMP: 1
SALES (est): 173.1K **Privately Held**
WEB: www.metrowoodworks.com
SIC: 2431 1522 Millwork; residential construction

(G-3204)
MF&B MAYPORT JOINT VENTURE
813 Industrial Ave (23324-2614)
PHONE....................757 222-4855
EMP: 1
SALES (est): 83K **Privately Held**
SIC: 3731 Shipbuilding/Repairing

(G-3205)
MIKROCOZE INC
1545 Crossways Blvd # 25 (23320-0205)
PHONE....................800 542-8715
Sukhmanjit Singh, *Ch of Bd*
EMP: 1 EST: 2016
SALES (est): 70.8K **Privately Held**
WEB: www.mikrocozeinc.com
SIC: 2511 5961 Wood household furniture; catalog & mail-order houses

(G-3206)
MINNIE ME MONOGRAMS
506 Aguila Ct (23322-7142)
PHONE....................423 331-1686
Brittany Hopkins, *Principal*
EMP: 1
SALES (est): 39.8K **Privately Held**
SIC: 2395 Embroidery & art needlework

(G-3207)
MITSUBISHI CHEMICAL AMER INC
401 Volvo Pkwy (23320-4611)
PHONE....................757 382-5750
John Canfield, *Senior VP*
Rick Harford, *Safety Mgr*
Mike Radom, *Safety Mgr*
Tom McPeak, *Maint Spvr*
Tim Hixson, *Plant Engr*
EMP: 8 **Privately Held**
WEB: www.mitsubishichemicalholdings.com
SIC: 3355 3444 Aluminum rolling & drawing; sheet metalwork
HQ: Mitsubishi Chemical America, Inc.
655 3rd Ave Fl 15
New York NY 10017
212 223-3043

(G-3208)
MITSUBISHI CHEMICAL COMPOSITES
Also Called: Alpolic Metal Composite Mtls
401 Volvo Pkwy (23320-4611)
PHONE....................757 548-7850
Eiichi Sato, *President*
Jim Moses, *Technical Mgr*
Shinichi Iguchi, *Treasurer*
Renee Etheridge, *Human Res Mgr*
Renee Mullins, *Marketing Staff*
◆ EMP: 106
SALES (est): 90MM **Privately Held**
WEB: www.alpolic-americas.com
SIC: 2819 5063 5051 Aluminum compounds; electrical apparatus & equipment; aluminum bars, rods, ingots, sheets, pipes, plates, etc.
HQ: Mitsubishi Chemical Corporation
1-1-1, Marunouchi
Chiyoda-Ku TKY 100-0

(G-3209)
MITSUBSHI CHEM HLDNGS AMER INC
Also Called: McHc
401 Volvo Pkwy (23320-4611)
PHONE....................757 382-5750
Dave Patel, *Research*
Steven Hadley, *Sales Staff*
John Canfield, *Manager*
EMP: 50 **Privately Held**
WEB: www.us.mitsubishi-chemical.com
SIC: 2819 Industrial inorganic chemicals

HQ: Mitsubishi Chemical Holdings America, Inc.
655 3rd Ave Fl 15
New York NY 10017

(G-3210)
MODEL A WOODWORKS
4710 Whaley Ct (23321-1440)
PHONE....................757 714-1126
EMP: 1 EST: 2019
SALES (est): 54.1K **Privately Held**
SIC: 2431 Millwork

(G-3211)
MOMS CHOICE LLC
732 Eden Way N Ste E (23320-2798)
PHONE....................757 410-9409
Bettie Youngs, *Principal*
Rachel Kiser, *Marketing Staff*
Roxanne Rask, *Director*
EMP: 2 EST: 2010
SALES (est): 147.2K **Privately Held**
WEB: www.momschoiceawards.com
SIC: 2741 Art copy & poster publishing

(G-3212)
MORTON SALT
4100 Buell St (23324-1004)
PHONE....................757 543-0148
D Vuylsteke, *Principal*
▲ EMP: 4 EST: 2001
SALES (est): 242.8K **Privately Held**
SIC: 2899 Salt

(G-3213)
MULTI-COLOR CORPORATION
1300 Cavalier Blvd (23323-1500)
PHONE....................757 487-2525
Phillip Draper, *CEO*
Rick Guyot, *Production*
Virginia Thayer-Smith, *Sales Staff*
EMP: 13 **Privately Held**
WEB: www.mcclabel.com
SIC: 2759 Labels & seals: printing
HQ: Multi-Color Corporation
4053 Clough Woods Dr
Batavia OH 45103
513 381-1480

(G-3214)
MURRAY BISCUIT COMPANY LLC
1335 Lindale Dr (23320-5981)
PHONE....................757 547-0249
Jim Mims, *Branch Mgr*
EMP: 138 **Publicly Held**
WEB: www.murrayfoods.com
SIC: 2052 Cookies
HQ: Murray Biscuit Company, L.L.C.
1550 Marvin Griffin Rd
Augusta GA 30906
706 798-8600

(G-3215)
MUSICIANS PUBLICATIONS
315 Great Bridge Blvd (23320-7012)
PHONE....................757 410-3111
Bill Holcombe Jr, *President*
EMP: 3
SALES (est): 149K **Privately Held**
WEB: www.billholcombe.com
SIC: 2759 Publication printing

(G-3216)
MUSTANG SPORTS RETAIL
357 Johnstown Rd Ste F (23322-5356)
PHONE....................757 679-2814
Christopher Marley, *Principal*
EMP: 2 EST: 2012
SALES (est): 161.1K **Privately Held**
SIC: 3949 Sporting & athletic goods

(G-3217)
NESTLE PIZZA COMPANY INC
Also Called: Kraft Foods
1512 Birch Leaf Rd (23320-8171)
PHONE....................757 479-1512
EMP: 11
SALES (corp-wide): 93.5B **Privately Held**
WEB: www.myfoodandfamily.com
SIC: 2038 Pizza, frozen
HQ: Nestle Pizza Company, Inc.
1 Kraft Ct
Glenview IL 60025
847 646-2000

(G-3218)
NICHE PUBLICATIONS LLC
36 N Kingsbridge Pl Apt A (23322-5696)
PHONE....................757 620-2631
Dorothy Suttmiller, *Principal*
EMP: 1 EST: 2008
SALES (est): 86.7K **Privately Held**
SIC: 2741 Miscellaneous publishing

(G-3219)
NITTO INC
809 Principal Ct (23320-3639)
PHONE....................757 436-5540
Myrna Cerwinski, *Enginr/R&D Asst*
Lisa Higgins, *Asst Mgr*
EMP: 4 **Privately Held**
WEB: www.nitto.com
SIC: 3714 Motor vehicle parts & accessories
HQ: Nitto, Inc.
1990 Rutgers Blvd
Lakewood NJ 08701
732 901-7905

(G-3220)
NOODLE GAMES
1105 Carriage Ct (23322-4654)
PHONE....................757 572-3849
Chad Triolet, *Owner*
EMP: 1
SALES (est): 110.5K **Privately Held**
WEB: www.noodlegames.net
SIC: 2098 Noodles (e.g. egg, plain & water), dry

(G-3221)
NORTHROP GRUMMAN CORPORATION
1320 Winfall Dr (23322-3946)
PHONE....................757 688-6850
Gilbert Vetere, *Branch Mgr*
EMP: 2 **Publicly Held**
WEB: www.northropgrumman.com
SIC: 3812 Search & navigation equipment
PA: Northrop Grumman Corporation
2980 Fairview Park Dr
Falls Church VA 22042

(G-3222)
NORTHROP GRUMMAN SYSTEMS CORP
Also Called: Sperry Marine Division
1500 Technology Dr # 104 (23320-5976)
PHONE....................757 312-8375
Bruce Begault, *Branch Mgr*
EMP: 5 **Publicly Held**
WEB: www.northropgrumman.com
SIC: 3812 Navigational systems & instruments
HQ: Northrop Grumman Systems Corporation
2980 Fairview Park Dr
Falls Church VA 22042
703 280-2900

(G-3223)
OCEAN IMPRESSIONS INC
3315 S Military Hwy (23323-3522)
PHONE....................757 485-3212
David Woods, *President*
EMP: 2
SALES (est): 145.6K **Privately Held**
SIC: 2261 Screen printing of cotton broadwoven fabrics

(G-3224)
OCEANEERING INTERNATIONAL INC
2155 Steppingstone Sq (23320-2517)
PHONE....................757 985-3800
Kyle Brocke, *Engineer*
Al Konetzni, *Branch Mgr*
EMP: 400 **Publicly Held**
WEB: www.oceaneering.com
SIC: 1389 Oil field services
PA: Oceaneering International Inc
11911 Fm 529 Rd
Houston TX 77041
713 329-4500

(G-3225)
OCEANEERING INTERNATIONAL INC
2155 Steppingstone Sq (23320-2517)
PHONE....................757 545-2200

Chris Klentzman, *Manager*
EMP: 290 **Publicly Held**
WEB: www.oceaneering.com
SIC: 3731 Submarine tenders, building & repairing
PA: Oceaneering International Inc
11911 Fm 529 Rd
Houston TX 77041
713 329-4500

(G-3226)
OFFICE ORGANIZERS
4208 Goldcrest Dr (23325-2212)
PHONE....................757 343-6860
Maggie Chandler, *Owner*
EMP: 1
SALES (est): 98.1K **Privately Held**
SIC: 3089 Organizers for closets, drawers, etc.: plastic

(G-3227)
OLD SOUL SIGNS LLC
1348 Danielle Ct (23320-8222)
PHONE....................757 256-5669
Margaret Pickles, *Principal*
EMP: 1
SALES (est): 50.6K **Privately Held**
SIC: 3993 Signs & advertising specialties

(G-3228)
ONEALS WELDING & REPAIR LLC
5145 Ballahack Rd (23322-3209)
PHONE....................757 421-0702
David Oneal, *Partner*
EMP: 8
SALES (est): 298.5K **Privately Held**
SIC: 7692 Welding repair

(G-3229)
OPEN PRINTS LLC
929 Ventures Way (23320-2858)
PHONE....................866 673-6110
Richard Stephenson, *Principal*
EMP: 2
SALES (est): 117.8K **Privately Held**
WEB: www.openprints.com
SIC: 2752 Commercial printing, lithographic

(G-3230)
OUT OF WOODWORK
713 Denham Arch (23322-6823)
PHONE....................757 814-8848
Jim Calder, *Principal*
EMP: 1 EST: 2011
SALES (est): 110.2K **Privately Held**
SIC: 2431 Millwork

(G-3231)
PAIGE SITTA & ASSOCIATES INC
Also Called: Paige Flrg Cverings Specialist
820 Greenbrier Cir Ste 10 (23320-2646)
PHONE....................757 420-5886
Heather Holloway, *Branch Mgr*
EMP: 20
SALES (corp-wide): 4.2MM **Privately Held**
WEB: www.paigefc.com
SIC: 3731 1752 Crew boats, building & repairing; ceramic floor tile installation
PA: Paige Sitta & Associates Inc
2050 Wilson Ave Ste B
National City CA 91950
619 233-5912

(G-3232)
PALE HORSE LLC
1296 Bttlfeld Blvd S Ste (23322)
PHONE....................757 576-0656
Donald Wingard, *CEO*
EMP: 10
SALES (est): 60K **Privately Held**
WEB: www.palehorsecoffee.com
SIC: 2095 Coffee roasting (except by wholesale grocers)

(G-3233)
PARENT RESOURCE CENTER
369 Battlefield Blvd S (23322-5366)
PHONE....................757 482-5923
James T Roberts, *Superintendent*
EMP: 2

SALES (est): 344.9K **Privately Held**
WEB: www.cpschools.com
SIC: **2752** Commercial printing, litho-
graphic

(G-3234)
PATRICIA MOORE
Also Called: Welcome Home Honey
3248 Old Mill Rd (23323-1812)
PHONE.....................................757 485-7414
Patricia Moore, *Owner*
Darrel Moore, *Co-Owner*
EMP: 2 EST: 2001
SALES (est): 157.5K **Privately Held**
WEB: www.welcomehomehoney.com
SIC: **3993** Signs & advertising specialties

(G-3235)
PATRIOT TOOLS LLC
2308 Smith Ave (23325-5026)
PHONE.....................................757 718-4591
EMP: 2
SALES (est): 81.4K **Privately Held**
SIC: **3599** Industrial machinery

(G-3236)
PERDUE FARMS INC
501 Barnes Rd (23324-1303)
PHONE.....................................757 494-5564
Kevin Brooks, *Opers Staff*
Jauncey Lewis, *Engineer*
Mike Barber, *Manager*
Charlie Cook, *Maintence Staff*
Scott Peterson, *Maintence Staff*
EMP: 100
SALES (corp-wide): 5.2B **Privately Held**
WEB: www.perduefarms.com
SIC: **2015** Chicken, processed: fresh;
ducks, processed: fresh
PA: Perdue Farms Inc.
31149 Old Ocean City Rd
Salisbury MD 21804
410 543-3000

(G-3237)
PETER KORER
120 Battlefield Blvd S (23322-5224)
PHONE.....................................702 460-2144
Peter Korer, *Principal*
EMP: 2
SALES (est): 90.5K **Privately Held**
WEB: www.thinkinkprinting.com
SIC: **2752** Commercial printing, offset

(G-3238)
**PHARMACEUTICAL SOURCE
LLC**
617 Flatrock Ln (23320-3292)
PHONE.....................................757 482-3512
Jean Dilday, *Treasurer*
Larry Dilday,
EMP: 2
SALES (est): 233.9K **Privately Held**
WEB: www.thepharmaceuticalsource.com
SIC: **2834** Pharmaceutical preparations

(G-3239)
PIEDMONT FABRICATION INC
1317 Cavalier Blvd (23323-1501)
PHONE.....................................757 543-5570
Thad Herron, *Sales Staff*
Rick Anderson, *Branch Mgr*
EMP: 15
SALES (corp-wide): 2.7MM **Privately
Held**
WEB: www.piedmontfabrication.com
SIC: **3441** Fabricated structural metal
PA: Piedmont Fabrication, Inc.
1624 Steel St
Chesapeake VA
757 543-5570

(G-3240)
PIONEER INDUSTRIES LLC
1056 Ballahack Rd (23322-2447)
PHONE.....................................757 432-8412
Theresa Shoulders, *Principal*
EMP: 1
SALES (est): 55.6K **Privately Held**
SIC: **3999** Manufacturing industries

(G-3241)
PJL MARINE ENTERPRISE LLC
3920 Trailwood Ct (23321-3336)
PHONE.....................................757 774-1050
Perry Lynch,

EMP: 4
SALES (est): 100K **Privately Held**
SIC: **3731** Shipbuilding & repairing

(G-3242)
**PLASSER AMERICAN
CORPORATION**
2001 Myers Rd (23324-3231)
P.O. Box 5464 (23324-0464)
PHONE.....................................757 543-3526
Joseph W Neuhofer, *President*
Robin R Laskowski, *Corp Secy*
Dr Gunther W Oblechner, *Vice Pres*
▲ EMP: 220 EST: 1970
SQ FT: 150,000
SALES (est): 81MM
SALES (corp-wide): 558.1MM **Privately
Held**
WEB: www.plasseramerican.com
SIC: **3531** Railway track equipment
HQ: Plasser & Theurer, Export Von Bahn-
baumaschinen, Gesellschaft M.B.H.
Johannesgasse 3
Wien 1010
151 572-0

(G-3243)
PPG INDUSTRIES INC
Also Called: PPG Prtctive Mar Coatings 9969
1416 Kelland Dr Ste F (23320-4447)
PHONE.....................................757 494-5116
Larry Best, *Branch Mgr*
EMP: 5
SALES (corp-wide): 15.3B **Publicly Held**
WEB: www.ppg.com
SIC: **2851** Shellac (protective coating)
PA: Ppg Industries, Inc.
1 Ppg Pl
Pittsburgh PA 15272
412 434-3131

(G-3244)
PRECISION PHARMACY LLC
Also Called: Genx Pharmacy
1101 Executive Blvd Ste A (23320-3634)
PHONE.....................................757 656-6560
Kimberly Owen, *Mng Member*
EMP: 13
SALES (est): 1.5MM **Privately Held**
SIC: **2834** Pharmaceutical preparations

(G-3245)
**PREMIER RESOURCES
EXPRESS LLC**
Also Called: PR Express
1320 Club House Dr (23322-8073)
P.O. Box 9383, Norfolk (23505-0383)
PHONE.....................................717 887-4003
Stacy Zepp,
EMP: 1
SALES (est): 120K **Privately Held**
SIC: **3842** Personal safety equipment

(G-3246)
PRESSURES ON
232 Centerville Tpke N (23320-3006)
PHONE.....................................757 681-8999
Ken Mills Jr, *President*
EMP: 2
SALES (est): 137.8K **Privately Held**
WEB: www.pressureson.com
SIC: **3589** High pressure cleaning equip-
ment

(G-3247)
**PRETTY UGLY DISTRIBUTION
LLC**
845 Battlefield Blvd S (23322-6610)
PHONE.....................................757 672-8958
Aaron Childers,
EMP: 1
SQ FT: 2,146
SALES (est): 43.5K **Privately Held**
SIC: **2082** Beer (alcoholic beverage)

(G-3248)
PRINTLINE GRAPHICS LLC
200 Tintern Ct Ste 105 (23320-4582)
PHONE.....................................757 547-3107
Lori Higgs, *President*
EMP: 5
SQ FT: 1,800
SALES (est): 594K **Privately Held**
WEB: www.printlinegraphics.com
SIC: **2752** Commercial printing, offset

(G-3249)
PRIORITY WIRE & CABLE INC
1403 Greenbrier Pkwy # 525 (23320-0006)
PHONE.....................................757 361-0207
▲ EMP: 2
SALES (est): 170K **Privately Held**
SIC: **3641** Mfg Electric Lamps

(G-3250)
**PROFESSIONAL PRINTING CTR
INC**
817 Yupo Ct (23320-3626)
PHONE.....................................757 547-1990
Norman E Ward, *President*
Brian R Ward, *President*
Barbara B Ward, *Corp Secy*
McBride Debbie, *Human Resources*
Lydia Spruill, *Cust Mgr*
EMP: 50 EST: 1977
SQ FT: 24,000
SALES (est): 11.6MM **Privately Held**
WEB: www.professionalprinting.com
SIC: **2752** Commercial printing, offset

(G-3251)
PROGRESSIVE DESIGNS
816 Old Bridge Ln (23320-3243)
PHONE.....................................757 547-9201
Linda Sullivan, *Owner*
Teresa Smither, *CFO*
EMP: 2
SALES (est): 173K **Privately Held**
SIC: **2434** Wood kitchen cabinets

(G-3252)
**QUALITY COATINGS VIRGINIA
INC**
3900 Holland Blvd (23323-1519)
P.O. Box 5443 (23324-0443)
PHONE.....................................757 494-0801
Warren R Weidrick, *President*
Donna Weidrick, *Vice Pres*
Shawn Lancaster, *Manager*
Douglas Williams, *Manager*
EMP: 27
SALES (est): 5MM **Privately Held**
WEB: www.qualitycoatingsofvirginia.com
SIC: **3731** Shipbuilding & repairing

(G-3253)
R & D WELDING SERVICES
4840 Condor Dr (23321-1355)
PHONE.....................................757 761-3499
Rodney Nagy, *Principal*
EMP: 1
SALES (est): 31.5K **Privately Held**
SIC: **7692** Welding repair

(G-3254)
R AND L MACHINE SHOP INC
2900 Yadkin Rd (23323-2296)
PHONE.....................................757 487-8879
Kenneth R Roth, *President*
Rex Roth, *Vice Pres*
EMP: 26 EST: 1965
SQ FT: 14,000
SALES (est): 2.1MM **Privately Held**
WEB: www.rlmachine.com
SIC: **3599 3441** Machine shop, jobbing &
repair; fabricated structural metal

(G-3255)
R&Y TRUCKING LLC
967 Geneva Ave (23323-4761)
PHONE.....................................404 781-1312
Yaritza Medina-Hernandez,
EMP: 1
SALES (est): 71K **Privately Held**
SIC: **3537** Industrial trucks & tractors

(G-3256)
RAYMOND GOLDEN
Also Called: Black Diamond Gold Fuel
836 Nottaway Dr (23320-4850)
PHONE.....................................757 549-1853
EMP: 1 EST: 2014
SALES (est): 67K **Privately Held**
SIC: **2899 7389** Mfg Chemical Prepara-
tions

(G-3257)
RAYTHEON COMPANY
1100 Intl Plz 100 (23323)
PHONE.....................................757 855-4394
Harland M Roberts, *Manager*

EMP: 205
SALES (corp-wide): 77B **Publicly Held**
WEB: www.rtx.com
SIC: **3812** Search & navigation equipment
HQ: Raytheon Company
870 Winter St
Waltham MA 02451
781 522-3000

(G-3258)
RAYTHEON COMPANY
1100 Intl Plz Ste 100 (23323)
PHONE.....................................310 647-9438
EMP: 5
SALES (corp-wide): 77B **Publicly Held**
WEB: www.rtx.com
SIC: **3812 3663 3761** Defense systems &
equipment; space satellite communications equipment; airborne radio communications equipment; guided missiles &
space vehicles, research & development;
rockets, space & military, complete
HQ: Raytheon Company
870 Winter St
Waltham MA 02451
781 522-3000

(G-3259)
RAYTHEON COMPANY
Relay Rd Rm Bldg 363 (23322)
PHONE.....................................757 421-8319
Larry Nelson, *Manager*
EMP: 500
SALES (corp-wide): 77B **Publicly Held**
WEB: www.rtx.com
SIC: **3812 3721 4581** Sonar systems &
equipment; nautical instruments; defense
systems & equipment; motorized aircraft;
airports, flying fields & services
HQ: Raytheon Company
870 Winter St
Waltham MA 02451
781 522-3000

(G-3260)
RC INDUSTRIES LLC
512 Winwood Dr (23323-3214)
PHONE.....................................757 839-5577
EMP: 1
SALES (est): 39.6K **Privately Held**
SIC: **3999** Manufacturing industries

(G-3261)
**REACH ORTHTIC PRSTHETIC
SVCS S**
4057 Taylor Rd Ste P (23321-5527)
PHONE.....................................757 673-2000
Matthew Zydron,
EMP: 2
SALES (est): 157.3K **Privately Held**
WEB: www.reachops.com
SIC: **3842 7251** Limbs, artificial; footwear,
custom made

(G-3262)
RECKLESS INC
1216 E Eva Blvd (23320-6210)
PHONE.....................................757 469-4416
Mario Daughtry, *CEO*
EMP: 5
SALES (est): 100K **Privately Held**
SIC: **2389 2759** Apparel & accessories;
screen printing

(G-3263)
REDISCOVER WOODWORK
3500 Douglas Rd (23322-3113)
PHONE.....................................757 813-0383
Robert Fisher, *Principal*
EMP: 1
SALES (est): 61.9K **Privately Held**
SIC: **2431** Millwork

(G-3264)
REDONO LLC
1448 Clearwater Ln (23322-3989)
PHONE.....................................757 553-2305
Apollos Hall, *CEO*
Kevin Stimpson, *COO*
Aaron Turner, *Marketing Staff*
EMP: 2
SALES (est): 85.2K **Privately Held**
SIC: **7372 7389** Application computer soft-
ware;

▲ = Import ▼=Export
◆ =Import/Export

(G-3265)
REFCO MFG
3835 Holland Blvd Ste B (23323-1533)
PHONE..............................757 487-2222
Reginald E Foley,
EMP: 4
SALES (est): 200K **Privately Held**
SIC: 3599 Machine shop, jobbing & repair

(G-3266)
REFCON SERVICES INC
813 Professional Pl W A110 (23320-3629)
P.O. Box 55088, Norfolk (23505-9068)
PHONE..............................757 616-0691
Celia Escobar, *President*
Joseph Chambers, *Director*
Amanda Smailes, *Director*
Allan Zeno, *Director*
Ruben Escobar, *Admin Sec*
EMP: 11
SQ FT: 2,000
SALES (est): 3MM **Privately Held**
WEB: www.refconservices.com
SIC: 3585 7623 Air conditioning units,
complete: domestic or industrial; refriger-
ation service & repair

(G-3267)
REFLECTIONS LIGHT BOXES
2801 Ashwood Dr (23321-4202)
PHONE..............................757 641-3192
Henry Whitener, *Owner*
EMP: 3
SALES (est): 219.4K **Privately Held**
WEB: www.reflectionslightboxes.com
SIC: 2531 Public building & related furni-
ture

(G-3268)
REGA ENTERPRISES INC
1889 Rosemary Ln (23321-3527)
PHONE..............................757 488-8056
Robert Alewine, *President*
Gail Thail, *Administration*
EMP: 2
SALES (est): 208.2K **Privately Held**
SIC: 3578 Accounting machines & cash
registers

(G-3269)
REQUISITES GALLERY
910 Star Ct (23322-3873)
PHONE..............................757 376-2754
Margaret Attkisson, *Principal*
EMP: 2
SALES (est): 129.5K **Privately Held**
WEB: www.requisitesgallery.com
SIC: 3999 Framed artwork

(G-3270)
**RICHARDSON ORNAMENTAL
IRON**
1136 S Military Hwy (23320-2351)
PHONE..............................757 420-1426
Gene Jennings, *Owner*
EMP: 6
SQ FT: 1,800
SALES (est): 148.6K **Privately Held**
WEB: www.richardsonsironco.com
SIC: 3446 Architectural metalwork

(G-3271)
ROAD & RAIL REPAIR INC
2233 Battery Park Rd (23323-5052)
PHONE..............................757 558-1920
Richard Green, *Principal*
EMP: 1 EST: 2007
SALES (est): 125.3K **Privately Held**
SIC: 3715 Truck trailers

(G-3272)
ROBERTS SCREEN PRINTING
337 Briarfield Dr (23322-5545)
PHONE..............................757 487-6285
Wilson G Roberts, *Owner*
EMP: 1
SALES (est): 60.5K **Privately Held**
SIC: 2759 Screen printing

(G-3273)
RODGERS PUDDINGS LLC
1410 Poindexter St (23324-2431)
PHONE..............................757 558-2657
Reginald Rodgers, *Mng Member*
Martha R Rodgers,

EMP: 2
SALES (est): 66.5K **Privately Held**
WEB: www.fridaysplaceinc.com
SIC: 2032 7389 Puddings, except meat:
packaged in cans, jars, etc.;

(G-3274)
ROL-LIFT INTERNATIONAL LLC
3955 S Military Hwy (23321-2914)
PHONE..............................757 650-2040
Brian Wheeler, *Principal*
Luther Wheeler, *Principal*
EMP: 1
SQ FT: 8,000
SALES (est): 116.2K **Privately Held**
WEB: www.rol-liftinternational.com
SIC: 3537 Lift trucks, industrial: fork, plat-
form, straddle, etc.

(G-3275)
**ROME RESEARCH
CORPORATION**
5102 Relay Rd Bldg 352 (23322-4408)
PHONE..............................757 421-8300
Stan Romes, *Branch Mgr*
EMP: 3 **Publicly Held**
WEB: www.pargovernment.com
SIC: 3663 Satellites, communications
HQ: Rome Research Corporation
421 Ridge St
Rome NY 13440
315 339-0491

(G-3276)
ROXANNAS CANDLES
3800 Conway Rd (23322-2802)
PHONE..............................804 243-9697
Roxanna Zook, *Principal*
EMP: 1
SALES (est): 39.6K **Privately Held**
SIC: 3999 Candles

(G-3277)
ROYALCANVASCOM
120 Bruton Ct (23322-4371)
PHONE..............................866 673-6110
EMP: 2
SALES (est): 60.9K **Privately Held**
WEB: www.royalcanvas.com
SIC: 2752 Commercial printing, litho-
graphic

(G-3278)
**ROYSTER PRINTING SERVICES
INC**
Also Called: Precision Printing
1300 Priority Ln (23324-1313)
PHONE..............................757 545-3019
Ray Grover, *Ch of Bd*
Jack Minks, *President*
Eva Kelly, *Sales Staff*
Cyndi Bindery, *Manager*
Maki Roppongi, *Graphic Designe*
EMP: 8
SQ FT: 8,000
SALES (est): 1.6MM **Privately Held**
WEB: www.precisionprintingva.com
SIC: 2752 Commercial printing, offset

(G-3279)
**RUGGED EVOLUTION
INCORPORATED**
424 Vespasian Cir (23322-6981)
PHONE..............................757 478-2430
Arrington Gavin, *President*
Dee Gavin, *Treasurer*
EMP: 4
SALES (est): 10K **Privately Held**
WEB: www.ruggedevo.com
SIC: 2844 Shaving preparations

(G-3280)
**S & S EQUIPMENT SLS & SVC
INC**
1753 West Rd (23323-6430)
PHONE..............................757 421-3000
Joe Spruill, *Owner*
EMP: 9
SALES (est): 1.2MM **Privately Held**
SIC: 3531 4213 Construction machinery;
heavy hauling

(G-3281)
**S3 MOBILE WELDING &
CUTTING**
300 Ewell Ln (23322-3829)
PHONE..............................757 647-0322
Lynn Sparck, *President*
EMP: 2
SALES (est): 70K **Privately Held**
SIC: 7692 Welding repair

(G-3282)
SALSA DE LOS FLORES INC
433 Mill Stone Rd (23322-4339)
PHONE..............................757 450-0796
Ivonne McNeese, *President*
EMP: 3 EST: 2010
SALES (est): 123.1K **Privately Held**
SIC: 2099 Dips, except cheese & sour
cream based

(G-3283)
SANDS 1B LLC
5421 Royal Tern Ct (23321-1379)
PHONE..............................757 673-1140
Kevin Prine, *Principal*
EMP: 2
SALES (est): 81.9K **Privately Held**
SIC: 1381 Drilling oil & gas wells

(G-3284)
SAVAGE TRANSPARENCY LLC
2458 Carnation Ln (23325-4641)
PHONE..............................760 218-6457
John Barkmeyer, *Mng Member*
EMP: 1
SALES (est): 320K **Privately Held**
SIC: 3469 3631 Household cooking &
kitchen utensils, porcelain enameled; bar-
becues, grills & braziers (outdoor cook-
ing)

(G-3285)
SAVY DESIGNS BY SYLVIA
805 Seabrooke Pt (23322-7040)
PHONE..............................757 547-7525
Claude B Blemmer, *Principal*
EMP: 1
SALES (est): 60K **Privately Held**
SIC: 3911 Jewelry, precious metal

(G-3286)
**SCAFFSALES INTERNATIONAL
LLC**
828 Seaboard Ave (23324-2645)
PHONE..............................757 545-5050
Richard C Mapp III, *Principal*
EMP: 8
SALES (est): 972.8K **Privately Held**
SIC: 2499 Scaffolds, wood

(G-3287)
**SCHLUMBERGER
TECHNOLOGY CORP**
510 Independence Pkwy (23320-5180)
PHONE..............................757 546-2472
EMP: 2 **Publicly Held**
SIC: 1389 Oil field services
HQ: Schlumberger Technology Corp
300 Schlumberger Dr
Sugar Land TX 77478
281 285-8500

(G-3288)
SCHOCK METAL AMERICA INC
1230 Scholastic Way (23323-1629)
PHONE..............................757 549-8300
Martin Schock, *President*
Jason Messenger, *Exec VP*
Muller Reinhard, *Vice Pres*
Helmut Fuchs, *CFO*
Erik Sanke, *Mng Member*
▲ EMP: 10
SQ FT: 15,000
SALES (est): 1.8MM
SALES (corp-wide): 355.8K **Privately
Held**
WEB: www.schockmetal.com
SIC: 3429 5072 Furniture hardware; hard-
ware; furniture hardware
HQ: Schock Metallwerk Gmbh
Siemensstr. 1-3
Urbach 73660
718 180-80

(G-3289)
SEAGER VALVE
925 Thatcher Way (23320-8510)
PHONE..............................757 478-0607
Steve Geer, *Owner*
EMP: 2
SALES (est): 126.6K **Privately Held**
SIC: 3491 Automatic regulating & control
valves

(G-3290)
SEMAD ENTERPRISES INC
2412 Featherbed Dr (23325-4620)
PHONE..............................757 424-6177
Anthony Dames, *President*
EMP: 1
SALES (est): 10K **Privately Held**
SIC: 3731 Shipbuilding & repairing

(G-3291)
**SHIP SSTNABILITY SOLUTIONS
LLC**
1012 Austenwood Ct (23322-9131)
PHONE..............................757 574-2436
Michael Kennedy,
EMP: 3
SALES (est): 139.1K **Privately Held**
SIC: 2821 3441 3731 7389 Plastics ma-
terials & resins; fabricated structural
metal; fabricated structural metal for
ships; shipbuilding & repairing; military
ships, building & repairing;

(G-3292)
**SHOFFNER INDUSTRIES
VIRGINIA**
3812 Cook Blvd (23323-1606)
PHONE..............................757 485-1132
Carroll Shoffner, *Principal*
EMP: 3 EST: 2016
SALES (est): 104.9K **Privately Held**
WEB: www.ufpi.com
SIC: 2439 Trusses, wooden roof

(G-3293)
SIHL USA INC
713 Fenway Ave Ste B (23323-3333)
PHONE..............................757 966-7180
Phil Hursh, *Principal*
Heather Skorski, *Cust Mgr*
Andreas Degroot, *Sales Staff*
Terry Greenberg, *Sales Staff*
David Gustafson, *Sales Staff*
▲ EMP: 5
SALES (est): 711.9K
SALES (corp-wide): 990.3K **Privately
Held**
WEB: www.sihlinc.com
SIC: 2679 Paper products, converted
PA: Diatec Holding Spa
Via Giosue' Carducci 11
Milano MI 20123

(G-3294)
**SIX PCKS ARTSAN RASTED COF
LLC**
1865 Shipyard Rd (23323-5506)
PHONE..............................757 337-0872
Nichol Pickerill, *Principal*
EMP: 2
SALES (est): 77.4K **Privately Held**
SIC: 2095 Roasted coffee

(G-3295)
SLEJS CUSTOM COATING LLC
1341 Thyme Trl (23320-2737)
PHONE..............................817 975-6274
Michael Harris, *Principal*
EMP: 2
SALES (est): 107.1K **Privately Held**
SIC: 3479 Metal coating & allied service

(G-3296)
SM INDUSTRIES LLC
3248 Bruin Dr (23321-4602)
PHONE..............................757 966-2343
Steven Moore, *Principal*
EMP: 3
SALES (est): 143.9K **Privately Held**
SIC: 3999 Manufacturing industries

GEOGRAPHIC

(G-3297)
SMALL ARMS MFG SOLUTIONS LLC
1033 Cavalier Blvd (23323-1509)
PHONE.................................757 673-7769
EMP: 2
SALES (est): 73.4K Privately Held
SIC: 3484 Small arms

(G-3298)
SMARTPHONE PHOTOBOOTH
254 Coventry Close # 201 (23320-4624)
PHONE.................................757 364-2403
EMP: 2
SALES (est): 73.2K Privately Held
SIC: 2759 Commercial printing

(G-3299)
SOLITE LLC
3900 Shannon St (23324-1054)
PHONE.................................757 494-5200
D Kirk Edens, President
EMP: 35
SALES (est): 2.5MM Privately Held
WEB: www.solitellc.com
SIC: 1081 Mine development, metal

(G-3300)
SOUNDS GREEK INC
1046 Windswept Cir (23320-5006)
PHONE.................................757 548-0062
Clyde Lacwell, President
EMP: 1
SALES (est): 60.8K Privately Held
SIC: 2395 Embroidery & art needlework

(G-3301)
SOUTHCOAST WELDING & MFG LLC
700 Rosemont Ave Bldg 3 (23324-1134)
PHONE.................................757 574-0090
EMP: 2 EST: 2019
SALES (est): 176.7K Privately Held
WEB: www.southcoastwelding.net
SIC: 3999 Manufacturing industries

(G-3302)
SOUTHERN ATL SCREENPRINT INC
3700 Profit Way (23323-1511)
PHONE.................................757 485-7800
EMP: 18
SQ FT: 7,200
SALES: 1.7MM Privately Held
SIC: 2759 Commercial Printing

(G-3303)
SOUTHERN PACKING CORPORATION
4004 Battlefield Blvd S (23322-2431)
PHONE.................................757 421-2131
Toll Free:.................................888 -
Hyman Brooke, President
B Benjamin Brooke, Vice Pres
L H Brooke, Treasurer
Margaret Norfleet, Bookkeeper
Ronald Brooke, Admin Sec
EMP: 34 EST: 1933
SQ FT: 15,300
SALES (est): 6.6MM Privately Held
WEB: www.southernpacking.com
SIC: 2011 2013 Meat packing plants; sausages & other prepared meats

(G-3304)
SOUTHERN TASTES LLC
237 Hanbury Rd E 17-325 (23322-6621)
PHONE.................................757 204-1414
David G Hanson, President
EMP: 2
SALES (est): 203K Privately Held
SIC: 2064 Candy & other confectionery products

(G-3305)
SPA GUY LLC
1228 Cavalier Blvd (23323-1540)
PHONE.................................757 855-0381
J Michael Kenny,
Chris Wagner, Master
▼ EMP: 1
SALES (est): 117.9K Privately Held
WEB: www.spaguyusa.com
SIC: 3949 5091 Swimming pools, plastic; swimming pools, equipment & supplies
PA: Futura Marketing Ltd
1228 Cavalier Blvd
Chesapeake VA 23323

(G-3306)
SPECIALTY MARINE INC
513 Freeman Ave (23324-1066)
PHONE.................................757 494-1199
William H J Fairing, President
Herrel L Gallop, Vice Pres
EMP: 10
SQ FT: 40,980
SALES (est): 1.3MM Privately Held
WEB: www.specialty-marine.com
SIC: 3731 Shipbuilding & repairing

(G-3307)
SPEDAPPS LLC
1550 Shell Rd (23323-6112)
PHONE.................................757 541-2663
Timothy Bond, Mng Member
EMP: 2
SALES (est): 100K Privately Held
SIC: 7372 Educational computer software

(G-3308)
SQUARE PENNY PUBLISHING LLC
1853 Burson Dr (23323-5405)
PHONE.................................757 348-2226
Tiffany Thompson, Principal
EMP: 2
SALES (est): 44.5K Privately Held
SIC: 2741 Miscellaneous publishing

(G-3309)
SRM LOGISTICS LLC
3201 Bruin Dr (23321-4601)
PHONE.................................757 232-9928
Shawn Mallory,
EMP: 1
SALES (est): 60K Privately Held
SIC: 3537 Truck trailers, used in plants, docks, terminals, etc.

(G-3310)
STAR OIL LLC
400 Freeman Ave Ste A (23324-1026)
PHONE.................................757 545-5100
Carolyn Moran, Manager
EMP: 2
SALES (est): 122.7K Privately Held
SIC: 2869 Fuels

(G-3311)
STAR PRINTING CO INC
413 Oak Lake Ter (23320-9507)
PHONE.................................757 625-7782
William G Duggan Jr, President
Darrell A Duggan, Principal
David A Duggan, Principal
Douglas Duggan, Principal
EMP: 5 EST: 1951
SALES (est): 724.8K Privately Held
SIC: 2752 Commercial printing, offset

(G-3312)
STEVE M SHEIL
508 Mustang Dr (23322-1309)
PHONE.................................757 482-2456
Steve M Sheil, Owner
EMP: 1
SALES (est): 54K Privately Held
SIC: 2511 Wood household furniture

(G-3313)
STITCHED LOOP LLC
433 Lake Crest Dr (23323-1774)
PHONE.................................678 467-1973
Lynette Horne, Principal
EMP: 1
SALES (est): 39.8K Privately Held
SIC: 2395 Embroidery & art needlework

(G-3314)
SUFFOLK WELDING & FAB
2051 Maywood St (23323-6001)
PHONE.................................757 544-4689
Rhonda Chappell, Principal
EMP: 1
SALES (est): 27.6K Privately Held
WEB: www.suffolkwelding.com
SIC: 7692 Welding repair

(G-3315)
SUPERIOR QUALITY MFG LLC
424 Network Sta (23320-3848)
PHONE.................................757 413-9100
Lawrence Cohen,
▲ EMP: 1
SALES (est): 6K
SALES (corp-wide): 173.1MM Privately Held
SIC: 3669 Highway signals, electric
HQ: Init Innovations In Transportation, Inc.
424 Network Sta
Chesapeake VA 23320

(G-3316)
SUPERNAL INDUSTRIES LLC
620 Mcrowland Way (23320-3274)
PHONE.................................804 380-1742
EMP: 1
SALES (est): 44.7K Privately Held
SIC: 3999 Manufacturing industries

(G-3317)
SUPPLY ONE CHESAPEAKE
3813 Cook Blvd (23323-1605)
PHONE.................................757 485-3570
Jennifer Mattern, Agent
EMP: 3
SALES (est): 120.7K Privately Held
SIC: 2653 Boxes, corrugated: made from purchased materials

(G-3318)
T/J ONE CORP
414 Rio Dr (23322-7144)
PHONE.................................757 548-0093
Teresa Philips, Owner
EMP: 2
SALES (est): 149.4K Privately Held
WEB: www.chileansculptor1.com
SIC: 2812 Alkalies & chlorine

(G-3319)
TACTICAL MARINE REPAIR INC
3737 Holland Blvd Ste C (23323-1532)
PHONE.................................757 967-8688
Raul Matos, Vice Pres
EMP: 3
SALES (est): 500K Privately Held
SIC: 3731 Shipbuilding & repairing

(G-3320)
TAMCO ENTERPRISES INC
1400 Kempsville Rd # 110 (23320-8188)
PHONE.................................757 627-9551
Tammy Barney, President
Robert R Barney, Exec VP
EMP: 6 EST: 1989
SQ FT: 8,500
SALES (est): 579K Privately Held
WEB: www.tamcopaint.com
SIC: 3999 Painting instrument dials

(G-3321)
TANTS MCH & FABRICATION INC
4001 Holland Blvd Ste D (23323-1551)
PHONE.................................757 434-9448
Juanita Tant, President
Ronald Tant Sr, Vice Pres
EMP: 2 EST: 2012
SALES (est): 235.1K Privately Held
WEB: www.mswodor.com
SIC: 3541 Lathes

(G-3322)
TAPIOCA GO
1434 Sams Dr Ste 106 (23320-4753)
PHONE.................................757 410-3836
Sarah Chan, General Mgr
EMP: 8
SALES (est): 43.5K Privately Held
SIC: 2046 5812 Tapioca; cafe

(G-3323)
TAYLORMADE WOODWORKING
4641 Captain Carter Cir (23321-1298)
PHONE.................................757 288-6256
Mark Didawick, Principal
EMP: 1
SALES (est): 54.1K Privately Held
SIC: 2431 Millwork

(G-3324)
TCTS TRUCKING LLC
200 Carver St (23320-6408)
PHONE.................................757 406-6323
Tavon Spence,
EMP: 1
SALES (est): 54.6K Privately Held
SIC: 3799 Transportation equipment

(G-3325)
TEAM CERAMIC INC
1500 Chasebury Pl Apt 107 (23320-3381)
PHONE.................................757 572-7725
Daniel A Dozier, Principal
EMP: 3
SALES (est): 197.6K Privately Held
WEB: www.teamceramic.com
SIC: 3269 Pottery products

(G-3326)
TECNICO CORPORATION (HQ)
831 Industrial Ave (23324-2614)
PHONE.................................757 545-4013
Raymond G Wittersheim, President
John Green, Division Mgr
Wray Bridger, General Mgr
Matthew Dewitt, Superintendent
Dave Horton, Superintendent
EMP: 375
SQ FT: 18,000
SALES (est): 112.4MM Privately Held
WEB: www.tecnicocorp.com
SIC: 3446 3441 3731 3444 Architectural metalwork; fabricated structural metal; shipbuilding & repairing; sheet metalwork; fabricated plate work (boiler shop)

(G-3327)
TEE TIME THREADS LLC
2711 Janice Lynn Ct (23323-2313)
PHONE.................................757 581-4507
Megan White, Owner
Megan V White,
EMP: 1
SALES (est): 45K Privately Held
SIC: 2396 Fabric printing & stamping

(G-3328)
TEE Z SPECIAL
4137 Lakeview Dr (23323-1622)
PHONE.................................757 488-2435
Wesley Burt, Owner
EMP: 1
SALES (est): 57K Privately Held
SIC: 2261 Screen printing of cotton broad-woven fabrics

(G-3329)
TEES & CO
645 Mill Landing Rd (23322-8330)
PHONE.................................757 744-9889
EMP: 2
SALES (est): 73.2K Privately Held
SIC: 2759 Screen printing

(G-3330)
TENT COMPANY OF NORFOLK LLC
Also Called: Norfolk Tent Company
3419 Bus Ctr Dr Ste B (23323)
PHONE.................................757 461-7330
EMP: 2
SALES (est): 129.5K Privately Held
SIC: 2393 Textile bags

(G-3331)
THERMAL SPRAY SOLUTIONS INC (PA)
1105 Intl Plz Ste B (23323)
PHONE.................................757 673-2468
Thomas S Giancoli, President
Chris Nichols, Vice Pres
Scott E Spruce, Vice Pres
EMP: 25
SQ FT: 55,000
SALES (est): 3.7MM Privately Held
WEB: www.thermalsprayusa.com
SIC: 3479 Coating of metals & formed products

(G-3332)
THINK INK PRINTING
1226 Executive Blvd # 103 (23320-2889)
PHONE.................................757 315-8565
Peter Korer, Principal

▲ = Import ▼=Export
◆ =Import/Export

EMP: 3
SALES (est): 101.5K **Privately Held**
WEB: www.thinkinkprinting.com
SIC: 2752 Commercial printing, offset

(G-3333)
THORN 10 PUBLISHING LLC
1205 Brassie Ct (23320-9456)
PHONE..........................757 277-9431
Gene Thornton, *Principal*
EMP: 2
SALES (est): 82.5K **Privately Held**
SIC: 2741 Miscellaneous publishing

(G-3334)
THRANE RGONAL WORKSHOP-MACKEY
209 Tintern Ct (23320-4515)
PHONE..........................757 410-3291
EMP: 2
SALES (est): 120K **Privately Held**
SIC: 3663 Mfg Radio/Tv Communication Equipment

(G-3335)
TI PRINTING OF VIRGINIA LLC
Also Called: Think Ink Printing
1226 Executive Blvd # 103 (23320-2889)
PHONE..........................757 315-8565
Julia Korer, *Managing Prtnr*
EMP: 3
SALES (est): 92.3K **Privately Held**
SIC: 2752 Commercial printing, lithographic

(G-3336)
TIDAL WAVE GRAPHICS
625 Innovation Dr Ste 101 (23320-3863)
PHONE..........................757 842-6269
Troy McDorman, *Principal*
EMP: 1 **EST**: 2007
SALES (est): 84.8K **Privately Held**
WEB: www.tidalwavegraphics.com
SIC: 3993 Signs & advertising specialties

(G-3337)
TIDEWATER AUTO ELEC SVCS II
940 Corporate Ln Ste A (23320-3679)
PHONE..........................757 523-5656
Anthony Knight, *President*
EMP: 5 **EST**: 1996
SQ FT: 1,918
SALES (est): 943.5K **Privately Held**
WEB: www.tidewaterautoelectric.com
SIC: 3699 Electrical equipment & supplies

(G-3338)
TIDEWATER GREEN
1500 Steel St (23323-6100)
PHONE..........................757 487-4736
James A Warren, *Owner*
EMP: 12
SALES (est): 710K **Privately Held**
WEB: www.tidewatergreen.com
SIC: 2952 4953 Asphalt felts & coatings; liquid waste, collection & disposal

(G-3339)
TIDEWATER TRADING POST INC
820 Greenbrier Cir Ste 33 (23320-2646)
P.O. Box 481, Hopewell (23860-0481)
PHONE..........................757 420-6117
EMP: 18
SQ FT: 2,000
SALES (est): 1.2MM **Privately Held**
SIC: 2741 2721 Publication Of Advertising Sheet

(G-3340)
TIDEWATER WLDG FABRICATION LLC
1336 Butts Station Rd (23320-3102)
PHONE..........................757 636-6630
Jasen Storberg,
EMP: 1
SALES (est): 98K **Privately Held**
SIC: 3317 7692 7389 Welded pipe & tubes; welding repair;

(G-3341)
TNL EMBROIDERY INC
500 Grayson Way (23320-3797)
PHONE..........................757 410-2671
EMP: 3

SALES: 800K **Privately Held**
SIC: 2395 Pleating/Stitching Services

(G-3342)
TNT GRAPHICS&SIGNS
2864 Wesley Rd (23323-2012)
PHONE..........................757 615-5936
William Ramsey, *Owner*
EMP: 1
SALES (est): 30K **Privately Held**
SIC: 3993 Signs & advertising specialties

(G-3343)
TNT PRINTING LLC
3648 Mill Bridge Way (23323-1219)
PHONE..........................757 818-5468
Todd Tucker, *Principal*
EMP: 1
SALES (est): 60.6K **Privately Held**
SIC: 2759 Business forms: printing

(G-3344)
TOP DRONE VIDEO
4319 Greenleaf Dr (23321-4212)
PHONE..........................757 288-1774
Barry Rowland, *Principal*
EMP: 2
SALES (est): 93.9K **Privately Held**
SIC: 3721 Motorized aircraft

(G-3345)
TOUCH HONEY DSGN PRINT PHOTG
31 King George Quay (23325-4749)
PHONE..........................757 606-0411
Wenona Fields, *Principal*
EMP: 4
SALES (est): 274K **Privately Held**
SIC: 2752 Commercial printing, lithographic

(G-3346)
TQ-SYSTEMS USA INC
424 Network Sta (23320-3848)
PHONE..........................757 503-3927
Frank Denk, *President*
EMP: 2
SALES (est): 90K
SALES (corp-wide): 135.7K **Privately Held**
SIC: 3674 3577 5045 Computer logic modules; computer peripheral equipment; computer software
HQ: Tq-Group Gmbh
Muhlstr. 2
Seefeld 82229
815 393-080

(G-3347)
TRACK PATCH 1 CORPORATION
134 Battlefield Blvd N (23320-3912)
PHONE..........................757 609-2842
EMP: 1
SALES (est): 41.1K **Privately Held**
SIC: 2395 Embroidery & art needlework

(G-3348)
TRADEMARK PRINTING LLC
460 Plummer Dr (23323-3116)
PHONE..........................757 803-7612
Becky Barlow, *Principal*
EMP: 4 **EST**: 2008
SALES (est): 291K **Privately Held**
SIC: 2752 Commercial printing, lithographic

(G-3349)
TRAINING SERVICES INC
Also Called: Tidewater Tech Aviation
2211 S Military Hwy Ste B (23320-5987)
PHONE..........................757 363-1800
Gerald Yagen, *Manager*
EMP: 11
SALES (corp-wide): 5MM **Privately Held**
WEB: www.fighterfactory.com
SIC: 3721 Aircraft
PA: Training Services, Inc.
4455 South Blvd Ste 500
Virginia Beach VA 23452
757 456-5065

(G-3350)
TRANE US INC
1100 Cavalier Blvd (23323-1506)
PHONE..........................757 485-7700

Bill Smith, *Branch Mgr*
EMP: 4 **Privately Held**
WEB: www.trane.com
SIC: 3585 Refrigeration & heating equipment
HQ: Trane U.S. Inc.
3600 Pammel Creek Rd
La Crosse WI 54601
608 787-2000

(G-3351)
TRIAX MUSIC INDUSTRIES
1511 Oleander Ave (23325-3741)
PHONE..........................757 839-1215
Randy Ladkau, *Owner*
EMP: 4
SALES (est): 209.8K **Privately Held**
SIC: 3999 Manufacturing industries

(G-3352)
TRUE SOUTHERN SMOKE BBQ LLC
205 Gregg St (23320-6317)
PHONE..........................757 816-0228
Jeffery Olando Brown, *CEO*
EMP: 1
SALES (est): 59K **Privately Held**
WEB: www.tssbbq.com
SIC: 2099 5812 Food preparations; caterers

(G-3353)
TWIN DISC INCORPORATED
Also Called: John Deere Authorized Dealer
3700 Profit Way (23323-1511)
PHONE..........................757 487-3670
Michael E Batten, *Branch Mgr*
EMP: 51 **Publicly Held**
WEB: www.twindisc.com
SIC: 3568 5082 Power transmission equipment; construction & mining machinery
PA: Twin Disc, Incorporated
1328 Racine St
Racine WI 53403
262 638-4000

(G-3354)
TWO N ONE FABRICATION LLC
2627 Cecilia Ter (23323-3805)
PHONE..........................757 642-2613
Daniel Lewis, *Mng Member*
EMP: 1 **EST**: 2016
SALES (est): 80K **Privately Held**
WEB: www.piedmontfabrication.com
SIC: 3441 Fabricated structural metal

(G-3355)
UFP MID-ATLANTIC LLC
Also Called: Universal Forest Products
3812 Cook Blvd (23323-1606)
PHONE..........................757 485-3190
Mark Campbell, *Manager*
EMP: 71
SALES (corp-wide): 4.4B **Publicly Held**
WEB: www.ufpi.com
SIC: 2439 Trusses, wooden roof
HQ: Ufp Mid-Atlantic, Llc
5631 S Nc Highway 62
Burlington NC 27215
336 226-9356

(G-3356)
USUI INTERNATIONAL CORPORATION
3824 Cook Blvd (23323-1630)
PHONE..........................757 558-7300
Bill Atteberry, *Vice Pres*
EMP: 270 **Privately Held**
WEB: www.usuiusa.com
SIC: 3317 3714 3564 Steel pipe & tubes; motor vehicle parts & accessories; blowers & fans
HQ: Usui International Corporation
44780 Helm St
Plymouth MI 48170
734 354-3626

(G-3357)
VA MEDICAL SUPPLY INC
5172 W Military Hwy Ste E (23321-1100)
PHONE..........................757 390-9000
Henry Powell, *President*
EMP: 1
SALES (est): 47.2K **Privately Held**
SIC: 2834 Pharmaceutical preparations

(G-3358)
VANWIN COATINGS VIRGINIA LLC (PA)
2601 Trade St Ste A (23323-3307)
P.O. Box 6859 (23323-0859)
PHONE..........................757 487-5080
John Byrd, *COO*
Edward Casper, *Opers Staff*
Skip Umphlett, *Production*
Jennifer Whitham, *Mng Member*
James A Whitham,
EMP: 25
SQ FT: 22,000
SALES (est): 4.3MM **Privately Held**
WEB: www.vanwincoatings.com
SIC: 3479 Coating of metals & formed products; coating, rust preventive

(G-3359)
VARIETY PRINTING INC
1014 Wadena Rd (23320-6028)
PHONE..........................757 480-1891
Thomas Wright, *President*
Nancy W Koonin, *Vice Pres*
EMP: 2
SQ FT: 1,550
SALES (est): 125K **Privately Held**
SIC: 2752 Commercial printing, offset

(G-3360)
VIRGINIA ELECTRIC AND POWER CO
Also Called: Dominion Energy Virginia
2837 S Military Hwy (23323-6203)
PHONE..........................757 558-5459
Frank Miller, *Manager*
EMP: 12
SALES (corp-wide): 16.5B **Publicly Held**
WEB: www.dominionenergy.com
SIC: 3511 4911 Turbines & turbine generator sets; electric services
HQ: Virginia Electric And Power Company
120 Tredegar St
Richmond VA 23219
804 819-2000

(G-3361)
VIRGINIA ELECTRONIC MONITORING
612 Ridge Cir (23320-4857)
PHONE..........................757 513-0942
Alfonso Porta, *CEO*
Demian Futterman, *President*
EMP: 2
SALES (est): 177.5K **Privately Held**
WEB: www.vemsystems.com
SIC: 3829 Measuring & controlling devices

(G-3362)
VIRGINIA MOBILE AC SYSTEMS INC
Also Called: Vmacs
704 Canal Dr (23323-4315)
PHONE..........................757 650-0957
Scott Faivre, *President*
Frank Van Deman, *E-Business*
Paula Faivre, *Admin Sec*
EMP: 4
SALES (est): 290K **Privately Held**
WEB: www.vmacs.net
SIC: 3599 Machine shop, jobbing & repair

(G-3363)
VISCOSITY LLC
120 Marina Reach (23320-3400)
PHONE..........................757 343-9071
Brian Eddy, *Principal*
EMP: 1
SALES (est): 71.9K **Privately Held**
SIC: 2911 5169 Oils, lubricating; greases, lubricating; oil additives

(G-3364)
VOLVO PENTA MARINE PDTS LLC (DH)
1300 Volvo Penta Dr (23320-4691)
P.O. Box 26248, Greensboro NC (27402-6248)
PHONE..........................757 436-2800
Lars Ljungquist, *Opers Staff*
Charles Martin, *VP Finance*
◆ **EMP**: 4

SALES (est): 30.9MM
SALES (corp-wide): 44.8B Privately Held
SIC: 3519 Marine engines

(G-3365)
VOLVO PENTA OF AMERICAS LLC
1300 Volvo Pkwy (23320-9419)
PHONE.................................757 436-2800
Clint Moore, *President*
EMP: 150
SALES (corp-wide): 44.8B Privately Held
WEB: www.volvopentastore.com
SIC: 3519 Marine engines
HQ: Volvo Penta Of The Americas, Llc
    1300 Volvo Penta Dr
    Chesapeake VA 23320

(G-3366)
VT MILCOM INC
Also Called: Fabrication Division
901 Professional Pl (23320-3618)
PHONE.................................757 548-2956
EMP: 75
SALES (corp-wide): 1.4B Privately Held
SIC: 3444 8711 1731 4813 Mfg Sheet
Metalwork Engineering Services Electrical
Contractor Telephone Communications
Mfg Radio/Tv Comm Equip
HQ: Vt Milcom Inc.
    448 Viking Dr Ste 350
    Virginia Beach VA 23452
    757 463-2800

(G-3367)
VULCAN CONSTRUCTION MTLS LLC
3900 Shannon St (23324-1054)
PHONE.................................757 545-0980
EMP: 60
SALES (corp-wide): 2.9B Publicly Held
SIC: 1422 Crushed/Broken Limestone
HQ: Vulcan Construction Materials, Llc
    1200 Urban Center Dr
    Vestavia AL 35242
    205 298-3000

(G-3368)
W D BARNETTE ENTERPRISE INC
Also Called: Barnette's Machine Shop
1332 Truxton St (23324-1325)
PHONE.................................757 494-0530
Daniel Barnette, *President*
William Barnette, *Vice Pres*
EMP: 3
SALES (est): 260K Privately Held
WEB: www.barnettesengines.com
SIC: 3599 Machine & other job shop work

(G-3369)
WALSH TOPS INC
1717 S Park Ct (23320-8911)
PHONE.................................757 523-1934
Thomas M Walsh, *President*
John Flach, *Manager*
EMP: 21
SQ FT: 8,800
SALES (est): 2.5MM Privately Held
WEB: www.walshtops.wordpress.com
SIC: 2434 Wood kitchen cabinets

(G-3370)
WALTER HEDGE
833 Principal Ln (23320-3638)
PHONE.................................757 548-4750
Walter Hedge, *Owner*
EMP: 4
SALES (est): 392.5K Privately Held
WEB: www.waltswaterworks.com
SIC: 3599 Water leak detectors

(G-3371)
WATERTREE PRESS LLC
512 Flax Mill Dr (23322-5847)
PHONE.................................757 512-5517
Charles Apperson, *Principal*
EMP: 2
SALES (est): 141K Privately Held
WEB: www.watertreepress.com
SIC: 2741 Miscellaneous publishing

(G-3372)
WB FRESH PRESS LLC
1009 Keltic Cir (23323-2738)
PHONE.................................757 485-3176
EMP: 2
SALES (est): 59.2K Privately Held
SIC: 2741 Miscellaneous publishing

(G-3373)
WELDING FABRICATION & DESIGN
720 Canal Dr (23323-4315)
PHONE.................................757 739-0025
Henry Green, *Owner*
EMP: 1
SALES (est): 50.7K Privately Held
SIC: 7692 Welding repair

(G-3374)
WELDPROTECH INC
801 Butler St Ste 6 (23323-3404)
PHONE.................................757 485-3293
Luis Diaz Cartagena, *President*
EMP: 2
SALES (est): 33.6K Privately Held
SIC: 7692 Welding repair

(G-3375)
WERRELL WOODWORKS
1716 S Park Ct (23320-8912)
PHONE.................................757 581-0131
EMP: 1
SALES (est): 54.1K Privately Held
WEB: www.staybycorisamuel.com
SIC: 2431 Millwork

(G-3376)
WHISPER TACTICAL LLC
517 Taryn Ct (23320-4095)
PHONE.................................757 645-5938
Charles Grimes, *CEO*
EMP: 1
SALES (est): 58.2K Privately Held
SIC: 3484 5099 Guns (firearms) or gun
parts, 30 mm. & below; machine guns

(G-3377)
WILLIAM K RAND III
824 Greenbrier Pkwy # 100 (23320-3697)
PHONE.................................757 410-7390
William Rand, *Owner*
EMP: 15 EST: 2008
SALES (est): 1.6MM Privately Held
WEB: www.ruetzelobgyn.com
SIC: 3131 Rands

(G-3378)
WINDING CREEK CANDLE CO LLC
740 Tyler Way (23322-1581)
PHONE.................................757 410-1991
Amy Paris, *Principal*
EMP: 1
SALES (est): 43.6K Privately Held
SIC: 3999 Candles

(G-3379)
WINNER MADE LLC
570 Marc Smiley Rd (23324-1483)
PHONE.................................757 828-7623
Rochon Washington, *Mng Member*
EMP: 2 EST: 2014
SALES (est): 40K Privately Held
WEB: www.winnermade.com
SIC: 2759 Screen printing

(G-3380)
WOOD TURNS
2525 Southern Pines Dr (23323-4316)
PHONE.................................904 303-8536
EMP: 1
SALES (est): 68.9K Privately Held
SIC: 2431 Millwork

(G-3381)
YUPO CORPORATION AMERICA
800 Yupo Ct (23320-3626)
PHONE.................................757 312-9876
Andre Fishback, *CEO*
Karen Zorumski, *Vice Pres*
Brad Whitlow, *Prdtn Mgr*
Reggie Coleman, *Mfg Staff*
John Hamilton, *Production*
▲ EMP: 149
SQ FT: 160,000

SALES (est): 63.1MM Privately Held
WEB: www.yupousa.com
SIC: 2621 4953 7389 Paper mills; med-
ical waste disposal; packaging & labeling
services
PA: Yupo Corporation
    4-3, Kandasurugadai
    Chiyoda-Ku TKY 101-0

Chester
Chesterfield County

(G-3382)
ADAMSON GLOBAL TECHNOLOGY CORP
13101 N Enon Church Rd # 15
(23836-3120)
PHONE.................................804 748-6453
Gordon Conti, *Branch Mgr*
EMP: 4 Privately Held
WEB: www.adamsontank.com
SIC: 3443 Industrial vessels, tanks & con-
tainers
PA: Adamson Global Technology Corp.
    2018 W Vemon Ave
    Kinston NC 28504

(G-3383)
ADVANSIX INC
4101 Bermuda Hundred Rd (23836-3245)
PHONE.................................804 530-6000
Michelle Blackwell, *Partner*
Michelle Davis, *Partner*
Christopher Gramm, *Vice Pres*
Daria Ferrell-White, *Cust Mgr*
Michelle Parr, *Cust Mgr*
EMP: 290
SALES (corp-wide): 1.3B Publicly Held
WEB: www.advansix.com
SIC: 2295 Resin or plastic coated fabrics
PA: Advansix Inc.
    300 Kimball Dr Ste 101
    Parsippany NJ 07054
    973 526-1800

(G-3384)
ALLIANCE SIGNS VIRGINIA LLC
12603 Green Garden Ter (23836-2754)
PHONE.................................804 530-1451
Misty Pisa, *Principal*
EMP: 1
SALES (est): 50.6K Privately Held
WEB: www.alliancesignsofva.com
SIC: 3993 Signs & advertising specialties

(G-3385)
ALTEC INDUSTRIES
13301 Great Coastal Dr (23836-2768)
PHONE.................................804 621-4080
EMP: 1
SALES (est): 60K Privately Held
SIC: 3531 Derricks, except oil & gas field

(G-3386)
AMCOR SPCLTY CRTONS AMRCAS
Lawson Mardon Richmond
701 Algroup Way (23836-2763)
PHONE.................................804 748-3470
Bryan Chekensen, *Manager*
EMP: 200
SALES (corp-wide): 12.4B Privately Held
WEB: www.amcor.com
SIC: 3081 Unsupported plastics film &
sheet
HQ: Amcor Specialty Cartons Americas Llc
    445 Dividend Dr
    Peachtree City GA 30269
    770 486-9095

(G-3387)
APPLES & BELLES LLC
1425 Chaplin Bay Dr (23836-5839)
PHONE.................................804 530-3180
EMP: 2
SALES (est): 90.9K Privately Held
SIC: 3571 Mfg Electronic Computers

(G-3388)
ASHTON CREEK VINEYARD LLC
14501 Jefferson Davis Hwy (23831-5345)
P.O. Box 1299, Colonial Heights (23834-
9299)
PHONE.................................804 896-1586
Lori Thibault, *President*
EMP: 6 EST: 2012
SALES (est): 322K Privately Held
WEB: www.ashtoncreekvineyard.com
SIC: 2084 Wines

(G-3389)
B & T LLC
Also Called: B & T Excavating
13701 Vance Dr (23836-5503)
PHONE.................................804 720-1758
Brock McAllister,
EMP: 6
SALES (est): 740K Privately Held
SIC: 3531 Construction machinery

(G-3390)
CARL ZEISS OPTICAL INC
13017 N Kingston Ave (23836-2743)
PHONE.................................804 530-8300
Alexandra Dreu, *Principal*
EMP: 4
SALES (est): 554.7K Privately Held
SIC: 3827 Optical instruments & lenses

(G-3391)
CARL ZEISS VISION INC
Southeastern Optical
13017 N Kingston Ave (23836-2743)
PHONE.................................800 456-0088
Robert Telecher, *Branch Mgr*
EMP: 80 Privately Held
WEB: www.vision.zeiss.com
SIC: 3827 Optical instruments & lenses
HQ: Carl Zeiss Vision Inc.
    12121 Scripps Summit Dr
    San Diego CA 92131

(G-3392)
CARTERS POWER EQUIPMENT INC
4807 W Hundred Rd Ste A (23831-1960)
PHONE.................................804 796-4895
Ralph Carter, *President*
Milette Carter, *Corp Secy*
EMP: 5
SALES (est): 672.8K Privately Held
WEB: www.carterspower.com
SIC: 3524 7699 Lawn & garden mowers &
accessories; lawn mower repair shop

(G-3393)
CEPHAS INDUSTRIES INC
13701 Allied Rd (23836-6441)
P.O. Box 6291, Glen Allen (23058-6291)
PHONE.................................804 641-1824
Morris Cephas, *Principal*
EMP: 1
SALES (est): 55.4K Privately Held
SIC: 3999 Manufacturing industries

(G-3394)
CHESTER RACEWAY
1900 W Hundred Rd (23836-2401)
PHONE.................................804 717-2330
Paresh Patel, *Owner*
EMP: 6
SALES (est): 350K Privately Held
SIC: 3644 Raceways

(G-3395)
CLASSIC ENGRAVERS
12821 Percival St (23831-4741)
PHONE.................................804 748-8717
Gary Helton, *Owner*
EMP: 1
SALES (est): 87.3K Privately Held
SIC: 3089 Engraving of plastic

(G-3396)
CONNER INDUSTRIES INC
12110 Old Stage Rd (23836-2411)
PHONE.................................804 706-4229
Bill Werner, *Branch Mgr*
EMP: 5

SALES (corp-wide): 171.2MM **Privately Held**
WEB: www.connerindustries.com
SIC: 2421 5031 Resawing lumber into smaller dimensions; lumber: rough, dressed & finished
PA: Conner Industries, Inc.
3800 Sandshell Dr Ste 235
Fort Worth TX 76137
800 413-8006

(G-3397)
CORDIAL CRICKET
3524 Festival Park Plz (23831-4449)
PHONE..............................804 931-8027
EMP: 2
SALES (est): 93.4K **Privately Held**
WEB: www.thecordialcricket.com
SIC: 3953 Stationery embossers, personal

(G-3398)
CUPPLES PRODUCTS INC
2001 Ware Btm Spring Rd (23836-2538)
PHONE..............................804 717-1971
Jay Berkowitz, *Manager*
EMP: 25
SALES (corp-wide): 155.9MM **Privately Held**
WEB: www.enclos.com
SIC: 3444 Sheet metal specialties, not stamped
HQ: Cupples Products, Inc
10733 Sunset Office Dr # 200
Saint Louis MO 63127

(G-3399)
CUSTOM BOOK BINDERY
Also Called: Koppee Shoppe
4441 Treely Rd (23831-6842)
PHONE..............................804 796-9520
A Wayne Markland, *Owner*
EMP: 2
SQ FT: 2,400
SALES (est): 200K **Privately Held**
SIC: 2789 7334 Bookbinding & repairing: trade, edition, library, etc.; photocopying & duplicating services

(G-3400)
CUSTOM EMBROIDERY & DESIGN
732 Okuma Dr (23836-5711)
PHONE..............................804 530-5238
Cindy B Partin, *President*
Partin John Boyd, *Vice Pres*
EMP: 1
SALES (est): 83.2K **Privately Held**
WEB: www.custom-emb.com
SIC: 2395 Embroidery products, except schiffli machine

(G-3401)
DANCING KILT BREWERY LLC
12912 Old Stage Rd (23836-2542)
PHONE..............................804 715-0695
Thomas Pakurar, *Principal*
EMP: 6 **EST:** 2014
SQ FT: 3,500
SALES (est): 527.3K **Privately Held**
WEB: www.dancingkiltbrewery.com
SIC: 2082 Ale (alcoholic beverage); beer (alcoholic beverage); stout (alcoholic beverage)

(G-3402)
DAWGBONE BANNERS & SIGNS
3900 Lanyard Ct (23831-7379)
PHONE..............................804 526-5734
David C Hopp, *President*
EMP: 1
SALES (est): 65.1K **Privately Held**
SIC: 3993 Signs & advertising specialties

(G-3403)
DB ENTERPRISES OF VA LLC
14213 Delamere Dr (23831-6588)
PHONE..............................804 931-7667
Jamari Minor,
EMP: 1
SALES (est): 54.6K **Privately Held**
SIC: 3799 Transportation equipment

(G-3404)
DIMENSION TOOL LLC
4001 Centralia Rd (23831-1132)
PHONE..............................804 350-9707

Timothy Clary,
EMP: 1
SALES (est): 160K **Privately Held**
SIC: 3544 Special dies & tools

(G-3405)
DIVINE LIFESTYLE PRINTING LLC
3307 Greenham Dr (23831-7153)
PHONE..............................804 219-3342
Alteria Smart, *Principal*
EMP: 2
SALES (est): 83.9K **Privately Held**
SIC: 2752 Commercial printing, lithographic

(G-3406)
DR FINNIE CARE LLC
1601 Carty Bay Dr (23836-5837)
PHONE..............................804 852-7998
EMP: 1
SALES (est): 57.5K **Privately Held**
SIC: 2676 Sanitary paper products

(G-3407)
DRAEGER SAFETY DIAGNOSTICS INC
12530 Iron Bridge Rd (23831-1599)
PHONE..............................804 768-4294
James Bentley, *Principal*
EMP: 3
SALES (corp-wide): 3B **Privately Held**
WEB: www.draegerinterlock.com
SIC: 3694 Engine electrical equipment
HQ: Draeger Safety Diagnostics, Inc.
4040 W Royal Ln Ste 136
Irving TX 75063
972 929-1100

(G-3408)
DU PONT TJIN FLMS US LTD PRTNR (PA)
3600 Discovery Dr (23836-6436)
PHONE..............................804 530-4076
Masaaki Hojo, *CEO*
Jean-Philippe Azoulay, *President*
John C Groves, *COO*
Mark Sagrans, *Counsel*
Sandra Kearney, *Production*
◆ **EMP:** 31
SALES (est): 227MM **Privately Held**
WEB: www.dupontteijinfilms.com
SIC: 3081 Unsupported plastics film & sheet

(G-3409)
DU PONT TJIN FLMS US LTD PRTNR
3600 Discovery Dr (23836-6436)
PHONE..............................804 530-4076
Wanda Watson, *Engineer*
Monica Filyaw, *Manager*
Jeff Bullock, *Supervisor*
EMP: 400
SALES (corp-wide): 227MM **Privately Held**
WEB: www.dupontteijinfilms.com
SIC: 3081 Plastic film & sheet
PA: Du Pont Teijin Films U.S. Limited Partnership
3600 Discovery Dr
Chester VA 23836
804 530-4076

(G-3410)
ELAINES CAKES INC
12921 Harrowgate Rd (23831-4520)
PHONE..............................804 748-2461
Elaine Elizabeth Flores, *President*
EMP: 1
SALES (est): 75.2K **Privately Held**
SIC: 2051 Cakes, bakery: except frozen

(G-3411)
EMBELLISHED EMBROIDERY
14620 Gimbel Dr (23836-6229)
PHONE..............................804 926-5785
Leslie Murray, *Owner*
EMP: 1
SALES (est): 68.5K **Privately Held**
SIC: 2395 Embroidery & art needlework

(G-3412)
EMBROIDERY EXPRESS LLC
2600 Bermuda Ave (23836-6407)
PHONE..............................804 458-5999
John F King, *Administration*
EMP: 2 **EST:** 2009
SALES (est): 119.8K **Privately Held**
SIC: 2395 Embroidery & art needlework

(G-3413)
ERICSONS INC
13300 Ramblewood Dr (23836-5515)
PHONE..............................770 505-6575
Mike Durbeck, *Branch Mgr*
EMP: 35
SALES (corp-wide): 13.9MM **Privately Held**
WEB: www.duratrench.com
SIC: 3082 Tubes, unsupported plastic
PA: Eric'sons, Inc.
574 Industrial Way N
Dallas GA 30132
770 505-6575

(G-3414)
EVANS CUSTOM PLAYSITES
14609 Gimbel Dr (23836-6230)
PHONE..............................804 615-3397
Eric Evans, *Owner*
EMP: 5
SALES (est): 250.8K **Privately Held**
SIC: 3949 Playground equipment

(G-3415)
EXPRESS SIGNS INC
11932 Centre St (23831-1701)
PHONE..............................804 796-5197
Oneill E Merlin Jr, *President*
Deborah R Oneill, *Corp Secy*
EMP: 4
SALES (est): 266.2K **Privately Held**
WEB: www.expresssigns.com
SIC: 3993 Signs & advertising specialties

(G-3416)
FLOORING ADVENTURES LLC
670 Hp Way (23836-2742)
PHONE..............................804 530-5004
Kelly Mortensen,
▼ **EMP:** 4
SQ FT: 11,000
SALES (est): 501.5K **Privately Held**
WEB: www.advantaflooring.com
SIC: 3996 Hard surface floor coverings

(G-3417)
FLUKE NETWORKS
524 Fairway Woods Dr (23836-8612)
PHONE..............................804 530-1826
EMP: 2
SALES (est): 112.5K **Privately Held**
SIC: 3825 Instruments to measure electricity

(G-3418)
G GIBBS PROJECT LLC
3701 Mineola Dr (23831-1345)
PHONE..............................804 638-9581
Gyovanne Gibbs, *Principal*
EMP: 2 **EST:** 2016
SALES (est): 67K **Privately Held**
SIC: 2326 5621 Men's & boys' work clothing; women's clothing stores

(G-3419)
GL HOLLOWELL PUBLISHING LLC
4336 Milsmith Rd (23831-4536)
PHONE..............................804 796-5968
EMP: 1
SALES (est): 65.1K **Privately Held**
SIC: 2741 Misc Publishing

(G-3420)
GREENLINE TRUCKING INC
611 Green Orchard Dr (23836-7910)
PHONE..............................804 638-1138
Louis Counter, *CEO*
EMP: 5
SALES (est): 230.7K **Privately Held**
SIC: 3537 Trucks, tractors, loaders, carriers & similar equipment

(G-3421)
HEAVENLY KAKES LLC
12417 Branner Way Apt 304 (23836-2807)
PHONE..............................804 874-3711
Matrice Lassiter,
EMP: 1
SALES (est): 39.5K **Privately Held**
SIC: 2051 Cakes, bakery: except frozen

(G-3422)
HONEYWELL INTERNATIONAL INC
4101 Bermuda Hundred Rd (23836-3245)
PHONE..............................804 530-6352
EMP: 350
SALES (corp-wide): 36.7B **Publicly Held**
WEB: www.honeywell.com
SIC: 3724 2821 Aircraft engines & engine parts; plastics materials & resins
PA: Honeywell International Inc.
300 S Tryon St
Charlotte NC 28202
704 627-6200

(G-3423)
HYDRO PREP & COATING INC
2401 Bermuda Ave (23836-6404)
PHONE..............................804 530-2178
Robert A Radcliff, *Principal*
EMP: 2
SALES (est): 228.1K **Privately Held**
SIC: 3479 Metal coating & allied service

(G-3424)
INFOCUS COATINGS INC
107 Crystal Downs Ct (23836-5785)
PHONE..............................804 530-4645
EMP: 2
SALES (est): 152.2K **Privately Held**
SIC: 3479 Coating/Engraving Service

(G-3425)
ITS ALL MX LLC
2400 Burgess Rd (23836-3409)
PHONE..............................540 785-6295
Janet Bahmer, *Mng Member*
EMP: 2
SALES (est): 100K **Privately Held**
SIC: 2674 Mothproof bags: made from purchased materials

(G-3426)
KATHERINE CHAIN
Also Called: Herbs of Happy Hill
14705 Happy Hill Rd (23831-7020)
PHONE..............................804 796-2762
Katherine Chain, *Owner*
EMP: 1
SALES (est): 72.5K **Privately Held**
SIC: 3999 5992 5261 Potpourri; plants, potted; garden supplies & tools

(G-3427)
LARRY WARD
Also Called: Klassic Tee's
13907 Old Hampstead Ln (23831-6538)
PHONE..............................804 778-7945
Larry Ward, *Owner*
Adrian Ward, *Principal*
EMP: 3
SALES (est): 111.8K **Privately Held**
SIC: 2759 Letterpress & screen printing

(G-3428)
LEGACY VULCAN LLC
Also Called: Dale Quarry
11520 Iron Bridge Rd (23831-1449)
PHONE..............................804 706-1773
Wayne Orr, *Manager*
EMP: 15 **Publicly Held**
WEB: www.vulcanmaterials.com
SIC: 1442 1423 Construction sand & gravel; crushed & broken granite
HQ: Legacy Vulcan, Llc
1200 Urban Center Dr
Vestavia AL 35242
205 298-3000

(G-3429)
LEGACY VULCAN LLC
12020 Old Stage Rd (23831)
PHONE..............................804 748-3695
EMP: 2 **Publicly Held**
WEB: www.vulcanmaterials.com
SIC: 1442 Construction sand & gravel

HQ: Legacy Vulcan, Llc
1200 Urban Center Dr
Vestavia AL 35242
205 298-3000

(G-3430)
LEGACY VULCAN LLC
5601 Ironbridge Pkwy (23831-7771)
PHONE..............................804 717-5770
Alan Townsend, *Foreman/Supr*
Wayne Banty, *Sales Staff*
Dick Reese, *Manager*
EMP: 18 **Publicly Held**
WEB: www.vulcanmaterials.com
SIC: 3273 Ready-mixed concrete
HQ: Legacy Vulcan, Llc
1200 Urban Center Dr
Vestavia AL 35242
205 298-3000

(G-3431)
M&M PRINTING LLC
3185 Poplar View Pl (23831-6935)
PHONE..............................804 621-4171
Malcolm Jones, *Principal*
EMP: 2
SALES (est): 101.5K **Privately Held**
SIC: 2752 Commercial printing, offset

(G-3432)
MABE DG & ASSOC INC
2140 E Hundred Rd (23836-3505)
PHONE..............................804 530-1406
David G Mabe Jr, *President*
EMP: 5
SQ FT: 3,000
SALES (est): 800.9K **Privately Held**
WEB: www.dgmabeandassociates.com
SIC: 3444 Sheet metal specialties, not stamped

(G-3433)
MERIT MEDICAL SYSTEMS INC
12701 N Kingston Ave (23836-2700)
PHONE..............................804 416-1030
Jon Chase, *Manager*
EMP: 100
SQ FT: 49,390
SALES (corp-wide): 994.8MM **Publicly Held**
WEB: www.merit.com
SIC: 3841 Surgical & medical instruments
PA: Merit Medical Systems, Inc.
1600 W Merit Pkwy
South Jordan UT 84095
801 253-1600

(G-3434)
MERIT MEDICAL SYSTEMS INC
837 Liberty Way (23836-2704)
PHONE..............................804 416-1069
EMP: 4
SALES (corp-wide): 994.8MM **Publicly Held**
WEB: www.merit.com
SIC: 3841 Surgical & medical instruments
PA: Merit Medical Systems, Inc.
1600 W Merit Pkwy
South Jordan UT 84095
801 253-1600

(G-3435)
MESSER LLC
921 Old Brmuda Hundred Rd
(23836-5626)
PHONE..............................804 796-5050
William Vincent, *Branch Mgr*
EMP: 28
SALES (corp-wide): 1.1B **Privately Held**
WEB: www.praxair.com
SIC: 2813 Industrial gases
HQ: Messer Llc
200 Somerset Corp Blvd # 7000
Bridgewater NJ 08807
908 464-8100

(G-3436)
METRO WATER PURIFICATION LLC
12508 Lewis Rd (23831-3808)
PHONE..............................804 366-2158
Vernice Pierce, *CEO*
James Pierce, *COO*
EMP: 1

SALES (est): 83K **Privately Held**
SIC: 3589 Water treatment equipment, industrial

(G-3437)
MINUTEMAN PRESS OF CHESTER
4100 W Hundred Rd (23831-1760)
PHONE..............................804 898-0050
David Smith, *Principal*
EMP: 1
SALES (est): 186.2K **Privately Held**
WEB: www.minutemanpress.com
SIC: 2752 Commercial printing, lithographic

(G-3438)
MOORE SIGN CORPORATION
901 Old Brmuda Hundred Rd
(23836-5626)
PHONE..............................804 748-5836
Thomas M Williams, *CEO*
Ralph S AST, *President*
Elizabeth Williams, *Vice Pres*
Marty Wells, *Sales Staff*
Diane Williams, *Admin Sec*
EMP: 29 **EST:** 1971
SQ FT: 21,750
SALES (est): 3.8MM **Privately Held**
WEB: www.mooresigncorp.com
SIC: 3993 1799 3446 3444 Electric signs; neon signs; sign installation & maintenance; architectural metalwork; sheet metalwork

(G-3439)
NEW LOOK PRESS LLC
305 Redbird Dr (23836-2661)
PHONE..............................804 530-0836
John Boyle, *Principal*
EMP: 2
SALES (est): 104.7K **Privately Held**
SIC: 2741 Miscellaneous publishing

(G-3440)
NIAGARA BOTTLING LLC
1700 Digital Dr (23836-2846)
PHONE..............................804 551-3923
EMP: 12 **EST:** 2017
SALES (est): 1.8MM **Privately Held**
WEB: www.niagarawater.com
SIC: 2086 Bottled & canned soft drinks

(G-3441)
NORTHROP GRUMMAN CORPORATION
11751 Meadowville Ln (23836-6315)
PHONE..............................804 416-6500
Gus Pilarte, *Project Mgr*
Steve Marshman, *Branch Mgr*
Jason Knaus, *Program Mgr*
Doug Bowmer, *Manager*
Paul Buscemi, *Technology*
EMP: 1 **Publicly Held**
WEB: www.northropgrumman.com
SIC: 3812 Search & navigation equipment
PA: Northrop Grumman Corporation
2980 Fairview Park Dr
Falls Church VA 22042

(G-3442)
PARK 500
4100 Bermuda Hundred Rd (23836-3245)
PHONE..............................804 751-2000
Louis Camilleri, *Principal*
EMP: 5
SALES (est): 810.3K **Privately Held**
SIC: 2141 Tobacco stemming & redrying

(G-3443)
PHILIP MORRIS USA INC
4100 Bermuda Hundred Rd (23836-3245)
P.O. Box 26603, Richmond (23261-6603)
PHONE..............................804 274-2000
Craig G Schwartz, *Senior VP*
EMP: 600 **Publicly Held**
WEB: www.philipmorrisusa.com
SIC: 2131 2141 Chewing & smoking tobacco; tobacco stemming & redrying
HQ: Philip Morris Usa Inc.
6601 W Brd St
Richmond VA 23230
804 274-2000

(G-3444)
PRE CON INC (PA)
6700 Courtyard Rd (23831-1430)
PHONE..............................804 732-0628
Mark Leslie Wauford, *President*
Jerry L Wauford, *Vice Pres*
Joyce Newcomb, *Purch Agent*
Lisa Wauford Tharp, *Treasurer*
Veronica B Wauford, *Admin Sec*
▲ **EMP:** 10
SQ FT: 2,000,000
SALES (est): 32MM **Privately Held**
WEB: www.wauford.com
SIC: 2821 2611 Polytetrafluoroethylene resins (teflon); pulp mills

(G-3445)
PRE CON INC
Also Called: Plant 4
13721 Jefferson Davis Hwy (23831-5329)
PHONE..............................804 748-5063
Ned Hopkins, *Branch Mgr*
EMP: 66
SALES (corp-wide): 32MM **Privately Held**
WEB: www.wauford.com
SIC: 2821 Polytetrafluoroethylene resins (teflon)
PA: Pre Con, Inc.
6700 Courtyard Rd
Chester VA 23831
804 732-0628

(G-3446)
PRE CON INC
Also Called: Plant 5
13751 Jefferson Davis Hwy (23831-5342)
PHONE..............................804 414-1560
Tom Troidle, *Branch Mgr*
EMP: 5
SALES (corp-wide): 32MM **Privately Held**
WEB: www.wauford.com
SIC: 2821 Polytetrafluoroethylene resins (teflon)
PA: Pre Con, Inc.
6700 Courtyard Rd
Chester VA 23831
804 732-0628

(G-3447)
PRE CON INC
Also Called: Plant 3
13701 Jefferson Davis Hwy (23831-5329)
PHONE..............................804 414-1560
Jeff Siffert, *Branch Mgr*
Tom Troidle, *Manager*
EMP: 26
SQ FT: 118,454
SALES (corp-wide): 32MM **Privately Held**
WEB: www.wauford.com
SIC: 2821 2679 Polytetrafluoroethylene resins (teflon); pressed fiber & molded pulp products except food products
PA: Pre Con, Inc.
6700 Courtyard Rd
Chester VA 23831
804 732-0628

(G-3448)
PROGRESSIVE MANUFACTURING CORP (PA)
Also Called: Progressive Engineering Co
1701 W Hundred Rd (23836-2536)
PHONE..............................804 717-5353
Melvin H Belcher, *President*
EMP: 36
SQ FT: 20,000
SALES (est): 5.8MM **Privately Held**
WEB: www.pecgears.com
SIC: 3599 7692 3568 3462 Machine shop, jobbing & repair; welding repair; power transmission equipment; iron & steel forgings; screw machine products; sheet metalwork

(G-3449)
PUBLISHING VILLAGE
11801 Centre St (23831-1781)
PHONE..............................804 425-5555
EMP: 3 **EST:** 2019
SALES (est): 72.6K **Privately Held**
SIC: 2711 Newspapers, publishing & printing

(G-3450)
REVERE MOLD & ENGINEERING INC
13221 Old Stage Rd (23836-5415)
PHONE..............................804 748-5059
H David Blake Jr, *President*
EMP: 10
SQ FT: 8,000
SALES (est): 1.1MM **Privately Held**
SIC: 3544 Forms (molds), for foundry & plastics working machinery; industrial molds

(G-3451)
RICHMOND CLB OF PRNT HSE CRFTS
12425 Percival St (23831-4434)
PHONE..............................804 748-3075
Alex Heggie, *Principal*
EMP: 12
SALES (est): 738.6K **Privately Held**
SIC: 2752 Commercial printing, lithographic

(G-3452)
RICHMOND SCHL HLTH & TECH INC
751 W Hundred Rd (23836-2516)
PHONE..............................804 751-9191
Debbie Harris, *Director*
EMP: 23
SALES (corp-wide): 5.6MM **Privately Held**
WEB: www.richmond.com
SIC: 2711 Newspapers, publishing & printing
PA: Richmond School Of Health And Technology, Inc.
713 W Hundred Rd
Chester VA 23836
804 425-5797

(G-3453)
RIVER CITY CABINETRY LLC
4102 Hilltop Farms Ter (23831-1166)
PHONE..............................804 397-7950
Joseph Winn Orr, *Administration*
EMP: 2
SALES (est): 98.6K **Privately Held**
WEB: www.rivercitycabinetryllc.com
SIC: 2434 Wood kitchen cabinets

(G-3454)
SHD LOGISTICS LLC
12020 Avaclaire Dr (23831-3732)
PHONE..............................804 405-4943
Shemeika Howard,
EMP: 3
SALES (est): 100K **Privately Held**
SIC: 3799 Transportation equipment

(G-3455)
SOUTHPARK HI LLC
2000 Ware Btm Spring Rd (23836-4200)
PHONE..............................804 777-9000
Neil Amin, *Principal*
EMP: 2
SALES (est): 114.6K **Privately Held**
SIC: 7372 Prepackaged software

(G-3456)
STAMPTECH INC (DH)
Also Called: AOC Metal Works
13140 Parkers Battery Rd (23836-5529)
P.O. Box 3870 (23831-8471)
PHONE..............................804 768-4658
Roger Dale McLawhorn Jr, *President*
Alan W Pettigrew, *Vice Pres*
Thomas Weed, *Vice Pres*
EMP: 15
SQ FT: 4,000
SALES (est): 6.6MM
SALES (corp-wide): 19.4MM **Privately Held**
WEB: www.aocmetals.com
SIC: 3441 Fabricated structural metal

(G-3457)
STRAIGHT LINE WELDING LLC
15520 Richmond St (23836-6431)
PHONE..............................804 837-0363
EMP: 1
SALES (est): 37.1K **Privately Held**
SIC: 7692 Welding Repair

(G-3458)
SWEET T&C KETTLE CORN LLC
12750 Jefferson Davis Hwy (23831-5308)
PHONE..................................804 840-0551
Kenny Hall, *Principal*
EMP: 3
SQ FT: 700
SALES (est): 121.6K **Privately Held**
SIC: 2096 Corn chips & other corn-based
snacks

(G-3459)
TEIJIN-DU PONT FILMS INC
3600 Discovery Dr (23836-6436)
PHONE..................................804 530-9310
Louis Tasquino, *Principal*
EMP: 78 **Privately Held**
WEB: www.teijin-dupontfilms.com
SIC: 3069 2821 Film, rubber; plastics ma-
terials & resins
PA: Teijin-Du Pont Films, Incorporated
1 Discovery Dr
Hopewell VA 23860

(G-3460)
TERESA BLOUNT
Also Called: Adoorable Ideas
13832 Greyledge Pl (23836-5794)
PHONE..................................804 402-1349
Teresa Blount, *Owner*
EMP: 1
SALES (est): 61.6K **Privately Held**
SIC: 3999 Wreaths, artificial

(G-3461)
TIMOTHY BREEDEN
10601 Greenyard Way (23831-1485)
PHONE..................................804 748-6433
Timothy M Breeden, *Principal*
EMP: 2
SALES (est): 264.6K **Privately Held**
WEB: www.drbreeden.com
SIC: 3843 Enamels, dentists'

(G-3462)
**TOTAL STITCH EMBROIDERY
INC**
10342 Iron Bridge Rd (23831-1425)
PHONE..................................804 748-9594
EMP: 2
SQ FT: 1,200
SALES (est): 170K **Privately Held**
SIC: 2397 Mfg Schiffli Embroideries

(G-3463)
UNISONCARE CORPORATION
1524 Anchor Landing Dr (23836-5406)
PHONE..................................804 721-3702
Javed Aleem, *President*
Shahana Ahmed, *Director*
EMP: 1
SALES (est): 85.4K **Privately Held**
WEB: www.unicharts.com
SIC: 7372 Prepackaged software

(G-3464)
**UNITED PRECAST FINISHER
LLC**
12426 Hogans Pl (23836-2766)
PHONE..................................804 386-6308
Jadson G Oliveira, *Principal*
EMP: 3
SALES (est): 202.7K **Privately Held**
SIC: 3272 Precast terrazo or concrete
products

(G-3465)
VALVOLINE INSTANT OIL
10850 Iron Bridge Rd (23831-1628)
PHONE..................................804 823-2104
EMP: 2
SALES (est): 81.9K **Privately Held**
SIC: 1382 Oil & gas exploration services

(G-3466)
VILLAGE PUBLISHING LLC
Also Called: Village News
4607 W Hundred Rd (23831-1743)
P.O. Box 2397 (23831-8446)
PHONE..................................804 751-0421
Mark Fausz, *Mng Member*
Linda Fausz, *Mng Member*
EMP: 4

SALES (est): 300K **Privately Held**
WEB: www.villagenewsonline.com
SIC: 2711 2721 Newspapers: publishing
only, not printed on site; comic books:
publishing only, not printed on site

(G-3467)
VIRGINIA TIMES
12100 Ganesh Ln (23836-3003)
PHONE..................................804 530-8540
Lokesh B Vuyyuru, *President*
EMP: 6
SALES (est): 216.2K **Privately Held**
SIC: 2711 Newspapers, publishing & print-
ing

(G-3468)
**WILSON GRAPHICS
INCORPORATED**
4405 Old Hundred Rd (23831-4233)
PHONE..................................804 748-0646
Larry Wilson, *Owner*
EMP: 3
SALES (est): 373.4K **Privately Held**
WEB: www.wilsongraphicsrva.com
SIC: 2796 7334 Photoengraving plates,
linecuts or halftones; photocopying & du-
plicating services

(G-3469)
**WREATHS GALORE AND MORE
LLC**
10649 Michmar Dr (23831-1207)
PHONE..................................804 312-6947
EMP: 4
SALES (est): 257.5K **Privately Held**
SIC: 3999 Wreaths, artificial

Chester Gap
Rappahannock County

(G-3470)
GIBSON SEWER WATER
8 Avery Dr (22623-2018)
PHONE..................................540 636-1131
Eddie Gibson, *Owner*
EMP: 1
SALES (est): 116.1K **Privately Held**
SIC: 3721 Aircraft

Chesterfield
Chesterfield County

(G-3471)
13 STITCHES LLC
13810 Brandy Oaks Pl (23832-2719)
PHONE..................................804 739-8982
Sally Hinski,
EMP: 1
SALES (est): 66K **Privately Held**
WEB: www.13stitches.us
SIC: 2395 Embroidery & art needlework

(G-3472)
**ACADEMY BOYS AND GIRLS
SOCCER**
6400 Belmont Rd (23832-8212)
PHONE..................................804 380-9005
Martin Hernandez, *CEO*
EMP: 2
SALES (est): 218.6K **Privately Held**
SIC: 3585 Refrigeration & heating equip-
ment

(G-3473)
**ADVANCED GRAPHICS TECH
LLC**
11120 Nash Rd (23838-6210)
PHONE..................................804 796-3399
John R Finger, *Partner*
Sean C Finger, *Partner*
EMP: 2
SALES (est): 50K **Privately Held**
SIC: 3699 Flight simulators (training aids),
electronic

(G-3474)
ALL THAT JAZ LLC
6000 Centralia Rd (23832-6515)
PHONE..................................800 224-8152

Jazmine Harris,
EMP: 1
SALES (est): 45K **Privately Held**
SIC: 3944 Craft & hobby kits & sets

(G-3475)
AP CANDLES LLC
4902 Ventura Rd (23832-8163)
PHONE..................................804 276-8681
Radiance Pulliam, *Principal*
EMP: 1
SALES (est): 39.6K **Privately Held**
SIC: 3999 Candles

(G-3476)
ARABELLE PUBLISHING LLC
10106 Krause Rd Ste 102 (23832-6503)
PHONE..................................804 298-5082
Diana Legere, *Principal*
EMP: 2
SQ FT: 200
SALES (est): 65.7K **Privately Held**
SIC: 2741 Miscellaneous publishing

(G-3477)
**BANTON CUSTOM
WOODWORKING LLC**
13712 Brandy Oaks Rd (23832-2704)
PHONE..................................804 334-4766
EMP: 1
SALES (est): 54.1K **Privately Held**
SIC: 2431 Millwork

(G-3478)
BATH SENSATIONS LLC
8207 Hampton Bluff Ter (23832-2036)
PHONE..................................804 832-4701
Tracey Anderson, *Principal*
EMP: 1
SALES (est): 8K **Privately Held**
SIC: 2841 7389 Soap & other detergents;
business services

(G-3479)
BAY WEST PAPER
11401 Carters Crossing Rd (23838-3037)
PHONE..................................804 639-3530
EMP: 3
SALES (est): 257.2K **Privately Held**
SIC: 3554 Mfg Paper Industrial Machinery

(G-3480)
BJ EMBROIDERY & DESIGNS
5304 Ridgerun Pl (23832-7154)
PHONE..................................804 605-4749
Joe Fagley, *Principal*
EMP: 1
SALES (est): 53.3K **Privately Held**
SIC: 2395 Embroidery & art needlework

(G-3481)
BOLVS LLC
9218 Scotts Bluff Ln (23832-9255)
PHONE..................................508 310-8682
Kwabena Ansong Denkyi,
EMP: 5
SALES (est): 300K **Privately Held**
SIC: 3011 Automobile tires, pneumatic

(G-3482)
BOTTLEHOOD OF VIRGINIA INC
8301 Macandrew Ter (23838-5307)
P.O. Box 1719 (23832-9107)
PHONE..................................804 454-0656
Tammy Mormando, *Exec Dir*
EMP: 1
SALES (est): 50K **Privately Held**
SIC: 3231 Products of purchased glass

(G-3483)
BRIGGS COMPANY
Also Called: Central Belting Hose & Rbr Co
5501 Fairpines Ct (23832-8283)
P.O. Box 11446, Wilmington DE (19850-
1446)
PHONE..................................804 233-0966
Frank Chamberlain, *Principal*
EMP: 1
SALES (corp-wide): 5.7MM **Privately
Held**
WEB: www.briggsco.net
SIC: 3061 Mechanical rubber goods

PA: The Briggs Company
3 Bellecor Dr
New Castle DE 19720
302 328-9471

(G-3484)
C A S SIGNS
6424 Mill River Trce (23832-9237)
PHONE..................................804 271-7580
EMP: 1
SALES (est): 59K **Privately Held**
SIC: 3993 Mfg Signs/Advertising Special-
ties

(G-3485)
CHC TRANSPORTS LLC
7719 Centerbrook Ln (23832-9229)
PHONE..................................804 398-8686
Jeffery Coins,
EMP: 1
SALES (est): 25K **Privately Held**
SIC: 3711 Truck tractors for highway use,
assembly of

(G-3486)
CHEYENNE AUTUMN ARTS
Also Called: Karselis Arts
7500 Hadley Ln (23832-7853)
PHONE..................................804 745-9561
Terence Karselis, *Owner*
Judith Karselis, *Co-Owner*
EMP: 2
SALES (est): 35.4K **Privately Held**
WEB: www.karselisarts.com
SIC: 3299 8999 Architectural sculptures:
gypsum, clay, papier mache, etc.; artists
& artists' studios

(G-3487)
CRAFTSMAN DISTILLERY LLC
8325 Regalia Pl (23838-5103)
PHONE..................................804 454-1514
Charles Kwarta, *Principal*
EMP: 2
SALES (est): 62.3K **Privately Held**
SIC: 2082 Malt beverages

(G-3488)
CRAZE SIGNS & GRAPHICS
8106 Gates Bluff Ct (23832-6344)
PHONE..................................804 748-9233
Larry M Craze, *Principal*
EMP: 2 **EST:** 2001
SALES (est): 177.5K **Privately Held**
SIC: 3993 Signs & advertising specialties

(G-3489)
**CREATE-A-PRINT AND SIGNS
LLC**
10406 Beachcrest Pl (23832-2751)
PHONE..................................804 920-8055
Emil Szabo, *Administration*
EMP: 2 **EST:** 2015
SALES (est): 74.2K **Privately Held**
SIC: 3993 Signs & advertising specialties

(G-3490)
**CROSSROAD DATA SOLUTIONS
LLC**
7305 Hancock Village Dr # 13
(23832-2771)
PHONE..................................804 302-4312
Amy Figard, *Opers Staff*
EMP: 1
SALES (corp-wide): 296K **Privately Held**
WEB: www.crossroaddata.com
SIC: 3861 Photographic equipment & sup-
plies
PA: Crossroad Data Solutions Llc
12730 Donegal Dr
Chesterfield VA 23832
804 302-4312

(G-3491)
**CUBBAGE CRANE
MAINTENANCE**
12500 Second Branch Rd (23838-2941)
PHONE..................................804 739-5459
Bruce Cubbage, *Owner*
EMP: 1
SALES (est): 111.5K **Privately Held**
WEB: www.cubbagecrane.com
SIC: 3531 Cranes, locomotive

(G-3492)
CULPEPPER
9107 Berry Patch Dr (23832-7585)
PHONE.............................804 276-1478
EMP: 1
SALES (est): 37.1K Privately Held
SIC: 7692 Welding repair

(G-3493)
DEPCO-DFNSE ENGNEERED PDTS LLC
7925 Cogbill Rd (23832-8031)
PHONE.............................804 271-7000
James Lauck, Principal
EMP: 1
SALES (est): 375K Privately Held
SIC: 3499 Machine bases, metal

(G-3494)
E I DU PONT DE NEMOURS & CO
13300 Carters Way Rd (23838-3031)
PHONE.............................804 383-4251
Kimberly Lee, Accounts Mgr
EMP: 339
SALES (corp-wide): 21.5B Publicly Held
WEB: www.dupont.com
SIC: 2879 Agricultural chemicals
HQ: E. I. Du Pont De Nemours And Company
974 Centre Rd Bldg 735
Wilmington DE 19805
302 485-3000

(G-3495)
E4 BEAUTY SUPPLY LLC
14431 Old Bond St (23832-4402)
PHONE.............................804 307-4941
Sabrina Merriman,
EMP: 3 EST: 2013
SQ FT: 1,500
SALES (est): 152.4K Privately Held
SIC: 3999 5999 Hair curlers, designed for beauty parlors; barber & beauty shop equipment; toiletries, cosmetics & perfumes

(G-3496)
ELLICE DARIEN LLC
10300 Sandy Ridge Dr (23832-6904)
PHONE.............................804 677-9145
Ellice Darien,
EMP: 1
SALES (est): 47.2K Privately Held
SIC: 2844 Cosmetic preparations

(G-3497)
EMCS INC
14413 Old Bond St (23832-4402)
PHONE.............................443 223-2335
EMP: 3
SALES (est): 104K Privately Held
SIC: 3572 Computer storage devices

(G-3498)
EUVANNA CHAYANNE COSMETICS LLC
14431 Old Bond St (23832-4402)
PHONE.............................804 307-4941
Euvanna Merriman, CEO
EMP: 1
SALES (est): 47.2K Privately Held
SIC: 2844 Lipsticks

(G-3499)
FANCY STITCHES
6201 Chstrfeld Meadows Dr (23832)
PHONE.............................804 796-6942
Stephen Weingarten, Owner
EMP: 2
SALES (est): 90K Privately Held
WEB: www.fancystitchz.com
SIC: 2395 Embroidery products, except schiffli machine

(G-3500)
FIRST LIGHT PUBLISHING INC
14402 Twickenham Pl (23832-2471)
PHONE.............................804 639-0659
Brian Rock, President
Mary L Rock, Vice Pres
EMP: 2
SALES (est): 133.6K Privately Held
SIC: 2741 Miscellaneous publishing

(G-3501)
FRIDLEYS WELDING SERVICE INC
5550 Quail Ridge Ter (23832-7567)
PHONE.............................804 674-1949
William Fridley, President
EMP: 1 EST: 2001
SALES (est): 60.8K Privately Held
SIC: 7692 Welding repair

(G-3502)
GENESIS PROFESSIONAL TRAINING
14503 Houghton St (23832-2487)
PHONE.............................804 818-3611
EMP: 1
SALES (est): 37.5K Privately Held
SIC: 2741 Miscellaneous publishing

(G-3503)
HEARTS DESIRE
11700 Beechwood Forest Dr (23838-3500)
PHONE.............................804 790-1336
Kathi Hodge, Owner
EMP: 1
SALES (est): 44K Privately Held
SIC: 2392 Household furnishings

(G-3504)
HEAVENLY GATES LLC
10200 Christina Rd (23832-3647)
PHONE.............................804 790-9840
Mildred Ridley, Principal
EMP: 2
SALES (est): 133.9K Privately Held
SIC: 2752 Commercial printing, lithographic

(G-3505)
INK IT ON ANYTHING
4141 Round Hill Dr (23832-7843)
PHONE.............................804 814-5890
Laurie Blath, Owner
EMP: 1
SALES (est): 91.2K Privately Held
SIC: 2759 7389 Commercial printing; business services

(G-3506)
ITZ ME CREATIONS
7607 Rolling Fields Pl (23832-2544)
PHONE.............................804 519-6023
Wanda Reynolds, Owner
EMP: 1
SALES (est): 24.4K Privately Held
SIC: 2395 Embroidery & art needlework

(G-3507)
JEWELERS SERVICES INC
6523 Centralia Rd (23832-6587)
PHONE.............................804 353-9612
Stephen Shaffner, President
Cunningham Robert E, Vice Pres
Jill La Piad, Vice Pres
Jill Laprad, Vice Pres
EMP: 14 EST: 1967
SQ FT: 2,000
SALES (est): 1.6MM Privately Held
WEB: www.j-s-i.com
SIC: 3911 7631 Jewelry, precious metal; jewelry repair services

(G-3508)
JOCO TRANSPORTATIONS LLC
7719 Centerbrook Ln (23832-9229)
PHONE.............................804 398-8686
Jeffery Coins, Mng Member
EMP: 2
SALES (est): 25K Privately Held
SIC: 3711 Truck tractors for highway use, assembly of

(G-3509)
JOSH MCDANIEL
7701 Rhodes Ln (23838-5908)
PHONE.............................804 748-4330
Josh McDaniel, CEO
EMP: 2 EST: 2017
SALES (est): 88.9K Privately Held
SIC: 3446 Architectural metalwork

(G-3510)
KEN MUSSELMAN & ASSOCIATES INC
12025 Trailbrook Dr (23838-2952)
PHONE.............................804 790-0302
Ken Musselman, President
Kathryn Musselman, Vice Pres
EMP: 2
SALES (est): 750K Privately Held
WEB: www.kenmusselmanassociates.com
SIC: 1481 7389 Mine & quarry services, nonmetallic minerals;

(G-3511)
KILPATRICK FRAMING AND ART
10607 Poachers Run (23832-7088)
PHONE.............................804 245-6824
Taneha Kilpatrick, Principal
EMP: 2
SALES (est): 90.1K Privately Held
SIC: 2499 Picture frame molding, finished

(G-3512)
LAKOTA JS CHOCOLATES CORP
15600 Chesdin Landing Ter (23838-3242)
PHONE.............................804 590-0010
Lakota Camp, Principal
EMP: 1
SALES (est): 47.9K Privately Held
SIC: 2064 7389 Candy & other confectionery products; business services

(G-3513)
MAIN GATE PUBLISHING CO LLC
10410 Genito Ln (23832-7284)
PHONE.............................804 744-2202
Wesley Richard, Principal
EMP: 2
SALES (est): 89.7K Privately Held
WEB: www.maingatepublishingcompany.com
SIC: 2741 Miscellaneous publishing

(G-3514)
MERRILL ST PHYSCIANS GROUP INC
13307 Corapeake Ter (23838-3264)
PHONE.............................804 441-1280
Eric Merrill, Director
EMP: 3
SALES (est): 76.2K Privately Held
SIC: 2711 Newspapers

(G-3515)
OLIVER PRINCESS
7118 Lake Caroline Dr (23832-8056)
PHONE.............................804 683-5779
Princess Oliver, Principal
EMP: 1 EST: 2018
SALES (est): 46K Privately Held
SIC: 3993 Signs & advertising specialties

(G-3516)
PACKED HEAD LLC
13241 Carters Way Rd (23838-3029)
PHONE.............................804 677-3603
Joseph Anderson,
EMP: 1 EST: 2017
SALES (est): 39.6K Privately Held
SIC: 3999 Manufacturing industries

(G-3517)
PATTY S PIECEWORKS
11913 Dunvegan Ct (23838-5178)
PHONE.............................804 796-3371
Patty Henry, Owner
EMP: 1 EST: 1993
SALES (est): 42.7K Privately Held
SIC: 2395 Quilting, for the trade

(G-3518)
PRISM INDUSTRIES LLC
6961 Slate Rd (23832-8350)
P.O. Box 6312, Richmond (23230-0312)
PHONE.............................804 916-0074
David Reinhardt, Principal
EMP: 3
SALES (est): 164.6K Privately Held
WEB: www.prism-industries.com
SIC: 3999 Manufacturing industries

(G-3519)
PUTT ARUND TOWN MINIATURE GOLF
13001 Carters Way Rd (23838-3064)
PHONE.............................804 317-6751
Hugh Smith, Owner
EMP: 1
SALES (est): 110K Privately Held
SIC: 3999 Miniatures

(G-3520)
RAY PAINTER SMALL
17312 Round Rock Pl (23838-6058)
PHONE.............................804 255-7050
Ray Small, Owner
Kristy Small, Co-Owner
EMP: 2 EST: 2016
SALES (est): 76.3K Privately Held
SIC: 2952 3281 5033 7389 Asphalt felts & coatings; cut stone & stone products; roofing, siding & insulation; business services

(G-3521)
SANOFI-AVENTIS US LLC
12407 Duntrune Ct (23838-5335)
PHONE.............................804 651-1595
EMP: 2 EST: 2018
SALES (est): 78.7K Privately Held
WEB: www.sanofi.us
SIC: 2834 Pharmaceutical preparations

(G-3522)
SCHOLL CUSTOM WD & MET CFT LLC
11420 Winterpock Rd (23838-2339)
PHONE.............................804 739-2390
Bill Scholl, Mng Member
EMP: 1
SALES (est): 120K Privately Held
SIC: 2411 Heading bolts, wood: hewn

(G-3523)
SEMETROL LLC
13312 Shore Lake Turn (23838-3252)
PHONE.............................804 536-7005
Daniel Johnstone, President
EMP: 1
SALES (est): 110.4K Privately Held
WEB: www.semetrol.com
SIC: 3674 3825 Semiconductors & related devices; instruments to measure electricity

(G-3524)
SIGNATURE DSIGNS CABINETRY LLC
11743 Burray Rd (23838-5155)
PHONE.............................804 614-0028
Shannon Tootle,
EMP: 1
SALES (est): 20K Privately Held
WEB: www.signaturedesigns.us.com
SIC: 2434 Wood kitchen cabinets

(G-3525)
SKETCHZ
6900 Woodpecker Rd (23838-5925)
PHONE.............................804 590-1234
Scott Williams, Owner
EMP: 1
SQ FT: 1,400
SALES (est): 84K Privately Held
WEB: www.sketchz.com
SIC: 2759 Screen printing

(G-3526)
SOUTHSIDE OIL
11800 Ivey Mill Rd (23838-3201)
PHONE.............................804 590-1684
Gail Green, Principal
EMP: 3
SALES (est): 147K Privately Held
SIC: 1311 Crude petroleum production

(G-3527)
SPADES & DIAMONDS CLOTHING CO
7733 Belmont Rd (23832-8002)
PHONE.............................804 271-0374
Robert M Barnes, Principal
EMP: 2
SALES (est): 80K Privately Held
SIC: 3496 Diamond cloth

(G-3528)
SPRING RUN VINEYARDS LLC
10700 Spring Run Rd (23832-3613)
PHONE.............................804 382-4529
EMP: 2
SALES (est): 81.7K **Privately Held**
WEB: www.springrunvineyards.com
SIC: 2084 Wines

(G-3529)
STEPHEN DUNNAVANT
11825 Riverpark Ter (23838-2185)
PHONE.............................804 337-3629
Stephen Dunnavant, *CEO*
EMP: 5
SALES (est): 510.1K **Privately Held**
WEB: www.dunnavantsteelworks.com
SIC: 7692 Welding repair

(G-3530)
SUPERIOR GLOBAL SOLUTIONS INC
9048 Mahogany Dr (23832-2677)
PHONE.............................804 794-3507
Sandra B Sylvester, *CEO*
EMP: 4
SALES (est): 1MM **Privately Held**
WEB: www.sgsinc.net
SIC: 7372 Educational computer software

(G-3531)
SUPERIOR PANEL TECHNOLOGY (PA)
7460 Airfield Dr F19 19 F (23838)
P.O. Box 1563 (23832-9105)
PHONE.............................562 776-9494
W Kenneth Whitaker, *Partner*
Warner Berry, *Partner*
EMP: 1
SQ FT: 800
SALES (est): 193.2K **Privately Held**
WEB: www.sptpanel.com
SIC: 3647 Aircraft lighting fixtures

(G-3532)
TIERA AVERETT
Also Called: Virgin Hair Group
10221 Krause Rd Unit 1472 (23832-1259)
PHONE.............................804 888-3721
Tiera Averett, *Owner*
EMP: 1
SALES (est): 30K **Privately Held**
SIC: 3999 Hair & hair-based products

(G-3533)
TORRANCE ENTERPRISES INC
9120 Waterfowl Flyway (23838-5259)
PHONE.............................804 748-5481
John Torrance, *President*
EMP: 2
SALES (est): 45K **Privately Held**
SIC: 3661 Fiber optics communications equipment

(G-3534)
TREXLO ENTERPRISES LLC
14404 Twickenham Pl (23832-2471)
PHONE.............................804 624-1977
EMP: 1
SALES (est): 62.9K **Privately Held**
SIC: 3993 Signs & advertising specialties

(G-3535)
TRK SYSTEMS INC
11306 Macandrew Dr (23838-5500)
PHONE.............................804 777-9445
Kevin Tortlriello, *President*
EMP: 2 EST: 2000
SALES (est): 97K **Privately Held**
SIC: 7372 Prepackaged software

(G-3536)
UPLIFT COLLECTIONS
9409 Snowbird Rd (23832-6820)
PHONE.............................804 319-9129
Joshua O Fatuyi, *CEO*
EMP: 1
SALES (est): 53.9K **Privately Held**
SIC: 2326 3161 2211 Men's & boys' work clothing; clothing & apparel carrying cases; apparel & outerwear fabrics, cotton

(G-3537)
UPLIFT COLLECTIONS LLC
9409 Snowbird Rd (23832-6820)
PHONE.............................804 319-9129
Joshua Fatuyi, *Manager*
EMP: 1
SALES (est): 42.5K **Privately Held**
SIC: 2326 2211 Men's & boys' work clothing; apparel & outerwear fabrics, cotton

(G-3538)
VALERIE PERKINS
Also Called: Vee's Accessories
14603 Ashlake Manor Dr (23832-2825)
PHONE.............................804 279-0011
Valerie Perkins, *Owner*
EMP: 1
SALES (est): 1.5K **Privately Held**
SIC: 2389 Apparel & accessories

(G-3539)
VIRGINIA GUIDE BAIT CO
7800 Woodpecker Rd (23838-5809)
P.O. Box 1375 (23832-9103)
PHONE.............................804 590-2991
Judith Henry, *Owner*
EMP: 3
SALES (est): 114.5K **Privately Held**
WEB: www.virginiaguidebaitco.com
SIC: 3949 5199 Lures, fishing: artificial; bait, fishing

(G-3540)
WADE M MARCITA
11631 Cedar Mill Ct (23838-3541)
PHONE.............................804 437-2066
Marcita Wade, *Owner*
EMP: 1
SALES (est): 19K **Privately Held**
SIC: 2844 Toilet preparations

(G-3541)
WHITE COLLAR 4 HIRE
10261 N Donegal Rd (23832-3874)
PHONE.............................804 212-4604
EMP: 2 EST: 2016
SALES (est): 88.3K **Privately Held**
SIC: 3625 Mfg Relays/Industrial Controls

(G-3542)
WILLIAM K WHITAKER
Also Called: Superior Panel Technology
8206 Fair Isle Ter (23838-5199)
P.O. Box 1563 (23832-9105)
PHONE.............................562 776-9494
William Whitaker, *Owner*
EMP: 2
SALES (est): 350.2K **Privately Held**
WEB: www.sptpanel.com
SIC: 3647 Aircraft lighting fixtures

(G-3543)
WOODEN CABOOSE INC
9418 Banff Ter (23838-5239)
PHONE.............................804 748-2101
Ross Dolbear, *President*
EMP: 1
SALES (est): 115.1K **Privately Held**
SIC: 2426 5945 Carvings, furniture: wood; hobby, toy & game shops

Chilhowie
Smyth County

(G-3544)
AMERICAN HIGHWALL MINING LLC
215 Kendall Ave (24319)
P.O. Box 1488 (24319-1488)
PHONE.............................276 646-5548
Paul Campbell,
EMP: 7
SALES (est): 345.2K **Privately Held**
WEB: www.americanhighwallsystems.com
SIC: 1241 Coal mining services

(G-3545)
AMERICAN HIGHWALL SYSTEMS
212 Kendall Ave (24319-5713)
P.O. Box 1539 (24319-1539)
PHONE.............................276 646-2004
E S Campbell, *CEO*

Paul Campbell, *COO*
EMP: 10
SALES (est): 942.3K **Privately Held**
WEB: www.americanhighwallsystems.com
SIC: 3578 Automatic teller machines (ATM)

(G-3546)
C & A CUTTER HEAD INC
212 Kendall Ave (24319-5713)
P.O. Box 5207 (24319-5207)
PHONE.............................276 646-5548
Clyde Huxtell, *President*
▲ EMP: 3
SALES (est): 374.1K **Privately Held**
WEB: www.cacutterhead.com
SIC: 3412 Metal barrels, drums & pails

(G-3547)
CHILHOWIE FENCE SUPPLY LLC
1517 Hwy 107 (24319)
P.O. Box 750 (24319-0750)
PHONE.............................276 780-0452
EMP: 10 EST: 2015
SALES (est): 1.1MM **Privately Held**
WEB: www.chilhowiefencesupply.com
SIC: 3089 Fences, gates & accessories: plastic

(G-3548)
CONFETTI ADVERTISING INC
1207 Horseshoe Bend Rd (24319-5443)
P.O. Box 1338 (24319-1338)
PHONE.............................276 646-5806
Gary L Heath, *President*
EMP: 2
SALES (est): 100K **Privately Held**
WEB: www.confettiadvertising.com
SIC: 2759 7311 Screen printing; advertising agencies

(G-3549)
CREGGERS CAKES & CATERING
1043 St Clairs Creek Rd (24319-5893)
PHONE.............................276 646-8739
Mary Alice Cregger, *Owner*
EMP: 1
SALES (est): 40K **Privately Held**
SIC: 2051 5999 Bakery: wholesale or wholesale/retail combined; alarm & safety equipment stores

(G-3550)
DOUGLAS VINCE JOHNER
Also Called: Johner's Contracting
1639 Whitetop Rd (24319-5676)
PHONE.............................276 780-2369
EMP: 5
SALES (est): 180K **Privately Held**
SIC: 3524 Mfg Lawn/Garden Equipment

(G-3551)
INNOVATIVE MILLWORK TECH LLC
370 Deer Valley Rd (24319-5498)
PHONE.............................276 646-8336
Scott Schnell,
EMP: 1
SQ FT: 146,000
SALES (est): 59.5K
SALES (corp-wide): 13.3MM **Privately Held**
SIC: 2431 Moldings, wood: unfinished & prefinished
PA: Evermark Llc
    1050 Northbrook Pkwy
    Suwanee GA 30024
    678 455-5188

(G-3552)
JACK CAMPBELL WIDNER
Also Called: Widner's Conveyor Belt
3479 Whitetop Rd (24319-5827)
PHONE.............................703 646-8841
Jack Widner, *Principal*
EMP: 2
SALES (est): 122K **Privately Held**
SIC: 3496 Conveyor belts

(G-3553)
JENSEN PROMOTIONAL ITEMS INC
1201 E Lee Hwy (24319-4667)
PHONE.............................276 521-0143
Thomas Jensen, *President*

Marie Jensen, *Office Mgr*
EMP: 1
SALES (corp-wide): 6.3MM **Privately Held**
WEB: www.jensenapparel.com
SIC: 2331 T-shirts & tops, women's: made from purchased materials
PA: Jensen Promotional Items, Inc.
    315 Great Bridge Blvd A
    Chesapeake VA 23320
    757 966-7608

(G-3554)
LONGWALL - ASSOCIATES INC
212 Kendall Ave (24319-5713)
P.O. Box 1488 (24319-1488)
PHONE.............................276 646-2004
Elmer Shelby Campbell, *CEO*
Lance A Campbell, *Vice Pres*
Jimmy Jensen, *Prdtn Mgr*
Lance Campbell, *Purch Mgr*
Tammy Kestner, *Purch Mgr*
◆ EMP: 175
SQ FT: 90,000
SALES (est): 54.2MM **Privately Held**
WEB: www.longwall.com
SIC: 3532 Mining machinery

(G-3555)
MAYS AUTO MACHINE SHOP INC
714 Belle Hollow Rd (24319-5973)
PHONE.............................276 646-3752
Michael May, *President*
EMP: 2
SALES (est): 218.2K **Privately Held**
SIC: 3519 Engines, diesel & semi-diesel or dual-fuel

(G-3556)
OAK HOLLOW WOODWORKING INC
1917 St Clairs Creek Rd (24319-5856)
PHONE.............................276 646-2476
Junior Reedy, *President*
Elizabeth Reedy, *Vice Pres*
EMP: 9
SALES (est): 1MM **Privately Held**
SIC: 2431 Woodwork, interior & ornamental

(G-3557)
PENNINGTONS LOGGING LLC
287 Jerrys Creek Rd (24319-5564)
PHONE.............................276 783-9374
Anthony Pennington,
EMP: 2
SALES (est): 235K **Privately Held**
SIC: 2411 Logging camps & contractors

(G-3558)
QUIKRETE COMPANIES LLC
671 Wadill Ln (24319)
P.O. Box 586 (24319-0586)
PHONE.............................276 646-8976
Dave McLaughlin, *Manager*
Joe Adkins, *Manager*
EMP: 30 **Privately Held**
WEB: www.quikrete.com
SIC: 3273 2899 Ready-mixed concrete; chemical preparations
HQ: The Quikrete Companies Llc
    5 Concourse Pkwy Ste 1900
    Atlanta GA 30328
    404 634-9100

(G-3559)
RUSSELL FRYE LLC
651 Colecrest Dr (24319-3638)
PHONE.............................276 646-1293
EMP: 2
SALES (est): 67.9K **Privately Held**
SIC: 3999 Manufacturing industries

(G-3560)
SHOWALL INC
212 Packing House Rd (24319-3617)
PHONE.............................276 646-8779
EMP: 2
SALES (est): 90.4K **Privately Held**
SIC: 2542 Mfg Partitions/Fixtures-Non-wood

Chincoteague
Accomack County

(G-3561)
CHINCTGUE ISLAND HSE JERKY LLC
6339 Maddox Blvd (23336-2616)
PHONE.....................215 353-6393
EMP: 2 EST: 2019
SALES (est): 68.6K **Privately Held**
WEB: www.chincoteagueislandhouseof-
jerky.com
SIC: 2013 Snack sticks, including jerky:
from purchased meat

(G-3562)
ISLAND DECOYS
6136 Maddox Blvd (23336-2612)
PHONE.....................757 336-5319
EMP: 3 EST: 1979
SALES (est): 102.5K **Privately Held**
SIC: 3949 Mfg Sporting/Athletic Goods

(G-3563)
REED SIGN CO
6445 Booth St (23336-1829)
PHONE.....................757 336-5505
Ollie J Reed, *Principal*
EMP: 2
SALES (est): 200.7K **Privately Held**
SIC: 3993 Signs & advertising specialties

(G-3564)
REFUGE GOLF & BUMPER BOATS
6528 Maddox Blvd (23336-2248)
P.O. Box 918, Chincoteague Island (23336-0918)
PHONE.....................757 336-5420
Stavros Katsetos, *President*
EMP: 3
SALES (est): 319.7K **Privately Held**
WEB: www.gotofunland.com
SIC: 3714 Bumpers & bumperettes, motor
vehicle

(G-3565)
RENEGADE CLASSICS
4102 Main St (23336-2408)
PHONE.....................757 336-6611
Kim Dranger, *Owner*
EMP: 3
SALES (est): 219K **Privately Held**
SIC: 2329 Riding clothes:, men's, youths' &
boys'

(G-3566)
STEVE S 2 EXPRESS
6761 Maddox Blvd (23336-2253)
PHONE.....................757 336-7377
Steve Katsetos, *Principal*
EMP: 2
SALES (est): 125K **Privately Held**
SIC: 2741 Miscellaneous publishing

Christiansburg
Montgomery County

(G-3567)
1 A LIFESAFER INC
175 Independence Blvd (24073-1448)
PHONE.....................800 634-3077
EMP: 1 **Privately Held**
WEB: www.lifesafer.com
SIC: 3829 Measuring & controlling devices
PA: 1 A Lifesafer, Inc.
3630 Park 42 Dr Ste 170f
Cincinnati OH 45241

(G-3568)
AMES TEXTILES INC
Also Called: Ames Textiles Synt Yarns Div
200 Industrial Dr (24073-2537)
P.O. Box 390 (24068-0390)
PHONE.....................540 382-8522
Richard Mercier, *CEO*
Mack McCarter, *General Mgr*
Jennifer Lucas, *Purchasing*
Eric Robert Baron, *Controller*
▲ EMP: 40 EST: 2012

SALES (est): 2MM **Privately Held**
WEB: www.3athrowing.com
SIC: 2281 Yarn spinning mills

(G-3569)
ARRINGTON SMITH HUNTER LEE
789 Talon Ln (24073-5644)
PHONE.....................540 230-4952
Hunter Smith, *Owner*
EMP: 1
SALES (est): 55K **Privately Held**
SIC: 2421 Resawing lumber into smaller
dimensions

(G-3570)
ATTIMO GROUP LLC
Also Called: Attimo Studio
4071 Childress Rd (24073-5968)
PHONE.....................540 838-1118
Richard J Obiso,
Melissa Obiso,
EMP: 11
SALES (est): 1.6MM **Privately Held**
WEB: www.whitebarrel.com
SIC: 2084 Wines

(G-3571)
ATTIMO WINERY
4025 Childress Rd (24073-5968)
PHONE.....................540 382-7619
Richard Obiso, *Owner*
EMP: 14
SALES (est): 1.4MM **Privately Held**
WEB: www.attimowinery.com
SIC: 2084 Wine cellars, bonded: engaged
in blending wines

(G-3572)
AVILA HERBALS LLC
4025 Childress Rd (24073-5968)
PHONE.....................540 838-1118
Richard Obiso, *Mng Member*
Theresa Obiso,
EMP: 5
SALES (est): 1MM **Privately Held**
SIC: 3999

(G-3573)
BETTER SIGNS
1035 Cambria St Ne Ste C (24073-1630)
PHONE.....................540 382-7446
Robert H Filippi, *Owner*
EMP: 2
SQ FT: 2,000
SALES (est): 100K **Privately Held**
WEB: www.bettersigns.com
SIC: 3993 7311 Signs & advertising spe-
cialties; advertising consultant

(G-3574)
BOUTIQUE QULTY BKS PUBG CO INC
960 Oaktree Blvd (24073-4749)
PHONE.....................678 316-4150
Terri Ann Leidich, *Admin Sec*
EMP: 2 EST: 2015
SALES (est): 45.4K **Privately Held**
SIC: 2741 Miscellaneous publishing

(G-3575)
BTMC HOLDINGS INC
Also Called: B T & M
795 Roanoke St (24073-3144)
PHONE.....................616 794-0100
Dave Harvey, *Branch Mgr*
EMP: 1
SALES (corp-wide): 3.4MM **Privately Held**
SIC: 3544 Special dies & tools
PA: Btmc Holdings, Inc.
1114 S Bridge St
Belding MI 48809
616 794-0100

(G-3576)
C I T C IMAGING
Also Called: Charge-It Toner Co.
405 N Franklin St (24073-3059)
PHONE.....................540 382-6557
Terry W Stike, *President*
Treena Stike, *Corp Secy*
EMP: 6

SALES (est): 500K **Privately Held**
SIC: 5943 Photographic equipment
& supplies; office forms & supplies

(G-3577)
CAMERON AUBERNON
405 Turpin Walk (24073-3621)
PHONE.....................540 251-4363
Cameron Aubernon, *Owner*
EMP: 1
SALES (est): 26K **Privately Held**
SIC: 2741

(G-3578)
CHANDLER CONCRETE PRODUCTS OF (PA)
Also Called: Marshal Concrete Products
700 Block Ln (24073-1384)
PHONE.....................540 382-1734
Steven A Marshall, *President*
Danny Marshall, *Exec VP*
George Kuhn, *Vice Pres*
David Stallings, *Vice Pres*
Nick Thomas, *Vice Pres*
EMP: 61 EST: 1979
SQ FT: 10,000
SALES (est): 7.2MM **Privately Held**
WEB: www.chandlerconcrete.com
SIC: 3271 3273 Blocks, concrete or cin-
der: standard; ready-mixed concrete

(G-3579)
CHANDLER CONCRETE VIRGINIA INC
Also Called: Marshall Concrete Products
700 Block Ln (24073-1384)
PHONE.....................540 382-1734
Thomas Chandler Jr, *President*
David Stallings, *Vice Pres*
EMP: 50
SALES (est): 7.4MM **Privately Held**
WEB: www.chandlerconcrete.com
SIC: 3273 Ready-mixed concrete

(G-3580)
CORNING INCORPORATED
3050 N Frank (24073)
PHONE.....................540 382-4921
Martin Ringelberg, *Plant Mgr*
Robert Robinson, *Facilities Mgr*
Guy Acciai, *Mfg Staff*
Patrick Tepesch, *Research*
Michele Holbrook, *Engineer*
EMP: 24
SALES (corp-wide): 11.5B **Publicly Held**
WEB: www.corning.com
SIC: 3229 Pressed & blown glass
PA: Corning Incorporated
1 Riverfront Plz
Corning NY 14831
607 974-9000

(G-3581)
CORNING INCORPORATED
3050 N Franklin St (24073-4014)
PHONE.....................540 382-4921
Ron Kovalcin, *General Mgr*
EMP: 60
SALES (corp-wide): 11.5B **Publicly Held**
WEB: www.corning.com
SIC: 3229 Pressed & blown glass
PA: Corning Incorporated
1 Riverfront Plz
Corning NY 14831
607 974-9000

(G-3582)
CREO INDUSTRIES
525 Silver Leaf Dr (24073-7651)
PHONE.....................804 385-2035
Casey Clark, *Finance Dir*
EMP: 2
SALES (est): 96.7K **Privately Held**
SIC: 2752 Commercial printing, litho-
graphic

(G-3583)
DICKERSON MACHINE AND DESIGN
3371 Zimmerman Ln (24073-6835)
PHONE.....................540 789-7945
Marion Dickerson, *President*
EMP: 3
SQ FT: 2,500

SALES (est): 300K **Privately Held**
SIC: 3599 Custom machinery; machine
shop, jobbing & repair

(G-3584)
DORSETT PUBLICATIONS LLC
Also Called: The Scale Cabinet Maker
630 Depot St Ne (24073-5506)
PHONE.....................540 382-6431
Margaret Dorsett, *President*
Carol Lindstrom, *Vice Pres*
EMP: 2 EST: 1975
SQ FT: 6,000
SALES (est): 135K **Privately Held**
WEB: www.cambriatoystation.com
SIC: 2721 Magazines: publishing only, not
printed on site

(G-3585)
DRAEGER SAFETY DIAGNOSTICS INC
Also Called: Unknown
415 N Franklin St (24073-2939)
PHONE.....................540 382-6650
John Dean, *Branch Mgr*
EMP: 2
SALES (corp-wide): 3B **Privately Held**
WEB: www.draegerinterlock.com
SIC: 3842 Surgical appliances & supplies
HQ: Draeger Safety Diagnostics, Inc.
4040 N Royal Ln Ste 136
Irving TX 75063
972 929-1100

(G-3586)
ELECTRIC WORKS
593 Smith Creek Rd (24073-8135)
PHONE.....................540 381-2917
Alan Brown, *Owner*
EMP: 1
SALES (est): 113K **Privately Held**
WEB: www.sfelectricworks.com
SIC: 7694 Electric motor repair

(G-3587)
ELITE FABRICATION & MACHINE
942 Radford St (24073-2828)
PHONE.....................540 392-6055
Travis Lancaster, *Principal*
EMP: 4 EST: 2007
SALES (est): 422.1K **Privately Held**
SIC: 3541 Machine tool replacement & re-
pair parts, metal cutting types

(G-3588)
FREEDOM HOMES
1340 W Main St (24073-4235)
PHONE.....................540 382-9015
Josh Morris, *Manager*
EMP: 2
SALES (est): 86.7K **Privately Held**
SIC: 2451 Mobile homes

(G-3589)
FRESH TWIST FOODS LLC
3145 N Franklin St (24073-4025)
PHONE.....................540 904-1291
Dan Steinberg,
EMP: 2
SALES (est): 62.3K **Privately Held**
SIC: 2099 Food preparations

(G-3590)
FULL FAT KITCHEN LLC
3145 N Franklin St (24073-4025)
PHONE.....................844 262-6629
Jason Johannessen, *Principal*
EMP: 6
SALES (est): 203.6K **Privately Held**
WEB: www.coconaise.com
SIC: 2099 Food preparations

(G-3591)
GO-RACE INC
1265 Moose Dr (24073-4253)
PHONE.....................540 392-0696
Travis Jones, *Principal*
EMP: 3 EST: 2008
SALES (est): 298.9K **Privately Held**
WEB: www.go-race.com
SIC: 3751 Motorcycles, bicycles & parts

▲ = Import ▼=Export
◆ =Import/Export

(G-3592)
GREGS FUN FOODS
1731 Hazelnut Rd (24073-7329)
PHONE..................................540 382-6267
Greg Feuchtenberger, *Principal*
EMP: 1
SALES (est): 53.9K **Privately Held**
SIC: 2024 Ice cream & frozen desserts

(G-3593)
HOLLYBROOK MULCH TRUCKING INC
Also Called: Americam Mulch
505 College St (24073-3326)
PHONE..................................540 381-7830
Daniel Bolt, *President*
Stacie Bolt, *CFO*
EMP: 7
SQ FT: 67,500
SALES (est): 861.4K **Privately Held**
WEB: www.americanmulchandmore.com
SIC: 2499 5199 Mulch, wood & bark; baling of wood shavings for mulch

(G-3594)
HUBBELL ENTERTAINMENT
2000 Electric Way (24073-2500)
PHONE..................................540 382-6111
Harvey Hazelwood, *Owner*
◆ **EMP:** 12
SALES (est): 1.2MM **Privately Held**
WEB: www.hubbellent.com
SIC: 3646 Commercial indusl & institutional electric lighting fixtures

(G-3595)
HUBBELL INCORPORATED
2000 Electric Way (24073-2500)
PHONE..................................540 394-2107
W M Brown, *Branch Mgr*
Nita Desrosiers, *Manager*
Connie Lyons, *Manager*
Daniel Mages, *Manager*
Don Ross, *Info Tech Dir*
EMP: 50
SQ FT: 1,000
SALES (corp-wide): 4.5B **Publicly Held**
WEB: www.hubbell.com
SIC: 3643 Current-carrying wiring devices
PA: Hubbell Incorporated
40 Waterview Dr
Shelton CT 06484
475 882-4000

(G-3596)
HUBBELL LIGHTING INC
2000 Electric Way (24073-2500)
PHONE..................................540 382-6111
Weston Brown, *Vice Pres*
Wes Thornton, *Vice Pres*
Scott Diel, *VP Opers*
Phillip Griffitts, *Plant Mgr*
Kelly Burnett, *Buyer*
EMP: 270
SALES (corp-wide): 4.5B **Publicly Held**
WEB: www.hubbell.com
SIC: 3646 Commercial indusl & institutional electric lighting fixtures
HQ: Hubbell Lighting, Inc.
701 Millennium Blvd
Greenville SC 29607

(G-3597)
HYPES CUSTOM WDWKG & HM IMPROV
465 School Ln (24073-2001)
PHONE..................................540 641-7419
Nathan Matthew, *Principal*
EMP: 1 **EST:** 2016
SALES (est): 59.5K **Privately Held**
SIC: 2431 Millwork

(G-3598)
INTERLUDE HOME INC
Also Called: Wieman Upholstery
135 Warren St (24073-1803)
PHONE..................................540 381-7745
Grant Campbell, *Branch Mgr*
EMP: 60
SALES (corp-wide): 35.5MM **Privately Held**
WEB: www.interludehome.com
SIC: 2512 Upholstered household furniture

PA: Interlude Home, Inc.
25 Trefoil Dr
Trumbull CT 06611
203 445-7617

(G-3599)
IV LABS INC
Also Called: Inorganic Ventures
300 Technology Dr (24073-7375)
PHONE..................................540 585-3030
Christopher Gaines, *CEO*
Paul R Gaines, *CEO*
William Marble, *Business Mgr*
Justin Yalung, *Vice Pres*
Laura Robinson, *Marketing Mgr*
EMP: 72
SQ FT: 40,000
SALES (est): 14.7MM **Privately Held**
WEB: www.inorganicventures.com
SIC: 3825 2819 Standards & calibrating equipment, laboratory; industrial inorganic chemicals

(G-3600)
J W ALTIZER
2255 Mud Pike (24073-7039)
PHONE..................................540 382-2652
Jim Altizer, *Owner*
EMP: 1
SALES (est): 81.9K **Privately Held**
SIC: 3423 Wrenches, hand tools

(G-3601)
JA ENGRAVING COMPANY LLC
100 Ash Dr (24073-4502)
PHONE..................................540 230-8490
Angelee King,
Jeffrey Shepherd,
EMP: 2
SALES (est): 76.9K **Privately Held**
SIC: 3479 Etching & engraving

(G-3602)
K L A ENTERPRISES LLC
Also Called: Sign-A-Rama
424 Peppers Fry Rd Nw (24073-5780)
PHONE..................................540 382-9444
Kevin Altizer, *Mng Member*
EMP: 4
SQ FT: 1,400
SALES (est): 546.3K **Privately Held**
WEB: www.signarama.com
SIC: 3993 Signs & advertising specialties

(G-3603)
LENZKES CLAMPING TOOLS INC
825 Radford St (24073-3306)
P.O. Box 660 (24068-0660)
PHONE..................................540 381-1533
Karl Lenzkes, *President*
Courtney Delong, *Sales Staff*
Brian Sisson, *Sales Staff*
Brian Wells, *Sales Staff*
Hebert Horstkoetter, *Admin Sec*
▲ **EMP:** 14
SQ FT: 11,000
SALES (est): 2MM **Privately Held**
WEB: www.lenzkesusa.com
SIC: 3544 Special dies & tools

(G-3604)
MACO TOOL INC
1015 Radford St (24073-2829)
PHONE..................................989 224-6723
EMP: 2
SALES (est): 164.1K **Privately Held**
WEB: www.macotool.com
SIC: 3544 Special dies & tools

(G-3605)
MEKATRONICH CORP
295 Industrial Dr (24073-2538)
PHONE..................................954 499-5794
Luis A Rodriguez, *President*
EMP: 5
SALES (est): 218.4K **Privately Held**
SIC: 3569 Robots, assembly line: industrial & commercial

(G-3606)
MELD MANUFACTURING CORPORATION
200 Technology Dr (24073-7384)
PHONE..................................540 951-3980

Nanci Hardwick, *CEO*
EMP: 8
SALES (est): 258.5K **Privately Held**
SALES (corp-wide): 3.7MM **Privately Held**
WEB: www.meldmanufacturing.com
SIC: 3999 Manufacturing industries
PA: Aeroprobe Corporation
200 Technology Dr
Christiansburg VA 24073
540 443-9215

(G-3607)
OLDTOWN PRINTING & COPYING
19 W Main St Ste E (24073-2968)
PHONE..................................540 382-6793
Ernest Bentley, *President*
Danielle Burcham, *Prdtn Mgr*
Suzanne Bentley, *Treasurer*
EMP: 5
SQ FT: 2,000
SALES (est): 621.3K **Privately Held**
WEB: www.otprint.com
SIC: 2759 2791 2789 2752 Screen printing; typesetting; bookbinding & related work; commercial printing, lithographic

(G-3608)
QUALITY WOOD PRODUCTS INC
820 Park St Ste G (24073-3260)
PHONE..................................540 750-1859
Robert Kincaid, *President*
EMP: 2 **EST:** 2015
SALES (est): 200K **Privately Held**
SIC: 2431 5031 Moldings & baseboards, ornamental & trim; molding, all materials

(G-3609)
SNAKECLAMP PRODUCTS LLC
5 Roanoke St (24073-3017)
PHONE..................................903 265-8001
Thomas Zuckerwar, *Principal*
Gerald Zuckerwar, *Principal*
▲ **EMP:** 3 **EST:** 2013
SALES (est): 121.3K **Privately Held**
WEB: www.snakeclamp.com
SIC: 3999 Manufacturing industries

(G-3610)
SOUTHLAND LOG HOMES INC
80 Hampton Blvd (24073-2708)
PHONE..................................540 268-2243
Walt Tayne, *Manager*
EMP: 5
SALES (corp-wide): 60MM **Privately Held**
WEB: www.southlandloghomes.com
SIC: 2452 Log cabins, prefabricated, wood
PA: Southland Log Homes, Inc.
7521 Broad River Rd
Irmo SC 29063
803 781-5100

(G-3611)
TECH EXPRESS INC
597 Depot St Ne A (24073-2066)
PHONE..................................540 382-9400
Mike Martin, *President*
Debra Martin, *Vice Pres*
EMP: 3 **EST:** 1992
SALES (est): 298.2K **Privately Held**
WEB: www.tech-express.com
SIC: 2752 Commercial printing, offset

(G-3612)
TERMINUS PRODUCTS INC
2240 Prospect Dr (24073-2541)
PHONE..................................585 546-4990
Timothy Seibold, *President*
John E Seibold Sr, *Admin Sec*
John Seibold, *Admin Sec*
EMP: 3
SALES (est): 221.1K **Privately Held**
WEB: www.terminusproducts.com
SIC: 3829 Measuring & controlling devices

(G-3613)
TIMBERTONE LLC
755 W Main St (24073-4225)
PHONE..................................540 381-9794
Robert Birchfield, *Owner*
EMP: 1
SALES (est): 7.2K **Privately Held**
WEB: www.timbertones.net
SIC: 2499 Decorative wood & woodwork

(G-3614)
TURMAN LUMBER COMPANY INC
3504 Mud Pike (24073-6312)
P.O. Box 209, Riner (24149-0210)
PHONE..................................540 639-1250
Truman Bolt, *Manager*
EMP: 50
SALES (corp-wide): 10.3MM **Privately Held**
WEB: www.turmanlumber.com
SIC: 2421 Lumber: rough, sawed or planed; wood household furniture; millwork
PA: Turman Lumber Company Inc
214 N Locust St
Floyd VA 24091
540 745-2041

(G-3615)
VALLEY GROUNDS INC
750 Den Hill Rd (24073-7720)
PHONE..................................540 382-6710
T Todd Walters, *President*
EMP: 25
SALES (est): 700K **Privately Held**
WEB: www.valleylandscapingva.com
SIC: 3523 Farm machinery & equipment

(G-3616)
VIRGINIA CUSTOM COACH BUILDERS
375 Bell Rd (24073-2401)
PHONE..................................540 381-0609
Mike Fitch, *Owner*
EMP: 1
SALES (est): 98.3K **Privately Held**
SIC: 3716 Motor homes

(G-3617)
WHITEBARREL WINERY
4025 Childress Rd (24073-5968)
PHONE..................................540 382-7619
Richard Obiso, *Owner*
Theresa Gallagher, *Co-Owner*
EMP: 4 **EST:** 2016
SALES (est): 134.4K **Privately Held**
WEB: www.whitebarrel.com
SIC: 2084 Wines

Church Road
Dinwiddie County

(G-3618)
SIGN SOLUTIONS
7406 Stanfield Farm Ln (23833-2566)
PHONE..................................804 691-1824
Major I Jones III, *Owner*
EMP: 1
SALES (est): 7.5K **Privately Held**
SIC: 3993 Signs & advertising specialties

Churchville
Augusta County

(G-3619)
AUGUSTA APPLE LLC
196 Wildwood Dr (24421-2131)
PHONE..................................540 337-7170
Trevor Wallace, *Principal*
EMP: 2 **EST:** 2017
SALES (est): 98.1K **Privately Held**
SIC: 3571 Electronic computers

(G-3620)
JET WELD INC
217 Union Church Rd (24421-2321)
PHONE..................................540 836-0163
Ledbetter Michael S, *Admin Sec*
EMP: 2
SALES (est): 106K **Privately Held**
WEB: www.jetweldinc.com
SIC: 7692 Welding repair

(G-3621)
VARNER LOGGING LLC
102 Crawford Dr (24421-2638)
PHONE..................................540 849-7451
Shad Varner, *Principal*
EMP: 2

SALES (est): 81.7K **Privately Held**
SIC: 2411 Logging

(G-3622)
VINEGAR HILL ACRES
553 Vinegar Hill Rd (24421-2505)
PHONE..................540 337-6839
Raymond L Grogg, *Principal*
EMP: 2
SALES (est): 140K **Privately Held**
SIC: 2099 Vinegar

(G-3623)
VIRGINIA MTAL FABRICATIONS LLC
174 Hankey Mountain Hwy (24421-2700)
PHONE..................540 292-0562
EMP: 1
SALES (est): 60K **Privately Held**
SIC: 7692 Welding Repair

Claremont
Surry County

(G-3624)
MATHOMANK VILLAGE TRIBE
68 Mancha Ave (23899)
PHONE..................757 504-5513
Rosa Holmes-Turner, *Chief*
EMP: 2
SALES (est): 86K **Privately Held**
SIC: 3731 3732 Shipbuilding & repairing;
  boat building & repairing

(G-3625)
SEWARD LUMBER COMPANY INC
2514 Spring Grove Rd (23899)
P.O. Box 398 (23899-0398)
PHONE..................757 866-8911
William E Seward IV, *President*
William Seward III, *Treasurer*
EMP: 28 EST: 1945
SQ FT: 1,000
SALES (est): 3.9MM **Privately Held**
WEB: www.sewardlumberco.com
SIC: 2421 Custom sawmill

Clarksville
Mecklenburg County

(G-3626)
AURU TECHNOLOGIES INC
101 Crescent Dr (23927-9003)
PHONE..................434 632-6978
Christopher Clarke, *CEO*
EMP: 1
SALES (est): 81.1K **Privately Held**
SIC: 3571 5734 Personal computers (microcomputers); modems, monitors, terminals & disk drives: computers; printers & plotters: computers; personal computers

(G-3627)
BUGGS ISLAND DOCK SERVICE
413 Virginia Ave (23927-9243)
PHONE..................434 374-8028
Michael Denton, *Owner*
Michael W Denton, *Owner*
EMP: 1
SQ FT: 43,000
SALES (est): 66K **Privately Held**
WEB: www.buggsislanddockservice.com
SIC: 2499 Floating docks, wood

(G-3628)
EAST COAST EMBROIDERY
43 Duskany Point Dr (23927-2450)
PHONE..................804 677-7584
Nicholas Romano, *Principal*
EMP: 1
SALES (est): 51.7K **Privately Held**
SIC: 2395 Pleating & stitching

(G-3629)
ELIXSYS VA LLC
356 Ulysses Way (23927-2655)
PHONE..................434 374-2398
Doreen Passmore, *Mng Member*
EMP: 3 EST: 2014

SALES (est): 105.8K **Privately Held**
WEB: www.elixsys.net
SIC: 1081 Metal mining services

(G-3630)
FOUR OAKS TIMBER COMPANY
126 Wilbourne Rd (23927-2615)
P.O. Box 1089 (23927-1089)
PHONE..................434 374-2669
Clifton Morgan Jr, *President*
Brenda J Morgan, *Corp Secy*
EMP: 2
SALES (est): 500K **Privately Held**
SIC: 2411 Logging camps & contractors

(G-3631)
J EUBANK SIGNS & DESIGNS
598 Buffalo Rd (23927-3024)
PHONE..................434 374-2364
Justin Eubank, *Owner*
EMP: 1
SALES (est): 98.1K **Privately Held**
WEB: www.southernsignworks.com
SIC: 3993 Signs & advertising specialties

(G-3632)
LAKESIDE STONE & LANDSCAPE SUP
Also Called: J & J Enterprises
300 Pamunkey Dr (23927-2325)
PHONE..................434 738-3204
Barbara J Stubbs, *Owner*
EMP: 5
SALES (est): 200.6K **Privately Held**
SIC: 3281 Granite, cut & shaped

(G-3633)
LURE LLC
171 Long Meadow Dr (23927-3404)
PHONE..................434 374-8559
Thomas Loftus, *Administration*
EMP: 2
SALES (est): 89.7K **Privately Held**
SIC: 3949 Lures, fishing: artificial

(G-3634)
MITI-GAIT LLC
211 Virginia Ave (23927-9205)
PHONE..................434 738-8632
EMP: 2
SALES (est): 113K **Privately Held**
WEB: www.mitigait.com
SIC: 3715 Trailers or vans for transporting horses

(G-3635)
STITCHES CORPORATE & CUSTOM EM
618 Virginia Ave (23927-9140)
P.O. Box 1737 (23927-1737)
PHONE..................434 374-5111
Joe Smith, *Principal*
EMP: 1
SALES (est): 76.8K **Privately Held**
WEB: www.stitchesweb.com
SIC: 2395 Embroidery & art needlework

(G-3636)
SUN PUBLISHING COMPANY
Also Called: Sun Newspaper
602 Virginia Ave (23927-9140)
P.O. Box 997 (23927-0997)
PHONE..................434 374-8152
Sylvia McLauglin, *President*
Tucker McLauglin, *Assistant VP*
Tom McLauglin, *Vice Pres*
EMP: 20 EST: 1976
SALES (est): 679.8K **Privately Held**
WEB: www.sovanow.com
SIC: 2711 Newspapers, publishing & printing

Claudville
Patrick County

(G-3637)
ALAN MITCHELL
Also Called: Dan Vally Farm
57 Dan Valley Farm Rd (24076-3538)
PHONE..................276 251-5077
Alan Mitchell, *Owner*
Linda Mitchell, *Co-Owner*
EMP: 3

SALES (est): 217.6K **Privately Held**
SIC: 2452 Farm & agricultural buildings, prefabricated wood

(G-3638)
MODULAR WOOD SYSTEMS INC
1805 Red Bank School Rd (24076-3327)
PHONE..................276 251-5300
Alvin Eckenrod, *President*
◆ EMP: 50
SQ FT: 83,000
SALES (est): 5.5MM **Privately Held**
SIC: 2542 2541 Partitions & fixtures, except wood; store fixtures, wood

(G-3639)
PANEL PROCESSING VIRGINIA INC
Also Called: Modular WD Systems Patrick Co
1805 Red Bank School Rd (24076-3327)
PHONE..................989 356-9007
Smith Eric G, *President*
Alan M Kelsey, *Admin Sec*
EMP: 1 EST: 2012
SALES (est): 8.2MM
SALES (corp-wide): 95.4MM **Privately Held**
WEB: www.panel.com
SIC: 2452 Modular homes, prefabricated, wood
PA: Panel Processing, Inc.
  120 N Industrial Hwy
  Alpena MI 49707
  800 433-7142

(G-3640)
RAYS WOODWORKS
1595 Dan Valley Farm Rd (24076-3460)
PHONE..................276 251-7297
EMP: 1
SALES (est): 71.8K **Privately Held**
SIC: 2431 Mfg Millwork

(G-3641)
TALL TOAD COSTUMES
276 Big Dan Lake Dr (24076-3306)
PHONE..................276 694-4636
Patricia Griffin, *Owner*
EMP: 1
SALES (est): 32K **Privately Held**
WEB: www.talltoad.net
SIC: 2389 Costumes

(G-3642)
YUM YUM CHOPPERS INC
7034 Dobyns Rd (24076-3265)
PHONE..................276 694-6152
Terry N Hill, *President*
EMP: 2
SALES (est): 145.8K **Privately Held**
SIC: 3751 Motorcycles & related parts

Clear Brook
Frederick County

(G-3643)
ALBAN TRACTOR CO INC
Also Called: Caterpillar Authorized Dealer
351 Zachary Ann Ln (22624-1565)
PHONE..................540 667-4200
Mike Williams, *Manager*
EMP: 13
SALES (corp-wide): 248.8MM **Privately Held**
WEB: www.albancat.com
SIC: 3523 5082 7353 Farm machinery & equipment; contractors' materials; heavy construction equipment rental
PA: Alban Tractor, Llc
  8531 Pulaski Hwy
  Baltimore MD 21237
  410 686-7777

(G-3644)
HAAS WOODWORKING
430 Hopewell Rd (22624-1735)
PHONE..................540 686-5837
EMP: 2
SALES (est): 160.9K **Privately Held**
SIC: 2431 Millwork

(G-3645)
HI-LITE SOLUTIONS INC
1285 Brucetown Rd (22624-1203)
P.O. Box 399 (22624-0399)
PHONE..................540 450-8375
John McNeely, *President*
Kelly Spinner, *Corp Secy*
Calvin McNeely, *Exec VP*
Linda McNeely, *Vice Pres*
Rhonda McNeely, *Vice Pres*
▼ EMP: 14
SALES (est): 2.7MM **Privately Held**
WEB: www.hi-lite.com
SIC: 2899 2842 Chemical preparations; degreasing solvent

(G-3646)
LESTER BUILDING SYSTEMS LLC
276 Woodbine Rd (22624-1400)
P.O. Box 129 (22624-0129)
PHONE..................540 665-0182
Kevin Conroy, *Senior Engr*
Bob Dovel, *Manager*
EMP: 20
SALES (corp-wide): 71MM **Privately Held**
WEB: www.lesterbuildings.com
SIC: 2452 Prefabricated buildings, wood
PA: Lester Building Systems, Llc
  1111 2nd Ave S
  Lester Prairie MN 55354
  320 395-5212

(G-3647)
MIC INDUSTRIES INC
4150 Martinsburg Pike (22624-1534)
PHONE..................540 678-2900
Richard Lindvig, *General Mgr*
Scott Way, *General Mgr*
Frank Lucostic, *Manager*
EMP: 12
SALES (corp-wide): 18MM **Privately Held**
WEB: www.micindustries.com
SIC: 3531 3549 Construction machinery; metalworking machinery
PA: M.I.C. Industries, Inc.
  4150 Martinsburg Pike
  Clear Brook VA 22624
  703 318-1900

(G-3648)
MIC INDUSTRIES INC (PA)
4150 Martinsburg Pike (22624-1534)
PHONE..................703 318-1900
Michael S Ansari, *President*
Eileen O Penland, *COO*
Syed Ahmed, *Vice Pres*
Sarah Daly, *Opers Mgr*
Tina Antonis, *Mktg Coord*
▲ EMP: 50
SQ FT: 15,000
SALES (est): 18MM **Privately Held**
WEB: www.micindustries.com
SIC: 3531 3549 Construction machinery; metalworking machinery

(G-3649)
O-N MINERALS CHEMSTONE COMPANY
Also Called: Carmeuse Lime & Stone
508 Quarry Ln (22624-1146)
P.O. Box 219 (22624-0219)
PHONE..................540 662-3855
Kevin Sutherly, *Maint Spvr*
Kyle Apple, *Manager*
Randy Miller, *Maintence Staff*
EMP: 40
SALES (corp-wide): 177.9K **Privately Held**
WEB: www.carmeuse.com
SIC: 1422 Crushed & broken limestone
HQ: O-N Minerals (Chemstone) Company
  11 Stanwix St Fl 21
  Pittsburgh PA 15222
  412 995-5500

(G-3650)
PYRAMID ALPACAS
240 John Deere Ct (22624-1144)
PHONE..................540 662-5501
Denise Price, *Principal*
EMP: 2

▲ = Import ▼=Export
◆ =Import/Export

SALES (est): 110.4K **Privately Held**
WEB: www.pyramidalpacas.com
SIC: 2231 Alpacas, mohair: woven

(G-3651)
SII INC
3470 Martinsburg Pike (22624-1548)
P.O. Box 362 (22624-0362)
PHONE................................540 722-6860
Paul Pond, *President*
Franck A March, *Shareholder*
◆ EMP: 5
SQ FT: 4,000
SALES (est): 1MM
SALES (corp-wide): 1MM **Privately Held**
SIC: 2821 Plastics materials & resins
PA: Shi, Inc.
    3470 Martinsburg Pike
    Clear Brook VA 22624
    540 722-6860

(G-3652)
TECHNICAL URETHANES INC
3470 Martinsburg Pike (22624-1548)
P.O. Box 98 (22624-0098)
PHONE................................540 667-1770
Robert Taylor, *Principal*
EMP: 4 EST: 2007
SALES (est): 326.9K **Privately Held**
SIC: 3479 Coating of metals & formed
products

(G-3653)
TRU-ADE COMPANY
800 Welltown Rd (22624-1723)
PHONE................................540 662-5484
Alec Bud Gunter, *President*
EMP: 1
SQ FT: 3,000
SALES (est): 95K **Privately Held**
SIC: 2086 Bottled & canned soft drinks

(G-3654)
WOOLEN MILLS GRILL
3416 Martinsburg Pike (22624-1548)
PHONE................................540 323-7552
EMP: 5
SALES (est): 428K **Privately Held**
WEB: www.woolenmillsgrill.com
SIC: 2231 Wool broadwoven fabrics

Cleveland
Russell County

(G-3655)
DICKENSON-RUSSELL COAL CO LLC
7546 Gravel Lick Rd (24225-7039)
P.O. Box 655, Norton (24273-0655)
PHONE................................276 889-6100
Stanley E Bateman, *Mng Member*
EMP: 300
SALES: 38.4K
SALES (corp-wide): 2.2B **Publicly Held**
SIC: 1241 Coal mining services
HQ: Alpha Natural Resources, Llc
    636 Shelby St Ste 1c
    Bristol TN 37620
    423 574-5100

(G-3656)
SAWMILL BOTTOM
11717 Sandy Ridge Rd (24225-2641)
PHONE................................276 880-2241
EMP: 2 EST: 2019
SALES (est): 101.2K **Privately Held**
SIC: 2411 Logging

Clifton
Fairfax County

(G-3657)
ATTN ERIC MINTON
13708 Springstone Ct (20124-2365)
PHONE................................703 868-4086
Eric Minton, *Principal*
EMP: 2
SALES (est): 102.3K **Privately Held**
WEB: www.shakespeareance.com
SIC: 2741 Miscellaneous publishing

(G-3658)
AVF SCREW MACHINE LLC
5754 Old Clifton Rd (20124-1023)
PHONE................................571 393-3099
Franky Nguyen,
EMP: 1
SALES (est): 129K **Privately Held**
WEB: www.avfdecolletage.com
SIC: 3599 Machine shop, jobbing & repair

(G-3659)
BUILD SOFTWARE LLC
11501 Henderson Rd (20124-2255)
PHONE................................703 629-2549
Brian Eubanks, *President*
EMP: 2
SALES (est): 140K **Privately Held**
WEB: www.brianeubanks.com
SIC: 7372 Prepackaged software

(G-3660)
CENTURION WOODWORKS LLC
13414 Cavalier Woods Dr (20124-1041)
PHONE................................703 594-2369
Kathleen Vorbau, *Principal*
EMP: 1
SALES (est): 59.5K **Privately Held**
SIC: 2431 Millwork

(G-3661)
CLIFTON CREEK PRESS INC
7500 Weymouth Hill Rd (20124-2821)
PHONE................................703 786-9180
Amy Waldrop, *Principal*
EMP: 2
SALES (est): 99.7K **Privately Held**
WEB: www.cliftonpark.org
SIC: 2741 Miscellaneous publishing

(G-3662)
CLIFTON LABORATORIES
7236 Clifton Rd (20124-1802)
PHONE................................703 830-0368
Jack Smith, *Owner*
EMP: 1
SALES (est): 181.4K **Privately Held**
WEB: www.dxengineering.com
SIC: 3825 Lab standards, electric: resist-
ance, inductance, capacitance

(G-3663)
EFFECTIVE COMM STRATEGIES LLC
6608 Ladyslipper Ln (20124-1637)
PHONE................................703 403-5345
Katherine Bricker, *CEO*
Paul Bricker, *Principal*
Youngbee Dale, *Consultant*
EMP: 6
SALES (est): 2.4MM **Privately Held**
WEB: www.ecommunicationstrategies.com
SIC: 3944 5961 Science kits: micro-
scopes, chemistry sets, etc.; educational
supplies & equipment, mail order

(G-3664)
EMINENCE JEWELERS
5756 Union Mill Rd (20124-1088)
PHONE................................703 815-1384
Chantha Hiep, *Principal*
Vattei Hiep, *Buyer*
EMP: 2
SALES (est): 150K **Privately Held**
WEB: www.eminencejewelers.com
SIC: 3911 5944 Jewelry, precious metal;
jewelry stores

(G-3665)
FOURTY4INDUSTRIES LLC
14002 Marleigh Ln (20124-2618)
PHONE................................703 266-0525
Kai Jackson, *Principal*
EMP: 1
SALES (est): 39.6K **Privately Held**
SIC: 3999 Manufacturing industries

(G-3666)
GENERAL MAGNETIC SCIENCES INC (PA)
Also Called: G M S
6420 Stonehaven Ct (20124-2460)
PHONE................................571 243-6887
Kenneth Beeks, *CEO*
John Menner, *Ch of Bd*
▲ EMP: 1

SALES (est): 850K **Privately Held**
SIC: 3669 7389 Emergency alarms; business services

(G-3667)
GRAPHIC COMM GROUP
6738 Bunkers Ct (20124-2556)
PHONE................................703 818-2700
Jeffrey Walter, *Principal*
EMP: 6
SALES (est): 615.7K **Privately Held**
WEB: www.e-gcg.com
SIC: 2752 Commercial printing, offset

(G-3668)
GRAVITTIONAL SYSTEMS ENGRG INC
Also Called: Alacrity Services
6400 Newman Rd (20124-1444)
PHONE................................312 224-8152
Gare Henderson, *Director*
EMP: 12
SALES (est): 994.4K **Privately Held**
WEB: www.gravitationalsystems.org
SIC: 3594 3561 3563 Fluid power pumps
& motors; industrial pumps & parts; air &
gas compressors including vacuum
pumps

(G-3669)
GREENESTEP LLC
5665 Lonesome Dove Ct (20124-0926)
PHONE................................703 546-4236
Sunil Kumar, *Mng Member*
EMP: 25
SALES (est): 456.2K **Privately Held**
WEB: www.greenestep.com
SIC: 7372 Business oriented computer
software

(G-3670)
HAMS ENTERPRISES LLC
7421 Beckwith Ln (20124-2824)
PHONE................................703 988-0992
Paul Harrity, *Principal*
EMP: 4
SALES (est): 254.3K **Privately Held**
SIC: 2013 Prepared pork products from
purchased pork

(G-3671)
HARRIS PUBLICATIONS
11403 Henderson Rd (20124-2202)
PHONE................................703 764-9279
Barbara Jacksier, *Principal*
EMP: 1
SALES (est): 33.3K **Privately Held**
SIC: 2731 Book publishing

(G-3672)
INNER PEACE WARRIORS LLC
12101 Beaver Creek Rd (20124-2116)
PHONE................................703 830-7680
EMP: 2
SALES (est): 88.3K **Privately Held**
SIC: 2741 Miscellaneous publishing

(G-3673)
IOS PRESS INC
6751 Tepper Dr (20124-1603)
PHONE................................703 830-6300
Barry Schneiderman, *Principal*
EMP: 3 EST: 2010
SALES (est): 169.6K **Privately Held**
WEB: www.iospress.nl
SIC: 2741 Miscellaneous publishing

(G-3674)
METHOD INNOVATION CORPORATION
13129 Twin Lakes Dr (20124-1214)
PHONE................................703 266-1115
EMP: 4 EST: 1996
SQ FT: 1,200
SALES: 400K **Privately Held**
SIC: 7372 Prepackaged Software Services

(G-3675)
PRESIDENTIAL COIN & ANTIQUE CO
Also Called: Pcac
12233 Chapel Rd (20124-1920)
P.O. Box 277 (20124-0277)
PHONE................................703 354-5454
H Joseph Levine, *President*

Alice H Levine, *Vice Pres*
EMP: 2
SQ FT: 1,710
SALES (est): 184.5K **Privately Held**
WEB: www.pcac.org
SIC: 3999 5932 Coins & tokens, non-cur-
rency; antiques

(G-3676)
SUB ROSA LLC
5762 Union Mill Rd (20124-1088)
PHONE................................703 338-3344
Evrim Dogu,
Erdogan Dogu,
EMP: 2
SQ FT: 1,440
SALES (est): 76.2K **Privately Held**
SIC: 2051 Bakery: wholesale or whole-
sale/retail combined

(G-3677)
TRANSFORMING DAILY LIVES
Also Called: Tdl
13836 Laurel Rock Ct (20124-2505)
PHONE................................916 990-2299
Zaneta Wooden, *Owner*
EMP: 1
SALES (est): 3.5K **Privately Held**
SIC: 2731 Books: publishing only

Clifton Forge
Alleghany County

(G-3678)
BOLIVIA LUMBER COMPANY LLC
101 Matthews Ln (24422-3126)
P.O. Box 25, Low Moor (24457-0025)
PHONE................................540 862-5228
Jack Gentry, *Manager*
EMP: 20
SALES (corp-wide): 11.7MM **Privately
Held**
WEB: www.bolivialumber.com
SIC: 2448 Pallets, wood
PA: Bolivia Lumber Company, Llc
    405 Old Mill Rd Ne
    Leland NC 28451
    910 371-2515

(G-3679)
BURSEY MACHINE & WELDING
1225 Grace Ave (24422-1415)
PHONE................................540 862-5033
John Bursey, *Owner*
EMP: 1
SALES (est): 61.8K **Privately Held**
SIC: 7692 Welding repair

(G-3680)
J & D PALLETS
2050 State Ave (24422-1983)
PHONE................................540 862-2448
Jeffrey Persinger, *President*
Melissa Persinger, *Vice Pres*
EMP: 25
SALES (est): 1MM **Privately Held**
SIC: 2448 Pallets, wood

(G-3681)
PICS BY KELS PHOTOGRAPHY LLC
505 Commercial Ave (24422-1120)
PHONE................................540 958-4944
Kelsey Meyer,
EMP: 1
SQ FT: 900
SALES (est): 85.5K **Privately Held**
WEB: www.picsbykelsphotography.pix-
ieset.com
SIC: 3861 Photographic equipment & sup-
plies

(G-3682)
POLYCHEM INC
2020 State Ave (24422-1983)
PHONE................................540 862-1321
George K Meszaros, *President*
EMP: 2
SQ FT: 3,000

SALES (est): 460K **Privately Held**
WEB: www.polychemusa.com
SIC: 2842 5048 Specialty cleaning preparations; optometric equipment & supplies

(G-3683)
WARBIRD TURKEY CALLS LLC
4123 Sharon Ln (24422-3506)
PHONE..........................540 968-0415
EMP: 2
SALES (est): 99.9K **Privately Held**
WEB: www.warbirdturkeycalls.com
SIC: 3949 Sporting & athletic goods

Clinchco
Dickenson County

(G-3684)
ALBRIGHT RECOVERY & CNSTR LLC
138 Dunrobin Rd (24226-8850)
PHONE..........................276 835-2026
Heather Lyall,
Rodney Albright,
EMP: 4 **EST:** 2014
SALES (est): 420.4K **Privately Held**
WEB: www.albrightrecoveryandconstruction.com
SIC: 2842 1389 1521 Specialty cleaning preparations; construction, repair & dismantling services; single-family housing construction

Clintwood
Dickenson County

(G-3685)
83 GAS & GROCERY INC
Rr 83 (24228)
PHONE..........................276 926-4388
Allen Compton, *President*
Jay Compton, *Vice Pres*
Elizabeth Kiazer, *Admin Sec*
EMP: 9
SQ FT: 18,000
SALES (est): 1MM **Privately Held**
SIC: 2869 Fuels

(G-3686)
ALLEGIANCE INC
182 Camp Jacob Rd (24228-2200)
PHONE..........................276 639-6884
Jeffery Mullins, *President*
Jordan Mullins, *Principal*
EMP: 9 **EST:** 2010
SALES (est): 1MM **Privately Held**
WEB: www.maritzcx.com
SIC: 3483 Ammunition components

(G-3687)
APPALACHIAN PROD SVCS INC (HQ)
Also Called: Appalachian Production Svcs
2487 Rose Rdg (24228-7740)
PHONE..........................276 619-4880
Frank Henderson, *President*
Jeannie Henderson, *Vice Pres*
EMP: 38
SQ FT: 3,500
SALES (est): 8.2MM
SALES (corp-wide): 53.6MM **Privately Held**
WEB: www.shalepro.com
SIC: 1389 Servicing oil & gas wells
PA: Shalepro Energy Services Llc
17 Lane Dr
Clarksburg WV 26301
304 709-7100

(G-3688)
DOUBLE T PUBLISHING INC
Also Called: Dickenson Star/Cmbrlnd Times
Main St Ste 202 (24228)
P.O. Box 707 (24228-0707)
PHONE..........................276 926-8816
Jenay Tate, *President*
EMP: 75

SALES (est): 2MM
SALES (corp-wide): 4.7MM **Privately Held**
WEB: www.dickensonstar.com
SIC: 2711 Commercial printing & newspaper publishing combined
PA: Coalfield Progress
725 Park Ave Sw
Norton VA 24273
276 679-1101

(G-3689)
MARAH BITAR LLC (PA)
419 Commanders Ln (24228-6822)
PHONE..........................856 630-4437
Joseph Aji, *Mng Member*
EMP: 2
SALES (est): 200K **Privately Held**
SIC: 2834 Ointments

(G-3690)
MCCLURE CONCRETE MATERIALS LLC
569 Happy Valley Dr (24228)
PHONE..........................276 964-9682
EMP: 3
SALES (corp-wide): 635.5K **Privately Held**
WEB: www.mcclureconcrete.com
SIC: 3273 Ready-mixed concrete
PA: Mcclure Concrete Materials Llc
1201 Iron St
Richlands VA 24641
276 964-9682

Clover
Halifax County

(G-3691)
CLOVER YARNS INC
1030 Tanyard Branch Rd (24534)
P.O. Box 354, Milford DE (19963-0354)
PHONE..........................434 454-7151
Harvey Vaughn, *Manager*
EMP: 200
SALES (corp-wide): 64.8MM **Privately Held**
WEB: www.cloveryarns.com
SIC: 2299 5949 2282 2281 Fibers, textile: recovery from textile mill waste & rags; knitting goods & supplies; throwing & winding mills; yarn spinning mills
PA: Clover Yarns, Inc.
715 S Washington St
Milford DE 19963
302 422-4518

(G-3692)
HUNTING CREEK VINEYARDS CO
2000 Addie Williams Trl (24534-3128)
PHONE..........................434 454-9219
Milton Lee McPherson Jr, *Principal*
EMP: 3
SALES (est): 232.3K **Privately Held**
WEB: www.hcvwines.com
SIC: 2084 Wines

Cloverdale
Botetourt County

(G-3693)
SOUTHERN STATES COOP INC
1796 Lee Hwy (24077-3105)
P.O. Box 459 (24077-0459)
PHONE..........................540 992-1100
Steve Kloser, *Manager*
EMP: 15
SALES (corp-wide): 2.1B **Privately Held**
WEB: www.southernstates.com
SIC: 2048 5999 Prepared feeds; feed & farm supply
PA: Southern States Cooperative, Incorporated
6606 W Broad St Ste B
Richmond VA 23230
804 281-1000

Cobbs Creek
Mathews County

(G-3694)
KAYJAE INC
323 Creek Ln (23035)
P.O. Box 95 (23035-0095)
PHONE..........................804 725-9664
Donald W Jaeger, *President*
Lynn Jaeger, *Vice Pres*
EMP: 4
SALES (est): 314.9K **Privately Held**
WEB: www.kayjae.com
SIC: 2499 Woodenware, kitchen & household

Coeburn
Wise County

(G-3695)
BIG D ENTERPRISES INC
195 Marigold Ln (24230-6369)
PHONE..........................276 679-1090
Darrell Stanley, *President*
EMP: 5
SALES (est): 425K **Privately Held**
SIC: 1221 Surface mining, bituminous

(G-3696)
CLAYTON HOMES INC
Also Called: Unknown
11416 Norton Coeburn Rd (24230-6448)
PHONE..........................276 395-7272
Glenn Tasley, *Branch Mgr*
Chris Hammonds, *Manager*
EMP: 2
SALES (corp-wide): 254.6B **Publicly Held**
WEB: www.claytonhomes.com
SIC: 2451 Mobile homes
HQ: Clayton Homes, Inc.
5000 Clayton Rd
Maryville TN 37804
865 380-3000

(G-3697)
CRESCENT PRINTERY LTD
307 2nd St Sw (24230-3422)
P.O. Box 39 (24230-0039)
PHONE..........................276 395-2101
William Pate, *President*
Helen Pate, *Vice Pres*
Jamie Nickels, *Admin Sec*
EMP: 3
SQ FT: 3,325
SALES (est): 432.3K **Privately Held**
SIC: 2752 Commercial printing, offset

(G-3698)
FAIRBANKS COAL CO INC
450 Front St W (24230-3604)
P.O. Box 950 (24230-0950)
PHONE..........................276 395-3354
Deborah Davis, *Corp Secy*
EMP: 5
SQ FT: 1,200
SALES (est): 610K **Privately Held**
SIC: 1221 Strip mining, bituminous

(G-3699)
HESSS BODY SHOP
303 2nd St Sw (24230-3422)
PHONE..........................276 395-7808
Silas Hess, *Owner*
EMP: 3
SALES (est): 60K **Privately Held**
SIC: 3714 Motor vehicle parts & accessories

(G-3700)
JORDAN SEPTIC TANK SERVICE
Old Coeburn Norton Hwy (24230)
PHONE..........................276 395-3938
Bill Hunsaker, *Owner*
EMP: 2
SQ FT: 1,500
SALES (est): 172.3K **Privately Held**
SIC: 3272 7699 Septic tanks, concrete; septic tank cleaning service

(G-3701)
MARTY CORPORATION (PA)
Also Called: Marty Materials
502a Front St W (24230-3606)
P.O. Box 310 (24230-0310)
PHONE..........................276 395-3326
Russell O Large, *President*
M Ruth Large, *Treasurer*
Rebecca Kilgore, *Admin Sec*
EMP: 7 **EST:** 1965
SQ FT: 2,000
SALES (est): 1.3MM **Privately Held**
WEB: www.martymaterials.com
SIC: 3273 Ready-mixed concrete

(G-3702)
SCRIPTED GATE SIGN CO LLC
3721 Dungannon Rd (24230-6013)
PHONE..........................276 219-3850
Andrea Denise Hicks, *Principal*
EMP: 1
SALES (est): 46K **Privately Held**
SIC: 3993 Signs & advertising specialties

(G-3703)
STANDARD CORE DRILLING CO INC
108 Quillen Ave Se (24230-4100)
P.O. Box 1526 (24230-1526)
PHONE..........................276 395-3391
Joel R Funk, *President*
EMP: 9 **EST:** 1955
SQ FT: 6,000
SALES (est): 483.1K **Privately Held**
SIC: 1241 1799 Coal mining services; core drilling & cutting

(G-3704)
WHATASEAT
10131 Pine Camp Rd (24230-6104)
P.O. Box 671, Norton (24273-0671)
PHONE..........................276 395-7887
EMP: 2
SALES (est): 108.1K **Privately Held**
WEB: www.what-a-seat.com
SIC: 3949 Sporting & athletic goods

(G-3705)
WISE COUNTY PSA
Also Called: Water Treatment Plant
3055 Carfax Rd (24230-5613)
PHONE..........................276 762-0159
Roy Markham, *Superintendent*
EMP: 4
SALES (est): 281K **Privately Held**
SIC: 3823 Water quality monitoring & control systems

Coleman Falls
Bedford County

(G-3706)
GRAYS WELDING LLC
1478 Fontella Rd (24536)
PHONE..........................434 401-4559
Shelton Gray,
EMP: 1
SALES (est): 50K **Privately Held**
SIC: 3599 Industrial machinery

(G-3707)
REAVES TIMBER CORPORATION
2957 Fontella Rd (24536-2549)
PHONE..........................434 299-5645
Donald Reaves, *President*
Lori Reaves, *Corp Secy*
Reaves Roy Edwin, *Vice Pres*
Roy Reaves, *Vice Pres*
EMP: 8 **EST:** 1951
SALES (est): 941.4K **Privately Held**
SIC: 2411 Timber, cut at logging camp; pulpwood contractors engaged in cutting

Collinsville
Henry County

(G-3708)
AMERICAN MARINE AND ENGINE
216 Ridge Rd (24078-2133)
PHONE..........................276 263-1211

EMP: 1
SALES (est): 60K Privately Held
SIC: 3519 Marine engines

(G-3709)
BOLDENS WELDING & TRAILOR SLS
Also Called: Bolden's Welding Shop
37 Turner Rd (24078-1667)
PHONE.....................276 647-8357
Bobby G Bolden, *Owner*
EMP: 2
SALES (est): 122.6K Privately Held
SIC: 7692 Welding repair

(G-3710)
COLLINSVILLE ENGRAVING LLC
3410 Virginia Ave (24078-2272)
P.O. Box 220 (24078-0220)
PHONE.....................276 647-8596
Pete Rakes, *President*
EMP: 2
SQ FT: 2,000
SALES (est): 237.7K Privately Held
SIC: 3914 Trophies

(G-3711)
FLOWERS BKG CO LYNCHBURG LLC
3416 Virginia Ave Ste 1 (24078-2240)
PHONE.....................276 647-8767
Linda Handy, *Manager*
EMP: 1
SALES (corp-wide): 4.1B Publicly Held
SIC: 2051 Bread, cake & related products
HQ: Flowers Baking Co. Of Lynchburg, Llc
1905 Hollins Mill Rd
Lynchburg VA 24503
434 528-0441

(G-3712)
HAVERLINE LABELS INC
11 Printers Ln (24078-1592)
PHONE.....................276 647-7785
Ben Copenhaver, *President*
EMP: 9
SQ FT: 16,000
SALES (est): 1.3MM Privately Held
SIC: 2759 Labels & seals: printing

(G-3713)
HOOKER PRINTING INC
11 Printers Ln (24078-1592)
PHONE.....................336 339-4802
James H Ford, *Administration*
EMP: 2
SALES (est): 96.5K Privately Held
SIC: 2752 Commercial printing, offset

(G-3714)
HUDDLE FURNITURE INC
3483 Virginia Ave (24078-2252)
P.O. Box 322, Martinsville (24114-0322)
PHONE.....................276 647-5129
Dwight Wright, *Manager*
EMP: 38
SALES (corp-wide): 29.6MM Privately Held
SIC: 2512 Upholstered household furniture
PA: Huddle Furniture, Inc.
1801 Main St E
Valdese NC 28690
828 874-8888

(G-3715)
REYNOLDS CONTAINER CORPORATION
2249 Virginia Ave (24078-2315)
P.O. Box 1129, Martinsville (24114-1129)
PHONE.....................276 647-8451
Robert C Hubble, *President*
Richard N Renz, *Vice Pres*
Nancy R Hubble, *Admin Sec*
EMP: 35
SQ FT: 30,000
SALES (est): 6.4MM Privately Held
SIC: 2653 2273 Boxes, corrugated: made from purchased materials; carpets & rugs

(G-3716)
SAN PAK INC
138 Parkwood Ct (24078-3037)
PHONE.....................276 647-5390
Paresh Patel, *Vice Pres*
EMP: 3

SALES (est): 50K Privately Held
SIC: 2321 Men's & boys' furnishings

(G-3717)
SUNBEAM BAKERIES
3416 Virginia Ave (24078-2240)
PHONE.....................276 647-8767
Linda Handy, *Principal*
EMP: 2
SALES (est): 77.2K Privately Held
SIC: 2051 Cakes, bakery: except frozen

(G-3718)
VIRGINIA BLOWER COMPANY (PA)
3677 Virginia Ave (24078-1723)
P.O. Box 215 (24078-0215)
PHONE.....................276 647-3804
Milford A Weaver, *President*
William N Galtress, *Senior VP*
Thomas F Harris, *Vice Pres*
Yolanda Smallwood, *Treasurer*
Milford Weaver, *Marketing Mgr*
EMP: 22
SQ FT: 14,164
SALES (est): 4.4MM Privately Held
WEB: www.virginiablowercompany.com
SIC: 3444 5075 1711 3585 Pipe, sheet metal; air conditioning & ventilation equipment & supplies; heating & air conditioning contractors; refrigeration & heating equipment; blowers & fans; heating equipment, except electric

Cologne
King William County

(G-3719)
HARTS WELDING & FABRICATION L
1358 Buena Vista Rd (23181-4009)
PHONE.....................804 785-3030
Sam Hart, *Principal*
EMP: 5
SALES (est): 183.1K Privately Held
SIC: 7692 Welding repair

Colonial Beach
Westmoreland County

(G-3720)
ALS CUSTOM SIGNS
2376 Longfield Rd (22443-5910)
PHONE.....................804 224-7105
Albert H Brown, *Owner*
EMP: 1 EST: 1981
SALES (est): 30K Privately Held
SIC: 3993 Signs, not made in custom sign painting shops

(G-3721)
BEACH BLOCK VENTURES LLC
215 Irving Ave N (22443-2327)
PHONE.....................540 848-0921
Sharon Markgraf, *CEO*
EMP: 2
SALES (est): 137.9K Privately Held
SIC: 2599 5812 Food wagons, restaurant; coffee shop

(G-3722)
BLACK PWDR ARTIFICER PRESS INC
1212 Monroe Bay Ave (22443-2920)
P.O. Box 575 (22443-0575)
PHONE.....................804 366-0562
William Tucker, *Principal*
EMP: 2 EST: 2013
SALES (est): 119.7K Privately Held
WEB: www.bpapress.com
SIC: 2741 Miscellaneous publishing

(G-3723)
COLONIAL BEACH BREWING LLC
215 Washington Ave Ste C (22443-2301)
PHONE.....................540 760-5661
Theodore Saffos, *Mng Member*
EMP: 7

SALES (est): 250K Privately Held
SIC: 2082 Beer (alcoholic beverage)

(G-3724)
DONLEY TECHNOLOGY
220 Garfield Ave (22443-2316)
P.O. Box 152 (22443-0152)
PHONE.....................804 224-9427
Elizabeth Donley, *Owner*
John Donley, *Editor*
Beth Donley, *Supervisor*
EMP: 2
SALES (est): 103K Privately Held
WEB: www.donleytech.com
SIC: 2741 8748 8641 Miscellaneous publishing; business consulting; environmental protection organization

(G-3725)
MOBILE TX/BOOKKEEPING PRTG LLC
420 Colonial Ave Ste B (22443-2210)
PHONE.....................804 224-8454
Bonnie Knott,
EMP: 2 EST: 2000
SALES (est): 167.2K Privately Held
SIC: 2759 Commercial printing

(G-3726)
POTOMAC ALTRNTOR BTRY SPCLISTS
321 1st St (22443-1802)
PHONE.....................804 224-2384
David Stinnette, *Partner*
Stacey Stinnette, *Partner*
EMP: 2
SALES (est): 185.7K Privately Held
WEB: www.wingsradio.com
SIC: 3694 5013 Automotive electrical equipment; alternators

(G-3727)
UBICABUS LLC
134 Washington Cir (22443-5082)
PHONE.....................804 512-5324
Robert Coates, *Mng Member*
Laura Bowie,
Fernando Flores,
Esteban Lubensky,
EMP: 16
SALES (est): 957.1K Privately Held
SIC: 7372 Business oriented computer software

(G-3728)
VENOM MOTORSPORTS
3793 Longfield Rd (22443-5927)
PHONE.....................804 347-7626
EMP: 2
SALES (est): 74.4K Privately Held
SIC: 2836 Venoms

(G-3729)
WESTMORELAND PALLET COMPAN
3941 Longfield Rd (22443-5925)
P.O. Box 370 (22443-0370)
PHONE.....................804 224-9450
James L Coates, *President*
Linda G Coates, *Corp Secy*
EMP: 3
SQ FT: 10,000
SALES (est): 120K Privately Held
SIC: 3531 Forestry related equipment

(G-3730)
WHICKER HOME INDUSTRIES LLC
Also Called: Whicker Home Services
1071 Shore Dr (22443-4213)
PHONE.....................703 675-7642
Maria Bell, *Owner*
Kevin Whicker, *Principal*
EMP: 2
SALES (est): 97.7K Privately Held
SIC: 3999 Manufacturing industries

Colonial Heights
Colonial Heights City County

(G-3731)
CARMEL TCTCAL SLTONS GROUP LLC
200 Lakeview Ave Ste B (23834-1502)
P.O. Box 125 (23834-0125)
PHONE.....................804 943-6121
Neil Kuchinsky, *Principal*
EMP: 5
SALES (est): 100K Privately Held
SIC: 3999 Manufacturing industries

(G-3732)
ELEMENTS OF GRACE LLC
220 Suffolk Ave (23834-3351)
PHONE.....................804 526-1482
Jada Campbell, *Principal*
EMP: 3 EST: 2017
SALES (est): 221.9K Privately Held
SIC: 2819 Industrial inorganic chemicals

(G-3733)
HARTMAN GRAPHICS & PRINT
3204 Glenview Ave (23834-1522)
PHONE.....................804 720-6549
Alex Hartman, *Principal*
EMP: 2 EST: 2017
SALES (est): 92.3K Privately Held
WEB: www.hartmangraphics.com
SIC: 2752 Commercial printing, lithographic

(G-3734)
HOUSE OF VONDRAKE LAVAR LLC
207 Archer Ave (23834-3705)
PHONE.....................804 295-6136
Lawrenroy Taylor, *CEO*
EMP: 8
SALES (est): 313.7K Privately Held
SIC: 3851 5099 5122 2844 Protective eyeware; sunglasses; toiletries; perfumes & colognes

(G-3735)
JAMES RIVER PRINTING LLC
2900 Cedar Ln Ste A (23834-1546)
PHONE.....................804 520-1000
James Smith, *President*
EMP: 3
SQ FT: 1,100
SALES (est): 372.2K Privately Held
WEB: www.jamesriverprinting.com
SIC: 2752 Commercial printing, offset

(G-3736)
JONATHAN CHANDLER
1208 Covington Rd (23834-2716)
P.O. Box 2707, Chesterfield (23832-9116)
PHONE.....................804 526-1148
Jonathan Chandler, *Partner*
EMP: 1 EST: 2016
SALES (est): 51.7K Privately Held
SIC: 3949 Sporting & athletic goods

(G-3737)
KEITHS BOAT SERVICE LLC
1147 Cumberland Dr (23834-1927)
PHONE.....................804 898-1644
Keith Kapinskis, *Principal*
EMP: 3
SALES (est): 266.7K Privately Held
SIC: 3732 Boat building & repairing

(G-3738)
MUNDET-HERMETITE INC (DH)
1106 W Roslyn Rd (23834-3900)
P.O. Box 70 (23834-0070)
PHONE.....................804 748-3319
Stephen F Young, *CEO*
G A Leedham, *Corp Secy*
Cyril Leonard, *Vice Pres*
◆ EMP: 85
SALES (est): 8.2MM
SALES (corp-wide): 1B Privately Held
WEB: www.delfortgroup.com
SIC: 2621 Filter paper

GEOGRAPHIC

(G-3739)
OFFSHORE CORPORATION
840 W Roslyn Rd Ste A (23834-3507)
PHONE..804 526-7665
Vicki Parks, *Principal*
EMP: 3
SALES (est): 170.7K **Privately Held**
SIC: 3731 Offshore supply boats, building
& repairing

(G-3740)
OLDE PETERSBURG PRINTERS
325 Shade Tree Dr (23834-1779)
PHONE..804 400-9644
EMP: 2
SALES (est): 83.9K **Privately Held**
SIC: 2752 Commercial printing, litho-
graphic

(G-3741)
P & C HEAVY TRUCK REPAIR
3117 Atlantic Ave (23834-2901)
PHONE..804 520-7619
Peggy Brough, *Partner*
Charles Brough, *Partner*
EMP: 3 EST: 1989
SALES (est): 122.4K **Privately Held**
SIC: 7692 Welding repair

(G-3742)
PROGRAM SERVICES LLC
Also Called: Military Newspapers of VA
114 Charlotte Ave (23834-3007)
PHONE..804 526-8656
Fax: 804 526-8692
EMP: 3 **Privately Held**
SIC: 2711 Newspapers-Publishing/Printing
HQ: Program Services, Llc
150 W Brambleton Ave
Norfolk VA 23510
757 222-3990

(G-3743)
REBECCA BURTON
Also Called: Becky Burton, Interpreter
1118 Peace Cliff Ct (23834-2200)
PHONE..804 526-3423
Rebecca Burton, *Owner*
EMP: 1
SALES (est): 56.7K **Privately Held**
SIC: 3993 Signs & advertising specialties

(G-3744)
RZ WOODWORKS LLC
526 Roslyn Ave (23834-3833)
PHONE..626 833-0628
Robert Zamaro, *Principal*
EMP: 2
SALES (est): 70.6K **Privately Held**
SIC: 2431 Millwork

(G-3745)
SABRA DIPPING COMPANY LLC
15881 Fort Waltall Ct (23834)
PHONE..804 526-5930
Imran Alli, *Branch Mgr*
EMP: 17
SQ FT: 25,000 **Privately Held**
WEB: www.sabra.com
SIC: 2099 5148 Salads, fresh or refriger-
ated; vegetables
PA: Sabra Dipping Company, Llc
777 Westchester Ave Fl 3
White Plains NY 10604

(G-3746)
**SAUNDERS CUSTOM
WOODWORK**
106 Waterfront Dr (23834-2180)
PHONE..804 520-4090
EMP: 2
SALES (est): 195.5K **Privately Held**
SIC: 2431 Mfg Millwork

(G-3747)
SIGN MANAGERS
2402 Boulevard Ste B (23834-2318)
PHONE..804 878-0555
Nathaniel Collier, *Principal*
EMP: 1 EST: 2017
SALES (est): 69.5K **Privately Held**
SIC: 3993 Signs & advertising specialties

(G-3748)
SPIRIT HALLOWEEN
342 Southpark Cir (23834-2965)
PHONE..804 513-2966
EMP: 2
SALES (est): 100.4K **Privately Held**
SIC: 2389 Masquerade costumes

(G-3749)
STYLES BY JAIMONIQUE LLC
2900 Cedar Ln Ste B (23834-1546)
PHONE..804 255-8581
Janeshia Swann,
EMP: 1
SALES (est): 39.6K **Privately Held**
SIC: 3999 Hair, dressing of, for the trade

(G-3750)
SUMNERS SCOREBOARDS
412 Waterfront Dr (23834-2152)
PHONE..804 526-7152
Mark Sumner, *Owner*
EMP: 1
SALES (est): 47.1K **Privately Held**
SIC: 3993 Signs & advertising specialties

(G-3751)
VIRGINIA WHEEL & RIM INC
105 Tudor Rd (23834-1150)
P.O. Box 1286 (23834-9286)
PHONE..804 526-9868
Linda Louise Knarr, *President*
EMP: 1
SALES (est): 86.8K **Privately Held**
WEB: www.customwheelsnc.com
SIC: 3714 Wheel rims, motor vehicle

Columbia
Goochland County

(G-3752)
KATHEZZ COMPOST LLC
351 Scenic River Dr (23038-3018)
PHONE..434 842-9395
Ken Droege, *Principal*
EMP: 3
SALES (est): 154.9K **Privately Held**
SIC: 2875 Compost

(G-3753)
NOTHING BUT NEON
351 Scenic River Dr (23038-3018)
PHONE..434 842-9395
EMP: 2
SALES (est): 106.4K **Privately Held**
SIC: 3993 Neon signs

Conaway
Buchanan County

(G-3754)
PEGGY SUES ADVERTISING INC
Also Called: Thompson Enterprises
Rr 460 (24603)
PHONE..276 530-7790
Peggy Thompson, *President*
Sherly Thompson, *Principal*
EMP: 2 EST: 1982
SQ FT: 1,370
SALES (est): 179.2K **Privately Held**
SIC: 2395 5199 Embroidery & art needle-
work; advertising specialties

Concord
Campbell County

(G-3755)
BALANCEMASTER INC
2246 Toll Gate Rd (24538-2206)
PHONE..434 258-5078
Harald M Collonia, *President*
Harald Michael, *General Mgr*
Charlotte Collonia, *CFO*
Charles Torbert, *Agent*
EMP: 7
SQ FT: 3,500
SALES (est): 1.5MM **Privately Held**
WEB: www.balancemaster.com
SIC: 3545 5046 Balancing machines (ma-
chine tool accessories); balances, exclud-
ing laboratory

(G-3756)
BLUE RIDGE MILLWORK
116 S And S Ln (24538-2294)
PHONE..434 993-1953
John Welch, *Principal*
EMP: 2
SALES (est): 226.7K **Privately Held**
WEB: www.blueridgemillwork.com
SIC: 2431 Millwork

(G-3757)
BOXLEY MATERIALS COMPANY
Also Called: Mt Athos Quarry
1299 Stage Rd (24538-3042)
P.O. Box 13527, Roanoke (24035-3527)
PHONE..540 777-7600
AB Boxley, *CEO*
EMP: 9
SALES (corp-wide): 2.2B **Publicly Held**
WEB: www.boxley.com
SIC: 1422 Crushed & broken limestone
HQ: Boxley Materials Company
15418 W Lynchburg Slem Tp
Blue Ridge VA 24064
540 777-7600

(G-3758)
CONCORD LOGGING
465 Toll Gate Rd (24538-2193)
PHONE..434 660-1889
EMP: 2
SALES (est): 81.7K **Privately Held**
SIC: 2411 Logging

(G-3759)
DEVAULT VINEYARDS LLC
247 Station Ln (24538-3059)
PHONE..434 993-0722
Terry Devault, *Principal*
EMP: 2
SALES (est): 183.7K **Privately Held**
WEB: www.devaultvineyards.com
SIC: 2084 Wines

(G-3760)
HI-TECH MACHINING LLC
1481 Doss Rd (24538-2278)
PHONE..434 993-3256
Jeffrey L Case,
EMP: 32
SQ FT: 12,000
SALES (est): 500K **Privately Held**
SIC: 3441 3599 Fabricated structural
metal; machine shop, jobbing & repair

(G-3761)
HI-TECH MACHINING LLC
1481 Doss Rd (24538-2278)
PHONE..434 993-3256
Jeff Case, *President*
EMP: 2
SALES (est): 137.9K **Privately Held**
SIC: 3599 Machine shop, jobbing & repair

(G-3762)
**ONYX COATING SOLUTIONS
LLC**
2668 Paradise Rd (24538-3508)
PHONE..434 660-4627
Tracey Burke, *Principal*
EMP: 2
SALES (est): 81.5K **Privately Held**
SIC: 3479 Metal coating & allied service

(G-3763)
SCRUB EXCHANGE LLC
5535 Spring Mill Rd (24538-2059)
PHONE..434 237-7778
EMP: 1
SALES (est): 87K **Privately Held**
SIC: 2326 5699 7213 7218 Mfg Men/Boy
Work Clothng Ret Misc Apparel/Access
Linen Supply Service Industrial Launderer

Copper Hill
Floyd County

(G-3764)
FABRIK
210 Daniels Run Rd Ne (24079-2575)
PHONE..540 651-4169
Michael Schaas, *Owner*
EMP: 2
SALES (est): 151.1K **Privately Held**
WEB: www.roidirect.com
SIC: 2519 Household furniture

(G-3765)
WINDRUSH FARM LLC
Also Called: Kenkashi
9046 Copper Hill Rd Ne (24079-2122)
PHONE..540 589-1878
Cassie Wilson, *Managing Dir*
EMP: 3
SALES (est): 190.2K **Privately Held**
WEB: www.windrushfarm.org
SIC: 2873 Nitrogenous fertilizers; fertiliz-
ers: natural (organic), except compost

Courtland
Southampton County

(G-3766)
ARKEMA INC
Also Called: Rubber Plas Div Frnkln/Crtland
27123 Shady Brook Trl (23837-2034)
PHONE..800 225-7788
Thierry Le H Naff, *CEO*
EMP: 123
SALES (corp-wide): 120.6MM **Privately
Held**
WEB: www.arkema-americas.com
SIC: 2819 Industrial inorganic chemicals
HQ: Arkema Inc.
900 First Ave
King Of Prussia PA 19406
610 205-7000

(G-3767)
CW MOORE & SONS LLC
23388 Lee St (23837-2160)
PHONE..757 653-9011
Timothy W Moore, *Mng Member*
EMP: 10
SALES (est): 942.8K **Privately Held**
SIC: 2411 Logging

(G-3768)
DBA JUS BCUZ
24291 Otter Dr (23837-2150)
PHONE..914 714-9327
Karen Butts, *Owner*
EMP: 3
SALES (est): 160.5K **Privately Held**
SIC: 2771 Greeting cards

(G-3769)
**EASTMAN CHEMICAL RESINS
INC**
27123 Shady Brook Trl (23837-2034)
PHONE..757 562-3121
Jeff Elliott, *Maintence Staff*
EMP: 9 **Publicly Held**
WEB: www.eastman.com
SIC: 2821 Plastics materials & resins
HQ: Eastman Chemical Resins, Inc.
200 S Wilcox Dr
Kingsport TN 37660
423 229-2000

(G-3770)
G&O LOGGING LLC
23191 Hanging Tree Rd (23837-1301)
PHONE..757 653-2181
Lewis H Davis Jr, *Principal*
EMP: 3
SALES (est): 406.5K **Privately Held**
SIC: 2411 Logging camps & contractors

(G-3771)
KITCHENS WELDING INC
22311 Southampton Pkwy (23837-2331)
P.O. Box 639 (23837-0639)
PHONE..757 653-2500
EMP: 4

▲ = Import ▼=Export
◆ =Import/Export

SQ FT: 6,000
SALES (est): 350K **Privately Held**
SIC: 3441 Fabricated Structural Metal

(G-3772)
LINWOOD L POPE
23120 Bryant Church Rd (23837-2400)
PHONE................................757 654-9397
EMP: 1 **EST:** 2001
SALES (est): 51K **Privately Held**
SIC: 2621 Supplying Copy Paper

(G-3773)
MOORE C W AND SONS LLC
24283 Moore Dr (23837-2207)
PHONE................................757 653-9121
Ronald L Moore, *Partner*
Samuel C Moore, *Partner*
Tim Moore, *Partner*
Hazel Moore, *Office Mgr*
Christian W Moore -Mng,
EMP: 6
SALES (est): 577.7K **Privately Held**
SIC: 2411 Logging camps & contractors

(G-3774)
**SOUTHEAST FIBER SUPPLY
INC**
23437 Jerusalem Rd (23837-2156)
P.O. Box 98 (23837-0098)
PHONE................................757 653-2318
Jerry Davies Rose Jr, *President*
Stephanie Blythe, *Vice Pres*
EMP: 5 **EST:** 2013
SALES (est): 407.2K **Privately Held**
SIC: 2411 Logging

Covesville
Albemarle County

(G-3775)
COVE CREEK INDUSTRIES INC
15 Mi S Of C VII On Us 29 (22931)
P.O. Box 68 (22931-0068)
PHONE................................434 293-6774
G Kevin Napier, *President*
Rhonda Napier, *Corp Secy*
E F Wiebolt Jr, *Director*
EMP: 4
SQ FT: 5,000
SALES (est): 350K **Privately Held**
WEB: www.covecreekindustries.com
SIC: 2499 Fencing, wood

Covington
Covington City County

(G-3776)
A & B BAKERY
4420 Johnson Creek Rd (24426-5438)
PHONE................................540 965-5500
Bonnie Barton, *Partner*
Aline Mattox, *Partner*
EMP: 3
SALES (est): 166.6K **Privately Held**
WEB:
www.453062187905966879.weebly.com
SIC: 2051 Bread, cake & related products

(G-3777)
ALLEGHANY PRINTING CO
Also Called: Alleghany Graphic Design Prtg
261 W Main St (24426-1542)
PHONE................................540 965-4246
James Eller, *Owner*
Bayly Dorothy M, *Vice Pres*
EMP: 2 **EST:** 1940
SQ FT: 2,000
SALES (est): 233.3K **Privately Held**
WEB: www.alleghanyprinting.com
SIC: 2752 Commercial printing, offset

(G-3778)
**BENNETT LOGGING & LUMBER
INC**
Also Called: Sawmill
6800 Rich Patch Rd (24426-6532)
PHONE................................540 862-7621
Stephen Bennett, *President*
David A Bennett, *Vice Pres*
Amy R Craft, *Vice Pres*

Drema Bennett, *Treasurer*
Karen C Carpenter, *Admin Sec*
EMP: 42
SALES (est): 6MM **Privately Held**
SIC: 2421 2411 Sawmills & planing mills,
general; logging

(G-3779)
BYER BROTHERS LOGGING INC
Also Called: Byer Bros Excvtg Alleghany Co
620 E Morris Hill Rd (24426-5708)
PHONE................................540 962-3071
Wallace H Byer, *President*
William Byer, *Vice Pres*
EMP: 2
SALES (est): 170K **Privately Held**
SIC: 2411 Logging camps & contractors

(G-3780)
CALLAGHAN MACHINE SHOP
4256 Callaghan Cir (24426-5417)
PHONE................................540 962-4779
Bob Moore, *Owner*
EMP: 1 **Privately Held**
SIC: 3599 Machine shop, jobbing & repair

(G-3781)
CHEM CORE INC
9300 Winterberry Ave (24426-6236)
PHONE................................540 862-2600
Keith Morris, *Principal*
EMP: 1 **EST:** 2017
SALES (est): 47.2K **Privately Held**
WEB: www.chemcore.net
SIC: 2841 Soap & other detergents

(G-3782)
**CHEMTRADE CHEMICALS US
LLC**
714 N Mill Rd (24426-1251)
PHONE................................540 962-6444
Kerry Fletcher, *Manager*
EMP: 2
SALES (corp-wide): 1.1B **Privately Held**
WEB: www.generalchem.com
SIC: 2819 Aluminum sulfate
HQ: Chemtrade Chemicals Us Llc
90 E Halsey Rd
Parsippany NJ 07054

(G-3783)
**CONSTRUCTION MATERIALS
COMPANY**
Also Called: Conrock
820 W Chestnut St (24426)
PHONE................................540 962-2139
Todd McCoy, *Exec VP*
James Coffey, *Manager*
EMP: 5 **Privately Held**
WEB: www.rockinghamredimix.com
SIC: 3273 Ready-mixed concrete
PA: Construction Materials Company
9 Memorial Ln
Lexington VA 24450

(G-3784)
COVINGTON VIRGINIAN INC
Also Called: Virginian Review
128 N Maple Ave (24426-1545)
P.O. Box 271 (24426-0271)
PHONE................................540 962-2121
Mary Ann Beirne, *President*
E Somers Beirne, *Vice Pres*
Beirne Ewell S, *Vice Pres*
Douglas Richard, *City Mgr*
EMP: 24 **EST:** 1914
SQ FT: 19,000
SALES (est): 157K **Privately Held**
WEB: www.thevirginianreview.com
SIC: 2711 Commercial printing & newspa-
per publishing combined

(G-3785)
CREATIVE FABRICATION INC
200 Industrial Ln (24426-6405)
P.O. Box 167 (24426-0167)
PHONE................................540 931-4877
Grayson Comer, *President*
Grayson Comer Jr, *General Mgr*
Fred Barnett, *Engineer*
Jaunice Brumit, *Admin Sec*
EMP: 30
SQ FT: 40,000

SALES (est): 6.5MM **Privately Held**
WEB: www.creatfab.com
SIC: 3443 3441 Fabricated plate work
(boiler shop); fabricated structural metal

(G-3786)
DAVID A BENNETT
6415 Rich Patch Rd (24426-6527)
PHONE................................540 862-5868
David Bennett, *Principal*
David A Bennett, *Principal*
EMP: 2
SALES (est): 260.4K **Privately Held**
SIC: 2411 Logging

(G-3787)
EAGLE AEROSPACE
713 Rose Ave (24426-6357)
PHONE................................540 965-9022
Lawrence Gilbert, *Owner*
EMP: 1
SALES (est): 85.6K **Privately Held**
SIC: 3721 Aircraft

(G-3788)
ERIC TUCKER
Also Called: Logging
2021 Rich Patch Rd (24426-6736)
PHONE................................540 747-5665
Eric Tucker, *Principal*
EMP: 3
SALES (est): 240.2K **Privately Held**
SIC: 2411 Logging

(G-3789)
FORMABLE GRABBER INC
4425 Midland Trl (24426-5422)
PHONE................................434 298-4722
Nicholas Morgan, *Principal*
EMP: 1
SALES (est): 76.4K **Privately Held**
WEB: www.formablegrabber.com
SIC: 3425 Saw blades & handsaws

(G-3790)
GEORGE THOMAS GARTEN
Also Called: Sign Express
201 W Locust St (24426-1558)
PHONE................................540 962-3633
George Thomas Garten, *Owner*
EMP: 3
SALES (est): 242K **Privately Held**
WEB: www.imageexpresscovington.com
SIC: 3993 Signs & advertising specialties

(G-3791)
**INGEVITY VIRGINIA
CORPORATION**
Specialty Chemicals Division
958 E Riverside St (24426-1072)
PHONE................................540 969-3700
John Luke, *CEO*
Cathie Symmes, *Manager*
EMP: 227
SALES (corp-wide): 1.2B **Publicly Held**
WEB: www.ingevity.com
SIC: 2819 Industrial inorganic chemicals
HQ: Virginia Ingevity Corporation
5255 Virginia Ave
North Charleston SC 29406
843 740-2300

(G-3792)
JC BRADLEY LUMBER CO
4500 Indian Draft Rd (24426-5607)
PHONE................................540 962-4446
John Bradley, *Owner*
EMP: 3
SALES (est): 151.1K **Privately Held**
SIC: 2421 5211 Sawmills & planing mills,
general; planing mill products & lumber

(G-3793)
**KEENS WELDING & ALUMINUM
WORKS**
1507 Mountain View Dr (24426-3013)
PHONE................................540 958-9600
EMP: 2
SALES (est): 104.4K **Privately Held**
SIC: 7692 Welding repair

(G-3794)
MAURICE LAMB
Also Called: R & T Woodworking
222 E Parrish St (24426-2635)
PHONE................................540 962-0903
Maurice Lamb, *Owner*
EMP: 1
SALES (est): 30K **Privately Held**
SIC: 2431 2521 Interior & ornamental
woodwork & trim; wood office filing cabi-
nets & bookcases

(G-3795)
ROCKY RIDGE ALPACAS VA LLC
6088 Indian Draft Rd (24426-5621)
PHONE................................540 962-6087
Pamela Thompson, *Principal*
EMP: 2
SALES (est): 97.6K **Privately Held**
SIC: 2231 Alpacas, mohair: woven

(G-3796)
RT DOOR CO LLC
222 E Parrish St (24426-2635)
PHONE................................540 962-0903
Maurice Wayne Lamb,
Jo Lamb,
EMP: 2 **Privately Held**
WEB: www.rtdoors.com
SIC: 2431 Doors, wood

(G-3797)
SMITTYS WELDING
5631 Johnson Creek Rd (24426-5241)
PHONE................................540 962-7550
Warren C Smith, *Owner*
Marlene Smith, *Co-Owner*
EMP: 2
SALES (est): 30K **Privately Held**
SIC: 7692 Welding repair

(G-3798)
SONOCO PRODUCTS COMPANY
9312 Winterberry Ave (24426-6236)
PHONE................................540 862-4135
Fred Richey, *Branch Mgr*
EMP: 30
SALES (corp-wide): 5.3B **Publicly Held**
WEB: www.sonoco.com
SIC: 2631 2655 Paperboard mills; fiber
cans, drums & similar products
PA: Sonoco Products Company
1 N 2nd St
Hartsville SC 29550
843 383-7000

(G-3799)
**STANDARD PRINTING
COMPANY INC**
Also Called: Standard Printing & Office Sup
356 W Main St (24426-1517)
PHONE................................540 965-1150
James N Garcia, *President*
EMP: 10 **EST:** 1940
SQ FT: 5,000
SALES (est): 1.3MM **Privately Held**
SIC: 2752 5943 Commercial printing, off-
set; office forms & supplies

(G-3800)
TAGHLEEF INDUSTRIES INC
Also Called: A E T
901 W Edgemont Dr (24426-2760)
PHONE................................540 962-1200
Joe Howard, *Manager*
EMP: 265 **Privately Held**
WEB: www.ti-films.com
SIC: 3081 Polypropylene film & sheet
HQ: Taghleef Industries Inc.
500 Creek View Rd Ste 301
Newark DE 19711
302 326-5500

(G-3801)
**UNION CHURCH MILLWORKS
INC**
6800 Rich Patch Rd (24426-6532)
PHONE................................540 862-0767
Stephen Bennett, *President*
Amy R Bennett, *Vice Pres*
David A Bennett, *Vice Pres*
Drema C Bennett, *Treasurer*
Karen Carpenter, *Admin Sec*
EMP: 10

GEOGRAPHIC

SALES (est): 1MM **Privately Held**
WEB: www.unionchurchmillworks.com
SIC: 2431 Millwork

(G-3802)
WAYNESBORO ALLOY WORKS INC
Also Called: Woiw
1607 N Alleghany Ave (24426-1066)
PHONE...................540 965-4038
EMP: 2
SALES (corp-wide): 2MM **Privately Held**
SIC: 3441 3599 3444 Structural Metal Fabrication Mfg Industrial Machinery Mfg Sheet Metalwork
PA: Waynesboro Alloy Works, Inc.
51 E Side Hwy
Waynesboro VA
540 949-8092

(G-3803)
WESTROCK MWV LLC
104 E Riverside St (24426-1238)
PHONE...................540 969-5230
EMP: 242
SALES (corp-wide): 17.5B **Publicly Held**
WEB: www.westrock.com
SIC: 2653 Boxes, corrugated: made from purchased materials
HQ: Westrock Mwv, Llc
501 S 5th St
Richmond VA 23219
804 444-1000

(G-3804)
WILLIAMS FABRICATION INC
Also Called: Jenfab
1201 Commerce Center Dr (24426-6351)
PHONE...................540 862-4200
Tony Williams, *President*
Ed Parrish, *Engineer*
Thurston Pam, *Sales Staff*
Amanda Williams, *Admin Sec*
Greg Taylor, *Administration*
EMP: 30
SQ FT: 1,500
SALES (est): 4MM **Privately Held**
WEB: www.williamsfabricationinc.com
SIC: 3444 3599 7692 Sheet metalwork; machine shop, jobbing & repair; welding repair

(G-3805)
WRKCO INC
Also Called: Covington Paperboard Mill
104 E Riverside St (24426-1238)
PHONE...................540 969-5000
Brenda Sickal, *Export Mgr*
Phillip Wright, *Maint Spvr*
Donald McCullough, *Engineer*
Lisa Bowles, *Marketing Staff*
Dan Dickerson, *Marketing Staff*
EMP: 450
SALES (corp-wide): 17.5B **Publicly Held**
WEB: www.ingevity.com
SIC: 2631 2621 2611 Linerboard; paper mills; pulp mills
HQ: Wrkco Inc.
1000 Abernathy Rd Ste 12
Atlanta GA 30328
770 448-2193

Craigsville
Augusta County

(G-3806)
HILLTOP HIDEAWAY ALPACAS LLC
511 Bennetts Springs Ln (24430-2220)
PHONE...................954 410-7238
Elaine Simpson, *Principal*
EMP: 2 EST: 2016
SALES (est): 115K **Privately Held**
WEB: www.hilltophideawayalpacas.com
SIC: 2231 Alpacas, mohair: woven

Crewe
Nottoway County

(G-3807)
AUDIO MART
436 Whitmore Town Rd (23930-3728)
PHONE...................434 645-8816
Walter Bender, *Owner*
EMP: 2
SALES (est): 280K **Privately Held**
SIC: 2721 Magazines: publishing only, not printed on site

(G-3808)
BINGHAM ENTERPRISES LLC
610 W Virginia Ave (23930-1115)
PHONE...................434 645-1731
Mikiala Bingham,
Ike Bingham,
EMP: 2
SALES (est): 130.9K **Privately Held**
SIC: 3441 Fabricated structural metal

(G-3809)
BRANDON JENKINS
Also Called: Aplus Networking
512 E Georgia Ave (23930-1516)
PHONE...................434 294-0917
Brandon Jenkins, *Owner*
EMP: 4
SALES (est): 855K **Privately Held**
SIC: 3825 Network analyzers

(G-3810)
CREWE BURKFIELD JOURNAL
Also Called: Crewe Chronicle
107 W Carolina Ave (23930-1803)
P.O. Box 108 (23930-0108)
PHONE...................434 645-7534
Rick Guter, *Owner*
EMP: 6
SALES (est): 165.6K **Privately Held**
SIC: 2711 Newspapers

(G-3811)
D & R PRO TOOLS LLC
683 Namozine Rd (23930-2947)
PHONE...................804 338-1754
David M Pavick, *Administration*
EMP: 2
SALES (est): 131.2K **Privately Held**
SIC: 3599 Industrial machinery

(G-3812)
E H PUBLISHING COMPANY IN
105 Guy Ave (23930-1301)
P.O. Box 108 (23930-0108)
PHONE...................434 645-1722
EMP: 1
SALES (est): 37.5K **Privately Held**
SIC: 2741 Miscellaneous publishing

(G-3813)
ITS MANUFACTURING INCORPORATED
1918 W Virginia Ave (23930-1032)
PHONE...................804 397-0504
Trace Shook, *Principal*
Tonya Mallory, *Principal*
EMP: 3 EST: 2014
SALES (est): 720.6K **Privately Held**
WEB: www.itsmachinemfg.com
SIC: 3541 Machine tools, metal cutting type

(G-3814)
M & S PUBLISHING CO INC
Also Called: Crewe Burkville Jounal
107 W Carolina Ave (23930-1803)
P.O. Box 108 (23930-0108)
PHONE...................434 645-7534
Rick Guter, *President*
Eanes Richard J, *Vice Pres*
EMP: 5
SALES (est): 375.5K **Privately Held**
WEB: www.creweburkevillechamber.com
SIC: 2711 2752 Commercial printing & newspaper publishing combined; commercial printing, lithographic

(G-3815)
S & D ADKINS LOGGING LLC
949 Piney Green Rd (23930-3109)
PHONE...................434 292-8882
Scott Adkins, *Principal*
EMP: 3 EST: 2014
SALES (est): 306.8K **Privately Held**
SIC: 2411 Logging camps & contractors

(G-3816)
SEJ PROPERTY LOGISTICS CO
310 Park Ave (23930-1432)
PHONE...................516 499-2549
Jermane Artwell, *CEO*
EMP: 5
SALES (est): 221K **Privately Held**
SIC: 1389 1521 1721 0782 Construction, repair & dismantling services; general remodeling, single-family houses; interior residential painting contractor; landscape contractors; interior decorating

(G-3817)
SHELTON LOGGING INC
2989 The Falls Rd (23930-3928)
PHONE...................434 294-1386
James T Franks, *Principal*
EMP: 3
SALES (est): 165.5K **Privately Held**
SIC: 2411 Logging camps & contractors

(G-3818)
TROUT RIVER LUMBER LLC
2600 Hudson Way (23930-3853)
PHONE...................434 645-2600
Dale Hudson, *General Mgr*
John Barber,
▲ EMP: 37 EST: 1998
SQ FT: 60,000
SALES (est): 7MM **Privately Held**
WEB: www.troutriverlumber.com
SIC: 2491 Flooring, treated wood block

(G-3819)
TYSON FOODS INC
Highway 360 (23930)
PHONE...................434 645-7791
Chuck Moore, *Manager*
Gary George,
EMP: 175
SALES (corp-wide): 43.1B **Publicly Held**
WEB: www.tysonfoods.com
SIC: 2015 Poultry slaughtering & processing
PA: Tyson Foods, Inc.
2200 W Don Tyson Pkwy
Springdale AR 72762
479 290-4000

(G-3820)
VIRGINIA CAROLINA BUILDINGS
210 S Fourth St (23930-2107)
PHONE...................434 645-7411
Eddie Bailey, *President*
Brad Bidgood, *Sales Staff*
Gene Lifsey, *Manager*
EMP: 10
SALES (est): 439.2K **Privately Held**
WEB: www.vacarolinabuildings.com
SIC: 3523 Barn stanchions & standards

Crimora
Augusta County

(G-3821)
HIDEAWAY TANNERY LLC
153 Thorofare Rd (24431-2416)
PHONE...................540 421-2640
Joshua Ribelin, *Principal*
EMP: 2
SALES (est): 105.5K **Privately Held**
SIC: 3111 Leather tanning & finishing

(G-3822)
RACER TEES
1819 East Side Hwy # 101 (24431-2442)
PHONE...................540 416-1320
EMP: 2
SALES (est): 136.6K **Privately Held**
WEB: www.racertees.com
SIC: 2759 Screen printing

Critz
Patrick County

(G-3823)
BH COOPER FARM & MILL INC
1268 Abram Penn Hwy (24082)
P.O. Box 126 (24082-0126)
PHONE...................276 694-6292
Mary S Terry, *Treasurer*
EMP: 1
SALES (est): 35K **Privately Held**
SIC: 3523 Balers, farm: hay, straw, cotton, etc.

(G-3824)
TATUMS CSTM EXHAUST & MET REPR
485 Hardin Reynolds Rd (24082)
PHONE...................276 692-4884
Darian Tatum, *Owner*
EMP: 1
SALES (est): 22.9K **Privately Held**
SIC: 7694 Motor repair services

Crockett
Wythe County

(G-3825)
JAVATEC INC
300 Chaney Branch Rd (24323-3150)
PHONE...................276 621-4572
James A Van Antwerp, *President*
Ivy Van Antwerp, *Corp Secy*
EMP: 3 EST: 1971
SALES (est): 250K **Privately Held**
WEB: www.javatec.net
SIC: 3625 7699 8742 Industrial controls: push button, selector switches, pilot; industrial machinery & equipment repair; business consultant

(G-3826)
S&T INDUSTRIES LLC
215 Scenic Trl (24323-3004)
PHONE...................276 686-4842
Shane McGrady, *Principal*
EMP: 2
SALES (est): 82.5K **Privately Held**
SIC: 3999 Manufacturing industries

Cross Junction
Frederick County

(G-3827)
SHAWNEE CANNING COMPANY INC (PA)
Also Called: Shawnee Springs Market
212 Cross Junction Rd (22625-2324)
P.O. Box 657 (22625-0657)
PHONE...................540 888-3429
Lisa Johnson, *CEO*
William L Whitacre, *President*
Scott Johnson, *General Mgr*
Debbie Ritter, *Vice Pres*
Bob Daniels, *Sales Mgr*
EMP: 6 EST: 1966
SQ FT: 12,000
SALES (est): **Privately Held**
WEB: www.shawneesprings.com
SIC: 2033 0175 0161 Fruits & fruit products in cans, jars, etc.; vegetables & vegetable products in cans, jars, etc.; deciduous tree fruits; vegetables & melons

Crozet
Albemarle County

(G-3828)
ALBEMARLE SIGNS
3921 Browns Gap Tpke (22932-1904)
PHONE...................434 823-1024
John White, *Owner*
Carrie White, *Co-Owner*
EMP: 2
SALES (est): 85K **Privately Held**
SIC: 3993 Signs & advertising specialties

(G-3829)
CO CONSTRUCT LLC
1814 Clay Dr (22932-2880)
PHONE.....................................434 326-0500
Donald Wyatt, *Principal*
Mesha Corey, *Vice Pres*
Gardiner Caroline, *Opers Staff*
David Cox, *Sales Staff*
Jay Scherr, *Sales Staff*
EMP: 1
SALES (est): 179.9K Privately Held
WEB: www.coconstruct.com
SIC: 7372 Application computer software

(G-3830)
CROZET BOPHARMA CONSULTING LLC
1041 Half Mile Branch Rd (22932-3306)
PHONE.....................................703 598-1940
Thomas Monath, *Partner*
Donald Heppner,
EMP: 2 EST: 2017
SALES (est): 78.7K Privately Held
SIC: 2836 Biological products, except diagnostic

(G-3831)
CROZET GAZETTE LLC
1335 Pleasant Green St (22932-3024)
PHONE.....................................434 823-2291
Mike Marshall, *Principal*
EMP: 4
SALES (est): 155.7K Privately Held
WEB: www.crozetgazette.com
SIC: 2711 Newspapers, publishing & printing

(G-3832)
FAT APPLE LLC
387 Grayrock Dr (22932-2866)
PHONE.....................................434 823-2481
EMP: 2
SALES (est): 85.9K Privately Held
SIC: 3571 Mfg Electronic Computers

(G-3833)
GRACE ESTATE WINERY LLC
5281 Mount Juliet Farm (22932-2417)
PHONE.....................................434 823-1486
Linda Clark,
EMP: 3 EST: 2013
SALES (est): 275.6K Privately Held
WEB: www.graceestatewinery.com
SIC: 2084 Wines

(G-3834)
H C SEXTON AND ASSOCIATES
6635 Highlander Way (22932-9722)
PHONE.....................................434 409-1073
Henry C Sexton V, *Principal*
EMP: 1
SALES (est): 231.2K Privately Held
WEB: www.hcsexton.com
SIC: 3553 Cabinet makers' machinery

(G-3835)
HALE MANU INC
1510 Seminole Trl (22932)
PHONE.....................................434 973-5850
EMP: 5
SALES (est): 220K Privately Held
SIC: 2097 Manufactured ice

(G-3836)
HALL WHITE VINEYARDS
5190 Sugar Ridge Rd (22932-2200)
PHONE.....................................434 823-8615
Anthony Champ, *Owner*
Lisa Champ, *Sales Mgr*
EMP: 6
SALES (est): 459.4K Privately Held
WEB: www.whitehallvineyards.com
SIC: 2084 5812 Wines; eating places

(G-3837)
HANDCRAFTERS OF ALBEMARLE LTD
5786 Three Notch D Rd C (22932-3107)
P.O. Box 3 (22932-0003)
PHONE.....................................434 823-4649
James M Webber, *Owner*
EMP: 4 EST: 1975
SQ FT: 6,000

SALES (est): 200K Privately Held
SIC: 2519 Furniture, household: glass, fiberglass & plastic

(G-3838)
HARLEQUIN CUSTOM DATABASES
5193 Three Notch D Rd (22932-3100)
PHONE.....................................434 823-6466
Anthony Potter, *Owner*
EMP: 3
SALES (est): 190K Privately Held
SIC: 7372 7371 Prepackaged software; computer software systems analysis & design, custom

(G-3839)
JR LAMB & SONS
5725 Locust Ln (22932-9314)
PHONE.....................................434 823-2320
Jim Lamb, *Owner*
EMP: 1
SALES (est): 84.2K Privately Held
SIC: 2519 Household furniture

(G-3840)
KING FAMILY VINEYARDS LLC
6550 Roseland Farm (22932-3336)
PHONE.....................................434 823-7800
David King,
▲ EMP: 2
SALES (est): 348.3K Privately Held
WEB: www.kingfamilyvineyards.com
SIC: 2084 Wines

(G-3841)
KWICKSILVER SYSTEMS LLC
5303 Ashlar Ave (22932-1548)
P.O. Box 428, Washington (22747-0428)
PHONE.....................................619 917-1067
EMP: 1
SALES (est): 47.2K Privately Held
WEB: www.kwicksilverusa.com
SIC: 2851 Removers & cleaners

(G-3842)
LETICIA E HELLEBY
1088 Old Trail Dr (22932-3341)
PHONE.....................................336 769-7920
Leticia Helleby, *Principal*
EMP: 1
SALES (est): 65K Privately Held
SIC: 2759 Invitation & stationery printing & engraving

(G-3843)
METALLUM3D LLC
1525 Old Trail Dr (22932-3356)
PHONE.....................................434 409-2401
Nelson Zambrana, *Principal*
EMP: 1
SALES (est): 72.4K Privately Held
SIC: 3569 8711 Assembly machines, non-metalworking; mechanical engineering

(G-3844)
MINT SPRINGS DESIGN
2069 Seal Rdg (22932-2517)
PHONE.....................................434 806-7303
Kim Connolly, *Owner*
EMP: 3
SALES (est): 500K Privately Held
SIC: 2541 Wood partitions & fixtures

(G-3845)
MOUNTFAIR VINEYARDS LLC
4875 Fox Mountain Rd (22932-1729)
PHONE.....................................434 823-7605
Lizzy Kellinger, *General Mgr*
Frederick Repich, *Principal*
EMP: 7
SALES (est): 610K Privately Held
WEB: www.mountfair.com
SIC: 2084 Wines

(G-3846)
PETER HENDERSON OIL CO (PA)
Also Called: Henderson Petroleum
5216 Rose Valley Farm (22932-2617)
P.O. Box 340 (22932-0340)
PHONE.....................................434 823-8608
Elizabeth R Henderson, *Owner*
EMP: 2
SQ FT: 1,500

SALES (est): 513.1K Privately Held
SIC: 1382 Oil & gas exploration services

(G-3847)
PINNELL CL CUSTOM LEATHER
1982 White Hall Rd (22932-2632)
P.O. Box 808 (22932-0805)
PHONE.....................................434 823-9800
Charles L Tinnell, *President*
Virginia Tinnell, *Vice Pres*
EMP: 2
SALES (est): 233.5K Privately Held
WEB: www.pinnellcustomleather.com
SIC: 3199 Leather goods

(G-3848)
PRESS START LLC
132 Grayrock Dr (22932-2864)
PHONE.....................................571 264-1220
Frances Berti, *Principal*
John Thomas, *Mng Member*
EMP: 2
SALES (est): 99K Privately Held
SIC: 2741 Miscellaneous publishing

(G-3849)
R A YANCEY LUMBER CORP
6317 Rockfish Gap Tpke (22932-3334)
P.O. Box 115 (22932-0115)
PHONE.....................................434 823-4107
Ed B Yancey, *President*
Sarah Y May, *Corp Secy*
Sarah Nay, *Corp Secy*
Donnie Rofe, *Vice Pres*
Ennett Yancey, *Vice Pres*
EMP: 55
SQ FT: 2,400
SALES (est): 8.6MM Privately Held
WEB: www.rayanceylumber.com
SIC: 2421 Sawmills & planing mills, general

(G-3850)
SMARTECH MARKETS PUBG LLC
2025 Library Ave Ste 402 (22932-3185)
P.O. Box 432 (22932-0432)
PHONE.....................................434 872-9008
Lawrence Gasman, *Principal*
Missy Wade, *Sales Staff*
EMP: 2 EST: 2012
SALES (est): 134.8K Privately Held
WEB: www.smartechanalysis.com
SIC: 2741 Miscellaneous publishing

(G-3851)
STARR HILL BREWING COMPANY
5391 Three Notch D Rd (22932-3181)
P.O. Box 283 (22932-0283)
PHONE.....................................434 823-5671
Mark Allan Thompson, *President*
Alisha Ames, *Manager*
Allie Hochman, *Technician*
▲ EMP: 3
SQ FT: 10,000
SALES (est): 613.8K Privately Held
WEB: www.starrhill.com
SIC: 2082 Beer (alcoholic beverage)

(G-3852)
THEBOXWORKS
4692 Browns Gap Tpke (22932-1608)
PHONE.....................................434 823-1004
Richard Sorensen, *Owner*
Leni Sorensen, *Engineer*
EMP: 2
SALES (est): 250K Privately Held
SIC: 2434 Wood kitchen cabinets

(G-3853)
UNIQUE CABINETS INC
3705 Browns Gap Tpke (22932-1902)
PHONE.....................................434 823-2188
Barry Easter, *President*
EMP: 2
SALES (est): 268.6K Privately Held
WEB: www.uniquecabinets.com
SIC: 2434 Wood kitchen cabinets

(G-3854)
US JOINER HOLDING COMPANY (PA)
5690 Three Notch D Rd # 200 (22932-3173)
PHONE.....................................434 220-8500
EMP: 6
SALES (est): 13MM Privately Held
SIC: 2531 3499 Public building & related furniture; furniture parts, metal

(G-3855)
WIGWAM INDUSTRIES
4950 Meeks Run (22932-2403)
PHONE.....................................434 823-4663
Gene Meeks, *Owner*
EMP: 2
SALES (est): 139.7K Privately Held
SIC: 3559 Paint making machinery

(G-3856)
WILLIAMSON WOOD
5623 Sugar Ridge Rd (22932-2205)
PHONE.....................................434 823-1882
Fred Williamson, *Owner*
EMP: 1
SALES (est): 123.5K Privately Held
WEB: www.wp.fredwilliamson.com
SIC: 3553 Woodworking machinery

Crozier
Goochland County

(G-3857)
CALLAHAN PAVING PRODUCTS INC
1850 Covington Rd (23039-2331)
PHONE.....................................434 589-9000
Terry Callahan, *President*
Brian Eberhark, *Vice Pres*
EMP: 2
SALES (est): 220.4K Privately Held
SIC: 3444 Concrete forms, sheet metal

(G-3858)
HYGISTICS LLC
1025 Hunters Woods (23039-2431)
P.O. Box 72, Goochland (23063-0072)
PHONE.....................................804 297-1504
Todd Scarola,
EMP: 2
SALES (est): 75.2K Privately Held
WEB: www.hygistics.com
SIC: 7372 Prepackaged software

Crystal Hill
Halifax County

(G-3859)
HUBER ENGINEERED WOODS LLC
1000 Chaney Ln (24539)
P.O. Box 38 (24539-0038)
PHONE.....................................434 476-6628
Jeremy Catron, *Manager*
EMP: 120
SALES (corp-wide): 898.2MM Privately Held
WEB: www.huberwood.com
SIC: 2493 2541 Reconstituted wood products; wood partitions & fixtures
HQ: Huber Engineered Woods Llc
10925 David Taylor Dr # 3
Charlotte NC 28262
800 933-9220

(G-3860)
JM HUBER CORPORATION
1000 Chaney Ln (24539)
P.O. Box 38 (24539-0038)
PHONE.....................................434 476-6628
Shannon Crews, *Maint Spvr*
Richard Holtman, *Branch Mgr*
Matt Staton, *Manager*
Kenny Irby, *Administration*
EMP: 150
SALES (corp-wide): 898.2MM Privately Held
WEB: www.huber.com
SIC: 2819 Industrial inorganic chemicals

GEOGRAPHIC

PA: J.M. Huber Corporation
499 Thornall St Ste 8
Edison NJ 08837
732 549-8600

Culpeper
Culpeper County

(G-3861)
A & A LOGGING LLC
2041 Leon Rd (22701-9169)
PHONE....................540 229-2830
Albert Jenkins, *Administration*
EMP: 2
SALES (est): 89.8K **Privately Held**
SIC: 2411 Logging camps & contractors

(G-3862)
AEROJET ROCKETDYNE INC
7499 Pine Stake Rd Bldg 5 (22701-8963)
PHONE....................540 854-2000
Terry Hall, *Principal*
Nicholas Brown, *Engineer*
Aaron Murphy, *Engineer*
John Sparks, *Engineer*
Vic Squire, *Instructor*
EMP: 151
SALES (corp-wide): 1.9B **Publicly Held**
WEB: www.rocket.com
SIC: 3764 Propulsion units for guided mis-
siles & space vehicles
HQ: Aerojet Rocketdyne, Inc.
2001 Aerojet Rd
Rancho Cordova CA 95742
916 355-4000

(G-3863)
**ALANS APARY HNEY BEES
SVCS LL**
205 S Main St 161 (22701-3113)
PHONE....................540 881-0405
EMP: 1
SALES (est): 63.3K **Privately Held**
SIC: 3999 Beekeepers' supplies

(G-3864)
**ALTERATIONS DONE
AFFORDABLY**
10150 Alum Springs Rd (22701-7001)
P.O. Box 586 (22701-0586)
PHONE....................540 423-2412
EMP: 1
SALES: 5K **Privately Held**
SIC: 3639 Household Appliances, Nec,
Nsk

(G-3865)
AM-CORCOM INC
14115 Lovers Ln Ste 157a (22701-4158)
P.O. Box 111, Elkwood (22718-0111)
PHONE....................540 349-5895
Angus W Macdonald, *President*
Marjorie Macdonald, *Manager*
EMP: 20
SALES (est): 2.2MM **Privately Held**
WEB: www.am-cor.com
SIC: 3441 Building components, structural
steel

(G-3866)
**APPALACHIAN
MANUFACTURING**
16184 Brandy Rd (22701-4622)
PHONE....................540 825-3522
Patty Livesay, *President*
EMP: 15
SQ FT: 20,000
SALES (est): 1.1MM **Privately Held**
SIC: 2391 2591 Draperies, plastic & tex-
tile: from purchased materials; window
shades

(G-3867)
APPLES CLOSET
203 N Main St (22701-2619)
PHONE....................540 825-9551
EMP: 2
SALES (est): 83K **Privately Held**
SIC: 3571 Mfg Electronic Computers

(G-3868)
ARDENT MILLS LLC
1900 Industry Dr (22701-4137)
P.O. Box 1476 (22701-6476)
PHONE....................540 825-1530
Karl Keller, *Prdtn Mgr*
EMP: 35
SALES (corp-wide): 524.6MM **Privately
Held**
WEB: www.ardentmills.com
SIC: 2041 Flour & other grain mill products
PA: Ardent Mills, Llc
1875 Lawrence St Ste 1400
Denver CO 80202
800 851-9618

(G-3869)
**ATLANTIC RESEARCH
CORPORATION**
Also Called: Aerojet
7499 Pine Stake Rd (22701-8963)
PHONE....................540 854-2000
Greg Jones, *Senior VP*
Jim Maser, *Senior VP*
John Schumacher, *Senior VP*
Steve Warren, *Vice Pres*
Diane Robinson, *Research*
EMP: 152
SALES (corp-wide): 3.3B **Publicly Held**
WEB: www.rocket.com
SIC: 3764 3694 3714 3511 Guided mis-
sile & space vehicle engines, research &
devel.; rocket motors, guided missiles;
propulsion units for guided missiles &
space vehicles; automotive electrical
equipment; motor vehicle parts & acces-
sories; turbines & turbine generator sets
HQ: Atlantic Research Corporation
5945 Wellington Rd
Gainesville VA 20155
703 754-5000

(G-3870)
BELMONT FARM DISTILLERY
13490 Cedar Run Rd (22701-7715)
PHONE....................540 825-3207
Chuck Miller, *Owner*
EMP: 2 EST: 2015
SALES (est): 45.9K **Privately Held**
WEB: www.belmontfarmdistillery.com
SIC: 2085 Distilled & blended liquors

(G-3871)
**BELMONT FARMS OF VIRGINIA
INC**
13490 Cedar Run Rd (22701-7715)
PHONE....................540 825-3207
Charles Miller, *President*
Jeanette Miller, *Corp Secy*
EMP: 4
SQ FT: 5,300
SALES (est): 396.8K **Privately Held**
WEB: www.belmontfarmdistillery.com
SIC: 2085 Corn whiskey

(G-3872)
BINGHAM & TAYLOR CORP
Also Called: B&T
601 Nalle Pl (22701)
P.O. Box 939 (22701-0939)
PHONE....................540 825-8334
Paul Perira, *General Mgr*
Brad Washburn, *Sales Mgr*
Brandon Wheeler, *Sales Staff*
EMP: 150
SALES (corp-wide): 51.9MM **Privately
Held**
WEB: www.binghamandtaylor.com
SIC: 3321 5051 Cast iron pipe & fittings;
foundry products
HQ: Bingham & Taylor Corp.
1022 Elm St
Rocky Hill CT 06067
540 825-8334

(G-3873)
BLACK FOREST SIGN INC
15373 Rocky Ridge Ln # 2 (22701-4226)
P.O. Box 703 (22701-0703)
PHONE....................540 825-0017
John Fink, *President*
Geraldine R Fink, *Admin Sec*
EMP: 13
SQ FT: 2,400

SALES (est): 1.3MM **Privately Held**
WEB: www.blackforestsign.com
SIC: 3993 Signs & advertising specialties

(G-3874)
**BLUE RIDGE CHORALE OF
CULPEPER**
754 Germanna Hwy (22701-3802)
P.O. Box 1871 (22701-6855)
PHONE....................540 717-5888
Carolyn Osborne, *Manager*
EMP: 3
SALES (est): 222.7K **Privately Held**
WEB: www.brcsings.com
SIC: 3842 Gynecological supplies & appli-
ances

(G-3875)
**BRANTNER AND ASSOCIATES
INC**
Also Called: Te Connectivity MOG
751 Old Brandy Rd (22701-2866)
PHONE....................540 825-2111
EMP: 3
SALES (corp-wide): 13.3B **Privately Held**
WEB: www.seaconworldwide.com
SIC: 3643 3678 Current-carrying wiring
devices; electronic connectors
HQ: Brantner And Associates, Inc.
1700 Gillespie Way
El Cajon CA 92020
619 562-7070

(G-3876)
BROWN RUSSEL
Also Called: Fabricraft Metal Works
20381 Dove Hill Rd (22701-8128)
PHONE....................540 547-3000
Russel Brown, *Owner*
Chris Brown, *General Mgr*
EMP: 5 **Privately Held**
WEB: www.oncampustsi.com
SIC: 3449 3444 Miscellaneous metalwork;
sheet metalwork

(G-3877)
CALHOUNS HAM HOUSE
Also Called: Tom's Meat Market
211 S East St (22701-3103)
PHONE....................540 825-8319
Tom Calhoun, *Owner*
Tracy Preziosi, *Co-Owner*
EMP: 6
SQ FT: 1,400
SALES (est): 430.1K **Privately Held**
WEB: www.calhounhams.com
SIC: 2011 5421 Meat packing plants; meat
markets, including freezer provisioners

(G-3878)
CANVAS EARTH LLC
403 Lesco Blvd Apt B (22701-1913)
PHONE....................540 522-9373
Kevin Brooks, *Principal*
EMP: 1
SALES (est): 50.4K **Privately Held**
SIC: 2211 Canvas

(G-3879)
**COLEMAN LUMBER CO INC
ROBERT S**
7019 Everona Rd (22701-9051)
PHONE....................540 854-5711
Robert S Coleman Jr, *President*
Sandra W Coleman, *Corp Secy*
James F Coleman, *Vice Pres*
▼ EMP: 39 EST: 1966
SQ FT: 900
SALES (est): 5.7MM **Privately Held**
WEB: www.rscolemanlumber.com
SIC: 2421 Lumber: rough, sawed or
planed; railroad ties, sawed

(G-3880)
**CONTINENTAL AUTO SYSTEMS
INC**
13456 Lovers Ln (22701-4152)
PHONE....................540 825-4100
Jeffrey Scott, *Plant Mgr*
Paul Cobleigh, *Mfg Mgr*
Michael Alves, *Engineer*
Matt Clawson, *Engineer*
Arvind Solanki, *Engineer*
EMP: 250

SALES (corp-wide): 49.2B **Privately Held**
WEB: www.continental-automotive.com
SIC: 3714 3511 3444 Motor vehicle brake
systems & parts; turbines & turbine generator sets; sheet metalwork
HQ: Continental Automotive Systems, Inc.
1 Continental Dr
Auburn Hills MI 48326
248 393-5300

(G-3881)
CONTINENTAL TEVES
13456 Lovers Ln (22701-4152)
PHONE....................540 825-4100
Paul Cobleigh, *Manager*
EMP: 11 EST: 2019
SALES (est): 1.8MM **Privately Held**
SIC: 3714 Motor vehicle parts & acces-
sories

(G-3882)
CUB CADET CULPEPER LLC
11332 James Monroe Hwy (22701-8023)
PHONE....................540 825-8381
EMP: 8
SALES (est): 820K **Privately Held**
SIC: 3524 Mfg Lawn/Garden Equipment

(G-3883)
**CULPEPER COMMERCIAL
PRINTERS**
122 W Spencer St (22701-2628)
PHONE....................540 825-0771
EMP: 1
SALES (est): 37.5K **Privately Held**
SIC: 2741 Miscellaneous publishing

(G-3884)
**CULPEPER FARMERS COOP INC
(PA)**
Also Called: CFC Farm & Home Center
15172 Brandy Rd (22701-2519)
P.O. Box 2002 (22701-6857)
PHONE....................540 825-2200
W A Spillman III, *President*
Richard Beard, *General Mgr*
W Stanley Hawkins, *Corp Secy*
Taylor E Gore, *Exec VP*
Byrd Inskeep, *Vice Pres*
EMP: 67 EST: 1932
SQ FT: 20,000
SALES (est): 33.5MM **Privately Held**
WEB: www.cfcfarmhome.net
SIC: 2048 2041 5191 Prepared feeds;
flour & other grain mill products; fertilizer
& fertilizer materials

(G-3885)
**CULPEPER MACHINE & SUPPLY
CO**
105 N Commerce St (22701-3033)
PHONE....................540 825-4644
Charles Feagan, *President*
Allen Feagan, *Vice Pres*
Valerie Feagan, *Treasurer*
EMP: 6 **Privately Held**
WEB: www.culpepetva.gov
SIC: 3599 Machine shop, jobbing & repair

(G-3886)
**CULPEPER ROANOKE RAPIDS
LLC**
15487 Braggs Corner Rd (22701-2536)
PHONE....................800 817-6215
EMP: 2
SALES (est): 69.3K **Privately Held**
WEB: www.culpeperwood.com
SIC: 2491 Wood preserving

(G-3887)
**CUSTOM FOAM AND CASES
LLC**
2565 Beahm Town Rd (22701-9184)
PHONE....................703 201-5908
Frank Kulesza,
EMP: 4
SALES (est): 168.3K **Privately Held**
SIC: 3086 Plastics foam products

(G-3888)
DATA RESEARCH GROUP CORP
233 E Davis St Ste 400 (22701-2169)
P.O. Box 1597 (22701-6597)
PHONE....................571 350-9590
Edward Burg, *President*

Rodney Larson, *Manager*
Joel Potter, *Technical Staff*
Erik Balderson, *Software Dev*
EMP: 7 Privately Held
WEB: www.datarg.com
SIC: 7372 Business oriented computer software

(G-3889)
DONOVAN PAT RACING ENTERPRISE
17525 Kibler Rd (22701-7641)
PHONE....................540 829-8396
Patrick Donovan, *Owner*
EMP: 3
SALES (est): 210K Privately Held
SIC: 3566 Torque converters, except automotive

(G-3890)
ELEMENT RADIUS LLC
15191 Montanus Dr (22701-1679)
PHONE....................540 229-6366
EMP: 2
SALES (est): 81.8K Privately Held
SIC: 2819 Elements

(G-3891)
FABRITECH
20381 Dove Hill Rd (22701-8128)
PHONE....................540 825-1544
EMP: 1
SALES (est): 56.4K Privately Held
SIC: 3449 Mfg Misc Structural Metalwork

(G-3892)
FINCHAM SIGNS
10255 Rixeyville Rd (22701-7158)
PHONE....................540 937-4634
Sue Fincham, *Owner*
EMP: 2
SALES (est): 74.3K Privately Held
SIC: 3993 Signs & advertising specialties

(G-3893)
GEORGETTE T HAWKINS
Also Called: Twisted Threads and More
12244 Hawkins Ln (22701-5225)
PHONE....................540 825-8928
Georgette Hawkins, *Owner*
EMP: 1 EST: 2007
SALES (est): 38.1K Privately Held
SIC: 2395 Embroidery & art needlework

(G-3894)
GET SOME SOCKS LLC
2180 Cottonwood Ln (22701-4179)
PHONE....................434 466-5054
EMP: 2
SALES (est): 73.4K Privately Held
SIC: 2252 Socks

(G-3895)
INNOVATIVE INDUSTRIES LLC
214 N East St (22701-2738)
PHONE....................540 317-1733
EMP: 1
SALES (est): 51.6K Privately Held
SIC: 3999 Manufacturing industries

(G-3896)
ITTY BITTY STITCHINGS LLC
13396 Chestnut Fork Rd (22701-4827)
PHONE....................540 829-9197
Catherine Hunter, *Principal*
EMP: 1
SALES (est): 36.6K Privately Held
SIC: 2395 Embroidery & art needlework

(G-3897)
JEFFERSON HOMEBUILDERS INC
15487 Braggs Corner Rd (22701-2536)
PHONE....................540 727-2240
Joshua Daniels, *Branch Mgr*
EMP: 70
SQ FT: 6,737
SALES (corp-wide): 72.7MM Privately Held
WEB: www.culpeperwood.com
SIC: 2491 Wood preserving
PA: Jefferson Homebuilders, Inc.
501 N Main St
Culpeper VA 22701
540 825-5898

(G-3898)
JEFFERSON HOMEBUILDERS INC (PA)
Also Called: Culpeper Wood Preservers
501 N Main St (22701-2607)
P.O. Box 1148 (22701-6148)
PHONE....................540 825-5898
Joseph R Daniel, *President*
Doris S Batiste, *Corp Secy*
Thomas Powell O Bannon, *Vice Pres*
Ronald Daniel, *Vice Pres*
B A Kerns, *Vice Pres*
EMP: 125 EST: 1972
SQ FT: 5,000
SALES (est): 72.7MM Privately Held
WEB: www.culpeperwood.com
SIC: 2491 1521 1522 Wood preserving; new construction, single-family houses; apartment building construction

(G-3899)
JEFFERSON HOMEBUILDERS INC
Also Called: Culpeper Wood Preservers
15487 Braggs Corner Rd (22701-2536)
PHONE....................540 825-5200
Jeff Lineberger, *Purchasing*
Joshua Daniels, *Branch Mgr*
EMP: 1
SALES (corp-wide): 72.7MM Privately Held
WEB: www.culpeperwood.com
SIC: 2491 Wood preserving
PA: Jefferson Homebuilders, Inc.
501 N Main St
Culpeper VA 22701
540 825-5898

(G-3900)
JENKINS LOGGING
3183 Meander Run Rd (22701-9156)
PHONE....................540 543-2079
Robert Jenkins, *Owner*
EMP: 1
SALES (est): 250K Privately Held
SIC: 2411 Logging camps & contractors

(G-3901)
JOE LONDON TRAINING LLC
8021 Olympic Way (22701-7259)
PHONE....................540 272-9205
EMP: 2
SALES (est): 118.9K Privately Held
WEB: www.joelondontraining.com
SIC: 3714 Motor vehicle parts & accessories

(G-3902)
JOHNNY SISK & SONS INC
1097 Leon Rd (22701-9188)
PHONE....................540 547-2202
EMP: 10
SALES (est): 1MM Privately Held
SIC: 2411 Logging

(G-3903)
K/R COMPANIES LLC
Also Called: Breeze Auto
19221 Rolling Hills Dr (22701-8342)
PHONE....................540 812-2422
Robin Kruczek, *Mng Member*
Kevin Kruczek,
EMP: 2
SALES (est): 107.1K Privately Held
WEB: www.breezeprinting-dpdesigns.com
SIC: 2754 Commercial printing, gravure

(G-3904)
KASH DESIGN
509 S Main St Ste 121 (22701-3155)
PHONE....................540 317-1473
Kathleen Abella, *Owner*
EMP: 2 EST: 2009
SALES (est): 122.6K Privately Held
WEB: www.kashdesign.com
SIC: 2759 Screen printing

(G-3905)
KEARNEY & ASSOCIATES INC
17477 Stevensburg Rd (22701-4476)
PHONE....................540 423-9511
Patrick Kearney, *President*
EMP: 12
SQ FT: 15,000

SALES (est): 1.3MM Privately Held
WEB: www.kearneyassoc.com
SIC: 2542 2531 Showcases (not refrigerated): except wood; public building & related furniture

(G-3906)
LAMMASU DEFENSE LLC
17476 Safe Haven Way (22701-6924)
PHONE....................540 229-7027
Derek McFarland, *Principal*
EMP: 2
SALES (est): 109.5K Privately Held
WEB: www.lammasudefense.com
SIC: 3812 Defense systems & equipment

(G-3907)
MASCO CABINETRY LLC
641 Maddox Dr (22701-4100)
P.O. Box 1387 (22701-6387)
PHONE....................540 727-7859
Kris Pierce, *Branch Mgr*
EMP: 224
SALES (corp-wide): 1.7B Privately Held
WEB: www.mascocabinetry.com
SIC: 2431 2434 Millwork; wood kitchen cabinets
HQ: Cabinetworks Group Michigan, Llc
4600 Arrowhead Dr
Ann Arbor MI 48105
734 205-4600

(G-3908)
MASSONE INDUSTRIES INC
14131 Inlet Rd (22701-5546)
PHONE....................540 825-7339
Anthony Thomas Mason, *Principal*
EMP: 2
SALES (est): 98.1K Privately Held
SIC: 3999 Manufacturing industries

(G-3909)
MINUTE MAN FARMS INC
18262 Alvere Rd (22701-7502)
PHONE....................540 423-1028
Timothy M Stegmaier, *President*
EMP: 2
SQ FT: 2,086
SALES (est): 392.6K Privately Held
SIC: 2752 Commercial printing, lithographic

(G-3910)
MORTON BUILDINGS INC
18478 Industrial Rd (22701-4148)
PHONE....................540 366-3705
Mike Ryan, *Manager*
EMP: 7
SALES (corp-wide): 558.4MM Privately Held
WEB: www.mortonbuildings.com
SIC: 3448 Prefabricated metal buildings
PA: Morton Buildings, Inc.
252 W Adams St
Morton IL 61550
800 447-7436

(G-3911)
MOUNTAIN RUN WINERY LLC
10753 Mountain Run Lk Rd (22701-8059)
PHONE....................703 638-5559
EMP: 2
SALES (est): 77.6K Privately Held
WEB: www.mountainrunwinery.com
SIC: 2084 Wines

(G-3912)
NORTH RIDGE
12501 Sherwood Forest Dr (22701-1665)
PHONE....................540 825-4275
EMP: 2
SALES (est): 105.7K Privately Held
SIC: 1311 Crude petroleum production

(G-3913)
OLD HOUSE VINEYARDS LLC
18351 Corkys Ln (22701-4413)
PHONE....................540 423-1032
Patrick Kearney,
Allyson Kearney,
EMP: 6 EST: 1998
SQ FT: 4,000
SALES (est): 240K Privately Held
WEB: www.oldhousevineyards.com
SIC: 2084 Wines

(G-3914)
PRECISION MACHINE WORKS INC
19028 Industrial Rd (22701-4149)
PHONE....................540 825-1882
Dewey Leon Fincher, *President*
Fincher Dewey L, *President*
Fincher Dianna B, *Vice Pres*
Daniel Lemelin, *Opers Mgr*
EMP: 18 EST: 1981
SQ FT: 20,000
SALES (est): 3.5MM Privately Held
WEB: www.precisionmachineworks.us
SIC: 3599 Machine shop, jobbing & repair

(G-3915)
RAMONEDA BROTHERS LLC (PA)
8100 Tinsley Pl (22701-9769)
P.O. Box 893 (22701-0893)
PHONE....................540 547-3168
Dick Ramoneda, *Mng Member*
Vincent L Ramoneda,
▼ **EMP: 9**
SALES (est): 600K Privately Held
SIC: 2429 Staves, barrel: sawed or split

(G-3916)
RAMONEDA BROTHERS LLC
13452 Rixeyville Rd (22701-5368)
P.O. Box 893 (22701-0893)
PHONE....................540 825-9166
Vic Ramaneda, *Manager*
EMP: 6
SALES (corp-wide): 600K Privately Held
SIC: 2429 Staves, barrel: sawed or split
PA: Ramoneda Brothers Llc
8100 Tinsley Pl
Culpeper VA 22701
540 547-3168

(G-3917)
RNG LLC
Also Called: Goodnight Jewelers
425 Meadowbrook Ctr (22701)
PHONE....................540 825-5322
EMP: 3
SALES (est): 137.9K Privately Held
SIC: 3911 Mfg Precious Metal Jewelry

(G-3918)
ROCK HILL LUMBER INC
2727 Leon Rd (22701-9119)
PHONE....................540 547-2889
James Sisk, *President*
Mary Lee Sisk, *Corp Secy*
Jason Corey Sisk, *Vice Pres*
Jeremy Sisk, *Vice Pres*
EMP: 29
SQ FT: 5,000
SALES (est): 5.3MM Privately Held
SIC: 2421 2431 2426 Sawmills & planing mills, general; millwork; hardwood dimension & flooring mills

(G-3919)
SHAMROCK SCREEN PRINT LLC
16139 Fox Chase Ln (22701-7318)
PHONE....................540 219-4337
EMP: 2
SALES (est): 87.9K Privately Held
SIC: 2752 Commercial printing, lithographic

(G-3920)
SIGN OF GOLDFISH
601 Germanna Hwy (22701-3800)
PHONE....................540 727-0008
EMP: 1
SALES (est): 52.3K Privately Held
SIC: 3993 Signs & advertising specialties

(G-3921)
SILVER LINING ASSISTANCE INC
Also Called: K&M Lawn Grdn & Arborist Sups
16033 Ira Hoffman Ln (22701-4290)
PHONE....................540 825-8371
David Silverman, *Principal*
Marcia Silverman, *Principal*
EMP: 16

SALES (est): 2.1MM **Privately Held**
SIC: 3524 7699 Lawn & garden tractors &
equipment; lawn & garden mowers & accessories; tractor repair; lawn mower repair shop

(G-3922)
STEEL MATES
16144 Bradford Rd (22701-4234)
PHONE...................................540 825-7333
Rodney Dixon, *Owner*
Amy Dixon, *Owner*
EMP: 2
SALES (est): 51K **Privately Held**
SIC: 7692 Welding repair

(G-3923)
TASTE OIL VINEGAR SPICE INC
122a E Davis St (22701-3012)
PHONE...................................540 825-8415
Janet Davis, *President*
EMP: 6
SALES (est): 500.6K **Privately Held**
WEB: www.tasteovs.com
SIC: 2099 Vinegar

(G-3924)
TE CONNECTIVITY
751 Old Brandy Rd (22701-2866)
PHONE...................................540 812-9126
EMP: 17
SALES (est): 3.6MM **Privately Held**
SIC: 3357 Nonferrous wiredrawing & insu-
lating

(G-3925)
**TLW SELF PUBLISHING
COMPANY**
12318 Osprey Ln (22701-3611)
PHONE...................................540 560-2507
Timothy Walker, *Principal*
EMP: 1
SALES (est): 37.5K **Privately Held**
WEB: www.tlwselfpublishingcompany.com
SIC: 2741 Miscellaneous publishing

(G-3926)
TRIPLE IMAGES INC
108 W Cameron St (22701-3004)
PHONE...................................540 829-1050
Thomas O'Connell, *President*
EMP: 1
SALES (est): 179.1K **Privately Held**
WEB: www.tripleimageva.info
SIC: 2759 Screen printing

(G-3927)
US GREENFIBER LLC
19028 Bleumont Ct (22701-8383)
PHONE...................................540 825-8000
Page Timberlake, *Branch Mgr*
EMP: 75 **Privately Held**
WEB: www.greenfiber.com
SIC: 2679 Building, insulating & packaging
paperboard
PA: Us Greenfiber, Llc
5500 77 Center Dr Ste 100
Charlotte NC 28217

(G-3928)
VENTAJAS PUBLICATIONS LLC
400 Southridge Pkwy (22701-3791)
PHONE...................................540 825-5337
Frances Goddard, *Principal*
EMP: 2 EST: 2009
SALES (est): 112.2K **Privately Held**
WEB: www.socialworkinfo.com
SIC: 2741 Miscellaneous publishing

(G-3929)
WALKER CUSTOM RIFLES
19234 Inglewood Rd (22701-6043)
PHONE...................................540 399-1632
EMP: 2 EST: 2019
SALES (est): 110.9K **Privately Held**
WEB: www.walkercustomrifles.com
SIC: 3069 Fabricated rubber products

(G-3930)
WALKER SAND STONE
19238 Inglewood Rd (22701-6043)
PHONE...................................540 775-5024
EMP: 2
SALES (est): 109.3K **Privately Held**
SIC: 1442 Construction sand & gravel

(G-3931)
WAUGHS LOGGING
5125 Bushy Mountain Rd (22701-9239)
PHONE...................................540 854-5676
John Waugh, *Owner*
EMP: 1 EST: 1984
SALES (est): 117.3K **Privately Held**
SIC: 2411 Logging camps & contractors

(G-3932)
WOOD TELEVISION LLC
Also Called: Culpeper Star Exponent
122 W Spencer St (22701-2628)
P.O. Box 1071 (22701-1071)
PHONE...................................540 825-4416
Cindy Algman, *Manager*
Jennifer Margerum, *Executive*
EMP: 75
SALES (corp-wide): 3B **Publicly Held**
WEB: www.woodtv.com
SIC: 2711 2752 Newspapers, publishing &
printing; commercial printing, lithographic
HQ: Wood Television Llc
120 College Ave Se
Grand Rapids MI 49503
616 456-8888

(G-3933)
XPRESS COPY & GRAPHICS
486 James Madison Hwy (22701-2322)
PHONE...................................540 829-1785
Jonathon James, *Owner*
EMP: 6
SALES (est): 826.6K **Privately Held**
WEB: www.xpress-copy.com
SIC: 2752 Commercial printing, offset

Cumberland
Cumberland County

(G-3934)
A FAMILY HEIRLOOM LLC
17 Booker Rd (23040-2420)
PHONE...................................434 607-1674
Ta'nesha Austin Lewis,
EMP: 2
SALES (est): 74.4K **Privately Held**
SIC: 2844 Hair preparations, including
shampoos

(G-3935)
JOHNNY ASAL LUMBER CO INC
118 Salem Church Rd (23040-2812)
PHONE...................................804 492-4884
Johnny Asal Jr, *President*
David M Asal, *Vice Pres*
EMP: 46 EST: 1960
SALES (est): 2.7MM **Privately Held**
SIC: 2421 5211 2426 Sawmills & planing
mills, general; planing mill products &
lumber; hardwood dimension & flooring
mills

(G-3936)
**MARION BROTHERS LOGGING
INC**
656 Anderson Hwy (23040-2126)
PHONE...................................804 492-3200
Curtis Franklin Marion, *President*
Stephanie Marion, *Administration*
EMP: 40
SALES (est): 1.3MM **Privately Held**
SIC: 2411 Logging camps & contractors

(G-3937)
SUSTAITA LAWN CARE
21 Schalow Rd (23040-2434)
PHONE...................................434 390-8118
Martin Sustaita, *Partner*
EMP: 2
SALES (est): 141.7K **Privately Held**
SIC: 3523 Grounds mowing equipment

Daleville
Botetourt County

(G-3938)
ALTEC INDUSTRIES INC
325 S Center Dr (24083-3031)
PHONE...................................540 992-5300
John Herrig, *Plant Mgr*

Andrew Dorr, *Engineer*
James Downing, *Engineer*
Zak Hilliard, *Engineer*
Chase House, *Engineer*
EMP: 200
SALES (corp-wide): 1.1B **Privately Held**
WEB: www.altec.com
SIC: 3531 3536 Cranes; cranes, overhead
traveling
HQ: Altec Industries, Inc.
210 Inverness Center Dr
Birmingham AL 35242
205 991-7733

(G-3939)
APEX INDUSTRIES INC
325 S Center Dr (24083-3031)
PHONE...................................540 992-5300
EMP: 1 EST: 2011
SALES (est): 41K **Privately Held**
SIC: 3999 Mfg Misc Products

(G-3940)
AUSTIN POWDER COMPANY
1432 Roanoke Rd (24083-2935)
P.O. Box 208 (24083-0208)
PHONE...................................540 992-6097
Jimmy Flinchum, *Principal*
EMP: 12
SALES (corp-wide): 509.6MM **Privately
Held**
WEB: www.austinpowder.com
SIC: 2892 Explosives
HQ: Austin Powder Company
25800 Science Park Dr # 300
Cleveland OH 44122
216 464-2400

(G-3941)
CUNNINGHAM DIGITAL INC
Also Called: Digital Image Printing
1615 Roanoke Rd (24083-2915)
PHONE...................................540 992-2219
Shirley Cunningham, *President*
EMP: 2
SALES (est): 350K **Privately Held**
WEB: www.digitalimageprinting.com
SIC: 2752 Commercial printing, offset

(G-3942)
CUPCAKE COTTAGE LLC
175 Cambridge Dr (24083-3537)
PHONE...................................540 330-8504
EMP: 8
SALES (est): 572.4K **Privately Held**
WEB: www.cupcakecottagesweets.com
SIC: 2051 Bread, cake & related products

(G-3943)
**ELDOR AUTO POWERTRAIN
USA LLC**
888 International Pkwy (24083-3216)
PHONE...................................540 855-1021
Stefano Concezzi, *CEO*
Christopher Atkins, *Buyer*
EMP: 150
SALES (est): 1.1MM **Privately Held**
SIC: 3694 Ignition coils, automotive
HQ: Eldor Corporation Spa
Via Don Paolo Berra 18
Orsenigo CO 22030
031 636-111

(G-3944)
**MOJO CUSTOM SPORTSWEAR
LLC**
1775 Roanoke Rd (24083-2916)
PHONE...................................540 632-2116
Steve Fralin Jr,
EMP: 4 EST: 2010
SALES (est): 422.6K **Privately Held**
WEB: www.mojosports.net
SIC: 2759 Screen printing

(G-3945)
NTELOS INC
1900 Roanoke Rd (24083-3102)
PHONE...................................540 992-2211
Duane Breeden, *Vice Pres*
EMP: 8 **Publicly Held**
WEB: www.ntelos.com
SIC: 7372 Prepackaged software
HQ: Ntelos Inc.
1154 Shenandoah Vlg Dr
Waynesboro VA 22980

Damascus
Washington County

(G-3946)
**COLUMBUS MCKINNON
CORPORATION**
22364 Jeb Stuart Hwy (24236-2504)
PHONE...................................276 475-3124
Richard Davidson, *Branch Mgr*
EMP: 198
SALES (corp-wide): 809.1MM **Publicly
Held**
WEB: www.columbusmckinnon.com
SIC: 3536 Hoists
PA: Columbus Mckinnon Corporation
205 Crosspoint Pkwy
Getzville NY 14068
716 689-5400

(G-3947)
DAMASCUS BREWERY
32173 Government Rd (24236-2611)
PHONE...................................276 475-5319
Adam Woodson, *Manager*
EMP: 2
SALES (est): 68.6K **Privately Held**
WEB: www.thedamascusbrewery.com
SIC: 2082 Malt beverages

(G-3948)
GARRETT CORPORATION
23215 Fisher Hollow Rd (24236)
P.O. Box 307 (24236-0307)
PHONE...................................276 475-3652
John Garrett, *Principal*
EMP: 5
SALES (est): 396.6K **Privately Held**
SIC: 3272 Monuments, concrete

(G-3949)
MILLIE B THOMPSON
23047 Bluff Hollow Rd (24236-2022)
PHONE...................................276 475-5940
Millie Thompson, *Principal*
EMP: 3
SALES (est): 238.1K **Privately Held**
WEB: www.eastman.com
SIC: 2821 Plastics materials & resins

(G-3950)
**SPECIAL T MANUFACTURING
CORP**
Also Called: Unique Properties
21250 Mccann Rd (24236-2738)
P.O. Box 187, Meadowview (24361-0187)
PHONE...................................276 475-5510
Bobby Blevins, *President*
EMP: 15 EST: 1997
SQ FT: 9,000
SALES (est): 1.1MM **Privately Held**
WEB: www.specialtmfg.com
SIC: 3677 Transformers power supply,
electronic type

Danville
Danville City County

(G-3951)
4L INC
329 Riverview Dr (24541-3451)
PHONE...................................434 792-0020
Lorraine P Womack, *President*
EMP: 3
SALES (est): 161.2K **Privately Held**
SIC: 2759 Commercial printing

(G-3952)
**A AND J HM IMPRV ANGELA
TOWLER**
208 Gatewood Ave (24541-6304)
PHONE...................................434 429-5087
Angela Towler, *Principal*
EMP: 1
SALES (est): 39.6K **Privately Held**
SIC: 3999 Candles

▲ = Import ▼=Export
◆ =Import/Export

(G-3953)
ALLGOOD PROMOTIONAL CONS
2323 Riverside Dr Ste K (24540-4271)
PHONE..................................434 793-6178
Kathy A Graves, *President*
EMP: 1
SALES (est): 95.9K **Privately Held**
SIC: 3993 Signs, not made in custom sign painting shops

(G-3954)
AMERICAN PHOENIX INC
121 Martha St (24541-6692)
PHONE..................................434 688-0662
Angela Martin, *Plant Mgr*
EMP: 35 **Privately Held**
WEB: www.apimix.net
SIC: 3069 Custom compounding of rubber materials
PA: American Phoenix, Inc.
5500 Wayzata Blvd # 1010
Golden Valley MN 55416

(G-3955)
AN ELECTRONIC INSTRUMENTATION
350 Slayton Ave (24540-5417)
PHONE..................................434 793-4870
Michael Duncan, *Branch Mgr*
EMP: 7
SALES (corp-wide): 71MM **Privately Held**
WEB: www.eit.com
SIC: 3679 Electronic circuits
PA: Electronic Instrumentation And Technology, Llc
309 Kellys Ford Plz Se
Leesburg VA 20175
703 478-0700

(G-3956)
ARISTA TUBES INC
Also Called: Tube Council, The
187 Cane Creek Blvd (24540-5609)
PHONE..................................434 793-0660
Jeremy Paul, *President*
Harish Anand, *Regional Mgr*
Ted Sojourner, *Vice Pres*
Pritam Chavan, *Manager*
Ben Stephens, *Director*
▲ EMP: 50
SQ FT: 150,000
SALES (est): 8.2MM **Privately Held**
WEB: www.esselpropack.com
SIC: 3082 Tubes, unsupported plastic
HQ: Epl Limited
Top Floor, Times Tower, Kamla City,
Mumbai MH 40001

(G-3957)
BGF INDUSTRIES INC (DH)
230 Slayton Ave 1a (24540-5195)
PHONE..................................843 537-3172
Philippe Porcher, *Ch of Bd*
Robby Dunnagan, *President*
Philippe R Dorier, *CFO*
◆ EMP: 75
SALES (est): 275.3MM
SALES (corp-wide): 2.6MM **Privately Held**
WEB: www.bgf.com
SIC: 2221 3624 2241 2295 Glass broadwoven fabrics; fibers, carbon & graphite; glass narrow fabrics; mats, varnished glass
HQ: Nvh Inc.
3802 Robert Porcher Way
Greensboro NC 27410
336 545-0011

(G-3958)
BIDGOOD ENTERPRISES
845 River Ridge Rd (24541-8301)
PHONE..................................434 489-4952
Barkley Bidgood, *President*
Lori Bidgood, *Vice Pres*
EMP: 2
SALES (est): 114.9K **Privately Held**
SIC: 2086 Iced tea & fruit drinks, bottled & canned

(G-3959)
BLUE RIDGE FIBERBOARD INC
Also Called: Celotex
250 Celotex Dr (24541)
PHONE..................................434 797-1321
James Dwyer, *CEO*
Matt Price, *President*
Mark Custer, *Plant Mgr*
Jerry Murrin, *CFO*
Holly Williams, *Sales Staff*
EMP: 70 EST: 2009
SALES (est): 19.7MM **Privately Held**
WEB: www.blueridgefiberboard.com
SIC: 2493 Fiberboard, other vegetable pulp

(G-3960)
BLUE RIDGE LOGGING CO INC
408 Vicar Rd (24540-1211)
PHONE..................................434 836-5663
Noah Wood, *President*
Ann Wood, *Corp Secy*
EMP: 7
SALES (est): 1MM **Privately Held**
SIC: 2411 Logging camps & contractors

(G-3961)
BLUE RIDGE SPRINGS INC
223 Riverview Dr Ste F (24541-3435)
P.O. Box 10254 (24543-5005)
PHONE..................................434 822-0006
Frank Meyer, *President*
EMP: 12 EST: 1994
SALES (est): 1.3MM **Privately Held**
WEB: www.blueridgespringsinc.com
SIC: 2086 Mineral water, carbonated: packaged in cans, bottles, etc.

(G-3962)
BOTTLING GROUP LLC
Also Called: Pepsi Beverages Company
1001 Riverside Dr (24540-4306)
PHONE..................................434 792-4512
Darin Ryding,
EMP: 75
SALES (est): 3.5MM **Privately Held**
SIC: 2086 Carbonated soft drinks, bottled & canned

(G-3963)
BROOKS SIGNS SCREEN PRINTING
101 Ripley Pl (24540-8255)
PHONE..................................434 728-3812
EMP: 2
SALES (est): 83.9K **Privately Held**
SIC: 2752 Commercial printing, lithographic

(G-3964)
CBN SECURE TECHNOLOGIES INC
350 Stinson Dr (24540-5396)
PHONE..................................434 799-9280
Ian Shaw, *President*
Marilou S Robinson, *Vice Pres*
Gordon C McKechnie, *Director*
Kimberly Allen, *Assistant*
EMP: 63
SQ FT: 27,000
SALES (est): 11.6MM
SALES (corp-wide): 306.1MM **Privately Held**
WEB: www.cbnco.com
SIC: 3089 Identification cards, plastic
PA: Canadian Bank Note Company, Limited
145 Richmond Rd
Ottawa ON K1Z 1
613 722-3421

(G-3965)
CHANDLER CONCRETE CO INC
1088 Industrial Ave (24541-3142)
PHONE..................................434 792-1233
James Turney, *Site Mgr*
Ronnie Sowers, *Manager*
EMP: 28
SALES (corp-wide): 50MM **Privately Held**
WEB: www.chandlerconcrete.com
SIC: 3273 Ready-mixed concrete
PA: Chandler Concrete Co., Inc.
1006 S Church St
Burlington NC 27215
336 226-1181

(G-3966)
CHARLES A BLISS JR
Also Called: Stoney Mill
1653 Stony Mill Rd (24540-6915)
PHONE..................................434 685-7311
Charles A Bliss Jr, *Owner*
EMP: 2
SALES (est): 126.7K **Privately Held**
SIC: 2048 Prepared feeds

(G-3967)
CITY OF DANVILLE
Also Called: Danville Wtr Pltion Ctrl Plant
229 Northside Dr (24540-4968)
PHONE..................................434 799-5137
Gary Manville, *Manager*
EMP: 23
SALES (corp-wide): 116.8MM **Privately Held**
WEB: www.danville-va.gov
SIC: 3589 9111 Water treatment equipment, industrial; mayors' offices
PA: City Of Danville
427 Patton St
Danville VA 24541
434 799-5100

(G-3968)
COASTAL WOOD IMPORTS INC
116 Walden Ct (24541-5162)
PHONE..................................434 799-1117
Harte J Whittle, *President*
Michael L Olmstead, *Vice Pres*
▲ EMP: 13
SALES (est): 1.7MM **Privately Held**
SIC: 2493 Reconstituted wood products

(G-3969)
COMMONWEALTH ORTHOTICS & PROST
413 Munt Cross Rd Ste 107 (24540)
PHONE..................................434 836-4736
Nick Argyrakis, *President*
EMP: 4
SALES (est): 284.4K **Privately Held**
SIC: 3842 Orthopedic appliances

(G-3970)
COMMONWLTH ORTHTICS PROSTHETIC
949 Piney Forest Rd Ste 1 (24540-1592)
PHONE..................................434 836-4736
T Nicholas Argyrakis, *President*
EMP: 4
SQ FT: 1,700
SALES (est): 458K **Privately Held**
SIC: 3842 5999 Prosthetic appliances; medical apparatus & supplies

(G-3971)
CONCEPT PRODUCTS INC
Also Called: R & R Service Center
338 Winston Cir (24540-4041)
P.O. Box 10552 (24543-5010)
PHONE..................................434 793-9952
Ronald Pritchett, *President*
▼ EMP: 2
SALES (est): 205.6K **Privately Held**
WEB: www.conceptsproducts.com
SIC: 2842 5531 Automobile polish; automotive parts

(G-3972)
CORNING INCORPORATED
265 Corning Dr (24541-6262)
PHONE..................................434 793-9511
EMP: 48
SALES (corp-wide): 7.8B **Publicly Held**
SIC: 3229 Mfg Pressed/Blown Glass
PA: Corning Incorporated
1 Riverfront Plz
Corning NY 14831
607 974-9000

(G-3973)
CREATIVE VISIONS WOODWORKS
146 Hayes Ct (24541-5510)
PHONE..................................434 822-0182
Alvin Payne, *Principal*
EMP: 2
SALES (est): 165.3K **Privately Held**
SIC: 2431 Millwork

(G-3974)
CUSTOM WOODWORK
1603 Halifax Rd (24540-5813)
PHONE..................................434 489-6991
Tom Allgood, *Owner*
Sam Grubb, *Project Mgr*
EMP: 8
SQ FT: 3,600
SALES (est): 350K **Privately Held**
SIC: 2541 2431 Cabinets, except refrigerated: show, display, etc.: wood; doors, wood

(G-3975)
DANCHEM TECHNOLOGIES INC
1975 Old Richmond Rd (24540-5725)
P.O. Box 400 (24543-0400)
PHONE..................................434 797-8120
John Zuppo, *President*
Kaushik Vashee, *Vice Pres*
Don Rowland, *QC Mgr*
George Austin LI, *VP Sales*
▲ EMP: 126
SQ FT: 136,000
SALES (est): 35.4MM
SALES (corp-wide): 39.6MM **Privately Held**
WEB: www.danchem.com
SIC: 2821 5169 Acrylic resins; industrial chemicals
PA: Edgewater Capital Partners, L.P.
5005 Rockside Rd Ste 840
Independence OH 44131
216 292-3838

(G-3976)
DANNY MARSHALL
1088 Industrial Ave (24541-3142)
PHONE..................................434 797-5861
Daniel Marshall, *Principal*
Danny Marshall, *Executive*
EMP: 4
SALES (est): 270.5K **Privately Held**
WEB: www.dannymarshall.com
SIC: 3089 Organizers for closets, drawers, etc.: plastic

(G-3977)
DANVILLE DENTAL LABORATORY
747 Main St (24541-1803)
PHONE..................................434 793-2225
Gary Haislip, *Principal*
EMP: 2 EST: 1959
SALES (est): 222.1K **Privately Held**
WEB: www.danvillegentledentistry.com
SIC: 3843 Dental equipment & supplies

(G-3978)
DANVILLE DONUTS LLC
111 Sandy Ct Ste C (24541-4175)
PHONE..................................434 835-4592
James G Simmons, *Mng Member*
EMP: 2
SALES (est): 62.3K **Privately Held**
SIC: 2051 Bakery: wholesale or wholesale/retail combined

(G-3979)
DANVILLE READY MIX
503 Wilkerson Rd (24540-0661)
P.O. Box 10368 (24543-5007)
PHONE..................................434 799-5818
Richard Tellitier, *Partner*
EMP: 10 EST: 2008
SALES (est): 1.4MM **Privately Held**
SIC: 3273 Ready-mixed concrete

(G-3980)
DAVCO FABRICATING & WELDING
2035 Woodlake Dr (24540-1489)
PHONE..................................434 836-0234
David Wooten, *Owner*
EMP: 4
SALES (est): 226.8K **Privately Held**
SIC: 3498 3443 Tube fabricating (contract bending & shaping); fabricated plate work (boiler shop)

(G-3981)
DENIM STAX INC
234 N Union St (24541-1030)
PHONE..................................434 429-6663
Debbie Bennett, *Principal*

EMP: 5 **EST:** 2010
SALES (est): 220.2K **Privately Held**
WEB: www.denimstax.storenvy.com
SIC: 2211 Denims

(G-3982)
DGI LINE INC (PA)
306 Updike Pl (24541-3357)
P.O. Box 1198 (24543-1198)
PHONE.................434 797-4114
Gerald Duffie, *President*
Phyllis Crews, *President*
▲ **EMP:** 60
SALES (est): 4.4MM **Privately Held**
WEB: www.dgiline.com
SIC: 2761 Computer forms, manifold or continuous

(G-3983)
DI-MAC OUTDOORS INC
166 Meadowbrook Cir (24541-7300)
PHONE.................434 489-3211
J Henry Sasser Sr, *Principal*
EMP: 2
SALES (est): 142.7K **Privately Held**
SIC: 3993 Signs & advertising specialties

(G-3984)
DIDC LLC
106 Willoughby Pl Apt B (24541-7401)
PHONE.................646 684-5861
Damien Banks,
EMP: 1
SALES (est): 41K **Privately Held**
SIC: 1389 Construction, repair & dismantling services

(G-3985)
DILLION LOGGING
169 Whitmore Dr (24540-6723)
PHONE.................434 685-1779
Allen Dillion, *Partner*
EMP: 2
SALES (est): 160K **Privately Held**
SIC: 2411 Logging camps & contractors

(G-3986)
DRAEGER SAFETY DIAGNOSTICS INC
3401 Westover Dr (24541-5469)
PHONE.................434 822-0820
EMP: 3
SALES (corp-wide): 3B **Privately Held**
WEB: www.draegerinterlock.com
SIC: 3829 Measuring & controlling devices
HQ: Draeger Safety Diagnostics, Inc.
4040 W Royal Ln Ste 136
Irving TX 75063
972 929-1100

(G-3987)
DT ENTERPRISES INC
418 Trade St (24541-3549)
PHONE.................434 799-3153
Debra Taylor, *Administration*
EMP: 1
SALES (est): 74.2K **Privately Held**
WEB: www.custommembroideryinc.com
SIC: 2759 Screen printing

(G-3988)
EBI LLC
745 Kentuck Rd (24540-5560)
PHONE.................434 797-9701
Lukasz Pol, *Opers Mgr*
Karol Michalaski, *Warehouse Mgr*
Stefan Tolwinski, *Purch Mgr*
John Reynolds, *Purchasing*
Pat Meyer, *CFO*
◆ **EMP:** 56
SALES (est): 11.2MM
SALES (corp-wide): 333.4MM **Privately Held**
WEB: www.ebillc.com
SIC: 2512 Upholstered household furniture
PA: Com40 Sp Z O O SpOlka Komandytowa
Ul. Podkocka 4b
Nowe Skalmierzyce 63-46
486 276-2952

(G-3989)
EFLAMELIGHTINGCOM INC
215 Wyndover Dr (24541-5555)
PHONE.................434 822-0632
Gignac Roy G, *President*

EMP: 4
SALES (est): 273.1K **Privately Held**
WEB: www.eflamelighting.com
SIC: 3648 Lighting equipment

(G-3990)
ELECTRONIC DEV LABS INC
Also Called: E D L
244 Oakland Dr (24540-7342)
PHONE.................434 799-0807
Donald N Polsky, *President*
Mary Polsky, *Corp Secy*
Kenneth Sloeneker, *Vice Pres*
Deanna Newton, *Manager*
EMP: 35
SQ FT: 25,000
SALES (est): 6.6MM **Privately Held**
WEB: www.edl-inc.com
SIC: 3823 3544 3826 Pyrometers, industrial process type; special dies, tools, jigs & fixtures; analytical instruments

(G-3991)
ENGINRED BOPHARMACEUTICALS INC
300 Ringgold Indus Pkwy (24540-5548)
PHONE.................860 730-3262
Carl Sahi, *President*
EMP: 2
SALES (est): 148.9K **Privately Held**
WEB: www.engbiopharm.com
SIC: 2834 Vitamin, nutrient & hematinic preparations for human use

(G-3992)
ENTWISTLE COMPANY
1940 Halifax Rd (24540-5820)
P.O. Box 1337 (24543-1337)
PHONE.................434 799-6186
Randy Gibson, *Principal*
Marylou Sullivan, *Technology*
Odelta Carvalho, *Admin Sec*
Diane Couture, *Admin Asst*
EMP: 40
SALES (corp-wide): 40MM **Privately Held**
WEB: www.entwistleco.com
SIC: 3489 3599 7692 3444 Ordnance & accessories; machine shop, jobbing & repair; welding repair; sheet metalwork; fabricated structural metal; missile silos & components, metal plate
HQ: The Entwistle Company
6 Bigelow St
Hudson MA 01749
508 481-4000

(G-3993)
EXCEL PRSTHETICS ORTHOTICS INC
312 S Main St (24541-2926)
PHONE.................434 797-1191
Hank Hinshaw, *Branch Mgr*
EMP: 1
SALES (corp-wide): 3.8MM **Privately Held**
WEB: www.excel-prosthetics.com
SIC: 3842 5999 Limbs, artificial; artificial limbs
PA: Excel Prosthetics & Orthotics, Inc.
115 Albemarle Ave Se
Roanoke VA 24013
540 982-0205

(G-3994)
FARLOW INDUSTRIES
1201 Piney Forest Rd (24540-1503)
PHONE.................434 836-4596
Jimmy Farlow, *CEO*
EMP: 1
SALES (est): 83.3K **Privately Held**
SIC: 3999 Manufacturing industries

(G-3995)
GARYS SIGN SERVICE
221 Franklin Tpke (24540-2057)
PHONE.................434 836-0248
Gary Horsley, *Principal*
EMP: 1
SALES (est): 131K **Privately Held**
SIC: 3993 Signs & advertising specialties

(G-3996)
GAS HOUSE CO
1414 Westover Dr (24541-5110)
PHONE.................434 822-1324

Ralph Walls, *Owner*
EMP: 1
SALES (est): 77.7K **Privately Held**
SIC: 3523 5541 Tractors, farm; filling stations, gasoline

(G-3997)
HARVILLE ENTPS OF DANVILLE VA
Also Called: J & K Screen Printing Company
260 Gilliland Dr (24541-5416)
PHONE.................434 822-2106
John C Harville, *President*
Kathy G Harville, *Treasurer*
EMP: 4
SQ FT: 4,200
SALES (est): 100K **Privately Held**
WEB: www.danvilleva.gov
SIC: 2759 2395 3993 2752 Screen printing; embroidery & art needlework; signs & advertising specialties; commercial printing, lithographic; automotive & apparel trimmings

(G-3998)
HUDSONS WELDING SHOP
1757 Westover Dr (24541-5044)
PHONE.................434 822-1452
Milton Hudson, *Owner*
EMP: 6
SALES (est): 500K **Privately Held**
WEB: www.hudsonvalleywelding.com
SIC: 7692 3443 Welding repair; tanks, standard or custom fabricated: metal plate

(G-3999)
IDEAL PRINTING LLC
180 Confederate Ave (24541-3202)
PHONE.................434 421-1000
Britney Hunt, *Mng Member*
EMP: 1
SALES (est): 40.9K **Privately Held**
SIC: 2396 Printing & embossing on plastics fabric articles

(G-4000)
INFINITY GLOBAL INC (PA)
501 Bridge St (24541-1405)
PHONE.................434 793-7570
Ronald Palmer, *President*
Sonya Summerfield, *Vice Pres*
Crystal Telfian, *Vice Pres*
Christine Palmer, *Opers Staff*
Dennis Johnson, *Purchasing*
▲ **EMP:** 42
SQ FT: 10,000
SALES (est): 15.8MM **Privately Held**
WEB: www.infinityrp.com
SIC: 2673 Plastic bags: made from purchased materials

(G-4001)
INIFINITY GLOBAL INC
1750 S Main St (24541-4093)
PHONE.................434 793-7570
EMP: 2
SALES (est): 90.7K **Privately Held**
SIC: 2673 Mfg Bags-Plastic/Coated Paper

(G-4002)
INTERTAPE POLYMER CORP
Intertape Polymer Group
1101 Eagle Springs Rd (24540-0631)
P.O. Box 3367 (24543-3367)
PHONE.................434 797-8273
Louis Ethier, *Principal*
EMP: 120
SALES (corp-wide): 1.1B **Privately Held**
WEB: www.itape.com
SIC: 2295 Tape, varnished: plastic & other coated (except magnetic)
HQ: Intertape Polymer Inc
9999 Boul Cavendish Bureau 200
Saint-Laurent QC H4M 2
514 731-7591

(G-4003)
IRFLEX CORPORATION
300 Ringgold Indus Pkwy (24540-5548)
PHONE.................434 483-4304
Francois Chenard, *President*
Robinson Kuis, *Principal*
Helen Gu, *Sales Mgr*
Angela Walker, *Admin Mgr*
David Mahan, *Technician*

EMP: 8
SALES (est): 1.5MM **Privately Held**
WEB: www.irflex.com
SIC: 3357 Fiber optic cable (insulated)

(G-4004)
ITG BRANDS
200 Kentuck Rd (24540-5055)
PHONE.................434 792-0521
Frank Warfield, *Branch Mgr*
EMP: 1
SALES (corp-wide): 40B **Privately Held**
WEB: www.itgbrands.com
SIC: 2111 Cigarettes
HQ: Itg Brands
714 Green Valley Rd
Greensboro NC 27408
336 335-7000

(G-4005)
J B WORSHAM
Also Called: Danville Sign Service
202 Nelson Ave (24540-1512)
PHONE.................434 836-9313
J B Worsham, *Owner*
EMP: 1
SALES (est): 84K **Privately Held**
WEB: www.denisekalacpiano.com
SIC: 3993 Signs, not made in custom sign painting shops

(G-4006)
JARRETT WELDING AND MCH INC (PA)
1212 Goodyear Blvd (24541-2150)
PHONE.................434 793-3717
John Carey, *President*
Jeremy Davis, *Project Mgr*
Kathy Harville, *Bookkeeper*
EMP: 13
SQ FT: 40,000
SALES (est): 2.7MM **Privately Held**
WEB: www.jarrettwelding.com
SIC: 3441 7692 Fabricated structural metal; welding repair

(G-4007)
JTI LEAF SERVICES (US) LLC (DH)
202 Stinson Dr (24540-5065)
PHONE.................434 799-3286
Masamichi Terabatake, *CEO*
Thomas A McCoy, *COO*
Mustafa Genis, *Engineer*
Michael Adkins, *Controller*
Debra Colby, *Human Res Mgr*
◆ **EMP:** 15
SALES (est): 70.2MM **Privately Held**
WEB: www.jti.com
SIC: 2131 Chewing & smoking tobacco
HQ: Jt International Sa
Rue Kazem-Radjavi 8
GenCve GE 1202
227 030-777

(G-4008)
K & A PRINTING
480 Peacock Acres Trl (24541-9648)
PHONE.................716 736-3250
EMP: 2 **EST:** 1996
SALES (est): 120K **Privately Held**
SIC: 2752 Lithographic Commercial Printing

(G-4009)
KANDD TRANSPORTATION SERVICE
3304 U S Highway 29 Ste C (24540-1488)
PHONE.................434 298-7716
Kenneth Ray Hood, *Principal*
EMP: 1
SALES (est): 250K **Privately Held**
SIC: 3715 Semitrailers for missile transportation

(G-4010)
KIRBY OF VA
547 Arnett Blvd (24540-2554)
PHONE.................434 835-4349
EMP: 2
SALES (est): 89K **Privately Held**
SIC: 3599 Mfg Industrial Machinery

(G-4011)
LEONARD ALUM UTLITY BLDNGS INC
1080 Riverside Dr (24540-4307)
PHONE................................434 792-8202
Matt Billion, *Manager*
EMP: 2
SALES (corp-wide): 88.2MM **Privately Held**
WEB: www.leonardusa.com
SIC: 3448 3713 3089 3714 Prefabricated metal buildings; truck tops; molding primary plastic; motor vehicle parts & accessories
PA: Leonard Aluminum Utility Buildings, Inc.
566 Holly Springs Rd
Mount Airy NC 27030
888 590-4769

(G-4012)
LEWIS INDUSTRIES LLC
4587 Horseshoe Rd (24541-9633)
PHONE................................434 203-7920
Zachary Michael Lewis, *Administration*
EMP: 2 EST: 2016
SALES (est): 161.8K **Privately Held**
SIC: 3999 Manufacturing industries

(G-4013)
LILLY LANE INCORPORATED
119 Mall Dr (24540-4069)
PHONE................................434 792-6387
Jacob B Patterson, *President*
EMP: 2 EST: 2016
SALES (est): 170.9K **Privately Held**
SIC: 2335 7299 Wedding gowns & dresses;

(G-4014)
LITEHOUSE INC
145 Cane Creek Blvd (24540-5609)
PHONE................................434 688-3100
Kelly Prior, *Branch Mgr*
EMP: 126
SQ FT: 132,000
SALES (corp-wide): 317.8MM **Privately Held**
WEB: www.litehousefoods.com
SIC: 2099 Food preparations
PA: Litehouse, Inc.
100 Litehouse Dr
Sandpoint ID 83864
208 920-2000

(G-4015)
MARSHALL CON PDTS OF DANVILLE (PA)
1088 Industrial Ave (24541-3142)
PHONE................................434 792-1233
Daniel W Marshall III, *President*
Steven Marshall, *President*
Dan R Canada, *Shareholder*
Nick R Thomas, *Shareholder*
EMP: 55
SQ FT: 3,000
SALES (est): 4.8MM **Privately Held**
WEB: www.danville-va.gov
SIC: 3273 Ready-mixed concrete

(G-4016)
NANOFACTORY CBN INC
350 Stinson Dr (24540-5396)
PHONE................................434 799-9280
Robert Freitas, *CEO*
Ralph Merkle, *President*
EMP: 26
SALES (est): 2.4MM **Privately Held**
SIC: 3761 Guided missiles & space vehicles

(G-4017)
NESTLE PREPARED FOODS COMPANY
Also Called: Nestle Prepared Foods Factory
201 Airside Dr (24540-5616)
PHONE................................434 822-4000
Don Nodtvedt, *Branch Mgr*
Ana Defendini, *Manager*
EMP: 100

SALES (corp-wide): 93.5B **Privately Held**
WEB: www.nestle.com
SIC: 2033 2098 2045 2035 Tomato purees: packaged in cans, jars, etc.; macaroni & spaghetti; prepared flour mixes & doughs; pickles, sauces & salad dressings
HQ: Nestle Prepared Foods Company
30003 Bainbridge Rd
Solon OH 44139
440 248-3600

(G-4018)
OAKES MEMORIALS & SIGNS INC
3676 Franklin Tpke (24540-8206)
PHONE................................434 836-5888
Gary C Oakes, *President*
Gail Oakes, *President*
EMP: 5
SQ FT: 3,000
SALES (est): 493.9K **Privately Held**
WEB: www.oakesmemorialsandsignsinc.com
SIC: 3281 Benches, cut stone; monument or burial stone, cut & shaped

(G-4019)
OLD 97 CHOPPERS
1010 S Boston Rd (24540-4804)
PHONE................................434 799-5400
Judy Purgason, *Principal*
EMP: 2
SALES (est): 88K **Privately Held**
SIC: 3545 Cutting tools for machine tools

(G-4020)
OXYSTRESS THERAPEUTICS LLC
918 Main St (24541-1810)
PHONE................................832 277-0270
Stephen R Wilson, *President*
EMP: 2
SALES (est): 136.4K **Privately Held**
SIC: 2834 Pharmaceutical preparations

(G-4021)
P AND H CASTERS CO INC
255 Stinson Dr (24540-5066)
PHONE................................817 312-1083
EMP: 2
SALES (est): 107.4K **Privately Held**
SIC: 3562 Casters

(G-4022)
P I P PRINTING 1156 INC
Also Called: PIP Printing
329 Riverview Dr (24541-3451)
PHONE................................434 792-0020
Lorraine Womack, *President*
EMP: 5
SALES (est): 693.6K **Privately Held**
SIC: 2752 2791 2789 2759 Commercial printing, offset; typesetting; bookbinding & related work; commercial printing

(G-4023)
PENNY SAVER
642 Worsham St (24540-4706)
PHONE................................434 857-5134
EMP: 3
SALES (est): 129.1K **Privately Held**
WEB: www.pennysaveronline.com
SIC: 2711 Newspapers, publishing & printing

(G-4024)
PEPSI-COLA METRO BTLG CO INC
1001 Riverside Dr (24540-4348)
PHONE................................434 792-4512
Philip Hubbard, *Business Mgr*
James Quesenberry, *Warehouse Mgr*
James Ellington, *Sales/Mktg Mgr*
EMP: 80
SALES (corp-wide): 67.1B **Publicly Held**
WEB: www.pepsico.com
SIC: 2086 Carbonated soft drinks, bottled & canned
HQ: Pepsi-Cola Metropolitan Bottling Company, Inc.
1111 Westchester Ave
White Plains NY 10604
914 767-6000

(G-4025)
PIEDMONT ENVIRONTMENTAL SYS
Also Called: Rainsoft Water Treatment
585 Woodrow Ln (24540-8079)
PHONE................................434 836-4547
Joseph Ray Carper, *President*
Belinda Carper, *Vice Pres*
EMP: 2
SALES (est): 197.8K **Privately Held**
SIC: 3589 Water treatment equipment, industrial

(G-4026)
PIEDMONT PALLET CORPORATION (PA)
2848 Blairmont Dr (24540-6134)
PHONE................................434 836-6730
Jeffrey Criswell, *President*
Jeffrey Scott Criswell, *President*
EMP: 9
SALES (est): 959.2K **Privately Held**
SIC: 2448 Pallets, wood

(G-4027)
PIEDMONT POWDER COATING INC
802 Mangrums Rd (24541-8528)
PHONE................................434 334-8434
Stanley Simpkins, *Principal*
EMP: 2 EST: 2011
SALES (est): 123.9K **Privately Held**
SIC: 3479 Metal coating & allied service

(G-4028)
PIEDMONT PRECISION MCH CO INC (PA)
150 Airside Dr (24540-5613)
P.O. Box 10309 (24543-5006)
PHONE................................434 793-0677
William J Gentry Jr, *President*
Darlene W Gibson, *Corp Secy*
Randy Shackelford, *Vice Pres*
Tammy Hammock, *CFO*
EMP: 80
SQ FT: 65,000
SALES (est): 15.2MM **Privately Held**
WEB: www.ppmmach.com
SIC: 3599 Machine shop, jobbing & repair

(G-4029)
PIEDMONT PRTG & GRAPHICS INC
521 Monroe St (24541-1017)
PHONE................................434 793-0026
Scott Chaney, *President*
EMP: 14 EST: 1989
SQ FT: 5,000
SALES (est): 2.5MM **Privately Held**
WEB: www.piedmontprintingandgraphics.com
SIC: 2759 Commercial printing

(G-4030)
PIEDMONT PUBLISHING INC
3157 Westover Dr (24541-5449)
PHONE................................434 822-1800
Kathy Crumpton, *President*
Alan Lingerfelt, *Vice Pres*
EMP: 12 EST: 2001
SQ FT: 1,200
SALES (est): 1MM **Privately Held**
WEB: www.piedmontshopper.com
SIC: 2721 Periodicals: publishing & printing

(G-4031)
POWERS SIGNS INCORPORATED
807 Industrial Ave (24541-2153)
PHONE................................434 793-6351
Thomas W Powers Sr, *President*
Linda Powers, *Corp Secy*
EMP: 10
SQ FT: 3,900
SALES (est): 912.4K **Privately Held**
WEB: www.powerssigns.com
SIC: 3993 Signs, not made in custom sign painting shops

(G-4032)
PRESERVE RESOURCES INC
901 Industrial Ave (24541-2443)
PHONE................................434 710-8131

Chuck Cooper, *President*
Joyce Standfield, *Director*
EMP: 25
SALES (est): 2.5MM **Privately Held**
WEB: www.preserveresources.com
SIC: 3089 Plastic processing

(G-4033)
PRO PUBLISHERS LLC
1200 Pinecroft Rd (24540-5399)
PHONE................................434 250-6463
William Teiper, *Principal*
EMP: 1
SALES (est): 27.9K **Privately Held**
SIC: 2741 Miscellaneous publishing

(G-4034)
RC TATE WOODWORKS
2876 Westover Dr (24541-5459)
PHONE................................434 822-0035
John Bell, *Owner*
EMP: 1
SALES (est): 88K **Privately Held**
WEB: www.wbyoungco.com
SIC: 2431 Millwork

(G-4035)
RIVERSIDE ROOF TRUSS LLC
733 River Park Dr (24540-5080)
PHONE................................434 793-0217
Keith Walden, *President*
Elizabeth Walden, *Corp Secy*
Tim Knight, *Controller*
Jenna Rudder, *Sales Staff*
Josh Clark, *Sales Associate*
EMP: 70
SALES (est): 11.9MM **Privately Held**
WEB: www.riversiderooftruss.net
SIC: 2439 Trusses, wooden roof

(G-4036)
ROBERT DEITRICH
251 Manor Pl (24541-2632)
PHONE................................804 793-8414
Robert Deitrich, *Administration*
EMP: 2 EST: 2016
SALES (est): 62.9K **Privately Held**
SIC: 2711 Newspapers

(G-4037)
ROUTE 58 RACEWAY INC
2203 S Boston Rd (24540-5532)
PHONE................................434 441-3903
Kirpal Singh, *Principal*
EMP: 6
SALES (est): 573.2K **Privately Held**
SIC: 3644 Raceways

(G-4038)
SETLIFF AND COMPANY LLC
560 Martin Rd (24541-6067)
PHONE................................434 793-1173
Mary Setliff, *Principal*
EMP: 4 EST: 2012
SALES (est): 453.4K **Privately Held**
SIC: 3567 Industrial furnaces & ovens

(G-4039)
TARS INC
3725 U S Highway 29 (24540-1423)
PHONE................................434 836-7890
John Kermit Farmer, *Principal*
EMP: 2
SALES (est): 224.1K **Privately Held**
SIC: 2865 Tar

(G-4040)
TAYLOR COMMUNICATIONS INC
5000 Riverside Dr (24541-5621)
PHONE................................434 822-1111
Kevin Keys, *Branch Mgr*
EMP: 1
SALES (corp-wide): 2.4B **Privately Held**
WEB: www.taylorcorp.com
SIC: 2761 Manifold business forms
HQ: Taylor Communications, Inc.
1725 Roe Crest Dr
North Mankato MN 56003
866 541-0937

(G-4041)
TIMINGWALLSTREET INC
Also Called: Wallstreetwindow
765 Piney Forest Rd (24540-2860)
P.O. Box 11658 (24543-5028)
PHONE................................434 489-2380

(PA)=Parent Co (HQ)=Headquarters (DH)=Div Headquarters
✪ = New Business established in last 2 years

2021 Virginia
Industrial Directory

143

GEOGRAPHIC

Mike Swanson, *Founder*
EMP: 2
SALES (est): 111.9K **Privately Held**
WEB: www.wallstreetwindow.com
SIC: 2741 Miscellaneous publishing

(G-4042)
TRANE US INC
104 Trade St Ste A (24541-3544)
PHONE..................................434 793-4822
Rodney Bryant, *Branch Mgr*
EMP: 5 **Privately Held**
WEB: www.trane.com
SIC: 3585 Refrigeration & heating equipment
HQ: Trane U.S. Inc.
　　3600 Pammel Creek Rd
　　La Crosse WI 54601
　　608 787-2000

(G-4043)
TYTON BIOSCIENCES LLC
Also Called: Tyton Bioenergy Systems
300 Ringgold Indus Pkwy (24540-5548)
PHONE..................................434 793-9100
Peter Majeranowski, *Director*
Sean Su, *Director*
Sue Jones, *Officer*
▲ EMP: 10
SALES (est): 1.8MM **Privately Held**
WEB: www.tytonbio.com
SIC: 2836 Biological products, except diagnostic

(G-4044)
UNARCO INDUSTRIES LLC
255 Stinson Dr (24540-5066)
PHONE..................................434 792-9531
Travis McClanahan, *Branch Mgr*
EMP: 200
SALES (corp-wide): 254.6B **Publicly Held**
WEB: www.unarco.com
SIC: 3496 Woven wire products
HQ: Unarco Industries Llc
　　400 Se 15th St
　　Wagoner OK 74467
　　918 485-9531

(G-4045)
V C ICE AND COLD STORAGE INC
Also Called: Consultant Contractors
333 Montague St (24541-2830)
PHONE..................................434 793-1441
Bud Smith, *President*
EMP: 3 EST: 1928
SALES (est): 156.6K **Privately Held**
SIC: 2097 4222 Manufactured ice; warehousing, cold storage or refrigerated

(G-4046)
VICTORY COACHWAYS
312 Bryant Ave (24540-4824)
PHONE..................................434 799-2569
EMP: 4
SALES (est): 176.4K **Privately Held**
SIC: 2741 Misc Publishing

(G-4047)
VIPLIFE ENT PUBLISHING LLC
1572 Kemper Road Ext (24541-4950)
PHONE..................................434 429-6037
Bricen McLaughlin, *Principal*
EMP: 1
SALES (est): 41.3K **Privately Held**
SIC: 2741 Miscellaneous publishing

(G-4048)
W R MEADOWS INC
250 Celotex Dr (24541)
PHONE..................................434 797-1321
Deborah Meadows, *Branch Mgr*
EMP: 4
SALES (corp-wide): 110.9MM **Privately Held**
WEB: www.wrmeadows.com
SIC: 2891 Adhesives & sealants
PA: W. R. Meadows, Inc.
　　300 Industrial Dr
　　Hampshire IL 60140
　　847 214-2100

(G-4049)
WAL-STAR INC
696 Inman Rd (24541-8048)
PHONE..................................434 685-1094
Dave Wall, *Owner*
Mary Wall, *Corp Secy*
EMP: 10
SQ FT: 8,200
SALES (est): 1.7MM **Privately Held**
WEB: www.wal-star.com
SIC: 3841 Surgical & medical instruments

(G-4050)
WEST GARAGE DOORS INC
1336 College Park Ext (24541-4000)
PHONE..................................434 799-4070
Francis L West II, *President*
EMP: 2
SALES (est): 290.7K **Privately Held**
SIC: 3442 7538 Garage doors, overhead: metal; general automotive repair shops

(G-4051)
WOOD TELEVISION LLC
Also Called: Danville Register & Bee
700 Monument St (24541-1512)
P.O. Box 331 (24543-0331)
PHONE..................................434 793-2311
James Randell, *Accounts Exec*
Winni Fred Grovley, *Manager*
Tony Canody, *Information Mgr*
EMP: 100
SALES (corp-wide): 3B **Publicly Held**
WEB: www.woodtv.com
SIC: 2711 Newspapers, publishing & printing
HQ: Wood Television Llc
　　120 College Ave Se
　　Grand Rapids MI 49503
　　616 456-8888

Dayton
Rockingham County

(G-4052)
BEERY BROTHERS
4840 Witmer Ln (22821-2546)
PHONE..................................540 879-2970
Sidney Beery, *Principal*
EMP: 2 EST: 1998
SALES (est): 194.4K **Privately Held**
SIC: 3523 Farm machinery & equipment

(G-4053)
CARGILL INCORPORATED
135 Huffman Dr (22821)
P.O. Box 158 (22821-0158)
PHONE..................................540 879-2521
Randy Watson, *Manager*
Laura Foltz, *Supervisor*
EMP: 293
SALES (corp-wide): 113.4B **Privately Held**
WEB: www.peterschocolate.com
SIC: 2015 Turkey, processed: fresh; turkey, processed: frozen
PA: Cargill, Incorporated
　　15407 Mcginty Rd W
　　Wayzata MN 55391
　　952 742-7575

(G-4054)
DOG WATCH OF SHENANDOAH
153 Clover Hill Rd (22821-2324)
PHONE..................................540 867-5124
Mark Reisenberg, *Owner*
EMP: 1
SALES (est): 70.7K **Privately Held**
WEB: www.dogwatchbymike.com
SIC: 2399 Pet collars, leashes, etc.: non-leather

(G-4055)
DOGWOOD RIDGE OUTDOORS INC
4253 Woodcock Ln (22821-2418)
PHONE..................................540 867-0764
Kevin Shank, *Principal*
EMP: 3
SALES (est): 283.8K **Privately Held**
WEB: www.naturefriendmagazine.com
SIC: 2721 Magazines: publishing & printing

(G-4056)
JOHN & LLOYD HORST
2667 W Dry River Rd (22821-2617)
PHONE..................................540 867-5655
John W Horst, *Partner*
Lloyd Horst, *Partner*
EMP: 4
SQ FT: 7,000
SALES (est): 314.6K **Privately Held**
WEB: www.journeyresearch.com
SIC: 3599 Machine shop, jobbing & repair

(G-4057)
KNICELY PLAINING MILL LLC
2015 Harness Shop Rd (22821-2749)
PHONE..................................540 879-2284
Lee Knicely,
EMP: 1
SALES (est): 147.7K **Privately Held**
WEB: www.knicelyandassociates.com
SIC: 2426 Turnings, furniture: wood

(G-4058)
NELSON MARTIN
Also Called: DAYTON LUMBER MILL
4826 Linhoss Rd (22821-2048)
PHONE..................................540 879-9016
Nelson Martin, *Owner*
Judith Martin, *Co-Owner*
EMP: 1
SQ FT: 3,000
SALES (est): 209.2K **Privately Held**
WEB: www.singerjewelersmiami.com
SIC: 2421 Sawmills & planing mills, general

(G-4059)
R & K WOODWORKING INC
2629 Shoreshill Rd (22821-2232)
PHONE..................................540 867-5975
Ray Shank, *President*
Isaac Shank, *Vice Pres*
Marsha Shank, *Admin Sec*
EMP: 3
SALES (est): 150K **Privately Held**
WEB: www.rkwood.wixsite.com
SIC: 2434 Wood kitchen cabinets

(G-4060)
REBARSOLUTIONS
3028 John Wayland Hwy (22821-2003)
PHONE..................................540 300-9975
Dale Wenger, *Manager*
William Robinson, *Manager*
EMP: 11
SQ FT: 14,000
SALES (est): 485.5K **Privately Held**
WEB: www.rebarsolutionsva.com
SIC: 3449 Bars, concrete reinforcing: fabricated steel

(G-4061)
ROCKINGHAM WELDING SVC LLC
3054 John Wayland Hwy (22821-2003)
PHONE..................................540 879-9500
Nathan Mathias, *Principal*
EMP: 1
SALES (est): 46.5K **Privately Held**
SIC: 7692 Welding repair

(G-4062)
SCHROCKS REPAIR
3599 Lumber Mill Rd (22821-3043)
PHONE..................................540 879-2406
David Schrock, *Owner*
EMP: 1
SALES (est): 57K **Privately Held**
SIC: 7692 7699 Welding repair; welding equipment repair

(G-4063)
SHICKEL PUBG CO DONNA LOU
5664 Ottobine Rd (22821-2913)
PHONE..................................540 879-3568
Donna Shickel, *Principal*
EMP: 2
SALES (est): 137.9K **Privately Held**
WEB: www.donnalou.com
SIC: 2741 Miscellaneous publishing

(G-4064)
SILVER LAKE WELDING SVC INC
2433 Silver Lake Rd (22821-2041)
PHONE..................................540 879-2591
Fred D Shank Sr, *President*
Fred Shank, *Vice Pres*
Fred D Shank Jr, *Vice Pres*
Dale Hevener, *Manager*
Helen L Shank, *Admin Sec*
EMP: 18
SQ FT: 11,800
SALES (est): 3.2MM **Privately Held**
WEB: www.slwsinc.com
SIC: 3444 3441 Sheet metalwork; fabricated structural metal

(G-4065)
SOUTHFORK ENTERPRISES
2567 Honey Run Rd (22821-2625)
PHONE..................................540 879-4372
Marlan R Showalter, *Partner*
Mariam Showalter, *Partner*
EMP: 2
SALES (est): 50K **Privately Held**
SIC: 7692 Welding repair

(G-4066)
SYCAMORE HOLLOW WELDING
4389 Bowman Rd (22821-2701)
PHONE..................................540 879-2266
Daniel Whitmer, *Owner*
EMP: 4 EST: 2011
SQ FT: 1,800
SALES (est): 144K **Privately Held**
SIC: 7692 Welding repair

(G-4067)
UMA INC
260 Main St (22821-9730)
P.O. Box 100 (22821-0100)
PHONE..................................540 879-2040
Awad Da'mes, *President*
Mu Dmes, *CFO*
Mu Awia Da'mes, *Treasurer*
Sharon Rathbun, *Sales Executive*
EMP: 25 EST: 1936
SQ FT: 7,500
SALES (est): 8.5MM **Privately Held**
WEB: www.umainstruments.com
SIC: 3841 3812 3845 3823 Surgical & medical instruments; aircraft control instruments; electromedical equipment; industrial instrmnts msrmnt display/control process variable; electrical equipment & supplies; machine tool accessories

(G-4068)
VALLEY COML INDUS SVCS LLC
240 Eastview St (22821-9521)
PHONE..................................540 908-1156
Joseph Lillis, *President*
EMP: 11 EST: 2018
SALES (est): 1.1MM **Privately Held**
WEB: www.valleycis.com
SIC: 3471 Sand blasting of metal parts

(G-4069)
VALLEY MEAT PROCESSORS INC
101 Meigs Ln (22821-2007)
PHONE..................................540 879-9041
Stacy Pangle, *President*
EMP: 4
SALES (est): 160K **Privately Held**
SIC: 2011 Meat packing plants

(G-4070)
VALLEY STRUCTURES INC (PA)
Rr 738 (22821)
PHONE..................................540 879-9454
Joe Zimmerman, *President*
Phyllis Zimmerman, *Vice Pres*
EMP: 16
SQ FT: 6,600
SALES (est): 2.9MM **Privately Held**
WEB: www.valleystructures.com
SIC: 2452 Prefabricated buildings, wood

(G-4071)
VISION PUBLISHERS LLC
1418 Hinton Rd (22821-2735)
PHONE..................................540 867-5302
EMP: 1

SALES (est): 56.1K **Privately Held**
SIC: 2741 Miscellaneous publishing

Delaplane
Fauquier County

(G-4072)
ASPEN DALE WINERY BARN
3180 Aspen Dale Ln (20144-2017)
PHONE.....................................540 364-1722
Shay McNeal, *Principal*
EMP: 2
SALES (est): 113.2K **Privately Held**
WEB: www.aspendalewinery.com
SIC: 2084 Wines

(G-4073)
BARREL OAK WINERY LLC
3623 Grove Ln (20144-2226)
PHONE.....................................540 364-6402
Brian Roeder, *Principal*
Sharon Roeder, *Principal*
Adale Henderson, *Director*
Eric Lucas, *Maintence Staff*
▲ EMP: 26
SALES (est): 4.6MM **Privately Held**
WEB: www.barreloak.com
SIC: 2084 Wines

(G-4074)
COBBLER MOUNTAIN CELLARS
5909 Long Fall Ln (20144-2172)
PHONE.....................................540 364-2802
Laura Louden,
Jeff Louden,
EMP: 3
SALES (est): 515.9K **Privately Held**
WEB: www.cobblermountain.com
SIC: 2084 Wines

(G-4075)
DELAPLANE SELLERS
2187 Winchester Rd (20144-1734)
PHONE.....................................540 592-7210
James Dolphin, *Principal*
EMP: 6
SALES (est): 139.2K **Privately Held**
WEB: www.delaplanecellars.com
SIC: 2084 Wines

(G-4076)
KEPPICK LLC KIM
3064 Lost Corner Rd (20144-2230)
PHONE.....................................540 364-3668
Kim Keppick, *Principal*
EMP: 2 EST: 2011
SALES (est): 112.5K **Privately Held**
SIC: 3462 Horseshoes

(G-4077)
**PIEDMONT STATION STUDIO
LLC**
10166 Glmpse Of Heaven Ln
(20144-1859)
PHONE.....................................540 364-4427
Kenneth Charles Rietz II,
EMP: 2 EST: 2010
SALES (est): 99.1K **Privately Held**
SIC: 2511 Wood household furniture

Deltaville
Middlesex County

(G-4078)
**CHESAPEAKE MARINE
RAILWAY**
548 Deagles Rd (23043-2058)
PHONE.....................................804 776-8833
Rick Farinholt, *Principal*
EMP: 3
SALES (est): 434.3K **Privately Held**
WEB: www.chesapeakeboatworks.com
SIC: 3732 Boat building & repairing

(G-4079)
GILLIE BOATWORKS
467 North End Rd (23043-2244)
PHONE.....................................804 370-4825
Thomas Gillie III, *Owner*
EMP: 2

SALES (est): 50K **Privately Held**
WEB: www.gillieboatworks.com
SIC: 3731 Shipbuilding & repairing

(G-4080)
**HARBOR HOUSE LAW PRESS
INC**
17456 General Puller Hwy (23043-2025)
P.O. Box 480, Hartfield (23071-0480)
PHONE.....................................804 776-7605
Pam Wright, *Owner*
Pete Wright, *Officer*
EMP: 5
SALES (est): 515.6K **Privately Held**
WEB: www.harborhouselaw.com
SIC: 2731 8111 Book publishing; legal
services

(G-4081)
HIGH TIDE PUBLICATIONS INC
1000 Bland Point Rd (23043-2283)
PHONE.....................................804 815-6805
Carl Johansen, *President*
EMP: 3
SALES (est): 105.4K **Privately Held**
WEB: www.hightidepublications.com
SIC: 2741 Miscellaneous publishing

(G-4082)
LATELL SAILMAKERS LLC
Also Called: Ullman Sails Virginia
17467 General Puller Hwy (23043-2025)
P.O. Box 297 (23043-0297)
PHONE.....................................804 776-6151
Jerry Latell,
EMP: 4
SQ FT: 3,000
SALES (est): 350K **Privately Held**
WEB: www.latellsails.com
SIC: 2394 Sails: made from purchased
materials

(G-4083)
MICHAEL MCKITTRICK
Also Called: Mikes Mobile Marine
358 Woods Creek Rd (23043-2380)
Rural Route 664 (23043)
PHONE.....................................804 695-7090
Michael McKittrick, *Owner*
EMP: 1 EST: 2015
SALES (est): 71.7K **Privately Held**
SIC: 3732 7389 Motorized boat, building &
repairing; business services

(G-4084)
**MILLERS CUSTOM METAL SVCS
LLC**
154 Hunton Creek Ln (23043-2239)
PHONE.....................................804 712-2588
Joshua Miller,
EMP: 3
SALES (est): 164.3K **Privately Held**
SIC: 3355 7692 Aluminum rail & structural
shapes; welding repair

(G-4085)
QUALITY EQUIPMENT REPAIR
512 Providence Rd (23043-2167)
PHONE.....................................804 815-2268
Robert L Burrell, *Principal*
EMP: 1
SALES (est): 25K **Privately Held**
SIC: 3841 Surgical & medical instruments

(G-4086)
RENDAS
1007 Robins Point Ave (23043-2139)
PHONE.....................................804 776-6215
Renda Kidwell, *Owner*
EMP: 1
SALES (est): 61K **Privately Held**
SIC: 3552 Knitting machines

(G-4087)
WALDENS MARINA INC
Also Called: Walden's Brother Marina
1224 Timberneck Rd (23043-2097)
PHONE.....................................804 776-9440
Mark Plakas, *President*
Chris Plakas, *Vice Pres*
Goldie Coxton, *Treasurer*
EMP: 5 EST: 1947 **Privately Held**
WEB: www.visitmiddlesexva.org
SIC: 3732 5551 4493 Boat kits, not mod-
els; marine supplies; marinas

(G-4088)
WATERWAY GUIDE MEDIA LLC
137 Neptune Ln (23043-2360)
P.O. Box 1125 (23043-1125)
PHONE.....................................804 776-8999
Jefferey Dons, *President*
John Dozier, *President*
Jeffery Jones, *Publisher*
Lisa Suhay, *Editor*
Heather Sadeg, *Sales Mgr*
▲ EMP: 21
SALES (est): 2.3MM **Privately Held**
WEB: www.waterwayguide.com
SIC: 2759 Publication printing

(G-4089)
WAVE RIDER MANUFACTURING
16294 General Puller Hwy (23043-2023)
PHONE.....................................804 654-9427
Richard Hundley, *Owner*
EMP: 6
SALES (est): 265.5K **Privately Held**
SIC: 2221 Fiberglass fabrics

(G-4090)
**ZIMMERMAN MARINE
INCORPORATED**
Also Called: John Deere Authorized Dealer
18691 Gen Puller Hwy (23043-2219)
PHONE.....................................804 776-0367
Adam Sadeg, *Branch Mgr*
EMP: 10
SALES (corp-wide): 3.5MM **Privately
Held**
WEB: www.zimmermanmarine.com
SIC: 3732 5091 Boat building & repairing;
boat accessories & parts
PA: Zimmerman Marine, Incorporated
59 Heron Point Rd
Cardinal VA
804 725-3440

Dendron
Surry County

(G-4091)
WINDSOR SURRY COMPANY
365 Commerce Dr (23839-2214)
PHONE.....................................757 294-0853
Craig Flynn, *President*
▲ EMP: 50
SALES (est): 6.7MM **Privately Held**
WEB: www.windsorone.com
SIC: 2431 Moldings, wood: unfinished &
prefinished

Dewitt
Dinwiddie County

(G-4092)
INDIGO SIGN CO
16189 Glebe Rd (23840-2904)
PHONE.....................................804 469-3233
EMP: 2
SALES (est): 70.2K **Privately Held**
SIC: 3993 Signs & advertising specialties

Diggs
Mathews County

(G-4093)
**OCEAN PRODUCTS RESEARCH
INC (PA)**
19 Butts Ln (23045-2136)
PHONE.....................................804 725-3406
James Monroe Hutson, *President*
Kathleen Powell Hutson, *Corp Secy*
Paul Hutson, *Vice Pres*
Allen Hudgins, *Info Tech Mgr*
EMP: 18
SQ FT: 23,400
SALES (est): 2.2MM **Privately Held**
WEB: www.opr-rope.com
SIC: 2298 5941 5091 Rope, except as-
bestos & wire; fishing equipment; fishing
equipment & supplies

Dillwyn
Buckingham County

(G-4094)
CURTIS WHARAM
Also Called: Wharam's Welding
273 Allens Lake Rd (23936-2010)
PHONE.....................................434 983-3904
Curtis Wharam, *Owner*
EMP: 2
SALES (est): 143.1K **Privately Held**
SIC: 7692 Welding repair

(G-4095)
EMERSON & CLEMENTS OFFICE
1097 Main St (23936-3247)
P.O. Box 171 (23936-0171)
PHONE.....................................434 983-5322
Mattie Clements, *President*
John Clements, *Admin Sec*
EMP: 8 EST: 1946
SALES (est): 720.2K **Privately Held**
SIC: 2611 Pulp mills

(G-4096)
KNABE LOGGING LLC
2072 Gravel Hill Rd (23936-2344)
PHONE.....................................434 547-9878
J Robert Snoddy III, *Administration*
EMP: 7
SALES (est): 144.7K **Privately Held**
SIC: 2411 Logging

(G-4097)
**KYANITE MINING
CORPORATION (PA)**
Also Called: Buffalo Wood Products Div
30 Willis Mtn Plant Ln (23936-3433)
PHONE.....................................434 983-2085
Guy Bishop Dixon, *President*
Joe Jones, *Vice Pres*
Barry Jones, *VP Opers*
Michael Edwards, *Opers Staff*
Kristin Gee, *Human Res Dir*
◆ EMP: 120 EST: 1928
SQ FT: 6,000
SALES (est): 46.6MM **Privately Held**
WEB: www.kyanite.com
SIC: 3295 Minerals, ground or treated

(G-4098)
**PIERCE & JOHNSON LUMBER
CO INC**
19135 N James Madison Hwy
(23936-2911)
P.O. Box 273 (23936-0273)
PHONE.....................................434 983-2586
Timothy W Pierce, *President*
Timothy Pierce, *President*
Foster L Pierce, *Vice Pres*
Helen J Pierce, *Admin Sec*
EMP: 25 **Privately Held**
SIC: 2421 Planing mills

(G-4099)
RANDY HAWTHORNE
Also Called: Mobile Welding & Fabrication
2982 Plank Rd (23936-2896)
PHONE.....................................434 547-3460
Randy Hawthorne, *Owner*
EMP: 1 EST: 2011
SALES (est): 44.6K **Privately Held**
SIC: 3469 Metal stampings

(G-4100)
**SILK TREE MANUFACTURING
INC**
1139 Spencer Rd (23936-2727)
PHONE.....................................434 983-1941
Henry Hagenau, *President*
EMP: 6
SALES (est): 110K **Privately Held**
WEB: www.silktree.com
SIC: 3523 Barn, silo, poultry, dairy & live-
stock machinery

(G-4101)
**STICKMANS WELDING SERVICE
LLC**
7474 Bell Rd (23936-2058)
PHONE.....................................434 547-9774
Daniel F Jamerson, *Administration*

G
E
O
G
R
A
P
H
I
C

EMP: 1 **EST:** 2012
SALES (est): 51K **Privately Held**
SIC: 7692 Welding repair

Disputanta
Prince George County

(G-4102)
35 PRINTING LLC
7069 Gregory Ln (23842-4216)
PHONE..............................804 926-5737
Shawn Goodwyn, *Principal*
EMP: 2
SALES (est): 94.6K **Privately Held**
SIC: 2752 Commercial printing, lithographic

(G-4103)
AG PACK LLC
9700 Robin Rd (23842-7250)
PHONE..............................804 514-9080
Gerhardus Van Rensburg, *Mng Member*
EMP: 5
SALES (est): 139.9K **Privately Held**
SIC: 2048 Prepared feeds

(G-4104)
ANDERSON ERLE P LUMBER COMPANY
15610 James River Dr (23842-8703)
PHONE..............................804 748-0500
Erl Anderson, *President*
Erle P Anderson, *President*
Willie Carter, *Corp Secy*
EMP: 22
SQ FT: 1,400
SALES (est): 2.1MM **Privately Held**
SIC: 2421 2426 Sawmills & planing mills, general; hardwood dimension & flooring mills

(G-4105)
CARTERS PUBLISHING COMPANY LLC
10300 Lamore Dr (23842-4601)
PHONE..............................804 590-4747
La-Tanya E Carter, *Principal*
EMP: 1
SALES (est): 41.3K **Privately Held**
SIC: 2741 Miscellaneous publishing

(G-4106)
DAILY SCRUB LLC
12090 Foxwood Dr (23842-4612)
PHONE..............................804 519-3696
Rachel Chieppa,
EMP: 1
SALES (est): 58.1K **Privately Held**
SIC: 2841 Soap & other detergents

(G-4107)
ERLE D ANDERSON LBR PDTS INC
15610 James River Dr (23842-8703)
PHONE..............................804 748-0500
Erle D Anderson, *President*
▼ **EMP:** 3
SQ FT: 1,400
SALES (est): 260K **Privately Held**
WEB: www.siltfencestakesupplier.com
SIC: 2499 Surveyors' stakes, wood

(G-4108)
HARDWOOD MULCH CORPORATION
15610 James River Dr (23842-8703)
PHONE..............................804 458-7500
Erle D Anderson, *President*
Garland Anderson, *Vice Pres*
Anderson M Garland, *Vice Pres*
EMP: 5
SQ FT: 100
SALES (est): 675.9K **Privately Held**
WEB:
www.hardwoodmulchcorporation.com
SIC: 2499 2421 Mulch, wood & bark; sawmills & planing mills, general

(G-4109)
JA LE CUSTOM CRAFTS
8900 Teakwood Dr (23842-8433)
PHONE..............................804 541-8957
EMP: 8

SALES (est): 440K **Privately Held**
SIC: 2434 Mfg Wood Cabinets

(G-4110)
JESSICA BURDETT
Also Called: Jessica Burdett Ind Conslt
12232 Prince George Dr (23842-4404)
PHONE..............................719 423-0582
Jessica Burdett, *Owner*
EMP: 1
SALES (est): 39.2K **Privately Held**
SIC: 2844 Face creams or lotions

(G-4111)
K O STITH HAULING LLC
6204 Oak Shades Park Dr (23842-4937)
PHONE..............................804 895-4617
Kelly Stith, *Principal*
EMP: 1
SALES (est): 67K **Privately Held**
SIC: 3715 Truck trailers

(G-4112)
LESCO INC
5045 County Dr (23842-4842)
PHONE..............................804 957-5516
Frank Vetter, *Manager*
EMP: 4
SALES (corp-wide): 39.2B **Publicly Held**
SIC: 3523 Spreaders, fertilizer
HQ: Lesco, Inc.
1385 E 36th St
Cleveland OH 44114
216 706-9250

(G-4113)
ROBERT E HORNE
Also Called: Washer Way Pressure Cleaning
10416 Lamore Dr (23842-4603)
PHONE..............................804 920-1847
EMP: 2
SALES: 30K **Privately Held**
SIC: 3589 Service Industry Machinery, Nec, Nsk

(G-4114)
THREE BROTHERS DISTILLERY INC
9935 County Line Rd (23842-7328)
PHONE..............................757 204-1357
David Reavis, *President*
Erica Hibner-Reavis, *Treasurer*
EMP: 2
SALES (est): 120K **Privately Held**
WEB: www.threebrotherswhiskey.com
SIC: 2085 Distilled & blended liquors

DOE Hill
Highland County

(G-4115)
NOEL I HULL
Also Called: Noel Hull Logging
7903 Doe Hill Rd (24433-2306)
PHONE..............................540 396-6225
Noel I Hull, *Owner*
EMP: 1
SALES (est): 107.2K **Privately Held**
SIC: 2411 Pulpwood contractors engaged in cutting

Dolphin
Brunswick County

(G-4116)
MACHINE WELDING PRITCHETT INC
3659 Liberty Rd (23843-2115)
PHONE..............................434 949-7239
James Pritchett, *President*
Linda Pritchett, *Vice Pres*
EMP: 3 **EST:** 1976
SALES (est): 155K **Privately Held**
SIC: 7692 Welding repair

Doran
Tazewell County

(G-4117)
JIF PALLETS LLC
3242 Kents Ridge Rd (24612)
P.O. Box 281 (24612-0281)
PHONE..............................276 963-6107
Judy Fuller, *Owner*
EMP: 5
SALES (est): 494.2K **Privately Held**
WEB: www.jifpallets.com
SIC: 2448 Pallets, wood & wood with metal

Doswell
Hanover County

(G-4118)
CASTLE GLEN ESTTES FRM WNERY L
18185 Narrow Path Trl (23047-1526)
PHONE..............................804 763-9677
Edward Cowdrey, *Principal*
EMP: 7
SQ FT: 2,620
SALES (est): 744.3K **Privately Held**
WEB: www.castleglenwine.com
SIC: 2084 Wines

(G-4119)
DCP HOLDINGS LLC
10351 Verdon Rd (23047-1600)
PHONE..............................804 876-3135
Geoff Baldwin, *President*
EMP: 23 **EST:** 2010
SALES (est): 5.1MM **Privately Held**
SIC: 2671 Bread wrappers, waxed or laminated: purchased material

(G-4120)
DOSWELL WATER TREATMENT PLANT
10076 Kings Dominion Blvd (23047-1915)
PHONE..............................804 876-3557
Jonathan England, *Superintendent*
EMP: 11
SALES (est): 1MM **Privately Held**
SIC: 3589 Water treatment equipment, industrial

(G-4121)
GRIFFIN INDUSTRIES LLC
Also Called: Bakery Feeds
16375 Doswell Park Rd (23047-1802)
P.O. Box 147 (23047-0147)
PHONE..............................804 876-3415
Gray Bradford, *General Mgr*
EMP: 10
SALES (corp-wide): 3.3B **Publicly Held**
WEB: www.griffinind.com
SIC: 2048 Prepared feeds
HQ: Griffin Industries Llc
4221 Alexandria Pike
Cold Spring KY 41076
859 781-2010

(G-4122)
HOUFF CORPORATION
10394 Doswell Rd (23047)
PHONE..............................540 234-9246
Justin Weimar, *Branch Mgr*
EMP: 3
SALES (corp-wide): 30.3MM **Privately Held**
WEB: www.houffcorp.com
SIC: 2873 5191 Nitrogenous fertilizers; farm supplies
HQ: Houff Corporation
97 Railside Dr
Weyers Cave VA 24486
540 234-8088

(G-4123)
METRIE INC
Also Called: Sauder Industries
10134 Kings Dominion Blvd (23047-1919)
PHONE..............................804 876-3588
Richard N McKerracher, *President*
Joe Fleming, *Sales Staff*
Bryce Amthor, *Manager*
Kent Hurley, *Manager*

Justin Struth, *Manager*
EMP: 55
SQ FT: 100,000
SALES (est): 8.1MM **Privately Held**
WEB: www.metrie.com
SIC: 2431 Moldings, wood: unfinished & prefinished

(G-4124)
SC&L OF VIRGINIA LLC
Also Called: Barricade Building Products
10351 Verdon Rd (23047-1600)
P.O. Box 2002 (23047-2002)
PHONE..............................804 876-3135
Geoff Baldwin, *President*
Mike Fields, *Vice Pres*
Dave Johnson, *Vice Pres*
Willam Berry, *CFO*
Bill Pugh, *Sales Mgr*
◆ **EMP:** 100
SQ FT: 250,000
SALES (est): 40.7MM **Privately Held**
WEB: www.barricadebp.com
SIC: 3089 5199 Plastic hardware & building products; packaging materials

(G-4125)
SOUND STRUCTURES VIRGINIA INC
17320 Washington Hwy (23047-1625)
P.O. Box 250 (23047-0250)
PHONE..............................804 876-3014
Eric Jones, *Vice Pres*
Stephen Jones, *Branch Mgr*
EMP: 4
SALES (corp-wide): 3.2MM **Privately Held**
WEB: www.soundstructures.com
SIC: 2491 Flooring, treated wood block
PA: Sound Structures Of Virginia, Inc.
126 S Lynnhaven Rd
Virginia Beach VA 23452
757 498-4448

(G-4126)
STRUCTURAL TECHNOLOGIES LLC
17320 Washington Hwy (23047-1625)
PHONE..............................888 616-0615
N Quercetti, *Manager*
EMP: 16
SALES (corp-wide): 16.6MM **Privately Held**
WEB: www.soundstructures.com
SIC: 2439 Trusses, wooden roof
HQ: Structural Technologies, L.L.C.
126 S Lynnhaven Rd
Virginia Beach VA 23452
757 498-4448

(G-4127)
WEABER INC
10134 Kings Dominion Blvd (23047-1919)
PHONE..............................804 876-3588
EMP: 2
SALES (corp-wide): 161MM **Privately Held**
WEB: www.weaberlumber.com
SIC: 2426 Hardwood dimension & flooring mills
HQ: Weaber, Inc.
1231 Mount Wilson Rd
Lebanon PA 17042
717 867-2212

(G-4128)
WISE MANUFACTURING INC
17182 Washington Hwy (23047-1623)
P.O. Box 90 (23047-0090)
PHONE..............................804 876-3335
Charles H Wise, *President*
EMP: 1
SALES (est): 170.8K **Privately Held**
WEB: www.wisemfginc.com
SIC: 2542 Pallet racks: except wood

(G-4129)
XTERIORS FACTORY OUTLETS INC (PA)
16401 International St (23047-1920)
PHONE..............................804 798-6300
Donald L Hall, *President*
Don Hall, *President*
EMP: 30
SQ FT: 1,000

▲ = Import ▼=Export
◆ =Import/Export

SALES (est): 3.5MM **Privately Held**
SIC: **3271** Blocks, concrete: landscape or retaining wall

Drakes Branch
Charlotte County

(G-4130)
BROWNS FOREST PRODUCTS INC
360 Craftons Gate Hwy (23937)
P.O. Box 362, Charlotte C H (23923-0362)
PHONE...............................434 735-8179
Samuel Brown, *President*
EMP: 11 EST: 1975
SALES (est): 1.8MM **Privately Held**
WEB: www.brownsforestproducts.com
SIC: **2421** Sawmills & planing mills, general

(G-4131)
CHARLOTTE PUBLISHING INC
Also Called: Charlotte Gazette
4789 Drakes Main St (23937-2934)
P.O. Box 214 (23937-0214)
PHONE...............................434 568-3341
Dorothy Tucker, *President*
Otis O Tucker Jr, *Principal*
EMP: 11 EST: 1946
SALES (est): 493.8K **Privately Held**
WEB: www.thecharlottegazette.com
SIC: **2711 2754** Job printing & newspaper publishing combined; job printing, gravure

(G-4132)
CUSTOM RODS & SUCH
4140 Westpoint Stevens Rd (23937-2826)
PHONE...............................434 736-9758
Sandra Lloyd, *Owner*
EMP: 1
SALES (est): 61K **Privately Held**
SIC: **3949** Fishing equipment

(G-4133)
INTERNATIONAL CARBIDE & ENGRG
5000 Drakes Main St (23937-2901)
PHONE...............................434 568-3311
Robert S Ponton, *President*
▲ EMP: 11
SALES (est): 1.4MM **Privately Held**
SIC: **3425 5084 5085 3494** Saw blades & handsaws; industrial machinery & equipment; industrial tools; valves & pipe fittings; abrasive products; synthetic rubber

(G-4134)
JAMES R NAPIER
Also Called: Napiers Extinguisher Sls & Svc
2299 Westpoint Stevens Rd (23937-2841)
PHONE...............................434 547-5511
James Napier, *Owner*
EMP: 1 EST: 2012
SALES (est): 48.5K **Privately Held**
SIC: **3999** Grenades, hand (fire extinguishers)

(G-4135)
JUDY A OBRIEN
Also Called: O'Brien's Supply
104 Bedford St (23937-2910)
PHONE...............................434 568-3148
Judy A O'Brien, *Owner*
EMP: 5 EST: 2005
SALES (est): 381.2K **Privately Held**
WEB: www.obriensk9supply.com
SIC: **2399** Horse & pet accessories, textile

(G-4136)
WAYNE HUDSON
Also Called: Hudson Logging
6900 Craftons Gate Hwy (23937-2849)
PHONE...............................434 568-6361
Wayne Hudson, *Owner*
EMP: 2
SALES (est): 200K **Privately Held**
SIC: **2411** Logging camps & contractors

Draper
Pulaski County

(G-4137)
VALLEY WELDING
2481 Wysor Hwy (24324-2986)
PHONE...............................276 733-7943
EMP: 1
SALES (est): 28.1K **Privately Held**
SIC: **7692** Welding repair

Drewryville
Southampton County

(G-4138)
ROYAL OAK PEANUTS LLC
13009 Cedar View Rd (23844-2001)
PHONE...............................434 658-9500
Stephanie Pope, *President*
Jeffrey Pope, *Vice Pres*
EMP: 1
SALES (est): 150.4K **Privately Held**
WEB: www.hopeandharmonyfarms.com
SIC: **2068** Salted & roasted nuts & seeds

(G-4139)
TC KUSTOMS
7220 Southampton Pkwy (23844-2051)
PHONE...............................434 348-3488
EMP: 4
SALES (est): 22K **Privately Held**
SIC: **3479** Painting of metal products

Dry Fork
Pittsylvania County

(G-4140)
DAVID R POWELL
584 Primitive Baptst Rd W (24549-3006)
PHONE...............................434 724-2642
David Powell, *Principal*
EMP: 2
SALES (est): 168.1K **Privately Held**
SIC: **3531** Backhoes

(G-4141)
ELITE FABRICATION LLC
8380 Franklin Tpke (24549-4909)
PHONE...............................434 251-2639
Christopher Coleman, *Mng Member*
EMP: 6
SALES (est): 788K **Privately Held**
WEB: www.elitefabrication.net
SIC: **3441 1799** Fabricated structural metal; welding on site

(G-4142)
GRAVLEY SAND WORKS
648 Flamingo Rd Fl 2 (24549-3428)
PHONE...............................434 724-7883
Dexter Gravley, *Owner*
EMP: 2
SALES (est): 163.2K **Privately Held**
WEB:
www.gravleysandworu.mfgpages.com
SIC: **1442** Sand mining

(G-4143)
PERFORMANCE CONSULTING INC
7912 Franklin Tpke (24549-4940)
PHONE...............................434 724-2904
Thomas D Ayers, *President*
David Ayers, *President*
Laura Ayers, *Corp Secy*
EMP: 1 EST: 1983
SQ FT: 3,200
SALES (est): 132.3K **Privately Held**
SIC: **3519** Internal combustion engines

Dryden
Lee County

(G-4144)
APPALACHIAN DRONE SERVIE LLC
422 Murphy Hobbs Rd (24243-8394)
PHONE...............................276 346-6350
Richard Hyde,
EMP: 3
SALES (est): 119.4K **Privately Held**
SIC: **3728** Target drones

(G-4145)
MAGNIFIED DUPLICATION PRTG INC
6345 Cave Springs Rd (24243-8257)
PHONE...............................276 393-3193
James G Sexton, *Principal*
EMP: 2 EST: 2016
SALES (est): 92.3K **Privately Held**
SIC: **2752** Commercial printing, lithographic

(G-4146)
STONE MOUNTAIN NATURALS LLC
215 Charles Calton Rd (24243-8345)
PHONE...............................276 415-5880
Latashia Carson, *Principal*
Mahlah Rowles, *Principal*
EMP: 2
SALES (est): 154.3K **Privately Held**
SIC: **2833** Drugs & herbs: grading, grinding & milling

Dublin
Pulaski County

(G-4147)
ALACRAN
5590 Bagging Plant Rd (24084-3490)
PHONE...............................540 629-6095
Ian Heyns, *CEO*
EMP: 3
SALES (corp-wide): 562.8K **Privately Held**
WEB: www.alacraninc.com
SIC: **3482 3559 8742** Small arms ammunition; ammunition & explosives, loading machinery; industrial & labor consulting services
PA: Alacran
2200 Kraft Dr Ste 2150
Blacksburg VA 24060
540 629-6095

(G-4148)
APPALACHIAN MACHINE INC
5304 Laboratory St (24084)
P.O. Box 1507 (24084-1507)
PHONE...............................540 674-1914
Jerry Ellis Jones, *President*
Eddie Farmer, *Vice Pres*
Don Gamblin, *Purch Agent*
Marge Tabor, *Purchasing*
Edgar Lee Farmer, *Treasurer*
▲ EMP: 19
SQ FT: 22,000
SALES (est): 3.6MM **Privately Held**
WEB: www.appalachianmachine.com
SIC: **3599 3441 3534 3444** Machine shop, jobbing & repair; fabricated structural metal; elevators & moving stairways; sheet metalwork

(G-4149)
AW ART LLC
208 Dunbar Ave Apt A (24084-3371)
PHONE...............................540 320-4565
Andrew Williams,
EMP: 1
SALES (est): 45.1K **Privately Held**
SIC: **3952** Canvas board, artists'

(G-4150)
CARDINAL QUARRIES LLC
5764 Wilderness Rd (24084-5641)
PHONE...............................540 674-5556
Mj O'Brien,
EMP: 18

SALES (est): 1MM **Privately Held**
WEB: www.salemstonecorp.com
SIC: **1422 7389** Crushed & broken limestone;

(G-4151)
CHANDLER CONCRETE PRODUCTS OF
5488 Bagging Plant Rd (24084-3400)
PHONE...............................540 674-4667
George Kuhn, *Finance Mgr*
EMP: 6
SALES (corp-wide): 7.2MM **Privately Held**
WEB: www.chandlerconcrete.com
SIC: **3271 3273** Concrete block & brick; ready-mixed concrete
PA: Chandler Concrete Products Of Christianberg Inc
700 Block Ln
Christiansburg VA 24073
540 382-1734

(G-4152)
CHESAPEAKE CARTRIDGE CORP
5366 Wilderness Rd (24084-3912)
PHONE...............................703 989-0903
Kris Dugger, *Officer*
Richmond H Dugger III, *Shareholder*
Kristopher R Dugger, *Shareholder*
EMP: 3
SALES (est): 188.3K **Privately Held**
WEB: www.chescart.com
SIC: **3482** Small arms ammunition

(G-4153)
COUNTRY HOUSE PRINTING
525 Church St (24084-2916)
PHONE...............................540 674-4616
EMP: 2
SALES (est): 199.8K **Privately Held**
SIC: **2752** Commercial printing, offset

(G-4154)
DUBLIN MACHINE INC
Also Called: Grey Wolf Machine Co.
98 Dublin Park Rd (24084-6085)
PHONE...............................540 674-9347
Edgar J Farmer, *President*
Beverly Terry, *Administration*
EMP: 5
SALES (est): 167.6K **Privately Held**
SIC: **3599** Machine shop, jobbing & repair

(G-4155)
ELECTROPLATE - RITE CORP
5529 Lee Hwy (24084-5897)
P.O. Box 160 (24084-0160)
PHONE...............................540 674-9363
John W Dickerson, *Ch of Bd*
Keith Dickerson, *President*
Louise V Dickerson, *Vice Pres*
Regina Morris, *Treasurer*
Ricky Morris, *Sales Staff*
EMP: 60
SQ FT: 35,000
SALES (est): 5.8MM **Privately Held**
WEB: www.electroplate-rite.com
SIC: **3471** Electroplating of metals or formed products

(G-4156)
FONTAINE MODIFICATION COMPANY
5135 Cougar Trail Rd (24084-3844)
PHONE...............................540 674-4638
Paul Kokalis, *Manager*
EMP: 25
SALES (corp-wide): 254.6B **Publicly Held**
WEB: www.fontainemodification.com
SIC: **3713 5013** Truck bodies & parts; truck parts & accessories
HQ: Fontaine Modification Company
9827 Mount Holly Rd
Charlotte NC 28214
704 392-8502

(G-4157)
HEYTEX USA INC
4090 Pepperell Way (24084-3800)
P.O. Box 729, Pulaski (24301-0729)
PHONE...............................540 674-9576
Ted Anderson, *President*

EMP: 25
SALES (corp-wide): 120.6MM **Privately Held**
WEB: www.bondcote.com
SIC: 2295 2297 2211 Coated fabrics, not rubberized; nonwoven fabrics; broadwoven fabric mills, cotton
HQ: Heytex Usa Inc.
　　509 Burgis Ave
　　Pulaski VA 24301

(G-4158)
HOLSTON RIVER QUARRY INC (PA)
Also Called: Salem Stone
5764 Wilderness Rd (24084-5641)
P.O. Box 1620 (24084-1620)
PHONE..................................540 380-5556
M J Obrien, *President*
EMP: 10
SQ FT: 4,200
SALES (est): 30MM **Privately Held**
WEB: www.salemstonecorp.com
SIC: 1422 Crushed & broken limestone

(G-4159)
IMPERIAL GROUP MFG INC
4969 Stepp Pl (24084-3833)
PHONE..................................540 674-1306
Jim Cox, *Branch Mgr*
EMP: 213
SALES (corp-wide): 529.1MM **Privately Held**
WEB: www.ironform.com
SIC: 3715 Trailer bodies
PA: Imperial Group Manufacturing, Inc.
　　4545 Airport Rd
　　Denton TX 76207
　　940 565-8505

(G-4160)
JERRY JOHNSTON
Also Called: Dublin Machine Enterprises
5015 Woodlyn St (24084-4406)
P.O. Box 1194 (24084-1194)
PHONE..................................540 674-0932
Jerry Johnston, *Owner*
EMP: 2
SQ FT: 2,400
SALES (est): 164.6K **Privately Held**
SIC: 3599 Machine shop, jobbing & repair

(G-4161)
KORONA CANDLES INC
3994 Pepperell Way (24084-3837)
PHONE..................................540 208-2440
Agnieszka Fafara, *President*
Traci Short, *Supervisor*
Marcin Hurylski, *Technical Staff*
▼ **EMP:** 200 **EST:** 2013
SQ FT: 165,000
SALES (est): 32MM
SALES (corp-wide): 2.6MM **Privately Held**
WEB: www.korona.info
SIC: 3999 Candles
HQ: Korona Candles Sp Z O O
　　Ul. Fabryczna 10
　　Wielun 98-30

(G-4162)
L H CORPORATION
4945 Stepp Pl (24084-3833)
PHONE..................................540 674-8803
Clemens Von Claparede, *President*
Barbara V Claparede, *Admin Sec*
EMP: 14
SQ FT: 5,500
SALES (est): 1MM **Privately Held**
WEB: www.lhcorp.net
SIC: 3599 Machine shop, jobbing & repair

(G-4163)
LANE ENTERPRISES INC
Also Called: Lane-Dublin Division
Rr 103 (24084)
P.O. Box 1146 (24084-1146)
PHONE..................................540 674-4645
Caroline McGee, *Manager*
EMP: 20

SALES (corp-wide): 68.7MM **Privately Held**
WEB: www.lane-enterprises.com
SIC: 3443 3444 3356 3312 Fabricated plate work (boiler shop); sheet metalwork; nonferrous rolling & drawing; blast furnaces & steel mills
PA: Lane Enterprises, Inc.
　　3905 Hartzdale Dr Ste 514
　　Camp Hill PA 17011
　　717 761-8175

(G-4164)
LIFELINEUSA
4085 Pepperell Way (24084-3810)
PHONE..................................540 251-2724
James Clay, *Principal*
EMP: 2
SALES (est): 163.8K **Privately Held**
SIC: 3714 Motor vehicle parts & accessories

(G-4165)
MAR-BAL INC
5400 Reserve Way (24084-3509)
PHONE..................................540 674-5320
Eric Stump, *Branch Mgr*
EMP: 175
SALES (corp-wide): 72.9MM **Privately Held**
WEB: www.mar-bal.com
SIC: 3089 2821 3699 Molding primary plastic; polyesters; electrical equipment & supplies
PA: Mar-Bal, Inc.
　　10095 Queens Way
　　Chagrin Falls OH 44023
　　440 543-7526

(G-4166)
MORRIS FINISHING CO
444 Church St (24084-2913)
PHONE..................................540 674-0079
Randall Mooris, *Owner*
EMP: 2
SALES (est): 122.3K **Privately Held**
WEB: www.morrisfinishing.com
SIC: 2421 Sawmills & planing mills, general

(G-4167)
NORMAN PRECISION MACHINING LLC
5015 Woodlyn St (24084-4406)
PHONE..................................540 674-0932
Kristofer Norman,
EMP: 1 **EST:** 2018
SALES (est): 51.7K **Privately Held**
SIC: 3599 Machine shop, jobbing & repair

(G-4168)
PHOENIX PACKG OPERATIONS LLC
Also Called: Grupo Phoenix
4800 Lina Ln (24084)
PHONE..................................540 307-4084
Alejandro Rodriguez, *Mfg Dir*
Felicia Fernandez, *Research*
John Mendez, *Project Engr*
Alberto Peisach, *Mng Member*
Nolan Hill, *Manager*
◆ **EMP:** 443
SALES (est): 188.6MM
SALES (corp-wide): 84.3MM **Privately Held**
WEB: www.grupophoenix.com
SIC: 2631 Container, packaging & boxboard
PA: Grupo Phoenix Corporate Services, Llc
　　18851 Ne 29th Ave Ste 601
　　Aventura FL 33180
　　954 241-0023

(G-4169)
PINE GLADE BUILDINGS LLC
4861 Cleburne Blvd (24084-4549)
P.O. Box 1441 (24084-1441)
PHONE..................................540 674-5229
Ray Miller, *Owner*
EMP: 4
SALES (est): 355.2K **Privately Held**
WEB: www.premierstructures.biz
SIC: 2452 Prefabricated wood buildings

(G-4170)
SALEM STONE CORPORATION (PA)
5764 Wilderness Rd (24084-5641)
P.O. Box 1620 (24084-1620)
PHONE..................................540 674-5556
M J O'Brein Jr, *President*
Kulis Kymberlee W, *Corp Secy*
Betsy Cook, *Controller*
EMP: 6
SALES (est): 34MM **Privately Held**
WEB: www.salemstonecorp.com
SIC: 1422 7389 Crushed & broken limestone;

(G-4171)
SISSON & RYAN QUARRY LLC
5764 Wilderness Rd (24084-5641)
P.O. Box 1620 (24084-1620)
PHONE..................................540 674-5556
Gary W Wright,
EMP: 20
SALES (est): 944.5K **Privately Held**
WEB: www.salemstonecorp.com
SIC: 1422 Crushed & broken limestone

(G-4172)
SOUTHSIDE MATERIALS LLC
5764 Wilderness Rd (24084-5641)
P.O. Box 1620 (24084-1620)
PHONE..................................540 674-5556
Mj O'Brien Jr, *Mng Member*
Jamie Collins, *Manager*
EMP: 30
SALES (est): 17.5MM **Privately Held**
WEB: www.salemstonecorp.com
SIC: 1422 Crushed & broken limestone

(G-4173)
VERTICAL INNOVATIONS LLC
5077 State Park Rd (24084-5669)
PHONE..................................540 616-6431
Terrance Dunn, *Principal*
EMP: 1
SALES (est): 129.9K **Privately Held**
SIC: 2591 Blinds vertical

(G-4174)
VOLVO GROUP NORTH AMERICA LLC
Volvo Trucks North America
4881 Cougar Trail Rd (24084-3918)
P.O. Box 1126 (24084-1126)
PHONE..................................336 393-2000
Tony Sims, *General Mgr*
Christopher Annunziato, *Counsel*
Vanessa Henley, *Opers Mgr*
Andrew Colon, *Parts Mgr*
Gilead Biggie, *Engineer*
EMP: 101
SALES (corp-wide): 44.8B **Privately Held**
WEB: www.macktrucks.com
SIC: 3711 3713 3537 Motor trucks, except off-highway, assembly of; truck & bus bodies; industrial trucks & tractors
HQ: Volvo Group North America, Llc
　　7900 National Service Rd
　　Greensboro NC 27409

Duffield
Scott County

(G-4175)
ANDY MEADE
Also Called: Andy's Small Engine Repairs
119 Mullins Dr (24244-2778)
PHONE..................................276 940-3000
Andy Meade, *Owner*
EMP: 1
SALES (est): 40K **Privately Held**
SIC: 3621 Motors & generators

(G-4176)
CHARIS MACHINE LLC
301 Dry Creek Rd (24244-8175)
PHONE..................................276 546-6675
Roger Edens,
EMP: 1
SALES (est): 100K **Privately Held**
SIC: 3541 Machine tools, metal cutting type

(G-4177)
DYNO NOBLE APPALACHIA INC (DH)
Hwy 23 N (24244)
P.O. Box 33 (24244-0033)
PHONE..................................276 940-2201
Cliff Wolford, *President*
EMP: 9
SQ FT: 8,000
SALES (est): 3.8MM **Privately Held**
SIC: 2892 Explosives
HQ: Dyno Nobel Inc.
　　6440 S Millrock Dr # 150
　　Salt Lake City UT 84121
　　801 364-4800

(G-4178)
GIBSON LOGGING ENTERPRISES LLC
185 Colfax Dr (24244-3965)
P.O. Box 103 (24244-0103)
PHONE..................................606 260-1889
Harold J Gibson, *Principal*
EMP: 5 **EST:** 2011
SALES (est): 531.7K **Privately Held**
SIC: 2411 Logging camps & contractors

(G-4179)
JOY GLOBAL UNDERGROUND MIN LLC
811 Boone Trail Rd (24244)
PHONE..................................276 431-2821
Richard Mullins, *Branch Mgr*
EMP: 146
SQ FT: 6,500 **Privately Held**
SIC: 3532 Mining machinery
HQ: Joy Global Underground Mining Llc
　　40 Pennwood Pl
　　Warrendale PA 15086
　　724 779-4500

(G-4180)
KYBO SALES LLC
4812 Boone Trail Rd (24244)
PHONE..................................276 431-2563
Wayne Bishop,
EMP: 1
SALES (est): 182.6K **Privately Held**
SIC: 3315 Steel wire & related products

(G-4181)
LEGACY VULCAN LLC
Dffield Va 24244 Rr 23 (24244)
PHONE..................................276 940-2741
EMP: 3 **Publicly Held**
WEB: www.vulcanmaterials.com
SIC: 3273 Ready-mixed concrete
HQ: Legacy Vulcan, Llc
　　1200 Urban Center Dr
　　Vestavia AL 35242
　　205 298-3000

(G-4182)
N S GILBERT LUMBER LLC
5102 Industrial Dr (24244)
P.O. Box 447 (24244-0447)
PHONE..................................276 431-4488
Keith Inman,
EMP: 78
SALES (est): 6.8MM **Privately Held**
SIC: 2435 Hardwood veneer & plywood

(G-4183)
PAIGE IRECO INC
Rr 23 (24244)
P.O. Box 33 (24244-0033)
PHONE..................................276 940-2201
Dave Pruitt, *President*
Robert Levan, *Vice Pres*
Richard Shea, *Admin Sec*
EMP: 8
SQ FT: 9,000
SALES (est): 667K **Privately Held**
SIC: 2892 Black powder (explosive)
HQ: Dyno Nobel Inc.
　　6440 S Millrock Dr # 150
　　Salt Lake City UT 84121
　　801 364-4800

(G-4184)
ROGERS FOAM CORPORATION
609 Boone Trail Rd (24244)
PHONE..................................276 431-2641
Jason Johnson, *Branch Mgr*
EMP: 2

▲ = Import ▼=Export
◆ =Import/Export

SALES (corp-wide): 233.8MM **Privately Held**
WEB: www.rogersfoam.com
SIC: 3086 Packaging & shipping materials, foamed plastic
PA: Rogers Foam Corporation
20 Vernon St Ste 1
Somerville MA 02145
617 623-3010

(G-4185)
TEMPUR PRODUCTION USA LLC (DH)
203 Tempur Pedic Dr # 102 (24244-5321)
P.O. Box 102 (24244-0102)
PHONE..................................276 431-7150
Robert Trussell Jr, *President*
Tom Bryant, *President*
William H Poche, *Corp Secy*
Lars Hansen, *Vice Pres*
Kenny Mitchell, *Plant Mgr*
▲ EMP: 133
SQ FT: 525,000
SALES (est): 99MM
SALES (corp-wide): 3.1B **Publicly Held**
WEB: www.tempursealy.com
SIC: 2515 Mattresses & foundations
HQ: Tempur World, Llc
1000 Tempur Way
Lexington KY 40511
859 455-1000

(G-4186)
TEMPUR-PEDIC TECHNOLOGIES LLC
203 Tempur Pedic Dr # 102 (24244-5321)
PHONE..................................276 431-7450
Scott L Thompson, *CEO*
Dale E Williams, *CFO*
William H Poche, *Treasurer*
Carrie Shell, *IT/INT Sup*
Evelyn S Dilsaver, *Director*
▲ EMP: 8
SALES (est): 1.1MM
SALES (corp-wide): 3.1B **Publicly Held**
WEB: www.tempurpedic.com
SIC: 2392 Household furnishings
PA: Tempur Sealy International, Inc.
1000 Tempur Way
Lexington KY 40511
800 878-8889

(G-4187)
VFP INC
402 Industrial Park Rd (24244)
P.O. Box 446 (24244-0446)
PHONE..................................276 431-4000
Brandon Sturgill, *Manager*
EMP: 170
SALES (corp-wide): 65MM **Privately Held**
WEB: www.vfpinc.com
SIC: 2452 3448 3272 Prefabricated wood buildings; prefabricated metal buildings; concrete products
PA: Vfp, Inc.
5410 Fallowater Ln
Roanoke VA 24018
540 977-0500

Dugspur
Carroll County

(G-4188)
FOGGY RIDGE CIDER
53 Chisholm Creek Rd (24325-3552)
PHONE..................................276 398-2337
Diane Flynt, *President*
John Troy, *Principal*
EMP: 5
SALES (est): 340.1K **Privately Held**
WEB: www.foggyridgecider.com
SIC: 2084 Wines

(G-4189)
MOORE LOGGING INC
1342 Double Cabin Rd (24325-3721)
PHONE..................................276 233-1693
Douglas Moore, *Principal*
EMP: 1
SALES (est): 109.5K **Privately Held**
SIC: 2411 Logging camps & contractors

(G-4190)
NARROGATE WOODWORKS INC
312 Narrogate Ln (24325-3946)
PHONE..................................276 728-3996
Arthur Wiggins, *Officer*
EMP: 1 EST: 2008
SALES (est): 117.5K **Privately Held**
WEB: www.narrogate.com
SIC: 2431 Millwork

Dulles
Loudoun County

(G-4191)
AIRLINE TARIFF PUBLISHING CO (PA)
Also Called: Atpco
45005 Aviation Dr Ste 400 (20166-7546)
PHONE..................................703 661-7400
Rolf Purzer, *CEO*
Robert Albert, *Exec VP*
Cathy Schroeder, *Production*
Vince Palmiere, *CFO*
Michelle Chan, *Controller*
▲ EMP: 380
SALES (est): 121.1MM **Privately Held**
WEB: www.atpco.net
SIC: 2721 7374 2731 Statistical reports (periodicals): publishing & printing; data processing service; book publishing

(G-4192)
AIROCARE INC
44330 Mercure Cir Ste 150 (20166-2024)
PHONE..................................703 788-1500
EMP: 11
SALES (est): 1MM **Privately Held**
SIC: 3564 Mfg Blowers/Fans

(G-4193)
BOOKS INTERNATIONAL INC
22841 Quicksilver Dr (20166-2019)
PHONE..................................703 661-1500
EMP: 1
SALES (est): 62.4K **Privately Held**
WEB: www.booksintl.presswarehouse.com
SIC: 2731 Book publishing

(G-4194)
BRIGHT YEAST LABS LLC
23600 Overland Dr Ste 150 (20166-4441)
PHONE..................................205 790-2544
Adriaan Akerboom, *Principal*
EMP: 1
SALES (est): 39.5K **Privately Held**
SIC: 2053 Yeast goods, sweet: frozen

(G-4195)
CHEMRING SNSORS ELCTRNIC SYSTE (DH)
Also Called: Cses
23031 Ladbrook Dr (20166-2098)
PHONE..................................703 661-0283
Thomas H Thebes Jr, *President*
Steven Cummings, *President*
Terrence Marsh, *President*
John Domitrovits, *Vice Pres*
Thomas Decrescente, *Buyer*
EMP: 160
SQ FT: 48,000
SALES (est): 34.8MM
SALES (corp-wide): 414.1MM **Privately Held**
WEB: www.chemring.co.uk
SIC: 3812 Infrared object detection equipment

(G-4196)
CONNECTED INTELLIGENCE LLC
43403 Stukely Dr (20166-2134)
PHONE..................................571 241-4540
Jacqueline Luo,
EMP: 1
SALES (est): 950K **Privately Held**
SIC: 3669 4812 Communications equipment; radio telephone communication

(G-4197)
DDI VA
1200 Severn Way (20166-8904)
PHONE..................................571 436-1378
Jacqueline Cole, *Buyer*
Mark Curry, *CFO*
EMP: 5
SALES (est): 622.3K **Privately Held**
SIC: 3672 Printed circuit boards

(G-4198)
DRS GLOBAL ENTP SOLUTIONS INC
Also Called: US Gov Vendor Drs Technologies
45975 Nokes Blvd Ste 145 (20166-6555)
PHONE..................................703 898-9233
EMP: 34
SALES (corp-wide): 9.9B **Privately Held**
WEB: www.leonardodrs.com
SIC: 3812 Search & navigation equipment
HQ: Drs Global Enterprise Solutions, Inc.
21345 Ridgetop Cir # 400
Dulles VA 20166
703 896-7100

(G-4199)
ENTERPRISING WOMEN
45685 Elmwood Ct (20166-4209)
PHONE..................................919 362-1551
Mike Clayton, *Manager*
EMP: 2
SALES (est): 73.1K **Privately Held**
WEB: www.enterprisingwomen.com
SIC: 2721 Periodicals

(G-4200)
EUREST RAYTHEON DULLES
22260 Pacific Blvd (20166-6916)
PHONE..................................571 250-1024
EMP: 2 EST: 2017
SALES (est): 77.4K **Privately Held**
WEB: www.rtx.com
SIC: 3812 Defense systems & equipment

(G-4201)
EXPLUS INC
44156 Mercure Cir (20166-2000)
PHONE..................................703 260-0780
Duncan T Burt, *President*
Lorrie Andrews, *General Mgr*
Mike Rayburn, *General Mgr*
Ronald L Beach, *Vice Pres*
Ken Edmonston, *Project Mgr*
▲ EMP: 80
SQ FT: 105,000
SALES (est): 11.9MM **Privately Held**
WEB: www.explusinc.com
SIC: 3999 3993 2542 Advertising display products; signs & advertising specialties; partitions & fixtures, except wood

(G-4202)
FALCO EMOTORS INC
100 Executive Dr Ste C (20166-9569)
PHONE..................................571 313-1154
Rakesh Dhawan, *President*
Bonita Dhawan, *Vice Pres*
EMP: 49
SQ FT: 10,000
SALES (est): 4.2MM **Privately Held**
WEB: www.falcoemotors.com
SIC: 3621 Motors, electric

(G-4203)
GAUGE WORKS INC
Also Called: Engineering Design Mfg
43671 Trade Center Pl # 156 (20166-2121)
PHONE..................................703 661-1300
Greg Day, *President*
EMP: 7
SALES (est): 760K **Privately Held**
SIC: 3089 Plastic containers, except foam

(G-4204)
GENESIC SEMICONDUCTOR INC
43670 Trade Center Pl # 15 (20166-2123)
PHONE..................................703 996-8200
Ranbir Singh, *CEO*
Sid Sundaresan, *Vice Pres*
Nathan Ostapovicz, *Asst Controller*
Siddarth Sundaresan, *Director*
EMP: 9
SQ FT: 5,900
SALES (est): 2.2MM **Privately Held**
WEB: www.genesicsemi.com
SIC: 3674 Semiconductors & related devices

(G-4205)
GIESECKE+DEVRIENT (DH)
Also Called: G&D America
45925 Horseshoe Dr # 100 (20166-6588)
PHONE..................................703 480-2000
James Petit, *President*
Dan Vacco, *District Mgr*
Martin Bauer, *Vice Pres*
Jeff Bowers, *Vice Pres*
Rajiv Gupta, *Vice Pres*
◆ EMP: 125 EST: 1990
SQ FT: 134,296
SALES (est): 115.9MM
SALES (corp-wide): 2.7B **Privately Held**
WEB: www.gi-de.com
SIC: 2672 5044 Coated & laminated paper; office equipment
HQ: Giesecke+Devrient Gesellschaft Mit Beschrankter Haftung
Prinzregentenstr. 159
Munchen 81677
894 119-0

(G-4206)
GUIDANCE SOFTWARE INC
21000 Atl Blvd Ste 750 (20166)
PHONE..................................703 433-5400
John Patzakis, *President*
Neil Condon, *Director*
EMP: 7
SALES (corp-wide): 3.1B **Privately Held**
WEB: www.guidancesoftware.com
SIC: 7372 Prepackaged software
HQ: Guidance Software, Inc.
1055 E Colo Blvd Ste 400
Pasadena CA 91106
626 229-9191

(G-4207)
L3HARRIS TECHNOLOGIES INC
Also Called: Evi Technology
44965 Aviation Dr Ste 400 (20166-7540)
PHONE..................................847 952-6120
EMP: 500
SALES (corp-wide): 6.8B **Publicly Held**
WEB: www.harris.com
SIC: 3823 Industrial instrmnts msrmnt display/control process variable
PA: L3harris Technologies, Inc.
1025 W Nasa Blvd
Melbourne FL 32919
321 727-9100

(G-4208)
MAHAWARA LLC
44330 Mercure Cir 100j (20166-2086)
PHONE..................................443 949-2602
Manpreet K Hundal,
EMP: 1
SALES (est): 300K **Privately Held**
SIC: 3999 Manufacturing industries

(G-4209)
MERCURY LEARNING AND INFO LLC (PA)
22883 Quicksilver Dr (20166-2019)
P.O. Box 605, Herndon (20172-0605)
PHONE..................................800 232-0223
David Pallai, *Mng Member*
▲ EMP: 4 EST: 2011
SQ FT: 4,000
SALES (est): 1MM **Privately Held**
WEB: www.merclearning.com
SIC: 2741 Miscellaneous publishing

(G-4210)
MVP PRESS LLC
43720 Trade Center Pl # 13 (20166-4480)
PHONE..................................703 661-6877
Theresa Ehlert,
EMP: 10
SALES (est): 198.3K **Privately Held**
WEB: www.mvppress.net
SIC: 2752 Commercial printing, offset

(G-4211)
N-MOLECULAR INC (PA)
Also Called: Zevacor
21000 Atl Blvd Ste 730 (20166)
PHONE..................................703 547-8161
Timothy Stone, *President*
EMP: 11
SQ FT: 7,800
SALES (est): 1.7MM **Privately Held**
WEB: www.zevacor.com
SIC: 2834 Pharmaceutical preparations

G E O G R A P H I C

(G-4212)
NORTHROP GRMMAN INNVTION SYSTE (HQ)
Also Called: Northrop Grmman Innvtion Syste
45101 Warp Dr (20166-6874)
PHONE.....................................703 406-5000
Kathy Warden, *Ch of Bd*
Frank L Culbertson, *President*
Blake E Larson, *President*
Alice Reed, *Principal*
Antonio L Elias, *Exec VP*
◆ EMP: 216
SQ FT: 80
SALES (est): 6.2B **Publicly Held**
WEB: www.northropgrumman.com
SIC: 3764 3812 3483 3482 Propulsion units for guided missiles & space vehicles; search & navigation equipment; warfare counter-measure equipment; detection apparatus: electronic/magnetic field, light/heat; ammunition, except for small arms; mortar shells, over 30 mm.; rockets (ammunition); bombs & parts; small arms ammunition; guns, howitzers, mortars & related equipment

(G-4213)
NORTHROP GRUMMAN SYSTEMS CORP
45101 Warp Dr (20166-6874)
PHONE.....................................703 406-5474
Alice Reed, *Principal*
Carl Claussen, *Mfg Staff*
Nancy Bertrand, *Senior Buyer*
Richard Calvin, *Engineer*
Segun Fontenot, *Engineer*
EMP: 2 **Publicly Held**
WEB: www.northropgrumman.com
SIC: 3812 Aircraft/aerospace flight instruments & guidance systems
HQ: Northrop Grumman Systems Corporation
2980 Fairview Park Dr
Falls Church VA 22042
703 280-2900

(G-4214)
ON OUR WAY INC
45449 Severn Way Ste 173 (20166-8918)
PHONE.....................................703 444-0007
Sharon Burke Lawson, *Principal*
EMP: 3
SALES (est): 227.6K **Privately Held**
WEB: www.dullesva.image360.com
SIC: 3993 Signs & advertising specialties

(G-4215)
ORBCOMM LLC
21700 Atl Blvd Ste 300 (20166)
PHONE.....................................703 433-6300
Wayne Cuddy, *President*
Marc J Eisenberg, *Branch Mgr*
EMP: 55
SALES (corp-wide): 272MM **Publicly Held**
WEB: www.orbcomm.com
SIC: 3663 Satellites, communications
HQ: Orbcomm Llc
395 W Passaic St Ste 3
Rochelle Park NJ 07662
703 433-6300

(G-4216)
ORBITAL SCIENCES CORPORATION
21830 Atlantic Blvd (20166-6849)
PHONE.....................................703 405-5012
Mike Tolbert, *Engineer*
James Cochran, *Manager*
Dave Detroye, *Manager*
Melinda Biegon, *Senior Mgr*
EMP: 463 **Publicly Held**
WEB: www.northropgrumman.com
SIC: 3812 Defense systems & equipment
HQ: Orbital Sciences Llc
45101 Warp Dr
Dulles VA 20166
703 406-5524

(G-4217)
ORBITAL SCIENCES LLC (DH)
Also Called: Orbital Sciences Corporation
45101 Warp Dr (20166-6874)
PHONE.....................................703 406-5524
David W Thompson, *Ch of Bd*

Ross Bridge, *Principal*
Alice Reed, *Principal*
Judith Kopp, *Business Mgr*
Antonio L Elias, *Exec VP*
◆ EMP: 900
SALES (est): 2.7B **Publicly Held**
WEB: www.northropgrumman.com
SIC: 3812 4899 7372 Defense systems & equipment; aircraft control systems, electronic; navigational systems & instruments; satellite earth stations; data communication services; prepackaged software

(G-4218)
ORBITAL SCIENCES LLC
Also Called: Space Systems Division
45101 Warp Dr (20166-6874)
PHONE.....................................703 406-5000
David Thomson, *President*
Michael Iwan, *Counsel*
Dennis Jackson, *Vice Pres*
Steve Bistline, *Engineer*
Austin Randolph, *Engineer*
EMP: 500 **Publicly Held**
WEB: www.northropgrumman.com
SIC: 3761 3728 3812 3769 Space vehicles, complete; research & dev by manuf., aircraft parts & auxiliary equip; search & navigation equipment; guided missile & space vehicle parts & auxiliary equipment
HQ: Orbital Sciences Llc
45101 Warp Dr
Dulles VA 20166
703 406-5524

(G-4219)
POTOMAC BOOKS INC
22841 Quicksilver Dr (20166-2019)
PHONE.....................................703 661-1548
Azad Ajamian, *President*
EMP: 12
SALES (est): 820K **Privately Held**
WEB: www.booksintl.presswarehouse.com
SIC: 2731 Books: publishing only

(G-4220)
PROTECTIVE SOLUTIONS INC
45064 Underwood Ln Ste B (20166-2304)
PHONE.....................................703 435-1115
Dave Duncan, *President*
EMP: 58
SALES (est): 11.4MM **Privately Held**
WEB: www.protectivesolutions.net
SIC: 3728 3312 Military aircraft equipment & armament; armor plate

(G-4221)
RAYTHEON COMPANY
22260 Pacific Blvd (20166-6916)
PHONE.....................................571 250-2260
Vince McKenzie, *Branch Mgr*
EMP: 1
SALES (corp-wide): 77B **Publicly Held**
WEB: www.rtx.com
SIC: 3812 Radar systems & equipment; sonar systems & equipment; fathometers; warfare counter-measure equipment
HQ: Raytheon Company
870 Winter St
Waltham MA 02451
781 522-3000

(G-4222)
RAYTHEON COMPANY
22265 Pacific Blvd (20166-6920)
PHONE.....................................571 250-1101
EMP: 2
SALES (corp-wide): 77B **Publicly Held**
WEB: www.rtx.com
SIC: 3812 3663 3761 Defense systems & equipment; space satellite communications equipment; airborne radio communications equipment; guided missiles & space vehicles, research & development; rockets, space & military, complete
HQ: Raytheon Company
870 Winter St
Waltham MA 02451
781 522-3000

(G-4223)
RAYTHEON COMPANY
22265 Pacific Blvd (20166-6920)
PHONE.....................................571 250-3421
Roger Duke, *Branch Mgr*

EMP: 100
SALES (corp-wide): 77B **Publicly Held**
WEB: www.rtx.com
SIC: 3812 Radar systems & equipment
HQ: Raytheon Company
870 Winter St
Waltham MA 02451
781 522-3000

(G-4224)
RAYTHEON COMPANY
22270 Pcf Blvd Ste 600 (20166)
PHONE.....................................972 272-0515
EMP: 5
SALES (corp-wide): 77B **Publicly Held**
WEB: www.rtx.com
SIC: 3728 Aircraft parts & equipment
HQ: Raytheon Company
870 Winter St
Waltham MA 02451
781 522-3000

(G-4225)
RAYTHEON COMPANY
22260 Pacific Blvd (20166-6916)
PHONE.....................................310 647-9438
Vinc Smith, *Manager*
EMP: 99
SALES (corp-wide): 77B **Publicly Held**
WEB: www.rtx.com
SIC: 3812 Search & navigation equipment
HQ: Raytheon Company
870 Winter St
Waltham MA 02451
781 522-3000

(G-4226)
SIX3 ADVANCED SYSTEMS INC (DH)
45200 Business Ct Ste 100 (20166-6715)
PHONE.....................................703 742-7660
J P London, *Ch of Bd*
John Mengucci, *President*
J William Koegel Jr, *Exec VP*
Tom Ladd, *Exec VP*
Rachel Dunn, *Purchasing*
EMP: 134 EST: 1999
SQ FT: 30,000
SALES (est): 148.9MM **Publicly Held**
WEB: www.bit-sys.com
SIC: 3825 4899 4789 Signal generators & averagers; data communication services; cargo loading & unloading services
HQ: Six3 Systems Holdings Ii, Inc.
1100 N Glebe Rd
Arlington VA 22201
703 841-7800

(G-4227)
SPACE LOGISTICS LLC
Also Called: Spacelogistics
45101 Warp Dr (20166-6874)
PHONE.....................................703 406-5474
Tom Wilson, *President*
Joseph Anderson, *Vice Pres*
Steven Mumma, *Director*
EMP: 3 EST: 2016
SALES (est): 948.8K **Publicly Held**
WEB: www.spacelogistics.net
SIC: 3761 Space vehicles, complete
HQ: Northrop Grumman Innovation Systems, Inc.
45101 Warp Dr
Dulles VA 20166

(G-4228)
TECHNLOGY ADVNCEMENT GROUP INC (PA)
22355 Tag Way (20166-9310)
PHONE.....................................703 406-3000
James McEwan, *CEO*
John A McEwan, *Ch of Bd*
Robert Jeffries, *Program Mgr*
Matthew Fedowitz, *Director*
EMP: 3
SALES (est): 23.8MM **Privately Held**
WEB: www.tag.com
SIC: 3571 7378 Electronic computers; computer maintenance & repair

(G-4229)
TEXTRON GROUND SUPPORT EQP INC
23941 Cargo Dr Bldg 1 (20166-7616)
PHONE.....................................703 572-5340

Bruce Haines, *Branch Mgr*
EMP: 3
SALES (corp-wide): 13.6B **Publicly Held**
WEB: www.tugtech.com
SIC: 3728 Aircraft parts & equipment
HQ: Textron Ground Support Equipment Inc.
1995 Duncan Dr Nw
Kennesaw GA 30144
770 422-7230

(G-4230)
UNISON VRTUAL ACQSTION OFF LLC
21251 Ridgetop Cir # 100 (20166-8532)
PHONE.....................................571 449-4188
Meghann Jeckell, *Accounts Mgr*
EMP: 1
SALES (est): 58K **Privately Held**
WEB: www.unisonglobal.com
SIC: 7372 Application computer software

(G-4231)
VELOCITY SYSTEMS LLC
45064 Underwood Ln Ste B (20166-2304)
PHONE.....................................703 707-6280
David Strum, *President*
Patrick Quinn, *Contract Law*
EMP: 10
SALES (est): 2MM **Privately Held**
WEB: www.velsyst.com
SIC: 3069 Dress shields, vulcanized rubber or rubberized fabric

(G-4232)
VERIDOS AMERICA INC
45925 Horseshoe Dr (20166-8533)
PHONE.....................................703 480-2025
Paul Mazzeo, *President*
Kathleen Synstegaard, *Sales Dir*
EMP: 8
SQ FT: 2,500
SALES (est): 336.4K **Privately Held**
SIC: 2759 3089 5043 Card printing & engraving, except greeting; identification cards, plastic; cameras & photographic equipment

---

Dumfries
Prince William County

(G-4233)
AMBUSH LLC
15702 Brandywine Rd (22025-1712)
PHONE.....................................480 338-5321
Patrick Broughton, *Principal*
◆ EMP: 5
SALES (est): 200K **Privately Held**
SIC: 2752 Commercial printing, lithographic

(G-4234)
ANTHONY BIEL
Also Called: A&M Designs
15049 Holleyside Dr (22025-3028)
PHONE.....................................703 307-8516
Anthony Biel, *Owner*
EMP: 3 EST: 2012
SALES (est): 110.6K **Privately Held**
WEB: www.anmdesignsva.net
SIC: 2396 2759 5699 5999 Fabric printing & stamping; letterpress & screen printing; T-shirts, custom printed; trophies & plaques;

(G-4235)
APPLIED MATERIALS INC
17539 Jefferson Davis Hwy (22026-2245)
PHONE.....................................540 583-0466
EMP: 2
SALES (est): 106K **Privately Held**
SIC: 3559 Semiconductor manufacturing machinery

(G-4236)
ARBAN PRECAST STONE LTD
19000 Colonial Port Rd (22026-2654)
P.O. Box 761 (22026-0761)
PHONE.....................................703 221-8005
Allen E Macey, *President*
Mark F Arban, *Vice Pres*
Joan M Arban, *Treasurer*
Leah Arban Macey, *Executive*
EMP: 40

SALES (est): 1.5MM **Privately Held**
WEB: www.arbanprecast.com
SIC: **3272** Concrete products, precast

(G-4237)
BOOM BASS CABINETS INC
17698d Main St (22026-3261)
PHONE.................................301 343-4918
Drue Williams, *President*
EMP: 1
SALES (est): 54K **Privately Held**
WEB: www.boombasscabinets.com
SIC: **3429** Cabinet hardware

(G-4238)
CEDAR INDUSTRY LLC
3042 Clancy Dr (22026-3337)
PHONE.................................571 402-4564
Abdulrehman Shahid, *CEO*
EMP: 20 EST: 2015
SALES (est): 197.5K **Privately Held**
SIC: **3199** Leather garments

(G-4239)
CHAPPELLE MECHANICAL
SVCS LLC
3701 Dalebrook Dr (22025-1807)
PHONE.................................240 299-3000
Luke Chappelle, *President*
EMP: 1
SALES (est): 61.4K **Privately Held**
SIC: **3585** Drinking fountains, mechanically refrigerated

(G-4240)
CONSTRUCTION SPECIALTIES
GROUP
15783 Crocus Ln (22025-1817)
PHONE.................................703 670-5300
Neil Savitth, *Owner*
EMP: 1
SALES (est): 140K **Privately Held**
SIC: **2899** Waterproofing compounds

(G-4241)
CREATIVE CRAFTY MOM LLC
17410 Glennville Dr (22026-3364)
PHONE.................................571 206-8570
Nimisha Patel,
EMP: 2
SALES (est): 15K **Privately Held**
SIC: **2499** Decorative wood & woodwork

(G-4242)
DANICAS S CROCHET CLUB
17432 Terri Ct (22026-3361)
PHONE.................................703 221-8574
Danica A Wheelock, *Principal*
EMP: 3
SALES (est): 168.6K **Privately Held**
SIC: **2399** 5411 Hand woven & crocheted products; grocery stores

(G-4243)
DRS CUSTOM FABRICATION
LLC
15017 Huntgate Ln (22025-1049)
PHONE.................................703 680-4259
Donald Stiles, *Principal*
EMP: 2
SALES (est): 152.1K **Privately Held**
WEB: www.drscustom.com
SIC: **3499** Novelties & giftware, including trophies

(G-4244)
EL COMERCIO NEWSPAPER
INC
17216 Larkin Dr (22026-2747)
P.O. Box 1132 (22026-9132)
PHONE.................................703 859-1554
EMP: 2
SALES (est): 62.9K **Privately Held**
SIC: **2711** Newspapers

(G-4245)
EMES LLC
15903 Cranberry Ct (22025-1708)
PHONE.................................703 680-0807
Matt Frank Jackson, *Owner*
EMP: 2
SALES (est): 130K **Privately Held**
SIC: **3571** Electronic computers

(G-4246)
EXTREME COMPUTER
SERVICES INC
15712 Cranberry Ct (22025-1710)
PHONE.................................703 730-8821
Przemyslaw Rosiak, *President*
EMP: 5
SALES (est): 400K **Privately Held**
WEB: www.ecs-info.com
SIC: **3571 7378** Electronic computers; computer maintenance & repair

(G-4247)
HEK LOGISTICS LLC
17615 Harpers Ferry Dr (22025-2029)
PHONE.................................757 637-8778
Harry Obeng Boafo,
EMP: 3
SALES (est): 138.9K **Privately Held**
SIC: **3537** Trucks: freight, baggage, etc.: industrial, except mining

(G-4248)
KASHAF SPICES
15407 Windsong Ln (22025-1134)
PHONE.................................571 572-5890
Nadeem Ahmad, *Owner*
EMP: 3
SALES (est): 60K **Privately Held**
SIC: **2099** Food preparations

(G-4249)
KERRIS KANDLES
15087 Lindenberry Ln (22025-3042)
PHONE.................................908 698-3968
EMP: 1 EST: 2016
SALES (est): 39.6K **Privately Held**
SIC: **3999** Candles

(G-4250)
LEGACY VULCAN LLC
217 Canal Rd (22026)
PHONE.................................800 732-3964
EMP: 2 **Publicly Held**
WEB: www. vulcanmaterials.com
SIC: **3273** Ready-mixed concrete
HQ: Legacy Vulcan, Llc
1200 Urban Center Dr
Vestavia AL 35242
205 298-3000

(G-4251)
LYONS SHARE LLC
4297 Mulcaster Ter (22025-3158)
PHONE.................................443 370-9514
Virginia Lyons, *Mng Member*
EMP: 2
SALES (est): 780K **Privately Held**
SIC: **3949** Sporting & athletic goods

(G-4252)
MECH WARRIOR INDUSTRIES
LLC
16124 Henderson Ln (22025-1755)
PHONE.................................703 670-5788
Anthony Wayne Jackson, *Principal*
EMP: 2
SALES (est): 74.6K **Privately Held**
SIC: **3999** Manufacturing industries

(G-4253)
ON THE DL CUSTOM PRINTS
LLC
17096 Belle Isle Dr (22026-3007)
PHONE.................................757 508-1609
EMP: 2 EST: 2018
SALES (est): 83.9K **Privately Held**
SIC: **2752** Commercial printing, lithographic

(G-4254)
OUR JOURNEY PUBLISHING
17204 Continental Dr (22026-3022)
PHONE.................................571 606-1574
Jasmine Sheffield, *Principal*
EMP: 1
SALES (est): 61.7K **Privately Held**
SIC: **2731 7389** Book publishing; business services

(G-4255)
ROCHON & ROCHON LLC A
FMLY CO
2472 Potomac River Blvd (22026-3002)
PHONE.................................571 331-4860
Dawn Bolden,
EMP: 1
SALES (est): 39.5K **Privately Held**
SIC: **2099** Food preparations

(G-4256)
SOCIAL DYNAMICS INDUSTRIES
17512 Denali Pl (22025-1975)
PHONE.................................703 441-2869
Eduardo Morales, *Principal*
EMP: 1 EST: 2014
SALES (est): 49.9K **Privately Held**
WEB: www.sdi-x.com
SIC: **3999** Manufacturing industries

(G-4257)
SPECTRA LAB LLC
17873 Main St Ste C (22026-2411)
P.O. Box 838 (22026-0838)
PHONE.................................703 634-5290
Sean Wallace, *Principal*
EMP: 5 EST: 2012
SALES (est): 544.3K **Privately Held**
WEB: www.spectralab.com
SIC: **3825** Instruments to measure electricity

(G-4258)
TALK IS LIFE LLC
17045 Gibson Mill Rd (22026-2286)
PHONE.................................703 951-3848
Antayah Abraham,
EMP: 1
SALES (est): 37.5K **Privately Held**
SIC: **2741**

(G-4259)
THEOREM PAINTING
4596 Bishop Pl (22025-1420)
PHONE.................................703 670-4330
David Henry, *Manager*
▲ EMP: 1
SALES (est): 42.7K **Privately Held**
SIC: **3944 8999** Craft & hobby kits & sets; artist

(G-4260)
THREADS INK LLC
2970 Myrtlewood Dr (22026-4534)
PHONE.................................703 221-0819
Christopher Long, *President*
EMP: 6
SQ FT: 1,500
SALES (est): 296.5K **Privately Held**
WEB: www.threads-ink.com
SIC: **2395** Embroidery products, except schiffli machine

(G-4261)
TITAN AMERICA LLC
3454 Canal Rd (22026-2393)
PHONE.................................703 221-2003
Mike Brooks, *General Mgr*
EMP: 31
SALES (corp-wide): 1.4MM **Privately Held**
WEB: www.titanamerica.com
SIC: **3273** Ready-mixed concrete
HQ: Titan America Llc
5700 Lake Wright Dr # 300
Norfolk VA 23502
757 858-6500

(G-4262)
WEALTHY SISTAS MEDIA
GROUP
4222 Fortuna Center Plz (22025-1515)
PHONE.................................800 917-9435
Deborah Hardnett, *CEO*
EMP: 1
SALES (est): 44.4K **Privately Held**
SIC: **2759 7336 8742 7389** Commercial printing; art design services; marketing consulting services; decoration service for special events; design services;

Dunn Loring
Fairfax County

(G-4263)
DAWNBREAKER
COMMUNICATIONS LLC
2178 Harithy Dr (22027-1059)
P.O. Box 85, Falls Church (22040-0085)
PHONE.................................202 288-0805
Gil Miller-Muro, *Marketing Staff*
EMP: 1
SALES (est): 100K **Privately Held**
WEB: www.dbchd.com
SIC: **3663** Radio & TV communications equipment

(G-4264)
KARAM WINERY
2139 Tysons Executive Ct (22027-1048)
PHONE.................................703 573-3886
EMP: 2 EST: 2013
SALES (est): 123.4K **Privately Held**
SIC: **2084** Wines

(G-4265)
MISSION DATA LLC
7875 Promontory Ct (22027-1173)
PHONE.................................513 298-1865
Ann Liu, *Branch Mgr*
EMP: 15
SALES (corp-wide): 1.2MM **Privately Held**
WEB: www.missiondata.com
SIC: **7372** Prepackaged software
PA: Mission Data, Llc
12910 Shelbyville Rd # 225
Louisville KY 40243
502 245-6756

(G-4266)
OPSENSE INC
7875 Promontory Ct (22027-1173)
PHONE.................................844 757-7578
Stuart Gavurin, *CEO*
EMP: 2
SQ FT: 1,000
SALES (est): 56.5K **Privately Held**
WEB: www.opsense.com
SIC: **7372 7371** Application computer software; computer software development & applications

Dunnsville
Essex County

(G-4267)
BRIZENDINE WELDING & REPR
INC
1790 Howerton Rd (22454-3337)
P.O. Box 193, Millers Tavern (23115-0193)
PHONE.................................804 443-1903
Temple Brizendine, *Owner*
EMP: 2
SALES (est): 103.3K **Privately Held**
WEB: www.dragonpulls.com
SIC: **7692** Welding repair

(G-4268)
CRAFTED CANVAS LLC
4097 Essex Mill Rd (22454-2345)
PHONE.................................917 426-8377
Janeen Richards,
EMP: 1 EST: 2012
SQ FT: 150
SALES (est): 85.1K **Privately Held**
WEB: www.craftedcanvas.com
SIC: **2394** Convertible tops, canvas or boat: from purchased materials

Dutton
Gloucester County

(G-4269)
BAYSIDE JOINERY CO LLC
51 Willow Oak Dr (23050-9783)
PHONE.................................804 551-3951
Rick Andrews, *Principal*
EMP: 2

SALES (est): 72K Privately Held
WEB: www.baysidejoinery.com
SIC: 2431 Millwork

(G-4270)
CUPCAKES BY CHERYL LLC
1937 Windsor Rd (23050-9725)
PHONE......................757 592-4185
Cheryl Bourgoin, *Principal*
EMP: 4
SALES (est): 160.2K Privately Held
SIC: 2051 Bread, cake & related products

(G-4271)
CUSTOM YACHT SERVICE INC
561 Wading Creek Rd (23050-9779)
P.O. Box 740, Irvington (22480-0740)
PHONE......................804 438-5563
Lester E Potter, *President*
Alissa Potter, *Corp Secy*
EMP: 12
SALES (est): 1.6MM Privately Held
WEB: www.customyachtsvc.com
SIC: 3732 5551 7699 Yachts, building &
repairing; marine supplies; boat repair

(G-4272)
EAST CAST CSTM SCREEN PRTG LLC
156 Ewellville Ln (23050-9721)
PHONE......................540 373-7576
Crystal Coons, *Principal*
EMP: 2
SALES (est): 83.9K Privately Held
SIC: 2752 Commercial printing, lithographic

(G-4273)
HUTSON HAULING
1795 Windsor Rd (23050-9727)
PHONE......................804 815-2421
Michael R Hutson, *Owner*
EMP: 2
SALES (est): 200K Privately Held
SIC: 2396 Automotive & apparel trimmings

(G-4274)
NORTH MACHINE SHOP
2036 Buckley Hall Rd (23050-9747)
PHONE......................804 725-5443
Juergen Metzger, *Owner*
EMP: 2
SQ FT: 1,000
SALES (est): 238.4K Privately Held
WEB: www.northmachine.biz
SIC: 3599 Machine shop, jobbing & repair

(G-4275)
ZOLL BROS PRIVATE CELLARS LLC
Also Called: Zoll Vineyards
9744 Dutton Rd (23050-9613)
PHONE......................857 498-1665
EMP: 10
SALES (est): 195.8K Privately Held
SIC: 2084 Wines

Dyke
Greene County

(G-4276)
MOSS VINEYARDS LLC (PA)
1849 Simmons Gap Rd (22935-1112)
PHONE......................434 990-0111
Barry Moss,
EMP: 4
SALES (est): 343.2K Privately Held
WEB: www.mossvineyards.net
SIC: 2084 Wines

(G-4277)
STONE MOUNTAIN VINEYARDS LLC
1376 Wyatt Mountain Rd (22935-1371)
PHONE......................434 990-9463
Christophe Breiner, *Principal*
EMP: 2
SALES (est): 202.9K Privately Held
WEB: www.stonemountainvineyards.com
SIC: 2084 Wines

Eagle Rock
Botetourt County

(G-4278)
ANDREW THURSTON LOGGING
561 Elburnell Dr (24085-3668)
PHONE......................540 521-6276
Andrew Thurston, *Owner*
EMP: 1 EST: 2002
SALES (est): 64.8K Privately Held
SIC: 2411 7389 Saw logs;

(G-4279)
BLUE RIDGE VINEYARD INC
1027 Shiloh Dr (24085-3710)
PHONE......................540 798-7642
Barbara J Kolb, *Principal*
EMP: 4 EST: 2009
SALES (est): 302.7K Privately Held
WEB: www.blueridgevineyard.com
SIC: 2084 Wines

(G-4280)
CABINETS DIRECT INC
907 Prices Bluff Rd (24085-3171)
PHONE......................540 884-2329
Ken Weaver, *President*
Elizabeth Weaver, *Vice Pres*
EMP: 2
SALES (est): 267.1K Privately Held
WEB: www.cabinetsdirectinc.com
SIC: 2434 Wood kitchen cabinets

(G-4281)
JEFF BRITT LOGGING
1063 Allen Branch Rd (24085-3716)
PHONE......................540 884-2499
Jeffrey Britt, *Principal*
EMP: 3
SALES (est): 259.9K Privately Held
SIC: 2411 Logging camps & contractors

(G-4282)
LEWIS A DUDLEY
Also Called: L.A. Dudley Welding
10115 Narrow Passage Rd (24085-3228)
PHONE......................540 884-2454
Lewis A Dudley, *Owner*
EMP: 1
SALES (est): 201.2K Privately Held
SIC: 7692 Welding repair

(G-4283)
SYSTEMS TECHNOLOGY VA LLC
Also Called: STI
130 Mount Moriah Rd (24085-3572)
PHONE......................540 884-1784
Howard Shawn Hylton, *Manager*
Karen Hylton, *Admin Sec*
Shawn Hylton,
▼ EMP: 6
SQ FT: 10,000
SALES (est): 400K Privately Held
SIC: 3599 8742 8711 7692 Custom machinery; machine shop, jobbing & repair;
automation & robotics consultant; engineering services; automotive welding

Earlysville
Albemarle County

(G-4284)
ALBION CABINETS STAIRS INC
395 Reas Ford Rd Ste 150 (22936-2461)
P.O. Box 305, Free Union (22940-0305)
PHONE......................434 974-4611
David Marshall, *President*
EMP: 4
SALES (est): 420K Privately Held
WEB: www.albioncabinets.com
SIC: 2434 1751 Wood kitchen cabinets;
cabinet & finish carpentry

(G-4285)
ANDREA PRESS
3558 Loftland Dr (22936-2452)
PHONE......................434 960-8026
EMP: 1
SALES (est): 37.5K Privately Held
SIC: 2741 Miscellaneous publishing

(G-4286)
ANN KITE
900 Reas Ford Rd (22936-2318)
PHONE......................434 989-4841
EMP: 1 EST: 2016
SALES (est): 44.4K Privately Held
WEB: www.annkite.com
SIC: 3944 Kites

(G-4287)
AXONDX LLC
Also Called: Axon Dx
379 Reas Ford Rd Ste 1 (22936-2407)
PHONE......................540 239-0668
Kent Murphy, *CEO*
Meeta Patnaik, *Principal*
Jeff Smith, *Principal*
Marc Hrovatic, *Vice Pres*
EMP: 8
SQ FT: 4,500
SALES (est): 765.9K Privately Held
WEB: www.axondx.com
SIC: 3826 Analytical instruments

(G-4288)
BLAISE GASTON INC
686 Fairhope Ave (22936-2241)
PHONE......................434 973-1801
Blaise Gaston, *President*
EMP: 2
SALES (est): 194.4K Privately Held
WEB: www.blaisegaston.com
SIC: 2511 Wood household furniture

(G-4289)
EZARA INC
1112 Frays Mountain Rd (22936-1826)
PHONE......................434 409-4232
Esther Zebley, *CEO*
EMP: 2
SALES (est): 50K Privately Held
SIC: 7372 Application computer software

(G-4290)
FISHER KNIVES INC
825 Norwood Ln (22936-9560)
PHONE......................434 242-3866
Robert E Fisher, *Principal*
EMP: 2
SALES (est): 129.8K Privately Held
WEB: www.fisherknives.com
SIC: 3999 Manufacturing industries

(G-4291)
MEADOWSEND FARM AND SAWMILL CO
325 Loftlands Farm (22936-9707)
PHONE......................434 975-6598
Robert French, *Principal*
EMP: 3
SALES (est): 176.9K Privately Held
SIC: 2421 Sawmills & planing mills, general

(G-4292)
MEMTEKS-USA INC
355 Mallard Ln Ste 200 (22936-9790)
PHONE......................434 973-9800
Yalcin Ozbey, *CEO*
Nina Lyn Ozbey, *Vice Pres*
▲ EMP: 353
SQ FT: 60,000
SALES (est): 17.2MM Privately Held
WEB: www.memteks-usa.com
SIC: 2254 2342 2339 5137 Underwear,
knit; brassieres; sportswear, women's;
sportswear, women's & children's;
women's & children's sportswear & swimsuits; underwear: women's, children's &
infants'

(G-4293)
MONSTER FIGHT CLUB LLC
395 Reas Ford Rd Ste 190 (22936-2464)
PHONE......................434 284-7258
John Kovaleski, *CEO*
EMP: 3
SQ FT: 5,767
SALES (est): 338.6K Privately Held
SIC: 3944 Board games, puzzles & models, except electronic

(G-4294)
ROCKYDALE CHRLOTTESVILLE QUARY
2430 Rio Mills Rd (22936-3026)
PHONE......................434 295-5700
R Thomas, *Owner*
John Basham, *Regl Sales Mgr*
Brian Wright, *Manager*
EMP: 2 EST: 2010
SALES (est): 131.2K Privately Held
SIC: 1422 Crushed & broken limestone

(G-4295)
TOM WILD PETROPHYSICAL SVCS
3785 Graemont Dr (22936-9104)
PHONE......................434 978-1269
Tom Wild, *Owner*
EMP: 1
SALES (est): 30K Privately Held
SIC: 1311 Crude petroleum & natural gas

Eastville
Northampton County

(G-4296)
PERDUE FARMS INC
Also Called: Eastville Farm 23/24
16121 Perdue Ln (23347)
PHONE......................757 787-5210
Bruce Roberts, *Branch Mgr*
EMP: 255
SALES (corp-wide): 5.2B Privately Held
WEB: www.perduefarms.com
SIC: 2015 Poultry slaughtering & processing
PA: Perdue Farms Inc.
31149 Old Ocean City Rd
Salisbury MD 21804
410 543-3000

(G-4297)
VANDENT DENTAL INC
14337 Harbor Ln (23347)
P.O. Box 1229 (23347-1229)
PHONE......................757 678-7973
Michael Arpino, *President*
EMP: 2
SALES (est): 120K Privately Held
WEB: www.vandent.com
SIC: 3843 8021 Hand pieces & parts, dental; offices & clinics of dentists

Ebony
Brunswick County

(G-4298)
ROBERT E CARROLL LOGGING INC
486 Robinson Ferry Rd (23845-2128)
P.O. Box 5 (23845-0005)
PHONE......................434 636-2168
Robert E Carroll, *President*
Michael W Carroll, *Vice Pres*
Robert E Carroll Jr, *Vice Pres*
Judith T Carroll, *Admin Sec*
EMP: 25
SALES (est): 1MM Privately Held
SIC: 2411 Logging camps & contractors

Edinburg
Shenandoah County

(G-4299)
BATTINO CONTG SOLUTIONS LLC
43674 Leesmill Sq (22824)
PHONE......................703 408-9162
Micah Battino, *Superintendent*
Francisco A Estevez, *Administration*
EMP: 6
SALES (est): 456.1K Privately Held
WEB: www.battinocontracting.com
SIC: 3825 Network analyzers

(G-4300)
BEC WELDING & MACHINE SHOP
16842 Senedo Rd (22824-2111)
PHONE..............................540 984-3793
EMP: 2
SALES (est): 110K **Privately Held**
SIC: 3599 Mfg Industrial Machinery

(G-4301)
COLEMAN MICROWAVE CO
109 Molineau Rd (22824-9656)
P.O. Box 247 (22824-0247)
PHONE..............................540 984-8848
Kenneth R Coleman Sr, *President*
Judith J Coleman, *Corp Secy*
EMP: 40 **EST:** 1973
SQ FT: 14,000
SALES (est): 4MM **Privately Held**
WEB: www.colemanmw.com
SIC: 3663 3812 Microwave communication equipment; radar systems & equipment

(G-4302)
DECAL MAGIC
2549 Palmyra Church Rd (22824-3411)
PHONE..............................540 984-3786
Katrine Defibaugh, *Owner*
EMP: 2
SALES (est): 150K **Privately Held**
SIC: 2396 Automotive & apparel trimmings

(G-4303)
EVERGREEN DESIGN INC
Also Called: Gold-Micro
520 Stoney Creek Blvd (22824-9142)
PHONE..............................540 984-4653
Norman Nelson, *President*
EMP: 3
SQ FT: 1,200
SALES (est): 68.4K **Privately Held**
SIC: 3571 8711 Electronic computers; engineering services

(G-4304)
FOLDER FACTORY
116 N High St (22824-3084)
P.O. Box 308, Mount Jackson (22842-0308)
PHONE..............................540 984-8852
EMP: 2 **EST:** 2011
SALES (est): 79K **Privately Held**
SIC: 2759 Commercial Printing

(G-4305)
GEORGES CHICKEN LLC (HQ)
Also Called: George's Chicken
19992 Senedo Rd (22824-3172)
PHONE..............................540 984-4121
David McClellan, *Vice Pres*
Troy Green, *Plant Mgr*
David Bright, *Purch Mgr*
Susan White, *CFO*
Steve Hilliard, *Controller*
▲ **EMP:** 58
SALES (est): 11.9MM
SALES (corp-wide): 1.6B **Privately Held**
WEB: www.georgesinc.com
SIC: 2015 Chicken slaughtering & processing
PA: George's, Inc.
402 W Robinson Ave
Springdale AR 72764
479 927-7000

(G-4306)
GJS CABINETRY INSTALLATION
2164 Dellinger Gap Rd (22824-2504)
PHONE..............................540 856-2726
George W Judd, *Principal*
EMP: 4
SALES (est): 282.9K **Privately Held**
SIC: 2434 Wood kitchen cabinets

(G-4307)
JOHNS MANVILLE CORPORATION
182 Johns Manville Dr (22824-3504)
PHONE..............................540 984-4171
John Lutz, *Principal*
EMP: 270

SALES (corp-wide): 254.6B **Publicly Held**
WEB: www.jm.com
SIC: 3296 3086 3069 2952 Fiberglass insulation; plastics foam products; roofing, membrane rubber; roofing materials; nonwoven fabrics; filters
HQ: Johns Manville Corporation
717 17th St Ste 800
Denver CO 80202
303 978-2000

(G-4308)
KENNEDY KONSTRUCTION KOMPANY (PA)
1634 Chapman Landing Rd (22824-2811)
PHONE..............................540 984-4191
Randall M Kennedy Sr, *President*
Martha Kennedy, *Corp Secy*
Brenda Dodson, *Purch Agent*
Erma Alkire, *Persnl Mgr*
EMP: 20
SALES (est): 2.2MM **Privately Held**
SIC: 2439 2452 3448 3441 Trusses, except roof: laminated lumber; panels & sections, prefabricated, wood; chicken coops, prefabricated, wood; farm buildings, prefabricated or portable: wood; prefabricated metal buildings; fabricated structural metal; hardwood veneer & plywood

(G-4309)
M L WELDING
525 Swover Creek Rd (22824-3077)
PHONE..............................540 984-4883
EMP: 1 **EST:** 2004
SALES (est): 77K **Privately Held**
SIC: 7692 Welding Repair

(G-4310)
MOUNTAIN VIEW RENDERING CO
173 Rocco Rd (22824-3145)
PHONE..............................540 984-4158
Robert Foory, *Manager*
EMP: 6 **Privately Held**
SIC: 2077 2048 Rendering; prepared feeds
PA: Mountain View Rendering Co
249 Allentown Rd
Souderton PA 18964

(G-4311)
SARA YANNUZZI
1857 Swover Creek Rd (22824-3215)
PHONE..............................703 955-2505
Sara Yannuzzi, *Owner*
EMP: 1
SALES (est): 59.5K **Privately Held**
SIC: 3949 Decoys, duck & other game birds

(G-4312)
SERVICING GREEN INC
370 Diana Dr (22824-2748)
PHONE..............................540 459-3812
Maida D Copp, *Principal*
EMP: 2
SALES (est): 137.6K **Privately Held**
SIC: 1389 Roustabout service

(G-4313)
SEVEN OAKS ALBEMARLE LLC
94 Landfill Rd (22824-9421)
PHONE..............................540 984-3829
Stephanie Bosseerman, *Mng Member*
Glenda Selvage, *Manager*
Jody Banks, *Admin Dir*
EMP: 6
SALES (est): 958.9K **Privately Held**
WEB: www.axiospress.com
SIC: 2731 Books: publishing only

(G-4314)
SHENANDOAH PUBLICATIONS INC
Also Called: Narrow Passage Press
18084 Old Valley Pike (22824-2807)
P.O. Box 777, Woodstock (22664-0777)
PHONE..............................540 459-4000
Keith A Stickley, *President*
Mona Casteel, *Editor*
David Stickley, *Editor*
Sonja Graham, *Receptionist*

EMP: 40
SQ FT: 5,200
SALES (est): 2.9MM **Privately Held**
WEB: www.ournewspaper.net
SIC: 2711 2752 Commercial printing & newspaper publishing combined; commercial printing, lithographic

(G-4315)
SPECIALTY MACHINING & FABG
531 Hillcrest Rd (22824-2960)
P.O. Box 190 (22824-0190)
PHONE..............................540 984-4265
Ronald Wilkins, *President*
EMP: 5
SALES (est): 504.1K **Privately Held**
SIC: 3599 8711 Machine shop, jobbing & repair; designing: ship, boat, machine & product

(G-4316)
WHOLESOME ENERGY LLC
986 S Ox Rd (22824-3071)
PHONE..............................540 984-8219
Wesley Pence, *Vice Pres*
Wesley Gray Pence, *Mng Member*
Nathan Pence,
EMP: 4
SALES (est): 298.5K **Privately Held**
WEB: www.wholesomeenergy.net
SIC: 2869 Fuels

(G-4317)
WILLARD ELLEDGE
123 Stout Rd (22824-3757)
PHONE..............................540 984-3375
Willard Elledge, *President*
EMP: 1
SALES (est): 52.5K **Privately Held**
SIC: 2084 Wines

Elberon
Surry County

(G-4318)
HAMPTON ROADS WINERY LLC
6074 New Design Rd (23846-2630)
PHONE..............................757 899-0203
David Sheldon, *Owner*
EMP: 6
SQ FT: 6,000
SALES (est): 344.9K **Privately Held**
WEB: www.hamptonroadswinery.com
SIC: 2084 Wines

(G-4319)
SHELTECH PLASTICS INC
6074 New Design Rd (23846-2630)
PHONE..............................978 794-2160
David R Sheldon, *President*
Diane P Sheldon, *Vice Pres*
John James, *Clerk*
EMP: 6
SQ FT: 12,000
SALES (est): 714.8K **Privately Held**
SIC: 3443 3089 Vacuum tunnels, metal plate; injection molded finished plastic products

---

Elk Creek
Grayson County

(G-4320)
COWDEN
2294 Elk View Rd (24326-2075)
PHONE..............................276 744-7120
Michael Cowden, *Owner*
EMP: 1
SALES (est): 99.5K **Privately Held**
SIC: 3321 Ductile iron castings

(G-4321)
SIGNS WORK
25 Wagon Wheel Rd (24326-2097)
PHONE..............................276 655-4047
Todd Price, *Owner*
EMP: 1
SALES (est): 70K **Privately Held**
WEB: www.entertainment-web.com
SIC: 3993 Electric signs

(G-4322)
TODD & GLORIA PRICE
25 Wagon Wheel Rd (24326-2097)
PHONE..............................276 655-4047
Todd Price, *Owner*
EMP: 1 **EST:** 1992
SALES (est): 46K **Privately Held**
SIC: 3993 Signs & advertising specialties

Elkton
Rockingham County

(G-4323)
COORS BREWING COMPANY
Rr 340 Box South (22827)
PHONE..............................540 289-8000
Robert Machado, *Manager*
EMP: 200
SALES (corp-wide): 10.5B **Publicly Held**
WEB: www.coors.com
SIC: 2082 5181 Beer (alcoholic beverage); beer & ale
HQ: Coors Brewing Company
17735 W 32nd Ave
Golden CO 80401

(G-4324)
CUPCAKE COMPANY
3391 Barbershop Ln (22827-3506)
PHONE..............................540 810-0795
EMP: 6
SALES (est): 182.3K **Privately Held**
SIC: 2051 Bread, cake & related products

(G-4325)
DOVE S DELIGHTS LLC
308 Hill Ave (22827-1020)
PHONE..............................540 298-7178
Amanda Dove, *Principal*
EMP: 4
SALES (est): 406.7K **Privately Held**
WEB: www.merck.com
SIC: 2834 Pharmaceutical preparations

(G-4326)
DWIGHT KITE
337 W Spring Ave (22827-1235)
PHONE..............................540 564-8858
Dwight Kite, *Principal*
EMP: 1
SALES (est): 45.1K **Privately Held**
SIC: 3944 Kites

(G-4327)
HAPPY LITTLE DUMPSTERS LLC
507 Mount Olivet Ch Rd (22827-3369)
PHONE..............................540 422-0272
Kyle Miller, *Principal*
EMP: 1 **EST:** 2016
SALES (est): 185K **Privately Held**
WEB: www.happylittledumpster.com
SIC: 3443 Dumpsters, garbage

(G-4328)
K & K MACHINING INCORPORATED
709 Shenandoah Ave (22827-3059)
P.O. Box 25 (22827-0025)
PHONE..............................540 298-1700
Kenneth Kite, *President*
EMP: 10
SQ FT: 4,200
SALES (est): 400K **Privately Held**
SIC: 3599 Machine shop, jobbing & repair

(G-4329)
KEYSTONE SUPPLY CO INC
2547 Waterloo Mill Ln (22827-3344)
PHONE..............................610 525-3654
EMP: 2
SALES (est): 77.5K **Privately Held**
SIC: 3842 Mfg Surgical Appliances/Supplies

(G-4330)
LEGACY VULCAN LLC
5967 Humes Run Rd (22827-2411)
PHONE..............................540 298-1237
EMP: 26 **Publicly Held**
WEB: www.vulcanmaterials.com
SIC: 3273 Ready-mixed concrete

HQ: Legacy Vulcan, Llc
1200 Urban Center Dr
Vestavia AL 35242
205 298-3000

(G-4331)
LETTER PERFECT
INCORPORATED
2454 North East Side Hwy # 8
(22827-2465)
PHONE..............................540 652-2022
Wayne Showalter, *President*
Amber Wampler, *Corp Secy*
Jayson Showalter, *Vice Pres*
EMP: 10
SALES (est): 400K **Privately Held**
WEB: www.letterperfectva.net
SIC: 3993 Signs, not made in custom sign
/ painting shops

(G-4332)
LYNIEL W KITE
3099 Carrier Ln (22827-2403)
PHONE..............................540 298-9657
Lyniel W Kite, *Principal*
EMP: 2
SALES (est): 128.9K **Privately Held**
SIC: 3944 Kites

(G-4333)
MILLER KITE HOUSE
310 E Rockingham St (22827-1506)
PHONE..............................540 298-5390
EMP: 1
SALES (est): 55.8K **Privately Held**
SIC: 3944 Kites

(G-4334)
ROCKINGHAM PUBLISHING
COMPANY
Also Called: Valley Banner, The
157 W Spotswood Ave (22827-1118)
P.O. Box 2068, Harrisonburg (22801-9504)
PHONE..............................540 298-9444
Thomas Byrd, *President*
Rebecca Penrod, *Accounts Exec*
EMP: 5
SQ FT: 3,000
SALES (est): 188.2K **Privately Held**
WEB: www.dnronline.com
SIC: 2711 Newspapers, publishing & print-
ing

(G-4335)
STONEWALL WOODWORKS LLC
47 Monger Hill Rd (22827-3008)
PHONE..............................540 298-1713
Joshua Myers, *Principal*
Joshua B Myers, *Principal*
EMP: 2
SALES (est): 187.7K **Privately Held**
SIC: 2431 Millwork

(G-4336)
VIRGINIA CABINETWORKS INC
416 W Spotswood Trl (22827-1126)
PHONE..............................540 298-9599
Daniel G Velker, *President*
EMP: 3
SALES (est): 305.2K **Privately Held**
WEB: www.vacab.com
SIC: 2434 Wood kitchen cabinets

(G-4337)
VIRGINIA INDUSTRIAL PLAS INC
Also Called: VIP Plastics
2454 North East Side Hwy (22827-2430)
PHONE..............................540 298-1515
Irvin R Mercer, *CEO*
Mercer William B, *President*
Edward Fisher, *President*
Brent Mercer, *President*
Larue Fisher, *Vice Pres*
▲ **EMP:** 18 **EST:** 1978
SQ FT: 85,000
SALES (est): 3.8MM
SALES (corp-wide): 2.8MM **Privately
Held**
WEB: www.vaplastic.com
SIC: 3082 3081 Rods, unsupported plas-
tic; tubes, unsupported plastic; plastic film
& sheet
PA: Ale Holdings, Inc.
177 Kensington Dr
Fishersville VA 22939
540 688-7031

(G-4338)
VIRGINIA INSTALLATIONS INC
104 N Fifth St (22827-1102)
PHONE..............................540 298-5300
James R Barrett, *President*
EMP: 8
SQ FT: 6,000
SALES (est): 593.5K **Privately Held**
WEB: www.virginiainstallations.com
SIC: 2541 Wood partitions & fixtures

(G-4339)
W P L INCORPORATED
185 W Spotswood Ave (22827-1118)
PHONE..............................540 298-0999
James C Powell, *President*
EMP: 7
SALES (est): 407.4K **Privately Held**
WEB: www.wplcorp.com
SIC: 1389 Oil consultants

Elkwood
Culpeper County

(G-4340)
AFFINITY WOODWORKS LLC
21457 Business Ct (22718-1757)
P.O. Box 83 (22718-0083)
PHONE..............................330 814-4950
Kevin Cromwell, *Principal*
EMP: 1 **EST:** 2017
SALES (est): 54.1K **Privately Held**
SIC: 2431 Millwork

(G-4341)
AMERICAN MANUFACTURING
CO INC (PA)
22011 Greenhouse Rd (22718)
P.O. Box 97 (22718-0097)
PHONE..............................540 825-7234
Robert B Mayer, *President*
Scott Locke, *President*
Bryan Allen, *General Mgr*
Paul Smith, *Plant Mgr*
Eric Valentine, *Sales Mgr*
EMP: 26
SQ FT: 10,000
SALES (est): 850.7K **Privately Held**
WEB: www.americanonsite.com
SIC: 3089 3613 3561 3494 Fittings for
pipe, plastic; shutters, plastic; switchgear
& switchboard apparatus; pumps & pump-
ing equipment; valves & pipe fittings

(G-4342)
ELKWOOD STONE & MULCH
LLC
13715 Berry Hill Rd (22718-1815)
PHONE..............................540 829-9273
James Andrew Kent Jr,
EMP: 2
SALES (est): 62.6K **Privately Held**
WEB: www.elkwoodstone.com
SIC: 3281 Cut stone & stone products

Elliston
Montgomery County

(G-4343)
BIG SPRING MILL INC
1931 Big Spring Dr (24087-3541)
P.O. Box 305 (24087-0305)
PHONE..............................540 268-2267
W Robert Long II, *Pres*
Long II William Robert, *President*
EMP: 30 **EST:** 1912
SQ FT: 12,000
SALES (est): 4.9MM **Privately Held**
WEB: www.bsmill.com
SIC: 2048 2041 Kelp meal & pellets: pre-
pared as animal feed; flour

(G-4344)
CLAYTON-MARCUS COMPANY
INC (HQ)
2121 Gardner St (24087-3055)
PHONE..............................540 389-8671
Vernon Bigsby, *President*
▲ **EMP:** 215
SQ FT: 307,000

SALES (est): 18.9MM **Privately Held**
SIC: 2512 Living room furniture: upholstered on wood frames

(G-4345)
FIREFLY HILL VINEYARDS LLC
4289 Northfork Rd (24087-3225)
PHONE..............................540 588-0231
EMP: 2
SALES (est): 7.5K **Privately Held**
WEB: www.fireflyhill.com
SIC: 2084 Wines, brandy & brandy spirits

(G-4346)
NOMAR CASTINGS INC
6563 Stones Keep Ln (24087-2313)
P.O. Box 351 (24087-0351)
PHONE..............................540 380-3394
Nolan Shipp, *President*
Jennifer Ship, *Vice Pres*
EMP: 15
SQ FT: 14,000
SALES (est): 2.4MM **Privately Held**
SIC: 3324 3321 3366 3365 Steel invest-
ment foundries; gray & ductile iron
foundries; brass foundry; aluminum
foundries

(G-4347)
PROCHEM INC
5100 Enterprise Dr (24087-3155)
P.O. Box 977 (24087-0977)
PHONE..............................540 268-9884
Barry Shelley, *President*
Laura Haggerty, *General Mgr*
Scott Buff, *Regional Mgr*
Brian Kidd, *Corp Secy*
Adam Parker, *Project Mgr*
◆ **EMP:** 50
SQ FT: 35,000
SALES (est): 12.8MM **Privately Held**
WEB: www.prochemwater.com
SIC: 3589 5169 2899 Water treatment
equipment, industrial; industrial chemi-
cals; water treating compounds

(G-4348)
ROWE FINE FURNITURE INC
(PA)
2121 Gardner St (24087-3055)
PHONE..............................540 444-7693
Bob Choppa, *CEO*
Tim Nugent, *CFO*
◆ **EMP:** 159
SALES (est): 181.5MM **Privately Held**
WEB: www.rowefurniture.com
SIC: 2512 2511 Upholstered household
furniture; wood household furniture

(G-4349)
ROWE FURNITURE INC
2121 Gardner St (24087-3055)
PHONE..............................540 389-8671
Gerald M Birnbach, *CEO*
Rowe Cos, *President*
Matt Mc Cabe, *Manager*
▼ **EMP:** 1500
SALES (est): 170.7MM
SALES (corp-wide): 6.9B **Privately Held**
WEB: www.rowefurniture.com
SIC: 2512 2511 2421 Upholstered house-
hold furniture; wood household furniture;
kiln drying of lumber
PA: Sun Capital Partners, Inc.
5200 Town Center Cir # 600
Boca Raton FL 33486
561 962-3400

(G-4350)
TURTLE HOUSE PRESS LLC
9662 Old Roanoke Rd (24087-3428)
PHONE..............................540 268-5487
Stewart Hill, *Principal*
EMP: 2
SALES (est): 87K **Privately Held**
SIC: 2741 Miscellaneous publishing

Emporia
Greensville County

(G-4351)
1A SMART START LLC
705 N Main St (23847-1274)
PHONE..............................434 336-1202

Ethelean Smart, *Principal*
EMP: 2 **Privately Held**
WEB: www.smartstartinc.com
SIC: 3694 Ignition apparatus & distributors
PA: 1a Smart Start Llc
500 E Dallas Rd Ste 100
Grapevine TX 76051

(G-4352)
A & R PRINTING
500 N Main St (23847-1236)
PHONE..............................434 829-2030
EMP: 4
SALES (est): 111.6K **Privately Held**
WEB: www.anrprinting.com
SIC: 2752 Commercial printing, litho-
graphic

(G-4353)
A TOUCH OF ELEGANCE LLC
339 Halifax St (23847-1709)
PHONE..............................434 634-4592
Darlene Cain, *Partner*
EMP: 4
SALES (est): 30K **Privately Held**
WEB: www.redbankredhot.com
SIC: 2099 Food preparations

(G-4354)
ALLIED CONCRETE PRODUCTS
LLC
120 Courtland Rd (23847-6550)
PHONE..............................434 634-6571
Rick Renner, *Manager*
EMP: 8
SALES (corp-wide): 30.6B **Privately Held**
WEB: www.alliedconcreteproductsusa.com
SIC: 3273 Ready-mixed concrete
HQ: Allied Concrete Products, Llc
3900 Shannon St
Chesapeake VA 23324

(G-4355)
BUTLER CUSTOM LOGGING
LLC
775 Mitchell Rd (23847-5239)
PHONE..............................434 634-5658
Robby Butler, *Principal*
EMP: 2
SALES (est): 217.6K **Privately Held**
SIC: 2411 Logging camps & contractors

(G-4356)
CROWN ON LLC
3001 Sussex Dr (23847-6325)
PHONE..............................202 427-3042
Myesha Tyler, *Principal*
EMP: 2
SALES (est): 67K **Privately Held**
SIC: 2389 Apparel & accessories

(G-4357)
DREAMS2REALITEES LLC
408 Wolfe St (23847-1544)
PHONE..............................434 594-6865
EMP: 2
SALES (est): 105.4K **Privately Held**
SIC: 2759 Screen printing

(G-4358)
FRANKLIN BRAID MFG CO
620 Davis St (23847-1405)
P.O. Box 711 (23847-0711)
PHONE..............................434 634-4142
James Woodruff, *President*
Franklin Braid, *Engineer*
Laura Diamond, *Treasurer*
Susan Gillam, *Manager*
Franklin A Milnes, *Admin Sec*
▲ **EMP:** 59
SQ FT: 70,000
SALES: 5.5MM
SALES (corp-wide): 15.4MM **Privately
Held**
WEB: www.franklinbraid.com
SIC: 2241 Braids, textile
HQ: Wayne Mills Company Inc
130 W Berkley St
Philadelphia PA 19144
215 842-2134

(G-4359)
GEORGIA-PACIFIC LLC
634 Davis St (23847-6460)
PHONE..............................434 634-5123

Joey Pate, *Manager*
Randy Harrison, *Manager*
EMP: 409
SALES (corp-wide): 38.9B **Privately Held**
WEB: www.gp.com
SIC: 2493 2435 2421 2436 Particleboard, plastic laminated; hardwood veneer & plywood; sawmills & planing mills, general; softwood veneer & plywood
HQ: Georgia-Pacific Llc
    133 Peachtree St Nw
    Atlanta GA 30303
    404 652-4000

(G-4360)
HEYCO WERK USA INC
300 Industrial Park Way (23847)
PHONE..............................434 634-8810
Karl Pieper, *Branch Mgr*
EMP: 3
SALES (corp-wide): 166.5MM **Privately Held**
SIC: 3089 Automotive parts, plastic
HQ: Heyco Werk Usa Inc.
    1310 Garlington Rd Ste F
    Greenville SC 29615
    973 718-9156

(G-4361)
J E MOORE LUMBER CO INC
1275 Brink Rd (23847-6008)
P.O. Box 979 (23847-0979)
PHONE..............................434 634-9740
David Moore, *President*
Frances Moore, *Admin Sec*
EMP: 13
SALES (est): 2.1MM **Privately Held**
SIC: 2421 Sawmills & planing mills, general

(G-4362)
KELLY SWENSON
552 N Main St (23847-1236)
PHONE..............................434 634-3926
Kelly B Swenson, *Principal*
EMP: 2
SALES (est): 107.4K **Privately Held**
SIC: 3599 Machine shop, jobbing & repair

(G-4363)
MARY A THOMAS
Also Called: P Pillar Printing & Promotions
195 Concord Ln (23847-7246)
PHONE..............................434 637-2016
Mary Thomas, *Owner*
EMP: 1
SALES (est): 53.2K **Privately Held**
SIC: 2752 Commercial printing, lithographic

(G-4364)
ORAN SAFETY GLASS INC
Also Called: Oran USA
48 Industrial Pkwy (23847-6335)
PHONE..............................434 336-1620
Daniel Cohen, *President*
Brandon Kindall, *Controller*
▲ **EMP:** 10
SALES (est): 4.2MM
SALES (corp-wide): 30.5MM **Privately Held**
WEB: www.osg.co.il
SIC: 3231 Products of purchased glass
PA: Oran-Palmach Tzuba Agricultural Cooperative Community Ltd
    Kibbutz
    Zova 90870
    257 061-00

(G-4365)
QUALITY CULVERT
34 Three Creek Dr (23847-6346)
PHONE..............................434 336-1468
EMP: 5
SALES (est): 190K **Privately Held**
SIC: 3272 Mfg Concrete Products

(G-4366)
RHOADES ENTERPRISE
3843 Slagles Lake Rd (23847-8023)
PHONE..............................804 347-2051
Samuel T Rhoades, *Principal*
EMP: 1
SALES (est): 97K **Privately Held**
SIC: 3861 Photographic equipment & supplies

(G-4367)
STEELFAB OF VIRGINIA INC
1510 Reese St (23847-6474)
P.O. Box 152 (23847-0152)
PHONE..............................434 348-9021
Wayne Lunceford, *Production*
Rob Burlington, *Branch Mgr*
Richard Pitt, *Manager*
EMP: 95
SALES (corp-wide): 445MM **Privately Held**
WEB: www.steelfab-inc.com
SIC: 3441 Building components, structural steel
HQ: Steelfab Of Virginia, Inc.
    5105 Bur Oak Cir Ste 100
    Raleigh NC 27612

(G-4368)
THORPE LOGGING INC
623 Belfield Rd (23847-8066)
PHONE..............................434 634-6050
Phillip B Thorpe, *President*
Wanda Thorpe, *Admin Sec*
EMP: 8
SALES (est): 500K **Privately Held**
SIC: 2411 Logging camps & contractors

(G-4369)
VALLEY PROTEINS (DE) INC
25170 Val Pro Dr (23847-6664)
P.O. Box 3588, Winchester (22604-2586)
PHONE..............................434 634-9475
Jim Biedenback, *Plant Mgr*
Tina Smith, *Purch Mgr*
Mike Anderson, *Manager*
EMP: 65
SALES (corp-wide): 501.1MM **Privately Held**
WEB: www.valleyproteins.com
SIC: 2048 Prepared feeds
PA: Valley Proteins (De), Inc.
    151 Valpro Dr
    Winchester VA 22603
    540 877-2533

(G-4370)
WESTERN EXPRESS INC
2296 Sussex Dr (23847-6308)
PHONE..............................434 348-0650
Fax: 434 348-1037
EMP: 7
SALES (corp-wide): 341.9MM **Privately Held**
SIC: 2741 Miscellaneous Publishing, Nsk
HQ: Western Express, Inc.
    7135 Centennial Pl
    Nashville TN 37209

(G-4371)
WOMACK PUBLISHING CO INC
111 Baker St (23847-1703)
P.O. Box 786 (23847-0786)
PHONE..............................434 432-1654
Brian Swart, *Branch Mgr*
EMP: 10
SALES (corp-wide): 33.3MM **Privately Held**
WEB: www.timesvirginian.com
SIC: 2711 Newspapers: publishing only, not printed on site
PA: Womack Publishing Co Inc
    28 N Main St
    Chatham VA 24531
    434 432-2791

Etlan
Madison County

(G-4372)
BLUE QUARTZ WINERY LLC
2861 S F T Valley Rd (22719-2000)
PHONE..............................540 923-4048
Christine Wallin, *Administration*
EMP: 4
SALES (est): 268.3K **Privately Held**
SIC: 2084 Wines

(G-4373)
FRYE DELANCE
Also Called: Hard Wind Farm
103 Champe Plain Rd (22719-1947)
PHONE..............................540 923-4581
Delance Frye, *Owner*

EMP: 1
SALES (est): 99.7K **Privately Held**
SIC: 3523 Balers, farm: hay, straw, cotton, etc.

Evington
Campbell County

(G-4374)
BENNETT MOTORSPORTS INC
Also Called: Pat Bennett Race Cars
314 Miles Ln (24550-4092)
PHONE..............................434 845-2277
Patrick Bennett, *President*
EMP: 6
SALES (est): 520K **Privately Held**
WEB: www.patbennettracecars.com
SIC: 3711 Automobile assembly, including specialty automobiles

(G-4375)
BURNOPP METAL LLC
189 Buffalo Ln (24550-3976)
PHONE..............................434 525-4746
Jake Burnopp,
EMP: 2
SALES (est): 400K **Privately Held**
SIC: 3499 1542 Aerosol valves, metal; commercial & office building, new construction

(G-4376)
DOME AND SPEAR DISTILLERY LLC
4529 Dearborn Rd (24550-1803)
PHONE..............................434 851-5477
EMP: 3
SALES (est): 135K **Privately Held**
SIC: 2085 Distilled & blended liquors

(G-4377)
HITEK POWDER COATING
314 Miles Ln (24550-4092)
PHONE..............................434 845-7000
Pat Bennett, *Principal*
EMP: 3
SALES (est): 143.8K **Privately Held**
WEB: www.patbennettracecars.com
SIC: 3479 Coating of metals & formed products

(G-4378)
LINE X CENTRAL VIRGINIA INC
1077 Sunburst Rd (24550-3618)
PHONE..............................434 525-8878
Amber Digges, *President*
John Boston, *President*
Amber Minso Digges, *Principal*
EMP: 3
SALES (est): 230K **Privately Held**
SIC: 2851 1752 Coating, air curing; floor laying & floor work

(G-4379)
MICHAELS WELDING
5268 Wards Rd (24550-1959)
PHONE..............................434 238-5302
Michael Ballowe, *Principal*
EMP: 1
SALES (est): 39.8K **Privately Held**
SIC: 7692 Welding repair

(G-4380)
MOS WELDING SHOP
600 Buffalo Mill Rd (24550-4119)
PHONE..............................434 525-1137
Morris Wright, *Owner*
EMP: 1
SALES (est): 48K **Privately Held**
SIC: 7692 Welding repair

(G-4381)
OAKS AT TIMBERLAKE
11 Sun Dr (24550-1732)
PHONE..............................434 525-7107
Lisa Ramsey, *Principal*
EMP: 2
SALES (est): 124.8K **Privately Held**
SIC: 3448 Buildings, portable: prefabricated metal

(G-4382)
OTTER RIVER FILTRATION PLANT
9625 Leesville Rd (24550-4241)
PHONE..............................434 821-8611
Mike Cameron, *Administration*
EMP: 5
SALES (est): 381.4K **Privately Held**
SIC: 2899 Water treating compounds

(G-4383)
PRECISION MILLWORK & CABINETS
3582 Evington Rd (24550-4181)
PHONE..............................434 525-6988
John W Mitchell Jr, *Owner*
Ronald Womach, *Vice Pres*
EMP: 2
SALES (est): 264.9K **Privately Held**
SIC: 2434 Wood kitchen cabinets

(G-4384)
SPEEDMTER CLBRTION SPECIALISTS
158 One Mile Rd (24550-2050)
PHONE..............................434 821-5374
Robert Evans, *Owner*
EMP: 1
SALES (est): 116.6K **Privately Held**
SIC: 3824 Speedometers

Ewing
Lee County

(G-4385)
LONESOME TRAILS ENTPS INC
227 Vrlin Hnsley Dr Ewing (24248)
PHONE..............................276 445-5443
Aaron Hensley, *CEO*
Jody Hensley, *Officer*
EMP: 2
SALES (est): 125K **Privately Held**
WEB: www.lonesometrails.org
SIC: 2865 Color lakes or toners

(G-4386)
M C CHADWELL
323 Old Bailey Dr (24248-8525)
PHONE..............................276 445-5495
M C Chdwell, *Owner*
EMP: 1
SALES (est): 1.2K **Privately Held**
SIC: 2048 Prepared feeds

Exmore
Northampton County

(G-4387)
WATERFORD PRINTING INC
12133 Bank Ave (23350)
P.O. Box 367 (23350-0367)
PHONE..............................757 442-5616
Hillary Little, *President*
Little Amy S, *Vice Pres*
Karen McCarter, *Treasurer*
EMP: 8
SQ FT: 1,200
SALES (est): 1.3MM **Privately Held**
WEB: www.waterfordprinting.com
SIC: 2752 Commercial printing, offset

Faber
Nelson County

(G-4388)
BRENT MANOR INN & VINEYARDS
100 Brent Manor Ln (22938-2538)
PHONE..............................540 226-5958
Brent Dcollier, *Principal*
EMP: 2
SALES (est): 176.4K **Privately Held**
WEB: www.brentmanorvineyards.com
SIC: 2084 Wines

(G-4389)
DELFOSSE VINEYARDS WINERY LLC
500 Del Fosse Winery Ln (22938-2465)
PHONE..................................434 263-6100
Michael Albers, *Mng Member*
EMP: 5
SALES (est): 150K **Privately Held**
WEB: www.delfossewine.com
SIC: 2084 Wines

(G-4390)
MOUNTAIN AND VINE LLC
Also Called: Delfosse Vinyrd Winery Nelson
500 Del Fosse Winery Ln (22938-2465)
PHONE..................................434 263-6100
Michael Albers, *Mng Member*
EMP: 2
SALES (est): 75.4K **Privately Held**
WEB: www.delfossewine.com
SIC: 2084 Wines

(G-4391)
STRUCTURES UNLIMITED
1625 River Rd (22938-2431)
PHONE..................................434 361-2294
Nancy Fletcher, *Owner*
EMP: 2
SALES (est): 141K **Privately Held**
SIC: 7692 Welding repair

(G-4392)
WOODS MILL DISTILLERY LLC
1625 River Rd (22938-2431)
PHONE..................................434 361-2294
EMP: 3
SALES (est): 158.4K **Privately Held**
WEB: www.nelsoncounty-va.gov
SIC: 2085 Distilled & blended liquors

Fairfax
Fairfax County

(G-4393)
1EARTHMATTERS LLC
12404b Liberty Bridge Rd (22033-6041)
PHONE..................................202 412-8882
Don Feil, *CEO*
EMP: 2
SQ FT: 3,000
SALES (est): 146.5K **Privately Held**
WEB: www.earthmattersllc.com
SIC: 3646 Commercial indusl & institutional electric lighting fixtures

(G-4394)
5GL SOFTWARE INC
4117 Marble Ln (22033-3129)
PHONE..................................703 861-3644
Janak Mathuria, *Principal*
EMP: 3
SALES (est): 104.2K **Privately Held**
SIC: 7372 Prepackaged software

(G-4395)
7M GRAPHIX INC
3160 Spring St Ste B (22031-2315)
P.O. Box 9523, Alexandria (22304-0523)
PHONE..................................703 751-6971
Fernando Acha, *President*
EMP: 3
SALES (est): 303.2K **Privately Held**
WEB: www.7mgraphix.com
SIC: 3993 Signs & advertising specialties

(G-4396)
A C GRAPHICS INC
2800 Dorr Ave Ste H (22031-1512)
P.O. Box 309, Linden (22642-0309)
PHONE..................................703 246-9466
EMP: 4 EST: 1997
SALES (est): 522K **Privately Held**
SIC: 2752 7336 Lithographic Commercial Printing Commercial Art/Graphic Design

(G-4397)
A REASON TO WRITE
3611 Deerberry Ct (22033-1227)
PHONE..................................703 481-3277
Ellen Weeren, *Owner*
EMP: 1 EST: 2007

SALES (est): 130K **Privately Held**
WEB: www.areasontowrite.com
SIC: 2771 Greeting cards

(G-4398)
AAACM GREEN WARRIOR INC
5215 Mornington Ct (22032-2621)
PHONE..................................703 865-5991
Lawrence D Liedtke, *President*
EMP: 1
SALES (est): 88.9K **Privately Held**
SIC: 2394 3444 Shades, canvas: made from purchased materials; awnings & canopies

(G-4399)
ABE LINCOLN FLAGS & BANNERS
8634 Lee Hwy (22031-2101)
PHONE..................................703 204-1116
Abe Lincoln, *Owner*
EMP: 1
SALES (est): 71K **Privately Held**
WEB: www.abeflags.net
SIC: 3993 Signs & advertising specialties

(G-4400)
AC CETERA INC
9812 Bacon Ct (22032-2801)
P.O. Box 900, Luxor PA (15662-0900)
PHONE..................................724 532-3363
Mark Tarshis, *President*
◆ EMP: 5
SQ FT: 2,000
SALES (est): 754K **Privately Held**
WEB: www.ac-cetera.com
SIC: 3651 7929 5099 Household audio equipment; entertainers & entertainment groups; musical instruments

(G-4401)
AERO CORPORATION
Also Called: Intermedia.aero
4000 Legato Rd Ste 1100 (22033-2893)
PHONE..................................703 896-7721
Richard Nelson, *CEO*
Joel Ratner, *COO*
EMP: 9
SQ FT: 1,000
SALES (est): 545.7K **Privately Held**
WEB: www.idc-tv.com
SIC: 3812 8731 7371 Instrument landing systems (ILS), airborne or ground; commercial physical research; energy research; electronic research; computer software development & applications

(G-4402)
AH LOVE OIL & VINEGAR
2910 District Ave Ste 165 (22031-2284)
PHONE..................................703 992-7000
EMP: 2
SALES (est): 62.3K **Privately Held**
SIC: 2099 Food Preparations, Nec, Nsk

(G-4403)
AI MACHINES INC
8226 Adenlee Ave Apt 101 (22031-4825)
PHONE..................................973 204-9772
Vishal Vadodaria, *CEO*
EMP: 1
SALES (est): 32.7K **Privately Held**
WEB: www.ai-machine.com
SIC: 7372 Application computer software; business oriented computer software

(G-4404)
ALPHA PRINTING INC
8451 Hilltop Rd Ste A (22031-4309)
PHONE..................................703 914-2800
Joseph Tucker, *Owner*
EMP: 2
SALES (est): 80.6K **Privately Held**
SIC: 2759 Commercial printing

(G-4405)
AMANDA GRACE HANDCRAFTED
Also Called: Amanda Grace Jewelry
12461 Hayes Ct Unit 101 (22033-4297)
PHONE..................................703 539-2151
Amanda Jarvis,
EMP: 2
SALES (est): 111.2K **Privately Held**
SIC: 3911 Pins (jewelry), precious metal

(G-4406)
AMATO INDUSTRIES
2801 Juniper St Ste 1 (22031-4418)
PHONE..................................703 534-1400
Sinclair Brian, *CEO*
Mary Boggs, *Opers Staff*
EMP: 2
SALES (est): 48K **Privately Held**
WEB: www.amatoind.com
SIC: 3999 Manufacturing industries

(G-4407)
AMF METAL ART INC
4315 Argonne Dr (22032-1406)
PHONE..................................703 354-1345
EMP: 2
SALES (est): 106.7K **Privately Held**
WEB: www.amfmetal.com
SIC: 3441 Fabricated structural metal

(G-4408)
ANNEX INC
10131 Zion Dr (22032-3209)
PHONE..................................703 239-8553
Darrell Steven Picard, *Principal*
EMP: 2
SALES (est): 152.1K **Privately Held**
WEB: www.annexinc.com
SIC: 3672 Printed circuit boards

(G-4409)
AQUABEAN LLC
8913 Glade Hill Rd (22031-3221)
PHONE..................................703 577-0315
Sonia Rehman, *CEO*
EMP: 1
SALES (est): 58.9K **Privately Held**
SIC: 3082 7389 Unsupported plastics profile shapes;

(G-4410)
ARABESQUE MEDIA
Also Called: Breek Media
4000 Legato Rd (22033-2892)
PHONE..................................703 745-5395
Marwan Ahmad,
EMP: 2
SQ FT: 500
SALES (est): 232.2K **Privately Held**
WEB: www.breekmedia.com
SIC: 2711 2721 2732 2741 Newspapers: publishing only, not printed on site; magazines: publishing only, not printed on site; pamphlets: printing only, not published on site; posters: publishing only, not printed on site; commercial art & graphic design; marketing consulting services

(G-4411)
ARCHEMATERIAL INC
9848b Main St (22031-3908)
PHONE..................................703 826-6820
Turker Aydemir, *Director*
EMP: 2
SALES (est): 143.1K **Privately Held**
SIC: 2759 Commercial printing

(G-4412)
ARGON ST INC (HQ)
12701 Fair Lakes Cir # 800 (22033-4910)
PHONE..................................703 322-0881
Ivan Mills, *General Mgr*
William Joe Carlin, *Vice Pres*
Kerry M Rowe, *Vice Pres*
Tanya Mayer, *Engineer*
John Holt, *CFO*
▼ EMP: 750
SQ FT: 165,000
SALES (est): 192.6MM
SALES (corp-wide): 76.5B **Publicly Held**
WEB: www.argonst.com
SIC: 3812 Navigational systems & instruments
PA: The Boeing Company
100 N Riverside Plz
Chicago IL 60606
312 544-2000

(G-4413)
ATS CORPORATION (DH)
Also Called: Ats Corporation of Virginia
4000 Legato Rd Ste 600 (22033-4055)
PHONE..................................571 766-2400
John Hassoun, *Co-CEO*
Leon C Perry, *COO*
Stuart R Lloyd, *Exec VP*

Jim Russell, *Senior VP*
Bob Pick, *Vice Pres*
EMP: 33
SALES (est): 43.8MM
SALES (corp-wide): 499.8MM **Privately Held**
WEB: www.salientcrgt.com
SIC: 7372 7379 8748 Business oriented computer software; computer related consulting services; business consulting

(G-4414)
AUTUMN PUBLISHING ENTERPRISES
4289 Country Squire Ln (22032-1611)
P.O. Box 1305 (22038-1305)
PHONE..................................703 978-2132
Pamela Barrett, *Principal*
EMP: 5
SALES (est): 234.6K **Privately Held**
SIC: 2731 5192 2721 Book publishing; books, periodicals & newspapers; statistical reports (periodicals): publishing only

(G-4415)
AVAYA FEDERAL SOLUTIONS INC
12730 Fair Lakes Cir (22033-4901)
PHONE..................................703 390-8333
Jeff Hansen, *President*
EMP: 25 **Publicly Held**
WEB: www.avaya.com
SIC: 3661 Telephone & telegraph apparatus
HQ: Avaya Federal Solutions, Inc.
12730 Fair Lakes Cir
Fairfax VA 22033

(G-4416)
AVAYA FEDERAL SOLUTIONS INC (DH)
12730 Fair Lakes Cir (22033-4901)
PHONE..................................703 653-8000
Michael Singer, *President*
Richard Coleman, *Vice Pres*
Dean Grayson, *Vice Pres*
Lori Molino, *Vice Pres*
Peter Hong, *Treasurer*
EMP: 15
SALES (est): 57.3MM **Publicly Held**
WEB: www.avaya.com
SIC: 3661 Telephone & telegraph apparatus
HQ: Avaya Inc.
4655 Great America Pkwy
Santa Clara CA 95054
908 953-6000

(G-4417)
BALTIMORE BUSINESS COMPANY LLC
12836 Point Pleasant Dr (22033-3215)
PHONE..................................301 848-7200
Saeed Movahedi, *Principal*
EMP: 5
SALES (est): 193.2K **Privately Held**
SIC: 2711 Newspapers, publishing & printing

(G-4418)
BANNER SINGS ETC
7252 Arlington Blvd (20151)
PHONE..................................703 698-5466
Ronald Holt, *Partner*
Alex Vann, *Partner*
EMP: 5
SALES (est): 323.6K **Privately Held**
SIC: 3993 Signs, not made in custom sign painting shops

(G-4419)
BASVIN SOFTWARE LLC
5531 Starboard Ct (22032-4012)
PHONE..................................703 537-0888
B Sathyanarayana, *Mng Member*
EMP: 3
SALES (est): 161K **Privately Held**
SIC: 7372 Prepackaged software

(G-4420)
BOP INTERNATIONAL INC
12128 Monument Dr # 236 (22033-5542)
PHONE..................................571 550-6669
Zane Farooq, *Principal*
EMP: 5 EST: 2010

▲ = Import ▼=Export
◆ =Import/Export

SALES (est): 357.5K **Privately Held**
WEB: www.bopintl.com
SIC: **1389** Oil field services

(G-4421)
BRIGGS & RILEY TRAVELWARE LLC
Also Called: Luggage Plus
11703 Lee Jackson Mem Hwy (22033)
PHONE.............................703 352-0713
Misty Zamora, *Branch Mgr*
EMP: 4
SALES (corp-wide): 11.6MM **Privately Held**
WEB: www.briggs-riley.com
SIC: **3199** Corners, luggage: leather
HQ: Briggs & Riley Travelware, Llc
400 Wireless Blvd Ste 1
Hauppauge NY 11788
631 434-7722

(G-4422)
C2-MASK INC
Also Called: Allegra Print & Imaging
2812 Merrilee Dr Ste E (22031-4439)
PHONE.............................703 698-7820
Oanh Henry, *President*
Brian Culbertson, *Shareholder*
EMP: 6
SALES (est): 971.8K **Privately Held**
WEB: www.allegramarketingprint.com
SIC: **2752** Commercial printing, offset

(G-4423)
CAPITAL BRANDWORKS LLC
3833 Pickett Rd (22031-3605)
PHONE.............................703 609-7010
Tyler Regehr,
EMP: 2 EST: 2015
SALES (est): 130.6K **Privately Held**
WEB: www.capitalbrandworks.com
SIC: **2326 2759 7389** Work apparel, except uniforms; letterpress & screen printing; advertising, promotional & trade show services

(G-4424)
CARDIAC DIAGNOSTICS LLC
9103 Vosger Ct (22031-2029)
PHONE.............................703 268-5751
Andrew Matoba,
EMP: 1
SALES (est): 83.9K **Privately Held**
SIC: **2835** In vitro & in vivo diagnostic substances

(G-4425)
CCI SCREENPRINTING INC
5003 Gadsen Dr (22032-3411)
PHONE.............................703 978-0257
Daniel Wallingford, *President*
Barbara Wallingford, *Admin Sec*
EMP: 8
SALES (est): 835.2K **Privately Held**
WEB: www.athleticunion.company
SIC: **2759** Screen printing

(G-4426)
CHADWICK INTERNATIONAL INC (PA)
8300 Arlington Blvd B2 (22031-5209)
PHONE.............................703 560-0970
Ronald Nocera, *Ch of Bd*
George S Henderson, *President*
David S Pikovsky, *Treasurer*
EMP: 16
SQ FT: 5,000
SALES (est): 1.1MM **Privately Held**
SIC: **2452** Prefabricated wood buildings

(G-4427)
CHAMPION BILLD & BAR STOOLS
13041 Fair Lk Shpg Ctr (22033-5179)
PHONE.............................703 631-8800
Mark Talinda, *Principal*
EMP: 2
SALES (est): 162.1K **Privately Held**
SIC: **2542 7999** Bar fixtures, except wood; billiard parlor

(G-4428)
CHOSUN ILBO WASHINGTON INC
9840 Main St Ste 100 (22031-3909)
PHONE.............................703 865-8310
EMP: 5
SALES (est): 261.2K **Privately Held**
WEB: www.chosunilbousa.com
SIC: **2711** Newspapers, publishing & printing

(G-4429)
COMPLETE SIGN INC
Also Called: Sign-A-Rama
2832 Dorr Ave Ste B (22031-1524)
PHONE.............................571 276-8407
John Martel, *President*
EMP: 8
SQ FT: 2,500
SALES (est): 961.6K **Privately Held**
WEB: www.completesign.net
SIC: **3993** Signs & advertising specialties

(G-4430)
CORPORATE SUPPLY TECHNOLOGY
3908 Plum Run Ct (22033-1447)
PHONE.............................703 932-3475
Linda Petrus, *Vice Pres*
EMP: 1
SALES (est): 60.1K **Privately Held**
SIC: **2522** Office chairs, benches & stools, except wood

(G-4431)
COUGAAR SOFTWARE INC
8260 Willow Oaks Corporat (22031-4523)
PHONE.............................703 506-1700
Dr Todd M Carrico, *President*
Melvin Sassoon, *Senior VP*
John Anderson, *Engineer*
Donna F Zuniga, *Human Resources*
Vassili Koriabine, *Software Engr*
EMP: 20 EST: 2001
SALES (est): 2.7MM **Privately Held**
WEB: www.cougaarsoftware.com
SIC: **7372** Prepackaged software

(G-4432)
CREATIVE DOCUMENT IMAGING INC (PA)
Also Called: CDI
8451 Hilltop Rd Ste I (22031-4309)
PHONE.............................703 208-2212
Luis Mendoza, *President*
Darryl Garland, *Regional Mgr*
Maurice Briddell, *Vice Pres*
Connie Hudson, *Facilities Mgr*
Dena Briddell, *Accounts Mgr*
EMP: 6
SALES (est): 957.2K **Privately Held**
WEB: www.creativedoc.net
SIC: **2752** Commercial printing, offset

(G-4433)
CROSS PRINTING SOLUTIONS LLC
8451 Hilltop Rd Ste B (22031-4309)
PHONE.............................703 208-2214
EMP: 2
SALES (est): 83.9K **Privately Held**
SIC: **2752** Commercial printing, lithographic

(G-4434)
CROSS STITCH LLC
4018 Royal Lytham Dr (22033-2013)
PHONE.............................703 961-1636
Ambrose Fernandez, *Principal*
EMP: 1
SALES (est): 37.3K **Privately Held**
SIC: **2395** Embroidery & art needlework

(G-4435)
DAILY DISTRIBUTIONS INC
10464 Malone Ct (22032-2377)
PHONE.............................703 577-8120
Abeed Azad, *Principal*
EMP: 4
SALES (est): 178.7K **Privately Held**
SIC: **2711** Newspapers, publishing & printing

(G-4436)
DANIELSON TRADING LLC
3992 White Clover Ct (22031-3854)
PHONE.............................703 764-0450
Chaya M Deitsch,
EMP: 2
SALES (est): 202.4K **Privately Held**
SIC: **2441** Boxes, wood

(G-4437)
DELL INC
8270 Wllw Oaks Crprte 3 (22031-4530)
PHONE.............................301 581-0513
George Omohundro, *Branch Mgr*
EMP: 670 **Publicly Held**
WEB: www.dell.com
SIC: **3571** Personal computers (microcomputers)
HQ: Dell Inc.
1 Dell Way
Round Rock TX 78682
800 289-3355

(G-4438)
DEXTALL INC
2720 Prosperity Ave # 400 (22031-4332)
PHONE.............................202 701-3208
Aurimas Sabulis, *CEO*
EMP: 1
SALES (est): 57.3K **Privately Held**
SIC: **2522** Office bookcases, wallcases & partitions, except wood

(G-4439)
DISTER INC
Also Called: BCT Virginia
2800 Juniper St Ste 5 (22031-4411)
PHONE.............................703 207-0201
Tom Defries, *Branch Mgr*
EMP: 40
SALES (corp-wide): 4MM **Privately Held**
WEB: www.bctvirginia.com
SIC: **2759 3953 2752 2396** Thermography; embossing seals & hand stamps; commercial printing, lithographic; automotive & apparel trimmings
PA: Dister Inc
925 Denison Ave
Norfolk VA 23513
757 857-1946

(G-4440)
DM ASSOCIATES LLC
4110 Whitacre Rd (22032-1144)
PHONE.............................571 406-2318
Miles Sanchez, *CEO*
EMP: 1
SALES (est): 50.1K **Privately Held**
SIC: **1041 7389** Placer gold mining;

(G-4441)
DR BANAJI GIRISH DDS PC
8505 Arlington Blvd # 370 (22031-4621)
PHONE.............................703 849-1300
Girish Banaji, *Owner*
EMP: 7
SALES (est): 777.8K **Privately Held**
WEB: www.banajidds.com
SIC: **3843** Enamels, dentists'

(G-4442)
E-KARE INC
Also Called: Ekare
3040 Williams Dr Ste 610 (22031-4618)
PHONE.............................844 443-5273
Patrick Cheng, *CEO*
Adil Alaoui, *Senior VP*
Emmanuel Wilson, *Opers Staff*
Kyle Wu, *Chief Mktg Ofcr*
Ozgur Guler, *CTO*
EMP: 2
SALES (est): 278.8K **Privately Held**
WEB: www.ekare.ai
SIC: **3845** Electromedical apparatus

(G-4443)
EDITEK INC
10907 Mddlgate Dr Fairfax (22032)
PHONE.............................703 652-9495
Raymond Cohen, *Principal*
Leonardo Cohen, *Consultant*
EMP: 2
SALES (est): 131.2K **Privately Held**
WEB: www.editek.com
SIC: **7372** Prepackaged software

(G-4444)
EINSTITUTE INC
Also Called: Game Institute, The
3929 Starters Ct (22033-2026)
PHONE.............................571 255-0530
EMP: 12
SALES (est): 37.4K **Privately Held**
SIC: **7372 7389** Prepackaged Software Services Business Services At Non-Commercial Site

(G-4445)
EK SCREEN PRINTS
3833 Pickett Rd (22031-3605)
PHONE.............................703 250-2556
Tyler Regehr, *Accountant*
Kristin Ross, *Manager*
EMP: 4
SALES (est): 512.9K **Privately Held**
WEB: www.eastlandscreenprints.com
SIC: **2759** Screen printing

(G-4446)
ENGRAVING AND PRINTING BUREAU
12116 Monu Dr Unit 310 (22033)
PHONE.............................202 997-9580
Neal Hambright, *Branch Mgr*
EMP: 2 **Publicly Held**
WEB: www.moneyfactory.gov
SIC: **2752** Commercial printing, lithographic
HQ: Bureau Of Engraving And Printing
14th And C St Sw
Washington DC 20228
202 874-2361

(G-4447)
ENTERPRISE ITECH CORP
10014 Manor Pl (22032-3628)
PHONE.............................703 731-7881
Palanisamy Nagaraj, *President*
EMP: 2 EST: 2000
SALES (est): 150K **Privately Held**
WEB: www.enterpriseitech.com
SIC: **7372** Prepackaged software

(G-4448)
ENTERTAINMENT SOFTWARE ASSOC
4025 Fair Ridge Dr # 250 (22033-2896)
PHONE.............................703 383-3976
EMP: 2
SALES (est): 130K **Privately Held**
SIC: **7372** Prepackaged Software

(G-4449)
EPIPHANY INC
3501 Stringfellow Ct (22033-1502)
PHONE.............................703 437-3133
Wassim Ghali, *President*
EMP: 8
SALES (est): 635.1K **Privately Held**
SIC: **2024** Ice cream & frozen desserts

(G-4450)
ESSENCE WOODWORKS LLC
13200 Goose Pond Ln (22033-5169)
PHONE.............................703 945-3108
EMP: 1
SALES (est): 54.1K **Privately Held**
SIC: **2431** Millwork

(G-4451)
ESSENTIAL SOFTWARE DEV LLC
9430 Silver King Ct # 302 (22031-4761)
PHONE.............................540 222-1254
Kingsley Klosson, *Mng Member*
EMP: 1
SALES (est): 180K **Privately Held**
SIC: **7372 7389** Prepackaged software; business services

(G-4452)
EURO DESIGN BUILDERS GROUP
12400 Stewarts Ford Ct (22033-2413)
PHONE.............................571 236-6189
Ali Nazhand, *Principal*
EMP: 4
SALES (est): 12K **Privately Held**
SIC: **3432** Plumbing fixture fittings & trim

GEOGRAPHIC

(G-4453)
EXPO BRANDERS
CORPORATION
9667 Main St Ste D (22031-3751)
PHONE................................703 865-7581
Amy Zydel, *President*
EMP: 5
SALES (est): 172.3K **Privately Held**
WEB: www.undercoverprinter.com
SIC: 2752 3993 7389 Commercial print-
ing, offset; signs & advertising specialties;
advertising, promotional & trade show
services

(G-4454)
EXPO CABINETRY
2940 Prosperity Ave B (22031-2209)
PHONE................................703 940-3800
EMP: 3
SALES (est): 289.4K **Privately Held**
SIC: 2434 Wood kitchen cabinets

(G-4455)
FAMILY TREE CARE INC
2913 Hideaway Rd (22031-1310)
P.O. Box 273, Easley SC (29641-0273)
PHONE................................703 280-1169
James Wentink, *President*
Elise Crosby, *Office Mgr*
EMP: 3
SALES (est): 300K **Privately Held**
WEB: www.familytreecare-va.com
SIC: 2499 0783 Mulch, wood & bark; re-
moval services, bush & tree

(G-4456)
FARAGE PRECISION LLC
10202 Aspen Willow Dr (22032-3600)
PHONE................................901 264-2422
Mark William Farage, *Administration*
EMP: 2
SALES (est): 156.3K **Privately Held**
WEB: www.farageprecision.com
SIC: 3599 Machine shop, jobbing & repair

(G-4457)
FINDERS KEEPERS
RECRUITING
4405 Fair Stone Dr # 301 (22033-5112)
PHONE................................703 963-0874
John Fimbel, *Principal*
EMP: 2
SALES (est): 85.9K **Privately Held**
WEB: www.finderskeepersrecruiting.com
SIC: 3571 Electronic computers

(G-4458)
FIXMEE LLC
4609 Luxberry Dr (22032-1930)
PHONE................................703 731-1444
EMP: 2
SALES (est): 68.5K **Privately Held**
WEB: www.fixmee.com
SIC: 7372 Prepackaged software

(G-4459)
FNA JEWELS
12309 Fox Lake Ct (22033-2863)
PHONE................................703 591-6817
EMP: 2
SALES (est): 92.7K **Privately Held**
WEB: www.fnajewels.com
SIC: 3577 Computer peripheral equipment

(G-4460)
G F I ASSOCIATES INC (HQ)
Also Called: Republic Electronics
8280 Willow Oaks Corp Dr (22031-4518)
PHONE................................703 533-8555
Michael W Ueltzen, *President*
EMP: 5
SALES (est): 456.6K
SALES (corp-wide): 10.7MM **Privately
Held**
WEB: www.therepublicgroup.com
SIC: 2731 Books: publishing only
PA: Republic Electronics Corporation
8280 Willow Oaks Corporat
Fairfax VA 22031
703 533-8555

(G-4461)
GARY SMITH
Also Called: Logical Decisions
9206 Saint Marks Pl (22031-3046)
PHONE................................703 218-1801
Gary Smith, *Owner*
EMP: 1
SALES (est): 500K **Privately Held**
WEB: www.logicaldecisions.com
SIC: 7372 7371 Business oriented com-
puter software; computer software sys-
tems analysis & design, custom

(G-4462)
GENERAL DYNAMICS
CORPORATION
12450 Fair Lkes Cir 200 (22033)
PHONE................................703 263-2835
Scott Butler, *Vice Pres*
Starlene Keppel, *Vice Pres*
Josh Richardson, *Project Mgr*
Shawn Yuroshek, *Facilities Mgr*
Mike Nobis, *Buyer*
EMP: 5
SALES (corp-wide): 39.3B **Publicly Held**
WEB: www.gdmissionsystems.com
SIC: 3812 Aircraft/aerospace flight instru-
ments & guidance systems
PA: General Dynamics Corporation
11011 Sunset Hills Rd
Reston VA 20190
703 876-3000

(G-4463)
GENERAL DYNMICS MSSION
SYSTEMS (HQ)
12450 Fair Lakes Cir (22033-3810)
PHONE................................877 449-0600
Christopher Brady, *President*
S Daniel Johnson, *Exec VP*
Mark C Roualet, *Exec VP*
Robert Lennox, *Senior VP*
Jim Stockdale, *Senior VP*
▲ EMP: 50
SALES (est): 2.3B
SALES (corp-wide): 39.3B **Publicly Held**
WEB: www.gdmissionsystems.com
SIC: 3571 Electronic computers
PA: General Dynamics Corporation
11011 Sunset Hills Rd
Reston VA 20190
703 876-3000

(G-4464)
GHTI CORPORATION
4100 Meadow Hill Ln (22033-3112)
PHONE................................703 802-8616
Jerry A Moore, *CEO*
EMP: 3
SALES (est): 139.8K **Privately Held**
SIC: 3231 Products of purchased glass

(G-4465)
GIANT LION SOFTWARE LLC
5075 Coleridge Dr (22032-2417)
PHONE................................703 764-8060
Neil M Baitinger, *Administration*
EMP: 2
SALES (est): 121.3K **Privately Held**
WEB: www.giantlionsoftware.com
SIC: 7372 Prepackaged software

(G-4466)
GIANT PRINTING
8400 Hilltop Rd (22031-4399)
PHONE................................703 525-1313
EMP: 2 EST: 2019
SALES (est): 83.9K **Privately Held**
SIC: 2752 Commercial printing, litho-
graphic

(G-4467)
GIANT PUBLISHING & CO
4107 Oak Village Ldg (22033-6229)
PHONE................................703 750-6447
EMP: 2
SALES (est): 43.3K **Privately Held**
WEB: www.giantdirectory.com
SIC: 2741 Miscellaneous publishing

(G-4468)
GILSTRAP INC JOHN
12758 Lavender Keep Cir (22033-2228)
PHONE................................703 961-9413
Joy B Gilstrap, *Principal*

EMP: 2 EST: 2009
SALES (est): 98.2K **Privately Held**
WEB: www.johngilstrap.com
SIC: 2741 Miscellaneous publishing

(G-4469)
GLOBAL DESIGN
CONTRACTORS INC
9253 Eljames Dr (22032-2110)
PHONE................................703 865-6064
Do Hee R Kim, *President*
EMP: 7
SALES (est): 70K **Privately Held**
SIC: 1221 Bituminous coal & lignite-sur-
face mining

(G-4470)
GOODER GROUP INC
2724 Dorr Ave Ste 103 (22031-4900)
PHONE................................703 698-7750
Fax: 703 698-8597
EMP: 15
SALES (est): 1.5MM **Privately Held**
SIC: 2741 2731 Publishes Newsletters &
Pamphlets

(G-4471)
GUPPY GROUP INC
3609 Prosperity Ave (22031-3336)
PHONE................................917 544-9749
Sanjib Kalita, *CEO*
EMP: 1
SALES (est): 32.7K **Privately Held**
WEB: www.guppy.ai
SIC: 7372 Application computer software

(G-4472)
H & A FINE WOODWORKING
10304 Nantucket Ct (22032-2326)
PHONE................................703 499-0944
Hasim Kockaya, *Branch Mgr*
EMP: 1 **Privately Held**
WEB: www.hawoodworking.com
SIC: 2431 Millwork
PA: H & A Fine Woodworking
7801 Loisdale Rd
Springfield VA 22150

(G-4473)
H&R PRINTING
4801 Great Heron Ter (22033-5403)
PHONE................................571 277-1454
EMP: 2
SALES (est): 163K **Privately Held**
WEB: www.printpluspromote.com
SIC: 2752 Commercial printing, offset

(G-4474)
HAIR STUDIO ORIE INC
12154 Penderview Ter # 1233
(22033-4786)
PHONE................................703 282-5390
Orie Hanrahan, *President*
EMP: 1
SALES (est): 39.6K **Privately Held**
SIC: 3999 Hair curlers, designed for
beauty parlors

(G-4475)
HARRODS NATURAL
RESOURCES (PA)
9675 Main St Ste C (22031-3762)
PHONE................................703 426-7200
Douglas R Marvin, *President*
EMP: 6
SALES (est): 781.5K **Privately Held**
SIC: 1381 Directional drilling oil & gas
wells

(G-4476)
HOMEACTIONS LLC
Also Called: Gooder Group
2724 Dorr Ave Ste 103 (22031-4900)
PHONE................................703 698-7750
EMP: 15
SALES (corp-wide): 3.9MM **Privately
Held**
WEB: www.checkpointmarketing.thomson-
reuters.com
SIC: 2741 2731 Newsletter publishing;
pamphlets: publishing & printing
PA: Homeactions, Llc
411 Wallnut St Ste 90124
Potomac MD 20854
301 947-1429

(G-4477)
HUFFS ARTISAN WOODWORK
3308 Sydenham St Apt 40 (22031-4808)
PHONE................................703 399-5493
Justin Huff, *Principal*
EMP: 1
SALES (est): 54.1K **Privately Held**
SIC: 2431 Millwork

(G-4478)
I SW LLC
2750 Prosperity Ave # 600 (22031-4312)
PHONE................................703 270-1540
EMP: 4 EST: 2015
SALES (est): 268.6K **Privately Held**
SIC: 3652 Pre-recorded records & tapes

(G-4479)
IN STOCK TODAY CABINETS
LLC
2817 Dorr Ave (22031-1576)
PHONE................................703 972-4030
Kamil Osmanjan, *CEO*
EMP: 17
SALES (est): 2.4MM **Privately Held**
WEB: www.istcabinets.com
SIC: 2434 Wood kitchen cabinets

(G-4480)
INTUS WINDOWS LLC
2720 Prosperity Ave # 400 (22031-4333)
PHONE................................202 450-4211
Aurimas Sabulis, *Mng Member*
Roland Talalas, *Mng Member*
Steve Tyson, *Business Dir*
▲ EMP: 10
SQ FT: 300
SALES (est): 3.5MM **Privately Held**
WEB: www.intuswindows.com
SIC: 3822 8748 Energy cutoff controls,
residential or commercial types; energy
conservation consultant

(G-4481)
IRON DOG METALSMITHS
9238 Kristin Ln (22032-1811)
PHONE................................703 503-9631
Brian Cunningham, *Principal*
EMP: 1
SALES (est): 57.4K **Privately Held**
SIC: 1011 Iron ores

(G-4482)
ITERIS INC
11781 Lee Jackson Memoria (22033-3319)
PHONE................................949 270-9400
EMP: 6 **Publicly Held**
WEB: www.iteris.com
SIC: 3669 Intercommunication systems,
electric
PA: Iteris, Inc.
1700 Carnegie Ave Ste 100
Santa Ana CA 92705
949 270-9400

(G-4483)
J K ENTERPRISE INC
Also Called: 1 Agrocare
3600 Ox Ridge Ct (22033-2586)
P.O. Box 80, Clifton (20124-0080)
PHONE................................703 352-1858
Jacob A Klitenic III, *President*
EMP: 3
SALES (est): 555.9K **Privately Held**
WEB: www.lumberjake.com
SIC: 2499 Mulch or sawdust products,
wood

(G-4484)
JAMI VENTURES INC
Also Called: Kwik Copy Printing
9653 Fairfax Blvd Ste 205 (22031-2314)
PHONE................................703 352-5679
Birjees J Javaid, *President*
Darlene Cicerchia, *Manager*
EMP: 5
SALES (est): 803.8K **Privately Held**
SIC: 2752 2791 2789 Commercial print-
ing, offset; typesetting; bookbinding & re-
lated work

(G-4485)
JANICE OSTHUS
Also Called: Janao
2862 Glenvale Dr (22031-1415)
PHONE....................................571 212-2247
Janice Osthus, *Owner*
EMP: 1
SALES (est): 52K **Privately Held**
SIC: 2741 Miscellaneous publishing

(G-4486)
**JOINT KNOWLEDGE SOFTWARE
I**
3996 Alcoa Dr (22033-1402)
PHONE....................................703 803-7470
EMP: 2 EST: 2008
SALES (est): 120K **Privately Held**
SIC: 7372 Prepackaged Software Services

(G-4487)
JUSTICE
11759l Fair Oaks Mall (22033-3304)
PHONE....................................703 352-8393
EMP: 2
SALES (est): 67K **Privately Held**
SIC: 2361 Girls' & children's dresses,
blouses & shirts

(G-4488)
K & Z INC
Also Called: Davic Drapery Company
2807 Merrilee Dr Ste D (22031-4414)
PHONE....................................703 876-1660
Sayeda Kazmi, *President*
Zaidi Mumtaz, *Vice Pres*
Bobby Kazmi, *Treasurer*
Kehkanshan Zaidi, *Admin Sec*
EMP: 6 EST: 1963
SQ FT: 4,000
SALES (est): 250K **Privately Held**
SIC: 2391 5714 Draperies, plastic & tex-
tile: from purchased materials; draperies

(G-4489)
KIHN SOLAR
10012 Manor Pl (22032-3628)
PHONE....................................703 425-2418
Ying Zhang, *Principal*
EMP: 3
SALES (est): 950K **Privately Held**
SIC: 3674 Semiconductors & related de-
vices

(G-4490)
**KLEPPINGER DESIGN GROUP
INC**
2809 Merrilee Dr (22031-4409)
PHONE....................................703 208-2208
C William Kleppinger, *President*
Kenneth Stocks, *Vice Pres*
Sandra Kleppinger, *Treasurer*
Elizabeth Alpert, *Consultant*
EMP: 12
SALES (est): 1.6MM **Privately Held**
WEB: www.kleppingerdesign.com
SIC: 2434 Wood kitchen cabinets

(G-4491)
KNOWLES FLOORING
3891 Fairfax Sq (22031-4200)
PHONE....................................571 224-3694
Donald James Knowles, *Owner*
EMP: 1
SALES (est): 75K **Privately Held**
WEB: www.knowlescontracting.com
SIC: 3996 Hard surface floor coverings

(G-4492)
KOLOZA LLC
10345 Latney Rd (22032-3238)
PHONE....................................301 204-9864
Frederik Koetje, *Administration*
EMP: 2
SALES (est): 118.4K **Privately Held**
WEB: www.koloza.com
SIC: 7372 Application computer software

(G-4493)
**KOREA EXPRESS WASHINGTON
INC**
Also Called: Korean Express
10944 Keys Ct (22032-3026)
P.O. Box 133, Fairfax Station (22039-0133)
PHONE....................................703 339-8201
Jeong Gyun Ju, *Owner*

▼ EMP: 2
SALES (est): 233K **Privately Held**
SIC: 3651 Electronic kits for home assem-
bly: radio, TV, phonograph

(G-4494)
KRYPTOWIRE LLC
5352 Brandon Ridge Way (22032-3282)
PHONE....................................571 314-0153
Tom Karygiannis, *Vice Pres*
Angelos Stavrou,
EMP: 3 **Privately Held**
WEB: www.kryptowire.com
SIC: 7372 Application computer software
PA: Kryptowire, Llc
8200 Greensboro Dr # 750
Tysons Corner VA 22102

(G-4495)
KUARY LLC
8901 Garden Gate Dr (22031-1475)
PHONE....................................703 980-3804
Travis Collins,
EMP: 1
SALES (est): 47.9K **Privately Held**
SIC: 7372 7389 Utility computer software;

(G-4496)
L & M PRINTING INC
2810 Dorr Ave Ste D (22031-1513)
PHONE....................................703 573-2257
Frank Leonard, *President*
Mary Leonard, *Corp Secy*
EMP: 6
SQ FT: 3,400
SALES (est): 976K **Privately Held**
WEB: www.landmprintinginc.com
SIC: 2752 Commercial printing, offset

(G-4497)
LASHME BY LESLIE LLC
13281c Leafcrest Ln # 304 (22033-4512)
PHONE....................................703 595-8628
Leslie Newton,
EMP: 1
SALES (est): 50K **Privately Held**
SIC: 3999 Eyelashes, artificial

(G-4498)
LEE HIGH SHEET METAL INC
8441 Lee Hwy (22031-2212)
PHONE....................................703 698-5168
Sharon Portch, *President*
John Bailey, *Manager*
EMP: 10
SQ FT: 5,000
SALES (est): 1.6MM **Privately Held**
WEB: www.indeglia.com
SIC: 3444 Sheet metalwork

(G-4499)
LFG GROUP INC
9320 Branch Side Ln (22031-6017)
PHONE....................................571 512-7446
EMP: 3
SALES (est): 142.6K **Privately Held**
SIC: 3993 Signs & advertising specialties

(G-4500)
M C SERVICES INC
4922 Princess Anne Ct (22032-2234)
PHONE....................................703 352-1711
Mark Cox, *President*
Jim Cerroni, *Natl Sales Mgr*
EMP: 2
SQ FT: 2,000
SALES (est): 300K **Privately Held**
SIC: 2759 Engraving

(G-4501)
MAGNOLIA WOODWORKING
8610 Crestview Dr (22031-2805)
PHONE....................................571 521-9041
Mark Christiansen, *Principal*
EMP: 2 EST: 2017
SALES (est): 85.2K **Privately Held**
SIC: 2431 Millwork

(G-4502)
**MANTECH ADVANCED DEV
GROUP INC (HQ)**
12015 Lee Jackson Mem Hwy
(22033-3300)
PHONE....................................703 218-6000
Kenneth J Farquhar, *President*

Donald Visnick, *Vice Pres*
EMP: 96
SQ FT: 6,000
SALES (est): 6.2MM
SALES (corp-wide): 2.2B **Publicly Held**
WEB: www.mantech.com
SIC: 7372 Educational computer software
PA: Mantech International Corporation
2251 Corp Park Dr Ste 600
Herndon VA 20171
703 218-6000

(G-4503)
MARTIN ELTHON
Also Called: Fairfax Plastics
2983 Prosperity Ave (22031-2208)
PHONE....................................703 853-1801
Martin Elthon, *Owner*
EMP: 1 EST: 2015
SQ FT: 1,500
SALES (est): 55K **Privately Held**
WEB: www.cdufresnemd.com
SIC: 3089 3443 Cases, plastic; industrial
vessels, tanks & containers

(G-4504)
MCCABE ENTERPRISES INC
Also Called: McCabes Printing Group
8451 Hilltop Rd Ste B (22031-4309)
PHONE....................................703 560-7755
Kevin McCabe, *President*
Cheryl McCabe, *Corp Secy*
EMP: 12 EST: 1980
SQ FT: 3,085
SALES (est): 2MM **Privately Held**
WEB: www.mccabesprinting.com
SIC: 2752 Commercial printing, offset

(G-4505)
MEDMARC
4000 Legato Rd Ste 800 (22033-4099)
PHONE....................................703 652-1305
George Ayd, *Assistant VP*
EMP: 2 EST: 2018
SALES (est): 86.6K **Privately Held**
SIC: 3841 Surgical & medical instruments

(G-4506)
MERRIFIELD METALS INC
2817 Dorr Ave Ste A (22031-1511)
PHONE....................................703 849-9100
Todd Peal, *President*
Terry Peal, *Assistant VP*
William Krasley, *Treasurer*
Brenda Peal, *Admin Sec*
EMP: 5
SALES (est): 600K **Privately Held**
WEB: www.merrifielddental.com
SIC: 3444 Sheet metalwork

(G-4507)
MESO SCALE DISCOVERY LLC
Also Called: Meso Scale Discoveries
4050 Legato Rd Fl 10 (22033-2895)
PHONE....................................571 318-5521
EMP: 3
SALES (corp-wide): 104.3MM **Privately
Held**
WEB: www.mesoscale.com
SIC: 3826 Analytical instruments
PA: Meso Scale Discovery Llc
1601 Research Blvd
Rockville MD 20850
240 314-2600

(G-4508)
MEZEH - FAIR OAKS LLC
11946l Fair Oaks Mall (22033-3306)
PHONE....................................703 310-9209
Sadiqa Mohamadi, *Controller*
Saleh Mohamadi, *Mng Member*
Tai Chiao, *Director*
EMP: 14
SALES (est): 499K **Privately Held**
SIC: 2099 5149 Food preparations; gro-
ceries & related products

(G-4509)
MG ENTERPRISE LLC
4927 Gainsborough Dr (22032-2317)
PHONE....................................703 646-2761
Matthew Gervais, *Mng Member*
EMP: 1
SALES (est): 130K **Privately Held**
SIC: 3541 7389 Home workshop machine
tools, metalworking;

(G-4510)
MIATA REALM LLC
9804 Laurel St (22032-1107)
PHONE....................................724 612-1029
Nathan Hadley, *Principal*
EMP: 1
SALES (est): 55.3K **Privately Held**
SIC: 3714 Motor vehicle parts & acces-
sories

(G-4511)
MICRON MANUFACTURING
2983 Prosperity Ave (22031-2208)
PHONE....................................703 853-1801
EMP: 1 EST: 2019
SALES (est): 39.6K **Privately Held**
SIC: 3999 Manufacturing industries

(G-4512)
MINTMESH INC
4012 Timber Oak Trl (22033-6222)
PHONE....................................703 222-0322
Neha Bhuradia, *Director*
EMP: 2
SALES (est): 128.7K **Privately Held**
WEB: www.mintmesh.com
SIC: 7372 Application computer software

(G-4513)
**MOBIL PETROCHEMICAL
HOLDINGS**
3225 Gallows Rd (22037-0001)
PHONE....................................703 846-3000
EMP: 2
SALES (est): 12.2K **Privately Held**
SIC: 3533 2911 Mfg Oil/Gas Field Machin-
ery Petroleum Refiner

(G-4514)
MODEL SIGN & GRAPHICS
4290 Birney Ln (22033-4333)
PHONE....................................703 527-2121
Raza Tahari, *Owner*
EMP: 5
SALES (est): 260K **Privately Held**
SIC: 3993 Signs & advertising specialties

(G-4515)
N-ASK INCORPORATED (PA)
4114 Legato Rd Ste 1100 (22033-3341)
PHONE....................................703 715-7909
Michael J Wheelock, *President*
Joey E Harris, *Vice Pres*
Brian Malone, *Vice Pres*
Byron Brigham, *Engineer*
Anthony Halley, *Engineer*
EMP: 52
SQ FT: 25,000
SALES (est): 11.8MM **Privately Held**
WEB: www.nask.world
SIC: 3571 Electronic computers

(G-4516)
NEOSYSTEMS CORP
3714 Valley Oaks Dr (22033-2224)
PHONE....................................571 234-4949
Rob Wilson, *COO*
EMP: 2
SALES (est): 147.2K **Privately Held**
SIC: 3577 Computer peripheral equipment

(G-4517)
NEW ERA TECHNOLOGY LLC
12190 Waveland St Apt 232 (22033-5569)
PHONE....................................571 308-8525
Fatih Demir, *Principal*
EMP: 1
SALES (est): 74.3K **Privately Held**
SIC: 3499 Machine bases, metal

(G-4518)
NINOSKA M MARCANO
2922 Fairhill Rd (22031-2119)
PHONE....................................202 604-8864
Ninoska M Marcano, *Owner*
EMP: 1 EST: 2015
SALES (est): 32.1K **Privately Held**
SIC: 2741 7389 Miscellaneous publishing;
translation services

(G-4519)
NIS INC
Also Called: Parent Institute , The
10505 Braddock Rd Ste B (22032-2243)
P.O. Box 7474, Fairfax Station (22039-7474)
PHONE....................703 323-9170
EMP: 25
SQ FT: 6,000
SALES (est): 3.1MM **Privately Held**
SIC: 2721 2731 7812 2741 Periodical-Publish/Print Book-Publishing/Printing Motion Pict/Video Prodtn Misc Publishing

(G-4520)
NORTHROP GRUMMAN INFO TECH
Also Called: Northrop Grumman Info Systems
12900 Fdral Systems Pk Dr (22033-4421)
PHONE....................703 968-1000
Jonathan Rankin, *General Mgr*
Frank Nadal, *Principal*
Derek Sampson, *Mfg Dir*
Mae Scott, *Opers Mgr*
Shou Chiang, *Research*
EMP: 49 **Publicly Held**
WEB: www.washingtontechnology.com
SIC: 3812 Search & navigation equipment
HQ: Northrop Grumman Information Technology, Inc.
7575 Colshire Dr
Mc Lean VA 22102
703 556-1144

(G-4521)
NOVA RETAIL LLC
3171d Spring St (22031-2300)
PHONE....................703 507-5220
Ali Zargarpur,
EMP: 4
SQ FT: 3,600
SALES (est): 750K **Privately Held**
SIC: 3993 5944 Signs & advertising specialties; watches

(G-4522)
NRC PUBLISHING VIRGINIA LLC
4000 Legato Rd (22033-2892)
PHONE....................703 407-0868
Shuekar Omar, *Principal*
EMP: 2 **EST:** 2010
SALES (est): 119.5K **Privately Held**
SIC: 2741 Miscellaneous publishing

(G-4523)
NUTTER CANDLE COMPANY LLC
5507 Cheshire Meadows Way
(22032-3226)
PHONE....................703 627-2561
Johna Nutter, *Principal*
EMP: 1
SALES (est): 41.1K **Privately Held**
SIC: 3999 Candles

(G-4524)
OASIS GLOBAL LLC
Also Called: Macabes Printing Group
8451 Hilltop Rd Ste B (22031-4309)
PHONE....................703 560-7755
Husni Safsaf, *President*
Howida Diab, *Principal*
EMP: 14
SALES (est): 732.3K **Privately Held**
WEB: www.mccabesprinting.com
SIC: 2752 7334 Commercial printing, offset; photocopying & duplicating services

(G-4525)
ONE ARM WOODWORKING LLC
9525 Jomar Dr (22032-2012)
PHONE....................703 203-9417
Jeffrey Sacknoff, *Principal*
EMP: 1
SALES (est): 54.1K **Privately Held**
SIC: 2431 Millwork

(G-4526)
ORTHOTIC PROSTHETIC CENTER (PA)
8330 Professional Hill Dr (22031-4681)
PHONE....................703 698-5007
Joan C Weintrob, *Ch of Bd*
Elliot Weintrob, *President*
Harry Weintrob, *Corp Secy*
Wanza Swann, *Office Mgr*
EMP: 1
SQ FT: 4,400
SALES (est): 2MM **Privately Held**
WEB: www.orthoticprostheticcenter.com
SIC: 3842 5999 Limbs, artificial; braces, orthopedic; medical apparatus & supplies

(G-4527)
ORTHOTIC SOLUTIONS L L C
2802 Merrilee Dr Ste 100 (22031-4410)
PHONE....................703 849-9200
Michael Malagari, *Principal*
Luke Stikeleather,
EMP: 9
SQ FT: 5,000
SALES (est): 200K **Privately Held**
WEB: www.orthoticsolutions.com
SIC: 3842 8011 Orthopedic appliances; offices & clinics of medical doctors

(G-4528)
PALLAS USA LTD
2719 Dorr Ave Ste B (22031-4991)
PHONE....................703 205-0007
EMP: 2
SALES (est): 77.4K **Privately Held**
WEB: www.pallasusa.com
SIC: 3081 Vinyl film & sheet

(G-4529)
PAPERCLIP MEDIA INC
Also Called: Parent Institute, The
10505 Braddock Rd Ste B (22032-2270)
P.O. Box 7474, Fairfax Station (22039-7474)
PHONE....................703 323-9170
Andrew McLaughlin, *President*
Marc Sasseville, *Manager*
EMP: 6
SALES (est): 274.6K **Privately Held**
WEB: www.parent-institute.com
SIC: 2741 Miscellaneous publishing

(G-4530)
PLATEAU SOFTWARE INC
2701 Prosperity Ave (22031-4313)
PHONE....................703 385-8300
Visshy Kizhapandal, *Branch Mgr*
EMP: 1
SALES (corp-wide): 950K **Privately Held**
WEB: www.plateauinc.com
SIC: 7372 Prepackaged software
PA: Plateau Software, Inc.
4580 Klahanie Dr Se
Sammamish WA 98029
425 985-1610

(G-4531)
PRESS OUT POVERTY
3805 Acosta Rd (22031-3803)
PHONE....................703 691-4329
Gary Jason Myers, *Principal*
EMP: 1 **EST:** 2018
SALES (est): 37.5K **Privately Held**
SIC: 2741 Miscellaneous publishing

(G-4532)
PRINTING AND SIGN SYSTEM INC
2808 Merrilee Dr Ste E (22031-4435)
PHONE....................703 280-1550
Sam Kaviani, *President*
EMP: 4
SQ FT: 1,800
SALES (est): 640.1K **Privately Held**
WEB: www.pssiweprint.com
SIC: 2752 7334 5099 5131 Commercial printing, offset; photocopying & duplicating services; signs, except electric; flags & banners; signs & advertising specialties; typesetting

(G-4533)
PRINTING IDEAS INC
9925 Main St (22031-3904)
PHONE....................703 591-1700
James Huie, *President*
Steve Huie, *Managing Prtnr*
Poysee Huie, *Vice Pres*
EMP: 6 **EST:** 1977
SQ FT: 2,700
SALES (est): 887.1K **Privately Held**
WEB: www.printingideas.com
SIC: 2752 Commercial printing, offset

(G-4534)
PROFIT FROM PUBLICITY LLC
5505 Talon Ct (22032-1737)
PHONE....................703 409-3630
George Anderson,
EMP: 2 **EST:** 2017
SALES (est): 65K **Privately Held**
SIC: 2741 Miscellaneous publishing

(G-4535)
R R DONNELLEY & SONS COMPANY
Also Called: Workflow Solutions
12150 Monument Dr Ste 100 (22033-4062)
PHONE....................703 279-1662
Arlene Saia, *Manager*
EMP: 25
SALES (corp-wide): 6.2B **Publicly Held**
WEB: www.rrd.com
SIC: 2759 2732 Commercial printing; book printing
PA: R. R. Donnelley & Sons Company
35 W Wacker Dr
Chicago IL 60601
312 326-8000

(G-4536)
RAINMAKER PUBLISHING LLC
9100 Hamilton Dr (22031-3081)
P.O. Box 3102, Oakton (22124-9102)
PHONE....................703 385-9761
Renee Dexter,
Michaela Gaaserud,
EMP: 2
SALES (est): 86.2K **Privately Held**
SIC: 2731 Books: publishing only

(G-4537)
RANDY EDWARDS
9371 Lee Hwy (22031-1801)
PHONE....................703 591-0545
Randy Edwards, *Principal*
EMP: 2
SALES (est): 62.9K **Privately Held**
SIC: 2711 Newspapers

(G-4538)
RED ACTION BLUE INFO LLC
2727 Merrilee Dr Apt 223 (22031-4449)
PHONE....................469 224-7673
JD Wilcox, *Branch Mgr*
EMP: 1
SALES (corp-wide): 374.4K **Privately Held**
SIC: 2389 Men's miscellaneous accessories
PA: Red Action Blue Information, Llc
6604 Chevy Chase Ave
Dallas TX 75225
469 224-7673

(G-4539)
RELATIONAL SYSTEMS DESIGN LTD
10712 Almond St (22032-3401)
P.O. Box 7189, Fairfax Station (22039-7189)
PHONE....................703 385-7073
Robert Garland, *President*
EMP: 5
SALES (est): 281.3K **Privately Held**
SIC: 7372 8748 Prepackaged software; business consulting

(G-4540)
REVOLUTION SOULTIONS VA LLC
12500 Fanleas Ct (22033)
PHONE....................804 539-5058
Fred West, *Manager*
Frederic Kemp West, *Administration*
EMP: 1 **EST:** 2015
SALES (est): 74.7K **Privately Held**
SIC: 3646 Commercial indusl & institutional electric lighting fixtures

(G-4541)
REYCO GLOBAL LLC
5213 Grinnell St (22032-3413)
PHONE....................719 321-6747
Emily Reyes,
EMP: 3
SALES (est): 121.7K **Privately Held**
SIC: 3812 Defense systems & equipment

(G-4542)
RIDAN PUBLISHING
9685 Lindenbrook St (22031-1132)
PHONE....................703 349-2028
EMP: 2
SALES (est): 94.8K **Privately Held**
WEB: www.ridanpublishing.com
SIC: 2741 Miscellaneous publishing

(G-4543)
RJM TECHNOLOGIES INC
9620 Maury Rd (22032-2833)
PHONE....................703 323-6677
Robert Main, *President*
John Dennis, *CFO*
EMP: 5
SALES (est): 424.8K **Privately Held**
WEB: www.rjmtechnologies.com
SIC: 7372 7363 Prepackaged software; employee leasing service

(G-4544)
ROLL OF HONOR FOUNDATION
3819 Hunt Manor Dr (22033-2217)
PHONE....................703 731-6109
Gerald Michaud, *Principal*
EMP: 1 **EST:** 2015
SALES (est): 63K **Privately Held**
SIC: 2741

(G-4545)
ROSE WINSTON DESIGNS
3801 Ridge Knoll Ct 3-A (22033-4611)
PHONE....................703 717-2264
Rose Winston, *Principal*
EMP: 1
SALES (est): 257.8K **Privately Held**
SIC: 2241 Narrow fabric mills

(G-4546)
ROUBIN AND JANEIRO INC
8550 Lee Hwy Ste 700 (22031-1594)
PHONE....................703 573-9350
Angel Roubin, *President*
EMP: 8
SALES (est): 547.8K **Privately Held**
SIC: 2951 Asphalt paving mixtures & blocks

(G-4547)
S K CIRCUITS INC
4094 Majestic Ln (22033-2104)
PHONE....................703 376-8718
EMP: 5
SALES (corp-wide): 1.6MM **Privately Held**
WEB: www.rkk.com
SIC: 3679 Electronic circuits
PA: S. K. Circuits Inc.
340 Rosewood Cir
Canastota NY 13032
703 376-8718

(G-4548)
SAN RODERIGO PUBLISHING LLC
4260 Jefferson Oaks Cir F (22033-4084)
PHONE....................703 968-9502
Elden Sodowsky, *Principal*
EMP: 2
SALES (est): 79.7K **Privately Held**
SIC: 2741 Miscellaneous publishing

(G-4549)
SCHNEDER ELC IT MSSION CRTCAL
3975 Fair Ridge Dr S21 (22033-2911)
PHONE....................703 968-0300
John C Lee IV, *CEO*
Molly L Rehm, *Vice Pres*
Neill A Blue, *Treasurer*
Stephanie Davis, *Financial Exec*
Russell Morrissey, *Admin Sec*
EMP: 312
SQ FT: 27,500
SALES (est): 39.3MM
SALES (corp-wide): 177.9K **Privately Held**
WEB: www.se.com
SIC: 3699 Electrical equipment & supplies
HQ: Schneider Electric Usa, Inc.
201 Wshington St Ste 2700
Boston MA 02108
978 975-9600

▲ = Import ▼=Export
◆ =Import/Export

(G-4550)
SCHNEIDER ELECTRIC USA INC
3975 Fair Ridge Dr S210 (22033-2911)
PHONE..................................703 968-0300
Hyatt Field, *Project Mgr*
John Lee, *Branch Mgr*
Claire Crawford, *Manager*
Mark Fugazzotto, *Manager*
EMP: 2
SALES (corp-wide): 177.9K **Privately Held**
WEB: www.ccagp.com
SIC: 3613 3643 Switches, electric power except snap, push button, etc.; bus bars (electrical conductors)
HQ: Schneider Electric Usa, Inc.
201 Wshington St Ste 2700
Boston MA 02108
978 975-9600

(G-4551)
SCOTT READY
4830 Gainsborough Dr (22032-2312)
PHONE..................................703 503-3374
Scott Ready, *Principal*
EMP: 4
SALES (est): 279.4K **Privately Held**
SIC: 3273 Ready-mixed concrete

(G-4552)
SCREEN PRTG TCHNCAL FOUNDATION
10015 Main St (22033-3403)
PHONE..................................703 359-1300
Dawn Hohl, *Principal*
Leanne Crowley,
EMP: 2 EST: 2008
SALES: 269.9K **Privately Held**
WEB: www.sgia.org
SIC: 2759 Screen printing

(G-4553)
SECOND SAMUEL INDUSTRIES INC
12734 Alder Woods Dr (22033-2220)
PHONE..................................703 715-2295
Ivan Leigh Mills, *Principal*
EMP: 1
SALES (est): 52.6K **Privately Held**
SIC: 3999 Manufacturing industries

(G-4554)
SILKSCREENING UNLIMITED INC
Also Called: T-Shirts Etc
10010 Mosby Rd (22032-1019)
PHONE..................................703 385-3212
Barbara Vogel, *President*
EMP: 5
SALES (est): 270K **Privately Held**
WEB: www.qccreations.com
SIC: 2396 5699 7389 Screen printing on fabric articles; T-shirts, custom printed; embroidering of advertising on shirts, etc.

(G-4555)
SILLY SPORT SOCKS
5414 Chatsworth Ct (22032-3912)
PHONE..................................703 926-5398
Amber Alfaro, *Principal*
EMP: 3
SALES (est): 204.6K **Privately Held**
SIC: 2252 Socks

(G-4556)
SILVERADO PRINTING LLC
13121 Penndale Ln (22033-3027)
PHONE..................................703 407-8720
Timothy McCarthy, *Principal*
Tanja Beahn, *Production*
Maggie Morris, *Manager*
EMP: 4
SALES (est): 222.2K **Privately Held**
WEB: www.silveradoprinting.com
SIC: 2752 Commercial printing, offset

(G-4557)
SOLEVENTS FLORAL LLC
4119 Middle Ridge Dr (22033-3227)
PHONE..................................571 221-5761
Soledad Soto, *Principal*
EMP: 2 EST: 2016
SALES (est): 95.1K **Privately Held**
SIC: 2911 Solvents

(G-4558)
SPARKZONE INC
4005 Stonewall Ave (22032-1016)
PHONE..................................703 861-0650
Jung Yi, *President*
Hyun Kim, *Vice Pres*
EMP: 6
SALES (est): 285K **Privately Held**
SIC: 3669 Intercommunication systems, electric

(G-4559)
SRG GOVERNMENT SOLUTIONS INC
Also Called: Systems Requirements Group
4323 Argonne Dr (22032-1406)
PHONE..................................703 609-7027
John Goddard, *President*
EMP: 2
SALES (est): 36K **Privately Held**
SIC: 7372 7371 Prepackaged software; custom computer programming services

(G-4560)
SRI SEVEN FAIR LAKES LLC
12500 Fair Lakes Cir (22033-3804)
PHONE..................................703 631-2350
James Cramp, *Project Mgr*
Amy Osterwalder, *Office Mgr*
Krishna Maddi, *Art Dir*
EMP: 7
SALES (est): 880K **Privately Held**
WEB: www.gdit.com
SIC: 3599 Carnival machines & equipment, amusement park

(G-4561)
STELLA STONE AND SEALANT LLC
8806 Southlea Ct (22031-3233)
PHONE..................................917 568-6489
EMP: 3 EST: 2018
SALES (est): 123.2K **Privately Held**
SIC: 2891 Sealants

(G-4562)
STRDEFENSE LLC
3975 Fair Ridge Dr D (22033-2911)
P.O. Box 41161, Baton Rouge LA (70835-1161)
PHONE..................................703 460-9000
Scott K Meyer,
Louis C Finch,
Robert J Fries,
EMP: 3
SQ FT: 1,500
SALES (est): 210K **Privately Held**
SIC: 3699 Flight simulators (training aids), electronic

(G-4563)
SUSTAINABLE GREEN PRTG PARTNR
10015 Main St (22031-3403)
PHONE..................................703 359-1376
Marcia Y Kinter, *Principal*
EMP: 2
SALES (est): 101.5K **Privately Held**
SIC: 2752 Commercial printing, lithographic

(G-4564)
SWAROVSKI NORTH AMERICA LTD
11750I Fair Oaks Mall (22033-3308)
PHONE..................................703 267-2332
Samar Saab, *Branch Mgr*
EMP: 3
SALES (corp-wide): 4.7B **Privately Held**
WEB: www.swarovski.com
SIC: 3961 Costume jewelry
HQ: Swarovski North America Limited
1 Kenney Dr
Cranston RI 02920
401 463-6400

(G-4565)
SWEET SUCCESS CUPCAKES
4613 Tara Dr (22032-2034)
PHONE..................................703 674-9442
Marissa Probst, *Principal*
EMP: 4 EST: 2014

SALES (est): 174.7K **Privately Held**
WEB: www.sweetsuccesscupcakes.com
SIC: 2051 Bakery: wholesale or wholesale/retail combined

(G-4566)
SYMMPLE TECHNOLOGIES
4325 Thomas Brigade Ln (22033-4280)
PHONE..................................703 591-7716
EMP: 2 EST: 2016
SALES (est): 85.9K **Privately Held**
SIC: 3571 Electronic Computers, Nsk

(G-4567)
SYNC OPTICS LLC
3723 Broadrun Dr (22033-2166)
PHONE..................................571 203-0580
Xiaoke Wan,
EMP: 1
SALES (est): 81K **Privately Held**
SIC: 3823 Infrared instruments, industrial process type

(G-4568)
TAPIOCA LLC
12353 Firestone Ct (22033-2581)
PHONE..................................703 715-8688
Nina Bui, *Principal*
EMP: 1
SALES (est): 69.1K **Privately Held**
SIC: 2046 Tapioca

(G-4569)
THOMAS HEGENS
Also Called: Comfort & Support
2750 Prosperity Ave # 120 (22031-4312)
PHONE..................................703 205-9000
Thomas Hegens, *Owner*
EMP: 10 EST: 2015
SQ FT: 500
SALES (est): 351.1K **Privately Held**
WEB: www.dcdowntownhotel.com
SIC: 3842 Braces, orthopedic; cervical collars; corsets, surgical; extension shoes, orthopedic

(G-4570)
TLC CLEANERS INC
9531 Braddock Rd (22032-2539)
PHONE..................................703 425-5577
HEI S Ahn, *President*
Nancy Ahn, *Vice Pres*
EMP: 11
SQ FT: 2,500
SALES (est): 2.2MM **Privately Held**
SIC: 2842 Drycleaning preparations

(G-4571)
TOPS OF TOWN VIRGINIA LLC
2800 Dorr Ave Ste L (22031-1512)
PHONE..................................703 242-8100
William Madden, *Owner*
William S Madden,
EMP: 2
SALES (est): 258.5K **Privately Held**
WEB: www.topsofthetownllc.com
SIC: 2434 1799 1521 Wood kitchen cabinets; counter top installation; single-family housing construction

(G-4572)
TOUCH 3 LLC
2888 Glenvale Dr (22031-1415)
PHONE..................................703 279-8130
Les McCarty, *Owner*
EMP: 4 EST: 1998
SALES (est): 289.1K **Privately Held**
WEB: www.touch3.com
SIC: 2741 7389 Miscellaneous publishing; apparel designers, commercial

(G-4573)
TRINGAPPS INC
3060 Williams Dr Ste 200 (22031-4642)
PHONE..................................703 698-6910
EMP: 2
SALES (est): 85.1K **Privately Held**
SIC: 7372 Prepackaged software

(G-4574)
UNIFORMED SERVICES ALMANAC
9342 Tovito Dr (22031-3825)
P.O. Box 4144, Falls Church (22044-0144)
PHONE..................................703 241-8100

Ron Hunter, *President*
Debra Hunter, *Vice Pres*
EMP: 5 EST: 1959
SQ FT: 1,900
SALES (est): 406.3K **Privately Held**
SIC: 2759 2731 Commercial printing; book publishing

(G-4575)
US 21 INC
Also Called: Us21
2721 Prosperity Ave # 300 (22031-4341)
PHONE..................................703 560-0021
Jennifer Saleh, *President*
Bahjat Saleh, *Vice Pres*
Brian Holder, *Sales Mgr*
Sondos Abumurra, *Accounts Mgr*
Garrett Grant, *Accounts Mgr*
◆ EMP: 55 EST: 1996
SQ FT: 8,000
SALES (est): 16.8MM **Privately Held**
WEB: www.us21.com
SIC: 3575 3577 5072 4899 Computer terminals; computer peripheral equipment; hardware; satellite earth stations

(G-4576)
USA CABINETS STORE
2832 Dorr Ave (22031-1523)
PHONE..................................703 204-3444
Emin Halac, *Principal*
EMP: 6
SALES (est): 1.3MM **Privately Held**
WEB: www.usacabinetstore.com
SIC: 2434 Wood kitchen cabinets

(G-4577)
USA TODAY
9208 Hamilton Dr (22031-3083)
PHONE..................................703 267-6964
Saverio Meddis, *Principal*
EMP: 3
SALES (est): 189.8K **Privately Held**
SIC: 2711 Newspapers, publishing & printing

(G-4578)
VEGA PRODUCTIONS & ASSOCIATES (PA)
Also Called: Hispanic Yellow Pages
2721 Prosperity Ave # 200 (22031-4318)
PHONE..................................703 908-9600
Francisco Vega Jr, *President*
Juan Vega, *Vice Pres*
▼ EMP: 8
SQ FT: 4,011
SALES (est): 1.4MM **Privately Held**
SIC: 2741 Directories, telephone: publishing only, not printed on site

(G-4579)
VINNELL CORP (PA)
12900 Fdral Systems Pk Dr (22033-4421)
PHONE..................................703 818-7903
A Thomas Fintel, *President*
Alan R Cox, *Vice Pres*
EMP: 9
SALES (est): 1.5MM **Privately Held**
SIC: 1481 Mine & quarry services, nonmetallic minerals

(G-4580)
WARRIOR TRAIL CONSULTING LLC (PA)
4000 Legato Rd Ste 1100 (22033-2893)
PHONE..................................703 349-1967
Lawrence Bronstein, *Exec Dir*
Della Bronstein,
EMP: 2
SALES (est): 236.2K **Privately Held**
WEB: www.warriortrail.com
SIC: 3949 8748 8742 Protective sporting equipment; safety training service; training & development consultant

(G-4581)
WHATS YOUR SIGN LLC
12500 Thompson Rd (22033-1608)
PHONE..................................703 860-2075
Patricia Rossini, *Principal*
EMP: 3 EST: 2008
SALES (est): 205.3K **Privately Held**
SIC: 3993 Signs & advertising specialties

GEOGRAPHIC

(G-4582)
WILSON INDUSTRIES & SVCS UN
10191 Wavell Rd (22032-2337)
PHONE........................703 472-6392
Les Clay, *Principal*
EMP: 1 EST: 2016
SALES (est): 39.6K **Privately Held**
SIC: 3999 Manufacturing industries

(G-4583)
WOLLEY SEGAP INTERNATIONAL
4369 Farm House Ln (22032-1616)
PHONE........................703 426-5164
EMP: 4
SALES (est): 300K **Privately Held**
SIC: 2731 Books-Publishing/Printing

(G-4584)
XARMR CORPORATION
8451 Hilltop Rd (22031-4309)
PHONE........................703 663-8711
EMP: 1
SALES (corp-wide): 1.4MM **Privately Held**
WEB: www.bb-armr.com
SIC: 3669 Transportation signaling devices
PA: Xarmr Corporation
5900 S Lake Forest Dr
Mckinney TX 75070
972 385-7899

(G-4585)
XLNT SOLUTIONS INC
3981 Woodberry Meadow Dr (22033-2498)
PHONE........................703 819-9265
Krishna Alluri, *Principal*
EMP: 2
SALES (est): 115.1K **Privately Held**
SIC: 7372 7389 Business oriented computer software;

(G-4586)
YUE XU
9423 Wrought Iron Ct (22032-1348)
PHONE........................703 503-9451
Yuching Hsu, *Executive*
EMP: 3
SALES (est): 90.5K **Privately Held**
WEB: www.verytech.net
SIC: 1099 Metal ores

Fairfax
Fairfax City County

(G-4587)
4GURUS LLC (PA)
Also Called: Event Guru Software
4169 Lower Park Dr (22030-8543)
PHONE........................703 520-5084
Mark Williams, *Business Mgr*
Christine Defrances,
Neal Burghardt,
Larry Defrances,
Charles Salem,
EMP: 4
SALES (est): 433.8K **Privately Held**
WEB: www.eventgurusoftware.com
SIC: 7372 7389 Business oriented computer software;

(G-4588)
4GURUS LLC
Also Called: Event Guru Software
4181 Lower Park Dr (22030-8544)
PHONE........................703 520-5084
Charles Salem, *Branch Mgr*
EMP: 1
SALES (corp-wide): 433.8K **Privately Held**
WEB: www.eventgurusoftware.com
SIC: 7372 Business oriented computer software
PA: 4gurus Llc
4169 Lower Park Dr
Fairfax VA 22030
703 520-5084

(G-4589)
ADVANCE SIGNS & GRAPHICS CO
10608 Orchard St (22030-3013)
PHONE........................703 359-8005
Julie Dabney, *Owner*
EMP: 2
SALES (est): 500K **Privately Held**
WEB: www.topdzines.com
SIC: 3993 Signs & advertising specialties

(G-4590)
ADVANCED RSPONSE CONCEPTS CORP (HQ)
11250 Waples Mill Rd (22030-7550)
PHONE........................703 246-8560
Daniel Turissini, *CEO*
Denise Finance, *President*
EMP: 5
SALES (est): 1MM **Publicly Held**
SIC: 7372 Business oriented computer software

(G-4591)
ALFA PRINT LLC
10370 Main St (22030-2412)
PHONE........................703 273-2061
Fadhel Alfadhli, *President*
EMP: 2
SALES (est): 111.6K **Privately Held**
SIC: 2752 Commercial printing, lithographic

(G-4592)
ANM FOOD SERVICES INC
Also Called: Wings Plus
11211 Lee Hwy Ste G (22030-5699)
PHONE........................703 865-4378
Ahmad Omar, *CEO*
EMP: 4
SALES (est): 100K **Privately Held**
SIC: 2099 Food preparations

(G-4593)
ANTMED CORPORATION
11092b Lee Hwy 104 (22030-5014)
PHONE........................703 239-3118
Molly Chen, *President*
EMP: 2
SALES (est): 120.3K **Privately Held**
SIC: 3069 3061 Atomizer bulbs, rubber; medical & surgical rubber tubing (extruded & lathe-cut)

(G-4594)
APPRENTICE PRESS
10605 Center St (22030-3115)
PHONE........................703 352-5005
EMP: 2
SALES (est): 94.6K **Privately Held**
SIC: 2741 Misc Publishing

(G-4595)
APRIZE SATELLITE INC
3554 Chain Bridge Rd # 103 (22030-2709)
PHONE........................703 273-7010
Dino Lorenzini, *President*
Mark Kanawaii, *Vice Pres*
EMP: 4
SQ FT: 5,500
SALES (est): 294.9K **Privately Held**
WEB: www.aprizesat.com
SIC: 3663 Satellites, communications

(G-4596)
ARETEC INC
Also Called: Data Science
10201 Fairfax Blvd # 223 (22030-2202)
PHONE........................703 539-8801
Anthony Rivera, *CEO*
Roby Luna, *President*
Luis Vicioso, *Managing Prtnr*
Steve Gaudreau, *Exec VP*
Cindy Elkins, *Opers Mgr*
EMP: 25
SQ FT: 2,200
SALES (est): 344.2K **Privately Held**
WEB: www.aretecinc.com
SIC: 3699 4899 7373 7371 Security control equipment & systems; communication signal enhancement network system; systems software development services; local area network (LAN) systems integrator; value-added resellers, computer systems; computer software writing services; computer software development; application computer software

(G-4597)
B & L BIOTECH USA INC
3959 Pender Dr Ste 350 (22030-7470)
PHONE........................703 272-7507
Bruce Shefsky, *Vice Pres*
Daniel Yang, *Vice Pres*
EMP: 4
SALES (est): 457K **Privately Held**
WEB: www.bnlbio.com
SIC: 7372 Application computer software

(G-4598)
BESPOKERY LLC
4126 Leonard Dr (22030-5118)
PHONE........................703 624-5024
EMP: 1
SALES (est): 76.5K **Privately Held**
SIC: 3999 Hosiery kits, sewing & mending

(G-4599)
BRADDOCK COMMUNICATIONS
4211 Ridge Top Rd # 3413 (22030-1100)
PHONE........................703 390-5870
Jason Stern, *President*
EMP: 1
SALES (est): 41.3K **Privately Held**
SIC: 2741 Miscellaneous publishing

(G-4600)
BROWN PRINTING COMPANY INC
11350 Random Hills Rd # 800 (22030-6044)
PHONE........................703 934-6078
Robin Mattson, *Owner*
EMP: 2
SALES (est): 196.5K **Privately Held**
SIC: 2752 Commercial printing, lithographic

(G-4601)
BUY CHIMES
3827 Jancie Rd (22030-4822)
PHONE........................703 293-6395
Carolyn Strong, *Principal*
EMP: 3
SALES (est): 240.4K **Privately Held**
WEB: www.buychimes.com
SIC: 3931 Musical instruments

(G-4602)
BYERLY TSHAWNA
4116 Lamarre Dr (22030-5163)
PHONE........................703 359-5598
Tshawna Byerly, *Owner*
EMP: 1
SALES (est): 51K **Privately Held**
SIC: 2741 Miscellaneous publishing

(G-4603)
C & S PRINTING ENTERPRISES
Also Called: Independent Speedy Printing
10408 Lee Hwy (22030)
PHONE........................703 385-4495
Drahm Arian, *President*
Sadeghi Fatemeh, *Vice Pres*
EMP: 6
SQ FT: 1,200
SALES (est): 876.1K **Privately Held**
SIC: 2752 5943 Commercial printing, offset; office forms & supplies

(G-4604)
CANDLELIGHT JEWELS
12101 Elm Forest Way (22030-7728)
PHONE........................305 301-2536
Donna Callahan, *Principal*
EMP: 2
SALES (est): 122.2K **Privately Held**
SIC: 3915 Jewel cutting, drilling, polishing, recutting or setting

(G-4605)
CAR WASH CARE INC
3809 Keith Ave (22030-3117)
PHONE........................703 385-9181
Philip A Warner, *President*
Emily Warner, *Vice Pres*
EMP: 2
SALES (est): 259.7K **Privately Held**
SIC: 3589 7699 Car washing machinery; aircraft & heavy equipment repair services

(G-4606)
CLIPPER MAGAZINE LLC
5709 Hampton Forest Way (22030-7222)
PHONE........................888 569-5100
Sandra Oskin, *Manager*
EMP: 1 **Publicly Held**
WEB: www.cmag.com
SIC: 2754 2621 Coupons: gravure printing; catalog, magazine & newsprint papers
HQ: Clipper Magazine, Llc
3708 Hempland Rd
Mountville PA 17554
717 569-5100

(G-4607)
COX MATTHEWS & ASSOCIATES INC (PA)
Also Called: Issues In Higher Education
10520 Warwick Ave Ste B8 (22030-3136)
P.O. Box 1305 (22038-1305)
PHONE........................703 385-2981
William E Cox Sr, *President*
William E Cox Jr, *Vice Pres*
Ralph Newell, *VP Bus Dvlpt*
Ndija Kakumba, *Adv Mgr*
Diane Remler, *Admin Asst*
EMP: 2
SQ FT: 6,500
SALES (est): 1.7MM **Privately Held**
WEB: www.diverseeducation.com
SIC: 2711 Newspapers

(G-4608)
CREATURE COMFORT CUSTOM CONCIE
3713 Burrows Ave (22030-3001)
PHONE........................703 609-7098
Kim Sheard, *Principal*
EMP: 2
SALES (est): 113.7K **Privately Held**
WEB: www.creaturecomfortva.com
SIC: 3999 Pet supplies

(G-4609)
CROWD ALMANAC LLC
10605 Cedar Ave (22030-3111)
PHONE........................703 385-6989
Jonathan Gessert, *Principal*
EMP: 3
SALES (est): 99.5K **Privately Held**
SIC: 2711 Newspapers

(G-4610)
CYPRESS WOODWORKING LLC
12221 Colchester Hunt Dr (22030-5937)
PHONE........................703 803-6254
EMP: 1 EST: 2007
SALES (est): 100K **Privately Held**
SIC: 2431 Mfg Millwork

(G-4611)
DEBEER PIANO SERVICE LLC
4907 Bentonbrook Dr (22030-5439)
PHONE........................703 727-4601
Leonard Debeer, *Mng Member*
EMP: 1
SALES (est): 51.6K **Privately Held**
SIC: 3931 Musical instruments

(G-4612)
DENIM TWIST INC
4800 Braddock Knoll Way (22030-4577)
PHONE........................703 273-3009
Gurpreet Singh, *Principal*
EMP: 1
SALES (est): 63.4K **Privately Held**
SIC: 2211 Denims

(G-4613)
DIGIGRAM INC
4035 Ridge Top Rd Ste 700 (22030-7411)
PHONE........................330 476-5247

EMP: 5
SALES (est): 444.8K
SALES (corp-wide): 6.7MM **Privately Held**
SIC: 3651 Mfg Home Audio/Video Equipment
PA: Digigram
82 84 Les Gemeaux
Montbonnot Saint Martin 75009
476 524-747

(G-4614)
DOROTHY PRNTICE ARMTHERAPY INC (PA)
11851 Monument Dr Apt 412 (22030-8741)
PHONE..................703 657-0160
Dorothy Prentice, *President*
◆ **EMP:** 3
SQ FT: 1,000
SALES (est): 330.8K **Privately Held**
WEB: www.dorothyprentice.com
SIC: 2844 5199 5719 Perfumes, natural or synthetic; colognes; toilet preparations; gift baskets; bath accessories

(G-4615)
EASTERN CHRSTN PBLICATIONS LLC
Also Called: Stauropegion
3574 University Dr (22030-2314)
P.O. Box 146 (22038-0146)
PHONE..................703 691-8862
John L Figel, *President*
EMP: 3
SALES (est): 305.8K **Privately Held**
WEB: www.ecpubs.com
SIC: 2721 2731 Periodicals; books: publishing only

(G-4616)
EASTERN CRANIAL AFFILIATES LLC (PA)
Also Called: Infinite Technologies O&P
10523 Main St (22030-3310)
PHONE..................703 807-5899
Hans Wolf, *CFO*
Charles Thorne, *Med Doctor*
Lower Burrell, *Manager*
Audrey Wood, *Director*
Joseph Terpenning,
EMP: 8
SQ FT: 3,100
SALES (est): 1.9MM **Privately Held**
WEB: www.infinitetech.org
SIC: 3842 5661 5999 Foot appliances, orthopedic; braces, orthopedic; corsets, surgical; adhesive tape & plasters, medicated or non-medicated; custom & orthopedic shoes; orthopedic & prosthesis applications

(G-4617)
ECOER INC
3900 Jermantown Rd # 150 (22030-4900)
PHONE..................703 348-2538
Ming LI, *President*
EMP: 1
SQ FT: 2,800
SALES (est): 2MM **Privately Held**
WEB: www.ecoer.com
SIC: 3585 Air conditioning equipment, complete
PA: Inhand Networks, Inc.
3900 Jermantown Rd # 150
Fairfax VA 22030
703 348-2988

(G-4618)
EOPUS INNOVATIONS LLC
3949 Pender Dr Ste 350 (22030-6003)
PHONE..................703 796-9882
Jongkook Park, *Principal*
EMP: 3
SALES (est): 209.4K **Privately Held**
SIC: 3674 Semiconductors & related devices

(G-4619)
EXECUTIVE PRESS INC
10412 Main St Ste 1 (22030-3325)
PHONE..................703 352-1337
Matthew C Stoeckel, *President*
Rebecca A Stoeckel, *President*
EMP: 5
SQ FT: 4,000

SALES (est): 855.6K **Privately Held**
SIC: 2752 Commercial printing, offset

(G-4620)
EYEGAZE INC
10363 Democracy Ln (22030-2505)
PHONE..................703 385-8800
Peter Norloff, *President*
Dixon Cleveland, *Vice Pres*
▼ **EMP:** 11
SQ FT: 4,000
SALES (est): 1.1MM **Privately Held**
WEB: www.eyegaze.com
SIC: 3669 7371 Visual communication systems; computer software development

(G-4621)
FAIRFAX PRINTERS INC
Also Called: David Jr Press
10608 Oliver St (22030-3989)
PHONE..................703 273-1220
Lehman H Young Sr, *President*
Mary Young, *Corp Secy*
Diana Mc Cormick, *Bookkeeper*
Lehman H Young Jr, *Shareholder*
EMP: 3
SQ FT: 2,800
SALES (est): 80K **Privately Held**
WEB: www.thevirginiapress.com
SIC: 2752 Commercial printing, offset

(G-4622)
FENNEC PUBLISHING LLC
9906 Great Oaks Way (22030-1607)
PHONE..................703 934-6781
Rafael Levy, *Principal*
EMP: 1
SALES (est): 37.5K **Privately Held**
SIC: 2741 Miscellaneous publishing

(G-4623)
FINTECH SYS INC
4095 River Forth Dr (22030-8565)
PHONE..................703 278-0606
Mike Kloak, *Principal*
EMP: 2
SALES (est): 188.7K **Privately Held**
WEB: www.fintechsystems.com
SIC: 7372 Prepackaged software

(G-4624)
FIRSTGUARD TECHNOLOGIES CORP
Also Called: Fgt
4031 University Dr # 100 (22030-3409)
PHONE..................703 267-6670
James Wolfe, *President*
David A Shaw, *Chairman*
Kenneth J Hintz, *Treasurer*
Jonathan D Kerness, *Admin Sec*
EMP: 5
SALES (est): 414.7K **Privately Held**
WEB: www.firstguardtech.com
SIC: 3679 8731 Electronic circuits; microwave components; commercial physical research; computer (hardware) development; engineering laboratory, except testing

(G-4625)
FIVE SIXTEEN SOLUTIONS
5510 Hampton Forest Way (22030-7205)
PHONE..................703 435-4247
Joseph Martinez, *Partner*
Nalini Martinez, *Partner*
EMP: 2
SALES (est): 138.2K **Privately Held**
SIC: 7372 Prepackaged software

(G-4626)
FRAMECAD AMERICA INC
3603 Mclean Ave (22030-3009)
PHONE..................703 615-2451
Mark Taylor, *President*
Kent Hutchings, *Chairman*
Nader Elhajj, *Director*
◆ **EMP:** 10 **EST:** 2012
SQ FT: 14,000
SALES (est): 1.9MM **Privately Held**
WEB: www.framecad.com
SIC: 3316 3272 8243 Cold finishing of steel shapes; concrete products; software training, computer
PA: Framecad Holdings Limited
99 Felton Mathew Avenue
Auckland 1072

(G-4627)
FREEDOM FLAG SIGN & BANNER CO
10608 Orchard St (22030-3013)
PHONE..................703 359-5353
Julie Dabney, *Owner*
EMP: 2
SALES (est): 85.9K **Privately Held**
SIC: 2399 Banners, pennants & flags

(G-4628)
GAS SENTINEL LLC
10340 Democracy Ln # 101 (22030-2518)
PHONE..................703 962-7151
John Pitchford, *Administration*
EMP: 3 **EST:** 2015
SALES (est): 209.2K **Privately Held**
WEB: www.gassentinel.com
SIC: 3823 Industrial instrmnts msrmnt display/control process variable

(G-4629)
GRAVITONUS
4031 University Dr (22030-3409)
PHONE..................571 321-2019
Eliot Norman, *Principal*
EMP: 2 **EST:** 2009
SALES (est): 143.2K **Privately Held**
WEB: www.gravitonus.com
SIC: 3571 Electronic computers

(G-4630)
HEALTHRX CORPORATION (PA)
4031 University Dr # 100 (22030-3400)
PHONE..................703 352-1760
Patrick Vandersluis, *President*
Jason A Ms, *Exec VP*
Jason Abell, *Exec VP*
Jackson Sunuwar, *Sr Software Eng*
EMP: 25
SALES (est): 1.5MM **Privately Held**
WEB: www.healthrx.com
SIC: 7372 Prepackaged software

(G-4631)
ICAROS INC (PA)
4100 Monu Crnr Dr Ste 520 (22030)
PHONE..................301 637-4324
Tom Bosanko, *CEO*
Daniel Abraham, *President*
Arik Nir, *COO*
Mitch Lindenfeldar, *CFO*
Jim Peters, *Director*
EMP: 15
SALES (est): 2.4MM **Privately Held**
WEB: www.icarosgeospatial.com
SIC: 3699 Electrical equipment & supplies

(G-4632)
ICE ENTERPRISES INC
10302 Eaton Pl Ste 100 (22030-2215)
PHONE..................703 934-4879
William A Owen III, *President*
Tammy Bagdasarian, *General Mgr*
Joe Jacob, *Engineer*
EMP: 12
SALES (est): 1.3MM **Privately Held**
WEB: www.ice-online.com
SIC: 3571 3577 Electronic computers; computer peripheral equipment

(G-4633)
INFORMATION ANALYSIS INC
11240 Waples Mill Rd # 201 (22030-6078)
PHONE..................703 383-3000
Sandor Rosenberg, *Ch of Bd*
Stanley A Reese, *COO*
Richard S Derose, *CFO*
Charles May, *Director*
Bonnie Wachtel, *Director*
EMP: 27
SQ FT: 4,434
SALES (est): 10.1MM **Privately Held**
WEB: www.infoa.com
SIC: 7372 7379 Application computer software; computer related consulting services

(G-4634)
INHAND NETWORKS INC (PA)
3900 Jermantown Rd # 150 (22030-4946)
PHONE..................703 348-2988
Ming LI, *President*
Thad Leingang, *Sales Staff*
EMP: 6 **EST:** 2013

SALES (est): 2MM **Privately Held**
WEB: www.inhandnetworks.com
SIC: 3571 5045 3663 Electronic computers; computers, peripherals & software; mobile communication equipment

(G-4635)
INNOVATIVE COMPUTER ENGRG INC
Also Called: Ice
10302 Eaton Pl Ste 200 (22030-2215)
PHONE..................703 934-4879
Richard Holley, *CEO*
David Parker, *Software Dev*
EMP: 9
SQ FT: 200
SALES (est): 1.8MM **Privately Held**
WEB: www.ice-online.com
SIC: 3577 7379 Computer peripheral equipment; computer related consulting services

(G-4636)
INNOVATIVE COMPUTER ENGRG INC
10302 Eaton Pl Ste 200 (22030-2215)
PHONE..................703 934-2782
Richard Holley, *CEO*
EMP: 7
SALES (est): 984.9K **Privately Held**
WEB: www.ice-online.com
SIC: 3577 Computer peripheral equipment

(G-4637)
INTEL FEDERAL LLC
4100 Monu Crnr Dr Ste 540 (22030)
PHONE..................703 633-0953
David Patterson, *Mng Member*
EMP: 20
SALES (est): 1.7MM **Privately Held**
SIC: 3674 Semiconductors & related devices

(G-4638)
INVINCEA INC
3975 University Dr # 460 (22030-2533)
PHONE..................703 352-7680
Anup Ghosh, *CEO*
Norm Laudermilch, *COO*
Chris Greamo, *Vice Pres*
Kristina Creque, *Project Mgr*
James Allen, *Opers Staff*
EMP: 102
SALES (est): 15.2MM
SALES (corp-wide): 1.2MM **Privately Held**
WEB: www.sophos.com
SIC: 7372 7382 Business oriented computer software; security systems services
HQ: Sophos Group Limited
1 Bartholomew Lane
London EC2N
123 555-9933

(G-4639)
IPAC INDUSTRIES LLC
11943 Goodwood Dr (22030-5710)
PHONE..................703 362-9090
Pamela Collins, *Principal*
EMP: 2
SALES (est): 123.2K **Privately Held**
SIC: 3999 Manufacturing industries

(G-4640)
JUSTINIAN POSTERS & PRINTS
3977 Chain Bridge Rd # 202 (22030-3308)
PHONE..................703 273-8049
EMP: 1
SALES (est): 45.8K **Privately Held**
SIC: 3952 Mfg Lead Pencils/Art Goods

(G-4641)
JWLBOOK LLC
11619 Fairfax Commons Dr (22030-8523)
PHONE..................571 287-0121
Ali Nadeem, *Manager*
EMP: 1
SALES (est): 41K **Privately Held**
SIC: 3911 Jewelry apparel

(G-4642)
KD PUPPETS
4212 Sideburn Rd (22030-3505)
PHONE..................703 385-4543
Dee Cardiff, *Owner*

GEOGRAPHIC

(PA)=Parent Co (HQ)=Headquarters (DH)=Div Headquarters
✿ = New Business established in last 2 years

EMP: 1
SALES (est): 56.2K **Privately Held**
WEB: www.kaydeepuppets.com
SIC: 3999 Furs

(G-4643)
KENNESAW HOLDING COMPANY
4231 Monu Wall Way 313 (22030)
PHONE..................603 866-6944
EMP: 1
SALES (est): 235K **Privately Held**
SIC: 3699 3949 6719 3484 Mfg Elec Mach/Equip/Supp Mfg Sport/Athletic Goods Holding Company Mfg Small Arms

(G-4644)
KUSTOMCOFFEE
Also Called: Kustomcoffee.com
10631 West Dr (22030-4229)
PHONE..................571 344-9030
Arka Chaudhuri, *Owner*
EMP: 1
SALES (est): 50K **Privately Held**
SIC: 2095 Coffee roasting (except by wholesale grocers)

(G-4645)
LEADERSHIP PERSPECTIVES INC
5701 Windsor Gate Ln (22030-5827)
PHONE..................703 629-8977
Jim Stryker, *Principal*
EMP: 4
SALES (est): 172.2K **Privately Held**
SIC: 2711 Newspapers, publishing & printing

(G-4646)
LEFT FIELD MEDIA
10815 Charles Dr (22030-5140)
PHONE..................703 980-4710
Glenn Arnold, *Owner*
EMP: 2
SALES (est): 109.7K **Privately Held**
WEB: www.leftfieldmedia.net
SIC: 2741 Miscellaneous publishing

(G-4647)
LI DDS PLLC TIN W
12289 Engelmann Oak Ln (22030-9069)
PHONE..................703 352-2500
Tin Wai LI, *Principal*
EMP: 4
SALES (est): 397K **Privately Held**
SIC: 3356 Tin

(G-4648)
LOCKHEED MARTIN
10530 Rosehaven St # 300 (22030-2840)
PHONE..................703 272-6061
Rob Robertson, *Branch Mgr*
EMP: 99 **Publicly Held**
WEB: www.lockheedmartin.com
SIC: 3812 Search & navigation equipment
HQ: Lockheed Martin Integrated Systems, Llc
6801 Rockledge Dr
Bethesda MD 20817

(G-4649)
LOCKHEED MARTIN CORPORATION
10530 Rosehaven St # 500 (22030-2840)
PHONE..................270 319-4600
EMP: 435 **Publicly Held**
WEB: www.lockheedmartin.com
SIC: 3812 Search & navigation equipment
PA: Lockheed Martin Corporation
6801 Rockledge Dr
Bethesda MD 20817

(G-4650)
MACRO SYSTEMS LLC
3867 Plaza Dr (22030-2512)
PHONE..................703 359-9211
Howard Cunningham,
EMP: 3
SQ FT: 1,500
SALES (est): 415.9K **Privately Held**
WEB: www.macrollc.com
SIC: 7372 7373 Prepackaged software; computer integrated systems design

(G-4651)
MANUFACTURING SYSTEM SVCS INC
Also Called: Barcoderental.com
10394 Democracy Ln (22030-2522)
PHONE..................800 428-8643
Bill Crumpecker, *President*
Linda Holthaus, *Treasurer*
William Campbell, *Controller*
EMP: 6
SQ FT: 1,784
SALES: 3.9MM **Privately Held**
WEB: www.mss-software.com
SIC: 7372 7371 7359 7379 Prepackaged software; computer software development; office machine rental, except computers; computer related maintenance services

(G-4652)
MECTS SERVICES JV
3877 Fairfax Ridge Rd 350n (22030-7449)
PHONE..................248 499-9243
Amy Hentgen, *Assistant*
EMP: 2 EST: 2013
SALES (est): 116.1K **Privately Held**
SIC: 3669 Intercommunication systems, electric

(G-4653)
MEDIA RELATIONS
4400 University Dr (22030-4422)
PHONE..................703 993-8780
Christine Lapaille, *Principal*
EMP: 2
SALES (est): 66.8K **Privately Held**
WEB: www.publicity.com
SIC: 2741 Miscellaneous publishing

(G-4654)
MERCURY SYSTEMS INC
3554 Chain Bridge Rd # 3 (22030-2709)
PHONE..................510 252-0870
Richard Fenoli, *Director*
EMP: 4 **Publicly Held**
WEB: www.mrcy.com
SIC: 3571 Electronic computers
PA: Mercury Systems, Inc.
50 Minuteman Rd
Andover MA 01810
978 256-1300

(G-4655)
METAWEAR LLC
3580 Jermantown Rd (22030-2944)
PHONE..................561 302-2010
Marci Zaroff, *CEO*
Tara Cappel, *Opers Staff*
EMP: 3
SALES (corp-wide): 1.5MM **Privately Held**
WEB: www.metawearorganic.com
SIC: 2253 Knit outerwear mills
PA: Metawear, Llc
610 W 42nd St Apt N53f
New York NY
561 302-2010

(G-4656)
NABIDAY LLC
10332 Main St Ste 309 (22030-2410)
PHONE..................703 625-8679
EMP: 1
SALES (est): 39.7K **Privately Held**
SIC: 7372 Application computer software

(G-4657)
NOVUS TECHNOLOGY INC
3818 Daniels Run Ct (22030-2452)
PHONE..................703 218-9801
Charles S Maples, *President*
Charles Maples, *Principal*
EMP: 5
SALES (est): 762.4K **Privately Held**
WEB: www.novustechnology.com
SIC: 3663 Radio & TV communications equipment

(G-4658)
PACIFIC VIEW INTERNATIONAL
5388 Ashleigh Rd (22030-7228)
PHONE..................703 631-8659
Steve Angeline, *Manager*
▲ EMP: 3

SALES (est): 100K **Privately Held**
WEB: www.pvicaps.com
SIC: 2353 Hats & caps

(G-4659)
PADDY PUBLICATIONS LLC
10332 Main St (22030-2410)
PHONE..................703 402-2233
John Sexton, *Principal*
EMP: 1
SALES (est): 39.8K **Privately Held**
SIC: 2741 Miscellaneous publishing

(G-4660)
PEER TECHNOLOGIES PLLC
Also Called: Peer Clinic For Back Pain Spine
4250 Chain Bridge Rd (22030-4214)
PHONE..................603 727-8692
Atiyya Mirza, *Branch Mgr*
EMP: 1
SALES (corp-wide): 450.1K **Privately Held**
WEB: www.peerclinic.com
SIC: 3841 Surgical instruments & apparatus
PA: Peer Technologies Pllc
378 Stoney Brook Rd
West Springfield NH 03284
603 727-6647

(G-4661)
PREFERRED PROFESSIONAL SVCS
13204 Austrian Pine Ct (22030-8248)
PHONE..................703 803-3563
Venkata Maddu, *President*
EMP: 2
SALES (est): 132.1K **Privately Held**
WEB: www.preferins.com
SIC: 3695 Computer software tape & disks: blank, rigid & floppy

(G-4662)
PRIVARIS INC
11200 Waples Mill Rd 10 (22030-7407)
PHONE..................703 592-1180
EMP: 2
SALES (est): 130K **Privately Held**
SIC: 3699 Mfg Electrical Equipment/Supplies

(G-4663)
PROVIDENCE PUBG GROUP LLC
11010 Fairchester Dr (22030-4836)
PHONE..................703 352-3152
Douglas Schauss, *Principal*
EMP: 2
SALES (est): 94.5K **Privately Held**
SIC: 2741 Miscellaneous publishing

(G-4664)
PSL AMERICA INC (PA)
Also Called: PSL America Group
11350 Random Hills Rd (22030-6044)
PHONE..................703 279-6426
Thomas Lee, *CEO*
Jeonghee Park, *CFO*
Jennie M Rhee, *Admin Sec*
EMP: 6
SALES (est): 2.1MM **Privately Held**
SIC: 3433 Solar heaters & collectors

(G-4665)
PTC ENTERPRISES LLC
11725 Lee Hwy (22030-8800)
PHONE..................703 352-9274
Vicky Pittman, *Principal*
EMP: 2
SALES (est): 121.9K **Privately Held**
SIC: 3999 Pet supplies

(G-4666)
PUBLICATION CERTIFIED
10301 Democracy Ln # 401 (22030-2545)
PHONE..................703 259-1936
R Nace, *Principal*
EMP: 2
SALES (est): 99.8K **Privately Held**
SIC: 2741 Miscellaneous publishing

(G-4667)
PUBLICATIONS PROFESSIONALS LLC
3603 Chain Bridge Rd A (22030-3244)
PHONE..................703 934-4499
Linda Stringer, *General Mgr*
Marcy Gessel, *Editor*
Barbara Hart,
EMP: 1
SALES (est): 69.1K **Privately Held**
WEB: www.pubspros.com
SIC: 2741 Miscellaneous publishing

(G-4668)
REAL ESTATE CONSULTANTS
10300 Eaton Pl Ste 120 (22030-2239)
PHONE..................949 212-1366
EMP: 2 EST: 2019
SALES (est): 88.3K **Privately Held**
SIC: 3699 Electrical equipment & supplies

(G-4669)
ROBBWORKS LLC
4182 Lord Culpeper Ln (22030-8123)
PHONE..................571 218-5532
Karl A Robb,
Angela Robb,
EMP: 2
SALES (est): 80K **Privately Held**
SIC: 2731 7389 Books: publishing only;

(G-4670)
ROGUE SOFTWARE LLC
3253 Arrowhead Cir (22030-7362)
PHONE..................703 945-9175
John Maitin, *Principal*
EMP: 2
SALES (est): 62.1K **Privately Held**
SIC: 7372 Prepackaged software

(G-4671)
ROLLSTREAM INC
3913 Old Lee Hwy Ste 33a (22030-2433)
PHONE..................703 277-2150
EMP: 2
SALES (est): 56.5K **Privately Held**
SIC: 7372 Prepackaged software

(G-4672)
SALIENTCONTENT LLC
5109 Brentwood Farm Dr (22030-6218)
PHONE..................571 286-8480
EMP: 3
SALES (est): 128.5K **Privately Held**
WEB: www.salientcontent.com
SIC: 2731 Book publishing

(G-4673)
SATIN SOLUTIONS LLC
10560 Main St (22030-7182)
PHONE..................703 218-3481
EMP: 1 EST: 2017
SALES (est): 46.5K **Privately Held**
SIC: 2221 Satins

(G-4674)
SCOTT COULTER
Also Called: Outdoor Excursions
10819 Warwick Ave (22030-3034)
P.O. Box 24, Boonsboro MD (21713-0024)
PHONE..................800 775-2925
Scott Coulter, *Principal*
EMP: 2
SALES (est): 155.4K **Privately Held**
WEB: www.outdoorexcursions.com
SIC: 2295 Tubing, textile: varnished

(G-4675)
SHINING LIGHTS LLC
12553 Cerromar Pl (22030-6654)
PHONE..................703 338-3820
EMP: 4 EST: 2009
SALES (est): 227.2K **Privately Held**
WEB: www.shining-lights.com
SIC: 2392 Bags, garment storage: except paper or plastic film

(G-4676)
SIGNS BY TOMORROW
11150 Fairfax Blvd # 104 (22030-5066)
PHONE..................703 591-2444
Michael Behn, *Principal*
EMP: 2

SALES (est): 194.9K **Privately Held**
WEB: www.signsbytomorrow.com
SIC: 3993 Signs & advertising specialties

(G-4677)
SIGNSATIONS LLC
11325 Random Hills Rd # 360
(22030-0972)
PHONE................................571 340-3330
Capers Brown, *General Mgr*
EMP: 4
SQ FT: 2,150
SALES (est): 75K **Privately Held**
WEB: www.signsationsrc.com
SIC: 3993 Signs, not made in custom sign painting shops

(G-4678)
SILENT CIRCLE AMERICAS LLC
4210 Fairfax Corner Ave W # 215
(22030-8627)
PHONE................................202 499-6427
EMP: 5
SALES (est): 400.8K **Privately Held**
WEB: www.silentcircle.com
SIC: 7372 Prepackaged software

(G-4679)
SOLEIL FOODS LTD LIABILITY CO (PA)
3900 Jermantown Rd # 300 (22030-4900)
PHONE................................201 920-1553
Abdelhalim Saad,
EMP: 8 EST: 2014
SQ FT: 200
SALES (est): 1.2MM **Privately Held**
SIC: 2034 Dates, dried

(G-4680)
SPACEQUEST LTD
3554 Chain Bridge Rd # 40 (22030-2709)
PHONE................................703 424-7801
Dino Lorenzini, *President*
Linda Jacobsen, *Vice Pres*
Patrick Shannon, *Vice Pres*
Glenn Richardson, *Engineer*
EMP: 10
SQ FT: 3,500
SALES (est): 3MM **Privately Held**
WEB: www.spacequest.com
SIC: 3663 4899 Space satellite communications equipment; satellite earth stations

(G-4681)
STEVE HOLLAR WDWKG & ENGRV
11648 Leehigh Dr (22030-5640)
PHONE................................703 273-0639
EMP: 2
SALES (est): 117.6K **Privately Held**
SIC: 2431 Millwork

(G-4682)
STILLHOUSE PRESS
4400 University Dr (22030-4422)
PHONE................................530 409-8179
EMP: 1 EST: 2018
SALES (est): 37.5K **Privately Held**
WEB: www.stillhousepress.org
SIC: 2741 Miscellaneous publishing

(G-4683)
STRUCTURED SOFTWARE INC
5369 Ashleigh Rd (22030-7231)
PHONE................................703 266-0588
EMP: 2 EST: 2001
SALES (est): 130K **Privately Held**
SIC: 7372 Prepackaged Software Services

(G-4684)
SUPPLIER SOLUTIONS INC
11350 Rndom Hlls Rd Ste 8 (22030)
P.O. Box 4928, Manassas (20108-4928)
PHONE................................703 791-7720
Nikolas Brisbin, *President*
Jeremy Traynor, *Project Mgr*
EMP: 15
SALES (est): 657.9K **Privately Held**
WEB: www.suppliersolutions.com
SIC: 7372 Application computer software

(G-4685)
TASCO USA CO INC
11315 Westbrook Mill Ln (22030-5672)
PHONE................................703 209-0193

Chun Young Tae, *President*
EMP: 2
SALES (est): 187.4K **Privately Held**
SIC: 3599 Machine shop, jobbing & repair

(G-4686)
TECH ENTERPRISES INC
11150 Fairfax Blvd # 402 (22030-5066)
PHONE................................703 352-0001
Ranjit Singh, *Principal*
EMP: 2
SALES (est): 160.6K **Privately Held**
SIC: 7372 Application computer software

(G-4687)
TEXTORE INC
4031 University Dr # 100 (22030-3409)
PHONE................................571 321-2013
Robert Stewart, *CEO*
Pat Little, *COO*
EMP: 10
SALES (est): 1.5MM **Privately Held**
WEB: www.textore.net
SIC: 7372 Business oriented computer software

(G-4688)
TODAYS SIGNS INC
Also Called: Fastsigns Fairfax
10341a Democracy Ln (22030)
PHONE................................703 352-6200
Cleopatra D Burke, *CEO*
James A Burke, *CFO*
EMP: 3
SQ FT: 1,800
SALES (est): 363K **Privately Held**
SIC: 3993 Signs & advertising specialties

(G-4689)
TRAFFICLAND INC
11325 Rndom Hlls Rd Ste 3 (22030)
PHONE................................703 591-1933
Lawrence Nelson, *CEO*
Jay Cohen, *Corp Comm Staff*
Walter Reed, *Manager*
Monica Cordero-Blanton, *Admin Sec*
EMP: 19
SALES (est): 3.5MM **Privately Held**
WEB: www.trafficland.com
SIC: 3669 Transportation signaling devices

(G-4690)
UNIFIEDONLINE INC (HQ)
4126 Leonard Dr (22030-5118)
PHONE................................816 679-1893
Robert M Howe III, *Ch of Bd*
EMP: 6
SALES (est): 924.4K **Publicly Held**
WEB: www.unifiedonline.net
SIC: 3572 7372 Computer storage devices; application computer software
PA: Unifiedonline Llc
4126 Leonard Dr
Fairfax VA 22030
816 679-1893

(G-4691)
UNIFIEDONLINE LLC (PA)
4126 Leonard Dr (22030-5118)
PHONE................................816 679-1893
Robert M Howe III, *Ch of Bd*
EMP: 2
SALES (est): 924.4K **Publicly Held**
SIC: 3572 7372 Computer storage devices; application computer software

(G-4692)
VARIETY PRESS LLC
3301 Spring Lake Ct (22030-2059)
PHONE................................703 359-0932
Albert Johnson, *Principal*
EMP: 1
SALES (est): 50.7K **Privately Held**
SIC: 2741 Miscellaneous publishing

(G-4693)
VERMARK GLOBAL SYSTEMS INC
Also Called: Vermark Gs
11216 Waples Mill Rd 102a (22030-6099)
PHONE................................703 629-1571
Audu Mark, *President*
EMP: 5
SALES (est): 275K **Privately Held**
SIC: 7372 Prepackaged software

(G-4694)
VORTEX INDUSTRIES LLC
4078 Fountainside Ln (22030-6089)
P.O. Box 2627, Merrifield (22116-2627)
PHONE................................703 732-5458
Saf Benouameur, *Principal*
EMP: 2
SALES (est): 93.1K **Privately Held**
SIC: 3999 Manufacturing industries

(G-4695)
WP COMPANY LLC
Also Called: Washington Post
3900 University Dr # 130 (22030-2513)
PHONE................................703 392-1303
Scott Patton, *Manager*
EMP: 5 **Privately Held**
WEB: www.washingtonpost.com
SIC: 2711 Newspapers, publishing & printing
HQ: Wp Company Llc
1301 K St Nw
Washington DC 20071

(G-4696)
YOBNUG LLC
3713 Burrows Ave (22030-3001)
PHONE................................703 385-1880
Henry Sheard, *Principal*
EMP: 2
SALES (est): 88.6K **Privately Held**
SIC: 3999 Pet supplies

(G-4697)
YOUR WAY SOFTWARE
10226 Raider Ln (22030-1909)
PHONE................................703 591-2064
David E Bryant, *Owner*
EMP: 2
SALES (est): 111.9K **Privately Held**
SIC: 7372 Prepackaged software

(G-4698)
ZINE GRAPHICS PRINT
10231 Stratford Ave (22030-2330)
P.O. Box 1166 (22038-1166)
PHONE................................703 591-4000
EMP: 2
SALES (est): 101.5K **Privately Held**
WEB: www.zinegraphics.com
SIC: 2752 Commercial printing, lithographic

Fairfax
Loudoun County

(G-4699)
SHOEBOX MEMORIES
25864 Flintonbridge Dr (20152-4802)
PHONE................................703 969-9290
Kevin Chin, *Owner*
EMP: 1
SALES (est): 94.5K **Privately Held**
WEB: www.shoeboxmemories.net
SIC: 3663 Digital encoders

Fairfax Station
Fairfax County

(G-4700)
A A BUSINESS FORMS & PRINTING
6007 Captain Marr Ct (22039-1304)
PHONE................................703 866-5544
EMP: 1
SALES (est): 46.4K **Privately Held**
SIC: 2782 Blankbooks & looseleaf binders

(G-4701)
CHESAPEAKE INTEGRATED BIOENRGY
7742 Clifton Rd (22039-1826)
PHONE................................202 253-5953
Raymond Crabbs, *Mng Member*
EMP: 1 EST: 2016
SALES (est): 92.8K **Privately Held**
SIC: 3519 Engines, diesel & semi-diesel or dual-fuel

(G-4702)
COMMONWEALTH GRAPHICS INC
8613 Mallard Vw (22039-3314)
PHONE................................703 495-0733
Kimberly Shaffer, *President*
Pat Shaffer, *Vice Pres*
EMP: 2
SALES (est): 178.9K **Privately Held**
WEB: www.commonwealthgraphics.com
SIC: 2759 Screen printing

(G-4703)
CONTEMPORARY WOODCRAFTS INC (PA)
7337 Wayfarer Dr (22039-1906)
PHONE................................703 787-9711
Rob Grant, *President*
EMP: 10
SQ FT: 8,500
SALES (est): 654K **Privately Held**
WEB: www.builtincabinet.com
SIC: 2434 Wood kitchen cabinets

(G-4704)
CREATIVE PERMUTATIONS LLC
9412 Englefield Ct (22039-3173)
PHONE................................703 628-3799
Roberta Breden,
EMP: 1
SALES (est): 39.6K **Privately Held**
SIC: 3999 Manufacturing industries

(G-4705)
DAGHIGH SOFTWARE CO INC
10622 Timberidge Rd (22039-2406)
PHONE................................703 323-7475
Shawn Daghigh, *Principal*
EMP: 2
SALES (est): 164.7K **Privately Held**
SIC: 7372 Prepackaged software

(G-4706)
DEEP-SPACE INTELLIGENT CONSTRU
11314 Robert Carter Rd (22039-1322)
PHONE................................571 247-7376
David Applin,
EMP: 2 EST: 2013
SALES (est): 129.5K **Privately Held**
SIC: 3769 Guided missile & space vehicle parts & aux eqpt, rsch & dev

(G-4707)
DEFENSE INSIGHTS LLC
9915 Evenstar Ln (22039-2501)
PHONE................................703 455-7880
Edward M Fortunato, *Administration*
EMP: 2 EST: 2010
SALES (est): 114.7K **Privately Held**
SIC: 3812 Defense systems & equipment

(G-4708)
DIVERGENCE SOFTWARE INC
8519 Oak Pointe Way (22039-3340)
PHONE................................703 690-9870
Christopher D Kryza, *Principal*
EMP: 2
SALES (est): 130.8K **Privately Held**
SIC: 7372 Prepackaged software

(G-4709)
DIXON MEDIATION GROUP LLC
10107 View Point Ct (22039-2978)
PHONE................................703 517-3556
Anna F Dixon,
EMP: 10
SALES (est): 950K **Privately Held**
WEB: www.dixonmediationgroup.com
SIC: 3624 Lighting carbons

(G-4710)
GRACENOTES
6309 Pohick Station Dr (22039-1649)
PHONE................................703 825-7922
Sarah Layman, *Principal*
EMP: 2
SALES (est): 99.9K **Privately Held**
WEB: www.gncm.org
SIC: 2741 Music book & sheet music publishing

GEOGRAPHIC

(G-4711)
GUARDIT TECHNOLOGIES LLC
9407 Braymore Cir (22039-3134)
PHONE..................................703 232-1132
Kristi Otto, *Principal*
EMP: 2 EST: 2011
SALES (est): 244.9K **Privately Held**
SIC: 3822 Thermostats & other environ-
　mental sensors

(G-4712)
GUNDLACH AEROSPACE LLC
11480 Robert Stephens Dr (22039-2329)
PHONE..................................703 303-0813
John Gundlach, *President*
EMP: 1
SALES (est): 128.7K **Privately Held**
SIC: 3721 Aircraft

(G-4713)
HEALTHY SNACKS DISTRS LTD
7103 Woodrise Ct (22039-2948)
PHONE..................................703 627-8578
John M Moore, *President*
EMP: 1
SALES (est): 200K **Privately Held**
SIC: 2024 Ice cream & frozen desserts

(G-4714)
JPS CONSULTING LLC
8311 Ivy Green Rd (22039-3224)
PHONE..................................571 334-0859
John P Schaub, *President*
EMP: 1
SALES (est): 50K **Privately Held**
SIC: 2023 Dietary supplements, dairy &
　non-dairy based

(G-4715)
**LANDMARK WOODWORKING
INC**
8304 Greenside Dr (22039-3222)
PHONE..................................703 424-3191
EMP: 2 EST: 2008
SALES (est): 120K **Privately Held**
SIC: 2431 Mfg Millwork

(G-4716)
LORD SIGN
10993 Centrepointe Way (22039-1415)
PHONE..................................301 316-7446
Mohammad Tabasi, *President*
EMP: 2
SALES (est): 121.4K **Privately Held**
WEB: www.lordsign.com
SIC: 3993 Signs & advertising specialties

(G-4717)
**MEKELEXX MANAGEMENT
SERVICES**
8649 Oak Chase Cir (22039-3332)
PHONE..................................561 644-8621
EMP: 1 EST: 2019
SALES (est): 46K **Privately Held**
SIC: 3993 Signs & advertising specialties

(G-4718)
MYTHIKOS MOMMY LLC
8607 Chase Glen Cir (22039-3308)
PHONE..................................703 568-7504
Charlotte Avery,
EMP: 1
SALES (est): 20K **Privately Held**
SIC: 2731 Book publishing

(G-4719)
NEW CENTURY SOFTWARE
6914 Wolf Run Shoals Rd (22039-1732)
PHONE..................................704 984-3135
Peter McConnell, *Manager*
EMP: 2
SALES (est): 62.1K **Privately Held**
WEB: www.choice-guide.com
SIC: 7372 Prepackaged software

(G-4720)
NORTH ARROW INC
11115 Flora Lee Dr (22039-1029)
PHONE..................................703 250-3215
Eric Henry, *Principal*
EMP: 2
SALES (est): 69.2K **Privately Held**
SIC: 2711 Newspapers

(G-4721)
**PHOENIX SECURITY GROUP
LTD**
7818 Ox Rd (22039-2520)
PHONE..................................703 323-4940
James Baker, *President*
Ira Weiss, *Treasurer*
EMP: 9
SALES (est): 990.8K **Privately Held**
WEB: www.phoenix-net.com
SIC: 3699 Security devices

(G-4722)
**REED ENVELOPE COMPANY
INC**
8630 Meadow Edge Ter (22039-3349)
PHONE..................................703 690-2249
Christopher Reed, *CEO*
EMP: 15
SQ FT: 16,000
SALES (est): 1.2MM **Privately Held**
SIC: 2759 2677 2752 Envelopes: printing;
　envelopes; commercial printing, litho-
　graphic

(G-4723)
ROCK XPRESS LLC
8602 Eagle Glen Ter (22039-2679)
PHONE..................................571 212-6689
EMP: 2 EST: 2010
SALES (est): 106.2K **Privately Held**
SIC: 1429 Crushed & broken stone

(G-4724)
SON1C WAX LLC
11515 Four Penny Ln (22039-1111)
PHONE..................................703 508-8188
Elias Andrew,
EMP: 1
SALES (est): 79.5K **Privately Held**
WEB: www.son1cwax.com
SIC: 2899 7542 Core wash or wax; wash-
　ing & polishing, automotive

(G-4725)
SWURLS LLC
8513 Century Oak Ct (22039-3343)
PHONE..................................571 423-9899
Arzin Alawi,
EMP: 1
SALES (est): 55.6K **Privately Held**
SIC: 2051 Cakes, pies & pastries

(G-4726)
VAULT TECHNOLOGIES LLC
9746 South Park Cir (22039-2941)
PHONE..................................703 283-2550
Max E Miller, *Mng Member*
Max Miller,
EMP: 2
SALES (est): 172.7K **Privately Held**
SIC: 3272 Burial vaults, concrete or pre-
　cast terrazzo

(G-4727)
WESTEND PRESS LLC
7140 Twelve Oaks Dr (22039-1500)
PHONE..................................703 992-6939
Nahid Sayah,
EMP: 2 EST: 2007
SALES (est): 227.1K **Privately Held**
WEB: www.westendpress.com
SIC: 2741 2759 7334 Miscellaneous pub-
　lishing; commercial printing; photocopying
　& duplicating services

(G-4728)
WICHAAR INC
6305 Travilah Ct (22039-1537)
PHONE..................................703 863-3451
Manzur Ejaz, *Principal*
EMP: 2
SALES (est): 112.8K **Privately Held**
WEB: www.wichaar.com
SIC: 2731 Book publishing

Fairfield
Rockbridge County

(G-4729)
BEA MAURER
6051 N Lee Hwy (24435-2505)
PHONE..................................540 377-5025
Lynne Gilbert, *Principal*
EMP: 2 EST: 1983
SALES (est): 158.2K **Privately Held**
WEB: www.beamaurer.com
SIC: 3999 Manufacturing industries

(G-4730)
**FITZGERALD LUMBER & LOG
CO INC**
5459 Northley Hwy (24435)
P.O. Box 141 (24435-0141)
PHONE..................................540 348-5199
Calvin Fitzgerald, *Branch Mgr*
EMP: 53
SALES (corp-wide): 19MM **Privately
Held**
WEB: www.fitzgeraldlumber.com
SIC: 2421 2426 Sawmills & planing mills,
　general; hardwood dimension & flooring
　mills
PA: Fitzgerald Lumber & Log Co., Inc.
　403 E 29th St
　Buena Vista VA 24416
　540 261-3430

(G-4731)
JARRETT MILLWORK
Also Called: Jarrett Millwork & Moldings
5987 N Lee Hwy (24435-2508)
PHONE..................................540 377-9173
David William Jarrett, *Owner*
EMP: 3
SQ FT: 10,000
SALES (est): 450K **Privately Held**
SIC: 2431 Millwork

(G-4732)
LEXINGTON PET WORLD
3920 N Lee Hwy (24435-2201)
PHONE..................................540 464-4141
Fax: 540 464-4143
EMP: 2
SALES (est): 13.3K **Privately Held**
SIC: 3999 5199 5999 Mfg Misc Products
　Whol Nondurable Goods Ret Misc Mer-
　chandise

(G-4733)
PHILIP BACK
Also Called: Back's Welding Service
2286 Borden Grant Trl (24435-2232)
PHONE..................................540 570-9353
Philip Back, *Principal*
EMP: 1
SALES (est): 50K **Privately Held**
SIC: 7692 Welding repair

(G-4734)
QUILTERY LLC
5661 N Lee Hwy (24435-2525)
PHONE..................................540 377-9191
Maureen Smart,
EMP: 3
SALES (est): 50K **Privately Held**
WEB: www.quilteryshop.com
SIC: 3496 Fabrics, woven wire

(G-4735)
RIDGE VALLEY ALPACAS
1458 Sterrett Rd (24435-2627)
PHONE..................................540 255-9200
EMP: 2
SALES (est): 132.3K **Privately Held**
WEB: www.ridgevalleyalpacas.com
SIC: 2231 Alpacas, mohair: woven

Fairlawn
Radford City County

(G-4736)
ELEVEN WEST INC
6598 New River Rd (24141-8532)
PHONE..................................540 639-9319
John H Giesen, *President*
Lee Wolf, *Technology*
Lisa Graham, *Executive*
Hope Galloway, *Admin Asst*
EMP: 20
SQ FT: 9,000
SALES (est): 2.7MM **Privately Held**
WEB: www.elevenwest.com
SIC: 2759 5199 2395 Screen printing; ad-
　vertising specialties; emblems, embroi-
　dered

(G-4737)
LYON ROOFING INC
7822 Peppers Ferry Blvd (24141-8656)
PHONE..................................540 633-0170
Bret Lyon, *Branch Mgr*
EMP: 5 **Privately Held**
WEB: www.lyonmetalroofing.com
SIC: 3444 2891 Sheet metalwork; adhe-
　sives
PA: Lyon Roofing, Inc.
　485 Industrial Park Rd
　Piney Flats TN 37686

(G-4738)
MS WHEELCHAIR VIRGINIA INC
7083 Hickman Cemetery Rd (24141-5811)
PHONE..................................540 838-5022
D B Robinson CPA, *President*
EMP: 2
SALES (est): 94.8K **Privately Held**
WEB: www.mswheelchairva.com
SIC: 3842 Wheelchairs

(G-4739)
**NEW RIVER VINEYARD &
WINERY**
6750 Falling Branch Rd (24141-8450)
PHONE..................................540 392-4870
Christy Wallen, *Principal*
EMP: 2
SALES (est): 93.8K **Privately Held**
WEB: www.nrvwine.com
SIC: 2084 Wines

(G-4740)
SIGN SYSTEMS INC
7084 Lee Hwy (24141-8416)
PHONE..................................540 639-0669
Jon T Wyatt, *CEO*
EMP: 8
SALES (est): 500K **Privately Held**
WEB: www.signsystemsinc.com
SIC: 3993 Signs & advertising specialties

Falls Church
Fairfax County

(G-4741)
AG ALMANAC LLC
Also Called: AlphaGraphics
2735 Hartland Rd Ste 101 (22043-3542)
PHONE..................................703 289-1200
Joe Huh, *Manager*
Sarah Huh,
EMP: 5 EST: 2011
SALES (est): 778K **Privately Held**
WEB: www.alphagraphics.com
SIC: 2752 Commercial printing, litho-
　graphic

(G-4742)
AL RAYANAH USA
3708 Sleepy Hollow Rd (22041-1022)
PHONE..................................703 941-1200
Dale Barnhard, *Partner*
Khalil Khatib, *Partner*
EMP: 2
SALES (est): 66.6K **Privately Held**
SIC: 3999 Fruits, artificial & preserved

(G-4743)
ALL KINDS OF SIGNS INC
1938 Pimmit Dr (22043-1100)
PHONE..................................703 321-6542
Jifeng LI, *Director*
EMP: 1
SALES (est): 46K **Privately Held**
SIC: 3993 Signs & advertising specialties

(G-4744)
ALLIANCE IN-HOME CARE LLC
6201 Leesburg Pike Ste 6 (22044-2201)
PHONE..................................703 825-1067
Priscilla Castillo-Hess, *Mng Member*
EMP: 7
SALES (est): 699.5K **Privately Held**
SIC: 3699 Automotive driving simulators
　(training aids), electronic

(G-4745)
AMANA U S A INCORPORATED
6669 Avignon Blvd (22043-1724)
PHONE..................................703 821-7501

▲ = Import ▼=Export
◆ =Import/Export

EMP: 2
SALES (est): 151.1K **Privately Held**
SIC: 3999 Mfg Misc Products

(G-4746)
AMBROSIA VINEYARDS
2825 Rosemary Ln (22042-1811)
PHONE..............................703 237-8717
EMP: 2
SALES (est): 72.6K **Privately Held**
SIC: 2084 Wines

(G-4747)
AMERICAN LOGO CORP
2190 Pimmit Dr Ste H (22043-2806)
PHONE..............................703 356-4709
Vihn Newgen, *President*
Lan Newgen, *Vice Pres*
EMP: 1
SQ FT: 2,500
SALES (est): 104.5K **Privately Held**
WEB: www.americanlogo.com
SIC: 2395 Embroidery products, except
schiffli machine

(G-4748)
**AMERICAN QUALITY
SOFTWARE INC**
2740 Pioneer Ln (22043-3411)
PHONE..............................571 730-4532
Anil Chagani, *Principal*
EMP: 2
SALES (est): 75K **Privately Held**
SIC: 7372 Prepackaged software

(G-4749)
AMERICAN SPIRIT LLC
Also Called: Hygenic Solutions
6302 Crosswoods Cir (22044-1302)
PHONE..............................703 914-1057
Joe Pisciotta, *President*
EMP: 2
SALES (est): 114.4K **Privately Held**
SIC: 2499 Seats, toilet

(G-4750)
ARMSTAR CORPORATION
3122 Patrick Henry Dr (22044-1823)
PHONE..............................703 241-8888
Benkt Linnander, *President*
Sarah Linnander, *Treasurer*
EMP: 2
SALES (est): 400K **Privately Held**
WEB: www.armstar.com
SIC: 3827 Optical instruments & lenses

(G-4751)
ATHENA SERVICES LLC
7000 Falls Reach Dr # 312 (22043-2335)
PHONE..............................201 232-9114
Venkat Subramaniam, *President*
EMP: 1
SALES (est): 100K **Privately Held**
SIC: 7372 7389 Application computer soft-
ware;

(G-4752)
AUSOME FOODS LLC
2251 Pimmit Dr Apt 214 (22043-2810)
PHONE..............................703 478-4866
Zeina Meng, *Principal*
EMP: 2
SALES (est): 146.8K **Privately Held**
SIC: 2021 Creamery butter

(G-4753)
**BACK POCKET PROVISIONS
LLC**
2908 Marshall St (22042-1917)
PHONE..............................703 585-3676
Jennifer G Beckman, *Administration*
Jennifer Beckman,
William Gray,
EMP: 2 EST: 2015
SALES (est): 98.7K **Privately Held**
SIC: 2033 Seasonings, tomato: packaged
in cans, jars, etc.

(G-4754)
BAE SYSTEMS INC (DH)
2941 Frview Pk Dr Ste 100 (22042)
PHONE..............................571 461-6000
Thomas A Arseneault, *CEO*
Guy Montminy, *President*
Alice Eldridge, *Senior VP*

Travis Garriss, *Senior VP*
Caitlin Hayden, *Senior VP*
▼ EMP: 152
SALES (est): 9.2B
WEB: www.baesystems.com
SIC: 3812 3728 Search & detection systems & instruments; navigational systems
& instruments; radar systems & equipment; missile guidance systems & equipment; countermeasure dispensers,
aircraft; chaff dispensers, aircraft

(G-4755)
**BAE SYSTEMS HOLDINGS INC
(HQ)**
2941 Frview Pk Dr Ste 100 (22042)
PHONE..............................571 461-6000
Thomas A Arseneault, *CEO*
Douglas Belair, *President*
Dennis Morris, *President*
Scott Obrien, *President*
Richard Schieffelin, *President*
◆ EMP: 400
SALES (est): 9.2B
SALES (corp-wide): 23.6B **Privately Held**
WEB: www.baesystems.com
SIC: 3699 3728 3812 Electrical equip-
ment & supplies; electronic training de-
vices; aircraft parts & equipment; search
& navigation equipment
PA: Bae Systems Plc
6 Carlton Gardens Stirling Square
London
125 237-3232

(G-4756)
**BAE SYSTEMS LAND
ARMAMENTS INC (DH)**
2941 Frview Pk Dr Ste 100 (22042)
PHONE..............................571 461-6000
Guy Montminy, *President*
James M Blue, *Treasurer*
◆ EMP: 40
SQ FT: 30,000
SALES (est): 784.3MM
SALES (corp-wide): 23.6B **Privately Held**
WEB: www.baesystems.com
SIC: 3721 3795 Aircraft; tanks & tank
components

(G-4757)
**BAE SYSTEMS LAND
ARMAMENTS LP (DH)**
2941 Frview Pk Dr Ste 100 (22042)
PHONE..............................571 461-6000
Erwin Bieber, *CEO*
◆ EMP: 60 EST: 1994
SALES (est): 889.5MM
SALES (corp-wide): 23.6B **Privately Held**
WEB: www.baesystems.com
SIC: 3795 3812 Tanks & tank compo-
nents; search & navigation equipment

(G-4758)
**BAE SYSTEMS LAND ARMMNTS
HLDNG**
2941 Frview Pk Dr Ste 100 (22042)
PHONE..............................571 461-6000
Thomas Rabaut, *President*
Francis Raborn, *CFO*
EMP: 60 EST: 1997
SALES (est): 4.5MM
SALES (corp-wide): 23.6B **Privately Held**
WEB: www.baesystems.com
SIC: 3795 Tanks & tank components
HQ: Bae Systems Land & Armaments Inc.
2941 Frview Pk Dr Ste 100
Falls Church VA 22042

(G-4759)
**BAE SYSTEMS TCTCAL VHCL
SYSTEM**
Also Called: Bae Systems Srvvbility Systems
2941 Frview Pk Dr Ste 100 (22042)
PHONE..............................571 461-6000
EMP: 25
SALES (corp-wide): 23.6B **Privately Held**
WEB: www.baesystems.com
SIC: 3711 3523 3561 Motor vehicles &
car bodies; fertilizing machinery, farm;
pumps, oil well & field

HQ: Bae Systems Tactical Vehicle Systems
Lp
2941 Frview Pk Dr Ste 100
Falls Church VA 22042

(G-4760)
**BAE SYSTEMS TCTCAL VHCL
SYSTEM (DH)**
2941 Frview Pk Dr Ste 100 (22042)
PHONE..............................571 461-6000
Keith Thompson, *Controller*
Erika Guerrero, *Administration*
◆ EMP: 3
SALES (est): 3MM
SALES (corp-wide): 23.6B **Privately Held**
WEB: www.baesystems.com
SIC: 3711 Military motor vehicle assembly

(G-4761)
BALMAR INC (HQ)
Also Called: Hbp
2818 Fallfax Dr (22042-2804)
PHONE..............................703 289-9000
John Snyder, *CEO*
James Morgan, *President*
Jim Morgan, *Division VP*
Mary K Humfel, *Treasurer*
Mike Edwads, *Mktg Dir*
▲ EMP: 36 EST: 1966
SQ FT: 30,000
SALES (est): 6.4MM
SALES (corp-wide): 18MM **Privately
Held**
WEB: www.hbp.com
SIC: 2752 Commercial printing, offset
PA: Hbp, Inc.
952 Frederick St
Hagerstown MD 21740
800 638-3508

(G-4762)
BCBG MAX AZRIA GROUP LLC
7907 Powers Blvd (22042)
PHONE..............................757 497-9575
EMP: 2
SALES (corp-wide): 1B **Privately Held**
SIC: 2335 Mfg Women's/Misses' Dresses
HQ: Bcbg Max Azria Group, Llc
2761 Fruitland Ave
Vernon CA 90058
323 589-2224

(G-4763)
BEAN COUNTERS
2833 Woodlawn Ave Apt 402 (22042-2045)
PHONE..............................703 534-1516
Robert Mansker, *President*
EMP: 2 EST: 2010
SALES (est): 237.4K **Privately Held**
SIC: 3131 Footwear cut stock

(G-4764)
BH MEDIA GROUP INC
Also Called: Tulsa World
3236 Spring Ln (22041-2608)
PHONE..............................703 241-2608
Jim Myers, *Principal*
EMP: 1
SALES (corp-wide): 254.6B **Publicly
Held**
WEB: www.tulsaworld.com
SIC: 2711 Newspapers, publishing & print-
ing
HQ: Bh Media Group, Inc.
315 S Boulder Ave
Tulsa OK 74103
918 583-2161

(G-4765)
BRADSHAW VIOLA
Also Called: Vi's Vtc Computer Consultant
5501 Seminary Rd Apt 807s (22041-3905)
PHONE..............................571 274-5244
Viola Bradshaw, *Owner*
EMP: 1
SALES (est): 79.3K **Privately Held**
SIC: 3571 Electronic computers

(G-4766)
BUTTER OF LIFE LLC
6166 Leesburg Pike B215 (22044-1840)
PHONE..............................703 507-5298
Marc Jacques-Louis, *Principal*
EMP: 1 EST: 2013

SALES (est): 66K **Privately Held**
SIC: 2844 8361 7389 Cosmetic preparations; residential care;

(G-4767)
CAMBIS LLC
5575 Seminary Rd Apt 306 (22041-3556)
PHONE..............................202 746-6124
Robert Coulson,
EMP: 4
SALES (est): 400K **Privately Held**
SIC: 7372 Prepackaged software

(G-4768)
CANVAS MARINE CO
2756 Cameron Rd (22042-2015)
PHONE..............................703 534-5886
William Shannon, *Principal*
EMP: 1
SALES (est): 68K **Privately Held**
SIC: 2394 Canvas & related products

(G-4769)
CAPITAL PUBLISHING CORP
3140 Graham Rd (22042-2506)
PHONE..............................571 214-1659
Nguyen Bui Thi, *Vice Pres*
EMP: 1
SALES (est): 50.5K **Privately Held**
SIC: 2741 Miscellaneous publishing

(G-4770)
**CAPITOL INFORMATION GROUP
INC**
Also Called: Kci Comminications
7600 A Lsburg Pike Ste 30 (22043)
PHONE..............................703 905-8000
Allie Ash, *President*
Steven Sturm, *Vice Pres*
Catherine Taylor, *Human Res Mgr*
Heather Rice, *Marketing Mgr*
Jennifer Brasler, *Marketing Staff*
EMP: 55
SALES (est): 7.6MM **Privately Held**
WEB: www.capinfogroup.com
SIC: 2721 8748 Magazines: publishing
only, not printed on site; periodicals: pub-
lishing only; business consulting; test de-
velopment & evaluation service

(G-4771)
**CAPITOL PUBLISHING
CORPORATION**
7290 Highland Estates Pl (22043-3008)
P.O. Box 743 (22040-0743)
PHONE..............................703 532-7535
Michelle Pena, *President*
EMP: 1 EST: 1999
SALES (est): 89.2K **Privately Held**
SIC: 2741 Miscellaneous publishing

(G-4772)
CAPITOL WOOD WORKS
6008 Kelsey Ct (22044-2944)
PHONE..............................703 237-2071
EMP: 2
SALES (est): 48.9K **Privately Held**
SIC: 2499 Mfg Wood Products

(G-4773)
CHA LUA NGOC HUNG
6799 Wilson Blvd Unit 2 (22044-3316)
PHONE..............................703 531-1868
Hiep Nguyen, *Owner*
EMP: 4
SALES (est): 315.1K **Privately Held**
WEB: www.edencenter.com
SIC: 2013 Ham, roasted: from purchased
meat

(G-4774)
CHARLIES WOODWORKS INC
7109 Carol Ln (22042-3713)
PHONE..............................703 944-0775
EMP: 2
SALES (est): 85.2K **Privately Held**
SIC: 2431 Millwork

(G-4775)
**CLEAN MARINE ELECTRONICS
INC**
1918 Anderson Rd (22043-1152)
P.O. Box 1101, Mc Lean (22101-1101)
PHONE..............................703 847-5142
Loretta Smith, *Vice Pres*

EMP: 2
SALES (est): 307K **Privately Held**
SIC: 3531 Marine related equipment

(G-4776)
COLOR SVC PRTG & GRAPHICS INC
2927 Gallows Rd Ste 101 (22042-1089)
PHONE..................................703 321-8100
Alwin Chan, *President*
▲ **EMP:** 2
SALES (est): 226.9K **Privately Held**
WEB: www.cspusa.net
SIC: 2752 Commercial printing, offset

(G-4777)
CONNECTUS INC
3419 Arnold Ln (22042-3505)
PHONE..................................703 560-7777
Stephen Su, *Principal*
EMP: 2 **EST:** 2001
SALES (est): 137.6K **Privately Held**
WEB: www.connectus.io
SIC: 7372 Application computer software

(G-4778)
CREATIVE EDUCATION & PUBG
3339 Ardley Ct (22041-2601)
PHONE..................................703 856-7005
EMP: 3 **EST:** 2008
SALES (est): 224.7K **Privately Held**
SIC: 2741 Miscellaneous publishing

(G-4779)
CSP PRODUCTIONS INC
Also Called: C S P Printing & Graphics
2927 Gallows Rd Ste 101 (22042-1089)
PHONE..................................703 321-8100
Ricky Chan, *President*
Alwin Chan, *Vice Pres*
▲ **EMP:** 6
SALES (est): 631.4K **Privately Held**
WEB: www.cspusa.net
SIC: 2752 Commercial printing, offset

(G-4780)
CUSTOM FLY GRIPS LLC
2231 Van Buren Ct (22043-1901)
PHONE..................................703 532-1189
Joseph Moriarity, *Principal*
EMP: 2
SALES (est): 169.4K **Privately Held**
WEB: www.customflygrips.com
SIC: 3949 Rods & rod parts, fishing

(G-4781)
D-ORBIT INC
6864 Frase Dr (22043-3066)
PHONE..................................703 533-5661
Robert Dean, *Owner*
EMP: 2
SALES (est): 102.9K **Privately Held**
WEB: www.dorbit.space
SIC: 7372 Prepackaged software

(G-4782)
DAVID A EINHORN
1944 Storm Dr (22043-1412)
PHONE..................................703 356-6218
David Einhorn, *Owner*
EMP: 1 **EST:** 2016
SALES (est): 33K **Privately Held**
SIC: 2741 Business service newsletters: publishing & printing

(G-4783)
DIGITAL CANVAS LLC
3218 Dashiell Rd (22042-4218)
PHONE..................................703 819-3543
Courtney Boger, *Principal*
EMP: 1
SALES (est): 46.5K **Privately Held**
SIC: 2211 Canvas

(G-4784)
DISKCOPY INC
Also Called: Discopy
6228 Lakeview Dr (22041-1322)
P.O. Box 422, Annandale (22003-0422)
PHONE..................................703 658-3539
Sylvia T Hadeed, *President*
EMP: 2
SQ FT: 1,000

SALES (est): 185.6K **Privately Held**
WEB: www.diskcopyinc.com
SIC: 7372 Prepackaged software

(G-4785)
DUPONT PRINTING SERVICE INC
3425 Payne St Side (22041-2037)
PHONE..................................703 931-1317
Ejac Malik, *President*
EMP: 6
SALES (est): 786.7K **Privately Held**
WEB: www.dupontprintingservices.com
SIC: 2752 Commercial printing, offset

(G-4786)
ECOZENITH USA INC
2230 George C Marshall Dr # 122 (22043-2529)
PHONE..................................703 992-6622
Jung Lee, *Vice Pres*
In Park, *Asst Director*
EMP: 9
SALES (est): 1.4MM **Privately Held**
WEB: www.ecozenithusa.com
SIC: 2656 Sanitary food containers

(G-4787)
ELCO COMPANY
3190 Fairview Park Dr (22042-4530)
PHONE..................................703 876-3000
EMP: 3
SALES (est): 145.1K
SALES (corp-wide): 30.9B **Publicly Held**
SIC: 3731 Mfg Submarines
PA: General Dynamics Corporation
　　2941 Frview Pk Dr Ste 100
　　Falls Church VA 20190
　　703 876-3000

(G-4788)
ENC ENTERPRISES
6014 Leesburg Pike (22041-2204)
PHONE..................................703 578-1924
Dhanbir Bedi, *Principal*
EMP: 1 **EST:** 2011
SALES (est): 74.1K **Privately Held**
SIC: 3578 Automatic teller machines (ATM)

(G-4789)
EXECWARE LLC
3440 S Jefferson St # 1125 (22041-3145)
PHONE..................................202 607-8904
Robert Listou, *Manager*
EMP: 2
SALES (est): 10K **Privately Held**
WEB: www.csr-reason.com
SIC: 7372 Prepackaged software

(G-4790)
FALLS CHURCH DISTILLERS LLC
6230 Cheryl Dr (22044-1805)
PHONE..................................703 858-9186
Michael Paluzzi, *Principal*
EMP: 1
SALES (est): 47.9K **Privately Held**
WEB: www.fcdistillers.com
SIC: 2085 Distillers' dried grains & solubles & alcohol

(G-4791)
FCW GOVERNMENT TECH GROUP
3110 Frview Pk Dr Ste 777 (22042)
PHONE..................................703 876-5100
Edith Holmes, *President*
Bloom Edward B, *Vice Pres*
EMP: 70
SALES (est): 2.7MM
SALES (corp-wide): 1.8MM **Privately Held**
WEB: www.fcw.com
SIC: 2721 Periodicals
HQ: Idg Communications, Inc.
　　5 Speen St
　　Framingham MA 01701
　　508 872-8200

(G-4792)
FCW MEDIA GROUP
3141 Frview Pk Dr Ste 777 (22042)
PHONE..................................703 876-5136
Neal Vitale, *President*
EMP: 75

SALES (est): 3.5MM **Privately Held**
SIC: 2721 Magazines: publishing only, not printed on site

(G-4793)
FLEXEL LLC
3225 Sherry Ct (22042-3719)
PHONE..................................301 314-1004
Jean Audebert, *CEO*
Lawrence Weinstein, *Research*
EMP: 12
SQ FT: 5,000
SALES (est): 1MM **Privately Held**
WEB: www.flexelinc.com
SIC: 3691 Batteries, rechargeable

(G-4794)
FREDERICK J DAY PC
5673 Columbia Pike # 100 (22041-2877)
PHONE..................................703 820-0110
Frederick Day, *Owner*
EMP: 2
SALES (est): 98.7K **Privately Held**
WEB: www.arlingtoncountylawfirm.com
SIC: 2759 Commercial printing

(G-4795)
GENERAL DYNMICS GVRNMENT SYSTE (HQ)
2941 Fairview Park Dr (22042-4522)
PHONE..................................703 876-3000
Kenneth C Dahlberg, *President*
Lisa Mills, *Regional Mgr*
Vincent Antonacci, *Vice Pres*
David Breen, *Vice Pres*
Michael Garrity, *Vice Pres*
◆ **EMP:** 1200
SQ FT: 800,000
SALES (est): 4.6B
SALES (corp-wide): 39.3B **Publicly Held**
WEB: www.gd.com
SIC: 3663 Radio & TV communications equipment
PA: General Dynamics Corporation
　　11011 Sunset Hills Rd
　　Reston VA 20190
　　703 876-3000

(G-4796)
GENERAL DYNMICS ONE SOURCE LLC
3150 Frview Pk Dr Ste 100 (22042)
PHONE..................................703 906-6397
Timothy J Turner, *Principal*
Kit Powell, *Manager*
Matthew Ryan, *Technology*
Kara Cook, *Director*
EMP: 10
SALES (est): 1.3MM
SALES (corp-wide): 39.3B **Publicly Held**
WEB: www.gdit.com
SIC: 3661 3663 8711 4899 Telephone & telegraph apparatus; radio & TV communications equipment; engineering services; data communication services; computer integrated systems design; computer related maintenance services
HQ: General Dynamics Information Technology, Inc.
　　3150 Frview Pk Dr Ste 100
　　Falls Church VA 22042
　　703 995-8700

(G-4797)
GENESIS GRAPHICS PRINTING
7635 Holmes Run Dr (22042-3345)
PHONE..................................703 560-8728
Jim Gasson, *President*
EMP: 2
SALES (est): 159.9K **Privately Held**
SIC: 2752 Commercial printing, lithographic

(G-4798)
GEOPLIANT LLC
2831 Summerfield Rd (22042-2062)
PHONE..................................888 273-7658
EMP: 2
SALES (est): 137.7K **Privately Held**
SIC: 7372 Prepackaged software

(G-4799)
GLOBAL HEALTH SOLUTIONS INC
2146 Kings Garden Way (22043-2593)
PHONE..................................703 848-2333
Xiaopo Batmanjhelidj, *President*
EMP: 3
SALES (est): 500K **Privately Held**
WEB: www.watercure.com
SIC: 2721 2731 Periodicals: publishing only; books: publishing only

(G-4800)
GREY MARKET LABS PBC
6446 Overbrook St (22043-1944)
PHONE..................................929 274-4465
Kristopher Schroeder, *CEO*
EMP: 6
SALES (est): 116.3K **Privately Held**
WEB: www.greymarketlabs.com
SIC: 7372 8731 Application computer software; electronic research

(G-4801)
GULFSTREAM AEROSPACE CORP
3150 Fairview Park Dr (22042-4504)
PHONE..................................301 967-9767
Arno Forehand, *Partner*
Buddy Sams, *Senior VP*
Alex Kolar, *Sales Staff*
Mena Wendling, *Manager*
EMP: 1691
SALES (corp-wide): 39.3B **Publicly Held**
WEB: www.gulfstream.com
SIC: 3721 4581 Aircraft; aircraft maintenance & repair services
HQ: Gulfstream Aerospace Corporation
　　500 Gulfstream Rd
　　Savannah GA 31408

(G-4802)
GULFSTREAM AEROSPACE CORP
2941 Fairview Park Dr (22042-4522)
PHONE..................................912 965-3000
Marvin Mathena, *Information Mgr*
EMP: 3
SALES (est): 177.8K **Privately Held**
WEB: www.gulfstream.com
SIC: 3721 Aircraft

(G-4803)
GULFSTREAM AEROSPACE CORP GA
3150 Fairview Park Dr (22042-4504)
PHONE..................................301 967-9767
Monroe Sams Jr, *Manager*
Kelly Peacock, *Officer*
Kelly Mirales, *Analyst*
EMP: 6
SALES (corp-wide): 39.3B **Publicly Held**
WEB: www.gulfstream.com
SIC: 3721 Aircraft
HQ: Gulfstream Aerospace Corporation (Georgia)
　　500 Gulfstream Rd
　　Savannah GA 31408
　　912 965-3000

(G-4804)
HEALTH E-LUNCH KIDS INC
7722 Willow Point Dr (22042-7531)
PHONE..................................703 402-9064
Monica Tomasso, *President*
EMP: 3
SALES (est): 400K **Privately Held**
SIC: 2099 Food preparations

(G-4805)
HENRYS COLOR GRAPHIC DESIGN
6269 Leesburg Pike (22044-1843)
PHONE..................................703 241-0101
Henry Mejia, *Owner*
EMP: 1
SALES (est): 75.3K **Privately Held**
WEB: www.henrycolor.com
SIC: 2752 Commercial printing, offset

(G-4806)
HTO INC
Also Called: Hodges Typographers
7603 Fisher Dr (22043-1226)
PHONE......................................703 533-0440
Carl Taliff, *President*
EMP: 3 EST: 1950
SQ FT: 1,000
SALES (est): 278.6K **Privately Held**
SIC: 2791 Photocomposition, for the printing trade

(G-4807)
I PATRIOT SHIPPING CORP
3190 Fairview Park Dr (22042-4530)
PHONE......................................703 876-3000
L H Redd, *President*
EMP: 2
SALES (est): 116.7K
SALES (corp-wide): 39.3B **Publicly Held**
SIC: 3731 Submarines, building & repairing
PA: General Dynamics Corporation
11011 Sunset Hills Rd
Reston VA 20190
703 876-3000

(G-4808)
IMAGINE IT DESIGNS LLC
6547 Orland St (22043-1813)
PHONE......................................703 795-6397
Michael P Doane,
EMP: 1
SALES (est): 100K **Privately Held**
WEB: www.imagineitdesigns.com
SIC: 2395 Pleating & stitching

(G-4809)
IWOAN LLC
3709 S George Mason Dr # 713
(22041-5700)
PHONE......................................347 606-0602
EMP: 2 EST: 2018
SALES (est): 62.3K **Privately Held**
SIC: 2034 5411 Dates, dried; frozen food & freezer plans, except meat

(G-4810)
IXIDOR LLC
Also Called: Smart Blocks
3705 S Grge Msn Dr 2315 (22041)
PHONE......................................571 332-3888
Mazin Badawi, *President*
EMP: 1
SALES (est): 50K **Privately Held**
SIC: 3952 Frames for artists' canvases

(G-4811)
JP NINO CORP
8116 Arlington Blvd 178 (22042-1002)
PHONE......................................775 636-8682
Paul Nino, *President*
Jamie Nino, *Manager*
EMP: 4
SALES (est): 267K **Privately Held**
SIC: 3357 Coaxial cable, nonferrous

(G-4812)
JUICE
2824 Fallfax Dr (22042-2804)
PHONE......................................202 280-0302
Jennifer Ngai, *Partner*
Shizu Okusa, *Partner*
EMP: 30
SALES (est): 1.2MM **Privately Held**
WEB: www.jrink.com
SIC: 2033 Vegetable juices: fresh

(G-4813)
JUICE&I LLC
2824 Fallfax Dr (22042-2804)
PHONE......................................202 280-0302
Jennifer Ngai,
Shizu Okusa,
EMP: 7
SALES (est): 324.3K **Privately Held**
SIC: 2033 Fruit juices: fresh; vegetable juices: fresh

(G-4814)
KAAH EXPRESS
5613 Leesburg Pike Ste 26 (22041-2912)
PHONE......................................703 379-0770
Byungsoo Park, *Principal*
EMP: 1

(G-4815)
KAJJO SIRWAN
Also Called: Crescent Communications
5597 Seminary Rd Apt 218 (22041-2686)
PHONE......................................202 569-1472
EMP: 1
SALES: 57K **Privately Held**
SIC: 3663 Mfg Radio/Tv Communication Equipment

(G-4816)
KISHBAUGH ENTERPRISES LLC
Also Called: Serenity Ridge Machining
6316 Castle Pl Ste 301 (22044-1906)
PHONE......................................571 375-2042
Greg Kishbaugh, *President*
Kerry Kishbaugh,
EMP: 1
SQ FT: 2,000
SALES (est): 1MM **Privately Held**
WEB: www.serenityridgemachining.com
SIC: 3599 Machine shop, jobbing & repair

(G-4817)
KLASSIC KREATURES
3105 Manor Rd (22042-2514)
PHONE......................................703 560-4409
Steve Klass, *Owner*
Sally Klass, *Co-Owner*
EMP: 2
SALES (est): 15K **Privately Held**
WEB: www.klassickreatures.com
SIC: 3961 5112 Pins (jewelry), except precious metal; pens &/or pencils

(G-4818)
KUSTERS ENGINEERING SEC INC
3190 Fairview Park Dr (22042-4530)
PHONE......................................703 967-1449
Eugene Denazza, *CEO*
Paul Vosbeek, *Principal*
EMP: 2
SALES (est): 30K **Privately Held**
SIC: 3579 Office machines

(G-4819)
KWIK KOPY
Also Called: Kwik Kopy Printing
3406 Casilear Rd (22042-3723)
PHONE......................................703 560-5042
Mike Pumphery, *Vice Pres*
EMP: 2
SALES (est): 92.3K **Privately Held**
SIC: 2759 Thermography

(G-4820)
LANGVAN
6787 Wilson Blvd (22044-3302)
PHONE......................................703 532-0466
Becky Win, *Owner*
EMP: 2
SALES (est): 161.4K **Privately Held**
SIC: 3825 Instruments to measure electricity

(G-4821)
LAS AMERICAS NEWSPAPER INC
Also Called: Las Americas Yellow Pages
3809 Bell Manor Ct (22041-1665)
PHONE......................................703 256-4200
Fernando Alvarez, *CEO*
EMP: 2 EST: 1999
SALES (est): 190.4K **Privately Held**
WEB: www.lasamericasnews.com
SIC: 2711 8661 Newspapers, publishing & printing; religious organizations

(G-4822)
LEGACY VULCAN LLC
7103 Gordons Rd (22043-3079)
PHONE......................................800 732-3964
EMP: 3 **Publicly Held**
WEB: www.vulcanmaterials.com
SIC: 3273 Ready-mixed concrete
HQ: Legacy Vulcan, Llc
1200 Urban Center Dr
Vestavia AL 35242
205 298-3000

(G-4823)
LIFT HILL MEDIA LLC
3320 Arnold Ln (22042-3603)
PHONE......................................703 408-4145
Michael Khaccheressian,
EMP: 1
SALES (est): 66.8K **Privately Held**
SIC: 2731 Book publishing

(G-4824)
LITTLE WARS INC
3033 Crane Dr (22042-3004)
PHONE......................................703 533-7942
EMP: 2 EST: 1997
SALES (est): 120K **Privately Held**
SIC: 3944 Mfg Games/Toys

(G-4825)
LNG PUBLISHING CO INC (PA)
7389 Lee Hwy Ste 300 (22042-1737)
PHONE......................................703 536-0800
Gloria Briskin, *President*
Lisa Tocci, *Vice Pres*
Nancy Demarco, *CFO*
Michele Persaud, *Manager*
Ricardo Lianez, *Art Dir*
EMP: 8
SALES (est): 761.8K **Privately Held**
WEB: www.lubesngreases.com
SIC: 2741 Miscellaneous publishing

(G-4826)
MACHINA DYNAMICA INC
8003 Chanute Pl Apt 10 (22042-1164)
PHONE......................................571 405-0709
EMP: 1 EST: 2018
SALES (est): 66.9K **Privately Held**
WEB: www.machinadynamica.com
SIC: 3651 Household audio & video equipment

(G-4827)
MASSTRANSIT PUBLISHING LLC
2260 Cartbridge Rd (22043-2933)
PHONE......................................703 205-2419
Denise Taranov, *Principal*
EMP: 1
SALES (est): 53.3K **Privately Held**
SIC: 2741 Miscellaneous publishing

(G-4828)
MECHANX CORP
Also Called: Auto Clinic
2858 Hartland Rd (22043-3526)
PHONE......................................703 698-7680
Pollick Benjamin D, *President*
EMP: 2
SALES (est): 170K **Privately Held**
WEB: www.autoclinic.com
SIC: 3694 7549 7539 Engine electrical equipment; high performance auto repair & service; automotive springs, rebuilding & repair

(G-4829)
MELVIN RILEY
Also Called: Metro Copier and Printer Svcs
5829 Seminary Rd (22041-3009)
PHONE......................................240 381-6111
EMP: 1 EST: 2012
SALES: 85K **Privately Held**
SIC: 3555 Mfg Printing Trades Machinery

(G-4830)
METROPOLITAN GENERAL CONTRS
3454 Quaker Ct (22042-3911)
PHONE......................................703 532-1606
Dave Miller, *President*
EMP: 1
SALES (est): 122.1K **Privately Held**
SIC: 1389 Construction, repair & dismantling services

(G-4831)
MILLER CREATIVE SOLUTIONS LLC
6182a Arlington Blvd (22044-2902)
PHONE......................................202 560-3718
Mohammed Omari,
EMP: 4
SALES (est): 310K **Privately Held**
SIC: 3993 Letters for signs, metal

(G-4832)
MIRANDA PUBLISHING COMPAN
7627 Trail Run Rd (22042-3417)
PHONE......................................703 207-9499
EMP: 2
SALES (est): 110K **Privately Held**
SIC: 2741 Misc Publishing

(G-4833)
MULTIMODAL ID
7799 Leesburg Pike # 500 (22043-2408)
PHONE......................................703 944-9000
Dennis Ackerman, *Principal*
EMP: 1
SALES (est): 57.4K **Privately Held**
WEB: www.citi-us.com
SIC: 7372 Prepackaged software

(G-4834)
NAPOLEAN MAGAZINE
7708 Willow Point Dr (22042-7531)
PHONE......................................703 641-9062
EMP: 2 EST: 2017
SALES (est): 73.1K **Privately Held**
SIC: 2721 Periodicals-Publishing/Printing

(G-4835)
NATIONAL INSTITUTE OF BUS MGT (PA)
Also Called: Nibm
7600a Leesburg Pike (22043-2000)
PHONE......................................703 394-4921
Phil Ash, *President*
Allie Ash, *President*
Adam Goldstein, *Publisher*
Elizabeth Hall, *Editor*
Steve Sturm, *Vice Pres*
EMP: 6
SALES (est): 844.8K **Privately Held**
WEB: www.businessmanagementdaily.com
SIC: 2741 Business service newsletters: publishing & printing

(G-4836)
NGC INTERNATIONAL INC (HQ)
2980 Fairview Park Dr (22042-4511)
PHONE......................................703 280-2900
Mark Rabinowitz, *President*
Wallace Jackson, *Opers Staff*
Robert Murphry, *Manager*
John Powers, *Senior Mgr*
John Page, *Administration*
EMP: 7
SALES (est): 1.8MM **Publicly Held**
WEB: www.northropgrumman.com
SIC: 3731 Shipbuilding & repairing

(G-4837)
NORTHERN VRGNIA PROF ASSOC INC
Also Called: Sir Speedy
6565 Arlington Blvd (22042-3013)
PHONE......................................703 525-5218
Gabriel Knowlton, *President*
EMP: 7
SQ FT: 3,500
SALES (est): 1.2MM **Privately Held**
WEB: www.sirspeedy.com
SIC: 2752 Commercial printing, lithographic

(G-4838)
NORTHROP GRMMAN / HNLULU - US
2980 Fairview Park Dr (22042-4511)
PHONE......................................808 529-9500
EMP: 3
SALES (est): 141.8K **Privately Held**
WEB: www.northropgrumman.com
SIC: 3812 Search & navigation equipment

(G-4839)
NORTHROP GRMMAN GDNCE ELEC INC (DH)
2980 Fairview Park Dr (22042-4511)
PHONE......................................703 280-2900
Wes Bush, *CEO*
Mark Rabinowitz, *President*
Kevin McCunn, *Manager*
◆ EMP: 29
SALES (est): 25.6MM **Publicly Held**
WEB: www.northropgrumman.com
SIC: 3812 3761 Search & navigation equipment; guided missiles & space vehicles

HQ: Northrop Grumman Systems Corporation
2980 Fairview Park Dr
Falls Church VA 22042
703 280-2900

(G-4840)
NORTHROP GRMMAN OVRSEAS HLDG I (HQ)
2980 Fairview Park Dr (22042-4511)
PHONE....................703 280-4069
Kathy J Warden, *Ch of Bd*
EMP: 5 EST: 1996
SALES (est): 10.3MM **Publicly Held**
WEB: www.northropgrumman.com
SIC: 3812 6719 Search & navigation equipment; personal holding companies, except banks

(G-4841)
NORTHROP GRUMMAN CORPORATION (PA)
2980 Fairview Park Dr (22042-4511)
PHONE....................703 280-2900
Kathy J Warden, *Ch of Bd*
Tom Alverson, *Exec VP*
Patrick M Antkowiak, *Vice Pres*
Martin Bernet, *Vice Pres*
Mark A Caylor, *Vice Pres*
EMP: 277
SALES (est): 33.8B **Publicly Held**
WEB: www.northropgrumman.com
SIC: 3812 Search & navigation equipment

(G-4842)
NORTHROP GRUMMAN GLOBAL SVCS
2980 Fairview Park Dr (22042-4511)
PHONE....................703 280-2900
Kathy J Warden, *Principal*
EMP: 2
SALES (est): 77.4K **Privately Held**
SIC: 3812 Search & navigation equipment

(G-4843)
NORTHROP GRUMMAN INTL INC (HQ)
2980 Fairview Park Dr (22042-4511)
PHONE....................703 280-2900
Ronald D Sugar, *CEO*
EMP: 42
SALES (est): 24MM **Publicly Held**
WEB: www.northropgrumman.com
SIC: 3812 Search & detection systems & instruments; radar systems & equipment; defense systems & equipment; warfare counter-measure equipment

(G-4844)
NORTHROP GRUMMAN INTL TRDG INC (DH)
2980 Fairview Park Dr (22042-4511)
PHONE....................703 280-2900
David T Perry, *President*
Talha A Zobair, *Vice Pres*
Steven Spiegel, *Treasurer*
Susie L Choung, *Admin Sec*
EMP: 5 EST: 2012
SALES (est): 1.5MM **Publicly Held**
WEB: www.northropgrumman.com
SIC: 3812 Search & navigation equipment
HQ: Northrop Grumman Overseas Holding, Inc.
2980 Fairview Park Dr
Falls Church VA 22042
703 280-4069

(G-4845)
NORTHROP GRUMMAN SYSTEMS CORP (HQ)
Also Called: Aerospace Systems
2980 Fairview Park Dr (22042-4511)
PHONE....................703 280-2900
Wesley G Bush, *CEO*
Mark Rabinowitz, *President*
James L Cameron, *Vice Pres*
Gary W Ervin, *Vice Pres*
Ed Halibozek, *Vice Pres*
◆ EMP: 277
SQ FT: 30,000

SALES (est): 5.9B **Publicly Held**
WEB: www.northropgrumman.com
SIC: 3721 3761 3728 3812 Airplanes, fixed or rotary wing; research & development on aircraft by the manufacturer; guided missiles, complete; guided missiles & space vehicles, research & development; fuselage assembly, aircraft; wing assemblies & parts, aircraft; research & dev by manuf., aircraft parts & auxiliary equip; inertial guidance systems; gyroscopes; warfare counter-measure equipment; search & detection systems & instruments; test equipment for electronic & electrical circuits; aircraft servicing & repairing

(G-4846)
NORTHROP GRUMMAN SYSTEMS CORP
Also Called: Northrop Gov't Relations Div
2980 Fairview Park Dr (22042-4511)
PHONE....................703 280-1220
Lee Tucker, *Mfg Staff*
Nastaran Avalos, *Engineer*
Kyle Sleeper, *Engineer*
Robert Helm, *Branch Mgr*
Mary Marine, *Technology*
EMP: 100 **Publicly Held**
WEB: www.northropgrumman.com
SIC: 3812 Search & navigation equipment
HQ: Northrop Grumman Systems Corporation
2980 Fairview Park Dr
Falls Church VA 22042
703 280-2900

(G-4847)
NOVA GREEN ENERGY LLC
3426 Lakeside View Dr (22041-2448)
PHONE....................571 210-0589
Michael Celley,
EMP: 1
SALES (est): 121.3K **Privately Held**
WEB: www.novagreenenergyllc.com
SIC: 3433 5211 1711 7389 Logs, gas fireplace; insulation & energy conservation products; hydronics heating contractor; heating & air conditioning contractors; solar energy contractor;

(G-4848)
OCTOPUS SOFTWARE SYSTEMS INC
6129 Lsburg Pike Apt 1009 (22041)
PHONE....................571 224-5283
Nihan Gunay, *President*
EMP: 2 EST: 2015
SALES (est): 86.2K **Privately Held**
SIC: 7372 Prepackaged software

(G-4849)
ODONNELL SUSANNAH CASSEDY
3215 Juniper Ln (22044-1608)
PHONE....................703 470-8572
Susannah O'Donnell, *Owner*
EMP: 1 EST: 2008
SALES (est): 36.4K **Privately Held**
SIC: 2741 Miscellaneous publishing

(G-4850)
OFF THE PRESS INC
6919 Westmoreland Rd (22042-2657)
PHONE....................703 533-1199
EMP: 2
SALES (est): 140K **Privately Held**
SIC: 2759 Commercial Printing

(G-4851)
ONE APERTURE LLC
3245 Rio Dr Apt 712 (22041-2124)
PHONE....................202 415-0416
Bun Kiat Lim,
EMP: 1
SALES (est): 75.5K **Privately Held**
SIC: 7372 7389 Prepackaged software;

(G-4852)
OPEN ROAD GRILL & ICEHOUSE
Also Called: Open Road Outfitters
8100 Lee Hwy (22042-1112)
PHONE....................571 395-4400
Dale Coyner, *President*
EMP: 2

SALES (est): 255.2K **Privately Held**
WEB: www.openroadgrill.com
SIC: 3751 Motorcycle accessories

(G-4853)
PAE-IMK INTERNATIONAL LLC
7799 Lsburg Pike Ste 300n (22043)
PHONE....................888 526-5416
John Heller, *Principal*
Greg Foley, *Principal*
EMP: 25
SALES (est): 767.9K **Privately Held**
WEB: www.pae.com
SIC: 2499 Picture frame molding, finished

(G-4854)
PARKGATE PRESS
7796 Marshall Heights Ct (22043-2553)
PHONE....................607 280-2364
EMP: 1 EST: 2013
SALES (est): 37.5K **Privately Held**
WEB: www.parkgatepress.com
SIC: 2741 Miscellaneous publishing

(G-4855)
PATRIOT IV SHIPPING CORP
2941 Frview Pk Dr Ste 100 (22042)
PHONE....................703 876-3000
EMP: 80 EST: 1952
SALES (est): 2.8MM
SALES (corp-wide): 30.9B **Publicly Held**
SIC: 3731 Mfg Submarines
PA: General Dynamics Corporation
2941 Frview Pk Dr Ste 100
Falls Church VA 20190
703 876-3000

(G-4856)
PERFECT IMAGE PRINTING
5616 Columbia Pike (22041-2716)
PHONE....................703 824-0010
Nhan Hoang, *President*
Minh Hoang, *Vice Pres*
Robert Hoang, *Manager*
EMP: 8
SQ FT: 900
SALES (est): 882.7K **Privately Held**
WEB: www.perfectimageprinting.us
SIC: 2752 Commercial printing, offset

(G-4857)
PRINT CITY
5908 Columbia Pike # 101 (22041-2034)
PHONE....................703 931-1114
SOO Park, *Owner*
EMP: 6
SQ FT: 6,000
SALES (est): 453.9K **Privately Held**
SIC: 2752 Commercial printing, lithographic

(G-4858)
PRINT STORE LLC
7115 Idylwood Rd (22043-1509)
PHONE....................703 821-2201
Leon Benikas, *Mng Member*
Ann Benikas, *Mng Member*
EMP: 3
SALES (est): 1.5MM **Privately Held**
SIC: 2741 Miscellaneous publishing

(G-4859)
PRODUCT SAFETY LETTER
2573 Holly Manor Dr (22043-3909)
PHONE....................703 247-3423
EMP: 2
SALES (est): 73.1K **Privately Held**
SIC: 2721 Periodicals-Publishing/Printing

(G-4860)
PUBLICITY WORKS LLC
2230 George C Marshall Dr (22043-2529)
PHONE....................703 876-0080
EMP: 2
SALES (est): 89K **Privately Held**
SIC: 2741 Misc Publishing

(G-4861)
QUANTUM TECHNOLOGIES INC
7635 Leesburg Pike Ste B (22043-2520)
PHONE....................703 214-9756
Arun Tewary, *President*
EMP: 5
SALES (est): 430.8K **Privately Held**
SIC: 3572 Computer storage devices

(G-4862)
RAPPAHANNOCK ENTP ASSOC INC
Also Called: Quick Silver Printing
3406 Casilear Rd (22042-3723)
PHONE....................703 560-5042
William Michael Pumphrey, *President*
Mike Pumphery, *Vice Pres*
David Pumphrey, *Treasurer*
EMP: 6
SALES (est): 650K **Privately Held**
SIC: 2752 2791 2789 7338 Commercial printing, offset; typesetting; bookbinding & related work; secretarial & court reporting

(G-4863)
RAYTHEON COMPANY
7700 Arlington Blvd (22042-2929)
PHONE....................703 661-7252
Corwin Butler, *Principal*
Robert Caracino, *Engineer*
Nicholas Desany, *Engineer*
Kieth Meyer, *Engineer*
John O'Neill, *Engineer*
EMP: 29
SALES (corp-wide): 77B **Publicly Held**
WEB: www.rtx.com
SIC: 3812 Defense systems & equipment
HQ: Raytheon Company
870 Winter St
Waltham MA 02451
781 522-3000

(G-4864)
REAL AMERICAN REVOLUTION
7124 Leesburg Pike (22043-2309)
PHONE....................703 732-9049
EMP: 1
SALES (est): 46.5K **Privately Held**
SIC: 2741 Miscellaneous publishing

(G-4865)
REDLINE PRODUCTIONS
2854 Cherry St Apt 306 (22042-6661)
PHONE....................703 861-8765
Adam Campbell, *Director*
EMP: 1
SALES (corp-wide): 946.6K **Privately Held**
SIC: 2741 Art copy: publishing & printing
PA: Redline Productions Media Group, Inc.
1875 Conn Ave Nw Fl 10
Washington DC 20009
703 861-8765

(G-4866)
REWARD HAPPINESS LLC
3409 Gallows Rd (22042-3308)
PHONE....................703 795-0746
Terrence Dunn,
EMP: 1
SALES (est): 33.3K **Privately Held**
SIC: 2731 Books: publishing & printing

(G-4867)
RISQUE CUSTOM CABINETRY
6640 Barrett Rd (22042-4228)
PHONE....................703 534-5319
EMP: 4 EST: 2009
SALES (est): 240K **Privately Held**
SIC: 2434 Mfg Wood Kitchen Cabinets

(G-4868)
ROCK INDUSTRIES LLC
7600 Lsburg Pike Ste 460e (22043)
PHONE....................703 637-8500
Jason Wakefield, *Principal*
EMP: 2
SALES (est): 91.5K **Privately Held**
SIC: 3999 Manufacturing industries

(G-4869)
RSI LLC
Also Called: Rsindustries
8135 Harper Valley Ln (22042-1266)
PHONE....................908 752-1496
Robert Szot, *Principal*
EMP: 1 EST: 2016
SALES (est): 61K **Privately Held**
SIC: 3999 Manufacturing industries

(G-4870)
RUFINA INC
6423 Crosswoods Dr (22044-1216)
PHONE....................703 577-2333

Kenneth Melero, *CEO*
EMP: 1
SALES (est): 59.9K **Privately Held**
SIC: 7372 8742 8748 7373 Prepackaged software; management consulting services; systems analysis & engineering consulting services; computer integrated systems design; computer software development

(G-4871)
SAGE DEFENSE LLC
7217 Hyde Rd (22043-2716)
PHONE................................703 485-5995
Brian David, *Principal*
EMP: 2
SALES (est): 216.2K **Privately Held**
WEB: www.sagedefense.com
SIC: 3812 Defense systems & equipment

(G-4872)
SANDHURST-AEC LLC
7653 Leesburg Pike (22043-2520)
PHONE................................703 533-1413
Kwafo Djan,
EMP: 1
SALES (est): 86.7K **Privately Held**
WEB: www.sandhurstaec.com
SIC: 1389 8711 8712 Construction, repair & dismantling services; engineering services; architectural services

(G-4873)
SCT PHOENIX OIL & GAS LLC
2202 Beacon Ln (22043-1742)
PHONE................................702 245-0269
Steve Tanner, *Principal*
EMP: 2 EST: 2015
SALES (est): 73.6K **Privately Held**
SIC: 1389 Oil & gas field services

(G-4874)
SILVIO ENTERPRISE LLC
3334 Kaywood Dr (22041-2532)
PHONE................................703 731-0147
Josemar Sejas, *Principal*
EMP: 2 EST: 2011
SALES (est): 229.1K **Privately Held**
SIC: 3537 Industrial trucks & tractors

(G-4875)
SIMPSON COMPANY LANDSCA
7800 Shreve Rd (22043-3312)
PHONE................................703 204-0453
Charles R Rainey Jr, *Administration*
EMP: 2
SALES (est): 160.2K **Privately Held**
WEB: www.simpsondoor.com
SIC: 2431 Millwork

(G-4876)
SMARTDOOR SYSTEMS INC
5711a Center Ln (22041-3001)
PHONE................................703 560-8093
EMP: 3
SALES (est): 2.4MM **Privately Held**
SIC: 3625 Manufacturer Of Electronic Door Control/Security Garage

(G-4877)
SPRINGBOARD RETAIL INC
3141 Fairview Park Dr (22042-4531)
PHONE................................888 347-2191
Gordon C Russell, *CEO*
Jay Stotz, *Principal*
Jennifer Raines-Loring, *Vice Pres*
Hannah Parker, *Finance*
Patric Caya, *Sales Staff*
EMP: 50
SALES (est): 559.7K **Privately Held**
WEB: www.heartlandretail.us
SIC: 7372 Business oriented computer software

(G-4878)
STUART-DEAN CO INC
5826 Seminary Rd Ste B (22041-3010)
PHONE................................703 578-1885
Joseph Gargrull, *CEO*
Savita Seth, *Human Res Dir*
Mark Christmas, *Marketing Staff*
EMP: 80

SALES (corp-wide): 65.4MM **Privately Held**
WEB: www.stuartdean.com
SIC: 3446 1741 3471 1743 Architectural metalwork; marble masonry, exterior construction; plating & polishing; terrazzo, tile, marble, mosaic work
PA: Stuart-Dean Co. Inc.
450 Fashion Ave Ste 3800
New York NY 10123
212 273-6900

(G-4879)
SUMMIT LDSCP & LAWN CARE LLC
2906 Lawrence Dr (22042-1405)
P.O. Box 472, Merrifield (22116-0472)
PHONE................................703 856-5353
Nigim Harb, *Principal*
EMP: 6
SALES (est): 481K **Privately Held**
WEB: www.summitlandscapeandlawncare.com
SIC: 3271 Blocks, concrete: landscape or retaining wall

(G-4880)
SUNNY DAY FUND SOLUTIONS INC
6003 Madison Overlook Ct (22041-3652)
PHONE................................703 622-1005
Siddhartha Pailla, *CEO*
EMP: 1
SALES (est): 85.5K **Privately Held**
SIC: 7372 Prepackaged software

(G-4881)
SWEET SVORY DELIGHTS BY VICKIE
3408 Haven Pl (22041-1705)
PHONE................................703 581-8499
EMP: 2
SALES (est): 62.3K **Privately Held**
SIC: 2064 Candy & other confectionery products

(G-4882)
THE FOR AMERICAN SOCIETY
2904 Bridgehampton Ct (22042-4436)
PHONE................................703 331-0075
Christine Alam, *Principal*
EMP: 2
SALES (est): 85.9K **Privately Held**
SIC: 3571 Electronic computers

(G-4883)
TIBCO SOFTWARE FEDERAL INC
3141 Frview Pk Dr Ste 600 (22042)
PHONE................................703 208-3900
Richard L Mortin, *CEO*
Joseph Kijewski, *Vice Pres*
Vernette Young, *Office Mgr*
EMP: 30
SALES: 1.8MM
SALES (corp-wide): 885.6MM **Privately Held**
SIC: 7372 Application computer software
HQ: Tibco Software Inc.
3307 Hillview Ave
Palo Alto CA 94304

(G-4884)
TOMMY V FOODS
6129 Lsburg Pike Apt 1006 (22041)
PHONE................................703 254-8764
Thomas T Venable Jr, *Principal*
EMP: 1
SALES (est): 15K **Privately Held**
SIC: 2099 Food preparations

(G-4885)
UHR CORPORATION
6705 Valley Brook Dr (22042-4020)
PHONE................................703 534-1250
C W Uhr Jr, *President*
Richard D Jones, *Vice Pres*
EMP: 3 **Privately Held**
SIC: 3822 Hardware for environmental regulators

(G-4886)
ULTIMATE WHEEL SVCS LLC
2106 Grayson Pl (22043-1618)
PHONE................................703 237-1044

Brian Dean, *Principal*
Brian P Dean, *Principal*
EMP: 2
SALES (est): 172.2K **Privately Held**
SIC: 3312 Blast furnaces & steel mills

(G-4887)
US CABINET & INTR DESIGN LLC
3210 Dashiell Rd (22042-4218)
PHONE................................202 740-0038
Sam Kaushal, *CEO*
EMP: 2
SALES (est): 181.4K **Privately Held**
SIC: 2434 7389 Wood kitchen cabinets; interior design services

(G-4888)
UTILITIES PRODUCTS INTL
7202 Arlington Blvd # 20 (22042-1859)
PHONE................................703 725-3150
Diane Beckerman, *Ch of Bd*
EMP: 2
SALES (est): 88.9K **Privately Held**
SIC: 3089 Plastics products

(G-4889)
VETSUSA II INC
307 Annandale Rd Ste 201 (22042-2454)
PHONE................................703 300-9874
Stephen Worthington, *Principal*
EMP: 42
SALES (est): 3.2MM **Privately Held**
SIC: 3281 Cut stone & stone products

(G-4890)
VINA EXPRESS INC
Also Called: Vina Xpress
6795 Wilson Blvd Ste 15 (22044-3313)
PHONE................................703 237-9398
Fran Yn, *President*
EMP: 4
SQ FT: 600
SALES (est): 336.8K **Privately Held**
WEB: www.edencenter.com
SIC: 3644 Noncurrent-carrying wiring services

(G-4891)
WELCOMEPOINT LLC
2260 Cartbridge Rd (22043-2933)
PHONE................................703 371-0499
Tim Taranov, *Principal*
Timofey Taranov, *Principal*
EMP: 1 EST: 2015
SALES (est): 49.3K **Privately Held**
SIC: 7372 Application computer software

(G-4892)
WILNER DESIGNS INC JANE
6051 Leesburg Pike Ste 9 (22041-2243)
PHONE................................703 998-2551
Natalie Torres, *President*
Suzanne Aton, *Vice Pres*
▲ **EMP:** 11
SQ FT: 1,600
SALES (est): 1.4MM **Privately Held**
WEB: www.janewilnerdesigns.com
SIC: 2299 Linen fabrics

(G-4893)
WORLDWIDE PAPERS INC
2160 Kings Garden Way (22043-2593)
PHONE................................703 883-8049
Shiv R Agarwal, *Principal*
EMP: 1
SALES (est): 154.1K **Privately Held**
SIC: 2621 Printing paper

(G-4894)
WYLIE WAGG OF TYSONS LLC
7505 Leesburg Pike (22043-2104)
PHONE................................703 748-0022
Alexis Rosenberg, *Principal*
EMP: 2
SALES (est): 139K **Privately Held**
SIC: 3999 Pet supplies

(G-4895)
YAYA LEARNING LLC
3720 Woodland Cir (22041-1124)
PHONE................................540 230-5051
Sofia Midkiff,
EMP: 2

SALES (est): 50K **Privately Held**
WEB: www.yayacards.com
SIC: 3944 Games, toys & children's vehicles

(G-4896)
ZA CONTRACTING LLC
3054 Patrick Henry Dr # 201 (22044-3435)
PHONE................................703 498-3531
Luis Martinez,
EMP: 2 EST: 2012
SALES (est): 121.1K **Privately Held**
SIC: 1241 Bituminous coal mining services, contract basis

(G-4897)
ZIMAR LLC
Also Called: Smakaball
5673 Columbia Pike # 201 (22041-2877)
PHONE................................703 688-3339
Rami Zein, *Mng Member*
▲ **EMP:** 1
SQ FT: 1,800
SALES (est): 250K **Privately Held**
WEB: www.smakaball.com
SIC: 3069 Toys, rubber

(G-4898)
ZIPNUT TECHNOLOGY LLC
7700 Lsburg Pike Ste 301n (22043)
PHONE................................703 442-7339
Hank Hulme, *Mng Member*
EMP: 2
SALES (est): 200K **Privately Held**
SIC: 3452 3503 Bolts, metal; shakers, tree: nuts, fruits, etc.

Falls Church
Falls Church City County

(G-4899)
ALLMOODS ENTERPRISES LLC
314 N Van Buren St (22046-3655)
PHONE................................703 241-8748
Evelyn Elgin, *Principal*
EMP: 2 EST: 2016
SALES (est): 129.8K **Privately Held**
WEB: www.allmoods.com
SIC: 2741 Miscellaneous publishing

(G-4900)
AMERICAN COURT COMM NEWSPAPERS
200 Little Falls St (22046-3393)
PHONE................................703 237-9806
EMP: 4
SALES: 70.1K **Privately Held**
SIC: 2711 Newspapers-Publishing/Printing

(G-4901)
B C R BOOKBINDING
707 W Broad St (22046-3221)
PHONE................................703 534-9181
Benjamin Flores, *Owner*
EMP: 2
SALES (est): 184.2K **Privately Held**
WEB: www.bcrbookbinding.com
SIC: 2789 Bookbinding & related work

(G-4902)
BLUE RIDGE DIGITAL PUBG LLC
426 E Columbia St (22046-3501)
PHONE................................703 785-3970
Rolf Anderson, *Principal*
EMP: 2 EST: 2017
SALES (est): 59.2K **Privately Held**
SIC: 2741 Miscellaneous publishing

(G-4903)
BTBYCB INC
2301 Brilyn Pl (22046-1809)
PHONE................................703 992-9041
Roberta K Carlson, *Owner*
EMP: 1
SALES (est): 70.3K **Privately Held**
SIC: 2621 Paper mills

(G-4904)
CBT SCREEN PRINTING LLC
310a S Washington St (22046-4423)
PHONE................................703 888-8539
EMP: 4

SALES (est): 231.1K **Privately Held**
SIC: 2752 Commercial printing, lithographic

(G-4905)
CLEAREDJOBSNET INC
1069 W Broad St Ste 775 (22046-4610)
PHONE..........................703 871-0037
John Nixon, *Exec VP*
Sara McMurrough, *Accounts Mgr*
Tracy Mitchell, *Accounts Mgr*
Shanon Raab, *Accounts Mgr*
Terri Langley, *Cust Mgr*
EMP: 5
SQ FT: 1,000
SALES (est): 650K **Privately Held**
WEB: www.clearedjobs.net
SIC: 2741

(G-4906)
CYBERSQUIRE LLC
511 Great Falls St (22046-2613)
PHONE..........................703 472-0283
Rebecca Masri, *Administration*
EMP: 1
SALES (est): 53K **Privately Held**
WEB: www.cybersquire.com
SIC: 3861 Photographic equipment & supplies

(G-4907)
DIGITAL DESIGN IMAGING SVC INC
100 W Jefferson St # 102 (22046-3400)
PHONE..........................703 534-7500
Curt Westergard, *President*
Inge Demey Westergard, *Comptroller*
Ryan Shuler, *Info Tech Mgr*
EMP: 3
SQ FT: 1,600
SALES (est): 364.1K **Privately Held**
WEB: www.airphotoslive.com
SIC: 3861 Aerial cameras

(G-4908)
DON ELTHON
Also Called: Elthon Enterprises
404 E Broad St (22046-3505)
PHONE..........................703 237-2521
Don Elthon, *Owner*
EMP: 2
SALES (est): 82K **Privately Held**
SIC: 2441 2452 2448 3545 Boxes, wood; prefabricated buildings, wood; skids, wood; precision measuring tools

(G-4909)
EDUCATIONAL OPTIONS INC
500 W Annandale Rd # 400 (22046-4205)
PHONE..........................480 777-7720
Ellen Moore, *Principal*
EMP: 3
SALES (est): 368.6K **Privately Held**
WEB: www.edmentum.com
SIC: 7372 Application computer software

(G-4910)
ELECTRAAERO INC
218 N Cherry St (22046-3520)
PHONE..........................540 660-2917
John S Langford, *Mng Member*
EMP: 3
SALES (est): 117.8K **Privately Held**
SIC: 3721 Aircraft

(G-4911)
EZ TOOL RENTAL
1103 W Broad St (22046-2115)
PHONE..........................703 531-4700
EMP: 2
SALES (est): 146K **Privately Held**
SIC: 3599 Machine shop, jobbing & repair

(G-4912)
FALLS CHURCH DISTILLERS LLC
442 S Washington St Ste A (22046-4420)
PHONE..........................703 858-9186
Michael E Paluzzi,
EMP: 10
SALES (est): 283.4K **Privately Held**
WEB: www.fcdistillers.com
SIC: 2085 Distilled & blended liquors

(G-4913)
FALLS CHURCH NEWS PRESS
200 Little Falls St # 508 (22046-4302)
PHONE..........................703 532-3267
Fax: 703 532-3396
EMP: 8
SALES (est): 390K **Privately Held**
SIC: 2711 Newspapers

(G-4914)
FINE PRINTS DESIGNS
7326 Ronald St (22046-1931)
PHONE..........................703 560-1519
EMP: 2
SALES (est): 154.4K **Privately Held**
SIC: 2752 Lithographic Commercial Printing

(G-4915)
GMA INDUSTRIES
313 Hillwood Ave (22046-2917)
PHONE..........................703 538-5100
EMP: 1 EST: 2017
SALES (est): 42.8K **Privately Held**
SIC: 3999 Mfg Misc Products

(G-4916)
GO4IT LLC
107 Hillier St (22046-3931)
PHONE..........................703 531-0586
Mary Anne J Carlson,
Raymond H Carlson,
Jill Heflinger,
EMP: 6
SALES (est): 320.8K **Privately Held**
SIC: 3999 Education aids, devices & supplies

(G-4917)
HOCKEY STICK BUILDS LLC
2345 Highland Ave (22046-2211)
PHONE..........................617 784-2918
Glenn Paul Tournier, *Principal*
EMP: 2
SALES (est): 137.6K **Privately Held**
SIC: 2519 Household furniture

(G-4918)
HODGES WATCH COMPANY LLC
204 Pennsylvania Ave (22046-3240)
PHONE..........................703 651-6440
Howie Hodges, *President*
EMP: 1
SALES (est): 69.8K **Privately Held**
WEB: www.hodgeswatch.com
SIC: 3873 Watches, clocks, watchcases & parts

(G-4919)
INFINITY RESOURCES CORPORATION
900 S Washington St B104 (22046-4010)
PHONE..........................830 822-4962
Yudianto Samsuhadi, *President*
EMP: 2 EST: 1996
SALES (est): 118.3K **Privately Held**
SIC: 3694 Distributors, motor vehicle engine

(G-4920)
KOMOREBI PRESS LLC
1069 W Broad St Ste 804 (22046-4610)
PHONE..........................301 910-5041
Victoria Smith,
EMP: 1
SALES (est): 34.4K **Privately Held**
SIC: 2731 Books: publishing & printing

(G-4921)
LYNK GLOBAL INC (PA)
510 N Washington St # 200 (22046-3571)
PHONE..........................937 367-8737
Margo Deckard, *CEO*
EMP: 7 EST: 2017
SALES (est): 959.7K **Privately Held**
SIC: 3663 Satellites, communications

(G-4922)
MEGA-TECH INC
701 W Broad St Ste 411 (22046-3220)
PHONE..........................703 534-1629
Dolores D Fisk, *President*
EMP: 21
SQ FT: 2,800

SALES (est): 2.5MM **Privately Held**
WEB: www.megatechinc.com
SIC: 7372 8711 7373 7371 Prepackaged software; engineering services; systems integration services; custom computer programming services; job training & vocational rehabilitation services

(G-4923)
NETWORK 12
116b W Broad St (22046-4201)
PHONE..........................703 532-2970
EMP: 2 EST: 2016
SALES (est): 91.3K **Privately Held**
SIC: 3273 Central-Mixed Concrete

(G-4924)
RELIANCE INDUSTRIES INC
140 Little Falls St # 208 (22046-3391)
PHONE..........................832 788-0108
Devandra Desai, *Branch Mgr*
EMP: 1
SALES (corp-wide): 3.4MM **Privately Held**
WEB: www.reliancemixers.com
SIC: 3556 Cutting, chopping, grinding, mixing & similar machinery
PA: Reliance Industries, Inc.
 1900 Fm 1092 Rd Ste A
 Missouri City TX 77459
 281 499-9926

(G-4925)
SHENANDOAH STONE SUPPLY CO
7139 Lee Hwy (22046-3725)
PHONE..........................703 532-0169
Steve Sislers, *Principal*
Connie Poling, *Office Mgr*
EMP: 4
SALES (corp-wide): 232.8K **Privately Held**
WEB: www.shenstonesupply.com
SIC: 1411 Sandstone, dimension-quarrying
PA: Shenandoah Stone Supply Company
 165 Bradstone Ln
 Harpers Ferry WV 25425
 304 725-5668

(G-4926)
TAX ANALYSTS
Also Called: Tax Analysts and Advocates
400 S Maple Ave Ste 400 # 400 (22046-4245)
PHONE..........................703 533-4400
Martin Lobel, *Ch of Bd*
Cara Griffith, *President*
David Brunori, *Publisher*
Mark Abbott, *Editor*
Roxanne Bland, *Editor*
EMP: 200
SQ FT: 37,414
SALES: 29.2MM **Privately Held**
WEB: www.taxnotes.com
SIC: 2731 2721 Book publishing; periodicals: publishing only

(G-4927)
WASHINGTON BUSINESS INFO INC
Also Called: Washington Drug Letter
300 N Washington St # 200 (22046-3438)
PHONE..........................703 538-7600
Cynthia Carter, *President*
Leslie Ramsey, *Editor*
Jodi Grizzel, *COO*
James Defalco, *Sales Dir*
William Tuttle, *Accounts Mgr*
EMP: 30
SQ FT: 8,800
SALES (est): 2.3MM
SALES (corp-wide): 92.2MM **Privately Held**
WEB: www.fdanews.com
SIC: 2741 Newsletter publishing
PA: Wirb - Copernicus Group, Inc.
 212 Carnegie Ctr Ste 301
 Princeton NJ 08540
 609 945-0101

(G-4928)
WELSH PRINTING CORPORATION
104 E Fairfax St (22046-2902)
P.O. Box 8975 (22041-8975)
PHONE..........................703 534-0232
Robert Welsh, *President*
Turner Rebecca, *Vice Pres*
EMP: 7 EST: 1960
SQ FT: 25,000
SALES (est): 1MM **Privately Held**
WEB: www.welshprinting.com
SIC: 2752 Commercial printing, offset

(G-4929)
WOODYS GOODYS LLC
2329 N Oak St (22046-2327)
PHONE..........................703 608-8533
Deborah Livingston, *Principal*
EMP: 1
SALES (est): 47.9K **Privately Held**
WEB: www.woodys-goodys.com
SIC: 2047 Dog & cat food

(G-4930)
WORKING SOFTWARE LLC
1301 Seaton Ln (22046-3822)
PHONE..........................703 992-6280
Fred Richards,
EMP: 1
SALES (est): 121.2K **Privately Held**
WEB: www.working-software.com
SIC: 7372 Business oriented computer software

Falls Mills
Tazewell County

(G-4931)
EXCEL TOOL INC
162 Tabor Ave (24613-9347)
P.O. Box 268 (24613-0268)
PHONE..........................276 322-0223
Fax: 276 322-0224
EMP: 14
SQ FT: 18,000
SALES: 1MM **Privately Held**
SIC: 3441 3545 Structural Metal Fabrication Mfg Machine Tool Accessories

Falmouth
Stafford County

(G-4932)
AGGREGATE INDUSTRIES - MWR INC
Also Called: Fredericksburg Plant
301 Warrenton Rd (22405-1330)
PHONE..........................540 379-0765
Brittany Conley, *Engineer*
EMP: 333
SALES (corp-wide): 1.7B **Privately Held**
WEB: www.lafargeholcim.us
SIC: 3273 1442 Ready-mixed concrete; construction sand & gravel
HQ: Aggregate Industries - Mwr, Inc.
 2815 Dodd Rd
 Eagan MN 55121

Fancy Gap
Carroll County

(G-4933)
BOBBY UTT CUSTOM CABINETS
2437 Greenberry Rd (24328-4216)
PHONE..........................276 728-9411
Bobby Utt, *Owner*
EMP: 2
SALES (est): 157.9K **Privately Held**
SIC: 2434 Wood kitchen cabinets

(G-4934)
DAVID S WELCH
162 Golden Leaves Dr (24328)
P.O. Box 69 (24328-0069)
PHONE..........................276 398-4024
David Welch, *Owner*
EMP: 1

▲ = Import ▼=Export
◆ =Import/Export

SALES (est): 77.3K **Privately Held**
SIC: 3563 7389 Air & gas compressors;
business services

(G-4935)
FANCY GAP WOODWORKS LLC
347 Forest Haven Dr (24328-2599)
PHONE...................................336 816-9881
Clyde Womble, *Principal*
EMP: 1
SALES (est): 54.1K **Privately Held**
SIC: 2431 Millwork

Farmville
Prince Edward County

(G-4936)
ABSOLUTE WELDING LLC
586 Hardtimes Rd (23901-5605)
PHONE...................................434 569-5351
James Cottrell, *Administration*
EMP: 1
SALES (est): 31.1K **Privately Held**
SIC: 7692 Welding repair

(G-4937)
BOLT SAWMILL
2524 Deer Run Rd (23901-7125)
PHONE...................................434 574-6732
Douglas Bolt, *Owner*
EMP: 4 EST: 1974
SALES (est): 232.8K **Privately Held**
SIC: 2421 Sawmills & planing mills, general

(G-4938)
CUMBERLAND COMPANY LP (PA)
113 E 2nd St Ste A (23901-1320)
PHONE...................................434 392-9911
E Plancaster Jr, *Owner*
◆ EMP: 3
SALES (est): 387K **Privately Held**
SIC: 2841 5169 Soap & other detergents;
detergents & soaps, except specialty
cleaning

(G-4939)
ELLETTS EMBROIDERY
Also Called: Creative Monogrim
1437 S Main St (23901-2531)
PHONE...................................434 392-2290
Wendy Ellett, *Owner*
EMP: 2
SALES (est): 135.4K **Privately Held**
WEB: www.ellettsemb.com
SIC: 2395 Embroidery products, except
schiffli machine

(G-4940)
FLOWERS BKG CO LYNCHBURG LLC
2799 W 3rd St (23901-2600)
PHONE...................................434 392-8134
Tj Estes, *Manager*
EMP: 2
SALES (corp-wide): 4.1B **Publicly Held**
SIC: 2051 Bread, cake & related products
HQ: Flowers Baking Co. Of Lynchburg, Llc
1905 Hollins Mill Rd
Lynchburg VA 24503
434 528-0441

(G-4941)
FRED B MEADOWS SONS LOGGI
1604 Briery Rd (23901-2552)
PHONE...................................434 392-5269
Lynn Meadows, *President*
Linda W Meadows, *Principal*
EMP: 9
SALES (est): 777.6K **Privately Held**
SIC: 2411 Logging

(G-4942)
GEMINI INCORPORATED
102 Hauschild Rd (23901-4032)
PHONE...................................434 315-0312
Robert Bednarski, *Vice Pres*
Steve Leonard, *Manager*
EMP: 60

SALES (corp-wide): 94.6MM **Privately Held**
WEB: www.geminisignproducts.com
SIC: 3993 Signs & advertising specialties
PA: Gemini, Incorporated
103 Mensing Way
Cannon Falls MN 55009
507 263-3957

(G-4943)
HICKS WELDING LLC RICHARD L
23 Raines Rd (23901-3818)
PHONE...................................434 392-9824
Richard Hicks, *Principal*
EMP: 1
SALES (est): 41.6K **Privately Held**
SIC: 7692 Welding repair

(G-4944)
JOE GILES SIGNS INC
1006 E 3rd St (23901-1612)
PHONE...................................434 391-9040
Joe Giles, *President*
EMP: 2
SALES (est): 192K **Privately Held**
WEB: www.joegilessigns.com
SIC: 3993 Signs & advertising specialties

(G-4945)
KINGDOM OBJECTIVES
Also Called: Eddie's Citrus Kicker
39 Bear Branch Rd (23901-4312)
PHONE...................................434 414-0808
Edward Ward, *Owner*
EMP: 1
SALES (est): 67.6K **Privately Held**
SIC: 2035 Seasonings, meat sauces (except tomato & dry)

(G-4946)
LAPP METALS LLC
304 Industrial Park Rd (23901-2661)
PHONE...................................434 392-3505
Stephen Lapp, *Mng Member*
EMP: 2
SALES (est): 131.7K **Privately Held**
WEB: www.lappmetals.org
SIC: 3441 Fabricated structural metal

(G-4947)
LINDSAY HARDWOODS INC
124 Sheppards Rd (23901-5464)
P.O. Box 343 (23901-0343)
PHONE...................................434 392-8615
Charles E Lindsay, *President*
C Eric Lindsay, *Vice Pres*
EMP: 17
SQ FT: 7,000
SALES (est): 3.7MM **Privately Held**
SIC: 2421 Sawmills & planing mills, general

(G-4948)
MAINLY CLAY LLC
217 N Main St (23901-1307)
PHONE...................................434 390-8138
Pamela Butler, *Mng Member*
EMP: 1
SALES (est): 100.4K **Privately Held**
WEB: www.mainlyclay.com
SIC: 3269 5049 Stoneware pottery products; precision tools

(G-4949)
MARGARET ATKINS
1547 Cumberland Rd (23901-4036)
P.O. Box 677 (23901-0677)
PHONE...................................434 315-3184
Margaret Atkins, *Owner*
EMP: 1
SALES (est): 49K **Privately Held**
SIC: 3479 Etching & engraving

(G-4950)
MEADOWS WELDING
5755 Farmville Rd (23901-5940)
PHONE...................................434 603-0000
EMP: 1 EST: 2017
SALES (est): 30K **Privately Held**
SIC: 7692 Welding repair

(G-4951)
MORRIS WOODWORKS LLC
305 River Rd (23901-3937)
PHONE...................................434 392-2285
EMP: 1 EST: 2013
SALES (est): 55K **Privately Held**
SIC: 2431 Mfg Millwork

(G-4952)
MOTTLEY FOILS INC
20 Mohele Rd (23901-7002)
PHONE...................................434 392-8347
EMP: 10
SALES (est): 710K **Privately Held**
SIC: 3353 2671 3497 3081 Mfg Aluminum Sheet/Foil Mfg Packaging
Paper/Film Mfg Metal Foil/Leaf Mfg Unsupport Plstc Film

(G-4953)
MSCBAKES LLC
1009 2nd Avenue Ext (23901-2204)
PHONE...................................434 214-0838
Maria Hamilton, *CEO*
EMP: 1
SALES (est): 47.9K **Privately Held**
SIC: 2051 Bread, cake & related products

(G-4954)
NORTH STREET ENTERPRISE INC
Also Called: Farmville Printing
127 North St (23901-1311)
P.O. Box 307 (23901-0307)
PHONE...................................434 392-4144
William B Wall Sr, *President*
Betty Ramsey, *Publisher*
Titus Mohler, *Editor*
Steven E Wall, *Vice Pres*
Edward Tracy, *Purch Mgr*
EMP: 41 EST: 1921
SQ FT: 10,000
SALES (est): 2.7MM **Privately Held**
WEB: www.farmvilleprinting.com
SIC: 2711 2752 2791 2789 Newspapers:
publishing only, not printed on site; commercial printing, offset; typesetting; bookbinding & related work

(G-4955)
PERFORMANCE COUNTS AUTOMOTIVE
3020 W 3rd St (23901-5418)
PHONE...................................434 392-3391
Ted Daves, *President*
EMP: 5 **Privately Held**
SIC: 3714 5531 Motor vehicle engines &
parts; automotive parts

(G-4956)
ROD & STAFF WELDING
2520 W 3rd St (23901-2655)
PHONE...................................434 392-3090
James Shanks, *Owner*
EMP: 3
SALES (est): 234.9K **Privately Held**
SIC: 7692 3599 1799 Welding repair; machine shop, jobbing & repair; welding on
site

(G-4957)
SMART START INC
3561 W 3rd St (23901-2995)
PHONE...................................434 392-3334
EMP: 2
SALES (est): 150.2K **Privately Held**
SIC: 3694 Ignition apparatus & distributors

(G-4958)
SMI-OWEN STEEL COMPANY INC
Also Called: CMC Steel Products
300 Smi Way (23901-3180)
PHONE...................................434 391-3903
EMP: 113
SALES (corp-wide): 5.9B **Publicly Held**
SIC: 3441 Structural Metal Fabrication
HQ: Smi-Owen Steel Company, Inc.
727 Mauney Dr
Columbia SC 29201
803 251-7680

(G-4959)
SUZIES ZOO INC
408 S Main St (23901-2074)
PHONE...................................434 547-4161
EMP: 2 EST: 2010
SALES (est): 122.4K **Privately Held**
SIC: 3999 Pet supplies

(G-4960)
TBRSP LLC
302 Dominion Dr (23901-2371)
P.O. Box 626, Dillwyn (23936-0626)
PHONE...................................434 315-5600
EMP: 2 EST: 1995
SALES (est): 99.4K **Privately Held**
SIC: 2542 Shelving, office & store: except
wood

(G-4961)
YAKATTACK LLC
100 Industrial Park Rd (23901-2659)
PHONE...................................434 392-3233
Luther Cifers III,
EMP: 2
SALES (est): 89.1K **Privately Held**
SIC: 3462 Gear & chain forgings

Farnham
Richmond County

(G-4962)
BG SMITH & SON OYSTER CO
70 Simonson Rd (22460-2117)
PHONE...................................804 394-2721
EMP: 3 EST: 2010
SALES (est): 201.3K **Privately Held**
SIC: 2091 Canned & cured fish & seafoods

(G-4963)
PROTECTED BY FAITH CNSTR LLC
282 Union Mill Rd (22460-2640)
PHONE...................................804 445-6888
Lavar Burton Rich,
EMP: 1
SALES (est): 41K **Privately Held**
SIC: 1389 Construction, repair & dismantling services

(G-4964)
RACHAEL A PEDEN ORIGINALS
826 Quinton Oak Ln (22460-2429)
PHONE...................................804 580-8709
Rachael A Peden, *Owner*
EMP: 3
SALES (est): 167.2K **Privately Held**
SIC: 2431 Woodwork, interior & ornamental

(G-4965)
SUPRAVISTA MEDICAL DSS LLC
514 Maon Rd (22460-2301)
PHONE...................................740 339-0080
Shirley Barrack, *Manager*
Jasvinder Kaur,
EMP: 2
SALES (est): 121.5K **Privately Held**
SIC: 7372 Prepackaged software

Ferrum
Franklin County

(G-4966)
ABSTRUSE TECHNICAL SERVICES
Also Called: Ats
635 Thompson Ridge Cir (24088-2678)
PHONE...................................540 489-8940
Everett Boone, *President*
EMP: 1
SQ FT: 2,000
SALES (est): 200K **Privately Held**
SIC: 3552 7699 8711 Textile machinery;
industrial machinery & equipment repair;
designing; ship, boat, machine & product

(G-4967)
AQUAO2 WASTEWATER
TREATMENT SY
5800 Prillaman Switch Rd (24088-3708)
P.O. Box 579 (24088-0579)
PHONE....................................540 365-0154
Lisa McKelvey, *President*
Michael McKelvey, *Officer*
EMP: 3 EST: 2015
SQ FT: 30,000
SALES (est): 270.9K **Privately Held**
WEB: www.aqua-o2.com
SIC: 3589 1629 Water treatment equipment, industrial; waste water & sewage treatment plant construction

(G-4968)
AQUAROBIC INTERNATIONAL
INC
5800 Prillaman Switch Rd (24088-3708)
PHONE....................................540 365-0154
Lisa McKelvey, *President*
Michael McKelvey, *Corp Secy*
Danny J Mangus, *Sales Mgr*
▼ EMP: 9
SQ FT: 52,000
SALES (est): 1.1MM **Privately Held**
WEB: www.aqua-o2.com
SIC: 3589 Water treatment equipment, industrial

(G-4969)
ARTWORKS
544 Running Brook Rd (24088-2553)
PHONE....................................540 420-3843
Freda Nichols, *Principal*
EMP: 2
SALES (est): 93K **Privately Held**
SIC: 2499 Picture frame molding, finished

(G-4970)
BELCHERS WOODWORKING
1544 King Richard Rd (24088-2839)
PHONE....................................540 365-7809
Anthony Belcher, *Owner*
EMP: 2
SALES (est): 150.4K **Privately Held**
SIC: 2499 Decorative wood & woodwork

(G-4971)
BLACKWATER BLDG CSTM
WDWKG LLC
50 Nelson St (24088-3040)
PHONE....................................540 493-1888
Logan Brubaker, *Principal*
EMP: 1
SALES (est): 54.1K **Privately Held**
SIC: 2431 Millwork

(G-4972)
BLUE RIDGE SHELVING CLOSET
LLC
Also Called: Gregory Wood Products
5800 Prillaman Switch Rd (24088-3708)
P.O. Box 39 (24088-0039)
PHONE....................................540 365-0150
Patrick Quinn, *Controller*
Margaret Quinn, *
EMP: 10 EST: 2006
SALES (est): 1.1MM **Privately Held**
WEB: www.gregorywoodproducts.com
SIC: 2599 Cabinets, factory

(G-4973)
BOWMAN WOODWORKING INC
6829 Providence Church Rd (24088-4253)
PHONE....................................540 483-1680
Gary Bowman, *President*
Nathan Bowman, *Vice Pres*
Greg Bowman, *Admin Sec*
EMP: 8
SQ FT: 8,200
SALES (est): 1.5MM **Privately Held**
WEB: www.bowmanswoodworking.com
SIC: 2434 Wood kitchen cabinets

(G-4974)
FOLEY LOGGING INC
1849 Henry Rd (24088-2769)
PHONE....................................540 365-3152
Lanny Foley, *President*
EMP: 2
SALES (est): 143.8K **Privately Held**
SIC: 2411 Logging

(G-4975)
KURVEZ GALORE BOUTIQUE
LLC
8394 Franklin St (24088-4410)
PHONE....................................336 901-5266
Katosha L Poindexter,
EMP: 1
SALES (est): 50K **Privately Held**
SIC: 3161 Clothing & apparel carrying cases

(G-4976)
NU-TEC OUTDOOR
INNOVATIONS LLC
10895 Franklin St (24088-3346)
PHONE....................................540 365-0551
EMP: 2
SALES (est): 135.9K **Privately Held**
WEB: www.nutecoutdoors.com
SIC: 3949 Sporting & athletic goods

(G-4977)
RAINBOW HILL FARM
Also Called: Norris Bowman Logging
1000 Skillet Rd (24088-4365)
P.O. Box 454 (24088-0454)
PHONE....................................540 365-7826
Norris Bowman, *Owner*
EMP: 6
SQ FT: 100
SALES (est): 360K **Privately Held**
WEB: www.rainbowhillfarm.org
SIC: 2411 Timber, cut at logging camp

(G-4978)
RICK BOYD STONE CABINET
1740 King Richard Rd (24088-2841)
P.O. Box 271 (24088-0271)
PHONE....................................540 365-2668
Rick Boyd, *Owner*
EMP: 6
SALES (est): 444.7K **Privately Held**
SIC: 2434 Wood kitchen cabinets

(G-4979)
ROCKY MOUNT HARDWOOD
INC
574 Franklin St (24088)
P.O. Box 18, Willis (24380-0018)
PHONE....................................540 483-1428
William Poff, *President*
John Turman, *Vice Pres*
William Layne, *Shareholder*
Brenda Poff, *Admin Sec*
EMP: 10
SQ FT: 9,400
SALES (est): 1.4MM **Privately Held**
WEB: www.rmhardwoods.com
SIC: 2421 Sawmills & planing mills, general

(G-4980)
SAW SHOP
1224 Thompson Ridge Rd (24088-2727)
PHONE....................................540 365-0745
Jess Sulther, *Owner*
EMP: 1 EST: 2010
SALES (est): 79.8K **Privately Held**
SIC: 2411 Saw logs

(G-4981)
SMITH RIVER BIOLOGICALS
9388 Charity Hwy (24088-3288)
PHONE....................................276 930-2369
David Roycraft, *Partner*
Dr Elizabeth Roycraft, *Partner*
EMP: 9
SQ FT: 6,700
SALES (est): 1.2MM **Privately Held**
WEB: www.smithriverbiologicals.com
SIC: 2835 Microbiology & virology diagnostic products

(G-4982)
SOUTHEASTERN LAND AND
LOGGING
2510 Old Ferrum Rd (24088-4302)
P.O. Box 885, Rocky Mount (24151-0885)
PHONE....................................540 489-1403
Robby Peters, *President*
Lori Peters, *Vice Pres*
EMP: 6
SALES (est): 568.3K **Privately Held**
SIC: 2411 Logging camps & contractors

(G-4983)
SOUTHERN PRIDE CABINETS
1990 Sawmill Rd (24088-2614)
PHONE....................................540 365-3227
James C Green, *President*
William Atkins, *Vice Pres*
EMP: 5
SALES (est): 235.5K **Privately Held**
WEB: www.southernpridecabinets.com
SIC: 2434 Wood kitchen cabinets

Fieldale
Henry County

(G-4984)
EASTMAN PERFORMANCE
FILMS LLC (DH)
Also Called: Solutias Performance Films Div
4210 The Great Rd (24089-3531)
PHONE....................................276 627-3000
Travis Smith, *President*
David Woodmansee, *Vice Pres*
Andrew Campbell, *Opers Staff*
Erin Packwood, *Human Resources*
John Sharpe, *Manager*
◆ EMP: 600
SQ FT: 420,000
SALES (est): 187.5MM **Publicly Held**
SIC: 2821 Plastics materials & resins
HQ: Solutia Inc.
575 Maryville Centre Dr
Saint Louis MO 63141
423 229-2000

(G-4985)
EASTMAN PERFORMANCE
FILMS LLC
4210 The Great Rd (24089-3531)
P.O. Box 5068, Martinsville (24115-5068)
PHONE....................................276 762-0242
EMP: 25 **Publicly Held**
SIC: 2821 Plastics materials & resins
HQ: Eastman Performance Films, Llc
4210 The Great Rd
Fieldale VA 24089
276 627-3000

(G-4986)
EASTMAN PERFORMANCE
FILMS LLC
4129 The Great Rd (24089-3532)
PHONE....................................276 627-3223
Joe Stultz, *Manager*
EMP: 15 **Publicly Held**
SIC: 2821 Plastics materials & resins
HQ: Eastman Performance Films, Llc
4210 The Great Rd
Fieldale VA 24089
276 627-3000

(G-4987)
HALLS MECHANICAL SERVICES
LLC
2216 John Baker Rd (24089-3321)
P.O. Box 589, Bassett (24055-0589)
PHONE....................................276 673-3300
Alan C Hall Jr, *Mng Member*
Alan Hall, *Mng Member*
EMP: 8
SQ FT: 2,500
SALES (est): 1.1MM **Privately Held**
WEB: www.hallsmechanical.com
SIC: 3444 Sheet metalwork

(G-4988)
HATCHER ENTERPRISES
67 Duke St (24089-3056)
PHONE....................................276 673-6077
Cecil Hatcher, *Owner*
EMP: 1
SALES (est): 87K **Privately Held**
SIC: 2752 7389 Commercial printing, offset; pay telephone network

(G-4989)
LAWLESS WLDG &
FABRICATION INC
3372 River Rd (24089-3480)
P.O. Box 520 (24089-0520)
PHONE....................................276 806-8077
Christopher Lawless, *President*
EMP: 4

SALES (est): 233.4K **Privately Held**
WEB: www.lawlessweldinginc.com
SIC: 7692 Welding repair

(G-4990)
NEW MINGLEWOOD MFG INC
191 Clyde Prillaman St (24089-3070)
PHONE....................................276 632-9107
Peter Ullstein, *Principal*
Todd Snyder, *Principal*
EMP: 4
SQ FT: 13,000
SALES (est): 478.8K **Privately Held**
SIC: 2521 Wood office furniture

(G-4991)
SOLUTIA INC
Also Called: Performance Films
4129 The Great Rd (24089-3532)
PHONE....................................314 674-3150
Dean Arrington, *Credit Mgr*
Amanda Chamov, *Branch Mgr*
EMP: 191 **Publicly Held**
WEB: www.eastman.com
SIC: 2821 Plastics materials & resins
HQ: Solutia Inc.
575 Maryville Centre Dr
Saint Louis MO 63141
423 229-2000

Fincastle
Botetourt County

(G-4992)
ATLANTIC QUALITY DESIGN INC
5815 Lee Ln (24090)
PHONE....................................540 966-4356
Hank Wallace, *President*
EMP: 1
SALES (est): 110K **Privately Held**
WEB: www.aqdi.com
SIC: 3695 8711 Computer software tape & disks: blank, rigid & floppy; engineering services

(G-4993)
CALDWELL MOUNTAIN COPPER
2391 Lees Gap Rd (24090-4110)
PHONE....................................540 473-2167
Porter Caldwell, *Owner*
Faye Caldwell, *Co-Owner*
EMP: 1
SALES (est): 115.8K **Privately Held**
WEB: www.caldwellmtncopper.com
SIC: 3499 Giftware, copper goods

(G-4994)
CALFEE PRINTING
92 Camp Eagle Rd (24090-3124)
PHONE....................................304 910-3475
Megan Calfee, *Principal*
EMP: 2
SALES (est): 83.9K **Privately Held**
SIC: 2752 Commercial printing, lithographic

(G-4995)
CARRIS REELS INC
Groggins, A Carris Div
64 W Wind Rd (24090-3671)
PHONE....................................540 473-2210
Brian Connell, *General Mgr*
EMP: 40 **Privately Held**
WEB: www.carris.com
SIC: 2499 3089 Spools, reels & pulleys: wood; injection molded finished plastic products
HQ: Carris Reels Inc
49 Main St
Proctor VT 05765
802 773-9111

(G-4996)
FINCASTLE VINEYARD &
WINERY
203 Maple Ridge Ln (24090-3243)
PHONE....................................540 591-9000
David Sawyer, *Owner*
EMP: 2
SALES (est): 151.7K **Privately Held**
WEB: www.fincastlewine.com
SIC: 2084 Wines

(G-4997)
PATTERN AND PRINT LLC
7691 Old Fincastle Rd (24090-3774)
PHONE..............................540 884-2660
Linda Lester, *Principal*
EMP: 2
SALES (est): 93.6K **Privately Held**
WEB: www.pattern-and-print.com
SIC: 2752 Commercial printing, lithographic

(G-4998)
RESCUE SYSTEMS INTL INC
755 Botetourt Rd (24090-3154)
PHONE..............................276 629-2900
Robert T Simmons, *President*
EMP: 2
SQ FT: 2,500
SALES (est): 86.6K **Privately Held**
SIC: 3842 5099 Personal safety equipment; safety equipment & supplies

(G-4999)
VIRGINIA MOUNTAIN VINEYARDS LL
4204 Old Fincastle Rd (24090-3559)
PHONE..............................540 473-2979
David Gibbs, *Principal*
EMP: 2
SALES (est): 144.1K **Privately Held**
WEB: www.vmvines.com
SIC: 2084 Wines

Fishersville
Augusta County

(G-5000)
ALPHA DEVELOPEMENT BUREAU
Also Called: Servocon Alpha
167 Expo Rd (22939-2308)
PHONE..............................540 337-4900
Richard A Coffman, *President*
Dale Carter, *Admin Sec*
EMP: 15
SQ FT: 5,000
SALES (est): 2.6MM **Privately Held**
WEB: www.servoconalpha.com
SIC: 3492 Fluid power valves & hose fittings

(G-5001)
BARREN RIDGE VINEYARDS LLC
984 Barrenridge Rd (22939-3026)
PHONE..............................540 248-3300
John R Higgs,
EMP: 2
SALES (est): 207.7K **Privately Held**
WEB: www.barrenridgevineyards.com
SIC: 2084 Wines

(G-5002)
COLE TOOL INC
124 Hickory Hill Ln (22939-2512)
PHONE..............................540 942-5174
EMP: 10 EST: 1950
SQ FT: 7,000
SALES (est): 530K **Privately Held**
SIC: 3599 Machine Shop

(G-5003)
GATEWAY GREEN ENERGY INC
65 Adin Cir (22939-3417)
P.O. Box 1116 (22939-1116)
PHONE..............................540 280-7475
Thomas Sikes, *President*
EMP: 2
SALES (est): 146.8K **Privately Held**
SIC: 3648 3229 2851 Floodlights; bulbs for electric lights; removers & cleaners

(G-5004)
HALL INDUSTRIES INC
162 Expo Rd (22939-2308)
P.O. Box 1137 (22939-1137)
PHONE..............................540 337-1210
Myles Truslow, *President*
EMP: 15
SQ FT: 55,000
SALES (est): 1.1MM **Privately Held**
SIC: 3599 Machine shop, jobbing & repair

(G-5005)
INDUSTRIAL FABRICATORS VA INC
48 Mule Academy Rd (22939-2254)
P.O. Box 518 (22939-0518)
PHONE..............................540 943-5885
John E Major, *President*
Linda A Major, *Corp Secy*
Scott M Childress, *Vice Pres*
EMP: 55
SQ FT: 35,000
SALES (est): 10.8MM **Privately Held**
WEB: www.industrialfabricatorsofva.com
SIC: 3441 3443 7699 5051 Fabricated structural metal; pipe, large diameter: metal plate; boiler repair shop; pipe & tubing, steel; machine shop, jobbing & repair; welding on site

(G-5006)
PENNY PLATE LLC
Also Called: Penny Plate of Virginia
286 Expo Rd (22939-2309)
PHONE..............................540 337-3777
Wayne Seal, *Manager*
EMP: 80
SALES (corp-wide): 294.6MM **Privately Held**
WEB: www.pennyplate.com
SIC: 3411 3354 Metal cans; aluminum extruded products
HQ: Penny Plate, Llc
1400 Horizon Way Ste 300
Mount Laurel NJ 08054
856 429-7583

(G-5007)
RDS CONTROL SYSTEMS INC
3 Joy Ln (22939-2103)
P.O. Box 298 (22939-0298)
PHONE..............................888 578-9428
Gordon McMurrain, *President*
Tim Bobsin, *Engineer*
Wendy Cullen-Lawhorne, *Manager*
David Matthews, *Manager*
Russell Neyman, *Manager*
EMP: 1 EST: 2011
SALES (est): 57.5K **Privately Held**
WEB: www.rdscontrol.com
SIC: 7372 Business oriented computer software

(G-5008)
SIGN MASTER
46 Tinkling Spring Rd (22939-2262)
PHONE..............................540 886-6900
Rob Griffin, *President*
EMP: 2 EST: 1998
SALES (est): 196.8K **Privately Held**
WEB: www.signmasterva.com
SIC: 3993 Signs, not made in custom sign painting shops

(G-5009)
STAFFORD HOME PRODUCTS
24 Lucas Rd (22939-2335)
PHONE..............................540 337-0068
EMP: 1
SALES (est): 40.9K **Privately Held**
SIC: 2392 Household furnishings

(G-5010)
VALLEY BEE SUPPLY INC
46 Tinkling Spring Rd (22939-2262)
PHONE..............................540 941-8127
Michael Shane Clatterbaugh, *President*
Sandy Fisher, *Admin Sec*
EMP: 3
SQ FT: 900
SALES (est): 306.2K **Privately Held**
WEB: www.valleybeesupply.com
SIC: 3999 Honeycomb foundations (beekeepers' supplies)

(G-5011)
VALLEY RESTAURANT REPAIR INC
46 Tinkling Spring Rd (22939-2262)
PHONE..............................540 294-1118
Shane Clatterbaugh, *President*
Sandy Fisher, *Admin Sec*
EMP: 5
SALES (est): 549K **Privately Held**
WEB: www.valleyrestaurantrepair.com
SIC: 3599 Industrial machinery

(G-5012)
VIRGINIA PROSTHETICS ORTHOTICS
1577 Jefferson Hwy # 101 (22939-2279)
PHONE..............................540 949-4248
EMP: 2
SALES (est): 112.8K **Privately Held**
SIC: 3842 Prosthetic appliances

(G-5013)
WILSON READY MIX LLC
46 Wilshire Ct (22939-2356)
P.O. Box 1347, Harrisonburg (22803-1347)
PHONE..............................540 324-0555
Mark Wilson,
EMP: 7
SALES (est): 1.2MM **Privately Held**
WEB: www.wilsonreadymix.com
SIC: 3273 Ready-mixed concrete

Flint Hill
Rappahannock County

(G-5014)
ARK WOODWORKING LLC
694 Zachary Taylor Hwy (22627-1726)
PHONE..............................540 272-7489
Benjamin Clemmer, *Administration*
EMP: 2
SALES (est): 59.5K **Privately Held**
SIC: 2431 Millwork

(G-5015)
CLC ENTERPRISES LLC
32 Mountain View Rd (22627-1856)
P.O. Box 195 (22627-0195)
PHONE..............................540 622-3488
Candace Clough, *President*
EMP: 2
SALES (est): 73.4K **Privately Held**
SIC: 3423 5072 5251 Hand & edge tools; hand tools; tools, hand

Floyd
Floyd County

(G-5016)
BETTY P HICKS
Also Called: David Hicks Logging
4427 Floyd Hwy N (24091-2706)
PHONE..............................540 745-5111
David Hicks, *Owner*
Betty Hicks, *Co-Owner*
EMP: 2
SALES (est): 202.6K **Privately Held**
SIC: 2411 Logging

(G-5017)
BRAD WARSTLER
Also Called: Northwind Woodworks
297 Sumner Ln Ne (24091-2056)
PHONE..............................540 745-3595
Brad Warstler, *Owner*
EMP: 1
SALES (est): 79.2K **Privately Held**
WEB: www.bradwarstler.com
SIC: 2426 Furniture stock & parts, hardwood

(G-5018)
CHATEAU MORRISETTE INC (PA)
287 Winery Rd Sw (24091-4033)
P.O. Box 766, Meadows of Dan (24120-0766)
PHONE..............................540 593-2865
David Morrisette, *President*
William F Morrisette Jr, *Vice Pres*
William Morrisette, *Vice Pres*
Sandra Vansutphin, *Treasurer*
Robert Longo, *Sales Mgr*
▲ EMP: 30
SQ FT: 50,000
SALES (est): 10.4MM **Privately Held**
WEB: www.thedogs.com
SIC: 2084 5921 5182 5812 Wines; wine; wine; cafe; drinking places

(G-5019)
COCOA MIA INC
109 E Main St (24091-2129)
P.O. Box 682 (24091-0682)
PHONE..............................540 695-0224
Linda Blair, *President*
EMP: 3
SALES (est): 100.5K **Privately Held**
SIC: 2064 Candy bars, including chocolate covered bars

(G-5020)
COCOA MIA INC
537 Needmore Ln Ne (24091-3804)
PHONE..............................540 493-4341
Linda Blair, *President*
EMP: 2
SALES (est): 68.6K **Privately Held**
SIC: 2026 Milk, chocolate

(G-5021)
CRENSHAW LIGHTING CORPORATION
115 Lighting Way (24091-1124)
PHONE..............................540 745-3900
William Crenshaw, *Principal*
Jason Selznick, *Vice Pres*
Mike Whitlock, *Prdtn Mgr*
Justin Burr, *Design Engr*
Drew Hubbard, *Design Engr*
EMP: 2
SALES (est): 452.4K **Privately Held**
WEB: www.crenshawlighting.com
SIC: 3646 Commercial indusl & institutional electric lighting fixtures

(G-5022)
DAVID W SLUSHER
717 Black Ridge Rd Sw (24091-4001)
PHONE..............................540 745-2485
David Slusher, *Principal*
EMP: 3
SALES (est): 212.8K **Privately Held**
SIC: 2411 Logging

(G-5023)
DEE K ENTERPRISES INC
220 Appalachian Rd (24091)
PHONE..............................540 745-3816
Kenneth Perry, *President*
EMP: 10
SQ FT: 30,000
SALES (est): 850K **Privately Held**
SIC: 2241 Elastic narrow fabrics, woven or braided

(G-5024)
EL CHARRO GRILL MEXICAN RES
302 S Locust St (24091-2320)
P.O. Box 305 (24091-0305)
PHONE..............................540 745-5303
Valentin Soto, *Principal*
EMP: 2 EST: 2008
SALES (est): 270.1K **Privately Held**
SIC: 2599 Bar, restaurant & cafeteria furniture

(G-5025)
FIVE MILE MOUNTAIN DISTILLERY
489 Floyd Hwy S (24091-3082)
PHONE..............................540 588-3158
Julie Arrington, *Principal*
EMP: 3 EST: 2015
SALES (est): 129.4K **Privately Held**
WEB: www.5milemountain.com
SIC: 2085 Distilled & blended liquors

(G-5026)
FLOYD PRESS INC
710 E Main St (24091-2620)
P.O. Box 155 (24091-0155)
PHONE..............................540 745-2127
Sam Cooper, *President*
Dorothy V Sumner, *President*
Wanda Combs, *Principal*
EMP: 7 EST: 1891
SQ FT: 3,000
SALES (est): 375.8K **Privately Held**
WEB: www.swvatoday.com
SIC: 2711 Newspapers, publishing & printing

(G-5027)
GRYPHON SOFTWARE
CORPORAT
120 W Main St (24091-2302)
PHONE................................814 486-3753
Pat Woodruff, *Principal*
EMP: 2 EST: 2013
SALES (est): 140K Privately Held
SIC: 7372 Prepackaged software

(G-5028)
HIGHLAND TIMBER FRAME INC
1019 Thunderstruck Rd Ne (24091-2058)
PHONE................................540 745-7411
James Callahan, *President*
EMP: 1
SALES (est): 119.2K Privately Held
WEB: www.highlandtimberframe.com
SIC: 2491 Structural lumber & timber,
treated wood

(G-5029)
HOLLINGSWORTH & VOSE
COMPANY
289 Parkview Rd Ne (24091-4180)
P.O. Box 199 (24091-0199)
PHONE................................540 745-7600
Tom Dinbinger, *Branch Mgr*
EMP: 150
SALES (corp-wide): 645.8MM Privately
Held
WEB: www.hollingsworth-vose.com
SIC: 2621 3053 Filter paper; gasket mate-
rials
PA: Hollingsworth & Vose Company
112 Washington St
East Walpole MA 02032
508 850-2000

(G-5030)
HUFFMAN TOOL CO
1367 Hcklbrry Ridge Rd Ne (24091-2036)
PHONE................................540 745-3359
Joe Huffman, *Partner*
Kenneth A Huffman, *Partner*
EMP: 5
SALES (est): 300K Privately Held
SIC: 3599 Machine shop, jobbing & repair

(G-5031)
LEONARD LOGGING INC
3172 Floyd Hwy S (24091-3061)
PHONE................................540 239-6991
Wallace Gregory Leonard, *Principal*
EMP: 3 EST: 2009
SALES (est): 182.7K Privately Held
SIC: 2411 Logging camps & contractors

(G-5032)
MOUNTAIN TOP LOGGING LLC
386 Silverleaf Ln Se (24091-2775)
PHONE................................540 745-6709
Emma Griffith, *Owner*
EMP: 3 EST: 2010
SALES (est): 306.6K Privately Held
SIC: 2411 Logging

(G-5033)
NATURAL WOODWORKING CO
1527 Franklin Pike Se (24091-2875)
PHONE................................540 745-2664
Donald H McBroom, *President*
Loreta Gibson, *Admin Sec*
EMP: 7
SALES (est): 250K Privately Held
WEB: www.naturalwoodworkingco.com
SIC: 2431 2519 Millwork; lawn & garden
furniture, except wood & metal

(G-5034)
POFF LOGGING LLC
493 Laurel Branch Rd Nw (24091-2353)
PHONE................................540 695-0060
William Poff, *Principal*
EMP: 3
SALES (est): 98.8K Privately Held
SIC: 2411 Logging

(G-5035)
PRESERVATION WOOD SALES
615 Cannady School Rd Se (24091-2689)
PHONE................................540 553-2023
Michael Whitlock, *Principal*
EMP: 2 EST: 2016

SALES (est): 134.9K Privately Held
SIC: 2511 Wood household furniture

(G-5036)
QUALITY LOGGING LLC
528 Laurel Branch Rd Nw (24091-2356)
PHONE................................540 493-7228
EMP: 3 EST: 2018
SALES (est): 98.8K Privately Held
SIC: 2411 Logging camps & contractors

(G-5037)
R & S STONE INC
1349 Shooting Creek Rd Se (24091-3384)
P.O. Box 203 (24091-0203)
PHONE................................540 745-6788
Terry G Reed, *President*
Terri Smith, *Vice Pres*
EMP: 16
SALES (est): 1.1MM Privately Held
SIC: 3281 Stone, quarrying & processing
of own stone products

(G-5038)
RITE PRINT SHOPPE & SUPPLY
126 N Locust St (24091-2103)
P.O. Box 717 (24091-0717)
PHONE................................540 745-3616
Jean Wright, *President*
Silveon Wright, *Corp Secy*
EMP: 2 Privately Held
SIC: 2752 Commercial printing, offset

(G-5039)
SLUSHERS LOGGING & SAWING
LLC
717 Black Ridge Rd Sw (24091-4001)
PHONE................................540 641-1378
EMP: 2
SALES (est): 81.7K Privately Held
SIC: 2411 Logging

(G-5040)
SOAPSTONE INC
139 Cannadays Gap Rd Se (24091-2958)
PHONE................................540 745-3492
Ray Braley, *Principal*
EMP: 2 EST: 2007
SALES (est): 130.4K Privately Held
SIC: 1499 Soapstone mining

(G-5041)
ST PIERRE INC
2081 Cannady School Rd Se (24091-2944)
PHONE................................540 797-3496
Bill St Pierre, *Principal*
EMP: 7
SALES (est): 430K Privately Held
WEB: www.stpierrewoodworking.com
SIC: 2499 Decorative wood & woodwork

(G-5042)
TURBO SALES & FABRICATION
INC
Also Called: Thomas Industrial Fabrication
296 Commerce Center Dr (24091-2556)
P.O. Box 79, Woolwine (24185-0079)
PHONE................................276 930-2422
Judy B Thomas, *President*
John Paul Thomas, *Vice Pres*
Sally Thomas Jenkins, *Treasurer*
EMP: 30
SQ FT: 12,000
SALES (est): 2.2MM Privately Held
WEB: www.thomasindfab.com
SIC: 3441 Fabricated structural metal

(G-5043)
TURMAN LUMBER COMPANY
INC (PA)
214 N Locust St (24091-2105)
P.O. Box 497 (24091-0497)
PHONE................................540 745-2041
John Michael Turman, *President*
Truman C Bolt Jr, *Corp Secy*
Douglas R Phillips, *Vice Pres*
Lena Gray, *Treasurer*
Al Galamore, *Office Mgr*
▼ EMP: 4
SQ FT: 1,500
SALES (est): 10.3MM Privately Held
WEB: www.turmanlumber.com
SIC: 2421 Sawmills & planing mills, gen-
eral

(G-5044)
UNLIMITED EMBROIDERY
181 Sams Rd Se (24091-2896)
PHONE................................540 745-3909
Vickie Wade, *Principal*
Jeff Wade, *Principal*
EMP: 2
SALES (est): 20K Privately Held
SIC: 2395 Embroidery products, except
schiffli machine

(G-5045)
VILLA APPALACCIA WINERY
752 Rock Castle Gorge (24091-4096)
PHONE................................540 593-3100
Stevan Haskell, *Owner*
Susanne Becker, *Co-Owner*
EMP: 2
SALES (est): 300K Privately Held
WEB: www.villaappalaccia.com
SIC: 2084 Wines

(G-5046)
WOODSONG INSTRUMENTS
1098 Dobbins Farm Rd Ne (24091-2001)
PHONE................................540 745-2708
EMP: 2
SALES (est): 97K Privately Held
SIC: 2491 Wood Preserving

Ford
Dinwiddie County

(G-5047)
SAMUEL L BROWN
Also Called: S Brown Trucking
10239 Colemans Lake Rd (23850-2433)
PHONE................................804 892-5629
Samuel L Brown, *Owner*
EMP: 1
SALES (est): 61.2K Privately Held
SIC: 3537 Industrial trucks & tractors

(G-5048)
SD DAVIS WELDING &
EQUIPMENT
Also Called: Doug
8221 White Oak Rd (23850-2647)
PHONE................................804 691-2112
Doug Davis, *Owner*
EMP: 1
SALES (est): 100K Privately Held
WEB: www.dougwestgroup.com
SIC: 7692 Welding repair

Forest
Bedford County

(G-5049)
ACCOUNTING TECHNOLOGY
LLC
106 Vista Centre Dr (24551-2600)
P.O. Box 2009 (24551-4409)
PHONE................................434 316-6000
Clay Coleman,
EMP: 13
SALES (est): 1.2MM Privately Held
SIC: 7372 Prepackaged software

(G-5050)
ANDREW CORPORATION
140 Vista Centre Dr (24551-3965)
PHONE................................434 386-5262
Van Hanson, *Senior VP*
Gary Brown, *Executive*
EMP: 8 EST: 2016
SALES (est): 624.2K Privately Held
WEB: www.commscope.com
SIC: 3663 Radio & TV communications
equipment

(G-5051)
ASPIRE MARKETING
CORPORATION (PA)
Also Called: Scentual Sun
1168 Everett Rd (24551-3874)
PHONE................................434 525-6191
Paul R Jaeger, *President*
EMP: 1

SALES (est): 250K Privately Held
SIC: 3999 5084 Sprays, artificial & preserved; paint spray equipment, industrial

(G-5052)
BARR LABORATORIES INC
2150 Perrowville Rd (24551-4129)
PHONE................................434 534-8600
Timmy Laughlin, *Research*
Mike Morrsade, *Manager*
Kevin Johnson, *Info Tech Mgr*
Ronald Moon, *Information Mgr*
Jerry Fain, *Technical Staff*
EMP: 90 Privately Held
WEB: www.tevagenerics.com
SIC: 2834 5122 Druggists' preparations
(pharmaceuticals); drugs acting on the
cardiovascular system, except diagnostic;
drugs affecting parasitic & infective dis-
eases; tranquilizers or mental drug prepa-
rations; patent medicines
HQ: Barr Laboratories, Inc.
400 Interpace Pkwy Ste A1
Parsippany NJ 07054
215 591-3000

(G-5053)
BEAU-GESTE INTERNATIONAL
INC (PA)
1835 Rocky Branch Dr (24551-4395)
PHONE................................434 534-0468
Wendy Sams-Tepper, *President*
Ivan H Tepper, *Corp Secy*
Janet Collins, *Exec VP*
EMP: 3
SALES (est): 300K Privately Held
SIC: 2399 2771 Military insignia, textile;
greeting cards

(G-5054)
BLACK JACKET LLC
1237 Smoketree Dr (24551-2351)
PHONE................................425 319-1014
Hans Andersen, *Mng Member*
EMP: 1 EST: 2013
SALES (est): 100K Privately Held
SIC: 2842 7699 3053 Leather dressings
& finishes; leather goods, cleaning & re-
pair; grease retainers, leather

(G-5055)
BOBBIN COIL SPEACIALISTS
INC
1185 Spring Creek Dr (24551-8213)
PHONE................................815 385-6205
Darlene Freeberg, *President*
EMP: 2 Privately Held
WEB: www.coilspecialists.com
SIC: 3677 Coil windings, electronic

(G-5056)
BRANCHES PUBLICATIONS LLC
1985 Colby Dr (24551-1822)
PHONE................................434 525-0432
Don Fanning, *Principal*
EMP: 2
SALES (est): 96.2K Privately Held
WEB: www.branchespublications.com
SIC: 2741 Miscellaneous publishing

(G-5057)
C & A AND SONS PAVING LLC
105 Dinlake Ct (24551-1415)
PHONE................................434 209-7357
Christopher Easley,
EMP: 4
SALES (est): 171.1K Privately Held
SIC: 2911 Asphalt or asphaltic materials,
made in refineries

(G-5058)
CALLOWAY ENTERPRISES INC
200 Britt Pl (24551-3004)
P.O. Box 349 (24551-0349)
PHONE................................434 525-1147
Randy Calloway, *President*
EMP: 4
SALES (est): 443.7K Privately Held
WEB: www.callowaytrash.com
SIC: 2851 Removers & cleaners

(G-5059)
CARRS FLOOR SERVICES
220 London Downs Dr (24551-3022)
PHONE................................434 525-8420

Allen Gillette, *Owner*
Teresa Gillette, *Co-Owner*
EMP: 3
SALES (est): 400K **Privately Held**
SIC: 3553 Sanding machines, except portable floor sanders: woodworking

(G-5060)
CLOUD RIDGE LABS LLC
Also Called: Cloudridge
1173 Research Way (24551-1870)
P.O. Box 2284 (24551-6284)
PHONE................................434 477-5060
Nathaniel Wade, *Principal*
EMP: 2
SALES (est): 68.4K **Privately Held**
WEB: www.cloudridgelabs.com
SIC: 7372 7371 7373 7374 Application computer software; computer software development; systems software development services; computer processing services; software training, computer

(G-5061)
COMMERCIAL WATER WORKS INC
1167 Greenbrook Ct (24551-2217)
PHONE................................434 534-8244
Gene Reed, *President*
EMP: 1
SALES (est): 79.4K **Privately Held**
SIC: 3523 Irrigation equipment, self-propelled

(G-5062)
COMMSCOPE TECHNOLOGIES LLC
140 Vista Centre Dr (24551-3965)
PHONE................................434 386-5300
Jim Burns, *Office Mgr*
EMP: 105 **Publicly Held**
SIC: 3663 3679 Cellular radio telephone; antennas, receiving
HQ: Commscope Technologies Llc
4 Westbrook Corporate Ctr
Westchester IL 60154
708 236-6600

(G-5063)
CONSTRAINED OPTIMIZATION INC
Also Called: Consopt
1033 S Oak Lawn Dr (24551-4657)
PHONE................................434 944-8564
Lisa Baumgartner, *CEO*
Wade Baumgartner, *President*
EMP: 2
SALES (est): 166.8K **Privately Held**
WEB: www.consopt.com
SIC: 3625 Control equipment, electric

(G-5064)
CONSULTING PRINTING SERVICES
1085 Vista Park Dr Ste A (24551-4253)
PHONE................................434 846-6510
Lindy Bryant, *Owner*
EMP: 12
SALES (est): 946.9K **Privately Held**
SIC: 2752 Commercial printing, offset

(G-5065)
CORNERSTONE CABINETS & DESIGN
171 Vista Centre Dr (24551-3964)
PHONE................................434 239-0976
Tracy Hanson, *President*
EMP: 8
SALES (est): 1MM **Privately Held**
WEB: www.cornerstonecabinetsandde-sign.com
SIC: 2434 Wood kitchen cabinets

(G-5066)
DFA DAIRY BRANDS FLUID LLC
12572 E Lynchburg Slem Tp (24551-3418)
PHONE................................336 714-9032
Michael Hardcastle, *Branch Mgr*
EMP: 7
SALES (corp-wide): 15.8B **Privately Held**
SIC: 2026 Fluid milk
HQ: Dfa Dairy Brands Fluid, Llc
1405 N 98th St
Kansas City KS 66111
816 801-6455

(G-5067)
DMT LLC (PA)
Also Called: D M T
1019 Dillard Dr (24551-2628)
P.O. Box 247 (24551-0247)
PHONE................................434 455-2460
Eddie Hughes, *Mng Member*
Ken Wallace,
EMP: 1
SALES (est): 1.1MM **Privately Held**
SIC: 3812 Search & detection systems & instruments

(G-5068)
EASTWIND SOFTWARE LLC
201 Eastwind Dr (24551-1847)
PHONE................................434 525-9241
Stephen L Fix, *Principal*
EMP: 1
SALES (est): 127.8K **Privately Held**
SIC: 7372 Prepackaged software

(G-5069)
ELCARE INNOVATIONS INC
1208 Rocky Branch Dr (24551-2930)
PHONE................................434 525-7685
Elroy T Cantrell, *Principal*
EMP: 3 **EST:** 2015
SALES (est): 197.7K **Privately Held**
WEB: www.scopecoinc.com
SIC: 3841 Surgical & medical instruments

(G-5070)
ELK CREEK WOODWORKING INC
4785 Bellevue Rd (24551-3534)
PHONE................................434 258-5142
Thomas A Twark, *President*
EMP: 2
SALES (est): 413.8K **Privately Held**
SIC: 3553 Woodworking machinery

(G-5071)
ELLIOTT OIL PRODUCTION LLC
519 Carriage Hill Dr (24551-2720)
PHONE................................434 525-3049
David Elliott, *Branch Mgr*
EMP: 1
SALES (corp-wide): 590K **Privately Held**
SIC: 2711 Newspapers, publishing & printing
PA: Elliott Oil Production, Llc
951 County Road 2050 E
Fairfield IL 62837
618 838-3441

(G-5072)
GENERAL SHALE BRICK INC
1085 Venture Dr (24551-2247)
PHONE................................800 414-4661
Corkey Clifton, *Regional Mgr*
EMP: 3
SALES (corp-wide): 3.8B **Privately Held**
WEB: www.generalshale.com
SIC: 3251 Brick & structural clay tile
HQ: General Shale Brick, Inc.
3015 Bristol Hwy
Johnson City TN 37601
423 282-4661

(G-5073)
HANWHA AZDEL INC
Lynchburg Facility, The
2000 Enterprise Dr (24551-2652)
PHONE................................434 385-6359
Paul Dicesare, *Branch Mgr*
EMP: 75 **Privately Held**
WEB: www.azdel.com
SIC: 3083 2851 Thermoplastic laminates: rods, tubes, plates & sheet; paints & allied products
HQ: Hanwha Azdel, Inc.
2000 Enterprise Dr
Forest VA 24551
434 385-6524

(G-5074)
INCANDESCENT TECHNOLOGIES
107 Cygnet Cir (24551-2651)
PHONE................................434 385-8825
EMP: 4
SALES (est): 180K **Privately Held**
SIC: 3679 Mfg Electronic Components

(G-5075)
INDEPENDENT DELIVERY EX INC
1436 Jefferson Dr W (24551-4419)
PHONE................................434 660-2389
Shawn Anderson, *President*
EMP: 1 **EST:** 2005
SALES (est): 400K **Privately Held**
SIC: 2542 Postal lock boxes, mail racks & related products

(G-5076)
INNERSPEC TECHNOLOGIES INC (PA)
2940 Perrowville Rd (24551-2225)
P.O. Box 369 (24551-0369)
PHONE................................434 948-1301
Borja Lopez, *CEO*
C L Christian III, *President*
Michael E Stinnett, *Corp Secy*
Daniel Geier, *Engineer*
David Mann, *Sales Staff*
EMP: 30
SQ FT: 24,000
SALES (est): 5.1MM **Privately Held**
WEB: www.innerspec.com
SIC: 3829 Measuring & controlling devices

(G-5077)
INNOVATIVE MACHINING INC
2104 Graves Mill Rd (24551-2662)
P.O. Box 220 (24551-0220)
PHONE................................804 385-4212
Carlton Mitchell, *President*
EMP: 31
SQ FT: 17,500
SALES (est): 4.2MM **Privately Held**
SIC: 3312 7692 3444 Tool & die steel & alloys; welding repair; sheet metalwork

(G-5078)
INTERCON INC
1222 Corporate Park Dr (24551-2277)
P.O. Box 647 (24551-0647)
PHONE................................434 525-3390
Ted F Counts, *President*
Joseph Stephens, *Vice Pres*
John Ruggiano, *Project Mgr*
Alison Richardson, *Opers Mgr*
Sharon Pfister, *Buyer*
▲ **EMP:** 73
SQ FT: 43,000
SALES (est): 17.7MM **Privately Held**
WEB: www.interconinc.com
SIC: 3679 Harness assemblies for electronic use: wire or cable

(G-5079)
L3HARRIS TECHNOLOGIES INC
12860 E Lynchburg Salem (24551-3416)
PHONE................................434 455-9390
EMP: 100
SALES (corp-wide): 6.8B **Publicly Held**
WEB: www.harris.com
SIC: 3812 3663 3699 3661 Search & navigation equipment; radio & TV communications equipment; security control equipment & systems; telephones & telephone apparatus; integrated circuits, semiconductor networks, etc.
PA: L3harris Technologies, Inc.
1025 W Nasa Blvd
Melbourne FL 32919
321 727-9100

(G-5080)
L3HARRIS TECHNOLOGIES INC
110 Vista Centre Dr Ste 4 (24551-2776)
PHONE................................434 455-6600
EMP: 40
SALES (corp-wide): 6.8B **Publicly Held**
WEB: www.harris.com
SIC: 3812 3663 3699 3661 Search & navigation equipment; radio & TV communications equipment; security control equipment & systems; telephones & telephone apparatus; integrated circuits, semiconductor networks, etc.
PA: L3harris Technologies, Inc.
1025 W Nasa Blvd
Melbourne FL 32919
321 727-9100

(G-5081)
LITESHEET SOLUTIONS LLC
1191 Venture Dr Ste A (24551-2273)
PHONE................................860 213-8311
Michael Pietras, *Buyer*
Shanita Kitts, *Manager*
Bob Byrne, *Administration*
EMP: 8
SALES (est): 1.4MM
SALES (corp-wide): 1.3MM **Privately Held**
WEB: www.litesheet.com
SIC: 3674 Light emitting diodes
PA: Liteideas, Llc
417 Mulberry Rd
Mansfield Center CT 06250
860 213-8311

(G-5082)
MCCRAW CABINETS
1075 London Dr (24551-2385)
PHONE................................434 238-2112
Becky McCraw, *Principal*
EMP: 2
SALES (est): 192.8K **Privately Held**
WEB: www.mccrawcabinets.com
SIC: 2434 Wood kitchen cabinets

(G-5083)
MIGHTY OAK INDUSTRIES
201 Locksley Pl (24551-4150)
PHONE................................434 426-7249
Joseph Hinson, *Principal*
EMP: 2
SALES (est): 114.1K **Privately Held**
SIC: 3999 Manufacturing industries

(G-5084)
MRP MUNUFACTURING INC
12660 E Lynchburg Salem (24551-3417)
PHONE................................434 525-1993
Louis Denaples, *President*
Johnnathan E Heffner, *Principal*
Stephen Soughery, *Principal*
Dominick Denaples, *Vice Pres*
▲ **EMP:** 50 **EST:** 1998
SALES (est): 10.2MM **Privately Held**
SIC: 3531 Construction machinery

(G-5085)
NANOTOUCH MATERIALS LLC
Also Called: Nanoseptic
1053 London Park Dr E (24551-2528)
PHONE................................888 411-6843
Mark Sisson, *Mng Member*
▼ **EMP:** 3
SQ FT: 2,000
SALES (est): 348.5K **Privately Held**
WEB: www.nanoseptic.com
SIC: 2842 Specialty cleaning preparations

(G-5086)
PARKLAND DIRECT INC
305 Enterprise Dr (24551-2645)
PHONE................................434 385-6225
Michael T Seckman, *President*
Vicki Y Seckman, *Senior VP*
Clint P Seckman, *Vice Pres*
Clint Seckman, *Vice Pres*
Michael Leleand Seckman, *Vice Pres*
EMP: 70
SQ FT: 58,000
SALES (est): 13.6MM **Privately Held**
WEB: www.parklanddirect.com
SIC: 2752 Commercial printing, offset

(G-5087)
PHASE II INC
Also Called: Fastsigns
14521 Forest Rd Ste G (24551-4079)
PHONE................................434 333-0808
Renae Adrian, *President*
Steve Adrian, *Vice Pres*
EMP: 5
SALES (est): 175K **Privately Held**
WEB: www.fastsigns.com
SIC: 3993 Signs & advertising specialties

(G-5088)
PRECISION PATTERNS INC
1010 Grand Oaks Dr (24551-4725)
PHONE................................434 385-4279
EMP: 8
SALES (est): 921.9K **Privately Held**
SIC: 3543 Mfg Industrial Patterns

GEOGRAPHIC

(G-5089)
RALPH RICE
Also Called: Ralph Rice Logging and Excvtg
2704 Elk Valley Rd (24551-4749)
PHONE..................................434 385-8614
Ralph Rice, *Owner*
EMP: 3
SALES (est): 142.3K **Privately Held**
SIC: 2411 Logging camps & contractors

(G-5090)
RIVER TECHNOLOGIES LLC
2107 Graves Mill Rd Ste A (24551-4293)
P.O. Box 822 (24551-0822)
PHONE..................................434 525-4734
Robert A Kozma, *COO*
Robert Cozma, *Officer*
Cheryl Ferguson,
EMP: 10
SQ FT: 1,800
SALES (est): 1.5MM **Privately Held**
WEB: www.rivertechnologies.biz
SIC: 3844 Nuclear irradiation equipment

(G-5091)
SE HOLDINGS LLC (PA)
Also Called: SIMPLIMATIC AUTOMATION
1046 W London Park Dr (24551-2164)
PHONE..................................434 385-9181
Paul McKinney, *Project Mgr*
Danny Hamilton, *Prdtn Mgr*
Woody Abbott, *Engineer*
Kamran Delavarpour, *Engineer*
Marc Keisler, *Engineer*
▲ EMP: 60
SQ FT: 50,000
SALES: 28.1MM **Privately Held**
WEB: www.simplimatic.com
SIC: 3535 Bulk handling conveyor systems

(G-5092)
SIMPLIMATIC AUTOMATION LLC
1046 W London Park Dr (24551-2164)
PHONE..................................434 385-9181
Sara Orange, *CFO*
Sabrina Carpenter, *Supervisor*
Jeremy Vaughan, *Director*
Elizabeth Dellinger, *General Counsel*
Thomas Dinardo,
EMP: 90
SQ FT: 60,000
SALES (est): 4.9MM **Privately Held**
WEB: www.simplimatic.com
SIC: 3549 3535 Assembly machines, in-
cluding robotic; conveyors & conveying
equipment
PA: Se Holdings Llc
1046 W London Park Dr
Forest VA 24551

(G-5093)
SKYBOSS DRONES LLC
1015 Helmsdale Dr (24551-4739)
PHONE..................................434 509-5028
Reinaldo Gonzalez, *Administration*
EMP: 3
SALES (est): 346.6K **Privately Held**
WEB: www.skybossdrones.com
SIC: 3721 Motorized aircraft

(G-5094)
SONYA DAVIS ENTERPRISES LLC
116 Valleywood Dr (24551-2804)
PHONE..................................703 264-0533
EMP: 2
SALES (est): 83.9K **Privately Held**
SIC: 2752 Commercial printing, litho-
graphic

(G-5095)
STAY IN TOUCH INC
1149 Vista Park Dr Ste D (24551-4685)
PHONE..................................434 239-7300
Gail Boswell, *President*
EMP: 18
SALES (est): 2.2MM **Privately Held**
WEB: www.stayintouchsystem.com
SIC: 2754 2771 Post cards, picture;
gravure printing; greeting cards

(G-5096)
STERLING BLOWER COMPANY (PA)
Also Called: Trucut Fabricators
135 Vista Centre Dr (24551-3964)
P.O. Box 2279 (24551-6279)
PHONE..................................434 316-5310
David R Snowman, *President*
Ron Pelletier, *Vice Pres*
Ronald Pelletier, *Vice Pres*
Greg Snowman, *Vice Pres*
Ron Frank, *Materials Mgr*
▲ EMP: 65
SQ FT: 60,000
SALES (est): 19.6MM **Privately Held**
WEB: www.sterlingblower.com
SIC: 3535 3559 Conveyors & conveying
equipment; recycling machinery

(G-5097)
STEVES SIGNWORX LLC
117 Vista Centre Dr Ste E (24551-2774)
PHONE..................................434 385-1000
Stephen Williams,
Richard Gilbert,
EMP: 5
SALES (est): 350K **Privately Held**
WEB: www.stevessignworx.com
SIC: 3993 Signs, not made in custom sign
painting shops

(G-5098)
STUBBORN PRESS AND COMPANY LLC
1070 Blane Dr (24551-1454)
PHONE..................................540 394-8412
EMP: 1
SALES (est): 54.1K **Privately Held**
WEB: www.stubbornpress.com
SIC: 2741 Miscellaneous publishing

(G-5099)
SUN MANUFACTURING LLC
1291 Burnbridge Rd (24551-4932)
PHONE..................................434 942-4626
Sonya Williams,
EMP: 3
SALES (est): 97.4K **Privately Held**
SIC: 3999 Manufacturing industries

(G-5100)
SYNTEC BUSINESS SYSTEMS INC
1134 Thomas Jefferson Rd (24551-2269)
PHONE..................................804 303-2864
Trevor Radke, *President*
EMP: 2
SALES (est): 178.7K **Privately Held**
WEB: www.salon-software.com
SIC: 7372 Prepackaged software

(G-5101)
TEVA PHARMACEUTICALS
2150 Perrowville Rd (24551-4129)
PHONE..................................888 838-2872
EMP: 27
SALES (est): 4.7MM **Privately Held**
WEB: www.tevagenerics.com
SIC: 2834 Pharmaceutical preparations

(G-5102)
TRIPLE S ENTERPRISES INC
Also Called: Scott's Cabinet Shop
14708 Forest Rd (24551-5000)
P.O. Box 703 (24551-0703)
PHONE..................................434 525-8400
Thomas Scott, *Corp Secy*
Clara Scott, *Admin Sec*
EMP: 17
SQ FT: 24,000
SALES (est): 1.7MM **Privately Held**
WEB: www.scottscabinet.com
SIC: 2434 Wood kitchen cabinets

(G-5103)
UTILITY ONE SOURCE FOR EQP LLC (HQ)
Also Called: Forestry Equipment of VA
12660 E Lynchburg (24551)
P.O. Box 15150, Lynchburg (24502-9015)
PHONE..................................434 525-2929
Mark B Sharman, *President*
Carla Hart, *Vice Pres*
Penny Fisher, *Purch Agent*
Nash Nicholson, *Engineer*
EMP: 69
SQ FT: 78,000
SALES (est): 33.6MM
SALES (corp-wide): 316MM **Privately Held**
WEB: www.uosforestry.com
SIC: 3537 7539 3089 Industrial trucks &
tractors; automotive repair shops; auto-
motive parts, plastic
PA: Custom Truck One Source, L.P.
7701 Independence Ave
Kansas City MO 64125
312 316-9520

(G-5104)
WEST WILLOW PUBG GROUP LLC
Also Called: Central Virginia Home Magazine
2058 Rocky Branch Dr (24551-2955)
PHONE..................................434 386-5667
Colleen Dougherty,
EMP: 2
SALES (est): 139K **Privately Held**
WEB: www.westwillowpublishing.com
SIC: 2721 Magazines: publishing only, not
printed on site

(G-5105)
WOODMSTERS CBNETS STR FIXS OF
4730 Waterlick Rd (24551-4248)
PHONE..................................434 525-4407
William Arthur Jr, *President*
Joycelyn Arthur, *Corp Secy*
Martha Arthur, *Vice Pres*
EMP: 3
SQ FT: 2,700
SALES (est): 275K **Privately Held**
SIC: 2541 Cabinets, except refrigerated:
show, display, etc.: wood

(G-5106)
WRACK-IT
103 Sailview Dr (24551-1843)
PHONE..................................434 258-4317
Tim Otis, *Principal*
EMP: 2
SALES (est): 130.1K **Privately Held**
WEB: www.wrack-it.com
SIC: 2431 Millwork

Fork Union
Fluvanna County

(G-5107)
AUSTIN POWDER COMPANY
Rr 6 (23055)
P.O. Box 74 (23055-0074)
PHONE..................................434 842-3589
John F Lamb, *Manager*
EMP: 14
SALES (corp-wide): 509.6MM **Privately Held**
WEB: www.austinpowder.com
SIC: 2892 5169 Explosives; explosives
HQ: Austin Powder Company
25800 Science Park Dr # 300
Cleveland OH 44122
216 464-2400

(G-5108)
AUTHENTIC KNITTING BOARD LLC
60 Carysbrook Rd (23055-2066)
PHONE..................................434 842-1180
Pat Novak,
▲ EMP: 4
SALES (est): 308.4K **Privately Held**
WEB: www.knittingboard.com
SIC: 3552 Knitting machines

(G-5109)
DIXIE WOODCRAFT INC
154 Red Bank Ln (23055-2047)
PHONE..................................434 842-3384
Mac Derry, *Principal*
EMP: 2
SALES (est): 137.4K **Privately Held**
SIC: 2511 Wood household furniture

(G-5110)
IN STITCHES
Rr 671 (23055)
P.O. Box 644 (23055-0644)
PHONE..................................434 842-2104
Cheryl L Falvella, *Owner*
EMP: 2
SALES (est): 75K **Privately Held**
WEB: www.in-stitches.com
SIC: 2395 Embroidery & art needlework

(G-5111)
INKLINGS INK
Also Called: Inklings Ink Screen Printing A
2053 East River Rd (23055-2059)
PHONE..................................434 842-2200
Susan Vonderbecke, *Owner*
EMP: 3 **Privately Held**
WEB: www.inklings-ink.com
SIC: 2759 7389 Screen printing; advertis-
ing, promotional & trade show services

(G-5112)
PIECES OF WOOD LLC
127 Holmhead Cir (23055-2061)
PHONE..................................434 842-3091
Fred Fhier, *Mng Member*
Hill Shainer, *Mng Member*
EMP: 1
SALES (est): 123.9K **Privately Held**
SIC: 2431 Woodwork, interior & ornamen-
tal

(G-5113)
THISTLE AND STAG MEADERY
2053 East River Rd (23055-2059)
PHONE..................................434 842-2200
EMP: 2
SALES (est): 85.9K **Privately Held**
WEB: www.thistleandstag.com
SIC: 2084 Wines

Fort Belvoir
Fairfax County

(G-5114)
DEFENSE THREAT
6200 Meade Rd (22060-5264)
PHONE..................................703 767-2798
EMP: 7
SALES (est): 543.8K **Privately Held**
WEB: www.dtra.mil
SIC: 3812 Defense systems & equipment

(G-5115)
GLOBAL INFO NETWRK SYSTEMS INC
6906 Inlet Cove Dr (22060-7433)
PHONE..................................703 409-4204
Moses B Whitlow Jr, *President*
EMP: 2
SALES (est): 114K **Privately Held**
SIC: 7372 Business oriented computer
software

(G-5116)
LEIDOS INC
8725 John J Kingman Rd # 6201
(22060-6217)
PHONE..................................703 676-7451
John Jumper, *CEO*
Lela Elliot, *Branch Mgr*
Thomas Brophy, *Manager*
Jake Prater, *Manager*
EMP: 200 **Publicly Held**
WEB: www.leidos.com
SIC: 3679 3674 7373 8742 Recording &
playback apparatus, including phono-
graph; integrated circuits, semiconductor
networks, etc.; systems engineering,
computer related; training & development
consultant
HQ: Leidos, Inc.
1750 Presidents St
Reston VA 20190
571 526-6000

(G-5117)
PINK PRESS DIOR LLC
5941 Halleck Blvd (22060-3230)
PHONE..................................703 781-0345
Shameko Johnson, *Principal*
EMP: 1 EST: 2017

SALES (est): 40.8K **Privately Held**
SIC: 2741 Miscellaneous publishing

(G-5118)
STORGE INDUSTRIES LLC
9325 Belvoir Rd (22060-8069)
PHONE..............................571 414-1413
Trilisa Burke, *Principal*
EMP: 2 **EST:** 2017
SALES (est): 66.1K **Privately Held**
SIC: 3999 Manufacturing industries

(G-5119)
UNITED STATES DEPT OF ARMY
Also Called: Army Pubg Directorate-Apd
9301 Chapek Rd Bldg 1458 (22060-5605)
PHONE..............................703 614-3727
Lanchi Tran, *Principal*
Lance Sumner, *IT/INT Sup*
EMP: 3 **Publicly Held**
WEB: www.us.army.mil
SIC: 2721 Periodicals
HQ: United States Dept Of The Army
101 Army Pentagon
Washington DC 20310

Fort Blackmore
Scott County

(G-5120)
BABB RAILROAD CONSTRUCTION
334 Taylor Town Rd (24250-3118)
P.O. Box 1312, Gate City (24251-1312)
PHONE..............................276 995-2090
Cheryl Babb, *Partner*
Denny Babb, *Partner*
EMP: 12
SQ FT: 260
SALES (est): 930K **Privately Held**
WEB: www.babbconstruction.com
SIC: 3462 Railroad, construction & mining forgings

(G-5121)
BENNY BABB
7585 Rye Cove Memorial Rd (24250-3152)
PHONE..............................276 995-2658
EMP: 2
SALES (est): 90K **Privately Held**
SIC: 3679 Electronic components

(G-5122)
JOHNNY HILLMAN LOGGING
Rr 1 (24250)
PHONE..............................276 467-2406
Johnny Hillman, *Owner*
EMP: 1
SALES (est): 116.7K **Privately Held**
SIC: 2411 Logging

(G-5123)
MICHAEL SANDERS
6841 Veterans Mem Hwy (24250-2727)
PHONE..............................276 452-2314
Michael Sanders, *Owner*
EMP: 1
SALES (est): 69.6K **Privately Held**
SIC: 2411 Logging

(G-5124)
SANDERS BROTHERS LOGGING INC
Rr 1 Box 87 (24250)
PHONE..............................276 995-2416
Edgar Sanders, *President*
EMP: 4
SALES (est): 384.7K **Privately Held**
SIC: 2411 Logging

(G-5125)
SAWYER LOGGING INC
11669 Veterans Mem Hwy (24250-2672)
PHONE..............................276 995-2522
EMP: 2
SALES (est): 89.8K **Privately Held**
SIC: 2411 Logging camps & contractors

Fort Eustis
Newport News City County

(G-5126)
DOCUMENT AUTOMATION & PRDTN
655 Williamson Ave (23604-5219)
PHONE..............................757 878-3389
Bernard Rice, *Director*
EMP: 2 **EST:** 2018
SALES (est): 83.9K **Privately Held**
SIC: 2752 Commercial printing, lithographic

(G-5127)
UNITED STATES DEPT OF ARMY
Also Called: Enterprise Multimedia Center
27502 Mcmahon St (23604-1337)
PHONE..............................757 878-4831
EMP: 5 **Publicly Held**
WEB: www.us.army.mil
SIC: 3572 Computer storage devices
HQ: United States Dept Of The Army
101 Army Pentagon
Washington DC 20310

Fort Lee
Prince George County

(G-5128)
DLA DOCUMENT SERVICES
2900 41st St (23801-1804)
PHONE..............................804 734-1791
Vicki Thurmond, *Director*
EMP: 4 **Publicly Held**
WEB: www.documentservices.dla.mil
SIC: 2752 9711 Commercial printing, lithographic; national security
HQ: Dla Document Services
5450 Carlisle Pike Bldg 9
Mechanicsburg PA 17050
717 605-2362

(G-5129)
FORCE FORGE
1803 Harrison Ct (23801-1311)
PHONE..............................804 454-5191
Andrew Farley, *Principal*
Shawn Larwson, *Principal*
EMP: 2
SALES (est): 140K **Privately Held**
SIC: 3648 Flashlights

(G-5130)
FT LEE WELCOME CENTER
500 Lee Ave (23801-1786)
PHONE..............................804 734-7488
Jamie Carson, *Editor*
EMP: 3
SALES (est): 107.5K **Privately Held**
WEB: www.fortleepresscenter.com
SIC: 2711 Newspapers

(G-5131)
GREEN TROPHY
373a Coral Sea Dr (23801-1330)
PHONE..............................619 387-6244
Rex Husband, *CEO*
EMP: 2
SALES (est): 75K **Privately Held**
SIC: 3599 Custom machinery

(G-5132)
SALLMAE LLC
542 Jackson Cir (23801-1068)
PHONE..............................931 472-9467
Sallmae Hester, *Principal*
EMP: 1
SALES (est): 75.2K **Privately Held**
WEB: www.goarmy.com
SIC: 3999 7389 Artificial flower arrangements;

Fort Monroe
Hampton City County

(G-5133)
OOZLEFINCH CRAFT BREWERY LLC
Also Called: Oozlefinch Beers & Blending
81 Patch Rd (23651-1052)
PHONE..............................757 224-7042
Russel Tinsley,
EMP: 3
SALES (est): 71K **Privately Held**
WEB: www.oozlefinchbeers.com
SIC: 2082 Malt beverages

Fort Valley
Shenandoah County

(G-5134)
ALTAR EGO PUBLICATIONS
928 Camp Roosevelt Rd (22652-3043)
PHONE..............................540 933-6530
Robert Bohm, *Principal*
EMP: 1
SALES (est): 57.1K **Privately Held**
SIC: 2741 Miscellaneous publishing

(G-5135)
NANCY STEPHENS
248 Habron Hollow Rd (22652-2730)
PHONE..............................540 933-6405
EMP: 3
SALES (est): 130K **Privately Held**
SIC: 1442 Construction Sand/Gravel

(G-5136)
VULCAN MACHINE CO
168 Cross Creek Ln (22652-2968)
PHONE..............................240 486-2685
Richard Xu, *President*
Joseph Wins, *Vice Pres*
Ashley Christopher, *Treasurer*
EMP: 3
SALES (est): 150K **Privately Held**
SIC: 3541 Numerically controlled metal cutting machine tools

Foster
Mathews County

(G-5137)
PODDERY
Rr 660 (23056)
PHONE..............................804 725-5956
Robert John Podd, *Owner*
EMP: 2
SALES (est): 100.5K **Privately Held**
WEB: www.thepoddery.com
SIC: 3269 Figures: pottery, china, earthenware & stoneware

Franklin
Franklin City County

(G-5138)
ALPHABET SOUP
111 E 2nd Ave (23851-1709)
PHONE..............................757 569-0110
Gerri Patnesky, *Owner*
EMP: 3
SQ FT: 675
SALES (est): 201.3K **Privately Held**
WEB: www.abcsoupva.com
SIC: 2395 5947 Embroidery products, except schiffli machine; gift shop

(G-5139)
BAR LOGGING LLC
22373 Sedley Rd (23851-3859)
PHONE..............................757 641-9269
Charles B Rowe, *Administration*
EMP: 3 **EST:** 2009
SALES (est): 204.3K **Privately Held**
SIC: 2411 Logging

(G-5140)
CARAUSTAR INDUSTRIAL AND CON
Also Called: Franklin, VA Tube Plant
1601 Carrsville Hwy (23851-3920)
PHONE..............................757 562-0345
Jeff Hemingway, *Branch Mgr*
EMP: 11
SALES (corp-wide): 4.6B **Publicly Held**
WEB: www.greif.com
SIC: 2655 Fiber spools, tubes & cones
HQ: Caraustar Industrial And Consumer Products Group Inc
5000 Austell Powder Ste
Austell GA 30106
803 548-5100

(G-5141)
DARDEN LOGGING LLC
19483 Drake Rd (23851-3749)
PHONE..............................757 647-9432
Phillip Darden, *Mng Member*
EMP: 6 **EST:** 2013
SALES (est): 563.6K **Privately Held**
SIC: 2411 Logging

(G-5142)
ENVIVA PELLETS SOUTHAMPTON LLC
26570 Rose Valley Rd (23851-5127)
PHONE..............................301 657-5560
John K Keppler, *CEO*
Sarah Gray, *Controller*
▲ **EMP:** 1
SALES (est): 120K **Publicly Held**
WEB: www.envivabiomass.com
SIC: 2421 Wood chips, produced at mill
PA: Enviva Partners, Lp
7200 Wscnsin Ave Ste 1000
Bethesda MD 20814
301 657-5560

(G-5143)
ERNEST BELTRAMI SR
31163 Beltrami Dr (23851-4912)
PHONE..............................757 516-8581
Ernest Beltrami Sr, *Principal*
EMP: 2
SALES (est): 160.4K **Privately Held**
SIC: 1311 Crude petroleum production

(G-5144)
FRANKLINE PAPER
34040 Union Camp Dr (23851-1575)
PHONE..............................757 569-4321
EMP: 1
SALES (est): 116.2K **Privately Held**
SIC: 2621 Paper mills

(G-5145)
INSIGHTS INTL HOLDINGS LLC
Also Called: Nantrak Industries
601 N Mechanic St Ste 414 (23851-1455)
PHONE..............................757 333-1291
Evan Parker,
EMP: 1 **EST:** 2010
SALES (est): 113.9K **Privately Held**
WEB: www.nantrak.com
SIC: 3949 Archery equipment, general; arrows, archery

(G-5146)
INTERNATIONAL PAPER COMPANY
34040 Union Camp Dr (23851-1575)
P.O. Box 178 (23851-0178)
PHONE..............................757 569-4321
Jeannine Siemdida, *Principal*
Tim Lass, *Manager*
Jennifer Railey, *Manager*
Linda Burkett, *Info Tech Mgr*
Stephen Lassiter, *Maintence Staff*
EMP: 140
SALES (corp-wide): 22.3B **Publicly Held**
WEB: www.internationalpaper.com
SIC: 2621 Paper mills
PA: International Paper Company
6400 Poplar Ave
Memphis TN 38197
901 419-9000

(G-5147)
KIMYAEASONWOOD
31030 Walters Hwy (23851-4065)
PHONE..............................757 502-5001

Kimya Wood, *Owner*
EMP: 1
SALES (est): 44.5K **Privately Held**
SIC: 3953 Seal presses, notary & hand

(G-5148)
LEGACY VULCAN CORP
Also Called: Franklin Yard
2001 Whitley Ln Ste B (23851-3910)
PHONE..................................757 562-5008
Fax: 757 562-7604
EMP: 2
SALES (corp-wide): 2.9B **Publicly Held**
SIC: 1442 Construction Sand/Gravel
HQ: Legacy Vulcan, Llc
　　1200 Urban Center Dr
　　Vestavia AL 35242
　　205 298-3000

(G-5149)
MOSENA ENTERPRISES INC
26460 Smiths Ferry Rd (23851-5102)
P.O. Box 175 (23851-0175)
PHONE..................................757 562-7033
Richard L Mosena, *President*
Dawn Mosena, *Admin Sec*
EMP: 5
SALES (est): 662.8K **Privately Held**
WEB: www.mosena.com
SIC: 3582 5087 3537 5084 Commercial
laundry equipment; laundry & dry clean-
ing equipment & supplies; forklift trucks;
lift trucks & parts; construction machinery;
construction & mining machinery

(G-5150)
NANTRAK TACTICAL LLC
601 N Mechanic St Ste 414 (23851-1455)
PHONE..................................757 517-2226
Evan Parker, *President*
EMP: 5
SQ FT: 800
SALES (est): 175K **Privately Held**
SIC: 3482 Small arms ammunition

(G-5151)
**OLD VIRGINIA MOLDING &
MLLWK**
100 W Jackson St (23851-1428)
PHONE..................................757 516-9055
Tomlin Cobb, *President*
Karen Cobb, *Vice Pres*
EMP: 2 **EST:** 1997
SALES (est): 220.9K **Privately Held**
WEB: www.oldevirginiamoulding.com
SIC: 2431 Millwork

(G-5152)
OLDE VIRGINIA MOULDING
100 W Jackson St (23851-1428)
PHONE..................................757 516-9055
Karen Cabb, *Owner*
EMP: 2
SALES (est): 182.6K **Privately Held**
WEB: www.oldevirginiamoulding.com
SIC: 2431 Millwork

(G-5153)
PB CRAVE OF NC LLC
32126 General Thomas Hwy (23851-5146)
PHONE..................................252 585-1744
EMP: 5
SALES (corp-wide): 1.1B **Privately Held**
WEB: www.pbcrave.com
SIC: 2099 Peanut butter
HQ: Pb Crave Of Nc, Llc
　　413 Main St
　　Severn NC 27877
　　252 585-1744

(G-5154)
PLASTICLAD LLC (PA)
131 Sachs Ave (23851-2411)
PHONE..................................757 562-5550
Michael W Tinder,
▲ **EMP:** 4
SALES (est): 972.5K **Privately Held**
WEB: www.plasticlad.com
SIC: 2821 Plastics materials & resins

(G-5155)
SHEET METAL PRODUCTS INC
2397 Carrsville Hwy (23851-4007)
P.O. Box 299 (23851-0299)
PHONE..................................757 562-1986
Edward Spivey, *President*

EMP: 18
SQ FT: 30,000
SALES (est): 1.8MM **Privately Held**
WEB: www.smphvac.com
SIC: 3444 Sheet metal specialties, not
stamped

(G-5156)
ST TISSUE LLC
34050 Union Camp Dr (23851-1575)
PHONE..................................757 304-5040
Sharad Tak, *CEO*
James Drewry, *Purchasing*
Jim Drewry, *Purchasing*
Mahendran Venkatachalam, *Purchasing*
Susan Hudgins, *Admin Asst*
EMP: 37 **EST:** 2012
SALES (est): 13.5MM **Privately Held**
WEB: www.stpaperllc.com
SIC: 2621 Towels, tissues & napkins:
paper & stock

(G-5157)
STEPHEN C MARSTON
Also Called: Midway Coatings Service
401 East St (23851-1405)
PHONE..................................757 562-0271
Stephen C Marston, *Owner*
Kim Ricks, *Sales Staff*
Janet Marston, *Office Mgr*
EMP: 4
SQ FT: 3,000
SALES (est): 262.2K **Privately Held**
SIC: 3479 Coating of metals & formed
products

(G-5158)
**TIDE WATER PULICATION LLC
(PA)**
Also Called: Tidewater News, The
1000 Armory Dr (23851-1852)
P.O. Box 497 (23851-0497)
PHONE..................................757 562-3187
Madden Cain, *Creative Dir*
Steve Stewart,
▲ **EMP:** 30 **EST:** 1905
SQ FT: 16,000
SALES (est): 6.1MM **Privately Held**
WEB: www.tidewaternews.com
SIC: 2711 Newspapers: publishing only,
not printed on site

(G-5159)
TIPS EAST LLC
Also Called: Domino's
1100 Armory Dr Ste 162 (23851-2460)
PHONE..................................757 562-7888
David Hess,
EMP: 79
SQ FT: 1,400
SALES (corp-wide): 7.4MM **Privately
Held**
WEB: www.dominos.com
SIC: 2099 Food preparations
PA: Tips East Llc
　　2010 Old Greenbrier Rd
　　Chesapeake VA 23320
　　720 202-0931

(G-5160)
UPON A ONCE STITCH LLC
35041 Lees Mill Rd (23851-3941)
PHONE..................................757 562-1900
Amy Baird, *Principal*
EMP: 1 **EST:** 2013
SALES (est): 49.9K **Privately Held**
SIC: 2395 Embroidery & art needlework

(G-5161)
VICS SIGNS & ENGRAVING
Also Called: Vic's Sign & Engraving
107 W 4th Ave (23851-1731)
PHONE..................................757 562-2243
Victor Story, *Owner*
EMP: 1
SQ FT: 15,000
SALES (est): 100K **Privately Held**
WEB: www.downtownfranklinva.org
SIC: 3993 Signs & advertising specialties

(G-5162)
WOODWORKS LLC
30443 Campbells Run (23851-5008)
PHONE..................................757 516-8405
Kenneth Behnken, *Owner*
EMP: 2

SALES (est): 156.7K **Privately Held**
SIC: 2431 Millwork

(G-5163)
WRITE LAB PRESS LLC
621 Pace St (23851-1905)
PHONE..................................757 390-1030
EMP: 1 **EST:** 2018
SALES (est): 37.5K **Privately Held**
SIC: 2741 Miscellaneous publishing

Franktown
Northampton County

(G-5164)
MERCURY PARTNERS USA LLC
Also Called: Mercury USA
6404 Holly Bluff Dr (23354)
PHONE..................................757 652-7067
Jonathan Bess,
EMP: 1
SALES (est): 39.9K **Privately Held**
SIC: 2711 8742 7371 7373 Newspapers;
management consulting services; custom
computer programming services; com-
puter integrated systems design; com-
puter facilities management; computer
related services

(G-5165)
NORTHAMPTON HOUSE PRE
7018 Wild Flower Ln (23354-2504)
PHONE..................................201 893-1826
EMP: 1 **EST:** 2018
SALES (est): 37.5K **Privately Held**
SIC: 2741 Miscellaneous publishing

Fredericksburg
*Fredericksburg City
County*

(G-5166)
2 HEARTS 1 DRESS LLC
614 Caroline St (22401-5902)
PHONE..................................540 300-0655
Stacey Thomas, *Principal*
EMP: 2 **EST:** 2016
SALES (est): 67K **Privately Held**
WEB: www.2hearts1dress.com
SIC: 2339 5621 Maternity clothing; mater-
nity wear; ready-to-wear apparel,
women's

(G-5167)
**ACUITY TECH HOLDG CO LLC
(PA)**
1191 Central Park Blvd (22401-4918)
PHONE..................................410 290-1411
Thomas Callahan III, *CEO*
Thomas Campbell, *Ch of Bd*
Lawrence Swift, *CFO*
Douglas Lake Jr, *Treasurer*
Teresa Dady, *Admin Sec*
EMP: 7
SALES (est): 12.8MM **Privately Held**
SIC: 3825 8711 Instruments to measure
electricity; engineering services

(G-5168)
**ADVANCE MEZZANINE
SYSTEMS LLC**
Also Called: AMS
1320 Alum Spring Rd (22401-7002)
PHONE..................................703 595-1460
EMP: 4
SALES: 381.9K **Privately Held**
SIC: 3441 Fabricated Structural Metal

(G-5169)
AIR TIGHT DUCT SYSTEMS INC
451 Central Rd Ste C (22401-7097)
PHONE..................................540 361-7888
David Robertson Jr, *President*
Terri Robertson, *General Mgr*
EMP: 5 **EST:** 2005
SALES (est): 340.3K **Privately Held**
SIC: 3444 Sheet metal specialties, not
stamped

(G-5170)
ARTISTEES
513 Jackson St (22401-5716)
PHONE..................................540 373-2888
EMP: 2 **EST:** 2009
SALES (est): 99.8K **Privately Held**
SIC: 2759 Screen printing

(G-5171)
ASPETTO INC
1691 Jefferson Davis Hwy (22401-4651)
PHONE..................................540 547-8487
Abbas Haider, *President*
Robert Davis, *COO*
EMP: 4
SALES (est): 602.5K **Privately Held**
WEB: www.aspetto.com
SIC: 2329 5699 8748 5049 Shirt & slack
suits: men's, youths' & boys'; military
goods & regalia; shirts, custom made;
systems engineering consultant, ex. com-
puter or professional; law enforcement
equipment & supplies

(G-5172)
BE READY ENTERPRISES LLC
Also Called: Be Ready Tactical
612 Lafayette Blvd # 200 (22401-6088)
P.O. Box 868, Spotsylvania (22553-0868)
PHONE..................................540 422-9210
Daniel Hinkson, *President*
EMP: 2
SQ FT: 200
SALES (est): 179.2K **Privately Held**
WEB: www.bereadytactical.com
SIC: 3484 8322 Guns (firearms) or gun
parts, 30 mm. & below; disaster service

(G-5173)
BENCHMARK DOORS
Also Called: General Products
310 Central Rd Ste 1 (22401-7092)
PHONE..................................540 898-5700
Bill Henshaw, *President*
Charles G McDaniels, *Admin Sec*
EMP: 385 **EST:** 1945
SQ FT: 16,600
SALES (est): 44.6MM **Privately Held**
WEB: www.mckcompany.com
SIC: 3442 3444 Garage doors, overhead:
metal; flues & pipes, stove or furnace:
sheet metal

(G-5174)
BOTANICA
811 Lafayette Blvd (22401-5614)
PHONE..................................540 899-5590
EMP: 1
SALES (est): 6.8K **Privately Held**
SIC: 2833 Mfg Medicinal/Botanical Prod-
ucts

(G-5175)
BREEZE-EASTERN LLC
1671 Jefferson Davis Hwy # 107
(22401-4684)
PHONE..................................973 602-1001
Brad Repp, *Branch Mgr*
EMP: 5
SALES (corp-wide): 5.1B **Publicly Held**
WEB: www.breeze-eastern.com
SIC: 3563 3531 3728 Air & gas compres-
sors including vacuum pumps; winches;
aircraft armament, except guns
HQ: Breeze-Eastern Llc
　　35 Melanie Ln
　　Whippany NJ 07981
　　973 602-1001

(G-5176)
CARICO INC
1300 Belman Rd (22401-7077)
PHONE..................................540 373-5983
Carey C Leitch, *President*
EMP: 28
SQ FT: 15,000
SALES (est): 4.2MM **Privately Held**
WEB: www.caricoinc.com
SIC: 3441 3446 3448 1799 Fabricated
structural metal; architectural metalwork;
sheet metalwork; welding on site

(G-5177)
CHERRY HILL CABINETRY (PA)
1320 Cntl Pk Blvd Ste 108 (22401)
PHONE..................................540 785-4333

▲ = Import ▼=Export
◆ =Import/Export

Pennie Ross, *Client Mgr*
Meredith Wearing, *Client Mgr*
EMP: 8 **EST:** 2010
SALES (est): 1MM **Privately Held**
WEB: www.cherryhillcabinetry.com
SIC: 2434 Wood kitchen cabinets

(G-5178)
CHRISTOPHER HAWKINS
Also Called: All American Mobility
1273 Central Park Blvd (22401-4912)
PHONE..............................540 361-1679
Christopher Hawkins, *Owner*
EMP: 8
SALES (est): 315.1K **Privately Held**
WEB: www.allamericanmobility.com
SIC: 3448 3534 5999 3999 Ramps: pre-fabricated metal; stair elevators, motor powered; wheelchair lifts; wheelchair lifts

(G-5179)
CLASSICO PUBLISHING LLC
119 Huntington Hills Ln (22401-5180)
PHONE..............................540 310-0067
Marianne Carey, *Principal*
EMP: 2 **EST:** 2011
SALES (est): 103.1K **Privately Held**
SIC: 2741 Miscellaneous publishing

(G-5180)
CROCHET BRAIDS BY TWANA LLC
1313 Walker Dr (22401-2629)
PHONE..............................571 201-7190
Twana Whitties, *Principal*
EMP: 2
SALES (est): 88.8K **Privately Held**
WEB: www.crochetbraidsbytwana.com
SIC: 2399 Hand woven & crocheted products

(G-5181)
CSL MEDIA LLC
2366 Plank Rd (22401-4900)
PHONE..............................540 785-3790
Phil Leonhardt, *Info Tech Mgr*
Phillip Leonhardt,
EMP: 1
SALES (est): 120K **Privately Held**
WEB: www.cslmediallc.com
SIC: 2752 2759 Commercial printing, off-set; post cards, picture: printing; promotional printing

(G-5182)
CURIOUS COMPASS LLC
1009 Hotchkiss Pl (22401-8404)
PHONE..............................540 735-5013
Carl Lawson Jr, *Owner*
EMP: 3
SALES (est): 100K **Privately Held**
WEB: www.curiouscompasses.com
SIC: 7372 Application computer software

(G-5183)
DOWLING SIGNS INC
1801 Princess Anne St (22401-3544)
P.O. Box 7125 (22404-7125)
PHONE..............................540 373-6675
Allen Malocha, *President*
Jane Malocha, *Treasurer*
EMP: 25 **EST:** 1936
SQ FT: 13,600
SALES (est): 2.9MM **Privately Held**
WEB: www.dowlingsignsinc.com
SIC: 3993 1799 Neon signs; electric signs; signs, not made in custom sign painting shops; sign installation & maintenance

(G-5184)
DOWNTOWN WRITING AND PRESS
1102 Prince Edward St (22401-3834)
PHONE..............................540 907-9732
Susan Morgan, *Administration*
EMP: 1
SALES (est): 43.3K **Privately Held**
WEB: www.downtownwritingandpress.com
SIC: 2741 Miscellaneous publishing

(G-5185)
FIVES N AMERCN COMBUSTN INC
2217 Princess Anne St 329-1 (22401-3353)
PHONE..............................540 735-8052
Steve Pope, *Branch Mgr*
EMP: 4
SALES (corp-wide): 2.1MM **Privately Held**
WEB: www.combustion.fivesgroup.com
SIC: 3433 Heating equipment, except electric
HQ: Fives North American Combustion, Inc.
4455 E 71st St
Cleveland OH 44105
216 271-6000

(G-5186)
FORSTLE LLC
1210 Walker Dr (22401-2622)
PHONE..............................540 424-6879
EMP: 1
SALES (est): 42.9K **Privately Held**
WEB: www.forstle.com
SIC: 2731 Book publishing

(G-5187)
FRASER WOOD ELEMENTS LLC
1023 Caroline St (22401-3813)
PHONE..............................540 373-0853
David Fraser, *Principal*
EMP: 5
SALES (est): 887.9K **Privately Held**
WEB: www.fraserwoodelements.com
SIC: 2819 Industrial inorganic chemicals

(G-5188)
FRED GOOD TIMES LLC
2011 Princess Anne St # 103 (22401-3456)
PHONE..............................540 372-7247
Kyle Matthew, *Principal*
EMP: 4
SALES (est): 101.4K **Privately Held**
WEB: www.fredgoodwill.org
SIC: 2711 Newspapers, publishing & printing

(G-5189)
FREDERICKSBURG MCH & STL LLC
2202 Airport Ave (22401-7220)
PHONE..............................540 373-7957
Luke Breivik, *Opers Mgr*
Don Breivik,
EMP: 8 **EST:** 1947
SQ FT: 8,000
SALES (est): 2MM **Privately Held**
WEB: www.fredericksburgmachine.com
SIC: 3599 3441 Machine shop, jobbing & repair; building components, structural steel

(G-5190)
FREE LANCE-STAR PUBLSHNG CO OF
Also Called: Free-Lance Star
1340 Cntl Pk Blvd Ste 100 (22401)
PHONE..............................540 374-5000
Dimitri Korvyakov, *Mng Member*
Gene M Carr,
EMP: 303
SALES (est): 34MM
SALES (corp-wide): 254.6B **Publicly Held**
WEB: www.freelancestar.com
SIC: 2711 4832 Newspapers: publishing only, not printed on site; radio broadcasting stations
HQ: Bh Media Group, Inc.
1314 Douglas St Ste 1500
Omaha NE 68102
402 444-1000

(G-5191)
FYLLO LLC
402 Hanover St (22401-5937)
PHONE..............................540 846-6441
Jonathan Mozena, *Principal*
EMP: 2
SALES (est): 56.5K **Privately Held**
SIC: 7372 Prepackaged software

(G-5192)
GOODLOE ASPHAULT LLC
102 Fauquier St (22401-3710)
PHONE..............................540 373-5863
Lucy Harman, *President*
EMP: 5
SALES (est): 558.7K **Privately Held**
SIC: 2951 Asphalt paving mixtures & blocks

(G-5193)
HAMS DOWN INC
2007 Plank Rd (22401-5103)
PHONE..............................540 374-1405
EMP: 6 **EST:** 2010
SALES (est): 469.9K **Privately Held**
SIC: 2013 Prepared pork products from purchased pork

(G-5194)
HARKNESS HALL LTD
10 Harkness Blvd (22401-7085)
PHONE..............................540 370-1590
Dennis Pacelli, *VP Sales*
Davis Burklinson, *Branch Mgr*
EMP: 8 **Privately Held**
WEB: www.harkness-screens.com
SIC: 3861 Photographic equipment & supplies
HQ: Harkness Screens (Uk) Limited
Unit A
Stevenage HERTS SG1 2

(G-5195)
HDT EXPEDITIONARY SYSTEMS INC
415 Wolfe St (22401-5947)
PHONE..............................540 373-1435
EMP: 1 **EST:** 2016
SALES (est): 65.9K **Privately Held**
SIC: 2394 2393 Mfg Canvas/Related Products Mfg Textile Bags
HQ: Hdt Expeditionary Systems, Inc.
30500 Aurora Rd Ste 100
Solon OH 44139
216 438-6111

(G-5196)
HOGUE
210 Amaret St (22401-3202)
PHONE..............................540 374-1144
R Hogue, *Principal*
EMP: 4
SALES (est): 367.3K **Privately Held**
SIC: 2389 Clergymen's vestments

(G-5197)
ITS JUST FURNITURE INC
1285 Central Park Blvd (22401-4912)
PHONE..............................703 357-6405
John Paul Wilder, *President*
EMP: 3
SQ FT: 1,500
SALES (est): 165.8K **Privately Held**
SIC: 2531 2521 5021 Public building & related furniture; wood office furniture; office & public building furniture; office furniture

(G-5198)
KAPOK PRESS LLC
1712 Augustine Ave (22401-4604)
PHONE..............................540 372-2033
Kristin Krill, *Principal*
EMP: 2
SALES (est): 106.6K **Privately Held**
SIC: 2741 Miscellaneous publishing

(G-5199)
KAYDEE PUPPETS
620 Wolfe St (22401-5736)
PHONE..............................804 347-6636
Lori Faris, *Principal*
EMP: 2
SALES (est): 86.1K **Privately Held**
WEB: www.kaydeepuppets.com
SIC: 3999 Furs

(G-5200)
KINGS MOBILE WELDING & FABRIC
446 Hanson Ave (22401-3167)
PHONE..............................571 620-4665
Lee King,
EMP: 1

SALES (est): 36.9K **Privately Held**
SIC: 7692 Welding repair

(G-5201)
LIBRARY CONSERVATION SERVICES
1431 Franklin St (22401-4503)
PHONE..............................540 372-9661
Ethel Hellman, *Owner*
EMP: 1
SALES (est): 60.9K **Privately Held**
SIC: 2789 Bookbinding & related work

(G-5202)
M-J PRINTERS INC
502 Kenmore Ave (22401-5741)
P.O. Box 681 (22404-0681)
PHONE..............................540 373-1878
John C Thomas, *President*
Mike Buckingham, *General Mgr*
Thomas Marie Antoinette, *Vice Pres*
EMP: 5 **EST:** 1961
SQ FT: 3,000
SALES (est): 200K **Privately Held**
SIC: 2752 2759 Commercial printing, off-set; letterpress printing

(G-5203)
MAXPCI LLC
1107 Walker Dr (22401-2625)
PHONE..............................703 565-3400
Susie Maxwell, *Director*
EMP: 3
SALES (est): 149K **Privately Held**
WEB: www.maxpcicomply.com
SIC: 7372 Prepackaged software

(G-5204)
MCA SYSTEMS INC
Also Called: Codehero
810 Caroline St Ste 202 (22401-5806)
PHONE..............................540 684-1617
G Szlyk, *President*
Gregory Szlyk, *President*
Don Carlton Forrester Jr, *Shareholder*
Richard Szlyk, *Shareholder*
EMP: 8
SALES (est): 623.9K **Privately Held**
WEB: www.mcasystemsllc.com
SIC: 7372 Application computer software

(G-5205)
MCGUFFIE HISTORY PUBLICATIONS
207 Pitt St (22401-3626)
P.O. Box 7812 (22404-7812)
PHONE..............................540 371-3659
Rebecca Light, *Principal*
EMP: 3
SALES (est): 76.2K **Privately Held**
SIC: 2711 Newspapers

(G-5206)
MERCER VAULT CO
1100 Summit St (22401-7033)
P.O. Box 636 (22404-0636)
PHONE..............................540 371-3666
James W Mercer Sr, *President*
Billie Lynn Mercer, *Corp Secy*
James W Mercer Jr, *Vice Pres*
Lynn Mercer, *Treasurer*
EMP: 7
SQ FT: 4,000
SALES (est): 1.1MM **Privately Held**
SIC: 3272 1799 Burial vaults, concrete or precast terrazzo; grave excavation

(G-5207)
MIRACLE PRINTS & MORE
1205 Graham Dr (22401-2687)
PHONE..............................540 656-9645
Breanna Holmes, *Principal*
EMP: 2 **EST:** 2018
SALES (est): 83.9K **Privately Held**
SIC: 2752 Commercial printing, lithographic

(G-5208)
NORFLEET ACQUISITION CO INC
105 Central Rd (22401-7003)
P.O. Box 743 (22404-0743)
PHONE..............................540 373-9481
Julia L Gross, *President*
EMP: 18

SQ FT: 10,000
SALES (est): 2.2MM **Privately Held**
SIC: 2499 Mulch, wood & bark

(G-5209)
NORFLEET QUALITY LLC
103 Central Rd (22401-7003)
PHONE..................................540 373-9481
Mark Palchak,
EMP: 6
SALES (est): 73.5K **Privately Held**
WEB: www.norfleetquality.com
SIC: 2499 Mulch or sawdust products,
wood

(G-5210)
ORACLE HEART & VASCULAR INC
1300 Hospital Dr Ste 302 (22401-8451)
PHONE..................................855 739-9953
Anna Czajka, *Vice Pres*
EMP: 3
SALES (est): 68.4K **Privately Held**
WEB: www.magnusheart.com
SIC: 7372 Prepackaged software

(G-5211)
PALLADION SOFTWARE
20 Pawnee Dr (22401-1111)
PHONE..................................540 429-0999
Tres Seaver, *Principal*
EMP: 2
SALES (est): 56.5K **Privately Held**
SIC: 7372 Prepackaged software

(G-5212)
PARTS MANUFACTURING VIRGINIA
1125 Summit St (22401-7032)
PHONE..................................540 845-3289
Emily L Terrill, *Principal*
EMP: 3
SALES (est): 100K **Privately Held**
WEB:
www.partsmanufacturingofvirginia.com
SIC: 3599 Machine shop, jobbing & repair

(G-5213)
PITTS AUTO PARTS INC (PA)
Also Called: Lane Auto Parts
316 Forbes St (22401-3152)
PHONE..................................540 373-3720
William E Pitts, *President*
Janet Pitts, *Corp Secy*
EMP: 16
SQ FT: 7,500
SALES (est): 325K **Privately Held**
SIC: 3599 5013 Machine shop, jobbing &
repair; automotive supplies & parts

(G-5214)
PROTOLAB INC
1511 Keeneland Rd (22401-5262)
PHONE..................................703 622-1889
Henry Wayne Gardner, *President*
EMP: 7
SQ FT: 2,800
SALES (est): 2MM
SALES (corp-wide): 2.6MM **Privately Held**
SIC: 3711 Military motor vehicle assembly
PA: Protolab Oy
Martinkylantie 52
Vantaa 01720
405 504-022

(G-5215)
PULP USA LLC
1312 Stafford Ave (22401-5344)
PHONE..................................540 907-0093
James Noll, *Principal*
EMP: 2
SALES (est): 77.6K **Privately Held**
SIC: 2741 Miscellaneous publishing

(G-5216)
QRC LLC (HQ)
Also Called: Qrc Technologies
1191 Central Park Blvd (22401-4918)
PHONE..................................540 446-2270
Larry Swift, *CEO*
Jeff Lazzuri, *Exec VP*
Nick Ortyl, *Vice Pres*
Michael Kovit, *Production*
Timothy Payne, *Production*

EMP: 38
SQ FT: 9,500
SALES (est): 8.5MM **Publicly Held**
WEB: www.qrctech.com
SIC: 3699 8711 Electrical equipment &
supplies; engineering services
PA: The Parsons Corporation
5875 Trinity Pkwy Ste 300
Centreville VA 20120
703 988-8500

(G-5217)
RAMBLETYPE LLC
500 Lafayette Blvd # 228 (22401-6070)
PHONE..................................540 440-1218
Christopher Muldrow,
Tamara Muldrow,
EMP: 2 EST: 2013
SALES (est): 121K **Privately Held**
WEB: www.rambletype.com
SIC: 2741 4841 Miscellaneous publishing;
cable & other pay television services

(G-5218)
RED STAR GLASS INC
Also Called: Red Star Construction
317 Bridgewater St (22401-3301)
PHONE..................................540 899-5779
EMP: 5
SALES (est): 240K **Privately Held**
SIC: 3231 Mfg Products-Purchased Glass

(G-5219)
RESCUE ME CLEANING SERVICE
106 Springwood Dr (22401-7027)
PHONE..................................540 370-0844
Terri Lopez, *Owner*
EMP: 1
SALES (est): 45.4K **Privately Held**
SIC: 2842 Specialty cleaning preparations

(G-5220)
SAVORY SUN VA LLC
242 Hillcrest Dr (22401-4010)
PHONE..................................540 898-0851
Kenneth E Brown, *Mng Member*
EMP: 20
SALES (est): 1.1MM **Privately Held**
SIC: 2023 2834 Dietary supplements,
dairy & non-dairy based; pharmaceutical
preparations

(G-5221)
SCENTER OF TOWN LLC
907 Charles St (22401-5809)
PHONE..................................540 372-4145
Susan R Wollam, *Administration*
EMP: 3
SALES (est): 308.8K **Privately Held**
WEB: www.thescenteroftown.com
SIC: 2911 Aromatic chemical products

(G-5222)
SHH STMLTING HEALTHY HAIR LLC
1889 C D Silver Pkwy 7 (22401)
PHONE..................................973 607-7138
Delia Fulcher, *Owner*
EMP: 1
SALES (est): 51.3K **Privately Held**
SIC: 3842 Prosthetic appliances

(G-5223)
SIGN CREATIONS LLC
1317 Alum Spring Rd (22401-7001)
PHONE..................................540 899-9555
Paul Gardner,
EMP: 1
SALES (est): 149.7K **Privately Held**
SIC: 3993 Signs, not made in custom sign
painting shops

(G-5224)
SIGN ENTERPRISE INC
1317 Alum Spring Rd (22401-7001)
PHONE..................................540 899-9555
Paul Gardner, *Principal*
Laurie Price, *Finance Mgr*
EMP: 6
SQ FT: 1,500

SALES (est): 630.9K **Privately Held**
WEB: www.signenterprise.com
SIC: 3993 3231 Electric signs; neon signs;
letters for signs, metal; reflector glass
beads, for highway signs or reflectors

(G-5225)
SOPHIA STREET STUDIO
1104 Sophia St (22401-3812)
PHONE..................................540 372-3459
Phillip V Chapman Trista, *Owner*
Trista Chapman, *Owner*
EMP: 1
SQ FT: 3,750
SALES (est): 42K **Privately Held**
WEB: www.sophiastreetstudios.com
SIC: 3269 5719 Pottery cooking & kitchen
articles; pottery

(G-5226)
SOUTHLAND LOG HOMES INC
1465 Carl D Silver Pkwy (22401-4922)
PHONE..................................540 548-1617
EMP: 2
SALES (corp-wide): 60MM **Privately Held**
WEB: www.southlandloghomes.com
SIC: 2452 Log cabins, prefabricated, wood
PA: Southland Log Homes, Inc.
7521 Broad River Rd
Irmo SC 29063
803 781-5100

(G-5227)
STAFFORD STONE WORKS LLC
1500 Howard Ave (22401-7230)
P.O. Box 698 (22404-0698)
PHONE..................................540 372-6601
Jennifer Sisco, *Manager*
Jesse V Hawthorne,
Jesse Hawthorne,
EMP: 23
SALES (est): 3.5MM **Privately Held**
WEB: www.staffordstoneworks.com
SIC: 3272 Cast stone, concrete

(G-5228)
SUGPIAT DEFENSE LLC
1320 Cntl Pk Blvd Ste 200 (22401)
PHONE..................................540 623-3626
Michael Bradshaw, *Mng Member*
EMP: 1 EST: 2018
SALES (est): 50.7K **Privately Held**
SIC: 3812 Defense systems & equipment

(G-5229)
SUPERSEAL CORP
313 Central Rd (22401-7007)
PHONE..................................540 645-1408
Michael P Shanks, *Office Mgr*
EMP: 4
SALES (est): 320.4K **Privately Held**
WEB: www.supersealofva.com
SIC: 3089 Injection molding of plastics

(G-5230)
TASTE OIL VINEGAR SPICE
815 Caroline St (22401-5805)
PHONE..................................540 373-1262
EMP: 3
SALES (est): 212.6K **Privately Held**
WEB: www.tasteovs.com
SIC: 2079 Olive oil

(G-5231)
TAYSTEESMOBILEFOODCOMPANY
905 Myrick St (22401-7128)
PHONE..................................240 310-6767
EMP: 2
SALES (est): 79K **Privately Held**
SIC: 2759 Screen printing

(G-5232)
VIRGINIA ARCHTECTURAL MTLS LLC
2202 Airport Ave (22401-7220)
PHONE..................................540 710-7701
Mike Rodrigue,
Betsy Rodrigue,
EMP: 7
SALES (est): 843K **Privately Held**
WEB: www.vametals.com
SIC: 3446 Ornamental metalwork

(G-5233)
VIRGINIA SEMICONDUCTOR INC
1501 Powhatan St (22401-4647)
PHONE..................................540 373-2900
Thomas G Digges Jr, *CEO*
Lana Ingram, *Vice Pres*
Lana I Digges, *Vice Pres*
John Langman, *Engineer*
Robert H Digges, *Admin Sec*
EMP: 40
SQ FT: 8,000
SALES (est): 7.3MM **Privately Held**
WEB: www.virginiasemi.com
SIC: 3339 3679 3674 Silicon refining (pri-
mary, over 99% pure); crystals & crystal
assemblies, radio; electronic circuits;
semiconductors & related devices

(G-5234)
VIRGINIA WINE PASS LLC
600 Princess Anne St (22404-1401)
PHONE..................................540 376-7902
EMP: 2
SALES (est): 108.5K **Privately Held**
WEB: www.virginiawinepass.com
SIC: 2084 Wines

(G-5235)
WEGNER METAL ARTS INC
Also Called: Ocean Bronze
520 Wolfe St (22401-5766)
P.O. Box 7861 (22404-7861)
PHONE..................................540 373-5662
Steven Wegner, *President*
Jane Wegner, *Corp Secy*
Stewart Wegner, *Vice Pres*
EMP: 6
SQ FT: 10,000
SALES (est): 872.7K **Privately Held**
WEB: www.worksbywegner.com
SIC: 3364 Brass & bronze die-castings

(G-5236)
WHITE PACKING CO INC-VA (PA)
1965 Jefferson Davis Hwy (22401-6213)
P.O. Box 7067 (22404-7067)
PHONE..................................540 373-9883
Karl White, *President*
Kris White, *Admin Sec*
EMP: 120
SQ FT: 60,000
SALES (est): 9.3MM **Privately Held**
SIC: 2013 2011 Bacon, side & sliced; from
purchased meat; meat packing plants

(G-5237)
WILLIAM O WILLS OD
1823 Charles St (22401-3530)
PHONE..................................540 371-9191
William O Wills Od, *President*
William O Wills, *President*
Joelle Wills, *Vice Pres*
EMP: 10 EST: 1971
SQ FT: 1,000
SALES (est): 730K **Privately Held**
WEB: www.williamwillsod.com
SIC: 3851 5048 8042 Lenses, oph-
thalmic; contact lenses; offices & clinics of
optometrists

(G-5238)
WM L MASON FINE STRING INSTRS
509 Jackson St 1 (22401-5716)
PHONE..................................540 645-7499
William Mason, *Partner*
Elaine Smith-Mason, *Partner*
EMP: 2
SALES (est): 15K **Privately Held**
SIC: 3931 Musical instruments

Fredericksburg
Spotsylvania County

(G-5239)
7430 BROKEN RIDGE LLC
11212 Carriage House Ct (22408-2449)
PHONE..................................571 354-0488
Marelis De La Cruz, *Partner*
EMP: 1 EST: 2011
SALES (est): 58.1K **Privately Held**
SIC: 2024 Ice cream & frozen desserts

(G-5240)
ACCURACY INTERNATIONAL N AMER
3410 Shannon Park Dr # 100 (22408-2373)
PHONE....................907 440-4024
Scott Seigmund, *Vice Pres*
Lance Strahl, *Sales Staff*
Todd Seigmund, *Marketing Staff*
EMP: 4
SALES (corp-wide): 19.6MM **Privately Held**
WEB: www.accuracyinternational.com
SIC: 3484 Guns (firearms) or gun parts, 30 mm. & below
PA: Accuracy International Limited
Po Box 81
Portsmouth HANTS PO3 5
239 267-1225

(G-5241)
ADVANCED COATING SOLUTIONS LLC
4915 Trade Center Dr (22408-2446)
PHONE....................540 898-9370
Richard Kettington, *Partner*
EMP: 2
SALES (est): 150K **Privately Held**
SIC: 3479 Coating of metals & formed products

(G-5242)
ALETHIA EMBROIDERY
6109 Fox Point Rd (22407-8332)
PHONE....................540 710-6560
Patricia Gray, *Principal*
EMP: 1
SALES (est): 60.6K **Privately Held**
WEB: www.nuwaveembroidery.com
SIC: 2395 Embroidery products, except schiffli machine

(G-5243)
ALVA RESTORATION & WATERPROOF
12209 Mcclain St (22407-6660)
PHONE....................540 785-0805
Richard Holley, *Owner*
EMP: 2
SALES (est): 177.5K **Privately Held**
SIC: 2385 Waterproof outerwear

(G-5244)
AMERICAN METAL FABRICATORS LLC
4932 Trade Center Dr (22408-2456)
PHONE....................540 834-2400
Joe Allen, *Mng Member*
EMP: 6
SALES (est): 482.5K **Privately Held**
SIC: 3444 Ducts, sheet metal

(G-5245)
ANGEL RIDES INC
11929 Gardenia Dr (22407-8564)
PHONE....................540 373-5540
Matthew Dickey, *President*
EMP: 3 EST: 2011
SALES (est): 385K **Privately Held**
SIC: 3842 Wheelchairs

(G-5246)
APPLE FRANKIES ENT INC
3217 Lancaster Ring Rd (22408-7723)
PHONE....................540 845-7372
EMP: 2
SALES (est): 85.9K **Privately Held**
SIC: 3571 Mfg Electronic Computers

(G-5247)
ARCO WELDING INC
329 Wallace Ln Ste A (22408-2417)
PHONE....................540 710-6944
Ray Wages, *President*
Audrey Hawkins, *Vice Pres*
EMP: 10
SALES (est): 1.6MM **Privately Held**
WEB: www.arcowelding.net
SIC: 7692 1629 Welding repair; chemical plant & refinery construction

(G-5248)
ARMSTRONG GREEN & EMBREY INC
Also Called: Quail Ridge
4821 Massaponax Church Rd (22407-8752)
PHONE....................540 898-7434
Ross Jones, *President*
EMP: 3 EST: 2010
SALES (est): 613.6K **Privately Held**
WEB: www.quailridgeproducts.com
SIC: 2499 2875 Mulch, wood & bark; compost

(G-5249)
ATLAS COPCO COMPRESSOR AIF VA
3905 Lancaster Ring Rd (22408-8767)
PHONE....................540 226-8655
Calvin Wallace, *Partner*
EMP: 1
SALES (est): 100K **Privately Held**
SIC: 3563 7389 Air & gas compressors including vacuum pumps;

(G-5250)
BADD NEWZ PUBLICATIONS LLC
4515 Kay Ct (22408-9212)
PHONE....................540 479-2848
EMP: 2
SALES (est): 67.1K **Privately Held**
SIC: 2711 Newspapers-Publishing/Printing

(G-5251)
BEACON
212 Freedom Ct Ste G (22408-2461)
PHONE....................540 408-2560
Craig Garvey, *Owner*
EMP: 1
SALES (est): 80.8K **Privately Held**
SIC: 2759 Posters, including billboards: printing

(G-5252)
BETTER FUELS OF VIRGINIA
12301 Dell Way (22407-6270)
PHONE....................540 693-4552
Lois Baird, *Principal*
EMP: 3 EST: 2014
SALES (est): 191.3K **Privately Held**
WEB: www.better-fuels.com
SIC: 2869 Fuels

(G-5253)
BILLY M SEARGEANT
4312 Mine Rd (22408-2559)
PHONE....................540 898-6396
Billy M Seargeant, *Owner*
EMP: 1
SALES (est): 56K **Privately Held**
SIC: 2311 Military uniforms, men's & youths': purchased materials

(G-5254)
BONRICK MOLDS
10701 Stoner Dr Ste 3 (22408-2621)
PHONE....................540 898-1512
EMP: 1 EST: 1978
SALES (est): 81K **Privately Held**
SIC: 3364 3363 Mfg Nonferrous Die-Castings Mfg Aluminum Die-Castings

(G-5255)
BOWMAN DISTILLERY INC A SMITH
Also Called: A Smith Bowman Distillery
1 Bowman Dr Ste 100 (22408-7350)
PHONE....................540 373-4555
Robert E Lee IV, *Ch of Bd*
John B Adams Jr, *President*
Tim S Brown, *Exec VP*
Kent Broussard, *CFO*
William Jones, *Supervisor*
▲ EMP: 12 EST: 1934
SQ FT: 250,000
SALES (est): 24.5MM
SALES (corp-wide): 336.9MM **Privately Held**
WEB: www.asmithbowman.com
SIC: 2085 Bourbon whiskey; vodka (alcoholic beverage); gin (alcoholic beverage); rum (alcoholic beverage)

PA: Sazerac Company, Inc.
101 Magazine St Fl 5
New Orleans LA 70130
866 729-3722

(G-5256)
C M C STEEL FABRICATORS INC
Also Called: CMC Rebar Virginia
9434 Crossroads Pkwy (22408-1734)
PHONE....................540 898-1111
Curtis Raven, *Manager*
EMP: 48
SQ FT: 435,600
SALES (corp-wide): 5.4B **Publicly Held**
WEB: www.cmc.com
SIC: 3441 Fabricated structural metal
HQ: C M C Steel Fabricators, Inc.
1 Steel Mill Dr
Seguin TX 78155
830 372-8200

(G-5257)
CC & MORE INC
3509 Shannon Park Dr # 117 (22408-2377)
PHONE....................540 786-7052
Donna Irvine, *President*
EMP: 5
SALES (est): 256.8K **Privately Held**
SIC: 2393 3171 Duffle bags, canvas: made from purchased materials; luggage; women's handbags & purses

(G-5258)
CELLOFOAM NORTH AMERICA INC
57 Joseph Mills Dr (22408-7304)
PHONE....................540 373-4596
EMP: 27
SALES (corp-wide): 119.7MM **Privately Held**
SIC: 3089 3086 Mfg Plastic Products Mfg Plastic Foam Products
PA: Cellofoam North America Inc.
1917 Rockdale Indstrl Blv
Conyers GA 30013
770 929-3688

(G-5259)
CELLOFOAM NORTH AMERICA INC
Also Called: Mid Atlantic Foam
57 Joseph Mills Dr (22408-7304)
P.O. Box 742 (22404-0742)
PHONE....................540 373-1800
Jeff Pepper, *COO*
Darren Burns, *Prdtn Mgr*
EMP: 37
SQ FT: 10,000
SALES (corp-wide): 143.4MM **Privately Held**
WEB: www.cellofoam.com
SIC: 3086 5033 Insulation or cushioning material, foamed plastic; insulation materials
PA: Cellofoam North America Inc.
1977 Weaver Ct
Conyers GA 30013
770 929-3688

(G-5260)
CHANEY ENTERPRISES LTD PARTNR
Also Called: Chaney Ent. Concrete
8520 Indian Hills Ct (22407-8737)
PHONE....................540 710-0075
David Meeks, *Manager*
EMP: 15
SALES (corp-wide): 124.2MM **Privately Held**
WEB: www.chaneyenterprises.com
SIC: 3273 5211 3272 Ready-mixed concrete; masonry materials & supplies; concrete products, precast
PA: Chaney Enterprises Limited Partnership
2410 Evergreen Rd Ste 201
Gambrills MD 21054
410 451-0197

(G-5261)
CHATTEM INC
Also Called: Chattem Consumer Products
11906 Rutherford Dr (22407-6721)
PHONE....................540 786-7970

PA: Sazerac Company, Inc.
101 Magazine St Fl 5
New Orleans LA 70130
866 729-3722

Roger Neff, *Manager*
EMP: 1 **Privately Held**
WEB: www.sanofi.us
SIC: 2834 2844 Proprietary drug products; toilet preparations; cosmetic preparations
HQ: Chattem, Inc.
1715 W 38th St
Chattanooga TN 37409
423 821-4571

(G-5262)
CLADDING FACADE SOLUTIONS LLC
5109 Commonwealth Dr (22407-9325)
PHONE....................571 748-7698
Philip Schwartz, *Principal*
EMP: 2
SALES (est): 145.9K **Privately Held**
WEB: www.claddingfacadesolutions.com
SIC: 3444 Sheet metalwork

(G-5263)
COCHRANE USA INC (PA)
3551 Lee Hill Dr (22408-7323)
PHONE....................202 434-8163
Ron Smith, *CEO*
Lusio Filiba, *Manager*
▲ EMP: 7
SALES (est): 15MM **Privately Held**
WEB: www.cochraneglobal.com
SIC: 3499 Barricades, metal

(G-5264)
COMBAT V TACTICAL
304 Laurel Ave (22408-1534)
PHONE....................540 604-0235
Mark Lisa Schaub, *Owner*
EMP: 2
SALES (est): 65.4K **Privately Held**
SIC: 2399 Fabricated textile products

(G-5265)
COMMONWEALTH PROVISIONS LLC
11720 Main St Ste 128 (22408-7367)
PHONE....................540 699-0222
Lucas Smith,
EMP: 1 EST: 2017
SALES (est): 128.7K **Privately Held**
SIC: 3999 Candles

(G-5266)
CONSOLIDATED WOOD PRODUCTS
11901 Bowman Dr Ste 101 (22408-7308)
P.O. Box 7786 (22404-7786)
PHONE....................540 374-1439
Andy Kidd, *President*
Michael Turner, *Vice Pres*
EMP: 1 EST: 1991
SALES (est): 122.7K **Privately Held**
SIC: 2449 Wood containers

(G-5267)
CREATIVE DIMENSION GROUP INC
11700 Shannon Dr (22408-7310)
PHONE....................540 891-1953
Deborah Sullivan, *President*
John W Johnson, *Corp Secy*
Jack Johnson, *Vice Pres*
George Keating, *Vice Pres*
EMP: 52
SQ FT: 35,000
SALES (est): 13.8MM **Privately Held**
WEB: www.creativedimensiongroup.com
SIC: 2541 2431 Cabinets, except refrigerated: show, display, etc.: wood; moldings, wood: unfinished & prefinished

(G-5268)
CSL MEDIA LLC
220 Industrial Dr (22408-2431)
PHONE....................540 785-3790
EMP: 2
SALES (est): 275.2K **Privately Held**
WEB: www.fredprint.com
SIC: 2752 Commercial printing, offset

(G-5269)
CUTHBERT PUBLISHING LLC
7416 N Katie Dr (22407-8687)
PHONE....................540 840-7218
Steven Neville, *Principal*
EMP: 1

SALES (est): 37.5K **Privately Held**
SIC: 2741 Miscellaneous publishing

(G-5270)
DAILY FRILLS LLC
8121 Twelfth Corps Dr (22407-1996)
PHONE...............................540 850-7909
EMP: 3
SALES (est): 118.6K **Privately Held**
WEB: www.dailyfrills.com
SIC: 2711 Newspapers, publishing & printing

(G-5271)
DATA FUSION SOLUTIONS INC
7218 River Rd (22407-2036)
P.O. Box 41194 (22404-1194)
PHONE...............................877 326-0034
Nina Willging, *CEO*
Patrick Willging, *Director*
EMP: 2 EST: 2015
SALES (est): 133.3K **Privately Held**
WEB: www.spotsylvania.va.us
SIC: 7372 7389 7371 Application computer software; ; computer software development

(G-5272)
DESIGNER SOFTWARE INC
Also Called: Ameridisc
4605 Carr Dr (22408-2683)
PHONE...............................540 842-8425
Robert M Butler, *CEO*
Carolyn R Butler, *Vice Pres*
EMP: 5
SALES (est): 585.8K **Privately Held**
SIC: 7372 Application computer software

(G-5273)
DICKERSON STUMP LLC
5618 Massaponax Church Rd
(22407-8704)
PHONE...............................540 898-9145
Norman Dickerson,
Leslie A Dickerson,
EMP: 4
SALES (est): 200K **Privately Held**
WEB: www.dickersonstump.vpweb.com
SIC: 2499 5261 Mulch, wood & bark; top soil

(G-5274)
DIGITAL MACHINING COMPANY
9200 Rapidan Dr (22407-1518)
PHONE...............................540 786-7138
Lawrence A Lang, *Owner*
EMP: 1
SALES (est): 101.3K **Privately Held**
SIC: 3443 Metal parts

(G-5275)
DISCUS N MORE LLC
6308 Sweetbriar Dr (22407-8322)
PHONE...............................609 678-6102
EMP: 4
SALES (est): 292.4K **Privately Held**
SIC: 3949 Sporting & athletic goods

(G-5276)
DOMINION STEEL INC
4920 Quality Dr (22408-2462)
P.O. Box 490, Hartwood (22471-0490)
PHONE...............................540 898-1249
Madeline Maitland, *Officer*
EMP: 17
SQ FT: 37,000
SALES (est): 4.4MM **Privately Held**
WEB: www.dominionsteelinc.com
SIC: 3441 5051 Fabricated structural metal; steel

(G-5277)
DREAM REELS INC
Also Called: Movie Time
6014 N Cranston Ln (22407-8391)
PHONE...............................540 891-9886
EMP: 30 EST: 1993
SALES (est): 2.3MM **Privately Held**
SIC: 3861 7841 Mfg Photographic Equipment/Supplies Video Tape Rental

(G-5278)
DS TEES LLC
6927 Versaille Dr (22407-2587)
PHONE...............................540 841-8831
Carla Goodman, *Principal*

EMP: 2 EST: 2017
SALES (est): 113.8K **Privately Held**
SIC: 2759 Screen printing

(G-5279)
E-Z AUTO SPECIALTIES
7102 River Rd (22407-2034)
PHONE...............................540 786-8111
Allayn Sheffield, *President*
Yolanda Sheffield, *Owner*
Rob Sheffield, *Principal*
EMP: 3
SALES (est): 160K **Privately Held**
WEB: www.e-zgroup.net
SIC: 3993 Signs & advertising specialties

(G-5280)
EL MORGAN COMPANY LLC
209 Green Arbor Dr (22407-6311)
PHONE...............................540 623-7086
Jose L Lopez Rivera, *Administration*
EMP: 2 EST: 2014
SALES (est): 88.5K **Privately Held**
SIC: 3931 Organs, all types: pipe, reed, hand, electronic, etc.

(G-5281)
ELEVATE HEARING AID CENTER
4903 Plank Rd Ste 101b (22407-6367)
PHONE...............................540 785-4676
EMP: 2
SALES (est): 92.6K **Privately Held**
SIC: 3842 Hearing aids

(G-5282)
EPIC LED
4513 Jefferson Davis Hwy (22408-4253)
PHONE...............................540 376-7183
EMP: 2
SALES (est): 142.4K **Privately Held**
WEB: www.epicled.com
SIC: 3993 Signs & advertising specialties

(G-5283)
ERIKSON DIVERSIFIED INDUSTRIES
5825 Plank Rd Ste 113 (22407-5207)
P.O. Box 7878 (22404-7878)
PHONE...............................703 216-5482
EMP: 1
SALES (est): 42.8K **Privately Held**
WEB: www.ediamerica.com
SIC: 3999 Manufacturing industries

(G-5284)
ERNIES WOODWORKING
800 Galway Ln (22407-6539)
PHONE...............................540 786-8959
EMP: 1 EST: 2011
SALES (est): 65K **Privately Held**
SIC: 2431 Mfg Millwork

(G-5285)
EVS GLASS CREATIONS LLC
4 Kendale Ln (22407-6532)
PHONE...............................540 412-8242
Evelyn Andrianos,
EMP: 1 EST: 2017
SALES (est): 39.7K **Privately Held**
WEB: www.evsglasscreations.com
SIC: 3231 Products of purchased glass

(G-5286)
FAUSTI USA SERVICE LLC
3509 Shannon Park Dr # 113 (22408-2377)
PHONE...............................540 371-3287
Steve Allen, *General Mgr*
Barbara Fausti, *Principal*
EMP: 3
SALES (est): 292.7K **Privately Held**
WEB: www.faustiusa.com
SIC: 3484 Shotguns or shotgun parts, 30 mm. & below

(G-5287)
FERGUSON CUSTOM SAWMILL LLC
1709 Nottingham Dr (22408-9674)
PHONE...............................540 903-8174
Kyle Ferguson, *Principal*
EMP: 3
SALES (est): 181.3K **Privately Held**
WEB: www.fergusoncustomsawmill.com
SIC: 2421 Custom sawmill

(G-5288)
FINCO INC
3401 Plank Rd (22407-4959)
PHONE...............................301 645-4538
Richard Finocchiaro Jr, *Principal*
EMP: 5
SALES (est): 430.5K **Privately Held**
SIC: 3556 Smokers, food processing equipment

(G-5289)
FLOWERS BKG CO LYNCHBURG LLC
230 Industrial Dr (22408-2448)
PHONE...............................540 371-1480
Meliton Garcia, *General Mgr*
EMP: 2
SALES (corp-wide): 4.1B **Publicly Held**
SIC: 2051 Bread, cake & related products
HQ: Flowers Baking Co. Of Lynchburg, Llc
1905 Hollins Mill Rd
Lynchburg VA 24503
434 528-0441

(G-5290)
FREDERICKSBURG FENCES LLC
4617 Mine Rd (22408-2613)
P.O. Box 1355, Spotsylvania (22553-1355)
PHONE...............................540 419-3910
Logan McNiel,
Joe Leonard,
EMP: 7
SALES (est): 100K **Privately Held**
WEB: www.fxbgfences.com
SIC: 3089 Fences, gates & accessories: plastic

(G-5291)
G5 EXAMINER LLC
10716 Lotus Ct (22407-1643)
PHONE...............................540 455-9186
Gerald W Knouff, *Principal*
EMP: 3
SALES (est): 137.9K **Privately Held**
SIC: 2711 Newspapers, publishing & printing

(G-5292)
GRACIES GOWNS INC
1919 Captain Dr (22408-9603)
PHONE...............................540 287-0143
Jessica Kidd, *President*
Patricia Franklin, *Vice Pres*
Stover Rebecca, *Treasurer*
Holly Williams, *Treasurer*
Wendy Carter, *Admin Sec*
EMP: 4
SALES (est): 315.5K **Privately Held**
WEB: www.graciesgowns.org
SIC: 2389 Hospital gowns

(G-5293)
GREENBROOK TMS NEUROHEALTH CTR
10304 Spotsylvania Ave # 106 (22408-8602)
PHONE...............................855 940-4867
EMP: 1
SALES (corp-wide): 2.7MM **Privately Held**
WEB: www.greenbrooktms.com
SIC: 3312 Blast furnaces & steel mills
PA: Greenbrook Tms Neurohealth Center
8405 Greensboro Dr # 120
Mc Lean VA 22102
703 356-1568

(G-5294)
H & S TACTICAL LLC
4920 Trade Center Dr (22408-2456)
PHONE...............................540 710-2715
Brian Hogeland, *Mng Member*
EMP: 4
SALES (est): 208.8K **Privately Held**
WEB: www.handstactical.com
SIC: 3489 Ordnance & accessories

(G-5295)
H20 PRO
12021 Dogwood Ave (22407-6581)
PHONE...............................540 785-6811
Michaeleal Seay, *Manager*
EMP: 2

SALES (est): 169.5K **Privately Held**
WEB:
www.fredericksburgwatertreatment.com
SIC: 3589 Water treatment equipment, industrial

(G-5296)
HAMMOND UNITED INDUSTRIES LLC
21 Noel Dr (22408-2501)
PHONE...............................571 306-9003
Julius Hammond, *Principal*
EMP: 2
SALES (est): 51.8K **Privately Held**
SIC: 3999 Manufacturing industries

(G-5297)
HIP OCCASIONS LLC
9504 Moores Creek Dr (22408-7788)
PHONE...............................540 695-8896
Angela J Moore, *CEO*
EMP: 1 EST: 2015
SALES (est): 51.1K **Privately Held**
SIC: 3999 Candles

(G-5298)
HOLLINGER METAL EDGE INC
9401 Northeast Dr (22408-8721)
PHONE...............................540 898-7300
Pete Hollinger, *President*
EMP: 15
SALES (corp-wide): 2.2MM **Privately Held**
WEB: www.hollingermetaledge.com
SIC: 2653 2675 Boxes, corrugated: made from purchased materials; folders, filing, die-cut: made from purchased materials
PA: Hollinger Metal Edge - Va Inc.
9401 Northeast Dr
Fredericksburg VA 22408
540 898-7300

(G-5299)
HOLLINGER METAL EDGE - VA INC (PA)
9401 Northeast Dr (22408-8721)
PHONE...............................540 898-7300
Mary Helen Hollinger, *Ch of Bd*
Robert J Henderson, *President*
Timothy Hollinger, *Vice Pres*
John Hollinger, *Admin Sec*
▼ EMP: 18
SQ FT: 53,000
SALES (est): 2.2MM **Privately Held**
WEB: www.hollingermetaledge.com
SIC: 2653 Boxes, corrugated: made from purchased materials

(G-5300)
HUNTER DEFENSE TECH INC
Also Called: Hdt Engineering Services
10300 Spotsylvania Ave # 100 (22408-2697)
PHONE...............................540 479-8100
Glen Brown, *Owner*
Robin Carney, *Manager*
Lynne Gilbert, *Manager*
EMP: 14 **Privately Held**
WEB: www.hdtglobal.com
SIC: 3714 Heaters, motor vehicle
PA: Hunter Defense Technologies, Inc.
30500 Aurora Rd Ste 100
Solon OH 44139

(G-5301)
IDX CORPORATION
Also Called: Idx Baltimore
11032 Tidewater Trl (22408-2043)
PHONE...............................410 551-3600
Jim Geary, *President*
Tom Delaitsch, *Branch Mgr*
EMP: 195
SALES (corp-wide): 4.4B **Publicly Held**
WEB: www.idxcorporation.com
SIC: 2542 2541 3993 Fixtures: display, office or store: except wood; store & office display cases & fixtures; signs & advertising specialties
HQ: Idx Corporation
13213 Corporate Exch Dr
Bridgeton MO 63044
314 739-4120

▲ = Import ▼=Export
◆ =Import/Export

(G-5302)
ILLUSIONS WRAP LLC
3719 Lafayette Blvd (22408-4156)
PHONE..................................540 710-9727
Ryan McGuirre,
EMP: 1 **EST:** 2016
SALES (est): 95.1K **Privately Held**
WEB: www.illusionswraps.com
SIC: 3993 Advertising artwork

(G-5303)
INSCRIBE PRESS LLC
12400 Regiment Ln (22407-5204)
PHONE..................................707 239-8404
Jeffrey Wayne Pelton, *Principal*
EMP: 1
SALES (est): 41.3K **Privately Held**
WEB: www.inscribepress.com
SIC: 2741 Miscellaneous publishing

(G-5304)
INVELOS SOFTWARE INC
12830 Mill Rd (22407-2220)
PHONE..................................540 786-8560
Kenneth Cole, *President*
EMP: 2
SALES (est): 72.2K **Privately Held**
SIC: 7372 Prepackaged software

(G-5305)
JACKED UP FOODS LLC
11403 Meadow Wood Ave (22407-7484)
PHONE..................................540 623-6313
Katherine Zalewski,
EMP: 2
SALES (est): 127.2K **Privately Held**
WEB: www.jackedupfoods.com
SIC: 2099 Food preparations

(G-5306)
**JEFFERSON HOMEBUILDERS
INC**
Also Called: Culpeper Wood Preservers
10229 Tidewater Trl (22408-9610)
PHONE..................................540 371-5338
Ryan Michnya, *Sales Staff*
Michele Rocha, *Manager*
EMP: 1
SALES (corp-wide): 72.7MM **Privately
Held**
WEB: www.culpeperwood.com
SIC: 2491 Wood preserving
PA: Jefferson Homebuilders, Inc.
501 N Main St
Culpeper VA 22701
540 825-5898

(G-5307)
JONATHAN PROMOTIONS INC
Also Called: Jonathan & Co Unlimited
4808 Jefferson Davis Hwy (22408-4258)
P.O. Box 8405 (22404-8405)
PHONE..................................540 891-7700
Jonathan R Burris, *President*
Carolyn Burris, *Vice Pres*
EMP: 8
SQ FT: 10,200
SALES (est): 1.2MM **Privately Held**
WEB: www.jonathanandco.com
SIC: 2759 2395 Screen printing; embroi-
dery & art needlework

(G-5308)
KELLER INDUSTRIES LLC
9321 Blue Pine Ln (22407-7392)
PHONE..................................573 452-4932
Namataka Heru, *Principal*
EMP: 1 **EST:** 2018
SALES (est): 39.6K **Privately Held**
SIC: 3999 Manufacturing industries

(G-5309)
KEYSTONE TECHNOLOGY LLC
6709 Willcher Ct (22407-1765)
PHONE..................................540 361-8318
Stephen Delacalzada-Delong, *CEO*
Steve Koeniger, *President*
EMP: 2
SALES (est): 62.1K **Privately Held**
SIC: 7372 7374 7371 7373 Prepackaged
software; data processing & preparation;
custom computer programming services;
systems software development services;
computer related maintenance services

(G-5310)
KITCHEN KRAFTERS INC
198 Wilcox St (22408-2696)
PHONE..................................540 891-7678
Dean Owens, *Manager*
EMP: 12 **Privately Held**
WEB: www.kitchenkraftersinc.com
SIC: 2541 Cabinets, except refrigerated:
show, display, etc.: wood
PA: Kitchen Krafters Inc
4134 Lafayette Blvd
Fredericksburg VA 22408

(G-5311)
KITCHEN KRAFTERS INC (PA)
4134 Lafayette Blvd (22408-4230)
PHONE..................................540 891-7678
Dean Owens, *President*
Dennis Williams, *Corp Secy*
Michael Shiflett, *Vice Pres*
EMP: 2
SQ FT: 1,050
SALES (est): 1.8MM **Privately Held**
WEB: www.kitchenkraftersinc.com
SIC: 2434 Wood kitchen cabinets

(G-5312)
LEGACY VULCAN LLC
9151 Luck Stone Ln (22407-5302)
PHONE..................................800 732-3964
EMP: 3 **Publicly Held**
WEB: www.vulcanmaterials.com
SIC: 3273 Ready-mixed concrete
HQ: Legacy Vulcan, Llc
1200 Urban Center Dr
Vestavia AL 35242
205 298-3000

(G-5313)
LL DISTRIBUTING INC
Also Called: Vault Printing, The
11417 Scott Dr (22407-6339)
PHONE..................................540 479-2221
Leslie Bauer, *CEO*
Cris Pollnow, *President*
Susan Stoddarb, *Opers Mgr*
EMP: 4 **EST:** 2004
SQ FT: 5,600
SALES (est): 400K **Privately Held**
SIC: 2759 Commercial printing

(G-5314)
**LOCKHEED MARTIN
CORPORATION**
4545 Empire Ct (22408-1949)
PHONE..................................540 891-5882
EMP: 2 **Publicly Held**
WEB: www.lockheedmartin.com
SIC: 3812 Search & navigation equipment
PA: Lockheed Martin Corporation
6801 Rockledge Dr
Bethesda MD 20817

(G-5315)
LOG HOMES BY CLORE BROS
Also Called: Garden Weddings By Clore Bros
5927 River Rd (22407-2244)
PHONE..................................540 786-7749
Gene Clore, *Owner*
EMP: 1
SALES (est): 500K **Privately Held**
WEB:
www.riversideweddingsandevents.com
SIC: 2452 Log cabins, prefabricated, wood

(G-5316)
LONGS EMBROIDERY
120 Falcon Dr Ste 8 (22408-1900)
PHONE..................................540 891-2880
Rick Long, *Principal*
EMP: 1 **EST:** 2005
SALES (est): 87.9K **Privately Held**
WEB: www.longsembroidery.net
SIC: 2395 Embroidery products, except
schiffli machine; embroidery & art needle-
work

(G-5317)
LUBAWA USA INC
10300 Ste 100 (22408)
PHONE..................................703 894-1909
John Longhouser, *President*
Stanistaw Litwin, *Director*
Marcin Kubica, *Admin Sec*
EMP: 2 **EST:** 2016

SALES (est): 175.2K **Privately Held**
WEB: www.lubawausa.com
SIC: 2842 Polishing preparations & related
products

(G-5318)
LUCK STONE CORPORATION
Also Called: Luck Stone - Spttsylvnia Plant
9100 Luck Stone Ln (22407-5302)
PHONE..................................540 898-6060
Foster Taliafer, *Branch Mgr*
EMP: 25
SALES (corp-wide): 824.7MM **Privately
Held**
WEB: www.luckstone.com
SIC: 3281 Cut stone & stone products
PA: Luck Stone Corporation
515 Stone Mill Dr
Manakin Sabot VA 23103
804 784-6300

(G-5319)
**MAPEI CORP
FREDERICKSBURG**
9420 Cosner Dr (22408-8708)
PHONE..................................540 710-5303
Gene Collis, *Manager*
EMP: 4 **EST:** 2011
SALES (est): 262.3K **Privately Held**
SIC: 2891 Adhesives

(G-5320)
MAPEI CORPORATION
9420 Cosner Dr (22408-8708)
PHONE..................................540 898-5124
Ray Hernandez, *General Mgr*
James Whitfield, *Technical Staff*
EMP: 72 **Privately Held**
WEB: www.mapei.com
SIC: 2891 Adhesives
HQ: Mapei Corporation
1144 E Newport Center Dr
Deerfield Beach FL 33442
954 246-8888

(G-5321)
**MARTIN MARIETTA MATERIALS
INC**
9100 Luck Stone Ln (22407-5302)
PHONE..................................540 894-5952
Bobby Boiling, *Branch Mgr*
EMP: 4 **Publicly Held**
WEB: www.martinmarietta.com
SIC: 1423 Crushed & broken granite
PA: Martin Marietta Materials Inc
2710 Wycliff Rd
Raleigh NC 27607

(G-5322)
**MASSAPONAX BLDG
COMPONENTS INC**
8737 Jefferson Davis Hwy (22407-8716)
PHONE..................................540 898-0013
Danny Chinault, *President*
EMP: 15 **EST:** 1977
SQ FT: 6,280
SALES (est): 223.4K **Privately Held**
SIC: 2439 Trusses, wooden roof

(G-5323)
MAVERICK WHEELS LLC
301 Butternut Dr (22408-1500)
PHONE..................................540 891-2681
Paul Humphreys, *Principal*
EMP: 2 **EST:** 2010
SALES (est): 125.8K **Privately Held**
SIC: 3312 Blast furnaces & steel mills

(G-5324)
MERCHANTS METALS LLC
Also Called: Meadow Burke Products
5115 Massaponax Church Rd
(22407-8755)
P.O. Box 960, Newington (22122-0960)
PHONE..................................877 518-7665
Kiki Kochel, *Manager*
EMP: 7
SALES (corp-wide): 6.1B **Publicly Held**
WEB: www.merchantsmetals.com
SIC: 3496 3452 Miscellaneous fabricated
wire products; bolts, nuts, rivets & wash-
ers

HQ: Merchants Metals Llc
211 Perimeter Center Pkwy
Atlanta GA 30346
770 741-0306

(G-5325)
METAL EDGE CO
9401 Northeast Dr (22408-8721)
PHONE..................................800 862-2228
EMP: 3 **EST:** 2019
SALES (est): 312.7K **Privately Held**
WEB: www.hollingermetaledge.com
SIC: 2653 Boxes, corrugated: made from
purchased materials

(G-5326)
MID-ATLANTIC RUBBER INC
Also Called: Mar
10707 Stoner Dr (22408-2620)
PHONE..................................540 710-5690
Scott Jacobs, *President*
EMP: 12
SQ FT: 5,000
SALES (est): 3MM **Privately Held**
WEB: www.mar-mfg.com
SIC: 3492 Hose & tube fittings & assem-
blies, hydraulic/pneumatic

(G-5327)
MIKES SIGNS4LESS
6010 Plank Rd (22407-6234)
PHONE..................................540 548-2940
Mike Neely, *Owner*
EMP: 2 **EST:** 2011
SALES (est): 10K **Privately Held**
WEB: www.mikessigns4less.net
SIC: 3993 Signs & advertising specialties

(G-5328)
MILGARD MANUFACTURING INC
Also Called: Milgard Windows
2000 Intl Pkwy Ste 101 (22408)
PHONE..................................540 834-0340
Fax: 540 834-0699
EMP: 8
SALES (corp-wide): 7.3B **Publicly Held**
SIC: 3089 3442 Mfg Plastic Products Mfg
Metal Doors/Sash/Trim
HQ: Milgard Manufacturing Incorporated
1010 54th Ave E
Fife WA 98424
253 922-6030

(G-5329)
**MORGAN RACE CARS LLC
JEFFREY**
2611 Melissa Ct (22408-8070)
PHONE..................................540 907-1205
EMP: 3
SALES (est): 253.7K **Privately Held**
SIC: 3711 Automobile assembly, including
specialty automobiles

(G-5330)
MY EXTRA HANDS LLC
Also Called: Spice Rack Chocolates
6320 Five Mile Centre Par (22407-5512)
PHONE..................................540 847-2063
Mary Schellhammer,
EMP: 2
SALES (est): 121.5K **Privately Held**
WEB: www.spicerackchocolates.com
SIC: 2064 Candy & other confectionery
products

(G-5331)
N2N SPECIALTY PRINTING LLC
7903 Westbury Manor Dr (22407-8653)
PHONE..................................540 786-5765
Edmond Noel, *Principal*
EMP: 2
SALES (est): 83.9K **Privately Held**
SIC: 2752 Commercial printing, litho-
graphic

(G-5332)
NETTALON INC
3324 Bourbon St (22408-7311)
PHONE..................................877 638-8256
Daniel Colin, *Principal*
EMP: 2
SALES (est): 164.6K **Privately Held**
WEB: www.nettalon.com
SIC: 3669 Communications equipment

(G-5333)
NETTALON SECURITY SYSTEMS INC
3304 Bourbon St Fl 3d (22408-7311)
PHONE....................540 368-5290
Daniel Collin, *President*
Ronald Dubois, *Corp Secy*
Denise Webster, *Office Mgr*
Donald R Jones Jr, *Director*
Spearman S Lancaste, *Director*
EMP: 10
SQ FT: 6,000
SALES (est): 1.8MM **Privately Held**
WEB: www.nettalon.com
SIC: 3669 3699 Fire detection systems, electric; security devices

(G-5334)
NEW HOMES MEDIA
11900 Main St Ste B114 (22408-7337)
PHONE....................540 654-5350
Chuck Smith, *Principal*
EMP: 1
SALES (est): 84.7K **Privately Held**
SIC: 3993 Signs & advertising specialties

(G-5335)
NEXGRID LLC
915 Maple Grove Dr # 200 (22407-6935)
PHONE....................833 639-4743
Costa Apostolakis, *CEO*
Joshua Holland, *Network Enginr*
Jim Devlin, *Director*
EMP: 26
SALES (est): 1.2MM **Privately Held**
WEB: www.intelagrid.com
SIC: 3825 Instruments to measure electricity

(G-5336)
NOTHING BUT CAKE INCORPORATED
5217 Sarah Ln (22407-7785)
PHONE....................540 322-7520
Jacob Miller, *CEO*
EMP: 1
SALES (est): 57.5K **Privately Held**
SIC: 2673 Food storage & trash bags (plastic)

(G-5337)
NUWAVE EMBROIDERY
5933 Plank Rd (22407-6231)
PHONE....................540 412-9799
Jessica Pearlman, *Owner*
EMP: 3
SALES (est): 20K **Privately Held**
WEB: www.nuwaveembroidery.com
SIC: 2395 Embroidery products, except schiffli machine; embroidery & art needlework

(G-5338)
ODIN SCNCE TECH INNOVATION LLC
1420 Hudgins Farm Cir (22408-4176)
PHONE....................850 582-0799
Eric Owen, *Mng Member*
EMP: 1
SALES (est): 90.5K **Privately Held**
SIC: 3679 Electronic circuits

(G-5339)
OLDCASTLE INFRASTRUCTURE INC
Also Called: Rotondo Precast
5115 Massaponax Church Rd (22407-8755)
PHONE....................540 898-6300
Sean Farmer, *Project Mgr*
Willie Clark, *Sales Staff*
Richard Rotondo, *Branch Mgr*
William Clark, *Technician*
EMP: 75
SQ FT: 1,199,206
SALES (corp-wide): 30.6B **Privately Held**
WEB: www.oldcastleinfrastructure.com
SIC: 3272 Concrete products
HQ: Oldcastle Infrastructure, Inc.
　　7000 Central Pkwy Ste 800
　　Atlanta GA 30328
　　470 602-2000

(G-5340)
OMEGA BLACK INCORPORATED
10711 Brice Ct (22407-7730)
PHONE....................240 416-1774
Derek Lee, *President*
EMP: 2
SALES (est): 50K **Privately Held**
SIC: 2836 Culture media

(G-5341)
ONDULINE NORTH AMERICA INC
Also Called: Onduvilla
4900 Ondura Dr (22407-8773)
PHONE....................540 898-7000
Mitch Sanner, *CEO*
Ed Harlin, *Vice Pres*
Sharrell Collier, *Purch Agent*
Gary Castellaw, *CFO*
Thomas Marshall, *Human Res Dir*
◆ EMP: 65
SQ FT: 55,000
SALES (est): 25.5MM **Privately Held**
WEB: www.us.ondoline.com
SIC: 2952 5032 Roofing materials; siding materials; concrete & cinder building products

(G-5342)
ONE ONE TOO LLC
9400 Braken Ct (22408-7746)
PHONE....................505 500-4749
Paul Weiland,
Susan Weiland,
EMP: 2
SALES (est): 94.3K **Privately Held**
SIC: 7372 Home entertainment computer software

(G-5343)
PATRIOT3 INC
11040 Pierson Dr (22408-2060)
PHONE....................540 891-7353
Charles P Fuqua, *CEO*
Mark Withiam, *Division Mgr*
Steve Kahre, *COO*
Steven Kahre, *Vice Pres*
Hunter Bryant, *Engineer*
◆ EMP: 20
SQ FT: 10,000
SALES (est): 5.9MM **Privately Held**
WEB: www.patriot3.com
SIC: 3812 Defense systems & equipment

(G-5344)
PEPSI-COLA METRO BTLG CO INC
11551 Shannon Dr (22408-7305)
PHONE....................540 361-4467
Laurie Engel, *Manager*
EMP: 56
SALES (corp-wide): 67.1B **Publicly Held**
WEB: www.pepsico.com
SIC: 2086 Carbonated soft drinks, bottled & canned
HQ: Pepsi-Cola Metropolitan Bottling Company, Inc.
　　1111 Westchester Ave
　　White Plains NY 10604
　　914 767-6000

(G-5345)
PERSONAL
11311 Glen Park Dr (22407-1763)
PHONE....................540 845-8771
Gary Tanner, *Principal*
EMP: 2
SALES (est): 104.8K **Privately Held**
SIC: 3441 Fabricated structural metal

(G-5346)
PINK CUPCAKE
11912 Hunting Ridge Dr (22407-7364)
PHONE....................801 349-6301
Nichole Tross, *Principal*
EMP: 4
SALES (est): 170.8K **Privately Held**
SIC: 2051 Bread, cake & related products

(G-5347)
PITNEY BOWES BUSINESS INSIGHT
7111 River Rd (22407-2035)
PHONE....................540 786-5744
Jesse Baldwin, *Principal*
EMP: 2
SALES (est): 119.9K **Privately Held**
SIC: 3579 Postage meters

(G-5348)
PRECISION DOORS & HARDWARE LLC
10941 Pierson Dr (22408-2070)
PHONE....................540 373-7300
Ronald Edwards, *Manager*
EMP: 12
SALES (corp-wide): 36.5MM **Privately Held**
WEB: www.cookandboardman.com
SIC: 2431 5719 5211 5251 Doors & door parts & trim, wood; bath accessories; door & window products; builders' hardware; builders' hardware
HQ: Precision Doors & Hardware, Llc
　　6295 Edsall Rd Ste 80
　　Alexandria VA 22312

(G-5349)
PREMONITION GAMES LLC
5011 Queensbury Cir (22408-1823)
PHONE....................586 404-7070
Bryant Kwiatkowski,
EMP: 1
SALES (est): 52.9K **Privately Held**
SIC: 3944 Games, toys & children's vehicles

(G-5350)
PRESSED 4 INK - CUSTOM APPAREL
325 Wallace Ln (22408-2417)
PHONE....................540 693-4023
EMP: 2
SALES (est): 83.9K **Privately Held**
SIC: 2752 Commercial printing, lithographic

(G-5351)
PRESSED 4 INK LLC
9716 Gunston Hall Rd (22408-9494)
PHONE....................540 834-0125
Charles Frye,
EMP: 5
SALES (est): 316.3K **Privately Held**
WEB: www.pressed4ink.com
SIC: 2759 Screen printing

(G-5352)
RADIO RECONNAISSANCE TECH INC (PA)
3328 Bourbon St (22408-7311)
PHONE....................540 752-7448
Nicholas Hoben, *President*
Ernie Gillespie, *Principal*
Clyde D Taylor, *Principal*
Kathy Yule, *Purch Mgr*
EMP: 2
SQ FT: 11,000
SALES (est): 3.8MM **Privately Held**
WEB: www.radiorecon.com
SIC: 3663 3812 7371 7379 Radio broadcasting & communications equipment; search & navigation equipment; custom computer programming services; computer related consulting services; educational services; electronic circuits; antennas, receiving; power supplies, all types: static

(G-5353)
RAPPAHANOCK SPORTS AND GRAPHIC
5100 Commonwealth Dr (22407-9360)
PHONE....................540 891-7662
James Donald, *Partner*
Layton Fairchild Jr, *Partner*
EMP: 3
SQ FT: 1,500
SALES (est): 366.6K **Privately Held**
WEB: www.rappsport.wixsite.com
SIC: 2759 Screen printing

(G-5354)
RESOURCE COLOR CONTROL TECH
11801 Main St Ste D (22408-7370)
PHONE....................540 548-1855
Robert Martin, *President*
EMP: 2
SQ FT: 300

(G-5355)
RIDGELINE INCORPORATED
4900 Ondura Dr (22407-8773)
PHONE....................540 898-7000
John A Adair Jr, *President*
L Paul Nelson II, *Senior VP*
Katherine D Adair, *Vice Pres*
Joseph Mehalko, *CFO*
EMP: 10 EST: 1991
SQ FT: 30,000
SALES (est): 853K **Privately Held**
WEB: www.ridgelineintl.com
SIC: 2952 Roofing materials

(G-5356)
ROWE CONCRETE SUPPLY STORE
8520 Indian Hills Ct (22407-8737)
PHONE....................540 710-7693
Jeff Slagle, *Principal*
EMP: 1
SALES (est): 90.1K **Privately Held**
WEB: www.chaneyenterprises.com
SIC: 3273 Ready-mixed concrete

(G-5357)
RWH INDUSTRIES INC
9430 Rapidan Dr (22407-1522)
PHONE....................540 736-8007
Robert Hall, *Principal*
EMP: 2 EST: 2016
SALES (est): 142.3K **Privately Held**
SIC: 3999 Manufacturing industries

(G-5358)
S&M TRUCKING INC
6025 Massaponax Dr (22407-1253)
PHONE....................540 842-1378
Stephen L Rollins, *President*
EMP: 1
SALES (est): 102.1K **Privately Held**
SIC: 3715 Truck trailers

(G-5359)
SCHLUMBERGER TECHNOLOGY CORP
11207 Sandusky Ct (22407-2514)
PHONE....................540 786-6419
EMP: 65 **Privately Held**
SIC: 1389 Oil/Gas Field Services
HQ: Schlumberger Technology Corp
　　100 Gillingham Ln
　　Sugar Land TX 77478
　　281 285-8500

(G-5360)
SHADE GREEN PUBLISHING
4408 Wexham Ct (22408-7731)
PHONE....................540 845-4780
Francine Dawkins, *Principal*
EMP: 2
SALES (est): 62.1K **Privately Held**
SIC: 2741 Miscellaneous publishing

(G-5361)
SHOCKEY BROS INC
Also Called: Shockey Precast Group
4717 Massaponax Church Rd (22408-8751)
P.O. Box 2530, Winchester (22604-1729)
PHONE....................540 667-7700
James D Shockey Jr, *President*
Wesley Garrett, *Manager*
Farrell Heishman, *Manager*
Robert Newlin, *Manager*
EMP: 80
SALES (corp-wide): 130.3MM **Privately Held**
WEB: www.shockeyprecast.com
SIC: 3272 Concrete products, precast
HQ: Shockey Bros., Inc.
　　219 Stine Ln
　　Winchester VA 22603
　　540 401-0101

(G-5362)
SMITH DISTRIBUTORS & MKTG LLC
12503 Argall Ln (22407-0121)
PHONE....................540 760-6833
Stacy Smith, *Principal*

EMP: 1 **EST:** 2017
SALES (est): 92.4K **Privately Held**
SIC: 3571 5045 Computers, digital, analog or hybrid; personal computers (microcomputers); computers & accessories, personal & home entertainment

(G-5363)
SNIFFAROO INC
11819 Switchback Ln (22407-1785)
PHONE..............................941 544-3529
Sean Dwyer, *Principal*
EMP: 2
SALES (est): 98.3K **Privately Held**
SIC: 2023 Dietary supplements, dairy & non-dairy based

(G-5364)
SOCIAL MUSIC LLC
11801 Hunting Ridge Dr (22407-7367)
PHONE..............................202 308-3249
EMP: 2 **EST:** 2015
SALES (est): 65.2K **Privately Held**
SIC: 2711 Newspapers

(G-5365)
SOLVENT INDUSTRIES INC
5316 Joshua Tree Cir (22407-9335)
Rural Route 5316 (22407)
PHONE..............................540 760-8611
Chris Hodge, *President*
Tony Buhr, *Director*
Lee Hodge, *Director*
EMP: 3
SALES (est): 83.9K **Privately Held**
SIC: 3999 Manufacturing industries

(G-5366)
SOURCE CONSULTING INC
5504 Heritage Hills Cir (22407-0103)
PHONE..............................540 785-0268
Dan Karcher, *General Mgr*
EMP: 3
SALES (est): 252.8K **Privately Held**
WEB: www.2sci.com
SIC: 7372 Prepackaged software

(G-5367)
SPOTCITY CUPCAKES LLC
5502 Joshua Tree Cir (22407-9343)
PHONE..............................703 587-4934
Eileen M Ramirez Mercado, *Administration*
EMP: 4 **EST:** 2012
SALES (est): 199.9K **Privately Held**
WEB: www.spotcitycupcakes.com
SIC: 2051 Bread, cake & related products

(G-5368)
SSB MANUFACTURING COMPANY
Also Called: Simmons Bedding Company
9601 Cosner Dr (22408-8733)
PHONE..............................540 891-0236
Rocco Poliseo, *Manager*
Lisa Del, *Manager*
EMP: 110 **Privately Held**
WEB: www.simmons.com
SIC: 2515 5712 Mattresses, innerspring or box spring; beds & accessories
HQ: Ssb Manufacturing Company
2451 Industry Ave
Doraville GA 30360
770 512-7700

(G-5369)
STROBER BUILDING SUPPLY
Also Called: Probuild Materials
5213 Jefferson Davis Hwy (22408-2605)
PHONE..............................540 834-2111
Jody Michniewicz, *Branch Mgr*
EMP: 9
SALES (corp-wide): 17.9MM **Privately Held**
SIC: 3275 Gypsum products
PA: Strober Building Supply
7811 Penn Western Ct
Upper Marlboro MD
301 967-9100

(G-5370)
STRUCTUREWORKS FABRICATION
3300 Dill Smith Dr (22408-7319)
PHONE..............................877 489-8064
Kim Whitt, *Business Mgr*

Andy Sears, *Vice Pres*
Neil O'Hare, *Sales Mgr*
Sam Perera, *Representative*
EMP: 2
SALES (est): 390.5K **Privately Held**
WEB: www.structureworksfab.com
SIC: 3444 Sheet metalwork

(G-5371)
SUMMER INTERIOR LLC
6501 Broad Creek Overlook (22407-3327)
PHONE..............................540 479-5145
Lisa Bonds,
EMP: 1
SALES (est): 81.8K **Privately Held**
SIC: 2519 Household furniture

(G-5372)
SYFTKOG
5503 Steeplechase Dr A (22407-7532)
PHONE..............................540 693-5875
Davie Hodge, *Principal*
EMP: 2
SALES (est): 110.9K **Privately Held**
WEB: www.syftkogtech.com
SIC: 7372 Prepackaged software

(G-5373)
T C CATLETT & SONS LUMBER CO
10315 Elys Ford Rd (22407-9650)
PHONE..............................540 786-2303
Robert E Catlett, *President*
T C Catlett, *Chairman*
Roger L Catlett, *Vice Pres*
Marie B Catlett, *Bookkeeper*
Allan Clay Catlett, *Admin Sec*
EMP: 22
SQ FT: 500
SALES (est): 2.9MM **Privately Held**
SIC: 2421 2426 2411 Sawmills & planing mills, general; hardwood dimension & flooring mills; logging

(G-5374)
TA TECHNICAL SERVICES LLC
5100 Windbreak Dr (22407-9323)
PHONE..............................540 429-5977
Terry Hester, *Principal*
EMP: 1 **EST:** 2012
SALES (est): 97.2K **Privately Held**
WEB: www.tatechnicalservices.com
SIC: 3695 Computer software tape & disks: blank, rigid & floppy

(G-5375)
TACTICAL MICRO
3509 Shannon Park Dr # 103 (22408-2377)
PHONE..............................540 907-0091
EMP: 2
SALES (est): 151.9K **Privately Held**
WEB: www.tacticalmicro.com
SIC: 3699 Electrical equipment & supplies

(G-5376)
TALLANT INDUSTRIES INC
4900 Ondura Dr (22407-8773)
PHONE..............................540 898-7000
John D Adair Jr, *CEO*
L Paul Nelson, *President*
Katherine D Adair, *Vice Pres*
Ed Harlin, *Vice Pres*
Allan Cowden, *Plant Engr*
EMP: 6
SALES (est): 1.1MM **Privately Held**
WEB: www.ondura.com
SIC: 2952 Roofing materials

(G-5377)
THERMO QUICK INC
11720 Main St Ste 100 (22408-7368)
PHONE..............................703 455-0040
Michael Anthony, *CEO*
EMP: 5
SALES (est): 500K **Privately Held**
WEB: www.thermoquickinc.com
SIC: 2752 Commercial printing, offset

(G-5378)
TITAN AMERICA LLC
10133 Tidewater Trl (22408-9609)
PHONE..............................540 372-8717
John Spivey, *Branch Mgr*
EMP: 5

SALES (corp-wide): 1.4MM **Privately Held**
WEB: www.titanamerica.com
SIC: 3273 Ready-mixed concrete
HQ: Titan America Llc
5700 Lake Wright Dr # 300
Norfolk VA 23502
757 858-6500

(G-5379)
TITAN SIGN CORPORATION
Also Called: Titan Sign & Awning
11001 Pierson Dr Ste H (22408-2079)
PHONE..............................540 899-5334
John G Lancto, *President*
Charles Lancto, *Treasurer*
EMP: 7
SQ FT: 5,000
SALES (est): 868.4K **Privately Held**
WEB: www.titansigncorp.com
SIC: 3993 5999 1799 Electric signs; neon signs; awnings; sign installation & maintenance

(G-5380)
TRANE INC
11205 New Albany Dr (22408-7352)
PHONE..............................540 376-3064
EMP: 2 **Privately Held**
WEB: www.trane.com
SIC: 3585 Refrigeration & heating equipment
HQ: Trane Inc.
1 Centennial Ave Ste 101
Piscataway NJ 08854
732 652-7100

(G-5381)
TRANE US INC
11205 New Albany Dr (22408-7352)
PHONE..............................540 376-3064
EMP: 2 **Privately Held**
WEB: www.trane.com
SIC: 3585 Refrigeration & heating equipment
HQ: Trane U.S. Inc.
3600 Pammel Creek Rd
La Crosse WI 54601
608 787-2000

(G-5382)
TRUSSWAY MANUFACTURING INC
11540 Shannon Dr (22408-7305)
PHONE..............................540 898-3477
Darren Hedrick, *Branch Mgr*
Rick Toledo, *Maintence Staff*
EMP: 90 **Privately Held**
WEB: www.trussway.com
SIC: 2439 Trusses, wooden roof
HQ: Trussway Manufacturing, Inc.
9411 Alcorn St
Houston TX 77093

(G-5383)
UNIQUE WREATHS
8610 Oldham Rd (22408-8756)
PHONE..............................540 322-9301
Tina Frame, *Principal*
EMP: 2
SALES (est): 62.5K **Privately Held**
SIC: 3999 Wreaths, artificial

(G-5384)
UNIVERSAL DYNAMICS INC
11700 Shannon Dr (22408-7310)
PHONE..............................703 490-7000
Paul Stafford, *Production*
Tom Martin, *Branch Mgr*
EMP: 6 **Privately Held**
WEB: www.unadyn.com
SIC: 3585 Dehumidifiers electric, except portable
HQ: Universal Dynamics, Inc.
13600 Dabney Rd
Woodbridge VA 22191
703 490-6114

(G-5385)
VA WOODWORKS LLC
105 Jubal St (22408-1901)
PHONE..............................540 903-6681
Brian Dykes, *Principal*
EMP: 2 **EST:** 2009
SALES (est): 145.8K **Privately Held**
SIC: 2431 Millwork

(G-5386)
VAULT
11047 Pierson Dr Ste A (22408-2062)
PHONE..............................540 479-2221
EMP: 3 **EST:** 2010
SALES (est): 150K **Privately Held**
SIC: 3272 Mfg Concrete Products

(G-5387)
VIRGINIA QUILTER
1 Murphy Ct (22407-6521)
P.O. Box 83 (22404-0083)
PHONE..............................540 548-3207
EMP: 1 **EST:** 1999
SALES (est): 52K **Privately Held**
SIC: 2395 5949 Pleating/Stitching Services Ret Sewing Supplies/Fabrics

(G-5388)
VULCAN MATERIALS COMPANY
Also Called: Cardinal Concrete
9201 Leavells Rd (22407)
PHONE..............................540 898-6210
Robert Miles, *Manager*
EMP: 12 **Publicly Held**
WEB: www.vulcanmaterials.com
SIC: 3273 Ready-mixed concrete
PA: Vulcan Materials Company
1200 Urban Center Dr
Vestavia AL 35242

(G-5389)
WALTON INDUSTRIES INC
Also Called: Minuteman Press
10699 Courthouse Rd (22407-7743)
PHONE..............................540 898-7888
Brenda L Walton, *President*
Douglas J Walton Jr, *Vice Pres*
EMP: 5
SALES (est): 578.2K **Privately Held**
WEB: www.minutemanpress.com
SIC: 2752 Commercial printing, lithographic

(G-5390)
WAVE PRINTING & GRAPHICS INC
220 Industrial Dr (22408-2431)
PHONE..............................540 373-1600
Wayne Whitley, *President*
Dave Whitley, *Vice Pres*
EMP: 5
SQ FT: 3,000
SALES (est): 488K **Privately Held**
WEB: www.wavepg.com
SIC: 2752 Commercial printing, offset

(G-5391)
WILKINSON WOODWORKING
4049 Woodside Dr (22407-4835)
PHONE..............................540 548-2029
Joseph Wilkinson, *Owner*
EMP: 1
SALES (est): 78K **Privately Held**
WEB: www.wilkinsonswoodworking.com
SIC: 2431 Millwork

(G-5392)
WIZARD
8700 Formation Dr (22407-5900)
PHONE..............................818 988-2283
EMP: 2
SALES (est): 88.6K **Privately Held**
SIC: 2759 Screen printing

(G-5393)
ZAKUFDM LLC
2413 Pittston Rd (22408-0282)
PHONE..............................330 338-0930
Ryan Scala, *Principal*
EMP: 1
SALES (est): 39.6K **Privately Held**
SIC: 3999 Manufacturing industries

(G-5394)
ZENTECH FREDERICKSBURG LLC
3361 Shannon Airport Cir (22408-2337)
PHONE..............................540 372-6500
Matt Turpin, *President*
Waleid Jabai, *Vice Pres*
Dorothy Shifflett, *Mfg Mgr*
Ginny Stevens, *Mfg Spvr*
Derrick Nabors, *Purch Agent*
EMP: 30 **EST:** 1982

GEOGRAPHIC

SQ FT: 25,000
SALES (est): 8.8MM
SALES (corp-wide): 56MM **Privately Held**
WEB: www.colonialassembly.com
SIC: 3672 Circuit boards, television & radio printed
PA: Zentech Manufacturing, Inc.
6980 Tudsbury Rd
Baltimore MD 21244
443 348-4500

Fredericksburg
Stafford County

(G-5395)
A TASTE OF LLC
33 Wellspring Dr (22405-2938)
PHONE....................................540 848-3186
Patrice Catlett,
EMP: 2
SALES (est): 62.3K **Privately Held**
SIC: 2051 Bakery, for home service delivery

(G-5396)
AGORA DATA SERVICES LLC
16 Ridge Pointe Ln (22405-2745)
PHONE....................................703 328-7758
Fred Kleibacker, *CEO*
Erika Kleibacker,
EMP: 1
SALES (est): 50.9K **Privately Held**
SIC: 7372 7379 Prepackaged software; computer related consulting services; data processing consultant

(G-5397)
ALL GLASS LLC
27 Utah Pl Ste 101 (22405-4528)
PHONE....................................540 288-8111
Edward Latendresse, *Marketing Mgr*
EMP: 4 EST: 2012
SALES (est): 141.1K **Privately Held**
WEB: www.allglassva.com
SIC: 3211 1793 5039 2431 Window glass, clear & colored; glass & glazing work; exterior flat glass: plate or window; louver windows, glass, wood frame; products of purchased glass

(G-5398)
AMERICAN TECH SLTONS INTL CORP (PA)
49 Bethany Way (22406-4452)
PHONE....................................540 907-5355
Patrick Regan, *President*
EMP: 31
SQ FT: 8,000
SALES (est): 13.7MM **Privately Held**
WEB: www.atsicorp.com
SIC: 3761 8748 8713 7379 Guided missiles & space vehicles; business consulting; surveying services; computer related consulting services; computer facilities management; geological consultant

(G-5399)
APOGEE POWER USA LLC
14 Little Field Dr (22405-1835)
PHONE....................................318 572-8967
Michael Parrish,
EMP: 15 EST: 2017
SALES (est): 436.7K **Privately Held**
WEB: www.apogeepower-usa.com
SIC: 3999 Manufacturing industries

(G-5400)
ART CONNECTED
181 Kings Hwy Ste 205 (22405-2683)
PHONE....................................540 628-2162
Freda Moore, *Manager*
EMP: 2 EST: 2010
SALES (est): 231.8K **Privately Held**
WEB: www.artconnectedgroup.com
SIC: 3552 Embroidery machines

(G-5401)
ATELIER FONTENEAU LLC
304 Interstate Bus Park (22405-1319)
PHONE....................................540 371-5074
Mickael Fonteneau, *Principal*
EMP: 4

SALES (est): 435.8K **Privately Held**
SIC: 3553 Cabinet makers' machinery

(G-5402)
BENZACO SCIENTIFIC INC (PA)
1406 Interstate Bus Park (22405-1308)
PHONE....................................540 371-5560
John Abalon, *President*
EMP: 2
SALES (est): 320.7K **Privately Held**
WEB: www.benzaco.com
SIC: 3823 8748 Pressure measurement instruments, industrial; environmental consultant

(G-5403)
BERNARD SPEED
Also Called: Family Power Washing
126 Cranes Corner Rd (22405-1477)
PHONE....................................540 514-9041
Bernard Speed, *Owner*
EMP: 2
SALES (est): 116.5K **Privately Held**
WEB: www.homeadvisors.com
SIC: 3589 Car washing machinery

(G-5404)
BOC GROUP DE
5 Rodney Ln (22405-2521)
PHONE....................................540 373-1782
Damon McMillion, *Principal*
EMP: 3 EST: 2014
SALES (est): 206.4K **Privately Held**
SIC: 2813 Industrial gases

(G-5405)
BRASS BULLET COFFEE CO VA LLC
500 Interstate Bus Park (22405-1315)
PHONE....................................540 373-2432
Eric Balough,
EMP: 10
SALES (est): 450K **Privately Held**
WEB: www.ricksroasters.com
SIC: 2095 Roasted coffee

(G-5406)
BYBEE STONE CO INC
210 England Pointe Dr (22406-6497)
PHONE....................................812 876-2215
Marybeth Haas, *Executive*
EMP: 2
SALES (est): 62.6K **Privately Held**
WEB: www.bybeestone.com
SIC: 3281 Cut stone & stone products

(G-5407)
CAMBER CORPORATION
30 Blackjack Rd (22405-4544)
PHONE....................................540 720-6294
EMP: 3
SALES (est): 87.1K **Publicly Held**
SIC: 3731 Military ships, building & repairing
PA: Huntington Ingalls Industries, Inc.
4101 Washington Ave
Newport News VA 23607

(G-5408)
CATHAY FOOD CORP
148 Basalt Dr (22406-7228)
PHONE....................................617 427-1507
EMP: 35
SQ FT: 21,000
SALES (est): 3.6MM **Privately Held**
SIC: 2099 2038 Mfg Food Preparations Mfg Frozen Specialties

(G-5409)
CAVE MMA LLC
1504 Interstate Bus Park (22405-1307)
PHONE....................................540 455-7623
EMP: 2
SALES (est): 121.5K **Privately Held**
SIC: 3949 Gloves, sport & athletic: boxing, handball, etc.

(G-5410)
CENTERLINE FABRICATORS
199 Tyler Von Way (22405-4514)
PHONE....................................540 318-6769
EMP: 2
SALES (est): 225.2K **Privately Held**
SIC: 3444 Sheet metalwork

(G-5411)
CHASE GROUP II A/C & HTG SVC
Also Called: Chase II, Raymond C
109 Ringgold Rd (22405-5719)
PHONE....................................571 245-7379
Raymond C Chase II, *Owner*
EMP: 1
SALES (est): 25K **Privately Held**
SIC: 3585 Refrigeration & heating equipment

(G-5412)
CLARKS LUMBER & MILLWORK INC
Also Called: C.L.m
1195 Intl Pkwy Ste 101 (22406)
PHONE....................................804 448-9985
Roger D Clark Jr, *President*
Scott McCrodden, *General Mgr*
Curley Williams, *Prgrmr*
EMP: 18
SQ FT: 10,000
SALES (est): 2.7MM **Privately Held**
WEB: www.clm-inc.com
SIC: 2431 Millwork

(G-5413)
COCA-COLA CONSOLIDATED INC
57 Commerce Pkwy (22406-1037)
PHONE....................................540 361-7500
Warren Woolfrey, *Manager*
EMP: 100
SALES (corp-wide): 4.8B **Publicly Held**
WEB: www.cokeconsolidated.com
SIC: 2086 Bottled & canned soft drinks
PA: Coca-Cola Consolidated, Inc.
4100 Coca Cola Plz # 100
Charlotte NC 28211
704 557-4400

(G-5414)
CORE PRINTS
1130 International Pkwy # 119 (22406-1220)
PHONE....................................540 356-9195
Russell Irby, *Principal*
EMP: 2 EST: 2018
SALES (est): 83.9K **Privately Held**
SIC: 2752 Commercial printing, lithographic

(G-5415)
COUNTRY CORNER LLC
155 Enon Rd (22405-5812)
PHONE....................................540 538-3763
Kim Haney,
EMP: 1
SALES (est): 105.2K **Privately Held**
SIC: 2426 5712 Carvings, furniture: wood; furniture stores

(G-5416)
CREATIVE SIGNS LTD
1231 Kings Hwy (22405-3909)
PHONE....................................540 899-0032
Phillip Lucas, *President*
Carol J Lucas, *Vice Pres*
EMP: 3
SQ FT: 1,200
SALES (est): 278.7K **Privately Held**
SIC: 3993 Signs, not made in custom sign painting shops

(G-5417)
CUSTOM SFTWR DSIGN SLTIONS LLC
Also Called: Csd Solutions
3 Gallagher Ln (22405-1780)
PHONE....................................888 423-4049
James Brewers, *President*
EMP: 1
SALES (est): 76.7K **Privately Held**
SIC: 7372 7371 Application computer software; computer software systems analysis & design, custom

(G-5418)
CYBER-CANVAS
19 Sanford Ferry Ct (22406-5446)
PHONE....................................540 692-9322
James Broad, *Principal*
EMP: 2

SALES (est): 100.6K **Privately Held**
WEB: www.cyber-canvas.com
SIC: 2211 Canvas

(G-5419)
DAVES MACHINE SHOP
34 New Hope Church Rd (22405-3610)
PHONE....................................540 903-0172
David Harrell, *Principal*
EMP: 2 EST: 2010
SALES (est): 143.2K **Privately Held**
SIC: 3599 Machine shop, jobbing & repair

(G-5420)
DOCKS CANVAS & UPHOLSTERY
371 Greenbank Rd (22405-5403)
PHONE....................................540 840-0440
EMP: 2
SALES (est): 73.4K **Privately Held**
SIC: 2211 Canvas

(G-5421)
DOMINION BLDG COMPONENTS LLC
68 Cool Spring Rd Ste B (22405-2656)
P.O. Box 9122 (22403-9122)
PHONE....................................540 371-2184
Sidney Allen Smith,
EMP: 6
SQ FT: 10,000
SALES (est): 793K **Privately Held**
SIC: 2439 Trusses, except roof: laminated lumber

(G-5422)
DWB DESIGN INC
91 Sandy Ridge Rd (22405-3551)
PHONE....................................540 371-0785
David W Ballard, *President*
EMP: 1
SALES (est): 95K **Privately Held**
SIC: 3672 Printed circuit boards

(G-5423)
DYNAMIC DESIGNS
40 Cool Spring Rd Ste 101 (22405-2694)
PHONE....................................540 371-7173
Bill Van Hoy, *Owner*
EMP: 2
SALES (est): 150.7K **Privately Held**
WEB: www.dynamicdesignsva.com
SIC: 3993 Signs & advertising specialties

(G-5424)
EAZY CONSTRUCTION INC
56 Antler Trl (22406-4632)
PHONE....................................571 220-8385
Paul Lowe, *CEO*
Zack Lowe, *Officer*
EMP: 1
SALES (est): 143.1K **Privately Held**
WEB: www.eazyconstructioninc.com
SIC: 2493 1761 1799 Insulation & roofing material, reconstituted wood; roofing, siding & sheet metal work; cleaning new buildings after construction

(G-5425)
EDGELIT DESIGNZ & ENGRV LLC
52 Colemans Mill Dr (22405-2183)
PHONE....................................540 373-8058
Shawn Shurina, *Principal*
EMP: 2 EST: 2016
SALES (est): 88.6K **Privately Held**
SIC: 2759 Commercial printing

(G-5426)
ELECTROMAGNETIC SHIELDING INC
115 Juliad Ct Ste 103 (22406-1100)
PHONE....................................540 286-3780
Debra Vitale, *CEO*
EMP: 2
SALES (est): 230K **Privately Held**
WEB: www.emishield.com
SIC: 3499 Magnetic shields, metal

(G-5427)
ELITE LAUNDRY AND CAR WASH LLC
312 Chatham Heights Rd (22405-2577)
PHONE....................................540 373-6150

Michael Newton, *Mng Member*
EMP: 4
SALES (est): 110K **Privately Held**
SIC: 3633 Laundry dryers, household or coin-operated

(G-5428)
ELS WHEELS LLC
30 Castlewood Dr (22406-8423)
PHONE..................................540 370-4397
Ellen Grady, *Principal*
EMP: 2
SALES (est): 180.8K **Privately Held**
SIC: 3312 Blast furnaces & steel mills

(G-5429)
ERIN WELDING SERVICE INC
1112 James Madison Cir (22405-1632)
PHONE..................................540 899-3970
James P McKelvey, *President*
EMP: 3
SQ FT: 3,000
SALES (est): 262K **Privately Held**
SIC: 7692 Welding repair

(G-5430)
FARMSTEAD FINDS SALVAGING
550 Long Meadow Dr (22406-4981)
PHONE..................................540 845-8200
Justin Doyle, *Principal*
EMP: 1
SALES (est): 54.1K **Privately Held**
SIC: 2431 Millwork

(G-5431)
FN AMERICA LLC
14 Hazel Park Ln (22405-4503)
PHONE..................................540 288-8002
Richard Adams, *Manager*
EMP: 4 **Privately Held**
WEB: www.fnamerica.com
SIC: 3484 Machine guns or machine gun parts, 30 mm. & below
HQ: Fn America, Llc
    7950 Jones Branch Dr
    Mc Lean VA 22102
    703 288-3500

(G-5432)
FRANK HAGERTY
Also Called: United Illumination
6 Westmoreland Pl (22405-3056)
PHONE..................................540 809-0589
Frank Hagerty, *Owner*
EMP: 1 **EST:** 2013
SALES (est): 53.7K **Privately Held**
WEB: www.hagerty.com
SIC: 3646 3648 Commercial indusl & institutional electric lighting fixtures; outdoor lighting equipment

(G-5433)
FTG CRCUITS FREDERICKSBURG INC
1026 Warrenton Rd (22406-6200)
PHONE..................................540 752-5511
Brad Bourne, *CEO*
Mark W Osborn, *President*
Paul Godbout, *General Mgr*
Roland E Murphy, *Corp Secy*
EMP: 65
SQ FT: 40,000
SALES (est): 11.2MM
SALES (corp-wide): 84.2MM **Privately Held**
WEB: www.colonialcircuits.com
SIC: 3672 Circuit boards, television & radio printed
PA: Firan Technology Group Corporation
    250 Finchdene Sq
    Toronto ON M1X 1
    416 299-4000

(G-5434)
GARY CLARK
Also Called: Gary Clark's Welding
61 Trails End Ln (22405-3458)
PHONE..................................540 373-4598
Gary Clark, *Owner*
Gary P Clark, *Owner*
EMP: 1
SALES (est): 110.3K **Privately Held**
SIC: 7692 Welding repair

(G-5435)
GLAMOROUS SWEET
210 Hartlake Dr (22406-4637)
PHONE..................................540 903-3683
Legg Natalie, *Owner*
EMP: 1
SALES (est): 51.9K **Privately Held**
SIC: 2052 Cookies & crackers

(G-5436)
GRAPEVINE
607 Payton Dr (22405-2252)
PHONE..................................540 371-4092
Linda Pulliam, *Owner*
EMP: 1
SALES (est): 63.7K **Privately Held**
SIC: 2449 Wood containers

(G-5437)
HARKNESS SCREENS (USA) LIMITED
100 Riverside Pkwy Ste 209 (22406)
P.O. Box 8480 (22404-8480)
PHONE..................................540 370-1590
Abby Jarrett, *Human Res Mgr*
David Burlinson, *Branch Mgr*
▲ **EMP:** 20 **Privately Held**
WEB: www.harkness-screens.com
SIC: 3861 Photographic paper & cloth, all types
HQ: Harkness Screens (Uk) Limited
    Unit A
    Stevenage HERTS SG1 2

(G-5438)
HARTWOOD LANDSCAPE INC
43 Debbie Dr (22406-4749)
PHONE..................................540 379-2650
Brian Way, *President*
EMP: 3
SALES (est): 450K **Privately Held**
WEB: www.hartwoodlandscape.com
SIC: 3523 Farm machinery & equipment

(G-5439)
HARTWOOD WINERY INC
345 Hartwood Rd (22406-4205)
PHONE..................................540 752-4893
James Livingston, *President*
Beverly Livingston, *General Mgr*
EMP: 2
SQ FT: 3,000
SALES (est): 180K **Privately Held**
WEB: www.hartwoodwineryva.com
SIC: 2084 Wines

(G-5440)
HEART STAR PRESS LLC
8 Yorktown Dr (22405-2989)
PHONE..................................540 479-6882
Alia Ann Reese, *Administration*
EMP: 2
SALES (est): 108.9K **Privately Held**
WEB: www.heartstarpress.com
SIC: 2741 Miscellaneous publishing

(G-5441)
INDIGENOUS INDUSTRIES LLC
110 Kellogg Mill Rd (22406-4300)
PHONE..................................540 847-9851
Joshua S Hobgood, *Manager*
EMP: 1
SALES (est): 39.6K **Privately Held**
SIC: 3999 Manufacturing industries

(G-5442)
INTUIT INC
110 Juliad Ct Ste 107 (22406-1170)
PHONE..................................540 752-6100
Alok Gulati, *Business Mgr*
Christine Stutzman, *Business Anlyst*
Bill Davidson, *Branch Mgr*
Dustin Phillips, *Manager*
Kayla Regetz, *Manager*
EMP: 240
SALES (corp-wide): 7.6B **Publicly Held**
WEB: www.intuit.com
SIC: 7372 Business oriented computer software
PA: Intuit Inc.
    2700 Coast Ave
    Mountain View CA 94043
    650 944-6000

(G-5443)
JERRY CANTRELL
1090 Truslow Rd (22406-5115)
PHONE..................................540 379-7689
Jerry Cantrell, *Owner*
EMP: 1
SALES (est): 62.4K **Privately Held**
SIC: 3523 Farm machinery & equipment

(G-5444)
JETTS SHEET METAL INC
211 Newton Rd (22405-3447)
PHONE..................................540 899-7725
Don Jett, *President*
EMP: 2
SQ FT: 1,200
SALES (est): 569K **Privately Held**
SIC: 3441 Fabricated structural metal

(G-5445)
JMR GAINES
17 N Pointe Dr (22405-2779)
PHONE..................................540 370-1723
James Gaines, *Principal*
EMP: 2 **EST:** 2017
SALES (est): 89.1K **Privately Held**
WEB: www.jmrgaines.com
SIC: 2741 Miscellaneous publishing

(G-5446)
JOHNSON & SON LUMBER INC
88 Storck Rd (22406-4725)
P.O. Box 259, Thornburg (22565-0259)
PHONE..................................540 752-5557
Douglas Johnson, *President*
Douglas F Johnson, *President*
Richard H Sorrell, *Vice Pres*
George Johnson, *Treasurer*
EMP: 30 **EST:** 1950
SALES (est): 3.6MM **Privately Held**
SIC: 2421 2426 Sawmills & planing mills, general; hardwood dimension & flooring mills

(G-5447)
KELKASE INC
30 Kinsley Ln (22406-4089)
PHONE..................................703 670-9443
EMP: 2 **EST:** 2010
SALES (est): 71K **Privately Held**
SIC: 3999 Mfg Misc Products

(G-5448)
LABELINK FLEXIBLES LLC
18 Blackjack Rd (22405-4531)
PHONE..................................703 348-4699
Stefan Bouchard,
EMP: 14 **EST:** 2018
SALES (est): 199.1K **Privately Held**
WEB: www.labelink.ca
SIC: 2752 Commercial printing, lithographic

(G-5449)
LESCO INC
115 Juliad Ct Ste 107 (22406-1100)
PHONE..................................540 752-1408
Ryan Swierk, *Branch Mgr*
EMP: 2
SALES (corp-wide): 39.2B **Publicly Held**
SIC: 2875 Fertilizers, mixing only
HQ: Lesco, Inc.
    1385 E 36th St
    Cleveland OH 44114
    216 706-9250

(G-5450)
LESDEN CORPORATION
802 Interstate Bus Park (22405-1314)
PHONE..................................540 373-4940
Leslie Wade, *President*
EMP: 3
SQ FT: 6,400
SALES (est): 467K **Privately Held**
SIC: 2431 1751 Millwork; cabinet & finish carpentry

(G-5451)
LEWIS EARL MILLS
1385 Truslow Rd (22406-5003)
PHONE..................................540 295-2061
Lewis Mills, *Principal*
EMP: 1
SALES (est): 55.1K **Privately Held**
SIC: 7692 Welding repair

(G-5452)
MAGIC BULLET SKATEBOARDS LLC
17 Argyle Hills Dr (22405-2855)
PHONE..................................703 371-0363
Brent C Eyestone, *Administration*
EMP: 4
SALES (est): 165.3K **Privately Held**
WEB: www.austinlucas.com
SIC: 3949 Skateboards

(G-5453)
MAPEI CORPORATION
300 Nelms Cir (22406-1120)
PHONE..................................540 361-1085
Eliezer Decote, *Warehouse Mgr*
Guido Trussardi, *Engineer*
Tom Montagu, *Branch Mgr*
Steve Tyrrell, *Manager*
EMP: 50
SQ FT: 70,374 **Privately Held**
WEB: www.mapei.com
SIC: 2891 2899 3255 Adhesives; chemical preparations; clay refractories
HQ: Mapei Corporation
    1144 E Newport Center Dr
    Deerfield Beach FL 33442
    954 246-8888

(G-5454)
MARKETFARE FOODS LLC
37 Mclane Dr (22406-1147)
P.O. Box 6107 (22403-6107)
PHONE..................................540 371-5110
Kent Zech, *Branch Mgr*
EMP: 200 **Privately Held**
WEB: www.taylorandfrancis.com
SIC: 2099 Sandwiches, assembled & packaged: for wholesale market
HQ: Marketfare Foods Llc
    222 Rosewood Dr Fl 2
    Danvers MA 01923
    978 716-2530

(G-5455)
MATTHEW MITCHELL
Also Called: Mitchell's Armory
93 Cedar Grove Rd (22406-4926)
PHONE..................................615 454-0787
Matthew Mitchell, *Owner*
EMP: 1
SALES (est): 49.5K **Privately Held**
SIC: 3484 Small arms

(G-5456)
MCKOON ZANETA
Also Called: Z Costumes
2000 Green Tree Rd (22406-1178)
PHONE..................................410 707-5701
Zaneta McKoon, *Owner*
EMP: 1
SALES (est): 45.5K **Privately Held**
SIC: 2389 Theatrical costumes

(G-5457)
MCQ INC
1545 Forbes St (22405-1606)
PHONE..................................540 361-4219
Tim Payne, *Branch Mgr*
EMP: 2
SALES (corp-wide): 1.6MM **Privately Held**
WEB: www.mcqinc.com
SIC: 3829 Surveying instruments & accessories
PA: Mcq Inc.
    1551 Forbes St
    Fredericksburg VA 22405
    540 373-2374

(G-5458)
MERRIMAN PUBLISHING LLC
29 Goldcup Dr (22406-1044)
PHONE..................................540 370-1852
Scott Merriman, *Principal*
EMP: 1
SALES (est): 44.7K **Privately Held**
WEB: www.merrimanpublishing.com
SIC: 2741 Miscellaneous publishing

(G-5459)
MINUTEMAN PRESS
2 Walton Way (22405-8402)
PHONE..................................703 220-7575
Brenda Walton, *Principal*

EMP: 2
SALES (est): 206.2K **Privately Held**
WEB: www.minutemanpress.com
SIC: 2752 Commercial printing, litho-
graphic

(G-5460)
MYRMIDON INDUSTRIES INC
1700 Sherwood Dr (22405-2219)
PHONE..................540 273-6414
Ellen Smith, *President*
Joey Cline, *Exec VP*
Jason Smith, *Exec VP*
EMP: 4
SALES (est): 230.5K **Privately Held**
WEB: www.myrmidoninc.com
SIC: 3999 Manufacturing industries

(G-5461)
NORTHERN VIRGINIA COMPUTE
754 Warrenton Rd (22406-1098)
PHONE..................540 479-4455
Tim Alexander, *President*
EMP: 5 **EST:** 2009
SALES (est): 708.1K **Privately Held**
SIC: 3577 Computer peripheral equipment

(G-5462)
**OBSIDIAN SOLUTIONS GROUP
LLC**
1130 Intl Pkwy Ste 127 (22406)
PHONE..................540 286-2266
Bruce E Lemaster, *Branch Mgr*
EMP: 10 **Privately Held**
WEB: www.obsidiansg.com
SIC: 3089 Injection molding of plastics;
plastic processing
PA: Obsidian Solutions Group Llc
1320 Cntl Pk Blvd Ste 304
Fredericksburg VA 22401

(G-5463)
**OLDE TOWNE WINDOW WORKS
INC**
204 Thompson Ave Ste 103 (22405-2565)
PHONE..................540 371-6987
Jonathan L Wilken, *President*
EMP: 30
SQ FT: 15,000
SALES (est): 3.2MM **Privately Held**
WEB: www.oldetownewindowworks.com
SIC: 2391 Draperies, plastic & textile: from
purchased materials; curtains, window:
made from purchased materials

(G-5464)
**ONE ASTERISK WOODWORKS
LLC**
157 Basalt Dr (22406-7228)
PHONE..................508 332-8151
Carl Shipley, *Principal*
EMP: 2
SALES (est): 85.2K **Privately Held**
SIC: 2431 Millwork

(G-5465)
OPTOMETRICS LLC
27 Blackberry Ln (22406-5440)
PHONE..................540 840-5802
Marie Nazario, *Principal*
EMP: 3
SALES (est): 222.2K **Privately Held**
WEB: www.dynasil.com
SIC: 3827 Optical instruments & lenses

(G-5466)
ORA INC
45 Commerce Pkwy (22406-1037)
P.O. Box 5010 (22403-0610)
PHONE..................540 368-3012
EMP: 6
SALES: 500K **Privately Held**
SIC: 3499 Mfg Misc Fabricated Metal
Products

(G-5467)
PARTY HEADQUARTERS INC
Also Called: Varsity Graphics & Awards
20 Rawlings Pl 123 (22405-4545)
PHONE..................703 494-5317
Tammy Da Silva, *CEO*
Fernando Da Silva Jr, *Principal*
EMP: 5

SALES (est): 659.4K **Privately Held**
WEB: www.varsitygraphicsandawards.com
SIC: 2396 2752 7336 Fabric printing &
stamping; promotional printing, lithographic; calendar & card printing, lithographic; commercial art & graphic design

(G-5468)
PC SHAREWARE INC
39 Brookstone Dr (22405-2794)
PHONE..................540 371-5746
Philip Kapusta, *President*
EMP: 1 **EST:** 1988
SALES (est): 76K **Privately Held**
SIC: 7372 Prepackaged software

(G-5469)
**PERSONAL SELLING POWER
INC (PA)**
1140 International Pkwy (22406-1126)
P.O. Box 5467 (22403-0467)
PHONE..................540 752-7000
Gerhard Gschwandtner, *President*
Laura Gschwandtner, *Chief*
Amanda David, *Web Dvlpr*
Lisa Gschwandtner, *Director*
Jane Flaherty, *Sr Consultant*
EMP: 30 **EST:** 1977
SQ FT: 10,000
SALES (est): 1.6MM **Privately Held**
WEB: www.sellingpower.com
SIC: 2721 2731 Periodicals: publishing
only; books: publishing only

(G-5470)
POTOMAC INDUSTRIES
209 Old Landing Ct (22405-3705)
P.O. Box 9183 (22403-9183)
PHONE..................540 940-7288
EMP: 1
SALES (est): 39.6K **Privately Held**
WEB: www.potomacindustries.com
SIC: 3999 Manufacturing industries

(G-5471)
**PRECISION MCH & FIREARM
SVC**
955 Ramoth Church Rd (22406-4519)
PHONE..................540 659-3037
Dan Rivenbark, *Principal*
EMP: 1
SALES (est): 96.5K **Privately Held**
SIC: 3599 Machine shop, jobbing & repair

(G-5472)
PRINT MAIL DIRECT LLC
12 Rapids Way (22405-2790)
PHONE..................540 899-6451
H Smith, *Principal*
EMP: 4
SALES (est): 337.3K **Privately Held**
SIC: 2752 Commercial printing, litho-
graphic

(G-5473)
PSYCHO PANDA
Also Called: Psycho Panda Streetwear
207 Clint Ln (22405-2785)
PHONE..................540 287-0588
Ralph A Kay Jr, *Owner*
EMP: 1
SALES (est): 45.3K **Privately Held**
SIC: 2329 Men's & boys' clothing

(G-5474)
PUBLISHERS ASSET LLC
48 Clarion Dr (22405-2819)
PHONE..................540 621-4422
Craig Byl,
EMP: 1
SALES (est): 39.4K **Privately Held**
WEB: www.pubasset.com
SIC: 2741 Micropublishing

(G-5475)
**RAPPAHANNOCK & POTOMAC
REP LLC**
Also Called: R & P Reps LLC
100 Hampton Dr (22405-3128)
PHONE..................540 373-9545
Joseph Mancini,
Joseph Pontarlelli,
EMP: 2
SALES (est): 110K **Privately Held**
SIC: 3651 Sound reproducing equipment

(G-5476)
**RECTORS REPAIR & WELDING
LLC**
92 Le Way Dr (22405-1030)
PHONE..................540 809-5683
James Ryan Rector, *Administration*
EMP: 1 **EST:** 2013
SALES (est): 87.5K **Privately Held**
WEB: www.rectorsrepair.com
SIC: 7692 Welding repair

(G-5477)
RICHARDSON LOGGING
85 Ringgold Rd (22405-5717)
PHONE..................540 373-5756
Kirk Richardson, *President*
EMP: 8
SALES (est): 905.9K **Privately Held**
SIC: 2411 Logging camps & contractors

(G-5478)
**RICK A DEBERNARD WELDING
INC**
186 Fisher Ln (22405-3730)
PHONE..................540 834-8348
Rick A Debernard, *President*
EMP: 2 **EST:** 1995
SALES (est): 259K **Privately Held**
WEB: www.superfoodtown531.com
SIC: 7692 Welding repair

(G-5479)
**RICKS ROASTERS COFFEE CO
LLC (PA)**
1304 Interstate Bus Park (22405-1309)
PHONE..................540 318-6850
Sean Ricks,
Keely Ricks,
EMP: 7
SALES (est): 1.4MM **Privately Held**
WEB: www.ricksroasters.com
SIC: 2095 Roasted coffee

(G-5480)
RIO TAKE BACK LLC
70 Sebring Dr (22406-8419)
PHONE..................540 371-3636
Jeff Small, *Administration*
EMP: 2
SALES (est): 138.5K **Privately Held**
WEB: www.riocarwash.com
SIC: 3589 Car washing machinery

(G-5481)
S&R PALS ENTERPRISES LLC
560 Celebrate Virginia Pk (22406-7298)
PHONE..................540 752-1900
EMP: 2
SALES: 150K **Privately Held**
SIC: 2741 8743 7313 4783 Misc Publish-
ing Public Relations Service Advertising
Rep Packing/Crating Service

(G-5482)
SAFETY SEAL PLASTICS LLC
18 Blackjack Rd Ste 101 (22405-4540)
PHONE..................703 348-4699
Michael Bedrosian,
EMP: 4
SALES (est): 155.5K
SALES (corp-wide): 9MM **Privately Held**
WEB: www.labelink.ca
SIC: 2891 Sealing compounds, synthetic
rubber or plastic
PA: Safety Seal Plastics Inc
400 Michener Rd Unit 1
Guelph ON
905 575-9699

(G-5483)
SAWMARK WOODWORKS
239 Lake Forest Dr (22406-4444)
PHONE..................540 657-4814
Richard Meadows, *Principal*
EMP: 2 **EST:** 2014
SALES (est): 88.1K **Privately Held**
SIC: 2431 Millwork

(G-5484)
SECOND CHANCE DOG RESCUE
1654 Truslow Rd (22406-5010)
PHONE..................540 752-1741
Lisa M Roosa, *Principal*
EMP: 2

SALES (est): 108.5K **Privately Held**
WEB: www.secondchancedog.com
SIC: 3999 Pet supplies

(G-5485)
**SHELLEY IMPRSSONS PRTG
COPYING**
20 Commerce Pkwy Ste 105 (22406-1089)
PHONE..................540 310-0766
Patrick M Reilly, *Owner*
EMP: 5
SALES (est): 478.8K **Privately Held**
WEB: www.shelleyimpressions.com
SIC: 2752 7334 Commercial printing, off-
set; photocopying & duplicating services

(G-5486)
SPARTANCORE INDUSTRIES
44 Charter Gate Dr (22406-8206)
PHONE..................540 322-7563
John Miller, *Principal*
EMP: 2
SALES (est): 113.7K **Privately Held**
SIC: 3999 Manufacturing industries

(G-5487)
SPORT SHACK INC
102 Castle Rock Dr (22405-2429)
PHONE..................540 372-3719
Fax: 540 372-3720
EMP: 4 **EST:** 1990
SQ FT: 1,350
SALES: 325K **Privately Held**
SIC: 2396 2395 7999 5941 Mfg Auto/Ap-
parel Trim Pleating/Stitching Svcs Amuse-
ment/Recreation Svc Ret Sport
Goods/Bicycles Whol Sporting
Goods/Supp

(G-5488)
STEFANIK SIGN SERVICE
1461 Warrenton Rd (22406-5030)
PHONE..................540 295-7248
Chris Stefanik, *Owner*
EMP: 1
SALES (est): 46K **Privately Held**
SIC: 3993 Signs & advertising specialties

(G-5489)
SWEET SERENITY GIFTS
1600 Hartwood Rd (22406-4010)
PHONE..................540 903-1964
EMP: 1
SQ FT: 3,062
SALES (est): 43.1K **Privately Held**
SIC: 3911 Mfg Precious Metal Jewelry

(G-5490)
SWEET SPRINKLES
16 Glen Oak Rd (22405-1773)
PHONE..................540 373-4750
Rhonda Schenck, *Principal*
EMP: 1 **EST:** 2011
SALES (est): 84.3K **Privately Held**
WEB: www.sweetsprinkles.org
SIC: 3421 Table & food cutlery, including
butchers'

(G-5491)
SYSTEM INNOVATIONS INC
Also Called: McQ
1551 Forbes St (22405-1603)
PHONE..................540 373-2374
John H McQuiddy, *President*
Gale A Ruskosky, *Treasurer*
EMP: 10
SQ FT: 10,500
SALES (est): 1.1MM
SALES (corp-wide): 1.6MM **Privately
Held**
WEB: www.mcqinc.com
SIC: 3829 3699 Measuring & controlling
devices; electrical equipment & supplies
PA: Mcq Inc.
1551 Forbes St
Fredericksburg VA 22405
540 373-2374

(G-5492)
TEREX CORPORATION
150 Rverside Pkwy Ste 203 (22406)
PHONE..................540 361-7755
Tom Manley, *Office Mgr*
EMP: 6

▲ = Import ▼=Export
◆ =Import/Export

SALES (corp-wide): 4.3B **Publicly Held**
WEB: www.terex.com
SIC: **3531 3537 6159** Construction machinery; industrial trucks & tractors; machinery & equipment finance leasing
PA: Terex Corporation
200 Nyala Farms Rd
Westport CT 06880
203 222-7170

(G-5493)
TIDEWTER EXHIBITS AG MLLWK MFG
678 Kings Hwy (22405-3156)
PHONE...................................540 379-1555
Deborah Sullivan, *Principal*
EMP: 1
SALES (est): 67.7K **Privately Held**
SIC: **2431** Millwork

(G-5494)
TIMOTHYS CUSTOM WOODWORKING
160 Newton Rd (22405-3442)
PHONE...................................540 408-4343
EMP: 1
SALES (est): 54.1K **Privately Held**
WEB: www.olearyswoodworking.com
SIC: **2431** Millwork

(G-5495)
TNT PIPING AND WELDING
45 Little Whim Rd (22405-1892)
PHONE...................................804 224-1634
EMP: 1
SALES (est): 48K **Privately Held**
SIC: **7692** Welding repair

(G-5496)
UNITED WELDING INC
34 Perchwood Dr (22405-4516)
PHONE...................................540 628-2286
Ira North, *President*
Kristin North, *Vice Pres*
EMP: 4 EST: 2011
SALES (est): 240K **Privately Held**
WEB: www.unitedweldinginc.com
SIC: **7692** Welding repair

(G-5497)
VELOCITY SERVICES CORPORATION
13 Myers Dr (22405-5767)
PHONE...................................540 368-2708
Tim Brewster, *President*
Timothy Brewster, *President*
Christie Wright, *Train & Dev Mgr*
EMP: 25
SALES (est): 1.4MM **Privately Held**
WEB: www.velocitysc.com
SIC: **7372** Business oriented computer software

(G-5498)
VIRGINIA T-SHIRT COMPANY LLC
418 Spotted Tavern Rd (22406-4027)
PHONE...................................540 752-8141
Russell Wayne Pearson, *Principal*
EMP: 3
SALES (est): 118.9K **Privately Held**
SIC: **2759** Screen printing

(G-5499)
W R GRACE & CO-CONN
1101 Intl Pkwy Ste 121 (22406)
PHONE...................................540 752-6048
EMP: 5
SALES (corp-wide): 1.7B **Publicly Held**
SIC: **2899** Mfg Chemical Preparations
HQ: W. R. Grace & Co.-Conn.
7500 Grace Dr
Columbia MD 21044
410 531-4000

(G-5500)
WANDA EUBANKS
Also Called: Notary On The Go
110 Cotton Blossom Ct (22405-1507)
PHONE...................................804 615-7095
Wanda Eubanks, *Owner*
EMP: 1
SALES (est): 43.9K **Privately Held**
SIC: **3953** Seal presses, notary & hand

(G-5501)
WEAPONS ANALYSIS LLC
118 Cleremont Dr (22405-3325)
PHONE...................................540 371-9134
Edward Hlywa, *Principal*
Ed Hlywa, *Opers Staff*
EMP: 3
SALES (est): 172.7K **Privately Held**
WEB: www.weaponsanalysis.com
SIC: **3812** Defense systems & equipment

(G-5502)
WELDING & FABRICATION LLC
1298 Warrenton Rd (22406-6205)
PHONE...................................540 907-7461
Max Luis Quinones, *Principal*
EMP: 1
SALES (est): 25.8K **Privately Held**
SIC: **7692** Welding repair

(G-5503)
WINE SAWMILL
1034 Truslow Rd (22406-5115)
PHONE...................................540 373-8328
Kenneth W Wine, *Owner*
EMP: 1
SALES (est): 54.2K **Privately Held**
SIC: **2421** Lumber: rough, sawed or planed

(G-5504)
WOODWRIGHT COMPANY
185 Hartwood Rd (22406-4201)
PHONE...................................540 764-2539
Tim Kelly, *Owner*
EMP: 3
SALES (est): 280K **Privately Held**
WEB: www.woodwrightco.com
SIC: **2541** Display fixtures, wood

(G-5505)
ZERK MOTORS LLC
43 Town And Country Dr (22405-8729)
PHONE...................................540 322-2003
Christopher Nacinovich,
EMP: 1
SALES (est): 27.8K **Privately Held**
SIC: **7694** Motor repair services

Free Union
Albemarle County

(G-5506)
FAITH MISSION HOME
Also Called: Mission Home Bake Shop
8239 Mission Home Rd (22940-2232)
PHONE...................................434 985-7177
Lloyd Miller, *Manager*
EMP: 17
SALES (est): 1.2MM **Privately Held**
WEB:
www.faithmissionhome.mennonite.net
SIC: **2051** Bakery products, partially cooked (except frozen)

(G-5507)
GLASS HOUSE WINERY LLC
5898 Free Union Rd (22940-1804)
PHONE...................................434 975-0094
Michelle Sanders, *Principal*
Janice Blanchard, *Manager*
EMP: 16
SALES (est): 1.6MM **Privately Held**
WEB: www.glasshousewinery.com
SIC: **2084** Wines

(G-5508)
LLC WILEY BROTHERS
4289 Free Union Rd (22940-2113)
P.O. Box 123 (22940-0123)
PHONE...................................434 806-9633
Marcus Wiley, *Principal*
EMP: 2
SALES (est): 130.7K **Privately Held**
WEB: www.wileybelts.com
SIC: **3199** Leather goods

(G-5509)
POTTERS CRAFT LLC
4699 Catterton Rd (22940-1903)
PHONE...................................850 528-6314
Daniel Potter,
Timothy Edmond,
EMP: 2 EST: 2010

SQ FT: 900
SALES (est): 162.3K **Privately Held**
WEB: www.potterscraftcider.com
SIC: **2084** Wine cellars, bonded: engaged in blending wines

(G-5510)
TRIDENT OIL CORP
2374 Buck Mountain Rd (22940-2123)
P.O. Box 182 (22940-0182)
PHONE...................................434 974-1401
Dennis Palmgren, *President*
EMP: 1
SALES (est): 178.7K **Privately Held**
SIC: **1311** Crude petroleum & natural gas

Freeman
Brunswick County

(G-5511)
DANIELS CERTIFIED WELDING
290 Powell Ln (23856-2511)
P.O. Box 60 (23856-0060)
PHONE...................................434 848-4911
Gale Daniel, *President*
EMP: 3
SALES (est): 1,000K **Privately Held**
SIC: **3599 1799 7692** Machine shop, jobbing & repair; welding on site; welding repair

(G-5512)
MARY TRUMAN
Also Called: Original Brunswick Stew Co.
18021 Gvrnor Hrrison Pkwy (23856-2533)
P.O. Box 52 (23856-0052)
PHONE...................................469 554-0655
Mary Truman, *Owner*
EMP: 3
SALES (est): 175.3K **Privately Held**
SIC: **2013** Beef stew from purchased meat

(G-5513)
VULCAN MATERIALS COMPANY
2500 Belfield Rd (23856-2534)
PHONE...................................434 848-4775
Travis Holman, *Plant Mgr*
Derek Harris, *Branch Mgr*
EMP: 14 **Publicly Held**
WEB: www.vulcanmaterials.com
SIC: **3273** Ready-mixed concrete
PA: Vulcan Materials Company
1200 Urban Center Dr
Vestavia AL 35242

Fries
Grayson County

(G-5514)
BACKWOODS WOODWORKING
144 Backwoods Farm Ln (24330-4315)
PHONE...................................276 237-2011
Shane Trimble, *Principal*
EMP: 1
SALES (est): 57.9K **Privately Held**
SIC: **2431** Millwork

(G-5515)
C & B LUMBER INC
3594 Turkey Knob Rd (24330-4238)
PHONE...................................276 744-3650
Terry Bond, *President*
EMP: 23
SALES (est): 3.2MM **Privately Held**
WEB: www.candblumber.com
SIC: **2421** Sawmills & planing mills, general

(G-5516)
EARL D PIERCE SAWMILL
5611 Ivanhoe Rd (24330-3591)
PHONE...................................276 744-7538
Earl D Pierce, *Owner*
EMP: 3
SALES (est): 350K **Privately Held**
SIC: **2421** Sawmills & planing mills, general

(G-5517)
RICHARD C IROLER
8703 Riverside Dr (24330-4382)
PHONE...................................276 236-3796
Richard C Iroler, *Owner*
EMP: 1
SALES (est): 69K **Privately Held**
SIC: **2411 2421** Logging; sawmills & planing mills, general

(G-5518)
STEWART FURNITURE DESIGN INC
2945 Scenic Rd (24330-4018)
PHONE...................................276 744-0186
James Stewart, *President*
EMP: 22
SQ FT: 26,000
SALES (est): 2MM **Privately Held**
WEB: www.stewartfurniture.com
SIC: **2512** Upholstered household furniture

Front Royal
Warren County

(G-5519)
AG LASERS TECHNOLOGIES LLC
1330 Progress Dr (22630-6425)
P.O. Box 630 (22630-0014)
PHONE...................................800 255-5515
Angelina Williams, *Principal*
EMP: 10
SQ FT: 22,000
SALES (est): 693.5K **Privately Held**
WEB: www.aglasertechnology.com
SIC: **3442 2522** Metal doors; filing boxes, cabinets & cases: except wood

(G-5520)
AIRPAC INC
888 Shenandoah Shores Rd (22630-6415)
PHONE...................................540 635-5011
Arthur Behnke, *President*
David Ring, *Production*
EMP: 9
SALES (est): 2.1MM **Privately Held**
WEB: www.airpacinc.com
SIC: **3585** Air conditioning units, complete: domestic or industrial

(G-5521)
AXALTA COATING SYSTEMS LLC
7961 Winchester Rd (22630-6901)
PHONE...................................540 622-2951
Kevin Hoffmaster, *Area Mgr*
Timothy Oconnell, *Opers Staff*
Gary Brown, *Engineer*
Michael Lewis, *Human Resources*
Jim Belson, *Manager*
EMP: 20
SALES (corp-wide): 4.4B **Publicly Held**
WEB: www.axalta.com
SIC: **2851** Paints: oil or alkyd vehicle or water thinned
HQ: Axalta Coating Systems, Llc
2001 Market St Ste 3600
Philadelphia PA 19103
855 547-1461

(G-5522)
B & H MACHINE WORKS
201b E 4th St (22630-4414)
PHONE...................................540 636-3366
William Cassone, *Owner*
EMP: 4
SALES (est): 485K **Privately Held**
WEB: www.scsplumbing.com
SIC: **3599** Machine shop, jobbing & repair

(G-5523)
BALENT-YOUNG PUBLISHING INC
951 Poca Bella Dr (22630-8349)
PHONE...................................540 636-2569
Karen Young, *Principal*
EMP: 2
SALES (est): 135.8K **Privately Held**
SIC: **2741** Miscellaneous publishing

(G-5524)
BLUE RIDGE SCIENTIFIC LLC
2392 Catlett Mountain Rd (22630-8264)
PHONE......................540 631-0356
Peter Morley,
EMP: 1
SALES (est): 54.6K **Privately Held**
SIC: 3721 Research & development on air-
craft by the manufacturer

(G-5525)
BOSCO INDUSTRIES
234 Cloud St (22630-3108)
PHONE......................540 671-8053
EMP: 1 EST: 2011
SALES (est): 42K **Privately Held**
SIC: 3999 Mfg Misc Products

(G-5526)
CAVITRONIX CORPORATION
830 John Marshall Hwy (22630-3743)
PHONE......................540 622-6240
Lickson Charles, *Principal*
EMP: 2
SALES (est): 99.2K **Privately Held**
WEB: www.letartliveon.com
SIC: 3599 Industrial machinery

(G-5527)
CREATIVE COATINGS INC
116 Success Rd (22630-6726)
P.O. Box 417 (22630-0009)
PHONE......................540 636-7911
Dale Miller, *President*
Brigitte Miller, *Vice Pres*
Kerri Wright, *Executive*
EMP: 15
SQ FT: 25,000
SALES (est): 1.9MM **Privately Held**
WEB: www.coatingsusa.com
SIC: 3479 Coating of metals & formed
products

(G-5528)
DANIEL PATRICK MCDERMOTT
Also Called: Warren County Report Newspa-
per
214 E Jackson St (22630-3175)
PHONE......................540 305-3000
Daniel McDermott, *Owner*
EMP: 1
SALES (est): 50.3K **Privately Held**
WEB: www.warrencountyva.com
SIC: 2711 Newspapers: publishing only,
not printed on site

(G-5529)
DAYTON DALICE
Also Called: Strictly Dtails Auto Detailing
218 E 4th St (22630-4413)
PHONE......................540 233-3657
Dalice Payton, *Owner*
EMP: 1
SALES (est): 60K **Privately Held**
SIC: 2842 Automobile polish

(G-5530)
DEFENSE HOLDINGS INC
999d Shenandoah Shores Rd
(22630-6464)
PHONE......................703 334-2858
Richard J Martin, *President*
EMP: 1 **Privately Held**
WEB: www.dh-inc.com
SIC: 3993 Signs & advertising specialties
PA: Defense Holdings, Inc.
9105b Owens Dr Ste 201
Manassas Park VA 20111

(G-5531)
E W SYSTEMS & DEVICES INC
100 Lakewood Dr (22630-5986)
PHONE......................540 635-5104
Lynwood A Cosby, *President*
Andrew Cosby, *Principal*
EMP: 2 **Privately Held**
SIC: 3679 Electronic circuits

(G-5532)
FRAGRANCES LTD
1724 N Shenandoah Ave (22630-3644)
PHONE......................540 636-8099
Ron Llwellyn, *President*
Charles Llwellyn, *Vice Pres*
EMP: 5

SALES (est): 803.9K **Privately Held**
WEB: www.qualityvacscents.com
SIC: 2842 Deodorants, nonpersonal

(G-5533)
GLEN MANOR VINEYARDS LLC
2244 Browntown Rd (22630-7632)
PHONE......................540 635-6324
Glen Manor, *General Mgr*
Jeff White,
EMP: 3
SALES (est): 290.1K **Privately Held**
WEB: www.glenmanorvineyards.com
SIC: 2084 Wines

(G-5534)
**GREENWORKS CSTM
CABINETRY LLC**
135 Morrison Ln (22630-6539)
PHONE......................540 635-5725
Paul Uhlenkott, *Principal*
EMP: 2
SALES (est): 240.7K **Privately Held**
SIC: 2434 Wood kitchen cabinets

(G-5535)
HANNA SIGN CO
20 Water St Ste 1 (22630-3084)
PHONE......................540 636-4877
Shae Parker, *Owner*
Richard Hanna, *Owner*
EMP: 1
SALES (est): 101.9K **Privately Held**
WEB: www.hannasigns.com
SIC: 3993 Electric signs

(G-5536)
HBH HOLDINGS LLC
Also Called: Blue Ridge Prestain
999 Shenandoah Shores Rd (22630-6418)
PHONE......................540 631-9555
Christopher Hawley, *Principal*
EMP: 12 **Privately Held**
SIC: 2851 Wood stains
PA: Hbh Holdings Llc
1223 E Arlington Rd
Arlington VT 05250

(G-5537)
INTERBAKE FOODS LLC
100 Baker Plz (22630-6766)
PHONE......................540 631-8100
Michael Cafferata, *Manager*
Mike Schlegel, *Director*
EMP: 298
SALES (corp-wide): 37.6B **Privately Held**
WEB: www.interbake.com
SIC: 2052 Cookies
HQ: Interbake Foods Llc
50 Maplehurst Dr
Brownsburg IN 46112
804 755-7107

(G-5538)
**JACKSON FURNITURE
COMPANY VA**
Jackson Upholstery
239 E 6th St (22630-3409)
P.O. Box 43 (22630-0061)
PHONE......................540 635-3187
Clark Devers, *Manager*
EMP: 130
SALES (corp-wide): 22.8MM **Privately
Held**
SIC: 2512 Upholstered household furniture
PA: Jackson Furniture Company Of Virginia
239 E 6th St
Front Royal VA 22630
540 635-3187

(G-5539)
KENDRAS COOKIES
116 Nottingham Ct (22630-4592)
P.O. Box 1881 (22630-0040)
PHONE......................540 660-5645
Kendra Allanson, *Owner*
EMP: 1
SALES (est): 4K **Privately Held**
SIC: 2052 Cookies & crackers

(G-5540)
KILN DOCTOR INC
100 E 8th St (22630-3414)
P.O. Box 721 (22630-0016)
PHONE......................540 636-6016

Michael Swauger, *President*
Arline Link, *Office Mgr*
EMP: 7
SALES (est): 1.2MM **Privately Held**
WEB: www.thekilndoctor.com
SIC: 3567 7629 5331 8299 Kilns; electri-
cal equipment repair services; variety
stores; ceramic school; ceramics sup-
plies; pottery making machinery

(G-5541)
LIFESITENEWS COM INC
4 Family Life Ln (22630-6453)
PHONE......................540 635-3131
Jon Fidero, *Vice Pres*
Clare Maagad, *Adv Mgr*
John Jalsevac, *Director*
Rebecca Fidero, *Administration*
EMP: 7
SQ FT: 20,000
SALES (est): 1MM **Privately Held**
WEB: www.lifesitenews.com
SIC: 2711 Newspapers, publishing & print-
ing

(G-5542)
MEDLENS INNOVATIONS LLC
1325 Progress Dr (22630-6425)
PHONE......................540 636-7976
Donald Sanders, *Mng Member*
Eric Marshall,
EMP: 9
SALES (est): 694.2K **Privately Held**
SIC: 3851 Ophthalmic goods

(G-5543)
MERCIERS WELDING
154 Easy Hollow Rd (22630-6890)
PHONE......................540 635-4175
Pierre Mercier, *Owner*
EMP: 1
SALES (est): 59.7K **Privately Held**
SIC: 7692 Welding repair

(G-5544)
MJ DISTRIBUTION
315 Poe Dr (22630-8065)
PHONE......................540 692-0062
Heather Silke, *Owner*
EMP: 1
SALES (est): 42.6K **Privately Held**
SIC: 2086 Bottled & canned soft drinks

(G-5545)
NC FOAM & SALES
508 Kendrick Ln 9 (22630-2907)
PHONE......................540 631-3363
Crystal Pope, *General Mgr*
EMP: 2
SALES (est): 100.8K **Privately Held**
SIC: 3086 Plastics foam products

(G-5546)
NORTHWEST HARDWOODS
7685 Winchester Rd (22630-6723)
PHONE......................540 631-3245
EMP: 2
SALES (est): 101K **Privately Held**
SIC: 2421 Sawmills & planing mills, gen-
eral

(G-5547)
OLIVE OIL SOAP COMPANY
306 Brown Ave (22630-2402)
PHONE......................540 671-6940
Candace Bulger, *Principal*
EMP: 2
SALES (est): 64.3K **Privately Held**
SIC: 2079 Olive oil

(G-5548)
PELICAN PRODUCTS
1390 Progress Dr (22630-6425)
PHONE......................540 636-1624
Antonio Napolitanao, *General Mgr*
A Napolitanao, *Manager*
EMP: 10
SALES (est): 862.9K **Privately Held**
WEB: www.pelican.com
SIC: 3089 Cases, plastic

(G-5549)
PRINTER FIX LLC
936 Bowling View Rd (22630-7481)
PHONE......................540 532-4948
EMP: 2

SALES (est): 101.5K **Privately Held**
SIC: 2752 Commercial printing, lithographic

(G-5550)
**ROANOKE CEMENT COMPANY
LLC**
33 Prezanis Way (22630-6990)
PHONE......................540 631-1335
Dwayne Whited, *Manager*
EMP: 2
SALES (corp-wide): 1.4MM **Privately
Held**
WEB: www.titanamerica.com
SIC: 3273 Ready-mixed concrete
HQ: Roanoke Cement Company Llc
6071 Catawba Rd
Troutville VA 24175

(G-5551)
RPS SHENANDOAH INC
Also Called: Reinforced Plastic Systems
211 E 4th St (22630-4414)
PHONE......................540 635-2131
Diane Ratcliffe, *President*
EMP: 15
SQ FT: 17,000
SALES (est): 3.2MM **Privately Held**
WEB: www.rpscomposites.com
SIC: 3498 Piping systems for pulp paper &
chemical industries

(G-5552)
SAFETY 1 INDUSTRIES LLC
1330 Progress Dr (22630-6425)
P.O. Box 630 (22630-0014)
PHONE......................540 635-4673
George K Williams, *President*
EMP: 2
SALES (est): 154.1K **Privately Held**
WEB: www.safety1industries.com
SIC: 3999 Manufacturing industries

(G-5553)
SAINT MARKS PUBLISHING
205 Windy Way (22630-6089)
PHONE......................540 551-3590
EMP: 1
SALES (est): 37.5K **Privately Held**
SIC: 2741 Misc Publishing

(G-5554)
SHENANDOAH CASTINGS LLC
100 Drummer Hill Rd (22630-6247)
PHONE......................540 551-5777
Dominic Ruggiero, *Principal*
EMP: 5
SALES (est): 385.8K **Privately Held**
WEB: www.shenandoahcastings.com
SIC: 3272 Concrete products

(G-5555)
**SPECTACULAR SPECTACLES
INC**
1211 N Shenandoah Ave (22630-3531)
PHONE......................540 636-2020
Cari Barisciano, *Principal*
EMP: 3
SALES (est): 302.7K **Privately Held**
SIC: 3851 Spectacles

(G-5556)
STITCHES & BOWS
1173 Wakeman Mill Rd (22630-8741)
PHONE......................678 876-1715
EMP: 1
SALES (est): 40.3K **Privately Held**
WEB: www.thestitchesandbows.com
SIC: 2395 Embroidery & art needlework

(G-5557)
TITAN AMERICA LLC
399 Kelly Dr (22630-6996)
PHONE......................540 622-2350
EMP: 180
SALES (corp-wide): 1.4MM **Privately
Held**
WEB: www.titanamerica.com
SIC: 3241 Cement, hydraulic
HQ: Titan America Llc
5700 Lake Wright Dr # 300
Norfolk VA 23502
757 858-6500

▲ = Import ▼=Export
◆ =Import/Export

(G-5558)
TORAY PLASTICS (AMERICA) INC
500 Toray Dr (22630-6762)
PHONE..................................540 636-3887
Michael Noll, *Vice Pres*
Chris Tomlinson, *Safety Mgr*
Monte Booher, *Purch Mgr*
Shelly Manners, *Buyer*
Jesse Baldwin, *Technical Mgr*
EMP: 1 Privately Held
WEB: www.toraytpa.com
SIC: 3081 2821 Polypropylene film & sheet; plastics materials & resins
HQ: Toray Plastics (America), Inc.
50 Belver Ave
North Kingstown RI 02852
401 294-4511

(G-5559)
TOTAL LIFT CARE LLC
300 Morrison Ln (22630-6540)
PHONE..................................540 631-0008
Charlene Foltz, *Mng Member*
Lawrence W Foltz,
EMP: 3
SALES (est): 323.8K Privately Held
SIC: 3537 7389 Forklift trucks;

(G-5560)
VALLEY REDI-MIX COMPANY INC
8867 Winchester Rd (22630-7003)
PHONE..................................540 631-9050
James Wilson, *President*
EMP: 20
SALES (corp-wide): 3.1MM Privately Held
SIC: 3272 Concrete products
PA: Valley Redi-Mix Company, Incorporated
333 Marlboro Rd
Stephens City VA 22655
540 869-1990

(G-5561)
VELVETEEN VIDEOS LLC
Also Called: Video Production
883 Wildcat Dr (22630-9234)
PHONE..................................703 229-3633
Gabrielle Altman, *Principal*
EMP: 1 EST: 2012
SALES (est): 98.1K Privately Held
SIC: 2211 Velveteens

(G-5562)
VISION BUSINESS SOLUTIONS
324 Jamestown Rd (22630-4222)
PHONE..................................540 622-6383
Chris Ryder, *Owner*
EMP: 1 EST: 1995
SALES (est): 83.7K Privately Held
SIC: 7372 Business oriented computer software

(G-5563)
WARREN SENTINEL
Also Called: Front Royal Warren Sentinel
429 N Royal Ave (22630-2619)
P.O. Box 1297 (22630-0027)
PHONE..................................540 635-4174
Thomas Byrd, *President*
Thomas T Byod, *President*
Kip Ritenour, *Editor*
EMP: 10
SALES (est): 585.9K Privately Held
SIC: 2711 Newspapers, publishing & printing

(G-5564)
WONDERLAND WOOD WORKS
148 Wonderland Ln (22630-7839)
PHONE..................................540 636-6158
EMP: 1 EST: 2019
SALES (est): 54.1K Privately Held
SIC: 2431 Millwork

Fulks Run
Rockingham County

(G-5565)
DONS WELDING
14238 Pine Crest Ln (22830-2112)
PHONE..................................540 896-3445

Donald W Reedy, *Principal*
EMP: 1
SALES (est): 63.5K Privately Held
SIC: 7692 Welding repair

(G-5566)
SPITZER MACHINE SHOP
16089 Lairs Run Rd (22830-2007)
PHONE..................................540 896-5827
Ken Spitzer, *Owner*
EMP: 2
SALES (est): 148.5K Privately Held
SIC: 3446 Architectural metalwork

Gainesville
Prince William County

(G-5567)
1TRYBE INC
15112 Windy Hollow Cir (20155-2846)
PHONE..................................540 270-6043
Wendy Watson, *CEO*
EMP: 3
SALES (est): 86.5K Privately Held
SIC: 2741

(G-5568)
ALFA PRINT LLC
8419 Holstein Pony Ct (20155-2968)
PHONE..................................703 754-2433
Fadhel Alfadhli, *Principal*
EMP: 2 EST: 2014
SALES (est): 115.2K Privately Held
SIC: 2752 Commercial printing, lithographic

(G-5569)
AMERICAN MANUFACTURING CO INC
5517 Wellington Rd (20155-1614)
PHONE..................................703 361-2210
EMP: 1
SALES (est): 39.6K Privately Held
WEB: www.americanonsite.com
SIC: 3999 Manufacturing industries

(G-5570)
AMPLIFY VENTURES LLC
Also Called: Sign-A-Rama
14305 Northbrook Ln (20155-3898)
PHONE..................................571 248-2282
Anthony Bashorun, *President*
Gbemisola Bashorun, *Principal*
EMP: 2
SALES (est): 60.1K Privately Held
WEB: www.signarama.com
SIC: 3993 2752 Signs & advertising specialties; promotional printing, lithographic

(G-5571)
ATLANTIC RESEARCH CORPORATION (DH)
5945 Wellington Rd (20155-1633)
PHONE..................................703 754-5000
John J Quicke, *President*
Armand F Lauzen, *President*
Paul Barchie, *Vice Pres*
Steven R Lowson, *Vice Pres*
Pat Jenkins, *CFO*
▲ **EMP: 700**
SQ FT: 347,000
SALES (est): 114.4MM
SALES (corp-wide): 3.3B Publicly Held
WEB: www.rocket.com
SIC: 3764 3694 Guided missile & space vehicle engines, research & devel.; rocket motors, guided missiles; propulsion units for guided missiles & space vehicles; automotive electrical equipment
HQ: Sequa Corporation
3999 Rca Blvd
Palm Beach Gardens FL 33410
561 935-3571

(G-5572)
BISON INC
5571 Pageland Ln (20155-1534)
PHONE..................................703 754-4190
Robert L Ait, *President*
Robert F Ait, *Vice Pres*
EMP: 6
SQ FT: 225

SALES (est): 1.6MM Privately Held
SIC: 1381 Directional drilling oil & gas wells

(G-5573)
BRIGHTVIEW PRESS LLC
13459 Brightview Way (20155-6636)
PHONE..................................703 743-1430
James Mosimann, *Principal*
EMP: 1
SALES (est): 48.9K Privately Held
SIC: 2741 Miscellaneous publishing

(G-5574)
C R BARD INC
14241 Clubhouse Rd (20155-2862)
PHONE..................................703 754-2848
Caitlin Turner, *Principal*
Gay Clark, *COO*
Cammi Van Gorkom, *Research*
Susan Gardner, *Branch Mgr*
Amy S Hutman, *Director*
EMP: 3 Privately Held
WEB: www.crbard.com
SIC: 3841 Surgical & medical instruments
HQ: C. R. Bard, Inc.
1 Becton Dr
Franklin Lakes NJ 07417
201 847-6800

(G-5575)
CATBERRIES LLC
15529 Tuxedo Ln (20155-3242)
PHONE..................................714 873-8245
Herbert Franklins, *Principal*
Binh-Minh Nguyen, *Principal*
EMP: 3
SALES (est): 77.7K Privately Held
SIC: 2395 Pleating & stitching

(G-5576)
CUSTOM INK
8171 Stonewall Shops Sq (20155-3891)
PHONE..................................703 884-2678
EMP: 2
SALES (est): 83.6K Privately Held
WEB: www.customink.com
SIC: 2759 Screen printing

(G-5577)
DAILY DEED LLC
4256 Lawnvale Dr (20155-1100)
PHONE..................................703 754-0644
Nathanael Minarik, *Principal*
EMP: 3
SALES (est): 111.6K Privately Held
SIC: 2711 Newspapers, publishing & printing

(G-5578)
DEBRA KROMER
Also Called: Pampered Chef, The
8053 Crimson Leaf Ct (20155-1738)
PHONE..................................571 248-4070
Debra Kromer, *Owner*
EMP: 1
SALES (est): 99.2K Privately Held
SIC: 3089 Plastics products

(G-5579)
DEFENSE INFORMATION TECH INC (PA)
8355 Roxborough Loop (20155-3210)
PHONE..................................703 628-0999
Helena Veltsistas, *Principal*
EMP: 1
SALES (est): 145K Privately Held
SIC: 3812 Defense systems & equipment

(G-5580)
DEMORAIS & ASSOCIATES PLLC
Also Called: Koket
8028 Montour Heights Dr (20155-3833)
PHONE..................................703 754-7991
Janet Morris, *Mng Member*
▲ **EMP: 7**
SALES (est): 588.9K Privately Held
WEB: www.bykoket.com
SIC: 3645 Garden, patio, walkway & yard lighting fixtures: electric

(G-5581)
EAGLE CONTRACTORS
12814 Lee Hwy (20155-1504)
PHONE..................................703 435-0004
Michael White, *Owner*
Angel Dodson, *Admin Mgr*
EMP: 8
SALES (est): 1.5MM Privately Held
WEB: www.eaglecontractors.net
SIC: 3089 Plastic containers, except foam

(G-5582)
ELVARIA LLC
7689 Limestone Dr Ste 125 (20155-4051)
PHONE..................................703 935-0041
Jeffrey Rydant, *President*
John Luongo, *Vice Pres*
Adam Rossi, *Mng Member*
▲ **EMP: 6**
SALES (est): 1MM Privately Held
WEB: www.elvaria.com
SIC: 3556 Ice cream manufacturing machinery

(G-5583)
FLI USA INC
15810 Spyglass Hill Loop (20155-3201)
PHONE..................................571 261-4174
Malcolm Wootton, *President*
Lesley Wootton, *Principal*
Rex Luzader, *Vice Pres*
EMP: 3
SALES (est): 236.2K Privately Held
WEB: www.fliuk.com
SIC: 3841 Surgical & medical instruments

(G-5584)
FORBZ HOUSE LLC
7371 Atlas Walk Way Ste 1 (20155-2992)
PHONE..................................703 216-1491
Cheryl Spangler, *CEO*
EMP: 1
SQ FT: 800
SALES (est): 50K Privately Held
SIC: 2731 Book publishing

(G-5585)
GARY BURNS
Also Called: Vista View Govt Solutions
15164 Windy Hollow Cir (20155-2847)
P.O. Box 121, Haymarket (20168-0121)
PHONE..................................703 992-4617
Gary Bruns, *Owner*
EMP: 2
SALES (est): 69.1K Privately Held
SIC: 2741 Miscellaneous publishing

(G-5586)
GLAZED & TWISTED LLC
5664 Shoal Creek Dr (20155)
PHONE..................................703 789-5522
Shawn Evans, *Partner*
EMP: 2 EST: 2013
SALES (est): 54.3K Privately Held
SIC: 2051 2045 Cakes, bakery: except frozen; bread & bread type roll mixes: from purchased flour

(G-5587)
GREENERBILLCOM
7371 Atlas Way Ste 337 (20155)
PHONE..................................703 898-5354
Andre Golanski,
EMP: 2
SALES (est): 100K Privately Held
SIC: 3674 Light emitting diodes

(G-5588)
H & L BROTHERS CONTRACTORS LLC
12250 Scarlet Maple Dr (20155-3873)
PHONE..................................703 856-1915
Luis Arteaga, *President*
EMP: 1
SALES (est): 100K Privately Held
SIC: 1389 Construction, repair & dismantling services

(G-5589)
HILLWOOD PARK INC
14280 Gardner Manor Pl (20155-3627)
PHONE..................................703 754-6105
Carl Gardner, *Principal*
EMP: 3

SALES (est): 180K **Privately Held**
WEB: www.hillwoodcamping.com
SIC: 3792 Camping trailers & chassis

(G-5590)
INERTIA PUBLISHING LLC
8405 Churchside Dr (20155-1798)
PHONE..................................703 754-9617
Gary Caruso, *Principal*
EMP: 2
SALES (est): 97.6K **Privately Held**
SIC: 2741 Music book & sheet music publishing

(G-5591)
IVORYS ESSENTIALS LLC
14100 Estate Manor Dr (20155-5816)
PHONE..................................571 201-6147
Naomie Nvodjo,
EMP: 1
SALES (est): 20K **Privately Held**
SIC: 2844 Hair preparations, including shampoos

(G-5592)
JKM SOFTWARE LLC
5446 Lick River Ln (20155-1385)
PHONE..................................703 754-9175
Sean Muir,
EMP: 1
SALES (est): 250K **Privately Held**
SIC: 7372 Prepackaged software

(G-5593)
KRAM INDUSTRIES INC
Also Called: Ezgo
4710 Angus Dr (20155-1217)
PHONE..................................571 220-9769
Mark Schmitt, *President*
EMP: 3
SALES (est): 255.3K **Privately Held**
SIC: 3999 Barber & beauty shop equipment

(G-5594)
LA FLEUR DE LIS LLC
5600 Artemus Rd (20155-1543)
PHONE..................................703 753-5690
Elisabeth Madison, *President*
EMP: 2
SALES (est): 129.8K **Privately Held**
SIC: 2732 Book printing

(G-5595)
LAVA INSTANT COFFEE LLC
14764 Soapstone Dr # 403 (20155-4800)
PHONE..................................703 239-0803
Mohammed A Zaqzouq, *Director*
EMP: 2
SALES (est): 62.3K **Privately Held**
SIC: 2095 Instant coffee

(G-5596)
LELO FABRICATION
5626 Lick River Ln (20155-1341)
PHONE..................................703 581-7852
EMP: 2
SALES (est): 130.4K **Privately Held**
SIC: 3441 Fabricated structural metal

(G-5597)
LONE WOLF SALSA
15070 Danehurst Cir (20155-4444)
PHONE..................................571 445-3499
Wolfgang Boeker, *Principal*
EMP: 3 EST: 2017
SALES (est): 109.2K **Privately Held**
SIC: 2099 Dips, except cheese & sour cream based

(G-5598)
MOJO CASTLE PRESS LLC
7008 Manahoac Pl (20155-1634)
PHONE..................................703 946-8946
Stephanie Kelsey, *Owner*
EMP: 4
SALES (est): 186.2K **Privately Held**
SIC: 2741 Miscellaneous publishing

(G-5599)
MPH DEVELOPMENT LLC
6853 Hollow Glen Ct (20155-1467)
PHONE..................................703 303-4838
Matthew Harrington, *COO*
EMP: 2

SALES (est): 151.2K **Privately Held**
WEB: www.mph-development.com
SIC: 7372 7389 Application computer software;

(G-5600)
NCS TECHNOLOGIES INC (PA)
Also Called: N C S
7669 Limestone Dr Ste 130 (20155-4038)
PHONE..................................703 743-8500
An Van Nguyen, *President*
Lauren Mayoral, *Partner*
Michael Brown, *Business Mgr*
Russell Smith, *Exec VP*
John Callahan, *Vice Pres*
▲ EMP: 108
SQ FT: 70,000
SALES (est): 47.7MM **Privately Held**
WEB: www.ncst.com
SIC: 3571 7373 Electronic computers; computer integrated systems design

(G-5601)
NO QUARTER LLC
15123 Windy Hollow Cir (20155-2849)
PHONE..................................703 753-0511
Dan Doherty, *Principal*
EMP: 1 EST: 2013
SALES (est): 128.6K **Privately Held**
SIC: 3131 Footwear cut stock

(G-5602)
NOMAD SOLUTIONS LLC
13575 Wellington Center C (20155-4060)
P.O. Box 70 (20156-0070)
PHONE..................................703 656-9100
Jeff Carroll, *COO*
Audrey Allen, *Human Res Dir*
Sean Arthur, *Mng Member*
EMP: 12
SALES (est): 2.4MM **Privately Held**
WEB: www.nomadsolutions.com
SIC: 3663 4899 7376 7373 Receivers, radio communications; satellite earth stations; communication signal enhancement network system; computer facilities management; local area network (LAN) systems integrator

(G-5603)
NORTHERN VIRGINIA WIRE WORKS
16001 Roland Park Pl (20155-1962)
PHONE..................................571 221-1882
Dustin Good, *Principal*
EMP: 2
SALES (est): 148.1K **Privately Held**
SIC: 3496 Miscellaneous fabricated wire products

(G-5604)
NORTHERN VRGNIA CAST STONE LLC
5406 Ancestry Ct (20155-1343)
PHONE..................................703 393-2777
Carl C Maine, *Administration*
EMP: 3 EST: 2010
SALES (est): 201.6K **Privately Held**
WEB: www.nvcast.com
SIC: 3272 Concrete products, precast

(G-5605)
OLDCASTLE APG NORTHEAST INC (DH)
Also Called: Anchor
13555 Wellington Cntr Cir (20155-4061)
PHONE..................................703 365-7070
Matt Lynch, *President*
Louis Mangiaracina, *Vice Pres*
Christopher Shermeyer, *Plant Mgr*
Michael Magalhaes, *Purch Agent*
Diane Damien, *Purchasing*
▲ EMP: 13 EST: 1945
SQ FT: 10,000
SALES (est): 94.9MM
SALES (corp-wide): 30.6B **Privately Held**
WEB: www.oldcastlemasonry.com
SIC: 3271 5032 Blocks, concrete or cinder: standard; brick, stone & related material
HQ: Crh Americas, Inc.
900 Ashwood Pkwy Ste 600
Atlanta GA 30338
770 804-3363

(G-5606)
ONYX INDUSTRIES LLC
8330 Roxborough Loop (20155-3208)
PHONE..................................425 269-7181
Michael Cadice,
EMP: 2
SALES (est): 88.9K **Privately Held**
SIC: 3999 Manufacturing industries

(G-5607)
PGB HANGERS LLC
7991 Turtle Creek Cir (20155-2204)
PHONE..................................703 851-4221
Deborah Dubrul,
James Saunders,
EMP: 4
SALES (est): 238.9K **Privately Held**
SIC: 3496 5199 3089 Garment hangers, made from purchased wire; clothes hangers; clothes hangers, plastic

(G-5608)
PIGTALE PRESS LLC
15207 Windy Hollow Cir (20155-2889)
PHONE..................................703 753-7572
Meritta White, *Principal*
EMP: 2
SALES (est): 101K **Privately Held**
WEB: www.pigtalepressllc.com
SIC: 2741 Miscellaneous publishing

(G-5609)
PURPLE INK PRESS
13525 Heritage Farms Dr (20155-1335)
PHONE..................................703 753-4638
Jan Maxwell, *Principal*
EMP: 1
SALES (est): 70.5K **Privately Held**
SIC: 2741 Miscellaneous publishing

(G-5610)
RECONCILIATION PRESS
6152 Ferrier Ct (20155-6679)
PHONE..................................703 743-2416
John Jenkins, *Principal*
EMP: 2
SALES (est): 107.4K **Privately Held**
SIC: 2731 8661 Book publishing; religious organizations

(G-5611)
SENTINEL PRESS LLC
13631 Hackamore Trl (20155-1781)
PHONE..................................703 753-5434
Lori Ransom, *Principal*
EMP: 3 EST: 2015
SALES (est): 92.2K **Privately Held**
SIC: 2711 Commercial printing & newspaper publishing combined

(G-5612)
SERENITY RIDGE MACHINING
4770 Angus Dr (20155-1217)
PHONE..................................571 261-2042
EMP: 2
SALES (est): 113.4K **Privately Held**
WEB: www.serenityridgemachining.com
SIC: 3599 Machine shop, jobbing & repair

(G-5613)
SOUTHPAW BREW CO LLC
8185 Tenbrook Dr (20155-3842)
PHONE..................................703 753-5986
Blane Perry, *Principal*
EMP: 2 EST: 2016
SALES (est): 62.3K **Privately Held**
SIC: 2082 Malt beverages

(G-5614)
SPARTAN VILLAGE LLC
15109 Anacortes Trl (20155-1987)
PHONE..................................661 724-6438
Nicholas Schmidt,
EMP: 1 EST: 2014
SALES (est): 66.4K **Privately Held**
SIC: 3812 Defense systems & equipment

(G-5615)
SSR FOODS LLC
Also Called: Wings-Pizza-N-things
8861 Yellow Hammer Dr (20155-5853)
PHONE..................................703 581-7260
Prashanti Nair, *Co-Owner*
EMP: 1

SALES (est): 99.7K **Privately Held**
SIC: 2099 5812 Food preparations; contract food services

(G-5616)
SYDRUS AEROSPACE LLC
8725 Ellis Mill Dr (20155-5935)
PHONE..................................831 402-5286
EMP: 2
SALES (est): 92.9K **Privately Held**
SIC: 3721 Aircraft

(G-5617)
THICK TO THIN LLC
7019 Little Thames Dr (20155-4010)
PHONE..................................607 427-1737
Andrea Kuchinski, *Administration*
EMP: 2
SALES (est): 123.5K **Privately Held**
WEB: www.thick-to-thin.com
SIC: 2323 Men's & boys' neckwear

(G-5618)
TONER & INK WAREHOUSE LLC
7371 Atlas Walk Way Ste 2 (20155-2992)
PHONE..................................301 332-2796
Reggie Carr, *Principal*
EMP: 2 EST: 2016
SALES (est): 95.2K **Privately Held**
SIC: 2893 Gravure ink

(G-5619)
TURNER PUBLIC AFFAIRS INC
8298 Roxborough Loop (20155-3207)
PHONE..................................703 489-7104
Caitlin Turner, *Principal*
EMP: 3 EST: 2013
SALES (est): 199.7K **Privately Held**
SIC: 3841 Surgical & medical instruments

(G-5620)
US 1 CABLE LLC
7371 Atlas Walk Way 260 (20155-2992)
PHONE..................................571 224-3955
Dinovan Siso,
EMP: 2
SQ FT: 110
SALES (est): 10K **Privately Held**
WEB: www.us1cable.com
SIC: 3661 Fiber optics communications equipment

(G-5621)
WESTON COMPANY
6303 Vint Hill Rd (20155)
P.O. Box 397 (20156-0397)
PHONE..................................540 349-1200
Thomas R Weston, *President*
William G Weston, *Vice Pres*
Christine Dingus, *Human Res Dir*
EMP: 40
SQ FT: 30,000
SALES (est): 8MM **Privately Held**
WEB: www.westoncompany.com
SIC: 3443 3441 Fabricated plate work (boiler shop); fabricated structural metal

(G-5622)
WINMAR BUSINESS GROUP
Also Called: Heroes Bottled Water
14109 Snickersville Dr (20155-4462)
PHONE..................................913 908-7413
Winston Jimenez, *Owner*
EMP: 1
SALES (est): 41.2K **Privately Held**
SIC: 2086 Bottled & canned soft drinks

(G-5623)
WOOD WORKS BY SNYDER LLC
14423 Woodwill Ln (20155-3894)
PHONE..................................703 203-6952
Corey Snyder, *Principal*
EMP: 1
SALES (est): 54.1K **Privately Held**
SIC: 2431 Millwork

(G-5624)
WOODCRAFTERS II LLC
13826 Estate Manor Dr (20155-5955)
PHONE..................................703 499-5418
Francisco J Cerpa, *Administration*
EMP: 3 EST: 2008
SALES (est): 204.9K **Privately Held**
SIC: 2511 Wood household furniture

(G-5625)
WORLD OF COLOR EXPO LLC
3507 Finish Line Dr (20155-1254)
PHONE.....................................703 754-3191
David Vernon, *Principal*
EMP: 1
SALES (est): 87.1K **Privately Held**
WEB: www.worldofcolorexpo.com
SIC: 3952 Paints, gold or bronze: artists'

Galax
Galax City County

(G-5626)
ALBANY INDUSTRIES-GALAX LLC
626 Creekview Dr (24333-5346)
PHONE.....................................276 236-0735
Mark Gosnell, *Manager*
▲ EMP: 80 EST: 2012
SALES (est): 11.3MM
SALES (corp-wide): 211.4MM **Privately Held**
SIC: 2512 Upholstered household furniture
HQ: Albany Industries, Llc
504 N Glenfield Rd
New Albany MS 38652

(G-5627)
AMERICAN MIRROR COMPANY INC
Also Called: Cavalier Mirror
300 E Grayson St (24333-2964)
PHONE.....................................276 236-5111
Rick L Gruber, *President*
◆ EMP: 152 EST: 1957
SQ FT: 93,000
SALES (est): 14.4MM **Privately Held**
WEB: www.americanmirror.net
SIC: 3231 Mirrored glass

(G-5628)
BLUE MOON CATERING CONCESSIONS
101 E Oldtown St (24333-3919)
PHONE.....................................276 236-8728
EMP: 2
SALES (est): 83.9K **Privately Held**
SIC: 2752 Commercial printing, lithographic

(G-5629)
BLUE RIDGE CREST LLC
301 Shaw St (24333-3120)
P.O. Box 716 (24333-0716)
PHONE.....................................276 236-7149
Douglas Vaught, *Manager*
EMP: 37
SALES (est): 2.3MM **Privately Held**
WEB: www.blueridgecrest.com
SIC: 2389 Apparel & accessories

(G-5630)
CARDINAL STONE COMPANY INC
2650 Fishers Gap Rd (24333-4340)
P.O. Box 1620, Dublin (24084-1620)
PHONE.....................................276 236-5457
Jay O'Brien, *President*
EMP: 18
SALES (est): 1.7MM **Privately Held**
WEB: www.hamptonhauling.net
SIC: 3281 1423 Stone, quarrying & processing of own stone products; crushed & broken granite

(G-5631)
CREATIVE SEATING LLC
1080 Grouse Hollow Ln (24333-3866)
PHONE.....................................276 236-3615
Lee Cates, *Principal*
Patricia G Rector,
EMP: 5
SQ FT: 2,000
SALES (est): 490.3K **Privately Held**
SIC: 2512 Upholstered household furniture

(G-5632)
CYNTHIA E COX
Also Called: Cox Printing
2867 Glendale Rd (24333-5003)
PHONE.....................................276 236-7697
Cynthia E Cox, *Owner*
EMP: 1
SALES (est): 43K **Privately Held**
SIC: 2759 Commercial printing

(G-5633)
FLOWERS BKG CO JAMESTOWN LLC
7599 Carrollton Pike A (24333-4269)
PHONE.....................................276 236-5009
EMP: 3
SALES (corp-wide): 4.1B **Publicly Held**
WEB: www.flowersfoods.com
SIC: 2051 Bakery: wholesale or wholesale/retail combined
HQ: Flowers Baking Co. Of Jamestown, Llc
801 W Main St
Jamestown NC 27282
336 841-8840

(G-5634)
GALLIMORE SAWMILL INC
3965 Coal Creek Rd (24333-6229)
PHONE.....................................276 236-5064
Verlin Gallimore, *President*
Gallimore Frieda, *Vice Pres*
Fridea Gallimore, *Admin Sec*
EMP: 15
SALES (est): 2MM **Privately Held**
SIC: 2421 Sawmills & planing mills, general

(G-5635)
GAZETTE NEWSPAPER
108 W Stuart Dr (24333-2114)
PHONE.....................................276 236-5178
Michael Abernathy, *Principal*
EMP: 5
SALES (est): 170.4K **Privately Held**
WEB: www.galaxgazette.com
SIC: 2711 Newspapers, publishing & printing

(G-5636)
GAZETTE PRESS INC
Also Called: Galax Office Supply
510 S Main St (24333-3918)
P.O. Box 186 (24333-0186)
PHONE.....................................276 236-4831
Roy B Lineberry, *President*
Robert Lineberry, *President*
Katherine L Patton, *Admin Sec*
EMP: 8 EST: 1963
SQ FT: 3,000
SALES (est): 500K **Privately Held**
SIC: 2752 5943 Commercial printing, offset; office forms & supplies

(G-5637)
GUARDIAN FABRICATION LLC
Also Called: Guardian Galax
110 Jack Guynn Dr (24333-2534)
PHONE.....................................276 236-5196
EMP: 125
SALES (corp-wide): 38.9B **Privately Held**
WEB: www.guardianglass.com
SIC: 3231 Products of purchased glass; mirrored glass
HQ: Guardian Fabrication, Llc
2300 Harmon Rd
Auburn Hills MI 48326
248 340-1800

(G-5638)
HANESBRANDS INC
1012 Glendale Rd (24333-2504)
PHONE.....................................276 236-5174
Steve Nichols, *Branch Mgr*
EMP: 1 **Publicly Held**
WEB: www.hanes.com
SIC: 2253 T-shirts & tops, knit
PA: Hanesbrands Inc.
1000 E Hanes Mill Rd
Winston Salem NC 27105

(G-5639)
HANSEN TURBINE ASSEMBLIES CORP
1056 Edmonds Rd (24333-3985)
PHONE.....................................276 236-7184
Helmar Neilson, *CEO*
Tim Parker, *General Mgr*
Chad Lawson, *Production*
David Smith, *Engineer*
Kevin Card, *Consultant*
▲ EMP: 26

SQ FT: 80,000
SALES (est): 5MM **Privately Held**
WEB: www.hansenturbine.com
SIC: 3621 2752 Power generators; photolithographic printing

(G-5640)
LANDMARK CMNTY NWSPPERS VA LLC (DH)
Also Called: Gazette, The
108 W Stuart Dr (24333-2114)
P.O. Box 68 (24333-0068)
PHONE.....................................276 236-5178
EMP: 13
SALES (est): 1MM **Privately Held**
WEB: www.galaxgazette.com
SIC: 2711 Commercial printing & newspaper publishing combined
HQ: Landmark Community Newspapers, Llc
601 Taylorsville Rd
Shelbyville KY 40065
502 633-4334

(G-5641)
MOOG INC
115 Jack Guynn Dr (24333-2536)
PHONE.....................................276 236-4921
Gary Guynn, *QC Mgr*
Travis Belton, *Manager*
EMP: 30
SALES (corp-wide): 2.8B **Publicly Held**
WEB: www.moog.com
SIC: 3672 Printed circuit boards
PA: Moog Inc.
400 Jamison Rd
Elma NY 14059
716 652-2000

(G-5642)
MOXLEY BROTHERS
419 State Shed Ln (24333-2058)
PHONE.....................................276 236-6580
Redd Moxley, *President*
Betty Moxley, *Owner*
Harold Moxley, *Co-Owner*
EMP: 2
SALES (est): 203.9K **Privately Held**
SIC: 3531 Graders, road (construction machinery)

(G-5643)
PARKDALE MILLS INCORPORATED
1012 Glendale Rd (24333-2504)
PHONE.....................................276 236-5174
Andy Messner, *Branch Mgr*
EMP: 4
SALES (corp-wide): 1.3B **Privately Held**
WEB: www.parkdalemills.com
SIC: 2281 Yarn spinning mills
HQ: Parkdale Mills, Incorporated
531 Cotton Blossom Cir
Gastonia NC 28054
704 874-5000

(G-5644)
PATTON SAND & CONCRETE
538 Rolling Wood Ln (24333-1859)
PHONE.....................................276 236-9362
Gary Patton, *Owner*
EMP: 1
SALES (est): 119K **Privately Held**
WEB: www.pattonsandandconcrete.com
SIC: 3273 5032 Ready-mixed concrete; brick, stone & related material

(G-5645)
PEPPERS SERVICES LLC
660 Blackberry Ln (24333-5914)
PHONE.....................................276 233-6464
Lauri Pepper, *Principal*
EMP: 3
SALES (est): 209.8K **Privately Held**
SIC: 2411 4212 7389 Logging; lumber (log) trucking, local;

(G-5646)
R G LOGGING
1373 Pipers Gap Rd (24333-6516)
PHONE.....................................276 233-9224
Ronnie Galyean, *Owner*
EMP: 1
SALES (est): 86.6K **Privately Held**
SIC: 2411 Timber, cut at logging camp

(G-5647)
RST MACHINE SERVICE LTD
466 Shepherd Pl (24333-5544)
PHONE.....................................276 236-8623
Sam Todd, *President*
Rhonda Todd, *Vice Pres*
EMP: 2
SQ FT: 1,800
SALES (est): 110K **Privately Held**
SIC: 3599 Machine shop, jobbing & repair

(G-5648)
SPRING VALLEY GRAPHICS
99 Bee Line Dr (24333-6135)
P.O. Box 442, Fries (24330-0442)
PHONE.....................................276 236-4357
Lesa Hines, *Managing Prtnr*
Sue Willie, *Partner*
EMP: 3
SQ FT: 2,500
SALES (est): 295.2K **Privately Held**
WEB: www.springvalleygraphics.com
SIC: 2396 7389 Screen printing on fabric articles; embroidering of advertising on shirts, etc.

(G-5649)
SUPREME EDGELIGHT DEVICES INC
682 Skyline Hwy (24333-3037)
PHONE.....................................276 236-3711
Darren Cuoghi, *President*
Marla Cuoghi, *Admin Sec*
EMP: 9 EST: 1952
SQ FT: 15,000
SALES (est): 210K **Privately Held**
SIC: 3647 Aircraft lighting fixtures

(G-5650)
TITAN TURF LLC
4140 Little River Rd (24333-4175)
PHONE.....................................276 768-7833
Jared Shaw, *Partner*
James Wilkinson, *Partner*
EMP: 2
SALES (est): 75K **Privately Held**
SIC: 3523 0782 Turf & grounds equipment; lawn services

(G-5651)
V-B/WILLIAMS FURNITURE CO INC
300 E Grayson St (24333-2964)
PHONE.....................................276 236-6161
John D Bassett III, *President*
Wayard Bassett, *President*
EMP: 450
SQ FT: 800,000
SALES (est): 125MM **Privately Held**
WEB: www.vaughan-bassett.com
SIC: 2511 Wood bedroom furniture; bedside stands: wood

(G-5652)
VAUGHAN FURNITURE COMPANY INC (PA)
816 Glendale Rd (24333-2311)
P.O. Box 1489 (24333-1489)
PHONE.....................................276 236-6111
Taylor C Vaughan, *President*
Michael E Stevens, *Senior VP*
Raymond L Hall Jr, *Treasurer*
David Vaughan, *Executive*
◆ EMP: 13 EST: 1923
SQ FT: 26,000
SALES: 6.8MM **Privately Held**
WEB: www.vaughanfurniture.com
SIC: 2511 Wood household furniture

(G-5653)
VAUGHAN-BASSETT FURN CO INC (PA)
300 E Grayson St (24333-2964)
PHONE.....................................276 236-6161
John D Bassett III, *CEO*
Wyatt P E Bassett, *President*
James Rector, *President*
James B Rector, *President*
J Douglas Bassett IV, *Vice Pres*
◆ EMP: 556 EST: 1919
SQ FT: 800,000

GEOGRAPHIC

SALES (est): 214.7MM **Privately Held**
WEB: www.vaughan-bassett.com
SIC: 2511 Bed frames, except water bed frames: wood; bedside stands: wood; dressers, household: wood; dining room furniture: wood

(G-5654)
WEBB FURNITURE ENTERPRISES INC (PA)
Also Called: American Mirror
117 Gillespie Ln (24333-2306)
P.O. Box 1277 (24333-1277)
PHONE.................................276 236-5111
John Bassett, *Ch of Bd*
Lee Houston, *President*
Robert Kirby, *Vice Pres*
Ervin Frazier, *Plant Mgr*
Hobert Bailey, *Purch Mgr*
◆ **EMP:** 80 **EST:** 1935
SQ FT: 600,000
SALES (est): 17.4MM **Privately Held**
WEB: www.americanmirror.net
SIC: 2493 Particleboard products

(G-5655)
WEBB FURNITURE ENTERPRISES INC
Also Called: Webb Particle Board
300 E Grayson St (24333-2964)
P.O. Box 1277 (24333-1277)
PHONE.................................276 236-6141
Eric Hess, *Manager*
EMP: 60
SALES (corp-wide): 17.4MM **Privately Held**
WEB: www.americanmirror.net
SIC: 2493 Particleboard products
PA: Webb Furniture Enterprises, Inc.
117 Gillespie Ln
Galax VA 24333
276 236-5111

Garrisonville
Stafford County

(G-5656)
LEGACY VULCAN LLC
Mideast Division
1012 Garrisonville Rd (22463)
P.O. Box 182 (22463-0182)
PHONE.................................540 659-3003
Martin Bischoff, *Manager*
EMP: 35 **Publicly Held**
WEB: www.vulcanmaterials.com
SIC: 1442 1423 Construction sand & gravel; crushed & broken granite
HQ: Legacy Vulcan, Llc
1200 Urban Center Dr
Vestavia AL 35242
205 298-3000

Gasburg
Brunswick County

(G-5657)
AUBREY L CLARY INC
2763 Ankum Rd (23857-2012)
PHONE.................................434 577-2724
Joyce W Clary, *President*
EMP: 42
SQ FT: 4,800
SALES (est): 3.3MM **Privately Held**
SIC: 2411 Logging camps & contractors

(G-5658)
CLARY TIMBER CO INC
3290 Ankum Rd (23857-2043)
PHONE.................................434 594-5055
Daryl Clary, *President*
Cheri Clary, *Admin Sec*
EMP: 11 **EST:** 1998
SALES (est): 1.2MM **Privately Held**
SIC: 2411 Logging camps & contractors

(G-5659)
M M WRIGHT INC (PA)
6894 Christanna Hwy (23857-2019)
PHONE.................................434 577-2101
Zenith Wright, *President*
Frank Myers, *Vice Pres*

Stephen Wright, *Vice Pres*
Stephen L Wright, *Vice Pres*
Stephen Wright, *Manager*
EMP: 70
SQ FT: 10,000
SALES (est): 6.4MM **Privately Held**
WEB: www.gasburgequipment.com
SIC: 2411 Logging camps & contractors

(G-5660)
S R JONES JR & SONS INC
8356 Christanna Hwy (23857-2031)
PHONE.................................434 577-2311
Nelvin R Jones, *President*
Thomas P Taylor, *Corp Secy*
JW Jones, *Vice Pres*
EMP: 35
SALES (est): 3.4MM **Privately Held**
SIC: 2411 4212 Logging camps & contractors; local trucking, without storage

Gate City
Scott County

(G-5661)
CLAUDE DAVID SANDERS
977 Nickelsville Hwy (24251-5301)
PHONE.................................276 386-6946
Claude David Sanders, *Principal*
EMP: 3
SALES (est): 169.1K **Privately Held**
SIC: 2411 Logging

(G-5662)
GATES CITY MACHINE AND REPAIR
111 Valleyview St (24251-3707)
PHONE.................................276 386-3456
Lee R Powers II, *Owner*
EMP: 3
SALES (est): 168.4K **Privately Held**
SIC: 3599 Machine shop, jobbing & repair

(G-5663)
HJS QWIK SIGNS
772 Filter Plant Frd (24251-2414)
PHONE.................................276 386-2696
Helen Sanders, *Owner*
EMP: 2
SALES (est): 146.9K **Privately Held**
SIC: 3993 Signs, not made in custom sign painting shops

(G-5664)
JIMMY DOCKERY LOGGING
206 Misty Morning Cir (24251-4346)
PHONE.................................276 225-0149
Jimmy Dockery, *Owner*
EMP: 4
SALES (est): 365.5K **Privately Held**
SIC: 2411 Logging camps & contractors

(G-5665)
PORTABLE SAWMILL SERVICE
Rr 1 (24251)
PHONE.................................276 940-4194
Larry France, *Owner*
EMP: 2
SALES (est): 99.1K **Privately Held**
SIC: 2421 Sawmills & planing mills, general

(G-5666)
RT LOGGING LLC
154 Belgian Dr (24251-3759)
PHONE.................................276 452-2258
Leonard Talbott, *President*
EMP: 2
SALES (est): 156.8K **Privately Held**
SIC: 2411 Logging camps & contractors

(G-5667)
SCOTT COUNTY HERALD VIRGINIAN
Also Called: Scott Printing Co
113 West Jackson St (24251-2930)
P.O. Box 218 (24251-0218)
PHONE.................................276 386-6300
Lisa McCarty, *President*
Daniel Barnette, *Director*
Rex E McCarty, *Admin Sec*
EMP: 8 **EST:** 1964
SQ FT: 1,600

SALES (est): 630.8K **Privately Held**
WEB: www.virginiastar.net
SIC: 2711 Job printing & newspaper publishing combined; newspapers: publishing only, not printed on site

(G-5668)
SPICEWATER ELECTRONIC HOME MON
168 Mcconnell St (24251-2935)
PHONE.................................276 690-4718
Jeffrey Spicer, *CEO*
Gregory Gillenwater, *CFO*
EMP: 2 **EST:** 2014
SALES (est): 145.5K **Privately Held**
SIC: 3663

Glade Hill
Franklin County

(G-5669)
AXEAMPS LLC
330 Housman Dr (24092-1792)
PHONE.................................540 484-0882
Robert Dower, *Principal*
EMP: 2
SALES (est): 87.2K **Privately Held**
SIC: 3931 Guitars & parts, electric & non-electric

(G-5670)
SHIVELY AND CARTER CABINETS
212 Smith Rd (24092-3702)
PHONE.................................540 483-4149
EMP: 2 **EST:** 2010
SALES (est): 89K **Privately Held**
SIC: 2434 Mfg Wood Kitchen Cabinets

(G-5671)
WLD LOGGING & CHIPPING INC
1444 Ayers Rd (24092-3768)
PHONE.................................540 483-1218
William L Davis Jr, *Exec Dir*
EMP: 3
SALES (est): 231.3K **Privately Held**
SIC: 2411 Logging camps & contractors

(G-5672)
WORDS ON WOOD SIGNS INC
199 Pine Grove Rd (24092-1782)
PHONE.................................540 493-9353
EMP: 1
SALES (est): 46K **Privately Held**
SIC: 3993 Signs & advertising specialties

Glade Spring
Washington County

(G-5673)
APPALACHIAN PLASTICS INC
34001 Glove Dr (24340-5141)
P.O. Box 1044 (24340-1044)
PHONE.................................276 429-2581
Betty F Debusk, *President*
Patricia Debusk, *Corp Secy*
D Allen Debusk, *Vice Pres*
EMP: 47
SQ FT: 96,000
SALES (est): 11.7MM **Privately Held**
WEB: www.appalachianplastics.com
SIC: 3089 Injection molded finished plastic products

(G-5674)
BLEEDING CANVAS
31208 Lee Hwy (24340-4816)
PHONE.................................276 623-2345
EMP: 2
SALES (est): 92.9K **Privately Held**
SIC: 2211 Cotton Broadwoven Fabric Mill

(G-5675)
GLADE MACHINE INC
13092 Old Monroe Rd (24340)
P.O. Box 1086 (24340-1086)
PHONE.................................276 429-2114
Ralph Sullivan, *President*
EMP: 12
SQ FT: 14,000

SALES (est): 1.9MM **Privately Held**
SIC: 3599 Machine shop, jobbing & repair

(G-5676)
GLADE STONE INC
14196 Monroe Rd (24340-4418)
PHONE.................................276 429-5241
John Wilkinson, *CEO*
Kenneth Taylor, *President*
Jerry Short, *Vice Pres*
Paul E Corum III, *Treasurer*
Charles Herman, *Admin Sec*
EMP: 15
SALES (est): 1.2MM **Privately Held**
SIC: 1422 Crushed & broken limestone

(G-5677)
GRAYMATTER INDUSTRIES LLC
13088 Prices Bridge Rd (24340-4508)
PHONE.................................276 429-2396
Jake Lester, *Principal*
EMP: 2 **EST:** 2011
SALES (est): 84.7K **Privately Held**
SIC: 3999 Manufacturing industries

(G-5678)
HIGHLANDS WELDING AND FABR
33438 Seven Springs Rd R (24340-5330)
P.O. Box 454 (24340-0454)
PHONE.................................276 429-4438
Jeffery Gobble, *Principal*
EMP: 2 **EST:** 2008
SALES (est): 119.5K **Privately Held**
SIC: 7692 Welding repair

(G-5679)
MOUNTAIN MATERIALS INC
14196 Monroe Rd (24340-4418)
PHONE.................................276 429-5241
John Wilkinson, *CEO*
EMP: 50
SALES (est): 5MM **Privately Held**
WEB: www.mountainmaterialsinc.com
SIC: 3273 Ready-mixed concrete

(G-5680)
PHASE II TRUCK BODY INC
33213 Lee Hwy (24340-4913)
P.O. Box 209, Abingdon (24212-0209)
PHONE.................................276 429-2026
EMP: 48
SALES (est): 4.4MM **Privately Held**
SIC: 3713 Mfg Truck/Bus Bodies

Gladstone
Nelson County

(G-5681)
BETHS EMBROIDERY LLC
589 Allens Creek Rd (24553-3092)
PHONE.................................434 933-8652
Beth Angus, *Principal*
EMP: 1
SALES (est): 48.4K **Privately Held**
SIC: 2395 Embroidery & art needlework

(G-5682)
BRYANT BROTHERS LOGGING L L C
2711 W James Anderson Hwy (24553-3506)
PHONE.................................434 933-8303
Buddy Bryant, *Partner*
EMP: 4
SALES (est): 500K **Privately Held**
SIC: 2411 Logging camps & contractors

(G-5683)
GREIF INC
861 Fiber Plant Rd (24553-3744)
P.O. Box 339, Amherst (24521-0339)
PHONE.................................434 933-4100
Andy Williams, *Purch Mgr*
Jim Bunch, *Engineer*
Randy Davis, *Engineer*
Brad Maines, *Project Engr*
Paul Pritchard, *Electrical Engi*
EMP: 150

SALES (corp-wide): 4.6B **Publicly Held**
WEB: www.deltacogroup.com
SIC: 2672 2621 Coated paper, except photographic, carbon or abrasive; paper mills
PA: Greif, Inc.
425 Winter Rd
Delaware OH 43015
740 549-6000

(G-5684)
HONAKER SON LOGGING
62 Old Thirteen Ln (24553-3017)
PHONE...................................434 933-8251
Mark Honaker, *Principal*
EMP: 3 EST: 2010
SALES (est): 216K Privately Held
SIC: 2411 Logging

(G-5685)
LLOYD D WELLS LOGGING CONTG
12789 Anderson Hwy (24553-3362)
PHONE...................................434 933-4316
Lloyd D Wells, *Owner*
EMP: 4
SALES (est): 500K Privately Held
SIC: 2411 Logging camps & contractors

(G-5686)
MARTIN RAILROAD TIE CO
220 Tye Yard Rd (24553-3309)
PHONE...................................434 933-4398
Greg Martin, *Owner*
EMP: 2
SQ FT: 200
SALES (est): 82K Privately Held
SIC: 2421 Railroad ties, sawed

(G-5687)
MCCORMICK JR LOGGING INC BD
424 Riverside Dr (24553-3254)
PHONE...................................434 238-3593
EMP: 3
SALES (est): 299.1K Privately Held
SIC: 2411 Logging

(G-5688)
STALLWORKS LLC
Also Called: Virginia Metalfab
9056 Oakville Rd (24553-3317)
PHONE...................................434 933-8939
Ron Martin, *President*
EMP: 37
SQ FT: 30,000
SALES (est): 3.8MM Privately Held
WEB: www.vametalfab.com
SIC: 3444 Sheet metalwork

(G-5689)
WESTERN DIGITAL CORPORATION
451 Cabin Ln (24553-3489)
P.O. Box 269 (24553)
PHONE...................................434 933-8162
EMP: 3 Publicly Held
WEB: www.westerndigital.com
SIC: 3572 Computer storage devices
PA: Western Digital Corporation
5601 Great Oaks Pkwy
San Jose CA 95119
408 717-6000

Gladys
Campbell County

(G-5690)
DIXIE PLASTICS & MACHINING
1802 Long Island Rd (24554-2752)
PHONE...................................434 283-3778
Dennis Elder, *Owner*
EMP: 3
SQ FT: 2,500
SALES (est): 150K Privately Held
SIC: 3599 Machine shop, jobbing & repair

(G-5691)
GEORGIA-PACIFIC LLC
Hwy 501 S (24554)
PHONE...................................434 283-1066
Wayne Bales, *Manager*
EMP: 125

SALES (corp-wide): 38.9B **Privately Held**
WEB: www.gp.com
SIC: 2493 2436 Strandboard, oriented; softwood veneer & plywood
HQ: Georgia-Pacific Llc
133 Peachtree St Nw
Atlanta GA 30303
404 652-4000

(G-5692)
GLADYS TIMBER PRODUCTS INC
8759 Brookneal Hwy (24554-3241)
P.O. Box 99 (24554-0099)
PHONE...................................434 283-4744
Bruce Wallace, *President*
Don Landis, *General Mgr*
EMP: 13
SALES (est): 1.6MM Privately Held
WEB: www.gladystimberproducts.com
SIC: 2491 Structural lumber & timber, treated wood

(G-5693)
JENNINGS STAINED GLASS INC
1802 Long Island Rd (24554-2752)
P.O. Box 100 (24554-0100)
PHONE...................................434 283-1301
Harold Jennings, *President*
EMP: 10
SALES (est): 902.9K Privately Held
WEB: www.jenningsstainedglass.net
SIC: 3231 Stained glass: made from purchased glass

(G-5694)
MANN LOGGING
611 County Airport Rd (24554-2044)
PHONE...................................434 283-5245
Debbie Mann, *Owner*
Donnie Mann, *Co-Owner*
EMP: 2
SALES (est): 125.2K Privately Held
SIC: 2411 Logging camps & contractors

(G-5695)
MELROSE BISON FARM
830 Dry Fork Rd (24554-2381)
PHONE...................................434 660-6036
Thomas Morris, *Owner*
EMP: 2
SALES (est): 50K Privately Held
SIC: 2011 Beef products from beef slaughtered on site

(G-5696)
SCHROCKS SLAUGHTERHOUSE
4141 Pigeon Run Rd (24554-2130)
PHONE...................................434 283-5400
Mark Schrock, *Owner*
EMP: 6
SALES (est): 240K Privately Held
WEB: www.schrocksh.com
SIC: 2011 Meat packing plants

(G-5697)
SWRD LLC
102 Dillards Ln (24554-1108)
PHONE...................................434 944-2558
Timron Debae Brown,
EMP: 1
SALES (est): 10K Privately Held
SIC: 3161 Clothing & apparel carrying cases

(G-5698)
WALTER PILLOW LOGGING
6231 Covered Bridge Rd (24554-2844)
PHONE...................................434 283-5449
Walter Pillow, *Owner*
EMP: 1
SALES (est): 59.6K Privately Held
SIC: 2411 Logging

Glasgow
Rockbridge County

(G-5699)
BURLINGTON INDUSTRIES INC
404 Anderson St (24555-2802)
PHONE...................................540 258-2811
David Speight, *Executive*
EMP: 1 EST: 2017

SALES (est): 83.2K **Privately Held**
SIC: 2273 Carpets & rugs

(G-5700)
MOHAWK INDUSTRIES INC
404 Anderson St (24555-2802)
PHONE...................................540 258-2811
Simmons Tim, *Vice Pres*
William Brown, *Opers Mgr*
Darryl Knick, *Safety Mgr*
Scotty Buchanan, *Production*
Smith Clint, *Production*
EMP: 10 **Publicly Held**
WEB: www.mohawkind.com
SIC: 2273 Finishers of tufted carpets & rugs
PA: Mohawk Industries, Inc.
160 S Industrial Blvd
Calhoun GA 30701

(G-5701)
ROCKBRIDGE STONE PRODUCTS INC (PA)
Hc 679 (24555)
P.O. Box 605 (24555-0605)
PHONE...................................540 258-2841
Roy Simmons, *President*
Barry Brubaker, *Corp Secy*
Allan Deleeuwerk, *Vice Pres*
EMP: 7
SALES (est): 881K Privately Held
SIC: 3281 5211 5032 1422 Stone, quarrying & processing of own stone products; sand & gravel; stone, crushed or broken; crushed & broken limestone

(G-5702)
ST CLAIR SIGNS INC
1630 Blue Ridge Rd (24555-2153)
P.O. Box 487 (24555-0487)
PHONE...................................540 258-2191
Danny St Clair, *President*
EMP: 1
SALES (est): 58.7K Privately Held
SIC: 3993 Signs & advertising specialties

Glen Allen
Henrico County

(G-5703)
ABLE MFG LLC
10487 Washington Hwy (23059-1964)
PHONE...................................804 550-4885
EMP: 3
SALES (est): 220K Privately Held
SIC: 2657 Mfg Folding Paperboard Boxes

(G-5704)
ABSOLUTE STONE DESIGN LLC
11200 Washington Hwy (23059-1976)
PHONE...................................804 752-2001
Emilio Peiro, *Sales Associate*
Val Ribeiro, *Mng Member*
Gray Lacy,
▲ **EMP: 23 EST:** 2008
SQ FT: 10,000
SALES (est): 3.3MM Privately Held
WEB: www.absolutestonedesign.com
SIC: 3281 Granite, cut & shaped; limestone, cut & shaped

(G-5705)
ATK CHAN INC
10444 Mountain Glen Pkwy (23060-4478)
PHONE...................................804 266-3428
Aung Thu Khine, *Principal*
EMP: 2 EST: 2009
SALES (est): 146.3K Privately Held
SIC: 3764 Propulsion units for guided missiles & space vehicles

(G-5706)
BAYONET
5219 Hickory Park Dr B (23059-2618)
PHONE...................................804 323-3204
EMP: 2
SALES (est): 75K Privately Held
WEB: www.carrieink.com
SIC: 7372 Prepackaged software

(G-5707)
BEST GREEN TECHNOLOGIES LLC
5208 Brockton Ct (23059-5583)
P.O. Box 19927, Denver CO (80219-0927)
PHONE...................................888 424-8432
Joseph Sullivan, *President*
Dennis Huyck, *COO*
▲ **EMP:** 12
SALES (est): 1.2MM Privately Held
SIC: 3433 Gas infrared heating units

(G-5708)
BIG PAPER RECORDS LLC
11318 Old Scotland Rd (23059-1858)
PHONE...................................804 381-9278
Jerome Spellman,
EMP: 1
SALES (est): 76K Privately Held
WEB: www.bigpaperrecords.com
SIC: 2741 7389 Music book & sheet music publishing;

(G-5709)
BIOSENSOR TECH LLC
4810 Garden Spring Ln # 206 (23059-7550)
PHONE...................................318 843-4479
Xinchuan Liu,
EMP: 1 EST: 2011
SALES (est): 79.6K Privately Held
SIC: 3845 Automated blood & body fluid analyzers, except laboratory

(G-5710)
BLACK ROOM PRESS LLC
4901 Olde Mill Pond Ln (23060-2860)
PHONE...................................804 929-8040
EMP: 2
SALES (est): 81.8K Privately Held
WEB: www.blackroompress.com
SIC: 2741 Miscellaneous publishing

(G-5711)
CAPITOL SIGNS INC
11214 Howards Mill Rd (23059-1536)
PHONE...................................804 749-3737
William L Akers Jr, *President*
Joel Howell, *Vice Pres*
Hudson T Mark, *Vice Pres*
EMP: 8
SQ FT: 1,500
SALES (est): 1MM Privately Held
WEB: www.capitolsigns.net
SIC: 3993 Signs & advertising specialties

(G-5712)
CHEF SOUS LLC
Also Called: Keep It Simple Syrup
4860 Cox Rd Ste 200 (23060-9248)
P.O. Box 6567 (23058-6567)
PHONE...................................804 938-5477
Susan Martinson, *Owner*
EMP: 1 EST: 2008
SALES (est): 102.4K Privately Held
WEB: www.keepitsimplesyrup.com
SIC: 2087 Beverage bases, concentrates, syrups, powders & mixes

(G-5713)
CHOCOLATE DMNDS PBLCATIONS LLC
708 Francis Rd (23059-4523)
PHONE...................................804 332-5117
Tiffany Harris, *Principal*
EMP: 2
SALES (est): 95.4K Privately Held
SIC: 2741 Miscellaneous publishing

(G-5714)
CHOICE PRINTING SERVICES
5504 Barnsley Ter (23059-3424)
P.O. Box 2054 (23058-2054)
PHONE...................................804 690-9064
Lainee Biliunas, *Owner*
EMP: 1
SALES (est): 141.5K Privately Held
WEB: www.choiceprintingonline.com
SIC: 2752 Commercial printing, offset

(G-5715)
COLFAX CORPORATION
Also Called: Unknown
10571 Telg Rd Ste 201 (23059)
PHONE...................................757 328-3987

GEOGRAPHIC

Robert Wilkinson, *Engineer*
Charles Hinckley, *Branch Mgr*
EMP: 2 **Publicly Held**
WEB: www.colfaxcorp.com
SIC: 3561 Pumps & pumping equipment
PA: Colfax Corporation
    420 Natl Bus Pkwy Ste 500
    Annapolis Junction MD 20701
    301 323-9000

(G-5716)
COLLEGE PUBLISHING
12309 Lynwood Dr (23059-7120)
PHONE..........................804 364-8410
Steven Mosberg, *Owner*
EMP: 1
SALES (est): 67.7K **Privately Held**
WEB: www.collegepublishing.us
SIC: 2731 Books: publishing only

(G-5717)
COMXI WORLD LLC
5231 Hickory Park Dr B (23059-2619)
PHONE..........................804 299-5234
Min Kim, *General Mgr*
Min Ho Lee, *Exec Dir*
EMP: 2
SQ FT: 200
SALES (est): 132K **Privately Held**
SIC: 3577 Input/output equipment, computer

(G-5718)
COX READY MIX INC SB (HQ)
12554 W Broad St (23058)
P.O. Box 5363 (23058-5363)
PHONE..........................804 364-0500
Morgan Nelson, *President*
Barbee Cox, *Vice Pres*
Kelli Mills, *Admin Asst*
EMP: 40
SALES (est): 10.3MM
SALES (corp-wide): 17.8MM **Privately Held**
WEB: www.coxreadymix.com
SIC: 3273 Ready-mixed concrete
PA: S. B. Cox, Incorporated
    901 Potomac St
    Richmond VA 23231
    804 222-2232

(G-5719)
CRAFTED FOR ME LLC
9412 Broad Meadows Rd (23060-3102)
PHONE..........................804 412-5273
Salve Lo, *Partner*
EMP: 1
SALES (est): 64.7K **Privately Held**
SIC: 3171 Women's handbags & purses

(G-5720)
CUSTOM ORNAMENTAL IRON INC
10412 Knotty Pine Ln (23059-1924)
P.O. Box 1583 (23060-1583)
PHONE..........................804 798-1991
John Price, *President*
James Call, *Vice Pres*
Nancy Call, *Vice Pres*
James Kramer, *Vice Pres*
Stephen Call, *Opers Staff*
EMP: 90
SQ FT: 6,200
SALES (est): 21.1MM **Privately Held**
WEB: www.customornamentaliron.com
SIC: 3444 3446 Sheet metalwork; stairs, fire escapes, balconies, railings & ladders

(G-5721)
DCSPORTS87 SPORT CARDS
9201 Dolmen Ct (23060-3520)
PHONE..........................571 334-3314
Zachary Camann,
EMP: 1
SALES (est): 51.7K **Privately Held**
SIC: 3949 Sporting & athletic goods

(G-5722)
DEMATOLOGY ASSOC VIRGINIA P
301 Cncourse Blvd Ste 190 (23059)
PHONE..........................804 549-4030
Laurra Phieffer, *President*
EMP: 2
SALES (est): 74.4K **Privately Held**
SIC: 2834 Dermatologicals

(G-5723)
DIEHAPPY LLC
14854 Elliot Ridge Way (23059-1571)
PHONE..........................804 283-6025
Shawn Boyer, *CEO*
EMP: 3
SALES (est): 150K **Privately Held**
SIC: 7372 Application computer software

(G-5724)
DISSE OUTDOOR GEAR LLC
5901 Herrick Pl (23059-7044)
PHONE..........................804 357-2860
EMP: 2
SALES (est): 104.8K **Privately Held**
WEB: www.dissegear.com
SIC: 2323 Men's & boys' neckwear

(G-5725)
DITCH WITCH OF VIRGINIA
11053 Washington Hwy (23059-1905)
PHONE..........................804 798-2590
EMP: 1
SALES (est): 60K **Privately Held**
WEB: www.ditchwitchva.com
SIC: 3531 Construction machinery

(G-5726)
DOORS & MORE WELDING
11196 Woodstock Hts Dr (23059-1766)
PHONE..........................804 798-4833
Stanley L Floyd Jr, *Owner*
EMP: 1 **EST:** 1986
SALES (est): 110.8K **Privately Held**
SIC: 7692 Welding repair

(G-5727)
DURABOOK FEDERAL INC
4860 Cox Rd Ste 200 (23060-9248)
PHONE..........................888 414-9844
Joseph W Guest, *President*
Chau Nguyen, *Principal*
EMP: 7
SALES (est): 279.3K **Privately Held**
SIC: 3571 Electronic computers

(G-5728)
EDUCREN INC
11535 Nuckols Rd Ste E (23059-5671)
PHONE..........................804 410-4305
Rajesh Singh, *President*
EMP: 4
SALES (est): 195.5K **Privately Held**
WEB: www.educren.com
SIC: 7372 Application computer software

(G-5729)
FAIR VALUE GAMES LLC
11608 Norwich Pkwy (23059-3414)
PHONE..........................804 307-9110
Charles Phelps, *Owner*
Roger Jones, *Principal*
EMP: 2 **EST:** 2012
SALES (est): 112.7K **Privately Held**
SIC: 7372 7389 Home entertainment computer software;

(G-5730)
FELTS SIGN CO
1501 Fauver Ave (23060-4003)
PHONE..........................804 262-1441
Clarence Felts Jr, *Owner*
EMP: 3
SQ FT: 700
SALES (est): 181.5K **Privately Held**
SIC: 3993 Signs & advertising specialties

(G-5731)
FIZE WORDSMITHING LLC
10001 Christiano Dr (23060-3708)
PHONE..........................804 756-8243
Finetta Milway, *Principal*
EMP: 2
SALES (est): 126.9K **Privately Held**
SIC: 3949 Playground equipment

(G-5732)
FOX RIVER DISTILLING COMPANY
2114 Liesfeld Pkwy (23060-5855)
PHONE..........................630 402-0027
Susan Leigh, *Exec Dir*
EMP: 6

SALES (est): 390.2K **Privately Held**
WEB: www.rabbitholedistillery.com
SIC: 2085 Distilled & blended liquors

(G-5733)
FRAYSER WELDING CO
11281 Cobbs Rd (23059-1803)
PHONE..........................804 798-8764
Richard Frayser, *Principal*
EMP: 1
SALES (est): 72.6K **Privately Held**
SIC: 7692 Welding repair

(G-5734)
G T WALLS CABINET SHOP
13527 Mountain Rd (23059-1742)
PHONE..........................804 798-6288
George T Walls Jr, *Owner*
EMP: 2 **EST:** 1960
SQ FT: 1,500
SALES (est): 203.7K **Privately Held**
SIC: 2434 2541 Wood kitchen cabinets; office fixtures, wood

(G-5735)
GENERAL CIGAR CO INC (HQ)
10900 Nuckols Rd Ste 100 (23059-9277)
PHONE..........................860 602-3500
Austin T McNamara, *President*
W Brent Currier, *Vice Pres*
Robert Loftus, *Vice Pres*
A Ross Wollen, *Asst Sec*
▼ **EMP:** 675
SALES (est): 71.5MM
SALES (corp-wide): 1B **Privately Held**
SIC: 2121 5199 0132 Cigars; smokers' supplies; lighters, cigarette & cigar; tobacco
PA: Scandinavian Tobacco Group A/S
    Sandtoften 9
    Gentofte 2820
    395 562-00

(G-5736)
GENERAL ELECTRIC COMPANY
4521 Highwoods Pkwy # 200 (23060-6148)
PHONE..........................804 965-1020
Karen Berry, *Branch Mgr*
EMP: 125
SALES (corp-wide): 95.2B **Publicly Held**
WEB: www.ge.com
SIC: 3641 Electric lamp (bulb) parts
PA: General Electric Company
    5 Necco St
    Boston MA 02210
    617 443-3000

(G-5737)
GLEN ALLEN PRESS LLC
Also Called: Objective Standard, The
4036 Cox Rd Ste D (23060-6704)
P.O. Box 5274 (23058-5274)
PHONE..........................804 747-1776
Craig Biddle, *Mng Member*
Jon Hersey, *Assoc Editor*
EMP: 2
SALES (est): 158.7K **Privately Held**
WEB: www.theobjectivestandard.com
SIC: 2741 Miscellaneous publishing

(G-5738)
GREENBROOK TMS NEUROHEALTH CTR
100 Eastshore Dr Ste 110 (23059-5758)
PHONE..........................804 980-7520
William Sauv, *Branch Mgr*
EMP: 3
SALES (corp-wide): 2.7MM **Privately Held**
WEB: www.greenbrooktms.com
SIC: 3312 Blast furnaces & steel mills
PA: Greenbrook Tms Neurohealth Center
    8405 Greensboro Dr # 120
    Mc Lean VA 22102
    703 356-1568

(G-5739)
HAMILTON BEACH BRANDS INC (HQ)
4421 Waterfront Dr (23060-3375)
PHONE..........................804 273-9777
Gregory H Trepp, *President*
Dana Sykes, *Counsel*
Gregory E Salyers, *Senior VP*
R Scott Tidey, *Senior VP*
Brian Brumbaugh, *Vice Pres*

◆ **EMP:** 295
SQ FT: 85,000
SALES (est): 226.1MM **Publicly Held**
WEB: www.hamiltonbeach.com
SIC: 3634 5719 Toasters, electric: household; ovens, portable: household; irons, electric: household; coffee makers, electric: household; kitchenware
PA: Hamilton Beach Brands Holding Company
    4421 Waterfront Dr
    Glen Allen VA 23060
    804 273-9777

(G-5740)
HAMILTON BEACH BRANDS HOLDG CO (PA)
4421 Waterfront Dr (23060-3375)
PHONE..........................804 273-9777
Alfred M Rankin Jr, *Ch of Bd*
Gregory H Trepp, *President*
Dana B Sykes, *Senior VP*
Arron Bryant, *Engineer*
Michelle O Mosier, *CFO*
▲ **EMP:** 19 **Publicly Held**
WEB: www.hamiltonbeachbrands.com
SIC: 3634 5719 Toasters, electric: household; kitchenware

(G-5741)
HASCO SALES INC
11725 Lincolnshire Ct (23059-3417)
PHONE..........................804 740-1869
Thomas Haeseker, *President*
Karen Haeseker, *Treasurer*
EMP: 4 **EST:** 1999
SALES (est): 38.4K **Privately Held**
WEB: www.hascosales.net
SIC: 3561 Pumps, domestic: water or sump

(G-5742)
HEYWARD INC VIRGINIA INC
10146 W Broad St (23060-3303)
P.O. Box 3270 (23058-3270)
PHONE..........................804 965-0086
James C Chastain III, *Administration*
EMP: 2
SALES (est): 143.8K **Privately Held**
WEB: www.heywardinc.com
SIC: 3589 Water treatment equipment, industrial

(G-5743)
HHH UNDERGROUND LLC
10353 Cedar Ln (23059-1925)
PHONE..........................804 365-6905
Janette Hanley, *President*
EMP: 16
SALES (est): 4.7MM **Privately Held**
WEB: www.mjwconstruction.net
SIC: 3532 1629 Drills & drilling equipment, mining (except oil & gas); drainage system construction

(G-5744)
HIBERNATE INC
14249 Big Apple Rd (23059-1663)
PHONE..........................804 513-1777
Kenneth Lowenstein, *President*
▲ **EMP:** 3
SALES (est): 3MM **Privately Held**
SIC: 2321 2331 5137 5136 Flannel shirts, except work: men's, youths' & boys'; T-shirts & tops, women's: made from purchased materials; women's & children's clothing; men's & boys' clothing

(G-5745)
HIGH CONCEPTS
9509 Brant Ln (23060-3876)
PHONE..........................804 683-2226
Jenny M High, *CEO*
EMP: 2
SALES (est): 126.4K **Privately Held**
SIC: 3911 Jewelry, precious metal

(G-5746)
HILL TOP DISTILLERY LLC
6020 Stonewick Ct (23059-7153)
PHONE..........................804 212-8645
EMP: 3
SALES (est): 68.6K **Privately Held**
SIC: 2085 Distilled & blended liquors

(G-5747)
HOME DECOR SEWING
5814 Shady Hills Way (23059-7069)
PHONE..................................804 364-8750
Kelly Parrish, *Owner*
EMP: 1
SALES (est): 56.4K **Privately Held**
SIC: 2284 Sewing thread

(G-5748)
HOWMEDICA OSTEONICS CORP
5500 Cox Rd Ste K (23060-9257)
PHONE..................................804 737-9426
Charlie Davis, *General Mgr*
Jeffrey Morley, *Sales Mgr*
Marc Verica, *Accounts Mgr*
Russ Bradshaw, *Sales Staff*
Frazer Orgain, *Sales Staff*
EMP: 8
SALES (corp-wide): 14.8B **Publicly Held**
SIC: 3842 Prosthetic appliances
HQ: Howmedica Osteonics Corp.
325 Corporate Dr
Mahwah NJ 07430
201 831-5000

(G-5749)
HYDRUS USA INC
5323 Stone Horse Rd (23059-5354)
PHONE..................................804 690-8158
Scott Frayser, *CEO*
EMP: 4
SALES (est): 165.7K **Privately Held**
SIC: 2842 Specialty cleaning, polishes & sanitation goods

(G-5750)
INDOFF INCORPORATED
12021 Wheat Ridge Ct (23059-5662)
PHONE..................................804 539-2425
EMP: 1
SALES (corp-wide): 269.3MM **Privately Held**
WEB: www.indoff.com
SIC: 2679 Tags & labels, paper
PA: Indoff, Incorporated
11816 Lackland Rd Ste 200
Saint Louis MO 63146
314 997-1122

(G-5751)
INK2WORK LLC
10307 W Broad St Ste 255 (23060-6716)
PHONE..................................605 202-9079
EMP: 1
SQ FT: 1,500
SALES (est): 46.9K **Privately Held**
SIC: 3955 Mfg Carbon Paper/Ink Ribbons

(G-5752)
IQ ENERGY LLC
4860 Cox Rd Ste 300 (23060-9250)
PHONE..................................804 747-8900
EMP: 6
SALES (est): 246.8K **Privately Held**
SIC: 2086 Mfg Industl Organic Chem Whol Groceries Mfg Soft Drinks

(G-5753)
ITEK SOFTWARE LLC
11604 Peavey St (23059-3435)
PHONE..................................312 404-3086
Suhasini Vuppala, *President*
EMP: 2
SALES (est): 62.1K **Privately Held**
SIC: 7372 Prepackaged software

(G-5754)
JAMES RIVER CELLARS INC
Also Called: James River Cellars Winery
11008 Washington Hwy (23059-1904)
PHONE..................................804 550-7516
Raymond F Lazarchic, *President*
Mitzi Patterson, *Principal*
EMP: 5
SALES (est): 520K **Privately Held**
WEB: www.jamesrivercellars.com
SIC: 2084 Wine cellars, bonded: engaged in blending wines

(G-5755)
JERRY KING
Also Called: Rack 'em Company
10477c Cobbs Rd (23059-1800)
PHONE..................................804 550-1243
Jerry King, *President*

Jerry Lee King, *Bookkeeper*
EMP: 5
SALES (est): 259K **Privately Held**
SIC: 3449 7549 2499 1799 Miscellaneous metalwork; automotive customizing services, non-factory basis; fencing, docks & other outdoor wood structural products; fence construction

(G-5756)
JM HUBER CORPORATION
5108 Old Forester Ln (23060-6382)
PHONE..................................804 357-3698
Jim Jenkins, *Branch Mgr*
EMP: 1
SALES (corp-wide): 898.2MM **Privately Held**
WEB: www.huber.com
SIC: 2819 Industrial inorganic chemicals
PA: J.M. Huber Corporation
499 Thornall St Ste 8
Edison NJ 08837
732 549-8600

(G-5757)
JORDO INC (PA)
4020 Gaelic Ln Apt Q (23060-6429)
PHONE..................................424 394-2986
Micheal Luce, *CEO*
EMP: 1
SALES (est): 129.4K **Privately Held**
SIC: 2241 7371 Lacings, textile; computer software development & applications

(G-5758)
JORDO INC
4990 Sadler Pl 30204 (23060-6122)
PHONE..................................424 394-2986
Micheal Luce, *CEO*
EMP: 1
SALES (corp-wide): 129.4K **Privately Held**
SIC: 2241 7371 Lacings, textile; computer software development & applications
PA: Jordo, Inc.
4020 Gaelic Ln Apt Q
Glen Allen VA 23060
424 394-2986

(G-5759)
K12EXCELLENCE INC
5318 Twin Hickory Rd (23059-5682)
PHONE..................................804 270-9600
Manoj Rewatkar, *CEO*
Aruna Kale, *President*
Sandra Oneal, *Vice Pres*
Brent Mullins, *Director*
EMP: 3
SALES (est): 195.3K **Privately Held**
WEB: www.k12excellence.com
SIC: 7372 7371 7373 Application computer software; educational computer software; computer software systems analysis & design, custom; computer software development & applications; systems integration services

(G-5760)
KANAWHA EAGLE COAL LLC (PA)
4701 Cox Rd Ste 285 (23060-6808)
PHONE..................................304 837-8587
Joseph W Bean, *Vice Pres*
Jim Bunn, *Mng Member*
EMP: 5
SALES (est): 5.9MM **Privately Held**
SIC: 1241 Coal mining services

(G-5761)
KEY MADE NOW
9811 Brook Rd (23059-4530)
PHONE..................................804 663-5192
EMP: 2 **EST:** 2012
SALES (est): 102.9K **Privately Held**
SIC: 3429 Keys, locks & related hardware

(G-5762)
LIFES A STITCH INC
3213 Forest Lodge Ct (23060-2640)
PHONE..................................804 672-7079
Debra A Hiltunen, *President*
EMP: 2
SALES (est): 20K **Privately Held**
WEB: www.lifesastitch.biz
SIC: 2395 Embroidery products, except schiffli machine

(G-5763)
LIGHT DESIGNS PUBLISHING CO
9915 Greenwood Rd Ste B (23060-4256)
PHONE..................................804 261-6900
EMP: 4
SALES (est): 210K **Privately Held**
SIC: 2741 Publishing

(G-5764)
LITTLEFIELD LOGGING
13534 Greenwood Rd (23059-1617)
PHONE..................................804 798-5590
Ann Littlefield, *Principal*
EMP: 3
SALES (est): 204.8K **Privately Held**
SIC: 2411 Logging

(G-5765)
LOU-VOISE
Also Called: Hospice Gowns By Lou-Voise
5417 Woolshire Dr (23059-3412)
PHONE..................................804 836-5601
Carole Moore, *Owner*
EMP: 1
SALES (est): 89.1K **Privately Held**
SIC: 2389 Apparel & accessories

(G-5766)
MACEMEDIA INC
Also Called: Fedweek
11551 Nuckols Rd Ste L (23059-5565)
PHONE..................................804 288-5321
Chris Mace, *President*
Michael Floyd, *Sales Staff*
Don Mace,
EMP: 10
SALES (est): 293.6K **Privately Held**
WEB: www.fedweek.com
SIC: 2741 Newsletter publishing

(G-5767)
MARKET THIS LLC
10808 Kittery Pl (23060-6485)
PHONE..................................804 382-9220
Lloyd R Leitstein,
EMP: 2
SALES (est): 175K **Privately Held**
SIC: 2721 2741 Magazines: publishing only, not printed on site; newsletter publishing

(G-5768)
MASTERS ENERGY INC
9601 Hastings Mill Dr (23060-3267)
PHONE..................................281 816-9991
Robert Fox, *CEO*
EMP: 27
SALES (est): 1.2MM **Privately Held**
WEB: www.mastersenergy.us
SIC: 2869 3699 1311 4213 Fuels; high-energy particle physics equipment; crude petroleum & natural gas; liquid petroleum transport, non-local

(G-5769)
MDC CAMDEN CLAYWORKS
11467 New Farrington Ct (23059-1629)
PHONE..................................804 798-4971
David Camden, *Owner*
EMP: 2
SALES (est): 95.6K **Privately Held**
WEB: www.camdenclayworks.com
SIC: 3269 Art & ornamental ware, pottery

(G-5770)
MICROSOFT CORPORATION
4301 Dominion Blvd # 200 (23060-6780)
PHONE..................................804 270-0146
Pam Goggins, *Accounts Exec*
Michael Perriello, *Accounts Exec*
Jodi Ovca, *Branch Mgr*
Art Akerman, *Manager*
Anne Lansing, *Manager*
EMP: 100
SALES (corp-wide): 143B **Publicly Held**
WEB: www.microsoft.com
SIC: 7372 Application computer software
PA: Microsoft Corporation
1 Microsoft Way
Redmond WA 98052
425 882-8080

(G-5771)
MO CAKES
3201 Lavecchia Way (23059-4830)
PHONE..................................804 349-8634
Monica Walker, *Owner*
EMP: 1
SALES (est): 14K **Privately Held**
SIC: 2051 Bread, cake & related products

(G-5772)
MOBILE RADIO PARTNERS INC (PA)
6573 Glenshaw Dr (23059-3408)
PHONE..................................804 364-1553
Michael Mazursky, *Principal*
EMP: 7
SALES (est): 1.8MM **Privately Held**
WEB: www.motorolasolutions.com
SIC: 3663 Radio & TV communications equipment

(G-5773)
MONUMENT32/THE SMYERS GROUP
4860 Cox Rd Ste 200 (23060-9248)
PHONE..................................804 217-8347
Matt Smyers, *Principal*
EMP: 3
SALES (est): 188.6K **Privately Held**
WEB: www.thesmyerslawfirm.com
SIC: 3272 Monuments & grave markers, except terrazo

(G-5774)
NARIAD PUBLISHING
426 Geese Lndg (23060-5877)
PHONE..................................973 650-8948
Meriel Martinez, *Principal*
EMP: 1
SALES (est): 39K **Privately Held**
SIC: 2741 Miscellaneous publishing

(G-5775)
OLD DOMINION MBL CANNING LLC
11300 Long Meadow Dr (23059-5115)
PHONE..................................804 517-1640
Philip Carter Strother, *Administration*
EMP: 4
SALES (est): 275.9K **Privately Held**
WEB: www.olddominionmobilecanning.com
SIC: 2082 Malt beverages

(G-5776)
OPPIYA LEARNING COMPANY LLC
5021 Parsons Walk Cir (23059-7575)
PHONE..................................804 296-0141
Nasser Chanda, *Mng Member*
EMP: 10
SALES (est): 348.8K **Privately Held**
WEB: www.oppiya.com
SIC: 2731 Book publishing

(G-5777)
OSAGE BIO ENERGY LLC (PA)
4991 Lake Brook Dr # 250 (23060-9290)
PHONE..................................804 612-8660
Shealy Isavel,
EMP: 20
SALES (est): 5MM **Privately Held**
WEB: www.osagebioenergy.com
SIC: 2869 8748 Fuels; energy conservation consultant

(G-5778)
PASSIONATE STITCHER
10908 Brunson Way (23060-6484)
PHONE..................................804 747-7141
Valerie Sepp, *Principal*
EMP: 3 **EST:** 2008
SALES (est): 214.6K **Privately Held**
SIC: 2241 Braids, textile

(G-5779)
PHILLIPS MEDICAL MANUFACTURER
2729 Maurice Walk Ct (23060-4427)
PHONE..................................804 475-9144
Todd Phillips, *Owner*
EMP: 2
SALES (est): 67K **Privately Held**
SIC: 2326 Medical & hospital uniforms, men's

GEOGRAPHIC

(G-5780)
POSITIVE PASTA PUBLISHING LLC
5505 Summer Creek Way (23059-7130)
PHONE..................................804 385-0151
Hemanki Doshi, *Principal*
EMP: 2 **EST:** 2017
SALES (est): 65.1K **Privately Held**
SIC: 2741 Miscellaneous publishing

(G-5781)
POWERUP PRINTING INC
12021 Wheat Ridge Ct (23059-5662)
PHONE..................................804 364-1353
EMP: 2
SALES (est): 116.4K **Privately Held**
SIC: 2752 Commercial printing, lithographic

(G-5782)
PREMIER PET PRODUCTS LLC
1054 Technology Park Dr (23059-4500)
PHONE..................................804 594-0613
Greg Birsinger, *CFO*
Sharon E Madere, *Mng Member*
Evan Wooton,
◆ **EMP:** 96
SQ FT: 72,000
SALES (est): 7.9MM **Privately Held**
WEB: www.premierpet.com
SIC: 2399 5199 Pet collars, leashes, etc.: non-leather; pet supplies
PA: Radio Systems Corporation
10427 Petsafe Way
Knoxville TN 37932

(G-5783)
PROFITOPTICS INC
4050 Innslake Dr Ste 375 (23060-3322)
PHONE..................................804 360-2776
Anthony J Pericle, *Principal*
Jon Ladle, *COO*
Jordan Hiatt, *Business Anlyst*
Nick Pericle, *IT/INT Sup*
Milan Ristic, *Software Dev*
EMP: 2 **EST:** 2009
SALES (est): 169.6K **Privately Held**
WEB: www.profitoptics.com
SIC: 7372 Prepackaged software

(G-5784)
PURYEAR GROUP & ASSOCIATES LLC
10307 W Broad St Unit 268 (23060-6716)
PHONE..................................202 327-3777
Glen Allen,
EMP: 3
SALES (est): 142.9K **Privately Held**
SIC: 2721 Magazines: publishing only, not printed on site

(G-5785)
R & S NAMEBADGE INC
10333 Old Courtney Rd (23060-3052)
PHONE..................................804 673-2842
Sue Kirkland, *President*
Rick Kirkland, *Admin Sec*
EMP: 2
SQ FT: 900
SALES (est): 120.5K **Privately Held**
WEB: www.rsnamebadge.com
SIC: 3993 7389 Signs & advertising specialties; engraving service

(G-5786)
R B M ENTERPRISES INC
Also Called: Minuteman Press
10148 W Broad St Ste 201 (23060-6670)
PHONE..................................804 290-4407
Robert B Maxwell III, *President*
Robert B Maxwell III, *President*
EMP: 4
SQ FT: 1,200
SALES (est): 360K **Privately Held**
WEB: www.minutemanpress.com
SIC: 2752 2399 2741 2731 Commercial printing, lithographic; banners, made from fabric; business service newsletters: publishing & printing; books: publishing & printing

(G-5787)
RICHMOND1040 LLC
9407 Meredith Creek Ln (23060-3428)
PHONE..................................407 538-3624

EMP: 2
SALES (est): 66.6K **Privately Held**
SIC: 2711 Newspapers, publishing & printing

(G-5788)
ROWING TEAM LLC
4435 Waterfront Dr # 300 (23060-6166)
PHONE..................................855 462-7238
Gemma Brooks,
Claire Herring,
Laura Howard,
EMP: 35
SALES (est): 206.4K **Privately Held**
WEB: www.blueoceanbrain.com
SIC: 7372 8742 8748 Business oriented computer software; management consulting services; human resource consulting services; training & development consultant; business consulting

(G-5789)
ROYAL PRINTING COMPANY
11058 Washington Hwy # 5 (23059-1955)
PHONE..................................804 798-8897
Deborah Vass, *President*
Roy Fama, *Admin Sec*
EMP: 3
SQ FT: 1,800
SALES (est): 600K **Privately Held**
WEB: www.royalprintingcompany.com
SIC: 2752 Commercial printing, offset

(G-5790)
SAS INSTITUTE INC
4860 Cox Rd Ste 200 (23060-9248)
PHONE..................................804 217-8352
Michael Sawyer, *Branch Mgr*
EMP: 5
SALES (corp-wide): 1.9B **Privately Held**
WEB: www.sas.com
SIC: 7372 Application computer software; business oriented computer software; educational computer software
PA: Sas Institute Inc.
100 Sas Campus Dr
Cary NC 27513
919 677-8000

(G-5791)
SCHRIBBLE INC
12012 Bennett Ct (23059-2503)
PHONE..................................804 869-6878
Chaun L Burnette, *CEO*
EMP: 1
SALES (est): 32.7K **Privately Held**
SIC: 7372 Educational computer software

(G-5792)
SCIENCE INFO LLC
4860 Cox Rd Ste 200 (23060-9248)
PHONE..................................804 332-5269
Jeya Chelliah,
EMP: 2
SALES (est): 65K **Privately Held**
WEB: www.escienceinfo.com
SIC: 2741 Miscellaneous publishing

(G-5793)
SCRUB SKINZ LLC
10816 Rimbey Ct (23060-6481)
PHONE..................................804 338-1350
Kristina Carol Bonovitch, *Administration*
EMP: 2 **EST:** 2013
SALES (est): 123.1K **Privately Held**
SIC: 3999 Manufacturing industries

(G-5794)
SENTIENT VISION SYSTEMS INC
4470 Cox Rd Ste 250 (23060-6765)
PHONE..................................703 531-8564
Paul Anthony Boxer, *President*
Stewart Day, *Admin Sec*
EMP: 2
SALES (est): 175.4K **Privately Held**
WEB: www.sentientvision.com
SIC: 7372 Prepackaged software

(G-5795)
SHERWIN-WILLIAMS COMPANY
1083 Virginia Center Pkwy (23059-4572)
PHONE..................................804 264-6156
EMP: 2

SALES (corp-wide): 17.9B **Publicly Held**
WEB: www.sherwin-williams.com
SIC: 2851 1721 Paints & allied products; residential painting
PA: The Sherwin-Williams Company
101 W Prospect Ave # 1020
Cleveland OH 44115
216 566-2000

(G-5796)
SIGN AND SEAL ASSOCIATES LLC
11905 Boulware Ct (23059-8029)
PHONE..................................804 266-0410
Tonya Davis, *Principal*
EMP: 1
SALES (est): 55K **Privately Held**
SIC: 3993 Signs & advertising specialties

(G-5797)
SIGN GYPSIES RICHMONDVA LLC
11808 Amberwood Ln (23059-7525)
PHONE..................................804 754-7345
Catherine Edmiston Curran, *Principal*
EMP: 1
SALES (est): 46K **Privately Held**
SIC: 3993 Signs & advertising specialties

(G-5798)
SIMPLE SCRIBES PUBG & DIST LLC
12420 Stone Horse Ct (23059-5324)
PHONE..................................804 364-3418
Paticia Delewski Hall, *Administration*
EMP: 2 **EST:** 2013
SALES (est): 110.6K **Privately Held**
SIC: 2741 Miscellaneous publishing

(G-5799)
SINK OF AMERICA INC
5000 Willows Green Rd (23059-5686)
PHONE..................................804 269-1111
Xudong Ye, *President*
EMP: 3 **EST:** 2010
SALES (est): 270.8K **Privately Held**
WEB: www.sinkofamerica.com
SIC: 3431 Sinks: enameled iron, cast iron or pressed metal

(G-5800)
SNC FOODS INC
4905 Merlin Ln (23060-4916)
PHONE..................................804 726-9907
Sarah N Cooper, *Principal*
EMP: 2
SALES (est): 70.3K **Privately Held**
SIC: 2099 Food preparations

(G-5801)
SOTER MARTIN OF VIRGINIA INC
713 Harmony Rd (23059-4539)
P.O. Box 15233, Richmond (23227-0633)
PHONE..................................804 550-2164
Charles R Martin, *President*
Mike Martin, *Vice Pres*
Deborah Martin, *Bookkeeper*
Dave Becker, *Sales Staff*
Rick Martin, *Sales Associate*
EMP: 2
SALES (est): 240.1K **Privately Held**
SIC: 3069 Plumbers' rubber goods

(G-5802)
STRING STALKER LLC
Also Called: Bow Hunting Lifestyle Apparel
10808 Arrowleaf Ct (23060-6741)
P.O. Box 4529 (23058-4529)
PHONE..................................727 430-7545
Jeffrey Kumper, *Principal*
EMP: 3
SALES (est): 500K **Privately Held**
WEB: www.stringstalker.com
SIC: 2326 5611 Overalls & coveralls; clothing accessories: men's & boys'

(G-5803)
SUPERIOR MAGNETIC PRODUCT
10424 Windam Hill Rd (23059-1754)
PHONE..................................804 752-7897
Wayne Willis, *Owner*
EMP: 1

SALES (est): 135K **Privately Held**
WEB: www.nailhound.com
SIC: 3423 Mechanics' hand tools

(G-5804)
SYNALLOY CORPORATION (PA)
4510 Cox Rd Ste 201 (23060-3394)
PHONE..................................804 822-3260
Christopher Hutter, *CEO*
Murray H Wright, *Ch of Bd*
Donald Cheatham, *Opers Staff*
Sally Cunningham, *CFO*
Dennis M Loughran, *CFO*
EMP: 84 **EST:** 1945
SQ FT: 5,911 **Publicly Held**
WEB: www.synalloy.com
SIC: 3317 3443 2865 2899 Steel pipe & tubes; process vessels, industrial: metal plate; color pigments, organic; chemical preparations; industrial organic chemicals

(G-5805)
TEAM SSP VENTURES INC
5105 Chappell Ridge Pl (23059-5654)
PHONE..................................804 273-9496
Scott P Johrde, *Principal*
EMP: 2 **EST:** 2016
SALES (est): 92K **Privately Held**
SIC: 3732 Boat building & repairing

(G-5806)
TEEN SCOTT TRUCKING INC
9717 Wendhurst Dr (23060-6332)
PHONE..................................804 833-9403
John R Scott, *Owner*
EMP: 4
SALES (est): 229.7K **Privately Held**
SIC: 3711 Truck & tractor truck assembly

(G-5807)
TENANT TURNER
4820 Lake Brook Dr # 125 (23060-9285)
PHONE..................................804 241-8810
EMP: 7
SALES (est): 457.9K **Privately Held**
SIC: 7372 Prepackaged software

(G-5808)
THE TINT
8820 Brook Rd Ste 12 (23060-4001)
PHONE..................................804 261-4081
EMP: 1 **EST:** 2011
SALES (est): 80K **Privately Held**
SIC: 3211 Mfg Flat Glass

(G-5809)
THERESA LUCAS SETELIN
Also Called: Trapper's Triangle
10001 Highview Ave (23059-4568)
PHONE..................................804 266-2324
Theresa Lucas Setelin, *Owner*
EMP: 2
SALES (est): 92.5K **Privately Held**
SIC: 3489 Ordnance & accessories

(G-5810)
THOMPSON MEDIA PACKAGING INC
1681 Mountain Rd (23060-4232)
P.O. Box 1283 (23060-1283)
PHONE..................................804 225-8146
Lon B Thompson, *President*
Beverly G Thompson, *Vice Pres*
EMP: 20
SALES (est): 2.3MM **Privately Held**
WEB: www.thompsonmediapackaging.com
SIC: 2782 Looseleaf binders & devices

(G-5811)
THOMSON REUTERS CORPORATION
4905 Riverplace Ct (23059-5655)
PHONE..................................804 346-5135
EMP: 1
SALES (corp-wide): 10.6B **Publicly Held**
WEB: www.thomsonreuters.com
SIC: 2731 Book publishing
HQ: Thomson Reuters Corporation
333 Bay St
Toronto ON M5H 2
416 687-7500

▲ = Import ▼=Export
◆ =Import/Export

(G-5812)
TIANGO FIELD SERVICES LLC
2400 Barda Cir (23060-4494)
PHONE.................................804 683-2067
Eugene Vango, *Principal*
EMP: 2
SALES (est): 81.9K **Privately Held**
SIC: 1311 Crude petroleum & natural gas

(G-5813)
TITAN PLASTICS LLC
9517 Country Way Rd (23060-3175)
PHONE.................................804 339-4464
John C Bowden IV,
EMP: 3
SALES (est): 25K **Privately Held**
SIC: 2673 Bags: plastic, laminated &
coated

(G-5814)
**TOWNSEND SCREEN PRINTING
LLC**
8679 Telegraph Rd (23060-4030)
PHONE.................................804 225-0716
Aaron Townsend,
EMP: 1
SALES (est): 120.8K **Privately Held**
WEB: www.townsendprinting.com
SIC: 2759 Screen printing

(G-5815)
TR PARTNERS LC
4190 Dominion Blvd (23060-3376)
PHONE.................................804 484-4091
Jason Richey,
EMP: 3
SQ FT: 24,000
SALES (est): 245.8K **Privately Held**
SIC: 3484 Guns (firearms) or gun parts, 30
mm. & below

(G-5816)
TRANLIN INC
Also Called: Vastly
4470 Cox Rd Ste 101 (23060-6746)
P.O. Box 6119 (23058-6119)
PHONE.................................866 215-8290
Zhiyuan Peng, *CEO*
John Stacey, *Senior VP*
Elizabeth Goldstein, *Vice Pres*
Richard Higby, *Vice Pres*
Jill Douthit, *CFO*
EMP: 4
SALES (est): 787.6K **Privately Held**
WEB: www.vastly.com
SIC: 2621 2873 Towels, tissues & napkins:
paper & stock; fertilizers: natural (or-
ganic), except compost

(G-5817)
TREXLO ENTERPRISES LLC
Also Called: Fastsigns
10817 W Broad St (23060-3367)
PHONE.................................804 270-7446
Carolyn Slappey, *Manager*
EMP: 2
SALES (corp-wide): 2.9MM **Privately
Held**
WEB: www.fastsigns.com
SIC: 3993 Signs & advertising specialties;
neon signs
PA: Trexlo Enterprises, Llc
2361a Greystone Ct Ste A
Rockville VA 23146
804 719-5900

(G-5818)
TRIMECH SOLUTIONS LLC (PA)
4461 Cox Rd Ste 302 (23060-3331)
PHONE.................................804 257-9965
Steve Pelham, *CEO*
Beth Fruehstorfer, *Business Mgr*
Tammy Pleasent, *Business Mgr*
Matthew Kokoski, *Technical Mgr*
Allen Miotke, *Technical Mgr*
EMP: 40
SALES (est): 24.5MM **Privately Held**
WEB: www.trimech.com
SIC: 7372 7373 Prepackaged software;
value-added resellers, computer systems

(G-5819)
TYSON FOODS INC
13264 Mountain Rd (23059-1737)
PHONE.................................804 798-8357

Bryan French, *Chairman*
Kendra Schmidt, *Human Resources*
James Drewery, *Maintence Staff*
EMP: 800
SALES (corp-wide): 43.1B **Publicly Held**
WEB: www.tysonfoods.com
SIC: 2015 Poultry, processed
PA: Tyson Foods, Inc.
2200 W Don Tyson Pkwy
Springdale AR 72762
479 290-4000

(G-5820)
UNIVERSAL IMPEX LLC
5615 Benoni Ct (23059-5964)
PHONE.................................202 322-4100
Asad Pervaiz, *Mng Member*
▼ EMP: 3
SQ FT: 2,200
SALES (est): 3MM **Privately Held**
SIC: 3341 Secondary nonferrous metals

(G-5821)
**UP AND GO TRANSPORTATION
LLC**
4870 Sadler Rd Ste 300 (23060-6294)
PHONE.................................443 859-0193
Chapelle Paige,
EMP: 1 **Privately Held**
SIC: 3799 Transportation equipment

(G-5822)
UTILISCOPE CORP
10367 Cedar Ln (23059-1925)
PHONE.................................804 550-5233
Paul J Hayes, *President*
Skip Clements, *Mfg Staff*
John Madsen, *Purchasing*
EMP: 10 EST: 1996
SALES (est): 1.2MM **Privately Held**
WEB: www.utiliscope.com
SIC: 3812 3531 Sonar systems & equip-
ment; construction machinery

(G-5823)
VENTURE APPS LLC
4717 Sadler Green Pl (23060-6161)
PHONE.................................804 747-3405
Ananto Amin, *Principal*
EMP: 2
SALES (est): 62.1K **Privately Held**
SIC: 7372 Prepackaged software

(G-5824)
VERDE CANDLES
10816 Rimbey Ct (23060-6481)
PHONE.................................804 338-1350
EMP: 1
SALES (est): 39.6K **Privately Held**
SIC: 3999 Candles

(G-5825)
VERTIV CORPORATION
1011 Technology Park Dr (23059-4500)
PHONE.................................804 747-6030
Richard Bralley, *General Mgr*
EMP: 10
SALES (corp-wide): 4.4B **Publicly Held**
WEB: www.vertiv.com
SIC: 3613 Regulators, power
HQ: Vertiv Corporation
1050 Dearborn Dr
Columbus OH 43085
614 888-0246

(G-5826)
VULCAN MATERIALS COMPANY
11460 Staples Mill Rd (23059-1926)
PHONE.................................804 270-5385
Jeff Rickey, *Plant Mgr*
EMP: 1 **Publicly Held**
WEB: www.vulcanmaterials.com
SIC: 3273 Ready-mixed concrete
PA: Vulcan Materials Company
1200 Urban Center Dr
Vestavia AL 35242

(G-5827)
WESTROCK MWV LLC
11013 W Broad St (23060-6017)
PHONE.................................804 201-2000
Linda Schreiner, *Vice Pres*
Mike Muller, *Manager*
EMP: 175

SALES (corp-wide): 17.5B **Publicly Held**
WEB: www.westrock.com
SIC: 2653 Boxes, corrugated: made from
purchased materials
HQ: Westrock Mwv, Llc
501 S 5th St
Richmond VA 23219
804 444-1000

(G-5828)
WILKINSON PRINTING CO INC
8704 Brook Rd (23060-4022)
PHONE.................................804 264-2524
EMP: 15 EST: 1953
SQ FT: 10,000
SALES (est): 163.2K **Privately Held**
SIC: 2752 7334 2759 2791 Lithographic
Coml Print Photocopying Service Com-
mercial Printing Typesetting Services

(G-5829)
WINEBOW INC
4800 Cox Rd Ste 300 (23060-6524)
PHONE.................................800 365-9463
Dean Ferrell, *President*
EMP: 2
SALES (est): 62.3K **Privately Held**
WEB: www.fatbastardwine.com
SIC: 2084 Wines

(G-5830)
ZO-ZOS JAMS
1408 Kennedy Station Pl (23060-3934)
PHONE.................................804 562-9867
Zoila L Harris, *Principal*
EMP: 3
SALES (est): 109K **Privately Held**
SIC: 2033 Jams, jellies & preserves: pack-
aged in cans, jars, etc.

(G-5831)
ZOMBIE DEFENSE
11330 Winfrey Rd (23059-4646)
PHONE.................................804 972-3991
EMP: 2
SALES (est): 115.1K **Privately Held**
SIC: 3812 Defense systems & equipment

Glen Lyn
Giles County

(G-5832)
**GE FAIRCHILD MINING
EQUIPMENT (PA)**
200 Fairchild Ln (24093-3530)
PHONE.................................540 921-8000
Jack Fairchild, *Principal*
▼ EMP: 55
SALES (est): 51.9MM **Privately Held**
SIC: 3532 3535 Mining machinery; con-
veyors & conveying equipment

(G-5833)
JUSTICE SIGNS LLC
205 Houston Ln (24093-3519)
P.O. Box 26 (24093-0026)
PHONE.................................304 898-2783
Elden Justice, *Administration*
EMP: 2
SALES (est): 55.2K **Privately Held**
SIC: 3993 Signs & advertising specialties

Gloucester
Gloucester County

(G-5834)
A HOPE SKIP AND A STITCH LLC
7914 Snow Haven Ln (23061-4195)
PHONE.................................804 684-5750
EMP: 1
SALES (est): 69.5K **Privately Held**
SIC: 2395 Embroidery products, except
schiffli machine

(G-5835)
**AGGREGATE INDUSTRIES MGT
INC**
Rr 17 (23061)
PHONE.................................804 693-2280
Bob Rapp, *Branch Mgr*
EMP: 8

SALES (corp-wide): 1.7B **Privately Held**
WEB: www.lafargeholcim.us
SIC: 3273 Ready-mixed concrete
HQ: Aggregate Industries Management,
Inc.
8700 W Bryn Mawr Ave # 300
Chicago IL 60631
773 372-1000

(G-5836)
B R PRODUCTS
6910 Tracey Ct (23061-4319)
P.O. Box 1673 (23061-1673)
PHONE.................................804 693-2639
William H Altemuf Jr,
Ray Rogers,
EMP: 2
SALES (est): 75K **Privately Held**
SIC: 3535 Belt conveyor systems, general
industrial use

(G-5837)
BATCH WOOD WORKS INC
7336 Wellford Ln (23061-5109)
P.O. Box 2305 (23061-2305)
PHONE.................................804 694-5767
EMP: 1
SALES (est): 64.7K **Privately Held**
WEB: www.batchwoodworksva.com
SIC: 2431 Millwork

(G-5838)
BLUEWATER PUBLISHING
7348 Main St (23061-5130)
PHONE.................................804 695-0400
Charles Lanning, *Principal*
EMP: 1
SALES (est): 68.4K **Privately Held**
WEB: www.buymycruisebook.com
SIC: 2741 Miscellaneous publishing

(G-5839)
**CANON ENVIRONMENTAL TECH
INC**
6000 Industrial Dr (23061-3767)
PHONE.................................804 695-7000
Yoroku Adachi, *Ch of Bd*
Toru Nishizawa, *President*
Roger Simpson, *General Mgr*
John Briggs, *Vice Pres*
Pamela Troutman, *Research*
▲ EMP: 300 EST: 1997
SALES (est): 32.3MM **Privately Held**
WEB: www.cvi.canon.com
SIC: 3861 Toners, prepared photographic
(not made in chemical plants)
HQ: Canon Virginia Inc
12000 Canon Blvd
Newport News VA 23606
757 881-6000

(G-5840)
CARLTON LOGGING LLC
5106 Chestnut Fork Rd (23061-3956)
PHONE.................................804 693-5193
David Carlton, *Principal*
EMP: 2
SALES (est): 81.7K **Privately Held**
SIC: 2411 Logging

(G-5841)
CHRISTOPHER AIKEN
Also Called: Images In Art Signs & Graphic
8209 Spring Hill Frm Rd W (23061-4184)
PHONE.................................804 693-6003
Christopher Aiken,
EMP: 2 EST: 1990
SALES (est): 90K **Privately Held**
SIC: 3993 Signs & advertising specialties

(G-5842)
CSL ENTERPRISES
7348 Main St (23061-5130)
PHONE.................................804 695-0400
Steve Lanning, *Principal*
EMP: 4
SALES (est): 333.4K **Privately Held**
SIC: 2731 Books: publishing only

(G-5843)
CUSTOM RESTORATIONS INC
Also Called: C R I
7264 Belroi Rd (23061-4324)
PHONE.................................804 693-6526
Pete Peterson, *President*
Avis K Peterson, *Treasurer*

EMP: 2
SQ FT: 1,200
SALES (est): 134.8K **Privately Held**
SIC: 3471 3479 Cleaning, polishing & finishing; finishing, metals or formed products; polishing, metals or formed products; painting, coating & hot dipping; coating of metals & formed products

(G-5844)
D & K EMBROIDERY
2212 Hickory Fork Rd (23061-4024)
PHONE..............................804 694-4747
Debbie Riddett, *Owner*
EMP: 1
SALES (est): 65.4K **Privately Held**
SIC: 2395 Embroidery & art needlework

(G-5845)
DEHARDIT PRESS
Also Called: Glo Quips
7339 Lewis Ave (23061-5184)
P.O. Box 675 (23061-0675)
PHONE..............................804 693-2795
William M Dehardit, *Partner*
Elizabeth Dehardit, *Partner*
EMP: 4 **EST:** 1959
SALES (est): 150K **Privately Held**
SIC: 2711 2752 Newspapers: publishing only, not printed on site; commercial printing, offset

(G-5846)
DS & RC ENTERPRISES LLC
Also Called: Colonial Awards
7576 South Shore Dr (23061-2580)
P.O. Box 1453 (23061-1453)
PHONE..............................804 824-5478
Ryan Cookson, *COO*
EMP: 2 **EST:** 2015
SALES (est): 94.2K **Privately Held**
WEB: www.colonialawards.com
SIC: 3499 7389 Novelties & giftware, including trophies;

(G-5847)
FOOD ALLERGY LIFESTYLE LLC
3608 Morris Farm Ln (23061-3386)
PHONE..............................757 509-3608
Gail Lavigne, *Principal*
EMP: 3 **EST:** 2010
SALES (est): 136.1K **Privately Held**
SIC: 2836 Allergens, allergenic extracts

(G-5848)
FRANCE NATURALS INC
7546 John Clayton Mem Hwy
(23061-5165)
PHONE..............................804 694-4777
Jean Jacques Jaouen, *Vice Pres*
Deborah Jaouen, *Officer*
▲ **EMP:** 3
SALES (est): 484.5K **Privately Held**
WEB: www.brittanysalt.com
SIC: 2844 Face creams or lotions

(G-5849)
GO 2 ROW INC
6494 Jenkins Ln (23061-2895)
PHONE..............................804 694-4868
Elizabeth Witt, *President*
EMP: 1 **EST:** 2008
SALES (est): 94.2K **Privately Held**
SIC: 2389 Men's miscellaneous accessories

(G-5850)
HBI CUSTOM FABRICATION LLC
4613 Pampa Rd (23061-2713)
PHONE..............................305 916-0161
Caryn Hogg,
EMP: 2
SALES (est): 86.6K **Privately Held**
SIC: 3441 Fabricated structural metal

(G-5851)
JEFFS TOOLS INC
6317 Ark Rd (23061-3357)
PHONE..............................804 694-6337
Jeffery Hamilton, *President*
EMP: 2
SALES (est): 219.3K **Privately Held**
SIC: 3312 Tool & die steel

(G-5852)
LASER ALIGNMENT SYSTEMS LLC
6718 Main St (23061-5143)
P.O. Box 2029 (23061-1903)
PHONE..............................410 507-6820
James Hall, *President*
Clyde Groover, *CFO*
EMP: 4
SALES (est): 345.7K **Privately Held**
SIC: 3821 Laser beam alignment devices

(G-5853)
LEATHEROOT LLC
6988 Indian Springs Ln (23061-6204)
PHONE..............................804 695-1604
Karin Clopper,
EMP: 1
SALES (est): 75K **Privately Held**
SIC: 3199 7389 Leather goods;

(G-5854)
MIKES MOBILE CANVAS
4719 Pampa Rd (23061-2712)
PHONE..............................804 815-2733
EMP: 1
SALES (est): 46.5K **Privately Held**
SIC: 2211 Canvas

(G-5855)
MODERN ENGRAVINGS LLC
8124 Founders Mill Way (23061-5280)
PHONE..............................757 876-3001
Christopher White,
EMP: 1
SALES (est): 83K **Privately Held**
SIC: 3993 Signs, not made in custom sign painting shops

(G-5856)
NATURAL BALANCE CONCEPTS LLC
7555 Springfield Trace Ln (23061-4189)
P.O. Box 151, Ark (23003-0151)
PHONE..............................804 693-5382
EMP: 1
SALES (est): 10K **Privately Held**
SIC: 2844 Mfg Toilet Preparations

(G-5857)
OAKTREE WOODWORKS
5392 Sleepy Hollow Ln (23061-3679)
PHONE..............................804 815-4669
Travis Jenkins, *Owner*
EMP: 1
SALES (est): 104.3K **Privately Held**
SIC: 3553 Woodworking machinery

(G-5858)
PRECISION FABRICATION LLC
7546 John Clayton Mem Hwy
(23061-5165)
PHONE..............................804 210-1613
Lambros Tzerefos,
▲ **EMP:** 5
SALES (est): 758.8K **Privately Held**
WEB: www.prefab-us.com
SIC: 3625 Numerical controls

(G-5859)
RIVER HOUSE CREATIONS LLC
2551 Red Bank Rd (23061-3163)
PHONE..............................757 509-2137
Annette Rowe,
EMP: 1
SALES (est): 50.9K **Privately Held**
SIC: 3231 5231 7389 Stained glass: made from purchased glass; glass, leaded or stained; business services

(G-5860)
RTH INNOVATIONS LLC
5276 Hickory Fork Rd (23061-3702)
PHONE..............................804 384-6767
Theodore Harder,
EMP: 2 **EST:** 2016
SALES (est): 102.8K **Privately Held**
WEB:
www.thebasicwindlasstourniquet.com
SIC: 3648 Decorative area lighting fixtures

(G-5861)
S & J INDUSTRIES LLC
5013 Chestnut Fork Rd (23061-3951)
PHONE..............................757 810-8399

Lloyd S Tucker, *Manager*
EMP: 2
SALES (est): 96.9K **Privately Held**
SIC: 3999 Manufacturing industries

(G-5862)
TIDEWATER NEWSPAPERS INC (PA)
Also Called: Gazette Journal
6625 Main St (23061-5194)
P.O. Box 2060 (23061-2060)
PHONE..............................804 693-3101
Elsa C Verbyla, *President*
Lisa Green, *Editor*
Giles B Cooke, *Vice Pres*
Giles Cooke, *Vice Pres*
Elsa Verbyla, *Vice Pres*
EMP: 43 **EST:** 1904
SQ FT: 16,360
SALES: 1.6MM **Privately Held**
WEB: www.gazettejournal.net
SIC: 2711 Commercial printing & newspaper publishing combined; newspapers, publishing & printing

(G-5863)
TRACY BARRETT
7791 Woodview Ln (23061-4115)
PHONE..............................757 342-3204
Tracy Barrett, *Principal*
EMP: 2
SALES (est): 87K **Privately Held**
SIC: 2741 Miscellaneous publishing

(G-5864)
VILLAGE BLACKSMITH LLC
6641 Gloucester St (23061-5104)
PHONE..............................804 824-2631
George Cramer, *Principal*
EMP: 1
SALES (est): 83.3K **Privately Held**
WEB: www.gloucesterblacksmith.com
SIC: 3199 Aprons: welders', blacksmiths', etc.: leather

(G-5865)
VIRGINIA WAVE INC
5439 White Hall Rd (23061-4623)
PHONE..............................804 693-4278
William E Mullis, *President*
EMP: 8
SALES (est): 670K **Privately Held**
SIC: 3531 Marine related equipment

(G-5866)
VULCAN MATERIALS COMPANY
5266 George Wash Mem Hwy
(23061-3760)
PHONE..............................804 693-3606
Thomas Hill, *Branch Mgr*
EMP: 36 **Publicly Held**
WEB: www.vulcanmaterials.com
SIC: 3273 5032 Ready-mixed concrete; masons' materials
PA: Vulcan Materials Company
   1200 Urban Center Dr
   Vestavia AL 35242

(G-5867)
VULCAN MATERIALS COMPANY
5266 George Washington Me (23061)
P.O. Box 520 (23061-0520)
PHONE..............................804 693-3606
Scott Finney, *Vice Pres*
Tyler B Johnson, *Vice Pres*
EMP: 2 **Publicly Held**
WEB: www.vulcanmaterials.com
SIC: 3273 Ready-mixed concrete
PA: Vulcan Materials Company
   1200 Urban Center Dr
   Vestavia AL 35242

(G-5868)
WILLIAM B CLARK
8456 Roaring Springs Rd (23061-4285)
PHONE..............................804 695-9950
EMP: 2
SALES: 18K **Privately Held**
SIC: 3812 Mfg Search/Navigation Equipment

(G-5869)
WILLIAMSBURG DISTILLERY INC
4683 Clay Bank Rd (23061-3513)
PHONE..............................757 676-7950
William Dodson, *Principal*
EMP: 2 **EST:** 2013
SQ FT: 1,800
SALES (est): 116K **Privately Held**
SIC: 2085 Distilled & blended liquors

(G-5870)
YORK RIVER GLASSWORKS LLC
7166 Purton Ln (23061-3226)
PHONE..............................804 815-0492
David Stifel,
EMP: 1 **EST:** 2017
SALES (est): 39.6K **Privately Held**
SIC: 3999 Manufacturing industries

Gloucester Point
Gloucester County

(G-5871)
AT THE POINT EMBROIDERY LLC
1758 Hoven Rd (23062-2120)
PHONE..............................804 684-9544
EMP: 1
SALES (est): 43K **Privately Held**
SIC: 2395 Pleating/Stitching Services

(G-5872)
BIG FRED PROMOTIONS INC
7554 Bellehaven Dr (23062-2411)
PHONE..............................804 832-5510
Fred Sparrow, *President*
EMP: 4
SALES (est): 323.6K **Privately Held**
SIC: 3993 Signs & advertising specialties

(G-5873)
MARS MACHINE WORKS INC
Hwy 17s (23062)
P.O. Box 190 (23062-0190)
PHONE..............................804 642-4760
Robert H Grow, *President*
David A Grow, *Corp Secy*
Linda Grow, *Vice Pres*
EMP: 3 **EST:** 1967
SQ FT: 4,800
SALES (est): 189.5K **Privately Held**
SIC: 3599 6513 Machine & other job shop work; apartment building operators

(G-5874)
MARTINS CUSTOM DESIGNS INC (PA)
Also Called: Scotty Signs
1707 Shane Rd (23062-2123)
PHONE..............................804 642-0235
Stacie L Martin, *President*
Paul H Martin, *Vice Pres*
EMP: 9
SALES (est): 1.3MM **Privately Held**
WEB: www.martinsdesign.com
SIC: 3993 Electric signs

(G-5875)
RACE TRAC PETROLEUM
1570 George Wash Mem Hwy
(23062-2526)
PHONE..............................804 694-9079
EMP: 2
SALES (est): 88.3K **Privately Held**
SIC: 3644 Raceways

(G-5876)
SEVERN WHARF CUSTOM RODS
8109 Yacht Haven Rd (23062-2124)
PHONE..............................804 642-0404
Neil Drumheller, *Principal*
EMP: 2
SALES (est): 96.5K **Privately Held**
SIC: 2048 Fish food

Goldvein
Fauquier County

(G-5877)
DRAGONSREALM VINEYARD LLC
3061 Heavenly Ln (22720-2215)
PHONE....................540 905-9679
Michael Schlosser, *Administration*
EMP: 2
SALES (est): 92.9K **Privately Held**
SIC: 2084 Wines

(G-5878)
FIREDOG FABRICATORS
13732 Blackwells Mill Rd (22720-1807)
PHONE....................540 809-7389
Richard Vestal, *Principal*
EMP: 2
SALES (est): 190K **Privately Held**
SIC: 3441 Fabricated structural metal

(G-5879)
TD & D UNLIMITED LLC
14273 Goldvein Rd (22720-1840)
PHONE....................703 946-9338
Brian Davis, *Principal*
EMP: 3
SALES (est): 460.3K **Privately Held**
WEB: www.tddunlimited.com
SIC: 2851 Removers & cleaners

Goochland
Goochland County

(G-5880)
BYRD CELLARS LLC
2442 Davis Mill Rd (23063-3300)
PHONE....................804 652-5663
Bruce Murray, *Mng Member*
EMP: 2
SALES (est): 164.3K **Privately Held**
WEB: www.byrdcellars.com
SIC: 2084 Wines

(G-5881)
CHOICE TACK
1680 Ragland Rd (23063-3426)
PHONE....................804 314-0787
Roberta Young, *Owner*
EMP: 1
SALES (est): 52.8K **Privately Held**
WEB: www.choicetack.com
SIC: 2099 Box lunches, for sale off premises

(G-5882)
ELK ISLAND WINERY
5759 River Rd W (23063-3312)
PHONE....................540 967-0944
Paul Klinefelter, *Principal*
EMP: 4 EST: 2013
SALES (est): 136.6K **Privately Held**
WEB: www.elkislandwinery.com
SIC: 2084 Wines

(G-5883)
GOLD SPOT
1940 Sandy Hook Rd # 101 (23063-3117)
PHONE....................804 708-0275
EMP: 1
SALES (est): 113.8K **Privately Held**
SIC: 3339 Precious metals

(G-5884)
GULP JUICERY LLC
2753 Dogtown Rd (23063-2424)
PHONE....................804 933-9483
Rachel Holmes,
EMP: 1
SQ FT: 15,000
SALES (est): 77K **Privately Held**
SIC: 3556 Juice extractors, fruit & vegetable: commercial type

(G-5885)
HERBSPICE LLC
2753 Dogtown Rd (23063-2424)
PHONE....................240 602-6525
EMP: 2
SALES (est): 62.3K **Privately Held**
SIC: 2099 Food preparations

(G-5886)
THEORY3 INC
Also Called: Tireflys
1940 Sandy Hook Rd Ste D (23063-3116)
PHONE....................804 335-1001
Wing Eng, *CEO*
Jason Barber, *President*
Russell Rothan, *Admin Sec*
EMP: 3
SQ FT: 1,300 **Privately Held**
SIC: 3647 Motor vehicle lighting equipment

(G-5887)
THREE HENS
1899 Haskin Rd (23063-3510)
PHONE....................804 787-3400
EMP: 2
SALES (est): 90K **Privately Held**
SIC: 3999 Candles

Goode
Bedford County

(G-5888)
3CATS PROMO
320 Hunting Ln (24556-1027)
PHONE....................540 586-7014
Marriane Bpyer, *President*
Marianne Boyer, *Owner*
Ronald Boyer, *Vice Pres*
EMP: 2
SALES (est): 72K **Privately Held**
WEB: www.3catspromo.com
SIC: 2759 7389 Screen printing; advertising, promotional & trade show services

(G-5889)
DOUBLE B TRAILERS
9145 Forest Rd (24556-3083)
PHONE....................540 586-0651
Jimmy Busch, *Owner*
EMP: 1
SQ FT: 3,000
SALES (est): 79.8K **Privately Held**
SIC: 7692 3714 Welding repair; trailer hitches, motor vehicle

(G-5890)
HUDGINS PLATING INC C R
6756 E Lynchburg Slem Tpk (24556-3021)
PHONE....................434 847-6647
Angela Renee Owen, *CEO*
James E Hudgins, *Ch of Bd*
Bobby R Robbins, *COO*
EMP: 65 EST: 1956
SALES (est): 6.8MM **Privately Held**
WEB: www.crhudgins.com
SIC: 3471 3479 Plating of metals or formed products; painting, coating & hot dipping

(G-5891)
JAN TANA INC
1208 Hideaway Rd (24556-1100)
PHONE....................540 586-8266
Jan Tana, *Principal*
EMP: 2
SALES (est): 181.2K **Privately Held**
WEB: www.jantana.com
SIC: 2844 Toilet preparations

(G-5892)
LEOGRAND VINYARDS
1343 Wingfield Dr (24556-2222)
PHONE....................540 586-4066
Norman Leogrand, *Principal*
EMP: 2
SALES (est): 100.6K **Privately Held**
SIC: 2084 Wines

(G-5893)
RICHARD A DAILY DR
Also Called: United Methodist Church
4171 Roaring Run Rd (24556-2796)
PHONE....................540 586-4030
Richard Daily, *Owner*
EMP: 1
SALES (est): 56K **Privately Held**
SIC: 2711 Newspapers, publishing & printing

Goodview
Bedford County

(G-5894)
BURNING BRITE CANDLE
502 Pleasure Point Dr (24095-2110)
PHONE....................540 904-6544
EMP: 1 EST: 2018
SALES (est): 39.6K **Privately Held**
SIC: 3999 Candles

(G-5895)
EPIC IMAGES
1750 Morris Rd (24095-2511)
PHONE....................540 537-2572
Ernie Lafebvre, *Owner*
EMP: 2
SALES (est): 112.3K **Privately Held**
SIC: 2221 Shirting fabrics, manmade fiber & silk

(G-5896)
LAVENMOON
1148 Red Horse Dr (24095-3022)
PHONE....................540 297-3274
EMP: 1
SALES (est): 58.8K **Privately Held**
SIC: 3999 Mfg Misc Products

(G-5897)
WINTEK CORPORATION
1201 Longview Estates Dr (24095-3266)
PHONE....................973 252-8200
EMP: 2
SALES (est): 129.1K **Privately Held**
SIC: 3559 Special industry machinery

Gordonsville
Orange County

(G-5898)
ATKINS CLEARING & TRUCKING
1856 Hanback Rd (22942-6014)
PHONE....................540 832-3128
Thomas H Atkins, *President*
Louise Atkins, *Corp Secy*
EMP: 6
SALES (est): 500K **Privately Held**
SIC: 2411 Logging camps & contractors

(G-5899)
AUTOMATED PROD MACHINING INC
300 Taylor St (22942-9213)
P.O. Box 1687 (22942-1687)
PHONE....................540 832-0835
David William Shaw, *President*
David Shaw, *General Mgr*
Joshua Shaw, *Treasurer*
Thomas Neff, *Office Mgr*
EMP: 11
SQ FT: 26,000
SALES (est): 2MM **Privately Held**
WEB: www.apmmfg.com
SIC: 3599 Machine shop, jobbing & repair

(G-5900)
BEDFORD FREEMAN & WORT
16365 James Madison Hwy (22942-8501)
PHONE....................651 330-8526
EMP: 1
SALES (est): 35.3K **Privately Held**
WEB: www.bfwpub.com
SIC: 2731 Book publishing

(G-5901)
BIOSTAR
1 Cleveland St Ste 800 (22942-7577)
PHONE....................800 686-9544
Rick Moore, *Principal*
EMP: 3
SALES (est): 210.9K **Privately Held**
WEB: www.biostarus.com
SIC: 2048 Prepared feeds

(G-5902)
BRANMAR LOGGING INC
8164 S Spotswood Trl (22942-6038)
PHONE....................540 832-5535
Andreas Riehn, *President*
Linda Marlene Riehn, *Corp Secy*
EMP: 3
SALES (est): 333.9K **Privately Held**
WEB: www.branmarforestproducts.com
SIC: 2411 5099 Wooden logs; logs, hewn ties, posts & poles

(G-5903)
CAMERON MOUNTAIN ALPACAS
18453 Cameron Rd (22942-8005)
PHONE....................540 832-3025
Roy Sjacobson, *Principal*
EMP: 2
SALES (est): 133.8K **Privately Held**
WEB: www.cameronmountain.com
SIC: 2231 Alpacas, mohair: woven

(G-5904)
CANOVA WOODWORKING LLC
758 Lightwood Rd (22942-7217)
PHONE....................434 422-0807
Wayne Canova, *Principal*
EMP: 2
SALES (est): 115.6K **Privately Held**
SIC: 2431 Millwork

(G-5905)
DARBYS BUILD AND DESIGN LLC
18147 Springer Ln (22942-6055)
PHONE....................434 989-5493
Megan Lookabaugh, *Principal*
EMP: 2
SALES (est): 85.2K **Privately Held**
SIC: 2431 Millwork

(G-5906)
DARBYS CUSTOM WOODWORKS
18147 Springer Ln (22942-6055)
PHONE....................434 989-5493
Michael Thomas Darby, *Principal*
EMP: 1
SALES (est): 54.1K **Privately Held**
SIC: 2431 Millwork

(G-5907)
HOLTZBRINCK PUBLISHERS LLC
16365 James Madison Hwy (22942-8501)
PHONE....................540 672-7600
Maureen Kevlahan, *Credit Staff*
John Sargent,
EMP: 1
SALES (corp-wide): 1.7B **Privately Held**
WEB: www.hayaleahmolnar.com
SIC: 2731 Book publishing
HQ: Holtzbrinck Publishers, Llc
175 5th Ave
New York NY 10010
646 307-5151

(G-5908)
HORTON CELLARS WINERY INC
Also Called: Horton Vineyards
6399 Spotswood Trl (22942-7735)
PHONE....................540 832-7440
Dennis Horton, *President*
EMP: 15
SALES (est): 450K **Privately Held**
WEB: www.hortonwine.com
SIC: 2084 Wines

(G-5909)
KLOCKNER PENTAPLAST AMER INC
Klockner Barrier Films
3585 Kloeckner Rd (22942-6148)
P.O. Box 500 (22942-0500)
PHONE....................540 832-3600
Jim Davis, *Site Mgr*
EMP: 500
SALES (corp-wide): 4.7MM **Privately Held**
WEB: www.kpfilms.com
SIC: 3081 Plastic film & sheet
HQ: Klockner Pentaplast Of America, Inc.
3585 Kloeckner Rd
Gordonsville VA 22942
540 832-1400

(G-5910)
KLOCKNER PENTAPLAST AMER INC (DH)
3585 Kloeckner Rd (22942-6148)
PHONE....................540 832-1400

Wayne Hewett, *Ch of Bd*
Michael P Ryan, *President*
Jurgen Bundschuh, *Business Mgr*
Justin Glass, *Business Mgr*
Tom Mucenski, *Business Mgr*
◆ **EMP:** 1318
SQ FT: 236,000
SALES (est): 1.3B
SALES (corp-wide): 4.7MM **Privately Held**
WEB: www.kpfilms.com
SIC: 3081 4213 Plastic film & sheet; trucking, except local

(G-5911)
KLOCKNER PENTAPLAST AMER INC
3758 Kloeckner Rd (22942-6152)
PHONE...................................540 832-7615
Vance Backe, *Maint Spvr*
Kim McClung, *Cust Mgr*
EMP: 3
SALES (corp-wide): 4.7MM **Privately Held**
WEB: www.kpfilms.com
SIC: 3081 4213 Plastic film & sheet; trucking, except local
HQ: Klockner Pentaplast Of America, Inc.
3585 Kloeckner Rd
Gordonsville VA 22942
540 832-1400

(G-5912)
LIBERTY PARK
1 Cleveland St Ste 13 (22942-7577)
PHONE...................................540 832-7680
Liberty Park, *Principal*
EMP: 2
SALES (est): 214.4K **Privately Held**
SIC: 3599 Amusement park equipment

(G-5913)
MACMILLAN HOLDINGS LLC
Also Called: MPS
16365 James Madison Hwy (22942-8501)
PHONE...................................888 330-8477
EMP: 28
SALES (corp-wide): 1.7B **Privately Held**
WEB: www.macmillanspeakers.com
SIC: 2741 Miscellaneous publishing
HQ: Macmillan Holdings, Llc
120 Broadway Fl 22
New York NY 10271

(G-5914)
MACOMA CAPITAL
204 N Main St (22942-9152)
PHONE...................................434 249-4580
Bradford Manning, *President*
Mark Betz, *Director*
EMP: 3
SALES (est): 158.8K **Privately Held**
WEB: www.perrigo.com
SIC: 2834 Pharmaceutical preparations

(G-5915)
MATT AND MOLLY TRADES LLC
101 Mt View Farm Rd (22942-6057)
PHONE...................................703 585-1858
Molly Wilshere,
EMP: 2
SALES (est): 62.5K **Privately Held**
SIC: 3999 Manufacturing industries

(G-5916)
NORFIELDS FARM INC
1982 James Madison Hwy (22942-6218)
PHONE...................................540 832-2952
Teresa Norton, *President*
EMP: 3
SALES (est): 205.9K **Privately Held**
SIC: 3523 Farm machinery & equipment

(G-5917)
VALLEY TIMBER SALES INC
Rr 15 (22942)
P.O. Box 969, Troy (22974-0969)
PHONE...................................540 832-3646
Michele Pascarella, *President*
Victor Pascarella, *President*
Michelle Pascarella-Gunn, *Vice Pres*
▲ **EMP:** 19 **EST:** 1980
SQ FT: 2,500
SALES (est): 3.4MM **Privately Held**
WEB: www.valleytimbersales.com
SIC: 2491 Wood preserving

(G-5918)
VELVET PILE CARPETS LLC
18558 Buzzard Hollow Rd (22942-7602)
PHONE...................................540 920-9473
Phillp Silva,
EMP: 2
SALES (est): 80.7K **Privately Held**
SIC: 2273 7389 Axminster carpets; wilton carpets; finishers of tufted carpets & rugs;

(G-5919)
WORTHINGTON MILLWORK LLC
Also Called: Worthngton Architectural Mllwk
1 Cleveland St Ste 920 (22942-7577)
PHONE...................................540 832-6391
Alycia Worthington, *Principal*
Jason Worthington, *Principal*
EMP: 5
SQ FT: 7,000
SALES (est): 252.5K **Privately Held**
WEB: www.wamillwork.com
SIC: 2434 5712 3993 2431 Wood kitchen cabinets; customized furniture & cabinets; letters for signs, metal; moldings & baseboards, ornamental & trim; wood office desks & tables

Gore
Frederick County

(G-5920)
BRAKE CONNECTIONS
135 Fletcher Rd (22637-2200)
P.O. Box 381 (22637-0381)
PHONE...................................540 247-9000
Jennifer Place, *Principal*
EMP: 2
SALES (est): 10K **Privately Held**
SIC: 3714 Motor vehicle parts & accessories

(G-5921)
COVIA HOLDINGS CORPORATION
334 Sand Mine Rd (22637)
P.O. Box 400 (22637-0400)
PHONE...................................540 858-3444
Steve Westmoreland, *Manager*
EMP: 31
SALES (corp-wide): 125.5MM **Privately Held**
WEB: www.coviacorp.com
SIC: 1446 Silica mining
HQ: Covia Holdings Corporation
3 Summit Park Dr Ste 700
Independence OH 44131
440 214-3284

(G-5922)
MCCORMICK & COMPANY INC
563 Fletcher Rd (22637-2204)
PHONE...................................540 858-2878
EMP: 3
SALES (corp-wide): 4.3B **Publicly Held**
SIC: 2099 Mfg Food Preparations
PA: Mccormick & Company Incorporated
18 Loveton Cir
Sparks MD 21031
410 771-7301

(G-5923)
TAMARA SMITH
Also Called: Household 6
1293 Hollow Rd (22637-2218)
PHONE...................................910 495-4404
Tamara Smith, *Owner*
EMP: 1
SALES (est): 57.5K **Privately Held**
SIC: 2841 2399 Soap & other detergents; hand woven & crocheted products

Goshen
Rockbridge County

(G-5924)
EDMUND DAVIDSON
3345 Virginia Ave (24439-2029)
PHONE...................................540 997-5651
Edmund Davidson, *Owner*
EMP: 1

SALES (est): 58.1K **Privately Held**
WEB: www.edmunddavidson.com
SIC: 3421 5941 Cutlery; sporting goods & bicycle shops

(G-5925)
ELYSSA E STRONG
Also Called: Black Oak Processing & Smoking
802 Railroad Ave (24439-2719)
PHONE...................................540 280-3982
Elyssa Strong, *Owner*
EMP: 3
SALES (est): 114.2K **Privately Held**
SIC: 2013 7389 Sausages & other prepared meats;

(G-5926)
NORTH FORK INC
Also Called: North Fork Lumber & Log Homes
250 N Fork Ln (24439)
P.O. Box 146 (24439-0146)
PHONE...................................540 997-5602
William L Harris III, *President*
Jane P Harris, *Corp Secy*
EMP: 35
SQ FT: 160,000
SALES (est): 4.4MM **Privately Held**
WEB: www.northforklumber.com
SIC: 2421 2411 Lumber: rough, sawed or planed; logging

(G-5927)
STELLA-JONES CORPORATION
Appalachian Div
9223 Maury River Rd (24439-2439)
P.O. Box 86 (24439-0086)
PHONE...................................540 997-9251
Doug Gentry, *Prdtn Mgr*
Eduardo Silva, *Supervisor*
EMP: 100
SALES (corp-wide): 1.6B **Privately Held**
WEB: www.babstcalland.com
SIC: 2491 3532 2452 2421 Wood products, creosoted; mining machinery; prefabricated wood buildings; sawmills & planing mills, general; logging
HQ: Stella-Jones Corporation
1000 Cliffmine Rd Ste 500
Pittsburgh PA 15275

(G-5928)
THELMA RETHFORD
Also Called: Rollarund Fshons For Hnd-capped
71 Furnace Hill Rd (24439-2419)
PHONE...................................540 997-9121
EMP: 2
SALES: 200K **Privately Held**
SIC: 2389 Mfg Apparel/Accessories

(G-5929)
THOMAS L ALPHIN INC
Also Called: Alphin Logging
260 Big River Rd (24439-2008)
PHONE...................................540 997-0611
Thomas Alphin, *President*
EMP: 2
SALES (est): 159.7K **Privately Held**
SIC: 2411 Logging camps & contractors

(G-5930)
TNT LOGGING LLC
735 Virginia Ave (24439-2004)
PHONE...................................540 997-0611
Thomas Vernon Alphin Jr, *Administration*
EMP: 7 **EST:** 2009
SALES (est): 821K **Privately Held**
SIC: 2411 Logging

Grafton
York County

(G-5931)
AUTOMATED MACHINE & TECH INC
Also Called: Amtech
125 Greene Dr (23692-4811)
PHONE...................................757 898-7844
Billy Benson Jr, *President*
Paul Bodkins, *Vice Pres*
Blair Guerreiro, *Purch Mgr*
Brian Harris, *Executive*
Brian Edmondson,

EMP: 25
SQ FT: 12,500
SALES (est): 5.5MM **Privately Held**
WEB: www.amtechmachine.com
SIC: 3599 7692 3541 Machine shop, jobbing & repair; welding repair; machine tools, metal cutting type

(G-5932)
THREADLINES INC
216 Henry Lee Ln (23692-2841)
PHONE...................................757 898-8355
Paulette Clement, *President*
Peter Clement, *Vice Pres*
EMP: 2
SALES (est): 88.8K **Privately Held**
SIC: 2395 Embroidery & art needlework

(G-5933)
YESTERDAYS TREASURES
103 Rustling Oak Rdg (23692-6161)
PHONE...................................757 877-5153
Sylvia Evenson, *Owner*
EMP: 1
SALES (est): 53.3K **Privately Held**
SIC: 3911 Jewelry, precious metal

Great Falls
Fairfax County

(G-5934)
AEROART INTERNATIONAL INC
Also Called: St Petersburg Collection, The
11797 Hollyview Dr (22066-1333)
PHONE...................................703 406-4376
Thor Johnson, *President*
Nikki Johnson, *Vice Pres*
EMP: 4
SALES (est): 373.6K **Privately Held**
WEB: www.aeroartinc.com
SIC: 3999 Miniatures

(G-5935)
AMAMA LTD (PA)
9505 Arnon Chapel Rd (22066-3914)
PHONE...................................703 759-9030
Meenakshi Bove, *President*
Paul Bove, *Vice Pres*
EMP: 3 **EST:** 1998
SALES (est): 184.5K **Privately Held**
WEB: www.amama.com
SIC: 2099 Seasonings & spices

(G-5936)
AMC INDUSTRIES INC
1108 Marlene Ln (22066-1806)
P.O. Box 1492 (22066-8492)
PHONE...................................410 320-5037
EMP: 1 **EST:** 2017
SALES (est): 58.4K **Privately Held**
SIC: 3999 Manufacturing industries

(G-5937)
ANDROMEDA3 INC
938 Leigh Mill Rd (22066-2301)
P.O. Box 118, Ashburn (20146-0118)
PHONE...................................240 246-5816
David McLaughlin, *President*
Bob Zambreny, *Principal*
EMP: 9 **EST:** 2015
SALES (est): 566.8K **Privately Held**
SIC: 7372 Application computer software

(G-5938)
ARTUSMODE SOFTWARE LLC
11529 Seneca Farm Way (22066-3050)
PHONE...................................703 794-6100
Andrew Norman, *CEO*
EMP: 2
SALES (est): 141.4K **Privately Held**
WEB: www.artusmode.com
SIC: 7372 7389 Business oriented computer software;

(G-5939)
BEADECKED INC (PA)
Also Called: Cotton Kids
10201 Brennanhill Ct (22066-2531)
PHONE...................................703 759-3725
Mrimalini R Anderson, *President*
Walter T Anderson, *Vice Pres*
▲ **EMP:** 1
SALES (est): 129.4K **Privately Held**
SIC: 2369 Girls' & children's outerwear

(G-5940)
BRIAN L LONGEST
10006 Minburn St (22066-2509)
PHONE................................703 759-3847
Brian Longest, *Principal*
EMP: 2
SALES (est): 158.9K **Privately Held**
SIC: 2899 Chemical preparations

(G-5941)
BROOKE STERLING CO
9102 White Chimney Ln (22066-2321)
PHONE................................850 650-8080
Kelly Price, *Principal*
EMP: 2
SALES (est): 116.6K **Privately Held**
WEB: www.sterlingbrooke.com
SIC: 2084 Wines, brandy & brandy spirits

(G-5942)
CAERUS LLC
204 Falcon Ridge Rd (22066-3519)
PHONE................................703 772-7688
Ashi Chaturvedula, *President*
EMP: 1
SALES (est): 40K **Privately Held**
WEB: www.caerustek.com
SIC: 7372 Business oriented computer software

(G-5943)
CAPITAL DESIGNS LLC
442 Seneca Rd (22066-1111)
PHONE................................703 444-2728
Brenda Onhaizer,
EMP: 2
SALES (est): 100K **Privately Held**
SIC: 3993 Signs & advertising specialties

(G-5944)
CARY PHARMACEUTICALS INC
9903 Windy Hollow Rd (22066-3550)
PHONE................................703 759-7460
Douglas B Cary, *President*
Lewellys F Barker MD, *Vice Pres*
Andrew R Menard, *Vice Pres*
Carl C Schwan, *Vice Pres*
EMP: 5
SQ FT: 1,500
SALES (est): 500K **Privately Held**
WEB: www.carypharma.com
SIC: 2834 8731 Druggists' preparations (pharmaceuticals); commercial physical research

(G-5945)
CECILIA M SCHULTZS
Also Called: Mrs Schultz's Marzipan
929 Hickory Run Ln (22066-1904)
P.O. Box 521 (22066-0521)
PHONE................................301 840-1283
EMP: 1
SALES (est): 56.6K **Privately Held**
SIC: 2064 Mfg Candy/Confectionery

(G-5946)
CHAOSWORKS INC
9844 Beach Mill Rd (22066-3709)
PHONE................................703 727-0772
Ali Fouladi, *President*
EMP: 1
SALES (est): 106.1K **Privately Held**
WEB: www.chaosworker.com
SIC: 3812 Search & navigation equipment

(G-5947)
CHARLES R PRESTON
Also Called: Quilt Doctor, The
9801 Georgetown Pike (22066-2662)
PHONE................................703 757-0495
Charles Preston, *Mng Member*
Charles R Preston, *Mng Member*
EMP: 8
SALES (est): 496.7K **Privately Held**
SIC: 2395 Quilting, for the trade

(G-5948)
CHRISTIAN FAMILY GAMES LLC
422 River Bend Rd (22066-4017)
PHONE................................703 863-6403
Eric Sapp, *Partner*
EMP: 2
SALES (est): 90.8K **Privately Held**
SIC: 3944 Electronic games & toys

(G-5949)
COMPUTING WITH KIDS
903 Falls Bridge Ln (22066-1347)
PHONE................................703 444-9005
Jinny Gudmundsen, *Principal*
EMP: 3
SALES (est): 115.2K **Privately Held**
WEB: www.techwithkids.com
SIC: 2721 Magazines: publishing & printing

(G-5950)
CORIOLIS WIND INC
1211 Trotting Horse Ln (22066-2011)
PHONE................................703 969-1257
EMP: 15
SALES (est): 970K **Privately Held**
SIC: 3511 Mfg Turbines/Generator Sets

(G-5951)
COZY CLOTHS
626 Philip Digges Dr (22066-2604)
P.O. Box 675 (22066-0675)
PHONE................................703 759-2420
Loni Parent, *Owner*
▲ EMP: 2 EST: 1998
SALES (est): 12K **Privately Held**
WEB: www.cozygift.com
SIC: 2211 Print cloths, cotton

(G-5952)
DAVID CERAMICS LLC
641 Kentland Dr (22066-1017)
PHONE................................703 430-2692
David T Cowdrill, *Administration*
EMP: 2
SALES (est): 88.7K **Privately Held**
SIC: 3269 Pottery products

(G-5953)
EMERGENCY ALERT SOLUTIONS GROU
Also Called: Emergency Lockdown Experts
10002 Park Royal Dr (22066-1847)
PHONE................................703 346-4787
Eric Morehouse, *President*
Kevin Cherven,
Brian Lyman,
EMP: 3
SALES (est): 146.7K **Privately Held**
WEB: www.emergencyalertgroup.com
SIC: 3669 Emergency alarms

(G-5954)
ERIC CARR WOODWORKS
934 Jaysmith St (22066-2404)
PHONE................................202 253-1010
Eric Carr, *Principal*
EMP: 1
SALES (est): 54.1K **Privately Held**
SIC: 2431 Millwork

(G-5955)
FOG LIGHT SOLUTIONS LLC
912 Jaysmith St (22066-2404)
PHONE................................703 201-0532
Deniz Johnson, *Principal*
EMP: 3
SALES (est): 221.5K **Privately Held**
SIC: 3647 Fog lights

(G-5956)
FRONTIER SYSTEMS LLC
805 Lake Windermere Ct (22066-1532)
PHONE................................314 221-2831
Patrick Arnold, *President*
Sarah Arnold,
EMP: 1
SALES (est): 58.8K
SALES (corp-wide): 340.9K **Privately Held**
SIC: 3695 7389 Computer software tape & disks: blank, rigid & floppy;
PA: Frontier Technical Solutions Llc
805 Lake Windermere Ct
Great Falls VA 22066
314 221-2831

(G-5957)
GOYAL GADGETS LLC
1193 Lees Meadow Ct (22066-1859)
PHONE................................703 757-8294
Ankit Goyal, *Principal*
EMP: 2

SALES (est): 102.1K **Privately Held**
SIC: 3915 Jewelers' materials & lapidary work

(G-5958)
GREAT DOGS GREAT FALLS LLC
9859 Georgetown Pike (22066-2617)
PHONE................................703 759-3601
Linda Waitkus, *Mng Member*
EMP: 3
SALES (est): 233K **Privately Held**
WEB: www.greatdogsofgreatfalls.com
SIC: 3999 0752 Pet supplies; grooming services, pet & animal specialties

(G-5959)
GREAT FALLS CREAMERY
766 Walker Rd (22066-2652)
PHONE................................703 272-7609
EMP: 5
SALES (est): 216.2K **Privately Held**
WEB: www.greatfallsconnection.com
SIC: 2021 Creamery butter

(G-5960)
GREAT FALLS TEA GARDEN LLC
901 Winstead St (22066-2547)
P.O. Box 505 (22066-0505)
PHONE................................703 757-6209
Laurie Bell,
EMP: 2
SALES (est): 103.1K **Privately Held**
WEB: www.greatfallsteagarden.com
SIC: 3999 Education aids, devices & supplies

(G-5961)
GTS DEFENSE MGT SVCS LLC
1129 Edward Dr Ste 100 (22066-2110)
PHONE................................832 326-7227
Marianne Sipple, *Principal*
Gregory Sipple,
EMP: 1
SALES (est): 950K **Privately Held**
SIC: 3663 Radio & TV communications equipment

(G-5962)
HR SOFTWARE LLC
752 Kentland Dr (22066-1012)
PHONE................................703 665-5134
Robert Might, *Principal*
EMP: 2 EST: 2013
SALES (est): 116.4K **Privately Held**
SIC: 7372 Prepackaged software

(G-5963)
KNOWLERA MEDIA LLC
774 Walker Rd Ste H (22066-2648)
PHONE................................703 757-5444
EMP: 1 EST: 2013
SALES (est): 93.2K **Privately Held**
SIC: 2741 Internet Publishing And Broadcasting

(G-5964)
LANZARA INDUSTRIES LLC
544 Springvale Rd (22066-3427)
PHONE................................703 759-6959
Helen Clanzara, *Principal*
EMP: 2
SALES (est): 141.8K **Privately Held**
SIC: 3999 Manufacturing industries

(G-5965)
LITTLE BIRDY BAGS LLC
10106 Nedra Dr (22066-2835)
PHONE................................703 757-6565
Marcus Roberts, *Principal*
EMP: 2
SALES (est): 126.8K **Privately Held**
WEB: www.littlebirdybags.com
SIC: 2323 Men's & boys' neckwear

(G-5966)
MICROBANX SYSTEMS LLC
10135 Colvin Run Rd # 101 (22066-1872)
PHONE................................703 757-1760
William C Moss,
EMP: 5
SQ FT: 2,000

SALES (est): 490K **Privately Held**
WEB: www.cobiscorp.com
SIC: 7372 Business oriented computer software

(G-5967)
MILL RUN SPECIALTIES
9830 Mill Run Dr (22066-1810)
PHONE................................703 759-3480
Maurice M Gettier Jr, *Owner*
EMP: 1
SALES (est): 93K **Privately Held**
SIC: 3599 Machine shop, jobbing & repair

(G-5968)
NEVINS & MOSS LLC
9708 Locust Hill Dr (22066-2030)
PHONE................................929 266-3640
Nevin Fahmy,
Maggdi Mossoba,
EMP: 2
SALES (est): 90K **Privately Held**
WEB: www.foglessbydesign.com
SIC: 2841 Soap & other detergents

(G-5969)
NUASIS CORP
1104 Great Passage Blvd (22066-1633)
PHONE................................571 230-8126
Craig Holms, *Principal*
EMP: 2
SALES (est): 56.5K **Privately Held**
SIC: 7372 Prepackaged software

(G-5970)
OPTIME SOFTWARE LLC
205 Carrwood Rd (22066-3720)
PHONE................................415 894-0314
Jon Schlegel, *Administration*
EMP: 2
SALES (est): 137.9K **Privately Held**
SIC: 7372 Prepackaged software

(G-5971)
PAULS SHOE REPAIR & LEA ACC
9903 Georgetown Pike (22066-2826)
P.O. Box 252 (22066-0252)
PHONE................................703 759-3735
EMP: 2 EST: 2016
SALES (est): 65.4K **Privately Held**
WEB: www.paulsleather.com
SIC: 3111 7251 Accessory products, leather; shoe repair shop

(G-5972)
PDH MOBILE INC
337 Walker Rd (22066-3503)
PHONE................................703 475-8223
Yuanlin Huang, *President*
EMP: 2
SALES (est): 50K **Privately Held**
SIC: 7372 Educational computer software

(G-5973)
PLAYCALL INC
395 Walker Rd (22066-3503)
PHONE................................571 385-6203
Mark Dumas, *CEO*
EMP: 1
SALES (est): 82.7K **Privately Held**
WEB: www.playcall.com
SIC: 7372 Home entertainment computer software

(G-5974)
POSHTIQUE
565 Nalls Dairy Ct (22066-1145)
PHONE................................703 404-2825
Laura Santini, *Owner*
EMP: 1
SALES (est): 89.7K **Privately Held**
SIC: 2392 Cushions & pillows

(G-5975)
POTOMAC LASER RECHARGE
11932 Holly Branch Ct (22066-1216)
PHONE................................703 430-0166
Richard A Cogan, *Owner*
EMP: 1
SALES (est): 25K **Privately Held**
SIC: 3955 Print cartridges for laser & other computer printers

(G-5976)
PRODUCTION MANUFACTURING INC
1114 Trotting Horse Ln (22066-2014)
PHONE..............................513 892-2331
Dale Henderson, *Financial Exec*
EMP: 2
SALES (est): 94.5K **Privately Held**
SIC: 3444 Sheet metalwork

(G-5977)
RED APPLE PUBLICATIONS
10908 Thimbleberry Ln (22066-3102)
PHONE..............................703 430-9272
Susan Blakely, *Principal*
EMP: 2
SALES (est): 137.5K **Privately Held**
SIC: 2741 Miscellaneous publishing

(G-5978)
ROYAL FERN PUBLISHING LLC
9603 Georgetown Pike (22066-2620)
PHONE..............................703 759-0264
Shaila Muralidhar, *Principal*
EMP: 2
SALES (est): 117.1K **Privately Held**
SIC: 2741 Miscellaneous publishing

(G-5979)
SERVHAWK LLC
177 River Park Dr (22066-3543)
PHONE..............................703 447-1456
Franz Jaggar, *Principal*
EMP: 2
SALES (est): 115.6K **Privately Held**
WEB: www.servhawk.com
SIC: 7372 Prepackaged software

(G-5980)
SOFTLOGISTICS LLC
337 Walker Rd (22066-3503)
PHONE..............................703 865-7965
Michael Y Huang,
EMP: 5
SQ FT: 950
SALES (est): 150K **Privately Held**
WEB: www.softlogistics.com
SIC: 3825 4783 Waveform measuring and/or analyzing equipment; packing goods for shipping

(G-5981)
SOFTWARE FLOW CORPORATION
727 Forest Park Rd (22066-2907)
PHONE..............................301 717-0331
Sarah Photowat, *CEO*
EMP: 1
SALES (est): 30K **Privately Held**
WEB: www.softwareflow.com
SIC: 7372 7371 Application computer software; computer software development

(G-5982)
TRAVELSERVER SOFTWARE INC (PA)
980 Old Holly Dr (22066-1325)
PHONE..............................703 406-7664
Joseph A Koshuta, *President*
EMP: 2
SALES (est): 231.1K **Privately Held**
WEB: www.travelserversoftware.com
SIC: 7372 Prepackaged software

(G-5983)
WASHINGTON INTERNATIONAL
967 Evonshire Ln (22066-1700)
P.O. Box 227 (22066-0227)
PHONE..............................703 757-5965
Patricia Keegan, *President*
David Layman, *Vice Pres*
Lloyd Holz, *Manager*
Dominiqu Wellington, *Administration*
EMP: 4
SALES (est): 216.4K **Privately Held**
WEB: www.washingtoninternational.com
SIC: 2741 Miscellaneous publishing

(G-5984)
WHILE SOFTWARE LLC
11697 Hollyview Dr (22066-1329)
PHONE..............................202 290-6705
EMP: 1

SALES (est): 73.4K **Privately Held**
SIC: 7372 7389 Prepackaged Software Services

(G-5985)
WHOOLEY INC
1059 Great Passage Blvd (22066-1643)
PHONE..............................703 307-4963
Tessa Husain, *CEO*
Najaf Husain, *Ch of Bd*
EMP: 4
SALES (est): 274.2K **Privately Held**
SIC: 7372 Application computer software

(G-5986)
ZINERVA PUBLISHING LLC
929 Holly Creek Dr (22066-1214)
PHONE..............................703 430-7629
Brent Glenn, *Principal*
EMP: 1
SALES (est): 64.1K **Privately Held**
SIC: 2741

Green Bay
Prince Edward County

(G-5987)
BARTON LOGGING INC
2503 Old Peach Tree Rd (23942-3022)
PHONE..............................434 390-8504
EMP: 2 EST: 2019
SALES (est): 81.7K **Privately Held**
SIC: 2411 Logging

(G-5988)
BUCK HALL LOGGING
864 Blankenship Pond Rd (23942-2113)
PHONE..............................434 696-1244
Eugene Hall, *Owner*
Windy Hall, *Admin Sec*
EMP: 6
SALES (est): 1.5MM **Privately Held**
SIC: 2411 Logging camps & contractors

(G-5989)
H & H LOGGING INC
864 Blankenship Pond Rd (23942-2113)
PHONE..............................434 321-9805
Hall Wendy, *Admin Sec*
EMP: 3
SALES (est): 228.8K **Privately Held**
SIC: 2411 Logging camps & contractors

(G-5990)
HIGH BRIDGE TRAIL STATE PARK
6888 Green Bay Rd (23942-2506)
PHONE..............................434 315-0457
Daniel Jordan, *General Mgr*
EMP: 10
SALES (est): 792K **Privately Held**
SIC: 2531 Picnic tables or benches, park

(G-5991)
RCT LOGGING LLC
3710 Schultz Mill Rd (23942-2427)
PHONE..............................434 767-4780
Jeanne B Roark, *Administration*
EMP: 11
SALES (est): 1.4MM **Privately Held**
SIC: 2411 Logging

Greenbackville
Accomack County

(G-5992)
EASTERN SHORE WLDG FABRICATION
2497 Captains Corridor (23356-2630)
PHONE..............................443 944-3451
Travis Carro, *Owner*
EMP: 2
SALES (est): 41.2K **Privately Held**
SIC: 7692 Welding repair

(G-5993)
ENGINEERED ENRGY SOLUTIONS LLC
Also Called: Delmarva Air Compressor
37434 Bayside Dr (23356-2816)
PHONE..............................443 299-2364
James Mottley, *President*
EMP: 3
SALES (est): 180K **Privately Held**
WEB: www.iiotconsultant.com
SIC: 3053 Packing: steam engines, pipe joints, air compressors, etc.

(G-5994)
KEYSTONE RUBBER CORPORATION
1539 Stockton Ave (23356)
PHONE..............................717 235-6863
EMP: 8
SQ FT: 20,000
SALES: 500K **Privately Held**
SIC: 3069 5085 Mfg Fabricated Rubber Products Whol Industrial Supplies

(G-5995)
LANCE STITCHER
3640 Captains Corridor (23356-2907)
PHONE..............................443 685-4829
Lance Evan Stitcher, *Administration*
EMP: 1 EST: 2016
SALES (est): 49.6K **Privately Held**
WEB: www.seasidevacations.rentals
SIC: 2395 Embroidery & art needlework

Greenbush
Accomack County

(G-5996)
JOHNSON WELDING SERVICE
21736 Parsons Rd (23357-2146)
P.O. Box 64 (23357-0064)
PHONE..............................757 787-4429
Gregory Johnson, *Partner*
Kristopher Johnson, *Partner*
EMP: 2
SQ FT: 10,000
SALES (est): 150K **Privately Held**
SIC: 7692 3599 Welding repair; machine shop, jobbing & repair

Greenville
Augusta County

(G-5997)
BOSSERMAN MURRY
2613 Cold Springs Rd (24440-1758)
PHONE..............................540 255-7949
Murry B Bosserman, *Owner*
EMP: 1
SALES (est): 96.2K **Privately Held**
SIC: 2411 Logging

(G-5998)
FIBERTECH VIRGINIA INC
340 Old Quarry Ln (24440-2010)
P.O. Box 546 (24440-0546)
PHONE..............................540 337-0916
Tish Folsom, *President*
EMP: 5
SALES (est): 479K **Privately Held**
WEB: www.fibertechva.com
SIC: 3229 Glass fiber products

(G-5999)
TOMLINSONS FARRIER SERVICE LLC
Also Called: Cross Tie Equine
1161 Broadhead School Rd (24440-1906)
PHONE..............................540 377-9195
William J Tomlinson, *Mng Member*
Heather S Tomlinson,
EMP: 2
SALES (est): 147K **Privately Held**
SIC: 3199 Boots, horse

Greenwood
Albemarle County

(G-6000)
SEVEN OAKS FARM LLC
Also Called: Septenary Winery
200 Seven Oaks Farm (22943-1912)
PHONE..............................303 653-3299
Sarah Zimmerman,
Todd Zimmerman,
EMP: 8
SQ FT: 2,400
SALES (est): 613.5K **Privately Held**
WEB: www.septenarywinery.com
SIC: 2084 7389 Wines; decoration service for special events

Gretna
Pittsylvania County

(G-6001)
ADAMS MACHINE SHOP INC
672 E Gretna Rd (24557-4605)
PHONE..............................434 656-2905
David Adams III, *President*
Martha Adams, *Vice Pres*
EMP: 3
SQ FT: 2,200
SALES (est): 104K **Privately Held**
SIC: 3599 Machine shop, jobbing & repair

(G-6002)
AMTHOR INTERNATIONAL INC
237 Indl Dr (24557)
PHONE..............................845 778-5576
Alice M Amthor, *President*
Butch Amthor, *President*
Mark Ageea, *General Mgr*
Amthor Arnold G, *Vice Pres*
Jack Green, *Purch Mgr*
▼ EMP: 65
SQ FT: 60,000
SALES: 25.8MM **Privately Held**
WEB: www.amthorinternational.com
SIC: 3713 3714 3443 Truck bodies & parts; motor vehicle parts & accessories; fabricated plate work (boiler shop)

(G-6003)
ASD BIOSYSTEMS INC
440 Johnson Farm Rd (24557-4910)
PHONE..............................804 545-3102
James J Tuite III, *CEO*
Lisa W Tuite, *Principal*
Peter E Andreotti, *Director*
EMP: 3
SQ FT: 500
SALES (est): 100K **Privately Held**
WEB: www.asdbiosystems.com
SIC: 2836 Biological products, except diagnostic

(G-6004)
BEARKERS WELDING
771 Mercury Rd (24557-3384)
PHONE..............................434 324-7616
Donnie Barker, *Principal*
EMP: 1
SALES (est): 34.9K **Privately Held**
SIC: 7692 Welding repair

(G-6005)
CAPPS SHOE COMPANY
224 Industrial Dr (24557-4091)
PHONE..............................434 528-3213
Olen Wilson, *Branch Mgr*
Tim Huffman, *Executive*
EMP: 110 **Privately Held**
WEB: www.usmadeshoes.com
SIC: 3143 3144 Men's footwear, except athletic; women's footwear, except athletic
PA: Capps Shoe Company
260 Fastener Dr
Lynchburg VA 24502

(G-6006)
CENTRAL VIRGINIA HARDWOOD PDTS
Also Called: Ceva Awards
3217 Renan Rd (24557-1864)
PHONE..............................434 335-5898
Philip Sanders, *President*
EMP: 8
SQ FT: 50,000
SALES (est): 1MM **Privately Held**
SIC: 3914 2511 Trophies, plated (all metals); wood household furniture

(G-6007)
CUSTER ICE SERVICE INC
202 Coffey St (24557-4093)
PHONE..............................434 656-2854
Roy Custer, *President*
Patricia Custer, *Vice Pres*
EMP: 4
SQ FT: 1,800
SALES (est): 84K **Privately Held**
SIC: 2097 Manufactured ice

(G-6008)
ELECTRONIC CANVAS
403 N Main St (24557-1500)
P.O. Box 267 (24557-0267)
PHONE..............................434 656-3070
Judy Simpson, *Owner*
EMP: 1
SQ FT: 1,000
SALES (est): 20K **Privately Held**
SIC: 2791 Typesetting, computer controlled

(G-6009)
RANDOLPH SCOTTS WELDING
Also Called: Scott's Randolph Welding
1193 Piney Grove Rd (24557-2085)
P.O. Box 30, Hurt (24563-0030)
PHONE..............................434 656-1471
Randolph Scott, *Owner*
EMP: 1
SALES (est): 63.4K **Privately Held**
SIC: 7692 Welding repair

(G-6010)
S & S BACKHOE & EXCVTR SVC LLC
1193 Player Rd (24557-4642)
PHONE..............................434 656-3184
Ronald Smith, *Principal*
EMP: 2
SALES (est): 72.6K **Privately Held**
SIC: 3531 Backhoes

Grottoes
Rockingham County

(G-6011)
2 BUSY BROOMS CLEANING SERVICE
779 Paine Run Rd (24441-5039)
PHONE..............................540 476-1190
Debbie Sorrels, *Owner*
EMP: 2
SALES (est): 121.8K **Privately Held**
SIC: 3635 Household vacuum cleaners

(G-6012)
ACCUAMP INCORPORATED
37 Auburn Dr (24441-5013)
PHONE..............................540 908-4079
Louis H Barker III, *President*
EMP: 2 EST: 2009
SALES (est): 170K **Privately Held**
WEB: www.accuamp.com
SIC: 3825 Instruments to measure electricity

(G-6013)
AGGREGATE INDUSTRIES MGT INC
Rr 340 (24441)
PHONE..............................540 249-5791
EMP: 13
SALES (corp-wide): 26.6B **Privately Held**
SIC: 1442 Construction Sand/Gravel

HQ: Aggregate Industries Management, Inc.
13900 Pney Metinghouse Rd
Rockville MD 60631
301 284-3600

(G-6014)
ALPHA INDUSTRIES
901 Dogwood Ave (24441-1851)
PHONE..............................540 249-4980
John Reir, *CFO*
EMP: 2
SALES (est): 88.9K **Privately Held**
SIC: 3089 Plastics products

(G-6015)
BATTARBEES CATERING
701b Elm Ave (24441-1752)
PHONE..............................540 249-9205
Margaret Battarbee, *Owner*
EMP: 1
SALES (est): 115.5K **Privately Held**
WEB: www.battarbeescatering.com
SIC: 2099 Food preparations

(G-6016)
BLUE RIDGE MACHINE WORKS INC
103 6th St (24441-2625)
P.O. Box 1212 (24441-1212)
PHONE..............................540 249-4640
Richard Shelton, *President*
EMP: 2
SQ FT: 10,000
SALES (est): 130K **Privately Held**
WEB: www.brmw-va.com
SIC: 3599 Machine shop, jobbing & repair

(G-6017)
CAKE BALLIN LLC
382 Trayfoot Rd (24441-5003)
PHONE..............................540 820-2938
Gina Wood,
EMP: 1
SALES (est): 67K **Privately Held**
SIC: 2099 Frosting mixes, dry: for cakes, cookies, etc.

(G-6018)
CUPP MANUFACTURING CO
73 Stonewall Ln (24441-4707)
PHONE..............................540 249-4011
Ray Cupp, *Owner*
EMP: 8
SALES (est): 674.8K **Privately Held**
SIC: 3599 2281 Machine shop, jobbing & repair; yarn spinning mills

(G-6019)
GIBSON GOOD TOOLS INC
402 5th St (24441-2623)
P.O. Box 11096, Savannah GA (31412-1296)
PHONE..............................540 249-5100
Leigh S Crumrine, *President*
EMP: 3 EST: 1935
SQ FT: 4,500
SALES (est): 308.7K **Privately Held**
WEB: www.gibsongoodtools.com
SIC: 3429 Manufactured hardware (general)

(G-6020)
GROTTOES PALLET CO INC
802 Edgewood St (24441-2419)
PHONE..............................540 249-4882
Barbara R Begoon, *President*
James T Begoon, *Corp Secy*
EMP: 8 EST: 1967
SQ FT: 4,000
SALES (est): 1MM **Privately Held**
SIC: 2448 Pallets, wood

(G-6021)
MACE LUMBER MILL
13189 Port Republic Rd (24441-5213)
PHONE..............................540 249-4458
Dale Mace, *Partner*
David Mace, *Partner*
EMP: 3
SQ FT: 500
SALES (est): 390.8K **Privately Held**
SIC: 2421 Sawmills & planing mills, general

(G-6022)
PETE BURR MACHINE WORKS INC
7 Pine Creek Ln (24441-4840)
PHONE..............................540 249-5693
Pat Burr, *President*
Penny Allen, *Vice Pres*
Joyce Burr, *Vice Pres*
Pete Burr, *Admin Sec*
EMP: 8 EST: 1981
SALES (est): 1MM **Privately Held**
WEB: www.peteburrmachineworks.com
SIC: 3599 Machine shop, jobbing & repair

(G-6023)
R & B CABINET SHOP
501 Aspen Ave (24441)
P.O. Box 485 (24441-0485)
PHONE..............................540 249-4507
Bob Alger, *Owner*
EMP: 3
SALES (est): 350K **Privately Held**
SIC: 2434 5712 Wood kitchen cabinets; furniture stores

(G-6024)
REYNOLDS CNSMR PDTS HLDNGS INC
149 Grand Caverns Dr (24441-1508)
PHONE..............................540 249-5711
Ronald Ritchie, *Purch Mgr*
Tim Shiflett, *Branch Mgr*
Lisa Sumption, *Director*
EMP: 223 **Privately Held**
WEB:
www.reynoldsconsumerproducts.com
SIC: 3353 3411 Aluminum sheet, plate & foil; aluminum cans
PA: Reynolds Consumer Products Holdings Llc
1900 W Field Ct
Lake Forest IL 60045

(G-6025)
TWP TRANSPORT LLC
1901 Cherry Ave Apt B (24441-2375)
PHONE..............................540 383-7995
Dakota Scott Conley,
EMP: 2
SALES (est): 260K **Privately Held**
SIC: 3799 Transportation equipment

(G-6026)
VALLEY TOOL & DESIGN INC
2307 Weyers Cave Rd (24441)
P.O. Box 68 (24441-0068)
PHONE..............................540 249-5710
Robert F Carr, *President*
Ann Carr, *Vice Pres*
Mary Ann Anderson, *Opers Mgr*
EMP: 6
SQ FT: 13,000
SALES (est): 1.1MM **Privately Held**
WEB: www.valleytool-design.com
SIC: 3443 Fabricated plate work (boiler shop)

Grundy
Buchanan County

(G-6027)
A B & J COAL COMPANY INC
237 Main St (24614)
P.O. Box 863 (24614-0863)
PHONE..............................276 530-7786
Elmer Fuller, *President*
Tony Lester, *Vice Pres*
EMP: 14
SALES (est): 1.4MM **Privately Held**
SIC: 1222 Bituminous coal-underground mining

(G-6028)
BRISTOL COAL CORPORATION
1021 Walnut St (24614)
P.O. Box 1426 (24614-1426)
PHONE..............................276 935-7562
Hank Matney, *President*
Fred Matney, *Corp Secy*
Rick Matney, *Vice Pres*
EMP: 15 **Privately Held**
SIC: 1241 Coal mining services

(G-6029)
COLE ELECTRIC OF VIRGINIA INC
20104 Riverside Dr (24614-6878)
P.O. Box 1560 (24614-1560)
PHONE..............................276 935-7562
Andy Cole, *President*
Bob Cole, *Corp Secy*
EMP: 6
SALES (est): 154.1K **Privately Held**
SIC: 7694 Electric motor repair

(G-6030)
DACOAL MINING INC
4014 Starbranch Rd (24614)
P.O. Box 1066 (24614-1066)
PHONE..............................276 531-8165
David Stevenson, *President*
EMP: 11
SALES (est): 662.6K **Privately Held**
SIC: 1241 Coal mining services

(G-6031)
EXCELLO OIL COMPANY INC (PA)
20813 Riverside Dr (24614-9596)
PHONE..............................276 935-2332
Roger Powers, *President*
EMP: 15
SALES (est): 1.1MM **Privately Held**
SIC: 1221 Bituminous coal & lignite-surface mining

(G-6032)
FLETCHERS HARDWARE & SPT CTR
100 Walnut St (24614)
P.O. Box 29, Vansant (24656-0029)
PHONE..............................276 935-8332
James A Fletcher, *Owner*
EMP: 5
SQ FT: 27,300
SALES (est): 200K **Privately Held**
SIC: 3949 Sporting & athletic goods

(G-6033)
GENESIS WELDING INC
1062 Alleghany Rd (24614-7141)
PHONE..............................276 935-2482
Charlie Deel, *President*
Regina Deel, *Admin Sec*
EMP: 3
SALES (est): 250K **Privately Held**
SIC: 7692 Welding repair

(G-6034)
H & H MINING COMPANY INC
1074 Stacy Hollow Rd (24614-5463)
PHONE..............................276 566-2105
Kathy Hurley, *President*
EMP: 2
SALES (est): 131K **Privately Held**
SIC: 1081 Draining or pumping of metal mines

(G-6035)
HORN CONSTRUCTION CO INC
Rr 83 (24614)
P.O. Box 815 (24614-0815)
PHONE..............................276 935-4749
EMP: 1
SALES (est): 120K **Privately Held**
SIC: 1221 Coal Mining

(G-6036)
MACKS TRANSFORMER SERVICE
Rr 460 Box E (24614)
P.O. Box 648 (24614-0648)
PHONE..............................276 935-4366
Mack Blankenship, *President*
EMP: 2
SQ FT: 2,400
SALES (est): 250K **Privately Held**
SIC: 3612 Power & distribution transformers

(G-6037)
MESCHER MANUFACTURING CO INC
24267 Riverside Dr (24614-6139)
PHONE..............................276 530-7856
Franklin J Matney, *President*
Harriet C Matney, *Corp Secy*

Jeff Horn, *Vice Pres*
Anne Mullins, *Vice Pres*
Jeneva Smith, *Data Proc Dir*
EMP: 12
SQ FT: 15,000
SALES (est): 2.2MM **Privately Held**
SIC: 3541 3532 Machine tools, metal cutting type; mine cars, plows, loaders, feeders & similar equipment

(G-6038)
MOUNTAINEER PUBLISHING CO INC
Also Called: Virginia Mountaineer
1200 Plaza Dr Ste 2400 (24614-9730)
P.O. Box 2040 (24614-2040)
PHONE..................................276 935-2123
Lodge Compton, *President*
Kathy St Clair, *Editor*
EMP: 9 **EST:** 1951
SALES (est): 633.6K **Privately Held**
SIC: 2711 2791 2759 2752 Newspapers, publishing & printing; typesetting; commercial printing; commercial printing, lithographic

(G-6039)
PAULS FAN COMPANY
2738 Home Creek Rd (24614-5243)
PHONE..................................276 530-7311
Gregory Todd Elswick, *President*
EMP: 58
SALES (est): 1.3MM **Privately Held**
WEB: www.paulsfans.com
SIC: 3999 Manufacturing industries

(G-6040)
PRITCHARD STUDIO
2749 Poplar Creek Rd (24614-6041)
PHONE..................................276 935-5829
EMP: 2
SALES (est): 83.9K **Privately Held**
SIC: 2752 Commercial printing, lithographic

(G-6041)
SYKES SIGNS INC
1182 Jim Rowe Hollow Rd (24614-9483)
PHONE..................................276 935-2772
Dewy Sykes, *President*
EMP: 1
SALES (est): 35K **Privately Held**
SIC: 3993 Signs & advertising specialties

(G-6042)
TRADITIONL SCRNPRNTG & MONOGRM
1402 Stable Dr (24614-6057)
PHONE..................................276 935-7110
Nora Cantrel, *Owner*
EMP: 2 **EST:** 2010
SALES (est): 193.4K **Privately Held**
SIC: 3552 Textile machinery

Gum Spring
Goochland County

(G-6043)
GRAYHAVEN WINERY
4675 E Grey Fox Rd (23065-2165)
PHONE..................................804 556-3917
Evelyn Peple,
Deon Abrams,
Charles Peple,
EMP: 5 **Privately Held**
WEB: www.grayhavenwinery.com
SIC: 2084 Wines

(G-6044)
SACO
4100 Lively Ln (23065-2042)
PHONE..................................804 457-3744
Keith Fellows, *Managing Dir*
▲ **EMP:** 4
SALES (est): 171.3K **Privately Held**
SIC: 3466 Bottle caps & tops, stamped metal

Gwynn
Mathews County

(G-6045)
D ATWOOD
35 Gwynnville Rd (23066)
P.O. Box 115 (23066-0115)
PHONE..................................703 508-5080
Donald J D Connolly, *Owner*
EMP: 2
SALES (est): 30K **Privately Held**
SIC: 3589 Service industry machinery

Hague
Westmoreland County

(G-6046)
GENERALS RIDGE VINEYARD
1618 Weldons Dr (22469-2418)
PHONE..................................804 472-3172
EMP: 2
SALES (est): 85.1K **Privately Held**
WEB: www.generalsridgevineyard.com
SIC: 2084 Wines

(G-6047)
HAGUE WINERY LLC
8268 Cople Hwy (22469-2523)
P.O. Box 141 (22469-0141)
PHONE..................................804 472-9235
Steven Madey, *President*
EMP: 2
SALES (est): 150K **Privately Held**
WEB: www.thehaguewinery.com
SIC: 2084 Wines, brandy & brandy spirits

Halifax
Halifax County

(G-6048)
ASW ALUMINUM
1105 Chaffin Trl (24558-3139)
PHONE..................................434 476-7557
Christopher T Lopez, *Owner*
EMP: 2
SALES (est): 50K **Privately Held**
WEB: www.aswaluminumproducts.com
SIC: 3999 Manufacturing industries

(G-6049)
HALIFAX MACHINE & WELDING INC
5043 Halifax Rd (24558-3185)
PHONE..................................434 572-3856
Butch Dawson, *President*
Joe Hall, *Vice Pres*
EMP: 4
SALES (est): 230K **Privately Held**
WEB: www.panoramicweb.com
SIC: 3599 1799 Machine shop, jobbing & repair; welding on site

(G-6050)
IN2 PRINT
3151 Chatham Rd (24558-2977)
PHONE..................................434 476-7996
Nadine Chalmers, *Principal*
EMP: 2
SALES (est): 83.9K **Privately Held**
SIC: 2752 Commercial printing, lithographic

(G-6051)
KEJAEH ENTERPRISES LLC
2121 Grubby Rd (24558-2435)
P.O. Box 1893 (24558-1893)
PHONE..................................434 476-1300
Don Bagwell Jr, *Mng Member*
EMP: 6
SALES (est): 602.4K **Privately Held**
SIC: 2491 Structural lumber & timber, treated wood

(G-6052)
SPRINGFIELD DISTILLERY LLC
9040 River Rd (24558-2344)
PHONE..................................434 572-1888
EMP: 4 **EST:** 2015

SALES (est): 217.5K **Privately Held**
WEB: www.springfielddistillery.com
SIC: 2085 Distilled & blended liquors

(G-6053)
SUNSHINE MILLS INC
100 Sunshine Dr (24558-2523)
P.O. Box 1060 (24558-1060)
PHONE..................................434 476-1451
Chris Melvin, *General Mgr*
Jamie Shelton, *Purch Mgr*
John Zeiner, *Research*
Adam Anderson, *Manager*
Ronald Spelman, *Manager*
EMP: 80
SQ FT: 95,000
SALES (corp-wide): 280MM **Privately Held**
WEB: www.sunshinemills.com
SIC: 2047 2048 Dog food; prepared feeds
PA: Sunshine Mills, Inc.
    500 6th St Sw
    Red Bay AL 35582
    256 356-9541

(G-6054)
SUNSHINE MILLS OF VIRGINIA
100 Salishan Dr (24558-9608)
PHONE..................................434 476-1451
Fred G Bostick, *Ch of Bd*
Alan O Bostick, *President*
O T Ray, *Corp Secy*
EMP: 100
SQ FT: 95,000
SALES (est): 10.1MM
SALES (corp-wide): 280MM **Privately Held**
WEB: www.sunshinemills.com
SIC: 2047 Dog food
PA: Sunshine Mills, Inc.
    500 6th St Sw
    Red Bay AL 35582
    256 356-9541

Hallwood
Accomack County

(G-6055)
STICK IT WELDING & FABRICATION
28035 Seaside Ave (23359-2655)
PHONE..................................757 710-5774
Allen Poulson, *Owner*
EMP: 1
SALES (est): 38K **Privately Held**
SIC: 7692 Automotive welding

Hamilton
Loudoun County

(G-6056)
DREAM CATCHER ENTERPRISES LLC
38409 Stone Eden Dr (20158-3455)
PHONE..................................540 338-8273
Steven Cox, *Manager*
EMP: 2 **EST:** 2016
SALES (est): 75.8K **Privately Held**
SIC: 2741

(G-6057)
EMBOSSING ETC
16919 Ivandale Rd (20158-9427)
PHONE..................................540 338-4520
Verla Page, *Owner*
EMP: 1
SALES (est): 30K **Privately Held**
WEB: www.store.embossing-etc.com
SIC: 3111 Embossing of leather

(G-6058)
GALLAGHER ESTATE VINEYARDS LLC
38547 Piggott Bottom Rd (20158-9463)
PHONE..................................301 252-3450
Brian Gallagher, *Principal*
EMP: 2
SALES (est): 78.8K **Privately Held**
SIC: 2084 Wines

(G-6059)
HAMILTON SAFETY CENTER INC
39071 E Colonial Hwy (20158-3111)
P.O. Box 549 (20159-0549)
PHONE..................................540 338-0500
EMP: 3
SALES: 250.6K **Privately Held**
WEB: www.harmonyhallva.com
SIC: 3711 Fire department vehicles (motor vehicles), assembly of

(G-6060)
HARMONY CREEK VINEYARDS LLC
18548 Harmony Church Rd (20158-3520)
PHONE..................................540 338-7677
Paula-Jean R Lawrence, *Principal*
EMP: 2
SALES (est): 62.3K **Privately Held**
SIC: 2084 Wines

(G-6061)
HUNTERS RUN WINERY LLC
40325 Charles Town Pike (20158-3217)
PHONE..................................703 926-4183
Catherine Nolan, *Principal*
EMP: 2
SALES (est): 133.7K **Privately Held**
WEB: www.huntersrunwinebarn.com
SIC: 2084 Wines

(G-6062)
OMNI TECHNOLOGY AND MFG LLC
40329 Charles Town Pike (20158-3217)
PHONE..................................703 929-8000
EMP: 2 **EST:** 2017
SALES (est): 71.4K **Privately Held**
SIC: 3999 Manufacturing industries

(G-6063)
PERSIMMON WOODWORKING
16714 Sommertime Ln (20158-3220)
PHONE..................................703 618-6909
Paul Rehm, *Owner*
EMP: 1
SALES (est): 56.1K **Privately Held**
SIC: 2431 5072 Millwork; shelf or light hardware

(G-6064)
QUAIL RUN SIGNS
43 E Colonial Hwy (20158-9010)
PHONE..................................540 338-8412
John Ralph, *Principal*
EMP: 4 **EST:** 2008
SALES (est): 519.6K **Privately Held**
WEB: www.quailrunsigns.com
SIC: 3993 Signs, not made in custom sign painting shops

Hampton
Hampton City County

(G-6065)
A & W MASONRY SPECIALISTS
2147 Cunningham Dr # 104 (23666-2520)
PHONE..................................757 327-3492
EMP: 2
SALES (est): 62.3K **Privately Held**
SIC: 2024 Yogurt desserts, frozen

(G-6066)
A J INDUSTRIES
307 Clay St (23663-2248)
PHONE..................................757 871-4109
EMP: 2
SALES (est): 132.6K **Privately Held**
SIC: 3999 Manufacturing industries

(G-6067)
AARON D CROUSE
Also Called: Welder For Hire
3308 W Lewis Rd (23666-3829)
PHONE..................................757 827-6123
Aaron D Crouse, *Owner*
EMP: 1
SALES (est): 40.2K **Privately Held**
SIC: 7692 1799 Welding repair; special trade contractors

(G-6068)
ACCESS PRIME TECHNCL SLTNS
616 Pelham Dr (23669-1639)
PHONE.................................757 651-6523
Bobby Harmon,
Roy Ayres,
John Caldwell,
Darlene Hill,
EMP: 4
SALES (est): 210K **Privately Held**
SIC: 3571 Electronic computers

(G-6069)
ACTION TOOL SERVICE INC
2202 Mingee Dr (23661-1033)
PHONE.................................757 838-4555
Larry D Franklin, *President*
David Franklin, *Vice Pres*
▲ EMP: 19 EST: 1978
SQ FT: 10,500
SALES (est): 3.7MM **Privately Held**
WEB: www.actiontoolservice.com
SIC: 3541 Machine tools, metal cutting type

(G-6070)
ACUTECH SIGNS & GRAPHICS INC
26 Research Dr (23666-1325)
PHONE.................................757 766-2627
William Watkins, *President*
EMP: 2
SALES (est): 90K **Privately Held**
WEB: www.primecaremedicalcenter.com
SIC: 3993 7532 Signs & advertising specialties; truck painting & lettering

(G-6071)
ADVANCED AIRCRAFT COMPANY LLC
1100 Exploration Way (23666-6264)
PHONE.................................757 325-6712
William Fredericks,
EMP: 2
SALES (est): 86K
SALES (corp-wide): 499K **Privately Held**
WEB: www.advancedaircraftcompany.com
SIC: 3721 Motorized aircraft
PA: Fredericks Aircraft Company
    1100 Exploration Way
    Hampton VA 23666
    757 727-3326

(G-6072)
ADVANCED CSTM COATINGS VA LLC
39 Leicester Ter (23666-2037)
PHONE.................................757 726-2628
Tony Logan,
EMP: 3
SALES (est): 500K **Privately Held**
WEB: www.advancedcustomcoatings.com
SIC: 3479 Coating of metals & formed products

(G-6073)
ADVEX CORPORATION
41 Research Dr (23666-1324)
PHONE.................................757 865-6660
George Hill, *President*
EMP: 30
SALES (corp-wide): 22.9MM **Privately Held**
WEB: www.advex.net
SIC: 3599 Machine shop, jobbing & repair
PA: Advex Corporation
    121 Floyd Thompson Blvd
    Hampton VA 23666
    757 865-0920

(G-6074)
AERO TRAINING CENTER
220 Hankins Dr (23669-3631)
PHONE.................................757 838-6570
Angela Goodloe, *Owner*
EMP: 3
SALES (est): 50K **Privately Held**
SIC: 3699 Flight simulators (training aids), electronic

(G-6075)
AEROSPACE & TECHNOLOGY
1 E Durand St (23681-2111)
PHONE.................................757 864-7227

Terry Hagen, *Principal*
EMP: 2 EST: 2016
SALES (est): 86K **Privately Held**
SIC: 3721 Aircraft

(G-6076)
AFFORDABLE PRINTING & COPIES
1926 E Pembroke Ave (23663-1326)
PHONE.................................757 728-9770
Tammy A Wright, *President*
James Wright, *Co-Owner*
Jim Wright, *Vice Pres*
EMP: 3
SALES (est): 581.2K **Privately Held**
WEB:
www.affordableprintingandcopies.com
SIC: 2752 Commercial printing, offset

(G-6077)
AFTER AFFECTS CUSTOM FURNITURE
32 Scotland Rd (23663-1430)
PHONE.................................504 510-1792
Clyde McClendon,
EMP: 2
SALES (est): 90.4K **Privately Held**
SIC: 2599 Furniture & fixtures

(G-6078)
AG CUSTOMS CREAT & DESIGNS LLC
21 E Big Sky Dr (23666-1585)
PHONE.................................757 927-7339
Andre Gillespie, *CEO*
EMP: 1
SALES (est): 72.5K **Privately Held**
SIC: 2389 Disposable garments & accessories

(G-6079)
AILEEN L BROWN
Also Called: Lillie's
2018 Laguard Dr (23661-2628)
PHONE.................................757 696-1814
Aileen Brown, *Owner*
EMP: 3
SALES (est): 99.8K **Privately Held**
SIC: 2099 5046 5145 Food preparations; commercial cooking & food service equipment; snack foods

(G-6080)
AKALINE CYLINDERS
2400 Aluminum Ave (23661-1236)
PHONE.................................757 896-9100
Gloria Harris, *Principal*
▲ EMP: 6
SALES (est): 558.7K **Privately Held**
WEB: www.catalinacylinders.com
SIC: 2813 Industrial gases

(G-6081)
ALT SERVICES INC
807 Sheffield St (23666-1980)
PHONE.................................757 806-1341
Alfonso Tundidor, *Principal*
EMP: 1
SALES (est): 64.9K **Privately Held**
WEB: www.altservicesinc.com
SIC: 3721 4581 4225 8742 Airplanes, fixed or rotary wing; aircraft maintenance & repair services; general warehousing & storage; administrative services consultant; management services

(G-6082)
AMERICAN GEN FABRICATION INC
915 Laredo Ct (23669-1227)
PHONE.................................757 329-4384
Edwin Billips, *President*
Willie May Billips, *Corp Secy*
EMP: 3
SQ FT: 2,710
SALES (est): 303.3K **Privately Held**
WEB: www.amgenfab.com
SIC: 3599 Machine shop, jobbing & repair

(G-6083)
AMES & AMES INC
95 Apollo Dr (23669-2005)
PHONE.................................757 851-4723
Beverly Ames, *Principal*
EMP: 3

SALES (est): 156.3K **Privately Held**
WEB: www.ames.k12.ia.us
SIC: 3494 Valves & pipe fittings

(G-6084)
AMES CLEANERS & FORMALS INC
Also Called: Ames Tuxedo
10 Town Center Way (23666-1999)
PHONE.................................757 825-3335
Chris Ames, *Manager*
EMP: 7
SALES (corp-wide): 1MM **Privately Held**
WEB: www.amestuxedos.com
SIC: 2311 5699 Men's & boys' suits & coats; formal wear
PA: Ames Cleaners & Formals, Inc.
    554 E Mercury Blvd
    Hampton VA 23663
    757 722-4301

(G-6085)
ARCONIC CBT
1 Howmet Dr (23661-1333)
PHONE.................................757 825-6870
Joel White, *Plant Mgr*
Jessica Carie, *Engineer*
Maureen Loughran, *Engineer*
Abraham Kulangara, *Controller*
Anna Gamache, *Financial Analy*
EMP: 6
SALES (est): 1.9MM **Privately Held**
WEB: www.arconic.com
SIC: 2834 Pharmaceutical preparations

(G-6086)
AUNT NOLAS PECAN PRALINES
7 Whipple Dr (23663-2419)
PHONE.................................757 723-1607
Chappell Joressa, *Owner*
EMP: 1
SALES (est): 56.7K **Privately Held**
SIC: 2064 Candy & other confectionery products

(G-6087)
B & C CUSTOM CANVAS
16 Hampshire Dr (23669-2130)
PHONE.................................757 870-0089
Christine M Griffin, *Owner*
EMP: 1
SALES (est): 2.5K **Privately Held**
WEB: www.bccustomcanvas.com
SIC: 2211 Canvas

(G-6088)
BATTS WOODWORKING
246 Bannon Ct (23666-3707)
PHONE.................................757 969-5824
EMP: 1 EST: 2015
SALES (est): 41.5K **Privately Held**
SIC: 2499 Mfg Wood Products

(G-6089)
BAY CUSTOM INC
407 Rotary St (23661-1318)
PHONE.................................757 971-4785
Robert Whelan, *President*
EMP: 9
SALES (est): 439.4K **Privately Held**
WEB: www.baycustommarine.com
SIC: 3732 Boat building & repairing

(G-6090)
BAY CUSTOM MAR FLEET REPR INC
407 Rotary St (23661-1318)
PHONE.................................757 224-3818
EMP: 15
SALES (est): 1.9MM **Privately Held**
SIC: 3732 Boatbuilding/Repairing

(G-6091)
BIG DADDYS SPORTS PRODUCTS
1 Cortez Ct (23666-2841)
PHONE.................................757 310-8565
Joseph Howard, *Principal*
EMP: 2
SALES (est): 94.4K **Privately Held**
SIC: 3949 Sporting & athletic goods

(G-6092)
BILLS YARD & LAWN SERVICE LLC
308 Brightwood Ave (23661-1643)
PHONE.................................757 871-4589
William Copeland,
EMP: 1
SALES (est): 105.9K **Privately Held**
SIC: 3271 7389 Blocks, concrete: landscape or retaining wall;

(G-6093)
BL & SON ENTERPRISES LLC
Also Called: Line-X of Chesapeake
4 Pirates Cv (23669-5224)
PHONE.................................757 938-9188
Brian Leffel, *Owner*
Brian S Leffel,
EMP: 5 EST: 2008
SALES (est): 862.3K **Privately Held**
WEB: www.linexofchesapeake.com
SIC: 2821 Plastics materials & resins

(G-6094)
BLACK ELEMENT LLC
1123 West Ave (23669-2728)
PHONE.................................757 224-6160
EMP: 3
SALES (est): 242.8K **Privately Held**
SIC: 2819 Mfg Industrial Inorganic Chemicals

(G-6095)
BLACKTAG SCREEN PRINTING INC
307 Ireland St (23663-2145)
PHONE.................................855 423-1680
Maria Lewis, *President*
EMP: 3 EST: 2015
SALES (est): 163.5K **Privately Held**
SIC: 2752 Commercial printing, lithographic

(G-6096)
BNC WELDING
125 Semple Farm Rd (23666-1459)
PHONE.................................757 706-2361
Steven Henderson, *Principal*
EMP: 1
SALES (est): 30K **Privately Held**
SIC: 7692 Welding repair

(G-6097)
BOBBY BURNS NOWLIN
Also Called: Nowlin Steelcraft
502 Copeland Dr (23661-1345)
PHONE.................................757 827-1588
Bob Nowlin, *President*
Cindy Nowlin, *Vice Pres*
EMP: 15
SQ FT: 6,500
SALES (est): 1.2MM **Privately Held**
SIC: 3446 3444 3441 Gates, ornamental metal; grillwork, ornamental metal; sheet metalwork; fabricated structural metal

(G-6098)
BOHO BAE & COMPANY LLC
1585 Briarfield Rd # 142 (23666-4833)
PHONE.................................757 344-9197
Alexis Riddick,
EMP: 1
SALES (est): 42.5K **Privately Held**
SIC: 2339 Women's & misses' accessories

(G-6099)
BOWLD FLAVORS LLC
1516 Denton Dr (23664-1014)
PHONE.................................757 952-4741
David Pickering,
EMP: 1
SALES (est): 20K **Privately Held**
SIC: 2499 Food handling & processing products, wood

(G-6100)
BYNUM
13 Neff Dr (23669-1123)
PHONE.................................757 224-1860
Freddie L Bynum, *Owner*
EMP: 1
SALES (est): 39.7K **Privately Held**
SIC: 3953 Embossing seals & hand stamps

(G-6101)
C AND F PROMOTIONS INC
83 W Mercury Blvd (23669-2508)
PHONE.............................757 912-5161
Christine Sparrow, *Principal*
EMP: 2
SALES (est): 124K **Privately Held**
WEB: www.vapromotions.com
SIC: 3993 Signs & advertising specialties

(G-6102)
CABRERA FAMILY MASONRY LLC
201 Courtney Dr (23669-2518)
PHONE.............................919 671-7623
Ricardo Gonzalez, *Principal*
EMP: 3
SALES (est): 72.6K **Privately Held**
SIC: 2024 Yogurt desserts, frozen

(G-6103)
CAFES D AFRIQUE LLC
81 Joynes Rd (23666-4571)
PHONE.............................757 725-1050
Jasmine Bryson, *Principal*
EMP: 2 EST: 2017
SALES (est): 65.4K **Privately Held**
SIC: 2095 7389 Roasted coffee;

(G-6104)
CANDLE EUPHORIA
10 Westminister Dr (23666-4331)
PHONE.............................757 327-8567
Crystal Fox, *Principal*
EMP: 2
SALES (est): 62.5K **Privately Held**
SIC: 3999 Candles

(G-6105)
CAP CITY INC
4809 W Mercury Blvd (23666-3727)
PHONE.............................757 827-0932
EMP: 3 EST: 1973
SQ FT: 1,500
SALES (est): 319.8K
SALES (corp-wide): 1MM **Privately Held**
SIC: 2386 5521 Mfg Leather Clothing Ret Used Automobiles
PA: Al Peak Distributors Inc
7831 N Military Hwy
Norfolk VA 23518
757 480-1870

(G-6106)
CAREPLEX PHARMACY
3000 Coliseum Dr Fl 2 (23666-5963)
PHONE.............................757 736-1215
Edward James Elzarian, *Principal*
EMP: 1
SALES (est): 167.3K **Privately Held**
WEB: www.careplexortho.com
SIC: 2834 Pharmaceutical preparations

(G-6107)
CARTER IRON AND STEEL CO
408 Industry Dr (23661-1313)
PHONE.............................757 826-4559
Wilson B Carter, *CEO*
Greg Carter, *President*
Barbara Carter, *Corp Secy*
EMP: 20
SQ FT: 5,000
SALES: 2.6MM **Privately Held**
WEB: www.carteriron.com
SIC: 3441 1791 Fabricated structural metal; structural steel erection

(G-6108)
CATALINA CYLINDERS
2400 Aluminum Ave (23661-1236)
PHONE.............................757 896-9100
Phillip Keeler, *Principal*
David Silva, *Business Mgr*
Joe Wolf, *Opers Staff*
Lorne Patterson, *Production*
Sharon Barbrey, *Buyer*
▲ EMP: 48
SALES (est): 17.6MM **Privately Held**
WEB: www.catalinacylinders.com
SIC: 3443 Fabricated plate work (boiler shop)

(G-6109)
CATALINA CYLINDERS INC
2400 Aluminum Ave (23661-1236)
PHONE.............................757 896-9100
Jeff Cunningham, *Manager*
EMP: 90
SALES (corp-wide): 25MM **Privately Held**
WEB: www.catalinacylinders.com
SIC: 3463 Aluminum forgings
PA: Catalina Cylinders, Inc.
7300 Anaconda Ave
Garden Grove CA 92841
714 890-0999

(G-6110)
CEGNA INC
Also Called: Graham Alliance
110 Clseum Crssing Ste 50 (23666)
PHONE.............................757 632-5000
Charles Graham, *CEO*
Tim Graham, *Vice Pres*
Tl Clark, *CFO*
▼ EMP: 40
SQ FT: 5,000
SALES (est): 2MM **Privately Held**
SIC: 2721 6531 Magazines: publishing only, not printed on site; real estate brokers & agents

(G-6111)
CENSUS CHANNEL
4410 Claiborne Sq E # 334 (23666-2071)
PHONE.............................757 838-3881
Anthony E Fairfax, *Owner*
EMP: 1
SALES (est): 63K **Privately Held**
SIC: 1389 Testing, measuring, surveying & analysis services

(G-6112)
CHASE FILTERS & COMPONENTS LLC
307 E St (23661-1209)
PHONE.............................757 327-0036
David Weeda, *Mng Member*
EMP: 20
SALES (est): 311.2K **Privately Held**
WEB: www.chasefiltercompany.com
SIC: 3569 Filters, general line: industrial

(G-6113)
CHRIS N CHRIS WOODWORKING LLC
5 Ashe Meadows Dr (23664-2069)
PHONE.............................757 810-4672
Christopher Lates, *Principal*
EMP: 1
SALES (est): 54.1K **Privately Held**
SIC: 2431 Millwork

(G-6114)
CME CONCRETE LLC
245 Loch Cir (23669-5530)
P.O. Box 9756 (23670-0756)
PHONE.............................757 713-0495
Sharon McGlone,
EMP: 6
SALES (est): 292.9K **Privately Held**
SIC: 3272 Paving materials, prefabricated concrete

(G-6115)
COLORFUL WORDS MEDIA LLC
2104 Newton Rd (23663-1023)
P.O. Box 7555 (23666-0555)
PHONE.............................757 268-9690
Latoya Debardelaben,
EMP: 1
SALES (est): 64.3K **Privately Held**
SIC: 2731 Book publishing

(G-6116)
COMMONWEALTH MECHANICAL INC
504 Rotary St (23661-1321)
PHONE.............................757 825-0740
Rommie Matthews, *Vice Pres*
EMP: 2
SALES (est): 94.5K **Privately Held**
SIC: 3444 Sheet metalwork

(G-6117)
COVAN WORLDIWDE MOVING & STOR
61 Basil Sawyer Dr (23666-1336)
PHONE.............................757 766-2305
Joyce Farish, *Manager*
▲ EMP: 2
SALES (est): 160K **Privately Held**
SIC: 3443 Fabricated plate work (boiler shop)

(G-6118)
CRAFT INDUSTRIAL INCORPORATED
2300 58th St (23661-1329)
PHONE.............................757 825-1195
David Schrum, *President*
▲ EMP: 25
SQ FT: 100,000
SALES (est): 6.4MM **Privately Held**
WEB: www.craftindustrial.com
SIC: 3554 7699 7629 Paper mill machinery: plating, slitting, waxing, etc.; pulp mill machinery; industrial machinery & equipment repair; electrical repair shops

(G-6119)
CRAFT MACHINE WORKS INC
2102 48th St (23661-1297)
PHONE.............................757 310-6011
Larry Schwoeri, *CEO*
Dannie L Schrum, *CEO*
Michael D Schrum, *President*
Michael D Cobb, *Vice Pres*
Karen Dougherty, *Buyer*
EMP: 100
SQ FT: 300,000
SALES (est): 26.5MM **Privately Held**
WEB: www.craftmachine.com
SIC: 3441 3599 Fabricated structural metal; custom machinery

(G-6120)
CRAFT MCH WRKS ACQUISITION LLC (DH)
2102 48th St (23661-1202)
PHONE.............................757 310-6011
Brent Willey, *Mng Member*
EMP: 35
SALES (est): 11.2MM
SALES (corp-wide): 810MM **Privately Held**
WEB: www.craftmachine.com
SIC: 3441 3599 Fabricated structural metal; custom machinery
HQ: Titanium Fabrication Corp
110 Lehigh Dr
Fairfield NJ 07004
973 227-5300

(G-6121)
CRAFT REPAIR INCORPORATED
550 Rotary St (23661-1321)
PHONE.............................757 838-0721
Wayne J Schrum, *President*
Michelle S Kelly, *Corp Secy*
EMP: 10
SQ FT: 16,000
SALES (est): 1.5MM **Privately Held**
WEB: www.craftrepair.com
SIC: 3599 5013 1799 Machine shop, jobbing & repair; wheels, motor vehicle; welding on site

(G-6122)
CROCHET BY GRAMMY
502 Marshall St (23669-3139)
PHONE.............................757 637-8416
Bobbie Shikle, *Principal*
EMP: 2
SALES (est): 83.2K **Privately Held**
SIC: 2399 Hand woven & crocheted products

(G-6123)
CROSSTOWN PAINT
125 Claremont Ave (23661-2705)
PHONE.............................757 817-7119
Angelique Bottomley, *Owner*
EMP: 2
SALES (est): 50K **Privately Held**
SIC: 2752 Commercial printing, lithographic

(G-6124)
CRYOSEL LLC
224 Salters Creek Rd (23661-1909)
PHONE.............................757 778-1854
Alex Martinez,
EMP: 2
SALES (est): 88.9K **Privately Held**
SIC: 3443 Cryogenic tanks, for liquids & gases

(G-6125)
CURRY INDUSTRIES LLC
1707 Neptune Dr (23669-3675)
PHONE.............................757 251-7559
Almondo Curry, *Principal*
EMP: 2
SALES (est): 87.6K **Privately Held**
SIC: 3999 Manufacturing industries

(G-6126)
CUSTOM KRAFT INC
213 Salters Creek Rd (23661-1908)
PHONE.............................757 265-2882
J P Williams Jr, *President*
James P Williams III, *Vice Pres*
Pauline Williams, *Treasurer*
EMP: 12
SQ FT: 10,000
SALES (est): 650K **Privately Held**
WEB: www.customkraftva.com
SIC: 2434 Wood kitchen cabinets

(G-6127)
DANDY POINT INDUSTRIES
326 Dandy Point Rd (23664-2121)
PHONE.............................757 851-3280
Noel D McCully, *Owner*
Florance J Mc Cully, *Co-Owner*
EMP: 2
SALES (est): 200K **Privately Held**
SIC: 3069 Brushes, rubber

(G-6128)
DFI SYSTEMS INC
2513 58th St (23661-1211)
PHONE.............................757 262-1057
James W Gravely, *Ch of Bd*
Marcus J Gravely, *President*
Robert J Sampere, *Vice Pres*
Mark A Wright, *Vice Pres*
Charley Freeman, *Manager*
EMP: 58
SQ FT: 138,000
SALES (est): 15.5MM **Privately Held**
WEB: www.dfisystems.com
SIC: 2452 Modular homes, prefabricated, wood

(G-6129)
DIVERSITY GRPHICS SLUTIONS LLC
1 Bounty Cir (23669-1371)
PHONE.............................757 812-3311
Katy Hanson,
Ellen Sorrel,
EMP: 6 EST: 2011
SALES (est): 385.3K **Privately Held**
SIC: 2759 Commercial printing

(G-6130)
DLBA ROBOTICS LTD
506 Industry Dr (23661-1315)
PHONE.............................757 288-0206
Doug Blount, *President*
Shirley Blount, *Vice Pres*
William Blount, *Vice Pres*
David Hoffman, *Treasurer*
Raul Flores, *Admin Sec*
EMP: 20
SQ FT: 30,000
SALES (est): 2.3MM **Privately Held**
WEB: www.dlbarobotics.com
SIC: 3543 Industrial patterns

(G-6131)
DOVE WELDING AND FABRICATION
2353 52nd St (23661-1334)
PHONE.............................757 262-0996
Randy Dove, *CEO*
David Chambers, *Vice Pres*
EMP: 11
SQ FT: 10,000
SALES (est): 2MM **Privately Held**
SIC: 3441 Fabricated structural metal

▲ = Import ▼=Export
◆ =Import/Export

(G-6132)
DOYLE SAILMAKERS VIRGINIA
4111 Kecoughtan Rd (23669-4536)
PHONE................................757 727-0750
EMP: 1
SALES (est): 54.7K **Privately Held**
SIC: 2394 Sails: made from purchased materials

(G-6133)
DR OZZ DAT DRIP BBQ SAUCE LLC
1585 Briarfield Rd # 112 (23666-4833)
PHONE................................757 597-4405
Ozzie Wilson,
EMP: 1
SALES (est): 39.5K **Privately Held**
SIC: 2099 Sauces: dry mixes

(G-6134)
DREAMBUILDERS USA LLC
603 Marcella Rd Apt 5 (23666-6412)
PHONE................................908 265-2621
Sanchez Blaise,
EMP: 2
SALES (est): 200K **Privately Held**
SIC: 2759 Screen printing

(G-6135)
EDWARD ALLEN PUBLISHING LLC
73 Terri Sue Ct (23666-8209)
PHONE................................757 768-5544
James S Price, *Administration*
EMP: 2 EST: 2012
SALES (est): 111.9K **Privately Held**
WEB: www.edwardallenpublishing.com
SIC: 2741 Miscellaneous publishing

(G-6136)
ELEKON INDUSTRIES USA INC
1000 Lucas Way (23666-1573)
PHONE................................757 766-1500
Thomas Dietiker, *President*
Wilma Dietiker, *Vice Pres*
EMP: 30
SQ FT: 8,000
SALES (est): 2.6MM
SALES (corp-wide): 13.3B **Privately Held**
SIC: 3577 5065 Optical scanning devices; electronic parts & equipment
HQ: Measurement Specialties, Inc.
1000 Lucas Way
Hampton VA 23666
757 766-1500

(G-6137)
ELEVEN ELEVEN CANDLES MORE LLC
4 Clydesdale Ct (23666-5329)
PHONE................................757 766-0687
Robin Friend, *Principal*
EMP: 1
SALES (est): 39.6K **Privately Held**
SIC: 3999 Candles

(G-6138)
ELIZABETH BALLARD-SPITZER
Also Called: Thread Connections
165 Wilderness Rd (23669-1441)
PHONE................................757 723-1194
Elizabeth Ballard-Spitzer, *Principal*
EMP: 1
SQ FT: 1,000
SALES (est): 50K **Privately Held**
WEB: www.threadconnections.net
SIC: 2395 Embroidery products, except schiffli machine; embroidery & art needlework

(G-6139)
EMEZRO LLC
203 Clay St (23663-2250)
PHONE................................757 327-2318
Ayeiza Perez Agosto,
EMP: 1
SALES (est): 50K **Privately Held**
SIC: 1389 Construction, repair & dismantling services

(G-6140)
EMPIRE INCORPORATED (PA)
615 N Back River Rd (23669-3335)
P.O. Box 216 (23669-0216)
PHONE................................757 723-6747

Oscar W Ward Jr, *President*
Bill Duke, *Vice Pres*
Kathleen Ward, *Vice Pres*
Cathrine E Ward, *Treasurer*
Oscar Ward III, *Admin Sec*
EMP: 20
SQ FT: 6,500
SALES (est): 1.7MM **Privately Held**
SIC: 3272 3271 Pipe, concrete or lined with concrete; blocks, concrete or cinder: standard

(G-6141)
ENTAN DEVICES LLC
1000 Lucas Way (23666-1573)
PHONE................................757 766-1500
Frank Guidone, *President*
EMP: 2
SALES (est): 194.8K
SALES (corp-wide): 13.3B **Privately Held**
SIC: 3829 Measuring & controlling devices
HQ: Measurement Specialties, Inc.
1000 Lucas Way
Hampton VA 23666
757 766-1500

(G-6142)
ENTERPRISE SIGNS & SVC
86 Tide Mill Ln (23666-2712)
PHONE................................757 338-0027
Richard Collins, *Principal*
EMP: 1
SALES (est): 83.3K **Privately Held**
SIC: 3993 Signs & advertising specialties

(G-6143)
EPIC
2520 58th St (23661-1228)
PHONE................................757 896-8464
Julie Palmer, *Principal*
Elyse Edge, *Project Mgr*
Jessie Hamilton, *Project Mgr*
Lauren Koehler, *Project Mgr*
Chris Langlie, *Project Mgr*
EMP: 1
SALES (est): 63.8K **Privately Held**
WEB: www.epic.com
SIC: 3944 Cars, play (children's vehicles)

(G-6144)
ERBOSOL PRINTING
17 Briarwood Dr (23666-4711)
PHONE................................757 325-9986
Eric Solomon, *President*
EMP: 2
SALES (est): 35K **Privately Held**
SIC: 2752 2396 7389 Commercial printing, lithographic; screen printing on fabric articles; embroidering of advertising on shirts, etc.

(G-6145)
ERN GRAPHIC DESIGN
203 Brooke Dr (23669-4627)
PHONE................................757 281-8801
Ernesto Santiago, *Owner*
EMP: 2
SALES (est): 75.6K **Privately Held**
SIC: 2791 7389 Typesetting, computer controlled;

(G-6146)
FAITH FIRST PRINTING LLC
5 Allison Sutton Dr (23669-4672)
PHONE................................757 723-7673
Tony Tootle, *Principal*
EMP: 2
SALES (est): 185.2K **Privately Held**
SIC: 2752 Commercial printing, offset

(G-6147)
FBGC JV LLC
135 Kings Way (23669-3500)
PHONE................................757 727-9442
Rayquan Miles,
EMP: 1
SALES (est): 72.1K **Privately Held**
SIC: 1389 Construction, repair & dismantling services

(G-6148)
FGP SENSORS INC
1000 Lucas Way (23666-1573)
PHONE................................757 766-1500
Don Fujihiara, *President*
EMP: 6

SALES (est): 510.2K **Privately Held**
WEB: www.te.com
SIC: 3829 Measuring & controlling devices

(G-6149)
FINISH LINE SHTMTAL & FBRICTNS
600 Copeland Dr (23661-1309)
PHONE................................757 262-1122
W Steven Causey, *Administration*
EMP: 2
SALES (est): 139.3K **Privately Held**
WEB: www.finishlinesheetmetal.com
SIC: 3499 Fabricated metal products

(G-6150)
FIRE SYSTEMS SERVICES INC
110 Coliseum Xing (23666-5971)
PHONE................................757 825-6379
Danny Lee Stox, *President*
Rian Keefe, *Vice Pres*
Jodi Gwalcney, *Manager*
EMP: 9
SALES (est): 750K **Privately Held**
SIC: 3569 Firefighting apparatus & related equipment

(G-6151)
FIXHER UPPER LLC
145 Lasalle Ave (23661-3541)
PHONE................................804 539-8816
EMP: 3
SALES (est): 175.7K **Privately Held**
SIC: 3131 Footwear cut stock

(G-6152)
FRANKLIN MACHINE SHOP
530 Aberdeen Rd Ste A (23661-1344)
PHONE................................757 241-6744
Jason Franklin, *President*
EMP: 3 EST: 2013
SALES (est): 406K **Privately Held**
WEB: www.franklinmachineshop.com
SIC: 3312 Tool & die steel

(G-6153)
FREDERICKS AIRCRAFT COMPANY (PA)
1100 Exploration Way (23666-6264)
PHONE................................757 727-3326
William Fredericks, *CEO*
EMP: 1 EST: 2015
SQ FT: 100
SALES (est): 499K **Privately Held**
WEB: www.advancedaircraftcompany.com
SIC: 3721 Motorized aircraft

(G-6154)
GARVEY PRCISION COMPONENTS LLC
2102 48th St (23661-1202)
PHONE................................757 310-6028
Lawerence Schwoeri, *CEO*
EMP: 42
SALES (est): 1.6MM **Privately Held**
SIC: 3599 Machine shop, jobbing & repair

(G-6155)
GARVEY PRECISION MACHINE INC
2102 48th St (23661-1202)
PHONE................................757 490-0498
Joseph Corr, *CEO*
John Ryan, *Vice Pres*
Janet Corr, *Admin Sec*
EMP: 22
SQ FT: 25,000
SALES (est): 3MM **Privately Held**
SIC: 3599 3593 Machine shop, jobbing & repair; fluid power cylinders & actuators

(G-6156)
GATELY JOHN
1 Sugarberry Run (23669-1073)
PHONE................................757 851-3085
John Gately, *Principal*
EMP: 2
SALES (est): 73.1K **Privately Held**
WEB: www.marketingmaverick.com
SIC: 2721 Periodicals

(G-6157)
GENERAL CIGAR CO INC
2105 Aluminum Ave (23661-1224)
PHONE................................757 825-7750

David Fleenor, *Branch Mgr*
EMP: 20
SALES (corp-wide): 1B **Privately Held**
SIC: 2121 Cigars
HQ: General Cigar Co., Inc.
10900 Nuckols Rd Ste 100
Glen Allen VA 23060

(G-6158)
GENESIS BOAT WORKS INC
8 Blackwater Ln (23669-1557)
PHONE................................757 869-0345
EMP: 1 EST: 2009
SALES (est): 6K **Privately Held**
WEB: www.genesisboatworks.com
SIC: 3732 Boat building & repairing

(G-6159)
GIVING LIGHT INC
15 Stephanies Rd (23666-2896)
PHONE................................757 236-2405
Carolyn McRae, *Principal*
EMP: 2
SALES (est): 164.9K **Privately Held**
WEB: www.givinglight.org
SIC: 3648 Lighting equipment

(G-6160)
GRAHAM AND ROLLINS INC
Also Called: Hampton Seafood Market
509 Bassette St (23669-3010)
PHONE................................757 755-1021
EMP: 23
SALES (corp-wide): 5MM **Privately Held**
WEB: www.grahamandrollins.com
SIC: 2091 Crabmeat: packaged in cans, jars, etc.
PA: Graham And Rollins, Incorporated
19 Rudd Ln
Hampton VA
757 723-3831

(G-6161)
GREEKS UNLIMITED
428 Greenbriar Ave (23661-2518)
PHONE................................804 368-1611
EMP: 4
SALES (est): 165.6K **Privately Held**
SIC: 2396 Mfg Auto/Apparel Trimming

(G-6162)
HAMPTON CANVAS AND RIGGING
Also Called: Quantum
4111 Kecoughtan Rd (23669-4536)
PHONE................................757 727-0750
James Miller, *President*
EMP: 3
SQ FT: 2,550
SALES (est): 212.6K **Privately Held**
SIC: 2394 Sails: made from purchased materials

(G-6163)
HAMPTON ROADS COMPONENT ASSEMB
58 Rotherham Ln (23666-1472)
PHONE................................757 236-8627
Katreen Elder, *President*
EMP: 1
SALES (est): 63.4K **Privately Held**
SIC: 3549 7389 Assembly machines, including robotic;

(G-6164)
HAMPTON UNIVERSITY
Also Called: Hampton Script
203 Stone Manor (23668-0001)
P.O. Box 6237
PHONE................................757 727-5385
Judith Malvaux, *Manager*
EMP: 1
SALES (corp-wide): 115.8MM **Privately Held**
WEB: www.hamptonu.edu
SIC: 2711 8221 Newspapers: publishing only, not printed on site; university
PA: Hampton University
200 William R Harvey Way
Hampton VA 23669
757 727-5000

GEOGRAPHIC

(G-6165)
HIBBARD IRON WORKS OF HAMPTON
Also Called: Hibbard's Iron Works
514 Aberdeen Rd (23661-1325)
PHONE................................757 826-5611
Clay Strader, *President*
Carol Strader, *Corp Secy*
EMP: 10 **EST:** 1958
SQ FT: 10,000
SALES (est): 1.2MM **Privately Held**
SIC: 3799 3792 Trailers & trailer equipment; trailer hitches; travel trailers & campers

(G-6166)
HIDEMAND SUPPLEMENTS LLC
299 Floyd Thompson Blvd (23666-6267)
PHONE................................757 224-3485
Kimber Johnson,
EMP: 1
SALES (est): 100K **Privately Held**
SIC: 2023 Dietary supplements, dairy & non-dairy based

(G-6167)
HILL BRENTON
Also Called: Tre 7 Entertainments
37 Kenilworth Dr (23666-1814)
PHONE................................757 560-9332
Brenton Hill, *Principal*
EMP: 4
SALES (est): 185.6K **Privately Held**
SIC: 3651 1731 7359 7389 Sound reproducing equipment; speaker systems; sound equipment specialization; sound & lighting equipment rental; ; entertainment service

(G-6168)
HOWMET CASTINGS & SERVICES INC
Also Called: Alcoa Howmet, Hampton
1 Howmet Dr (23661-1333)
P.O. Box 9365 (23670-0365)
PHONE................................757 838-4680
Greg Pfeifer, *Counsel*
Clarence McCaskill, *Transportation*
Heath Huczel, *Opers Staff*
Gil Fryer, *Mfg Staff*
Janet Moskal, *Buyer*
EMP: 400 **Publicly Held**
WEB: www.alcoa.com
SIC: 3324 Commercial investment castings, ferrous
HQ: Howmet Castings & Services, Inc.
    1616 Harvard Ave
    Newburgh Heights OH 44105
    216 641-4400

(G-6169)
HOWMET CORPORATION
1 Howmet Dr (23661-1381)
P.O. Box 9365 (23670-0365)
PHONE................................757 838-4680
Gary Baldwin, *Manager*
EMP: 158 **Publicly Held**
WEB: www.theplayhouseatwhitelake.org
SIC: 3324 Commercial investment castings, ferrous
HQ: Howmet Corporation
    1 Misco Dr
    Whitehall MI 49461
    231 894-5686

(G-6170)
HST GLOBAL INC
150 Research Dr (23666-1339)
PHONE................................757 766-6100
Ronald R Howell, *Ch of Bd*
EMP: 1
SALES (est): 121.5K **Privately Held**
WEB: www.hstglobal.com
SIC: 2834 Pharmaceutical preparations

(G-6171)
HUNTINGTON INGALLS INC
100 E St (23661-1207)
PHONE................................757 380-4982
Mike Petters, *Branch Mgr*
EMP: 3984 **Publicly Held**
WEB: www.huntingtoningalls.com
SIC: 3731 Shipbuilding & repairing

HQ: Huntington Ingalls Incorporated
    4101 Washington Ave
    Newport News VA 23607
    757 380-2000

(G-6172)
HUNTINGTON INGALLS INDS INC
2175 Aluminum Ave (23661-1224)
PHONE................................757 380-2000
EMP: 13 **Publicly Held**
WEB: www.huntingtoningalls.com
SIC: 3731 Military ships, building & repairing
PA: Huntington Ingalls Industries, Inc.
    4101 Washington Ave
    Newport News VA 23607

(G-6173)
HY-MARK CYLINDERS INC
530 Aberdeen Rd Ste C (23661-1344)
PHONE................................757 251-6744
Wayne Franklin, *President*
Sergio Cosio, *Vice Pres*
EMP: 33 **EST:** 2000
SALES (est): 5.2MM **Privately Held**
WEB: www.catalinacylinders.com
SIC: 3354 3841 3443 Aluminum extruded products; surgical & medical instruments; fabricated plate work (boiler shop)

(G-6174)
I LOVE ART BOUTIQUE LLC
110 Coliseum Xing # 6092 (23666-5971)
PHONE................................757 204-1260
Kiawana Newell,
EMP: 1
SALES (est): 40.9K **Privately Held**
SIC: 2394 Canvas & related products

(G-6175)
INEVITABLE ENTERTAINMENT LLC
221 Bryson Cir (23666-4353)
PHONE................................757 470-1521
Vern Watkins,
EMP: 1
SALES (est): 33.3K **Privately Held**
SIC: 2731 Book publishing

(G-6176)
INTERLOCK PAVING SYSTEMS INC
802 W Pembroke Ave (23669-3327)
P.O. Box 486 (23669-0486)
PHONE................................757 722-2591
Thomas Hunnicutt III, *President*
Ann N Hunnicutt, *Vice Pres*
Jim Hassell, *VP Sales*
EMP: 8
SQ FT: 3,000
SALES (est): 600K **Privately Held**
WEB: www.interlockpavingsystems.com
SIC: 3281 Paving blocks, cut stone

(G-6177)
JACK CLAMP SALES CO INC
4116 W Mercury Blvd (23666-3248)
PHONE................................757 827-6704
Dois I Rosser Jr, *President*
Steve Adams, *Vice Pres*
EMP: 3
SALES (est): 200.3K **Privately Held**
SIC: 3429 Marine hardware

(G-6178)
KAROLINA DE LOS SANTOS
Also Called: Amor De Beauty
339 Kinsmen Way (23666-3676)
PHONE................................757 597-4315
Karolina De Los Santos, *Owner*
EMP: 1
SALES (est): 20K **Privately Held**
SIC: 3999 Hair & hair-based products

(G-6179)
KASINOF & ASSOCIATES
Also Called: National Optometry
2040 Coliseum Dr Ste 33 (23666-3200)
PHONE................................757 827-6530
Gwen Smith, *Manager*
EMP: 4

SALES (corp-wide): 1.8MM **Privately Held**
WEB: www.myeyedr.com
SIC: 3851 Eyeglasses, lenses & frames
PA: Kasinof & Associates
    17301 Valley Mall Rd # 106
    Hagerstown MD

(G-6180)
KISS KROWN LLC
102 Doolittle Rd (23669-2648)
PHONE................................757 776-6518
Telisha Banks, *CEO*
EMP: 2
SALES (est): 111.7K **Privately Held**
SIC: 2399 Hand woven & crocheted products

(G-6181)
KOBAYASHI WINERY
660 Pennsylvania Ave (23661-2349)
PHONE................................757 644-4464
EMP: 15
SALES (est): 950K **Privately Held**
SIC: 2082 Mfg Malt Beverages

(G-6182)
L C PEMBROKE MANUFACTURING
756 N First St (23664-1504)
PHONE................................757 723-3435
M P Lowe, *Administration*
EMP: 2
SALES (est): 83.6K **Privately Held**
SIC: 3999 Manufacturing industries

(G-6183)
LIFAC INC
505 Howmet Dr (23661-1310)
PHONE................................757 826-6051
Bruce Snyder, *Manager*
EMP: 10
SALES (est): 688K **Privately Held**
SIC: 3731 Military ships, building & repairing

(G-6184)
LIL GUY PRINTING
7 Camellia Ln (23663-1198)
PHONE................................757 995-5705
Justin Vias, *Principal*
EMP: 2
SALES (est): 83.9K **Privately Held**
SIC: 2752 Commercial printing, lithographic

(G-6185)
LOCKHEED MARTIN CORPORATION
22 Enterprise Pkwy # 120 (23666-5844)
PHONE................................757 896-4860
Jay Sledge, *Branch Mgr*
EMP: 1018 **Publicly Held**
WEB: www.lockheedmartin.com
SIC: 3812 Search & navigation equipment
PA: Lockheed Martin Corporation
    6801 Rockledge Dr
    Bethesda MD 20817

(G-6186)
LRJ PUBLISHING GROUP LLC
Also Called: Daydream Writing
2104 Newton Rd (23663-1023)
PHONE................................757 788-6163
Latoya Debardelaben, *CEO*
Latoya A Debardelaben, *Administration*
EMP: 1
SALES (est): 52.3K **Privately Held**
SIC: 2731 Book publishing

(G-6187)
MACHINE & FABG SPECIALISTS INC
Also Called: G&R Metals
810 Kiwanis St (23661-1737)
PHONE................................757 244-5693
Jay Mayo, *President*
Sarah Bruce, *Vice Pres*
EMP: 43
SQ FT: 24,500
SALES (est): 6.4MM **Privately Held**
WEB: www.gandrmetals.com
SIC: 7692 3441 3599 Welding repair; fabricated structural metal; machine shop, jobbing & repair

(G-6188)
MAIDA DEVELOPMENT COMPANY (PA)
201 S Mallory St (23663-1817)
P.O. Box 3529 (23663-0529)
PHONE................................757 723-0785
Edward T Maida, *President*
David Smith, *General Mgr*
Susan Maida, *Corp Secy*
Nancy M Hoffman, *Treasurer*
Cindy Bowens, *Human Res Mgr*
▲ **EMP:** 100 **EST:** 1947
SQ FT: 102,000
SALES (est): 13.3MM **Privately Held**
WEB: www.maida.com
SIC: 3559 Electronic component making machinery

(G-6189)
MAIDA DEVELOPMENT COMPANY
9 Williams St (23663-1822)
PHONE................................757 719-3038
Edward Maida, *Sales Mgr*
EMP: 50
SALES (corp-wide): 13.3MM **Privately Held**
WEB: www.maida.com
SIC: 3559 Electronic component making machinery
PA: Maida Development Company
    201 S Mallory St
    Hampton VA 23663
    757 723-0785

(G-6190)
MAKES SENSE TO ME SOFTWARE LLC
303 Gaines Mill Ln (23669-1427)
PHONE................................757 771-5289
Thomas Long, *Principal*
EMP: 2
SALES (est): 94.3K **Privately Held**
SIC: 7372 Prepackaged software

(G-6191)
MATRIC KOLOR
905 G St (23661-1752)
PHONE................................757 310-6764
EMP: 2 **EST:** 2009
SALES (est): 120K **Privately Held**
SIC: 2752 Lithographic Commercial Printing

(G-6192)
MAXX MATERIAL SYSTEMS LLC
315 E St (23661-1209)
PHONE................................757 637-4026
Mark Hogan,
EMP: 40
SQ FT: 44,000
SALES (est): 8.9MM
SALES (corp-wide): 843.2MM **Privately Held**
SIC: 3496 5084 3535 Conveyor belts; materials handling machinery; conveyors & conveying equipment
HQ: Duravant Llc
    3500 Lacey Rd Ste 290
    Downers Grove IL 60515

(G-6193)
MAZZELLA JHH COMPANY INC
Also Called: J Henry Holland
402 Aberdeen Rd (23661-1324)
PHONE................................757 827-9600
Larry Lusk, *Vice Pres*
EMP: 8 **Privately Held**
WEB: www.jhenryholland.com
SIC: 3496 Miscellaneous fabricated wire products
HQ: Mazzella Jhh Company, Inc.
    5931 Thurston Ave
    Virginia Beach VA 23455
    757 460-3300

(G-6194)
MEASUREMENT SPECIALTIES INC (HQ)
Also Called: Te Connectivity
1000 Lucas Way (23666-1573)
PHONE................................757 766-1500
Frank D Guidone, *President*
Devin Brock, *General Mgr*
Jolly MA, *General Mgr*

▲ = Import ▼=Export
◆ =Import/Export

Bob Kill, *Business Mgr*
Joe Gleeson, *COO*
◆ **EMP:** 150 **EST:** 1981
SALES (est): 549.2MM
SALES (corp-wide): 13.3B **Privately Held**
WEB: www.te.com
SIC: 3829 Photopitometers
PA: Te Connectivity Ltd.
　　Muhlenstrasse 26
　　Schaffhausen SH 8200
　　526 336-677

(G-6195)
MEISSNER CSTM KNIVES PENS LLC
205 Ian Ct (23666-1982)
PHONE.............................321 693-2392
Bryan Meissner,
EMP: 2
SALES (est): 124.6K **Privately Held**
SIC: 2499 3421 Carved & turned wood; cutlery

(G-6196)
METALS OF DISTINCTION INC
Also Called: Gilliam Welding
532 E Mercury Blvd (23663-2229)
PHONE.............................757 727-0773
Andre Gilliam, *President*
EMP: 8
SALES (est): 610K **Privately Held**
WEB: www.gilliamwelding.com
SIC: 7692 Welding repair

(G-6197)
MICHAEL REISS LLC
8 Templewood Dr (23666-1824)
PHONE.............................757 826-4277
Michael Reiss, *Principal*
EMP: 2
SALES (est): 118K **Privately Held**
SIC: 3931 Musical instruments

(G-6198)
MICHELLE ERICKSON POTTERY
18 N Mallory St (23663-1744)
PHONE.............................757 727-9139
Michelle M Erickson, *President*
EMP: 3
SALES (est): 200K **Privately Held**
WEB: www.michelleericksonceramics.com
SIC: 3269 5719 Art & ornamental ware, pottery; figures: pottery, china, earthenware & stoneware; pottery

(G-6199)
MICRONERGY LLC
1100 Exploration Way (23666-6264)
PHONE.............................757 325-6973
James Hubbard, *COO*
EMP: 4
SALES (est): 212.3K **Privately Held**
WEB: www.micronergy.com
SIC: 3674 Semiconductors & related devices

(G-6200)
MID ATLNTIC MTAL SOLUTIONS INC
502 Copeland Dr (23661-1345)
PHONE.............................757 827-1588
Derek Nowlin, *President*
Bob Nowlin, *Principal*
EMP: 8
SALES (est): 1MM **Privately Held**
WEB: www.midatlanticmetalsolutions.com
SIC: 3441 Fabricated structural metal

(G-6201)
MIGHTY MANN INC
406 Aberdeen Rd Ste B (23661-1348)
PHONE.............................757 945-8056
Robert Mann, *President*
EMP: 12
SALES (est): 907.8K **Privately Held**
SIC: 3537 Industrial trucks & tractors

(G-6202)
MISSING LYNK PUBLISHING LLC
621 Houston Ave (23669-1612)
PHONE.............................757 851-1766
Michael Wade Lynk,
EMP: 1

SALES (est): 66.7K **Privately Held**
SIC: 2731 Books: publishing only

(G-6203)
MOROSE BRAND LLC
110 Coliseum Xing 6054 (23666-5971)
PHONE.............................747 346-1550
Monica Rosario, *Mng Member*
EMP: 5
SALES (est): 203.2K **Privately Held**
SIC: 3161 Clothing & apparel carrying cases

(G-6204)
MOTHER TERESAS COTTAGE
112 N Sixth St (23664-1310)
PHONE.............................757 850-0350
Patricia Postlik, *Principal*
EMP: 2 **EST:** 2007
SALES (est): 80K **Privately Held**
SIC: 2339 Maternity clothing

(G-6205)
MOUNIR E SHAHEEN
Also Called: T Body Shirts
1962 E Pembroke Ave (23663-1326)
PHONE.............................757 723-4445
Mounir E Shaheen, *Owner*
EMP: 5 **EST:** 1980
SQ FT: 5,000
SALES (est): 160K **Privately Held**
WEB: www.tbodypromotions.com
SIC: 2395 2396 5199 Embroidery & art needlework; screen printing on fabric articles; advertising specialties

(G-6206)
NCG LLC
Also Called: Newport Cutter Grinding
302 Aberdeen Rd (23661-1716)
PHONE.............................757 838-3224
Jeff Duncan, *Mng Member*
EMP: 10 **EST:** 2001
SALES (est): 3.4MM **Privately Held**
WEB: www.ncgmfg.com
SIC: 3441 Fabricated structural metal

(G-6207)
NEWPORT CUTTER GRINDING CO INC
Also Called: N C G
302 Aberdeen Rd (23661-1716)
PHONE.............................757 838-3224
Jeff D Duncan, *President*
Gloria W Duncan, *Treasurer*
EMP: 10
SQ FT: 10,000
SALES (est): 1.5MM **Privately Held**
WEB: www.ncgmfg.com
SIC: 3549 3544 3599 Wiredrawing & fabricating machinery & equipment, ex. die; special dies, tools, jigs & fixtures; machine shop, jobbing & repair

(G-6208)
NOIR X JOJO LLC
136 Semple Farm Rd # 207 (23666-1886)
PHONE.............................757 756-9134
Whitney Harris,
EMP: 1
SALES (est): 150K **Privately Held**
SIC: 2339 Women's & misses' athletic clothing & sportswear

(G-6209)
NOKYEM NATURALS LLC
6 Mill Creek Ter (23663-1820)
PHONE.............................757 218-1794
EMP: 2
SALES (est): 91.7K **Privately Held**
WEB: www.nokyem.com
SIC: 2844 Toilet preparations

(G-6210)
NORTH SAILS HAMPTON INC
Also Called: Performance Rigging
86 Algonquin Rd (23661-3454)
PHONE.............................757 723-6280
Ken Saylor, *President*
M Andria Saylor, *President*
EMP: 5
SQ FT: 3,000
SALES (est): 533.4K **Privately Held**
SIC: 2394 7699 Sails: made from purchased materials; nautical repair services

(G-6211)
NORTHROP GRUMMAN CORPORATION
21 Enterprise Pkwy # 210 (23666-6413)
PHONE.............................757 838-7221
Richard Phillips, *Branch Mgr*
EMP: 735 **Publicly Held**
WEB: www.northropgrumman.com
SIC: 3812 Aircraft/aerospace flight instruments & guidance systems
PA: Northrop Grumman Corporation
　　2980 Fairview Park Dr
　　Falls Church VA 22042

(G-6212)
PALACE INTERIORS
15 N Mallory St (23663-1743)
PHONE.............................757 592-1509
Karyn Thomason, *Owner*
EMP: 1
SALES (est): 10K **Privately Held**
SIC: 2531 Public building & related furniture

(G-6213)
PARKWAY MANUFACTURING COMPANY
707 Industry Dr (23661-1002)
PHONE.............................757 896-9712
Walter Schultz, *President*
Barbara Mastj, *Vice Pres*
Barbara Schultz, *Treasurer*
EMP: 18
SALES (est): 3MM **Privately Held**
WEB: www.parkwaymfg.com
SIC: 3441 Fabricated structural metal

(G-6214)
PEEBLES WELDING & FABRICATION
738 Plum Ave (23661-1739)
PHONE.............................757 880-5332
EMP: 2
SALES (est): 86.6K **Privately Held**
WEB:
www.peeblesweldingandfabrication.com
SIC: 3441 Fabricated structural metal

(G-6215)
PETERS MELVIN CABINET SHOP INC
416 Rotary St (23661-1319)
PHONE.............................757 826-7317
Darrell Harrah, *President*
Donna Harrah, *President*
EMP: 5 **EST:** 1955
SQ FT: 5,000
SALES (est): 472K **Privately Held**
SIC: 2434 Wood kitchen cabinets

(G-6216)
PG GAMES PUBLISHING LLC
3510 Matoaka Rd (23661-1645)
PHONE.............................870 637-4380
Pierce Gaithe, *Principal*
EMP: 2
SALES (est): 59.2K **Privately Held**
SIC: 2741 Miscellaneous publishing

(G-6217)
PRECISION SHTMTL FBRCATION LLC
211 Challenger Way (23666-1369)
PHONE.............................757 865-2508
Gregory Simmons,
EMP: 2
SQ FT: 7,800
SALES (est): 312.9K **Privately Held**
WEB: www.precision-sheet-metal.net
SIC: 3444 Sheet metal specialties, not stamped

(G-6218)
PREMO WELDING
Also Called: Primo Welding
1421 Todds Ln (23666-2944)
PHONE.............................757 880-6951
Marvin Degutis, *Owner*
EMP: 1
SALES (est): 74.7K **Privately Held**
SIC: 7692 1799 Welding repair; welding on site

(G-6219)
PRESSURE SYSTEMS INC
Also Called: P S I
1000 Lucas Way (23666-1573)
PHONE.............................757 766-4464
Richard Brad Lawrence, *CEO*
Steve Yakshe, *President*
Rich La Rose, *Purchasing*
EMP: 116
SQ FT: 24,000
SALES (est): 15.2MM
SALES (corp-wide): 13.3B **Privately Held**
WEB: www.te.com
SIC: 3829 3823 Measuring & controlling devices; pressure measurement instruments, industrial
HQ: Measurement Specialties, Inc.
　　1000 Lucas Way
　　Hampton VA 23666
　　757 766-1500

(G-6220)
PRESTIGE PRESS INC
610 Rotary St (23661-1396)
PHONE.............................757 826-5881
Marvin J Malish, *President*
Amber Malish Jones, *Vice Pres*
Michael Sconyers, *Accounts Exec*
EMP: 25 **EST:** 1955
SQ FT: 2,000
SALES (est): 3.7MM **Privately Held**
WEB: www.prestigepress.com
SIC: 2752 2791 2789 2759 Commercial printing, offset; typesetting; bookbinding & related work; commercial printing

(G-6221)
PRICE GOLDSMITH CO
47 E Queens Way Ste 202 (23669-4092)
PHONE.............................757 722-3210
Jim Dreisigacker, *COO*
EMP: 1
SALES (est): 46.1K **Privately Held**
WEB: www.dreisigacker.com
SIC: 3911 Jewelry, precious metal

(G-6222)
PRO-TEK INC
4410 Claiborne Sq E # 400 (23666-2071)
PHONE.............................757 813-9820
Seung Kim, *President*
EMP: 1
SALES (est): 60.7K **Privately Held**
SIC: 2541 Wood partitions & fixtures

(G-6223)
PROTON SYSTEMS LLC (PA)
35 Research Dr (23666-1324)
PHONE.............................757 224-5685
Shawn Lednick, *President*
EMP: 1 **EST:** 2013
SQ FT: 10,000
SALES (est): 292.9K **Privately Held**
WEB: www.protonsystems.com
SIC: 3599 Machine & other job shop work; custom machinery; machine shop, jobbing & repair

(G-6224)
QUALITY MACHINE SHOP
336 Rip Rap Rd (23669-3031)
PHONE.............................757 722-6077
Rommie L Head Jr, *President*
EMP: 3 **EST:** 1971
SQ FT: 2,000
SALES (est): 160K **Privately Held**
WEB: www.qualitymachineshop.com
SIC: 3599 Machine shop, jobbing & repair

(G-6225)
RAYTHEON TECHNOLOGIES CORP
2101 Executive Dr Ste 610 (23666-3092)
PHONE.............................757 838-7980
Timothy Forsythe, *Branch Mgr*
EMP: 4
SALES (corp-wide): 77B **Publicly Held**
WEB: www.rtx.com
SIC: 3721 Helicopters
PA: Raytheon Technologies Corporation
　　870 Winter St
　　Waltham MA 02451
　　781 522-3000

GEOGRAPHIC

(G-6226)
RED MOON PARTNERS LLC
Also Called: International Replica Arms Co
34 Research Dr Ste 300 (23666-1325)
PHONE........................757 240-4305
James Crawford, *President*
EMP: 6
SALES (est): 316.4K Privately Held
WEB: www.threattec.com
SIC: 3489 Depth charge release pistols &
projectors, over 30 mm.

(G-6227)
RENTURY SOLUTIONS LLC
216 N First St (23664-1402)
PHONE........................757 453-5763
Elias Oxendine IV, *COO*
William Randolph,
EMP: 2
SALES (est): 57K Privately Held
SIC: 2741

(G-6228)
RIGGINS COMPANY LLC
410 Rotary St (23661-1375)
PHONE........................757 826-0525
Dustin Brown, *Plant Mgr*
Ben Butler, *Project Mgr*
Todd Strong, *Project Mgr*
Andrea Jordan, *Purchasing*
Kelly Topp, *Engrg Mgr*
EMP: 70
SQ FT: 21,500
SALES (est): 20.1MM Privately Held
WEB: www.rigginscompany.com
SIC: 3443 1711 1791 3498 Fabricated
plate work (boiler shop); mechanical con-
tractor; structural steel erection; mani-
folds, pipe: fabricated from purchased
pipe

(G-6229)
**ROAD RNNER MBL WLDG
FBRCTION L**
Also Called: Roadrnner MBL Wldg Fabrica-
tion
506 Copeland Dr Ste C (23661-1343)
PHONE........................757 915-2077
Loren A Mangubat, *Principal*
EMP: 2 EST: 2018
SALES (est): 212.8K Privately Held
WEB: www.roadrunnerwelds.com
SIC: 7692 Welding repair

(G-6230)
ROBERT FURR CABINET SHOP
2542 W Pembroke Ave (23661-1710)
PHONE........................757 244-1267
Robert N Furr, *Owner*
EMP: 5
SQ FT: 6,000
SALES (est): 240K Privately Held
WEB: www.robertfurrcabinets.com
SIC: 2434 2541 2517 Wood kitchen cabi-
nets; wood partitions & fixtures; wood tel-
evision & radio cabinets

(G-6231)
S&R TRANSPORT LLC
9 Pelican Shores Dr (23666-5232)
PHONE........................757 344-0251
Shawn Banks,
EMP: 4
SALES (est): 101K Privately Held
SIC: 3537 Trucks, tractors, loaders, carri-
ers & similar equipment

(G-6232)
SENTINEL SELF-DEFENSE LLC
670 Downey Green St # 410 (23666-2283)
PHONE........................757 234-2501
Sean Spofford,
EMP: 3 EST: 2017
SALES (est): 145.3K Privately Held
SIC: 3812 Defense systems & equipment

(G-6233)
SHANTANU TANK
9 Henrys Fork Dr (23666-1587)
PHONE........................757 766-3829
EMP: 3
SALES (est): 168.3K Privately Held
SIC: 3443 Industrial vessels, tanks & con-
tainers

(G-6234)
SIEMENS INDUSTRY INC
103 Research Dr (23666-1340)
PHONE........................757 766-4190
Urusla Pickert, *Principal*
EMP: 3
SALES (corp-wide): 67.4B Privately Held
WEB: www.new.siemens.com
SIC: 3511 Turbines & turbine generator
sets
HQ: Siemens Industry, Inc.
1000 Deerfield Pkwy
Buffalo Grove IL 60089
847 215-1000

(G-6235)
SIGN WITH ME VA
81 Madison Chase (23666-6119)
PHONE........................757 969-9876
Diann Shorter, *Principal*
EMP: 1
SALES (est): 50.5K Privately Held
WEB: www.signwithmeva.com
SIC: 3993 Signs & advertising specialties

(G-6236)
**SIGNATURE CANVASMAKERS
LLC**
102 N Hope St (23663-1749)
PHONE........................757 788-8890
Charlene Clark, *Mng Member*
Chandler Clark,
EMP: 3
SQ FT: 2,000
SALES (est): 125K Privately Held
WEB: www.signaturecanvasmakers.com
SIC: 2394 Canvas awnings & canopies;
canvas boat seats

(G-6237)
SIGNMEDIA INC
2109 Mingee Dr (23661-1031)
PHONE........................757 826-7128
Mike Burnett, *President*
Jeff Green, *President*
Jonny Cassells, *Sales Staff*
EMP: 34 EST: 1967
SQ FT: 12,000
SALES (est): 1MM Privately Held
WEB: www.signmediainc.com
SIC: 3993 7389 Electric signs; neon signs;
interior design services

(G-6238)
**SIMPLY PANACHE PRODUCTS
LLC**
100 Glica Ct (23666-5699)
PHONE........................757 358-7062
Lakesha Brown-Renfro,
Nzinga Teule-Hekima,
Tanecia Willis,
EMP: 4
SALES (est): 347.1K Privately Held
WEB: www.amangoparty.com
SIC: 2033 7389 Jams, jellies & preserves:
packaged in cans, jars, etc.;

(G-6239)
**SKF LBRICATION SYSTEMS USA
INC**
Also Called: SKF Lubrication Solutions
2115 Aluminum Ave (23661-1224)
PHONE........................757 951-0370
Matti Lopponen, *President*
Mack Owens, *Facilities Mgr*
Debra Blair, *QC Mgr*
Robert Fort, *Sales Staff*
Billy Coleman, *Supervisor*
▲ EMP: 64
SQ FT: 50,000
SALES (est): 19.8MM
SALES (corp-wide): 8.9B Privately Held
WEB: www.skf.com
SIC: 3714 5084 3569 3561 Lubrication
systems & parts, motor vehicle; industrial
machinery & equipment; lubricating
equipment; pumps & pumping equipment
HQ: Skf Usa Inc.
890 Forty Foot Rd
Lansdale PA 19446
267 436-6000

(G-6240)
SOAPLIGHT LLC
110 Coliseum Xing 5130 (23666-5971)
PHONE........................518 898-3441
Arndrel Chatmon,
EMP: 1
SALES (est): 47.2K Privately Held
SIC: 2841 Soap & other detergents

(G-6241)
SORBILITE INC
1 Reflection Ln (23666-2386)
P.O. Box 7272 (23666-0272)
PHONE........................757 460-7330
Andrew Peter Pohl, *President*
Brigitte Pohl, *Treasurer*
EMP: 3
SQ FT: 5,000
SALES (est): 7.5MM Privately Held
WEB: www.sorbilite.com
SIC: 2542 Office & store showcases & dis-
play fixtures

(G-6242)
SPEEDY SIGN-A-RAMA USA INC
3303 W Mercury Blvd (23666-3806)
PHONE........................757 838-7446
Sam Lackey, *President*
Bonnie Lackey, *Vice Pres*
EMP: 3
SALES (est): 220K Privately Held
WEB: www.signarama.com
SIC: 3993 7532 7389 7331 Signs & ad-
vertising specialties; truck painting & let-
tering; mailbox rental & related service;
mailing service; corrugated & solid fiber
boxes; agents, shipping

(G-6243)
STAHMER INC
Also Called: Sign Central
3003 W Mercury Blvd (23666-3930)
PHONE........................757 838-4200
Dawn Stahmer, *President*
EMP: 1
SALES (est): 97K Privately Held
WEB: www.signcentral-va.com
SIC: 3993 Signs & advertising specialties

(G-6244)
STC CATALYSTS INC
21 Enterprise Pkwy # 150 (23666-6413)
PHONE........................757 766-5810
Chand Deepak, *President*
Adarsh Deepak, *Chairman*
Rink C Wood, *Vice Pres*
EMP: 5
SALES (est): 848K Privately Held
WEB: www.stcnet.com
SIC: 2819 Industrial inorganic chemicals

(G-6245)
SWAGG JUICES LLC
96 Tudor Ct (23669-2859)
PHONE........................757 254-6754
Ashlee Smith, *Mng Member*
EMP: 2
SALES (est): 62.3K Privately Held
SIC: 2037 Fruit juices

(G-6246)
SWEETBRIAR SCENTS LLC
106 Horsley Dr (23666-2272)
PHONE........................757 358-6815
Clinton Reese, *Principal*
EMP: 3
SALES (est): 177.9K Privately Held
SIC: 2844 Toilet preparations

(G-6247)
SWIFT MOBILE WELDING LLC
1315 Quash St (23669-2715)
PHONE........................757 367-9060
Daryl Swift,
EMP: 1
SALES (est): 40.2K Privately Held
SIC: 7692 Welding repair

(G-6248)
T-BODY PROMOTIONS LLC
1962 E Pembroke Ave (23663-1326)
PHONE........................757 723-4445
EMP: 2
SALES (est): 95.9K Privately Held
WEB: www.tbodypromotions.com
SIC: 2789 Bookbinding & related work

(G-6249)
TAYLOR MFG & DESIGN LLC
3425 Old Armistead Ave (23666-1691)
PHONE........................757 902-1820
Gregory C Taylor, *President*
Wendy Taylor, *Vice Pres*
EMP: 2
SALES (est): 81.4K Privately Held
SIC: 3599 Industrial machinery

(G-6250)
TELEDYNE INSTRUMENTS INC
Also Called: Teledyne Hastings Instruments
804 Newcombe Ave (23669-4539)
PHONE........................757 723-6531
Peggy Van Hook, *General Mgr*
Jeff Kudlock, *Opers Mgr*
Keith Parcetich, *Opers Staff*
Anthony D Williams, *VP Engrg*
Kevin Brewer, *QC Mgr*
EMP: 70
SALES (corp-wide): 3.1B Publicly Held
WEB: www.teledyne.com
SIC: 3823 3824 3545 Flow instruments,
industrial process type; fluid meters &
counting devices; machine tool acces-
sories
HQ: Teledyne Instruments, Inc.
1049 Camino Dos Rios
Thousand Oaks CA 91360
805 373-4545

(G-6251)
TEQUILLA BATTLE
Also Called: Tequila With Leroy Home Imprv
233 Lantana Ln B (23669-2567)
PHONE........................757 769-1595
Tequilla Battle, *Owner*
EMP: 1
SALES (est): 50K Privately Held
SIC: 1389 Construction, repair & disman-
tling services

(G-6252)
TERRY PLYMOUTH
Also Called: Plymtech Welding & Assembly
19 Ducette Dr (23666-2984)
PHONE........................757 838-2718
Terry Plymouth, *Owner*
EMP: 2
SALES (est): 105.4K Privately Held
SIC: 7692 Welding repair

(G-6253)
TROTTER JAMIL
Also Called: Mj-Squared
1025 W Pembroke Ave (23669-3811)
PHONE........................757 251-8754
Jamil Trotter, *Owner*
EMP: 1
SQ FT: 900
SALES (est): 51K Privately Held
SIC: 2024 2211 2656 5137 Ice cream &
frozen desserts; apparel & outerwear fab-
rics, cotton; frozen food & ice cream con-
tainers; apparel belts, women's &
children's; teenage apparel

(G-6254)
TUT & TITI LLC
215b Settlers Landing Rd (23669-3959)
PHONE........................757 761-1921
Cedric Middleton,
EMP: 4
SALES (est): 125.1K Privately Held
SIC: 3999 Hair & hair-based products

(G-6255)
TYPE FACTORY INC
615 Regional Dr Ste B (23661-1843)
PHONE........................757 826-6055
Paula Fuller, *President*
Donald Fuller, *Vice Pres*
Jennifer Brown, *Sales Mgr*
EMP: 5
SQ FT: 1,300
SALES (est): 300K Privately Held
SIC: 2791 7336 Typesetting; graphic arts
& related design

(G-6256)
UNIVERSITY PRIDE & PRESTIGE
126 Diggs Dr (23666-1729)
PHONE........................757 766-2590
Ray Erickson, *Owner*
EMP: 1

SALES (est): 74.3K **Privately Held**
SIC: 2261 Finishing plants, cotton

(G-6257)
UNMANNED AERIAL PROP SYSTMS
Also Called: Uaps
100 Exploration Way (23666-6266)
PHONE....................................757 325-6792
Maxwell Depiro, *President*
EMP: 2
SALES (est): 86K **Privately Held**
SIC: 3721 Aircraft

(G-6258)
VALENTINECHERRY CREATIONS
26 Brough Ln (23669-3200)
PHONE....................................757 848-6137
Priscilla Holmes, *Owner*
EMP: 1
SALES (est): 50.4K **Privately Held**
SIC: 3999 5999 Artificial trees & flowers; artificial flowers

(G-6259)
VALEO NORTH AMERICA INC
Also Called: Transmissions Dv
301 W Park Ln (23666-5035)
PHONE....................................757 827-0310
Bruce Clutton, *General Mgr*
Renato Barbi, *Business Mgr*
Allen Traylor, *Plant Mgr*
Steven Kidd, *Maint Spvr*
Pat Ingram, *Purch Mgr*
EMP: 165
SALES (corp-wide): 177.9K **Privately Held**
SIC: 3714 Radiators & radiator shells & cores, motor vehicle
HQ: Valeo North America, Inc.
150 Stephenson Hwy
Troy MI 48083

(G-6260)
VANGUARD BREWPUB & DISTILLERY
504 N King St (23669-3057)
PHONE....................................757 224-1807
EMP: 3
SALES (est): 68.6K **Privately Held**
WEB: www.thevanguard757.com
SIC: 2085 Distilled & blended liquors

(G-6261)
VIBE CANDLE CO LLC
2104 Pridgen Rd (23663-1030)
PHONE....................................757 589-3274
Kendra Johnson, *Mng Member*
EMP: 1
SALES (est): 5K **Privately Held**
SIC: 3999 Candles

(G-6262)
VICIOUS CREATIONS LLC
76 Tide Mill Ln (23666-2712)
PHONE....................................256 479-7689
Tara Cunningham, *CEO*
Duane Cunningham,
EMP: 4
SALES (est): 14.4K **Privately Held**
SIC: 3679 8243 7629 Electronic circuits; repair training, computer; circuit board repair

(G-6263)
VIRGINIA PRINTING SERVICES INC
Also Called: Sir Speedy
60 W Mercury Blvd (23669-2509)
PHONE....................................757 838-5500
Brad Brooks, *President*
Carol Darby, *Principal*
EMP: 12
SQ FT: 8,000
SALES (est): 1.7MM **Privately Held**
WEB: www.sirspeedy.com
SIC: 2752 7331 5199 5999 Commercial printing, lithographic; mailing service; advertising specialties; banners, flags, decals & posters

(G-6264)
VISION MACHINE AND FABRICATION
2100 Mingee Dr (23661-1032)
PHONE....................................757 865-1234
Adam Panholzer, *President*
Amy Panholzer, *Vice Pres*
EMP: 8
SQ FT: 6,000
SALES (est): 625.5K **Privately Held**
WEB: www.visionmfc.com
SIC: 3599 Machine shop, jobbing & repair

(G-6265)
VLH TRANSPORTATION INC
107 Bowen Dr (23666-4707)
P.O. Box 9365 (23670-0365)
PHONE....................................757 880-5772
Vincent Hawthorne, *President*
EMP: 3
SALES (est): 250K **Privately Held**
SIC: 3799 Transportation equipment

(G-6266)
VOGEL LUBRICATION
2115 Aluminum Ave (23661-1224)
PHONE....................................757 380-8585
Robert Amann, *Principal*
Dorothy Owen, *Purch Mgr*
Ricardo Gomez, *Manager*
EMP: 15
SALES (est): 2.5MM **Privately Held**
SIC: 3569 Lubricating equipment

(G-6267)
WALBERG AEROSPACE
49 W Queens Way (23669-4011)
PHONE....................................321 634-6349
Wayne Fuller, *Principal*
EMP: 2
SALES (est): 86K **Privately Held**
WEB: www.cdmmiami.com
SIC: 3721 Aircraft

(G-6268)
WANDERERS HIDEAWAY
405 N Second St (23664-1410)
PHONE....................................904 480-6117
Mia Rodriguez,
EMP: 1
SALES (est): 32.7K **Privately Held**
SIC: 7372 Application computer software

(G-6269)
WARD ENTP FABRICATION LLC
31 Regal Way (23669-4680)
PHONE....................................757 675-5712
Kenneth Ward, *President*
EMP: 1
SALES (est): 65.1K **Privately Held**
SIC: 3449 Miscellaneous metalwork

(G-6270)
WARDS SOUL FOOD KITCHEN
2710 N Armistead Ave F (23666-1687)
PHONE....................................757 865-7069
Melvin Ward, *Principal*
Mary Ward, *Vice Pres*
EMP: 2
SALES (est): 165.1K **Privately Held**
SIC: 2353 Silk hats

(G-6271)
WDFUP LLC
1708 Todds Ln Unit B2 (23666-3123)
PHONE....................................757 309-6214
Lamarco Williams, *Principal*
EMP: 4
SALES (est): 430.2K **Privately Held**
SIC: 2899 Oils & essential oils

(G-6272)
WESTON SOLUTIONS INC
2 Eaton St Ste 603 (23669-4055)
PHONE....................................757 819-5300
Anthony Pace, *Project Mgr*
Todd Liebig, *Branch Mgr*
EMP: 6
SALES (corp-wide): 451MM **Privately Held**
WEB: www.westonsolutions.com
SIC: 1389 8742 Construction, repair & dismantling services; management consulting services

HQ: Weston Solutions, Inc.
1400 Weston Way
West Chester PA 19380
610 701-3000

(G-6273)
WORDS TO PONDER PUBG CO LLC
91 Snug Harbor Dr (23661-3429)
P.O. Box 1394 (23661-0394)
PHONE....................................803 567-3692
Jessica Lee, *General Mgr*
Trefus Lee,
Melissa Lee, *Administration*
Florenza Lee,
EMP: 4
SALES (est): 109.8K **Privately Held**
SIC: 2731 Book publishing

(G-6274)
YOUR LIFE UNCORKED
79 Tide Mill Ln (23666-2713)
PHONE....................................757 218-8495
Lisa Smith, *Owner*
Billy Leudesdorf, *Branch Mgr*
EMP: 2
SALES (est): 155.9K **Privately Held**
WEB: www.yourlifeuncorked.com
SIC: 3993 Signs & advertising specialties

Hampton
Newport News City County

(G-6275)
LABEL
56 Newmarket Sq (23605-2721)
PHONE....................................757 236-8434
EMP: 2
SALES (est): 119.2K **Privately Held**
SIC: 2679 Labels, paper: made from purchased material

Hampton
Poquoson City County

(G-6276)
JOEYS SIGN & LETTER INC
128 Church St (23662-2204)
PHONE....................................757 868-7166
Kathy Hanberry, *Principal*
EMP: 2
SALES (est): 236.4K **Privately Held**
SIC: 3993 5091 Letters for signs, metal; boat accessories & parts

Hampton
York County

(G-6277)
COASTAL SCREEN PRINTING
12 Provider Ct (23665-2576)
PHONE....................................541 441-6358
Ben Schram, *Principal*
EMP: 2
SALES (est): 83.9K **Privately Held**
SIC: 2752 Commercial printing, lithographic

(G-6278)
LOCKHEED MARTIN CORPORATION
87 Oak St (23665-2105)
PHONE....................................757 766-3282
EMP: 2 **Publicly Held**
WEB: www.lockheedmartin.com
SIC: 3812 Search & navigation equipment
PA: Lockheed Martin Corporation
6801 Rockledge Dr
Bethesda MD 20817

(G-6279)
US DEPT OF THE AIR FORCE
Also Called: Langley Afb
34 Elm St (23665-2008)
PHONE....................................757 764-5616
Sammy Davis Jr, *Chief*
EMP: 5 **Publicly Held**
WEB: www.af.mil

SIC: 2741 Music books: publishing & printing
HQ: United States Department Of The Air Force
1000 Air Force Pentagon
Washington DC 20330

Hanover
Hanover County

(G-6280)
BISHOP STONE AND MET ARTS LLC
8001 Cadys Mill Rd (23069-1612)
PHONE....................................804 240-1030
Justin Bishop,
EMP: 1
SALES (est): 90K **Privately Held**
WEB: www.bishopstoneandmetal.com
SIC: 3281 Cut stone & stone products

(G-6281)
HANOVER WOODWORKING STUDIO LLC
8032 Cadys Mill Rd (23069-1612)
PHONE....................................804 625-5679
Timothy Christensen, *Principal*
EMP: 2
SALES (est): 67.8K **Privately Held**
SIC: 2431 Millwork

(G-6282)
MACS SMACK LLC
13278 Depot Rd (23069-1526)
PHONE....................................804 913-9126
McKenzie Payne, *Owner*
EMP: 2 **EST:** 2011
SALES (est): 132.3K **Privately Held**
WEB: www.macssmack.com
SIC: 3469 Kitchen fixtures & equipment: metal, except cast aluminum

(G-6283)
ROMAINE PRINTING
897 Edgar Rd (23069-2312)
PHONE....................................804 994-2213
Lisa Romaine, *Owner*
EMP: 2 **EST:** 1998
SALES (est): 166.2K **Privately Held**
WEB: www.viviennepdx.com
SIC: 2759 Invitation & stationery printing & engraving

(G-6284)
ROOM THE WISHING INC
Also Called: Wish Book Press
5422 Triangle Ln (23069-1842)
P.O. Box 58, Studley (23162-0058)
PHONE....................................804 746-0375
EMP: 3
SQ FT: 2,250
SALES (est): 164K **Privately Held**
SIC: 2731 Books-Publishing/Printing

Hardy
Franklin County

(G-6285)
ADVERTISING SPC & PROMOTIONS
41 Turtleback Path Rd (24101-3311)
PHONE....................................540 537-4121
Kimberly White, *Owner*
EMP: 4
SALES (est): 50K **Privately Held**
SIC: 3993 Signs & advertising specialties

(G-6286)
DENEALS CABINETS INC (PA)
2650 Edwardsville Rd (24101-4910)
PHONE....................................540 721-8005
David Deneal, *President*
Deneal Daniel R, *Vice Pres*
EMP: 6
SALES (est): 385K **Privately Held**
WEB: www.denealscabinets.com
SIC: 2434 5031 1751 Wood kitchen cabinets; kitchen cabinets; cabinet & finish carpentry

GEOGRAPHIC

(G-6287)
DISCOVER SML MAGAZINE (PA)
40 Village Springs Dr (24101-3982)
PHONE...............................540 719-7881
Dany Turner, *Principal*
EMP: 5
SALES (est): 782.3K **Privately Held**
WEB:
www.discoversmithmountainlake.com
SIC: 2721 Magazines: publishing only, not
printed on site

(G-6288)
Q C VENEER & LOGS LLC
525 N Church Dr (24101-2678)
PHONE...............................540 719-4349
▼ EMP: 6
SALES (est): 290K **Privately Held**
SIC: 2411 Veneer logs

(G-6289)
**RICHARDS BUILDING SUPPLY
CO**
Also Called: Cabinet Gallery, The
66 Builders Pride Rd (24101-3949)
PHONE...............................540 719-0128
Connie Hall, *Owner*
EMP: 1
SALES (corp-wide): 112.6MM **Privately
Held**
WEB: www.richards-supply.com
SIC: 2541 5712 Cabinets, except refriger-
ated: show, display, etc.: wood; cabinets,
except custom made: kitchen
PA: Richards Building Supply Co.
12070 W 159th St
Homer Glen IL 60491
773 586-7777

Harrisonburg
Harrisonburg City County

(G-6290)
AKG INC
1730 Dealton Ave (22801-2723)
P.O. Box 128, Bridgewater (22812-0128)
PHONE...............................540 574-0760
Jerry Sweeten, *President*
EMP: 6
SALES (est): 140K **Privately Held**
WEB: www.akg-inc.com
SIC: 3643 Current-carrying wiring devices

(G-6291)
ALLGOODS CLEANING SERVICE
429 Eastover Dr (22801-4409)
PHONE...............................540 434-1511
Fred Allgood Jr, *Partner*
Casandra Allgood, *Partner*
Natalia Allgood, *Partner*
Sheldon Allgood, *Partner*
EMP: 6
SALES (est): 554.1K **Privately Held**
WEB: www.lakeshoresoftware.com
SIC: 2842 7349 Specialty cleaning prepa-
rations; building maintenance services

(G-6292)
AMERICAST INC (HQ)
210 Stone Spring Rd (22801-9651)
PHONE...............................540 434-6979
Tichacek Jr William J, *President*
McNeely Grayson C, *Vice Pres*
McNeely IV C Wilson, *Vice Pres*
Woody Livesay, *CFO*
Livesay L Woodward, *Treasurer*
▲ EMP: 50
SALES (est): 46.4MM
SALES (corp-wide): 200.4MM **Privately
Held**
SIC: 3272 Concrete products, precast
PA: Eagle Corporation
1020 Harris St
Charlottesville VA 22903
434 971-2686

(G-6293)
ARIAKE USA INC (HQ)
Also Called: Gourmet Royol
1711 N Liberty St (22802-4518)
PHONE...............................540 432-6550
Haruhisa Ohta, *President*
Jamie R Eanes, *Treasurer*

◆ EMP: 60
SQ FT: 31,000
SALES (est): 10.1MM **Privately Held**
WEB: www.ariakeusa.com
SIC: 2015 Poultry slaughtering & process-
ing

(G-6294)
AURALOG INC
135 W Market St (22801-3710)
PHONE...............................602 470-0300
Nagi Sioufi, *President*
Christophe Pralong, *Vice Pres*
Penny C Williams, *Administration*
▲ EMP: 350
SQ FT: 15,000
SALES (est): 13.5MM **Privately Held**
WEB: www.rosettastone.co.uk
SIC: 7372 Prepackaged software
HQ: Rosetta Stone
14 Rue Du Fort De Saint Cyr
Montigny Le Bretonneux 78180
130 071-212

(G-6295)
**BLUE RIDGE MCH
MOTORSPORTS LLC**
Also Called: B R M M
971 Acorn Dr (22802-2400)
PHONE...............................540 432-6560
James Hall Jr,
EMP: 2 EST: 2007
SALES (est): 130K **Privately Held**
WEB: www.brmmharrisonburg.com
SIC: 3751 Motorcycles, bicycles & parts

(G-6296)
**BLUE RIDGE PROSTHETICS &
ORTHO**
1951 Evelyn Byrd Ave E (22801-3483)
PHONE...............................540 242-4499
EMP: 2
SALES (est): 93.5K **Privately Held**
SIC: 3842 Prosthetic appliances

(G-6297)
BOC GASES
940 S High St (22801-1602)
PHONE...............................540 433-1029
Garry Snow, *President*
EMP: 2
SALES (est): 81.9K **Privately Held**
SIC: 1311 Crude petroleum & natural gas

(G-6298)
**CARGILL TURKEY PRODUCTION
LLC (HQ)**
1 Kratzer Ave (22802-4567)
PHONE...............................540 568-1400
John Niemann, *President*
Timothy Maupin, *Vice Pres*
Jay Kroese, *Admin Sec*
EMP: 10
SALES (est): 2.2MM
SALES (corp-wide): 113.4B **Privately
Held**
WEB: www.sugarmesweetcupcakery.com
SIC: 2099 Food preparations
PA: Cargill, Incorporated
15407 Mcginty Rd W
Wayzata MN 55391
952 742-7575

(G-6299)
CASSCO CORPORATION
125 W Bruce St (22801-3615)
PHONE...............................540 433-2751
Charles N Broaddus, *Principal*
EMP: 3
SALES (est): 162.4K **Privately Held**
SIC: 2097 Manufactured ice

(G-6300)
**CHRISTIAN LIGHT
PUBLICATIONS (PA)**
1051 Mount Clinton Pike (22802-2479)
P.O. Box 1212 (22803-1212)
PHONE...............................540 434-0768
Richard Shank, *President*
Leon Yoder, *Chairman*
Ben Bergen, *Regional Mgr*
John Hartzler, *Treasurer*
Frieda Thiessen, *Consultant*
▼ EMP: 46
SQ FT: 40,000

SALES: 4.8MM **Privately Held**
WEB: www.clp.org
SIC: 2741 2752 2732 2731 Miscellaneous publishing; commercial printing,
lithographic; book printing; book publishing

(G-6301)
CLAUDIA & CO
Also Called: Claudia Hand Painted
40 W Washington St (22802-4558)
P.O. Box 85 (22803-0085)
PHONE...............................540 433-1140
Claudia M McClean, *President*
▲ EMP: 2
SALES (est): 190K **Privately Held**
WEB: www.claudiaco.com
SIC: 2253 Dresses, hand knit

(G-6302)
**COLLEGE AND UNIVERSITY
EDUCATI**
Also Called: Cued-In
343 W Bruce St (22801-1922)
PHONE...............................540 820-7384
Seth Marsh, *Exec Dir*
EMP: 4 EST: 2017
SALES (est): 238.2K **Privately Held**
SIC: 7372 8222 8299 Educational com-
puter software; community college; edu-
cational services

(G-6303)
COLOR QUEST LLC
105 Newman Ave (22801-4003)
PHONE...............................540 433-4890
EMP: 2
SALES (est): 88.6K **Privately Held**
WEB: www.colorquestprinting.com
SIC: 2759 2752 Commercial printing;
commercial printing, lithographic

(G-6304)
COLOR QUEST LLC
300 Waterman Dr Ste 100 (22802-5301)
P.O. Box 713 (22803-0713)
PHONE...............................540 896-8186
EMP: 2
SALES (est): 111.4K **Privately Held**
SIC: 2752 Commercial printing, offset

(G-6305)
**COMMONWEALTH RESCUE
SYSTEMS**
615 Pleasant Valley Rd (22801-9624)
PHONE...............................540 438-8972
Kevin Rogers, *President*
EMP: 5 EST: 1997
SQ FT: 1,000
SALES (est): 567.4K **Privately Held**
WEB: www.commonwealthrescue.com
SIC: 3569 Firefighting apparatus & related
equipment

(G-6306)
COMSONICS INC (PA)
1350 Port Republic Rd (22801-3563)
P.O. Box 1106 (22803-1106)
PHONE...............................540 434-5965
Dennis A Zimmermann, *President*
Berry Grant, *General Mgr*
Bill Groseclose, *General Mgr*
Bill Grossclose, *General Mgr*
Robert Norris, *General Mgr*
▲ EMP: 65
SQ FT: 25,000
SALES (est): 37.6MM **Privately Held**
WEB: www.comsonics.com
SIC: 3663 7629 Cable television equip-
ment; electrical equipment repair services

(G-6307)
CP INSTRUMENTS LLC
2322 Blue Stone Hills Dr (22801-5403)
PHONE...............................540 558-8596
Marc Hrovatic, *Vice Pres*
Kent Murphy,
EMP: 1
SALES (est): 98.1K **Privately Held**
SIC: 3823 Industrial instrmnts msrmnt dis-
play/control process variable

(G-6308)
DAILY NEWS RECORD (HQ)
231 S Liberty St (22801-3621)
PHONE...............................540 574-6200
Peter Yates, *President*
Phillips Mike, *Marketing Staff*
Penny Anderson, *Manager*
Delores Hammer, *Consultant*
EMP: 12
SQ FT: 30,000
SALES (est): 2.7MM
SALES (corp-wide): 13MM **Privately
Held**
WEB: www.dnronline.com
SIC: 2711 Newspapers, publishing & print-
ing
PA: Rockingham Publishing Co, Inc
231 S Liberty St
Harrisonburg VA 22801
540 574-6200

(G-6309)
DK PHARMA GROUP LLC
947 Summit Ave (22802-2318)
PHONE...............................540 574-4651
Deryl G Kennel, *Administration*
EMP: 3
SALES (est): 174.3K **Privately Held**
SIC: 2834 Pharmaceutical preparations

(G-6310)
DRAGONS LAIR GLASS STUDIO
814 Spotswood Dr (22802-5045)
PHONE...............................540 564-0318
Jackson Brennon, *Owner*
EMP: 3
SALES (est): 123.6K **Privately Held**
SIC: 3211 Flat glass

(G-6311)
DUPONT CREDIT UNION
1820 S High St (22801-8501)
PHONE...............................540 868-8714
EMP: 2
SALES (est): 74.4K **Privately Held**
SIC: 2879 Agricultural chemicals

(G-6312)
EDWARDS EDDIE SIGNS INC
119 Pleasant Hill Rd (22801-5712)
PHONE...............................540 434-8589
Chris Runion, *Principal*
EMP: 1
SALES (est): 78.8K **Privately Held**
WEB: www.eesigns.biz
SIC: 3993 Signs, not made in custom sign
painting shops

(G-6313)
ELKS CLUB 450
Also Called: 123945495max Gun Shop
482 S Main St (22801-3626)
PHONE...............................540 434-3673
Don Kidd, *Principal*
Milton Werner, *Principal*
EMP: 3
SALES (est): 144K **Privately Held**
WEB: www.elkslodge450.com
SIC: 2389 5941 5813 Lodge costumes;
firearms; drinking places

(G-6314)
EXHIBIT FOUNDRY
794 N Main St (22802-4623)
PHONE...............................540 705-0055
EMP: 1 EST: 2016
SALES (est): 60K **Privately Held**
WEB: www.exhibitfoundry.com
SIC: 3993 Signs & advertising specialties

(G-6315)
**EXTREME EXPOSURE MEDIA
LLC**
847 Martin Luther King Jr (22801-4393)
PHONE...............................540 434-0811
Edwin Clamp,
Jason Clamp,
EMP: 10
SALES (est): 659.8K **Privately Held**
SIC: 3861 Blueprint reproduction machines
& equipment

(G-6316)
FLOWERS BKG CO LYNCHBURG LLC
Also Called: Flowers Bakery Outlet
60 Charles St (22802-4608)
PHONE..................................540 434-4439
Wilson Randolph, *Manager*
EMP: 6
SALES (corp-wide): 4.1B **Publicly Held**
SIC: 2051 Bread, cake & related products
HQ: Flowers Baking Co. Of Lynchburg, Llc
1905 Hollins Mill Rd
Lynchburg VA 24503
434 528-0441

(G-6317)
FRAZIER QUARRY INCORPORATED (PA)
75 Waterman Dr (22802-2111)
P.O. Box 588 (22803-0588)
PHONE..................................540 434-6192
Robert B Frazier, *President*
Robert Y Frazier, *Chairman*
Bibb Y Frazier, *Exec VP*
James Riggleman, *Foreman/Supr*
Cyril Frazier, *Sales Staff*
▲ EMP: 25
SQ FT: 4,500
SALES: 16.4M **Privately Held**
WEB: www.frazierquarry.com
SIC: 1422 1442 3274 1429 Limestones, ground; construction sand & gravel; agricultural lime; riprap quarrying

(G-6318)
FRITO-LAY NORTH AMERICA INC
455 Pleasant Valley Rd (22801-9738)
PHONE..................................540 434-2426
Roy Varner, *Manager*
EMP: 20
SALES (corp-wide): 67.1B **Publicly Held**
WEB: www.fritolay.com
SIC: 2096 2099 Potato chips & other potato-based snacks; food preparations
HQ: Frito-Lay North America, Inc.
7701 Legacy Dr
Plano TX 75024

(G-6319)
GARRISON PRESS LLC
164 Waterman Dr (22802-2112)
P.O. Box 123 (22803-0123)
PHONE..................................540 434-2333
Angie Barker, *Partner*
EMP: 7 EST: 1914
SQ FT: 6,500
SALES (est): 1.1MM **Privately Held**
WEB: www.garrisonpress.com
SIC: 2752 Commercial printing, offset

(G-6320)
GEMINI COATING OF VIRGINIA
3333 Willow Spring Rd (22801-9732)
PHONE..................................540 434-4201
Michael Smith, *President*
Roger Woolery, *President*
EMP: 11
SQ FT: 18,000
SALES (est): 116.4K
SALES (corp-wide): 1.6MM **Privately Held**
SIC: 2851 Lacquer: bases, dopes, thinner; stains: varnish, oil or wax
PA: Gemini Industries, Inc.
421 Se 27th St
El Reno OK 73036
405 262-5710

(G-6321)
GEMINI COATINGS INC
3333 Willow Spring Rd (22801-9732)
PHONE..................................540 434-4201
Mike Filler, *General Mgr*
EMP: 13
SALES (corp-wide): 1.6MM **Privately Held**
WEB: www.gemini-coatings.com
SIC: 2851 Lacquers, varnishes, enamels & other coatings
HQ: Gemini Coatings, Inc.
421 Se 27th St
El Reno OK 73036
405 262-5710

(G-6322)
GEORGES INC
Also Called: Geroge's
501 N Liberty St (22802-3917)
PHONE..................................540 433-0720
Brenda Thompson, *Site Mgr*
Tammy Smith, *Buyer*
EMP: 860
SALES (corp-wide): 1.6B **Privately Held**
WEB: www.georgesinc.com
SIC: 2015 Poultry slaughtering & processing
PA: George's, Inc.
402 W Robinson Ave
Springdale AR 72764
479 927-7000

(G-6323)
GEORGES CHICKEN LLC
Also Called: Chicken Farms Division
1620 S Main St (22801-2729)
PHONE..................................540 434-7394
Marc White, *Manager*
EMP: 10
SALES (corp-wide): 1.6B **Privately Held**
WEB: www.georgesinc.com
SIC: 2015 Poultry slaughtering & processing
HQ: Georges Chicken Llc
19992 Senedo Rd
Edinburg VA 22824
540 984-4121

(G-6324)
GILMER INDUSTRIES INC
560 Stone Spring Rd (22801-9661)
P.O. Box 1247 (22803-1247)
PHONE..................................540 434-8877
Robert Gilmer, *President*
Robert G Gilmer III, *Vice Pres*
Pamela L Gilmer, *Treasurer*
Linda M Gilmer, *Admin Sec*
EMP: 20 EST: 1974
SALES (est): 7.3MM **Privately Held**
WEB: www.gilmerindustries.com
SIC: 2819 5169 Industrial inorganic chemicals; sanitation preparations

(G-6325)
GRAHAM PACKG PLASTIC PDTS INC
291 W Wolfe St (22802-3816)
PHONE..................................540 564-1000
Steve Tigpen, *Branch Mgr*
EMP: 150
SALES (corp-wide): 177.9K **Privately Held**
WEB: www.grahampackaging.com
SIC: 3089 3085 Pallets, plastic; plastics bottles
HQ: Graham Packaging Plastic Products Inc.
1 Seagate
Toledo OH 43604
717 849-8500

(G-6326)
GRIFFITH BAG COMPANY
510 Waterman Dr (22802-5305)
PHONE..................................540 433-2615
Greg Griffith, *President*
F Lynn Griffith, *Chairman*
Betty Griffith, *Shareholder*
▲ EMP: 7
SQ FT: 15,000
SALES (est): 1MM **Privately Held**
WEB: www.griffithbagco.com
SIC: 2221 5261 Polypropylene broadwoven fabrics; lawn & garden supplies

(G-6327)
HEIDI YODER
Also Called: Seams Like Home
920 Smithland Rd (22802-9339)
PHONE..................................540 432-5598
Heidi Yoder, *Owner*
EMP: 1
SALES (est): 54.5K **Privately Held**
SIC: 2391 2591 7389 Curtains & draperies; drapery hardware & blinds & shades; window blinds;

(G-6328)
HERALD PRESS
Also Called: Nenno Media
1251 Virginia Ave (22802-2434)
P.O. Box 866 (22803-0866)
PHONE..................................540 434-6701
Kimberly Metzler, *Accountant*
Russ Eanes, *Exec Dir*
Barbara Finnegan, *Director*
Aileen Esau,
EMP: 17 EST: 2011
SALES (est): 874.4K **Privately Held**
WEB: www.mennomedia.org
SIC: 2741 Miscellaneous publishing

(G-6329)
HOUGHTON MIFFLIN HARCOURT PUBG
Also Called: Great Source Education Group
1170 S Dogwood Dr (22801-1535)
PHONE..................................540 434-0137
Betty Shreckhise, *Manager*
EMP: 1 **Publicly Held**
WEB: www.hmhco.com
SIC: 2731 Book publishing
HQ: Houghton Mifflin Harcourt Publishing Company
125 High St Ste 900
Boston MA 02110
617 351-5000

(G-6330)
HUGO KOHL LLC
217 S Liberty St Ste 103 (22801-3675)
PHONE..................................540 564-2755
Hugo Kohl, *Principal*
EMP: 2
SALES (est): 112.1K **Privately Held**
WEB: www.hugokohl.com
SIC: 3911 Jewelry, precious metal

(G-6331)
INNOVATIVE SOLID SURFACES LLC
1021 W Market St (22801-9064)
PHONE..................................540 560-0747
Anton Kalashmikob, *Manager*
EMP: 2 EST: 2012
SALES (est): 222.9K **Privately Held**
WEB: www.innovativesolidsurface.com
SIC: 2541 Counter & sink tops

(G-6332)
JAH ROOTZ INDUSTRIES LLC
26 Pleasant Hill Rd (22801-5709)
PHONE..................................512 925-1109
Joshua Spencer, *Manager*
EMP: 2
SALES (est): 74.4K **Privately Held**
SIC: 2869 5149 Industrial organic chemicals; natural & organic foods

(G-6333)
JENZABAR INC
Also Called: C M D S
181 S Liberty St (22801-3619)
PHONE..................................540 432-5200
Kelly Ganoe, *General Mgr*
Mimi Flanagan, *Vice Pres*
Sashi Parthasarathi, *Vice Pres*
Jennifer Saunders, *Project Mgr*
Chris Myers, *Engineer*
EMP: 150
SALES (corp-wide): 1.5MM **Privately Held**
WEB: www.jenzabar.com
SIC: 7372 Prepackaged software
PA: Jenzabar, Inc.
101 Huntington Ave # 2200
Boston MA 02199
617 492-9099

(G-6334)
JON MARTIN WOODWORKING LLC
1230 Harmony Dr Apt A (22802-6158)
PHONE..................................540 560-3721
Jonathan Ruel Martin, *Principal*
EMP: 1
SALES (est): 58.3K **Privately Held**
SIC: 2431 Millwork

(G-6335)
KAWNEER COMPANY INC
2031 Deyerle Ave (22801-3489)
PHONE..................................540 433-2711
Tom Leach, *Data Proc Staff*
EMP: 100
SALES (corp-wide): 7.2B **Publicly Held**
WEB: www.alcoa.com
SIC: 3442 Metal doors
HQ: Kawneer Company, Inc.
555 Guthridge Ct
Norcross GA 30092
770 449-5555

(G-6336)
LANTZ CUSTOM WOODWORKING
641 Acorn Dr (22802-2474)
PHONE..................................540 438-1819
Doug Lantz, *Partner*
EMP: 5
SQ FT: 5,100
SALES (est): 782.6K **Privately Held**
WEB: www.lantzwoodworking.com
SIC: 2434 Wood kitchen cabinets

(G-6337)
LEXIA LEARNING SYSTEMS INC
135 W Market St (22801-3710)
PHONE..................................978 405-6242
Ruth Curry, *Principal*
EMP: 5
SALES (est): 248.8K **Privately Held**
SIC: 7372 Prepackaged software

(G-6338)
LIBERTY PRESS INC
300 Waterman Dr (22802-5301)
PHONE..................................540 434-5513
Scott T Barnard, *President*
Micheal Fornaddle, *Vice Pres*
EMP: 20
SQ FT: 5,000
SALES (est): 2.6MM **Privately Held**
SIC: 2752 Commercial printing, offset

(G-6339)
LINSEY ECHOWATER SYSTEM
105 Newman Ave (22801-4003)
PHONE..................................540 434-0212
Paul Labadie, *Owner*
EMP: 1 EST: 2010
SALES (est): 73.8K **Privately Held**
SIC: 3949 Water skis

(G-6340)
LLOYD ELC CO HARRISONBURG INC
870 N Liberty St (22802-4502)
PHONE..................................540 433-5335
Robert Lloyd, *President*
Kobi Lloyd, *Vice Pres*
EMP: 7
SALES (est): 1.2MM **Privately Held**
WEB: www.lloydelectric.net
SIC: 7694 Electric motor repair

(G-6341)
LSC COMMUNICATIONS US LLC
1025 Willow Spring Rd (22801-9793)
PHONE..................................540 564-3900
EMP: 7
SALES (corp-wide): 6.1B **Publicly Held**
WEB: www.lsccom.com
SIC: 2721 Magazines: publishing & printing
HQ: Lsc Communications Us, Llc
191 N Wacker Dr Ste 1400
Chicago IL 60606
844 572-5720

(G-6342)
MAGNES INDUSTRIES LLC
1034 Betsy Ross Ct (22802-6520)
PHONE..................................540 246-6088
EMP: 2
SALES (est): 85.9K **Privately Held**
SIC: 3999 Manufacturing industries

(G-6343)
MARK-IT
125 W Water St (22801-3612)
PHONE..................................540 434-4824
Todd McCoy, *Owner*
EMP: 3
SQ FT: 3,000

SALES (est): 279.1K **Privately Held**
WEB: www.themarkithva.com
SIC: 2759 Screen printing

(G-6344)
MB WELD LLC
815 Grant St (22802-5608)
PHONE..............................540 434-4042
Mario Bianchi, *Principal*
EMP: 5
SALES (est): 490.8K **Privately Held**
WEB: www.mbweld.com
SIC: 7692 Welding repair

(G-6345)
MILLER CABINETS INC
1910 S High St (22801-8562)
PHONE..............................540 434-4835
Mervyl Miller, *President*
Alan B Ritchie, *Vice Pres*
EMP: 4 EST: 1964
SQ FT: 8,400
SALES (est): 657K **Privately Held**
WEB: www.millercabinetsinc.com
SIC: 2431 5712 Millwork; cabinet work,
custom

(G-6346)
MIX IT UP LLC
64 Maplehurst Ave (22801-3030)
PHONE..............................540 434-9868
John Jackson Broaddus, *Administration*
EMP: 3
SALES (est): 160.4K **Privately Held**
SIC: 3273 Ready-mixed concrete

(G-6347)
MODUS WORKSHOP LLC
449 Sunrise Ave (22801-1652)
P.O. Box 668 (22803-0668)
PHONE..............................800 376-5735
Nathan Cooper, *Administration*
EMP: 3
SALES (est): 150K **Privately Held**
WEB: www.modusworkshop.com
SIC: 2431 Millwork

(G-6348)
MONTEBELLO PACKAGING INC
Also Called: MONTEBELLO PACKAGING,
INC.
812 N Main St (22802-4625)
PHONE..............................540 437-0119
Lane Jackson, *Manager*
EMP: 142
SALES (corp-wide): 1.5MM **Privately
Held**
WEB: www.montebellopkg.com
SIC: 3354 Aluminum pipe & tube
HQ: Montebello Packaging Inc.
650 Indl Dr
Lebanon KY 40033

(G-6349)
MUDDY FEET LLC
2061 Evelyn Byrd Ave E (22801-3442)
PHONE..............................540 830-0342
Todd Dofflemyer, *Owner*
EMP: 7
SALES (est): 405.7K **Privately Held**
WEB: www.muddyfeetgraphics.com
SIC: 3993 Signs, not made in custom sign
painting shops

(G-6350)
**MY MEXICO FOODS & DISTRS
INC**
1555 Red Oak St (22802-8395)
PHONE..............................540 560-3587
Margarita Rendon, *Admin Sec*
EMP: 6
SALES (est): 355.4K **Privately Held**
SIC: 2041 Flour & other grain mill products

(G-6351)
**PACKAGING CORPORATION
AMERICA**
Also Called: PCA / Harrisonburg, 333
930 Pleasant Valley Rd (22801-9744)
PHONE..............................540 434-0785
Dan Kirkpatrick, *General Mgr*
Eric Dean, *Project Mgr*
Randy Moats, *Project Mgr*
Tom Jenkins, *Safety Mgr*
Brian Wilson, *Production*

EMP: 315 **Publicly Held**
WEB: www.packagingcorp.com
SIC: 2653 Boxes, corrugated: made from
purchased materials
PA: Packaging Corporation Of America
1 N Field Ct
Lake Forest IL 60045
847 482-3000

(G-6352)
**PACKAGING CORPORATION
AMERICA**
21 Warehouse Rd (22801-9704)
PHONE..............................540 432-1353
EMP: 2 **Publicly Held**
WEB: www.packagingcorp.com
SIC: 2653 Boxes, corrugated: made from
purchased materials
PA: Packaging Corporation Of America
1 N Field Ct
Lake Forest IL 60045
847 482-3000

(G-6353)
**PACKAGING CORPORATION
AMERICA**
Also Called: Pca/Mid-Atlantic Area
2262 Blue Stone Hills Dr C (22801-5434)
PHONE..............................540 438-8504
Jim Mc Kee, *Manager*
EMP: 7 **Publicly Held**
WEB: www.packagingcorp.com
SIC: 2653 Boxes, corrugated: made from
purchased materials
PA: Packaging Corporation Of America
1 N Field Ct
Lake Forest IL 60045
847 482-3000

(G-6354)
PHO HA VIETNAMESE NOODLE
1015 Port Republic Rd (22801-3507)
PHONE..............................540 438-0999
EMP: 4
SALES (est): 171.1K **Privately Held**
SIC: 2098 Macaroni And Spaghetti

(G-6355)
**PILGRIMS PRIDE
CORPORATION**
Also Called: Harrisonburg Feed Mill
590 Mount Clinton Pike (22802-2500)
PHONE..............................540 564-6070
Scott Wilkins, *Controller*
Mike Ellington, *Manager*
EMP: 29
SALES (corp-wide): 177.9K **Publicly
Held**
WEB: www.pilgrims.com
SIC: 2015 Poultry slaughtering & process-
ing
HQ: Pilgrim's Pride Corporation
1770 Promontory Cir
Greeley CO 80634
970 506-8000

(G-6356)
PRINTING EXPRESS INC
21 Warehouse Rd (22801-9704)
PHONE..............................540 433-1237
Aaron Smith, *Opers Mgr*
Tim Meredith, *Prdtn Mgr*
Tom Legg, *Executive*
Mike Meredith,
EMP: 48
SALES (est): 1.2MM **Privately Held**
WEB: www.theprintingexpress.com
SIC: 2752 Commercial printing, offset

(G-6357)
PRINTING SERVICES
116 Laurel St (22801-2761)
PHONE..............................540 434-5783
Jim Spitzer, *Owner*
EMP: 1
SQ FT: 1,000
SALES (est): 103.7K **Privately Held**
SIC: 2752 Commercial printing, offset

(G-6358)
**R R DONNELLEY & SONS
COMPANY**
1400 Kratzer Rd (22802-8301)
PHONE..............................540 434-8833
John Reichard, *Manager*

EMP: 6
SALES (corp-wide): 6.2B **Publicly Held**
WEB: www.rrd.com
SIC: 2759 Commercial printing
PA: R. R. Donnelley & Sons Company
35 W Wacker Dr
Chicago IL 60601
312 326-8000

(G-6359)
**R R DONNELLEY & SONS
COMPANY**
Banta Book Group
1025 Willow Spring Rd (22801-9793)
PHONE..............................540 564-3900
Devone Philips, *Manager*
EMP: 300
SALES (corp-wide): 6.2B **Publicly Held**
WEB: www.rrd.com
SIC: 2752 2731 Commercial printing, litho-
graphic; book publishing
PA: R. R. Donnelley & Sons Company
35 W Wacker Dr
Chicago IL 60601
312 326-8000

(G-6360)
RAINCROW STUDIOS LLC
128 W Bruce St (22801-3663)
PHONE..............................540 746-8696
Travis Fox, *CEO*
Daniel Hanlon, *Ch Credit Ofcr*
EMP: 5 EST: 2011
SALES (est): 5K **Privately Held**
WEB: www.raincrowstudios.com
SIC: 7372 Home entertainment computer
software

(G-6361)
REDDY ICE CORPORATION
610 Pleasant Valley Rd (22801-9623)
P.O. Box 2217 (22801-9507)
PHONE..............................540 433-2751
Norbert Garcia, *Branch Mgr*
EMP: 30 **Privately Held**
WEB: www.reddyice.com
SIC: 2097 Manufactured ice
HQ: Reddy Ice Corporation
5720 Lyndon B Johnson Fwy # 200
Dallas TX 75240
214 526-6740

(G-6362)
ROCCO SPECIALTY FOODS INC
1 Kratzer Ave (22802-4567)
PHONE..............................540 432-1060
James J Darazsdi, *President*
Patrick Evick, *Plant Mgr*
EMP: 10
SALES (est): 1.3MM **Privately Held**
SIC: 2099 Food preparations

(G-6363)
**ROCKINGHAM PUBLISHING CO
INC (PA)**
Also Called: Daily News Record
231 S Liberty St (22801-3621)
P.O. Box 193 (22803-0193)
PHONE..............................540 574-6200
Thomas T Byrd, *President*
Craig Bartoldson, *Publisher*
Beverly Byrd, *Principal*
Jim Sacco, *Editor*
Harry F Byrd III, *Vice Pres*
EMP: 115
SQ FT: 35,000
SALES (est): 13MM **Privately Held**
WEB: www.dnronline.com
SIC: 2711 2752 Newspapers, publishing &
printing; commercial printing, lithographic

(G-6364)
ROCKINGHAM REDI-MIX INC
380 Waterman Dr (22802-5301)
P.O. Box 1347 (22803-1347)
PHONE..............................540 433-9128
Roy Simmons, *Branch Mgr*
EMP: 3
SALES (corp-wide): 8.7MM **Privately
Held**
WEB: www.rockinghamredimix.com
SIC: 3273 Ready-mixed concrete
PA: Rockingham Redi-Mix, Inc.
1557 Garbers Church Rd
Rockingham VA 22801
540 433-9128

(G-6365)
ROSETTA STONE LTD (DH)
135 W Market St (22801-3710)
PHONE..............................540 432-6166
John Hass, *CEO*
Catherine Runion, *General Mgr*
Sean Hartford, *Vice Pres*
Mark Moseley Jr, *Vice Pres*
Jeff Farnsworth, *Buyer*
◆ EMP: 360
SALES (est): 108.1MM
SALES (corp-wide): 39.2MM **Privately
Held**
WEB: www.rosettastone.com
SIC: 7372 Educational computer software

(G-6366)
SAIFLAVOR
310 Cedar St (22801-1512)
PHONE..............................304 520-9464
SAI Hill, *Partner*
Jonathan Hill, *Partner*
EMP: 1
SALES (est): 44.5K **Privately Held**
SIC: 2499 7389 Food handling & process-
ing products, wood;

(G-6367)
SCOUTCO LLC
3610 S Main St (22801-9762)
PHONE..............................540 433-5136
Michael Moore, *Branch Mgr*
EMP: 2 **Privately Held**
WEB: www.scoutcoproducts.com
SIC: 3993 Signs & advertising specialties
PA: Scoutco Llc
9201 Centerville Rd
Bridgewater VA 22812

(G-6368)
SENIOR MOBILITY LLC
141 S Carlton St (22801-4326)
PHONE..............................540 574-0215
Steven Ray, *Principal*
EMP: 2
SALES (est): 155.9K **Privately Held**
SIC: 3842 Walkers; wheelchairs

(G-6369)
SHALOM FOUNDATION INC
Also Called: Together Newspaper
1251 Virginia Ave (22802-2434)
PHONE..............................540 433-5351
Richard L Benner, *Director*
EMP: 3
SALES: 42.2K **Privately Held**
WEB: www.churchoutreach.com
SIC: 2711 Newspapers, publishing & print-
ing

(G-6370)
SIGNFIELD INC
Also Called: Sign Pro
1550a E Market St (22801-5108)
PHONE..............................540 574-3032
Kerry Cofield, *President*
EMP: 5
SALES (est): 290K **Privately Held**
WEB: www.mysignpros.net
SIC: 3993 Signs & advertising specialties

(G-6371)
SIGNS USA INC
21 Terri Dr (22802-8854)
PHONE..............................540 432-6166
James L Anderson, *President*
Jodie W Anderson, *Vice Pres*
EMP: 4
SQ FT: 4,000
SALES (est): 561.9K **Privately Held**
WEB: www.signsusava.com
SIC: 3993 Neon signs

(G-6372)
SNOWSHOE RETREATS LLC
129 University Blvd (22801-3751)
PHONE..............................540 442-6144
Maria Hernandez, *Principal*
EMP: 2
SALES (est): 93.4K **Privately Held**
SIC: 3949 Snowshoes

(G-6373)
SPECIAL FLEET SERVICES INC (PA)
875 Waterman Dr (22802-5632)
P.O. Box 990 (22803-0990)
PHONE..........................540 434-4488
M Gregory Weaver, *President*
Winston Weaver, *Vice Pres*
John Sinnett, *Plant Mgr*
Winston O Weaver Jr, *Treasurer*
Ralph EBY, *Finance Mgr*
EMP: 95
SQ FT: 18,000
SALES (est): 20.1MM **Privately Held**
WEB: www.specialfleet.com
SIC: 1389 5072 8734 Derrick building, repairing & dismantling; power tools & accessories; product testing laboratory, safety or performance

(G-6374)
SPECIAL FLEET SERVICES INC
2500 S Main St (22801-2611)
PHONE..........................540 433-7727
Aaron Swope, *Purch Agent*
Jim Killen, *Sales Staff*
Loren Mast, *Branch Mgr*
EMP: 35
SALES (corp-wide): 20.1MM **Privately Held**
WEB: www.specialfleet.com
SIC: 1389 5072 Construction, repair & dismantling services; hardware
PA: Special Fleet Services, Inc.
875 Waterman Dr
Harrisonburg VA 22802
540 434-4488

(G-6375)
SUMI LLC
1271 Stonechris Dr (22802-0884)
PHONE..........................571 287-9480
EMP: 2
SALES (est): 94.6K **Privately Held**
WEB: www.sumiprinting.com
SIC: 2752 Commercial printing, lithographic

(G-6376)
SUN RNR OF VIRGINIA INC
Also Called: Sunrunr
865 Neyland Dr (22801-1759)
PHONE..........................540 271-3403
Jennifer French, *President*
Alan Mattichak, *Vice Pres*
Scott French, *Treasurer*
EMP: 3
SALES (est): 500.2K **Privately Held**
WEB: www.sunrnr.com
SIC: 3433 5074 4911 Solar heaters & collectors; heating equipment & panels, solar; generation, electric power

(G-6377)
SUPERIOR CONCRETE INC
1526 Country Club Rd (22802-5071)
P.O. Box 1147 (22803-1147)
PHONE..........................540 433-2482
Lawrence Wilt, *President*
Kim Diehl, *Executive*
Scott Boshart, *Associate*
EMP: 40 **EST:** 1953
SQ FT: 2,500
SALES (est): 6.2MM **Privately Held**
WEB: www.superiorconcreteinc.com
SIC: 3273 Ready-mixed concrete

(G-6378)
SUTERS CABINET SHOP INC (PA)
Also Called: Suter's Handcrafted Furniture
2610 S Main St (22801-2613)
PHONE..........................540 434-2131
Carol Michael, *President*
Michael Carol Suter, *Vice Pres*
EMP: 19
SQ FT: 10,200
SALES (est): 2.4MM **Privately Held**
WEB: www.suters.com
SIC: 2511 5712 Wood household furniture; furniture stores

(G-6379)
TENNECO AUTOMOTIVE OPER CO INC
3160 Abbott Ln (22801-9708)
PHONE..........................540 432-3545
Chris McHugh, *Branch Mgr*
EMP: 600
SALES (corp-wide): 17.4B **Publicly Held**
SIC: 3714 Exhaust systems & parts, motor vehicle
HQ: Tenneco Automotive Operating Company, Inc.
500 N Field Dr
Lake Forest IL 60045
847 482-5000

(G-6380)
TENNECO AUTOMOTIVE OPER CO INC
3160 Abbott Ln (22801-9708)
PHONE..........................540 434-2461
Kirk Wine, *Engineer*
Mark Perfora, *Branch Mgr*
EMP: 24
SALES (corp-wide): 17.4B **Publicly Held**
SIC: 3714 Shock absorbers, motor vehicle
HQ: Tenneco Automotive Operating Company, Inc.
500 N Field Dr
Lake Forest IL 60045
847 482-5000

(G-6381)
TIM LACEY BUILDERS
301 Stoneleigh Dr (22801-9003)
PHONE..........................540 434-3372
EMP: 6 **EST:** 1996
SALES: 500K **Privately Held**
SIC: 1389 Oil/Gas Field Services

(G-6382)
TIMBERVILLE DRUG STORE
33 Emery St (22801-2705)
PHONE..........................540 434-2379
EMP: 2
SALES (est): 86.6K **Privately Held**
SIC: 3841 Surgical & medical instruments

(G-6383)
VALLEY BUILDING SUPPLY INC (HQ)
Also Called: Valley Blox and Bldg Mtls Div
210 Stone Spring Rd (22801-9651)
PHONE..........................540 434-6725
Thomas J Dawson, *President*
William H Bolton, *Treasurer*
EMP: 150
SQ FT: 25,000
SALES: 32.1MM
SALES (corp-wide): 200.4MM **Privately Held**
WEB: www.valleybuildingsupply.com
SIC: 3272 3271 5211 1411 Concrete products, precast; blocks, concrete or cinder: standard; concrete & cinder block; limestone, dimension-quarrying; trusses, wooden roof; millwork
PA: Eagle Corporation
1020 Harris St
Charlottesville VA 22903
434 971-2686

(G-6384)
VILLAGE TO VILLAGE PRESS LLC
1510 College Ave (22802-5509)
PHONE..........................267 416-0375
EMP: 1
SALES (est): 37.5K **Privately Held**
WEB: www.villagetovillagepress.com
SIC: 2741 Miscellaneous publishing

(G-6385)
VIRGINIA NEEDLE ART INC
940 Mockingbird Dr (22802-4963)
PHONE..........................540 433-8070
Loretta Eklund, *President*
George F Eklund, *Vice Pres*
EMP: 2
SALES (est): 126.9K **Privately Held**
SIC: 2395 Art goods for embroidering, stamped: purchased materials

(G-6386)
VISION PUBLISHERS INC
755 Cantrell Ave Ste C (22801-4366)
P.O. Box 190 (22803-0190)
PHONE..........................540 437-1967
Harold Campbell, *President*
Lonnie D Yoder, *Corp Secy*
EMP: 2
SQ FT: 1,900
SALES (est): 100K **Privately Held**
WEB: www.vision-publishers.com
SIC: 2741 Miscellaneous publishing

(G-6387)
WHITE BRICK MUSIC
206 Divot Dr (22802-8779)
PHONE..........................323 821-9449
EMP: 1
SALES (est): 37.5K **Privately Held**
SIC: 2741 Misc Publishing

(G-6388)
YOUVE GOT IT MADE LLC
486 Myers Ave (22801-4212)
PHONE..........................410 840-8744
Jennifer Matthaei,
EMP: 1
SALES (est): 88K **Privately Held**
WEB: www.youvegotitmade.org
SIC: 3993 Advertising novelties

(G-6389)
ZOOK AVIATION INC
1866 E Market St 312c (22801-5111)
PHONE..........................540 217-4471
Reuben Zook, *CEO*
EMP: 1
SALES (est): 75.7K **Privately Held**
WEB: www.zookaviation.com
SIC: 2741 Miscellaneous publishing

Hartfield
Middlesex County

(G-6390)
HENLEY CABINETRY INC
10880 General Puller Hwy I (23071-3140)
PHONE..........................804 776-0016
EMP: 4
SALES (est): 213.4K **Privately Held**
WEB: www.henleycabinetry.com
SIC: 2434 Wood kitchen cabinets

(G-6391)
STAMPERS BAY PUBLISHING LLC
550 Stampers Bay Rd (23071-3136)
PHONE..........................804 776-9122
Wayne Usry,
Mead Usry,
EMP: 3 **EST:** 2015
SALES (est): 118K **Privately Held**
WEB: www.stampersbay.com
SIC: 2731 Book publishing

Hartwood
Stafford County

(G-6392)
SPEARS & ASSOCIATE
97 Timberidge Dr (22471)
PHONE..........................540 752-5577
Dennis Spears, *Owner*
EMP: 2
SALES (est): 113K **Privately Held**
SIC: 3444 Sheet metalwork

Hayes
Gloucester County

(G-6393)
ADVANCED FINISHING SYSTEMS
2954 George Wash Mem Hwy (23072-3429)
P.O. Box 1172 (23072-1172)
PHONE..........................804 642-7669
Christopher Green, *President*
EMP: 18
SQ FT: 7,500
SALES (est): 2.1MM **Privately Held**
WEB: www.advanced-finishing.com
SIC: 3471 Electroplating of metals or formed products

(G-6394)
ALWAYS IN STITCHES
6622 Powhatan Dr (23072-3216)
PHONE..........................804 642-0800
Diane L Hoegero, *Owner*
EMP: 1
SALES (est): 117.4K **Privately Held**
SIC: 2281 Embroidery yarn, spun

(G-6395)
ANTEX USA INC
4914 Ste B Grge Wshngtn M (23072)
PHONE..........................804 693-0831
EMP: 5 **EST:** 2007
SALES (est): 339.6K **Privately Held**
SIC: 3423 Mfg Hand/Edge Tools
HQ: Antex (Electronics) Limited
4 Darklake View
Plymouth PL6 7
175 269-5756

(G-6396)
BIG ISLAND OYSTERS
Also Called: Tidewater Oyster Farms
9817 Misty Ln (23072-4037)
PHONE..........................804 389-9589
EMP: 2
SALES (est): 62.3K **Privately Held**
SIC: 2091 Seafood products: packaged in cans, jars, etc.

(G-6397)
BRICKHOUSE INDUSTRIES LLC
8465 Little England Rd (23072-3874)
PHONE..........................757 880-7249
Stephanie Bonniville, *President*
EMP: 2
SALES (est): 90.6K **Privately Held**
SIC: 3999 Manufacturing industries

(G-6398)
CANVAS DOCKTORS LLC
2784 Pigeon Hill Rd (23072-3403)
PHONE..........................757 759-7108
Jan Fiehler, *Principal*
EMP: 1 **EST:** 2014
SALES (est): 46.5K **Privately Held**
WEB: www.canvasdocktors.com
SIC: 2211 Canvas

(G-6399)
H & H ENTERPRISES INC
Also Called: Triad Machine Shop
2950 George Wash Mem Hwy (23072-3429)
PHONE..........................804 684-5901
Amy Lawing, *President*
Michael Lawing, *Vice Pres*
Donna Lawing, *Director*
Jordan Lawing, *Director*
EMP: 8
SALES (est): 377.2K **Privately Held**
WEB: www.triadmachineshop.com
SIC: 3599 Machine shop, jobbing & repair

(G-6400)
HAYES CUSTOM SAILS INC
4104 George Wash Mem Hwy (23072-2932)
PHONE..........................804 642-6496
Rod Hayes, *President*
George R Hayes, *Treasurer*
EMP: 5
SQ FT: 2,200
SALES (est): 568.2K **Privately Held**
SIC: 2394 Sails: made from purchased materials

(G-6401)
MICHAELS CATERING
6450 Hickory Fork Rd (23072-2515)
PHONE..........................804 815-6985
Michael Davis, *Owner*
EMP: 5
SALES (est): 246.7K **Privately Held**
SIC: 2099 Food preparations

GEOGRAPHIC

(G-6402)
MILLCREEK WOOD WORKS
9969 Bonniville Rd (23072-4103)
PHONE..............................804 642-4792
EMP: 2
SALES (est): 155.1K **Privately Held**
SIC: 2431 Millwork

(G-6403)
NORTHWIND ASSOCIATES
8770 Little England Rd (23072-3867)
PHONE..............................757 871-8215
Jacqueline Outten, *Owner*
EMP: 2
SALES (est): 17K **Privately Held**
WEB: www.northwindassociates.com
SIC: 2499 Signboards, wood

(G-6404)
PERFORMANCE SUPPORT SYSTEMS
8270 Little England Rd (23072-3850)
PHONE..............................757 873-3700
Dennis E Coates, *CEO*
Meredith M Bell, *President*
Paula Y Schlauch, *CFO*
Paula Schlauch, *CFO*
EMP: 5
SALES (est): 360.5K **Privately Held**
WEB: www.strongforperformance.com
SIC: 7372 8742 Prepackaged software;
management consulting services

(G-6405)
RONALD PAUL GARDNER
Also Called: Foh Sounds
1818 Creekwood Ct (23072-3814)
PHONE..............................804 815-6529
Ronald Paul Gardner, *Owner*
EMP: 1
SALES (est): 50K **Privately Held**
SIC: 3861 Sound recording & reproducing
equipment, motion picture

(G-6406)
S & S MIXED SIGNS INC
4041 George Wash Mem Hwy
(23072-2930)
PHONE..............................804 642-2641
Sherry Elston, *President*
EMP: 2
SALES (est): 158.2K **Privately Held**
WEB: www.ssmixedsigns.com
SIC: 3993 Signs & advertising specialties

(G-6407)
SAWMILL CREEK WDWORKERS FORUMS
8770 Little England Rd (23072-3867)
PHONE..............................757 871-8214
Aaron Koehl, *Executive*
EMP: 1
SALES (est): 54.1K **Privately Held**
WEB: www.freedompens.org
SIC: 2431 Millwork

(G-6408)
SEVERN YACHTING LLC
Also Called: Severn Yachting Center
3398 Stonewall Rd (23072-4552)
PHONE..............................804 642-6969
Shawn Gordon, *Branch Mgr*
EMP: 1
SALES (corp-wide): 513.3K **Privately Held**
WEB: www.severnyc.com
SIC: 3732 Boat building & repairing
PA: Severn Yachting Llc
295 Enon Hall Rd
White Stone VA 22578
804 642-6969

(G-6409)
SHADEWORKS LLC
7979 Starkey Dr (23072-3642)
PHONE..............................804 642-2618
Robin Sukhai, *President*
EMP: 1
SALES (est): 122K **Privately Held**
SIC: 2591 Blinds vertical

(G-6410)
SISTERS IN STITCHES LLC
7333 Joseph Lewis Rd (23072-3533)
PHONE..............................757 660-0871
Patricia Donoflio, *Principal*
EMP: 1
SALES (est): 45.5K **Privately Held**
SIC: 2395 Embroidery & art needlework

Haymarket
Prince William County

(G-6411)
ABOVE RIM LLC
14505 Holshire Way (20169-2697)
PHONE..............................703 407-9398
Benny McKee,
EMP: 1
SALES (est): 250K **Privately Held**
SIC: 3711 Motor vehicles & car bodies

(G-6412)
ACRO SOFTWARE INC
5331 Chaffins Farm Ct (20169-4518)
P.O. Box 575 (20168-0575)
PHONE..............................703 753-7508
Ching Luo, *President*
Yumin Tan, *Treasurer*
EMP: 5
SQ FT: 1,000
SALES (est): 810K **Privately Held**
WEB: www.acrosoftware.com
SIC: 7372 Business oriented computer
software

(G-6413)
ADAPTIVE ELEMENTS LLC
15143 La Jolla Ct (20169-3142)
PHONE..............................571 261-3671
Gary Brown, *Principal*
EMP: 3 EST: 2013
SALES (est): 186.8K **Privately Held**
SIC: 2819 Industrial inorganic chemicals

(G-6414)
AT SIGN LLC
5008 Warwick Hills Ct (20169-3185)
PHONE..............................703 895-7035
Josiah Ferguson, *Principal*
EMP: 1
SALES (est): 46K **Privately Held**
SIC: 3993 Signs & advertising specialties

(G-6415)
BEETS & APPLES
5049 Burnside Farm Pl (20169-2581)
PHONE..............................703 743-4112
GA Yeong Pak, *Principal*
EMP: 2 EST: 2017
SALES (est): 168.1K **Privately Held**
SIC: 3571 Electronic computers

(G-6416)
BUILT IN STYLE LLC
6021 Empire Lakes Ct (20169-6105)
PHONE..............................703 753-8518
Hyojon Joshua Robbins,
EMP: 2
SALES (est): 192.4K **Privately Held**
WEB: www.builtinstyle.com
SIC: 2673 Wardrobe bags (closet acces-
sories): from purchased materials

(G-6417)
CENTURY STAIR COMPANY
15175 Washington St (20169-2951)
PHONE..............................703 754-4163
Donald G Costello, *President*
Jeff Held, *Vice Pres*
Brett Olinger, *Accounts Mgr*
Jeff Rife, *Accounts Mgr*
Melissa Penn, *Assistant*
EMP: 90 EST: 1976
SQ FT: 50,000
SALES (est): 9.9MM **Privately Held**
WEB: www.houzz.com
SIC: 2431 5211 3446 Staircases & stairs,
wood; millwork & lumber; architectural
metalwork

(G-6418)
DEATRICK & ASSOCIATES INC
5618 Swift Creek Ct (20169-5423)
PHONE..............................703 753-1040
Peter Buchan, *President*
EMP: 3 **Privately Held**
SIC: 2834 Chlorination tablets & kits (water
purification)

(G-6419)
DIRECTIVE SYSTEMS AND ENG LLC
2702 Rodgers Ter (20169-1628)
PHONE..............................703 754-3876
Terrence Price, *Mng Member*
Marjorie Price, *Mng Member*
EMP: 2 EST: 2013
SALES (est): 100K **Privately Held**
WEB: www.directivesystems.com
SIC: 3663 Antennas, transmitting & com-
munications

(G-6420)
E-Z TREAT INC
16211 Thoroughfare Rd (20168)
P.O. Box 176 (20168-0176)
PHONE..............................703 753-4770
Carlos Perry, *President*
Francine Perry, *Vice Pres*
EMP: 10
SQ FT: 20,000
SALES (est): 1.9MM **Privately Held**
WEB: www.eztreat.net
SIC: 3089 3088 Injection molding of plas-
tics; plastics plumbing fixtures

(G-6421)
EAST TOOLS INC
4187 Benvenue Rd (20169-2443)
PHONE..............................703 754-1931
Jeffery East, *Principal*
EMP: 2
SALES (est): 130.7K **Privately Held**
SIC: 3599 Industrial machinery

(G-6422)
EMBEDDED SYSTEMS LLC
15714 Victorias Crest Pl (20169-8122)
PHONE..............................860 269-8148
Bhal R Tulpule, *President*
EMP: 1
SQ FT: 1,000
SALES (est): 250K **Privately Held**
SIC: 3571 Electronic computers

(G-6423)
ENVIRONMENTAL LTG SOLUTIONS
6312 Cullen Pl (20169-5400)
PHONE..............................202 361-2686
David Hall, *Principal*
▲ EMP: 1
SALES (est): 70.7K **Privately Held**
SIC: 3648 Lighting equipment

(G-6424)
FUR PERSONS RESCUE FUND
3097 James Madison Hwy (20169-2024)
PHONE..............................703 754-7474
Helen E Marmoll Esq, *Principal*
EMP: 2
SALES (est): 68.2K **Privately Held**
SIC: 3999 Furs

(G-6425)
GEZA GEAR INC
5501 Merchants View Sq # 211
(20169-5439)
PHONE..............................703 327-9844
Tom Cseri, *President*
EMP: 25
SALES (est): 2.1MM **Privately Held**
WEB: www.gezagear.com
SIC: 3751 5571 Motorcycle accessories;
motorcycle parts & accessories

(G-6426)
IDEZINE LLC
15755 Cool Spring Dr (20169-5420)
PHONE..............................703 946-3490
Macrina Singleton, *Principal*
EMP: 2
SALES (est): 217.4K **Privately Held**
SIC: 2752 Commercial printing, litho-
graphic

(G-6427)
INSPIRE LIVING INC
13815 Piedmont Vista Dr (20169-3219)
PHONE..............................703 991-0451
Kristi Otto, *CEO*
EMP: 2
SALES (est): 141.2K **Privately Held**
WEB: www.inspirelivinginc.com
SIC: 3845 Patient monitoring apparatus

(G-6428)
JUNK IN MY TRUNK LLC
6864 Jockey Club Ln (20169-2967)
PHONE..............................703 753-7505
William Tanner, *Principal*
EMP: 3
SALES (est): 193.7K **Privately Held**
SIC: 3443 Dumpsters, garbage

(G-6429)
LELO FABRICATION LLC
1518 Duffey Dr (20169-1351)
PHONE..............................703 754-1141
Jeffrey Huff, *Principal*
EMP: 2
SALES (est): 135.9K **Privately Held**
WEB: www.lelofabrication.com
SIC: 3441 Fabricated structural metal

(G-6430)
N ZONE SPORTS
15104 Championship Dr (20169-6200)
PHONE..............................703 743-2848
EMP: 1 EST: 2016
SALES (est): 75.6K **Privately Held**
SIC: 3949 Sporting & athletic goods

(G-6431)
NORTHERN VIRGINIA INSULATION
4518 Jennifer Ln (20169-2206)
PHONE..............................703 753-7249
Charles Clendenny, *Owner*
EMP: 1
SALES (est): 50.2K **Privately Held**
SIC: 3292 Boiler covering (heat insulating
material), except felt

(G-6432)
OWEN CO LLC
5320 Trevino Dr (20169-3159)
PHONE..............................571 261-1316
Tommy Owen, *Principal*
EMP: 2
SALES (est): 204.9K **Privately Held**
WEB: www.owenironworks.com
SIC: 7692 Welding repair

(G-6433)
PARACHUTERIGGERUS LLC
2350 Youngs Dr (20169-1560)
PHONE..............................703 753-9265
James Wine, *Principal*
EMP: 2
SALES (est): 102.2K **Privately Held**
WEB: www.parachuterigger.us
SIC: 2221 Parachute fabrics

(G-6434)
PARTFINITI INC
5501 Merchants View Sq (20169-5439)
PHONE..............................703 679-7278
Geoffrey Laycock, *President*
EMP: 10 EST: 2010
SQ FT: 200
SALES (est): 96.5K **Privately Held**
WEB: www.partfiniti.com
SIC: 7372 Prepackaged software

(G-6435)
PEAC LLC
14646 Celeste Ct (20169-3285)
PHONE..............................571 261-1527
Mimi Zugel, *Principal*
EMP: 2
SALES (est): 52.2K **Privately Held**
SIC: 2711 Newspapers, publishing & print-
ing

(G-6436)
PIKE WOODWORKS
5649 Wheelwright Way (20169-3182)
PHONE..............................571 329-4377
Michael Pike, *Principal*
EMP: 2 EST: 2016
SALES (est): 85.2K **Privately Held**
SIC: 2431 Millwork

▲ = Import ▼=Export
◆ =Import/Export

(G-6437)
POOF INC
Also Called: Ahh Products
15911 Waterfall Rd (20169-2128)
PHONE....................703 298-7516
Ngoc Nguyen, *CEO*
EMP: 1
SALES (est): 837.2K **Privately Held**
WEB: www.ahhprods.com
SIC: 2519 2522 Household furniture, except wood or metal: upholstered; office furniture, except wood

(G-6438)
PWC WINERY LLC
4970 Antioch Rd (20169-2259)
PHONE....................703 753-9360
Chris Pearmund, *Principal*
▲ **EMP:** 2
SQ FT: 7,673
SALES (est): 194.2K **Privately Held**
WEB: www.wineryatlagrange.com
SIC: 2084 Wines

(G-6439)
R & B COMMUNICATIONS LLC
15670 Alderbrook Dr (20169-6128)
PHONE....................703 348-7088
Ronald Clatterbuck,
EMP: 2 EST: 2011
SALES (est): 240.3K **Privately Held**
SIC: 2752 Commercial printing, offset

(G-6440)
R T SALES INC
14524 Brinestone Pl (20169-2640)
PHONE....................703 542-5862
Sue Allen Thornbro, *President*
William Schwickrath, *Director*
EMP: 5
SQ FT: 1,800
SALES (est): 1.2MM **Privately Held**
WEB: www.rtsales.net
SIC: 3572 Computer tape drives & components

(G-6441)
RKI INSTRUMENTS INC
6227 Olga Ct (20169-2504)
PHONE....................703 753-3333
EMP: 2
SALES (est): 104.2K **Privately Held**
SIC: 3826 Analytical instruments

(G-6442)
SERUM INSTITUTE INDIA PVT LLC
15213 Brier Creek Dr (20169-6206)
PHONE....................571 248-0911
Francois M Laforce, *Principal*
EMP: 2
SALES (est): 74.4K **Privately Held**
SIC: 2836 Serums

(G-6443)
SEWCIAL STITCH
4626 Hull Dr (20169-8182)
PHONE....................813 786-2966
Mandi Persell, *Principal*
EMP: 1
SALES (est): 40.3K **Privately Held**
SIC: 2395 Embroidery & art needlework

(G-6444)
SHEFFIELD WOODWORKING
15244 Weiskopf Ct (20169-6122)
PHONE....................571 261-4904
EMP: 2
SALES (est): 164.9K **Privately Held**
SIC: 2431 Mfg Millwork

(G-6445)
SIGNS FOR YOU LLC
6153 Popes Creek Pl (20169-5435)
PHONE....................703 653-4353
Pritpal Singh, *Principal*
EMP: 3 EST: 2015
SALES (est): 57.9K **Privately Held**
SIC: 3993 Signs & advertising specialties

(G-6446)
SOPHIE GS CANDLES LLC
15412 Rosemont Manor Dr (20169-6240)
PHONE....................202 253-7798
Sophia Young, *Principal*
EMP: 1
SALES (est): 41.9K **Privately Held**
SIC: 3999 Candles

(G-6447)
SPOTLIGHT DANCE LLC
13920 Shelter Manor Dr (20169-2447)
PHONE....................703 753-9173
Lisa Hayes, *Principal*
EMP: 2
SALES (est): 125.8K **Privately Held**
SIC: 3648 Lighting equipment

(G-6448)
STACK LABS INC
Also Called: Stack Lighting
5501 Merchants View Sq (20169-5439)
PHONE....................503 453-5172
Nigel Mould, *CEO*
Niel Joseph, *Chairman*
Jack McFarland, *CFO*
Pedraam Behroozi, *Technical Staff*
EMP: 20
SQ FT: 5,000
SALES (est): 7.5MM **Privately Held**
WEB: www.stack.care
SIC: 3646 Commercial indusl & institutional electric lighting fixtures

(G-6449)
STRATEGIC PRINT SOLUTIONS LLC
15320 Turning Leaf Pl (20169-8132)
PHONE....................703 272-3440
Kristin McClellan, *Vice Pres*
Timothy J McClellan,
EMP: 6
SALES (est): 685.5K **Privately Held**
WEB: www.integrasynergy.com
SIC: 2752 Commercial printing, lithographic

(G-6450)
TOTAL WELDING SOLUTIONS LLC
16000 Tiffany Ln (20169-1620)
PHONE....................703 898-8720
Valerie Strawser,
Timothy Strawser,
EMP: 1
SALES (est): 62.4K **Privately Held**
SIC: 7692 7699 7389 Welding repair; welding equipment repair;

(G-6451)
TRANSONIC POWER CONTROLS & SVC
14004 Dan Ct (20169-1201)
PHONE....................703 754-8943
William D Neely, *Owner*
EMP: 5
SALES (est): 576.2K **Privately Held**
WEB: www.oltvweb.com
SIC: 7694 Electric motor repair

(G-6452)
TRM INC (PA)
Also Called: Warvel Products
5365 Antioch Ridge Dr (20169-3196)
PHONE....................920 855-2194
Timothy R Meharry, *President*
Sherry R Meharry, *Admin Sec*
◆ **EMP:** 35 EST: 1985
SQ FT: 72,000
SALES (est): 16.1MM **Privately Held**
SIC: 2435 5031 2431 Hardwood veneer & plywood; building materials, interior; millwork

(G-6453)
VISION ACADEMY PUBLISHING LLC
13771 Oakland Ridge Rd (20169-2466)
PHONE....................703 753-0710
Jennifer Georgia, *Principal*
EMP: 1 EST: 2017
SALES (est): 41.3K **Privately Held**
SIC: 2741 Miscellaneous publishing

(G-6454)
WINERY AT LAGRANGE
4970 Antioch Rd (20169-2259)
PHONE....................703 753-9360
Paige Lyman, *Principal*
EMP: 6

SALES (est): 716.7K **Privately Held**
WEB: www.wineryatlagrange.com
SIC: 2084 Wines

(G-6455)
WOODWORK & CABINETS LLC
5425 Bowers Hill Dr (20169-4506)
PHONE....................703 881-1915
Jose Flores, *Principal*
EMP: 1 EST: 2016 **Privately Held**
SIC: 2431 Millwork

(G-6456)
XTREME DIAMOND LLC
6868 Jockey Club Ln (20169-2967)
PHONE....................703 753-0567
Daniel Pumphrey, *President*
EMP: 2
SALES (est): 165.7K **Privately Held**
SIC: 3545 Diamond cutting tools for turning, boring, burnishing, etc.

Haysi
Dickenson County

(G-6457)
BROKEN NEEDLE EMBROIDERY
252 Pressley Br (24256-6275)
PHONE....................276 865-4654
EMP: 1
SALES (est): 31.2K **Privately Held**
SIC: 2395 Embroidery & art needlework

(G-6458)
SUPERIOR FABRICATION LLC
1680 Breaks Park Rd (24256)
P.O. Box 651 (24256-0651)
PHONE....................276 865-4000
David Cole,
EMP: 10 EST: 2011
SQ FT: 34,620
SALES (est): 2MM **Privately Held**
WEB: www.superiorfabrication.us
SIC: 3441 Fabricated structural metal

Heathsville
Northumberland County

(G-6459)
BECKETT CONSULTING INC
129 Bowsprit Ln (22473-4553)
PHONE....................804 580-4164
EMP: 3 **Privately Held**
WEB: www.newsontheneck.com
SIC: 2711 Newspapers, publishing & printing
PA: Beckett Consulting Inc
238 Hill Valley Ln
Heathsville VA 22473

(G-6460)
CLINPAK TECHNOLOGIES LLC
358 Sandy Beach Rd (22473-2234)
PHONE....................410 357-4454
Neil Bryant,
Mark Sassler,
EMP: 6
SALES (est): 629.6K **Privately Held**
SIC: 2834 Pharmaceutical preparations

(G-6461)
CUTTING EDGE MILLWORKS LLC
1334 Sampsons Wharf Rd (22473-3773)
PHONE....................804 580-7270
Angela O'Neill, *Principal*
EMP: 2
SALES (est): 55.2K **Privately Held**
SIC: 2499 Wood products

(G-6462)
FROST INDUSTRIES INC
157 Miskimon Rd (22473-3821)
PHONE....................804 724-0330
Christina Frost, *President*
EMP: 2 EST: 2013
SALES (est): 176.4K **Privately Held**
SIC: 3441 Fabricated structural metal

(G-6463)
PHILOMEN FASHION AND DESIGNS
826 Indian Valley Rd (22473-3544)
PHONE....................703 966-5680
Michael Richards, *Partner*
Kimberly Clarke, *Partner*
Rosalina Clarke, *Partner*
EMP: 5
SALES (est): 264.4K **Privately Held**
WEB: www.philomenfashion.com
SIC: 2393 5699 Canvas bags; bags & containers, except sleeping bags: textile; designers, apparel

(G-6464)
ROYAL STANDARD MINERALS INC
3258 Mob Neck Rd (22473-2306)
PHONE....................804 580-8107
Roland Larsen, *President*
EMP: 2 EST: 1995
SALES (est): 105.2K **Privately Held**
SIC: 1499 Mineral abrasives mining

(G-6465)
SHARPE RESOURCES CORP (PA)
Also Called: Sharpe Energy Company
3258 Mob Neck Rd (22473-2306)
P.O. Box 72, Burgess (22432-0072)
PHONE....................804 580-8107
Roland M Larsen, *President*
Jim Dunlop, *Director*
Kimberly Koener, *Director*
EMP: 2
SQ FT: 3,500
SALES (est): 540K **Privately Held**
WEB:
www.sharperesourcescorporation.com
SIC: 1382 Oil & gas exploration services

(G-6466)
SIGN DESIGNS
1938 Walnut Point Rd (22473-2906)
PHONE....................804 580-7446
Jessica Guy-Haynie, *Owner*
EMP: 1
SALES (est): 84.9K **Privately Held**
WEB: www.signdesignsbyjessica.com
SIC: 3993 Signs & advertising specialties

(G-6467)
THAT DAMN MARY BREWING LLC
148 Skipjack Dr (22473-4543)
PHONE....................804 761-1085
Mary Anderson-Leichty, *Principal*
EMP: 2
SALES (est): 62.3K **Privately Held**
SIC: 2082 Malt beverages

Henrico
Henrico County

(G-6468)
3314 MONUMENT AVE LLC
607 Baldwin Rd (23229-6815)
PHONE....................804 285-9770
Paul Kastelberg, *Principal*
EMP: 2
SALES (est): 91.3K **Privately Held**
SIC: 3272 Monuments & grave markers, except terrazo

(G-6469)
A & R CABINET CO INC
10190 Purcell Rd (23228-1112)
PHONE....................804 261-4098
Raymond T Easter Jr, *Ch of Bd*
Donna Etinsley, *President*
Raymond Easter III, *Vice Pres*
EMP: 6
SQ FT: 4,100
SALES (est): 625.6K **Privately Held**
WEB: www.aandrcabinet.com
SIC: 2434 Wood kitchen cabinets

(G-6470)
AFGD INC
6200 Gorman Rd (23231-6037)
PHONE....................804 222-0120

EMP: 1 EST: 2016
SALES (est): 67.6K Privately Held
SIC: 3229 Mfg Pressed/Blown Glass

(G-6471)
AGC FLAT GLASS NORTH AMER INC
6200 Gorman Rd (23231-6037)
PHONE..................................804 222-0120
EMP: 2 Privately Held
WEB: www.agc.com
SIC: 3231 Safety glass: made from purchased glass
HQ: Agc Flat Glass North America, Inc.
11175 Cicero Dr Ste 400
Alpharetta GA 30022
404 446-4200

(G-6472)
ALCOLOCK VA INC
8143 Staples Mill Rd (23228-2751)
PHONE..................................804 515-0022
Felix J E Comeau, *President*
Bruce Bailey, *Treasurer*
EMP: 5 EST: 2009
SALES (est): 311.2K
SALES (corp-wide): 1.3MM Privately Held
SIC: 3694 Ignition apparatus & distributors
PA: Alcolock Tx Inc
60 International Boulevard
Toronto ON M9W 6
416 619-3500

(G-6473)
ANORD MARDIX (USA) INC
2704 Seven Hills Blvd (23231-6012)
PHONE..................................800 228-4689
Rob Sweaney, *President*
Alan Cooling, *Corp Secy*
John Day, *Vice Pres*
Kris Morgheim, *Project Mgr*
Jay Biggers, *Purch Mgr*
◆ **EMP: 2**
SALES (est): 1MM
SALES (corp-wide): 1.7MM Privately Held
WEB: www.anordmardix.com
SIC: 3613 Switchgear & switchboard apparatus
HQ: Anord Mardix (Ireland) Limited
Unit 17
Dundalk
429 320-500

(G-6474)
ANXIOUS BENCH MUSIC INC
2207 Fon Du Lac Rd (23229-3319)
PHONE..................................757 813-4389
Mark Hayward, *Principal*
EMP: 1
SALES (est): 47.2K Privately Held
SIC: 2741 Miscellaneous publishing

(G-6475)
APRIL PRESS
2507 Waldo Ln (23228-5146)
PHONE..................................804 551-8463
EMP: 1 EST: 2017
SALES (est): 37.5K Privately Held
SIC: 2741 Misc Publishing

(G-6476)
ART GUILD INC
8433 Glazebrook Ave (23228-2804)
P.O. Box 6621, Richmond (23230-0621)
PHONE..................................804 282-5434
Violet O Swann, *President*
EMP: 12 EST: 1945
SALES (est): 1MM Privately Held
WEB: www.banner-express.com
SIC: 2759 7336 Screen printing; commercial art & illustration

(G-6477)
ARTEFFECTS
5606 Greendale Rd (23228-5816)
PHONE..................................804 266-7691
Richard Reinhard, *Owner*
EMP: 2
SALES (est): 73.2K Privately Held
SIC: 2759 Commercial printing

(G-6478)
ATLANTIC EMBROIDERY WORKS LLC
1507 N Parham Rd (23229-4604)
PHONE..................................804 282-5027
Amy Ellif, *Accountant*
Craig Mayhew, *Mng Member*
EMP: 6
SALES (est): 350K Privately Held
WEB: www.atlanticembroideryworks.com
SIC: 2396 2395 Screen printing on fabric articles; embroidery & art needlework

(G-6479)
AUTHENTIC PRINTING COMPANY LLC
9020 Shewalt Dr (23228-2347)
PHONE..................................804 672-6659
Jason Ford, *Principal*
EMP: 2
SALES (est): 92.3K Privately Held
SIC: 2752 Commercial printing, offset

(G-6480)
BABYPIPSCOM LLC
3900 Westerre Pkwy # 300 (23233-1478)
PHONE..................................866 674-9258
EMP: 1
SALES (est): 294.2K Privately Held
SIC: 2711 Newspapers, publishing & printing

(G-6481)
BERGER AND BURROW ENTPS INC (PA)
Also Called: Dynamic Mobile Imaging
2301 N Parham Rd Ste 4 (23229-3171)
P.O. Box 17588, Richmond (23226-7588)
PHONE..................................804 282-9729
Deborah A Berger, *Principal*
Dean Berger, *COO*
Sue Bartholomew, *Accounts Mgr*
Heather Emmer, *Accounts Mgr*
EMP: 50
SALES (est): 15.7MM Privately Held
WEB: www.dynamicmobileimaging.com
SIC: 3844 Radiographic X-ray apparatus & tubes

(G-6482)
BERKLEY LATASHA
Also Called: Kingdom Jewelry, The
4530 Kings Hill Rd (23231-1959)
PHONE..................................804 572-6394
Latasha Berkley, *Owner*
EMP: 1
SALES (est): 41K Privately Held
SIC: 2399 5139 7389 Hand woven & crocheted products; footwear; business services

(G-6483)
BMG METALS INC
6301 Gorman Rd (23231-6050)
P.O. Box 7536 (23231-0036)
PHONE..................................804 622-9452
Wayne Galleher, *Manager*
EMP: 7
SALES (corp-wide): 7MM Privately Held
WEB: www.bmgmetals.com
SIC: 3599 Air intake filters, internal combustion engine, except auto
HQ: Bmg Metals, Inc.
950 Masonic Ln
Richmond VA 23223
804 226-1024

(G-6484)
BOOMERANG AIR SPORTS
11512 Bridgetender Dr (23233-1782)
PHONE..................................804 360-0320
Robert Lupica, *Principal*
EMP: 1
SALES (est): 47K Privately Held
WEB: www.boomerangairsports.com
SIC: 3949 Boomerangs

(G-6485)
BORGWALDT KC INCORPORATED
2800 Charles City Rd (23231-4532)
PHONE..................................804 271-6471
Michael Connor, *President*
Martin Hermann, *Director*
Andreas Panz, *Director*

◆ **EMP: 35**
SQ FT: 22,000
SALES (est): 6.6MM
SALES (corp-wide): 2MM Privately Held
WEB: www.borgwaldt.hauni.com
SIC: 3823 Industrial instrmnts msrmnt display/control process variable
HQ: Hauni Maschinenbau Gmbh
Kurt-A.-Korber-Chaussee 8-32
Hamburg 21033
407 250-01

(G-6486)
BUNZL CAROLINAS AND VIRGINIA
2400 Distribution Dr (23231-5407)
PHONE..................................804 236-5000
EMP: 3
SALES (est): 99.8K Privately Held
WEB: www.bunzldistribution.com
SIC: 2671 Packaging paper & plastics film, coated & laminated

(G-6487)
CAB-POOL INC
Also Called: A Cab-Pool
11838 Chase Wellesley Dr # 416 (23233-7754)
PHONE..................................804 218-8294
Barbara Burton, *CEO*
Brian Littler, *President*
EMP: 11
SALES (est): 992.6K Privately Held
SIC: 2431 Millwork

(G-6488)
CARRIAGE HOUSE PRODUCTS INC
5511 Lakeside Ave (23228-5718)
PHONE..................................804 615-2400
Timothy Dowdy, *President*
Anthony Oley, *Treasurer*
EMP: 4
SALES (est): 354.9K Privately Held
WEB: www.carriagehouseproducts.com
SIC: 2051 Bakery: wholesale or wholesale/retail combined

(G-6489)
CAVE SYSTEMS INC
113 Williamson Ct (23229-7763)
P.O. Box 68, Keswick (22947-0068)
PHONE..................................877 344-2283
Jason Tuckley, *President*
EMP: 1
SQ FT: 2,000
SALES (est): 1MM Privately Held
WEB: www.cavesystems.com
SIC: 3441 Fabricated structural metal

(G-6490)
CDA USA INC
4310 Eubank Rd (23231-4315)
PHONE..................................804 918-3707
Pascal P Delrieu, *President*
Delrieu Pascal P J, *President*
Remi Langlois, *Business Mgr*
Remi Lauglois, *Vice Pres*
Adam Hanig, *Sales Engr*
▲ **EMP: 5 EST: 2012**
SALES (est): 1.2MM Privately Held
WEB: www.cda-usa.com
SIC: 3565 Packaging machinery

(G-6491)
CERVANTES MASONRY
8408 Spalding Dr (23229-5736)
PHONE..................................804 741-7271
EMP: 2
SALES (est): 62.3K Privately Held
SIC: 2024 Yogurt desserts, frozen

(G-6492)
CHUCKS CONCRETE PUMPING LLC
6717 Whitelake Dr (23231-6568)
P.O. Box 70205, Richmond (23255-0205)
PHONE..................................804 347-3986
Antwon Vaughn,
EMP: 3
SALES (est): 485.8K Privately Held
WEB: www.chucksconcretepumping.com
SIC: 3531 Construction machinery

(G-6493)
CITIWOOD URBAN FOREST PRODUCTS
5454 Charles City Rd (23231-6550)
PHONE..................................804 795-9220
Edward Bath, *Owner*
EMP: 1
SALES (est): 62.1K Privately Held
WEB: www.citiwood.com
SIC: 2499 Wood products

(G-6494)
CORPORATE IMPRINTS
6920 Lakeside Ave Ste C (23228-5247)
PHONE..................................804 965-9838
Bobbie E Griffin, *President*
Cindi Cosby, *Corp Secy*
EMP: 8
SALES (est): 953.5K Privately Held
WEB: www.corporateimprints.com
SIC: 2759 Screen printing

(G-6495)
CUPRON INC
4329 November Ave (23231-4309)
P.O. Box 85073, Richmond (23285-5073)
PHONE..................................804 322-3650
Danny Lustiger, *CEO*
Christopher Andrews, *General Mgr*
Jason L Ellis, *General Mgr*
Paul F Rocheleau, *Chairman*
Dennis Cavender, *Vice Pres*
▲ **EMP: 11 Privately Held**
WEB: www.cupron.com
SIC: 2299 Textile mill waste & remnant processing

(G-6496)
CUSTOM ENGRAVING AND SIGNS LLC
9120 Crystalwood Ln (23294-5925)
PHONE..................................804 270-1272
Steve Shepherd, *Opers Staff*
EMP: 1
SALES (est): 46K Privately Held
SIC: 3993 Signs & advertising specialties

(G-6497)
CUSTOM WINDOWS
2238 Cresthaven Ct (23238-3218)
PHONE..................................804 262-1621
EMP: 1
SALES (est): 49K Privately Held
SIC: 2391 5023 Mfg Curtains/Draperies Whol Homefurnishings

(G-6498)
CYNTHERAPY SCENTED CANDLES LLC
3312 Hawkins Rd (23228-3434)
PHONE..................................804 901-2681
Cynthia Edwards, *Administration*
EMP: 1
SALES (est): 52.9K Privately Held
WEB: www.cyntherapyscentedcandles.com
SIC: 3999 Candles

(G-6499)
DEFAZIO INDUSTRIES LLC
3900 Westerre Pkwy # 300 (23233-1339)
PHONE..................................703 399-1494
Rick Defazio, *Principal*
EMP: 5 EST: 2015
SALES (est): 211K Privately Held
WEB: www.defaziollc.com
SIC: 3999 Manufacturing industries

(G-6500)
DIAMOND SCREEN GRAPHICS INC
4305 Sarellen Rd (23231-4311)
PHONE..................................804 249-4414
Alexander N Simon, *Administration*
EMP: 2
SALES (est): 107.2K Privately Held
WEB: www.diamondscreengraphics.com
SIC: 2759 Commercial printing

(G-6501)
DIAZ CERAMICS
2406 Skeet St (23294-3502)
PHONE..................................804 672-7161
EMP: 1 EST: 2013

SALES (est): 50.9K **Privately Held**
SIC: 3269 Mfg Pottery Products

(G-6502)
DIMENSIONU INC
1895 Billingsgate Cir B (23238-4229)
PHONE......................................804 447-4220
Steven Hoy, *CEO*
Ntiedo Etuk, *Ch of Bd*
EMP: 39
SALES (est): 950K **Privately Held**
WEB: www.dimensionu.com
SIC: 3571 Electronic computers

(G-6503)
DRIVING 4 DOLLARS
1300 Oakland Rd (23231-4764)
PHONE......................................757 609-1298
Johnie Hopkins, *Principal*
James Sheppard, *Principal*
EMP: 2
SALES (est): 110K **Privately Held**
SIC: 7372 Application computer software

(G-6504)
DURATION PRODUCTS LLC
8568 Sanford Dr (23228-2813)
PHONE......................................804 651-1700
Peter J Barossi, *President*
Bill Pittman,
EMP: 1
SALES (est): 118K **Privately Held**
SIC: 2891 Epoxy adhesives

(G-6505)
DYSERT CUSTOM WOODWORK
11201 Pinewood Ct (23238-5314)
PHONE......................................804 741-4712
Scott Dysert, *Principal*
EMP: 1
SALES (est): 57.4K **Privately Held**
WEB: www.dysertcw.com
SIC: 2431 Millwork

(G-6506)
EDWARDS KRETZ LOHR & ASSOC
2215 Cox Rd (23233-2766)
PHONE......................................804 673-9666
John Edwards, *President*
EMP: 15
SALES (est): 1.9MM **Privately Held**
WEB: www.edwardskretzlohr.com
SIC: 3531 Rakes, land clearing: mechanical

(G-6507)
ENRICH COMPOST LLC
2509 Burnley Ave (23228-5123)
PHONE......................................518 410-2402
Kelsey Marie Ryan, *Principal*
EMP: 2
SALES (est): 81.8K **Privately Held**
SIC: 2875 Compost

(G-6508)
EXHIBIT DESIGN & PROD SVCS LLC
4300 Eubank Rd (23231-4315)
PHONE......................................804 347-0924
James Bandelean, *Principal*
Michael Pittman, *VP Bus Dvlpt*
EMP: 1
SALES (est): 97K **Privately Held**
WEB: www.designtechexhibits.com
SIC: 3577 Graphic displays, except graphic terminals

(G-6509)
FEEDRVA INC
2601 Lafayette Ave (23228-4516)
PHONE......................................804 513-3100
Karen L Atkinso, *President*
EMP: 2
SALES (est): 67.9K **Privately Held**
WEB: www.rvamag.com
SIC: 2711 Newspapers

(G-6510)
FINITE WISDOM
8212 Cobbler Ct (23228-3124)
PHONE......................................804 794-9585
EMP: 3

SALES (est): 162.2K **Privately Held**
WEB: www.finitewisdom.com
SIC: 3652 Pre-recorded records & tapes

(G-6511)
FIVE PONDS PRESS
10210 Windbluff Dr (23238-3823)
PHONE......................................804 740-5867
EMP: 1
SALES (est): 42.4K **Privately Held**
SIC: 2741 Miscellaneous publishing

(G-6512)
FLINT GROUP US LLC
8000 Villa Park Dr (23228-6500)
PHONE......................................804 270-1328
Ken Smith, *Manager*
EMP: 2
SALES (corp-wide): 53.9B **Publicly Held**
WEB: www.flintgrp.com
SIC: 2893 Printing ink
HQ: Flint Group Us Llc
17177 N Laurel Park Dr # 300
Livonia MI 48152
734 781-4600

(G-6513)
FMP INC
11217 Eastborough Ct (23233-1839)
PHONE......................................434 392-3222
Rithie Misher, *Principal*
EMP: 4
SALES (est): 192.2K **Privately Held**
SIC: 2051 Bread, cake & related products

(G-6514)
FOR RENT MAGAZINE
3923 Deep Rock Rd (23233-1416)
PHONE......................................305 305-0494
EMP: 2
SALES (est): 78.1K **Privately Held**
SIC: 2721 Magazines: publishing only, not printed on site

(G-6515)
FREEDOM RESPIRATORY
2852 E Parham Rd (23228-2918)
PHONE......................................804 266-2002
EMP: 2
SALES (est): 86.6K **Privately Held**
SIC: 3841 Surgical & medical instruments

(G-6516)
GARRET INDUSTRIES LLC
7453 Willson Rd (23231-5849)
PHONE......................................804 795-1650
Howard Troy Garrett, *Principal*
EMP: 1
SALES (est): 39.6K **Privately Held**
SIC: 3999 Manufacturing industries

(G-6517)
GHEK INDUSTRIES LLC
1204 Middleberry Dr (23231-4761)
PHONE......................................804 955-0710
Gregory Kopf, *Principal*
EMP: 2 EST: 2017
SALES (est): 124.2K **Privately Held**
SIC: 3999 Manufacturing industries

(G-6518)
GOULET PEN COMPANY LLC
1590 E Parham Rd (23228-2360)
PHONE......................................804 368-0482
Brian Goulet, *CEO*
Rachel Goulet, *Officer*
EMP: 21 EST: 2009
SQ FT: 12,000
SALES (est): 3.4MM **Privately Held**
WEB: www.gouletpens.com
SIC: 3951 Fountain pens & fountain pen desk sets

(G-6519)
GST MICRO LLC
8356 Town Hall Ct (23231-7591)
PHONE......................................203 271-0830
Debra Tillotson, *Principal*
EMP: 4 EST: 2016
SALES (est): 335.9K **Privately Held**
WEB: www.gstmicro.com
SIC: 2834 Pharmaceutical preparations

(G-6520)
HEAVENLY AROMAS LLC
118 N Cedar Ave (23075-1429)
PHONE......................................804 651-6250
Alexis Harris, *Mng Member*
EMP: 10
SALES (est): 10K **Privately Held**
SIC: 3999 Candles

(G-6521)
HENRICO
3426 Pump Rd (23233-1111)
PHONE......................................434 202-2331
Tomella Bowles, *Supervisor*
Barbara Bonner, *Assistant*
Tyler League, *Assistant*
Tim Sanders, *Assistant*
John Marshall, *Associate*
EMP: 2
SALES (est): 69.2K **Privately Held**
SIC: 2711 Newspapers, publishing & printing

(G-6522)
HSS INC
10514 Gayton Rd (23238-4104)
PHONE......................................610 444-7409
Hughes Owen L, *Principal*
EMP: 3
SALES (est): 139.6K **Privately Held**
SIC: 7372 Prepackaged software

(G-6523)
HUGHES POSTERS LLC
Also Called: PHD Posters
1704 Tunbridge Dr (23238-4127)
PHONE......................................304 615-3433
Charlotte Dauphin,
Brett Hugher,
EMP: 2
SALES (est): 127.1K **Privately Held**
SIC: 2759 Posters, including billboards: printing

(G-6524)
ITEK SOFTWARE LLC
5402 Glenside Dr Ste D (23228-3994)
PHONE......................................804 505-4835
EMP: 2
SALES (est): 33.6K **Privately Held**
WEB: www.itek-software.com
SIC: 7372 Prepackaged software

(G-6525)
J M FRY COMPANY (PA)
Also Called: J.M. Fry Printing Inks
4329 Eubank Rd (23231-4314)
P.O. Box 7719 (23231-0219)
PHONE......................................804 236-8100
Robert A Hodges, *President*
Billy J Hodges, *Vice Pres*
James H Hodges, *Vice Pres*
David Parker, *Sales Staff*
Brian Duncan, *Info Tech Mgr*
▼ EMP: 50 EST: 1938
SQ FT: 42,000
SALES (est): 21MM **Privately Held**
WEB: www.jmfryinks.com
SIC: 2893 Printing ink

(G-6526)
JAMES RIVER PUBLISHING INC
11202 Pinewood Ct (23238-5310)
PHONE......................................804 740-0729
Cindi Graesser, *Principal*
EMP: 2
SALES (est): 69.1K **Privately Held**
SIC: 2711 Newspapers

(G-6527)
KIMBERLY GILBERT
11213 Halbrooke Ct (23233-1840)
PHONE......................................804 201-6591
EMP: 1
SALES: 35K **Privately Held**
SIC: 3931 Musical Instruments And Parts, Nec

(G-6528)
KOOLNUT LLC
2115 Clarke St (23228-5741)
PHONE......................................213 349-0196
Safdar Nazir,
EMP: 1

SALES (est): 50K **Privately Held**
SIC: 3263 Kitchen articles, semivitreous earthenware

(G-6529)
KORMAN SIGNS INC
3029 Lincoln Ave (23228-4209)
PHONE......................................804 262-6050
Dan Kirk, *Sales Staff*
EMP: 1
SALES (est): 50.6K **Privately Held**
SIC: 3993 Signs & advertising specialties

(G-6530)
LINEAGE MECHANICAL LLC
113 N Kalmia Ave (23075-1809)
PHONE......................................804 687-5649
Ashley Walker, *Owner*
EMP: 1
SALES (est): 220K **Privately Held**
WEB: www.lineagemechanical.com
SIC: 7694 Electric motor repair

(G-6531)
LORON INC
Also Called: Pgfx
3 Alexis Dr (23231-6440)
PHONE......................................804 780-0000
Ron Sprouse, *President*
EMP: 5 EST: 1998
SALES (est): 370K **Privately Held**
SIC: 2754 Photogravure & rotogravure printing

(G-6532)
MANAN LLC
Also Called: Gyrus Systems
5400 Glenside Dr Ste B (23228-3996)
PHONE......................................804 320-1414
Trey Moyer, *Sales Staff*
Viren Kapadia,
Smita Kapadia,
EMP: 12
SQ FT: 3,100
SALES (est): 1.1MM **Privately Held**
WEB: www.gyrus.com
SIC: 7372 Educational computer software

(G-6533)
MARILYN CARTER
Also Called: Printing Professionals
2531 Lkfeld Mews Ct Apt G (23231)
PHONE......................................804 901-4757
Marilyn Carter, *Principal*
EMP: 1
SALES (est): 93.3K **Privately Held**
SIC: 2759 Commercial printing

(G-6534)
MCCOY WATER FILTER INC
8441 Varina Rd (23231-8243)
P.O. Box 590, Sandston (23150-0590)
PHONE......................................804 222-2089
Brian A McCoy, *President*
EMP: 3
SALES (est): 362.3K **Privately Held**
WEB: www.mccoywaterfilter.com
SIC: 3589 Water filters & softeners, household type

(G-6535)
MOBILE RADIO PARTNERS INC
1420 N Parham Rd Ste Q107 (23229-5513)
PHONE......................................804 525-4013
Michael Mazursky, *Branch Mgr*
EMP: 16
SALES (corp-wide): 1.8MM **Privately Held**
WEB: www.motorolasolutions.com
SIC: 3663 Radio & TV communications equipment
PA: Mobile Radio Partners, Inc.
6573 Glenshaw Dr
Glen Allen VA 23059
804 364-1553

(G-6536)
MOLINS RICHMOND INC
1470 E Parham Rd (23228-2300)
PHONE......................................804 887-2525
Tom Lavinka, *President*
Jim Klein, *Sales Staff*
▲ EMP: 100
SQ FT: 86,500

SALES (est): 18.1MM
SALES (corp-wide): 114.7MM **Privately Held**
WEB: www.molins.com
SIC: 3559 Broom making machinery
HQ: Molins Machine Company, Inc.
1470 E Parham Rd
Richmond VA
804 887-2100

(G-6537)
MS KATHLEEN B WATKINS
9084 Hoke Brady Rd (23231-8234)
PHONE..................................804 741-0388
EMP: 2 EST: 2017
SALES (est): 95.3K **Privately Held**
SIC: 3669 Communications equipment

(G-6538)
MSC IMAGING TECH LLC
2530 Gayton Centre Dr (23238-6912)
PHONE..................................804 593-0689
Adarshvir Singh,
EMP: 3
SALES (est): 98.2K **Privately Held**
SIC: 2759 Commercial printing

(G-6539)
NEIGHBORHOOD FLAGS
13317 Teasdale Ct (23233-1026)
PHONE..................................804 360-3398
Steve Nelson, *Vice Pres*
EMP: 2
SALES (est): 104.7K **Privately Held**
WEB: www.neighborhoodflags.com
SIC: 2241 Braids, textile

(G-6540)
NEUTRA-GREEN CLG SOLUTIONS LLC
2221 E Parham Rd Ste C (23228-2239)
PHONE..................................804 447-8010
Laura West, *Principal*
Jemma Cox, *Principal*
EMP: 3
SALES (est): 123.2K **Privately Held**
SIC: 2879 Agricultural chemicals

(G-6541)
NEW HEALTH ANALYTICS LLC
200 Westgate Pkwy Ste 104 (23233-7794)
PHONE..................................804 245-8240
Todd Nuckols, *CEO*
Larry Hoffheimer, *COO*
James Dameron, *CTO*
EMP: 12 EST: 2017
SALES (est): 256K
SALES (corp-wide): 2.5MM **Privately Held**
WEB: www.newhealthanalytics.com
SIC: 7372 Business oriented computer software
PA: Enterbridge Technologies, Inc.
200 Westgate Pkwy Ste 104
Henrico VA 23233
804 234-8100

(G-6542)
NEW LOOK PRESSURE WASHING LLC
1300 Oakland Rd (23231-4764)
PHONE..................................804 476-2000
EMP: 1
SALES: 50K **Privately Held**
SIC: 3589 Mfg Service Industry Machinery

(G-6543)
NEWCOMB WOODWORKS LLC
2206 Oakwood Ln (23228-5612)
PHONE..................................804 370-0441
EMP: 1
SALES (est): 41.5K **Privately Held**
SIC: 2499 Wood products

(G-6544)
NIGHTINGALE INC
8903 Three Chopt Rd (23229-4614)
PHONE..................................804 332-7018
Hannah Pollack, *President*
EMP: 6
SQ FT: 2,000
SALES (est): 185.1K **Privately Held**
SIC: 2024 2052 Ice cream, packaged: molded, on sticks, etc.; cookies & crackers

(G-6545)
NUTRIATI INC (PA)
9722 Gayton Rd (23238-4907)
PHONE..................................804 562-2322
Michael Todd, *CEO*
EMP: 18
SALES (est): 5.5MM **Privately Held**
WEB: www.nutriati.com
SIC: 2099 Food preparations

(G-6546)
PATRICK PIERCE
4900 E Leyburn Ct Apt 102 (23228-4848)
PHONE..................................804 833-1800
Patrick Pierce, *Co-Owner*
▲ EMP: 1
SALES (est): 70.6K **Privately Held**
SIC: 3421 7699 Table & food cutlery, including butchers'; surgical instrument repair

(G-6547)
PAUL OWENS
Also Called: Budget Printing Services Ng
6925 Fox Downs Dr (23231-5226)
PHONE..................................804 393-2475
Paul Owens, *Owner*
Kymie Owens, *Principal*
EMP: 1
SALES (est): 77K **Privately Held**
SIC: 2752 Commercial printing, lithographic

(G-6548)
PIVOTAL GEAR LLC
2701 Emerywood Pkwy # 101 (23294-3722)
PHONE..................................804 726-1328
Leighton Klevana, *Principal*
EMP: 2
SALES (est): 150.1K **Privately Held**
WEB: www.dynamicbrands.com
SIC: 3949 Sporting & athletic goods

(G-6549)
PLUG ELECTRICAL
6512 Marleigh Ct (23231-7900)
PHONE..................................804 873-8688
Brandon Burrell, *Principal*
EMP: 2
SALES (est): 88.3K **Privately Held**
SIC: 3643 Plugs, electric

(G-6550)
PRINT TENT LLC
4911 Mulford Rd (23231-2619)
PHONE..................................804 852-9750
Alonzo Robinson, *President*
EMP: 2
SALES (est): 99.8K **Privately Held**
WEB: www.theprinttent.com
SIC: 2759 Letterpress & screen printing

(G-6551)
PRINTER GATHERER LLC
1519 Baysdale Ln (23229-4702)
PHONE..................................540 420-2426
Emily Striffler, *Principal*
EMP: 2
SALES (est): 122.4K **Privately Held**
WEB: www.printergatherer.com
SIC: 2752 Commercial printing, lithographic

(G-6552)
PROSTRIDE ORTHOTICS LLC
9609 Gayton Rd Ste 102 (23238-4900)
PHONE..................................804 310-3894
EMP: 1
SALES (corp-wide): 314.2K **Privately Held**
WEB: www.prostrideorthotics.com
SIC: 3842 Orthopedic appliances
PA: Prostride Orthotics, Llc
5366 Twin Hickory Rd B
Glen Allen VA

(G-6553)
PUZZLE HOMES LLC
2290 N Parham Rd (23229-3159)
PHONE..................................804 247-7256
EMP: 1
SALES (est): 41K **Privately Held**
SIC: 3944 Puzzles

(G-6554)
RAIN FOREST SHOWER SYSTEM LLC
10001 Patterson Ave # 207 (23238-5126)
PHONE..................................804 432-8930
Spilman Short, *President*
Jody Short, *Mng Member*
▲ EMP: 3 EST: 2012
SALES (est): 10K **Privately Held**
WEB: www.rainforestshower.com
SIC: 3431 Shower stalls, metal

(G-6555)
RAVE ON INDUSTRIES LLC
9504 Gayton Rd (23229-5320)
PHONE..................................804 308-0898
Ray Harrison Vaughan III, *Principal*
EMP: 1
SALES (est): 39.6K **Privately Held**
SIC: 3999 Manufacturing industries

(G-6556)
REESES AMAZING PRINTING SVCS
405 Sherilyn Dr (23075-2007)
PHONE..................................804 325-0947
Teresa Auston,
EMP: 1
SALES (est): 60.8K **Privately Held**
SIC: 2759 2754 2752 2741 Calendars: printing; post cards, picture: printing; invitation & stationery printing & engraving; stationery & invitation printing, gravure; calendar & card printing, lithographic; posters: publishing & printing

(G-6557)
REGINALDS HOMEMADE LLC
8104 Greystone East Cir (23229-7272)
PHONE..................................804 972-4040
Andrew M Lohmann, *Administration*
EMP: 6
SALES (est): 279.7K **Privately Held**
WEB: www.reginaldshomemade.com
SIC: 2099 Peanut butter

(G-6558)
RICHMOND DEFENSE FIRM
4124 E Parham Rd (23228-3745)
PHONE..................................804 977-0764
EMP: 2
SALES (est): 87.4K **Privately Held**
WEB: www.virginiacriminallawyernow.com
SIC: 3812 Defense systems & equipment

(G-6559)
RING FIRE MANUFACTURING LLC
7642 Phillips Woods Dr (23231-6344)
PHONE..................................804 617-9288
David Elliott, *Administration*
EMP: 2 EST: 2016
SALES (est): 71.4K **Privately Held**
WEB: www.ringoffiremfg.com
SIC: 3999 Manufacturing industries

(G-6560)
RIVANNA NATURAL DESIGNS INC
3009 Lincoln Ave (23228-4209)
PHONE..................................434 244-3447
Crystal Mario, *President*
Admir Hasanovic, *Opers Mgr*
Gretchen Wirth, *Sales Executive*
Ashley Sisti, *Technology*
EMP: 7
SQ FT: 4,007
SALES (est): 276K **Privately Held**
WEB: www.rivannadesigns.com
SIC: 2491 Wood products, creosoted

(G-6561)
RIVERCITY COMMUNICATIONS
Also Called: David Aponte Sr
7311 Osborne Tpke (23231-6749)
PHONE..................................804 304-9590
David Aponte, *Partner*
EMP: 3
SALES (est): 35K **Privately Held**
WEB: www.rivercitycommunications.net
SIC: 3651 Household audio & video equipment

(G-6562)
RVA SWEETS LLC
3943 Waterville Ct Apt 14 (23233-1252)
PHONE..................................540 748-9298
Robin Holland,
EMP: 1
SALES (est): 10K **Privately Held**
SIC: 2099 Food preparations

(G-6563)
RVA WOODWORK LLC
5880 Charles City Rd (23231-6623)
PHONE..................................804 840-2345
Evan Howard, *Principal*
EMP: 2 EST: 2014
SALES (est): 91.2K **Privately Held**
SIC: 2431 Millwork

(G-6564)
S4 WOOD WORKS LLC
2820 Hardings Trace Ln (23233-7002)
PHONE..................................804 299-0454
EMP: 1
SALES (est): 59.5K **Privately Held**
SIC: 2431 Millwork

(G-6565)
SAN-J INTERNATIONAL INC (DH)
6200 Gorman Rd (23231-6072)
PHONE..................................804 226-8333
Takashi Sato, *President*
Christina Hurst, *Human Resources*
Lisa Newcomb, *Sales Staff*
◆ EMP: 36 EST: 1978
SQ FT: 44,000
SALES (est): 8.7MM **Privately Held**
WEB: www.san-j.com
SIC: 2035 1541 Soy sauce; food products manufacturing or packing plant construction

(G-6566)
SEMA WRAY
7205 Pinetree Rd (23229-7510)
PHONE..................................804 282-3609
EMP: 2 EST: 2017
SALES (est): 109.6K **Privately Held**
WEB: www.semawray.com
SIC: 2741 Miscellaneous publishing

(G-6567)
SIGN BIZ LLC
9020 Quioccasin Rd (23229-5515)
PHONE..................................804 741-7446
EMP: 1
SALES (est): 46K **Privately Held**
WEB: www.signbiz.com
SIC: 3993 Signs & advertising specialties

(G-6568)
SIGN SCAPES INC
7519 Ranco Rd (23228-3751)
PHONE..................................804 980-7111
Jennifer Tompkins, *Principal*
Amber Watts, *Graphic Designe*
EMP: 3
SALES (est): 326.8K **Privately Held**
WEB: www.richmondsignscapes.com
SIC: 3993 Signs & advertising specialties

(G-6569)
SIGN SOURCE
7509 Lisa Ln (23294-4607)
PHONE..................................804 270-3252
Gino M Scarpa, *Principal*
EMP: 2
SALES (est): 160.1K **Privately Held**
WEB: www.signsourcesigns.com
SIC: 3993 Signs & advertising specialties

(G-6570)
SIGNARAMA
Also Called: Sign-A-Rama
3712 West End Dr (23294-5832)
PHONE..................................804 967-3768
EMP: 1
SALES (est): 52.1K **Privately Held**
WEB: www.signarama.com
SIC: 3993 Signs & advertising specialties

(G-6571)
SISKO DUEL FUEL SYSTEM
7800 Wood Mill Dr (23231-7341)
PHONE..................................804 795-1634

▲ = Import ▼=Export
◆ =Import/Export

EMP: 4
SALES (est): 306K **Privately Held**
SIC: 2869 Fuels

(G-6572)
SOUTH ANNA INC
3603 Mayland Ct (23233-1409)
P.O. Box 3568, Glen Allen (23058-3568)
PHONE.............................804 316-9660
Stephanie Jeter, *CEO*
EMP: 9
SALES (est): 818.1K **Privately Held**
WEB: www.southanna.com
SIC: 7372 7379 Application computer software; data processing consultant

(G-6573)
SPECIALTY TOOLING LLC
8656 Staples Mill Rd (23228-2719)
PHONE.............................804 912-1158
R Jefferson Garnett, *Mng Member*
EMP: 2
SALES (est): 276.5K **Privately Held**
SIC: 3545 Machine tool accessories

(G-6574)
SPECTRA QUEST INC
8227 Hermitage Rd (23228-3031)
PHONE.............................804 261-3300
Surendra N Ganeriwala, *President*
Jim Lowe, *Design Engr*
EMP: 15
SQ FT: 17,500
SALES (est): 4.2MM **Privately Held**
WEB: www.spectraquest.com
SIC: 3531 8711 3829 Construction machinery; industrial engineers; kinematic test & measuring equipment

(G-6575)
STACEY A PEETS
Also Called: Government Sign Solution
2706a Enterprise Pkwy (23294-6334)
PHONE.............................847 707-3112
Stacey Peets, *Owner*
EMP: 1
SALES (est): 46.8K **Privately Held**
SIC: 3993 7389 Signs & advertising specialties; business services

(G-6576)
SUPERB CLEANING SOLUTONS
1408 Nanassas Ct (23231-5116)
PHONE.............................804 908-9018
Larry Snead Jr, *Principal*
EMP: 1
SALES (est): 25K **Privately Held**
SIC: 2842 Specialty cleaning, polishes & sanitation goods

(G-6577)
SWEET HEAT CANDLES
8343 Strath Rd (23231-7421)
PHONE.............................804 921-8233
EMP: 1
SALES (est): 39.6K **Privately Held**
SIC: 3999 Candles

(G-6578)
TAPE-TAB LP
10125 Idlebrook Dr (23238-3708)
PHONE.............................804 404-6855
Linnette Kirill, *Managing Prtnr*
EMP: 2 EST: 2016
SALES (est): 112.9K **Privately Held**
SIC: 3842 Tape, adhesive: medicated or non-medicated

(G-6579)
TAYLYNN MANUFACTURING LLC (PA)
Also Called: Ziptip
3900 Westerre Pkwy # 300 (23233-1478)
PHONE.............................804 727-0103
Thomas T Medsker,
EMP: 1
SQ FT: 400
SALES (est): 9.7K **Privately Held**
SIC: 3965 Zipper

(G-6580)
TETELESTAI INDUSTRIES LLC
2113 Turtle Creek Dr # 8 (23233-3662)
PHONE.............................804 596-5232
Joseph Capri, *Principal*

EMP: 2 EST: 2012
SALES (est): 103K **Privately Held**
SIC: 3999 Manufacturing industries

(G-6581)
THUMBPRINT EVENTS BY
20 Skipwith Green Cir (23294-3432)
PHONE.............................703 720-1000
Sandra Marsh, *Principal*
EMP: 2
SALES (est): 87.9K **Privately Held**
SIC: 2752 Commercial printing, lithographic

(G-6582)
TIFFANYS BY SHARON INC
1517 N Parham Rd Ste D (23229-4651)
PHONE.............................804 273-6303
Sharon T Townsend, *Administration*
EMP: 2 EST: 2009
SALES (est): 167.7K **Privately Held**
WEB: www.tiffanysbridal.com
SIC: 2311 Tuxedos: made from purchased materials

(G-6583)
TOMS WILD GAME PRODUCTS
11200 Ashford Lake Pl # 1 (23233-1292)
PHONE.............................540 598-3900
Harvey T Gardner, *Principal*
EMP: 1
SALES (est): 75K **Privately Held**
SIC: 2013 Snack sticks, including jerky: from purchased meat

(G-6584)
TREO ENTERPRISE SOLUTIONS INC
6380 Beulah Rd (23231-6119)
PHONE.............................804 977-9862
Felicia Matthews, *President*
EMP: 12
SALES (est): 85K **Privately Held**
WEB: www.treoes.com
SIC: 2431 Planing mill, millwork

(G-6585)
TRIAL EXHIBITS INC
2727 Entp Pkwy Ste 109 (23294)
PHONE.............................804 672-0880
Jack Stein, *Owner*
EMP: 1
SALES (corp-wide): 2.7MM **Privately Held**
WEB: www.trialexhibitsinc.com
SIC: 3999 Preparation of slides & exhibits
PA: Trial Exhibits Inc
1177 W Cass St
Tampa FL 33606
813 258-6153

(G-6586)
TRIPLE OG PUBLISHING LLC
5101 Eanes Ln (23231-3912)
PHONE.............................804 252-0856
EMP: 2
SALES (est): 98.2K **Privately Held**
SIC: 2741 Miscellaneous publishing

(G-6587)
TUMORPIX LLC
9909 Carrington Pl (23238-5573)
PHONE.............................804 754-3961
Dharamdas Ramnani, *Owner*
EMP: 2 EST: 2012
SALES (est): 118K **Privately Held**
SIC: 7372 Educational computer software

(G-6588)
UNITED TECHNOLOGIES I LLC
7804 Balineen Ct (23228-6425)
PHONE.............................804 553-3116
EMP: 3
SALES (est): 157K **Privately Held**
SIC: 3812 Search & navigation equipment

(G-6589)
VIE LA PUBLISHING HOUSE LLC
1707 Foxcreek Cir (23238-4209)
PHONE.............................804 741-2670
EMP: 1
SALES (est): 37.5K **Privately Held**
WEB: www.vielapublishing.com
SIC: 2741 Miscellaneous publishing

(G-6590)
VIRGINIA WOODCRAFTERS LLC
8609 Oakview Ave (23228-2819)
PHONE.............................804 276-2766
Nisab Cirkic, *Mng Member*
EMP: 8
SQ FT: 7,500
SALES (est): 1.2MM **Privately Held**
WEB: www.virginiawoodcrafters.com
SIC: 2434 Wood kitchen cabinets

(G-6591)
WHITE KNIGHT PRESS
9704 Old Club Trce (23238-5733)
PHONE.............................757 814-7192
EMP: 1
SALES (est): 39.7K **Privately Held**
WEB: www.whiteknightpress.com
SIC: 2741 Miscellaneous publishing

(G-6592)
WORTH BABY PRODUCTS LLC
Also Called: Baby Fanatic
302 Hollyport Rd (23229-7623)
PHONE.............................804 644-4707
Darrell Jervey, *Marketing Mgr*
Patricia Woodson,
◆ EMP: 10 **Privately Held**
WEB: www.babyfanatic.com
SIC: 3944 5999 Carriages, baby; children's furniture

(G-6593)
ZOSARO LLC
Also Called: ZOSARO'S BAKERY
6920 Lakeside Ave Ste D (23228-5247)
PHONE.............................804 564-9450
Lisa Ratliff, *President*
EMP: 4 EST: 2014
SQ FT: 1,000
SALES (est): 40K **Privately Held**
WEB: www.zosarosbakery.com
SIC: 2051 Cakes, bakery: except frozen

Henry
Franklin County

(G-6594)
CUSTOM FABRICATION SVCS INC
3399 Providence Church Rd (24102-3310)
PHONE.............................540 483-8809
David Philpott, *Principal*
EMP: 1
SALES (est): 131.2K **Privately Held**
SIC: 3499 Novelties & giftware, including trophies

(G-6595)
EXTREME POWDER WORKS LLC
24102 Providence Ch Rd (24102)
PHONE.............................540 483-2684
Travis Young, *Principal*
EMP: 1
SALES (est): 98.3K **Privately Held**
SIC: 3479 Metal coating & allied service

(G-6596)
NAFF WELDING & MACH WORKS
949 Lillian Naff Dr (24102-3208)
PHONE.............................276 629-1129
David Naff, *Owner*
EMP: 1
SALES (est): 26.3K **Privately Held**
SIC: 7692 Welding repair

(G-6597)
STEVE STONE
Also Called: Stone Welding
303 Pintail Ln (24102-3391)
PHONE.............................276 956-8451
Steve Stone, *Owner*
EMP: 1
SALES (est): 98.2K **Privately Held**
WEB: www.stonewelding.com
SIC: 7692 Welding repair

Herndon
Fairfax County

(G-6598)
3D HERNDON
761a Monroe St (20170-4645)
PHONE.............................202 746-6176
Ran Farmer, *Principal*
EMP: 2 EST: 2017 **Privately Held**
WEB: www.3dherndon.com
SIC: 2752 Commercial printing, lithographic

(G-6599)
3D IMGING SMLTION CORP AMRICAS
Also Called: 3disc
365 Herndon Pkwy Ste 18 (20170-6236)
PHONE.............................800 570-0363
Sigrid Smitt Jeppesen, *CEO*
EMP: 5
SALES (est): 138.7K **Privately Held**
WEB: www.3disc.com
SIC: 3826 Analytical instruments
PA: Digiray Corp.
142 Ilsan-Ro, Ilsandong-Gu
Goyang-Si 10442

(G-6600)
A & T PARTNERS INC
298 Sunset Park Dr (20170-5219)
PHONE.............................703 707-8246
EMP: 1
SALES (est): 61K **Privately Held**
SIC: 3421 Mfg Cutlery

(G-6601)
AACA EMBROIDERY SCREEN PRTG
13200 Lazy Glen Ln (20171-2348)
PHONE.............................703 880-9872
Alphonse Alix, *Principal*
EMP: 2
SALES (est): 161.4K **Privately Held**
SIC: 2752 Commercial printing, lithographic

(G-6602)
ABC IMAGING OF WASHINGTON
601 Carlisle Dr (20170-4806)
PHONE.............................571 514-1033
EMP: 11
SALES (corp-wide): 144.4MM **Privately Held**
WEB: www.abcimaging.com
SIC: 2759 Advertising literature: printing
PA: Abc Imaging Of Washington, Inc
5290 Shawnee Rd Ste 300
Alexandria VA 22312
202 429-8870

(G-6603)
ACCORDING TO PLAN LLC
2503 James Madison Cir (20171-4477)
PHONE.............................703 953-1584
Marilyn L Smith, *Mng Member*
EMP: 1 **Privately Held**
SIC: 2395 Embroidery & art needlework

(G-6604)
AFTERSHOCK ADVISORS LLC
560 Herndon Pkwy Ste 130 (20170-5277)
PHONE.............................703 787-0139
Nancy McSally, *Director*
David Wiedemer John, *Administration*
Jennifer Schoenefeldt, *Admin Asst*
EMP: 4
SALES (est): 324.4K **Privately Held**
WEB: www.aftershockpublishing.com
SIC: 2741 Miscellaneous publishing

(G-6605)
AIRBUS A300 LEASING INC
198 Van Buren St Ste 300 (20170-5338)
PHONE.............................703 834-3400
Fabrice Brgier, *President*
EMP: 1
SALES (est): 45.2K
SALES (corp-wide): 77.9B **Privately Held**
WEB: www.airbus.com
SIC: 3721 Aircraft

HQ: Airbus Americas, Inc.
2550 Wasser Ter Ste 9100
Herndon VA 20171
703 834-3400

(G-6606)
AIRBUS AMERICAS INC (DH)
Also Called: Aina Holdings
2550 Wasser Ter Ste 9100 (20171-6381)
PHONE..................................703 834-3400
Guillaume Faury, *CEO*
Jonathan Williams, *General Mgr*
Leslie Shigaki, *Counsel*
Klaus Richter, *Exec VP*
Lindsay Cunningham, *Vice Pres*
▲ **EMP:** 75
SQ FT: 30,000
SALES (est): 114.9MM
SALES (corp-wide): 77.9B **Privately Held**
WEB: www.airbus.com
SIC: 3721 Aircraft

(G-6607)
AIRBUS DEF SPACE HOLDINGS INC
2550 Wasser Ter Ste 9000 (20171-6128)
PHONE..................................703 466-5600
Michael Cosentino, *President*
Marc Bouvier, *Vice Pres*
Dennis Burnett, *Vice Pres*
Guy M Hicks, *Vice Pres*
Corinne Kaplan, *Vice Pres*
▲ **EMP:** 1702 **EST:** 1956
SQ FT: 25,000
SALES (est): 3MM
SALES (corp-wide): 77.9B **Privately Held**
WEB: www.airbus.com
SIC: 3721 Aircraft
PA: Airbus Se
Mendelweg 30
Leiden
715 245-600

(G-6608)
AIRBUS GROUP INC (DH)
2550 Wasser Ter Ste 9000 (20171-6128)
PHONE..................................703 466-5600
Allan McArtor, *CEO*
Robert Lekites, *Exec VP*
Guy Hicks, *Vice Pres*
Michael Stewart, *Sales Staff*
Dirk Erat, *Corp Comm Staff*
EMP: 33 **EST:** 2014
SALES (est): 3.2MM
SALES (corp-wide): 77.9B **Privately Held**
SIC: 3721 Aircraft
HQ: Airbus U.S. Space & Defense, Inc.
2550 Wasser Ter Ste 9000
Herndon VA 20171
703 466-5600

(G-6609)
ALL TRAFFIC SOLUTIONS INC (PA)
12950 Worldgate Dr # 310 (20170-6004)
PHONE..................................814 237-9005
Michael Souders, *CEO*
Scott Johnson, *President*
Carrie Fedders, *VP Sales*
▼ **EMP:** 17 **EST:** 1999
SQ FT: 5,000
SALES (est): 3.3MM **Privately Held**
WEB: www.alltrafficsolutions.com
SIC: 3669 3993 7372 Traffic signals, electric; transportation signaling devices; electric signs; prepackaged software

(G-6610)
ALLEN MANAGEMENT COMPANY INC
Also Called: Sign-A-Rama
316 Victory Dr (20170-5216)
PHONE..................................703 481-8858
Henry Allen, *CEO*
EMP: 5
SQ FT: 2,200 **Privately Held**
WEB: www.signarama.com
SIC: 3993 Signs & advertising specialties

(G-6611)
AM TUNESHOP LLC
12481 Manderley Way (20171-1800)
PHONE..................................703 758-9193
C Anderson, *Principal*
EMP: 2

SALES (est): 147.3K **Privately Held**
WEB: www.amtuneshop.com
SIC: 2731 Book music: publishing only, not printed on site

(G-6612)
AMOGH CONSULTANTS INC
2440 Dakota Lakes Dr (20171-2969)
PHONE..................................469 867-1583
Vinit Patankar, *President*
Sharda Divekar, *Director*
EMP: 1
SALES (est): 94.3K **Privately Held**
WEB: www.amoghconsultants.com
SIC: 7372 7371 Application computer software; custom computer programming services

(G-6613)
APOGEE COMMUNICATIONS
900 Mcdaniel Ct (20170-3206)
PHONE..................................703 481-1622
Alied Van Doren, *Owner*
EMP: 1
SALES (est): 76.4K **Privately Held**
SIC: 3663 Studio equipment, radio & television broadcasting

(G-6614)
APPLIED VSUAL CMMNICATIONS INC
450 Springpark Pl # 1200 (20170-5271)
PHONE..................................703 787-6668
Carole Peters, *CEO*
Thomas Peters, *President*
William Seifert, *Vice Pres*
EMP: 47
SQ FT: 4,500
SALES (est): 11.8MM **Privately Held**
WEB:
www.appliedvisualcommunications.com
SIC: 3651 3669 Audio electronic systems; visual communication systems

(G-6615)
APRIL A PHILLIPS POTTERY
11296 Fairwind Way (20190-4246)
PHONE..................................703 464-1283
EMP: 1
SALES (est): 36K **Privately Held**
SIC: 3269 Mfg Pottery Products

(G-6616)
AUTOMBILI LAMBORGHINI AMER LLC (HQ)
2200 Ferdinand Porsche Dr (20171-6243)
PHONE..................................866 681-6276
Wolfgang Hoffmann, *President*
Alessandro Sarmeschi, *COO*
Marco Schiavo, *Buyer*
Costanza Malservisi, *Marketing Staff*
Daniele Fancello, *Manager*
EMP: 12
SALES (est): 1.5MM
SALES (corp-wide): 279.5B **Privately Held**
WEB: www.lamborghini.com
SIC: 3069 Rubber automotive products
PA: Volkswagen Ag
Berliner Ring 2
Wolfsburg 38440
536 190-

(G-6617)
AXIOS SYSTEMS INC
2411 Dulles Corner Park # 475 (20171-5605)
PHONE..................................703 326-1357
Marylin Bell, *Partner*
Markos Symeonides, *Vice Pres*
Allison Brant, *Opers Staff*
Lynda Robertson, *Finance*
Kirstie Lingel, *Marketing Staff*
EMP: 20
SALES (est): 3.2MM
SALES (corp-wide): 25.8MM **Privately Held**
WEB: www.axiossystems.com
SIC: 7372 Prepackaged software
PA: Axios Systems Public Limited Company
Axios House
Edinburgh EH3 7
131 220-4748

(G-6618)
B K PRINTING
Also Called: Kwik Kopy Printing
605 Carlisle Dr (20170-4806)
PHONE..................................703 435-5502
V J Patel, *Owner*
Dan Barton, *Graphic Designe*
Demetrius Driscoll, *Graphic Designe*
EMP: 6
SQ FT: 1,700
SALES (est): 500K **Privately Held**
WEB: www.kwikkopyhouston.com
SIC: 2752 2791 2789 Commercial printing, offset; typesetting; bookbinding & related work

(G-6619)
BARISMIL LLC
2517 James Maury Dr (20171-4352)
PHONE..................................703 622-4550
Mohammad Ismail, *Principal*
EMP: 1
SALES (est): 121.8K **Privately Held**
SIC: 3144 3199 3559 3143 Boots, canvas or leather: women's; dress shoes, women's; boots, horse; boots, shoes & leather working machinery; dress shoes, men's

(G-6620)
BATTS INDUSTRIES LLC
715 Alabama Dr (20170-5405)
PHONE..................................202 669-6015
Norvell Batts, *Principal*
EMP: 3 **EST:** 2015
SALES (est): 126.2K **Privately Held**
SIC: 3999 Manufacturing industries

(G-6621)
BE BOLD SIGN STUDIO
1204 Sunrise Ct (20170-4118)
PHONE..................................678 520-1029
Andrea Francois, *Principal*
EMP: 1 **EST:** 2016
SALES (est): 49K **Privately Held**
SIC: 3993 Signs & advertising specialties

(G-6622)
BEADECKED INC
342 Victory Dr (20170-5216)
PHONE..................................703 435-5663
EMP: 1
SALES (corp-wide): 129.4K **Privately Held**
SIC: 2369 5137 Girls' & children's outerwear; children's goods
PA: Beadecked Inc
10201 Brennanhill Ct
Great Falls VA 22066
703 759-3725

(G-6623)
BETA CONTRACTORS LLC
Also Called: Dorcas Electric Services
3304 Applegrove Ct (20171-3941)
PHONE..................................703 424-1940
Shih-Kuan Lin,
EMP: 1
SALES (est): 50K **Privately Held**
SIC: 3585 Refrigeration & heating equipment

(G-6624)
BIGEYE DIRECT INC
13860 Redskin Dr (20171-3208)
PHONE..................................703 955-3017
Mark Karl, *CEO*
Damon Smith, *President*
Michael J Calder, *COO*
Kendrick Kimberly, *Treasurer*
Jake Brown, *Accounts Exec*
EMP: 100
SQ FT: 32,000
SALES (est): 16.1MM **Privately Held**
WEB: www.bigeyedirect.com
SIC: 2752 2759 7374 Commercial printing, offset; laser printing; data processing & preparation

(G-6625)
BLACKSKY HOLDINGS INC (PA)
13241 Wdlnd Pk Rd Ste 300 (20171)
PHONE..................................703 935-1930
Brian O'Toole, *CEO*
Nick Merski, *Vice Pres*
Catherine Fitch, *Engineer*

Eric Lund, *Engineer*
Jodi Sorensen, *VP Mktg*
EMP: 29
SQ FT: 17,000
SALES (est): 17.1MM **Privately Held**
WEB: www.spaceflight.com
SIC: 3761 8731 3764 Guided missiles & space vehicles, research & development; commercial physical research; guided missile & space vehicle engines, research & devel.

(G-6626)
BLOCKMASTER SECURITY INC
2325 Dulles Corn (20171)
PHONE..................................703 788-6809
EMP: 70
SQ FT: 2,000
SALES (est): 2.5MM **Privately Held**
SIC: 3695 Magnetic And Optical Recording Media

(G-6627)
BMC SOFTWARE INC
2201 Coop Way Ste 200 (20171)
PHONE..................................703 404-0230
Sean McDermott, *President*
EMP: 27
SALES (corp-wide): 1.3B **Privately Held**
WEB: www.bmc.com
SIC: 7372 Prepackaged software
PA: Bmc Software, Inc.
2103 Citywest Blvd # 2100
Houston TX 77042
713 918-8800

(G-6628)
BOEING COMPANY
460 Herndon Pkwy Ste 300 (20170-5280)
PHONE..................................703 467-2534
Francis Odiase, *Engineer*
Stephen Givinski, *Manager*
EMP: 25
SALES (corp-wide): 76.5B **Publicly Held**
WEB: www.boeing.com
SIC: 3663 Satellites, communications; space satellite communications equipment
PA: The Boeing Company
100 N Riverside Plz
Chicago IL 60606
312 544-2000

(G-6629)
BOSHKINS SOFTWARE CORPORATION
2507 Branding Iron Ct (20171-2947)
PHONE..................................703 318-7785
Anatoly Boshkin, *Principal*
EMP: 2
SALES (est): 163.8K **Privately Held**
SIC: 7372 Prepackaged software

(G-6630)
BRAD & MOO MERCHANTS LLC
2703 Robaleed Way (20171-2472)
PHONE..................................434 738-1130
Kristen Altobello,
EMP: 2
SALES (est): 25K **Privately Held**
SIC: 3999 Pet supplies

(G-6631)
BRANDIMAGE LLC
1156 Cypress Tree Pl (20170-4130)
PHONE..................................703 855-5401
Ramin Mohammad,
EMP: 2
SALES (est): 104.8K **Privately Held**
SIC: 2844 Toilet preparations

(G-6632)
CA INC
Also Called: CA Technologies A Broadcom Co
2291 Wood Oak Dr Ste 200 (20171-6007)
PHONE..................................800 225-5224
Mike Miller, *Vice Pres*
EMP: 300
SALES (corp-wide): 22.6B **Publicly Held**
WEB: www.broadcom.com
SIC: 7372 Application computer software
HQ: Ca, Inc.
520 Madison Ave
New York NY 10022
800 225-5224

▲ = Import ▼=Export
◆ =Import/Export

(G-6633)
CAPO SOFTWARE
13064 Monterey Estates Dr (20171-2637)
PHONE...................................571 205-8695
Michael Stoddard, *Principal*
EMP: 2 EST: 2008
SALES (est): 130K **Privately Held**
SIC: 7372 Prepackaged software

(G-6634)
CARDINAL CONCRETE COMPANY
13880 Dulles Corner Ln (20171-4685)
PHONE...................................703 550-7650
Thompson S Baker, *Ch of Bd*
Hank Nehilla, *President*
Dennis Frick, *Admin Sec*
Wyatt Susie A, *Asst Sec*
EMP: 209
SQ FT: 7,500
SALES (est): 32.5MM **Publicly Held**
SIC: 3273 Ready-mixed concrete
HQ: Legacy Vulcan, Llc
1200 Urban Center Dr
Vestavia AL 35242
205 298-3000

(G-6635)
CARLAS CUPCAKES LLC
13229 Pleasant Glen Ct (20171-2344)
PHONE...................................703 582-7615
Carla Mangone, *Principal*
EMP: 4 EST: 2011
SALES (est): 194.1K **Privately Held**
WEB: www.carlas-cupcakes.com
SIC: 2051 Bread, cake & related products

(G-6636)
CASTLEMANS COMPOST LLC
12421 Rock Ridge Rd (20170-5725)
PHONE...................................571 283-3030
David Castleman, *Principal*
EMP: 2
SALES (est): 74.4K **Privately Held**
SIC: 2875 Compost

(G-6637)
CAZADOR LLC
2553 Dulles View Dr (20171-5226)
PHONE...................................719 387-7450
David Hoy, *President*
Nicholas Estep, *Project Mgr*
Robert Smith, *Project Mgr*
Mark Dias, *Opers Staff*
Munya Makanda, *Controller*
▼ EMP: 56
SALES (est): 15.7MM
SALES (corp-wide): 1.1B **Privately Held**
WEB: www.cazador.biz
SIC: 2542 Partitions & fixtures, except wood
HQ: Akima, Llc
2553 Dulles View Dr # 700
Herndon VA 20171
571 323-5200

(G-6638)
CENTRIPETAL NETWORKS INC (PA)
2251 Corp Park Dr Ste 150 (20171-5806)
PHONE...................................571 252-5080
Steven Rogers, *CEO*
Brett Claydon, *Vice Pres*
Pierre Mallett, *Vice Pres*
Neel Price, *Vice Pres*
Neil Price, *Vice Pres*
EMP: 35
SQ FT: 9,000
SALES (est): 1MM **Privately Held**
WEB: www.centripetalnetworks.com
SIC: 3571 3669 7373 7371 Electronic computers; intercommunication systems, electric; computer systems analysis & design; systems engineering, computer related; computer software development & applications; physical research, noncommercial; commercial physical research; computer (hardware) development; electronic research

(G-6639)
CHANTILLY PRTG & GRAPHICS INC
13808 Redskin Dr (20171-3208)
PHONE...................................703 471-2800
James Swiatocha, *President*
EMP: 8
SQ FT: 7,500
SALES (est): 1.2MM **Privately Held**
WEB: www.chantillyprinting.com
SIC: 2752 Commercial printing, offset

(G-6640)
CIPHERCLOUD INC
560 Herndon Pkwy Ste 100 (20170-5239)
PHONE...................................703 659-0533
Pravin Kothari, *CEO*
Tyler Owen, *Director*
EMP: 4 **Privately Held**
WEB: www.ciphercloud.com
SIC: 7372 Prepackaged software
PA: Ciphercloud, Inc.
2581 Junction Ave Ste 200
San Jose CA 95134

(G-6641)
CISCO SYSTEMS INC
13600 Dulles Tech Dr (20171-4602)
PHONE...................................703 484-5500
Chuck Robbins, *CEO*
William Gessaman, *Partner*
Justin Cashman, *General Mgr*
Steve Seasholtz, *Regional Mgr*
Tina Swallow, *Regional Mgr*
EMP: 95 **Publicly Held**
WEB: www.cisco.com
SIC: 3577 Computer peripheral equipment
PA: Cisco Systems, Inc.
170 W Tasman Dr
San Jose CA 95134
408 526-4000

(G-6642)
CITAPEI COMMUNICATIONS INC
2755 Viking Dr (20171-2408)
PHONE...................................703 620-2316
Ron Wagner, *President*
Lisa M Kauffman, *Vice Pres*
EMP: 6
SQ FT: 3,500
SALES (est): 4MM **Privately Held**
WEB: www.globalunity.com
SIC: 2731 7371 Books: publishing only; custom computer programming services

(G-6643)
COBWEB INDUSTRIES LLC
1506 Coat Ridge Rd (20170-2723)
PHONE...................................703 834-1000
Paul Scott, *Administration*
EMP: 2
SALES (est): 68.3K **Privately Held**
SIC: 3999 Manufacturing industries

(G-6644)
CONNOISSEUR PUBLISHING
12905 Centre Park Cir (20171-5813)
PHONE...................................303 437-5099
EMP: 1 EST: 2016
SALES (est): 41.6K **Privately Held**
WEB: www.winesconnoisseur.com
SIC: 2741 Miscellaneous publishing

(G-6645)
COOP SYSTEMS INC
2201 Coop Way Ste 600 (20171)
PHONE...................................703 581-6364
Christopher Alvord, *CEO*
Vicki Alvord, *COO*
William Escobar, *Accounting Mgr*
Jocelyne Dao, *Account Dir*
Michael Brinn, *Executive*
EMP: 25
SQ FT: 1,700
SALES (est): 2.7MM **Privately Held**
WEB: www.coop-systems.com
SIC: 7372 Application computer software

(G-6646)
CORE ENGINEERED SOLUTIONS INC
620 Herndon Pkwy Ste 120 (20170-5400)
PHONE...................................703 563-0320
Frank Evans, *President*
Eugene O'Brien, *Vice Pres*
Deborah Ulbrick, *Vice Pres*
Jeanne Murck, *VP Opers*
Chuck Nance, *Project Mgr*
▼ EMP: 14
SQ FT: 3,600
SALES (est): 7.9MM **Privately Held**
WEB: www.core-es.com
SIC: 3443 5084 5999 Fuel tanks (oil, gas, etc.): metal plate; safety equipment; safety supplies & equipment

(G-6647)
CORNING INCORPORATED
13221 Wdlnd Pk Rd Ste 400 (20171)
PHONE...................................703 448-1095
Ron Kaiser, *CEO*
EMP: 8
SALES (corp-wide): 11.5B **Publicly Held**
WEB: www.corning.com
SIC: 3229 Pressed & blown glass
PA: Corning Incorporated
1 Riverfront Plz
Corning NY 14831
607 974-9000

(G-6648)
CORNING OPTCAL CMMNCATIONS LLC
13221 Woodland Park Rd (20171-5503)
PHONE...................................703 848-0200
Ann Widder, *Branch Mgr*
EMP: 2
SALES (corp-wide): 11.5B **Publicly Held**
WEB: www.corning.com
SIC: 3669 Intercommunication systems, electric
HQ: Corning Optical Communications Llc
4200 Corning Pl
Charlotte NC 28216
828 901-5000

(G-6649)
COTTAGE INDUSTRIES EXPOSITION
2831 Mustang Dr (20171-3533)
PHONE...................................703 834-0055
Wajahat Qureshi, *Owner*
EMP: 2
SALES (est): 72K **Privately Held**
SIC: 3999 Manufacturing industries

(G-6650)
CUSTOM HOPE CHESTS VA LLC
1521 Powells Tavern Pl (20170-2832)
PHONE...................................703 850-5019
Lawrence Gambee, *Principal*
EMP: 2
SALES (est): 116K **Privately Held**
SIC: 2441 Chests & trunks, wood

(G-6651)
CYBEREX CORPORATION
520 Herndon Pkwy Ste H (20170-6218)
PHONE...................................703 904-0980
Ali A Eshgh, *President*
▲ EMP: 2 EST: 2000
SQ FT: 1,500
SALES (est): 172.2K **Privately Held**
SIC: 7372 5032 Prepackaged software; marble building stone; granite building stone

(G-6652)
CYNTHIA GRAY
12313 Delevan Dr (20171-2001)
PHONE...................................703 860-5711
EMP: 2
SALES (est): 56.5K **Privately Held**
SIC: 7372 Prepackaged Software Services

(G-6653)
DAVID BIRKENSTOCK
Also Called: Birkenstock Aerospace
13577 Big Boulder Rd (20171-5002)
PHONE...................................703 343-5718
David Birkenstock, *Owner*
EMP: 1
SALES (est): 26K **Privately Held**
WEB: www.birkenstockaerospace.com
SIC: 3721 Aircraft

(G-6654)
DELICIOUS BEVERAGE LLC
760 Palmer Dr (20170-5459)
PHONE...................................703 517-0216
EMP: 3
SALES (est): 150K **Privately Held**
SIC: 2086 Mfg Bottled/Canned Soft Drinks

(G-6655)
DELTEK SYSTEMS INC
13880 Dulles Corner Ln # 400 (20171-4685)
PHONE...................................703 734-8606
Kevin T Parker, *CEO*
Deb Fitzgerald, *President*
Dwight Smith, *Principal*
David Schwiesow, *Senior VP*
Tim Hannon, *Vice Pres*
EMP: 2
SALES (est): 170K **Privately Held**
WEB: www.deltek.com
SIC: 7372 Prepackaged software

(G-6656)
DELTEK SYSTEMS INC
2291 Wood Oak Dr (20171-6006)
PHONE...................................800 456-2009
Daren Fontenot, *Managing Dir*
Peter Dimarzio, *Business Mgr*
Susanna Finger, *Research*
Nicholas Fisher, *Research*
Jennifer Sakole, *Research*
EMP: 3 EST: 2019
SALES (est): 33.8K **Privately Held**
WEB: www.deltek.com
SIC: 7372 Prepackaged software

(G-6657)
DIGITAL DOCUMENTS INC
Also Called: Express Printing
12529 Misty Water Dr (20170-5704)
PHONE...................................571 434-0341
EMP: 3
SQ FT: 3,500
SALES: 200K **Privately Held**
SIC: 2752 Lithographic Commercial Printing

(G-6658)
DISPERSIVE TECHNOLOGIES INC
3076 Centreville Rd # 114 (20171-3737)
PHONE...................................252 725-0874
Thomas Dougherty, *Branch Mgr*
EMP: 1 **Privately Held**
WEB: www.dispersive.io
SIC: 7372 Prepackaged software
PA: Dispersive Technologies, Inc.
3290 W Shadowlawn Ave Ne
Atlanta GA 30305

(G-6659)
DPTL INC
Also Called: Fairfax Screen Printing
623 Carlisle Dr (20170-4806)
PHONE...................................703 435-2291
David M Haas, *President*
Patricia K Haas, *Partner*
Taeo Haas, *Vice Pres*
Andrew Raines, *Graphic Designe*
EMP: 12 EST: 1975
SQ FT: 5,000
SALES (est): 1.1MM **Privately Held**
WEB: www.fairfaxscreenprinting.com
SIC: 2261 2395 Screen printing of cotton broadwoven fabrics; embroidery & art needlework

(G-6660)
DREAMVISION SOFTWARE LLC
13800 Coppermine Rd # 305 (20171-6163)
PHONE...................................703 378-7191
EMP: 2
SALES (est): 190.8K **Privately Held**
SIC: 7372 Prepackaged Software Services

(G-6661)
DRS C3 & AVIATION COMPANY
12930 Worldgate Dr # 700 (20170-6011)
PHONE...................................571 346-7700
Alan Dietrich, *Principal*
Paul Franklin, *Manager*
EMP: 2
SALES (est): 195.4K **Privately Held**
WEB: www.leonardodrs.com
SIC: 3812 Search & navigation equipment

(G-6662)
DRS LEONARDO INC
1033 Sterling Rd Ste 104 (20170-3837)
PHONE...................................703 260-7979
Damodar R Gumamaudpu, *Branch Mgr*
EMP: 4

SALES (corp-wide): 9.9B **Privately Held**
WEB: www.leonardodrs.com
SIC: 3812 Search & navigation equipment
HQ: Leonardo Drs, Inc.
2345 Crystal Dr Ste 1000
Arlington VA 22202
703 416-8000

(G-6663)
DTC COMMUNICATIONS INC (HQ)
2303 Dulles Station Blvd # 205
(20171-6356)
PHONE...................727 471-6900
Juan Navarro, *President*
Tom Thebes, *CFO*
EMP: 28
SQ FT: 30,000
SALES (est): 15MM **Privately Held**
WEB: www.domotactical.com
SIC: 3663 Radio & TV communications
equipment; radio broadcasting & commu-
nications equipment

(G-6664)
E PRIMERA ENABLE CORP
Also Called: Evolve Solutions Group
12358 Marionwood Ct (20171-2133)
PHONE...................703 476-2270
Shirley Kuder, *President*
EMP: 14
SQ FT: 2,100
SALES (est): 3.2MM **Privately Held**
SIC: 7372 Prepackaged software

(G-6665)
EDULINKED LLC
13390 Spofford Rd Apt 303 (20171-4555)
PHONE...................703 869-2228
Punnaiah Chalasani,
Raghuveera Chalasani,
EMP: 2
SALES (est): 97.8K **Privately Held**
SIC: 7372 8243 Educational computer
software; software training, computer

(G-6666)
ELECTRIFY AMERICA LLC
2200 Ferdinand Porsche Dr (20171-6243)
PHONE...................703 364-7000
Mark McNabb, *CEO*
Giovanni Palazzo, *COO*
Chip T Tietze, *Purch Mgr*
Swapan Das, *Manager*
Matthew Nelson, *Director*
EMP: 74
SALES (est): 3.2MM
SALES (corp-wide): 279.5B **Privately Held**
SIC: 3799 Recreational vehicles
HQ: Volkswagen Group Of America, Inc.
2200 Ferdinand Porsche Dr
Herndon VA 20171
703 364-7000

(G-6667)
ERISYS LLC
13800 Coppermine Rd (20171-6163)
PHONE...................660 864-4474
David Erisman, *Mng Member*
EMP: 4
SALES (corp-wide): 791K **Privately Held**
SIC: 3663 Radio broadcasting & communi-
cations equipment
PA: Erisys Llc
707 S Warren St
Warrensburg MO 64093
660 864-4474

(G-6668)
ERP CLOUD TECHNOLOGIES LLC
2551 Dulles View Dr (20171-5298)
PHONE...................727 723-0801
Sreedhar Veeramachaneni, *CEO*
EMP: 5
SALES (est): 138.7K **Privately Held**
SIC: 7372 7371 Application computer soft-
ware; computer software systems analy-
sis & design, custom

(G-6669)
ETL SYSTEMS INC
297 Herndon Pkwy Ste 303 (20170-4469)
PHONE...................703 657-0411
Ian Hilditch, *President*

EMP: 3 EST: 2010
SALES (est): 394.6K
SALES (corp-wide): 143.6B **Privately Held**
WEB: www.etlsystems.com
SIC: 3663 Radio broadcasting & communi-
cations equipment
HQ: Etl Systems Limited
Coldwell Radio Station
Hereford HR2 9

(G-6670)
EUTOPIA MAGAZINE GUELPH PRESS
2579 John Milton Dr # 105 (20171-2563)
PHONE...................703 938-6077
Mary Grussmeyer, *Principal*
EMP: 2
SALES (est): 98.2K **Privately Held**
SIC: 2721 Periodicals

(G-6671)
EXCELETICS INC
2707 Floris Ln (20171-3608)
PHONE...................703 405-5479
Todd Hutson, *CEO*
EMP: 1
SALES (est): 93K **Privately Held**
SIC: 3669 Communications equipment

(G-6672)
EXECUTIVE GLASS SERVICES INC
3305 Wellhouse Ct (20171-3328)
PHONE...................703 689-2178
William H Raines, *Principal*
EMP: 1
SALES (est): 88.4K **Privately Held**
SIC: 3231 Products of purchased glass

(G-6673)
FAMILY MAGAZINE NETWORK INC
485 Springpark Pl (20170-5289)
PHONE...................703 298-0601
Brenda Mills Hyde, *Principal*
EMP: 3
SALES (est): 186.8K **Privately Held**
WEB: www.washingtonfamily.com
SIC: 2721 Magazines: publishing only, not
printed on site

(G-6674)
FAST SIGNS OF HERNDON
Also Called: Fastsigns
2465 Centreville Rd J20 (20171-4586)
PHONE...................703 713-0743
Ron Kelly, *Principal*
EMP: 1
SALES (est): 80.3K **Privately Held**
WEB: www.fastsigns.com
SIC: 3993 Signs & advertising specialties

(G-6675)
FIDDLEHAND INC
2620 Viking Dr (20171-2419)
PHONE...................703 340-9806
Kalani Matthews, *Principal*
Steve Connell, *COO*
Sherrill Stamey II,
EMP: 3 EST: 2012
SALES (est): 134.8K **Privately Held**
WEB: www.fiddlehand.com
SIC: 3999 7371 7373 8731 Identification
tags, except paper; custom computer pro-
gramming services; systems engineering,
computer related; electronic research;
business services

(G-6676)
FINAL RESOURCE INC
12103 Courtney Ct (20170-2438)
PHONE...................703 404-8740
EMP: 2
SALES (est): 88.3K **Privately Held**
SIC: 3669 Communications equipment

(G-6677)
FREEPORT TECHNOLOGIES INC
470 Springpark Pl Ste 100 (20170-5252)
PHONE...................571 262-0400
John McGreevy, *President*
Don Orndorff, *COO*
Richard W Tucker, *Vice Pres*
Charles Dulaney, *Engineer*

Ruth Ann Hoel, *Human Resources*
EMP: 17
SQ FT: 7,450
SALES (est): 4.3MM **Privately Held**
WEB: www.freeporttech.com
SIC: 3699 Security devices

(G-6678)
GANLEYS
2615 John Milton Dr (20171-2545)
PHONE...................703 476-8864
EMP: 2
SALES (est): 85.9K **Privately Held**
SIC: 3577 Mfg Computer Peripheral Equip-

(G-6679)
GATHERSBURG CABNTRY
1130 Elden St (20170-5501)
PHONE...................703 742-8472
EMP: 1 EST: 2010
SALES (est): 106.2K **Privately Held**
SIC: 3553 Cabinet makers' machinery

(G-6680)
GENERAL DYNAMICS CORPORATION
540 Huntmar Park Dr Ste E (20170-5154)
PHONE...................703 925-8636
Steve Bershader, *Branch Mgr*
EMP: 4
SALES (corp-wide): 39.3B **Publicly Held**
WEB: www.gdmissionsystems.com
SIC: 3812 Search & navigation equipment
PA: General Dynamics Corporation
11011 Sunset Hills Rd
Reston VA 20190
703 876-3000

(G-6681)
GENERAL DYNAMICS INFO TECH INC
13857 Mclearen Rd (20171-3210)
PHONE...................703 268-7000
Tiffany Berry, *Project Mgr*
Andrew Laprade, *Engineer*
Thomas Pierce, *Senior Engr*
Pam Atorick, *Finance Mgr*
Pamela Howden, *Finance Mgr*
EMP: 60
SALES (corp-wide): 39.3B **Publicly Held**
WEB: www.gdit.com
SIC: 3661 Telephone & telegraph appara-
tus
HQ: General Dynamics Information Tech-
nology, Inc.
3150 Frview Pk Dr Ste 100
Falls Church VA 22042
703 995-8700

(G-6682)
GENESIS INFOSOLUTIONS INC
2613 Tarleton Corner Dr (20171-4497)
PHONE...................703 835-4469
Gopal Pinnamareddy, *Vice Pres*
EMP: 3
SALES (est): 135.2K **Privately Held**
SIC: 7372 7371 Application computer soft-
ware; custom computer programming
services

(G-6683)
GET AURA INC
2553 Dulles View Dr Fl 4 (20171-5226)
PHONE...................703 801-4382
Hari Ravichandran, *CEO*
EMP: 7
SALES (est): 100K **Privately Held**
SIC: 7372 Application computer software

(G-6684)
GILBERT IDELKHANI
862 Dogwood Ct (20170-5446)
PHONE...................703 399-1225
Gilbert Idelkhani, *Principal*
EMP: 2
SALES (est): 147.2K **Privately Held**
WEB: www.gilbertidelkhani.com
SIC: 2844 Hair coloring preparations

(G-6685)
GLENCOURSE PRESS
2170 Glencourse Ln (20191-1344)
PHONE...................703 860-2416
EMP: 2

SALES (est): 96.9K **Privately Held**
SIC: 2741 Misc Publishing

(G-6686)
GLOBAL OLED TECHNOLOGY LLC
13873 Park Center Rd # 330 (20171-3223)
PHONE...................703 870-3282
Paul Parkins, *Mng Member*
Juan Gisone, *Director*
Brandon Kim, *Analyst*
EMP: 10
SALES (est): 1MM **Privately Held**
WEB: www.globaloledtech.com
SIC: 3674 Light emitting diodes

(G-6687)
GOLD BRAND SOFTWARE LLC
1282 Mason Mill Ct (20170-5739)
PHONE...................703 450-1321
Goldfedder Brandon, *Administration*
EMP: 3 EST: 2009
SALES (est): 181.4K **Privately Held**
SIC: 7372 Prepackaged software

(G-6688)
GOV PANDA LLC
409 Spring St (20170-6223)
PHONE...................571 275-6370
EMP: 1 EST: 2019
SALES (est): 44.8K **Privately Held**
SIC: 2741 Miscellaneous publishing

(G-6689)
GRAPHIC PRINTS INC
12707 Fantasia Dr (20170-2942)
PHONE...................703 787-3880
Kyle McKibbin, *Principal*
Chrissy McKibbin, *Info Tech Mgr*
EMP: 4 EST: 2009
SALES (est): 333.7K **Privately Held**
WEB: www.graphicprints.biz
SIC: 2752 Commercial printing, offset

(G-6690)
GRASSROOTS ENTERPRISE INC (DH)
13005 Bankfoot Ct (20171-2300)
PHONE...................703 354-1177
Bill McIntyre, *CEO*
Robert Florian, *Exec VP*
Kevin McCann, *Exec VP*
EMP: 13
SQ FT: 3,500
SALES (est): 1.5MM
SALES (corp-wide): 428.9MM **Privately Held**
SIC: 2711 7375 Newspapers; on-line data
base information retrieval
HQ: Daniel J. Edelman, Inc.
200 E Randolph St Fl 63
Chicago IL 60601
312 240-3000

(G-6691)
GREEN POINT
12155 Eddyspark Dr (20170-2548)
PHONE...................703 391-5006
Jaime Spigner, *Principal*
EMP: 1 EST: 2014
SALES (est): 113.7K **Privately Held**
WEB: www.gpi-solutions.com
SIC: 3498 Fabricated pipe & fittings

(G-6692)
GREKTEK LLC
13520 Mclearen Rd (20171-8000)
PHONE...................202 607-4734
Tom Klaff, *CEO*
Greg Eoyang, *President*
EMP: 2
SALES (est): 56.5K **Privately Held**
SIC: 7372 Application computer software

(G-6693)
GS PHARMACEUTICALS INC (PA)
2301 Woodland Crossing Dr (20171-5893)
PHONE...................703 789-3344
Saber Saleem, *President*
EMP: 4 EST: 2012
SALES (est): 600K **Privately Held**
WEB: www.hygieniq.com
SIC: 2834 Pharmaceutical preparations

(G-6694)
HARRIS COMMUNICATIONS AND IN
2235 Monroe St (20171-2824)
PHONE......................703 668-7256
William Ostrowski, *Director*
Kimberly Withers,
EMP: 50
SALES (est): 1.5MM **Privately Held**
WEB: www.harris.com
SIC: 3812 Aircraft/aerospace flight instruments & guidance systems

(G-6695)
HARRIS CORPORATION
Also Called: Exelis C4i
2235 Monroe St (20171-2824)
PHONE......................571 203-7605
EMP: 5
SALES (corp-wide): 6.1B **Publicly Held**
SIC: 3823 3812 Manufactures Process Control Instruments And Search Or Navigation Equipment
PA: Harris Corporation
1025 W Nasa Blvd
Melbourne FL 32919
321 727-9100

(G-6696)
HERITAGE INTERIORS LLC
2553 Dulles View Dr (20171-5226)
PHONE......................571 323-5200
Scott Mackie,
EMP: 2
SALES (est): 95.7K **Privately Held**
WEB: www.heritageinteriorsllc.com
SIC: 2542 Partitions & fixtures, except wood

(G-6697)
HERNDON PUBLISHING CO INC
Also Called: Observer Newspapers
1043 Sterling Rd Ste 104 (20170-3842)
P.O. Box 109 (20172-0109)
PHONE......................703 689-0111
Thomas Grein, *President*
Elizabeth Grein, *Vice Pres*
Christopher Moore, *Manager*
EMP: 14
SQ FT: 2,000
SALES (est): 751.8K **Privately Held**
WEB: www.mascotbooks.com
SIC: 2711 Newspapers: publishing only, not printed on site

(G-6698)
HEWLETT-PACKARD FEDERAL LLC
13600 Eds Dr (20171-3225)
PHONE......................800 727-5472
Antonio Neri, *CEO*
Faye Staten Brown, *Administration*
EMP: 27
SALES (est): 7.2MM
SALES (corp-wide): 26.9B **Publicly Held**
SIC: 3571 Electronic computers
PA: Hewlett Packard Enterprise Company
6280 America Center Dr
San Jose CA 95002
650 687-5817

(G-6699)
HISPANIC NEWSPAPER INC
761c Monroe St Ste 200 (20170-4675)
PHONE......................703 478-6806
Daniel Alvarado, *CEO*
EMP: 7
SALES (est): 70K **Privately Held**
SIC: 2711 Newspapers

(G-6700)
HITACHI VANTARA LLC
2201 Coop Way Ste 300 (20171)
PHONE......................405 593-3783
EMP: 3 **Privately Held**
WEB: www.hitachivantara.com
SIC: 3572 Computer storage devices
HQ: Hitachi Vantara Llc
2535 Augustine Dr
Santa Clara CA 95054
408 970-1000

(G-6701)
HJK CONTRACTING INC
12504 Nathaniel Oaks Dr (20171-1730)
PHONE......................703 793-8127
Hyo Kim, *President*
EMP: 3
SALES (est): 203.8K **Privately Held**
SIC: 1389 Construction, repair & dismantling services

(G-6702)
HM TRUCKING
1358 Rock Chapel Rd (20170-2039)
PHONE......................703 932-7058
Hector Medrano, *Owner*
EMP: 1
SALES (est): 44.2K **Privately Held**
SIC: 3531 Snow plow attachments

(G-6703)
HONEYWELL INTERNATIONAL INC
400 Herndon Pkwy Ste 100 (20170-5299)
PHONE......................703 879-9951
Eric Ball, *Branch Mgr*
EMP: 14
SALES (corp-wide): 36.7B **Publicly Held**
WEB: www.honeywell.com
SIC: 3724 Aircraft engines & engine parts
PA: Honeywell International Inc.
300 S Tryon St
Charlotte NC 28202
704 627-6200

(G-6704)
HUANG SHANG JEO
13025 Rose Petal Cir (20171-4815)
PHONE......................703 471-4457
Jeo Shang, *Principal*
EMP: 2
SALES (est): 81K **Privately Held**
SIC: 2731 Book publishing

(G-6705)
IDIRECT GOVERNMENT LLC (DH)
Also Called: Igt
13921 Park Center Rd # 600 (20171-3236)
PHONE......................703 648-8118
John Ratigan, *President*
Richard Gallivan, *Principal*
Greg Walker, *Senior VP*
Karl Fuchs, *Vice Pres*
Jim Hanlon, *Vice Pres*
EMP: 55
SALES (est): 15.8MM **Privately Held**
WEB: www.idirectgov.com
SIC: 3663 Satellites, communications

(G-6706)
INDEX SYSTEMS INC
13503 Copper Bed Rd (20171-3528)
PHONE......................571 420-4600
Chinna Nemelidinne, *President*
Indira Nemelidinne,
EMP: 2
SALES (est): 235.1K **Privately Held**
WEB: www.indexsystemsinc.com
SIC: 7372 8712 8711 7373 Prepackaged software; architectural services; engineering services; computer systems analysis & design; management consulting services; software training, computer

(G-6707)
INDUSTRIAL COMMERCIAL WLDG LLC
1456 Winterberry Ct (20170-3930)
PHONE......................703 707-6347
Carlos A Herrera-Zans, *Principal*
EMP: 1
SALES (est): 30K **Privately Held**
SIC: 7692 Welding repair

(G-6708)
INFOBLOX FEDERAL INC
13454 Snrs Vly Dr Ste 570 (20171-5405)
PHONE......................703 672-2607
Ralph Havens, *President*
Chhaya Choudhary, *Engineer*
Norm Proffitt, *Engineer*
Michael Fancher, *Treasurer*
Daniel Dalton, *Manager*
EMP: 20
SQ FT: 3,400

SALES (est): 1.8MM
SALES (corp-wide): 235MM **Privately Held**
WEB: www.infoblox.de
SIC: 3825 Network analyzers
HQ: Infoblox Inc.
3111 Coronado Dr
Santa Clara CA 95054
408 986-4000

(G-6709)
INFORCE GROUP LLC
6601 Coop Way Set 600 600 Set (20171)
PHONE......................703 788-6835
Alexander Pyntikov, *CEO*
Natalia Pyntikova, *COO*
EMP: 7
SALES (est): 138.8K **Privately Held**
SIC: 7372 Application computer software

(G-6710)
INNOVATIVE DYNAMIC SOLUTIONS
12808 Pinecrest Rd (20171-2604)
PHONE......................703 234-5282
Babu Vinayagam, *Principal*
EMP: 2 EST: 2011
SALES (est): 121.8K **Privately Held**
WEB: www.idsglobalinc.com
SIC: 7372 Application computer software

(G-6711)
INVIZER LLC
2552 James Maury Dr (20171-4355)
PHONE......................410 903-2507
Muthukumar Vasudevan, *Manager*
EMP: 2
SALES (est): 139.5K **Privately Held**
WEB: www.invizer.com
SIC: 7372 Business oriented computer software

(G-6712)
IRON BOW HOLDINGS INC (PA)
2303 Dulles Station Blvd # 400 (20171-6447)
PHONE......................703 279-3000
Rene B Lavigne, *President*
Suzanne McGhee, *Partner*
John Meier, *General Mgr*
Marc Mercilliott, *Senior VP*
Stu Strang, *Senior VP*
EMP: 120
SQ FT: 25,626
SALES (est): 950MM **Privately Held**
WEB: www.ironbow.com
SIC: 3571 Electronic computers

(G-6713)
ITL NA INC
1175 Herndon Pkwy Ste 350 (20170-5550)
PHONE......................703 435-6700
Stephanie Norrell, *President*
EMP: 3
SALES (est): 303.5K **Privately Held**
WEB: www.itl.pl
SIC: 3841 Surgical & medical instruments

(G-6714)
ITS ABOUT GOLF
649 Alabama Dr (20170-5403)
PHONE......................703 437-1527
Robert Tressler, *Owner*
EMP: 1 EST: 1998
SALES (est): 70K **Privately Held**
SIC: 3949 Shafts, golf club

(G-6715)
J & V PUBLISHING LLC
2427 Little Current Dr # 2722 (20171-4615)
PHONE......................571 318-1700
Veronica Halliburton, *Principal*
EMP: 2
SALES (est): 62.9K **Privately Held**
SIC: 2711 Newspapers

(G-6716)
JAMES DOCTOR PRESS INC
3311 Bywater Ct (20171-3938)
PHONE......................703 476-0579
Chris Colston, *Principal*
EMP: 4 EST: 2010
SALES (est): 203.8K **Privately Held**
SIC: 2741 Miscellaneous publishing

(G-6717)
JLT AEROSPACE (NORTH AM
13873 Park Center Rd # 201 (20171-3223)
PHONE......................703 459-2380
S A Cameron, *Insurance Agent*
EMP: 2
SALES (est): 188.5K **Privately Held**
SIC: 3721 Aircraft

(G-6718)
JNET DIRECT INC
1555 Coomber Ct (20170-2573)
P.O. Box 404 (20172-0404)
PHONE......................703 629-6406
EMP: 2
SALES (est): 127.2K **Privately Held**
WEB: www.jnetdirect.com
SIC: 7372 Prepackaged software

(G-6719)
JORDAN CONSULTING AND RESEARCH
13230 Pleasant Glen Ct (20171-2342)
PHONE......................703 597-7812
Stephen Jordan, *Principal*
EMP: 2
SALES (est): 165K **Privately Held**
SIC: 3463 Missile & ordnance forgings

(G-6720)
JS SOFTWARE INC
1158 Millwood Pond Dr (20170-2365)
PHONE......................214 924-3179
Jaygan Vederey, *Owner*
EMP: 2
SALES (est): 167.4K **Privately Held**
SIC: 7372 Prepackaged software

(G-6721)
JUNIPER NETWORKS (US) INC
2251 Corp Park Dr Ste 200 (20171-4840)
PHONE......................571 203-1700
Rami Rahim, *CEO*
EMP: 150 **Publicly Held**
WEB: www.juniper.net
SIC: 3577 Computer peripheral equipment
HQ: Juniper Networks (Us), Inc.
1133 Innovation Way
Sunnyvale CA 94089

(G-6722)
KENNEY INC
916 Barker Hill Rd (20170-3014)
PHONE......................703 731-9208
Francis Kenney Jr, *President*
EMP: 4
SALES (est): 177.9K **Privately Held**
SIC: 2591 5999 Drapery hardware & blinds & shades; miscellaneous retail stores

(G-6723)
KINEMETRX INCORPORATED
309 Senate Ct (20170-5488)
PHONE......................703 596-5095
Mark Gianturco, *President*
EMP: 5 EST: 2016
SALES (est): 156K **Privately Held**
SIC: 7372 7371 7389 Application computer software; computer software development & applications;

(G-6724)
KINKOS COPIES
Also Called: Kinko's
13085 Worldgate Dr (20170-4374)
PHONE......................703 689-0004
David Bradchew, *Manager*
EMP: 2 EST: 2015
SALES (est): 124.1K **Privately Held**
SIC: 2752 Commercial printing, lithographic

(G-6725)
KPW VENTURES INC
1116 Clinch Rd (20170-2411)
PHONE......................703 725-6482
Meyer Olivier S, *President*
EMP: 2
SALES (est): 134.7K **Privately Held**
SIC: 2752 Commercial printing, offset

(PA)=Parent Co (HQ)=Headquarters (DH)=Div Headquarters
✪ = New Business established in last 2 years

2021 Virginia
Industrial Directory

229

GEOGRAPHIC

(G-6726)
KWICK HELP LLC
1043 Sterling Rd Ste 102 (20170-3842)
PHONE....................................703 499-7223
Ahsan Kazmi,
EMP: 2
SALES (est): 56.5K **Privately Held**
SIC: 7372 Application computer software

(G-6727)
L 3 MARITIME SYSTEMS
2235 Monroe St (20171-2824)
PHONE....................................703 443-1700
Robert Gaylord, *President*
EMP: 80
SALES (est): 7.4MM **Privately Held**
WEB: www.l-3mps.com
SIC: 3629 Electronic generation equipment

(G-6728)
L3HARRIS TECHNOLOGIES INC
12975 Worldgate Dr (20170-6008)
PHONE....................................703 668-6239
Dave Melcher, *Manager*
EMP: 385
SALES (corp-wide): 6.8B **Publicly Held**
WEB: www.harris.com
SIC: 3823 3812 Industrial instrmnts
msrmnt display/control process variable;
search & navigation equipment
PA: L3harris Technologies, Inc.
1025 W Nasa Blvd
Melbourne FL 32919
321 727-9100

(G-6729)
L3HARRIS TECHNOLOGIES INC
12975 Worldgate Dr (20170-6008)
PHONE....................................703 668-6000
EMP: 7
SALES (corp-wide): 6.8B **Publicly Held**
WEB: www.harris.com
SIC: 3812 Search & navigation equipment
PA: L3harris Technologies, Inc.
1025 W Nasa Blvd
Melbourne FL 32919
321 727-9100

(G-6730)
L3HARRIS TECHNOLOGIES INC
2235 Monroe St (20171-2824)
PHONE....................................703 668-7256
Kimberly Withers,
EMP: 25
SALES (corp-wide): 6.8B **Publicly Held**
WEB: www.harris.com
SIC: 3663 Radio & TV communications
equipment
PA: L3harris Technologies, Inc.
1025 W Nasa Blvd
Melbourne FL 32919
321 727-9100

(G-6731)
LAFARGE NORTH AMERICA INC
12950 Worldgate Dr # 500 (20170-6001)
PHONE....................................505 471-6456
Colleen Lacivita, *General Mgr*
Eric Bender, *Area Mgr*
Ken Cathcart, *Vice Pres*
Carlos Espina, *Vice Pres*
Emmanuel Mazeaud, *Vice Pres*
EMP: 3
SALES (corp-wide): 1.7B **Privately Held**
WEB: www.lafarge-na.com
SIC: 3241 Cement, hydraulic
HQ: Lafarge North America Inc.
8700 W Bryn Mawr Ave
Chicago IL 60631
773 372-1000

(G-6732)
LASH AND GLOW BY TESS LLC
384 Elden St (20170-4818)
PHONE....................................571 732-1080
Tess Potter, *Principal*
EMP: 2
SALES (est): 88.4K **Privately Held**
WEB: www.lashandglowbytess.com
SIC: 3999 Manufacturing industries

(G-6733)
LED SOLAR AND LIGHT COMPANY
1312 Yellow Tavern Ct (20170-2056)
PHONE....................................703 201-3250
Micheal Arnone, *CFO*
▲ **EMP:** 5
SALES (est): 589.1K **Privately Held**
WEB: www.ledsolarandlightcompany.com
SIC: 3648 Lighting equipment

(G-6734)
LISAS CANDLES
13395 Coppermine Rd # 204 (20171-5394)
PHONE....................................703 940-6733
Lisa Ruth Morin, *Principal*
EMP: 2
SALES (est): 68K **Privately Held**
SIC: 3999 Candles

(G-6735)
LOCKHEED MARTIN CORPORATION
13530 Dulles Tech Dr # 300 (20171-4641)
PHONE....................................703 403-9829
Tom Gordon, *Vice Pres*
Scott Nibbe, *Engineer*
Stan Brown, *Software Dev*
Girard Andres, *Director*
Scharline Hart,
EMP: 1437 **Publicly Held**
WEB: www.lockheedmartin.com
SIC: 3812 Search & navigation equipment
PA: Lockheed Martin Corporation
6801 Rockledge Dr
Bethesda MD 20817

(G-6736)
LOCKHEED MARTIN CORPORATION
13560 Dulles Tech Dr (20171-3414)
PHONE....................................703 466-3000
Ricky Ensslen, *President*
Marc Berkowitz, *Vice Pres*
Patrick Hanley, *Engineer*
EMP: 3000 **Publicly Held**
WEB: www.lockheedmartin.com
SIC: 3812 Search & navigation equipment
PA: Lockheed Martin Corporation
6801 Rockledge Dr
Bethesda MD 20817

(G-6737)
LOCKHEED MARTIN CORPORATION
2245 Monroe St (20171-2824)
PHONE....................................703 787-4027
Michael Oliver, *Business Dir*
Sean Patton, *Business Dir*
EMP: 435 **Publicly Held**
WEB: www.lockheedmartin.com
SIC: 3812 Search & navigation equipment
PA: Lockheed Martin Corporation
6801 Rockledge Dr
Bethesda MD 20817

(G-6738)
LOOSELY COUPLED SOFTWARE LLC
13218 Lazy Glen Ln (20171-2348)
PHONE....................................703 707-9235
Thomas W Philpott, *Administration*
EMP: 2
SALES (est): 141K **Privately Held**
WEB: www.looselycoupledsoftware.com
SIC: 7372 Business oriented computer
software

(G-6739)
MADISON EDGECNNEX HOLDINGS LLC
2201 Coop Way Ste 200 (20171)
PHONE....................................703 880-5404
EMP: 2
SALES (est): 56.5K **Privately Held**
WEB: www.edgeconnex.com
SIC: 7372 Business oriented computer
software

(G-6740)
MAGNET FORENSICS USA INC (PA)
2250 Corp Park Dr Ste 130 (20171-4837)
PHONE....................................519 342-0195

Adam Belsher, *CEO*
Jad Saliba, *President*
Chuck Cobb, *Vice Pres*
EMP: 9 **EST:** 2013
SALES (est): 1.7MM **Privately Held**
WEB: www.magnetforensics.com
SIC: 7372 8243 Application computer soft-
ware; operator training, computer

(G-6741)
MAN DIESEL & TURBO N AMER INC
2200 Ferdinand Porsche Dr (20171-6243)
PHONE....................................703 373-0690
EMP: 3
SALES (corp-wide): 272B **Privately Held**
SIC: 3519 3621 Mfg Internal Combustion
Engines Mfg Motors/Generators
HQ: Man Diesel & Turbo North America Inc.
1600 Brittmoore Rd Ste A
Houston TX 77423
713 780-4200

(G-6742)
MANTAS
13650 Dulles Tech Dr (20171-4649)
PHONE....................................703 322-4917
Ramakrishnan Subramanian, *CEO*
EMP: 7
SALES (est): 482.3K **Publicly Held**
SIC: 7372 Prepackaged software
HQ: Oracle Financial Services Software
Limited
Oracle Park, Off Western Express
Highway,
Mumbai MH 40006

(G-6743)
MARY JO KIRWAN
Also Called: Practical Aplicat Solutions
2616 Stone Mountain Ct (20170-2883)
PHONE....................................703 421-1919
Mary Jo Kirwan, *Owner*
EMP: 1 **EST:** 1998
SALES (est): 80.3K **Privately Held**
SIC: 3272 Concrete products

(G-6744)
MAV6 LLC (PA)
1071 Cedar Chase Ct (20170-2477)
PHONE....................................601 619-7722
Buford Blount, *CEO*
Adam Jay Harrison, *President*
Dave Deptula, *Principal*
EMP: 30
SALES (est): 7.8MM **Privately Held**
SIC: 3812 8742 Defense systems &
equipment; productivity improvement con-
sultant

(G-6745)
MELLANOX FEDERAL SYSTEMS LLC
575 Herndon Pkwy Ste 130 (20170-5282)
PHONE....................................703 969-5735
Charles Peri, *Engineer*
Kyle Maida, *Sales Staff*
Dale Dalessio, *Mng Member*
Dawn Beazer, *Associate*
EMP: 12
SALES (est): 414.2K **Publicly Held**
WEB: www.mellanoxfederal.com
SIC: 3577 5045 5734 Computer periph-
eral equipment; computer peripheral
equipment; computer peripheral equip-
ment
HQ: Mellanox Technologies, Inc.
350 Oakmead Pkwy
Sunnyvale CA 94085
408 970-3400

(G-6746)
MELTINGEARTH
12644 Stoa Ct (20170-2861)
PHONE....................................703 395-5855
EMP: 1
SALES (est): 53.4K **Privately Held**
WEB: www.meltingearth.com
SIC: 2741 Miscellaneous publishing

(G-6747)
MINUTEMAN PRESS
319 Sunset Park Dr (20170-5222)
PHONE....................................703 439-2160
EMP: 2 **EST:** 2018

SALES (est): 83.9K **Privately Held**
WEB: www.minutemanpress.com
SIC: 2752 Commercial printing, litho-
graphic

(G-6748)
MKRS CORPORATION
11905 Crayton Ct (20170-2453)
PHONE....................................203 349-1149
Rohit Sharma, *President*
EMP: 45
SALES (est): 122.7K **Privately Held**
SIC: 2711 Newspapers

(G-6749)
NANO SOLUTIONS INC
3215 Greenstone Ct (20171-3301)
PHONE....................................703 481-3321
David Dowgiallo, *President*
Edward Dowgiallo, *Vice Pres*
EMP: 2
SALES (est): 133.4K **Privately Held**
SIC: 3691 Storage batteries

(G-6750)
NASOTECH LLC
2467 Iron Forge Rd (20171-2917)
PHONE....................................703 493-0436
Sangeetha Dorairajan, *Administration*
EMP: 2
SALES (est): 176.7K **Privately Held**
WEB: www.nasotech.com
SIC: 7372 Application computer software

(G-6751)
NEMESYS SOFTWARE
1007 Hertford St (20170-3118)
PHONE....................................703 435-0508
Laurent Daudelin, *Owner*
EMP: 1
SALES (est): 70.8K **Privately Held**
WEB: www.nemesys-soft.com
SIC: 7372 Prepackaged software

(G-6752)
NEOPATH SYSTEMS LLC
3202 Brynwood Pl (20171-3923)
PHONE....................................571 238-1333
Binesh Gummadi, *Mng Member*
Lakshmi Priya Gummadi,
EMP: 1
SALES (est): 32.7K **Privately Held**
SIC: 7372 7389 Application computer soft-
ware; business services

(G-6753)
NERVVE TECHNOLOGIES INC
505 Huntmar Park Dr # 325 (20170-5103)
PHONE....................................703 334-1488
Robert Robey, *Manager*
EMP: 2
SALES (corp-wide): 3.7MM **Privately
Held**
WEB: www.nervve.com
SIC: 7372 8711 Application computer soft-
ware; electrical or electronic engineering
PA: Nervve Technologies, Inc.
450 Park Ave Fl 30
New York NY 10022
716 800-2250

(G-6754)
NETQOS INC (DH)
Also Called: CA
2291 Wood Oak Dr Ste 140 (20171-6008)
PHONE....................................703 708-3699
Joel Trammell, *President*
George Janis, *Regional Mgr*
Stan Rynex, *Regional Mgr*
Pamela Liou, *Counsel*
Joseph Page, *Senior VP*
EMP: 170
SQ FT: 75,000
SALES (est): 20.6MM
SALES (corp-wide): 22.6B **Publicly Held**
WEB: www.broadcom.com
SIC: 7372 Prepackaged software
HQ: Ca, Inc.
520 Madison Ave
New York NY 10022
800 225-5224

(G-6755)
NIKA SOFTWARE INC
2452 Dakota Lakes Dr (20171-2969)
PHONE....................................703 992-5318

Yelimati Srikanth, *President*
Srikanth Yelimati, *Principal*
EMP: 2 **EST:** 2011
SALES (est): 152.3K **Privately Held**
WEB: www.nika-software.com
SIC: 7372 Prepackaged software

(G-6756)
**NORTHROP GRMMAN
WORLDWIDE ENTP (DH)**
2340 Dulles Corner Blvd (20171-3400)
PHONE..................703 713-4096
George Petteys, *Principal*
EMP: 5
SALES (est): 570.3K **Publicly Held**
WEB: www.northropgrumman.com
SIC: 3812 Search & navigation equipment
HQ: Northrop Grumman Technical Services, Inc.
7575 Colshire Dr
Mc Lean VA 22102
703 556-1144

(G-6757)
**NORTHROP GRUMMAN
CORPORATION**
2340 Dulles Corner Blvd (20171-3400)
PHONE..................703 713-4096
Bill Daus, *Business Mgr*
Mark Skinner, *Vice Pres*
Louise Ussery, *Vice Pres*
Shaun Miller, *Facilities Mgr*
Mark Plummer, *Production*
EMP: 11 **Publicly Held**
WEB: www.northropgrumman.com
SIC: 3812 Search & navigation equipment
PA: Northrop Grumman Corporation
2980 Fairview Park Dr
Falls Church VA 22042

(G-6758)
**NORTHROP GRUMMAN
SYSTEMS CORP**
Also Called: Northrop Grumman Info Systems
2340 Dulles Corner Blvd (20171-3400)
PHONE..................703 968-1000
Jack M Martin Jr, *Director*
EMP: 326 **Publicly Held**
WEB: www.northropgrumman.com
SIC: 3721 Airplanes, fixed or rotary wing
HQ: Northrop Grumman Systems Corporation
2980 Fairview Park Dr
Falls Church VA 22042
703 280-2900

(G-6759)
**NORTHROP GRUMMAN
SYSTEMS CORP**
Also Called: Northrop Grumman Info Systems
2340 Dulles Corner Blvd (20171-3400)
PHONE..................703 968-1000
Mike Twyman, *Manager*
EMP: 116 **Publicly Held**
WEB: www.northropgrumman.com
SIC: 3812 Search & navigation equipment
HQ: Northrop Grumman Systems Corporation
2980 Fairview Park Dr
Falls Church VA 22042
703 280-2900

(G-6760)
**NORTHROP GRUMMAN
SYSTEMS CORP**
Also Called: Northrop Grumman Info Systems
13825 Sunrise Valley Dr # 200
(20171-3539)
PHONE..................703 968-1100
Bart Bailey, *Branch Mgr*
Heather Jones, *Director*
EMP: 229 **Publicly Held**
WEB: www.northropgrumman.com
SIC: 3812 Search & navigation equipment
HQ: Northrop Grumman Systems Corporation
2980 Fairview Park Dr
Falls Church VA 22042
703 280-2900

(G-6761)
NYLA LLC
1201 Bond St (20170-3528)
PHONE..................800 916-8326
Vivian Zalami,

EMP: 2
SALES (est): 103.6K **Privately Held**
SIC: 2337 Women's & misses' suits & coats

(G-6762)
O2O SOFTWARE INC
1548 Coomber Ct (20170-2573)
PHONE..................571 234-3243
Ummey Hossain, *Ch of Bd*
Syed A Hossain, *President*
EMP: 2
SALES (est): 136.8K **Privately Held**
WEB: www.o2osoft.com
SIC: 7372 8742 Prepackaged software; management consulting services

(G-6763)
**OBJECTIVE INTRFACE
SYSTEMS INC**
Also Called: Ois
220 Spring St Ste 530 (20170-6201)
PHONE..................703 295-6500
R William Beckwith, *President*
Joseph M Jacob, *Vice Pres*
James Crowe, *Opers Staff*
Joe Cordani, *Engineer*
Jeff Nguyen, *Engineer*
▼ **EMP:** 55
SQ FT: 7,300
SALES (est): 7.1MM **Privately Held**
WEB: www.ois.com
SIC: 7372 8731 Prepackaged software; commercial physical research

(G-6764)
OCEAN SOFTWARE US LLC
2553 Dulles View Dr Ste 2 (20171-5226)
PHONE..................703 796-1300
Adam Hogan, *Vice Pres*
EMP: 4
SALES (est): 284.1K **Privately Held**
WEB: www.oceansoftwareus.com
SIC: 7372 Prepackaged software

(G-6765)
OLDE WOOLEN MILL LLC
11499 White Oak Ct (20170-2413)
PHONE..................571 926-9604
Laxmi N Kesari, *Administration*
EMP: 2
SALES (est): 199.2K **Privately Held**
SIC: 2231 Wool broadwoven fabrics

(G-6766)
OSGOODE MEDIA INC
13450 Farmcrest Ct # 636 (20171-3152)
PHONE..................866 573-0754
Joseph Stallard, *CEO*
Joseph Andrew Stallard, *CEO*
EMP: 1
SALES (est): 49.7K **Privately Held**
SIC: 7372 Home entertainment computer software

(G-6767)
PARAGON AVIATION SERVICES
447 Carlisle Dr Ste B (20170-5605)
PHONE..................703 787-8800
Julie Obrien, *General Mgr*
Ken Weiss, *Principal*
EMP: 1 **EST:** 2001
SALES (est): 85.4K **Privately Held**
SIC: 3721 Aircraft

(G-6768)
PCPURSUIT INC
2214 Rock Hill Rd Ste 270 (20170-4214)
PHONE..................425 890-5495
Robert Walker, *President*
EMP: 2
SALES (est): 56.5K **Privately Held**
WEB: www.vendors46.wixsite.com
SIC: 7372 Business oriented computer software

(G-6769)
**PERATON CMMNCTONS
HOLDINGS LLC**
12975 Worldgate Dr (20170-6008)
PHONE..................703 668-6001
David Myers, *President*
EMP: 1

SALES (est): 126.4K
SALES (corp-wide): 2.3B **Privately Held**
WEB: www.peraton.com
SIC: 3663 Satellites, communications
HQ: Peraton Corp.
12975 Worldgate Dr # 100
Herndon VA 20170
703 668-6000

(G-6770)
PERATON INC
12975 Worldgate Dr # 100 (20170-6010)
PHONE..................719 599-1500
Alan Stewart, *Branch Mgr*
EMP: 58
SALES (corp-wide): 2.3B **Privately Held**
WEB: www.peraton.com
SIC: 3625 Control equipment, electric
HQ: Peraton Inc.
12975 Worldgate Dr # 100
Herndon VA 20170

(G-6771)
PERATON INC
12975 Worldgate Dr # 100 (20170-6010)
PHONE..................703 668-6000
Jermey Wensinger, *Branch Mgr*
EMP: 185
SALES (corp-wide): 2.3B **Privately Held**
WEB: www.peraton.com
SIC: 3625 Relays & industrial controls
HQ: Peraton Inc.
12975 Worldgate Dr # 100
Herndon VA 20170

(G-6772)
PEXIP INC
13461 Sunrise Valley Dr (20171-3283)
PHONE..................703 480-3181
EMP: 2
SALES (corp-wide): 40.4MM **Privately Held**
WEB: www.pexip.com
SIC: 7372 Application computer software
HQ: Pexip, Inc.
240 W 35th St Ste 400
New York NY 10001
703 338-3544

(G-6773)
PINKY & FACE INC
13300 Franklin Farm Rd F (20171-4096)
PHONE..................703 478-2708
Long Vu, *Owner*
EMP: 2
SALES (est): 83.5K **Privately Held**
SIC: 2844 Manicure preparations

(G-6774)
PIXIA CORP
2350 Corp Park Dr Ste 400 (20171-4851)
PHONE..................571 203-9665
Rudi Ernst, *CEO*
Patrick Ernst, *COO*
Mark Sarojak, *Vice Pres*
Heather Fields, *Admin Asst*
Michele Holley, *Administration*
EMP: 40
SQ FT: 17,023
SALES (est): 6.4MM **Privately Held**
WEB: www.pixia.com
SIC: 7372 Prepackaged software

(G-6775)
PLEXUS INC
13554 Virginia Randlh Ave (20171-4445)
PHONE..................703 474-0383
EMP: 3
SALES (est): 140.2K **Privately Held**
WEB: www.plexusmedica.com
SIC: 3841 Surgical & medical instruments

(G-6776)
POMS CORPORATION (PA)
Also Called: Incode
196 Van Buren St Ste 200 (20170-5337)
PHONE..................703 574-9901
Curt Grina, *President*
EMP: 125
SALES (est): 13.2MM **Privately Held**
WEB: www.poms.com
SIC: 2834 Pharmaceutical preparations

(G-6777)
**POTOMAC SHORES CABINETRY
LLC**
2712 Fox Mill Rd (20171-2011)
PHONE..................703 476-5658
Eric Smith, *Principal*
EMP: 2
SALES (est): 107K **Privately Held**
SIC: 2434 Wood kitchen cabinets

(G-6778)
**PRAGER UNIVERSITY
FOUNDATION**
Also Called: Prageru
2325 Dulles Corner Blvd # 670
(20171-4674)
PHONE..................323 577-2437
Allen Estrin, *CEO*
Marissa Streit, *COO*
Laurie Dorr, *Administration*
EMP: 3 **EST:** 2010
SALES (est): 471.4K **Privately Held**
WEB: www.prageru.com
SIC: 7372 Educational computer software

(G-6779)
PROVISIONING INC
12906 Tarragon Ct (20171-2281)
PHONE..................571 451-3134
Jinping Zheng, *Principal*
EMP: 2
SALES (est): 107.2K **Privately Held**
WEB: www.tamrieljournal.com
SIC: 2741 Miscellaneous publishing

(G-6780)
**PUBLISHERS SERVICE ASSOC
INC**
453 Carlisle Dr Ste B (20170-5611)
PHONE..................570 322-7848
Samantha Detulleo, *Art Dir*
EMP: 1
SALES (est): 37.5K **Privately Held**
SIC: 2741 Miscellaneous publishing

(G-6781)
**QUADRAMED CORPORATION
(DH)**
Also Called: Harris Healthcare
2300 Corp Park Dr Ste 400 (20171-4843)
P.O. Box 710 (20172-0710)
PHONE..................703 709-2300
Duncan W James, *CEO*
Daniel Desaulniers, *President*
Dianna Van Riper, *Principal*
David L Piazza, *COO*
Jim Dowling, *Exec VP*
EMP: 122
SQ FT: 70,750
SALES (est): 68.1MM
SALES (corp-wide): 3.4B **Privately Held**
WEB: www.quadramed.com
SIC: 7372 Business oriented computer software
HQ: N. Harris Computer Corporation
1 Antares Dr Suite 400
Nepean ON K2E 8
613 226-5511

(G-6782)
QUANG D NGUYEN
2817 Gibson Oaks Dr (20171-2287)
PHONE..................703 715-2244
Quang D Nguyen, *Principal*
EMP: 3
SALES (est): 333.2K **Privately Held**
SIC: 3585 Heat pumps, electric

(G-6783)
QUANTA SYSTEMS LLC
Data Control Systems
510 Spring St Ste 200 (20170-5148)
PHONE..................703 885-7900
EMP: 4
SALES (corp-wide): 774.6MM **Publicly Held**
SIC: 3677 Mfg Byte Telemetry Synco Decoms
HQ: Quanta Systems, Llc
510 Spring St Ste 200
Herndon VA 20170

(G-6784)
QUANTUM CONNECT LLC
2350 Corp Park Dr Ste 110 (20171-4849)
PHONE....................................703 251-3342
EMP: 2
SALES (est): 85.9K Privately Held
SIC: 3572 Computer storage devices

(G-6785)
RAASTECH SOFTWARE LLC
2201 Coop Way Ste 600 (20171)
PHONE....................................888 565-3397
Ahmed Aboulnaga, *Mng Member*
Harold Dost III,
EMP: 2
SALES (est): 111.7K Privately Held
WEB: www.raastech.com
SIC: 7372 Business oriented computer
   software

(G-6786)
REDLAND QUARRIES NY INC
12950 Worldgate Dr Ste 50 (20170-6001)
PHONE....................................703 480-3600
Dokani Khaled, *President*
Wole Adeleke, *Finance Dir*
Travis Carpenter, *Branch Mgr*
EMP: 5
SALES (est): 156.2K Privately Held
WEB: www.lafarge-na.com
SIC: 1422 Crushed & broken limestone

(G-6787)
**RESEARCH SERVICE BUREAU
LLC**
3118 Ashburton Ave (20171-2354)
PHONE....................................703 593-7507
John Dixon,
EMP: 1
SALES (est): 100K Privately Held
WEB: www.rsb-inc.com
SIC: 3694 7389 Automotive electrical
   equipment;

(G-6788)
RESTON COPY CENTER ✪
605 Carlisle Dr (20170-4806)
PHONE....................................703 860-9600
EMP: 2 EST: 2020
SALES (est): 101.5K Privately Held
SIC: 2752 Commercial printing, offset

(G-6789)
RESTORTECH INC
13849 Park Center Rd A (20171-3285)
P.O. Box 710660 (20171-0660)
PHONE....................................703 204-0401
John Pletcher, *President*
Salley Pletcher, *Vice Pres*
EMP: 10
SQ FT: 3,500
SALES (est): 1.2MM Privately Held
WEB: www.restortech.com
SIC: 3471 Cleaning, polishing & finishing

(G-6790)
RESULTS SOFTWARE
12334 Folkstone Dr (20171-1817)
PHONE....................................703 713-9100
Sam Saab, *President*
EMP: 2
SALES (est): 120.8K Privately Held
WEB: www.abacusnext.com
SIC: 7372 Business oriented computer
   software

(G-6791)
REVERSE IONIZER LLC
360 Herndon Pkwy Ste 1400 (20170-4865)
PHONE....................................703 403-7256
Patrick Hughes,
EMP: 2
SALES (est): 126.1K Privately Held
WEB: www.reverseionizer.com
SIC: 3823 Water quality monitoring & con-
   trol systems

(G-6792)
RIGEL SYSTEMS INC
2492 Quick St Apt 101 (20171-4574)
PHONE....................................215 715-8950
EMP: 2
SALES (est): 167.6K Privately Held
SIC: 3827 Optical instruments & lenses

(G-6793)
ROAD RUNNER HOLD CO LLC
13241 Woodland Park Rd (20171-6400)
PHONE....................................703 345-2400
EMP: 2
SALES (est): 77.2K Privately Held
WEB: www.rr.com
SIC: 2741 Miscellaneous publishing

(G-6794)
ROBERT DENTON
790 Station St (20170-4663)
PHONE....................................703 435-6960
Robert Denton, *Principal*
EMP: 2 EST: 2014
SALES (est): 134.3K Privately Held
SIC: 3825 Instruments to measure electric-
   ity

(G-6795)
ROTO RAYS INC
722 Park Ave (20170-3232)
PHONE....................................703 437-3353
Richard V Slepetz, *President*
Linda Slepetz, *Corp Secy*
EMP: 2 EST: 1979
SALES (est): 170K Privately Held
SIC: 3648 Lighting fixtures, except electric:
   residential; floodlights

(G-6796)
**ROX CHOX & WOODWORKING
LLC**
1008 Charlton Pl (20170-3203)
PHONE....................................703 378-1313
EMP: 2
SALES (est): 153.6K Privately Held
SIC: 2431 Mfg Millwork

(G-6797)
RUBINS COMPANY MJ INC
1129 Artic Quill Rd (20170-3603)
PHONE....................................571 437-7298
Silbina Correa, *President*
David Rubin, *Advisor*
EMP: 12
SALES (est): 30K Privately Held
WEB: www.rubinscomp.com
SIC: 2389 Costumes

(G-6798)
SALEM INFOTECH INC
2201 Coop Way Ste 600 (20171)
PHONE....................................703 731-9711
Wordsworth Ayyadurai, *Principal*
EMP: 10
SALES (est): 495K Privately Held
WEB: www.saleminfotech.com
SIC: 7372 7389 Application computer soft-
   ware;

(G-6799)
SALUS LLC
3008 Hughsmith Ct (20171-4058)
PHONE....................................475 222-3784
Amy Nicewick, *CEO*
EMP: 1 EST: 2016
SALES (est): 56.7K Privately Held
WEB: www.salushomecare.com
SIC: 7372 Business oriented computer
   software

(G-6800)
SANDBOX ENTERPRISES
2457 Terra Cotta Cir (20171-4694)
PHONE....................................410 999-4666
Sandra J Krebs, *Owner*
EMP: 2
SALES (est): 114.9K Privately Held
WEB: www.agrainofsand.com
SIC: 2653 Corrugated & solid fiber boxes

(G-6801)
SAPR3 ASSOCIATES INC
13598 Cedar Run Ln (20171-3262)
PHONE....................................501 256-8645
Prabhakera Pusapati, *President*
EMP: 1
SALES (est): 79.9K Privately Held
SIC: 7372 Business oriented computer
   software

(G-6802)
SCILUCENT LLC
Also Called: Osborne, Carl G.
585 Grove St Ste 300 (20170-4790)
PHONE....................................703 435-0033
Carl G Osborne, *Mng Member*
Kelley Boyer, *Manager*
Cynthia A Fink, *Manager*
Cynthia Fink, *Manager*
Bonnie Sadow, *Manager*
EMP: 12 EST: 1998
SALES (est): 2.6MM Privately Held
WEB: www.scilucent.com
SIC: 2834 8999 Pharmaceutical prepara-
   tions; chemical consultant

(G-6803)
**SECURE ELEMENTS
INCORPORATED**
13221 Wdlnd Pk Rd Ste 110 (20171)
PHONE....................................703 234-7840
EMP: 25
SALES (est): 1.4MM Privately Held
SIC: 7372 Prepackaged Software Services

(G-6804)
SENSTAR INC (HQ)
13800 Coppermine Rd Fl 2 (20171-6269)
PHONE....................................703 463-3088
James Quick, *President*
Nilton Costa, *Vice Pres*
Bill Hodgins, *Vice Pres*
Alicia Kelly, *Vice Pres*
Gord Loney, *Vice Pres*
EMP: 9
SQ FT: 5,000
SALES (est): 1.9MM Privately Held
WEB: www.senstar.com
SIC: 3669 3829 3812 Burglar alarm appa-
   ratus, electric; measuring & controlling
   devices; search & navigation equipment

(G-6805)
**SGV SOFTWARE AUTOMTN RES
CORP**
907 Broad Oaks Dr (20170-3674)
PHONE....................................703 904-0678
Vikas Joshi, *CEO*
EMP: 30
SALES (est): 1.5MM Privately Held
WEB: www.sgvsarc.com
SIC: 7372 Prepackaged software

(G-6806)
SIGN & PRINT
1056 Elden St (20170-3803)
PHONE....................................703 707-8556
EMP: 2
SALES (est): 92.3K Privately Held
SIC: 2752 Commercial printing, offset

(G-6807)
**SIGNS OF THE TIMES
APOSTOLATE**
360 Herndon Pkwy Ste 1100 (20170-4824)
P.O. Box 345 (20172-0345)
PHONE....................................703 707-0799
Maureen Flynn, *Exec Dir*
EMP: 8
SQ FT: 5,400
SALES: 345.4K Privately Held
WEB: www.sign.org
SIC: 2732 5942 5961 Book printing; book
   stores; book & record clubs

(G-6808)
SIMPLICIKEY LLC
13873 Park Center Rd # 500 (20171-3223)
PHONE....................................703 904-5010
Dvell Garrison, *Vice Pres*
Jason Pizzillo,
Jason Pizzillio,
▲ EMP: 25
SQ FT: 1,000
SALES (est): 2MM Privately Held
WEB: www.simplicikey.com
SIC: 3429 Locks or lock sets

(G-6809)
SINA CORP
1056 Elden St (20170-3803)
PHONE....................................703 707-8556
Mehrdad Khosrowdad, *President*
EMP: 2
SQ FT: 900

SALES (est): 130K Privately Held
SIC: 2759 Advertising literature: printing

(G-6810)
SIP-TONE
196 Van Buren St (20170-5346)
PHONE....................................703 480-0228
Carl Kelly, *Principal*
EMP: 2 EST: 2009
SALES (est): 88.7K Privately Held
SIC: 7372 Prepackaged software

(G-6811)
**SOLARWINDS NORTH AMERICA
INC**
2250 Corp Park Dr Ste 210 (20171-4836)
PHONE....................................877 946-3751
Michael McDowell, *Engineer*
Eric Quitugua, *Engineer*
David Ianetta, *Sales Engr*
Ryan Macia, *Business Anlyst*
Kevin B Thompson, *Branch Mgr*
EMP: 5
SALES (corp-wide): 932.5MM Publicly
Held
WEB: www.solarwinds.com
SIC: 7372 Prepackaged software
HQ: Solarwinds North America, Inc.
   7171 Southwest Pkwy
   Austin TX 78735
   512 682-9300

(G-6812)
SOLSTIK
13163 Fox Hunt Ln Apt 411 (20171-5373)
PHONE....................................571 348-4277
Derran Eaddy, *Owner*
EMP: 1
SALES (est): 47.2K Privately Held
SIC: 2836 Culture media

(G-6813)
SPEED AND ACCURACY LLC
13100 Weather Vane Way (20171-2944)
PHONE....................................405 375-3432
EMP: 1
SALES (est): 58.4K Privately Held
SIC: 3299 Nonmetallic mineral products

(G-6814)
**ST ENGINEERING IDIRECT INC
(DH)**
13861 Sunrise Valley Dr # 300
   (20171-6126)
PHONE....................................703 648-8002
Kevin Steen, *President*
Ramkumar Bangaru, *Engineer*
Christopher Pearson, *Engineer*
Chris Sell, *Engineer*
Przemyslaw Siedlecki, *Engineer*
◆ EMP: 450
SQ FT: 103,016
SALES (est): 207.5MM Privately Held
WEB: www.idirect.net
SIC: 3663 Radio & TV communications
   equipment

(G-6815)
STEM TECHNOLOGIES LLC
13126 Deer Wood Way (20171-5365)
PHONE....................................703 787-4654
Aruna Sannala, *Principal*
EMP: 2
SALES (est): 93.3K Privately Held
SIC: 2834 Pharmaceutical preparations

(G-6816)
SUGARLAND RUN PANTRIES
1019 Monroe St (20170-3212)
PHONE....................................571 216-8565
Marrianne M Henle, *Owner*
EMP: 1
SALES (est): 57.3K Privately Held
SIC: 2053 Frozen bakery products, except
   bread

(G-6817)
**SUNMICRO SOFTWARE
INCORPORATED**
2372 Stone Fence Ln (20171-5358)
PHONE....................................703 587-9362
R Kumar Ayyalasomayajula, *President*
EMP: 2
SALES (est): 89.7K Privately Held
SIC: 7372 Prepackaged software

(G-6818)
SVM SERVICES LLC
13423 Pocono Ct (20170-4045)
PHONE.................................703 389-5100
EMP: 1 EST: 2001
SALES (est): 42.4K **Privately Held**
SIC: 3674 Semiconductors & related devices

(G-6819)
SWEETPEAS BY SHAFER DOBRY
12812 Tewksbury Dr (20171-2427)
PHONE.................................703 476-6787
EMP: 1 EST: 1989
SALES (est): 81K **Privately Held**
SIC: 3842 2329 Mfg Surgical Appliances/Supplies Mfg Men's/Boy's Clothing

(G-6820)
SYNTERAS LLC
2553 Dulles View Dr # 70 (20171-5226)
PHONE.................................703 766-6222
Craig Robinson, *Mng Member*
Jay Jayamohan, *Mng Member*
Matthew Jesinsky,
EMP: 3 EST: 2001
SQ FT: 5,800
SALES (est): 7.6MM
SALES (corp-wide): 1.1B **Privately Held**
WEB: www.synteras.com
SIC: 7372 8742 7375 Application computer software; management information systems consultant; data base information retrieval
HQ: Akima, Llc
2553 Dulles View Dr # 700
Herndon VA 20171
571 323-5200

(G-6821)
T SHIRT BROKER
12521 Arnsley Ct (20171-2550)
PHONE.................................703 362-9297
John Zarou, *Owner*
EMP: 1
SALES (est): 200K **Privately Held**
SIC: 2759 Screen printing

(G-6822)
TALU LLC
2553 Dulles (20171)
PHONE.................................571 323-5200
Eric Woller, *Sr Exec VP*
Scott Mackie, *Manager*
David Hoy, *Manager*
Greg Petersen, *Manager*
Lila Poingue, *Manager*
EMP: 2
SQ FT: 1,200
SALES (est): 406K
SALES (corp-wide): 1.1B **Privately Held**
WEB: www.talullc.com
SIC: 2531 Public building & related furniture
HQ: Akima, Llc
2553 Dulles View Dr # 700
Herndon VA 20171
571 323-5200

(G-6823)
TAYLOR COMMUNICATIONS INC
11715 Bowman Green Dr (20190-3507)
PHONE.................................703 904-0133
EMP: 3
SALES (corp-wide): 2.4B **Privately Held**
WEB: www.taylorcorp.com
SIC: 2761 Manifold business forms
HQ: Taylor Communications, Inc.
1725 Roe Crest Dr
North Mankato MN 56003
866 541-0937

(G-6824)
TCONNEX INC
580 Herndon Pkwy Ste 105 (20170-6239)
PHONE.................................703 910-3400
Larry Liu, *President*
EMP: 3
SQ FT: 150,000
SALES (est): 221K **Privately Held**
WEB: www.tconnex.com
SIC: 7372 Application computer software

(G-6825)
TERRALIGN GROUP INC
441 Carlisle Dr Ste C (20170-4837)
P.O. Box 1905, Ashburn (20146-1905)
PHONE.................................571 388-4990
EMP: 5
SALES (est): 773.9K **Privately Held**
SIC: 7372 8742 Prepackaged Software Services Management Consulting Services

(G-6826)
TIENDA HERNDON INC
1020 Elden St Ste 101 (20170-3800)
PHONE.................................703 478-0478
Jose A Zelaza, *Principal*
EMP: 2 EST: 2009
SALES (est): 136.8K **Privately Held**
SIC: 3861 Photographic equipment & supplies

(G-6827)
TOP IT OFF HATS
1432 Valley Mill Ct (20170-2050)
PHONE.................................703 988-1839
Joyce Bready, *Principal*
EMP: 2
SALES (est): 110.1K **Privately Held**
SIC: 2353 Hats, caps & millinery

(G-6828)
TOPAM LLC
1338 Cassia St (20170-2500)
PHONE.................................703 444-4240
Denis Descour, *Principal*
EMP: 4 EST: 2012
SALES (est): 365.1K **Privately Held**
SIC: 2834 Pharmaceutical preparations

(G-6829)
TOPOATLAS LLC
12706 Kettering Dr (20171-2448)
PHONE.................................703 476-5256
Ralph Smith, *Principal*
EMP: 2 EST: 2012
SALES (est): 117K **Privately Held**
WEB: www.topoatlas.com
SIC: 2741

(G-6830)
TOY RAY GUN
106 Elden St (20170-4872)
PHONE.................................703 662-3348
EMP: 1
SALES (est): 41K **Privately Held**
SIC: 3944 Mfg Games/Toys

(G-6831)
TRISEC ASSOC INC
2905 Parklawn Ct (20171-2349)
P.O. Box 710097 (20171-0097)
PHONE.................................703 471-6564
Allen Bozorth, *President*
Bradley Harris, *Vice Pres*
EMP: 4
SALES (est): 269K **Privately Held**
WEB: www.trisecassociates.com
SIC: 7372 Prepackaged software

(G-6832)
TROJAN DEFENSE LLC
2417 Mill Heights Dr (20171-2983)
PHONE.................................703 981-8710
Matthew Schor, *President*
EMP: 2
SALES (est): 206.3K **Privately Held**
WEB: www.flipzchipz.com
SIC: 3674 Semiconductors & related devices

(G-6833)
TRUSTEDCOM LLC
12930 Worldgate Dr # 300 (20170-6011)
PHONE.................................440 725-1115
Mefide Veseli, *Program Mgr*
Sunil Kalahasti, *Manager*
Bekim Veseli,
Tom Geretz, *Sr Consultant*
EMP: 8
SQ FT: 8,500
SALES (est): 1MM **Privately Held**
WEB: www.trusted.com
SIC: 3695 Computer software tape & disks: blank, rigid & floppy

(G-6834)
TWO BLUE CANDLE CO LLC
12555 Rock Ridge Rd (20170-2888)
PHONE.................................786 301-3371
EMP: 1
SALES (est): 42.4K **Privately Held**
SIC: 3999 Candles

(G-6835)
VAN VIERSSEN MARCEL
Also Called: Potomac Computer Consulting
481 Carlisle Dr Ste 6 (20170-4830)
PHONE.................................703 471-0393
Marcel Van Vierssen, *Owner*
EMP: 3
SQ FT: 1,000
SALES (est): 208K **Privately Held**
WEB:
www.potomaccomputerconsulting.com
SIC: 7372 Prepackaged software

(G-6836)
VENUS TECH LLC
12925 Centre Park Cir # 111 (20171-5933)
PHONE.................................703 389-5557
Vengaiah Mutthineni,
EMP: 2
SALES (est): 133.6K **Privately Held**
WEB: www.venustechinc.com
SIC: 3612 Generator voltage regulators

(G-6837)
VERTEXUSA LLC
12913 Alton Sq (20170-5885)
PHONE.................................213 294-9072
EMP: 1
SALES (corp-wide): 500K **Privately Held**
SIC: 3999 5199 Mannequins; clothes hangers
PA: Vertexusa, Llc
44330 Mercure Cir Ste 309
Sterling VA 20166
213 294-3072

(G-6838)
VIDAR SYSTEMS CORPORATION
Also Called: 3d Systems
365 Herndon Pkwy Ste 105 (20170-6236)
PHONE.................................703 471-7070
Greg Elfering, *Vice Pres*
Brian Loch, *Research*
Jeffrey B Laughlin, *CFO*
Jin Jung, *Sales Mgr*
◆ EMP: 40
SQ FT: 27,800
SALES (est): 9.5MM **Publicly Held**
WEB: www.vidar.com
SIC: 3577 2834 3844 Optical scanning devices; digitalis pharmaceutical preparations; X-ray apparatus & tubes
PA: 3d Systems Corporation
333 Three D Systems Cir
Rock Hill SC 29730

(G-6839)
VIENNA PT RESTON/HERNDON 04
Also Called: Benjamin Moore Authorized Ret
282 Sunset Park Dr (20170-5219)
PHONE.................................703 733-3899
EMP: 1
SALES (est): 56.3K **Privately Held**
WEB: www.viennapaints.com
SIC: 2851 5231 Paints & allied products; paint, glass & wallpaper

(G-6840)
VIRGINIA CABINETS LLC
2465 Centreville Rd J21 (20171-4586)
PHONE.................................703 793-8307
Kemal K Boyraz, *Administration*
EMP: 2
SALES (est): 84.7K **Privately Held**
WEB: www.virginiacabinets.com
SIC: 2434 Wood kitchen cabinets

(G-6841)
VIRGINIA CONCRETE COMPANY LLC (DH)
13880 Dulles Corner Ln # 450 (20171-4685)
PHONE.................................703 354-7100
Clarron Render, *President*
Diggs S Bishop, *President*

Michele Saenz, *Assoc VP*
Hoai Nguyen, *Asst Controller*
Mat Morgan, *Marketing Staff*
EMP: 134
SQ FT: 7,500
SALES (est): 47.1MM **Publicly Held**
WEB: www.wrightsconcrete.net
SIC: 3273 Ready-mixed concrete
HQ: Legacy Vulcan, Llc
1200 Urban Center Dr
Vestavia AL 35242
205 298-3000

(G-6842)
VK PRINTING
605 Carlisle Dr (20170-4806)
PHONE.................................703 435-5502
Manish Patel, *Principal*
EMP: 2
SALES (est): 134.7K **Privately Held**
SIC: 2759 7334 Commercial printing; photocopying & duplicating services

(G-6843)
WAVESET
171 Elden St (20170-4875)
PHONE.................................703 904-7411
Shawn Denson, *Manager*
EMP: 2
SALES (est): 101.3K **Privately Held**
SIC: 7372 Prepackaged software

(G-6844)
WINPRO LLC
11544 Southington Ln (20170-2445)
PHONE.................................703 450-7904
Vijay Aggarwal, *Principal*
EMP: 2
SALES (est): 120.4K **Privately Held**
WEB: www.formtekgroup.com
SIC: 3599 Machine shop, jobbing & repair

(G-6845)
WRIGHT EXPRESS
1807 Michael Faraday Ct (20190-5303)
PHONE.................................703 467-5738
EMP: 1
SALES (est): 61K **Privately Held**
SIC: 2741 Misc Publishing

(G-6846)
XCEEDIUM INC
2291 Wood Oak Dr Ste 200 (20171-6007)
PHONE.................................703 539-5410
Glenn C Hazard, *CEO*
Ken Ammon, *Principal*
Mordecai Rosen, *COO*
Jay Zimmet, *Exec VP*
Richard Rose, *CFO*
EMP: 21 EST: 2011
SALES (est): 6.8MM
SALES (corp-wide): 22.6B **Publicly Held**
WEB: www.broadcom.com
SIC: 3825 Network analyzers
HQ: Ca, Inc.
520 Madison Ave
New York NY 10022
800 225-5224

(G-6847)
ZEN SPORTS PRODUCTS LLC
2500 Tallyrand Ct (20171-2700)
PHONE.................................703 925-0118
John Bull, *Principal*
EMP: 2
SALES (est): 122.3K **Privately Held**
WEB: www.mbzen.com
SIC: 3949 Sporting & athletic goods

(G-6848)
ZINGIFY LLC
1502 Kings Valley Ct (20170-2749)
P.O. Box 1175 (20172-1175)
PHONE.................................703 689-3636
Stacy B Schalk, *Mng Member*
EMP: 1 EST: 1997
SALES (est): 250K **Privately Held**
WEB: www.zingify.com
SIC: 3993 7389 Signs & advertising specialties; advertising, promotional & trade show services

(G-6849)
ZOIL JEWELRY LLC
605 Center St Apt T1 (20170-5006)
PHONE.................................571 340-2256

Benjamin D Szoko,
▲ EMP: 1
SALES (est): 63K **Privately Held**
SIC: 3961 5632 7389 Costume jewelry;
costume jewelry;

Highland Springs
Henrico County

(G-6850)
BLACK MAGAZINE LLC
828 Wales Dr (23075-1525)
PHONE..........................804 306-6735
Tatyanna Dickerson,
EMP: 1
SALES (est): 46.5K **Privately Held**
SIC: 2759 Magazines: printing

(G-6851)
BOWMAN NAKIA
Also Called: K Tonyale The Brand
1415 Renee Ln (23075-2526)
PHONE..........................804 263-2181
Nakia Bowman, *Owner*
EMP: 4
SALES (est): 75K **Privately Held**
SIC: 3999 Hair & hair-based products

(G-6852)
FIRST R & R CO INC
125 S Cedar Ave (23075-1310)
PHONE..........................804 737-4400
Mark Roetke, *President*
EMP: 1
SALES (est): 81.8K **Privately Held**
SIC: 2591 1799 Drapery hardware &
blinds & shades; window treatment instal-
lation

(G-6853)
FREDRICK ALLEN MURPHEY
Also Called: On-Site Fire Extngsher Sls Svc
319 S Kalmia Ave (23075-1617)
PHONE..........................804 385-1650
Fredrick Murphey, *Owner*
EMP: 1
SALES (est): 86.6K **Privately Held**
SIC: 3999 Grenades, hand (fire extinguish-
ers)

(G-6854)
MILLER PUBLISHING
1901 Repp St (23075-2417)
PHONE..........................804 901-2315
L Disheka, *Principal*
EMP: 1
SALES (est): 38.3K **Privately Held**
SIC: 2741 Miscellaneous publishing

(G-6855)
**PRINTED CIRCUITS
INTERNATIONAL**
Also Called: PCI
407 Lee Ave (23075-1514)
PHONE..........................804 737-7979
Stephen Conner, *President*
EMP: 2 EST: 1972
SALES (est): 197.6K **Privately Held**
SIC: 3672 3679 Circuit boards, television
& radio printed; liquid crystal displays
(LCD)

(G-6856)
**RICHMOND POWDER COATING
INC**
504 Babcock Rd (23075-1208)
PHONE..........................804 226-4111
Virgil G Jones, *Principal*
EMP: 2
SALES (est): 112.7K **Privately Held**
SIC: 3479 Metal coating & allied service

(G-6857)
TATUMS FLOOR SERVICE
118 N Daisy Ave (23075-1423)
PHONE..........................804 737-3328
George Tatum, *Owner*
EMP: 2
SALES (est): 165K **Privately Held**
SIC: 2426 Flooring, hardwood

(G-6858)
V & S XPRESS LLC
204 N Beech Ave (23075-1410)
PHONE..........................804 714-4259
Valerie Jordan,
EMP: 2
SALES (est): 95.5K **Privately Held**
SIC: 3537 Trucks, tractors, loaders, carri-
ers & similar equipment

Hillsboro
Loudoun County

(G-6859)
ABSOLUTE SIGNS INC
15573 Woodgrove Rd (20132-2716)
PHONE..........................540 668-6807
Dixiane Hallaj, *Principal*
EMP: 1
SALES (est): 51K **Privately Held**
SIC: 3993 Signs & advertising specialties

(G-6860)
BREAUX VINEYARDS LTD
36888 Breaux Vineyards Ln (20132-1748)
PHONE..........................540 668-6299
Paul Breaux, *President*
Jennifer Breaux, *Vice Pres*
Whitney Gerritzen, *Manager*
Gonzalo Ortiz, *Manager*
EMP: 7
SALES (est): 739.4K **Privately Held**
WEB: www.breauxvineyards.com
SIC: 2084 Wines

(G-6861)
**CONTINENTAL COMMERCIAL
CORP**
Also Called: Hillsborough Vineyards
36716 Charles Town Pike (20132-2743)
PHONE..........................540 668-6216
Bora Baki, *President*
EMP: 2
SALES (est): 279K **Privately Held**
WEB: www.hillsboroughwine.com
SIC: 2084 Wines

(G-6862)
CREATIVEXPOSURE LLC
36388 Charles Town Pike (20132-2780)
PHONE..........................540 668-9070
Kenneth C Stewart, *Administration*
EMP: 2
SALES (est): 106.4K **Privately Held**
SIC: 3861 Photographic equipment & sup-
plies

(G-6863)
CRUSHED CELLARS LLC
37938 Charles Town Pike (20132-2931)
P.O. Box 261, Purcellville (20134-0261)
PHONE..........................571 374-9463
Kalok Robert, *Administration*
EMP: 4
SALES (est): 216.6K **Privately Held**
WEB: www.crushedcellars.com
SIC: 2084 Wines

(G-6864)
DOUKENIE WINERY
14727 Mountain Rd (20132-3638)
PHONE..........................540 668-6464
Sebastien Marquet, *General Mgr*
Nicki Bazaco, *Principal*
Bill Travis, *Manager*
EMP: 2
SALES (est): 231.2K **Privately Held**
WEB: www.doukeniewinery.com
SIC: 2084 Wines

(G-6865)
EMERALD LAKE VINEYARD
12138 Harpers Ferry Rd (20132-2608)
PHONE..........................540 270-3399
Mark A Malick, *Owner*
EMP: 2
SQ FT: 3,524
SALES (est): 77.2K **Privately Held**
WEB: www.maggiemalickwinecaves.com
SIC: 2084 Wines

(G-6866)
FEDOR VENTURES LLC
Also Called: North Gate Vineyard
16110 Mountain Ridge Ln (20132-2813)
PHONE..........................540 668-6248
Mark Fedor, *Principal*
EMP: 2 EST: 2007
SALES (est): 178K **Privately Held**
WEB: www.northgatevineyard.mobi
SIC: 2084 Wines

(G-6867)
FREEDOM FORGE PRESS LLC
35700 Bowen Pl (20132-2560)
PHONE..........................757 784-1038
Eric Egger, *Principal*
EMP: 2
SALES (est): 85.2K **Privately Held**
WEB: www.freedomforgepress.com
SIC: 2741 Miscellaneous publishing

(G-6868)
FRUIT FOR YOU INC
37488 Chartwell Ln (20132-2990)
PHONE..........................540 668-7750
Diane Fisher, *Principal*
EMP: 3
SALES (est): 249.1K **Privately Held**
SIC: 2253 Knit outerwear mills

(G-6869)
GOODBOY LLC
36559 Vineyard View Pl (20132-1760)
PHONE..........................540 421-6712
Richard Scherzinger, *Principal*
EMP: 2 EST: 2012
SALES (est): 98.2K **Privately Held**
WEB: www.locovapor.com
SIC: 2084 Wines

(G-6870)
HOPE CRUSHED VINEYARD LLC
12970 Harpers Ferry Rd (20132-2627)
PHONE..........................540 668-6587
Brad Robertson, *Principal*
EMP: 2 EST: 2011
SALES (est): 88.9K **Privately Held**
SIC: 2084 Wines

(G-6871)
HUNT COUNTRY JEWELERS INC
36955 Charles Town Pike (20132-2784)
PHONE..........................540 338-8050
Ed Cutshall, *President*
Claire Cutshall, *Vice Pres*
EMP: 2
SQ FT: 700
SALES (est): 475K **Privately Held**
WEB: www.huntcountry.com
SIC: 3911 5944 Jewelry, precious metal;
jewelry, precious stones & precious met-
als

(G-6872)
IE W RAILWAY SUPPLY
38200 Charles Town Pike (20132-2927)
PHONE..........................540 882-3886
James Stapleton, *Owner*
EMP: 1
SALES (est): 63.4K **Privately Held**
SIC: 3743 Railroad equipment

(G-6873)
KALERO VINEYARD LLC
13141 Sagle Rd (20132-1832)
PHONE..........................703 216-9036
EMP: 2
SALES (est): 101.2K **Privately Held**
WEB: www.kalerovineyard.com
SIC: 2084 Wines

(G-6874)
KEHOE ENTERPRISES LLC
15971 Charter House Ln (20132-2861)
PHONE..........................540 668-9080
Peter Kehoe,
Louise Cantrell Kehoe,
EMP: 2
SALES (est): 80K **Privately Held**
WEB: www.reboundhoofpack.com
SIC: 2834 5999 Veterinary pharmaceutical
preparations; feed & farm supply

(G-6875)
**MAGGIE MALICK WINE CAVES
LLC**
12138 Harpers Ferry Rd (20132-2608)
PHONE..........................540 905-2921
Maggie Beth Malick, *Administration*
EMP: 2
SALES (est): 156.9K **Privately Held**
WEB: www.maggiemalickwinecaves.com
SIC: 2084 Wines

(G-6876)
MARK SOFTWARE LLC
37433 Hidden Springs Ln (20132-2802)
PHONE..........................703 409-4605
Mark D Johnson, *Administration*
Mark Johnson, *Administration*
EMP: 2 EST: 2013
SALES (est): 93.2K **Privately Held**
SIC: 7372 Prepackaged software

(G-6877)
NOTAVIVA VINEYARDS
13274 Sagle Rd (20132-1829)
PHONE..........................540 668-6756
Stephen Mackey, *Principal*
EMP: 5
SQ FT: 1,008
SALES (est): 425.1K **Privately Held**
WEB: www.notavivavineyards.com
SIC: 2084 Wines

(G-6878)
S AND H PUBLISHING INC
15573 Woodgrove Rd (20132-2716)
PHONE..........................703 915-0913
Dixiane Hallaj, *Editor*
Peter Bair, *Administration*
EMP: 2
SALES (est): 65.9K **Privately Held**
WEB: www.sandhbooks.com
SIC: 2741 Miscellaneous publishing

(G-6879)
SILHOUETTE VINEYARDS LLC
Also Called: 868 Estate Vineyards
14001 Harpers Ferry Rd (20132-1729)
PHONE..........................540 668-6000
Thomas Orme, *Principal*
▲ EMP: 7
SALES (est): 877.7K **Privately Held**
WEB: www.868estatevineyards.com
SIC: 2084 Wines

(G-6880)
**TWO TWISTED POSTS WINERY
LLC**
12970 Harpers Ferry Rd (20132-2627)
PHONE..........................540 668-6587
Theresa Robertson, *Principal*
Lynda Dattilio, *Manager*
EMP: 3 EST: 2011
SALES (est): 275.8K **Privately Held**
WEB: www.twotwistedposts.com
SIC: 2084 Wines

(G-6881)
**WINDHAM WINERY ON
WINDHAM FARM**
14727 Mountain Rd (20132-3638)
PHONE..........................540 668-6464
George Bazaco, *President*
Nicki Bazaco, *Vice Pres*
EMP: 7
SALES (est): 606.8K **Privately Held**
WEB: www.doukeniewinery.com
SIC: 2084 Wines

Hillsville
Carroll County

(G-6882)
**ADAMS PUBLISHING GROUP
LLC**
Also Called: Carroll News, The
804 N Main St (24343-1443)
PHONE..........................276 728-7311
EMP: 1

▲ = Import ▼=Export
◆ =Import/Export

SALES (corp-wide): 251.7MM **Privately Held**
WEB: www.stardem.com
SIC: 2711 Newspapers, publishing & printing
PA: Adams Publishing Group, Llc
103 W Summer St
Greeneville TN 37743
218 348-3391

(G-6883)
APPALACHIAN ALPACA FIBR CO LLC
5197 Snake Creek Rd (24343-4145)
PHONE................................276 728-2349
Audrey McCarter, *Principal*
EMP: 2 EST: 2014
SALES (est): 115.8K **Privately Held**
SIC: 2231 Alpacas, mohair: woven

(G-6884)
B & G BANDMILL
Also Called: Blue Ridge Hearts Pine Floors
931 Deerfield Rd (24343-4436)
PHONE................................276 766-4280
Bob Gill, *Owner*
EMP: 1
SALES (est): 105.4K **Privately Held**
WEB: www.blueridgeheartpinefloors.com
SIC: 2421 Sawmills & planing mills, general

(G-6885)
B MICROFARADS INC
Also Called: Barker Microfarads
205 Mill St (24343-1300)
P.O. Box 697 (24343-0697)
PHONE................................276 728-9121
Enrique Sanchez, *President*
Isaac Murrell, *Executive*
▲ EMP: 110
SQ FT: 12,000
SALES (est): 20.2MM **Privately Held**
WEB: www.bmicaps.com
SIC: 3675 Electronic capacitors
PA: Nueva Generacion Manufacturas, S.A. De C.V.
Av. Tezozomoc No. 239
Ciudad De Mexico CDMX 02760

(G-6886)
BLUE RIDGE COLD PRESS COMPANY
4373 Greenberry Rd (24343-5449)
PHONE................................276 229-1661
Kermit Hundley, *President*
Joe Sutfin, *COO*
Hayden Weaver, *CFO*
EMP: 3
SALES (est): 85.6K **Privately Held**
SIC: 2741 Miscellaneous publishing

(G-6887)
BURKS FORK LOG HOMES
5058 Sylvatus Hwy (24343-5323)
PHONE................................276 766-0350
Jeff Johnson, *Owner*
EMP: 1
SALES (est): 69K **Privately Held**
WEB: www.burksforkloghomes.com
SIC: 2499 Applicators, wood

(G-6888)
CARROLL PUBLISHING CORP
Also Called: Carroll News
1192 W Stuart Dr (24343-1520)
P.O. Box 487 (24343-0487)
PHONE................................276 728-7311
Wayne Brockborough, *President*
INA Horton, *Publisher*
EMP: 11
SALES (est): 482.6K **Privately Held**
WEB: www.thecarrollnews.com
SIC: 2711 Newspapers, publishing & printing

(G-6889)
CLASSIC CREATIONS SCREEN PRTG
358 Industrial Park Dr (24343-3884)
PHONE................................276 728-0540
Keith Sanders, *Owner*
EMP: 2
SALES (est): 168.6K **Privately Held**
SIC: 2759 Screen printing

(G-6890)
DUTCH MADE CABINETS
620 Island Creek Dr (24343-5251)
PHONE................................276 728-5700
Shawn Beachy, *Owner*
EMP: 4
SALES (est): 290K **Privately Held**
SIC: 2434 Wood kitchen cabinets

(G-6891)
F & M CONSTRUCTION CORP
927 Training Center Rd (24343-5607)
P.O. Box 546 (24343-0546)
PHONE................................276 728-2255
Forest E Crowder, *President*
Marty F Crowder, *Vice Pres*
EMP: 15 EST: 1972
SALES (est): 600K
SALES (corp-wide): 1MM **Privately Held**
SIC: 3273 1422 Ready-mixed concrete; limestones, ground
PA: H D Crowder & Sons Inc
Rr 958
Hillsville VA 24343
276 728-2255

(G-6892)
GRAPHIC COMM INC
2340 Island Creek Dr (24343-5166)
PHONE................................301 599-9127
M Bbroquet, *Director*
EMP: 2
SALES (est): 83.9K **Privately Held**
SIC: 2752 Commercial printing, lithographic

(G-6893)
GRAPHIC COMMUNICATIONS INC
2340 Island Creek Dr (24343-5166)
PHONE................................301 599-2020
Jerry Randall, *President*
James Randall, *Corp Secy*
EMP: 18
SQ FT: 48,000
SALES (est): 2.5MM **Privately Held**
WEB: www.gciprint.com
SIC: 2752 2789 Commercial printing, offset; bookbinding & related work

(G-6894)
H & F BODY & CABINET SHOP
4191 Fancy Gap Hwy (24343-3537)
PHONE................................276 728-9404
William Horton, *Partner*
Greg Fariss, *Partner*
EMP: 2
SALES (est): 258.9K **Privately Held**
SIC: 3713 5712 Truck beds; cabinet work, custom

(G-6895)
L&F LOGGING INC
395 Hardscuffle Rd (24343-4868)
PHONE................................276 728-5773
Leonard Branscome, *President*
Ricky Marshall, *Admin Sec*
EMP: 7
SALES (est): 375K **Privately Held**
SIC: 2411 Logging camps & contractors

(G-6896)
MCMILLAN WELDING INC
802 Snake Creek Rd (24343-1742)
PHONE................................276 728-1031
Martin E McMillan, *President*
EMP: 1
SALES (est): 144.3K **Privately Held**
WEB: www.boyntonbeachchauffeur.com
SIC: 7692 Welding repair

(G-6897)
MOHAWK INDUSTRIES INC
351 Floyd Pike (24343-1693)
PHONE................................276 728-2141
Mickey Wilcox, *Branch Mgr*
EMP: 156 **Publicly Held**
WEB: www.mohawkind.com
SIC: 2273 3253 Finishers of tufted carpets & rugs; ceramic wall & floor tile
PA: Mohawk Industries, Inc.
160 S Industrial Blvd
Calhoun GA 30701

(G-6898)
PARKDALE MILLS INCORPORATED
Also Called: Parkdale Plants 32 33 34 & 35
1 Advanced Technology Dr (24343-2701)
PHONE................................276 728-1001
Anderson Warlick, *Branch Mgr*
EMP: 106
SALES (corp-wide): 1.3B **Privately Held**
WEB: www.parkdalemills.com
SIC: 2281 Cotton yarn, spun
HQ: Parkdale Mills, Incorporated
531 Cotton Blossom Cir
Gastonia NC 28054
704 874-5000

(G-6899)
SALEM STONE CORPORATION
456 Wysor Hwy (24343-4540)
PHONE................................276 766-3449
Betsy Cook, *General Mgr*
Roger Ramey, *Manager*
EMP: 20
SALES (corp-wide): 34MM **Privately Held**
WEB: www.salemstonecorp.com
SIC: 1423 1422 Crushed & broken granite; crushed & broken limestone
PA: Salem Stone Corporation
5764 Wilderness Rd
Dublin VA 24084
540 674-5556

(G-6900)
TIMOTHY C VASS
3882 Stable Rd (24343-5100)
PHONE................................276 728-7753
Timothy C Vass, *Owner*
EMP: 2
SALES (est): 176.1K **Privately Held**
SIC: 3523 0139 Cattle feeding, handling & watering equipment; hay farm

(G-6901)
TURMAN SAWMILL INC (PA)
555 Expansion Dr (24343-3777)
P.O. Box 475 (24343-0475)
PHONE................................276 728-3752
John Michael Turman, *President*
Mike Turman, *Principal*
Lena Gray, *Corp Secy*
Mason Thomas, *Manager*
▼ EMP: 52 EST: 1971
SQ FT: 1,900
SALES (est): 10.9MM **Privately Held**
WEB: www.theturmangroup.com
SIC: 2421 Lumber: rough, sawed or planed

(G-6902)
TURMAN-MERCER SAWMILLS LLC (PA)
Also Called: Turman Group, The
555 Expansion Dr (24343-3777)
P.O. Box 475 (24343-0475)
PHONE................................276 728-7974
Mike Turman, *President*
Bob Jackson, *Buyer*
Lee Daugherty, *Manager*
▼ EMP: 10
SALES (est): 36.6MM **Privately Held**
WEB: www.theturmangroup.com
SIC: 2421 Sawmills & planing mills, general

(G-6903)
VAUGHANS CUSTOM CABINETS-HOME
250 Retrievers Run (24343-3984)
PHONE................................276 398-2440
Darryl Vaughan, *Owner*
EMP: 4
SALES (est): 287.6K **Privately Held**
SIC: 2434 Wood kitchen cabinets

Hiltons
Scott County

(G-6904)
BELLAMY MFG & REPR CO
Also Called: Bellamy Manufacturing & Repair
170 Academy Rd Ste 101 (24258-6698)
P.O. Box 55 (24258-0055)
PHONE................................276 386-7273

Harvey Lee Bellamy, *President*
Pamela Bellamy, *Corp Secy*
EMP: 2 EST: 1954
SQ FT: 65,000
SALES (est): 227K **Privately Held**
SIC: 3713 7538 Truck bodies (motor vehicles); truck engine repair, except industrial

Hinton
Rockingham County

(G-6905)
RAWLEY PIKE WELDING LLC
6009 Rawley Pike (22831-2211)
PHONE................................540 867-5335
Douglas W Shank,
EMP: 2
SQ FT: 4,000
SALES (est): 33K **Privately Held**
SIC: 7692 Welding repair

(G-6906)
VIRGINIA PLTY GROWERS COOP INC (PA)
Also Called: Vpgc
6349 Rawley Pike (22831-2001)
P.O. Box 228 (22831-0228)
PHONE................................540 867-4000
Steve Bazzle, *Ch of Bd*
James Mason, *President*
Jim Mason, *President*
John King, *Vice Pres*
David Price, *Sales Dir*
EMP: 500
SQ FT: 200,000
SALES (est): 87MM **Privately Held**
WEB: www.vapoultrygrowers.com
SIC: 2015 Chicken slaughtering & processing

(G-6907)
VPGC LLC (PA)
Also Called: Virginia Plty Grwers Rckingham
6349 Rawley Pike (22831-2001)
P.O. Box 1287, Harrisonburg (22803-1287)
PHONE................................540 867-4000
James Mason, *President*
John A King II, *Vice Pres*
EMP: 2
SALES (est): 605.2K **Privately Held**
SIC: 2015 Poultry slaughtering & processing

Hiwassee
Pulaski County

(G-6908)
ACCURACY GEAR LLC
4988 Lead Mine Rd (24347-2816)
PHONE................................540 230-0257
William Alexander,
EMP: 1
SALES (est): 43.2K **Privately Held**
SIC: 3999 Manufacturing industries

(G-6909)
APPALCHIAN LEICESTER LONGWOOLS
4615 Mountain Pride Rd (24347-2101)
PHONE................................540 639-3077
Gail Groot, *Partner*
EMP: 8
SALES (est): 364.1K **Privately Held**
SIC: 2231 7389 Dyeing & finishing: wool or similar fibers;

(G-6910)
BLUEWIRE PROTOTYPES INC
6309 Old Ferry Rd (24347-2435)
PHONE................................540 200-3200
Michael H Harris, *President*
EMP: 3
SALES (est): 291.5K **Privately Held**
WEB: www.bluewireproto.com
SIC: 3679 Electronic circuits

(G-6911)
CATHAY INDUSTRIES INC
2170 Julia Simpkins Rd (24347-2200)
P.O. Box 218 (24347-0218)
PHONE....................................224 629-4210
EMP: 1 EST: 2018
SALES (est): 39.6K **Privately Held**
WEB: www.cathayindusa.com
SIC: 3999 Manufacturing industries

(G-6912)
HOOVER COLOR CORPORATION
2170 Julia Simpkins Rd (24347-2200)
P.O. Box 218 (24347-0218)
PHONE....................................540 980-7233
Charles E Hoover, *President*
Burl D Bowman, *Vice Pres*
Melissa Zienius, *VP Persnl*
Steve Haimann, *Director*
Melissa L Zienius, *Admin Sec*
◆ EMP: 4 EST: 1924
SQ FT: 140,000
SALES (est): 6.8MM **Privately Held**
WEB: www.hoovercolor.com
SIC: 2816 Inorganic pigments
HQ: Cathay Industries (Usa) Inc.
2340 Kenyon Rd
Bartlett IL 60103

(G-6913)
NEXT GENERATION WOODS INC
4615 Mountain Pride Rd (24347-2101)
PHONE....................................540 639-3077
Harry Groot, *President*
EMP: 2
SALES (est): 210.3K **Privately Held**
WEB: www.nextgenwoods.com
SIC: 2421 Sawmills & planing mills, general

Honaker
Russell County

(G-6914)
HAROLD KEENE COAL CO INC
Also Called: Keene Carpet
Rr 67 (24260)
P.O. Box 929 (24260-0929)
PHONE....................................276 873-5437
Harold Lynn Keene, *President*
Larry Stinson, *Admin Sec*
EMP: 7 EST: 1974
SALES (est): 969.2K **Publicly Held**
SIC: 1241 5052 Coal mining services; coal
PA: Suncoke Energy, Inc.
1011 Warrenville Rd # 600
Lisle IL 60532

(G-6915)
MDJ LOGGING INC
5929 New Garden Rd (24260-6180)
PHONE....................................276 889-4658
Milton Harris, *Principal*
EMP: 6
SALES (est): 286.2K **Privately Held**
SIC: 2411 Logging

Hopewell
Hopewell City County

(G-6916)
ACE BATH BOMBS LLC
207 S 9th Ave (23860-3810)
PHONE....................................804 839-8639
EMP: 2
SALES (est): 69.6K **Privately Held**
SIC: 2844 Bath salts

(G-6917)
ADVANSIX INC
905 E Randolph Rd (23860-2413)
PHONE....................................804 541-5000
Christopher Rock, *Engineer*
Steven Baker, *Project Engr*
Jeffrey Taylor, *Electrical Engi*
Connor Robison, *Accountant*
Erik Jiang, *Marketing Staff*
EMP: 750

SALES (corp-wide): 1.3B **Publicly Held**
WEB: www.advansix.com
SIC: 2899 Chemical preparations
PA: Advansix Inc.
300 Kimball Dr Ste 101
Parsippany NJ 07054
973 526-1800

(G-6918)
ARROMAN INDUSTRIES CORP
609 Elm Ct (23860-5251)
PHONE....................................804 317-4737
Aaron Cummings, *Principal*
EMP: 3
SALES (est): 199.5K **Privately Held**
SIC: 3999 Manufacturing industries

(G-6919)
CHEMTRADE CHEMICALS US LLC
511 Plant St (23860-5226)
P.O. Box 759 (23860-0759)
PHONE....................................804 541-0261
Arthur Grammar, *Branch Mgr*
Tim Link, *Manager*
EMP: 10
SALES (corp-wide): 1.1B **Privately Held**
WEB: www.generalchem.com
SIC: 2819 Industrial inorganic chemicals
HQ: Chemtrade Chemicals Us Llc
90 E Halsey Rd
Parsippany NJ 07054

(G-6920)
COOKING WILLIAMS GOOD
3102 Sussex Dr (23860-4140)
PHONE....................................804 931-6643
Claude Williams,
EMP: 3
SALES (est): 282.6K **Privately Held**
SIC: 2599 Food wagons, restaurant

(G-6921)
CUSTOM COMFORT BY WINN LTD
15 Rev Cw Harris St (23860-2942)
P.O. Box 1676 (23860-1180)
PHONE....................................804 452-0929
Winn Butterworth, *President*
Charles Lynch, *Vice Pres*
Floyd Roberts, *Vice Pres*
EMP: 10
SQ FT: 30,000
SALES (est): 1.4MM **Privately Held**
WEB: www.winndom.com
SIC: 2515 Mattresses & foundations; box springs, assembled

(G-6922)
DAVIDS MOBILE SERVICE LLC
3213 Clay St (23860-4807)
PHONE....................................804 481-1647
David Waselchalk,
EMP: 5 EST: 2013
SALES (est): 317.4K **Privately Held**
SIC: 3465 5013 2992 Body parts, automobile: stamped metal; automobile service station equipment; brake fluid (hydraulic): made from purchased materials

(G-6923)
DETERMINED LLC
105 S Mesa Dr (23860-2049)
PHONE....................................804 829-7229
Trinity Beveridge,
EMP: 5
SALES (est): 186.2K **Privately Held**
SIC: 2335 Women's, juniors' & misses' dresses

(G-6924)
E I DU PONT DE NEMOURS & CO
Also Called: Dupont
1 Discovery Dr (23860)
PHONE....................................804 530-9300
Christina Tippett, *Buyer*
Jan Lariviere, *Research*
Peter Neuschul, *Manager*
Steven Crisp, *Executive*
Smith Ginnie, *Contractor*
EMP: 50
SALES (corp-wide): 21.5B **Publicly Held**
WEB: www.dupont.com
SIC: 2821 3081 Plastics materials & resins; unsupported plastics film & sheet

HQ: E. I. Du Pont De Nemours And Company
974 Centre Rd Bldg 735
Wilmington DE 19805
302 485-3000

(G-6925)
EVONIK CORPORATION
914 E Randolph Rd (23860-2458)
PHONE....................................804 541-8658
Ken Bittner, *Vice Pres*
Derek Dagostino, *Plant Mgr*
Bryan Brown, *Production*
Dave McCue, *Production*
Chris Earnest, *Buyer*
EMP: 123
SALES (corp-wide): 1.7B **Privately Held**
WEB: www.sorry.evonik.com
SIC: 2869 Industrial organic chemicals
HQ: Evonik Corporation
299 Jefferson Rd
Parsippany NJ 07054
973 929-8000

(G-6926)
EVONIK GOLDSCHMIDT CORPORATION
914 E Randolph Rd (23860-2458)
P.O. Box 1299 (23860-1299)
PHONE....................................804 541-8658
Reinhold Brand, *President*
Werner Bischoff, *COO*
Thomas Hermann, *COO*
Michael Immich, *COO*
Wolfgang Kaster, *COO*
◆ EMP: 550
SQ FT: 100,000
SALES (est): 73.1K
SALES (corp-wide): 1.7B **Privately Held**
SIC: 2869 2819 Industrial organic chemicals; silicones; industrial inorganic chemicals
HQ: Evonik Corporation
299 Jefferson Rd
Parsippany NJ 07054
973 929-8000

(G-6927)
GREEN PLAINS HOPEWELL LLC
701 S 6th St (23860-3819)
PHONE....................................804 668-0013
Michael Wierzbicki, *Facilities Mgr*
EMP: 8
SALES (est): 1.2MM **Publicly Held**
SIC: 2869 Ethyl alcohol, ethanol
PA: Green Plains Inc.
1811 Aksarben Dr
Omaha NE 68106
402 884-8700

(G-6928)
HERCULES INC
1111 Hercules Rd (23860-5245)
PHONE....................................804 541-4545
Mark Jones, *Principal*
Ken Peek, *Engineer*
EMP: 4 EST: 2016
SALES (est): 201.7K **Privately Held**
WEB: www.hercules.se
SIC: 2869 Industrial organic chemicals

(G-6929)
HONEY HALEYS MEADERY LLC
235 E Broadway (23860-2809)
P.O. Box 1628 (23860-1174)
PHONE....................................804 668-5943
EMP: 2
SALES (est): 90.5K **Privately Held**
WEB: www.haleyshoneymeadery.com
SIC: 2084 Wines

(G-6930)
HONEYWELL INTERNATIONAL INC
105 Winston Churchill Dr (23860-5235)
P.O. Box 831 (23860-0831)
PHONE....................................804 458-7649
Mike Andrews, *Program Mgr*
Edward Mills, *Executive*
EMP: 256
SALES (corp-wide): 36.7B **Publicly Held**
WEB: www.honeywell.com
SIC: 3724 Aircraft engines & engine parts

PA: Honeywell International Inc.
300 S Tryon St
Charlotte NC 28202
704 627-6200

(G-6931)
HONEYWELL INTERNATIONAL INC
905 E Randolph Rd (23860-2413)
P.O. Box 761 (23860-0761)
PHONE....................................804 541-5000
Ahmadou Tanko, *President*
Rick Higbie, *Systems Mgr*
EMP: 4
SALES (corp-wide): 36.7B **Publicly Held**
WEB: www.honeywell.com
SIC: 2824 2869 2819 Organic fibers, non-cellulosic; industrial organic chemicals; industrial inorganic chemicals
PA: Honeywell International Inc.
300 S Tryon St
Charlotte NC 28202
704 627-6200

(G-6932)
HONEYWELL INTERNATIONAL INC
7006 Laprade St (23860)
PHONE....................................804 541-5618
Asa Booti, *Manager*
EMP: 40
SALES (corp-wide): 36.7B **Publicly Held**
WEB: www.honeywell.com
SIC: 3724 Aircraft engines & engine parts
PA: Honeywell International Inc.
300 S Tryon St
Charlotte NC 28202
704 627-6200

(G-6933)
HONEYWELL RESINS & CHEM LLC (HQ)
905 E Randolph Rd Bldg 97 (23860-2413)
P.O. Box 761 (23860-0761)
PHONE....................................804 541-5000
Walter Hubbard,
Anthony Dilucente,
James V Gelly,
John M Quitmeyer,
◆ EMP: 100
SALES (est): 28.9MM
SALES (corp-wide): 36.7B **Publicly Held**
WEB: www.honeywell.com
SIC: 2824 2869 2819 Organic fibers, non-cellulosic; industrial organic chemicals; industrial inorganic chemicals
PA: Honeywell International Inc.
300 S Tryon St
Charlotte NC 28202
704 627-6200

(G-6934)
HOPEWELL PUBLISHING COMPANY
Also Called: Tri City Advertiser, The
516 E Randolph Rd (23860-2652)
P.O. Box 481 (23860-0481)
PHONE....................................804 452-6127
James D Lancaster, *President*
Marion Lancaster, *Vice Pres*
White Barney W, *Vice Pres*
James D Lancaster Jr, *Admin Sec*
EMP: 35 EST: 1925
SQ FT: 12,800
SALES (est): 2MM **Privately Held**
WEB: www.hopepubs.com
SIC: 2711 2791 2789 2752 Newspapers, publishing & printing; typesetting; bookbinding & related work; commercial printing, lithographic

(G-6935)
IMPERIAL SIGN CO
111 S Main St (23860-3914)
PHONE....................................804 541-8545
Glen Conner, *Owner*
EMP: 1
SALES (est): 65K **Privately Held**
WEB: www.imperialsign.com
SIC: 3993 Signs & advertising specialties

(G-6936)
JET PAC LLC
215 E Randolph Rd (23860-2727)
PHONE....................................804 334-5216

George J Kranitzky, *Administration*
EMP: 3 **EST:** 2016
SALES (est): 246.5K **Privately Held**
SIC: 3724 Aircraft engines & engine parts

(G-6937)
JOHNSON PRINTING SERVICE INC
404 E Poythress St (23860-7803)
P.O. Box 1403 (23860-1403)
PHONE..................................804 541-3635
Keith Johnson, *President*
Keithjohnson President, *Principal*
EMP: 6
SQ FT: 2,500
SALES (est): 761.8K **Privately Held**
SIC: 2752 Commercial printing, offset

(G-6938)
LINDE INC
Also Called: Praxair
107 Industrial St (23860-7824)
PHONE..................................804 452-3181
EMP: 3 **Privately Held**
WEB: www.praxair.com
SIC: 2813 Industrial gases
HQ: Linde Inc.
    10 Riverview Dr
    Danbury CT 06810
    203 837-2000

(G-6939)
MESSER LLC
221 Hopewell St (23860-7808)
PHONE..................................804 458-0928
Nelson Samot, *Branch Mgr*
EMP: 22
SALES (corp-wide): 1.1B **Privately Held**
WEB: www.praxair.com
SIC: 2813 Nitrogen; oxygen, compressed or liquefied
HQ: Messer Llc
    200 Somerset Corp Blvd # 7000
    Bridgewater NJ 08807
    908 464-8100

(G-6940)
MYSTICAL CREATIONS
2802 Grant St (23860-2041)
PHONE..................................804 943-8386
Kristi Ambroise, *Owner*
EMP: 1
SALES (est): 41K **Privately Held**
SIC: 3944 5945 Craft & hobby kits & sets; arts & crafts supplies

(G-6941)
TEGO CHEMIE SVC USADIV OF GOLD
914 E Randolph Rd (23860-2458)
PHONE..................................804 541-8658
Sam Shermer, *Principal*
EMP: 1
SALES (est): 92.3K **Privately Held**
SIC: 2869 Industrial organic chemicals

(G-6942)
TEIJIN-DU PONT FILMS INC (PA)
1 Discovery Dr (23860)
P.O. Box 411 (23860-0411)
PHONE..................................804 530-9310
Henry Voigt, *President*
David Obarski, *Corp Secy*
Steven Crisp, *Accountant*
▲ **EMP:** 2
SALES (est): 19.7MM **Privately Held**
WEB: www.teijin-dupontfilms.com
SIC: 3081 5099 Film base, cellulose acetate or nitrocellulose plastic; video cassettes, accessories & supplies

(G-6943)
WALKERS CERTIFIED WELDING INC
1102 Plant Rd (23860-5206)
P.O. Box 1502 (23860-1113)
PHONE..................................804 541-2612
Nancy Walker, *President*
Nancy E Walker, *Treasurer*
EMP: 6
SALES (est): 680.4K **Privately Held**
SIC: 7692 Welding repair

(G-6944)
WESTROCK CP LLC
910 Industrial St (23860-7826)
PHONE..................................804 541-9600
Chuck Bogatie, *Manager*
EMP: 436
SALES (corp-wide): 17.5B **Publicly Held**
WEB: www.westrock.com
SIC: 2631 2621 Kraft linerboard; paper mills
HQ: Westrock Cp, Llc
    1000 Abernathy Rd Ste 125
    Atlanta GA 30328

Hot Springs
Bath County

(G-6945)
B & H EXCAVATING
1266 Shady Ln (24445-2785)
P.O. Box 1004 (24445-0766)
PHONE..................................540 839-2107
Joseph Tuning, *Owner*
EMP: 1
SALES (est): 74.2K **Privately Held**
SIC: 1389 Excavating slush pits & cellars

(G-6946)
HMT PUBLISHERS LLC
11328 Sam Snead Hwy (24445-2742)
PHONE..................................540 839-5628
Steven W Cauley, *Administration*
EMP: 2
SALES (est): 50K **Privately Held**
SIC: 2741 Miscellaneous publishing

(G-6947)
LOUIE DUFOUR
5456 Sam Snead Hwy (24445-2428)
PHONE..................................540 839-5232
Louie Dufour, *Principal*
EMP: 2
SALES (est): 92.6K **Privately Held**
SIC: 7692 Automotive welding

(G-6948)
LOUIES WELDING AND FABRICATION
5456 Sam Snead Hwy (24445-2428)
PHONE..................................540 839-5232
EMP: 1
SALES (est): 27.6K **Privately Held**
SIC: 7692 Welding repair

(G-6949)
PE CREW LLC
9530 Sam Snead Hwy (24445-2920)
PHONE..................................540 839-5999
Robert Donze,
EMP: 2 **EST:** 2017
SALES (est): 40K **Privately Held**
SIC: 3721 Research & development on aircraft by the manufacturer

(G-6950)
WARM SPRINGS MTN WOODWORKS
71 Besley Ln (24445-2706)
PHONE..................................540 839-9747
Peter Judah, *Principal*
EMP: 2 **EST:** 2011
SALES (est): 194.2K **Privately Held**
WEB: www.warmspringsmountainwoodworks.com
SIC: 2431 Millwork

Howardsville
Buckingham County

(G-6951)
HORSESHOE BEND IMPRVS LLC
1253 Axtell Rd (24562-4132)
PHONE..................................434 969-1672
Eber A Rhodes, *Administration*
EMP: 2
SALES (est): 147.4K **Privately Held**
WEB:
www.horseshoebendimprovements.com
SIC: 3462 Horseshoes

Huddleston
Bedford County

(G-6952)
BL NICHOLS LOGGING INC
1895 Preston Mill Rd (24104-8000)
PHONE..................................540 875-8690
Bobby Nichols, *President*
Ella Nichols, *Treasurer*
EMP: 9
SALES (est): 1.2MM **Privately Held**
SIC: 2411 Logging camps & contractors

(G-6953)
EASYLOADER MANUFACTURING LLC
207 Byway Rd (24104-3298)
PHONE..................................540 297-2601
Timothy S Bird, *Administration*
EMP: 2
SALES (est): 84.3K **Privately Held**
SIC: 3999 Manufacturing industries

(G-6954)
K & J LOGGING INC
4468 Dundee Rd (24104-3442)
PHONE..................................540 330-9812
Howell Kenneth G, *Principal*
EMP: 3
SALES (est): 98.8K **Privately Held**
SIC: 2411 Logging camps & contractors

(G-6955)
LEE SAVOY INC
1822 Echo Forest Way (24104-3946)
PHONE..................................540 297-9275
EMP: 2
SALES (est): 130K **Privately Held**
SIC: 2084 Mfg Wines/Brandy/Spirits

(G-6956)
NICHOLS LOGGING INC
1433 Preston Mill Rd (24104-3841)
PHONE..................................540 297-3246
EMP: 2
SALES (est): 110.7K **Privately Held**
SIC: 2411 Logging camps & contractors

(G-6957)
PRECISION COMPONENTS INC
1337 Thornbird Pl (24104-3803)
PHONE..................................540 297-1853
Betty L Callahan, *President*
David T Callahan, *Vice Pres*
David Callahan, *Vice Pres*
EMP: 2
SALES (est): 160K **Privately Held**
SIC: 3714 Brake drums, motor vehicle

(G-6958)
SMITH MOUNTAIN LAND & LBR INC
2868 Crab Orchard Rd (24104-4230)
PHONE..................................540 297-1205
Monty A Burnette, *President*
Malcolm B Burnette, *Vice Pres*
EMP: 13
SALES (est): 2.1MM **Privately Held**
WEB: www.smithmtnlandandlumberinc.com
SIC: 2421 5031 Sawmills & planing mills, general; lumber: rough, dressed & finished

(G-6959)
STONE MOUNTAIN VENTURES INC
1597 Eagle Point Rd (24104-3759)
PHONE..................................888 244-9306
William H Jennings, *President*
Sherri Hodnett, *Accountant*
Matt Kidd, *Sales Staff*
EMP: 10
SALES (est): 1.4MM **Privately Held**
WEB: www.stonemountainltd.com
SIC: 3651 Microphones

Hume
Fauquier County

(G-6960)
DESERT ROSE RANCH & WINERY LLC
13726 Hume Rd (22639-1713)
PHONE..................................540 635-3200
Robert W Claymier,
Linda Claymier,
EMP: 2 **EST:** 2014
SALES (est): 195.5K **Privately Held**
WEB: www.desertrosewinery.com
SIC: 2084 Wines

(G-6961)
FOUR CALLING BIRDS LTD
6160 Keyser Rd (22639-1908)
PHONE..................................540 317-5761
Gail I Crouthamel, *Administration*
EMP: 2
SALES (est): 161.3K **Privately Held**
SIC: 3999 Framed artwork

(G-6962)
LAUREL RUN LLC
11171 Hume Rd (22639-1815)
PHONE..................................540 364-1238
EMP: 2
SALES (est): 101.7K **Privately Held**
SIC: 1221 Bituminous Coal/Lignite Surface Mining

(G-6963)
STILLHOUSE VINEYARDS LLC
Also Called: Philip Carter Winery
4366 Stillhouse Rd (22639-1825)
PHONE..................................434 293-8221
Philip Strother, *Mng Member*
Jose Luis Antonio, *Manager*
EMP: 4
SALES (est): 178.2K **Privately Held**
WEB: www.stillhousevineyards.com
SIC: 2084 Wines

Huntly
Rappahannock County

(G-6964)
CANA CELLARS INC
Also Called: Rappahannock Cellars
14437 Hume Rd (22640-3134)
PHONE..................................540 635-9398
John Delmare, *President*
Allan Delmare, *Treasurer*
Kelly Knight, *Manager*
Marialisa Delmare, *Admin Sec*
▲ **EMP:** 10
SALES (est): 556.8K **Privately Held**
WEB: www.rappahannockcellars.com
SIC: 2084 Wines

(G-6965)
PRESTON AEROSPACE INC
187 Resettlement Rd (22640-3016)
PHONE..................................540 675-3474
Charles Preston, *President*
EMP: 1
SALES (est): 113.1K **Privately Held**
WEB: www.prestonaerospace.com
SIC: 3721 Aircraft

(G-6966)
RICKS CUSTOM WELDING INC
62 Homestead Knoll Ln (22640-3104)
PHONE..................................540 675-1888
Richard Nawrocki, *President*
EMP: 2 **EST:** 1998
SQ FT: 2,700
SALES (est): 254.6K **Privately Held**
WEB: www.rickscustomwelding.com
SIC: 7692 Welding repair

(G-6967)
WHITE OAK FORGE LTD
31 Shootz Hollow Rd (22640-3122)
PHONE..................................540 636-4545
Oliver D Putnam, *President*
EMP: 1
SQ FT: 1,575

GEOGRAPHIC

SALES (est): 80K **Privately Held**
WEB: www.white-oak-forge-ltd.huntly.va.amfibi.company
SIC: 3462 Ornamental metal forgings, ferrous

Hurley
Buchanan County

(G-6968)
ALLIANCE RESOURCE PARTNERS LP
Hwy 643 (24620)
P.O. Box 196 (24620-0196)
PHONE..............................276 566-8516
Charles Keen, *Branch Mgr*
EMP: 59 **Publicly Held**
WEB: www.arlp.com
SIC: 1222 Underground mining, subbituminous
HQ: Alliance Resource Partners Lp
  1717 S Boulder Ave # 400
  Tulsa OK 74119
  918 295-7600

(G-6969)
LAYNE LOGGING
8287 Hurley Rd (24620-8505)
PHONE..............................276 312-1665
Morgan Layne, *Principal*
EMP: 2
SALES (est): 81.7K **Privately Held**
SIC: 2411 Logging

Hurt
Pittsylvania County

(G-6970)
ALTILLO VINEYARDS & WINERY
620 Level Run Rd (24563-3344)
PHONE..............................434 324-4160
Eric Schenkel, *Principal*
EMP: 2
SALES (est): 82.3K **Privately Held**
WEB: www.altillovineyards.com
SIC: 2084 Wines

(G-6971)
B & S XPRESS LLC
14241 Rockford School Rd (24563-3801)
PHONE..............................434 851-2695
Teresa Wiegand, *Administration*
EMP: 2
SALES (est): 126.9K **Privately Held**
SIC: 2741 Miscellaneous publishing

(G-6972)
CLAYS MACHINE SHOP & WELDING
2357 Pocket Rd (24563-2429)
P.O. Box 473 (24563-0473)
PHONE..............................434 324-4997
Ervin Clay, *Owner*
EMP: 3
SALES (est): 217K **Privately Held**
SIC: 3599 Machine shop, jobbing & repair

(G-6973)
CLEAN AND BLESS
2044 Shula Dr (24563-3450)
PHONE..............................434 324-7129
Patsy Clements, *Owner*
EMP: 1
SALES (est): 84.1K **Privately Held**
SIC: 2044 Rice milling

(G-6974)
DINKLE ENTERPRISES
Also Called: Dinkle, C W Enterprises
2440 Roark Mill Rd (24563-3556)
PHONE..............................434 324-8508
Carroll Dinkle, *Owner*
EMP: 1
SALES (est): 62.5K **Privately Held**
SIC: 1442 7033 Gravel mining; trailer park

(G-6975)
FIELSIDE WOODWORKIG
1657 Spring Rd (24563-3847)
PHONE..............................434 203-5530
Jacque Oakes, *Principal*

EMP: 1
SALES (est): 54.1K **Privately Held**
SIC: 2431 Millwork

(G-6976)
PRODUCTION SYSTEMS SOLUTIONS
1720 Pocket Rd (24563-2416)
P.O. Box 700 (24563-0700)
PHONE..............................434 324-7843
Curt Keesee, *President*
Anita Ireland, *Corp Secy*
EMP: 3
SQ FT: 3,000
SALES (est): 419.9K **Privately Held**
WEB: www.pss-inc.biz
SIC: 3625 Industrial electrical relays & switches

(G-6977)
ROBERTSON LUMBER INC
3900 Dews Rd (24563-3207)
PHONE..............................434 335-5100
Michael Robertson, *President*
Robertson Earl Leon, *Vice Pres*
EMP: 12
SALES (est): 2MM **Privately Held**
SIC: 2421 Sawmills & planing mills, general

(G-6978)
SOUTHERN AIRBRUSHES
1381 Shula Dr (24563-8101)
PHONE..............................434 324-4049
Rick Perkins, *Owner*
Cheryl Perkins, *Manager*
EMP: 2 EST: 1999
SALES (est): 90.1K **Privately Held**
WEB: www.southern-airbrushing.business.site
SIC: 3952 Brushes, air, artists'

Independence
Grayson County

(G-6979)
CHARLIE WARD
2267 Riverside Dr (24348-4815)
PHONE..............................276 768-7266
Charlie Ward, *Owner*
EMP: 1
SALES (est): 94.7K **Privately Held**
SIC: 3711 Snow plows (motor vehicles), assembly of

(G-6980)
CORE HEALTH & FITNESS LLC
Also Called: Star Trac
709 Powerhouse Rd (24348-3782)
PHONE..............................714 669-1660
EMP: 22
SALES (corp-wide): 240.5MM **Privately Held**
WEB: www.corehandf.com
SIC: 3949 Exercise equipment
PA: Core Health & Fitness, Llc
  4400 Ne 77th Ave Ste 300
  Vancouver WA 98662
  360 326-4090

(G-6981)
DARCO SOUTHERN LLC
253 Darco Dr (24348)
P.O. Box 454 (24348-0454)
PHONE..............................276 773-2711
David Durnovich, *President*
Brian Humphrey, *Purch Agent*
Ashley Cooper, *Sales Staff*
Mike Shumate, *Sales Staff*
▲ EMP: 25
SQ FT: 30,500
SALES (est): 4.2MM **Privately Held**
WEB: www.darcosouthern.com
SIC: 3053 2221 Packing, rubber; gaskets, all materials; fiberglass fabrics

(G-6982)
EMBROIDERYVILLE
229 Black Rock Mtn Ln (24348-4690)
P.O. Box 68 (24348-0068)
PHONE..............................276 768-9727
EMP: 1
SALES (est): 35K **Privately Held**
SIC: 2395 Pleating/Stitching Services

(G-6983)
GRAYSON EXPRESS
2686 Graystone Rd (24348-3609)
PHONE..............................276 773-9173
Ronnie Jones, *Owner*
EMP: 4
SALES (est): 290.4K **Privately Held**
WEB: www.graysoncountyva.com
SIC: 2741 Miscellaneous publishing

(G-6984)
GRAYSON MILLWORKS COMPANY INC
315 W Main St (24348)
P.O. Box 804 (24348-0804)
PHONE..............................276 773-8590
Richard B Hill, *President*
EMP: 2 EST: 2008
SALES (est): 321.8K **Privately Held**
WEB: www.graysonmillworks.com
SIC: 2431 Millwork

(G-6985)
HOFFMAN POTTERY
100 Driftwood Ln (24348-4314)
PHONE..............................276 773-3546
David Hoffman, *Owner*
Sherry Hoffman, *Co-Owner*
EMP: 3
SALES (est): 90K **Privately Held**
WEB: www.hoffmanpottery.com
SIC: 3269 5719 Stoneware pottery products; pottery

(G-6986)
I T F CIRCLE
173 Rainbow Cir (24348-3998)
P.O. Box 590 (24348-0590)
PHONE..............................276 773-3114
W Alexander McAllister III, *President*
William McAllister Jr, *Corp Secy*
J B Macdonald, *Vice Pres*
Mercier Pierre, *Vice Pres*
McAllister Mills, *Shareholder*
EMP: 30
SQ FT: 8,000
SALES (est): 2.9MM **Privately Held**
SIC: 3229 Yarn, fiberglass

(G-6987)
INDEPENDENCE LUMBER INC
407 Lumber Ln (24348-4057)
PHONE..............................276 773-3744
Eller Randall, *President*
Nelson D Weaver, *Exec VP*
Damon Eller, *Vice Pres*
Eller Damon Randell, *Vice Pres*
Greg Wyatt, *Maint Spvr*
EMP: 100
SQ FT: 12,000
SALES (est): 21.8MM **Privately Held**
WEB: www.independencelumberinc.com
SIC: 2421 Lumber: rough, sawed or planed

(G-6988)
INDIAN RIVER CANOE MFG
Also Called: New River Canoe Manufacturing
832 E Main St (24348-3830)
PHONE..............................276 773-3124
Ruell Holeton, *Owner*
EMP: 2
SALES (est): 154.7K **Privately Held**
WEB: www.mohawkpaddles.com
SIC: 3732 Canoes, building & repairing

(G-6989)
MCALLISTER MILLS INC
173 Rainbow Cir (24348-3998)
P.O. Box 590 (24348-0590)
PHONE..............................276 773-3114
William A McAllister III, *President*
William A McAllister Jr, *Corp Secy*
Carol D McAllister, *Vice Pres*
▲ EMP: 31
SQ FT: 35,000
SALES (est): 6.6MM **Privately Held**
WEB: www.mcallistermills.com
SIC: 2298 2295 Cordage & twine; coated fabrics, not rubberized

(G-6990)
MCKEE BREWER
469 Brewers Ln (24348-4292)
PHONE..............................276 579-2048
Ellis Brewer, *Principal*

EMP: 5
SALES (est): 274.1K **Privately Held**
SIC: 2411 Logging

(G-6991)
MOUNTAIN MARIMBA INC
431 E Main St (24348-3910)
P.O. Box 224 (24348-0224)
PHONE..............................276 773-3899
Sandra L Venzie, *Principal*
EMP: 2
SALES (est): 130.1K **Privately Held**
SIC: 3931 Marimbas

(G-6992)
NAUTILUS INTERNATIONAL INC
709 Powerhouse Rd (24348-3782)
P.O. Box 708 (24348-0708)
PHONE..............................276 773-2881
Irwin Maddery, *President*
Michelle Fink, *Purch Mgr*
Greg Webb, *VP Engrg*
▲ EMP: 200
SALES (est): 14.4MM **Privately Held**
WEB: www.deltaapparel.com
SIC: 3949 Racket sports equipment
PA: Delta Woodside Industries Inc
  700 N Woods Dr
  Fountain Inn SC 29644
  864 255-4100

(G-6993)
RIVER RIDGE MEATS LLC
226 Industrial Ln (24348-3994)
PHONE..............................276 773-2191
Richard Brantley Ivey,
Sharon Hale, *Admin Asst*
EMP: 4 EST: 2016
SQ FT: 7,000
SALES (est): 145.8K **Privately Held**
WEB: www.landcraftedfood.com
SIC: 2013 Prepared beef products from purchased beef

(G-6994)
SAFE GUARD SECURITY SERVICE
1165 N Independence Ave (24348-5056)
P.O. Box 4882, Martinsville (24115-4882)
PHONE..............................276 773-2866
Dick Wilcox, *Corp Secy*
EMP: 2
SALES (est): 100K **Privately Held**
SIC: 3699 Security devices

(G-6995)
SHAKLEE AUTHORIZED DISTRI
383 Doe Run Rd (24348-4848)
PHONE..............................276 744-3546
Brenda Grabley, *Owner*
EMP: 1
SALES (est): 55K **Privately Held**
SIC: 2023 Dietary supplements, dairy & non-dairy based

(G-6996)
TRITEX LLC
60 Corporate Ln (24348)
P.O. Box 370 (24348-0370)
PHONE..............................276 773-0593
William A McAllister III,
EMP: 14
SALES (est): 1.6MM **Privately Held**
WEB: www.tritexllc.com
SIC: 2295 Chemically coated & treated fabrics

(G-6997)
UNITED CNTRY CLLINS ASSOC REAL
155 W Main St (24348-4002)
PHONE..............................407 233-4377
EMP: 2
SALES (est): 74.4K **Privately Held**
WEB:
www.graysonmountainrealestate.com
SIC: 2842 Specialty cleaning, polishes & sanitation goods

Indian Valley
Floyd County

(G-6998)
VAUGHANS MILL INC
1318 Vaughns Mill Rd Nw (24105-3069)
PHONE.................................540 789-7144
Jeff Vaughn, *President*
Danny Vaughan, *Vice Pres*
EMP: 3
SALES (est): 162.8K **Privately Held**
SIC: 2041 2048 Grain mills (except rice); prepared feeds

Iron Gate
Alleghany County

(G-6999)
IRON GATE VLNTR FIRE DEPT INC
300 Third St (24448)
P.O. Box 146 (24448-0146)
PHONE.................................540 862-5700
Robert Daniels Sr, *President*
Robert Boyd, *Chief*
EMP: 26
SQ FT: 4,520
SALES: 110K **Privately Held**
SIC: 3711 Fire department vehicles (motor vehicles), assembly of

Irvington
Lancaster County

(G-7000)
CREATIVE DESIGNS OF VIRGINIA
63 Rappahannock Rd (22480-2503)
PHONE.................................804 435-2382
Sandra Matthews, *Owner*
EMP: 1
SALES (est): 130.4K **Privately Held**
WEB: www.cdva.com
SIC: 3993 Signs & advertising specialties

(G-7001)
ENTERPRISE HIVE LLC
4507 Irvington Rd Ste 200 (22480-2119)
P.O. Box 685 (22480-0685)
PHONE.................................804 438-9393
Vicki Tambellini, *CEO*
EMP: 7
SALES (est): 504.1K **Privately Held**
WEB: www.enterprisehive.com
SIC: 7372 Business oriented computer software

(G-7002)
WOODWRIGHTS LLC
48 Steamboat Rd (22480-2211)
PHONE.................................804 761-0775
Matson C Terry II, *Administration*
EMP: 3
SALES (est): 177.7K **Privately Held**
WEB: www.lumbersmith.com
SIC: 2421 Sawmills & planing mills, general

Ivanhoe
Wythe County

(G-7003)
COMMONWEALTH MFG & DEV
5226 Ivanhoe Rd (24350-3565)
PHONE.................................276 699-2089
Dan Good, *President*
Peggy Good, *Vice Pres*
EMP: 10
SALES (est): 1MM **Privately Held**
WEB: www.cmdinc.us
SIC: 3069 Molded rubber products

(G-7004)
COMMONWEALTH RECYCLING SVCS
5226 Ivanhoe Rd (24350-3565)
PHONE.................................931 289-3645
EMP: 2
SALES (est): 77.4K **Privately Held**
SIC: 3069 Fabricated rubber products

(G-7005)
CROSS MACHINE WELDING
137 Rakestown Rd (24350-3021)
PHONE.................................276 699-1974
Maurice Porter, *Principal*
EMP: 1
SALES (est): 81K **Privately Held**
SIC: 7692 Welding repair

(G-7006)
WASHING ON WHEELS INC
216 River Bluff Dr (24350-3571)
PHONE.................................276 699-6275
Timothy Blair, *Principal*
EMP: 2
SALES (est): 142K **Privately Held**
SIC: 3312 Blast furnaces & steel mills

Ivor
Southampton County

(G-7007)
WPD INC
38082 Broadwater Rd (23866-2904)
PHONE.................................757 859-9498
Wayne Copeland, *Owner*
EMP: 1
SALES (est): 121.9K **Privately Held**
SIC: 3715 Truck trailers

Jamaica
Middlesex County

(G-7008)
CRAZY CLOVER BUTCHER SHOP
1176 Briery Swamp Rd (23079-2066)
PHONE.................................804 370-5291
David Wayne Burch, *Owner*
EMP: 8
SALES (est): 289.8K **Privately Held**
SIC: 2011 Meat packing plants

Jarratt
Greensville County

(G-7009)
A PLACE CALLED THERE WITH SIGN
2050 Aberdour Rd (23867-8728)
PHONE.................................434 594-5576
Junius Broadnax, *Vice Pres*
EMP: 1
SALES (est): 46K **Privately Held**
SIC: 3993 Signs & advertising specialties

(G-7010)
HERCULES STEEL COMPANY INC
305 Jarratt Ave (23867-9055)
P.O. Box 248 (23867-0248)
PHONE.................................434 535-8571
Cheryl McBee, *Manager*
EMP: 1
SALES (corp-wide): 6.5MM **Privately Held**
WEB: www.herculessteelco.com
SIC: 3441 Fabricated structural metal
PA: Hercules Steel Company Inc
950 Country Club Dr
Fayetteville NC 28301
910 488-5110

Java
Pittsylvania County

(G-7011)
GREGORY LUMBER INC
12121 Halifax Rd (24565-3011)
PHONE.................................434 432-1000
John M Gregory, *President*
Mary Gregory, *Vice Pres*
EMP: 35 **EST:** 1987
SQ FT: 44,000
SALES (est): 7MM **Privately Held**
SIC: 2421 5031 Sawmills & planing mills, general; lumber, plywood & millwork

Jeffersonton
Culpeper County

(G-7012)
FRESH PRINTZ LLC
19248 Walnut Hills Rd (22724-2251)
PHONE.................................540 937-3017
Linda Debruhl, *Principal*
EMP: 1
SALES (est): 54.1K **Privately Held**
WEB: www.athleticunion.company
SIC: 2395 2396 7389 7335 Embroidery & art needlework; screen printing on fabric articles; embroidering of advertising on shirts, etc.; commercial photography; commercial art & graphic design

(G-7013)
GROVES CABINETRY INC
19253 Hillcrest Ln (22724-2029)
PHONE.................................540 341-7309
D Scott Groves, *Principal*
EMP: 2
SALES (est): 139.9K **Privately Held**
SIC: 2434 Wood kitchen cabinets

(G-7014)
WRAP BUDDIES LLC
3118 Somerset Dr (22724-1798)
PHONE.................................855 644-2783
Bret D Wortman,
EMP: 1
SALES (est): 175K **Privately Held**
SIC: 2679 Gift wrap & novelties, paper

Jetersville
Amelia County

(G-7015)
SWIFT CREEK FOREST PRODUCTS
20200 Patrick Henry Hwy (23083-2118)
P.O. Box 507, Amelia Court House (23002-0507)
PHONE.................................804 561-1751
Jerry G Long, *President*
Brenda Long, *Corp Secy*
EMP: 50
SQ FT: 8,000
SALES (est): 6.6MM **Privately Held**
SIC: 2448 2441 Pallets, wood; nailed wood boxes & shook

(G-7016)
TYSON FOODS INC
23065 St James Rd (23083-2502)
PHONE.................................804 561-2187
Ronald L Baptist, *Branch Mgr*
Ronald Baptist, *Branch Mgr*
EMP: 581
SALES (corp-wide): 43.1B **Publicly Held**
WEB: www.tysonfoods.com
SIC: 2015 Chicken, processed; frozen
PA: Tyson Foods, Inc.
2200 W Don Tyson Pkwy
Springdale AR 72762
479 290-4000

(G-7017)
TYSON FOODS INC
1938 Patrick Henry Hwy (23083-2869)
PHONE.................................434 645-7791
Don Tyson, *Branch Mgr*
EMP: 161

SALES (corp-wide): 43.1B **Publicly Held**
WEB: www.tysonfoods.com
SIC: 2011 2015 Pork products from pork slaughtered on site; chicken slaughtering & processing
PA: Tyson Foods, Inc.
2200 W Don Tyson Pkwy
Springdale AR 72762
479 290-4000

Jonesville
Lee County

(G-7018)
BARBER LOGGING LLC
444 Henry Gibbons Rd (24263-7179)
PHONE.................................276 346-4638
Waylon Barber,
EMP: 2
SALES (est): 225K **Privately Held**
SIC: 2411 Logging camps & contractors

(G-7019)
CARTER WELDING LLC
365 Cowboy Ln (24263-7104)
Rural Route 2 Box 2396 (24263)
PHONE.................................276 346-1873
EMP: 1 **EST:** 2010
SALES (est): 96.3K **Privately Held**
SIC: 7692 Welding repair

(G-7020)
CURTIS RUSSELL LUMBER CO INC
Rr 2 Box 2312 (24263)
P.O. Box 930 (24263-0930)
PHONE.................................276 346-1958
Gary Russell, *President*
Curtis Russell, *President*
Ola Russell, *Corp Secy*
EMP: 42
SQ FT: 10,000
SALES (est): 4.9MM **Privately Held**
SIC: 2448 2421 Pallets, wood; sawmills & planing mills, general

(G-7021)
CUSTOM BUILT CABINETS AND
598 Living Waters Dr (24263)
PHONE.................................812 427-9733
Raymond Byler, *Owner*
EMP: 3
SALES (est): 246.4K **Privately Held**
SIC: 2434 Wood kitchen cabinets

(G-7022)
JIM L CLARK
Also Called: Clark's Custom Cut Sawmill
1220 Cox Rd (24263-6516)
PHONE.................................276 393-2359
Jim Clark, *Owner*
EMP: 1 **EST:** 2013
SALES (est): 73K **Privately Held**
SIC: 2421 7389 Sawmills & planing mills, general; business services

(G-7023)
ROOP WELDING & GENERAL REPAIR
Rr 4 (24263)
P.O. Box 206 (24263-0206)
PHONE.................................276 346-3338
Don G Roop, *President*
Wanda Roop, *Corp Secy*
EMP: 4
SQ FT: 2,400
SALES (est): 200K **Privately Held**
SIC: 7692 Welding repair

(G-7024)
WILMAS WOODWORKING
1282 State Route 70 (24263-7642)
PHONE.................................276 346-3611
Wilma Young, *Principal*
EMP: 1
SALES (est): 90.9K **Privately Held**
SIC: 2431 Millwork

GEOGRAPHIC

Keeling
Pittsylvania County

(G-7025)
J D SHELTON
Also Called: Shelton Logging
18465 Old Richmond Rd (24566-4135)
PHONE..............................434 797-4403
J D Shelton, *Owner*
EMP: 8
SALES (est): 490K **Privately Held**
SIC: 2411 Logging camps & contractors

Keezletown
Rockingham County

(G-7026)
AKL ASSOCIATES LTD
Also Called: Window Architecture
1213 Indian Trail Rd (22832-2348)
PHONE..............................540 269-8228
Howard G Davis, *President*
EMP: 2
SALES (est): 170K **Privately Held**
SIC: 2591 Window shades

(G-7027)
DANDEE PRINTING CO
1881 Mountain Valley Rd (22832-2001)
PHONE..............................540 828-4457
Dale Burkholder, *Principal*
Karen Burkholder, *Principal*
EMP: 2
SALES (est): 316K **Privately Held**
SIC: 2752 Commercial printing, offset

(G-7028)
MACS MACHINE SHOP
3420 Rush Ln (22832-2361)
PHONE..............................540 269-2222
George Coffman, *Owner*
EMP: 1
SALES (est): 25K **Privately Held**
SIC: 3599 Machine shop, jobbing & repair

(G-7029)
RONALD STEPHEN RHODES
2937 Minie Ball Ln (22832-2262)
PHONE..............................540 435-1441
Ronald Rhodes, *Owner*
EMP: 3 **EST:** 2015
SALES (est): 158.5K **Privately Held**
SIC: 3523 Grounds mowing equipment

(G-7030)
STAFFORD SALAD COMPANY LLC
2924 Keezletown Rd (22832-2330)
PHONE..............................540 269-2462
David Engle, *Principal*
EMP: 3
SALES (est): 128.8K **Privately Held**
SIC: 2099 Salads, fresh or refrigerated

(G-7031)
SUCCESSFUL MIX LLC
1968 Mountain Valley Rd (22832-2008)
PHONE..............................540 269-6904
Sue Sternberg, *Owner*
EMP: 3 **EST:** 2010
SALES (est): 193.4K **Privately Held**
WEB: www.thesuccessfulmix.com
SIC: 3273 Ready-mixed concrete

Kenbridge
Lunenburg County

(G-7032)
BARNES MANUFACTURING COMPANY
621 Main St (23944-2097)
P.O. Box 439 (23944-0439)
PHONE..............................434 676-8210
Franklin Barnes, *President*
Thomas C Barnes Jr, *Admin Sec*
▼ **EMP:** 50 **EST:** 1941
SQ FT: 2,000

SALES (est): 5MM **Privately Held**
SIC: 2421 Sawmills & planing mills, general

(G-7033)
HINKLE WELDING & FABRICATION
1415 Hinkle Rd (23944-2903)
PHONE..............................434 447-2770
Shannon Hinkle, *Principal*
EMP: 1 **EST:** 2017
SALES (est): 45.8K **Privately Held**
SIC: 7692 Welding repair

(G-7034)
LIGNETICS OF VIRGINIA INC
11068 South Hill Rd (23944-3229)
PHONE..............................434 676-4800
Kenneth R Tucker, *President*
Ted Hartshorn, *Admin Sec*
EMP: 20 **EST:** 2007
SQ FT: 12,000
SALES (est): 3.1MM
SALES (corp-wide): 28.8MM **Privately Held**
WEB: www.lignetics.com
SIC: 2448 Wood pallets & skids
HQ: Lignetics, Inc.
   Hwy 200 E
   Kootenai ID 83840

(G-7035)
TRI-COUNTY OPE
123 Main St (23944-2093)
PHONE..............................434 676-4441
Darlene Pettit, *Principal*
EMP: 4
SQ FT: 2,100
SALES (est): 431.3K **Privately Held**
SIC: 3524 7699 Lawn & garden mowers & accessories; professional instrument repair services

(G-7036)
WALKER BRANCH LUMBER
276 Hite Ln (23944-3225)
PHONE..............................434 676-3199
Nelson Swartzenruber,
Naomi Swartzenruber,
EMP: 2
SALES (est): 195.7K **Privately Held**
SIC: 2431 Panel work, wood

(G-7037)
WORTHAM MACHINE AND WELDING
532 Main St (23944-2001)
P.O. Box 263 (23944-0263)
PHONE..............................434 676-8080
Scott Wortham, *President*
Pam Smith, *Admin Sec*
▲ **EMP:** 12
SQ FT: 12,500
SALES (est): 1.6MM **Privately Held**
SIC: 3599 7692 Machine shop, jobbing & repair; welding repair

Kents Store
Fluvanna County

(G-7038)
DECOTEC INC
1172 Perkins Rd (23084-2345)
PHONE..............................434 589-0881
William D Weisenburger Sr, *President*
EMP: 3
SQ FT: 3,500
SALES (est): 100K **Privately Held**
SIC: 3699 8732 8742 Security control equipment & systems; market analysis or research; industry specialist consultants

(G-7039)
JAMES RIVER BEVERAGE CO LLC
1111 Dogwood Dr (23084-2431)
PHONE..............................434 589-2798
Connie Stevens,
EMP: 1
SALES (est): 43.5K **Privately Held**
WEB: www.jrbeverage.com
SIC: 2082 Beer (alcoholic beverage)

Keokee
Lee County

(G-7040)
H & B MACHINE
1289 Rocklick Rd (24265)
PHONE..............................276 546-5307
Betty Fleenor, *Principal*
EMP: 3
SALES (est): 127.2K **Privately Held**
SIC: 3399 3429 7389 Laminating steel; clamps, metal; business services

Keswick
Albemarle County

(G-7041)
ADIAL CORPORATION
4098 Wood Ln (22947-2900)
PHONE..............................434 243-0570
Bankole Johnson, *Principal*
EMP: 3
SALES (est): 153.5K **Privately Held**
WEB: www.adialcorp.com
SIC: 2834 Pharmaceutical preparations

(G-7042)
ADULT MEDICAL PREDICTIVE DEVIC
1406 Sandown Ln (22947-9184)
PHONE..............................434 996-1203
Matthew Clark, *CFO*
EMP: 1
SALES (est): 82.3K **Privately Held**
SIC: 3841 Surgical & medical instruments

(G-7043)
AXON CELLS INC
756 Club Dr (22947-2616)
PHONE..............................434 987-4460
Cynthia M Barber PHD, *President*
EMP: 5
SALES (est): 293.2K **Privately Held**
WEB: www.axoncells.com
SIC: 2834 Pharmaceutical preparations

(G-7044)
BULLET ENTERPRISES INC
4985 Richmond Rd (22947-3109)
PHONE..............................757 897-9100
M Stewart Felty, *President*
EMP: 1
SALES (est): 100K **Privately Held**
SIC: 3441 Fabricated structural metal

(G-7045)
DR KINGS LITTLE LUXURIES LLC
640 Bunker Hill Ln (22947-2419)
PHONE..............................434 293-8515
Eva M King, *Mng Member*
EMP: 1 **EST:** 2015
SALES (est): 10K **Privately Held**
WEB: www.drevaskincare.com
SIC: 2844 5999 Toilet preparations; toiletries, cosmetics & perfumes

(G-7046)
DYNAMIC LITERACY LLC
265 Campbell Rd (22947-2109)
P.O. Box 388, Lake Junaluska NC (28745-0388)
PHONE..............................888 696-8597
Jerry Bailey, *Asst Director*
Eric A Schmitz,
Gerald V Bailey,
Dr Thomas H Estes,
Dr David Larrick,
EMP: 5
SQ FT: 2,100
SALES (est): 436.8K **Privately Held**
WEB: www.dynamicliteracy.com
SIC: 7372 2731 Educational computer software; book publishing

(G-7047)
GLADSTONE MEDIA CORPORATION
214 Clarks Tract (22947-2318)
PHONE..............................434 293-8471

Leonard G Phillips, *President*
EMP: 1
SALES (est): 425K **Privately Held**
WEB: www.gladstonemedia.shop.musictoday.com
SIC: 2741 Miscellaneous publishing

(G-7048)
KESWICK GOURMET FOODS LLC
1726 Downing Ct (22947-9200)
PHONE..............................610 585-2688
Kathy Larrabee, *Mng Member*
David Larrabee,
EMP: 2
SALES (est): 124.1K **Privately Held**
WEB: www.keswick.com
SIC: 2035 Pickles, sauces & salad dressings

(G-7049)
KESWICK VINEYARD
6131 Gordonsville Rd (22947-1802)
PHONE..............................434 295-1834
Albert Schornberg, *Principal*
Stephen Barnard, *Marketing Mgr*
EMP: 2 **EST:** 2007
SALES (est): 145.5K **Privately Held**
WEB: www.keswickvineyards.com
SIC: 2084 Wines

(G-7050)
KESWICK VINEYARDS LLC
1575 Winery Dr (22947-1822)
PHONE..............................434 244-3341
J D Dunn, *Principal*
Stephen Barnard, *Marketing Mgr*
Albert Schornberg,
EMP: 13
SALES (est): 1.6MM **Privately Held**
WEB: www.keswickvineyards.com
SIC: 2084 Wines

(G-7051)
KESWICK WINERY LLC
1575 Keswick Winery Dr (22947-1833)
PHONE..............................434 244-3341
Al Schornberg, *Mng Member*
Cindy Schornberg, *Manager*
EMP: 3
SALES (est): 341.8K **Privately Held**
WEB: www.keswickvineyards.com
SIC: 2084 Wines

(G-7052)
LUMACYTE LLC
1145 River Rd Ste 16 (22947)
PHONE..............................888 472-9295
Sean Jeffrey Hart,
EMP: 15
SALES (est): 475.7K **Privately Held**
WEB: www.lumacyte.com
SIC: 3826 8731 Analytical instruments; commercial physical research

(G-7053)
OLAN DE MEXICO SA DE CV
2450 Pendower Ln (22947-9192)
PHONE..............................804 365-8344
EMP: 3 **Privately Held**
SIC: 3086 Mfg Plastic Products
PA: Olan De Mexico, S.A. De C.V.
   Calle 3 No. 200
   Naucalpan EDOMEX.
   555 576-7122

Keysville
Charlotte County

(G-7054)
ALL-N-LOGGING LLC
450 Walton Rd (23947-3841)
PHONE..............................434 547-3550
Andrew Ryan Barton, *Administration*
EMP: 5
SALES (est): 580.2K **Privately Held**
SIC: 2411 Logging camps & contractors

(G-7055)
COUNTY LINE LLC
8818 Church St (23947-3615)
P.O. Box 909 (23947-0909)
PHONE..............................434 736-8405

Garet K Bosiger, *Mng Member*
▲ EMP: 55
SQ FT: 250,000
SALES (est): 25.5K
SALES (corp-wide): 83.2MM **Privately Held**
WEB: www.countylinellcair.com
SIC: 3469 2426 Furniture components, porcelain enameled; hardwood dimension & flooring mills
PA: Genesis Products, Llc
2608 Almac Ct
Elkhart IN 46514
877 266-8292

(G-7056)
DER LLC
161 Kings Hwy (23947-4538)
P.O. Box 270 (23947-0270)
PHONE..................................434 736-9100
Lewis E Wilkerson Jr,
Lewis Wilkerson,
EMP: 4
SALES (est): 517.8K **Privately Held**
SIC: 3537 Truck trailers, used in plants, docks, terminals, etc.

(G-7057)
GOLDEN LEAF TOBACCO COMPANY
3662 Ontario Rd Ste B (23947-2710)
PHONE..................................434 736-2130
Steven A Abailey, *Vice Pres*
Beverley Bailey, *Executive*
EMP: 5
SALES (est): 207.6K **Privately Held**
WEB: www.gltobacco.com
SIC: 2111 Cigarettes

(G-7058)
GOT SCENTS & SOVA CANDLES
245 Tech Ln (23947-3562)
PHONE..................................434 736-9394
Lesley Ferranto, *Principal*
EMP: 2 EST: 2014
SALES (est): 56K **Privately Held**
WEB: www.sovacandles.com
SIC: 3999 Candles

(G-7059)
HEIDI HO INC
8322 George Wash Hwy (23947-3909)
P.O. Box 9, Charlotte C H (23923-0009)
PHONE..................................434 736-8763
David C Watkins, *President*
EMP: 45
SQ FT: 12,000
SALES (est): 500K **Privately Held**
SIC: 2361 2339 Dresses: girls', children's & infants'; blouses: girls', children's & infants'; women's & misses' outerwear

(G-7060)
LEWIS WELDING & CNSTR WORKS
523 Lunenburg County Rd (23947-3113)
PHONE..................................434 696-5527
Wayne Lewis, *President*
EMP: 6
SALES (est): 250K **Privately Held**
WEB: www.lewisweldingconstruction.com
SIC: 3548 1542 1522 Welding wire, bare & coated; commercial & office building contractors; residential construction

(G-7061)
ONTARIO HARDWOOD COMPANY INC (PA)
3828 Horseshoe Bend Rd (23947-4594)
PHONE..................................434 736-9291
Richard H Hogan, *CEO*
Clarke Hogan, *President*
Jane Hogan, *Corp Secy*
EMP: 33
SQ FT: 1,800
SALES (est): 5.9MM **Privately Held**
WEB: www.ontariohardwood.com
SIC: 2421 2426 Lumber: rough, sawed or planed; hardwood dimension & flooring mills

(G-7062)
PULPWOOD AND LOGGING INC
191 King St (23947-3679)
P.O. Box 599 (23947-0599)
PHONE..................................434 736-9440
Lealon M Vassar, *President*
Brenda N Vassar, *Corp Secy*
EMP: 3
SALES (est): 338.9K **Privately Held**
SIC: 2411 Pulpwood contractors engaged in cutting

(G-7063)
SOUTHERN VIRGINIA EQUIPMENT
2033 Old Kings Hwy (23947-3512)
PHONE..................................434 390-0318
Linda Perkinson, *Owner*
EMP: 4
SALES (est): 382.8K **Privately Held**
SIC: 3537 Industrial trucks & tractors

(G-7064)
TUCKER TIMBER PRODUCTS INC
200 Spaulding Ave (23947)
P.O. Box 630 (23947-0630)
PHONE..................................434 736-9661
Timothy B Tucker, *President*
Patricia Tucker, *Corp Secy*
EMP: 15
SQ FT: 25,000
SALES (est): 1.9MM **Privately Held**
WEB: www.tuckertimberproducts.com
SIC: 2421 Sawmills & planing mills, general

(G-7065)
WESTROCK CP LLC
6367 Kings Hwy (23947-3681)
PHONE..................................434 736-8505
Ervine Dilmyer, *Principal*
EMP: 7
SALES (corp-wide): 17.5B **Publicly Held**
WEB: www.westrock.com
SIC: 2653 Boxes, corrugated: made from purchased materials
HQ: Westrock Cp, Llc
1000 Abernathy Rd Ste 125
Atlanta GA 30328

(G-7066)
WRIGHT LOGGING LLC
214 Henderson Rd (23947-5006)
PHONE..................................434 547-4525
Christopher Wright,
EMP: 7
SALES (est): 835.2K **Privately Held**
SIC: 2411 Timber, cut at logging camp

(G-7067)
WST PRODUCTS LLC
131 Kings Hwy (23947-4538)
P.O. Box 270 (23947-0270)
PHONE..................................434 736-9100
Lewis E Wilkerson,
EMP: 6
SALES (est): 830.7K **Privately Held**
SIC: 2411 Logging

Kilmarnock
Lancaster County

(G-7068)
AMERICAN DIESEL CORP
101 American Dr (22482)
P.O. Box 1838 (22482-1838)
PHONE..................................804 435-3107
Robert F Smith, *President*
Smith Brian E, *Vice Pres*
Gale D Smith, *Treasurer*
◆ EMP: 5
SQ FT: 12,000
SALES (est): 860.3K **Privately Held**
WEB: www.americandieselcorp.com
SIC: 3519 7538 3429 Marine engines; general automotive repair shops; manufactured hardware (general)

(G-7069)
D & T AKERS CORPORATION
Also Called: Beatley Custom Cabinets
1281 Goodluck Rd (22482)
P.O. Box 1731 (22482-1731)
PHONE..................................804 435-2709
Daniel Akers, *President*
EMP: 6
SALES (est): 620.2K **Privately Held**
SIC: 2599 Cabinets, factory

(G-7070)
ILMARNOCK LETTERING CO LLC
31 Tartan Village Dr (22482-3867)
PHONE..................................804 435-6956
Paul Stamm, *Principal*
EMP: 3
SALES (est): 240K **Privately Held**
WEB: www.klcsigns.com
SIC: 3993 Signs & advertising specialties

(G-7071)
KEANE WRITERS PUBLISHING LLC
87 Mariners Watch Ln (22482-3726)
PHONE..................................804 435-2618
EMP: 2 EST: 2010
SALES (est): 108.1K **Privately Held**
SIC: 2741 Misc Publishing

(G-7072)
MANUFACTURING TECHNIQUES
180 Technology Park Dr (22482-3906)
PHONE..................................804 436-9000
EMP: 1
SALES (est): 53.6K **Privately Held**
WEB: www.us.qinetiq.com
SIC: 3999 Manufacturing industries

(G-7073)
MOUBRAY COMPANY
31 Tartan Village Dr (22482-3867)
PHONE..................................804 435-6334
Randy Moubray, *Owner*
EMP: 6
SALES (est): 540.8K **Privately Held**
SIC: 3089 1761 Plastic boats & other marine equipment; architectural sheet metal work

(G-7074)
PERDUE FARMS INC
1671 Waverly Ave (22482-3818)
PHONE..................................804 453-4656
EMP: 4
SALES (corp-wide): 5.7B **Privately Held**
SIC: 2015 Poultry Processing
PA: Perdue Farms Inc.
31149 Old Ocean City Rd
Salisbury MD 21804
410 543-3000

(G-7075)
QINETIQ INC
Also Called: Mteq
160 Technology Park Dr (22482-3837)
PHONE..................................804 436-9000
Mary Williams, *President*
EMP: 8 **Privately Held**
WEB: www.us.qinetiq.com
SIC: 3679 Harness assemblies for electronic use: wire or cable
HQ: Qinetiq Inc.
10440 Furnace Rd Ste 204
Lorton VA 22079

(G-7076)
RAPPAHANNOCK RECORD
Also Called: Estate of J E Currell The
27 N Main St (22482-8501)
P.O. Box 400 (22482-0400)
PHONE..................................804 435-1701
Fred Gaskins, *President*
Fred Gaskin, *President*
Bettie Lee Gaskin, *Corp Secy*
Susan Simmons, *Production*
Bettie L Gaskins, *Treasurer*
EMP: 18 EST: 1916
SALES (est): 1.1MM **Privately Held**
WEB: www.rrecord.com
SIC: 2711 2791 2752 Newspapers: publishing only, not printed on site; typesetting; commercial printing, lithographic

(G-7077)
USA SECURITY SOLUTION CORP
180 Technology Park Dr C (22482-3906)
P.O. Box 276, Irvington (22480-0276)
PHONE..................................804 435-9999
Alberto Toledo, *President*
William Thorpe, *COO*
▲ EMP: 2
SQ FT: 2,500
SALES (est): 173.1K **Privately Held**
WEB: www.usa-ssc.com
SIC: 7372 Prepackaged software

(G-7078)
VIRGINIA BODIESEL REFINERY LLC
1676 Waverly Ave (22482-3818)
P.O. Box 426 (22482-0426)
PHONE..................................804 435-1126
Ryan Faulkner, *General Mgr*
Norm F Faulkner, *Mng Member*
EMP: 7 EST: 2009
SALES (est): 969.6K **Privately Held**
SIC: 2911 5172 Diesel fuels; diesel fuel

(G-7079)
WATERLINE NNK LLC
80 S Main St (22482-9537)
PHONE..................................804 577-4160
EMP: 3
SALES (est): 146.1K **Privately Held**
SIC: 3443 Water tanks, metal plate

King George
King George County

(G-7080)
AGGREGATE INDUSTRIES - MWR INC
Med Atlantic Materials
15141 Cleve Dr (22485-2419)
PHONE..................................540 775-7600
Michael Macher, *Branch Mgr*
EMP: 30
SALES (corp-wide): 1.7B **Privately Held**
WEB: www.lafargeholcim.us
SIC: 1442 Construction sand mining; gravel mining
HQ: Aggregate Industries - Mwr, Inc.
2815 Dodd Rd
Eagan MN 55121

(G-7081)
B & B WELDING & FABRICATION
6261 Saint Pauls Rd (22485-5445)
PHONE..................................540 663-5949
Suzi Bernett, *Owner*
EMP: 1
SALES (est): 42.9K **Privately Held**
SIC: 7692 1799 Welding repair; welding on site

(G-7082)
CBD SOLUTIONS LLC
9052 Mullen Rd (22485-6767)
PHONE..................................757 286-8733
Gary E Carrer, *Principal*
EMP: 3
SALES (est): 100.1K **Privately Held**
SIC: 3999

(G-7083)
CHARLES COUNTY SAND & GRAV CO
Also Called: Chaney Enterprises
13250 James Madison Pkwy (22485-3207)
PHONE..................................540 775-9550
EMP: 1
SALES (corp-wide): 16.3K **Privately Held**
WEB: www.chaneyenterprises.com
SIC: 3273 Ready-mixed concrete
PA: Charles County Sand & Gravel Co Inc
2410 Evergreen Rd Ste 201
Gambrills MD 21054
301 932-5000

(G-7084)
COMMERCIAL METALS COMPANY
Also Called: CMC King George
10924 Dennis W Kerns Pkwy (22485-6665)
PHONE..................540 775-8501
Heather Lear, *Manager*
EMP: 45
SALES (corp-wide): 5.4B **Publicly Held**
WEB: www.cmc.com
SIC: 3312 3449 3315 Hot-rolled iron & steel products; bars & bar shapes, steel, hot-rolled; structural shapes & pilings, steel; bars, concrete reinforcing: fabricated steel; spikes, steel: wire or cut; welded steel wire fabric; nails, steel: wire or cut
PA: Commercial Metals Company
6565 N Macarthur Blvd # 800
Irving TX 75039
214 689-4300

(G-7085)
CUSTOM MARINE CANVAS
6099 Marineview Rd (22485-7404)
PHONE..................540 775-6699
Charles Wilkerson, *Principal*
EMP: 2
SALES (est): 128K **Privately Held**
SIC: 2211 Canvas

(G-7086)
DEBRA HEWITT
Also Called: Shadow River Books
7147 Peppermill Rd (22485-5426)
P.O. Box 378 (22485-0378)
PHONE..................540 809-6281
Debra Hewitt, *Owner*
EMP: 1 EST: 2016
SALES (est): 36.6K **Privately Held**
WEB: www.shadowriverbooks.com
SIC: 2731 7389 Books: publishing only;

(G-7087)
DKS MACHINE SHOP INC
15079 Sunset Ln (22485-3239)
PHONE..................540 775-9648
Richard Hagaman, *President*
EMP: 3
SALES (est): 254.2K **Privately Held**
SIC: 2299 3599 Linen fabrics; industrial machinery

(G-7088)
E Z DATA INC
7981 Caledon Rd (22485-7375)
PHONE..................540 775-2961
Stephen Despres, *President*
Cathy Despres, *Vice Pres*
EMP: 2
SALES (est): 180K **Privately Held**
SIC: 7372 7379 Prepackaged software; computer related consulting services

(G-7089)
EAST COAST HEMP COMPANY LLC
2259 Kings Hwy Ste 102 (22485-6638)
PHONE..................540 740-7099
EMP: 2
SALES (est): 73.4K **Privately Held**
SIC: 2299 Hemp yarn, thread, roving & textiles

(G-7090)
GE ENERGY MANUFACTURING INC
10900 Birchwood Dr (22485-6653)
PHONE..................540 775-6308
Bill Hutchins, *Branch Mgr*
EMP: 4
SALES (corp-wide): 95.2B **Publicly Held**
WEB: www.ge.com
SIC: 3621 Power generators
HQ: Ge Energy Manufacturing, Inc.
1333 West Loop S Ste 700
Houston TX 77027
713 803-0900

(G-7091)
GENERAL DYNAMICS INFO TECH INC
16501 Commerce Dr Ste 300 (22485-5858)
P.O. Box 1000, Dahlgren (22448-1000)
PHONE..................540 663-1000
Jim Coggin, *Vice Pres*
Brian Roush, *Branch Mgr*
EMP: 30
SALES (corp-wide): 39.3B **Publicly Held**
WEB: www.gdit.com
SIC: 3731 Submarines, building & repairing
HQ: General Dynamics Information Technology, Inc.
3150 Frview Pk Dr Ste 100
Falls Church VA 22042
703 995-8700

(G-7092)
GEORGE KING WELDING INC
13417 Poplar Neck Rd (22485-4923)
PHONE..................540 379-3407
Amy Ackerman, *Administration*
EMP: 4 EST: 2012
SALES (est): 416.7K **Privately Held**
SIC: 7692 Welding repair

(G-7093)
HAYWOOD MACHINE INC
6484 Landing Rd (22485-5239)
PHONE..................540 663-2606
William G Reeson, *Director*
EMP: 3
SALES (est): 240.3K **Privately Held**
WEB: www.haywoodmachine.com
SIC: 3599 Machine shop, jobbing & repair

(G-7094)
HUSSMANN CORPORATION
6095 Marineview Rd (22485-7404)
PHONE..................540 775-2502
Michael Meyer, *Branch Mgr*
EMP: 2 **Privately Held**
WEB: www.hussmann.com
SIC: 3585 Refrigeration & heating equipment
HQ: Hussmann Corporation
12999 St Charles Rock Rd
Bridgeton MO 63044
314 291-2000

(G-7095)
JESSE DUDLEY JR
Also Called: J D Welding
16084 Dudley Dr (22485-5046)
PHONE..................540 663-3773
Jesse Dudley Jr, *Owner*
EMP: 1
SALES (est): 30K **Privately Held**
SIC: 7692 Welding repair

(G-7096)
JTS BLINDS INSTALLATION LLC
4385 Navigator Ln (22485-5982)
PHONE..................240 682-1009
EMP: 1
SALES (est): 57.3K **Privately Held**
SIC: 2591 Window blinds

(G-7097)
KG SPORTS
Also Called: Kg-Sports
14130 Ryan Ln (22485-4624)
PHONE..................540 538-7216
Herbert Ferro, *Owner*
EMP: 2
SALES (est): 10K **Privately Held**
WEB: www.kgyaa.org
SIC: 3949 Sporting & athletic goods

(G-7098)
KORA CONFECTIONS LLC
Also Called: Kora Confections
6193 Curtis Cir (22485-7160)
PHONE..................240 478-2222
Omarelis Rivera,
EMP: 1
SALES (est): 50.6K **Privately Held**
SIC: 2051 7389 Pies, bakery: except frozen;

(G-7099)
LANE CUSTOM HEARING
10988 Laforce Ln (22485-6547)
PHONE..................540 775-5999
Troy Steinc, *Owner*
EMP: 1
SALES (est): 73.4K **Privately Held**
WEB: www.lanecustomhearing.com
SIC: 3842 Hearing aids

(G-7100)
LOCKHEED MARTIN CORPORATION
16539 Commerce Dr Ste 10 (22485-5847)
PHONE..................540 644-2830
Nick Scharf, *Vice Pres*
EMP: 435 **Publicly Held**
WEB: www.lockheedmartin.com
SIC: 3812 Search & navigation equipment
PA: Lockheed Martin Corporation
6801 Rockledge Dr
Bethesda MD 20817

(G-7101)
LOCKHEED MARTIN CORPORATION
5323 Windsor Dr (22485)
P.O. Box 1779, Dahlgren (22448-1779)
PHONE..................540 663-3337
Richard Walsh, *Manager*
EMP: 100 **Publicly Held**
WEB: www.lockheedmartin.com
SIC: 3812 Search & navigation equipment
PA: Lockheed Martin Corporation
6801 Rockledge Dr
Bethesda MD 20817

(G-7102)
MCKEAN DEFENSE GROUP LLC
17006 Dahlgren Rd (22485-5812)
PHONE..................540 413-1202
EMP: 3 **Privately Held**
WEB: www.mckean-defense.com
SIC: 3812 Defense systems & equipment
PA: Mckean Defense Group, Llc
1 Crescent Dr Ste 400
Philadelphia PA 19112

(G-7103)
MR INDUSTRIES LLC
3521 White Hall Rd (22485-6858)
PHONE..................484 838-9154
Rudy Wilson, *Principal*
EMP: 2 EST: 2018
SALES (est): 74.6K **Privately Held**
SIC: 3999 Manufacturing industries

(G-7104)
NORTHROP GRUMMAN CORPORATION
16480 Commerce Dr Ste 100 (22485-5860)
PHONE..................540 469-9647
Greg Billick, *Principal*
EMP: 702 **Publicly Held**
WEB: www.northropgrumman.com
SIC: 3812 Defense systems & equipment
PA: Northrop Grumman Corporation
2980 Fairview Park Dr
Falls Church VA 22042

(G-7105)
OAK CREST VINEYARD & WINERY
8215 Oak Crest Dr (22485-5047)
P.O. Box 1778, Pound (24279-1778)
PHONE..................540 663-2813
Kevin Brandts, *President*
Conrad Brandts, *Partner*
EMP: 2
SALES (est): 163.2K **Privately Held**
WEB: www.oakcrestwinery.com
SIC: 2084 Wines

(G-7106)
QUALITYCROCHETBYBARB LLC
5356 Potomac Dr (22485-6106)
PHONE..................202 596-7301
Barb Newberry, *Principal*
EMP: 2
SALES (est): 88.7K **Privately Held**
SIC: 2399 Hand woven & crocheted products

(G-7107)
REAPER PRECISION LLC
16283 Round Hill Rd (22485-4418)
PHONE..................540 841-0028
Christopher Elko,
EMP: 1
SALES (est): 39.6K **Privately Held**
SIC: 3999 Manufacturing industries

(G-7108)
ROCKY TOP EMBROIDERY & MORE
7821 Dolleys Ct (22485-7085)
PHONE..................540 775-9564
Beckey Gallamore, *Owner*
EMP: 6 EST: 2007
SALES (est): 225K **Privately Held**
WEB: www.rockytoponline.com
SIC: 2395 Embroidery products, except schiffli machine; embroidery & art needlework

(G-7109)
RODGERS SERVICES LLC
5327 N Williams Creek Dr (22485-6210)
PHONE..................301 848-6384
Joseph Rodgers,
EMP: 1 EST: 2013
SALES (est): 122.1K **Privately Held**
SIC: 3582 7389 Commercial laundry equipment;

(G-7110)
ROGER K WILLIAMS
8621 Bloomsbury Rd (22485-6846)
PHONE..................540 775-3192
Roger Williams, *Owner*
EMP: 3
SALES (est): 210K **Privately Held**
SIC: 2411 Wooden logs

(G-7111)
ROGERS - MAST-R-WOODWORK LLC
7389 Passapatanzy Dr (22485-7656)
PHONE..................540 273-1460
Gary Rogers, *Administration*
EMP: 2
SALES (est): 138.4K **Privately Held**
SIC: 2431 Millwork

(G-7112)
RY FABRICATING LLC
9191 Lambs Creek Ch Rd (22485-6900)
PHONE..................571 835-0567
Robert Young,
EMP: 1 EST: 2017
SALES (est): 60.8K **Privately Held**
SIC: 7692 Welding repair

(G-7113)
SIGNWORKS OF KING GEORGE
8755 Dahlgren Rd (22485-3505)
PHONE..................540 709-7483
EMP: 1
SALES (est): 69.4K **Privately Held**
WEB: www.lr-signs.com
SIC: 3993 Signs & advertising specialties

(G-7114)
SPUR DEFENSE SYSTEMS
8324 Reagan Dr (22485-7149)
PHONE..................540 742-8394
John Johnston, *Owner*
EMP: 2
SALES (est): 94.9K **Privately Held**
SIC: 3577 3571 Computer peripheral equipment; mainframe computers

(G-7115)
TOTAL MACHINE LLC (PA)
11034 Bloomsbury Rd (22485-6668)
PHONE..................540 775-2375
Lemoyne Emory,
Larry Emory,
EMP: 6
SQ FT: 6,000
SALES (est): 250K **Privately Held**
WEB: www.totalmachineva.com
SIC: 3599 Machine shop, jobbing & repair

(G-7116)
TURNERS WELDING
4326 Turkey Acres Rd (22485-6917)
PHONE..................540 373-1107

EMP: 1
SALES (est): 51.7K **Privately Held**
SIC: 7692 Welding repair

(G-7117)
TZ INDUSTRIES LLC
11034 Bloomsbury Rd (22485-6668)
PHONE.................................540 903-7210
Tyler Emory, *Principal*
EMP: 1
SQ FT: 1,000
SALES (est): 67K **Privately Held**
SIC: 3479 Galvanizing of iron, steel or end-
formed products

(G-7118)
UNITED DEFENSE
4485 Danube Dr Ste 1 (22485-5756)
PHONE.................................540 663-9291
EMP: 4 EST: 2007
SALES (est): 180K **Privately Held**
SIC: 3795 Mfg Tanks/Tank Components

(G-7119)
VINYL VISIONS LLC
9495 Inaugural Dr (22485-7035)
PHONE.................................540 369-5244
Andrew Pomeroy, *Principal*
EMP: 2
SALES (est): 165.3K **Privately Held**
WEB: www.vinylvisionsllc.com
SIC: 3993 Signs & advertising specialties

(G-7120)
VITAL SIGNS & DISPLAYS LLC
4307 Island View Ln (22485-8507)
PHONE.................................540 656-8303
Joseph Paul Bristow, *Administration*
EMP: 2
SALES (est): 107.7K **Privately Held**
SIC: 3993 Signs & advertising specialties

(G-7121)
W & M BACKHOE SERVICE
7296 Passapatanzy Dr (22485-7652)
PHONE.................................540 775-7185
William L Hamm, *Owner*
EMP: 1
SALES (est): 146.5K **Privately Held**
SIC: 3531 Backhoes

(G-7122)
WALKER SAND & STONE INC
12542 James Madison Pkwy (22485-3203)
PHONE.................................540 775-5024
Lewis C Walker, *President*
John Walker, *Vice Pres*
Dorothy R Walker, *Treasurer*
EMP: 30
SALES (est): 953.6K **Privately Held**
WEB: www.walkersand.com
SIC: 3273 Ready-mixed concrete

(G-7123)
WILLIAMS & SON INC HL
8621 Bloomsbury Rd (22485-6846)
PHONE.................................540 775-3192
Roger K Williams, *President*
Michelle Williams, *Corp Secy*
Herbert L Williams, *Shareholder*
EMP: 9
SALES (est): 975.7K **Privately Held**
SIC: 2411 Logging camps & contractors

(G-7124)
WORDSMITH INDEXING SERVICES
8112 Harrison Dr (22485-2051)
PHONE.................................540 775-3012
Kara Pekar, *Owner*
EMP: 1
SALES (est): 68.2K **Privately Held**
WEB: www.wordsmith.org
SIC: 2675 Index cards, die-cut: made from
purchased materials

King Queen Ch
King And Queen County

(G-7125)
COLONIAL COMMERCIAL ELEC CO
832 Court Hse Landing Rd (23085-2003)
PHONE.................................804 720-2455
James Lee, *Owner*
EMP: 5
SALES (est): 418.7K **Privately Held**
SIC: 3369 Nonferrous foundries

(G-7126)
GIBSON LOGGING INC
12853 The Trail (23085-2064)
PHONE.................................804 769-1130
Richard Gibson, *CEO*
EMP: 5
SALES (est): 602.3K **Privately Held**
SIC: 2411 Logging camps & contractors

(G-7127)
MIKE GIBSON & SONS LOGGING
847 Shilo Rd (23085-2041)
PHONE.................................804 769-3510
Mike Gibson, *Principal*
EMP: 6
SALES (est): 615.8K **Privately Held**
SIC: 2411 Logging camps & contractors

King William
King William County

(G-7128)
CUSHING METALS LLC
733 Kelley Ln (23086-3339)
PHONE.................................804 339-1114
Randy Jennings,
EMP: 1
SALES (est): 65.9K **Privately Held**
SIC: 3444 3499 5039 3443 Metal hous-
ings, enclosures, casings & other contain-
ers; metal ladders; metal guardrails; metal
parts

(G-7129)
DOBBS & ASSOCIATES
191 Powhatan Trl (23086-2631)
PHONE.................................804 769-4266
Chris Dobbs, *Principal*
EMP: 1
SALES (est): 113.7K **Privately Held**
WEB: www.dobbsandassociates.com
SIC: 3553 Cabinet makers' machinery

(G-7130)
NESTLE PURINA PETCARE COMPANY
Also Called: Nestle Purina Factory
931 Dunluce Rd (23086-3418)
PHONE.................................804 769-1266
Jim Baugh, *Branch Mgr*
Chuck Dixon, *Technician*
EMP: 95
SALES (corp-wide): 93.5B **Privately Held**
WEB: www.purina.com
SIC: 2047 Dog & cat food
HQ: Nestle Purina Petcare Company
1 Checkerboard Sq
Saint Louis MO 63164
314 982-1000

(G-7131)
SUPERIOR GARNITURE COMPONENTS
812 Sharon Rd (23086-3629)
PHONE.................................804 769-4319
EMP: 3
SALES (est): 239.3K **Privately Held**
SIC: 3559 Mfg Misc Industry Machinery

(G-7132)
VIRGINIA TAG SERVICE INC
Also Called: Virginia Tag Service
2862 East River Rd (23086-3043)
PHONE.................................804 690-7304
William R Cooper, *President*
EMP: 1

SALES (est): 50K **Privately Held**
WEB: www.engravedplastics.com
SIC: 2759 Labels & seals: printing

Kinsale
Westmoreland County

(G-7133)
BEVANS OYSTER COMPANY (PA)
Also Called: Yeocomico Oyster Co
1090 Skipjack Rd (22488-2051)
PHONE.................................804 472-2331
Ronald W Bevans, *President*
Stanley E Bevans, *Vice Pres*
Shirley E Bevans, *Admin Sec*
▲ EMP: 85
SQ FT: 10,700
SALES (est): 13MM **Privately Held**
WEB: www.bevansoyster.com
SIC: 2091 2092 Oysters: packaged in
cans, jars, etc.; seafoods, fresh: prepared

(G-7134)
BEVANS OYSTER COMPANY
Also Called: Yeocomico Oyster Co
1090 Skipjack Rd 610 (22488-2051)
PHONE.................................804 472-2331
Ronald W Bevans, *President*
EMP: 2
SALES (corp-wide): 13MM **Privately Held**
WEB: www.bevansoyster.com
SIC: 2092 2091 Seafoods, fresh: pre-
pared; oysters: packaged in cans, jars,
etc.
PA: Bevans Oyster Company
1090 Skipjack Rd
Kinsale VA 22488
804 472-2331

(G-7135)
ITS HOMEADE LLC
Also Called: Scratch Brand Foods
Rr 203 Box 309 (22488)
P.O. Box 1585, Ashland (23005-4585)
PHONE.................................804 641-8248
David Gilmore, *Co-Owner*
Jane M Gilmore,
EMP: 1
SALES (est): 51.6K **Privately Held**
WEB: www.scratchbrand.com
SIC: 2051 Bakery products, partially
cooked (except frozen)

(G-7136)
POTOMAC SUPPLY LLC
1398 Kinsale Rd (22488-2435)
PHONE.................................804 472-2527
William T Carden, *CEO*
Lisa McGinness, *Sales Staff*
▼ EMP: 68
SALES (est): 14.2MM **Privately Held**
WEB: www.potomacsupply.com
SIC: 2491 2448 2426 Wood preserving;
pallets, wood; hardwood dimension &
flooring mills

(G-7137)
RIVAH VINEYARDS AT GROVE LLC
751 Kinsale Bridge Rd (22488-2308)
PHONE.................................804 472-3734
William Taylor, *Principal*
Susan Taylor, *Administration*
EMP: 3
SALES (est): 183.5K **Privately Held**
WEB: www.rivahvineyards.com
SIC: 2084 Wines

(G-7138)
VAULT FIELD VINEYARDS LLC
2953 Kings Mill Rd (22488-2411)
P.O. Box 128 (22488-0128)
PHONE.................................804 472-4430
EMP: 3
SALES (est): 290.3K **Privately Held**
WEB: www.vaultfield.com
SIC: 2084 Wines

La Crosse
Mecklenburg County

(G-7139)
AMERICAN BUILDINGS COMPANY
501 Golden Eagle Dr (23950-2217)
P.O. Box 100 (23950-0100)
PHONE.................................434 757-2220
J Byerley, *Sales Mgr*
Kris Kutterer, *Sales Mgr*
Dennis Dozier, *Manager*
Wayne Adler, *Manager*
EMP: 200
SALES (corp-wide): 22.5B **Publicly Held**
WEB: www.americanbuildings.com
SIC: 3448 3449 3479 8711 Prefabricated
metal buildings; miscellaneous metal-
work; coating of metals & formed prod-
ucts; engineering services; trucking,
except local
HQ: American Buildings Company
1150 State Docks Rd
Eufaula AL 36027
334 687-2032

(G-7140)
BOYTERS WELDING & FABRICATION
1695 Reed Rd (23950-2315)
PHONE.................................434 636-5974
Penny Boyter, *Principal*
EMP: 1
SALES (est): 52.4K **Privately Held**
SIC: 7692 Welding repair

(G-7141)
CAVAN SALES LO
3334 Country Club Rd (23950-1617)
P.O. Box 130 (23950-0130)
PHONE.................................434 757-1680
Hunter Cavan, *Owner*
EMP: 1
SALES (est): 61.7K **Privately Held**
SIC: 2391 Curtains & draperies

(G-7142)
CHRIS ELLIS SIGNS & AIRBRUSH
1399 N Mecklenburg Ave (23950-1719)
PHONE.................................434 447-8013
Chris Ellis, *Owner*
EMP: 1
SALES (est): 43.5K **Privately Held**
SIC: 3993 Signs & advertising specialties

(G-7143)
ELLIS SIGNS AND CUSTOM PNTG
105 Clover Rd (23950-1553)
PHONE.................................434 584-0032
Chris Ellis, *Owner*
EMP: 1 EST: 2007
SALES (est): 98.5K **Privately Held**
SIC: 3993 Signs & advertising specialties

(G-7144)
EXPRESS YOURSELF INC (PA)
223 Moseley St (23950-2128)
P.O. Box 66 (23950-0066)
PHONE.................................434 757-1099
Sandra F Tanner, *President*
Thomas C Tanner, *Vice Pres*
EMP: 1
SALES (est): 90.1K **Privately Held**
WEB: www.expressyourselfinc.com
SIC: 2395 Embroidery products, except
schiffli machine

(G-7145)
GALAXY PLASTIC INDUSTRIES INC
539 Golden Eagle Dr (23950-2217)
P.O. Box 190 (23950-0190)
PHONE.................................434 757-7200
Hilary Thor, *Principal*
EMP: 8
SALES (est): 1.3MM **Privately Held**
WEB: www.galaxyplastic.com
SIC: 3089 Injection molding of plastics

(G-7146)
MARTIN TONYA
Also Called: Sweets 4 The Sweet
1432 Wray Rd (23950-1770)
P.O. Box 4004, Chester (23831-8474)
PHONE..........................804 742-8721
Hattie Martin, *Principal*
EMP: 2 **EST:** 2013
SALES (est): 70.5K **Privately Held**
SIC: 2051 7389 Bakery: wholesale or
wholesale/retail combined; business serv-
ices

(G-7147)
NEWELL LOGGING
938 Alvis Rd (23950-2014)
PHONE..........................434 636-2743
Sterling Newell, *Principal*
EMP: 3
SALES (est): 202.6K **Privately Held**
SIC: 2411 Logging

(G-7148)
PIEDMONT WELDING &
MAINTENANCE
845 Canaan Church Rd (23950-2104)
PHONE..........................434 447-6600
Randall King, *Principal*
EMP: 2
SALES (est): 89.1K **Privately Held**
WEB: www.piedmontwelding.com
SIC: 7692 Welding repair

(G-7149)
PIEDMONT WLDG & MAINT SVC
LLC
336 Union Mill Rd (23950-1528)
PHONE..........................434 447-6600
Russell Thompson, *Principal*
EMP: 1
SALES (est): 164K **Privately Held**
WEB: www.piedmontwelding.com
SIC: 3599 Machine shop, jobbing & repair

(G-7150)
ROSEMONT OF VIRGINIA LLC
Also Called: Rosemont Vineyards
1050 Blackridge Rd (23950-2915)
PHONE..........................434 636-4372
Justin Rose, *General Mgr*
R Stephen Rose, *Mng Member*
EMP: 5
SALES (est): 498.5K **Privately Held**
WEB: www.rosemontofvirginia.com
SIC: 2084 Wines

(G-7151)
TAYLOR MADE CUSTOM
EMBROIDERY
2220 Hall Rd (23950-2741)
PHONE..........................434 636-0660
Joyce Taylor, *Principal*
EMP: 1
SALES (est): 69.9K **Privately Held**
SIC: 2395 Embroidery & art needlework

(G-7152)
VIRGINIA QUILTING INC (PA)
100 S Main St (23950-1834)
P.O. Box 99 (23950-0099)
PHONE..........................434 757-1809
John W McAden Sr, *President*
Sybil McFarland, *Principal*
John W McAden Jr, *Vice Pres*
Tonya Morris, *Sales Staff*
Cindy Clevinger, *Manager*
EMP: 200 **EST:** 1975
SQ FT: 22,500
SALES (est): 14.9MM **Privately Held**
WEB: www.vqcinc.com
SIC: 2392 2391 2395 Bedspreads & bed
sets: made from purchased materials;
draperies, plastic & textile: from pur-
chased materials; pleating & stitching

(G-7153)
YORK FABRICATION
549 Bracey Pl (23950-2614)
PHONE..........................804 241-0136
William York, *Principal*
EMP: 4
SALES (est): 425.9K **Privately Held**
SIC: 3441 Fabricated structural metal

Ladysmith
Caroline County

(G-7154)
AMERICAN STONE VIRGINIA
LLC
8179 Arba Ave (22501)
P.O. Box 25 (22501-0025)
PHONE..........................804 448-9460
S Dino Diana, *President*
EMP: 64 **EST:** 1957
SQ FT: 2,400
SALES (est): 10.6MM **Privately Held**
WEB: www.asiprecast.com
SIC: 3272 Concrete products, precast

Lake Frederick
Warren County

(G-7155)
CHRISTIAN POTIER USA INC
113 Flycatcher Way (22630-2268)
PHONE..........................330 815-2202
EMP: 2
SALES (est): 62.3K **Privately Held**
SIC: 2099 Sauces: gravy, dressing & dip
mixes

Lake Ridge
Prince William County

(G-7156)
INTERNTIONAL REGISTRATION
PLAN
4196 Merchant Plz (22192-5085)
PHONE..........................502 845-0398
EMP: 2
SALES: 1.7MM **Privately Held**
WEB: www.irponline.org
SIC: 7372 Business oriented computer
software

(G-7157)
SAK CONSULTING
13016 Sturbridge Rd (22192-3730)
PHONE..........................703 220-2020
Sikirat Adediran, *CEO*
EMP: 1
SALES (est): 55K **Privately Held**
SIC: 3845 Ultrasonic medical equipment,
except cleaning

Lancaster
Lancaster County

(G-7158)
ANDRA ONEIL SMITH
2561 Morattico Rd (22503-3131)
PHONE..........................804 436-3764
Andre Smith, *Owner*
EMP: 1
SALES (est): 37.5K **Privately Held**
SIC: 2741 Art copy & poster publishing

(G-7159)
DOBYNS FAMILY LLC
525 Colinbrook Way 1 (22503-2622)
PHONE..........................804 462-5554
Anita Tadlock,
EMP: 2
SALES (est): 87.1K **Privately Held**
SIC: 2411 0831 0722 0811 Logging; for-
est products; crop harvesting; timber
tracts; business services

(G-7160)
E J CONRAD & SONS SEAFOOD
INC
1947 Rocky Neck Rd (22503-3430)
PHONE..........................804 462-7400
EMP: 50
SQ FT: 5,000
SALES (est): 4.3MM **Privately Held**
SIC: 2092 Mfg Fresh/Frozen Packaged
Fish

(G-7161)
FAIRWAY PRODUCTS INC
5459 Mary Ball Rd (22503-2630)
PHONE..........................804 462-0123
EMP: 2 **EST:** 2008
SALES (est): 100K **Privately Held**
SIC: 2759 Commercial Printing

(G-7162)
HEARTSTRINGS PRESS LLC
Also Called: Grandloving
49 Starview Pl (22503-4149)
PHONE..........................804 462-0884
Susan S Johnson, *Mng Member*
EMP: 2
SALES (est): 10K **Privately Held**
WEB: www.grandloving.com
SIC: 2741 Miscellaneous publishing

(G-7163)
TRUSS SYSTEMS INC
2831 Murry Hill Rd (22503)
P.O. Box 755 (22503-0755)
PHONE..........................804 462-5963
Bruce Pflugradt, *President*
Tara Pflugradt, *Vice Pres*
EMP: 5
SQ FT: 6,000
SALES (est): 500K **Privately Held**
WEB: www.trusssystemsva.com
SIC: 2439 Trusses, wooden roof

Lanexa
New Kent County

(G-7164)
CREATIVE CABINET WORKS
15980 Kentflatts Ln (23089-5346)
PHONE..........................757 220-1941
EMP: 4
SALES (est): 347.8K **Privately Held**
SIC: 2434 Mfg Wood Kitchen Cabinets

(G-7165)
DOUBLE D S WLDG &
FABRICATION
Also Called: Double Ds Welding & Fabricati
3931 Ropers Church Rd (23089-5642)
PHONE..........................757 566-0019
Robert Downin, *President*
EMP: 1
SALES (est): 68.5K **Privately Held**
SIC: 7692 Welding repair

(G-7166)
EMBRACE EMBROIDERY LP
16101 Diascund Shores Ln (23089-5654)
PHONE..........................757 784-3874
EMP: 1 **EST:** 2009
SALES (est): 35.1K **Privately Held**
SIC: 2395 Embroidery & art needlework

(G-7167)
LINDAS WELDING & MECH LLC
7251 Otey Dr (23089-9428)
PHONE..........................757 719-1567
EMP: 1
SALES (est): 30.6K **Privately Held**
SIC: 7692 Welding repair

(G-7168)
M&M ENGRAVING SERVICES
INC
16601 Cooks Mill Rd (23089-5120)
PHONE..........................804 843-3212
Monty Mills, *President*
EMP: 2
SALES (est): 38K **Privately Held**
SIC: 2759 Engraving

(G-7169)
WHIMSICAL EXPRESSIONS
4875 Colby Dr (23089-5950)
PHONE..........................804 239-6550
Lisa Walker, *Owner*
EMP: 1
SALES (est): 10K **Privately Held**
SIC: 2499 Picture & mirror frames, wood

Lansdowne
Loudoun County

(G-7170)
FINEST ART & FRAMING LLC
19358 Diamond Lake Dr (20176-6574)
PHONE..........................703 945-9000
Waleed Sabri,
Masoud Sabri,
EMP: 3
SALES (est): 188K **Privately Held**
WEB: www.finestartframing.com
SIC: 2499 5023 5719 8742 Picture & mir-
ror frames, wood; frames & framing, pic-
ture & mirror; pictures & mirrors;
management consulting services; picture
framing, custom

(G-7171)
LEESBURG TODAY INC
19301 Winmeade Dr Ste 224 (20176-6503)
P.O. Box 591, Leesburg (20178-0591)
PHONE..........................703 771-8800
Gene M Carr, *CEO*
EMP: 3
SALES (est): 187.3K **Privately Held**
WEB: www.loudounnow.com
SIC: 2711 Newspapers, publishing & print-
ing

(G-7172)
LOUDOUN BUSINESS INC
19301 Winmeade Dr Ste 21 (20176-6503)
PHONE..........................703 777-2176
Gene M Carr, *Principal*
Levent Durmus, *Vice Pres*
K Repage, *Program Mgr*
Ashley Krimmel, *Manager*
Tricia Worden, *Consultant*
EMP: 3
SALES (est): 128.9K **Privately Held**
WEB: www.loudounchamber.org
SIC: 2711 Newspapers, publishing & print-
ing

(G-7173)
SOYWICK CANDLES LLC
18772 Upper Meadow Dr (20176-1801)
PHONE..........................571 333-4750
Julianne Ireland, *Principal*
EMP: 2
SALES (est): 87K **Privately Held**
SIC: 3999 Candles

(G-7174)
TRAVELSERVER SOFTWARE
INC
19415 Drfield Ave Ste 204 (20176)
PHONE..........................571 209-5907
EMP: 1
SALES (corp-wide): 231.1K **Privately**
Held
WEB: www.travelserversoftware.com
SIC: 7372 Prepackaged software
PA: Travelserver Software Inc
980 Old Holly Dr
Great Falls VA 22066
703 406-7664

Laurel Fork
Carroll County

(G-7175)
ROUND MEADOWS CABINET
SHOP
1886 Fireside Dr (24352-3838)
PHONE..........................276 398-1153
EMP: 1 **EST:** 2007
SALES (est): 64K **Privately Held**
SIC: 2434 Mfg Wood Kitchen Cabinets

Lawrenceville
Brunswick County

(G-7176)
A L BAIRD INC
Also Called: A L Baird Trucking
12679 Christanna Hwy (23868-3914)
PHONE..........................434 848-2129

▲ = Import ▼=Export
◆ =Import/Export

A L Baird Jr, *President*
EMP: 19 **EST:** 1960
SALES (est): 1.2MM **Privately Held**
WEB: www.brunswickspeedway.com
SIC: 2411 Logging camps & contractors

(G-7177)
BENEATH THE BARK INC
3711 Planters Rd (23868-2829)
PHONE..................................434 848-3995
Robert Davis, *President*
EMP: 2
SALES (est): 239.5K **Privately Held**
WEB: www.beneaththebark.net
SIC: 2421 Custom sawmill

(G-7178)
BRUNSWICK ICE AND COAL CO INC
514 New St (23868-1612)
P.O. Box 538 (23868-0538)
PHONE..................................434 848-2615
Robert F Pecht Jr, *President*
Sue Sumpter, *Corp Secy*
Robert F Pecht III, *Exec VP*
EMP: 20 **EST:** 1929
SQ FT: 2,250
SALES (est): 2MM **Privately Held**
WEB: www.purifiedice.com
SIC: 2097 Manufactured ice

(G-7179)
EDMONDS PRTG / CLOR IMAGES INC
13770 Christanna Hwy (23868-3901)
PHONE..................................434 848-2264
Aubrey B Edmonds, *President*
Calvin R Edmonds, *Vice Pres*
Kerry Wayne Edmonds, *Treasurer*
EMP: 7
SQ FT: 8,000
SALES (est): 850K **Privately Held**
WEB: www.edmondsprinting.net
SIC: 2752 Commercial printing, offset

(G-7180)
FELTON BROTHERS TRNST MIX INC
301 South St (23868-2016)
P.O. Box 231 (23868-0231)
PHONE..................................434 848-3966
Fred Maslin, *Manager*
EMP: 5
SALES (corp-wide): 3.3MM **Privately Held**
WEB: www.feltonbrothers.com
SIC: 3273 Ready-mixed concrete
PA: Felton Brothers Transit Mix, Incorporated
1 Edmunds St
South Boston VA 24592
434 572-2665

(G-7181)
HYPONEX CORPORATION
Also Called: Scotts Hyponex
3175 Bright Leaf Rd (23868-3231)
PHONE..................................434 848-2727
Don Dugger, *Branch Mgr*
EMP: 44
SALES (corp-wide): 4.1B **Publicly Held**
WEB: www.scotts.com
SIC: 2873 2875 Fertilizers: natural (organic), except compost; fertilizers, mixing only
HQ: Hyponex Corporation
14111 Scottslawn Rd
Marysville OH 43040
937 644-0011

(G-7182)
LAWRENCEVILLE BRICK INC
16144 Gvrnor Hrrison Pkwy (23868)
PHONE..................................434 848-3151
Benjamin B Powell, *Vice Pres*
Leon F Williams, *Vice Pres*
Richard B Davenport, *Treasurer*
Glenn N Johnson, *Admin Sec*
▲ **EMP:** 67 **EST:** 1946
SQ FT: 330,000
SALES (est): 8.1MM **Privately Held**
WEB: www.glengery.com
SIC: 3251 Brick & structural clay tile

(G-7183)
REDLAND BRICK
16144 Gvrnor Hrrison Pkwy (23868)
P.O. Box 45 (23868-0045)
PHONE..................................434 848-2397
Benjamin Powell, *Principal*
Brian Moseley,
EMP: 1
SALES (est): 39.7K **Privately Held**
SIC: 3251 Brick & structural clay tile

(G-7184)
SCOTTS COMPANY LLC
3175 Bright Leaf Rd (23868-3231)
PHONE..................................434 848-2727
Janet Thomas, *Vice Pres*
Laura Beaver, *Office Mgr*
Dun Dugger, *Branch Mgr*
EMP: 20
SALES (corp-wide): 4.1B **Publicly Held**
WEB: www.scotts.com
SIC: 2879 Pesticides, agricultural or household
HQ: The Scotts Company Llc
14111 Scottslawn Rd
Marysville OH 43040
937 644-0011

(G-7185)
SOPKO MANUFACTURING INC
Also Called: Lawrenceville Machine Shop
320 W 5th Ave (23868-2004)
P.O. Box 5 (23868-0005)
PHONE..................................434 848-3460
Jerry S Sopko, *President*
EMP: 13
SQ FT: 4,500
SALES (est): 948.7K **Privately Held**
SIC: 7692 3531 3599 Welding repair; logging equipment; machine shop, jobbing & repair

(G-7186)
TIDE WATER PULICATION LLC
Also Called: Brunswick Times Gazette
213 N Main St (23868-1807)
P.O. Box 250 (23868-0250)
PHONE..................................434 848-2114
Sylvia Allen, *Branch Mgr*
EMP: 3
SALES (corp-wide): 6.1MM **Privately Held**
WEB: www.tidewaternews.com
SIC: 2711 Newspapers: publishing only, not printed on site
PA: Tide Water Pulication Llc
1000 Armory Dr
Franklin VA 23851
757 562-3187

(G-7187)
VIRGINIA PALLETS & WOOD LLC
852 Planters Rd (23868-3362)
PHONE..................................434 515-2221
James Davenport Lucy,
EMP: 4
SQ FT: 50,000
SALES (est): 1MM **Privately Held**
SIC: 2448 5031 Pallets, wood; pallets, wood

Lebanon
Russell County

(G-7188)
AUTOMOTION INC
942 E Main St (24266-5010)
PHONE..................................276 889-3715
William Castle, *President*
EMP: 1
SALES (est): 98.1K **Privately Held**
SIC: 3711 Motor vehicles & car bodies

(G-7189)
BRECMO LLC
12262 U S Highway 19 (24266-4571)
PHONE..................................276 202-7381
Brenton Moseley,
EMP: 2 **EST:** 2010
SALES (est): 141.1K **Privately Held**
SIC: 1389 Well logging

(G-7190)
CHAMBERS WELDING INC CARL
4353 N 71 (24266-3431)
PHONE..................................276 794-7170
Carl Chambers, *Principal*
EMP: 1
SALES (est): 44.2K **Privately Held**
SIC: 7692 Welding repair

(G-7191)
DEVIN CLARK
Also Called: Clark Print Shop
63 Old Fincastle Rd (24266)
P.O. Box 1329 (24266-1329)
PHONE..................................276 889-3426
Devin Clark, *Owner*
EMP: 2 **EST:** 1998
SALES (est): 161.8K **Privately Held**
WEB: www.clarkprintshop.com
SIC: 2752 Commercial printing, offset

(G-7192)
GERALDS TOOLS INC
3304 N 71 (24266-6004)
P.O. Box 2241 (24266-2241)
PHONE..................................276 889-2964
EMP: 1
SALES (est): 92.3K **Privately Held**
SIC: 3423 Mfg Hand/Edge Tools

(G-7193)
HEIRLOOM CANDLE COMPANY LLC
2313 E Main St (24266-7027)
PHONE..................................276 889-2505
Traci Gilmer, *Principal*
EMP: 1 **EST:** 2013
SALES (est): 55.7K **Privately Held**
SIC: 3999 Candles

(G-7194)
JOHN J HECKFORD
Also Called: Heckford, Artisan of Wood
Rr 1 Box Creekside (24266)
PHONE..................................276 889-5646
John J Heckford, *Owner*
EMP: 3
SALES (est): 195K **Privately Held**
SIC: 2431 2511 Staircases & stairs, wood; mantels, wood; wood desks, bookcases & magazine racks

(G-7195)
JONES LOGGING
Rr 3 (24266)
PHONE..................................276 794-9510
Danny Jones, *Principal*
EMP: 3
SALES (est): 199.1K **Privately Held**
SIC: 2411 Logging camps & contractors

(G-7196)
KCI SERVICES LLC
1731 Pioneer Dr (24266-5380)
PHONE..................................276 623-7404
EMP: 2
SALES (est): 90.4K **Privately Held**
SIC: 2599 Hospital beds

(G-7197)
LEBANON APPAREL CORPORATION
Also Called: Three Creek Apparel
70 Thornhill Dr (24266-6093)
PHONE..................................276 889-3656
Bodenhorst Jeoffrey B, *President*
Dan L Vipperman, *President*
Bodenhorst Mary Alice T, *Corp Secy*
Evelyn O Dinunzio, *Asst Treas*
▲ **EMP:** 150
SQ FT: 72,000
SALES (est): 15.9MM **Privately Held**
WEB: www.lacorpusa.com
SIC: 2337 2339 2326 Uniforms, except athletic: women's, misses' & juniors'; women's & misses' outerwear; work uniforms

(G-7198)
LEBANON NEWS INC
308 Clinch Mountain Ave (24266-4200)
P.O. Box 1268 (24266-1268)
PHONE..................................276 889-2112
A G Griffith Jr, *President*

Robert Hillman, *Principal*
Jerry Larke, *Editor*
EMP: 15
SALES (est): 729K **Privately Held**
WEB: www.thelebanonnews.com
SIC: 2711 Newspapers, publishing & printing

(G-7199)
LUDAIRE FINE WOOD FLOORS INC
644 Clydes Way Dr (24266)
PHONE..................................276 889-3072
EMP: 6
SALES (est): 400K **Privately Held**
SIC: 2426 Hardwood Dimension/Floor Mill

(G-7200)
MCCLURE CONCRETE
13761 U S Highway 19 (24266-4355)
PHONE..................................276 889-2289
Jason Herndon, *Principal*
EMP: 2
SALES (est): 133.4K **Privately Held**
WEB: www.mcclureconcrete.com
SIC: 3273 Ready-mixed concrete

(G-7201)
MCCLURE CONCRETE PRODUCTS INC
Lebanon Concrete
Hwy Rte 19 (24266)
PHONE..................................276 889-3496
James Asbur, *Manager*
EMP: 3 **Privately Held**
WEB: www.mcclureconcrete.com
SIC: 3273 Ready-mixed concrete
PA: Mcclure Concrete Products, Inc.
1201 Iron St
Richlands VA 24641

(G-7202)
NORFIELD-FOGLEMAN CABINETS
Rr 19 (24266)
PHONE..................................276 889-1333
Charles Fogleman, *Owner*
EMP: 2
SQ FT: 1,500
SALES (est): 125K **Privately Held**
SIC: 2434 Vanities, bathroom: wood

(G-7203)
P & P FARM MACHINERY INC
28601 U S Highway 58 (24266-5690)
PHONE..................................276 794-7806
Arthur A Purcell, *President*
EMP: 7
SALES (est): 823.1K **Privately Held**
SIC: 3523 Farm machinery & equipment

(G-7204)
POLYCAP LLC
219 Joe Gillespie Dr (24266-1129)
P.O. Box 566 (24266-0566)
PHONE..................................276 883-5700
EMP: 4 **EST:** 2018
SALES (est): 169.2K **Privately Held**
SIC: 3089 Caps, plastic

(G-7205)
RATLIFF
449 Valley View Est (24266-5592)
PHONE..................................276 794-7377
Robert P Pierce, *Owner*
EMP: 1
SALES (est): 109.3K **Privately Held**
SIC: 1241 Bituminous coal mining services, contract basis

(G-7206)
SAMUEL SON & CO (USA) INC
58 Samuel Way Dr (24266-1105)
PHONE..................................276 415-9970
Bill Kahl, *Branch Mgr*
EMP: 248
SALES (corp-wide): 1.8B **Privately Held**
WEB: www.samuel.com
SIC: 3443 Industrial vessels, tanks & containers; tanks, standard or custom fabricated: metal plate; vessels, process or storage (from boiler shops): metal plate

HQ: Samuel, Son & Co. (Usa) Inc.
1401 Davey Rd Ste 300
Woodridge IL 60517
630 783-8900

(G-7207)
STEEL FAB
58 Samuel Way Dr (24266-1105)
PHONE.....................................276 628-3843
Misty Teaster, *Opers Dir*
EMP: 2
SALES (est): 95.2K **Privately Held**
SIC: 3441 Fabricated structural metal

(G-7208)
STONE MOUNTAIN DISTILLING LLC
2219 E Main St (24266-7190)
PHONE.....................................276 970-4081
EMP: 3
SALES (est): 147.9K **Privately Held**
SIC: 2085 Distilled & blended liquors

(G-7209)
TIM PRICE WOODWORKING LLC
356 Church Hill Rd (24266-5955)
PHONE.....................................276 794-9405
Tim Price, *Administration*
EMP: 4
SALES (est): 341.5K **Privately Held**
SIC: 2431 Millwork

(G-7210)
VINCENTS VINEYARD INC
2313 E Main St (24266-7027)
PHONE.....................................276 889-2505
Vincent J Gilmer, *President*
EMP: 2
SALES (est): 125.7K **Privately Held**
WEB: www.vincentsvineyard.com
SIC: 2084 Wines

(G-7211)
WAYRICK INC
1722 U S Highway 19 (24266-5395)
P.O. Box 190, Pounding Mill (24637-0190)
PHONE.....................................276 988-8091
EMP: 4
SALES (est): 464.1K **Privately Held**
SIC: 3531 Forestry related equipment

Leesburg
Loudoun County

(G-7212)
21ST CENTURY SCIENCE ASSOC INC
60 Sycolin Rd Se Ste 203 (20175-4105)
PHONE.....................................703 777-6943
Marsha Freeman, *President*
EMP: 2
SALES (est): 116.2K **Privately Held**
WEB: www.21sci-tech.com
SIC: 2721 Magazines: publishing only, not printed on site

(G-7213)
ACCELERATED PRINTING CORP INC
41636 Carter Ridge Ln (20176-6057)
PHONE.....................................703 437-1084
Joseph Giuliano, *President*
EMP: 7
SQ FT: 4,800
SALES (est): 869.5K **Privately Held**
WEB: www.acceleratedprinting.com
SIC: 2752 2789 7334 Commercial printing, offset; binding & repair of books, magazines & pamphlets; photocopying & duplicating services

(G-7214)
ADIDAS NORTH AMERICA INC
Also Called: Adidas Outlet Store Leesburg
241 Fort Evans Rd Ne # 897 (20176-4038)
PHONE.....................................703 771-6925
Rhoel Zapata, *Manager*
EMP: 5
SALES (corp-wide): 26.1B **Privately Held**
WEB: www.adidas-group.com
SIC: 2329 Athletic (warmup, sweat & jogging) suits: men's & boys'

HQ: Adidas North America, Inc.
3449 N Anchor St Ste 500
Portland OR 97217
971 234-2300

(G-7215)
ADVANCED BIOIP LLC
41655 Catoctin Springs Ct (20176-5866)
PHONE.....................................301 646-3640
Dorothy Glodek, *Mng Member*
EMP: 1
SALES (est): 55K **Privately Held**
SIC: 3841 Surgical & medical instruments

(G-7216)
AMNION LLC
Also Called: Amdrop
14980 Limestone School Rd (20176-5636)
PHONE.....................................267 255-6700
Erik Melling, *Mng Member*
EMP: 1
SALES (est): 500K **Privately Held**
SIC: 2836 Biological products, except diagnostic

(G-7217)
AN ELECTRONIC INSTRUMENTATION (PA)
Also Called: E I T
309 Kellys Ford Plz Se (20175-5442)
PHONE.....................................703 478-0700
Joe T May, *Ch of Bd*
David Faliskie, *President*
Jalil Faieq, *Vice Pres*
Billy Lemaster, *VP Prdtn*
Tiffany Joyner, *Project Mgr*
▲ EMP: 180
SQ FT: 70,000
SALES (est): 71MM **Privately Held**
WEB: www.eit.com
SIC: 3679 3672 3829 3823 Electronic circuits; printed circuit boards; measuring & controlling devices; industrial instrmnts msrmnt display/control process variable; controllers for process variables, all types

(G-7218)
ANATOMY HOME INSPECTION SVC
15200 James Monroe Hwy (20176-5729)
PHONE.....................................703 771-1568
John Enright, *Principal*
EMP: 1
SALES (est): 100.6K **Privately Held**
WEB: www.anatomyhome.com
SIC: 1389 Construction, repair & dismantling services

(G-7219)
APPLE-POLISHERS LLC
1212 Cannon Ct Ne (20176-4807)
PHONE.....................................571 918-1027
Paul A Christensen, *Administration*
EMP: 2 EST: 2012
SALES (est): 112.7K **Privately Held**
SIC: 3571 Electronic computers

(G-7220)
APPLIED VISUAL SCIENCES INC (PA)
525 E Market St 116k (20176-4121)
PHONE.....................................703 539-6190
William J Donovan, *Ch of Bd*
Gregory E Hare, *CFO*
Sean W Kennedy, *CTO*
EMP: 4
SALES (est): 776.8K **Publicly Held**
WEB: www.appliedvs.com
SIC: 7372 Application computer software; business oriented computer software

(G-7221)
ARCWORX WELDING LLC
40949 Pearce Cir (20176-7110)
PHONE.....................................540 394-1494
Daniel Malof, *Principal*
EMP: 1
SALES (est): 25K **Privately Held**
SIC: 7692 Welding repair

(G-7222)
ARMSTRONG FAMILY
43271 Meadowood Ct (20176-5130)
PHONE.....................................703 737-6188
EMP: 2

SALES (est): 65.5K **Privately Held**
SIC: 1389 Oil/Gas Field Services

(G-7223)
ARUNDEL WOODWORKS
525 E Market St (20176-4121)
PHONE.....................................202 713-8781
EMP: 1
SALES (est): 70.5K **Privately Held**
SIC: 2431 Millwork

(G-7224)
ATLAS DEFENSE PLATFORM LLC
19186 Charandy Dr (20175-7216)
PHONE.....................................703 737-6112
William Inman, *Principal*
EMP: 3
SALES (est): 159.6K **Privately Held**
SIC: 3812 Defense systems & equipment

(G-7225)
ATOMIC ARMOR INC
202 Church St Se Ste 524 (20175-3033)
PHONE.....................................703 400-3954
Michael D Miller, *President*
Michael Miller, *President*
EMP: 1
SALES (est): 106.5K **Privately Held**
WEB: www.atomictrampoline.com
SIC: 2851 Coating, air curing

(G-7226)
BAGIRA SYSTEMS USA LLC
44001 Indian Fields Ct (20176-1641)
PHONE.....................................571 278-1989
Peter Muller, *Mng Member*
John Daniele, *Mng Member*
EMP: 2
SALES (est): 100K **Privately Held**
WEB: www.bagirasys.com
SIC: 3699 Electronic training devices

(G-7227)
BARRY ENTERPRISES INTL LLC
18256 Oak Lake Ct (20176-6809)
PHONE.....................................202 812-6822
Elhadj N Barry, *Administration*
EMP: 3
SALES (est): 86.5K **Privately Held**
SIC: 2066 Chocolate

(G-7228)
BECKLEY LLC
Also Called: Beckley & Company
18313 Buccaneer Ter (20176-8476)
PHONE.....................................843 822-8091
J Beckley, *Administration*
EMP: 2
SALES (est): 154.3K **Privately Held**
SIC: 3663 Radio & TV communications equipment

(G-7229)
BEETLEBUG SOFTWARE LLC
43103 Nrthlake Ovrlook Te (20176-6825)
PHONE.....................................571 223-5041
EMP: 2 EST: 2009
SALES (est): 104.8K **Privately Held**
WEB: www.beetlebugsoftware.com
SIC: 7372 Prepackaged software

(G-7230)
BIGBRASSBAND LLC
15 N King St Fl 3 (20176-2827)
PHONE.....................................571 223-7137
Adam Wride, *CEO*
EMP: 20
SALES (est): 2.7MM **Privately Held**
WEB: www.bigbrassband.com
SIC: 7372 Prepackaged software

(G-7231)
BISHOP MONTANA ENT
706 Amber Ct Ne (20176-4920)
PHONE.....................................703 777-8248
John Stanley, *Owner*
EMP: 2
SALES (est): 20K **Privately Held**
SIC: 2741 Miscellaneous publishing

(G-7232)
BLACK HOOF BREWING COMPANY LLC
11 S King St (20175-2903)
P.O. Box 319 Lake Vw Nw (20176)
PHONE.....................................571 707-8014
Bill Haase, *Mng Member*
EMP: 2
SQ FT: 2,000
SALES (est): 300K **Privately Held**
WEB: www.cbcgordonville.org
SIC: 2082 Beer (alcoholic beverage)

(G-7233)
BLACKFISH SOFTWARE LLC (PA)
335 Whipp Dr Se (20175-6141)
PHONE.....................................703 779-9649
Michael Beard, *Principal*
EMP: 3
SALES (est): 307K **Privately Held**
SIC: 7372 Prepackaged software

(G-7234)
BLUEPRINT INC
503 Meade Dr Sw (20175-5010)
PHONE.....................................703 771-9256
Sharon Hickman, *Principal*
EMP: 2
SALES (est): 87.3K **Privately Held**
SIC: 2752 Commercial printing, lithographic

(G-7235)
BND SOFTWARE
17190 Silver Charm Pl (20176-7156)
PHONE.....................................202 997-1070
Sean Kennedy,
EMP: 2
SALES (est): 105.3K **Privately Held**
WEB: www.bndsoftware.com
SIC: 7372 Business oriented computer software

(G-7236)
BP INVESTMENTS LTD
43531 Firestone Pl (20176-3921)
PHONE.....................................580 795-3364
Richard D Phillips, *Partner*
Patti Denman, *Partner*
Annette Sparks, *Partner*
EMP: 4
SALES (est): 380.2K **Privately Held**
SIC: 1311 Crude petroleum production

(G-7237)
BROOK HIDDEN WINERY LLC
43301 Spinks Ferry Rd (20176-5631)
PHONE.....................................703 737-3935
Eric Hauck, *Principal*
EMP: 2
SALES (est): 155.6K **Privately Held**
WEB: www.hiddenbrookwinery.com
SIC: 2084 Wines

(G-7238)
CARAVELLE INDUSTRIES INC
60 Sycolin Rd Se (20175-4105)
P.O. Box 3008 (20177-7984)
PHONE.....................................434 432-2331
J Micheal Roncaglione, *Manager*
EMP: 5
SALES (corp-wide): 1.8MM **Privately Held**
WEB: www.caravellewash.com
SIC: 3589 Car washing machinery
PA: Caravelle Industries, Inc
2045 U S Hwy 29 N
Chatham VA 24531
434 432-2331

(G-7239)
CARAVELLE WESTERN INDS INC
60a Sycolin Rd Se (20175-4105)
P.O. Box 3008 (20177-7984)
PHONE.....................................703 777-9412
Roncaglione J W, *President*
James Roncaglione, *President*
EMP: 2
SALES (est): 146.3K **Privately Held**
SIC: 3599 Machine shop, jobbing & repair

▲ = Import ▼=Export
◆ =Import/Export

(G-7240)
CARDINAL PARK UNIT OWNERS
12 Cardinal Park Dr Se # 107
(20175-4436)
PHONE................................703 777-2311
Scott Goulet, *Partner*
EMP: 1
SQ FT: 4,644
SALES (est): 99.5K **Privately Held**
SIC: 3432 Plumbing fixture fittings & trim

(G-7241)
CASANEL VINEYARDS
17956 Canby Rd (20175-6912)
PHONE................................540 751-1776
De Nelson, *Owner*
EMP: 7
SALES (est): 747.7K **Privately Held**
WEB: www.casanelvineyards.com
SIC: 2084 Wines

(G-7242)
CASEY TRAXLER
Also Called: Tier 1 Operations
15600 Malvosin Pl (20176-7632)
PHONE................................703 402-0745
Casey Traxler, *Owner*
EMP: 1
SALES (est): 46.6K **Privately Held**
SIC: 3484 7389 Small arms; business
services

(G-7243)
CHUKA LLC
1501 Balch Dr S Apt 310 (20175-4705)
PHONE................................443 837-5522
Dustin Rauch,
Gabriela Rauch,
EMP: 2
SALES (est): 190.8K **Privately Held**
SIC: 2522 Office furniture, except wood

(G-7244)
CLEAN POWER & SERVICE LLC
20413 Crimson Pl (20175-6362)
PHONE................................703 443-1717
Shelly Illig,
John Younts,
EMP: 2
SALES (est): 126.4K **Privately Held**
SIC: 3612 3699 7948 Transformers, ex-
cept electric; waveguide pressurization
equipment; race track operation

(G-7245)
CLOVER LLC
202 Church St Se Ste 210 (20175-3031)
PHONE................................703 771-4286
Julie S Kyle,
EMP: 2 EST: 2018
SALES (est): 68.6K **Privately Held**
SIC: 7372 7371 Prepackaged software;
computer software development

(G-7246)
CNC MODELS LLC
620 Marshall Dr Ne (20176-2398)
PHONE................................703 669-0709
Charles Huet, *Administration*
EMP: 2
SALES (est): 158K **Privately Held**
SIC: 3599 Machine shop, jobbing & repair

(G-7247)
COASTAL PRECAST SYSTEMS
227 Town Branch Ter Sw (20175-2707)
PHONE................................571 442-8648
EMP: 2 EST: 2015
SALES (est): 120.1K **Privately Held**
SIC: 3272 Precast terrazo or concrete
products

(G-7248)
CRAFTY STITCHER LLC
18943 Canoe Landing Ct (20176-8218)
PHONE................................703 855-2736
Karen Sullivan, *Principal*
EMP: 1
SALES (est): 68.7K **Privately Held**
SIC: 2395 Embroidery & art needlework

(G-7249)
CREATIVE FRAMING GALLERY
525 E Market St Ste M (20176-4171)
PHONE................................703 771-6354
David Hankins, *Principal*
EMP: 1
SALES (est): 53.5K **Privately Held**
WEB: www.creativeframingoakland.com
SIC: 2499 Picture frame molding, finished

(G-7250)
CUSTOM INK
1019a Edwards Ferry Rd Ne (20176-3347)
PHONE................................703 884-2680
EMP: 2
SALES (est): 84.8K **Privately Held**
WEB: www.custom ink.com
SIC: 2759 Screen printing

(G-7251)
**CUTIE PIES CLAY PRINT
KEEPSKES**
18420 Mill Run Ct (20176-6818)
PHONE................................703 533-3313
Forrest Jones, *Principal*
EMP: 2
SALES (est): 100K **Privately Held**
WEB: www.cutiepieskeepsakes.com
SIC: 2752 Commercial printing, litho-
graphic

(G-7252)
DAILY PRODUCTIONS INC
18592 Colston Ct (20176-5153)
PHONE................................703 477-8444
Sherrill Daily, *Principal*
EMP: 4
SALES (est): 210.1K **Privately Held**
SIC: 2711 Newspapers, publishing & print-
ing

(G-7253)
**DENTAL EQUIPMENT SERVICES
LLC**
18111 Gore Ln (20175-6927)
PHONE................................703 927-1837
Mark McDonald, *Principal*
EMP: 2 EST: 2015
SALES (est): 104.8K **Privately Held**
SIC: 3843 Dental equipment

(G-7254)
DESIGNER GOLDSMITH INC
39272 Mount Gilead Rd (20175-6727)
PHONE................................703 777-7661
Les Thompson, *President*
EMP: 3
SALES (est): 200K **Privately Held**
WEB: www.designergoldsmith.com
SIC: 3961 5944 Costume jewelry, ex. pre-
cious metal & semiprecious stones; jew-
elry, precious stones & precious metals

(G-7255)
DESIGNER GOLDSMITH INC
203 Harrison St Se Ste A (20175-3747)
PHONE................................703 777-7661
Stephanie Dodge, *Principal*
EMP: 1
SALES (est): 45.1K **Privately Held**
SIC: 3961 Costume jewelry

(G-7256)
DET ENTERPRISES INC
40742 Greyhouse Pl (20175-4857)
PHONE................................310 429-3234
Sivanandam Chitra, *Director*
EMP: 5
SALES (est): 374.1K **Privately Held**
SIC: 2082 Malt beverages

(G-7257)
DI COLA LLC CIRO SCHIANO
19537 Emerald Park Dr (20175-9006)
PHONE................................703 779-0212
Ciro Schiano Di Cola, *Administration*
EMP: 3
SALES (est): 159.1K **Privately Held**
SIC: 2086 Soft drinks: packaged in cans,
bottles, etc.

(G-7258)
DISRUPT6 INC
18625 Darden Ct (20176-5148)
PHONE................................571 721-1155
Joseph Klein, *Principal*
Wendy Fox, *Principal*
EMP: 2

SALES (est): 113.6K **Privately Held**
WEB: www.disrupt6.com
SIC: 3577 7371 7379 7389 Computer
peripheral equipment; custom computer
programming services; computer related
maintenance services;

(G-7259)
DRACULAS TOKENS LLC
19449 Xerox Dr (20176-6559)
PHONE................................717 818-5687
Christopher Hunsicker,
EMP: 1
SALES (est): 39.6K **Privately Held**
SIC: 3999 Manufacturing industries

(G-7260)
DRAPERY HOUSE INC
18 Sycolin Rd Se (20175-4105)
PHONE................................703 669-9622
Denise Gaquin, *CEO*
Julie Smead, *Accounting Mgr*
EMP: 3 EST: 2008
SALES (est): 210K **Privately Held**
WEB: www.draperyhousedesigncenter.com
SIC: 2391 5714 Curtains & draperies;
drapery & upholstery stores

(G-7261)
DRY MILL RD LLC
102 Dry Mill Rd Sw # 101 (20175-2635)
PHONE................................703 737-3697
Katharine M Ayers, *Administration*
EMP: 2
SALES (est): 117.3K **Privately Held**
WEB: www.drymillwine.com
SIC: 2084 Wines

(G-7262)
DUNDEE MINIATURES LLC
40371 Foxfield Ln (20175-9021)
PHONE................................703 669-5591
Robert Krivanek, *Principal*
EMP: 2
SALES (est): 140.2K **Privately Held**
SIC: 3999 Miniatures

(G-7263)
EDUCATION ONLINE
205 Colleen Ct Ne (20176-4826)
PHONE................................571 242-6986
John Leddo, *President*
EMP: 10
SALES (est): 795K **Privately Held**
SIC: 3695 Computer software tape &
disks: blank, rigid & floppy

(G-7264)
EIR NEWS SERVICE INC
62 Sycolin Rd Se (20175-4105)
P.O. Box 17390, Washington DC (20041-
0390)
PHONE................................703 777-4494
Linda De Hoyos, *President*
Scott Thompson, *Officer*
Susan Ulanowski, *Admin Sec*
EMP: 100
SALES (est): 4.4MM **Privately Held**
WEB: www.larouchepub.com
SIC: 2711 7383 Newspapers, publishing &
printing; news reporting services for
newspapers & periodicals

(G-7265)
EKAGRA PARTNERS LLC
161 Fort Evans Rd Ne # 200 (20176-3373)
PHONE................................571 421-1100
Kalpesh Patel, *President*
EMP: 10
SALES (est): 1.9MM **Privately Held**
WEB: www.ekagra.com
SIC: 7372 7371 7379 7373 Prepackaged
software; computer software systems
analysis & design, custom; computer software development & applications; computer related maintenance services;
computer related consulting services;
computer systems analysis & design

(G-7266)
ELEMENT ONE LLC
105 Courier Ct Ne (20176-4972)
PHONE................................901 292-7721
Marcus Oliver, *Principal*
EMP: 1

SALES (est): 64.8K **Privately Held**
SIC: 2819 Elements

(G-7267)
**EMERGENCY TRACTION
DEVICE LLC**
40002 Thomas Mill Rd (20175-6936)
PHONE................................703 771-1025
Palmer E Robeson, *Mng Member*
EMP: 2
SALES (est): 74.8K **Privately Held**
SIC: 2399 Tire covers

(G-7268)
ENERGY SHERLOCK LLC
Also Called: Energysherlock
40692 Manor House Rd (20175-6515)
PHONE................................703 346-7584
Tim Reichert, *CEO*
Soraya C Reichert,
EMP: 2
SALES (est): 206.2K **Privately Held**
WEB: www.energysherlock.com
SIC: 3646 Commercial indusl & institu-
tional electric lighting fixtures

(G-7269)
EQUESTRIAN FORGE INC
Also Called: National Trust Foundry
222 S King St Ste 4 (20175-3020)
P.O. Box 1950 (20177-1950)
PHONE................................703 777-2110
Alexander Bigler, *President*
Bigler Alexander, *Vice Pres*
EMP: 1
SQ FT: 4,000
SALES (est): 162.6K **Privately Held**
SIC: 3369 Castings, except die-castings,
precision

(G-7270)
ERP INITIATIVES LLC
21868 Foxden Ln (20175-6357)
PHONE................................703 439-9352
Paul Romanoski, *Principal*
EMP: 2
SALES (est): 145.8K **Privately Held**
WEB: www.erpinitiatives.com
SIC: 3652 Pre-recorded records & tapes

(G-7271)
FABBIOLI CELLARS
15669 Limestone School Rd (20176-5905)
PHONE................................703 771-1197
Doug Fabbioli, *Principal*
EMP: 3
SALES (est): 336.4K **Privately Held**
WEB: www.fabbioliwines.com
SIC: 2084 Wines

(G-7272)
FASTSIGNS
934 Edwards Ferry Rd Ne (20176-3324)
PHONE................................571 510-0400
Michelle Messich, *Principal*
EMP: 1 EST: 2018
SALES (est): 46K **Privately Held**
WEB: www.fastsigns.com
SIC: 3993 Signs & advertising specialties

(G-7273)
FERRERA GROUP USA INC
673 Potomac Station Dr Ne # 141
(20176-1819)
PHONE................................703 340-8300
EMP: 5
SALES: 1MM **Privately Held**
SIC: 2035 Mfg Pickles/Sauces/Dressing

(G-7274)
**FLEETWOOD FARM WINERY
LLC**
23075 Evergreen Mills Rd (20175-6411)
PHONE................................703 722-2124
John Edgemond, *Principal*
EMP: 25
SALES (est): 2.2MM **Privately Held**
WEB: www.fleetwoodfarmwinery.com
SIC: 2084 Wines

(G-7275)
FSO MISSION SUPPORT LLC
43830 Lost Corner Rd (20176-5225)
PHONE................................571 528-3507
Peyton Hutton, *General Mgr*

EMP: 1 EST: 2014
SALES (est): 88.3K Privately Held
WEB: www.fso-academy.com
SIC: 2759 7382 8742 Commercial printing; security systems services; management consulting services

(G-7276)
GADFLY LLC
288 Wood Trestle Ter Se (20175-3755)
P.O. Box 147 (20178-0147)
PHONE..................................703 282-9448
Jill Ryan, General Mgr
Andrew M Ryan, Mng Member
EMP: 2 EST: 2007
SALES (est): 125.1K Privately Held
WEB: www.gadflyllc.com
SIC: 2731 8748 8742 7371 Book publishing; business consulting; publishing consultant; management consulting services; marketing consulting services; computer software systems analysis & design, custom; computer systems analysis & design

(G-7277)
GEE PHARMA LLC
200 Lawson Rd Se (20175-4476)
PHONE..................................703 669-8055
Theophilus Gana, Principal
EMP: 2
SALES (est): 78.7K Privately Held
SIC: 2834 Pharmaceutical preparations

(G-7278)
GIGASHEET INC
17359 Cannonade Dr (20176-7195)
PHONE..................................703 231-8758
Jason Hines, Principal
EMP: 3
SALES (est): 71.1K Privately Held
SIC: 7372 Prepackaged software

(G-7279)
GLOBAL POLISHING SYSTEM LLC
28 W Market St (20176-2805)
P.O. Box 2128, Ashland (23005-5128)
PHONE..................................937 534-1538
EMP: 7
SALES (est): 466.9K Privately Held
SIC: 3471 Polishing, metals or formed products

(G-7280)
GLORY DAYS PRESS LLC
19875 Evergreen Mills Rd (20175-8740)
PHONE..................................703 443-1964
Andrea Alexander, Principal
EMP: 2 EST: 2016
SALES (est): 62.9K Privately Held
SIC: 2711 Newspapers

(G-7281)
GM INTERNATIONAL LTD COMPANY
43194 Parkers Ridge Dr (20176-5133)
PHONE..................................703 577-0829
Davinder Hanjan, President
EMP: 3
SALES (est): 855K Privately Held
WEB: www.gm-international.us
SIC: 3451 3541 3544 Screw machine products; machine tools, metal cutting type; special dies, tools, jigs & fixtures

(G-7282)
GRACE UPON GRACE LLC
Also Called: Cooper's Cookie Company
775 Gteway Dr Se Apt 1111 (20175)
PHONE..................................703 999-6678
Mary Shepherd,
EMP: 1
SALES (est): 64.8K Privately Held
SIC: 2047 Dog food

(G-7283)
HARMONY RDS LLC
44050 Woodridge Pkwy (20176-5103)
PHONE..................................304 433-2188
Zhonghua Ci,
EMP: 5
SALES (est): 50K Privately Held
SIC: 2023 Dietary supplements, dairy & non-dairy based

(G-7284)
HENRY SAINT-DENIS LLC
404 Ayrlee Ave Nw (20176-2001)
PHONE..................................540 547-6657
Harry Denis, Principal
EMP: 3
SALES (est): 152.4K Privately Held
SIC: 2339 Women's & misses' accessories

(G-7285)
ICARE CLINICAL TECH LLC
41655 Catoctin Springs Ct (20176-5866)
PHONE..................................301 646-3640
Dorothy Glodek, Mng Member
EMP: 4
SALES (est): 149.2K Privately Held
SIC: 3841 Surgical & medical instruments

(G-7286)
ICE SCRAPER CARD INC
40503 Dogwood Run Ln (20175-6013)
PHONE..................................703 327-4622
Jay Bradshaw, President
EMP: 2
SALES (est): 124.4K Privately Held
WEB: www.icecard.com
SIC: 3993 Advertising novelties

(G-7287)
INOVITECH LLC
205 Wildman St Ne (20176-2319)
PHONE..................................877 429-0377
Debra Rozier,
EMP: 7 EST: 2011
SALES (est): 409.5K Privately Held
WEB: www.inovitech.com
SIC: 7372 7389 Application computer software;

(G-7288)
INTERNTNAL SOC FOR CMPTTNAL BI
Also Called: Iscb
525k E Market St Rm 330 (20176-4113)
PHONE..................................571 293-2113
Thomas Lengauer, President
Bonnie Berger, Vice Pres
Terry Gaasterland, Vice Pres
Janet Kelso, Vice Pres
Christine Orengo, Vice Pres
EMP: 4
SALES: 1.6MM Privately Held
WEB: www.iscb.org
SIC: 2721 Magazines: publishing & printing

(G-7289)
IXTHOS INC
741 Miller Dr Se Ste D1 (20175-8994)
PHONE..................................703 779-7800
Jeffry Milrod, Principal
EMP: 2
SALES (est): 136.1K Privately Held
SIC: 3829 Measuring & controlling devices

(G-7290)
J & J WELDING LLC
15770 Temple Hall Ln (20176-5912)
PHONE..................................703 431-1044
John Moore, Principal
EMP: 1 EST: 2011
SALES (est): 121.9K Privately Held
WEB: www.jandjweldingllc.com
SIC: 7692 Welding repair

(G-7291)
JAE EL INCORPORATED
42305 Green Meadow Ln (20176-6294)
PHONE..................................540 535-5210
John R Lampl, Director
EMP: 3 EST: 2010
SALES (est): 363.3K Privately Held
SIC: 3559 Automotive related machinery

(G-7292)
JUST PRINT IT LLC
41250 Stone School Ln (20175-6459)
PHONE..................................703 327-2060
Alfred Ziviello, Principal
EMP: 2 EST: 2009
SALES (est): 152.8K Privately Held
WEB: www.justprintitva.com
SIC: 2752 Commercial printing, offset

(G-7293)
JV-RM HOLDINGS INC
Also Called: Sign
525 E Market St Ste D (20176-4171)
PHONE..................................703 669-3333
John Voigt, President
EMP: 6
SALES (est): 300K Privately Held
WEB: www.leesburgsign.com
SIC: 3993 Electric signs

(G-7294)
K & S PEWTER INC
42403 Stumptown Rd (20176-5539)
P.O. Box 319, Round Hill (20142-0319)
PHONE..................................540 751-0505
Fax: 540 751-0506
EMP: 2
SALES: 115K Privately Held
SIC: 3914 5719 5961 Mfg Retail Mail Order Of Pewter Plates Bowles Goblets & Related Products

(G-7295)
K2M GROUP HOLDINGS INC
600 Hope Pkwy Se (20175-4428)
PHONE..................................703 777-3155
Eric D Major, Ch of Bd
Lane Major, COO
Sandra Gilbert, Vice Pres
Warren Gitt, Vice Pres
Gianluca Iasci, Vice Pres
EMP: 286 EST: 2004
SQ FT: 146,000
SALES: 258MM
SALES (corp-wide): 14.8B Publicly Held
WEB: www.k2m.com
SIC: 3842 Surgical appliances & supplies
PA: Stryker Corporation
2825 Airview Blvd
Portage MI 49002
269 385-2600

(G-7296)
KESSLER SOILS ENGRG PDTS INC (PA)
Also Called: Kse
17775 Running Colt Pl (20175-7110)
PHONE..................................571 291-2284
Virginia Aiken, President
Virginia Aicken, Vice Pres
Gary Aiken, Admin Sec
▲ EMP: 7
SALES (est): 900K Privately Held
WEB: www.kesslerdcp.com
SIC: 2899 5032 5082 Soil testing kits; asphalt mixture; concrete processing equipment

(G-7297)
LE REVE BRIDAL INC
Also Called: Le Reve Bridal & Tuxedo Wear
213 Loudoun St Se (20175-3115)
PHONE..................................703 777-3757
Sonia Sibay, President
EMP: 11
SALES (est): 672.3K Privately Held
WEB: www.lerevebridal.com
SIC: 2335 5621 Wedding gowns & dresses; bridal shops

(G-7298)
LEXADYNE PUBLISHING INC
525k E Market St Ste 240 (20176-4113)
P.O. Box 4498 (20177-8564)
PHONE..................................703 779-4998
Roger Crutchfield, President
EMP: 1 EST: 1997
SALES (est): 85.1K Privately Held
WEB: www.englishvocabulary.com
SIC: 2731 Books: publishing only

(G-7299)
LIGHTHOUSE CABINETS INC
110 Richard Dr Se (20175-6128)
PHONE..................................571 293-1064
Ted R White, Administration
EMP: 2 EST: 2013
SALES (est): 115.6K Privately Held
SIC: 2434 Wood kitchen cabinets

(G-7300)
LIGHTHOUSE CONCEPTS LLC
114 Courier Ct Ne (20176-4972)
PHONE..................................703 779-9617
Kathy Renton, Administration
EMP: 2
SALES (est): 233.4K Privately Held
WEB: www.lhconcepts.com
SIC: 2759 Screen printing

(G-7301)
LIMATHERM USA INC
960 Sycolin Rd Se Ste 155 (20175-7606)
PHONE..................................540 402-4060
Wojciech Fizyta, President
Adam Fizyta, Vice Pres
Alicja Fizyta, Vice Pres
EMP: 5
SALES (est): 748K
SALES (corp-wide): 1.4MM Privately Held
SIC: 3363 Aluminum die-castings
HQ: Limatherm S A
Ul. Tarnowska 1
Limanowa 34-60
481 833-7982

(G-7302)
LOCKHEED MARTIN CORPORATION
825 E Market St (20176-4404)
PHONE..................................703 771-3515
Kenneth Clayton, Manager
EMP: 5 Publicly Held
WEB: www.lockheedmartin.com
SIC: 3812 Search & navigation equipment
PA: Lockheed Martin Corporation
6801 Rockledge Dr
Bethesda MD 20817

(G-7303)
LOCO BEANS — FRESH ROASTED
1003 Rollins Dr Sw (20175-4333)
PHONE..................................703 851-5997
Attilio Modolo Paul, Administration
EMP: 3
SALES (est): 146.9K Privately Held
WEB: www.locobeanscoffee.com
SIC: 2095 Roasted coffee

(G-7304)
LOST CREEK VINEYARD
43277 Spinks Ferry Rd (20176-5629)
PHONE..................................703 443-9836
Aimee Henkle, Mng Member
Susan Mitchell, Manager
Todd Henkle,
EMP: 12
SQ FT: 3,608
SALES (est): 408K Privately Held
WEB: www.lostcreekwinery.com
SIC: 2084 Wines

(G-7305)
LOUDOUN COUNTY ASPHALT
42050 Cochran Mill Rd (20175-4642)
PHONE..................................703 669-9001
Mike Day, Principal
EMP: 3
SQ FT: 1,600
SALES (est): 356.1K Privately Held
WEB: www.loudoun.gov
SIC: 2951 Asphalt paving mixtures & blocks

(G-7306)
LOUDOUN MEDICAL GROUP PC
116 Edwards Ferry Rd Ne (20176-2301)
PHONE..................................703 669-6118
EMP: 43 Privately Held
WEB: www.lmgdoctors.com
SIC: 2834 8011 Medicines, capsuled or ampuled; offices & clinics of medical doctors
PA: Loudoun Medical Group, P.C.
224d Cornwall St Nw # 40
Leesburg VA 20176

(G-7307)
LOUDOUN NOW
15 N King St Ste 101 (20176-2827)
PHONE..................................703 770-9723
EMP: 4
SALES (est): 215K Privately Held
WEB: www.loudounnow.com
SIC: 2711 Newspapers, publishing & printing

(G-7308)
LOUDOUN SIGNS INC
Also Called: Sign-A-Rama
525 E Market St Ste D (20176-4171)
PHONE....................703 669-3333
Mark A Carlson, *President*
Melissa A Carlson, *Vice Pres*
EMP: 4
SQ FT: 1,480
SALES (est): 317.7K **Privately Held**
WEB: www.leesburgsign.com
SIC: 3993 Signs & advertising specialties

(G-7309)
MANNY WEBER
Also Called: Aunt Becky's Candle Shoppe
207 Rosemeade Pl Sw (20175-2519)
P.O. Box 4316 (20177-8424)
PHONE....................703 819-3338
Manny D Weber, *Owner*
EMP: 2
SALES (est): 10K **Privately Held**
WEB: www.auntbeckyscandleshoppe.com
SIC: 3999 Candles

(G-7310)
**MDR PERFORMANCE ENGINES
LLC**
18896 Woodburn Rd (20175-9032)
PHONE....................540 338-1001
Alan Jackson, *Principal*
EMP: 3
SALES (est): 313.9K **Privately Held**
WEB: www.mdrengines.com
SIC: 3519 Internal combustion engines

(G-7311)
MEDIA AFRICA INC
30 Catoctin Cir Se Ste C (20175-3044)
PHONE....................703 260-6494
Sossina Tafari, *CEO*
EMP: 4 EST: 2017
SQ FT: 10,000
SALES (est): 98.7K **Privately Held**
SIC: 2741

(G-7312)
MERCURY SOLUTIONS LLC
19300 Creek Field Cir (20176-1620)
PHONE....................703 474-9456
Sean Murrell, *Principal*
EMP: 2
SALES (est): 132.3K **Privately Held**
SIC: 3577 Computer peripheral equipment

(G-7313)
MERIDIAN TECH SYSTEMS INC
880 Harrison St Se # 260 (20175-4526)
PHONE....................301 606-6490
Daemon Price, *CEO*
EMP: 3
SALES (corp-wide): 647.3K **Privately
Held**
WEB: www.meridiantsi.com
SIC: 3812 3572 3577 8731 Search &
navigation equipment; computer storage
devices; computer peripheral equipment;
commercial physical research
PA: Meridian Technology Systems, Inc.
4539 Metropolitan Ct
Frederick MD 21704
301 360-3510

(G-7314)
MICRO TECH INDUSTRIES INC
709 Vermillion Dr Ne (20176-3622)
PHONE....................703 674-9647
Leila Sarabi, *Principal*
EMP: 2
SALES (est): 110.5K **Privately Held**
SIC: 3999 Manufacturing industries

(G-7315)
MIGUEL SOTO
Also Called: Miguel's Snow Removal
195 Alpine Dr Se (20175-6172)
PHONE....................571 274-3790
Miguel Soto, *Owner*
EMP: 2
SALES (est): 109.9K **Privately Held**
SIC: 3531 7389 Plows: construction, exca-
vating & grading; business services

(G-7316)
MOTOROLA SOLUTIONS INC
44330 Woodridge Pkwy (20176-5143)
PHONE....................703 724-8000
Michael Harris, *Manager*
Earl Delk, *Manager*
EMP: 200 **Publicly Held**
WEB: www.motorolasolutions.com
SIC: 3663 Radio & TV communications
equipment
PA: Motorola Solutions, Inc.
500 W Monroe St Ste 4400
Chicago IL 60661
847 576-5000

(G-7317)
MYBODYMYWORSHIP
102 Oakcrest Manor Dr Ne (20176-2219)
PHONE....................703 669-2901
EMP: 1 EST: 2019
SALES (est): 37.5K **Privately Held**
SIC: 2741 Miscellaneous publishing

(G-7318)
NATIONAL AFFL MKTG CO INC
Also Called: Intellirf Systems
19355 Wrenbury Ln (20175-8886)
PHONE....................703 297-7316
T Brent Chapel, *CEO*
EMP: 45
SALES (est): 950K **Privately Held**
WEB: www.intellirf.com
SIC: 3825 Radio frequency measuring
equipment

(G-7319)
NATIONAL VACCINE INFORMAT
726 Tonquin Pl Ne (20176-3671)
PHONE....................703 777-3736
EMP: 2
SALES (est): 81.8K **Privately Held**
SIC: 2836 Vaccines

(G-7320)
NEW TECH INNOVATIONS
43074 Northlake Blvd (20176-5193)
PHONE....................703 731-8160
Christopher Farmer, *Partner*
EMP: 1
SALES (est): 43.1K **Privately Held**
SIC: 7372 Prepackaged software

(G-7321)
**NORTH STAR SOFTWARE
CONSULTING**
908 Octorora Pl Ne (20176-6656)
PHONE....................703 628-8564
Jorgen Jensen, *Administration*
EMP: 2
SALES (est): 100.9K **Privately Held**
WEB: www.emeraldstarsoftware.com
SIC: 7372 Prepackaged software

(G-7322)
OSTRICH PRESS LLC
154 Connery Ter Sw (20175-5039)
PHONE....................703 779-7580
EMP: 1
SALES (est): 57.7K **Privately Held**
SIC: 2741 Misc Publishing

(G-7323)
**PAINTING PAGES PUBLISHING
LLC**
687 Mcleary Sq Se (20175-5651)
PHONE....................571 266-9529
Virginlan Hicks, *Principal*
EMP: 2
SALES (est): 106.8K **Privately Held**
SIC: 2741 Miscellaneous publishing

(G-7324)
PEOPLE INTERACT LLC
43067 Lake Ridge Pl (20176-6811)
PHONE....................571 223-5888
Srinivas Sharadaih, *Principal*
EMP: 2
SALES (est): 102.9K **Privately Held**
WEB: www.peopleinteract.com
SIC: 7372 Prepackaged software

(G-7325)
PERFECT BLIND
43106 Kingsport Dr (20176-1803)
PHONE....................703 675-4111
EMP: 1
SALES (est): 57.3K **Privately Held**
SIC: 2591 Window blinds

(G-7326)
**POTOMAC PRINTING
SOLUTIONS INC**
19441 Golf Vista Plz # 250 (20176-8271)
PHONE....................703 723-2511
Kevin J Pehlke, *President*
Kristi Muse, *Office Mgr*
Caitlin Meehan,
EMP: 65
SQ FT: 3,000
SALES (est): 7.6MM **Privately Held**
WEB: www.potomacprint.com
SIC: 2752 Commercial printing, offset

(G-7327)
**PRALL SOFTWARE
CONSULTING LLC**
511 Valley View Ave Sw (20175-3817)
PHONE....................703 777-8423
Craig Prall,
EMP: 1 EST: 2001 **Privately Held**
WEB: www.pcweenie.com
SIC: 7372 Prepackaged software

(G-7328)
**PRODUCT DEV MFG & PACKG
(PA)**
Also Called: P D M P
105 Loudoun St Sw (20175-2910)
PHONE....................703 777-8400
William Teringo, *President*
EMP: 6
SQ FT: 4,000
SALES (est): 1.2MM **Privately Held**
WEB: www.pdmpantiqueprints.com
SIC: 3089 3663 3841 Plastic containers,
except foam; antennas, transmitting &
communications; diagnostic apparatus,
medical

(G-7329)
QBEAM INC
19490 Sandridge Way # 330 (20176-3468)
PHONE....................703 574-5330
Eugene Estinto, *President*
Eugenio Estinto, *Administration*
EMP: 2 EST: 2015
SALES (est): 234.3K **Privately Held**
WEB: www.qbeaminc.com
SIC: 3827 Optical instruments & apparatus

(G-7330)
QUANTUM COMPUTING INC
215 Depot Ct Se Ste 215 # 215
(20175-3017)
PHONE....................703 436-2161
Robert Liscouski, *Ch of Bd*
Christopher Roberts, *CFO*
EMP: 7
SQ FT: 350
SALES (est): 484.1K **Privately Held**
WEB: www.quantumcomputinginc.com
SIC: 7372 Prepackaged software

(G-7331)
RAFFY WELDING LLC
14072 Gusty Knoll Ln (20176-6035)
PHONE....................703 945-0554
Ryan Raffensperger, *Administration*
EMP: 1 EST: 2015
SALES (est): 37.3K **Privately Held**
WEB: www.raffywelding.com
SIC: 7692 Welding repair

(G-7332)
RAPHAEL PRESS LLC
19370 Magnolia Grove Sq (20176-6886)
PHONE....................703 771-7571
Laura J Bobrow, *Principal*
EMP: 1 EST: 2019
SALES (est): 37.5K **Privately Held**
WEB: www.laurajbobrow.com
SIC: 2741 Miscellaneous publishing

(G-7333)
REHAU AUTOMOTIVE LLC (HQ)
1501 Edwards Ferry Rd Ne (20176-6680)
PHONE....................703 777-5255
Holm Riepenhausen, *Principal*
Chris Hauser, *Engineer*
Debora Jones, *Treasurer*

Reiner Leifhelm, *Mng Member*
▲ EMP: 2
SALES (est): 1.2MM **Privately Held**
WEB: www.rehau.com
SIC: 3089 Plastic processing

(G-7334)
**REHAU CONSTRUCTION LLC
(HQ)**
1501 Edwards Ferry Rd Ne (20176-6680)
PHONE....................800 247-9445
Miranda Bowling, *Purch Agent*
Mac McCarty, *Buyer*
Christian Fabian, *Mng Member*
Michael Hoshor, *Supervisor*
Sandi Breinig, *Executive Asst*
◆ EMP: 36
SQ FT: 10,000
SALES (est): 24MM **Privately Held**
WEB: www.rehau.com
SIC: 3089 Plastic processing

(G-7335)
REHAU INCORPORATED (PA)
1501 Edwards Ferry Rd Ne (20176-6680)
PHONE....................703 777-5255
Kathleen Saylor, *CEO*
Christian Fabian, *CEO*
Paul Thompson, *Area Mgr*
Brian Murphy, *Business Mgr*
Terry Barnaby, *Vice Pres*
▲ EMP: 175
SQ FT: 70,000
SALES (est): 224.8MM **Privately Held**
WEB: www.rehau.com
SIC: 3089 Plastic processing

(G-7336)
REHAU INDUSTRIES LLC
1501 Edwards Ferry Rd Ne (20176-6680)
PHONE....................703 777-5255
Christian K Fabian, *Mng Member*
◆ EMP: 2
SALES (est): 664.9K **Privately Held**
WEB: www.rehau.com
SIC: 3089 Plastic processing
PA: Rehau Incorporated
1501 Edwards Ferry Rd Ne
Leesburg VA 20176

(G-7337)
RIVERLAND SOLUTIONS CORP
42993 Buna Mae Ln (20176-5641)
PHONE....................571 247-2382
Gary Moreland, *CEO*
EMP: 1
SALES (est): 35.9K **Privately Held**
SIC: 7372 7371 8733 Application com-
puter software; computer software sys-
tems analysis & design, custom; scientific
research agency

(G-7338)
ROBERT MONTGOMERY
319 E Market St (20176-4102)
PHONE....................703 737-0491
EMP: 2
SALES (est): 128.1K **Privately Held**
SIC: 3444 Mfg Sheet Metalwork

(G-7339)
ROOT GROUP LLC
41125 Grenata Preserve Pl (20175-8716)
PHONE....................703 595-7008
EMP: 4
SALES (est): 295.6K **Privately Held**
SIC: 2741 Miscellaneous publishing

(G-7340)
**RPI AAR RAILROAD TANK CAR
PRJ**
13541 Taylorstown Rd (20176-6165)
PHONE....................540 822-4800
Todd Treichel, *Principal*
EMP: 1
SALES (est): 70.5K **Privately Held**
SIC: 3462 Railroad, construction & mining
forgings

(G-7341)
**SAM HOME IMPROVEMENTS
LLC**
43239 Lecroy Cir (20176-3849)
PHONE....................703 372-6000
Muhammad Saleem,

EMP: 2
SALES (est): 30K **Privately Held**
SIC: **1389** Construction, repair & dismantling services

(G-7342)
SAWARMOR LLC
1306 Hawling Pl Sw (20175-5021)
PHONE..............................703 779-7719
Thomas Bendien, *Principal*
EMP: 1
SALES (est): 50K **Privately Held**
WEB: www.sawarmor.com
SIC: **3825 7389** Electrical power measuring equipment;

(G-7343)
SCRIYB LLC
109 N King St Ste B (20176-2837)
PHONE..............................202 549-7070
Christopher Etesse,
EMP: 10 EST: 2014
SALES (est): 500K **Privately Held**
WEB: www.scriyb.com
SIC: **7372** Educational computer software

(G-7344)
SEHER RESOURCES INC
42837 Forest Spring Dr (20176-6842)
PHONE..............................703 771-7170
Fida M Malik, *President*
EMP: 2
SALES (est): 200K **Privately Held**
SIC: **3444** Wells, light: sheet metal

(G-7345)
SEMATRON LLC
17623 Canby Rd (20175-6907)
PHONE..............................919 360-5806
Anthony R Tinkle,
EMP: 1 EST: 2010
SALES (est): 113.7K **Privately Held**
SIC: **3829 8999** Geophysical or meteorological electronic equipment; geophysical consultant

(G-7346)
SENTIENTRF
22643 Watson Rd (20175-6443)
PHONE..............................503 467-8026
EMP: 2
SALES (est): 140.8K **Privately Held**
SIC: **3825** Instruments To Measure Electricity

(G-7347)
SERENDIPITME LLC
673 Potomac Station Dr Ne # 223
(20176-1819)
PHONE..............................301 370-2466
Lawrence Stanley,
EMP: 1
SALES (est): 60.1K **Privately Held**
SIC: **7372** Business oriented computer software

(G-7348)
SIGNS BY DAVE
103 Pershing Ave Nw (20176-2036)
PHONE..............................703 777-2870
David Payne, *Owner*
Linda Payne, *Owner*
EMP: 2
SALES (est): 150.8K **Privately Held**
WEB: www.signsbydave.com
SIC: **3993** Signs & advertising specialties

(G-7349)
SLIPSTREAM AVIATION SFTWR INC
202 Church St Se Ste 311 (20175-3032)
PHONE..............................703 729-6535
Ira Gershkoff, *President*
EMP: 1
SALES (est): 200K **Privately Held**
WEB: www.slipstreamsoftware.com
SIC: **7372** Prepackaged software

(G-7350)
SOFTWARE SECURITY CONS LLC
41154 Grenata Preserve Pl (20175-8715)
PHONE..............................571 234-3663
Bahar Limaye, *Principal*
EMP: 1

SALES (est): 117.8K **Privately Held**
SIC: **7372** Application computer software

(G-7351)
STAR HOME THEATER LLC
Also Called: Sht Technologies
42714 Cool Breeze Sq (20176-6856)
PHONE..............................855 978-2748
Binh Nguyen,
EMP: 2
SALES (est): 266K **Privately Held**
WEB: www.starht.com
SIC: **3651** Household audio & video equipment

(G-7352)
STRYKER CORPORATION
Stryker Spine
600 Hope Pkwy Se (20175-4428)
PHONE..............................571 919-2000
Spencer S Stiles, *President*
Samuel Lee, *Opers Staff*
EMP: 4
SALES (corp-wide): 14.8B **Publicly Held**
WEB: www.stryker.com
SIC: **3842** Surgical appliances & supplies
PA: Stryker Corporation
2825 Airview Blvd
Portage MI 49002
269 385-2600

(G-7353)
STRYKER CORPORATION
Also Called: Stryker Spine
610 Hope Pkwy Se (20175-4428)
PHONE..............................571 919-2345
EMP: 2
SALES (est): 93.5K **Privately Held**
SIC: **3841** Surgical & medical instruments

(G-7354)
SUB ROSA PRESS LTD
313 Lounsbury Ct Ne (20176-2335)
PHONE..............................703 777-1157
David L Phillips, *Principal*
EMP: 2
SALES (est): 92.9K **Privately Held**
SIC: **2741** Miscellaneous publishing

(G-7355)
SUPREME CONCRETE BLOCKS INC
42824 Durham Ct (20175-4715)
PHONE..............................703 478-1988
Andrew Person, *Principal*
EMP: 2
SALES (est): 108.4K **Privately Held**
SIC: **3271** Blocks, concrete or cinder: standard

(G-7356)
SURA SOLUTIONS INC
705 Invermere Dr Ne (20176-3615)
PHONE..............................703 973-1939
Srinivas Manam, *Principal*
EMP: 3 EST: 2010
SALES (est): 212.2K **Privately Held**
WEB: www.sura-solutions.com
SIC: **3695** Computer software tape & disks: blank, rigid & floppy

(G-7357)
T-SHIRT COMPANY LLC
521 Currant Ter Ne (20176-2453)
PHONE..............................703 669-4619
Stephanie Bills, *Principal*
EMP: 2
SALES (est): 113.2K **Privately Held**
WEB: www.customink.com
SIC: **2759** Screen printing

(G-7358)
TALON INC
Also Called: Riverbend Sawmill
42217 Cochran Mill Rd (20175-4613)
PHONE..............................703 777-3600
Jean Webb, *President*
Randy Webb, *Vice Pres*
EMP: 17
SQ FT: 700 **Privately Held**
SIC: **2421** Lumber: rough, sawed or planed

(G-7359)
TARARA
Also Called: Tarara Winery
13648 Tarara Ln (20176-5236)
PHONE..............................703 771-7100
Ralph Hubert, *Partner*
Michael Hubert, *Partner*
Margret Russell, *Manager*
EMP: 14
SQ FT: 1,200
SALES (est): 2.4MM **Privately Held**
WEB: www.tarara.com
SIC: **2084** Wines

(G-7360)
TEN COMPANIES LLC
161 Fort Evans Rd Ne (20176-3369)
PHONE..............................703 669-1008
EMP: 1
SALES (est): 81.9K **Privately Held**
SIC: **3651** Household audio & video equipment

(G-7361)
TIMES COMMUNITY MEDIA
1602 Village Market Blvd (20175-4721)
PHONE..............................703 777-1111
Donna Hirsch, *Executive*
EMP: 2 EST: 2018
SALES (est): 69.2K **Privately Held**
WEB: www.loudountimes.com
SIC: **2711** Newspapers, publishing & printing

(G-7362)
TITAS NENE BICOL ATCHARA LLC
19110 Dalton Points Pl (20176-3837)
PHONE..............................571 501-8599
Robert Villar, *Principal*
EMP: 2
SALES (est): 4K **Privately Held**
SIC: **2035** Pickles, sauces & salad dressings

(G-7363)
TNT LASER WORKS LLC
22 1/2 Pershing Ave Nw (20176-2019)
PHONE..............................571 214-7517
Theodore Wysocki,
EMP: 1 EST: 2015
SALES (est): 97.9K **Privately Held**
SIC: **3699** Laser welding, drilling & cutting equipment

(G-7364)
TODD INDUSTRIES
18981 Coreopsis Ter (20176-8463)
PHONE..............................571 275-2782
EMP: 2
SALES (est): 75K **Privately Held**
SIC: **3999** Mfg Misc Products

(G-7365)
TRIPLE C WOODWORKING LLC
41335 Shreve Mill Rd (20175-6301)
PHONE..............................703 779-9966
Robert Mock, *Principal*
EMP: 2
SALES (est): 130.4K **Privately Held**
WEB: www.triplecwoodworking.com
SIC: **2431** Millwork

(G-7366)
U3 SOLUTIONS INC
Also Called: AlphaGraphics Loudoun
604 S King St Ste 100 (20175-3926)
PHONE..............................703 777-5020
Cynthia Urbano, *Owner*
EMP: 6 EST: 2011
SALES (est): 1MM **Privately Held**
WEB: www.alphagraphics.com
SIC: **2752 2759** Commercial printing, lithographic; commercial printing

(G-7367)
UNITED INK PRESS
19235 Gooseview Ct (20176-1268)
PHONE..............................703 966-6343
Frank Deldjoui, *Owner*
EMP: 1 EST: 2010
SALES (est): 113.7K **Privately Held**
SIC: **2759** Commercial printing

(G-7368)
UNIVERSAL COMPOSITION SVCS LLC
14347 Newvalle Church Rd (20175)
PHONE..............................202 255-7995
Altaf Ullah Khan, *Administration*
EMP: 2 EST: 2010
SALES (est): 116.5K **Privately Held**
WEB: www.exporealtors.com
SIC: **2791** Typesetting

(G-7369)
VANHUSS FAMILY CELLARS LLC
Also Called: Dry Mill Vineyards and Winery
18195 Dry Mill Rd (20175-7024)
PHONE..............................703 737-3930
Dean Vanhuss, *President*
Sherrill D Vanhuss, *Vice Pres*
EMP: 5
SALES (est): 350K **Privately Held**
WEB: www.drymillwine.com
SIC: **2084 5921 5182** Wines; wine; wine

(G-7370)
VETERAN MADE LLC
15 E Market St Unit 567 (20178-8020)
PHONE..............................703 328-2570
Jeffrey M Macintyre,
EMP: 1
SALES (est): 5K **Privately Held**
SIC: **3999** Manufacturing industries

(G-7371)
VIDRIO TECHNOLOGIES
18541 Bear Creek Ter (20176-7424)
PHONE..............................703 405-4944
Bruce Kimmel, *Principal*
EMP: 2 EST: 2014
SALES (est): 117.5K **Privately Held**
SIC: **1389** Oil field services

(G-7372)
VIRGINIA NEWS GROUP LLC
108 Church St Se Ste C (20175-3045)
PHONE..............................703 777-1111
Peter Arundel, *Branch Mgr*
EMP: 1
SALES (corp-wide): 14.9MM **Privately Held**
WEB: www.loudountimes.com
SIC: **2711** Commercial printing & newspaper publishing combined
PA: Virginia News Group, Llc
1602 Village Market Blvd
Leesburg VA 20175
703 777-1111

(G-7373)
VIRGINIA NEWS GROUP LLC (PA)
1602 Village Market Blvd (20175-4721)
PHONE..............................703 777-1111
Peter Arundel, *President*
Bonnie Keyes, *Credit Staff*
EMP: 3
SQ FT: 5,900
SALES (est): 14.9MM **Privately Held**
WEB: www.loudountimes.com
SIC: **2711** Commercial printing & newspaper publishing combined; newspapers, publishing & printing

(G-7374)
VOICE SOFTWARE LLC
43277 Overview Pl (20176-3681)
PHONE..............................571 331-2861
Nathaniel Cooper,
EMP: 1
SALES (est): 69.3K **Privately Held**
WEB: www.thevoicesoftware.com
SIC: **7372 7371** Prepackaged software; computer software systems analysis & design, custom

(G-7375)
WEIBEL EQUIPMENT INC
44001 Indian Fields Ct (20176-1641)
PHONE..............................571 278-1989
Peder Pedersen, *Principal*
Peter Muller, *Vice Pres*
EMP: 3

▲ = Import ▼=Export
◆ =Import/Export

SALES (est): 1MM **Privately Held**
WEB: www.weibel.dk
SIC: 3812 Navigational systems & instruments

(G-7376)
WEIDER HISTORY GROUP INC
19300 Promenade Dr (20176-6500)
PHONE.................................703 779-8388
EMP: 55
SQ FT: 9,711
SALES (est): 7.8MM **Privately Held**
SIC: 2721 Periodicals-Publishing/Printing

(G-7377)
WHITEBOARD APPLICATIONS INC
518 Deermeadow Pl Sw (20175-5829)
P.O. Box 336 (20178-0336)
PHONE.................................703 297-2835
Gary Kedda, *CFO*
David Taliaferro, *Director*
Charles Swisher, *Director*
EMP: 3
SALES (est): 71.1K **Privately Held**
SIC: 7372 7389 Application computer software;

(G-7378)
WIGGLESWORTH GRANOLA LLC
1423 Hague Dr Sw (20175-5013)
PHONE.................................703 443-0130
Laura K Wigglesworth, *Administration*
EMP: 1 EST: 2015
SALES (est): 54.4K **Privately Held**
SIC: 2043 Granola & muesli, except bars & clusters

(G-7379)
WILLOWCROFT FARM VINEYARDS
38906 Mount Gilead Rd (20175-6721)
PHONE.................................703 777-8161
Lewis Parker, *Owner*
Kim Hawkins, *Manager*
EMP: 3
SQ FT: 3,668
SALES (est): 221K **Privately Held**
WEB: www.willowcroftwine.com
SIC: 2084 Wines

(G-7380)
WINE WITH EVERYTHING LLC
341 Caldwell Ter Se (20175-5689)
PHONE.................................703 777-4899
Sherri L Dodson, *Mng Member*
Vonda Driscoll,
Pamela Holmes,
Carol Vaught,
EMP: 4
SALES (est): 256.6K **Privately Held**
SIC: 3999 5199 7389 Candles; candles;

(G-7381)
WP COMPANY LLC
Also Called: Washington Post
305 Harrison St Se 100a (20175-3729)
PHONE.................................703 771-1491
EMP: 12 **Privately Held**
SIC: 2711 Newspapers-Publishing/Printing
HQ: Wp Company Llc
1301 K St Nw
Washington DC 20071

(G-7382)
YUMMY IN MY TUMMY INC
609 Bluff Ct Ne (20176-6607)
PHONE.................................703 209-1516
Waheed Shareef, *President*
EMP: 8
SALES (est): 612.8K **Privately Held**
SIC: 2024 Yogurt desserts, frozen

(G-7383)
ZAKAA COUTURE LLC
19390 Diamond Lake Dr (20176-6560)
PHONE.................................703 554-7506
Asma Zaka, *Administration*
EMP: 5
SALES (est): 99K **Privately Held**
SIC: 2335 Bridal & formal gowns

Lewisetta
Northumberland County

(G-7384)
ORBAN
973 Coan Haven Rd (22511-2650)
PHONE.................................804 529-6283
I Orban, *Principal*
EMP: 1
SALES (est): 77.2K **Privately Held**
SIC: 3663 Radio & TV communications equipment

Lexington
Lexington City County

(G-7385)
141 REPELLENT INC
1 High Meadow Dr (24450-3733)
P.O. Box 96, Pink Hill NC (28572-0096)
PHONE.................................540 421-3956
Dennis Tracz, *CEO*
EMP: 2 EST: 2009
SALES (est): 108.7K **Privately Held**
SIC: 2899 Chemical preparations

(G-7386)
A & S SCREEN PRINTING
Also Called: A & S Screen Printing and EMB
176 W Midland Trl (24450-4000)
PHONE.................................540 464-9042
Sheila Minnick, *Owner*
Allen Minnick, *Co-Owner*
EMP: 2
SALES (est): 164.8K **Privately Held**
SIC: 2759 Screen printing

(G-7387)
B & D TRUCKING OF VIRGINIA
2970 W Midland Trl (24450-6313)
PHONE.................................540 463-3035
Doris Sibold, *President*
Phil Sibold, *Corp Secy*
David Sibold, *Vice Pres*
EMP: 8
SALES (est): 1.2MM **Privately Held**
SIC: 2499 Mulch, wood & bark

(G-7388)
BARGER SON CNSTR INC CHARLES W
Hwy 60 E (24450)
P.O. Box 778 (24450-0778)
PHONE.................................540 463-2106
Beatrice Doss, *Ch of Bd*
Charles W Barger III, *President*
EMP: 65
SQ FT: 7,500
SALES (est): 7.6MM **Privately Held**
WEB: www.cwbargerandson.com
SIC: 3273 1622 1411 1422 Ready-mixed concrete; highway construction, elevated; bridge construction; limestone, dimension-quarrying; crushed & broken limestone

(G-7389)
CHINOOK & CO LLC
151 Pullen Rd (24450-7025)
PHONE.................................540 463-9556
Tenney Rudge,
EMP: 1
SALES (est): 93.4K **Privately Held**
WEB: www.breakawaycollar.com
SIC: 2399 Pet collars, leashes, etc.: non-leather

(G-7390)
CHRISTIAN OBSERVER
56 Robinson Ln (24450-4104)
P.O. Box 1371 (24450-1371)
PHONE.................................540 464-3570
Bob Williams, *Principal*
EMP: 3
SALES (est): 159K **Privately Held**
WEB: www.christianobserver.org
SIC: 2711 Newspapers, publishing & printing

(G-7391)
CONSTRUCTION MATERIALS COMPANY
Also Called: Conrock
9 Memorial Ln (24450-5722)
PHONE.................................540 463-3441
James Coffey, *Branch Mgr*
EMP: 8 **Privately Held**
WEB: www.rockinghamredimix.com
SIC: 3273 Ready-mixed concrete
PA: Construction Materials Company
9 Memorial Ln
Lexington VA 24450

(G-7392)
CONSTRUCTION MATERIALS COMPANY (PA)
Also Called: Conrock
9 Memorial Ln (24450-5722)
P.O. Box 1347, Harrisonburg (22803-1347)
PHONE.................................540 433-9043
Roy D Simmons Jr, *President*
Alan Deleeuwerk, *Corp Secy*
Edward Harris, *Vice Pres*
EMP: 15
SALES (est): 11.6MM **Privately Held**
WEB: www.rockinghamredimix.com
SIC: 3273 Ready-mixed concrete

(G-7393)
CRIMPHAVEN ALPACAS LLC
4165 W Midland Trl (24450-6474)
PHONE.................................540 463-4063
EMP: 2
SALES (est): 142.2K **Privately Held**
SIC: 2231 Wool Broadwoven Fabric Mill

(G-7394)
DARK HOLLOW LLC
513 Beatty Holw (24450-4033)
PHONE.................................540 355-8218
Lucas Tyree, *Manager*
EMP: 1
SALES (est): 57.2K **Privately Held**
SIC: 2879 Trace elements (agricultural chemicals)

(G-7395)
DONALDS MEAT PROCESSING LLC
194 Mccorkle Dr (24450-2995)
P.O. Box 752 (24450-0752)
PHONE.................................540 463-2333
Charles A Potter Jr, *Administration*
EMP: 10 EST: 2009
SALES (est): 832.7K **Privately Held**
WEB: www.donaldsmeats.com
SIC: 2011 Meat packing plants

(G-7396)
JAMES ALLEN PRINTING CO
145 E Midland Trl (24450-5700)
PHONE.................................540 463-9232
James Allen, *President*
Chad Allen, *Principal*
Jamie Allen, *Principal*
EMP: 6 EST: 1970
SQ FT: 3,200
SALES (est): 577.5K **Privately Held**
WEB: www.jamesallenprinting.com
SIC: 2752 2759 Commercial printing, offset; letterpress printing

(G-7397)
LEXINGTON MEASUREMENT TECH
25 Meadow Heights Ln (24450-7338)
PHONE.................................540 261-3966
Joseph R Blandino, *Owner*
EMP: 2
SALES (est): 10K **Privately Held**
SIC: 3829 Measuring & controlling devices

(G-7398)
LEXINGTON PAPAGALLO INC
23 N Main St (24450-2520)
PHONE.................................540 463-5988
EMP: 2
SALES (est): 85.1K **Privately Held**
SIC: 3161 Clothing & apparel carrying cases

(G-7399)
MARVIN DUDLEY LOGGING
785 Bunker Hill Mill Rd (24450-7334)
PHONE.................................540 784-3098
EMP: 2
SALES (est): 81.7K **Privately Held**
SIC: 2411 Logging

(G-7400)
MAURY RIVER OIL COMPANY
172 Old Buena Vista Rd (24450-3701)
PHONE.................................540 463-2233
EMP: 3
SALES (est): 174.8K **Privately Held**
SIC: 1311 Crude petroleum & natural gas

(G-7401)
MAURYWOOD LLC
317 Jackson Ave (24450-2009)
PHONE.................................540 463-6209
Mary Gilliam, *President*
EMP: 2 EST: 2015
SALES (est): 55.2K **Privately Held**
SIC: 2499 Wood products

(G-7402)
MODINE MANUFACTURING COMPANY
360 Collierstown Rd (24450-6047)
PHONE.................................540 464-3640
EMP: 2
SALES (corp-wide): 1.9B **Publicly Held**
WEB: www.modine.com
SIC: 3443 Air preheaters, nonrotating: plate type
PA: Modine Manufacturing Company Inc
1500 Dekoven Ave
Racine WI 53403
262 636-1200

(G-7403)
MOORMAN SHICKRAM & STEPHEN
30 Crossing Ln (24450-6354)
PHONE.................................540 463-3146
Laurence Stephen, *President*
EMP: 2
SALES (est): 121K **Privately Held**
SIC: 1481 Nonmetallic mineral services

(G-7404)
MOUNTAIN VIEW BREWERY LLC
Also Called: Devils Backbone Brewing Co
50 Northwind Ln (24450-3303)
PHONE.................................540 462-6200
Hayes Humphreys, *COO*
Brystal Silvious, *Manager*
Megan Tuttle, *Director*
Steve Crandall,
Brittany Crandall, *Analyst*
▲ EMP: 200
SALES (est): 23.4MM **Privately Held**
WEB: www.dbbrewingcompany.com
SIC: 2082 7371 Malt beverages; computer software development & applications

(G-7405)
MTN MAN WELDING
1460 Blacks Creek Rd (24450-6711)
PHONE.................................540 463-9352
EMP: 1
SALES (est): 44.2K **Privately Held**
SIC: 7692 Welding repair

(G-7406)
NAPOLEON BOOKS
616 Little Dry Holw (24450-6936)
PHONE.................................540 463-6804
Roberta Wiener, *Owner*
James R Arnold, *Co-Owner*
▲ EMP: 2
SALES (est): 12K **Privately Held**
WEB: www.napoleonbooks.com
SIC: 2731 7389 Book publishing; business services

(G-7407)
NEW STUDENT CHRONICLE
308 Jackson Ave (24450-2010)
PHONE.................................540 463-4000
James Worth, *Principal*
EMP: 3

GEOGRAPHIC

SALES (est): 113.5K **Privately Held**
SIC: 2711 Newspapers, publishing & printing

(G-7408)
NEWS-GAZETTE CORPORATION
Also Called: News Gazette Print Shop
109 S Jefferson St (24450-2026)
PHONE.............................540 463-3116
Matt Paxton, *Owner*
EMP: 30
SALES (corp-wide): 1.1MM **Privately Held**
WEB: www.thenews-gazette.com
SIC: 2711 Newspapers, publishing & printing
PA: The News-Gazette Corporation
　20 W Nelson St
　Lexington VA
　540 463-3113

(G-7409)
OAXACA EMBROIDERY LLC
104 Johnstone St (24450-1818)
PHONE.............................540 463-3808
Rolland Moore, *Principal*
EMP: 1 EST: 2012
SALES (est): 46.6K **Privately Held**
WEB: www.oaxacaembroidery.com
SIC: 2395 Embroidery & art needlework

(G-7410)
ONLINE PUBLISHING & MKTG LLC
1545 N Lee Hwy Ste 4 (24450-3449)
P.O. Box 1076 (24450-1076)
PHONE.............................540 463-2057
Joe Ackerson, *Office Mgr*
Lee Euler, *Mng Member*
EMP: 7 EST: 2009
SALES (est): 434.8K **Privately Held**
WEB: www.cancerdefeated.com
SIC: 2741 Miscellaneous publishing

(G-7411)
PAINTER MACHINE SHOP INC
170 Turkey Hill Rd (24450-3436)
PHONE.............................540 463-5854
Mark Painter, *President*
EMP: 1 EST: 1978
SALES (est): 231.8K **Privately Held**
WEB: www.indusprayusa.com
SIC: 3599 Machine shop, jobbing & repair

(G-7412)
PRESS ENDURING
14 Link Rd (24450-2204)
PHONE.............................540 462-2920
David Shreve, *Principal*
EMP: 2
SALES (est): 114.6K **Privately Held**
WEB: www.enduringpress.com
SIC: 2741 Miscellaneous publishing

(G-7413)
RAILS END WOOD & MET CRAFTERS
227 Mclaughlin St (24450-2001)
PHONE.............................540 463-9565
J Mark Jones, *Owner*
EMP: 4 EST: 1974
SQ FT: 3,700
SALES (est): 250K **Privately Held**
SIC: 7692 Welding repair

(G-7414)
RAMSEY BROTHERS LOGGING INC
935 Sugar Creek Rd (24450-6218)
P.O. Box 1325 (24450-1325)
PHONE.............................540 463-5044
Larry Ramsey, *Principal*
EMP: 3
SALES (est): 315.4K **Privately Held**
SIC: 2411 Logging camps & contractors

(G-7415)
RICK ROBBINS BAMBOO FLY RODS
974 Sugar Creek Rd (24450-6218)
PHONE.............................540 463-2864
Rick Robbins, *Principal*
EMP: 2

SALES (est): 130K **Privately Held**
WEB: www.rickrobbinsbambooflyrods.com
SIC: 3949 Rods & rod parts, fishing

(G-7416)
SHENANDOAH SPECIALTY PUBG LLC (PA)
Also Called: Shenandoah Valley Guide
158 S Main St (24450-2316)
P.O. Box 2425, Staunton (24402-2425)
PHONE.............................540 463-2319
Patricia F Gibson, *Publisher*
James Putbrest,
Robert Hubbard,
Eric Mogensen,
James Putbrese,
EMP: 8
SQ FT: 1,200
SALES (est): 240K **Privately Held**
WEB: www.shenandoahvalleyguide.com
SIC: 2721 7374 Magazines: publishing & printing; computer graphics service

(G-7417)
SHUMATE INC GEORGE C
81 Tranquility Ln (24450-3640)
PHONE.............................540 463-2244
George C Shumate, *President*
EMP: 32
SQ FT: 4,000
SALES (est): 8MM **Privately Held**
SIC: 2426 2421 2411 Lumber, hardwood dimension; sawmills & planing mills, general; logging

(G-7418)
SUGAR SPRING PRESS
802 Sunset Dr (24450-1842)
PHONE.............................540 463-4094
Cleveland Hickman, *Professor*
EMP: 1 EST: 2012
SALES (est): 56.9K **Privately Held**
WEB: www.galapagosmarine.com
SIC: 2741 Miscellaneous publishing

(G-7419)
TALMADGE FIX
Also Called: Cherrywood
1402 Mountain View Rd (24450-3214)
PHONE.............................540 463-9629
Talmadge Fix, *Owner*
EMP: 1
SALES (est): 60K **Privately Held**
WEB: www.cherrywoodshop.com
SIC: 2434 Wood kitchen cabinets

(G-7420)
TUMBLEWEED LLC
80 Forge Rd (24450-5830)
PHONE.............................540 261-7404
Keith Holland, *Partner*
EMP: 2
SALES (est): 126.3K **Privately Held**
SIC: 3089 Tumblers, plastic

(G-7421)
UNDER RADAR LLC
409 Honeysuckle Hl (24450-1721)
PHONE.............................540 348-8996
Quinton Robinson Wm, *Principal*
EMP: 3
SALES (est): 122.5K **Privately Held**
SIC: 2721 Magazines: publishing & printing

(G-7422)
W R DEACON & SONS TIMBER INC
209 Sawmill Ln (24450-6817)
PHONE.............................540 463-3832
W R Deacon, *President*
Jerry Deacon, *Corp Secy*
Philip W Deacon, *Vice Pres*
Stuart Deacon, *Vice Pres*
EMP: 27 EST: 1974
SQ FT: 1,600
SALES (est): 4.6MM **Privately Held**
SIC: 2421 2426 Sawmills & planing mills, general; hardwood dimension & flooring mills

(G-7423)
WEBSAUCE SOFTWARE LLC
20 W Washington St (24450-2100)
PHONE.............................540 319-4002
Stephen Steiner, *Engineer*

Steve Steiner,
EMP: 2
SALES (est): 107.1K **Privately Held**
WEB: www.websaucesoftware.com
SIC: 7372 Business oriented computer software

(G-7424)
WEST MIDLAND TIMBER LLC
4370 W Midland Trl (24450-6467)
PHONE.............................540 570-5969
Matthew Spencer,
Paul Fox,
EMP: 2 EST: 2013
SALES (est): 131.7K **Privately Held**
SIC: 2411 Logging

Lignum
Culpeper County

(G-7425)
JSD MILL WORK LLC
24022 Batna Rd (22726-1914)
PHONE.............................703 863-7183
Hakam M Abu-Gharbieh, *Administration*
EMP: 2
SALES (est): 115.7K **Privately Held**
SIC: 2431 Millwork

(G-7426)
WINN INDUSTRIES LLC
22037 Jacobs Ford Rd (22726-2158)
PHONE.............................571 334-2676
Steven Michael Winn, *Administration*
EMP: 2 EST: 2016
SALES (est): 110.2K **Privately Held**
SIC: 3999 Manufacturing industries

Linden
Warren County

(G-7427)
CONVERGENT CROSSFIT
698 Jonathan Rd (22642-6043)
PHONE.............................703 385-5400
EMP: 2
SALES (est): 101.6K **Privately Held**
WEB: www.convergentcrossfit.com
SIC: 3674 Semiconductors & related devices

(G-7428)
FOX MEADOW FARMS LLC
3310 Freezeland Rd (22642-5368)
PHONE.............................540 636-6777
Robert Mortland, *Principal*
EMP: 1
SALES (est): 135.2K **Privately Held**
WEB: www.foxmeadowwinery.com
SIC: 2084 Wines

(G-7429)
JOHN M RUSSELL
139 Henry Way (22642-5133)
PHONE.............................540 622-6281
John M Russell, *Owner*
EMP: 1
SALES (est): 100K **Privately Held**
WEB: www.johnmrussell.com
SIC: 3944 Craft & hobby kits & sets

(G-7430)
LAURET COMPANY
13386 John Marshall Hwy (22642-1732)
PHONE.............................540 635-1670
Katie Sullivan, *Partner*
William Sullivan, *Partner*
EMP: 3
SALES (est): 191.7K **Privately Held**
SIC: 3914 Pewter ware

(G-7431)
LINDEN WOODWORK LLC
60 Redmile Ct (22642-5618)
PHONE.............................540 636-3345
Leslie Williamosn, *Principal*
EMP: 4
SALES (est): 457.6K **Privately Held**
SIC: 2431 Millwork

(G-7432)
QUARLES FOOD STOP
4697 John Marshall Hwy (22642-6501)
PHONE.............................540 635-1899
Rose Hicks, *Principal*
EMP: 3
SALES (est): 121.5K **Privately Held**
SIC: 2099 Food preparations

(G-7433)
STRONG OAKS WOODSHOP
847 Jonathan Rd (22642-6041)
PHONE.............................540 683-2316
Mike Schmiedicke, *Principal*
EMP: 3
SALES (est): 333.7K **Privately Held**
WEB: www.strongoakswoodshop.com
SIC: 2499 Decorative wood & woodwork

Linville
Rockingham County

(G-7434)
COUNTRY WOOD CRAFTS
Also Called: Country Woodcrafts
8997 Mount Zion Rd (22834-2602)
PHONE.............................540 833-4985
Lowell Haarer, *Owner*
EMP: 1
SALES (est): 66.6K **Privately Held**
SIC: 3489 Guns or gun parts, over 30 mm.

(G-7435)
JOGLEX CORPORATION
5239 Williamsburg Rd (22834-2202)
PHONE.............................540 833-2444
John E Hostetler, *President*
Janet Hospetler, *Corp Secy*
Peter Hostetler, *Admin Sec*
EMP: 3
SALES (est): 500K **Privately Held**
WEB: www.joglex-corporation.linville.va.amfibi.company
SIC: 3523 1542 Cattle feeding, handling & watering equipment; nonresidential construction

(G-7436)
VALLEY PROTEINS INC
6230 Kratzer Rd (22834-2359)
PHONE.............................540 833-6641
Roger Vance, *Plant Mgr*
Gary Nolt, *Safety Mgr*
Kim Spitzer, *Purch Mgr*
Hobie Halterman, *Manager*
Garry Hassett, *Manager*
EMP: 75
SALES (corp-wide): 501.1MM **Privately Held**
WEB: www.valleyproteins.com
SIC: 2048 2077 Poultry feeds; animal & marine fats & oils
PA: Valley Proteins (De), Inc.
　151 Valpro Dr
　Winchester VA 22603
　540 877-2533

(G-7437)
VALLEY PROTEINS INC
6331 Val Pro Dr (22834-2321)
PHONE.............................540 833-8322
Hobie Halterman, *Manager*
Alan Holland, *Manager*
EMP: 100
SALES (corp-wide): 501.1MM **Privately Held**
WEB: www.valleyproteins.com
SIC: 2048 Poultry feeds
PA: Valley Proteins (De), Inc.
　151 Valpro Dr
　Winchester VA 22603
　540 877-2533

(G-7438)
WELDING UNLIMITED
6220 Grist Mill Rd (22834-2408)
PHONE.............................540 833-4146
Rachel Fitzwater, *Principal*
EMP: 1
SALES (est): 47.3K **Privately Held**
SIC: 7692 Welding repair

▲ = Import ▼ =Export
◆ =Import/Export

Lively
Lancaster County

(G-7439)
BAY ETCHING & IMPRINTING INC
Also Called: Arton Glass & Crmic Decorators
43 Lively Oaks Rd (22507)
PHONE..................................800 925-2877
Arthur Roberts, *President*
Maureen Roberts, *Vice Pres*
Lisa Roman, *Sales Mgr*
Mary McCloud, *Manager*
EMP: 25
SALES (est): 3.9MM **Privately Held**
WEB: www.artonproducts.com
SIC: 3231 2396 Decorated glassware:
chipped, engraved, etched, etc.; automotive & apparel trimmings

Locust Dale
Madison County

(G-7440)
CASTLE GRUEN VNYRDS WINERY LLC
1272 Meander Run Rd (22948-4810)
PHONE..................................540 229-2498
Jeanne Gruenburg, *Principal*
EMP: 5 EST: 2007
SALES (est): 338.5K **Privately Held**
WEB: www.castlegruenwinery.com
SIC: 2084 Wines

Locust Grove
Orange County

(G-7441)
BRITE LITE INC
205 Monticello Cir (22508-5638)
P.O. Box 249 (22508-0249)
PHONE..................................540 972-0212
Marlene E Passmore, *Principal*
EMP: 2
SALES (est): 142.5K **Privately Held**
WEB: www.britelitegas.com
SIC: 3648 Gas lighting fixtures

(G-7442)
CUSTOM CABINET WORKS
223 Battlefield Rd (22508-5717)
PHONE..................................540 972-1734
EMP: 1 EST: 1989
SALES (est): 85.4K **Privately Held**
SIC: 3553 Cabinet makers' machinery

(G-7443)
CUSTOM COMPUTER SOFTWARE
135 Green St (22508-5444)
PHONE..................................540 972-3027
James Hopkins, *Owner*
Jim Hopkins, *Director*
EMP: 1
SALES (est): 65K **Privately Held**
WEB: www.jimhopkins.com
SIC: 7372 Prepackaged software

(G-7444)
GOLD CANYON CANDLES
104 Hillside Dr (22508-5233)
PHONE..................................540 972-1266
Alayna Stiffler, *Manager*
EMP: 1
SALES (est): 53.6K **Privately Held**
WEB: www.lovefreecandles.com
SIC: 3999 Candles

(G-7445)
GRIT PACK CALLS LLC/GP CALLS L
34435 Parker Rd (22508-2934)
PHONE..................................540 735-5391
Teddy Carr Carr, *Principal*
EMP: 2
SALES (est): 117.8K **Privately Held**
WEB: www.gpcalls.com
SIC: 3949 Sporting & athletic goods

(G-7446)
HORSEMANS KNIVES LLC
6317 Louisianna Rd (22508-2734)
PHONE..................................540 854-6975
Michael Zummo,
EMP: 1
SALES (est): 74.5K **Privately Held**
WEB: www.horsemansknives.com
SIC: 3421 Knife blades & blanks

(G-7447)
LARRY GRAVES
Also Called: AB
1514 Lakeview Pkwy (22508-5318)
PHONE..................................540 972-5320
Larry Graves, *Owner*
EMP: 1 EST: 2010
SALES (est): 61.9K **Privately Held**
SIC: 2759 Security certificates: engraved

(G-7448)
MICHAEL NEELY
225 Washington St (22508-5137)
PHONE..................................540 972-3265
EMP: 2
SALES (est): 149.5K **Privately Held**
SIC: 3993 Mfg Signs/Advertising Specialties

(G-7449)
MID ATLANTIC SOLID SURFACE
124 Republic Ave (22508-5146)
PHONE..................................540 972-3050
EMP: 2
SALES (est): 130K **Privately Held**
SIC: 2541 Mfg Wood Partitions/Fixtures

(G-7450)
POISONED PUBLISHING
407 Birchside Cir (22508-5440)
PHONE..................................540 755-2956
EMP: 2
SALES (est): 59.2K **Privately Held**
SIC: 2741 Miscellaneous publishing

(G-7451)
SOUTH WINDS BINDERY LLC
30521 Mine Run Rd (22508-9605)
PHONE..................................540 661-7637
Anna Sawyer,
EMP: 1 EST: 2015
SALES (est): 70.1K **Privately Held**
WEB: www.southwindsbindery.com
SIC: 2789 Bookbinding & repairing: trade, edition, library, etc.

(G-7452)
SURE SITE SATELLITE INC
31350 Zoar Rd (22508-2503)
P.O. Box 280 (22508-0280)
PHONE..................................540 948-5880
Devin Van Lieu, *President*
Katie E Van Lieu, *Admin Sec*
EMP: 6
SALES (est): 416.6K **Privately Held**
WEB: www.suresitesatellite.com
SIC: 3663 Satellites, communications

Locust Hill
Middlesex County

(G-7453)
JD GORDON TOOL COMPANY LLC
139 Bennett Crest Dr (23092-9748)
PHONE..................................804 832-9907
Jason D Gordon,
EMP: 2 EST: 2015
SALES (est): 108.4K **Privately Held**
SIC: 3599 Industrial machinery

(G-7454)
SIMPLY CLSSIC CBNETS CNSTR LLC
137 Heron Ct (23092-9724)
PHONE..................................804 815-3283
Rebecca Eanes,
EMP: 3
SALES (est): 190.4K **Privately Held**
SIC: 2434 Wood kitchen cabinets

(G-7455)
SUTHERLINS LOGGING INC
Rr 619 (23092)
P.O. Box 202, Hartfield (23071-0202)
PHONE..................................804 366-3871
Thomas Sutherlin, *President*
Thomas Sutherlins, *President*
Linda Sutherlins, *Admin Sec*
EMP: 3
SALES (est): 700K **Privately Held**
SIC: 2411 Logging camps & contractors

Lorton
Fairfax County

(G-7456)
5TH ELEMENT CO
8534 Terminal Rd (22079-1428)
PHONE..................................800 684-3144
EMP: 4 EST: 2018
SALES (est): 261.5K **Privately Held**
SIC: 2819 Industrial inorganic chemicals

(G-7457)
AB LIGHTING AND PRODUCTION LLC
8249 Backlick Rd Ste F (22079-1464)
PHONE..................................703 550-7707
Fred Elting, *Principal*
Mutsa Elting, *Info Tech Mgr*
EMP: 5 EST: 2011
SALES (est): 651.4K **Privately Held**
SIC: 3534 Escalators, passenger & freight

(G-7458)
ACTION MACHINING
7240 Telegraph Square Dr (22079-1557)
PHONE..................................703 339-7232
Jeff Drake, *Owner*
EMP: 1
SQ FT: 1,500
SALES (est): 139.4K **Privately Held**
WEB: www.actionmachining.net
SIC: 3599 Machine shop, jobbing & repair

(G-7459)
ALEXANDRIA COATINGS LLC
Also Called: Alexandria Metal Finishers
9418 Gunston Cove Rd (22079-2314)
PHONE..................................703 643-1636
Walter Prichard, *President*
Larry Capoccia, *Vice Pres*
Greg Prichard,
EMP: 40
SQ FT: 46,000
SALES (est): 4.7MM **Privately Held**
WEB: www.alexandriametalfinishers.com
SIC: 3471 Electroplating of metals or formed products

(G-7460)
ALPACA + KNITWEAR
8257 Singleleaf Ln (22079-5635)
PHONE..................................703 994-3346
Rosa Estevez, *Principal*
EMP: 2
SALES (est): 96.5K **Privately Held**
SIC: 2231 Alpacas, mohair: woven

(G-7461)
AMPAK SPORTSWEAR INC
8253 Backlick Rd Ste B (22079-1463)
PHONE..................................703 550-1300
Salim Raza, *President*
EMP: 5
SQ FT: 1,800
SALES (est): 382.4K **Privately Held**
WEB: www.ampaksportswear.com
SIC: 2395 Embroidery products, except schiffli machine

(G-7462)
ANSEAL INC
8532u Terminal Rd (22079-1428)
PHONE..................................571 642-0680
Alejandro Soto, *President*
EMP: 3
SALES (est): 200K **Privately Held**
SIC: 3281 Cut stone & stone products

(G-7463)
ANTONIO PUDUCAY
Also Called: Epic Band
8179 Douglas Fir Dr (22079-5656)
PHONE..................................703 927-2953
Antonio Puducay, *Owner*
EMP: 6
SALES (est): 200K **Privately Held**
SIC: 3931 Synthesizers, music

(G-7464)
B & G STAINLESS WORKS INC
8538 Terminal Rd Ste Hjk (22079-1428)
PHONE..................................703 339-6002
Isaac Gonzalez, *President*
EMP: 7
SQ FT: 4,500
SALES: 367.8K **Privately Held**
WEB: www.bgstainlessworks.com
SIC: 3444 7692 Sheet metalwork; welding repair

(G-7465)
BARNETT CONSULTING LLC
9253 Plaskett Ln (22079-2925)
PHONE..................................703 655-1635
James Barnett,
EMP: 1
SALES (est): 73.1K **Privately Held**
WEB: www.thomaspmbarnett.com
SIC: 3812 Search & navigation equipment

(G-7466)
BENSON FINE WOODCRAFTING LLC
10842 Greene Dr (22079-3530)
PHONE..................................703 372-1871
Jonathan Benson,
EMP: 1
SALES (est): 120K **Privately Held**
WEB: www.bensonfinewoodcrafting.com
SIC: 2499 Wood products

(G-7467)
BILTCO LLC
7402 Lockport Pl Ste C (22079-1575)
PHONE..................................703 372-5940
Luis F Lamas, *Principal*
EMP: 1 EST: 2008
SALES (est): 185.5K **Privately Held**
WEB: www.biltco-us.com
SIC: 2499 Decorative wood & woodwork

(G-7468)
BOTTLING GROUP LLC
Also Called: Pepsico
8550 Terminal Rd (22079-1428)
PHONE..................................703 339-5640
EMP: 14
SALES (corp-wide): 67.1B **Publicly Held**
WEB: www.pepsico.com
SIC: 2086 Carbonated soft drinks, bottled & canned
HQ: Bottling Group, Llc
   1111 Westchester Ave
   White Plains NY 10604
   914 253-2000

(G-7469)
CANAAN WELDING LLC
Also Called: Vortex Iron Works
7002 Newington Rd Ste A (22079-1148)
PHONE..................................703 339-7799
Seung Hyun Kim, *Mng Member*
EMP: 7 EST: 2019
SALES (est): 128.1K **Privately Held**
WEB: www.vortexiw.com
SIC: 7692 Welding repair

(G-7470)
CAPITAL SCREEN PRTG UNLIMITED
Also Called: CSP Unlimited
8382 Terminal Rd Ste A (22079-1422)
P.O. Box 251, Newington (22122-0251)
PHONE..................................703 550-0033
Mohammad Zakir, *President*
EMP: 6
SQ FT: 25,000
SALES (est): 649.1K **Privately Held**
SIC: 2759 2752 2395 7336 Screen printing; commercial printing, offset; embroidery & art needlework; commercial art & graphic design

(G-7471)
CHEFIT LLC
9151 Furey Rd (22079-2966)
PHONE..........................202 769-6049
Travis Coleman,
EMP: 1
SALES (est): 39.5K Privately Held
SIC: 2099 Food preparations

(G-7472)
CHEMTRON INC (PA)
7350 Lockport Pl Ste C (22079-1573)
P.O. Box 383 (22199-0383)
PHONE..........................703 550-7772
Blake Young, President
Shannon Young, Corp Secy
William Easley Smith, Vice Pres
EMP: 9
SQ FT: 20,000
SALES (est): 2.9MM Privately Held
WEB: www.chemtroninc.com
SIC: 2842 2841 Laundry cleaning preparations; soap & other detergents

(G-7473)
CIRCLEPOINT PUBLISHING LLC
10824 Anita Dr (22079-3520)
PHONE..........................703 339-1580
EMP: 2 EST: 2008
SALES (est): 110K Privately Held
SIC: 2741 Misc Publishing

(G-7474)
CLOSET PIONEERS LLC
7300 Lockport Pl Ste 11 (22079-1572)
PHONE..........................703 844-0400
EMP: 1
SALES (est): 59.5K Privately Held
WEB: www.closetpioneers.com
SIC: 2431 Millwork

(G-7475)
COLD FRONT MUSIC LLC
7317 Ardglass Dr (22079-1547)
PHONE..........................703 398-6187
Tony Craddock Jr, Principal
EMP: 2 EST: 2018
SALES (est): 80.7K Privately Held
WEB: www.tonycraddockjr.com
SIC: 2741 Miscellaneous publishing

(G-7476)
CONFERO FOODS LLC
8176 Mccauley Way (22079-2970)
PHONE..........................703 334-7516
Hector Quinteros,
▲ EMP: 2
SALES (est): 140.9K Privately Held
SIC: 2032 Spanish foods: packaged in cans, jars, etc.

(G-7477)
CONSERVTION RESOURCES INTL LLC
7350 Lockport Pl Ste A (22079-1573)
PHONE..........................703 321-7730
William Hollinger, President
Lavonia Hollinger, Vice Pres
Rob Hull, Train & Dev Mgr
EMP: 20
SALES (est): 5.7MM Privately Held
WEB: www.conservationresources.com
SIC: 2679 Pressed & molded pulp products, purchased material

(G-7478)
DDK GROUP LLC
8115 Bluebonnet Dr (22079-5630)
PHONE..........................201 726-2535
Dahesh A Khalil, Mng Member
EMP: 2 EST: 2014
SQ FT: 2,000
SALES (est): 350K Privately Held
SIC: 3944 Automobiles & trucks, toy

(G-7479)
DELONG LITHOGRAPHICS SERVICES
7205 Lockport Pl Ste D (22079-1533)
P.O. Box 1529 (22199-1529)
PHONE..........................703 550-2110
Fred J Delong, President
Marcia Delong, Vice Pres
Steve Delong, Treasurer
EMP: 6
SQ FT: 3,150
SALES (est): 500K Privately Held
WEB: www.delonglitho.com
SIC: 2752 Commercial printing, offset

(G-7480)
DELULLO SOFTWARE LLC
8528 Blue Rock Ln (22079-3063)
PHONE..........................570 419-6736
Anthony Delullo, Principal
EMP: 2
SALES (est): 101.7K Privately Held
WEB: www.tonyandjoanie.com
SIC: 7372 Prepackaged software

(G-7481)
DISCOUNT FRAMES INC (PA)
Also Called: Adlers Art & Frame
7200 Telegraph Square Dr (22079-1551)
PHONE..........................703 550-0000
Ron Adler, President
EMP: 4
SQ FT: 3,000
SALES (est): 3.7MM Privately Held
WEB: www.adlersartandframe.com
SIC: 2499 5999 Picture & mirror frames, wood; art, picture frames & decorations

(G-7482)
E-TRON SYSTEMS INC
Also Called: Wild Flour Bread Mill
9406 Gunston Cove Rd F (22079-2301)
PHONE..........................703 690-2731
James Rogan, Director
▲ EMP: 40
SQ FT: 5,000
SALES: 2.1MM Privately Held
WEB: www.etronsystems.com
SIC: 3679 5461 Electronic circuits; bakeries

(G-7483)
EARTH SCIENCE TECHNOLOGY LLC
6747 Newington Rd (22079-1111)
PHONE..........................703 584-8533
Colin Cookes, Director
Kurt Kleess, Director
EMP: 2 EST: 2015
SALES (est): 138.7K Privately Held
SIC: 3829 7389 Geophysical or meteorological electronic equipment; business services

(G-7484)
ELITE DEFENSE INC
6823 Silver Ann Dr (22079-1311)
PHONE..........................703 339-0749
Joseph Darling, Principal
EMP: 2
SALES (est): 157K Privately Held
WEB: www.elitedefenseinc.com
SIC: 3812 Defense systems & equipment

(G-7485)
EVANS CORPORATE SERVICES LLC
7985 Almeda Ct (22079-2363)
PHONE..........................703 344-3678
Michael Evans,
Tawanna Evans,
EMP: 10
SALES (est): 1.2MM Privately Held
WEB: www.evanscorporateservices.com
SIC: 2522 2531 4214 Office furniture, except wood; panel systems & partitions, office: except wood; public building & related furniture; furniture moving & storage, local

(G-7486)
EXTREME POWDER COATING LLC
8384b Terminal Rd (22079-1422)
PHONE..........................703 339-8233
Gary Lamb, Owner
EMP: 2
SALES (est): 223.3K Privately Held
WEB: www.extremepowdercoating.com
SIC: 3479 Coating of metals & formed products

(G-7487)
FALCK SCHMIDT DEF SYSTEMS CORP
Also Called: Corporation Trust Co, The
8534f Terminal Rd (22079-1428)
PHONE..........................805 689-1739
Joseph M Blanco, CFO
EMP: 5
SALES (est): 419.4K Privately Held
SIC: 3443 Missile silos & components, metal plate

(G-7488)
FED REACH INC
9024 Haywood Ave (22079-3248)
PHONE..........................703 507-8822
A Zaman Khan, President
EMP: 1
SALES (est): 250K Privately Held
WEB: www.fedreach.com
SIC: 3571 Electronic computers

(G-7489)
FIGURE ENGINEERING LLC
8580 Cinder Bed Rd # 1000 (22079-1489)
PHONE..........................540 818-5034
Loren Edwards,
EMP: 2
SALES (est): 312.2K Privately Held
WEB: www.figureengineering.com
SIC: 3444 Sheet metalwork

(G-7490)
FMD LLC
7200 Telegraph Square Dr (22079-1551)
P.O. Box 1500 (22199-1500)
PHONE..........................703 339-8881
Yousry Faragalla,
EMP: 6
SQ FT: 4,200
SALES (est): 793.1K Privately Held
WEB: www.fmdco.com
SIC: 3841 Medical instruments & equipment, blood & bone work

(G-7491)
GOOATS LLC
8538 Terminal Rd Ste O (22079-1428)
PHONE..........................267 997-7789
Nahum Jeannot, Mng Member
EMP: 1
SQ FT: 5,000
SALES (est): 43.5K Privately Held
WEB: www.gooats.life
SIC: 2043 Oatmeal: prepared as cereal breakfast food

(G-7492)
HAWKINS GLASS WHOLESALERS LLC
9712 Gunston Cove Rd J (22079-2374)
PHONE..........................703 372-2990
Brad Kingsbury, Sales Staff
Jason Rickards, Manager
Virgil L Smith,
Mary Agnes Smith,
Mary Smith,
EMP: 48 EST: 1957
SQ FT: 70,000
SALES (est): 8.2MM Privately Held
WEB: www.hawkinsglass.com
SIC: 3211 3231 3083 3711 Laminated glass; structural glass; products of purchased glass; plastic finished products, laminated; cars, armored, assembly of

(G-7493)
HILLTOP SAND AND GRAVEL CO INC
8245 Backlick Rd Ste D2 (22079-1462)
PHONE..........................571 322-0389
William A Fritz Jr, Branch Mgr
EMP: 3
SALES (corp-wide): 4.9MM Privately Held
WEB: www.hilltoplandfill.com
SIC: 1442 Construction sand & gravel
PA: Hilltop Sand And Gravel Company, Incorporated
7950 Telegraph Rd
Alexandria VA 22315
571 322-0392

(G-7494)
I & I SLING INC
7403 Lockport Pl Ste A (22079-1153)
PHONE..........................703 550-9405
Salina Hill, Manager
EMP: 4
SALES (corp-wide): 19.7MM Privately Held
WEB: www.iandisling.com
SIC: 3496 Miscellaneous fabricated wire products
PA: I & I Sling, Inc.
205 Bridgewater Rd
Aston PA 19014
610 485-8500

(G-7495)
IMPRINT ID LTD
7960 Conell Ct (22079-1013)
PHONE..........................877 385-7785
EMP: 2
SALES (est): 180.5K Privately Held
WEB: www.imprintid.com
SIC: 2759 Commercial printing

(G-7496)
INKWELL DUCK INC
7607 Surry Grove Ct (22079-1705)
PHONE..........................703 550-1344
Tracey Wood, President
EMP: 1
SALES (est): 65K Privately Held
WEB: www.inkwellduck.com
SIC: 2752 Commercial printing, lithographic

(G-7497)
ITI GROUP
8245 Backlick Rd Ste D (22079-1462)
PHONE..........................703 339-5388
Bill Wong, CEO
EMP: 2
SALES (est): 125.1K Privately Held
SIC: 2899 Chemical preparations

(G-7498)
ITT LLC
6012 Chapman Rd (22079-4138)
PHONE..........................703 550-2594
Allison Mills, Branch Mgr
EMP: 6 Publicly Held
WEB: www.itt.com
SIC: 3625 Control equipment, electric
HQ: Itt Llc
1133 Westchester Ave N-100
White Plains NY 10604
914 641-2000

(G-7499)
JIMS ELECTRIC MOTOR CO INC
8811 Telegraph Rd (22079-1530)
PHONE..........................703 550-8624
James L Still, President
EMP: 15
SQ FT: 12,500
SALES (est): 2.2MM Privately Held
WEB: www.jimselectricmotor.com
SIC: 7694 1731 5063 Electric motor repair; electrical work; motors, electric

(G-7500)
KANAN WELDING
8538 Terminal Rd (22079-1428)
PHONE..........................703 339-7799
Sung Kim, Owner
EMP: 2
SALES (est): 73.3K Privately Held
SIC: 7692 Welding repair

(G-7501)
KASHAF SPICES INC
10595 Furnace Rd (22079-2638)
PHONE..........................703 232-3529
EMP: 3 EST: 2018
SALES (est): 154.8K Privately Held
SIC: 2099 Food preparations

(G-7502)
KIBELA PRINT LLC
7464 Wounded Knee Rd (22079-1854)
PHONE..........................703 436-1646
Ivaylo Mechkarov,
EMP: 1 EST: 2015

▲ = Import ▼=Export
◆ =Import/Export

SALES (est): 105.6K **Privately Held**
WEB: www.kibelaprint.com
SIC: 2752 Commercial printing, offset; promotional printing, lithographic; business form & card printing, lithographic

(G-7503)
KRYSTAL CLEAR
8865 Cherokee Rose Way (22079-5633)
PHONE....................................703 944-2066
Waleed Osman, *Principal*
EMP: 2
SALES (est): 18K **Privately Held**
SIC: 2842 Specialty cleaning, polishes & sanitation goods

(G-7504)
LEGACY VULCAN LLC
Mideast Division
10000 Ox Rd (22079-3433)
P.O. Box E, Occoquan (22125-0135)
PHONE....................................703 690-1172
Mark Doebel, *Plant Mgr*
Jim Cooter, *Branch Mgr*
John Hurst, *Maintence Staff*
EMP: 45 **Publicly Held**
WEB: www.vulcanmaterials.com
SIC: 1442 Construction sand & gravel
HQ: Legacy Vulcan, Llc
1200 Urban Center Dr
Vestavia AL 35242
205 298-3000

(G-7505)
LEGACY VULCAN LLC
8402 Terminal Rd (22079-1424)
PHONE....................................800 732-3964
EMP: 2 **Publicly Held**
SIC: 3273 Ready-mixed concrete
HQ: Legacy Vulcan, Llc
1200 Urban Center Dr
Vestavia AL 35242
205 298-3000

(G-7506)
LEGACY VULCAN LLC
8413 Terminal Rd Q (22079-1425)
PHONE....................................800 732-3964
EMP: 3 **Publicly Held**
WEB: www.vulcanmaterials.com
SIC: 3273 Ready-mixed concrete
HQ: Legacy Vulcan, Llc
1200 Urban Center Dr
Vestavia AL 35242
205 298-3000

(G-7507)
LIBERTY PRINTING HOUSE INC
7300 Lockport Pl Ste 2 (22079-1572)
PHONE....................................202 664-7702
Samer Zaiber, *President*
Ahmad Al-Sammarie, *Principal*
EMP: 4
SQ FT: 2,200
SALES (est): 311.8K **Privately Held**
WEB: www.libertyprintinghouse.com
SIC: 2752 Commercial printing, offset

(G-7508)
LOCKHEED MARTIN
10505 Furnace Rd Ste 101 (22079-2635)
PHONE....................................703 982-9008
Edwin Bouton, *Branch Mgr*
EMP: 100 **Publicly Held**
WEB: www.lockheedmartin.com
SIC: 3812 Search & navigation equipment
HQ: Lockheed Martin Integrated Systems, Llc
6801 Rockledge Dr
Bethesda MD 20817

(G-7509)
LORTON ENTERPRISES
8254 Laurel Heights Loop (22079-5650)
PHONE....................................703 725-2933
Erik Lorton, *Principal*
EMP: 3
SALES (est): 234K **Privately Held**
WEB: www.chaneyenterprises.com
SIC: 3273 Ready-mixed concrete

(G-7510)
M & S FABRICATORS
8249 Backlick Rd Ste G (22079-1464)
PHONE....................................703 550-3900

Frank Mc Lary, *Owner*
EMP: 2
SALES (est): 170K **Privately Held**
SIC: 3441 Fabricated structural metal

(G-7511)
MERRILL FINE ARTS ENGRV INC
Also Called: Fine Arts Engraving Company
8270 Cinder Bed Rd (22079-1102)
PHONE....................................703 339-3900
Fax: 703 339-1900
EMP: 25
SALES (corp-wide): 579.3MM **Privately Held**
SIC: 3479 Coating/Engraving Service
HQ: Merrill Fine Arts Engraving, Inc.
311 S Wacker Dr Ste 300
Chicago IL 60606
312 786-6300

(G-7512)
MOON CABINET INC
9022 Telegraph Rd Ste D (22079-1583)
PHONE....................................703 339-8097
EMP: 2 EST: 2007
SALES (est): 120K **Privately Held**
SIC: 2434 Mfg Wood Kitchen Cabinets

(G-7513)
NATIONWIDE LAMINATING INC
Also Called: Nationwide Laminating & Finshg
8208 Cinder Bed Rd Ste C (22079-1150)
P.O. Box 1267, Lexington (24450-1267)
PHONE....................................703 550-8400
Brian Hills, *President*
Reavis Swett, *Vice Pres*
Natalie Hills, *Treasurer*
Michael Hills, *Admin Sec*
EMP: 11
SQ FT: 10,000
SALES (est): 2.1MM **Privately Held**
WEB: www.nationwidelaminating.com
SIC: 3089 7389 Identification cards, plastic; laminating service

(G-7514)
NETSTYLE CORP
7960 Conell Ct (22079-1013)
PHONE....................................703 717-9706
Aminul Siddiqui, *Director*
▲ EMP: 2
SQ FT: 400
SALES (est): 106.4K **Privately Held**
SIC: 3999 Identification badges & insignia

(G-7515)
NEW HOME MEDIA
9408 Gunston Cove Rd E (22079-2302)
P.O. Box 1126 (22199-1126)
PHONE....................................703 550-2233
Charles B Smith Jr, *President*
Russ Steele, *Prdtn Mgr*
Debbie Blevins, *Accounting Dir*
Omar Ahmad, *Manager*
Lori Lewellyn, *Director*
EMP: 178
SALES (est): 22MM **Privately Held**
WEB: www.newhomemedia.net
SIC: 3993 1799 Signs, not made in custom sign painting shops; sign installation & maintenance

(G-7516)
NGUYEN & PHAN LLC
8220 Laurel Heights Loop (22079-5650)
PHONE....................................571 730-9948
Thanh Nguyen, *Principal*
EMP: 4 EST: 2013
SALES (est): 279.8K **Privately Held**
WEB: www.123cartao.com.br
SIC: 7372 Prepackaged software

(G-7517)
NHM INC
9408 Gunston Cove Rd E (22079-2302)
P.O. Box 1126 (22199-1126)
PHONE....................................703 550-2233
EMP: 5
SALES (est): 489.9K **Privately Held**
WEB: www.newhomemedia.net
SIC: 3993 Signs & advertising specialties

(G-7518)
NOMADIC DISPLAY LLC
10505 Furnace Rd Ste 108 (22079-2635)
PHONE....................................800 336-5019

Franklin Gaskins, *Principal*
EMP: 5
SALES (est): 309.9K **Privately Held**
WEB: www.nomadicdisplay.com
SIC: 3993 Signs & advertising specialties

(G-7519)
OPTIMIZE PRINT SOLUTIONS LLC
9435 Lorton Market St # 266 (22079-1963)
PHONE....................................703 856-7386
Rex Nowell, *Owner*
EMP: 2
SALES (est): 158.2K **Privately Held**
WEB: www.optimizeprintsolutions.com
SIC: 2752 Commercial printing, lithographic

(G-7520)
OPTX IMAGING SYSTEMS LLC
10716 Richmond Hwy # 201 (22079-2644)
PHONE....................................703 398-1432
Roy Littleton, *CEO*
Jay Vizgaitis, *Principal*
EMP: 15
SALES (est): 2.4MM **Privately Held**
WEB: www.optximaging.com
SIC: 3827 8711 Optical instruments & lenses; engineering services

(G-7521)
PONDECA INDUSTRIES INC
8807 Carpenters Hall Dr (22079-4719)
PHONE....................................703 599-4375
Lloyd Pondeca, *President*
EMP: 1
SALES (est): 39.6K **Privately Held**
SIC: 3999 Manufacturing industries

(G-7522)
PUZZLE CUTS LLC
8192 Mistletoe Ln (22079-5619)
PHONE....................................703 470-9333
EMP: 1
SALES (est): 41K **Privately Held**
WEB: www.puzzlecuts.com
SIC: 3944 Puzzles

(G-7523)
QINETIQ INC
Also Called: Technical Services Division
10440 Furnace Rd Ste 204 (22079-2630)
PHONE....................................540 658-2720
Mary Williams, *General Mgr*
Shannon Thornton, *Production*
Jorge Ortiz, *Branch Mgr*
Jacqueline Judge, *Sr Software Eng*
EMP: 35 **Privately Held**
WEB: www.us.qinetiq.com
SIC: 3679 8733 Harness assemblies for electronic use: wire or cable; physical research, noncommercial
HQ: Qinetiq Inc.
10440 Furnace Rd Ste 204
Lorton VA 22079

(G-7524)
QINETIQ INC (HQ)
Also Called: Mteq
10440 Furnace Rd Ste 204 (22079-2630)
PHONE....................................540 658-2720
Mary Williams, *President*
Greg Demeo, *General Mgr*
Gregory A Williams, *Senior VP*
Charles A Taylor, *Vice Pres*
Samuel Schack, *Project Mgr*
EMP: 40
SALES (est): 54.3MM **Privately Held**
WEB: www.us.qinetiq.com
SIC: 3679 8733 Harness assemblies for electronic use: wire or cable; physical research, noncommercial

(G-7525)
REAMCO INC
6826 Hill Park Dr (22079-1010)
PHONE....................................703 690-2000
Tom Edger, *Manager*
EMP: 3
SALES (est): 238.8K **Privately Held**
WEB: www.reamco.com
SIC: 3533 Oil & gas field machinery

(G-7526)
RIGGING BOX INC
8180 Newington Rd (22079-1130)
PHONE....................................703 339-7575
Selina Conrad, *President*
Dawn Walker, *Principal*
EMP: 9
SQ FT: 1,200
SALES (est): 1.3MM **Privately Held**
WEB: www.theriggingbox.com
SIC: 2298 Wire rope centers

(G-7527)
RONART ASSOCIATES
6805 Bulkley Rd (22079-1120)
PHONE....................................703 362-5373
Ronald R Douquette, *Owner*
EMP: 1
SALES (est): 99.7K **Privately Held**
SIC: 3679 Recording heads, speech & musical equipment

(G-7528)
SANI LLC
7361 Lockport Pl Ste D (22079-1595)
PHONE....................................703 596-2296
Belal Aljaradat, *Mng Member*
EMP: 5
SALES (est): 139.9K **Privately Held**
SIC: 2051 Bakery: wholesale or wholesale/retail combined

(G-7529)
SANITECH CORP (PA)
7207 Lockport Pl Ste H (22079-1534)
PHONE....................................703 339-7001
Bill Hannigan, *CEO*
Mano R Sharma, *President*
J R Bhalla, *Vice Pres*
William A Hannigan Jr, *Vice Pres*
Pradip Kar, *Vice Pres*
EMP: 30
SQ FT: 10,000
SALES (est): 6.4MM **Privately Held**
WEB: www.sanitechcorp.com
SIC: 3589 Commercial cleaning equipment

(G-7530)
SNOW HILL CLASSICS INC
6124 River Dr (22079-4124)
PHONE....................................703 339-6278
Diana York, *President*
James York, *Treasurer*
EMP: 2
SALES (est): 35K **Privately Held**
WEB: www.snowhillclassicsllc.exposuremanager.com
SIC: 2329 Athletic (warmup, sweat & jogging) suits: men's & boys'

(G-7531)
SNYDERS-LANCE INC
8900 Telegraph Rd Ste B (22079-1590)
PHONE....................................703 339-0541
Brian Reach, *Branch Mgr*
EMP: 282
SALES (corp-wide): 8.6B **Publicly Held**
WEB: www.snyderslance.com
SIC: 2052 Cookies
HQ: Snyder's-Lance, Inc.
13515 Balntyn Corp Pl
Charlotte NC 28277
704 554-1421

(G-7532)
SPRINGFIELD CUSTOM AUTO MCH
8532v Terminal Rd (22079-1428)
PHONE....................................703 339-0999
EMP: 3
SQ FT: 1,500
SALES (est): 340K **Privately Held**
SIC: 3764 Engine Parts Remanufacturer

(G-7533)
SRN SOFTWARE LLC
8608 Monacan Ct (22079-3093)
PHONE....................................703 646-5186
Sandeep Khosla, *Administration*
EMP: 2
SALES (est): 95.2K **Privately Held**
SIC: 7372 Prepackaged software

G E O G R A P H I C

(G-7534)
STATICE QUO LLC
8202 Catbird Cir Unit 101 (22079-4649)
PHONE..................................703 646-5411
Lori Craddock, *Principal*
EMP: 2 **EST:** 2012
SALES (est): 96.2K **Privately Held**
WEB: www.appalachianedie.com
SIC: 2084 Wines

(G-7535)
STONE DEPOT GRANITE
7300 Lockport Pl Ste 13 (22079-1572)
PHONE..................................703 926-3844
Julia Papalaskaris, *Owner*
EMP: 10
SALES (est): 742.4K **Privately Held**
WEB: www.stonedepotllc-va.com
SIC: 3281 Granite, cut & shaped

(G-7536)
TEK-AM CORP
7405 Lockport Pl Ste A (22079-1581)
PHONE..................................703 321-9144
Neil J Keefe, *President*
Sina Sabet, *General Mgr*
Bobbie Keefe, *Corp Secy*
EMP: 12
SQ FT: 5,000
SALES (est): 800K **Privately Held**
WEB: www.phoenixcompaniesllc.com
SIC: 3599 3444 Machine shop, jobbing & repair; sheet metalwork; forming machine work, sheet metal

(G-7537)
TERRENCE SMITH
9712 Gunston Cove Rd (22079-2373)
PHONE..................................703 339-2194
Terrence Smith, *Principal*
EMP: 1
SALES (est): 45.5K **Privately Held**
SIC: 3229 Glass fiber products

(G-7538)
VIET BAO INC
Also Called: Vb Printing
8394 Terminal Rd Ste C2 (22079-1432)
PHONE..................................703 339-9852
Suong Truong, *President*
Tuyen Giang, *President*
EMP: 4
SALES (est): 200K **Privately Held**
SIC: 2711 Newspapers, publishing & printing

(G-7539)
VILOQUINNE LLC
9246 Mccarty Rd (22079-2926)
PHONE..................................703 493-8864
Teniecia Robinson, *Principal*
EMP: 4
SALES (est): 340.2K **Privately Held**
WEB: www.viloquinne.com
SIC: 2844 Toilet preparations

(G-7540)
VINYLITE WINDOWS PRODUCTS INC
Also Called: Vinyl Lite Window Factory
8815 Telegraph Rd (22079-1530)
PHONE..................................703 550-7766
Michael Bouchery, *President*
Wayne Bouchery, *Vice Pres*
EMP: 37
SQ FT: 10,000
SALES (est): 7.6MM **Privately Held**
WEB: www.vinyl-lite.com
SIC: 3442 1751 5031 3231 Window & door frames; window & door (prefabricated) installation; lumber, plywood & millwork; products of purchased glass

(G-7541)
WF MED
8245 Backlick Rd Ste V (22079-1462)
PHONE..................................703 339-5388
EMP: 2
SALES (est): 112.8K **Privately Held**
WEB: www.wfmed.com
SIC: 3999 Candles

(G-7542)
WHISPER PRAYERS DAILY
9212 Marovelli Forest Dr (22079-3454)
PHONE..................................703 690-1184
Cynthia Snyder, *Principal*
EMP: 3
SALES (est): 76.2K **Privately Held**
SIC: 2711 Newspapers, publishing & printing

Lottsburg
Northumberland County

(G-7543)
LAKE PACKING CO INC
755 Lake Landing Dr (22511-2503)
PHONE..................................804 529-6101
Samuel Lake Cowart Sr, *President*
Samuel Lake Cowart Jr, *Vice Pres*
Mary B Cowart, *Treasurer*
Pat Basye, *Office Mgr*
Ellen W Cowart, *Asst Sec*
EMP: 15 **EST:** 1948
SQ FT: 60,000
SALES (est): 2.1MM **Privately Held**
WEB: www.manningshominy.com
SIC: 2033 2091 Hominy: packaged in cans, jars, etc.; herring: packaged in cans, jars, etc.

(G-7544)
THOMAS E LEWIS
2804 Lake Rd (22511-2510)
PHONE..................................804 529-7526
Thomas Lewis, *Owner*
EMP: 2
SALES (est): 70K **Privately Held**
SIC: 3999 Grasses, artificial & preserved

Louisa
Louisa County

(G-7545)
ALLIED BRASS INC
195 Duke St (23093-4142)
PHONE..................................540 967-5970
Robert Andris, *President*
▲ **EMP:** 40 **EST:** 1965
SQ FT: 35,000
SALES (est): 5.7MM **Privately Held**
WEB: www.alliedbrass.com
SIC: 3431 3432 Bathroom fixtures, including sinks; plumbing fixture fittings & trim

(G-7546)
BROCKS WELDING SERVICE
321 Lakeside Dr (23093-3159)
PHONE..................................540 967-3258
Brock Baker, *Owner*
EMP: 1
SALES (est): 200K **Privately Held**
WEB: www.brocksweldingservice.com
SIC: 7692 Welding repair

(G-7547)
BUSADA MANUFACTURING CORP
78 Rescue Ln (23093-4105)
PHONE..................................540 967-2882
Jean B Jones, *President*
John Busada, *Principal*
Charels J Busada, *Vice Pres*
Darrell Jones, *Vice Pres*
EMP: 11 **EST:** 1951
SQ FT: 20,000
SALES (est): 1.7MM **Privately Held**
WEB: www.busada.com
SIC: 3089 Injection molding of plastics

(G-7548)
C&S CUSTOM CABINETS INC
215 Cedar Creek Rd (23093-5025)
PHONE..................................540 273-5450
Weimer Marcia Nevins, *Admin Sec*
EMP: 3 **EST:** 2013
SALES (est): 194.8K **Privately Held**
SIC: 2434 Wood kitchen cabinets

(G-7549)
CENTURION TOOLS LLC
637 Industrial Dr (23093-4137)
PHONE..................................540 967-5402
Ken Fritz, *Vice Pres*
Fred Fitzsimmons,
Kenneth Fritz,
EMP: 10 **EST:** 1997
SQ FT: 5,000
SALES (est): 726K **Privately Held**
WEB: www.centuriontools.com
SIC: 3541 Machine tools, metal cutting type

(G-7550)
COOPER VINEYARDS LLC
13372 Shannon Hill Rd (23093-3929)
PHONE..................................540 894-5474
David Drillock,
EMP: 1
SALES (est): 119.4K **Privately Held**
WEB: www.coopervineyards.com
SIC: 2084 Wines

(G-7551)
CREATIVE DESIGNS LLC
1134 Kents Mill Rd (23093-5007)
PHONE..................................540 223-0083
Yvonne Agee,
EMP: 1
SALES (est): 115.8K **Privately Held**
SIC: 2759 Commercial printing

(G-7552)
CROSSROADS EXPRESS INC
358 Bybee Rd (23093-2815)
P.O. Box 1018, Troy (22974-1018)
PHONE..................................434 882-0320
James G Brochu Jr, *President*
EMP: 5
SALES (est): 402.7K **Privately Held**
SIC: 1442 Construction sand & gravel

(G-7553)
CROSSROADS FARRIER INC
67 Rollins Ln (23093-2861)
PHONE..................................434 589-4501
Jeff Denn, *Principal*
EMP: 3
SALES (est): 274.9K **Privately Held**
WEB: www.crossroadsfarriersupply.com
SIC: 3462 Horseshoes

(G-7554)
CV CORPORATION OF VIRGINIA (PA)
Also Called: Central Virginian, The
89 Rescue Ln (23093-4105)
P.O. Box 464 (23093-0464)
PHONE..................................540 967-0368
Budgie Duke, *President*
G B Duke, *President*
John E Thomasson, *Vice Pres*
Harold K Richardson, *Treasurer*
Cathy Collins, *Manager*
EMP: 15
SQ FT: 950
SALES (est): 1.4MM **Privately Held**
WEB: www.thecentralvirginian.com
SIC: 2711 Newspapers: publishing only, not printed on site

(G-7555)
D CARTER INC
5159 W Old Mountain Rd (23093-6404)
PHONE..................................540 967-1506
Ernest T Carter, *President*
Dianna K Carter, *Corp Secy*
EMP: 2
SALES (est): 122.9K **Privately Held**
SIC: 2331 2311 2361 Women's & misses' blouses & shirts; men's & boys' suits & coats; girls' & children's dresses, blouses & shirts

(G-7556)
HMB INC
Also Called: Piedmont Metal Fabricators
119 Jefferson Hwy (23093-6520)
P.O. Box 1690 (23093-1690)
PHONE..................................540 967-1060
Gregory Brindle, *President*
▼ **EMP:** 60
SQ FT: 65,000
SALES (est): 13.3MM **Privately Held**
WEB: www.piedmontmetalfab.com
SIC: 3559 3444 Tobacco products machinery; sheet metalwork

(G-7557)
JNLK INC
358 Bybee Rd (23093-2815)
P.O. Box 1018, Troy (22974-1018)
PHONE..................................434 566-1037
James G Brochu, *President*
EMP: 1
SALES (est): 150K **Privately Held**
SIC: 3281 Cut stone & stone products

(G-7558)
MAGNIFAZINE LLC
730 Carter Ln (23093-2660)
PHONE..................................248 224-1137
Cynthia Winn, *President*
EMP: 1 **EST:** 2014
SALES (est): 72.1K **Privately Held**
SIC: 2392 7389 Table mats, plastic & textile;

(G-7559)
MANAGEMENT SOLUTIONS LC
Also Called: Esstech Engineering
348 Industrial Dr (23093-4130)
PHONE..................................540 967-9600
Ellen Stadtler, *President*
Matt Granger, *General Mgr*
Stacey Harrington, *Vice Pres*
Don Stadtler, *Vice Pres*
EMP: 8
SQ FT: 3,750
SALES (est): 1.9MM **Privately Held**
SIC: 3629 Electronic generation equipment

(G-7560)
MICHAEL W GILLESPIE
Also Called: Windmill Nursery
4583 E Old Mountain Rd (23093-2420)
PHONE..................................540 894-0288
Michael W Gillespie, *Owner*
EMP: 1
SALES (est): 30K **Privately Held**
WEB: www.expertmetalworks.com
SIC: 3499 Fire- or burglary-resistive products

(G-7561)
MUSEUMRAILS LLC
19564 Louisa Rd (23093-4421)
P.O. Box 738 (23093-0738)
PHONE..................................540 603-2414
Michael Remorenko, *Mng Member*
EMP: 3
SALES (est): 250K **Privately Held**
WEB: www.museumrails.com
SIC: 2542 Partitions & fixtures, except wood

(G-7562)
NORTH STAR PRESS
186 Harris Creek Rd (23093-4201)
P.O. Box 1752 (23093-1752)
PHONE..................................540 967-5093
EMP: 1 **EST:** 2018
SALES (est): 37.5K **Privately Held**
SIC: 2741 Miscellaneous publishing

(G-7563)
PORCUPINE LOGGING LLC
2366 Waltons Store Rd (23093-2345)
PHONE..................................540 894-1675
Ronald Pendleton,
EMP: 4
SALES (est): 500K **Privately Held**
SIC: 2411 Logging camps & contractors

(G-7564)
RAG BAG AERO WORKS INC
198 Locust Dr (23093-5760)
PHONE..................................540 967-5400
Dennis Harbin, *President*
Patricia Harbin, *Exec VP*
EMP: 5
SQ FT: 1,900
SALES (est): 547.8K **Privately Held**
WEB: www.rag-bag-aero-works.myshopify.com
SIC: 2395 Embroidery & art needlework

(G-7565)
RENAISSANCE CABINET SHOP
1844 Courthouse Rd (23093-2600)
PHONE.....................540 967-0422
Hank Bilek, *Owner*
EMP: 2
SALES (est): 198.9K **Privately Held**
WEB: www.renaissancecabinetshop.com
SIC: 2434 Wood kitchen cabinets

(G-7566)
SHAW LLC
2484 Oakland Rd (23093-4912)
PHONE.....................540 967-9783
EMP: 1
SALES (est): 77.1K **Privately Held**
SIC: 7692 Welding Repair

(G-7567)
SIGNAFAB LLC
464 Deep Woods Rd (23093-5241)
PHONE.....................703 489-8572
Todd Polanowski, *General Mgr*
Daniel Garbers,
EMP: 2
SALES (est): 224.7K **Privately Held**
WEB: www.signafab.com
SIC: 3663 7373 8748 Mobile communica-
tion equipment; systems integration serv-
ices; systems analysis & engineering
consulting services

(G-7568)
SPARKS ELECTRIC
35 Loudin Ln (23093-4260)
PHONE.....................540 967-0436
Melissa B Merritt, *Administration*
EMP: 2
SALES (est): 114.9K **Privately Held**
SIC: 3699 1731 Electrical equipment &
supplies; electrical work

(G-7569)
**SUGAR MAPLE LN
WOODWORKER LLC**
38 Sugar Maple Ln (23093-6152)
PHONE.....................434 962-6494
James F Tanner, *Administration*
EMP: 2
SALES (est): 163.3K **Privately Held**
SIC: 2431 Millwork

(G-7570)
SUPRACITY PUBLISHING LLC
5014 Sand Trap Cir (23093-2234)
PHONE.....................804 301-9370
Barry L Brown, *Administration*
EMP: 2
SALES (est): 124.8K **Privately Held**
WEB: www.supracity.com
SIC: 2741 Miscellaneous publishing

(G-7571)
TETRA PAK TUBEX INC
193 Industrial Dr (23093-4182)
P.O. Box 1547 (23093-1547)
PHONE.....................540 967-0733
Dan H Scott, *President*
Jorgen Bengtsson, *Vice Pres*
Bengtsson Jorgen, *Vice Pres*
Lawrence Johnson, *Manager*
Michael Hawkinson, *Director*
◆ EMP: 45
SALES (est): 13MM **Privately Held**
SIC: 3556 Food products machinery

(G-7572)
TRI-DIM FILTER CORPORATION
675 Industrial Dr (23093-4137)
PHONE.....................540 967-2600
EMP: 4
SALES (corp-wide): 4.6B **Privately Held**
WEB: www.tridim.com
SIC: 3569 Filters
HQ: Tri-Dim Filter Corporation
93 Industrial Dr
Louisa VA 23093
540 967-2600

(G-7573)
**TRI-DIM FILTER CORPORATION
(DH)**
93 Industrial Dr (23093-4126)
PHONE.....................540 967-2600
Mark E King, *President*

Mark King, *Exec VP*
Connie Madison, *Vice Pres*
Margaret Bingman, *Prdtn Mgr*
Joyce Delgratta, *Materials Mgr*
◆ EMP: 140
SQ FT: 115,000
SALES: 137.3MM
SALES (corp-wide): 4.6B **Privately Held**
WEB: www.tridim.com
SIC: 3564 Filters, air: furnaces, air condi-
tioning equipment, etc.
HQ: Mann + Hummel, Inc.
6400 S Sprinkle Rd
Portage MI 49002
269 329-3900

(G-7574)
**VIRGINIA VERMICULITE LLC
(PA)**
13341 Louisa Rd (23093-4707)
P.O. Box 70 (23093-0070)
PHONE.....................540 967-2266
Diane Jablonski, *Marketing Staff*
Ned Gumble, *Mng Member*
Ned K Gumble, *Manager*
▼ EMP: 43
SQ FT: 8,000
SALES (est): 4.7MM **Privately Held**
WEB: www.vermiculite.org
SIC: 3295 Vermiculite, exfoliated

(G-7575)
WOOLFOLK BROTHERS LLC
578 Bloomington Ln (23093-6222)
PHONE.....................540 967-0664
Cosby L Woolfolk, *Principal*
EMP: 3
SALES (est): 250.9K **Privately Held**
SIC: 2411 Logging

(G-7576)
WOOLFOLK ENTERPRISES
578 Bloomington Ln (23093-6222)
PHONE.....................540 967-0664
Kaulsy Woolfolk, *Manager*
EMP: 3
SALES (est): 204.1K **Privately Held**
SIC: 2411 Logging

Lovettsville
Loudoun County

(G-7577)
CREEKS EDGE WINERY
41255 Annas Ln (20180-2280)
PHONE.....................540 822-3825
Spenser Wempe, *Principal*
EMP: 2 EST: 2017
SALES (est): 176.9K **Privately Held**
WEB: www.creeksedgewinery.com
SIC: 2084 Wines

(G-7578)
DONATY SOFTWARE INC
39891 Honeysuckle Ct (20180-1923)
PHONE.....................540 822-5496
Robert Donaty, *President*
EMP: 1 EST: 1998
SALES (est): 60K **Privately Held**
SIC: 7372 Prepackaged software

(G-7579)
J & J WELDING LLC
11760 Armistead Filler Ln (20180-1915)
PHONE.....................571 271-3337
Jack Moore, *Principal*
EMP: 1
SALES (est): 25K **Privately Held**
SIC: 7692 Welding repair

(G-7580)
JJOJAY LLC
11 Stocks St (20180-8641)
PHONE.....................240 660-6146
Nana Yaa Asante, *CEO*
Eastwood Asante, *CFO*
EMP: 2
SALES (est): 62.3K **Privately Held**
SIC: 2099 Seasonings & spices

(G-7581)
KRISTA HAWK LLC
22 Mills Ct (20180-8514)
PHONE.....................703 554-7654
Krista Hawk, *Administration*
EMP: 2
SALES (est): 59.5K **Privately Held**
SIC: 2711 Newspapers, publishing & printing

(G-7582)
LOUDOUN COMMUNITY BAND
39604 Rickard Rd (20180-3302)
PHONE.....................540 882-3838
Brian Loch, *Research*
Richard W Denney Jr, *Administration*
EMP: 3
SALES (est): 131.2K **Privately Held**
WEB: www.loudountimes.com
SIC: 2711 Newspapers, publishing & print-
ing

(G-7583)
LOUDOUN METAL & MORE
11811 Berlin Tpke (20180-1831)
PHONE.....................540 668-5067
Norman K Styer, *Publisher*
EMP: 2
SALES (est): 269.9K **Privately Held**
WEB: www.loudounnow.com
SIC: 2711 Newspapers, publishing & print-
ing

(G-7584)
ONEILL DISTILLERY LLC TF
12264 Sedgeway Ln (20180-2758)
PHONE.....................540 822-5812
Jenna Strayhand, *Division Mgr*
Timothy Oneill, *Principal*
Clay Dotson, *Manager*
Janet Hammer, *Manager*
Phillip Castro, *Director*
EMP: 2
SALES (est): 84K **Privately Held**
SIC: 2085 Distilled & blended liquors

(G-7585)
P&L WOODWORKS
38111 Long Ln (20180-1707)
PHONE.....................240 676-8648
Perry Jackman, *Principal*
EMP: 1
SALES (est): 54.1K **Privately Held**
SIC: 2431 Millwork

(G-7586)
**SHIELD TECHNOLOGY
CORPORATION**
13439 Milltown Rd (20180-3511)
PHONE.....................540 882-3254
Rex Bambling, *President*
Jay Shupe, *Software Engr*
EMP: 4
SQ FT: 4,000
SALES (est): 306.8K **Privately Held**
WEB: www.shieldware.com
SIC: 7372 Application computer software

(G-7587)
THERMO-OPTICAL GROUP LLC
12260 Elvan Rd (20180-2731)
P.O. Box 182 (20180-0182)
PHONE.....................540 822-9481
EMP: 6
SALES (est): 264.9K
SALES (corp-wide): 1MM **Privately Held**
SIC: 3812 Mfg Search/Navigation Equip-
ment
PA: Embedded Control Systems, Inc.
106 S Clow Intl Pkwy
Bolingbrook IL

Lovingston
Nelson County

(G-7588)
**ATOMIZED PRODUCTS GROUP
INC (PA)**
885 Freshwater Cove Ln (22949-2008)
PHONE.....................434 263-4551
Janet S Puckett, *President*
Edward Puckett, *Corp Secy*
▲ EMP: 2

SALES (est): 2.4MM **Privately Held**
WEB: www.atomizedproductsgroup.com
SIC: 3341 Secondary nonferrous metals

(G-7589)
BOOKWRIGHTS PRESS
1060 Old Ridge Rd (22949-2552)
PHONE.....................434 263-4818
Mayapriya Long, *Owner*
EMP: 1
SQ FT: 300
SALES (est): 96.8K **Privately Held**
WEB: www.bookwrights.com
SIC: 2679 Book covers, paper

(G-7590)
HARVEY LOGGING CO INC
116 Cannery Loop (22949-2319)
PHONE.....................434 263-5942
Franklin Harvey, *President*
James Harvey, *Vice Pres*
Carroll Harvey, *Treasurer*
Virginia Harvey, *Admin Sec*
EMP: 4
SALES (est): 600K **Privately Held**
SIC: 2411 Logging camps & contractors

(G-7591)
LA ABRA FARM & WINERY INC
Also Called: Mountain Cove Vineyards
1362 Fortunes Cove Ln (22949-2226)
PHONE.....................434 263-5392
Albert Charles Weed II, *President*
EMP: 3
SALES (est): 190K **Privately Held**
WEB: www.mountaincovevineyards.com
SIC: 2084 0172 0212 Brandy; grapes;
beef cattle except feedlots

(G-7592)
LOVINGTON WINERY LLC
885 Freshwater Cove Ln (22949-2008)
PHONE.....................434 263-8467
Ed Tuckett, *Owner*
Janet Tuckett, *Co-Owner*
EMP: 2
SALES (est): 138.4K **Privately Held**
WEB: www.lovingstonwinery.com
SIC: 2084 Wines

(G-7593)
VIRGINIA DISTILLERY CO LLC
299 Eades Ln (22949-2325)
PHONE.....................434 285-2900
John McCray,
▲ EMP: 1
SALES (est): 257K **Privately Held**
WEB: www.vadistillery.com
SIC: 2085 Grain alcohol for beverage pur-
poses

(G-7594)
**WILBUR FREDERICK - WOOD
CARVER**
14332 James River Rd (22949-2341)
P.O. Box 425 (22949-0425)
PHONE.....................434 263-4827
Frederick C Wilbur, *Owner*
EMP: 1
SALES (est): 55.4K **Privately Held**
SIC: 2499 Laundry products, wood

Lowesville
Nelson County

(G-7595)
J R PLASTICS & MACHINING INC
2820 Lowesville Rd (22922-6025)
PHONE.....................434 277-8334
Raymond H Schneider, *President*
Jerie Schneider, *Vice Pres*
Pamela Trent, *Vice Pres*
EMP: 6
SALES (est): 819.2K **Privately Held**
WEB: www.jrplasticsva.com
SIC: 3089 Injection molding of plastics

(G-7596)
LESTER VIAR
261 Gunter Hollow Rd (22967-2819)
PHONE.....................434 277-5504
Viar Lester, *Owner*
EMP: 2

SALES (est): 87K **Privately Held**
SIC: 2411 Timber, cut at logging camp

(G-7597)
NELLIE HARRIS
Also Called: Ram Company, The
512 Dillard Hill Rd (22967-6016)
PHONE............................434 277-8511
Nellie Harris, *Owner*
Terry Harris, *Co-Owner*
EMP: 2 EST: 1976
SALES (est): 45K **Privately Held**
WEB: www.theramcompany.com
SIC: 3561 3433 5169 Industrial pumps & parts; solar heaters & collectors; chemicals & allied products

Lowmoor
Alleghany County

(G-7598)
BOXLEY MATERIALS COMPANY
Also Called: Rich Patch Quarry
7612 Rich Patch Rd (24457)
P.O. Box 13527, Roanoke (24035-3527)
PHONE............................540 777-7600
Abney S Boxley III, *Branch Mgr*
EMP: 6
SALES (corp-wide): 2.2B **Publicly Held**
WEB: www.boxley.com
SIC: 1422 Crushed & broken limestone
HQ: Boxley Materials Company
15418 W Lynchburg Slem Tp
Blue Ridge VA 24064
540 777-7600

(G-7599)
WESTROCK MWV LLC
300 Westvaco Rd (24457)
PHONE............................540 863-2300
Al Millbenberger, *Manager*
EMP: 250
SALES (corp-wide): 17.5B **Publicly Held**
WEB: www.westrock.com
SIC: 2631 Linerboard
HQ: Westrock Mwv, Llc
501 S 5th St
Richmond VA 23219
804 444-1000

Luray
Page County

(G-7600)
ALANS FACTORY OUTLET
128 Hill House Ln (22835-2118)
P.O. Box 646 (22835-0646)
PHONE............................540 860-1035
Alan Bernau Jr, *Owner*
EMP: 5
SALES (est): 462K **Privately Held**
WEB: www.alansfactoryoutlet.com
SIC: 3448 Prefabricated metal buildings

(G-7601)
BLUE RIDGE HOMESTEAD LLC
1773 E Rocky Branch Rd (22835-4140)
PHONE............................540 743-2374
Toll Free:............................877
Bucky Thomas,
Teresa Thomas,
EMP: 2
SALES (est): 160K **Privately Held**
SIC: 2452 Log cabins, prefabricated, wood

(G-7602)
BLUE RIDGE PORTABLE SAWMILL
3729 Ida Rd (22835-7423)
PHONE............................540 743-2520
David Shenk, *Principal*
EMP: 1
SALES (est): 89.3K **Privately Held**
SIC: 2421 Sawmills & planing mills, general

(G-7603)
BRASS AGE RESTORATIONS
1631 Stonyman Rd (22835-5417)
PHONE............................540 743-4674
William Edwin Price, *President*

John Lineberger, *Opers Staff*
EMP: 3
SALES (est): 187.7K **Privately Held**
SIC: 3471 Plating of metals or formed products

(G-7604)
CASTLE VINEYARDS LLC
2150 Mims Rd (22835-3411)
PHONE............................571 283-7150
Jeremy McCoy, *Principal*
EMP: 2 EST: 2017
SALES (est): 85.7K **Privately Held**
SIC: 2084 Wines

(G-7605)
CURTIS E HARRELL
223 Wilson Ave (22835-2016)
PHONE............................540 843-2027
Curtis Harrell, *Owner*
Curtis E Harrell, *Principal*
EMP: 1
SALES (est): 68.1K **Privately Held**
SIC: 1422 Lime rock, ground

(G-7606)
DAILY NEWS RECORD
Also Called: Page News & Courier
1113 E Main St (22835-1623)
P.O. Box 707 (22835-0707)
PHONE............................540 743-5123
Randy Arrington, *Branch Mgr*
EMP: 13
SALES (corp-wide): 13MM **Privately Held**
WEB: www.dnronline.com
SIC: 2711 Newspapers, publishing & printing
HQ: Daily News Record
231 S Liberty St
Harrisonburg VA 22801
540 574-6200

(G-7607)
EDIBLE PRINTING LLC
329 Mechanic St (22835-1807)
PHONE............................212 203-8275
EMP: 2
SALES (est): 122.1K **Privately Held**
WEB: www.edibleprinting.com
SIC: 2752 Commercial printing, offset

(G-7608)
EERKINS INC
1134 E Main St (22835-1624)
PHONE............................703 626-6248
Naeem Jan, *Vice Pres*
EMP: 5
SALES (est): 75.4K **Privately Held**
SIC: 2086 5084 6799 Carbonated soft drinks, bottled & canned; food product manufacturing machinery; commodity contract trading companies

(G-7609)
EMCO ENTERPRISES INC
Also Called: Andersen
31 Stoney Brook Ln (22835-9066)
PHONE............................540 843-7900
Carey Verba, *Principal*
Dennis McLaughlin, *IT/INT Sup*
Charlie Elbon, *Analyst*
Roberta Randall, *Associate*
EMP: 350
SALES (corp-wide): 2.7B **Privately Held**
WEB: www.andersenwindows.com
SIC: 3442 Storm doors or windows, metal
HQ: Emco Enterprises, Inc.
2121 E Walnut St
Des Moines IA 50317
515 264-4283

(G-7610)
EVERGREEN OUTFITTERS LLC
18 E Main St (22835-1901)
PHONE............................540 843-2576
Howard Thompson, *Principal*
EMP: 2
SALES (est): 110K **Privately Held**
SIC: 3949 Camping equipment & supplies

(G-7611)
FAITHBROOKE BARN VINEYARDS LLC
4468 Us Highway 340 N (22835-3434)
PHONE............................540 743-1207

Melinda Jenkins, *Principal*
EMP: 1
SALES (est): 87.3K **Privately Held**
WEB: www.faithbrooke.com
SIC: 2084 Wines

(G-7612)
FIRST FOREST FURNITURE & MLLWK
1079 Us Highway 211 W (22835-5245)
PHONE............................540 743-2051
Joanne Coleman, *President*
John Coleman, *Director*
EMP: 2
SQ FT: 3,600
SALES (est): 169.3K **Privately Held**
WEB: www.awesomewood.com
SIC: 2434 Wood kitchen cabinets

(G-7613)
GLENN F KITE
11 Meadow Ln (22835-1676)
PHONE............................540 743-6124
Glenn Kite, *Principal*
EMP: 2 EST: 2010
SALES (est): 175.9K **Privately Held**
SIC: 3944 Kites

(G-7614)
JOSHS WELDING & FABRICATION
2532 Stonyman Rd (22835-6952)
PHONE............................540 244-9950
EMP: 1
SALES (est): 28.1K **Privately Held**
SIC: 7692 Welding repair

(G-7615)
LOG HOME LOVERS
903 E Main St (22835-1619)
PHONE............................540 743-7355
David Foster, *Owner*
EMP: 2
SALES (est): 129.4K **Privately Held**
SIC: 2452 Log cabins, prefabricated, wood

(G-7616)
LURAY COPY SERVICES INC
27 E Main St (22835-1902)
PHONE............................540 743-3433
Earl Racer, *President*
Nancy K Racer, *Admin Sec*
EMP: 4
SALES (est): 499.4K **Privately Held**
WEB: www.luraycopyservice.com
SIC: 2752 2759 Commercial printing, offset; letterpress printing

(G-7617)
MARATHON MILLWORK INC
119 Planning Mill Rd (22835-1909)
PHONE............................540 743-1721
Michael Rowles, *President*
Sheri Rowles, *Vice Pres*
EMP: 4
SALES (est): 462.9K **Privately Held**
WEB: www.marathonmillwork.com
SIC: 2499 Decorative wood & woodwork

(G-7618)
MOYER BROTHERS CONTRACTING INC
Also Called: Moyer Bros Contracting
467 Somers Rd (22835-7445)
PHONE............................540 743-7864
Kevin Moyer, *President*
EMP: 3 EST: 2015
SALES (est): 184.9K **Privately Held**
SIC: 3531 1629 0761 Plows: construction, excavating & grading; land clearing contractor; crew leaders, farm labor: contracting services

(G-7619)
MUSIC AT MONUMENT
50 Cottage Dr (22835-9201)
PHONE............................202 570-7800
Judy Xanthopoulos, *Principal*
EMP: 2
SALES (est): 47.1K **Privately Held**
WEB: www.musicatthemonument.org
SIC: 3272 Monuments & grave markers, except terrazo

(G-7620)
NICHOLS CABINETRY LLC
229 Fairview Rd (22835-1605)
PHONE............................540 860-9252
Jason Nichols, *Principal*
EMP: 1
SALES (est): 132.2K **Privately Held**
SIC: 2434 Wood kitchen cabinets

(G-7621)
PAGE PRINTING CONNECTION
297 Rhodes Way (22835-3534)
PHONE............................540 743-7746
EMP: 2
SALES (est): 87.9K **Privately Held**
WEB: www.pageprintingconnection.com
SIC: 2752 Commercial printing, offset

(G-7622)
ROCKINGHAM REDI-MIX INC
20 Fairlane Dr (22835-1752)
PHONE............................540 743-5940
Rick Kite, *Manager*
EMP: 3
SALES (corp-wide): 8.7MM **Privately Held**
WEB: www.rockinghamredimix.com
SIC: 3273 Ready-mixed concrete
PA: Rockingham Redi-Mix, Inc.
1557 Garbers Church Rd
Rockingham VA 22801
540 433-9128

(G-7623)
SIGN DOCTOR SALES & SERVICE
24 Zerkel St (22835-1913)
P.O. Box 254 (22835-0254)
PHONE............................540 743-5200
Reginald Desper Judd Jr, *President*
Jennifer Judd, *Admin Sec*
EMP: 5
SALES (est): 230K **Privately Held**
WEB: www.signdoctor.biz
SIC: 3993 Electric signs

(G-7624)
TONYA SHERIDAN CROP ORGANIZER
130 Stuart Ct (22835-9613)
PHONE............................540 860-0528
Tonya Sheridan, *Owner*
EMP: 2
SALES (est): 123K **Privately Held**
WEB: www.sassycrops.com
SIC: 2782 Scrapbooks

(G-7625)
WILLIAM L JUDD POT & CHINA CO
2904 Us Highway 211 W (22835-5142)
PHONE............................540 743-3294
Wiallam Judd, *Owner*
EMP: 3
SALES (est): 236.3K **Privately Held**
SIC: 3086 Cups & plates, foamed plastic

(G-7626)
YATES ABBATTOIR
3027 Farmview Rd (22835-7014)
PHONE............................540 778-2123
Jim Yates, *Principal*
EMP: 5
SALES (est): 180K **Privately Held**
SIC: 2011 Meat packing plants

Lynch Station
Campbell County

(G-7627)
COTTLE MULTI MEDIA INC
3390 Mount Airy Rd (24571-3054)
PHONE............................434 263-5447
John D Cottle Jr, *Owner*
Kimberly A Cottle, *Vice Pres*
EMP: 8
SQ FT: 2,400
SALES (est): 50K **Privately Held**
WEB: www.cottlemultimedia.com
SIC: 3993 Signs, not made in custom sign painting shops

(G-7628)
P&B PALLET CO
2783 Wileman Rd (24571-2006)
P.O. Box 158, Hurt (24563-0158)
PHONE..............................434 309-1028
Perry Brockwell, *Principal*
EMP: 4
SALES (est): 421.5K **Privately Held**
SIC: 2448 Pallets, wood

(G-7629)
VA FOODS LLC
6313 Bedford Hwy (24571-3048)
PHONE..............................434 221-1456
Cheri Goldsmith,
Kyle Goldsmith,
EMP: 1 EST: 2014
SALES (est): 72.2K **Privately Held**
SIC: 2099 2043 Pancake syrup, blended
& mixed; oatmeal: prepared as cereal
breakfast food

Lynchburg
Lynchburg City County

(G-7630)
ABLCOMP LLC
147 Mill Ridge Rd Ste 138 (24502-4341)
PHONE..............................434 942-5325
Sarah Pratt, *Office Mgr*
William Johnston,
EMP: 3
SQ FT: 3,000
SALES (est): 1MM **Privately Held**
WEB: www.ablcomp.com
SIC: 3599 Machine shop, jobbing & repair

(G-7631)
ACCESS REPORTS INC
1624 Dogwood Ln (24503-1924)
PHONE..............................434 384-5334
Harry A Hammitt, *President*
Katherine L Morland, *Treasurer*
EMP: 2
SALES (est): 50K **Privately Held**
WEB: www.accessreports.com
SIC: 2741 2721 Newsletter publishing; pe-
riodicals

(G-7632)
ACCUTECH FABRICATION INC
910 Orchard St (24501-1728)
PHONE..............................434 528-4858
Ron Sagle, *President*
Mary Dawn Slagle, *Principal*
Vance Wilkins, *Corp Secy*
Mary Slagle, *Vice Pres*
Geoff Jones, *Sales Staff*
EMP: 16 EST: 2000
SQ FT: 1,800
SALES (est): 3.6MM **Privately Held**
WEB: www.accutechfab.com
SIC: 3444 Sheet metalwork

(G-7633)
ADVANCED MFG TECH INC
Also Called: Amti
28 Millrace Dr (24502-4342)
PHONE..............................434 385-7197
Larry Hatch Sr, *President*
Ryan Blank, *President*
Jose Rodriguez, *Mfg Staff*
Melody Boyd, *Buyer*
Amanda Hart, *QC Mgr*
EMP: 75
SQ FT: 45,000
SALES (est): 24.4MM **Privately Held**
WEB: www.advmanufacturing.com
SIC: 3672 Printed circuit boards

(G-7634)
ADVANTAGE PUCK GROUP INC
Also Called: Advantage Puck Technologies
109 Ramsey Pl (24501-6722)
PHONE..............................434 385-9181
Kurt Sieber, *President*
Dan Ceglia, *COO*
Frank Williams, *Vice Pres*
Eddie Craig, *Engineer*
EMP: 21
SQ FT: 25,000
SALES (est): 2.1MM **Privately Held**
WEB: www.simplimatic.com
SIC: 3089 Injection molding of plastics

(G-7635)
AERO CLEAN TECHNOLOGIES LLC
1320 Stephenson Ave (24501-5732)
PHONE..............................434 381-0699
John Burdsall,
Elizabeth Burdsall,
EMP: 2
SQ FT: 16,000 **Privately Held**
WEB: www.aerocleantechnologies.com
SIC: 2841 Textile soap

(G-7636)
AFTER CURFEW INC
97 Mesena Dr Apt 302 (24502-7346)
PHONE..............................608 214-1289
Stephen Cook, *Principal*
EMP: 1
SALES (est): 0 **Privately Held**
SIC: 2741 Miscellaneous publishing

(G-7637)
AIR & LIQUID SYSTEMS CORP
Also Called: Aerofin
4621 Murray Pl (24502-2235)
P.O. Box 10819 (24506-0819)
PHONE..............................434 845-7081
Kenny Terrence W, *President*
Gavin E Divers, *President*
Paul Robert A, *Chairman*
Geoffrey Steadman, *COO*
Gavin Divers, *Exec VP*
▲ EMP: 200 EST: 1923
SQ FT: 200,000
SALES (est): 51.2MM
SALES (corp-wide): 397.9MM **Publicly Held**
WEB: www.aerofin.com
SIC: 3443 Heat exchangers, condensers &
components
PA: Ampco-Pittsburgh Corporation
726 Bell Ave Ste 301
Carnegie PA 15106
412 456-4400

(G-7638)
ALLIANCE INDUSTRIAL CORP
208 Tomahawk Indus Park (24502-4153)
PHONE..............................434 239-2641
Gary Garner, *President*
David Booker, *Project Mgr*
Wilson Jeff, *Opers Mgr*
Pat McCarron, *Purchasing*
Reynolds Jackson, *Research*
EMP: 27
SALES (est): 11.4MM **Privately Held**
WEB: www.allianceindustrial.com
SIC: 3535 Conveyors & conveying equip-
ment

(G-7639)
AMERICAN HOFMANN CORPORATION (HQ)
3700 Cohen Pl (24501-5046)
P.O. Box 10369 (24506-0369)
PHONE..............................434 522-0300
Simon Lott, *President*
William Brabant, *Regional Mgr*
Russell Holdridge, *Regional Mgr*
Frank Jack, *Vice Pres*
Steven Prance, *Vice Pres*
▲ EMP: 80
SQ FT: 90,000
SALES (est): 14.5MM
SALES (corp-wide): 21.6MM **Privately Held**
WEB: www.hofmann-global.com
SIC: 3823 3825 3829 Industrial instrmnts
msrmnt display/control process variable;
instruments to measure electricity; meas-
uring & controlling devices
PA: Hofmann Mondial, Inc.
3700 Cohen Pl
Lynchburg VA
434 522-0300

(G-7640)
AMG INC
301 Jefferson Ridge Pkwy (24501-6950)
P.O. Box 4321 (24502-0321)
PHONE..............................434 385-7525
Greg Morris, *President*
Gayle Davise, *General Mgr*
John Hannell, *Vice Pres*
Michael Pingstock, *Vice Pres*

Adam Fenwick, *Foreman/Supr*
EMP: 83
SQ FT: 44,000
SALES (est): 16MM **Privately Held**
WEB: www.amg-inc.net
SIC: 3599 7692 Machine shop, jobbing &
repair; welding repair

(G-7641)
APICAL WOODWORKS & NURSERY LLC
1010 Pioneer Ct (24503-4728)
PHONE..............................434 384-0525
Charles Boaz, *Principal*
EMP: 1
SALES (est): 59.2K **Privately Held**
SIC: 2431 Millwork

(G-7642)
APPS OF ALL NATIONS LLC
1506 Hamilton Dr (24503-2304)
PHONE..............................434 851-0651
Isabelle Duston,
EMP: 2
SALES (est): 93.4K **Privately Held**
WEB: www.appsofallnations.com
SIC: 2731 Book publishing

(G-7643)
ARMES PRCSION MCHNING FBRCTION
173 Fastener Dr (24502-3954)
PHONE..............................434 237-4552
Tom Armes, *President*
EMP: 7
SALES (est): 1.1MM **Privately Held**
WEB: www.armesprecision.com
SIC: 3599 Machine shop, jobbing & repair

(G-7644)
ATCC GLOBAL (PA)
6015 Fort Ave Ste 23 (24502-1922)
PHONE..............................434 237-6861
Raymond H Cypess, *President*
John L Child, *Treasurer*
Renee Randall, *Director*
James S Burns, *Admin Sec*
EMP: 5
SALES (est): 99.6MM **Privately Held**
SIC: 2836 Plasmas

(G-7645)
AUTOMATED CONVEYOR SYSTEMS INC
Also Called: ACS
6 Millrace Dr (24502-4342)
PHONE..............................434 385-6699
Michael G Shenigo, *CEO*
David M Smith, *President*
Jeff Smeathers, *Vice Pres*
William R Toms, *Vice Pres*
Shannah Wilbun, *Purch Mgr*
▲ EMP: 145
SQ FT: 145,000
SALES (est): 52.5MM **Privately Held**
WEB: www.acsconveyor.com
SIC: 3535 Conveyors & conveying equip-
ment

(G-7646)
AVIATION COMPONENT SVCS INC
18245 Forest Rd (24502-4355)
PHONE..............................434 237-7077
Kelli Marten, *CEO*
EMP: 3
SALES (est): 117.8K **Privately Held**
SIC: 3728 Aircraft parts & equipment

(G-7647)
B & M MACHINERY INC
449 Old Plantation Dr (24502-6908)
PHONE..............................434 525-1498
EMP: 7
SALES: 650K **Privately Held**
SIC: 3541 Mfg Carbide Cutting Tools

(G-7648)
BANKER STEEL CO LLC (HQ)
1619 Wythe Rd Ste B (24501-3461)
P.O. Box 10875 (24506-0875)
PHONE..............................434 847-4575
Donald Banker, *CEO*
Greg Nichols, *President*
Charles Mehalic, *General Mgr*

Chet McPhatter, *COO*
Richard Plant, *VP Opers*
▲ EMP: 105
SQ FT: 100,000
SALES (est): 52.4MM
SALES (corp-wide): 6.1B **Publicly Held**
WEB: www.bankersteel.com
SIC: 3441 Fabricated structural metal
PA: Atlas Holdings, Llc
100 Northfield St
Greenwich CT 06830
203 622-9138

(G-7649)
BARRY-WHMLLER CONT SYSTEMS INC
Also Called: Bw Container Systems
1320 Wards Ferry Rd (24502-2908)
PHONE..............................434 582-1200
Mike Dierker, *Engineer*
Victor Romero, *Engineer*
Eric Collier, *Sales Staff*
Scott Smith, *Marketing Staff*
Russ Garrett, *Manager*
EMP: 90 **Privately Held**
WEB: www.bwintegratedsystems.com
SIC: 3535 Conveyors & conveying equip-
ment
HQ: Barry-Wehmiller Container Systems,
Inc.
1305 Lakeview Dr
Romeoville IL 60446

(G-7650)
BAUSCH & LOMB INCORPORATED
1501 Graves Mill Rd (24502-4328)
PHONE..............................434 385-0407
Sarah McCoy, *Transportation*
Allen Barr, *Manager*
Satish Nair, *Manager*
EMP: 120
SALES (corp-wide): 8.6B **Privately Held**
WEB: www.bausch.com
SIC: 3851 Ophthalmic goods
HQ: Bausch & Lomb Incorporated
400 Somerset Corp Blvd
Bridgewater NJ 08807
585 338-6000

(G-7651)
BEESWAX CANDLE COMPANY LLC
109 13th St (24504-1825)
PHONE..............................434 528-9885
Kathy Shaw, *Owner*
EMP: 1
SALES (est): 106.1K **Privately Held**
WEB: www.beeswaxcandleco.com
SIC: 3999 Candles

(G-7652)
BELVAC PRODUCTION MCHY INC
237 Graves Mill Rd (24502-4203)
PHONE..............................434 239-0358
Richard S Steigerwald, *President*
David J Mammolenti, *Exec VP*
David Mammolenti, *Vice Pres*
Daniel Metzger, *Vice Pres*
Gene Oliver, *Materials Mgr*
◆ EMP: 200 EST: 1962
SQ FT: 100,000
SALES (est): 105MM
SALES (corp-wide): 7.1B **Publicly Held**
WEB: www.belvac.com
SIC: 3565 Canning machinery, food
PA: Dover Corporation
3005 Highland Pkwy # 200
Downers Grove IL 60515
630 541-1540

(G-7653)
BG INDUSTRIES INC
107 Woodberry Ln (24502-4455)
PHONE..............................434 369-2128
EMP: 2 EST: 2009
SALES (est): 91K **Privately Held**
SIC: 3999 Manufacturing industries

(G-7654)
BIMBO BAKERIES USA
20446 Lynchburg Hwy (24502-4074)
PHONE..............................434 525-2947
EMP: 4

SALES (est): 130K **Privately Held**
SIC: 2051 Mfg Bread/Related Products

(G-7655)
BLUE RIDGE MARBLE MFRS LLC
147 Mill Ridge Rd 234b (24502-4341)
PHONE..............................434 582-6139
EMP: 2
SALES (est): 12.6K **Privately Held**
SIC: 3599 Mfg Industrial Machinery

(G-7656)
BLUE RIDGE STONE CORP
762 Lawyers Rd (24501-7156)
PHONE..............................434 239-9249
Jack McCarthy, *Manager*
▲ EMP: 2
SALES (est): 122.9K **Privately Held**
SIC: 1481 Mine & quarry services, non-metallic minerals

(G-7657)
BOHLING STEEL INC
Also Called: Cavalier Steel
3410 Forest Brook Rd (24501-6802)
PHONE..............................434 385-5175
Mark Bohling, *President*
Edward Natt, *Principal*
Tom Ballowe, *Project Mgr*
Danny Devier, *Project Mgr*
Allan Walls, *Project Mgr*
EMP: 20
SQ FT: 19,500
SALES (est): 5.7MM **Privately Held**
WEB: www.bohlingsteel.com
SIC: 3441 5039 Building components, structural steel; joists; wire fence, gates & accessories

(G-7658)
BOXLEY MATERIALS COMPANY
Also Called: Lawyers Road Quarry
762 Lawyers Rd (24501-7156)
P.O. Box 13527, Roanoke (24035-3527)
PHONE..............................540 777-7600
AB Boxley, *CEO*
Donald Barricks, *Superintendent*
George Honeycutt, *Engineer*
Tim Mauzy, *Engineer*
Melissa Wood, *Accounting Mgr*
EMP: 32
SALES (corp-wide): 2.2B **Publicly Held**
WEB: www.boxley.com
SIC: 1422 Crushed & broken limestone
HQ: Boxley Materials Company
    15418 W Lynchburg Slem Tp
    Blue Ridge VA 24064
    540 777-7600

(G-7659)
BOXLEY MATERIALS COMPANY
Also Called: Lynchburg Plant
3535 John Capron Rd (24501-5045)
P.O. Box 13527, Roanoke (24035-3527)
PHONE..............................540 777-7600
Abney S Boxley III, *Branch Mgr*
EMP: 17
SALES (corp-wide): 2.2B **Publicly Held**
WEB: www.boxley.com
SIC: 2951 Asphalt paving mixtures & blocks
HQ: Boxley Materials Company
    15418 W Lynchburg Slem Tp
    Blue Ridge VA 24064
    540 777-7600

(G-7660)
BRISON INDUSTRIES INC
512 Ivanhoe Trl (24504-5445)
PHONE..............................434 665-2231
Alison Creasy, *President*
Franklin Taylor, *Sales Associate*
EMP: 2 EST: 2008
SALES (est): 33K **Privately Held**
WEB: www.brisoninc.com
SIC: 3599 Machine shop, jobbing & repair

(G-7661)
BROOK BRINDERS LIMITED
Also Called: Warthen, C W Company
311 Rivermont Ave Ste A (24504-2354)
PHONE..............................434 845-1231
Harold B Brooks Jr, *President*
Greg Brooks, *Vice Pres*
EMP: 6

SQ FT: 23,000
SALES (est): 330K **Privately Held**
WEB: www.cwarthen.com
SIC: 2789 5112 1721 Bookbinding & related work; stationery & office supplies; stationery; painting & paper hanging

(G-7662)
BUBBLES WRECKER SERVICE
903 Buchanan St (24501-1346)
PHONE..............................434 845-2411
Gary Vaughan, *Owner*
EMP: 1 EST: 1973
SALES (est): 60K **Privately Held**
SIC: 3711 7549 Wreckers (tow truck), assembly of; towing services

(G-7663)
BVM PRINT VA LLC
1709 Memorial Ave (24501-1714)
PHONE..............................434 845-1153
Nikunj Patel,
EMP: 8
SALES (est): 313.6K **Privately Held**
SIC: 2752 Commercial printing, offset

(G-7664)
BWX TECHNOLOGIES INC
109 Ramsey Pl (24501-6722)
PHONE..............................434 385-2535
Larry Fannon, *Supervisor*
EMP: 3 **Publicly Held**
WEB: www.bwxt.com
SIC: 3621 Power generators
PA: Bwx Technologies, Inc.
    800 Main St Ste 4
    Lynchburg VA 24504

(G-7665)
BWX TECHNOLOGIES INC
110 Ramsey Pl (24501-3997)
PHONE..............................434 316-7638
Jay Fetherolk, *Engineer*
Karen Hemmerlein, *Software Engr*
EMP: 14 **Publicly Held**
WEB: www.bwxt.com
SIC: 3621 Power generators
PA: Bwx Technologies, Inc.
    800 Main St Ste 4
    Lynchburg VA 24504

(G-7666)
BWX TECHNOLOGIES INC
Also Called: Nuclear Products
800 Main St (24504-1533)
PHONE..............................434 522-6000
Brandon Bethards, *President*
EMP: 6 **Publicly Held**
WEB: www.bwxt.com
SIC: 3443 Nuclear core structurals, metal plate
PA: Bwx Technologies, Inc.
    800 Main St Ste 4
    Lynchburg VA 24504

(G-7667)
BWX TECHNOLOGIES INC (PA)
Also Called: Bwxt
800 Main St Ste 4 (24504-1533)
PHONE..............................980 365-4300
John A Fees, *Ch of Bd*
Rex D Geveden, *President*
Joseph G Henry, *President*
Jim Bittner, *General Mgr*
Joann Beehler, *Principal*
EMP: 242 **Publicly Held**
WEB: www.bwxt.com
SIC: 3621 3829 Power generators; nuclear instrument modules

(G-7668)
BWXT GOVERNMENT GROUP INC (DH)
2016 Mount Athos Rd (24504-5447)
PHONE..............................434 522-6000
Mary Salomone, *CEO*
Dara Glass, *Regional Mgr*
Benjamin H Bash, *Senior VP*
James D Canafax, *Senior VP*
Regina W Carter, *Vice Pres*
▲ EMP: 206
SALES (est): 1.2B **Publicly Held**
WEB: www.bwxt.com
SIC: 3443 Nuclear core structurals, metal plate

(G-7669)
BWXT NCLEAR OPRTIONS GROUP INC (DH)
2016 Mount Athos Rd (24504-5447)
PHONE..............................434 522-6000
Joseph Henry, *President*
Nate Foote, *General Mgr*
Rod Woolsey, *Vice Pres*
Jason Mardian, *Project Mgr*
Erin Culver, *Engineer*
EMP: 276
SALES (est): 613.4MM **Publicly Held**
WEB: www.bwxt.com
SIC: 3443 Fabricated plate work (boiler shop)
HQ: Bwxt Government Group, Inc.
    2016 Mount Athos Rd
    Lynchburg VA 24504
    434 522-6000

(G-7670)
BWXT Y - 12 LLC (HQ)
109 Ramsey Pl (24501-6722)
PHONE..............................434 316-7633
Kenneth R Camplin, *President*
Kirt J Kubbs, *Treasurer*
Robert B Hancock, *Controller*
William R Hull, *Manager*
Terry Chalker, *Director*
EMP: 6
SALES (est): 1.9MM **Publicly Held**
WEB: www.bwxt.com
SIC: 3483 3761 Missile warheads; guided missiles & space vehicles

(G-7671)
C B FLEET COMPANY INC (HQ)
Also Called: Boudreaux's Butt Paste
4615 Murray Pl (24502-2235)
P.O. Box 11349 (24506-1349)
PHONE..............................434 528-4000
Steve Lamonte, *Ch of Bd*
Jeffrey R Rowan, *President*
Terisa Watlington, *General Mgr*
Douglas Davis, *Vice Pres*
Lori Kumar, *Vice Pres*
▼ EMP: 200 EST: 1916
SQ FT: 300,000
SALES (est): 72.2MM **Publicly Held**
WEB: www.prestigebrands.com
SIC: 2834 Pharmaceutical preparations
PA: Prestige Consumer Healthcare Inc.
    660 White Plains Rd # 250
    Tarrytown NY 10591
    914 524-6800

(G-7672)
CANLINE USA CORPORATION
1030 Mcconville Rd Ste 1 (24502-4555)
PHONE..............................540 380-8585
Kevin Oddo, *Principal*
EMP: 15 EST: 2013
SALES (est): 2.9MM **Privately Held**
WEB: www.canline.com
SIC: 3542 Magnetic forming machines

(G-7673)
CAPPS SHOE COMPANY (PA)
260 Fastener Dr (24502-6810)
PHONE..............................434 528-3213
Tom Capps, *President*
John C Glover, *Vice Pres*
John G Glover, *Vice Pres*
John Glover, *VP Opers*
Kim Hall, *Controller*
▲ EMP: 10
SQ FT: 50,000
SALES (est): 16MM **Privately Held**
WEB: www.usmadeshoes.com
SIC: 3144 3143 Women's footwear, except athletic; men's footwear, except athletic

(G-7674)
CARLA WILKES
1010 9th St (24504-3321)
PHONE..............................434 228-1427
Carla Wilkes, *Owner*
EMP: 2
SALES (est): 99.6K **Privately Held**
SIC: 2759 Commercial printing

(G-7675)
CASPIAN INC
3813 Wards Rd Ste B (24502-2970)
PHONE..............................434 237-1900

Dave Casper, *Principal*
EMP: 8
SALES (est): 420K **Privately Held**
WEB: www.caspiantattoo.com
SIC: 3423 Jewelers' hand tools

(G-7676)
CATAPULT SOLUTIONS INC
104 Cupola St (24502-5281)
PHONE..............................434 401-1077
EMP: 2 EST: 2015
SALES (est): 97.7K **Privately Held**
SIC: 3599 Catapults

(G-7677)
CHARTER OF LYNCHBURG INC
Also Called: Charter Time Furniture
139 Winebarger Cir (24501-7143)
P.O. Box 11988 (24506-1988)
PHONE..............................434 239-2671
Waldemar Oelschlager, *CEO*
EMP: 75 EST: 1997
SQ FT: 210,000
SALES (est): 8.6MM **Privately Held**
WEB: www.charterinc.com
SIC: 2599 Hotel furniture

(G-7678)
CHOICE ADHESIVES CORPORATION
2500 Carroll Ave (24501-5924)
PHONE..............................434 847-5671
Mark A Brown, *President*
Paul Nicolai, *CFO*
◆ EMP: 30 EST: 1934
SQ FT: 60,000
SALES (est): 12.6MM
SALES (corp-wide): 1.8MM **Privately Held**
WEB: www.choiceadhesivescorp.com
SIC: 2891 Adhesives
PA: Choice Slocum Holdings, Llc
    666 Redna Ter Ste 600
    Cincinnati OH 45215
    800 330-5566

(G-7679)
CLEARVIEW SOFTWARE CORPORATION
1607a Enterprise Dr (24502-5797)
PHONE..............................804 381-6300
John McPherson, *Manager*
Matt Pantana, *CTO*
EMP: 4 EST: 2015
SALES (est): 163.6K **Privately Held**
WEB: www.unanet.com
SIC: 7372 Prepackaged software

(G-7680)
COLUMBUS WOODWORKS
905a Graves Mill Rd (24502-4260)
P.O. Box 11284 (24506-1284)
PHONE..............................434 528-1052
Tim Columbus, *Owner*
EMP: 5
SALES (est): 447.9K **Privately Held**
WEB: www.columbuswoodworks.com
SIC: 2431 Millwork

(G-7681)
COMMONWEALTH HAMS INC
Also Called: Heavenly Ham
3700 Candlers Mountain Rd (24502-2228)
PHONE..............................434 846-4267
Barbara Ragland, *President*
EMP: 6
SALES (est): 510K **Privately Held**
SIC: 2013 Prepared pork products from purchased pork

(G-7682)
COMMONWEALTH REPROGRAPHICS
Also Called: Cri Mutual Press
58 9th St (24504-1423)
P.O. Box 632 (24505-0632)
PHONE..............................434 845-1203
Patrick R Donahue, *President*
Amy R Donahue, *Vice Pres*
Donahue Amy Roark, *Vice Pres*
EMP: 11
SQ FT: 3,000

SALES (est): 1.7MM **Privately Held**
WEB: www.cridigitalva.com
SIC: 2752 7334 Commercial printing, off-set; blueprinting service

(G-7683)
CONTINENTAL BRICK COMPANY (PA)
1000 Church St (24504-4655)
P.O. Box 638 (24505-0638)
PHONE......................434 845-5918
C Lynch Christian III, *President*
Laura McCraw, *Corp Secy*
EMP: 2
SQ FT: 1,500
SALES (est): 20.3MM **Privately Held**
WEB: www.continentalbrick.com
SIC: 3255 Brick, clay refractory

(G-7684)
COPY DOG PRINTING
3022 Memorial Ave (24501-3728)
PHONE......................434 528-4134
EMP: 2
SALES (est): 92.3K **Privately Held**
WEB: www.copydogprinting.com
SIC: 2752 Commercial printing, offset

(G-7685)
COTTAGE STILL ROOM/BEES WAX CN
31 Cabell St (24504-1208)
P.O. Box 3472 (24503-0472)
PHONE......................434 846-4398
Aline C Bowles, *Owner*
EMP: 3
SALES (est): 100K **Privately Held**
WEB: www.cottagestillroom.com
SIC: 3999 5947 Candles; gift, novelty & souvenir shop

(G-7686)
COTTON CONNECTION
416 Main St (24504-1318)
PHONE......................434 528-1416
H Atkinson, *Principal*
Amanda Flower, *Manager*
EMP: 6 EST: 1998
SALES (est): 547.1K **Privately Held**
WEB: www.cottoncnx.com
SIC: 2759 Screen printing

(G-7687)
CRISWELL INC
Also Called: PIP Printing
1709 Memorial Ave (24501-1714)
PHONE......................434 845-0439
Lynda F Criswell, *President*
John A Criswell, *Vice Pres*
EMP: 16
SQ FT: 7,000
SALES: 1MM **Privately Held**
WEB: www.pip.com
SIC: 2752 2796 2791 2789 Commercial printing, offset; platemaking services; typesetting; bookbinding & related work

(G-7688)
CRYSTALS OF HOPE
527 Capstone Dr (24502-5171)
PHONE......................434 525-7279
Nancy McKee, *President*
Jay McKee, *Vice Pres*
EMP: 2
SALES (est): 120.1K **Privately Held**
SIC: 3911 5944 5094 Jewelry apparel; jewelry, precious stones & precious metals; jewelry

(G-7689)
CUSTOM CONCESSIONS INC
115 Rowse Dr (24502-5366)
PHONE......................800 910-8533
Marie D Williams, *CEO*
James Williams, *Vice Pres*
Derese Stith, *Admin Sec*
EMP: 7
SALES (est): 1.6MM **Privately Held**
WEB: www.customconcessionsusa.com
SIC: 3792 Travel trailers & campers

(G-7690)
CUSTOM EMB & SCREEN PRTG
528a Crowell Ln (24502-5570)
PHONE......................434 239-2144

Stan Maschal, *Owner*
EMP: 3
SALES (est): 132K **Privately Held**
WEB: www.custommembsp.com
SIC: 2395 Embroidery products, except schiffli machine

(G-7691)
CUSTOM MACHINE INCORPORATED
7249 Richmond Hwy (24504-4015)
PHONE......................434 846-8987
Willard White, *President*
Rod Bryant, *Vice Pres*
Carolyn White, *Admin Sec*
EMP: 3
SQ FT: 1,950
SALES (est): 400K **Privately Held**
SIC: 3599 Machine shop, jobbing & repair

(G-7692)
DANIEL CRANFORD RECOVERY
Also Called: DC Recovery
132 Fredonia Ave (24503-1612)
PHONE......................434 382-8409
Daniel Cranford, *Owner*
EMP: 1
SALES (est): 72.1K **Privately Held**
SIC: 3711 Wreckers (tow truck), assembly of

(G-7693)
DATACUT PRECISION MACHINING
200 Airpark Dr (24502-4970)
P.O. Box 11911 (24506-1911)
PHONE......................434 237-8320
Terry Thompson, *President*
EMP: 3
SQ FT: 2,500
SALES (est): 300K **Privately Held**
SIC: 3469 Machine parts, stamped or pressed metal

(G-7694)
DATAPRIVIA INC
1942 Thmson Dr Lwer Level Lower Level (24501)
PHONE......................855 477-4842
Jeff Hurley, *CEO*
EMP: 10 EST: 2013
SQ FT: 3,000
SALES (est): 996.5K **Privately Held**
WEB: www.dataprivia.com
SIC: 3699 7382 Security devices; security systems services

(G-7695)
DAVIS-FROST INC (PA)
Also Called: James T Davis
3416 Candlers Mountain Rd (24502-2214)
P.O. Box 10578 (24506-0578)
PHONE......................434 846-2721
Calvin C Henning, *CEO*
Caleb Falls, *General Mgr*
David E Boie, *Vice Pres*
Denise Henning, *Vice Pres*
Jerry Simpson, *Vice Pres*
EMP: 8 EST: 1938
SQ FT: 20,000
SALES (est): 18.3MM **Privately Held**
WEB: www.jamestdavis.com
SIC: 2851 5231 Varnishes; paint, glass & wallpaper

(G-7696)
DIVERSIFIED SOLUTION LLC
101 Duncraig Dr Unit 209 (24502-5795)
P.O. Box 4709 (24502-0709)
PHONE......................434 845-5100
Kimberly Smith,
EMP: 2
SALES (est): 125.5K **Privately Held**
WEB: www.diversifiedsolutionllc.com
SIC: 2389 Apparel & accessories

(G-7697)
DR PEPPER BOTTLERS LYNCHBURG
121 Bradley Dr (24501-4950)
PHONE......................434 528-5107
Karen Davis, *Director*
EMP: 3

SALES (est): 110.1K **Privately Held**
SIC: 2086 Soft drinks: packaged in cans, bottles, etc.

(G-7698)
EAST COAST CANDLE CO
220 Mcconville Rd Apt 58 (24502-4545)
PHONE......................781 718-9466
EMP: 1
SALES (est): 43.6K **Privately Held**
SIC: 3999 Mfg Misc Products

(G-7699)
EAST CRLINA METAL TREATING INC
Also Called: Virginia Metal Treating
3117 Odd Fellows Rd (24501-5009)
PHONE......................434 333-4412
EMP: 1
SALES (corp-wide): 4.6MM **Privately Held**
WEB: www.ecmtinc.com
SIC: 3398 Metal heat treating
PA: East Carolina Metal Treating, Inc.
  1117 Capital Blvd
  Raleigh NC 27603
  919 834-2100

(G-7700)
ELECTRMCHNCAL CTRL SYSTEMS INC
Also Called: Emcs
1409 Waterlick Rd Unit B (24501-7259)
PHONE......................434 610-5747
John Watson, *CEO*
EMP: 4
SALES (est): 94.5K **Privately Held**
SIC: 3572 Computer storage devices

(G-7701)
ELECTRONIC DESIGN & MFG CO
Also Called: E D M
31 Millrace Dr (24502-4343)
PHONE......................434 385-0046
Robert C Roberts, *CEO*
Georgeann Snead, *President*
Rebekah Taylor, *Business Mgr*
Dave McAden, *Vice Pres*
Teresa Angel, *Purch Mgr*
▲ EMP: 55
SQ FT: 35,000
SALES (est): 18.4MM **Privately Held**
WEB: www.edmva.com
SIC: 3672 Circuit boards, television & radio printed

(G-7702)
EMERGENCY VEHICLE OUTFITTERS
Also Called: Evo
448 Crowell Ln (24502-3613)
PHONE......................571 228-2837
Dean Albertson,
EMP: 2
SALES (est): 40K **Privately Held**
SIC: 3647 Vehicular lighting equipment

(G-7703)
EMGE NATURALS LLC
109 Chadwick Dr (24502-4668)
PHONE......................434 660-6907
Myscha Hargett-Gaines, *Principal*
EMP: 2
SALES (est): 108.4K **Privately Held**
SIC: 2844 Toilet preparations

(G-7704)
ERICSSON INC
314 Jefferson Ridge Pkwy (24501-6954)
PHONE......................434 592-5610
Mans Ulvestahl, *Manager*
EMP: 100
SALES (corp-wide): 23.5B **Privately Held**
WEB: www.ericsson.com
SIC: 3663 Radio broadcasting & communications equipment; cellular radio telephone; mobile communication equipment
HQ: Ericsson Inc.
  6300 Legacy Dr
  Plano TX 75024
  972 583-0000

(G-7705)
ERICSSON INC
5061d Fort Ave (24502-1601)
PHONE......................434 528-7000
Per-Arne Sandsto, *Principal*
EMP: 3
SALES (corp-wide): 23.5B **Privately Held**
WEB: www.ericsson.com
SIC: 3663 5065 Cellular radio telephone; electronic parts & equipment
HQ: Ericsson Inc.
  6300 Legacy Dr
  Plano TX 75024
  972 583-0000

(G-7706)
EXCEL PRSTHETICS ORTHOTICS INC
2201 Langhorne Rd Ste A (24501-1125)
PHONE......................434 528-3695
Michael Vogt, *Branch Mgr*
EMP: 2
SALES (corp-wide): 3.8MM **Privately Held**
WEB: www.excel-prosthetics.com
SIC: 3842 5999 Limbs, artificial; artificial limbs
PA: Excel Prosthetics & Orthotics, Inc.
  115 Albemarle Ave Se
  Roanoke VA 24013
  540 982-0205

(G-7707)
FINLY CORPORATION
3401 Forest Brook Rd (24501-6801)
P.O. Box 4237 (24502-0237)
PHONE......................434 385-5028
Royal E Fariss, *President*
Steven Hill, *Vice Pres*
Adam Fariss, *Plant Mgr*
Ann Fariss, *Treasurer*
Bennie Martin, *Sales Mgr*
EMP: 28 EST: 1971
SALES (est): 4.4MM **Privately Held**
WEB: www.finlycorporation.com
SIC: 3273 3272 7699 Ready-mixed concrete; septic tanks, concrete; septic tank cleaning service

(G-7708)
FLEET INTERNATIONAL INC C B (DH)
4615 Murray Pl (24502-2235)
P.O. Box 11349 (24506-1349)
PHONE......................866 255-6960
Doug Bellaire, *President*
William R Chambers, *President*
Robert Lemon, *Corp Secy*
EMP: 50
SQ FT: 33,000
SALES (est): 11.2MM **Publicly Held**
WEB: www.prestigebrands.com
SIC: 2844 Deodorants, personal
HQ: C. B. Fleet Company, Incorporated
  4615 Murray Pl
  Lynchburg VA 24502
  434 528-4000

(G-7709)
FLIPS GRAPHIX DESIGN
14413 Wards Rd (24502-4834)
PHONE......................434 237-3547
Flip Holbrook, *Principal*
EMP: 1
SALES (est): 110.2K **Privately Held**
SIC: 3993 Signs & advertising specialties

(G-7710)
FLOWERS BKG CO LYNCHBURG LLC (HQ)
Also Called: Flowers Bakery
1905 Hollins Mill Rd (24503-2761)
P.O. Box 3307 (24503-0307)
PHONE......................434 528-0441
J Forrest,
EMP: 100
SQ FT: 54,000
SALES (est): 39.6MM
SALES (corp-wide): 4.1B **Publicly Held**
SIC: 2051 Bakery: wholesale or wholesale/retail combined
PA: Flowers Foods, Inc.
  1919 Flowers Cir
  Thomasville GA 31757
  912 226-9110

(G-7711)
FLOWERS BKG CO LYNCHBURG LLC
3301 Odd Fellows Rd (24501-5013)
PHONE..................................434 528-0441
Allen Branscome, *Manager*
EMP: 28
SALES (corp-wide): 4.1B **Publicly Held**
SIC: 2051 Bread, all types (white, wheat, rye, etc): fresh or frozen
HQ: Flowers Baking Co. Of Lynchburg, Llc
1905 Hollins Mill Rd
Lynchburg VA 24503
434 528-0441

(G-7712)
FLOWERS BKG CO LYNCHBURG LLC
2120 Lakeside Dr (24501-6804)
PHONE..................................434 385-5044
Gill Reid, *Human Res Mgr*
Ralph Garrett, *Branch Mgr*
EMP: 1
SALES (corp-wide): 4.1B **Publicly Held**
WEB: www.lynchburgregion.org
SIC: 2051 Bread, cake & related products
HQ: Flowers Baking Co. Of Lynchburg, Llc
1905 Hollins Mill Rd
Lynchburg VA 24503
434 528-0441

(G-7713)
FLOWSERVE CORPORATION
5114 Woodall Rd (24502-2248)
P.O. Box 11318 (24506-1318)
PHONE..................................434 528-4400
Bill Fath, *Vice Pres*
Louis Bessiere, *Vice Pres*
Catherine Lee, *Opers Staff*
John Thilking, *Senior Engr*
Mark Knowles, *Controller*
EMP: 250
SALES (corp-wide): 3.9B **Publicly Held**
WEB: www.flowserve.com
SIC: 3561 Industrial pumps & parts
PA: Flowserve Corporation
5215 N Ocnnor Blvd Ste 23 Connor
Irving TX 75039
972 443-6500

(G-7714)
FRAMATOME INC
Also Called: Manufacturing Plant
1724 Mount Athos Rd (24504-5477)
PHONE..................................434 832-5000
Jere Laplatney, *Vice Pres*
Jim Murtha, *Project Mgr*
Cynthia Scruggs, *Buyer*
Jamie Campbell, *Engineer*
Jennifer Nelson, *Engineer*
EMP: 200
SALES (corp-wide): 4.2MM **Privately Held**
WEB: www.framatome.com
SIC: 2819 Nuclear fuel & cores, inorganic
HQ: Framatome Inc.
3315 Old Forest Rd
Lynchburg VA 24501

(G-7715)
FRAMATOME INC
7207 Ibm Dr (24501)
PHONE..................................434 832-3000
Chris Hamilton, *Opers Staff*
Judy Steele, *Buyer*
Michael W Rencheck, *Branch Mgr*
Joan Moore, *Administration*
Dixie Reichard, *Administration*
EMP: 500
SALES (corp-wide): 4.2MM **Privately Held**
WEB: www.orano.group
SIC: 1094 Uranium ore mining
HQ: Framatome Inc.
3315 Old Forest Rd
Lynchburg VA 24501

(G-7716)
FRAMATOME INC (DH)
3315 Old Forest Rd (24501-2912)
PHONE..................................434 832-3000
Gary Mignogna, *CEO*
George B Beam, *Senior VP*
Rick Walsh, *Project Mgr*
Kathy Williams, *CFO*

Laurie S Harris, *Treasurer*
◆ EMP: 500
SQ FT: 300,000
SALES (est): 910.3MM
SALES (corp-wide): 4.2MM **Privately Held**
WEB: www.framatome.com
SIC: 3823 3829 8711 5085 Industrial instrmnts msrmnt display/control process variable; measuring & controlling devices; engineering services; industrial supplies; valves & fittings; pumps & pumping equipment; industrial inorganic chemicals

(G-7717)
FRAMERY AND ARTS CORP
2703 Memorial Ave (24501-2625)
PHONE..................................434 525-0444
Jerry Shores, *President*
EMP: 4
SQ FT: 2,400
SALES (est): 110K **Privately Held**
WEB: www.framery-art-gallery.business.site
SIC: 3952 5999 Canvas, prepared on frames: artists'; artists' supplies & materials; picture frames, ready made; art dealers

(G-7718)
FRED FAUBER
258 Whispering Stream Ln (24501-7306)
PHONE..................................434 845-0303
Fred Fauber, *Owner*
EMP: 2
SALES (est): 164.1K **Privately Held**
SIC: 2411 0782 Logging; landscape contractors

(G-7719)
GALLAGHER-STONE INCORPORATED (PA)
2103 Wiggington Rd (24502-4667)
PHONE..................................434 528-5181
Michael J Stone, *President*
Gallagher Doris B, *Vice Pres*
Fred L Gallagher Jr, *Vice Pres*
EMP: 6
SQ FT: 1,200
SALES (est): 740.3K **Privately Held**
SIC: 3821 Laboratory equipment: fume hoods, distillation racks, etc.; laboratory furniture

(G-7720)
GATORGUARD LLC
3604 Montridge Pl (24501-3130)
PHONE..................................434 942-0245
Jeff Kirkland, *Partner*
EMP: 2
SALES (est): 100K **Privately Held**
SIC: 2952 Asphalt felts & coatings

(G-7721)
GLOBAL GOSPEL PUBLISHERS
221 Farley Branch Dr (24502-2364)
PHONE..................................434 582-5049
EMP: 1
SALES (est): 37.5K **Privately Held**
SIC: 2741 Miscellaneous publishing

(G-7722)
GODS COMPASS MOVIE LLC
1608 Linden Ave (24503-2409)
PHONE..................................434 219-6865
Stephan Schultze, *Principal*
EMP: 3
SALES (est): 126.9K **Privately Held**
WEB: www.wset.com
SIC: 2711 Newspapers

(G-7723)
GRAYSON FERGUSON WDWKG INC
2920 Sackett St (24501-4956)
PHONE..................................434 528-3405
Grayson Ferguson, *President*
EMP: 8
SALES (est): 1MM **Privately Held**
WEB: www.graysonferguson.com
SIC: 2431 Millwork

(G-7724)
GREAT WHITE BUFFALO ENTPS LLC
107 Jordan Dr (24502-3615)
PHONE..................................434 329-1150
Thomas Seamster,
EMP: 2
SALES (est): 100K **Privately Held**
SIC: 3441 Fabricated structural metal

(G-7725)
GRIFFIN PIPE PRODUCTS CO LLC
10 Adams St (24504-1446)
PHONE..................................434 845-8021
Scott Diestelkamp, *Branch Mgr*
EMP: 5
SALES (corp-wide): 1.5B **Publicly Held**
SIC: 3585 Refrigeration & heating equipment
HQ: Griffin Pipe Products Co., Llc
1011 Warrenville Rd # 550
Lisle IL 60532

(G-7726)
GRILLETECH LLC
3022 Memorial Ave (24501-3728)
PHONE..................................434 941-7129
Chris Driver,
Ben Boswell,
EMP: 2
SALES (est): 420K **Privately Held**
SIC: 3429 Motor vehicle hardware

(G-7727)
HANGER PRSTHETCS & ORTHO INC
Also Called: Lynchburg Orthopedic Lab
2015 Tate Springs Rd # 1 (24501-1100)
PHONE..................................434 846-1803
Terry Loveless, *Manager*
EMP: 6
SQ FT: 1,500
SALES (corp-wide): 1.1B **Publicly Held**
WEB: www.hangerclinic.com
SIC: 3842 8093 Limbs, artificial; specialty outpatient clinics
HQ: Hanger Prosthetics & Orthotics, Inc.
10910 Domain Dr Ste 300
Austin TX 78758
512 777-3800

(G-7728)
HANSON INDUSTRIES INC
19 Millrace Dr (24502-4343)
PHONE..................................434 845-9091
Robert B Harris Jr, *President*
Kennthe R Horner, *CFO*
EMP: 2
SALES (est): 225K **Privately Held**
WEB: www.hansonindinc.com
SIC: 3441 3469 Fabricated structural metal; cooking ware, porcelain enameled

(G-7729)
HARRINGTON CORPORATION (PA)
Also Called: Harco
3721 Cohen Pl (24501-5047)
P.O. Box 10335 (24506-0335)
PHONE..................................434 845-7094
Michael B Harrington, *President*
Kathy Baker, *Superintendent*
Steve Baily, *Vice Pres*
Eichmann E C, *Vice Pres*
Steven C Harrington, *Vice Pres*
◆ EMP: 103
SALES (est): 22.9MM **Privately Held**
WEB: www.harcofittings.com
SIC: 3089 3498 Fittings for pipe, plastic; fabricated pipe & fittings

(G-7730)
HARTNESS INTERNATIONAL A DIV
2250 Murrell Rd (24501-2141)
PHONE..................................434 455-0357
Greg Burns, *Principal*
Chad Jones, *Sales Staff*
EMP: 100
SALES (corp-wide): 14.9MM **Privately Held**
WEB: www.hartness.com
SIC: 3565 Packaging machinery

PA: Hartness International A Division Of Illinois Tool Works, Inc.
500 Hartness Dr
Greenville SC 29615
864 297-1200

(G-7731)
HEARTH PROS
20451 Timberlake Rd (24502-7204)
PHONE..................................434 237-5913
Mary Davis, *Treasurer*
EMP: 2 EST: 2012
SALES (est): 136K **Privately Held**
WEB: www.aquapros.com
SIC: 3272 Fireplace & chimney material: concrete

(G-7732)
HICKORY FRAME CORP
1400 Thurman Ave (24501-3428)
P.O. Box 11585 (24506-1585)
PHONE..................................434 847-8489
Jeff Bechtel Jr, *President*
EMP: 6
SQ FT: 30,000
SALES (est): 793K **Privately Held**
WEB: www.tablelegs4u.com
SIC: 2426 2439 Furniture stock & parts, hardwood; structural wood members

(G-7733)
HIGH GROUND PARTNERS LLC
1423 Robin Hood Pl (24503-2517)
PHONE..................................434 944-8254
Vaden L Cobb,
Roger W Beeker,
EMP: 1
SALES (est): 129.2K **Privately Held**
SIC: 3714 Motor vehicle parts & accessories

(G-7734)
HIP-HOP SPOT 24/7 LLC
100 Holmes Cir Apt 4 (24501-3009)
PHONE..................................434 660-3166
Kevin Stone,
EMP: 2
SALES (est): 81.9K **Privately Held**
SIC: 3993 7929 7389 Advertising novelties; musical entertainers; entertainment service;

(G-7735)
HOLCOMB ROCK COMPANY
4839 Holcomb Rock Rd (24503-6525)
P.O. Box 13, Coleman Falls (24536-0013)
PHONE..................................434 386-6050
Rick Kaster, *Partner*
Byron Wenger, *Partner*
EMP: 4
SALES (est): 496.6K **Privately Held**
SIC: 3621 Power generators

(G-7736)
HOMETOWN CREATIONS
1059 Coronado Ln (24502-1719)
PHONE..................................434 237-2364
Donna Tucker, *Owner*
EMP: 1 EST: 1996
SALES (est): 45.7K **Privately Held**
SIC: 2395 Emblems, embroidered

(G-7737)
ILLINOIS TOOL WORKS INC
ITW Packtron
1205 Mcconville Rd (24502-4535)
P.O. Box 4539 (24502-0539)
PHONE..................................434 239-6941
Ian Clelland, *Branch Mgr*
EMP: 72
SALES (corp-wide): 14.1B **Publicly Held**
WEB: www.itw.com
SIC: 3679 3675 Electronic circuits; electronic capacitors
PA: Illinois Tool Works Inc.
155 Harlem Ave
Glenview IL 60025
847 724-7500

(G-7738)
INDUSTRIAL PLATING CORP
318 Crowell Ln (24502-5567)
P.O. Box 318 (24505-0318)
PHONE..................................434 582-1920
Dave Doss, *Principal*
EMP: 9

SALES (est): 904.7K **Privately Held**
WEB: www.industrialplatingcorp.com
SIC: 3471 Electroplating of metals or
formed products

(G-7739)
**INNOVATIO SEALING TECH
CORP**
4925 Boonsboro Rd Pmb 212
(24503-2240)
PHONE..............................434 238-2397
Katrina Fields, *Principal*
Jason Brown, *Principal*
▲ EMP: 2
SALES (est): 124.7K **Privately Held**
SIC: 3053 Gaskets, all materials

(G-7740)
INNOVATIVE TECH INTL INC
Also Called: Novatech
220 Jefferson Ridge Pkwy (24501-6953)
PHONE..............................434 239-1979
Richard F Rochow, *President*
Lew Walton, *Vice Pres*
Mike Trepanitis, *VP Mfg*
Bobby Rowland, *Opers Staff*
Anne Austin, *Engineer*
EMP: 34
SQ FT: 14,000
SALES (est): 7.6MM **Privately Held**
WEB: www.novatechusa.com
SIC: 3441 8711 3537 Fabricated struc-
tural metal; engineering services; trucks,
tractors, loaders, carriers & similar equip-
ment

(G-7741)
**INNOVATIVE WIRELESS TECH
INC**
Also Called: I W T
1100 Main St Ste 202 (24504-1715)
PHONE..............................434 316-5230
Eric Hansen, *President*
Phil Carrier, *Vice Pres*
Steve Harrison, *Vice Pres*
Jim Silverstrim, *Vice Pres*
Peter Bronner, *Engineer*
EMP: 41
SQ FT: 5,068
SALES (est): 12.3MM **Privately Held**
WEB: www.iwtwireless.com
SIC: 3531 3532 Construction machinery;
mining machinery

(G-7742)
INSTANT REPLAY
2052 Garfield Ave (24501-6417)
PHONE..............................434 941-2568
Lee Luther, *Owner*
EMP: 1
SALES (est): 59.8K **Privately Held**
SIC: 2752 Commercial printing, litho-
graphic

(G-7743)
INTEGRA MUSIC GROUP
105 Cupola St (24502-5282)
PHONE..............................434 821-3796
EMP: 1
SALES: 15K **Privately Held**
SIC: 2741 Miscellaneous Publishing, Nsk

(G-7744)
INTERMET FOUNDRIES INC
1132 Mount Athos Rd (24504-5484)
PHONE..............................434 528-8721
EMP: 2 EST: 2018
SALES (est): 167.7K **Privately Held**
WEB: www.lynchburgva.gov
SIC: 3315 Steel wire & related products

(G-7745)
**INTERNATIONAL PAPER
COMPANY**
3491 Mayflower Dr (24501-5018)
PHONE..............................434 845-6071
Parcher Louie, *Mfg Mgr*
Donna McDaniel, *Purchasing*
Dave Olsen, *Branch Mgr*
Ron Anderson, *Executive*
Andy Johnson, *Maintence Staff*
EMP: 185
SALES (corp-wide): 22.3B **Publicly Held**
WEB: www.internationalpaper.com
SIC: 2621 Paper mills

PA: International Paper Company
6400 Poplar Ave
Memphis TN 38197
901 419-9000

(G-7746)
INTOUCH FOR INMATES LLC
212 Mountain Laurel Dr (24503-3756)
PHONE..............................862 246-6283
Lucas Dollarhite, *CEO*
EMP: 2 EST: 2016
SALES (est): 56.5K **Privately Held**
WEB: www.intouchforinmates.com
SIC: 7372 7389 Business oriented com-
puter software;

(G-7747)
JACK EINREINHOF
Also Called: Bingo Bugle Newspaper
136 Yorkshire Cir (24502-2757)
PHONE..............................434 239-3072
Jack Einreinhof, *Director*
EMP: 1
SALES (est): 58.1K **Privately Held**
WEB: www.bingobugle.com
SIC: 2711 Newspapers, publishing & print-
ing

(G-7748)
JAMES RIVER INDUSTRIES BT
300 Lucado Pl (24504-5483)
PHONE..............................702 515-9937
EMP: 3
SALES (est): 214K **Privately Held**
SIC: 3531 Construction Machinery, Nsk

(G-7749)
**KAYS PHOTOGRAPHY AND
PRINTS**
1560 Caroline St (24501-5402)
PHONE..............................757 344-4817
Kay Reid, *Principal*
EMP: 2 EST: 2018
SALES (est): 83.9K **Privately Held**
WEB: www.kayreidphotography.net
SIC: 2752 Commercial printing, litho-
graphic

(G-7750)
KDC US HOLDING INC (DH)
Also Called: Kdc Lynchburg
1000 Robins Rd (24504-3516)
P.O. Box 10341 (24506-0341)
PHONE..............................434 845-7073
Ian Kalinosky, *President*
Ian Kalinoski, *President*
David Wardach, *Vice Pres*
Arturo Fernandez, *Engineer*
Eric Shultz, *Engineer*
▲ EMP: 180
SQ FT: 200,000
SALES (est): 49.2MM
SALES (corp-wide): 1.1B **Privately Held**
WEB: www.kdc-one.com
SIC: 2844 2085 Cosmetic preparations;
grain alcohol for medicinal purposes
HQ: Knowlton Development Corporation
Inc
375 Boul Roland-Therrien
Longueuil QC J4H 4
450 243-2000

(G-7751)
**KERSCHBAMER
WOODWORKING LLC**
1701 12th St (24501-1953)
PHONE..............................434 455-2508
EMP: 1
SALES (est): 88K **Privately Held**
WEB: www.kerschbamer.com
SIC: 2431 Millwork

(G-7752)
L & R PRECISION TOOLING INC
3720 Cohen Pl (24501-5046)
PHONE..............................434 525-4120
Allen S Leath, *President*
Clay Leath, *President*
Mark White, *Accounts Mgr*
Jackie Satterfield, *Admin Sec*
EMP: 37
SALES (est): 6.2MM **Privately Held**
WEB: www.lrprecisiontooling.com
SIC: 3599 3398 3544 Machine shop, job-
bing & repair; metal heat treating; special
dies, tools, jigs & fixtures

(G-7753)
L3HARRIS TECHNOLOGIES INC
Also Called: Harris Corporation
221 Jefferson Ridge Pkwy (24501-6952)
PHONE..............................434 455-6600
Phil Beeson, *Counsel*
Emily Carden, *Engineer*
Brian McQueen, *Engineer*
Grady Powers, *Engineer*
Charles Shaughussy, *Branch Mgr*
EMP: 441
SALES (corp-wide): 6.8B **Publicly Held**
WEB: www.harris.com
SIC: 3663 Radio & TV communications
equipment
PA: L3harris Technologies, Inc.
1025 W Nasa Blvd
Melbourne FL 32919
321 727-9100

(G-7754)
LABYRINTH WOODWORKS LLC
66 North Princeton Cir (24503-1547)
PHONE..............................206 235-6272
Marc Mehrotra, *Principal*
EMP: 1
SALES (est): 54.1K **Privately Held**
SIC: 2431 Millwork

(G-7755)
LARK PRINTING INC
485 Hopkins Rd (24502-4839)
PHONE..............................434 237-4449
EMP: 2 EST: 2001
SALES (est): 204.5K **Privately Held**
SIC: 2752 Lithographic Commercial Print-
ing

(G-7756)
**LEONARD ALUM UTLITY
BLDNGS INC**
20530 Timberlake Rd (24502-7211)
PHONE..............................434 237-5301
Jack Swicher, *Manager*
EMP: 3
SALES (corp-wide): 88.2MM **Privately
Held**
WEB: www.leonardusa.com
SIC: 3448 Farm & utility buildings
PA: Leonard Aluminum Utility Buildings, Inc.
566 Holly Springs Rd
Mount Airy NC 27030
888 590-4769

(G-7757)
LINCOLN INDUSTRIES LLC
2925 Rivermont Ave (24503-1400)
PHONE..............................434 509-7191
Abraham Hebert, *Principal*
EMP: 2
SALES (est): 74.6K **Privately Held**
SIC: 3999 Manufacturing industries

(G-7758)
LIVE TRENDY OR DIE LLC
1615 Spottswood Pl (24503-2323)
PHONE..............................856 371-7638
Stephanie Atkinson, *Principal*
EMP: 2
SALES (est): 113.6K **Privately Held**
WEB: www.livetrendyordie.com
SIC: 3544 Special dies & tools

(G-7759)
LUCIA COATES
Also Called: Montana Plains Bread Co
4925 Boonsboro Rd (24503-2240)
PHONE..............................434 384-1779
Lucia Coates, *Owner*
EMP: 3
SALES (est): 188.5K **Privately Held**
SIC: 2051 Bread, cake & related products

(G-7760)
LYNCHBURG FABRICATION LLC
503 Old Plantation Dr (24502-6963)
PHONE..............................434 660-0935
Gould Thorpe, *Co-Owner*
Frederick Wilson,
EMP: 5 EST: 2011
SALES (est): 826.6K **Privately Held**
WEB: www.lynfab.com
SIC: 3441 Fabricated structural metal

(G-7761)
**LYNCHBURG FABRICATION INC
VA**
2824 Carroll Ave (24501-4911)
P.O. Box 10306 (24506-0306)
PHONE..............................434 473-7291
Freddie Wilson, *President*
Matt Gluldthorpe, *President*
EMP: 10
SALES (est): 1MM **Privately Held**
WEB: www.lynfab.com
SIC: 3441 Fabricated structural metal

(G-7762)
LYNCHBURG MACHINING LLC
120 Bradley Dr (24501-4949)
PHONE..............................434 846-7327
Greg White, *Opers Mgr*
James Ferguson, *Mng Member*
Jason Rice,
Katherine Rice,
EMP: 13 EST: 2014
SQ FT: 20,000
SALES (est): 2MM **Privately Held**
WEB: www.lynchburgmachining.com
SIC: 3541 3543 3366 Machine tools,
metal cutting type; industrial patterns;
castings (except die)

(G-7763)
**LYNCHBURG POWDER
COATING**
Also Called: Lynchburg Pwdr Cting Mdia Blst
317 Crowell Ln (24502-5568)
PHONE..............................434 239-8454
Edward Litchford, *Owner*
EMP: 3
SALES (est): 218K **Privately Held**
WEB: www.lynchburgpowdercoating.com
SIC: 3479 Coating of metals & formed
products

(G-7764)
**LYNCHBURG READY-MIX CON
CO INC (PA)**
100 Halsey Rd (24501-2540)
P.O. Box 10066 (24506-0066)
PHONE..............................434 846-6563
Robert M O'Brian, *President*
Sydney Burns, *General Mgr*
O'Brian Rebecca Holt, *Vice Pres*
John Wegener, *Plant Mgr*
Kevin Wegener, *Plant Mgr*
EMP: 35
SQ FT: 2,500
SALES (est): 3.7MM **Privately Held**
WEB: www.lrmcc.com
SIC: 3273 3272 Ready-mixed concrete;
concrete products

(G-7765)
LYNCHBURG WRAPS
1053 Cottontown Rd (24503-4961)
PHONE..............................434 385-1370
Greg Harrison, *Principal*
EMP: 1
SALES (est): 57K **Privately Held**
WEB: www.outtasightwraps.com
SIC: 3993 Signs & advertising specialties

(G-7766)
LYNDON STEEL COMPANY LLC
99 Woodberry Ln Ste E (24502-4459)
PHONE..............................434 660-0829
EMP: 3
SALES (corp-wide): 1B **Privately Held**
WEB: www.lyndonsteel.com
SIC: 3441 Fabricated structural metal
HQ: Lyndon Steel Company Llc
1947 Union Cross Rd
Winston Salem NC 27107
336 785-0848

(G-7767)
M MCGUIRE WOODWORKS
407 Howard Dr (24503-1716)
PHONE..............................434 841-3702
EMP: 1
SALES (est): 54.1K **Privately Held**
SIC: 2431 Millwork

(G-7768)
MAGNIGEN LLC
1318 Eyrie View Dr (24503-6570)
PHONE..............................434 420-1435

G
E
O
G
R
A
P
H
I
C

William A Hunter Jr, *Administration*
EMP: 5
SALES (est): 340.5K **Privately Held**
WEB: www.magnigen.com
SIC: 7372 Prepackaged software

(G-7769)
MAYSTEEL PORTERS LLC
3726 Cohen Pl (24501-5046)
PHONE.............................434 846-7412
Todd Van Noordtt, *Purch Agent*
Jim Smith, *Manager*
Stephanie Hensler, *Senior Mgr*
Mike Worth, *Info Tech Mgr*
EMP: 110
SALES (corp-wide): 33.1MM **Privately Held**
WEB: www.portersfab.com
SIC: 3578 Automatic teller machines (ATM)
HQ: Maysteel Porters, Llc
6199 County Rd W
Allenton WI 53002
262 251-1632

(G-7770)
MELOS MANUFACTURING
917 Old Trents Ferry Rd (24503-1111)
PHONE.............................434 401-9496
Richard Melos, *Principal*
EMP: 2
SALES (est): 84.6K **Privately Held**
WEB: www.melosmfrg.com
SIC: 3599 Machine shop, jobbing & repair

(G-7771)
MERCURY HOUR
283 Gardenpark Ave (24502-2397)
PHONE.............................434 237-4011
Edith Custer, *Owner*
EMP: 3 **EST:** 1974
SALES (est): 125.8K **Privately Held**
SIC: 2721 Periodicals

(G-7772)
MICROWAVE CIRCUITS INC
1611 Kemper St (24501-2033)
PHONE.............................434 455-2800
Carl Hofferberth, *CEO*
EMP: 2
SALES (est): 113.2K **Privately Held**
WEB: www.diplexers.com
SIC: 3679 Electronic circuits

(G-7773)
MIGHTY OAKS TREE TRIMING & LOG
507 Cornerstone St (24502-5342)
PHONE.............................585 471-0213
Thomas Parmiter, *Principal*
EMP: 2
SALES (est): 88.6K **Privately Held**
SIC: 2411 Logging

(G-7774)
MLD PUBLISHING
1504 Longview Rd Apt 200 (24501-6340)
PHONE.............................434 535-6008
Jermal Word, *Owner*
EMP: 5
SALES (est): 980K **Privately Held**
SIC: 2721 Periodicals

(G-7775)
MOUNTAIN PLAINS INDUSTRIES
1088 Macon Loop (24503-6326)
PHONE.............................434 386-0100
James H Wilson, *Owner*
EMP: 1
SALES (est): 71K **Privately Held**
WEB: www.precisionplustargets.com
SIC: 3949 Targets, archery & rifle shooting

(G-7776)
NHANCE TECHNOLOGIES INC
122 Cornerstone St (24502-5346)
PHONE.............................434 582-6110
Todd Sneed, *President*
EMP: 10
SQ FT: 2,400
SALES (est): 820K **Privately Held**
WEB: www.nhancetech.com
SIC: 3699 Countermeasure simulators, electric

(G-7777)
NORCRAFT COMPANIES LP
Also Called: Kitchen & Bath Ideas
1 Macel Dr (24502-2274)
PHONE.............................434 385-7500
Amy Carpenter, *Materials Mgr*
Becky Campbell, *Purchasing*
Michael Dunn, *Manager*
EMP: 300
SALES (corp-wide): 5.7B **Publicly Held**
WEB: www.norcraftcompanies.com
SIC: 2434 Wood kitchen cabinets
HQ: Norcraft Companies, L.P.
1 Masterbrand Cabinets Dr
Jasper IN 47546
651 234-3300

(G-7778)
OLD DOMINION WOOD PRODUCTS INC
Also Called: Old Dominion Furniture
800 Craddock St (24501-1700)
P.O. Box 11226 (24506-1226)
PHONE.............................434 845-5511
George R Harris, *President*
Ann S Harris, *Treasurer*
Laura Morgan, *Sales Staff*
Whitney Perrow, *Sales Staff*
Barbara Wood, *Director*
◆ **EMP:** 20
SQ FT: 60,000
SALES (est): 3.8MM **Privately Held**
WEB: www.olddominionfurniture.com
SIC: 2599 2511 Restaurant furniture, wood or metal; wood household furniture

(G-7779)
OUTTHINK CORPORATION
2001 Autumn Dr (24502-1941)
PHONE.............................434 426-7706
EMP: 2
SALES (est): 104.7K **Privately Held**
WEB: www.outthinkgroup.com
SIC: 2741 Miscellaneous publishing

(G-7780)
PAC BRIDGE LLC
Also Called: SIGNS BY TOMORROW LYNCHBURG
3406 Forest Brook Rd (24501-6802)
PHONE.............................434 385-8070
Arthur Pike, *President*
EMP: 4
SQ FT: 2,800
SALES (est): 125.8K **Privately Held**
SIC: 3993 Signs & advertising specialties

(G-7781)
PAPERBUZZ
18 West Princeton Cir # 85 (24503-1465)
PHONE.............................434 528-2899
Natalie Langley, *Owner*
EMP: 2
SALES (est): 214.6K **Privately Held**
SIC: 2759 Invitation & stationery printing & engraving

(G-7782)
PARKER-HANNIFIN CORPORATION
Integrated Sealing Systems Div
3700 Mayflower Dr (24501-5023)
PHONE.............................434 846-6541
Jason Brown, *General Mgr*
Steven Margules, *General Mgr*
Rainbow Wang, *Mfg Mgr*
Donnie Gilbert, *Safety Mgr*
Michael Littrell, *Buyer*
EMP: 400
SALES (corp-wide): 14.3B **Publicly Held**
WEB: www.phtruck.com
SIC: 3053 Gaskets, all materials
PA: Parker-Hannifin Corporation
6035 Parkland Blvd
Cleveland OH 44124
216 896-3000

(G-7783)
PATRON ID INC
828 Main St Ste 1402 (24504-1548)
PHONE.............................954 282-6636
Sabbato Avello, *CEO*
John Donges, *CFO*
Micah Gaudio, *CIO*
EMP: 3

SALES (est): 500K **Privately Held**
SIC: 7372 Prepackaged software

(G-7784)
PEARSON EQUIPMENT COMPANY
Also Called: Bobcat of Lynchburg
3904 Harris Ln (24501-5054)
PHONE.............................434 845-3171
Tim Carrico, *Principal*
Michael Bradshaw, *Manager*
EMP: 6 **Privately Held**
WEB: www.pearsonequipment.com
SIC: 3531 Construction machinery
PA: Pearson Equipment Company
3900 Harris Ln
Lynchburg VA 24501

(G-7785)
PEPSI-COLA METRO BTLG CO INC
121 Bradley Dr (24501-4950)
PHONE.............................434 528-5107
Sean Councell, *Manager*
EMP: 54
SQ FT: 100,000
SALES (corp-wide): 67.1B **Publicly Held**
WEB: www.pepsico.com
SIC: 2086 5149 Soft drinks: packaged in cans, bottles, etc.; soft drinks
HQ: Pepsi-Cola Metropolitan Bottling Company, Inc.
1111 Westchester Ave
White Plains NY 10604
914 767-6000

(G-7786)
PIERCE PUBLISHING
100 Earls Ct (24503-2149)
PHONE.............................434 386-5667
Julie Pierce, *Owner*
EMP: 1
SALES (est): 72.2K **Privately Held**
SIC: 2741 Miscellaneous publishing

(G-7787)
PRESS OIL & VINEGAR LLC
1005 Grand View Cir (24502-2316)
PHONE.............................434 534-2915
Jennifer Blankenstein, *Principal*
EMP: 4
SALES (est): 88.3K **Privately Held**
SIC: 2099 Vinegar

(G-7788)
PRINT SQUAD LLC
6412 Pawnee Dr (24502-5214)
PHONE.............................434 609-3335
Brian Long, *Principal*
EMP: 2
SALES (est): 101.5K **Privately Held**
SIC: 2752 Commercial printing, offset

(G-7789)
PRINT WORLD INC
701 Leesville Rd (24502-2813)
PHONE.............................434 237-2200
William A James, *President*
Nancy M James, *Vice Pres*
EMP: 14 **EST:** 1979
SQ FT: 7,000
SALES (est): 1.2MM **Privately Held**
WEB: www.printworksva.com
SIC: 2752 Commercial printing, offset

(G-7790)
PROGRESS PRINTING COMPANY (PA)
Also Called: Progress Printing Plus
2677 Waterlick Rd (24502-4861)
PHONE.............................434 239-9213
Michael A Thornton, *CEO*
Thornton Michael A, *President*
Dickie Beale, *President*
Sherrill Wright, *President*
Deidra B Eland, *Vice Pres*
EMP: 95 **EST:** 1962
SQ FT: 212,000
SALES (est): 43.9MM **Privately Held**
WEB: www.progressprintplus.com
SIC: 2796 2752 2789 2759 Platemaking services; commercial printing, offset; bookbinding & related work; commercial printing

(G-7791)
PROGRESSIVE MACHINE WORKS
1359 Waterlick Rd (24501-7224)
PHONE.............................434 237-5517
Kirk Nuckols, *Owner*
EMP: 1 **EST:** 2001
SALES (est): 130.2K **Privately Held**
SIC: 3599 Machine shop, jobbing & repair

(G-7792)
PROLIFIC PURCHASING PROPERTIES
1302 Hendricks Ave (24501-5712)
PHONE.............................434 329-1476
Andy Cooper, *Principal*
EMP: 1
SALES (est): 37.5K **Privately Held**
SIC: 2741 Miscellaneous publishing

(G-7793)
PROTOTEC INC
1431 Waterlick Rd (24501-7259)
PHONE.............................434 832-7440
Daniel S Moon, *President*
Theresa G Moon, *Vice Pres*
EMP: 5
SQ FT: 2,000
SALES (est): 300K **Privately Held**
WEB: www.prototec2000.com
SIC: 3549 Metalworking machinery

(G-7794)
PURE EARTH RECYCLING TECH INC
1009 Misty Mountain Rd # 1613 (24502-5184)
PHONE.............................434 944-6262
Michael Mongelli, *President*
Leslie J Colby, *Vice Pres*
Leslie Kozera, *Vice Pres*
EMP: 2
SQ FT: 13,600
SALES (est): 361.8K **Privately Held**
SIC: 2611 Pulp mills, mechanical & recycling processing

(G-7795)
Q P I INC
Also Called: Royal County Arts
1000 Commerce St (24504-1702)
P.O. Box 853 (24505-0853)
PHONE.............................434 528-0092
J C Davis Jr, *President*
Audrey Davis, *Corp Secy*
Timothy S Davis, *Vice Pres*
EMP: 5
SALES (est): 662.1K **Privately Held**
SIC: 2899 8999 Chemical preparations; art related services

(G-7796)
QPI
548 Oakley Ave (24501-3649)
PHONE.............................434 528-0092
EMP: 3
SALES (est): 198.7K **Privately Held**
SIC: 2869 Industrial organic chemicals

(G-7797)
R R DONNELLEY & SONS COMPANY
Also Called: R R Donnelley Printing
4201 Murray Pl (24501-5099)
P.O. Box 11829 (24506-1829)
PHONE.............................434 846-7371
Horst Fleck, *Manager*
EMP: 860
SALES (corp-wide): 6.2B **Publicly Held**
WEB: www.rrd.com
SIC: 2759 Commercial printing
PA: R. R. Donnelley & Sons Company
35 W Wacker Dr
Chicago IL 60601
312 326-8000

(G-7798)
RADER CABINETS
183 Brookwood Dr (24501-7429)
PHONE.............................434 610-1954
Jim Rader, *Principal*
EMP: 2
SALES (est): 131.2K **Privately Held**
SIC: 2434 Wood kitchen cabinets

▲ = Import ▼=Export
◆ =Import/Export

(G-7799)
REDDZWAY LLC
218 Mill View Ln (24502-4232)
PHONE..............................434 515-0791
Kristie Rucker, *Owner*
EMP: 1
SALES (est): 39.6K **Privately Held**
SIC: 3999 Hair & hair-based products

(G-7800)
REEDS CARBIDE SAW SERVICE
Also Called: Reeds Carbide Saw and Tool
1315 Commerce St (24504-1803)
PHONE..............................434 846-6436
Scott Murphy, *President*
EMP: 15 EST: 1974
SQ FT: 7,500
SALES (est): 2MM **Privately Held**
SIC: 3425 7699 3545 Saw blades &
handsaws; tool repair services; drill bits,
metalworking

(G-7801)
RELIANT CEM SERVICES INC
630 Wyndhurst Dr Apt C (24502-3454)
PHONE..............................717 459-4990
Michael Kinard, *President*
Steven Scannapieco, *Vice Pres*
Arlene Rettew, *CFO*
EMP: 4
SQ FT: 800
SALES (est): 666.7K **Privately Held**
WEB: www.reliantcemservices.com
SIC: 3829 Instrument board gauges, auto-
motive: computerized

(G-7802)
**RIVERSEDGE FURNITURE CO
INC (PA)**
107 Hexham Dr (24502-3012)
PHONE..............................434 847-4155
James McCloskey, *President*
Mark L Stubstad, *President*
Glenn Damiani, *Manager*
Amy Jones, *Admin Asst*
▲ EMP: 27
SQ FT: 6,000
SALES (est): 2.2MM **Privately Held**
WEB: www.riversedgeusa.net
SIC: 2512 Upholstered household furniture

(G-7803)
**RMJ MACHINE TECHNOLOGIES
INC**
171 Jordan Dr (24502-3615)
P.O. Box 15145 (24502-9015)
PHONE..............................434 582-4719
Roger Cash, *President*
Melissa Cash, *Vice Pres*
EMP: 14
SQ FT: 7,000
SALES (est): 1MM **Privately Held**
WEB: www.rmjmachine.com
SIC: 3599 Machine shop, jobbing & repair

(G-7804)
SAJAMES PUBLICATIONS LLC
71 Timber Ct (24501-2950)
PHONE..............................434 509-5331
Stephanie James, *Principal*
EMP: 1
SALES (est): 37.5K **Privately Held**
SIC: 2741 Miscellaneous publishing

(G-7805)
SALT CEDAR PUBLICATIONS
116 Temple Cir (24502-2416)
PHONE..............................434 258-5333
Davis Charmaine, *Principal*
EMP: 1
SALES (est): 73.4K **Privately Held**
SIC: 2741 Miscellaneous publishing

(G-7806)
**SERVICE PRINTING OF
LYNCHBURG**
Also Called: Service Printing Co
1201 Commerce St (24504-1801)
PHONE..............................434 845-3681
Alan Layne, *President*
Mary J G Layne, *Vice Pres*
EMP: 6 EST: 1922
SQ FT: 5,600

SALES (est): 648.7K **Privately Held**
WEB: www.serviceprinting.net
SIC: 2752 Commercial printing, offset

(G-7807)
SIMPLY CANDLES & GIFTS
1009 Misty Mountain Rd # 1323
(24502-5184)
PHONE..............................315 806-4204
Susie Lake, *Principal*
EMP: 1 EST: 2018
SALES (est): 39.6K **Privately Held**
SIC: 3999 Candles

(G-7808)
SML PACKAGING LLC
117 Greystone Dr (24502-4893)
P.O. Box 11405 (24506-1405)
PHONE..............................434 528-3640
Mark Wojdyla, *Mng Member*
EMP: 12
SQ FT: 6,000
SALES (est): 3.5MM **Privately Held**
WEB: www.smlpkg.com
SIC: 3565 Packaging machinery

(G-7809)
SOUTHERN AIR SHEET METAL
5 Millrace Dr (24502-4343)
PHONE..............................434 907-2268
EMP: 2
SALES (est): 207.2K **Privately Held**
SIC: 3444 Sheet metalwork

(G-7810)
SOUTHERN FIRE & SAFETY CO
185 Lakehaven Pl (24502-6898)
PHONE..............................434 546-6774
Christi O'Daniel, *Owner*
EMP: 2
SALES (est): 69K **Privately Held**
SIC: 3999 7389 Grenades, hand (fire ex-
tinguishers);

(G-7811)
SPLENDOR PUBLISHING
308 Kenyon St (24501-3336)
PHONE..............................434 665-2339
Sandra Thomas, *Principal*
EMP: 2
SALES (est): 59.2K **Privately Held**
SIC: 2741 Miscellaneous publishing

(G-7812)
STAMPTECH INC
19 Millrace Dr (24502-4343)
PHONE..............................434 845-9091
Roger Dale McLawhorn Jr, *President*
EMP: 3
SALES (corp-wide): 19.4MM **Privately
Held**
WEB: www.aocmetals.com
SIC: 3469 Metal stampings
HQ: Stamptech, Inc.
13140 Parkers Battery Rd
Chester VA 23836

(G-7813)
STARMARK CABINETRY
1 Macel Dr (24502-2274)
PHONE..............................434 385-7500
John Widseth, *Branch Mgr*
EMP: 10
SQ FT: 127,000
SALES (corp-wide): 5.7B **Publicly Held**
WEB: www.starmarkcabinetry.com
SIC: 2434 Vanities, bathroom: wood
HQ: Starmark Cabinetry
600 E 48th St N
Sioux Falls SD 57104
800 755-7789

(G-7814)
STYLEWIRE LLC
1309 Eyrie View Dr (24503-6571)
PHONE..............................770 841-1300
Sam Avello, *Managing Prtnr*
Gregory Tautkus, *Managing Prtnr*
EMP: 2 EST: 2012
SALES (est): 141.9K **Privately Held**
SIC: 3944 Electronic toys

(G-7815)
**SUGARLOAF ALPACA
COMPANY LLC**
2021 Rivermont Ave (24503-4120)
PHONE..............................240 500-0007
Nancy Brandt,
EMP: 2
SALES (est): 131.5K **Privately Held**
SIC: 2231 Alpacas, mohair: woven

(G-7816)
SUNNY SLOPE LLC
4716 John Scott Dr (24503-1004)
PHONE..............................434 384-8994
EMP: 1
SALES (est): 39.6K **Privately Held**
SIC: 3999 Manufacturing industries

(G-7817)
T5 GROUP LLC
213 Two Creek Dr (24502-5138)
PHONE..............................704 575-7721
Kenneth H Terrell, *Administration*
EMP: 5
SALES (est): 467.6K **Privately Held**
WEB: www.t5groupllc.com
SIC: 7372 Prepackaged software

(G-7818)
TABB ENTERPRISE LLC
6221 Pawtucket Dr (24502-5215)
PHONE..............................434 238-7196
Sampson Tabb,
EMP: 10
SALES (est): 120K **Privately Held**
SIC: 3589 Commercial cleaning equipment

(G-7819)
TESSY PLASTICS LLC
231 Jefferson Ridge Pkwy (24501-6952)
PHONE..............................434 385-5700
Kenneth Beck, *President*
▲ EMP: 200
SALES (est): 33.8MM
SALES (corp-wide): 393.5MM **Privately
Held**
WEB: www.tessyva.com
SIC: 3089 Injection molded finished plastic
products
PA: Tessy Plastics Corp.
700 Visions Dr
Skaneateles NY 13152
315 689-3924

(G-7820)
TESSY PLASTICS CORP
231 Jefferson Ridge Pkwy (24501-6952)
PHONE..............................434 385-5700
Doug Jobe, *Opers Mgr*
George Smith, *QC Dir*
Bev Burford, *QC Mgr*
Ron Desalis, *Engineer*
Charles McClendon, *Engineer*
EMP: 140
SALES (corp-wide): 393.5MM **Privately
Held**
WEB: www.tessy.com
SIC: 3089 3549 Injection molded finished
plastic products; metalworking machinery
PA: Tessy Plastics Corp.
700 Visions Dr
Skaneateles NY 13152
315 689-3924

(G-7821)
TETGRAPHIC INC
3616 Campbell Ave Apt 1 (24501-4523)
PHONE..............................434 845-4450
Lloyd Pusey, *President*
Ella Wqz, *Admin Sec*
EMP: 4 EST: 1976
SALES (est): 300K **Privately Held**
WEB: www.tetragraphicsinc.com
SIC: 2759 Commercial printing

(G-7822)
TETRA GRAPHICS INC
3616 Campbell Ave (24501-4523)
PHONE..............................434 845-4450
Lloyd Pusey, *President*
Lloyd J Pusey, *President*
Ella W Pusey, *Treasurer*
EMP: 2 EST: 1974
SQ FT: 4,400

SALES (est): 100K **Privately Held**
WEB: www.tetragraphicsinc.com
SIC: 2796 7336 Lithographic plates, posi-
tives or negatives; color separations for
printing; art design services

(G-7823)
THEODORE TURPIN
Also Called: Quality Home Improvements
1008 Polk St (24504-3025)
PHONE..............................434 485-6600
Theodore Turpin, *Owner*
EMP: 3 EST: 2011
SALES (est): 213.3K **Privately Held**
SIC: 2841 Soap & other detergents

(G-7824)
TOOL WAGON LLC
1114 Templeton Mill Rd (24503-6451)
PHONE..............................434 610-9664
Richard Lee Brown II,
EMP: 1
SALES (est): 568.8K **Privately Held**
SIC: 2451 Mobile homes

(G-7825)
**TORRENT LOADING SYSTEMS
LLC**
406 Oakridge Blvd (24502-4722)
PHONE..............................434 509-7307
Paul Shaskan, *Principal*
EMP: 6 EST: 2013
SALES (est): 503.5K **Privately Held**
WEB: www.torrentloadingsystems.com
SIC: 3812 Defense systems & equipment

(G-7826)
**TRAX INTERNATIONAL
CORPORATION**
Also Called: Trax Energy Solutions
5061 Fort Ave (24502-1601)
PHONE..............................434 485-7100
F Craig Wilson, *Branch Mgr*
EMP: 4
SALES (corp-wide): 215.9MM **Privately
Held**
WEB: www.traxintl.com
SIC: 7372 Prepackaged software
PA: Trax International Corporation
8337 W Sunset Rd Ste 250
Las Vegas NV 89113
702 216-4455

(G-7827)
TREVOR LLC
Also Called: American Electric Motors
3701 Mayflower Dr (24501-5024)
PHONE..............................434 528-3884
Chris Carwile,
Wendell Carwile,
▲ EMP: 2
SQ FT: 10,000
SALES (est): 200K **Privately Held**
SIC: 7694 Electric motor repair

(G-7828)
TRI-TECH LABORATORIES LLC
Also Called: Knowlton Packaging
1000 Robins Rd (24504-3516)
PHONE..............................434 845-7073
EMP: 2
SALES (est): 104.2K **Privately Held**
SIC: 2844 2085 Toilet preparations; grain
alcohol for medicinal purposes

(G-7829)
UNSEEN TECHNOLOGIES INC
22664 Timberlake Rd (24502-7304)
PHONE..............................704 207-7391
Todd Zak, *President*
EMP: 2
SALES (est): 116.1K **Privately Held**
SIC: 7372 7389 Business oriented com-
puter software;

(G-7830)
UPSCALE TIME LLC
20911 Timberlake Rd Ste F (24502-7243)
PHONE..............................434 832-0101
Darrell Spencer, *Principal*
EMP: 4
SALES (est): 27.1K **Privately Held**
WEB: www.upscaletime.com
SIC: 3915 Jewelry soldering for the trade

GEOGRAPHIC

(G-7831)
V T R INTERNATIONAL INC
19206 Forest Rd (24502-4478)
PHONE......................................434 385-5300
Joseph Nuccioh, *President*
EMP: 4 EST: 2001
SALES (est): 414.6K **Privately Held**
WEB: www.repairedbyvtr.com
SIC: 3663 Radio broadcasting & communications equipment

(G-7832)
VENOMOUS SCENTS & NOVELTIES
918 Pierce St (24501-1831)
PHONE......................................434 660-1164
Shanna Berryman, *Owner*
EMP: 1
SALES (est): 92.8K **Privately Held**
SIC: 3679 Electronic loads & power supplies

(G-7833)
VIRGINIA BLADE INC
5177 Boonsboro Rd (24503-2116)
PHONE......................................434 384-1282
Duke Dudley, *Principal*
EMP: 2
SALES (est): 161.1K **Privately Held**
WEB: www.va-blade.myshopify.com
SIC: 3421 Knives: butchers', hunting, pocket, etc.

(G-7834)
VIRGINIA STEEL & BUILDING SPC
713 Jefferson St (24504-1409)
P.O. Box 1536 (24505-1536)
PHONE......................................434 528-4302
Michael A Suchodolski, *President*
Tina Fleshman, *Corp Secy*
Fleshman Tina Dalton, *Vice Pres*
EMP: 10
SQ FT: 20,000
SALES (est): 1.4MM **Privately Held**
SIC: 3441 5051 Building components, structural steel; iron & steel (ferrous) products

(G-7835)
WAHOO INDUSTRIES
3000 Lennox St (24501-4923)
PHONE......................................434 929-2466
EMP: 2
SALES (est): 110.3K **Privately Held**
WEB: www.wahooindustries.net
SIC: 3441 Fabricated structural metal

(G-7836)
WARWICK PUBLISHERS INC
Also Called: Warwick House Publishers
720 Court St (24504-1406)
PHONE......................................434 846-1200
Peter Houck, *President*
Joyce Maddox, *Manager*
Leighton Houck, *Admin Sec*
EMP: 3
SQ FT: 1,200
SALES (est): 172.5K **Privately Held**
WEB: www.warwickpublishers.com
SIC: 2731 Book publishing

(G-7837)
WEGMANN USA INC (DH)
30 Millrace Dr (24502-4342)
P.O. Box 11648 (24506-1648)
PHONE......................................434 385-1580
Charles Troy Warren, *President*
Ashwell Danny Davis, *Vice Pres*
Bryan Lowe, *Engineer*
Ashwell Davis, *VP Finance*
Bonnie McCafferty, *Admin Asst*
◆ EMP: 100
SQ FT: 35,000
SALES (est): 19.8MM
SALES (corp-wide): 2.5B **Privately Held**
WEB: www.wegmannusa.com
SIC: 3462 3489 8331 3444 Iron & steel forgings; projectors: depth charge, grenade, rocket, etc.; job training services; sheet metalwork; partitions & fixtures, except wood

HQ: Krauss-Maffei Wegmann Gmbh & Co.
Kg
Krauss-Maffei-Str. 11
Munchen 80997
898 140-50

(G-7838)
WESTOVER DAIRY
2801 Fort Ave (24501-3309)
PHONE......................................434 528-2560
Roger Miller, *Principal*
EMP: 1
SALES (est): 127.9MM **Publicly Held**
SIC: 2099 Food preparations
PA: The Kroger Co
1014 Vine St Ste 1000
Cincinnati OH 45202
513 762-4000

(G-7839)
WHEELS TRACKS & SAFETY LLC
134 Grist Mill Rd (24501-7715)
PHONE......................................434 846-8975
EMP: 3
SALES (est): 311.9K **Privately Held**
SIC: 3312 Blast Furnace-Steel Works

(G-7840)
WOOD TELEVISION LLC
Also Called: The News & Advance
101 Wyndale Dr (24501-6710)
P.O. Box 10129 (24506-0129)
PHONE......................................434 385-5400
Kelly E Mirt, *Publisher*
Dean Smith, *General Mgr*
Logan Anderson, *Editor*
Matt Busse, *Editor*
Emily Wood, *Controller*
EMP: 162
SALES (corp-wide): 3B **Publicly Held**
WEB: www.woodtv.com
SIC: 2711 2752 Newspapers, publishing & printing; commercial printing, lithographic
HQ: Wood Television Llc
120 College Ave Se
Grand Rapids MI 49503
616 456-8888

Lyndhurst
Augusta County

(G-7841)
BACKROADS PUBLICATIONS
1461 Love Rd (22952-2808)
PHONE......................................540 949-0329
Lynn Coffey, *Owner*
EMP: 1
SALES (est): 52.3K **Privately Held**
WEB: www.backroadsbooks.com
SIC: 2731 Book publishing

(G-7842)
BLUE RIDGE PALLET LLC
17 Commonwealth Dr (22952-2529)
PHONE......................................540 836-8115
Sean Skally, *Manager*
Karl Millsap,
EMP: 14
SALES (est): 3.1MM **Privately Held**
WEB: www.blueridgepallet.com
SIC: 3537 Platforms, stands, tables, pallets & similar equipment

(G-7843)
DEXTER W ESTES
Also Called: Estes Construction
70 Blackwell Ln (22952-2433)
PHONE......................................434 996-8068
Dexter Estes, *Owner*
EMP: 3
SQ FT: 24,000
SALES (est): 171.1K **Privately Held**
WEB: www.bigdsdumpsters.com
SIC: 3531 Bulldozers (construction machinery)

(G-7844)
RE MAX ADVANTAGE
49 Georganna Dr (22952-2507)
PHONE......................................540 241-2499
EMP: 1
SALES (est): 36K **Privately Held**
SIC: 2066 Mfg Chocolate/Cocoa Products

Machipongo
Northampton County

(G-7845)
CAKE PASSION CUSTOM CAKES LLC
14093 Jordan Rd (23405-1530)
PHONE......................................757 982-0928
Joanne Jones,
EMP: 1
SALES (est): 39.5K **Privately Held**
SIC: 2051 Cakes, bakery: except frozen

(G-7846)
CHATHAM VINEYARDS LLC
9232 Chatham Rd (23405-2727)
PHONE......................................757 678-5588
Jonathan Wehner,
EMP: 9 EST: 2014
SQ FT: 9,600
SALES (est): 660.4K **Privately Held**
WEB: www.chathamvineyards.com
SIC: 2084 Wines

(G-7847)
HECLYN PRECISION GEAR COMPANY
Also Called: Williamson Gear & Machine
3350 Vaucluse Ln (23405-2300)
P.O. Box 3729, Philadelphia PA (19125-0729)
PHONE......................................215 739-7094
David Rogers, *President*
Linda Rogers, *Shareholder*
EMP: 15 EST: 1947
SALES (est): 2.2MM **Privately Held**
SIC: 3566 Gears, power transmission, except automotive

(G-7848)
RA RESKY WOODSMITH LLC
11331 Sparrow Point Rd (23405-2505)
PHONE......................................757 678-7555
Maryann Resky, *Principal*
EMP: 3
SALES (est): 211.3K **Privately Held**
SIC: 2411 Wooden logs

Madison
Madison County

(G-7849)
BLACKPEARL SOAPSTONE
2858 N Seminole Trl (22727-4042)
PHONE......................................813 909-8400
EMP: 3
SALES (est): 90.5K **Privately Held**
SIC: 1411 Dimension stone

(G-7850)
DEANE LOGGING CO INC
4771 S Seminole Trl (22727-2517)
P.O. Box 97 (22727-0097)
PHONE......................................540 718-3676
Wayne Deane, *President*
Anthony Dean, *Vice Pres*
Leona Deane, *Admin Sec*
EMP: 4
SALES (est): 16.3K **Privately Held**
SIC: 2411 Logging camps & contractors

(G-7851)
E A CLORE SONS INC
303 Clore Pl (22727-2881)
P.O. Box 765 (22727-0765)
PHONE......................................540 948-5821
W A Coppage, *President*
Sara C Utz, *Corp Secy*
Troy K Coppage, *Vice Pres*
Troy Coppage, *Vice Pres*
Suzanne Kavanaugh, *Manager*
EMP: 52 EST: 1914
SALES (est): 3.3MM **Privately Held**
WEB: www.eaclore.com
SIC: 2511 Wood household furniture

(G-7852)
FORK MOUNTAIN RACEWAY LLC
3943 Hebron Valley Rd (22727-3126)
PHONE......................................540 229-1828
French H Grimes, *Administration*
EMP: 3 EST: 2009
SALES (est): 137.2K **Privately Held**
SIC: 3644 Raceways

(G-7853)
GRIMES FRENCH RACE SYSTEMS
3943 Hebron Valley Rd (22727-3126)
PHONE......................................540 923-4541
French Grimes, *Owner*
EMP: 3
SQ FT: 7,500
SALES (est): 238.8K **Privately Held**
WEB: www.frenchgrimes.com
SIC: 3714 3694 Fuel systems & parts, motor vehicle; ignition systems, high frequency

(G-7854)
HILL WELDING SERVICES CORP
162 Duet Rd (22727-2920)
P.O. Box 1035 (22727-1035)
PHONE......................................540 923-4474
EMP: 1
SALES (est): 140.4K **Privately Held**
SIC: 7692 Welding Repair

(G-7855)
L INDUSTRIES
140 Fairground Rd (22727-3078)
PHONE......................................540 948-4806
Teresa Lambrich, *General Mgr*
Teresa Diane Lambrich, *Principal*
Ronnie Lambrich, *Vice Pres*
EMP: 6 EST: 2009
SALES (est): 579.6K **Privately Held**
WEB: www.lsindustriesinc.net
SIC: 3599 Machine shop, jobbing & repair

(G-7856)
L S INDUSTRIES INC
140 Fairground Rd (22727-3078)
PHONE......................................540 948-4806
Ronnie Lambrich, *President*
EMP: 12
SQ FT: 10,000
SALES (est): 559.9K **Privately Held**
WEB: www.lsindustriesinc.net
SIC: 3599 Machine shop, jobbing & repair

(G-7857)
LEROY WOODWARD
168 Garth Run Rd (22727-3305)
P.O. Box 836 (22727-0836)
PHONE......................................540 948-6335
Leroy Woodward, *Co-Owner*
Carolyn Woodard, *Co-Owner*
EMP: 4
SALES (est): 300K **Privately Held**
SIC: 2411 Logging camps & contractors

(G-7858)
MADISON COUNTY WINES LLC
Also Called: Early Mountain Vineyards
6109 Wolftown Hood Rd (22727-2582)
PHONE......................................540 948-9005
Peter Hoehn, *CEO*
Patrick Eagan, *Sales Staff*
Rachel Caggiano, *Marketing Staff*
Aileen Sevier, *Marketing Staff*
Doneva Wolf, *Executive Asst*
EMP: 15
SALES (est): 2.2MM **Privately Held**
WEB: www.earlymountain.com
SIC: 2084 Wines

(G-7859)
MADISON FLOORING COMPANY INC
333 Oak Park Rd (22727-4204)
PHONE......................................540 948-4498
EMP: 19 EST: 1947
SQ FT: 800
SALES (est): 1.7MM **Privately Held**
SIC: 2426 Hardwood Dimension/Floor Mill

▲ = Import ▼=Export
◆ =Import/Export

(G-7860)
PHINEAS ROSE WOOD JOINERY LLC
1112 Graves Mill Rd (22727-2598)
PHONE..................540 948-4248
Richard Gordon, *Partner*
Ninika Clark Gordon, *Partner*
EMP: 2
SALES (est): 80K **Privately Held**
WEB: www.phineasrose.com
SIC: 2511 Wood household furniture

(G-7861)
PRESS-WELL SERVICES INC
915 Whippoorwill Rd (22727-2994)
PHONE..................540 923-4799
Joseph May III, *President*
EMP: 8 EST: 1998
SQ FT: 5,200
SALES (est): 969.8K **Privately Held**
SIC: 2752 Commercial printing, offset

(G-7862)
SOUTHERN STATES COOP INC
1295 N Main St (22719)
P.O. Box 130 (22727-0130)
PHONE..................540 948-5691
EMP: 35
SALES (corp-wide): 909.6MM **Privately Held**
SIC: 2048 Mfg & Whol Feedsseeds & Fertilizer & Whol Fuls & Farm Supplies & Ret Farm Home &Garden Supplies &Petroleum Product
PA: Southern States Cooperative, Incorporated
6606 W Broad St Ste B
Richmond VA 23230
804 281-1000

(G-7863)
SWEELY ESTATE WINERY
6109 Wolftown Hood Rd (22727-2582)
PHONE..................540 948-7603
Delores Coppedge, *Manager*
Melissa Rice, *Director*
EMP: 5 EST: 2010
SALES (est): 262.1K **Privately Held**
WEB: www.earlymountain.com
SIC: 2084 Wines

(G-7864)
VIRTUE SOLAR LLC
367 N White Oak Dr (22727-5048)
P.O. Box 525 (22727-0525)
PHONE..................540 407-8353
Matt Powers, *Mng Member*
Matthew Powers, *Administration*
EMP: 1
SALES (est): 160.4K **Privately Held**
WEB: www.virtuesolar.com
SIC: 3674 Semiconductors & related devices

(G-7865)
WOOD TELEVISION LLC
Also Called: Madison County Eagle
201 Main St (22727)
P.O. Box 325 (22727-0325)
PHONE..................540 948-5121
Greg Glassner, *Branch Mgr*
EMP: 4
SALES (corp-wide): 3B **Publicly Held**
WEB: www.woodtv.com
SIC: 2711 Newspapers, publishing & printing
HQ: Wood Television Llc
120 College Ave Se
Grand Rapids MI 49503
616 456-8888

Madison Heights
Amherst County

(G-7866)
ABC PRINTING
184 Scottsmill Rd (24572-2368)
PHONE..................434 847-7468
Carleton Phipps Sr, *Owner*
Tova Phipps, *Co-Owner*
Georgina Davis, *Human Res Dir*
EMP: 2
SALES (est): 186.9K **Privately Held**
SIC: 2752 Commercial printing, offset

(G-7867)
AMHERST ARMS AND SUPPLY LLC
4811 S Amherst Hwy (24572-2497)
PHONE..................434 929-1978
Bryan Barber,
EMP: 4
SALES (est): 120K **Privately Held**
WEB: www.amherstarms.com
SIC: 3484 3949 Small arms; archery equipment, general

(G-7868)
BERNIES FURN & CABINETRY INC
186 Meadowview Ln (24572-3501)
PHONE..................434 846-6883
Bernard Campbell, *President*
EMP: 2
SALES (est): 64.3K **Privately Held**
WEB: www.berniescustomfurniture.com
SIC: 2434 Wood kitchen cabinets

(G-7869)
CLEAR WATER MANUFACTURING
161 Crennel Dr (24572-2584)
PHONE..................434 582-9511
EMP: 2
SALES (est): 67.4K **Privately Held**
WEB: www.clrwtr.net
SIC: 3999 Manufacturing industries

(G-7870)
COUNTRYSIDE MACHINING INC
494 Possum Island Rd (24572-4637)
PHONE..................434 929-0065
Laura Campbell, *President*
Dirk Campbell, *Vice Pres*
EMP: 2
SALES (est): 50K **Privately Held**
SIC: 7692 Welding repair

(G-7871)
ENGLAND STOVE WORKS
100 W Progress Ln (24572-3769)
PHONE..................434 929-0120
▲ EMP: 3
SALES (est): 281.6K **Privately Held**
SIC: 3433 Heating equipment, except electric

(G-7872)
EP COMPUTER SERVICE
121 Penn Ln (24572-3521)
PHONE..................804 592-7272
Gary Penn, *Partner*
EMP: 2
SALES (est): 1K **Privately Held**
SIC: 2752 Commercial printing, lithographic

(G-7873)
HARMONY LIGHTS CANDLE
1088 Monacan Park Rd (24572-3441)
PHONE..................434 384-5549
Malachi Lord, *Owner*
EMP: 2
SALES (est): 71.2K **Privately Held**
WEB: www.harmonylights.com
SIC: 3999 Candles

(G-7874)
HICKEY ELECTRIC CO INC
Also Called: Hickey Electric Heating and A
4262 S Amherst Hwy # 100 (24572-5363)
PHONE..................434 384-1896
Fred Hickey, *Owner*
EMP: 14
SALES (est): 2.2MM **Privately Held**
WEB: www.hickeyelectricco.com
SIC: 3646 Commercial indusl & institutional electric lighting fixtures

(G-7875)
I H MCBRIDE SIGN COMPANY INC
5493 S Amherst Hwy (24572)
P.O. Box 622, Lynchburg (24505-0622)
PHONE..................434 847-4151
Tony McBride, *President*
Lynn Mayberry, *Opers Staff*
EMP: 11
SQ FT: 20,000

SALES (est): 1.7MM **Privately Held**
WEB: www.mcbridesigns.com
SIC: 3993 Signs, not made in custom sign painting shops

(G-7876)
LASERMARX INC
Also Called: Quality Archery Designs
301 E Progress Ln (24572-3771)
P.O. Box 940 (24572-0940)
PHONE..................434 528-1044
Daniel Summers, *President*
Kevin Fry, *Marketing Staff*
▲ EMP: 7
SALES (est): 872.3K **Privately Held**
WEB: www.qadinc.com
SIC: 3949 Archery equipment, general

(G-7877)
MONUMENTAL SERVICES
174 Sunset Cir (24572-2602)
PHONE..................434 847-6630
Joseph Sanzone, *President*
EMP: 3
SALES (est): 273.2K **Privately Held**
SIC: 3272 Monuments & grave markers, except terrazo

(G-7878)
NI PHI THACH
Also Called: Jesse Nails and Spa
4573 S Amherst Hwy (24572-5343)
PHONE..................434 386-8852
Ni PHI Thach, *Owner*
EMP: 2
SALES (est): 94.4K **Privately Held**
SIC: 3421 Clippers, fingernail & toenail

(G-7879)
O D B MACHINE CO
Also Called: Odb Machine Co
271 Mitchell Bell Rd (24572-2579)
P.O. Box 680, Lynchburg (24505-0680)
PHONE..................434 929-4002
Mike Buhler, *President*
Wayne Lankford, *Admin Sec*
▲ EMP: 10
SALES (est): 670K **Privately Held**
WEB: www.olddominionbox.com
SIC: 3599 Machine shop, jobbing & repair

(G-7880)
OLD DOMINION BOX CO INC (PA)
300 Elon Rd (24572-2587)
P.O. Box 680, Lynchburg (24505-0680)
PHONE..................434 929-6701
Frank H Buhler, *Ch of Bd*
Michael O Buhler, *President*
T Wayne Lankford, *Vice Pres*
Amy B Scott, *Vice Pres*
Thomas B Scott, *Treasurer*
▲ EMP: 20
SQ FT: 174,000
SALES: 10.9K **Privately Held**
WEB: www.olddominionbox.com
SIC: 2652 2657 2653 Setup paperboard boxes; folding paperboard boxes; boxes, corrugated: made from purchased materials

(G-7881)
OLD DOMINION BOX CO INC
Also Called: Old Dominion Machinery Company
186 Dillard Rd (24572-2528)
P.O. Box 680, Lynchburg (24505-0680)
PHONE..................434 929-6701
Tom Scott, *Vice Pres*
EMP: 50
SALES (corp-wide): 10.9K **Privately Held**
WEB: www.olddominionbox.com
SIC: 2652 2657 2653 Setup paperboard boxes; folding paperboard boxes; corrugated & solid fiber boxes
PA: The Old Dominion Box Co Inc
300 Elon Rd
Madison Heights VA 24572
434 929-6701

(G-7882)
PHILLIPS WELDING SERVICE INC
130 Laurel Dr (24572-3638)
PHONE..................434 989-7236
Mae Phillips, *President*

Alfred Phillips, *Principal*
EMP: 2 EST: 2015
SALES (est): 137.2K **Privately Held**
SIC: 3548 Spot welding apparatus, electric

(G-7883)
RIVERINE JET BOATS
122 Rocky Hill Rd (24572-2249)
PHONE..................434 258-5874
EMP: 2 EST: 2013
SALES (est): 123.8K **Privately Held**
WEB: www.riverroadjetboats.com
SIC: 3732 Boat building & repairing

(G-7884)
SHE SIGNS
221 Melwood Dr (24572-3115)
PHONE..................434 509-3173
Christine Black, *Principal*
EMP: 1
SALES (est): 46K **Privately Held**
SIC: 3993 Signs & advertising specialties

(G-7885)
THAYER DESIGN INC
Also Called: Dana Thayer Design
5066 S Amherst Hwy # 102 (24572-2442)
PHONE..................434 528-3850
John Marc Waller, *President*
Paula K Waller, *Admin Sec*
EMP: 4
SQ FT: 2,000
SALES (est): 400K **Privately Held**
WEB: www.thayerdesign.com
SIC: 3999 7336 Advertising display products; graphic arts & related design

(G-7886)
TOMORROWS RESOURCES UNLIMITED
131 Crennel Dr (24572-2584)
PHONE..................434 929-2800
Greg Summers, *President*
Benjamin Summers, *Marketing Staff*
Margaret Summers, *Admin Sec*
EMP: 20
SALES (est): 1.7MM **Privately Held**
WEB: www.truball.com
SIC: 2411 Logging

Maidens
Goochland County

(G-7887)
CMG IMPRESSIONS INC
2746 Maidens Loop Ste F (23102-2630)
PHONE..................804 556-2551
Christopher M Garland, *President*
EMP: 2
SALES (est): 247.7K **Privately Held**
WEB: www.cmgprint.com
SIC: 2752 Commercial printing, offset

(G-7888)
COURTHOUSE CREEK CIDER
1581 Maidens Rd (23102-2601)
PHONE..................804 543-3157
EMP: 2
SALES (est): 80.3K **Privately Held**
WEB: www.courthousecreek.com
SIC: 2084 Wines

(G-7889)
CREATIVE CORP
Also Called: Custom Design Products
2353 Country Ln (23102-2418)
PHONE..................804 556-4839
Tone A Delpapa, *President*
Rita Delpappa, *Corp Secy*
EMP: 3
SQ FT: 1,800
SALES (est): 294.5K **Privately Held**
SIC: 3089 Laminating of plastic

(G-7890)
DO-DA INNOVATIONS LLC
2415 Two Turtles Rd (23102-2238)
PHONE..................804 556-6645
Karron Myrick, *President*
EMP: 1
SALES (est): 63.3K **Privately Held**
WEB: www.dodainnovations.com
SIC: 2099 5149 Maple syrup; condiments

GEOGRAPHIC

(G-7891)
K & R TREE CARE LLC
2750 River Rd W (23102-2610)
PHONE...................................804 767-0695
Kimberly Burrell,
EMP: 1
SALES (est): 93.6K Privately Held
WEB: www.kandrtreecare.com
SIC: 2411 0783 Stumps, wood; planting, pruning & trimming services

(G-7892)
RED EAGLE CREATIONS
2161 Maidens Rd (23102-2218)
PHONE...................................804 556-2041
Suzanne Harris, *Principal*
EMP: 1
SALES (est): 41.1K Privately Held
WEB: www.redeaglecreations.com
SIC: 2395 Embroidery products, except schiffli machine

(G-7893)
WALTON WIRING INC
2278 Pony Farm Rd (23102-2063)
PHONE...................................804 556-3104
Raymond Walton, *President*
EMP: 1 EST: 1999
SALES (est): 143.6K Privately Held
SIC: 3357 Communication wire

Manakin Sabot
Goochland County

(G-7894)
AMBOY ENTERPRISES LLC
561 Hill Grove Rd (23103-2918)
PHONE...................................804 708-0945
Donald Fitzsimmons, *Administration*
EMP: 2
SALES (est): 169.6K Privately Held
WEB: www.pakmailvirginia.com
SIC: 2499 Wood products

(G-7895)
ARCHITECTURAL CUSTOM WDWRK INC
Also Called: A C W
44 Plaza Dr (23103-2247)
PHONE...................................804 784-2283
Douglas L Cone, *President*
EMP: 8
SQ FT: 6,500
SALES (est): 871.9K Privately Held
WEB: www.acwkitchens.com
SIC: 2431 5211 Millwork; millwork & lumber

(G-7896)
BUF CREAMERY LLC
931 Dover Farm Rd (23103-3034)
PHONE...................................434 466-7110
Grant Grayson, *Principal*
EMP: 4
SALES (est): 210.5K Privately Held
SIC: 2021 Creamery butter

(G-7897)
CARBIDE SPECIALTIES INC
573 Fords Rd (23103-2141)
PHONE...................................804 346-3314
Debanko John, *President*
EMP: 3
SALES (est): 224.9K Privately Held
SIC: 2819 Carbides

(G-7898)
DEMENTI MILESTONE PUBG INC
1530 Oak Grove Dr (23103-2224)
PHONE...................................804 784-5151
EMP: 1
SALES (est): 41.3K Privately Held
WEB:
www.dementimilestonepublishing.com
SIC: 2741 Miscellaneous publishing

(G-7899)
DIRECT CUT LAWN TREE SVC LLC
1657 Manakin Rd (23103-2633)
PHONE...................................804 516-7771
EMP: 1 EST: 2016

SALES (est): 58.5K Privately Held
WEB: www.directcutlawntreeservice.com
SIC: 3524 Lawn & garden mowers & accessories

(G-7900)
KAPSTONE
1900 Manakin Rd Ste H (23103-2252)
PHONE...................................804 708-0083
John Caplice, *Principal*
EMP: 2 EST: 2012
SALES (est): 185.6K Privately Held
SIC: 2679 Paper products, converted

(G-7901)
LUCK STONE CORPORATION (PA)
Also Called: Luck Stone Luck Stone Cmpanies
515 Stone Mill Dr (23103-3261)
P.O. Box 29682, Richmond (23242-0682)
PHONE...................................804 784-6300
Charles S Luck III, *Ch of Bd*
John A Legore, *President*
Charles S Luck IV, *President*
Britten Parker, *Partner*
Matt Rise, *Partner*
◆ EMP: 75
SQ FT: 40,000
SALES (est): 824.7MM Privately Held
WEB: www.luckstone.com
SIC: 1423 2899 3281 5211 Crushed & broken granite; chemical preparations; cut stone & stone products; masonry materials & supplies; management services

(G-7902)
LUCK STONE CORPORATION
Also Called: Luck Stone-Boscobel Plant
485 Boscobel Rd (23103)
P.O. Box 128 (23103-0128)
PHONE...................................804 784-4652
Rod Gardner, *Manager*
EMP: 24
SALES (corp-wide): 824.7MM Privately Held
WEB: www.luckstone.com
SIC: 1423 Crushed & broken granite
PA: Luck Stone Corporation
515 Stone Mill Dr
Manakin Sabot VA 23103
804 784-6300

(G-7903)
MANAKIN INDUSTRIES LLC
758 Double Oak Ln (23103-3045)
PHONE...................................804 784-5514
Todd M Lutterbein,
Thomas Bowden,
▲ EMP: 7
SALES (est): 671.4K Privately Held
WEB: www.manakinind.com
SIC: 3353 3842 5047 Aluminum sheet, plate & foil; surgical appliances & supplies; medical equipment & supplies

(G-7904)
RG BOATWORKS LLC
110 Alice Run (23103-3116)
PHONE...................................804 784-1991
David Lingerfelt, *Principal*
EMP: 2
SALES (est): 103.6K Privately Held
SIC: 3732 Boat building & repairing

(G-7905)
THISTLEDOWN ALPACAS INC
489 Manakin Ferry Rd (23103-3321)
PHONE...................................804 784-4837
Jane A Christie, *Principal*
EMP: 2 EST: 2009
SALES (est): 131.6K Privately Held
WEB: www.thistledownalpacas.com
SIC: 2231 Alpacas, mohair: woven

(G-7906)
VIRGINIA CUSTOM BUILDINGS (PA)
Also Called: Gouchland Custom Buildings
280 Broad Street Rd (23103-2220)
PHONE...................................804 784-3816
Rodney W Harrison, *President*
Sonya Richards, *Bookkeeper*
EMP: 12
SQ FT: 3,000

SALES (est): 1.1MM Privately Held
WEB: www.shedsandbuildings.com
SIC: 2452 2511 Prefabricated buildings, wood; lawn furniture: wood

(G-7907)
WATKINS INDUSTRIES LLC
1200 Dover Creek Ln (23103-2531)
PHONE...................................540 371-5007
John Watkins, *Principal*
EMP: 3 EST: 2010
SALES (est): 196.2K Privately Held
WEB: www.watkinsawnings.com
SIC: 3999 Manufacturing industries

Manassas
Manassas City County

(G-7908)
1A SMART START
10400 Morias Ct Unit A (20110-4175)
PHONE...................................703 330-1372
EMP: 1
SALES (est): 72.7K Privately Held
SIC: 3714 Motor vehicle parts & accessories

(G-7909)
ABC IMAGING OF WASHINGTON
10498 Colonel Ct (20110-6793)
PHONE...................................703 396-9081
Andrew Jones, *Branch Mgr*
EMP: 33
SALES (corp-wide): 144.4MM Privately Held
WEB: www.abcimaging.com
SIC: 2759 Commercial printing
PA: Abc Imaging Of Washington, Inc
5290 Shawnee Rd Ste 300
Alexandria VA 22312
202 429-8870

(G-7910)
AMERICAN BIODIESEL CORPORATION
9562 Oakenshaw Dr (20110-5803)
PHONE...................................703 906-9434
Stephen Johnson, *President*
EMP: 4
SALES (est): 4.5MM Privately Held
SIC: 2911 Diesel fuels

(G-7911)
ARRINGTON & SONS INC
10500 Dumfries Rd (20110-7961)
P.O. Box 462 (20108-0462)
PHONE...................................703 368-1462
Nancy Arrington, *President*
Richard W Arrington, *Vice Pres*
Paul H Arrington, *Treasurer*
EMP: 9
SQ FT: 2,700
SALES (est): 750K Privately Held
WEB: www.arringtonsons.com
SIC: 2789 2759 Paper cutting; embossing on paper

(G-7912)
ART CREATIONS COMPANY INC
8492b Signal Hill Rd (20110-8701)
PHONE...................................703 257-9510
EMP: 2 EST: 1994
SALES: 400K Privately Held
SIC: 2431 Mfg Custom Woodwork And Display Cases

(G-7913)
ART&CREATION INC
Also Called: Millwork
8492b Signal Hill Rd (20110-8701)
PHONE...................................571 606-8999
Iulian Ene, *President*
Julian Ene, *Manager*
EMP: 1 EST: 2017
SALES (est): 76.4K Privately Held
SIC: 2431 Planing mill, millwork

(G-7914)
ASCP SOLUTIONS LLC
8629 Mathis Ave (20110-5270)
PHONE...................................410 782-1122
Alonzo Nixon, *Info Tech Mgr*
Andrew Calvert,

EMP: 10
SQ FT: 5,100
SALES (est): 685.2K Privately Held
WEB: www.aspcsolutions.com
SIC: 3842 Surgical appliances & supplies

(G-7915)
ASTRO LLC
9705 Liberia Ave Ste 299 (20110-1744)
PHONE...................................888 401-1003
Ahmet Aksoylu,
EMP: 3
SALES (est): 123.2K Privately Held
SIC: 2899 Chemical preparations

(G-7916)
AURORA FLIGHT SCIENCES CORP (HQ)
9950 Wakeman Dr (20110-2702)
PHONE...................................703 369-3633
Per Beith, *CEO*
Mark C Cherry, *President*
Jeanine Boyle, *Vice Pres*
Joseph Granata, *Vice Pres*
Brian Yutko, *Vice Pres*
▲ EMP: 140
SQ FT: 70,000
SALES (est): 146.7MM
SALES (corp-wide): 76.5B Publicly Held
WEB: www.aurora.aero
SIC: 3728 Aircraft parts & equipment
PA: The Boeing Company
100 N Riverside Plz
Chicago IL 60606
312 544-2000

(G-7917)
BADWOLF BREWERY LLC
9776 Center St (20110-4128)
PHONE...................................571 208-1064
Douglas Webb,
EMP: 3
SALES (est): 80K Privately Held
SIC: 2082 Beer (alcoholic beverage)

(G-7918)
BAE SYSTEMS INFO & ELEC SYS
9300 Wellington Rd 110 (20110-4122)
PHONE...................................703 361-1471
Bin LI, *Engineer*
Daniel Pirkl, *Engineer*
Randy Zeger, *Engineer*
Jamie Bernard, *Electrical Engi*
Ken Knowles, *Electrical Engi*
EMP: 296
SALES (corp-wide): 23.6B Privately Held
WEB: www.baesystems.com
SIC: 3812 Search & navigation equipment
HQ: Bae Systems Information And Electronic Systems Integration Inc.
65 Spit Brook Rd
Nashua NH 03060
603 885-4321

(G-7919)
BAM BAMS LLC
10498 Colonel Ct Ste 104 (20110-6794)
PHONE...................................703 372-1940
Damien Siggia, *CFO*
Benn Chazan, *Sales Mgr*
Sarah Cole, *Cust Mgr*
Brian Nutt, *Cust Mgr*
Jon McLean, *Accounts Exec*
▲ EMP: 30
SALES (est): 3.7MM Privately Held
WEB: www.bambams.com
SIC: 3993 Signs & advertising specialties

(G-7920)
BBK CNSLDTED SLUTIONS SVCS LLC
8688 Carlton Dr (20110-6307)
PHONE...................................571 229-2276
Kimmy Lisenby,
EMP: 1
SALES (est): 37.5K Privately Held
SIC: 2741

(G-7921)
BOWMAN TERESSA
8464 Georgian Ct (20110-4564)
PHONE...................................240 601-9982
Teressa Bowman, *Principal*
EMP: 2

▲ = Import ▼=Export
◆ =Import/Export

SALES (est): 83.9K **Privately Held**
SIC: 2752 Commercial printing, lithographic

(G-7922)
BRUCE MOORE PRINTING CO
Also Called: Power Quote Software
9239 Bayberry Ave (20110-4611)
P.O. Box 1605 (20108-1605)
PHONE..................703 361-0369
Bruce Moore, *President*
EMP: 2
SALES (est): 235.3K **Privately Held**
WEB: www.pqprintestimating.com
SIC: 2759 Commercial printing

(G-7923)
C4 EXPLOSIVE SPT TRAINING LLC
10219 Nokesville Rd (20110-4133)
PHONE..................571 379-7955
EMP: 2
SALES (est): 74.4K **Privately Held**
SIC: 2892 Explosives

(G-7924)
CASSANDRAS GRMET CLASSICS CORP
Also Called: Island Treasure's Gourmet
10681 Wakeman Ct (20110-2026)
P.O. Box 6806, Woodbridge (22195-6806)
PHONE..................703 590-7900
Cassandra L Craig, *President*
Kenneth S Craig, *Treasurer*
Isaac Lartey, *Sales Mgr*
Ken Craig, *Manager*
▲ EMP: 11
SQ FT: 5,000
SALES (est): 200K **Privately Held**
WEB: www.cassandrasgourmet.com
SIC: 2051 Cakes, bakery: except frozen

(G-7925)
COMCAST TECH CENTER
9450 Innovation Dr (20110-2214)
PHONE..................571 229-9112
Christine Shartzer, *Principal*
EMP: 2
SALES (est): 142.1K **Privately Held**
SIC: 3663 Mobile communication equipment

(G-7926)
CONTROP USA INC
9720 Capital Ct Ste 301 (20110-2051)
PHONE..................301 605-4499
EMP: 2 EST: 2019
SALES (est): 99K **Privately Held**
WEB: www.contropuas.com
SIC: 3674 Semiconductors & related devices

(G-7927)
CRYPTO RESERVE INC
9809 Cockrell Rd (20110-4111)
PHONE..................571 229-0826
Anthony Tran, *President*
EMP: 1
SALES (est): 39.6K **Privately Held**
SIC: 3999 Cigarette & cigar products & accessories

(G-7928)
CUSTOM QUALITY WOODWORKING
9603 Clover Hill Rd (20110-2753)
PHONE..................703 368-8010
EMP: 2
SALES (est): 147K **Privately Held**
SIC: 2431 Millwork

(G-7929)
D-STAR INSTRUMENTS
8424 Quarry Rd Ste 203 (20110-5388)
PHONE..................703 335-0770
Donald B Kenworthy, *President*
EMP: 6
SALES (est): 213.1K **Privately Held**
WEB: www.d-star.com
SIC: 3826 Analytical instruments

(G-7930)
DEEM PRINTING COMPANY INC
9052 Euclid Ave (20110-5308)
PHONE..................703 335-2422

Michael Deem, *President*
Lawrence Deem, *Vice Pres*
Jerry Deem, *VP Sales*
EMP: 9
SALES (est): 1.2MM **Privately Held**
WEB: www.deemprintingmanassas.com
SIC: 2752 Commercial printing, offset

(G-7931)
DELTA Q DYNAMICS LLC
8347 Tillett Loop (20110-8313)
P.O. Box 2513 (20108-0855)
PHONE..................703 980-9449
Gary Harmon,
EMP: 1
SALES (est): 480K **Privately Held**
SIC: 3764 8731 8748 Guided missile & space vehicle propulsion unit parts; engineering laboratory, except testing; electronic research; systems analysis or design; systems engineering consultant, ex. computer or professional

(G-7932)
DEMORAIS INTERNATIONAL INC
9255 Center St Ste 200 (20110-5079)
PHONE..................703 369-3326
Janet Morais, *President*
EMP: 1
SALES (est): 46.2K **Privately Held**
WEB: www.demoraisinternational.com
SIC: 2514 Household furniture: upholstered on metal frames

(G-7933)
E-AGREE LLC (PA)
8577 Sudley Rd Ste D (20110-3860)
PHONE..................571 358-8012
Thomas Ervin, *Mng Member*
Mike Meier, *Manager*
Rich Armandi, *Associate*
Karyn Brooks, *Associate*
Norma Krech, *Associate*
EMP: 10
SQ FT: 800
SALES (est): 531.8K **Privately Held**
WEB: www.topreglazing.com
SIC: 7372 Prepackaged software

(G-7934)
EAHEART EQUIPMENT INC
10413 Dumfries Rd (20110-7959)
PHONE..................703 366-3880
Jerry Sutphin, *Manager*
EMP: 10
SALES (corp-wide): 3.7MM **Privately Held**
SIC: 3524 Lawn & garden mowers & accessories
PA: Eaheart Equipment, Inc.
8326 Meetze Rd
Warrenton VA 20187
540 347-2880

(G-7935)
EAST TO WEST EMB & DESIGN
9153 Key Commons Ct (20110-5300)
PHONE..................703 335-2397
Kristina Evans, *President*
Glenn Evans, *Vice Pres*
EMP: 4
SQ FT: 1,800
SALES (est): 614K **Privately Held**
WEB: www.easttowest.com
SIC: 2395 Embroidery products, except schiffli machine

(G-7936)
EL CHAMO PRINTING
8501 Bucyrus Ct Ste 104 (20110-5354)
PHONE..................703 582-5782
Jorge Suarez, *Administration*
EMP: 2
SALES (est): 101.5K **Privately Held**
WEB: www.elchamoprinting.com
SIC: 2759 Screen printing

(G-7937)
ELLIS PAGE COMPANY LLC
10481 Colonel Ct (20110-4173)
PHONE..................703 464-9404
Roy E Page,
EMP: 20

SALES (est): 2.8MM **Privately Held**
WEB: www.elliscodesign.com
SIC: 2541 Counter & sink tops

(G-7938)
EMERGENCY RESPONSE TECH LLC
9532 Liberia Ave Ste 716 (20110-1719)
PHONE..................703 932-1118
Patricia K Gilham,
Gary Gilham,
EMP: 2
SALES (est): 50K **Privately Held**
SIC: 3669 Communications equipment

(G-7939)
EPIC LED
9314 Witch Hazel Way (20110-5985)
PHONE..................703 499-4485
Tinika Shellington, *Owner*
▲ EMP: 3
SALES (est): 150K **Privately Held**
WEB: www.epicled.com
SIC: 3674 7389 Light emitting diodes; business services

(G-7940)
FH SHEET METAL INC
9011 Centreville Rd # 56 (20110-8438)
PHONE..................703 408-4622
EMP: 2
SALES (est): 136.4K **Privately Held**
SIC: 3444 Sheet metalwork

(G-7941)
FLIGHT PRODUCT CENTER INC
9998 Wakeman Dr (20110-2702)
PHONE..................703 361-2915
EMP: 3 EST: 2012
SALES (est): 110K **Privately Held**
SIC: 3812 Mfg Search/Navigation Equipment

(G-7942)
FORTUNE NAILS LLC
9401 Liberia Ave (20110-1718)
PHONE..................703 330-1306
Lucy Nguyen,
EMP: 6
SALES (est): 175.4K **Privately Held**
SIC: 3999 Fingernails, artificial

(G-7943)
GENERAL DISPLAY COMPANY LLC
10390 Central Park Dr (20110-4196)
PHONE..................703 335-9292
J D Griffith, *Mng Member*
EMP: 1
SALES (est): 86.6K **Privately Held**
WEB: www.generaldisplaycompany.com
SIC: 3993 7389 5199 3086 Displays & cutouts, window & lobby; displays, paint process; design, commercial & industrial; advertising specialties; plastics foam products; catalog & mail-order houses

(G-7944)
GENERAL MAGNETIC SCIENCES INC
Also Called: G M S
9518 Technology Dr (20110-4149)
PHONE..................571 243-6887
Kenneth Beeks, *Branch Mgr*
EMP: 1 **Privately Held**
SIC: 3669 Emergency alarms
PA: General Magnetic Sciences, Inc.
6420 Stonehaven Ct
Clifton VA 20124

(G-7945)
GEORATOR CORPORATION
9617 Center St (20110-5521)
PHONE..................703 368-2101
George J Ripol, *President*
Peggy Barkley, *General Mgr*
Karl L Cagle, *Vice Pres*
Mike Katsarelis, *Plant Mgr*
Linda Lugiano, *Purch Mgr*
▲ EMP: 14 EST: 1950
SQ FT: 25,000
SALES (est): 3.4MM **Privately Held**
WEB: www.georator.com
SIC: 3621 5063 Generators & sets, electric; electrical apparatus & equipment

(G-7946)
GLEN-GERY CORPORATION
Also Called: Glen-Gery Capital Plant
9905 Godwin Dr (20110-4156)
PHONE..................703 368-3178
Fay Henry, *Safety Mgr*
Allen Gunn, *Opers-Prdtn-Mfg*
Paula Good, *Manager*
EMP: 94
SQ FT: 5,000 **Privately Held**
WEB: www.glengery.com
SIC: 3251 5211 Brick & structural clay tile; brick
HQ: Glen-Gery Corporation
1166 Spring St
Reading PA 19610
610 374-4011

(G-7947)
GLOBAL CODE USA INC
Also Called: Stone Flex USA
8620 Rolling Rd (20110-3828)
PHONE..................908 764-5818
EMP: 4
SALES (est): 153.8K **Privately Held**
SIC: 2493 Marbleboard (stone face hard board)

(G-7948)
GRANITE TOP LLC
10498 Business Center Ct (20110-4178)
PHONE..................703 257-0714
EMP: 3
SALES (est): 152.2K **Privately Held**
SIC: 3281 Mfg Cut Stone/Products

(G-7949)
GREEN PHYSICS CORPORATION
9411 Main St Ste 204a (20110-5447)
P.O. Box 10054 (20108-0614)
PHONE..................703 989-6706
John Schultz, *President*
EMP: 2
SQ FT: 168
SALES (est): 125K **Privately Held**
SIC: 7372 8748 7389 Application computer software; systems engineering consultant, ex. computer or professional;

(G-7950)
HEARTH & HOME TECHNOLOGIES LLC
10126 Hrry J Parrish Blvd (20110-7813)
PHONE..................703 367-9413
Larry Boido, *Branch Mgr*
James Gilstrap, *Representative*
EMP: 8
SALES (corp-wide): 2.2B **Publicly Held**
WEB: www.fireside.com
SIC: 3429 5023 5719 Fireplace equipment, hardware; andirons, grates, screens; fireplace equipment & accessories; fireplaces & wood burning stoves
HQ: Hearth & Home Technologies, Llc
7571 215th St W
Lakeville MN 55044

(G-7951)
HECHOS VIOS PUBLISHING INC
8711 Plntn Ln Ste 301 (20110)
PHONE..................703 496-7019
Osman Lazarte, *Principal*
EMP: 4
SALES (est): 164.7K **Privately Held**
SIC: 2741 Miscellaneous publishing

(G-7952)
HERFF JONES LLC
Also Called: Scholastic Services
9426 Robnel Ave (20110-2525)
P.O. Box 170 (20108-0170)
PHONE..................703 368-9550
Tom Young, *Manager*
EMP: 8
SALES (corp-wide): 1.1B **Privately Held**
WEB: www.yearbookdiscoveries.com
SIC: 3911 Rings, finger: precious metal
HQ: Herff Jones, Llc
4501 W 62nd St
Indianapolis IN 46268
800 419-5462

(G-7953)
INTERPRETIVE WDWRK DESIGN INC
8513 Phoenix Dr (20110-8410)
PHONE................................703 330-6105
Stanley Negvesky, *President*
Michael Negvesky, *Corp Secy*
EMP: 3
SQ FT: 10,000
SALES (est): 500K **Privately Held**
WEB: www.iwd-i.com
SIC: 2431 2521 2499 Millwork; wood office furniture; decorative wood & woodwork

(G-7954)
JOY-PAGE COMPANY INC
10481 Colonel Ct (20110-4173)
PHONE................................703 464-9404
Roy E Page, *President*
Sharon Page, *CFO*
EMP: 10
SQ FT: 7,000
SALES (est): 570K **Privately Held**
SIC: 2541 Counter & sink tops

(G-7955)
KEYSTONE SOFTWARE INC
10707 Dabshire Way (20110-2757)
PHONE................................703 866-1593
Ralph Saunders, *President*
EMP: 1
SALES (est): 400K **Privately Held**
SIC: 7372 Business oriented computer software

(G-7956)
KO DISTILLING
10381 Central Park Dr (20110-4182)
PHONE................................571 292-1115
John O'Mara, *Principal*
EMP: 7
SALES (est): 419.6K **Privately Held**
WEB: www.kodistilling.com
SIC: 2084 5182 Brandy spirits; brandy & brandy spirits

(G-7957)
L H GAITHER CO INC
10402 Johnson Dr (20110-2731)
PHONE................................703 335-2300
Larry H Gaither, *President*
Terri Gaither, *Admin Sec*
EMP: 4
SALES (est): 357.4K **Privately Held**
SIC: 3599 Machine shop, jobbing & repair

(G-7958)
L-3 COMMUNICATIONS CORP
9507 Oakenshaw Dr (20110-5896)
PHONE................................703 375-4911
EMP: 2
SALES (est): 88.3K **Privately Held**
SIC: 3663 Mfg Radio/Tv Communication Equipment

(G-7959)
LAKE LITHOGRAPH COMPANY
10371 Central Park Dr (20110-4197)
PHONE................................703 361-8030
Howard Lake, *CEO*
Pam Lake Pell, *President*
Mildred Lake, *Corp Secy*
Jere Gill, *Vice Pres*
EMP: 53
SQ FT: 45,000
SALES (est): 6.2MM **Privately Held**
SIC: 2752 2789 Commercial printing, offset; bookbinding & related work

(G-7960)
LAMBERT METAL SERVICES LLC
10476 Godwin Ct (20110-4167)
PHONE................................571 261-5811
Bob Lambert, *Principal*
EMP: 1
SALES (est): 188.2K **Privately Held**
WEB: www.lambertmetalservices.com
SIC: 1081 Metal mining exploration & development services

(G-7961)
LAND VENTURE TWO LC
8303 Quarry Rd (20110-5313)
PHONE................................703 367-9456
Thomas J Knight, *Principal*
Manuel B Vilaca,
EMP: 6
SALES (est): 57.4K **Privately Held**
SIC: 3281 Stone, quarrying & processing of own stone products

(G-7962)
LESCO INC
8420 Kao Cir (20110-1728)
PHONE................................703 257-9015
EMP: 3
SALES (corp-wide): 26.6B **Publicly Held**
SIC: 2875 Mfg Fertilizers-Mix Only
HQ: Lesco, Inc.
　1385 E 36th St
　Cleveland OH 44114
　216 706-9250

(G-7963)
LEVEL UP FUN CORPORATION
10512 Coral Berry Dr (20110-2775)
PHONE................................703 365-8071
EMP: 2 EST: 2017
SALES (est): 121K **Privately Held**
SIC: 7372 Application computer software

(G-7964)
LIFESAFER
8512 Bucyrus Ct (20110-5351)
PHONE................................571 379-5575
EMP: 2
SALES (est): 94.7K **Privately Held**
SIC: 3694 Ignition apparatus & distributors

(G-7965)
LOCKHEED MARTIN CORPORATION
9500 Godwin Dr (20110-4166)
PHONE................................703 367-2121
Amy Spaulding, *General Mgr*
Michael Zieser, *Business Mgr*
Matthew Berinato, *Purchasing*
David Hunn, *Chief Engr*
Sam Angeles, *Engineer*
EMP: 1261 **Publicly Held**
WEB: www.lockheedmartin.com
SIC: 3812 Search & navigation equipment
PA: Lockheed Martin Corporation
　6801 Rockledge Dr
　Bethesda MD 20817

(G-7966)
LOCKHEED MARTIN CORPORATION
9500 Godwin Dr (20110-4166)
PHONE................................703 367-2121
Dale Hutchinson, *Manager*
EMP: 250 **Publicly Held**
WEB: www.lockheedmartin.com
SIC: 3761 3812 3699 3577 Guided missiles, complete; defense systems & equipment; flight simulators (training aids), electronic; computer peripheral equipment; prepackaged software; electronic computers
PA: Lockheed Martin Corporation
　6801 Rockledge Dr
　Bethesda MD 20817

(G-7967)
LOCKHEED MARTIN CORPORATION
9500 Godwin Dr (20110-4166)
PHONE................................813 855-5711
Richard Martin, *Branch Mgr*
EMP: 380 **Publicly Held**
WEB: www.lockheedmartin.com
SIC: 3812 Search & navigation equipment
PA: Lockheed Martin Corporation
　6801 Rockledge Dr
　Bethesda MD 20817

(G-7968)
LOCKHEED MARTIN CORPORATION
9500 Godwin Dr (20110-4166)
PHONE................................703 367-2121
Mike Berdeguez, *Branch Mgr*
EMP: 2 **Publicly Held**
WEB: www.lockheedmartin.com

SIC: 3812 3761 Search & navigation equipment; guided missiles & space vehicles
PA: Lockheed Martin Corporation
　6801 Rockledge Dr
　Bethesda MD 20817

(G-7969)
LOCKHEED MARTIN INTEGRTD SYSTM
9500 Godwin Dr (20110-4166)
PHONE................................703 367-2121
Mike Berdeguez, *Branch Mgr*
EMP: 30 **Publicly Held**
WEB: www.lockheedmartin.com
SIC: 3812 Search & navigation equipment
HQ: Lockheed Martin Integrated Systems, Llc
　6801 Rockledge Dr
　Bethesda MD 20817

(G-7970)
LOGIS-TECH INC
9450 Innovation Dr Ste 1 (20110-2214)
PHONE................................703 393-4840
Roland E Berg, *CEO*
James K Bounds, *President*
Jean Berg, *Corp Secy*
Barry Fitzgerald, *Opers Dir*
Michael Colburn, *Opers Staff*
▼ EMP: 139
SQ FT: 18,000
SALES: 19.9MM **Privately Held**
WEB: www.logis-tech.com
SIC: 3829 Measuring & controlling devices

(G-7971)
LOYAL SERVICE SYSTEMS
8709 Quarry Rd (20110-5357)
PHONE................................703 361-7888
EMP: 1
SALES (est): 39.6K **Privately Held**
WEB: www.loyalhygiene.com
SIC: 3999 Manufacturing industries

(G-7972)
MANASSAS ICE & FUEL CO INC (PA)
9009 Center St Ste 1 (20110-5455)
PHONE................................703 368-3121
Harry J Parrish II, *President*
Mattie C Parrish, *Vice Pres*
John W Fraber, *Controller*
Nancy P Lawson, *Admin Sec*
EMP: 9
SQ FT: 5,500
SALES (est): 708.6K **Privately Held**
WEB: www.manassascity.org
SIC: 2097 Manufactured ice

(G-7973)
MASTERBRAND CABINETS INC
8424 Kao Cir (20110-1728)
PHONE................................703 396-7804
Joe Rhodes, *Branch Mgr*
EMP: 229
SALES (corp-wide): 5.7B **Publicly Held**
WEB: www.masterbrand.com
SIC: 2434 Wood kitchen cabinets
HQ: Masterbrand Cabinets, Inc.
　1 Masterbrand Cabinets Dr
　Jasper IN 47546
　812 482-2527

(G-7974)
MEDLIMINAL LLC (PA)
9385 Innovation Dr (20110-2224)
P.O. Box 3610 (20108-0973)
PHONE................................571 719-6837
Amy Westmoreland, *Database Admin*
James Natoli,
EMP: 10 EST: 2013
SQ FT: 17,399
SALES (est): 3.4MM **Privately Held**
WEB: www.medliminal.com
SIC: 7372 Application computer software

(G-7975)
MICRON TECHNOLOGY INC
9600 Godwin Dr (20110-4162)
PHONE................................703 396-1000
Massimiliano Ippoliti, *Area Mgr*
Wayne Allen, *Plant Mgr*
Jason Deborde, *Opers Staff*
Mignon Bliss, *Production*
Brenda Herndon, *Purchasing*

EMP: 100
SALES (corp-wide): 21.4B **Publicly Held**
WEB: www.micron.com
SIC: 3674 Random access memory (RAM)
PA: Micron Technology, Inc.
　8000 S Federal Way
　Boise ID 83716
　208 368-4000

(G-7976)
MILESTONE SOFTWARE INC
9532 Liberia Ave Ste 722 (20110-1719)
PHONE................................703 217-4262
EMP: 2 EST: 2011
SALES (est): 83K **Privately Held**
SIC: 7372 Prepackaged Software Services

(G-7977)
MR1 CONSTRUCTION LLC
9837 Buckner Rd (20110-5901)
PHONE................................301 748-6078
Maximo Barrales, *Principal*
EMP: 2
SALES (est): 142.8K **Privately Held**
SIC: 1389 1799 7389 Construction, repair & dismantling services; construction site cleanup;

(G-7978)
MUMBLE WRAPS LLC
10472 Business Center Ct (20110-4178)
PHONE................................571 358-5388
William Schwarz,
EMP: 1
SALES (est): 40.9K **Privately Held**
SIC: 2399 Automotive covers, except seat & tire covers

(G-7979)
N A D C
10438 Business Center Ct (20110-4178)
PHONE................................703 331-5611
Dianne Braley, *Principal*
Jason Riley, *Opers Staff*
Peter Braley, *CIO*
EMP: 4
SALES (est): 446.3K **Privately Held**
WEB: www.nadc.com
SIC: 3575 Computer terminals

(G-7980)
NATURAL STONES INC
9109 Euclid Ave Ste 107 (20110-1715)
PHONE................................703 408-8801
Liliana Patricia Ferrel, *Administration*
EMP: 2 EST: 2012
SALES (est): 143.9K **Privately Held**
WEB: www.naturalstonesinc.com
SIC: 2541 Counter & sink tops

(G-7981)
NCS TECHNOLOGIES INC
9490 Innovation Dr (20110-2214)
PHONE................................703 743-8500
Timothy Shanahan, *Engrg Dir*
Allen Shorey, *Engineer*
Scott Sinclair, *Sales Staff*
Jacob Kim, *Branch Mgr*
Greg Britt, *Manager*
EMP: 3 **Privately Held**
WEB: www.ncst.com
SIC: 3571 Electronic computers
PA: Ncs Technologies, Inc.
　7669 Limestone Dr Ste 130
　Gainesville VA 20155

(G-7982)
NEEVARPT PRODUCTIONS LLC
8603 Dutchman Ct (20110-7803)
PHONE................................571 549-1169
Praveen Thaivalappil,
EMP: 1
SALES (est): 37.5K **Privately Held**
WEB: www.neevarpt.com
SIC: 2741 5961 ;

(G-7983)
NVA SIGNS & STRIPING LLC
10448 Business Center Ct (20110-4178)
PHONE................................703 263-1940
Tim Skelly,
EMP: 1
SALES (est): 155.7K **Privately Held**
WEB: www.stores.inksoft.com
SIC: 3993 Signs, not made in custom sign painting shops

▲ = Import ▼=Export
◆ =Import/Export

(G-7984)
OLD DOMINION SHAKER BOXES
9010 Longstreet Dr (20110-4905)
PHONE.............................703 470-7921
Doug Bell, *Principal*
EMP: 2
SALES (est): 105.9K **Privately Held**
WEB: www.odshakerboxes.wordpress.com
SIC: 2499 Decorative wood & woodwork

(G-7985)
ONEIDOS LLC
8569 Sudley Rd Ste C (20110-3863)
PHONE.............................703 819-3860
Helleni Moon,
EMP: 2
SALES (est): 52.5K **Privately Held**
SIC: 2731 Book publishing

(G-7986)
OPTICAL AIR DATA SYSTEMS LLC
Also Called: Oads
10781 James Payne Ct (20110-2042)
PHONE.............................703 393-0754
Phil Rogers, *President*
Alisa Rogers, *Vice Pres*
Beth Dakin, *Program Mgr*
EMP: 30
SQ FT: 2,500
SALES (est): 5.5MM **Privately Held**
WEB: www.oads.com
SIC: 3699 Laser systems & equipment

(G-7987)
PAQUETERIA EXPRESS INC
9019 Church St (20110-5433)
PHONE.............................703 330-4580
Jose G Solis, *CEO*
EMP: 2
SALES (est): 134.3K **Privately Held**
SIC: 2741 Miscellaneous publishing

(G-7988)
PAYNE PUBLISHERS INC
8707 Quarry Rd Ste B (20110-1722)
PHONE.............................703 631-9033
John Barbour, *President*
Daniel Fink, *Vice Pres*
Glenda Licausi, *Accountant*
Patricia Molina, *Cust Mgr*
Keith Jones, *Manager*
◆ EMP: 75
SALES (est): 8.1MM **Privately Held**
WEB: www.paynepub.com
SIC: 3993 2789 2759 2741 Signs & advertising specialties; bookbinding & related work; commercial printing; directories: publishing & printing

(G-7989)
PK HOT SAUCE LLC
8191 Oakglen Rd (20110-4622)
PHONE.............................703 629-0920
Parviz Kamali, *Mng Member*
EMP: 1
SALES (est): 25K **Privately Held**
SIC: 2033 6531 7389 Chili sauce, tomato: packaged in cans, jars, etc.; real estate agents & managers;

(G-7990)
PROFILE MACHINEWORKS LLC
8510 Rolling Rd (20110-3645)
PHONE.............................571 991-6331
Susan Doster, *Administration*
EMP: 1
SALES (est): 82.1K **Privately Held**
SIC: 3599 Machine shop, jobbing & repair

(G-7991)
PURE BLEND ORGANICS
9420 Beauregard Ave (20110-2504)
PHONE.............................703 476-1414
EMP: 1
SALES (est): 43.3K **Privately Held**
SIC: 2048 Mfg Prepared Feeds

(G-7992)
QUICK SIGNS INC
Also Called: Signs By Tomorrow
8695 Sudley Rd (20110-4588)
PHONE.............................703 606-3008
Carl Casey, *President*
Dawn Fraioli, *Vice Pres*

EMP: 3
SALES (est): 500K **Privately Held**
WEB: www.signsbytomorrow.com
SIC: 3993 Signs & advertising specialties

(G-7993)
R3 BLADES LLC
10289 Winged Elm Cir (20110-2712)
PHONE.............................571 234-3068
Ramfis Rosa,
EMP: 1
SALES (est): 46.6K **Privately Held**
SIC: 3421 Cutlery

(G-7994)
RANDALL PUBLICATION INC
Also Called: Old Bridge Observer
8803 Sudley Rd Ste 201 (20110-4718)
P.O. Box 1146 (20108-1146)
PHONE.............................703 369-0741
Randy Reid, *President*
EMP: 10
SALES (est): 576.6K **Privately Held**
WEB: www.bullrunnow.com
SIC: 2711 Newspapers: publishing only, not printed on site

(G-7995)
RECONCILIATION PRESS INC
9028 West St (20110-5044)
PHONE.............................703 369-6132
Mark Weaver, *Owner*
EMP: 1
SALES (est): 56.6K **Privately Held**
SIC: 2741 Miscellaneous publishing

(G-7996)
REUSEIT SOFTWARE INC
10512 Coral Berry Dr (20110-2775)
PHONE.............................703 365-8071
William Willis, *Principal*
EMP: 2
SALES (est): 137.7K **Privately Held**
SIC: 7372 Prepackaged software

(G-7997)
ROXEN INCORPORATED
Also Called: MINUTEMAN PRESS
9774 Center St (20110-4128)
PHONE.............................571 208-0782
Michael Rodzianko, *CEO*
Michael Rodziamko, *CEO*
Oksana Rodziamko, *Treasurer*
EMP: 5 EST: 2013
SQ FT: 1,100
SALES: 505.8K **Privately Held**
WEB: www.minutemanpress.com
SIC: 2752 Commercial printing, lithographic

(G-7998)
S&C GLOBAL PRODUCTS LLC
Also Called: Truckclaws
10363 Piper Ln (20110-2053)
PHONE.............................703 499-3635
Brent Simpson,
Mike Curry,
EMP: 7
SQ FT: 2,000
SALES (est): 140.5K **Privately Held**
WEB: www.truckclaws.com
SIC: 3713 5013 Utility truck bodies; truck parts & accessories

(G-7999)
SEVA PUBLISHING LLC
10327 Cabin Ridge Ct (20110-6924)
PHONE.............................757 556-1965
Patricia Hill,
EMP: 1
SALES (est): 25K **Privately Held**
SIC: 2741 Miscellaneous publishing

(G-8000)
SIGN GRAPHX INC
9091 Euclid Ave (20110-5309)
PHONE.............................703 335-7446
Charles Ledpold, *President*
James Dempsey, *Opers Mgr*
EMP: 10 EST: 2001
SALES (est): 1.5MM **Privately Held**
WEB: www.signgraphx.com
SIC: 3993 1799 Electric signs; sign installation & maintenance

(G-8001)
SUBURBAN CONTRACTORS LLC
10090 Market St (20110-2130)
PHONE.............................703 739-5600
Nikolaos Kollas, *President*
Jennifer Kollas, *Principal*
EMP: 43
SALES (est): 2.5MM **Privately Held**
SIC: 3443 1721 1799 Water tanks, metal plate; industrial painting; exterior cleaning, including sandblasting

(G-8002)
T BC
8635 Mahogany Ct (20110-8404)
PHONE.............................703 969-8221
EMP: 2
SALES (est): 106.8K **Privately Held**
SIC: 2752 Commercial printing, lithographic

(G-8003)
TMN LLC
Also Called: Tin Man Shtmtl Fabrication
9218 Prince William St (20110-5617)
PHONE.............................703 335-8191
David Simpson, *CEO*
EMP: 10
SALES (est): 1MM **Privately Held**
WEB: www.tinmansheetmetallc.com
SIC: 3444 Sheet metal specialties, not stamped

(G-8004)
TOKYO ELECTRON AMERICA INC
9501 Innovation Dr (20110-2225)
PHONE.............................703 257-2211
Glen Schwartz, *Manager*
EMP: 45 **Privately Held**
WEB: www.tel.com
SIC: 3674 Semiconductors & related devices
HQ: Tokyo Electron America, Inc.
2400 Grove Blvd
Austin TX 78741
512 424-1000

(G-8005)
TOWER HILL CORP
8707 Quarry Rd Ste F (20110-1722)
PHONE.............................703 368-7727
Leo J Haberman, *President*
Janet M Sablon, *Principal*
Thomas E Sablonm Sr, *Principal*
Ruth Ann Haberman, *Treasurer*
EMP: 20
SQ FT: 30,000
SALES (est): 3.2MM **Privately Held**
SIC: 3444 5039 Sheet metal specialties, not stamped; air ducts, sheet metal

(G-8006)
TYCOSYS LLC
9720 Capital Ct Ste 100 (20110-2049)
PHONE.............................571 278-5300
Alaaeldin Elshaer, *President*
EMP: 1 EST: 2013
SALES (est): 74K **Privately Held**
WEB: www.tycosys.com
SIC: 3841 Medical instruments & equipment, blood & bone work

(G-8007)
US PARCEL & COPY CENTER INC
10450 Dumfries Rd (20110-7958)
PHONE.............................703 365-7999
Bill Whitaker, *Owner*
EMP: 2
SQ FT: 1,600
SALES (est): 280.8K **Privately Held**
WEB: www.dominionpawn.com
SIC: 2752 4783 7331 Commercial printing, lithographic; packing & crating; mailing service

(G-8008)
UTRON KINETICS LLC
9441 Innovation Dr (20110-2215)
PHONE.............................703 369-5552
Tesa Bell, *Prdtn Mgr*
Dennis Massey,
Per Bong Jenson,

EMP: 7
SALES (est): 3.1MM **Privately Held**
WEB: www.utronkinetics.com
SIC: 3499 Metal household articles

(G-8009)
V & P INVESTMENT LLC (PA)
Also Called: Discover Granite & Marble
9067 Jerrys Cir (20110-5356)
PHONE.............................703 365-7835
Parvin Ismayilov, *CEO*
EMP: 13
SQ FT: 7,100
SALES (est): 1.2MM **Privately Held**
WEB: www.discovergranite.com
SIC: 3281 2541 Cut stone & stone products; counter & sink tops

(G-8010)
VERTICAL ROCK INC
10225 Nokesville Rd (20110-4133)
PHONE.............................855 822-5462
Ian Colton, *President*
Lindsy Colton, *Vice Pres*
EMP: 5
SALES (est): 23.8K **Privately Held**
WEB: www.climb-va.com
SIC: 2591 Blinds vertical

(G-8011)
WHISKYWRIGHT FINE HANDCRAFTED
9305 Witch Hazel Way (20110-5987)
PHONE.............................703 398-0121
Edwin Wright, *Owner*
Horatio Roberson, *Vice Pres*
EMP: 2 EST: 2017
SALES (est): 97K **Privately Held**
SIC: 2085 Distilled & blended liquors

(G-8012)
WILCOX WOODWORKS INC
10687 Wakeman Ct (20110-2026)
PHONE.............................703 369-3455
Daniel Curtis Wilcox, *President*
Rocky Malamphy, *Opers Mgr*
Gretchen K Wilcox, *Manager*
Jason Wills, *Manager*
Gretchen Wilcox, *Admin Sec*
EMP: 15
SQ FT: 18,668
SALES: 2.5MM **Privately Held**
WEB: www.wilcoxwoodworks.com
SIC: 2499 2521 Decorative wood & woodwork; cabinets, office: wood

(G-8013)
WOLFFINZ LLC
Also Called: Public House Kitchen & Brewry
9406 Battle St (20110-5431)
P.O. Box 330 (20108-0330)
PHONE.............................571 292-1427
Sarah Meyers, *Mng Member*
Jonathan Kibben, *Mng Member*
Jeremy Meyers, *Mng Member*
Christopher Sellers, *Mng Member*
EMP: 30
SALES (est): 1MM **Privately Held**
SIC: 2082 5812 Beer (alcoholic beverage); restaurant, family: independent

(G-8014)
WOOD TELEVISION LLC
Also Called: Potomac News
9028 Prince William St F (20110-5679)
PHONE.............................703 368-9268
L McConnell, *Branch Mgr*
EMP: 9
SALES (corp-wide): 3B **Publicly Held**
WEB: www.woodtv.com
SIC: 2711 Newspapers: publishing only, not printed on site
HQ: Wood Television Llc
120 College Ave Se
Grand Rapids MI 49503
616 456-8888

(G-8015)
ZOTZ
9126 Taylor St (20110-5043)
PHONE.............................703 330-2305
Keating Carrier, *Owner*
EMP: 1
SALES (est): 50K **Privately Held**
SIC: 2399 Horse blankets

GEOGRAPHIC

Manassas
Prince William County

(G-8016)
3 GYPSIES CANDLE COMPANY LLC
9663 Janet Rose Ct (20111-2537)
PHONE..................................703 300-2307
EMP: 2 EST: 2015
SALES (est): 59.2K **Privately Held**
SIC: 3999 Candles

(G-8017)
ABC IMAGING
8480 Virginia Meadows Dr (20109-4860)
PHONE..................................571 379-4299
EMP: 2
SALES (est): 78.2K **Privately Held**
SIC: 2759 Publication printing

(G-8018)
ABSOLUTE SIGNS INC
11900 Livingston Rd # 161 (20109-8306)
PHONE..................................703 229-9436
James Hallaj, *Principal*
EMP: 3 EST: 2010
SALES (est): 201.9K **Privately Held**
WEB: www.absolutesigns.com
SIC: 3993 Electric signs

(G-8019)
ACI PARTNERS LLC
Also Called: Award Crafters
8854 Rixlew Ln (20109-3733)
PHONE..................................703 818-0500
James Munden,
Michele Munden,
Joseph Whitcraft,
Kathleen Whitcraft,
EMP: 12 EST: 1964
SQ FT: 7,500
SALES (est): 1.8MM **Privately Held**
WEB: www.awardcrafters.com
SIC: 3999 5999 Plaques, picture, laminated; trophies & plaques

(G-8020)
**AGGREGATE INDUSTRIES -
MWR INC**
Also Called: Centerville Concrete
9321 Developers Dr (20109-3985)
PHONE..................................703 361-2276
Tony Fabian, *Manager*
EMP: 30
SALES (corp-wide): 1.7B **Privately Held**
WEB: www.lafargeholcim.us
SIC: 3273 Ready-mixed concrete
HQ: Aggregate Industries - Mwr, Inc.
2815 Dodd Rd
Eagan MN 55121

(G-8021)
AJ TRIM LLC
7750 Wellingford Dr (20109-5223)
P.O. Box 1158 (20108-1158)
PHONE..................................703 330-1212
Alberto Pereira, *Administration*
EMP: 3
SALES (est): 155.6K **Privately Held**
SIC: 2431 Millwork

(G-8022)
ALL AMERICAN LOGISTIC CO
9110 Forestview Dr (20112-3361)
PHONE..................................571 237-6039
Awad Farah, *President*
EMP: 2
SALES (est): 90K **Privately Held**
SIC: 2542 Carrier cases & tables, mail: except wood

(G-8023)
ALLIGATORTALEZ
7892 English St (20112-3672)
PHONE..................................703 791-4238
EMP: 2
SALES (est): 85.9K **Privately Held**
SIC: 3571 Electronic computers

(G-8024)
AMEE BAY LLC
10440 Balls Ford Rd (20109-2501)
PHONE..................................703 365-0450
EMP: 3
SALES (corp-wide): 63.2MM **Privately Held**
WEB: www.ameebay.com
SIC: 3731 Shipbuilding & repairing
HQ: Amee Bay, Llc
2702 Denali St Ste 104
Anchorage AK 99503

(G-8025)
AMELIA LAWRENCE LLC
12837 Mill Race Ct (20112-4679)
PHONE..................................703 493-9095
Amy Pugh, *Principal*
EMP: 2
SALES (est): 139K **Privately Held**
SIC: 3911 Jewelry apparel

(G-8026)
AMERICA FURNITURE LLC
8328 Shoppers Sq (20111-2174)
PHONE..................................703 939-3678
Darilh Vallecillo,
EMP: 1 **Privately Held**
SIC: 2211 Furniture denim

(G-8027)
ANTHONY AMUSEMENTS
5973 Twin Rivers Dr (20112-3069)
PHONE..................................703 670-2681
Anthony Bado, *Owner*
EMP: 1
SALES (est): 50K **Privately Held**
SIC: 3999 Coin-operated amusement machines

(G-8028)
APPLIED MATERIALS INC
7900 Sudley Rd Ste 303 (20109-2806)
PHONE..................................703 331-1476
Peter Schuler, *Manager*
EMP: 40
SALES (corp-wide): 17.2B **Publicly Held**
WEB: www.appliedmaterials.com
SIC: 3674 Semiconductors & related devices
PA: Applied Materials, Inc.
3050 Bowers Ave Bldg 1
Santa Clara CA 95054
408 727-5555

(G-8029)
ARIC LYNN LLC
Also Called: Aric Lynn Co
11033 Wooldridge Dr (20111-2901)
PHONE..................................571 505-7657
Roger Aric Rogers, *Principal*
EMP: 1 EST: 2005
SALES (est): 30K **Privately Held**
SIC: 2521 Wood office furniture

(G-8030)
AUTUMN PUBLISHING INC
7219 Nathan Ct (20109-2436)
PHONE..................................703 368-4857
EMP: 4
SQ FT: 1,800
SALES (est): 260K **Privately Held**
SIC: 2721 Publishers Newspaper

(G-8031)
AVM SHEET METAL INC
12041 Coloriver Rd (20112-8610)
PHONE..................................703 975-7715
EMP: 2
SALES (est): 119.4K **Privately Held**
SIC: 3444 Sheet metalwork

(G-8032)
AXCELIS TECHNOLOGIES INC
8140 Flannery Ct (20109-2733)
PHONE..................................571 921-1493
Todd Stull, *Manager*
EMP: 400
SALES (corp-wide): 342.9MM **Publicly Held**
WEB: www.axcelis.com
SIC: 3829 Measuring & controlling devices
PA: Axcelis Technologies, Inc.
108 Cherry Hill Dr
Beverly MA 01915
978 787-4000

(G-8033)
BAJJ USA INC
8025 Towering Oak Way (20111-5212)
PHONE..................................703 953-1541
Rana S Ahmed, *CEO*
EMP: 2
SALES (est): 178.1K **Privately Held**
SIC: 2329 Men's & boys' sportswear & athletic clothing

(G-8034)
BAKEFULLY YOURS LLC
8136 Flannery Ct (20109-2733)
PHONE..................................301 276-4972
EMP: 2
SALES (est): 62.3K **Privately Held**
SIC: 2051 Bakery: wholesale or wholesale/retail combined

(G-8035)
BANNERWORKS SIGNS & GRAPHICS
11900 Livingston Rd # 139 (20109-8304)
PHONE..................................571 292-2567
Carl Casey, *Owner*
EMP: 3
SALES (est): 500K **Privately Held**
WEB: www.bannerworx.com
SIC: 3993 Signs & advertising specialties

(G-8036)
BEAR-KAT MANUFACTURING LLC
12351 Randolph Ridge Ln (20109-5213)
PHONE..................................800 442-9700
South T Patterson, *Administration*
EMP: 2 EST: 2011
SALES (est): 95.3K **Privately Held**
WEB: www.atlanticemergency.com
SIC: 3999 Manufacturing industries

(G-8037)
BELTSVILLE CONSTRUCTION SUPPLY
10337 Balls Ford Rd (20109-2603)
PHONE..................................703 392-8588
Tom Eveler, *Principal*
EMP: 2
SALES (est): 130K **Privately Held**
WEB: www.beltsvillesupply.com
SIC: 3524 Lawn & garden equipment

(G-8038)
BETTER GRANITE GARCIA LLC
6954 Wellington Rd 3 (20109-2708)
PHONE..................................703 624-9912
Heriberto Contreras-Garcia, *President*
EMP: 10
SQ FT: 7,000
SALES (est): 636.8K **Privately Held**
WEB: www.bettergranitegarcia.com
SIC: 3281 Curbing, granite or stone

(G-8039)
BIOLOGICS INC
8761 Virginia Meadows Dr (20109-7826)
PHONE..................................703 367-9020
Denise Scarpato, *CEO*
Michael A Zervoudis, *President*
Hill Peter, *Technical Staff*
EMP: 19
SQ FT: 11,200
SALES (est): 1.4MM **Privately Held**
WEB: www.biologics-inc.com
SIC: 3821 Laboratory apparatus & furniture

(G-8040)
BKC INDUSTRIES INC
11220 Assett Loop Ste 210 (20109-7914)
PHONE..................................856 694-9400
Karen Harrison-Carter, *Principal*
Bernard Carter, *Principal*
Alvin Harrison, *Principal*
EMP: 5
SALES (est): 150.7K **Privately Held**
SIC: 3999 Manufacturing industries

(G-8041)
BOW INDUSTRIES OF VIRGINIA
10349 Balls Ford Rd (20109-2603)
PHONE..................................703 361-7704
Dale Whysong, *President*
EMP: 5 EST: 1969
SQ FT: 3,000
SALES (est): 540K **Privately Held**
WEB: www.bowindustries.com
SIC: 3577 Computer peripheral equipment

(G-8042)
BRADY CONTRACTING SERVICE
10920 Peninsula Ct (20111-4363)
PHONE..................................703 864-9207
William Brady, *President*
EMP: 1
SALES (est): 130.5K **Privately Held**
SIC: 3699 3449 Electrical equipment & supplies; miscellaneous metalwork

(G-8043)
C Y J ENTERPRISES CORP
Also Called: C J Steel
7121 Gary Rd (20109-2649)
PHONE..................................703 367-7722
EMP: 2 EST: 2006
SALES (est): 170K **Privately Held**
SIC: 3441 Structural Metal Fabrication

(G-8044)
CAPITOL EXHIBIT SERVICES INC
Also Called: Capitol Trade Show Services
12299 Livingston Rd (20109-2772)
PHONE..................................703 330-9000
Dehart Ray, *President*
Amanda Coggins, *Vice Pres*
Chuck Farmer, *Vice Pres*
Yvette Holland, *Vice Pres*
Bruce Swanson, *Vice Pres*
▲ EMP: 50
SQ FT: 98,000
SALES (est): 9.2MM **Privately Held**
WEB: www.capitolmuseumservices.com
SIC: 3993 Signs & advertising specialties

(G-8045)
CAPSTONE INDUSTRIES LLC
Also Called: Cnc Metal Design
7728 Beckham Ct (20111-8221)
PHONE..................................703 966-6718
Phillip Caplinger,
EMP: 1
SALES (est): 135.8K **Privately Held**
WEB: www.cncmetaldesign.com
SIC: 3541 3444 2514 Plasma process metal cutting machines; sheet metalwork; bins, prefabricated sheet metal; metal lawn & garden furniture

(G-8046)
CARBURETORS UNLIMITED
10369 Balls Ford Rd (20109-2603)
PHONE..................................703 273-0751
EMP: 2
SALES (est): 85.9K **Privately Held**
SIC: 3592 Carburetors, Pistons, Rings, Valves, Nsk

(G-8047)
CASSANDRAS CUSTOM DESIGNS LLC
7856 Rebel Walk Dr (20109-7733)
PHONE..................................571 229-0389
Cassandra Nicole, *Principal*
EMP: 2 EST: 2017
SALES (est): 109.4K **Privately Held**
SIC: 2759 Screen printing

(G-8048)
CENTURY PRESS INC
10443 Balls Ford Rd (20109-2640)
PHONE..................................703 335-5663
Tory Wadel, *CEO*
Dolly Alexander, *President*
Costello Darlene M, *Vice Pres*
EMP: 6
SQ FT: 2,700
SALES (est): 897.8K **Privately Held**
WEB: www.centurypressinc.com
SIC: 2752 Commercial printing, offset

(G-8049)
CIO CONTROLS INC
8140 Ashton Ave Ste 210 (20109-5701)
PHONE..................................703 365-2227
Sharad Gupta, *President*
EMP: 2
SALES (est): 950K **Privately Held**
SIC: 7372 Prepackaged software

▲ = Import ▼=Export
◆ =Import/Export

(G-8050)
CITADEL STUDIOS INC
11571 Purse Dr (20112-7562)
PHONE..................................407 766-6302
EMP: 2
SALES (est): 110.6K **Privately Held**
WEB: www.citadelstudios.net
SIC: 3652 Pre-recorded records & tapes

(G-8051)
COMMERCIAL TECH INC
Also Called: Commercial Hvacr
8986 Mike Garcia Dr (20109-5455)
PHONE..................................703 468-1339
Manpreet Nijjer, *President*
Mandeep Nijjer, *Principal*
EMP: 4
SALES (est): 434.3K **Privately Held**
WEB: www.mycommercialtech.com
SIC: 3585 1711 Refrigeration & heating
equipment; boiler maintenance contractor; heating & air conditioning contractors; refrigeration contractor; heating systems repair & maintenance

(G-8052)
CORNING INCORPORATED
9345 Discovery Blvd (20109-3992)
PHONE..................................703 471-5955
EMP: 2
SALES (corp-wide): 11.5B **Publicly Held**
WEB: www.corning.com
SIC: 3357 Nonferrous wiredrawing & insulating
PA: Corning Incorporated
1 Riverfront Plz
Corning NY 14831
607 974-9000

(G-8053)
CROWN INTERNATIONAL INC
8508 Virginia Meadows Dr (20109-4861)
PHONE..................................703 335-0066
Stoyan I Bakalov, *Ch of Bd*
Sultana Bakalov, *Exec VP*
EMP: 12
SQ FT: 6,000
SALES (est): 924.9K **Privately Held**
WEB: www.crowninternationalinc.us
SIC: 1241 5012 5013 5531 Bituminous
coal mining services, contract basis; automobiles & other motor vehicles; automotive supplies & parts; automobile & truck equipment & parts; ; gas analyzing equipment

(G-8054)
DAVIS BRIANNA
7105 Signal Hill Rd (20111-4203)
PHONE..................................703 220-4791
Brianna Davis, *Consultant*
EMP: 1 EST: 2014
SALES (est): 65.5K **Privately Held**
SIC: 1389 Surveying wells

(G-8055)
DEEM PRINTING COMPANY INC
7519 Presidential Ln (20109-2629)
PHONE..................................703 335-5422
EMP: 2
SALES (est): 90.5K **Privately Held**
WEB: www.deemprinting.com
SIC: 2752 Commercial printing, offset

(G-8056)
DELMER-VA INC
11149 Wortham Crest Cir (20109-5690)
PHONE..................................571 447-1413
Paul Bhatt, *Director*
EMP: 1 EST: 2017
SALES (est): 44.9K **Privately Held**
SIC: 3911 Jewelry, precious metal

(G-8057)
DEPORTER DOMINICK & ASSOC LLC
7853 Coppermine Dr Ste C (20109-2505)
PHONE..................................703 530-9255
Henry Wilson,
EMP: 2
SALES (est): 196.6K **Privately Held**
SIC: 3646 Commercial indusl & institutional electric lighting fixtures

(G-8058)
DIVINELY INSPIRED PRESS LLC
5764 Laurel Glen Ct (20112-3057)
PHONE..................................703 763-3790
Marie Woods, *Principal*
EMP: 1 EST: 2014
SALES (est): 59.8K **Privately Held**
SIC: 2741 Miscellaneous publishing

(G-8059)
DIZZY PIG LLC
8763 Virginia Meadows Dr (20109-7826)
PHONE..................................571 379-4884
Rodrigo Izquierdo, *Prdtn Mgr*
Chris Capell, *Mng Member*
EMP: 5
SALES (est): 556.2K **Privately Held**
WEB: www.dizzypigbbq.com
SIC: 2099 Seasonings & spices

(G-8060)
E G D SHEET METAL LLC
10262 Cub Run Ct (20109-3501)
PHONE..................................571 577-1647
EMP: 2 EST: 2018
SALES (est): 114.4K **Privately Held**
SIC: 3444 Sheet metalwork

(G-8061)
EARTHWALK COMMUNICATIONS INC
10511 Battleview Pkwy (20109-2343)
PHONE..................................703 393-1940
Evan T McConnell, *CEO*
Peggi McConnell, *President*
Facundo Alberdi, *Vice Pres*
Robert Vanderlip, *Vice Pres*
Abdi Karbassi, *Opers Mgr*
◆ EMP: 60
SQ FT: 40,000
SALES (est): 15.3MM **Privately Held**
WEB: www.earthwalk.com
SIC: 3999 8748 Education aids, devices & supplies; educational consultant

(G-8062)
EAST COAST CUSTOM COACHES INC
Also Called: East Coast MBL Bus Launchpad
11900 Livingston Rd # 119 (20109-8304)
PHONE..................................571 292-1583
Eduardo Bocock, *President*
Jason Tipton, *COO*
▼ EMP: 15
SQ FT: 2,500
SALES (est): 2.2MM **Privately Held**
WEB: www.eastcoastlaunchpad.com
SIC: 3537 Trucks, tractors, loaders, carriers & similar equipment

(G-8063)
ELECTROMOTIVE INC
8754 Virginia Meadows Dr (20109-7820)
PHONE..................................703 331-0100
Fred Schuettler, *President*
Patti Dove, *Vice Pres*
Stephanie Brewer, *Office Mgr*
Frank Cowles, *Shareholder*
EMP: 22 EST: 1981
SQ FT: 52,000
SALES (est): 3MM **Privately Held**
WEB: www.electromotive.com
SIC: 3694 3823 3625 Engine electrical equipment; industrial instrmnts msrmnt display/control process variable; relays & industrial controls

(G-8064)
ENDEAVOR CONSULTING GROUP LLC
10632 Tattersall Dr (20112-2411)
PHONE..................................202 599-7437
Eric Holder,
Ebony Karim,
EMP: 1
SALES (est): 39.6K **Privately Held**
SIC: 3999 Manufacturing industries

(G-8065)
ENNSTONE
9321 Developers Dr (20109-3985)
PHONE..................................703 335-2650
Ken Creswick, *Principal*
EMP: 4

SALES (est): 230.2K **Privately Held**
SIC: 3273 Ready-mixed concrete

(G-8066)
EVOLUTION PRINTING INC
7200 S Hill Dr (20109-2609)
PHONE..................................571 292-1213
Michael Greg Turley, *President*
EMP: 3
SALES (est): 315.2K **Privately Held**
WEB: www.evoprinting.com
SIC: 2752 Commercial printing, offset

(G-8067)
EYE DOLLZ LASHES BUTY BAR LLC
10432 Balls Ford Rd (20109-2514)
PHONE..................................703 480-7899
Kristi Barnett,
EMP: 1
SALES (est): 57.1K **Privately Held**
SIC: 3999 Eyelashes, artificial

(G-8068)
FAIRFAX WOODWORKING INC
12042 Cadet Ct (20109-7897)
PHONE..................................571 292-2220
EMP: 4
SALES (est): 300K **Privately Held**
SIC: 2431 Mfg Millwork

(G-8069)
FASTSIGNS
7612 Stream Walk Ln (20109-2465)
PHONE..................................703 392-7446
EMP: 1 EST: 2018
SALES (est): 46K **Privately Held**
WEB: www.fastsigns.com
SIC: 3993 Signs & advertising specialties

(G-8070)
FASTWARE INC
8474 Virginia Meadows Dr (20109-4860)
PHONE..................................703 680-5050
John Rigot, *President*
EMP: 1 EST: 2002
SALES (est): 205.7K **Privately Held**
WEB: www.fastwareinc.com
SIC: 3429 Manufactured hardware (general)

(G-8071)
FUN WITH CANVAS
7008 Tech Cir (20109-7314)
PHONE..................................724 689-5821
EMP: 1
SALES (est): 51.2K **Privately Held**
WEB: www.funwithcanvas.com
SIC: 2211 Canvas

(G-8072)
GEEK KEEP LLC
11560 Temple Loop (20112-7590)
PHONE..................................703 867-9867
Andrea Bryant, *Principal*
Michelle Matthews, *Principal*
Thor Anthony Matthews, *Administration*
EMP: 4 EST: 2015
SALES (est): 244.8K **Privately Held**
SIC: 3944 5734 Video game machines, except coin-operated; software, computer games

(G-8073)
GENERAL SHEET METAL CO INC
10814 Valley Falls Ct (20112-5868)
PHONE..................................571 221-3270
OH Yong Yul, *Principal*
EMP: 6 EST: 2014
SALES (est): 411.2K **Privately Held**
SIC: 3444 Sheet metalwork

(G-8074)
GGB LLC
7516 Aruba Ct (20109-7100)
PHONE..................................571 234-9597
Kevin Gordon,
EMP: 4
SALES (est): 229K **Privately Held**
SIC: 3568 Power transmission equipment

(G-8075)
GIFTED EDUCATION PRESS
10201 Yuma Ct (20109-2935)
PHONE..................................703 369-5017
Maurice D Fischer, *Owner*
Eugenia Fischer, *Co-Owner*
EMP: 2 EST: 1980
SALES (est): 88K **Privately Held**
WEB: www.giftededpress.com
SIC: 2741 Miscellaneous publishing

(G-8076)
GRANITE DESIGN INC
6954 Wellingford Dr (20109)
PHONE..................................703 530-1223
Florian Dimashi, *President*
EMP: 3
SQ FT: 9,000
SALES (est): 275.8K **Privately Held**
SIC: 3281 Granite, cut & shaped

(G-8077)
GRC ENTERPRISES INC
Also Called: Grc Direct
9203 Mike Garcia Dr (20109-5466)
PHONE..................................540 428-7000
Arvind K Gupta, *President*
Vinay Kumar, *Vice Pres*
Jim Slater, *Technology*
EMP: 38
SQ FT: 38,000
SALES (est): 5.6MM **Privately Held**
WEB: www.grassrootcommunication.com
SIC: 2752 7334 Commercial printing, offset; photocopying & duplicating services

(G-8078)
HLK CUSTOM STAINLESS INC
10476 Godwin Dr (20112-2730)
PHONE..................................571 261-5811
Teresa Lambert, *President*
Darrell Lambert, *Product Mgr*
EMP: 6
SQ FT: 1,000
SALES (est): 318.6K **Privately Held**
SIC: 3446 Railings, bannisters, guards, etc.: made from metal pipe

(G-8079)
IBS MILLWORK CORPORATION
8501 Buckeye Timber Dr (20109-3803)
PHONE..................................703 631-4011
Beth Walton, *Purch Agent*
Mike Chambers, *Sales Staff*
Patricia Brinkley, *Manager*
Rachel Dean, *Administration*
EMP: 2
SALES (est): 90.2K **Privately Held**
WEB: www.usa-millwork.com
SIC: 2431 Millwork

(G-8080)
INDUKO INC
7012 Trappers Ct (20111-4378)
PHONE..................................703 217-4262
Jeremy Wills, *CEO*
EMP: 2
SALES (est): 950K **Privately Held**
SIC: 7372 Prepackaged software

(G-8081)
INSTITUTE OF NAVIGATION (DC)
8551 Rixlew Ln Ste 360 (20109-4278)
PHONE..................................703 366-2723
Lisa Beaty, *President*
Kenneth Esthus, *Director*
Megan Andrews, *Meeting Planner*
EMP: 8
SALES: 3.9MM **Privately Held**
WEB: www.ion.org
SIC: 2721 8621 Trade journals: publishing only, not printed on site; scientific membership association

(G-8082)
INTEGRA MANAGEMENT GROUP LLC
Also Called: Integra Drapes
7819 Abbey Oaks Ct (20112-4683)
PHONE..................................703 791-2007
Julie E Barns,
EMP: 15
SALES (est): 600K **Privately Held**
WEB: www.integramanagementgroup.com
SIC: 2391 Curtains & draperies

(G-8083)

INTERIOR BUILDING SYSTEMS CORP

Also Called: Fidelity Contracting Company
8501 Buckeye Timber Dr (20109-3803)
PHONE.................................703 335-9655
Paul V Bell, *President*
Patricia Brinkley, *Vice Pres*
Luciano Pusterla, *Project Mgr*
Neal Packer, *Purchasing*
Drew Sonnek, *Engineer*
EMP: 77
SQ FT: 50,000
SALES (est): 14.7MM **Privately Held**
WEB: www.usa-millwork.com
SIC: 2521 2431 1751 2434 Cabinets, office: wood; millwork; finish & trim carpentry; wood kitchen cabinets

(G-8084)

INTERNATIONAL APPAREL LTD

Also Called: Corporate Identity
13711 Dumfries Rd (20112-3728)
PHONE.................................571 643-0100
C Robert Brewer, *President*
Sharenik Jain, *Partner*
Vikrant Sharma, *Vice Pres*
▲ **EMP:** 25 **EST:** 1995
SQ FT: 4,000
SALES (est): 1.9MM **Privately Held**
SIC: 2321 Men's & boys' furnishings

(G-8085)

INTUITIVE GLOBAL LLC

12701 Crystal Lake Ct (20112-3299)
PHONE.................................571 388-6183
John Kolb, *President*
Caroline Kolb,
EMP: 2 **EST:** 2014
SALES (est): 129.5K **Privately Held**
SIC: 3599 Crankshafts & camshafts, machining

(G-8086)

INVISION INC

10432 Balls Ford Rd # 300 (20109-2517)
PHONE.................................703 774-3881
EMP: 15
SALES (corp-wide): 66.9MM **Privately Held**
WEB: www.invisionapp.com
SIC: 7372 Application computer software
HQ: Invision Inc.
25 W 43rd St Ste 609
New York NY 10036

(G-8087)

ISOMET CORPORATION (PA)

10342 Battleview Pkwy (20109-2338)
PHONE.................................703 321-8301
Michael Hillier, *President*
Robert G Bonner, *Exec VP*
Scotty Johnson, *Opers Staff*
D Tyndall, *Purchasing*
Donald Chamaj, *Engineer*
EMP: 30 **EST:** 1956
SQ FT: 25,974
SALES (est): 3.2MM **Privately Held**
WEB: www.isomet.com
SIC: 3826 3827 3825 3823 Laser scientific & engineering instruments; optical instruments & lenses; instruments to measure electricity; industrial instrmnts msrmnt display/control process variable; electrical equipment & supplies; computer peripheral equipment

(G-8088)

ISOTHRIVE LLC

9385 Discovery Blvd (20109-3998)
PHONE.................................855 552-5572
Jack Oswald, *CEO*
Lee R Madsen II, *Vice Pres*
Peter Swann, *Chief Mktg Ofcr*
EMP: 2
SALES (est): 74.4K **Privately Held**
WEB: www.isothrive.com
SIC: 2834 Extracts of botanicals: powdered, pilular, solid or fluid

(G-8089)

JAMES J ROBERTS

7808 Lake Dr (20111-1947)
PHONE.................................703 330-0448
James Roberts, *Owner*
EMP: 2 **EST:** 2008

SALES (est): 161K **Privately Held**
SIC: 2759 Engraving

(G-8090)

JUGGERNAUT INDUSTRIES

8700 Virginia Meadows Dr (20109-7820)
PHONE.................................703 686-0191
Kim Kollins, *Partner*
EMP: 2
SALES (est): 142.1K **Privately Held**
WEB: www.juggernautindusa.com
SIC: 3999 Manufacturing industries

(G-8091)

K & J WOODWORKING/ CASH

7230 Yates Ford Rd (20111-3906)
PHONE.................................703 369-7161
Davis Kemp, *Principal*
EMP: 2
SALES (est): 144.1K **Privately Held**
SIC: 2431 Millwork

(G-8092)

KARMA GROUP INC

10497 Labrador Loop (20112-2734)
PHONE.................................717 253-9379
John Kovaleski, *Principal*
EMP: 4
SALES (est): 395.8K **Privately Held**
SIC: 3555 Typesetting machines: linotype, monotype, intertype, etc.

(G-8093)

KENNETH LEE WOODS

8216 Birch St (20111-2235)
PHONE.................................703 361-7390
EMP: 2
SALES (est): 83.9K **Privately Held**
SIC: 2752 Commercial printing, lithographic

(G-8094)

KILMARTIN JONES GROUP LLC

5555 Old Farm Ln (20109-2118)
PHONE.................................703 232-1531
Paul Kilmartin, *Chief*
Margaret Jones,
EMP: 2
SALES (est): 160.5K **Privately Held**
WEB: www.worldtechtoday.com
SIC: 2741 7389 Miscellaneous publishing;

(G-8095)

L-1 STANDARDS AND TECH INC

10364 Battleview Pkwy (20109-2338)
PHONE.................................571 428-2227
Steven R Lorentz, *President*
EMP: 9
SQ FT: 7,500
SALES (est): 1.7MM **Privately Held**
WEB: www.l-1.biz
SIC: 3829 Meteorological instruments

(G-8096)

LA PRINCESA

8388 Centreville Rd (20111-2224)
PHONE.................................703 330-2400
Gloria Velasquez, *Owner*
EMP: 3
SALES (est): 295K **Privately Held**
WEB: www.azprincesa.com
SIC: 2335 Wedding gowns & dresses

(G-8097)

LABRADOR TECHNOLOGY

12219 Vista Brooke Dr (20112-7532)
PHONE.................................703 791-7660
Mark Baker, *Principal*
EMP: 1
SALES (est): 120K **Privately Held**
SIC: 3674 Light emitting diodes

(G-8098)

LAURIE GRUSHA ZIPF

Also Called: Zipf Patterns
7030 Gray Fox Trl (20112-3231)
PHONE.................................703 794-9497
Laurie Zipf Grusha, *Owner*
EMP: 1
SALES (est): 160K **Privately Held**
SIC: 3553 Pattern makers' machinery, woodworking

(G-8099)

LEGACY VULCAN LLC

Mideast Division
8537 Vulcan Ln (20109-3947)
PHONE.................................703 368-2475
Chris Carroll, *Manager*
George McCall, *Maintence Staff*
EMP: 76
SQ FT: 2,000 **Publicly Held**
WEB: www.vulcanmaterials.com
SIC: 3273 Ready-mixed concrete
HQ: Legacy Vulcan, Llc
1200 Urban Center Dr
Vestavia AL 35242
205 298-3000

(G-8100)

LIGHT GREY INDUSTRIES

10346 Portsmouth Rd (20109-8007)
PHONE.................................703 330-1339
EMP: 1
SALES (est): 67.1K **Privately Held**
SIC: 3999 Manufacturing industries

(G-8101)

LITTON GUITAR WORKS LLC

9716 Manassas Forge Dr (20111-2576)
PHONE.................................703 966-0571
Michael Litton,
EMP: 1
SALES (est): 77.5K **Privately Held**
SIC: 3931 Guitars & parts, electric & non-electric

(G-8102)

M&M WELDING LLC

8010 Ashland Ave Apt 3 (20109-8010)
PHONE.................................703 201-4066
Jose Rosa,
EMP: 1
SALES (est): 89.7K **Privately Held**
SIC: 7692 Automotive welding

(G-8103)

M2M LLC

10262 Battleview Pkwy (20109-2336)
PHONE.................................816 204-0938
John Morrison, *Mng Member*
Evan McConnell,
Margaret McConnell,
EMP: 3
SALES (est): 29K **Privately Held**
SIC: 3429 Fireplace equipment, hardware: andirons, grates, screens

(G-8104)

MANASSAS CONSULTING SVCS INC

12788 Lost Creek Ct (20112-3452)
PHONE.................................703 346-1358
John Silva, *CEO*
EMP: 1
SALES (est): 90K **Privately Held**
WEB:
www.manassasconsultingservices.com
SIC: 2741 7389 Miscellaneous publishing;

(G-8105)

MATERIALS DEVELOPMENT CORP

12169 Balls Ford Rd (20109-2449)
PHONE.................................703 257-1500
Amy Triggs, *Office Mgr*
Art Torres, *Branch Mgr*
EMP: 1 **Privately Held**
WEB: www.materialsdevelopment.com
SIC: 3577 Computer peripheral equipment
PA: Materials Development Corp
12832 Ne Tillamook St
Portland OR

(G-8106)

MEDIATECH INC (HQ)

Also Called: Corning
9345 Discovery Blvd (20109-3992)
PHONE.................................703 471-5955
Lydia A Kenton Walsh, *President*
John Elliott Jr, *Exec VP*
Jason Walsh, *Vice Pres*
Peter Stangeby, *CFO*
Robert P Vanni, *Treasurer*
EMP: 20
SQ FT: 50,000

SALES (est): 14.9MM
SALES (corp-wide): 11.5B **Publicly Held**
WEB: www.cellgro.com
SIC: 2836 Biological products, except diagnostic
PA: Corning Incorporated
1 Riverfront Plz
Corning NY 14831
607 974-9000

(G-8107)

MEMORIAL WELDING LLC

7804 Signal Hill Rd (20111-2514)
PHONE.................................703 369-2428
Jose German Fernandez, *Principal*
EMP: 1 **EST:** 2018
SALES (est): 25K **Privately Held**
SIC: 7692 Welding repair

(G-8108)

MGKE CONSTRUCTION LLC

7523 Alleghany Rd (20111-4146)
PHONE.................................571 282-8415
Miguel Portillo, *Director*
EMP: 2
SALES (est): 97.2K **Privately Held**
SIC: 3612 7389 Current limiting reactors, electrical;

(G-8109)

MNG ONLINE LLC

Also Called: My African Bikini
8105 Porter Ridge Ln # 9 (20109-8105)
PHONE.................................571 247-8276
Gabriel Mahia, *Principal*
EMP: 1
SALES (est): 109.4K **Privately Held**
SIC: 2211 2339 7389 2221 Apparel & outerwear fabrics, cotton; women's & misses' athletic clothing & sportswear; translation services; ; apparel & outerwear fabric, manmade fiber or silk; apparel & outerwear broadwoven fabrics

(G-8110)

MOBILE CUSTOMS LLC

11850 Livingston Rd # 105 (20109-8308)
PHONE.................................757 903-5092
EMP: 2
SALES (est): 87.2K **Privately Held**
SIC: 3715 Truck trailers

(G-8111)

MONSTRACITY PRESS

14124 Walton Dr (20112-3701)
PHONE.................................703 791-2759
Andrew Fox, *Principal*
EMP: 1
SALES (est): 54.1K **Privately Held**
WEB: www.fantasticalandrewfox.com
SIC: 2741 Miscellaneous publishing

(G-8112)

MONTI TOOLS INC

7677 Coppermine Dr (20109-2668)
PHONE.................................832 623-7970
Michael Fischer, *President*
◆ **EMP:** 4
SALES (est): 409.5K
SALES (corp-wide): 242.1K **Privately Held**
WEB: www.monti.de
SIC: 3546 5251 5072 Power-driven handtools; tools, power; power tools & accessories
HQ: M O N T I - Werkzeuge Gmbh
Reisertstr. 21
Hennef (Sieg) 53773
224 290-9063

(G-8113)

MR GRAPHICS PRINT SHOP LLC

7537 Gary Rd (20109-2608)
PHONE.................................703 980-8239
Daniel Go,
EMP: 3
SALES (est): 300K **Privately Held**
SIC: 2752 Commercial printing, offset

(G-8114)

MU-DEL ELECTRONICS LLC

7430 Merritt Park Dr # 140 (20109-8315)
PHONE.................................703 368-8900
Souren Hakopian, *President*
Sami Antrazi, *General Mgr*
Jim Guinaw, *Exec VP*

▲ = Import ▼=Export
◆ =Import/Export

Trey Middleton, *Opers Staff*
Thomas Gilboy, *CFO*
EMP: 15
SALES (est) 3.4MM **Privately Held**
WEB: www.mu-del.com
SIC: 3663 7382 8711 7373 Radio & TV communications equipment; protective devices, security; mechanical engineering; systems integration services; household audio & video equipment

(G-8115)
NATIONAL TARS
10620 Crestwood Dr Ste B (20109-4403)
PHONE.................................703 368-4220
Barbara Gilbert, *Owner*
EMP: 2
SALES (est) 118.5K **Privately Held**
WEB: www.teenagerepublicans.org
SIC: 2865 Tar

(G-8116)
NEUROTECH NA INC
11220 Assett Loop Ste 101 (20109-7914)
PHONE.................................888 980-1197
John Velure, *President*
J Christopher McAuliffe, *COO*
EMP: 6 EST: 2009
SQ FT: 1,500
SALES (est) 919.5K **Privately Held**
WEB: www.kneehab.com
SIC: 3841 Surgical & medical instruments
PA: Bio-Medical Research Limited
Bmr House
Galway

(G-8117)
NEW CREATION SOURCING INC
8830 Rixlew Ln (20109-3733)
P.O. Box 324, Mineral (23117-0324)
PHONE.................................703 330-5314
Christopher J Hilburn, *President*
Betsy Oxendine, *Vice Pres*
Sharon Schwartz, *Art Dir*
April Ashcraft, *Administration*
▲ **EMP:** 15
SQ FT: 2,200
SALES (est) 18MM **Privately Held**
WEB: www.newcreationinc.com
SIC: 2329 Men's & boys' sportswear & athletic clothing

(G-8118)
NOTALVISION INC
7717 Coppermine Dr (20109-2506)
PHONE.................................703 953-3339
Quinton Oswald, *CEO*
Barbara Benedict, *Vice Pres*
Courtney Goodwin, *Director*
Jon Johnson, *Director*
EMP: 80
SALES (est) 10MM **Privately Held**
WEB: www.notalvision.com
SIC: 3826 Perimeters (optical instruments)

(G-8119)
NV CAST STONE
11900 Livingston Rd # 147 (20109-8310)
PHONE.................................703 393-2777
Carl Maine, *Principal*
EMP: 10 EST: 2008
SALES (est) 1.4MM **Privately Held**
WEB: www.nvcast.com
SIC: 3272 Concrete products

(G-8120)
OKOS SOLUTIONS LLC
7036 Tech Cir (20109-7314)
PHONE.................................703 880-3039
Stephen McDonough, *Sales Staff*
Harinath Polu, *Mng Member*
Hari Polu, *Administration*
◆ **EMP:** 25
SQ FT: 7,200
SALES (est) 4.5MM **Privately Held**
WEB: www.okos.com
SIC: 3825 Test equipment for electronic & electrical circuits

(G-8121)
OLIVE MANASSAS OIL CO
10016 Moore Dr (20111-2507)
PHONE.................................703 543-9206
EMP: 3 EST: 2015

SALES (est) 158.8K **Privately Held**
WEB: www.manassasoliveoil.com
SIC: 2079 Olive oil

(G-8122)
ORION APPLIED SCIENCE TECH LLC
10432 Balls Ford Rd # 300 (20109-2514)
PHONE.................................571 393-1942
Alvin J Alexander II,
EMP: 1
SQ FT: 1,000
SALES (est) 116K **Privately Held**
WEB: www.orionast.com
SIC: 3663 7373 8742 Satellites, communications; computer integrated systems design; systems engineering, computer related; systems integration services; management consulting services; general management consultant

(G-8123)
ORLANDO GARZON CUELLAR
9105 Mineola Ct (20111-8261)
PHONE.................................571 274-6913
Orlando Garzon Cuellar, *Principal*
EMP: 2
SALES (est) 148.4K **Privately Held**
SIC: 3639 7389 Floor waxers & polishers, electric: household;

(G-8124)
OUR FAMILYS OLIVE OIL LLC
Also Called: Laconiko
9239 Mike Garcia Dr (20109-5466)
PHONE.................................571 292-1394
Dino Pierrakos,
Diamantis Pierrakos,
▲ **EMP:** 2
SALES (est) 360K **Privately Held**
WEB: www.laconiko.com
SIC: 2079 Olive oil

(G-8125)
OUTDOOR LEISURE (PA)
10364 Balls Ford Rd (20109-2618)
PHONE.................................703 349-1965
Greg Harsh, *Principal*
EMP: 4
SALES (est) 680.6K **Privately Held**
WEB: www.hottubsandpooltablesoutlet.com
SIC: 3999 Hot tubs

(G-8126)
PAUL V BELL
8501 Buckeye Timber Dr (20109-3803)
PHONE.................................703 631-4011
Paul V Bell, *Principal*
EMP: 3
SALES (est) 148.8K **Privately Held**
WEB: www.paulvi.net
SIC: 2431 Millwork

(G-8127)
PERRY RAILWORKS INC
13573 Den Hollow Ct (20112-5545)
PHONE.................................703 794-0507
William R Perry, *President*
Melissa G Perry, *Admin Sec*
EMP: 5
SQ FT: 1,500
SALES (est) 540K **Privately Held**
WEB: www.perryrailworks.com
SIC: 2431 Stair railings, wood

(G-8128)
PINE CREEK STRUCTURES
14195 Dumfries Rd (20112-3718)
PHONE.................................703 791-5700
EMP: 1
SALES (est) 59.6K **Privately Held**
WEB: www.storageshedspa.com
SIC: 2511 Wood household furniture

(G-8129)
PIONK ENTERPRISES INTL LLC
Also Called: Pei
6138 River Forest Dr (20112-3075)
PHONE.................................571 425-8179
Jerome Pionk,
Michelle Pionk,
EMP: 2
SALES (est) 92.9K **Privately Held**
SIC: 2741 Miscellaneous publishing

(G-8130)
PIXEL DESIGNS & PRINTING
7410 Bull Run Rd (20111-1530)
PHONE.................................571 359-6080
Antonia Casillas, *Principal*
EMP: 2
SALES (est) 83.9K **Privately Held**
SIC: 2752 Commercial printing, lithographic

(G-8131)
PRECISE FREIGHT SOLUTIONS
8072 Stonewall Brigade Ct (20109-2759)
PHONE.................................703 627-1327
Otis Williams, *President*
EMP: 1
SALES (est) 15K **Privately Held**
SIC: 3743 Freight cars & equipment

(G-8132)
PRECISION BRICK CUTTING LTD
11900 Livingston Rd # 147 (20109-8304)
PHONE.................................703 393-2777
Carl Naine, *Principal*
EMP: 3
SALES (est) 270.1K **Privately Held**
SIC: 3251 Brick clay: common face, glazed, vitrified or hollow

(G-8133)
PRFWMPRO FIRE FIGHTERS
8510 Virginia Meadows Dr (20109-4861)
PHONE.................................703 393-2598
EMP: 2 EST: 2007
SALES (est) 164.7K **Privately Held**
SIC: 3711 Fire department vehicles (motor vehicles), assembly of

(G-8134)
PRINCE WILLIAM ORTHOTICS & PRS
10322 Battleview Pkwy (20109-2338)
PHONE.................................703 368-7967
Albert J Garney,
EMP: 4 EST: 2008
SALES (est) 563K **Privately Held**
WEB: www.pwop.net
SIC: 3842 Limbs, artificial

(G-8135)
PUZZLE PALOOZA ETC INC
9551 Fostern Ln (20112-4427)
PHONE.................................703 368-3619
EMP: 2
SALES (est) 150.2K **Privately Held**
SIC: 3944 Mfg Games/Toys

(G-8136)
QUALITY PRECAST STONE
8138 Bethlehem Rd (20109-2727)
PHONE.................................703 244-4551
Jaime Argandona, *President*
EMP: 5 EST: 2013
SALES (est) 459.8K **Privately Held**
WEB: www.qualityprecaststone.com
SIC: 3272 Concrete products, precast

(G-8137)
R GONZALEZ SHEETMETAL LLC
8831 Flatbush Ct (20109-4807)
PHONE.................................571 316-8241
EMP: 2 EST: 2019
SALES (est) 125.7K **Privately Held**
SIC: 3444 Sheet metalwork

(G-8138)
RAINBOW CUSTOM WOODWORKING
7700 Wellingford Dr (20109-2477)
PHONE.................................571 379-5500
Bang W Yang, *President*
EMP: 25
SQ FT: 20,000
SALES (est) 2MM **Privately Held**
SIC: 2431 1751 Millwork; carpentry work

(G-8139)
RAPISCAN SYSTEMS INC
Also Called: Rapiscan Counterbomber Tech
7301 Gateway Ct Ste 7321 (20109-7310)
PHONE.................................703 257-3429
Peter Kent, *Branch Mgr*
EMP: 11 **Publicly Held**
WEB: www.rapiscansystems.com

SIC: 3699 Security control equipment & systems
HQ: Rapiscan Systems, Inc.
2805 Columbia St
Torrance CA 90503

(G-8140)
READY TO COVER INC
Also Called: RTC
10429 Balls Ford Rd (20109-2660)
PHONE.................................571 379-5766
David Slager, *President*
Bryan Slager, *Vice Pres*
EMP: 3
SQ FT: 1,200
SALES (est) 88K **Privately Held**
WEB: www.readytocover.com
SIC: 2511 Wood household furniture

(G-8141)
RED STITCH TACTICAL LLC
Also Called: Red Stitch Targets
9349 Mike Garcia Dr (20109-5470)
PHONE.................................703 798-4385
Darin Morrell,
EMP: 2
SQ FT: 2,200
SALES (est) 206.5K **Privately Held**
WEB: www.redstitchtargets.com
SIC: 3443 Metal parts

(G-8142)
RELATIONAL DATA SOLUTIONS INC
10805 Gambril Dr (20109-6510)
PHONE.................................703 369-3580
Victor McDonnell, *Principal*
EMP: 2 EST: 2018
SALES (est) 78.4K **Privately Held**
SIC: 7372 Prepackaged software

(G-8143)
RENMUS TECHNOLOGIES INC
7226 Nathan Ct Ste 200 (20109-2435)
PHONE.................................703 624-9144
EMP: 2
SALES (est) 87.4K **Privately Held**
WEB: www.renmustechnologies.com
SIC: 3652 Pre-recorded records & tapes

(G-8144)
RESURFACE INCORPORATED
11517 Robertson Dr (20109-5446)
PHONE.................................703 335-1950
Sommer Robinson, *President*
Mark Trego, *Project Mgr*
Matt Pelow, *Director*
EMP: 15
SALES (est) 5.9MM **Privately Held**
WEB: www.resurfaceva.com
SIC: 2952 Asphalt saturated board

(G-8145)
RIVERAS TORTILLAS
10953 Lute Ct (20109-2438)
PHONE.................................703 368-1249
Jesus Perez, *Principal*
EMP: 6
SALES (est) 250K **Privately Held**
WEB: www.riverasfactory.com
SIC: 2099 Food preparations

(G-8146)
ROCKSTAR WRAPS LLC
8060 Flannery Ct (20109-2872)
PHONE.................................703 392-7625
Brian Saunders, *President*
EMP: 4
SALES (est) 367.9K **Privately Held**
WEB: www.rockstarwraps.com
SIC: 3993 Signs & advertising specialties

(G-8147)
RODEO WELDING LLC
9201 Amelia Ct (20111-4145)
PHONE.................................571 379-4179
Arnoldo Medrano, *Administration*
EMP: 1
SALES (est) 56.6K **Privately Held**
SIC: 7692 Welding repair

(G-8148)
RSK INC
10384 Portsmouth Rd (20109-8007)
PHONE.................................703 330-1959

Kawal Kapoor, *Owner*
EMP: 3
SALES (est): 172.2K **Privately Held**
SIC: 3089 Injection molding of plastics

(G-8149)
SANS SCREENPRINT INC
7014 Wellington Rd (20109-2710)
PHONE..................................703 368-6700
Sixto Naranjo, *CEO*
EMP: 40
SALES (est): 1.7MM **Privately Held**
WEB: www.sansscreenprint.com
SIC: 2759 Screen printing

(G-8150)
SAVAGE THRUST INDUSTRIES LLC
8449 Mary Jane Dr (20112-4710)
PHONE..................................702 405-1045
EMP: 2
SALES (est): 84.9K **Privately Held**
SIC: 3999 Manufacturing industries

(G-8151)
SCHIEBEL AIRCRAFT INC (HQ)
Also Called: Schiebel Technology, Inc
8464 Virginia Meadows Dr (20109-4860)
PHONE..................................540 351-1731
Hans Schiebel, *President*
Natalie Seehofer, *Manager*
EMP: 10
SQ FT: 6,000
SALES (est): 806.7K
SALES (corp-wide): 55.8MM **Privately Held**
WEB: www.schiebel.net
SIC: 3812 Search & detection systems & instruments
PA: Schiebel Industries Ag
  MargaretenstraBe 112
  Wien 1050
  154 626-0

(G-8152)
SCSI4ME CORPORATION
12034 Cadet Ct (20109-7897)
PHONE..................................571 229-9723
Huiping Dong, *Administration*
EMP: 2
SALES (est): 88.6K **Privately Held**
WEB: www.scsi4me.com
SIC: 2759 Publication printing

(G-8153)
SES
9251 Industrial Ct 101 (20109-3938)
PHONE..................................540 428-3919
Rob Fields, *Principal*
EMP: 3 **EST:** 2010
SALES (est): 300K **Privately Held**
WEB: www.ses-company.com
SIC: 3826 Environmental testing equipment

(G-8154)
SHIBUYA HOPPMANN CORPORATION (HQ)
7849 Coppermine Dr (20109-2505)
PHONE..................................540 829-2564
Mark Flanagan, *President*
Hirotoshi Shibuya, *President*
Mike East, *Exec VP*
Yoshi Izumi, *Exec VP*
Yoshitatsu Izumi, *Exec VP*
▲ **EMP:** 55 **EST:** 1955
SQ FT: 48,000
SALES (est): 17.2MM **Privately Held**
WEB: www.shibuyahoppmann.com
SIC: 3565 Packaging machinery

(G-8155)
SHIGOL MAKKOLI WINERY
7083 Gary Rd (20109-2651)
PHONE..................................646 594-7405
EMP: 2
SALES (est): 62.3K **Privately Held**
SIC: 2084 Wines

(G-8156)
SLOPERS STITCH HOUSE
10560 Associates Ct (20109-3457)
PHONE..................................703 368-7197
Troy Sloper, *Owner*
EMP: 7 **EST:** 2001

SALES (est): 716.3K **Privately Held**
WEB: www.stitchhouse.com
SIC: 2395 Embroidery products, except schiffli machine; embroidery & art needlework

(G-8157)
SMARTCELL INC
14142 Walton Dr (20112-3701)
PHONE..................................703 989-5887
Thomas Hafley, *President*
EMP: 1
SALES (est): 50K **Privately Held**
SIC: 3663 8748 Mobile communication equipment; telecommunications consultant

(G-8158)
SMBLTC CORP
Also Called: Waggy Pups
6227 Gwendolyn Dr (20112-3830)
PHONE..................................703 596-5218
Shannon Bunn, *CEO*
EMP: 1
SALES (est): 55.3K **Privately Held**
SIC: 2399 Pet collars, leashes, etc.: non-leather

(G-8159)
SOL SHINING
8084 Flannery Ct (20109-2872)
PHONE..................................571 719-3957
Pete Evick, *Administration*
EMP: 2
SALES (est): 122.6K **Privately Held**
WEB: www.shiningsol.com
SIC: 3999 Candles

(G-8160)
SPEEDPRO IMAGING - CENTREVILLE
8108 Flannery Ct (20109-2733)
PHONE..................................571 719-3161
EMP: 2
SALES (est): 107.9K **Privately Held**
WEB: www.speedpro.com
SIC: 3993 Signs & advertising specialties

(G-8161)
STAIR STORE INC
13573 Den Hollow Ct (20112-5545)
PHONE..................................703 794-0507
Melissa Perry, *President*
EMP: 12
SALES (corp-wide): 983.3K **Privately Held**
WEB: www.thestairstore.net
SIC: 2431 Staircases & stairs, wood
PA: The Stair Store Inc
  100 Henshaw Rd
  Bunker Hill WV 25413
  703 794-0507

(G-8162)
STEVEN ALSAHI
10630 Crestwood Dr Ste A (20109-4405)
PHONE..................................703 369-0099
Steven Alsahi, *Principal*
EMP: 2
SALES (est): 122.9K **Privately Held**
SIC: 3843 Enamels, dentists'

(G-8163)
SUREFIRE AUTO DETAILING
9511 Damascus Dr (20109-3329)
PHONE..................................703 361-2369
Paul Zorich, *Principal*
EMP: 2
SALES (est): 137.2K **Privately Held**
SIC: 3842 Surgical appliances & supplies

(G-8164)
SWEETBAY PUBLISHING LLC
8391 Jill Brenda Ct (20112-3569)
PHONE..................................703 203-9130
Debbie Wykowski, *Principal*
EMP: 1
SALES (est): 39.9K **Privately Held**
SIC: 2741 Miscellaneous publishing

(G-8165)
TEAM MARKETING
8120 Shane Ct (20112-3537)
PHONE..................................703 405-0576
EMP: 2 **EST:** 2016

SALES (est): 87.2K **Privately Held**
SIC: 3711 Mfg Motor Vehicle/Car Bodies

(G-8166)
TEENDRIVINGSTICKERCOM LLC
9550 Birmingham Dr (20111-2410)
PHONE..................................571 643-6956
Robert Fabian,
Jeffrey Fabian,
EMP: 2
SALES (est): 112.7K **Privately Held**
SIC: 7372 Application computer software

(G-8167)
TIMELESS TOUCH LLC
11501 Albrite Ct (20112-8634)
PHONE..................................703 986-0096
Paulina Le, *Mng Member*
◆ **EMP:** 3
SQ FT: 4,700
SALES (est): 500K **Privately Held**
SIC: 2023 Dietary supplements, dairy & non-dairy based

(G-8168)
TOTAL MILLWORK LLC
7700 Wellingford Dr (20109-2477)
PHONE..................................571 379-5500
Joseph Yang, *Mng Member*
Greg Deweese,
EMP: 44
SQ FT: 30,000
SALES (est): 7.8MM **Privately Held**
WEB: www.wellingford.net
SIC: 2521 Filing cabinets (boxes), office: wood

(G-8169)
TOWERS CUSTOM WOODWORK LLC C A
7828 Signal Hill Rd (20111-2513)
PHONE..................................703 330-7107
C Towers, *Principal*
EMP: 2
SALES (est): 115.7K **Privately Held**
SIC: 2431 Millwork

(G-8170)
TRAFFIC SYSTEMS LLC
Also Called: Traffic Systems & Technology
7390 Merritt Park Dr # 160 (20109-8316)
PHONE..................................703 530-9655
Randy Dominick, *President*
Samuel J Dominick, *Senior VP*
Jon Bondanella, *Vice Pres*
Walt Britton, *Vice Pres*
Maura Florimonte, *Project Mgr*
EMP: 10 **EST:** 2000
SALES: 19MM **Privately Held**
WEB: www.trafficsystems.us
SIC: 3648 3669 Lighting equipment; traffic signals, electric

(G-8171)
TRU SPORTS LLC
9133 Mulder Ct (20111-8267)
PHONE..................................571 266-5059
Marieo Foster, *Co-Owner*
EMP: 2
SALES (est): 74.1K **Privately Held**
SIC: 3949 Baseball, softball & cricket sports equipment

(G-8172)
TRULY CRAFTED WOODWORKING LLC
5595 Websters Way (20112-3487)
PHONE..................................571 268-0834
Justin Edwards,
EMP: 2
SALES (est): 148.9K **Privately Held**
SIC: 2431 Millwork

(G-8173)
UNITED FEDERAL SYSTEMS INC
10432 Balls Ford Rd # 30 (20109-2514)
PHONE..................................703 881-7777
James Elder, *President*
EMP: 12

SALES (est): 1.3MM **Privately Held**
WEB: www.ufsi.com
SIC: 3571 7371 8711 Electronic computers; custom computer programming services; engineering services

(G-8174)
VERTU CORP
Also Called: C-More Competition
7555 Gary Rd (20109-2608)
P.O. Box 340, Warrenton (20188-0340)
PHONE..................................540 341-3006
Ira Kay, *President*
Gayle A Kay, *Corp Secy*
EMP: 30
SALES (est): 3.8MM **Privately Held**
WEB: www.cmorecomp.com
SIC: 3484 Guns (firearms) or gun parts, 30 mm. & below

(G-8175)
VETERANS PRINTING LLC
7515 Presidential Ln (20109-2628)
PHONE..................................571 208-0074
Therese Smith,
EMP: 3
SALES (est): 120K **Privately Held**
WEB: www.veteransprintingusa.com
SIC: 2752 Commercial printing, offset

(G-8176)
VIRGINIA SIGN AND LIGHTING CO
11116 Industrial Rd (20109-3909)
PHONE..................................703 222-5670
Carol Fernandez, *President*
EMP: 6 **EST:** 2009
SALES (est): 999.4K **Privately Held**
SIC: 3993 Signs & advertising specialties

(G-8177)
WESTERN BRANCH DIESEL INC
Also Called: John Deere Authorized Dealer
12011 Balls Ford Rd (20109-2408)
PHONE..................................703 369-5005
Gary Trainum, *Branch Mgr*
EMP: 50
SALES (corp-wide): 201.3MM **Privately Held**
WEB: www.westernbranchdiesel.com
SIC: 3519 7537 5082 Diesel engine rebuilding; automotive transmission repair shops; construction & mining machinery
HQ: Western Branch Diesel, Llc
  3504 Shipwright St
  Portsmouth VA 23703
  757 673-7000

(G-8178)
WILLIAMS BRIDGE COMPANY (HQ)
Also Called: Williams Industries
8624 J D Reading Dr (20109-3943)
P.O. Box 1770 (20108-1770)
PHONE..................................703 335-7800
Frank E Williams III, *Ch of Bd*
Danny C Dunlap, *President*
Christ Manos, *Corp Secy*
Dan Maller, *COO*
Richard N Johnson, *Vice Pres*
EMP: 25
SQ FT: 50,000
SALES (est): 13.6MM
SALES (corp-wide): 77.4MM **Privately Held**
WEB: www.wmsi.com
SIC: 3441 Fabricated structural metal for bridges
PA: Williams Industries Incorporated
  1128 Tyler Farms Dr
  Raleigh NC 27603
  919 604-1746

(G-8179)
WISAKON WOODS
10001 Wisakon Trl (20111-2663)
P.O. Box 282, Leslie AR (72645-0282)
PHONE..................................571 332-9844
Mary Maguire, *Principal*
EMP: 4
SALES (est): 350.4K **Privately Held**
WEB: www.wisakonwoods.com
SIC: 2431 Millwork

(G-8180)
XEROX
7890 Notes Dr (20109-2432)
PHONE..............................703 330-4044
Kimberly Mulgrew, *Supervisor*
EMP: 2
SALES (est): 65.4K Privately Held
SIC: 3861 Photographic equipment & supplies

(G-8181)
YORK PUBLISHING COMPANY LLC
8140 Raphiel Ct (20112-3707)
PHONE..............................571 226-0221
Todd Fontaine, *Principal*
EMP: 2
SALES (est): 81.6K Privately Held
WEB: www.prayer-ring.com
SIC: 2741 Miscellaneous publishing

(G-8182)
ZEB WOODWORKS LLC
7876 Knightshayes Dr (20111-2992)
PHONE..............................703 361-2842
Greg Ochs, *Principal*
EMP: 2
SALES (est): 63.4K Privately Held
SIC: 2431 Millwork

(G-8183)
ZENPURE CORPORATION (DH)
Also Called: Zenpure Americas
12030 Cadet Ct (20109-7897)
PHONE..............................703 335-9910
Zhenwu Lin, *President*
Ken Adrian, *Vice Pres*
Yue Zhang, *Treasurer*
Jenny Peterson, *Project Leader*
Carl Attardo, *Admin Sec*
▲ EMP: 5
SALES (est): 4MM
SALES (corp-wide): 328.4MM Privately Held
WEB: www.zenpure.com
SIC: 3589 Water filters & softeners, household type

(G-8184)
ZESTRON CORPORATION
11285 Assett Loop (20109-3994)
PHONE..............................703 393-9880
Harald Wack, *President*
Ralph Hoeckle, *General Mgr*
James Yeoh, *General Mgr*
Peter Nicholas Lalos, *Corp Secy*
Mark McNeill, *Exec VP*
▲ EMP: 30
SQ FT: 11,500
SALES (est): 10.5MM Privately Held
WEB: www.zestron.com
SIC: 2899 Chemical preparations

Manassas Park
Prince William County

(G-8185)
1 A LIFESAFER INC
9108 Manassas Dr Ste A (20111-5234)
PHONE..............................800 634-3077
EMP: 1 Privately Held
WEB: www.lifesafer.com
SIC: 3829 Measuring & controlling devices
PA: 1 A Lifesafer, Inc.
    3630 Park 42 Dr Ste 170f
    Cincinnati OH 45241

(G-8186)
ALEGRIA JOHN
Also Called: Alegria Furniture Restoration
8395 Euclid Ave Ste S (20111-5215)
PHONE..............................703 398-6009
John Alegria, *Owner*
EMP: 2
SALES (est): 8.8K Privately Held
WEB: www.alegriafurniturerestoration.com
SIC: 3425 Saws, hand: metalworking or woodworking

(G-8187)
ALLIANCE STL FABRICATIONS INC
9106 Manassas Dr (20111-2366)
P.O. Box 11008, Manassas (20113-0008)
PHONE..............................703 631-2355
Ken Harrington, *President*
Lieu Nguyen, *Vice Pres*
Thomas O Nutt Jr, *Admin Sec*
EMP: 15
SQ FT: 5,000
SALES (est): 3.4MM Privately Held
SIC: 3441 3446 1799 Fabricated structural metal; architectural metalwork; welding on site

(G-8188)
AMERICAN STRIPPING COMPANY
9205 Vassau Ct (20111-4830)
PHONE..............................703 368-9922
James E Sejd, *President*
John D Alewine, *Vice Pres*
EMP: 30 EST: 1980
SQ FT: 68,000
SALES (est): 3.7MM Privately Held
WEB: www.ascoweb.com
SIC: 3471 3479 Cleaning & descaling metal products; painting of metal products

(G-8189)
AROMA KANDLES LLC
9407 Silver Meteor Ct (20111-3002)
PHONE..............................202 525-1550
EMP: 1 EST: 2016
SALES (est): 39.6K Privately Held
SIC: 3999 Candles

(G-8190)
BEECHHURST INDUSTRIES INC
9203 Enterprise Ct Ste J (20111-4834)
PHONE..............................703 334-6703
Frank Scully, *General Mgr*
EMP: 5
SQ FT: 3,500
SALES (est): 460K Privately Held
SIC: 3728 5088 Aircraft parts & equipment; aircraft equipment & supplies

(G-8191)
BLACK SAND SOLUTIONS LLC
9323 Brandon St (20111-8203)
PHONE..............................703 393-1127
Robert Howe, *Principal*
EMP: 2 EST: 2016
SALES (est): 66K Privately Held
SIC: 1442 Construction sand & gravel

(G-8192)
C & M LURES LLC
9428 Wilcoxen Dr (20111-8219)
PHONE..............................703 369-3060
EMP: 2
SALES (est): 89K Privately Held
SIC: 3949 Bobsleds

(G-8193)
CABINET & MORE
9207 Enterprise Ct (20111-4846)
PHONE..............................571 719-5040
EMP: 1 EST: 2016
SALES (est): 59.1K Privately Held
WEB: www.candm.us
SIC: 2434 Wood kitchen cabinets

(G-8194)
CABINET MASTERS
9107 Industry Dr (20111-4847)
PHONE..............................703 331-5781
EMP: 1
SALES (est): 109.7K Privately Held
WEB: www.cabinetmastersva.com
SIC: 3553 Cabinet makers' machinery

(G-8195)
CAPITOL LEATHER LLC
125 Market St (20111-3212)
PHONE..............................434 229-8467
Jonathan Kia, *Principal*
EMP: 2
SALES (est): 145.9K Privately Held
SIC: 3199 Leather goods

(G-8196)
COIL EXCHANGE INC
9203 Enterprise Ct Ste B (20111-4834)
PHONE..............................703 369-7150
Bruce Chestnutt, *President*
EMP: 5
SQ FT: 3,600
SALES (est): 620.4K Privately Held
WEB: www.coilexchange.com
SIC: 3443 Heat exchangers, plate type

(G-8197)
CONAWAYS WOODWORKING LLC
9201 Fairway Ct (20111-3050)
PHONE..............................703 530-8725
David Conaway, *Principal*
EMP: 1 EST: 2017
SALES (est): 57.6K Privately Held
SIC: 2431 Millwork

(G-8198)
DAVE CLEARY
9313 Cougar Ct (20111-3062)
PHONE..............................727 327-5118
Dave Cleary, *Principal*
EMP: 2
SALES (est): 69.9K Privately Held
WEB: www.clearysystems.com
SIC: 3471 Plating & polishing

(G-8199)
DIMITRIOS & CO INC
9203 Enterprise Ct Ste U (20111-4834)
PHONE..............................703 368-1757
Dimitrios Louvros, *President*
Perry Louvros, *Vice Pres*
◆ EMP: 4
SQ FT: 3,800
SALES (est): 330K Privately Held
WEB: www.dimitriosandcompany.com
SIC: 2499 5021 Decorative wood & woodwork; bookcases

(G-8200)
GARY A WATKINS CONSTRUCTION
9204 Vassau Ct Ste C (20111-4849)
PHONE..............................703 367-0477
Gary A Watkins, *President*
EMP: 7
SALES (est): 352.3K Privately Held
WEB: www.builtincabinet.com
SIC: 2434 Wood kitchen cabinets

(G-8201)
HEARTWOOD SOLID SURFACES INC
8198 Euclid Ct (20111-4811)
PHONE..............................703 369-0045
Donald Carr, *President*
EMP: 15
SQ FT: 15,000
SALES (est): 2MM Privately Held
WEB: www.hwss.comcastbiz.net
SIC: 2541 Table or counter tops, plastic laminated; counter & sink tops

(G-8202)
JAMES LEE HERNDON
164 Colburn Dr (20111-1846)
PHONE..............................703 549-2585
James Lee Herndon, *Principal*
EMP: 2
SALES (est): 143K Privately Held
SIC: 2752 Commercial printing, lithographic

(G-8203)
JD CONCRETE LLC
9207 Enterprise Ct (20111-4846)
PHONE..............................703 331-2155
Jose Espinal,
EMP: 15 EST: 2015
SALES (est): 1.5MM Privately Held
WEB: www.jdconcretellcva.com
SIC: 3444 Concrete forms, sheet metal

(G-8204)
LMR-INC COM
9104 Manassas Dr Ste N (20111-5211)
PHONE..............................518 253-9220
Sonnie Donaby, *Principal*
EMP: 3 EST: 2016

SALES (est): 85.7K Privately Held
SIC: 2721 Periodicals

(G-8205)
METRO SIGN & DESIGN INC
8197 Euclid Ct (20111-4810)
PHONE..............................703 631-1866
Robert B Anderson III, *President*
Maureen Anderson, *Corp Secy*
Bob Anderson, *Vice Pres*
EMP: 20
SQ FT: 2,500
SALES (est): 2.6MM Privately Held
WEB: www.metrosign.com
SIC: 3993 3443 Electric signs; signs, not made in custom sign painting shops; fabricated plate work (boiler shop)

(G-8206)
POTOMAC SIGNS INC
9102 Industry Dr Ste F (20111-4850)
PHONE..............................703 425-7000
Hwan Kim, *President*
EMP: 2 EST: 2011
SALES (est): 129.7K Privately Held
WEB: www.potomacsigns.com
SIC: 3993 Signs & advertising specialties

(G-8207)
PROFILE MACHINEWORKS LLC
9199 Enterprise Ct Unit B (20111-4829)
PHONE..............................703 361-2959
Susan Doster, *General Mgr*
Martin W Utt,
EMP: 5 EST: 2010
SALES (est): 561.5K Privately Held
WEB: www.profilemachineworks.com
SIC: 3599 Machine shop, jobbing & repair

(G-8208)
QMT ASSOCIATES INC
Also Called: Arias Windchimes
9204 Vassau Ct Ste H (20111-4849)
PHONE..............................703 368-4920
Michael Throne, *President*
Theresa Miles, *Executive Asst*
EMP: 135 Privately Held
WEB: www.qmtwindchimes.com
SIC: 3999 Wind chimes
PA: Qmt Associates Inc.
    8431 Euclid Ave
    Manassas Park VA

(G-8209)
S & K INDUSTRIES INC
Also Called: Abuelita Mexican Foods
9209 Enterprise Ct (20111-4809)
PHONE..............................703 369-0232
Eugene F Suarez, *President*
Eugene F Suarez Jr, *Vice Pres*
Marie Forman, *Admin Sec*
EMP: 46 EST: 1971
SQ FT: 26,500
SALES (est): 8.9MM Privately Held
WEB: www.abuelita.com
SIC: 2099 Tortillas, fresh or refrigerated

(G-8210)
S J PRINTING INC
9105 Owens Dr (20111-4802)
PHONE..............................703 378-7142
Ronald Jenkins, *President*
EMP: 3
SALES (est): 195.6K Privately Held
SIC: 2752 Commercial printing, offset

(G-8211)
SOLAR SHEET METAL INC
121 Martin Dr (20111-2019)
PHONE..............................770 256-2618
Mary Yessika Bonilla, *President*
EMP: 2
SALES (est): 128.7K Privately Held
SIC: 3444 Metal housings, enclosures, casings & other containers

(G-8212)
SSA FABRICATION LLC
9107 Industry Dr Ste B (20111-4847)
PHONE..............................703 479-7377
EMP: 2 EST: 2018
SALES (est): 113.3K Privately Held
SIC: 3599 Machine shop, jobbing & repair

(G-8213)
VAULT44 LLC
9201 Zachary Ct (20111-2490)
PHONE..................................202 758-6228
Paul De Souza,
EMP: 2 EST: 2017
SALES (est): 91.3K Privately Held
SIC: 3272 Concrete products

Mannboro
Amelia County

(G-8214)
C DCAP MODEM LINE
3800 Richmond Rd (23105-9900)
PHONE..................................804 561-6267
EMP: 3
SALES (est): 140.2K Privately Held
SIC: 3661 Modems

Manquin
King William County

(G-8215)
CYCLE MACHINE LLC
116d Commerce Park Dr (23106-2564)
PHONE..................................804 779-0055
James Carroll, Principal
EMP: 2 EST: 2007
SALES (est): 145.1K Privately Held
SIC: 3599 Machine & other job shop work

(G-8216)
IVY SOFTWARE INC
1146 Richmond Tapp Hwy (23106-2558)
P.O. Box 15776, Richmond (23227-5776)
PHONE..................................804 769-7193
Robert Holt, President
Ferebee Smith, Marketing Staff
Rob Holt, Creative Dir
EMP: 5
SQ FT: 2,300
SALES (est): 583K Privately Held
WEB: www.ivysoftware.com
SIC: 7372 Business oriented computer
software

(G-8217)
NEAULT LLC
Also Called: Leo Paul & Associates
7839 Dabneys Mill Rd (23106-2108)
PHONE..................................804 283-5948
Christopher P Neault,
EMP: 1
SALES (est): 88K Privately Held
WEB: www.leopaulandassociates.com
SIC: 3599 Industrial machinery

Mappsville
Accomack County

(G-8218)
EASTERN SHORE SEAFOOD PDTS LLC
Also Called: Myers Clamdock
13249 Lankford Hwy (23407)
P.O. Box 38 (23407-0038)
PHONE..................................757 854-4422
Arthur R Myers III, President
Mary Jane Myers, Corp Secy
EMP: 2
SQ FT: 160,000
SALES (est): 217.6K Privately Held
SIC: 2092 4492 2091 2038 Fresh or
frozen packaged fish; docking of ocean
vessels; canned & cured fish & seafoods;
frozen specialties

Marion
Smyth County

(G-8219)
A B PRINTING LLC
425 S Main St (24354-2411)
PHONE..................................276 783-2837
Dean Tucker, Principal

EMP: 6
SALES (est): 695.4K Privately Held
SIC: 2752 Commercial printing, offset

(G-8220)
ALL THINGS WELDED
1341 Matson Dr (24354-3609)
PHONE..................................423 492-0880
Davud Hayes, President
EMP: 5 EST: 2017
SALES (est): 74.4K Privately Held
WEB: www.allthingswelded.com
SIC: 7692 Welding repair

(G-8221)
AMARVEDA
Also Called: Rejuvination Center
221 W Main St (24354-2530)
P.O. Box 883 (24354-0883)
PHONE..................................276 782-1819
S K Gandhi, Owner
▲ EMP: 24 EST: 1991
SALES (est): 1.5MM Privately Held
WEB: www.liveto108.com
SIC: 2844 5999 Toilet preparations; cos-
metics

(G-8222)
AMERICAN WOOD FIBERS INC
514 Lee Hwy (24354-6160)
PHONE..................................276 646-3075
Marvin Lundsford, Vice Pres
Wildy Dolinger, Opers Mgr
EMP: 47 Privately Held
WEB: www.awf.com
SIC: 2431 Millwork
PA: American Wood Fibers, Inc.
9740 Patuxent Woods Dr # 500
Columbia MD 21046

(G-8223)
CATRON MACHINE & WELDING INC
138 Harris Ln (24354-6376)
PHONE..................................276 783-6826
James F Catron Jr, President
John Catron, Vice Pres
Cora Lee Catron, Admin Sec
EMP: 5
SQ FT: 2,600 Privately Held
SIC: 3599 5261 7699 7389 Machine
shop, jobbing & repair; lawnmowers &
tractors; knife, saw & tool sharpening &
repair; lawn mower repair shop; crane &
aerial lift service

(G-8224)
CENTURYLINK SWITCH ROOM
132 W Main St (24354-2532)
PHONE..................................276 646-8000
EMP: 2
SALES (est): 127.1K Privately Held
SIC: 3679 Mfg Electronic Components

(G-8225)
COFFMAN STAIRS LLC (PA)
138 E Main St 1 (24354-3106)
PHONE..................................276 783-7251
Lowry E Hobbs, Mng Member
▲ EMP: 400 EST: 1874
SQ FT: 12,000
SALES (est): 24MM Privately Held
SIC: 2431 3231 Staircases, stairs & rail-
ings; doors & door parts & trim, wood;
woodwork, interior & ornamental; leaded
glass

(G-8226)
DONALD F ROUSE
219 Autumn Ln 21 (24354-6169)
PHONE..................................276 783-7569
EMP: 1
SALES (est): 69K Privately Held
SIC: 2431 Mfg Millwork

(G-8227)
GENERAL DYNAMICS MISSION
150 Johnston Rd (24354-4324)
P.O. Box 1072 (24354-1072)
PHONE..................................276 783-3121
Dawn Archer, Prdtn Mgr
William Finch, QC Mgr
Jim Losse, Sales Staff
Jeff Vancleef, Branch Mgr
Dana McIntyre, Security Mgr
EMP: 375

SALES (corp-wide): 39.3B Publicly Held
WEB: www.gdmissionsystems.com
SIC: 3089 3448 Prefabricated plastic
buildings; prefabricated metal buildings
HQ: General Dynamics Mission Systems,
Inc.
12450 Fair Lakes Cir
Fairfax VA 22033
877 449-0600

(G-8228)
GENERAL DYNAMICS OTS CAL INC
325 Brunswick Ln (24354-3903)
PHONE..................................276 783-3121
Bruce Howard, Principal
EMP: 1
SALES (corp-wide): 39.3B Publicly Held
WEB: www.gd-ots.com
SIC: 3728 Aircraft parts & equipment
HQ: General Dynamics Ots (California),
Inc.
11399 16th Ct N Ste 200
Saint Petersburg FL 33716
727 578-8100

(G-8229)
HUDSON JEWELRY CO INC
570 Lee Hwy (24354-6160)
P.O. Box 1398, Chilhowie (24319-1398)
PHONE..................................276 646-5565
Vicki C Wilson, President
Roy F Cullop, Treasurer
EMP: 4
SALES (est): 670K Privately Held
SIC: 3911 5094 Jewelry, precious metal;
jewelry & precious stones

(G-8230)
LAURA COPENHAVER INDUSTRIES
Also Called: Rosemont Industries
114 W Main St (24354-2514)
P.O. Box 149 (24354-0149)
PHONE..................................276 783-4663
Tom Copenhaver, President
EMP: 7
SALES (est): 450K Privately Held
SIC: 2392 5719 5961 Bedspreads & bed
sets; made from purchased materials;
bedding (sheets, blankets, spreads & pil-
lows); catalog & mail-order houses

(G-8231)
LLTS PAVING
506 Horne Ave (24354-1639)
PHONE..................................276 782-9550
Levi Turner Jr, Owner
EMP: 5
SALES (est): 220K Privately Held
SIC: 2951 Asphalt paving mixtures &
blocks

(G-8232)
M & P SAWMILL CO INC
1762 Stoney Battery Rd (24354-6890)
PHONE..................................276 783-5585
Carolyn R McClellan, President
EMP: 1
SALES (est): 68.1K Privately Held
WEB: www.putinbayfuels.com
SIC: 2426 Hardwood dimension & flooring
mills

(G-8233)
MARION ELECTRIC COMPANY
440 1/2 N Main St (24354-3344)
PHONE..................................276 783-4765
Roger Shields, Owner
EMP: 1
SALES (est): 59.9K Privately Held
WEB: www.marion-electric.com
SIC: 7694 1731 Electric motor repair;
electrical work

(G-8234)
MARION MOLD & TOOL INC
176 Rifton Dr (24354-6786)
P.O. Box 967 (24354-0967)
PHONE..................................276 783-6101
David Martin, President
Lori Kalber, Partner
Frank Yarber, Vice Pres
Janet Blevins, Sales Staff
Robyn Rowland, Manager
◆ EMP: 46 EST: 1957

SQ FT: 25,500
SALES (est): 8.2MM Privately Held
WEB: www.marionmold.com
SIC: 3544 3354 3769 Special dies &
tools; industrial molds; jigs & fixtures; aluminum extruded products; guided missile
& space vehicle parts & auxiliary equipment

(G-8235)
MARION OPERATIONS
150 Johnston Rd (24354-4324)
PHONE..................................276 783-3121
EMP: 2
SALES (est): 88.9K Privately Held
SIC: 3089 Plastics products

(G-8236)
MICKEY NORRIS LOGGING
630 Highwood Ln (24354-6085)
PHONE..................................276 206-3959
EMP: 2
SALES (est): 81.7K Privately Held
SIC: 2411 Logging

(G-8237)
MIDWAY TELEMETRY
122 S Fork Rd (24354-6833)
PHONE..................................276 378-5933
EMP: 2
SALES (est): 111.9K Privately Held
WEB: www.midwaytelemetry.com
SIC: 3999 Pet supplies

(G-8238)
NANNAS CNDLES UNIQUE GIFTS LLC
704 Matson Dr (24354-3710)
PHONE..................................276 780-2513
Brenda Jackson, Principal
EMP: 1
SALES (est): 39.6K Privately Held
SIC: 3999 Candles

(G-8239)
PEPSI-COLA GENERAL BOTTLERS
Also Called: Pepsico
211 Washington Ave (24354-2364)
PHONE..................................276 783-7232
EMP: 3
SALES (est): 116.3K Privately Held
SIC: 2086 Carbonated soft drinks, bottled
& canned

(G-8240)
PEPSICO INC
Also Called: Frito-Lay
223 Browns Subdivision Rd (24354-6657)
PHONE..................................276 781-2177
EMP: 3
SALES (corp-wide): 67.1B Publicly Held
WEB: www.pepsico.com
SIC: 2086 Carbonated soft drinks, bottled
& canned
PA: Pepsico, Inc.
700 Anderson Hill Rd
Purchase NY 10577
914 253-2000

(G-8241)
PUBLISHERS TEABERRY FEILDS
169 Teaberry Ln (24354-7069)
PHONE..................................276 783-2546
Lavina Gass, Owner
EMP: 1
SALES (est): 27.7K Privately Held
SIC: 2741 Miscellaneous publishing

(G-8242)
ROYAL GROUP INC
Also Called: Royal Building Products
135 Bear Creek Rd (24354-4447)
PHONE..................................276 783-8161
Susan M Ehrlich, Partner
Jessica R Schwartz, Partner
Steve Testerman, Production
Larry Wallace, Research
Felicia Osborne, Finance
EMP: 24 Publicly Held
WEB: www.royalbuildingproducts.com
SIC: 3272 Concrete stuctural support &
building material

▲ = Import ▼=Export
◆ =Import/Export

HQ: Royal Group, Inc
91 Royal Group Cres
Woodbridge ON L4H 1
905 264-0701

(G-8243)
SMYTH COUNTY NEWS
119 S Sheffey St (24354-2523)
P.O. Box 640 (24354-0640)
PHONE..................276 783-5121
Debbie Maxwell, *Principal*
EMP: 8
SALES (est): 593K **Privately Held**
WEB: www.swvatoday.com
SIC: 2711 Newspapers, publishing & printing

(G-8244)
SUMMIT BEVERAGE GROUP LLC
211 Washington Ave (24354-2364)
PHONE..................276 781-0671
Rohan Soares, *Production*
Geoffrey Soares, *Mng Member*
John Carson, *Mng Member*
Abner James, *Director*
Debbie Atchison, *Administration*
EMP: 4
SQ FT: 102,000
SALES (est): 1MM **Privately Held**
WEB: www.summitbeveragegroup.com
SIC: 3565 Bottling machinery: filling, capping, labeling

(G-8245)
WM COFFMAN RESOURCES LLC
138 E Main St Ste 1 (24354-3106)
PHONE..................800 810-9204
Mike Jackson, *President*
EMP: 1
SALES (corp-wide): 4.5MM **Privately Held**
WEB: www.wm-coffman.com
SIC: 3446 Stairs, staircases, stair treads: prefabricated metal
PA: Wm Coffman Resources Llc
2603 Technology Dr
Plano TX 75074
800 810-9204

(G-8246)
WOODGRAIN MILLWORK INC
Hwy 11 E (24354)
P.O. Box 948 (24354-0948)
PHONE..................208 452-3801
Charles Hitch, *General Mgr*
Megan Pack, *Human Res Mgr*
Michael Stanley, *Master*
EMP: 130 **Privately Held**
WEB: www.apinepro.com
SIC: 2431 Millwork
HQ: Woodgrain Inc.
300 Nw 16th St
Fruitland ID 83619
208 452-3801

Markham
Fauquier County

(G-8247)
CHATEAU OBRIEN AT NORTH POINT
3238 Railstop Rd (22643-1841)
PHONE..................540 364-6441
Howard O'Brien, *Owner*
Pascal Valadier, *Manager*
EMP: 3
SALES (est): 258.6K **Privately Held**
WEB: www.chateauobrien.com
SIC: 2084 Wines

(G-8248)
WINDING ROAD CELLARS LLC
4289 Leeds Manor Rd (22643-1908)
PHONE..................540 364-1025
Linda Culver,
EMP: 3
SALES (est): 209K **Privately Held**
WEB: www.windingroadcellars.com
SIC: 2084 Wines

Marshall
Fauquier County

(G-8249)
AIR ROUTE OPTIMIZER INC
5649 John Barton Payne Rd (20115-2529)
PHONE..................540 364-3470
Suzette Matthews, *Principal*
EMP: 5
SALES (est): 1K **Privately Held**
SIC: 3812 8732 Air traffic control systems & equipment, electronic; research services, except laboratory

(G-8250)
BAKEFULLY YOURS LLC
10398 Brenna Ct (20115-2376)
PHONE..................540 229-6232
Sarah Seligman,
EMP: 5
SALES (est): 200K **Privately Held**
WEB: www.bakefully.com
SIC: 2051 Bakery: wholesale or wholesale/retail combined

(G-8251)
COMMERCIAL TOOL & DIE INC
7591 E Main St (20115-3359)
PHONE..................540 364-3922
Jeff Symanski, *President*
Laura Symanski, *Corp Secy*
EMP: 7
SQ FT: 6,000
SALES (est): 750K **Privately Held**
WEB: www.commercialtoolanddie.com
SIC: 3599 Machine shop, jobbing & repair

(G-8252)
FORGING THE WARRIOR SPIRIT
Also Called: Ftwsa
6566 Chimney Oaks Ct (20115-2483)
PHONE..................703 851-4789
Bill Barkovic, *CEO*
EMP: 1
SALES (est): 46.6K **Privately Held**
SIC: 3484 8742 Guns (firearms) or gun parts, 30 mm. & below; management consulting services

(G-8253)
FOUR HATS INC
5967 Moore Rd (20115-2533)
PHONE..................571 926-4303
EMP: 2 **EST:** 2014
SALES (est): 84.6K **Privately Held**
SIC: 2353 Hats, caps & millinery

(G-8254)
FUNES PROJECT LLC
8302 E Main St (20115-3228)
PHONE..................540 364-8054
EMP: 2 **EST:** 2013
SALES (est): 97.8K **Privately Held**
WEB: www.funescustomupholstery.net
SIC: 2531 Public building & related furniture

(G-8255)
HAGERSTOWN BLOCK COMPANY
Also Called: Marshall Division
8244 E Main St (20115-3227)
P.O. Box 8 (20116-0008)
PHONE..................540 364-1531
Doug Gray, *Manager*
EMP: 7
SALES (corp-wide): 9MM **Privately Held**
WEB: www.hagerstownblock.com
SIC: 3271 Blocks, concrete or cinder: standard
PA: The Hagerstown Block Company
860 Oak St
Hagerstown MD 21740
301 733-3510

(G-8256)
HORSE SENSE BALANCED
4292 Belvoir Rd (20115-3316)
P.O. Box 2071, Middleburg (20118-2071)
PHONE..................540 253-9987
Andrea M Weyer, *Mng Member*
Carl Donaghy,
EMP: 7

SQ FT: 1,600
SALES (est): 700K **Privately Held**
SIC: 2048 Mineral feed supplements

(G-8257)
KLING RESEARCH AND SFTWR INC
3233 Fortune Mountain Rd (20115-3324)
PHONE..................540 364-2524
Ronald Kling, *President*
Susan Kling, *Principal*
EMP: 2
SALES (est): 180.9K **Privately Held**
WEB: www.rlkling.com
SIC: 7372 Business oriented computer software

(G-8258)
PIEDMONT WOODWORKS LLC
3803 Rectortown Rd (20115-3338)
P.O. Box 145, Rectortown (20140-0145)
PHONE..................540 364-1849
Pete Piske, *Principal*
EMP: 2
SALES (est): 154.9K **Privately Held**
WEB: www.piedmontwoodworks.com
SIC: 2431 Millwork

(G-8259)
RURAL SQUIRREL LLC
4003 Whiting Rd (20115-3346)
PHONE..................540 364-2281
EMP: 2
SALES (est): 100.2K **Privately Held**
SIC: 3999 Candles

(G-8260)
SNOW 39S WOODWORK
7041 Olinger Rd (20115-2468)
PHONE..................540 428-1762
EMP: 1
SALES (est): 54.1K **Privately Held**
SIC: 2431 Millwork

(G-8261)
SNOWS CUSTOM WOODWORK
7041 Olinger Rd (20115-2468)
PHONE..................540 428-1763
Warren Snow, *Owner*
EMP: 1
SALES (est): 7.9K **Privately Held**
SIC: 2499 Decorative wood & woodwork

Martinsville
Martinsville City County

(G-8262)
A1 FINISHING INC
100a Tensbury Dr (24112-0677)
P.O. Box 484, Collinsville (24078-0484)
PHONE..................276 632-2121
Al Powell, *President*
Monroe Boothe, *Vice Pres*
EMP: 12
SQ FT: 20,000
SALES (est): 800K **Privately Held**
WEB: www.a1finishinginc.com
SIC: 2599 7641 Hotel furniture; furniture repair & maintenance

(G-8263)
ADKINS CUSTOM WOODWORKING
928 Foxfire Rd (24112-8573)
PHONE..................276 638-8198
Karen Adkins, *Principal*
EMP: 4 **EST:** 2009
SALES (est): 190K **Privately Held**
SIC: 2431 Millwork

(G-8264)
ADVANCED AIR SYSTEMS INC
113 E Main St (24112-2813)
P.O. Box 5544 (24115-5544)
PHONE..................276 666-8829
Patrick Dowling, *President*
EMP: 90
SQ FT: 30,000
SALES (est): 14MM
SALES (corp-wide): 24.2MM **Privately Held**
SIC: 3535 Pneumatic tube conveyor systems

PA: Ohio Blow Pipe Company
446 E 131st St
Cleveland OH 44108
216 681-7379

(G-8265)
ALL-SIGNS
140 Rosenwall Dr (24112-0776)
PHONE..................276 632-6733
Anthony Lawson, *Owner*
EMP: 4
SALES (est): 150K **Privately Held**
WEB: www.bannersexpress.com
SIC: 3993 Signs & advertising specialties

(G-8266)
ANDREA DARCELL LLC
712 3rd St (24112-4024)
PHONE..................980 533-5128
Andrea Martin,
EMP: 1
SALES (est): 100K **Privately Held**
SIC: 2335 Gowns, formal

(G-8267)
APPLIED FELTS INC
450 College Dr (24112-6790)
PHONE..................276 656-1904
Hecter Rawson, *Ch of Bd*
Alex Johnson, *President*
Mark Sanders, *General Mgr*
Justin Hancock, *Opers Mgr*
Joven Millner, *Manager*
◆ **EMP:** 70
SQ FT: 84,000
SALES (est): 16.5MM **Privately Held**
WEB: www.novapipe.com
SIC: 3498 Fabricated pipe & fittings

(G-8268)
AUTOINSTRUMENTS CORP
47 Ford St (24112-2713)
PHONE..................276 647-5550
Jengry Zitmyers, *President*
EMP: 6
SALES (est): 563.7K **Privately Held**
WEB: www.autoinstruments.com
SIC: 3694 Automotive electrical equipment

(G-8269)
BEAVER CREEK WIPERS
2201 Appalachian Dr (24112-7273)
PHONE..................276 632-3033
EMP: 1
SALES (est): 40.9K **Privately Held**
SIC: 2392 Household furnishings

(G-8270)
BLUE RIDGE PACKAGING CORP
355 Industrial Park Dr (24115)
P.O. Box 4027 (24115-4027)
PHONE..................276 638-1413
Stephen L Dashoff, *President*
Scott Jones, *Office Mgr*
Judith N Dashoff, *Admin Sec*
EMP: 25
SQ FT: 60,000
SALES (est): 5.5MM **Privately Held**
WEB: www.blueridgebox.com
SIC: 2653 3412 Boxes, corrugated: made from purchased materials; metal barrels, drums & pails

(G-8271)
BOXLEY MATERIALS COMPANY
Also Called: Martinsville Plant
201 Koehler Rd (24112-7729)
P.O. Box 13527, Roanoke (24035-3527)
PHONE..................540 777-7600
AB Boxley, *CEO*
EMP: 11
SALES (corp-wide): 2.2B **Publicly Held**
WEB: www.boxley.com
SIC: 3273 Ready-mixed concrete
HQ: Boxley Materials Company
15418 W Lynchburg Slem Tp
Blue Ridge VA 24064
540 777-7600

(G-8272)
BOXLEY MATERIALS COMPANY
Also Called: Fieldale Quarry
3785 Carver Rd (24112-7678)
P.O. Box 13527, Roanoke (24035-3527)
PHONE..................540 777-7600
K D Ramsey, *Manager*

EMP: 18
SALES (corp-wide): 2.2B **Publicly Held**
WEB: www.boxley.com
SIC: 1423 Crushed & broken granite
HQ: Boxley Materials Company
15418 W Lynchburg Slem Tp
Blue Ridge VA 24064
540 777-7600

(G-8273)
BURR FOX SPECIALIZED
WDWKG
373 Old Liberty Dr (24112-0419)
PHONE...............................276 666-0127
Burr Fox, *President*
Lori Fox, *Vice Pres*
EMP: 13
SALES (est): 1.6MM **Privately Held**
WEB: www.burrfox.net
SIC: 2499 Decorative wood & woodwork

(G-8274)
CASSON ART & FRAME
Also Called: Casson Art
2000 N Fork Rd (24112-1598)
P.O. Box 4187 (24115-4187)
PHONE...............................276 638-1450
EMP: 5
SALES: 350K **Privately Held**
SIC: 2499 5023 5999 8999 Mfg Wood
Products Whol Homefurnishings Ret Misc
Merchandise Services-Misc

(G-8275)
CM HARRIS INDUSTRIES LLC
2191 Greenhill Dr (24112-7840)
PHONE...............................276 632-8438
Regina Harris, *Principal*
EMP: 2
SALES (est): 81.1K **Privately Held**
SIC: 3999 Manufacturing industries

(G-8276)
COLLINSVILLE PRINTING CO
79 Beaver Creek Dr (24112-2051)
P.O. Box 505, Collinsville (24078-0505)
PHONE...............................276 666-4400
Jesse S Bowles, *President*
Gary Gibson, *Treasurer*
Smith Steve, *Manager*
Carol Gibson, *Admin Sec*
EMP: 39
SQ FT: 60,000
SALES: 4.3MM **Privately Held**
WEB: www.collinsvilleprinting.com
SIC: 2759 2752 2732 Screen printing;
commercial printing, offset; book printing

(G-8277)
CP FILMS INC
1450 Beaver Creek Dr (24112-2145)
PHONE...............................276 632-4991
EMP: 3
SALES (est): 189.2K **Privately Held**
SIC: 3679 Electronic components

(G-8278)
CUSTOM CAMSHAFT COMPANY
INC
67 Motorsports Dr (24112-7599)
PHONE...............................276 666-6767
Joey Arrington, *President*
Jeanette Arrington, *Admin Sec*
EMP: 3
SALES (est): 453.3K **Privately Held**
SIC: 3714 Camshafts, motor vehicle

(G-8279)
DOMINION QUIKRETE INC
930 Meadowood Trl (24112-6814)
PHONE...............................276 957-3235
EMP: 20
SALES (corp-wide): 5.6MM **Privately
Held**
SIC: 3241 5032 3273 3255 Cement, hy-
draulic; cement; ready-mixed concrete;
clay refractories; industrial sand
PA: Dominion Quikrete, Inc.
932 Professional Pl
Chesapeake VA 23320
757 547-9411

(G-8280)
DRAEGER SAFETY
DIAGNOSTICS INC
176 Tensbury Dr (24112-0677)
PHONE...............................434 770-5594
EMP: 3
SALES (corp-wide): 3B **Privately Held**
WEB: www.draegerinterlock.com
SIC: 3829 Measuring & controlling devices
HQ: Draeger Safety Diagnostics, Inc.
4040 W Royal Ln Ste 136
Irving TX 75063
972 929-1100

(G-8281)
DRY FORK FRUIT DISTILLERY
LLC
1355 Mount Olivet Rd (24112-6034)
P.O. Box 953, Meadows of Dan (24120-
0953)
PHONE...............................276 952-1222
EMP: 3
SALES (est): 145.5K **Privately Held**
WEB: www.dryforkfruitdistillery.com
SIC: 2082 Malt beverages

(G-8282)
EASTMAN CHEMICAL COMPANY
345 Beaver Creek Dr (24112-2090)
PHONE...............................276 632-4991
Sandy Penn, *President*
Shelby Swhite, *Technical Staff*
EMP: 8 **Publicly Held**
WEB: www.eastman.com
SIC: 2821 Plastics materials & resins
PA: Eastman Chemical Company
200 S Wilcox Dr
Kingsport TN 37660

(G-8283)
EASTMAN PERFORMANCE
FILMS LLC
1450 Beaver Creek Dr (24112-2145)
PHONE...............................423 224-7768
Jeff Quinn, *President*
EMP: 100 **Publicly Held**
SIC: 3479 3399 3083 3089 Painting,
coating & hot dipping; laminating steel;
laminated plastics plate & sheet; window
frames & sash, plastic
HQ: Eastman Performance Films, Llc
4210 The Great Rd
Fieldale VA 24089
276 627-3000

(G-8284)
EASTMAN PERFORMANCE
FILMS LLC
140 Hollie Dr (24112-1343)
PHONE...............................276 627-3355
Susie Ramsey, *Principal*
EMP: 2 **Publicly Held**
SIC: 2821 Plastics materials & resins
HQ: Eastman Performance Films, Llc
4210 The Great Rd
Fieldale VA 24089
276 627-3000

(G-8285)
EXCELSCION MED CDING
BLLING LL
314 Fairy Street Ext B (24112-1913)
PHONE...............................561 866-1000
EMP: 1
SALES (est): 60K **Privately Held**
SIC: 3536 Hoists, cranes & monorails

(G-8286)
EXQUISITE INVITATIONS INC
1010 Foxfire Rd (24112-8500)
PHONE...............................276 666-0168
Tammy Keen, *President*
EMP: 1
SALES (est): 126.9K **Privately Held**
SIC: 2759 Invitation & stationery printing &
engraving

(G-8287)
FLOWERS BKG CO LYNCHBURG
LLC
309 Lavinder St (24112-3520)
PHONE...............................276 666-2008
D Connor, *Branch Mgr*
EMP: 1

SALES (corp-wide): 4.1B **Publicly Held**
SIC: 2051 Bread, cake & related products
HQ: Flowers Baking Co. Of Lynchburg, Llc
1905 Hollins Mill Rd
Lynchburg VA 24503
434 528-0441

(G-8288)
GCSEAC INC
200 Sellers St (24112-3537)
P.O. Box 5151 (24115-5151)
PHONE...............................276 632-9700
Giles Smith, *Owner.*
Kevin Miles, *Manager*
Cameron Adkins, *Admin Asst*
EMP: 3
SQ FT: 40,000
SALES (est): 540.6K **Privately Held**
WEB: www.gcseac.com
SIC: 3663 8748 Carrier equipment, radio
communications; antennas, transmitting &
communications; microwave communica-
tion equipment; telecommunications con-
sultant

(G-8289)
GILDAN DELAWARE INC (HQ)
3375 Joseph Martin Hwy (24112-0495)
PHONE...............................276 956-2305
Michael Hoffman, *President*
Gregg Webb, *Plant Mgr*
Randall Ferguson, *Engineer*
Shannon Preston, *VP Human Res*
Ken Tincher, *Natl Sales Mgr*
▲ **EMP:** 13
SALES (est): 412.6MM
SALES (corp-wide): 2.8B **Privately Held**
SIC: 2252 2254 Socks; underwear, knit
PA: Gildan Activewear Inc
600 Boul De Maisonneuve O 33eme
etage
Montreal QC H3A 3
514 735-2023

(G-8290)
GLOBAL TRADING OF
MARTINSVILLE
240 Stonewall Jackson Trl (24112-0607)
PHONE...............................276 666-0236
John G Mitchell, *President*
Phyllis H Mitchell, *Vice Pres*
▲ **EMP:** 2
SALES (est): 200K **Privately Held**
WEB: www.martinsville.com
SIC: 3069 5169 Rubber coated fabrics &
clothing; synthetic resins, rubber & plastic
materials

(G-8291)
GOURMET MANUFACTURING
INC
400 Starling Ave (24112-3732)
PHONE...............................276 638-2367
John Gregory, *Principal*
EMP: 2 **EST:** 2007
SALES (est): 97.6K **Privately Held**
SIC: 3999 Manufacturing industries

(G-8292)
GREENE COMPANY OF
VIRGINIA INC
2075 Stultz Rd (24112-1074)
P.O. Box 711 (24114-0711)
PHONE...............................276 638-7101
Edith K Greene, *President*
Barry Greene, *Corp Secy*
Sandy Burnette, *VP Mfg*
Amanda Ala Fountain, *Accountant*
◆ **EMP:** 9
SQ FT: 20,000
SALES: 4.2MM **Privately Held**
WEB: www.thegreenecompany.com
SIC: 2321 2339 Men's & boys' furnishings;
women's & misses' outerwear

(G-8293)
HANESBRANDS INC
Also Called: Canada Bread
380 Beaver Creek Dr (24112-2002)
P.O. Box 4626 (24115-4626)
PHONE...............................276 670-4500
Brent Corns, *Opers Staff*
Bernie Chitwood, *Manager*
EMP: 300 **Publicly Held**
WEB: www.hanes.com

SIC: 2341 2322 Women's & children's undergarments; men's & boys' underwear &
nightwear
PA: Hanesbrands Inc.
1000 E Hanes Mill Rd
Winston Salem NC 27105

(G-8294)
HASKELL INVESTMENT
COMPANY INC (DH)
204 Broad St (24112-3704)
P.O. Box 3711 (24115-3711)
PHONE...............................276 638-8801
George H Harris Jr, *President*
Heidi Roberson, *Admin Sec*
EMP: 75
SQ FT: 100,000
SALES (est): 5.2MM
SALES (corp-wide): 254.6B **Publicly
Held**
WEB: www.martinsvillebulletin.com
SIC: 2711 Commercial printing & newspa-
per publishing combined
HQ: Bh Media Group, Inc.
1314 Douglas St Ste 1500
Omaha NE 68102
402 444-1000

(G-8295)
HICKORY RIDGE DESIGNS INC
1103 Brookdale St Ste A (24112-4531)
PHONE...............................888 236-8431
Janice Dortch, *Branch Mgr*
EMP: 1
SALES (corp-wide): 129.4K **Privately
Held**
WEB: www.hickoryridgedesigns.com
SIC: 2395 Embroidery & art needlework
PA: Hickory Ridge Designs Inc
106 Winter Hawk Rd
Martinsville VA

(G-8296)
HONEST ABE LOG HOMES INC
200 Meadowood Trl (24112-7210)
PHONE...............................800 231-3695
EMP: 1
SALES (corp-wide): 11.4MM **Privately
Held**
WEB: www.honestabe.com
SIC: 2452 Log cabins, prefabricated, wood
PA: Honest Abe Log Homes, Inc.
9995 Clay County Hwy
Moss TN 38575
931 258-3648

(G-8297)
HOOKER FURNITURE
CORPORATION (PA)
440 Commonwealth Blvd E (24112-2040)
P.O. Box 4708 (24115-4708)
PHONE...............................276 632-2133
Paul B Toms Jr, *Ch of Bd*
D Lee Boone, *President*
Jeremy R Hoff, *President*
Douglas Townsend, *President*
Paul A Huckfeldt, *CFO*
◆ **EMP:** 208 **EST:** 1924
SALES: 610.8MM **Publicly Held**
WEB: www.hookerfurniture.com
SIC: 2512 2517 2521 2511 Upholstered
household furniture; home entertainment
unit cabinets, wood; wood office furniture;
wood bedroom furniture

(G-8298)
HOOKER FURNITURE
CORPORATION
Also Called: Martinsville Plant
850 Hooker St (24112)
P.O. Box 4708 (24115-4708)
PHONE...............................276 632-1763
Mike Pennington, *Manager*
EMP: 200
SALES (corp-wide): 610.8MM **Publicly
Held**
WEB: www.modusfurniture.com
SIC: 2517 2511 Home entertainment unit
cabinets, wood; wood desks, bookcases
& magazine racks
PA: Hooker Furniture Corporation
440 Commonwealth Blvd E
Martinsville VA 24112
276 632-2133

▲ = Import ▼=Export
◆ =Import/Export

(G-8299)
HUDDLE FURNITURE INC
225 Beaver Creek Dr (24112-1342)
PHONE....................828 874-8888
Bree Creel, *Merchandising*
EMP: 54
SALES (corp-wide): 29.6MM **Privately Held**
SIC: 2512 Upholstered household furniture
PA: Huddle Furniture, Inc.
1801 Main St E
Valdese NC 28690
828 874-8888

(G-8300)
INNOVATIVE YARNS INC
820 Roy St (24112-4139)
P.O. Box 4101 (24115-4101)
PHONE....................305 294-7244
Francis M Campbell, *President*
Robert Cabe, *Treasurer*
EMP: 50
SALES (est): 2MM **Privately Held**
WEB: www.thelittlegallery.net
SIC: 2281 Manmade & synthetic fiber yarns, spun

(G-8301)
INVISTA CAPITAL MANAGEMENT LLC
1008 Dupont Rd (24112-4600)
PHONE....................276 656-0500
EMP: 44
SALES (corp-wide): 38.9B **Privately Held**
WEB: www.invista.com
SIC: 2821 Plastics materials & resins
HQ: Invista Capital Management, Llc
2801 Centerville Rd
Wilmington DE 19808
302 683-3000

(G-8302)
INVISTA PRECISION CONCEPTS
1008 Dupont Rd (24112-4600)
PHONE....................276 656-0504
EMP: 2 **EST:** 2015
SALES (est): 289.9K **Privately Held**
WEB: www.invista.com
SIC: 3519 Parts & accessories, internal combustion engines

(G-8303)
J LYNETTE BUTY & BUNDLES LLC
707 Berkshire Pl (24112-5401)
PHONE....................276 790-9510
Jessica Wingfield,
EMP: 1
SALES (est): 65K **Privately Held**
SIC: 3999 Hair & hair-based products

(G-8304)
KEITH SANDERS
Also Called: Classic Creations
1216 Mulberry Rd (24112-5510)
PHONE....................276 728-0540
Keith Sanders, *Owner*
EMP: 2
SALES (est): 162.4K **Privately Held**
SIC: 2396 Screen printing on fabric articles

(G-8305)
KNAUSS SNACK FOOD & CO LLC
200 Knauss Dr (24112-1958)
PHONE....................276 656-3500
EMP: 2
SALES (est): 103.8K **Privately Held**
SIC: 2013 Sausages & other prepared meats

(G-8306)
LOVELL LOGGING INC
1124 Windy Ridge Rd (24112-7933)
PHONE....................276 632-5191
James Lovell, *President*
EMP: 2
SALES (est): 110K **Privately Held**
SIC: 2411 Logging

(G-8307)
MARBROOKE PRINTING INC
Also Called: Service Printing
20 Bridge St S (24112-6202)
PHONE....................276 632-7115

William David Martin, *President*
EMP: 1 **EST:** 2009
SALES (est): 91.5K **Privately Held**
SIC: 2752 Commercial printing, offset

(G-8308)
MARTINSVILLE CONCRETE PRODUCTS
530 Hairston St (24112-4318)
P.O. Box 3351 (24115-3351)
PHONE....................276 632-6416
William Sapp, *President*
William E Sapp, *President*
Margaret Adams, *Admin Sec*
EMP: 21
SQ FT: 10,000
SALES (est): 3.3MM **Privately Held**
WEB: www.martinsvilleconcrete.com
SIC: 3271 3272 Blocks, concrete or cinder: standard; concrete products

(G-8309)
MARTINSVILLE FINANCE & INV (PA)
184 Tensbury Dr (24112-0677)
PHONE....................276 632-9500
Robert L Wilson, *President*
Alec C Wilson Jr, *Vice Pres*
EMP: 5 **EST:** 1930
SQ FT: 2,000
SALES (est): 3.8MM **Privately Held**
SIC: 1423 3273 Crushed & broken granite; ready-mixed concrete

(G-8310)
MARTINSVILLE MACHINE WORKS
1106 Memorial Blvd S (24112-4725)
P.O. Box 3847 (24115-3847)
PHONE....................276 632-6491
Daniel K Critz, *President*
Katie Cox, *Admin Sec*
EMP: 5
SQ FT: 25,000
SALES (est): 1.1MM **Privately Held**
WEB: www.martinsvillemachine.com
SIC: 3599 Machine shop, jobbing & repair

(G-8311)
MEHLER INC (DH)
175 Mehler Ln (24112-2037)
PHONE....................276 638-6166
Fried Moeller, *President*
Ulrich Goeth, *CFO*
Andreas M Schulze Ising, *Admin Sec*
Gray Sullivan, *Admin Sec*
▲ **EMP:** 75
SALES (est): 15MM
SALES (corp-wide): 412.4MM **Privately Held**
WEB: www.mehlerinc.com
SIC: 2281 Needle & handicraft yarns, spun
HQ: Mehler Engineered Products Gmbh
Edelzeller Str. 44
Fulda 36043
661 103-0

(G-8312)
MEHLER INC
Also Called: Mehler Engineered Products
175 Mehler Ln (24112-2037)
PHONE....................276 638-6166
Paul Bleisteiner, *President*
EMP: 60
SALES (corp-wide): 412.4MM **Privately Held**
WEB: www.mehlerinc.com
SIC: 3052 2296 Automobile hose, rubber; tire cord & fabrics
HQ: Mehler, Inc.
175 Mehler Ln
Martinsville VA 24112
276 638-6166

(G-8313)
MEHLER ENGINEERED PRODUCTS INC
175 Mehler Ln (24112-2037)
PHONE....................276 638-6166
Richard Grobauer, *President*
Gray Sullivan, *Exec VP*
Jerry Adams, *Vice Pres*
◆ **EMP:** 58
SQ FT: 148,800

SALES (est): 11.5MM
SALES (corp-wide): 412.4MM **Privately Held**
WEB: www.mehler-ep.com
SIC: 2281 Needle & handicraft yarns, spun
PA: Kap Ag
Edelzeller Str. 44
Fulda 36043
661 103-0

(G-8314)
MOTRAK MODELS
717 Windsor Ln (24112-4512)
PHONE....................813 476-4784
Jeffrey Adam, *Principal*
EMP: 2
SALES (est): 134.5K **Privately Held**
WEB: www.motrakmodelsusa.com
SIC: 3944 Games, toys & children's vehicles

(G-8315)
ORALIGN BABY LLC
19 Cleveland Ave (24112-2925)
PHONE....................540 492-0453
John Davis,
EMP: 1
SQ FT: 3,300
SALES (est): 101.4K **Privately Held**
SIC: 2676 Infant & baby paper products

(G-8316)
PATRICK HAWKS
Also Called: Pac Custom Wdwkg & Cnc Routing
212 Franklin St (24112-2706)
PHONE....................276 618-2055
Patrick Hawks, *Principal*
EMP: 1
SALES (est): 47.6K **Privately Held**
SIC: 2431 Millwork

(G-8317)
PERFORMANCE LIVESTOCK & FEED C
11 Redd Level Plant Rd (24112-1104)
PHONE....................888 777-5912
EMP: 2
SALES (est): 68.6K **Privately Held**
WEB: www.performancelivestock.com
SIC: 2048 Livestock feeds

(G-8318)
PINE PRODUCTS INC
315 Carver Rd (24112-7552)
P.O. Box 5471 (24115-5471)
PHONE....................276 957-2222
Ronald Wood, *President*
Ruth R Aaron, *Corp Secy*
William C Smith, *Vice Pres*
Ruth Aaron, *Admin Sec*
EMP: 44
SQ FT: 3,000
SALES (est): 7.8MM **Privately Held**
WEB: www.pineproductslumber.com
SIC: 2421 Sawmills & planing mills, general

(G-8319)
PINE PRODUCTS LLC
315 Carver Rd (24112-7552)
PHONE....................276 957-2222
EMP: 2
SALES (est): 121.1K **Privately Held**
SIC: 2421 Sawmills & planing mills, general

(G-8320)
PRESTON RDGE WNERY BREWING INC
4105 Preston Rd (24112-7100)
PHONE....................276 634-8752
Lawrence Penn, *President*
EMP: 1
SALES (est): 108.6K **Privately Held**
WEB: www.southlakeproperty.com
SIC: 2084 Wines

(G-8321)
PRO-GRAPHX
405 Walker Rd (24112-2195)
PHONE....................844 777-0288
Carson Stone, *Principal*
EMP: 2 **EST:** 2018

SALES (est): 206.2K **Privately Held**
WEB: www.pro-graphx.com
SIC: 2752 Commercial printing, lithographic

(G-8322)
QUALITY PRINTING
706 Memorial Blvd S (24112-6415)
PHONE....................276 632-1415
Larry Thurman, *Owner*
EMP: 5
SQ FT: 5,000
SALES (est): 400K **Privately Held**
WEB: www.qualityprintingva.com
SIC: 2752 2759 Commercial printing, offset; letterpress printing

(G-8323)
RESTORATION BOOKS & PUBLISHING
203 Emmett St (24112-4240)
PHONE....................276 224-7244
Debra Turner, *Principal*
EMP: 1
SALES (est): 37.5K **Privately Held**
SIC: 2741 Miscellaneous publishing

(G-8324)
RONBUILT CORPORATION
175 Ward Rd (24112-0478)
P.O. Box 1081 (24114-1081)
PHONE....................276 638-2090
Ronald A Ressel Jr, *President*
EMP: 8 **EST:** 1975
SQ FT: 27,000
SALES (est): 1MM **Privately Held**
WEB: www.ronbuiltcorp.com
SIC: 2512 2431 1521 Upholstered household furniture; millwork; new construction, single-family houses

(G-8325)
SAMS GUTTER SHOP
1025 Liberty St (24112-1340)
PHONE....................276 632-6522
Randy Rowland, *Owner*
Samuel Rolands, *Partner*
EMP: 1
SQ FT: 4,800
SALES (est): 500K **Privately Held**
WEB: www.danielperry.tel
SIC: 3444 1761 Gutters, sheet metal; gutter & downspout contractor

(G-8326)
SANWELL PRINTING CO INC
900 Starling Ave (24112-6435)
P.O. Box 4427 (24115-4427)
PHONE....................276 638-3772
Lowell T Roberts, *President*
EMP: 5
SQ FT: 10,000
SALES (est): 651.6K **Privately Held**
SIC: 2759 5943 Letterpress printing; office forms & supplies

(G-8327)
SEIDLE MOTORSPORTS
1615 Virginia Ave (24112-9541)
PHONE....................276 632-2255
Chris Seidle, *Owner*
EMP: 1 **EST:** 2010
SALES (est): 50K **Privately Held**
WEB: www.prohemiperformance.com
SIC: 3751 Motorcycles & related parts

(G-8328)
SHORE TRADERS LLC
1208 Knollwood Pl (24112-5506)
PHONE....................276 632-5073
Sergio Amato,
EMP: 2
SALES (est): 103.3K **Privately Held**
SIC: 2221 Apparel & outerwear fabric, manmade fiber or silk

(G-8329)
SIGNODE INDUSTRIAL GROUP LLC
Also Called: Multi Wall Packaging
50 Multi Wall Dr (24112-2041)
P.O. Box 4631 (24115-4631)
PHONE....................276 632-2352
Charlie Lawless, *Manager*
Charley Lawless, *Manager*

EMP: 220
SQ FT: 4,500
SALES (corp-wide): 11.6B Publicly Held
WEB: www.signode.com
SIC: 2631 2671 2621 Packaging board; packaging paper & plastics film, coated & laminated; specialty papers
HQ: Signode Industrial Group Llc
    3650 W Lake Ave
    Glenview IL 60026
    847 724-7500

(G-8330)
SMITH MOUNTAIN INDUSTRIES LTD
125 Cedar Run (24112-6115)
PHONE..................540 576-3117
Carlile Robertson, Principal
EMP: 2 EST: 2010
SALES (est): 132.3K Privately Held
SIC: 3999 Manufacturing industries

(G-8331)
SOLID STONE FABRICS INC
405 Walker Rd (24112-2195)
PHONE..................276 634-0115
David Stone, President
Jon Alba, Vice Pres
Luke Harris, VP Mfg
Carson Stone, Engineer
Leath Patti, Sales Staff
▲ EMP: 12 EST: 2003
SQ FT: 24,000
SALES (est): 2.5MM Privately Held
WEB: www.solidstonefabrics.com
SIC: 2297 Nonwoven fabrics

(G-8332)
SOUTHEASTERN WOOD PRODUCTS INC
1801 Rivermont Hts (24112-5034)
PHONE..................276 632-9025
James Michael Grogan, President
Kathleen Semones, Corp Secy
Thomas Snipes, Vice Pres
▲ EMP: 18
SQ FT: 10,000
SALES (est): 2.8MM Privately Held
WEB: www.southeasternwood.com
SIC: 2511 2426 5072 Wood household furniture; hardwood dimension & flooring mills; saw blades

(G-8333)
SOUTHERN FINISHING COMPANY INC
801 E Church St (24112-3108)
P.O. Box 4221 (24115-4221)
PHONE..................276 632-4901
Carl W Via, Manager
Joan Fulcher, Supervisor
Wade Hartman, Technician
EMP: 32
SALES (corp-wide): 70.6MM Privately Held
WEB: www.southernfinishing.com
SIC: 2499 2511 Furniture inlays (veneers); wood household furniture
PA: The Southern Finishing Company Incorporated
    100 W Main St
    Stoneville NC 27048
    336 573-3741

(G-8334)
SOUTHPRINT INC (PA)
Also Called: Checkered Flag Sports
545 Hollie Dr (24112-1386)
PHONE..................276 666-3000
Raul Alvarez, CEO
Richard Lawhon, Exec VP
Rich Elliott, Plant Mgr
Shane Pinkston, Director
Sharon Collins, Executive
▲ EMP: 100
SQ FT: 100,000
SALES (est): 24.6MM Privately Held
WEB: www.store.checkeredflagsports.com
SIC: 2759 Screen printing

(G-8335)
SPANX INC
229 Hollie Dr (24112-1383)
PHONE..................888 806-7311
Michelle Burke, Manager

Kathleen De Goede, Manager
Stewart Eulisa, Manager
Anne Satterthwaite, Manager
Natalya Gritsevich, Senior Mgr
EMP: 3 Privately Held
WEB: www.spanx.com
SIC: 2251 Women's hosiery, except socks
PA: Spanx, Inc.
    3035 Peachtree Rd Ne # 200
    Atlanta GA 30305

(G-8336)
SPARTAN INDS MARTINSVILLE
2201 Appalachian Dr (24112-3001)
P.O. Box 127, Collinsville (24078-0127)
PHONE..................276 632-3033
Lewis Barnes, Principal
EMP: 1 EST: 2001
SALES (est): 72.6K Privately Held
SIC: 3999 Manufacturing industries

(G-8337)
SPRINGS GLOBAL US INC
460 Beaver Creek Dr (24112-2036)
PHONE..................276 670-3440
Amos King, Engineer
Fred Laxton, Manager
Sheri Cochran, Clerk
EMP: 50
SALES (corp-wide): 42.3MM Privately Held
WEB: www.ir.springs.com
SIC: 2392 Household furnishings
HQ: Springs Global Us, Inc.
    205 N White St
    Fort Mill SC 29715

(G-8338)
STONE DYNAMICS INC
1220 Memorial Blvd S (24112-4807)
PHONE..................276 638-7755
Robert Lankford, President
L Donavant, Vice Pres
▲ EMP: 21
SALES (est): 3.3MM Privately Held
WEB: www.stonedynamics.com
SIC: 3281 Marble, building: cut & shaped

(G-8339)
SUNTEK HOLDING COMPANY
Also Called: Commonwalth Laminating Coating
345 Beaver Creek Dr (24112-2090)
PHONE..................276 632-4991
Ashley Reynolds, Principal
EMP: 100
SALES (est): 12.4MM Publicly Held
WEB: www.suntekfilms.com
SIC: 3479 Painting, coating & hot dipping
PA: Eastman Chemical Company
    200 S Wilcox Dr
    Kingsport TN 37660

(G-8340)
TECHNICAL MACHINE SERVICE INC
101 Evening Star Ln (24112-0701)
PHONE..................276 638-2105
Jerry S Wood, President
Joanne Wood, Corp Secy
Walter Wood, Shareholder
EMP: 3
SQ FT: 5,000
SALES (est): 447.1K Privately Held
SIC: 3599 Machine shop, jobbing & repair

(G-8341)
TECHNICAL MOTOR SERVICE LLC
141 Dye Plant Rd (24112-0668)
PHONE..................276 638-1135
Jerry Wood, Mng Member
Duke Seacrest,
John Tibbetts,
EMP: 7
SQ FT: 15,000
SALES (est): 571.4K Privately Held
SIC: 3621 Electric motor & generator parts

(G-8342)
TEXTURING SERVICES LLC
Also Called: Tsi Yarns
615 Walker Rd (24112-2165)
P.O. Box 3631 (24115-3631)
PHONE..................276 632-3130
Roger Hutchins, President

Gray Sullivan, General Mgr
William Vernon, Opers Mgr
Ken Carder, CFO
Mike Stanley, Maintence Staff
▲ EMP: 130
SQ FT: 91,602
SALES (est): 22.6MM Privately Held
WEB: www.tsiyarns.com
SIC: 2282 2281 Textured yarn; yarn spinning mills
PA: Hamilton International, Llc
    2233 Peachtree Rd Ne # 305
    Atlanta GA 30309

(G-8343)
THIRTY SEVEN CENT MACHINE
156 Hodges Farm Rd (24112-6838)
PHONE..................276 673-1400
S Kenneth Staples, Principal
Soloman Staples, Principal
EMP: 2
SALES (est): 195.9K Privately Held
SIC: 3541 Machine tool replacement & repair parts, metal cutting types

(G-8344)
TOKYO EXPRESS
1170 Memorial Blvd N (24112-2435)
PHONE..................276 632-7599
Nhieu Tran, Principal
EMP: 4
SALES (est): 321.9K Privately Held
WEB: www.tokyoexpressva.com
SIC: 2741 Miscellaneous publishing

(G-8345)
VF IMAGEWEAR (EAST) INC
3375 Joseph Martin Hwy (24112-0495)
P.O. Box 5423 (24115-5423)
PHONE..................276 956-7200
George N Derhofer, President
Sue Minter, Data Proc Exec
▲ EMP: 4180
SALES (est): 25.2MM Publicly Held
SIC: 2253 2321 Jogging & warm-up suits, knit; jackets, knit; T-shirts & tops, knit; men's & boys' furnishings
PA: V.F. Corporation
    1551 Wewatta St
    Greenwood Village CO 80110
    720 778-4000

(G-8346)
VICTORIA AUSTIN
519 Glendale St (24112-1709)
PHONE..................276 632-1742
Michael Austin, Owner
EMP: 2
SALES (est): 83.9K Privately Held
SIC: 2752 Commercial printing, lithographic

(G-8347)
VIRGINIA MIRROR COMPANY INC (PA)
300 Moss St S (24112-3697)
P.O. Box 5431 (24115-5431)
PHONE..................276 956-3131
Chris Beeler, CEO
John D Korff, President
W C Beeler Jr, Chairman
Benjamin D Beeler, Exec VP
J J Abercrombie, Vice Pres
▼ EMP: 52 EST: 1913
SQ FT: 273,000
SALES (est): 27.3MM Privately Held
WEB: www.va-glass.com
SIC: 3231 3211 Mirrored glass; tempered glass

(G-8348)
VIRGINIA MIRROR COMPANY INC
Also Called: Virginia Glass
300 Moss St S (24112-3697)
PHONE..................276 632-9816
John D Korff, Branch Mgr
EMP: 1
SALES (corp-wide): 27.3MM Privately Held
WEB: www.va-glass.com
SIC: 3231 3211 Mirrored glass; tempered glass

PA: Virginia Mirror Company, Incorporated
    300 Moss St S
    Martinsville VA 24112
    276 956-3131

(G-8349)
VIRGINIA REAL ESTATE REVIEWS
228 Oxford Dr (24112-0059)
PHONE..................276 956-5900
Callie Martin, President
EMP: 5
SALES (est): 417.2K Privately Held
WEB: www.virginiarealestatereviews.com
SIC: 2721 Periodicals

(G-8350)
WASHBURN SIGN SERVICES INC
10970 Sontag Rd (24112-8911)
PHONE..................540 483-5784
EMP: 1
SALES (est): 50.6K Privately Held
SIC: 3993 Signs & advertising specialties

(G-8351)
WATER FILTRATION PLANT
302 Clearview Dr (24112-1704)
PHONE..................276 656-5137
Doug Wood, Manager
EMP: 11
SALES (est): 840K Privately Held
SIC: 3589 Water treatment equipment, industrial

(G-8352)
WESTROCK CP LLC
588 Industrial Park Dr (24115)
P.O. Box 5231 (24115-5231)
PHONE..................276 632-2176
Rod Anderson, Manager
EMP: 151
SALES (corp-wide): 17.5B Publicly Held
WEB: www.westrock.com
SIC: 2653 Boxes, corrugated: made from purchased materials
HQ: Westrock Cp, Llc
    1000 Abernathy Rd Ste 125
    Atlanta GA 30328

(G-8353)
WHATS YOUR SIGN
27 E Church St (24112-6207)
PHONE..................276 632-0576
Heather Webb, Partner
EMP: 2
SALES (est): 35K Privately Held
SIC: 3993 7389 2396 2752 Signs & advertising specialties; embroidering of advertising on shirts, etc.; screen printing on fabric articles; business form & card printing, lithographic

(G-8354)
WREATHS BOWS & BLESSINGS
2157 Figsboro Rd (24112-8230)
PHONE..................276 340-2380
Wanda Ashley, Principal
EMP: 2
SALES (est): 102.9K Privately Held
SIC: 3999 Wreaths, artificial

Mathews
Mathews County

(G-8355)
HAWKEYE INSPECTION SERVICE
116 Williamsdale Ln (23109-2125)
P.O. Box 267 (23109-0267)
PHONE..................804 725-9751
Robin Thompson, President
Robert Thompson, Vice Pres
EMP: 2
SALES (est): 25K Privately Held
WEB: www.hawkeyeinspects.com
SIC: 1389 7389 Construction, repair & dismantling services; building inspection service

▲ = Import ▼=Export
◆ =Import/Export

(G-8356)
LOUIS G BALL & SON INC
1203 Callis Field Ln (23109-2168)
P.O. Box 761 (23109-0761)
PHONE..................................804 725-5202
Louis G Ball, *President*
Daniel Scott Ball, *Director*
EMP: 2
SQ FT: 2,500
SALES (est): 250K **Privately Held**
WEB: www.finecabinetsandmore.com
SIC: 2434 Wood kitchen cabinets

Mattaponi
King And Queen County

(G-8357)
ASB GREENWORLD INC
496 Airport Rd (23110-2159)
P.O. Box Q, West Point (23181-1709)
PHONE..................................804 785-9260
Helmut Auranz, *President*
Robert Bollinger, *Vice Pres*
▲ **EMP:** 49
SALES (est): 6.9MM
SALES (corp-wide): 68.1MM **Privately Held**
WEB: www.asbgreenworld.com
SIC: 2875 Compost; potting soil, mixed
HQ: Asb Grunland Helmut Aurenz Gmbh
    Mittlerer Pfad 19
    Stuttgart 70499
    711 215-760

(G-8358)
F3 TECHNOLOGIES LLC
1776 Patriot Way (23110-2147)
PHONE..................................804 785-1017
Stanley Wood,
Kelly McDougall,
Mary McDougall,
Scott Richman,
Michael Zinanni,
EMP: 3 **EST:** 2014
SQ FT: 150
SALES (est): 159.2K **Privately Held**
WEB: www.fulcrumconceptsllc.com
SIC: 3728 Military aircraft equipment & armament

(G-8359)
GEMTEK ELECTRONIC COMPONE
Also Called: Gemtek Electronic Component
30 Rundlith Hill Rd (23110)
PHONE..................................603 218-3902
EMP: 3 **EST:** 2009
SALES (est): 160K **Privately Held**
SIC: 3679 Mfg Electronic Components

Maurertown
Shenandoah County

(G-8360)
CARLTON ORNDORFF
5271 Zepp Rd (22644-1727)
PHONE..................................540 436-3543
Carlton Orndorff, *Owner*
EMP: 2
SALES (est): 204.2K **Privately Held**
SIC: 2421 Sawmills & planing mills, general

(G-8361)
FINE LINE INC
25118 Old Valley Pike (22644-2530)
PHONE..................................540 436-3626
Harald E Huttner, *President*
Cheryl Huttner, *Corp Secy*
EMP: 5
SQ FT: 6,000
SALES (est): 462.4K **Privately Held**
WEB: www.finelinesigns.net
SIC: 3993 Signs & advertising specialties

(G-8362)
FINE LINE LLC
25118 Old Valley Pike (22644-2530)
PHONE..................................540 436-3626
Wasim Talib, *CEO*
EMP: 4

SALES (est): 110.6K **Privately Held**
SIC: 3993 8742 Signs & advertising specialties; marketing consulting services

(G-8363)
FOSTER JACKSON LLC
Also Called: North Mountain Vineyard
4374 Swartz Rd (22644-2322)
PHONE..................................540 436-9463
Brad Foster,
John Jackson,
Krista Jacksonfoster,
EMP: 3
SALES (est): 140K **Privately Held**
WEB: www.northmountainvineyard.com
SIC: 2084 Wines

(G-8364)
TIMOTHY L HOSEY
Also Called: Automated Panels
6814 Back Rd (22644-2110)
PHONE..................................270 339-0016
Timothy Hosey, *Owner*
Timothy L Hosey, *Principal*
EMP: 1
SALES (est): 31.2K **Privately Held**
SIC: 2741 7371 1623 ; custom computer programming services; software programming applications; transmitting tower (telecommunication) construction

Max Meadows
Wythe County

(G-8365)
ARCHER CONSTRUCTION
156 Rome Rd (24360-3452)
PHONE..................................276 637-6905
Christopher Archer, *Owner*
EMP: 3
SALES (est): 198.3K **Privately Held**
SIC: 3531 7389 Road construction & maintenance machinery;

(G-8366)
BODY CREATIONS
162 Acorn Ln (24360-3708)
PHONE..................................276 620-9989
Melissa Aker, *Principal*
EMP: 1
SALES (est): 72.1K **Privately Held**
SIC: 2342 Brassieres

(G-8367)
DMMT GLISAN INC
Also Called: Extreme Signs and Graphics
4450 E Lee Hwy (24360-3434)
PHONE..................................276 620-0298
Douglas Glisan, *President*
EMP: 3 **EST:** 2001
SALES (est): 212.9K **Privately Held**
SIC: 3993 Signs & advertising specialties

(G-8368)
FORT CHISWELL MACHINE TL PDTS
324 Apache Run (24360-3308)
PHONE..................................276 637-3022
Clarence A Aker, *President*
Emma T Aker, *Vice Pres*
EMP: 7
SALES (est): 821.5K **Privately Held**
WEB: www.fcmtp.webs.com
SIC: 3599 Machine shop, jobbing & repair

(G-8369)
MICROFAB LLC
5156 E Lee Hwy (24360-3424)
PHONE..................................276 620-7200
Brooke Stewart, *Co-Owner*
Johnny Stewart, *Mng Member*
Johnny L Stewart,
EMP: 2
SQ FT: 1,250
SALES (est): 15K **Privately Held**
SIC: 3541 Machine tools, metal cutting type

(G-8370)
VIRGINIA FIRE PROTECTION SVCS
7893 Peppers Ferry Rd (24360-3343)
PHONE..................................276 637-1012

Matthew Martin, *Principal*
EMP: 1
SALES (est): 107K **Privately Held**
WEB: www.virginiafps.com
SIC: 2899 7389 5099 3999 Fire extinguisher charges; fire extinguisher servicing; fire extinguishers; fire extinguishers, portable; fire extinguishers

(G-8371)
WEST WIND FARM INC
Also Called: West Wind Farm Vinyrd & Winery
2228 Fort Chiswell Rd (24360-3036)
PHONE..................................276 699-2020
Paul J Hric, *President*
EMP: 2
SALES (est): 194.6K **Privately Held**
WEB: www.westwindwine.com
SIC: 2084 Wines

Maxie
Buchanan County

(G-8372)
LOONEYS BIT SERVICE INC
Rr 609 (24628)
P.O. Box 77 (24628-0077)
PHONE..................................276 531-8767
Randall Lee Looney, *President*
EMP: 3
SALES (est): 303.1K **Privately Held**
SIC: 3532 Drills, bits & similar equipment

Mc Clure
Dickenson County

(G-8373)
CONTURA ENERGY SERVICES LLC
1465 Herndon Rd (24269-7076)
PHONE..................................276 835-8041
EMP: 5
SALES (est): 266.9K **Privately Held**
SIC: 1241 Coal mining services

Mc Dowell
Highland County

(G-8374)
HARTENSHIELD GROUP INC
321 Davis Run Rd (24458-2282)
PHONE..................................302 388-4023
William Copper, *Principal*
EMP: 2 **EST:** 2011
SALES (est): 93.3K **Privately Held**
WEB: www.hartenshield.com
SIC: 2731 Book music: publishing only, not printed on site

(G-8375)
OBAUGH WELDING LLC
1183 Doe Hill Rd (24458-2219)
PHONE..................................540 396-6151
Kyle Obaugh,
EMP: 3
SALES (est): 200K **Privately Held**
SIC: 3441 Fabricated structural metal

(G-8376)
SUGAR TREE COUNTRY STORE
185 Mansion House Rd (24458-2100)
P.O. Box 19 (24458-0019)
PHONE..................................540 396-3469
Glen Heatwole, *President*
Fern Heatwole, *Vice Pres*
EMP: 5
SALES (est): 150K **Privately Held**
WEB: www.sugartreecountrystore.com
SIC: 2099 Maple syrup

Mc Gaheysville
Rockingham County

(G-8377)
BRIX AND COLUMNS VINEYARDS LLC
1501 Dave Berry Rd (22840-2391)
PHONE..................................540 810-0566
EMP: 7
SALES (est): 233.4K **Privately Held**
WEB: www.brixandcolumns.com
SIC: 2084 Wines

(G-8378)
NOVARTIS CORPORATION
5138 Lawyer Rd (22840-3707)
PHONE..................................540 435-1836
Charles Cruse, *Branch Mgr*
Charles E Cruse, *Administration*
EMP: 2
SALES (corp-wide): 47.5B **Privately Held**
WEB: www.us.novartis.com
SIC: 2834 Pharmaceutical preparations
HQ: Novartis Corporation
    1 S Ridgedale Ave Ste 1 # 1
    East Hanover NJ 07936
    212 307-1122

Mc Kenney
Dinwiddie County

(G-8379)
EDMUNDS WASTE REMOVAL INC
8507 Mckenney Hwy (23872-3439)
PHONE..................................804 478-4688
Susan Edmunds, *President*
Tommy Edmunds, *General Mgr*
Edwards Susan C, *Vice Pres*
Thomas F Edmunds, *Vice Pres*
EMP: 8
SALES (est): 880K **Privately Held**
WEB: www.edmundswasteremoval.com
SIC: 3089 7359 Toilets, portable chemical: plastic; portable toilet rental

(G-8380)
KAISA USA INC
20520 Unico Rd (23872-2704)
PHONE..................................206 228-7711
Wen Hua, *President*
Harry McCants, *Director*
Rudy Shepherd, *Director*
▲ **EMP:** 5
SQ FT: 248,000
SALES (est): 26MM **Privately Held**
SIC: 2678 Memorandum books, notebooks & looseleaf filler paper

(G-8381)
LEWIS BROTHERS LOGGING
21108 Westover Dr (23872-2502)
PHONE..................................804 478-4243
Walter S Lewis, *Partner*
Gary R Lewis, *Partner*
EMP: 9 **Privately Held**
SIC: 2411 Logging camps & contractors

(G-8382)
OLD HICKORY CANDLE COMPANY
26125 Ridge Ln (23872-2053)
PHONE..................................804 400-8602
George F Marable III, *Principal*
EMP: 1
SALES (est): 39.6K **Privately Held**
SIC: 3999 Candles

Mc Lean
Fairfax County

(G-8383)
4C NORTH AMERICA INC
1765 Grnsboro Stn Pl 90 (22102-3467)
PHONE..................................540 850-8470
Michael Coss, *President*
David Hazlett, *CFO*
EMP: 3

SALES (est): 78.2K **Privately Held**
WEB: www.4cstrategies.com
SIC: 7372 7371 Application computer software; computer software development & applications

(G-8384)
ACINTYO INC
7423 Old Maple Sq (22102-2824)
PHONE................................703 349-3400
Pradeep Singh, *President*
EMP: 7
SALES (est): 367.4K **Privately Held**
SIC: 7372 7371 Application computer software; software programming applications

(G-8385)
ACORN PRESS LLC
1110 Brook Valley Ln (22102-1532)
PHONE................................703 760-0920
Ann Fritz Hackett, *Administration*
EMP: 1
SALES (est): 53.3K **Privately Held**
SIC: 2741 Miscellaneous publishing

(G-8386)
ADOBE INC
7930 Jones Branch Dr Fl 5 (22102-3396)
PHONE................................571 765-5400
David Mathew, *Opers Staff*
Nick Gatz,
EMP: 70
SALES (corp-wide): 11.1B **Publicly Held**
WEB: www.adobe.com
SIC: 7372 Prepackaged software
PA: Adobe Inc.
　345 Park Ave
　San Jose CA 95110
　408 536-6000

(G-8387)
ADOBE SYSTEMS FEDERAL LLC
7930 Jones Branch Dr # 500 (22102-3388)
PHONE................................571 765-5523
Shantanu Narayen, *Ch of Bd*
Michael Barr, *Sales Dir*
Jennie Strobeck, *Sales Staff*
Andrea Green Carvajal, *Manager*
Amy Marra, *Manager*
EMP: 39
SALES (est): 5MM
SALES (corp-wide): 11.1B **Publicly Held**
SIC: 7372 Prepackaged software
PA: Adobe Inc.
　345 Park Ave
　San Jose CA 95110
　408 536-6000

(G-8388)
ADV3NTUS SOFTWARE LLC
8201 Greensboro Dr Ste 71 (22102-3810)
PHONE................................703 288-3380
Christopher Weiler, *Principal*
EMP: 2
SALES (est): 115.5K **Privately Held**
SIC: 7372 Prepackaged software

(G-8389)
AERO DESIGN & MFG CO IN
7930 Jones Branch Dr # 900 (22102-3388)
PHONE................................218 722-1927
EMP: 1
SALES (est): 39.6K **Privately Held**
SIC: 3999 Manufacturing industries

(G-8390)
AIR BARGE COMPANY
5840 Bermuda Ct (22101-3301)
PHONE................................310 378-2928
EMP: 2
SALES (est): 118.3K **Privately Held**
SIC: 3599 Mfg Proprietary Jacks & Air Cushion Mobility Equipment

(G-8391)
ALL EXPORT IMPORT USA LLC
1350 Beverly Rd 115-334 (22101-3961)
PHONE................................571 242-2250
Sasan Oghlidos, *Bookkeeper*
May Safari,
EMP: 1
SALES (est): 81.1K **Privately Held**
SIC: 2844 Cosmetic preparations

(G-8392)
AMERICAN INSTITUTE RES INC
6825 Redmond Dr Ste I (22101-3715)
PHONE................................703 470-1037
Warren Polk, *President*
Lloyd Woodward, *Vice Pres*
EMP: 3
SQ FT: 2,000
SALES (est): 122.8K **Privately Held**
SIC: 7372 Educational computer software

(G-8393)
APPIAN CORPORATION (PA)
7950 Jones Branch Dr (22102-3302)
PHONE................................703 442-8844
Matthew Calkins, *Ch of Bd*
Robert C Kramer, *General Mgr*
Robert Kramer, *General Mgr*
Chris Stern, *Counsel*
David Mitchell, *Senior VP*
EMP: 148
SQ FT: 210,000
SALES: 260.3MM **Publicly Held**
WEB: www.appian.com
SIC: 7372 Prepackaged software

(G-8394)
APTIFY CORPORATION
7901 Jones Branch Dr Fl 5 (22102-3309)
PHONE................................202 223-2600
EMP: 2 **Privately Held**
WEB: www.aptify.com
SIC: 7372 Prepackaged software
PA: Aptify Corporation
　7900 Wstpk Dr 5th Fl Atrm # 5
　Tysons Corner VA 22102

(G-8395)
AQUANTA INC
1775 Tysons Blvd Fl 5 (22102-4285)
PHONE................................703 286-0923
Matt Carlson, *CEO*
Arnoud Van Houten, *President*
Arnoud Van, *Manager*
EMP: 3
SALES (est): 348.3K **Privately Held**
WEB: www.aquanta.io
SIC: 3674 Solar cells

(G-8396)
ARK COMMERCIAL SERVICES LLC
1775 Tysons Blvd (22102-4284)
PHONE................................202 807-6211
Durim Tafilaj,
EMP: 12 **EST:** 2018 **Privately Held**
SIC: 3822 Building services monitoring controls, automatic

(G-8397)
ATI-ENDYNA JV LLC
7926 Jones Branch Dr # 620 (22102-3303)
PHONE................................410 992-3424
Kishan Amarasekera,
EMP: 1
SALES (est): 80.2K **Privately Held**
WEB: www.endyna.com
SIC: 3312 Stainless steel

(G-8398)
BIG MIND PUBLISHING INC
940 Swinks Mill Rd (22102-2127)
PHONE................................703 734-8359
Elizabeth N Russell, *Principal*
EMP: 2
SALES (est): 109.8K **Privately Held**
WEB: www.polestarstrategies.com
SIC: 2741 Miscellaneous publishing

(G-8399)
BISSELL
6125 Long Meadow Rd (22101-2312)
PHONE................................703 827-5769
Richard E Bissell, *Principal*
EMP: 2
SALES (est): 134.1K **Privately Held**
SIC: 3589 Service industry machinery

(G-8400)
BLACK TREE LLC
8200 Greensboro Dr # 404 (22102-3891)
PHONE................................703 669-0178
EMP: 7
SQ FT: 1,600

SALES: 4.3MM **Privately Held**
SIC: 3812 Mfg Search/Navigation Equipment

(G-8401)
BLULOGIX LLC
1356 Beverly Rd Ste 300 (22101-3640)
PHONE................................443 333-4100
Timothy Cook, *CEO*
Youssef Yaghmour, *COO*
Jennifer Halstead, *Controller*
Jackie Kindig, *Accounts Mgr*
Ahmad Omari, *Director*
EMP: 30
SALES (est): 1.6MM **Privately Held**
WEB: www.blulogix.com
SIC: 7372 Business oriented computer software

(G-8402)
BMC SOFTWARE INC
8401 Greensboro Dr # 100 (22102-5100)
PHONE................................713 918-8800
Kevin Orr, *VP Sales*
Arthur Kelley, *Sales Staff*
Trey Rowan, *Sales Staff*
Patrick Flynn, *Marketing Staff*
Lisa Gallagher, *Marketing Staff*
EMP: 10
SALES (corp-wide): 1.3B **Privately Held**
WEB: www.bmc.com
SIC: 7372 Prepackaged software
PA: Bmc Software, Inc.
　2103 Citywest Blvd # 2100
　Houston TX 77042
　713 918-8800

(G-8403)
BOXWOOD TECHNOLOGY INC
1430 Spring Hill Rd Fl 6 (22102-3000)
PHONE................................703 707-8686
John Bell, *CEO*
Orang Firoozi, *Opers Staff*
April Dunnett, *Accounts Mgr*
Kevin Fitzgerald, *Accounts Mgr*
Richard Eberhart, *Manager*
EMP: 10 **Privately Held**
WEB: www.naylor.com
SIC: 7372 Business oriented computer software
HQ: Boxwood Technology Incorporated
　11350 Mccormick Ep 1 Rd
　Hunt Valley MD 21031
　877 262-2470

(G-8404)
BRANTLEY T JOLLY JR
1539 Brookhaven Dr (22101-4128)
PHONE................................703 447-6897
Brantley Jolly, *Owner*
EMP: 1
SALES (est): 82.5K **Privately Held**
SIC: 3699 Security devices

(G-8405)
CHERRY HILL CABINETRY
6232 Old Dominion Dr (22101-4217)
PHONE................................703 942-6053
EMP: 5
SALES (corp-wide): 1MM **Privately Held**
WEB: www.cherryhillcabinetry.com
SIC: 2434 Wood kitchen cabinets
PA: Cherry Hill Cabinetry
　1320 Cntl Pk Blvd Ste 108
　Fredericksburg VA 22401
　540 785-4333

(G-8406)
CHRISTIAN PUBLICATIONS
1504 Lincoln Way Unit 305 (22102-5856)
P.O. Box 9124 (22102-0124)
PHONE................................703 568-4300
William Koenig, *Principal*
EMP: 1
SALES: 106.8K **Privately Held**
SIC: 2741 Miscellaneous publishing

(G-8407)
COMFORTRAC INC
7901 Jones Branch Dr 6th (22102-3338)
P.O. Box 3800, Oakton (22124-8800)
PHONE................................703 891-0455
Christian Hunt, *President*
EMP: 4

SALES (est): 19.1K **Privately Held**
WEB: www.comfortrac.net
SIC: 3842 Traction apparatus

(G-8408)
CONCILIO LABS INC
1640 Boro Pl 400 (22102-3612)
PHONE................................571 282-4248
Terri Mille, *CEO*
Lindy Rider, *Project Leader*
EMP: 1 **EST:** 2014
SALES (est): 74.1K **Privately Held**
WEB: www.conciliolabs.com
SIC: 7372 Application computer software

(G-8409)
CONTACTENGINE INC
6849 Old Dominion Dr # 315 (22101-3733)
PHONE................................571 348-3220
Giles Bryan, *CEO*
EMP: 9
SALES (est): 3.1MM **Privately Held**
WEB: www.contactengine.com
SIC: 7372 Application computer software

(G-8410)
CORASCLOUD INC
7918 Jones Branch Dr # 800 (22102-3337)
PHONE................................703 797-1881
Moe Jafari, *President*
Michelle Jafari, *Senior VP*
Kevin Reed, *Comms Dir*
Dasha Fedorova, *Software Engr*
John Bassham, *Software Dev*
EMP: 36
SQ FT: 3,600
SALES: 5.3MM **Privately Held**
WEB: www.coras.com
SIC: 7372 7374 Prepackaged software; data processing & preparation
PA: Humantouch Llc
　7918 Jones Branch Dr # 800
　Mc Lean VA 22102

(G-8411)
CORCE COLLEC BUSINESS SYSTEM (DH)
7927 Jones Branch Dr # 3200 (22102-3322)
PHONE................................703 790-7272
Douglas W Clark, *President*
Matt Clark, *COO*
Dave Lindeen, *Senior VP*
Rob Devincent, *Vice Pres*
Jeff Grygiel, *Vice Pres*
EMP: 26
SQ FT: 7,536
SALES (est): 535.9MM
SALES (corp-wide): 90MM **Publicly Held**
WEB: www.corcentric.com
SIC: 7372 Prepackaged software
HQ: Corcentric, Llc
　62861 Cllctons Ctr Drv 60
　Chicago IL 60693
　800 608-0809

(G-8412)
CREATIVE OCCASIONS
1312 Chain Bridge Rd # 3 (22101-3968)
PHONE................................703 821-3210
EMP: 5
SALES (est): 280K **Privately Held**
SIC: 2759 Commercial Printing

(G-8413)
CVENT INC
8180 Greensboro Dr # 900 (22102-3876)
PHONE................................571 830-2301
EMP: 1
SALES (est): 1.1MM **Privately Held**
WEB: www.cvent.com
SIC: 7372 Business oriented computer software

(G-8414)
D-FEND INC
1640 Boro Pl (22102-3612)
PHONE................................703 728-4283
Terry Divittorio, *General Mgr*
EMP: 1
SALES (est): 54.6K **Privately Held**
SIC: 3728 Target drones

(G-8415)
DAQ BATS LLC
6147 Tompkins Dr (22101-3236)
PHONE..................................202 365-3246
Steve D'Aquila, *Principal*
EMP: 2
SALES (est): 162.7K **Privately Held**
WEB: www.daqbats.com
SIC: 3949 Sporting & athletic goods

(G-8416)
DATABLINK INC (HQ)
7921 Jones Branch Dr # 101 (22102-3332)
PHONE..................................703 639-0600
Alexandre Cagnoni, *CEO*
Shlomo Yanay, *President*
Gomes Da Silva, *Admin Sec*
EMP: 8 EST: 2014
SALES (est): 671.5K **Privately Held**
WEB: www.datablink.com
SIC: 7372 Business oriented computer
   software

(G-8417)
DEFENSOR HOLSTERS LLC
6205 Long Meadow Rd (22101-2312)
PHONE..................................703 409-4865
Dennis Defensor, *Principal*
EMP: 2
SALES (est): 87.6K **Privately Held**
SIC: 3199 Holsters, leather

(G-8418)
DETAIL MAXX LLC
1544 Spring Hill Rd (22102-0009)
PHONE..................................703 942-8965
Kamy Aazami,
EMP: 6
SALES (est): 700K **Privately Held**
SIC: 3589 Car washing machinery

(G-8419)
DIFFERENTIAL BRANDS GROUP INC
2001 International Dr (22102-4605)
PHONE..................................703 448-9985
EMP: 1
SALES (corp-wide): 80.2MM **Publicly Held**
SIC: 2337 Apparel And Other Finished
   Products
PA: Differential Brands Group Inc.
   1231 S Gerhart Ave
   Commerce CA 10118
   323 890-1800

(G-8420)
DMKP INC
Also Called: Balfour of Northern VA
1340 Old Chain Bridge Rd (22101-3955)
PHONE..................................703 941-1436
Donato Pasquarelli, *President*
Mike Flotz, *Principal*
EMP: 1
SALES (est): 106.5K **Privately Held**
SIC: 3911 Jewelry, precious metal

(G-8421)
DREAMPAK LLC
7901 Jones Branch Dr # 420 (22102-3300)
PHONE..................................703 751-3511
Joe Kaiser, *Production*
Stephon Smallwood, *Research*
Daniel G Zenner, *Controller*
Daniel Zenner, *Controller*
Tarick Gamay, *Sales Staff*
EMP: 10
SALES (corp-wide): 8.9MM **Privately Held**
WEB: www.dreampak.com
SIC: 2833 Vitamins, natural or synthetic:
   bulk, uncompounded
PA: Dreampak, Llc
   17100 W Ryerson Rd
   New Berlin WI 53151
   262 780-2982

(G-8422)
E PERFORMANCE INC
6657 Chilton Ct (22101-4422)
PHONE..................................703 217-6885
Tim Hughes, *Principal*
Mitchell Kieron, *CFO*
Charles Bryant, *Supervisor*
EMP: 4

SALES (est): 273.7K **Privately Held**
SIC: 2834 Pharmaceutical preparations

(G-8423)
EMC CORPORATION
8444 Westpark Dr Ste 100 (22102-5122)
PHONE..................................703 749-2260
Jeremy Whitfield, *Engineer*
Scott Manley, *Senior Engr*
Chris Richards, *Senior Engr*
John Terry, *Senior Engr*
Scott Casavant, *Finance*
EMP: 20 **Publicly Held**
WEB: www.emc.com
SIC: 3572 Computer storage devices
HQ: Emc Corporation
   176 South St
   Hopkinton MA 01748
   508 435-1000

(G-8424)
EVERLASTING LIFE PRODUCT
6812 Dean Dr (22101-5443)
PHONE..................................703 761-4900
Joseph Lee, *Owner*
EMP: 2
SALES (est): 92.8K **Privately Held**
SIC: 2844 5499 Toothpastes or powders,
   dentifrices; health & dietetic food stores

(G-8425)
EXPONENTIAL BIOTHERAPIES INC
7921 Jones Branch Dr # 133 (22102-3332)
PHONE..................................703 288-3710
Zsolt Harsanyi, *President*
Bob S Berns, *Vice Pres*
Roger Kirman, *Admin Sec*
EMP: 5
SALES (est): 40K **Privately Held**
WEB: www.expobio.com
SIC: 2834 Pharmaceutical preparations

(G-8426)
FALCON LAB INC
1765 Greensboro Station P (22102-3468)
PHONE..................................703 442-0124
Borzou Azabdaftari, *President*
EMP: 5
SQ FT: 1,200
SALES (est): 1MM **Privately Held**
WEB: www.thefalconlab.com
SIC: 2752 3993 7336 8742 Commercial
   printing, offset; advertising novelties;
   commercial art & graphic design; market-
   ing consulting services

(G-8427)
FEDERAL DATA CORPORATION
7575 Colshire Dr (22102-7508)
PHONE..................................703 734-3773
EMP: 2 EST: 1986
SQ FT: 1,178
SALES (est): 250K **Privately Held**
SIC: 7372 Prepackaged Software Services

(G-8428)
FEDERATED PUBLICATIONS INC
7950 Jones Branch Dr (22102-3302)
PHONE..................................703 854-6000
Karen Levy, *Admin Sec*
EMP: 99
SALES (est): 950K **Publicly Held**
SIC: 2741 Miscellaneous publishing
HQ: Gannett Media Corp.
   7950 Jones Branch Dr
   Mc Lean VA 22102
   703 854-6000

(G-8429)
FILENET CORPORATION
8401 Greensboro Dr # 400 (22102-3598)
PHONE..................................703 312-1500
EMP: 15
SALES (corp-wide): 99.7B **Publicly Held**
SIC: 7372 Prepackaged Software
HQ: Filenet Corporation
   3565 Harbor Blvd
   Costa Mesa CA 92626
   800 345-3638

(G-8430)
FINE LEATHER WORKS LLC
8201 Greensboro Dr # 300 (22102-3810)
PHONE..................................703 200-1953
EMP: 2
SALES (est): 72.1K **Privately Held**
SIC: 3199 Leather goods

(G-8431)
FIRST RENAISSANCE VENTURES
1915 Chain Bridge Rd 500b (22102-4401)
PHONE..................................703 408-6961
Martin Erim, *President*
Annie Brossard, *Managing Prtnr*
John Clemens, *Managing Prtnr*
Harald Ritzau, *Managing Prtnr*
EMP: 4
SQ FT: 1,500
SALES (est): 438.9K **Privately Held**
SIC: 3663 7389 Carrier equipment, radio
   communications; financial services

(G-8432)
FISHHAT INC
6823 Old Dominion Dr (22101-3711)
PHONE..................................703 827-0990
Edward David Danoff, *Principal*
EMP: 3
SALES (est): 304.2K **Privately Held**
SIC: 2836 Vaccines & other immunizing
   products

(G-8433)
FLAGSTONE OPRTING PARTNERS LLC
8448 Holly Leaf Dr (22102-2225)
PHONE..................................703 532-6238
Andrew Ambrose, *Principal*
EMP: 2 EST: 2015
SALES (est): 72.6K **Privately Held**
SIC: 3281 Flagstones

(G-8434)
FN AMERICA LLC (DH)
Also Called: Fnh USA
7950 Jones Branch Dr (22102-3302)
P.O. Box 9424 (22102-0424)
PHONE..................................703 288-3500
Jim Oldham, *Vice Pres*
Scot Fischer, *Opers Staff*
Bryon Cox, *Mfg Staff*
John Beville, *Engineer*
David Brosey, *Engineer*
▲ EMP: 190
SALES (est): 98.7MM **Privately Held**
WEB: www.fnamerica.com
SIC: 3484 Machine guns or machine gun
   parts, 30 mm. & below; rifles or rifle parts,
   30 mm. & below
HQ: Fn Herstal
   Voie De Liege 33
   Herstal 4040
   424 081-11

(G-8435)
FORTIFY SOFTWARE
9004 Old Dominion Dr (22102-1014)
PHONE..................................571 286-6320
EMP: 2
SALES (est): 56.5K **Privately Held**
SIC: 7372 Prepackaged software

(G-8436)
FRANGIPANI INC
Also Called: Cleaning Up
1155 Daleview Dr (22102-1513)
P.O. Box 6944 (22106-6944)
PHONE..................................703 903-0099
Paula Parker, *President*
EMP: 1
SALES (est): 75.6K **Privately Held**
SIC: 3911 5094 Jewel settings & mount-
   ings, precious metal; jewelry

(G-8437)
FUELCOR DEVELOPMENT LLC
906 Ridge Dr (22101-1632)
PHONE..................................703 740-0071
EMP: 2
SALES (est): 92.5K **Privately Held**
SIC: 2911 3699 Petroleum Refining Mfg
   Elec Mach/Equip/Supp

(G-8438)
GANNETT CO INC (PA)
7950 Jones Branch Dr (22102-3302)
PHONE..................................703 854-6000
Michael E Reed, *Ch of Bd*
Kurt Madden, *Editor*
Kelly Andresen, *Vice Pres*
Orestes Baez, *Vice Pres*
Bill Bolger, *Vice Pres*
EMP: 300 **Publicly Held**
WEB: www.gannett.com
SIC: 2711 7373 Newspapers, publishing &
   printing; systems integration services

(G-8439)
GANNETT HOLDINGS LLC (HQ)
7950 Jones Branch Dr (22102-3302)
PHONE..................................703 854-6000
Paul J Bascobert, *President*
EMP: 2
SALES (est): 2.9B **Publicly Held**
SIC: 2711 Newspapers, publishing & print-
   ing
PA: Gannett Co., Inc.
   7950 Jones Branch Dr
   Mc Lean VA 22102
   703 854-6000

(G-8440)
GANNETT MEDIA CORP (DH)
7950 Jones Branch Dr (22102-3302)
PHONE..................................703 854-6000
John Jeffry Louis, *Ch of Bd*
Paul J Bascobert, *President*
Maribel Perez Wadsworth, *President*
Cynthia W Barrows, *Editor*
Richard Mardekian, *Chief*
▲ EMP: 215
SQ FT: 178,551
SALES: 2.9B **Publicly Held**
WEB: www.gannett.com
SIC: 2711 7375 Newspapers, publishing &
   printing; information retrieval services
HQ: Gannett Holdings Llc
   7950 Jones Branch Dr
   Mc Lean VA 22102
   703 854-6000

(G-8441)
GANNETT OFFSET
7950 Jones Branch Dr (22107-0002)
PHONE..................................781 551-2923
EMP: 2
SALES (est): 113K **Privately Held**
WEB: www.gannett.com
SIC: 2752 Commercial printing, offset

(G-8442)
GANNETT PUBLISHING SVCS LLC (DH)
7950 Jones Branch Dr (22102-3302)
PHONE..................................703 854-6000
Mike Christopher, *General Mgr*
Dale Carpenter, *Vice Pres*
Mike Donohue, *Vice Pres*
Greg Fiorito, *Vice Pres*
Jack Saunders, *Vice Pres*
EMP: 19
SALES (est): 4.8MM **Publicly Held**
WEB: www.gannett.com
SIC: 2711 Commercial printing & newspa-
   per publishing combined
HQ: Gannett Media Corp.
   7950 Jones Branch Dr
   Mc Lean VA 22102
   703 854-6000

(G-8443)
GANNETT RIVER STATES PUBG CORP (DH)
Also Called: Arkansas Gazette, The
7950 Jones Branch Dr (22102-3302)
PHONE..................................703 284-6000
William T Malone, *Ch of Bd*
Hugh B Patterson, *Vice Ch Bd*
Craig A Moon, *President*
Donald Davis, *Vice Pres*
Ronald Krengel, *Vice Pres*
◆ EMP: 900
SALES (est): 240.3MM **Publicly Held**
WEB: www.gannett.com
SIC: 2711 2741 Newspapers, publishing &
   printing; miscellaneous publishing

HQ: Gannett Media Corp.
7950 Jones Branch Dr
Mc Lean VA 22102
703 854-6000

(G-8444)
GANNETT STLLITE INFO NTWRK LLC (DH)
Also Called: USA Today
7950 Jones Branch Dr (22102-3302)
PHONE....................703 854-6000
Douglas H Mc Corkindale, *CEO*
Tom Beusse, *President*
Robert J Dickey, *President*
Emily Bahor, *Partner*
John Bacon, *Editor*
◆ EMP: 600
SQ FT: 800,000
SALES (est): 517.7MM **Publicly Held**
WEB: www.gannett.com
SIC: 2711 Commercial printing & newspaper publishing combined
HQ: Gannett Media Corp.
7950 Jones Branch Dr
Mc Lean VA 22102
703 854-6000

(G-8445)
GCOE LLC
7950 Jones Branch Dr (22102-3302)
PHONE....................703 854-6000
EMP: 1
SALES (est): 184.9K **Publicly Held**
SIC: 2711 Newspapers, publishing & printing
HQ: Gannett Media Corp.
7950 Jones Branch Dr
Mc Lean VA 22102
703 854-6000

(G-8446)
GEEBO INC
1350 Beverly Rd Apt 218 (22101-3900)
PHONE....................888 439-3113
Greg Collier, *Principal*
EMP: 3 EST: 2010
SALES (est): 200K **Privately Held**
WEB: www.geebo.com
SIC: 3532 Classifiers (metallurgical or mining machinery)

(G-8447)
GENFORMAX LLC
7918 Jones Branch Dr # 540 (22102-3366)
PHONE....................703 346-7445
EMP: 2
SALES (est): 99.7K **Privately Held**
WEB: www.genformax.com
SIC: 3652 Pre-recorded records & tapes

(G-8448)
GETSAT NORTH AMERICA INC
1750 Tysons Blvd Ste 1500 (22102-4200)
PHONE....................571 308-2451
Kfir Benjamin, *Director*
Mark Klein, *Administration*
EMP: 20
SQ FT: 100
SALES (est): 977.5K **Privately Held**
WEB: www.getsat.com
SIC: 3663 Space satellite communications equipment
PA: Get Sat Communications Ltd
27 Eli Hurvitz
Rehovot 76088

(G-8449)
GLOBAL TELECOM GROUP INC (PA)
8220 Crestwood Heights Dr # 1401 (22102-3138)
PHONE....................571 291-9631
Ahmed Farrukh, *Principal*
EMP: 7
SALES (est): 16.3MM **Privately Held**
WEB: www.globaltelecomgroup.com
SIC: 2079 Edible fats & oils

(G-8450)
GLOBAL X PRESS
660 Chain Bridge Rd (22101-1810)
PHONE....................202 417-2070
EMP: 2
SALES (est): 62.9K **Privately Held**
SIC: 2711 Newspapers

(G-8451)
GO VIVACE INC
1616 Anderson Rd Ste 303 (22102-1602)
PHONE....................703 869-9463
Magendre Goel, *CEO*
Vandana Goel, *President*
EMP: 3
SALES (est): 500K **Privately Held**
WEB: www.govivace.com
SIC: 7372 7389 Educational computer software; business services

(G-8452)
GORMANLEE INDUSTRIES LLC
1021 Savile Ln (22101-1830)
PHONE....................703 448-1948
Andrew Lee, *Principal*
EMP: 2 EST: 2014
SALES (est): 80.5K **Privately Held**
SIC: 3999 Manufacturing industries

(G-8453)
GRADIENT DYNAMICS LLC
604 Boyle Ln (22102-1404)
PHONE....................865 207-9052
Dendy Young,
EMP: 3
SALES (est): 305.3K **Privately Held**
SIC: 3812 7389 Antennas, radar or communications; business services

(G-8454)
GWEN GRABER & ASSOCIATES
1617 Bryan Branch Rd (22101-4102)
PHONE....................703 356-9239
Gwen Graber, *Owner*
EMP: 2
SALES (est): 100K **Privately Held**
SIC: 2741 Miscellaneous publishing

(G-8455)
H MOSS DESIGN
1208 Old Stable Rd (22102-2419)
PHONE....................703 356-7824
Harriet Moss, *Owner*
EMP: 1
SALES (est): 94.9K **Privately Held**
SIC: 2253 Sweaters & sweater coats, knit

(G-8456)
HEALTHY CHEF CREATIONS
5922 Autumn Dr (22101-2502)
PHONE....................407 339-2433
John Procacci, *President*
Shannon Grayer, *Manager*
EMP: 20 EST: 2011
SALES (est): 2.4MM **Privately Held**
WEB: www.healthychefcreations.com
SIC: 2048 Prepared feeds

(G-8457)
HENRY SCHEIN
1420 Beverly Rd Ste 350 (22101-3730)
PHONE....................703 883-8031
EMP: 2
SALES (est): 115.8K **Privately Held**
SIC: 3843 Dental equipment & supplies

(G-8458)
HEYTOPIA LLC
8421 Broad St Unit 1516 (22102-3768)
PHONE....................703 794-3082
EMP: 2
SALES (est): 56.5K **Privately Held**
SIC: 7372 7371 Application computer software; computer software development & applications

(G-8459)
HOTBED TECHNOLOGIES INC
6718 Whittier Ave Ste 100 (22101-4531)
PHONE....................703 462-2350
Don Eckrod, *CEO*
EMP: 13 EST: 2010
SALES (est): 1MM **Privately Held**
WEB: www.hotbedtech.com
SIC: 7372 Prepackaged software

(G-8460)
IAEVA MERCANTILE LLC
6611 Denny Pl (22101-5505)
PHONE....................301 523-6566
Evert McDowell,
EMP: 1 EST: 2017

SALES (est): 51.2K **Privately Held**
SIC: 3483 Ammunition, except for small arms

(G-8461)
IDS PUBLISHING CORPORATION
7730 Bridle Path Ln (22102-2523)
P.O. Box 389, Worthington OH (43085-0389)
PHONE....................703 821-2323
Maggi Reiss, *President*
Michel Reiss, *Vice Pres*
Benjamin Reiss, *Admin Sec*
EMP: 1
SALES (est): 250K **Privately Held**
WEB: www.idspublishing.com
SIC: 2741 7372 2731 Miscellaneous publishing; prepackaged software; books: publishing only

(G-8462)
IFEXO LLC
7902 Tysons One Pl (22102-5202)
PHONE....................443 856-7705
Vitaliy Hayda,
EMP: 1
SALES (est): 35.8K **Privately Held**
SIC: 7372 Business oriented computer software

(G-8463)
IG PETROLEUM LLC
1420 Spring Hill Rd # 600 (22102-3030)
P.O. Box 4229 (22103-4229)
PHONE....................703 749-1780
Robert Hallmark, *Mng Member*
EMP: 12
SALES (est): 1.4MM **Privately Held**
SIC: 2999 Coke

(G-8464)
ILEEN SHEFFERMAN DESIGNS
Also Called: Wearable Art
6460 Madison Ct (22101-4137)
PHONE....................703 821-3261
Iileen Shefferman, *Owner*
EMP: 1
SALES (est): 41.2K **Privately Held**
SIC: 3961 Jewelry apparel, non-precious metals

(G-8465)
INT DIAGNOSTIC SYST
7730 Bridle Path Ln (22102-2523)
PHONE....................414 477-8035
EMP: 2
SALES (est): 79.8K **Privately Held**
SIC: 2741 Miscellaneous publishing

(G-8466)
INTELLIGENT SOFTWARE DESIGN
6728 Pine Creek Ct (22101-5519)
PHONE....................703 731-9091
Mikhail Velikovich, *President*
EMP: 2
SALES (est): 121.5K **Privately Held**
SIC: 7372 Prepackaged software

(G-8467)
INTER-AMERICAN GROUP INC
1800 Old Meadow Rd # 1002 (22102-1823)
PHONE....................202 255-4528
Augusto Sanabria, *Administration*
EMP: 2 EST: 2012
SALES (est): 89K **Privately Held**
SIC: 2741 Miscellaneous publishing

(G-8468)
INTERNATIONAL WINE REVIEW HQ
6625 Old Chesterbrook Rd (22101-4612)
PHONE....................703 448-5566
Mike Potashnik, *Publisher*
Don Winkler, *Editor*
Donald Winkler, *Editor*
EMP: 2 EST: 2017
SALES (est): 69.2K **Privately Held**
WEB: www.i-winereview.com
SIC: 2084 Wines, brandy & brandy spirits

(G-8469)
IRIDIUM COMMUNICATIONS INC (PA)
1750 Tysons Blvd Ste 1400 (22102-4244)
PHONE....................703 287-7400
Matthew J Desch, *CEO*
Robert H Niehaus, *Ch of Bd*
Suzanne E McBride, *COO*
Bryan J Hartin, *Exec VP*
Scott T Scheimreif, *Exec VP*
EMP: 31
SQ FT: 30,600
SALES (est): 560.4MM **Publicly Held**
WEB: www.iridium.com
SIC: 3663 4899 Radio & TV communications equipment; data communication services

(G-8470)
IRIDIUM HOLDINGS LLC (HQ)
1750 Tysons Blvd Ste 1400 (22102-4244)
PHONE....................703 287-7400
Matthew J Desch, *CEO*
Michael Smith, *Exec Dir*
EMP: 3
SALES (est): 35.2MM **Publicly Held**
WEB: www.iridium.com
SIC: 3663 Radio & TV communications equipment

(G-8471)
IRIDIUM SATELLITE LLC (DH)
1750 Tysons Blvd Ste 1400 (22102-4244)
PHONE....................703 356-0484
Matthew J Desch, *CEO*
S Scott Smith, *COO*
Bryan J Hartin, *Exec VP*
Scott T Scheimreif, *Exec VP*
Timothy Kapalka, *Vice Pres*
▲ EMP: 27
SALES (est): 35.2MM **Publicly Held**
WEB: www.iridium.com
SIC: 3663 Satellites, communications

(G-8472)
ISELFSCHOOLING
1202 Buchanan St (22101-2943)
PHONE....................703 821-3282
EMP: 2 EST: 2017
SALES (est): 97.2K **Privately Held**
WEB: www.iselfschooling.com
SIC: 7372 Prepackaged software

(G-8473)
ISKOYISAL INC
1648 Westwind Way (22102-1604)
PHONE....................703 992-6629
EMP: 2
SALES (est): 96.8K **Privately Held**
SIC: 7372 Prepackaged software

(G-8474)
ITT DEFENSE & ELECTRONICS
1650 Tysons Blvd Ste 1700 (22102-4827)
PHONE....................703 790-6300
Marvin R Sambur, *CEO*
Henry Driese, *President*
Karl Pierson, *VP Admin*
Jack Murrel, *Vice Pres*
Mark Lang, *CFO*
EMP: 1148
SQ FT: 120,000
SALES (est): 91.5MM **Publicly Held**
WEB: www.harris.com
SIC: 3679 3678 3674 3769 Electronic circuits; electronic connectors; semiconductors & related devices; guided missile & space vehicle parts & auxiliary equipment; ordnance & accessories
HQ: Itt Llc
1133 Westchester Ave N-100
White Plains NY 10604
914 641-2000

(G-8475)
JOE PRODUCTS INC
1350 Beverly Rd 115-416 (22101-3961)
PHONE....................314 409-4477
Dan Kliska, *CEO*
EMP: 3
SALES (est): 220K **Privately Held**
SIC: 3999 Hair & hair-based products

(G-8476)
JR BERNARD HEARN
Also Called: Rare-Rocks Curation
958 Saigon Rd (22102-2119)
PHONE.................703 821-1373
Bernard Carter Hearn Jr, *Owner*
EMP: 1
SALES (est): 76.9K **Privately Held**
SIC: 2819 Industrial inorganic chemicals

(G-8477)
KALEIDOSCOPE PUBLISHING LTD
1420 Spring Hill Rd # 490 (22102-3006)
PHONE.................703 821-0571
Declan Bransfield, *Owner*
EMP: 20
SALES (est): 638.7K **Privately Held**
SIC: 2741 Newsletter publishing

(G-8478)
KATZ HADRIAN
1324 Lancia Dr (22102-2204)
PHONE.................202 942-5707
EMP: 2
SALES (est): 90K **Privately Held**
SIC: 3679 Mfg Electronic Components

(G-8479)
KEY BRIDGE GLOBAL LLC
8416 Holly Leaf Dr (22102-2224)
PHONE.................703 414-3500
Jesse Caulfield, *Administration*
EMP: 2
SALES (est): 158.2K **Privately Held**
WEB: www.keybridgeglobal.com
SIC: 3441 4813 7371 3663 Tower sections, radio & television transmission; ; computer software development & applications; radio receiver networks

(G-8480)
KIMBERLYS
7022 Old Dominion Dr (22101-2647)
PHONE.................703 448-7298
Kim Kovanic, *Owner*
EMP: 2 **EST:** 2017
SALES (est): 62.3K **Privately Held**
SIC: 2051 Bread, cake & related products

(G-8481)
L3HARRIS TECHNOLOGIES INC
Also Called: Exelis
1650 Tysons Blvd (22102-4856)
P.O. Box 9007, Melbourne FL (32902-9007)
PHONE.................703 790-6300
Matt Griffin, *Engrg Dir*
Edward Mienko, *Chief Engr*
Jeffery Schweiger, *Engineer*
Douglas Turnipseed, *IT/INT Sup*
EMP: 163
SALES (corp-wide): 6.8B **Publicly Held**
WEB: www.harris.com
SIC: 3812 Space vehicle guidance systems & equipment
PA: L3harris Technologies, Inc.
1025 W Nasa Blvd
Melbourne FL 32919
321 727-9100

(G-8482)
LAUREN E THRONSON
1944 Valleywood Rd (22101-4930)
PHONE.................703 536-3625
Lauren Thronson, *Owner*
EMP: 1
SALES (est): 37.5K **Privately Held**
SIC: 2741 Miscellaneous publishing

(G-8483)
LEE TALBOT ASSOCIATES INC
Also Called: T R A
6656 Chilton Ct (22101-4422)
PHONE.................703 734-8576
Lee Talbot, *President*
Martha Talbot, *Admin Sec*
EMP: 2
SALES (est): 172.2K **Privately Held**
SIC: 3799 Off-road automobiles, except recreational vehicles

(G-8484)
LEHR INC (PA)
Also Called: McLean Copy
1356 Beverly Rd Ste 180 (22101-3625)
PHONE.................703 821-2679
Gregory Lehr, *President*
EMP: 3
SQ FT: 900
SALES (est): 325K **Privately Held**
WEB: www.mcleancopy.com
SIC: 2752 Commercial printing, offset

(G-8485)
LEIDOS INC
7927 Jones Branch Dr # 200 (22102-3322)
PHONE.................703 734-5315
Gary Lusriu, *Manager*
EMP: 38 **Publicly Held**
WEB: www.leidos.com
SIC: 3577 Computer peripheral equipment
HQ: Leidos, Inc.
1750 Presidents St
Reston VA 20190
571 526-6000

(G-8486)
LEIGH ANN CARRASCO
Also Called: Womeldorf Press
7107 Sea Cliff Rd (22101-5031)
PHONE.................703 725-4680
Leigh Ann Carrasco, *Owner*
EMP: 1
SALES (est): 39.6K **Privately Held**
SIC: 2731 7389 Books: publishing only;

(G-8487)
LOCAL ENERGY TECHNOLOGIES
Also Called: Let Global
1111 Wimbledon Dr (22101-2937)
PHONE.................717 371-0041
Luke Schoenfelder, *Principal*
EMP: 5
SALES (est): 217.9K **Privately Held**
SIC: 3577 3825 4931 Computer peripheral equipment; instruments to measure electricity; electric & other services combined

(G-8488)
LOCATION BSED SVCS CONTENT LLC
1419 Mayhurst Blvd (22102-2236)
PHONE.................703 622-1490
Charles Dimeglio,
EMP: 1
SALES (est): 76.5K **Privately Held**
SIC: 7372 Business oriented computer software

(G-8489)
LOCKWOOD SOFTWARE ENGRG INC
1409 Mayhurst Blvd (22102-2236)
PHONE.................202 494-7886
Shirley Lockwood, *President*
Jerard Lockwood, *Vice Pres*
EMP: 13
SALES (est): 849.9K **Privately Held**
WEB: www.lockwoodsoftware.com
SIC: 7372 7371 Prepackaged software; computer software systems analysis & design, custom

(G-8490)
LUNANO INC
6602 Mclean Ct (22101-4001)
PHONE.................202 594-2959
Bradley Kevin Duckworth, *President*
EMP: 3
SALES (est): 123.2K **Privately Held**
SIC: 2842 Disinfectants, household or industrial plant

(G-8491)
MARS INCORPORATED (PA)
6885 Elm St Ste 1 (22101-6038)
PHONE.................703 821-4900
Grant Reid, *President*
Tracey Massey, *President*
Lisa Sabatino, *President*
Helen Mills, *Vice Pres*
Marc Turcan, *Vice Pres*
◆ **EMP:** 300 **EST:** 1952
SQ FT: 30,000

SALES (est): 48.6B **Privately Held**
WEB: www.mars.com
SIC: 2024 2066 2064 5812 Ice cream, packaged: molded, on sticks, etc.; chocolate candy, solid; candy & other confectionery products; chocolate candy, except solid chocolate; candy bars, including chocolate covered bars; caterers; pet foods; pet food

(G-8492)
MARS LOGIC LLC
6507 Smoot Dr (22101-4003)
PHONE.................510 220-7117
Sivakumar Dandamudi, *Principal*
EMP: 2
SALES (est): 95.5K **Privately Held**
WEB: www.mars.com
SIC: 2064 Candy & other confectionery products

(G-8493)
MARS OVERSEAS HOLDINGS INC (HQ)
Also Called: Effem Food
6885 Elm St Ste 1 (22101-6038)
PHONE.................703 821-4900
Forrest Mars, *President*
Lance Black, *Accounts Mgr*
Pat Heffern, *Manager*
Catherine Terwilliger, *Manager*
Jennifer Bongiovanni, *Executive Asst*
EMP: 9
SALES (est): 19.5MM
SALES (corp-wide): 48.6B **Privately Held**
WEB: www.mars.com
SIC: 2047 Dog food
PA: Mars, Incorporated
6885 Elm St Ste 1
Mc Lean VA 22101
703 821-4900

(G-8494)
MARS PETCARE US INC
6885 Elm St (22101-6031)
PHONE.................703 821-4900
EMP: 64
SALES (corp-wide): 48.6B **Privately Held**
WEB: www.williamsonchamber.com
SIC: 2047 Cat food
HQ: Mars Petcare Us, Inc.
2013 Ovation Pkwy
Franklin TN 37067
615 807-4626

(G-8495)
MATRE INC (HQ)
6885 Elm St (22101-6031)
PHONE.................703 821-4927
Alberto Mora, *President*
O C Goudet, *Vice Pres*
EMP: 4
SALES (est): 12.8MM
SALES (corp-wide): 48.6B **Privately Held**
SIC: 2064 Lollipops & other hard candy
PA: Mars, Incorporated
6885 Elm St Ste 1
Mc Lean VA 22101
703 821-4900

(G-8496)
MAUREEN MELVILLE
1909 Massachusetts Ave (22101-4908)
PHONE.................703 533-2448
EMP: 1
SALES (est): 67.8K **Privately Held**
SIC: 3231 Mfg Products-Purchased Glass

(G-8497)
MEAT & WOOL NEW ZEALAND LTD
1483 Chain Bridge Rd # 300 (22101-5703)
PHONE.................703 927-4817
EMP: 2
SALES (est): 62.3K **Privately Held**
SIC: 2011 Meat packing plants

(G-8498)
MEMORYBLUE
7925 Jones Branch Dr # 4100 (22102-3382)
PHONE.................703 891-3840
EMP: 7
SALES (est): 506.6K **Privately Held**
WEB: www.memoryblue.com
SIC: 3652 Pre-recorded records & tapes

(G-8499)
METOCEAN TELEMATICS INC
1750 Tysons Blvd Ste 1500 (22102-4200)
PHONE.................902 468-2505
Tony Chedrawy, *CEO*
EMP: 4
SALES (est): 208.8K **Privately Held**
WEB: www.metocean.com
SIC: 3679 Electronic circuits

(G-8500)
MFGS INC
1430 Spring Hill Rd # 401 (22102-3000)
PHONE.................844 267-9266
Craig Abod, *Principal*
EMP: 6
SALES (est): 598K **Privately Held**
WEB: www.mfgsinc.com
SIC: 3999 Manufacturing industries

(G-8501)
MILLERS FURS INC
Also Called: Furseller
7921 Jones Branch Dr LI2 (22102-3306)
PHONE.................703 772-4593
Mark Miller, *President*
EMP: 1 **EST:** 2004
SALES (est): 110K **Privately Held**
WEB: www.furseller.com
SIC: 2371 5621 Apparel, fur; maternity wear

(G-8502)
MINUTEMAN PRESS OF MC LEAN
6821 Tennyson Dr (22101-4547)
PHONE.................703 356-6612
David Coyle, *Principal*
EMP: 4
SQ FT: 1,000
SALES (est): 475.5K **Privately Held**
WEB: www.minutemanpress.com
SIC: 2752 7334 2759 7336 Commercial printing, lithographic; photocopying & duplicating services; promotional printing; commercial art & graphic design; advertising, promotional & trade show services; marketing consulting services

(G-8503)
MISRA PUBLISHING LLC
1258 Beverly Rd (22101-2833)
PHONE.................703 821-2985
Nancy Bracy, *Administration*
EMP: 1
SALES (est): 80.7K **Privately Held**
SIC: 2741 Miscellaneous publishing

(G-8504)
MOBITRUM CORPORATION
6875 Churchill Rd (22101-2832)
PHONE.................301 793-4728
Ray Wang, *CEO*
EMP: 5
SQ FT: 2,000
SALES (est): 400K **Privately Held**
WEB: www.mobitrum.com
SIC: 3661 Telephone cords, jacks, adapters, etc.

(G-8505)
MOLDING LIGHT LLC
6902 Lemon Rd (22101-5423)
PHONE.................703 847-0232
Martha Galvin, *Principal*
EMP: 3 **EST:** 2012
SALES (est): 177.7K **Privately Held**
SIC: 3089 Molding primary plastic

(G-8506)
MOON CONSORTIUM LLC
6628 Ivy Hill Dr (22101-5206)
PHONE.................571 408-9570
Sun-Chan Moon,
EMP: 1
SALES (est): 37.5K **Privately Held**
SIC: 2741

(G-8507)
MORRIS MOUNTAINEER OIL GAS LLC
1411 Mayflower Dr (22101-5613)
PHONE.................703 283-9700
Mark B Van Kirk, *Principal*
EMP: 2 **EST:** 2016

(PA)=Parent Co (HQ)=Headquarters (DH)=Div Headquarters
✪ = New Business established in last 2 years

2021 Virginia
Industrial Directory

287

GEOGRAPHIC

SALES (est): 126.5K **Privately Held**
SIC: 1389 Oil & gas field services

(G-8508)
N A D A SERVICES CORPORATION
8400 Westpark Dr Ste 1 (22102-3522)
PHONE......................................703 821-7000
Phillip Brady, *President*
Terri Collins, *Manager*
RE Malaise, *MIS Staff*
Melissa Wolpert, *Director*
Reinaldo Funes, *Representative*
EMP: 200
SQ FT: 168,000
SALES (est): 15.4MM
SALES (corp-wide): 90.2MM **Privately Held**
WEB: www.nada.org
SIC: 2741 8111 Guides: publishing only, not printed on site; newsletter publishing; legal services
PA: National Automobile Dealers Association
8484 Westpark Dr Ste 500
Tysons VA 22102
800 557-6232

(G-8509)
NAJ ENTERPRISES LLP
1857 Massachusetts Ave (22101-4906)
PHONE......................................202 251-7821
Nancy Najarian, *Partner*
K George Najarian, *Partner*
▼ EMP: 1
SALES (est): 80K **Privately Held**
WEB: www.clipitsystems.com
SIC: 3089 5162 8742 8748 Closures, plastic; plastics materials & basic shapes; management consulting services; administrative services consultant; communications consulting

(G-8510)
NAYLOR CMG
1430 Spring Hill Rd Fl 6 (22102-3000)
PHONE......................................703 934-4714
Alex Debarr, *Principal*
Tom Aley, *Vice Pres*
EMP: 2
SALES (est): 124.5K **Privately Held**
WEB: www.naylor.com
SIC: 2741 Miscellaneous publishing

(G-8511)
NORTHROP GRUMMAN CORPORATION
Also Called: Northrop Grumman Info Systems
7575 Colshire Dr (22102-7508)
PHONE......................................703 556-1144
Linda A Mills, *Division Pres*
Rich Boak, *Vice Pres*
Charlton Walker, *Vice Pres*
James Beins, *Engineer*
Adrienne Mallett, *Engineer*
EMP: 6 **Publicly Held**
WEB: www.northropgrumman.com
SIC: 3812 Search & navigation equipment
PA: Northrop Grumman Corporation
2980 Fairview Park Dr
Falls Church VA 22042

(G-8512)
NORTHROP GRUMMAN INTL INC
7575 Colshire Dr (22102-7508)
PHONE......................................703 556-1144
Dan Shoemaker, *Branch Mgr*
EMP: 8 **Publicly Held**
WEB: www.northropgrumman.com
SIC: 3812 Search & navigation equipment
HQ: Northrop Grumman International, Inc.
2980 Fairview Park Dr
Falls Church VA 22042

(G-8513)
NORTHROP GRUMMAN SYSTEMS CORP
Also Called: Defense Group
7575 Colshire Dr (22102-7508)
PHONE......................................703 556-1144
Janet Chilson, *Sr Associate*
Josh Cantor, *Associate*
Joni Frank, *Associate*
EMP: 73 **Publicly Held**
WEB: www.northropgrumman.com

SIC: 3812 Search & navigation equipment
HQ: Northrop Grumman Systems Corporation
2980 Fairview Park Dr
Falls Church VA 22042
703 280-2900

(G-8514)
NORTHROP GRUMMAN SYSTEMS CORP
Also Called: Idiq Pmo
7575 Colshire Dr (22102-7508)
PHONE......................................703 556-1144
EMP: 310 **Publicly Held**
WEB: www.northropgrumman.com
SIC: 3812 Search & navigation equipment
HQ: Northrop Grumman Systems Corporation
2980 Fairview Park Dr
Falls Church VA 22042
703 280-2900

(G-8515)
NORTHROP GRUMMAN SYSTEMS CORP
Also Called: Civilian Agencies
7575 Colshire Dr (22102-7508)
PHONE......................................703 556-1144
Robert Tagg, *Branch Mgr*
EMP: 172 **Publicly Held**
WEB: www.northropgrumman.com
SIC: 3812 Search & navigation equipment
HQ: Northrop Grumman Systems Corporation
2980 Fairview Park Dr
Falls Church VA 22042
703 280-2900

(G-8516)
NORTHROP GRUMMAN SYSTEMS CORP
Also Called: Defense Systems Sector
7575 Colshire Dr (22102-7508)
PHONE......................................703 556-1144
Mark Eichin, *Engineer*
Aaron Henry, *Engineer*
Michael Ray, *Engineer*
Kimberly Knechtly, *Manager*
Steve Marietti, *Manager*
EMP: 30 **Publicly Held**
WEB: www.northropgrumman.com
SIC: 3812 Search & navigation equipment
HQ: Northrop Grumman Systems Corporation
2980 Fairview Park Dr
Falls Church VA 22042
703 280-2900

(G-8517)
NORTHROP GRUMMAN SYSTEMS CORP
Also Called: Northrop Grumman Info Systems
7575 Colshire Dr (22102-7508)
PHONE......................................703 556-1144
Jim Myers, *Manager*
EMP: 326 **Publicly Held**
WEB: www.northropgrumman.com
SIC: 3721 Airplanes, fixed or rotary wing
HQ: Northrop Grumman Systems Corporation
2980 Fairview Park Dr
Falls Church VA 22042
703 280-2900

(G-8518)
NORTHROP GRUMMAN SYSTEMS CORP
Also Called: Northrop Grumman Info Systems
7575 Colshire Dr (22102-7508)
PHONE......................................703 556-1144
Jim Myers, *Manager*
EMP: 229 **Publicly Held**
WEB: www.northropgrumman.com
SIC: 3812 Search & navigation equipment
HQ: Northrop Grumman Systems Corporation
2980 Fairview Park Dr
Falls Church VA 22042
703 280-2900

(G-8519)
NORTONLIFELOCK INC
Also Called: Symantec
8180 Greensboro Dr # 575 (22102-3888)
PHONE......................................703 883-0180

EMP: 2
SALES (corp-wide): 2.4B **Publicly Held**
WEB: www.broadcom.com
SIC: 7372 Prepackaged software
PA: Nortonlifelock Inc.
60 E Rio Salado Pkwy # 1
Tempe AZ 85281
650 527-8000

(G-8520)
OBJECTVIDEO LABS LLC
8281 Greensboro Dr # 100 (22102-5211)
PHONE......................................571 327-3673
Jeff Bedell, *President*
Catherine Scavello,
EMP: 28
SALES (est): 70.8K
SALES (corp-wide): 502.3MM **Publicly Held**
WEB: www.objectvideolabs.com
SIC: 7372 Prepackaged software
PA: Alarm.Com Holdings, Inc.
8281 Greensboro Dr # 100
Tysons VA 22102
877 389-4033

(G-8521)
OTERO KUCBEL ENTERPRISES INC
1350 Snow Meadow Ln (22102-2528)
PHONE......................................703 734-0209
Gladies Kucbel, *President*
EMP: 2
SALES (est): 111K **Privately Held**
SIC: 3914 Silverware, sterling silver

(G-8522)
PACIFIC AND SOUTHERN COMPANY
7950 Jones Branch Dr (22102-3302)
PHONE......................................703 854-6899
Dave Lougee, *Principal*
Linda Carducci, *Manager*
EMP: 99
SALES (est): 950K **Privately Held**
WEB: www.guampdn.com
SIC: 3663 Studio equipment, radio & television broadcasting

(G-8523)
PAPER & PACKAGING BOARD
8200 Greensboro Dr # 1175 (22102-3841)
PHONE......................................703 935-5386
Mary Anne Hansan, *President*
Steven Voorhees, *Chairman*
Kevin Burkum, *Senior VP*
Jill Seibert, *CFO*
Jennifer L Miller, *Treasurer*
EMP: 3
SALES (est): 291.9K **Privately Held**
WEB: www.paperandpackaging.org
SIC: 2621 Wrapping & packaging papers; packaging paper; condenser paper

(G-8524)
PB & J PUBLISHING LLC
7714 Carlton Pl (22102-2149)
PHONE......................................703 903-9561
Stuart Stein, *Principal*
EMP: 2
SALES (est): 104.8K **Privately Held**
SIC: 2741 Miscellaneous publishing

(G-8525)
PERMISSIONBIT INC
1750 Tysons Blvd Ste 1500 (22102-4200)
PHONE......................................703 278-3832
Ronnie Mainieri, *CEO*
EMP: 4
SALES (est): 198.4K **Privately Held**
WEB: www.permissionbit.com
SIC: 7372 Business oriented computer software

(G-8526)
PERSONAM INC
1420 Spring Hill Rd # 525 (22102-3006)
PHONE......................................571 297-9371
John Kauffman, *CEO*
Thad Scheer, *President*
Theresa Smith, *Treasurer*
Erik Stein, *Admin Sec*
EMP: 1
SQ FT: 7,500

SALES (est): 80.4K **Privately Held**
WEB: www.personaminc.com
SIC: 7372 Business oriented computer software

(G-8527)
PGENOMEX INC
1557 Mary Ellen Ct (22101-5022)
PHONE......................................703 343-3282
John F Deeken, *CEO*
EMP: 2
SALES (est): 126.4K **Privately Held**
SIC: 2835 In vitro & in vivo diagnostic substances

(G-8528)
PHILIP MILES
1532 Lincoln Way Apt 303 (22102-5886)
PHONE......................................703 760-9832
EMP: 1 EST: 2017
SALES (est): 37.5K **Privately Held**
SIC: 2741 Miscellaneous Publishing, Nsk

(G-8529)
PHOTO FINALE INC
1420 Spring Hill Rd # 600 (22102-3006)
PHONE......................................703 564-3400
Stephen Giordano, *Principal*
Jason Pareti, *CTO*
EMP: 19 EST: 2013
SALES (est): 1.6MM **Privately Held**
WEB: www.photofinale.com
SIC: 7372 Prepackaged software

(G-8530)
PLAYER PURSUITS LLC
1308 Vincent Pl Fl 2 (22101-3614)
PHONE......................................202 207-6000
Jeffrey D Hokenson,
EMP: 2
SALES (est): 25K **Privately Held**
SIC: 7372 Publishers' computer software

(G-8531)
PRIMATICS FINANCIAL LLC (HQ)
8401 Greensboro Dr # 300 (22102-5126)
PHONE......................................703 342-0040
Kevin J Hesselbirg, *CEO*
Nabil Qureshi, *Business Mgr*
Jeff Sant, *Exec VP*
Umar Syyid, *Exec VP*
Michael Therrien, *Exec VP*
EMP: 99
SALES (est): 38.2MM
SALES (corp-wide): 4.6B **Publicly Held**
WEB: www.primaticsfinancial.com
SIC: 7372 Prepackaged software
PA: Ss&C Technologies Holdings, Inc.
80 Lamberton Rd
Windsor CT 06095
860 298-4500

(G-8532)
RAPID MAT GROUP LLC
1600 Tysons Blvd Fl 8 (22102-4872)
PHONE......................................703 629-2426
EMP: 3 EST: 2011
SALES (est): 260K **Privately Held**
SIC: 3339 Primary Nonferrous Metal Producer

(G-8533)
RAYTHEON APPLIED SGNAL TECH IN
7925 Jones Branch Dr # 1200 (22102-3365)
PHONE......................................571 484-9373
Michael Liggett, *President*
EMP: 6
SALES (corp-wide): 77B **Publicly Held**
WEB: www.rtx.com
SIC: 3812 Search & navigation equipment
HQ: Raytheon Applied Signal Technology, Inc.
460 W California Ave
Sunnyvale CA 94086
408 749-1888

(G-8534)
READSPEAKER LLC
1600 Tysons Blvd Fl 8 (22102-4872)
PHONE......................................703 462-8738
Paul Kim, *Business Mgr*
Joop Heijenrath, *COO*
Charles Meyer, *Engineer*
Riccardo Vanzetti, *Sales Staff*

Lotta Bergstrom, *Office Mgr*
EMP: 3 **EST:** 2019
SALES (est): 123.4K **Privately Held**
SIC: 7372 Prepackaged software

(G-8535)
RED ACTION BLUE INFO LLC
7911 Westpark Dr Apt 2501 (22102-4319)
PHONE..........................703 474-2617
Justin B Li, *Branch Mgr*
EMP: 1
SALES (corp-wide): 374.4K **Privately Held**
SIC: 2389 Men's miscellaneous accessories
PA: Red Action Blue Information, Llc
6604 Chevy Chase Ave
Dallas TX 75225
469 224-7673

(G-8536)
RED HAT INC
8260 Greensboro Dr # 300 (22102-4901)
PHONE..........................703 748-2201
Lynne Chamberlain, *VP Bus Dvlpt*
William Zewe, *Branch Mgr*
Kyle Jensen, *Manager*
Christopher Basquez, *Director*
Rita Carroll, *Director*
EMP: 15
SALES (corp-wide): 77.1B **Publicly Held**
WEB: www.redhat.com
SIC: 7372 Operating systems computer software
HQ: Red Hat, Inc.
100 E Davie St
Raleigh NC 27601

(G-8537)
RET CORP
8300 Greensboro Dr # 620 (22102-3605)
PHONE..........................703 471-8108
Donald Maffei, *Vice Pres*
EMP: 1
SALES (est): 114.4K **Privately Held**
WEB: www.maffeifinancial.com
SIC: 3572 Computer storage devices

(G-8538)
RISING EDGE TECHNOLOGIES INC
8300 Greensboro Dr # 620 (22102-3605)
PHONE..........................703 471-8108
Don Maffei, *President*
Michael Lewis, *Vice Pres*
EMP: 6
SQ FT: 8,000
SALES (est): 768.4K **Privately Held**
WEB: www.risingedge.com
SIC: 3572 7371 Computer storage devices; custom computer programming services

(G-8539)
RIVERLAND INC
Also Called: Fastsigns
1980 Chain Bridge Rd (22102-4002)
PHONE..........................703 760-9300
Charles Manns, *President*
Chuck Manns, *Human Res Mgr*
Sarah Manns, *Manager*
EMP: 6
SALES (est): 738.4K **Privately Held**
WEB: www.fastsigns.com
SIC: 3993 Signs & advertising specialties

(G-8540)
ROCAMED INC
2010 Corp Rdg Ste 700 (22102)
PHONE..........................703 503-3616
Laurent Donchegay, *President*
EMP: 2
SALES (est): 127.5K **Privately Held**
SIC: 3841 Surgical & medical instruments

(G-8541)
S SOFTWARE DEVELOPMENT SYSTEM
1359 Northwyck Ct (22102-2614)
PHONE..........................571 633-0554
EMP: 2
SALES (est): 56.5K **Privately Held**
SIC: 7372 Prepackaged software

(G-8542)
SAGE SOFTWARE INC
1750 Old Madow Rd Ste 300 (22102)
PHONE..........................503 439-5271
Chrystina Aros-Portillo, *Partner*
Daniel Brookbanks, *Sales Staff*
Kimberly Creamore, *Marketing Staff*
Geoff Merten, *Marketing Staff*
Shari Lawrence, *Branch Mgr*
EMP: 4
SALES (corp-wide): 2.4B **Privately Held**
WEB: www.na.sage.com
SIC: 7372 Business oriented computer software
HQ: Sage Software, Inc.
271 17th St Nw Ste 1100
Atlanta GA 30363
866 996-7243

(G-8543)
SALSA ROOM
1524 Spring Hill Rd (22102-3007)
PHONE..........................571 489-8422
EMP: 3
SALES (est): 173.4K **Privately Held**
SIC: 2099 Dips, except cheese & sour cream based

(G-8544)
SAMBUQCOM INC
1600 Tysons Blvd Ste 800 (22102-4872)
PHONE..........................703 980-8669
Ganesh Rajagopal, *CEO*
EMP: 2
SALES (est): 71.9K **Privately Held**
SIC: 2741

(G-8545)
SAPENTIA LLC
8220 Crestwood Heights Dr (22102-3119)
PHONE..........................703 269-7191
John Dunbar, *Mng Member*
Yeon O Dunbar,
EMP: 2 **EST:** 2015
SALES (est): 350K **Privately Held**
SIC: 3724 7389 Aircraft engines & engine parts;

(G-8546)
SHENOX PHARMACEUTICALS LLC
1765 Greensboro Sta (22102-3467)
PHONE..........................732 309-2419
Hock Tan,
EMP: 2
SALES (est): 79.5K **Privately Held**
SIC: 2834 Pharmaceutical preparations

(G-8547)
SIR SPEEDY PRINTING CTR 7411
8616 Old Dominion Dr (22102-1216)
PHONE..........................703 821-8781
Robert Kenny, *Principal*
EMP: 2
SALES (est): 146.6K **Privately Held**
WEB: www.sirspeedy.com
SIC: 2752 Commercial printing, lithographic

(G-8548)
SMITH CABINETS
1441 Colleen Ln (22101-3106)
PHONE..........................703 790-9896
Harold Smith, *Owner*
Mary Smith, *Treasurer*
EMP: 2
SALES (est): 115.9K **Privately Held**
SIC: 2599 Cabinets, factory

(G-8549)
SOCCER BRIDGE
6627 Tucker Ave (22101-5272)
PHONE..........................703 356-0462
Susan Gordon Castle, *Co-Owner*
EMP: 2
SALES (est): 117.5K **Privately Held**
SIC: 3949 8699 Team sports equipment; charitable organization

(G-8550)
SOFT EDGE INC
6888 Elm St Ste 2c (22101-3829)
P.O. Box 460 (22101-0460)
PHONE..........................703 442-8353
Robert Zehnder, *President*

Ben Russell, *Sales Staff*
EMP: 5
SALES (est): 587.7K **Privately Held**
WEB: www.thesoftedge.com
SIC: 7372 Business oriented computer software

(G-8551)
SOFTCHOICE CORPORATION
7900 Westpark Dr Ste T400 (22102-4273)
PHONE..........................703 480-1952
Nash Hickman, *Accounts Exec*
Chris Healing, *Manager*
John Rudolf, *Executive*
EMP: 5
SQ FT: 3,800
SALES (corp-wide): 4.2MM **Privately Held**
WEB: www.softchoice.com
SIC: 7372 Prepackaged software
HQ: Softchoice Corporation
314 W Superior St Ste 400
Chicago IL 60654

(G-8552)
SOVEREIGN MEDIA
6731 Whittier Ave C100 (22101-4525)
PHONE..........................703 964-0361
Mark Hintz, *CEO*
EMP: 5
SALES (est): 289.4K **Privately Held**
WEB: www.sovhomestead.com
SIC: 2721 Periodicals: publishing only

(G-8553)
SPARKS COMPANIES INC
6862 Elm St (22101-3897)
PHONE..........................703 734-8787
EMP: 1
SALES (est): 37.5K **Privately Held**
SIC: 2741 Miscellaneous publishing

(G-8554)
SPECTRUM CENTER INC
Also Called: Atdi
1451 Dolley Madison Blvd (22101-3879)
PHONE..........................703 848-4750
Pierre Missud, *President*
Clara Yang, *General Mgr*
Jin Hwang, *Managing Dir*
David Missud, *Exec VP*
Martin Rais, *Project Mgr*
EMP: 10 **EST:** 1999
SALES (est): 3.2MM
SALES (corp-wide): 2.2MM **Privately Held**
WEB: www.atdi.us.com
SIC: 7372 Prepackaged software
PA: Advanced Topographic Development & Images
11 Boulevard Malesherbes
Paris 75008
153 308-141

(G-8555)
SPENCE PUBLISHING CO INC
6708 Lupine Ln (22101-1577)
PHONE..........................214 939-1700
Thomas Spence, *President*
Mitchell Muncy, *Vice Pres*
EMP: 4
SQ FT: 9,000
SALES (est): 260K **Privately Held**
SIC: 2731 Books: publishing only

(G-8556)
SPOTTED HAWK DEVELOPMENT LLC
Also Called: SHD Oil & Gas
1650 Tysons Blvd Ste 900 (22102-4826)
PHONE..........................703 286-1450
Joyce McEwen, *Mng Member*
Demarco Bell,
Edgar Rios,
EMP: 11
SALES (est): 8.1MM **Privately Held**
SIC: 1382 Oil & gas exploration services

(G-8557)
SPRITELOGIC LLC
1027 Northwoods Trl (22102-1320)
PHONE..........................703 568-0468
Yuan Ding, *CEO*
EMP: 1

SALES (est): 56.8K **Privately Held**
SIC: 7372 7389 Home entertainment computer software;

(G-8558)
SPYDRSAFE MOBILE SECURITY INC
1616 Anderson Rd (22102-1602)
PHONE..........................703 286-0750
Fax: 703 890-3135
EMP: 5
SALES (est): 100K **Privately Held**
SIC: 7372 Prepackaged Software Services

(G-8559)
STEEP LLC
1750 Tysons Blvd Ste 1500 (22102-4200)
PHONE..........................571 271-5690
Matthias Moeseler, *CEO*
EMP: 1
SALES (est): 62.4K **Privately Held**
SIC: 3679 Electronic components

(G-8560)
SUGARFINA INC
1961 Chain Bridge Rd (22102-4501)
PHONE..........................703 844-0049
EMP: 2
SALES (est): 91.1K **Privately Held**
SIC: 2064 Candy & other confectionery products

(G-8561)
SWAROVSKI NORTH AMERICA LTD
8017 Tysons Corner Ctr (22102-4505)
PHONE..........................571 633-1800
Samar Saab, *Branch Mgr*
EMP: 3
SALES (corp-wide): 4.7B **Privately Held**
WEB: www.swarovski.com
SIC: 3961 Costume jewelry
HQ: Swarovski North America Limited
1 Kenney Dr
Cranston RI 02920
401 463-6400

(G-8562)
SYNAPTEIN SOLUTIONS INC (PA)
Also Called: Synapone
1568 Spring Hill Rd # 402 (22102-3024)
PHONE..........................703 209-2350
Sharad Dayma, *CEO*
Gangadhar Douri, *CTO*
EMP: 12 **EST:** 2011
SQ FT: 2,000
SALES (est): 970K **Privately Held**
WEB: www.synapteinsolutions.com
SIC: 7372 2741 7371 8742 Prepackaged software; ; custom computer programming services; management consulting services; management services

(G-8563)
T3B LLC
8360 Greensboro Dr # 810 (22102-3511)
PHONE..........................202 550-4475
Irish Barbour, *Principal*
EMP: 2 **EST:** 2016
SALES (est): 85.9K **Privately Held**
SIC: 3571 Electronic computers

(G-8564)
TAXLAW20 LLC
1750 Tysons Blvd Ste 1500 (22102-4200)
PHONE..........................202 470-3980
EMP: 2
SALES (est): 85.9K **Privately Held**
SIC: 3571 Electronic computers

(G-8565)
TEA LADY PILLOWS
1034 Northwoods Trl (22102-1322)
PHONE..........................703 448-0033
Jeffery Martin, *Principal*
EMP: 2
SALES (est): 122.6K **Privately Held**
SIC: 2299 Pillow fillings: curled hair, cotton waste, moss, hemp tow

GEOGRAPHIC

(G-8566)
THORIUM POWER INC
Also Called: Radkowsky Thorium Power
8300 Greensboro Dr # 800 (22102-3605)
PHONE................703 918-4904
Seth Grae, *President*
EMP: 6 **EST:** 1992
SALES (est): 492.8K **Publicly Held**
WEB: www.thoriumpower.com
SIC: 3443 Nuclear reactors, military or industrial
PA: Lightbridge Corporation
　11710 Plaza America Dr # 200
　Reston VA 20190

(G-8567)
THOUGHT & EXPRESSION CO LLC (PA)
6841 Elm St Unit J (22101-8006)
P.O. Box J (22101-0770)
PHONE................405 919-0068
Chris Lavernge, *Mng Member*
Ed Lavernge,
EMP: 28
SQ FT: 600
SALES (est): 2.3MM **Privately Held**
SIC: 2731 Book clubs: publishing & printing

(G-8568)
TITANIUM 3 LLC
7001 Arbor Ln (22101-1545)
PHONE................617 417-9288
Matthew Fincher, *Principal*
Dennis Weppner,
EMP: 2
SALES (est): 108.5K **Privately Held**
SIC: 3356 Titanium

(G-8569)
TURNING POINT SOFTWARE INC
1910 Hyannis Ct Apt 201 (22102-1976)
PHONE................703 448-6672
Darrin Schmidt, *Project Mgr*
EMP: 2
SALES (est): 163.4K **Privately Held**
SIC: 7372 Prepackaged software

(G-8570)
UAS TECHNOLOGIES INC
1750 Tysons Blvd Ste 1500 (22102-4200)
PHONE................703 822-4382
Amir Snir, *CEO*
EMP: 1
SALES (est): 96.1K
SALES (corp-wide): 488.9K **Privately Held**
WEB: www.uastec.com
SIC: 3721 Research & development on aircraft by the manufacturer
PA: Unmanned Aerospace Technologies Ltd
　9 Hasnunit
　Kadima
　375 633-33

(G-8571)
USA TODAY INTERNATIONAL CORP (DH)
7950 Jones Branch Dr (22102-3302)
PHONE................703 854-3400
Craig Moon, *President*
Jeff Webber, *Publisher*
Susan Lavington, *Senior VP*
Ken Paulson, *Senior VP*
Brett Wilson, *Senior VP*
EMP: 14
SQ FT: 4,000
SALES (est): 11MM **Publicly Held**
WEB: www.gannett.com
SIC: 2711 Newspapers, publishing & printing
HQ: Gannett Media Corp.
　7950 Jones Branch Dr
　Mc Lean VA 22102
　703 854-6000

(G-8572)
USA TODAY SPT MEDIA GROUP LLC (DH)
7950 Jones Branch Dr (22102-3302)
PHONE................703 854-6000
Tali Bental, *Executive*
EMP: 8

SALES (est): 13.8MM **Publicly Held**
SIC: 2711 Newspapers, publishing & printing
HQ: Gannett Media Corp.
　7950 Jones Branch Dr
　Mc Lean VA 22102
　703 854-6000

(G-8573)
USA WEEKEND INC
7950 Jones Branch Dr (22102-3302)
PHONE................703 854-6000
Marcia Bullard, *President*
Dave Hunke, *Publisher*
David Baratz, *Editor*
Rob Harrison, *Vice Pres*
Crystal Shaw, *Manager*
EMP: 130
SALES (est): 24MM **Publicly Held**
WEB: www.reachlocal.com
SIC: 2711 Newspapers: publishing only, not printed on site
HQ: Gannett Media Corp.
　7950 Jones Branch Dr
　Mc Lean VA 22102
　703 854-6000

(G-8574)
VANS INC
7921 Tysons Corner Ctr (22102-4526)
PHONE................703 442-0161
EMP: 10 **Publicly Held**
WEB: www.vans.com
SIC: 3021 Canvas shoes, rubber soled
HQ: Vans, Inc.
　1588 S Coast Dr
　Costa Mesa CA 92626
　855 909-8267

(G-8575)
VEAMEA INC
1364 Beverly Rd Ste 105 (22101-3627)
PHONE................703 382-2288
EMP: 9
SALES (est): 950K **Privately Held**
SIC: 7372 4813 Prepackaged Software Services Telephone Communications

(G-8576)
VIENNA QUILT SHOP
6724 Curran St (22101-3803)
PHONE................703 281-4091
Nancy Preston, *Owner*
EMP: 5
SQ FT: 800
SALES (est): 260K **Privately Held**
WEB: www.quiltdoctor.com
SIC: 2395 5949 5947 Quilting, for the trade; quilting materials & supplies; gift shop

(G-8577)
VOLARRE INC
1350 Beverly Rd 115-197 (22101-3961)
PHONE................202 258-2640
Nicholas Kingston, *Managing Dir*
Scott Schaffter, *Principal*
EMP: 5
SALES (est): 191.8K **Privately Held**
SIC: 7372 Educational computer software

(G-8578)
WELLZONE INC
8270 Greensboro Dr (22102-3800)
PHONE................703 770-2861
Sreedhar Potarazu, *President*
EMP: 4
SALES (est): 195.6K **Privately Held**
WEB: www.wellzone.com
SIC: 2741

(G-8579)
WINDY HILL COLLECTIONS LLC
1343 Gunnell Ct (22102-1517)
PHONE................703 848-8888
Nancy Bao, *Marketing Staff*
Andy Bao,
EMP: 2 **EST:** 2012
SALES (est): 110.2K **Privately Held**
WEB: www.windyhillcollection.com
SIC: 2392 Household furnishings

(G-8580)
WIRELESS VENTURES USA INC
7900b Westpark Dr 200t (22102-4202)
PHONE................703 852-1350

George E Gonzalez, *CEO*
▲ **EMP:** 15
SALES (est): 1.7MM **Privately Held**
SIC: 3663 Satellites, communications

(G-8581)
XEROX ALUMNI ASSOCIATION INC
1536 Hampton Hill Cir (22101-6025)
PHONE................703 848-0624
EMP: 2
SALES (est): 85.9K **Privately Held**
SIC: 3577 Computer peripheral equipment

(G-8582)
XYKEN LLC
7921 Jones Branch Dr # 392 (22102-3334)
PHONE................703 288-1601
Steven Yi,
EMP: 7
SALES (est): 720.4K **Privately Held**
WEB: www.xyken.com
SIC: 3845 Electromedical equipment

McGaheysville
Rockingham County

(G-8583)
ATLANTIC CONTAINMENT LLC
806 Island Ford Rd (22840-2306)
P.O. Box 335 (22840-0335)
PHONE................540 289-5051
Lisa Hopkins,
EMP: 21
SALES (est): 815.1K **Privately Held**
WEB: www.atlanticcontainment.com
SIC: 3499 Fabricated metal products

(G-8584)
CAVE HILL CORPORATION
Also Called: Cave Hill Mech & Maint Svc
806 Island Ford Rd (22840-2306)
P.O. Box 335 (22840-0335)
PHONE................540 289-5051
Walter M Hopkins, *President*
EMP: 40
SQ FT: 30,000
SALES (est): 8MM **Privately Held**
WEB: www.cavehillfarms.com
SIC: 3441 7389 7699 Fabricated structural metal; crane & aerial lift service; construction equipment repair; industrial machinery & equipment repair

(G-8585)
TURNING 65 INC
1942 Cemetery Rd (22840-2651)
PHONE................540 289-5768
Jennifer Norton, *Principal*
EMP: 2 **EST:** 2017
SALES (est): 97.3K **Privately Held**
SIC: 3599 Machine shop, jobbing & repair

Mclean
Fairfax County

(G-8586)
GANNETT GP MEDIA INC
7950 Jones Branch Dr (22101)
P.O. Box 677589, Dallas TX (75267-7589)
PHONE................703 854-6000
Gracia C Martore, *President*
Michael A Hart, *Treasurer*
Kevin Polchow, *Treasurer*
Michael B Witwer, *Treasurer*
Patrick Burke, *Marketing Staff*
EMP: 1
SALES (est): 184.9K **Publicly Held**
WEB: www.gannett.com
SIC: 2711 Newspapers, publishing & printing
HQ: Gannett Media Corp.
　7950 Jones Branch Dr
　Mc Lean VA 22102
　703 854-6000

(G-8587)
GOVSEARCH LLC
Also Called: Leadconnector LLC
1861 Intl Dr Ste 270 (22102)
PHONE................703 340-1308

Ashish Khot,
EMP: 24
SALES (est): 646.6K
SALES (corp-wide): 4MM **Privately Held**
SIC: 2741 Directories: publishing only, not printed on site
PA: Technomile Llc
　1861 Intl Dr Ste 270
　Mclean VA 22102
　703 340-1308

(G-8588)
MULTINATIONAL DEFENSE SVCS LLC
1660 Intl Dr Ste 200 (22102)
PHONE................727 333-7290
Angelo Saitta, *Mng Member*
Edmundo Apodaca, *Mng Member*
EMP: 2
SALES (est): 114.4K **Privately Held**
WEB: www.multinationaldefense.com
SIC: 3483 Ammunition, except for small arms

(G-8589)
WORK SCENE MEDIA LLC
2010 Corp Rdg Ste 700 (22102)
PHONE................703 910-5959
Michael Webb,
EMP: 10
SALES (est): 261K **Privately Held**
WEB: www.workscene.com
SIC: 2741

Meadows of Dan
Patrick County

(G-8590)
AERIAL MACHINE & TOOL CORP (HQ)
Also Called: Capewell Aerial Systems
4298 Jeb Stuart Hwy (24120-4530)
PHONE................276 952-2006
John Marcaccio, *CEO*
Joseph Goins, *Manager*
Cathy Roberts, *Manager*
Mike Hardin, *Exec Dir*
▲ **EMP:** 68 **EST:** 1926
SQ FT: 34,500
SALES (est): 20MM
SALES (corp-wide): 45.4MM **Privately Held**
WEB: www.capewellaerialsystems.com
SIC: 3549 3429 3728 Metalworking machinery; aircraft & marine hardware, inc. pulleys & similar items; aircraft parts & equipment
PA: Capewell Aerial Systems Llc
　105 Nutmeg Rd S
　South Windsor CT 06074
　860 610-0700

(G-8591)
HORSE PASTURE MFG LLC
Also Called: Liisu Yarns
1202 Luke Helms Rd (24120-3757)
P.O. Box 143 (24120-0143)
PHONE................276 952-2558
EMP: 2 **EST:** 2000
SALES: 30K **Privately Held**
SIC: 3449 Mfg Misc Structural Metalwork

(G-8592)
KREAGER WOODWORKING INC
9412 Jeb Stuart Hwy (24120-3827)
PHONE................276 952-2052
Larry Kreager, *President*
Daryl Kreager, *Vice Pres*
EMP: 46
SQ FT: 15,000
SALES (est): 5.4MM **Privately Held**
SIC: 2426 Frames for upholstered furniture, wood

(G-8593)
ROTO-DIE COMPANY INC
Also Called: Rotometric Group, The
225 Jeb Stuart Hwy (24120-4136)
PHONE................276 952-2026
Terry Harris, *Vice Pres*
Corey Inman, *Buyer*
Carolyn Robinson, *Buyer*
Ken McInnis, *Purchasing*

Travis Turnbough, *Design Engr*
EMP: 300
SALES (corp-wide): 190.8MM **Privately Held**
WEB: www.rotometrics.com
SIC: 3544 Die sets for metal stamping (presses)
PA: Roto-Die Company, Inc.
800 Howerton Ln
Eureka MO 63025
636 587-3600

Meadowview
Washington County

(G-8594)
COMMERCIAL MACHINE & FABG
28219 Robindale Rd (24361-4103)
P.O. Box 219 (24361-0219)
PHONE........................276 944-3643
Johnny M Johnson, *President*
EMP: 6
SQ FT: 6,600
SALES (est): 802.2K **Privately Held**
SIC: 3599 Machine shop, jobbing & repair

(G-8595)
HUBS AND WHEELS EMORY INC
28435 Blaine St (24361-3705)
P.O. Box 27, Emory (24327-0027)
PHONE........................276 944-4900
Donald Coulthard, *President*
Sally Wann, *Vice Pres*
▼ **EMP:** 16
SALES (est): 3.2MM **Privately Held**
WEB: www.hubsandwheelsofemory.com
SIC: 3312 Wheels

(G-8596)
STANDARD BANNER COAL CORP
29059 Rivermont Dr (24361-2847)
PHONE........................276 944-5603
Conrad Mc Nire, *President*
EMP: 4
SALES (est): 271.4K **Privately Held**
SIC: 1221 Bituminous coal & lignite-surface mining

Mears
Accomack County

(G-8597)
STANDARD MARINE INC
27066 Turkey Run Rd (23409-2434)
PHONE........................757 824-0293
Chase Byrd, *President*
EMP: 10
SALES (est): 1.8MM **Privately Held**
SIC: 3499 Machine bases, metal

Mechanicsville
Hanover County

(G-8598)
A BETTER DRIVING SCHOOL LLC
Also Called: A Better Ceaning Service
9011 Brigadier Rd (23116-6565)
PHONE........................804 874-5521
Erica Frye,
EMP: 2
SALES (est): 1.5K **Privately Held**
SIC: 2842 Specialty cleaning, polishes & sanitation goods

(G-8599)
ABC PETWEAR INC
8005 Strawhorn Dr (23116-3832)
PHONE........................804 730-3890
Brenda Watkinson, *President*
Wayne Watkinson, *Vice Pres*
EMP: 2
SALES (est): 178.8K **Privately Held**
WEB: www.abcpetwear.com
SIC: 2399 Horse & pet accessories, textile

(G-8600)
AD VICE INC
Also Called: Advice Sign Consultants
6400 Mechanicsville Tpke Trpk2 (23111-4579)
PHONE........................804 730-0503
David Goodwin, *President*
Bronski Linda, *Traffic Mgr*
Kat McDonald,
EMP: 7 **EST:** 1997
SQ FT: 2,000
SALES (est): 869.4K **Privately Held**
WEB: www.advicestudios.com
SIC: 3993 8742 Electric signs; management consulting services

(G-8601)
AMF BOWLING WORLDWIDE INC
8100 Amf Dr (23111-3700)
P.O. Box 15060 (23111)
PHONE........................804 730-4000
Pricilla Tinnell, *Branch Mgr*
EMP: 9
SALES (corp-wide): 341.2MM **Privately Held**
WEB: www.amf.com
SIC: 3949 Bowling equipment & supplies
HQ: Amf Bowling Worldwide, Inc.
7313 Bell Creek Rd
Mechanicsville VA 23111

(G-8602)
AMF BOWLING WORLDWIDE INC (DH)
7313 Bell Creek Rd (23111-3551)
PHONE........................804 730-4000
Frederick R Hipp, *President*
Paul Riar, *Principal*
Merrell C Wreden, *Vice Pres*
Stephen D Satterwhite, *CFO*
Rachel S Labrecque, *Controller*
◆ **EMP:** 17
SQ FT: 360,000
SALES (est): 480.5MM
SALES (corp-wide): 341.2MM **Privately Held**
WEB: www.amf.com
SIC: 3949 7933 Bowling equipment & supplies; bowling centers

(G-8603)
AMH PRINT GROUP LLC
7286 Hanover Green Dr C (23111-1710)
PHONE........................804 286-6166
Chad Hollins,
Dennis Ashcraft,
Kyle Martin,
EMP: 8
SALES (est): 530.7K **Privately Held**
SIC: 2752 Commercial printing, lithographic

(G-8604)
ANNABS GLUTEN FREE LLC
10198 Summer Hill Rd (23116-6610)
P.O. Box 26, Studley (23162-0026)
PHONE........................804 491-9288
Angela EBY, *Principal*
EMP: 7
SALES (est): 659.6K **Privately Held**
WEB: www.annabsglutenfree.com
SIC: 2051 Bread, cake & related products

(G-8605)
ARLINGTON MCH FABRICATION INC
8444 Erle Rd (23116-1500)
P.O. Box 247 (23111-0247)
PHONE........................804 559-2500
Bruce Chamberlain, *President*
Clint Chamberlain, *Info Tech Mgr*
EMP: 2 **EST:** 2012
SALES (est): 295.2K **Privately Held**
WEB: www.arlingtonmachineinc.com
SIC: 3599 Machine shop, jobbing & repair

(G-8606)
BAS CONTROL SYSTEMS LLC
8420 Meadowbridge Rd C (23116-1505)
PHONE........................804 569-2473
Nick Gosslin, *Mng Member*
EMP: 5

SALES (est): 170K **Privately Held**
WEB: www.bas-cs.com
SIC: 3822 8711 1731 Hydronic pressure or temperature controls; temperature controls, automatic; heating & ventilation engineering; lighting contractor

(G-8607)
BLAKBUNNI
6012 Saber Ct (23111-4571)
PHONE........................347 239-5139
Kenneth Skelton, *CEO*
EMP: 2
SALES (est): 75K **Privately Held**
SIC: 2131 Smoking tobacco

(G-8608)
BURCHAM PRINTS INC
8340 Sherton Ct (23116-2840)
PHONE........................804 559-7724
EMP: 2
SALES (est): 170K **Privately Held**
SIC: 2752 Lithographic Commercial Printing

(G-8609)
BUSINESS
7481 Tangle Ridge Dr (23111-5940)
PHONE........................804 559-8770
Paul Rush, *Owner*
Clayton Medford, *Vice Pres*
EMP: 1
SALES (est): 110.9K **Privately Held**
WEB: www.novachamber.org
SIC: 2791 Typesetting

(G-8610)
C & C PUBLISHING INC (PA)
Also Called: Powhatan Today
8460 Times Dispatch Blvd (23116-2029)
P.O. Box 10, Powhatan (23139-0010)
PHONE........................804 598-4305
David Cole, *President*
Jim McConnell, *Editor*
Roslyn McNally, *Editor*
Cary Martin, *CFO*
Sharon Cole, *Admin Sec*
EMP: 9
SALES (est): 442.3K **Privately Held**
WEB: www.richmond.com
SIC: 2711 2721 Newspapers: publishing only, not printed on site; periodicals

(G-8611)
CITY PUBLICATIONS RICHMOND
8106 S Mayfield Ln (23111-2230)
PHONE........................804 621-0911
Rob Norman, *President*
EMP: 1 **EST:** 2017
SALES (est): 41.3K **Privately Held**
WEB: www.citypubnationwide.com
SIC: 2741 Miscellaneous publishing

(G-8612)
CLEANVENT DRYER EXHUST SPCLSTS
6115 Silverbell Ln (23111-7510)
PHONE........................804 730-1754
Gil Calkins, *Owner*
EMP: 2
SALES (est): 201K **Privately Held**
WEB: www.safedryer.com
SIC: 3634 7533 5087 Fans, exhaust & ventilating, electric: household; auto exhaust system repair shops; cleaning & maintenance equipment & supplies

(G-8613)
COMPUTING TECHNOLOGIES INC (PA)
Also Called: COTS
6372 Mechanicsville Tpke # 112 (23111-4705)
PHONE........................703 280-8800
Manuel Sosa Jr, *President*
James Gill, *Vice Pres*
David Neault, *Vice Pres*
Mary Sosa, *Vice Pres*
Ann Marie Gillikin, *CFO*
EMP: 3
SQ FT: 700
SALES: 865.5K **Privately Held**
WEB: www.cots.com
SIC: 7372 4813 Prepackaged software; telephone communication, except radio

(G-8614)
CONSUTECH SYSTEMS LLC
8407 Erle Rd (23116-1507)
P.O. Box 15119, Richmond (23227-0519)
PHONE........................804 746-4120
Robert S Lee, *President*
David P Richardson, *Treasurer*
▼ **EMP:** 25
SQ FT: 80,000
SALES (est): 4MM **Privately Held**
WEB: www.consutech.com
SIC: 3567

(G-8615)
COPY CAT PRINTING LLC
5516 Mechanicsville Tpke (23111-4563)
P.O. Box 460 (23111-0460)
PHONE........................804 746-0008
Lewis Redford, *Manager*
William Smithson,
EMP: 6
SALES (est): 963.8K **Privately Held**
WEB: www.copycatprinting.net
SIC: 2752 Commercial printing, offset

(G-8616)
CTW PRINTING CONCEPTS
8388 Shady Grove Rd (23116-2300)
PHONE........................804 559-5020
Cheryl Tinsley-Wilkerson, *Principal*
EMP: 2
SALES (est): 126.2K **Privately Held**
SIC: 2752 Commercial printing, offset

(G-8617)
DDG SUPPLY INC
9480 Shelley Dr (23116-5449)
PHONE........................804 730-0118
Danny Gillis, *President*
EMP: 3
SALES (est): 210.5K **Privately Held**
SIC: 3643 Current-carrying wiring devices

(G-8618)
DOMETIC CORPORATION
Also Called: Dometic Environmental Systems
8433 Erle Rd (23116-1507)
P.O. Box 15299, Richmond (23227-0699)
PHONE........................804 746-1313
Charlie Barefoot, *President*
Charlie Baresote, *Manager*
EMP: 130
SALES (corp-wide): 1.9B **Privately Held**
WEB: www.dometic.com
SIC: 3585 3629 3429 Air conditioning, motor vehicle; battery chargers, rectifying or nonrotating; manufactured hardware (general)
HQ: Dometic Corporation
5155 Verdant St
Elkhart IN 46516

(G-8619)
DSIGNS
8529 Meadowbridge Rd (23116-1508)
PHONE........................804 559-5884
EMP: 1 **EST:** 2019
SALES (est): 50.6K **Privately Held**
SIC: 3993 Signs & advertising specialties

(G-8620)
E C B CONSTRUCTION COMPANY
Also Called: ECB Security Co
8390 Brittewood Cir (23116-2925)
PHONE........................804 730-2057
Winnie Rymer, *President*
Daymond Rymer, *Vice Pres*
Don Rymer, *Treasurer*
EMP: 4
SALES (est): 551.6K **Privately Held**
WEB: www.ecbsecurity.com
SIC: 3699 Security devices

(G-8621)
ENVIRONMENTAL EQUIPMENT INC
Also Called: Environmental Equipment Engrg
8418 Erle Rd (23116-1500)
P.O. Box 389 (23111-0389)
PHONE........................804 730-1280
Pamela Mentz, *President*
H C Mentz, *Vice Pres*
Mentz Hubert C, *Vice Pres*
EMP: 5

GEOGRAPHIC

SQ FT: 6,000
SALES (est): 650K Privately Held
WEB: www.eeeusa.net
SIC: 3823 Industrial instrmnts msrmnt display/control process variable

(G-8622)
FIBER CONSULTING SERVICES
8134 Ashty Pl (23116)
PHONE......................804 746-2357
James Dunbar, *President*
▲ **EMP:** 2
SALES (est): 146.4K Privately Held
SIC: 3559 Fiber optics strand coating machinery

(G-8623)
FIREWALL LLC (PA)
7045 Mechanicsville Tpke (23111-7100)
PHONE......................804 977-8777
Ashraf Yacout, *Mng Member*
EMP: 4
SALES (est): 1.6MM Privately Held
WEB: www.firewallllc.com
SIC: 3491 Industrial valves

(G-8624)
FLYNNS FOODS INC
4152 Peppertown Rd (23111-4941)
PHONE......................804 779-3205
Richard Ryder, *CEO*
Marlene Lowery, *President*
EMP: 7
SALES (est): 554.7K Privately Held
SIC: 2099 Sauces: dry mixes

(G-8625)
FROST PROPERTY SOLUTIONS LLC (PA)
11137 Countryside Ln (23116-3193)
PHONE......................804 571-2147
Mack Frost Jr, *President*
EMP: 1
SALES (est): 15.5K Privately Held
SIC: 7372 6531 8742 Business oriented computer software; real estate leasing & rentals; real estate consultant

(G-8626)
GAME DAY PUBLICATIONS LLC
9073 Winter Spring Dr (23116-2826)
PHONE......................804 314-7526
Daniel Steiner, *Principal*
EMP: 2 **EST:** 2009
SALES (est): 103.7K Privately Held
SIC: 2741 Miscellaneous publishing

(G-8627)
GEARMAXUSA LTD
10137 Spring Ivy Ln (23116-5144)
P.O. Box 2814 (23116-0022)
PHONE......................804 521-4320
▲ **EMP:** 4
SALES (est): 600K Privately Held
SIC: 3161 Mfg Luggage

(G-8628)
GOODROW HOLDINGS INC
9431 Studley Plntn Dr (23116-6660)
PHONE......................804 543-2136
Kenneth Goodrow, *President*
Joanne Goodrow, *Admin Sec*
▲ **EMP:** 2
SALES (est): 1.8MM Privately Held
WEB: www.emsco-inc.com
SIC: 3679 Electronic circuits

(G-8629)
GRAMMERS WELDING
6269 Fieldshire Ct (23111-6561)
PHONE......................804 730-7296
Charlotte Grammer, *Principal*
EMP: 1
SALES (est): 80.5K Privately Held
SIC: 7692 Welding repair

(G-8630)
GRAPHIC ARTS ADHESIVES
9102 Knight Dr (23116-5421)
PHONE......................804 779-3304
Michael D Hurley, *President*
EMP: 5
SALES (est): 538.8K Privately Held
WEB: www.graphicartsadhesives.com
SIC: 2891 Adhesives

(G-8631)
GREEN EDGE LIGHTING LLC
8436 Erle Rd (23116-1500)
PHONE......................804 462-0221
Richard Gill,
EMP: 2
SALES (est): 163.4K Privately Held
SIC: 3641 Electric lamps

(G-8632)
GREEN FUEL OF VA
8104 Cypresstree Ln (23111-4677)
PHONE......................804 304-4564
Thomas Stewart, *Principal*
EMP: 3 **EST:** 2010
SALES (est): 211.1K Privately Held
SIC: 2869 Fuels

(G-8633)
GYRFALCON AERIAL SYSTEMS LLC
Also Called: Gyrfalcon Arial Systems Hnover
9211 Trumpet Ct (23116-3190)
PHONE......................757 724-1861
Keith Paquin,
EMP: 4 **EST:** 2016
SALES (est): 10K Privately Held
WEB: www.gyrfalconas.com
SIC: 3499 7389 Target drones, for use by ships: metal;

(G-8634)
HANOVER BRASSFOUNDRY
5155 Cold Harbor Rd (23111-6916)
PHONE......................804 781-1864
Heresa Williams, *Owner*
EMP: 2
SALES (est): 160.8K Privately Held
WEB: www.hanoverbrass.com
SIC: 3366 Copper foundries

(G-8635)
HANOVER MACHINE & TOOL CO INC
8059 Elm Dr (23111-1160)
PHONE......................804 746-4156
Siegfried Leise, *President*
James Huber, *Vice Pres*
Patricia Huber, *Admin Sec*
EMP: 14
SQ FT: 16,000
SALES (est): 2.1MM Privately Held
WEB: www.hanovermachineandtool.com
SIC: 3599 Machine shop, jobbing & repair

(G-8636)
HIGHER LVING PUBLICATIONS CORP
8290 Carrolton Ridge Pl (23111-6525)
PHONE......................804 789-0592
Frederick M Wyatt III, *Principal*
EMP: 2 **EST:** 2010
SALES (est): 76K Privately Held
SIC: 2741 Miscellaneous publishing

(G-8637)
HILLCRAFT MACHINE & WELDING
Also Called: Hillcraft Machine Company
1069 Old Church Rd (23111-6029)
P.O. Box 270 (23111-0270)
PHONE......................804 779-2280
Howard Garner, *President*
EMP: 6
SQ FT: 3,500
SALES (est): 350K Privately Held
SIC: 3599 1799 Machine shop, jobbing & repair; welding on site

(G-8638)
HONE BLADE LLC
9014 Brigadier Rd (23116-6565)
PHONE......................804 370-8598
EMP: 2 **EST:** 2017
SALES (est): 62.6K Privately Held
SIC: 3291 Hones

(G-8639)
IMAGE PACKAGING
7204 History Ln (23111-5026)
PHONE......................804 730-7358
Carl Milletary, *Owner*
Desiree Williams, *Admin Sec*
EMP: 1

SALES (est): 74.4K Privately Held
SIC: 2673 Plastic bags: made from purchased materials

(G-8640)
IMPRESSION AN EVERLASTING INC
6274 Banshire Dr (23111-6569)
PHONE......................804 363-7185
Wayne Doggett, *President*
EMP: 15
SALES (est): 1.1MM Privately Held
SIC: 3651 1521 7389 Household audio & video equipment; general remodeling, single-family houses;

(G-8641)
INSUL INDUSTRIES INC
10287 Still Spring Ct (23116-5109)
PHONE......................804 550-1933
Thomas U Potts, *President*
EMP: 10
SQ FT: 1,500
SALES (est): 942K Privately Held
SIC: 2891 3089 8742 Caulking compounds; plastic hardware & building products; marketing consulting services

(G-8642)
INTERNATIONAL ROLL-CALL CORP
8346 Old Richfood Rd C (23116-2004)
PHONE......................804 730-9600
William C Schaeffer, *President*
Tyler Schaeffer, *Vice Pres*
Deborah B Ward, *Vice Pres*
David Ward Jr, *Manager*
Robert Feidt, *Data Proc Dir*
EMP: 21 **EST:** 1936
SALES (est): 4.7MM Privately Held
WEB: www.roll-call.com
SIC: 3579 Voting machines

(G-8643)
ITKM SYSTEMS LLC
9220 Stephens Manor Dr (23116-5174)
PHONE......................502 370-6488
EMP: 2
SALES (est): 115.8K Privately Held
WEB: www.itkmsystems.com
SIC: 3652 Pre-recorded records & tapes

(G-8644)
JENNIFER REYNOLDS
Also Called: J Reynolds Welding & Repair
9234 Fair Hill Ct (23116-3156)
PHONE......................804 229-1697
Jennifer Reynolds, *Owner*
EMP: 1 **EST:** 2016
SALES (est): 44.4K Privately Held
SIC: 7692 7389 Welding repair;

(G-8645)
JGTSENTERPRISE INC
9073 Brevet Ln (23116-6591)
PHONE......................804 677-4578
EMP: 2
SALES (est): 104.7K Privately Held
SIC: 3732 Boat building & repairing

(G-8646)
JOSEPH L BURRUSS BURIAL VAULTS
8171 Elm Dr (23111-1212)
P.O. Box 385 (23111-0385)
PHONE......................804 746-8250
William Naumann, *Owner*
Janet B Naumann, *Vice Pres*
EMP: 18
SALES (est): 1.7MM Privately Held
SIC: 3272 Burial vaults, concrete or precast terrazzo

(G-8647)
JUST DESSERTS
9468 Crescent View Dr (23116-2703)
PHONE......................804 310-5958
Nell Curtis, *Principal*
EMP: 3
SALES (est): 147K Privately Held
SIC: 2024 Ice cream & frozen desserts

(G-8648)
KENDALL/HUNT PUBLISHING CO
9037 Gold Ridge Ln (23116-5821)
PHONE......................804 285-9411
Curts Ross, *Branch Mgr*
EMP: 2
SALES (corp-wide): 70.4MM Privately Held
WEB: www.kendallhunt.com
SIC: 2731 Books: publishing & printing
PA: Kendall/Hunt Publishing Company
4050 Westmark Dr
Dubuque IA 52002
563 589-1000

(G-8649)
KLUG SERVICING LLC
4372 River Rd (23116-6604)
PHONE......................804 310-5866
Daniel Klug, *Principal*
EMP: 2
SALES (est): 134.7K Privately Held
SIC: 1389 Roustabout service

(G-8650)
LAI OF RICHMOND LLC
8106 Academy Dr (23116-3853)
PHONE......................804 746-2739
Curtis D Gordon, *Administration*
EMP: 3
SALES (est): 94.3K Privately Held
WEB: www.richmond.com
SIC: 2711 Newspapers, publishing & printing

(G-8651)
LEGACY PRINTING INC
8051 Ellerson Station Dr (23111-1897)
PHONE......................804 730-1834
Amanda L Evans, *Principal*
EMP: 2
SALES (est): 230.7K Privately Held
WEB: www.legacyprinting.biz
SIC: 2752 Commercial printing, offset

(G-8652)
LEGACY VULCAN LLC
6385 Power Rd (23111-5362)
PHONE......................804 730-1008
EMP: 3 **Publicly Held**
WEB: www.vulcanmaterials.com
SIC: 3273 Ready-mixed concrete
HQ: Legacy Vulcan, Llc
1200 Urban Center Dr
Vestavia AL 35242
205 298-3000

(G-8653)
LLC LINK MASTERS
7201 Trench Trl (23111-5081)
PHONE......................804 241-3962
Harold Coorens, *Mng Member*
EMP: 1
SALES (est): 90.2K Privately Held
WEB: www.linkmastersllc.com
SIC: 3541 Electrochemical milling machines

(G-8654)
LOGGING NINJA INC
6088 Green Haven Dr (23111-7552)
PHONE......................804 569-6054
Donald Foss, *Principal*
EMP: 2
SALES (est): 81.7K Privately Held
SIC: 2411 Logging

(G-8655)
LOVINGS WELDING & FABRICATING
8175 Newman Dr (23116-1825)
PHONE......................804 370-3084
Roland C Loving, *Administration*
EMP: 1
SALES (est): 45.5K Privately Held
SIC: 7692 Welding repair

(G-8656)
MASSEY WOOD & WEST INC
Also Called: National Sliding Door Frame Co
8404 Erle Rd (23116-1500)
PHONE......................804 746-2800
Gerald W Bradley, *Owner*
EMP: 20 **Privately Held**

WEB: www.masseywoodandwest.com
SIC: 2431 3231 Millwork; products of purchased glass
PA: Massey, Wood & West, Incorporated
1713 Westwood Ave
Richmond VA 23227
804 355-1721

(G-8657)
**MECHANICSVILLE METAL
WORKS INC**
8029 Industrial Park Rd (23116-1514)
P.O. Box 247 (23111-0247)
PHONE..................................804 266-5055
Bruce Wayne, *President*
Doug Williams, *Vice Pres*
EMP: 15 EST: 2016
SALES (est): 760.9K **Privately Held**
WEB: www.mechanicsvillemetals.com
SIC: 3449 Bars, concrete reinforcing: fabri-
cated steel

(G-8658)
MECHANICSVILLE PALLETS INC
7494 Industrial Park Rd (23116-1510)
PHONE..................................804 746-4658
Kenneth W Blackwell, *President*
Mary Hobson, *Treasurer*
EMP: 14 EST: 1976
SQ FT: 9,600
SALES (est): 2.7MM **Privately Held**
SIC: 2448 Pallets, wood

(G-8659)
**MECHANICSVILLE UNITED
FUTBOL**
2035 Retreat Dr (23111-6080)
PHONE..................................804 647-6557
Manuel L Tavares, *Principal*
Patrick Wood, *Comms Dir*
EMP: 2 EST: 2010
SALES (est): 141.2K **Privately Held**
WEB:
www.mechanicsvilleunitedsoccer.com
SIC: 3949 Sporting & athletic goods

(G-8660)
**MEDIA SERVICES OF
RICHMOND**
7991 Ellerson Station Dr (23111-1801)
PHONE..................................804 559-1000
Charlie Shields, *President*
EMP: 2
SALES (est): 145.5K **Privately Held**
WEB: www.richmond.com
SIC: 2752 Commercial printing, litho-
graphic

(G-8661)
**MERICA TACTICAL INDUSTRIES
LLC**
7099 Foxbernie Dr (23111-5646)
PHONE..................................804 516-0435
Justin Eastland,
EMP: 2
SALES (est): 77K **Privately Held**
SIC: 3999 Manufacturing industries

(G-8662)
MILLER ROLL GRINDING & MFG
8150 Elm Dr (23111-1213)
PHONE..................................804 559-5745
Mary R Miller, *President*
David Miller, *Manager*
EMP: 5
SQ FT: 3,600
SALES (est): 593.7K **Privately Held**
SIC: 3599 Machine shop, jobbing & repair

(G-8663)
MKM COATINGS LLC
9127 Sycamore Hill Pl (23116-5806)
PHONE..................................804 514-3506
Mark Stewart, *Owner*
EMP: 3
SALES (est): 234K **Privately Held**
SIC: 2851 Paints & allied products

(G-8664)
N&J SALES & SERVICES
7172 Mill Valley Rd (23111-5234)
PHONE..................................804 559-7172
Nicole E Coggins, *Owner*
EMP: 1

SALES (est): 34.5K **Privately Held**
WEB: www.cogginscustomapparel.com
SIC: 2759 Screen printing

(G-8665)
NOVELTY SIGN WORKS LLC
6273 Tammy Ln (23111-5333)
PHONE..................................804 559-2009
Timothy Boggs, *Principal*
EMP: 2
SALES (est): 136.2K **Privately Held**
SIC: 3993 Signs & advertising specialties

(G-8666)
ONE VOLT ASSOCIATES (PA)
6372 Mchncsvlle Tpke Ste (23111)
PHONE..................................301 565-3930
Pete Peek, *President*
EMP: 11
SALES (est): 982.6K **Privately Held**
WEB: www.1volt.com
SIC: 3829 Surveying instruments & acces-
sories

(G-8667)
PERMAGUARD COATINGS LLC
9245 Rural Point Dr (23116-4179)
PHONE..................................929 352-5665
Denis R Goulet, *Administration*
EMP: 2
SALES (est): 150.2K **Privately Held**
SIC: 3479 Metal coating & allied service

(G-8668)
PRINTPROS LLC
9489 Hartford Oaks Dr (23116-6524)
PHONE..................................804 789-8884
EMP: 2
SALES (est): 100.1K **Privately Held**
SIC: 2752 Commercial printing, litho-
graphic

(G-8669)
**QUBICAAMF WORLDWIDE LLC
(HQ)**
8100 Amf Dr (23111-3700)
PHONE..................................804 569-1000
Patrick Ciniello, *Ch of Bd*
Emanuele Govani, *President*
Emanuele Govoni, *President*
Roberto Vaioli, *Chief*
Luca Drusiani, *COO*
◆ EMP: 297
SQ FT: 355,000
SALES (est): 123.3MM
SALES (corp-wide): 30.9MM **Privately
Held**
WEB: www.qubicaamf.com
SIC: 3949 7933 Bowling equipment & sup-
plies; bowling balls; bowling centers
PA: Qubicaamf Europe Spa
Via Della Croce Coperta 15
Bologna BO 40128
051 419-2611

(G-8670)
RECYCLED PALLETS INC
8029 Industrial Park Rd (23116-1514)
P.O. Box 2846 (23116-0023)
PHONE..................................804 400-9931
Thomas Fisher, *President*
Joy Fisher, *Corp Secy*
EMP: 6
SQ FT: 10,000
SALES (est): 567K **Privately Held**
SIC: 2448 4213 Pallets, wood; trucking,
except local

(G-8671)
ROBERT K MONTGOMERY II
8561 Anderson Ct (23116-3101)
PHONE..................................804 730-0361
Robert Montgomery, *Principal*
EMP: 2
SALES (est): 141.4K **Privately Held**
SIC: 1382 Oil & gas exploration services

(G-8672)
RVA WOODWORK LLC
2545 Westwood Rd (23111-6263)
PHONE..................................804 840-2345
Evan Howard, *Principal*
EMP: 1
SALES (est): 54.1K **Privately Held**
SIC: 2431 Millwork

(G-8673)
RVA WOODWORKS LLC
9353 Kings Charter Dr (23116-5117)
PHONE..................................804 303-3820
Terry Wright, *Principal*
EMP: 1
SALES (est): 57K **Privately Held**
WEB: www.rvawoodworks.com
SIC: 2431 Millwork

(G-8674)
**SANDY HOBSON T/A S H
MONOGRAMS**
7111 Mechanicsville Tpke (23111-3626)
PHONE..................................804 730-7211
Sandy Hobson, *Owner*
EMP: 2
SQ FT: 500
SALES (est): 74.4K **Privately Held**
SIC: 2395 Embroidery products, except
schiffli machine

(G-8675)
SB WOODWORKS
7400 Pine Dr (23111-4427)
PHONE..................................804 417-7729
Samuel Bond, *Principal*
EMP: 2 EST: 2017
SALES (est): 65.4K **Privately Held**
WEB: www.sbwoodworks.bigcartel.com
SIC: 2431 Millwork

(G-8676)
SIMMS SIGN CO/CASH
7485 Cold Harbor Rd (23111-1625)
PHONE..................................804 746-0595
Joseph Simms, *Principal*
EMP: 2
SALES (est): 163.9K **Privately Held**
SIC: 3993 Signs & advertising specialties

(G-8677)
SJP CONSULTING LLC
7210 Trench Trl (23111-5081)
PHONE..................................804 277-8153
Shawna J Perry,
EMP: 2
SALES (est): 25K **Privately Held**
SIC: 3442 Metal doors, sash & trim

(G-8678)
**SOCIITERRA INTERNATIONAL
LLC**
Also Called: Beez Nuts Balms
10451 Pollard Creek Rd (23116-4794)
P.O. Box 488, Boone NC (28607-0488)
PHONE..................................804 461-1876
Jonathan Noggle, *President*
Kevin Duke, *Vice Pres*
EMP: 2
SALES (est): 81.8K **Privately Held**
SIC: 2844 5122 Hair preparations, includ-
ing shampoos; face creams or lotions; lip-
sticks; suntan lotions & oils; toilet
preparations

(G-8679)
SPECIALTY ENTERPRISES INC
5176 Farmer Dr (23111-6937)
PHONE..................................804 781-0314
Harvey L Farmer, *President*
EMP: 1 EST: 1973
SALES (est): 146.7K **Privately Held**
SIC: 3441 Fabricated structural metal

(G-8680)
SPORTSTITCH
6371 Yellowrose Ln (23111-7531)
PHONE..................................804 387-5127
EMP: 2
SALES (est): 93.3K **Privately Held**
WEB: www.sportstitch.info
SIC: 2759 Screen printing

(G-8681)
STEPHEN W MAST
8403 Kaye Dr (23116-2444)
PHONE..................................804 467-3608
Stephen W Mast, *Owner*
EMP: 1
SALES (est): 95K **Privately Held**
SIC: 3537 2531 Trucks: freight, baggage,
etc.: industrial, except mining; bleacher
seating, portable

(G-8682)
STEVE D GILNETT
Also Called: A To Z Lettering
7160 Catlin Rd (23111-1927)
PHONE..................................804 746-5497
Steve Gilnett, *Principal*
EMP: 1
SALES (est): 61.8K **Privately Held**
SIC: 3993 Signs & advertising specialties

(G-8683)
STRONGTOWER INC
6803 Rural Point Rd (23116-6535)
PHONE..................................804 723-8050
Jeffrey Marano, *President*
EMP: 2
SALES (est): 100K **Privately Held**
WEB: www.shunleepalacecharlotte.com
SIC: 2024 Ice cream & frozen desserts

(G-8684)
**STUART MATHEWS
ENGINEERING**
4356 Sandy Valley Rd (23111-6416)
PHONE..................................804 779-2976
Mathews Stuart, *Owner*
EMP: 3
SALES (est): 200K **Privately Held**
SIC: 3714 7538 Rebuilding engines &
transmissions, factory basis; general au-
tomotive repair shops

(G-8685)
THEME QUEEN LLC
7435 Rural Point Rd (23116-4770)
PHONE..................................804 439-0854
EMP: 1
SALES (est): 90K **Privately Held**
SIC: 2611 Plastic Recycle

(G-8686)
TORCHS MOBILE WELDING
8243 S Mayfield Ln (23111-2244)
PHONE..................................804 216-0412
Marcus Thomas, *Principal*
EMP: 1
SALES (est): 42K **Privately Held**
SIC: 7692 Welding repair

(G-8687)
TRC DESIGN INC
8307 Little Florida Rd (23111-6446)
P.O. Box 456 (23111-0456)
PHONE..................................804 779-3383
Glenn Crider, *President*
EMP: 1
SALES (est): 175.8K **Privately Held**
WEB: www.oldworldchristmas.com
SIC: 3634 5947 Housewares, excluding
cooking appliances & utensils; gift, nov-
elty & souvenir shop

(G-8688)
TRINITY PUBLICATIONS LLC
7409 Flannigan Mill Rd (23111-6056)
PHONE..................................804 779-3499
Kari Smith, *Principal*
EMP: 2 EST: 2018
SALES (est): 59.2K **Privately Held**
SIC: 2741 Miscellaneous publishing

(G-8689)
TRIPLE Z TRANSPORT LLC
7986 Wynbrook Ln (23111-3538)
PHONE..................................804 335-5962
Rashawn Hoggard,
EMP: 1
SALES (est): 100K **Privately Held**
SIC: 3537 Trucks: freight, baggage, etc.:
industrial, except mining

(G-8690)
TRISHS BOOKS
Also Called: Dbt Publications
10330 Agecroft Manor Ct (23116-5110)
PHONE..................................804 550-2954
Patricia H Lyons, *Owner*
EMP: 1
SALES (est): 68.8K **Privately Held**
SIC: 2741 Guides: publishing only, not
printed on site

GEOGRAPHIC

(G-8691)
UPPER DECKS LLC
6997 Brooking Way (23111-3389)
PHONE..................................804 789-0946
EMP: 3 EST: 2009
SALES (est): 335K Privately Held
SIC: 3131 Mfg Footwear Cut Stock

(G-8692)
VH DRONES LLC
10984 Milestone Dr (23116-5858)
PHONE..................................804 938-9713
EMP: 2
SALES (est): 139.8K Privately Held
SIC: 3721 Motorized aircraft

(G-8693)
VICTOR RANDALL LOGGING LLC
9829 Kingsrock Ln (23116-8727)
P.O. Box 230, New Kent (23124-0230)
PHONE..................................804 241-6630
Victor K Randall Sr,
EMP: 6
SALES (est): 530K Privately Held
SIC: 2411 Logging camps & contractors

(G-8694)
VIRGINIA CUSTOM PLATING INC
9203 Royal Grant Dr (23116-4195)
P.O. Box 1797 (23116-0005)
PHONE..................................804 789-0719
Thomas Brummell, Principal
EMP: 3
SALES (est): 203.1K Privately Held
WEB: www.vcplating.com
SIC: 3471 Plating of metals or formed products

(G-8695)
VIRGINIA ENGINEER
Also Called: Virginia Engineer, The
7401 Flannigan Mill Rd (23111-6056)
PHONE..................................804 779-3527
Richard Carden II, President
EMP: 5
SALES (est): 319.6K Privately Held
WEB: www.vaeng.com
SIC: 2731 7336 Book publishing; commercial art & graphic design

(G-8696)
VISTA-GRAPHICS INC
7003 Mechanicsville Tpke # 1016
(23111-7100)
PHONE..................................804 559-6140
Randy Thompson, President
EMP: 1
SALES (corp-wide): 9MM Privately Held
WEB: www.vistagraphicsinc.com
SIC: 2721 Periodicals
PA: Vista-Graphics Inc
1264 Perimeter Pkwy
Virginia Beach VA 23454
757 422-8979

(G-8697)
VISUAL GRAPHICS&DESIGNS
8283 Wetherden Dr (23111-5606)
PHONE..................................804 221-6983
Lenora Smith, Principal
EMP: 2 EST: 2015
SALES (est): 83.9K Privately Held
SIC: 2752 Commercial printing, lithographic

(G-8698)
WILSON MECHANICAL REPAIR SERVI
9302 Blagdon Dr (23116-4104)
PHONE..................................804 317-4919
Wendell Wilson, Manager
EMP: 3
SALES (est): 298K Privately Held
SIC: 3585 Refrigeration & heating equipment

(G-8699)
WINDSHIELD RPS BY RALPH SMILEY
7415 Amesbury Cir (23111-2101)
PHONE..................................804 690-7517
Ralph J Smiley, President

EMP: 1
SALES (est): 100K Privately Held
WEB: www.windshieldrepairsbyralphsmiley.com
SIC: 3714 7536 Windshield wiper systems, motor vehicle; automotive glass replacement shops

(G-8700)
WOOD TELEVISION LLC
Also Called: Richmond Times Dispatch
8460 Times Dispatch Blvd (23116-2029)
PHONE..................................804 559-8207
Daniel L Criner, Accounts Exec
Tappy August, Manager
Lonnie Briggs, Manager
Gregory N Whitlow, Manager
EMP: 200
SALES (corp-wide): 3B Publicly Held
WEB: www.woodtv.com
SIC: 2711 Newspapers, publishing & printing
HQ: Wood Television Llc
120 College Ave Se
Grand Rapids MI 49503
616 456-8888

(G-8701)
WOODMARK DESIGNS
6091 Terry Ville Ter (23111)
PHONE..................................804 921-9454
James Holt, President
EMP: 1
SALES (est): 18K Privately Held
SIC: 2499 Laundry products, wood

(G-8702)
WOODWORKS LLC
8548 Anderson Ct (23116-3101)
P.O. Box 1504 (23116-0001)
PHONE..................................804 730-0631
Matthew Wood, Administration
EMP: 2
SALES (est): 72K Privately Held
SIC: 2431 Millwork

(G-8703)
WORLD MEDIA ENTERPRISES INC
Also Called: World Media Pubg Solutions
8460 Times Dispatch Blvd (23116-2029)
PHONE..................................804 559-8261
Kristin Jones, Principal
Sam Hightower, Vice Pres
Lance Pryor, Vice Pres
EMP: 10
SALES (est): 629.9K Privately Held
WEB: www.worldmediapublishingsolutions.com
SIC: 2711 Newspapers, publishing & printing

Meherrin
Prince Edward County

(G-8704)
A CUT ABOVE LOGGING LLC
3608 Crymes Rd (23954-2008)
P.O. Box 333, Keysville (23947-0333)
PHONE..................................434 547-5979
Jerry Wallace Amos, Principal
EMP: 6
SALES (est): 715K Privately Held
SIC: 2411 Logging

(G-8705)
CENTRAL REDI-MIX CONCRETE INC
3907 Patrick Henry Hwy (23954-5021)
PHONE..................................434 736-0091
Caraletta S Orton, President
David C Orton, Corp Secy
EMP: 5
SQ FT: 480
SALES (est): 539.3K Privately Held
SIC: 3273 Ready-mixed concrete

(G-8706)
MOUNTAIN CREEK INDUSTRIES LLC
286 Rr Eppes Rd (23954-3134)
PHONE..................................804 432-1601
Jeff Pelkey,

EMP: 2
SALES (est): 83.1K Privately Held
SIC: 3999 Manufacturing industries

(G-8707)
YOUNG AND HEALTHY MKTG LLC
396 Watson Blvd (23954-3240)
PHONE..................................214 945-5816
John Watson,
EMP: 1 EST: 2017
SALES (est): 32.7K Privately Held
WEB: www.truckers-trip-planning-app.com
SIC: 7372 Prepackaged software

Melfa
Accomack County

(G-8708)
BOGGS WATER & SEWAGE INC
28367 Railroad Ave (23410)
P.O. Box 333 (23410-0333)
PHONE..................................757 787-4000
Phil Dunn, President
Nathan L Thornton, Vice Pres
EMP: 29
SQ FT: 10,000
SALES (est): 4.2MM Privately Held
SIC: 3272 5039 1781 1623 Septic tanks, concrete; septic tanks; water well drilling; water, sewer & utility lines

(G-8709)
COASTAL AEROSPACE INC
21419 Fair Oaks Rd (23410-2433)
PHONE..................................757 787-3704
Bruce E Freeman, President
EMP: 7
SQ FT: 7,000
SALES (est): 1.2MM Privately Held
WEB: www.coastalaerospace.com
SIC: 3728 Aircraft parts & equipment

(G-8710)
INTERAD LIMITED LLC
18321 Parkway Rd (23410-3017)
PHONE..................................757 787-7610
EMP: 15 EST: 1970
SQ FT: 20,000
SALES (est): 1.2MM Privately Held
SIC: 3812 Mfg Search/Navigation Equipment

(G-8711)
LUMINARY AIR GROUP LLC
18321 Parkway (23410-3023)
PHONE..................................757 655-0705
David Lumgair, Managing Prtnr
Lee Trainum, Principal
EMP: 1
SALES (est): 215K Privately Held
WEB: www.luminary.aero
SIC: 3728 Aircraft parts & equipment

(G-8712)
TRUSS-TECH INC
18541 Parkway (23410-3021)
PHONE..................................757 787-3014
Thomas J Hill, President
EMP: 37
SQ FT: 18,000
SALES (est): 5.8MM Privately Held
WEB: www.trusstech.net
SIC: 2439 Trusses, wooden roof

(G-8713)
TURNER SCULPTURE LTD
27316 Lankford Hwy (23410-2862)
P.O. Box 128, Onley (23418-0128)
PHONE..................................757 787-2818
David Turner, President
William H Turner, Vice Pres
Melvin Drummond Jr, Treasurer
Brenda Thornton, Admin Sec
EMP: 24
SQ FT: 6,000
SALES (est): 2.8MM Privately Held
WEB: www.turnersculpture.com
SIC: 3366 8999 7999 3463 Bronze foundry; sculptor's studio; art gallery, commercial; nonferrous forgings

Middlebrook
Augusta County

(G-8714)
WALKERS CREEK CABINET WORKS
3906 Walkers Creek Rd (24459-2004)
PHONE..................................540 348-5810
Donald Campbell, Principal
EMP: 6
SALES (est): 549.6K Privately Held
SIC: 2434 Wood kitchen cabinets

Middleburg
Loudoun County

(G-8715)
50 WEST VINEYARDS
39060 John Mosby Hwy (20117-2918)
PHONE..................................571 367-4760
EMP: 2
SALES (est): 76.4K Privately Held
WEB: www.50westvineyards.com
SIC: 2084 Wines

(G-8716)
BOXWOOD WINERY LLC
2042 Burrland Rd (20118)
P.O. Box 1887 (20118-1887)
PHONE..................................540 687-8778
Sean Martin, Vice Pres
Rita Cooke, Manager
Dorothy Vaccaro, Manager
John K Cook,
Rita Cook, Admin Sec
EMP: 5
SALES (est): 577.2K Privately Held
WEB: www.boxwoodwinery.com
SIC: 2084 Wines

(G-8717)
CANA VINEYARDS WINERY
38600 John Mosby Hwy (20117-2916)
PHONE..................................703 348-2458
EMP: 2 EST: 2015
SALES (est): 158.1K Privately Held
WEB: www.canavineyards.com
SIC: 2084 Wines

(G-8718)
CHRONICLE OF THE HORSE LLC
Also Called: Chronicle of The Horse, The
108 The Plains Rd (20117-2686)
P.O. Box 46 (20118-0046)
PHONE..................................540 687-6341
Sharon Rose, Editor
Beth Honcharski, Production
Patricia Boyce, Manager
Kat Netzler, Senior Editor
Mark Bellissimo,
EMP: 20 EST: 1937
SALES (est): 2.3MM
SALES (corp-wide): 21.8MM Privately Held
WEB: www.chronofhorse.com
SIC: 2721 Magazines: publishing only, not printed on site
PA: Vistan Corporation
3870 Halfway Rd
The Plains VA 20198
540 253-5540

(G-8719)
DIVERSIFIED EDUCTL SYSTEMS
205 E Washington St (20118)
P.O. Box 368 (20118-0368)
PHONE..................................540 687-7060
Mark Wyatt, President
Mark E Wyatt, President
Amy Mann, Purch Agent
Mary Sue Pierce, Administration
Ray Lanham,
EMP: 40
SQ FT: 1,600
SALES (est): 18MM Privately Held
WEB: www.des.com
SIC: 3821 Laboratory apparatus & furniture

(G-8720)
GDM INTERNATIONAL SERVICES INC (PA)
22456 Sam Fred Rd (20117-3208)
PHONE..................540 687-6687
Mary Ann Hebard, *President*
James F Hebard, *Vice Pres*
EMP: 2
SALES (est): 492.2K **Privately Held**
WEB: www.gdmis.com
SIC: 3571 Computers, digital, analog or hybrid

(G-8721)
GREENHILL WINERY AND VINEYARDS
23595 Winery Ln (20117-2847)
PHONE..................540 687-6968
David Greenhill, *Owner*
Sebastien Marquet, *General Mgr*
Rebekah Pizana, *Marketing Staff*
EMP: 7
SALES (est): 540.4K **Privately Held**
WEB: www.greenhillvineyards.com
SIC: 2084 Wines

(G-8722)
HELLEN SYSTEMS LLC
9 N Liberty St (20117)
P.O. Box 193 (20118-0193)
PHONE..................571 276-7730
Trowbridge Littleton, *President*
EMP: 3 EST: 2016
SALES (est): 228.2K **Privately Held**
SIC: 3812 Search & navigation equipment

(G-8723)
IMPERIAL REVIVAL LLC
8 Orange Dr (20117)
P.O. Box 1997 (20118-1997)
PHONE..................540 326-8189
Jessica Miller,
EMP: 2
SALES (est): 250K **Privately Held**
SIC: 2084 Wines

(G-8724)
INSTANT TRANSACTIONS CORP
35396 Millville Rd (20117-3628)
PHONE..................540 687-3151
Michael W Hall, *Principal*
EMP: 2
SALES (est): 164.2K **Privately Held**
SIC: 2752 Commercial printing, lithographic

(G-8725)
JOURNEYMEN SADDLERS LTD
2 W Federal St (20117)
P.O. Box 1288 (20118-1288)
PHONE..................540 687-5888
Dorothy Lee, *President*
EMP: 10 EST: 1978
SQ FT: 1,700
SALES (est): 1MM **Privately Held**
SIC: 3111 5611 5621 Equestrian leather products; men's & boys' clothing stores; women's clothing stores

(G-8726)
LOCKSLEY ESTATE FRMSTEAD CHESE
23876 Champe Ford Rd (20117-2942)
PHONE..................703 926-4759
Jennifer McCloud, *Principal*
EMP: 8
SALES (est): 200K **Privately Held**
SIC: 2022 Natural cheese

(G-8727)
LOUDOUN CONSTRUCTION LLC
37256 Mountville Rd (20117-3328)
P.O. Box 364 (20118-0364)
PHONE..................703 895-7242
Ryan Michels,
EMP: 3
SALES (est): 257.7K **Privately Held**
SIC: 2499 1521 Fencing, wood; general remodeling, single-family houses

(G-8728)
MARKET SALAMANDER
200 W Washington St (20117)
P.O. Box 1767 (20118-1767)
PHONE..................540 687-8011

Shiela Johnson, *President*
EMP: 20
SQ FT: 3,392
SALES (est): 1.7MM **Privately Held**
WEB: www.salamanderresort.com
SIC: 2392 Laundry, garment & storage bags

(G-8729)
MIDDLEBURG PRINTERS LLC
5 E Federal St (20118)
P.O. Box 1121 (20118-1121)
PHONE..................540 687-5710
Vince Perricone,
EMP: 5
SQ FT: 1,800
SALES (est): 619.1K **Privately Held**
SIC: 2752 Commercial printing, offset

(G-8730)
MIDDLEBURG TACK EXCHANGE LTD
103 W Federal St (20117)
P.O. Box 190 (20118-0190)
PHONE..................540 687-6608
Josephine Motion, *President*
EMP: 6
SQ FT: 2,250 **Privately Held**
WEB: www.middleburgtack.com
SIC: 3111 5941 5699 Saddlery leather; specialty sport supplies; western apparel

(G-8731)
PATRICIA GAVIN
Also Called: Washington DC Lndmark Card Fnd
23776 Champe Ford Rd (20117-2940)
PHONE..................703 439-4403
Patricia Gavin, *Owner*
EMP: 1 EST: 2015
SALES (est): 69.1K **Privately Held**
WEB: www.wdclc.com
SIC: 2771 5112 7812 Greeting cards; social stationery & greeting cards; educational motion picture production

(G-8732)
PINNACLE OIL CO
10 N Jay St (20118)
P.O. Box 796 (20118-0796)
PHONE..................540 687-6351
Guy O Dove III, *President*
Karen Chen, *Controller*
EMP: 3
SALES (est): 127.4K **Privately Held**
WEB: www.pinnacleoil.com
SIC: 1389 Oil field services

(G-8733)
POPCORN MONKEY LLC (PA)
101 W Federal St (20117)
PHONE..................540 687-6539
Deltone Moore, *Mng Member*
EMP: 4
SALES (est): 934.9K **Privately Held**
WEB: www.popcornmonkeyllc.com
SIC: 2064 Popcorn balls or other treated popcorn products

(G-8734)
TERRABUILT CORP INTERNATIONAL
1073 W Federal St (20117)
PHONE..................540 687-4211
EMP: 1
SALES (est): 92K **Privately Held**
SIC: 3531 Mfg Of Green Machines

(G-8735)
WW MONOGRAMS LLC
35653 Millville Rd (20117-3635)
PHONE..................540 687-6510
EMP: 1
SALES (est): 40.3K **Privately Held**
SIC: 2395 Embroidery & art needlework

Middletown
Frederick County

(G-8736)
BDL PROTOTYPE & AUTOMATION LLC
621 Klines Mill Rd Bldg B (22645-1737)
P.O. Box 1510, Stephens City (22655-1510)
PHONE..................540 868-2577
David Monroe,
William Snoberger,
EMP: 3
SALES (est): 350K **Privately Held**
WEB: www.nicolasfelizolaphoto.com
SIC: 3599 Machine shop, jobbing & repair

(G-8737)
DIXIE PLATE GL & MIRROR CO LLC
6773 Valley Pike (22645-1719)
PHONE..................540 869-4400
Martha Downes, *Mng Member*
EMP: 8
SQ FT: 8,500
SALES (est): 500K **Privately Held**
SIC: 3231 1793 3229 3211 Insulating glass: made from purchased glass; glass & glazing work; pressed & blown glass; flat glass

(G-8738)
FORMALLY YOURS
160 Headley Rd (22645-1614)
PHONE..................540 974-3071
Alan Gray,
EMP: 1
SALES (est): 5K **Privately Held**
WEB: www.formallyyoursga.com
SIC: 2335 Women's, juniors' & misses' dresses

(G-8739)
GRYPHON TILE LLC
106 Crest River Dr (22645-3565)
PHONE..................540 868-2953
Cindy Rodriguez, *Mng Member*
Bunny Funk, *Office Admin*
Efrain Rodriguez,
EMP: 7
SALES (est): 669.9K **Privately Held**
WEB: www.gryphontile.com
SIC: 3253 7389 Ceramic wall & floor tile;

(G-8740)
HIGGINS INC
Also Called: Higgins & Associates
2091 Guard Hill Rd (22645-3953)
P.O. Box 1334, Front Royal (22630-0028)
PHONE..................540 636-3756
Gene Higgins, *President*
EMP: 13
SQ FT: 9,000
SALES (est): 1.5MM **Privately Held**
SIC: 3211 Window glass, clear & colored

(G-8741)
O-N MINERALS CHEMSTONE COMPANY
Also Called: Carmeuse Lime & Stone
351 Mccune Rd (22645-1942)
PHONE..................540 869-1066
EMP: 172
SALES (corp-wide): 177.9K **Privately Held**
WEB: www.carmeuse.com
SIC: 1422 Crushed & broken limestone
HQ: O-N Minerals (Chemstone) Company
11 Stanwix St Fl 21
Pittsburgh PA 15222
412 995-5500

(G-8742)
PRINT A PROMO LLC
362 Reliance Woods Dr (22645-3882)
PHONE..................800 675-6869
Kevin Williams, *Principal*
EMP: 2
SALES (est): 182K **Privately Held**
SIC: 2752 Commercial printing, lithographic

(G-8743)
SPECIALIST MANUFACTURE
325 Westernview Dr (22645-2073)
PHONE..................540 974-0780
Donald Hopkins, *Principal*
EMP: 2
SALES (est): 223.9K **Privately Held**
SIC: 3441 Fabricated structural metal

(G-8744)
THERMO FISHER SCIENTIFIC INC
8365 Valley Pike (22645-1905)
PHONE..................540 869-3200
Jerry Needles, *Mfg Staff*
Carl Snider, *Mfg Staff*
Phillip Parker, *Engineer*
Davis Richard, *Engineer*
Diana Patton, *Financial Analy*
EMP: 307
SALES (corp-wide): 25.5B **Publicly Held**
WEB: www.thermofisher.com
SIC: 3826 Analytical instruments
PA: Thermo Fisher Scientific Inc.
168 3rd Ave
Waltham MA 02451
781 622-1000

(G-8745)
UNLIMITED WELDING LLC
1736 Reliance Rd (22645-3720)
PHONE..................540 683-4776
Michael Edwin Garrett, *Mng Member*
EMP: 1
SALES (est): 74K **Privately Held**
SIC: 7692 Welding repair

(G-8746)
VALLEY INDUSTRIAL PLASTICS INC
6953 Middle Rd (22645-2116)
PHONE..................540 723-8855
James J Lantz, *President*
Tom Keenan, *Principal*
Alan Toxopeus, *Principal*
Jeffry Dawson, *Vice Pres*
Joann B Lantz, *CFO*
EMP: 90
SQ FT: 31,000
SALES (est): 11.2MM **Privately Held**
WEB: www.vipva.com
SIC: 3089 Injection molding of plastics

(G-8747)
VALLEY TRADER THE INC
8503 Valley Pike (22645-1913)
P.O. Box 126, Stephens City (22655-0126)
PHONE..................540 869-5132
Charles M Pittman, *CEO*
EMP: 12
SALES (est): 1MM **Privately Held**
WEB: www.valleytraderpaper.com
SIC: 2711 Newspapers: publishing only, not printed on site

(G-8748)
VIRGINIA CITIZENS DEFENSE
2329 Third St (22645-9587)
PHONE..................703 944-4845
EMP: 2 EST: 2018
SALES (est): 77.4K **Privately Held**
SIC: 3812 Defense systems & equipment

Midland
Fauquier County

(G-8749)
CHEMETRICS INC
4295 Catlett Rd (22728-2003)
PHONE..................540 788-9026
Gordon A Rampy, *Ch of Bd*
Bruce H Rampy, *President*
Shirley Ward, *Business Mgr*
Henry Castaneda, *Vice Pres*
Teresa Neale, *Vice Pres*
▲ EMP: 56
SQ FT: 19,000
SALES (est): 14.8MM **Privately Held**
WEB: www.chemetrics.com
SIC: 3826 8734 3823 Water testing apparatus; testing laboratories; industrial instrmnts msrmnt display/control process variable

(G-8750)
COW PIE COMPOST LLC
10337 Messick Rd (22728-1940)
PHONE.....................540 272-2854
James B Messick, *Administration*
EMP: 3
SALES (est): 239.5K **Privately Held**
SIC: 2875 Compost

(G-8751)
CWC PUBLISHING CO LLC
10466 Old Carolina Rd (22728-2140)
PHONE.....................540 439-3851
Charles Cooke, *Owner*
EMP: 1
SALES (est): 51.5K **Privately Held**
SIC: 2741 Miscellaneous publishing

(G-8752)
DIRECT BUY MATTRESS LLC
8819 Commerce St (22728)
PHONE.....................703 346-0323
Barry Phipps,
EMP: 2 EST: 2017
SALES (est): 88.2K **Privately Held**
SIC: 2515 Mattresses & bedsprings

(G-8753)
DOUBLE JJ ALPACAS LLC
12480 Tower Hill Rd (22728-9642)
PHONE.....................540 286-0992
John Kleindl, *Principal*
EMP: 2
SALES (est): 169.7K **Privately Held**
WEB: www.doublejjalpacas.com
SIC: 2231 Alpacas, mohair: woven

(G-8754)
DSG TEC USA INC
4818 Midland Rd (22728-2225)
PHONE.....................619 757-5430
Jeff Williams, *CEO*
Sareit Crabtree, *Director*
EMP: 2
SALES (est): 83.8K **Privately Held**
WEB: www.dsgtec.com
SIC: 3482 Small arms ammunition

(G-8755)
FREEPORT PRESS
5206 Hunt Crossing Ln (22728-1828)
PHONE.....................540 788-9745
Robin Mattson, *Executive*
EMP: 2 EST: 2016
SALES (est): 63.8K **Privately Held**
SIC: 2741 Miscellaneous publishing

(G-8756)
FUN WITH CANVAS
4522 Catlett Rd (22728-2017)
PHONE.....................540 272-2436
EMP: 2
SALES (est): 78.2K **Privately Held**
SIC: 2211 Canvas

(G-8757)
FUZZYPRINTS
4681 Midland Rd (22728-2228)
PHONE.....................571 989-3899
Dale Furr, *Principal*
EMP: 2
SALES (est): 83.9K **Privately Held**
SIC: 2752 Commercial printing, lithographic

(G-8758)
INTERNATIONAL TRADE & TECH INC (PA)
Also Called: IT&t
4818 Midland Rd (22728-2225)
PHONE.....................703 929-0595
Sung Giu Chung, *President*
SOO Chung, *Manager*
SOO Young Chung, *Admin Sec*
EMP: 7
SQ FT: 1,000
SALES (est): 482.4K **Privately Held**
WEB: www.inter2t.com
SIC: 3827 3812 8742 Gun sights, optical; defense systems & equipment; foreign trade consultant

(G-8759)
KELMAR INC
5212 Midland Rd (22728-2131)
P.O. Box 60 (22728-0060)
PHONE.....................540 439-8952
Glenn Kelly, *President*
Gail Vignoe, *Vice Pres*
▼ EMP: 13
SQ FT: 25,000
SALES (est): 1.8MM **Privately Held**
WEB: www.kelmarsystems.com
SIC: 3599 Machine shop, jobbing & repair

(G-8760)
KING AVIATION
6555 Stoney Rd (22728-1747)
PHONE.....................540 439-8621
John King, *Principal*
EMP: 2
SQ FT: 5,034
SALES (est): 171.8K **Privately Held**
SIC: 3721 Airplanes, fixed or rotary wing

(G-8761)
PRECISION EXPLOSIVES LLC
4818 Midland Rd (22728)
PHONE.....................833 338-6628
Kenneth Wilber, *Branch Mgr*
EMP: 2
SALES (corp-wide): 343.2K **Privately Held**
SIC: 2892 Explosives
PA: Precision Explosives Llc
7964 Baileys Joy Ln
Warrenton VA

(G-8762)
ROSS INDUSTRIES INC (PA)
5321 Midland Rd (22728-2135)
PHONE.....................540 439-3271
Jamie Usrey, *President*
James T McFarland, *Vice Pres*
Salvatore Sparacino, *Vice Pres*
Douglas Hinkle, *Inv Control Mgr*
Allen Snow, *QC Mgr*
◆ EMP: 135
SQ FT: 46,500
SALES (est): 25MM **Privately Held**
WEB: www.rossindinc.com
SIC: 3556 3565 Meat, poultry & seafood processing machinery; packaging machinery

(G-8763)
SMITH-MIDLAND CORPORATION
5119 Catlett Rd (22728-2113)
P.O. Box 300 (22728-0300)
PHONE.....................540 439-3266
Ashley B Smith, *President*
Wesley A Taylor, *VP Admin*
EMP: 100 EST: 1960
SQ FT: 33,000
SALES (est): 9MM **Publicly Held**
WEB: www.smithmidland.com
SIC: 3272 Concrete products, precast
PA: Smith-Midland Corporation
5119 Catlett Rd
Midland VA 22728

(G-8764)
SMITH-MIDLAND CORPORATION (PA)
5119 Catlett Rd (22728-2113)
P.O. Box 300 (22728-0300)
PHONE.....................540 439-3266
Rodney I Smith, *Ch of Bd*
Ashley B Smith, *President*
Bobby Rochester, *General Mgr*
Adam J Krick, *CFO*
Estelle Cardenas-Mcclin, *Human Res Mgr*
EMP: 137
SQ FT: 44,000
SALES (est): 46.6MM **Publicly Held**
WEB: www.smithmidland.com
SIC: 3272 Concrete products, precast

(G-8765)
TAYLOR BOYZ LLC
9886 Rogues Rd (22728-1824)
PHONE.....................540 347-2443
Jeff Taylor, *CEO*
Nicole Taylor, *Admin Sec*
EMP: 2
SALES (est): 320.4K **Privately Held**
WEB: www.taylorboyz.com
SIC: 3799 Horse trailers, except fifth-wheel type

Midlothian
Chesterfield County

(G-8766)
A 1 PAINTING OF RICHMOND
13817 Barnes Spring Rd (23112-4251)
PHONE.....................804 237-9939
Andrew Leivas, *Principal*
EMP: 4
SALES (est): 191.8K **Privately Held**
WEB: www.richmond.com
SIC: 2711 Newspapers, publishing & printing

(G-8767)
A WILLIAMS TRANSPORT LLC
13926 Hull Street Rd # 1083 (23112-2004)
PHONE.....................804 896-5878
Anecia Williams, *Mng Member*
EMP: 1
SALES (est): 60K **Privately Held**
SIC: 3537 Trucks, tractors, loaders, carriers & similar equipment

(G-8768)
ADIS AMERICA
1309 Walton Creek Dr (23114-7148)
PHONE.....................804 794-2848
Greg Beckwith, *Principal*
EMP: 3
SALES (est): 195.9K **Privately Held**
SIC: 2329 Men's & boys' sportswear & athletic clothing

(G-8769)
AGILE WRITER PRESS
13620 Cradle Hill Rd (23112-4020)
PHONE.....................804 986-2985
Greg Smith, *Principal*
EMP: 2
SALES (est): 41.3K **Privately Held**
WEB: www.agilewriters.com
SIC: 2741 Miscellaneous publishing

(G-8770)
ALLEN DISPLAY & STORE EQP INC
14301 Sommerville Ct (23113-6837)
PHONE.....................804 794-6032
Hope Allen, *President*
Steve H Allen, *President*
Steve Allen, *General Mgr*
Stuart F Allen, *Exec VP*
Stuart Allen, *Vice Pres*
▲ EMP: 19
SQ FT: 8,200
SALES (est): 3.4MM **Privately Held**
WEB: www.allendisplay.com
SIC: 2542 5046 Fixtures, store: except wood; store fixtures

(G-8771)
ALSTOM RENEWABLE US LLC
2800 Waterford Lake Dr (23112-3981)
PHONE.....................804 763-2196
Richard D Austin,
EMP: 40
SQ FT: 6,000
SALES (est): 3.7MM
SALES (corp-wide): 95.2B **Publicly Held**
SIC: 3629 3511 Thermo-electric generators; turbines & turbine generator sets
HQ: Ge Steam Power, Inc.
200 Great Pond Dr
Windsor CT 06095
866 257-8664

(G-8772)
AO HATHAWAY PUBLISHING LLC
14241 Midlothian Tpke (23113-6500)
PHONE.....................804 305-9832
Gwynne Elliott, *Principal*
EMP: 2
SALES (est): 86K **Privately Held**
SIC: 2741 Miscellaneous publishing

(G-8773)
APEX MOBILE APP LLC
8834 Buffalo Nickel Turn (23112-6839)
P.O. Box 4415 (23112-0008)
PHONE.....................804 245-0471
EMP: 2
SALES (est): 62.1K **Privately Held**
SIC: 7372 Application computer software

(G-8774)
ARGOS USA LLC
Also Called: Ready Mix Concrete Company
3636 Warbro Rd (23112-3900)
P.O. Box 11063, Richmond (23230-1063)
PHONE.....................804 763-6112
Sterling Durham, *Manager*
EMP: 11 **Privately Held**
WEB: www.argos-us.com
SIC: 3273 Ready-mixed concrete
HQ: Argos Usa Llc
3015 Windward Plz Ste 300
Alpharetta GA 30005
678 368-4300

(G-8775)
ASCENSION PUBLISHING LLC
13330 Thornridge Ln (23112-4838)
PHONE.....................804 212-5347
Christopher Allen, *Principal*
EMP: 2 EST: 2015
SALES (est): 50K **Privately Held**
SIC: 2741 Miscellaneous publishing

(G-8776)
BASIC CONVERTING EQUIPMENT
2310 Conte Dr (23113-2361)
PHONE.....................804 794-2090
Walt Goetschius, *President*
Goetschlus Alberta Frances, *Vice Pres*
EMP: 4 EST: 1991
SQ FT: 2,400
SALES (est): 355.9K **Privately Held**
SIC: 3599 Machine shop, jobbing & repair

(G-8777)
BEAM GLOBAL SPIRITS AND
5309 Commonwealth Ctr (23112-2633)
PHONE.....................804 763-2823
Kyle Salus, *President*
EMP: 2
SALES (est): 67.4K **Privately Held**
WEB: www.beamsuntory.com
SIC: 2085 Distilled & blended liquors

(G-8778)
BECTON DICKINSON AND COMPANY
11300 Longtown Dr (23112-1677)
PHONE.....................804 744-4495
EMP: 2 **Publicly Held**
WEB: www.crbard.com
SIC: 3841 Surgical & medical instruments
PA: Becton, Dickinson And Company
1 Becton Dr
Franklin Lakes NJ 07417
201 847-6800

(G-8779)
BEJOI LLC
12613 Village School Ln (23112-3282)
PHONE.....................804 319-7369
Brittany Conroy,
EMP: 1 EST: 2015
SALES (est): 30K **Privately Held**
SIC: 2841 Soap & other detergents

(G-8780)
BLOOMBEAMS LLC
5316 Clipper Cove Rd (23112-6235)
PHONE.....................804 822-1022
Stephen M Bloom, *Mng Member*
EMP: 1
SALES (est): 93.1K **Privately Held**
WEB: www.bloombeams.com
SIC: 3648 7389 Outdoor lighting equipment; business services

(G-8781)
BOND INTERNATIONAL SFTWR INC
15871 City View Dr (23113-7304)
PHONE.....................804 601-4640
David Perotti, *Branch Mgr*
EMP: 2

▲ = Import ▼=Export
◆ =Import/Export

SALES (corp-wide): 34.8MM **Privately Held**
WEB: www.erecruit.com
SIC: 7372 Prepackaged software
HQ: Bond International Software, Inc.
1805 Old Alabama Rd # 340
Roswell GA 30076

(G-8782)
BRANDERVISIONS
Also Called: Bvs
13507 E Boundary Rd Ste A (23112-3939)
PHONE..........................804 744-1705
Fax: 804 744-6169
EMP: 5 **EST:** 1981
SQ FT: 1,200
SALES (est): 380K **Privately Held**
SIC: 3825 7629 Mfg Electrical Measuring Instruments Electrical Repair

(G-8783)
BRAUN & ASSOC INC
5904 Eastbluff Ct (23112-2043)
P.O. Box 36698, North Chesterfield (23235-8014)
PHONE..........................804 739-8616
Steve Braun, *President*
EMP: 1
SALES (est): 153.9K **Privately Held**
WEB: www.braunpackaging.com
SIC: 3086 Packaging & shipping materials, foamed plastic

(G-8784)
BROKEN WING ENTERPRISES INC
3632 Derby Ridge Way (23113-3726)
P.O. Box 368 (23113-0368)
PHONE..........................804 378-0136
EMP: 3 **EST:** 2009
SALES (est): 185.9K **Privately Held**
WEB: www.tateandtini.com
SIC: 2711 Newspapers, publishing & printing

(G-8785)
C & G FLOORING LLC
5141 Craig Rath Blvd (23112-6258)
PHONE..........................804 318-0927
David W Armentrout,
EMP: 9
SALES (est): 950K **Privately Held**
SIC: 2273 Carpets & rugs

(G-8786)
C THOMPSON ENTERPRISES ALL
1701 Winterfield Rd (23113-4136)
PHONE..........................804 794-3407
Cecil Thompson, *Principal*
EMP: 4
SALES (est): 248.3K **Privately Held**
SIC: 3699 Security control equipment & systems

(G-8787)
CABINET KINGDOM LLC
9025 Hidden Nest Dr (23112-6869)
PHONE..........................804 514-9546
Jason Kellum, *Principal*
EMP: 2 **EST:** 2007
SALES (est): 217.9K **Privately Held**
WEB: www.cabinetkingdomllc.com
SIC: 2434 Wood kitchen cabinets

(G-8788)
CAMERA CLUB OF RICHMOND
16301 Midlothian Tpke (23113-7326)
PHONE..........................804 380-9218
Douglas Turner, *Treasurer*
EMP: 3
SALES (est): 126.6K **Privately Held**
WEB: www.richmond.com
SIC: 2711 Newspapers, publishing & printing

(G-8789)
CAPITAL LINEN SERVICES INC
2430 Oak Lake Blvd (23112-7901)
PHONE..........................804 744-3334
Bernard Rixey, *President*
EMP: 19

SALES (est): 1.2MM **Privately Held**
SIC: 2299 5719 3582 Batting, wadding, padding & fillings; linens; commercial laundry equipment

(G-8790)
CAPITOL GRANITE LLC
1700 Oak Lake Blvd E (23112-3995)
PHONE..........................804 379-2641
Chris Kidd, *Regional Mgr*
Mike Avery, *Prdtn Mgr*
Melissa Morris, *Sales Staff*
Paul Menninger, *Mng Member*
Travis Bowling, *Manager*
EMP: 45
SQ FT: 20,000
SALES (est): 7.2MM **Privately Held**
WEB: www.capitolgranite.net
SIC: 3281 1743 Granite, cut & shaped; marble installation, interior

(G-8791)
CARGOTRIKE CUPCAKES
713 Colony Oak Ln (23114-4684)
PHONE..........................804 245-0786
EMP: 1
SALES (est): 3K **Privately Held**
SIC: 2051 Bread, Cake, And Related Products

(G-8792)
CARYS MILL WOODWORKING
12742 Spectrim Ln (23112-3957)
PHONE..........................804 639-2946
Rick Hudson, *Principal*
EMP: 9 **EST:** 2011
SALES (est): 1.2MM **Privately Held**
WEB: www.carysmill.com
SIC: 2434 Wood kitchen cabinets

(G-8793)
CEMARK INC
13531 E Boundary Rd Ste A (23112-3953)
PHONE..........................804 763-4100
Gilbert W Chapman Jr, *CEO*
Karen Halder, *General Mgr*
EMP: 15
SQ FT: 2,500 **Privately Held**
WEB: www.cemarkinc.com
SIC: 2731 5999 Textbooks: publishing only, not printed on site; education aids, devices & supplies

(G-8794)
CHESAPEAKE OUTDOOR DESIGNS INC
1600 Sville Chase Turn Ln (23112-4587)
PHONE..........................804 632-1900
Frank Legg, *President*
▼ **EMP:** 18
SALES (est): 2.2MM **Privately Held**
SIC: 2431 Panel work, wood

(G-8795)
CLASSIC EDGE LLC
14300 Midlothian Tpke E (23113-6561)
PHONE..........................804 794-4256
Robert Appleby,
EMP: 4 **EST:** 2009
SALES (est): 337.1K **Privately Held**
WEB: www.theclassicedge.com
SIC: 3421 Cutlery

(G-8796)
CLASSIC GRANITE AND MARBLE INC
14301 Justice Rd (23113-6841)
PHONE..........................804 404-8004
Tony Kilic, *Principal*
▲ **EMP:** 17 **EST:** 2012
SALES (est): 2.7MM **Privately Held**
WEB: www.classicgranite.com
SIC: 3281 5032 Granite, cut & shaped; marble building stone

(G-8797)
CLODFELTER MACHINE INC
3017 Warbro Rd (23112-3946)
PHONE..........................804 744-3848
Charles K Clodfelter, *President*
Carol Clodfelter, *Vice Pres*
EMP: 11 **EST:** 1977
SQ FT: 10,800
SALES (est): 1.9MM **Privately Held**
SIC: 3599 Machine shop, jobbing & repair

(G-8798)
CMC PRINTING AND GRAPHICS INC
13513 E Boundary Rd Ste A (23112-3938)
PHONE..........................804 744-5821
Dan Woods, *President*
Frank Shortall, *Vice Pres*
EMP: 4
SALES (est): 450.5K **Privately Held**
WEB: www.cmcprint.com
SIC: 2752 Commercial printing, offset
PA: Collegiate Marketing Concepts Inc
13513 E Boundary Rd Ste B
Midlothian VA

(G-8799)
COGHILL COMPOSITION CO INC
10801 Tealby Ct (23112-1580)
PHONE..........................804 714-1100
John H Coghill, *President*
James M Coghill, *Vice Pres*
Jimmy Coghill, *Vice Pres*
Robin Gillespie, *CFO*
William Coghill, *Treasurer*
EMP: 17 **EST:** 1960
SALES (est): 1.2MM **Privately Held**
WEB: www.coghillcomposition.com
SIC: 2791 7338 Typesetting; secretarial & court reporting

(G-8800)
COLONIAL APPS LLC
4438 Old Fox Trl (23112-4734)
PHONE..........................804 744-8535
Doug Clementson, *Principal*
EMP: 2
SALES (est): 106.3K **Privately Held**
WEB: www.colonialapps.com
SIC: 7372 Prepackaged software

(G-8801)
COMMONWLTH SOCCER PROGRAMS LLC
1153 Huguenot Trl (23113-9113)
PHONE..........................804 794-2092
Steve Lovgren, *Mng Member*
EMP: 1
SALES (est): 98.8K **Privately Held**
WEB: www.cspsoccer.net
SIC: 3949 Soccer equipment & supplies

(G-8802)
COMPOST RVA LLC
6607 Southshore Dr (23112-2054)
PHONE..........................804 639-0363
Bruno Welsh, *Principal*
EMP: 3
SALES (est): 170.6K **Privately Held**
SIC: 2875 Compost

(G-8803)
COMPUTATIONAL SYSTEMS INC
Also Called: Emerson Process Management
201 Wylderose Dr (23113-6845)
PHONE..........................804 858-5800
EMP: 2
SALES (corp-wide): 18.3B **Publicly Held**
WEB: www.emerson.com
SIC: 3823 Industrial instrmnts msrmnt display/control process variable
HQ: Computational Systems, Incorporated
8000 West Florissant Ave
Saint Louis MO 63136
314 553-2000

(G-8804)
CR8TIVE SIGN WORKS
5613 Promontory Pointe Rd (23112-2023)
PHONE..........................804 608-8698
Carol Halsaver, *Principal*
EMP: 2
SALES (est): 100K **Privately Held**
SIC: 3993 Signs & advertising specialties

(G-8805)
CREATIATE
14007 Shadow Ridge Rd (23112-4113)
PHONE..........................609 703-2378
Sarah Patro, *Principal*
EMP: 2 **EST:** 2016
SALES (est): 72.3K **Privately Held**
WEB: www.creatiate.com
SIC: 3069 Fabricated rubber products

(G-8806)
CRISMAN WOODWORKS
5509 Chestnut Bluff Rd (23112-6309)
PHONE..........................804 317-1446
Tasha Crisman, *Principal*
EMP: 2
SALES (est): 117.3K **Privately Held**
WEB: www.crismanwoodworks.com
SIC: 2431 Millwork

(G-8807)
D3COMPANIES INC
201 Wylderose Dr (23113-6845)
PHONE..........................804 358-2020
Robert Hazelton, *President*
Christy Hunter, *Finance*
Beth Cato, *Exec Sec*
EMP: 1
SALES (est): 49.5K **Privately Held**
SIC: 2392 Household furnishings

(G-8808)
DAVIDSON BEAUTY SYSTEMS
10917 Hull Street Rd (23112-3317)
PHONE..........................804 674-4875
Sally Wilson, *Principal*
EMP: 2 **EST:** 2010
SALES (est): 109.6K **Privately Held**
SIC: 2844 Perfumes & colognes

(G-8809)
DIVINE NTRE & ANTNG MNSTS INC
14301 Trophy Buck Ct (23112-7603)
PHONE..........................757 240-8939
Patience Dean, *President*
EMP: 1
SALES (est): 35K **Privately Held**
SIC: 2731 7389 Book publishing;

(G-8810)
DOMINION TAPING & REELING INC
3930 Castle Rock Rd Ste D (23112-2947)
PHONE..........................804 763-2700
Lesa Beatty, *CEO*
Thomas Beatty, *President*
Richard Keyser, *Vice Pres*
Friend Wells, *Vice Pres*
EMP: 5
SQ FT: 1,100
SALES (est): 366K **Privately Held**
WEB: www.dominiontapeandreel.com
SIC: 3679 7389 Electronic circuits; packaging & labeling services

(G-8811)
DREAM IT & DO IT LLC
14451 W Salisbury Rd (23113-6453)
PHONE..........................804 379-5474
John Darrell Davis, *Administration*
EMP: 2 **EST:** 2014
SALES (est): 116.6K **Privately Held**
SIC: 2841 Textile soap

(G-8812)
EAST END RESOURCES GROUP LLC
2920 Polo Pkwy (23113-1453)
PHONE..........................804 677-3207
Juhan Kim, *Branch Mgr*
EMP: 1 **Privately Held**
SIC: 1382 Oil & gas exploration services
PA: East End Resources Group Llc
3912 Meadowdale Blvd
North Chesterfield VA

(G-8813)
EDGE MCS LLC
14321 Sommerville Ct (23113-6910)
P.O. Box 345 (23113-0345)
PHONE..........................804 379-6772
Jerry Grothendick, *President*
EMP: 1 **EST:** 2015
SQ FT: 25,000
SALES (est): 76.5K **Privately Held**
WEB: www.edgemcs.com
SIC: 3621 3629 3694 3511 Generators for storage battery chargers; battery chargers, rectifying or nonrotating; battery charging alternators & generators; turbines & turbine generator sets; switchgear; switchgear & switchboard apparatus

(G-8814)
ERIC WALKER
2931 Polo Pkwy (23113-1453)
PHONE.....................804 439-2880
Eric Walker, *Principal*
EMP: 1
SALES (est): 46K **Privately Held**
WEB: www.ericwalker.strikingly.com
SIC: 3993 Signs & advertising specialties

(G-8815)
EXCELSIA INDUSTRIES LLC
14218 Chimney House Rd (23112-4304)
PHONE.....................804 347-7626
Lars Douglas, *Administration*
EMP: 2
SALES (est): 85.2K **Privately Held**
SIC: 3999 Manufacturing industries

(G-8816)
EXIDE TECHNOLOGIES
Also Called: Exide Transportation Group
14231 Riverdowns South Dr (23113-3797)
PHONE.....................678 566-9000
Bob Carusso, *President*
EMP: 5
SALES (est): 776.3K **Privately Held**
WEB: www.exide.com
SIC: 3699 Electrical equipment & supplies

(G-8817)
FALLING CREEK METAL PRODUCTS
3909 Bellson Park Dr (23112-2911)
PHONE.....................804 744-1061
Jay Howard Smith III, *President*
James H Smith Jr, *Admin Sec*
EMP: 7 **EST:** 1970
SQ FT: 18,000
SALES (est): 943.2K **Privately Held**
SIC: 3599 Custom machinery

(G-8818)
FIRSTMARK CORP (HQ)
2742 Live Oak Ln (23113-3100)
PHONE.....................724 759-2850
Chris Disantis, *CEO*
David Devine, *Exec VP*
Matt Isley, *Exec VP*
EMP: 11
SALES (est): 15.5MM
SALES (corp-wide): 192.1MM **Privately Held**
WEB: www.firstmarkcorp.com
SIC: 3728 3812 Aircraft parts & equipment; acceleration indicators & systems components, aerospace
PA: Ontic Engineering And Manufacturing, Inc.
20400 Plummer St
Chatsworth CA 91311
818 678-6555

(G-8819)
FLEXI-DENT INC
1256 Sycamore Sq Ste 201 (23113-4255)
PHONE.....................804 897-2455
Gerard Mosca, *President*
EMP: 2 **EST:** 1997
SALES (est): 165K **Privately Held**
WEB: www.flexident.biz
SIC: 3843 Dental equipment & supplies

(G-8820)
FT COMMUNICATIONS INC
Also Called: APT Finders Free Locaters Svc
15431 Houndmaster Ter (23112-6518)
P.O. Box 1495 (23113-8495)
PHONE.....................804 739-8555
Michael Bognar, *President*
EMP: 3 **EST:** 1993
SALES (est): 366.1K **Privately Held**
SIC: 2741 Miscellaneous publishing

(G-8821)
GANPAT ENTERPRISE INC
Also Called: Yummo Frz Yogurt Chesterfield
13623 Genito Rd (23112-4002)
PHONE.....................804 763-2405
Ramesh C Bhatia, *President*
Raju Sarwal, *Vice Pres*
EMP: 5
SALES (est): 455.1K **Privately Held**
SIC: 2023 Yogurt mix

(G-8822)
GLOBAL PARTNERS VIRGINIA LLC
Also Called: Global Embroidery
3005 E Boundary Ter Ste G (23112-4067)
PHONE.....................804 744-8112
Norman Falkner, *Mng Member*
EMP: 2
SALES (est): 157K **Privately Held**
WEB: www.globalpromosonline.com
SIC: 2395 Embroidery products, except schiffli machine

(G-8823)
GLOBAL PROMOS
3005 E Boundary Ter Ste G (23112-4067)
PHONE.....................804 744-8112
EMP: 2
SALES (est): 108.2K **Privately Held**
WEB: www.globalpromosonline.com
SIC: 2759 Screen printing

(G-8824)
H & M CABINETRY
2940 Queenswood Rd (23113-6304)
PHONE.....................804 338-9504
Harriet Marks, *Administration*
EMP: 2
SALES (est): 142.5K **Privately Held**
SIC: 2434 Wood kitchen cabinets

(G-8825)
HALLMARK SYSTEMS
13600 Winterberry Ridge (23112-4946)
PHONE.....................804 744-2694
Robert Hall II, *Owner*
EMP: 1 **EST:** 1996
SALES (est): 89.4K **Privately Held**
SIC: 2796 Platemaking services

(G-8826)
HAYES LUMBER INSPECTION SVC
5414 Meadow Chase Rd (23112-6316)
PHONE.....................804 739-0739
Dale Hayes, *Owner*
EMP: 2
SALES (est): 95.6K **Privately Held**
SIC: 1389 Construction, repair & dismantling services

(G-8827)
HOMES & LAND OF RICHMOND
Also Called: State and Homes Magazine
1811 Huguenot Rd Ste 201 (23113-5601)
PHONE.....................804 794-8494
Michael Jones, *Owner*
EMP: 3
SALES (est): 218.7K **Privately Held**
WEB:
www.estatesandhomesmagazine.com
SIC: 2721 Magazines: publishing only, not printed on site

(G-8828)
HOMES & LAND OF VIRGINIA LLC
15764 Wc Main St (23113-7328)
PHONE.....................804 357-7005
Marsha Williams,
EMP: 1 **EST:** 2016
SALES (est): 60.5K **Privately Held**
SIC: 2721 Magazines: publishing only, not printed on site

(G-8829)
HUNTER INDUSTRIES INCORPORATED
13808 Cannonade Ln (23112-6181)
PHONE.....................804 739-8978
EMP: 3 **Privately Held**
SIC: 3432 Mfg Plastic Sprinkler Heads Valves & Control Products
PA: Hunter Industries Incorporated
1940 Diamond St
San Marcos CA 92078

(G-8830)
HY-TECH USA INC
14501 Charter Walk Ln (23114-4698)
P.O. Box 488 (23113-0488)
PHONE.....................804 647-2048
Ashwin Mondkar, *President*
Darshan Mondkar, *Shareholder*
EMP: 2
SALES (est): 177.7K **Privately Held**
WEB: www.hytechgroup.com
SIC: 3492 Valves, hydraulic, aircraft

(G-8831)
HYBERNATIONS LLC
2801 Sagecreek Ct (23112-4237)
PHONE.....................804 744-3580
Kevin Solley, *Principal*
EMP: 3
SALES (est): 211.8K **Privately Held**
SIC: 2331 2211 Women's & misses' blouses & shirts; shirting fabrics, cotton

(G-8832)
INNOVATIVE HOME MEDIA LLC
12319 Swift Crossing Dr (23113-3143)
PHONE.....................804 513-4784
EMP: 1
SALES (est): 75K **Privately Held**
SIC: 3651 Household Audio And Video

(G-8833)
INTEGRATED GLOBAL SERVICES INC
Also Called: Metal Spray
2713 Oak Lake Blvd (23112-3991)
PHONE.....................804 897-0326
Iain Hall, *Manager*
EMP: 3 **Privately Held**
WEB: www.integratedglobal.com
SIC: 3999 Sprays, artificial & preserved
PA: Integrated Global Services, Inc.
7600 Whitepine Rd
North Chesterfield VA 23237

(G-8834)
INTERPROME MARKETING INC
3005 E Boundary Ter Ste J (23112-4067)
PHONE.....................804 744-2922
Cory Holden Philpott, *President*
Shirley Marie Philpott, *Admin Sec*
▲ **EMP:** 2
SALES (est): 302.7K **Privately Held**
WEB: www.interprome.com
SIC: 2899 Chemical preparations

(G-8835)
J&A INNOVATIONS LLC
1925 Regiment Ter (23113-7230)
PHONE.....................804 387-6466
Allen Bancroft, *Principal*
EMP: 2 **EST:** 2013
SALES (est): 157.3K **Privately Held**
SIC: 3949 Sporting & athletic goods

(G-8836)
JEDI PRINTS LLC
13905 Deer Thicket Ln (23112-1996)
PHONE.....................757 869-4267
Ashlee Allard, *Principal*
EMP: 2
SALES (est): 90.8K **Privately Held**
SIC: 2752 Commercial printing, lithographic

(G-8837)
JEREMIAHS WOODWORK LLC
3003 Cove Ridge Rd (23112-4353)
PHONE.....................804 519-0984
Vanessa Cabrera, *Principal*
EMP: 2
SALES (est): 85.2K **Privately Held**
SIC: 2431 Millwork

(G-8838)
JINKS MOTOR CARRIERS INC
12220 Chattanooga Plz (23112-4865)
PHONE.....................804 921-3121
Alexander Jinks, *President*
EMP: 2 **EST:** 2016
SALES (est): 113.6K **Privately Held**
WEB: www.jinks-motor-carriers-towing-and-recovery-inc.business.site
SIC: 3711 Motor vehicles & car bodies

(G-8839)
KINDRED BROTHERS INC
3124 Queens Grant Dr (23113-3778)
PHONE.....................210 334-7723
EMP: 3
SALES (est): 73.3K **Privately Held**
SIC: 2082 Malt beverages

(G-8840)
KLDS CLIENT SERVICES LLC
2118 Tomahawk Ridge Pl (23112-4284)
PHONE.....................804 586-7538
Kerry Stutt, *Principal*
EMP: 3
SALES (est): 163.9K **Privately Held**
WEB: www.kldsclientservices.com
SIC: 2131 Chewing & smoking tobacco

(G-8841)
KROWN LLC
5131 Morning Dove Mews (23112-3157)
PHONE.....................804 307-9722
K J Anderson, *Mng Member*
Kaleeta Johnson Anderson, *Mng Member*
EMP: 1
SALES (est): 62.8K **Privately Held**
SIC: 2261 Printing of cotton broadwoven fabrics

(G-8842)
KUYKENDALL LLC DAVID
2511 Whispering Oaks Ct (23112-4203)
PHONE.....................804 622-2439
EMP: 2
SALES (est): 128.3K **Privately Held**
SIC: 2731 Books-Publishing/Printing

(G-8843)
LAGNIAPPE PUBLISHING LLC
5624 Beacon Hill Dr (23112-6530)
PHONE.....................804 739-0795
Benjamin Dehaven, *Principal*
EMP: 2
SALES (est): 102.2K **Privately Held**
WEB: www.lagniappepub.com
SIC: 2741 Miscellaneous publishing

(G-8844)
LATHAM ARCHITECTURAL PDTS INC
13912 Two Notch Pl (23113-4119)
P.O. Box 1718 (23113-1718)
PHONE.....................804 308-2205
Gary P Latham, *President*
Anne Elizabeth Latham, *Treasurer*
EMP: 3
SQ FT: 900
SALES (est): 289.1K **Privately Held**
SIC: 3354 Aluminum extruded products

(G-8845)
LAZY DAYS WINERY
3816 Old Gun Rd W (23113-2020)
PHONE.....................804 437-3453
John Fitzhugh, *Principal*
EMP: 2 **EST:** 2016
SALES (est): 89.3K **Privately Held**
WEB: www.lazydayswinery.com
SIC: 2084 Wines

(G-8846)
LEAPFROG SOFTWARE LLC
1611 Oakengate Ln (23113-4077)
PHONE.....................804 677-7051
David Johnson, *Partner*
EMP: 1
SALES (est): 97K **Privately Held**
SIC: 7372 Prepackaged software

(G-8847)
LEGACY PRODUCTS LLC
12727 Spectrim Ln (23112-3957)
PHONE.....................804 739-9333
Devin Granback, *Mng Member*
EMP: 20
SALES (est): 2.8MM **Privately Held**
WEB: www.legacy-products.com
SIC: 3089 5031 2431 Windows, plastic; windows; millwork; windows, wood

(G-8848)
LEVITON MANUFACTURING C
1607 Upperbury Dr (23114-5157)
PHONE.....................804 461-8293
David Hutchens, *Principal*
EMP: 1
SALES (est): 39.6K **Privately Held**
SIC: 3999 Manufacturing industries

(G-8849)
LIMITORQUE CORP
15407 Fox Crest Ln (23112-6349)
PHONE.....................804 639-0529

Woody Lawman, *Principal*
EMP: 1
SALES (est): 86.8K **Privately Held**
SIC: 3541 Milling machines

(G-8850)
LIZIS JAMS
13717 Cannonade Ln (23112-6180)
PHONE..................................804 837-1904
Elizabeth Egan, *Principal*
EMP: 3
SALES (est): 164.8K **Privately Held**
SIC: 2033 Jams, jellies & preserves: packaged in cans, jars, etc.

(G-8851)
LUCIA RICHIE
13000 E Coal Hopper Ln (23113-4602)
PHONE..................................804 878-8969
EMP: 1
SALES (est): 62K **Privately Held**
SIC: 3911 Mfg Precious Metal Jewelry

(G-8852)
MARTIN MARIETTA MATERIALS INC
1 Parkwest Cir (23114)
PHONE..................................804 674-9517
Bob Rysinski, *Branch Mgr*
EMP: 11 **Publicly Held**
WEB: www.martinmarietta.com
SIC: 3273 Ready-mixed concrete
PA: Martin Marietta Materials Inc
2710 Wycliff Rd
Raleigh NC 27607

(G-8853)
MARTIN MARIETTA MATERIALS INC
Also Called: Midlothian Quarry
3636 Warbro Rd (23112-3900)
P.O. Box 1709 (23113-1709)
PHONE..................................804 744-1130
Steve Choew, *Manager*
EMP: 22 **Publicly Held**
WEB: www.martinmarietta.com
SIC: 1422 Crushed & broken limestone
PA: Martin Marietta Materials Inc
2710 Wycliff Rd
Raleigh NC 27607

(G-8854)
MATTHEWS HOME DECOR
13102 Dawnwood Ter (23114-4400)
PHONE..................................804 379-2640
EMP: 2 **EST:** 2018
SALES (est): 88.3K **Privately Held**
SIC: 3634 Mfg Electric Housewares/Fans

(G-8855)
MC PROMOTIONS LLC
14419 Michaux Wood Way (23113-6868)
PHONE..................................804 386-7073
Monica Radford, *Partner*
EMP: 1
SALES (est): 100K **Privately Held**
WEB:
www.richmondpromotionalproducts.com
SIC: 2395 Embroidery products, except schiffli machine

(G-8856)
METALSPRAY INTERNATIONAL INC
2725 Oak Lake Blvd (23112-3991)
PHONE..................................804 794-1646
Frank B Easterly, *President*
Marcel Jimenez, *Controller*
EMP: 100 **EST:** 1989
SALES (est): 5.2MM **Privately Held**
WEB: www.integratedglobal.com
SIC: 3479 Coating, rust preventive

(G-8857)
METALSPRAY UNITED INC (PA)
2725 Oak Lake Blvd (23112-3991)
PHONE..................................804 794-1646
Frank B Easterly, *CEO*
Paul Strauss, *Vice Pres*
EMP: 12
SQ FT: 6,000
SALES (est): 6.7MM **Privately Held**
SIC: 3479 Coating, rust preventive

(G-8858)
MID-ATLANTIC BACKHOE INC
2131 Swamp Fox Rd (23112-5305)
PHONE..................................804 897-3443
Brian Norge, *Principal*
EMP: 3
SALES (est): 401.8K **Privately Held**
SIC: 3531 Backhoes

(G-8859)
MIDLOTHIAN CUSTOM WORKSHOP LLC
14208 Aldengate Rd (23114-6501)
PHONE..................................804 937-1184
Erik Thompson, *CEO*
EMP: 1
SALES (est): 50.9K **Privately Held**
SIC: 2511 Wood desks, bookcases & magazine racks

(G-8860)
MIELATA LLC
12910 Grove Hill Rd # 203 (23114-5558)
PHONE..................................804 245-1227
Forikh Shamsiev,
EMP: 1
SALES (est): 39.5K **Privately Held**
SIC: 2099 7389 Honey, strained & bottled;

(G-8861)
MOBILE INK LLC
12760 Forest Mill Dr (23112-7023)
P.O. Box 200, Richmond (23218-0200)
PHONE..................................804 218-8384
Karen Parker,
EMP: 10
SALES (est): 624.6K **Privately Held**
SIC: 2752 Commercial printing, offset

(G-8862)
MOSS MARKETING COMPANY INC
Also Called: Rsvp Richmond
14451 Chepstow Rd (23113-4174)
PHONE..................................804 794-0654
Winston Moss, *President*
EMP: 1
SALES (est): 56.3K **Privately Held**
SIC: 2741 Miscellaneous publishing

(G-8863)
MS MONOGRAM LLC
13510 Midlothian Tpke (23113-2626)
PHONE..................................804 502-3551
Brittany Krebs, *Principal*
EMP: 1
SALES (est): 41K **Privately Held**
SIC: 2395 Embroidery & art needlework

(G-8864)
MTF RESOURCES LLC
14201 Leafield Dr (23113-6003)
PHONE..................................804 240-5335
EMP: 2
SALES (est): 65.5K **Privately Held**
SIC: 1389 Oil & gas field services

(G-8865)
MVMT INC
2711 Ellesmere Dr (23113-3804)
PHONE..................................804 356-6520
EMP: 2
SALES (est): 118.6K **Privately Held**
SIC: 2741 Miscellaneous publishing

(G-8866)
MYBOYS3 PRESS
14400 Roberts Mill Ct (23113-6339)
P.O. Box 2555 (23113-8555)
PHONE..................................804 379-6964
Steven Smith, *Principal*
EMP: 1
SALES (est): 73K **Privately Held**
WEB: www.myboys3.com
SIC: 2741 Miscellaneous publishing

(G-8867)
NECTAR OF GODS CORPORATION
1601 Black Heath Rd (23113-2506)
PHONE..................................703 582-0856
EMP: 2
SALES (est): 64.1K **Privately Held**
SIC: 2084 Wines, brandy & brandy spirits

(G-8868)
NERD ALERT TEES LLC
14101 Thorney Ct (23113-6056)
PHONE..................................804 938-9375
James Carragher, *Principal*
EMP: 2
SALES (est): 90.3K **Privately Held**
SIC: 2759 Screen printing

(G-8869)
OBDRILLERS PROSHOP
200 Old Otterdale Rd (23114)
PHONE..................................804 897-3708
Brian Funnell, *Owner*
EMP: 1 **EST:** 2008
SALES (est): 61.7K **Privately Held**
WEB: www.orbdrillersproshop.com
SIC: 3949 Bowling alleys & accessories

(G-8870)
OBSERVER INC
Also Called: Chesterfield Observer
4600 Market Square Ln (23112-4875)
P.O. Box 1616 (23113-1616)
PHONE..................................804 545-7500
Gregory Pearson, *President*
EMP: 9
SALES (est): 526.4K **Privately Held**
WEB: www.chesterfieldobserver.com
SIC: 2711 Commercial printing & newspaper publishing combined; newspapers, publishing & printing

(G-8871)
OLIVE OIL TAMPROOM LLC
11400 W Huguenot Rd # 116 (23113-1193)
PHONE..................................804 897-6464
Shauna Wells, *Principal*
EMP: 4
SALES (est): 269.9K **Privately Held**
WEB: www.theoliveoiltaproom.com
SIC: 2079 Olive oil

(G-8872)
ONE OF A KIND KID
1811 Huguenot Rd (23113-5600)
PHONE..................................800 276-0054
EMP: 1
SALES (est): 42.5K **Privately Held**
WEB: www.oneofakindkid.com
SIC: 2369 Girls' & children's outerwear

(G-8873)
OUT ON A LIMB QUILTWORKS
5620 Beacon Hill Dr (23112-6531)
PHONE..................................804 739-7901
Cindy Hubbard, *Principal*
EMP: 3
SALES (est): 222.8K **Privately Held**
SIC: 3842 Limbs, artificial

(G-8874)
PAL ENTERPRISES
2707 Sutters Mill Ct (23112-4017)
PHONE..................................804 763-1769
Patricia Knalls, *Owner*
Lewis Knalls, *Co-Owner*
EMP: 2
SALES (est): 126K **Privately Held**
SIC: 3944 Craft & hobby kits & sets

(G-8875)
PANDY CO INC
13603 Quail Hollow Ct (23112-4452)
PHONE..................................804 744-1563
Penny Gilliand, *President*
EMP: 2
SALES (est): 50K **Privately Held**
SIC: 3999 Education aids, devices & supplies

(G-8876)
PARI RESPIRATORY EQUIPMENT INC (HQ)
2412 Pari Way (23112-3858)
PHONE..................................804 897-3311
Geoff Hunziker, *President*
Juan Guerra, *Vice Pres*
Julio Mendoza, *Engineer*
Leslie Rounds, *Accounting Mgr*
September Staten, *Accountant*
▲ **EMP:** 19
SQ FT: 14,295

SALES (est): 8.1MM
SALES (corp-wide): 12.2MM **Privately Held**
WEB: www.paripals.com
SIC: 3841 5047 Inhalators, surgical & medical; hospital equipment & furniture
PA: Pre Holdings, Inc.
2412 Pari Way
Midlothian VA 23112
804 253-7274

(G-8877)
PEABODY COALTRADE LLC
1500 Huguenot Rd Ste 108 (23113-2478)
PHONE..................................804 378-4655
EMP: 2
SALES (est): 1.4MM
SALES (corp-wide): 5.5B **Publicly Held**
SIC: 1241 Coal Mining Services
PA: Peabody Energy Corporation
701 Market St
Saint Louis MO 63101
314 342-3400

(G-8878)
PEGS EMBROIDERY INC
11814 Murray Olds Ct (23114-2658)
PHONE..................................804 378-2053
Patricia E Rice, *President*
Patricia A Hamilton, *Corp Secy*
EMP: 7
SQ FT: 2,500
SALES (est): 564.4K **Privately Held**
WEB: www.pegsembroidery.com
SIC: 2395 Embroidery products, except schiffli machine; embroidery & art needlework

(G-8879)
PIPER PUBLISHING LLC
2221 Huguenot Springs Rd (23113-7202)
PHONE..................................804 432-9015
John Guzak, *Principal*
Lisa Guzak, *Principal*
EMP: 2
SALES (est): 70.7K **Privately Held**
SIC: 2741 Miscellaneous publishing

(G-8880)
PIPET REPAIR SERVICE INC
5324 Houndmaster Rd (23112-6524)
PHONE..................................804 739-3720
Cathie Beavers, *President*
EMP: 5
SALES (est): 715.6K **Privately Held**
WEB: www.pipetterepairservice.com
SIC: 3821 7699 3825 8734 Pipettes, hemocytometer; balances, laboratory; laboratory instrument repair; scale repair service; standards & calibrating equipment, laboratory; calibration & certification

(G-8881)
PRE HOLDINGS INC (PA)
Also Called: Pari
2412 Pari Way (23112-3858)
PHONE..................................804 253-7274
Jeoff Hunzicker, *President*
Eloy Fernandez, *Business Mgr*
Mike Shutt, *Treasurer*
Barbara Allan, *Mktg Coord*
Kane Furey, *Manager*
▲ **EMP:** 7 **EST:** 1998
SALES (est): 12.2MM **Privately Held**
WEB: www.pari.com
SIC: 3841 Inhalators, surgical & medical

(G-8882)
PREMIER CABINETS VIRGINIA LLC
2350 Winterfield Rd (23113-4146)
PHONE..................................804 335-7354
Landon Edwards, *Mng Member*
EMP: 1
SALES (est): 85.1K **Privately Held**
WEB: www.premiercabsva.com
SIC: 2434 Wood kitchen cabinets

(G-8883)
PRODUCT ENGINEERED SYSTEMS
1303 Cedar Crossing Trl (23114-3148)
PHONE..................................804 794-3586
Kenneth A Odom, *President*
Angela Odom, *Vice Pres*
EMP: 6

GEOGRAPHIC

SQ FT: 10,000
SALES (est): 200K **Privately Held**
SIC: 3559 3599 Tobacco products machinery; custom machinery

(G-8884)
PUPPET NEIGHBORHOOD
1000 Ashbrook Landing Ter (23114-3137)
PHONE......................................804 794-2899
Mary V Simmons, *Principal*
Mary Simmons, *Principal*
EMP: 1
SALES (est): 88.6K **Privately Held**
SIC: 3999 Puppets & marionettes

(G-8885)
R A HANDY TITLE EXAMINER
Also Called: Richard Handy Title Examiner
6814 Sika Ct (23112-1938)
PHONE......................................804 739-9520
Richard Handy, *Owner*
EMP: 1
SALES (est): 67.6K **Privately Held**
SIC: 2711 Newspapers, publishing & printing

(G-8886)
RECOGNITION WORKS
2837 Cove View Ln (23112-4344)
PHONE......................................804 739-1483
Jeff Gunther, *Principal*
EMP: 2
SALES (est): 159K **Privately Held**
WEB: www.vcu.edu
SIC: 2499 Trophy bases, wood

(G-8887)
RENOVATED RICHMOND LLC
2020 Christendom Dr (23113-6008)
PHONE......................................804 467-5470
Lisa Pulsifer, *Principal*
EMP: 3
SALES (est): 114.3K **Privately Held**
SIC: 2711 Newspapers, publishing & printing

(G-8888)
RICHMOND REFACING
6302 Willow Glen Rd (23112-2232)
PHONE......................................804 739-9222
Christopher Harrison, *Owner*
EMP: 2 EST: 2010
SALES (est): 126.8K **Privately Held**
WEB: www.richmondrefacing.com
SIC: 2434 Wood kitchen cabinets

(G-8889)
RINEHART TECHNOLOGY SVCS LLC
2740 Ionis Ln (23112-3426)
PHONE......................................804 744-7891
Donald Rinehart Jr,
EMP: 1
SALES (est): 3K **Privately Held**
SIC: 3825 Instruments to measure electricity

(G-8890)
RIVER CITY CHOCOLATE LLC
12613 Village School Ln (23112-3282)
PHONE......................................804 317-8161
Edward Conroy, *Principal*
EMP: 1
SALES (est): 80.4K **Privately Held**
SIC: 2051 5441 5461 Bakery: wholesale or wholesale/retail combined; confectionery produced for direct sale on the premises; cakes

(G-8891)
RIVER CITY SIGN COMPANY
14430 W Salisbury Rd (23113-6452)
PHONE......................................804 687-1466
Collins Doyle, *Principal*
EMP: 1
SALES (est): 50.6K **Privately Held**
SIC: 3993 Signs & advertising specialties

(G-8892)
RIVER CITY WRAP LLC
3912 Mill Manor Dr (23112-7003)
PHONE......................................804 914-7325
EMP: 5

SALES (est): 441.4K **Privately Held**
WEB: www.rivercitywrap.com
SIC: 3272 Concrete products used to facilitate drainage

(G-8893)
ROCKHILL RESOURCES LLC
1851 Castlebridge Rd (23113-4002)
P.O. Box 846 (23113-0846)
PHONE......................................804 794-6259
David C Nelson, *Mng Member*
EMP: 2
SQ FT: 1,600
SALES (est): 240K **Privately Held**
SIC: 1311 Crude petroleum production

(G-8894)
ROYS COPIES
13531 E Boundary Rd Ste B (23112-3953)
PHONE......................................804 744-6200
Roy Hipwell, *Principal*
EMP: 3
SALES (est): 294.7K **Privately Held**
WEB: www.royscopies.com
SIC: 2752 Commercial printing, offset

(G-8895)
SAFEGUARD PRINTING PROMO
1520 Huguenot Rd Ste 114 (23113-2477)
PHONE......................................804 378-2166
EMP: 2
SALES (est): 83.9K **Privately Held**
WEB: www.thinkmarketink.com
SIC: 2752 Commercial printing, lithographic

(G-8896)
SEW MY MONOGRAM LLC
12016 Suthshore Pointe Rd (23112)
PHONE......................................804 739-2407
EMP: 1
SALES (est): 54.3K **Privately Held**
WEB: www.sewmymonogram.com
SIC: 2395 Embroidery products, except schiffli machine

(G-8897)
SHOP GUYS
1518 Unison Dr (23113-2831)
PHONE......................................804 317-9440
Paul Cole, *Partner*
Morgan Wiseman, *Partner*
EMP: 2
SALES (est): 140.5K **Privately Held**
SIC: 3537 7699 3569 Forklift trucks; lift trucks, industrial: fork, platform, straddle, etc.; loading docks: portable, adjustable & hydraulic; pallet loaders & unloaders; hydraulic equipment repair; jacks, hydraulic

(G-8898)
SIERRA TANNERY LLC
4400 Old Gun Rd E (23113-1358)
PHONE......................................804 323-5898
Michael L Jones, *Administration*
EMP: 2
SALES (est): 125.4K **Privately Held**
SIC: 3111 Tanneries, leather

(G-8899)
SIGN & ENGRAVING TECHNOLOGY
3905 Bellson Park Dr (23112-2911)
PHONE......................................804 744-7749
Clifton Williams, *Owner*
EMP: 10
SALES (est): 322K **Privately Held**
WEB: www.getmeasign.com
SIC: 3993 Signs & advertising specialties

(G-8900)
SIGN CRAFTERS INC
800 Murray Olds Dr (23114-2657)
PHONE......................................804 379-2004
Chris Isenberg, *Branch Mgr*
EMP: 1
SALES (corp-wide): 5MM **Privately Held**
WEB: www.signcrafters-inc.com
SIC: 3993 Signs, not made in custom sign painting shops
PA: Sign Crafters Inc
        1508 Stringtown Rd
        Evansville IN 47711
        812 424-9011

(G-8901)
SILICON EQUIPMENT CONS LLC
543 Watch Hill Rd (23114-3036)
PHONE......................................804 357-8926
Bryan Nicoll,
EMP: 1
SALES (est): 50K **Privately Held**
SIC: 3825 Instruments to measure electricity

(G-8902)
SIMPSONS EXPRESS PAINTIN
14710 Genito Rd (23112-5006)
PHONE......................................804 744-8587
Mike Simpsons, *Owner*
EMP: 1
SALES (est): 96.5K **Privately Held**
SIC: 3479 Painting, coating & hot dipping

(G-8903)
SJM AGENCY INC
1700 Huguenot Rd Ste D (23113-2397)
PHONE......................................703 754-3073
Steve Miller, *President*
Joan Miller, *Corp Secy*
EMP: 6
SALES (est): 900K **Privately Held**
SIC: 3993 Signs & advertising specialties

(G-8904)
SOLA RICHMOND LLC
1920 Normandstone Dr (23113-9668)
P.O. Box 703 (23113-0703)
PHONE......................................804 302-4498
David Aschheim,
EMP: 5
SALES (est): 291.7K **Privately Held**
WEB: www.richmond.com
SIC: 2711 Newspapers, publishing & printing

(G-8905)
SOUTHERN ACCENT EMBROIDERY
11906 Nevis Dr (23114-5303)
PHONE......................................843 991-4910
Jennifer Davis, *Principal*
EMP: 2 EST: 2015
SALES (est): 61.2K **Privately Held**
WEB: www.southernaccentembroidery.com
SIC: 2395 Embroidery & art needlework

(G-8906)
SPEC-TRIM MFG CO INC
12727 Spectrim Ln (23112-3957)
PHONE......................................804 739-9333
John F Webb, *President*
Karen G Webb, *Vice Pres*
EMP: 70
SQ FT: 65,000
SALES (est): 7.3MM **Privately Held**
SIC: 2431 Louver doors, wood

(G-8907)
SPECIALTY VHCL SOLUTIONS LLC
Also Called: Manufacturing
3930 Castle Rock Rd Ste H (23112-2947)
PHONE......................................609 882-1900
J Michael Burke, *CEO*
Brian Tomchik, *Principal*
Michael Burke, *Manager*
▼ EMP: 25
SALES (est): 3.6MM **Privately Held**
WEB: www.svs-us.com
SIC: 3711 Bus & other large specialty vehicle assembly

(G-8908)
SPECTRUM METAL SERVICES INC
1624 Oak Lake Blvd E (23112-3985)
PHONE......................................804 744-0387
Meredith Tullos, *President*
Jason Jenkins, *Vice Pres*
Michelle Jenkins, *Admin Sec*
EMP: 3
SALES (est): 505K **Privately Held**
WEB: www.spectrummetalservices.com
SIC: 3441 Fabricated structural metal

(G-8909)
SPOTLIGHT ON SPORTS LLC
2103 Carbon Hill Pl (23113-2510)
PHONE......................................804 615-3284

EMP: 2
SALES (est): 124K **Privately Held**
SIC: 3648 Lighting equipment

(G-8910)
STITCH MAKERS EMBROIDERY
1404 Quiet Lake Loop (23114-3258)
PHONE......................................804 794-4523
Judith Harvick, *Principal*
EMP: 1
SALES (est): 37.3K **Privately Held**
SIC: 2395 Embroidery & art needlework

(G-8911)
T E L PAK INC
2251 Banstead Rd (23113-4102)
PHONE......................................804 794-9529
Thomas E Loeper, *President*
EMP: 3
SALES (est): 1MM **Privately Held**
SIC: 3089 Molding primary plastic

(G-8912)
TECHLINE MFG LLC
3669 Speeks Dr (23112-7309)
PHONE......................................804 986-8285
John D Allen,
EMP: 1 EST: 2009
SALES (est): 15K **Privately Held**
SIC: 2844 Toilet preparations

(G-8913)
TIMMONS & KELLEY ARCHITECTS
14005 Steeplestone Dr D (23113-7602)
PHONE......................................804 897-5636
Jeff Timmon, *President*
Malcolm Kelley, *Partner*
EMP: 5
SALES (est): 421.2K **Privately Held**
WEB: www.timmonskelleyarchitects.com
SIC: 3446 8712 Architectural metalwork; architectural services

(G-8914)
TINKERS TREASURES
707 Coralview Ter (23114-3321)
PHONE......................................708 633-0710
EMP: 1
SALES (est): 41.5K **Privately Held**
SIC: 2499 Mfg Wood Products

(G-8915)
TWFUTURES INC
Also Called: Schd
14311 W Salisbury Rd (23113-6446)
PHONE......................................804 301-6629
Michael Roberts, *President*
Ryan Wilson, *Principal*
Jonathan D Tester, *Vice Pres*
EMP: 5 **Privately Held**
SIC: 2519 Garden furniture, except wood, metal, stone or concrete

(G-8916)
UNIQUES LLC
Also Called: Line Riders Custom Lures
3601 Muirfield Green Pl (23112-4529)
PHONE......................................804 307-0902
Patricia Boyle, *Principal*
William Boyle, *Manager*
EMP: 2
SALES (est): 97.6K **Privately Held**
SIC: 3949 Lures, fishing: artificial

(G-8917)
UROLOGICS LLC
5609 Promontory Pointe Rd (23112-2023)
PHONE......................................757 419-1463
Xuejun Wen, *Partner*
Kenneth Wynne, *Administration*
EMP: 2 EST: 2014
SALES (est): 122.9K **Privately Held**
WEB: www.urologics.com
SIC: 3841 3842 Catheters; surgical appliances & supplies

(G-8918)
VIRGINIA BREEZE ALPACAS LLC
13300 Hensley Rd (23112-1206)
PHONE......................................804 641-4811
Patricia Hamilton, *Principal*
EMP: 2

SALES (est): 106.3K **Privately Held**
WEB: www.alpacafacts.com
SIC: 2231 Alpacas, mohair: woven

(G-8919)
VMEK GROUP LLC
Also Called: Vmek Sorting Technology
2719 Oak Lake Blvd (23112-3991)
PHONE................................804 380-1831
Adriana Lovvorn, *President*
John Gardiner, *Production*
EMP: 5
SALES (est): 514.5K **Privately Held**
WEB: www.vmek.com
SIC: 3523 3569 Grading, cleaning, sorting machines, fruit, grain, vegetable; robots, assembly line: industrial & commercial

(G-8920)
WEST SHORE CABINETRY
14301 West Shore Ln (23112-6227)
PHONE................................804 739-2985
Lester Cmcghee, *Principal*
EMP: 2
SALES (est): 170.7K **Privately Held**
SIC: 2434 Wood kitchen cabinets

(G-8921)
WESTSIDE METAL FABRICATORS
1624 Oak Lake Blvd E (23112-3985)
PHONE................................804 744-0387
Brian Tullos, *President*
Meredith Tullos, *Vice Pres*
EMP: 7
SQ FT: 3,200
SALES (est): 790K **Privately Held**
WEB: www.spectrummetalservices.com
SIC: 3444 Sheet metalwork

(G-8922)
WOERNER WELDING & FABRICATION
3825 Hendricks Rd (23112-7334)
PHONE................................804 349-6563
EMP: 1
SALES (est): 25K **Privately Held**
SIC: 7692 Welding repair

(G-8923)
WRAP PACK INDUSTRIES INC
3106 Handley Rd (23113-3677)
PHONE................................804 897-1351
Michael Falcone, *Owner*
EMP: 2
SALES (est): 128.7K **Privately Held**
SIC: 3999 Manufacturing industries

(G-8924)
WYNNVISION LLC
5609 Promontory Pointe Rd (23112-2023)
PHONE................................757 419-1463
Kenneth Wynne, *President*
EMP: 1
SALES (est): 51.9K **Privately Held**
SIC: 2821 Plasticizer/additive based plastic materials

(G-8925)
XYMID LLC (PA)
5141 Craig Rath Blvd (23112-6258)
PHONE................................804 423-5798
John Strang, *Business Mgr*
Eric Teagan, *Vice Pres*
Craig Blvd, *Mfg Staff*
Frank Rehorst, *Technical Mgr*
Bill Mann, *Manager*
▲ EMP: 21 EST: 1998
SALES (est): 4.6MM **Privately Held**
WEB: www.xymidllc.com
SIC: 2394 2732 2823 2297 Cloth, drop (fabric): made from purchased materials; book printing; cellulosic manmade fibers; nonwoven fabrics

(G-8926)
YESCO OF RICHMOND
12730 Spectrim Ln Ste F (23112-7900)
PHONE................................804 302-4391
EMP: 3 EST: 2013
SALES (est): 245.7K **Privately Held**
WEB: www.yesco.com
SIC: 3993 Signs & advertising specialties

(G-8927)
ZYFLEX LLC
5141 Craig Rath Blvd (23112-6258)
PHONE................................804 306-6333
William Spencer,
Susan Spencer,
EMP: 1 EST: 2000
SALES (est): 450K
SALES (corp-wide): 4.6MM **Privately Held**
WEB: www.sportsactivewear.com
SIC: 2329 Men's & boys' sportswear & athletic clothing
PA: Xymid, Llc
5141 Craig Rath Blvd
Midlothian VA 23112
804 423-5798

Milford
Caroline County

(G-8928)
BEASLEY CONCRETE INC
Also Called: RR Beasley Beasley Concreting
16090 Aspen Rd (22514-2161)
P.O. Box 322 (22514-0322)
PHONE................................804 633-9626
Ray Beasley, *President*
William C Beasley, *Vice Pres*
EMP: 29 EST: 1992
SALES (est): 3.8MM **Privately Held**
WEB: www.beasleyconcrete.com
SIC: 3272 3273 Concrete products, precast; ready-mixed concrete

(G-8929)
CRH AMERICAS INC
16326 Industrial Dr (22514-2153)
P.O. Box 238 (22514-0238)
PHONE................................804 633-9841
Terrance McClain, *Branch Mgr*
EMP: 4
SALES (corp-wide): 30.6B **Privately Held**
WEB: www.crhamericas.com
SIC: 3273 Ready-mixed concrete
HQ: Crh Americas, Inc.
900 Ashwood Pkwy Ste 600
Atlanta GA 30338
770 804-3363

(G-8930)
DEJARNETTE LUMBER COMPANY
17186 Alliance Dr (22514-2170)
P.O. Box 67 (22514-0067)
PHONE................................804 633-9821
Terry Bullock, *President*
EMP: 17 EST: 1925
SALES (est): 2.3MM **Privately Held**
WEB: www.mineolascreenprint.net
SIC: 2421 5211 2426 Planing mills; planing mill products & lumber; hardwood dimension & flooring mills

(G-8931)
JCI JONES CHEMICALS INC
16248 Industrial Dr (22514-2139)
PHONE................................804 633-5066
Arlene Harris, *Manager*
EMP: 17
SQ FT: 19,822
SALES (corp-wide): 196.9MM **Privately Held**
WEB: www.jcichem.com
SIC: 2812 Chlorine, compressed or liquefied
PA: Jci Jones Chemicals, Inc.
1765 Ringling Blvd # 200
Sarasota FL 34236
941 330-1537

(G-8932)
NUTRIEN AG SOLUTIONS INC
15679 Colonial Rd (22514-2158)
PHONE................................540 775-2985
Duke McBroom, *Manager*
EMP: 9
SALES (corp-wide): 20B **Privately Held**
WEB: www.nutrienagsolutions.com
SIC: 2875 5191 2048 5261 Fertilizers, mixing only; pesticides; insecticides; chemicals, agricultural; prepared feeds; bird food, prepared; fertilizer

HQ: Nutrien Ag Solutions, Inc.
3005 Rocky Mountain Ave
Loveland CO 80538
970 685-3300

(G-8933)
R R BEASLEY INC
16090 Aspen Rd (22514-2161)
P.O. Box 322 (22514-0322)
PHONE................................804 633-9626
Ray Beasley, *Manager*
Judy Tidwell, *Manager*
EMP: 25
SALES (corp-wide): 5MM **Privately Held**
WEB: www.beasleyconcrete.com
SIC: 3272 Septic tanks, concrete
PA: R. R. Beasley, Inc.
16944 Richmond Rd
Callao VA 22435
804 529-6470

Millboro
Bath County

(G-8934)
BLUEGRASS WOODS INC
223 Millboro Indus Rd (24460-2136)
PHONE................................540 997-0174
Glenn Cauley, *President*
Vickie Ryder, *Vice Pres*
◆ EMP: 10
SALES (est): 500K **Privately Held**
WEB: www.bluegrasswoods.com
SIC: 2499 Fencing, docks & other outdoor wood structural products

(G-8935)
DEEDS BROTHERS INCORPORATED
8286 Douthat State Pk Rd (24460-3010)
PHONE................................540 862-7837
Daniel B Deeds, *President*
Judy M Deeds, *Corp Secy*
David L Deeds, *Vice Pres*
EMP: 5
SALES (est): 600K **Privately Held**
SIC: 2411 Logging

(G-8936)
KOOL-DRI INC
33640 Mountain Valley Rd (24460-2170)
PHONE................................540 997-9241
Earl M Myers, *President*
Kenneth Stewart, *Corp Secy*
John Bergman, *Vice Pres*
EMP: 12
SQ FT: 28,000
SALES (est): 704K
SALES (corp-wide): 1.6MM **Privately Held**
WEB:
www.countyofbathchamber.dw1.bytejam.com
SIC: 2385 Raincoats, except vulcanized rubber: purchased materials
PA: Keystone Nitewear Co Inc
550 W Route 897
Reinholds PA 17569
717 336-7534

(G-8937)
MIKES WRECKER SERVICE & BDY SP
21793 Mountain Valley Rd (24460-2832)
PHONE................................540 996-4152
Michael C Tennant, *Owner*
EMP: 3
SALES (est): 108.8K **Privately Held**
SIC: 7692 7532 Welding repair; body shop, automotive

(G-8938)
PETER ADAMS
Also Called: Adams Trucking
11131 Douthat State Pk Rd (24460-3000)
PHONE................................540 960-0241
Peter Adams, *Owner*
EMP: 2
SALES (est): 85.3K **Privately Held**
SIC: 1481 Overburden removal, nonmetallic minerals

Millers Tavern
Essex County

(G-8939)
BALL LUMBER CO INC
7343 Rchmond Tpphnnock Hw (23115)
P.O. Box 10 (23115-0010)
PHONE................................804 443-5555
John H Ball Jr, *Ch of Bd*
John P Ball, *President*
E Gary Ball, *Vice Pres*
Lewis H Ball, *Treasurer*
Esther P Beazley, *Admin Sec*
EMP: 60 EST: 1963
SQ FT: 4,000
SALES (est): 10.2MM **Privately Held**
WEB: www.balllumber.com
SIC: 2421 2426 Lumber: rough, sawed or planed; hardwood dimension & flooring mills

(G-8940)
HOLLAND LUMBER CO INC
Hwy 360 (23115)
PHONE................................804 443-4200
Richard E Holland Jr, *President*
Richard Holland, *President*
Jean S Holland, *Corp Secy*
Canfield Glenda Holland, *Vice Pres*
Linda Allen, *Shareholder*
EMP: 23
SALES (est): 1.7MM **Privately Held**
SIC: 2421 2426 Planing mills; hardwood dimension & flooring mills

Mine Run
Orange County

(G-8941)
WATSON WOOD YARD (PA)
11237 Dulin Ln (22508-9713)
PHONE................................540 854-7703
Lewis Watson, *Owner*
Ronnie Watson, *Co-Owner*
EMP: 1
SALES (est): 167.8K **Privately Held**
WEB: www.watsonsmulchtopsoil.com
SIC: 2499 Mulch or sawdust products, wood

Mineral
Louisa County

(G-8942)
BRYAN VOSSEKUIL
5501 Hickory Tree Ln (23117-9102)
PHONE................................540 854-9067
Bryan Vossekuil, *Principal*
EMP: 2
SALES (est): 157.3K **Privately Held**
SIC: 3699 Security control equipment & systems

(G-8943)
CANDLES MAKE SCENTS LLC
36 Derby Ridge Rd (23117-4879)
PHONE................................540 223-3972
George Perry, *Principal*
EMP: 1
SALES (est): 43.6K **Privately Held**
SIC: 3999 Candles

(G-8944)
CARDINALS LOGGING
4617 Old Frdericksburg Rd (23117-2129)
PHONE................................804 457-3543
Clifton Cardinal, *Principal*
EMP: 3 EST: 2011
SALES (est): 257.7K **Privately Held**
SIC: 2411 Logging camps & contractors

(G-8945)
CUNNING RUNNING SOFTWARE INC
Also Called: Crsi
668 Windway Ln (23117-4867)
PHONE................................703 926-5864
Chris Barrington Brown, *CEO*
Joanna Meletis, *President*

EMP: 2 EST: 2012
SALES (est): 127.6K **Privately Held**
SIC: 7372 7389 Application computer software;

(G-8946)
CUSTOM DESIGNS & MORE
121b Mineral Ave (23117)
PHONE.....................................540 894-5050
EMP: 3
SALES: 70K **Privately Held**
SIC: 2395 Embroidery

(G-8947)
CUSTOM DSIGNS EMB PRINT WR LLC
5600 Dogwood Tree Ln (23117-9114)
P.O. Box 840 (23117-0840)
PHONE.....................................540 748-5455
Cheryl A Fick, *Administration*
EMP: 2 EST: 2012
SALES (est): 147.6K **Privately Held**
SIC: 2752 Commercial printing, lithographic

(G-8948)
FOURTH CORPORATION
6018 Stubbs Bridge Rd (23117-9643)
P.O. Box 2652, Springfield (22152-0652)
PHONE.....................................703 229-6222
Jose Prats, *Treasurer*
Jose J Prats, *Marketing Staff*
EMP: 1 EST: 2000
SALES (est): 84.5K **Privately Held**
WEB: www.4thcorp.com
SIC: 7372 Prepackaged software

(G-8949)
HARRIS COMPANY INC
252 Poplar Ave (23117-4133)
PHONE.....................................540 894-4413
Samuel D Harris, *President*
Shirley A Harris, *Corp Secy*
EMP: 2
SQ FT: 6,000
SALES (est): 80K **Privately Held**
WEB: www.harris.com
SIC: 3523 Farm machinery & equipment

(G-8950)
MONTICELLO SOFTWARE INC
6411 Carter Ln (23117-9692)
PHONE.....................................540 854-4200
EMP: 8
SALES: 1.4MM **Privately Held**
SIC: 7372 7371 Prepackaged Software Services

(G-8951)
PAN CUSTOM MOLDING INC
112 Midpoint Dr Ste Br (23117-2122)
PHONE.....................................804 787-3821
EMP: 1
SALES (est): 95.4K **Privately Held**
WEB: www.panmould.com
SIC: 2431 Millwork

(G-8952)
WALTON LUMBER CO INC
2463 Pendleton Rd (23117-3915)
PHONE.....................................540 894-5444
Hidmore H Walton Jr, *President*
H H Walton III, *President*
EMP: 18 EST: 1939
SQ FT: 15,000
SALES (est): 2.8MM **Privately Held**
WEB: www.waltonlumber.com
SIC: 2421 Planing mills

(G-8953)
WELDMENT DYNAMICS LLC
112 Mdpoint Dr Unit A2 A3 (23117)
PHONE.....................................540 840-7866
Ryan Hatfield,
EMP: 1 EST: 2018
SALES (est): 90K **Privately Held**
SIC: 7692 3441 Welding repair; fabricated structural metal

Mitchells
Culpeper County

(G-8954)
CEDAR MOUNTAIN STONE CORP
10496 Quarry Dr (22729)
P.O. Box 12 (22729-0012)
PHONE.....................................540 825-3370
Edward C Dalrymple Jr, *Vice Pres*
David J Dalrymple, *Treasurer*
Robert H Dalrymple, *Admin Sec*
▲ EMP: 31
SQ FT: 4,000
SALES (est): 6.7MM
SALES (corp-wide): 110.7MM **Privately Held**
WEB: www.cedarmtnstone.com
SIC: 1422 Crushed & broken limestone
PA: Dalrymple Holding Corp
　　2105 S Broadway
　　Pine City NY 14871
　　607 737-6200

Moneta
Bedford County

(G-8955)
A PROEHL
9505 Stewartsville Rd (24121-4759)
PHONE.....................................540 890-6096
A Proehl, *Principal*
EMP: 2
SALES (est): 66.5K **Privately Held**
SIC: 2711 Newspapers, publishing & printing

(G-8956)
ADVANCED NANO ADHESIVES INC
360 Firstwatch Dr (24121-4018)
PHONE.....................................919 247-6411
EMP: 2
SALES (est): 86.7K **Privately Held**
SIC: 2435 Hardwood Veneer And Plywood, Nsk

(G-8957)
BLUE RIDGE WOOD PRESERVING INC
1220 Hendricks Store Rd (24121-6112)
P.O. Box 39 (24121-0039)
PHONE.....................................540 297-6607
Eldridge J Wimmer, *President*
Edward A Snodgrass, *Admin Sec*
EMP: 12
SQ FT: 10,000
SALES (est): 1.8MM **Privately Held**
SIC: 2491 Millwork, treated wood

(G-8958)
CHANDLER CONCRETE INC
14418 Moneta Rd (24121-5879)
PHONE.....................................540 297-4369
Frank Caldwell, *Site Mgr*
EMP: 5 **Privately Held**
WEB: www.chandlerconcrete.com
SIC: 3273 Ready-mixed concrete
PA: Chandler Concrete Inc
　　1006 S Church St
　　Burlington NC 27215

(G-8959)
CLARKE INC
1110 Benni Ct (24121-3543)
P.O. Box 10936, Lynchburg (24506-0936)
PHONE.....................................434 847-5561
Victor Clarke, *President*
Robin Clarke, *Vice Pres*
George P Sax, *Vice Pres*
Deborah Harris, *Manager*
EMP: 15
SALES (est): 2.1MM **Privately Held**
WEB: www.bebetterdomore.com
SIC: 2752 2789 2759 Commercial printing, offset; bookbinding & related work; commercial printing

(G-8960)
CLINE WOODWORKS LLC
5137 Scruggs Rd (24121-5216)
PHONE.....................................540 721-2286
Nelson W Cline, *Administration*
EMP: 4
SALES (est): 427.5K **Privately Held**
SIC: 2431 Millwork

(G-8961)
EXPRESS CONTRACT FULLMEN
477 Backnine Dr (24121)
PHONE.....................................540 719-2100
Valerie Sell, *Principal*
EMP: 2
SALES (est): 89.2K **Privately Held**
SIC: 3999 Novelties, bric-a-brac & hobby kits

(G-8962)
FERGUSON LOGGING INC
289 Shoreline Marina Cir # 110 (24121-2383)
PHONE.....................................540 721-3408
Edward S Ferguson Sr, *President*
EMP: 2
SALES (est): 141.9K **Privately Held**
SIC: 2411 Logging

(G-8963)
GSE INDUSTRIES LLC
321 Spinnaker Sail Ct (24121-3299)
PHONE.....................................832 633-9864
Susan English, *Principal*
EMP: 1
SALES (est): 52.1K **Privately Held**
SIC: 3999 Manufacturing industries

(G-8964)
HALES PAINTING INC
74 Scruggs Rd (24121-6329)
P.O. Box 805, Hardy (24101-0805)
PHONE.....................................540 719-1972
Nathan Hale, *President*
Kim Eaton, *Vice Pres*
EMP: 25
SALES (est): 182.3K **Privately Held**
SIC: 3479 Painting, coating & hot dipping

(G-8965)
HICKORY HILL VINEYARDS LLC
1722 Hickory Cove Ln (24121-4559)
PHONE.....................................540 296-1393
Roger Furrow, *Principal*
Furrow Judy, *Sales Dir*
Furrow Roger, *Sales Dir*
EMP: 4
SALES (est): 474.4K **Privately Held**
WEB: www.smlwine.com
SIC: 2084 Wines

(G-8966)
INDUSTRIAL MINERALS INC
208 Red Oak Rd (24121-2639)
P.O. Box 626 (24121-0626)
PHONE.....................................540 297-8667
Wolfgang Schmiel, *President*
◆ EMP: 2
SALES (est): 101.3K **Privately Held**
SIC: 3295 Minerals, ground or treated

(G-8967)
INTERNTIONAL ABRASIVE PDTS INC
413 Hillcrest Heights Dr (24121-4941)
PHONE.....................................540 797-7821
William Gordon Pringle Jr, *Principal*
EMP: 5 EST: 2009
SALES (est): 347.2K **Privately Held**
SIC: 3291 Abrasive products

(G-8968)
KLEARWALL INDUSTRIES
530 Anchor Dr (24121-2309)
PHONE.....................................203 689-5404
James Evans, *Software Dev*
EMP: 2
SALES (est): 156.5K **Privately Held**
WEB: www.klearwall.com
SIC: 3999 Manufacturing industries

(G-8969)
LAKE MANUFACTURING INC
Also Called: Lake Machine
2586 Tuck Rd (24121-4536)
PHONE.....................................540 297-2957
James Bowman, *President*
Lisa Pollard, *Manager*
EMP: 13
SALES (est): 684.9K **Privately Held**
WEB: www.lakemarineinc.com
SIC: 3599 Machine shop, jobbing & repair

(G-8970)
LAKESIDE EMBROIDERY
70 Scruggs Rd Ste 103 (24121-5199)
PHONE.....................................540 719-2600
Tuck Stevens, *Owner*
EMP: 1 EST: 2009
SALES (est): 65K **Privately Held**
WEB: www.lakesideembroidery.com
SIC: 2395 Embroidery products, except schiffli machine

(G-8971)
MARCUS COX & SONS INC
Also Called: W J Cox & Sons Lumber Co
3743 White House Rd (24121-4411)
PHONE.....................................540 297-5818
Wendell J Cox, *President*
Margaret Cox, *Corp Secy*
EMP: 10 EST: 1928
SQ FT: 1,000
SALES (est): 870K **Privately Held**
SIC: 2421 5021 Sawmills & planing mills, general; furniture

(G-8972)
MARSHALL CONCRETE PRODUCTS
14418 Moneta Rd (24121-5879)
P.O. Box 362 (24121-0362)
PHONE.....................................540 297-4369
Danny Marshall, *President*
EMP: 14
SALES (est): 1.1MM **Privately Held**
WEB: www.chandlerconcrete.com
SIC: 3273 Ready-mixed concrete

(G-8973)
NORTHWESTERN PA OPT CLINIC
Also Called: N W P O C
147 Windmere Trl (24121-3216)
PHONE.....................................540 721-6017
Richard J Wenzel, *CEO*
James R George, *Exec Dir*
EMP: 2
SALES (est): 36.4K **Privately Held**
SIC: 3851 8399 Eyeglasses, lenses & frames; social services

(G-8974)
PRINT-N-PAPER INC
70 Scruggs Rd Ste 104 (24121-5199)
PHONE.....................................540 719-7277
Teresa Schoonover, *President*
EMP: 3
SALES (est): 397.3K **Privately Held**
WEB: www.printnpaper.com
SIC: 2752 Commercial printing, offset

(G-8975)
PRINTERS RESEARCH CO
2455 Merriman Way Rd (24121-3164)
P.O. Box 787 (24121-0787)
PHONE.....................................540 721-9916
Lewis E Bondurnt, *Owner*
EMP: 3
SALES (est): 170K **Privately Held**
SIC: 2752 Commercial printing, lithographic

(G-8976)
SHANE HARPER
1074 Joyful Dr (24121-6078)
PHONE.....................................540 297-4800
Shane Harper, *Principal*
EMP: 2
SALES (est): 309.2K **Privately Held**
WEB: www.shaneharperplumbing.com
SIC: 3561 Industrial pumps & parts

(G-8977)
SIGN STUDIO
1280 Bremble Dr Apt C (24121-2687)
PHONE.................................540 789-4200
EMP: 1
SALES (est): 59.9K **Privately Held**
SIC: 3993 Mfg Signs/Advertising Specialties

(G-8978)
SKY DYNAMICS CORPORATION
1900 Skyway Dr (24121-4469)
PHONE.................................540 297-6754
Kevin Murray, *President*
Martha Murray, *Treasurer*
EMP: 6
SQ FT: 4,000
SALES (est): 480K **Privately Held**
WEB: www.skydynamics.com
SIC: 3728 5599 5088 Aircraft parts & equipment; aircraft instruments, equipment or parts; aircraft equipment & supplies

(G-8979)
SML SIGNS & MORE LLC
74 Scruggs Rd Ste 102 (24121-6330)
PHONE.................................540 719-7446
EMP: 3
SALES (est): 227.4K **Privately Held**
WEB: www.smlsignsandmore.com
SIC: 3993 Signs, not made in custom sign painting shops

(G-8980)
SML WATER SKI CLUB INC
425 Baywood Dr (24121-5394)
PHONE.................................540 328-0425
Tom Tanner, *Principal*
EMP: 1
SALES (est): 87K **Privately Held**
WEB: www.smlwaterski.org
SIC: 3949 Water skis

(G-8981)
SPRING GROVE INC
82 Park Way Ave (24121-6314)
PHONE.................................540 721-1502
W Goforth, *Owner*
EMP: 2 EST: 2018
SALES (est): 106K **Privately Held**
SIC: 3559 Special industry machinery

(G-8982)
THERMO-FLEX TECHNOLOGIES INC
360 Firstwatch Dr (24121-4018)
PHONE.................................919 247-6411
EMP: 2
SALES (est): 106K **Privately Held**
SIC: 3552 Textile Machinery, Nsk

(G-8983)
VALHALLA HOLSTERS LLC
1093 Cranberry Ct (24121-6356)
PHONE.................................540 529-4520
Ludwell Fairchild, *Principal*
EMP: 2
SALES (est): 95.6K **Privately Held**
SIC: 3199 Holsters, leather

(G-8984)
VALVE SAFE SOLUTIONS LLC
125 Larboard Dr (24121-2313)
PHONE.................................540 721-7808
Dennis Amos, *Principal*
EMP: 2
SALES (est): 140.9K **Privately Held**
WEB: www.valvesafesolutions.com
SIC: 3592 Valves

(G-8985)
WILDERNESS PRINTS
2416 Scenic View Rd (24121-4746)
PHONE.................................540 309-6803
EMP: 2
SALES (est): 81K **Privately Held**
SIC: 2752 Lithographic Commercial Printing

Monroe
Amherst County

(G-8986)
AAVERA ENGINEERING LLC
596 Ashby Woods Rd (24574-3107)
PHONE.................................434 922-7525
Jonathan Schjonning,
Warren Schjonning,
EMP: 4 EST: 2009
SALES (est): 302.1K **Privately Held**
WEB: www.aavera.com
SIC: 3694 Engine electrical equipment

(G-8987)
BLUE RIDGE WOODWORKS VA INC
130 Oakview Dr (24574-3344)
PHONE.................................434 477-0313
John B Price III, *CEO*
EMP: 1
SALES (est): 59.5K **Privately Held**
SIC: 2431 2434 2511 Millwork; wood kitchen cabinets; vanities, bathroom: wood; wood household furniture

(G-8988)
COOPER STEEL OF VIRGINIA LLC
275 Francis Ave (24574-2758)
P.O. Box 149, Shelbyville TN (37162-0149)
PHONE.................................931 205-6117
Jordan Cooper,
EMP: 32
SQ FT: 90,000
SALES (est): 69.7K **Privately Held**
WEB: www.coopersteel.com
SIC: 3441 Building components, structural steel

(G-8989)
ENGLANDS STOVE WORKS INC
Also Called: Englander
589 S Five Forks Rd (24574-2821)
P.O. Box 206 (24574-0206)
PHONE.................................434 929-0120
Carroll Hudson, *CEO*
Ronald G England, *CEO*
Robert C Dillard, *Vice Pres*
Chris Terrell, *Vice Pres*
Michael Speight, *Purch Mgr*
▲ EMP: 160
SQ FT: 55,000
SALES (est): 48.4MM **Privately Held**
WEB: www.heatredefined.com
SIC: 3433 Stoves, wood & coal burning

(G-8990)
GREEN VALLEY MEAT PROCESSORS
2494 W Perch Rd (24574-3172)
PHONE.................................434 299-5529
Joseph Albert, *Owner*
EMP: 1
SALES (est): 54K **Privately Held**
WEB: www.greenvalleymeatprocessors.com
SIC: 2011 Meat packing plants

(G-8991)
H & R LOGGING
Also Called: H and R Logging
111 Dancing Creek Rd (24574-3061)
PHONE.................................434 922-7417
Harold T Lloyd, *President*
Raymond Lloyd, *Principal*
EMP: 2
SALES (est): 140K **Privately Held**
SIC: 2411 Logging camps & contractors

(G-8992)
IMCO INC
767 Wilderness Creek Rd (24574-2934)
PHONE.................................434 299-5919
EMP: 25
SALES (est): 800K **Privately Held**
SIC: 3531 Mfg Construction Machinery

(G-8993)
J W BIBB SHOOTING BAGS
923 Ambrose Rucker Rd (24574-2178)
PHONE.................................434 384-9431
Jeff Bibb, *Principal*

EMP: 2
SALES (est): 126K **Privately Held**
WEB: www.jeffbibbpouchesandhorns.com
SIC: 3949 Shooting equipment & supplies, general

(G-8994)
OUTLAW WELDING LLC
258 Woodrow Ave (24574-2108)
PHONE.................................434 929-4734
Gregory Cyrus Jr, *Principal*
EMP: 2 EST: 2011
SALES (est): 96K **Privately Held**
SIC: 7692 Welding repair

(G-8995)
SAMS LOGGING INC
281 Foxcroft Dr (24574-2721)
PHONE.................................434 661-7137
Dalmase J Goff Jr, *President*
EMP: 2
SALES (est): 196.5K **Privately Held**
SIC: 2411 Logging camps & contractors

(G-8996)
TRI STATE GENERATORS LLC
2524 Elon Rd (24574-2904)
PHONE.................................434 660-3851
William Hickey, *Principal*
Robert Payne, *Mng Member*
EMP: 10
SALES (est): 957.8K **Privately Held**
WEB: www.tristategens.com
SIC: 3621 Generators & sets, electric

Montclair
Prince William County

(G-8997)
DOROTHY WHIBLEY
Also Called: Frank's Engraving Service
15443 Beachview Dr (22025-1024)
PHONE.................................703 892-6612
Dorothy J Whibley, *Owner*
Richard Whibley, *Owner*
EMP: 2
SALES (est): 330K **Privately Held**
WEB: www.franksengraving.com
SIC: 2796 7389 Engraving platemaking services; business services

(G-8998)
GIANT GRADALL AND EQP RENTL
16006 Prestwick Ct (22025-1732)
PHONE.................................703 878-3032
Gary Gaddy, *Owner*
EMP: 6
SALES (est): 1MM **Privately Held**
SIC: 3531 Cranes

(G-8999)
MACMURRAY GRAPHICS & PRTG INC
4177 Waterway Dr (22025-1602)
PHONE.................................703 680-4847
Joanne M Macmurray, *Owner*
EMP: 2
SALES (est): 250K **Privately Held**
WEB: www.mgpi.biz
SIC: 2752 7336 Commercial printing, offset; graphic arts & related design

Monterey
Highland County

(G-9000)
ALLEGHANY HIGHLANDS AG CTR LLC
Also Called: Alleghany Meats
6095 Potomac River Rd (24465-2715)
PHONE.................................540 474-2422
Caroline Smith, *Ch of Bd*
EMP: 6
SQ FT: 3,900
SALES (est): 418.2K **Privately Held**
WEB: www.alleghanymeats.com
SIC: 2015 2011 Poultry slaughtering & processing; meat packing plants

(G-9001)
ALLEGHENY INSTRUMENTS INC
1509 Jackson River Rd (24465-2407)
P.O. Box 8, Mc Dowell (24458-0008)
PHONE.................................540 468-3740
R Cotten Brown, *President*
▼ EMP: 7
SQ FT: 3,200
SALES (est): 899.9K **Privately Held**
WEB: www.alleghenyinstruments.com
SIC: 3861 Cameras & related equipment

(G-9002)
AMERICAN IMMGRTION CTRL FNDTIO
224 W Main St (24465)
P.O. Box 525 (24465-0525)
PHONE.................................540 468-2022
John Vinson, *President*
EMP: 2
SALES (est): 723.2K **Privately Held**
WEB: www.aicfoundation.com
SIC: 2741 Newsletter publishing

(G-9003)
BIG FISH CIDER CO
59 Spruce St (24465)
P.O. Box 523 (24465-0523)
PHONE.................................540 468-2322
L Kirk Billingsley, *President*
EMP: 4
SALES (est): 116.1K **Privately Held**
WEB: www.bigfishcider.com
SIC: 2099 Cider, nonalcoholic

(G-9004)
BRIGHTWAY INC
80 Potomac River Rd (24465-2227)
P.O. Box 32 (24465-0032)
PHONE.................................540 468-2510
Mark W Waybright, *President*
EMP: 4
SALES (est): 327.4K **Privately Held**
WEB: www.brightway.com
SIC: 1389 Gas field services

(G-9005)
DAVID BLANCHARD WOODWORKING
132 W Main St (24465-2754)
PHONE.................................540 468-3900
David Blanchard, *Principal*
EMP: 2
SALES (est): 210.9K **Privately Held**
SIC: 2431 Millwork

(G-9006)
HIGHLAND WLDG FABRICATION LLC
5221 Potomac River Rd (24465-2255)
PHONE.................................540 474-3105
Stephen F Good, *Administration*
Steve Good, *Administration*
EMP: 2
SALES (est): 136.5K **Privately Held**
WEB: www.htcnet.org
SIC: 7692 Welding repair

(G-9007)
HOOKE BROTHERS LUMBER CO LLC
Hwy 84 17 Miles W (24465)
PHONE.................................540 499-2540
Jerry Hooke,
John Hooke,
EMP: 17
SQ FT: 5,000
SALES (est): 199.9K **Privately Held**
SIC: 2421 Sawmills & planing mills, general

(G-9008)
KIDDOS LLC
27 W Main St (24465-2752)
P.O. Box 73, Cartersville (23027-0073)
PHONE.................................540 468-2700
Monica Baber, *President*
EMP: 3
SQ FT: 3,500

SALES (est): 178K **Privately Held**
SIC: **2038** 5142 5149 Dinners, frozen &
packaged; lunches, frozen & packaged;
packaged frozen goods; natural & organic
foods

(G-9009)
KING SIGNS AND GRAPHICS
3858 Jackson River Rd (24465-2676)
PHONE................540 468-2932
Terry King, *Owner*
Aaron King, *Co-Owner*
Vicki King, *Co-Owner*
EMP: 3
SQ FT: 1,440
SALES (est): 214.2K **Privately Held**
SIC: **3993** Signs & advertising specialties

(G-9010)
MOUNTAINTOP LOGGING LLC
151 Collins Run Ln (24465-2724)
PHONE................540 468-3059
Herbert Fisher, *Principal*
EMP: 2 **EST:** 2016
SALES (est): 104K **Privately Held**
SIC: **2411** Logging

(G-9011)
MOYERS LOGGING
10677 Mountain Tpke (24465-2599)
PHONE................540 468-2289
Ronald Moyers, *Owner*
EMP: 2
SALES (est): 150.2K **Privately Held**
SIC: **2411** Logging

(G-9012)
RECORDER PUBLISHING OF VA INC
Also Called: Recorder The
3 Water St (24465-2706)
P.O. Box 10 (24465-0010)
PHONE................540 468-2147
P Lea Campbell Jr, *President*
Claudia Campbell, *Vice Pres*
EMP: 13 **EST:** 1877
SALES (est): 400K **Privately Held**
WEB: www.therecorderonline.com
SIC: **2752** 2711 Commercial printing, off-
set; newspapers, publishing & printing

(G-9013)
REXRODE TIMBER & EXCAVATION
6492 Potomac River Rd (24465-2265)
PHONE................540 474-5892
Glen A Rexrode, *President*
Karen Rexode, *Vice Pres*
EMP: 2
SALES (est): 100K **Privately Held**
SIC: **2411** 1794 Logging camps & contrac-
tors; excavation work

(G-9014)
WESTROCK MWV LLC
6162 Potomac River Rd (24465-2263)
PHONE................540 474-5811
Trent Burkheldor, *Manager*
EMP: 4
SALES (corp-wide): 17.5B **Publicly Held**
WEB: www.westrock.com
SIC: **2631** Paperboard mills
HQ: Westrock Mwv, Llc
501 S 5th St
Richmond VA 23219
804 444-1000

Montpelier
Hanover County

(G-9015)
CLEARIMAGE CREATIONS
16253 Wild Cherry Ln (23192-2753)
PHONE................804 883-0199
Marlin Fegely, *Owner*
EMP: 2
SALES (est): 139.5K **Privately Held**
SIC: **3993** Signs & advertising specialties

(G-9016)
EDITORIAL INSPIRATIONS LLC
15086 Brown Pleasants Rd (23192-2642)
PHONE................703 627-0023

April Michelle Davis,
EMP: 1
SALES (est): 78.1K **Privately Held**
WEB: www.editorialinspirations.com
SIC: **2741** Miscellaneous publishing

(G-9017)
JONES LUMBER COMPANY J E
17055 Mountain Rd (23192-2549)
PHONE................804 883-6331
J E Jones Jr, *President*
J E Jones III, *President*
Barbara Segle Jones, *Treasurer*
EMP: 20 **EST:** 1932
SALES: 1.8MM **Privately Held**
SIC: **2421** 2426 Planing mills; hardwood
dimension & flooring mills

(G-9018)
MITCHELL MEDICAL LLC
16060 Saint Peters Ch Rd (23192-3012)
PHONE................804 640-4851
Tim C Mitchell, *Principal*
Dana Mitchell, *Principal*
Ed Mitchell, *Principal*
Jane Mitchell, *Principal*
Tim Mitchell, *Principal*
EMP: 5
SALES (est): 198.4K **Privately Held**
SIC: **3842** Surgical appliances & supplies

(G-9019)
R L BECKLEY SAWMILL INC
737 Windyknight Rd (23192-4015)
PHONE................540 872-3621
Robert L Beckley Sr, *President*
EMP: 14
SALES (est): 1.6MM **Privately Held**
SIC: **2421** Custom sawmill

(G-9020)
SCRATCHERGURU LLC
16193 Derby Ridge Rd (23192-2735)
PHONE................804 239-8629
Michael Pence, *CEO*
EMP: 2 **EST:** 2014
SALES (est): 110.9K **Privately Held**
SIC: **7372** 7389 Application computer soft-
ware;

(G-9021)
SELBY LLC
16060 Saint Peters Ch Rd (23192-3012)
PHONE................804 640-4851
EMP: 2
SALES (est): 89.9K **Privately Held**
WEB: www.janekennedymitchell.com
SIC: **2741** Miscellaneous publishing

(G-9022)
U S SILICA COMPANY
17359 Taylors Creek Rd (23192-2501)
PHONE................804 883-6700
Al Gwizdala, *Manager*
EMP: 33
SALES (corp-wide): 1.4B **Publicly Held**
WEB: www.ussilica.com
SIC: **1446** Industrial sand
HQ: U. S. Silica Company
24275 Katy Fwy Ste 100
Katy TX 77494
301 682-0600

Montross
Westmoreland County

(G-9023)
A & A PRECISION MACHINING LLC
80 Industrial Park Rd (22520)
PHONE................804 493-8416
Arthur Albertsen,
Susan Albertsen,
EMP: 8 **EST:** 1961
SQ FT: 5,600
SALES (est): 485K **Privately Held**
WEB: www.aandaprecision.com
SIC: **3599** 3829 3812 3728 Machine
shop, jobbing & repair; measuring & con-
trolling devices; search & navigation
equipment; aircraft parts & equipment
HQ: Qinetiq Inc.
10440 Furnace Rd Ste 204
Lorton VA 22079

(G-9024)
CABINET WORKS OF N N
17503 Kings Hwy (22520-2923)
PHONE................804 493-8102
EMP: 1
SALES (est): 60.7K **Privately Held**
SIC: **2434** Wood kitchen cabinets

(G-9025)
CAPTAIN FAUNCE SEAFOOD INC
2811 Cople Hwy (22520-3110)
P.O. Box 397 (22520-0397)
PHONE................804 493-8690
Joseph W Howeth, *President*
EMP: 20
SQ FT: 4,800
SALES (est): 500K **Privately Held**
SIC: **2092** 5146 5421 Fish, frozen: pre-
pared; crab meat, fresh: packaged in non-
sealed containers; seafoods; meat & fish
markets

(G-9026)
CLARKS DIRECTIONAL BORING
47 Glenn St (22520-2744)
P.O. Box 175 (22520-0175)
PHONE................804 493-7475
Donald Clark Jr, *President*
EMP: 5 **EST:** 2000
SALES (est): 1.2MM **Privately Held**
WEB: www.clarksdirectionalboringinc.com
SIC: **1381** Directional drilling oil & gas
wells

(G-9027)
ROBERT C REED
296 Federal Farm Rd (22520-3515)
PHONE................804 493-7297
Robert C Reed, *Owner*
EMP: 2
SALES (est): 98.2K **Privately Held**
SIC: **3524** Snowblowers & throwers, resi-
dential

(G-9028)
WALMER ENTERPRISES
39 Monument Dr (22520-8717)
PHONE................703 461-9330
Lorraine Horbaly, *President*
David Hogue, *Vice Pres*
Maegan Hogue, *Vice Pres*
Judd Horbaly, *Vice Pres*
Horbaly Judd, *Vice Pres*
EMP: 26
SALES (est): 1.8MM **Privately Held**
WEB: www.walmerenterprises.com
SIC: **2541** 3944 2517 Cabinets, except
refrigerated: show, display, etc.: wood;
games, toys & children's vehicles; wood
television & radio cabinets

Montvale
Bedford County

(G-9029)
E Z MOUNT BRACKET CO INC
Also Called: E-Z Fasteners
1307 Price St (24122-2820)
P.O. Box 295 (24122-0295)
PHONE................540 947-5500
Polly Medlin, *Vice Pres*
Lewis B Medlin Sr,
EMP: 17
SQ FT: 5,625
SALES (est): 2.1MM **Privately Held**
SIC: **3965** Fasteners

(G-9030)
SOUTH WESTERN SERVICES INC
Also Called: United States Precious Met Co
11871 W Lynchburg Rd (24122)
P.O. Box 538 (24122-0538)
PHONE................540 947-5407
Allen Woody, *President*
Barry Driskill, *Corp Secy*
EMP: 2
SQ FT: 12,000
SALES (est): 900K **Privately Held**
SIC: **3341** Secondary nonferrous metals

Moon
Mathews County

(G-9031)
ALCAT PRECAST INC
125 Blue Crab Dr (23119-2136)
P.O. Box 301 (23119-0301)
PHONE................804 725-4080
EMP: 3
SALES (est): 249.2K **Privately Held**
WEB: www.alcatprecast.com
SIC: **3272** Precast terrazo or concrete
products

Moseley
Chesterfield County

(G-9032)
AA RENWBLE ENRGY HYDRO SYS INC
4101 Hobblebush Ter (23120-1250)
P.O. Box 35952, North Chesterfield
(23235-0952)
PHONE................804 739-0045
Maurice Smith, *CEO*
Jermaine Smith, *Vice Pres*
EMP: 7
SALES (est): 555.3K **Privately Held**
WEB: www.aarenewablehydroenergy.com
SIC: **3612** 7389 Specialty transformers;

(G-9033)
BACKWOODS SECURITY LLC
5300 Otterdale Rd (23120-2201)
PHONE................804 641-0674
Matthew McClure,
EMP: 1
SALES (est): 86.3K **Privately Held**
SIC: **3484** 7389 Guns (firearms) or gun
parts, 30 mm. & below;

(G-9034)
BATONBIO LLC
7055 Golden Aster Dr (23120-1664)
PHONE................347 491-0189
Paul Yarabe,
EMP: 1
SALES (est): 47.2K **Privately Held**
SIC: **2834** Pharmaceutical preparations

(G-9035)
COUNTY LINE CUSTOM WDWKG LLC
21311 Genito Rd (23120-1004)
PHONE................804 338-8436
Andrew Lindberg, *Principal*
EMP: 2
SALES (est): 85.2K **Privately Held**
SIC: **2431** Millwork

(G-9036)
CPS CONTRACTORS INC
17707 Hull Street Rd (23120-1469)
P.O. Box 25, Jetersville (23083-0001)
PHONE................804 561-6834
Kathy Osborne, *Office Mgr*
Kathryn Osborne, *Manager*
EMP: 5
SQ FT: 1,300
SALES (est): 288.5K **Privately Held**
WEB: www.cpscontractorsinc.com
SIC: **3088** 3261 3432 1711 Plastics
plumbing fixtures; vitreous plumbing fix-
tures; plastic plumbing fixture fittings, as-
sembly; heating & air conditioning
contractors; packing & crating

(G-9037)
CROSSROADS CABINETS LLC
7607 Rock Cress Dr (23120-1787)
PHONE................319 431-1588
EMP: 1
SALES (est): 53.7K **Privately Held**
SIC: **2434** Wood kitchen cabinets

(G-9038)
DESALES INC
21411 Genito Rd (23120-1067)
PHONE................804 794-8187
John Pennington, *President*
EMP: 2

SALES (est): 96.4K **Privately Held**
SIC: 2299 Ramie yarn, thread, roving & textiles

(G-9039)
DOWNUNDER HATS VIRGINIA LLC
6600 Glen Falls Xing (23120-1796)
PHONE......................................804 334-7476
William Locke, *Principal*
EMP: 2
SALES (est): 82.6K **Privately Held**
WEB: www.downunderhats.com
SIC: 2353 Hats, caps & millinery

(G-9040)
HOLLYWOOD GRAPHICS AND SIGNS
1135 Bradbury Rd (23120-1044)
PHONE......................................804 382-2199
Ryan Wilbourne, *Principal*
EMP: 1
SALES (est): 70.9K **Privately Held**
WEB: www.teamhollywoodgraphics.com
SIC: 3993 Signs & advertising specialties

(G-9041)
L C M B INC
16801 Starlee Ct (23120-2214)
PHONE......................................804 639-1429
Leanne Bank, *Principal*
EMP: 2
SALES (est): 79.5K **Privately Held**
SIC: 2731 Book publishing

(G-9042)
LA PUBLISHING
6100 Otterdale Rd (23120-1285)
PHONE......................................757 650-8364
Pam Wiggins, *Principal*
EMP: 1
SALES (est): 37.5K **Privately Held**
WEB: www.lapllc.com
SIC: 2741 Miscellaneous publishing

(G-9043)
MONDAY MORNING PRESS LLC
6313 Knotgrass Aly (23120-2277)
PHONE......................................804 869-5020
EMP: 1
SALES (est): 41.3K **Privately Held**
SIC: 2741 Miscellaneous publishing

(G-9044)
PHILOSOPHY WORLDWIDE APPAREL
4010 Hunters Ridge Dr (23120-1243)
PHONE......................................804 767-0308
Jesse Arroyo, *Partner*
EMP: 2
SALES (est): 10K **Privately Held**
SIC: 2389 Apparel & accessories

(G-9045)
PN LABS
1179 Bradbury Rd (23120-1044)
PHONE......................................804 938-1600
Robert Ylimaki, *CEO*
EMP: 2
SQ FT: 30,000
SALES (est): 114.6K **Privately Held**
SIC: 3699 Linear accelerators

(G-9046)
RICHMOND WOODWORKS LLC
19701 Genito Rd (23120-1069)
PHONE......................................804 510-3747
Robert Shumaker, *Principal*
EMP: 1
SALES (est): 45.6K **Privately Held**
SIC: 2499 Wood products

(G-9047)
SANDY FARNHAM
Also Called: Scoops
20521 Skinquarter Rd (23120-1504)
PHONE......................................804 310-6171
Sandy Farnham, *Owner*
EMP: 1
SALES (est): 39.5K **Privately Held**
SIC: 2024 Ice cream & frozen desserts

(G-9048)
SOUTHERN PLUMBING & BACKHOE IN
2021 Genito Rd (23120-1073)
PHONE......................................804 598-7470
Stephen L Francisco, *Principal*
EMP: 6
SALES (est): 1MM **Privately Held**
SIC: 3531 Backhoes

(G-9049)
TKO PROMOS
5337 Fox Lake Ter (23120-1611)
PHONE......................................804 564-1683
Tracy Ebert, *Owner*
Pistana Jim, *Marketing Mgr*
EMP: 1
SALES (est): 140K **Privately Held**
SIC: 3993 Signs & advertising specialties

(G-9050)
TRADEMARK BRANDERS
16902 Hull Street Rd (23120-1460)
P.O. Box 1692, Midlothian (23113-1692)
PHONE......................................804 277-4428
Michael Lynn, *Principal*
EMP: 3 EST: 2016
SALES (est): 137.2K **Privately Held**
WEB: www.trademarkbranders.com
SIC: 2323 Men's & boys' neckwear

Mount Crawford
Rockingham County

(G-9051)
CARGILL INCORPORATED
5688 S Valley Pike (22841-2346)
P.O. Box 549, Harrisonburg (22803-0549)
PHONE......................................540 432-5700
Neal Snoddy, *Branch Mgr*
EMP: 30
SALES (corp-wide): 113.4B **Privately Held**
WEB: www.peterschocolate.com
SIC: 2015 Turkey, processed: fresh
PA: Cargill, Incorporated
15407 Mcginty Rd W
Wayzata MN 55391
952 742-7575

(G-9052)
CARGILL MEAT SOLUTIONS CORP
5688 S Valley Pike (22841-2346)
PHONE......................................540 437-8000
Patrick Evick, *Plant Mgr*
EMP: 8
SALES (corp-wide): 113.4B **Privately Held**
WEB: www.cargillmeatsolutions.com
SIC: 2011 Meat packing plants
HQ: Cargill Meat Solutions Corp
151 N Main St Ste 900
Wichita KS 67202
316 291-2500

(G-9053)
CROSS KEYS VINEYARDS LLC
6011 E Timber Ridge Rd (22841-2550)
PHONE......................................540 234-0505
Nikoo Rafat,
Bob Bakhtair,
▲ EMP: 14 EST: 2002
SQ FT: 22,000
SALES (est): 2.2MM **Privately Held**
WEB: www.crosskeysvineyards.com
SIC: 2084 Wines

(G-9054)
EASTERN BIOPLASTICS LLC
100 White Picket Trl (22841-2372)
P.O. Box 1845, Harrisonburg (22801-9500)
PHONE......................................540 437-1984
Cecil E Meyerhoeffer Jr, *Mng Member*
EMP: 8
SQ FT: 12,500
SALES (est): 1.3MM **Privately Held**
WEB: www.easternbioplastics.com
SIC: 2821 Plastics materials & resins

(G-9055)
INTRAPAC (HARRISONBURG) INC
4850 Crowe Dr (22841-2221)
PHONE......................................540 434-1703
Rami Younes, *President*
Joe Forelich, *Vice Pres*
Randy Churchill, *Plant Mgr*
David Stanlick, *Opers Mgr*
Tim Cox, *Manager*
◆ EMP: 260
SQ FT: 142,575
SALES (est): 50.1MM
SALES (corp-wide): 158MM **Privately Held**
WEB: www.intrapacinternational.com
SIC: 3499 3089 Metal household articles; plastic containers, except foam
PA: Intrapac International Llc
136 Fairview Rd Ste 320
Mooresville NC 28117
704 360-8923

(G-9056)
MARCELINE VINEYARDS LLC
5887 Cross Keys Rd (22841-2552)
PHONE......................................540 212-9798
J Burns Earle III, *Administration*
EMP: 1
SALES (est): 78.3K **Privately Held**
WEB: www.marcelinevineyards.com
SIC: 2084 Wine cellars, bonded: engaged in blending wines

(G-9057)
POWER MONITORS INC (PA)
800 N Main St (22841-2325)
PHONE......................................540 432-3077
Walter Curt, *CEO*
Wayne Bruffy, *President*
Chris Mullins, *President*
Dale Partlow, *Engineer*
Wayne Lafleur, *Senior Engr*
EMP: 24
SQ FT: 8,000
SALES: 7.9K **Privately Held**
WEB: www.powermonitors.com
SIC: 3829 Measuring & controlling devices

(G-9058)
RIDDLEBERGER BROTHERS INC
Also Called: Honeywell Authorized Dealer
6127 S Valley Pike (22841-2352)
P.O. Box 27 (22841-0027)
PHONE......................................540 434-1731
James P Young, *CEO*
Wayne Gibson, *General Mgr*
Daniel Blosser, *Vice Pres*
Charles E Cline, *Vice Pres*
William George, *Vice Pres*
EMP: 400
SQ FT: 35,000
SALES (est): 36.5MM
SALES (corp-wide): 2.1B **Publicly Held**
WEB: www.rbiva.com
SIC: 3444 1711 Sheet metalwork; mechanical contractor
PA: Comfort Systems Usa, Inc.
675 Bering Dr Ste 400
Houston TX 77057
713 830-9600

(G-9059)
RIVER VALLEY CUSTOM MILLWORK
975 Cottontail Trl (22841-2171)
PHONE......................................540 438-0208
EMP: 1
SALES (est): 54.1K **Privately Held**
SIC: 2431 Millwork

(G-9060)
TODD HUFFMAN INSTALLS LLC
Also Called: Thi
6257a S Valley Pike (22841-2324)
PHONE......................................540 271-4221
Todd Huffman, *CEO*
EMP: 1
SQ FT: 1,600
SALES (est): 60.9K **Privately Held**
WEB: www.thinstalls.com
SIC: 3714 Motor vehicle parts & accessories

(G-9061)
TRIPLE S PALLETS LLC
950 Cottontail Trl (22841-2171)
P.O. Box 129 (22841-0129)
PHONE......................................540 810-4581
Kenneth Lehmon, *Mng Member*
Hans Lehmon,
EMP: 25
SALES (est): 275K **Privately Held**
SIC: 2448 3271 Pallets, wood; blocks, concrete: landscape or retaining wall

(G-9062)
VALLEY HEIRLOOMS LLC
4752 Landis Ln (22841-2538)
PHONE......................................540 234-0251
Anita Riggleman, *Principal*
EMP: 2 EST: 2016
SALES (est): 56K **Privately Held**
WEB: www.valleyheirlooms.com
SIC: 2511 Wood household furniture

(G-9063)
WWF OPERATING COMPANY
Also Called: Whitewave Foods
6364 S Valley Pike (22841-2370)
P.O. Box 218 (22841-0218)
PHONE......................................540 434-7328
Andy Morris, *Manager*
EMP: 309
SALES (corp-wide): 656MM **Privately Held**
WEB: www.whitewave.com
SIC: 2026 Milk processing (pasteurizing, homogenizing, bottling)
HQ: Wwf Operating Company
12002 Airport Way
Broomfield CO 80021
214 303-3400

Mount Jackson
Shenandoah County

(G-9064)
ANDROS BOWMAN PRODUCTS LLC (DH)
Also Called: Andros Foods North America
10119 Old Valley Pike (22842-9565)
P.O. Box 817 (22842-0817)
PHONE......................................540 217-4100
Terry Stoehr, *CEO*
Jean-Luc Heymans, *President*
Todd Fisher, *Vice Pres*
Julian Lahaye, *Vice Pres*
Jason Simpson, *Vice Pres*
◆ EMP: 90 EST: 1939
SQ FT: 3,000,000
SALES (est): 150MM **Privately Held**
WEB: www.androsna.com
SIC: 2033 2099 2037 Fruit juices: packaged in cans, jars, etc.; apple sauce: packaged in cans, jars, etc.; fruit juices: fresh; jams, jellies & preserves: packaged in cans, jars, etc.; food preparations; frozen fruits & vegetables
HQ: Andros
Bonne Maman Andros France Boin
Biars Sur Cere 46130
565 100-625

(G-9065)
APPALACHIAN GROWTH LOGGING LLC
2782 Supinlick Ridge Rd (22842-3524)
PHONE......................................540 336-2674
Alan Elmer Gleske, *Principal*
EMP: 2 EST: 2018
SALES (est): 81.7K **Privately Held**
SIC: 2411 Logging

(G-9066)
BOBBY AND PJS JERKY SHACK
1849 Kelly Rd (22842-3329)
PHONE......................................540 856-2415
EMP: 3
SALES (est): 144.7K **Privately Held**
SIC: 2013 Snack sticks, including jerky: from purchased meat

(G-9067)
CANTEL MEDICAL CORP
5569 Main St (22842-9411)
PHONE......................................800 633-3080

EMP: 6
SALES (corp-wide): 1B **Publicly Held**
WEB: www.cantelmedical.com
SIC: **3569** Filters
PA: Cantel Medical Corp.
150 Clove Rd Ste 36
Little Falls NJ 07424
973 890-7220

(G-9068)
CORNERSTONE TECH SOLUTIONS INC
Also Called: Cornerstone Protection Svcs
5421 Main St Ste 400 (22842-9537)
P.O. Box 648 (22842-0648)
PHONE..................540 477-2180
David Moore, *President*
Kim Eaton, *Manager*
EMP: 5
SQ FT: 1,000
SALES (est): 933.9K **Privately Held**
WEB: www.cornerstonetech.net
SIC: **3699** 5063 1731 Security control equipment & systems; fire alarm systems; communications specialization

(G-9069)
DUCK PALLET CO LLC
738 Conicville Rd (22842-2415)
PHONE..................540 477-2771
Trevor Moyers, *Principal*
EMP: 3
SALES (est): 119.9K **Privately Held**
SIC: **2448** Pallets, wood & wood with metal

(G-9070)
GEORGES FAMILY FARMS LLC
560 Caverns Rd (22842)
PHONE..................540 477-3181
Gary George,
Ancel McClane,
EMP: 26
SALES (est): 4.9MM **Privately Held**
SIC: **3556** Mills, food

(G-9071)
GOING FORWARD IMPORTS LLC
266 Wunder St (22842-9303)
PHONE..................301 693-1562
Gavin Simpson,
EMP: 1
SALES (est): 50K **Privately Held**
SIC: **2899** Salt

(G-9072)
HERALD SQUARE LLC
3691 Conicville Rd (22842-2704)
PHONE..................540 477-2019
Donald H Albright, *Administration*
EMP: 2
SALES (est): 82.3K **Privately Held**
SIC: **2711** Newspapers, publishing & printing

(G-9073)
JAMES PIRTLE
10817 Senedo Rd (22842-2316)
P.O. Box 364 (22842-0364)
PHONE..................540 477-2647
James Pirtle, *Owner*
Tina Pirtle, *Owner*
EMP: 4
SALES (est): 295.4K **Privately Held**
SIC: **3423** Carpenters' hand tools, except saws: levels, chisels, etc.

(G-9074)
KINDRED POINTE STABLES LLC
3575 Conicville Rd (22842-2703)
PHONE..................540 477-3570
Amy B Helsley,
EMP: 1
SALES (est): 84.5K **Privately Held**
WEB: www.kindredpointe.com
SIC: **2084** Wines

(G-9075)
LUTZ FARM & SERVICES
Also Called: Conicville Ostrich
14144 Senedo Rd (22842-2406)
PHONE..................540 477-3574
Willard Lutz, *Owner*
Lorna Lutz, *Co-Owner*
EMP: 2

SALES (est): 100.4K **Privately Held**
WEB: www.lutzfarmservices.net
SIC: **2033** Jams, jellies & preserves: packaged in cans, jars, etc.

(G-9076)
MASCO CABINETRY LLC
1325 Industrial Park Rd (22842-2040)
P.O. Box 719 (22842-0719)
PHONE..................540 477-2961
Andy Blugerman, *CEO*
EMP: 431
SALES (corp-wide): 1.7B **Privately Held**
WEB: www.mascocabinetry.com
SIC: **2434** Wood kitchen cabinets
HQ: Cabinetworks Group Michigan, Llc
4600 Arrowhead Dr
Ann Arbor MI 48105
734 205-4600

(G-9077)
RICHARDS-WILBERT INC
330 Nelson St (22842-9505)
P.O. Box 411 (22842-0411)
PHONE..................540 477-3842
Ronald Burner, *Principal*
EMP: 6
SALES (corp-wide): 39.9K **Privately Held**
WEB: www.richardswilbert.com
SIC: **3272** Burial vaults, concrete or precast terrazzo
PA: Richards-Wilbert, Inc.
1481 Salem Ave
Hagerstown MD 21740
301 790-0124

(G-9078)
SMALL FRY INC
Also Called: Route 11 Potato Chips
11 Edwards Way (22842-2037)
PHONE..................540 477-9664
Sarah D Cohen, *President*
Michael S Connelly, *Vice Pres*
Mike Connelly, *Vice Pres*
▼ EMP: 40 EST: 2007
SQ FT: 25,000
SALES (est): 6.6MM **Privately Held**
WEB: www.rt11.com
SIC: **2096** Potato chips & other potato-based snacks

(G-9079)
SMYTH-RILEY
5998 Main St Ofc (22842-9402)
PHONE..................540 477-9652
Sherry Zimmer, *Owner*
EMP: 8
SALES (est): 690.8K **Privately Held**
WEB: www.smithandriley.com
SIC: **2499** Picture & mirror frames, wood

(G-9080)
SUGANIT BIO-RENEWABLES LLC
377 Industrial Park Rd (22842-2042)
PHONE..................703 736-0634
Praveen Paripati,
Anupama Paripati,
EMP: 12
SALES (est): 553.1K **Privately Held**
SIC: **2869** 2899 Industrial organic chemicals; chemical preparations

(G-9081)
TABARD CORPORATION
Also Called: Route 11 Potato Chips
11 Edwards Way (22842-2037)
PHONE..................540 477-9664
Sarah Cohen, *President*
EMP: 30
SALES (corp-wide): 4.1MM **Privately Held**
WEB: www.tabardinn.com
SIC: **2034** 2096 Potato products, dried & dehydrated; potato chips & similar snacks
PA: Tabard Corporation
1739 N St Nw
Washington DC 20036
202 331-8528

(G-9082)
VALLEY ICE LLC
123 Business Park Ln (22842)
P.O. Box 41 (22842-0041)
PHONE..................540 477-4447
W T Holtzman, *General Mgr*

William T Holtzman, *Manager*
Todd Holtzman,
EMP: 15
SALES (est): 1.3MM **Privately Held**
WEB: www.valleyice.net
SIC: **2097** Manufactured ice

(G-9083)
WINERY AT KINDRED POINTE LLC
3575 Conicville Rd (22842-2703)
PHONE..................540 481-6016
Amy B Helsley,
EMP: 1
SALES (est): 150K **Privately Held**
WEB: www.kindredpointe.com
SIC: **2084** Wines

Mount Sidney
Augusta County

(G-9084)
RDK LLC
2309 Lee Hwy (24467-2201)
P.O. Box 327 (24467-0327)
PHONE..................540 446-8327
Thomas Cline,
EMP: 6
SALES (est): 346.4K **Privately Held**
SIC: **3651** Household audio & video equipment

(G-9085)
TRUSS IT INC
391 Mount Pisgah Rd (24467-2414)
PHONE..................540 248-2177
EMP: 2
SALES (est): 131.1K **Privately Held**
SIC: **2439** Mfg Structural Wood Members

Mount Solon
Augusta County

(G-9086)
DUPONT AERO LLC
205 Lookout Mountain Ln (22843-3213)
PHONE..................540 350-4306
Samuel Francis Dupont, *Principal*
EMP: 2
SALES (est): 74.4K **Privately Held**
SIC: **2879** Agricultural chemicals

(G-9087)
EYEGLASS REPAIR SHOPPE
141 Bear Trap Farm Rd (22843-2327)
PHONE..................903 509-1517
Curt Paul, *Owner*
EMP: 1
SALES (est): 30K **Privately Held**
SIC: **3851** 5995 Eyeglasses, lenses & frames; optical goods stores

(G-9088)
MARY KAY INC
69 Reeves Rd (22843-2109)
PHONE..................770 497-8800
Jeff Porter, *Manager*
EMP: 2
SALES (est): 107.3K **Privately Held**
SIC: **3679** Electronic components

(G-9089)
MOUNT SLON WLDG FBRICATION LLC
1908 N River Rd (22843-2307)
PHONE..................540 350-2733
Doug W Fifer, *Principal*
EMP: 2
SALES (est): 93.9K **Privately Held**
SIC: **7692** Welding repair

(G-9090)
SULLIVAN MACHINE SHOP
17 Buckland Dr (22843-2500)
PHONE..................540 350-2549
Wallace Sullivan, *Owner*
EMP: 1
SALES (est): 83.4K **Privately Held**
SIC: **3599** Machine shop, jobbing & repair

Mouth of Wilson
Grayson County

(G-9091)
BLUERIDGE SAND INC
9916 Wilson Hwy (24363-3120)
P.O. Box 87 (24363-0087)
PHONE..................276 579-2007
Dennis Gary Lovell Jr, *President*
EMP: 3
SALES (est): 170K **Privately Held**
SIC: **1241** Coal mining services

(G-9092)
CABIN CREEK MUSICAL INSTRS
290 Bakers Branch Rd (24363-3537)
PHONE..................276 388-3202
Walter T Messick, *Owner*
EMP: 1
SALES (est): 37K **Privately Held**
WEB: www.cabincreekmusic.com
SIC: **3931** 5736 Musical instruments; musical instrument stores

(G-9093)
HUFFMAN & HUFFMAN INC
Also Called: Virginia & Carolina Concrete
4621 Potato Creek Rd (24363-3252)
PHONE..................276 579-2373
Ted Huffman, *President*
EMP: 7
SQ FT: 2,000
SALES (est): 826K **Privately Held**
SIC: **3272** 3273 Septic tanks, concrete; ready-mixed concrete

(G-9094)
LUMINAIRE TECHNOLOGIES INC
Also Called: L T I
9932 Wilson Hwy (24363-3120)
P.O. Box 13, Coleman Falls (24536-0013)
PHONE..................276 579-2007
Mark Fendig, *President*
EMP: 3
SQ FT: 2,500
SALES (est): 522.9K **Privately Held**
WEB: www.lblocker.com
SIC: **3648** 4911 Outdoor lighting equipment; generation, electric power

(G-9095)
MOUNTAIN MTLS MUTH WLSON PLANT
4648 Potato Creek Rd (24363-3256)
PHONE..................276 579-6351
Jerry Lewis, *Principal*
EMP: 2
SALES (est): 129.5K **Privately Held**
SIC: **1422** Crushed & broken limestone

Narrows
Giles County

(G-9096)
CELANESE ACETATE LLC
3520 Virginia Ave (24124-2409)
PHONE..................540 921-1111
David Weidman, *COO*
EMP: 26 EST: 1997
SALES (est): 3.3MM **Privately Held**
SIC: **2281** Manmade & synthetic fiber yarns, spun

(G-9097)
CELANESE AMERICAS LLC
3520 Virginia Ave (24124-2409)
P.O. Box 1000 (24124-0600)
PHONE..................540 921-6540
Roy Fahl, *Controller*
BEK Humelsine, *Branch Mgr*
Regina Blankenship, *Property Mgr*
Anthony Valencic, *Manager*
Bill Batson, *MIS Mgr*
EMP: 90
SALES (corp-wide): 6.3B **Publicly Held**
WEB: www.celanese.com
SIC: **2819** Industrial inorganic chemicals

HQ: Celanese Americas Llc
222 Colinas Blvd W # 900
Irving TX 75039
972 443-4000

(G-9098)
PRECISION MACHINE & DESIGN
211 Main St Ste 116 (24124-1339)
PHONE..................................540 726-8229
Johnny W Lucas, *President*
EMP: 2
SALES (est): 188.2K **Privately Held**
WEB: www.brianallendentistry.com
SIC: 3599 Machine shop, jobbing & repair

(G-9099)
WILLIAMS DEBURRING SMALL PARTS
602 College St (24124-2164)
PHONE..................................540 726-7485
Bobby Williams, *Owner*
EMP: 1 **Privately Held**
SIC: 3541 Deburring machines

Nassawadox
Northampton County

(G-9100)
FRANCIS C JAMES JR
Also Called: F C James Company
10198 Shell St (23413)
P.O. Box 282 (23413-0282)
PHONE..................................757 442-3630
Francis C James Jr, *Owner*
EMP: 1
SQ FT: 2,280
SALES (est): 130.6K **Privately Held**
SIC: 2434 5211 5999 Wood kitchen cabinets; cabinets, kitchen; monuments & tombstones

(G-9101)
NORTHAMPTON CUSTOM MILLING LLC
10168 Shell St (23413)
P.O. Box 135 (23413-0135)
PHONE..................................757 442-4747
Paula Paschaol, *Principal*
EMP: 1
SALES (est): 125.3K **Privately Held**
WEB: www.northamptoncustommilling.com
SIC: 2431 Millwork

Nathalie
Halifax County

(G-9102)
BRIGHT MEADOWS FARM
1181 Nathalie Rd (24577-3917)
PHONE..................................434 349-9463
Boyd Archer, *Principal*
EMP: 2
SALES (est): 187.3K **Privately Held**
WEB: www.brightmeadowsfarm.com
SIC: 2084 Wines

(G-9103)
JAMES D CREWS LOGGING
Also Called: Crews James D
3030 Armistead Rd (24577-3154)
PHONE..................................434 349-1999
James Crews, *Owner*
EMP: 3 EST: 1998
SALES (est): 278.5K **Privately Held**
SIC: 2411 Logging camps & contractors

(G-9104)
WALLER BROTHERS TROPHY SHOP
1074 Jesses Ln (24577-3812)
PHONE..................................434 376-5465
Andy Waller, *President*
H T Waller, *Corp Secy*
EMP: 7
SALES (est): 908K **Privately Held**
SIC: 3499 5941 Trophies, metal, except silver; sporting goods & bicycle shops

Natural Bridge
Rockbridge County

(G-9105)
ERP ENVIRONMENTAL FUND INC
15 Appledore Ln (24578-3602)
P.O. Box 305, Madison WV (25130-0305)
PHONE..................................304 369-8113
EMP: 6 EST: 2015
SALES (est): 452.4K **Privately Held**
SIC: 1241 Coal mining services

(G-9106)
HCG INDUSTRIES LLC
1575 Wert Faulkner Hwy (24578)
P.O. Box 88, Naturl BR STA (24579-0088)
PHONE..................................540 291-2674
Hank Gleisberg,
EMP: 4
SALES (est): 301.7K **Privately Held**
SIC: 3999 Manufacturing industries

(G-9107)
J & V KITCHEN INC
Also Called: Fancy Hill Jams and Jellies
9 Surrey Ln (24578-3583)
PHONE..................................540 291-2794
Pamela Lydick, *President*
EMP: 3
SALES (est): 263.5K **Privately Held**
SIC: 2099 Jelly, corncob (gelatin)

Natural Bridge Stati
Rockbridge County

(G-9108)
BARR MARINE BY E D M
100 Douglas Way (24579)
P.O. Box 190, Naturl BR STA (24579-0190)
PHONE..................................540 291-4180
▲ **EMP:** 3
SALES (est): 200K **Privately Held**
SIC: 3519 Mfg Internal Combustion Engines

(G-9109)
FEI LTD
37 Rock Bridge Indus Park (24579)
PHONE..................................540 291-3398
Dave Hunt, *President*
Mike Osullivan, *CFO*
EMP: 16
SALES (est): 3.9MM
SALES (corp-wide): 34.8MM **Privately Held**
SIC: 3441 Fabricated structural metal
PA: The Berlin Steel Construction Company
76 Depot Rd
Kensington CT 06037
860 828-3531

Naturl BR STA
Rockbridge County

(G-9110)
CHARLIE WATTS SIGNS
856 Petites Gap Rd (24579-3063)
PHONE..................................540 291-3211
Charlie Watts, *Owner*
EMP: 1
SALES (est): 69.7K **Privately Held**
SIC: 3993 Signs & advertising specialties

(G-9111)
CLARENCE D CAMPBELL
Also Called: C D Campbell Logging
33 Cedar Bottom Rd (24579-3033)
PHONE..................................540 291-2740
Clarance D Campbell, *Owner*
EMP: 3
SALES (est): 181.1K **Privately Held**
SIC: 2411 2611 Timber, cut at logging camp; pulp mills

(G-9112)
SAYRE ENTERPRISES INC (PA)
45 Natural Bridge Schl Rd (24579-1500)
PHONE..................................540 291-3808
Scott Sayre, *President*
Mary B Sayre, *Vice Pres*
▲ **EMP:** 120
SQ FT: 30,000
SALES (est): 15.3MM **Privately Held**
WEB: www.sayreinc.com
SIC: 2389 2395 2759 Men's miscellaneous accessories; suspenders; arm bands, elastic; embroidery & art needlework; screen printing

Nellysford
Nelson County

(G-9113)
HILL TOP BERRY FRM & WINERY LC
2800 Berry Hill Rd (22958-2034)
PHONE..................................434 361-1266
Kimberly Allen Pugh, *Principal*
Gregory Pugh, *Principal*
Irma Allen,
Marlyn Allen,
EMP: 11
SALES (est): 581.6K **Privately Held**
WEB: www.hilltopberrywine.com
SIC: 2084 0171 Wines; berry crops

(G-9114)
WINTERGREEN WINERY LTD
Winery Ln Rr 462 (22958)
PHONE..................................434 325-2200
Jeff Stone, *President*
EMP: 6
SALES (est): 500K **Privately Held**
WEB: www.wintergreenwinery.com
SIC: 2084 5921 Wines; wine

(G-9115)
WOODWORK CAREER ALIANCE N AMER
189 Dogwood Ln (22958-3044)
PHONE..................................434 298-4650
Scott Nelson, *Principal*
EMP: 2 EST: 2009
SALES: 95.3K **Privately Held**
WEB: www.woodworkcareer.org
SIC: 2431 Millwork

Nelson
Mecklenburg County

(G-9116)
WELLS BELCHER PAVING SERVICE
Also Called: Belcher Wells Paving
747 Winston Rd (24580-2541)
P.O. Box 652, Buffalo Junction (24529-0652)
PHONE..................................434 374-5518
Belcher Wells, *Owner*
Jackie Wells, *Co-Owner*
EMP: 2 EST: 1979
SALES (est): 146.3K **Privately Held**
SIC: 2951 Asphalt paving mixtures & blocks

New Canton
Buckingham County

(G-9117)
JIMS ORNA FABRICATION & WLDG
2553 Cartersville Rd (23123-2057)
PHONE..................................434 581-1420
James Cook, *Owner*
EMP: 1
SALES (est): 42.5K **Privately Held**
SIC: 7692 Welding repair

(G-9118)
ML MANUFACTURING
521 Social Hall Rd (23123-2036)
PHONE..................................434 581-2000
Laveda Case,
Mark Schneider,
EMP: 2 EST: 2010

SALES (est): 213.2K **Privately Held**
WEB: www.mlmanufacturing.net
SIC: 3531 5082 3536 7353 Cranes; cranes, construction; hoists, cranes & monorails; cranes & aerial lift equipment, rental or leasing; manufactured hardware (general)

(G-9119)
S&SPRINTING
29661 N James Madison Hwy (23123-2229)
PHONE..................................434 581-1983
George Jefferies, *Principal*
EMP: 2
SALES (est): 83.9K **Privately Held**
SIC: 2752 Commercial printing, lithographic

New Castle
Craig County

(G-9120)
GS PLASTICS LLC
23580 Craigs Creek Rd (24127-6263)
P.O. Box 247 (24127-0247)
PHONE..................................276 629-7981
Terry Cundiff, *Vice Pres*
Herbert Como,
▲ **EMP:** 4
SQ FT: 20,000
SALES (est): 650K **Privately Held**
WEB: www.gsplasticsllc.com
SIC: 3087 Custom compound purchased resins

(G-9121)
KO SYNTHETICS CORP
96 12th St (24127-6014)
PHONE..................................540 580-1760
Barry Owens, *President*
EMP: 3
SALES (est): 383.9K **Privately Held**
WEB: www.barryowens.com
SIC: 2822 Cyclo rubbers, synthetic

(G-9122)
MET MACHINE INC
Hc 34 Box 352 (24127)
PHONE..................................540 864-6007
Micheal Logan, *President*
EMP: 4 EST: 1996
SQ FT: 7,000
SALES (est): 655.1K **Privately Held**
SIC: 3599 Custom machinery

(G-9123)
ROSE WELDING INC
322 Red Brush Rd (24127-7013)
PHONE..................................540 312-0138
Chris E Rose, *President*
EMP: 4
SALES (est): 129.1K **Privately Held**
SIC: 3999 Manufacturing industries

(G-9124)
STRAUCH FIBER EQUIPMENT C
10319 Johns Creek Rd (24127-6807)
PHONE..................................540 864-8869
Otto Strauch, *Principal*
EMP: 5
SALES (est): 406.8K **Privately Held**
WEB: www.strauchfiber.com
SIC: 3999 Manufacturing industries

New Church
Accomack County

(G-9125)
KMX CHEMICAL CORP (PA)
30474 Energy Dr (23415)
P.O. Box 280 (23415-0280)
PHONE..................................757 824-3600
Dr Hubert L Fleming, *Principal*
Jill Harris, *COO*
Neil Harwoods, *Vice Pres*
Jerry Union, *Vice Pres*
◆ **EMP:** 23
SALES (est): 5MM **Privately Held**
WEB: www.kmxchemical.com
SIC: 2899 7389 Chemical preparations; brokers' services

(PA)=Parent Co (HQ)=Headquarters (DH)=Div Headquarters
✿ = New Business established in last 2 years

(G-9126)
KMX CHEMICAL CORP
30474 Energy Dr (23415-3125)
PHONE 757 824-3600
Todd Godwin, *Opers Staff*
EMP: 15
SALES (corp-wide): 5MM **Privately Held**
WEB: www.kmxchemical.com
SIC: 2899 Chemical preparations
PA: Kmx Chemical Corp.
   30474 Energy Dr
   New Church VA 23415
   757 824-3600

(G-9127)
PARSONS PRESSURE WASHING
7077 Fleming Rd (23415-2447)
PHONE 757 894-3110
Richard Parsons, *Principal*
EMP: 2
SALES (est): 150.9K **Privately Held**
SIC: 3589 High pressure cleaning equipment

New Kent
New Kent County

(G-9128)
ALLIED PALLET COMPANY (PA)
7151 Poindexter Rd (23124-2201)
PHONE 804 966-5597
William C Newman, *President*
Kosal Som, *General Mgr*
EMP: 250
SQ FT: 200,000
SALES (est): 29.2MM **Privately Held**
WEB: www.alliedpalletcompany.com
SIC: 2448 Pallets, wood

(G-9129)
COLONIAL RAIL SYSTEMS LLC
9000 Deer Trace Ln (23124-2447)
PHONE 804 932-5200
Mark Clifford, *President*
EMP: 4
SQ FT: 12,000
SALES (est): 632.7K **Privately Held**
WEB: www.dmbgroup.biz
SIC: 3312 1751 1521 Rails, steel or iron; cabinet building & installation; general remodeling, single-family houses

(G-9130)
DOMBROSKI VINEYARDS LLC
8400 Old Church Rd (23124-2700)
P.O. Box 188 (23124-0188)
PHONE 804 932-8240
Joe Dombroski,
Jo Anna Dombroksi,
EMP: 4
SALES (est): 523K **Privately Held**
WEB: www.tidewaterreview.com
SIC: 2084 Wines

(G-9131)
ECLIPSE SCROLL SAW
11700 Lock Ln (23124-3400)
PHONE 804 779-3549
Ernesto Mellon, *Owner*
EMP: 3
SALES (est): 100K **Privately Held**
WEB: www.eclipsesaw.com
SIC: 3553 3546 Woodworking machinery; power-driven handtools

(G-9132)
FLIP-N-HAUL LLC
5627 Gentry Dr (23124-2855)
PHONE 804 932-4372
Gregory Haaser, *Mng Member*
EMP: 1
SALES (est): 82.7K **Privately Held**
SIC: 3499 Ladders, portable: metal

(G-9133)
GLORIAS GLASS
9500 New Kent Hwy (23124-2331)
PHONE 804 357-0676
Gloria Hanchey, *Owner*
EMP: 1
SALES (est): 27K **Privately Held**
WEB: www.gloriasglass.com
SIC: 3231 Windshields, glass: made from purchased glass

(G-9134)
JOHNSON ENTERPRISES LLC
5752 Mako Rd (23124-2883)
PHONE 804 432-0469
EMP: 1
SALES (est): 74.9K **Privately Held**
SIC: 3482 Small arms ammunition

(G-9135)
KEO-CORP LLC
8535 Red Juniper Ln (23124-3027)
PHONE 636 515-5549
Richard F Rogers, *President*
EMP: 1
SALES (est): 56K **Privately Held**
SIC: 3699 3544 3443 3541 Electrical equipment & supplies; special dies, tools, jigs & fixtures; fabricated plate work (boiler shop); machine tools, metal cutting type

(G-9136)
NEON GUITAR
11941 Steel Trap Rd (23124-3203)
PHONE 804 932-3716
Claude Heath Jr, *Principal*
EMP: 2
SALES (est): 101K **Privately Held**
SIC: 2813 Neon

(G-9137)
OLD MILL MECHANICAL INC
8600 Historical Path Rd (23124-2727)
P.O. Box 328, Providence Forge (23140-0328)
PHONE 804 932-5060
Louanna Martin, *President*
Chris Martin, *Director*
EMP: 3
SALES (est): 483.9K **Privately Held**
SIC: 3433 Heating equipment, except electric

(G-9138)
RISSER FARMS INC
8266 E Lord Btetourt Loop (23124-2872)
PHONE 804 387-8584
Kortlynd Risser, *President*
EMP: 1
SALES (est): 66.6K **Privately Held**
SIC: 2015 Egg processing

(G-9139)
WOODDUCKS ODD JOBS LAWN SVC LL
8844 Greenwood Blvd (23124-2800)
PHONE 804 932-4612
EMP: 2
SALES (est): 50.2K **Privately Held**
SIC: 2499 Mfg Wood Products

New Market
Shenandoah County

(G-9140)
BILL KLINCK PUBLISHING
140 Rocky Mountain Ln (22844-3214)
PHONE 540 740-3034
Bill Klinck, *Owner*
EMP: 2
SALES (est): 103.2K **Privately Held**
SIC: 2741 Miscellaneous publishing

(G-9141)
CHAMPION VENTURES LLC
358 Jackson Ave (22844-9540)
PHONE 540 975-0791
EMP: 2
SALES (est): 89.8K **Privately Held**
SIC: 2411 Logging

(G-9142)
FRENCHS AUTO PARTS INC
Rr 11 (22844)
P.O. Box 567 (22844-0567)
PHONE 540 740-3676
Kirk French, *Vice Pres*
EMP: 5
SALES (est): 377.1K **Privately Held**
WEB: www.frenchsautoparts.com
SIC: 3714 Motor vehicle parts & accessories

(G-9143)
JEFF FLEISHER
645 Highview Rd (22844-3509)
PHONE 703 955-6873
EMP: 1
SALES (est): 76.4K **Privately Held**
WEB: www.mtnviews.net
SIC: 2431 Millwork

(G-9144)
KENNAMETAL INC
450 New Market Depot Rd (22844-2065)
PHONE 540 740-3128
Paul Smith, *Opers Dir*
Tom Baker, *Facilities Mgr*
James Small, *Branch Mgr*
Kathy McNeal, *Executive*
EMP: 125 **Publicly Held**
WEB: www.kennametal.com
SIC: 3545 Cutting tools for machine tools
PA: Kennametal Inc.
   525 William Penn Pl # 3300
   Pittsburgh PA 15219
   412 248-8000

(G-9145)
NEW MARKET POULTRY LLC
145 E Old Cross Rd (22844-9535)
PHONE 540 740-4260
Brad Respess, *President*
Charlie Singleton, *CFO*
EMP: 200
SALES (est): 10.7MM
SALES (corp-wide): 278MM **Privately Held**
WEB: www.tiptoppoultry.com
SIC: 2015 Poultry, processed: fresh
PA: Tip Top Poultry, Inc.
   327 Wallace Rd
   Marietta GA 30062
   770 973-8070

(G-9146)
OCTOPUS AROSPC SOLUTIONS LLC
Also Called: Oas Intel
9706 Fairway Dr (22844-9634)
PHONE 866 244-4500
Robert Thompson,
Bryan Ingram,
Gabriel Leoni,
EMP: 3
SALES (est): 117.8K **Privately Held**
SIC: 3728 Aircraft parts & equipment

(G-9147)
PALAWAN BLADE LLC
3670 Smith Creek Rd (22844-3244)
PHONE 434 294-2065
Christopher George,
EMP: 1 EST: 2017
SALES (est): 71.1K **Privately Held**
WEB: www.palawanblade.com
SIC: 3421 Cutlery

(G-9148)
SHENANDOAH DRONES LLC
9706 Fairway Dr (22844-9634)
PHONE 540 421-3116
EMP: 2
SALES (est): 121.2K **Privately Held**
WEB: www.shenandoahdrones.com
SIC: 3721 Motorized aircraft

(G-9149)
TOTAL BLISS GOURMET SOAP LLC
1872 E Lee Hwy (22844-3221)
P.O. Box 456 (22844-0456)
PHONE 540 740-8823
Brenda Ritchie, *Principal*
EMP: 2
SALES (est): 148.7K **Privately Held**
WEB: www.totalblissgourmetsoap.com
SIC: 2841 Soap: granulated, liquid, cake, flaked or chip

(G-9150)
TYSON FOODS INC
361 Smith Creek Rd (22844-3833)
PHONE 540 740-3118
S Merrill Ware, *President*
EMP: 7
SALES (corp-wide): 43.1B **Publicly Held**
WEB: www.tysonfoods.com
SIC: 2015 Poultry slaughtering & processing
PA: Tyson Foods, Inc.
   2200 W Don Tyson Pkwy
   Springdale AR 72762
   479 290-4000

New River
Pulaski County

(G-9151)
MOTION CONTROL SYSTEMS INC
6701 Viscoe Rd (24129)
P.O. Box 115 (24129-0115)
PHONE 540 731-0540
William Harris, *President*
Harris William M, *President*
Worth Burruss, *Engineer*
Allen Canterbury, *Engineer*
Bob Dapper, *Engineer*
EMP: 60
SQ FT: 30,000
SALES (est): 12.8MM **Privately Held**
WEB: www.motioncontrol.com
SIC: 3625 Motor controls & accessories

Newington
Fairfax County

(G-9152)
ALLIANT TCHSYSTEMS OPRTONS LLC
8560 Cinderbed Rd Ste 700 (22122)
PHONE 703 254-2454
Francine Kull, *Branch Mgr*
EMP: 50 **Publicly Held**
WEB: www.northropgrumman.com
SIC: 3812 Search & navigation equipment
HQ: Alliant Techsystems Operations Llc
   601 Carlson Pkwy Ste 600
   Minnetonka MN 55305

(G-9153)
DAD13 INC
8401 Terminal Rd (22122)
P.O. Box 1467 (22122-1467)
PHONE 703 550-9555
David Dickens, *President*
Bob Stone, *Vice Pres*
Bryan Gunther, *Accounts Mgr*
Derek Thompson, *Accounts Mgr*
Zach Beeler, *Sales Staff*
EMP: 115 EST: 1971
SQ FT: 80,000
SALES (est): 19.4MM
SALES (corp-wide): 97.5MM **Privately Held**
WEB: www.master-print.com
SIC: 2752 2789 2761 Commercial printing, offset; lithographing on metal; bookbinding & related work; manifold business forms
PA: Vomela Specialty Company
   845 Minnehaha Ave E
   Saint Paul MN 55106
   651 228-2200

Newport News
Newport News City County

(G-9154)
4 KEES INC
744 Village Green Pkwy (23602-7034)
PHONE 757 249-2584
Margaret Lee R Keesecker, *President*
EMP: 2
SALES (est): 157.2K **Privately Held**
SIC: 2221 Upholstery, tapestry & wall covering fabrics

(G-9155)
A & J SEAMLESS GUTTERS INC
122 Tazewell Rd (23608-3012)
PHONE..............................757 291-6890
Allen Whitley, *President*
EMP: 3
SALES (est): 100K **Privately Held**
SIC: 3444 Sheet metalwork

(G-9156)
A PINCH OF CHARM
805 Ashley Pl (23608-3391)
PHONE..............................757 262-7820
Ashley Rybin, *Principal*
EMP: 2 EST: 2010
SALES (est): 112.2K **Privately Held**
SIC: 2335 Wedding gowns & dresses

(G-9157)
ADF UNIT TRUST INC
11815 Ftn Way Ste 300 (23606)
PHONE..............................757 926-5252
Joan Phoenix French, *President*
EMP: 5
SALES (est): 100MM **Privately Held**
SIC: 1081 7389 Metal mining services; financial services

(G-9158)
ADVANCE TECHNOLOGY INC
316 49th St (23607-2516)
PHONE..............................757 223-6566
Charles K Bennett, *President*
Charles Bennett, *President*
Dana Drawsand, *CFO*
EMP: 100
SQ FT: 2,000
SALES (est): 5MM **Privately Held**
WEB: www.advancedtechnologyinc.com
SIC: 3731 Shipbuilding & repairing

(G-9159)
ADVANCED TECHNOLOGIES INC
875 City Center Blvd (23606-3078)
PHONE..............................757 873-3017
R Toby Roberts, *President*
Michael Kane, *Vice Pres*
Paul Thomeer, *Vice Pres*
Phillip Wieting, *Manager*
EMP: 85
SQ FT: 85,000
SALES (est): 11.4MM **Privately Held**
WEB: www.advancedtechnologiesinc.com
SIC: 3829 8711 Measuring & controlling devices; aviation &/or aeronautical engineering

(G-9160)
AERY AVIATION LLC
305 Cherokee Dr (23602-4437)
PHONE..............................757 271-1600
Joshua Walton, *Vice Pres*
Leslie Walton, *Mng Member*
Scott Beale,
Robert Dynan,
EMP: 16
SALES (est): 9.2MM **Privately Held**
WEB: www.rickaviation.com
SIC: 3721 8711 8741 Aircraft; aviation &/or aeronautical engineering; management services

(G-9161)
ALL ABOUT SECURITY INC
229 Gate House Rd (23608-5022)
PHONE..............................757 887-6700
Timothy Daniels, *President*
EMP: 2 EST: 2001
SALES (est): 253.2K **Privately Held**
WEB: www.newportnewshomesecurity-company.com
SIC: 3699 Security devices

(G-9162)
ALL AFFAIRS TRANSPORTATION LLC
724 City Center Blvd C (23606-3081)
PHONE..............................757 342-2474
Bradford Jones, *Mng Member*
▲ EMP: 6
SQ FT: 8,000

SALES (est): 800K **Privately Held**
WEB: www.granitekitchenbath.com
SIC: 3281 2434 Marble, building: cut & shaped; table tops, marble; paving blocks, cut stone; wood kitchen cabinets

(G-9163)
ALLENDE-EL PUBLISHING CO LLC
304 Windy Ridge Ln (23602-6851)
PHONE..............................757 528-9997
Kerry Andre Allende-El,
EMP: 1
SALES (est): 37.5K **Privately Held**
SIC: 2741 Miscellaneous publishing

(G-9164)
ALLIED AEROSPACE SERVICES LLC
703 City Center Blvd (23606-2551)
PHONE..............................757 873-1344
William E Jacobson,
EMP: 20
SALES (est): 1MM **Privately Held**
SIC: 3728 Aircraft parts & equipment

(G-9165)
ALLIED AEROSPACE UAV LLC
Also Called: Allied Aerospace Indutries
703 City Center Blvd (23606-2551)
PHONE..............................757 873-1344
Kenneth J McNamara,
Christopher Lacovara,
Thomas Miller,
Mark Thomson,
Evan Wildstein,
EMP: 3
SALES (est): 188.8K **Privately Held**
SIC: 3728 Aircraft parts & equipment

(G-9166)
ALTERNTIVE ENERGYWAVE TECH LLC
16 Bosch Ln (23606-2665)
PHONE..............................757 897-1312
Patrick Boland,
EMP: 1
SALES (est): 76.2K **Privately Held**
SIC: 3634 Electric housewares & fans

(G-9167)
ANNIE LEE TRAFFIC PATROL
1187 Old Denbigh Blvd (23602-2077)
PHONE..............................888 682-5882
EMP: 1
SALES (est): 92K **Privately Held**
SIC: 3669 Mfg Communications Equipment

(G-9168)
ANTHONY LAMON WILLIAMS
Also Called: A & A
231 Lochaven Dr (23602-7037)
PHONE..............................757 927-8141
Anthony Lamon Williams, *Owner*
EMP: 4
SALES (est): 150K **Privately Held**
SIC: 3537 Trucks, tractors, loaders, carriers & similar equipment

(G-9169)
APOLLO PRESS INC
708 Thimble Shoals Blvd # 1 (23606-4547)
PHONE..............................757 247-9002
John W Taylor, *President*
Robert Dent Jr, *General Mgr*
Robert Edward Dent Jr, *Vice Pres*
EMP: 41
SQ FT: 25,000
SALES (est): 4MM **Privately Held**
WEB: www.dailypress.com
SIC: 2791 2759 2789 2752 Typesetting; commercial printing; bookbinding & related work; commercial printing, lithographic

(G-9170)
ARCAMAX PUBLISHING INC
11830 Canon Blvd Ste A (23606-2568)
PHONE..............................757 596-9730
Scott Wolf, *CEO*
Roy J Jay, *Ch of Bd*
Andy Summerlin, *Vice Pres*
Charles Strauss, *Accountant*
Allison Johnston, *Advt Staff*

EMP: 5
SALES (est): 550K **Privately Held**
WEB: www.arcamax.com
SIC: 2741 Miscellaneous publishing

(G-9171)
AS CLEAN AS A WHISTLE
304 Belray Dr (23601-1423)
PHONE..............................757 753-0600
Richard Langston, *Principal*
EMP: 2 EST: 2003
SALES (est): 139.5K **Privately Held**
SIC: 3999 Whistles

(G-9172)
ASHTON GREEN SEAFOOD
203 Sunrise Ct (23608-3814)
PHONE..............................757 887-3551
Min Suk Chon, *President*
EMP: 2
SALES (est): 126.7K **Privately Held**
WEB: www.dsofbartlett.com
SIC: 2091 2092 Fish & seafood soups, stews, chowders: canned or packaged; seafoods, fresh: prepared

(G-9173)
ATLANTIC TEXTILE GROUP INC
Also Called: Fox Screen Print
499 Muller Ln (23606-1303)
PHONE..............................757 249-7777
Jeffrey Fox, *President*
Michael Fox, *Corp Secy*
Gregory Scott Worth, *Director*
Walter Wainwright, *Art Dir*
EMP: 14
SQ FT: 10,000
SALES (est): 1.2MM **Privately Held**
WEB: www.foxscreenprint.com
SIC: 2759 Screen printing

(G-9174)
AUTOMATED PRECISION INC
Also Called: API Services
750 City Center Blvd (23606-2693)
PHONE..............................757 223-4157
Ronald Hicks, *Vice Pres*
Dr Kam Lau, *Mng Member*
John Gross, *Manager*
Aaron Goodman, *Technology*
EMP: 11
SQ FT: 6,000
SALES (est): 2.5MM **Privately Held**
WEB: www.apisensor.com
SIC: 3823 7374 3827 4581 Combustion control instruments; optical scanning data service; optical test & inspection equipment; aircraft servicing & repairing

(G-9175)
B QUEEN NATION LLC
169 Colony Rd (23602-6645)
PHONE..............................678 507-4445
Tia Canady, *Mng Member*
EMP: 1
SALES (est): 150K **Privately Held**
SIC: 2331 Women's & misses' blouses & shirts

(G-9176)
BANVERA LLC
Also Called: Medicap
956 J Clyde Morris Blvd (23601-1043)
PHONE..............................757 599-9643
Banyo Ndanga, *Mng Member*
EMP: 22 EST: 2007
SQ FT: 3,000
SALES (est): 3.1MM **Privately Held**
SIC: 2836 5122 Vaccines & other immunizing products; pharmaceuticals

(G-9177)
BERING SEA ENVIRONMENTAL LLC
606 Thimble Shoals Blvd B2 (23606-4530)
PHONE..............................757 223-1446
Robert Dean Hughes, *President*
B Smith, *Branch Mgr*
EMP: 1
SALES (corp-wide): 184.1MM **Privately Held**
WEB: www.bsenv.com
SIC: 3731 Shipbuilding & repairing

HQ: Bering Sea Environmental, Llc
3601 C St Ste 1000
Anchorage AK 99503
907 278-2311

(G-9178)
BERTS INC
108 Nicewood Dr (23602-6504)
P.O. Box 2575 (23609-0575)
PHONE..............................757 865-8040
Joey Agee, *Principal*
EMP: 4
SALES (est): 450K **Privately Held**
WEB: www.bertsinc.com
SIC: 3585 Refrigeration & heating equipment

(G-9179)
BIBLE TRUTH MUSIC
709 Willow Dr (23605-1035)
P.O. Box 1881 (23601-0881)
PHONE..............................757 365-9956
Byron Foxx, *Founder*
EMP: 2
SALES (est): 118.9K **Privately Held**
WEB: www.bibletruthmusic.com
SIC: 2741 8661 Music, sheet: publishing only, not printed on site; religious organizations

(G-9180)
BIG D WOODWORKING
314 Mona Dr (23608-1609)
PHONE..............................757 753-4814
Miller Doland, *Principal*
EMP: 2
SALES (est): 93.8K **Privately Held**
SIC: 2431 Millwork

(G-9181)
BLACK GOLD INDUSTRIES LLC
12844 Daybreak Cir (23602-9511)
PHONE..............................757 768-4674
Keri Nichols,
EMP: 1
SALES (est): 39.6K **Privately Held**
SIC: 3999 Manufacturing industries

(G-9182)
BNNT LLC
300 Ed Wright Ln Ste A (23606-4384)
PHONE..............................757 369-1939
R Roy Whitney PHD, *President*
EMP: 4
SALES (est): 526.5K **Privately Held**
WEB: www.bnnt.com
SIC: 2819 Boron compounds, not from mines

(G-9183)
BORFSKI PRESS
1000 University Pl (23606-3061)
PHONE..............................571 439-9093
Dagney Palmer, *Principal*
Shawn Hatfield, *Senior Editor*
EMP: 1 EST: 2017
SALES (est): 41.3K **Privately Held**
SIC: 2741 Miscellaneous publishing

(G-9184)
BRAIDING STATION INC
Also Called: Beauty & Beyond Salon
1386 Washington Blvd (23604-1281)
PHONE..............................804 898-2255
Debra Vasquez, *Vice Pres*
EMP: 4 EST: 2015
SQ FT: 12,513
SALES (est): 172.3K **Privately Held**
SIC: 2844 Shampoos, rinses, conditioners: hair

(G-9185)
BREAKFAST LADY LLC
833 41st St (23607-2340)
PHONE..............................302 241-7400
Tr'ier Davis, *Mng Member*
EMP: 1
SALES (est): 39.5K **Privately Held**
SIC: 2043 Cereal breakfast foods

(G-9186)
BRYANT ENERGY CORP
250 Picketts Line (23603-1366)
PHONE..............................757 887-2181
Martha Bryant, *President*
Dwight Bryant, *Vice Pres*

EMP: 4 EST: 2011
SQ FT: 40,000
SALES (est): 417.3K **Privately Held**
SIC: 2411 Wooden logs

(G-9187)
BWX TECHNOLOGIES INC
Babcock and Wilcox
11864 Canon Blvd Ste 105 (23606-4253)
PHONE .... (757) 595-7982
Lisa Tomlin, *Research*
David Drabison, *Draft/Design*
Steve Killmeyer, *Draft/Design*
Chris Marshall, *Draft/Design*
Scott Marchand, *Accounting Mgr*
EMP: 32 Publicly Held
WEB: www.bwxt.com
SIC: 3822 7389 7371 3625 Auto controls
regulating residntl & coml environmt & ap-
plncs; air pollution measuring service;
custom computer programming services;
relays & industrial controls; blowers &
fans
PA: Bwx Technologies, Inc.
800 Main St Ste 4
Lynchburg VA 24504

(G-9188)
CA JONES INC
11832 Fishing Point Dr # 100 (23606-2564)
PHONE .... (757) 595-0005
Michael Warnke, *President*
Seth Nogiec, *General Mgr*
Nick Beaver, *Manager*
EMP: 1
SALES (est): 500K **Privately Held**
WEB: www.cajshop.com
SIC: 3599 3731 Machine shop, jobbing &
repair; shipbuilding & repairing

(G-9189)
CALSPAN SYSTEMS CORPORATION (HQ)
Also Called: Allied Aerospace
703 City Center Blvd (23606-2551)
PHONE .... (757) 873-1344
Louis Knotts, *CEO*
Douglas Rog, *Engineer*
Peter Sauer, *CFO*
Gerald Britt, *Prgrmr*
Charles Masser, *Director*
EMP: 120 EST: 1971
SQ FT: 91,000
SALES (est): 35.1MM
SALES (corp-wide): 78MM **Privately Held**
WEB: www.calspan.com
SIC: 3721 3769 Research & development
on aircraft by the manufacturer; guided
missile & space vehicle parts & auxiliary
equipment
PA: Calspan Holdings, Llc
4455 Genesee St Ste 1000
Buffalo NY 14225
716 631-6955

(G-9190)
CANDYLICIOUS CRAFTS LLC
442 Winterhaven Dr (23606-2533)
P.O. Box 6083 (23606-0083)
PHONE .... (757) 915-5542
Soniea Hall,
EMP: 1
SALES (est): 81.2K **Privately Held**
SIC: 3999 7389 Boutiquing: decorating gift
items with sequins, fruit, etc.;

(G-9191)
CANNON ENTERPRISES LLC
459 Old Colonial Way # 104 (23608-2039)
PHONE .... (757) 876-3463
Dexter Cannon, *Mng Member*
Sabrina Cannon, *Mng Member*
EMP: 1
SALES (est): 60K **Privately Held**
SIC: 3537 Trucks, tractors, loaders, carri-
ers & similar equipment

(G-9192)
CANON VIRGINIA INC (DH)
12000 Canon Blvd (23606-4201)
PHONE .... (757) 881-6000
Toru Nishizawa, *President*
Roland Brown, *Managing Dir*
Shields Natsuko, *Business Mgr*
Akira Machida, *Exec VP*

John Briggs, *Senior VP*
◆ **EMP:** 1500
SQ FT: 2,000,000
SALES (est): 297MM **Privately Held**
WEB: www.cvi.canon.com
SIC: 3861 3577 3555 Photographic
equipment & supplies; computer periph-
eral equipment; printing trades machinery
HQ: Canon U.S.A., Inc.
1 Canon Park
Melville NY 11747
516 328-5000

(G-9193)
CASE MECHANICAL LLC
110 Stonewall Pl (23606-1136)
PHONE .... (757) 272-6050
Ryan Daniel, *Agent*
EMP: 1
SALES (est): 54.5K **Privately Held**
SIC: 3523 Farm machinery & equipment

(G-9194)
CASHMERE HANDRAILS INC
27 Milford Rd (23601-3940)
PHONE .... (757) 838-2307
EMP: 2 EST: 2010
SALES (est): 164K **Privately Held**
SIC: 3312 Structural shapes & pilings,
steel

(G-9195)
CATHERINE RACHEL BRAXTON
Also Called: Cathy's Specialty
818 26th St (23607-4635)
P.O. Box 5672 (23605-0672)
PHONE .... (757) 244-7531
Catherine Braxton, *Owner*
EMP: 6
SALES (est): 241.8K **Privately Held**
SIC: 2369 Girls' & children's outerwear

(G-9196)
CHAMPS
12300 Jefferson Ave # 415 (23602-0009)
PHONE .... (800) 991-6813
EMP: 1
SALES (est): 58K **Privately Held**
SIC: 3949 Mfg Sporting/Athletic Goods

(G-9197)
CHAMPS CREATE A BOOK
960 Willbrook Rd (23602-9101)
PHONE .... (757) 369-3879
Valarie Miller, *Owner*
EMP: 1
SALES (est): 43K **Privately Held**
SIC: 2732 Book printing

(G-9198)
CHESAPEAKE BAY PACKING LLC
Also Called: Processing Plant
703 Jefferson Ave (23607-6115)
PHONE .... (757) 244-8400
Terence D Molloy, *General Mgr*
Teresa Anthony, *Controller*
EMP: 21 Privately Held
WEB: www.chesapeakebaypacking.com
SIC: 2092 Seafoods, fresh: prepared
PA: Chesapeake Bay Packing, Llc
800 Terminal Ave
Newport News VA 23607

(G-9199)
CHESAPEAKE BAY PACKING LLC (PA)
Also Called: Cbp
800 Terminal Ave (23607-6142)
PHONE .... (757) 244-8440
Norman Hardee, *Managing Prtnr*
◆ **EMP:** 28
SQ FT: 50,000
SALES (est): 48MM **Privately Held**
WEB: www.chesapeakebaypacking.com
SIC: 2092 2091 5421 Seafoods, fresh:
prepared; canned & cured fish &
seafoods; meat & fish markets

(G-9200)
CLEAR VISION PUBLISHING
103 Wreck Shoal Dr (23606-1945)
PHONE .... (757) 753-9422
EMP: 2 EST: 2017

SALES (est): 59.2K **Privately Held**
SIC: 2741 Miscellaneous publishing

(G-9201)
COASTAL PRSTTICS ORTHOTICS LLC
11818 Rock Landing Dr # 104
(23606-4230)
PHONE .... (757) 240-4228
Harry Edmond Bright, *Principal*
EMP: 1
SALES (corp-wide): 306.4K **Privately Held**
WEB: www.coastalpando.com
SIC: 3842 Limbs, artificial
PA: Coastal Prostetics And Orthotics Llc
433 Network Sta
Chesapeake VA 23320
757 892-5300

(G-9202)
COASTAL SCREEN PRINTING
909 Bickerton Ct (23608-9365)
PHONE .... (757) 764-1409
Ben Schrambow, *Principal*
EMP: 2
SALES (est): 83.9K **Privately Held**
SIC: 2752 Commercial printing, litho-
graphic

(G-9203)
COLLIER RESEARCH AND DEV CORP (PA)
760 Pilot House Dr Ste A (23606-2068)
PHONE .... (757) 825-0000
Craig Collier, *President*
Danielle Ko, *General Mgr*
Ivonne Collier, *CFO*
Gina Doughty, *Marketing Staff*
John Maitin, *Software Engr*
▼ **EMP:** 15
SQ FT: 2,680
SALES (est): 4MM **Privately Held**
WEB: www.hypersizer.com
SIC: 7372 7371 8711 Application com-
puter software; custom computer pro-
gramming services; aviation &/or
aeronautical engineering; structural engi-
neering

(G-9204)
CONTINENTAL AUTO SYSTEMS INC
Also Called: Synerject
615 Bland Blvd (23602-4309)
PHONE .... (757) 890-4900
Elmar Degenhart, *CEO*
Bret Sauerwein, *Vice Pres*
Todd Detweiler, *Project Mgr*
Erik Gibbs, *Opers Mgr*
Carsten Berndt, *Engineer*
EMP: 65
SALES (corp-wide): 49.2B **Privately Held**
WEB: www.continental-automotive.com
SIC: 3714 Motor vehicle parts & acces-
sories
HQ: Continental Automotive Systems, Inc.
1 Continental Dr
Auburn Hills MI 48326
248 393-5300

(G-9205)
COOK & BOARDMAN GROUP LLC
700 Flag Stone Way Ste C (23608-5203)
P.O. Box 2395 (23609-0395)
PHONE .... (757) 873-3979
Jill Bandmann, *Project Mgr*
Bruce Barber, *Branch Mgr*
EMP: 8
SALES (corp-wide): 36.5MM **Privately Held**
WEB: www.cookandboardman.com
SIC: 3272 Building materials, except block
or brick: concrete
HQ: The Cook & Boardman Group Llc
3916 Westpoint Blvd
Winston Salem NC 27103
336 768-8872

(G-9206)
COTTAGE GROVE CANDLES
639 Nansemond Dr (23605-2965)
PHONE .... (757) 751-8333
Stacy Masters, *Principal*

EMP: 1
SALES (est): 39.6K **Privately Held**
SIC: 3999 Candles

(G-9207)
COUTURE INTUITION LLC
909 Forest Lake Ct # 303 (23605-3028)
PHONE .... (757) 570-8126
Shavonda El,
EMP: 1
SALES (est): 39.6K **Privately Held**
SIC: 3999 Candles

(G-9208)
CRAFT BEARING COMPANY INC
5000 Chestnut Ave (23605-2108)
PHONE .... (757) 247-6000
Donald L Moore, *CEO*
Ian Hadden, *President*
Robert Kerwin, *General Mgr*
Dannie L Schrum, *Chairman*
Dave Moss, *COO*
▲ **EMP:** 30
SALES (est): 5.8MM **Privately Held**
WEB: www.craftbearing.com
SIC: 3463 Bearing & bearing race forgings,
nonferrous

(G-9209)
CUSTOM VINYL PRODUCTS LLC
260 Enterprise Dr (23603-1300)
PHONE .... (757) 887-3194
Doanld Peinado, *Plant Mgr*
Carolyn Taylor, *Human Resources*
Jon Middleton, *Sales Staff*
Barry Taylor, *Mng Member*
EMP: 40
SQ FT: 40,000
SALES (est): 6.7MM **Privately Held**
WEB: www.customvinyl.net
SIC: 2452 Prefabricated wood buildings

(G-9210)
CUZ TO CUZ TRUCKING
1211 73rd St (23605-1815)
PHONE .... (757) 806-0358
Garland Hooker, *CEO*
EMP: 1
SALES (est): 70K **Privately Held**
SIC: 3531 Trucks, off-highway

(G-9211)
CYCLE SPECIALIST
11115 Jefferson Ave (23601-2528)
PHONE .... (757) 599-5236
Larry McBride, *Owner*
Kathie McBride, *Co-Owner*
EMP: 3
SQ FT: 6,000
SALES (est): 300K **Privately Held**
WEB: www.larrymcbride.com
SIC: 3599 7699 5571 Machine shop, job-
bing & repair; motorcycle repair service;
motorcycle parts & accessories

(G-9212)
D P WELDING INC
834 Wyemouth Dr (23602-8915)
PHONE .... (757) 232-0460
John Dennis Prillaman, *President*
EMP: 2
SALES (est): 132.2K **Privately Held**
WEB: www.site.dpweldinginc.com
SIC: 7692 Welding repair

(G-9213)
DAILY PRESS INC (HQ)
703 Mariners Row (23606-4432)
P.O. Box 2820, Norfolk (23501-2820)
PHONE .... (757) 245-3737
Digby A Solomon Diez, *President*
Gregory Pedersen, *Vice Pres*
Ann Wilson, *CFO*
EMP: 11
SQ FT: 100,000
SALES (est): 135.1MM **Publicly Held**
WEB: www.dailypress.com
SIC: 2711 Job printing & newspaper pub-
lishing combined; newspapers, publishing
& printing
PA: Tribune Publishing Company
160 N Stetson Ave
Chicago IL 60601
312 222-9100

▲ = Import ▼=Export
◆ =Import/Export

(G-9214)
DAP INCORPORATED
11015 Warwick Blvd (23601-3225)
P.O. Box 2302, Williamsburg (23187-2302)
PHONE..................................757 921-3576
Alexus Sundy, *Principal*
EMP: 3
SALES (est): 135.1K Privately Held
WEB: www.dap.com
SIC: 2261 2396 2621 2741 Printing of cotton broadwoven fabrics; fabric printing & stamping; book, bond & printing papers; art copy: publishing & printing; commercial printing, offset

(G-9215)
DARLIN MONOGRAMS LLC
241 Petersburg Ct (23606-1645)
PHONE..................................757 930-8786
Karen Wilcox, *Principal*
EMP: 1
SALES (est): 48.8K Privately Held
SIC: 2395 Embroidery & art needlework

(G-9216)
DILON TECHNOLOGIES INC
12050 Jefferson Ave # 340 (23606-4471)
PHONE..................................757 269-4910
Robert G Moussa, *President*
Robert Moussa, *President*
Benjamin L Welch, *Vice Pres*
Shari Hicks, *Manager*
Steve Moen, *Manager*
EMP: 32 EST: 1996
SQ FT: 3,000
SALES (est): 5.5MM Privately Held
WEB: www.dilon.com
SIC: 3844 Gamma ray irradiation equipment

(G-9217)
DIXIE FUEL COMPANY
512 Muller Ln Ste B (23606-1370)
P.O. Box 1160, Grafton (23692-1160)
PHONE..................................757 249-1264
Michael Kerlin, *President*
EMP: 4
SALES (est): 510K Privately Held
WEB: www.quarlesinc.com
SIC: 1321 7389 Natural gas liquids;

(G-9218)
DW SALTWATER FLIES LLC
928 Lacon Dr (23608-2525)
PHONE..................................757 874-1859
Milton D Waller, *Principal*
EMP: 1
SALES (est): 56.2K Privately Held
SIC: 1389 7389 Impounding & storing salt water, oil & gas field; business services

(G-9219)
EAGLE AVIATION TECH LLC
7505 Warwick Blvd (23607-1517)
PHONE..................................757 224-6269
Emitt Wallace, *CEO*
Bruce Bailey, *Vice Pres*
Adam Qureshi, *Engineer*
Mia C Copeland,
EMP: 82
SQ FT: 210,000
SALES (est): 13.3MM Privately Held
WEB: www.eagleaviationtech.com
SIC: 3724 3721 8711 3599 Research & development on aircraft engines & parts; aircraft; helicopters; engineering services; machine & other job shop work

(G-9220)
ECONOMY SIGNS
168 Little John Pl (23602-6550)
PHONE..................................757 877-5082
Susan Connor, *Partner*
Vernie Connor, *Partner*
EMP: 2
SALES (est): 86.7K Privately Held
SIC: 3993 Signs & advertising specialties

(G-9221)
EVERETTE PUBLISHING LLC
106 Tillerson Dr (23602-4011)
PHONE..................................757 344-9092
Priscilla Burnett,
EMP: 1
SALES (est): 3.5K Privately Held
SIC: 2731 Books: publishing only

(G-9222)
EXECUTIVE LIFESTYLE MAG INC
703 Juniper Dr (23601-3511)
PHONE..................................757 438-5582
William Dittmar, *Owner*
EMP: 3
SALES (est): 208.1K Privately Held
SIC: 2721 Periodicals

(G-9223)
FAIRLEAD BOATWORKS INC
99 Jefferson Ave (23607-6102)
P.O. Box 7008, Portsmouth (23707-0008)
PHONE..................................757 247-0101
Jerrold L Miller, *Principal*
Daniel Wood, *Treasurer*
EMP: 56
SQ FT: 10,780
SALES: 12MM Privately Held
WEB: www.fairleadint.com
SIC: 3732 3731 Boat building & repairing; shipbuilding & repairing

(G-9224)
FAMM PROJECT LLC
9601 Warwick Blvd (23601-4540)
PHONE..................................757 975-6492
Tristan Jackson,
EMP: 4
SALES (est): 156.7K Privately Held
SIC: 2836 Culture media

(G-9225)
FEAT LITTLE PUBLISHING LLC
46 Hopkins St (23601-4026)
PHONE..................................757 594-9265
EMP: 1
SALES (est): 37.5K Privately Held
SIC: 2741 Miscellaneous publishing

(G-9226)
FIBERGLASS CUSTOMS INC
7826 Warwick Blvd (23607-1524)
PHONE..................................757 244-0610
EMP: 3
SALES (est): 388.5K Privately Held
SIC: 3061 3732 7699 7532 Mfg Mechanical Rubber Gd Boatbuilding/Repairing Repair Services Auto Body Repair/Paint

(G-9227)
FIDOUGH HOMEMADE DOG TREATS
767 Terrace Dr (23601-4608)
PHONE..................................757 876-4548
Theresa Smith, *Owner*
EMP: 1 EST: 2014
SALES (est): 128.6K Privately Held
SIC: 2047 Dog food

(G-9228)
FIGURE FREIGHT LLC
550 Pavilion Pl Apt 8b (23606-3214)
PHONE..................................757 814-3610
Jamal Frink,
EMP: 1
SALES (est): 60K Privately Held
SIC: 3537 Trucks, tractors, loaders, carriers & similar equipment

(G-9229)
FITZGERALDS CABINET SHOP INC
13191 Warwick Blvd (23602-8345)
PHONE..................................757 877-2538
Brenda Peters, *President*
EMP: 7
SALES (est): 420K Privately Held
WEB: www.fitzgeraldcabinetshop.com
SIC: 2599 1751 5031 2531 Cabinets, factory; cabinet building & installation; kitchen cabinets; public building & related furniture; wood kitchen cabinets

(G-9230)
FLEET WAVEGUIDES LLC
700 Tech Center Pkwy # 200 (23606-3075)
PHONE..................................757 337-3311
Nicolas Middleton,
EMP: 2
SALES (est): 500K Privately Held
SIC: 3679 Waveguides & fittings

(G-9231)
FLOWERS BAKING CO NORFOLK LLC
Also Called: Flowers Baking Co Norfolk Whse
808 City Center Blvd (23606-2899)
PHONE..................................757 873-0066
EMP: 4
SALES (corp-wide): 4.1B Publicly Held
SIC: 2051 Bread, cake & related products
HQ: Flowers Baking Co. Of Norfolk, Llc
1209 Corprew Ave
Norfolk VA 23504
757 622-6317

(G-9232)
FORRLACE INC (PA)
Also Called: Signs By Tomorrow
11712 Jefferson Ave Ste A (23606-4406)
PHONE..................................757 873-5777
Linda Bassett, *President*
Forest Bassett, *Vice Pres*
Joe Mauldin, *Director*
EMP: 8
SQ FT: 3,600
SALES (est): 1MM Privately Held
WEB: www.signsbytomorrow.com
SIC: 3993 Signs & advertising specialties

(G-9233)
FULLMAN IMAN
Also Called: Iman Fullman Mua
13224 Margaux Cir Apt 4 (23608-1212)
PHONE..................................908 627-3376
Iman Fullman, *CEO*
EMP: 1 EST: 2016
SALES (est): 51.9K Privately Held
SIC: 2844 Hair preparations, including shampoos

(G-9234)
GE ENERGY
11864 Canon Blvd Ste 105 (23606-4253)
PHONE..................................757 595-7982
EMP: 1
SALES (est): 65.8K Privately Held
SIC: 3564 Blowers & fans

(G-9235)
GET IT RIGHT ENTERPRISE
213 Piez Ave (23601-4017)
PHONE..................................757 869-1736
Edward Davignon, *Owner*
EMP: 2
SALES (est): 107.5K Privately Held
WEB: www.getitrightenterprise.com
SIC: 2311 Military uniforms, men's & youths': purchased materials

(G-9236)
GOLCO LOGISTICS LLC
300 Continental Pkwy # 315 (23602-4542)
PHONE..................................571 234-3466
Emmanuel K Baffour Senkyire,
EMP: 1
SALES (est): 240K Privately Held
SIC: 3537 Trucks: freight, baggage, etc.: industrial, except mining

(G-9237)
GOODLION MUSIC & PUBLISHING
701 Industrial Park Dr B (23608-1467)
PHONE..................................757 875-0000
EMP: 1
SALES (est): 68K Privately Held
SIC: 2741 Misc Publishing

(G-9238)
GRANITE COUNTERTOP EXPERTS LLC
Also Called: USA Stone Experts
5875 Jefferson Ave Bldg B (23605-3219)
PHONE..................................757 826-9316
Natalie Lago, *Mng Member*
EMP: 2
SQ FT: 7,500
SALES (est): 193.8K Privately Held
WEB: www.granitecountertopexperts.com
SIC: 3281 1743 5099 Cut stone & stone products; terrazzo, tile, marble, mosaic work; monuments & grave markers

(G-9239)
GRAPHIC PRINTS
311 Poplar Ave (23607-4940)
PHONE..................................757 244-3753
EMP: 2
SALES (est): 83.9K Privately Held
SIC: 2752 Lithographic Commercial Printing

(G-9240)
HAMPTON MACHINE SHOP INC
900 39th St (23607-3142)
PHONE..................................757 245-9243
James E Wilson, *President*
James Wilson, *General Mgr*
Diane Beilharz, *Vice Pres*
Laurie Backley, *Opers Mgr*
Sheri Lanning, *Opers Mgr*
EMP: 45 EST: 1973
SQ FT: 42,000
SALES (est): 7.9MM Privately Held
WEB: www.hampmach.com
SIC: 3599 Machine shop, jobbing & repair

(G-9241)
HAMPTON ROADS BINDERY INC
15466 Warwick Blvd (23608-1506)
PHONE..................................757 369-5671
Phillip Gibson, *President*
EMP: 8
SALES (est): 518.2K Privately Held
WEB: www.hamptonroadsbindery.com
SIC: 2789 2759 Binding only: books, pamphlets, magazines, etc.; commercial printing

(G-9242)
HAMPTON SHEET METAL INC
509 Muller Ln (23606-1305)
PHONE..................................757 249-1629
Ronald T Nelsen, *President*
Linda Block, *General Mgr*
Linda S Block, *Vice Pres*
Scott Grimm, *Project Mgr*
Justin Dudney, *Prdtn Mgr*
EMP: 23 EST: 1975
SQ FT: 8,000
SALES (est): 1.3MM Privately Held
WEB: www.hamptonsheetmetalinc.com
SIC: 3312 3353 Stainless steel; aluminum sheet, plate & foil

(G-9243)
HANGER PRSTHETCS & ORTHO INC
704 Thmble Shls Blvd 400b (23606-4544)
PHONE..................................757 873-1984
Joe Carideo, *Manager*
EMP: 6
SALES (corp-wide): 1.1B Publicly Held
WEB: www.hangerclinic.com
SIC: 3842 5999 Prosthetic appliances; orthopedic appliances; artificial limbs
HQ: Hanger Prosthetics & Orthotics, Inc.
10910 Domain Dr Ste 300
Austin TX 78758
512 777-3800

(G-9244)
HANGUK RICE CAKE MARK
15320 Warwick Blvd (23608-2651)
PHONE..................................757 874-4150
EMP: 4
SALES (est): 75.4K Privately Held
SIC: 2052 Rice cakes

(G-9245)
HAPPY YARD SIGNS
813 Olive Dr (23601-1415)
PHONE..................................757 599-5171
Charles Williams, *Owner*
EMP: 2 EST: 2015
SALES (est): 61.3K Privately Held
WEB: www.happyyardsigns.com
SIC: 3993 Signs & advertising specialties

(G-9246)
HARTZ CONTRACTORS INC
424 Skipjack Rd (23602-6254)
PHONE..................................757 870-2978
Jim Hartzheim, *President*
EMP: 7
SALES (est): 250K Privately Held
SIC: 3448 Sunrooms, prefabricated metal

(G-9247)
HII UNMNNED MRTIME SYSTEMS INC (HQ)
Also Called: Undersea Solutions Corporation
4101 Washington Ave (23607-2700)
PHONE..............................757 688-5672
James F Hughes, *President*
Michael H Burton, *Asst Treas*
Stephen R Powell, *Asst Treas*
Stephen Powell, *Asst Treas*
Dianna P Yoko, *Asst Treas*
EMP: 30
SQ FT: 500
SALES (est): 8.8MM **Publicly Held**
WEB: www.huntingtoningalls.com
SIC: 3731 Military ships, building & repairing

(G-9248)
HR KIDS LLC
188 Arthur Way (23602-9443)
PHONE..............................210 341-7783
EMP: 1
SALES (est): 49.1K **Privately Held**
SIC: 3873 Watches, clocks, watchcases & parts

(G-9249)
HUNTINGTON INGALLS INC (HQ)
4101 Washington Ave (23607-2700)
PHONE..............................757 380-2000
Matt Mulherin, *President*
Bill Ermatinger, *Exec VP*
Alene Kaufman, *Vice Pres*
Barbara A Niland, *Vice Pres*
Robin Penley, *Research*
▲ EMP: 277
SALES (est): 4.2B **Publicly Held**
WEB: www.huntingtoningalls.com
SIC: 3731 Submarines, building & repairing

(G-9250)
HUNTINGTON INGALLS INC
Also Called: Apprentice School-Newport News
4101 Washington Ave (23607-2700)
PHONE..............................757 380-2000
Mike Petters, *CEO*
Xavier Beale, *Vice Pres*
Don Godwin, *Vice Pres*
Matt Needy, *Vice Pres*
Bill Smith, *Vice Pres*
EMP: 9 **Publicly Held**
WEB: www.huntingtoningalls.com
SIC: 3731 Combat vessels, building & repairing
HQ: Huntington Ingalls Incorporated
4101 Washington Ave
Newport News VA 23607
757 380-2000

(G-9251)
HUNTINGTON INGALLS INC
4101 Washington Ave (23607-2734)
PHONE..............................757 688-1411
Matthew J Mulherin, *Manager*
EMP: 3984 **Publicly Held**
WEB: www.huntingtoningalls.com
SIC: 3731 Shipbuilding & repairing
HQ: Huntington Ingalls Incorporated
4101 Washington Ave
Newport News VA 23607
757 380-2000

(G-9252)
HUNTINGTON INGALLS INDS INC
Also Called: Newport News Shipbuilding
230 41st St Fl 2521 (23607-2709)
PHONE..............................757 380-7053
EMP: 60 **Publicly Held**
WEB: www.huntingtoningalls.com
SIC: 3731 Military ships, building & repairing
PA: Huntington Ingalls Industries, Inc.
4101 Washington Ave
Newport News VA 23607

(G-9253)
HUNTINGTON INGALLS INDS INC
Northrop Grumman Newport News
3100 Washington Ave (23607-3329)
PHONE..............................757 380-2000

Mike Petters, *President*
Bill Bell, *Vice Pres*
Brian Fields, *Vice Pres*
Barbara A Niland, *CFO*
Peter Wong, *Director*
EMP: 18 **Publicly Held**
WEB: www.huntingtoningalls.com
SIC: 3731 Landing ships, building & repairing
PA: Huntington Ingalls Industries, Inc.
4101 Washington Ave
Newport News VA 23607

(G-9254)
HUNTINGTON INGALLS INDS INC (PA)
4101 Washington Ave (23607-2700)
PHONE..............................757 380-2000
Kirkland H Donald, *Ch of Bd*
C Michael Petters, *President*
Bharat B Amin, *Exec VP*
Jennifer R Boykin, *Exec VP*
Brian J Cuccias, *Exec VP*
EMP: 253
SALES: 8.9B **Publicly Held**
WEB: www.huntingtoningalls.com
SIC: 3731 Military ships, building & repairing

(G-9255)
I10CARTEL RECORDS LLC
3802 Woodbridge Dr (23608-8277)
PHONE..............................713 979-8182
Olander Albright, *CEO*
EMP: 3
SALES (est): 121.3K **Privately Held**
SIC: 3651 Music distribution apparatus

(G-9256)
INDIANA PACKERS CORPORATION
603 Pilot House Dr Fl 4th (23606-1904)
PHONE..............................270 926-2324
Bonita Then, *Branch Mgr*
EMP: 2 **Privately Held**
WEB: www.specialtyfoodsgroup.com
SIC: 2013 Prepared beef products from purchased beef
HQ: Indiana Packers Corporation
6755 W 100 N
Delphi IN 46923

(G-9257)
INFINITY PUBLISHING GROUP LLC
394 Deputy Ln (23608-2921)
PHONE..............................757 874-0135
Winter Giovanni, *Principal*
EMP: 5
SALES (est): 419.1K **Privately Held**
SIC: 2741 Miscellaneous publishing

(G-9258)
INKD OUT ELECTRICAL SVC LLC
719 Industrial Park Dr C (23608-1358)
PHONE..............................757 369-9827
Duane Crosby, *Mng Member*
EMP: 12
SALES (est): 373.7K **Privately Held**
WEB: www.inkedoutllc.com
SIC: 3993 Signs & advertising specialties

(G-9259)
INKD OUT LLC
719 Industrial Park Dr C (23608-1358)
PHONE..............................757 369-9827
Joshua Barnett, *Vice Pres*
Terry Harris,
EMP: 1
SALES (est): 128.2K **Privately Held**
WEB: www.inkedoutllc.com
SIC: 3993 5131 7389 Letters for signs, metal; flags & banners; sign painting & lettering shop

(G-9260)
INNOVATED MACHINE & TL CO INC
250 Picketts Line (23603-1366)
PHONE..............................757 887-2181
Dwight Bryant, *CEO*
Cameron Bryant, *President*
Kirsten Gastoukian, *Principal*
Dana Powell, *Vice Pres*

Linwood Joyner, *Production*
EMP: 50
SQ FT: 60,000
SALES (est): 14.6MM **Privately Held**
WEB: www.innovatedmachine.com
SIC: 3599 Machine shop, jobbing & repair

(G-9261)
ITT EXELIS
11830 Canon Blvd Ste J (23606-2568)
PHONE..............................757 594-1600
Cliff Motley, *Manager*
EMP: 3
SALES (est): 212.5K **Privately Held**
SIC: 3812 Search & navigation equipment

(G-9262)
IVWATCH LLC
700 Tech Center Pkwy # 300 (23606-3075)
PHONE..............................855 489-2824
Jaclyn Lautz, *COO*
Laurie Swicegood, *Controller*
Mendy Chilton, *Accounts Mgr*
Gary Warren, *Mng Member*
Jason Naramore, *CTO*
EMP: 40
SQ FT: 7,200
SALES (est): 6.4MM **Privately Held**
WEB: www.ivwatch.com
SIC: 3845 Electromedical equipment

(G-9263)
J FRED DOWIS
Also Called: Sign Engineering
15454 Warwick Blvd (23608-1506)
PHONE..............................757 874-7446
J Fred Dowis, *Owner*
EMP: 1 EST: 1970
SQ FT: 6,000
SALES (est): 61K **Privately Held**
WEB: www.sign-engineer.com
SIC: 3993 7389 1799 Electric signs; sign painting & lettering shop; sign installation & maintenance

(G-9264)
JACKSON POINTE LLC
Also Called: Jefferson Labs
628 Hofstadter Rd Ste 6 (23606-3060)
PHONE..............................757 269-7100
Peter Bjonerud, *Mng Member*
▲ EMP: 2
SALES (est): 670K **Privately Held**
WEB: www.jlab.org
SIC: 3821 Laboratory apparatus & furniture

(G-9265)
JAMES LASSITER
725 Arrowhead Dr (23601-1640)
PHONE..............................757 595-4242
James Lassiter, *Owner*
EMP: 6
SALES (est): 234.5K **Privately Held**
SIC: 3942 Dolls & stuffed toys

(G-9266)
JAMES RIVER SIGNS INC
724 City Center Blvd A (23606-3081)
PHONE..............................757 870-3368
Dave Gupta, *Director*
EMP: 2
SALES (est): 67.2K **Privately Held**
WEB: www.jamesriversigns.com
SIC: 3993 Signs & advertising specialties

(G-9267)
JANICE MARTIN-FREEMAN
Also Called: Wing Tips & Unique Gifts EMB
30 Holloway Rd (23602-7375)
PHONE..............................757 234-0056
Janice Martin-Freeman, *Owner*
EMP: 1
SALES (est): 57.2K **Privately Held**
WEB: www.wingtips.us
SIC: 2395 Embroidery products, except schiffli machine; embroidery & art needlework

(G-9268)
JAY DOUGLAS CARPER
Also Called: Atlantic Vent
200 Old Marina Ln (23602-7571)
P.O. Box 1715 (23601-0715)
PHONE..............................757 595-7660
Jay Douglas Carper, *Owner*
EMP: 1

SALES (est): 42.3K **Privately Held**
SIC: 3564 Ventilating fans: industrial or commercial

(G-9269)
JEFFS MOBILE WELDING INC
415 Oakwood Pl (23608-1341)
PHONE..............................757 870-7049
Jeff Judd, *Principal*
EMP: 1
SALES (est): 37.2K **Privately Held**
SIC: 7692 Welding repair

(G-9270)
JR EVERETT WOODSON
Also Called: Deep Clean Carpet & Upholstery
213 Picard Dr (23602-5246)
PHONE..............................757 867-3478
Everett Woodson Jr, *Owner*
EMP: 1
SALES (est): 68.4K **Privately Held**
SIC: 2819 Iodides

(G-9271)
K AND M INDUSTRIES LLC
471 Dunmore Dr (23602-6440)
PHONE..............................757 328-0227
David Canaday, *Principal*
EMP: 1 EST: 2018
SALES (est): 49.1K **Privately Held**
SIC: 3999 Manufacturing industries

(G-9272)
KANDY GIRL KNDY APPLES BERRIES
57 Otsego Dr (23602-2071)
PHONE..............................719 200-1662
Leasha Williams, *Principal*
EMP: 2
SALES (est): 77.2K **Privately Held**
SIC: 2064 Fruit & fruit peel confections

(G-9273)
KANGS EMBROIDERY
15525 Warwick Blvd (23608-1580)
PHONE..............................757 887-5232
EMP: 1 EST: 2010
SALES (est): 42K **Privately Held**
SIC: 2395 Pleating/Stitching Services

(G-9274)
KELVIN INTERNATIONAL CORP
742 Bluecrab Rd (23606-2549)
PHONE..............................757 833-1011
Al Guerra, *CEO*
Paul Guerra, *Engineer*
Janice Sherwood, *CFO*
◆ EMP: 10
SQ FT: 8,100
SALES (est): 2.7MM **Privately Held**
WEB: www.kelvinic.com
SIC: 3569 8711 3443 Generators: steam, liquid oxygen or nitrogen; industrial engineers; cryogenic tanks, for liquids & gases

(G-9275)
KEMPSVILLE BUILDING MTLS INC
814 Chapman Way (23608-1302)
PHONE..............................757 875-1850
Bob Gentry, *Manager*
EMP: 6
SALES (corp-wide): 1.5B **Privately Held**
WEB: www.kempsvillebuilding.com
SIC: 2431 2439 5211 Millwork; trusses, except roof: laminated lumber; lumber & other building materials
HQ: Kempsville Building Materials, Incorporated
3300 Business Center Dr
Chesapeake VA 23323
757 485-0782

(G-9276)
KINYO VIRGINIA INC
290 Enterprise Dr (23603-1300)
PHONE..............................757 888-2221
Kazuo Nakamura, *President*
Steven Vanover, *Engineer*
Neryn Reyes, *Maintenance Staff*
◆ EMP: 110
SQ FT: 153,000

▲ = Import ▼=Export
◆ =Import/Export

SALES: 16.2MM **Privately Held**
WEB: www.kinyova.com
SIC: **3069** 3555 2796 Medical & laboratory rubber sundries & related products; printing trades machinery; platemaking services
PA: Kinyosha Co., Ltd.
1-2-2, Osaki
Shinagawa-Ku TKY 141-0

(G-9277)
L & L TOOL AND MACHINE INC
505 Edwards Ct (23608-8635)
PHONE......................757 224-3445
Anna Lloyd, *President*
Kim Lloyd, *Vice Pres*
EMP: 1
SALES (est): 190.7K **Privately Held**
WEB: www.landltool.com
SIC: **3599** Machine shop, jobbing & repair

(G-9278)
L3HARRIS TECHNOLOGIES INC
Also Called: Exelis Systems Corp - Folbos
11830 Canon Blvd (23606-2568)
PHONE......................757 594-1607
Marykay Tomlinson, *Branch Mgr*
EMP: 247
SALES (corp-wide): 6.8B **Publicly Held**
WEB: www.harris.com
SIC: **3812** 3823 3669 Search & navigation equipment; industrial instrmnts msrmnt display/control process variable; burglar alarm apparatus, electric
PA: L3harris Technologies, Inc.
1025 W Nasa Blvd
Melbourne FL 32919
321 727-9100

(G-9279)
LAWRENCE CUSTOM CABINETS
S
53 Buxton Ave (23607-6030)
PHONE......................757 380-0817
Lawrence Britt, *Principal*
EMP: 2
SALES (est): 169.1K **Privately Held**
SIC: **2434** Wood kitchen cabinets

(G-9280)
LEGACY VULCAN LLC
Also Called: Skiffes Creek Yard and Recycle
313 O Hara Ln (23602)
PHONE......................757 888-2982
Jeanie Clay, *Manager*
EMP: 5 **Publicly Held**
WEB: www.vulcanmaterials.com
SIC: **3273** Ready-mixed concrete
HQ: Legacy Vulcan, Llc
1200 Urban Center Dr
Vestavia AL 35242
205 298-3000

(G-9281)
LEHIGH CEMENT COMPANY LLC
21 Stanley Dr (23608)
PHONE......................757 928-1559
Charles Whitten, *Branch Mgr*
EMP: 3
SALES (corp-wide): 20.8B **Privately Held**
WEB: www.lehighhanson.com
SIC: **3273** Ready-mixed concrete
HQ: Lehigh Cement Company Llc
300 E John Carpenter Fwy
Irving TX 75062
877 534-4442

(G-9282)
LESS THAN LADYLIKE CANDLE LLC
80 Meredith Way (23606-1179)
PHONE......................757 817-0616
Lianne Michelle Hedden, *Principal*
EMP: 1
SALES (est): 43.6K **Privately Held**
SIC: **3999** Candles

(G-9283)
LIFESAFER INC
11849 Tug Boat Ln (23606-3067)
PHONE......................757 595-8800
EMP: 2
SALES (est): 144.1K **Privately Held**
SIC: **3694** Ignition apparatus & distributors

(G-9284)
LIGHTSMOKECHILL CANDLE CO LLC
109 Jefferson Point Ln 2d (23602-8140)
PHONE......................347 720-2596
Dominique Benneth, *Mng Member*
EMP: 1
SALES (est): 39.6K **Privately Held**
SIC: **3999** Candles

(G-9285)
LISA A MCLAIN
905 Pine Mill Ct (23602-9468)
PHONE......................757 788-1781
Lisa A McLain, *Owner*
EMP: 1
SALES (est): 30.5K **Privately Held**
SIC: **3999** Hair, dressing of, for the trade

(G-9286)
LITTLE BLACK DOG DESIGNS
910 Healey Dr (23608-2409)
PHONE......................757 874-0928
Deborah Green, *Owner*
Robert Green, *Co-Owner*
EMP: 3
SALES (est): 134.3K **Privately Held**
SIC: **2782** Scrapbooks

(G-9287)
LUCK STONE CORPORATION
538 Oyster Point Rd (23602-6920)
PHONE......................757 566-8676
EMP: 4
SALES (corp-wide): 824.7MM **Privately Held**
WEB: www.luckstone.com
SIC: **3281** Cut stone & stone products
PA: Luck Stone Corporation
515 Stone Mill Dr
Manakin Sabot VA 23103
804 784-6300

(G-9288)
M & B DIESEL SUPPLY LLC
725 Industrial Park Dr (23608-1358)
PHONE......................757 903-8146
Robert Kappesser,
EMP: 2
SQ FT: 5,500
SALES (est): 104K **Privately Held**
SIC: **3519** Diesel, semi-diesel or duel-fuel engines, including marine; marine engines; diesel engine rebuilding

(G-9289)
MAOLA MILK AND ICE CREAM CO (HQ)
5500 Chestnut Ave (23605-2118)
PHONE......................252 638-1131
Steve Nicoll, *General Mgr*
Tony Norbut, *Sales Staff*
Harold Littlefield, *Supervisor*
John Hardesty,
Jay Bryant,
EMP: 83 EST: 1935
SQ FT: 150,000
SALES (est): 68.6MM
SALES (corp-wide): 1.3B **Privately Held**
WEB: www.maolamilk.com
SIC: **2026** 2024 Fluid milk; ice cream, bulk
PA: Maryland And Virginia Milk Producers Cooperative Association, Incorporated
1985 Isaac Newton Sq W
Reston VA 20190
703 742-6800

(G-9290)
MARCY BOYS MUSIC
3013 Williams St (23607-3731)
PHONE......................:757 247-6222
Marcia Epps, *Partner*
Larry Binns, *Partner*
EMP: 4
SALES (est): 75K **Privately Held**
SIC: **2731** Book music: publishing & printing

(G-9291)
MARTINS CUSTOM DESIGNS INC
340 Ed Wright Ln (23606-4369)
PHONE......................757 245-7129
Paul Martin, *Vice Pres*
EMP: 18

SALES (corp-wide): 1.3MM **Privately Held**
WEB: www.martinsdesign.com
SIC: **3993** Electric signs
PA: Martin's Custom Designs, Inc.
1707 Shane Rd
Gloucester Point VA 23062
804 642-0235

(G-9292)
MARYLAND AND VIRGINIA MILK PR
Marva Maid Dairy
5500 Chestnut Ave (23605-2118)
P.O. Box 5145 (23605-0145)
PHONE......................757 245-3857
Danny Lovell, *Manager*
Greg Deaver, *Manager*
EMP: 200
SALES (corp-wide): 1.3B **Privately Held**
WEB: www.mdvamilk.com
SIC: **2026** 5143 5451 2086 Milk processing (pasteurizing, homogenizing, bottling); dairy products, except dried or canned; dairy products stores; bottled & canned soft drinks; canned fruits & specialties; dry, condensed, evaporated dairy products
PA: Maryland And Virginia Milk Producers Cooperative Association, Incorporated
1985 Isaac Newton Sq W
Reston VA 20190
703 742-6800

(G-9293)
MASTER MACHINE & AUTO LLC
Also Called: Dunkum's Machine Shop
5823 Jefferson Ave (23605-3219)
P.O. Box 5027 (23605-0027)
PHONE......................757 244-8401
Gary McMurray, *President*
EMP: 6
SQ FT: 6,500
SALES (est): 600K **Privately Held**
WEB: www.dunkums.com
SIC: **3599** 5013 Machine shop, jobbing & repair; automotive supplies & parts

(G-9294)
MASTER MACHINE & TOOL CO INC
5857 Jefferson Ave (23605-3219)
P.O. Box 5027 (23605-0027)
PHONE......................757 245-6653
Gary E McMurray, *President*
David Revere, *General Mgr*
Penelope Rich, *General Mgr*
David A Revere, *Vice Pres*
▼ EMP: 19
SQ FT: 16,000
SALES (est): 2.6MM **Privately Held**
WEB: www.master-machine.com
SIC: **3599** Machine shop, jobbing & repair

(G-9295)
MASTER MOLD OF VIRGINIA LLC
5857 Jefferson Ave (23605-3219)
P.O. Box 5027 (23605-0027)
PHONE......................757 868-8283
Sue Fountain, *Mng Member*
EMP: 5
SALES (est): 394.3K **Privately Held**
WEB: www.master-machine.com
SIC: **3599** Machine shop, jobbing & repair

(G-9296)
MATTHIAS ENTERPRISES INC
Also Called: Applied Electronics
722 Bluecrab Rd Ste A (23606-2582)
PHONE......................757 591-9371
Scott Humphrey, *President*
Mike Ramemeyer, *COO*
Max Wilson, *VP Sales*
Jack Brown, *Sales Mgr*
Ernie Laviolette, *Sales Staff*
◆ EMP: 42
SQ FT: 40,000
SALES (est): 15.3MM **Privately Held**
WEB: www.appliednn.com
SIC: **3448** 7922 Trusses & framing: prefabricated metal; lighting, theatrical

(G-9297)
MAVERICK FABRICATION
5931 Marshall Ave (23605-2335)
PHONE......................321 210-9004
Barton Drummond, *Principal*
EMP: 1
SALES (est): 39.6K **Privately Held**
SIC: **3999** Manufacturing industries

(G-9298)
MET OF HAMPTON ROADS INC
Also Called: Fox Screen Print & Embroidery
499 Muller Ln (23606-1303)
PHONE......................757 249-7777
Michael J Fox, *Corp Secy*
EMP: 2 EST: 2011
SALES (est): 225.4K **Privately Held**
WEB: www.foxscreenprint.com
SIC: **2759** Screen printing

(G-9299)
MICA CO OF CANADA INC
900 Jefferson Ave (23607-6120)
P.O. Box 318 (23607-0318)
PHONE......................757 244-7311
James Turbish, *President*
EMP: 6 EST: 1966
SQ FT: 36,000
SALES (est): 4.8MM
SALES (corp-wide): 5MM **Privately Held**
WEB: www.ashevillemica.com
SIC: **3644** 3498 3469 Insulators & insulation materials, electrical; fabricated pipe & fittings; metal stampings
PA: Asheville-Schoonmaker Mica Co., Llc
900 Jefferson Ave
Newport News VA
757 244-7311

(G-9300)
MICHAEL BURNETTE
1406 Riversedge Rd (23606-2037)
PHONE......................757 478-8585
Michael Burnette, *Principal*
EMP: 2
SALES (est): 85.9K **Privately Held**
SIC: **3577** Computer peripheral equipment

(G-9301)
MID ATLANTIC IMAGING CENTERS
750 Mcguire Pl Ste A (23601-1675)
PHONE......................757 223-5059
Barbara Miller, *Administration*
EMP: 2
SALES (est): 176K **Privately Held**
SIC: **3826** Magnetic resonance imaging apparatus

(G-9302)
MK INDUSTRIES INC
6060 Jefferson Ave LI16 (23605-3014)
PHONE......................757 245-0007
Lenny Mattos, *Branch Mgr*
EMP: 17 **Privately Held**
WEB: www.mkpro.com
SIC: **3731** 7361 Shipbuilding & repairing; employment agencies
PA: M.K. Industries, Inc.
253 Indigo Dr
Brunswick GA 31525

(G-9303)
MODERN MACHINE AND TOOL CO INC
11844 Jefferson Ave (23606-2506)
PHONE......................757 873-1212
Brent G Meadors, *President*
Jarell Lane, *Vice Pres*
Naresh Patel, *Vice Pres*
Randy Kirt, *Engineer*
Yousuf Mohammed, *Engineer*
EMP: 75 EST: 1947
SQ FT: 53,000
SALES (est): 15.5MM **Privately Held**
WEB: www.mmtool.com
SIC: **3829** Measuring & controlling devices

(G-9304)
MODULAR DESIGN INSTALLATIONS
2107 Marshall Ave (23607-5253)
PHONE......................757 871-8885
Paul William Jones Jr, *Owner*
EMP: 1

SALES (est): 61.4K **Privately Held**
SIC: 2522 Office furniture, except wood

(G-9305)
MOORE METAL
540 Burcher Rd (23606-1502)
PHONE..................................757 930-0849
David Moore, *Owner*
EMP: 4
SALES (est): 520.5K **Privately Held**
SIC: 3399 Primary metal products

(G-9306)
NORTHROP GRUMMAN NEWPORT NEWS (DH)
Also Called: Newport News Shipbuilding
4101 Washington Ave (23607-2700)
PHONE..................................757 380-2000
Mike Petters, *President*
Bharat Amin, *Vice Pres*
Ray Bagley, *Vice Pres*
Fields Brian, *Vice Pres*
Mary Cullen, *Vice Pres*
◆ **EMP:** 18000
SALES (est): 68.9K **Publicly Held**
WEB: www.nns.huntingtoningalls.com
SIC: 3731 Submarines, building & repair-
ing
HQ: Titan Ii Inc.
4101 Washington Ave
Newport News VA 23607
757 380-2000

(G-9307)
NORTHROP GRUMMAN SYSTEMS CORP
4101 Washington Ave (23607-2700)
PHONE..................................757 380-2612
Rebecca Hughson, *Project Mgr*
Stacey Leach, *Project Mgr*
Lisa Grosgebauer, *QC Mgr*
Myong Chung, *Engineer*
Christie Circle, *Engineer*
EMP: 7 **Publicly Held**
WEB: www.northropgrumman.com
SIC: 3812 Search & navigation equipment
HQ: Northrop Grumman Systems Corpora-
tion
2980 Fairview Park Dr
Falls Church VA 22042
703 280-2900

(G-9308)
OLD POINT PACKING INC (PA)
Also Called: Old Point Seafoods
817 Jefferson Ave (23607-6117)
P.O. Box 13 (23607-0013)
PHONE..................................757 247-0557
Tim Daniels, *President*
EMP: 10
SQ FT: 15,000
SALES (est): 848.3K **Privately Held**
WEB: www.oldpointpacking.com
SIC: 2092 Fresh or frozen packaged fish

(G-9309)
PANDORAS BOX
10171 Jefferson Ave D10 (23605-1046)
PHONE..................................757 719-6669
EMP: 1
SALES (est): 38K **Privately Held**
SIC: 3961 Mfg Costume Jewelry

(G-9310)
PARASITX LLC
11849 Tug Boat Ln Ste A (23606-3067)
PHONE..................................757 653-6179
EMP: 3
SALES (est): 109.9K **Privately Held**
WEB: www.thebeerbug.com
SIC: 2082 Malt beverages

(G-9311)
PEPSI-COLA METRO BTLG CO INC
17200 Warwick Blvd (23603-1312)
PHONE..................................757 887-2310
William Reeser, *Vice Pres*
Todd Thomas, *Plant Mgr*
Annamaria Bugos, *Manager*
Stuart Adkins, *Info Tech Mgr*
Phyllis Thompson, *Info Tech Mgr*
EMP: 200

SALES (corp-wide): 67.1B **Publicly Held**
WEB: www.pepsico.com
SIC: 2086 Carbonated soft drinks, bottled
& canned
HQ: Pepsi-Cola Metropolitan Bottling Company, Inc.
1111 Westchester Ave
White Plains NY 10604
914 767-6000

(G-9312)
PERATON INC
11830 Canon Blvd Ste H (23606-2568)
PHONE..................................315 838-7009
Alan Stewart, *CFO*
Gloria Kleaka, *Contract Law*
EMP: 6
SALES (corp-wide): 2.3B **Privately Held**
WEB: www.peraton.com
SIC: 3812 Radar systems & equipment
HQ: Peraton Inc.
12975 Worldgate Dr # 100
Herndon VA 20170

(G-9313)
PILGRIM INTERNATIONAL
Also Called: Pilgrim Wireless
13294 Warwick Blvd (23602-6722)
P.O. Box 8087, Yorktown (23693-8087)
PHONE..................................757 989-5045
▲ **EMP:** 3
SALES (est): 250K **Privately Held**
SIC: 2673 Mfg Bags-Plastic/Coated Paper

(G-9314)
PLYMKRAFT INC (PA)
281 Picketts Line (23603-1367)
PHONE..................................757 595-0364
Doug Southard, *CEO*
Southard Douglas K, *CEO*
Daniel Singer, *Division Mgr*
Steve Zajac, *Vice Pres*
Alan Cross, *Safety Dir*
▲ **EMP:** 50
SQ FT: 98,000
SALES (est): 17.2MM **Privately Held**
WEB: www.plymkraft.com
SIC: 2282 2621 2241 2671 Throwing &
winding mills; paper mills; cords, fabric;
packaging paper & plastics film, coated &
laminated

(G-9315)
PRATT & WHITNEY ENG SVCS INC
11837 Rock Landing Dr (23606-4491)
PHONE..................................757 838-7980
Timothy Forsythe, *General Mgr*
Stan Steven, *Manager*
Stanley Stevens, *Manager*
EMP: 3
SALES (corp-wide): 77B **Publicly Held**
WEB: www.rtx.com
SIC: 3724 Aircraft engines & engine parts
HQ: Pratt & Whitney Engine Services, Inc.
1525 Midway Park Rd
Bridgeport WV 26330
304 842-5421

(G-9316)
PRINT LLC
57 Post St (23601-3950)
PHONE..................................757 746-5708
John Runner, *Principal*
EMP: 2
SALES (est): 83.9K **Privately Held**
SIC: 2752 Commercial printing, litho-
graphic

(G-9317)
PRINTINGWRIGHT LLC
12458a Warwick Blvd (23606-3042)
PHONE..................................757 591-0771
Adam Wright,
EMP: 2
SALES (est): 190K **Privately Held**
WEB: www.printingwright.com
SIC: 2759 Screen printing

(G-9318)
PROLOGUE
250 Picketts Line (23603-1366)
PHONE..................................757 871-3708
William L Gouger Jr, *Administration*
EMP: 1

SALES (est): 68.1K **Privately Held**
WEB: www.prologue-firelogs.com
SIC: 2499 Wood products

(G-9319)
PROV31 PUBLISHING LLC
14511 Old Courthouse Way (23608-2803)
PHONE..................................804 536-0436
Tequila Connors, *Principal*
EMP: 1
SALES (est): 37.5K **Privately Held**
SIC: 2741 Miscellaneous publishing

(G-9320)
PUZZLE PEACE PUBLICATIONS LLC
630 Saint Andrews Ln # 104 (23608-8021)
PHONE..................................973 766-5282
Tamika Foster, *Mng Member*
Iman Foster, *Mng Member*
EMP: 1
SALES (est): 37.5K **Privately Held**
SIC: 2741 Miscellaneous publishing

(G-9321)
REACH ORTHOTIC PROSTHETIC SVCS
Also Called: Silhouette Mastectomy Boutique
12715 Warwick Blvd Ste V (23606-1800)
PHONE..................................757 930-0139
Julie C Beach, *Principal*
EMP: 1 **EST:** 2011
SALES (est): 104.6K **Privately Held**
WEB: www.reachops.com
SIC: 3842 Orthopedic appliances

(G-9322)
REEF ROOM
1a Lyliston Ln (23601-3125)
PHONE..................................757 592-0955
Dale Cordle, *Principal*
EMP: 1
SALES (est): 46K **Privately Held**
SIC: 3731 Submarine tenders, building &
repairing

(G-9323)
REINHART CUSTOM CABINETS INC
605 Industrial Park Dr B (23608-1383)
PHONE..................................757 303-1438
EMP: 1
SALES (est): 59.1K **Privately Held**
SIC: 2434 Wood kitchen cabinets

(G-9324)
RESIDUAL SENSE MARKETING LLC
423 Lester Rd Apt 1 (23601-2260)
PHONE..................................757 595-0278
Dewayne Perry, *Principal*
EMP: 3
SALES (est): 202.3K **Privately Held**
SIC: 2911 Residues

(G-9325)
REWINED LLC
708 Windy Way Unit 308 (23602-5681)
PHONE..................................757 877-3480
Christopher Lane, *Principal*
EMP: 2
SALES (est): 65.3K **Privately Held**
SIC: 2084 Wines, brandy & brandy spirits

(G-9326)
REX COMPANIES INC
725 City Center Blvd (23606-3085)
PHONE..................................757 873-5452
Mathias Grob, *President*
Markus Baumeler, *Vice Pres*
Thomas Kellis, *Vice Pres*
Marcia Rowe, *Purch Agent*
Dale Barrows, *Manager*
◆ **EMP:** 31
SQ FT: 6,000
SALES (est): 9.7MM
SALES (corp-wide): 426.9MM **Privately
Held**
WEB: www.rexcompanies.com
SIC: 3536 Hoists, cranes & monorails
PA: Grapha-Holding Ag
Sonnenbergstrasse 13
Hergiswil NW 6052
416 326-868

(G-9327)
RIBBONS & SWEET MEMORIES
685 Turnberry Blvd # 15362 (23608-0290)
PHONE..................................757 874-1871
Debra Harrison, *Owner*
EMP: 3
SALES (corp-wide): 137.2K **Privately
Held**
WEB: www.ribbonsbiz.com
SIC: 2759 Invitation & stationery printing &
engraving
PA: Ribbons & Sweet Memories
685 Turnberry Blvd
Newport News VA 23608
757 874-1871

(G-9328)
RIVERSIDE HEALTHCARE ASSN INC
Also Called: Riverside Diagnostic Center
895 Middle Ground Blvd (23606-4250)
PHONE..................................757 594-3900
Suzanne Riley, *Branch Mgr*
EMP: 1 **Privately Held**
WEB: www.riversideonline.com
SIC: 3841 Diagnostic apparatus, medical
PA: Riverside Healthcare Association, Inc.
701 Town Center Dr # 1000
Newport News VA 23606
757 534-7000

(G-9329)
ROBIN STIPPICH
Also Called: Tgihm Thank Gdness Its HM
Made
317 55th St (23607-2009)
PHONE..................................757 692-5744
Robin Stippich, *Owner*
EMP: 1
SALES (est): 60.2K **Privately Held**
WEB: www.huntingtonhouseva.com
SIC: 2051 2064 Cakes, bakery: except
frozen; candy & other confectionery prod-
ucts

(G-9330)
SALSA PICANTE BORI
915 Birchwood Ct (23608-1133)
PHONE..................................256 874-4074
Socrates Montesdeoca, *Principal*
EMP: 2 **EST:** 2018
SALES (est): 70.4K **Privately Held**
SIC: 2099 Dips, except cheese & sour
cream based

(G-9331)
SCENTS BY SCALES
14346 Warwick Blvd # 366 (23602-3810)
PHONE..................................757 234-3380
Anthony Scales, *Principal*
EMP: 2
SALES (est): 177.2K **Privately Held**
WEB: www.scentsbyscales.com
SIC: 2844 Toilet preparations

(G-9332)
SCOTTYS SIGN INC
Also Called: Scotty's Sign Service
340 Ed Wright Ln (23606-4369)
PHONE..................................757 245-7129
Howard C McKay, *President*
Douglas Collins, *Vice Pres*
Amos C McKay, *Treasurer*
EMP: 19
SQ FT: 8,500
SALES (est): 2.3MM **Privately Held**
WEB: www.scottysigns.com
SIC: 3993 1799 Signs, not made in cus-
tom sign painting shops; sign installation
& maintenance

(G-9333)
SEA TECHNOLOGY LTD
95 Tyler Ave Ste I (23601-4330)
PHONE..................................804 642-3568
McClanahan Ingles, *President*
Karen Hudgins, *Office Mgr*
EMP: 10
SALES (est): 92.5K **Privately Held**
WEB: www.seatechpower.com
SIC: 3731 Shipbuilding & repairing

(G-9334)
SEMMATERIALS LP
801 Terminal Ave (23607-6141)
PHONE.....................................757 244-6545
Tom Kivisto, *Manager*
EMP: 7
SQ FT: 5,000 **Publicly Held**
WEB: www.semgroup.com
SIC: 2951 Asphalt paving mixtures &
blocks
HQ: Semmaterials, L.P.
6520 S Yale Ave Ste 700
Tulsa OK 74136

(G-9335)
SHANTELL C YOUNG
563 Ayrshire Way Apt C (23602-4335)
PHONE.....................................251 348-7247
Shantell Young, *Owner*
EMP: 1
SALES (est): 58.2K **Privately Held**
SIC: 3531 Construction machinery

(G-9336)
SHINE BEAUTY COMPANY
252 Nantucket Pl (23606-3547)
P.O. Box 6325 (23606-0325)
PHONE.....................................757 509-7338
Marcus R Callahan, *Owner*
EMP: 1
SALES (est): 55K **Privately Held**
SIC: 3999 Barber & beauty shop equip-
ment

(G-9337)
SIEMENS AG
11827 Canon Blvd (23606-3071)
PHONE.....................................757 875-7000
Keith Schorr, *Engineer*
EMP: 5
SALES (est): 126.8K **Privately Held**
WEB: www.new.siemens.com
SIC: 3661 Telephones & telephone appara-
tus

(G-9338)
SIEMENS INDUSTRY SOFTWARE INC
11827 Canon Blvd Ste 400 (23606-3071)
PHONE.....................................757 591-6633
Michael Baltes, *Director*
EMP: 32
SALES (corp-wide): 67.4B **Privately Held**
WEB: www.new.siemens.com
SIC: 7372 Business oriented computer
software
HQ: Siemens Industry Software Inc.
5800 Granite Pkwy Ste 600
Plano TX 75024
972 987-3000

(G-9339)
SIGN SHOP OF NEWPORT NEWS
Also Called: Sign Shop The
715 Bluecrab Rd Ste A (23606-2687)
PHONE.....................................757 873-1157
Sherri Bullock, *President*
EMP: 5
SALES (est): 453.7K **Privately Held**
WEB: www.signshop-va.com
SIC: 3993 Signs & advertising specialties

(G-9340)
SIGN SOLUTIONS
133 Harpersville Rd (23601-2323)
PHONE.....................................757 594-9688
Robert Lumpkin, *Owner*
EMP: 2
SALES (est): 80K **Privately Held**
SIC: 3993 Signs & advertising specialties

(G-9341)
SIGN-N-DATE MOBILE NOTARY LLC
26 Wendfield Cir (23601-1025)
PHONE.....................................757 285-9619
Michelle Johnson, *Principal*
EMP: 1
SALES (est): 70.4K **Privately Held**
WEB: www.sign-n-datemobilenotary.com
SIC: 3993 Signs & advertising specialties

(G-9342)
SILVAS HEAT & AIR
6 Rutledge Rd (23601-2423)
PHONE.....................................757 596-5991
Bobby Silva, *Owner*
EMP: 1
SALES (est): 80.2K **Privately Held**
WEB: www.silvasheatandair.com
SIC: 3585 Refrigeration & heating equip-
ment

(G-9343)
SMITHFIELD FOODS INC
121 Harwood Dr (23603-1371)
PHONE.....................................757 933-2977
C Larry Pope, *Branch Mgr*
April Johnson, *Manager*
EMP: 574 **Privately Held**
WEB: www.smithfieldfoods.com
SIC: 2011 Meat packing plants
HQ: Smithfield Foods, Inc.
200 Commerce St
Smithfield VA 23430
757 365-3000

(G-9344)
SP SMOOTHIES INC
4191 William Styron Sq N (23606-2870)
PHONE.....................................757 595-0600
EMP: 3
SALES (est): 136.8K **Privately Held**
SIC: 2037 Frozen fruits & vegetables

(G-9345)
SPECTRUM
1 Bayport Way Ste 300 (23606-4560)
PHONE.....................................757 224-7500
Cynthia Smith, *Principal*
Michael Nickerson, *Vice Pres*
Bruce Fritz, *Research*
Ellen Briggs, *Finance Mgr*
Luci Wister, *Finance Asst*
EMP: 4
SALES (est): 543.8K **Privately Held**
WEB: www.sptrm.com
SIC: 3663 Receivers, radio communica-
tions

(G-9346)
STANLEY ACCESS TECH LLC
126 Sloane Pl (23606-4021)
PHONE.....................................804 598-0502
George Allen, *Manager*
EMP: 6
SALES (corp-wide): 14.4B **Publicly Held**
WEB: www.stanleyaccess.com
SIC: 3699 Door opening & closing devices,
electrical
HQ: Stanley Access Technologies Llc
65 Scott Swamp Rd
Farmington CT 06032

(G-9347)
STEVE K JONES
Also Called: Warwick Custom Kitchens
74 Maxwell Ln (23606-1641)
PHONE.....................................757 930-0217
Steve K Jones, *Owner*
EMP: 8
SQ FT: 10,000
SALES (est): 359.2K **Privately Held**
SIC: 2434 Wood kitchen cabinets

(G-9348)
STONE QUARRY
371 Chatham Dr (23602-4382)
PHONE.....................................757 722-9653
EMP: 2
SALES (est): 133.7K **Privately Held**
SIC: 3999 Lawn ornaments

(G-9349)
SUMMA LLC
396 Francisco Way (23601-3819)
PHONE.....................................757 254-1000
Stephanie Pfeifer,
EMP: 1
SALES (est): 30K **Privately Held**
SIC: 2514 Novelty furniture, household:
metal

(G-9350)
SUNGLOW INDUSTRIES INC
11861 Canon Blvd Ste B (23606-4245)
PHONE.....................................703 870-9918
Graham Reed, *Principal*
EMP: 1
SALES (est): 57.2K **Privately Held**
WEB: www.sunglowind.com
SIC: 3999 Manufacturing industries

(G-9351)
T3J ENTERPRISES LLC
345 Rivers Ridge Cir (23608-5301)
P.O. Box 2316 (23609-0316)
PHONE.....................................757 768-0528
James Stewart,
Tamara Stewart,
EMP: 2
SALES (est): 1K **Privately Held**
WEB: www.t3jent.com
SIC: 2759 7389 Letterpress & screen
printing;

(G-9352)
TCS MATERIALS LLC
700 Shields Rd (23608-1319)
PHONE.....................................757 874-5575
Louis Petrillo, *Branch Mgr*
EMP: 15 **Publicly Held**
SIC: 3273 Ready-mixed concrete
HQ: Tcs Materials, Llc
2100 Deepwater Trml Rd
Richmond VA 23234
804 232-1200

(G-9353)
TEXTRON INC
1001 Providence Blvd (23602-8701)
PHONE.....................................757 874-8100
EMP: 6
SALES (corp-wide): 13.6B **Publicly Held**
WEB: www.textron.com
SIC: 3721 Aircraft
PA: Textron Inc.
40 Westminster St
Providence RI 02903
401 421-2800

(G-9354)
TEXTURE SAND TRESSES
183 Pine Bluff Dr (23602-8367)
PHONE.....................................757 369-3033
EMP: 2
SALES (est): 66K **Privately Held**
SIC: 1442 Construction Sand/Gravel

(G-9355)
TIDEWATER PRINTERS INC
Also Called: Cardwell Printing & Advg
15470 Warwick Blvd (23608-1506)
PHONE.....................................757 888-0674
Phillip Gibson, *President*
Danette Cardwell-Gibson, *Vice Pres*
EMP: 15
SQ FT: 7,000
SALES (est): 3.5MM **Privately Held**
WEB: www.cardwellprinting.com
SIC: 2752 Commercial printing, offset

(G-9356)
TINDAHAN
621 Stoney Creek Ln Ste 2 (23608-0064)
PHONE.....................................757 243-8207
Amy Austria, *Owner*
EMP: 1 EST: 2009
SALES (est): 96.3K **Privately Held**
SIC: 2032 Mexican foods: packaged in
cans, jars, etc.

(G-9357)
TIRE KINGS
5302 Jefferson Ave (23605-3210)
PHONE.....................................757 586-5206
Jorge A Cabrera, *Owner*
EMP: 3
SALES (est): 50K **Privately Held**
SIC: 3011 Tires & inner tubes

(G-9358)
TITAN II INC (HQ)
4101 Washington Ave (23607-2700)
PHONE.....................................757 380-2000
Mike Petters, *CEO*
Jerri Fuller Dickseski, *Vice Pres*
Bruce N Hawthorne, *Vice Pres*
Alexis C Livanos, *Vice Pres*
Jennifer C McGarey, *Vice Pres*
◆ EMP: 91
SQ FT: 30,000

SALES (est): 2.9B **Publicly Held**
WEB: www.huntingtoningalls.com
SIC: 3728 3761 7373 3721 Aircraft parts
& equipment; guided missiles, complete;
guided missiles & space vehicles, research & development; computer integrated systems design; airplanes, fixed or
rotary wing; research & development on
aircraft by the manufacturer; aircraft servicing & repairing; search & detection systems & instruments; radar systems &
equipment; defense systems & equipment; warfare counter-measure equipment

(G-9359)
TORRES GRAPHICS AND SIGNS INC
Also Called: Signs By Tomorrow
11712 Jefferson Ave Ste A (23606-4406)
PHONE.....................................757 873-5777
Clarissa Torres, *President*
Joshuah Torres, *Vice Pres*
EMP: 4
SALES (est): 162.8K **Privately Held**
WEB: www.signsbytomorrow.com
SIC: 3993 Signs & advertising specialties

(G-9360)
TOUCH CLASS CONSTRUCTION CORP
817 48th St (23607-2205)
PHONE.....................................757 728-3647
Elizabeth Washington, *CEO*
Gary Washington, *Principal*
EMP: 6
SALES (est): 248.7K **Privately Held**
WEB: www.tocconstruct.com
SIC: 3315 1521 2431 1761 Chain link
fencing; patio & deck construction & re-
pair; staircases, stairs & railings; roofing,
siding & sheet metal work

(G-9361)
TPP ENTERPRISES LLC
324 57th St (23607-2050)
PHONE.....................................757 247-0016
Timothy Dolon,
EMP: 1 EST: 2011
SALES (est): 68.4K **Privately Held**
SIC: 3172 Personal leather goods

(G-9362)
TRIBE 9 LLC
340 Witness Ln Unit B (23608-2977)
PHONE.....................................757 542-5348
Richelle Thomas,
EMP: 4
SALES (est): 53.9K **Privately Held**
SIC: 7692 Welding repair

(G-9363)
TRIGG INDUSTRIES LLC
716 Bluecrab Rd Ste B (23606-2678)
PHONE.....................................757 223-7522
Harry E Trigg, *President*
Dorothy F Trigg, *Corp Secy*
Amy James, *Office Mgr*
EMP: 4 EST: 1975
SALES (est): 679.2K **Privately Held**
WEB: www.triggindustries.com
SIC: 3669 3824 Traffic signals, electric;
fluid meters & counting devices

(G-9364)
TRITON INDUSTRIES INC
250 Enterprise Dr (23603-1300)
PHONE.....................................757 887-1956
Michael Atalay, *President*
EMP: 22
SQ FT: 24,000
SALES: 1.7MM **Privately Held**
WEB: www.triton.us.com
SIC: 3544 Special dies & tools

(G-9365)
TRUSWOOD INC
501 Truswood Ln (23608-8637)
PHONE.....................................757 833-5300
Brian O'Connor, *Manager*
EMP: 75
SALES (corp-wide): 20.3MM **Privately Held**
WEB: www.truswood.com
SIC: 2439 Trusses, wooden roof; trusses,
except roof: laminated lumber

PA: Truswood, Inc.
8816 Running Oak Dr
Raleigh NC 27617
800 473-8787

(G-9366)
TWISTED EROTICA PUBLISHING LLC
1075 Willow Green Dr (23602-7159)
PHONE..........................757 344-7364
Brenda Hurley, *Principal*
EMP: 1
SALES (est): 52.9K **Privately Held**
SIC: 2741 Miscellaneous publishing

(G-9367)
TYPICAL TEES LLC
172 Alan Dr (23602-4126)
PHONE..........................757 641-6514
Tamara Cooke, *Principal*
EMP: 3
SALES (est): 159K **Privately Held**
SIC: 2759 Screen printing

(G-9368)
UAV COMMUNICATIONS INC (HQ)
Also Called: Mag Aerospace
1 Bayport Way Ste 250 (23606-4572)
PHONE..........................757 271-3428
Sam Sblendorio, *President*
Matt Twiggs, *General Mgr*
Joseph Paull, *COO*
Daniel M Enoch, *Vice Pres*
Leonard Mygatt, *Engineer*
EMP: 30
SQ FT: 20,000
SALES (est): 26.5MM **Privately Held**
SIC: 3499 8711 3724 Target drones, for use by ships: metal; structural engineering; electrical or electronic engineering; aircraft engines & engine parts

(G-9369)
UNITED STATES DEPT OF NAVY
Also Called: Supervisor Shipbuilding Conver
4101 Washington Ave (23607-2700)
PHONE..........................757 380-4223
Jim Taylor, *Vice Pres*
Michael McMahon, *Branch Mgr*
Thomas Frankfurt, *Officer*
EMP: 500 **Publicly Held**
WEB: www.sealiftcommand.com
SIC: 3731 9711 Shipbuilding & repairing; Navy;
HQ: United States Department Of Navy
1200 Navy Pentagon
Washington DC 20350

(G-9370)
UTZ QUALITY FOODS LLC
330 Ed Wright Ln (23606-4369)
PHONE..........................757 249-0568
Mike Rice, *Branch Mgr*
EMP: 1
SALES (corp-wide): 845MM **Privately Held**
WEB: www.utzsnacks.com
SIC: 2096 Potato chips & similar snacks
PA: Utz Quality Foods, Llc
900 High St
Hanover PA 17331
800 367-7629

(G-9371)
VA EPOXY DESIGNS LLC
21 Old Oyster Point Rd (23602-7118)
PHONE..........................757 947-6249
Tevin Gaillard,
EMP: 1
SALES (est): 80K **Privately Held**
SIC: 2426 Hardwood dimension & flooring mills

(G-9372)
VANS INC
12300 Jefferson Ave # 813 (23602-0005)
PHONE..........................757 249-0802
EMP: 2 **Publicly Held**
WEB: www.vans.com
SIC: 3021 Rubber & plastics footwear
HQ: Vans, Inc.
1588 S Coast Dr
Costa Mesa CA 92626
855 909-8267

(G-9373)
VIRGINIA GAZETTE COMPANIES LLC
Also Called: Chicago Tribune
703 Mariners Row (23606-4432)
PHONE..........................757 220-1736
Donna Amory, *Principal*
EMP: 2
SALES (est): 241.8K
SALES (corp-wide): 3B **Publicly Held**
WEB: www.vagazette.com
SIC: 2711 2759 2752 Newspapers, publishing & printing; commercial printing; commercial printing, lithographic
HQ: Tribune Media Company
515 N State St Ste 2400
Chicago IL 60654
312 222-3394

(G-9374)
VIRGINIA MACHINE & SUP CO INC
900 39th St (23607-3142)
PHONE..........................757 380-8500
Ann H Wilson, *President*
Kimberly Riley, *Vice Pres*
Denise Thomas, *Purch Agent*
James E Wilson, *Admin Sec*
EMP: 20 **EST:** 1981
SQ FT: 4,500
SALES (est): 2.7MM **Privately Held**
WEB: www.hampmach.com
SIC: 3599 Machine shop, jobbing & repair

(G-9375)
VIRGINIA SILVER PLATING INC
3201a Warwick Blvd (23607-3419)
PHONE..........................757 244-3645
John Michaels, *President*
EMP: 6
SQ FT: 3,400
SALES (est): 450K **Privately Held**
SIC: 3471 Chromium plating of metals or formed products; electroplating of metals or formed products; plating of metals or formed products; rechroming auto bumpers

(G-9376)
VITESCO TECHNOLOGIES USA LLC
615 Bland Blvd (23602-4309)
PHONE..........................757 875-7000
Mike Dallmeyer, *Engineer*
Ulf Dreier, *Engineer*
Clark Gresham, *Engineer*
Mark Mosser, *Engineer*
Alberto Marinai, *Branch Mgr*
EMP: 755
SALES (corp-wide): 23.9MM **Privately Held**
WEB: www.continental.com
SIC: 3714 Motor vehicle parts & accessories
HQ: Vitesco Technologies Usa, Llc
2400 Executive Hills Dr
Auburn Hills MI 48326
248 209-4000

(G-9377)
VULCAN MATERIALS COMPANY
700 Shields Rd (23608-1319)
PHONE..........................757 874-5575
Darren Robinson, *Plant Mgr*
EMP: 17 **Publicly Held**
WEB: www.vulcanmaterials.com
SIC: 3273 Ready-mixed concrete
PA: Vulcan Materials Company
1200 Urban Center Dr
Vestavia AL 35242

(G-9378)
WALKER VIRGINIA
Also Called: Ginnys Ink
346 Circuit Ln (23608-4904)
PHONE..........................757 652-0430
Virginia Walker, *Owner*
EMP: 1
SALES (est): 19.9K **Privately Held**
SIC: 3993 3999 Signs & advertising specialties; advertising display products

(G-9379)
WILLIE GATLING JR
Also Called: Atomic Dog Mobile Catering
1108 75th St (23605-1914)
PHONE..........................757 236-5206
Willie Gatling Jr, *Owner*
EMP: 1
SALES (est): 60K **Privately Held**
SIC: 2599 Food wagons, restaurant

(G-9380)
WOLF EQUIPMENT INC
Also Called: Wolf Contracting
473 Wolf Dr (23601-1900)
PHONE..........................757 596-1660
Dwight Scott Wolf, *President*
Taylor R Wyant, *Vice Pres*
Andrea Laronde, *Admin Sec*
EMP: 40 **EST:** 1995
SALES (est): 4MM **Privately Held**
WEB: www.wolfinc.com
SIC: 3589 Cooking equipment, commercial

(G-9381)
WOODWORKING SHOP INC
713 Industrial Park Dr (23608-1358)
PHONE..........................757 872-0890
William Peters, *President*
Scotty Peters, *Corp Secy*
Peters Melvin Robert, *Vice Pres*
EMP: 5
SQ FT: 4,000
SALES (est): 700K **Privately Held**
WEB: www.woodworkingcabinetshop.com
SIC: 2434 5031 Wood kitchen cabinets; kitchen cabinets

(G-9382)
YARDSALESHEADQUARTERSC OM LLC
11712 Jefferson Ave C-4 (23606-4406)
PHONE..........................757 503-0940
EMP: 2
SALES (est): 57.1K **Privately Held**
WEB: www.yardsalesheadquarters.com
SIC: 2741 Miscellaneous publishing

(G-9383)
YESCO SIGN & LIGHTING SERVICE
719 Industrial Park Dr C (23608-1358)
PHONE..........................757 369-9827
EMP: 1
SALES (est): 46K **Privately Held**
WEB: www.yesco.com
SIC: 3993 Signs & advertising specialties

Nickelsville
Scott County

(G-9384)
CUSTOM SCULPTURE & SIGN CO
127 Wampler St (24271-1200)
PHONE..........................860 876-7529
EMP: 1
SALES (est): 46K **Privately Held**
WEB: www.sculpturalsigns.com
SIC: 3993 Signs & advertising specialties

(G-9385)
SALYER LOGGING
165 Thunder Dr (24271-2816)
PHONE..........................276 690-0688
EMP: 3
SALES (est): 217.9K **Privately Held**
SIC: 2411 Logging

(G-9386)
TAYLORED INFORMATION TECH LLC
5996 Nickelsville Hwy (24271-3102)
PHONE..........................276 479-2122
Mitch Taylor,
EMP: 1
SALES (est): 91K **Privately Held**
WEB: www.tayloredit.net
SIC: 3674 Integrated circuits, semiconductor networks, etc.

Ninde
King George County

(G-9387)
BURNS MACHINE INC
16475 Ridge Rd (22526)
PHONE..........................815 434-3131
Kirk Burns, *President*
EMP: 5
SQ FT: 4,000
SALES (est): 360.9K **Privately Held**
WEB: www.burnsmachine.com
SIC: 3599 Machine shop, jobbing & repair

Nokesville
Prince William County

(G-9388)
ACTION IRON LLC
14250 Fitzwater Dr (20181-1919)
P.O. Box 1967, Woodbridge (22195-1967)
PHONE..........................703 594-2909
Margaret Bell, *Partner*
Larry Bell, *Vice Pres*
EMP: 6
SALES (est): 309K **Privately Held**
WEB: www.actionironllc.com
SIC: 7692 Welding repair

(G-9389)
BAKER BUILDERS LLC
Also Called: Advision Sign Co.
7329 Foster Ln (20181-5813)
PHONE..........................703 753-4904
Kathy Baker, *General Mgr*
EMP: 2
SALES (est): 250K **Privately Held**
WEB: www.advisionsignco.com
SIC: 3993 Signs & advertising specialties

(G-9390)
CEDAR FOREST CABINETRY & MILLW
4224 Ringwood Rd (20181-3549)
PHONE..........................703 753-0644
Forest Cedar, *Principal*
EMP: 3
SALES (est): 308.1K **Privately Held**
WEB: www.cedarforestcabinetry.com
SIC: 2434 Wood kitchen cabinets

(G-9391)
ECO-FRIENDLY LUMBER LLC
13413 Vint Hill Rd (20181-3620)
PHONE..........................703 881-1966
EMP: 2
SALES (est): 191.7K **Privately Held**
WEB: www.ecofriendlylumber.com
SIC: 2431 Millwork

(G-9392)
G&M SIGNS LLC
13760 Vint Hill Rd (20181-1319)
PHONE..........................540 405-3232
Carlos Eugene Clement, *Administration*
EMP: 1 **EST:** 2016
SALES (est): 55.7K **Privately Held**
SIC: 3993 Signs & advertising specialties

(G-9393)
GEO ENTERPRISE INC
10456 Lonesome Rd (20181-1532)
P.O. Box 238 (20182-0238)
PHONE..........................703 594-3816
EMP: 2
SALES (est): 157.2K **Privately Held**
SIC: 1382 4212 Oil/Gas Exploration Services Local Trucking Operator

(G-9394)
HP METAL FABRICATION LLC
13615 Carriage Ford Rd (20181-2422)
PHONE..........................571 499-0298
Natalie Plada, *Principal*
EMP: 1
SALES (est): 54.3K **Privately Held**
SIC: 3499 Fabricated metal products

(G-9395)
KDL SOLUTIONS LLC
10845 Crockett Rd (20181-3443)
PHONE........................703 216-2201
Karen Matteo, *Agent*
EMP: 2
SALES (est): 74.4K **Privately Held**
SIC: 2899 Chemical preparations

(G-9396)
MONDAYS CHILD
10109 Burwell Rd (20181-1114)
PHONE........................703 754-9048
Peggy Poston, *Owner*
EMP: 1
SALES (est): 44.2K **Privately Held**
WEB: www.lanedentalsociety.org
SIC: 3942 Dolls & stuffed toys

(G-9397)
QUEENS GUITAR SHOP
10316 Reid Ln (20181-3619)
PHONE........................703 754-4330
Thomas Queen, *Owner*
EMP: 1
SALES (est): 56K **Privately Held**
SIC: 3931 Musical instruments

(G-9398)
**R A ONIJS CLASSIC
WOODWORK**
10301 Schaeffer Ln (20181-1710)
PHONE........................703 594-3304
Ronald Albert, *Principal*
EMP: 2
SALES (est): 149.4K **Privately Held**
SIC: 2431 Millwork

(G-9399)
SERPIN PHARMA LLC
14645 Sulky Run Ct (20181-2952)
PHONE........................703 343-3258
Cohava Gelber, *Manager*
Soren Mogelsvang, *Info Tech Mgr*
EMP: 3
SALES (est): 354K **Privately Held**
WEB: www.serpinpharma.com
SIC: 2834 Pharmaceutical preparations

(G-9400)
TECHNI COMM
8627 Arbee Ct (20181-3200)
PHONE........................703 231-6475
EMP: 2
SALES (est): 98.7K **Privately Held**
SIC: 3949 Sporting & athletic goods

(G-9401)
**TRUE PRECISION MACHINING
INC**
11921 Airlea Dr (20181-2302)
PHONE........................703 314-7071
Jason Thornton, *President*
EMP: 3
SALES (est): 100K **Privately Held**
WEB: www.trueprecisioninc.com
SIC: 3599 Machine shop, jobbing & repair

(G-9402)
**TWOMORROWS YESTERDAYS
LLC**
10105 Oxford Ct (20181-1612)
PHONE........................571 292-2930
EMP: 2
SALES (est): 49K **Privately Held**
SIC: 2741 Miscellaneous publishing

(G-9403)
VIRTUAL EA INC
12164 Rain Slicker Pl (20181-3660)
PHONE........................703 855-9593
Nita S Shah, *Principal*
EMP: 2
SALES (est): 72.1K **Privately Held**
SIC: 7372 Prepackaged software

(G-9404)
WATERS GROUP INC
9641 Leeta Cornus Ln (20181-3120)
PHONE........................703 791-3607
George Waters, *President*
EMP: 1 EST: 1997
SALES (est): 109K **Privately Held**
WEB: www.waters.com
SIC: 2819 Heavy water

(G-9405)
**WONDERFULLY MADE
CERAMICS**
10079 Greenwich Wood Dr (20181-1430)
PHONE........................571 261-1633
Pamela McCracken, *Principal*
EMP: 2
SALES (est): 122.5K **Privately Held**
SIC: 3269 Pottery products

(G-9406)
YUP CANDLES LLC
15090 Spittle Ln (20181-1138)
PHONE........................571 248-6772
Scott Andrew Rinderle, *Administration*
EMP: 2 EST: 2016
SALES (est): 75.6K **Privately Held**
SIC: 3999 Candles

Nora
Dickenson County

(G-9407)
BLANDS WELDING & FABG CO
5880 Brushy Ridge Rd (24272-7038)
PHONE........................276 495-8132
Weldon Bland, *Owner*
EMP: 1
SALES (est): 42K **Privately Held**
SIC: 7692 Welding repair

(G-9408)
JWT WELL SERVICES INC
3992 Dante Mountain Rd (24272)
P.O. Box 429 (24272-0429)
PHONE........................276 835-8793
Carl Rose, *President*
Janice Rose, *Corp Secy*
Michael Rose, *Vice Pres*
EMP: 28
SALES (est): 6.8MM **Privately Held**
SIC: 1381 Drilling oil & gas wells

Norfolk
Norfolk City County

(G-9409)
**1 HOUR A 24 HR ER A VA BCH
LCK**
313 W Bute St (23510-1301)
PHONE........................757 295-8288
EMP: 2 EST: 2007
SALES (est): 110K **Privately Held**
SIC: 3599 Mfg Industrial Machinery

(G-9410)
10 10 LLC
Also Called: Minuteman Press
259 W York St (23510-1520)
PHONE........................757 627-4311
Gayle Patrick, *Principal*
EMP: 2 EST: 2014
SALES (est): 224.2K **Privately Held**
WEB: www.minutemanpress.com
SIC: 2752 2741 Commercial printing, litho-
graphic; business service newsletters:
publishing & printing

(G-9411)
**2308 GRANBY STREET ASSOC
LLC**
2308 Granby St (23517-1420)
PHONE........................757 627-4844
Michael Ricks,
EMP: 1
SALES (est): 76.5K **Privately Held**
SIC: 2599 Ship furniture

(G-9412)
3DXTREMES
501 Boush St Ste B (23510-1400)
PHONE........................757 741-8671
Blade Taylor, *Principal*
EMP: 2
SALES (est): 108.9K **Privately Held**
WEB: www.3dxtremes.com
SIC: 3599 Machine shop, jobbing & repair

(G-9413)
A CREATIVE MIND LLC
Also Called: N2 Publishing
1939 Kingston Ave (23503-2611)
PHONE........................757 450-2899
David Owen Bowling, *Administration*
EMP: 1 EST: 2014
SALES (est): 58.7K **Privately Held**
SIC: 2741 Miscellaneous publishing

(G-9414)
A DESCAL MATIC CORP
1518 Springmeadow Blvd (23518-4814)
PHONE........................757 858-5593
Ernest J Florestano, *President*
Mary A Florestano, *Corp Secy*
EMP: 6
SQ FT: 9,000
SALES (est): 1.1MM **Privately Held**
WEB: www.descal-a-matic.com
SIC: 3589 5074 5999 2899 Water treat-
ment equipment, industrial; plumbing &
hydronic heating supplies; water purifica-
tion equipment; water treating compounds

(G-9415)
**AARD-ALLTUF
SCREENPRINTERS**
Also Called: Aard/Altuf Screen Printers
4625 E Princess Anne Rd (23502-1615)
PHONE........................757 853-7641
Brooks Ross Clements, *President*
Gary Tuthill, *Vice Pres*
▲ EMP: 35 EST: 1981
SQ FT: 20,000
SALES (est): 5.4MM **Privately Held**
WEB: www.aardalltuf.com
SIC: 2261 Screen printing of cotton broad-
woven fabrics

(G-9416)
ACCENT SIGNING COMPANY
2704 Arkansas Ave (23513-4404)
PHONE........................757 857-8800
Fax: 757 857-1200
EMP: 4
SALES (est): 251.7K **Privately Held**
SIC: 3993 Mfg Signs/Advertising Special-
ties

(G-9417)
**ACCOUNTING EXECUTIVE SVCS
LLC**
1813 While Ln (23518-4933)
PHONE........................757 406-1127
Karen Dzupinka,
EMP: 1
SALES (est): 91.2K **Privately Held**
SIC: 3578 Calculating & accounting equip-
ment

(G-9418)
ACCURATE MACHINE INC
3317 Tait Ter (23513-4427)
PHONE........................757 853-2136
Mariah Gurecki, *Owner*
Phillip Gurecki, *Treasurer*
Bill Sutton, *Prgrmr*
EMP: 5
SQ FT: 9,000
SALES (est): 617.5K **Privately Held**
WEB: www.accmachine.com
SIC: 3829 3444 3429 3443 Medical diag-
nostic systems, nuclear; sheet metalwork;
metal fasteners; metal parts; machine &
other job shop work; machine shop, job-
bing & repair

(G-9419)
ACESUR NORTH AMERICA INC
Also Called: Italica Imports
981 Scott St Ste 100 (23502-3165)
PHONE........................757 664-2390
Juanita Elder, *Vice Pres*
EMP: 25
SQ FT: 50,000
SALES (corp-wide): 8.6MM **Privately
Held**
WEB: www.acesurnorthamerica.com
SIC: 2033 Olives: packaged in cans, jars,
etc.
PA: Acesur North America, Inc.
2700 Westchester Ave # 105
Purchase NY
914 925-0450

(G-9420)
ACO CORPORATION
1430 Ballentine Blvd (23504-3810)
PHONE........................757 480-2875
Vladimir Gordiyenko, *Manager*
EMP: 5
SALES (corp-wide): 1MM **Privately Held**
WEB: www.acocorp.com
SIC: 2426 Furniture stock & parts, hard-
wood
PA: Aco Corporation
3500 Virginia Beach Blvd # 200
Virginia Beach VA 23452
757 480-2875

(G-9421)
**ADESSO PRECISION MACHINE
CO**
3517 Argonne Ave (23509-2156)
PHONE........................757 857-5544
David K Meador, *President*
Margaret F Meador, *Corp Secy*
Peggy Meador, *Vice Pres*
Margaret Meador, *Info Tech Mgr*
EMP: 7
SQ FT: 12,500
SALES (est): 397K **Privately Held**
WEB: www.adessomachine.com
SIC: 3599 1799 Machine shop, jobbing &
repair; welding on site

(G-9422)
ADMIRAL SIGNWORKS CORP
1531 Early St (23502-1603)
PHONE........................757 422-6700
Greg De Valdes, *President*
EMP: 12 **Privately Held**
WEB: www.admiralsignworks.com
SIC: 3993 7389 Neon signs; sign painting
& lettering shop

(G-9423)
**ADVANCED INTEGRATED TECH
LLC**
2427 Ingleside Rd (23513-4525)
PHONE........................757 416-7407
Kerry Slane, *Business Mgr*
Patrick Lemery, *Project Mgr*
Ken Bates, *Production*
Stuart Carlson, *Purchasing*
Carl Spraberry, *Mng Member*
EMP: 67
SQ FT: 6,500
SALES (est): 17.7MM **Privately Held**
WEB: www.ait-marine.com
SIC: 3731 Shipbuilding & repairing

(G-9424)
ADVANCING EYECARE (HQ)
5358 Robin Hood Rd (23513-2430)
PHONE........................757 853-8888
Brad Staley, *CEO*
EMP: 37
SALES (est): 6.5MM **Privately Held**
SIC: 3841 Eye examining instruments &
apparatus

(G-9425)
**ADVERTISING SERVICE
AGENCY**
807 Granby St (23510-2003)
PHONE........................757 622-3429
Reuben G Prescott, *President*
Alan Prescott, *Vice Pres*
Hazel R Prescott, *Vice Pres*
EMP: 4
SQ FT: 2,625
SALES (est): 180K **Privately Held**
SIC: 2752 7331 Commercial printing, off-
set; mailing service

(G-9426)
ADVOCATE-DEMOCRAT
440 Bank St (23510-2401)
PHONE........................423 337-7101
Leslie Eder, *Financial Exec*
EMP: 2
SALES (est): 66K **Privately Held**
SIC: 2711 Newspapers, publishing & print-
ing

(G-9427)
AERIAL AND AQUATIC ROBOTICS
1138 Bolling Ave Apt 221a (23508-1550)
PHONE....................757 932-0909
Davis D Moore, *Owner*
Davis Moore, *Principal*
Cate Turner, *Principal*
EMP: 2 **EST:** 2016
SALES (est): 80.9K **Privately Held**
SIC: 3721 Aircraft

(G-9428)
AFTERMARKET PARTS SOLUTIONS
6336 E Virginia Bch Blvd (23502-2827)
PHONE....................757 227-3166
EMP: 4 **EST:** 2010
SALES (est): 220K **Privately Held**
SIC: 3465 Body parts, automobile: stamped metal

(G-9429)
AIR WISONSIN AIRLINES CORP
6170 Miller Store Rd (23502-5506)
PHONE....................757 853-8215
EMP: 2
SALES (est): 200.2K **Privately Held**
SIC: 3721 Aircraft

(G-9430)
ALI BABA HANDWROUGHT JEWELRY
333 Waterside Dr 312 (23510-3202)
PHONE....................757 622-5007
Terry R Wright, *Owner*
EMP: 4
SQ FT: 12,000
SALES (est): 210.2K **Privately Held**
SIC: 3911 5944 Jewelry, precious metal; jewelry, precious stones & precious metals

(G-9431)
ALL CARE TRAINING & SERVICES
801 E 26th St (23504-1943)
PHONE....................757 346-2703
Lillie D Hayes, *Principal*
EMP: 1
SALES (est): 39.6K **Privately Held**
SIC: 3999 Education aids, devices & supplies

(G-9432)
ALLEGRA NETWORK LLC
879 Poplar Hall Dr (23502-3715)
PHONE....................757 448-8271
EMP: 8
SALES (corp-wide): 44.2MM **Privately Held**
WEB: www.valuemyprintbusiness.com
SIC: 2752 Commercial printing, offset
HQ: Allegra Network Llc
47585 Galleon Dr
Plymouth MI 48170
248 596-8600

(G-9433)
ALLERGAN SALES LLC
999 Waterside Dr Ste 2000 (23510-3307)
PHONE....................757 624-5320
April Amory, *Principal*
EMP: 4 **Privately Held**
WEB: www.bystolic.com
SIC: 2834 Pharmaceutical preparations
HQ: Allergan Sales, Llc
2525 Dupont Dr
Irvine CA 92612

(G-9434)
ALLIANCE PRESRVNG HSTRY WWII
5922 Powhatan Ave (23508-1050)
PHONE....................757 423-1429
Ping Tcheng, *Director*
Gene Hou, *Director*
EMP: 9
SALES (est): 568.7K **Privately Held**
SIC: 2491 8412 Wood preserving; museum

(G-9435)
ALLIANCE TECHNICAL SVCS INC (PA)
900 Granby St Ste 228 (23510-2568)
PHONE....................757 628-9500
Larry A Wade, *President*
Rita Lake, *CFO*
EMP: 83
SALES (est): 16.3MM **Privately Held**
WEB: www.atsnorfolk.com
SIC: 3731 Shipbuilding & repairing

(G-9436)
ALLINDER PRINTING
7565 Buttercup Cir (23518-4600)
PHONE....................757 672-4918
EMP: 2
SALES (est): 101.5K **Privately Held**
SIC: 2752 Commercial printing, lithographic

(G-9437)
AMERICA HEAVY INDUSTRY
2635 Nevada Ave (23513-4410)
PHONE....................757 858-2000
William George, *Principal*
EMP: 2
SALES (est): 180.8K **Privately Held**
SIC: 3534 Elevators & moving stairways

(G-9438)
AMERICAN INTERIORS LTD
833 W 21st St (23517-1513)
PHONE....................757 627-0248
Gary Hermann, *President*
EMP: 5
SQ FT: 12,000
SALES (est): 649.6K **Privately Held**
WEB: www.americaninteriorsltd.com
SIC: 2511 5712 5719 7641 Wood household furniture; furniture stores; lamps & lamp shades; pictures & mirrors; reupholstery; antiques

(G-9439)
AMERICAN SHEET METAL & WELDING
2713 Colley Ave (23517-1137)
PHONE....................757 627-9203
EMP: 5 **EST:** 2011
SALES (est): 240K **Privately Held**
SIC: 7692 Welding Repair

(G-9440)
AMERICOMM LLC (PA)
Also Called: Americomm Direct Marketing
1048 W 27th St (23517-1019)
PHONE....................757 622-2724
David Craig, *Mng Member*
Thomas G Spalding, *Principal*
EMP: 100 **EST:** 2000
SALES (est): 44.7MM **Privately Held**
WEB: www.americomm.net
SIC: 2791 7331 Typesetting; direct mail advertising services

(G-9441)
AMILCAR S SHEET METAL LLC
1548 Chela Ave (23503-1007)
PHONE....................571 330-8371
Amilcar Medrano, *Administration*
EMP: 2 **EST:** 2014
SALES (est): 112.3K **Privately Held**
SIC: 3444 Sheet metalwork

(G-9442)
ANOINTED FOR PURPOSE
328 E Ingram Ct (23505-1377)
PHONE....................804 651-4427
EMP: 1
SALES (est): 37.5K **Privately Held**
SIC: 2741 Miscellaneous publishing

(G-9443)
APPLIED PRESSURES DIAMOND
7425 Sewells Point Rd (23513-1700)
PHONE....................757 967-7006
EMP: 2 **EST:** 2019
SALES (est): 73.2K **Privately Held**
SIC: 2759 Commercial printing

(G-9444)
ARIF WINTER
Also Called: Ksquared Cupcakes
1455 Mellwood Ct Ste B (23513-1522)
PHONE....................757 515-9940
Winter Arif, *Owner*
EMP: 1
SALES (est): 60.2K **Privately Held**
WEB: www.ksquaredcupcakes.com
SIC: 2051 Cakes, bakery: except frozen

(G-9445)
ARTFX LLC (HQ)
Also Called: Artfx, Inc.
1125 Azalea Garden Rd (23502-5601)
PHONE....................757 853-1703
Lucille C Groce, *President*
Thomas A Groce, *Principal*
Susan Simmons, *Human Res Mgr*
Adam Tennant, *Art Dir*
▲ **EMP:** 125
SQ FT: 45,000
SALES (est): 47.5MM
SALES (corp-wide): 164.6MM **Privately Held**
WEB: www.artfx.com
SIC: 2261 7389 7336 4731 Screen printing of cotton broadwoven fabrics; packaging & labeling services; package design; freight forwarding
PA: Tegra Llc
211 Prmter Ctr Park Ste 9
Atlanta GA 30346
470 705-1280

(G-9446)
ARTWOLF SIGNS & GRAPHICS
1131 Smith St (23510-3127)
PHONE....................757 567-8122
Sam Knight, *Principal*
EMP: 2
SALES (est): 97.9K **Privately Held**
SIC: 3993 Signs & advertising specialties

(G-9447)
AURA LLC
5018 E Princess Anne Rd (23502-1715)
PHONE....................757 965-8400
EMP: 2 **EST:** 2013
SALES (est): 140K **Privately Held**
SIC: 2015 5812 4213 Poultry Processing Eating Place Trucking Operator-Nonlocal

(G-9448)
B & B CLEANING SERVICE
301 Naval Base Rd # 702 (23505-3615)
PHONE....................757 667-9528
Meocia Broussard, *Partner*
Myisha Brooks, *Partner*
EMP: 2
SALES (est): 120.1K **Privately Held**
SIC: 2842 Specialty cleaning preparations

(G-9449)
B & L MCH & FABRICATION INC
3411 Amherst St (23513-4057)
PHONE....................757 853-1800
Gilbert Lozano, *President*
Liliana Hanes, *Vice Pres*
Blanca Lozano, *Treasurer*
EMP: 21
SQ FT: 12,230
SALES (est): 2.5MM **Privately Held**
WEB: www.blmachine-fab.com
SIC: 3441 Fabricated structural metal

(G-9450)
B TEAM PUBLICATIONS LLC
9516 26th Bay St (23518-1814)
PHONE....................757 362-3006
John Michael Bredehoft, *Administration*
EMP: 1
SALES (est): 52.1K **Privately Held**
SIC: 2741 Miscellaneous publishing

(G-9451)
BADGERDOG LITERARY PUBLISHING
500 E Main St Ste 1300 (23510-2206)
PHONE....................757 627-2315
Deborah Stearns, *Senior VP*
EMP: 1
SALES (est): 37.5K **Privately Held**
SIC: 2741 Miscellaneous publishing

(G-9452)
BAE SYSTEMS NRFOLK SHIP REPR I
Also Called: Norshipco
750 W Berkley Ave (23523-1032)
PHONE....................757 494-4000
William Clifford, *President*
Joe Campbell, *Vice Pres*
Thomas Seitz, *Vice Pres*
Robert Ward, *Engineer*
Lauren Sedlak, *Financial Analy*
◆ **EMP:** 1200 **EST:** 1915
SQ FT: 500,000
SALES (est): 225.7MM
SALES (corp-wide): 23.6B **Privately Held**
WEB: www.baesystems.com
SIC: 3731 Shipbuilding & repairing; barges, building & repairing; lighters, marine: building & repairing; ferryboats, building & repairing
HQ: Bae Systems Ship Repair Inc.
750 W Berkley Ave
Norfolk VA 23523
757 494-4000

(G-9453)
BAE SYSTEMS SHIP REPAIR INC (DH)
750 W Berkley Ave (23523-1032)
PHONE....................757 494-4000
Moseley Erin, *President*
Dana Harris, *Superintendent*
Herr David, *Vice Pres*
Geneva Lee, *Vice Pres*
Brad Moyer, *Vice Pres*
EMP: 1000
SQ FT: 10,000
SALES (est): 472.3MM
SALES (corp-wide): 23.6B **Privately Held**
WEB: www.virginiashiprepair.org
SIC: 3731 3732 Shipbuilding & repairing; barges, building & repairing; lighters, marine: building & repairing; ferryboats, building & repairing; yachts, building & repairing

(G-9454)
BAKER SHEET METAL CORPORATION
3541 Argonne Ave (23509-2156)
P.O. Box 7340 (23509-0340)
PHONE....................757 853-4325
Rufus E Baker, *President*
John A Faircloth, *Vice Pres*
Paul Johnson, *Mfg Spvr*
Randy L Bristow, *Treasurer*
Randy Bristow, *Treasurer*
EMP: 90
SQ FT: 55,000
SALES (est): 9.3MM **Privately Held**
WEB: www.bakersheetmetal.com
SIC: 3444 Sheet metal specialties, not stamped

(G-9455)
BASKETBALL PRODUCTS INTL LLC
2406 Colley Ave B (23517-1128)
P.O. Box 3082 (23514-3082)
PHONE....................757 626-3865
Kevin Murphy,
EMP: 1
SALES (est): 144.8K **Privately Held**
WEB: www.basketballproductsinternational.com
SIC: 3949 Sporting & athletic goods

(G-9456)
BATH IRON WORKS CORPORATION
9727 Avionics Loop (23511-3731)
PHONE....................757 855-4182
Michael Deamato, *Manager*
EMP: 17
SALES (corp-wide): 39.3B **Publicly Held**
WEB: www.gdbiw.com
SIC: 3731 Shipbuilding & repairing
HQ: Bath Iron Works Corporation
700 Washington St Stop 1
Bath ME 04530
207 443-3311

(G-9457)
BAUER COMPRESSORS INC
1340 Azalea Garden Rd (23502-1904)
PHONE..................................757 855-6006
EMP: 2
SALES (corp-wide): 71.5MM **Privately Held**
WEB: www.bauercomp.com
SIC: 3563 Air & gas compressors
PA: Bauer Compressors, Inc.
1328 Azalea Garden Rd
Norfolk VA 23502
757 855-6006

(G-9458)
BAUER COMPRESSORS INC (PA)
1328 Azalea Garden Rd (23502-1944)
PHONE..................................757 855-6006
Heinz Bauer, Ch of Bd
Anthony Bayat, President
Jan Von Dobeneck, President
Paula Hebert, Business Mgr
Leslie R Rhue, Corp Secy
◆ EMP: 240
SQ FT: 130,000
SALES (est): 71.5MM **Privately Held**
WEB: www.bauercomp.com
SIC: 3563 Air & gas compressors including vacuum pumps

(G-9459)
BAY BREEZE PUBLISHING LLC
4839 Coventry Ln (23518-1636)
PHONE..................................757 535-1580
Sarah Parrott, Principal
EMP: 3
SALES (est): 69.2K **Privately Held**
SIC: 2711 Newspapers, publishing & printing

(G-9460)
BEAUTY POP LLC
313 Dixie Dr (23505-1505)
PHONE..................................757 416-5858
Shantel Walz,
EMP: 1
SALES (est): 39.6K **Privately Held**
SIC: 3999 Barber & beauty shop equipment

(G-9461)
BECKETT CORPORATION (PA)
3321 E Princess Anne Rd (23502-1502)
P.O. Box 2196, Virginia Beach (23450-2196)
PHONE..................................757 857-0153
William Arnold, President
Wingate Sung, COO
▲ EMP: 23 EST: 1974
SQ FT: 700,000
SALES (est): 2.9MM **Privately Held**
SIC: 2519 3561 Lawn & garden furniture, except wood & metal; industrial pumps & parts

(G-9462)
BIRSCH INDUSTRIES INC
3412 Strathmore Ave (23504-4613)
PHONE..................................757 622-0355
Diana Leonie, COO
EMP: 2
SALES (est): 74.4K **Privately Held**
SIC: 2842 Specialty cleaning, polishes & sanitation goods

(G-9463)
BISHOP DISTRIBUTORS LLC
150 S Military Hwy (23502-5229)
PHONE..................................757 618-6401
EMP: 5
SALES (est): 290K **Privately Held**
SIC: 3559 Automotive Maintenance Equipment

(G-9464)
BISHOP II INC
Also Called: No Burn Technology
2325 Palmyra St (23513-4320)
PHONE..................................757 855-7137
Delbert Bishop Emery, President
Jerry Bishop Richard, Vice Pres
Sharon Jane Weitzel, Admin Sec
EMP: 3

SALES (est): 236.7K **Privately Held**
SIC: 2899 Fire retardant chemicals

(G-9465)
BLACK RABBIT DELIGHTS LLC
1702 Bellevue Ave (23509-1104)
PHONE..................................757 453-3359
Charmayne Nikia Clark,
EMP: 1
SALES (est): 20K **Privately Held**
SIC: 2051 Bakery: wholesale or wholesale/retail combined

(G-9466)
BLACKOUT TINTING LLC
1533 Azalea Garden Rd (23502-1671)
PHONE..................................757 416-5658
Samuel Crawford,
EMP: 5
SALES (est): 280K **Privately Held**
WEB: www.blackoutxclusive.com
SIC: 3211 Window glass, clear & colored

(G-9467)
BLOOM PUBLICATION
417 W 20th St (23517-1363)
PHONE..................................757 373-4402
Danielle Leibovici, Principal
EMP: 1
SALES (est): 70.9K **Privately Held**
SIC: 2741 Miscellaneous publishing

(G-9468)
BLUCLOUDRADIO LLC
259 Granby St (23510-1810)
PHONE..................................757 812-2380
Calvin Clark, CEO
EMP: 2
SALES (est): 59.2K **Privately Held**
SIC: 2741

(G-9469)
BOEING COMPANY
5700 Lake Wright Dr # 204 (23502-1859)
PHONE..................................757 461-5206
Louis Lalli, Manager
EMP: 831
SALES (corp-wide): 76.5B **Publicly Held**
WEB: www.boeing.com
SIC: 3721 Aircraft
PA: The Boeing Company
100 N Riverside Plz
Chicago IL 60606
312 544-2000

(G-9470)
BURNSBOKS PUBG - PSTSHIRTS LLC
7409 W Kenmore Dr Apt 4 (23505-3552)
PHONE..................................404 354-6082
Alfonso Burney, Principal
EMP: 1
SALES (est): 37.5K **Privately Held**
SIC: 2741 Miscellaneous publishing

(G-9471)
C&M INDUSTRIES INC
3425 Westminster Ave (23504-4618)
PHONE..................................757 626-1141
Earl Edwards, Manager
EMP: 1
SALES (est): 114.3K **Privately Held**
SIC: 3999 Manufacturing industries

(G-9472)
CABINETS TO GO LLC
416 Campostella Rd (23523-2206)
PHONE..................................814 688-7584
EMP: 2
SALES (corp-wide): 40.6MM **Privately Held**
WEB: www.cabinetstogo.com
SIC: 2434 Wood kitchen cabinets
PA: Cabinets To Go, Llc
2350 Wo Smith Dr
Lawrenceburg TN 38464
909 646-5900

(G-9473)
CABLE SYSTEMS
3411 Progress Rd (23502-1929)
PHONE..................................757 853-6313
Norman Caroon, President
EMP: 2

SALES (est): 210K **Privately Held**
WEB: www.r7krecon.com
SIC: 3357 Aluminum wire & cable

(G-9474)
CAMCO
3424 Azalea Garden Rd (23513-4902)
PHONE..................................757 855-5890
Larry Campbell, Principal
EMP: 3
SALES (est): 301.6K **Privately Held**
SIC: 2399 5013 7532 Seat covers, automobile; automotive supplies & parts; upholstery & trim shop, automotive

(G-9475)
CAMPOSTELLA BUILDERS AND SUP
1109 Poppleton St (23523-2434)
PHONE..................................757 545-3212
Frank Palmer, President
Ann Palmer, Corp Secy
Doyle Palmer, Exec VP
James Ambrose, Project Mgr
Peyton Palmer, Project Mgr
EMP: 47 EST: 1947
SQ FT: 20,000
SALES (est): 7.7MM **Privately Held**
WEB: www.campostellabuilders.com
SIC: 2431 Millwork

(G-9476)
CANDLE UTOPIA INCORPORATED
2400 Myrtle Ave (23504-3928)
PHONE..................................757 274-2406
Gerald Lee Walton, Principal
EMP: 1
SALES (est): 39.6K **Privately Held**
SIC: 3999 Candles

(G-9477)
CAPITAL CONCRETE INC (PA)
400 Stapleton St (23504-4630)
P.O. Box 1137 (23501-1137)
PHONE..................................757 627-0630
Elizabeth A Twohy, President
Boo Twohy, President
Kenny Harvey, Vice Pres
Jim Simons, Vice Pres
Sarah Beasley, VP Opers
EMP: 2
SQ FT: 3,000
SALES (est): 11.7MM **Privately Held**
WEB: www.capitalconcreteinc.com
SIC: 3273 Ready-mixed concrete

(G-9478)
CATCH SURFBOARD CO LLC
Also Called: Catch Surf Norfolk
1416 Ballentine Blvd (23504-3810)
PHONE..................................949 218-0428
EMP: 1
SALES (est): 62.6K **Privately Held**
SIC: 3949 Surfboards

(G-9479)
CC WIRELESS CORPORATION
Also Called: C C Wireless
956 E Little Creek Rd (23518-3843)
PHONE..................................757 802-8140
Yanghee Chae, Administration
EMP: 2 EST: 2014
SALES (est): 129.4K **Privately Held**
SIC: 3663 7389 Cellular radio telephone; telephone services

(G-9480)
CERBERUS SKATEBOARD CO LLC
241 Granby St (23510-1841)
PHONE..................................757 715-2225
Sean Pepe, Principal
EMP: 2
SALES (est): 109.8K **Privately Held**
SIC: 3949 Skateboards

(G-9481)
CHEMTEQ
600 W 24th St Ste B (23517-1208)
PHONE..................................757 622-2223
K S Kirollos, CEO
Jessica Guzman, Vice Pres
EMP: 10 EST: 2010

SALES (est): 537.1K **Privately Held**
WEB: www.chemteq.net
SIC: 3841 3677 Diagnostic apparatus, medical; filtration devices, electronic

(G-9482)
CHESAPEAKE CONNECTOR & CABLE
5248 Cape Henry Ave (23513-2502)
PHONE..................................757 855-5504
Kenny Thompson, President
Diane Thompson, Vice Pres
EMP: 2
SALES (est): 270K **Privately Held**
SIC: 3678 Electronic connectors

(G-9483)
CHRISTINA BENNETT
Also Called: Love Rugby Company
122 E Randall Ave (23503-4420)
P.O. Box 230477, Centreville (20120-0477)
PHONE..................................703 489-9018
Christina Bennett,
EMP: 2
SALES (est): 300K **Privately Held**
WEB: www.loverugbycompany.com
SIC: 3949 Sporting & athletic goods

(G-9484)
CHRISTOPHER PHILLIP & MOSS LLC
532 W 35th St Ste C (23508-3102)
PHONE..................................757 525-0683
Carim Phillip,
EMP: 10 EST: 2013
SALES (est): 331.8K **Privately Held**
SIC: 2329 Men's & boys' sportswear & athletic clothing

(G-9485)
CHURCH TRUCKING LLC
5328 Bellefield Rd (23502-2302)
PHONE..................................757 386-1761
Antjuan Church,
EMP: 1
SALES (est): 54.6K **Privately Held**
SIC: 3743 Freight cars & equipment

(G-9486)
CITY CONNECTION MAGAZINE LLC
900 Granby St Ste 249 (23510-2577)
PHONE..................................757 570-9249
Javone Johnson, President
Mica Powell, Director
EMP: 2
SQ FT: 200
SALES (est): 204.7K **Privately Held**
SIC: 2721 Magazines: publishing only, not printed on site

(G-9487)
CLARK & CLARK LLC
Also Called: Creations By Clark & Clark
7474 N Shore Rd (23505-1756)
P.O. Box 6314 (23508-0314)
PHONE..................................757 264-9000
Michelle Clark, Administration
Chris Clark,
EMP: 2
SALES (est): 108.1K **Privately Held**
SIC: 3911 Jewelry, precious metal

(G-9488)
CLASSIC WOODCRAFT
884 E Little Creek Rd (23518-3741)
PHONE..................................757 631-9354
Martin Willis, Owner
EMP: 1
SALES (est): 110.8K **Privately Held**
WEB: www.classicwoodcraft.net
SIC: 2434 Wood kitchen cabinets

(G-9489)
COCA-COLA CONSOLIDATED INC
2000 Monticello Ave (23517-2341)
PHONE..................................757 890-8700
Steve Lam, Manager
EMP: 100
SALES (corp-wide): 4.8B **Publicly Held**
WEB: www.cokeconsolidated.com
SIC: 2086 Bottled & canned soft drinks

PA: Coca-Cola Consolidated, Inc.
4100 Coca Cola Plz # 100
Charlotte NC 28211
704 557-4400

(G-9490)
COCA-COLA CONSOLIDATED INC
2000 Monticello Ave (23517-2341)
PHONE..................757 446-3000
Jess Howe, *Branch Mgr*
EMP: 160
SALES (corp-wide): 4.8B **Publicly Held**
WEB: www.cokeconsolidated.com
SIC: 2086 Bottled & canned soft drinks
PA: Coca-Cola Consolidated, Inc.
4100 Coca Cola Plz # 100
Charlotte NC 28211
704 557-4400

(G-9491)
COLD COMPANY LLC
2804 Colchester Cres (23504-4022)
PHONE..................757 589-7034
Cornelius Drummond,
EMP: 1
SALES (est): 13K **Privately Held**
SIC: 2211 Apparel & outerwear fabrics, cotton

(G-9492)
COLD PRESS II LLC
1902 Colley Ave (23517-1613)
PHONE..................757 227-0809
EMP: 3
SALES (est): 78.9K **Privately Held**
SIC: 2711 Newspapers

(G-9493)
COLONIAL CHEVROLET COMPANY LP
6252 E Virginia Bch Blvd (23502-2856)
P.O. Box 12529 (23541-0529)
PHONE..................757 455-4500
J R Hendrick III, *Principal*
Jeremy Jordan, *Sales Mgr*
EMP: 500
SALES (est): 62MM **Privately Held**
WEB: www.rhchevynorfolk.com
SIC: 3714 Motor vehicle parts & accessories

(G-9494)
COLONIAL WLDG FABRICATION INC
5801 Curlew Dr (23502-4626)
PHONE..................757 459-2680
Cheryl A Sundstrom, *President*
John E Sundstrom, *Corp Secy*
Dan McAdoo, *Vice Pres*
Jeff McAdoo, *Vice Pres*
EMP: 25
SQ FT: 24,000
SALES (est): 4.5MM **Privately Held**
WEB: www.colonialwelding.com
SIC: 3444 3441 Sheet metalwork; fabricated structural metal

(G-9495)
COLONNAS SHIP YARD INC (PA)
Also Called: Steel America
400 E Indian River Rd (23523-1799)
PHONE..................757 545-2414
Willoughby W Colonna Jr, *Ch of Bd*
Thomas W Godfrey Jr, *President*
Wanda Drees, *General Mgr*
Gary Daughety, *Superintendent*
Robert Boyd, *Principal*
▲ **EMP:** 565 **EST:** 1875
SALES (est): 150MM **Privately Held**
WEB: www.colonnaship.com
SIC: 3731 3443 3499 Shipbuilding & repairing; fabricated plate work (boiler shop); fire- or burglary-resistive products

(G-9496)
COLONNAS SHIP YARD INC
Also Called: Steel America
400 E Indian River Rd (23523-1799)
PHONE..................757 545-5311
Ken Mebane, *Branch Mgr*
EMP: 300

SALES (corp-wide): 150MM **Privately Held**
WEB: www.colonnaship.com
SIC: 3731 3441 Commercial cargo ships, building & repairing; tugboats, building & repairing; cargo vessels, building & repairing; military ships, building & repairing; fabricated structural metal
PA: Ship Colonna's Yard Incorporated
400 E Indian River Rd
Norfolk VA 23523
757 545-2414

(G-9497)
COLONNAS SHIP YARD INC
Also Called: Weld America
400 E Indian River Rd (23523-1799)
PHONE..................757 545-2414
Thomas W Godfrey Jr, *President*
EMP: 750
SALES (est): 15.3MM **Privately Held**
WEB: www.colonnaship.com
SIC: 3731 3443 Shipbuilding & repairing; fabricated plate work (boiler shop); fabricated metal products

(G-9498)
COLONNAS SHIPYARD
150 S Main St (23523-1130)
PHONE..................757 962-0508
EMP: 2
SALES (est): 244.4K **Privately Held**
WEB: www.colonnaship.com
SIC: 3731 Shipbuilding & repairing

(G-9499)
COMMERCIAL METALS COMPANY
Also Called: CMC Rebar Virginia
1344 Ballentine Blvd (23504-3808)
P.O. Box 7229 (23509-0229)
PHONE..................757 625-4201
EMP: 10
SALES (corp-wide): 7B **Publicly Held**
SIC: 3312 Blast Furnace-Steel Work
PA: Commercial Metals Company
6565 N Mcarthr Blvd # 800
Irving TX 75039
214 689-4300

(G-9500)
COMPUTERIZED IMAGING REFERENCE
900 Asbury Ave (23513-2865)
PHONE..................757 855-1127
Mark Devlin, *President*
Rene Bois, *COO*
Moustafa Zerhouni, *Chief Engr*
Ted Lynch, *Engineer*
Merouane Lamari, *Electrical Engi*
EMP: 30
SQ FT: 25,000
SALES (est): 5MM **Privately Held**
WEB: www.cirsinc.com
SIC: 3841 Medical instruments & equipment, blood & bone work

(G-9501)
COMSACO INC
3737 E Virginia Bch Blvd (23502-3217)
PHONE..................757 466-9188
Walter W Westhoff, *President*
Felicia Gower, *Purch Agent*
Brian Lineberry, *QC Mgr*
Randy Fowler, *Design Engr*
Ted Karch, *Manager*
EMP: 30
SQ FT: 20,000
SALES (est): 6.2MM **Privately Held**
WEB: www.comsaco.com
SIC: 3699 Electrical equipment & supplies

(G-9502)
CONFORMA LABORATORIES INC
Also Called: Conforma Contact Lenses
4707 Colley Ave (23508-2034)
P.O. Box 2693 (23501-2693)
PHONE..................757 321-0200
Kevin Sanford, *President*
Teri Mackley, *Vice Pres*
Terry Sanford, *Sales Staff*
Randy Campbell, *Consultant*
Bita Scope, *Technology*
EMP: 20

SALES (est): 2.7MM **Privately Held**
WEB: www.conforma.com
SIC: 3851 3827 Contact lenses; optical instruments & lenses

(G-9503)
CONSOLIDATED WELDING LLC
5948 Jerry Rd (23502-5212)
PHONE..................757 348-6304
John Tipton, *Principal*
EMP: 1
SALES (est): 28.8K **Privately Held**
SIC: 7692 Welding repair

(G-9504)
CONTRA SURPLUS LLC
222 W 21st St Ste F621 (23517-2200)
PHONE..................757 337-9971
Joseph Cherry, *Mng Member*
EMP: 5
SALES (est): 400K **Privately Held**
SIC: 3799 4789 Transportation equipment; cargo loading & unloading services

(G-9505)
COPY CONNECTION
236 E Main St (23510-1608)
PHONE..................757 627-4701
Karen Bohrer, *Partner*
EMP: 6
SQ FT: 984
SALES (est): 773K **Privately Held**
WEB: www.copyconnectionnorfolkva.com
SIC: 2752 Commercial printing, offset

(G-9506)
COPY CONNECTION LLC
236 E Main St (23510-1608)
PHONE..................757 627-4701
Karen Bohrer, *Owner*
EMP: 3
SALES (est): 141.8K **Privately Held**
SIC: 2752 Commercial printing, lithographic

(G-9507)
CORONET GROUP INC
809 Brandon Ave Ste 302 (23517-1676)
PHONE..................757 488-4800
Lawrence L Ashinoff, *President*
Carol Ashinoff, *Vice Pres*
Moss Friedman, *Vice Pres*
Flip Atkinson, *Manager*
EMP: 90 **EST:** 1955
SQ FT: 60,000
SALES (est): 4.1MM **Privately Held**
SIC: 2321 Sport shirts, men's & boys': from purchased materials

(G-9508)
COVA SHIP REPAIR INC
2131 Cromwell Rd (23504-3103)
PHONE..................757 390-2177
Andrew Smith, *CEO*
EMP: 15
SALES (est): 751K **Privately Held**
SIC: 3731 Shipbuilding & repairing

(G-9509)
CREATIVE SIGN BUILDERS LLC
2401 Fawn St (23504-1917)
PHONE..................757 622-5591
Roger E Harp, *Partner*
Brian Strode, *Partner*
EMP: 3
SQ FT: 4,100
SALES (est): 284.8K **Privately Held**
WEB: www.drdaynaburnett.net
SIC: 3993 Electric signs

(G-9510)
CTRL-PAD INC
1543 Bolling Ave (23508-1359)
PHONE..................757 216-9170
EMP: 5
SALES (est): 348.7K **Privately Held**
SIC: 7372 8741 Prepackaged Software Services/Asset Mgmt

(G-9511)
CUSTOM MADE SPRINGS INC
822 W 40th St (23508-2514)
P.O. Box 6024 (23508-0024)
PHONE..................757 489-8202
Louis A Schmitt, *President*
EMP: 1

SQ FT: 1,000
SALES (est): 300K **Privately Held**
SIC: 3495 Wire springs

(G-9512)
CUSTOM RAILING SOLUTIONS INC
5875 Adderley St (23502-4601)
PHONE..................757 455-8501
EMP: 3
SALES (est): 283.6K **Privately Held**
SIC: 3446 Architectural metalwork

(G-9513)
D & G SIGNS INC
Also Called: Signet Signs
2640 Arkansas Ave (23513-4402)
PHONE..................757 858-2140
Don Galvin, *President*
Barbara D'Ambrosio, *Corp Secy*
EMP: 9
SALES (est): 1MM **Privately Held**
SIC: 3993 Signs, not made in custom sign painting shops

(G-9514)
D W BOYD CORPORATION
4003 Colley Ave (23508-2601)
PHONE..................757 423-2268
Dennis Boyd, *President*
Marlo Williams, *Principal*
EMP: 7
SQ FT: 9,000
SALES (est): 1.5MM **Privately Held**
WEB: www.dwboyd.com
SIC: 3731 7699 7623 Shipbuilding & repairing; industrial machinery & equipment repair; air conditioning repair

(G-9515)
DALLAS-KATEC INCORPORATED (PA)
4511 Maiden Ln (23518-1718)
P.O. Box 3399, Virginia Beach (23454-9466)
PHONE..................757 428-8822
Michael C Campbell, *President*
EMP: 3
SQ FT: 4,500
SALES (est): 300K **Privately Held**
WEB: www.aerosolv.com
SIC: 3559 Recycling machinery

(G-9516)
DANTE INDUSTRIES INC
1324 Ballentine Blvd (23504-3808)
PHONE..................757 605-6100
Lisa Papini, *President*
EMP: 4
SALES (est): 250.6K **Privately Held**
WEB: www.dantevalve.com
SIC: 3494 Valves & pipe fittings

(G-9517)
DATAONE SOFTWARE
150 Granby St (23510-1604)
PHONE..................877 438-8467
Jacob Maki, *Principal*
EMP: 2
SALES (est): 116K **Privately Held**
WEB: www.dataonesoftware.com
SIC: 7372 Prepackaged software

(G-9518)
DAVIS CHETIA
Also Called: Chetia Plugg Publication
8426 Tidewater Dr Apt 7 (23518-2535)
PHONE..................757 575-9225
Chetia Davis, *Owner*
EMP: 1
SALES (est): 26K **Privately Held**
SIC: 2711 Newspapers, publishing & printing

(G-9519)
DEAD RECKONING DISTILLERY
312 W 24th St (23517-1306)
PHONE..................757 535-9864
EMP: 4
SALES (est): 278.4K **Privately Held**
SIC: 2085 Distilled & blended liquors

(G-9520)
DEADLINE TYPESETTING INC
Also Called: Deadline Digital Printing
1048b W 27th St (23517-1019)
PHONE......................757 625-5883
Cheryl Scott, *President*
Jeryl Barnett, *Vice Pres*
EMP: 6
SQ FT: 2,500
SALES (est): 625K **Privately Held**
WEB: www.printingbydeadline.com
SIC: 2791 2759 Typesetting; commercial printing; advertising literature: printing

(G-9521)
DEBORAH E ROSS
Also Called: Ross Enterprise
6830 Orangewood Ave (23513-1121)
PHONE......................757 857-6140
Deborah E Ross, *Owner*
EMP: 1
SALES (est): 52.3K **Privately Held**
SIC: 2331 Blouses, women's & juniors': made from purchased material

(G-9522)
DECIPHER INC
259 Granby St Ste 100 (23510-1810)
PHONE......................757 664-1111
Warren L Holland Jr, *Principal*
▲ **EMP:** 100
SALES (est): 11.2MM **Privately Held**
WEB: www.decipher.com
SIC: 3944 Games, toys & children's vehicles

(G-9523)
DECISION POINT TECH LLC
7407 Muirfield Rd (23505-1753)
PHONE......................757 286-1065
James Phillips, *Principal*
EMP: 2
SALES (est): 99K **Privately Held**
SIC: 2741 Miscellaneous publishing

(G-9524)
DEGEN ENTERPRISES INC
Also Called: Kay Gee Plastics
2532 Ingleside Rd (23513-4543)
PHONE......................757 853-7651
Gunther Degen, *CEO*
Lore Degen, *Principal*
Gordon H Degen, *Vice Pres*
EMP: 3
SQ FT: 5,000
SALES (est): 513.2K **Privately Held**
WEB: www.kaygeeplastics.weebly.com
SIC: 3089 Windshields, plastic; plastic processing

(G-9525)
DISTER INC (PA)
Also Called: BCT Virginia
925 Denison Ave (23513-2811)
P.O. Box 10390 (23513-0390)
PHONE......................757 857-1946
Arthur C Dister, *CEO*
Bill Dister, *President*
Tiffany Coffman, *Manager*
Kelly George, *Officer*
EMP: 40
SQ FT: 9,000
SALES (est): 4MM **Privately Held**
WEB: www.bctvirginia.com
SIC: 2759 3953 2752 2396 Thermography; embossing seals & hand stamps; commercial printing, lithographic; automotive & apparel trimmings

(G-9526)
DLA DOCUMENT SERVICES
1279 Franklin St Rm 129 (23511-2406)
PHONE......................757 855-0300
Sherrall L Fonner, *Manager*
EMP: 10 **Publicly Held**
WEB: www.documentservices.dla.mil
SIC: 2752 9711 Commercial printing, lithographic; national security
HQ: Dla Document Services
5450 Carlisle Pike Bldg 9
Mechanicsburg PA 17050
717 605-2362

(G-9527)
DLA DOCUMENT SERVICES
1641 Morris St Bldg Kbb (23511-2809)
PHONE......................757 444-7068
Earl Waddell, *Manager*
EMP: 48 **Publicly Held**
WEB: www.documentservices.dla.mil
SIC: 2752 9711 Commercial printing, lithographic; national security;
HQ: Dla Document Services
5450 Carlisle Pike Bldg 9
Mechanicsburg PA 17050
717 605-2362

(G-9528)
DOMINION DISTRIBUTION SVCS INC (DH)
150 Granby St (23510-1604)
PHONE......................757 351-7000
Jim Cattan, *President*
Ray Buchanan, *Director*
EMP: 12 **EST:** 2008
SALES (est): 4.9MM **Privately Held**
WEB: www.dominionenterprises.com
SIC: 2721 Periodicals: publishing only
HQ: United Advertising Publications, Inc.
1331 L St Nw Ste 2
Washington DC 20005
210 377-3116

(G-9529)
DOMINION ENTERPRISES
150 Granby St Ste 150 (23510-1688)
PHONE......................757 351-7000
EMP: 50
SALES (corp-wide): 800MM **Privately Held**
SIC: 2741 2721 Misc Publishing Periodicals-Publishing/Printing
HQ: Dominion Enterprises
4460 Corp Ln Ste 317
Virginia Beach VA 23510
757 351-7000

(G-9530)
DOMINION ENTERPRISES
413 W York St (23510-1114)
PHONE......................757 226-9440
Beth Campbell, *Director*
EMP: 3 **Privately Held**
WEB: www.dominionenterprises.com
SIC: 2721 Periodicals
HQ: Dominion Enterprises
150 Granby St
Norfolk VA 23510

(G-9531)
DONNASATTICOFCRAFTS
4566 Kennebeck Ave (23513-3677)
PHONE......................757 855-0559
EMP: 2
SALES (est): 90.8K **Privately Held**
SIC: 3312 Blast Furnaces And Steel Mills, Nsk

(G-9532)
DOUGS MOBILE ELECTRIC
1062 W 37th St (23508-2612)
PHONE......................757 438-6045
EMP: 1 **EST:** 1998
SALES (est): 37K **Privately Held**
SIC: 7694 Armature Rewinding

(G-9533)
DUROLINE NORTH AMERICA INC
4414 Killam Ave Unit A (23508-2068)
PHONE......................757 447-6290
Rafael Mazzochi, *Vice Pres*
▲ **EMP:** 4
SALES (est): 70K **Privately Held**
SIC: 3069 Brake linings, rubber

(G-9534)
DYNAMIC TOWING EQP & MFG INC
1120 E Brambleton Ave (23504-3415)
PHONE......................757 624-1360
Anthony Gentile, *President*
Shelly Schultz, *Vice Pres*
Joseph Gentile, *Admin Sec*
EMP: 35
SQ FT: 40,000
SALES (est): 6.9MM **Privately Held**
WEB: www.dynamicmfg.com
SIC: 3711 Wreckers (tow truck), assembly of

(G-9535)
EAST CAST REPR FABRICATION LLC (PA)
5803 Curlew Dr (23502-4626)
P.O. Box 13687, Chesapeake (23325-0687)
PHONE......................757 455-9600
Richard Faulkenberry, *Vice Pres*
Andrew Hetzner, *Project Mgr*
Bonnie Englant, *Buyer*
Erin Oneil, *Human Resources*
Jacob Dinmore, *Manager*
EMP: 126 **EST:** 2008
SQ FT: 18,000
SALES (est): 30.8MM **Privately Held**
WEB: www.ecrfab.com
SIC: 3731 3732 3441 Shipbuilding & repairing; boat building & repairing; fabricated structural metal

(G-9536)
EAST CAST REPR FABRICATION LLC
5803 Curlew Dr Ste D (23502-4626)
P.O. Box 13687, Chesapeake (23325-0687)
PHONE......................757 455-9600
Jorge Luis Rivera, *Branch Mgr*
EMP: 99
SALES (corp-wide): 30.8MM **Privately Held**
WEB: www.ecrfab.com
SIC: 3732 3731 8711 Boat building & repairing; shipbuilding & repairing; engineering services
PA: East Coast Repair & Fabrication, L.L.C.
5803 Curlew Dr
Norfolk VA 23502
757 455-9600

(G-9537)
EAST COAST BRAKE RBLDRS CORP
Also Called: East Coast Brake & Rebuilders
5812 Curlew Dr (23502-4627)
PHONE......................757 466-1308
Claude K Gregory, *President*
CK Gregory Jr, *Vice Pres*
Arthur Cardente, *Sales Mgr*
Casey Gregory, *Sales Staff*
Courtney Gregory, *Office Mgr*
▲ **EMP:** 15
SQ FT: 19,500
SALES (est): 3.7MM **Privately Held**
WEB: www.eastcoastbrakes.com
SIC: 3714 Motor vehicle brake systems & parts

(G-9538)
ECHO PUBLISHING INC
2910 Church St (23504-1618)
PHONE......................757 603-3774
Darly Antoine, *President*
EMP: 9 **EST:** 2011
SALES (est): 665.5K **Privately Held**
WEB: www.thegoodprinters.com
SIC: 2752 Commercial printing, lithographic

(G-9539)
ECOLOCHEM INTERNATIONAL INC
4545 Patent Rd (23502-5604)
PHONE......................757 855-9000
Lyman Dickerson, *Chairman*
EMP: 3
SALES (est): 141.1K **Privately Held**
WEB: www.ecolochem.com
SIC: 3559 Special industry machinery

(G-9540)
EDGECONNEX INC
3800 Village Ave (23502-5613)
PHONE......................757 855-0351
EMP: 3 **Privately Held**
WEB: www.edgeconnex.com
SIC: 3511 Turbines & turbine generator sets
PA: Edgeconnex, Inc.
2201 Coop Way Ste 400
Herndon VA 20171

(G-9541)
EDIGNAS FASHION
547 E Little Creek Rd (23505-2817)
PHONE......................757 588-4958
EMP: 1
SALES (est): 46K **Privately Held**
SIC: 2299 Mfg Textile Goods

(G-9542)
EGGLESTON MINOR
Also Called: Black Ark Art & Design Studio
616 Naval Base Rd Ste 1 (23505-3651)
PHONE......................757 819-4958
Minor Eggleston, *Owner*
EMP: 1 **EST:** 2016
SALES (est): 49.3K **Privately Held**
WEB: www.blackarkstudio.net
SIC: 2759 3993 Post cards, picture: printing; promotional printing; screen printing; displays & cutouts, window & lobby; displays, paint process

(G-9543)
ELECTRO TECHS LLC
9524 Sherwood Pl (23503-2917)
PHONE......................704 900-1911
Joe Getz,
EMP: 3
SALES (est): 50K **Privately Held**
WEB: www.electrotechs.net
SIC: 3663 Radio & TV communications equipment

(G-9544)
ESSENTIAL EATS LLC
1031 Quail St (23513-3215)
PHONE......................757 304-2393
Daniel Kealiinohomoku, *Administration*
EMP: 2
SALES (est): 173.6K **Privately Held**
WEB: www.essentialeatsllc.com
SIC: 2899 Salt

(G-9545)
FACE CONSTRUCTION TECHNOLOGIES
Also Called: Face Companies, The
427 W 35th St (23508-3201)
P.O. Box 6300 (23508-0300)
PHONE......................757 624-2121
Bradbury Robinson Face, *President*
EMP: 3
SQ FT: 7,000
SALES (est): 600K **Privately Held**
WEB: www.dipstick.com
SIC: 3829 7371 Measuring & controlling devices; custom computer programming services

(G-9546)
FACE ELECTRONICS LC
427 W 35th St (23508-3201)
PHONE......................757 624-2121
J Douglas Sorensen, *Principal*
Jeff Rogers, *Engineer*
Christine Busacco, *CFO*
Alfredo Carazo,
EMP: 23
SALES (est): 1.6MM **Privately Held**
WEB: www.transoner.com
SIC: 3679 Electronic circuits

(G-9547)
FACE X LLC
427 W 35th St (23508-3201)
PHONE......................757 624-2121
Bradbury R Face,
EMP: 2
SALES (est): 88.3K **Privately Held**
SIC: 3612 Power & distribution transformers

(G-9548)
FAIRBANKS MORSE LLC
981 Scott St Ste A (23502-3165)
PHONE......................757 623-2711
Vickie Reynolds, *General Mgr*
Robert Beckwith, *Manager*
Brian Cauley, *Supervisor*
EMP: 1

GEOGRAPHIC

SALES (corp-wide): 98.9MM **Privately Held**
WEB: www.fairbanksmorse.com
SIC: 3519 Diesel, semi-diesel or duel-fuel engines, including marine
HQ: Fairbanks Morse, Llc
　　701 White Ave
　　Beloit WI 53511
　　800 356-6955

(G-9549)
FAIRVIEW PLACE LLC
1232 Westover Ave (23507-1336)
PHONE.............................330 257-1138
Ashley Mars, *Mng Member*
EMP: 1
SALES (est): 59.3K **Privately Held**
SIC: 3999 Artificial flower arrangements

(G-9550)
FASTSIGNS NORFOLK
2000 Colonial Ave (23517-1908)
PHONE.............................757 274-3344
Jene Knolack, *Principal*
EMP: 2
SALES (est): 256.1K **Privately Held**
WEB: www.fastsigns.com
SIC: 3993 Signs & advertising specialties

(G-9551)
FELLERS INC
930 Denison Ave (23513-2825)
PHONE.............................757 853-1363
EMP: 2
SALES (corp-wide): 70.9MM **Privately Held**
SIC: 3993 Mfg Signs/Advertising Specialties
PA: Fellers Inc
　　6566 E Skelly Dr
　　Tulsa OK 74145
　　918 621-4400

(G-9552)
FIBER FOODS INC
2400 Florida Ave (23513-4520)
PHONE.............................757 853-2888
Lidan Zou, *CEO*
Qing Xia, *President*
EMP: 5
SQ FT: 20,000
SALES (est): 360K **Privately Held**
WEB: www.fiber-foods.com
SIC: 2099 2098 Noodles, uncooked: packaged with other ingredients; noodles (e.g. egg, plain & water), dry

(G-9553)
FIRST CLASS CHARIOTS LLC
6352 E Virginia Bch Blvd (23502-2827)
PHONE.............................757 334-7298
Jeanette Clifton, *Principal*
EMP: 2
SALES (est): 218.9K **Privately Held**
WEB: www.firstclasschariots.com
SIC: 2335 Wedding gowns & dresses

(G-9554)
FIRST OBJECTIVE SOFTWARE INC
1185 Pineridge Rd (23502-2043)
PHONE.............................757 855-0191
EMP: 1
SALES (corp-wide): 160K **Privately Held**
WEB: www.firstobject.com
SIC: 7372 Prepackaged software
PA: First Objective Software Inc
　　6238 Split Creek Ln
　　Alexandria VA 22312
　　703 751-9406

(G-9555)
FLAGSHIP INC
Also Called: Flagship, The
150 W Brambleton Ave (23510-2018)
PHONE.............................757 222-3965
Pat Richardson, *President*
Amber Schmidt, *Controller*
Guy R Friddell III, *Admin Sec*
EMP: 35
SALES (est): 3MM **Publicly Held**
WEB: www.militarynews.com
SIC: 2711 Newspapers, publishing & printing

HQ: Virginian-Pilot Media Companies, Llc
　　5429 Greenwich Rd
　　Virginia Beach VA 23462
　　757 446-9000

(G-9556)
FLEET SERVICES INC
Also Called: Fleet Printing
712 W 20th St (23517-1904)
P.O. Box 11191 (23517-0191)
PHONE.............................757 625-4214
J D Blankenship, *President*
EMP: 10
SQ FT: 12,000
SALES (est): 1.7MM **Privately Held**
WEB: www.fleetprinting.net
SIC: 2752 Commercial printing, offset

(G-9557)
FLOWERS BAKING CO NORFOLK LLC (HQ)
Also Called: Flowers Bakery
1209 Corprew Ave (23504-3403)
P.O. Box 2860 (23501-2860)
PHONE.............................757 622-6317
Josh Stoddard, *Superintendent*
David Dodge, *Vice Pres*
Abel Menchaca, *Vice Pres*
Bruce Wyatt, *Vice Pres*
Gary Cook, *Facilities Mgr*
EMP: 115 EST: 1902
SQ FT: 40,000
SALES (est): 11.9MM
SALES (corp-wide): 4.1B **Publicly Held**
SIC: 2051 Breads, rolls & buns
PA: Flowers Foods, Inc.
　　1919 Flowers Cir
　　Thomasville GA 31757
　　912 226-9110

(G-9558)
FORERUNNER FEDERATION
520 W 21st St (23517-1950)
PHONE.............................757 639-6576
E Andrew Balas, *Principal*
EMP: 4 EST: 2010
SALES (est): 17.2K **Privately Held**
WEB: www.forerunnerfederation.org
SIC: 2836 Culture media

(G-9559)
FRESHWTER PARL MEDIA GROUP LLC
Also Called: We Socialize For You
3577 Norland Ct (23513-4019)
PHONE.............................757 785-5483
Theresa Ferrell, *President*
EMP: 1
SALES (est): 43.7K **Privately Held**
SIC: 2741 8742 8299 ; management consulting services; marketing consulting services; personal development school; educational services

(G-9560)
FROG INDUSTRIES LLC
3905 Granby St (23504-1201)
PHONE.............................757 995-2359
Teikeshia Melton, *Principal*
EMP: 1
SALES (est): 39.6K **Privately Held**
SIC: 3999 Manufacturing industries

(G-9561)
GEORGE PEREZ
Also Called: PC Unlimited
9609 Dolphin Run (23518-2020)
PHONE.............................757 362-3131
George Perez, *Owner*
EMP: 1
SALES (est): 93K **Privately Held**
WEB: www.pcuinfo.com
SIC: 3575 7378 7372 Computer terminals; computer maintenance & repair; prepackaged software

(G-9562)
GERLOFF INC CHARLES W
2622 Cromwell Rd (23509-2308)
PHONE.............................757 853-5232
Joseph Gerloff, *President*
Cynthia Gerloff, *Corp Secy*
Donet J Gerloff, *Vice Pres*
Gerloff Donet James, *Vice Pres*
EMP: 6
SQ FT: 2,400

SALES (est): 805.2K **Privately Held**
WEB: www.gerloffwelding.com
SIC: 7692 Automotive welding; brazing

(G-9563)
GLOBAL YACHT FUEL LLC
5353 E Princess Anne Rd F (23502-1861)
PHONE.............................954 462-6050
EMP: 6
SALES (est): 697.8K **Privately Held**
SIC: 2869 Fuels

(G-9564)
GOON SQUAD APPS LLC
3218a Pretty Lake Ave (23518-1322)
PHONE.............................706 410-6139
Alston Harper, *Principal*
EMP: 3
SALES (est): 117.4K **Privately Held**
SIC: 7372 Application computer software

(G-9565)
GREEN AIR ENVIRONMENTAL SVCS
Also Called: Biocide USA
8508 Benjamin Ave (23518-2102)
PHONE.............................757 739-1349
EMP: 2
SALES (est): 72.7K **Privately Held**
SIC: 2842 Polishes And Sanitation Goods

(G-9566)
GREENBRIER CUSTOM CABINETS
Also Called: Custom Bars & Entrmt Systems
535 W 25th St Ste B (23517-1268)
PHONE.............................757 438-5475
Charles Stewart, *President*
EMP: 8
SALES (est): 638K **Privately Held**
SIC: 2434 Wood kitchen cabinets

(G-9567)
GRYPHON THREADS LLC
2232 Corbett Ave (23518-2104)
PHONE.............................707 320-7865
Megan Lord, *Partner*
Ian Lord,
EMP: 2
SALES (est): 90.3K **Privately Held**
SIC: 2395 Embroidery & art needlework

(G-9568)
HAMILTON PERKINS COLLECTN LLC
201 W Tazewell St Apt 312 (23510-1319)
PHONE.............................757 544-7161
Hamilton Perkins, *Mng Member*
EMP: 1
SALES (est): 101.8K **Privately Held**
WEB: www.hamiltonperkins.com
SIC: 3111 Accessory products, leather; bag leather

(G-9569)
HAMPTON ROADS BAKING CO LLC
1209 Corprew Ave (23504-3403)
PHONE.............................757 622-0347
Richard Holder, *Principal*
EMP: 2
SALES (est): 166.8K **Privately Held**
SIC: 2051 Biscuits, baked: baking powder & raised

(G-9570)
HAMPTON ROADS GREEN CLEAN LLC
Also Called: Hrgc LLC
1328 Bolton St (23504-2803)
P.O. Box 1125, Chesapeake (23327-1125)
PHONE.............................757 515-8183
Tonya Foreman, *CEO*
EMP: 10
SALES (est): 409.5K **Privately Held**
WEB: www.greencleanautowash.com
SIC: 2842 Specialty cleaning preparations

(G-9571)
HARBINGER TECH SOLUTIONS LLC
Also Called: Arcsys
2014 Granby St Ste 200 (23517-2331)
PHONE.............................757 962-6130

Michael Umscheid, *President*
Dean Rodil, *COO*
Kaleigh Wells, *Mktg Dir*
Justin Umscheid, *Technology*
EMP: 14
SALES (est): 207.5K **Privately Held**
WEB: www.arcsysonline.com
SIC: 7372 Prepackaged software

(G-9572)
HARRIS CONNECT LLC
6315 N Center Dr (23502-4006)
PHONE.............................757 965-8000
Bob Brian, *Director*
EMP: 500
SALES (corp-wide): 102.6MM **Privately Held**
WEB: www.harrisconnect.com
SIC: 2741 7389 Directories: publishing only, not printed on site; telemarketing services
HQ: Harris Connect, Llc
　　1400 Crossways Blvd # 114
　　Chesapeake VA 23320
　　757 965-8000

(G-9573)
HAVE HAPPYFEET
609 Obendorfer Rd (23523-1636)
PHONE.............................757 339-0833
Brian Alexander, *President*
EMP: 3
SALES (est): 186.1K **Privately Held**
SIC: 3842 Surgical appliances & supplies

(G-9574)
HAYWARD TRMT & PEST CTRL LLC
8422 Tidewater Dr Ste B (23518-2563)
PHONE.............................757 263-7858
Marcus W-Hayward, *Owner*
EMP: 1 EST: 2013
SALES (est): 61.8K **Privately Held**
SIC: 2879 7389 Insecticides & pesticides;

(G-9575)
HEALTHY BY CHOICE
3534 Humboldt St (23513-2120)
PHONE.............................810 449-5999
Jessica Kellaway, *Principal*
EMP: 1 EST: 2018
SALES (est): 42.8K **Privately Held**
SIC: 2499 Wood products

(G-9576)
HEALTHY LABRADORS
440 Monticello Ave # 1900 (23510-2571)
PHONE.............................757 740-0681
EMP: 2
SALES (est): 86.6K **Privately Held**
SIC: 3841 Surgical & medical instruments

(G-9577)
HEARTFELT STITCH CO
3568 Ladd Ave (23502-4217)
PHONE.............................757 828-6036
Desiree Smith, *Principal*
EMP: 1
SALES (est): 47.7K **Privately Held**
SIC: 2395 Embroidery & art needlework

(G-9578)
HECO SLINGS CORPORATION
4570 Progress Rd (23502-1911)
PHONE.............................757 855-7139
Harvey L Howlett Jr, *President*
Cheryl West, *Purchasing*
Conrad Eiban, *Sales Staff*
Bonita Lyons, *Sales Staff*
Janice Sorrell, *Receptionist*
EMP: 12
SQ FT: 12,000
SALES: 6.1MM **Privately Held**
WEB: www.hecoslings.com
SIC: 3496 Miscellaneous fabricated wire products

(G-9579)
HELIOS ACQUISITION LLC
543 E Indian River Rd (23523-1717)
PHONE.............................757 545-6400
Thomas Epley, *Mng Member*
Victor Brannon,
EMP: 99
SALES (est): 3MM **Privately Held**
SIC: 3731 Shipbuilding & repairing

▲ = Import ▼=Export
◆ =Import/Export

(G-9580)
HEREISURSIGN LLC
169 W Ocean Ave (23503-4337)
PHONE............................757 277-8487
Eric Hovik, *Principal*
EMP: 1
SALES (est): 49.1K **Privately Held**
WEB: www.hereisursign.com
SIC: 3993 Signs & advertising specialties

(G-9581)
HIGHLAND BEARS AND MORE
8263 Simons Dr (23505-1644)
PHONE............................757 480-1125
William T Snow, *Owner*
EMP: 2 EST: 1997
SALES (est): 92.6K **Privately Held**
SIC: 3942 3961 Stuffed toys, including animals; jewelry apparel, non-precious metals

(G-9582)
HOME BREWUSA (PA)
5802 E Virginia Bch Blvd (23502-2475)
PHONE............................757 459-2739
Neal Erschens, *Owner*
Elizabeth Erschens, *Co-Owner*
EMP: 8 EST: 2007
SALES (est): 700K **Privately Held**
WEB: www.homebrewusa.com
SIC: 2085 Distilled & blended liquors

(G-9583)
HOWMET AEROSPACE INC
5610 E Virginia Bch Blvd (23502-2420)
PHONE............................757 461-1360
Steve Henderson, *Manager*
EMP: 2 **Publicly Held**
WEB: www.howmet.com
SIC: 3353 Aluminum sheet & strip
PA: Howmet Aerospace Inc.
201 Isabella St Ste 200
Pittsburgh PA 15212
412 992-2500

(G-9584)
HUNTER COMPANY HB (HQ)
981 Scott St Ste 100 (23502-3165)
P.O. Box 1599 (23501-1599)
PHONE............................757 664-5200
Lucy Halperin, *CEO*
William D Barrett, *President*
Josh Davis, *Prdtn Mgr*
John S Gilbert, *Controller*
◆ EMP: 12
SQ FT: 35,000
SALES (est): 3.1MM
SALES (corp-wide): 8.6MM **Privately Held**
SIC: 2033 2035 Fruits: packaged in cans, jars, etc.; maraschino cherries: packaged in cans, jars, etc.; olives: packaged in cans, jars, etc.; pickles, sauces & salad dressings; mustard, prepared (wet); onions, pickled
PA: Acesur North America, Inc.
2700 Westchester Ave # 105
Purchase NY
914 925-0450

(G-9585)
HUNTINGTON INGALLS INC
9727 Avionics Loop Ste M (23511-3731)
PHONE............................757 440-5390
Ryan Norris, *Vice Pres*
Dave Demers, *Manager*
Brent Gooding, *Exec Dir*
Damon Saetre, *Planning*
EMP: 12 **Publicly Held**
WEB: www.huntingtoningalls.com
SIC: 3731 Shipbuilding & repairing
HQ: Huntington Ingalls Incorporated
4101 Washington Ave
Newport News VA 23607
757 380-2000

(G-9586)
HUSTEADS CANVAS CREATIONS INC
628 W 24th St (23517-1208)
PHONE............................757 627-6912
Patricia Butler, *President*
Dennis Hustead, *Corp Secy*
EMP: 20
SQ FT: 12,000
SALES (est): 2.1MM **Privately Held**
WEB: www.husteadscanvascreations.com
SIC: 2394 Awnings, fabric: made from purchased materials

(G-9587)
HWTE TIN HAN
850 Kempsville Rd (23502-3920)
PHONE............................757 261-5963
EMP: 3
SALES (est): 172.7K **Privately Held**
SIC: 3356 Tin

(G-9588)
I A WELDING LLC
5875 Adderley St (23502-4601)
PHONE............................757 455-8500
EMP: 1
SALES (est): 25K **Privately Held**
SIC: 7692 Welding repair

(G-9589)
IHS PRESS
222 W 21st St Ste F122 (23517-2200)
PHONE............................877 447-7737
John Sharpe, *Chairman*
Randa Sharpe, *Admin Sec*
EMP: 2
SALES (est): 29.6K **Privately Held**
WEB: www.ihspress.com
SIC: 2731 Books: publishing only

(G-9590)
IM EMBROIDERY
415 W York St (23510-1117)
P.O. Box 3214 (23514-3214)
PHONE............................757 533-5397
EMP: 2 EST: 2014
SALES (est): 58.5K **Privately Held**
SIC: 2395 Embroidery products, except schiffli machine

(G-9591)
IMPERIAL CLEANERS
9311 Sloane St (23503-4329)
PHONE............................757 531-1125
Rick Ortega, *Owner*
EMP: 1
SALES (est): 82.8K **Privately Held**
SIC: 2211 Draperies & drapery fabrics, cotton

(G-9592)
INDUSTRIAL ALLOY WELDING LLC
5875 Adderley St (23502-4601)
PHONE............................757 573-8496
Mike Robinson, *General Mgr*
Michael Robinson,
EMP: 1
SALES (est): 341.9K **Privately Held**
WEB: www.industrialalloywelding.com
SIC: 7692 7389 Welding repair;

(G-9593)
INSTANT SYSTEMS
5505 Robin Hood Rd Ste A (23513-2423)
P.O. Box 11570 (23517-0570)
PHONE............................757 200-5494
Gerald Ramsey, *Ch of Bd*
Burley Kimber, *Vice Pres*
Kim Peck, *Executive Asst*
EMP: 7
SALES (est): 828.1K **Privately Held**
WEB: www.instantsystems.com
SIC: 3086 Packaging & shipping materials, foamed plastic

(G-9594)
INTERCO PRINT LLC
150 Granby St (23510-1604)
PHONE............................757 351-7000
Jack J Ross, *President*
EMP: 9
SALES (est): 718.8K **Privately Held**
SIC: 2752 Commercial printing, lithographic

(G-9595)
INTERNATIONAL PAINT LLC
Also Called: Akzo Nobel
981 Scott St Ste 100 (23502-3165)
PHONE............................757 466-0705
Robert Keenan, *General Mgr*
EMP: 9

SALES (corp-wide): 10.2B **Privately Held**
WEB: www.akzonobel.com
SIC: 2851 Paints & allied products
HQ: International Paint Llc
6001 Antoine Dr
Houston TX 77091
713 682-1711

(G-9596)
INTUIT YOUR LIFE NETWORK LLC
8100 Simons Dr Ste 100 (23505-1608)
PHONE............................757 588-0533
Daryl Ketner, *Principal*
EMP: 2
SALES (est): 20K **Privately Held**
SIC: 3634 Massage machines, electric, except for beauty/barber shops

(G-9597)
J & R PARTNERS
2000 Colonial Ave (23517-1908)
PHONE............................757 274-3344
Jene Knolack, *Owner*
EMP: 1 **Privately Held**
WEB: www.fastsigns.com
SIC: 3993 Signs & advertising specialties
PA: J & R Partners
4780 Euclid Rd
Virginia Beach VA 23462

(G-9598)
J H MILES CO INC (PA)
902 Southampton Ave (23510-1016)
P.O. Box 178 (23501-0178)
PHONE............................757 622-9264
John R Miles, *CEO*
Roy Parker, *President*
Larry Lusk, *Vice Pres*
Richard D Miles, *Vice Pres*
Elizabeth P Riley, *CFO*
▼ EMP: 32 EST: 1900
SQ FT: 20,000
SALES (est): 11.1MM **Privately Held**
WEB: www.jhmiles.com
SIC: 2092 Fresh or frozen packaged fish

(G-9599)
JACK CARTER CABINET MAKER
125 E Severn Rd (23505-4827)
PHONE............................757 622-9414
Jack Carter, *Owner*
EMP: 1
SALES (est): 86.3K **Privately Held**
SIC: 2521 2511 Cabinets, office: wood; wood household furniture

(G-9600)
JAMMAC CORPORATION
Also Called: American Cartridge Charge
6610 E Virginia Bch Blvd (23502-3014)
PHONE............................757 855-5474
Michael J Vastano, *President*
Marie Ann Vastano, *President*
Vastand Michael B, *Vice Pres*
Michael B Vastano Jr, *Vice Pres*
Joseph Vastano, *Treasurer*
EMP: 9
SQ FT: 4,450
SALES (est): 1.7MM **Privately Held**
WEB: www.virginiaprintingandsigns.com
SIC: 2752 Commercial printing, offset

(G-9601)
JARCAM SPORTS
3174 E Ocean View Ave (23518-1359)
PHONE............................678 995-4607
James McCombs, *President*
EMP: 1
SALES (est): 79.3K **Privately Held**
SIC: 7372 7032 Prepackaged software; sporting camps

(G-9602)
JEANETTE ANN SMITH
Also Called: Handy Bus Shipg & Prtg Svc
3535 Tidewater Dr (23509-1333)
PHONE............................757 622-0182
Jeanette Smith, *Owner*
EMP: 3
SALES (est): 105.2K **Privately Held**
SIC: 2732 2752 4783 7331 Pamphlets: printing only, not published on site; business form & card printing, lithographic; packing goods for shipping; mailing list compilers; mailing service

(G-9603)
JH ENTERPRISE INC
233 W 30th St (23504-1519)
PHONE............................757 639-5049
Jerome Harriell, *CEO*
EMP: 1
SALES (est): 184.4K **Privately Held**
SIC: 2522 Office furniture, except wood

(G-9604)
JODYS INC (PA)
Also Called: Jody's Popcorn
2842 Cromwell Rd (23509-2408)
P.O. Box 1290, Virginia Beach (23451-0290)
PHONE............................757 422-8646
Jody M Wagner, *President*
Alan Wagner, *Vice Pres*
Melvin Hudson, *Plant Mgr*
Stephanie Herndon, *Bookkeeper*
Amanda Atkins, *Director*
▼ EMP: 17
SQ FT: 8,000
SALES (est): 1.2MM **Privately Held**
WEB: www.jodyspopcorn.com
SIC: 2064 Popcorn balls or other treated popcorn products; fudge (candy)

(G-9605)
JOHNSON CONTROLS
3750 Progress Rd (23502-1908)
PHONE............................757 853-6611
Jim Collins, *Manager*
EMP: 70 **Privately Held**
WEB: www.tycosimplexgrinnell.com
SIC: 3669 5087 Emergency alarms; fire-fighting equipment
HQ: Johnson Controls Fire Protection Lp
6600 Congress Ave
Boca Raton FL 33487
561 988-7200

(G-9606)
JONDA ENTERPRISE INC
1725 Canton Ave (23523-2307)
PHONE............................757 559-5793
Tara Davis, *Vice Pres*
EMP: 2
SALES (est): 116.7K **Privately Held**
SIC: 3731 7699 Lighters, marine: building & repairing; marine engine repair; marine propeller repair

(G-9607)
JOY VIRGINN-PLOT FUND FNDATION
150 W Brambleton Ave (23510-2018)
PHONE............................757 446-2000
EMP: 3
SALES (est): 347.8K **Privately Held**
WEB: www.pilotonline.com
SIC: 2711 Newspapers, publishing & printing

(G-9608)
JULIAN SWAIN BUILDERS INC
5618 E Virginia Bch Blvd (23502-2420)
PHONE............................757 490-0211
Susan B Swain, *CEO*
Julian Swain, *President*
Cynthia Jensen, *Treasurer*
EMP: 29
SQ FT: 20,000
SALES (est): 3.6MM **Privately Held**
WEB: www.julianswainbuilders.com
SIC: 2434 Wood kitchen cabinets

(G-9609)
JUPTIERS VAULT
5920 Adderley St (23502-4630)
PHONE............................757 404-9535
EMP: 3
SALES (est): 130K **Privately Held**
SIC: 3272 Mfg Concrete Products

(G-9610)
K HART HOLDING INC
938 Sutton St (23504-2534)
PHONE............................800 294-5348
Kenneth Hart, *President*
EMP: 3
SALES (est): 100.5K **Privately Held**
SIC: 3993 Signs, not made in custom sign painting shops

GEOGRAPHIC

(G-9611)
KAY KOLLECTIONS LLC
311 Walker Ave (23523-1538)
PHONE................757 901-7710
Lakeisha Keene, *Mng Member*
EMP: 5
SALES (est): 35K **Privately Held**
SIC: 3999 Hair, dressing of, for the trade

(G-9612)
KINGDOM MARKETPLACE INTL LLC (PA)
999 Waterside Dr Ste 2525 (23510-3316)
PHONE................757 524-4948
Bernard S Harrison, *Mng Member*
EMP: 2
SALES (est): 50K **Privately Held**
SIC: 2759 Advertising literature: printing

(G-9613)
KOMBUCHICK INC
2500 Church St (23504-1610)
PHONE................757 818-7703
EMP: 3 EST: 2015
SALES (est): 117.7K **Privately Held**
SIC: 2082 Malt beverages

(G-9614)
KRATOS TECH TRNING SLTIONS INC
5700 Lake Wright Dr # 103 (23502-1859)
PHONE................757 466-3660
EMP: 6 **Publicly Held**
SIC: 7372 8711 Prepackaged Software Services Engineering Services
HQ: Kratos Technology & Training Solutions, Inc.
4820 Estgate Mall Ste 200
San Diego CA 92131
858 812-7300

(G-9615)
LANDMARK COMMUNITY NEWSPAPERS
150 Granby St Fl 19 (23510-1604)
PHONE................502 633-4334
Michael G Abernathy, *Manager*
EMP: 1 EST: 1997
SALES (est): 58.5K **Privately Held**
SIC: 2711 Newspapers, publishing & printing
HQ: Landmark Community Newspapers, Llc
601 Taylorsville Rd
Shelbyville KY 40065
502 633-4334

(G-9616)
LANDMARK MEDIA ENTERPRISES LLC (PA)
150 Granby St (23510-1604)
PHONE................757 351-7000
Frank Batten Jr, *Ch of Bd*
Jack J Ross, *President*
Guy R Friddell III, *Exec VP*
Ritaf Graves, *Assistant VP*
Teresa F Blevins, *CFO*
EMP: 700
SQ FT: 500,000
SALES (est): 800MM **Privately Held**
WEB: www.landmarkmediaenterprises.com
SIC: 2711 5045 2721 6531 Commercial printing & newspaper publishing combined; computer software; periodicals; real estate listing services

(G-9617)
LANDMARK MILITARY NEWSPAPERS
150 W Brambleton Ave (23510-2018)
PHONE................254 690-9000
Dayle Izenvice, *President*
EMP: 1
SALES (est): 92.1K **Privately Held**
WEB: www.militarynews.com
SIC: 2711 Newspapers, publishing & printing

(G-9618)
LIFE PROTECT 24/7 INC
6160 Commander Pkwy (23502-5518)
PHONE................888 864-8403
Brad Peterson, *President*
EMP: 1

SALES (est): 165.7K **Privately Held**
WEB: www.lifeprotect247.com
SIC: 3669 8011 Emergency alarms; free-standing emergency medical center

(G-9619)
LIL DIVAS MOBILE SPA LLC
229 W 30th St Apt D (23504-1511)
PHONE................757 386-1455
Monica Mitchell,
EMP: 3
SALES (est): 80K **Privately Held**
SIC: 3421 Clippers, fingernail & toenail

(G-9620)
LISKEY & SONS INC
Also Called: Liskey and Sons Printing
1228 Ballentine Blvd (23504-3806)
PHONE................757 627-8712
Lee R Liskey, *President*
Ann P Liskey, *Exec VP*
Jeffrey Liskey, *Vice Pres*
Guy Liskey, *Treasurer*
Melissa Julian, *Manager*
▲ EMP: 14
SQ FT: 15,000
SALES (est): 2.4MM **Privately Held**
SIC: 2752 Commercial printing, offset

(G-9621)
LOKRING MID-ATLANTIC INC
2715 Monticello Ave Ste C (23517-1401)
P.O. Box 213 (23501-0213)
PHONE................757 423-2784
Matthew Nimershiem, *President*
David Schatz, *Technical Staff*
EMP: 1
SALES (est): 400K **Privately Held**
SIC: 3498 Fabricated pipe & fittings

(G-9622)
LONGS-ROULLET BOOKBINDERS INC
2800 Monticello Ave (23504-1620)
PHONE................757 623-4244
Alain A Roullet, *President*
Eileen Roullet, *Vice Pres*
EMP: 7 EST: 1975
SALES (est): 708.6K **Privately Held**
WEB: www.longs-roullet.com
SIC: 2789 Binding only: books, pamphlets, magazines, etc.

(G-9623)
LOYALTY DOCTORS LLC
Also Called: Mobile App Builder
182 Blades St (23503-4704)
PHONE................757 675-8283
Robert Farthing,
EMP: 2
SALES (est): 250K **Privately Held**
WEB: www.loyaltydoctors.com
SIC: 7372 Application computer software

(G-9624)
LUCK STONE CORPORATION
Also Called: Berkley Yard
508 E Indian River Rd (23523-1765)
PHONE................757 545-2020
Jim Herber, *Branch Mgr*
EMP: 21
SALES (corp-wide): 824.7MM **Privately Held**
WEB: www.luckstone.com
SIC: 1423 Crushed & broken granite
PA: Luck Stone Corporation
515 Stone Mill Dr
Manakin Sabot VA 23103
804 784-6300

(G-9625)
LYON SHIPYARD INC
1818 Brown Ave (23504-4458)
PHONE................757 622-4661
George Lyon, *President*
Ann Ackiss, *Principal*
Johnny E Gaskins, *Vice Pres*
Ken Kimball, *Vice Pres*
Douglas Boss, *Safety Mgr*
EMP: 303 EST: 1928
SQ FT: 30,000
SALES (est): 82.6MM **Privately Held**
WEB: www.lyonshipyard.com
SIC: 3731 Shipbuilding & repairing

(G-9626)
LYON SHIPYARD INC
1818 Brown Ave (23504-4458)
P.O. Box 2180 (23501-2180)
PHONE................757 622-4661
Fax: 757 623-4751
EMP: 21
SALES (est): 5.3MM **Privately Held**
SIC: 3731 Shipbuilding/Repairing

(G-9627)
M SHIELDS STUDIO INC
9628 18th Bay St (23518-1504)
PHONE................757 340-1670
Mark Shields, *Owner*
EMP: 1
SALES (est): 45.1K **Privately Held**
WEB: www.mshields.com
SIC: 3911 Jewelry, precious metal

(G-9628)
MACK MIMSEY
1319 Melrose Pkwy (23508-1703)
PHONE................757 777-6333
Mimsey Taylor, *CEO*
EMP: 2
SALES (est): 64.6K **Privately Held**
WEB: www.mimseymaccormack.com
SIC: 3931 Musical instruments

(G-9629)
MADE BY SANDY
1865 Branchwood St (23518-3121)
PHONE................757 588-1123
Sandy Dyer, *Owner*
EMP: 1
SALES (est): 42.2K **Privately Held**
SIC: 3944 Craft & hobby kits & sets

(G-9630)
MAERSK OIL TRADING INC
Also Called: Maersk Fluid Technology, Inc.
1 Commercial Pl (23510-2101)
PHONE................757 857-4800
Klaus Werner, *President*
Vijay Yalangi, *Superintendent*
Stacy Jarrell, *Production*
Susan Jackson, *Purch Agent*
Jeff Lee, *Purchasing*
EMP: 5
SALES (est): 269.6K
SALES (corp-wide): 1.9MM **Privately Held**
WEB: www.maersklinelimited.com
SIC: 3594 Motors: hydraulic, fluid power or air
HQ: Maersk Oil Trading And Investments A/S
Esplanaden 50
KObenhavn 1263
336 333-63

(G-9631)
MARCELL SGNTURE SCNTED CANDLES
9642 Sherwood Pl Apt 1 (23503-1737)
PHONE................757 502-5236
Virginia Purvis, *Principal*
EMP: 1
SALES (est): 39.6K **Privately Held**
SIC: 3999 Candles

(G-9632)
MARINE HYDRAULICS INTL LLC (HQ)
Also Called: Mhi Ship Repair & Services
543 E Indian River Rd (23523-1797)
PHONE................757 545-6400
Thomas Epley, *President*
Iftrue Homas Epley, *Exec VP*
Kim Lauterbach, *Vice Pres*
Michael E Walker, *Vice Pres*
Morris Maka, *Project Mgr*
EMP: 91
SQ FT: 60,000
SALES (est): 41.5MM **Privately Held**
WEB: www.mhi-shiprepair.com
SIC: 3731 7629 Military ships, building & repairing; electrical repair shops

(G-9633)
MASA CORPORATION (PA)
5445 Hennemon Dr Ste 200 (23513-2415)
P.O. Box 10263 (23513-0263)
PHONE................757 855-3013

Fraim Jr Thomas E, *CEO*
Wayne Prince, *COO*
Yulonda Robinson, *Purch Agent*
Ted Brackman, *Sales Mgr*
Bob Fowler, *Sales Staff*
▲ EMP: 65 EST: 1961
SQ FT: 25,000
SALES (est): 25MM **Privately Held**
WEB: www.masacorp.com
SIC: 2621 2672 5113 5199 Poster & art papers; coated & laminated paper; labels (unprinted), gummed: made from purchased materials; tape, pressure sensitive: made from purchased materials; shipping supplies; packaging materials; marking devices; chemical preparations

(G-9634)
MASA CORPORATION OF VIRGINIA (HQ)
5445 Hennemon Dr Ste 200 (23513-2415)
P.O. Box 10263 (23513-0263)
PHONE................757 855-3013
Thomas E Fraim, *President*
▲ EMP: 6
SQ FT: 12,000
SALES (est): 1.3MM
SALES (corp-wide): 25MM **Privately Held**
WEB: www.masacorp.com
SIC: 3555 Printing presses
PA: The Masa Corporation
5445 Hennemon Dr Ste 200
Norfolk VA 23513
757 855-3013

(G-9635)
MAZZIKA LLC
4800 Colley Ave Ste D (23508-2162)
PHONE................757 489-0028
EMP: 1
SALES (est): 102.5K **Privately Held**
SIC: 3421 Table & food cutlery, including butchers'

(G-9636)
MEDICAL LABORATORY SOLUTIONS
5635 Raby Rd Ste H (23502-2465)
PHONE................414 425-8605
EMP: 2
SALES (est): 181.7K **Privately Held**
WEB: www.medtestdx.com
SIC: 3826 Analytical instruments

(G-9637)
MEETINGSPHERE INC
440 Monticello Ave # 1875 (23510-2571)
PHONE................703 348-0725
Neal Bastick, *President*
Wolfram Hoegel, *Vice Pres*
Tim Burgess, *Accounting Mgr*
EMP: 20
SALES (est): 1.1MM **Privately Held**
WEB: www.meetingsphere.com
SIC: 7372 Business oriented computer software

(G-9638)
MERIDIAN PRINTING & PUBLISHING
1228 Ballentine Blvd (23504-3806)
PHONE................757 627-8712
Theresa Liskey, *President*
Luchie Rogers, *Plant Mgr*
Terri Liskey, *Sales Mgr*
EMP: 1
SALES (est): 113.2K **Privately Held**
WEB: www.liskeyprinting.com
SIC: 2752 Commercial printing, offset

(G-9639)
MERMAID VINEYARD & WINERY LLC
330 W 22nd St Ste 106 (23517-2136)
PHONE................757 233-4155
Jennifer Eichert, *Principal*
EMP: 5
SALES (est): 512K **Privately Held**
WEB: www.mermaidwinery.com
SIC: 2084 Wines

▲ = Import ▼=Export
◆ =Import/Export

(G-9640)
MERWINS AFFORDABLE GRINDING
5412 Pine Grove Ave (23502-4925)
PHONE.................................757 461-3405
Jeffrey Merwin, *Principal*
▲ EMP: 2
SALES (est): 128.1K **Privately Held**
SIC: 3599 Grinding castings for the trade

(G-9641)
METRO MACHINE CORP (HQ)
Also Called: General Dynmics Nassco-Norfolk
200 Ligon St (23523-1000)
P.O. Box 1860 (23501-1860)
PHONE.................................757 543-6801
Frederick J Harris, *President*
Steve Miley, *General Mgr*
John Stram, *General Mgr*
Wade Hyatt, *Project Mgr*
Dave Rogalski, *Buyer*
▲ EMP: 400 EST: 1963
SALES (est): 260.1MM
SALES (corp-wide): 39.3B **Publicly Held**
WEB: www.nassconorfolk.com
SIC: 3731 Military ships, building & repairing
PA: General Dynamics Corporation
11011 Sunset Hills Rd
Reston VA 20190
703 876-3000

(G-9642)
MHI HOLDINGS LLC
543 E Indian River Rd (23523-1717)
PHONE.................................757 545-6400
Victor Brannon,
EMP: 328
SQ FT: 30,000
SALES (est): 189.8K
SALES (corp-wide): 3.3B **Publicly Held**
WEB: www.mhi-shiprepair.com
SIC: 3731 Shipbuilding & repairing
HQ: Vigor Industrial Llc
5555 N Channel Ave # 71
Portland OR 97217
503 247-1777

(G-9643)
MID VALLEY PRODUCTS
902 Cooke Ave (23504-3438)
PHONE.................................757 625-0780
▼ EMP: 1
SALES (est): 88.1K **Privately Held**
SIC: 3496 Mfg Misc Fabricated Wire Products

(G-9644)
MIL-SPEC ABRASIVES LLC
3306 Peterson St (23509-2415)
PHONE.................................757 927-6699
Jerrold Miller,
Daniel Wood,
EMP: 10
SALES (est): 1MM **Privately Held**
WEB: www.milspecabrasives.us
SIC: 3291 Abrasive products

(G-9645)
MINDFUL MEDIA LLC
914 Gates Ave (23517-1621)
PHONE.................................757 627-5151
Ellen Fitzenrider,
EMP: 1
SALES (est): 74K **Privately Held**
SIC: 2731 Book publishing

(G-9646)
MINUTE MAN PRESS
2961 Heutte Dr (23518-4624)
PHONE.................................757 464-6509
EMP: 2
SALES (est): 83.9K **Privately Held**
WEB: www.minutemanpress.com
SIC: 2752 Commercial printing, lithographic

(G-9647)
MOBILE LINK VIRGINA LLC
7862 Tidewater Dr Ste 109 (23505-3711)
PHONE.................................757 583-8300
EMP: 1
SALES (est): 73.7K **Privately Held**
SIC: 3949 Cricket equipment, general

(G-9648)
MONARCH MANUFACTURING WORKS
101 W Main St Ste 900 (23510-1653)
PHONE.................................757 640-3727
Joel Weaver, *Principal*
EMP: 2 **EST:** 2010
SALES (est): 78K **Privately Held**
SIC: 3999 Manufacturing industries

(G-9649)
MR LUCK INC
619 Baldwin Ave (23517-1811)
P.O. Box 246, Greentown PA (18426-0246)
PHONE.................................570 766-8734
Michael Luck, *Principal*
EMP: 5 **EST:** 2008
SALES (est): 454.5K **Privately Held**
SIC: 2452 Log cabins, prefabricated, wood

(G-9650)
MSP GROUP LLC
3490 E Virginia Bch Blvd (23502-3123)
PHONE.................................757 855-5416
Scott Samter, *Mng Member*
EMP: 8 **EST:** 2013
SALES (est): 1MM **Privately Held**
WEB: www.mspdesigngroup.com
SIC: 3552 Textile machinery

(G-9651)
MUSE WRITERS CENTER
2200 Colonial Ave Ste 3 (23517-1915)
PHONE.................................757 818-9880
EMP: 1
SALES (est): 61.3K **Privately Held**
WEB: www.the-muse.org
SIC: 2741 Miscellaneous publishing

(G-9652)
MYSTIQUE QUEEN PUBLISHING LLC
915 Briar Hill Rd (23502-3520)
PHONE.................................484 250-1131
Danika Wright,
EMP: 1
SALES (est): 5K **Privately Held**
SIC: 2731 Books: publishing only

(G-9653)
NATASHA MATTHEW
Also Called: Zenobiabooks
713 Stanwix Sq (23502-3905)
PHONE.................................757 407-1897
Natasha Matthew, *Principal*
EMP: 2
SALES (est): 56.5K **Privately Held**
SIC: 2731 Books: publishing & printing

(G-9654)
NEON DISTRICT
759 Granby St (23510-2010)
PHONE.................................757 663-6970
EMP: 3
SALES (est): 123.2K **Privately Held**
WEB: www.downtownnorfolk.org
SIC: 2813 Neon

(G-9655)
NEON NIGHTS
2640 Arkansas Ave (23513-4402)
PHONE.................................757 857-6366
James Tolbert, *Owner*
EMP: 2
SALES (est): 155.1K **Privately Held**
WEB: www.neon-nights.net
SIC: 3993 Neon signs

(G-9656)
NEON NIGHTS INC
1555 Shelton Ave (23502-1728)
PHONE.................................757 248-5676
EMP: 1 **EST:** 2017
SALES (est): 46K **Privately Held**
SIC: 3993 Mfg Signs/Advertising Specialties

(G-9657)
NETS PIX & THINGS LLC
132 Kidd Blvd (23502-5214)
PHONE.................................757 466-1337
Jeanette Artis,
Stanley Artis,
EMP: 2

SALES (est): 85K **Privately Held**
SIC: 2759 Screen printing

(G-9658)
NEU AGE SPORTSWEAR
7502 Rosefield Dr (23513-1020)
PHONE.................................757 581-8333
Stanley Walden, *Principal*
EMP: 2
SALES (est): 130K **Privately Held**
SIC: 2329 7389 Men's & boys' sportswear & athletic clothing; business services

(G-9659)
NEW AGE REPR & FABRICATION LLC
871 Cedar St Apt 307 (23523-1857)
PHONE.................................757 819-3887
Kenyatta Headen,
EMP: 1
SALES (est): 59.9K **Privately Held**
SIC: 7692 7389 3731 Welding repair; brazing; ; barges, building & repairing

(G-9660)
NEW JOURNAL AND GUIDE INC
5127 E Virginia Beach Blv (23502-3489)
P.O. Box 209 (23501-0209)
PHONE.................................757 543-6531
Brenda Andrews, *President*
EMP: 14
SQ FT: 2,200
SALES (est): 790.6K **Privately Held**
WEB: www.thenewjournalandguide.com
SIC: 2711 Newspapers, publishing & printing

(G-9661)
NEW PARADIGM PUBLISHING LLC
609 W Little Creek Rd (23505-2021)
PHONE.................................757 423-3385
Laura Jackson Loo, *Principal*
EMP: 1
SALES (est): 37.5K **Privately Held**
SIC: 2741 Miscellaneous publishing

(G-9662)
NEW WAVE THRIFTY LLC
710 Sycamore St (23523-2346)
PHONE.................................904 400-8539
James Rivers III,
EMP: 1
SALES (est): 125K **Privately Held**
SIC: 2519 Furniture, household: glass, fiberglass & plastic

(G-9663)
NEWPORT INDUSTRIES LTD
416 Boush St (23510-1252)
PHONE.................................440 208-3322
EMP: 1
SALES (est): 49.1K **Privately Held**
SIC: 3999 Manufacturing industries

(G-9664)
NEXT LEVEL PRINTING
833 W 41st St (23508-2517)
P.O. Box 6133 (23508-0133)
PHONE.................................757 288-1399
Lundy T Shannel, *Principal*
EMP: 2 **EST:** 2014
SALES (est): 122.8K **Privately Held**
WEB: www.nextlevelprintingva.com
SIC: 2752 Commercial printing, offset

(G-9665)
NO LIMITS LLC
7862 Tidewater Dr (23505-3711)
PHONE.................................757 729-5612
EMP: 2 **EST:** 2012
SALES (est): 111.9K **Privately Held**
SIC: 2326 Men's & boys' work clothing

(G-9666)
NORFOLK MACHINE AND WLDG INC
1028 W 27th St (23517-1019)
P.O. Box 11173 (23517-0173)
PHONE.................................757 489-0330
Mallard M Josephine, *CEO*
Bobby H Mallard, *President*
M Josephine Mallard, *Vice Pres*
Peter F McCoy, *Vice Pres*
EMP: 27

SALES (est): 4.4MM **Privately Held**
WEB: www.norfolkmachine.com
SIC: 3599 7699 7692 Machine shop, jobbing & repair; industrial machinery & equipment repair; welding repair

(G-9667)
NORFOLK PRINTING CO
805 Granby St (23510-2003)
PHONE.................................757 627-1302
Michael Phelps, *President*
Donnie Parker, *President*
EMP: 8 **EST:** 1933
SQ FT: 2,500
SALES (est): 1.1MM **Privately Held**
WEB: www.norfolkprintingcompany.com
SIC: 2752 Commercial printing, offset

(G-9668)
NORFOLK TENT COMPANY INC
2633 Wyoming Ave (23513-4437)
P.O. Box 6978, Chesapeake (23323-0978)
PHONE.................................757 461-7330
Lisa S Trainor, *President*
Tim Trainer, *Vice Pres*
▲ EMP: 10
SQ FT: 11,000
SALES (est): 550K **Privately Held**
WEB: www.norfolktents.com
SIC: 2394 Tents: made from purchased materials

(G-9669)
NORTHFIELD MEDICAL MFG LLC (PA)
Also Called: Oshakits
5505 Robin Hood Rd Ste B (23513-2423)
PHONE.................................800 270-0153
Carter Smith, *Engineer*
Owen Griffin, *Mng Member*
EMP: 23
SALES (est): 5.1MM **Privately Held**
WEB: www.northfieldmanufacturing.com
SIC: 3841 5999 3851 3842 Surgical & medical instruments; cleaning equipment & supplies; protective eyeware; clothing, fire resistant & protective; medical equipment & supplies

(G-9670)
NORVA PLASTICS INC
3911 Killam Ave (23508-2632)
P.O. Box 6226 (23508-0226)
PHONE.................................757 622-9281
Howard H Everton, *President*
EMP: 16 **EST:** 1975
SQ FT: 38,500
SALES (est): 3.1MM **Privately Held**
WEB: www.norvaplastics.com
SIC: 3089 Injection molding of plastics

(G-9671)
OCEAN MARINE LLC
543 E Indian River Rd (23523-1717)
PHONE.................................757 222-1306
M Walker, *CEO*
EMP: 2
SALES (est): 136.7K **Privately Held**
SIC: 3731 Shipbuilding & repairing

(G-9672)
OFFICE ELECTRONICS INC
225 W Olney Rd (23510-1523)
PHONE.................................757 622-8001
Chris Smith, *Principal*
EMP: 2 **EST:** 2016
SALES (est): 73.2K **Privately Held**
SIC: 2759 Commercial printing

(G-9673)
OFFICE FURNITURE OUTLET INC (PA)
5595 Raby Rd Ste 3 (23502-2460)
PHONE.................................757 855-5522
Lawrence E Iverson, *President*
Susan Boatwright, *Vice Pres*
Liz Boatwright, *Sales Staff*
EMP: 7
SQ FT: 65,000
SALES (est): 2.8MM **Privately Held**
WEB: www.ofova.com
SIC: 2522 2521 2542 Office furniture, except wood; wood office furniture; partitions & fixtures, except wood

GEOGRAPHIC

(G-9674)
OLD COOTS LLC
6032 Prince Ave (23502-2625)
PHONE..................................757 713-2888
Henry Wedderburn, *Principal*
EMP: 2
SALES (est): 56.9K **Privately Held**
WEB: www.oldcootsbbq.com
SIC: 2033 5149 Barbecue sauce: packaged in cans, jars, etc.; sauces

(G-9675)
OLD WORLD LABS LLC
888 Magazine Ln Apt 3d (23510-2031)
PHONE..................................800 282-0386
Nicholas Liverman, *Principal*
EMP: 2
SALES (est): 266.1K **Privately Held**
WEB: www.oldworldlabs.com
SIC: 3555 7372 3577 Printing trades machinery; application computer software; computer peripheral equipment

(G-9676)
OMNI REPAIR COMPANY
3313 Tait Ter (23513-4427)
PHONE..................................757 853-1220
Malcolm V Burns, *Owner*
EMP: 4
SQ FT: 2,500
SALES (est): 250K **Privately Held**
SIC: 3599 Machine shop, jobbing & repair

(G-9677)
OPTA (USA) INC
902 Cooke Ave (23504-3438)
PHONE..................................843 296-7074
Daniel Bancroft, *Sales Staff*
James Wilson, *Branch Mgr*
EMP: 4
SALES (corp-wide): 1.1B **Privately Held**
WEB: www.optagroupllc.com
SIC: 3295 3356 3325 Minerals, ground or treated; magnesium; steel foundries
HQ: Opta (Usa) Inc.
   300 Corporate Pkwy
   Amherst NY 14226
   716 446-8914

(G-9678)
OUT OF PRINT LLC
1449 Westover Ave (23507-1027)
PHONE..................................919 368-0980
Joseph Clayton Hoyt, *Administration*
EMP: 2
SALES (est): 92.3K **Privately Held**
SIC: 2752 Commercial printing, lithographic

(G-9679)
OVER 9000 MEDIA LLC
1360 Hilton St Apt 6 (23518-4048)
PHONE..................................850 210-7114
Faraji F Jackson,
Jason Eugene,
David J Washington,
EMP: 3 EST: 2014
SALES (est): 103K **Privately Held**
SIC: 2759 7336 7374 Commercial printing; graphic arts & related design; computer graphics service

(G-9680)
PALIDORI LLC
901 Goff St Apt 170 (23504-2749)
PHONE..................................757 609-1134
Raeven Spady,
EMP: 1
SALES (est): 42.5K **Privately Held**
SIC: 2326 Men's & boys' work clothing

(G-9681)
PANDA KITCHEN AND BATH VA LLC
Also Called: Panda Kitchen & Bath
3587 Argonne Ave (23509-2156)
PHONE..................................757 889-9888
Eddie Siu, *Manager*
EMP: 1 **Privately Held**
WEB: www.pandakitchenva.com
SIC: 2434 Wood kitchen cabinets
PA: Panda Kitchen And Bath Of Virginia Llc
   3852 Virginia Beach Blvd
   Virginia Beach VA 23452

(G-9682)
PARAMOUNT INDUS COMPANIES INC
Also Called: Paramount Sleep
1112 Kingwood Ave (23502-5603)
PHONE..................................757 855-3321
Arthur Diamonstein, *Ch of Bd*
Richard Fleck, *President*
Richard Diamonstein, *Managing Dir*
◆ EMP: 125 EST: 1935
SQ FT: 70,000
SALES (est): 22.9MM **Privately Held**
WEB: www.paramountsleep.com
SIC: 2515 Mattresses, innerspring or box spring

(G-9683)
PEPSI BEVERAGES COMPANY
1194 Pineridge Rd (23502-2025)
PHONE..................................757 857-1251
EMP: 7
SALES (est): 461.9K **Privately Held**
WEB: www.pepsico.com
SIC: 2086 Carbonated soft drinks, bottled & canned

(G-9684)
PEPSI-COLA METRO BTLG CO INC
1194 Pineridge Rd (23502-2025)
PHONE..................................757 857-1251
Dave Fitts, *Sales/Mktg Mgr*
Mark Henley, *Sales Staff*
Lawrence Majette, *Sales Staff*
Kenneth Burroughs, *Supervisor*
EMP: 155
SALES (corp-wide): 67.1B **Publicly Held**
WEB: www.pepsico.com
SIC: 2086 Carbonated soft drinks, bottled & canned
HQ: Pepsi-Cola Metropolitan Bottling Company, Inc.
   1111 Westchester Ave
   White Plains NY 10604
   914 767-6000

(G-9685)
PERATON INC
5365 Robin Hood Rd Ste A3 (23513-2416)
PHONE..................................757 857-0099
James Conkle, *Manager*
EMP: 20
SALES (corp-wide): 2.3B **Privately Held**
WEB: www.peraton.com
SIC: 3663 Radio & TV communications equipment
HQ: Peraton Inc.
   12975 Worldgate Dr # 100
   Herndon VA 20170

(G-9686)
PHIL MORGAN
Also Called: Installers
3 Interstate Corp Ctr (23502)
PHONE..................................757 455-9475
Phil Morgan, *Owner*
Jackie Shaw, *Info Tech Mgr*
EMP: 1
SALES (est): 73.8K **Privately Held**
SIC: 1389 Construction, repair & dismantling services

(G-9687)
PHILADELPHIA RIVERBOAT LLC
870 N Military Hwy # 200 (23502-3638)
PHONE..................................757 640-9205
Thomas J Damato, *Manager*
EMP: 5
SALES (est): 410K **Privately Held**
SIC: 7372 Prepackaged software

(G-9688)
PIERSIDE MARINE INDUSTRIES
2614 Wyoming Ave (23513-4438)
PHONE..................................757 852-9571
▲ EMP: 20
SQ FT: 7,500
SALES (est): 1.2MM **Privately Held**
SIC: 3731 Ship Repair

(G-9689)
PILOT MEDIA
Also Called: Home Search Magazine
150 W Brambleton Ave (23510-2018)
PHONE..................................757 446-2000
Linda Garner, *Principal*
Corey Kenner, *Sales Staff*
Barbara Curtiss, *Manager*
Carol Young, *Executive*
EMP: 2
SALES (est): 233.3K **Privately Held**
WEB: www.mypilotmedia.com
SIC: 2711 Newspapers, publishing & printing

(G-9690)
PITNEY BOWES INC
5301 Robin Hood Rd (23513-2419)
PHONE..................................757 322-8000
George Flamman, *Manager*
EMP: 35
SALES (corp-wide): 3.2B **Publicly Held**
WEB: www.pitneybowes.com
SIC: 3579 7359 Postage meters; business machine & electronic equipment rental services
PA: Pitney Bowes Inc.
   3001 Summer St
   Stamford CT 06905
   203 356-5000

(G-9691)
POETICA PUBLISHING COMPANY
900 Granby St Ste 122 (23510-2503)
PHONE..................................757 617-0821
EMP: 1 EST: 2017
SALES (est): 52.1K **Privately Held**
WEB: www.poeticamagazine.com
SIC: 2741 Miscellaneous publishing

(G-9692)
POSTAL MECHANICAL SYSTEMS
3460 Trant Ave (23502-3117)
PHONE..................................757 424-2872
Raul Matos, *General Mgr*
Ralph Bollinger, *Mng Member*
EMP: 18
SALES (est): 1MM **Privately Held**
SIC: 3731 Shipbuilding & repairing

(G-9693)
POWER CATCH INC
2715 Monticello Ave Ste A (23517-1401)
PHONE..................................757 962-0999
Fadi Debbas, *President*
EMP: 3
SALES (est): 332.3K **Privately Held**
WEB: www.powercatch.net
SIC: 3612 Transformers, except electric

(G-9694)
PRECISION SHEETMETAL INC
3200 S Cape Henry Ave (23504-3156)
PHONE..................................757 389-5730
Kristin Holiman-Brown, *Principal*
EMP: 8
SALES (est): 1.3MM **Privately Held**
WEB: www.precisionsheetmetalva.com
SIC: 3444 Sheet metalwork

(G-9695)
PRIME 3 SOFTWARE INC
201 E City Hall Ave (23510-1797)
PHONE..................................757 763-8560
Christopher Ruddick, *CEO*
EMP: 1
SALES (est): 72.5K **Privately Held**
WEB: www.prime3software.com
SIC: 7372 7373 Prepackaged software; computer systems analysis & design; systems software development services; systems integration services; systems engineering, computer related

(G-9696)
PRIVATEER INDUSTRIES LLC
4600 Village Ave Ste 100 (23502-2060)
PHONE..................................757 857-7273
L Scott Seymour, *Administration*
EMP: 2
SALES (est): 96.5K **Privately Held**
SIC: 3999 Manufacturing industries

(G-9697)
PROFESSIONAL WELDING SVC INC
2300 Florida Ave (23513-4518)
PHONE..................................757 853-9371
Kathy Downs, *President*
Warren Downs, *Vice Pres*
EMP: 9
SALES (est): 300K **Privately Held**
WEB: www.professionalweldinginc.com
SIC: 7692 3441 3444 Welding repair; fabricated structural metal; sheet metalwork

(G-9698)
PROGRAM SERVICES LLC (DH)
Also Called: Northstar Training
150 W Brambleton Ave (23510-2018)
PHONE..................................757 222-3990
EMP: 8
SQ FT: 20,000
SALES (est): 4.1MM **Publicly Held**
WEB: www.militarynews.com
SIC: 2711 2791 2789 2759 Newspapers: publishing only, not printed on site; typesetting; bookbinding & related work; commercial printing; commercial printing, lithographic
HQ: Virginian-Pilot Media Companies, Llc
   5429 Greenwich Rd
   Virginia Beach VA 23462
   757 446-9000

(G-9699)
PROVIA BIOLOGICS LTD
124 E 40th St (23504-1006)
PHONE..................................757 305-9263
Dean Troyer, *Partner*
Margaret Troyer, *Partner*
EMP: 2
SALES (est): 100K **Privately Held**
WEB: www.proviabiologics.com
SIC: 2835 Cytology & histology diagnostic agents; in vitro diagnostics

(G-9700)
QUALITY STAMP CO
3338 Cromwell Dr (23509-2640)
PHONE..................................757 858-0653
Joseph R Kaplan, *Owner*
EMP: 1
SQ FT: 1,500
SALES (est): 54.4K **Privately Held**
WEB: www.qualitystampco.com
SIC: 3953 2752 5943 Textile marking stamps, hand: rubber or metal; commercial printing, offset; office forms & supplies

(G-9701)
RAMSEY MANUFACTURING LLC
Also Called: US Float Tanks
431 W 25th St (23517-1243)
PHONE..................................757 232-9034
James Ramsey, *Partner*
Steven Ramsey, *Partner*
EMP: 4
SALES (est): 340K **Privately Held**
WEB: www.superiorfloattanks.com
SIC: 3841 Surgical & medical instruments

(G-9702)
REAL IS RARE LABEL LLC
854 48th St (23508-2016)
PHONE..................................757 705-1850
Devante Batts,
EMP: 1
SALES (est): 10K **Privately Held**
SIC: 2782 Record albums

(G-9703)
REALTA LIFE SCIENCES INC
5665 Lowery Rd Ste 100 (23502-2246)
PHONE..................................757 418-4842
Ulrich Thienel, *CEO*
Kenji Cunnion, *Principal*
Neel Krishna, *Principal*
Thomas McCarter, *Principal*
EMP: 3
SALES (est): 465.9K **Privately Held**
WEB: www.realtalifesciences.com
SIC: 2834 Pharmaceutical preparations

(G-9704)
REDDY ICE CORPORATION
1129 Production Rd (23502-1917)
PHONE..................................757 855-6065
John Dillon, *Manager*
Gilbert Segovia, *Analyst*
EMP: 21 **Privately Held**
WEB: www.reddyice.com
SIC: 2097 Manufactured ice

HQ: Reddy Ice Corporation
5720 Lyndon B Johnson Fwy # 200
Dallas TX 75240
214 526-6740

(G-9705)
REESE KYNDAL
Also Called: Getxlaced
130 Brooke Ave Apt 213 (23510-1842)
PHONE...................................757 718-0525
Kyndal Reese, *Owner*
EMP: 1
SALES (est): 50K **Privately Held**
SIC: 3999 Hair & hair-based products

(G-9706)
REIGNFOREST SPICES & TEA LLC
2704 Westminster Ave (23504-4528)
PHONE...................................757 716-5205
Tiquerra Brown,
EMP: 2
SALES (est): 62.3K **Privately Held**
SIC: 2099 Tea blending

(G-9707)
RH CERAMICS
8500 Tidewater Dr Apt 36 (23503-5557)
PHONE...................................760 880-4088
Richard Holk, *Owner*
EMP: 1
SALES (est): 39.7K **Privately Held**
SIC: 3229 Tableware, glass or glass ceramic

(G-9708)
RIFLE BUILDING LLC
8168 Ships Crossing Rd (23518-3589)
PHONE...................................518 879-9195
Wesley Hitt,
EMP: 2 EST: 2017
SALES (est): 73.4K **Privately Held**
SIC: 3484 Small arms

(G-9709)
ROLAND VAULT LTD
Also Called: Roland Vault Limited
1159 Harmony Rd (23502-2356)
PHONE...................................757 466-8800
Tom Roland, *President*
EMP: 21
SQ FT: 24,200
SALES (est): 2.5MM **Privately Held**
WEB: www.rolandvaults.com
SIC: 3272 Burial vaults, concrete or precast terrazzo

(G-9710)
ROSEANN COMBS
Also Called: Northstar Industrial Electric
3407 Chesapeake Blvd (23513-4040)
PHONE...................................757 228-1795
Roseann Combs, *Owner*
EMP: 6
SALES (est): 150K **Privately Held**
SIC: 3699 1731 Electrical equipment & supplies; electrical work

(G-9711)
ROYAL SILVER MFG CO INC
3300 Chesapeake Blvd (23513-4099)
PHONE...................................757 855-6004
Lloyd M Gilbert Jr, *President*
Anne G Morgan, *Corp Secy*
EMP: 10 EST: 1907
SQ FT: 36,000
SALES (est): 1MM **Privately Held**
WEB: www.rschrome.com
SIC: 3471 3914 3949 Plating of metals or formed products; flatware, stainless steel; lures, fishing: artificial

(G-9712)
RUBINAS ADORNMENTS INC
712 Michigan Ave (23508-2925)
PHONE...................................757 623-4246
Anna Prather, *Principal*
EMP: 2
SALES (est): 97.2K **Privately Held**
SIC: 3911 Jewelry, precious metal

(G-9713)
S&D INDUSTRIES LLC
1070 Joyner St (23513-1836)
PHONE...................................901 208-5036

Erica Maina,
EMP: 1
SALES (est): 39.6K **Privately Held**
SIC: 3999 Manufacturing industries

(G-9714)
SAN FRANCISCO BAY PRESS
522 Spotswood Ave Apt C5 (23517-2046)
PHONE...................................757 412-5642
EMP: 1
SALES (est): 37.5K **Privately Held**
SIC: 2741 Miscellaneous publishing

(G-9715)
SC MEDICAL OVERSEAS INC
Also Called: Orfit Industries America
810 Ford Dr Ste A (23523-2406)
P.O. Box 6, Trenton TN (38382-0006)
PHONE...................................516 935-8500
Steven A Cuypres, *President*
Martin Ratner, *Vice Pres*
◆ EMP: 9
SALES (est): 780K **Privately Held**
WEB: www.orfit.com
SIC: 2821 Plastics materials & resins

(G-9716)
SEA MARINE LLC
1301 Monticello Ave (23510-2613)
P.O. Box 66206, Virginia Beach (23466-6206)
PHONE...................................757 528-9869
Denardo Christia,
EMP: 10
SALES (est): 100.8K **Privately Held**
SIC: 7692 Welding repair

(G-9717)
SENIOR PUBL FREE SENIORITY
Also Called: Commonwealth Printing
143 Granby St (23510-1611)
PHONE...................................757 222-3900
EMP: 25
SALES (est): 1.2MM **Privately Held**
SIC: 2721 Periodicals

(G-9718)
SEVEN SEVENS INC
Also Called: Best Printing
879 Poplar Hall Dr (23502-3715)
PHONE...................................757 340-1300
Curtis Hoessly, *President*
Donetta Elrod, *Accountant*
Megan Zelinko, *Graphic Designe*
EMP: 4
SALES (est): 459.5K **Privately Held**
WEB: www.allegramarketingprint.com
SIC: 2752 Commercial printing, offset

(G-9719)
SEXTANT SOLUTIONS GROUP LLC
501 Boush St Ste B (23510-1400)
PHONE...................................757 797-4353
Brian Donegan, *Principal*
EMP: 4
SALES (est): 184.8K **Privately Held**
SIC: 3812 Sextants

(G-9720)
SFI PARTNERS CLUB
225 W Olney Rd Ste 300 (23510-1523)
PHONE...................................757 622-8001
Timothy Schriner, *Principal*
EMP: 1
SALES (est): 99.7K **Privately Held**
SIC: 2679 Paper products, converted

(G-9721)
SHARON SOLOMON
Also Called: Just Braids By Sharon Solomon
5417 Beckner St (23509-2122)
PHONE...................................757 515-2325
Sharon Solomon, *Owner*
EMP: 1
SALES (est): 30K **Privately Held**
SIC: 3999 Hair, dressing of, for the trade

(G-9722)
SHORE DRIVE SELF STORAGE CORP
8110 Shore Dr (23518-2431)
PHONE...................................757 587-6000
Charles L Bashara, *President*
EMP: 1

SALES (est): 132K **Privately Held**
SIC: 2511 Storage chests, household: wood

(G-9723)
SIEMENS INDUSTRY INC
Also Called: Siemens Building Technologies
5301 Robin Hood Rd # 118 (23513-2419)
PHONE...................................757 490-6026
Jeff Suber, *Engineer*
Jason Sanker, *Manager*
Tom Krotzer, *Manager*
Mike Tasch, *Manager*
Nick Cassevah, *Executive*
EMP: 55
SALES (corp-wide): 67.4B **Privately Held**
WEB: www.new.siemens.com
SIC: 3822 3585 Auto controls regulating residntl & coml environmt & applncs; refrigeration & heating equipment
HQ: Siemens Industry, Inc.
1000 Deerfield Pkwy
Buffalo Grove IL 60089
847 215-1000

(G-9724)
SIFCO APPLIED SRFC CNCEPTS LLC
Also Called: Sifco Selective Plating
1333 Azalea Garden Rd F (23502-1933)
PHONE...................................757 855-4305
John Quiocho, *Manager*
EMP: 4
SALES (corp-wide): 7.1MM **Privately Held**
WEB: www.sifcoasc.com
SIC: 3471 Electroplating of metals or formed products
PA: Sifco Applied Surface Concepts, Llc
5708 E Schaaf Rd
Cleveland OH 44131
216 524-0099

(G-9725)
SIGNS TO GO
645 Church St Ste 102 (23510-1712)
PHONE...................................757 622-7446
Antoine Dee, *President*
EMP: 1 EST: 2018
SALES (est): 46K **Privately Held**
SIC: 3993 Signs & advertising specialties

(G-9726)
SMITHFIELD PACKAGED MEATS CORP
435 E Indian River Rd (23523-1755)
PHONE...................................757 357-4321
W F Rushing, *General Mgr*
Darden Hurt, *Business Mgr*
EMP: 70 **Privately Held**
WEB: www.johnmorrell.com
SIC: 2011 Meat packing plants
HQ: Smithfield Packaged Meats Corp.
805 E Kemper Rd
Cincinnati OH 45246
513 782-3800

(G-9727)
SNIPS OF VIRGINIA BEACH INC
Also Called: Snips of Vb Coast To Coast
888 Norfolk Sq (23502-3210)
PHONE...................................888 634-5008
Mike Miller, *President*
EMP: 11
SQ FT: 6,000
SALES (est): 1.2MM **Privately Held**
WEB: www.snipsofvb.com
SIC: 2261 2395 Screen printing of cotton broadwoven fabrics; embroidery & art needlework

(G-9728)
SOAP N SUDS LAUDROMATS
2515 Colley Ave (23517-1129)
PHONE...................................757 313-0515
Anthony Polozos, *Principal*
EMP: 2
SALES (est): 134.4K **Privately Held**
SIC: 3589 Car washing machinery

(G-9729)
SOC LLC
5426 Robin Hood Rd (23513-2447)
PHONE...................................757 857-6400
Mike Littlejohn, *General Mgr*
Dave Williams, *General Mgr*

Jason Eubank, *Program Mgr*
George H Warren,
▼ EMP: 10
SALES (est): 750K
SALES (corp-wide): 1.7B **Privately Held**
SIC: 3731 1541 Military ships, building & repairing; renovation, remodeling & repairs: industrial buildings
PA: The Day & Zimmermann Group Inc
1500 Spring Garden St
Philadelphia PA 19130
215 299-8000

(G-9730)
SORRENTINO MARIANI & COMPANY (PA)
2701 Saint Julian Ave (23504-2619)
PHONE...................................757 624-9025
Virgil R Mariani, *CEO*
Felicia Mariani, *Ch of Bd*
Jon Turner, *Prdtn Mgr*
Allen Nichols, *Warehouse Mgr*
David Mariani, *Engineer*
▲ EMP: 53 EST: 1996
SQ FT: 60,000
SALES (est): 8MM **Privately Held**
WEB: www.smfurniture.com
SIC: 2599 Hotel furniture

(G-9731)
SOUTH BAY INDUSTRIES INC
415 W 24th St (23517-1204)
PHONE...................................757 489-9344
Robert Jennette, *President*
EMP: 4
SALES (est): 594.9K **Privately Held**
WEB: www.southbayny.com
SIC: 2599 8742 Ship furniture; industry specialist consultants

(G-9732)
SOUTHERN CASTING LLC
1159 Lance Rd Ste B (23502-2472)
PHONE...................................757 233-1700
William Edwards, *Administration*
EMP: 6
SALES (est): 821K **Privately Held**
SIC: 3369 Nonferrous foundries

(G-9733)
STANDARD WELDING CORP
830 W 40th St (23508-2514)
PHONE...................................757 423-0470
Ralph Davis Jr, *President*
Ronald Davis, *Treasurer*
EMP: 3
SALES (est): 348.3K **Privately Held**
WEB: www.standardweldingcorp.com
SIC: 7692 Welding repair

(G-9734)
STEFFAN LOTT
Also Called: Bdrc USA LLC
326 W Mcginnis Cir (23502-5223)
PHONE...................................786 366-9494
Steffan Lott, *Owner*
EMP: 1
SALES (est): 120K **Privately Held**
SIC: 2211 Apparel & outerwear fabrics, cotton

(G-9735)
STRONG INDUSTRIES LLC
1001 W 27th St (23517-1018)
PHONE...................................757 533-9100
EMP: 2
SALES (est): 91.4K **Privately Held**
SIC: 3949 Sporting & athletic goods

(G-9736)
STUDIO 29
125 College Pl Ste 29 (23510-1907)
PHONE...................................757 624-1445
Mark McFarlane, *Owner*
EMP: 1
SQ FT: 350
SALES (est): 55.5K **Privately Held**
SIC: 3911 Jewelry, precious metal

(G-9737)
SUEZ WTS SERVICES USA INC (DH)
Also Called: Suez Water Tech & Solutions
4545 Patent Rd (23502-5604)
PHONE...................................757 855-9000

Heinrich Markhoff, *President*
Thomas Johnston, *Chairman*
Ashim Gupta, *Vice Pres*
David Collins, *Supervisor*
Glynn Key, *Admin Sec*
◆ **EMP:** 130
SQ FT: 52,000
SALES (est): 158.4MM
SALES (corp-wide): 100.8MM **Privately Held**
WEB: www.ge.com
SIC: 3589 Water treatment equipment, industrial
HQ: Suez Wts Systems Usa, Inc.
4636 Somerton Rd
Trevose PA 19053
215 355-3300

(G-9738)
SUPERIOR FLOAT TANKS LLC
431 W 25th St (23517-1243)
PHONE...................................757 966-6350
James Ramsey, *CEO*
Steven Ramsey, *COO*
EMP: 7
SALES (est): 350.8K **Privately Held**
WEB: www.superiorfloattanks.com
SIC: 3599 Custom machinery

(G-9739)
TABET MANUFACTURING CO INC
1336 Ballentine Blvd (23504-3808)
PHONE...................................757 627-1855
Jeffrey Jaycox, *President*
Paul Sullivan, *Vice Pres*
Chuck Woods, *Safety Mgr*
Anio Galdenzi, *Purchasing*
David Nickens, *Project Engr*
EMP: 45 **EST:** 1995
SQ FT: 40,000
SALES (est): 12.1MM **Privately Held**
WEB: www.tabetmfg.com
SIC: 3669 3663 3444 Intercommunication systems, electric; radio & TV communications equipment; sheet metalwork

(G-9740)
TANGERS ELECTRONICS LLC
1527 Magnolia Ave (23508-1105)
PHONE...................................757 215-5117
Shu Xiao, *Principal*
EMP: 1
SALES (est): 94.7K **Privately Held**
SIC: 3699 Pulse amplifiers

(G-9741)
TARGET ADVERTISING INC
Also Called: The Downtowner Newspaper
1439 Mallory Ct (23507-1020)
PHONE...................................757 627-2216
Jack Armistead, *President*
EMP: 6
SALES (est): 338.2K **Privately Held**
WEB: www.downtowneronline.com
SIC: 2711 Newspapers, publishing & printing

(G-9742)
TARMAC FLORIDA INC
1151 Azalea Garden Rd (23502-5601)
PHONE...................................757 858-6500
John D Carr, *President*
Russell A Fink, *Vice Pres*
EMP: 154
SQ FT: 30,000
SALES (est): 18.5MM
SALES (corp-wide): 1.4MM **Privately Held**
WEB: www.titanamerica.com
SIC: 3273 3271 5032 Ready-mixed concrete; concrete block & brick; concrete building products
HQ: Titan America Llc
5700 Lake Wright Dr # 300
Norfolk VA 23502
757 858-6500

(G-9743)
TARMAC MID-ATLANTIC INC
1151 Azalea Garden Rd (23502-5601)
PHONE...................................757 858-6500
John D Carr, *President*
Russell A Fink, *Admin Sec*
EMP: 1062
SQ FT: 12,000

SALES (est): 72.8MM
SALES (corp-wide): 1.4MM **Privately Held**
WEB: www.titanamerica.com
SIC: 3273 1442 3272 3271 Ready-mixed concrete; construction sand & gravel; concrete products; pipe, concrete or lined with concrete; blocks, concrete or cinder: standard
HQ: Titan America Llc
5700 Lake Wright Dr # 300
Norfolk VA 23502
757 858-6500

(G-9744)
TEAGLE & LITTLE INCORPORATED
1048 W 27th St (23517-1019)
PHONE...................................757 622-5793
A Deck Jordan, *Ch of Bd*
Ralph Gregory Jordan, *President*
Sid Cherry, *Vice Pres*
Drury Jordan, *Vice Pres*
Alan Smith, *Vice Pres*
EMP: 60
SQ FT: 45,000
SALES (est): 8.5MM **Privately Held**
WEB: www.teagle.co.uk
SIC: 2752 Commercial printing, offset

(G-9745)
TEAM 1 TRUCKING LLC
1117 Valley Dr (23502-2414)
PHONE...................................800 296-9740
Dion Sparrow,
EMP: 3
SALES (est): 100K **Privately Held**
SIC: 3537 Trucks, tractors, loaders, carriers & similar equipment

(G-9746)
TEGRA LLC
3801 E Princess Anne Rd (23502-1539)
PHONE...................................470 705-1280
Steven Cochran, *CEO*
EMP: 1
SALES (corp-wide): 164.6MM **Privately Held**
WEB: www.tegraglobal.com
SIC: 2329 Men's & boys' athletic uniforms
PA: Tegra Llc
211 Prmter Ctr Park Ste 9
Atlanta GA 30346
470 705-1280

(G-9747)
THELMAS INTERIORS INC
1523 Azalea Garden Rd (23502-1601)
P.O. Box 64265, Virginia Beach (23467-4265)
PHONE...................................757 855-0280
Kim Tharp, *President*
Brehm Carolyn A, *Vice Pres*
Carol Breham, *Admin Sec*
EMP: 4
SQ FT: 2,300
SALES (est): 205K **Privately Held**
SIC: 2391 Draperies, plastic & textile: from purchased materials

(G-9748)
THERMCOR INC
2601 Colley Ave (23517-1131)
PHONE...................................757 622-7881
Walter Dixon, *President*
Ron Dixon, *COO*
Ronald Dixon, *COO*
William Bolean, *Vice Pres*
Timothy Bolean, *Project Mgr*
EMP: 60
SQ FT: 6,400
SALES (est): 16.8MM **Privately Held**
WEB: www.thermcorinc.com
SIC: 3731 Military ships, building & repairing

(G-9749)
THRIFTY TRUNK
3747 Dare Cir (23513-5302)
PHONE...................................757 478-7836
Michele Lefebvre, *Principal*
EMP: 3
SALES (est): 185.4K **Privately Held**
SIC: 3161 Trunks

(G-9750)
TI ASSOCIATES INC
5401 Henneman Dr (23513-2439)
PHONE...................................757 857-6266
Richard H Love, *CEO*
Eunice W Love, *Corp Secy*
Bruce Barton, *Vice Pres*
Denise Love, *Sales Staff*
EMP: 60
SQ FT: 14,080
SALES (est): 8.7MM **Privately Held**
WEB: www.tiassoc.com
SIC: 2211 7389 2391 Draperies & drapery fabrics, cotton; interior designer; curtains & draperies

(G-9751)
TIDAL CORROSION SERVICES LLC
1158 Pickett Rd 1160 (23502-2317)
PHONE...................................757 216-4011
Denise Koch, *Mng Member*
Kenneth Koch,
Lisa Lafreniere,
EMP: 5
SQ FT: 15,000
SALES (est): 706.9K **Privately Held**
SIC: 3479 1721 Painting of metal products; commercial painting

(G-9752)
TIDEWATER FOODS INC
5714 Curlew Dr (23502-4625)
PHONE...................................757 410-2498
Steve A Paden, *President*
Galen Paden, *Admin Sec*
EMP: 2
SALES (est): 227.4K **Privately Held**
WEB: www.tidewaterfoodsinc.com
SIC: 2092 5146 Fresh or frozen fish or seafood chowders, soups & stews; fish & seafoods

(G-9753)
TIDEWATER GRAPHICS AND SIGNS
645 Church St Ste 102 (23510-1712)
PHONE...................................757 622-7446
Darly Antoine, *Owner*
EMP: 9
SQ FT: 2,000 **Privately Held**
SIC: 3993 7336 Signs & advertising specialties; graphic arts & related design

(G-9754)
TIDEWATER PALLETS
2608 Wyoming Ave (23513-4438)
PHONE...................................757 962-0020
Greg Rogers, *Principal*
EMP: 7
SALES (est): 458.2K **Privately Held**
WEB: www.tidewaterpallets.weebly.com
SIC: 2448 Pallets, wood

(G-9755)
TIDEWATER PARENT
150 W Brambleton Ave (23510-2018)
PHONE...................................757 222-3900
Jeanne Melton, *Principal*
EMP: 1
SALES (est): 73.3K **Privately Held**
WEB: www.pilotonline.com
SIC: 2711 Newspapers, publishing & printing

(G-9756)
TIDEWATER PROSTHETIC CENTER
6363 Center Dr Ste 100 (23502-4103)
PHONE...................................757 925-4844
Rick Stapleton, *Branch Mgr*
EMP: 2
SALES (corp-wide): 1.1B **Publicly Held**
WEB: www.hangerclinic.com
SIC: 3842 Limbs, artificial
HQ: Tidewater Prosthetic Center, Inc
150 Burnetts Way Ste 300
Suffolk VA 23434
757 925-4844

(G-9757)
TIFFANY INC
200 W 22nd St (23517-2231)
PHONE...................................757 622-2915
Anne McRae, *President*

Cary Petzinger, *Vice Pres*
▲ **EMP:** 5
SQ FT: 4,000
SALES (est): 240K **Privately Held**
WEB: www.certificatesbytiffany.com
SIC: 2741 Miscellaneous publishing

(G-9758)
TITAN AMERICA LLC
Also Called: Tarmac Titan
2125 Kimball Ter (23504-4417)
PHONE...................................757 533-7152
Jay Trefry, *Opers Mgr*
Greg Nikitas, *Branch Mgr*
EMP: 1
SALES (corp-wide): 1.4MM **Privately Held**
WEB: www.titanamerica.com
SIC: 3273 3271 5032 Ready-mixed concrete; concrete block & brick; concrete building products
HQ: Titan America Llc
5700 Lake Wright Dr # 300
Norfolk VA 23502
757 858-6500

(G-9759)
TITANIUM PRODUCTIONS INC
101 W Plume St (23510-1619)
P.O. Box 99092 (23509-9092)
PHONE...................................757 351-2526
Henri Lejacques Parks, *Principal*
EMP: 4
SALES (est): 385.3K **Privately Held**
SIC: 3356 Titanium

(G-9760)
TOM JAMES COMPANY
500 E Plume St Ste 405 (23510-2315)
PHONE...................................757 394-3205
Jim Thomas, *Branch Mgr*
EMP: 11
SALES (corp-wide): 574.6MM **Privately Held**
WEB: www.tomjames.com
SIC: 2311 Suits, men's & boys': made from purchased materials
PA: Tom James Company
263 Seaboard Ln
Franklin TN 37067
615 771-1122

(G-9761)
TONYS UNISEX BARBER
731 Monticello Ave (23510-2508)
PHONE...................................757 237-7049
Tony Lankford,
EMP: 4
SQ FT: 1,800
SALES (est): 151.4K **Privately Held**
SIC: 3999 Sterilizers, barber & beauty shop

(G-9762)
TOP SHOP ONESIES & APPAREL
406 W 34th St (23508-3225)
PHONE...................................757 202-3371
Jaleah Hood, *Owner*
EMP: 1
SALES (est): 42.5K **Privately Held**
SIC: 2335 Women's, juniors' & misses' dresses

(G-9763)
TRACK PATCH 1 CORPORATION
501 Boush St Ste B (23510-1400)
PHONE...................................757 289-5870
John Reese, *CEO*
EMP: 3
SALES (est): 121.3K **Privately Held**
SIC: 3634 Personal electrical appliances

(G-9764)
TRADITION CANDLE LLC
426 Granby St Apt 3c (23510-1958)
PHONE...................................630 881-7194
Preston Reilly, *Principal*
EMP: 1
SALES (est): 43.6K **Privately Held**
SIC: 3999 Candles

(G-9765)
TRANTER INC
2401 Church St (23504-1607)
PHONE...................................757 533-9185
EMP: 2 **EST:** 2011

SALES (est): 158.4K **Privately Held**
SIC: 3585 Heating equipment, complete

(G-9766)
TRAVEL GUIDE LLC
Also Called: Travel Media Group
150 Granby St (23510-1604)
PHONE..........................757 351-7000
Jeffrey Littlejohn, *Exec VP*
EMP: 20 EST: 2011
SALES (est): 1.4MM **Privately Held**
SIC: 2721 Periodicals

(G-9767)
TRI-ED DISTRIBUTION INC
2500 Almeda Ave Ste 107 (23513-2403)
PHONE..........................757 852-3780
EMP: 2
SALES (est): 88.3K **Privately Held**
WEB: www.tri-ed.com
SIC: 3669 Communications equipment

(G-9768)
TRINITY CONSTRUCTION SVCS INC
2043 Church St (23504-2332)
PHONE..........................757 455-8660
Preston A Thomas, *President*
Tommy Thompson, *Corp Secy*
EMP: 7
SALES (est): 640K **Privately Held**
SIC: 3545 Milling cutters

(G-9769)
TST FABRICATIONS LLC (HQ)
Also Called: Metal Concepts
1075 W 35th St (23508-3012)
PHONE..........................757 627-9101
Russell Turner, *CEO*
Shawn Kuhle,
EMP: 5
SALES (est): 1.8MM **Privately Held**
WEB: www.tstvb.com
SIC: 3441 Fabricated structural metal

(G-9770)
TST FABRICATIONS LLC
Also Called: Metal Concepts
1075 W 35th St (23508-3012)
PHONE..........................757 627-9101
Janie Kennedy, *Branch Mgr*
EMP: 18 **Privately Held**
WEB: www.tstvb.com
SIC: 3444 Sheet metal specialties, not stamped
HQ: Tst Fabrications, Llc
1075 W 35th St
Norfolk VA 23508
757 627-9101

(G-9771)
TYNES FIBERGLASS COMPANY INC
1202 N Shore Rd (23505-3012)
PHONE..........................757 423-0222
Richard Tynes, *President*
EMP: 5
SQ FT: 1,500
SALES (est): 250K **Privately Held**
SIC: 3732 7699 Boat building & repairing; boat repair

(G-9772)
U S GRAPHICS INC
1125 Azalea Garden Rd (23502-5601)
PHONE..........................757 855-2600
Tom Groce, *President*
Lisa Radsell, *CTO*
EMP: 8
SQ FT: 1,000
SALES (est): 739.6K **Privately Held**
WEB: www.usgraphicsinc.com
SIC: 2759 Screen printing

(G-9773)
UNITED STATES GYPSUM COMPANY
1424 S Main St (23523-1218)
PHONE..........................757 494-8100
Phil Reale, *Foreman/Supr*
Duane Van Duuren, *Engineer*
William Brown, *Supervisor*
Mike Phillips, *Systems Staff*
EMP: 150

SALES (corp-wide): 8.2B **Privately Held**
WEB: www.usg.com
SIC: 3275 Gypsum products
HQ: United States Gypsum Company
550 W Adams St Ste 1300
Chicago IL 60661
312 606-4000

(G-9774)
UNIVERSAL AIR PRODUCTS CORP (PA)
Also Called: Universal Air & Gas Products
1140 Kingwood Ave (23502-5603)
PHONE..........................757 461-0077
Toll Free:..........................888 -
Kurt Kondas, *President*
Peter Briggs, *VP Opers*
◆ EMP: 38 EST: 1962
SQ FT: 25,000
SALES (est): 11MM **Privately Held**
WEB: www.uapc.com
SIC: 3563 3564 Air & gas compressors; blowers & fans

(G-9775)
UP-N-COMING MAGAZINE
860 Meads Rd (23505-1454)
PHONE..........................757 343-8829
Dorcas A Carter, *Owner*
EMP: 1
SALES (est): 71K **Privately Held**
SIC: 2721 Magazines: publishing only, not printed on site

(G-9776)
USO PATH FINDER
1510 Gilbert St (23511-2738)
P.O. Box 15324 (23511-0324)
PHONE..........................757 395-4270
M Stephenson- Galvez, *Owner*
Michelle Stephenson- Galvez, *Principal*
EMP: 4 EST: 2016
SALES (est): 366.2K **Privately Held**
SIC: 2843 Processing assistants

(G-9777)
VA DESIGNS AND CNSTR LLC
6360 Glenoak Dr (23513-3359)
PHONE..........................757 651-8909
James Hoffler, *Principal*
Anna Knight, *Principal*
EMP: 2
SALES (est): 100K **Privately Held**
SIC: 1389 7389 Construction, repair & dismantling services; business services

(G-9778)
VANGUARD INDUSTRIES EAST INC (PA)
1172 Azalea Garden Rd (23502-5612)
PHONE..........................757 665-8405
William M Gershen, *President*
John McClain, *General Mgr*
Michael Harrison, *Vice Pres*
Betty Ramos, *Accounting Mgr*
Warren Dunlap, *Accounts Exec*
▲ EMP: 125
SQ FT: 40,000
SALES (est): 12.9MM **Privately Held**
WEB: www.vanguardmil.com
SIC: 2399 2396 3452 3295 Military insignia, textile; apparel findings & trimmings; bolts, nuts, rivets & washers; pleating & stitching

(G-9779)
VBK PUBLISHING
1644 Kingsway Rd (23518-4347)
PHONE..........................757 587-1741
Kevin Rogers, *Principal*
EMP: 1
SALES (est): 62.9K **Privately Held**
SIC: 2741 Miscellaneous publishing

(G-9780)
VELLA MAC INDUSTRIES INC
1109 Campostella Rd (23523-2103)
P.O. Box 4515 (23523-0515)
PHONE..........................757 724-0026
Annie Ford, *CEO*
Frederick McRae, *Principal*
EMP: 15
SALES (est): 474K **Privately Held**
SIC: 3999 Manufacturing industries

(G-9781)
VETERAN FREELANCER
3571 Riverside Dr (23502-4224)
PHONE..........................484 772-5931
Jessica Walcott,
EMP: 1
SALES (est): 37.5K **Privately Held**
SIC: 2741

(G-9782)
VIRGINIA BEACH GUIDE MAGAZINE
Also Called: Vb Guide
1228 Ballentine Blvd (23504-3806)
PHONE..........................757 627-8712
Terri Litzky, *Owner*
Guy Litzky, *Owner*
EMP: 2 EST: 2001
SALES (est): 198.9K **Privately Held**
WEB: www.vbschools.com
SIC: 2721 Magazines: publishing only, not printed on site

(G-9783)
VIRGINIA CAROLINA STEEL INC
2411 Ingleside Rd (23513-4525)
P.O. Box 7128 (23509-0128)
PHONE..........................757 853-7403
Sidney A Martin Jr, *President*
Stephen N Nicholas, *Vice Pres*
Linda Martin, *Treasurer*
EMP: 26
SQ FT: 3,300
SALES (est): 2.6MM **Privately Held**
SIC: 3441 Building components, structural steel

(G-9784)
VIRGINIA MATERIALS INC (DH)
3306 Peterson St (23509-2415)
PHONE..........................800 321-2282
Jeremy N Kendall, *Ch of Bd*
David Kruse, *President*
Steven Bromley, *Corp Secy*
▲ EMP: 4 EST: 2001
SQ FT: 1,000
SALES (est): 2.4MM
SALES (corp-wide): 1.1B **Privately Held**
WEB: www.optaminerals.com
SIC: 3291 5032 5084 Abrasive products; brick, stone & related material; industrial machinery & equipment

(G-9785)
VULCAN CONSTRUCTION MTLS LLC
954 Ballentine Blvd (23504-4102)
PHONE..........................757 494-3202
John Barnes, *Manager*
EMP: 3 **Publicly Held**
WEB: www.vulcanmaterials.com
SIC: 3273 Ready-mixed concrete
HQ: Vulcan Construction Materials, Llc
1200 Urban Center Dr
Vestavia AL 35242
205 298-3000

(G-9786)
VULCAN CONSTRUCTION MTLS LLC
1151 Azalea Garden Rd (23502-5601)
P.O. Box 2016 (23501-2016)
PHONE..........................757 858-6500
Ed Pittman, *Vice Pres*
EMP: 40 **Publicly Held**
WEB: www.vulcanmaterials.com
SIC: 3273 Ready-mixed concrete
HQ: Vulcan Construction Materials, Llc
1200 Urban Center Dr
Vestavia AL 35242
205 298-3000

(G-9787)
VULCAN MATERIALS COMPANY
954 Ballentine Blvd (23504-4102)
PHONE..........................757 622-4110
Ed Rider, *Safety Mgr*
Robert Breland, *Sales Staff*
John Barnes, *Branch Mgr*
EMP: 6 **Publicly Held**
WEB: www.vulcanmaterials.com
SIC: 1442 Construction sand & gravel
PA: Vulcan Materials Company
1200 Urban Center Dr
Vestavia AL 35242

(G-9788)
W T BROWNLEY CO INC
523 W 24th St (23517-1206)
P.O. Box 8254 (23503-0254)
PHONE..........................757 622-7589
Fax: 757 627-4189
EMP: 2
SQ FT: 995
SALES: 350K **Privately Held**
SIC: 3812 Mfg Search/Navigation Equipment

(G-9789)
WALASHEK HOLDINGS INC (PA)
3411 Amherst St (23513-4057)
PHONE..........................757 853-6007
Frank Walashek, *President*
Paula Walashek, *Vice Pres*
EMP: 3 EST: 2016
SALES (est): 29.3MM **Privately Held**
WEB: www.walashek.com
SIC: 3731 1711 Shipbuilding & repairing; heating systems repair & maintenance

(G-9790)
WALASHEK INDUSTRIAL & MAR INC
3411 Amherst St (23513-4057)
PHONE..........................757 853-6007
Gail Walashek, *President*
Frank Walashek, *Manager*
EMP: 34
SALES (corp-wide): 29.3MM **Privately Held**
WEB: www.walashek.com
SIC: 3731 Shipbuilding & repairing
HQ: Walashek Industrial & Marine, Inc.
3411 Amherst St
Norfolk VA 23513

(G-9791)
WALASHEK INDUSTRIAL & MAR INC (HQ)
3411 Amherst St (23513-4057)
PHONE..........................202 624-2880
Frank Walashek, *President*
Paula Walashek, *Vice Pres*
EMP: 17
SALES (est): 29.3MM **Privately Held**
WEB: www.walashek.com
SIC: 3731 Shipbuilding & repairing
PA: Walashek Holdings, Inc.
3411 Amherst St
Norfolk VA 23513
757 853-6007

(G-9792)
WALLPAPER FITTED CLOTHING CO
1035 W 25th St Ste F1 (23517-1000)
PHONE..........................757 639-8531
Kaneisha Heckstall, *Partner*
EMP: 2
SALES (est): 45K **Privately Held**
SIC: 2331 Women's & misses' blouses & shirts

(G-9793)
WATKINS PRODUCTS
1172 Janaf Pl (23502-2671)
PHONE..........................757 461-2800
Virginia Campbell, *Principal*
EMP: 1
SALES (est): 106.8K **Privately Held**
SIC: 3421 Table & food cutlery, including butchers'

(G-9794)
WESTMONT WOODWORKING INC
421 E Westmont Ave (23503-5334)
PHONE..........................757 287-2442
Charles Daniel Harris, *Administration*
EMP: 1 EST: 2017
SALES (est): 59.5K **Privately Held**
SIC: 2431 Millwork

(G-9795)
WINDSHIELD WIZARD
946 Avenue H (23513-1714)
PHONE..........................757 714-1642
David Askew Sr, *Owner*
EMP: 2

SALES (est): 25K **Privately Held**
SIC: 3714 Motor vehicle parts & accessories

(G-9796)
WINTER GIOVANNI LLC
1317 Olinger St Apt 2 (23523-2243)
PHONE.....................................757 343-9100
Winter Giovanni,
Yvette Morton,
EMP: 5
SALES (est): 300K **Privately Held**
SIC: 2731 Book publishing

(G-9797)
XVD BOARD SPORTS LLC
852 44th St (23508-2086)
P.O. Box 6009 (23508-0009)
PHONE.....................................757 504-0006
EMP: 2
SALES (est): 118.1K **Privately Held**
SIC: 3949 Skateboards

(G-9798)
YELLOW DOG SOFTWARE LLC
965 Norfolk Sq (23502-3227)
PHONE.....................................757 818-9360
Padric Toman, *Managing Dir*
Jay Livingood, *Principal*
David Lawrence, *Consultant*
Matt Lynn, *Technology*
EMP: 5 EST: 2009
SALES (est): 577K **Privately Held**
WEB: www.yellowdogsoftware.com
SIC: 7372 Application computer software

(G-9799)
YORGEA INC
2412 E Va Beach Blvd 10h (23504-3665)
PHONE.....................................704 431-8252
Calvin Saunders, *CEO*
EMP: 5 EST: 2009
SALES (est): 4.7K **Privately Held**
WEB: www.yorgea.com
SIC: 2741 4213 Miscellaneous publishing; trucking, except local

(G-9800)
ZENMAN TECHNOLOGY LLC
1116 Redgate Ave (23507-1425)
PHONE.....................................757 679-6703
Steven Nelson, *President*
EMP: 1
SALES (est): 63.9K **Privately Held**
SIC: 3511 Steam turbines

(G-9801)
ZRAMICS MTLS SCIENCE TECH LLC
2713 Colley Ave (23517-1133)
PHONE.....................................757 955-0493
Matthew Rippard, *Managing Prtnr*
George Karpin, *Development*
EMP: 2
SALES (est): 111.8K **Privately Held**
SIC: 2752 2754 2759 Commercial printing, lithographic; circulars: gravure printing; commercial printing

North
Mathews County

(G-9802)
DAVIS LOGGING
827 Bookers Ln (23128-2017)
PHONE.....................................804 725-7988
EMP: 3 EST: 2010
SALES (est): 110K **Privately Held**
SIC: 2411 Logging

(G-9803)
HOWARDS SIGNS LLC
14296 John Clyton Mem Hwy (23128-2073)
PHONE.....................................804 815-8333
EMP: 1
SALES (est): 50.6K **Privately Held**
WEB: www.howardssigns.com
SIC: 3993 Signs & advertising specialties

North Chesterfield
Chesterfield County

(G-9804)
A TOAST TO CANVAS
10272 Cherylann Rd (23236-1926)
PHONE.....................................804 363-4395
Holly Seon-Wilson, *Principal*
EMP: 1
SALES (est): 51.2K **Privately Held**
WEB: www.atoasttocanvas.com
SIC: 2211 Canvas

(G-9805)
ADVANTA FLOORING INC
7518 Whitepine Rd (23237-2217)
PHONE.....................................804 530-5004
Kent Choi, *President*
Kelly Mortensen, *Vice Pres*
EMP: 3
SALES (est): 1.2MM **Privately Held**
WEB: www.advantaflooring.com
SIC: 3996 5023 Hard surface floor coverings; floor coverings

(G-9806)
ADVANTAGE ACCNTNG BKKPING LLC
8121 Virginia Pine Ct (23237-2299)
PHONE.....................................434 989-0443
Katelyn Offield, *Administration*
EMP: 2
SALES (est): 90.8K **Privately Held**
SIC: 2782 Account books

(G-9807)
AFFORDABLE AUDIO RENTAL
5624 Gilling Rd (23234-5242)
PHONE.....................................804 305-6664
Cy Taggart, *Owner*
EMP: 1
SALES (est): 73.5K **Privately Held**
WEB: www.affordableaudio.com
SIC: 3699 Electric sound equipment

(G-9808)
AIR & BEYOND LLC
2100 Breezy Point Cir # 204 (23235-4299)
PHONE.....................................804 229-9450
J'Von Spruell,
EMP: 2
SALES (est): 65.5K **Privately Held**
SIC: 1389 Construction, repair & dismantling services

(G-9809)
AIRGAS USA LLC
Also Called: Air Liquid America
5901 Jefferson Davis Hwy (23234-5115)
P.O. Box 34404 (23234-0404)
PHONE.....................................804 743-0661
Larry Recard, *Principal*
EMP: 12
SALES (corp-wide): 129.8MM **Privately Held**
WEB: www.airgas.com
SIC: 2813 5169 5984 5171 Industrial gases; industrial gases; liquefied petroleum gas dealers; petroleum bulk stations & terminals
HQ: Airgas Usa, Llc
259 N Radnor Chester Rd
Radnor PA 19087
610 687-5253

(G-9810)
ALERIS ROLLED PRODUCTS INC
1801 Reymet Rd (23237-3725)
PHONE.....................................804 714-2100
Larry Allen, *General Mgr*
Beth McDade, *Human Res Mgr*
EMP: 59 **Privately Held**
WEB: www.aleris.com
SIC: 3341 Secondary nonferrous metals
HQ: Aleris Rolled Products, Inc.
25825 Science Park Dr # 400
Beachwood OH 44122
216 910-3400

(G-9811)
ALERIS ROLLED PRODUCTS INC
1701 Reymet Rd (23237-3727)
PHONE.....................................804 714-2180
Brian McCallie, *Branch Mgr*
EMP: 100 **Privately Held**
WEB: www.aleris.com
SIC: 3353 Aluminum sheet, plate & foil
HQ: Aleris Rolled Products, Inc.
25825 Science Park Dr # 400
Beachwood OH 44122
216 910-3400

(G-9812)
ALLEN SISSON PUBLISHERS REP
2102 Ramsgate Sq (23236-1551)
PHONE.....................................804 745-0903
Allen Sisson, *Owner*
EMP: 1
SALES (est): 90.9K **Privately Held**
SIC: 2741 Miscellaneous publishing

(G-9813)
ALLIED CONCRETE COMPANY
Also Called: Allied Concrete Products
1231 Willis Rd (23237-2920)
PHONE.....................................804 279-7501
Gary Madden, *Manager*
EMP: 45
SALES (corp-wide): 200.4MM **Privately Held**
WEB: www.alliedconcrete.com
SIC: 3273 Ready-mixed concrete
HQ: Allied Concrete Company
1000 Harris St
Charlottesville VA 22903
434 296-7181

(G-9814)
AMARQUIS PUBLICATIONS LLC
3915 Berrybrook Dr (23234-5504)
PHONE.....................................804 464-7203
Shannon I Smith, *Administration*
EMP: 5
SALES (est): 102K **Privately Held**
SIC: 2741 Miscellaneous publishing

(G-9815)
AMERICAN FLOORS
1249 Raynor Dr (23235-6141)
PHONE.....................................804 745-8932
Tina Pates, *Owner*
EMP: 3
SALES (est): 203.3K **Privately Held**
WEB: www.americanfloorsrichmond.com
SIC: 2426 Flooring, hardwood

(G-9816)
AMERICAN GASKET & SEAL TECH
Also Called: AGS
7400 Whitepine Rd (23237-2219)
PHONE.....................................804 271-0020
Troy K Martin, *President*
Karen K Jacobs, *Admin Sec*
EMP: 14
SQ FT: 14,000
SALES (est): 1.9MM **Privately Held**
WEB: www.ags-health.com
SIC: 3053 Gaskets, all materials

(G-9817)
ANALYTIC STRESS RELIEVING INC
7523 Whitepine Rd (23237-2216)
PHONE.....................................804 271-5447
K Martin, *Branch Mgr*
EMP: 5
SALES (corp-wide): 224.8MM **Privately Held**
WEB: www.analyticstress.com
SIC: 3398 Metal heat treating
PA: Analytic Stress Relieving, Inc.
3118 W Pinhook Rd Ste 202
Lafayette LA 70508
337 237-8790

(G-9818)
ANDREA LEWIS
Also Called: Scorpio Jungle
6526 Iron Bridge Rd (23234-5206)
PHONE.....................................804 933-4161
EMP: 2

SALES (est): 78.3K **Privately Held**
SIC: 3999 7389 Mfg Misc Products

(G-9819)
ARE YOU WIRED LLC
2737 Perlock Rd (23237-4611)
PHONE.....................................804 512-3990
Scott Wiener, *Principal*
EMP: 4
SALES (est): 337.9K **Privately Held**
SIC: 3663 Space satellite communications equipment

(G-9820)
ARROW MACHINE INC
309 Ruthers Rd (23235-5335)
PHONE.....................................804 272-0202
Bobby Fletcher, *President*
Judy Fletcher, *Vice Pres*
EMP: 7 EST: 1979
SQ FT: 90,000
SALES (est): 500K **Privately Held**
SIC: 3599 Machine shop, jobbing & repair

(G-9821)
ASSEMBLY & DESIGN INC
425 Southlake Blvd Ste 1b (23236-3064)
PHONE.....................................804 379-5432
Douglas Bronnenberg, *President*
Marcia Lewis, *Vice Pres*
EMP: 10
SQ FT: 3,000
SALES (est): 1.5MM **Privately Held**
WEB: www.assemblyanddesign.com
SIC: 3672 Circuit boards, television & radio printed

(G-9822)
AVCOM OF VIRGINIA INC
500 Southlake Blvd (23236-3043)
PHONE.....................................804 794-2500
Robert Hatfield, *Branch Mgr*
EMP: 1
SALES (corp-wide): 5.4MM **Privately Held**
WEB: www.avcomofva.com
SIC: 3621 Motors & generators
PA: Avcom Of Virginia, Inc.
7729 Pocoshock Way
North Chesterfield VA 23235
804 794-2500

(G-9823)
AVCOM OF VIRGINIA INC (PA)
7729 Pocoshock Way (23235-6483)
PHONE.....................................804 794-2500
Jay Evans, *President*
Chris Blyseth, *Engineer*
EMP: 25 EST: 1980
SALES (est): 5.4MM **Privately Held**
WEB: www.avcomofva.com
SIC: 3663 3829 3827 3825 Satellites, communications; measuring & controlling devices; optical instruments & lenses; instruments to measure electricity

(G-9824)
B & B PRINTING COMPANY INC
Also Called: B&B
521 Research Rd (23236-3046)
PHONE.....................................804 794-8273
Michael Bland, *President*
Steve Vanhuss, *Sales Staff*
Laura M Bland, *Admin Sec*
EMP: 120
SQ FT: 38,000
SALES (est): 21.1MM **Privately Held**
WEB: www.bbsmartsolutions.com
SIC: 2752 Commercial printing, offset

(G-9825)
B & J CABINET CO INC
7600 Dalebrook Dr (23237-1008)
PHONE.....................................804 271-0192
Ernie J Brownie, *President*
Glen Matthew Brownie, *Admin Sec*
EMP: 20 EST: 1957
SALES (est): 1.2MM **Privately Held**
SIC: 2434 2541 Wood kitchen cabinets; wood partitions & fixtures

(G-9826)
BALLOUS SIGNS AND DESIGNS INC
2501 Foxberry Cir (23235-6507)
PHONE.....................................804 986-6635

Richard S Ballou Sr, *President*
EMP: 2
SALES (est): 162.2K **Privately Held**
SIC: 3993 Signs & advertising specialties

(G-9827)
BAREFOOT SPAS LLC
8401 Fort Darling Rd (23237-1368)
PHONE..................................804 298-3939
Richard French, *Mng Member*
EMP: 50
SALES (est): 1.5MM **Privately Held**
WEB: www.shop.barefootspas.com
SIC: 3088 Plastics plumbing fixtures

(G-9828)
BARRON CONSTRUCTION LLC
6209 Tandem Ct (23234-4545)
PHONE..................................804 400-5569
Nicolas Barron, *Owner*
Baltazar Barron,
Adela De Barron,
EMP: 4
SALES (est): 284.3K **Privately Held**
SIC: 3271 Paving blocks, concrete

(G-9829)
BEC
8012 Midlothian Tpke # 200 (23235-5279)
PHONE..................................804 330-2500
D Satterfield, *Accounts Mgr*
EMP: 1
SALES (est): 43.6K **Privately Held**
WEB: www.becplasticcard.com
SIC: 3999 Manufacturing industries

(G-9830)
BEST IMAGE PRINTERS LTD
2735 Buford Rd (23235-2423)
PHONE..................................804 272-1006
Randolph C Raine, *President*
Stephen Raine, *Principal*
EMP: 10
SQ FT: 2,600
SALES (est): 1.5MM **Privately Held**
WEB: www.bestimageprinters.net
SIC: 2752 Commercial printing, offset

(G-9831)
BIG FACE BENJI MUSIC GROUP LLC
2100 Breezy Point Cir # 204 (23235-4299)
PHONE..................................804 229-9450
Jvon Spruell,
EMP: 1 **Privately Held**
SIC: 2782 Record albums

(G-9832)
BIG IMAGE GRAPHICS INC
800 Gordon School Pl (23236-2566)
PHONE..................................804 379-9910
William D Johnston, *President*
Richard A Combs, *Vice Pres*
De Ann Fipz, *Manager*
EMP: 20 EST: 1997
SALES (est): 1.7MM **Privately Held**
WEB: www.bigartgraphics.com
SIC: 2759 Commercial printing

(G-9833)
BON AIR CRAFTSMAN LLC
1806 Buford Rd (23235-4272)
PHONE..................................804 745-0130
Kevin Baker, *Principal*
EMP: 2
SALES (est): 150.4K **Privately Held**
WEB: www.bonaircraftsman.com
SIC: 2431 Millwork

(G-9834)
BRAIN BASED LEARNING INC
Also Called: Mind Attuned
725 Twinridge Ln (23235-5270)
PHONE..................................804 320-0158
Virginia L Sandford, *President*
EMP: 2
SALES (est): 112.8K **Privately Held**
SIC: 7372 Educational computer software

(G-9835)
BROWN WELDING INC
3206 Old Courthouse Rd (23236-1410)
PHONE..................................804 240-3094
Archie W Brown, *President*
EMP: 4

SALES (est): 240K **Privately Held**
SIC: 7692 Cracked casting repair

(G-9836)
BUTLER WOODCRAFTERS INC
569 Southlake Blvd Ste B (23236-3237)
PHONE..................................203 241-9753
EMP: 3
SALES (corp-wide): 490.5MM **Privately Held**
WEB: www.butlerhumanservices.com
SIC: 2421 Lumber: rough, sawed or planed
HQ: Butler Woodcrafters, Inc.
413 Branchway Rd Ste A
North Chesterfield VA 23236
877 852-0784

(G-9837)
BUTLER WOODCRAFTERS INC (DH)
413 Branchway Rd Ste A (23236-3264)
PHONE..................................877 852-0784
Lawrence Giaimo, *President*
Douglas P Cross, *Corp Secy*
Bill McMackin, *Sales Staff*
Mary Ellen Giaimo, *Marketing Staff*
Tyler Hickey, *Manager*
▲ EMP: 50
SQ FT: 75,000
SALES (est): 8.4MM
SALES (corp-wide): 490.5MM **Privately Held**
WEB: www.butlerhumanservices.com
SIC: 2511 Wood household furniture
HQ: Sauder Manufacturing Co.
930 W Barre Rd
Archbold OH 43502
419 445-7670

(G-9838)
C S LEWIS & SONS LLC
3940 Evelake Rd (23237-2726)
PHONE..................................804 275-6879
Cs Lewis,
EMP: 5
SALES (est): 250K **Privately Held**
SIC: 3315 3496 Steel wire & related products; miscellaneous fabricated wire products

(G-9839)
CANAAN PRINTING INC
4820 Jefferson Davis Hwy (23234-3155)
PHONE..................................804 271-4820
Carolyn Misenheimer, *President*
Brock Misenheimer, *COO*
Debbie Hise, *Bookkeeper*
Mari Varner, *Account Dir*
EMP: 20 EST: 1975
SQ FT: 5,000
SALES (est): 3.2MM **Privately Held**
WEB: www.canaanprinting.net
SIC: 2752 2789 Commercial printing, offset; bookbinding & related work

(G-9840)
CASEYS WELDING SERVICE
6429 Iron Bridge Rd (23234-5203)
PHONE..................................804 275-7960
EMP: 1
SALES (est): 56K **Privately Held**
SIC: 7692 Welding Repair

(G-9841)
CDK INDUSTRIES LLC
11318 W Providence Rd (23236-5226)
PHONE..................................804 551-3085
Christopher Lane, *Principal*
EMP: 1 EST: 2017
SALES (est): 39.6K **Privately Held**
SIC: 3999 Manufacturing industries

(G-9842)
CHAZ & REETAS CREATIONS
8642 Pine Glade Ln (23237-2640)
P.O. Box 37244 (23234-7244)
PHONE..................................804 248-4933
Marquetta C Fisher, *Owner*
EMP: 2
SALES (est): 5K **Privately Held**
SIC: 3999 Manufacturing industries

(G-9843)
CHRISTIAN FELLOWSHIP PUBLS
11515 Allecingie Pkwy (23235-4301)
PHONE..................................804 794-5333
Stephen Kaung, *President*
John Blanchard, *Treasurer*
Herbert L Fader, *Admin Sec*
EMP: 2
SALES (est): 173.2K **Privately Held**
WEB: www.c-f-p.com
SIC: 2731 8661 Books: publishing only; religious organizations

(G-9844)
CHT USA INC
8021 Reycan Rd (23237-2264)
PHONE..................................804 271-9010
Ginger Goodspeed, *Sales Staff*
Tera Hickman, *Branch Mgr*
EMP: 17
SALES (corp-wide): 144.1K **Privately Held**
WEB: www.icmproducts.com
SIC: 2821 Plastics materials & resins
HQ: Cht Usa Inc.
805 Wolfe Ave
Cassopolis MI 49031
269 445-0847

(G-9845)
CHT USA INC
Also Called: Quantum Silicones
7820 Whitepine Rd (23237-2211)
PHONE..................................800 852-3147
Phil McDermott, *Vice Pres*
Anna Clark, *Safety Dir*
Chris Ouglas, *Opers Mgr*
Linda Duva, *Buyer*
Teresa Sollowin, *Engineer*
▲ EMP: 42
SQ FT: 28,000
SALES (est): 11.7MM
SALES (corp-wide): 144.1K **Privately Held**
WEB: www.quantumsilicones.com
SIC: 2821 Plastics materials & resins
HQ: Cht Usa Inc.
805 Wolfe Ave
Cassopolis MI 49031
269 445-0847

(G-9846)
CLINE AUTOMOTIVE INC
Also Called: Advance Engine Design
2530 Willis Rd (23237-4606)
PHONE..................................804 271-9107
John Dickey, *President*
▲ EMP: 10
SQ FT: 9,000
SALES (est): 1.9MM **Privately Held**
WEB: www.aedperformance.com
SIC: 3714 5013 Fuel systems & parts, motor vehicle; automotive supplies & parts

(G-9847)
CNK MACHINE MANUFACTURING INC
615 Moorefield Park Dr A (23236-3685)
PHONE..................................804 320-1082
Carl Norman Kite, *President*
Diana H Kite, *Corp Secy*
Keith Anderson, *Manager*
Norman Kite, *CIO*
Linda Jessee, *Officer*
EMP: 15
SQ FT: 10,000
SALES (est): 2.5MM **Privately Held**
WEB: www.cnkmachinemfg.com
SIC: 3599 Machine shop, jobbing & repair

(G-9848)
COLD ROLL STEEL MCH & MFG LLC
8808c Metro Ct (23237-2944)
PHONE..................................804 275-9229
Terry Winfree,
EMP: 11 EST: 2014
SQ FT: 10,000
SALES (est): 714K **Privately Held**
SIC: 3599 Machine shop, jobbing & repair

(G-9849)
COLEMAN AND COLEMAN SOFTWARE
8108 Surreywood Dr (23235-5744)
PHONE..................................804 276-5372
Morton Coleman, *Principal*
Mort Coleman, *Prgrmr*
EMP: 1
SALES (est): 100K **Privately Held**
WEB: www.mactiques.com
SIC: 7372 Prepackaged software

(G-9850)
COMMODORE SALES LLC
11002 Trade Rd (23236-3910)
P.O. Box 35688 (23235-0688)
PHONE..................................804 794-1992
Kim Swagger, *Mng Member*
EMP: 26
SALES (est): 3.5MM **Privately Held**
WEB: www.commodorecoatings.us
SIC: 2899 Chemical preparations

(G-9851)
COMMONWEALTH SURGICAL SOLUTION
720 Mrfield Pk Dr Ste 105 (23236)
PHONE..................................804 330-0988
Daniel J Lawrence, *Principal*
EMP: 4
SALES (est): 402.8K **Privately Held**
WEB: www.commonwealthcounseling.com
SIC: 3842 Prosthetic appliances

(G-9852)
COVINGTONS SCRUBS WITH LOVE
4912 Burnt Oak Dr (23234-2987)
PHONE..................................804 503-8061
Lydia Covington, *Principal*
EMP: 2 EST: 2013
SALES (est): 99.4K **Privately Held**
WEB: www.cscrubswithlove.com
SIC: 2844 Toilet preparations

(G-9853)
CREED APPAREL
4902 Whetstone Rd (23234-4318)
PHONE..................................804 219-3291
Dominique Anderson, *CEO*
EMP: 4
SALES (est): 100K **Privately Held**
SIC: 1389 Construction, repair & dismantling services

(G-9854)
CRESPO URBAN DEFENSE LLC
1725 Creek Bottom Way (23236-5308)
PHONE..................................804 562-7566
George Crespo, *Principal*
EMP: 2
SALES (est): 133.6K **Privately Held**
SIC: 3812 Defense systems & equipment

(G-9855)
CUSTOM METAL FABRICATORS INC
7601 Whitepine Rd (23237-2214)
P.O. Box 98, Chesterfield (23832-0001)
PHONE..................................804 271-6094
Joseph D Johnson, *President*
Adam Wood, *President*
Gary K Johnson, *Vice Pres*
Joan Clarke, *Admin Sec*
Sue Graves, *Admin Sec*
EMP: 16 EST: 1969
SQ FT: 14,500
SALES (est): 3.5MM **Privately Held**
WEB: www.custommetalfabricators.com
SIC: 3444 3599 Sheet metal specialties, not stamped; machine shop, jobbing & repair

(G-9856)
CUSTOM PACKAGING SERVICE
2220 Station Rd (23234-5133)
PHONE..................................804 279-7225
John Fraim, *Principal*
EMP: 1
SALES (est): 83.6K **Privately Held**
SIC: 2631 Container, packaging & boxboard

(G-9857)
DELTA CIRCLE INDUSTRIES INC
8001 Reycan Rd (23237-2264)
PHONE.................................804 743-3500
Dennis H Owens Sr, *President*
Dennis Owens, *Vice Pres*
Sissi Hengle, *Sales Mgr*
EMP: 15
SALES (est): 2.2MM **Privately Held**
WEB: www.deltacircle.com
SIC: 3089 Injection molding of plastics

(G-9858)
DESTINY 11 PUBLICATIONS LLC
10401 Crooked Branch Ter (23237-4066)
PHONE.................................804 814-3019
Alicia Hill Jones, *Administration*
EMP: 2
SALES (est): 84.1K **Privately Held**
SIC: 2741 Miscellaneous publishing

(G-9859)
DETECTIVE COATING LLC
10910 Southlake Ct Ste H (23236-3938)
PHONE.................................804 893-3313
EMP: 3 EST: 2014
SALES (est): 184.4K **Privately Held**
WEB: www.detectivecoating.com
SIC: 3479 Coating of metals & formed products

(G-9860)
DREAM OF ME BOWTIQUE
9411 Kennesaw Rd (23236-2310)
PHONE.................................804 955-5908
Stephanie Cruz, *Owner*
EMP: 1
SALES (est): 42.5K **Privately Held**
SIC: 2369 7389 Headwear: girls', children's & infants'; business services

(G-9861)
DRUMSTICKS INC
6042 Jessup Rd (23234-4110)
PHONE.................................804 743-9356
Lee Brumright, *President*
Patricia Brumright, *Principal*
EMP: 1
SALES (est): 69K **Privately Held**
SIC: 2394 5311 Tarpaulins, fabric: made from purchased materials; department stores

(G-9862)
DU PONT TJIN FLMS US LTD PRTNR
5401 Jefferson Davis Hwy (23234-2257)
PHONE.................................804 530-9339
EMP: 2
SALES (est): 310K **Privately Held**
SIC: 3081 Unsupported Plastics Film And Sheet, Nsk

(G-9863)
DUPONT DE NEMOURS INC
3905 Beulah Rd (23237-1455)
PHONE.................................804 549-4747
Blair Andrews, *Branch Mgr*
▲ EMP: 4
SALES (corp-wide): 21.5B **Publicly Held**
WEB: www.usa.dupont.com
SIC: 2879 Agricultural chemicals
PA: Dupont De Nemours, Inc.
974 Centre Rd
Wilmington DE 19805
302 774-3034

(G-9864)
DUPONT JAMES RIVER GYPS FCILTY
1202 Bellwood Rd (23237-1334)
PHONE.................................804 714-3362
EMP: 2
SALES (est): 74.4K **Privately Held**
WEB: www.grancominerals.com
SIC: 2879 Agricultural chemicals

(G-9865)
DUPONT SPECIALTY PDTS USA LLC
5401 Jefferson Davis Hwy (23234-2257)
PHONE.................................804 383-2000
Arnold Raymond, *Partner*

Nikeya Clarkson, *General Mgr*
Rich Eagles, *General Mgr*
Susan Henshaw, *General Mgr*
L Kent Lewis, *General Mgr*
EMP: 145
SALES (corp-wide): 21.5B **Publicly Held**
WEB: www.dupont.com
SIC: 2819 Industrial inorganic chemicals
HQ: Dupont Specialty Products Usa, Llc
974 Centre Rd
Wilmington DE 19805
302 774-3034

(G-9866)
E H LAIL MILLWORK INC
3040 Goolsby Ave (23234-4442)
PHONE.................................804 271-1111
Ruth Lail, *President*
E H Lail III, *Exec VP*
Jeffrey W Brand, *Vice Pres*
Wanda Stewart, *Treasurer*
EMP: 16 EST: 1982
SQ FT: 30,000
SALES (est): 2.4MM **Privately Held**
WEB: www.lailmillwork.com
SIC: 2431 5031 Doors, wood; millwork

(G-9867)
EAST COAST INTERIORS INC
11000 Trade Rd (23236-3939)
PHONE.................................804 423-2554
Christopher R Baslick, *President*
EMP: 20
SALES (est): 2.6MM **Privately Held**
SIC: 1081 Metal mining services

(G-9868)
EVONIK CORPORATION
Also Called: Care & Surface Specialties
7801 Whitepine Rd (23237-2210)
P.O. Box 34628 (23234-0628)
PHONE.................................804 727-0711
Philip Munson, *Principal*
Steve Peloso, *Controller*
Andrea Alquicira, *Marketing Staff*
Serdar Ayvedi, *Manager*
Melissa Jones, *Manager*
EMP: 161
SALES (corp-wide): 1.7B **Privately Held**
WEB: www.sorry.evonik.com
SIC: 2869 Industrial organic chemicals
HQ: Evonik Corporation
299 Jefferson Rd
Parsippany NJ 07054
973 929-8000

(G-9869)
EXPRESS RACING & MACHINE
9740 Jefferson Davis Hwy (23237-4620)
PHONE.................................804 521-7891
EMP: 5
SALES (est): 380K **Privately Held**
SIC: 3714 Mfg Motor Vehicle Parts/Accessories

(G-9870)
FAITH PRINTING
7814 Midlothian Tpke (23235-5228)
PHONE.................................804 745-0667
Wilbert Davis, *Owner*
EMP: 2
SALES (est): 73.2K **Privately Held**
WEB: www.faithprintingonline.com
SIC: 2752 Commercial printing, offset

(G-9871)
FAT MLTONS STHERN SWETS TREATS
8908 Talon Ln (23237-4318)
PHONE.................................804 248-4175
Milton L Burch, *President*
Lawanda Burch, *Admin Sec*
EMP: 2
SALES (est): 101.4K **Privately Held**
SIC: 2053 Cakes, bakery: frozen

(G-9872)
FEEFEES CABINET LLC
2530 Noel St (23237-4417)
PHONE.................................804 647-0297
Felicia Ann Baldwin, *Principal*
EMP: 1
SALES (est): 53.7K **Privately Held**
SIC: 2434 Wood kitchen cabinets

(G-9873)
FINAL TOUCH II MFG LLC
2545 Bellwood Rd Ste 305 (23237-4481)
PHONE.................................804 389-3899
John Allen, *President*
EMP: 1
SALES (est): 57.1K **Privately Held**
SIC: 2844 Toilet preparations

(G-9874)
FISHER PUBLICATIONS INC
9918 Midlothian Tpke (23235-4814)
P.O. Box 1380, Midlothian (23113-8380)
PHONE.................................804 323-6252
Alan R Hunter, *President*
EMP: 2
SQ FT: 1,300
SALES (est): 110K **Privately Held**
SIC: 2752 Commercial printing, offset

(G-9875)
FISHER-ROSEMOUNT SYSTEMS INC
8130 Virginia Pine Ct (23237-2203)
PHONE.................................804 714-1400
John Carlo, *Manager*
Jim Holubar, *Manager*
EMP: 9
SALES (corp-wide): 18.3B **Publicly Held**
WEB: www.emerson.com
SIC: 3823 Industrial instrmnts msrmnt display/control process variable
HQ: Fisher-Rosemount Systems, Inc.
1100 W Louis Henna Blvd
Round Rock TX 78681

(G-9876)
FLEXIBLE CONVEYOR SYSTEMS INC
11310 Business Center Dr (23236-3068)
PHONE.................................804 897-9572
Carlo O'Keefe, *President*
Michelle Leipold, *Engineer*
EMP: 10
SQ FT: 10,000
SALES (est): 2MM **Privately Held**
WEB: www.flexibleconveyorsystems.com
SIC: 3535 Conveyors & conveying equipment

(G-9877)
FLOWSERVE CORPORATION
7445 Whitepine Rd (23237-2261)
PHONE.................................804 271-4031
Greg Peters, *Branch Mgr*
EMP: 1
SALES (corp-wide): 3.9B **Publicly Held**
WEB: www.flowserve.com
SIC: 3561 Pumps & pumping equipment
PA: Flowserve Corporation
5215 N Ocnnor Blvd Ste 23 Connor
Irving TX 75039
972 443-6500

(G-9878)
FOBBS QUALITY SIGNS LLC
7013 Irongate Dr (23234-2846)
PHONE.................................804 714-0102
James Andrew Fobbs Jr, *Principal*
EMP: 1
SALES (est): 46K **Privately Held**
WEB: www.fobbsqualitysigns.com
SIC: 3993 Signs & advertising specialties

(G-9879)
FOUNTAINHEAD SYSTEMS LTD
8950 Cardiff Rd (23236-1524)
PHONE.................................804 320-0527
Phillip R Scanlon, *Principal*
EMP: 1
SALES (est): 71.2K **Privately Held**
SIC: 7372 7373 Prepackaged software; computer integrated systems design

(G-9880)
FRITZ KEN TOOLING & DESIGN
1324 Hybla Rd (23236-2009)
PHONE.................................804 721-2319
Kenneth E Fritz, *President*
EMP: 20
SALES (est): 3.7MM **Privately Held**
SIC: 2679 5031 Pressed fiber & molded pulp products except food products; molding, all materials

(G-9881)
GREEN GRAPHIC SIGNS LLC
8807 Elkview Ct (23236-1315)
PHONE.................................804 229-3351
Edward Hierholzer, *Mng Member*
EMP: 3
SALES (est): 900K **Privately Held**
WEB: www.greengraphicsigns.com
SIC: 3993 7389 Signs & advertising specialties

(G-9882)
GRID2020 INC (PA)
7405 Whitepine Rd (23237-2218)
PHONE.................................804 918-1982
Alan Snook, *President*
Sergio Angeli, *Senior VP*
Dan Hermes, *Vice Pres*
Daniel Hermes, *Vice Pres*
Scott Bussing, *VP Sales*
EMP: 17
SQ FT: 3,000
SALES (est): 2.3MM **Privately Held**
WEB: www.grid2020.com
SIC: 3825 Instruments to measure electricity

(G-9883)
HERBAL ORIGINS LLC
11650 Belvdr Vista Ln # 103 (23235-4356)
PHONE.................................804 715-0015
Shaunta Henderson,
EMP: 1
SALES (est): 450K **Privately Held**
SIC: 3999 Hair & hair-based products

(G-9884)
HERITAGE ELECTRICAL CORP
7725 Whitepine Rd (23237-2212)
PHONE.................................804 743-4614
Ronald L Daugherty, *President*
Robert Perrot, *Vice Pres*
Teresa Daugherty, *Treasurer*
EMP: 13
SQ FT: 20,000
SALES (est): 2.2MM **Privately Held**
WEB: www.hec-corp.com
SIC: 3625 1731 Control equipment, electric; electrical work

(G-9885)
HERMETIC NETWORKS INC
7637 Hull Street Rd # 201 (23235-6437)
PHONE.................................804 545-3173
Bailey Mikhail, *President*
Jeff Hughes, *CFO*
EMP: 2
SALES (est): 333.6K **Privately Held**
WEB: www.hermeticnetworks.com
SIC: 3825 Network analyzers

(G-9886)
HILL PHOENIX INC
1301 Battery Brooke Pkwy (23237-3018)
PHONE.................................800 283-1109
Marcy Combs, *Engineer*
Bryan Ruby, *Regl Sales Mgr*
Jamie Williams, *Representative*
EMP: 9
SALES (corp-wide): 7.1B **Publicly Held**
WEB: www.hillphoenix.com
SIC: 3632 Household refrigerators & freezers
HQ: Hill Phoenix, Inc.
2016 Gees Mill Rd Ne
Conyers GA 30013

(G-9887)
HO-HO-KUS INCORPORATED
10911 Southlake Ct (23236-3913)
PHONE.................................206 552-4559
Steve Sucharski, *Vice Pres*
EMP: 78
SALES (est): 2.3MM **Privately Held**
WEB: www.hohokusinc.com
SIC: 3724 Research & development on aircraft engines & parts

(G-9888)
HUGHIE C ROSE
Also Called: Rose Paving and Seal Coating
6919 Jefferson Davis Hwy (23237-1547)
PHONE.................................540 423-5240
Hughie C Rose, *Owner*
EMP: 1

SALES (est): 25K **Privately Held**
SIC: 2951 Asphalt & asphaltic paving mixtures (not from refineries)

(G-9889)
IMAGE 360
11605 Busy St (23236-4059)
PHONE....................................804 897-8500
Bruce Bloomquest, *Principal*
EMP: 2
SALES (est): 172K **Privately Held**
SIC: 3993 Signs & advertising specialties

(G-9890)
IMMCO LLC
Also Called: Industrial Machine Mfg
7516 Whitepine Rd (23237-2217)
PHONE....................................804 271-6979
John Menendez, *Vice Pres*
Brenda Colbert, *Admin Mgr*
Russ Martin,
Billy Teal, *Technician*
EMP: 12
SALES (est): 1.7MM **Privately Held**
WEB: www.uniflow.works
SIC: 3462 Machinery forgings, ferrous

(G-9891)
IMPERIAL MACHINE COMPANY INC
7631 Whitepine Rd (23237-2380)
PHONE....................................804 271-6022
Pauline G Pace, *President*
Pace Brandon, *Engineer*
EMP: 8
SQ FT: 24,000
SALES (est): 640K **Privately Held**
WEB: www.imperialmachine.us
SIC: 3599 Machine shop, jobbing & repair

(G-9892)
INDUSTRIAL MACHINE MFG INC
8140 Virginia Pine Ct (23237-2203)
PHONE....................................804 271-6979
Marvin Garrett, *President*
Leo Moore, *Vice Pres*
EMP: 20 EST: 1956
SQ FT: 19,600 **Privately Held**
WEB: www.uniflow.works
SIC: 3559 3599 Refinery, chemical processing & similar machinery; machine shop, jobbing & repair

(G-9893)
INDUSTRIAL WELDING & MECH INC
2401 Bellwood Rd (23237-1309)
PHONE....................................804 744-8812
Paul Duncan, *President*
Donald Munden, *Vice Pres*
Pamela Munden, *Treasurer*
Lynn Mello-Frizzell, *Office Mgr*
Cindy Duncan, *Asst Sec*
EMP: 12
SALES (est): 1.5MM **Privately Held**
WEB: www.theanchoragecamp.org
SIC: 7692 Welding repair

(G-9894)
INFINITY PRINTING INC
11025 Research Ct (23236-3942)
PHONE....................................804 378-8656
EMP: 2 EST: 1997
SALES (est): 130K **Privately Held**
SIC: 2752 Lithographic Commercial Printing

(G-9895)
INFORMATION SYSTEMS GROUP
605 N Courthouse Rd # 201 (23236-4068)
PHONE....................................804 526-4220
William T Bandy, *President*
EMP: 2
SALES (est): 204.9K **Privately Held**
WEB: www.bandyworks.com
SIC: 3663 Radio & TV communications equipment

(G-9896)
INGERSOLL RAND INC
540 Southlake Blvd (23236-3084)
PHONE....................................804 214-7054
EMP: 2 **Publicly Held**
WEB: www.gardnerdenver.com

SIC: 3563 Air & gas compressors
PA: Ingersoll Rand Inc.
800 Beaty St Ste A
Davidson NC 28036
704 655-4000

(G-9897)
INSOURCE SFTWR SOLUTIONS INC (PA)
Also Called: Insource Solutions
11321 Business Center Dr (23236-3069)
PHONE....................................804 378-8981
Ann P Croom, *President*
Thomas Barczak, *Vice Pres*
Aaron Evans, *Vice Pres*
Julie Joyce, *Vice Pres*
Scott E Miller, *Vice Pres*
EMP: 22
SQ FT: 10,000
SALES (est): 34MM **Privately Held**
WEB: www.insource.solutions
SIC: 7372 8742 Prepackaged software; manufacturing management consultant

(G-9898)
INTEGRATED GLOBAL SERVICES INC (PA)
7600 Whitepine Rd (23237-2215)
PHONE....................................804 794-1646
Richard Crawford, *President*
Reichert Hunter J, *Chairman*
Iain Hall, *Vice Pres*
Jeff Shelton, *Vice Pres*
Phillip Critchfield, *Safety Mgr*
◆ EMP: 100
SALES (est): 29.3MM **Privately Held**
WEB: www.integratedglobal.com
SIC: 3479 Coating, rust preventive

(G-9899)
INTERNATIONAL DESIGNS LLC
8310 Shell Rd Ste 102 (23237-1341)
PHONE....................................804 275-1044
Carl R Jones,
EMP: 1
SALES (est): 126.7K **Privately Held**
SIC: 3469 3599 Machine parts, stamped or pressed metal; machine shop, jobbing & repair

(G-9900)
IVANS INC
9740 Jefferson Davis Hwy (23237-4620)
PHONE....................................804 271-0477
EMP: 2
SALES (est): 80.3K **Privately Held**
SIC: 7372 Home entertainment computer software

(G-9901)
JACATAI VENDING
9643 Ransom Hills Ter (23237-3470)
PHONE....................................804 317-2526
Taivia Armstrong, *Owner*
EMP: 1
SALES (est): 63.7K **Privately Held**
SIC: 3581 Automatic vending machines

(G-9902)
JESSICA RADELLANT DESIGNS LLC
735 Hartford Ln (23236-4501)
PHONE....................................804 301-3994
Jessica Radellant,
EMP: 1 EST: 2015
SALES (est): 44.6K **Privately Held**
SIC: 2389 Disposable garments & accessories

(G-9903)
JOVIC EMBROIDERY LLC
9517 Chipping Dr (23237-3842)
PHONE....................................804 748-2598
Vickie H Aprile,
EMP: 2
SALES (est): 132.4K **Privately Held**
WEB: www.jovicemb.com
SIC: 2395 Embroidery products, except schiffli machine; embroidery & art needlework

(G-9904)
KAISER ALUMINUM CORPORATION
1901 Reymet Rd (23237-3723)
PHONE....................................804 743-6405
Jeff Chalkley, *Opers Staff*
Jack Hockema, *Branch Mgr*
Jerry Rolison, *Manager*
Teno Bratton, *Administration*
EMP: 450
SALES (corp-wide): 1.5B **Publicly Held**
WEB: www.kaiseraluminum.com
SIC: 3354 Aluminum extruded products
PA: Kaiser Aluminum Corporation
27422 Portola Pkwy # 350
Foothill Ranch CA 92610
949 614-1740

(G-9905)
KAISER BELLWOOD CORPORATION
Also Called: Kaiser Aluminum & Chemical
1901 Reymet Rd (23237-3723)
PHONE....................................804 743-6300
Jack A Hockema, *President*
EMP: 100 EST: 1997
SQ FT: 45,000
SALES (est): 17.9MM
SALES (corp-wide): 1.5B **Publicly Held**
SIC: 3354 Pipe, extruded, aluminum
HQ: Kaiser Aluminum Fabricated Products, Llc
27422 Portola Pkwy # 200
Foothill Ranch CA 92610

(G-9906)
KEC ASSOCIATES LTD
Also Called: Smart Marketing Services
467 Southlake Blvd (23236-3044)
PHONE....................................804 404-2601
Randall Copeland, *President*
▼ EMP: 6
SQ FT: 1,800
SALES (est): 490K **Privately Held**
SIC: 2434 Wood kitchen cabinets

(G-9907)
KENNLEY CORPORATION
8808b Metro Ct (23237-2944)
P.O. Box 790, Chesterfield (23832-0011)
PHONE....................................804 275-9088
Ken Guthrie, *President*
Reggie Stanfield, *Corp Secy*
Philip A Roberts Jr, *Vice Pres*
Bonnie Fletcher, *Accounts Mgr*
▼ EMP: 8
SQ FT: 2,800
SALES (est): 1.9MM **Privately Held**
WEB: www.kennley.com
SIC: 3469 Machine parts, stamped or pressed metal

(G-9908)
KLM RACE LLC
10910 Southlake Ct (23236-3938)
PHONE....................................804 594-6187
EMP: 3
SALES (est): 244.3K **Privately Held**
SIC: 1389 Construction, repair & dismantling services

(G-9909)
KNOCKAWE WOODWORKING LLC
301 Brighton Dr (23235-5003)
PHONE....................................804 928-3506
Glen Davis, *Mng Member*
EMP: 2
SALES (est): 176.7K **Privately Held**
SIC: 2431 Millwork

(G-9910)
KWIK SIGNS INC
611 Research Rd Ste B (23236-3948)
PHONE....................................804 897-5945
Darlene Herrington, *Owner*
EMP: 1
SALES (est): 106K **Privately Held**
WEB: www.kwiksignsrva.com
SIC: 3993 Signs, not made in custom sign painting shops

(G-9911)
LA MICHOACANA III LLC
9110 Jefferson Davis Hwy (23237-4632)
PHONE....................................804 275-0011
EMP: 3
SALES (est): 174.9K **Privately Held**
SIC: 2024 Ice cream, bulk

(G-9912)
LA PRADE ENTERPRISES
5260 Ronson Rd (23234-4677)
PHONE....................................804 271-9899
James E La Prade, *Owner*
EMP: 1
SALES (est): 109.6K **Privately Held**
SIC: 2541 2511 2434 Cabinets, except refrigerated: show, display, etc.: wood; display fixtures, wood; bed frames, except water bed frames: wood; wood kitchen cabinets

(G-9913)
LARSCO LLC
830 Montour Dr (23236-3644)
PHONE....................................804 400-0667
Lawrence N Ferguson, *Administration*
EMP: 2
SALES (est): 71.2K **Privately Held**
SIC: 3489 Ordnance & accessories

(G-9914)
LUXEMANES LLC
Also Called: Scalpscratchers
10819 Trade Rd (23236-3036)
PHONE....................................804 922-1410
Adeyemi Kayode,
EMP: 10
SALES (est): 785.9K **Privately Held**
WEB: www.scalpscratchers.com
SIC: 3999 Hair & hair-based products

(G-9915)
M&Q WELDING LLC
2306 Ives Ln (23235-6346)
PHONE....................................804 564-8864
Michael Allen Titley, *President*
Michael Allen Tilley, *Mng Member*
EMP: 1
SALES (est): 44.1K **Privately Held**
SIC: 7692 Welding repair

(G-9916)
MACTAVISH MACHINE MFG CO
Also Called: Evans Mactavis Agregrats
7429 Whitepine Rd (23237-2255)
PHONE....................................804 264-6109
Donald I Evans, *President*
Charles Evans, *Vice Pres*
Hendrik Van Dorp, *Draft/Design*
Francis Smith, *Treasurer*
Beverly Lanham, *VP Sales*
EMP: 8
SQ FT: 100,000
SALES (est): 1.4MM **Privately Held**
WEB: www.mactavish.com
SIC: 3559 3556 Tobacco products machinery; food products machinery; ovens, bakery

(G-9917)
MADGAR ENTERPRISES LLC
Also Called: Bend The Bare Vents
4673 Melody Rd (23234-3532)
PHONE....................................540 760-6946
Alex Madgar,
EMP: 1
SALES (est): 50K **Privately Held**
SIC: 7372 Application computer software

(G-9918)
MADINAH PUBLS & DISTRS INC
2308 Lancashire Dr (23235-5728)
PHONE....................................804 839-8073
Ayman Abualrub, *Principal*
EMP: 2
SALES (est): 60K **Privately Held**
SIC: 2741 Miscellaneous publishing

(G-9919)
MAGNIFOAM DELAWARE INC
8020 Whitepine Rd (23237-2263)
PHONE....................................804 564-9700
Jason Anderson, *Manager*
EMP: 2

SALES (est): 93.7K **Privately Held**
WEB: www.magnifoam.com
SIC: **3086** Plastics foam products

(G-9920)
MAGSS IDEAS & CONCEPTS
8959 Cardiff Rd (23236-1523)
PHONE.............................804 304-6324
Evelyn Hall Harris, *Owner*
EMP: 2
SALES (est): 71.6K **Privately Held**
SIC: **3944** Board games, children's & adults'

(G-9921)
MARCO MACHINE & DESIGN INC
7740 Whitepine Rd (23237-2213)
PHONE.............................804 275-5555
Donald Lawson, *President*
Pat Lawson, *Treasurer*
EMP: 16
SQ FT: 20,700
SALES (est): 2.2MM **Privately Held**
WEB: www.marcomachine.com
SIC: **3599 3549 3541** Machine shop, jobbing & repair; metalworking machinery; machine tools, metal cutting type

(G-9922)
MARKHAM BURIAL VAULT SERVICE (PA)
Also Called: Markham Wilbert
8400 Jefferson Davis Hwy (23237-1342)
PHONE.............................804 271-1441
Earnie O Markham, *President*
Betty J Markham, *Chairman*
John S Markham, *Corp Secy*
EMP: 40
SQ FT: 12,000
SALES (est): 5.4MM **Privately Held**
WEB: www.markhamvault.com
SIC: **3272** Burial vaults, concrete or precast terrazzo

(G-9923)
MARLOR INC
Also Called: Auntie Anne's Hand Rolled Pret
11500 Mdlthn Tpke 470 (23235)
PHONE.............................804 378-5071
Loren B Garner, *President*
Marthetta M Garner, *Vice Pres*
EMP: 14
SQ FT: 500
SALES (est): 1.1MM **Privately Held**
SIC: **2052 5461** Pretzels; pretzels

(G-9924)
MARUCHAN VIRGINIA INC
8101 Whitepine Rd (23237-2288)
PHONE.............................804 275-2800
Oda Mutsumiko, *President*
Hiro Matsushita, *Plant Mgr*
Sharon Bryant, *Human Res Mgr*
Mike Snyder, *Manager*
Hiroshige Tsubaki, *Admin Sec*
◆ EMP: 185
SALES (est): 51.7MM **Privately Held**
SIC: **2098 2099** Noodles (e.g. egg, plain & water), dry; food preparations
HQ: Maruchan, Inc.
　15800 Laguna Canyon Rd
　Irvine CA 92618
　949 789-2300

(G-9925)
MASA CORPORATION OF VIRGINIA
Also Called: Label Systems
2203 Station Rd (23234-5132)
PHONE.............................804 271-8102
John Fraim, *General Mgr*
EMP: 3
SALES (corp-wide): 25MM **Privately Held**
WEB: www.masacorp.com
SIC: **3565** Labeling machines, industrial
HQ: The Masa Corporation Of Virginia
　5445 Henneman Dr Ste 200
　Norfolk VA 23513
　757 855-3013

(G-9926)
MASTER BUSINESS SOLUTIONS INC
Also Called: Lexacom
400 Southlake Blvd Ste C (23236-3061)
P.O. Box 35993 (23235-0993)
PHONE.............................804 378-5470
Kevin Chaplin, *President*
Lisa Chaplin, *Vice Pres*
EMP: 3 EST: 1989
SQ FT: 900
SALES (est): 276.2K **Privately Held**
SIC: **7372** Application computer software

(G-9927)
MCC ABATEMENT LLC
7511 Troycott Rd (23237-4404)
PHONE.............................804 731-4238
EMP: 2
SALES (est): 62.6K **Privately Held**
WEB: www.mccabatementcollcva.com
SIC: **3292** Asbestos products

(G-9928)
MELVIN CRUTCHFIELD
Also Called: Mobile-Tel
3301 Clearview Dr (23234-4887)
PHONE.............................804 440-3547
Melvin Crutchfield, *Owner*
EMP: 2
SALES (est): 85K **Privately Held**
WEB: www.mobiletelusa.com
SIC: **3661** Telephone & telegraph apparatus

(G-9929)
METROPOLITAN EQUIPMENT GROUP
611 Moorefield Park Dr A (23236-3667)
PHONE.............................804 744-4774
Rick Mullis, *Office Mgr*
EMP: 2
SALES (est): 160.8K **Privately Held**
WEB: www.meghvac.com
SIC: **3585** Heating & air conditioning combination units

(G-9930)
MG INDUSTRIES
5901 Jefferson Davis Hwy (23234-5115)
PHONE.............................804 743-0661
Tim Tyree, *Manager*
Tyree Tim, *Manager*
EMP: 2
SALES (est): 128.4K **Privately Held**
SIC: **3999** Manufacturing industries

(G-9931)
MID-ATLANTIC ENERGY LLC
812 Moorefield Park Dr # 310 (23236-3674)
PHONE.............................804 213-2500
Harry Newton, *Mng Member*
Bruce McDaniel, *Mng Member*
EMP: 3
SALES (est): 2MM **Privately Held**
WEB: www.mid-atlanticenergy.com
SIC: **1321** Natural gas liquids

(G-9932)
MINGLEWOOD TRADING
2604 Teaberry Dr (23236-1655)
PHONE.............................804 245-6162
Christopher Sheehy, *Partner*
Shannon Sheehy, *Partner*
EMP: 2
SALES (est): 80.6K **Privately Held**
WEB: www.minglewoodtrading.com
SIC: **2759 7336 5699** Poster & decal printing & engraving; commercial art & graphic design; T-shirts, custom printed

(G-9933)
MOTH LLC
5807 Gloryvine Ct 105-11 (23234-6918)
PHONE.............................804 655-8216
Javon Mack,
EMP: 5
SALES (est): 229.7K **Privately Held**
SIC: **2899** Essential oils

(G-9934)
MR ROBOT INC
10220 Robious Rd (23235-4434)
P.O. Box 974, Midlothian (23113-0974)
PHONE.............................804 426-3394
John Wellon, *CEO*
EMP: 3
SALES (est): 300.2K **Privately Held**
SIC: **3559** Robots, molding & forming plastics

(G-9935)
MTG ENTERPRISES INC
4603 Jacobs Glenn Dr (23236-4718)
PHONE.............................804 269-5218
Gilbert Mark, *President*
EMP: 1
SALES (est): 88.2K **Privately Held**
SIC: **3732** Boat building & repairing

(G-9936)
MUNCIE POWER PRODUCTS INC
9407 Burge Ave (23237-3034)
PHONE.............................804 275-6724
Ray Chambers, *Branch Mgr*
EMP: 131
SALES (corp-wide): 109.4MM **Privately Held**
WEB: www.munciepower.com
SIC: **3714** Motor vehicle parts & accessories
HQ: Muncie Power Products, Inc.
　201 E Jackson St Ste 500
　Muncie IN 47305
　765 284-7721

(G-9937)
NABINA PUBLICATIONS
11304 Prvidence Creek Ter (23236-5269)
P.O. Box 4091, Midlothian (23112-0001)
PHONE.............................804 276-0454
Nanaa Biney-Amissah, *Owner*
EMP: 1
SALES (est): 72.5K **Privately Held**
SIC: **2759** Publication printing

(G-9938)
NELSONS CABINETRY
543 Southlake Blvd (23236-3042)
PHONE.............................804 363-5800
Marshall Nelson, *President*
EMP: 5
SALES (est): 375K **Privately Held**
WEB: www.nelsoncabinetry.net
SIC: **2434** Wood kitchen cabinets

(G-9939)
NELSONS CABINETRY INC
10501 Ashburn Rd (23235-2605)
PHONE.............................804 560-4785
Marshall Budd Nelson, *Principal*
EMP: 1
SALES (est): 53.7K **Privately Held**
SIC: **2434** Wood kitchen cabinets

(G-9940)
NORTHROP GRUMMAN CORPORATION
101 Gateway Centre Pkwy # 300 (23235-5173)
PHONE.............................804 272-1321
Devon Giuliano, *Project Mgr*
Louis Piper, *Chief Engr*
Jackie Henley, *Accountant*
Mary Fitzgerald, *Branch Mgr*
Linda Bollinger, *Manager*
EMP: 735 **Publicly Held**
WEB: www.northropgrumman.com
SIC: **3812** Search & detection systems & instruments
PA: Northrop Grumman Corporation
　2980 Fairview Park Dr
　Falls Church VA 22042

(G-9941)
NUCOR CORPORATION
Also Called: Vulcraft Division
559 Southlake Blvd (23236-3073)
PHONE.............................804 379-3704
Scott Askew, *General Mgr*
EMP: 3
SALES (corp-wide): 22.5B **Publicly Held**
WEB: www.nucor.com
SIC: **3312** Blast furnaces & steel mills

PA: Nucor Corporation
　1915 Rexford Rd Ste 400
　Charlotte NC 28211
　704 366-7000

(G-9942)
O DEPUY
720 Mrfield Pk Dr Ste 105 (23236)
PHONE.............................804 330-0988
Fax: 804 330-5421
EMP: 3
SALES (est): 197.1K **Privately Held**
SIC: **3842** Mfg Surgical Appliances/Supplies

(G-9943)
OFFICIAL TEE BLANCO LLC
4106 Laurelwood Rd (23234-3438)
PHONE.............................804 418-0218
Tiandra Threat, *Owner*
EMP: 1
SALES (est): 59.1K **Privately Held**
SIC: **2759 7231** Screen printing; cosmetologist

(G-9944)
OUTER BANKS WOODWORKS INC
9701 W Providence Rd (23236-3848)
PHONE.............................804 937-4330
William Bayliss, *Principal*
EMP: 2
SALES (est): 171.8K **Privately Held**
WEB: www.outerbankswoodworks.com
SIC: **2431** Millwork

(G-9945)
PARKER HANNIFEN SPORLAN DIV
605 Research Rd Ste C (23236-3933)
PHONE.............................804 379-8551
EMP: 2
SALES (est): 178.7K **Privately Held**
SIC: **3822** Mfg Environmental Controls

(G-9946)
PARTNERSHIP FOR SUCCESS
211 Ruthers Rd Ste 103 (23235-5396)
PHONE.............................804 363-3380
Linda Coles, *Owner*
EMP: 4
SALES (est): 201.2K **Privately Held**
SIC: **3089** Organizers for closets, drawers, etc.; plastic

(G-9947)
PHAT DADDYS POLISH SHOP
8706 S Boones Trail Rd (23236-4735)
PHONE.............................804 405-5301
Kevin Ferguson, *Owner*
EMP: 1
SALES (est): 30K **Privately Held**
SIC: **3751 5999** Motorcycles & related parts; alarm & safety equipment stores

(G-9948)
PHIL GUNN MACHINE CO INC
7801 Redpine Rd Ste A (23237-2290)
PHONE.............................804 271-7059
Phil Gunn, *President*
EMP: 7
SQ FT: 3,000
SALES (est): 768.3K **Privately Held**
WEB: www.philgunnmachine.com
SIC: **3599** Machine shop, jobbing & repair

(G-9949)
PHILIP MORRIS USA INC
9201 Arboretum Pkwy Fl 2 (23236-5403)
PHONE.............................804 253-8464
Sam Bowen, *Manager*
EMP: 130 **Publicly Held**
WEB: www.philipmorrisusa.com
SIC: **2111** Cigarettes
HQ: Philip Morris Usa Inc.
　6601 W Brd St
　Richmond VA 23230
　804 274-2000

(G-9950)
POPS SNACKS LLC
Also Called: Grand Pop's Best
11609 Busy St (23236-4059)
PHONE.............................804 594-7290
Aslam Gilani,

▲ = Import ▼=Export
◆ =Import/Export

Ashley Gilani,
EMP: 3
SQ FT: 3,000
SALES (est): 150K **Privately Held**
WEB: www.grandpopsbest.com
SIC: 2099 Popcorn, packaged: except already popped

(G-9951)
POREX TECHNOLOGIES CORPORATION
7400 Whitepine Rd (23237-2219)
PHONE..............................804 275-2631
Martin Caulfield, *President*
EMP: 150
SALES (corp-wide): 327.7MM **Privately Held**
WEB: www.porex.com
SIC: 3999 3951 2823 Cigarette filters; pens & mechanical pencils; cigarette tow, cellulosic fiber
HQ: Porex Technologies Corp.
1625 Ashton Park Dr Ste A
South Chesterfield VA 23834
804 524-4983

(G-9952)
POSIE PRESS LLC
1218 Traway Dr (23235-5557)
PHONE..............................804 276-0716
Nancy Beasley, *Principal*
EMP: 3
SALES (est): 141.5K **Privately Held**
SIC: 2711 Newspapers, publishing & printing

(G-9953)
PRECISION MACHINE CO INC
8011 Whitebark Ter (23237-2206)
P.O. Box 6892, Richmond (23230-0892)
PHONE..............................804 359-5758
Joe Price, *President*
EMP: 8 **EST:** 1960
SQ FT: 7,333
SALES (est): 740K **Privately Held**
WEB: www.precisionmachineco.com
SIC: 3599 7692 Machine shop, jobbing & repair; welding repair

(G-9954)
PRICEWALKER INC
Also Called: Precision Machine Co.
8011 Whitebark Ter (23237-2206)
PHONE..............................804 359-5758
Joseph Price, *President*
Harold Walker, *Vice Pres*
EMP: 8
SQ FT: 6,500
SALES (est): 932.6K **Privately Held**
WEB: www.precisionmachineco.com
SIC: 3599 Machine shop, jobbing & repair

(G-9955)
R & B DISTRIBUTING INC
535 Branchway Rd (23236-3032)
P.O. Box 3955 (23235-7955)
PHONE..............................804 794-5848
Lee R Green, *President*
Betty Green, *Corp Secy*
▲ **EMP:** 60
SQ FT: 20,000
SALES (est): 6.3MM **Privately Held**
SIC: 2353 Uniform hats & caps

(G-9956)
R AND N EXPRESS LLC
Also Called: Nelson Rogue
6517 Old Zion Hill Rd (23234-5843)
PHONE..............................804 909-3761
Nelson Rogue,
EMP: 2
SALES (est): 145.9K **Privately Held**
SIC: 3711 Personnel carriers (motor vehicles), assembly of

(G-9957)
RAVEN MACHINE
3015 Falling Creek Ave (23234-3924)
P.O. Box 37332 (23234-7332)
PHONE..............................804 271-6001
John Chandler, *Owner*
EMP: 7
SQ FT: 7,000

SALES (est): 842.3K **Privately Held**
WEB: www.ravenmachine.com
SIC: 3599 7692 Machine shop, jobbing & repair; welding repair

(G-9958)
RESOUNDING LLC
1905 Huguenot Rd Ste 200 (23235-4312)
PHONE..............................804 677-0947
Christopher Gatewood, *President*
Harper Trow, *Vice Pres*
EMP: 2
SQ FT: 1,100
SALES (est): 75.2K **Privately Held**
SIC: 7372 Business oriented computer software

(G-9959)
REYNOLDS CONSUMER PRODUCTS LLC
2101 Reymet Rd (23237-3719)
PHONE..............................804 743-6000
William Handlos, *General Mgr*
Douglas Crigger, *Engineer*
Thomas Degnan, *Branch Mgr*
Robert Reisch, *Director*
EMP: 14 **Privately Held**
WEB:
www.reynoldsconsumerproducts.com
SIC: 3353 Aluminum sheet, plate & foil
HQ: Reynolds Consumer Products Llc
1900 W Field Ct
Lake Forest IL 60045

(G-9960)
RICHARD RHEA INDUSTRIES LLC
10005 Cutter Dr (23235-4513)
PHONE..............................804 320-6575
Carmen Hoge, *Principal*
EMP: 2
SALES (est): 86.4K **Privately Held**
SIC: 3999 Manufacturing industries

(G-9961)
RICHMOND LIGHT CO (PA)
2301 Falkirk Dr (23236-1650)
PHONE..............................804 276-0559
Alex M Clarke, *President*
Ronald K Hale, *Corp Secy*
EMP: 5
SQ FT: 3,000
SALES (est): 450.1K **Privately Held**
WEB: www.trlc.com
SIC: 3841 8011 Medical instruments & equipment, blood & bone work; offices & clinics of medical doctors

(G-9962)
RICHMOND LIGHT CO
9840 Oxbridge Pl Ste 200 (23236-4230)
PHONE..............................804 276-0559
Alex Clark, *President*
EMP: 5
SALES (corp-wide): 450.1K **Privately Held**
WEB: www.trlc.com
SIC: 3841 Medical instruments & equipment, blood & bone work
PA: The Richmond Light Co
2301 Falkirk Dr
North Chesterfield VA 23236
804 276-0559

(G-9963)
RICHMOND PINBALL COLLECTIVE
9550 Midlothian Tpke # 112 (23235-4900)
PHONE..............................301 652-8000
EMP: 3 **EST:** 2017
SALES (est): 136.8K **Privately Held**
WEB: www.richmond.com
SIC: 2711 Newspapers, publishing & printing

(G-9964)
RICHMOND VENTURES LLC
2510 Cherrytree Ln (23235-2924)
PHONE..............................804 282-5901
Herman C Daniel III, *Administration*
EMP: 2
SALES (est): 71K **Privately Held**
SIC: 2711 Newspapers, publishing & printing

(G-9965)
ROLLING WITH CLASS LLC
4413 Deertrail Dr (23234-6603)
PHONE..............................804 836-9760
Charles Archer Jr, *Mng Member*
EMP: 1
SALES (est): 60K **Privately Held**
SIC: 3537 Trucks: freight, baggage, etc.: industrial, except mining

(G-9966)
ROSS PUBLISHING INC
Also Called: Seniors Housing Guide
711 Moorefield Park Dr H (23236-3669)
P.O. Box 35026 (23235-0026)
PHONE..............................804 674-5004
John Ross, *President*
Lori Ross, *Publisher*
Shannon Tippette, *Publisher*
Brian Ross, *COO*
Katharine Ross, *VP Sales*
EMP: 7
SALES (est): 998.2K **Privately Held**
WEB: www.seniorsguideonline.com
SIC: 2741 Guides: publishing only, not printed on site

(G-9967)
RRB INDUSTRIES INC
8808 Metro Ct (23237-2944)
PHONE..............................804 396-3270
Ramesh Bridgmohan, *Principal*
▼ **EMP:** 6
SQ FT: 1,000
SALES (est): 455K **Privately Held**
SIC: 3451 Screw machine products

(G-9968)
RVMF INC
Also Called: Original Mattress Factory, The
8401 Midlothian Tpke (23235-5121)
PHONE..............................614 921-1223
Ronald E Trzcinski, *President*
Cheryl Trzcinski, *Corp Secy*
David Coupland, *Vice Pres*
Tim Matthews, *Vice Pres*
EMP: 3
SALES (est): 442.3K **Privately Held**
WEB: www.originalmattress.com
SIC: 2515 5712 Mattresses & foundations; bedding & bedsprings

(G-9969)
SAUDER MANUFACTURING CO
413 Branchway Rd Ste A (23236-3264)
PHONE..............................804 897-3400
Shawn Shepherd, *Principal*
EMP: 2
SALES (est): 90.4K **Privately Held**
WEB: www.saudermfg.com
SIC: 2599 Furniture & fixtures

(G-9970)
SAVANNAH PUBLICATIONS
11302 Prvdence Creek Mews (23236-5268)
PHONE..............................804 674-1937
Susan Garnett, *Principal*
EMP: 2 **EST:** 2010
SALES (est): 101.7K **Privately Held**
WEB: www.thesavannahjpublications.com
SIC: 2741 Miscellaneous publishing

(G-9971)
SAXSMO PUBLISHING LLC
6401 Octagon Dr (23234-6145)
PHONE..............................804 269-0473
James Gates, *Principal*
EMP: 3
SALES (est): 92.2K **Privately Held**
SIC: 2711 Newspapers, publishing & printing

(G-9972)
SCHNEIDER AUTOMATION INC
7630 Whitepine Rd (23237-2215)
PHONE..............................804 271-7700
Billie Robinson, *Manager*
EMP: 7
SALES (corp-wide): 177.9K **Privately Held**
WEB: www.se.com
SIC: 3699 Electrical equipment & supplies

HQ: Schneider Automation Inc.
800 Federal St
Andover MA 01810
978 794-0800

(G-9973)
SEABOARD CONCRETE PRODUCTS CO
5000 Castlewood Rd (23234-3800)
P.O. Box 24001, Richmond (23224-0001)
PHONE..............................804 275-0802
Randy Daniel, *President*
EMP: 30 **EST:** 1979
SQ FT: 20,000
SALES (est): 4.5MM **Privately Held**
WEB: www.seaboardconcrete.com
SIC: 3272 Concrete products, precast

(G-9974)
SEALPAC USA LLC
2301 Chancellor Rd (23235-2713)
PHONE..............................804 261-0580
Kristina Kuzel-Meyer, *Office Mgr*
Carsten Fouget, *Mng Member*
Carsten Fouquet, *Mng Member*
▲ **EMP:** 5
SALES (est): 592K **Privately Held**
WEB: www.sealpac-us.com
SIC: 3565 Packaging machinery

(G-9975)
SEPARATION UNLIMITED INC
11501 Allecingie Pkwy (23235-4301)
PHONE..............................804 794-4864
Glenn Pfluger Sr, *President*
Didanna Pfluger, *Corp Secy*
EMP: 15
SQ FT: 5,500
SALES (est): 1.7MM **Privately Held**
WEB: www.interseps.com
SIC: 2759 2796 Commercial printing; color separations for printing

(G-9976)
SHAKESPEAREINK INC
2609 Wicklow Loop (23236-1364)
PHONE..............................804 381-8237
Catherine Alexander, *President*
EMP: 15 **EST:** 2017
SALES (est): 453.4K **Privately Held**
SIC: 2721 Periodicals

(G-9977)
SHELTON PLUMBING & HEATING LLC
4779 Stornoway Dr (23234-3757)
PHONE..............................804 539-8080
Londell Shelton,
EMP: 2
SALES (est): 85.1K **Privately Held**
WEB: www.sheltonplumbingandheating.org
SIC: 3088 Plastics plumbing fixtures

(G-9978)
SHERRIE & SCOTT EMBROIDERY
7031 Bridgeside Pl (23234-8229)
PHONE..............................804 271-2024
EMP: 1
SALES (est): 50.4K **Privately Held**
SIC: 2395 Embroidery & art needlework

(G-9979)
SIGNARAMA RICHMOND
705 Johnston Willis Dr (23236-3953)
PHONE..............................804 301-9317
EMP: 2
SALES (est): 83.9K **Privately Held**
WEB: www.powerplayimaging.com
SIC: 2752 Commercial printing, lithographic

(G-9980)
SIGNS AT WORK
641 Johnston Willis Dr (23236-3954)
PHONE..............................804 338-7716
EMP: 1
SALES (est): 50.6K **Privately Held**
SIC: 3993 Signs & advertising specialties

(G-9981)
SIGNS WORK INC
641 Johnston Willis Dr (23236-3954)
PHONE..............................804 338-7716
Alan Sloan, *President*

GEOGRAPHIC

EMP: 1
SALES (est): 125K **Privately Held**
SIC: 2759 Decals: printing

(G-9982)
SOFOREAL ENTERTAINMENT (PA)
Also Called: Crazy Tees
9550 Midlothian Tpke (23235-4900)
PHONE..................................804 442-6850
Dexter Carmon, *CEO*
EMP: 1
SALES (est): 50K **Privately Held**
WEB: www.crazyteesrva.com
SIC: 2261 Printing of cotton broadwoven fabrics

(G-9983)
SOLO PER TE BAKED GOODS INC
704 Sunrise Five Way E (23236-3751)
PHONE..................................804 277-9010
Mrs Lydia Johnson, *Principal*
EMP: 1
SALES (est): 39.5K **Privately Held**
SIC: 2051 Bread, cake & related products

(G-9984)
SOLUTIONS WISE GROUP
9565 Chipping Dr (23237-3842)
PHONE..................................804 748-0205
Glen Kemp, *Principal*
EMP: 2
SALES (est): 152K **Privately Held**
SIC: 7372 Prepackaged software

(G-9985)
SOUTHERNS M&P LLC
7607 Midlothian Tpke (23235-5223)
PHONE..................................804 330-2407
Gregory Ballengee, *President*
Wayne Miles Jr, *Vice Pres*
EMP: 2
SQ FT: 900
SALES (est): 107.8K **Privately Held**
SIC: 3999 5099 5661 5999 Badges, metal: policemen, firemen, etc.; firearms & ammunition, except sporting; men's boots; women's boots; police supply stores

(G-9986)
SPECTRUM OPTOMETRIC
8709 Forest Hill Ave (23235-2459)
PHONE..................................804 457-8733
EMP: 2
SALES (est): 104.2K **Privately Held**
WEB: www.spectrumoptometric.info
SIC: 3827 Optical instruments & lenses

(G-9987)
SPHINX INDUSTRIES INC
7101 Bridgeside Ct (23234-8230)
PHONE..................................804 279-8894
Jeff Randolph, *Principal*
EMP: 2
SALES (est): 92.7K **Privately Held**
SIC: 3999 Manufacturing industries

(G-9988)
SPORTS SUPPLEMENTS SOUTH INC
477 Southlake Blvd (23236-3044)
PHONE..................................804 379-6410
Steve Tapscott, *President*
EMP: 8
SQ FT: 10,000
SALES (est): 2.1MM **Privately Held**
WEB: www.sssva.com
SIC: 2023 Dietary supplements, dairy & non-dairy based

(G-9989)
SPRECHER & SCHUH INC
Also Called: Sprecher Schuh
821 Southlake Blvd (23236-3917)
PHONE..................................804 379-6065
Brian Schofner, *President*
EMP: 17 **Publicly Held**
WEB: www.sprecherschuh.com
SIC: 3625 4225 Motor controls, electric; general warehousing & storage

HQ: Sprecher & Schuh, Inc.
15910 Intl Plz Dr
Houston TX 77032
281 442-9000

(G-9990)
STARTUP VIRGINIA
1712 Buford Rd (23235-4270)
PHONE..................................804 502-3131
William Loving, *Ch of Bd*
Bryan Bostic, *Exec Dir*
Bradley Cummings, *Director*
EMP: 3
SQ FT: 5,000
SALES (est): 101.8K **Privately Held**
WEB: www.richmond.com
SIC: 2711 Newspapers, publishing & printing

(G-9991)
STELLAR DAY PRODUCTS CORP
9565 Chipping Dr (23237-3842)
PHONE..................................804 748-8086
Mary Kemp, *Principal*
EMP: 2
SALES (est): 112.9K **Privately Held**
WEB: www.churchkeeper.com
SIC: 7372 Prepackaged software

(G-9992)
SUPER RAD COILS LTD PARTNR
451 Southlake Blvd (23235-3044)
P.O. Box 73450 (23235-8041)
PHONE..................................804 794-2887
Louis Rogerson, *General Mgr*
Matt Holland, *Vice Pres*
Brooke Hughes, *Vice Pres*
Mark Schuch, *Vice Pres*
Ralf Schulze, *Design Engr*
EMP: 130
SALES (corp-wide): 52.2MM **Privately Held**
WEB: www.superradiatorcoils.com
SIC: 3443 5075 3585 3498 Heat exchangers: coolers (after, inter), condensers, etc.; warm air heating equipment & supplies; refrigeration & heating equipment; fabricated pipe & fittings; heating equipment, except electric
PA: Super Radiator Coils Limited Partnership
104 Peavey Rd
Chaska MN 55318
952 556-3330

(G-9993)
SUPERIOR SIGNS LLC
2510 Willis Rd (23237-4606)
PHONE..................................804 271-5685
Allen Twedt, *Managing Prtnr*
David Goad, *Mng Member*
Carin Elmore, *Executive*
Annie Moore,
David Moore,
EMP: 26
SQ FT: 3,000
SALES (est): 3MM **Privately Held**
WEB: www.superiorsignsrva.com
SIC: 3993 7389 Signs, not made in custom sign painting shops; sign painting & lettering shop

(G-9994)
SWAMI SHRIJI LLC
6206 Faulkner Dr (23234-6177)
PHONE..................................804 322-9644
Kaushal Patel,
EMP: 1 EST: 2013
SALES (est): 200K **Privately Held**
SIC: 7372 8742 7371 7389 Application computer software; management information systems consultant; software programming applications;

(G-9995)
SWEET & SAVORY BY EMILY LLC
1301 Elmart Ln (23235-6203)
PHONE..................................804 248-8252
Emily Taylor, *Principal*
EMP: 1 EST: 2016
SALES (est): 10K **Privately Held**
SIC: 2066 2024 Chocolate; non-dairy based frozen desserts

(G-9996)
SYLVAN SPIRIT
2339 Jimmy Winters Rd (23235-2929)
PHONE..................................804 330-5454
Rebecca Worth, *President*
EMP: 2
SALES (est): 125.5K **Privately Held**
WEB: www.sylvanspirit.com
SIC: 3911 Jewelry, precious metal

(G-9997)
SYMMETRIC SYSTEMS INC
Also Called: Boom Media Services
9225 Chatham Grove Ln D (23236-1185)
P.O. Box 4085, Midlothian (23112-0001)
PHONE..................................804 276-7202
Richard A Ott, *President*
EMP: 1
SQ FT: 1,200
SALES (est): 128.4K **Privately Held**
SIC: 2752 8742 Commercial printing, offset; marketing consulting services

(G-9998)
TARKETT USA INC
301 Southlake Blvd (23236-3085)
PHONE..................................804 594-0500
EMP: 5
SALES (corp-wide): 589.6K **Privately Held**
WEB: www.commercial.tarkett.com
SIC: 2273 Carpets & rugs
HQ: Tarkett Usa Inc.
30000 Aurora Rd
Solon OH 44139
440 543-8916

(G-9999)
TECHNISERVICES INC
8800 Metro Ct (23237-2944)
PHONE..................................804 275-9207
J D McCoy, *President*
EMP: 3
SALES (est): 504.9K **Privately Held**
SIC: 3679 Harness assemblies for electronic use: wire or cable

(G-10000)
TEXT ART PRINT
6405 Octagon Dr Apt 3a (23234-6164)
PHONE..................................908 619-2809
John Joseph Neely, *Principal*
EMP: 2 EST: 2010
SALES (est): 12.8K **Privately Held**
SIC: 2752 Commercial printing, lithographic

(G-10001)
THOMPSON FIXTURE INSTALLATION
530 Southlake Blvd Ste D (23236-3067)
PHONE..................................804 378-9352
Paul Thompson, *President*
Rich Hord, *Superintendent*
Kimberly Thompson, *Vice Pres*
Paul Pollak, *Opers Staff*
Mike Cole, *Sr Project Mgr*
EMP: 18
SALES (est): 2.5MM **Privately Held**
WEB: www.tfinstall.com
SIC: 2542 Fixtures: display, office or store: except wood

(G-10002)
THREE CROSSES DISTLG CO LLC
11620 Drysdale Dr (23236-4039)
PHONE..................................804 818-6330
EMP: 2
SALES (est): 68.2K **Privately Held**
WEB: www.threecrossesdistilling.com
SIC: 2085 Distilled & blended liquors

(G-10003)
TOTAL STITCH EMBROIDERY INC
8612 Hunterstand Ct (23237-2352)
PHONE..................................804 275-4853
EMP: 2 EST: 2009
SALES (est): 92K **Privately Held**
SIC: 2395 Pleating/Stitching Services

(G-10004)
TREXLO ENTERPRISES LLC
Also Called: Fastsigns
11523 Midlothian Tpke C (23235-4762)
PHONE..................................804 272-7446
Chris Howard, *Manager*
Christopher Robertson, *Manager*
EMP: 2
SALES (corp-wide): 2.9MM **Privately Held**
WEB: www.fastsigns.com
SIC: 3993 Signs & advertising specialties
PA: Trexlo Enterprises, Llc
2361a Greystone Ct Ste A
Rockville VA 23146
804 719-5900

(G-10005)
TS BY EXTREME LLC
Also Called: Fetti Bear Apparel and ACC
7331 Summertree Dr (23234-5935)
PHONE..................................804 335-0260
Eddie Cook, *Principal*
EMP: 3
SALES (est): 113.3K **Privately Held**
SIC: 2389 Apparel & accessories

(G-10006)
TYPE & ART
1905 Huguenot Rd Ste 104 (23235-4312)
PHONE..................................804 794-3375
Judson C Anderson, *Owner*
EMP: 2
SQ FT: 3,000
SALES (est): 76K **Privately Held**
SIC: 2791 7336 Typesetting; commercial art & illustration

(G-10007)
UNITED ARMAMENT LLC
425 Southlake Blvd Ste 1b (23236-3064)
PHONE..................................804 839-1800
EMP: 2
SALES (est): 136.7K **Privately Held**
SIC: 3482 Small arms ammunition

(G-10008)
VERDEX TECHNOLOGIES INC
9305 Burge Ave (23237-3036)
PHONE..................................804 491-9733
Bradford Higgins, *CEO*
Damien Deehan, *President*
EMP: 1
SQ FT: 5,000
SALES (est): 102.4K **Privately Held**
WEB: www.verdextech.com
SIC: 3569 Filters
PA: Sosventures Llc
485 Jessie St
San Francisco CA 94103

(G-10009)
VIRGINIA HEAD AND NECK THERAPE
10149 Bon Air Crest Dr (23235-4868)
PHONE..................................804 837-9594
Jeffrey Ward Cash DDS, *Principal*
EMP: 3
SALES (est): 174.3K **Privately Held**
SIC: 2834 Pharmaceutical preparations

(G-10010)
WARRIORWARE LLC
8825 Lyndale Dr (23235-6047)
P.O. Box 74144 (23236-0003)
PHONE..................................804 338-9431
John J Rogers, *President*
EMP: 1
SALES (est): 58.8K **Privately Held**
SIC: 2253 Knit outerwear mills

(G-10011)
WIGLANCE LLC
7119 Koufax Ct (23234-8217)
PHONE..................................866 301-3662
Ronald Quarrles,
EMP: 3 EST: 2016
SALES (est): 96.5K **Privately Held**
SIC: 3769 Guided missile & space vehicle parts & aux eqpt, rsch & dev

(G-10012)
WILSONS ELITE EXPRESS LLC
6105 Rosenblum Ct Apt 1b (23234-0020)
PHONE..................................804 517-4276

Kareem Wilson,
EMP: 2
SALES (est): 100K **Privately Held**
SIC: 3743 Freight cars & equipment

(G-10013)
WINTERLOCH PUBLISHING LLC
2400 Loch Braemar Dr (23236-1609)
P.O. Box 35368 (23235-0368)
PHONE................804 571-2782
Lori Justice, *Publisher*
Therese Silvius, *Principal*
EMP: 2
SALES (est): 91.5K **Privately Held**
WEB: www.winterlochpublishing.com
SIC: 2731 7389 Books: publishing only;

(G-10014)
WOP HAIR LLC
7018 Walmsley Blvd (23235-5814)
PHONE................804 277-4666
Antwan Harris, *Mng Member*
EMP: 1
SALES (est): 39.6K **Privately Held**
SIC: 3999 Hair & hair-based products

(G-10015)
XP MANUFACTURING LLC
107 Hempstead Way (23236-2476)
PHONE................804 833-1411
EMP: 1
SALES (est): 39.6K **Privately Held**
SIC: 3999 Manufacturing industries

North Chesterfield
Richmond City County

(G-10016)
ALR TECHNOLOGIES INC
7400 Beaufont Spring Dr # 3 (23225-5556)
PHONE................804 554-3500
Sidney Chan, *Ch of Bd*
▲ **EMP:** 1 **EST:** 1987
SALES (est): 168.4K **Privately Held**
WEB: www.alrt.com
SIC: 3841 3845 Surgical & medical instruments; electromedical equipment; electromedical apparatus

(G-10017)
CUSTOM VAULT CORPORATION
1011 Boulder Springs Dr (23225-4950)
PHONE................804 303-1741
EMP: 2 **EST:** 2016
SALES (est): 113.2K **Privately Held**
SIC: 3272 Burial vaults, concrete or precast terrazzo

(G-10018)
DOMINION AMMUNITION MFG INC
106 Turner Rd (23225-6414)
PHONE................804 276-2851
Jerry Thompson, *Principal*
EMP: 2
SALES (est): 67K **Privately Held**
SIC: 3999 Manufacturing industries

(G-10019)
ECOLOCHEM INC
7400 Beaufont Spring Dr # 3 (23225-5556)
PHONE................804 327-6846
EMP: 60
SALES (est): 87.9K **Privately Held**
SIC: 3589 Service industry machinery

(G-10020)
IDEAPHORIA PRESS LLC
7758 Yarmouth Dr (23225-2147)
PHONE................804 272-6231
William York III, *Principal*
EMP: 2
SALES (est): 71.5K **Privately Held**
WEB: www.ideaphoriapress.com
SIC: 2741 Miscellaneous publishing

(G-10021)
PLATINUM POINT LLC
7518 Elkhardt Rd (23225-6910)
PHONE................804 357-3337
EMP: 3

SALES (est): 78.8K **Privately Held**
WEB: www.platinumpointpublishing.com
SIC: 2711 Newspapers

(G-10022)
RIDE-AWAY INC
Also Called: Mobilityworks
7450 Midlothian Tpke (23225-5419)
PHONE................804 233-8267
William Koeblitz, *President*
Peter Lanzo, *Manager*
Katie Walter, *Consultant*
EMP: 10
SALES (corp-wide): 564.6MM **Privately Held**
WEB: www.mobilityworks.com
SIC: 3999 7532 5047 Wheelchair lifts; van conversion; medical & hospital equipment
HQ: Ride-Away, Inc.
54 Wentworth Ave
Londonderry NH 03053
603 437-4444

(G-10023)
S JOYE & SON INC
2612 Goodes Bridge Rd C (23224-2567)
P.O. Box 34385 (23234-0385)
PHONE................804 745-2419
John L Joye, *President*
John T Joye Jr, *Vice Pres*
EMP: 2
SALES (est): 170K **Privately Held**
SIC: 3444 Sheet metalwork

(G-10024)
SOLAR ELECTRIC AMERICA LLC
Also Called: Solar Elc Amer Richmond Ci
7530 Yarmouth Dr (23225-2143)
PHONE................804 332-6358
Charles Bush, *CEO*
EMP: 1
SALES (est): 121K **Privately Held**
WEB: www.solarelectricamerica.com
SIC: 3433 Solar heaters & collectors

(G-10025)
TAYLOR COMMUNICATIONS INC
1001 Boulders Pkwy # 440 (23225-5522)
PHONE................937 221-1000
George Keller, *Manager*
EMP: 13
SALES (corp-wide): 2.4B **Privately Held**
WEB: www.taylorcommunications.com
SIC: 2761 Manifold business forms
HQ: Taylor Communications, Inc
111 W 1st St Ste 910
Dayton OH 45402
937 221-1000

(G-10026)
TG HOLDINGS INTERNATIONAL CV
1100 Boulders Pkwy (23225-4036)
PHONE................804 330-1000
Charles Ewell, *Principal*
EMP: 1
SALES (est): 110K **Privately Held**
WEB: www.tredegar.com
SIC: 3081 Plastic film & sheet

(G-10027)
TORISHIMA PUMP MFG CO LTD
7400 Beaufont Spring Dr # 3 (23225-5556)
PHONE................866 374-1130
EMP: 1
SALES (est): 43.6K **Privately Held**
SIC: 3999 Manufacturing industries

(G-10028)
TREDEGAR CONSUMER DESIGNS INC
1100 Boulders Pkwy # 200 (23225-4064)
PHONE................804 330-1000
John Gottwald, *President*
Michael Francis, *Opers Staff*
Steve Bruce, *Research*
Brandon Smith, *Finance Mgr*
EMP: 1
SALES (est): 98.6K **Publicly Held**
WEB: www.tredegar.com
SIC: 3081 Unsupported plastics film & sheet

PA: Tredegar Corporation
1100 Boulders Pkwy # 200
North Chesterfield VA 23225

(G-10029)
TREDEGAR CORPORATION (PA)
1100 Boulders Pkwy # 200 (23225-4064)
PHONE................804 330-1000
William M Gottwald, *Ch of Bd*
John M Steitz, *President*
Rosana Godoi, *Business Mgr*
Douglas Monk, *COO*
Michael J Schewel, *Vice Pres*
◆ **EMP:** 100
SALES: 1B **Publicly Held**
WEB: www.tredegar.com
SIC: 3081 2671 3083 3354 Plastic film & sheet; plastic film, coated or laminated for packaging; laminated plastics plate & sheet; aluminum extruded products

(G-10030)
TREDEGAR CORPORATION
Tredegar Film Products Div
1100 Boulders Pkwy # 200 (23225-4064)
PHONE................804 330-1000
EMP: 150 **Publicly Held**
WEB: www.tredegar.com
SIC: 3354 3081 Aluminum extruded products; plastic film & sheet
PA: Tredegar Corporation
1100 Boulders Pkwy # 200
North Chesterfield VA 23225

(G-10031)
TREDEGAR FAR EAST CORPORATION (HQ)
1100 Boulders Pkwy # 200 (23225-4064)
PHONE................804 330-1000
Gregory Williams, *CEO*
EMP: 1
SALES (est): 2MM **Publicly Held**
WEB: www.tredegar.com
SIC: 3081 Unsupported plastics film & sheet

(G-10032)
TREDEGAR FILM PRODUCTS CORP
1100 Boulders Pkwy # 200 (23225-4064)
PHONE................847 438-2111
Tim Rogers, *Production*
Carol Gillespie, *Purch Mgr*
Becky Bailey, *Technical Staff*
EMP: 170 **Publicly Held**
WEB: www.tredegar.com
SIC: 3081 3089 Polyethylene film; plastic processing
HQ: Tredegar Film Products Corporation
1100 Boulders Pkwy # 200
North Chesterfield VA 23225

(G-10033)
TREDEGAR FILM PRODUCTS CORP (HQ)
1100 Boulders Pkwy # 200 (23225-4064)
PHONE................804 330-1000
Mary Jane Hellyar, *President*
Mary Anderson, *Counsel*
Carole Gillespie, *Purchasing*
Wayne Meaker, *Senior Mgr*
◆ **EMP:** 121
SALES (est): 233.4MM **Publicly Held**
WEB: www.tredegar.com
SIC: 3081 Unsupported plastics film & sheet

(G-10034)
TREDEGAR FILM PRODUCTS LATIN
1100 Boulders Pkwy # 200 (23225-4064)
PHONE................804 330-1000
EMP: 1 **EST:** 2015
SALES (est): 103.4K **Publicly Held**
WEB: www.tredegarfilms.com
SIC: 3081 Plastic film & sheet
PA: Tredegar Corporation
1100 Boulders Pkwy # 200
North Chesterfield VA 23225

(G-10035)
TREDEGAR FILM PRODUCTS US LLC
1100 Boulders Pkwy # 200 (23225-4064)
PHONE................804 330-1000

John Gottwald, *Principal*
EMP: 277
SALES (est): 634.7K **Publicly Held**
WEB: www.tredegarsurfaceprotection.com
SIC: 3081 Unsupported plastics film & sheet
HQ: Tredegar Film Products Corporation
1100 Boulders Pkwy # 200
North Chesterfield VA 23225

(G-10036)
TREDEGAR FILMS DEVELOPMENT INC
1100 Boulders Pkwy # 200 (23225-4064)
PHONE................804 330-1000
Mary Jane Hellyar, *President*
A Brent King, *Vice Pres*
Kevin A O'Leary, *Treasurer*
EMP: 1
SALES (est): 82K **Publicly Held**
WEB: www.tredegar.com
SIC: 3081 Unsupported plastics film & sheet
PA: Tredegar Corporation
1100 Boulders Pkwy # 200
North Chesterfield VA 23225

(G-10037)
TREDEGAR FILMS RS CONVERTING
1100 Boulders Pkwy # 200 (23225-4064)
PHONE................804 330-1000
EMP: 208
SALES (est): 179K **Publicly Held**
WEB: www.tredegarfilms.com
SIC: 3081 Unsupported plastics film & sheet
HQ: Tredegar Film Products Corporation
1100 Boulders Pkwy # 200
North Chesterfield VA 23225

(G-10038)
TREDEGAR PERFORMANCE FILMS INC
1100 Boulders Pkwy # 200 (23225-4064)
PHONE................804 330-1000
Douglas O'Connell, *President*
EMP: 346
SALES (est): 422.9K **Publicly Held**
WEB: www.tredegarfilms.com
SIC: 3081 Unsupported plastics film & sheet
HQ: Tredegar Film Products Corporation
1100 Boulders Pkwy # 200
North Chesterfield VA 23225

(G-10039)
TREDEGAR PERSONAL CARE LLC
1100 Boulders Pkwy # 200 (23225-4064)
PHONE................804 330-1000
EMP: 1
SALES (est): 46.8K **Publicly Held**
SIC: 2389 Disposable garments & accessories
PA: Tredegar Corporation
1100 Boulders Pkwy # 200
North Chesterfield VA 23225

(G-10040)
TREDEGAR PETROLEUM CORPORATION
1100 Boulders Pkwy # 200 (23225-4064)
PHONE................804 330-1000
EMP: 1
SALES (est): 91.1K **Publicly Held**
WEB: www.tredegar.com
SIC: 1382 Oil & gas exploration services
PA: Tredegar Corporation
1100 Boulders Pkwy # 200
North Chesterfield VA 23225

(G-10041)
TREDEGAR SURFC PROTECTION LLC (HQ)
1100 Boulders Pkwy # 200 (23225-4064)
PHONE................804 330-1000
EMP: 1
SALES (est): 110.2K **Publicly Held**
WEB: www.tredegarsurfaceprotection.com
SIC: 3827 Optical instruments & lenses

GEOGRAPHIC

(G-10042)
URIEL WIND INC (HQ)
7400 Beaufont Springs Dr # 300
(23225-5556)
PHONE..............................804 672-4471
Felix Morales, *President*
Ignacio Huarte, *Chairman*
EMP: 4 EST: 2008
SQ FT: 1,000
SALES (est): 384.7K
**SALES (corp-wide): 3.7MM Privately
Held**
WEB: www.urielwind.com
SIC: 3621 Power generators
PA: Uriel Inversiones Sa
    Paseo Castellana, 116 - Planta 8
    Madrid 28046
    915 641-861

(G-10043)
**VIRGINIA MTALS FABRICATION
LLC**
2471 Goodes Bridge Rd (23224-2521)
PHONE..............................804 622-2900
EMP: 2
SALES (est): 160.5K Privately Held
WEB: www.virginiametalsystems.com
SIC: 3499 Fabricated metal products

(G-10044)
WHEATLEY RACING
6600 Parliament Rd (23224-4330)
PHONE..............................804 276-3670
EMP: 1
SALES (est): 90.7K Privately Held
SIC: 3519 Mfg Internal Combustion En-
gines

(G-10045)
**WILLIAM L BONNELL COMPANY
INC (PA)**
1100 Boulders Pkwy (23225-4036)
PHONE..............................804 330-1147
McAlister C Marshall II, *Vice Pres*
EMP: 7
SALES (est): 90.2MM Privately Held
SIC: 3354 Aluminum extruded products

(G-10046)
**YOUNG MOVAR & ASSOC
MRKTNG**
300 Turner Rd Ste C (23225-6431)
PHONE..............................804 320-5860
Gladys Young, *Principal*
EMP: 2 EST: 2012
SALES (est): 94.3K Privately Held
SIC: 2741 Miscellaneous publishing

North Dinwiddie
Petersburg City County

(G-10047)
**ARLENE NANCYS MEALS ON
WHEELS**
8709 Squirrel Level Rd (23803-7725)
PHONE..............................404 940-8995
Nabranna Beasley, *CEO*
EMP: 1
SALES (est): 57.3K Privately Held
SIC: 2599 Food wagons, restaurant

(G-10048)
BISHOP CUSTOM CABINETS
10500 Duncan Rd (23803-9036)
PHONE..............................804 469-7549
Donald Bishop, *Owner*
Barbara Hammond, *Principal*
EMP: 1
SALES (est): 121.5K Privately Held
WEB: www.bishopcustomcabinets.com
SIC: 2434 Wood kitchen cabinets

(G-10049)
CHAPARRAL (VIRGINIA) INC
Also Called: Gerdau Ameristeel Dinwiddie Co
25801 Hofmeier Way (23803-8905)
PHONE..............................972 647-7915
Cy Wang, *President*
Marcos Cresencio, *Vice Pres*
Ruben Trevino, *Engineer*
Dana Warren, *Controller*
Connie Jones, *Manager*

▲ **EMP:** 410
SALES (est): 330MM Privately Held
WEB: www.gerdau.com
SIC: 3312 Blast furnaces & steel mills
HQ: Gerdau Ameristeel Us Inc.
    4221 W Boy Scout Blvd # 600
    Tampa FL 33607
    813 286-8383

(G-10050)
DAVES CABINET SHOP INC
22418 Cox Rd (23803-6900)
PHONE..............................804 861-9275
David Roane, *President*
Patrick Casale, *Corp Secy*
EMP: 2
SQ FT: 8,000
SALES (est): 180K Privately Held
SIC: 2434 Wood kitchen cabinets

(G-10051)
GERDAU AMERISTEEL US INC
25801 Hofheimer Way (23803-8905)
PHONE..............................804 520-0286
Robert Simcoe, *Manager*
EMP: 232 Privately Held
WEB: www.gerdau.com
SIC: 3312 Blast furnaces & steel mills
HQ: Gerdau Ameristeel Us Inc.
    4221 W Boy Scout Blvd # 600
    Tampa FL 33607
    813 286-8383

(G-10052)
HERITAGE CABINETS INC
23024 Airpark Dr (23803-6926)
PHONE..............................804 861-5251
Charles Mullis, *President*
EMP: 5
SALES (est): 623.8K Privately Held
SIC: 2434 Wood kitchen cabinets

(G-10053)
**HILLCREST TRANSPORTATION
INC (PA)**
25452 Hofheimer Way (23803-8937)
PHONE..............................804 861-1100
John P Edmunds, *CEO*
EMP: 32
SALES (est): 5.4MM Privately Held
WEB: www.hillcresttransportation.com
SIC: 3715 Truck trailers

(G-10054)
JACK STONE QUARRY
23308 Cox Rd (23803-6834)
PHONE..............................804 862-6669
Jeff Rickey, *Principal*
EMP: 3 EST: 2011
SALES (est): 155.8K Privately Held
SIC: 1422 Crushed & broken limestone

(G-10055)
JWS WELDING & REPAIR
11735 Old Stage Rd (23805-9505)
PHONE..............................804 720-2523
James M Walker Jr, *Owner*
EMP: 2
SALES (est): 97K Privately Held
SIC: 7692 Welding repair

(G-10056)
LEGACY VULCAN LLC
26505 Simpson Rd (23803-8934)
PHONE..............................804 863-4565
EMP: 3 Publicly Held
WEB: www.vulcanmaterials.com
SIC: 3273 Ready-mixed concrete
HQ: Legacy Vulcan, Llc
    1200 Urban Center Dr
    Vestavia AL 35242
    205 298-3000

(G-10057)
LEMAC CORPORATION
22909 Airpark Dr (23803-6969)
PHONE..............................804 862-8481
Frank G Coleman, *President*
Paul Smith, *Vice Pres*
◆ **EMP: 21**
SQ FT: 6,000
SALES (est): 5.7MM Privately Held
WEB: www.lemaconline.com
SIC: 3531 Construction machinery attach-
ments; backhoe mounted, hydraulically
powered attachments

(G-10058)
LIFE EVAC
23301 Airport Rd (23803-6727)
PHONE..............................804 652-0171
Jay Love Lady, *Director*
Chris Stevenson, *Director*
EMP: 50
SALES (est): 3.5MM Privately Held
SIC: 3711 Ambulances (motor vehicles),
assembly of

(G-10059)
LITTLEBIRD JAMS AND JELLIES
25321 Cox Rd (23803-6507)
PHONE..............................804 586-4420
Marcia Williams, *Principal*
EMP: 3
SALES (est): 147.2K Privately Held
SIC: 2033 Jams, jellies & preserves: pack-
aged in cans, jars, etc.

(G-10060)
MAXINES CHEESECAKES LLC
8771 Lake Jordan Way (23803-6594)
PHONE..............................804 586-5135
Maxine Dixon, *Principal*
EMP: 2
SALES (est): 123.2K Privately Held
WEB: www.maxinescheesecakes.com
SIC: 2591 Window blinds

(G-10061)
PAGE PUBLICATIONS INC
23212 Airport St (23803-6912)
PHONE..............................804 733-8636
Byerly Hanes, *Owner*
EMP: 2
SALES (est): 62.9K Privately Held
SIC: 2711 Newspapers

(G-10062)
QUEST INDUSTRIES LLC
22909 Airpark Dr (23803-6969)
PHONE..............................804 862-8481
Ken Wiseman, *Principal*
◆ **EMP: 2**
SALES (est): 82K Privately Held
WEB: www.questattachments.com
SIC: 3999 Manufacturing industries

(G-10063)
**RICHARDSON ENTERPRISES
INC**
Also Called: Hollywood Signs
23202 Airport St (23803-6912)
PHONE..............................804 733-8956
Lee Richardson, *President*
EMP: 2
SQ FT: 2,500
SALES (est): 180K Privately Held
SIC: 3993 Signs, not made in custom sign
painting shops

(G-10064)
TCS MATERIALS CORP
26505 Simpson Rd (23803-8934)
P.O. Box 1008, Petersburg (23804-1008)
PHONE..............................804 863-4525
EMP: 11
SALES (corp-wide): 2.7B Publicly Held
SIC: 3272 Mfg Concrete Products
HQ: Tcs Materials Corp
    2100 Deepwater Trml Rd
    Richmond VA 23234
    804 232-1200

(G-10065)
TINDALL CORPORATION
Also Called: Tindall Concrete Virginia
5400 Olgers Rd (23803-6884)
P.O. Box 711, Petersburg (23804-0711)
PHONE..............................804 861-8447
Chuck Wynings, *Branch Mgr*
EMP: 200
**SALES (corp-wide): 425.6MM Privately
Held**
WEB: www.tindallrecruiting.com
SIC: 3272 Concrete products, precast
PA: Tindall Corporation
    3076 N Blackstock Rd
    Spartanburg SC 29301
    864 576-3230

(G-10066)
TMS INTERNATIONAL LLC
25805 Hofheimer Way (23803-8905)
PHONE..............................804 957-9611
Michael J Connolly, *Vice Pres*
EMP: 7 Privately Held
WEB: www.tmsinternational.com
SIC: 3312 Blast furnaces & steel mills
HQ: Tms International, Llc
    Southside Wrks Bldg 1 3f
    Pittsburgh PA 15203
    412 678-6141

(G-10067)
**TYE CUSTOM METAL
FABRICATORS**
22508 Cox Rd (23803-6902)
PHONE..............................804 863-2551
Terry Frank, *Owner*
EMP: 1
SALES (est): 89.7K Privately Held
SIC: 3441 Fabricated structural metal

(G-10068)
VIRGINIA SCREEN PRINTING
24108 River Rd (23803-8316)
PHONE..............................804 295-7440
Virginia Williams, *Principal*
EMP: 2
SALES (est): 83.9K Privately Held
SIC: 2752 Commercial printing, litho-
graphic

(G-10069)
**VULCAN CONSTRUCTION MTLS
LLC**
23308 Cox Rd (23803-6834)
PHONE..............................804 862-6665
Jeff Ricky, *Branch Mgr*
EMP: 28
SQ FT: 1,700 Publicly Held
WEB: www.vulcanmaterials.com
SIC: 3273 Ready-mixed concrete
HQ: Vulcan Construction Materials, Llc
    1200 Urban Center Dr
    Vestavia AL 35242
    205 298-3000

(G-10070)
WESTERN SHEET METAL INC
23610 Airport Rd (23803-6728)
PHONE..............................804 732-0230
Mike Junell, *President*
EMP: 8 Privately Held
SIC: 3444 Sheet metal specialties, not
stamped

(G-10071)
**WILSON & WILSON
INTERNATIONAL**
5111 Yellowstone Dr (23803-8736)
PHONE..............................804 733-3180
Cie Wilson, *Owner*
▲ **EMP: 2**
SALES (est): 80.2K Privately Held
SIC: 3944 7389 Chessmen & chess-
boards;

(G-10072)
WILSON ENTERPRISES INC
23011 Airpark Dr (23803-6927)
P.O. Box 100, Disputanta (23842-0100)
PHONE..............................804 732-6884
Ben B Wilson Jr, *President*
EMP: 12
SALES (est): 1.6MM Privately Held
SIC: 2048 Feed supplements

(G-10073)
WILSON WAREHOUSE
23011 Airpark Dr (23803-6927)
PHONE..............................804 991-2163
Ben Wilson, *Owner*
EMP: 5
SALES (est): 452.7K Privately Held
SIC: 2833 Animal based products

▲ = Import ▼=Export
◆ =Import/Export

North Garden
Albemarle County

(G-10074)
**CAMPBELL LUMBER CO INC
(PA)**
4195 Plank Rd (22959-2048)
P.O. Box 239 (22959-0239)
PHONE..................................434 293-3021
Harry D Campbell, *President*
Tinsley Campbell, *Vice Pres*
Sandy Austin, *Admin Sec*
EMP: 17
SQ FT: 14,500
SALES (est): 2.2MM **Privately Held**
SIC: 2421 Sawmills & planing mills, general

(G-10075)
HANKS INDEXING
2049 Middlebranch Dr (22959-1546)
PHONE..................................434 960-6805
Bonnie Hanks, *Owner*
EMP: 1
SALES (est): 42.5K **Privately Held**
SIC: 2731 Book publishing

(G-10076)
HARRIS WOODWORKING
2857 Southern Hills Dr (22959-1638)
PHONE..................................434 295-4316
EMP: 1
SALES (est): 54.1K **Privately Held**
SIC: 2431 Millwork

(G-10077)
JMY JAMS LLC
4410 Monacan Trail Rd (22959-1933)
P.O. Box 115 (22959-0115)
PHONE..................................434 906-0256
EMP: 2 EST: 2014
SALES (est): 147.8K **Privately Held**
SIC: 2033 Jams, jellies & preserves: packaged in cans, jars, etc.

(G-10078)
KOKUA JOHN LLC
2833 Southern Hills Dr (22959-1638)
PHONE..................................509 270-3454
EMP: 1
SALES (est): 80.4K **Privately Held**
SIC: 3069 Mfg Fabricated Rubber Products

(G-10079)
LAIRD & COMPANY
3638 Laird Ln (22959-2016)
PHONE..................................434 296-6058
Lester Clements, *Branch Mgr*
EMP: 3
SALES (corp-wide): 43.7MM **Privately
Held**
WEB: www.lairdandcompany.com
SIC: 2084 Brandy & brandy spirits
PA: Laird & Company
1 Laird Rd
Eatontown NJ 07724
732 542-0312

(G-10080)
**MARTIN MARIETTA MATERIALS
INC**
Also Called: Martin Marietta Aggregates
2625 Red Hill Rd (22959-1814)
P.O. Box 86 (22959-0086)
PHONE..................................434 296-5562
Chanbe Allen, *Branch Mgr*
James Jordan, *Manager*
EMP: 10 **Publicly Held**
WEB: www.martinmarietta.com
SIC: 1422 Crushed & broken limestone
PA: Martin Marietta Materials Inc
2710 Wycliff Rd
Raleigh NC 27607

(G-10081)
PETTIGREW
2435 Rock Branch Ln (22959-1724)
PHONE..................................434 979-0018
Alex Pettigrew, *Principal*
EMP: 2
SALES (est): 191.2K **Privately Held**
SIC: 2431 Millwork

(G-10082)
**PIPPIN HL FRM & VINEYARDS
LLC**
5022 Plank Rd (22959-1616)
PHONE..................................434 202-8063
Dean P Andrews, *Owner*
Eric Moody, *Business Mgr*
Matt Lovelady, *Manager*
EMP: 5
SALES (est): 628.7K **Privately Held**
WEB: www.pippinhillfarm.com
SIC: 2084 Wines

(G-10083)
SUGARLEAF VINEYARDS
3613 Walnut Branch Ln (22959-2104)
PHONE..................................434 984-4272
Jerry Bias, *Principal*
EMP: 2
SALES (est): 105.2K **Privately Held**
WEB: www.wisdomoakwinery.com
SIC: 2084 Wines

(G-10084)
WISDOM OAK WINERY
Also Called: Wisdom Oak Winery
3613 Walnut Branch Ln (22959-2104)
PHONE..................................434 984-4272
Jason Lavallee, *CEO*
Jason Lavalle, *CEO*
Laura Lavallee, *President*
EMP: 5 EST: 2016
SALES (est): 216.6K **Privately Held**
WEB: www.wisdomoakwinery.com
SIC: 2084 Wines

(G-10085)
ZEPHYR WOODWORKS LLC
4285 Burton Rd (22959-1622)
PHONE..................................434 979-4425
Rose Zavada, *Principal*
EMP: 2 EST: 2007
SALES (est): 143.3K **Privately Held**
SIC: 2431 Millwork

North Prince George
Hopewell City County

(G-10086)
ANCHOR WOODWORKS
2607 Douglas Ln (23860-7775)
PHONE..................................804 458-6443
James Koontz, *Owner*
EMP: 2 **Privately Held**
WEB:
www.anchorwoodworks.wordpress.com
SIC: 2431 Millwork

(G-10087)
FEDERAL PRISON INDUSTRIES
Also Called: Unicor
1100 River Rd (23860-1659)
PHONE..................................804 733-7881
Charles Bender, *Branch Mgr*
EMP: 1 **Publicly Held**
WEB: www.bop.gov
SIC: 2299 9223 Batting, wadding, padding
& fillings; correctional institutions;
HQ: Federal Prison Industries, Inc
320 1st St Nw
Washington DC 20534

(G-10088)
**HOPEWELL HARDWOOD SALES
INC**
13513 Old Stage Rd (23860-9156)
P.O. Box 281, Hopewell (23860-0281)
PHONE..................................804 458-5178
Fax: 804 541-8849
▼ **EMP:** 32
SQ FT: 1,000
SALES (est): 3.8MM **Privately Held**
SIC: 2421 Sawmill/Planing Mill

(G-10089)
MGI FUEL EXPRESS LLC
5002 Oaklawn Blvd (23860-7332)
PHONE..................................804 541-0299
Inderjit Singh, *Principal*
EMP: 3
SALES (est): 307.1K **Privately Held**
SIC: 3578 Automatic teller machines (ATM)

(G-10090)
MONSANTO TAMANTHA
1121 Collingwood Dr (23860-7628)
PHONE..................................434 517-0013
EMP: 2
SALES (est): 74.4K **Privately Held**
SIC: 2879 Agricultural chemicals

(G-10091)
REIERSON WOODWORKING
11008 Jenny Creek Dr (23860-7625)
PHONE..................................804 541-1945
Clint Reierson, *Principal*
EMP: 2
SALES (est): 90K **Privately Held**
SIC: 2431 Millwork

(G-10092)
**STRIKE FORCE
MANUFACTURING INC**
10006 Brighton Dr (23860-8861)
PHONE..................................804 731-0831
Donald W Piacentini, *Administration*
EMP: 2 EST: 2011
SALES (est): 109.5K **Privately Held**
WEB: www.toddjarrett.com
SIC: 3999 Manufacturing industries

North Tazewell
Tazewell County

(G-10093)
**BAPTIST VALLEY MACHINE SP
LLC**
4958 Baptist Valley Rd (24630-8600)
PHONE..................................276 988-8284
Jeffrey C Duty, *Principal*
EMP: 2
SALES (est): 81.4K **Privately Held**
SIC: 3599 Machine shop, jobbing & repair

(G-10094)
BARG-N-FINDERS INC
Also Called: Bargain Finders Marketplace
30672 Gvrnor G C Pery Hwy (24630-9193)
P.O. Box 947, Tazewell (24651-0947)
PHONE..................................276 988-4953
George Cole, *Owner*
EMP: 8
SALES (est): 904.1K **Privately Held**
WEB: www.bargnfinders.com
SIC: 2752 Publication printing, lithographic

(G-10095)
BRADLEY ADKINS
Also Called: B and D Welding & Fabrication
205 Walnut St Ste D (24630-9584)
PHONE..................................304 910-6553
Bradley Adkins, *Principal*
EMP: 1
SALES (est): 46.9K **Privately Held**
SIC: 7692 Welding repair

(G-10096)
**CLINCH VALLEY PRINTING
COMPANY**
205 Walnut St (24630-9584)
P.O. Box 746 (24630-0746)
PHONE..................................276 988-5410
Doyle W Rasnick, *President*
Linda Rasnick, *Office Mgr*
EMP: 16 EST: 1976
SQ FT: 5,000
SALES (est): 2.7MM **Privately Held**
WEB: www.clinchvalleyprinting.com
SIC: 2752 Commercial printing, offset

(G-10097)
CUSTOM METALSMITH INC
205 Walnut St (24630-9584)
PHONE..................................276 988-0330
David Wayne Baker, *President*
EMP: 2
SALES (est): 314.1K **Privately Held**
SIC: 3441 Fabricated structural metal

(G-10098)
ECKO INCORPORATED
Also Called: Ecko Fire Protections
Tazewell Industrial Park (24630)
P.O. Box 448 (24630-0448)
PHONE..................................276 988-7943
Delbert R White, *President*
Donald Graves, *Corp Secy*
Lennie D White, *Vice Pres*
EMP: 17 EST: 1976
SALES (est): 2.6MM **Privately Held**
WEB: www.ecko.com
SIC: 3669 1731 3663 Fire detection systems, electric; communications specialization; fire detection & burglar alarm systems specialization; mobile communication equipment

(G-10099)
F & R ELECTRIC INC
29835 Gvrnor G C Pery Hwy (24630-8347)
PHONE..................................276 979-8480
Frank Starling, *President*
Tammy Jeffers, *Corp Secy*
Richard Starling, *Vice Pres*
EMP: 15
SQ FT: 5,450
SALES (est): 2.1MM **Privately Held**
WEB: www.fandrelectric.com
SIC: 7694 Electric motor repair

(G-10100)
HARRY JONES ENTERPRISES
35240 Gvrnor G C Pery Hwy (24630-8002)
PHONE..................................276 322-5096
Harry Jones, *Owner*
EMP: 1 EST: 1975
SALES (est): 110K **Privately Held**
SIC: 2048 Livestock feeds

(G-10101)
I C E
205 Walnut St (24630-9584)
PHONE..................................276 988-0330
Peter Dahlquist, *President*
EMP: 6
SALES (est): 463.3K **Privately Held**
SIC: 3444 Sheet metalwork

(G-10102)
LONNIE L SPARKS
Also Called: Dryfork Mine Supply
135 Sparks Hollow Rd (24630-8772)
PHONE..................................276 988-4298
Lonnie L Sparks, *Owner*
EMP: 1
SALES (est): 50K **Privately Held**
SIC: 1241 Coal mining services

(G-10103)
MEFCOR INCORPORATED
33049 Gvrnor G C Pery Hwy (24630-7971)
P.O. Box 818, Bluefield (24605-0818)
PHONE..................................276 322-5021
Charlene B Hurt, *President*
Kyle Hurt, *Treasurer*
EMP: 6
SQ FT: 5,000
SALES (est): 1.2MM **Privately Held**
WEB: www.mefcoroutdoors.com
SIC: 3532 3823 3643 3625 Mining machinery; industrial instrmnts msrmnt display/control process variable; current-carrying wiring devices; relays & industrial controls; pumps & pumping equipment

(G-10104)
**PHOENIX SPORTS AND ADVG
INC**
146 Shire Ln (24630-5044)
PHONE..................................276 988-9709
Ralph Hayton, *President*
Barry White, *Corp Secy*
EMP: 4
SQ FT: 4,800
SALES (est): 250K **Privately Held**
SIC: 2261 5199 5941 5999 Screen printing of cotton broadwoven fabrics; advertising specialties; sporting goods & bicycle shops; trophies & plaques

(G-10105)
**PYOTT-BOONE ELECTRONICS
INC (PA)**
Also Called: P B E Group
1459 Wittens Mill Rd (24630-8373)
PHONE..................................276 988-5505
S De Crespigny, *CEO*
Stuart J Champion De Crespigny, *CEO*
John Craig, *Business Mgr*
Christa Glassburn, *COO*

GEOGRAPHIC

Peter Ryan, *Exec VP*
◆ **EMP:** 101 **EST:** 1971
SQ FT: 43,324
SALES (est): 23MM **Privately Held**
WEB: www.pbegrp.com
SIC: 3661 8734 3672 3663 Telephone & telegraph apparatus; testing laboratories; printed circuit boards; radio & TV communications equipment; nonferrous wire-drawing & insulating

(G-10106)
S & K WELDING INC
8596 Baptist Valley Rd (24630-9260)
PHONE............................276 988-5591
Barnes Lee Kidd, *Principal*
Linda G Kidd, *Corp Secy*
EMP: 3 **EST:** 1974
SQ FT: 7,500
SALES (est): 319.6K **Privately Held**
SIC: 3441 Fabricated structural metal

(G-10107)
STUBBY STEVES
27860 Gvrnor G C Pery Hwy (24630-8586)
P.O. Box 1268 (24630-1268)
PHONE............................276 988-2915
Steven Munsey, *Owner*
EMP: 7
SQ FT: 1,980
SALES (est): 10K **Privately Held**
SIC: 3949 Fishing equipment

(G-10108)
TAZZ CONVEYOR CORPORATION
294 Walnut St (24630-9584)
PHONE............................276 988-4883
Malcom Browning, *President*
▲ **EMP:** 11
SALES (est): 2.4MM **Privately Held**
WEB: www.tazzconveyor.com
SIC: 3535 5084 Conveyors & conveying equipment; overhead conveyor systems; conveyor systems

(G-10109)
TECHNIFAB OF VIRGINIA INC
30014 Gvrnor G C Prry Hwy (24630)
P.O. Box 1256 (24630-1256)
PHONE............................276 988-7517
Shirley Buchanan, *President*
Deborah Ball, *Corp Secy*
Harry Carter, *Vice Pres*
EMP: 22
SQ FT: 17,000
SALES (est): 3.4MM **Privately Held**
WEB: www.technifabva.com
SIC: 3444 3446 3443 3441 Sheet metal specialties, not stamped; architectural metalwork; fabricated plate work (boiler shop); fabricated structural metal

(G-10110)
VALLEY SUPPLY AND SERVICES LLC
174 Stansbury Ln (24630-8961)
PHONE............................276 979-4547
Melissa Cline, *Principal*
EMP: 2
SQ FT: 12,000
SALES (est): 94.8K **Privately Held**
SIC: 3492 3548 Hose & tube couplings, hydraulic/pneumatic; seam welding apparatus, electric

(G-10111)
WILLIAM G SEXTON
Also Called: J L Sexton & Son
29587 Gov G C Peery Hwy (24630)
P.O. Box 1267 (24630-1267)
PHONE............................276 988-9012
William G Sexton, *Owner*
Joshua Sexton, *Principal*
EMP: 2
SALES (est): 250K **Privately Held**
SIC: 1381 1241 1382 1081 Drilling oil & gas wells; coal mining exploration & test boring; geological exploration, oil & gas field; metal mining exploration & development services; geothermal drilling

Norton
Norton City County

(G-10112)
AMERICAN ENERGY LLC
Phillips Crk (24273)
P.O. Box 917, Abingdon (24212-0917)
PHONE............................276 935-7562
Irvin Stiltner, *Mng Member*
Keith Stiltner,
EMP: 50
SQ FT: 1,200
SALES (est): 10MM **Privately Held**
SIC: 1241 Coal mining services

(G-10113)
BLUFF SPUR COAL LLC
Also Called: Cumberland Resources
5703 Crutchfield Dr (24273-3902)
PHONE............................276 679-6962
Richard B Gilliam, *President*
Jodi Marco, *Manager*
Leslie Gilliam,
Marvin Gilliam,
EMP: 25 **EST:** 2000
SALES (est): 2.4MM **Privately Held**
SIC: 1241 Coal mining services

(G-10114)
C&J WELL SERVICES INC
580 Hawthorne Dr Ne (24273-2959)
PHONE............................276 679-5860
Larry Van Hoorebeke, *Principal*
EMP: 6 **Publicly Held**
WEB: www.nabors.com
SIC: 1389 Oil field services
HQ: C&J Well Services, Inc.
　　3990 Rogerdale Rd
　　Houston TX 77042

(G-10115)
COALFIELD PROGRESS (PA)
725 Park Ave Sw (24273-1926)
P.O. Box 380 (24273-0380)
PHONE............................276 679-1101
Michael Tate, *President*
Carol Robbie Tate, *Vice Pres*
Moore Jeff, *Vice Pres*
Johnny Teglas, *Vice Pres*
Jenay Tate, *Treasurer*
EMP: 75 **EST:** 1923
SQ FT: 10,000
SALES (est): 4.7MM **Privately Held**
WEB: www.thecoalfieldprogress.com
SIC: 2711 2759 2752 Commercial printing & newspaper publishing combined; commercial printing; commercial printing, lithographic

(G-10116)
CULBERTSON LUMBER COMPANY INC
4637 Overlook Rd (24273-4200)
PHONE............................276 679-7620
Donald K Culbertson, *President*
Connie Culbertson, *Treasurer*
EMP: 9
SALES (est): 590K **Privately Held**
SIC: 2421 Lumber: rough, sawed or planed

(G-10117)
EASTMAN CHEMICAL COMPANY
500 Hawthorne Ave (24273-2959)
PHONE............................276 679-1800
EMP: 53
SALES (corp-wide): 9.5B **Publicly Held**
SIC: 2821 Mfg Plastic Materials/Resins
PA: Eastman Chemical Company
　　200 S Wilcox Dr
　　Kingsport TN 37660
　　423 229-2000

(G-10118)
ELITE COALS INC
5465 Kent Junction Rd (24273-4801)
PHONE............................276 679-4070
Carter Long, *President*
EMP: 7
SQ FT: 1,000
SALES (est): 584.1K **Privately Held**
SIC: 1221 Bituminous coal surface mining

(G-10119)
GREATER WISE INCORPORATED
State Rte 610 (24273)
P.O. Box 668 (24273-0668)
PHONE............................276 679-1400
Bill D Humphrey, *Ch of Bd*
Bill G Humphrey, *Ch of Bd*
Deborah H Thomas, *Corp Secy*
Danny Humphrey, *Vice Pres*
Ron Mc Call, *VP Finance*
EMP: 55
SQ FT: 1,000
SALES (est): 4.9MM **Privately Held**
SIC: 1221 6519 Unit train loading facility, bituminous or lignite; real property lessors

(G-10120)
HUMPHREYS ENTERPRISES INC
6999 Polk Rd (24273)
P.O. Box 668 (24273-0668)
PHONE............................276 679-1400
James M Thomas, *President*
Jim N Humphrey, *Corp Secy*
William D Humphreys, *Vice Pres*
Edward Clapp, *Safety Dir*
John Miller, *Controller*
EMP: 18
SQ FT: 1,500
SALES (est): 4.3MM **Privately Held**
WEB: www.humphreyenterprises.com
SIC: 1221 Strip mining, bituminous

(G-10121)
IMPRESSIONS OF NORTON INC
832 Park Ave Nw (24273-1924)
P.O. Box 4149, Wise (24293-4149)
PHONE............................276 679-1560
Danny Rowland, *President*
Henrietta Dotson, *Vice Pres*
EMP: 4 **EST:** 1997
SQ FT: 4,800
SALES (est): 400K **Privately Held**
SIC: 2759 2395 Screen printing; art goods for embroidering, stamped: purchased materials

(G-10122)
INNOVATIVE GRAPHICS & DESIGN
55 15th St Nw (24273-1617)
PHONE............................276 679-2340
Gary Burgess, *President*
Linda Burgess, *Vice Pres*
David S Burgess, *Treasurer*
EMP: 5
SALES (est): 590.7K **Privately Held**
WEB: www.inngraphicsdesign.com
SIC: 2759 Screen printing

(G-10123)
JOY GLOBAL UNDERGROUND MIN LLC
722 Kentucky Ave Sw (24273-2508)
PHONE............................276 679-1082
James Swoager, *Director*
EMP: 13 **Privately Held**
WEB: www.mining.komatsu
SIC: 3532 Mining machinery
HQ: Joy Global Underground Mining Llc
　　40 Pennwood Pl
　　Warrendale PA 15086
　　724 779-4500

(G-10124)
LONESOME PINE BEVERAGE COMPANY
213 6th St Nw (24273-1905)
P.O. Box 98 (24273-0098)
PHONE............................276 679-2332
Rebecca Dorton, *President*
EMP: 6
SALES (est): 350K **Privately Held**
SIC: 2086 Carbonated beverages, nonalcoholic: bottled & canned

(G-10125)
MARTY CORPORATION
Also Called: Marty Materials
465 Industrial Way (24273)
PHONE............................276 679-3477
Bill Evans, *Manager*
EMP: 4

SALES (corp-wide): 1.3MM **Privately Held**
WEB: www.martymaterials.com
SIC: 3273 Ready-mixed concrete
PA: Marty Corporation
　　502a Front St W
　　Coeburn VA 24230
　　276 395-3326

(G-10126)
MAXXIM REBUILD CO LLC (DH)
5703 Crutchfield Dr (24273-3902)
PHONE............................276 679-7020
Richard H Verheij,
Wanda Fields,
Tracy Ford,
James Hartough,
Anthony Keaton,
◆ **EMP:** 1800
SALES (est): 147.3MM
SALES (corp-wide): 2.2B **Publicly Held**
WEB: www.conturaenergy.com
SIC: 1241 Coal mining services
HQ: Alpha Natural Resources, Llc
　　636 Shelby St Ste 1c
　　Bristol TN 37620
　　423 574-5100

(G-10127)
MAXXIM SHARED SERVICES LLC
Also Called: Spectrum Laboratories
5703 Crutchfield Dr (24273-3902)
PHONE............................276 679-7020
Eddie Bateman,
EMP: 1
SALES (est): 140.4K
SALES (corp-wide): 2.2B **Publicly Held**
SIC: 1222 Bituminous coal-underground mining
HQ: Alpha Natural Resources, Inc.
　　636 Shelby St Ste 1c
　　Bristol TN 37620
　　423 574-5100

(G-10128)
MCCLURE CONCRETE MATERIALS LLC
465 Industrial Park Rd (24273-4073)
PHONE............................276 679-3477
EMP: 4
SALES (corp-wide): 635.5K **Privately Held**
WEB: www.mcclureconcrete.com
SIC: 3273 Ready-mixed concrete
PA: Mcclure Concrete Materials Llc
　　1201 Iron St
　　Richlands VA 24641
　　276 964-9682

(G-10129)
MOUNTAIN ENERGY RESOURCES INC
150 Coeburn Ave Sw (24273-2600)
PHONE............................276 679-3593
Dale Stanley, *President*
EMP: 1
SALES (est): 91.3K **Privately Held**
WEB: www.mtneri.com
SIC: 1241 4731 Coal mining services; transportation agents & brokers

(G-10130)
MULLICAN FLOORING LP
Also Called: Mullican Lumber & Mfg Co
Blackwood Indus Pk Rd (24273)
P.O. Box 99 (24273-0099)
PHONE............................276 679-2924
Jim Myers, *COO*
Jake Harman, *Vice Pres*
Ryan Brainard, *Supervisor*
EMP: 240
SALES (corp-wide): 339MM **Privately Held**
WEB: www.mullicanflooring.com
SIC: 2421 2426 Sawmills & planing mills, general; hardwood dimension & flooring mills
HQ: Mullican Flooring, L.P.
　　655 Woodlyn Rd
　　Johnson City TN 37601
　　423 262-8440

▲ = Import ▼=Export
◆ =Import/Export

(G-10131)
NORRISBILT FBRCTION MBL WLDG L
520 Kentucky Ave Sw (24273-2504)
PHONE..........................276 325-0269
Ronald Norris, *Principal*
Tiffany Norris, *Principal*
EMP: 33 EST: 2014
SALES (est): 1.7MM **Privately Held**
WEB: www.norrisbuiltfab.com
SIC: 7692 Welding repair

(G-10132)
PARAMONT CONTURA LLC
5703 Crutchfield Dr (24273-3902)
PHONE..........................276 679-7020
EMP: 1 EST: 2016
SALES (est): 518.1K
SALES (corp-wide): 2.2B **Publicly Held**
SIC: 1221 Bituminous coal & lignite-surface mining
PA: Contura Energy, Inc.
340 Mrtin Lther King Jr B
Bristol TN 37620
423 573-0300

(G-10133)
PARDEE COAL COMPANY INC
Rr 610 (24273)
PHONE..........................276 679-1400
William Doug Humphrey, *President*
Jim N Humphrey, *Vice Pres*
Ron Mc Call, *Vice Pres*
James Michael Thomas, *Vice Pres*
John Miller, *Controller*
EMP: 6
SQ FT: 1,000
SALES (est): 415K **Privately Held**
SIC: 1241 1221 Coal mining services; bituminous coal & lignite-surface mining

(G-10134)
PEPSI COLA BTLG INC NORTON VA (PA)
Also Called: Pepsico
12th St At Park Ave (24273)
P.O. Box 158 (24273-0158)
PHONE..........................276 679-1122
George Edward Hunnicutt Jr, *President*
Joseph Hunnicutt, *Vice Pres*
Jordan Snyder, *Sales Associate*
Gregory Jones, *Manager*
Clara Funk, *Admin Sec*
EMP: 75 EST: 1914
SQ FT: 120,000
SALES (est): 21.1MM **Privately Held**
WEB: www.pepsico.com
SIC: 2086 Carbonated soft drinks, bottled & canned

Oak Hill
Fairfax County

(G-10135)
ASTROCOMM TECHNOLOGIES LLC
2702 Copper Creek Rd (20171-3520)
PHONE..........................703 606-2022
Shabbir Parvez, *Principal*
Mohammad Rehman, *Principal*
Scott Dunnihoo, *CFO*
EMP: 4 EST: 2014
SALES (est): 270K **Privately Held**
WEB: www.astrocommtech.com
SIC: 3663 Amplifiers, RF power & IF; satellites, communications

(G-10136)
BALLAS LLC
13610 Old Dairy Rd (20171-4015)
PHONE..........................703 689-9644
Stan Ballas, *Senior Engr*
EMP: 1
SALES (est): 250K **Privately Held**
WEB: www.ballasllc.com
SIC: 3663 Satellites, communications

(G-10137)
IRON FORGE SOFTWARE LLC
2608 Iron Forge Rd (20171-2918)
PHONE..........................571 263-6540
Gustavo Verdun,
EMP: 1 EST: 2010

SALES (est): 69.8K **Privately Held**
SIC: 7372 7389 Prepackaged software;

(G-10138)
PUTTING TGTHER PZZLE PECES LLC
3014 Gatepost Ln (20171-2246)
PHONE..........................703 391-1754
Robin E Moyher, *Principal*
EMP: 2
SALES (est): 90.3K **Privately Held**
SIC: 3944 Puzzles

(G-10139)
THERMOHALT TECHNOLOGY LLC
3002 Hughsmith Ct (20171-4058)
PHONE..........................703 880-6697
Gerard Eldering,
EMP: 1
SALES (est): 93.7K **Privately Held**
SIC: 3825 Test equipment for electronic & electric measurement

Oakton
Fairfax County

(G-10140)
AETAS MOBILE LLC
11002 Vale Rd (22124-1418)
PHONE..........................704 258-9159
Matthew Maroofi,
EMP: 2
SALES (est): 56.5K **Privately Held**
SIC: 7372 Application computer software

(G-10141)
AVERIA HEALTH SOLUTIONS LLC
3401 Waples Glen Ct (22124-2036)
PHONE..........................703 716-0791
Rohan Suri, *CEO*
EMP: 1
SALES (est): 35.9K **Privately Held**
SIC: 7372 Application computer software

(G-10142)
CAE SOFTWARE SOLUTIONS LLC
Also Called: C-Sol
11313 Lapham Dr (22124-1318)
PHONE..........................734 417-6991
Stuart Kerr, *President*
Neil Bishop,
Tamra Lynn Caserio,
Betty-Anne Kerr,
Karl Sweitzer,
EMP: 4
SALES (est): 177.1K
SALES (corp-wide): 4.1B **Privately Held**
SIC: 7372 7371 Prepackaged software; computer software development
HQ: Caefatigue Ltd
Cedar House
Cobham

(G-10143)
DEXCO POLYMERS LP
3438 Valewood Dr (22124-2226)
PHONE..........................703 846-2193
EMP: 2
SALES (est): 80.3K **Privately Held**
SIC: 2821 Plastics materials & resins

(G-10144)
DOUCRAFT SERVICES
Also Called: Harriet Craft
3603 Twilight Ct (22124-2103)
PHONE..........................703 620-4965
Harriett Craft, *Owner*
EMP: 1
SALES (est): 82K **Privately Held**
SIC: 7372 Application computer software

(G-10145)
DTC PRESS LLC
2979 Westhurst Ln (22124-1739)
PHONE..........................703 255-9891
Rosemary Lauer, *President*
EMP: 2
SALES (est): 68.7K **Privately Held**
WEB: www.dtcpress.com
SIC: 2741 Miscellaneous publishing

(G-10146)
EAGLE SUNRISE VINEYARD LLC
11214 Country Pl (22124-1303)
PHONE..........................703 648-3258
William Chambers, *Principal*
EMP: 2
SALES (est): 106K **Privately Held**
SIC: 2084 Wines, brandy & brandy spirits

(G-10147)
ERSH-ENTERPRISES INC
Also Called: PIP Printing
3003 Westhurst Ct A101 (22124-1751)
PHONE..........................703 866-1988
Ernie Lederer, *President*
EMP: 10
SALES (est): 1.2MM **Privately Held**
SIC: 2752 2791 2789 Commercial printing, offset; typesetting; bookbinding & related work

(G-10148)
GENERAL DYNAMICS GOVT SYST
Also Called: General Dynamics Advanced Info
10455 White Granite Dr (22124-2764)
PHONE..........................703 383-3605
EMP: 26
SALES (corp-wide): 39.3B **Publicly Held**
WEB: www.gd.com
SIC: 3661 Telephone & telegraph apparatus
HQ: General Dynamics Government Systems Corporation
2941 Fairview Park Dr
Falls Church VA 22042
703 876-3000

(G-10149)
HANA TONIC LLC
11232 Sorrel Ridge Ln (22124-1322)
PHONE..........................804 993-4262
Renee Louis-Charles, *Branch Mgr*
EMP: 1
SQ FT: 500
SALES (corp-wide): 820.9K **Privately Held**
WEB: www.hanatonic.com
SIC: 2833 Vitamins, natural or synthetic: bulk, uncompounded
PA: Hana Tonic, Llc
11232 Sorrel Ridge Ln
Oakton VA 22124
808 281-5853

(G-10150)
HOTRODZ PERFORMANCE & MOTOR
2961a Hunter Mill Rd # 106 (22124-1704)
PHONE..........................571 337-2988
Carrie Litten,
EMP: 7
SALES (est): 455.4K **Privately Held**
SIC: 3559 Automotive related machinery

(G-10151)
HYDROGEN MOTORS INC
3600 Twilight Ct (22124-2103)
PHONE..........................703 407-9802
Dmitry Shvenderman, *Principal*
EMP: 3
SALES (est): 206.2K **Privately Held**
SIC: 3621 Motors, electric

(G-10152)
J-ALM PUBLISHING
3403 Miller Heights Rd (22124-1925)
PHONE..........................703 385-9766
Michael McCarey, *Principal*
EMP: 2
SALES (est): 128.6K **Privately Held**
SIC: 2741 Miscellaneous publishing

(G-10153)
KEVINS WELDING
10218 Bushman Dr Apt 103 (22124-2820)
PHONE..........................703 242-8649
EMP: 1
SALES (est): 56.4K **Privately Held**
SIC: 3449 Miscellaneous metalwork

(G-10154)
LIVE CASES
3102 Borge St (22124-2807)
PHONE..........................703 627-0994
EMP: 1
SALES (est): 54.5K **Privately Held**
WEB: www.livecases.com
SIC: 3523 Farm machinery & equipment

(G-10155)
MAGIC AND MEMORIES PRESS LLC
11300 Hunt Farm Ln (22124-1201)
PHONE..........................703 849-0921
Kari Walker, *Principal*
EMP: 1
SALES (est): 37.5K **Privately Held**
SIC: 2741 Miscellaneous publishing

(G-10156)
MANDYLION RESEARCH LABS LLC
10611 Hannah Farm Rd (22124-1527)
PHONE..........................703 628-4284
Joseph S Grajewski, *President*
David Schoenbrot, *Vice Pres*
Gene Leone, *Director*
▲ EMP: 20
SALES (est): 2.1MM **Privately Held**
WEB: www.mandylionlabs.com
SIC: 3571 8721 7371 8731 Electronic computers; accounting, auditing & bookkeeping; computer software writing services; commercial physical research

(G-10157)
MARK PEARSON
3104 Bandol Ln (22124-2355)
PHONE..........................703 648-2568
Mark Pearson, *Owner*
EMP: 1
SALES (est): 88K **Privately Held**
SIC: 3695 5045 Computer software tape & disks: blank, rigid & floppy; computer software

(G-10158)
MID ATLANTIC WOOD WORKS LLC
10133 Palmer Dr (22124-2622)
PHONE..........................703 281-4376
Emil Ravesteijn, *Principal*
EMP: 1
SALES (est): 124.4K **Privately Held**
SIC: 2431 Millwork

(G-10159)
MYTHOS PUBLISHING LLC
12016 Wandabury Rd (22124-2334)
PHONE..........................703 531-0795
Tim Henriques, *Principal*
EMP: 2
SALES (est): 59.2K **Privately Held**
SIC: 2741 Miscellaneous publishing

(G-10160)
NORTH STAR SCIENCE & TECH LLC
3105 Windsong Dr (22124-1832)
P.O. Box 438, King George (22485-0438)
PHONE..........................410 961-6692
Blake Henke, *Managing Prtnr*
Michael Blake Henke,
EMP: 5
SALES (est): 600K **Privately Held**
WEB: www.northstarst.com
SIC: 3699 Electric sound equipment

(G-10161)
OAKTON PRESS
11151 Conestoga Ct (22124-1904)
PHONE..........................703 359-6800
James Hood, *President*
EMP: 1
SALES (est): 70.8K **Privately Held**
SIC: 2741 Miscellaneous publishing

(G-10162)
THOUGHTWEB USA INC
2961a Hunter Mill Rd (22124-1704)
PHONE..........................575 639-1726
Murray G Christopher, *President*
EMP: 1 **Privately Held**
SIC: 7372 Prepackaged software

GEOGRAPHIC

(G-10163)
US TACTICAL INC
2735 Valestra Cir (22124-1422)
PHONE....................................703 217-8781
Jeffrey C May, *President*
EMP: 1
SALES (est): 87K **Privately Held**
WEB: www.ustacticalusa.com
SIC: 3484 7699 Guns (firearms) or gun
parts, 30 mm. & below; gunsmith shop

(G-10164)
WEBB-MASON INC
2448 Fairhunt Ct (22124-1042)
PHONE....................................703 391-0626
Doug Traxler, *Branch Mgr*
EMP: 2 **Privately Held**
WEB: www.webbmason.com
SIC: 2752 Commercial printing, offset
PA: Webb-Mason, Inc.
10830 Gilroy Rd
Hunt Valley MD 21031

Oakwood
Buchanan County

(G-10165)
COCHRAN INDS INC -
WYTHEVILLE
8112 Riverside Dr (24631-8903)
PHONE....................................276 498-3836
Constance Y Ratliff, *Administration*
EMP: 1
SALES (est): 62.3K **Privately Held**
SIC: 3999 Manufacturing industries

(G-10166)
COCHRAN INDUSTRIES INC - VA
(PA)
8112 Riverside Dr (24631-8903)
PHONE....................................276 498-3836
Zachary Cochran, *President*
Constance Ratliff, *Corp Secy*
Gary Cochran, *Vice Pres*
EMP: 4 EST: 1948
SQ FT: 1,000
SALES (est): 384.7K **Privately Held**
SIC: 3271 Blocks, concrete or cinder: stan-
dard

(G-10167)
DOMINION COAL CORP
15498 Riverside Dr (24631-8913)
PHONE....................................276 935-8810
James Mullins, *Principal*
Jeffery Patton, *Plant Engr*
EMP: 2
SALES (est): 70.4K **Privately Held**
SIC: 1221 Bituminous coal & lignite-sur-
face mining

(G-10168)
HORN WELL DRILLING INC
NOAH
1070 Sandy Valley Ln (24631-9651)
P.O. Box 269, Vansant (24656-0269)
PHONE....................................276 935-5902
Jeffery A Horn, *President*
Boyd Leon, *Vice Pres*
Matthew McClanahan, *Warehouse Mgr*
Marianne H Gibson, *Treasurer*
Johnson Susan H, *Admin Sec*
EMP: 150
SQ FT: 14,000
SALES (est): 22.4MM **Privately Held**
WEB: www.noahhorn.com
SIC: 1381 1781 Directional drilling oil &
gas wells; water well drilling

(G-10169)
JAKE LITTLE CONSTRUCTION
INC
2862 Wilderness Rd (24631-8735)
P.O. Box 768, Grundy (24614-0768)
PHONE....................................276 498-7462
Robert Pierce Ratliff, *President*
Rufus Ray, *Corp Secy*
Debbie Webb, *Accountant*
EMP: 30
SALES (est): 4.3MM **Privately Held**
SIC: 1241 Mine preparation services

(G-10170)
JEWELL SMOKELESS COAL
CORP (DH)
1029 Miners Rd (24631-8926)
PHONE....................................276 935-8810
Denise R Cade, *President*
Michael J Thomson, *President*
Dennis B Taylor, *CFO*
Earl Humber, *Treasurer*
Michael H Dingus, *Director*
EMP: 20 EST: 1971
SALES (est): 49.9MM **Publicly Held**
SIC: 1222 Bituminous coal-underground
mining
HQ: Jewell Resources Corporation
1011 Warrenville Rd # 600
Lisle IL 60532
276 935-8810

(G-10171)
WEST RIVER CONVEYORS &
MCHY CO (PA)
8936 Dismal River Rd (24631-9643)
PHONE....................................276 259-5353
Jerry Roulett, *President*
J B Roulette, *President*
Joe G Street, *Corp Secy*
Joe Street, *Vice Pres*
EMP: 25
SQ FT: 14,000
SALES (est): 10.5MM **Privately Held**
WEB: www.westriverconveyors.com
SIC: 3535 Conveyors & conveying equip-
ment

Occoquan
Prince William County

(G-10172)
EAST AMBER LLC
1435 Occoquan Heights Ct (22125-7742)
P.O. Box 286 (22125-0286)
PHONE....................................703 414-9409
Reanna Pettigrew,
EMP: 1
SALES (est): 56.3K **Privately Held**
SIC: 2844 Face creams or lotions

(G-10173)
HITCHCOCK PAPER CO
125 Mill St (22125-7732)
PHONE....................................571 398-6601
Sarah Burzio, *Principal*
EMP: 3 EST: 2019
SALES (est): 196.2K **Privately Held**
WEB: www.hitchckpaper.com
SIC: 2621 Paper mills

(G-10174)
PUZZLE PALOOZA ECT
403 Mill St (22125-7736)
PHONE....................................703 494-0579
Holly Vandenheuvel, *Owner*
EMP: 1
SALES (est): 45.1K **Privately Held**
WEB: www.puzzlepaloozaetc.com
SIC: 3944 Puzzles

(G-10175)
SO OLIVE LLC
125 Mill St Unit 10 (22125-7732)
PHONE....................................571 398-2377
Charleen Cox,
EMP: 3
SALES (est): 100K **Privately Held**
WEB: www.soolive.com
SIC: 2079 7389 Olive oil;

Oilville
Goochland County

(G-10176)
BERKLE WELDING &
FABRICATION
1146 Tricounty Dr Ste B (23129-2222)
PHONE....................................804 708-0662
Darlene Berkle, *President*
Kenney Berkle, *Admin Sec*
EMP: 10

SALES (est): 1.1MM **Privately Held**
SIC: 7692 Welding repair

(G-10177)
COPYRIGHT PRINTING
1393 Broad Street Rd (23129-2101)
PHONE....................................804 784-4760
David Goode, *Owner*
EMP: 1
SALES (est): 101.3K **Privately Held**
SIC: 2752 Commercial printing, offset

(G-10178)
GOOCHLAND TEES INC
1390 Broad Street Rd C (23129-2100)
PHONE....................................804 708-2041
Darlene Bobbio, *President*
EMP: 3
SALES (est): 150K **Privately Held**
WEB: www.goochlandtees.com
SIC: 2759 Screen printing

(G-10179)
HARRIS MACHINE PRODUCTS
INC
1075 Merchants Ln (23129-2210)
PHONE....................................804 784-4511
Raymond Harris, *President*
EMP: 3
SQ FT: 2,000
SALES (est): 274.7K **Privately Held**
WEB: www.harrismachineproducts.com
SIC: 3599 Machine shop, jobbing & repair

(G-10180)
IMPRESSION OBSESSION
2546 Turkey Creek Rd (23129-2011)
PHONE....................................804 749-3580
Mitra Friant, *Owner*
EMP: 8 EST: 1998
SALES (est): 474.2K **Privately Held**
WEB: www.iostamps.com
SIC: 3953 Marking devices

(G-10181)
L & N WOOD PRODUCTS INC
2055 Valpark Dr (23129-2223)
PHONE....................................804 784-4734
Scott Valentine, *President*
EMP: 1
SALES (est): 80.9K **Privately Held**
SIC: 3523 Grading, cleaning, sorting ma-
chines, fruit, grain, vegetable

(G-10182)
LETTERPRESS DIRECT
1146 Tricounty Dr (23129-2222)
PHONE....................................804 285-8020
EMP: 2 EST: 2008
SALES (est): 80K **Privately Held**
SIC: 2759 Commercial Printing

(G-10183)
MID-ATLANTIC
MANUFACTURING INC
2559 Turkey Creek Rd (23129-2011)
P.O. Box 6384, Ashland (23005-6384)
PHONE....................................804 798-7462
Laurent Claudel, *President*
Gena Claudel, *Admin Sec*
EMP: 21
SALES (est): 3.8MM **Privately Held**
WEB: www.midatlanticsurfaces.com
SIC: 2541 1799 2493 Table or counter
tops, plastic laminated; counter top instal-
lation; particleboard, plastic laminated

(G-10184)
STRICKLAND MFG LLC
1070 Merchants Ln (23129-2209)
PHONE....................................866 929-3388
Sean O'Reilly, *General Mgr*
▲ EMP: 2
SALES (est): 400.1K **Privately Held**
WEB: www.stricklandus.com
SIC: 2449 Wood pails, buckets, & vats:
coopered

(G-10185)
TKL PRODUCTS CORP
2551 Rte 1200 (23129)
P.O. Box 215 (23129-0215)
PHONE....................................804 749-8300
Thomas D Dougherty, *President*
Donna M Dougherty, *Vice Pres*

Jose Elizondo, *Materials Mgr*
Donna Dougherty, *VP Finance*
Linda Alexander, *Accounting Mgr*
▲ EMP: 40
SQ FT: 64,000
SALES (est): 8MM **Privately Held**
WEB: www.tkl.com
SIC: 3161 5736 Cases, carrying; musical
instrument stores

(G-10186)
UNIQUECOAT TECHNOLOGIES
LLC
2071 Valpark Dr (23129-2223)
PHONE....................................804 784-0997
Enrw Verstak, *Partner*
Viatcheslav Baranovski, *Mng Member*
Slava Baranovski, *Info Tech Mgr*
Andrew Baranovski,
David Jewell,
▼ EMP: 6
SQ FT: 3,000
SALES (est): 2.6MM **Privately Held**
WEB: www.uniquecoat.com
SIC: 3479 Coating of metals & formed
products

(G-10187)
WEST END FABRICATORS INC
1173 Tricounty Dr (23129-2222)
PHONE....................................804 360-2106
Hillman W Rice, *President*
Elba S Rice, *Corp Secy*
EMP: 7
SQ FT: 1,800
SALES (est): 1MM **Privately Held**
SIC: 3312 Structural shapes & pilings,
steel

Onancock
Accomack County

(G-10188)
ADCO SIGNS INC
165 Market St Ste 1 (23417-4233)
P.O. Box 316 (23417-0316)
PHONE....................................757 787-1393
Karl M Stiegelbauer, *President*
Karl Stiegelbauer, *President*
Sara Stuart, *Vice Pres*
Linda Meyers, *Office Mgr*
EMP: 4
SALES (est): 900K **Privately Held**
WEB: www.adcosigns.wix.com
SIC: 3993 3999 Signs & advertising spe-
cialties; theatrical scenery

(G-10189)
AOK QUALITY SOLUTIONS
25137 Serenity Ln (23417-1636)
PHONE....................................757 710-9844
Anne G Kellam, *Owner*
EMP: 2
SALES (est): 87.5K **Privately Held**
WEB: www.jasonotoolerealestate.com
SIC: 3949 Sporting & athletic goods

(G-10190)
ART-A-METAL LLC
20485 Market St (23417-4316)
PHONE....................................757 787-1574
Chris Beauchamp, *Manager*
EMP: 2
SALES (est): 88.9K **Privately Held**
SIC: 3446 Architectural metalwork

(G-10191)
BBJ LLC
152 Market St (23417-4225)
P.O. Box 212, Wachapreague (23480-
0212)
PHONE....................................757 787-4646
Ben Byrd,
EMP: 3
SQ FT: 6,000
SALES (est): 300K **Privately Held**
SIC: 2752 Commercial printing, litho-
graphic

(G-10192)
CHESAPEAKE CABINET &
FINISH CO
25110 Nottingham Ln (23417-3145)
PHONE.....................757 787-9422
J Morris, *Principal*
EMP: 2
SALES (est): 149.2K **Privately Held**
SIC: 2434 Wood kitchen cabinets

(G-10193)
CHESAPEAKE DISTRIBUTORS
LLC
15068 Holly St (23417-3000)
PHONE.....................757 302-1108
EMP: 2
SALES (est): 75K **Privately Held**
SIC: 2329 Mfg Men's/Boy's Clothing

(G-10194)
COVE ANTIQUES
18368 Hermitage Rd (23417-2005)
PHONE.....................757 787-3881
Kevin Daley, *Owner*
EMP: 5
SALES (est): 451.1K **Privately Held**
SIC: 2434 Wood kitchen cabinets

(G-10195)
CRYSTAL BEACH STUDIO
16383 Crystal Beach Rd (23417-2649)
PHONE.....................757 787-4605
Miguel M Bizzotto, *Owner*
EMP: 3
SALES (est): 221K **Privately Held**
SIC: 3171 3172 5199 5948 Handbags, women's; personal leather goods; leather, leather goods & furs; luggage, except footlockers & trunks

(G-10196)
EASTERN SHORE SEAFOOD CO
INC
21325 Bayside Rd (23417-2107)
PHONE.....................757 787-7539
EMP: 25 **EST:** 1948
SQ FT: 4,400
SALES (est): 2.4MM **Privately Held**
SIC: 2092 2091 Mfg Fresh/Frozen Fish Mfg Canned/Cured Seafood

(G-10197)
SHOOTING STAR GALLERY LLC
60 Hill St (23417-1622)
PHONE.....................757 787-4536
Brenda Wright, *Mng Member*
EMP: 2
SALES (est): 149.1K **Privately Held**
WEB: www.shooting-star-gallery.com
SIC: 3999 5999 Framed artwork; picture frames, ready made

(G-10198)
TRUITTS WELDING SERVICE
22 Liberty St (23417-1800)
PHONE.....................757 787-7290
M Truitt, *Principal*
EMP: 2
SALES (est): 176K **Privately Held**
SIC: 7692 Welding repair

(G-10199)
VERTICAL SUNSET
17487 Northside Rd (23417-2523)
PHONE.....................757 787-7595
EMP: 2
SALES (est): 130K **Privately Held**
SIC: 2591 Mfg Drapery Hardware/Blinds

Onley
Accomack County

(G-10200)
EASTERN SHORE POST INC
24391 Lankford Hwy (23418-2610)
P.O. Box 517 (23418-0517)
PHONE.....................757 789-7678
Cheryl Nowak, *President*
Bill Massty, *Corp Secy*
Angela Crutchley, *Executive*
EMP: 5
SQ FT: 4,000

SALES (est): 325.5K **Privately Held**
WEB: www.easternshorepost.com
SIC: 2711 Newspapers, publishing & printing

(G-10201)
T&W BLOCK INCORPORATED
(PA)
21075 Washington St (23418)
P.O. Box 487 (23418-0487)
PHONE.....................757 787-2646
Wendy Walker, *CEO*
Genevieve W Switzer, *President*
Tammy Hill, *Vice Pres*
EMP: 20
SQ FT: 26,000
SALES (est): 3MM **Privately Held**
WEB: www.twblock.com
SIC: 3273 3271 5032 5211 Ready-mixed concrete; blocks, concrete or cinder: standard; brick, except refractory; paving stones; construction sand & gravel

Orange
Orange County

(G-10202)
AMERICAN WOODMARK
CORPORATION
281 Kentucky Rd (22960-1200)
P.O. Box 351 (22960-0206)
PHONE.....................540 672-3707
Adam Kell, *Plant Mgr*
Alan Davis, *Manager*
Mike Filicko, *Regional*
EMP: 200 **Publicly Held**
WEB: www.americanwoodmark.com
SIC: 2431 2426 2434 Millwork; hardwood dimension & flooring mills; vanities, bathroom: wood
PA: American Woodmark Corporation
561 Shady Elm Rd
Winchester VA 22602
540 665-9100

(G-10203)
APG ELECTRONICS
15339 Kerby Dr (22960-3220)
PHONE.....................540 672-7252
Patricia Frenzel, *Owner*
EMP: 1
SALES (est): 72.8K **Privately Held**
SIC: 3629 Electronic generation equipment

(G-10204)
BAILEY & SONS PUBLISHING
CO D
197 E Main St (22960-1656)
PHONE.....................434 990-9291
Denis A Bailey, *President*
EMP: 1
SALES (est): 84.9K **Privately Held**
SIC: 2741 Miscellaneous publishing

(G-10205)
CF SMITH & SONS
12243 Mayhurst Ln (22960-2844)
PHONE.....................540 672-3291
James P Smith, *Partner*
EMP: 3
SALES (est): 24.3K **Privately Held**
SIC: 2411 Logging

(G-10206)
CHATEAU MERRILLANNE LLC
16234 Marquis Rd (22960-3704)
PHONE.....................540 656-6177
Kenneth Anthony White, *Administration*
EMP: 2
SALES (est): 146.3K **Privately Held**
WEB: www.chateaumerrillanne.com
SIC: 2084 Wines

(G-10207)
CORNER CABINET SHOP INC
315 Caroline St (22960-1510)
PHONE.....................540 672-9460
David Gallihugh, *President*
EMP: 3 **EST:** 1999 **Privately Held**
WEB: www.cornercabinetshop.com
SIC: 2434 Wood kitchen cabinets

(G-10208)
CUSTOM PRINTING
124 Chapman St (22960-1617)
PHONE.....................540 672-2281
Ron Smith, *Owner*
EMP: 2 **EST:** 1972
SQ FT: 2,400
SALES (est): 169.2K **Privately Held**
SIC: 2752 Commercial printing, offset

(G-10209)
D & S CONSTRUCTION
15187 Buena Vista Dr (22960-2942)
PHONE.....................540 718-5303
Jeff Dodson, *Owner*
EMP: 2
SALES (est): 142.2K **Privately Held**
SIC: 3993 Signs & advertising specialties

(G-10210)
DAILY PROGRESS
Also Called: Orange County Review
146 Byrd St (22960-1631)
PHONE.....................540 672-1266
Jeff Poole, *General Mgr*
Jenny Rector, *Editor*
Karla Hernandez, *Executive*
Sondra Key, *Representative*
EMP: 2 **EST:** 2012
SALES (est): 10K **Privately Held**
WEB: www.dailyprogress.com
SIC: 2711 Newspapers, publishing & printing

(G-10211)
DIPPED IN ICE LLC
18539 Brick Church Rd (22960-4420)
PHONE.....................540 845-3567
A'Miaya Poindexter,
EMP: 1
SALES (est): 42.5K **Privately Held**
SIC: 2339 Women's & misses' accessories

(G-10212)
EAGLE EYE ELECTRIC
11281 Rapidan Rd (22960-4619)
PHONE.....................540 672-1673
Jimmy Dix, *Owner*
EMP: 4
SALES (est): 260K **Privately Held**
SIC: 3625 Relays & industrial controls

(G-10213)
FOODS FOR THOUGHT INC
13418 Old Gordonsville Rd (22960-2915)
PHONE.....................434 242-4996
Rob Harrison, *Treasurer*
William Harris,
EMP: 1
SALES (est): 53.2K **Privately Held**
WEB: www.foodsforthoughtinc.com
SIC: 2011 Beef products from beef slaughtered on site

(G-10214)
GLASS FRONTS INC
215 Red Hill Rd (22960-1112)
PHONE.....................540 672-4410
John C Paisley, *President*
Ruth Anne Paisley, *Corp Secy*
EMP: 10
SALES (est): 618.8K **Privately Held**
WEB: www.glassfronts.com
SIC: 3211 Structural glass

(G-10215)
IBA LED
12046 Spicers Mill Rd (22960-2104)
PHONE.....................434 566-2109
Chuck Meehan, *Principal*
EMP: 6
SALES (est): 963.6K **Privately Held**
SIC: 3646 Commercial indusl & institutional electric lighting fixtures

(G-10216)
JASON HAMMOND ALDOUS
Also Called: Hammond Printing Company
127 Berry Hill Rd (22960-1632)
PHONE.....................540 672-5050
Jason A Hammond, *Owner*
Jason Hammond, *Owner*
EMP: 5
SQ FT: 5,000

SALES (est): 56.2K **Privately Held**
WEB: www.hammondmfg.com
SIC: 2752 Commercial printing, offset

(G-10217)
JOHNNY PORTER CANDLE CO
211 Morton St (22960-1415)
PHONE.....................540 406-1608
EMP: 1
SALES (est): 48K **Privately Held**
SIC: 3999 Candles

(G-10218)
KOPPERS INDUSTRIES INC
110 Walker St (22960-1649)
PHONE.....................540 672-3802
Larry Sappington, *Branch Mgr*
EMP: 2 **Publicly Held**
WEB: www.koppers.com
SIC: 3272 2421 Concrete products; railroad ties, sawed
HQ: Koppers Industries Of Delaware Inc.
436 7th Ave Ste 2026
Pittsburgh PA 15219

(G-10219)
LOHMANN SPECIALTY
COATINGS LLC
14218 Litchfield Dr (22960-2574)
PHONE.....................859 334-4900
Paula Roberts, *Buyer*
Steven Dejong,
▲ **EMP:** 7
SALES (est): 1.5MM
SALES (corp-wide): 677MM **Privately Held**
WEB: www.softstickadhesive.com
SIC: 3479 Coating of metals & formed products
HQ: Lohmann Corporation
3000 Earhart Ct Ste 155
Hebron KY 41048
859 334-4900

(G-10220)
MLS LOGGING LLC
11423 Westwind Dr (22960-2430)
PHONE.....................540 223-0394
Michael Smith, *Principal*
EMP: 2
SALES (est): 89.8K **Privately Held**
WEB: www.mslsoggingandexcavating.com
SIC: 2411 Logging

(G-10221)
MPS RETURN CENTER
14301 Litchfield Dr (22960-2570)
PHONE.....................540 672-0792
EMP: 2
SALES (est): 144.2K **Privately Held**
SIC: 2741 Catalogs: publishing & printing

(G-10222)
PROTO-TECHNICS INC
180 S Almond St (22960-1643)
PHONE.....................540 672-5193
Robert M Shreve, *Treasurer*
Richard West, *Treasurer*
EMP: 24
SALES (est): 1.7MM **Privately Held**
SIC: 3585 Refrigeration & heating equipment

(G-10223)
PUBLISHERS PRESS
INCORPORATED
Also Called: North-South Trader
256 E Main St (22960-1721)
P.O. Box 631 (22960-0370)
PHONE.....................540 672-4845
Stephen W Sylvia, *President*
EMP: 2
SALES (est): 220.5K **Privately Held**
WEB: www.nstcivilwar.com
SIC: 2721 Magazines: publishing only, not printed on site

(G-10224)
Q B ENTERPRISES INC
13164 James Madison Hwy (22960-2808)
PHONE.....................540 825-2950
Rebecca Kube, *President*
Roger Kube, *Vice Pres*
▲ **EMP:** 2

SALES (est): 309.9K **Privately Held**
WEB: www.quickdrytowels.com
SIC: 3589 Car washing machinery

(G-10225)
RACERS CUSTOM CABINETS INC
227 Byrd St (22960-1630)
PHONE......................540 672-4231
Steve M Racer, *President*
Christine Racer, *Corp Secy*
Racer Christine J, *Vice Pres*
EMP: 4
SALES (est): 180K **Privately Held**
SIC: 2434 Wood kitchen cabinets

(G-10226)
RIDGE TOOL COMPANY
14100 Old Gordonsville Rd (22960-2921)
P.O. Box 150 (22960-0086)
PHONE......................540 672-5150
Allen Hoffman, *Branch Mgr*
EMP: 170
SQ FT: 88,000
SALES (corp-wide): 18.3B **Publicly Held**
WEB: www.ridgidpumps.com
SIC: 3541 3545 Machine tools, metal cutting type; machine tool accessories
HQ: Ridge Tool Company
400 Clark St
Elyria OH 44035
440 323-5581

(G-10227)
ROLLINS MEAT PROCESSING
17212 Rollins Rd (22960-3038)
P.O. Box 706 (22960-0806)
PHONE......................540 672-5177
Charles Rollins, *Owner*
Stuart Rollins, *Partner*
EMP: 4
SALES (est): 295.6K **Privately Held**
SIC: 2011 Meat packing plants

(G-10228)
TERRAPIN SPORTS SUPPLY INC
125 Madison Rd (22960-1409)
PHONE......................540 672-9370
Walter Gipson, *President*
EMP: 1
SALES (est): 69K **Privately Held**
SIC: 3949 Sporting & athletic goods

(G-10229)
VIRGINIA AROMATICS LTD COMPANY
12493 Spicewood Rd (22960-2201)
PHONE......................540 672-2847
Kerensa Bertolino, *Principal*
EMP: 4 **EST:** 2012
SALES (est): 339.8K **Privately Held**
WEB: www.luxaromatica.com
SIC: 2844 Toilet preparations

(G-10230)
VON HOLTZBRINCK PUBLISHING
14301 Litchfield Dr (22960-2570)
PHONE......................540 672-9311
Thomas Talley, *Principal*
EMP: 2
SALES (est): 130.9K **Privately Held**
WEB: www.skaneatelesproperties.com
SIC: 2741 Miscellaneous publishing

(G-10231)
WHEELER TEMBER
Also Called: Michael Wheeler
10386 Larmond Rd (22960-4657)
PHONE......................540 672-4186
Michael S Wheeler, *Owner*
EMP: 1
SALES (est): 109.3K **Privately Held**
SIC: 2411 4212 Logging camps & contractors; local trucking, without storage

(G-10232)
WOOD TELEVISION LLC
Also Called: Orange County Review
110 Berry Hill Rd (22960-1673)
P.O. Box 589 (22960-0345)
PHONE......................540 672-1266
Nancy Embree, *Manager*
EMP: 30

SALES (corp-wide): 3B **Publicly Held**
WEB: www.woodtv.com
SIC: 2711 2796 2791 2759 Newspapers, publishing & printing; platemaking services; typesetting; commercial printing; commercial printing, lithographic
HQ: Wood Television Llc
120 College Ave Se
Grand Rapids MI 49503
616 456-8888

(G-10233)
WOODBERRY FARM INC
6005 Woodberry Farm Rd (22960-3048)
PHONE......................540 854-6967
Robert Smithdeal, *President*
Deborah Smithdeal, *Admin Sec*
EMP: 2
SALES (est): 321.3K **Privately Held**
WEB: www.woodberryfarmsinc.com
SIC: 2421 Sawdust & shavings

(G-10234)
WRIGHT LOOK
190 Caroline St Ste F (22960-1508)
PHONE......................540 672-5085
Sherrie Page, *Owner*
EMP: 3
SALES (est): 294.6K **Privately Held**
SIC: 3648 Sun tanning equipment, incl. tanning beds

(G-10235)
WRIGHTS IRON INC
13160 James Madison Hwy (22960-2808)
P.O. Box 831 (22960-0493)
PHONE......................540 661-1089
Hugh Rasworth Wright Jr, *President*
EMP: 2
SALES (est): 284.3K **Privately Held**
WEB: www.wrightsiron.com
SIC: 7692 3499 Welding repair; fabricated metal products

Ordinary
Gloucester County

(G-10236)
BAHAMA BREEZE SHUTTER AWNG LLC
3759 George Wash Mem Hwy (23131)
P.O. Box 387 (23131-0387)
PHONE......................757 592-0265
Rodney Hockaday, *Partner*
Robin Sukhai, *Partner*
EMP: 2 **EST:** 2012
SALES (est): 114.3K **Privately Held**
SIC: 2394 2431 3442 Canvas awnings & canopies; awnings, blinds & shutters, wood; louvers, shutters, jalousies & similar items

(G-10237)
TURLINGTON SONS SPTIC TANK SVC
7007 Ernest Ln (23131)
P.O. Box 335 (23131-0335)
PHONE......................804 642-9538
Peter A Turlington, *President*
Jacqueline E Turlington, *Vice Pres*
EMP: 5 **EST:** 1970
SQ FT: 1,000
SALES (est): 425.7K **Privately Held**
WEB: www.turlingtonseptic.com
SIC: 3272 1711 Septic tanks, concrete; septic system construction

Paeonian Springs
Loudoun County

(G-10238)
CUSTOM GRAPHICS INC
16552 Clarkes Gap Rd (20129-1707)
P.O. Box 304, Purcellville (20134-0304)
PHONE......................540 882-3488
Robert A Farkas, *President*
Linda Farkas, *Vice Pres*
EMP: 2 **EST:** 1973

SALES (est): 200K **Privately Held**
SIC: 2791 8999 7336 7335 Typesetting; editorial service; graphic arts & related design; commercial photography; brokers, contract services

(G-10239)
SEALANTS AND COATINGS TECH (PA)
16955 Simpson Cir (20129-1731)
PHONE......................812 256-3378
James F McCain, *President*
EMP: 4 **EST:** 1982
SALES (est): 330.9K **Privately Held**
SIC: 2452 Log cabins, prefabricated, wood

Painter
Accomack County

(G-10240)
EASTERN SHORE REBUILDERS
31378 Pennyville Rd (23420-4244)
PHONE......................757 709-1250
Jon McCleish, *Owner*
EMP: 1
SQ FT: 600
SALES (est): 92.8K **Privately Held**
SIC: 3694 Alternators, automotive; ignition apparatus & distributors

(G-10241)
OLD DOMINION PIPE COMPANY LLC
19465 Pungo Creek Ln (23420)
P.O. Box 69 (23420-0069)
PHONE......................757 710-2681
Robert Savage, *Principal*
EMP: 2
SALES (est): 43.6K **Privately Held**
WEB: www.olddominionpipe.com
SIC: 3999 Tobacco pipes, pipestems & bits

(G-10242)
PLUS IS ME
16282 Savagetown Rd (23420-3431)
PHONE......................757 693-1505
Candice Turner, *CEO*
EMP: 2
SALES (est): 50K **Privately Held**
SIC: 2331 Women's & misses' blouses & shirts

Palmyra
Fluvanna County

(G-10243)
AGEE CATERING SERVICES
56 Agee Ln (22963-5315)
PHONE......................434 960-8906
Eric Agee, *Owner*
Chef Eric Agee, *Owner*
EMP: 1 **EST:** 2015
SALES (est): 37K **Privately Held**
SIC: 2043 7699 Oatmeal: prepared as cereal breakfast food; tank truck cleaning service

(G-10244)
BOOKY BIZ LLC
37 Burns Plz (22963-3170)
PHONE......................434 207-3715
EMP: 2 **EST:** 2014
SALES (est): 99.9K **Privately Held**
SIC: 2741 Miscellaneous publishing

(G-10245)
BUCKINGHAM BEACON
2987 Lake Monticello Rd (22963-4820)
P.O. Box 59 (22963-0059)
PHONE......................434 591-1000
Carlos Santos, *Owner*
EMP: 2
SALES (est): 64K **Privately Held**
WEB: www.fluvannareview.com
SIC: 2711 Newspapers, publishing & printing

(G-10246)
CH KRAMMES & CO INC
3794 Haden Martin Rd (22963-5428)
PHONE......................434 589-1663

Clifford H Krammes, *President*
Chris Krammes, *Vice Pres*
▲ **EMP:** 9
SQ FT: 800
SALES (est): 1.5MM **Privately Held**
WEB: www.krammes.com
SIC: 3599 Machine shop, jobbing & repair

(G-10247)
CUNNINGHAM CREEK WINERY LLC
3304 Ruritan Lake Rd (22963-5281)
PHONE......................434 207-3907
Bruce Deal, *Principal*
EMP: 3
SALES (est): 68.6K **Privately Held**
WEB: www.cunninghamcreek.wine
SIC: 2084 Wines

(G-10248)
DUN INC
374 White Oak Dr (22963-4278)
PHONE......................804 240-4183
Roy Larimer, *President*
EMP: 2
SALES (est): 150K **Privately Held**
WEB: www.duninc.com
SIC: 3861 7335 Photographic equipment & supplies; commercial photography

(G-10249)
GJA LLC
Also Called: Glenmore Life
2 Putt Cir (22963-2520)
PHONE......................434 218-0216
Josephine Andersen, *Principal*
EMP: 2 **EST:** 2013
SALES (est): 60K **Privately Held**
SIC: 2721 Magazines: publishing & printing

(G-10250)
JOHNSONS POSTCARDS
9 Corn Pone Ln (22963-2136)
PHONE......................434 589-7605
Nathaniel Britton Johnson, *Owner*
EMP: 2
SALES (est): 176.2K **Privately Held**
SIC: 2752 Post cards, picture: lithographed

(G-10251)
NEWSWISE INC
265 Turkeysag Trl Ste 102 (22963-2654)
PHONE......................434 296-9417
Jessica Johnson, *CEO*
Lisa Freyer, *Sales Staff*
Lucas Clugston, *Producer*
EMP: 20
SALES (est): 2.2MM **Privately Held**
WEB: www.newswise.com
SIC: 2741 Miscellaneous publishing

(G-10252)
PALMYRA PRESS INC
2185 Haden Martin Rd (22963-5419)
PHONE......................434 589-6634
Barbara Clarke, *President*
Sam Y Clarke, *Vice Pres*
EMP: 2
SALES (est): 192.5K **Privately Held**
SIC: 2721 Periodicals

(G-10253)
PARMLY JR LAND LOGGING & TIMBE
2460 Shores Rd (22963-5230)
PHONE......................434 842-2900
P Parmly, *Principal*
EMP: 3
SALES (est): 250.9K **Privately Held**
SIC: 2411 Logging camps & contractors

(G-10254)
PERRONE PUBLISHING LLC
37 Morewood Pl (22963-2750)
PHONE......................434 962-6694
Darlene Perrone, *Principal*
EMP: 2 **EST:** 2007
SALES (est): 79K **Privately Held**
SIC: 2741 Miscellaneous publishing

(G-10255)
PICKERS GRIP LLC
265 Turkeysag Trl 102-2 (22963-2654)
PHONE......................434 260-3366
EMP: 2

▲ = Import ▼=Export
◆ =Import/Export

SALES (est): 112.7K **Privately Held**
WEB: www.pickersgrip.com
SIC: 3949 Sporting & athletic goods

(G-10256)
PREMIER EMBROIDERY AND DESIGN
8 Wedge Ter (22963-2315)
PHONE....................434 242-2801
Gary L Baughn, *Owner*
EMP: 1
SALES (est): 5K **Privately Held**
SIC: 2395 Embroidery & art needlework

(G-10257)
QUALATEE
117 Union Church Rd (22963-5330)
PHONE....................434 842-3530
EMP: 8
SALES (est): 914.9K **Privately Held**
WEB: www.qualatee.com
SIC: 2759 Screen printing

(G-10258)
TROOPMASTER SOFTWARE INC
Also Called: T S I
5 Fleetwood Dr (22963-2652)
P.O. Box 416 (22963-0416)
PHONE....................434 589-6788
Robert Edwards, *President*
Kelly Robbins, *Vice Pres*
EMP: 4
SALES (est): 493.4K **Privately Held**
WEB: www.troopmaster.com
SIC: 7372 Business oriented computer
   software

(G-10259)
VALLEY PUBLISHING CORPORATION
Also Called: Fluvanna Review The
Crofton Plz Bldg 106ste (22963)
P.O. Box 59 (22963-0059)
PHONE....................434 591-1000
Carlos Santos, *President*
Kathleen Zeek, *Manager*
EMP: 4 EST: 1995
SALES (est): 20.9K **Privately Held**
WEB: www.fluvannareview.com
SIC: 2711 Newspapers

(G-10260)
WHISPERING PINES WELD & IRON
532 Deep Creek Rd (22963-3600)
PHONE....................434 465-0704
Betty Shiflett, *Principal*
EMP: 1
SALES (est): 25K **Privately Held**
SIC: 7692 Welding repair

Parksley
Accomack County

(G-10261)
D & V ENTERPRISES INC
Also Called: Parksley Sign Company
18475 Dunne Ave (23421)
P.O. Box 163 (23421-0163)
PHONE....................757 665-5202
EMP: 4
SALES: 100K **Privately Held**
SIC: 3993 Signage/Business
   Cards/Screenprinting

(G-10262)
GOHRING COMPONENTS CORP
24013 Bennett St (23421-2922)
PHONE....................757 665-4110
William Gohring Jr, *President*
EMP: 2
SQ FT: 5,000
SALES (est): 145K **Privately Held**
SIC: 3559 Pharmaceutical machinery

Partlow
Spotsylvania County

(G-10263)
ALPHA
10700 Edenton Rd (22534-9643)
PHONE....................540 895-5731
Richard Lafferty, *Owner*
Sharon Lafferty, *Co-Owner*
EMP: 2
SALES (est): 182.8K **Privately Held**
SIC: 2844 5431 0782 5261 Shaving
   preparations; vegetable stands or mar-
   kets; landscape contractors; nurseries

(G-10264)
BRUSH 10
9200 Thurston Ln (22534-9593)
PHONE....................540 582-3820
EMP: 2
SALES (est): 107.4K **Privately Held**
SIC: 3647 Vehicular Lighting Equipment

(G-10265)
CROSS-LAND CONVEYORS LLC
10909 Astarita Ave (22534-9718)
PHONE....................540 287-9150
Ratliff Ray, *Manager*
Kennith Ray Ratliff,
EMP: 2
SALES (est): 191.9K **Privately Held**
WEB: www.almasjewelryandnovelties.com
SIC: 3535 Conveyors & conveying equip-
   ment

(G-10266)
IMANI M X-ORTIZ
Also Called: Imani M X-Ortiz Og Distributor
5405 Partlow Rd (22534-9693)
PHONE....................540 582-5898
EMP: 1
SALES (est): 33K **Privately Held**
SIC: 2095 Mfg Roasted Coffee

(G-10267)
MARK T GOODMAN
4300 Partlow Rd (22534-9686)
PHONE....................540 582-2328
Mark T Goodman, *Owner*
EMP: 1 EST: 2010
SALES (est): 64.5K **Privately Held**
SIC: 3524 7389 Snowblowers & throwers,
   residential; business services

(G-10268)
U S MINING INC
10909 Astarita Ave (22534-9718)
PHONE....................804 769-7222
Matthew O Heldreth, *President*
EMP: 1
SALES (est): 41.4K **Privately Held**
SIC: 1011 Underground iron ore mining

Patrick Springs
Patrick County

(G-10269)
BRADS WLDG & ALIGN BORING LLC
74 Holt Valley Ln Trlr 4 (24133-3889)
P.O. Box 463 (24133-0463)
PHONE....................276 340-1605
Brad Holt, *Principal*
EMP: 2
SALES (est): 148.4K **Privately Held**
SIC: 3548 Resistance welders, electric

(G-10270)
FOLLEY FENCING SERVICE
1542 Koger Mill Rd (24133-3238)
PHONE....................276 629-8487
William Folley, *Owner*
EMP: 1
SALES (est): 82.6K **Privately Held**
SIC: 3446 Architectural metalwork

Pearisburg
Giles County

(G-10271)
APM ENTERPRISES INC
205 N Main St (24134-1611)
PHONE....................540 921-3399
Eric Price, *Principal*
EMP: 7 EST: 2008
SALES (est): 824.3K **Privately Held**
WEB: www.apmenterprises.com
SIC: 3599 Machine shop, jobbing & repair

(G-10272)
B & B POWDER INC
212 Sugar Run Rd (24134-2646)
PHONE....................540 921-1158
James H Brown Jr, *President*
EMP: 5
SALES (est): 600K **Privately Held**
SIC: 3479 Painting, coating & hot dipping

(G-10273)
B AND B POWDER COATING
212 Sugar Run Rd (24134-2646)
PHONE....................540 921-1158
Harvey Brown, *Owner*
EMP: 1
SALES (est): 400K **Privately Held**
WEB: www.bbpowder.com
SIC: 3479 Coating of metals & formed
   products

(G-10274)
EZ CUT BANDMILLS
175 Rose Bush Ln (24134-2892)
PHONE....................540 931-2410
EMP: 2
SALES (est): 120.7K **Privately Held**
SIC: 3999 Manufacturing industries

(G-10275)
J&S FISHER LLC
Also Called: J&S Creations
301 Forest Hill Dr (24134-1105)
PHONE....................540 921-3197
Jeffrey Fisher,
Elizabeth Fisher,
EMP: 2 EST: 2014
SALES (est): 96.1K **Privately Held**
SIC: 3961 Costume jewelry, ex. precious
   metal & semiprecious stones

(G-10276)
ROCKY RIDGE FURNITURE
125 Rose Bush Ln (24134-2892)
PHONE....................419 512-0067
Aaron Kinsinger, *Owner*
EMP: 1
SALES (est): 431.5K **Privately Held**
SIC: 2511 Wood lawn & garden furniture

(G-10277)
SIMPLICITY PURE BATH & BDY LLC
216 Fairview Ave (24134-1124)
PHONE....................540 922-9287
Sherri Janney,
EMP: 1
SALES (est): 87.3K **Privately Held**
SIC: 2841 5122 5999 7389 Soap & other
   detergents; cosmetics; cosmetics; busi-
   ness services

(G-10278)
UFP MID-ATLANTIC LLC
Also Called: Universal Forest Products
152 Industrial Park Dr (24134-2689)
PHONE....................540 921-1286
EMP: 60
SALES (corp-wide): 4.4B **Publicly Held**
WEB: www.ufpi.com
SIC: 2439 Trusses, wooden roof; trusses,
   except roof: laminated lumber
HQ: Ufp Mid-Atlantic, Llc
   5631 S Nc Highway 62
   Burlington NC 27215
   336 226-9356

(G-10279)
VIRGINIAN LEADER CORP
511 Mountain Lake Ave (24134-1629)
PHONE....................540 921-3434

Kenneth L Rakes, *President*
Kenneth Rakes, *President*
Amy Burdette, *Manager*
EMP: 14 EST: 1961
SQ FT: 5,400
SALES (est): 700K **Privately Held**
WEB: www.virginianleader.com
SIC: 2711 2759 Newspapers: publishing
   only, not printed on site; commercial print-
   ing

Pembroke
Giles County

(G-10280)
20-X INDUSTRIES LLC
186 Doe Creek Rd (24136-3061)
PHONE....................540 922-0005
Lorne Bowman, *Principal*
EMP: 2
SALES (est): 147.3K **Privately Held**
SIC: 3999 Manufacturing industries

(G-10281)
AMISH HEIRLOOMS OF VRGN
619 Snidow St (24136-3489)
PHONE....................540 626-8587
Tom Spangler, *Principal*
EMP: 2
SALES (est): 156.8K **Privately Held**
SIC: 2511 Wood household furniture

(G-10282)
NUTRITION SUPPORT SERVICES
477 New Zion Rd (24136-3156)
PHONE....................540 626-3081
Susan Donoghue Dvm, *President*
EMP: 1
SALES (est): 64.6K **Privately Held**
SIC: 2836 7338 8049 Veterinary biologi-
   cal products; editing service; nutrition
   specialist

(G-10283)
POWELLS PAVING SEALING LLC
208 Painter School Rd (24136-3438)
PHONE....................540 921-2455
James J Powell, *Mng Member*
EMP: 1
SALES (est): 101K **Privately Held**
SIC: 2951 Asphalt paving mixtures &
   blocks

(G-10284)
SNIDER & SONS INC
378 Eggleston Rd (24136-3145)
PHONE....................540 626-5849
John Grant Snider, *President*
EMP: 3
SALES (est): 189.5K **Privately Held**
SIC: 3599 7692 Machine shop, jobbing &
   repair; welding repair

Penhook
Franklin County

(G-10285)
SWINSON MEDICAL LLC
180 Island View Dr (24137-5020)
P.O. Box 289 (24137-0289)
PHONE....................540 576-1719
Phil L Swinson, *Mng Member*
Janet Swinson,
EMP: 4
SALES (est): 350K **Privately Held**
WEB: www.swinsonmedical.com
SIC: 2599 3841 Hospital furniture, except
   beds; surgical & medical instruments

(G-10286)
TWEEDIES REPAIR SERVICE
14775 Snow Creek Rd (24137-1144)
PHONE....................540 576-2617
Harold Tweedie, *Owner*
EMP: 1
SALES (est): 66.1K **Privately Held**
SIC: 7692 Welding repair

GEOGRAPHIC

Penn Laird
Rockingham County

(G-10287)
ABINGTON SUNSHADE &
BLINDS CO
7680 Kathleen Ct (22846-9546)
PHONE...........................540 435-6450
Louis Cabrera, *President*
EMP: 10
SQ FT: 5,000
SALES (est): 1MM **Privately Held**
WEB: www.abingtonsunshade.com
SIC: 2591 5023 Window shade rollers &
fittings; home furnishings

(G-10288)
EMBROIDERY DEPOT LTD
7372 Mountain Grove Rd (22846-9505)
PHONE...........................540 289-5044
Dennis D Trobaugh, *CEO*
EMP: 2
SALES (est): 33K **Privately Held**
SIC: 2395 Embroidery products, except
schiffli machine

(G-10289)
JACOBS POWDER COATING
LLC
8253 Spotswood Trl (22846-9503)
PHONE...........................540 208-7762
Monica Waugh, *Administration*
EMP: 2
SALES (est): 140.2K **Privately Held**
SIC: 3479 Coating of metals & formed
products

(G-10290)
VALLEY DOORS UNLIMITED LLC
5001 Spotswood Trl (22846-2002)
PHONE...........................540 638-0167
Mark Pinnow,
EMP: 2 EST: 2016
SALES (est): 107.5K **Privately Held**
SIC: 3429 5072 Keys, locks & related
hardware; builders' hardware

Pennington Gap
Lee County

(G-10291)
AMERICAN CONCRETE GROUP
LLC
515 Industrial Dr (24277)
P.O. Box 708 (24277-0708)
PHONE...........................276 546-1633
Charles Litton, *President*
EMP: 8
SQ FT: 6,000
SALES (est): 801.4K **Privately Held**
SIC: 3271 3273 Concrete block & brick;
ready-mixed concrete

(G-10292)
AMERICAN CONCRETE GROUP
LLC (PA)
R-2 Woodway (24277)
P.O. Box 708 (24277-0708)
PHONE...........................276 546-1666
Charles Litton,
EMP: 4
SALES (est): 959.1K **Privately Held**
SIC: 2899 Concrete curing & hardening
compounds

(G-10293)
APPALCHIAN AFRCAN AMRCN
CNTER
Also Called: Appalchian Afrcan Amrcn Cltral
265 Leona St (24277-1319)
PHONE...........................276 546-5144
Kevin Carson, *Ch of Bd*
Elizabeth Catte, *Ch of Bd*
Michael Gilley, *Ch of Bd*
William Isom, *Ch of Bd*
Sue Ella Kobak, *Ch of Bd*
EMP: 40
SALES (est): 10K **Privately Held**
WEB: www.aaaculturalcenter.org
SIC: 2836 Culture media

(G-10294)
COREY ELY LOGGING LLC
370 Ely Pucketts Creek Rd (24277-7097)
PHONE...........................423 579-3436
Corey Ely, *President*
EMP: 8
SALES (est): 175.1K **Privately Held**
SIC: 2411 Logging

(G-10295)
MARK A HARBER
Also Called: Moonlite Septic Service
2097 Ward Hill Rd (24277-8017)
PHONE...........................276 546-6051
Mark Harber, *Owner*
EMP: 2
SALES (est): 107.4K **Privately Held**
SIC: 3561 7389 Pumps & pumping equip-
ment; business services

(G-10296)
OLD VRGINIA HAND HEWN LOG
HOMES
Us Hwy 58 Rr 2 (24277)
PHONE...........................276 546-5647
Judy Williams, *President*
Jacqueline Kelly, *Admin Sec*
EMP: 10
SQ FT: 5,000
SALES (est): 1.4MM **Privately Held**
WEB: www.oldvirginialoghomes.com
SIC: 2452 1521 Log cabins, prefabricated,
wood; single-family housing construction

(G-10297)
POWELL VALLEY PRINTING
COMPANY
Also Called: Powell Valley News
41798 E Morgan Ave (24277-3216)
P.O. Box 459 (24277-0459)
PHONE...........................276 546-1210
Shirley R Watson, *President*
Rick Watson, *Vice Pres*
EMP: 14 EST: 1956
SQ FT: 28,000
SALES (est): 974.9K **Privately Held**
WEB: www.powellvalleybank.com
SIC: 2711 2752 Job printing & newspaper
publishing combined; commercial printing,
lithographic

(G-10298)
POWELL VALLEY STONE CO
INC
43115 Wilderness Rd (24277-8322)
P.O. Box 10, Dryden (24243-0010)
PHONE...........................276 546-2550
Renee Jessee, *President*
Kellee Jessee, *Treasurer*
Nicole Gordon, *Admin Asst*
EMP: 10 EST: 1978
SQ FT: 3,267,000
SALES (est): 1MM **Privately Held**
WEB: www.powellvalleybank.com
SIC: 1422 Limestones, ground

(G-10299)
PULLIN INK
179 N Kentucky St (24277-2223)
PHONE...........................276 546-2760
Ann Hall, *Owner*
EMP: 3
SALES (est): 100K **Privately Held**
WEB: www.pullinink.com
SIC: 2261 Screen printing of cotton broad-
woven fabrics

(G-10300)
SYNERGY BIOFUELS LLC
334 Guy Walton Dr (24277-7746)
P.O. Box 515 (24277-0515)
PHONE...........................276 546-5226
Ankit Patel, *Mng Member*
EMP: 5
SQ FT: 450,000
SALES (est): 560.9K **Privately Held**
WEB: www.synergybiofuels.com
SIC: 2911 Diesel fuels

Petersburg
Petersburg City County

(G-10301)
ADVANTUS CORP
1818 Dock St (23803-2847)
PHONE...........................804 324-7169
EMP: 63
SALES (corp-wide): 83.7MM **Privately
Held**
WEB: www.advantus.com
SIC: 3429 Metal fasteners
PA: Advantus, Corp.
12276 San Jose Blvd # 618
Jacksonville FL 32223
904 482-0091

(G-10302)
AMPAC FINE CHEMICALS VA
LLC
2820 Normandy Dr (23805-9372)
PHONE...........................804 504-8600
Dwayne Ash, *Engineer*
John V Sobchak, *CFO*
Aslan Malik, *Mng Member*
Scott Roberts, *Maintence Staff*
EMP: 20
SQ FT: 35,000
SALES (est): 50MM **Privately Held**
WEB: www.ampacfinechemicals.com
SIC: 2834 Pharmaceutical preparations
HQ: Ampac Fine Chemicals Llc
Highway 50 Hzel Ave Bldg
Rancho Cordova CA 95741
916 357-6880

(G-10303)
AMSTED RAIL COMPANY INC
Amsted Rail Brenco- Petersburg
2580 Frontage Rd (23805-9309)
PHONE...........................804 732-0202
McIntyre Louthan, *COO*
EMP: 450
SALES (corp-wide): 2.2B **Privately Held**
WEB: www.amstedrail.com
SIC: 3743 Railroad equipment
HQ: Amsted Rail Company, Inc.
311 S Wacker Dr Ste 5300
Chicago IL 60606

(G-10304)
ANKH & LOTUS LLC
704 High St (23803-3039)
PHONE...........................313 333-5138
Jordan Redwine,
EMP: 1
SALES (est): 46.5K **Privately Held**
SIC: 2211 Apparel & outerwear fabrics,
cotton

(G-10305)
ANTONIO ROBINSON
Also Called: Robinson's Lawn Care
2773 Meadowbrook St (23803-7928)
PHONE...........................804 368-9889
Antonio Robinson, *Owner*
EMP: 3
SALES (est): 118.7K **Privately Held**
SIC: 3524 Lawnmowers, residential: hand
or power

(G-10306)
ART PRINTING SOLUTIONS LLC
219 Nansemond St (23803-3705)
PHONE...........................804 387-3203
Bryan Rodriguez, *Principal*
EMP: 2
SALES (est): 83.9K **Privately Held**
SIC: 2752 Commercial printing, litho-
graphic

(G-10307)
ATLANTIC STAIRCRAFTERS
1133 Triad Pkwy (23803-7900)
PHONE...........................804 732-3323
Charlie Shaylor, *Owner*
EMP: 14
SQ FT: 3,000
SALES (est): 1MM **Privately Held**
SIC: 2431 Staircases & stairs, wood

(G-10308)
ATTIC ZIPPER
2214 W Washington St (23803-2758)
PHONE...........................804 518-5094
EMP: 2
SALES (est): 78.2K **Privately Held**
WEB: www.attichatchcover.com
SIC: 3965 Zipper

(G-10309)
BATH SON AND SONS
ASSOCIATES
2016 W Washington St (23803-2878)
PHONE...........................804 722-0687
Balbir Singh, *Principal*
EMP: 2
SALES (est): 179.3K **Privately Held**
SIC: 2591 Venetian blinds

(G-10310)
BOEHRINGER INGELHEIM CORP
2820 Normandy Dr (23805-9372)
PHONE...........................804 862-8316
Agnieszka Abeyta, *Manager*
Elizabe Hildebrandt, *Technology*
EMP: 1
SALES (corp-wide): 21B **Privately Held**
WEB: www.boehringer-ingelheim.com
SIC: 2834 Pharmaceutical preparations
HQ: Boehringer Ingelheim Corporation
900 Ridgebury Rd
Ridgefield CT 06877
203 798-9988

(G-10311)
CHESAPEAKE BIOFUELS
1925 Puddledock Rd (23803-3614)
PHONE...........................804 482-1784
Anders Blixt, *Principal*
EMP: 2
SALES (est): 131.2K **Privately Held**
SIC: 2429 Special product sawmills

(G-10312)
COLONIAL IRON WORKS INC
215 N South St (23803-3027)
PHONE...........................804 862-4141
Joseph F Michael Jr, *President*
EMP: 5
SALES (est): 240K **Privately Held**
SIC: 3446 Ornamental metalwork

(G-10313)
COLONIAL TAILORS CHALK
2041 Midway Ave (23803-2879)
PHONE...........................850 622-2270
Christopher M Robin, *Owner*
EMP: 6 EST: 2012
SALES (est): 453.2K **Privately Held**
WEB: www.colonialtailorschalk.com
SIC: 3952 Crayons: chalk, gypsum, char-
coal, fusains, pastel, wax, etc.

(G-10314)
COLONIAL TAILORS CHALK INC
Also Called: Ctc FL
2041 Midway Ave (23803-2879)
PHONE...........................757 291-2445
Christopher Robin, *President*
Linda Herr, *Vice Pres*
EMP: 6
SALES (est): 771.1K **Privately Held**
WEB: www.colonialtailorschalk.com
SIC: 3952 Crayons: chalk, gypsum, char-
coal, fusains, pastel, wax, etc.; chalk: car-
penters', blackboard, marking, tailors',
etc.

(G-10315)
CRICKET PRODUCTS INC
Also Called: Glenna Jean Manufacturing
1921 Anchor Ave (23803-2827)
P.O. Box 2187 (23804-1487)
PHONE...........................804 861-0687
Kramer Glenna S, *President*
Stuart Ashley Kramer, *Vice Pres*
Kramer Whitney Page, *Vice Pres*
Tracy Harrison, *Credit Mgr*
Wanda Elliot, *Human Res Dir*
▲ EMP: 26
SQ FT: 30,000
SALES (est): 490.1K **Privately Held**
WEB: www.glennajean.com
SIC: 2392 2395 Household furnishings;
quilting, for the trade

(G-10316)
DESIGN SYSTEMS & SERVICES CORP
318 E Wythe St (23803-4351)
P.O. Box 5757, Virginia Beach (23471-0757)
PHONE..............................804 722-0396
Scott Moore, *Principal*
Mike Blasiole, *Principal*
Jr Chestnutt, *Principal*
EMP: 50
SQ FT: 6,000
SALES (est): 5MM **Privately Held**
WEB: www.dss-corporation.com
SIC: 3699 Electrical welding equipment

(G-10317)
DISCOUNTCRYO CO
2200 E Washington St (23803-3726)
PHONE..............................804 733-3229
Jimmy Lee Jobe, *Principal*
EMP: 2
SALES (est): 158.9K **Privately Held**
SIC: 3559 Cryogenic machinery, industrial

(G-10318)
EIW GROUP
203 N Davis St (23803-3817)
PHONE..............................804 677-6214
Edward Ward, *Owner*
EMP: 2
SALES (est): 85.7K **Privately Held**
WEB: www.rentpetersburg.com
SIC: 3695 Magnetic & optical recording media

(G-10319)
EMPRESS PUBLISHING LLC
300 Addison Way Apt 13-2i (23805-9375)
PHONE..............................856 630-8198
Karen Bryant, *Principal*
EMP: 1
SALES (est): 37.5K **Privately Held**
SIC: 2741 Miscellaneous publishing

(G-10320)
FLOW DYNAMICS INC
1620 Berkeley Ave (23805-2810)
PHONE..............................804 835-9740
EMP: 2
SALES (est): 130K **Privately Held**
SIC: 3491 Mfg Industrial Valves

(G-10321)
GALE WELDING AND MCH CO INC
415 E Bank St (23803-3301)
PHONE..............................804 732-4521
James Herbert Williams, *President*
Cynthia W Bailey, *Admin Sec*
Cynthia Bailey, *Admin Sec*
EMP: 10
SQ FT: 5,000
SALES (est): 1.5MM **Privately Held**
WEB: www.galewelding.com
SIC: 7692 3599 Welding repair; machine shop, jobbing & repair

(G-10322)
GATEHOUSE MEDIA LLC
Also Called: Progress Index, The
15 Franklin St (23803-4503)
P.O. Box 71 (23804-0071)
PHONE..............................804 732-3456
Craig Richards, *Publisher*
Leilia Magee, *Editor*
Mike Robbins, *Manager*
Bob Seals, *Director*
EMP: 27 **Publicly Held**
WEB: www.gannett.com
SIC: 2711 Newspapers, publishing & printing
HQ: Gatehouse Media, Llc
175 Sullys Trl Fl 3
Pittsford NY 14534
585 598-0030

(G-10323)
GATEHUSE MEDIA VA HOLDINGS INC
15 Franklin St (23803-4503)
PHONE..............................585 598-0030
Garrett J Cummings,
EMP: 1

SALES (est): 76.4K **Publicly Held**
WEB: www.progress-index.com
SIC: 2711 Commercial printing & newspaper publishing combined
PA: Gannett Co., Inc.
7950 Jones Branch Dr
Mc Lean VA 22102
703 854-6000

(G-10324)
HONEYWELL INTERNATIONAL INC
220 Perry St (23803-4202)
PHONE..............................804 518-2351
Brian Puse, *Branch Mgr*
EMP: 699
SALES (corp-wide): 36.7B **Publicly Held**
WEB: www.honeywell.com
SIC: 3724 Aircraft engines & engine parts
PA: Honeywell International Inc.
300 S Tryon St
Charlotte NC 28202
704 627-6200

(G-10325)
INDUSTRIAL GLVANIZERS AMER INC (HQ)
Also Called: Valmont Coatings
3535 Halifax Rd Ste A (23805-1113)
PHONE..............................804 763-1760
Richard Cornish, *President*
Kelly Smith, *Manager*
EMP: 2
SALES (est): 13.3MM **Privately Held**
WEB: www.valmontcoatings.com
SIC: 3479 Etching & engraving

(G-10326)
INTERNATIONAL PAPER COMPANY
2333 Wells Rd (23805-8925)
PHONE..............................804 861-8164
John Svanda, *General Mgr*
EMP: 95
SQ FT: 100,000
SALES (corp-wide): 22.3B **Publicly Held**
WEB: www.internationalpaper.com
SIC: 2653 Boxes, corrugated: made from purchased materials
PA: International Paper Company
6400 Poplar Ave
Memphis TN 38197
901 419-9000

(G-10327)
JIM WAREHIME
Also Called: Wooden Leg Van Shop
214a Grove Ave (23803-3240)
PHONE..............................804 861-5255
Jim Warehime, *Owner*
EMP: 1
SQ FT: 2,000
SALES (est): 50K **Privately Held**
SIC: 3211 Window glass, clear & colored

(G-10328)
JS MONOGRAMMING
1781 Anchor Ave (23803-2822)
PHONE..............................804 862-4324
Hak Lee, *Owner*
EMP: 2
SALES (est): 87.3K **Privately Held**
SIC: 2395 Embroidery & art needlework

(G-10329)
L B FOSTER COMPANY
26401 Hofheimer Way (23804)
PHONE..............................804 722-0398
John Knapp, *Manager*
Regina Dennis, *Admin Asst*
EMP: 9
SALES (corp-wide): 655MM **Publicly Held**
WEB: www.lbfoster.com
SIC: 3449 Bars, concrete reinforcing: fabricated steel
PA: L. B. Foster Company
415 Holiday Dr Ste 1
Pittsburgh PA 15220
412 928-3400

(G-10330)
MERCURY LUGGAGE MFG CO
1818 Dock St (23803-2847)
PHONE..............................804 733-5222

EMP: 100
SALES (corp-wide): 39.5MM **Privately Held**
SIC: 3161 Luggage
PA: Mercury Luggage Manufacturing Company
12276 San Jose Blvd # 618
Jacksonville FL 32223
904 733-9595

(G-10331)
OLD MANSION INC
Also Called: Old Mansion Foods
3811 Corporate Rd (23805-9288)
P.O. Box 1838 (23805-0838)
PHONE..............................804 862-9889
J Dale Patton, *President*
W Allen Patton Jr, *Vice Pres*
Diana Evans, *Purchasing*
John Mento, *Sales Staff*
Laura Palombo, *Manager*
◆ EMP: 40
SQ FT: 50,000
SALES (est): 7MM **Privately Held**
WEB: www.oldmansion.com
SIC: 2099 2095 Tea blending; spices, including grinding; bread crumbs, not made in bakeries; coffee, ground: mixed with grain or chicory

(G-10332)
PARAMOUNT WOODWORKING
3951 S Crater Rd Ste C (23805-9290)
PHONE..............................804 862-2432
Charles W Perkinson, *Owner*
EMP: 1
SALES (est): 78.6K **Privately Held**
SIC: 2499 Trophy bases, wood

(G-10333)
PATRICK MARRIETTA
Also Called: Designs By Ms. Rita
2029 Colston St (23803-2724)
PHONE..............................804 479-9791
Marrietta Patrick, *Principal*
EMP: 1
SALES (est): 53.2K **Privately Held**
SIC: 3911 Jewelry, precious metal

(G-10334)
PEGRAMS TRANSPORTING SVCS LLC
930 W Washington St (23803-4004)
PHONE..............................804 295-1798
Calvin Pegram,
EMP: 2
SALES (est): 86.6K **Privately Held**
SIC: 3441 Railroad car racks, for transporting vehicles: steel

(G-10335)
POWELL MANUFACTURING CO LLC
230 E Bank St (23803-3322)
PHONE..............................804 677-5728
John McCormack, *Principal*
EMP: 2 EST: 2007
SALES (est): 146.3K **Privately Held**
SIC: 3999 Manufacturing industries

(G-10336)
PRE CON INC
Also Called: Brown Street Plant
319 Brown St (23803-4228)
PHONE..............................804 732-1253
Gene Voss, *Branch Mgr*
EMP: 85
SALES (corp-wide): 32MM **Privately Held**
WEB: www.wauford.com
SIC: 2821 3272 Polytetrafluoroethylene resins (teflon); precast terrazo or concrete products
PA: Pre Con, Inc.
6700 Courtyard Rd
Chester VA 23831
804 732-0628

(G-10337)
PRE CON INC
Also Called: Bag Plant Warehouse & Maint
110 Perry St (23803-4135)
PHONE..............................804 861-0282
Mike Blackard, *Branch Mgr*
EMP: 11

SALES (corp-wide): 32MM **Privately Held**
WEB: www.wauford.com
SIC: 2821 2393 Polytetrafluoroethylene resins (teflon); bags & containers, except sleeping bags: textile
PA: Pre Con, Inc.
6700 Courtyard Rd
Chester VA 23831
804 732-0628

(G-10338)
RICKS MACHINE SHOP
124 S Chappell St (23803-3911)
PHONE..............................804 518-5266
EMP: 2
SALES (est): 81.4K **Privately Held**
SIC: 3599 Machine shop, jobbing & repair

(G-10339)
RMAE INC
601 E Washington St (23803-4403)
PHONE..............................804 651-6911
Matthew A Eads, *Administration*
EMP: 2
SALES (est): 127.5K **Privately Held**
SIC: 2752 Commercial printing, offset

(G-10340)
SAICOMP LLC
216 Wisteria Ln Apt 3d (23805-9167)
P.O. Box 3538 (23805-3538)
PHONE..............................714 421-8967
Vamin Cha, *Principal*
EMP: 2
SALES (est): 68.4K **Privately Held**
SIC: 7372 7373 8721 Application computer software; word processing computer software; systems engineering, computer related; accounting services, except auditing

(G-10341)
SHORT RUN STAMPING COMPANY INC
539 N West St (23803-2964)
PHONE..............................804 861-6872
Dave Orecchio, *Manager*
EMP: 56
SQ FT: 10,000
SALES (corp-wide): 28.8MM **Privately Held**
WEB: www.shortrun.com
SIC: 3469 Stamping metal for the trade
PA: The Short Run Stamping Company Inc
925 E Linden Ave
Linden NJ 07036
908 862-1070

(G-10342)
SHOTZ FROM HEART LLC
1810 Randolph Ave (23803-2852)
PHONE..............................804 898-5635
Ebony Leach, *Principal*
EMP: 2
SALES (est): 73.2K **Privately Held**
SIC: 2759 Screen printing

(G-10343)
SO AMAZING PUBLICATIONS
301 Crestfall Ct (23805-1288)
PHONE..............................804 412-5224
EMP: 1
SALES (est): 37.5K **Privately Held**
SIC: 2741 Miscellaneous publishing

(G-10344)
SOUTH DISTRIBUTORS LLC
Also Called: Plastic Container City
216 N South St (23803-3030)
PHONE..............................718 258-0200
▼ EMP: 5 EST: 2010
SALES (est): 485.8K **Privately Held**
SIC: 3089 Mfg Plastic Products

(G-10345)
TEMPLE-INLAND INC
2333 Wells Rd (23805-8925)
PHONE..............................804 861-8164
Tom Jester, *Personnel Exec*
EMP: 7 EST: 2015
SALES (est): 606.6K **Privately Held**
SIC: 2653 Corrugated & solid fiber boxes

(G-10346)
TRAPEZIUM BREWING LLC
230 E Bank St (23803-3322)
PHONE..804 677-5728
John David Mc Cormick Jr,
EMP: 1
SALES (est): 74K Privately Held
WEB: www.trapeziumlofts.com
SIC: 2082 Beer (alcoholic beverage)

(G-10347)
**TUBULAR FABRICATORS
INDUST INC**
Also Called: Tfi Health Care
600 W Wythe St (23803-4138)
PHONE..804 733-4000
Joseph Battiston, President
▲ EMP: 49 EST: 1979
SQ FT: 70,000
SALES (est): 7.1MM Privately Held
WEB: www.tfihealthcare.com
SIC: 2511 3842 Commodes; walkers

(G-10348)
VALMONT INDUSTRIES INC
Also Called: Industrial Galvanizers VA
3535 Halifax Rd (23805-1113)
PHONE..804 733-0808
John Schrider, Principal
Brian Wright, Opers Mgr
Lloyd Roduner, Engineer
Brian Foyt, Plant Engr
Eva Snow, Sales Mgr
EMP: 35 Publicly Held
WEB: www.valmont.com
SIC: 3441 Fabricated structural metal
PA: Valmont Industries, Inc.
　1 Valmont Plz Ste 500
　Omaha NE 68154
　402 963-1000

(G-10349)
**VIRGINIA ABRASIVES
CORPORATION**
2851 Service Rd (23805-9347)
PHONE..804 732-0058
R G Jenks Jr, Corp Secy
Spencer V Perkins III, Vice Pres
Karl Stafflinger, Vice Pres
Bert Stinebaugh, Vice Pres
Joe Cortese, Accounting Mgr
◆ EMP: 65
SQ FT: 60,000
SALES (est): 11.5MM
SALES (corp-wide): 151.6MM Privately
Held
WEB: www.virginiaabrasives.com
SIC: 3291 5085 Coated abrasive prod-
ucts; abrasives
PA: Barton Mines Company, L.L.C.
　6 Warren St
　Glens Falls NY 12801
　518 798-5462

(G-10350)
WHEELS N MOTION
3297 S Crater Rd (23805-9384)
PHONE..804 991-3090
Ronald Small, Principal
EMP: 3
SALES (est): 153.4K Privately Held
WEB: www.phoenixpeace.com
SIC: 3465 Hub caps, automobile: stamped
metal

(G-10351)
WILLIAM R SMITH COMPANY
Also Called: Dietz Press
930 Winfield Rd (23803-4748)
PHONE..804 733-0123
Robert B Smith, President
▲ EMP: 24
SQ FT: 8,000
SALES (est): 3MM Privately Held
WEB: www.dietzpress.com
SIC: 2752 2796 2791 2789 Commercial
printing, offset; platemaking services;
typesetting; bookbinding & related work

(G-10352)
**WYATT SIGN & PAINTING
COMPANY**
1307 Hinton St (23803-2925)
PHONE..804 733-5251
Wayne Wyatt, Owner

EMP: 3
SQ FT: 3,000
SALES (est): 250K Privately Held
WEB: www.wyattsigns.com
SIC: 3993 Signs & advertising specialties

(G-10353)
**XTERIORS MANUFACTURING
LLC**
420 High St Apt 409 (23803-3827)
PHONE..804 445-3597
Donald L Hall, Mng Member
EMP: 12 EST: 2007
SALES (est): 1.7MM Privately Held
WEB: www.xteriorspavers.com
SIC: 3281 Curbing, paving & walkway
stone

Phenix
Charlotte County

(G-10354)
ALMA MATER LLC
6655 Red House Rd (23959-3101)
PHONE..434 248-5465
Trisha Durbin, Principal
EMP: 2
SALES (est): 69.5K Privately Held
SIC: 2752 Commercial printing, litho-
graphic

(G-10355)
SHORE HOLDERS
2122 Stockdale Rd (23959)
P.O. Box 27 (23959-0027)
PHONE..434 542-4105
Arthur G Sinnott, Owner
Arthur Sinnott, Owner
Nancy E Fraser, Manager
Nancy Fraser, Manager
EMP: 10 EST: 1979
SQ FT: 10,000
SALES (est): 1MM Privately Held
WEB: www.shoreholders.com
SIC: 3643 5063 Sockets, electric; electri-
cal apparatus & equipment

Pilot
Montgomery County

(G-10356)
BLUE RIDGE YURTS LLC
369 Parkway Ln S (24138)
PHONE..540 651-8422
Kathy Anderson, Opers Staff
EMP: 4
SALES (est): 150K Privately Held
WEB: www.blueridgeyurts.com
SIC: 3999 Barber & beauty shop equip-
ment

(G-10357)
OMIS GNOME HATS
1033 Huffville Rd Ne (24138-1658)
PHONE..540 230-0258
Patricia Spino-Freudenthal, Principal
EMP: 2
SALES (est): 87.5K Privately Held
WEB: www.omisgnomehats.com
SIC: 2353 Hats, caps & millinery

(G-10358)
SIGN WISE LLC
1478 High Rock Hill Rd (24138-1404)
PHONE..540 382-8343
Craig Simpkins, Principal
EMP: 1
SALES (est): 46K Privately Held
SIC: 3993 Signs & advertising specialties

(G-10359)
SMITHS WELDING
147 Smith Run Ne (24138-1529)
PHONE..540 651-2382
EMP: 1
SALES (est): 35.3K Privately Held
SIC: 7692 Welding repair

Piney River
Nelson County

(G-10360)
ABSOLUTE ANESTHESIA
3818 Patrick Henry Hwy (22964-2101)
P.O. Box 2 (22964-0002)
PHONE..434 277-9360
Mitch J Madison, Owner
Mitchell J Madison, Owner
EMP: 2
SQ FT: 1,200
SALES (est): 450K Privately Held
WEB: www.absoluteanesthesiaco.com
SIC: 3841 Veterinarians' instruments & ap-
paratus

(G-10361)
KERRY SCOTT
Also Called: Nero Gate Tracking
3136 Patrick Henry Hwy (22964)
P.O. Box 8 (22964-0008)
PHONE..434 277-9337
Kerry Scott, President
Marlies Scott, Vice Pres
EMP: 4
SALES (est): 200K Privately Held
SIC: 2399 Horse blankets

Pittsville
Pittsylvania County

(G-10362)
GRAVES
973 Court Rd (24139-2839)
PHONE..434 656-2491
Oscar Graves, Principal
EMP: 2
SALES (est): 150K Privately Held
SIC: 3531 Automobile wrecker hoists

Poquoson
Poquoson City County

(G-10363)
A SPECIAL OCCASION LLC
110 Lee Ave (23662-1238)
PHONE..757 868-3160
EMP: 2
SALES (est): 81K Privately Held
SIC: 2335 Mfg Women's/Misses' Dresses

(G-10364)
ALC TRAINING GROUP LLC
Also Called: Blue Line Yoga Virginia
8 Valasia Rd (23662-1550)
PHONE..757 746-0428
EMP: 2
SALES (est): 78K Privately Held
SIC: 2844 Lipsticks

(G-10365)
C B C CORPORATION
657 Poquoson Ave (23662-1607)
PHONE..757 868-6571
Eugene L Manning, President
EMP: 4
SALES (est): 465.4K Privately Held
SIC: 3272 Burial vaults, concrete or pre-
cast terrazzo

(G-10366)
CELISE LLC
8 Freeman Dr (23662-1712)
PHONE..757 771-5176
Cameron Ross, Principal
EMP: 2 EST: 2018
SALES (est): 150K Privately Held
SIC: 2821 Plastics materials & resins

(G-10367)
**COASTAL HMPTON RADS
VLLYBALL C**
102 Ct Deayllon (23662-2241)
PHONE..757 759-0204
Chad Hagen, President
EMP: 2

SALES (est): 450K Privately Held
SIC: 3949 Nets: badminton, volleyball, tennis, etc.

(G-10368)
CREATIONS AT PLAY LLC
129 Bennett Rd (23662-1703)
PHONE..757 541-8226
Georgette Phillips, Principal
EMP: 1 EST: 2012
SALES (est): 72.2K Privately Held
SIC: 3993 2399 7389 Signs, not made in
custom sign painting shops; letters for
signs, metal; emblems, badges & in-
signia; lettering & sign painting services

(G-10369)
DORIS ANDERSON
Also Called: Embroidery By Design
17 Emmaus Rd (23662-1217)
PHONE..877 869-1543
EMP: 1
SALES (est): 33K Privately Held
SIC: 2395 Pleating And Stitching, Nsk

(G-10370)
**EDGYASH PADDLEBOARDS
LLC**
4 Roberts Landing Dr (23662-1026)
PHONE..717 404-6073
Lance Proctor,
EMP: 1 EST: 2014
SALES (est): 63K Privately Held
SIC: 2499 Oars & paddles, wood

(G-10371)
FUHGIDDABOWDIT INDUSTRIES
547 Wythe Creek Rd (23662-1545)
PHONE..757 598-0331
EMP: 1 EST: 2010
SALES (est): 41K Privately Held
SIC: 3999 Mfg Misc Products

(G-10372)
GARY L LAWSON
Also Called: Altist Welding & Fabrication
1026 Poquoson Ave (23662-1720)
PHONE..757 848-7003
Gary Lawson, Principal
EMP: 1 EST: 2008
SALES (est): 75K Privately Held
WEB: www.altistwelding.com
SIC: 7692 Welding repair

(G-10373)
**INTERNATIONAL MACHINE
SERVICE**
19 Phillips Rd (23662-1135)
P.O. Box 2395 (23662-0395)
PHONE..757 868-8487
Margit Kaiser, President
Helmut H Kaiser, President
EMP: 3
SALES (est): 278.4K Privately Held
WEB: www.machineserviceinc.com
SIC: 3599 7699 Machine shop, jobbing &
repair; industrial machinery & equipment
repair

(G-10374)
POAMAX LLC
17 Alphus St (23662-2015)
PHONE..757 871-7196
Michael Palmer, Mng Member
EMP: 2
SALES (est): 173.8K Privately Held
SIC: 3841 Surgical & medical instruments

(G-10375)
POQUOSON ENTERPRISES
Also Called: Poquoson Carts
306 Wythe Creek Rd (23662-1900)
PHONE..757 876-6655
James Seidnitzer, Owner
EMP: 3
SALES (est): 114.3K Privately Held
WEB: www.ci.poquoson.va.us
SIC: 3423 Soldering irons or coppers

(G-10376)
SHIP POINT OYSTER COMPANY
1115 Poquoson Ave (23662-1843)
PHONE..757 848-3557
Ethan Currie, Principal
EMP: 4

▲ = Import ▼=Export
◆ =Import/Export

SALES (est): 75.4K Privately Held
SIC: 2091 Oysters, preserved & cured

(G-10377)
TEAMS IT
41 Valmoore Dr (23662-1247)
PHONE..............................757 868-1129
EMP: 2
SALES (est): 85.9K Privately Held
SIC: 3577 Computer Peripheral Equipment, Nec

(G-10378)
VAN ROSENDALE JOHN
Also Called: Vr Technologies
104 Sandy Bay Dr (23662-1030)
PHONE..............................757 868-8593
John Van Rosendale, Owner
EMP: 1
SALES (est): 175K Privately Held
SIC: 3577 Computer peripheral equipment

(G-10379)
YORK BOX & BARREL MFG CO
163 Little Florida Rd (23662-2038)
PHONE..............................757 868-9411
Gordon Helsel, President
EMP: 5
SQ FT: 13,000
SALES (est): 814.7K Privately Held
SIC: 2653 Boxes, corrugated: made from purchased materials

(G-10380)
ZENTOX CORPORATION
538 Wythe Creek Rd (23662-1569)
PHONE..............................757 868-0870
EMP: 17
SQ FT: 45,000
SALES (est): 2.1MM Privately Held
SIC: 3564 7389 Mfg Blowers/Fans Business Services

Port Haywood
Mathews County

(G-10381)
ASIP PUBLISHING INC
1275 Lighthouse Rd (23138-2153)
PHONE..............................804 725-4613
William Johnson, Principal
EMP: 1
SALES (est): 37.5K Privately Held
SIC: 2741 Miscellaneous publishing

(G-10382)
CHESAPEAKE THERMITE WLDG LLC
Also Called: CTW
1065 Possum Point Rd (23138)
P.O. Box 129 (23138-0129)
PHONE..............................804 725-1111
Donna Anderson,
EMP: 4
SALES (est): 250K Privately Held
SIC: 7692 Welding repair

Port Republic
Rockingham County

(G-10383)
DALMATIAN HILL ENGNEERING
7190 Charlie Town Rd (24471-2604)
PHONE..............................540 289-5079
Larry Meyerhoeffer, Owner
EMP: 1
SALES (est): 70K Privately Held
SIC: 3441 7538 Fabricated structural metal; general automotive repair shops

(G-10384)
IHS COMPUTER SERVICE INC
7991 Port Republic Rd (24471-2651)
P.O. Box 36 (24471-0036)
PHONE..............................540 249-4833
Daniel Sweger, President
Nathan Miller, Corp Secy
EMP: 2
SALES (est): 100K Privately Held
SIC: 7372 Prepackaged software

Port Royal
Caroline County

(G-10385)
AMERICAN SOC FOR ENGRG EDUCATN
Computers In Education Div
68 Port Royal Sq Unit 68 (22535)
PHONE..............................804 742-5611
W W Everett Jr, Managing Dir
EMP: 1
SALES (corp-wide): 84.2MM Privately Held
WEB: www.asee.org
SIC: 7372 Publishers' computer software
PA: American Society For Engineering Education
1818 N St Nw Ste 600
Washington DC 20036
202 331-3500

Portsmouth
Portsmouth City County

(G-10386)
3 DEGREES PUBLISHING LLC
3806 Banstr Rvr Rch Apt D (23703-5417)
PHONE..............................757 634-3164
Erica Veal,
EMP: 1
SALES (est): 44.8K Privately Held
SIC: 2741 Miscellaneous publishing

(G-10387)
A & L TRANSPORT LLC
509 Delham Rd (23701-2122)
PHONE..............................757 735-0047
Anthony Clements, CEO
EMP: 2
SALES (est): 132.7K Privately Held
SIC: 3537 Trucks, tractors, loaders, carriers & similar equipment

(G-10388)
ADVANTAGE MACHINE & ENGRG
2043 Ponderosa St (23701-2633)
PHONE..............................757 488-5085
Donnie Simpson, President
Sharon Simposon, Vice Pres
EMP: 13
SQ FT: 900
SALES (est): 2.6MM Privately Held
SIC: 3549 Metalworking machinery

(G-10389)
ALBERTS ASSOCIATES INC
5220 Cobble Hill Rd (23703-4110)
PHONE..............................757 638-3352
Russel Alberts, President
EMP: 2 EST: 1976
SALES (est): 45K Privately Held
SIC: 3621 Power generators

(G-10390)
ALERE INC
1342 Court St (23704-3660)
PHONE..............................800 340-4029
Katie Scott, Director
EMP: 7
SALES (corp-wide): 31.9B Publicly Held
WEB: www.alere.com
SIC: 2835 In vitro & in vivo diagnostic substances
HQ: Alere Inc.
51 Sawyer Rd Ste 200
Waltham MA 02453
781 647-3900

(G-10391)
AMERICAN ASSEMBLY LLC
2746 Greenwood Dr (23702-1612)
PHONE..............................757 639-6040
Christopher Hirst,
Darla Hirst,
EMP: 2
SALES (est): 162.3K Privately Held
SIC: 2599 Furniture & fixtures

(G-10392)
AMERICAN CEMETERY SUPPLIES INC
2001 Laigh Rd (23701-2630)
PHONE..............................757 488-0018
Frank Doleman Jr, President
Del Doleman, Vice Pres
Delphia Doleman, Vice Pres
▼ EMP: 16
SQ FT: 19,000
SALES (est): 2.2MM Privately Held
WEB: www.acsupplies.com
SIC: 2394 Tents: made from purchased materials

(G-10393)
ARTCRAFT FABRICATORS INC (PA)
Also Called: Collins Machine Works
2707 Syer Rd (23707-4743)
PHONE..............................757 399-7777
Robert D Twine Sr, President
Kent Oslund, General Mgr
Charles Riemann, Prdtn Mgr
Keith Sharp, Safety Mgr
Morgan McDowall, Buyer
▲ EMP: 60
SQ FT: 30,000
SALES (est): 23MM Privately Held
WEB: www.collinsmachine.net
SIC: 3599 7699 Air intake filters, internal combustion engine, except auto; pumps & pumping equipment repair

(G-10394)
ATLANTIC FABRICATION & BOILER
1 Beechwood Ct (23702-2313)
P.O. Box 6390, Chesapeake (23323-0390)
PHONE..............................757 494-0597
David Dunn, President
William Slade, Vice Pres
Robert Mc Million, Treasurer
Michael Moore, Admin Sec
EMP: 19
SALES: 3.4MM Privately Held
WEB: www.afbsinc.com
SIC: 3444 Ventilators, sheet metal

(G-10395)
ATLANTIC WOOD INDUSTRIES INC
Also Called: Atlantic Metrocast
3904 Burtons Point Rd (23704-7107)
P.O. Box 340 (23705-0340)
PHONE..............................757 397-2317
Bernard E Monroe Jr, Sales/Mktg Mgr
EMP: 27
SALES (corp-wide): 79MM Privately Held
WEB: www.atlantic.joshuawells.com
SIC: 2491 3272 Poles & pole crossarms, treated wood; structural lumber & timber, treated wood; concrete products
PA: Atlantic Wood Industries, Inc.
405 E Perry St
Savannah GA 31401
912 966-7008

(G-10396)
BANDER COMPUTERS
Also Called: Home Town Computers
722 County St (23704-3428)
PHONE..............................757 398-3443
Andrew Bander, Owner
EMP: 2
SALES (est): 100K Privately Held
SIC: 3571 Personal computers (microcomputers)

(G-10397)
BATTLE KING INC
309 Ansell Ave Apt F (23702-1436)
PHONE..............................757 324-1854
Eric Cominski Jr, President
EMP: 1
SALES (est): 42.5K Privately Held
WEB: www.battlekingllc.com
SIC: 2329 Men's & boys' clothing

(G-10398)
BELLVUE CORP
Also Called: Cigs and Sodas
3810 George Wash Hwy (23702-1413)
PHONE..............................276 806-4418
Nicholas Moyer, Manager
EMP: 4
SALES (corp-wide): 1.5MM Privately Held
SIC: 3999 2086 Cigarette filters; bottled & canned soft drinks
PA: Bellvue Corp.
351 N Main St
Suffolk VA

(G-10399)
BENCHMARK WOODWORKS INC
2517 Turnpike Rd (23707-4719)
PHONE..............................757 971-3380
Donnie Robuck, President
Logan Collins, Project Mgr
EMP: 11
SALES (est): 1.4MM Privately Held
WEB: www.benchmarkww.com
SIC: 2431 Millwork

(G-10400)
BETTER VISION EYEGLASS CENTER
3235 Academy Ave Ste 200 (23703-3200)
PHONE..............................757 397-2020
Bob Vernon, Owner
Tide Watereye, Owner
EMP: 4
SALES (est): 251.8K Privately Held
WEB: www.tnisleep.com
SIC: 3851 5999 Eyeglasses, lenses & frames; sunglasses

(G-10401)
BLACKHAWK RUBBER & GASKET INC
4105 Kalona Rd (23703-2065)
PHONE..............................888 703-9060
Ronald Kiitinger, President
Dave Miller, Vice Pres
▲ EMP: 2
SQ FT: 1,300
SALES (est): 400K Privately Held
WEB: www.gasketsnseals.com
SIC: 3053 Gaskets, all materials

(G-10402)
C & F PLUMBING
5816 Brookmere Ln (23703-1608)
PHONE..............................757 606-3124
Clarence Sylvester Hunt, Owner
EMP: 1
SALES (est): 10K Privately Held
SIC: 3432 Plumbing fixture fittings & trim

(G-10403)
C AND J FABRICATION INC
Also Called: T/A United Sheet Metal
1023 Virginia Ave (23707-2134)
PHONE..............................757 399-3340
Carlton Miller, President
EMP: 5
SQ FT: 12,400
SALES (est): 221.8K Privately Held
SIC: 3444 Sheet metalwork

(G-10404)
CANDLE FETISH
1025 City Park Ave (23701-1932)
PHONE..............................757 535-3105
EMP: 1
SALES (est): 39.6K Privately Held
SIC: 3999 Candles

(G-10405)
CBG LLC
4013 Seaboard Ct Ste A3 (23701-2632)
PHONE..............................757 465-0333
Kenith D Guthrie, Mng Member
Deborah Lee, Consultant
EMP: 2
SQ FT: 2,500
SALES (est): 220K Privately Held
WEB: www.brokenbolts.com
SIC: 3541 Machine tool replacement & repair parts, metal cutting types

(G-10406)
CC & C DESKTOP PUBLISHING &
25 Beacon Rd (23702-1209)
PHONE..............................757 393-3606
Carllette Parker, Owner

EMP: 1
SALES (est): 46.8K **Privately Held**
SIC: 2741 Miscellaneous publishing

(G-10407)
CHARTMAN PUBLICATIONS LLC
3908 Clifford St (23707-2914)
P.O. Box 912, Avon NC (27915-0912)
PHONE..............................252 489-0151
Charles Michael Johnson Sr, *Administration*
EMP: 2
SALES (est): 90.4K **Privately Held**
WEB: www.chartmanpublications.com
SIC: 2741 Miscellaneous publishing

(G-10408)
CLEAN WAY SERVICES LLC
1121 High St (23704-3339)
P.O. Box 477 (23705-0477)
PHONE..............................757 606-1840
Steven Carl, *President*
EMP: 26
SALES (est): 5.7MM **Privately Held**
WEB: www.progressive.com
SIC: 3731 Shipbuilding & repairing

(G-10409)
COPPER AND OAK CFT SPIRITS LLC
739a High St (23704-3425)
PHONE..............................309 255-2001
Skyler Pittman,
EMP: 1 **EST:** 2017
SALES (est): 39.6K **Privately Held**
SIC: 3999 Manufacturing industries

(G-10410)
COSMETICS BY MAKEENA
17 Rodgers Pl (23702-3108)
PHONE..............................757 737-8402
Makeena C Stephens, *Owner*
EMP: 1
SALES (est): 63.8K **Privately Held**
SIC: 2844 Toilet preparations

(G-10411)
COUNTRY SCENTS CANDLES
925 Martin Ave (23701-1805)
PHONE..............................757 359-8730
Joshua Asble, *Principal*
EMP: 2
SALES (est): 62.5K **Privately Held**
SIC: 3999 Candles

(G-10412)
CRAVING SENSATIONS LLC
2606 Gothic St (23704-4729)
PHONE..............................757 609-5038
Oriel Rivers,
EMP: 1
SALES (est): 47.2K **Privately Held**
SIC: 2844 Cosmetic preparations

(G-10413)
CRISPERY OF VIRGINIA LLC
Also Called: Crispery, The
2728 Sterling Point Dr (23703-5225)
PHONE..............................757 673-5234
Steven Soldinger, *President*
Judy Soldinger, *Treasurer*
EMP: 2
SQ FT: 2,500
SALES (est): 6MM **Privately Held**
WEB: www.thecrispery.com
SIC: 2052 Cookies & crackers

(G-10414)
DAMSEL DETECTORS
4417 Faigle Rd (23703-4814)
PHONE..............................757 268-4128
Kelley REA, *Principal*
EMP: 2
SALES (est): 102.9K **Privately Held**
SIC: 3669 Communications equipment

(G-10415)
DESIGN ASSSTNCE CNSTR SYSTEMS
Also Called: Dacs
900 Port Centre Pkwy (23704-6700)
PHONE..............................757 393-0704
John T Henning, *President*
Clark Avery, *COO*
Bert Y Culpepper Jr, *Treasurer*
Gary Smith, *VP Sales*

Troy L Culpepper, *Admin Sec*
EMP: 43 **EST:** 1987
SQ FT: 73
SALES (est): 9.5MM **Privately Held**
WEB: www.fluekeeper.com
SIC: 3444 Roof deck, sheet metal

(G-10416)
DODD CUSTOM CANVAS LLC
828 Pacific Ave (23707-1419)
PHONE..............................757 717-4436
David Dodd, *Administration*
EMP: 1
SALES (est): 99.7K **Privately Held**
SIC: 2394 Canvas & related products

(G-10417)
DRAKE WELDING SERVICES INC
202 Monitor Rd (23707-1020)
PHONE..............................757 399-7705
Nancy W Drake, *President*
Guy W Drake, *President*
Nancy Drake, *President*
EMP: 4
SALES (est): 302.3K **Privately Held**
SIC: 7692 Welding repair

(G-10418)
EARL ENERGY LLC
650 Chautauqua Ave (23707-2106)
PHONE..............................757 606-2034
Joshua W Prueher, *CEO*
Daniel Wood, *Finance*
Jerrold L Miller,
EMP: 27
SALES (est): 3MM **Privately Held**
WEB: www.fairleadint.com
SIC: 3612 3823 Control transformers; distribution transformers, electric; voltage regulators, transmission & distribution; controllers for process variables, all types

(G-10419)
ECONOMY PRINTING INC
4519 George Wash Hwy (23702-2403)
PHONE..............................757 485-4445
Grace Smith, *President*
Scott Smith, *Vice Pres*
EMP: 6 **EST:** 1971
SQ FT: 1,200
SALES (est): 400K **Privately Held**
WEB: www.economyprinting.us
SIC: 2752 Commercial printing, offset

(G-10420)
ELEMENTS OF HEALING LLC
3706 Princeton Pl Apt I3 (23707-2430)
PHONE..............................757 951-7155
Kimberly Johnson, *Principal*
EMP: 3
SALES (est): 204.4K **Privately Held**
SIC: 2819 Industrial inorganic chemicals

(G-10421)
ELFINSMITH LTD INC
Also Called: Elfinsmith's
610 Virginia Ave (23707-2130)
PHONE..............................757 399-4788
Bill Bailey, *President*
Janet Brown, *General Mgr*
Rhonda Bailey, *Corp Secy*
Jennie Brown, *Manager*
C Didio, *Administration*
EMP: 3
SQ FT: 6,000
SALES (est): 547.3K **Privately Held**
WEB: www.elfinsmiths.com
SIC: 3089 3469 3993 Novelties, plastic; metal stampings; signs & advertising specialties

(G-10422)
ELITE WELDERS LLC
900 Broad St (23707-2047)
PHONE..............................757 613-1345
Wilbert McNair Jr,
EMP: 7
SQ FT: 1,950
SALES (est): 116.6K **Privately Held**
SIC: 7692 Welding repair

(G-10423)
ENGINE SCOUT PROFESSIONALS LLC
3009 Ballard Ave Ste B (23701-2733)
PHONE..............................757 621-8526
Bob Russek, *President*
Robert Russek, *President*
EMP: 4
SALES (est): 50K **Privately Held**
SIC: 7694 8748 Motor repair services; business consulting

(G-10424)
EXTRACT ATTRACT INC
201 Edison Ave (23702-1325)
PHONE..............................757 751-0671
Shana Jones, *Principal*
EMP: 2
SALES (est): 74.4K **Privately Held**
SIC: 2836 Extracts

(G-10425)
FAIRLEAD INTEGRATED LLC (PA)
650 Chautauqua Ave (23707-2106)
P.O. Box 7008 (23707-0008)
PHONE..............................757 384-1957
Fred Pasquine, *President*
Daniel Wood, *Vice Pres*
Kevin Morrozoff, *CFO*
Stacie Bailey, *Human Resources*
Jerry Miller, *Mng Member*
EMP: 111 **EST:** 2012
SALES (est): 25.7MM **Privately Held**
WEB: www.fairleadint.com
SIC: 3731 3441 Shipbuilding & repairing; fabricated structural metal for ships; ship sections, prefabricated metal

(G-10426)
FAIRLEAD INTEGRATED LLC
176 Lincoln St (23704-4910)
PHONE..............................757 606-2034
Daniel Wood, *Vice Pres*
EMP: 80
SALES (corp-wide): 25.7MM **Privately Held**
WEB: www.fairleadint.com
SIC: 3731 Shipbuilding & repairing
PA: Fairlead Integrated, Llc
650 Chautauqua Ave
Portsmouth VA 23707
757 384-1957

(G-10427)
FAIRLEAD INTGRTED PWR CNTRLS L
Also Called: Fairlead IPC
650 Chautauqua Ave (23707-2106)
PHONE..............................757 384-1957
David Bruce, *Finance*
Jerry Miller, *Mng Member*
Ashley Brown, *Manager*
Jerry Seymour, *Manager*
Bill Miller, *Administration*
EMP: 14
SALES (est): 3.1MM
SALES (corp-wide): 25.7MM **Privately Held**
WEB: www.fairleadint.com
SIC: 3731 3441 Shipbuilding & repairing; fabricated structural metal for ships
PA: Fairlead Integrated, Llc
650 Chautauqua Ave
Portsmouth VA 23707
757 384-1957

(G-10428)
FAIRLEAD MARINE INC
650 Chautauqua Ave (23707-2106)
PHONE..............................757 606-2034
Jerrold Miller, *President*
Caleb Rietveld, *QC Mgr*
Daniel Wood, *Finance*
Challis Nierman, *Program Mgr*
Kevin Morrozoff, *Director*
EMP: 3
SQ FT: 500
SALES (est): 218.4K **Privately Held**
WEB: www.fairleadint.com
SIC: 3731 Shipbuilding & repairing; barges, building & repairing; fishing vessels, large: building & repairing; trawlers, building & repairing

(G-10429)
FAIRLEAD PRCSION MFG INTGRTION
Also Called: Fairlead PMI
750 Chautauqua Ave (23707-2108)
PHONE..............................757 384-1957
Jerry Miller, *Mng Member*
EMP: 1
SALES (est): 22.5MM
SALES (corp-wide): 25.7MM **Privately Held**
WEB: www.fairleadint.com
SIC: 3731 3441 Shipbuilding & repairing; fabricated structural metal for ships
PA: Fairlead Integrated, Llc
650 Chautauqua Ave
Portsmouth VA 23707
757 384-1957

(G-10430)
FAIRLEAD PRECISION MFG
933 Broad St Unit 7008 (23707-1242)
PHONE..............................757 606-2033
EMP: 2 **EST:** 2015
SALES (est): 75.6K **Privately Held**
WEB: www.fairleadint.com
SIC: 3999 Manufacturing industries

(G-10431)
FLEET SVCS & INSTALLATIONS LLC (PA)
3535 Elmhurst Ln (23701-2612)
PHONE..............................757 405-1405
Duke Ingraham,
EMP: 4
SALES (est): 384.7K **Privately Held**
SIC: 3281 Cut stone & stone products

(G-10432)
FOOD PORTIONS LLC
1805 High St (23704-3105)
PHONE..............................757 839-3265
Daryl Corbett, *President*
Aretha Corbett,
EMP: 3
SQ FT: 2,000
SALES (est): 15.9K **Privately Held**
SIC: 2038 Pizza, frozen

(G-10433)
FREDA MARSHALL
5210 Forestdale Dr (23703-4111)
PHONE..............................757 632-1364
Freda Marshall, *Owner*
EMP: 3
SALES (est): 91.3K **Privately Held**
SIC: 2024 Ice cream & frozen desserts

(G-10434)
GENERAL DYNAMICS
Also Called: Ucc
650 Chautauqua Ave (23707-2106)
PHONE..............................757 398-0785
Warren Kennedy, *Director*
Kerri Linkenhoker,
Lee D Murphy,
EMP: 80
SALES (est): 25K **Privately Held**
WEB: www.nassconorfolk.com
SIC: 3479 Painting, coating & hot dipping

(G-10435)
GOOD NEWS NETWORK
3850 Broadway St (23703-2435)
PHONE..............................757 638-3289
Jene Oley, *Principal*
EMP: 4
SALES (est): 195.5K **Privately Held**
WEB: www.goodnewsnetwork.org
SIC: 2711 Newspapers, publishing & printing

(G-10436)
GRATISPICKS INC
50 Beechdale Rd (23702-2399)
PHONE..............................757 739-4143
EMP: 1
SQ FT: 144
SALES (est): 83K **Privately Held**
SIC: 3572 Mfg Computer Storage Devices

(G-10437)
GRIMSLEYS HOUSE TOOLS INC
355 Crawford St Ste 620 (23704-2823)
P.O. Box 699 (23705-0699)
PHONE.....................................757 399-4438
Stephen Trent, *President*
Adam Trent, *Vice Pres*
Rebecca Trent, *Treasurer*
EMP: 5
SQ FT: 1,000
SALES (est): 594.9K **Privately Held**
WEB: www.grimsleystools.com
SIC: 3545 Machine tool accessories

(G-10438)
GRUBB PRINTING & STAMP CO INC
3303 Airline Blvd Ste 1g (23701-2665)
PHONE.....................................757 295-8061
Patricia Cochran, *President*
Steve Stanley, *Production*
Andrew Goff, *Manager*
EMP: 13 EST: 1872
SQ FT: 7,500
SALES (est): 2.1MM **Privately Held**
WEB: www.grubbprint.com
SIC: 2752 2759 5112 2796 Commercial printing, offset; letterpress printing; business forms; platemaking services

(G-10439)
GWENDOLYN H SPEAR
2508 Oakleaf Pl Apt 201 (23707-2611)
PHONE.....................................757 725-2747
Gwendolyn Spear, *Owner*
EMP: 2 EST: 2016
SALES (est): 82.2K **Privately Held**
SIC: 3471 Cleaning, polishing & finishing

(G-10440)
HAMPTON ROADS PROCESSORS INC
4500 Norman Rd (23703-4925)
PHONE.....................................757 285-8811
Graham Whitehurst, *President*
EMP: 1
SALES (est): 145.2K **Privately Held**
SIC: 3714 Motor vehicle parts & accessories

(G-10441)
HEALTHCARE SIMULATIONS LLC
200 High St Ste 405 (23704-3721)
PHONE.....................................757 399-4502
Johnny Garcia, *President*
George Dieffenbach,
EMP: 6
SQ FT: 1,000
SALES (est): 286.4K **Privately Held**
WEB: www.learnwithaims.com
SIC: 7372 Educational computer software
PA: Simis, Inc.
1040 University Blvd # 310
Portsmouth VA 23703

(G-10442)
HIGHSTAR INDUSTRIAL TECH
1410 Court St (23704-3663)
PHONE.....................................757 398-9300
Larry Murphy, *CEO*
Blake Murphy, *Vice Pres*
EMP: 12
SQ FT: 15,000
SALES (est): 1.9MM **Privately Held**
SIC: 3599 Machine shop, jobbing & repair

(G-10443)
HOT WORX INC
230 Sandpiper Dr (23704-1506)
PHONE.....................................757 967-9809
Brenda Thacker, *President*
Roger W Thacker, *President*
EMP: 3
SALES (est): 74.7K **Privately Held**
WEB: www.hotworxinc.com
SIC: 7692 Welding repair

(G-10444)
INTERNATIONAL PAPER COMPANY
3100 Elmhurst Ln (23701-2735)
PHONE.....................................757 405-3046
EMP: 4
SQ FT: 81,375

SALES (corp-wide): 22.3B **Publicly Held**
WEB: www.internationalpaper.com
SIC: 2653 2656 2621 Boxes, corrugated: made from purchased materials; food containers (liquid tight), including milk cartons; cartons, milk: made from purchased material; printing paper
PA: International Paper Company
6400 Poplar Ave
Memphis TN 38197
901 419-9000

(G-10445)
IRON PEN WEB DESIGN & PRINTING
707 North St (23704-2447)
PHONE.....................................757 645-9945
Kecia Jackson, *Principal*
EMP: 2
SALES (est): 83.9K **Privately Held**
SIC: 2752 Commercial printing, lithographic

(G-10446)
JANE HFL GRESHAM
212 Chautauqua Ave (23707-1702)
PHONE.....................................757 397-2208
EMP: 2 EST: 2001
SALES (est): 96K **Privately Held**
SIC: 3639 Mfg Household Appliances

(G-10447)
JHA LLC
151 Florida Ave (23707-1522)
PHONE.....................................757 535-2724
John W Higgins, *Partner*
EMP: 1
SALES (est): 93.7K **Privately Held**
SIC: 3826 Analytical instruments

(G-10448)
JONES TONJA
Also Called: Jewl's N' Gems By Tonja
5809 Dunkirk St (23703-3127)
PHONE.....................................757 773-9475
Tonja Jones, *Owner*
EMP: 1
SALES (est): 41K **Privately Held**
SIC: 3911 Jewelry apparel

(G-10449)
JUMA BROTHERS INC
Also Called: Mr Wholesale Cigar Master
3325 Victory Blvd (23701-4319)
PHONE.....................................757 312-0544
Mousa Juma, *President*
EMP: 6
SALES (est): 425.3K **Privately Held**
WEB: www.jumabros.com
SIC: 3231 2064 Novelties, glass: fruit, foliage, flowers, animals, etc.; candy & other confectionery products

(G-10450)
K & E LEGACY INCORPORATED
3303 Airline Blvd Ste 3g (23701-2635)
PHONE.....................................757 328-4609
Beverly Joyner, *CEO*
Alisha L Bazemore, *Manager*
EMP: 6 EST: 2010
SALES (est): 300K **Privately Held**
SIC: 3731 Shipbuilding & repairing

(G-10451)
KALMAR USA INC
3115 Watson St (23707-3443)
PHONE.....................................757 465-7995
Howard Case, *President*
EMP: 14
SQ FT: 9,740
SALES (corp-wide): 4B **Privately Held**
WEB: www.kalmarusa.com
SIC: 3537 Trucks, tractors, loaders, carriers & similar equipment
HQ: Kalmar Usa Inc.
415 E Dundee St
Ottawa KS 66067
785 242-2200

(G-10452)
KAWOOD LLC
300 Saunders Dr (23701-1042)
PHONE.....................................757 488-4658
James Underwood, *Principal*
EMP: 1

SALES (est): 41.5K **Privately Held**
SIC: 2499 Wood products

(G-10453)
LINX INDUSTRIES INC
2600 Airline Blvd (23701-2701)
PHONE.....................................757 488-1144
Michael Price, *Branch Mgr*
EMP: 7
SQ FT: 58,820
SALES (corp-wide): 53.6MM **Privately Held**
WEB: www.li-hvac.com
SIC: 3312 Iron & steel: galvanized, pipes, plates, sheets, etc.
HQ: Linx Industries, Inc.
2600 Airline Blvd
Portsmouth VA 23701

(G-10454)
LIVIN COLOR LLC
215 Chautauqua Ave (23707-1701)
PHONE.....................................757 582-6030
Eboni Gaskins,
EMP: 1
SALES (est): 42.5K **Privately Held**
SIC: 2389 Apparel & accessories

(G-10455)
LYNX BREWING COMPANY LLC
33 Aylwin Rd (23702-2105)
PHONE.....................................773 819-8748
Kymbrieyell Johnson,
EMP: 1
SALES (est): 39.5K **Privately Held**
SIC: 2082 Beer (alcoholic beverage)

(G-10456)
M & S MARINE & INDUSTRIAL SVCS
702 Fifth St (23704-6760)
PHONE.....................................757 405-9623
Kenneth Wright, *President*
EMP: 80
SQ FT: 8,000
SALES (est): 8.4MM **Privately Held**
SIC: 3731 3732 Shipbuilding & repairing; boat building & repairing

(G-10457)
MARCOM SERVICES LLC
620 Lincoln St (23704-4818)
PHONE.....................................757 963-1851
Lee Murphy, *President*
Tim Wise, *Vice Pres*
EMP: 3
SALES (est): 646.4K **Privately Held**
WEB: www.marcomserv.com
SIC: 3731 Shipbuilding & repairing

(G-10458)
MASSIMO ZANETTI BEV USA INC
1200 Court St (23704-3642)
PHONE.....................................757 215-7409
EMP: 3
SALES (corp-wide): 257.5K **Privately Held**
WEB: www.mzb-usa.com
SIC: 2095 Roasted coffee
HQ: Massimo Zanetti Beverage Usa, Inc.
1370 Progress Rd
Suffolk VA 23434

(G-10459)
MAVERICK BUS SOLUTIONS LLC
46 Candlelight Ln (23703-2266)
PHONE.....................................757 870-8489
Bradley Murrell,
EMP: 4
SALES (est): 130.9K **Privately Held**
SIC: 7372 7389 Business oriented computer software; financial services

(G-10460)
METAL PRODUCTS SPECIALIST INC
420 Virginia Ave (23707-2126)
PHONE.....................................757 398-9214
David Horen, *President*
Brian Horen, *Vice Pres*
EMP: 8
SQ FT: 4,400

SALES (est): 2MM **Privately Held**
SIC: 3441 Fabricated structural metal

(G-10461)
METRO MACHINE CORP
2 Harper Rd (23707-1819)
PHONE.....................................757 397-1039
EMP: 142
SALES (corp-wide): 39.3B **Publicly Held**
WEB: www.nassconorfolk.com
SIC: 3731 Shipbuilding & repairing
HQ: Metro Machine Corp.
200 Ligon St
Norfolk VA 23523
757 543-6801

(G-10462)
METRO MACHINE CORP
3132 Victory Blvd (23702-1830)
PHONE.....................................757 392-3703
Melissa Thomas, *Branch Mgr*
EMP: 142
SALES (corp-wide): 39.3B **Publicly Held**
WEB: www.nassconorfolk.com
SIC: 3731 Shipbuilding & repairing
HQ: Metro Machine Corp.
200 Ligon St
Norfolk VA 23523
757 543-6801

(G-10463)
MYSTICAL MIRRORS & GLASS
21 Maupin Ave (23702-1021)
PHONE.....................................757 399-4682
Joseph Lavin; *Owner*
EMP: 1
SALES (est): 58.6K **Privately Held**
SIC: 3088 Shower stalls, fiberglass & plastic

(G-10464)
ONDECK HOME SOLUTIONS LLC
1906 Richmond Ave (23704-5545)
PHONE.....................................757 535-3771
Eboni McNulty,
EMP: 1
SALES (est): 41K **Privately Held**
SIC: 1389 Construction, repair & dismantling services

(G-10465)
ONTHEFLY PICTURES LLC
3651 Gateway Dr Apt 2b (23703-5048)
PHONE.....................................757 339-1520
Tommy Boswell, *Mng Member*
EMP: 3
SALES (est): 95.1K **Privately Held**
SIC: 2741 7812 Miscellaneous publishing; video production

(G-10466)
OSBORNE WELDING INC
9 Beechwood Ct (23702-2313)
P.O. Box 3576 (23701-0576)
PHONE.....................................757 487-0900
W Keith Osborne, *President*
Andy Rich, *Project Mgr*
Lori Asbury, *Office Mgr*
Megan Osborne, *Agent*
EMP: 30
SQ FT: 8,000
SALES (est): 9.1MM **Privately Held**
WEB: www.osborneweldinginc.com
SIC: 3441 3312 Building components, structural steel; blast furnaces & steel mills

(G-10467)
PERFORMNCE MTAL FBRICATORS INC
3901 Alexander St (23701-2711)
P.O. Box 9798, Chesapeake (23321-9798)
PHONE.....................................757 465-8622
John Parsons, *President*
Deborah Parsons, *Vice Pres*
EMP: 9
SQ FT: 26,000
SALES: 1.7MM
SALES (corp-wide): 77B **Publicly Held**
WEB: www.performancemetalfab.com
SIC: 3441 3499 Fabricated structural metal; furniture parts, metal
HQ: Rockwell Collins, Inc.
400 Collins Rd Ne
Cedar Rapids IA 52498

(G-10468)
PERSON ENTERPRISES INC
Also Called: The Printing Center
6008 High St W (23703-4508)
PHONE..................................757 483-6252
J E Person, *President*
Julia W Person, *Corp Secy*
EMP: 7
SQ FT: 1,325
SALES (est): 270K **Privately Held**
WEB: www.personcottage.com
SIC: 2752 Commercial printing, offset

(G-10469)
PMA IT SOLUTIONS INC
Also Called: Incuhub, The
100 7th St Ste 104 (23704-4800)
PHONE..................................571 336-2408
Marko Frigelj, *Principal*
EMP: 1 **EST:** 2014
SALES (est): 109.3K **Privately Held**
SIC: 7372 Home entertainment computer
software

(G-10470)
PORTSMOUTH FIRE MARSHALS OFC
645 Broad St (23707-2042)
PHONE..................................757 393-8123
Regina Humphrey, *Office Mgr*
EMP: 2
SALES (est): 130.3K **Privately Held**
WEB: www.fire.portsmouthva.gov
SIC: 3711 Fire department vehicles (motor
vehicles), assembly of

(G-10471)
PORTSMOUTH LUMBER CORPORATION
2511 High St (23707-3601)
PHONE..................................757 397-4646
C Paul Hanbury Jr, *President*
Mike Jones, *Vice Pres*
Paul Hanbury, *Purchasing*
John Motley, *Treasurer*
Vicki Marshall, *Train & Dev Mgr*
EMP: 19 **EST:** 1914
SQ FT: 2,000
SALES (est): 3.7MM **Privately Held**
WEB: www.portsmouthlumber.com
SIC: 2431 5211 2439 2426 Moldings,
wood: unfinished & prefinished; lumber
products; structural wood members; hard-
wood dimension & flooring mills

(G-10472)
PREMIER MANUFACTURING INC
500 Premier Pl (23704-4801)
PHONE..................................757 967-9959
Kent Woodward, *President*
EMP: 36
SALES (est): 2.4MM **Privately Held**
SIC: 3429 Marine hardware

(G-10473)
PRINTCRAFT PRESS INCORPORATED
305 Columbia St (23704-3714)
P.O. Box 1224, Suffolk (23439-1224)
PHONE..................................757 397-0759
Ray Johnson, *President*
EMP: 21 **EST:** 1840
SQ FT: 12,900
SALES (est): 2.4MM **Privately Held**
SIC: 2752 2791 2789 Commercial print-
ing, offset; typesetting; bookbinding & re-
lated work

(G-10474)
RANDOLPH-BUNDY INCORPORATED
4012 Seaboard Ct (23701-2611)
P.O. Box 2618, Norfolk (23501-2618)
PHONE..................................757 625-2556
R D Randolph, *CEO*
Thomas Randolph, *President*
Joey Boozer, *Purch Agent*
David Randolph, *Treasurer*
EMP: 40
SQ FT: 68,000

SALES (est): 6.7MM **Privately Held**
WEB: www.randolph-bundy.com
SIC: 2431 5031 Doors, wood; millwork;
building materials, exterior; building materials, interior

(G-10475)
REBECCA ORTIZSANCHEZ
113 Niagra St (23702-2428)
PHONE..................................315 532-4439
Rebecca Ortizsanchez, *Owner*
EMP: 1
SALES (est): 10K **Privately Held**
SIC: 2841 Soap & other detergents

(G-10476)
ROBERTS SCREEN PRINTING
684 Military Rd (23702-2310)
PHONE..................................757 487-6285
EMP: 2
SALES (est): 89.8K **Privately Held**
WEB: www.rscreenprint.com
SIC: 2759 Screen printing

(G-10477)
SANDRA SIGNS LLC
141 Monitor Rd (23707-1000)
PHONE..................................757 397-4321
Daniel D Dickenson III, *Administration*
EMP: 1
SALES (est): 50.6K **Privately Held**
SIC: 3993 Signs & advertising specialties

(G-10478)
SCADCO PUBLISHING LLC
3613 Pine Rd (23703-3547)
PHONE..................................757 484-4878
William Spivey, *Principal*
EMP: 3 **EST:** 2016
SALES (est): 94.9K **Privately Held**
SIC: 2711 Newspapers, publishing & print-
ing

(G-10479)
SHEPHERD ENTERPRISES ANCHOR RM
102 Pine Blf (23701-1235)
PHONE..................................757 641-7829
EMP: 3 **EST:** 2015
SALES (est): 195.9K **Privately Held**
WEB: www.anchor-room.com
SIC: 3999 Manufacturing industries

(G-10480)
SHIP SHAPE CLEANING LLC
400 W Road Portsmouth (23707)
PHONE..................................757 769-3845
Janet Williams,
EMP: 1
SALES (est): 70.8K **Privately Held**
SIC: 3582 7217 7349 Rug cleaning, dry-
ing or napping machines: commercial;
carpet & upholstery cleaning; building &
office cleaning services

(G-10481)
SHYANNE BRANCH
Also Called: Divine Creations
3714 Bamboo Rd (23703-2605)
PHONE..................................757 532-4951
Shyanne Branch, *Owner*
EMP: 1
SALES (est): 50K **Privately Held**
SIC: 3944 Craft & hobby kits & sets

(G-10482)
SIGN EXPRESS INC
6075 High St W (23703-4507)
PHONE..................................757 686-3010
Tamara P Holland, *President*
Raymond Jay Holland, *Vice Pres*
Tammy Holland, *Manager*
EMP: 2
SQ FT: 1,000
SALES (est): 90K **Privately Held**
WEB: www.signexpresshr.com
SIC: 3993 Signs, not made in custom sign
painting shops

(G-10483)
SMITH BROTHERS CAR WASH INC
3523 Western Branch Blvd (23707-3135)
PHONE..................................757 397-7711
Terry Schultz, *President*

EMP: 3
SALES (est): 130K **Privately Held**
SIC: 3589 Car washing machinery

(G-10484)
SMITH MAINTENANCE SERVICES LLC
924 Tazewell St (23701-3230)
PHONE..................................252 640-5016
Antonio Smith,
EMP: 1
SALES (est): 41K **Privately Held**
SIC: 1389 Construction, repair & disman-
tling services

(G-10485)
STATE LINE CONTROLS INC
3420 Wilshire Rd (23703-3940)
PHONE..................................757 969-8527
Kent Stokes, *President*
EMP: 5
SALES (est): 958.8K **Privately Held**
SIC: 3822 Building services monitoring
controls, automatic

(G-10486)
STOREY MILL PUBLISHING
42 Cooper Dr (23702-2267)
PHONE..................................757 399-4969
Esther Kitchens Gifford, *Principal*
EMP: 2
SALES (est): 94.2K **Privately Held**
SIC: 2741 Miscellaneous publishing

(G-10487)
STOWE INC A D
450 Virginia Ave (23707-2126)
P.O. Box 7247 (23707-0247)
PHONE..................................757 397-1842
Lynn Williams, *Branch Mgr*
EMP: 12
SALES (corp-wide): 4MM **Privately Held**
WEB: www.adstowe.com
SIC: 3275 Plaster & plasterboard, gypsum
PA: Stowe, Inc., A. D.
2504 Detroit St
Portsmouth VA 23707
757 397-1842

(G-10488)
SUPA PRODUCER PUBLISHING
5604 Gregory Ct (23703-1637)
PHONE..................................757 484-2495
Anthony Richardson, *Principal*
EMP: 2
SALES (est): 104.5K **Privately Held**
SIC: 2741 Miscellaneous publishing

(G-10489)
SUPERIOR AWNING SERVICE INC
2901 Deep Creek Blvd (23704-6205)
PHONE..................................757 399-8161
Roger D Schiefer, *President*
Schiefer Roger Byron, *Vice Pres*
Geraldine Schiefer, *Admin Sec*
EMP: 5
SQ FT: 3,000
SALES (est): 550K **Privately Held**
SIC: 3444 1799 Awnings, sheet metal;
awning installation

(G-10490)
SWEETB DESIGNS LLC
2705 Roanoke Ave (23704-6333)
PHONE..................................757 550-0436
Cynthia Tyler,
EMP: 1
SALES (est): 63.5K **Privately Held**
SIC: 2329 2339 2399 7389 Riding
clothes; men's, youths' & boys'; service
apparel, washable: women's; hand woven
apparel; textile & apparel services; styling
of fashions, apparel, furniture, textiles,
etc.;

(G-10491)
TIDEWATER CASTINGS INC
2401 Wesley St (23707-1716)
PHONE..................................757 399-0679
Fax: 757 399-2218
EMP: 9
SQ FT: 16,000
SALES (est): 540K **Privately Held**
SIC: 3369 Foundry

(G-10492)
TRADEMARK PRINTING LLC
3564 Western Branch Blvd (23707-3134)
PHONE..................................757 410-1800
EMP: 2
SALES (est): 83.9K **Privately Held**
SIC: 2752 Commercial printing, litho-
graphic

(G-10493)
TRADEMARK PRINTING LLC
3111 Ballard Ave (23701-2723)
PHONE..................................757 465-1736
EMP: 2
SALES (est): 116K **Privately Held**
SIC: 2759 Commercial Printing

(G-10494)
U S FLAG & SIGNAL COMPANY
802 Fifth St (23704-6762)
P.O. Box 62205, Virginia Beach (23466-
2205)
PHONE..................................757 497-8947
Doris Widman Wilgus, *President*
Ed Capps, *Vice Pres*
EMP: 28
SQ FT: 9,000
SALES (est): 2.6MM **Privately Held**
WEB: www.flagmaker.com
SIC: 2399 5099 5999 Flags, fabric; ban-
ners, made from fabric; flag poles; flags;
banners

(G-10495)
UNITED STATES DEPT OF NAVY
Also Called: Norfolk Naval Shipyard
Norfolk Naval Shipyard (23709)
PHONE..................................757 396-8615
Gregory Thomas, *Branch Mgr*
EMP: 924 **Publicly Held**
WEB: www.sealiftcommand.com
SIC: 3731 Combat vessels, building & re-
pairing
HQ: United States Department Of Navy
1200 Navy Pentagon
Washington DC 20350

(G-10496)
US AMINES (PORTSMOUTH) LLC
3230 W Norfolk Rd (23703-2432)
PHONE..................................757 638-2614
Randall Fillingim, *Plant Mgr*
Mitch Davis, *Safety Mgr*
Randy Fillingim, *Manager*
James H Allen,
▲ **EMP:** 9
SALES (est): 1.2MM **Privately Held**
WEB: www.usamines.com
SIC: 2819 Industrial inorganic chemicals

(G-10497)
VAPORT INC
1510 Columbus Ave (23704-3906)
PHONE..................................757 397-1397
Andrew S Auerbach, *Principal*
EMP: 7
SQ FT: 30,000
SALES (est): 998.7K **Privately Held**
WEB: www.vaport.com
SIC: 2079 2077 Vegetable refined oils (ex-
cept corn oil); animal fats, oils & meals

(G-10498)
VISTAPRINT
3823 Springbloom Dr (23703-2513)
PHONE..................................757 483-2357
Jean Desert, *Principal*
EMP: 2
SALES (est): 83.9K **Privately Held**
SIC: 2752 Commercial printing, litho-
graphic

(G-10499)
VRENP LLC
3916 Deep Creek Blvd (23702-1636)
PHONE..................................757 510-7770
Vernon Jones,
EMP: 5
SALES (est): 500K **Privately Held**
SIC: 3537 Trucks, tractors, loaders, carri-
ers & similar equipment

(G-10500)
W & O SUPPLY INC
500 Premier Pl (23704-4801)
PHONE..................................757 967-9959

▲ = Import ▼=Export
◆ =Import/Export

Bill Duffy, *General Mgr*
EMP: 30
SALES (corp-wide): 1.9B **Privately Held**
WEB: www.wandosupply.com
SIC: 3356 Nickel & nickel alloy pipe, plates, sheets, etc.
HQ: W. & O. Supply, Inc.
2677 Port Industrial Dr
Jacksonville FL 32226
904 354-3800

(G-10501)
WHATS YOUR GRIND LLC
300 Plover Dr (23704-1640)
PHONE................................757 447-8506
Charles Munyi, *Principal*
EMP: 2
SALES (est): 106.8K **Privately Held**
SIC: 3599 Grinding castings for the trade

(G-10502)
WILBAR TRUCK EQUIPMENT INC
2808 Frederick Blvd (23704-6820)
PHONE................................757 397-3200
Keith S Cichorz, *Opers-Prdtn-Mfg*
EMP: 21
SQ FT: 9,000
SALES (corp-wide): 6.3MM **Privately Held**
WEB: www.wilbar.com
SIC: 3713 3711 5531 5014 Truck bodies (motor vehicles); motor vehicles & car bodies; truck equipment & parts; truck tires & tubes; automotive servicing equipment; industrial trucks & tractors
PA: Wilbar Truck Equipment, Incorporated
2808 Frederick Blvd
Portsmouth VA
757 397-3200

(G-10503)
WILLIAMS INCORPORATED T O
300 Wythe St (23704-5208)
P.O. Box C (23705-0080)
PHONE................................757 397-0771
Huyn Jong Chay, *President*
Diane N Chay, *Vice Pres*
Peter J Chay, *Vice Pres*
Tracy Harris, *VP Opers*
Matt Hemler, *Engineer*
EMP: 35
SQ FT: 13,500
SALES (est): 2.7MM **Privately Held**
WEB: www.vasausage.com
SIC: 2013 Cured meats from purchased meat

(G-10504)
WIMBROUGH & SONS INC
1420 King St (23704-3232)
PHONE................................757 399-1242
Kenneth L Wimbrough, *President*
Carl T Wimbrough, *Corp Secy*
Wimbrough Robert E, *Vice Pres*
EMP: 8 **EST:** 1923
SQ FT: 7,500
SALES (est): 1.5MM **Privately Held**
SIC: 3272 Burial vaults, concrete or pre-cast terrazzo

(G-10505)
WINN STONE PRODUCTS INC
62 Sandie Point Ln (23701-1154)
PHONE................................757 465-5363
Susan Winn, *President*
Allan Winn, *Corp Secy*
Robert Winn, *Vice Pres*
EMP: 7
SQ FT: 3,500
SALES (est): 772.5K **Privately Held**
WEB: www.winnstone.com
SIC: 3281 5999 1799 Marble, building: cut & shaped; granite, cut & shaped; monuments & tombstones; counter top installation

(G-10506)
YEATES MFG INC
Also Called: Portsmouth Tent & Awning
3923 Victory Blvd (23701-2811)
PHONE................................757 465-7772
George Jordan, *President*
David A Jordan, *Vice Pres*
Alice J Strange, *Vice Pres*
EMP: 5

SQ FT: 14,500
SALES (est): 300K **Privately Held**
SIC: 2394 Tents: made from purchased materials

(G-10507)
YOCUMS SIGNATURE HOT RODS
400 Cumberland Ave (23707-3224)
PHONE................................757 393-0700
EMP: 2
SALES (est): 110K **Privately Held**
SIC: 3312 Blast Furnace-Steel Works

Potomac Falls
Loudoun County

(G-10508)
CLIFFORD AEROWORKS LLC
42 Whittingham Cir (20165-6237)
P.O. Box 157, Midland (22728-0157)
PHONE................................703 304-3675
John Clifford, *Mng Member*
EMP: 5 **EST:** 2009
SALES (est): 250K **Privately Held**
SIC: 3999 Airplane models, except toy

(G-10509)
IIS RAYTHEON
47737 League Ct (20165-7416)
PHONE................................561 212-2954
EMP: 2
SALES (est): 77.4K **Privately Held**
SIC: 3812 Defense systems & equipment

(G-10510)
WEARMAX INC
Also Called: Wholesale
20398 Rupert Island Pl (20165-5112)
PHONE................................631 361-7222
Ovais Sheikh, *President*
▲ **EMP:** 2 **EST:** 1996
SALES (est): 217.5K **Privately Held**
WEB: www.wearmaxamerica.net
SIC: 2393 5131 Textile bags; textiles, woven

Pound
Wise County

(G-10511)
D L S & ASSOCIATES
8205 S Mountain Rd (24279-4827)
PHONE................................276 796-5275
Donna M Sturgill, *President*
Royce H Sturgill Jr, *Vice Pres*
EMP: 9
SALES (est): 350K **Privately Held**
SIC: 1389 Oil consultants

(G-10512)
DANE MEADES SHOP
9334 Clintwood Hwy (24279-4218)
PHONE................................276 926-4847
EMP: 1
SALES (est): 90.4K **Privately Held**
SIC: 3532 Mfg Mining Machinery

(G-10513)
GLR WELDING & FABRICATION
5831 Luray Ln (24279-4520)
PHONE................................276 337-1401
Gary Rutherford, *Principal*
EMP: 1
SALES (est): 33.4K **Privately Held**
SIC: 7692 Welding repair

(G-10514)
TRUE ENERGY FUELS
7652 S Fork Rd (24279-3018)
PHONE................................276 796-4003
David Ison, *Superintendent*
Michael R Castle, *CFO*
EMP: 3 **EST:** 2010
SALES (est): 292.2K **Privately Held**
SIC: 2869 Fuels

Pounding Mill
Tazewell County

(G-10515)
BLACK EYED TEES
772 Thru Dr (24637-4114)
PHONE................................276 971-1219
Miranda Hill, *Principal*
EMP: 2 **EST:** 2017
SALES (est): 108.5K **Privately Held**
SIC: 2759 Screen printing

(G-10516)
BUC-DOE TECTOR OUTDOORS LLC
126 Sunshine Ln (24637-3773)
PHONE................................276 971-1383
Monte L Lambert, *Principal*
Monte S Lambert,
EMP: 2
SALES (est): 117.8K **Privately Held**
WEB: www.bucknutdeerscents.com
SIC: 3949 Sporting & athletic goods

(G-10517)
CLINCH VALLEY REPAIR SERVICE
2737 Pounding Mill Br Rd (24637-3890)
PHONE................................276 964-5191
Tom Tillie, *President*
Sheila Tillie, *Vice Pres*
EMP: 2
SALES (est): 50K **Privately Held**
SIC: 3255 Fire clay blocks, bricks, tile or special shapes

(G-10518)
DOODADD SHOP
155 Legend St (24637-3698)
PHONE................................276 964-2389
Eddie Vandyke, *Owner*
EMP: 2
SALES (est): 106.7K **Privately Held**
SIC: 2499 Decorative wood & woodwork

(G-10519)
FRANK CALANDRA INC
258 Kappa Dr (24637)
PHONE................................276 964-7023
Larry McCoy, *Branch Mgr*
EMP: 9
SALES (corp-wide): 753.2MM **Privately Held**
WEB: www.jennmar.com
SIC: 3532 Mining machinery
PA: Calandra Frank Inc
258 Kappa Dr
Pittsburgh PA 15238
412 963-9071

(G-10520)
HENDERSON PUBLISHING
811 Evas Walk (24637-3688)
PHONE................................276 964-2291
Kenneth Henderson, *Owner*
Marie Henderson, *Co-Owner*
EMP: 2
SALES (est): 85.1K **Privately Held**
SIC: 2731 Book publishing

(G-10521)
INDEPENDENT HOLINESS PUBLI
175 Green Mountain Rd (24637-4257)
PHONE................................276 964-2824
Matthew Vance, *Principal*
EMP: 3 **EST:** 2009
SALES (est): 242.2K **Privately Held**
SIC: 2741 Miscellaneous publishing

(G-10522)
LAPORTE AMERICA LLC
129 Post St (24637-4003)
P.O. Box 492 (24637-0492)
PHONE................................800 335-8727
EMP: 1
SALES (est): 69.9K **Privately Held**
WEB: www.laporte.biz
SIC: 3949 Sporting & athletic goods

(G-10523)
LAPORTE USA
14463 Gvrnor G C Pery Hwy (24637-4292)
P.O. Box 188 (24637-0188)
PHONE................................276 964-5566
Michael McGlothlin, *President*
▲ **EMP:** 6 **EST:** 1997
SALES (est): 400.3K **Privately Held**
WEB: www.laporte.biz
SIC: 3949 Target shooting equipment

(G-10524)
MIKES SCREEN PRINTING
405 Cedar Creek Dr (24637-3552)
PHONE................................276 971-9274
EMP: 2 **EST:** 2019
SALES (est): 83.9K **Privately Held**
SIC: 2752 Commercial printing, lithographic

(G-10525)
QUIKRETE COMPANIES LLC
Hwy 19 Rr 460 Rt 460 (24637)
P.O. Box 134 (24637-0134)
PHONE................................276 964-6755
Mike Scutella, *Branch Mgr*
EMP: 30 **Privately Held**
WEB: www.quikrete.com
SIC: 3272 Concrete products
HQ: The Quikrete Companies Llc
5 Concourse Pkwy Ste 1900
Atlanta GA 30328
404 634-9100

(G-10526)
VANCE GRAPHICS LLC
175 Green Mountain Rd (24637-4257)
PHONE................................276 964-2822
Matthew Vance, *Mng Member*
EMP: 6 **EST:** 2010
SQ FT: 4,500
SALES (est): 200K **Privately Held**
WEB: www.vancegraphic.com
SIC: 3993 Signs & advertising specialties

Powhatan
Powhatan County

(G-10527)
3D DESIGN AND MFG LLC
2620 Farmington Ln (23139-5222)
PHONE................................804 214-3229
Shirley M Modlin,
David Modlin,
EMP: 2
SALES (est): 150K **Privately Held**
WEB: www.3ddesignandmanufacturing.com
SIC: 3449 Miscellaneous metalwork

(G-10528)
AAE INC
1352 Anderson Hwy Ste G (23139-8055)
PHONE................................804 427-1111
EMP: 4
SALES (est): 486K **Privately Held**
WEB: www.aaellc.com
SIC: 3824 Speedometers

(G-10529)
ALL TOOLS INC
1885 Hope Meadow Way (23139-7061)
PHONE................................804 598-1549
William Mottley, *President*
EMP: 2
SALES (est): 100K **Privately Held**
SIC: 3423 Masons' hand tools

(G-10530)
AMERICAN HANDS LLC
3611 Maidens Rd (23139-4021)
PHONE................................804 349-8974
Craig O'Gallagher,
EMP: 1
SALES (est): 86K **Privately Held**
SIC: 2426 7389 3645 5063 Carvings, furniture: wood; ; residential lighting fixtures; receptacles, electrical; general electrical contractor

(G-10531)
AWARE INC
4300 Spoonbill Ct (23139-6900)
PHONE..........................804 598-1016
Susan Shepperson, *Principal*
EMP: 4 **Publicly Held**
WEB: www.aware.com
SIC: 3674 Semiconductors & related de-
vices
PA: Aware, Inc.
   40 Middlesex Tpke
   Bedford MA 01730
   781 276-4000

(G-10532)
BEST OF LANDSCAPING
4662 Bell Rd (23139-4701)
PHONE..........................804 253-4014
Stacy Jackson, *Owner*
EMP: 1
SALES (est): 50K **Privately Held**
SIC: 1442 Construction sand & gravel

(G-10533)
BIG SKY DRONE SERVICES LLC
1730 Calais Trl (23139-4522)
PHONE..........................804 378-2970
James Lyles, *Principal*
EMP: 2
SALES (est): 100.2K **Privately Held**
SIC: 3721 Motorized aircraft

(G-10534)
BODIE VINEYARDS LLC
1809 May Way Dr (23139-7422)
PHONE..........................804 598-2240
Clyde Bodie, *Principal*
EMP: 3
SALES (est): 174.8K **Privately Held**
WEB: www.bodievineyards.com
SIC: 2084 Wines

(G-10535)
BRET HAMILTON ENTERPRISES
2025 New Dorset Rd (23139-7540)
PHONE..........................804 598-8246
Tina Hamilton, *President*
Bret Hamilton, *Vice Pres*
EMP: 2
SQ FT: 6,000
SALES (est): 200K **Privately Held**
SIC: 3711 Automobile assembly, including
specialty automobiles

(G-10536)
C & C PUBLISHING INC
725 Petersburg Rd (23139-8114)
P.O. Box 215 (23139-0215)
PHONE..........................804 598-4035
Billy Davis, *Branch Mgr*
EMP: 4
SALES (corp-wide): 442.3K **Privately
Held**
WEB: www.richmond.com
SIC: 2711 Newspapers, publishing & print-
ing
PA: C & C Publishing Inc
   8460 Times Dispatch Blvd
   Mechanicsville VA 23116
   804 598-4305

(G-10537)
CENTREX FAB
4010 Jefferson Woods Dr (23139-4851)
PHONE..........................804 598-6000
William Pritchard, *Manager*
EMP: 2 EST: 2017
SALES (est): 91.1K **Privately Held**
SIC: 3499 Fabricated metal products

(G-10538)
**CLARK HARDWOOD FLR
REFINISHING**
2340 Mosby Rd (23139-5437)
PHONE..........................804 350-8871
Steve Clark, *Principal*
EMP: 1 EST: 2007
SALES (est): 114K **Privately Held**
WEB: www.clarkhardwoodfloors.com
SIC: 2426 1771 1752 Flooring, hardwood;
flooring contractor; floor laying & floor
work

(G-10539)
CLEMENTS BACKHOE LLC
1886 Nichols Rd (23139-6631)
PHONE..........................804 598-6230
Charles Clements Jr, *Principal*
EMP: 1 EST: 2011
SALES (est): 146.4K **Privately Held**
SIC: 3531 Backhoes

(G-10540)
**COLONY CONSTRUCTION ASP
LLC (PA)**
2333 Anderson Hwy (23139-7504)
PHONE..........................804 598-1400
Catherine Claud, *Mng Member*
Scott Claud,
Harry King Jr,
EMP: 18
SALES (est): 2.9MM **Privately Held**
WEB: www.colonypaving.com
SIC: 2951 Asphalt paving mixtures &
blocks

(G-10541)
**CRAZY ROOSTER BREWING CO
LLC**
1560 Oakbridge Dr (23139-8063)
PHONE..........................804 464-2958
Timothy Torrez, *Mng Member*
EMP: 5
SALES (est): 264K **Privately Held**
SIC: 2082 Beer (alcoholic beverage)

(G-10542)
DOMINION LEASING SOFTWARE
1545 Standing Ridge Dr B (23139-8062)
PHONE..........................804 378-2204
Joann Weinstein, *Principal*
Donna Kivikko, *Manager*
EMP: 2
SALES (est): 256.9K **Privately Held**
WEB: www.domls.com
SIC: 7372 Prepackaged software

(G-10543)
DUTCH GAP STRIPING INC
1939a Woodberry Mill Rd (23139-5300)
PHONE..........................804 594-0069
EMP: 3
SALES: 170K **Privately Held**
SIC: 3069 Mfg Fabricated Rubber Prod-
ucts

(G-10544)
ETHERIDGE ELECTRIC INC
Also Called: Etheridge Automation
2430 New Dorset Ter (23139-7549)
P.O. Box 685, Midlothian (23113-0685)
PHONE..........................804 372-6428
Johnny Etheridge, *CEO*
Matthew G Etheridge, *President*
Emily E Starks, *Vice Pres*
Diane Wood, *Office Mgr*
EMP: 8
SQ FT: 2,100
SALES (est): 2.1MM **Privately Held**
WEB: www.etheridgeautomation.com
SIC: 3625 Relays & industrial controls

(G-10545)
GARRIS SIGNS INC
Also Called: Garris Sign Company
4250 Pierce Rd (23139-6915)
P.O. Box 927 (23139-0927)
PHONE..........................804 598-1127
Coy Garris, *President*
EMP: 3
SALES (est): 301.7K **Privately Held**
WEB: www.garrissigns.net
SIC: 3993 Signs & advertising specialties

(G-10546)
GHOST WIND LLC
1545 Meade Point Dr (23139-8042)
PHONE..........................561 624-1141
EMP: 2
SALES (est): 113.7K **Privately Held**
WEB: www.retrofitmedical.com
SIC: 3944 Games, toys & children's vehi-
cles

(G-10547)
GREENLEAF FILTRATION LLC
1500 Stavemill Ter Ste D (23139-8057)
P.O. Box 992, Midlothian (23113-0992)
PHONE..........................804 378-7744
Joseph Schumann, *President*
Karen Schumann, *General Mgr*
EMP: 8
SALES (est): 2.5MM **Privately Held**
WEB: www.greenleaffilters.net
SIC: 3677 Filtration devices, electronic

(G-10548)
HARPER AND TAYLOR CUSTOM
1408 Stavemill Rd (23139-7903)
PHONE..........................804 658-8753
EMP: 1 EST: 2018
SALES (est): 64.6K **Privately Held**
SIC: 2431 Millwork

(G-10549)
HERFF JONES LLC
2020 New Dorset Rd (23139-7540)
P.O. Box 245, Midlothian (23113-0245)
PHONE..........................804 598-0971
Jay Radabush, *Manager*
EMP: 14
SALES (corp-wide): 1.1B **Privately Held**
WEB: www.yearbookdiscoveries.com
SIC: 2752 Commercial printing, litho-
graphic
HQ: Herff Jones, Llc
   4501 W 62nd St
   Indianapolis IN 46268
   800 419-5462

(G-10550)
**HYDROPOWER TURBINE
SYSTEMS**
Also Called: Hts
1940 Flint Lock Ct (23139-6143)
PHONE..........................804 360-7992
Alfred Patzig, *Executive*
▲ EMP: 2
SALES (est): 160K **Privately Held**
WEB:
www.harmonytechnologyservices.com
SIC: 3511 5084 Turbines & turbine gener-
ator sets; screening machinery & equip-
ment

(G-10551)
INTERIOR 2000
2434 New Dorset Cir (23139-7500)
PHONE..........................804 598-0340
David Dowdy, *Owner*
EMP: 2
SALES (est): 90K **Privately Held**
WEB: www.interior2kva.com
SIC: 3231 5231 1751 Silvered glass:
made from purchased glass; glass; car-
pentry work

(G-10552)
INTL PRINTERS WORLD
3887 Old Buckingham Rd (23139-7020)
PHONE..........................804 403-3940
EMP: 2
SALES (est): 98K **Privately Held**
SIC: 2752 Lithographic Commercial Print-
ing

(G-10553)
**JAMES A KENNEDY & ASSOC
INC**
4529 Mattox Crossing Ct (23139-6939)
PHONE..........................804 241-6836
James A Kennedy, *CEO*
Michael Damico, *Treasurer*
Richard A Harsh, *Admin Sec*
EMP: 5 EST: 2010
SALES (est): 6.8K **Privately Held**
WEB: www.jamesakennedy.com
SIC: 2037 2038 5149 2013 Frozen fruits
& vegetables; frozen specialties; gro-
ceries & related products; sausages &
other prepared meats; meat & fish mar-
kets;

(G-10554)
JD GOODMAN WELDING
2559 Walkers Ridge Cir (23139-7842)
P.O. Box 1168 (23139-1168)
PHONE..........................804 598-1070
EMP: 1

SALES (est): 133.5K **Privately Held**
SIC: 7692 Welding Repair

(G-10555)
L A BOWLES LOGGING INC
2120 Ballsville Rd (23139-6322)
PHONE..........................804 492-3103
Lawrence A Bowles, *President*
Juanita Bowles, *Admin Sec*
EMP: 8
SALES (est): 360K **Privately Held**
SIC: 2411 Logging camps & contrac-
tors; pulp mills

(G-10556)
LINETREE WOODWORKS
1870 Lower Mill Rd (23139-7082)
PHONE..........................919 619-3013
Craig Debussey, *Principal*
EMP: 1 EST: 2018
SALES (est): 54.1K **Privately Held**
SIC: 2431 Millwork

(G-10557)
MARK FOUR INC
Also Called: First Impressions
1837 High Hill Dr (23139-7628)
PHONE..........................804 330-0765
Allen D Simon, *President*
Alan Simon, *Sales Staff*
EMP: 2
SALES (est): 400K **Privately Held**
SIC: 2752 Commercial printing, offset

(G-10558)
MEDICOR TECHNOLOGIES LLC
2970 Palaver Blf (23139-4866)
PHONE..........................804 616-8895
Charles Faison,
EMP: 1
SALES (est): 92.1K **Privately Held**
SIC: 3699 Cleaning equipment, ultrasonic,
except medical & dental

(G-10559)
MOBOTREX INC
1550 Standing Ridge Dr (23139-8051)
PHONE..........................804 794-1592
Paul Thompson, *Branch Mgr*
EMP: 15
SALES (corp-wide): 32MM **Privately
Held**
WEB: www.mobotrex.com
SIC: 3669 Transportation signaling devices
PA: Mobotrex, Inc.
   109 W 55th St
   Davenport IA 52806
   563 323-0009

(G-10560)
MOON RIVER PRINT CO
1346 Stavemill Rd (23139-7901)
PHONE..........................804 350-2647
EMP: 2
SALES (est): 83.9K **Privately Held**
SIC: 2752 Commercial printing, litho-
graphic

(G-10561)
**MOSLOW WOOD PRODUCTS
INC**
3450 Maidens Rd (23139-4015)
PHONE..........................804 598-5579
James Moslow, *President*
Bill Moslow, *Vice Pres*
William Moslow Jr, *Vice Pres*
▲ EMP: 56
SQ FT: 45,000
SALES (est): 10.2MM **Privately Held**
WEB: www.moslowwood.com
SIC: 2499 Decorative wood & woodwork;
trophy bases, wood

(G-10562)
PENGUIN WOODWORKING LLC
2144b Tower Hill Rd (23139-6007)
PHONE..........................804 502-2656
EMP: 1
SALES (est): 54.1K **Privately Held**
SIC: 2431 Millwork

▲ = Import ▼=Export
◆ =Import/Export

(G-10563)
PERFORMANCE CSTM CABINETS LLC
3573 Archers Rdg (23139-4233)
PHONE...............................804 382-3870
Henry Scott,
EMP: 1
SALES (est): 150K **Privately Held**
WEB: www.securevehiclesolutions.com
SIC: 3714 Motor vehicle parts & accessories

(G-10564)
PHOTOLIVELY LLC
3358 John Tree Hill Rd (23139-4520)
PHONE...............................804 937-0896
Wendy McSweeney, *Mng Member*
EMP: 2
SALES (est): 75K **Privately Held**
WEB: www.photolively.com
SIC: 2782 Scrapbooks, albums & diaries

(G-10565)
PIQUANT PRESS LLC
1801 Hillenwood Dr (23139-7626)
PHONE...............................804 379-3856
Rodney D Butterworth, *Administration*
EMP: 1
SALES (est): 62.1K **Privately Held**
SIC: 2741 Miscellaneous publishing

(G-10566)
PK PLUMBING INC
3385 Trenholm Rd (23139-4613)
PHONE...............................804 909-4160
Stephanie Keuther, *President*
EMP: 2
SALES (est): 226.9K **Privately Held**
SIC: 3432 Plumbing fixture fittings & trim

(G-10567)
POWER CLEAN INDUSTRIES LLC
1815 Dorset Ridge Way (23139-7543)
PHONE...............................804 372-6838
Jennifer Reynolds, *Principal*
EMP: 1
SALES (est): 50.1K **Privately Held**
SIC: 3999 Manufacturing industries

(G-10568)
PRESIDIUM ATHLETICS LLC
1500 Oakbridge Ter Ste A (23139-8057)
PHONE...............................800 618-9661
Michael Perez, *Mng Member*
EMP: 5
SALES (est): 265.1K **Privately Held**
WEB: www.ooblock.com
SIC: 3949 Sporting & athletic goods

(G-10569)
R F TECH SOLUTIONS INC
1570 Hollow Log Dr (23139-6954)
PHONE...............................804 241-5250
EMP: 4
SALES (est): 75K **Privately Held**
SIC: 3812 Mfg Search/Navigation Equipment

(G-10570)
RAPID MANUFACTURING INC
4347 Anderson Hwy (23139-5604)
PHONE...............................804 598-7467
Deborah C Llewellyn, *CEO*
Ronald H Oliver Jr, *President*
Ronald Oliver, *Opers Staff*
Debbie Llewellyn, *CFO*
Comer Jeremy, *Software Dev*
EMP: 20
SQ FT: 18,000
SALES (est): 5MM **Privately Held**
WEB: www.rapidva.com
SIC: 3599 3711 Machine shop, jobbing & repair; automobile assembly, including specialty automobiles

(G-10571)
RGA LLC
1550 Standing Ridge Dr (23139-8051)
PHONE...............................804 794-1592
Paul Thomson, *President*
Stuart Swift, *Sales Staff*
Marc Merkel, *Manager*
Cindy Denoon, *Admin Asst*
▲ **EMP:** 17

SQ FT: 7,000
SALES (est): 5.6MM
SALES (corp-wide): 32MM **Privately Held**
WEB: www.mobotrex.com
SIC: 3669 5063 Traffic signals, electric; signaling equipment, electrical
PA: Mobotrex, Inc.
109 W 55th St
Davenport IA 52806
563 323-0009

(G-10572)
SB COX READY MIX INC
1918a Anderson Hwy (23139-7918)
PHONE...............................804 364-0500
EMP: 10
SALES (corp-wide): 6.3MM **Privately Held**
WEB: www.coxreadymix.com
SIC: 3273 Ready-mixed concrete
PA: Sb Cox Ready Mix Inc
2160 Lanier Ln
Rockville VA

(G-10573)
SCT WOODWORKS LLC
2492 Royce Ct (23139-5837)
PHONE...............................804 310-1908
Seth Thomas, *Principal*
EMP: 1
SALES (est): 54.1K **Privately Held**
SIC: 2431 Millwork

(G-10574)
SHIRLEYS STITCHES LLC
3130 Blue Bell Farms Rd (23139-4328)
PHONE...............................804 370-7182
Shirley Hoskin, *Principal*
EMP: 1
SALES (est): 33.7K **Privately Held**
SIC: 2395 Embroidery & art needlework

(G-10575)
SHUTTERBOOTH
2621 Glenalmond Ct (23139-4333)
PHONE...............................804 662-0471
EMP: 3
SALES (est): 137K **Privately Held**
SIC: 3442 Shutters, door or window: metal

(G-10576)
SIGN DESIGN OF VA LLC
1901 Anderson Hwy Ste F (23139-7932)
PHONE...............................804 794-1689
Lonnie Leslie Jr, *President*
Derek Graham,
EMP: 2
SALES (est): 153.5K **Privately Held**
SIC: 3993 Signs & advertising specialties

(G-10577)
SIGN DESIGNS OF POWHATAN INC
1901 Anderson Hwy Ste B (23139-7932)
PHONE...............................804 794-1689
Lonnie Leslie Jr, *President*
EMP: 4
SALES (est): 344.1K **Privately Held**
WEB: www.trucklettering.com
SIC: 3993 Signs & advertising specialties

(G-10578)
SKIPPERS CREEK VINEYARD LLC
965 Rocky Ford Rd (23139-7204)
PHONE...............................804 598-7291
EMP: 2
SALES (est): 158.9K **Privately Held**
WEB: www.skipperscreekvineyard.com
SIC: 2084 Wines

(G-10579)
STREETWERKZ CUSTOMS
1695 Bracketts Bend (23139-6712)
PHONE...............................804 921-6483
EMP: 1 **EST:** 2013
SALES (est): 103.4K **Privately Held**
SIC: 7692 Welding repair

(G-10580)
THORE SIGNS
2212 French Hill Ter (23139-4535)
PHONE...............................804 513-5621
Kathleen Walker, *Principal*

EMP: 1
SALES (est): 50.6K **Privately Held**
SIC: 3993 Signs & advertising specialties

(G-10581)
THREE CROSSES DISTILLING CO LL
3835 Old Buckingham Rd (23139-7020)
PHONE...............................804 512-9690
EMP: 3
SALES (est): 160.2K **Privately Held**
SIC: 2085 Distilled & blended liquors

(G-10582)
TRINITY STEEL ERECTION INC
1349 Pine Creek Ridge Dr (23139-7945)
P.O. Box 774 (23139-0774)
PHONE...............................804 598-8811
Elizabeth Belcher, *President*
Michael D Belcher, *Vice Pres*
Danny Belcher, *Project Mgr*
Dennis Mickles, *Project Mgr*
Mike Johnson, *Opers Staff*
EMP: 35
SALES (est): 2.9MM **Privately Held**
WEB: www.trinitysteelerection.com
SIC: 3441 Fabricated structural metal

(G-10583)
WATSON MACHINE CORPORATION
2052 New Dorset Rd (23139-7540)
PHONE...............................804 598-1500
David L Watson Sr, *President*
Marie Watson, *Corp Secy*
Samuel H Watson, *Vice Pres*
Justin Antrobius, *VP Opers*
EMP: 12
SALES (est): 1.6MM **Privately Held**
WEB: www.watsonmachine.com
SIC: 3699 Teaching machines & aids, electronic

(G-10584)
WEIGHTPACK INC
3490 Anderson Hwy (23139-5801)
P.O. Box 27 (23139-0027)
PHONE...............................804 598-4512
Gianguido Corniani, *CEO*
Teresa Whitlock, *CFO*
Sabrina Capitani, *Accounting Mgr*
Angela Conigliaro, *Manager*
Mark Hayes, *Manager*
▲ **EMP:** 29
SALES (est): 10MM **Privately Held**
WEB: www.weightpack.com
SIC: 3565 Bottling machinery: filling, capping, labeling

(G-10585)
WHITLEYS WELDING INC
2548 Liberty Hill Rd (23139-5205)
PHONE...............................804 350-6203
Allen Whitley, *President*
EMP: 2
SALES (est): 117.4K **Privately Held**
SIC: 7692 1799 Welding repair; welding on site

Prince George
Prince George County

(G-10586)
460 MACHINE COMPANY
6104 Hardware Dr (23875-3049)
PHONE...............................804 861-8787
Steven Westermann, *President*
Sandra Wallace, *Vice Pres*
EMP: 9
SQ FT: 6,000
SALES (est): 814.7K **Privately Held**
WEB: www.460machine.com
SIC: 3599 Machine shop, jobbing & repair

(G-10587)
BIG EZ PRINTS
4550 Jefferson Pointe Ln (23875-1475)
PHONE...............................804 929-3479
Alesia Bassett, *Principal*
EMP: 2
SALES (est): 83.9K **Privately Held**
SIC: 2752 Commercial printing, lithographic

(G-10588)
CAROLINA CONTAINER COMPANY
Also Called: Digital High Point
5701 Quality Way (23875-3047)
P.O. Box 2166, High Point NC (27261-2166)
PHONE...............................804 458-4700
Jerry Carden, *Branch Mgr*
EMP: 13
SALES (corp-wide): 242.4MM **Privately Held**
WEB: www.carolinacontainer.com
SIC: 2653 Boxes, corrugated: made from purchased materials
HQ: Carolina Container Llc
909 Prospect St
High Point NC 27260
336 883-7146

(G-10589)
COYENT
5117 Courthouse Rd (23875-3204)
PHONE...............................804 861-3323
EMP: 1
SALES (est): 46K **Privately Held**
SIC: 2499 Mfg Wood Products

(G-10590)
CROP PRODUCTION SVC
5025 E Whitehill Ct (23875-1250)
PHONE...............................804 732-6166
EMP: 2 **EST:** 2019
SALES (est): 74.4K **Privately Held**
SIC: 2873 Nitrogenous fertilizers

(G-10591)
DESSIES DELICIOUS DESSERTS LLC
213 Wren St (23875-3443)
PHONE...............................804 822-7482
Felecia Gonzalez,
EMP: 1
SALES (est): 75.7K **Privately Held**
SIC: 2051 Cakes, bakery: except frozen; bakery, for home service delivery

(G-10592)
DIRTY DEEDS POWER WASHING
7355 Trailing Rock Rd (23875-2679)
P.O. Box 1234 (23875-0901)
PHONE...............................804 731-2739
Larry Hildreth, *Owner*
EMP: 1
SALES (est): 6.4K **Privately Held**
WEB: www.dirtydeedspowerwashing.com
SIC: 2211 Washcloths

(G-10593)
EDWARDS CONSULTING
2801 Irwin Rd (23875-1136)
PHONE...............................804 733-2506
EMP: 3
SALES (est): 130K **Privately Held**
SIC: 2522 Mfg Office Furniture-Nonwood

(G-10594)
FRED SISSON
Also Called: Deal Products
5497 Snow Creek Ct (23875-2539)
P.O. Box 80896, Charleston SC (29416-0896)
PHONE...............................843 641-7155
Fred Sisson Jr, *Owner*
EMP: 4
SALES (est): 275K **Privately Held**
SIC: 3341 3356 Secondary nonferrous metals; lead & lead alloy bars, pipe, plates, shapes, etc.

(G-10595)
GREEN WASTE ORGANICS LLC
5333 Hall Farm Rd (23875-2139)
P.O. Box 89, Surry (23883-0089)
PHONE...............................804 929-8505
Wade Taylor, *Owner*
Tamara Tolley,
EMP: 3
SALES (est): 213.9K **Privately Held**
SIC: 2611 Pulp mills, mechanical & recycling processing

(G-10596)
INK & MORE
7106 Courthouse Rd (23875-2541)
PHONE..................................804 794-3437
Doris Pennington, *Owner*
EMP: 2
SALES (est): 25K **Privately Held**
SIC: 2262 Screen printing: manmade fiber & silk broadwoven fabrics

(G-10597)
KID FUELED KCO LLC
7100 Whispering Winds Dr (23875-2759)
PHONE..................................804 720-4091
Tracy Taliaferro, *Principal*
EMP: 3
SALES (est): 192.1K **Privately Held**
SIC: 2869 Fuels

(G-10598)
KWE PUBLISHING LLC
5015 Takach Rd (23875-2426)
PHONE..................................804 458-4789
Kimberley Eley, *Principal*
EMP: 5
SALES (est): 91.4K **Privately Held**
WEB: www.kwepub.com
SIC: 2711 Newspapers, publishing & printing

(G-10599)
MACROSEAL MECHANICAL LLC
2122 E Whitehill Rd (23875-1252)
PHONE..................................804 458-5655
Linda B Holdsworth,
EMP: 10
SALES (est): 1.2MM **Privately Held**
WEB: www.macroseal.com
SIC: 3053 Gaskets, packing & sealing devices

(G-10600)
MARK BRIC DISPLAY CORP
4740 Chudoba Pkwy (23875-3039)
PHONE..................................800 742-6275
Lars Carlsson, *CEO*
Edgardo Marquez, *President*
John Diaz, *Vice Pres*
Eva Romeling, *Vice Pres*
Alfred L Schiele, *Treasurer*
▲ EMP: 34
SQ FT: 17,500
SALES (est): 3.3MM
SALES (corp-wide): 20.6MM **Privately Held**
WEB: www.markbric.com
SIC: 3999 7389 Advertising display products; advertising, promotional & trade show services
PA: Mark Bric Inc.
4740 Chudoba Pkwy
Prince George VA 23875
804 863-2331

(G-10601)
MILLENNIUM SERVICES INC
1520 Fine St (23875-1207)
PHONE..................................804 733-8505
Reina Pellegrini, *President*
Michael Pellegrini, *Vice Pres*
EMP: 10
SALES (est): 470.2K **Privately Held**
WEB: www.millenniumpower.net
SIC: 3599 Machine shop, jobbing & repair

(G-10602)
MUD PUPPY CUSTOM LURES LLC
9629 Shadywood Rd (23875-1940)
PHONE..................................804 895-1489
EMP: 1
SALES (est): 51.7K **Privately Held**
SIC: 3949 Lures, fishing: artificial

(G-10603)
NCI GROUP INC
6001 Quality Way (23875-3038)
PHONE..................................804 957-6811
Keith Brown, *Site Mgr*
Tim Johnson, *Maint Spvr*
Chuck Reynolds, *Manager*
Bill Wilkinson, *Manager*
Cynthia Gray, *Office Admin*
EMP: 70

SALES (corp-wide): 4.8B **Publicly Held**
WEB: www.metal-prep.com
SIC: 3448 Panels for prefabricated metal buildings
HQ: Nci Group, Inc.
10943 N Sam Huston Pkwy W
Houston TX 77064
281 897-7788

(G-10604)
PERDUE FARMS INC
5155 Chudoba Pkwy (23875-3000)
P.O. Box 1537, Salisbury MD (21802-1537)
PHONE..................................804 722-1276
Cherie Hall, *Engineer*
Kevin Hurst, *Branch Mgr*
Adolfo Hernandez, *IT/INT Sup*
Donna Shupe, *Data Proc Exec*
Debbie Barnes, *Executive Asst*
EMP: 400
SALES (corp-wide): 5.2B **Privately Held**
WEB: www.perdue.com
SIC: 2015 Chicken, processed: fresh
PA: Perdue Farms Inc.
31149 Old Ocean City Rd
Salisbury MD 21804
410 543-3000

(G-10605)
PRECISION SOLUTIONS INC
7520 Harvest Rd (23875-1930)
PHONE..................................804 452-2217
Samuel Mellichampe, *President*
Samuel A Mellichampe, *President*
Candace R Mellichampe, *Vice Pres*
EMP: 7
SQ FT: 19,000
SALES (est): 952.6K **Privately Held**
WEB: www.cti1.net
SIC: 3599 Machine shop, jobbing & repair

(G-10606)
ROLLS-ROYCE CROSSPOINTE LLC (DH)
8800 Wells Station Rd (23875-3055)
PHONE..................................877 787-6247
James M Guyette, *CEO*
Thomas A Bell, *President*
Thomas P Dale, *Exec VP*
Stephen B Plummer, *Exec VP*
William T Powers III, *Exec VP*
▲ EMP: 15
SALES (est): 1.9MM
SALES (corp-wide): 21.4B **Privately Held**
WEB: www.rolls-royce.com
SIC: 3365 3728 Aerospace castings, aluminum; aircraft power transmission equipment
HQ: Rolls-Royce North America Inc.
1900 Reston Metro Plz # 4
Reston VA 20190
703 834-1700

(G-10607)
SERVICE CENTER METALS LLC
5850 Quality Way (23875-3040)
PHONE..................................804 518-1550
R Scott Kelly, *CEO*
Chip Dollins Jr, *Vice Pres*
Randy Weis, *Vice Pres*
Calvin Wiggins, *Mfg Dir*
Dustin Stell, *QC Mgr*
◆ EMP: 247
SALES (est): 37.4MM **Privately Held**
WEB: www.servicecentermetals.com
SIC: 3354 Aluminum extruded products
PA: Scm Industries Llc
800 E Canal St Ste 1900
Richmond VA 23219
804 363-8762

(G-10608)
TERRY BROWN
Also Called: Brown's Heating & Air
5305 Oak Leaf Ln (23875-2691)
PHONE..................................804 721-6667
Terry Brown, *Owner*
EMP: 3 EST: 2015
SALES (est): 151.4K **Privately Held**
SIC: 3585 7389 Parts for heating, cooling & refrigerating equipment;

(G-10609)
VULCAN CONSTRUCTION MTLS LLC
4120 Puddledock Rd (23875-1309)
PHONE..................................804 862-6660
Andy Price, *Branch Mgr*
EMP: 37 **Publicly Held**
WEB: www.vulcanmaterials.com
SIC: 1422 1442 Crushed & broken limestone; construction sand & gravel
HQ: Vulcan Construction Materials, Llc
1200 Urban Center Dr
Vestavia AL 35242
205 298-3000

(G-10610)
WELLS CABINET SHOP
3926 Puddledock Rd (23875-1305)
PHONE..................................804 861-8325
William A Wells Sr, *Owner*
EMP: 9
SQ FT: 3,500
SALES (est): 718.7K **Privately Held**
SIC: 2434 Wood kitchen cabinets

(G-10611)
WSS RICHMOND
6750 Hardware Dr (23875-3044)
PHONE..................................804 722-0150
EMP: 2
SALES (est): 438.7K **Privately Held**
SIC: 2752 Commercial printing, lithographic

Prospect
Prince Edward County

(G-10612)
HOPE SPRINGS MEDIA
Also Called: Resource Management Strategies
988 Sulphur Spring Rd (23960-8105)
PHONE..................................434 574-2031
Paul Hoffman, *Owner*
EMP: 2 EST: 2010
SALES (est): 134.4K **Privately Held**
WEB: www.hopespringsmedia.com
SIC: 2731 Book publishing

(G-10613)
JENNINGS LOGGING LLC
178 Jennings Farm Ln (23960-8184)
PHONE..................................434 248-6876
Brian Jennings, *Principal*
EMP: 3
SALES (est): 163.6K **Privately Held**
SIC: 2411 Logging

(G-10614)
SIGND AND SEALD
107 S Hardtimes Dr (23960-7975)
PHONE..................................814 460-2547
EMP: 2
SALES (est): 134.9K **Privately Held**
SIC: 3993 Signs & advertising specialties

(G-10615)
VILLAGE CABINET CO
226 Prospect Rd (23960-2161)
P.O. Box 204 (23960-0204)
PHONE..................................434 574-6263
Gary Paris, *Owner*
EMP: 4
SALES (est): 500K **Privately Held**
SIC: 2434 Wood kitchen cabinets

(G-10616)
WILCKS LAKE STORAGE SHEDS INC
Also Called: Wilcks Lake Sheds
10316 Prince Edward Hwy (23960-8152)
PHONE..................................434 574-5131
Norman Eli Troyer, *President*
Alethea Stringfellow, *Office Mgr*
Barbara Troyer, *Admin Sec*
EMP: 14
SQ FT: 80,000
SALES (est): 1.8MM **Privately Held**
WEB: www.wilckslakesheds.com
SIC: 2452 Prefabricated buildings, wood

Providence Forge
New Kent County

(G-10617)
A JOHNSON LINWOOD
Also Called: Johnson's Logging
7141 S Lott Cary Rd (23140-2510)
PHONE..................................804 829-5364
Linwood A Johnson, *Owner*
EMP: 6
SALES (est): 378.3K **Privately Held**
SIC: 2411 Logging

(G-10618)
ARES SELF DEFENSE INC
11537 Winding River Rd (23140-4447)
PHONE..................................757 561-3538
Richard Brent McGhee Sr, *President*
EMP: 3
SALES (est): 162.1K **Privately Held**
SIC: 3812 Defense systems & equipment

(G-10619)
C H EVELYN PILING COMPANY INC
2200 Barnetts Rd (23140-2104)
P.O. Box 366 (23140-0366)
PHONE..................................804 966-2273
Charles H Evelyn Jr, *President*
Chrales Eevyn III, *Vice Pres*
Benjamin Evelyn, *Treasurer*
William Evelyn, *Admin Sec*
EMP: 15 EST: 1958
SQ FT: 4,000
SALES (est): 1.8MM **Privately Held**
WEB: www.evelynpiling.com
SIC: 2411 2491 2499 Piling, wood: untreated; pilings, treated wood; poles, wood

(G-10620)
CHARLES CITY FOREST PRODUCTS
2200 Roxbury Rd (23140-2100)
PHONE..................................804 966-2336
Thomas Evelyn, *President*
Charles H Evelyn Jr, *Vice Pres*
▲ EMP: 30
SQ FT: 5,000
SALES (est): 5.1MM **Privately Held**
WEB: www.ccforestproducts.com
SIC: 2421 2448 2435 2426 Lumber: rough, sawed or planed; wood pallets & skids; hardwood veneer & plywood; hardwood dimension & flooring mills

(G-10621)
CHARLES CITY TIMBER AND MAT
2200 Barnetts Rd (23140-2104)
PHONE..................................804 512-8150
Patrick Evelyn, *Branch Mgr*
EMP: 3 **Privately Held**
WEB: www.cctimberandmat.com
SIC: 2273 Mats & matting
PA: Charles City Timber And Mat, Inc
2221 Barnetts Rd
Providence Forge VA 23140

(G-10622)
CHARLES CITY TIMBER AND MAT (PA)
2221 Barnetts Rd (23140-2104)
P.O. Box 458 (23140-0458)
PHONE..................................804 966-8313
Patrick Evelyn, *President*
Evelyn Patric, *President*
Evelyn Emily Anne, *Director*
EMP: 32
SALES (est): 4.3MM **Privately Held**
WEB: www.cctimberandmat.com
SIC: 2273 Mats & matting

(G-10623)
EMERGENCY WELDING INC
8231 Courthouse Rd (23140-2533)
PHONE..................................804 829-2976
William L Lewis, *Principal*
EMP: 2 EST: 2009
SALES (est): 96.4K **Privately Held**
SIC: 7692 Welding repair

(G-10624)
FIRST COLONY TECHNOLOGY LLC
4603 Black Rail Ct (23140-3734)
PHONE..................................434 579-3655
Chris Gowdy, *Principal*
EMP: 2 EST: 2013
SALES (est): 137.9K Privately Held
WEB: www.firstcolonytechnology.com
SIC: 3571 Electronic computers

(G-10625)
GARTHRGHT LAND CLEARING INC TW
4665 Bailey Rd (23140-3538)
PHONE..................................804 370-5408
Nancy Garthright, *Principal*
EMP: 3 EST: 2010
SALES (est): 287.2K Privately Held
SIC: 2411 Logging

(G-10626)
JAMES RIVER ENVIROMENTAL INC
8075 Long Reach Rd (23140-3255)
PHONE..................................804 966-7609
Jason M Flippo, *Principal*
EMP: 2
SALES (est): 129.5K Privately Held
SIC: 2833 Botanical products, medicinal: ground, graded or milled

(G-10627)
OFFROADARROWCOM LLC
12717 Tylers Ridge Ct (23140-2611)
PHONE..................................804 920-2529
Timothy Morris, *Owner*
EMP: 2
SALES (est): 128.4K Privately Held
SIC: 3949 Arrows, archery

(G-10628)
SURFSTROKE LLC
11400 Brickshire Park (23140-4415)
PHONE..................................804 437-2032
Richard Bowman, *President*
EMP: 1
SALES (est): 63K Privately Held
SIC: 3949 Exercise equipment

(G-10629)
T SHIRT UNIQUE INC
9014 Boulevard Rd (23140-3722)
PHONE..................................804 557-2989
EMP: 1
SALES (est): 65K Privately Held
SIC: 2262 Manmade Fiber & Silk Finishing Plant

Pulaski
Pulaski County

(G-10630)
ARTISTIC DESIGN
4616 Newbern Heights Dr (24301-6906)
PHONE..................................540 980-1598
Roger Cardell, *Owner*
Linda Cardell, *Co-Owner*
EMP: 2 Privately Held
SIC: 3993 Signs & advertising specialties

(G-10631)
BONDCOTE HOLDINGS INC
509 Burgis Ave (24301-5305)
P.O. Box 729 (24301-0729)
PHONE..................................540 980-2640
Micheal Steinback, *Ch of Bd*
Ted Anderson, *President*
◆ EMP: 150
SQ FT: 90,000
SALES (est): 45MM Privately Held
WEB: www.bondcote.com
SIC: 2295 Coated fabrics, not rubberized

(G-10632)
CENTELLAX INC
1740 Smith Ln (24301-2006)
PHONE..................................540 980-2905
EMP: 2 EST: 2010
SALES (est): 68K Privately Held
SIC: 3931 Mfg Musical Instruments

(G-10633)
CREATIVE CABINET DESIGNS LLC
5295 Crossbow Dr (24301-6094)
PHONE..................................703 644-1090
Brent Harral, *Principal*
EMP: 4
SALES (est): 306.6K Privately Held
WEB: www.brentharral.com
SIC: 2434 Wood kitchen cabinets

(G-10634)
DECOR LIGHTING & ELEC CO
620 Jefferson Ave N (24301-3624)
PHONE..................................540 320-8382
EMP: 3 EST: 2008
SALES (est): 140K Privately Held
SIC: 3699 Mfg Electrical Equipment/Supplies

(G-10635)
EAST PENN MANUFACTURING CO
4769 Wurno Rd (24301-7010)
PHONE..................................540 980-1174
Donna Edwards, *Manager*
Ed Miller, *Manager*
EMP: 7
SALES (corp-wide): 2.8B Privately Held
WEB: www.eastpennmanufacturing.com
SIC: 3691 Storage batteries
PA: East Penn Manufacturing Co.
102 Deka Rd
Lyon Station PA 19536
610 682-6361

(G-10636)
FALLS STAMPING & WELDING CO
28 Jefferson Ave S (24301-5625)
PHONE..................................330 928-1191
Dave Fisher, *Branch Mgr*
EMP: 25
SALES (corp-wide): 47.2MM Privately Held
WEB: www.falls-stamping.com
SIC: 7692 Welding repair
PA: Falls Stamping & Welding Company
2900 Vincent St
Cuyahoga Falls OH 44221
330 928-1191

(G-10637)
HEYTEX USA INC (DH)
Also Called: Bond Cote
509 Burgis Ave (24301-5305)
P.O. Box 729 (24301-0729)
PHONE..................................540 980-2640
Theodore Anderson, *President*
Diane Lynch, *CFO*
Dan Christian, *Info Tech Mgr*
Paula Military, *Admin Asst*
◆ EMP: 76
SQ FT: 90,000
SALES (est): 35MM
SALES (corp-wide): 120.6MM Privately Held
WEB: www.bondcote.com
SIC: 2295 Resin or plastic coated fabrics
HQ: Heytex Bramsche Gmbh
Heywinkelstr. 1
Bramsche 49565
546 877-740

(G-10638)
HURD MACHINE SHOP INC
224 12th St Nw (24301-3132)
PHONE..................................540 980-6265
Roger D Hurd, *Principal*
EMP: 2
SALES (est): 137.6K Privately Held
SIC: 3599 Machine shop, jobbing & repair

(G-10639)
JAMES HARDIE BUILDING PDTS INC
1000 James Hardy Way (24301-3472)
PHONE..................................540 980-9143
Louis Gries, *President*
Mike Mitchell, *Engineer*
Matthew Marsh, *Treasurer*
Lance Gardner, *Controller*
Joseph C Blasko, *Admin Sec*
▲ EMP: 60

SALES (est): 23.7MM Privately Held
WEB: www.jhcareercenter.com
SIC: 3292 Siding, asbestos cement

(G-10640)
M & H PARAGON INC
64 1st St Ne (24301-5744)
P.O. Box 311 (24301-0311)
PHONE..................................540 994-0080
Rick Warden, *President*
Bill Warden, *Vice Pres*
EMP: 6
SQ FT: 15,000
SALES (est): 575K Privately Held
WEB: www.paragonmh.com
SIC: 3556 Food products machinery

(G-10641)
MAMAS FUDGE
5344 Thornspring Rd (24301-6061)
PHONE..................................540 980-8444
Brenda Prosser, *Principal*
EMP: 2 EST: 2018
SALES (est): 79.4K Privately Held
SIC: 2064 Fudge (candy)

(G-10642)
MARVELOUS GREEN LLC
4250 Mcfall Hollow Rd (24301-7510)
PHONE..................................540 577-6967
Adam Drummonds,
EMP: 1
SALES (est): 39.6K Privately Held
SIC: 3999 Manufacturing industries

(G-10643)
MCCREADY LUMBER COMPANY INC
4801 Wurno Rd (24301-7009)
PHONE..................................540 980-8700
Howard McCready, *President*
Karen McCready, *Corp Secy*
EMP: 6
SQ FT: 30,000
SALES (est): 647.2K Privately Held
SIC: 2491 Millwork, treated wood

(G-10644)
PLANET CARE INC
4102 Bob White Blvd (24301-7093)
PHONE..................................540 980-2420
Bill Tobin, *President*
EMP: 2
SALES (est): 236.5K Privately Held
WEB: www.eco-purewastewatersystems.com
SIC: 3589 3677 Water treatment equipment, industrial; water purification equipment, household type; filtration devices, electronic

(G-10645)
RICK USA STAMPING CORPORATION
4783 Wurno Rd (24301-7010)
PHONE..................................540 980-1327
Marcio Cremar, *President*
EMP: 8 EST: 2014
SALES (est): 306.1K Privately Held
WEB: www.rick-usa.com
SIC: 3469 Stamping metal for the trade

(G-10646)
SOUTHPAW MECHANICAL LLC (PA)
306 1st St Ne (24301-5750)
PHONE..................................540 577-6967
Adam Drummonds, *Mng Member*
EMP: 1
SALES (est): 39.6K Privately Held
SIC: 3999 Manufacturing industries

(G-10647)
SOUTHWEST PUBLISHER LLC (PA)
Also Called: Southwest Times
34 5th St Ne (24301-4608)
P.O. Box 391 (24301-0391)
PHONE..................................540 980-5220
Ray Carhart, *President*
Susan Holley, *Publisher*
Jeremy Norman, *Publisher*
David Gravely, *Editor*
Melinda Williams, *Editor*
EMP: 24

SALES (est): 1.5MM Privately Held
WEB: www.southwesttimes.com
SIC: 2711 2752 Commercial printing & newspaper publishing combined; commercial printing, lithographic

(G-10648)
THOMAS BROTHERS SOFTWARE CORP
5680 Jill Dr (24301-7071)
PHONE..................................540 320-3505
P Keith Thomas, *Principal*
EMP: 2 EST: 2009
SALES: 166.7K Privately Held
WEB: www.thomasbrothers.net
SIC: 7372 Prepackaged software

(G-10649)
WARDEN SHACKLE EXPRESS
601 1st St Ne (24301-5823)
P.O. Box 2217 (24301-1932)
PHONE..................................540 980-2056
Rick Warden, *Owner*
EMP: 2
SQ FT: 4,000
SALES (est): 200K Privately Held
SIC: 3443 Fabricated plate work (boiler shop)

Pungoteague
Accomack County

(G-10650)
HIGHPOINT GLASS WORKS
30389 Bobtown Rd (23422)
P.O. Box 437 (23422-0437)
PHONE..................................757 442-7155
Kenneth Platt, *Owner*
EMP: 2
SALES (est): 141.2K Privately Held
WEB: www.highpointglassworks.com
SIC: 3229 Pressed & blown glass

Purcellville
Loudoun County

(G-10651)
BAP LLC
425 Crosman Ct (20132-3446)
PHONE..................................800 507-9728
Pepper Fernandez, *CEO*
Emily Bonnett, *Bd of Directors*
Scott Major, *Bd of Directors*
Jon Platt, *Bd of Directors*
EMP: 4
SALES (est): 226.3K Privately Held
SIC: 7372 Prepackaged software

(G-10652)
BLUE RIDGE LEADER
Also Called: Blue Rdge Leader Loudoun Today
128 S 20th St (20132-3301)
P.O. Box 325 (20134-0325)
PHONE..................................540 338-6200
Phillip Y Hahn, *President*
Philip Hahn, *Publisher*
EMP: 6
SALES (est): 464.9K Privately Held
WEB: www.blueridgeleader.com
SIC: 2621 Newsprint paper

(G-10653)
CATOCTIN CREEK CUSTOM RODS LLC
201 N 18th St (20132-3174)
PHONE..................................540 751-1482
Mark Burks, *Principal*
Scott Harris, *Manager*
Rebecca Harris, *Info Tech Mgr*
EMP: 2
SALES (est): 126.9K Privately Held
WEB: www.catoctincreekdistilling.com
SIC: 2085 Distilled & blended liquors

(G-10654)
CATOCTIN CREEK DISTLG CO LLC
120 W Main St (20132-3023)
PHONE..................................540 751-8404
Rebecca L Harris, *Mng Member*

GEOGRAPHIC

Scott E Harris,
EMP: 2
SALES (est): 180K **Publicly Held**
WEB: www.catoctincreekdistilling.com
SIC: 2085 Distilled & blended liquors
PA: Constellation Brands, Inc.
207 High Point Dr # 100
Victor NY 14564
585 678-7100

(G-10655)
CATOCTIN EDGES LLC
901 W Main St (20132-3016)
PHONE....................540 687-1244
Tony Castelhano,
EMP: 1
SALES (est): 80.6K **Privately Held**
WEB: www.catoctinedges.com
SIC: 3421 7699 Scissors, shears, clippers, snips & similar tools; knife, saw & tool sharpening & repair

(G-10656)
COMMERCIAL FUELING 24/7 INC
115 E Main St (20132-3175)
PHONE....................540 338-6457
William Murphy, *President*
Mary Murphy Jones, *Vice Pres*
EMP: 2
SALES (est): 146K **Privately Held**
WEB: www.valleyenergy.org
SIC: 2869 Fuels

(G-10657)
COQUINA PRESS LLC
19682 Telegraph Sprng Rd (20132-4228)
PHONE....................571 577-7550
Barbara Leary, *Principal*
EMP: 2
SALES (est): 59.2K **Privately Held**
WEB: www.coquinapress.com
SIC: 2741 Miscellaneous publishing

(G-10658)
DANIEL ORENZUK
37519 Oak Green Ln (20132-4064)
PHONE....................410 570-1362
Daniel Orenzuk, *Owner*
EMP: 1
SALES (est): 59.2K **Privately Held**
SIC: 2834 7389 Druggists' preparations (pharmaceuticals); business services

(G-10659)
DESANTIS DESIGN INC
105 E Cornwell Ln (20132-3076)
PHONE....................540 751-9014
Tim Desantis, *Principal*
EMP: 3
SALES (est): 266.9K **Privately Held**
WEB: www.desantisdesigns.com
SIC: 2511 Wood household furniture

(G-10660)
DRAEGER SAFETY DIAGNOSTICS INC
Also Called: Draeger Ignition Interlock
37251 E Richardson Ln (20132-3505)
PHONE....................703 517-0974
EMP: 3
SALES (corp-wide): 3B **Privately Held**
WEB: www.draegerinterlock.com
SIC: 3829 3999 Measuring & controlling devices; barber & beauty shop equipment
HQ: Draeger Safety Diagnostics, Inc.
4040 W Royal Ln Ste 136
Irving TX 75063
972 929-1100

(G-10661)
FRANKS WELDING INC
14181 Paris Breeze Pl (20132-1784)
PHONE....................540 668-6185
EMP: 1 **EST:** 2011
SALES (est): 41K **Privately Held**
SIC: 7692 Welding Repair

(G-10662)
GIDGETS BEAUTY BOX LLC
550 E Main St (20132-3171)
PHONE....................303 859-5914
Allison Cremona, *Branch Mgr*
EMP: 1

SALES (corp-wide): 103.9K **Privately Held**
WEB: www.gidgetsbeautybox.com
SIC: 2844 Toilet preparations
PA: Gidget's Beauty Box Llc
14 Jackson Ave
Round Hill VA

(G-10663)
GOOSE CREEK FARMS & WINERY LLC
18050 Tranquility Rd (20132-9031)
PHONE....................540 338-2056
Thomas D Page, *Administration*
EMP: 3
SALES (est): 230.3K **Privately Held**
WEB: www.bauerempire.com
SIC: 2084 Wines

(G-10664)
HAYES STAIR CO INC
121 N Bailey Ln (20132-3085)
PHONE....................540 751-0201
Joseph L Hayes, *President*
James C Hayes, *Vice Pres*
Michael T Hubbard, *Treasurer*
Barbara J Griffin, *Admin Sec*
EMP: 25
SALES (est): 3.8MM **Privately Held**
WEB: www.hayesstair.com
SIC: 2431 Staircases & stairs, wood; stair railings, wood

(G-10665)
LEGACY WOODWORKING LLC
205 Ken Culbert Ln (20132-6170)
PHONE....................703 431-8811
Thomas Johns, *Owner*
EMP: 4
SALES (est): 250.9K **Privately Held**
SIC: 2431 Millwork

(G-10666)
LINCOLN WOODWORKING
37612 Chappelle Hill Rd (20132-4004)
PHONE....................703 297-7512
Joseph Andrews, *Principal*
EMP: 1 **EST:** 2015
SALES (est): 59.5K **Privately Held**
WEB: www.lincolnwoodworking.com
SIC: 2431 Millwork

(G-10667)
LITTLE ENTERPRISES LLC
18600 Telegraph Sprng Rd (20132-4107)
PHONE....................804 869-8612
Robert Little,
EMP: 3
SALES (est): 302.7K **Privately Held**
WEB: www.little-enterprises.com
SIC: 3599 1799 8711 Machine shop, job-bing & repair; welding on site; engineering services

(G-10668)
LOST CLIPPER ENTERPRISES LLC
18113 Linden Grove Ct (20132-4085)
PHONE....................310 386-0972
Guy Noffsinger,
EMP: 1
SALES (est): 54.2K **Privately Held**
WEB: www.lostclipper.com
SIC: 2741 Miscellaneous publishing

(G-10669)
LOUDOUN CLASSICAL SCHOOL
441 E Main St (20132-3170)
PHONE....................540 338-6101
EMP: 3 **EST:** 2019
SALES (est): 121.7K **Privately Held**
WEB: www.loudounnow.com
SIC: 2711 Newspapers, publishing & print-ing

(G-10670)
LOUDOUN STAIRS INC
341 N Maple Ave (20132-3139)
PHONE....................703 478-8800
Brent Mercke, *President*
Gina Hope, *General Mgr*
Gina Elkins Hope, *General Mgr*
Michael R Mercke, *Vice Pres*
Michael Mercke, *Vice Pres*
EMP: 50

SALES (est): 9.2MM **Privately Held**
WEB: www.loudounstairs.com
SIC: 2431 1751 Staircases & stairs, wood; stair railings, wood; woodwork, interior & ornamental; finish & trim carpentry

(G-10671)
MR PRINT
501 E Main St (20132-3172)
PHONE....................540 338-5900
Nolan Barzee, *Owner*
Albert Patterson, *Sales Associate*
EMP: 5
SQ FT: 4,800
SALES (est): 563.7K **Privately Held**
WEB: www.mrprint.net
SIC: 2752 7334 Commercial printing, off-set; photocopying & duplicating services

(G-10672)
NET6DEGREES LLC
19570 Greggsville Rd (20132-4348)
PHONE....................703 201-4480
Michael Kilrain, *Principal*
Craig Gilley, *Principal*
EMP: 2
SALES (est): 115.3K **Privately Held**
SIC: 7372 7389 Business oriented com-puter software;

(G-10673)
POLIBAK PLASTICS AMERICA INC
36942 Snickersville Tpke (20132-4917)
PHONE....................703 709-3004
Polga Baki, *President*
Tolga Baki, *Vice Pres*
Erdogan Alkan, *Prdtn Mgr*
▲ **EMP:** 5
SALES (est): 901.3K **Privately Held**
WEB: www.polibakusa.com
SIC: 2821 Plastics materials & resins

(G-10674)
PREPARE HIM ROOM PUBG LLC
221 S 12th St (20132-3384)
PHONE....................703 909-1147
Wayne Ruckman, *Principal*
EMP: 1
SALES (est): 37.5K **Privately Held**
SIC: 2741 Miscellaneous publishing

(G-10675)
RI SOFTWARE CORP
905 Towering Oak Ct (20132-7219)
PHONE....................301 537-1593
Karel Alvarez, *Principal*
EMP: 2 **EST:** 2010
SALES (est): 126.6K **Privately Held**
WEB: www.risoftwarecorp.com
SIC: 7372 Prepackaged software

(G-10676)
SEQUOIA VIEW VINEYARD LLC
14914 Manor View Ln (20132-2769)
PHONE....................540 668-6245
EMP: 2 **EST:** 2013
SALES (est): 94.7K **Privately Held**
SIC: 2084 Mfg Wines/Brandy/Spirits

(G-10677)
SIGN DESIGN INC
142 E Main St (20132-3162)
PHONE....................540 338-5614
Patti House, *President*
EMP: 1
SALES (est): 100K **Privately Held**
WEB: www.signdesigninc.net
SIC: 3993 Signs & advertising specialties

(G-10678)
SIGNARAMA
Also Called: Sign-A-Rama
36936 Snickersville Tpke (20132-4917)
PHONE....................703 743-9424
James Butler, *Principal*
EMP: 3
SALES (est): 80.9K **Privately Held**
WEB: www.signarama.com
SIC: 3993 Signs & advertising specialties

(G-10679)
SPOTLIGHT STUDIO
300 S Orchard Dr (20132-3257)
P.O. Box 92 (20134-0092)
PHONE....................540 338-2690
EMP: 2 **EST:** 2010
SALES (est): 160K **Privately Held**
SIC: 3648 Mfg Lighting Equipment

(G-10680)
STUDIO B GRAPHICS
520 S 11th St (20132-3385)
PHONE....................703 777-8755
Diana Bridges, *Owner*
EMP: 1
SALES (est): 75.1K **Privately Held**
SIC: 3993 Signs & advertising specialties

(G-10681)
SUNSET HILLS VINEYARD LLC
38295 Fremont Overlook Ln (20132-2980)
PHONE....................540 882-4560
Sydney Smith, *Manager*
Diane Canney,
EMP: 6
SALES (est): 660.5K **Privately Held**
WEB: www.sunsethillsvineyard.com
SIC: 2084 Wines

(G-10682)
TROPQ CREAMERY LLC
721 E Main St (20132-3178)
PHONE....................540 680-0916
EMP: 3
SALES (est): 150.6K **Privately Held**
WEB: www.tropq.com
SIC: 2021 Creamery butter

(G-10683)
ULTRACOMM LLC
413 Gatepost Ct (20132-7205)
PHONE....................703 622-6397
David Digirolamo, *CEO*
EMP: 2 **EST:** 2012
SALES (est): 170.9K **Privately Held**
WEB: www.ultracomminc.com
SIC: 3651 7389 Household audio & video equipment;

(G-10684)
VALLEY WELDING INC
37241 E Richardson Ln (20132-3505)
P.O. Box 1237 (20134-1237)
PHONE....................540 338-5323
Mark Miller, *President*
Kim Mikker, *Vice Pres*
EMP: 1
SALES (est): 150K **Privately Held**
SIC: 7692 Welding repair

(G-10685)
VETERANS CHOICE MED SUP LLC
38211 Highland Farm Pl (20132-9672)
PHONE....................571 244-4358
David Fries,
EMP: 1
SALES (est): 100.4K **Privately Held**
SIC: 3841 Surgical & medical instruments

(G-10686)
WALKERS WELDING
16560 Chstnut Overlook Dr (20132-2869)
PHONE....................214 779-0089
Kiecemon Walker, *Principal*
EMP: 1
SALES (est): 37.4K **Privately Held**
SIC: 7692 Welding repair

(G-10687)
WOLFSBANE INDUSTRIES LLC
37756 Drawbridge Way (20132-3189)
PHONE....................703 972-5072
EMP: 1
SALES (est): 54.6K **Privately Held**
SIC: 3999 Manufacturing industries

Quantico
Prince William County

(G-10688)
DLA DOCUMENT SERVICES
1001 Barnett Ave Code40 (22134-5102)
PHONE......................703 784-2208
EMP: 7 **Publicly Held**
WEB: www.documentservices.dla.mil
SIC: 2752 9711 Commercial printing, lithographic; national security;
HQ: Dla Document Services
5450 Carlisle Pike Bldg 9
Mechanicsburg PA 17050
717 605-2362

(G-10689)
JEAN LEE INC
Also Called: Quantico's Best
334 Potomac Ave (22134-3498)
PHONE......................703 630-0276
Sang Lee, *President*
Taehwan Lee, *General Mgr*
EMP: 3 **EST:** 2010
SALES (est): 80K **Privately Held**
WEB: www.quanticosbest.com
SIC: 2395 2211 Embroidery & art needlework; print cloths, cotton

(G-10690)
LION-VALLEY INDUSTRIES
1999 Hill Ave (22134-5141)
PHONE......................703 630-3123
EMP: 1
SALES (est): 58.5K **Privately Held**
SIC: 3999 Manufacturing industries

(G-10691)
SUMMIT DRONES INC
13159 Adams St (22134-4201)
PHONE......................724 961-9197
Zachary Herbison, *Principal*
EMP: 2
SALES (est): 119.5K **Privately Held**
WEB: www.flysummitdrones.com
SIC: 3721 Motorized aircraft

Quicksburg
Shenandoah County

(G-10692)
APPLE RIDGE PUBLISHERS
217 Bob White Ln (22847-1437)
PHONE......................703 597-8523
EMP: 1
SALES (est): 41.3K **Privately Held**
WEB: www.appleridgepublishers.com
SIC: 2741 Miscellaneous publishing

(G-10693)
POLKS LOGGING & LUMBER
2133 Pinewoods Rd (22847-1323)
PHONE......................540 477-3376
Robert Polk, *Owner*
EMP: 1
SALES (est): 121.3K **Privately Held**
SIC: 2411 Logging camps & contractors

Quinton
New Kent County

(G-10694)
DRIFTWOOD GALLERY
2800 Brianwood Ct (23141-1616)
P.O. Box 681 (23141-0681)
PHONE......................804 932-3318
John Brammer, *Owner*
EMP: 2
SALES (est): 108.3K **Privately Held**
SIC: 2499 Decorative wood & woodwork

(G-10695)
EPIC BOOKS PRESS
1921 Ellyson Ct (23141-1841)
PHONE......................804 557-3111
Kurt Herbel, *Principal*
EMP: 2
SALES (est): 59.2K **Privately Held**
SIC: 2741 Miscellaneous publishing

(G-10696)
HAISLIP FARMS LLC
2831 New Kent Hwy (23141-1737)
PHONE......................801 932-4087
Lawrence Haislip, *Vice Pres*
EMP: 1
SALES (est): 78.4K **Privately Held**
SIC: 3531 Drags, road (construction & road maintenance equipment)

(G-10697)
HARRIS CUSTOM WOODWORKING
1637 Arrowhead Rd (23141-1803)
PHONE......................804 241-9525
Thad Harris, *Owner*
EMP: 2
SALES (est): 200K **Privately Held**
SIC: 2599 Furniture & fixtures

(G-10698)
IDU OPTICS LLC
7012 N Hairpin Dr (23141-1541)
PHONE......................707 845-4996
Du Cheng, *Principal*
Paula Schanes,
EMP: 2 **EST:** 2015
SQ FT: 400
SALES (est): 20K **Privately Held**
WEB: www.ilabcam.com
SIC: 3827 Optical instruments & lenses

(G-10699)
RICHMOND RAMPS INC
7414 Club Dr (23141-1604)
PHONE......................804 932-8507
James Walker, *Principal*
EMP: 2
SALES (est): 122.6K **Privately Held**
WEB: www.richmondramps.com
SIC: 3999 Wheelchair lifts

(G-10700)
SWORD & SHIELD COACHING LLC
4105 Old Nottingham Rd (23141-2300)
PHONE......................804 557-3937
EMP: 1
SALES (est): 46.6K **Privately Held**
SIC: 3421 Mfg Cutlery

(G-10701)
VIRTUAL REALTY
7472 Pinehurst Dr (23141-1550)
PHONE......................757 718-2633
Preston Johnson, *Executive*
EMP: 2
SALES (est): 87.2K **Privately Held**
SIC: 3716 Motor homes

Radford
Radford City County

(G-10702)
ACE INDUSTRIES VIRGINIA LLC
609 E Main St Apt C (24141-1707)
PHONE......................757 292-3321
Aaron Davis, *Mng Member*
EMP: 1
SALES (est): 39.6K **Privately Held**
SIC: 3999 Manufacturing industries

(G-10703)
ALEXANDER INDUSTRIES INC (PA)
Also Called: Alexander Arms
Us Army Rdford Arsnal 104 (24141)
P.O. Box 1 (24143-0001)
PHONE......................540 443-9250
James Reddish, *President*
Melissa Spittle, *Opers Mgr*
Bill Alexander, *Officer*
EMP: 8
SQ FT: 2,500
SALES (est): 1MM **Privately Held**
WEB: www.alexanderarms.com
SIC: 3484 5099 Guns (firearms) or gun parts, 30 mm. & below; firearms, except sporting

(G-10704)
ASPEN MOTION TECHNOLOGIES INC
Also Called: Moog Aspen Motion Technologies
1120 W Rock Rd (24141-3362)
PHONE......................540 639-4440
Randall Hogan, *Ch of Bd*
Delton D Nickel, *President*
Phil Pejovich, *President*
Moe Barani, *Vice Pres*
Steve Chlupsa, *Vice Pres*
▲ **EMP:** 270
SQ FT: 68,000
SALES (est): 36.4MM
SALES (corp-wide): 2.8B **Publicly Held**
WEB: www.aspenmotiontech.com
SIC: 3621 Motors, electric
PA: Moog Inc.
400 Jamison Rd
Elma NY 14059
716 652-2000

(G-10705)
BALLPARK SIGNS INC
105 Harrison St (24141-1723)
PHONE......................540 239-7677
Michelle Beale, *President*
EMP: 2
SALES (est): 300K **Privately Held**
WEB: www.ballparksigns.com
SIC: 3993 Signs & advertising specialties

(G-10706)
CWI MARKETING & PRINTING
800 Wadsworth St (24141-2920)
PHONE......................540 295-5139
EMP: 2 **EST:** 2017
SALES (est): 83.9K **Privately Held**
SIC: 2752 Commercial printing, lithographic

(G-10707)
D & S TOOL INC
1303 W Main St (24141-1671)
P.O. Box 3246 (24143-3246)
PHONE......................540 731-1463
Charles Vest, *President*
EMP: 3
SALES (est): 243.1K **Privately Held**
SIC: 3545 3599 Precision tools, machinists'; machine shop, jobbing & repair

(G-10708)
D J R ENTERPRISES INC
Also Called: Trade Route International
1012 W Main St (24141-1663)
P.O. Box 3158 (24143-3158)
PHONE......................540 639-9386
Eleanor B McDaniel, *President*
David A McDaniel, *Vice Pres*
EMP: 14 **EST:** 1971
SQ FT: 18,000
SALES (est): 1MM **Privately Held**
WEB: www.djrpromo.com
SIC: 2395 5621 5136 5137 Embroidery & art needlework; women's sportswear; sportswear, men's & boys'; sportswear, women's & children's; screen printing

(G-10709)
DANAHER CORPORATION
501 W Main St (24141-1590)
PHONE......................540 639-9046
EMP: 3
SALES (est): 240.1K **Privately Held**
SIC: 3621 Motors & generators

(G-10710)
DANAHER MOTION
501 W Main St (24141-1590)
PHONE......................540 639-9046
EMP: 4 **EST:** 2019
SALES (est): 172.7K **Privately Held**
WEB: www.kollmorgen.com
SIC: 3621 Motors & generators

(G-10711)
DANNY COLTRANE
Also Called: Coltrane Welding & Fabrication
8259 Sawgrass Way (24141-6998)
PHONE......................540 629-3814
Danny Coltrane, *Owner*
EMP: 10
SQ FT: 5,000

SALES (est): 991.9K **Privately Held**
SIC: 3441 Fabricated structural metal

(G-10712)
EDDIES MIND INC
1000 Stockton St (24141-1728)
PHONE......................540 731-9304
Eddie Boes, *Principal*
EMP: 2
SALES (est): 248.8K **Privately Held**
WEB: www.eddiesmind.com
SIC: 3446 Architectural metalwork

(G-10713)
EMOTION US LLC
201 W Rock Rd (24141-4026)
PHONE......................540 639-9045
Michael Jellen, *General Mgr*
EMP: 14
SALES (est): 2.2MM **Privately Held**
SIC: 3621 Motors & generators
HQ: Zapi, Inc.
267 Hein Dr
Garner NC 27529
919 789-4588

(G-10714)
GAME QUEST INC
1085 E Main St (24141-1747)
PHONE......................540 639-6547
Robert F Roy, *President*
Annette Roy, *Vice Pres*
EMP: 3
SALES (est): 60K **Privately Held**
WEB: www.gamequestinc.com
SIC: 3944 5942 5945 Games, toys & children's vehicles; comic books; models, toy & hobby

(G-10715)
GREDE RADFORD LLC
1701 W Main St (24141-1684)
PHONE......................248 727-1800
David C Dauch, *Ch of Bd*
EMP: 72
SALES (est): 1.5MM
SALES (corp-wide): 683.9MM **Privately Held**
SIC: 3714 3711 Motor vehicle parts & accessories; motor vehicles & car bodies
HQ: Grede Ii Llc
20750 Civic Center Dr # 100
Southfield MI 48076
248 727-1800

(G-10716)
HUNTINGTON FOAM LLC
Also Called: Huntington Solutions Radva Div
604 17th St (24141-3423)
PHONE......................540 731-3700
Ed Flynn, *Branch Mgr*
EMP: 67 **Privately Held**
WEB: www.hunt-sol.com
SIC: 3086 2821 Packaging & shipping materials, foamed plastic; plastics materials & resins
PA: Huntington Foam, Llc
125 Caliber Ridge Dr # 200
Greer SC 29651

(G-10717)
INDUSTRIAL DRIVES
201 W Rock Rd (24141-4026)
PHONE......................540 639-2495
Willy Vergrugghe, *Principal*
EMP: 6
SALES (est): 783.2K **Privately Held**
SIC: 3621 Motors & generators

(G-10718)
JOHN A TREESE
Also Called: Custom Fab & Finish
4805 Shelburne Rd (24141-8061)
PHONE......................540 731-0250
John A Treese, *Owner*
EMP: 1
SALES (est): 25K **Privately Held**
WEB: www.cffpowder.com
SIC: 3479 Coating of metals & formed products

(G-10719)
JOHN E HILTON
1151 E Main St Ste A (24141-1761)
PHONE......................540 639-1674
J E Hilton Jr, *Principal*

EMP: 2
SALES (est): 249.4K Privately Held
WEB: www.radfordfamilydental.com
SIC: 3843 Enamels, dentists'

(G-10720)
KOLLMORGEN CORPORATION (HQ)
203a W Rock Rd (24141-4026)
PHONE..................................540 639-9045
Daniel Wen St Martin, *President*
Gary Matteson, *Regional Mgr*
James Davison, *Vice Pres*
Dennis Gallagher, *Vice Pres*
Tom Hill, *Vice Pres*
▲ EMP: 600 EST: 1916
SALES (est): 353.2MM
SALES (corp-wide): 1.8B Publicly Held
WEB: www.kollmorgen.com
SIC: 3825 3827 3861 3621 Test equipment for electronic & electrical circuits; periscopes; densitometers; servomotors, electric
PA: Altra Industrial Motion Corp.
300 Granite St Ste 201
Braintree MA 02184
781 917-0600

(G-10721)
KOLLMORGEN CORPORATION
501 W Main St (24141-1590)
PHONE..................................540 633-3536
Cliff Walters, *Area Mgr*
Jeanine St Pierre, *Buyer*
Peter Benoit, *Engineer*
Matt Frauenthal, *Engineer*
Jessie Rafferty, *Engineer*
EMP: 400
SQ FT: 140,000
SALES (corp-wide): 1.8B Publicly Held
WEB: www.kollmorgen.com
SIC: 3625 3621 3593 3651 Relays & industrial controls; motors, electric; fluid power cylinders & actuators; household audio & video equipment; search & navigation equipment
HQ: Kollmorgen Corporation
203a W Rock Rd
Radford VA 24141
540 639-9045

(G-10722)
KOLLMORGEN CORPORATION
Also Called: Danaher Motion
201 W Rock Rd (24141-4026)
PHONE..................................540 639-9045
John Boyland, *President*
Robert Caddick, *Vice Pres*
James Davison, *Vice Pres*
Dennis Gallagher, *Vice Pres*
Jeff Lemons, *Vice Pres*
EMP: 500
SALES (corp-wide): 1.8B Publicly Held
WEB: www.kollmorgen.com
SIC: 3621 Motors, electric
HQ: Kollmorgen Corporation
203a W Rock Rd
Radford VA 24141
540 639-9045

(G-10723)
KOLLMORGEN CORPORATION
Danaher Motion Acquisition Ctr
203a W Rock Rd (24141-4026)
PHONE..................................540 633-3400
John Flynn Jr, *Accountant*
Annette D Gorga, *Branch Mgr*
Robert Murphy, *Administration*
Raymond Testerman, *Maintence Staff*
EMP: 50
SALES (corp-wide): 1.8B Publicly Held
WEB: www.kollmorgen.com
SIC: 3621 Servomotors, electric
HQ: Kollmorgen Corporation
203a W Rock Rd
Radford VA 24141
540 639-9045

(G-10724)
METAL PROCESSING INC
6693 Viscoe Rd (24141-6903)
PHONE..................................540 731-0008
Kelley Nunley, *President*
Grace Nunley, *Admin Sec*
▲ EMP: 14

SALES (est): 2MM Privately Held
WEB: www.metal-processing.com
SIC: 3599 Machine shop, jobbing & repair

(G-10725)
MICROXACT INC
6580 Valley Center Dr # 312 (24141-5696)
PHONE..................................540 394-4040
Vladimir Kochergin, *President*
Elena Kochergina, *CFO*
Yelena Antipova, *Shareholder*
David Klein, *Shareholder*
David Lambeth, *Shareholder*
EMP: 8
SQ FT: 5,500
SALES: 705.6K Privately Held
WEB: www.microxact.com
SIC: 3825 8731 Test equipment for electronic & electric measurement; commercial physical research

(G-10726)
NEW RIVER CONCRETE SUPPLY CO
Also Called: Conrock
10 Forest Ave (24141)
PHONE..................................540 639-9679
EMP: 15
SALES (est): 1MM Privately Held
SIC: 3273 3272 Mfg Ready-Mixed Concrete Mfg Concrete Products

(G-10727)
NEW RIVER ENERGETICS INC (DH)
State Rte 114 (24143)
P.O. Box 6 (24143-0006)
PHONE..................................703 406-5695
Nicholas Vlchakis, *President*
EMP: 1
SALES (est): 316.2K Publicly Held
SIC: 2892 Gunpowder

(G-10728)
NIPPON PULSE AMERICA INC
4 Corporate Dr (24141-5100)
PHONE..................................540 633-1677
Mat Masuda, *President*
▲ EMP: 8 EST: 2002
SQ FT: 5,000
SALES (est): 1.4MM Privately Held
WEB: www.nipponpulse.com
SIC: 3621 Electric motor & generator parts; motors, electric
PA: Nippon Pulse Motor Co., Ltd.
2-16-13, Hongo
Bunkyo-Ku TKY 113-0

(G-10729)
NORTHROP GRMMAN INNVTION SYSTE
1304 Tyler Ave Apt G (24141-3842)
P.O. Box 1 (24143-0001)
PHONE..................................540 639-7631
Victor Wells, *Branch Mgr*
EMP: 7 Publicly Held
WEB: www.northropgrumman.com
SIC: 3764 Propulsion units for guided missiles & space vehicles
HQ: Northrop Grumman Innovation Systems, Inc.
45101 Warp Dr
Dulles VA 20166

(G-10730)
NORTHROP GRUMMAN CORPORATION
State Rte 114 (24143)
PHONE..................................703 406-5695
EMP: 2 Publicly Held
WEB: www.northropgrumman.com
SIC: 3812 Search & navigation equipment
PA: Northrop Grumman Corporation
2980 Fairview Park Dr
Falls Church VA 22042

(G-10731)
NORTHROP GRUMMAN INNOVATION
State Rte 114 (24141)
P.O. Box 6 (24143-0006)
PHONE..................................540 831-4788
David Thompson, *CEO*
M D McGregor, *General Mgr*
EMP: 14 Publicly Held

WEB: www.northropgrumman.com
SIC: 3812 Search & navigation equipment
HQ: Northrop Grumman Innovation Systems, Inc.
45101 Warp Dr
Dulles VA 20166

(G-10732)
NORTHROP GRUMMAN SYSTEMS CORP
Also Called: Weapons System Division
415 Cnstttion Rd Bldg 229 (24141)
PHONE..................................304 726-5030
Alice Reed, *Principal*
Matt Dillow, *Branch Mgr*
EMP: 4 Publicly Held
WEB: www.northropgrumman.com
SIC: 3812 Search & navigation equipment
HQ: Northrop Grumman Systems Corporation
2980 Fairview Park Dr
Falls Church VA 22042
703 280-2900

(G-10733)
PACIFIC SCIENTIFIC COMPANY
Motor Products Division
201 W Rock Rd (24141-4026)
PHONE..................................815 226-3100
EMP: 10
SQ FT: 8,000
SALES (corp-wide): 2.6B Privately Held
SIC: 3825 3823 3625 Mfg Process Cntrl Instr Mfg Relay/Indstl Control
HQ: Pacific Scientific Company Inc
1785 Voyager Ave
Simi Valley CA 93063
805 526-5700

(G-10734)
PATTERN SVCS & FABRICATION LLC
51 Wadsworth St (24141-1435)
PHONE..................................540 731-4891
Bill Sowers,
Calvin Hall,
EMP: 2
SQ FT: 7,300
SALES (est): 240K Privately Held
SIC: 3543 Foundry patternmaking

(G-10735)
PRS TOWING & RECOVERY
1422 W Main St (24141-1672)
PHONE..................................540 838-2388
EMP: 1
SALES (est): 37.5K Privately Held
SIC: 2741 Miscellaneous publishing

(G-10736)
PYROTECHNIQUE BY GRUCCI INC
Rfaap Rte 114 Pep Fer Rd (24143)
P.O. Box 1 (24143-0001)
PHONE..................................540 639-8800
Butler Donna Grucci, *Vice Pres*
Melanie Orey, *Purch Mgr*
Randall Sumner, *Manager*
EMP: 70
SALES (corp-wide): 38.5MM Privately Held
WEB: www.grucci.com
SIC: 2899 2892 Flares, fireworks & similar preparations; explosives
PA: Pyrotechnique By Grucci, Inc.
20 Pinehurst Dr
Bellport NY 11713
631 286-0088

(G-10737)
RADFORD WLDG & FABRICATION LLC
Also Called: Calvin G. Hall
500 Unruh Dr (24141-1534)
PHONE..................................540 731-4891
Calvin Hall,
EMP: 1 EST: 2016
SQ FT: 1,500 Privately Held
WEB: www.radfordwelding.com

WEB: www.northropgrumman.com
SIC: 3812 Search & navigation equipment
HQ: Northrop Grumman Innovation Systems, Inc.
45101 Warp Dr
Dulles VA 20166

SIC: 7692 3548 2899 3441 Welding repair; cracked casting repair; arc welding generators, alternating current & direct current; spot welding apparatus, electric; fluxes: brazing, soldering, galvanizing & welding; building components, structural steel

(G-10738)
RIVER COMPANY REST & BREWRY I
6580 Valley Center Dr # 322 (24141-5691)
PHONE..................................540 633-6731
Mark Hall, *Principal*
EMP: 4
SALES (est): 146.9K Privately Held
WEB: www.rivercobeef.com
SIC: 2082 Malt beverages

(G-10739)
S&S ELECTRIC MOTOR SERVICE INC
6784 Beach Dr (24141-8318)
PHONE..................................540 577-7366
EMP: 6 EST: 2017
SALES (est): 574.7K Privately Held
SIC: 7694 Electric motor repair

(G-10740)
TECHLAB INC
20 Corporate Dr (24141-5100)
PHONE..................................540 953-1664
Charlie Pennington, *Branch Mgr*
EMP: 65
SALES (corp-wide): 44.2MM Privately Held
WEB: www.techlab.com
SIC: 3821 Laboratory apparatus & furniture
HQ: Techlab, Inc.
2001 Kraft Dr
Blacksburg VA 24060

(G-10741)
THE CITY OF RADFORD
Also Called: Water Treatment Plant
20 Forest Ave (24141-4411)
PHONE..................................540 731-3662
Lawrence Rice, *Director*
EMP: 12
SALES (corp-wide): 27.1MM Privately Held
WEB: www.radfordva.gov
SIC: 3589 9111 Sewage & water treatment equipment; city & town managers' offices
PA: The City Of Radford
10 Robertson St
Radford VA 24141
540 731-5501

(G-10742)
THERMASTEEL INC
609 W Rock Rd (24141-4034)
PHONE..................................540 633-5000
ADI Ben-Senior, *CEO*
EMP: 3
SALES (est): 541.4K Privately Held
WEB: www.thermasteelinc.com
SIC: 3441 Fabricated structural metal

(G-10743)
THERMASTEEL RP LTD
609 W Rock Rd (24141-4034)
PHONE..................................540 633-5000
Donald Hanshew, *General Mgr*
EMP: 2
SALES (est): 323.2K Privately Held
WEB: www.thermasteelinc.com
SIC: 3444 Sheet metalwork

(G-10744)
THIRD SECURITY RNR LLC
1881 Grove Ave (24141-1628)
PHONE..................................540 633-7900
Randal J Kirk, *Mng Member*
EMP: 6 EST: 1999
SALES (est): 710.7K Privately Held
WEB: www.thirdsecurity.com
SIC: 2834 Pharmaceutical preparations

(G-10745)
THOMSON INDUSTRIES INC
203a W Rock Rd (24141-4026)
PHONE..................................540 633-3549
Ellen Hollingsworth, *Engineer*
Greg Elter, *Finance*

▲ = Import ▼=Export
◆ =Import/Export

Ann Svederborn, *Human Res Mgr*
Greg Goetz, *Accounts Mgr*
Kyle Stephens, *Accounts Mgr*
EMP: 2
SALES (est): 100.3K **Privately Held**
WEB: www.thomsonlinear.com
SIC: 3599 Industrial machinery

(G-10746)
TSC CORPORATION
609 W Rock Rd (24141-4034)
PHONE.................................540 633-5000
Tuncer Mary Mills, *President*
Kaya Tuncer, *President*
▼ **EMP:** 25
SALES (est): 4.7MM **Privately Held**
SIC: 3448 Prefabricated metal buildings

Randolph
Charlotte County

(G-10747)
CHARLOTTE PRINTING LLC
22950 Kings Hwy (23962-4001)
PHONE.................................434 738-7155
Walter David Tucker, *Administration*
EMP: 2 **EST:** 2017
SALES (est): 101K **Privately Held**
SIC: 2752 Commercial printing, offset

(G-10748)
FOSTER LOGGING
6121 Clover Rd (23962-3009)
PHONE.................................434 454-7946
Jeffrey Foster, *Principal*
EMP: 6
SALES (est): 551.6K **Privately Held**
SIC: 2411 Logging camps & contractors

Raphine
Rockbridge County

(G-10749)
**GOOSE CREEK WOODWORKS
LLC**
579 Davis Rd (24472-2308)
PHONE.................................540 348-4163
Spencer A Golladay, *Owner*
EMP: 2 **EST:** 2009
SALES (est): 133.8K **Privately Held**
SIC: 2431 Millwork

(G-10750)
ROCKBRIDGE VINEYARD INC
35 Hillview Ln (24472-2403)
PHONE.................................540 377-6204
Parke Shepherd Rouse III, *President*
Elizabeth Jane Millott-Rouse, *Vice Pres*
EMP: 12
SQ FT: 4,000
SALES (est): 400K **Privately Held**
WEB: www.rockbridgevineyard.com
SIC: 2084 Wines

(G-10751)
WADES MILL INC
Also Called: Wades Flour Mill
55 Kennedy Wdes Mill Loop (24472-2107)
PHONE.................................540 348-1400
Jim F Young, *President*
Georgiana Young, *Treasurer*
EMP: 4
SQ FT: 6,000
SALES (est): 100K **Privately Held**
WEB: www.wadesmill.com
SIC: 2041 5719 5947 Flour; kitchenware;
gift shop

(G-10752)
WESTROCK MWV LLC
Also Called: Cdc Lofton Warehouse
271 Lofton Rd (24472-2800)
PHONE.................................540 377-9745
Will Author, *Branch Mgr*
EMP: 70
SALES (corp-wide): 17.5B **Publicly Held**
WEB: www.westrock.com
SIC: 2631 Paperboard mills

HQ: Westrock Mwv, Llc
501 S 5th St
Richmond VA 23219
804 444-1000

Rapidan
Culpeper County

(G-10753)
LEGACY VULCAN LLC
11454 Quarry Dr (22733)
PHONE.................................800 732-3964
EMP: 4 **Publicly Held**
WEB: www.vulcanmaterials.com
SIC: 3273 Ready-mixed concrete
HQ: Legacy Vulcan, Llc
1200 Urban Center Dr
Vestavia AL 35242
205 298-3000

(G-10754)
VIRGINIA MIST GRANITE CORP
11235 Muddy Bottom Ln (22733-2335)
PHONE.................................540 661-0030
Fabrizio Ponzanelli, *Principal*
▲ **EMP:** 3
SALES (est): 314.9K **Privately Held**
SIC: 1411 Granite dimension stone

(G-10755)
VIRGINIA MIST GROUP INC
11235 Muddy Bottom Ln (22733-2335)
PHONE.................................540 661-0030
Marc Lalancette, *Vice Pres*
▲ **EMP:** 18
SALES (est): 2.4MM **Privately Held**
WEB: www.virginiamist.com
SIC: 1411 Granite, dimension-quarrying

Raven
Buchanan County

(G-10756)
**KNOX CREEK COAL
CORPORATION**
2295 Gvrnor G C Pery Hwy (24639)
PHONE.................................276 964-4333
David Kramer, *President*
Richard H Verheij, *Vice Pres*
Tony Honaker, *Purchasing*
EMP: 450
SALES (est): 28.7MM
SALES (corp-wide): 2.2B **Publicly Held**
SIC: 1222 Bituminous coal-underground
mining
HQ: Appalachia Holding Company
1 Alpha Pl
Bristol VA 24202
276 619-4410

(G-10757)
SILVER SPUR CONVEYORS
578 Raven Rd (24639)
P.O. Box 1327, Cedar Bluff (24609-1327)
PHONE.................................276 596-9414
Greg Smith, *President*
▲ **EMP:** 6
SQ FT: 100,000
SALES (est): 861.2K **Privately Held**
WEB: www.silverspurconveyor.com
SIC: 3496 Conveyor belts

(G-10758)
SKYLINE FABRICATING INC
1112 Contrary Creek Rd (24639-8646)
P.O. Box 663, Oakwood (24631-0663)
PHONE.................................276 498-3560
Kenneth Horne, *President*
EMP: 2
SALES (est): 99.9K **Privately Held**
SIC: 3317 3353 7692 3548 Conduit:
welded, lock joint or heavy riveted; tubes,
wrought: welded or lock joint; tubes,
welded, aluminum; automotive welding;
electric welding equipment

Red Oak
Charlotte County

(G-10759)
**MORGAN LUMBER COMPANY
INC**
628 Jeb Stuart Hwy (23964)
P.O. Box 25 (23964-0025)
PHONE.................................434 735-8151
John W Morgan, *President*
Julian K Morgan Jr, *President*
Clarissa Ferrell, *Vice Pres*
J Kenneth Morgan Jr, *Treasurer*
Mary R Morgan, *Treasurer*
EMP: 48
SQ FT: 1,000
SALES (est): 13.1MM **Privately Held**
WEB: www.morganlumber.com
SIC: 2421 Planing mills

(G-10760)
SOUTHSIDE UTILITIES & MAINT
1839 Jeb Stuart Hwy (23964-3068)
P.O. Box 23 (23964-0023)
PHONE.................................434 735-8853
EMP: 20
SALES (est): 1.9MM **Privately Held**
SIC: 2491 Treatment And Inspection Of
Poles

Reedville
Northumberland County

(G-10761)
FLEETON MACHINE WORKS INC
890 Main St (22539-4427)
PHONE.................................804 453-6130
John E Shelton, *President*
EMP: 2 **EST:** 1921
SQ FT: 5,000
SALES (est): 242K **Privately Held**
SIC: 3599 Machine shop, jobbing & repair

(G-10762)
JENNINGS BOAT YARD INC
169 Boatyard Rd (22539-4315)
PHONE.................................804 453-7181
John L Jennings, *President*
Sharon E Jennings, *Treasurer*
EMP: 4
SALES (est): 407.8K **Privately Held**
SIC: 3732 Fishing boats: lobster, crab, oys-
ter, etc.: small

(G-10763)
OMEGA PROTEIN INC (DH)
Also Called: Nutegrity Northumberland Co
610 Menhaden Rd (22539-4126)
PHONE.................................804 453-6262
Bret D Scholtes, *CEO*
Gary R Goodwin, *Ch of Bd*
Matthew Phillips, *President*
◆ **EMP:** 50
SALES (est): 13.7MM
SALES (corp-wide): 268.6MM **Privately
Held**
WEB: www.omegaprotein.com
SIC: 2077 Fish oil
HQ: Omega Protein Corporation
610 Menhaden Rd
Reedville VA 22539
804 453-6262

(G-10764)
OMEGA PROTEIN INC
Also Called: Omega Prtein - Hlth Scence Ctr
243 Menhaden Rd (22539-4124)
PHONE.................................804 453-4923
Jane Crowther, *Branch Mgr*
EMP: 1
SALES (corp-wide): 268.6MM **Privately
Held**
WEB: www.omegaprotein.com
SIC: 2077 Fish oil
HQ: Omega Protein, Inc.
610 Menhaden Rd
Reedville VA 22539
804 453-6262

(G-10765)
**OMEGA PROTEIN
CORPORATION (HQ)**
610 Menhaden Rd (22539-4126)
PHONE.................................804 453-6262
Bret D Scholtes, *President*
Scott Springwer, *General Mgr*
John D Held, *Exec VP*
John Held, *Exec VP*
Montgomery Deihl, *Vice Pres*
◆ **EMP:** 50
SALES (est): 235.7MM
SALES (corp-wide): 268.6MM **Privately
Held**
WEB: www.omegaprotein.com
SIC: 2077 5199 Fish meal, except as ani-
mal feed; fish oil; oils, animal or vegetable
PA: Cooke Inc
669 Main St
Blacks Harbour NB E5H 1
506 456-6600

(G-10766)
PLUM SUMMER LLC
110 Whaley Ln (22539-3401)
P.O. Box 476, Burgess (22432-0476)
PHONE.................................804 519-0009
Carol A Muratore, *Principal*
EMP: 2
SALES (est): 193.2K **Privately Held**
WEB: www.plumsummer.com
SIC: 2591 Drapery hardware & blinds &
shades

Remington
Fauquier County

(G-10767)
CANAM UWH
23231 Hubbards Rd (22734-1803)
PHONE.................................906 399-7857
David Kennedy, *Principal*
EMP: 1
SALES (est): 53.1K **Privately Held**
WEB: www.canamuwhgear.com
SIC: 3949 Sporting & athletic goods

(G-10768)
DK CONSULTING LLC
Also Called: Canam Underwater Hockey
Gear
23231 Hubbards Rd (22734-1803)
PHONE.................................224 402-3333
David Kennedy, *Mng Member*
EMP: 2
SALES (est): 122.6K **Privately Held**
WEB: www.canamuwhgear.com
SIC: 3949 Hockey equipment & supplies,
general

(G-10769)
MJS WOODWORKING LLC
7083 Helm Dr (22734-9415)
PHONE.................................571 233-4991
Joseph Spina, *Principal*
EMP: 1 **EST:** 2017
SALES (est): 54.1K **Privately Held**
SIC: 2431 Millwork

(G-10770)
MOOTHRU LLC
11402 James Madison Hwy (22734-2101)
PHONE.................................540 439-6455
Kenneth Smith, *President*
Ken Smith, *General Mgr*
Emily Julian, *Opers Staff*
EMP: 5
SALES (est): 189.1K **Privately Held**
WEB: www.moothru.com
SIC: 2024 5963 5812 Ice cream, pack-
aged: molded, on sticks, etc.; ice cream
wagon; snack bar

(G-10771)
QUADD INC
Also Called: Quadd Building Systems
11610 Lucky Hill Rd (22734-9460)
PHONE.................................540 439-2148
Jimmy E Defnall, *President*
Shawn Hyson, *General Mgr*
Lynne Defnall, *Treasurer*
John Defnall, *Supervisor*
EMP: 9

GEOGRAPHIC

SQ FT: 60,000
SALES (est): 535K **Privately Held**
WEB: www.quaddbs.com
SIC: 2439 5211 Trusses, wooden roof;
concrete & cinder block

(G-10772)
QUADD BUILDING SYSTEMS LLC
11610 Lucky Hill Rd (22734-9460)
PHONE.....................................540 439-2148
Jim Defnall, *President*
Kenny Shiffled, *Mng Member*
Shawn Hyson, *Manager*
EMP: 50
SALES (est): 169K **Privately Held**
WEB: www.quaddbs.com
SIC: 2439 5031 5211 Trusses, wooden
roof; lumber, plywood & millwork; roofing
material

(G-10773)
THREAT PROT WRD WIDE SVCS LLC
6997 Justin Ct E (22734-9464)
P.O. Box 110, Herndon (20172-0110)
PHONE.....................................703 795-2445
Mark Schmidt,
Brian Ferguson,
John Savelsberg,
EMP: 3 EST: 2013
SALES (est): 178K **Privately Held**
WEB: www.tp-ws.com
SIC: 3795 7536 Specialized tank compo-
nents, military; automotive glass replace-
ment shops

(G-10774)
TRADITIONAL IRON & WOODWORKING
12636 Tin Pot Run Ln (22734-9691)
P.O. Box 203 (22734-0203)
PHONE.....................................540 439-6911
Charles R Walker, *Owner*
EMP: 1
SALES (est): 94.6K **Privately Held**
SIC: 2499 Decorative wood & woodwork

(G-10775)
U S PIPE FABRICATION
11622 Lucky Hill Rd (22734-9460)
PHONE.....................................540 439-7373
George Lewis, *Manager*
EMP: 10
SALES (est): 1.4MM **Privately Held**
WEB: www.uspipe.com
SIC: 3498 Fabricated pipe & fittings

(G-10776)
UNITED STATES PIPE FNDRY LLC
11622 Lucky Hill Rd (22734-9460)
PHONE.....................................540 439-7373
Sean Sullivan, *Branch Mgr*
▲ EMP: 10
SALES (corp-wide): 1.5B **Publicly Held**
WEB: www.uspipe.com
SIC: 3498 Tube fabricating (contract bend-
ing & shaping)
HQ: United States Pipe And Foundry Com-
pany Llc
2 Chase Corporate Dr # 200
Hoover AL 35244
205 263-8540

Reston
Fairfax County

(G-10777)
ACTIVE NAVIGATION INC
11720 Plaza America Dr # 150
(20190-6709)
PHONE.....................................571 346-7607
Peter Baumann, *President*
John Cofrancesco, *President*
Steve Matthews, *Principal*
Rich Hale, *CTO*
Dean Gonsowski, *Risk Mgmt Dir*
EMP: 12

SALES (est): 4MM
SALES (corp-wide): 4.3MM **Privately Held**
WEB: www.activenavigation.com
SIC: 7372 Business oriented computer
software
PA: Data Discovery Solutions Ltd
St Georges Chambers
Winchester HANTS SO23
196 228-0161

(G-10778)
ADNET SYSTEMS INC
11260 Roger Bacon Dr # 403 (20190-5227)
PHONE.....................................571 313-1356
Ashok Jha, *Branch Mgr*
EMP: 10 **Privately Held**
WEB: www.adnet-sys.com
SIC: 7372 Prepackaged software
PA: Adnet Systems, Inc.
6720b Rockledge Dr # 504
Bethesda MD 20817

(G-10779)
AEH DESIGNS
10721 Oldfield Dr (20191-5215)
PHONE.....................................703 860-3204
Anna Hayoz, *Owner*
EMP: 1
SALES (est): 59.5K **Privately Held**
SIC: 2273 Art squares, textile fiber

(G-10780)
AGMA LLC
12158 Chancery Stn Cir (20190-5803)
PHONE.....................................703 689-3458
Anurag Sharma, *Principal*
EMP: 3
SALES (est): 92.2K **Privately Held**
WEB: www.agma.glass
SIC: 2711 Newspapers

(G-10781)
AGUSTAWESTLANDBELL LLC
11700 Plaza America Dr # 900
(20190-4751)
PHONE.....................................703 373-1613
Cathy Wong, *Controller*
Robert Labell, *Mng Member*
Cymele Founders, *Manager*
Mike Nuwell,
EMP: 2
SALES (est): 25K
SALES (corp-wide): 9.9B **Privately Held**
SIC: 3721 Aircraft
HQ: Agustawestland North America, Inc.
2345 Crystal Dr Ste 906
Arlington VA 22202
703 373-8000

(G-10782)
AIGIS BLAST PROTECTION
11710 Plaza America Dr # 2000
(20190-4742)
PHONE.....................................703 871-5173
Eamonn Cooney, *President*
EMP: 3
SALES (est): 250.1K **Privately Held**
SIC: 3443 Fabricated plate work (boiler
shop)

(G-10783)
AKAMAI TECHNOLOGIES INC
11111 Sunset Hills Rd # 250 (20190-5374)
PHONE.....................................877 425-2624
John Bean, *Accounts Exec*
Blair Vorgang, *Branch Mgr*
Nick Marcou, *Manager*
Jonathan Anderson, *Technology*
Sopha Dos, *Database Admin*
EMP: 20 **Publicly Held**
WEB: www.akamai.com
SIC: 7372 Prepackaged software
PA: Akamai Technologies, Inc.
145 Broadway
Cambridge MA 02142
617 444-3000

(G-10784)
ALLEN WATSON
Also Called: Innovative Industries
11017 Howland Dr (20191-4912)
PHONE.....................................703 620-5350
Allen Watson, *Owner*
EMP: 4

SALES (est): 181.3K **Privately Held**
SIC: 3089 Plastics products

(G-10785)
ALVARIAN PRESS
11517 Olde Tiverton Cir (20194-1922)
PHONE.....................................703 864-8018
Thomas Kurek, *Principal*
EMP: 2
SALES (est): 62.9K **Privately Held**
SIC: 2711 Newspapers

(G-10786)
AMERICAN INST ARNTICS ASTRNTIC (PA)
Also Called: AIAA
12700 Sunrise Valley Dr # 2 (20191-5805)
PHONE.....................................703 264-7500
John S Langford, *President*
Rich Hem, *Managing Dir*
Ben Iannotta, *Chief*
William Seymore, *Treasurer*
Michele McDonald, *Corp Comm Staff*
EMP: 72
SQ FT: 16,600
SALES: 22.3MM **Privately Held**
WEB: www.aiaa.org
SIC: 2731 Books: publishing only

(G-10787)
AMERICAN RHEINMETALL DEF INC (PA)
11180 Sunrise Valley Dr (20191-5464)
PHONE.....................................571 867-0047
Stephen Hedger, *President*
Patrick Thoms, *Manager*
EMP: 3
SALES (est): 9MM **Privately Held**
WEB: www.rheinmetall.com
SIC: 3827 Optical instruments & lenses

(G-10788)
ANNANDALE TIMES
1760 Reston Pkwy (20190-3388)
PHONE.....................................703 437-5400
EMP: 2
SALES (est): 71K **Privately Held**
SIC: 2711 Newspapers, publishing & print-
ing

(G-10789)
ANNOAI INC
11951 Freedom Dr Fl 15 (20190-5640)
PHONE.....................................571 490-5316
Steven Witt, *CEO*
Michael Mohamed, *President*
EMP: 6
SALES (est): 78.2K **Privately Held**
SIC: 7372 7389 Application computer soft-
ware;

(G-10790)
ANTHEON SOLUTIONS INC
1712 Clubhouse Rd Ste 122 (20190-4502)
PHONE.....................................703 298-1891
Hermia Johnson, *CEO*
Gregory Sieber, *CFO*
EMP: 1
SALES (est): 32.7K **Privately Held**
SIC: 7372 7373 8742 8748 Application
computer software; systems engineering,
computer related; business consultant;
systems engineering consultant, ex. computer or professional; custom computer
programming services

(G-10791)
ARHAT MEDIA INC
11901 Escalante Ct (20191-1833)
PHONE.....................................703 716-5662
Robert Hand, *Principal*
EMP: 1 EST: 2011
SALES (est): 52.6K **Privately Held**
WEB: www.arhatmedia.com
SIC: 2741 Miscellaneous publishing

(G-10792)
ASCALON INTERNATIONAL INC
11951 Freedom Dr Fl 13 (20190-5686)
PHONE.....................................703 926-4343
Michael Mulcahy, *CEO*
EMP: 1
SALES (est): 61.5K **Privately Held**
SIC: 2842 Disinfectants, household or in-
dustrial plant

(G-10793)
ASSOCIATION FOR PRINT TECH
1899 Preston White Dr (20191-5458)
PHONE.....................................703 264-7200
EMP: 2
SALES (est): 64.5K **Privately Held**
WEB: www.printtechnologies.org
SIC: 2396 Fabric printing & stamping

(G-10794)
ATHENAS WORKSHOP INC
11115 Glade Dr (20191-4706)
PHONE.....................................703 615-4429
Helen Levy-Myers, *CEO*
EMP: 2
SALES (est): 141.5K **Privately Held**
WEB: www.athenasworkshop.com
SIC: 7372 Application computer software

(G-10795)
AVOID EVADE COUNTER LLC
2332 Archdale Rd (20191-1602)
PHONE.....................................703 593-1951
George H Danzer, *Administration*
EMP: 3
SALES (est): 206.5K **Privately Held**
SIC: 3131 Counters

(G-10796)
AXON MEDCHEM LLC
12020 Sunrise Valley Dr (20191-3440)
PHONE.....................................703 650-9359
EMP: 7
SALES (est): 627.4K **Privately Held**
WEB: www.axonmedchem.com
SIC: 2834 Pharmaceutical preparations

(G-10797)
BAE SYSTEMS INFO & ELEC SYS
Also Called: Cnir
11487 Sunset Hills Rd (20190-5228)
PHONE.....................................703 668-4000
Thomas N Maxwell, *Engineer*
Leonard Digregorio, *Director*
Alaina Hacker, *Analyst*
EMP: 200
SALES (corp-wide): 23.6B **Privately Held**
WEB: www.baesystems.com
SIC: 3812 Search & navigation equipment
HQ: Bae Systems Information And Elec-
tronic Systems Integration Inc.
65 Spit Brook Rd
Nashua NH 03060
603 885-4321

(G-10798)
BEST SOFTWARE INC
11413 Isaac Newton Sq S (20190-5005)
PHONE.....................................949 753-1222
Lia McChesney, *Principal*
Judy Stucki, *Executive Asst*
EMP: 2
SALES (est): 134.8K **Privately Held**
SIC: 7372 Prepackaged software

(G-10799)
BIBLE BELIEVERS PRESS
11692 Generation Ct (20191-3028)
P.O. Box 3333 (20195-1333)
PHONE.....................................703 476-0125
EMP: 2
SALES (est): 59.2K **Privately Held**
SIC: 2741 Miscellaneous publishing

(G-10800)
BIZWHAZEE LLC
11600 Sunrise Valley Dr # 300
(20191-1412)
PHONE.....................................703 889-8499
EMP: 2
SALES (est): 90K **Privately Held**
WEB: www.bizwhazee.com
SIC: 7372 Prepackaged software

(G-10801)
BLACKBOARD CONNECT INC
11720 Plaza America Dr # 11 (20190-4757)
PHONE.....................................919 841-0175
John Diaz, *Vice Pres*
EMP: 5 **Privately Held**
WEB: www.blackboardconnect.com
SIC: 7372 Business oriented computer
software

HQ: Blackboard Connect Inc.
1111 19th St Nw Fl 9
Washington DC
202 303-9000

(G-10802)
BLACKBOARD HOLDINGS INC
11720 Plaza America Dr # 6 (20190-6705)
PHONE.....................202 463-4860
William Ballhaus, *Principal*
EMP: 2379
SALES (est): 276.6MM **Privately Held**
SIC: 7372 6719 Educational computer
software; investment holding companies,
except banks
HQ: Blackboard Super Holdco, Inc
11720 Plaza America Dr # 11
Reston VA 20190
202 463-4860

(G-10803)
BLACKBOARD INC (HQ)
11720 Plaza America Dr # 11 (20190-4757)
PHONE.....................202 463-4860
William L Ballhaus, *CEO*
Lee Blakemore, *President*
Mark Gruzin, *President*
Kevin Guyton, *Vice Pres*
Mike Neuhauser, *Vice Pres*
EMP: 175
SQ FT: 134,000
SALES (est): 280.6MM **Privately Held**
WEB: www.blackboard.com
SIC: 7372 Educational computer software;
business oriented computer software

(G-10804)
BLACKBOARD INC
11720 Plaza America Dr # 11 (20190-4757)
PHONE.....................512 474-8363
EMP: 3 **Privately Held**
WEB: www.blackboard.com
SIC: 7372 Business oriented computer
software
HQ: Blackboard Inc.
11720 Plaza America Dr # 11
Reston VA 20190
202 463-4860

(G-10805)
BLACKBOARD INC
11720 Plaza America Dr # 11 (20190-4757)
PHONE.....................254 251-3203
George Guidry, *Professor*
EMP: 4 **Privately Held**
WEB: www.blackboard.com
SIC: 7372 Business oriented computer
software
HQ: Blackboard Inc.
11720 Plaza America Dr # 11
Reston VA 20190
202 463-4860

(G-10806)
BLACKBOARD INC
1807 Michael Faraday Ct (20190-5303)
PHONE.....................202 463-4860
Jason Niesz, *Branch Mgr*
EMP: 4 **Privately Held**
WEB: www.blackboard.com
SIC: 7372 Educational computer software
HQ: Blackboard Inc.
11720 Plaza America Dr # 11
Reston VA 20190
202 463-4860

(G-10807)
BLACKBOARD SUPER HOLDCO INC (HQ)
11720 Plaza America Dr # 11 (20190-4757)
PHONE.....................202 463-4860
William Ballhaus, *Principal*
EMP: 3
SALES (est): 24.1MM **Privately Held**
SIC: 7372 6719 Educational computer
software; investment holding companies,
except banks

(G-10808)
BLEHERT
11919 Moss Point Ln (20194-1728)
PHONE.....................703 471-7907
Pamela Blehert, *Principal*
EMP: 2 EST: 2009

SALES (est): 94.6K **Privately Held**
WEB: www.blehert.com
SIC: 2741 Miscellaneous publishing

(G-10809)
BLIND INDUSTRIES
12310 Sunrise Valley Dr (20190-3414)
PHONE.....................703 390-9221
Marcus Taylor, *President*
EMP: 1
SALES (est): 70.1K **Privately Held**
WEB: www.bism.org
SIC: 3999 Manufacturing industries

(G-10810)
BOEHRINGER INGELHEIM CORP
1780 Business Center Dr (20190-5318)
PHONE.....................703 759-0630
Paul Boehringer, *Branch Mgr*
EMP: 4
SALES (corp-wide): 21B **Privately Held**
WEB: www.boehringer-ingelheim.com
SIC: 2834 Pharmaceutical preparations
HQ: Boehringer Ingelheim Corporation
900 Ridgebury Rd
Ridgefield CT 06877
203 798-9988

(G-10811)
BOEING COMPANY
11720 Sunrise Valley Dr (20191-1444)
PHONE.....................571 814-4103
Marilyn K Riseley, *President*
Kevin Mastropaolo, *Engineer*
Adam Roberts, *Engineer*
Terry Saylor, *Engineer*
Catherine Case, *Business Anlyst*
EMP: 258
SALES (corp-wide): 76.5B **Publicly Held**
WEB: www.boeing.com
SIC: 3721 Aircraft
PA: The Boeing Company
100 N Riverside Plz
Chicago IL 60606
312 544-2000

(G-10812)
BRITEMOVES LLC
1900 Campus Commons Dr (20191-1561)
PHONE.....................703 629-6391
Judy White, *Sales Staff*
Terry Saeger, *Exec Dir*
Deborah Lanuti, *Director*
Leslie Fuller, *Administration*
EMP: 12
SALES (est): 500K **Privately Held**
WEB: www.nterone.com
SIC: 3993 Signs & advertising specialties

(G-10813)
BULLETIN NEWS NETWORK INC
Also Called: Bulletinnews
11190 Sunrise Valley Dr # 20 (20191-4393)
PHONE.....................703 749-0040
Paul D Roellig, *President*
Erik McGunnigle, *Vice Pres*
EMP: 48
SALES (est): 2.9MM **Privately Held**
WEB: www.bulletinmedia.com
SIC: 2741 2711 Miscellaneous publishing;
newspapers

(G-10814)
CACI NSS INC
Also Called: Stratis Division
11955 Fredom Dr Ste 12000 (20190)
PHONE.....................703 434-4000
Anthony Smeraglinolo, *CEO*
EMP: 33 **Publicly Held**
WEB: www.l3asa.com
SIC: 3663 Radio & TV communications
equipment
HQ: Caci Nss, Llc
11955 Freedom Dr Fl 2
Reston VA 20190
703 434-4000

(G-10815)
CACI PRODUCTS COMPANY
2100 Reston Pkwy Ste 500 (20191-1235)
PHONE.....................973 437-9800
J Mengucci, *Branch Mgr*
EMP: 3 **Publicly Held**
SIC: 7372 8742 Prepackaged software;
management consulting services

HQ: Caci Products Company
1100 N Glebe Rd Ste 200
Arlington VA 22201

(G-10816)
CANVAS SOLUTIONS INC (PA)
11911 Freedom Dr Ste 850 (20190-6243)
PHONE.....................703 436-8069
James Quigley, *CEO*
Michael Benedict, *Vice Pres*
Reggie Gaither, *Vice Pres*
Joseph Gatto, *Vice Pres*
Jason Good, *Vice Pres*
EMP: 4
SALES (est): 1.4MM **Privately Held**
WEB: www.gocanvas.com
SIC: 7372 Application computer software

(G-10817)
CANVAS SOLUTIONS INC
1801 Old Reston Ave (20190-3389)
PHONE.....................703 564-8564
EMP: 1 EST: 2012
SALES (est): 48K **Privately Held**
SIC: 2211 Cotton Broadwoven Fabric Mill

(G-10818)
CARDINAL CONTROL SYSTEMS INC
1529 Park Glen Ct (20190-4913)
PHONE.....................703 437-0437
Martin Dapot, *President*
Susan Dapot, *Admin Sec*
▲ EMP: 9
SQ FT: 1,500
SALES (est): 1.2MM **Privately Held**
WEB: www.cardinalcontrolsystems.com
SIC: 3625 Electric controls & control ac-
cessories, industrial

(G-10819)
CAREFUSION SOLUTIONS LLC
12120 Sunset Hills Rd # 300 (20190-3231)
PHONE.....................571 521-8900
Kenneth Tighe, *Branch Mgr*
EMP: 50 **Publicly Held**
WEB: www.bd.com
SIC: 3841 Surgical & medical instruments
HQ: Carefusion Solutions, Llc
3750 Torrey View Ct
San Diego CA 92130

(G-10820)
CEE CORPORATION
11250 Roger Bacon Dr 2a (20190-5202)
PHONE.....................571 526-4447
EMP: 2
SALES (est): 116.1K **Privately Held**
WEB: www.ceesl.com
SIC: 3652 Pre-recorded records & tapes

(G-10821)
CHARLIE MOSELEY
11400 Washington Plz W # 102
(20190-4306)
PHONE.....................571 235-3206
EMP: 2 EST: 2011
SQ FT: 21,000
SALES (est): 70.8K **Privately Held**
SIC: 3944 Mfg Games/Toys

(G-10822)
COLIN K EAGEN
1893 Preston White Dr (20191-5470)
PHONE.....................703 716-7505
Colin K Eagen, *Principal*
EMP: 1
SALES (est): 73.1K **Privately Held**
WEB: www.starproducts.com
SIC: 1311 Crude petroleum & natural gas

(G-10823)
COMMUNICATIONS-APPLIED TECH CO (PA)
11250 Roger Bacon Dr # 14 (20190-5202)
PHONE.....................703 481-0068
Seth Leyman, *President*
Rona Leyman, *Treasurer*
▼ EMP: 17
SQ FT: 2,000
SALES (est): 2.4MM **Privately Held**
WEB: www.c-at.com
SIC: 3663 Satellites, communications

(G-10824)
COMSCORE INC (PA)
11950 Democracy Dr # 600 (20190-5653)
PHONE.....................703 438-2000
Bill Livek, *CEO*
Brent D Rosenthal, *Ch of Bd*
Sarah Hofstetter, *President*
Jaime Agullo, *General Mgr*
Cameron Meierhoefer, *COO*
EMP: 170
SQ FT: 111,000 **Publicly Held**
WEB: www.comscore.com
SIC: 7372 Business oriented computer
software; application computer software

(G-10825)
CONGERO TECHNOLOGY GROUP INC
12110 Sunset Hills Rd (20190-5852)
PHONE.....................434 266-4376
Thomas Cong, *CEO*
EMP: 20
SALES (est): 204.4K **Privately Held**
WEB: www.congerotechnology.com
SIC: 7372 Application computer software

(G-10826)
CONNECT SOFTWARE LLC
11654 Plaza America Dr (20190-4700)
PHONE.....................706 974-8300
Nicole Bass,
EMP: 1
SALES (est): 32.7K **Privately Held**
SIC: 7372 Prepackaged software

(G-10827)
CORILLIAN PAYMENT SOLUTIONS (DH)
11600 Sunrise Valley Dr # 100
(20191-1412)
PHONE.....................703 259-3000
Karen Kracher, *President*
EMP: 21
SQ FT: 25,200
SALES (est): 2.3MM
SALES (corp-wide): 10.1B **Publicly Held**
SIC: 7372 Prepackaged software
HQ: Corillian Corporation
3400 Ne John Olsen Ave
Hillsboro OR 97124
503 746-0600

(G-10828)
COVATA USA INC
11190 Sunrise Valley Dr # 140
(20191-4393)
PHONE.....................703 657-5260
Trent Telford, *CEO*
Charles Archer, *Ch of Bd*
Jenny Song, *VP Mktg*
Semion Smushkevich, *Admin Sec*
EMP: 5
SQ FT: 5,000
SALES (est): 547.3K **Privately Held**
WEB: www.cipherpoint.com
SIC: 7372 Publishers' computer software

(G-10829)
CRAFTER SOFTWARE
1800 Alexander Bell Dr (20191-5465)
PHONE.....................703 955-3480
Mike Vertal, *President*
Alex Kraus, *Sales Staff*
EMP: 4
SALES (est): 121.9K **Privately Held**
WEB: www.craftersoftware.com
SIC: 7372 Prepackaged software

(G-10830)
CUSTOM INK
11130i South Lakes Dr (20191-4327)
PHONE.....................703 957-1648
EMP: 2
SALES (est): 72.1K **Privately Held**
WEB: www.customink.com
SIC: 2759 Screen printing

(G-10831)
DAILY MONEY MATTERS LLC
1935 Crescent Park Dr (20190-3291)
PHONE.....................703 904-9157
Wendy G Pohanka, *Administration*
EMP: 3

SALES (est): 111.3K **Privately Held**
SIC: 2711 Newspapers, publishing & printing

(G-10832)
DAR BE DAR LLC
11058 Aldbury Ct (20194-1430)
PHONE.................................703 244-1599
Tala Raassi,
EMP: 2 EST: 2011
SALES (est): 141.7K **Privately Held**
WEB: www.talaraassi.com
SIC: 2369 Girls' & children's outerwear

(G-10833)
DATABASICS INC
12700 Sunrise Valley Dr # 102
(20191-5806)
PHONE.................................703 262-0097
Alan L Tyson, *President*
Shirley Tyson, *Corp Secy*
Ryan Vaz, *Administration*
EMP: 22
SALES (est): 3.2MM **Privately Held**
WEB: www.data-basics.com
SIC: 7372 Business oriented computer
software

(G-10834)
DBSD NORTH AMERICA INC
11700 Plaza America Dr (20190-4751)
PHONE.................................703 964-1400
EMP: 90
SALES (est): 1.3MM **Publicly Held**
SIC: 3663 Radio & TV communications
equipment
PA: Dish Network Corporation
9601 S Meridian Blvd
Englewood CO 80112

(G-10835)
DDC CONNECTIONS INC
2434 Brussels Ct (20191-2508)
PHONE.................................703 858-0326
Man M Ngo, *President*
EMP: 2 EST: 2002
SALES (est): 210K **Privately Held**
SIC: 3822 Auto controls regulating residntl
& coml environmt & applncs

(G-10836)
DECKS DOWN UNDER LLC
2054 Chadds Ford Dr (20191-4012)
PHONE.................................703 758-2572
James A Burkart Jr,
EMP: 3
SALES (est): 277K **Privately Held**
SIC: 3089 2394 Awnings, fiberglass &
plastic combination; canvas & related
products

(G-10837)
DEFENSATIVE LLC
Also Called: Netwatcher
1861 Wiehle Ave Ste 250 (20190-5216)
PHONE.................................202 557-6937
Scott Suhy, *CEO*
Lauren Sexton, *Director*
EMP: 18
SQ FT: 2,500
SALES (est): 188.8K **Privately Held**
WEB: www.netwatcher.com
SIC: 7372 Business oriented computer
software

(G-10838)
DELICIOUS DAINTIES LLC
2351 Millennium Ln (20191-2957)
PHONE.................................240 620-7581
Prabha Iyer, *Owner*
EMP: 2
SALES (est): 93K **Privately Held**
SIC: 2064 Chocolate candy, except solid
chocolate; fruit, chocolate covered (ex-
cept dates); candy bars, including choco-
late covered bars

(G-10839)
DELL EMC
10700 Parkridge Blvd (20191-5452)
PHONE.................................301 897-1400
EMP: 2
SALES (est): 85.9K **Privately Held**
SIC: 3572 Computer storage devices

(G-10840)
DENNINGTON WDWRK SOLUTIONS LLC
2211 Lofty Heights Pl (20191-1716)
PHONE.................................571 414-6917
EMP: 1
SALES (est): 54.1K **Privately Held**
SIC: 2431 Millwork

(G-10841)
DI9 EQUITY INVESTORS
11710 Plaza America Dr (20190-4742)
PHONE.................................703 860-0901
EMP: 2
SALES (est): 86.7K **Privately Held**
SIC: 2451 Mobile homes

(G-10842)
DKL INTERNATIONAL INC
11921 Freedom Dr Ste 550 (20190-5635)
PHONE.................................703 938-6700
▼ EMP: 6 EST: 1998
SQ FT: 1,000
SALES (est): 422K **Privately Held**
SIC: 3825 5065 Mfg Instruments To Meas-
ure Electricity Whol Electronic Parts &
Equipment

(G-10843)
DOSKOCIL MFG CO INC
11801 Riders Ln (20191-4230)
PHONE.................................218 766-2558
Ann Bruestle, *Director*
EMP: 2
SALES (est): 74.6K **Privately Held**
SIC: 3999 Manufacturing industries

(G-10844)
DSD LABORATORIES INC
11921 Freedom Dr Ste 550 (20190-5635)
PHONE.................................703 904-4384
Bill Krebs, *Finance Mgr*
EMP: 10
SALES (corp-wide): 27.4MM **Privately Held**
WEB: www.dsdlabs.com
SIC: 3695 Computer software tape &
disks: blank, rigid & floppy
PA: Dsd Laboratories, Inc.
75 Union Ave Ste 200
Sudbury MA 01776
978 443-9700

(G-10845)
E C A
12100 Sunset Hills Rd (20190-3233)
PHONE.................................703 234-4142
EMP: 2
SALES (est): 402.1K **Privately Held**
SIC: 3679 5065 Electronic Components,
Nec, Nsk

(G-10846)
ENERGYTECH SOLUTIONS LLC
10877 Hunter Gate Way (20194-1447)
PHONE.................................703 269-8172
Khanh Ho-Si,
EMP: 3
SALES (est): 201.1K **Privately Held**
SIC: 3822 Auto controls regulating residntl
& coml environmt & applncs

(G-10847)
ENGILITY LLC
Also Called: Command & Control Systems
11955 Freedom Dr Ste 2000 (20190-5651)
PHONE.................................703 434-4000
David Tockl, *Finance Dir*
Walker Craig, *Manager*
Jillian Onstad, *Analyst*
EMP: 1500
SALES (corp-wide): 6.3B **Publicly Held**
WEB: www.engility.com
SIC: 3663 7373 7379 8734 Space satel-
lite communications equipment; systems
engineering, computer related; computer
related consulting services; testing labo-
ratories
HQ: Engility Llc
4803 Stonecroft Blvd
Chantilly VA 20151
703 708-1400

(G-10848)
ENVITIA INC
11710 Plaza America Dr # 2000
(20190-4742)
PHONE.................................703 871-5255
Sharon L Looper, *President*
Robin Parrish, *Principal*
Maurice C Scott, *Admin Sec*
EMP: 2
SQ FT: 800
SALES (est): 360K
SALES (corp-wide): 7.8MM **Privately Held**
WEB: www.envitia.com
SIC: 7372 Application computer software
PA: Envitia Group Plc
North Heath Lane Industrial Estate
Horsham W SUSSEX RH12
140 327-3173

(G-10849)
ETZ LLC
1938 Upper Lake Dr (20191-3620)
PHONE.................................703 620-3014
Judith Newcomb, *Principal*
EMP: 3
SALES (est): 226.5K **Privately Held**
SIC: 3273 Ready-mixed concrete

(G-10850)
FAIRFAX STATION TIMES
1920 Assn Dr Ste 500 (20191)
PHONE.................................703 437-5400
Steve Cahill, *Principal*
EMP: 7 EST: 2010
SALES (est): 414.6K **Privately Held**
WEB: www.fairfaxtimes.com
SIC: 2711 Newspapers, publishing & print-
ing

(G-10851)
FINCH COMPUTING
12018 Sunrise Valley Dr (20191-3432)
PHONE.................................571 599-7480
EMP: 6 EST: 2016
SALES (est): 284K **Privately Held**
WEB: www.finchcomputing.com
SIC: 7372 Prepackaged software

(G-10852)
FINISH AGENT INC
1318 Sundial Dr (20194-2000)
PHONE.................................703 437-7822
Gina Hiatt, *Administration*
EMP: 2 EST: 2011
SALES (est): 167.9K **Privately Held**
SIC: 2843 Finishing agents

(G-10853)
FLEXPROTECT LLC
11911 Freedom Dr Ste 850 (20190-6243)
PHONE.................................703 957-8648
Terry Prime, *Mng Member*
John Lakey,
EMP: 5
SALES (est): 100K
SALES (corp-wide): 929.4K **Privately Held**
SIC: 3812 7372 Navigational systems &
instruments; application computer soft-
ware
PA: Elastic M2m Inc.
11911 Freedom Dr Ste 850
Reston VA 20190
703 957-8649

(G-10854)
FROGUE
11303 Geddys Ct Ste F (20191-3606)
PHONE.................................703 679-7003
V Dwarapudi,
EMP: 11 EST: 2013
SQ FT: 220
SALES (est): 529.9K **Privately Held**
WEB: www.frogueclark.com
SIC: 3843 8731 8742 Dental equipment &
supplies; biotechnical research, commer-
cial; productivity improvement consultant

(G-10855)
GALLAS FOODS INC
12051 Summer Meadow Ln (20194-2740)
PHONE.................................703 593-9957
Jim Gallas, *Vice Pres*
EMP: 3

SALES (est): 100K **Privately Held**
SIC: 2035 5812 Dressings, salad: raw &
cooked (except dry mixes); eating places

(G-10856)
GBP SOFTWARE LLC
Also Called: Cluetrust
11654 Plaza America Dr # 214
(20190-4700)
PHONE.................................703 967-3896
Gaige B Paulsen,
EMP: 4
SALES (est): 286.2K **Privately Held**
WEB: www.cluetrust.com
SIC: 7372 Prepackaged software

(G-10857)
GENERAL DYNAMICS CORPORATION (PA)
11011 Sunset Hills Rd (20190-5311)
PHONE.................................703 876-3000
Phebe N Novakovic, *Ch of Bd*
Catherine Razzano, *Counsel*
John Casey, *Exec VP*
Gregory S Gallopoulos, *Senior VP*
Paul Besson, *Vice Pres*
▲ EMP: 175 EST: 1952
SALES (est): 39.3B **Publicly Held**
WEB: www.generaldynamics.com
SIC: 3721 3731 3795 3711 Aircraft; sub-
marines, building & repairing; combat
vessels, building & repairing; tanks, mili-
tary, including factory rebuilding; recon-
naissance cars, assembly of; search &
navigation equipment; search & detection
systems & instruments

(G-10858)
GENERAL DYNMICS WRLDWIDE HLDNG (HQ)
11011 Sunset Hills Rd (20190-5311)
PHONE.................................703 876-3000
EMP: 5
SALES (est): 2.7MM
SALES (corp-wide): 39.3B **Publicly Held**
SIC: 3731 Submarines, building & repair-
ing
PA: General Dynamics Corporation
11011 Sunset Hills Rd
Reston VA 20190
703 876-3000

(G-10859)
GIT R DONE INC
11710 Plaza America Dr # 2000
(20190-4742)
PHONE.................................703 843-8697
Aliah Fatima Warmund, *Principal*
Malene Nilsson, *Human Res Mgr*
EMP: 2
SALES (est): 101.1K **Privately Held**
SIC: 3949 Batons

(G-10860)
GOLLYGEE SOFTWARE INC
1474 Northpoint Vlg Ctr (20194-1190)
PHONE.................................703 437-3751
Johnathan Blockson, *President*
Ronald Blockson, *Vice Pres*
EMP: 2 EST: 1997
SALES (est): 127.8K **Privately Held**
WEB: www.gollygee.com
SIC: 7372 7371 Prepackaged software;
custom computer programming services

(G-10861)
GOOD HUMOR ICE CREAM LLC
1612 Becontree Ln Apt 3a (20190-4084)
PHONE.................................703 898-5516
Amar Magoub, *Mng Member*
EMP: 2
SALES (est): 62.3K **Privately Held**
SIC: 2024 Ice cream & ice milk

(G-10862)
GRAPHUS INC
11111 Chessington Pl (20194-1457)
PHONE.................................703 481-8861
Manoj Kumar Srivastavva, *Principal*
EMP: 3 EST: 2015
SALES (est): 153K **Privately Held**
WEB: www.graphus.ai
SIC: 3861 Photographic equipment & sup-
plies

(G-10863)
GREENVISION SYSTEMS INC
11710 Plaza America Dr # 2000
(20190-4742)
PHONE....................703 467-8784
Danny Moshe, *CEO*
EMP: 2
SALES (est): 137.4K **Privately Held**
WEB: www.greenvs.com
SIC: 3826 Analytical instruments

(G-10864)
HIPRO CALL INC
11921 Freedom Dr (20190-5667)
PHONE....................703 397-5155
EMP: 2
SALES (est): 156.2K **Privately Held**
SIC: 3651 Audio electronic systems

(G-10865)
**HITACHI VANTARA FEDERAL
CORP**
11950 Democracy Dr # 200 (20190-6285)
PHONE....................703 787-2900
David Turner, *President*
Mark A Serway, *CFO*
Jay Benedicto, *Manager*
Mike Schutz, *Consultant*
David Funk, *General Counsel*
EMP: 118
SALES (est): 100MM **Privately Held**
WEB: www.hitachivantarafederal.com
SIC: 3571 3572 5045 7372 Electronic
  computers; computer storage devices;
  computers, peripherals & software;
  prepackaged software; computer mainte-
  nance & repair
HQ: Hitachi Vantara Corporation
  2535 Augustine Dr
  Santa Clara CA 95054
  408 970-1000

(G-10866)
ICEBERRY INC (PA)
11990 Market St Ste C (20190-6021)
PHONE....................703 481-0670
Jung Haekwang, *Principal*
EMP: 6
SALES (est): 939K **Privately Held**
WEB: www.iceberryus.com
SIC: 2026 Yogurt

(G-10867)
IDEMIA AMERICA CORP
11951 Freedom Dr Ste 1800 (20190-5642)
PHONE....................703 263-0100
EMP: 4
SALES (corp-wide): 8.1B **Privately Held**
WEB: www.idemia.com
SIC: 3578 Calculating & accounting equip-
  ment
HQ: Idemia America Corp.
  296 Concord Rd Ste 300
  Billerica MA 01821
  978 215-2400

(G-10868)
IKANOW LLC
11921 Freedom Dr Ste 550 (20190-5635)
P.O. Box 682775, Park City UT (84068-
2775)
PHONE....................619 884-4434
David Camarata,
Audrey Lelevier,
Christopher Morgan,
EMP: 25
SQ FT: 3,000
SALES (est): 1MM **Privately Held**
WEB: www.ikanow.com
SIC: 7372 Application computer software

(G-10869)
**ILS INTRNTONAL LAUNCH SVCS
INC**
12110 Sunset Hills Rd # 4 (20190-5852)
PHONE....................703 435-5689
Tiphaine Louradour, *President*
Russell Prytula, *Business Mgr*
Jim Kramer, *Vice Pres*
Larry Berrios, *Technology*
Kimberly Kho-Knee, *Admin Sec*
EMP: 60
SALES (est): 9.1MM **Privately Held**
WEB: www.ilslaunch.com
SIC: 3663 Satellites, communications

(G-10870)
**IMPACT SOFTWARE SOUTIONS
INC**
12001 Creekbend Dr (20194-5629)
PHONE....................703 615-5212
Bradley Hummel, *Administration*
EMP: 2
SALES (est): 123.5K **Privately Held**
WEB: www.impactsolutions-inc.com
SIC: 7372 Prepackaged software

(G-10871)
**INFOITION NEWS SERVICES
INC**
1900 Cmpus Cmmons Dr Ste (20191)
PHONE....................703 853-8857
Jeff Trexel, *President*
Josh Witt, *Project Mgr*
Charles Poulson, *Info Tech Mgr*
Jennifer Santiago, *Officer*
Steve Mock, *Analyst*
EMP: 17
SALES (est): 977.9K **Privately Held**
WEB: www.infoition.com
SIC: 2711 Newspapers: publishing only,
  not printed on site

(G-10872)
INFORMATICA CORP
Also Called: Informatica Federal Sales Div
11710 Plaza America Dr # 2000
(20190-4742)
PHONE....................703 234-8500
Sohaib Abbasi, *CEO*
James Pruden, *President*
EMP: 3 EST: 2007
SALES (est): 87.9K **Privately Held**
WEB: www.informatica.com
SIC: 7372 Prepackaged software
PA: Informatica Llc
  2100 Seaport Blvd
  Redwood City CA 94063

(G-10873)
INFRASCALE INC (PA)
Also Called: SOS Hosting
12110 Sunset Hills Rd # 600 (20190-5916)
PHONE....................703 520-7072
Russell P Reeder, *CEO*
Michael Bell, *President*
Taylor Berger, *Partner*
Nicholas Hill, *Partner*
Davide De Vellis, *Vice Pres*
EMP: 137
SALES (est): 14MM **Privately Held**
WEB: www.infrascale.com
SIC: 7372 5045 Business oriented com-
  puter software; computers, peripherals &
  software; computer software

(G-10874)
**INTEGRATED SOFTWARE
SOLUTIONS**
1800 Alexander Bell Dr (20191-5465)
PHONE....................703 255-1130
EMP: 7
SALES (est): 860K **Privately Held**
SIC: 7372 7371 Prepackaged & Custom
  Software

(G-10875)
INTEL FEDERAL LLC
11911 Freedom Dr (20190-5668)
PHONE....................302 644-3756
EMP: 2
SALES (est): 90K **Privately Held**
SIC: 3674 Microprocessors

(G-10876)
**INTELLIGENT BUS PLATFORMS
LLC**
12020 Sunrise Valley Dr (20191-3440)
PHONE....................202 640-8868
Aditya Watal, *President*
EMP: 40
SQ FT: 300
SALES (est): 4.8MM **Privately Held**
SIC: 7372 5734 Application computer soft-
  ware; computer software & accessories

(G-10877)
**INTELLIGIZE INCORPORATED
(DH)**
1920 Assn Dr Ste 200 (20191)
PHONE....................888 925-8627
Todd Hicks, *CEO*
Joanne Ferrara, *VP Mktg*
Conrad Fair, *Director*
EMP: 2
SALES (est): 2.9MM
SALES (corp-wide): 10.1B **Privately Held**
WEB: www.intelligize.com
SIC: 7372 Business oriented computer
  software
HQ: Relx Inc.
  230 Park Ave Ste 700
  New York NY 10169
  212 309-8100

(G-10878)
INTEX LLC
11409 Fieldstone Ln (20191-3920)
PHONE....................703 899-3336
Janos Nagy, *Principal*
EMP: 3
SALES (est): 219.2K **Privately Held**
SIC: 3577 Computer peripheral equipment

(G-10879)
ITFORESIGHT LLC
11561 North Shore Dr # 21 (20190-4321)
PHONE....................703 829-7283
EMP: 2
SALES (est): 83.2K **Privately Held**
SIC: 1221 Bituminous coal & lignite-sur-
  face mining

(G-10880)
JDDR FOODS INC
12255 Angel Wing Ct (20191-1102)
PHONE....................571 356-0165
Jeremy De La Rocha, *President*
Darien Rich-Forner, *Vice Pres*
EMP: 2
SALES (est): 106.5K **Privately Held**
SIC: 2033 2095 Chili sauce, tomato: pack-
  aged in cans, jars, etc.; instant coffee

(G-10881)
JJJ INC
Also Called: Donnelly's Printing & Graphics
11250 Roger Bacon Dr (20190-5219)
PHONE....................703 938-0565
James Donnelly, *President*
Jeffrey Donnelly, *Vice Pres*
EMP: 4
SQ FT: 2,600
SALES (est): 440K **Privately Held**
WEB: www.donnprint.com
SIC: 2759 Commercial printing

(G-10882)
LAFARGE NORTH AMERICA INC
12018 Sunrise Valley Dr # 5 (20191-3432)
PHONE....................703 480-3600
Thomas Farrell, *Exec VP*
James Obrien, *Marketing Staff*
EMP: 6
SALES (est): 1.3MM **Privately Held**
SIC: 3273 Ready-mixed concrete

(G-10883)
**LASER LIGHT
COMMUNICATIONS INC**
1818 Library St Ste 500 (20190-6274)
PHONE....................571 346-7623
Robert H Brumley II, *President*
Fletcher Brumley, *Vice Pres*
EMP: 2
SALES (est): 159.1K **Privately Held**
WEB: www.laserlightcomms.com
SIC: 3663 Satellites, communications

(G-10884)
LASER LIGHT FEDERAL LLC
1818 Library St Ste 500 (20190-6274)
PHONE....................703 283-0659
Robert H Brumley III, *Principal*
Henry Dubouis, *Principal*
EMP: 4
SALES (est): 203.1K **Privately Held**
WEB: www.laserlightcomms.com
SIC: 3674 Semiconductors & related de-
  vices

(G-10885)
LAVA FLOW YOGA LLC
1970 Winterport Cluster (20191-3600)
PHONE....................703 264-1638
EMP: 2
SALES (est): 77.4K **Privately Held**
SIC: 3069 Fabricated rubber products

(G-10886)
LEASEACCELERATOR INC (PA)
10740 Parkridge Blvd # 70 (20191-5422)
PHONE....................866 446-0980
Michael J Keeler, *CEO*
Tracy Henriques, *Vice Pres*
Steve Keifer, *Vice Pres*
Leonard Neuhaus, *Vice Pres*
Rob Esche, *Project Mgr*
EMP: 15
SALES (est): 4MM **Privately Held**
WEB: www.explore.leaseaccelerator.com
SIC: 7372 Business oriented computer
  software

(G-10887)
LIFE TRANSFORMATIONS LLC
11490 Waterhaven Ct (20190-4462)
PHONE....................703 624-0130
Joanne Aaronson,
EMP: 1
SALES (est): 72.3K **Privately Held**
WEB: www.lifetransformations-kc.com
SIC: 2335 Wedding gowns & dresses

(G-10888)
**LIGADO NETWORKS INC
VIRGINIA**
Also Called: Lightsquared Inc of Virginia
10802 Parkridge Blvd (20191-4334)
PHONE....................877 678-2920
Sanjiv Ahuja, *CEO*
EMP: 350 **Privately Held**
WEB: www.ligado.com
SIC: 3663 Satellites, communications

(G-10889)
**LOOKINGGLASS CYBER
SLUTION INC (PA)**
10740 Parkridge Blvd # 200 (20191-5428)
PHONE....................703 351-1000
Brian Garmey, *Vice Pres*
Jay Denison, *Engineer*
Stewart Curley, *CFO*
Alyssa Shames, *Marketing Staff*
Haresh Ghoghari, *Manager*
EMP: 78
SQ FT: 10,000
SALES (est): 40.1MM **Privately Held**
WEB: www.lookingglasscyber.com
SIC: 7372 7374 Prepackaged software;
  data processing & preparation

(G-10890)
LOZIER CORP
11961 Grey Squirrel Ln (20194-1726)
PHONE....................703 742-4098
Ken Cooper, *Principal*
EMP: 2
SALES (est): 129.5K **Privately Held**
SIC: 2542 Partitions & fixtures, except
  wood

(G-10891)
LULULEMON ATHLETICA
11957 Market St (20190-5664)
PHONE....................703 787-8327
EMP: 1
SALES (est): 42.5K **Privately Held**
SIC: 2389 Apparel & accessories

(G-10892)
MADERA FLOORS LLC
1908 Reston Metro Plz # 1119
(20190-5932)
PHONE....................703 855-6847
Olmo Alatorre, *Principal*
Javier Flores,
EMP: 2
SALES (est): 210.1K **Privately Held**
WEB: www.maderafloors.com
SIC: 2426 Hardwood dimension & flooring
  mills

GEOGRAPHIC

(G-10893)
MAGPIE DESIGN LLC
2312 Toddsbury Pl (20191-1623)
PHONE.................................703 975-5818
Kristin Jett,
EMP: 1
SALES (est): 54K **Privately Held**
SIC: 2741 7336 Yearbooks: publishing &
printing; graphic arts & related design

(G-10894)
MANTIS NETWORKS LLC
11160 South Lakes Dr # 190 (20191-4327)
PHONE.................................571 306-1234
Kevin Fecher,
Elliott Starin,
EMP: 2
SALES (est): 162.6K **Privately Held**
WEB: www.mantisnet.com
SIC: 3357 3577 5045 Communication
wire; fiber optic cable (insulated);
input/output equipment, computer; com-
puter software

(G-10895)
MARK TONER LLC
1507 Inlet Ct (20190-4421)
PHONE.................................703 689-0609
EMP: 3
SALES (est): 101.8K **Privately Held**
WEB: www.marktoner.com
SIC: 2711 Newspapers

(G-10896)
MCAFEE LLC
11911 Freedom Dr Ste 400 (20190-5671)
PHONE.................................571 449-4600
Steve Mercier, Branch Mgr
EMP: 9 **Privately Held**
WEB: www.mcafee.com
SIC: 7372 Prepackaged software
HQ: Mcafee, Llc
6220 America Center Dr
San Jose CA 95002

(G-10897)
MEGAPHONE LLC (HQ)
1900 Reston Metro Plz # 3 (20190-5218)
PHONE.................................703 594-7623
Cameron Jones, CEO
Brendan Monaghan, CEO
Lindsay Herron, Manager
EMP: 20 EST: 2016
SQ FT: 21,000
SALES (est): 4.2MM **Publicly Held**
WEB: www.megaphone.fm
SIC: 2741
PA: Graham Holdings Company
1300 17th St N Fl 17
Arlington VA 22209
703 345-6300

(G-10898)
MENDOZA SERVICES INC
11307 Sunset Hills Rd (20190-5281)
PHONE.................................703 860-9600
Jose F Mendoza, Administration
EMP: 2
SALES (est): 112.7K **Privately Held**
SIC: 2759 Post cards, picture: printing

(G-10899)
METRO PRINTING CENTER INC
11870 Snrise Valy Dr Ste (20191)
PHONE.................................703 620-3532
Arjun Nowlakha, President
EMP: 3
SALES (est): 540K **Privately Held**
WEB: www.metroprintingcenter.com
SIC: 2752 Commercial printing, offset

(G-10900)
MEZEH-RESTON LLC
12120 Sunset Hills Rd # 1 (20190-5853)
PHONE.................................703 310-9209
Sadiqa Mohamadi, Controller
Saleh Mohamadi, Mng Member
Tai Chiao, Director
EMP: 11
SALES (est): 822.3K **Privately Held**
SIC: 2099 5149 Food preparations; gro-
ceries & related products

(G-10901)
MICROSOFT CORPORATION
12012 Sunset Hills Rd (20190-5869)
PHONE.................................703 673-7600
Christina Treacy, Partner
Bob De Haven, General Mgr
Yagy Gaur, General Mgr
Brian McKenzie, General Mgr
Melissa Ranslem, General Mgr
EMP: 740
SALES (corp-wide): 143B **Publicly Held**
WEB: www.microsoft.com
SIC: 7372 Application computer software
PA: Microsoft Corporation
1 Microsoft Way
Redmond WA 98052
425 882-8080

(G-10902)
MINUTEMAN PRESS INTL INC
11317 Sunset Hills Rd (20190-5205)
PHONE.................................703 787-6506
Swamy Karnam, President
Stephen Aten, Production
EMP: 4
SALES (corp-wide): 23.4MM **Privately
Held**
WEB: www.chanhassen-mn.minuteman-
press.com
SIC: 2752 7389 Commercial printing, litho-
graphic; photo-offset printing; business
form & card printing, lithographic;
PA: Minuteman Press International, Inc.
61 Executive Blvd
Farmingdale NY 11735
631 249-1370

(G-10903)
MOGO INC
Also Called: AlphaGraphics 584
12343 Sunrise Valley Dr C (20191-3476)
PHONE.................................703 476-8595
Mohamed Osman, President
Joey Cunanan, Manager
EMP: 5
SALES (est): 518.7K **Privately Held**
WEB: www.alphagraphics.com
SIC: 2752 Commercial printing, litho-
graphic

(G-10904)
MUHAMMAD ISLAM
12006 Starboard Dr # 304 (20194-4312)
PHONE.................................631 569-8325
Muhammad Islam, Owner
EMP: 1
SALES (est): 85.3K **Privately Held**
SIC: 3663 Studio equipment, radio & tele-
vision broadcasting

(G-10905)
**MULTIMDAL IDNTFCATION TECH
LLC**
11921 Freedom Dr Ste 550 (20190-5635)
PHONE.................................818 729-1954
Ross McKinnon,
EMP: 1
SALES (est): 56.5K **Privately Held**
SIC: 3577 Data conversion equipment,
media-to-media: computer

(G-10906)
NEIGHBORHOODS VI LLC
1881 Campus Commons Dr (20191-1519)
PHONE.................................703 964-5000
EMP: 1
SALES (est): 47.7K **Privately Held**
SIC: 2519 Household furniture
HQ: Stanley-Martin Communities, Llc
11710 Plaza America Dr # 1100
Reston VA 20190
703 988-6537

(G-10907)
NEW TOWN HOLDINGS INC
11440 Isaac Newton Sq N (20190-5008)
PHONE.................................703 471-6666
EMP: 2
SALES (est): 87K **Privately Held**
SIC: 2741 Misc Publishing

(G-10908)
NEXTFLIGHT JETS LLC
1908 Reston Metro Plz # 1915
(20190-5237)
PHONE.................................703 392-6500
Alan Cook,
EMP: 2
SALES (est): 86K **Privately Held**
SIC: 3721 Aircraft

(G-10909)
NOMAD GEOSCIENCES
11429 Purple Beech Dr (20191-1325)
PHONE.................................703 390-1147
Al Taylor, Owner
EMP: 1
SALES (est): 85K **Privately Held**
WEB: www.nomadgeosciences.com
SIC: 1382 Oil & gas exploration services

(G-10910)
NTT AMERICA SOLUTIONS INC
12120 Sunset Hills Rd # 5 (20190-5853)
PHONE.................................571 203-4032
Wes Johnston, Manager
EMP: 26 **Privately Held**
WEB: www.hello.global.ntt
SIC: 7372 7373 Application computer soft-
ware; systems integration services
HQ: Ntt America Solutions, Inc.
1 Penn Plz Fl 18
New York NY 10119
704 969-2784

(G-10911)
NVIS INC
11495 Sunset Hills Rd # 106 (20190-5257)
PHONE.................................571 201-8095
Marc Foglia, President
Minoo Bablani, Vice Pres
EMP: 10
SQ FT: 1,600
SALES (est): 1.9MM **Publicly Held**
WEB: www.nvisinc.com
SIC: 3571 Electronic computers
PA: Kopin Corporation
125 North Dr
Westborough MA 01581
508 870-5959

(G-10912)
**OCEUS ENTERPRISE
SOLUTIONS LLC**
1895 Preston White Dr # 300 (20191-5449)
PHONE.................................703 234-9200
Rose Gazarek, Principal
Barrie Burnick, Vice Pres
EMP: 99
SQ FT: 600
SALES (est): 4.7MM
SALES (corp-wide): 21.8MM **Privately
Held**
WEB: www.oceusnetworks.com
SIC: 3663 Transmitter-receivers, radio
HQ: Oceus Networks, Llc
1895 Preston White Dr # 300
Reston VA 20191

(G-10913)
OGC INC (PA)
11800 Sunrise Valley Dr # 3 (20191-5300)
PHONE.................................703 860-3736
Edward Blum, President
Robert Larson, Vice Pres
EMP: 2
SQ FT: 1,000
SALES (est): 2MM **Privately Held**
WEB: www.ogc.org
SIC: 1389 Gas field services

(G-10914)
ONLINE BIOSE INC
Also Called: Temprotect
10801 Oldfield Dr (20191-5207)
PHONE.................................703 758-6672
Richard Smith, President
EMP: 2 EST: 1999
SALES (est): 108.6K **Privately Held**
WEB: www.temprotect.com
SIC: 2741 3823 Miscellaneous publishing;
humidity instruments, industrial process
type

(G-10915)
ORACLE AMERICA INC
1900 Oracle Way (20190-4733)
PHONE.................................703 478-9000
Leonard Pomata, Branch Mgr
EMP: 100 **Publicly Held**
WEB: www.ea.com
SIC: 7372 Prepackaged software
HQ: Oracle America, Inc.
500 Oracle Pkwy
Redwood City CA 94065
650 506-7000

(G-10916)
**ORACLE SYSTEMS
CORPORATION**
1910 Oracle Way (20190-4735)
PHONE.................................703 478-9000
Gary Emge, President
Christo Andonyadis, Principal
Sanjai Bhargava, Engineer
Jay Nussbaum, Principal
Dan McMurrer, Manager
EMP: 800 **Publicly Held**
SIC: 7372 7379 7371 5734 Educational
computer software; computer related con-
sulting services; custom computer pro-
gramming services; computer & software
stores; computers, peripherals & software
HQ: Oracle Systems Corporation
500 Oracle Pkwy
Redwood City CA 94065

(G-10917)
PACKET DYNAMICS LLC
11110 Sunset Hills Rd (20190-9997)
P.O. Box 2309 (20195-0309)
PHONE.................................703 597-1413
Daniel Conner, President
Rich Heffner, COO
EMP: 1
SALES (est): 107.5K **Privately Held**
WEB: www.packet-dynamics.com
SIC: 3663 Radio & TV communications
equipment

(G-10918)
**PALO ALTO NTWRKS PUB
SCTOR LLC (HQ)**
12110 Sunset Hills Rd (20190-5852)
PHONE.................................240 328-3016
Jeff True, President
Mark McLaughlin, Principal
Steffan Tomlinson, Principal
Meredith Hannah, Business Mgr
Phillip Egelston,
EMP: 14
SQ FT: 19,618
SALES (est): 2.3MM **Publicly Held**
WEB: www.paloaltonetworks.com
SIC: 3577 Computer peripheral equipment
PA: Palo Alto Networks Inc.
3000 Tannery Way
Santa Clara CA 95054
408 753-4000

(G-10919)
PANTHEON INTEGRATION LLC
11654 Plaza America Dr # 631
(20190-4700)
PHONE.................................571 732-1570
Derreck Barber, Principal
EMP: 2
SALES (est): 110K **Privately Held**
SIC: 7372 Prepackaged software

(G-10920)
PARABON COMPUTATION INC
11260 Roger Bacon Dr # 406 (20190-5227)
PHONE.................................703 689-9689
Steven Armentrout, President
Mario Bulhoes, Vice Pres
Paula Armentrout, Admin Sec
EMP: 15
SALES (est): 1.6MM **Privately Held**
WEB: www.parabon-nanolabs.com
SIC: 7372 7371 Prepackaged software;
custom computer programming services

(G-10921)
PARABON NANOLABS INC
11260 Roger Bacon Dr # 40 (20190-5227)
PHONE.................................703 689-9689
Steven Armentrout, President
Sarah Carlson, Sr Software Eng

▲ = Import ▼=Export
◆ =Import/Export

Paula Armentrout, *Admin Sec*
EMP: 25
SALES (est): 4MM **Privately Held**
WEB: www.parabon-nanolabs.com
SIC: 7372 8731 8999 Prepackaged software; commercial physical research; services

(G-10922)
PAYA INC (DH)
12120 Sunset Hills Rd # 500 (20190-5858)
PHONE.................................800 261-0240
Jeffrey Hack, *CEO*
Greg Cohen, *President*
Brad Pendley, *Partner*
Jenn Boutwell, *Vice Pres*
Lori Carney, *Vice Pres*
EMP: 13
SALES (est): 3.6MM
SALES (corp-wide): 271.4MM **Privately Held**
WEB: www.paya.com
SIC: 7372 Business oriented computer software
HQ: Gtcr Ultra Holdings, Llc
300 N La Salle Dr # 5600
Chicago IL 60654
312 382-2200

(G-10923)
PBP SOLUTIONS LLC
11790 Indian Ridge Rd (20191-3527)
PHONE.................................202 999-8101
Roy McIntosh, *Principal*
Linh Nguyen, *Principal*
Tony Mazza, *Exec Dir*
Anthony Mazzsa, *Exec Dir*
EMP: 4
SALES (est): 186.9K **Privately Held**
SIC: 3571 3572 4813 2741 Computers, digital, analog or hybrid; computer auxiliary storage units; ; ; commercial physical research;

(G-10924)
PHARMACEUTICAL RES ASSOC INC
12120 Sunset Hills Rd # 6 (20190-5853)
PHONE.................................703 464-6300
Terrance Bieker, *Principal*
David Dockhorn, *Exec VP*
EMP: 1
SALES (est): 41.3K
SALES (corp-wide): 3B **Publicly Held**
SIC: 2834 Pharmaceutical preparations
PA: Pra Health Sciences, Inc.
4130 Parklake Ave Ste 400
Raleigh NC 27612
919 786-8200

(G-10925)
PICCADILLY CIRCUITS
11560 Shadbush Ct (20191-3010)
PHONE.................................703 860-5426
EMP: 2 EST: 2010
SALES (est): 110K **Privately Held**
SIC: 3679 Mfg Electronic Components

(G-10926)
PLEASANT VLY BUS SOLUTIONS LLC
1801 Alexander Bell Dr # 520 (20191-4344)
PHONE.................................703 391-0977
Bernard Mustafa, *CEO*
Pedro Diaz, *Partner*
Sean Mohan, *Vice Pres*
Adil Nowsherwan, *Vice Pres*
Paul Skurpski, *Vice Pres*
EMP: 30
SQ FT: 11,000
SALES (est): 4.2MM **Privately Held**
WEB: www.govcon365.com
SIC: 7372 7373 Business oriented computer software; value-added resellers, computer systems
HQ: Xtivia, Inc.
304 S 8th St Ste 201
Colorado Springs CO 80905
719 685-3100

(G-10927)
PONS CORP
11406 Windleaf Ct Unit M (20194-2047)
PHONE.................................786 270-7774
Ricardo Aponte, *President*

EMP: 1
SALES (est): 70K **Privately Held**
SIC: 3812 Search & navigation equipment

(G-10928)
POTOMAC DEFENSE LLC
1818 Library St Ste 500 (20190-6274)
PHONE.................................703 253-3441
Michael R Shattuck, *President*
EMP: 1
SALES (est): 54K
SALES (corp-wide): 2.6MM **Privately Held**
SIC: 3812 Defense systems & equipment
PA: The Shattuck Group Llc
13800 Coppermine Rd Fl 2
Herndon VA 20171
703 234-4161

(G-10929)
POTOMAC HEALTH SOLUTIONS INC (PA)
Also Called: Zone2
1800 Alexander Bell Dr # 400 (20191-5465)
PHONE.................................703 774-8278
Kenneth J Gordon, *President*
Kenneth Gordon, *CEO*
Paul Guthrie, *Ch of Bd*
EMP: 4 EST: 2016
SALES (est): 384.7K **Privately Held**
WEB: www.zone2.org
SIC: 3949 Exercise equipment

(G-10930)
PRESS GO BUTTON LLC
11766 Great Owl Cir (20194-1169)
PHONE.................................703 709-5839
Carla Brown, *Principal*
EMP: 3
SALES (est): 160.7K **Privately Held**
WEB: www.pressthegobutton.com
SIC: 2711 Newspapers

(G-10931)
PROGRM FOR THE ARCHTCTRL WDWRK
1952 Isaac Newton Sq W (20190-5001)
PHONE.................................978 468-5141
EMP: 1 EST: 2018
SALES (est): 54.1K **Privately Held**
SIC: 2431 Millwork

(G-10932)
PROTECTEDBYAI INC
1900 Reston Metro Plz # 6 (20190-5218)
PHONE.................................571 489-6906
Jt Kostman PHD, *CEO*
Brian Gallagher, *President*
EMP: 2
SALES (est): 68.4K **Privately Held**
SIC: 7372 Prepackaged software

(G-10933)
PROXY TECHNOLOGIES INC
11718 Bowman Green Dr # 200 (20190-3596)
PHONE.................................703 665-5152
Jonathan Merril, *CEO*
Thomas A Corcoran, *Ch of Bd*
Chris Hamilton, *Exec VP*
Marc M Herman, *CFO*
EMP: 10
SALES (est): 870.6K **Privately Held**
WEB: www.proxy.com
SIC: 3812 Aircraft control instruments

(G-10934)
PUBLIC UTILITIES REPORTS INC
11410 Isaac Newton Sq N # 220 (20190-5045)
PHONE.................................703 847-7720
Bruce W Radford, *President*
Angela Hawkinson, *Editor*
Steve Mitnick, *Chief*
Phillip Cross, *Vice Pres*
Joseph Paparello, *Sales Staff*
EMP: 18
SQ FT: 8,500
SALES (est): 5MM **Privately Held**
WEB: www.purinc.com
SIC: 2731 2721 Book publishing; trade journals: publishing & printing

(G-10935)
QUEST SOFTWARE INC
11400 Commerce Park Dr (20191-1516)
PHONE.................................703 234-3000
Tim Randall, *Marketing Staff*
Eva Cohen, *Manager*
EMP: 15
SALES (corp-wide): 1.1B **Privately Held**
WEB: www.quest.com
SIC: 7372 Prepackaged software
HQ: Quest Software, Inc.
4 Polaris Way
Aliso Viejo CA 92656
949 754-8000

(G-10936)
REGULA FORENSICS INC
1800 Alexander Bell Dr # 400 (20191-5465)
PHONE.................................703 473-2625
Arif A Mamedov, *President*
Nikita Kolesnev, *Chairman*
EMP: 2
SALES (est): 355.7K **Privately Held**
WEB: www.regula.us
SIC: 3826 3829 3842 5043 Environmental testing equipment; measuring & controlling devices; surgical appliances & supplies; photographic equipment & supplies

(G-10937)
RESERVATION GATEWAY INC
11654 Plaza America Dr # 64 (20190-4700)
PHONE.................................703 286-5331
EMP: 2
SALES (est): 113.2K **Privately Held**
WEB: www.rezgateway.com
SIC: 7372 Prepackaged software

(G-10938)
RESTON COPY CENTER INC
11307 Sunset Hills Rd B3 (20190-5279)
PHONE.................................703 860-9600
Frank Mendoza, *President*
EMP: 4
SQ FT: 2,000
SALES (est): 517.2K **Privately Held**
WEB: www.restoncopycenter.com
SIC: 2752 Commercial printing, offset

(G-10939)
RESTON SOFTWARE LLC
12200 Dark Star Ct (20191-2610)
PHONE.................................703 234-2932
Ion A Neag, *Principal*
EMP: 5
SALES (est): 318.4K **Privately Held**
WEB: www.restonsoftware.com
SIC: 7372 Business oriented computer software

(G-10940)
REZGATEWAY
11654 Plaza America Dr # 64 (20190-4700)
PHONE.................................703 286-5331
Mesfin W Eyob, *CEO*
EMP: 1
SALES (est): 89.2K **Privately Held**
WEB: www.rezgateway.com
SIC: 3652 7371 Pre-recorded records & tapes; software programming applications

(G-10941)
RIDGE BUSINESS SOLUTIONS LLC
11890 Sunrise Valley Dr # 2 (20191-3302)
PHONE.................................571 241-8714
Nalini Kurre, *Mng Member*
Raju Ip, *Consultant*
EMP: 23
SALES (est): 172.6K **Privately Held**
WEB: www.ridge-bsol.com
SIC: 7372 7379 Prepackaged software; computer related consulting services

(G-10942)
ROMAC PUBLISHING LLC
11578 Lake Newport Rd (20194-1208)
PHONE.................................703 478-9794
Romey McPherson, *Principal*
EMP: 1 EST: 2007
SALES (est): 60.9K **Privately Held**
WEB: www.romacpublishing.com
SIC: 2741 Miscellaneous publishing

(G-10943)
SAILPLAN INC
1589 Regatta Ln (20194-1218)
PHONE.................................703 217-9658
Jacob Ruytenbeek, *CEO*
EMP: 1
SALES (est): 49.1K **Privately Held**
SIC: 3812 Navigational systems & instruments

(G-10944)
SAMVIT SOLUTIONS LLC
11654 Plaza America Dr # 740 (20190-4700)
PHONE.................................703 481-1274
Smita Hastak, *CEO*
EMP: 6
SALES (est): 324.8K **Privately Held**
WEB: www.samvit-solutions.com
SIC: 7372 Operating systems computer software

(G-10945)
SCIENCELOGIC INC (PA)
10700 Parkridge Blvd # 150 (20191-5324)
PHONE.................................703 354-1010
David Link, *CEO*
Susan Rogers, *Partner*
Mike Denning, *COO*
Don Pyle, *COO*
Richard Chart, *Exec VP*
EMP: 109
SQ FT: 28,000
SALES (est): 45.7MM **Privately Held**
WEB: www.sciencelogic.com
SIC: 7372 Business oriented computer software

(G-10946)
SELEX COMMUNICATIONS INC
1801 Robert Fulton Dr # 400 (20191-4347)
PHONE.................................703 547-6280
Antoine Cortezi, *President*
Dave O'Brien, *Business Mgr*
Alan Kaplan, *CFO*
Dave Obrien, *Director*
EMP: 10
SQ FT: 4,000
SALES (est): 15MM
SALES (corp-wide): 9.9B **Privately Held**
SIC: 3663 Radio broadcasting & communications equipment
HQ: Selex Elsag Limited
Lambda House
Basildon
126 882-3400

(G-10947)
SENSOR NETWORKS LLC
1472 Roundleaf Ct (20190-4054)
PHONE.................................703 481-2224
George Royal, *Managing Prtnr*
Diane Royal, *General Ptnr*
EMP: 2
SALES (est): 189.3K **Privately Held**
WEB: www.sensornetworkscorp.com
SIC: 3571 7373 7371 Electronic computers; systems software development services; computer software systems analysis & design, custom

(G-10948)
SHARESTREAM EDCATN RSURCES LLC
11600 Sunrise Valley Dr # 4 (20191-1412)
P.O. Box 4230, Gaithersburg MD (20885-4230)
PHONE.................................301 208-8000
Allan M Weinstein, *Chairman*
Bill Dipietro, *Director*
Gayraud A Townsend, *Director*
David J Weinstein,
Paul Kline,
EMP: 10
SALES (est): 399.3K **Privately Held**
WEB: www.sharestream.com
SIC: 7372 Educational computer software

(G-10949)
SHELTON GLOBAL ASSOC
2003 Wethersfield Ct (20191-3602)
PHONE.................................202 841-8463
EMP: 2
SALES (est): 87K **Privately Held**
SIC: 2741 Miscellaneous publishing

GEOGRAPHIC

(G-10950)
SIMULYZE INC
12020 Sunrise Valley Dr # 300
(20191-3852)
PHONE..................................703 391-7001
Kevin Gallagher, *President*
Steven R Newman, *Vice Pres*
EMP: 14
SALES (est): 1.4MM **Privately Held**
WEB: www.simulyze.com
SIC: 7372 Prepackaged software
PA: Smz Holdings, Inc.
　12020 Sunrise Valley Dr
　Reston VA 20191
　703 391-7001

(G-10951)
SINGH EXPRESS CORP
12020 Sunrise Valley Dr (20191-3440)
PHONE..................................202 816-8686
Gurdial Singh, *President*
EMP: 3 EST: 2016
SALES (est): 109.4K **Privately Held**
SIC: 2711 Newspapers, publishing & print-
ing

(G-10952)
SJ DOBERT
12401 Melmark Ct (20191-1615)
PHONE..................................301 847-5000
EMP: 2
SALES (est): 85.9K **Privately Held**
SIC: 3577 Mfg Computer Peripheral Equip-
ment

(G-10953)
SKYMATE INC
11890 Sunrise Valley Dr # 100
(20191-3302)
PHONE..................................703 961-5800
John Tandler, *President*
Marshall Bohannon, *Vice Pres*
Craig Myers, *Manager*
EMP: 8
SALES (est): 941.2K **Privately Held**
WEB: www.skymate.com
SIC: 3663 Satellites, communications

(G-10954)
**SMC HOLDINGS & INVESTMENT
CORP**
11710 Plaza America Dr (20190-4742)
PHONE..................................703 860-0901
EMP: 2
SALES (est): 86.7K **Privately Held**
SIC: 2451 Mobile homes

(G-10955)
SMITHS DETECTION INC
11190 Sunrise Valley Dr (20191-4393)
PHONE..................................571 346-3400
Nathan Lefebvre, *Sales Staff*
EMP: 145
SALES (corp-wide): 3.1B **Privately Held**
WEB: www.smithsdetection.com
SIC: 3812 Detection apparatus: elec-
tronic/magnetic field, light/heat
HQ: Smiths Detection Inc.
　2202 Lakeside Blvd
　Edgewood MD 21040
　410 612-2625

(G-10956)
SNOWBIRD HOLDINGS INC
11921 Freedom Dr Ste 1120 (20190-5634)
PHONE..................................703 796-0445
EMP: 1
SALES: 5MM **Privately Held**
SIC: 7372 Public Finance/Taxation/Mone-
tary Policy Prepackaged Software Serv-
ices

(G-10957)
**SOCIETY NCLEAR MDCINE
MLCLAR I**
1850 Samuel Morse Dr (20190-5316)
PHONE..................................703 708-9000
Virginia M Pappas, *CEO*
Gary L Dillehay, *President*
Frederic H Fahey, *President*
Peter Herscovitch, *President*
Alan B Packard, *President*
EMP: 52
SQ FT: 22,000

SALES: 10.3MM **Privately Held**
WEB: www.snmmi.org
SIC: 2721 8621 Periodicals; scientific
membership association

(G-10958)
SOFTWARE AG INC
11700 Plaza America Dr # 700
(20190-4739)
PHONE..................................703 480-1860
Al Arebalo, *Manager*
EMP: 17
SALES (corp-wide): 985.3MM **Privately
Held**
WEB: www.softwareag.com
SIC: 7372 Application computer software
HQ: Software Ag, Inc.
　11700 Plaza America Dr # 700
　Reston VA 20190
　703 860-5050

(G-10959)
SOFTWARE AG INC (HQ)
11700 Plaza America Dr # 700
(20190-4739)
PHONE..................................703 860-5050
Mark Edwards, *President*
Johnson Jay, *Principal*
Dan Cox, *Vice Pres*
Amy Farrant, *Vice Pres*
Larry McGhaw, *Vice Pres*
EMP: 250
SQ FT: 70,000
SALES (est): 303.5MM
SALES (corp-wide): 985.3MM **Privately
Held**
WEB: www.softwareag.com
SIC: 7372 Application computer software;
business oriented computer software; op-
erating systems computer software; word
processing computer software
PA: Software Ag
　Uhlandstr. 12
　Darmstadt 64297
　615 192-0

(G-10960)
**SOFTWARE QUALITY EXPERTS
LLC**
1910 Assn Dr Ste 101 (20191)
PHONE..................................703 291-4641
Bhashwar Satwik, *Principal*
Seema Mittal, *Human Res Mgr*
EMP: 4
SALES (est): 143.9K **Privately Held**
WEB: www.sqexperts.com
SIC: 7372 Prepackaged software

(G-10961)
SPIDER SUPPORT SYSTEMS
11654 Plaza America Dr # 180
(20190-4700)
PHONE..................................703 758-0699
Charles Kendall, *President*
EMP: 2
SALES (est): 188.6K **Privately Held**
WEB: www.spidersupport.com
SIC: 3861 Tripods, camera & projector

(G-10962)
SPORTS UNSTOPPABLE LLC
1818 Library St Ste 500 (20190-6274)
PHONE..................................571 346-7622
Kevin Lucido, *CEO*
William Trommelen, *COO*
EMP: 1
SALES (est): 73.2K **Privately Held**
WEB: www.sportsunstoppable.com
SIC: 2741 Miscellaneous publishing

(G-10963)
SPRINGFIELD TIMES
1760 Reston Pkwy (20190-3388)
PHONE..................................703 437-5400
Arthur Arundel, *Principal*
EMP: 2 EST: 2010
SALES (est): 110.9K **Privately Held**
WEB: www.springfieldtimes.net
SIC: 2711 Newspapers

(G-10964)
SPROUTING STAR PRESS
2034 Golf Course Dr (20191-3819)
PHONE..................................703 860-0958
Laurel Wanrow, *Principal*
EMP: 2

SALES (est): 62.9K **Privately Held**
SIC: 2711 Newspapers

(G-10965)
STEALTHPATH LLC
10700 Parkridge Blvd # 30 (20191-5452)
PHONE..................................571 888-6772
Andrew Gordon, *CEO*
Mike Clark, *Exec VP*
EMP: 6
SALES (est): 293.2K **Privately Held**
SIC: 3699 Security control equipment &
systems

(G-10966)
STERLING FLYERS INC
11621 Vantage Hill Rd (20190-3424)
PHONE..................................571 830-4476
Marcia Davidson, *Principal*
EMP: 2
SALES (est): 150.5K **Privately Held**
SIC: 2752 Commercial printing, litho-
graphic

(G-10967)
STRIVE COMMUNICATIONS LLC
Also Called: Strive3
11921 Freedom Dr Ste 550 (20190-5635)
PHONE..................................703 925-5900
Patrick Mason, *Director*
Victor Rogers,
EMP: 4
SQ FT: 205
SALES (est): 500K **Privately Held**
WEB: www.strive3.com
SIC: 2741 7336 7812 7331 Business
service newsletters: publishing & printing;
commercial art & graphic design; motion
picture & video production; direct mail ad-
vertising services

(G-10968)
**SUGANIT BIO-RENEWABLES
LLC**
10903 Hunt Club Rd (20190-3912)
PHONE..................................703 736-0634
Praveen Paripati, *Mng Member*
EMP: 5
SALES (est): 5MM **Privately Held**
WEB: www.suganit.com
SIC: 2869 Industrial organic chemicals

(G-10969)
SYNCDOG INC
1818 Library St Ste 500 (20190-6274)
PHONE..................................800 430-1268
EMP: 2
SALES (est): 139.3K **Privately Held**
WEB: www.syncdog.com
SIC: 7372 Prepackaged software

(G-10970)
TEDS BULLETIN
11948 Market St (20190-5614)
PHONE..................................571 313-8961
Ryan Dunn, *Principal*
EMP: 3
SALES (est): 176.8K **Privately Held**
WEB: www.tedsbulletin.com
SIC: 2041 5812 Farina (except breakfast
food); eating places

(G-10971)
TEKALIGN INC
Also Called: Tod Methods
11654 Plaza America Dr # 181
(20190-4700)
PHONE..................................703 757-6690
EMP: 15
SQ FT: 2,500
SALES (est): 908.7K **Privately Held**
SIC: 3663 Mfg Radio/Tv Communication
Equipment

(G-10972)
**TERRYS CUSTOM
WOODWORKS**
11158 Saffold Way (20190-3823)
PHONE..................................703 963-7116
EMP: 1
SALES (est): 54.1K **Privately Held**
WEB: www.fairfaxcabinets.com
SIC: 2431 Millwork

(G-10973)
TIAN CORPORATION
11955 Freedom Dr (20190-5673)
PHONE..................................703 434-4000
Laura Strafer, *Principal*
EMP: 2
SALES (est): 574.8K **Privately Held**
SIC: 3663 Radio & TV communications
equipment

(G-10974)
TIPPERS LLC
11859 Abercorn Ct (20191-2702)
PHONE..................................703 391-7232
Sarah Bury, *Principal*
EMP: 2
SALES (est): 100.3K **Privately Held**
WEB: www.columbiacorp.com
SIC: 3999 Manufacturing industries

(G-10975)
TMI USA INC
Also Called: TMI-Orion
11491 Sunset Hills Rd # 301 (20190-5244)
PHONE..................................703 668-0114
Jean-Luc Favre, *President*
Michael Welsh, *General Mgr*
Guillaume Favre, *Vice Pres*
EMP: 5
SALES (est): 1.1MM **Privately Held**
WEB: www.tmi-orion.com
SIC: 3829 Thermometers & temperature
sensors

(G-10976)
TRIBLIO INC
11600 Sunrise Valley Dr # 100
(20191-1400)
PHONE..................................703 942-9557
Mohamad Ali, *CEO*
David Nelson, *Adv Board Mem*
Andrew Mahr, *Vice Pres*
Dawn Orr, *CFO*
Justin Hinders, *Sales Staff*
EMP: 10
SALES (est): 1.1MM
SALES (corp-wide): 1.8MM **Privately
Held**
WEB: www.triblio.com
SIC: 7372 Business oriented computer
software
HQ: Idg Communications, Inc.
　5 Speen St
　Framingham MA 01701
　508 872-8200

(G-10977)
UNIFYIA INC
11710 Plaza America Dr # 200
(20190-4742)
PHONE..................................703 344-6758
Gurpreet Singh, *CEO*
EMP: 10 EST: 2017
SALES (est): 42.8K **Privately Held**
WEB: www.unifyia.com
SIC: 7372 Prepackaged software

(G-10978)
**UNITED DEFENSE SYSTEMS
INC**
11850 Freedom Dr Apt 2001 (20190-6083)
P.O. Box 171, Exeter RI (02822-0502)
PHONE..................................401 304-9100
Richard Volomino, *President*
EMP: 3
SALES (est): 121.7K **Privately Held**
SIC: 3812 7382 Defense systems &
equipment; confinement surveillance sys-
tems maintenance & monitoring

(G-10979)
UNITEDSLICKMART LLC
12020 Sunrise Valley Dr # 1 (20191-3440)
PHONE..................................800 714-0532
Nitin Masih,
EMP: 3
SALES (est): 121.3K **Privately Held**
SIC: 3631 Household cooking equipment

(G-10980)
UZIO INC
12355 Sunrise Valley Dr # 300
(20191-3497)
P.O. Box 1010, Great Falls (22066-9010)
PHONE..................................800 984-7952

▲ = Import ▼=Export
◆ =Import/Export

Sanjay Singh, *CEO*
EMP: 113
SALES (est): 8.3M **Privately Held**
WEB: www.uzio.com
SIC: 7372 Application computer software

(G-10981)
VARIANCE MEDIA ENTERPRISES LLC
11741 Dry River Ct (20191-2946)
PHONE..................202 770-1701
Travis Johnson,
EMP: 1
SALES (est): 46.4K **Privately Held**
SIC: 2721 Comic books: publishing only, not printed on site

(G-10982)
VELOCITY LLC
11465 Washington Plz W (20190-4311)
PHONE..................703 304-6152
Deborah Macdougall, *Principal*
EMP: 2 **EST:** 2018
SALES (est): 100.3K **Privately Held**
WEB: www.velsyst.com
SIC: 3999 Manufacturing industries

(G-10983)
VERINT SYSTEMS INC
11950 Democracy Dr # 250 (20190-6284)
PHONE..................703 481-9326
Greg Stock, *Branch Mgr*
EMP: 2 **Publicly Held**
WEB: www.verint.com
SIC: 7372 Prepackaged software
PA: Verint Systems Inc.
175 Broadhollow Rd # 100
Melville NY 11747

(G-10984)
VIBRANT PRINTS LLC
12000 Market St Apt 60 (20190-5694)
PHONE..................843 425-2506
Khaliah El-Amin, *Principal*
EMP: 2
SALES (est): 92.3K **Privately Held**
SIC: 2752 Commercial printing, lithographic

(G-10985)
VIRGINIA NEWS GROUP LLC
Also Called: Times Community Newspaper
1760 Reston Pkwy Ste 411 (20190-3360)
PHONE..................703 437-5400
Nia Lewis, *Branch Mgr*
EMP: 44
SALES (corp-wide): 14.9MM **Privately Held**
WEB: www.loudountimes.com
SIC: 2711 Newspapers, publishing & printing
PA: Virginia News Group, Llc
1602 Village Market Blvd
Leesburg VA 20175
703 777-1111

(G-10986)
VIRGINIA TEK INC
2516 Farrier Ln (20191-2116)
PHONE..................703 391-8877
Hussein Ezzat, *President*
Mohammed El Ezaby, *Chairman*
EMP: 12
SQ FT: 5,000
SALES (est): 1.1MM **Privately Held**
WEB: www.teksynap.com
SIC: 3679 7373 Electronic circuits; computer-aided manufacturing (CAM) systems service

(G-10987)
WAVELAB INC
12007 Sunrise Valley Dr (20191-3479)
PHONE..................703 860-9321
Guobao Zheng, *President*
Jatries Hsu, *President*
Mike Engle, *Vice Pres*
EMP: 8
SQ FT: 5,000
SALES (est): 1.8MM **Privately Held**
WEB: www.wave-lab.com
SIC: 3663 Radio & TV communications equipment

(G-10988)
WEBB-MASON INC
1897 Preston White Dr # 300 (20191-5479)
PHONE..................703 242-7278
Jamie Harding, *Marketing Staff*
Sarkis Hagopian, *Manager*
EMP: 23 **Privately Held**
WEB: www.webbmason.com
SIC: 2752 Business form & card printing, lithographic
PA: Webb-Mason, Inc.
10830 Gilroy Rd
Hunt Valley MD 21031

(G-10989)
WEISS SONI
Also Called: Auggie Company
2158 Cartwright Pl (20191-1907)
PHONE..................703 264-5848
Sondra Weiss, *President*
EMP: 2
SALES (est): 190K **Privately Held**
WEB: www.soniweiss.com
SIC: 3429 Clamps, metal

(G-10990)
WELLSKY HUMN SOCIAL SVCS CORP (HQ)
11700 Plaza America Dr # 100 (20190-4751)
PHONE..................703 674-5100
Rob Weber, *Exec VP*
Randy French, *Vice Pres*
David McMillan, *Vice Pres*
Victoria Winters, *Opers Staff*
Dave McEwan, *Engineer*
EMP: 75
SALES (est): 18MM
SALES (corp-wide): 115.1MM **Privately Held**
SIC: 7372 Business oriented computer software
PA: Wellsky Corporation
11300 Switzer St
Overland Park KS 66210
913 307-1000

(G-10991)
WINDROSE MEDIA LLC
11236 Chestnut Grove Sq (20190-5118)
PHONE..................703 464-1274
David Corsino,
EMP: 1
SALES (est): 125K **Privately Held**
WEB: www.windrosemedia.com
SIC: 3695 Magnetic & optical recording media

(G-10992)
WISE LA TINA PUBLISHING
2402 Alsop Ct (20191-3022)
PHONE..................202 425-1129
Jenny Sarabia, *Principal*
EMP: 2
SALES (est): 114.7K **Privately Held**
SIC: 2741 Miscellaneous publishing

(G-10993)
WOODCRAFTERS INC
11735 Summerchase Cir # 1735 (20194-1143)
PHONE..................703 736-2825
Gary Carsten, *Principal*
EMP: 2
SALES (est): 92.9K **Privately Held**
SIC: 2511 Wood household furniture

(G-10994)
WORKDYNAMICS TECHNOLOGIES INC
11710 Plaza America Dr # 2000 (20190-4742)
PHONE..................703 481-9874
Grant Bifolchi, *Principal*
Don Harrod, *Vice Pres*
EMP: 25
SALES (est): 952.7K
SALES (corp-wide): 3.3MM **Privately Held**
SIC: 7372 7371 5045 Prepackaged software; computer software systems analysis & design, custom; computers, peripherals & software

PA: Workdynamics Technologies Inc
50 Hines Rd Suite 220
Kanata ON K2K 2
613 254-9125

(G-10995)
WORKHORSE PRINT SOLUTIONS LLC
1298 Golden Eagle Dr (20194-1105)
PHONE..................703 707-1648
James Ellis, *Principal*
EMP: 2 **EST:** 2007
SALES (est): 117.5K **Privately Held**
SIC: 2752 Commercial printing, lithographic

(G-10996)
X-COM SYSTEMS LLC (HQ)
1875 Cmpus Cmmons Dr Ste (20191)
PHONE..................703 390-1087
Mark Johnson, *CEO*
Dennis Morgan, *CFO*
▼ **EMP:** 22
SQ FT: 9,000
SALES (est): 2.5MM **Privately Held**
WEB: www.birdrf.com
SIC: 3812 Defense systems & equipment

(G-10997)
YUZHNOYE-US LLC
1800 Jonathan Way # 1223 (20190-3592)
PHONE..................321 537-2720
John Isella, *Managing Dir*
EMP: 4
SALES (est): 189.2K **Privately Held**
SIC: 3761 3764 Rockets, space & military, complete; guided missiles & space vehicles, research & development; propulsion units for guided missiles & space vehicles

(G-10998)
ZEURIX LLC
11710 Plaza America Dr # 2000 (20190-4742)
PHONE..................571 297-9460
Naha Kayani,
EMP: 4 **EST:** 2017
SALES (est): 145K **Privately Held**
WEB: www.zeurix.com
SIC: 7372 7371 Business oriented computer software; custom computer programming services; computer software systems analysis & design, custom; computer software writing services; computer software development & applications

Reva
Madison County

(G-10999)
BF WISE & SONS LC
3890 Ridgeview Rd (22735-3749)
PHONE..................540 547-2918
Shirley Wise, *Principal*
EMP: 2
SALES (est): 178.9K **Privately Held**
SIC: 3011 Tires & inner tubes

(G-11000)
ERIC S WELDING SERVICE
6121 Duncan Trl (22735-2025)
PHONE..................540 717-3256
Eric Dovell, *CEO*
EMP: 1
SALES (est): 52.8K **Privately Held**
WEB: www.ericsweldingservice.com
SIC: 7692 Welding repair

(G-11001)
SUNSHINE HILL PRESS LLC
2937 Novum Rd (22735-3550)
PHONE..................571 451-8448
Robert J Shade, *Principal*
EMP: 1 **EST:** 2018
SALES (est): 37.5K **Privately Held**
SIC: 2741 Miscellaneous publishing

(G-11002)
TRIPLE YOLK LLC
1224 Desert Rd (22735-3920)
PHONE..................540 923-4040
Sara Tung, *Mng Member*
Todd Crames,

EMP: 2
SALES (est): 195.1K **Privately Held**
WEB: www.tripleyolk.com
SIC: 7372 8999 7389 Application computer software; commercial & literary writings;

(G-11003)
W W BURTON
16272 Reva Rd (22735-1941)
PHONE..................540 547-4668
Walter Burton, *Owner*
EMP: 2
SQ FT: 2,448
SALES (est): 113.9K **Privately Held**
WEB: www.wwburtonco.com
SIC: 3993 Neon signs

Rice
Prince Edward County

(G-11004)
CASSICAN PRESS LLC
746 Gates Bass Rd (23966-2456)
PHONE..................434 392-4832
EMP: 1
SALES (est): 37.5K **Privately Held**
SIC: 2741 Miscellaneous publishing

(G-11005)
JOHN P HINES LOGGING
Rr 460 (23966)
PHONE..................434 392-3861
John P Hines, *Owner*
EMP: 7
SALES (est): 410.2K **Privately Held**
SIC: 2411 Logging

(G-11006)
SHORTYS BREADING COMPANY LLC
Also Called: Shortys Fish and Fowl Breading
10885 Green Bay Rd (23966-2406)
PHONE..................434 390-1772
Nash Osborn, *President*
EMP: 3
SALES (est): 183.3K **Privately Held**
WEB: www.shortysbreading.com
SIC: 2015 2092 Poultry slaughtering & processing; fish fillets

Rich Creek
Giles County

(G-11007)
JENNMAR CORPORATION
Also Called: JM USA
101 Powell Mountain Rd (24147-3017)
PHONE..................540 726-2326
Greg Ratcliff, *Plant Mgr*
Dennis Richards, *Engineer*
Teresa Altizer, *Sales Staff*
EMP: 80
SALES (corp-wide): 753.2MM **Privately Held**
WEB: www.jennmar.com
SIC: 3532 1081 Mining machinery; metal mining exploration & development services
HQ: Jennmar Of Pennsylvania, Llc
258 Kappa Dr
Pittsburgh PA 15238
412 963-9071

(G-11008)
SMITH VALLEY MEATS
Church St (24147)
P.O. Box C (24147-0337)
PHONE..................540 726-3992
G Dale Smith, *Partner*
Brenda Smith, *Partner*
EMP: 6
SALES (est): 500K **Privately Held**
SIC: 2011 5147 5421 Meat packing plants; meats, fresh; meat markets, including freezer provisioners

Richardsville
Culpeper County

(G-11009)
BIG DOG WOODWORKING LLC
21066 White Rock Dr (22736-1755)
PHONE.............................540 359-1056
Thomas Ranneberger, *Principal*
EMP: 2
SALES (est): 87.1K Privately Held
SIC: 2431 Millwork

(G-11010)
H&L BACKHOE SERVICE INC
21025 White Rock Dr (22736-1762)
PHONE.............................540 399-5013
William Leary, *Principal*
EMP: 4
SALES (est): 240.7K Privately Held
SIC: 3531 Backhoes

(G-11011)
LIVINGSTON RESOURCES INC
Also Called: Ameridarts
21009 Walkers Ln (22736-1977)
PHONE.............................704 892-1989
David Holt, *President*
Janis Cromer, *Treasurer*
EMP: 2 EST: 1996
SQ FT: 3,500
SALES (est): 204.7K Privately Held
SIC: 3949 Sporting & athletic goods

Richlands
Tazewell County

(G-11012)
**APPALACHIAN MINERAL
SERVICES**
Also Called: AM Services
113 Augusta Ave (24641-2706)
PHONE.............................276 345-4610
Rufus E Gilbert, *President*
EMP: 5 EST: 2016
SALES (est): 234K Privately Held
SIC: 3999 Atomizers, toiletry

(G-11013)
**BAKER HUGHES HOLDINGS
LLC**
2652 Chestnut St (24641-2727)
PHONE.............................276 963-0106
EMP: 2
SALES (corp-wide): 23.8B Publicly Held
WEB: www.bakerhughes.com
SIC: 1389 Oil field services
HQ: Baker Hughes Holdings Llc
　17021 Aldine Westfield Rd
　Houston TX 77073
　713 439-8600

(G-11014)
**BROCK ENTERPRISES VIRGINIA
LLC**
Also Called: Four Wheel Supply
1400 Iron St (24641-2829)
PHONE.............................276 971-4549
Mitchell R Null, *Mng Member*
Charles F Lawson,
EMP: 6
SQ FT: 3,000
SALES (est): 241.5K Privately Held
WEB: www.fourwheelsupply.net
SIC: 3545 Machine tool accessories

(G-11015)
CAL SYD INC
Also Called: Cline Chemicals
2111 3rd St (24641-2259)
PHONE.............................276 963-3640
Andy Altever, *President*
Peggy Altazer, *Corp Secy*
EMP: 2 EST: 1969
SALES (est): 311.3K Privately Held
SIC: 2842 Specialty cleaning preparations

(G-11016)
G&G WELDING & FABRICATING
113 Augusta Ave (24641-2706)
PHONE.............................276 202-3815
Rufus Gilbert, *Principal*
EMP: 1
SALES (est): 35.2K Privately Held
SIC: 7692 Welding repair

(G-11017)
JACKIE SCREEN PRINTING
2401 Front St (24641-2214)
PHONE.............................276 963-0964
Jack Mullins Jr, *Owner*
EMP: 1
SQ FT: 2,000
SALES (est): 80K Privately Held
SIC: 2261 3993 2396 Screen printing of
cotton broadwoven fabrics; signs & adver-
tising specialties; automotive & apparel
trimmings

(G-11018)
**MCCLURE CONCRETE
MATERIALS LLC (PA)**
1201 Iron St (24641-2855)
P.O. Box 338 (24641-0338)
PHONE.............................276 964-9682
Jason Herndon, *President*
EMP: 4
SALES (est): 635.5K Privately Held
WEB: www.mcclureconcrete.com
SIC: 3273 Ready-mixed concrete

(G-11019)
**MCCLURE CONCRETE
PRODUCTS INC (PA)**
Also Called: Richlands Concrete
1201 Iron St (24641-2855)
P.O. Box 338 (24641-0338)
PHONE.............................276 964-9682
Kenneth Herndon, *President*
Jason K Herndon, *Vice Pres*
B O Cyne, *Manager*
EMP: 8
SALES (est): 3.9MM Privately Held
WEB: www.mcclureconcrete.com
SIC: 3273 Ready-mixed concrete

(G-11020)
**TADANO MANTIS
CORPORATION**
2680 S Front St (24641-2751)
PHONE.............................800 272-3325
Andrew Cowden, *Engineer*
Thomas Wallace, *Engineer*
Steve B Atherton, *Manager*
Peter Blinn, *Technician*
Tim Vaillancourt, *Technician*
EMP: 25 Privately Held
WEB: www.mantiscranes.com
SIC: 3531 Cranes
HQ: Tadano Mantis Corporation
　1705 Columbia Ave Ste 200
　Franklin TN 37064
　615 794-4556

(G-11021)
ULTRA PETROLEUM LLC
1400 5th St (24641-2499)
P.O. Box 429 (24641-0429)
PHONE.............................276 964-6118
Stanford Mullins,
EMP: 7
SALES (est): 1.5MM Privately Held
WEB: www.ultrapetrollc.com
SIC: 2999 Coke (not from refineries), pe-
troleum

(G-11022)
VALLEY WHEEL CO INC
Also Called: Valley Wheel & Machine
101 Bedford Ave (24641-2708)
P.O. Box 1007 (24641-1007)
PHONE.............................276 964-5013
John N Buskill, *President*
EMP: 2
SQ FT: 8,000
SALES (est): 161.6K Privately Held
SIC: 3462 Railroad wheels, axles, frogs or
other equipment: forged

Richmond
Chesterfield County

(G-11023)
ALTRIA CLIENT SERVICES LLC
Also Called: Altria Group
2325 Bells Rd (23234-2274)
PHONE.............................804 274-2000
EMP: 4
SALES (est): 320.6K Publicly Held
SIC: 2111 Cigarettes
PA: Altria Group, Inc.
　6601 W Broad St
　Richmond VA 23230
　804 274-2200

(G-11024)
ALTRIA GROUP INC
4201 Commerce Rd (23234-2269)
PHONE.............................804 335-2703
EMP: 12 Publicly Held
WEB: www.altria.com
SIC: 2111 Cigarettes
PA: Altria Group, Inc.
　6601 W Broad St
　Richmond VA 23230
　804 274-2200

(G-11025)
**AMERICAN MACHINE CO
RICHMOND**
2200 Commerce Rd (23234-1849)
PHONE.............................804 231-1157
Ralph Bauwins, *President*
Elsie Williams, *Office Mgr*
Kim Hargett, *Manager*
Billy Carty, *Info Tech Mgr*
EMP: 12
SQ FT: 20,000
SALES (est): 2.1MM Privately Held
WEB: www.americanmachineco.com
SIC: 3599 Machine shop, jobbing & repair

(G-11026)
**AMERICAN MTAL
FABRICATIONS INC**
2512 Sisco Ave (23234-2732)
P.O. Box 34280, North Chesterfield
(23234-0280)
PHONE.............................804 271-8355
Garland Moss, *President*
Evelyn Moss, *Admin Sec*
Darrell Moss, *Administration*
EMP: 20
SQ FT: 9,000
SALES (est): 4.5MM Privately Held
WEB: www.americanmetalfabrications.com
SIC: 3441 Fabricated structural metal for
ships

(G-11027)
**ATLANTIC CORRUGATED BOX
CO INC**
1701 Ruffin Rd (23234-1830)
PHONE.............................804 231-4050
Edward D Barlow II, *President*
Vika Smahina, *HR Admin*
Gina Melendez, *Sales Staff*
Nita Nicholson, *Admin Asst*
Bonnie Wright,
EMP: 23
SQ FT: 60,000
SALES (est): 7.1MM Privately Held
WEB: www.acbc-inc.com
SIC: 2653 Boxes, corrugated: made from
purchased materials

(G-11028)
BARA PRINTING SERVICES
2944 Bells Rd (23234-1606)
PHONE.............................804 303-8615
EMP: 2
SALES (est): 73.2K Privately Held
SIC: 2759 Publication printing

(G-11029)
BELIEVE MAGAZINE
4131 Dorset Rd (23234-3638)
PHONE.............................804 291-7509
Emily Maxey, *Principal*
EMP: 3
SALES (est): 172.3K Privately Held
SIC: 2721 Periodicals

(G-11030)
BURROUGHS QIANA
Also Called: Ana's House Braids and Styles
8842 Proctors Run Dr (23237-2773)
PHONE.............................804 218-4031
Qiana Burroughs, *Owner*
EMP: 1
SALES (est): 17K Privately Held
SIC: 2844 Hair preparations, including
shampoos

(G-11031)
CARPENTER CO
2400 Jefferson Davis Hwy (23234-1122)
P.O. Box 34526, North Chesterfield
(23234-0526)
PHONE.............................804 359-0800
Allan Skagg, *Branch Mgr*
EMP: 300
SQ FT: 642,496
SALES (corp-wide): 1.8B Privately Held
WEB: www.carpenterftp.com
SIC: 3086 Plastics foam products
PA: Carpenter Co.
　5016 Monument Ave
　Richmond VA 23230
　804 359-0800

(G-11032)
CARPENTER CO
Also Called: M H Reinhart Technical Center
2600 Jefferson Davis Hwy (23234-1126)
P.O. Box 34546, North Chesterfield
(23234-0546)
PHONE.............................804 233-0606
Terry Thiem, *Branch Mgr*
EMP: 60
SALES (corp-wide): 1.8B Privately Held
WEB: www.carpenterftp.com
SIC: 3086 1311 2869 Insulation or cush-
ioning material, foamed plastic; carpet &
rug cushions, foamed plastic; padding,
foamed plastic; crude petroleum & natural
gas; industrial organic chemicals
PA: Carpenter Co.
　5016 Monument Ave
　Richmond VA 23230
　804 359-0800

(G-11033)
**CAVALIER PRINTING INK CO INC
(PA)**
Also Called: Cavalier Ink & Coatings
2807 Transport St (23234-1648)
P.O. Box 24538 (23224-0538)
PHONE.............................804 271-4214
Samuel Johnson, *President*
Linda Lightfoot, *Corp Secy*
▲ EMP: 5 EST: 1970
SQ FT: 25,570
SALES (est): 5.9MM Privately Held
WEB: www.cavalierinksandcoatings.com
SIC: 2893 Gravure ink

(G-11034)
CK GRAPHICWEAR LLC
4001 Garden Rd (23235-1126)
PHONE.............................804 464-1258
Christie Owens, *Principal*
EMP: 6
SALES (est): 493.2K Privately Held
WEB: www.ckgraphicwear.com
SIC: 2759 Screen printing

(G-11035)
CMC INTERIORS LLC
2110 Ruffin Rd (23234-6521)
PHONE.............................804 883-5671
Curtis M Clingenpeel,
EMP: 10 EST: 1989
SQ FT: 3,500
SALES (est): 225K Privately Held
SIC: 2521 3131 Cabinets, office: wood;
counters

(G-11036)
**CREATIVE WOODWORKING
SPECIALIS**
10501 Hobby Hill Rd (23235-1702)
PHONE.............................804 514-9066
EMP: 2
SALES (est): 171.2K Privately Held
SIC: 2431 Mfg Millwork

(G-11037)
CROP PRODUCTION SERVICES INC
Also Called: CPS
804 Mrfield Pk Dr Ste 210 (23236)
PHONE....................................804 282-7115
EMP: 2
SALES (corp-wide): 16B Privately Held
SIC: 2875 5191 2048 Mfg Fertilizers Whol Pesticides Insecticides & Agricultural Chemicals & Mixes & Mfg Grass & Bird Seed
HQ: Crop Production Services, Inc.
3005 Rocky Mountain Ave
Loveland CO 80538
970 685-3300

(G-11038)
CUSHING MANUFACTURING & EQP CO
Also Called: Cushing Manufacturing Company
2901 Commerce Rd (23234-1809)
P.O. Box 24365 (23224-0365)
PHONE....................................804 231-1161
Richard Farrell, CEO
W Ross Jennings III, President
Randy Jennings, Exec VP
▲ EMP: 27
SQ FT: 28,000
SALES (est): 5.6MM Privately Held
WEB: www.cushingmanufacturing.com
SIC: 3444 3448 Sheet metal specialties, not stamped; prefabricated metal buildings

(G-11039)
DANVILLE LEAF TOBACCO CO INC (HQ)
9201 Forest Hill Ave Fl 1 (23235-6865)
P.O. Box 25099 (23260-5099)
PHONE....................................804 359-9311
◆ EMP: 120
SQ FT: 45,000
SALES (est): 554.9MM
SALES (corp-wide): 2B Publicly Held
SIC: 2141 Tobacco Stemming/Redrying
PA: Universal Corporation
9201 Forest Hill Ave
Richmond VA 23235
804 359-9311

(G-11040)
DEEP CORPORATION
Also Called: American Pallet
2500 Deepwater Trml Rd (23234-1820)
P.O. Box 17615 (23226-7615)
PHONE....................................804 751-1826
William Deep, CEO
J Russell Brown, General Mgr
EMP: 15
SALES (est): 2.6MM Privately Held
WEB: www.americanpalletinc.com
SIC: 2448 Pallets, wood

(G-11041)
DILORETO PARTNERS INC
Also Called: Acf Environmental
5005 Castlewood Rd (23234)
PHONE....................................804 271-2363
EMP: 2
SALES (corp-wide): 38MM Privately Held
WEB: www.acfenvironmental.com
SIC: 3531 Construction machinery
PA: Diloreto Partners, Inc.
2831 Cardwell Rd
North Chesterfield VA 23234
757 665-8564

(G-11042)
DOZIER TANK AND WELDING CO
2212 Deepwater Trml Rd (23234-1817)
PHONE....................................804 232-0092
David T Dozier, President
EMP: 1
SALES (est): 52.6K Privately Held
WEB: www.doziertank.com
SIC: 7692 Welding repair

(G-11043)
GREGORY WAYNETTE
62221 Leopold Cir (23234)
PHONE....................................804 239-0230

Waynette Gregory, Owner
EMP: 1
SALES (est): 37K Privately Held
SIC: 2844 Toilet preparations

(G-11044)
HELP CONSTRUCTION RICHMOND LLC
2520 Prof Rd Ste A (23235)
PHONE....................................804 320-3220
Rick Bishop,
EMP: 2
SALES (est): 100K Privately Held
WEB: www.richmond.com
SIC: 2711 Newspapers, publishing & printing

(G-11045)
HERITAGE PRINTING LLC
11331 Bsneva Ctr Dr Ste C (23236)
PHONE....................................804 378-1196
Georgianna Rogers, Principal
EMP: 6
SALES (est): 702.8K Privately Held
SIC: 2752 Commercial printing, lithographic

(G-11046)
INTERNATIONAL PAPER COMPANY
3100 Hopkins Rd (23234-2016)
PHONE....................................804 232-4937
EMP: 2
SALES (est): 90.7K
SALES (corp-wide): 21.7B Publicly Held
SIC: 2621 Paper Mills
PA: International Paper Company
6400 Poplar Ave
Memphis TN 38197
901 419-9000

(G-11047)
JOHN MIDDLETON CO (DH)
2325 Bells Rd (23234-2274)
PHONE....................................610 792-8000
William Gofford Jr, CEO
Wynette Valentine, Supervisor
◆ EMP: 3 EST: 1856
SQ FT: 100,000
SALES (est): 47.1MM Publicly Held
WEB: www.johnmiddletonco.com
SIC: 2131 2121 Smoking tobacco; cigars
HQ: Philip Morris Usa Inc.
6601 W Brd St
Richmond VA 23230
804 274-2000

(G-11048)
JONETTE D MEADE
2917 Monteith Rd (23235-2150)
PHONE....................................804 247-0639
Jonette Meade, President
Willie Barley, Business Mgr
EMP: 2
SALES (est): 64.6K Privately Held
SIC: 3953 7299 Seal presses, notary & hand; party planning service

(G-11049)
KII INDUSTRIES LLC
2916 Glenan Dr (23234-1414)
PHONE....................................804 232-5791
Monica Esparza, Administration
EMP: 2 EST: 2010
SALES (est): 93K Privately Held
SIC: 3999 Manufacturing industries

(G-11050)
MID ATLANTIC WELDING TECH (PA)
3018 W Martins Grant Cir (23235-2108)
PHONE....................................804 330-8191
S Craig Lane, Administration
EMP: 4
SALES (est): 484K Privately Held
SIC: 7692 Welding repair

(G-11051)
MILLER MANUFACTURING CO INC (PA)
Also Called: Miller Group , The
3301 Castlewood Rd (23234-2111)
P.O. Box 1356 (23218-1356)
PHONE....................................804 232-4551
Ron Barsalou, President

S Tucker Grigg Jr, Principal
◆ EMP: 58 EST: 1897
SQ FT: 650,000
SALES (est): 14.7MM Privately Held
WEB: www.miller-group.com
SIC: 2541 Showcases, except refrigerated: wood

(G-11052)
MINERS OIL COMPANY INC
3737 Belt Blvd (23234-1524)
PHONE....................................804 230-5769
Richard Bays, President
EMP: 1
SQ FT: 900
SALES (est): 64.2K Privately Held
SIC: 1389 Oil field services

(G-11053)
MISS LIZZIES LOOT
9941 Maplested Ln (23235-2239)
PHONE....................................804 484-4212
Carolyn McCracken, Principal
EMP: 1
SALES (est): 39.6K Privately Held
SIC: 3999 Candles

(G-11054)
NAMAX MUSIC LLC
4102 Castlewood Rd (23234-2708)
P.O. Box 24162 (23224-0162)
PHONE....................................804 271-9535
M Brown, President
EMP: 6
SALES (est): 371.5K Privately Held
SIC: 2741 Miscellaneous publishing

(G-11055)
PALLET EMPIRE
2820 Bells Rd Ste D (23234-1659)
PHONE....................................804 389-3604
Geri Filatov, Principal
EMP: 4
SALES (est): 281.3K Privately Held
SIC: 2448 Pallets, wood

(G-11056)
PEPSICO INC
1608 Willis Rd (23237)
PHONE....................................804 714-1382
EMP: 2
SALES (corp-wide): 67.1B Publicly Held
WEB: www.pepsico.com
SIC: 2086 Carbonated soft drinks, bottled & canned
PA: Pepsico, Inc.
700 Anderson Hill Rd
Purchase NY 10577
914 253-2000

(G-11057)
PETERS PALLETS INC
2700 Jefferson Davis Hwy (23234-1222)
PHONE....................................410 647-8094
Harry King, President
EMP: 1 Privately Held
WEB: www.peterspallets.net
SIC: 2448 Pallets, wood
PA: Peters Pallets, Inc.
8221 Ritchie Hwy Ste 105
Pasadena MD 21122

(G-11058)
PHILIP MORRIS USA INC
3601 Commerce Rd (23234-2272)
P.O. Box 26603 (23261-6603)
PHONE....................................804 274-2000
Art Bell, Principal
Craig G Schwartz, Senior VP
EMP: 24 Publicly Held
WEB: www.philipmorrisusa.com
SIC: 2111 Cigarettes
HQ: Philip Morris Usa Inc.
6601 W Brd St
Richmond VA 23230
804 274-2000

(G-11059)
PHIPPS & BIRD INC
2924 Bells Rd (23234-1606)
P.O. Box 7475 (23221-0475)
PHONE....................................804 254-2737
Wes Skaperdas, President
Patricia L Skaperdas, Exec VP
Kevin Brown, Chief Engr
▼ EMP: 13 EST: 1990

SQ FT: 30,000 Privately Held
WEB: www.phippsbird.com
SIC: 3826 3821 3499 3841 Analytical instruments; laboratory apparatus & furniture; furniture parts, metal; medical instruments & equipment, blood & bone work

(G-11060)
PLAN B DESIGN FABRICATION INC (PA)
4210 Castlewood Rd (23234-2710)
PHONE....................................804 271-5200
Norman Elliott, President
▲ EMP: 19
SQ FT: 6,500
SALES (est): 1.5MM Privately Held
WEB: www.planbdesignandfab.com
SIC: 3441 Fabricated structural metal

(G-11061)
PPG INDUSTRIES INC
Also Called: PPG 9424
11351 Intl Dr Ste B (23236)
PHONE....................................804 794-5331
Rick Hull, Branch Mgr
EMP: 3
SALES (corp-wide): 15.3B Publicly Held
WEB: www.ppg.com
SIC: 2851 Paints & allied products
PA: Ppg Industries, Inc.
1 Ppg Pl
Pittsburgh PA 15272
412 434-3131

(G-11062)
ROCKWELL AUTOMATION INC
9020 Stony Point Pkwy (23235-1947)
PHONE....................................804 560-6444
Bruce C Freer, Regional Mgr
David Eckert, Project Mgr
Leilani Yoshida, Opers Staff
Steve Cisler, Engineer
Jessica Drda, Engineer
EMP: 67 Publicly Held
WEB: www.rockwellautomation.com
SIC: 3625 Relays & industrial controls
PA: Rockwell Automation, Inc.
1201 S 2nd St
Milwaukee WI 53204

(G-11063)
SECURITAS INC
4228 N Huguenot Rd (23235-1614)
PHONE....................................800 705-4545
Don Carpenter, President
Smokie Sizemore, Admin Sec
▲ EMP: 9
SQ FT: 1,200
SALES (est): 1MM Privately Held
WEB: www.no-shank.com
SIC: 2844 3952 3951 Shampoos, rinses, conditioners: hair; shaving preparations; deodorants, personal; toothpastes or powders, dentifrices; pencils & pencil parts, artists'; ball point pens & parts

(G-11064)
SLIM STRENGTH INC
2419 Wendell Ln (23234-1341)
PHONE....................................804 715-3080
Lydia Johnson,
Cornelius Johnson,
EMP: 2
SALES (est): 94.4K Privately Held
WEB: www.slimstrength.com
SIC: 2396 7389 Linings, apparel: made from purchased materials;

(G-11065)
TCS MATERIALS LLC (DH)
2100 Deepwater Trml Rd (23234-1816)
PHONE....................................804 232-1200
George Hossenlopt, President
Adamson W B, Vice Pres
Eileen M Bierlien, Admin Sec
EMP: 60
SQ FT: 6,000
SALES (est): 6.5MM Publicly Held
SIC: 3273 Ready-mixed concrete
HQ: Legacy Vulcan, Llc
1200 Urban Center Dr
Vestavia AL 35242
205 298-3000

(G-11066)
UNIVERSAL LEAF TOBACCO CO INC (HQ)
Also Called: Thorpe & Ricks
9201 Frest Hl Ave Stony P (23235)
P.O. Box 25099 (23260-5099)
PHONE.....................804 359-9311
George C Freeman III, *CEO*
Airton L Hentschke, *COO*
Preston D Wigner, *Senior VP*
Michael Haymore, *Vice Pres*
Jim Nagy, *Vice Pres*
◆ EMP: 72
SQ FT: 45,000
SALES (est): 51.4MM **Publicly Held**
WEB: www.universalleaf.com
SIC: 2141 Tobacco stemming & redrying
PA: Universal Corporation
9201 Forest Hill Ave
Richmond VA 23235
804 359-9311

(G-11067)
WORTHEN INDUSTRIES INC
Also Called: Upaco Adhesives
4107 Castlewood Rd (23234-2707)
PHONE.....................804 275-9231
Dale Huff, *Opers Staff*
Gary A Groat, *Manager*
EMP: 25 **Privately Held**
WEB: www.worthenind.com
SIC: 2891 Adhesives
HQ: Worthen Industries, Inc.
3 E Spit Brook Rd
Nashua NH 03060
603 888-5443

(G-11068)
WORTHEN INDUSTRIES INC
Also Called: Upaco Adhesive Division
4105 Castlewood Rd (23234-2707)
PHONE.....................804 275-9231
EMP: 20 **Privately Held**
WEB: www.worthenind.com
SIC: 2891 2295 Adhesives; coated fabrics, not rubberized
HQ: Worthen Industries, Inc.
3 E Spit Brook Rd
Nashua NH 03060
603 888-5443

Richmond
Henrico County

(G-11069)
10FOLD WALLETS LLC
1329 Amherst Ave (23227-4020)
PHONE.....................804 982-0003
EMP: 1
SALES (est): 49.1K **Privately Held**
SIC: 3172 Wallets

(G-11070)
1ST STOP ELECTRONICS LLC
1209 Garber St (23231-3510)
PHONE.....................804 931-0517
Clinton Parker,
EMP: 1
SQ FT: 1,000
SALES (est): 72.2K **Privately Held**
SIC: 3999 5045 3577 1731 Badges, metal: policemen, firemen, etc.; computers, peripherals & software; printers, computer; computer installation; electronic computers

(G-11071)
2 P PRODUCTS
8205 Costin Dr (23229-3251)
PHONE.....................804 273-9822
EMP: 3 EST: 2001
SALES (est): 190K **Privately Held**
SIC: 2891 Mfg Adhesives/Sealants

(G-11072)
2R2S INC
1421 Greycourt Ave (23227-4045)
PHONE.....................804 262-6922
Meredith Harriss, *Principal*
EMP: 2
SALES (est): 104.8K **Privately Held**
SIC: 3589 High pressure cleaning equipment

(G-11073)
3MP1RE CLOTHING CO
5642 Trafalgar Park (23228-1818)
PHONE.....................540 892-3484
Keith Wheeler, *Principal*
EMP: 1
SALES (est): 36.5K **Privately Held**
SIC: 2361 2331 5699 3144 T-shirts & tops: girls', children's & infants'; T-shirts & tops, women's: made from purchased materials; T-shirts, custom printed; dress shoes, women's; women's shoes; business services

(G-11074)
4 SHORES TRNSPRTING LGSTIX LLC
1304 Elmshadow Dr (23231-4727)
PHONE.....................804 319-6247
Kimberly Robinson, *CEO*
John Robinson, *CFO*
EMP: 4 EST: 2016
SALES (est): 135.7K **Privately Held**
SIC: 3441 8211 4213 8742 Railroad car racks, for transporting vehicles: steel; specialty education; less-than-truckload (LTL) transport; materials mgmt. (purchasing, handling, inventory) consultant

(G-11075)
A & V PRECISION MACHINE INC
5710 Charles City Cir (23231-4502)
PHONE.....................804 222-9466
Kimh Tran, *President*
Tommy Bear, *Admin Sec*
EMP: 8
SQ FT: 2,400
SALES (est): 275K **Privately Held**
SIC: 3599 Machine shop, jobbing & repair

(G-11076)
A BETTER IMAGE
2317 Westwood Ave Ste 213 (23230-4020)
PHONE.....................804 358-9912
EMP: 1
SALES (est): 104.6K **Privately Held**
SIC: 3861 Photographic Equipment And Supplies

(G-11077)
A SORTED AFFIAR RICHMOND LLC
8605 Seldondale Ln (23229-7241)
PHONE.....................804 464-9820
EMP: 3
SALES (est): 117.2K **Privately Held**
WEB: www.richmond.com
SIC: 2711 Newspapers, publishing & printing

(G-11078)
A-1 SECURITY MFG CORP
3001 Moore St (23230-4507)
PHONE.....................804 359-9003
▲ EMP: 14
SQ FT: 10,000
SALES (est): 970K **Privately Held**
SIC: 3429 3589 Mfg Locksmith Tools And Supplies & Industrial Dust Collection Supplies

(G-11079)
ABB POWER PROTECTION LLC (DH)
Also Called: J T Packard
5900 Eastport Blvd Ste V (23231-4459)
PHONE.....................804 236-3300
Christian M Tecca, *President*
Pedro Mendieta, *General Mgr*
Harry Tillery, *Vice Pres*
James Brown, *Engineer*
Chris Hackman, *Engineer*
▲ EMP: 156
SQ FT: 60,000
SALES (est): 99MM
SALES (corp-wide): 27.9B **Privately Held**
WEB: www.electrification.us.abb.com
SIC: 3629 Power conversion units, a.c. to d.c.: static-electric
HQ: Abb Installation Products Inc.
860 Ridge Lake Blvd
Memphis TN 38120
901 252-5000

(G-11080)
ACE HARDWOOD
11105 Woodbaron Ct (23233-1268)
PHONE.....................804 270-4260
Aaron K Hollister, *Principal*
EMP: 3
SALES (est): 236.1K **Privately Held**
SIC: 3272 Floor slabs & tiles, precast concrete

(G-11081)
ACORN SALES COMPANY INC
Also Called: Acorn Sign Manufacturing
1506 Tomlynn St (23230-3313)
P.O. Box 6971 (23230-0971)
PHONE.....................804 359-0505
J Daniel Raidabaugh Jr, *President*
Holly Raidabaugh, *Vice Pres*
EMP: 17
SQ FT: 10,000
SALES (est): 2.3MM **Privately Held**
WEB: www.acornsales.com
SIC: 2499 3953 Signboards, wood; embossing seals & hand stamps

(G-11082)
ACORN SIGN GRAPHICS INC
4109 W Clay St (23230-3307)
P.O. Box 11664 (23230-0064)
PHONE.....................804 726-6999
Tj Daly, *CEO*
Beth J Gillispie, *President*
Owen Taylor, *General Mgr*
Adam Canady, *Business Mgr*
Ann Taylor, *Business Mgr*
EMP: 44
SALES (est): 6.4MM **Privately Held**
WEB: www.acornsign.com
SIC: 3993 Signs, not made in custom sign painting shops

(G-11083)
ACTION DIGITAL INC
2317 Westwood Ave Ste 101 (23230-4019)
PHONE.....................804 358-7289
Albert D Seim II, *President*
Lawrence I Seim, *Corp Secy*
Margaret R Seim, *Exec VP*
EMP: 5 EST: 1995
SQ FT: 1,300
SALES (est): 476.3K **Privately Held**
SIC: 3625 3651 3577 Electric controls & control accessories, industrial; household audio & video equipment; computer peripheral equipment

(G-11084)
ACTION TSHIRTS LLC
2926 W Marshall St Lowr (23230-4832)
PHONE.....................804 359-4645
Ernest Ferguson, *Mng Member*
EMP: 1 EST: 1980
SQ FT: 2,400
SALES (est): 38.7K **Privately Held**
WEB: www.actiont-shirts.com
SIC: 2759 Screen printing

(G-11085)
ADAMANTINE PRECISION TOOLS
3117 Aspen Ave (23228-4902)
PHONE.....................804 354-9118
Jason Fields, *Owner*
EMP: 8
SALES (est): 1MM **Privately Held**
WEB: www.texasleatherworks.com
SIC: 3599 Machine shop, jobbing & repair

(G-11086)
ADVANCED CABINETS & TOPS INC
1726 Arlington Rd (23230-4202)
PHONE.....................804 355-5541
Benny Verdi, *President*
Susan Verdi, *Vice Pres*
EMP: 5
SQ FT: 10,000
SALES (est): 661.6K **Privately Held**
WEB: www.actccu.com
SIC: 2434 Wood kitchen cabinets

(G-11087)
ADVERTECH PRESS LLC
701 Erin Crescent St (23231-1218)
PHONE.....................804 404-8560
Terrance Bellock, *Principal*
EMP: 1
SALES (est): 46.6K **Privately Held**
SIC: 2741 Miscellaneous publishing

(G-11088)
ADVERTISING IMAGES & EMB
5608 W Marshall St (23230-2612)
PHONE.....................703 447-4282
EMP: 1
SALES (est): 31.2K **Privately Held**
SIC: 2395 Pleating & stitching

(G-11089)
AGENT MEDICAL LLC
1145 Gaskins Rd Ste 102 (23238-5236)
PHONE.....................804 562-9469
EMP: 4 EST: 2013
SALES (est): 183.1K **Privately Held**
SIC: 3841 Mfg Surgical/Medical Instruments

(G-11090)
AHF PUBLISHING LLC
411 Libbie Ave (23226-2655)
PHONE.....................804 282-6170
Matthew Farley, *Principal*
EMP: 1
SALES (est): 55.5K **Privately Held**
SIC: 2741 Miscellaneous publishing

(G-11091)
AIR METAL CORP
7608 Compton Rd (23228-3618)
PHONE.....................804 262-1004
Douglas D Smith, *President*
Gladys F Smith, *Corp Secy*
Deborah A Rosser, *Vice Pres*
EMP: 7
SQ FT: 6,000
SALES (est): 1.2MM **Privately Held**
SIC: 3444 Ducts, sheet metal

(G-11092)
ALBEMARLE CORPORATION
5721 Gulfstream Rd (23250-2422)
PHONE.....................225 388-8011
Jeffrey Gardner, *Manager*
Jon Huckels, *Manager*
Andrew Ray, *Info Tech Mgr*
Ray A Kozakewicz, *Director*
EMP: 245 **Publicly Held**
WEB: www.albemarle.com
SIC: 2821 2834 2819 2812 Plastics materials & resins; pharmaceutical preparations; bromine, elemental; alkalies & chlorine; industrial organic chemicals; fire retardant chemicals
PA: Albemarle Corporation
4250 Congress St Ste 900
Charlotte NC 28209

(G-11093)
ALDRIDGE INSTALLATIONS LLC
2142 Tomlynn St (23230-3338)
PHONE.....................804 658-1035
Wallace Aldridge, *Principal*
EMP: 5
SALES (est): 559.9K **Privately Held**
WEB: www.richmondshowerdoorsandmore.com
SIC: 3089 5211 Doors, folding: plastic or plastic coated fabric; bathroom fixtures, equipment & supplies; closets, interiors & accessories

(G-11094)
ALFA LAVAL CHAMP LLC
5400 Intl Trade Dr (23231)
PHONE.....................866 253-2528
Steve Allmond, *Project Mgr*
Edie Hall, *Executive Asst*
EMP: 2
SALES (est): 117K **Privately Held**
SIC: 3491 Industrial valves

(G-11095)
ALFA LAVAL INC (HQ)
5400 Intl Trade Dr (23231)
PHONE.....................866 253-2528
Joakim Vilson, *Ch of Bd*
Jo Vanhoren, *President*
Christine Casey, *Regional Mgr*
Alfredo Fernandez, *Business Mgr*
Tobias Vernersson, *Business Mgr*
◆ EMP: 250 EST: 1885

▲ = Import ▼=Export
◆ =Import/Export

SQ FT: 180,000
SALES (est): 215.5MM **Privately Held**
SIC: 3491 3433 3585 3569 Industrial valves; heating equipment, except electric; refrigeration & heating equipment; assembly machines, non-metalworking; laboratory apparatus & furniture

(G-11096)
ALFA LAVAL US HOLDING INC (DH)
5400 Intl Trade Dr (23231)
P.O. Box 7731 (23231-0231)
PHONE...................................804 222-5300
John Atanasio, *President*
Nish Patel, *Chairman*
Mark Larsen, *Vice Pres*
Jeff Sharbaugh, *Vice Pres*
Joseph M Lawrence, *Treasurer*
◆ EMP: 64
SALES (est): 376.4MM **Privately Held**
WEB: www.alfalaval.com
SIC: 3569 5085 Centrifuges, industrial; valves & fittings
HQ: Alfa Laval Usa Inc.
5400 Intl Trade Dr
Richmond VA 23231
804 222-5300

(G-11097)
ALFA LAVAL USA INC (DH)
5400 Intl Trade Dr (23231)
PHONE...................................804 222-5300
John Atanasio, *President*
Nish Patel, *Chairman*
Cecilie Ogara, *Business Mgr*
Ester Codina, *Senior VP*
John Piazza, *Vice Pres*
◆ EMP: 29
SALES (est): 258.7MM **Privately Held**
WEB: www.alfalaval.com
SIC: 3443 3585 Finned tubes, for heat transfer; evaporative condensers, heat transfer equipment
HQ: Alfa Laval Corporate Ab
Rudeboksvagen 3
Lund 226 5
463 665-00

(G-11098)
ALICESA FOSTER GRAVES LLC
7414 Griffin Ave (23227-1805)
PHONE...................................804 658-0092
Alicesa Foster, *President*
EMP: 1
SALES (est): 52.8K **Privately Held**
SIC: 3999 5999 Manufacturing industries; miscellaneous retail stores

(G-11099)
ALTAMONT RECORDERS LLC
1710 Altamont Ave (23230-4504)
PHONE...................................804 814-2310
Maynard Sipe, *Principal*
EMP: 1
SALES (est): 45.1K **Privately Held**
SIC: 3931 Musical instruments

(G-11100)
ALTRIA
6601 W Broad St (23230-1723)
PHONE...................................804 274-2100
EMP: 320
SALES (est): 29.6MM **Privately Held**
SIC: 3999 Mfg Misc Products

(G-11101)
ALTRIA CLIENT SERVICES LLC
Also Called: Altria Ventures
6601 W Broad St (23230-1723)
P.O. Box 85088 (23285-5088)
PHONE...................................804 274-2000
Jonathan Watson, *Engineer*
Billy Gifford, *Mng Member*
Scott Scofield, *Director*
Patricia Womack, *Analyst*
EMP: 10 EST: 2013
SALES (est): 845.2K **Publicly Held**
WEB: www.altria.com
SIC: 2111 2121 Cigarettes; cigars
PA: Altria Group, Inc.
6601 W Broad St
Richmond VA 23230
804 274-2200

(G-11102)
ALTRIA ENTERPRISES II LLC (DH)
6601 W Broad St (23230-1723)
PHONE...................................804 274-2200
EMP: 100
SALES (est): 5.7MM **Publicly Held**
WEB: www.altria.com
SIC: 2111 Cigarettes
HQ: Philip Morris Usa Inc.
6601 W Brd St
Richmond VA 23230
804 274-2000

(G-11103)
ALTRIA GROUP INC
6603 W Broad St (23230-1711)
P.O. Box 26603 (23261-6603)
PHONE...................................804 274-2000
Craig A Johnson, *President*
EMP: 11 **Publicly Held**
WEB: www.altria.com
SIC: 2111 Cigarettes
PA: Altria Group, Inc.
6601 W Broad St
Richmond VA 23230
804 274-2200

(G-11104)
ALTRIA GROUP INC
5720 Gulfstream Rd (23250-2422)
PHONE...................................804 274-2000
Dave Trickey, *COO*
EMP: 7 **Publicly Held**
WEB: www.altria.com
SIC: 2111 Cigarettes
PA: Altria Group, Inc.
6601 W Broad St
Richmond VA 23230
804 274-2200

(G-11105)
ALTRIA GROUP INC (PA)
6601 W Broad St (23230-1723)
PHONE...................................804 274-2200
Howard A Willard III, *CEO*
James Browne, *General Mgr*
Nat Sherman, *General Mgr*
Thomas Farrell, *Chairman*
Paul Cunningham, *District Mgr*
EMP: 1400 **Publicly Held**
WEB: www.altria.com
SIC: 2111 2084 Cigarettes; wines

(G-11106)
ALTRIA VENTURES INC (HQ)
6601 W Broad St (23230-1723)
PHONE...................................804 274-2000
EMP: 6
SALES (est): 2.8MM **Publicly Held**
WEB: www.altria.com
SIC: 2111 Cigarettes
PA: Altria Group, Inc.
6601 W Broad St
Richmond VA 23230
804 274-2200

(G-11107)
AMERICAN CMG SERVICES INC
Also Called: American Orthtic Prsthetic Ctr
2000 Bremo Rd Ste 205 (23226-2440)
PHONE...................................804 353-9077
Cynthia Smith, *President*
Michael Norton, *Manager*
EMP: 4 **Privately Held**
WEB: www.americanopc.com
SIC: 3842 5999 Prosthetic appliances; artificial limbs
PA: American Cmg Services, Inc.
1521 Technology Dr
Chesapeake VA 23320

(G-11108)
AMERICAN DRUM INC
2800 Seven Hills Blvd (23231-6033)
PHONE...................................804 226-1778
George Jacob, *President*
George Jacobs, *President*
▲ EMP: 5
SQ FT: 6,620
SALES (est): 529K **Privately Held**
WEB: www.americandrum.com
SIC: 3931 Musical instruments

(G-11109)
AMERICAN LASER CENTERS
2004 Bremo Rd (23226-2442)
PHONE...................................804 200-5000
Mary Taylor, *Manager*
EMP: 2 EST: 2007
SALES (est): 129.1K **Privately Held**
SIC: 2759 Laser printing

(G-11110)
AMF AUTOMATION TECH LLC (PA)
2115 W Laburnum Ave (23227-4396)
PHONE...................................804 355-7961
Russell Hembree, *CEO*
Lauren McFadyen, *General Mgr*
Jason Ward, *Exec VP*
Fabiano Malara, *Vice Pres*
Federico Martinez, *Vice Pres*
◆ EMP: 234
SQ FT: 167,000
SALES (est): 126MM **Privately Held**
WEB: www.amfbakery.com
SIC: 3556 Bakery machinery

(G-11111)
AMF BAKERY SYSTEMS CORP
2115 W Laburnum Ave (23227-4396)
PHONE...................................800 225-3771
Scott Bieker, *Vice Pres*
EMP: 2
SALES (est): 192K **Privately Held**
WEB: www.amfbakery.com
SIC: 3556 Food products machinery

(G-11112)
AMS SERVICES LLC
2014 Skipwith Rd (23294-3536)
PHONE...................................804 869-4777
Adam Stewart, *Principal*
EMP: 1 EST: 2011
SALES (est): 73.8K **Privately Held**
SIC: 7372 Prepackaged software

(G-11113)
AMSCIEN INSTRUMENT
4408 Hungary Glen Ter (23294-6048)
PHONE...................................804 301-0797
Shugen Zhang, *President*
Caiting Fu, *Principal*
EMP: 6
SALES (est): 100K **Privately Held**
WEB: www.amscien.com
SIC: 3826 Analytical instruments

(G-11114)
ANNE CHAPMAN CASTING
2939 W Marshall St (23230-4810)
PHONE...................................804 728-1300
Anne Chapman, *Principal*
EMP: 1 EST: 2015
SALES (est): 84.7K **Privately Held**
WEB: www.annechapmancasting.com
SIC: 3366 Copper foundries

(G-11115)
APPLIED POLYMER LLC
12840 River Rd (23238-7205)
PHONE...................................804 615-5105
David Pendergrast,
EMP: 1 EST: 2009
SALES (est): 400K **Privately Held**
SIC: 2822 Ethylene-propylene rubbers, EPDM polymers

(G-11116)
ARCHITECTURAL SYSTEMS VIRGINIA (PA)
9522 Downing St (23238-4444)
P.O. Box 70351 (23255-0351)
PHONE...................................804 270-0477
Tom Burke, *CEO*
Sean Burke, *Project Mgr*
EMP: 4
SALES (est): 1.5MM **Privately Held**
WEB: www.arch-systems.net
SIC: 3231 5033 Products of purchased glass; roofing, siding & insulation

(G-11117)
ARDEENS DESIGNS INC
4610 Lkfeld Mews Pl Apt G (23231)
PHONE...................................804 562-3840
EMP: 1

SALES (est): 64.9K **Privately Held**
SIC: 2335 Womens, Juniors, And Misses Dresses

(G-11118)
ARGON
3805 Cutshaw Ave (23230-3943)
PHONE...................................804 365-5628
EMP: 3
SALES (est): 135.2K **Privately Held**
WEB: www.argonapartments.com
SIC: 2813 Argon

(G-11119)
ASSOCIATED PRINTING SVCS INC
2504 Brookstone Ln (23233-6914)
P.O. Box 5967, Glen Allen (23058-5967)
PHONE...................................804 360-5770
James J Palmer, *President*
EMP: 2
SALES (est): 700K **Privately Held**
WEB: www.associatedprintingservices.com
SIC: 3567 Industrial furnaces & ovens

(G-11120)
ASTELLAS PHARMA US INC
9701 Electra Ln (23228-1424)
PHONE...................................804 262-3197
Spencer Eddy, *Principal*
EMP: 1 **Privately Held**
WEB: www.astellas.com
SIC: 2834 Pharmaceutical preparations
HQ: Astellas Pharma Us, Inc.
1 Astellas Way
Northbrook IL 60062

(G-11121)
BARKER COLLISION PRECISION LLC
1123 Penobscot Rd (23227-1252)
PHONE...................................716 481-8253
Richard Dibble, *Administration*
EMP: 2
SALES (est): 79.5K **Privately Held**
SIC: 3489 Ordnance & accessories

(G-11122)
BAXTER HEALTHCARE CORPORATION
5800 S Laburnum Ave (23231-4423)
PHONE...................................804 226-1962
Kristie Zinselmeier, *Vice Pres*
Ken Lober, *Branch Mgr*
Ross Disney, *Manager*
EMP: 4
SALES (corp-wide): 11.3B **Publicly Held**
WEB: www.baxter.com
SIC: 3841 Surgical & medical instruments
HQ: Baxter Healthcare Corporation
1 Baxter Pkwy
Deerfield IL 60015
224 948-2000

(G-11123)
BELL PRINTING INC
1720 E Parham Rd (23228-2202)
PHONE...................................804 261-1776
Annabella D Bell, *Principal*
EMP: 4
SALES (est): 292K **Privately Held**
SIC: 2752 Commercial printing, lithographic

(G-11124)
BFI WASTE SERVICES LLC
Also Called: BFI Waste Services of Richmond
2490 Charles City Rd (23231-4402)
PHONE...................................804 222-1152
Zack Hanson, *Manager*
EMP: 50 **Publicly Held**
WEB: www.republicservices.com
SIC: 3639 Trash compactors, household
HQ: Bfi Waste Services, Llc
18500 N Allied Way # 100
Phoenix AZ 85054
480 627-2700

(G-11125)
BINGO TRIBUNE INC
6500 Barcroft Ln (23226-3103)
PHONE...................................804 221-9049
Benjamin Freedlander, *Principal*
EMP: 4

SALES (est): 194K **Privately Held**
WEB: www.bingotribune.com
SIC: **2711** Newspapers, publishing & printing

(G-11126)
BIOMASS ENGLISH PARTNERS LLC
2890 Seven Hills Blvd (23231-6033)
P.O. Box 50218 (23250-0218)
PHONE.................................804 226-8227
Doug Padgett, *Project Mgr*
Johnnie English,
EMP: 4 EST: 2010
SALES (est): 420K **Privately Held**
WEB: www.englishboiler.com
SIC: **3443** Boiler shop products: boilers, smokestacks, steel tanks

(G-11127)
BIOMATERIALS USA LLC
2405 Westwood Ave Ste 203 (23230-4017)
PHONE.................................843 442-4789
Xuejun Wen,
EMP: 3
SALES (est): 215.3K **Privately Held**
WEB: www.biomaterialsusa.com
SIC: **3842** Implants, surgical

(G-11128)
BLUE BEE CIDER LLC
1320 Summit Ave (23230-4710)
PHONE.................................804 231-0280
Courtney Mailey, *Mng Member*
Amy Shumaker, *Manager*
EMP: 15
SALES (est): 504.9K **Privately Held**
WEB: www.bluebeecider.com
SIC: **2084** 5169 5921 Wine cellars, bonded: engaged in blending wines; alcohols; liquor stores

(G-11129)
BLUEBIRD CABINETRY
7333 Strath Rd (23231-7110)
PHONE.................................804 937-5429
Andrew Olsen, *Owner*
EMP: 1
SALES (est): 141.5K **Privately Held**
SIC: **2434** Wood kitchen cabinets

(G-11130)
BLYTHE
11713 W Broad St (23233-1006)
PHONE.................................804 364-1717
EMP: 2
SALES (est): 74.5K **Privately Held**
WEB: www.shopatblythe.com
SIC: **2323** Men's & boys' neckwear

(G-11131)
BRASS BEDS OF VIRGINIA INC
3210 W Marshall St Ste B (23230-4635)
PHONE.................................804 353-3503
Pat Hudgins, *President*
EMP: 30
SQ FT: 23,000
SALES (est): 3.3MM **Privately Held**
WEB: www.brassbedofva.com
SIC: **2514** 5712 2515 2511 Metal household furniture; furniture stores; mattresses & bedsprings; wood household furniture

(G-11132)
BRAZILIAN BEST GRANITE INC (PA)
Also Called: Bbg
6512 W Broad St (23230-2014)
PHONE.................................804 562-3022
Fernando Sobreira, *President*
Trey Monday, *COO*
Tanya Rigsby, *Office Mgr*
Tanya Martin, *Manager*
Best Granite, *Products*
▲ EMP: 4
SALES (est): 2.4MM **Privately Held**
WEB: www.bbggranite.com
SIC: **3281** 1799 Granite, cut & shaped; table tops, marble; counter top installation

(G-11133)
BRIDGETOWN LLC
9020 Michaux Ln (23229-6342)
PHONE.................................804 741-0648
Carl Girard,

EMP: 1
SALES (est): 25K **Privately Held**
SIC: **2844** Toilet preparations

(G-11134)
BRIGHTWORK BOAT CO
7601 Fourdale Ln (23231-7132)
PHONE.................................804 795-9080
William F Patterson, *Owner*
EMP: 1
SALES (est): 68K **Privately Held**
SIC: **3732** Boats, fiberglass: building & repairing

(G-11135)
BROAD STREET SIGNS INC
3000 Impala Pl (23228-4206)
PHONE.................................804 262-1007
EMP: 1
SALES (est): 48.8K **Privately Held**
SIC: **3993** Mfg Signs/Advertising Specialties

(G-11136)
BRODIES NATURALS LLC
8037 Stonemeade Dr (23231-8944)
PHONE.................................804 507-0542
Brodie Janie, *Principal*
EMP: 2
SALES (est): 117.6K **Privately Held**
WEB: www.herbalbodyblessings.com
SIC: **2844** Toilet preparations

(G-11137)
BRUSH HOLDINGS INC (PA)
110 Tuckahoe Blvd (23226-2225)
PHONE.................................804 226-4433
Timothy B Brizzolara, *President*
Dennis Duke Brizzolara, *Vice Pres*
Duke Brizzolara, *Vice Pres*
April Boykin, *Sales Staff*
Patricia Vernon, *Sales Associate*
◆ EMP: 89 EST: 1910
SALES (est): 9.8MM **Privately Held**
WEB: www.odbco.com
SIC: **3991** Brooms & brushes

(G-11138)
BUILDERS CABINET CO INC
959 Myers St Ste C (23230-4800)
P.O. Box 11833 (23230-8033)
PHONE.................................804 358-7789
Joey Bryant, *President*
EMP: 7 EST: 1975
SQ FT: 10,000
SALES (est): 1MM **Privately Held**
SIC: **2541** Counter & sink tops

(G-11139)
BUSH RIVER CORPORATION
Also Called: AMF
8100 Amf Dr (23227)
PHONE.................................804 730-4000
Steve Satterwhite, *President*
EMP: 1
SALES (est): 66.2K
SALES (corp-wide): 341.2MM **Privately Held**
WEB: www.amfbakery.com
SIC: **3949** Bowling equipment & supplies
HQ: Amf Bowling Centers Holdings Inc.
7313 Bell Creek Rd
Mechanicsville VA 23111

(G-11140)
BUSINESS PRESS
Also Called: Business Center
2112 Spencer Rd (23230-2624)
PHONE.................................804 282-3150
E J Barbour, *Owner*
EMP: 12
SQ FT: 5,000
SALES (est): 1.4MM **Privately Held**
WEB: www.flashcolorimaging.com
SIC: **2752** Commercial printing, offset

(G-11141)
BUSKEY CIDER
2910 W Leigh St (23230-4528)
PHONE.................................901 626-0535
William Correll, *Owner*
Julie Britland, *Sales Staff*
Andrew Coffin, *Manager*
EMP: 1 EST: 2015

SALES (est): 126.9K **Privately Held**
WEB: www.buskeycider.com
SIC: **2099** Cider, nonalcoholic

(G-11142)
BXI INC
Also Called: Art Guild Signs & Graphics
2111 Lake Ave (23230-2636)
P.O. Box 6621 (23230-0621)
PHONE.................................804 282-5434
Clyde Willis, *Branch Mgr*
EMP: 8
SQ FT: 9,792
SALES (corp-wide): 3.3MM **Privately Held**
WEB: www.banner-express.com
SIC: **2759** 7336 3993 2752 Screen printing; commercial art & illustration; signs & advertising specialties; commercial printing, lithographic; automotive & apparel trimmings; broadwoven fabric mills, manmade
PA: Bxi Inc
8416 Staples Mill Rd
Henrico VA 23228
804 285-7575

(G-11143)
CABINETS TO GO LLC
2305 Westwood Ave (23230-4011)
PHONE.................................804 325-4775
EMP: 2
SALES (corp-wide): 40.6MM **Privately Held**
WEB: www.cabinetstogo.com
SIC: **2434** Wood kitchen cabinets
PA: Cabinets To Go, Llc
2350 Wo Smith Dr
Lawrenceburg TN 38464
909 646-5900

(G-11144)
CAMPBELL GRAPHICS INC
Also Called: AlphaGraphics
2904 W Clay St (23230-4807)
P.O. Box 8587 (23226-0587)
PHONE.................................804 353-7292
Craig H Campbell, *President*
Craig Campbell Jr, *Vice Pres*
Jason Campbell, *Graphic Designe*
EMP: 5 EST: 2000
SALES (est): 698.9K **Privately Held**
WEB: www.dnstore.com
SIC: **2752** Commercial printing, lithographic

(G-11145)
CANE CONNECTION
6941 Lakeside Ave (23228-5234)
PHONE.................................804 261-6555
Stephen Culler, *Owner*
EMP: 1
SALES (est): 317.4K **Privately Held**
WEB: www.thecaneconnection.com
SIC: **3553** Furniture makers' machinery, woodworking

(G-11146)
CARPENTER CO (PA)
5016 Monument Ave (23230-3620)
P.O. Box 27205 (23261-7205)
PHONE.................................804 359-0800
Stanley F Pauley, *Ch of Bd*
Mike Lowery, *President*
Roger Wilcox, *Regional Mgr*
J A Hacker, *Exec VP*
Ryan Doyle, *Prdtn Mgr*
◆ EMP: 175
SQ FT: 60,000
SALES (est): 1.8B **Privately Held**
WEB: www.carpenterftp.com
SIC: **3086** 1311 2869 2297 Insulation or cushioning material, foamed plastic; carpet & rug cushions, foamed plastic; padding, foamed plastic; crude petroleum & natural gas; industrial organic chemicals; bonded-fiber fabrics, except felt; household furnishings; plastics materials & resins

(G-11147)
CARPENTER CO
5016 Monument Ave (23230-3620)
PHONE.................................804 359-0800
Mike McKenrick, *Manager*
EMP: 55

SQ FT: 50,000
SALES (corp-wide): 1.8B **Privately Held**
WEB: www.carpenterftp.com
SIC: **3086** 5199 Padding, foamed plastic; foams & rubber
PA: Carpenter Co.
5016 Monument Ave
Richmond VA 23230
804 359-0800

(G-11148)
CARPENTER HOLDINGS INC (HQ)
5016 Monument Ave (23230-3620)
PHONE.................................804 359-0800
Stanley F Pauley, *Ch of Bd*
Michael Lowery, *President*
Holly Powell, *CFO*
Herbert Claiborne, *Admin Sec*
EMP: 4
SQ FT: 10,000
SALES (est): 259.7MM
SALES (corp-wide): 1.8B **Privately Held**
WEB: www.carpenter.com
SIC: **3086** Insulation or cushioning material, foamed plastic
PA: Carpenter Co.
5016 Monument Ave
Richmond VA 23230
804 359-0800

(G-11149)
CARTER COMPOSITION CORPORATION
Also Called: Carter Printing Co
2007 N Hamilton St (23230-4103)
P.O. Box 6901 (23230-0901)
PHONE.................................804 359-9206
Wayne R Carter, *President*
Carter Wayne R, *President*
Carter Jr Wayne Russell, *Vice Pres*
Bob Lindenzweig, *VP Sales*
Nichole Elkins, *Accounts Mgr*
▲ EMP: 125
SQ FT: 42,000
SALES (est): 19.4MM **Privately Held**
WEB: www.carterprinting.com
SIC: **2791** 2752 2796 Photocomposition, for the printing trade; commercial printing, offset; platemaking services

(G-11150)
CARTER JDUB MUSIC
315 Flicker Dr (23227-3629)
PHONE.................................804 329-1815
Joseph William Carter IV, *Principal*
EMP: 1
SALES (est): 37.5K **Privately Held**
SIC: **2741** Miscellaneous publishing

(G-11151)
CASE MECHANICAL
2512 Grenoble Rd (23294-3614)
PHONE.................................804 501-0003
EMP: 1
SALES (est): 54.5K **Privately Held**
SIC: **3523** Farm machinery & equipment

(G-11152)
CATHOLIC VIRGINIAN PRESS INC
7800 Carousel Ln (23294-4201)
P.O. Box 26843 (23261-6843)
PHONE.................................804 358-3625
Francis Dalorenzo, *President*
EMP: 4
SALES (est): 1.4MM **Privately Held**
WEB: www.catholicvirginian.org
SIC: **2711** Newspapers, publishing & printing

(G-11153)
CCF/SWISS INC
313 Berwickshire Dr (23229-7301)
PHONE.................................804 622-4277
EMP: 1
SALES (est): 52.5K **Privately Held**
SIC: **3489** Ordnance & accessories

(G-11154)
CHEM STATION OF VIRGINIA
5745 Charles City Cir (23231-4501)
PHONE.................................804 236-0090
Dave Fritter, *President*
EMP: 2

SALES (est): 215.3K **Privately Held**
SIC: 2841 Soap & other detergents

(G-11155)
CHEMICAL SUPPLY INC
1600 Roseneath Rd Ste B (23230-4452)
P.O. Box 3503, North Chesterfield (23235-7503)
PHONE...................................804 353-2971
Randolph B Lassiter, *President*
EMP: 4
SQ FT: 1,500 **Privately Held**
SIC: 2899 Water treating compounds

(G-11156)
CHESAPEAKE PROPELLER LLC
6331 River Rd (23229-8524)
PHONE...................................804 421-7991
EMP: 2
SALES (est): 120K **Privately Held**
SIC: 3366 Copper Foundry

(G-11157)
CHOW TIME LLC
2117 Tuckaway Ln (23229-4507)
PHONE...................................804 934-9305
Sherry Maynard, *Principal*
EMP: 1 EST: 2008
SALES (est): 6.9K **Privately Held**
SIC: 3581 Automatic vending machines

(G-11158)
CLASSIC KITCHENS OF VIRGINIA
12535 Patterson Ave (23238-6414)
PHONE...................................804 784-5075
Morris E Gunn Jr, *President*
Brenda C Gunn, *Corp Secy*
Michael D Elliott, *Vice Pres*
EMP: 16
SQ FT: 2,500
SALES (est): 1.7MM **Privately Held**
WEB: www.classickitchensofva.com
SIC: 2434 Wood kitchen cabinets

(G-11159)
CLOSED LOOP LLC
1801 Libbie Ave (23226-1836)
PHONE...................................804 648-4802
Joseph Hernandez,
EMP: 1
SALES (est): 82.1K **Privately Held**
SIC: 3845 Patient monitoring apparatus

(G-11160)
COCA-COLA CONSOLIDATED INC
4530 Oakleys Ln (23231-2912)
PHONE...................................804 328-5300
David McNeil, *Manager*
EMP: 91
SALES (corp-wide): 4.8B **Publicly Held**
WEB: www.cokeconsolidated.com
SIC: 2086 Bottled & canned soft drinks
PA: Coca-Cola Consolidated, Inc.
4100 Coca Cola Plz # 100
Charlotte NC 28211
704 557-4400

(G-11161)
COLLABRTIVE TECH CMMNCTONS COR
Also Called: Collaborative AV
12830 West Creek Pkwy F (23238-1126)
PHONE...................................804 477-8695
Richard Tedrow, *Principal*
EMP: 8 EST: 2015
SALES (est): 417.8K **Privately Held**
WEB: www.collaborative-av.com
SIC: 3651 7389 Household audio & video equipment;

(G-11162)
COLLECTING CONCEPTS INC
Also Called: White's Guide To Collecting
8100 Three Chopt Rd # 226 (23229-4833)
PHONE...................................804 285-0994
EMP: 31
SALES (est): 1.1MM **Privately Held**
SIC: 2741 5961 2721 Misc Publishing Ret Mail-Order House Periodicals-Publishing/Printing

(G-11163)
COMMONWALTH GIRL SCOUT COUNCIL
4900 Augusta Ave (23230-3626)
PHONE...................................804 340-2835
Lillie Branch, *President*
EMP: 2 EST: 2001
SALES: 4.2MM **Privately Held**
WEB: www.comgirlscouts.org
SIC: 2361 8322 Girls' & children's dresses, blouses & shirts; youth center

(G-11164)
COMPASS COAL SERVICES LLC
9 Stonehurst Grn (23226-3214)
PHONE...................................804 218-8880
William E Massey Jr, *President*
EMP: 1
SALES (est): 63.6K **Privately Held**
SIC: 1241 Coal mining services

(G-11165)
CONTRACTORS INSTITUTE LLC
1100 Welborne Dr Ste 103 (23229-5656)
PHONE...................................804 250-6750
Clayton Turner,
EMP: 1
SALES (corp-wide): 199.8K **Privately Held**
WEB: www.contractortrainingcenter.com
SIC: 2731 8331 Book publishing; job counseling
PA: Contractors Institute, Llc
5911 W Broad St Ste 103
Richmond VA 23230
804 556-5518

(G-11166)
CONTRACTORS INSTITUTE LLC
1100 Welborne Dr Ste 103 (23229-5656)
PHONE...................................804 556-5518
Fax: 804 556-3410
EMP: 3
SALES: 1MM **Privately Held**
SIC: 2731 8331 Books-Publishing/Printing Job Training/Related Services

(G-11167)
CONVERGENT BUS SOLUTIONS LLC
13316 College Valley Ln (23233-7682)
PHONE...................................804 360-0251
John Nelms, *Principal*
EMP: 3
SALES (est): 204.6K **Privately Held**
SIC: 3674 Semiconductors & related devices

(G-11168)
COSTUME SHOP
1503 Bellevue Ave (23227-4006)
PHONE...................................804 421-7361
Leslie Winn, *Partner*
Ivy Austin, *Partner*
EMP: 2 EST: 1982
SALES (est): 100K **Privately Held**
WEB: www.thecostumeshoprichmond.com
SIC: 2389 Costumes

(G-11169)
CREATIVE MNDS PUBLICATIONS LLC
2325 Crowncrest Dr (23233-2607)
PHONE...................................804 740-6010
Kathryn Starke, *Principal*
EMP: 3 EST: 2014
SALES (est): 142.6K **Privately Held**
WEB: www.creativemindspublications.com
SIC: 2741 Miscellaneous publishing

(G-11170)
CUNNINGHAM ENTPS LLC DANIEL
Also Called: Mark It Plus
2211 Dickens Rd Ste A (23230-2020)
PHONE...................................804 359-2180
Kathy Barnes, *Vice Pres*
Kathy Burns, *VP Opers*
Daniel Cunnighman,
EMP: 3

SALES (est): 472.8K **Privately Held**
WEB: www.markitplus.com
SIC: 2679 Tags, paper (unprinted): made from purchased paper

(G-11171)
CUPCAKES AND MORE LLC
1504 Southbury Ave (23231-5252)
PHONE...................................804 305-2350
Stacie Page, *Principal*
EMP: 8 EST: 2012
SALES (est): 477.1K **Privately Held**
SIC: 2051 Bread, cake & related products

(G-11172)
CUSTOM ENGRAVING & SIGNS LLC
8427 Glazebrook Ave (23228-2804)
PHONE...................................804 545-3961
Steve Shepherd, *Opers Staff*
Florence Shepherd,
Donald Shepherd,
EMP: 3
SALES (est): 100K **Privately Held**
WEB: www.traillifeawards.com
SIC: 3993 Signs & advertising specialties

(G-11173)
CUSTOM LOGOS
3108 N Parham Rd Ste 600a (23294-4417)
PHONE...................................804 967-0111
Micheal R Dickerson, *Owner*
EMP: 2
SALES (est): 150K **Privately Held**
WEB: www.customlogosva.com
SIC: 2395 5699 2759 Embroidery products, except schiffli machine; sports apparel; promotional printing

(G-11174)
CUSTOM PRINTING
1720 E Parham Rd (23228-2202)
PHONE...................................804 261-1776
Alfred Diez, *Principal*
EMP: 2
SALES (est): 220.9K **Privately Held**
SIC: 2752 Commercial printing, offset

(G-11175)
CUSTOM SIGN SHOP LLC
1016 Nth Blvd (23230)
PHONE...................................804 353-2768
Andrew Rapisarda,
EMP: 3
SALES (est): 264K **Privately Held**
WEB: www.thecustomsign.com
SIC: 3993 Signs, not made in custom sign painting shops

(G-11176)
CUT AND BLEED LLC
1600 Roseneath Rd (23230-4454)
PHONE...................................804 937-0006
EMP: 2
SALES (est): 73.2K **Privately Held**
SIC: 2759 Posters, including billboards: printing

(G-11177)
DAILY GRUB HOSPITALITY INC
4912 W Marshall St Ste C (23230-3127)
PHONE...................................804 221-5323
Cedric Boatwright, *Principal*
EMP: 2
SALES (est): 62.9K **Privately Held**
SIC: 2711 Newspapers, publishing & printing

(G-11178)
DATABRANDS LLC
1910 Byrd Ave Ste 131 (23230-3034)
PHONE...................................804 282-7890
EMP: 2
SALES (est): 204K **Privately Held**
SIC: 2752 Lithographic Commercial Printing

(G-11179)
DAVID M TENCH FINE CRAFTE
6218 Ellis Ave (23228-5227)
PHONE...................................804 261-3628
David Tench, *Principal*
EMP: 3
SALES (est): 182.5K **Privately Held**
SIC: 3993 Signs & advertising specialties

(G-11180)
DD&T CUSTOM WOODWORKING INC
12109 Glastonbury Pl (23233-7072)
PHONE...................................804 360-2714
Dusan Lemaic, *President*
EMP: 4
SALES (est): 385.5K **Privately Held**
SIC: 2431 Millwork

(G-11181)
DENIM
4748 Finlay St (23231-2754)
PHONE...................................804 918-2361
EMP: 1
SALES (est): 46.5K **Privately Held**
SIC: 2211 Denims

(G-11182)
DENNIS H FREDRICK
Also Called: Colonial Metal Crafts
7940 Blueberry Hill Ct (23229-6600)
PHONE...................................804 358-6000
Dennis H Fredrick, *Owner*
EMP: 3
SQ FT: 1,184
SALES (est): 160K **Privately Held**
WEB: www.colonialmetalcrafts.com
SIC: 3645 Residential lighting fixtures

(G-11183)
DESIGNS IN WOOD LLC
3410 W Leigh St (23230-4442)
PHONE...................................804 517-1414
Samuel I Jordan,
EMP: 2
SALES (est): 120K **Privately Held**
WEB: www.designsinwoodllc.us
SIC: 2434 Wood kitchen cabinets

(G-11184)
DETECTAMET INC
5111 Glen Alden Dr (23231-4318)
PHONE...................................804 303-1983
Angela Musson-Smith, *President*
EMP: 13
SALES (est): 2.2MM **Privately Held**
WEB: www.detectamet.com
SIC: 2821 Plastics materials & resins
PA: Detectamet Ltd
Prospect House
York YO42

(G-11185)
DIAMOND SOURCE OF VIRGINIA
12813 Fox Meadow Dr (23233-2296)
PHONE...................................804 360-3373
EMP: 2
SALES (est): 90.8K **Privately Held**
SIC: 3312 Blast furnaces & steel mills

(G-11186)
DOGTOWN LIGHTS LLC
1600 Roseneath Rd Ste I (23230-4449)
PHONE...................................804 334-5088
Jay Kemp, *Owner*
EMP: 2 EST: 2015
SALES (est): 117.6K **Privately Held**
WEB: www.dogtownlights.com
SIC: 3648 Lighting equipment

(G-11187)
DOMINION ENERGY INC
2901 Charles City Rd (23231-4527)
P.O. Box 26666 (23261-6666)
PHONE...................................804 771-3000
William C Hall, *Vice Pres*
Morenike Miles, *Vice Pres*
Thomas Capps, *Manager*
Bristow Venable, *Manager*
Rob Roland, *Supervisor*
EMP: 82
SALES (corp-wide): 16.5B **Publicly Held**
WEB: www.dominionenergy.com
SIC: 1311 4922 4911 8741 Natural gas production; natural gas transmission; transmission, electric power; management services; investors; subdividers & developers
PA: Dominion Energy, Inc.
120 Tredegar St
Richmond VA 23219
804 819-2000

(G-11188)
DOMINION GRAPHICS INC
3110 W Leigh St (23230-4408)
PHONE................................804 353-3755
Richard Keyser, *President*
John Ondra, *Vice Pres*
EMP: 5
SQ FT: 3,300
SALES (est): 637.8K **Privately Held**
WEB: www.keyserprinting.com
SIC: 2752 7336 Commercial printing, off-set; commercial art & graphic design

(G-11189)
DOMINION WATER PRODUCTS INC (PA)
5707 S Laburnum Ave (23231-4420)
PHONE................................804 236-9480
EMP: 20
SQ FT: 4,675
SALES (est): 1.7MM **Privately Held**
SIC: 3589 7389 5074 Mfg Service Industry Machinery Business Services Whol Plumbing Equipment/Supplies

(G-11190)
DRAGON DEFENSE MFG
8526 Sanford Dr (23228-2813)
PHONE................................804 986-6635
EMP: 1 EST: 2012
SALES (est): 46K **Privately Held**
SIC: 3999 Mfg Misc Products

(G-11191)
DRILLING J
2610 Pine Grove Dr (23294-6221)
PHONE................................804 303-5517
EMP: 2
SALES (est): 133.3K **Privately Held**
SIC: 1381 Service well drilling

(G-11192)
DSH SIGNS LLC
Also Called: Signs By Tomorrow
2036 Dabney Rd (23230-3362)
PHONE................................804 270-4003
Scotty Hager, *Sales Mgr*
Dorothy M Hager, *Mng Member*
Dorothy Hager,
EMP: 16
SQ FT: 2,800
SALES (est): 3.3MM **Privately Held**
WEB: www.signsbytomorrow.com
SIC: 3993 Signs & advertising specialties

(G-11193)
DUCK PUBLISHING LLC
13129 Middle Ridge Way (23233-7551)
PHONE................................609 636-8431
Charles Obrien, *Principal*
EMP: 1 EST: 2016
SALES (est): 39.1K **Privately Held**
SIC: 2741 Miscellaneous publishing

(G-11194)
DYNAMIC MOTION LLC
Also Called: Larktale
2701 Emerywood Pkwy # 10 (23294-3722)
PHONE................................804 433-2294
Leighton Klevana, *Mng Member*
Mark Zehfuss, *Mng Member*
EMP: 5
SALES (est): 214.9K **Privately Held**
WEB: www.larktale.com
SIC: 3944 Strollers, baby (vehicle)

(G-11195)
EASTERN SLEEP PRODUCTS COMPANY
Also Called: Symbol Mattress
4901 Fitzhugh Ave Ste 300 (23230-3531)
P.O. Box 11045 (23230-1045)
PHONE................................804 353-8965
Terry Byrd, *Plant Mgr*
Dick Jacobs, *Controller*
Barbara Nordblom, *Human Res Mgr*
Vernon Byrd, *Manager*
James Sams, *Manager*
EMP: 175
SALES (corp-wide): 105.8MM **Privately Held**
WEB: www.symbolmattress.com
SIC: 2515 Box springs, assembled; mattresses & foundations

PA: Eastern Sleep Products Company
4901 Fitzhugh Ave
Richmond VA 23230
804 254-1711

(G-11196)
ECP INC
5725 Charles City Cir (23231-4501)
PHONE................................804 222-2460
Jeff Willis, *President*
Charles Norris, *Vice Pres*
EMP: 2
SQ FT: 2,000
SALES (est): 27K **Privately Held**
SIC: 3599 Machine shop, jobbing & repair

(G-11197)
ELECTRICAL MECH RESOURCES INC
Also Called: Electrical & Mech Resources
4640 Intl Trade Ct (23231)
P.O. Box 38400 (23231-0600)
PHONE................................804 226-1600
William H Overton, *President*
Susan B Overton, *Vice Pres*
EMP: 20
SQ FT: 20,000
SALES (est): 4.4MM **Privately Held**
WEB: www.emrva.com
SIC: 3621 5063 Motors & generators; electrical apparatus & equipment

(G-11198)
ELECTRO-LUMINX LIGHTING CORP
Also Called: Light Tape
1320 N Arthur Ashe Blvd (23230-4522)
PHONE................................804 355-1692
Steve Pendlebury, *President*
▲ EMP: 8
SALES (est): 1.5MM **Privately Held**
WEB: www.lighttape.com
SIC: 3646 5063 Commercial indusl & institutional electric lighting fixtures; light bulbs & related supplies; lighting fittings & accessories; lighting fixtures, commercial & industrial; lighting fixtures, residential

(G-11199)
ELEGANCE MEETS DESIGNS LLC
9300 Golden Way Ct Apt P (23294-6423)
P.O. Box 3171, Glen Allen (23058-3171)
PHONE................................347 567-6348
Ketura Israel,
EMP: 3 EST: 2014
SALES (est): 86.4K **Privately Held**
WEB: www.elegancemeetsdesigns.com
SIC: 2339 7389 Women's & misses' accessories;

(G-11200)
ELEGANT DRAPERIES LTD (PA)
1831 Boulevard W (23230-4325)
PHONE................................804 353-4268
Grace Oeters Medford, *Owner*
Grace Oeters-Medford, *Manager*
Kim Baughan, *Technology*
▲ EMP: 14
SQ FT: 8,000
SALES (est): 1.5MM **Privately Held**
WEB: www.elegantdraperies.com
SIC: 2391 5023 Curtains & draperies; draperies

(G-11201)
EMBROIDERY BARNYARD
7704 Lampworth Ter (23231-7321)
PHONE................................804 795-1555
Sherry Baber, *Principal*
EMP: 1
SALES (est): 63.6K **Privately Held**
SIC: 2395 Embroidery & art needlework

(G-11202)
EMC METAL FABRICATION
1855 Boulevard W (23230-4325)
PHONE................................804 355-1030
Jack Woodfin Jr, *CEO*
Martha Jones, *Administration*
EMP: 2
SALES (est): 85.9K **Privately Held**
SIC: 3572 Computer storage devices

(G-11203)
ENDOWED EXPRESSIONS LLC
2801 Goldeneye Ct (23231-7599)
P.O. Box 11604, Norfolk (23517-0604)
PHONE................................804 638-5459
Sumiko Brown, *Principal*
EMP: 2
SALES (est): 98.2K **Privately Held**
SIC: 2391 Curtains & draperies

(G-11204)
ENVIRONMENTAL STONEWORKS LLC
9051 Hermitage Rd (23228-2808)
PHONE................................804 553-9560
Esther Mattick, *Regional Mgr*
Ron Loyd, *Vice Pres*
Chad Karst, *Accounts Mgr*
EMP: 49
SALES (corp-wide): 14.3MM **Privately Held**
WEB: www.estoneworks.com
SIC: 3281 Granite, cut & shaped
PA: Environmental Stoneworks Llc
98 Pheasant Run Rd
Orwigsburg PA 17961
570 366-6460

(G-11205)
ERODEX INC
5727 S Laburnum Ave (23231-4431)
PHONE................................804 525-6609
John Rolinson, *President*
EMP: 9 EST: 2016
SALES (est): 1.1MM **Privately Held**
SIC: 3599 Machine shop, jobbing & repair

(G-11206)
EVERYTHING GOS LLC
801 Windomere Ave (23227-2925)
PHONE................................804 290-3870
Charity Cardoza, *Owner*
Denell Garner, *Owner*
EMP: 1 EST: 2012
SALES (est): 58.7K **Privately Held**
SIC: 3949 5131 7389 Bowling pins; piece goods & notions;

(G-11207)
EZL SOFTWARE LLC
110 Countryside Ln (23229-7342)
PHONE................................804 288-0748
Mark Fonville, *Principal*
EMP: 2
SALES (est): 153.8K **Privately Held**
WEB: www.ezlsoftware.com
SIC: 7372 Application computer software

(G-11208)
FANTABULOUS CHEF SERVICE
1719 Winesap Dr (23231-5147)
PHONE................................804 245-4492
Alonzo Langley,
EMP: 1
SALES (est): 82.7K **Privately Held**
SIC: 3589 7389 Commercial cooking & foodwarming equipment;

(G-11209)
FERGUSSON PRINTING
Also Called: Allegra Richmond Henrico Co
4109 Jacque St (23230-3213)
P.O. Box 11103 (23230-1103)
PHONE................................804 355-8621
John Fergusson, *Branch Mgr*
EMP: 1 **Privately Held**
WEB: www.allegramarketingprint.com
SIC: 2752 Commercial printing, offset
PA: Fergusson Printing, Design & Marketing, Inc.
4109 Jacque St
Richmond VA

(G-11210)
FINANCIAL PRESS LLC
9702 Gayton Rd (23238-4907)
PHONE................................804 928-6366
George M Lee, *Principal*
EMP: 2 EST: 2011
SALES (est): 97K **Privately Held**
SIC: 2741 Miscellaneous publishing

(G-11211)
FLEXICELL INC
4329 November Ave (23231-4309)
PHONE................................804 550-7300
EMP: 2 EST: 2019
SALES (est): 107.4K **Privately Held**
WEB: www.flexicell.com
SIC: 3565 Packaging machinery

(G-11212)
FRANK FOR ALL INGNITIONS KEYS
8001 W Broad St (23294-4213)
PHONE................................804 663-5222
Kevin Ford, *Principal*
EMP: 2 EST: 2012
SALES (est): 101K **Privately Held**
SIC: 3429 Keys, locks & related hardware

(G-11213)
FRESHII
1700 Willow Lawn Dr (23230-3003)
PHONE................................804 223-8027
EMP: 4
SALES (est): 163.7K **Privately Held**
WEB: www.richmond.com
SIC: 2711 Newspapers, publishing & printing

(G-11214)
GARBUIO INC
2800 Charles City Rd (23231-4532)
P.O. Box 7898, Henrico (23231-0398)
PHONE................................804 279-0020
David Heath, *President*
▲ EMP: 5
SQ FT: 3,300
SALES (est): 958.5K
SALES (corp-wide): 2MM **Privately Held**
WEB: www.garbuio.com
SIC: 3559 Tobacco products machinery
HQ: Garbuio Spa
Via Enrico Azzi 1
Paese TV 31038
042 243-1140

(G-11215)
GENERAL MARBLE & GRANITE CO
2118 Lake Ave (23230-2635)
PHONE................................804 353-2761
Barbara Stanley, *President*
▲ EMP: 5
SALES (est): 464.4K **Privately Held**
WEB: www.generalmarbleandgranite.com
SIC: 3281 3253 5999 5032 Marble, building: cut & shaped; ceramic wall & floor tile; monuments & tombstones; marble building stone; counter top installation

(G-11216)
GENERAL MEDICAL MFG CO
1601 Willow Lawn Dr (23230-3427)
P.O. Box 7475 (23221-0475)
PHONE................................804 254-2737
EMP: 1
SALES (est): 39.6K **Privately Held**
SIC: 3999 Manufacturing industries

(G-11217)
GENERATOR INTERLOCK TECH LLC
1735 Arlington Rd (23230-4201)
PHONE................................804 726-2448
Justin Grubb, *Manager*
EMP: 2
SALES (est): 97.2K **Privately Held**
WEB: www.interlockkit.com
SIC: 3694 Engine electrical equipment

(G-11218)
GENIK INCORPORATED
6119 Miller Rd (23231-6058)
P.O. Box 50037 (23250-0037)
PHONE................................804 226-2907
Buck L Kesler, *President*
Buck Kesler, *Consultant*
EMP: 6 EST: 1982
SQ FT: 14,000
SALES (est): 1.2MM **Privately Held**
WEB: www.genik.biz
SIC: 3554 3555 Paper industries machinery; printing trades machinery

(G-11219)
GLO 4 ITCOM
5104 Wythe Ave (23226-1505)
PHONE..................................804 527-7608
Gloria Barnes, *Principal*
EMP: 2 EST: 2016
SALES (est): 87.2K **Privately Held**
SIC: 3711 Motor vehicles & car bodies

(G-11220)
GOLDEN SQUEEGEE INC
Also Called: Goldensqueegee
1508 Belleville St (23230-4438)
PHONE..................................804 355-8018
Ross Flippen, *President*
EMP: 4
SQ FT: 9,000
SALES (est): 374.5K **Privately Held**
WEB: www.goldensqueegee.com
SIC: 2396 2759 Screen printing on fabric
articles; screen printing

(G-11221)
**GREATER RICHMOND DANCE
PROJECT**
5470 W Broad St (23230-2630)
PHONE..................................804 302-4338
Tim Robertson, *President*
EMP: 12
SALES (est): 397.9K **Privately Held**
WEB: www.richmond.com
SIC: 2711 Newspapers, publishing & print-
ing

(G-11222)
GREEN APPLE ASSOC A VIRGIN
2238 John Rolfe Pkwy (23233-6913)
PHONE..................................804 551-5040
EMP: 2
SALES (est): 85.9K **Privately Held**
SIC: 3571 Mfg Electronic Computers

(G-11223)
**GREENDALE RAILING
COMPANY**
2031a Westwood Ave (23230-4114)
PHONE..................................804 363-7809
Jerry Lee Mayers, *President*
EMP: 22
SQ FT: 5,000
SALES (est): 4.8MM **Privately Held**
WEB: www.greendalerailing.com
SIC: 3446 3444 Architectural metalwork;
sheet metalwork

(G-11224)
GREGORY BRIGGS
Also Called: Alpha & Omega Towel Washing
Co
6006 Westbourne Dr (23230-2314)
PHONE..................................804 402-6867
Barbara Briggs, *Owner*
EMP: 2
SALES (est): 50K **Privately Held**
SIC: 2842 Specialty cleaning preparations

(G-11225)
**GREGORY MCRRAE
PUBLISHING**
3600 W Broad St Unit 537 (23230-4948)
PHONE..................................808 238-9907
Gregory McRae, *Principal*
EMP: 1
SALES (est): 41.3K **Privately Held**
SIC: 2741 Miscellaneous publishing

(G-11226)
GROOVIN GEARS
1600 Roseneath Rd Ste H (23230-4449)
PHONE..................................804 729-4177
EMP: 2
SALES (est): 115.9K **Privately Held**
SIC: 3566 Speed changers, drives & gears

(G-11227)
**GTP VENTURES
INCORPORATED**
Also Called: Dominion Sign Company
3825 Gaskins Rd (23233-1436)
PHONE..................................804 346-8922
Faiz Oley, *President*
EMP: 2

WEB: www.dominionsigns.com
SIC: 3993 Signs & advertising specialties

(G-11228)
GUYNN GROUP LLC
8140 Greystone East Cir (23229-7272)
PHONE..................................804 288-0191
Sally Guynn, *Principal*
EMP: 4
SALES (est): 190.1K **Privately Held**
WEB: www.sallyguynnartandbooks.com
SIC: 2741 Miscellaneous publishing

(G-11229)
**HAAS MACHINERY AMER INC
FRANZ**
Also Called: Haas Franz Machinery America
6207 Settler Rd (23231-6044)
PHONE..................................804 222-6022
Johann Haas, *President*
Josef Haas, *Vice Pres*
Margarete Jiraschek, *Vice Pres*
Roger Atkins, *Purch Mgr*
Michael A Fleetwood, *Treasurer*
◆ EMP: 10
SQ FT: 25,000
SALES (est): 2.9MM
SALES (corp-wide): 153.2MM **Privately
Held**
WEB: www.buhlergroup.com
SIC: 3556 Bakery machinery
HQ: Buhler Food Equipment Gmbh
Franz Haas-StraBe 1
Leobendorf 2100
226 260-00

(G-11230)
HALEY PEARSALL INC
Also Called: Haley Pearsall Cabinet Makers
12601 River Rd (23238-6169)
P.O. Box 40, Manakin Sabot (23103-0040)
PHONE..................................804 784-3438
Fax: 804 784-3441
EMP: 8 EST: 1977
SALES (est): 580K **Privately Held**
SIC: 2434 1751 2431 Mfg Wood Kitchen
Cabinets Carpentry Contractor Mfg Mill-
work

(G-11231)
HAND SIGNS LLC
2002 National St (23231-3424)
PHONE..................................804 482-3568
Joseph Trimmer, *Principal*
EMP: 1 EST: 2014
SALES (est): 60.8K **Privately Held**
WEB: www.surehandsigns.com
SIC: 3993 Signs & advertising specialties

(G-11232)
**HANG MEN HIGH HEATING &
COOLG**
Also Called: Wig Splitters
109 Norman Dr (23227-2017)
PHONE..................................804 651-3320
Jonathan A West, *President*
EMP: 6 EST: 2014
SALES (est): 99.4K **Privately Held**
SIC: 3585 Heating & air conditioning com-
bination units

(G-11233)
**HANKINS & JOHANN
INCORPORATED**
Also Called: H&J
7609 Compton Rd (23228-3617)
P.O. Box 28390, Henrico (23228-0390)
PHONE..................................804 266-2421
Fax: 804 262-9898
EMP: 9 EST: 1919
SQ FT: 50,000
SALES (est): 1.4MM **Privately Held**
SIC: 3471 3442 Plating/Polishing Svcs
Mfg Metal Door/Sash/Trim

(G-11234)
HAUNI RICHMOND INC
2800 Charles City Rd (23231-4500)
PHONE..................................804 222-5259
John L Miller, *President*
Dr Martin Herman, *Principal*
Jrgen Spykman, *Principal*
Christopher Somm, *Chairman*
Peter Moderegger, *Vice Pres*

▲ EMP: 120
SQ FT: 150,000
SALES (est): 29.5MM
SALES (corp-wide): 2MM **Privately Held**
WEB: www.haunirichmond.com
SIC: 3559 5084 3565 Tobacco products
machinery; industrial machinery & equip-
ment; bread wrapping machinery
HQ: Hauni Maschinenbau Gmbh
Kurt-A.-Korber-Chaussee 8-32
Hamburg 21033
407 250-01

(G-11235)
HELIX INNOVATIONS LLC
6603 W Broad St (23230-1711)
PHONE..................................804 274-2000
Jody Begley, *Manager*
Jhonny Cedeno, *Manager*
Shannon Leistra, *Manager*
Allison Bolyard,
Darren C Broughton,
EMP: 6
SALES (est): 668.1K **Privately Held**
SIC: 2121 Cigars

(G-11236)
HENKEL US OPERATIONS CORP
4414 Sarellen Rd (23231-4440)
PHONE..................................804 222-6100
Kenneth Gaspar, *Branch Mgr*
EMP: 17
SALES (corp-wide): 22.2B **Privately Held**
WEB: www.henkel.com
SIC: 2046 2821 2869 2891 Industrial
starch; edible starch; plastics materials &
resins; industrial organic chemicals; fla-
vors or flavoring materials, synthetic; per-
fume materials, synthetic; fatty acid
esters, aminos, etc.; adhesives
HQ: Henkel Us Operations Corporation
1 Henkel Way
Rocky Hill CT 06067
860 571-5100

(G-11237)
HENRICO CHUBBYS
6016 W Broad St (23230-2222)
PHONE..................................804 285-4469
H Patel, *Principal*
EMP: 2
SALES (est): 142.7K **Privately Held**
SIC: 3589 Car washing machinery

(G-11238)
HI-TECH PHARMACAL CO INC
9878 Maryland Dr (23233)
PHONE..................................804 935-7220
Claiborne Robins Jr, *Branch Mgr*
EMP: 3
SALES (corp-wide): 682.4MM **Privately
Held**
WEB: www.ecrobins.com
SIC: 2834 Pharmaceutical preparations
HQ: Hi-Tech Pharmacal Co., Inc.
369 Bayview Ave
Amityville NY 11701
631 789-8228

(G-11239)
**HIGH IMPACT MUSIC FOR YOU
LLC**
630 Windomere Ave (23227-2955)
PHONE..................................757 915-8696
Priscilla Warren, *Principal*
EMP: 1
SALES (est): 74.9K **Privately Held**
WEB: www.highimpact.com
SIC: 2741 Miscellaneous publishing

(G-11240)
HOLLAWOOD PUBLISHING LLC
2317 Westwood Ave 201a (23230-4007)
PHONE..................................804 353-3310
Linwood Butler, *Principal*
EMP: 2
SALES (est): 95.9K **Privately Held**
SIC: 2741 Miscellaneous publishing

(G-11241)
**HONEYWELL INTERNATIONAL
INC**
7870 Villa Park Dr # 900 (23228-6508)
PHONE..................................804 515-1500
Wayne Verlander, *Branch Mgr*

Bobby Hall, *Supervisor*
EMP: 40
SALES (corp-wide): 36.7B **Publicly Held**
WEB: www.honeywell.com
SIC: 3724 Aircraft engines & engine parts
PA: Honeywell International Inc.
300 S Tryon St
Charlotte NC 28202
704 627-6200

(G-11242)
**HOUGHTALING ASSOCIATES
INC**
2830 Ackley Ave Ste 101 (23228-2135)
PHONE..................................804 740-7098
Thomas P Houghtaling, *President*
Scott Houghtaling, *Manager*
EMP: 3 EST: 1976
SQ FT: 1,500 **Privately Held**
WEB: www.haiboiler.com
SIC: 3433 5074 Burners, furnaces, boilers
& stokers; heating equipment (hydronic)

(G-11243)
HOWMET AEROSPACE INC
6603 W Broad St (23230-1711)
PHONE..................................804 281-2262
Charles Cox, *Partner*
Pennye Arana, *Sales Staff*
Steve Mudd, *Chief Mktg Ofcr*
Brienne Neisewander, *Marketing Staff*
Greg Heroux, *Manager*
EMP: 250 **Publicly Held**
WEB: www.howmet.com
SIC: 3334 Primary aluminum
PA: Howmet Aerospace Inc.
201 Isabella St Ste 200
Pittsburgh PA 15212
412 992-2500

(G-11244)
HUDSON INDUSTRIES INC
Also Called: Hudson Medical
5250 Klockner Dr (23231-4335)
PHONE..................................804 226-1155
Gary C Hudson, *President*
James Cocuzza, *Managing Prtnr*
Mark Hudson, *COO*
Michael Corswandt, *VP Sales*
▲ EMP: 60 EST: 1976
SQ FT: 90,000
SALES (est): 6.6MM **Privately Held**
WEB: www.hudsonindustries.com
SIC: 2821 2392 3086 Plastics materials &
resins; pillows, bed: made from pur-
chased materials; plastics foam products

(G-11245)
HUGER EMBROIDERY
11 1/2 Tapoan Rd (23226-3218)
PHONE..................................804 304-8808
Sarah Gibson Wiley, *Principal*
EMP: 1
SALES (est): 65.7K **Privately Held**
WEB: www.hugermemories.com
SIC: 2395 Embroidery & art needlework

(G-11246)
**INDEPENDENCE PUBLISHING
TLR**
10011 Palace Ct Apt A (23238-5674)
P.O. Box 9261 (23227-0261)
PHONE..................................757 761-8579
EMP: 1 EST: 2017
SALES (est): 37.5K **Privately Held**
SIC: 2741 Miscellaneous publishing

(G-11247)
INFILCO DEGREMONT INC
8007 Discovery Dr (23229-8605)
PHONE..................................804 756-7600
Shyam Bhan, *CEO*
P Ballard, *CIO*
Sean Leonard, *Technology*
Chris Desmottes, *Executive Asst*
Becky Korb, *Assistant*
EMP: 31
SALES (est): 6.4MM **Privately Held**
WEB: www.awpt.com
SIC: 3589 Water treatment equipment, in-
dustrial

(G-11248)
INFLUENCES OF ZION
8114 Presquile Rd (23231-7403)
PHONE..................................804 248-4758

Sherri Marchan, *Owner*
EMP: 1
SALES (est): 42.5K **Privately Held**
SIC: 2389 5632 Apparel & accessories;
apparel accessories

(G-11249)
INR ENERGY LLC
7275 Glen Forest Dr # 206 (23226-3777)
PHONE.............................804 282-0369
Gary Rogliano,
Stephen D Williams,
EMP: 7 **EST:** 2007
SALES (est): 500.8K **Privately Held**
WEB: www.nrillc.com
SIC: 1241 Coal mining services

(G-11250)
INTERALIGN LLC
1711 Charles St (23226-3503)
PHONE.............................804 314-4713
John Romeo, *President*
EMP: 2
SALES (est): 169.9K **Privately Held**
SIC: 3161 Attache cases

(G-11251)
INTERNATIONAL WINE SPIRITS LTD
6603 W Broad St (23230-1711)
PHONE.............................804 274-1432
Vincent Gierer, *Ch of Bd*
Theodor P Baseler, *President*
Douglas N Gore, *Senior VP*
Shila A Newlands, *Senior VP*
Glen D Yaffa, *Senior VP*
◆ **EMP:** 855
SALES (est): 252.6K **Publicly Held**
WEB: www.iws-fla.com
SIC: 2084 Wines
HQ: Altria Enterprises Ii Llc
6601 W Broad St
Richmond VA 23230

(G-11252)
ISLEY BREWING COMPANY
1715 Summit Ave (23230-4515)
P.O. Box 11294 (23230-1294)
PHONE.............................804 499-0721
Michael Isley, *President*
EMP: 2
SALES (est): 176K **Privately Held**
WEB: www.isleybrewingcompany.com
SIC: 2082 Beer (alcoholic beverage); ale
(alcoholic beverage); porter (alcoholic
beverage); stout (alcoholic beverage)

(G-11253)
JARVIS SIGN COMPANY
109 Maple Ave (23226-2350)
PHONE.............................804 514-9879
Robert B Jarvis, *President*
EMP: 2
SALES (est): 147.4K **Privately Held**
SIC: 3993 Electric signs

(G-11254)
JBT AEROTECH
5300 Federal Rd (23250-2410)
PHONE.............................336 254-4104
EMP: 3
SALES (est): 168.9K **Privately Held**
SIC: 3556 Food products machinery

(G-11255)
JENNIFER OMOHUNDRO
Also Called: Commonwealth Toner and Ink
10309 Wilkes Ridge Pl (23233-7397)
P.O. Box 71212 (23255-1212)
PHONE.............................804 937-9308
Jennifer Omohundro, *Owner*
EMP: 2
SALES (est): 104.1K **Privately Held**
WEB: www.cticartridges.com
SIC: 3955 Print cartridges for laser & other
computer printers

(G-11256)
JOHNS MANVILLE CORPORATION
Johns Manville
7400 Ranco Rd (23228-3702)
PHONE.............................804 261-7400
Paul Fudala, *Branch Mgr*
Tony Moore, *Info Tech Mgr*

Chris Griffin, *Director*
EMP: 270
SALES (corp-wide): 254.6B **Publicly Held**
WEB: www.jm.com
SIC: 2952 3296 2891 Roofing materials;
mineral wool; adhesives & sealants
HQ: Johns Manville Corporation
717 17th St Ste 800
Denver CO 80202
303 978-2000

(G-11257)
JOHNSON CONTROLS
8555 Magellan Pkwy # 1000 (23227-1333)
PHONE.............................804 727-3890
Paul Bratton, *Principal*
Graydon Bohn, *Sales Staff*
William Comer, *Sales Staff*
James Lewis, *Sales Staff*
Alex Sinclair, *Sales Staff*
EMP: 5 **Privately Held**
WEB: www.tycosimplexgrinnell.com
SIC: 3669 1731 1711 Emergency alarms;
fire detection & burglar alarm systems
specialization; fire sprinkler system instal-
lation
HQ: Johnson Controls Fire Protection Lp
6600 Congress Ave
Boca Raton FL 33487
561 988-7200

(G-11258)
JUST HANDLE IT LLC
1903 West Club Ln (23226-2417)
PHONE.............................804 285-0786
Colleen Warner, *Principal*
EMP: 2 **EST:** 2014
SALES (est): 121.2K **Privately Held**
SIC: 2499 Handles, wood

(G-11259)
KENMORE ENVELOPE COMPANY INC
4641 Intl Trade Ct (23231)
PHONE.............................804 271-2100
D Rhett Riddle Jr, *President*
Carolyn M Riddle, *Corp Secy*
Scott Evans, *Vice Pres*
Derek Zbyszinski, *CFO*
Justin Snow, *Accounts Mgr*
EMP: 105
SQ FT: 110,000
SALES (est): 38MM **Privately Held**
WEB: www.kenmore-envelope.com
SIC: 2677 2759 2752 Envelopes; en-
velopes: printing; commercial printing,
lithographic

(G-11260)
KEYSER COLLECTION
509 N Gaskins Rd (23238-5505)
PHONE.............................804 740-3237
Helen Keyser, *Owner*
EMP: 2
SALES (est): 20K **Privately Held**
WEB: www.keysercollection.com
SIC: 2499 Picture & mirror frames, wood

(G-11261)
KHEM PRECISION MACHINING LLC
3007 W Clay St Ste D (23230-4735)
PHONE.............................804 915-8922
Thorn Khem, *Mng Member*
EMP: 3
SQ FT: 12,000
SALES (est): 600K **Privately Held**
WEB: www.khemprecision.com
SIC: 3561 3599 7539 3565 Industrial
pumps & parts; machine shop, jobbing &
repair; machine shop, automotive; pack-
aging machinery

(G-11262)
KINDRED BROTHERS INC
Also Called: Kindred Spirit Brewing
12830 West Creek Pkwy (23238-1126)
PHONE.............................803 318-5097
Joe Trottier, *CEO*
Jason Trottier, *General Mgr*
John Barefoot, *Principal*
Heather Barefoot, *Opers Mgr*
EMP: 8

SALES (est): 600K **Privately Held**
WEB: www.kindredspiritbrewing.com
SIC: 2082 7372 Beer (alcoholic bever-
age); application computer software

(G-11263)
KNITTING INFORMATION
7809 Wanymala Rd (23229-4254)
PHONE.............................804 288-4754
EMP: 2
SALES (est): 110K **Privately Held**
SIC: 2731 Books-Publishing/Printing

(G-11264)
KORMAN SIGNS INC
3029 Lincoln Ave (23228-4209)
PHONE.............................804 262-6050
Bill Korman Jr, *President*
John Murra, *Exec VP*
Dale P McDonough, *Vice Pres*
Joan A Murray, *Vice Pres*
Dale McDough, *VP Opers*
▲ **EMP:** 50
SQ FT: 50,000
SALES (est): 13.2MM **Privately Held**
WEB: www.kormansigns.com
SIC: 3993 3669 Signs, not made in cus-
tom sign painting shops; traffic signals,
electric

(G-11265)
KSB AMERICA CORPORATION (DH)
4415 Sarellen Rd (23231-4428)
PHONE.............................804 222-1818
William A Leech, *Principal*
Karen M Wood, *Corp Secy*
Paul Boroughs, *Vice Pres*
Wolfgang Schmitt, *Director*
◆ **EMP:** 1
SALES (est): 163.4MM
SALES (corp-wide): 144.1K **Privately Held**
SIC: 3561 3494 3625 5084 Industrial
pumps & parts; pipe fittings; actuators, in-
dustrial; pumps & pumping equipment
HQ: Pab Pumpen- Und Armaturen- Beteili-
gungsgesellschaft Mit Beschrankter
Haftung
Johann-Klein-Str. 9
Frankenthal (Pfalz)
623 386-0

(G-11266)
LASERSERV INC
2317 Westwood Ave Ste 114 (23230-4019)
P.O. Box 6846 (23230-0846)
PHONE.............................804 359-6188
Richard Grosch, *President*
Gloria Grosch, *Corp Secy*
Jeffrey S Grosch, *Vice Pres*
EMP: 21
SQ FT: 8,000
SALES (est): 3.8MM **Privately Held**
WEB: www.laserserv.net
SIC: 3577 3571 7699 Printers & plotters;
electronic computers; printing trades ma-
chinery & equipment repair

(G-11267)
LATIMER JULIAN MANUFACTURING
101 Eisenhower Dr (23227-2011)
PHONE.............................804 405-6851
Julian Latimer, *Partner*
EMP: 2
SALES (est): 93.3K **Privately Held**
SIC: 3433 Heating equipment, except elec-
tric

(G-11268)
LEGACY VULCAN LLC
Also Called: Lower Dock Yard
5600 Old Osborne Tpke (23231-3025)
PHONE.............................804 236-4160
Robert Parkinson, *Manager*
EMP: 1 **Publicly Held**
WEB: www.vulcanmaterials.com
SIC: 3273 Ready-mixed concrete
HQ: Legacy Vulcan, Llc
1200 Urban Center Dr
Vestavia AL 35242
205 298-3000

(G-11269)
LES PETALES INC
401 Old Locke Ln (23226-1716)
PHONE.............................804 254-7863
Cary Goodstein, *CEO*
Jeff Goodstein, *Admin Sec*
EMP: 1
SALES (est): 70.5K **Privately Held**
SIC: 3999 Artificial flower arrangements

(G-11270)
LINE-X OF RICHMOND
6405 Dickens Pl Ste F (23230-2018)
PHONE.............................804 321-9166
Dale King, *Principal*
EMP: 3
SALES (est): 376.5K **Privately Held**
WEB: www.linexofrichmond.com
SIC: 2821 Plastics materials & resins

(G-11271)
LINEAR ROTARY BEARINGS INC
6417 Rigsby Rd (23226-2916)
PHONE.............................540 261-1375
Garnette S Teass, *President*
Gerard F Dunne, *Admin Sec*
EMP: 6
SALES (est): 939K **Privately Held**
WEB: www.e-lrb.com
SIC: 3562 Ball & roller bearings

(G-11272)
LIPHART STEEL COMPANY INC (PA)
3308 Rosedale Ave (23230-4290)
P.O. Box 6326 (23230-0326)
PHONE.............................804 355-7481
Mark A Teachey, *President*
Ben Hey, *Superintendent*
R N Ruby, *Exec VP*
Robert A Kerr, *Vice Pres*
Mike Teachey, *Vice Pres*
EMP: 68
SQ FT: 5,000
SALES: 36.7MM **Privately Held**
WEB: www.liphartsteel.com
SIC: 3441 1791 Building components,
structural steel; iron work, structural

(G-11273)
LLOYD ENTERPRISES INC
Also Called: AAA-Bar Printing & Forms Co
5407 Lakeside Ave Ste 3 (23228-6061)
P.O. Box 9133 (23227-0133)
PHONE.............................804 266-1185
Elizabeth G Lloyd, *President*
Janice L Banks, *Corp Secy*
Lucy H Lloyd, *Corp Secy*
EMP: 3
SQ FT: 1,200
SALES (est): 350.7K **Privately Held**
SIC: 2754 Business form & card printing,
gravure

(G-11274)
LOVELLS REPLAY SPORTSTOP LLC
2550 New Market Rd (23231-7011)
PHONE.............................804 507-0271
EMP: 2
SALES (est): 132.9K **Privately Held**
SIC: 3949 Sporting & athletic goods

(G-11275)
LUMINOUS AUDIO TECHNOLOGY
8705 W Broad St (23294-6207)
PHONE.............................804 741-5826
Tim D Stinson, *President*
EMP: 3 **EST:** 1992
SALES (est): 115K **Privately Held**
WEB: www.luminousaudio.com
SIC: 3651 5099 Audio electronic systems;
video & audio equipment

(G-11276)
LUSCIOUS LOVEZZ LLC
1806 Smmit Ave Ste 30010 (23230)
PHONE.............................804 538-4151
Shaquita Christian,
EMP: 1
SALES (est): 30K **Privately Held**
SIC: 3999 Hair & hair-based products

▲ = Import ▼=Export
◆ =Import/Export

(G-11277)
LYDELL GROUP INCORPORATED
Also Called: AlphaGraphics
3007 Lincoln Ave (23228-4209)
PHONE..................804 627-0500
Bill Cozens, *President*
Jackie Cozens, *Vice Pres*
EMP: 8
SALES (est): 1.2MM *Privately Held*
WEB: www.alphagraphics.com
SIC: 2752 2759 2789 2791 Commercial printing, lithographic; ready prints; bookbinding & related work; typesetting; photocopying & duplicating services

(G-11278)
MAC BONE INDUSTRIES LTD
9301 Old Staples Mill Rd (23228-2011)
PHONE..................804 264-3603
L Jeremy Crews, *President*
John Sniffin, *Vice Pres*
Ned Sniffin, *Vice Pres*
John R Sniffin, *CFO*
Ned H Sniffin, *Manager*
EMP: 3
SQ FT: 12,000
SALES (est): 1.2MM *Privately Held*
WEB: www.macbone.com
SIC: 3585 3594 3567 Air conditioning equipment, complete; fluid power pumps & motors; industrial furnaces & ovens

(G-11279)
MACLAREN ENDEAVORS LLC
Also Called: Printegration Henrico Co
8000 Villa Park Dr (23228-6500)
PHONE..................804 358-3493
EMP: 30
SALES: 5MM *Privately Held*
SIC: 2752 2759 7331 Lithographic Commercial Printing Commercial Printing Direct Mail Advertising Services

(G-11280)
MACOY PUBG MASONIC SUP CO INC
Also Called: Macoy Pubg & Masonic Sup Co
3011 Dumbarton Rd (23228-5831)
PHONE..................804 262-6551
John Emory, *President*
Hope Lindsey, *Office Mgr*
▲ EMP: 38 EST: 1849
SQ FT: 22,000
SALES (est): 4.1MM *Privately Held*
WEB: www.macoy.com
SIC: 2389 5699 2731 Regalia; customized clothing & apparel; books: publishing & printing

(G-11281)
MAFCO CONSOLIDATED GROUP INC
Also Called: Mafco Natural Products
4400 Williamsburg Ave (23231-1210)
P.O. Box 24 (23218-0024)
PHONE..................804 222-1600
Frank Adao, *Manager*
EMP: 11
SQ FT: 65,000 *Publicly Held*
WEB: www.macandrewsandforbes.com
SIC: 2099 2087 Spices, including grinding; flavoring extracts & syrups
HQ: Mafco Consolidated Group Inc
35 E 62nd St
New York NY 10065

(G-11282)
MAJESTIC MARKETING LLC
1806 Smmit Ave Ste 30010 (23230)
PHONE..................804 210-7667
Irvin Mines, *Mng Member*
EMP: 1
SALES (est): 50K *Privately Held*
SIC: 2741

(G-11283)
MANCHESTER INDUSTRIES INC VA (HQ)
200 Orleans St (23231-3005)
PHONE..................804 226-4250
Debbie Brown, *General Mgr*
Deborah Brown, *Vice Pres*
Tom Harris, *Vice Pres*
Keith Tyre, *Sales Mgr*
▲ EMP: 50
SQ FT: 100,000
SALES (est): 35.3MM *Publicly Held*
WEB: www.manind.com
SIC: 2679 Paperboard products, converted

(G-11284)
MATCH AMMO LLC
6020 W Broad St (23230-2222)
PHONE..................804 266-2666
EMP: 2
SALES (est): 84.1K *Privately Held*
SIC: 3482 Small arms ammunition

(G-11285)
MATTRESS DEAL LLC
7601 W Broad St (23294-3641)
PHONE..................804 869-3387
Minh Huynh,
EMP: 2
SALES (est): 200K *Privately Held*
SIC: 2515 Mattresses & bedsprings

(G-11286)
MCKINNON AND HARRIS INC (PA)
1722 Arlington Rd (23230-4202)
PHONE..................804 358-2385
William Massie Jr, *President*
Ken Dail, *COO*
Annie H Massie, *Vice Pres*
Annie Massie, *Vice Pres*
Matthew Browne, *Engineer*
▲ EMP: 35
SQ FT: 36,628
SALES (est): 5.5MM *Privately Held*
WEB: www.mckinnonharris.com
SIC: 2514 Garden furniture, metal

(G-11287)
MERCK & CO INC
5504 Millwheel Ln (23228-2049)
PHONE..................804 363-0876
Laura Fravel, *Principal*
EMP: 3 *Publicly Held*
WEB: www.merck.com
SIC: 2834 Pharmaceutical preparations
PA: Merck & Co., Inc.
2000 Galloping Hill Rd
Kenilworth NJ 07033
908 740-4000

(G-11288)
METHOD WOOD WORKING
3410 W Leigh St (23230-4442)
PHONE..................804 332-3715
EMP: 4 EST: 2015
SALES (est): 471.2K *Privately Held*
SIC: 2431 Millwork

(G-11289)
METRO SIGNS & GRAPHICS INC
3807 Alston Ln (23294-5410)
PHONE..................804 747-1918
David Bentley, *President*
EMP: 3
SQ FT: 1,500
SALES (est): 175K *Privately Held*
SIC: 3993 Signs, not made in custom sign painting shops

(G-11290)
METROMONT CORPORATION
Also Called: Structural Concrete Products
1650 Darbytown Rd (23231-4021)
PHONE..................804 222-6770
C Pastorious, *General Mgr*
EMP: 100
SALES (corp-wide): 130.3MM *Privately Held*
WEB: www.metromont.com
SIC: 3272 Concrete products, precast
PA: Metromont Corporation
2802 White Horse Rd
Greenville SC 29611
804 222-6770

(G-11291)
MICRO SERVICES COMPANY
8545 Patterson Ave # 206 (23229-6455)
PHONE..................804 741-5000
George Cummings, *Owner*
EMP: 3
SQ FT: 600

SALES (est): 163.3K *Privately Held*
SIC: 7372 5734 Prepackaged software; computer & software stores

(G-11292)
MINUTEMAN PRESS
1720 E Parham Rd (23228-2202)
PHONE..................804 441-9761
EMP: 2
SALES (est): 92.3K *Privately Held*
WEB: www.minutemanpress.com
SIC: 2752 Commercial printing, lithographic

(G-11293)
MISSION REALTY GROUP
7204 Glen Forest Dr # 206 (23226-3782)
PHONE..................804 545-6651
Rick Nichols, *Vice Pres*
Mary Soroka, *Buyer*
Sarah Hutchinson, *Sales Mgr*
Clayton E Gits, *Director*
EMP: 2
SALES (est): 109.4K *Privately Held*
WEB: www.missionrealty.com
SIC: 2451 Mobile homes

(G-11294)
MK INTERIORS INC
6011 W Broad St (23230-2221)
PHONE..................804 288-2819
EMP: 2
SALES (est): 110K *Privately Held*
SIC: 2391 Mfg Curtains/Draperies

(G-11295)
MOBJACK BINNACLE PRODUCTS LLC
5809 York Rd (23226-2162)
PHONE..................804 814-4077
John Belniak,
EMP: 3 EST: 2014
SQ FT: 500
SALES (est): 175.2K *Privately Held*
WEB: www.mobjackbp.org
SIC: 2821 Molding compounds, plastics

(G-11296)
MORGAN E MCKINNEY
4814 Rodney Rd (23230-2509)
PHONE..................804 389-9371
Morgan E McKinney, *Principal*
EMP: 2
SALES (est): 106.2K *Privately Held*
WEB: www.morganmckinney.com
SIC: 3479 Painting, coating & hot dipping

(G-11297)
MULLER MARTINI CORP
503 Waveny Rd (23229-6741)
PHONE..................804 282-4802
Randy Shannon, *Manager*
EMP: 1
SALES (corp-wide): 426.9MM *Privately Held*
WEB: www.mullermartini.com
SIC: 3555 Printing trades machinery
HQ: Muller Martini Corp.
456 Wheeler Rd
Hauppauge NY 11788
631 582-4343

(G-11298)
MYERS REPAIR COMPANY
3105 Gay Ave (23231-2219)
PHONE..................804 222-3674
Thomas A Myers, *President*
Donald Myers, *Chairman*
EMP: 1
SQ FT: 6,000
SALES (est): 69.6K *Privately Held*
SIC: 7692 7539 Welding repair; automotive repair shops

(G-11299)
NATIONAL MARKING PRODUCTS INC
5606 Greendale Rd (23228-5816)
P.O. Box 9705 (23228-0705)
PHONE..................804 266-7691
Richard A Reinhard, *President*
Rick Reinhard, *General Mgr*
Robert Reinhard, *Chairman*
Shirley C Reinhard, *Admin Sec*
▲ EMP: 21 EST: 1891

SQ FT: 7,500
SALES (est): 3.6MM *Privately Held*
WEB: www.nationalmarking.com
SIC: 3953 2759 Embossing seals & hand stamps; cancelling stamps, hand: rubber or metal; embossing seals, corporate & official; screen printing

(G-11300)
NATURAL RESOURCES INTL LLC
7275 Glen Forest Dr # 206 (23226-3777)
PHONE..................804 282-0369
Gary R Rogliano, *CEO*
EMP: 8
SALES (est): 439.4K *Privately Held*
WEB: www.nrillc.com
SIC: 1241 Coal mining services

(G-11301)
NECTAR OF THE GODS CORP
1313 Altamont Ave (23230-4713)
PHONE..................703 582-0856
EMP: 2
SALES (est): 124.7K *Privately Held*
SIC: 2084 Wines, brandy & brandy spirits

(G-11302)
NEIGHBORHOOD SPORTS LLC
Also Called: Neighborhood Sports Magazine
824 Arlington Cir (23229-6508)
P.O. Box 70162 (23255-0162)
PHONE..................804 282-8033
David Kearny,
Jane Kearny,
EMP: 2 EST: 1998
SALES (est): 179.8K *Privately Held*
WEB: www.neighborhoodsportsmagazine.com
SIC: 2721 2741 Magazines: publishing & printing; miscellaneous publishing

(G-11303)
NEWELL BRANDS INC
2042 Westmoreland St (23230-3245)
PHONE..................800 241-1848
David Boardman, *Branch Mgr*
EMP: 2
SALES (corp-wide): 9.7B *Publicly Held*
WEB: www.newellbrands.com
SIC: 3944 Games, toys & children's vehicles
PA: Newell Brands Inc.
6655 Pachtree Dunwoody Rd
Atlanta GA 30328
770 418-7000

(G-11304)
NEXTDAY CABINETS OF VA LLC
3985 Deep Rock Rd (23233-1413)
PHONE..................703 291-8935
Sevket S Keskin, *Branch Mgr*
EMP: 2
SALES (corp-wide): 5.7MM *Privately Held*
WEB: www.nextdaycabinets.com
SIC: 2434 Wood kitchen cabinets
PA: Nextday Cabinets Of Va, Llc
14000k Thunderbolt Pl
Chantilly VA 20151
703 291-8935

(G-11305)
NICOL CANDY
10211 Pepperhill Ln (23238-3813)
PHONE..................804 740-2378
Marilyn Nicol, *Owner*
EMP: 1
SALES (est): 61.1K *Privately Held*
WEB: www.nicolcandy.com
SIC: 2064 Candy & other confectionery products

(G-11306)
NORTH OF JAMES
3122 W Clay St Apt 6 (23230-4725)
P.O. Box 9225 (23227-0225)
PHONE..................804 218-5265
Charles McGuigan, *Owner*
EMP: 1
SALES (est): 63K *Privately Held*
SIC: 2711 Newspapers

(G-11307)
NORTH SOUTH PARTNERS LLC
Also Called: Old World Prints
8080 Villa Park Dr (23228-6500)
PHONE..................................804 213-0600
Julie Holland, *Director*
Scott Elles,
Alicia Ludwig, *Graphic Designe*
Becky Bryant, *Assistant*
EMP: 40
SALES (est): 4.3MM **Privately Held**
WEB: www.theworldartgroup.com
SIC: 2741 Art copy: publishing & printing

(G-11308)
NORTHEAST SOLITE CORPORATION
4801 Hermitage Rd Ste 105 (23227-3332)
PHONE..................................804 262-8119
Philip M Nesmith, *Branch Mgr*
EMP: 2
SALES (corp-wide): 16.2MM **Privately Held**
WEB: www.nesolite.com
SIC: 3295 Perlite, aggregate or expanded
PA: Northeast Solite Corporation
　　1135 Kings Hwy
　　Saugerties NY 12477
　　845 246-2646

(G-11309)
NUNA MED LLC
9702 Gayton Rd Ste 183 (23238-4907)
PHONE..................................707 373-7171
Ali Barta, *Mng Member*
EMP: 1
SALES (est): 97.5K **Privately Held**
SIC: 2833 Drugs & herbs: grading, grinding & milling

(G-11310)
NUTRI-BLEND INC
2353 Charles City Rd (23231-4303)
P.O. Box 38060 (23231-0860)
PHONE..................................804 222-1675
John J Simons, *President*
Lawrence R Mathews, *Vice Pres*
EMP: 15
SQ FT: 1,000
SALES (est): 1.6MM **Privately Held**
WEB: www.nutri-blend.com
SIC: 2873 Fertilizers: natural (organic), except compost

(G-11311)
OAKLEA PRESS INC
Also Called: Stephen Hawley Martin
41 Old Mill Rd (23226-3111)
PHONE..................................804 288-2683
Stephen H Martin, *President*
EMP: 3
SQ FT: 10,000
SALES (est): 500K **Privately Held**
WEB: www.oakleapress.com
SIC: 2741 Miscellaneous publishing

(G-11312)
OLD DOMINION 4 WHL DRV CLB INC
2308 Carrollwood Ct (23238-3032)
PHONE..................................804 750-2349
Mike Morris, *Principal*
EMP: 2
SALES (est): 132.7K **Privately Held**
SIC: 3312 Wheels

(G-11313)
OLD DOMINION BRUSH COMPANY INC
Also Called: Odb
5118 Glen Alden Dr (23231-4319)
PHONE..................................800 446-9823
Ronald A Robinson, *President*
EMP: 4
SALES (est): 5MM **Publicly Held**
WEB: www.odbco.com
SIC: 3991 3589 Brushes, household or industrial; vacuum cleaners & sweepers, electric: industrial
PA: Alamo Group Inc.
　　1627 E Walnut St
　　Seguin TX 78155
　　830 379-1480

(G-11314)
OLDE VIRGINIA CIDERY LLC
2910 W Leigh St (23230-4528)
PHONE..................................901 626-0535
William Correll, *Owner*
EMP: 2 EST: 2016
SALES (est): 138.3K **Privately Held**
SIC: 2084 Wines

(G-11315)
OMEGA ALPHA II INC
Also Called: Advanced Printing & Graphics
3817 Gaskins Rd (23233-1436)
PHONE..................................804 747-7705
Anne Weisenburg, *President*
Joseph Galeski, *Vice Pres*
Alex Weiss, *Admin Sec*
EMP: 10
SQ FT: 4,279
SALES (est): 1MM **Privately Held**
SIC: 2752 7374 7334 2791 Commercial printing, offset; computer processing services; photocopying & duplicating services; typesetting, computer controlled

(G-11316)
ORACLE AMERICA INC
Also Called: Sun Microsystems
2701 Emerywood Pkwy 108 (23294-3722)
PHONE..................................804 672-0998
Jim Mecktly, *Branch Mgr*
EMP: 16 **Publicly Held**
WEB: www.ea.com
SIC: 7372 Prepackaged software
HQ: Oracle America, Inc.
　　500 Oracle Pkwy
　　Redwood City CA 94065
　　650 506-7000

(G-11317)
OUTRAGEOUS SHINE LLC
11204 Patterson Ave (23238-5011)
PHONE..................................804 741-9274
EMP: 2
SALES (est): 140.6K **Privately Held**
SIC: 3589 Car washing machinery

(G-11318)
PAN CUSTOM MOLDING INC
10137 Grand Oaks Dr (23233-2040)
PHONE..................................804 787-3820
EMP: 4
SALES (est): 200.2K **Privately Held**
SIC: 3089 Molding primary plastic

(G-11319)
PARKER MANUFACTURING LLC
5734 Charles City Cir (23231-4502)
P.O. Box 977, Sandston (23150-0977)
PHONE..................................804 507-0593
Kenneth Parker, *Mng Member*
EMP: 5
SALES (est): 768.1K **Privately Held**
WEB: www.parkermftg.com
SIC: 3549 Metalworking machinery

(G-11320)
PAUL VALENTINE ORTHOTICS
2139 Staples Mill Rd (23230-2905)
PHONE..................................804 355-0283
Paul L Valentine, *Owner*
EMP: 7
SQ FT: 4,598
SALES (est): 720.4K **Privately Held**
WEB: www.valentineorthotics.com
SIC: 3842 5999 Limbs, artificial; orthopedic & prosthesis applications

(G-11321)
PFIZER INC
Also Called: Wyeth
2300 Darbytown Rd (23231-5406)
P.O. Box 26609 (23261-6609)
PHONE..................................804 652-6782
Carl De Rubeis, *Branch Mgr*
Mallik Karamsetty, *Technology*
Nikhil Gadre, *Director*
Sarah Karchere, *Director*
Paul Martini, *Director*
EMP: 150
SALES (corp-wide): 51.7B **Publicly Held**
WEB: www.pfizer.com
SIC: 2834 Pharmaceutical preparations

PA: Pfizer Inc.
　　235 E 42nd St Rm 107
　　New York NY 10017
　　212 733-2323

(G-11322)
PHILIP MORRIS DUTY FREE INC
6601 W Broad St (23230-1723)
P.O. Box 85086 (23285-5086)
PHONE..................................804 274-2000
Joseph H Workman, *General Mgr*
▲ EMP: 100
SALES (est): 12MM **Publicly Held**
WEB: www.altria.com
SIC: 2111 Cigarettes
HQ: Philip Morris Usa Inc.
　　6601 W Brd St
　　Richmond VA 23230
　　804 274-2000

(G-11323)
PHILIP MORRIS USA INC (HQ)
6601 W Brd St (23230)
P.O. Box 26603 (23261-6603)
PHONE..................................804 274-2000
John R Nelson, *President*
David R Beran, *Exec VP*
Craig G Schwartz, *Senior VP*
Harry G Steele, *Senior VP*
David Campbell, *Vice Pres*
◆ EMP: 600 EST: 1919
SALES (est): 2.3B **Publicly Held**
WEB: www.philipmorrisusa.com
SIC: 2111 2141 5194 Cigarettes; tobacco stemming & redrying; cigarettes
PA: Altria Group, Inc.
　　6601 W Broad St
　　Richmond VA 23230
　　804 274-2200

(G-11324)
PHOTONBLUE LLC
3627 Springsberry Pl (23233-1846)
PHONE..................................804 747-7412
Steven Ashworth, *Principal*
EMP: 3
SALES (est): 201.1K **Privately Held**
SIC: 3661 Fiber optics communications equipment

(G-11325)
PIF INDUSTRIES LLC
3113 W Marshall St (23230-4730)
PHONE..................................804 677-2945
EMP: 2 EST: 2010
SALES (est): 82.4K **Privately Held**
SIC: 3999 Manufacturing industries

(G-11326)
PINNACLE CABINETRY DESIGN LLC
5418 Lakeside Ave (23228-6057)
PHONE..................................804 262-7356
Steven Huber, *Mng Member*
EMP: 2
SALES (est): 200K **Privately Held**
WEB: www.pinnaclecabinetry.net
SIC: 2434 Wood kitchen cabinets

(G-11327)
PITTSTON MINERALS GROUP INC (HQ)
1801 Bayberry Ct Fl 4 (23226-3771)
P.O. Box 18100 (23226-8100)
PHONE..................................804 289-9600
James Hartough, *Vice Pres*
Austin F Reed, *Vice Pres*
Robert T Ritter, *CFO*
James B Hartough, *VP Finance*
Frank T Lennon, *Administration*
EMP: 150
SQ FT: 40,000
SALES (est): 30.3MM
SALES (corp-wide): 3.6B **Publicly Held**
SIC: 1221 1222 Bituminous coal & lignite-surface mining; bituminous coal-underground mining
PA: The Brink's Company
　　1801 Bayberry Ct
　　Richmond VA 23226
　　804 289-9600

(G-11328)
POWER SYSTEMS & CONTROLS INC
3206 Lanvale Ave (23230-4219)
P.O. Box 27306 (23261-7306)
PHONE..................................804 355-2803
Thomas J Delano, *President*
Daniel M Connor, *President*
Douglas R Watson, *Vice Pres*
Ed Dehaven, *Engineer*
Dan Connor, *Controller*
◆ EMP: 75
SQ FT: 50,000 **Privately Held**
WEB: www.pscpower.com
SIC: 3625 5063 Electric controls & control accessories, industrial; electrical apparatus & equipment

(G-11329)
PRECEPT MEDICAL PRODUCTS INC
5666 Eastport Blvd (23231-4442)
PHONE..................................804 236-1010
EMP: 5
SALES (corp-wide): 17.9MM **Privately Held**
SIC: 3842 Mfg Surgical Appliances/Supplies
PA: Precept Medical Products, Inc.
　　370 Airport Rd
　　Arden NC 28704
　　828 681-0209

(G-11330)
PRECISION PRINT & COPY LLC
10623 Patterson Ave (23238-4701)
PHONE..................................804 740-3514
Tanju I Tanir, *Principal*
EMP: 3
SQ FT: 1,100
SALES (est): 355.6K **Privately Held**
SIC: 2752 Commercial printing, offset

(G-11331)
PREMIUM MED SUPPLY LLC
3200 Rckbrdge St Unit 302 (23230)
PHONE..................................888 506-6367
Wendy Scelia,
EMP: 6
SALES (est): 216.7K **Privately Held**
SIC: 2389 Disposable garments & accessories

(G-11332)
PRESTIGE INC
Also Called: Prestige Cabinets Countertops
5805 School Ave Ste C (23228-5444)
PHONE..................................804 266-1000
Michael J Waller, *President*
John Lassiter, *Vice Pres*
Rex Collins, *Admin Sec*
EMP: 16 EST: 1999
SQ FT: 12,000
SALES (est): 2.2MM **Privately Held**
WEB: www.prestigecabinetsva.com
SIC: 2434 Wood kitchen cabinets

(G-11333)
PRINTERSMARK INC
6010 N Crestwood Ave F (23230-2200)
P.O. Box 27402 (23261-7402)
PHONE..................................804 353-2324
Mark Charle Henderson, *President*
EMP: 5
SQ FT: 15,000
SALES (est): 987.3K **Privately Held**
WEB: www.printersmark.com
SIC: 2752 Commercial printing, offset

(G-11334)
PRINTING DEPARTMENT INC
Also Called: Mailing Resources
2108 Spencer Rd (23230-2624)
PHONE..................................804 282-2739
Merle E Robertson, *President*
Merle Robertson III, *Vice Pres*
Betty Robertson, *Treasurer*
EMP: 6
SQ FT: 3,100
SALES (est): 1MM **Privately Held**
WEB: www.pdiprint.com
SIC: 2752 Commercial printing, offset

(G-11335)
PRINTING DEPT INC
6521 Kensington Ave (23226-3029)
PHONE................804 673-1904
EMP: 2
SALES (est): 83.9K **Privately Held**
SIC: 2752 Commercial printing, lithographic

(G-11336)
PRODUCT IDENTIFICATION
8532 Sanford Dr (23228-2813)
PHONE................804 264-4434
Toll Free:................888
Cary Wright, *Manager*
Irene Cook, *Manager*
Michael Maceranka, *Info Tech Dir*
EMP: 3
SALES (corp-wide): 1.9MM **Privately Held**
WEB: www.pips.com
SIC: 2269 7389 5045 2679 Labels, cotton: printed; packaging & labeling services; computers; labels, paper: made from purchased material
PA: Product Identification & Processing Systems, Inc.
10 Midland Ave Ste M-02
Port Chester NY
212 996-6000

(G-11337)
PROFESSIONAL BUSINESS PRTG INC
Also Called: Sterns Printing and Engrv Co
8770 Park Central Dr (23227-1146)
PHONE................804 423-1355
Samuel Bennett Harper, *President*
EMP: 1
SALES (est): 148.1K **Privately Held**
WEB: www.worthiggins.com
SIC: 2752 Commercial printing, offset

(G-11338)
PROPER PIE CO LLC
4301 Masonic Ln (23231-2025)
PHONE................804 343-7437
EMP: 6
SALES (est): 552.9K **Privately Held**
WEB: www.properpieco.com
SIC: 2051 Bread, cake & related products

(G-11339)
PS ITS LEATHER
9028 Horrigan Ct (23294-5015)
PHONE................804 762-9489
Paul Beverly, *Owner*
Sandy Dyche, *Co-Owner*
EMP: 2
SALES (est): 155.3K **Privately Held**
WEB: www.psitsleather.blogspot.com
SIC: 3199 Leather garments

(G-11340)
PULMOFLOW INC
3900 Westerre Pkwy # 300 (23233-1478)
PHONE................831 206-8659
Jan Zimmerman, *Principal*
Dale Anderson, *Finance*
EMP: 2
SALES (est): 130K **Privately Held**
SIC: 3841 Surgical & medical instruments

(G-11341)
PURER AIR
9609 Georges Bluff Rd (23229-7677)
PHONE................804 921-8234
Debbie Davis, *Owner*
EMP: 1
SALES (est): 100K **Privately Held**
WEB: www.purerair.com
SIC: 3564 Air purification equipment

(G-11342)
Q STITCHED LLC
10206 Maremont Cir (23238-3604)
PHONE................757 621-6025
Lindsay Susan, *Principal*
EMP: 1
SALES (est): 43.9K **Privately Held**
SIC: 2395 Embroidery & art needlework

(G-11343)
QG LLC
Also Called: Worldcolor Richmond
7400 Impala Dr (23228-3741)
PHONE................804 264-3866
Steve Eggleston, *Branch Mgr*
EMP: 178
SALES (corp-wide): 3.9B **Publicly Held**
WEB: www.quad.com
SIC: 2752 Commercial printing, offset
HQ: Qg, Llc
N61w23044 Harrys Way
Sussex WI 53089

(G-11344)
RACE TECHNOLOGY USA LLC
2317 Westwood Ave Ste 101 (23230-4019)
PHONE................804 358-7289
Albert Seim,
Albert D Seim,
EMP: 3
SALES (est): 231.1K **Privately Held**
WEB: www.race-technology.com
SIC: 3829 Measuring & controlling devices

(G-11345)
RAND WORLDWIDE INC
8100 Three Chopt Rd (23229-4833)
PHONE................804 290-8850
Louise L Foster, *Branch Mgr*
EMP: 1 **Publicly Held**
WEB: www.rand.com
SIC: 7372 Prepackaged software
PA: Rand Worldwide, Inc.
11201 Dlfeld Blvd Ste 112
Owings Mills MD 21117
410 581-8080

(G-11346)
RAVEN ENTERPRISES LLC
Also Called: Historic Organ Study Tours
3217 Brook Rd (23227-4803)
P.O. Box 25111 (23260-5111)
PHONE................804 355-6386
William Vanpelt,
EMP: 1
SALES (est): 179.1K **Privately Held**
WEB: www.ravencd.com
SIC: 3652 Pre-recorded records & tapes

(G-11347)
RBR TACTICAL INC
Also Called: Rbr Tactical Armor
3113 Aspen Ave (23228-4902)
PHONE................804 564-6787
James Scovell, *President*
Paul Fishwick, *Vice Pres*
EMP: 6
SQ FT: 7,000
SALES (est): 12MM **Privately Held**
SIC: 2311 Military uniforms, men's & youths': purchased materials

(G-11348)
READY SET READ LLC
202 Ralston Rd (23229-8026)
PHONE................804 673-8764
Kimberly Gorenflo, *Principal*
EMP: 3
SALES (est): 205.9K **Privately Held**
SIC: 3273 Ready-mixed concrete

(G-11349)
RED TIE GROUP INC
5616 Eastport Blvd (23231-4443)
P.O. Box 3301, Henrico (23228-9706)
PHONE................804 236-4632
Carlton McMichael, *Manager*
David Wiskman, *Manager*
EMP: 6
SALES (corp-wide): 26.1MM **Privately Held**
WEB: www.wikoff.com
SIC: 2893 5084 Printing ink; printing trades machinery, equipment & supplies
PA: Red Tie Group, Inc.
4521 Industrial Pkwy
Cleveland OH 44135

(G-11350)
RENTBOT LLC
29 Lexington Rd (23226-1625)
PHONE................844 473-6826
Nathan Markey, *President*
EMP: 1

SALES (est): 63.2K **Privately Held**
WEB: www.rentbot.co
SIC: 7372 7389 Business oriented computer software;

(G-11351)
RESERVOIR DISTILLERY LLC
1800 Summit Ave (23230-4314)
PHONE................804 912-2621
Grant H Ancarrow, *President*
James Carpenter,
David Cuttino,
EMP: 1
SALES (est): 105.1K **Privately Held**
WEB: www.reservoirdistillery.com
SIC: 2085 Distilled & blended liquors

(G-11352)
REYNOLDS FOOD PACKAGING LLC (DH)
6601 W Broad St (23230-1723)
PHONE................800 446-3020
Rebecca Leibert, *Mng Member*
Sandy Drummonds, *Manager*
Bob Stasicky, *Manager*
Beryl Holzbach, *Technology*
◆ EMP: 41
SALES (est): 45.1MM **Publicly Held**
WEB: www.reynoldsconsumerproducts.com
SIC: 3081 2621 Plastic film & sheet; packaging paper

(G-11353)
REYNOLDS METALS COMPANY LLC
6641 W Broad St (23230-1700)
PHONE................804 746-6723
EMP: 2
SALES (corp-wide): 9.3B **Publicly Held**
SIC: 3411 Mfg Metal Cans
HQ: Reynolds Metals Company, Llc
390 Park Ave
New York NY 10022
212 518-5400

(G-11354)
RICHMOND DISTRIBUTORS LLC
959 Myers St Ste A (23230-4800)
PHONE................804 497-0713
EMP: 2
SALES (est): 252.8K **Privately Held**
SIC: 2111 Cigarettes

(G-11355)
RICHMOND EQUITY VENTURES LLC
6806 Paragon Pl Ste 300 (23230-1824)
PHONE................804 837-3523
EMP: 3 EST: 2018
SALES (est): 142.2K **Privately Held**
WEB: www.richmond.com
SIC: 2711 Newspapers, publishing & printing

(G-11356)
RICHMOND LIVING LLC
2607 Cottage Cove Dr (23233-3317)
PHONE................804 266-5202
Dana Hennesey, *Principal*
EMP: 3 EST: 2017
SALES (est):126.5K **Privately Held**
WEB: www.richmondmagazine.com
SIC: 2721 Magazines: publishing only, not printed on site

(G-11357)
RICHMOND NEWSPAPER INC
5742 Charles City Cir (23231-4502)
PHONE................804 261-1101
EMP: 4
SALES (est): 143.4K **Privately Held**
SIC: 2711 Newspapers, publishing & printing

(G-11358)
RICHMOND PHILHARMONIC INC
8100 Three Chopt Rd # 209 (23229-4833)
PHONE................804 673-7400
J Durwood Felton, *President*
Merrybeth Hall, *Vice Pres*
Tom Carson, *Treasurer*
Ruth Auman, *Admin Sec*
EMP: 1

SALES (est): 30.9K **Privately Held**
WEB: www.richmondphilharmonic.org
SIC: 3931 Musical instruments

(G-11359)
RICHMOND PUBLISHING
8010 Ridge Rd Ste F (23229-7288)
PHONE................804 229-6267
Angela Lehman-Rios, *Editor*
EMP: 2 EST: 2018
SALES (est): 69.2K **Privately Held**
SIC: 2711 Newspapers, publishing & printing

(G-11360)
RICHMOND STEEL INC
2031 Westwood Ave (23230-4114)
P.O. Box 9405 (23228-0405)
PHONE................804 355-8080
Toll Free:................888
Fred T Mayers, *Ch of Bd*
Fred T Mayers Jr, *President*
Fred T Mayers III, *President*
Mark A Mayers, *Vice Pres*
Christine Mayers, *Treasurer*
EMP: 36 EST: 1944
SQ FT: 3,500
SALES (est): 9.8MM **Privately Held**
WEB: www.richmondsteelinc.com
SIC: 3441 5039 Fabricated structural metal; joists

(G-11361)
RICHMOND STEEL BOAT WORKS INC
9303 Wishart Rd (23229-7046)
PHONE................804 741-0432
Stuart P Tansill, *President*
EMP: 2
SALES (est): 172.2K **Privately Held**
SIC: 3732 Boat building & repairing

(G-11362)
RICHMOND TOP MOVING CO
8500 Jesse Senior Dr (23229-5700)
PHONE................804 441-9702
Cheryl Ferris, *Manager*
EMP: 3
SALES (est): 104.6K **Privately Held**
WEB: www.richmond.com
SIC: 2711 Newspapers, publishing & printing

(G-11363)
RICHMOND YELLOWPAGES COM
3604 Monument Ave (23230-4900)
PHONE................804 565-9170
EMP: 1
SALES (est): 56K **Privately Held**
SIC: 2741 Misc Publishing

(G-11364)
RICHS STITCHES INC
4013 Macarthur Ave (23227-4050)
PHONE................804 262-3477
Cecilia Rich, *President*
Andrew Rich, *Corp Secy*
Rich Christine Anne, *Vice Pres*
Christine Rich, *Vice Pres*
Chris Rich, *Sales Staff*
EMP: 3
SQ FT: 1,800
SALES (est): 320K **Privately Held**
WEB: www.richsstitches.com
SIC: 2395 Embroidery products, except schiffli machine

(G-11365)
ROCKING HORSE VENTURES INC
10607 Patterson Ave (23238-4743)
PHONE................804 784-5830
Barbara Pedersen, *Principal*
EMP: 3
SALES (est): 212.8K **Privately Held**
SIC: 3944 Rocking horses

(G-11366)
RODRIGUEZ GUITARS
929 Myers St (23230-4812)
PHONE................804 358-6324
Thomas Rodriguez, *Owner*
EMP: 1

SALES (est): 70.7K **Privately Held**
WEB: www.rodriguezguitars.com
SIC: 3931 5736 5099 Guitars & parts, electric & nonelectric; musical instrument stores; musical instruments

(G-11367)
ROYAL TEE LLC
2014 N Parham Rd (23229-4110)
PHONE 540 892-7694
Shanteea Onike Childress, *Principal*
EMP: 2
SALES (est): 73.2K **Privately Held**
SIC: 2759 Screen printing

(G-11368)
RVA BOATWORKS LLC
9950 Hoke Brady Rd (23231-8333)
PHONE 804 937-7448
Jason Taylor, *Principal*
EMP: 2 **EST:** 2017
SALES (est): 125.9K **Privately Held**
SIC: 3732 Boat building & repairing

(G-11369)
SAI KRISHNA LLC
2115 Dabney Rd (23230-3324)
PHONE 804 442-7140
Suchit Gandhi, *President*
EMP: 6
SALES (est): 433.6K **Privately Held**
SIC: 3052 Hose, pneumatic: rubber or rubberized fabric

(G-11370)
SAM ENGLISH OF VA
2890 Seven Hills Blvd (23231-6033)
P.O. Box 50025 (23250-0025)
PHONE 804 222-7114
William Dunlap IV, *Principal*
EMP: 25
SALES (est): 950K **Privately Held**
WEB: www.samenglishofva.com
SIC: 3312 3443 Blast furnaces & steel mills; boilers: industrial, power, or marine

(G-11371)
SAMPSON COATINGS INCORPORATED
1900 Ellen Rd (23230-4213)
PHONE 804 359-5011
EMP: 1
SALES (est): 51.9K **Privately Held**
SIC: 2851 Paints & allied products

(G-11372)
SARA CAMPBELL LTD
306 Libbie Ave (23226-2614)
PHONE 617 423-3134
EMP: 1
SALES (corp-wide): 4.2MM **Privately Held**
WEB: www.saracampbell.com
SIC: 2337 Women's & misses' suits & coats
PA: Sara Campbell, Ltd.
67 Kemble St Ste 4
Boston MA 02119
617 423-3134

(G-11373)
SB PRINTING LLC
2107 Dabney Rd (23230-3324)
PHONE 804 247-2404
EMP: 2
SALES (est): 92.3K **Privately Held**
SIC: 2752 Commercial printing, lithographic

(G-11374)
SCREEN CRAFTS INC
2915 Moore St (23230-4529)
PHONE 804 355-4156
Janet Williams, *President*
Dwayne Gary, *Vice Pres*
Todd Gary, *Treasurer*
EMP: 20
SQ FT: 30,000
SALES (est): 4MM **Privately Held**
WEB: www.screencraftsinc.com
SIC: 2759 2396 Screen printing; screen printing on fabric articles

(G-11375)
SEABOARD SERVICE OF VA INC
5707 Old Osborne Tpke (23231-3059)
PHONE 804 643-5112
EMP: 3
SALES (est): 354.3K **Privately Held**
SIC: 3272 Concrete products

(G-11376)
SEMICONDUCTOR TECHNOLOGY RES
Also Called: Str
1607 Swinton Ln (23238-4054)
PHONE 804 304-8092
Yuri Makarov, *President*
EMP: 3
SALES (est): 450K **Privately Held**
WEB: www.str-soft.com
SIC: 3674 Semiconductors & related devices

(G-11377)
SERENE SUDS LLC
6414 Engel Rd (23226-2810)
PHONE 804 433-8032
Isara Serene, *Principal*
EMP: 1
SALES (est): 78.6K **Privately Held**
SIC: 2841 Soap & other detergents

(G-11378)
SHADE MANN-KIDWELL CORP
Also Called: Mann-Kdwell Intr Win Tratments
6011 W Broad St (23230-2221)
PHONE 804 288-2819
Andrew L Kidwell III, *President*
EMP: 8 **EST:** 1967
SQ FT: 4,125
SALES (est): 1.1MM **Privately Held**
WEB: www.mannkidwell.com
SIC: 2591 2391 5719 Venetian blinds; draperies, plastic & textile: from purchased materials; venetian blinds

(G-11379)
SHOWBEST FIXTURE CORP (PA)
4112 Sarellen Rd (23231-4327)
PHONE 804 222-5535
Jim Schubert, *President*
Colleen Brooks, *Vice Pres*
Edward A Meyer, *Vice Pres*
Ned Meyer, *Vice Pres*
Scott Schubert, *VP Mfg*
▲ **EMP:** 88
SQ FT: 115,000
SALES (est): 23.9MM **Privately Held**
WEB: www.showbest.com
SIC: 2542 Fixtures, store: except wood

(G-11380)
SIEMENS INDUSTRY INC
5106 Glen Alden Dr (23231-4319)
PHONE 804 222-6680
Dan Clark, *District Mgr*
John Nickels, *Engineer*
Joseph Byrd, *Manager*
Kenneth Cossaboon, *Manager*
EMP: 56
SALES (corp-wide): 67.4B **Privately Held**
WEB: www.new.siemens.com
SIC: 3822 5075 Air conditioning & refrigeration controls; air conditioning equipment, except room units
HQ: Siemens Industry, Inc.
1000 Deerfield Pkwy
Buffalo Grove IL 60089
847 215-1000

(G-11381)
SIGN MANAGERS LLC
2920 W Broad St (23230-5103)
PHONE 804 381-5198
Austin McDaniel, *Principal*
EMP: 1 **EST:** 2015
SALES (est): 50.6K **Privately Held**
SIC: 3993 Signs & advertising specialties

(G-11382)
SILVERWOOD PRESS LLC
1620 Nottoway Ave (23227-3963)
PHONE 804 833-0595
Hannah Koca, *Principal*
EMP: 1

SALES (est): 41.3K **Privately Held**
WEB: www.silverwoodpress.com
SIC: 2741 Miscellaneous publishing

(G-11383)
SINGLECOMM LLC
3200 Rockbridge St # 202 (23230-4333)
PHONE 203 559-5486
Ross Krisel, *Exec VP*
Robert Ragland, *Senior VP*
Bret McAllister, *Vice Pres*
Paul Levasseur, *VP Opers*
Kurt Maschoff, *VP Opers*
EMP: 10
SQ FT: 100,000
SALES (est): 690.1K **Privately Held**
WEB: www.singlecomm.com
SIC: 7372 4813 Business oriented computer software; voice telephone communications

(G-11384)
SLATE & SHELL LLC
1425 Westshire Ln (23238-3907)
PHONE 804 381-8713
William Cobb,
EMP: 1
SALES (est): 66.3K **Privately Held**
WEB: www.slateandshell.com
SIC: 2731 Books: publishing only

(G-11385)
SMART START OF GLEN ALLEN
2201 Dickens Rd (23230-2024)
PHONE 804 447-7642
EMP: 4 **EST:** 2009
SALES (est): 257.5K **Privately Held**
SIC: 3357 Automotive wire & cable, except ignition sets: nonferrous

(G-11386)
SOURCE PUBLISHING INC
2316 Persimmon Trek (23233-2738)
P.O. Box 8327 (23226-0327)
PHONE 804 747-4080
EMP: 2 **EST:** 2009
SALES (est): 86K **Privately Held**
SIC: 2741 Misc Publishing

(G-11387)
SOUTHERN GRAVURE SERVICE INC
2891 Sprouse Dr (23231-6040)
PHONE 804 226-2490
Larry M White, *President*
Tim Moore, *Regl Sales Mgr*
Scott Thompson, *Director*
EMP: 2
SALES (est): 193.2K **Privately Held**
WEB: www.sgsintl.com
SIC: 3555 Printing trades machinery

(G-11388)
SOUTHERN STAMP INCORPORATED
1506 Tomlynn St (23230-3313)
PHONE 804 359-0531
Adam Raidabaugh, *Principal*
EMP: 2
SALES (est): 130.5K **Privately Held**
WEB: www.southernstamp.com
SIC: 3953 Marking devices

(G-11389)
SOUTHERN STATES COOP INC (PA)
Also Called: Agway
6606 W Broad St Ste B (23230-1731)
P.O. Box 26234 (23260-6234)
PHONE 804 281-1000
Jeff Stroburg, *President*
Steve Patterson, *Vice Pres*
Curry A Roberts, *Vice Pres*
Karen Thomas, *Vice Pres*
Fred Jezouit, *CFO*
▲ **EMP:** 300
SQ FT: 200,000
SALES (est): 2.1B **Privately Held**
WEB: www.southernstates.com
SIC: 2048 0181 2873 2874 Prepared feeds; bulbs & seeds; nitrogenous fertilizers; phosphatic fertilizers; farm supplies; feed; seeds & bulbs; fertilizer & fertilizer materials; petroleum products

(G-11390)
SOUTHERN STATES COOP INC
Also Called: Williamsburg Rd Serv
3119 Williamsburg Rd (23231-2231)
P.O. Box 69, Goochland (23063-0069)
PHONE 804 226-2758
Lucas Householder, *Manager*
EMP: 17
SALES (corp-wide): 2.1B **Privately Held**
WEB: www.southernstates.com
SIC: 2048 2873 0181 2874 Prepared feeds; nitrogenous fertilizers; bulbs & seeds; phosphatic fertilizers; animal feeds; saws & sawing equipment
PA: Southern States Cooperative, Incorporated
6606 W Broad St Ste B
Richmond VA 23230
804 281-1000

(G-11391)
SOUTHWEST PLASTIC BINDING CO
6601 S Laburnum Ave (23231-5000)
PHONE 804 226-0400
Don Barks, *Manager*
EMP: 27
SALES (corp-wide): 12.1MM **Privately Held**
WEB: www.swbindinglaminating.com
SIC: 2789 Bookbinding & related work
PA: Southwest Plastic Binding Co.
109 Millwell Dr
Maryland Heights MO 63043
314 739-4400

(G-11392)
SPOT COOLERS INC
5742 Charles City Cir (23231-4502)
PHONE 804 222-5530
Ken Swanson, *Branch Mgr*
EMP: 4
SALES (corp-wide): 77B **Publicly Held**
WEB: www.spot-coolers.com
SIC: 3585 Heating & air conditioning combination units
HQ: Spot Coolers, Inc.
444 E Palmetto Park Rd
Boca Raton FL 33432
561 394-6455

(G-11393)
SPOTSPOT CO
5407 Patterson Ave 200a (23226-2040)
PHONE 804 909-7353
David Vogeleer, *Director*
Fletcher Padgett, *Director*
Kevin Power, *Director*
Thiago Balzano, *Officer*
John Mills, *Officer*
EMP: 7 **EST:** 2013
SQ FT: 300
SALES (est): 274.8K **Privately Held**
SIC: 7372 Application computer software

(G-11394)
SPRAYING SYSTEMS CO
13605 Swanhollow Dr (23233-7623)
PHONE 804 364-0095
Rudi Schick, *Vice Pres*
Mark W Lacroix, *Project Engr*
Frank Brooks, *Sales Mgr*
Mathieu Proteau, *Sales Engr*
Peter Bonnevie, *Branch Mgr*
EMP: 6
SALES (corp-wide): 351.1MM **Privately Held**
WEB: www.spray.com
SIC: 3499 Nozzles, spray: aerosol, paint or insecticide
PA: Spraying Systems Co.
200 W North Ave
Glendale Heights IL 60139
630 665-5000

(G-11395)
SPRING MOSES INC
6414 Horsepen Rd (23226-2906)
PHONE 804 321-0156
Dana Longenderfer, *President*
Mark Longenderfer, *Vice Pres*
Longederfer Mark, *Vice Pres*
▲ **EMP:** 3
SQ FT: 5,000

SALES (est): 220K Privately Held
SIC: 3299 5092 3645 Non-metallic mineral statuary & other decorative products; arts & crafts equipment & supplies; residential lighting fixtures

(G-11396)
SPRINT SIGNS
9020 Quioccasin Rd Ste C (23229-5515)
PHONE.....................804 741-7446
Jonathan Francis, *Owner*
EMP: 3
SALES (est): 150K Privately Held
WEB: www.sprintsigns.biz
SIC: 3993 Signs & advertising specialties

(G-11397)
STAR US PRECISION INDUSTRY LTD
3781 Westerre Pkwy Ste F (23233-1328)
PHONE.....................804 747-8948
Neil Song, *CEO*
Allen Tan, *President*
▲ **EMP: 3**
SQ FT: 1,200
SALES (est): 199.6K Privately Held
SIC: 3544 Special dies & tools

(G-11398)
STEPHAN BURGER FINE WDWKG
5001 W Leigh St (23230-2810)
PHONE.....................434 960-5440
Stephan Burger, *Principal*
EMP: 1 EST: 2016
SALES (est): 88.5K Privately Held
SIC: 2431 Millwork

(G-11399)
STRATOS LLC
2920 W Broad St Ste 100 (23230-5103)
PHONE.....................800 213-4705
Ryan Leach, *CEO*
Aaron Ludin, *Shareholder*
Gonzalo Trevino, *Shareholder*
EMP: 1
SQ FT: 56
SALES (est): 64.7K Privately Held
SIC: 3411 Food & beverage containers

(G-11400)
STUARTS AC & REFRIGERATION
1535 Westshire Ln (23238-3039)
P.O. Box 6789 (23230-0789)
PHONE.....................804 405-0960
Stuart Weger, *President*
Donna Weger, *Vice Pres*
EMP: 2
SALES (est): 150K Privately Held
SIC: 3822 Air conditioning & refrigeration controls

(G-11401)
SUDDEN SERVICE INC
8351 Brook Rd (23227-1105)
PHONE.....................804 266-6200
EMP: 2 EST: 2015
SALES (est): 89.6K Privately Held
WEB: www.taylorsuddenservice.com
SIC: 3599 Industrial machinery

(G-11402)
SUPERIOR BOILER LLC
2890 Seven Hills Blvd (23231-6033)
P.O. Box 50218 (23250-0218)
PHONE.....................804 226-8227
Rosa Garcia, *Bookkeeper*
Marshall Parker, *Manager*
Bart Bergman, *Manager*
John English, *Manager*
Richard English, *Manager*
EMP: 50 EST: 2016
SQ FT: 121,705
SALES (est): 1.1MM Privately Held
WEB: www.englishboiler.com
SIC: 3443 Boiler & boiler shop work

(G-11403)
SUPERIOR METAL FABRICATORS
4217 Sarellen Rd (23231-4320)
P.O. Box 7567 (23231-0067)
PHONE.....................804 236-3266
Winfred C Smith, *President*

Robert Smith, *Treasurer*
EMP: 10
SQ FT: 10,000
SALES (est): 1.2MM Privately Held
WEB: www.superiormetalfabinc.com
SIC: 3599 1799 Machine & other job shop work; welding on site

(G-11404)
T3 MEDIA LLC
Also Called: Henrico Citizen
6924 Lakeside Ave (23228-5240)
PHONE.....................804 262-1700
Sarah Story, *Editor*
George Weltmer, *Accounts Exec*
Thomas Lappas, *Mng Member*
EMP: 3
SALES (est): 268.9K Privately Held
WEB: www.henricocitizen.com
SIC: 2711 Newspapers, publishing & printing

(G-11405)
TACTICAL DPLOYMENT SYSTEMS LLC
Also Called: Lightwav
2111b Spencer Rd (23230-2657)
P.O. Box 28928 (23228-8928)
PHONE.....................804 672-8426
Mullsteff David, *Bd of Directors*
EMP: 3 EST: 2012
SALES (est): 276.9K Privately Held
WEB: www.tacreadydeploy.com
SIC: 3679 Harness assemblies for electronic use: wire or cable

(G-11406)
TAICCO FUEL INC
805 E Parham Rd (23227-1107)
PHONE.....................571 405-7700
Ayaz Ahmed, *Administration*
EMP: 3
SALES (est): 173.5K Privately Held
SIC: 2869 Fuels

(G-11407)
TAYLOR COMMUNICATIONS INC
1518 Willow Lawn Dr Fl 3 (23230-3419)
PHONE.....................804 612-7597
EMP: 3
SALES (corp-wide): 2.4B Privately Held
WEB: www.taylorcorp.com
SIC: 2754 Commercial printing, gravure
HQ: Taylor Communications, Inc.
  1725 Roe Crest Dr
  North Mankato MN 56003
  866 541-0937

(G-11408)
TENSION ENVELOPE CORP
5803 S Crestwood Ave (23226-1801)
PHONE.....................540 615-5372
EMP: 2 EST: 2019
SALES (est): 77.5K Privately Held
WEB: www.tensionenvelope.com
SIC: 2759 Commercial printing

(G-11409)
THALHIMER HEADWEAR CORPORATION
4825 Radford Ave Ste 100 (23230-3532)
PHONE.....................804 355-1200
Harry R Thalhimer, *President*
Paul S Isaac III, *Vice Pres*
EMP: 3
SQ FT: 3,000
SALES (est): 404.6K Privately Held
WEB: www.thalhimerheadwear.com
SIC: 2261 Screen printing of cotton broadwoven fabrics

(G-11410)
THOR SYSTEMS INC
3621 Saunders Ave (23227-4354)
PHONE.....................804 353-7477
Robert Van Sickle, *President*
Vansickle Robert, *Exec VP*
Tom Armstrong, *Vice Pres*
Brenda Murray, *Office Mgr*
EMP: 5
SALES (est): 420K Privately Held
WEB: www.thorsystems.us
SIC: 3643 Lightning protection equipment

(G-11411)
THURSTON SIGN & GRAPHIC
2325 Lenora Ln (23230-2108)
PHONE.....................804 285-4617
Wayne Thurston, *Owner*
EMP: 1
SALES (est): 66.8K Privately Held
WEB: www.thurstonsign.com
SIC: 3993 Signs & advertising specialties

(G-11412)
TITAN AMERICA LLC
Also Called: Titan Virginia Ready Mix
4305 Sarellen Rd (23231-4311)
P.O. Box 7892 (23231-0392)
PHONE.....................804 236-4122
Dan Osborne, *General Mgr*
EMP: 14
SALES (corp-wide): 1.4MM Privately Held
WEB: www.titanamerica.com
SIC: 1422 3241 3273 Crushed & broken limestone; cement, hydraulic; ready-mixed concrete
HQ: Titan America Llc
  5700 Lake Wright Dr # 300
  Norfolk VA 23502
  757 858-6500

(G-11413)
TOBACCO PROCESSORS INC
1501 N Hamilton St (23230-3925)
PHONE.....................804 359-9311
Ray Paul, *President*
Mike Ligon, *Vice Pres*
Karen M L Whelan, *Treasurer*
Robert Peebles, *Controller*
George Freeman III, *Admin Sec*
EMP: 4
SQ FT: 48,000
SALES (est): 418.4K Publicly Held
WEB: www.universalcorp.com
SIC: 2141 Tobacco stemming; tobacco redrying
HQ: Universal Leaf Tobacco Company, Incorporated
  9201 Frest Hl Ave Stony P
  Richmond VA 23235

(G-11414)
TOPCRAFTERS OF VIRGINIA INC
4415 Augusta Ave (23230-3815)
PHONE.....................804 353-1797
Margaret D Bucker, *President*
Beverly A Bucker, *Corp Secy*
EMP: 5
SALES (est): 398.5K Privately Held
SIC: 2541 Counter & sink tops

(G-11415)
TORTILLERIA SAN LUIS LLC
9027 Quioccasin Rd (23229-5522)
PHONE.....................804 901-1501
Facundo Samuel, *Principal*
EMP: 3 EST: 2010
SALES (est): 152.5K Privately Held
SIC: 2099 Tortillas, fresh or refrigerated

(G-11416)
TOTAL PRINTING CO INC
4401 Sarellen Rd (23231-4428)
PHONE.....................804 222-3813
Gary L Williams Jr, *President*
Gary Williams Jr, *President*
Dale B Williams, *Vice Pres*
Bo Williams III, *Treasurer*
Drew Pugh, *Sales Executive*
EMP: 25
SQ FT: 20,000
SALES (est): 2.5MM Privately Held
WEB: www.total-printing.com
SIC: 2752 2759 2791 2789 Commercial printing, offset; letterpress printing; typesetting; bookbinding & related work

(G-11417)
TRADEMARK WOODWORKING LLC
3108 W Marshall St (23230-4706)
P.O. Box 71195 (23255-1195)
PHONE.....................804 346-5999
Marc Hawn, *Mng Member*
Marc L Cohen,
EMP: 3
SQ FT: 4,800

SALES (est): 366.4K Privately Held
WEB: www.trademarkww.com
SIC: 2434 Wood kitchen cabinets

(G-11418)
TREDEGAR CORPORATION
Tredegar Film Products
5700 Eastport Blvd Ste A (23231-4441)
PHONE.....................804 523-3001
John Gottwald, *President*
EMP: 1 Publicly Held
WEB: www.tredegar.com
SIC: 2671 Plastic film, coated or laminated for packaging
PA: Tredegar Corporation
  1100 Boulders Pkwy # 200
  North Chesterfield VA 23225

(G-11419)
TRIDENT PLASTICS INC
5608 Charles City Cir (23231-4539)
PHONE.....................804 236-8705
William A Thomas, *President*
Thyra Cadic, *Corp Secy*
Ronald Cadic, *Vice Pres*
John Ravia, *Sales Staff*
EMP: 10
SQ FT: 15,000
SALES (est): 1.8MM Privately Held
WEB: www.tridentplastics.com
SIC: 3089 Injection molding of plastics

(G-11420)
TRINITEE GROUP LLC
1597 Heritage Hill Dr (23238-4327)
PHONE.....................757 268-9694
Latorria Mason, *Principal*
EMP: 6
SALES (est): 376K Privately Held
SIC: 2086 Soft drinks: packaged in cans, bottles, etc.

(G-11421)
TROMP GROUP AMERICAS LLC
2115 W Laburnum Ave (23227-4315)
PHONE.....................800 225-3771
EMP: 2 EST: 2014
SALES (est): 107K
SALES (corp-wide): 9.5B Publicly Held
SIC: 3556 Bakery machinery
PA: Markel Corporation
  4521 Highwoods Pkwy # 200
  Glen Allen VA 23060
  804 747-0136

(G-11422)
TRU POINT DESIGN
3302 Williamsburg Rd (23231-2355)
PHONE.....................804 477-0976
James Henley, *Principal*
EMP: 1
SALES (est): 2K Privately Held
SIC: 2759 Commercial printing

(G-11423)
TT & J HAULING
560 Creekmore Rd (23238-7107)
PHONE.....................804 647-0375
Timothy Dickerson, *Owner*
EMP: 1
SQ FT: 600
SALES (est): 160K Privately Held
WEB: www.ttandjhauling.net
SIC: 1389 Haulage, oil field

(G-11424)
TWO SWORDS STRATEGIES LLC
6219 Jeffrey Rd (23226-2518)
PHONE.....................804 337-3103
Adam Paul Short, *Principal*
EMP: 1
SALES (est): 62.8K Privately Held
SIC: 3421 Cutlery

(G-11425)
U S SMOKELESS TOB BRANDS INC
6603 W Broad St (23230-1711)
PHONE.....................804 274-2000
Brian W Quigley, *President*
EMP: 5
SALES (est): 290.7K Publicly Held
SIC: 2131 Chewing & smoking tobacco

HQ: U.S. Smokeless Tobacco Company
6603 W Broad St
Richmond VA 23230
804 274-2000

(G-11426)
UB-04 SOFTWARE INC
404 Walsing Dr (23229-7645)
PHONE..............................804 754-2708
Stephen J Szuchy, *Director*
EMP: 2
SALES (est): 147.1K **Privately Held**
WEB: www.ub04software.com
SIC: 7372 Application computer software

(G-11427)
ULTIMATE WOODWORKS
1313 Grumman Dr (23229-5416)
PHONE..............................804 938-8987
EMP: 2
SALES (est): 161.7K **Privately Held**
WEB: www.ultimatewoodworks.com
SIC: 2431 Millwork

(G-11428)
UPPER WEYANOKE LLC
14 Tapoan Rd (23226-3222)
PHONE..............................804 288-7333
Lawrence Gray, *Principal*
EMP: 3
SALES (est): 142.7K **Privately Held**
SIC: 3131 Footwear cut stock

(G-11429)
URBAN VIEWS WEEKLY LLC
6802 Paragon Pl Ste 410 (23230-1655)
PHONE..............................804 441-6255
Ervin Clarke, *Publisher*
Ervin B Clarke, *Principal*
Shelia Shaw, *Accounts Exec*
EMP: 6
SALES (est): 337.8K **Privately Held**
WEB: www.urbanviewsweekly.com
SIC: 2711 Newspapers, publishing & printing

(G-11430)
**US SMOKELESS TOBACCO
COMPANY (HQ)**
6603 W Broad St (23230-1711)
PHONE..............................804 274-2000
Brian Quigley,
▼ EMP: 27 EST: 2009
SALES (est): 113.8MM **Publicly Held**
WEB: www.altria.com
SIC: 2131 Chewing & smoking tobacco
PA: Altria Group, Inc.
6601 W Broad St
Richmond VA 23230
804 274-2200

(G-11431)
UTS FENDRAG PUBLISHING CO
4606 Brook Rd (23227-3707)
PHONE..............................804 266-9108
Stew Gardner, *President*
EMP: 4
SALES (est): 304K **Privately Held**
SIC: 2741 Miscellaneous publishing

(G-11432)
VAN KY TROUNG
Also Called: Van's Printing Services
4109 Jacque St (23230-3213)
P.O. Box 11103 (23230-1103)
PHONE..............................804 612-6151
KY Troung Van, *Owner*
EMP: 2
SQ FT: 2,500
SALES (est): 84.2K **Privately Held**
WEB: www.vansprintingservices.com
SIC: 2759 Commercial printing

(G-11433)
VANGARDE WOODWORKS INC
2121 N Hamilton St Ste F (23230-4124)
PHONE..............................804 355-4917
Dave Gunter, *Vice Pres*
EMP: 1 EST: 2015
SALES (est): 173.2K **Privately Held**
WEB: www.vangarde.com
SIC: 2434 3553 Wood kitchen cabinets;
woodworking machinery

(G-11434)
VANGUARD PLASTICS
2800 Sprouse Dr (23231-6039)
PHONE..............................804 222-2012
David Booher, *Principal*
EMP: 6
SALES (est): 990.4K **Privately Held**
SIC: 2673 Bags: plastic, laminated &
coated

(G-11435)
VENTUREWISE LLC
13709 Milbranch Ct (23233-7638)
PHONE..............................804 277-9564
EMP: 3
SALES (est): 211.2K **Privately Held**
WEB: www.iclarityoptics.com
SIC: 3827 Optical instruments & lenses

(G-11436)
VETERANS WELDING LLC
2501 Hickory Knoll Ln (23230-2129)
PHONE..............................804 904-7951
Luke Chasteen, *CEO*
EMP: 1
SALES (est): 27.5K **Privately Held**
SIC: 7692 Welding repair

(G-11437)
VILA PIMENTA IMPORTS LLC
3420 Pump Rd Ste 157 (23233-1111)
PHONE..............................610 533-3278
Arielle Finer, *President*
EMP: 4
SQ FT: 5,000
SALES (est): 176.1K **Privately Held**
SIC: 2084 Wines, brandy & brandy spirits

(G-11438)
VINCI CO LLC
2715 Entp Pkwy Ste A (23294)
PHONE..............................888 529-6864
Peter John Vinci, *CEO*
Peter William Vinci, *President*
Joanne Vinci, *Vice Pres*
EMP: 6
SALES (est): 253.2K **Privately Held**
WEB: www.vincipro.com
SIC: 3949 Balls: baseball, football, basket-
ball, etc.

(G-11439)
VIRGINIA CUSTOM SIGNS CORP
4808 Leonard Pkwy (23226-1340)
PHONE..............................804 278-8788
Kevin Kenny, *President*
EMP: 1
SALES (est): 93.7K **Privately Held**
WEB: www.vacustomsigns.com
SIC: 3993 Signs, not made in custom sign
painting shops

(G-11440)
VIRGINIA DENTAL SC INC
Also Called: Dentalpartshaus
1803 Lakecrest Ct (23238-3811)
PHONE..............................804 422-1888
Perry Levenson, *President*
EMP: 6
SALES (est): 950K **Privately Held**
WEB: www.dentalpartshaus.com
SIC: 3843 7699 Dental equipment; dental
instrument repair

(G-11441)
VOICE 1 COMMUNICATION LLC
3828 Pheasant Chase Dr (23231-7578)
PHONE..............................804 795-7503
Roger Hicks,
EMP: 1
SALES (est): 134.8K **Privately Held**
SIC: 3661 Telephone & telegraph appara-
tus

(G-11442)
W W DISTRIBUTORS
Also Called: Revolution X
4901 W Leigh St (23230-2808)
PHONE..............................804 301-2308
Whit Whitley, *President*
EMP: 2 EST: 1993
SALES (est): 62K **Privately Held**
WEB: www.phantasticpoes.com
SIC: 2099 Syrups

(G-11443)
WE ALL SCREAM
4023 Macarthur Ave (23227-4050)
PHONE..............................804 716-1157
Charles H Zimmerman III, *Administration*
EMP: 5 EST: 2008
SALES (est): 286.7K **Privately Held**
SIC: 2024 Ice cream, bulk

(G-11444)
WE SULLIVAN CO
3751 Westerre Pkwy Ste B (23233-1472)
PHONE..............................804 273-0905
Bruce Sullivan, *Principal*
EMP: 2
SALES (est): 149.4K **Privately Held**
WEB: www.wesullivanco.com
SIC: 3699 Electrical equipment & supplies

(G-11445)
WELDONE INC
480 Hylton Rd Ste D (23238-6450)
PHONE..............................804 784-8860
James Bowler, *President*
Patricia Campbell, *Vice Pres*
EMP: 2 EST: 2001
SQ FT: 4,000
SALES (est): 70K **Privately Held**
SIC: 7692 Welding repair

(G-11446)
**WEST END MACHINE &
WELDING**
6804 School Ave (23228-4920)
P.O. Box 9444 (23228-0444)
PHONE..............................804 266-9631
John A Rueger Jr, *CEO*
Michael F Mitchell, *Vice Pres*
Richard A Minardi Jr, *Admin Sec*
EMP: 20 EST: 1953
SQ FT: 12,000
SALES (est): 1.6MM **Privately Held**
WEB: www.westendmachine.com
SIC: 3599 7692 Machine shop, jobbing &
repair; welding repair

(G-11447)
WESTROCK CP LLC
2900 Sprouse Dr (23231-6041)
PHONE..............................804 222-6380
Rich Slamm, *Owner*
EMP: 150
SALES (corp-wide): 17.5B **Publicly Held**
WEB: www.westrock.com
SIC: 2653 Boxes, corrugated: made from
purchased materials
HQ: Westrock Cp, Llc
1000 Abernathy Rd Ste 125
Atlanta GA 30328

(G-11448)
WESTROCK CP LLC
Westrock Company
5710 S Laburnum Ave (23231-4421)
PHONE..............................804 226-5840
Pete Widolff, *Manager*
EMP: 166
SQ FT: 147,000
SALES (corp-wide): 17.5B **Publicly Held**
WEB: www.westrock.com
SIC: 2653 5113 Boxes, corrugated: made
from purchased materials; corrugated &
solid fiber boxes
HQ: Westrock Cp, Llc
1000 Abernathy Rd Ste 125
Atlanta GA 30328

(G-11449)
**WHITE FOREST RESOURCES
INC**
6800 Paragon Pl Ste 440 (23230-1652)
PHONE..............................804 410-9231
Jeff Wilson, *President*
EMP: 2
SALES (est): 66K **Privately Held**
SIC: 1241 5052 Coal mining services; coal

(G-11450)
WILLIAM BUTLER ALUMINUM
3103 Kenbridge St (23231-2221)
PHONE..............................804 393-1046
EMP: 1
SALES (est): 66K **Privately Held**
SIC: 3479 Coating/Engraving Service

(G-11451)
**WILLIAM MOWRY
WOODWORKING**
7108 Brigham Rd (23226-3725)
PHONE..............................804 282-3831
William Mowry, *Principal*
EMP: 1
SALES (est): 82K **Privately Held**
SIC: 2431 Millwork

(G-11452)
WIMABI PRESS LLC
7102 Lakewood Dr (23229-7532)
PHONE..............................804 282-3227
Charles Bice, *Principal*
EMP: 2
SALES (est): 113.4K **Privately Held**
SIC: 2741 Miscellaneous publishing

(G-11453)
WOBANC DANFORTH
6954 Wildwood St (23231-5637)
PHONE..............................804 222-7877
EMP: 2
SALES (est): 120K **Privately Held**
SIC: 3469 Mfg Metal Stampings

(G-11454)
WOOD CREATIONS LLC
2911 Maplewood Rd (23228-5027)
PHONE..............................804 553-1862
Michael Goettl,
EMP: 3
SALES (est): 306.4K **Privately Held**
SIC: 2431 Millwork

(G-11455)
WOODWRIGHTS COOPERATIVE
3202 Rosedale Ave (23230-4223)
P.O. Box 6832 (23230-0832)
PHONE..............................804 358-4800
O B Yancey III, *Owner*
EMP: 5
SQ FT: 5,000
SALES (est): 285K **Privately Held**
SIC: 2521 2541 1751 Cabinets, office:
wood; cabinets, except refrigerated:
show, display, etc.: wood; cabinet & finish
carpentry

(G-11456)
WORSE LLC
Also Called: Worse For Wear
3012 W Broad St (23230-5105)
PHONE..............................512 506-0057
Laura Smith,
Michael Saunders,
EMP: 2
SALES (est): 73.1K **Privately Held**
WEB: www.worsewear.com
SIC: 2339 Jeans: women's, misses' & jun-
iors'

(G-11457)
**WORTH HIGGINS &
ASSOCIATES INC**
8770 Park Central Dr (23227-1146)
PHONE..............................804 353-0607
EMP: 20
SALES (corp-wide): 45MM **Privately
Held**
WEB: www.whaprint.com
SIC: 3993 Signs & advertising specialties
PA: Worth Higgins & Associates, Inc.
8770 Park Central Dr
Richmond VA 23227
804 264-2304

(G-11458)
**WORTH HIGGINS &
ASSOCIATES INC**
Signs Unlimited
8770 Park Central Dr (23227-1146)
PHONE..............................804 353-0607
Courtlin Lareau, *Manager*
EMP: 30
SALES (corp-wide): 45MM **Privately
Held**
WEB: www.whaprint.com
SIC: 3993 Signs & advertising specialties
PA: Worth Higgins & Associates, Inc.
8770 Park Central Dr
Richmond VA 23227
804 264-2304

▲ = Import ▼=Export
◆ =Import/Export

(G-11459)
WYETH PHARMACEUTICALS LLC
2248 Darbytown Rd (23231-5404)
P.O. Box 26609 (23261-6609)
PHONE................................804 652-6000
Scott Denicourt, *Branch Mgr*
EMP: 217
SALES (corp-wide): 51.7B **Publicly Held**
WEB: www.pfizer.com
SIC: 2834 Pharmaceutical preparations
HQ: Wyeth Pharmaceuticals Llc
500 Arcola Rd
Collegeville PA 19426
484 865-5000

(G-11460)
XPLOR INDUSTRIES
9702 Gayton Rd (23238-4907)
PHONE................................804 306-6621
EMP: 2
SALES (est): 124.2K **Privately Held**
WEB: www.xplorind.com
SIC: 3999 Manufacturing industries

(G-11461)
YAMCO LLC
9113 Derbyshire Rd Unit G (23229-7056)
P.O. Box 295, Timnath CO (80547-0295)
PHONE................................804 749-0480
EMP: 2 EST: 2009
SALES (est): 130K **Privately Held**
SIC: 7372 Prepackaged Software Services

(G-11462)
ZATARA PRESS LLC
10805 N Bank Rd (23238-3522)
PHONE................................804 754-8682
Andrew Fedynak, *Principal*
EMP: 3
SALES (est): 74.9K **Privately Held**
SIC: 2741 Miscellaneous publishing

(G-11463)
ZELLER + GMELIN CORPORATION (HQ)
4801 Audubon Dr (23231-2786)
PHONE................................800 848-8465
Andreas Mahlich, *President*
Damon Geer, *Vice Pres*
Stephen L Lazure, *Vice Pres*
Frank Glunt, *Sales Mgr*
David Saiz, *Accounts Mgr*
▲ EMP: 69
SQ FT: 83,000
SALES (est): 21.5MM
SALES (corp-wide): 266.8MM **Privately Held**
WEB: www.zeller-gmelin.com
SIC: 2893 5085 2899 Printing ink; ink,
printers'; ink or writing fluids
PA: Zeller + Gmelin Gmbh & Co. Kg
SchloBstr. 20
Eislingen/Fils 73054
716 180-20

(G-11464)
ZOOOM PRINTING LLC
2042 Westmoreland St (23230-3245)
PHONE................................804 343-0009
Nora Rossi, *Vice Pres*
Leighann Boone, *Prdtn Mgr*
Connie Billings, *Manager*
Joann C Rossi, *Manager*
Nick Phouthakhanty, *Technician*
◆ EMP: 13
SALES (est): 2.4MM **Privately Held**
WEB: www.zooomprinting.com
SIC: 2752 Commercial printing, offset

Richmond
Richmond City County

(G-11465)
501 FRANKLIN LLC
Also Called: Moxy Richmond Downtown
501 E Franklin St (23219-2322)
PHONE................................804 777-9000
Neil Amin,
Pramod C Amin,
Bhagirath N Shah,
Jay Shah,
EMP: 10

SALES (est): 238.9K **Privately Held**
WEB: www.richmond.com
SIC: 2711 Newspapers, publishing & printing

(G-11466)
64 WAYS TRUCKING/HAULING LLC
2101 Decatur St (23224-3713)
PHONE................................804 801-5330
Shareef Atkins, *Mng Member*
Jermaine Greene,
EMP: 14 EST: 2016
SALES (est): 800K **Privately Held**
SIC: 1429 1442 Riprap quarrying; construction sand & gravel; construction sand mining

(G-11467)
AARON S WALTERS
1021 E Cary St (23219-0020)
PHONE................................804 783-6925
EMP: 3
SALES (est): 205.1K **Privately Held**
SIC: 3442 Mfg Metal Doors/Sash/Trim

(G-11468)
ABORIGINAL PRINTS LLC
4248 Oakleys Ct Ste C (23223-5973)
PHONE................................804 994-1987
Solomon Bey, *Mng Member*
EMP: 1
SALES (est): 82.1K **Privately Held**
SIC: 2752 Commercial printing, lithographic

(G-11469)
ACCESS PUBLISHING CO
413 Stuart Cir Unit 3d (23220-3741)
P.O. Box 7439 (23221-0439)
PHONE................................804 358-0163
Stanley Stillman, *Principal*
EMP: 1
SALES (est): 66.5K **Privately Held**
SIC: 2741 Miscellaneous publishing

(G-11470)
ACI-STRICKLAND LLC
Also Called: Strickland Machine Company
2400 Magnolia Ct (23223-2332)
PHONE................................804 643-7483
Matt McGee, *President*
Richard Frisbie, *Manager*
EMP: 30
SALES (est): 1.1MM **Privately Held**
WEB: www.stricklandmachine.com
SIC: 3599 Crankshafts & camshafts, machining

(G-11471)
ACTIONSTEP INC
919 E Main St Ste 1155 (23219-4624)
PHONE................................540 809-9326
Edward Stanley Jordan, *President*
EMP: 2
SALES (est): 123.9K **Privately Held**
WEB: www.actionstep.com
SIC: 7372 Prepackaged software

(G-11472)
ACUITY BRANDS LIGHTING INC
Also Called: ACUITY BRANDS LIGHTING, INC.
7311 Riverside Dr (23225-1242)
PHONE................................804 320-3444
Becky Edwards, *Branch Mgr*
EMP: 1
SALES (corp-wide): 3.3B **Publicly Held**
WEB: www.lithonia.acuitybrands.com
SIC: 3646 Commercial indusl & institutional electric lighting fixtures
HQ: Acuity Brands Lighting, Inc.
1 Acuity Way
Conyers GA 30012

(G-11473)
ADIVA NATURALS LLC
1802 E Franklin St Us (23223-6950)
PHONE................................804 683-3738
Nadira Naja Chase,
EMP: 3
SALES (est): 150K **Privately Held**
WEB: www.adivanaturals.com
SIC: 2844 Cosmetic preparations

(G-11474)
ADVANCED CGNITIVE SYSTEMS CORP
Also Called: ACS
2601 The Terrace (23222-3645)
PHONE................................804 397-3373
Kim Franklin, *Ch of Bd*
EMP: 1
SALES (est): 73.7K **Privately Held**
SIC: 2911 6211 6799 Jet fuels; bond dealers & brokers; commodity contract pool operators

(G-11475)
AFTON CHEMICAL ADDITIVES CORP (DH)
330 S 4th St (23219-4350)
P.O. Box 2189 (23218-2189)
PHONE................................804 788-5000
Thomas E Gottwald, *President*
Wayne C Drinkwater, *Treasurer*
Steven M Mayer, *Admin Sec*
EMP: 15
SALES (est): 2.4MM
SALES (corp-wide): 2.1B **Publicly Held**
WEB: www.ethyl.com
SIC: 2869 Industrial organic chemicals
HQ: Afton Chemical Corporation
500 Spring St
Richmond VA 23219
804 788-5800

(G-11476)
AFTON CHEMICAL CORPORATION (HQ)
500 Spring St (23219-4300)
P.O. Box 2158 (23218-2158)
PHONE................................804 788-5800
Regina A Harm, *President*
Alan Horwitz, *Managing Dir*
Lindsay Tycer, *Business Mgr*
Robert A Shama, *Vice Pres*
Kevin Keller, *Mfg Dir*
◆ EMP: 394
SALES (est): 1.1B
SALES (corp-wide): 2.1B **Publicly Held**
WEB: www.aftonchemical.com
SIC: 2899 2999 3999 Oil treating compounds; waxes, petroleum: not produced in petroleum refineries; atomizers, toiletry
PA: Newmarket Corporation
330 S 4th St
Richmond VA 23219
804 788-5000

(G-11477)
AFTON CHEMICAL CORPORATION
101 E Byrd St (23219-3728)
PHONE................................804 788-5250
Maria Kobrinetz, *Branch Mgr*
EMP: 1
SALES (corp-wide): 2.1B **Publicly Held**
WEB: www.aftonchemical.com
SIC: 2899 Oil treating compounds
HQ: Afton Chemical Corporation
500 Spring St
Richmond VA 23219
804 788-5800

(G-11478)
AFTON CHEMICAL CORPORATION
330 S 4th St (23219-4350)
PHONE................................804 788-5800
Warren Huang, *President*
Andrew Martin, *Opers Staff*
Philip Boegner, *Engineer*
Mike Malfer, *Sales Staff*
Kelley Foster, *Mktg Coord*
EMP: 7
SALES (corp-wide): 2.1B **Publicly Held**
WEB: www.aftonchemical.com
SIC: 2899 Chemical preparations
HQ: Afton Chemical Corporation
500 Spring St
Richmond VA 23219
804 788-5800

(G-11479)
AG ESSENCE INC
1601 Overbrook Rd Ste C (23220-1300)
PHONE................................804 915-6650
Bella Wingfield, *President*
Robert Boyd, *Vice Pres*

Bill Wingfield, *Officer*
EMP: 8 EST: 2011
SQ FT: 10,000
SALES (est): 500K **Privately Held**
WEB: www.ag21healthsciences.com
SIC: 2834 Pharmaceutical preparations

(G-11480)
AGAINST ALL ODDZ PUBLICATIONS
2500 Chamberlayne Ave (23222-4215)
PHONE................................757 300-4645
Larry Johnson, *Principal*
EMP: 1
SALES (est): 37.5K **Privately Held**
SIC: 2741 Miscellaneous publishing

(G-11481)
ALL A BOARD INC
395 Dabbs House Rd (23223-4820)
PHONE................................804 652-0020
Walter C Etheridge Jr, *President*
William Burford, *Vice Pres*
Kenneth W Harris Jr, *Treasurer*
Andrew Barth, *VP Sales*
Susan Wells, *Sales Staff*
EMP: 19
SQ FT: 35,789
SALES (est): 3.1MM **Privately Held**
WEB: www.allaboardinc.com
SIC: 2511 2531 Wood household furniture; public building & related furniture

(G-11482)
ALL TYED UP
516 S Pine St Apt 2 (23220-6250)
PHONE................................804 855-7158
Forest Hayward, *Owner*
EMP: 1 EST: 2016
SALES (est): 49.1K **Privately Held**
SIC: 2326 7389 Men's & boys' work clothing; business services

(G-11483)
ALLSPARK INDUSTRIAL LLC
2605 W Main St (23220-4312)
PHONE................................804 977-2732
Tom Click,
EMP: 3
SALES (est): 121.3K **Privately Held**
SIC: 3644 5063 Electric conduits & fittings; cable conduit

(G-11484)
AMERICAN NEXUS LLC
1700 E Marshall St # 114 (23223-6336)
PHONE................................804 405-5443
Brandon Fuller, *President*
Elliott Fausz, *Principal*
EMP: 2
SALES (est): 117.3K **Privately Held**
SIC: 3621 5063 5072 Electric motor & generator parts; electrical apparatus & equipment; hardware

(G-11485)
ANIMATE SYSTEMS INC
4700 Devonshire Rd (23225-3136)
PHONE................................804 233-8085
James A Brown, *Principal*
EMP: 2
SALES (est): 70.9K **Privately Held**
SIC: 7372 7371 Prepackaged software; custom computer programming services

(G-11486)
AQUEOUS SOLUTIONS GLOBAL LLC
2828 Cofer Rd (23224-7102)
PHONE................................410 710-7736
Alden Badge, *Ch of Bd*
Timothy Badger, *President*
EMP: 2
SALES (est): 157.4K **Privately Held**
WEB: www.aqueoussolutionsglobal.com
SIC: 2899 Water treating compounds

(G-11487)
ARBOLEDA CABINETS INC
Also Called: Arboleda Counter Tops
5421 Distributor Dr (23225-6105)
P.O. Box 35188, North Chesterfield (23235-0188)
PHONE................................804 230-0733
Giullermo Arboleda, *President*

Julio Arboleda, *Vice Pres*
EMP: 12 **EST:** 1992
SQ FT: 5,000
SALES (est): 1.7MM **Privately Held**
WEB: www.arboledacabinets.com
SIC: 2434 2541 Wood kitchen cabinets;
counter & sink tops

(G-11488)
ARMATA PHARMACEUTICALS INC
800 E Leigh St Ste 54 (23219-1598)
PHONE..............................804 827-3010
Joe Anderson, *Manager*
EMP: 3 **Publicly Held**
WEB: www.armatapharma.com
SIC: 2836 Biological products, except diagnostic
PA: Armata Pharmaceuticals, Inc.
4503 Glencoe Ave
Marina Del Rey CA 90292

(G-11489)
ARMSTEAD HAULING INC
2906 Stockton St (23224-3548)
PHONE..............................804 675-8221
Caliph Armstead, *Principal*
EMP: 1
SALES (est): 131.5K **Privately Held**
SIC: 3537 7389 Trucks: freight, baggage,
etc.: industrial, except mining;

(G-11490)
ASHE KUSTOMZ LLC
3806 Alma Ave (23222-1931)
PHONE..............................804 997-6406
Candice Tyler, *CFO*
Troy Davis, *Mng Member*
EMP: 2
SALES (est): 83.9K **Privately Held**
SIC: 2752 Commercial printing, lithographic

(G-11491)
ASHFORD COURT LLC
5915 Midlothian Tpke (23225-5917)
PHONE..............................804 743-0700
▲ **EMP:** 76
SQ FT: 122,000
SALES: 5MM **Privately Held**
SIC: 2392 Mfg Home Decorating Items

(G-11492)
ASIAN AMERICAN COAL INC
4 N 4th St Apt 100 (23219-2230)
PHONE..............................804 648-1611
▲ **EMP:** 4
SALES (est): 219.5K **Privately Held**
SIC: 1241 Coal mining services

(G-11493)
ASTRA DESIGN INC
16 S Allen Ave (23220-5302)
P.O. Box 4714 (23220-8714)
PHONE..............................804 257-5467
Louise Ellis, *President*
Tom Chenoweth, *Assistant VP*
EMP: 2
SALES (est): 205.3K **Privately Held**
WEB: www.astradesign-usa.com
SIC: 3441 Fabricated structural metal

(G-11494)
AUSTIN INDUSTRIAL SERVICES LLC
Also Called: Ais Industrial Services
1001 E 4th St (23224-5507)
PHONE..............................804 232-8940
Ron Hedlund, *Opers Staff*
Larry Austin,
Bernadale Witherspoon, *Assistant*
EMP: 10
SQ FT: 25,000
SALES (est): 1.6MM **Privately Held**
WEB: www.aisindustrial.com
SIC: 7694 Electric motor repair

(G-11495)
AUTOPARTSOURCE LLC (HQ)
4605 Carolina Ave (23222-1420)
PHONE..............................804 329-3000
John Amalfe, *President*
Christopher Kern, *Managing Dir*
Christophe Kern, *Vice Pres*
Tammy Branch, *Purchasing*

Vicky Poarch, *Finance*
▲ **EMP:** 40
SQ FT: 100
SALES (est): 6.4MM
SALES (corp-wide): 16.2MM **Privately
Held**
WEB: www.autopartsource.com
SIC: 3841 5013 Surgical & medical instruments; automotive supplies & parts
PA: Momentum Usa, Inc.
120 Fieldcrest Ave
Edison NJ 08837
844 300-1553

(G-11496)
AZIZA BEAUTY LLC
Also Called: Aziza Beauty Supply
3406 Wellington St (23222-2851)
P.O. Box 608, Sandston (23150-0608)
PHONE..............................804 525-9989
Darshall Banks, *Principal*
EMP: 3
SALES (est): 284K **Privately Held**
SIC: 2841 5999 Textile soap; toiletries,
cosmetics & perfumes

(G-11497)
B & R REBAR
950 Masonic Ln (23223-5545)
PHONE..............................800 526-1024
Tom Gay, *President*
EMP: 12
SALES (est): 1MM **Privately Held**
SIC: 3449 Bars, concrete reinforcing: fabricated steel

(G-11498)
B H COBB LUMBER CO
2300 Hermitage Rd Ste B (23220-1353)
PHONE..............................804 358-3801
James H Clifton, *Principal*
EMP: 6
SALES (est): 579.5K **Privately Held**
WEB: www.cobblumber.net
SIC: 2491 5211 5031 Structural lumber &
timber, treated wood; lumber & other
building materials; lumber, plywood & millwork; lumber: rough, dressed & finished

(G-11499)
BAGGESEN J RAND
7101 Jahnke Rd (23225-4017)
PHONE..............................804 560-0490
Philip Moeller, *Principal*
EMP: 1
SALES (est): 91.1K **Privately Held**
WEB: www.executive.md
SIC: 3131 Rands

(G-11500)
BAHASHEM SOAP COMPANY LLC
1221a Hull St (23224-3918)
PHONE..............................804 398-0982
Diana Gaston,
EMP: 1
SQ FT: 1,100
SALES (est): 113.7K **Privately Held**
SIC: 2841 Soap & other detergents

(G-11501)
BATTLE MONUMENT PARTNERS
530 E Main St Ste 1000 (23219-2415)
PHONE..............................804 644-4924
William Oliver, *Administration*
EMP: 3 **EST:** 2017
SALES (est): 290.4K **Privately Held**
WEB: www.battlemonument.com
SIC: 3272 Monuments & grave markers,
except terrazo

(G-11502)
BBR PRINT INC
Also Called: Bambooink
807 Oliver Hill Way (23219-1622)
P.O. Box 398 (23218-0398)
PHONE..............................804 230-4515
Brooke B Rhodes, *President*
Robert A Rhodes III, *Corp Secy*
EMP: 18
SQ FT: 10,000
SALES (est): 1.6MM **Privately Held**
WEB: www.bambooink.com
SIC: 2752 Commercial printing, offset

(G-11503)
BELLE ISLE CRAFT SPIRITS INC
Also Called: Belle Isle Cft Sprits Rchmond
615 Maury St (23224-4121)
PHONE..............................518 265-7221
Riggi Vincent, *President*
Erica Jacobs, *Sales Staff*
EMP: 4
SALES (est): 612.2K **Privately Held**
WEB: www.belleislecraftspirits.com
SIC: 2085 Cocktails, alcoholic

(G-11504)
BENJAMIN FRANKLIN PRINTING CO
1528 High St (23220-2314)
PHONE..............................804 648-6361
John R Overbey Jr, *President*
Ken Wood, *Director*
EMP: 15 **EST:** 1925
SQ FT: 6,000
SALES (est): 2.1MM **Privately Held**
WEB: www.benjfranklinprinting.com
SIC: 2752 2759 Commercial printing, offset; letterpress printing

(G-11505)
BLACK BUSINESS TODAY INC
201 W Marshall St Apt 204 (23220-3952)
PHONE..............................804 528-7407
Razan Garland, *CEO*
EMP: 1
SALES (est): 50K **Privately Held**
SIC: 3714 Motor vehicle engines & parts

(G-11506)
BOROUGHBRIDGE METAL & WLDG LLC
903 Boroughbridge Rd (23225-4438)
PHONE..............................804 387-3510
John Dragnich, *Principal*
EMP: 1 **EST:** 2016
SALES (est): 59.3K **Privately Held**
SIC: 7692 Welding repair

(G-11507)
BRANCH HOUSE SIGNATURE PDTS
2501 Monument Ave (23220-2618)
PHONE..............................804 644-3041
Robert Pogue, *President*
EMP: 2
SQ FT: 19,366
SALES (est): 184K **Privately Held**
SIC: 2851 5231 Coating, air curing; paint

(G-11508)
BRANDITO LLC
2601 Mury St Whse 28 Spac 28 Whse (23224)
PHONE..............................804 747-6721
Krissy Keener, *Opers Staff*
Anna Harris, *Accounts Mgr*
Alex Palmer, *Accounts Mgr*
Lauren Radow, *Accounts Mgr*
Mary Loving, *Accounts Exec*
EMP: 23
SQ FT: 1,500
SALES (est): 816.6K **Privately Held**
WEB: www.brandito.net
SIC: 2759 Promotional printing

(G-11509)
BRANDYLANE PUBLISHERS INC
5 S 1st St (23219-3716)
PHONE..............................804 644-3090
Robert H Pruett, *President*
EMP: 2
SQ FT: 1,000
SALES (est): 200K **Privately Held**
WEB: www.brandylanepublishers.com
SIC: 2731 Books: publishing only

(G-11510)
BROOKS GRAY SIGN COMPANY
Also Called: Brooks-Gray Sign Company
2661 Hull St (23224-3673)
PHONE..............................804 233-4343
Brian Kelmar, *President*
EMP: 15 **EST:** 1943
SQ FT: 7,000

SALES (est): 3.8MM **Privately Held**
WEB: www.signenterprise.com
SIC: 3993 1799 Electric signs; neon signs;
signs, not made in custom sign painting
shops; sign installation & maintenance

(G-11511)
BROOKS STITCH & FOLD LLC
711 N Sheppard St (23221-1713)
PHONE..............................804 367-7979
Devon Shavel Chester, *Administration*
Devon Chester,
EMP: 2 **EST:** 2017
SALES (est): 120.3K **Privately Held**
WEB: www.brooksstitchfold.com
SIC: 2395 Embroidery & art needlework

(G-11512)
BROWN ENTERPRISE PALLETS LLC
2601 Maury St (23224-3665)
PHONE..............................804 447-0485
Raymon Brown,
EMP: 8 **EST:** 2015
SALES (est): 257K **Privately Held**
SIC: 2448 Pallets, wood

(G-11513)
BUERLEIN & CO LLC
6767 Frest Hl Ave Ste 315 (23225)
PHONE..............................804 355-1758
Robert A Buerlein,
EMP: 6
SALES (est): 874.4K **Privately Held**
SIC: 3499 Fabricated metal products

(G-11514)
BURKE PUBLICATIONS
2822 Griffin Ave (23222-3629)
PHONE..............................804 321-1756
Elisa Burke, *Principal*
EMP: 1
SALES (est): 55.6K **Privately Held**
SIC: 2741 Miscellaneous publishing

(G-11515)
BYD MUSIC PUBLISHING LLC
1504 Bowen St (23224-7814)
PHONE..............................305 423-9577
EMP: 2
SALES (est): 55K **Privately Held**
SIC: 2741 Miscellaneous publishing

(G-11516)
CABINETRY & CONSTRUCTION INC
18 S Thompson St Ste 162 (23221-2721)
PHONE..............................804 497-3491
Connie Browski, *Principal*
EMP: 3 **EST:** 2007
SALES (est): 758.3K **Privately Held**
WEB: www.cabinetry-construction.com
SIC: 2434 Wood kitchen cabinets

(G-11517)
CANADA DRY POTOMAC CORPORATION
Also Called: 7 Up Bottling
3100 N Hopkins Rd Ste 102 (23224-6631)
P.O. Box 42010 (23224-9010)
PHONE..............................804 231-7777
Phil Sutton, *General Mgr*
EMP: 50
SALES (corp-wide): 79.2MM **Privately
Held**
WEB: www.cdpotomac.com
SIC: 2086 Bottled & canned soft drinks
PA: Canada Dry Potomac Corporation
3600 Pennsy Dr
Hyattsville MD 20785
301 773-5500

(G-11518)
CANDY APPLES AND FAVORS LLC
2907 Matisse Ln (23224-5949)
PHONE..............................804 674-4061
Dejaneece Arriell Fisher, *Principal*
EMP: 2
SALES (est): 124.5K **Privately Held**
SIC: 3571 Electronic computers

▲ = Import ▼ =Export
◆ =Import/Export

(G-11519)
CANVAS ASL LLC
13 S 15th St Ste A (23219-4264)
PHONE................................804 269-0851
EMP: 1
SALES (corp-wide): 343.2K **Privately Held**
SIC: 2211 Canvas
PA: Canvas Asl, Llc
1517 Nottoway Ave
Richmond VA

(G-11520)
CANVAS SALON LLC
212 E Clay St (23219-1358)
PHONE................................804 926-5518
Christopher Way, *Administration*
EMP: 2
SALES (est): 62K **Privately Held**
SIC: 2211 Canvas

(G-11521)
CAPE FEAR PUBLISHING COMPANY
Also Called: Richmond Guide
109 E Cary St (23219-3742)
PHONE................................804 343-7539
John-Lawrence Smith, *President*
Kim Benson, *Manager*
Kenny Kane, *Director*
EMP: 12
SQ FT: 1,800
SALES (est): 1.5MM **Privately Held**
WEB: www.capefear.capefearpublish-ingco.com
SIC: 2721 Magazines: publishing only, not printed on site

(G-11522)
CARRYTHEWHATREPLICATIONS LLC
Also Called: 3d Central
1308 W Main St (23220-4827)
PHONE................................804 254-2933
Cynthia Laird, *Principal*
EMP: 3
SALES (est): 145.7K **Privately Held**
WEB: www.3dcentralva.com
SIC: 3599 Machine & other job shop work

(G-11523)
CC RICHMOND II LP
11 S 12th St Ste 115 (23219-4053)
PHONE................................804 213-2706
Dan Magder, *Partner*
Greg Shron, *Partner*
EMP: 5
SALES (est): 187.6K **Privately Held**
SIC: 2711 Newspapers, publishing & printing

(G-11524)
CHARM SCHOOL LLC
311 W Broad St (23220-4218)
PHONE................................415 999-9496
Alex Zavaleta,
Meryl Hillerson,
EMP: 2
SQ FT: 2,967
SALES (est): 68.6K **Privately Held**
WEB: www.charmschoolrva.com
SIC: 2051 2052 Bakery: wholesale or wholesale/retail combined; cones, ice cream

(G-11525)
CHASE ARCHITECTURAL METAL LLC
500 Albany Ave (23224-5512)
PHONE................................804 230-1136
Robert Chase, *Mng Member*
EMP: 6
SQ FT: 14,000
SALES (est): 1MM **Privately Held**
WEB: www.chasearchitecturalmetal.com
SIC: 3446 Architectural metalwork

(G-11526)
CHECKPOINT SYSTEMS INC
Checkview
6829 Atmore Dr Ste A (23225-5638)
PHONE................................804 745-0010
Frances Rohloff-Murdock, *Credit Staff*
Bryan Austin, *Manager*
Alice Brown, *Manager*

Jennifer Cruz, *Administration*
John Watson, *Administration*
EMP: 40
SALES (corp-wide): 4B **Privately Held**
WEB: www.checkpointsystems.com
SIC: 3699 Security control equipment & systems
HQ: Checkpoint Systems, Inc.
101 Wolf Dr
West Deptford NJ 08086
800 257-5540

(G-11527)
CHEP (USA) INC
Also Called: Ifco Systems
3707 Nine Mile Rd (23223-4813)
PHONE................................804 226-0229
Gerald Hughes, *Manager*
EMP: 65 **Privately Held**
WEB: www.chep.com
SIC: 2448 Pallets, wood
HQ: Chep (U.S.A.) Inc.
5897 Windward Pkwy
Alpharetta GA 30005
770 668-8100

(G-11528)
CHESAPEAKE MANUFACTURING INC
506 Maury St (23224-4120)
PHONE................................804 716-2035
Dick Westbrook, *President*
EMP: 3 EST: 2013
SALES (est): 265.8K **Privately Held**
SIC: 3999 Manufacturing industries

(G-11529)
CHIEF PRINTING COMPANY
11 S 21st St (23223-7365)
PHONE................................515 480-6577
Whitehead Stephen R, *Director*
EMP: 2
SALES (est): 142.6K **Privately Held**
SIC: 2752 Commercial printing, offset

(G-11530)
CHILLI RICHMOND LLC
Also Called: River Cy & Flame Sauces & Rubs
109 W Lancaster Rd (23222-3640)
PHONE................................804 329-2262
Paulette Horne,
EMP: 1
SALES (est): 52.6K **Privately Held**
SIC: 2035 Pickles, sauces & salad dressings

(G-11531)
CHURCH HILL GUN CLUB PUBG LLC
500 N 29th St (23223-7314)
PHONE................................804 236-0802
Matthew Elmes, *Principal*
EMP: 2
SALES (est): 76.6K **Privately Held**
WEB: www.chpn.net
SIC: 2741 Miscellaneous publishing

(G-11532)
COLONIAL PLATING SHOP
Also Called: Colonial Brass
9 S 1st St (23219-3716)
PHONE................................804 648-6276
Dan Rowe, *Owner*
EMP: 2
SQ FT: 1,855
SALES (est): 112.3K **Privately Held**
SIC: 3471 7699 Plating of metals or formed products; general household repair services

(G-11533)
COMMERCIAL CUSTOM CABINET INC
1606 Magnolia St (23222-4034)
PHONE................................804 228-2100
Gary Carlton, *President*
Becky Carlton, *Vice Pres*
Eric Deglau, *Project Mgr*
EMP: 24 EST: 1993
SQ FT: 21,000
SALES: 890.5K **Privately Held**
WEB: www.commercialcustomcabinetinc.com
SIC: 2434 Wood kitchen cabinets

(G-11534)
COMMERCIAL MACHINE INC
2706 Rady St (23222-4016)
PHONE................................804 329-5405
Robert L Jones, *President*
Julie J Rice, *Admin Sec*
EMP: 17
SQ FT: 22,000
SALES: 2.2MM **Privately Held**
WEB: www.commercialmachine.com
SIC: 3599 7692 Machine shop, jobbing & repair; welding repair

(G-11535)
COMMONWEALTH SIGN & DESIGN
2025 W Broad St (23220-2005)
PHONE................................804 358-5507
Sabah I Zaki, *President*
Brenda R Zaki, *Vice Pres*
Nasser S Zaki, *Admin Sec*
EMP: 1
SQ FT: 1,246
SALES (est): 120.6K **Privately Held**
SIC: 3993 Signs & advertising specialties

(G-11536)
COMMONWEALTH TIMES
817 W Broad St (23284-9104)
PHONE................................804 828-1058
Mark Robinson, *Principal*
EMP: 5 EST: 2010
SALES (est): 141.8K **Privately Held**
WEB: www.commonwealthtimes.org
SIC: 2711 Commercial printing & newspaper publishing combined

(G-11537)
COMPLEX PRINTS LLC
12 W Broad St (23220-4213)
PHONE................................804 274-0266
Jonathan Armstead,
EMP: 2
SALES (est): 73.2K **Privately Held**
SIC: 2759 Screen printing

(G-11538)
COMPUTER SOLUTION CO OF VA INC
Also Called: Tcsc
200 S 10th St Ste 900 (23219-4064)
PHONE................................804 794-3491
David P Romig II, *President*
Kevin Carter, *Vice Pres*
Marceline A Romig, *Treasurer*
Chet Ubowski, *Program Mgr*
Eric Eklund, *Manager*
EMP: 30
SQ FT: 11,000
SALES (est): 4.3MM **Privately Held**
SIC: 7372 7379 Business oriented computer software; computer related consulting services

(G-11539)
CONSOLIDATED NATURAL GAS CO (HQ)
120 Tredegar St (23219-4306)
PHONE................................804 819-2000
Thomas F Farrell II, *President*
Steven A Rogers, *Vice Pres*
Thomas N Chewning, *CFO*
EMP: 350 EST: 1999
SALES (est): 3.5MM
SALES (corp-wide): 16.5B **Publicly Held**
SIC: 1311 4922 4924 Natural gas production; natural gas transmission; natural gas distribution
PA: Dominion Energy, Inc.
120 Tredegar St
Richmond VA 23219
804 819-2000

(G-11540)
CONVERSATIONS PUBLISHING LLC
100 Shockoe Slip (23219-4164)
PHONE................................804 698-5922
Sarah Warner, *Principal*
Kaseorg Matthias, *VP Human Res*
Martin Conn, *Shareholder*
Laura Hooe, *Associate*
EMP: 2 EST: 2008

SALES (est): 70.6K **Privately Held**
WEB: www.moranreevesconn.com
SIC: 2741 Miscellaneous publishing

(G-11541)
CORPORATE & MUSEUM FRAME INC
301 W Broad St (23220-4218)
PHONE................................804 643-6858
Joseph Johnson, *President*
EMP: 2
SQ FT: 3,000
SALES (est): 232.9K **Privately Held**
WEB: www.corporatemuseumframe.com
SIC: 2499 7699 Picture & mirror frames, wood; picture framing, custom

(G-11542)
CORPORATE FURN SVCS VA LLC
5717 Oakleys Pl (23223-5957)
PHONE................................804 928-1143
Keith Stith, *President*
EMP: 1
SQ FT: 100
SALES (est): 118.7K **Privately Held**
SIC: 2522 Panel systems & partitions, office: except wood

(G-11543)
COUGARBEARBOBCAT LLC
Also Called: Shelf Tagger
3400 Ellwood Ave (23221-2708)
P.O. Box 14680 (23221-0680)
PHONE................................804 690-8006
Robert Barrowclift,
David Hawes,
EMP: 2
SALES (est): 132.3K **Privately Held**
SIC: 7372 7374 7371 Application computer software; data processing & preparation; computer software development & applications

(G-11544)
COURTNEY PRESS
19 E Main St (23219-2109)
PHONE................................804 266-8359
Michael G Picano, *Owner*
EMP: 1 EST: 1971
SQ FT: 1,900
SALES (est): 69.4K **Privately Held**
SIC: 2752 2759 Commercial printing, offset; letterpress printing

(G-11545)
COZINO ENTERPRISE INC
2402 Decatur St (23224-3604)
PHONE................................804 921-1896
Neil Cozino, *Principal*
EMP: 7
SALES (est): 733.3K **Privately Held**
SIC: 3629 Power conversion units, a.c. to d.c.: static-electric

(G-11546)
CRENSHAW OF RICHMOND INC
Also Called: Crenshaw Equipment
1700 Commerce Rd (23224-7504)
P.O. Box 24217 (23224-0217)
PHONE................................804 231-6241
C W Crenshaw, *President*
Robert Ashby, *President*
Leroy Crenshaw, *Vice Pres*
EMP: 52
SALES (est): 8.3MM **Privately Held**
WEB: www.crenshawcorp.com
SIC: 3714 5012 5531 5013 Motor vehicle brake systems & parts; truck bodies; truck equipment & parts; truck parts & accessories

(G-11547)
CRUST & CREAM
4610 Forest Hill Ave (23225-3246)
PHONE................................804 230-5555
EMP: 5
SALES (est): 315.1K **Privately Held**
SIC: 2024 Ice cream, bulk

(G-11548)
CUPCAKES ON MOVE LLC
4212 Seamore St (23223-2261)
PHONE................................804 477-6754
Keith Oneal Scott, *Administration*

GEOGRAPHIC

EMP: 4
SALES (est): 139.8K **Privately Held**
SIC: 2051 Bread, cake & related products

(G-11549)
CUSTOM CANDYY LLC
120 E Roanoke St (23224-1348)
PHONE..................................804 447-8179
Shari Pryor, *Co-Owner*
Carmen Bragg, *Co-Owner*
EMP: 12 EST: 2016
SALES (est): 634.6K **Privately Held**
WEB: www.customcandyy.com
SIC: 2064 7389 Candy bars, including
chocolate covered bars;

(G-11550)
CUSTOM INK
3401 W Cary St (23221-2726)
PHONE..................................804 419-5651
EMP: 2
SALES (est): 90.8K **Privately Held**
WEB: www.customink.com
SIC: 2759 Screen printing

(G-11551)
CUSTOM PACKAGING INC
1003 Commerce Rd (23224-7007)
PHONE..................................804 232-3299
Ed Beadles, *President*
EMP: 12
SQ FT: 30,000
SALES (est): 2.4MM **Privately Held**
SIC: 2653 5113 5199 Boxes, corrugated:
made from purchased materials; shipping
supplies; packaging materials

(G-11552)
CUSTOM PRINTS LLC
3505 Austin Ave (23222-3403)
PHONE..................................804 839-0749
Parth Patel,
EMP: 2
SALES (est): 95.8K **Privately Held**
SIC: 2752 Commercial printing, litho-
graphic

(G-11553)
**CUSTOM STAGE CURTAIN
FBRCTRS**
9 W Cary St (23220-5609)
PHONE..................................804 264-3700
Tony Lovette, *Owner*
Scott Macfadyen, *Sales Mgr*
EMP: 1
SALES (est): 39.6K **Privately Held**
SIC: 3999 Manufacturing industries

(G-11554)
DAYLIGHT CABINETRY LLC
5203 New Kent Rd (23225-3029)
PHONE..................................804 432-4954
Robert J Baughan Jr, *Administration*
EMP: 1
SALES (est): 127K **Privately Held**
SIC: 2434 Wood kitchen cabinets

(G-11555)
DEAN FOODS COMPANY (PA)
2000 W Broad St (23220-2006)
P.O. Box 27366 (23261-7366)
PHONE..................................804 359-5786
Conrad F Sauer IV, *President*
Mark A Sauer, *Vice Pres*
Gregory Wolljung, *Vice Pres*
Gary Rahlfs, *CFO*
William F Uhlik, *CFO*
EMP: 190 EST: 1910
SQ FT: 80,000
SALES (est): 24MM **Privately Held**
WEB: www.deanfoods.com
SIC: 2079 Margarine & margarine oils

(G-11556)
DEBBIE BELT
Also Called: Mascotcandy.com
5302 Caledonia Rd (23225-3010)
PHONE..................................912 856-9476
Debbie Belt, *Owner*
EMP: 5
SALES (est): 253.1K **Privately Held**
SIC: 3999 5145 Manufacturing industries;
candy

(G-11557)
DEER DUPLICATING SVC INC
15 N 3rd St (23219-2207)
PHONE..................................804 648-6509
EMP: 2
SALES (est): 92.3K **Privately Held**
SIC: 2752 Commercial printing, offset

(G-11558)
DEFENSE UNITED STATES DEPT
400 N 8th St Ste 584 (23219-4802)
PHONE..................................804 292-5642
EMP: 5 **Publicly Held**
WEB: www.defense.gov
SIC: 3812 Defense systems & equipment
HQ: United States Department Of Defense
1000 Defense Pentagon # 3
Washington DC 20301
703 692-7100

(G-11559)
**DEFENSECOAT INDUSTRIES
LLC**
5511a Biggs Rd (23224-1014)
PHONE..................................804 356-5316
Robert Madison, *President*
Clay Rathburn, *Vice Pres*
EMP: 3
SQ FT: 3,000
SALES (est): 105.7K **Privately Held**
WEB: www.defensecoat.com
SIC: 3479 Metal coating & allied service

(G-11560)
DELIGHTFUL SCENTS
6823 W Carnation St Apt E (23225-5265)
PHONE..................................804 245-6999
Raquel Tharpe, *Principal*
EMP: 2
SALES (est): 94K **Privately Held**
SIC: 2844 Toilet preparations

(G-11561)
DELIVERY JUNKIES
5710 Dendron Dr (23223-6163)
PHONE..................................540 329-9060
Warren McCall, *CEO*
EMP: 15
SALES (est): 748.6K **Privately Held**
SIC: 3537 Trucks, tractors, loaders, carri-
ers & similar equipment

(G-11562)
DOLAN LLC
Also Called: Virginia Lawyers Media
801 E Main St Ste 302 (23219-2918)
P.O. Box 86, Minneapolis MN (55486-
0086)
PHONE..................................804 783-0770
Paul Fletcher, *Branch Mgr*
EMP: 12
SALES (corp-wide): 519.8MM **Privately
Held**
WEB: www.bridgetowermedia.com
SIC: 2711 Newspapers, publishing & print-
ing
HQ: Dolan Llc
222 S 9th St Ste 2300
Minneapolis MN 55402

(G-11563)
DOMINION INK LLC
1111 Carrolton St (23221-3907)
PHONE..................................804 350-7996
EMP: 2 EST: 2016
SALES (est): 129.2K **Privately Held**
SIC: 2752 Commercial printing, offset

(G-11564)
DOMINION PRODUCTION
1421 Rogers St (23223-4318)
PHONE..................................804 247-4106
Michael Kenneth Ross, *Owner*
EMP: 1
SALES (est): 49K **Privately Held**
SIC: 2741 Music book & sheet music pub-
lishing

(G-11565)
DOSE GUARDIAN LLC (PA)
6130 Midlothian Tpke (23225-5922)
PHONE..................................804 726-5448
James B Gibson,
Merri Beth Gibson,
EMP: 3

SALES (est): 50K **Privately Held**
WEB: www.topbizbuys.com
SIC: 3999 Manufacturing industries

(G-11566)
DOT BLUE
303 W 30th St (23225-3719)
PHONE..................................804 564-2563
Chopper Dawson, *Principal*
EMP: 1
SALES (est): 54.6K **Privately Held**
SIC: 3751 Motorcycles & related parts

(G-11567)
**DOVER PLANK ENTERPRISES
LLC**
2315 Rosewood Ave (23220-5716)
PHONE..................................757 286-6772
Patrick Mahloy,
EMP: 1
SALES (est): 54.1K **Privately Held**
SIC: 2431 Woodwork, interior & ornamen-
tal

(G-11568)
DRAFT DOCTOR
1901 Cedarhurst Dr (23225-2315)
P.O. Box 9054 (23225-0754)
PHONE..................................804 986-6588
Dennis Cullender, *Owner*
EMP: 1
SALES (est): 100K **Privately Held**
WEB: www.thedraftdoctor.com
SIC: 3585 Beer dispensing equipment

(G-11569)
DRG IMPORTS LLC
Also Called: Nicola Biscardo Selections
1535 West Ave (23220-3726)
PHONE..................................786 246-6548
Nicola Biscardo, *Mng Member*
▲ EMP: 1
SALES (est): 82.4K **Privately Held**
SIC: 2084 Wines

(G-11570)
DUST GOLD PUBLISHING LLC
3126 W Cary St (23221-3504)
PHONE..................................540 828-5110
EMP: 1
SALES (est): 47.8K **Privately Held**
WEB: www.gdws.co
SIC: 2741 Miscellaneous publishing

(G-11571)
E T MOORE JR CO INC
3100 N Hopkins Rd Ste 101 (23224-6631)
PHONE..................................804 231-1823
Edwin T Moore Jr, *President*
Kristine Moore, *Vice Pres*
EMP: 18
SQ FT: 37,500
SALES (est): 1.5MM **Privately Held**
WEB: www.etmoore.com
SIC: 2431 Woodwork, interior & ornamen-
tal

(G-11572)
**ECONOMIC DEV AUTH CY
RICHMOND**
501 E Franklin St (23219-2322)
PHONE..................................804 521-4002
Dale Fickett, *Exec Dir*
EMP: 3
SALES (est): 141.5K **Privately Held**
WEB: www.richmond.com
SIC: 2711 Newspapers, publishing & print-
ing

(G-11573)
ELLIOTT MFG
4232 Oakleys Ct (23223-5966)
PHONE..................................804 737-1475
EMP: 1
SALES (est): 44.7K **Privately Held**
SIC: 3999 Manufacturing industries

(G-11574)
**EMPIRE MARBLE & GRANITE
CO**
1717 Rhoadmiller St (23220-1108)
P.O. Box 5221 (23220-0221)
PHONE..................................804 359-2004
Stephen Broocks, *President*
Jerry L Nixon, *Vice Pres*

Corinne K Barnes, *Admin Sec*
EMP: 6
SALES (est): 494.8K **Privately Held**
WEB: www.empiremarblegranite.com
SIC: 3281 5999 5032 5031 Stone, quarrying & processing of own stone products;
monuments & tombstones; marble building stone; kitchen cabinets; counter top
installation

(G-11575)
**EMPIRE PUBLISHING
CORPORATION**
5 E Clay St (23219-1329)
P.O. Box 71703 (23255-1703)
PHONE..................................804 440-5379
EMP: 2
SALES (est): 73.7K **Privately Held**
SIC: 2741 Miscellaneous publishing

(G-11576)
ENERGY 11 LP
814 E Main St (23219-3306)
PHONE..................................804 344-8121
EMP: 2
SALES (est): 140K **Privately Held**
SIC: 1311 Crude petroleum & natural gas

(G-11577)
ENERGY RESOURCES 12 LP
814 E Main St (23219-3306)
PHONE..................................804 344-8121
EMP: 2
SALES (est): 74.8K **Privately Held**
WEB: www.energyresources12.com
SIC: 1311 Crude petroleum & natural gas

(G-11578)
ENGINE AND FRAME LLC
608 Commerce Rd (23224-5416)
PHONE..................................757 407-0134
Cory Manning, *Principal*
EMP: 3
SALES (est): 300.8K **Privately Held**
WEB: www.engineandframe.com
SIC: 3599 Machine shop, jobbing & repair

(G-11579)
ENNIS-FLINT INC
4400 Vawter Ave (23222-1406)
PHONE..................................804 309-3199
Elias Certa, *Manager*
EMP: 20
SQ FT: 38,399
SALES (corp-wide): 162.8MM **Privately
Held**
WEB: www.ennisflintamericas.com
SIC: 2851 5198 2952 Paints & allied
products; paints; asphalt felts & coatings
HQ: Ennis-Flint, Inc.
4161 Piedmont Pkwy # 370
Greensboro NC 27410
800 331-8118

(G-11580)
ETHYL CORPORATION (HQ)
330 S 4th St (23219-4304)
P.O. Box 2189 (23218-2189)
PHONE..................................804 788-5000
Thomas E Gottwald, *CEO*
Azfar A Choudhury, *President*
Russell L Gottwald Jr, *President*
T E Gottwald, *Chairman*
W C Drinkwater, *Vice Pres*
◆ EMP: 5 EST: 1887
SQ FT: 420,000
SALES (est): 127.1MM
SALES (corp-wide): 2.1B **Publicly Held**
WEB: www.ethyl.com
SIC: 2869 5169 2899 2841 Industrial or-
ganic chemicals; chemicals & allied prod-
ucts; corrosion preventive lubricant; soap
& other detergents; cyclic crudes & inter-
mediates
PA: Newmarket Corporation
330 S 4th St
Richmond VA 23219
804 788-5000

(G-11581)
**EVERGREEN ENTERPRISES
INC**
Also Called: Cypress Home
5915 Midlothian Tpke (23225-5917)
PHONE..................................804 231-1800
Frank Qiu, *Branch Mgr*

EMP: 150 **Privately Held**
WEB: www.myevergreen.com
SIC: 3253 Ceramic wall & floor tile
PA: Evergreen Enterprises, Inc.
5915 Midlothian Tpke
Richmond VA 23225

(G-11582)
EVERGREEN ENTERPRISES
INC (PA)
Also Called: Ashford Court Richmond Ci
5915 Midlothian Tpke (23225-5917)
P.O. Box 602961, Charlotte NC (28260-2961)
PHONE..............................804 231-1800
Frank Qiu, *CEO*
Ting Xu, *Ch of Bd*
John Toler, *President*
David Earle, *Vice Pres*
Brittany Toler, *Vice Pres*
◆ EMP: 200
SALES (est): 137.6MM **Privately Held**
WEB: www.myevergreen.com
SIC: 2399 3253 5193 5999 Flags, fabric; ceramic wall & floor tile; flowers & florists' supplies; banners, flags, decals & posters

(G-11583)
EVERGREEN ENTERPRISES VA
LLC
5915 Midlothian Tpke (23225-5917)
PHONE..............................804 231-1800
Fei Qui, *CEO*
Ting Xu, *President*
John Toler, *COO*
Bettye Columbo, *Manager*
Shelley Dumais, *Manager*
EMP: 1
SALES (est): 102.6K **Privately Held**
WEB: www.myevergreenonline.com
SIC: 2399 Banners, pennants & flags

(G-11584)
EXTREMEHT2COM
522 Rossmore Rd (23225-4248)
PHONE..............................804 665-6304
EMP: 2
SALES (est): 170.9K **Privately Held**
SIC: 3699 3641 Security devices; electric lamps & parts for specialized applications

(G-11585)
FAST RA XPRESS LLC
5003 Colwyck Dr (23223-5912)
PHONE..............................804 514-5696
EMP: 2
SALES (est): 83K **Privately Held**
SIC: 2741 Misc Publishing

(G-11586)
FESTIVAL DESIGN INC
Also Called: Festival Flags
309 N Monroe St (23220-4232)
PHONE..............................804 643-5247
David Edwards, *President*
Hong Edwards, *Supervisor*
EMP: 2 EST: 1971
SQ FT: 3,000
SALES (est): 250K **Privately Held**
WEB: www.festivalflags.com
SIC: 2399 Flags, fabric

(G-11587)
FIBRXL PERFORMANCE INC
4590 Vawter Ave (23222-1412)
PHONE..............................804 329-0491
Stephen M Bassett, *President*
Benno Ter Horst, *Vice Pres*
▲ EMP: 25
SALES (est): 2.5MM **Privately Held**
WEB: www.dominionfiber.com
SIC: 2281 Yarn spinning mills

(G-11588)
FILTROIL LLC
2600 E Cary St Apt 5102 (23223-7893)
PHONE..............................804 359-9125
Jeremy D Leahman, *President*
Jaime Patino, *Sales Staff*
▲ EMP: 20
SALES (est): 3.8MM **Privately Held**
WEB: www.filtroil.com
SIC: 3569 Filters

(G-11589)
FINISH LINE DIE CUTTING
800 W Leigh St (23220-3136)
P.O. Box 5036 (23220-0036)
PHONE..............................804 342-8000
Wendy Vick,
Shelly McDowell,
EMP: 15
SALES (est): 1MM **Privately Held**
WEB: www.finishlinedc.com
SIC: 2789 Bookbinding & related work

(G-11590)
FIREMANS SHIELD LLC
5915 Midlothian Tpke (23225-5917)
PHONE..............................804 231-1800
EMP: 2
SALES (est): 140K **Privately Held**
SIC: 3842 Mfg Surgical Appliances/Supplies

(G-11591)
FLIPCLEAN CORP
2102 Decatur St (23224-3714)
PHONE..............................804 233-4845
Reed Carter, *President*
Don Faye, *Vice Pres*
Faye Donald L, *Vice Pres*
EMP: 2
SQ FT: 600
SALES (est): 252.9K **Privately Held**
WEB: www.flipcleanguttersystems.com
SIC: 3444 Downspouts, sheet metal

(G-11592)
FLIPPEN & SONS INC
2100 Porter St (23225-3945)
PHONE..............................804 233-1461
George Flippen, *President*
Kenneth Flippen, *Corp Secy*
EMP: 9
SQ FT: 6,600
SALES (est): 1.4MM **Privately Held**
SIC: 3444 1761 1711 Sheet metal specialties, not stamped; sheet metalwork; heating & air conditioning contractors

(G-11593)
FORMEX LLC
2800 Cofer Rd (23224-7102)
PHONE..............................804 231-1988
John Skiles, *Mng Member*
Theresa Skiles,
EMP: 10
SQ FT: 28,000
SALES (est): 1.7MM **Privately Held**
WEB: www.formex.net
SIC: 3441 Fabricated structural metal

(G-11594)
FREDERICK ENTERPRISES LLC
1505 Cummings Dr (23220-1121)
PHONE..............................804 405-4976
Greg Frederick, *Mng Member*
EMP: 25
SALES (est): 3MM **Privately Held**
WEB: www.architecturaloutfitters.net
SIC: 2431 1751 Interior & ornamental woodwork & trim; cabinet building & installation

(G-11595)
FRIT SMALL DOLLAR TWAI
701 E Byrd St (23219-3921)
PHONE..............................804 697-3968
Lon Zanetta, *Principal*
EMP: 4
SALES (est): 474.3K **Privately Held**
SIC: 2899 Frit

(G-11596)
G I K OF VIRGINIA INC
Also Called: Sir Speedy
1638 Ownby Ln (23220-1317)
PHONE..............................804 358-8500
Lloyd Newton, *President*
EMP: 5
SALES (est): 825.7K **Privately Held**
WEB: www.sirspeedy.com
SIC: 2752 Commercial printing, lithographic

(G-11597)
G-FORCE EVENTS INC
4245 Carolina Ave (23222-1403)
P.O. Box 488, Mechanicsville (23111-0488)
PHONE..............................804 228-0188
Jason A Yarema, *Administration*
EMP: 2 EST: 2013
SALES (est): 171.9K **Privately Held**
WEB: www.gforcekarts.com
SIC: 3999 Music boxes

(G-11598)
GEL FORMATIONS LLC
800 E Leigh St (23219-1551)
PHONE..............................704 706-4606
Bryan Toton,
EMP: 3
SALES (est): 94.1K **Privately Held**
SIC: 3296 Insulation: rock wool, slag & silica minerals

(G-11599)
GENERAL CIGAR CO INC
2100 E Cary St Fl 2 (23223-7270)
PHONE..............................804 935-2800
EMP: 2 **Privately Held**
WEB: www.cigarworld.com
SIC: 2121 Whol Tobacco Products

(G-11600)
GILGIT PRESS LLC
2309 Monument Ave (23220-2603)
PHONE..............................804 359-2524
Jack Spain,
EMP: 2
SALES (est): 77.8K **Privately Held**
WEB: www.studiosofrichmond.net
SIC: 2741 Miscellaneous publishing

(G-11601)
GIVE MORE MEDIA INC
Also Called: Inspireyourpeople.com
115 S 15th St Ste 502 (23219-4254)
PHONE..............................804 762-4500
Samuel L Parker, *President*
James Gould, *Vice Pres*
Emily Kittrell, *Recruiter*
EMP: 8 EST: 1998
SQ FT: 4,500
SALES (est): 1MM **Privately Held**
WEB: www.inspireyourpeople.com
SIC: 2741 8249 8742 ; business training services; human resource consulting services; training & development consultant

(G-11602)
GLENNA JEAN MFG CO
119 Shockoe Slip (23219-4121)
PHONE..............................804 783-1490
Glenna Kramer, *Principal*
EMP: 1
SALES (est): 68.8K **Privately Held**
SIC: 3999 Manufacturing industries

(G-11603)
GLOBAL BUSINESS PAGES
6820 Atmore Dr (23225-5631)
PHONE..............................855 825-2124
Vin Cees, *Owner*
EMP: 1
SALES (est): 37.5K **Privately Held**
SIC: 2741 Miscellaneous publishing

(G-11604)
GRAND INVESTMENT LLC
3823 Creighton Rd (23223-2246)
PHONE..............................804 939-9473
Maquita Johnson,
EMP: 1
SALES (est): 50K **Privately Held**
SIC: 2842 Sanitation preparations, disinfectants & deodorants

(G-11605)
GREEN SOLUTIONS LIGHTING
LLC
206 Oxford Cir W (23221-3251)
PHONE..............................804 334-2705
Thomas Stallings,
EMP: 1
SALES (est): 100K **Privately Held**
SIC: 3646 Commercial indusl & institutional electric lighting fixtures

(G-11606)
GUARDIAN PUBLISHING HOUSE
3319 Hanes Ave (23222-2654)
PHONE..............................804 321-2139
David Carter, *Partner*
EMP: 2
SALES (est): 70.3K **Privately Held**
WEB: www.davidcarterbooks.com
SIC: 2731 Book publishing

(G-11607)
HALLMARK FABRICATORS INC
601 Gordon Ave (23224-7000)
PHONE..............................804 230-0880
William D Edwards, *President*
Donald Edwards, *Vice Pres*
EMP: 7
SQ FT: 25,000
SALES (est): 1.2MM **Privately Held**
SIC: 3499 Machine bases, metal

(G-11608)
HAVERDASH
2100 Decatur St (23224-3714)
PHONE..............................804 371-1107
Britt Sebastian, *Owner*
EMP: 2
SALES (est): 140.7K **Privately Held**
WEB: www.haberdash.shop
SIC: 2211 Print cloths, cotton

(G-11609)
HENRICO TOOL & DIE CO INC
405 Dabbs House Rd (23223-4818)
PHONE..............................804 222-5017
James Hepper, *President*
Jim Hepper, *President*
EMP: 8 EST: 1965
SQ FT: 7,000
SALES (est): 901.5K **Privately Held**
WEB: www.henrico.us
SIC: 3599 Machine shop, jobbing & repair; chemical milling job shop; custom machinery

(G-11610)
HERITAGE PRINTING SERVICE
INC
2611 Decatur St (23224-3600)
PHONE..............................804 233-3024
Lindsey Yates, *President*
Stephanie Anderson, *Vice Pres*
Will Yates, *Sales Executive*
Gary Bright, *Manager*
EMP: 16 EST: 1945
SQ FT: 18,000
SALES (est): 2.5MM **Privately Held**
WEB: www.heritageps.com
SIC: 2752 Commercial printing, offset

(G-11611)
HEROES APPAREL LLC
1614 Ownby Ln (23220-1317)
PHONE..............................804 304-1001
Paul Hartsoe, *Mng Member*
Donald Lee Smoyer,
Donald Smoyer,
EMP: 7
SALES (est): 1MM **Privately Held**
WEB: www.heroesapparel.com
SIC: 2311 Policemen's uniforms: made from purchased materials

(G-11612)
IJ THERAPEUTICS LLC
111 Virginia St Ste 300 (23219-4159)
PHONE..............................804 543-6360
EMP: 3 EST: 2018
SALES (est): 182.9K **Privately Held**
SIC: 2834 Pharmaceutical preparations

(G-11613)
IMAGENATION DESIGN & PRTG
LLC
4226 Riding Place Rd (23223-4952)
PHONE..............................804 687-3581
Uronda Burrell, *Administration*
EMP: 2
SALES (est): 101.5K **Privately Held**
SIC: 2752 Commercial printing, lithographic

(G-11614)
IMAGINE THIS COMPANY
5331 Distributor Dr (23225-6103)
PHONE.....................................804 232-1300
Michael Moss, *President*
Bev Moss, *Vice Pres*
Lewis S Broad, *Treasurer*
Beverly Moss, *Officer*
Nicole Scott, *Graphic Designe*
EMP: 10
SQ FT: 2,800
SALES (est): 1.3MM **Privately Held**
WEB: www.imaginethiscompany.com
SIC: 3993 2759 Signs, not made in custom sign painting shops; screen printing

(G-11615)
IMMUNARRAY USA INC (HQ)
737 N 5th St Ste 304 (23219-1441)
PHONE.....................................804 212-2975
Steve Wallace, *COO*
Donna Edmonds, *Treasurer*
Joseph Bs, *Technical Staff*
EMP: 1 EST: 2010
SQ FT: 1,200
SALES (est): 858.9K
SALES (corp-wide): 5.2MM **Privately Held**
WEB: www.immunarray.com
SIC: 2835 In vitro diagnostics
PA: Immunarray Ltd
12 Hamada
Rehovot 76703
893 657-27

(G-11616)
IN YOUR ELEMENT COMMERCE INC
3425 W Cary St (23221-2726)
PHONE.....................................804 426-6914
Sherry Burgess, *President*
EMP: 2
SALES (est): 165.3K **Privately Held**
SIC: 2844 Lotions, shaving

(G-11617)
IN10M LLC
700 E Main St 2487 (23219-2619)
PHONE.....................................202 779-7977
Jamall Alajmi,
EMP: 1
SALES (est): 64.3K **Privately Held**
SIC: 3822 Incinerator control systems, residential & commercial type

(G-11618)
INCH BY INCH LLC
200 N 21st St (23223-7012)
PHONE.....................................804 678-8271
April Scott,
EMP: 1
SQ FT: 1,200
SALES (est): 51.4K **Privately Held**
SIC: 2361 Girls' & children's dresses, blouses & shirts

(G-11619)
INTERBAKE FOODS LLC
900 Terminal Pl (23220-1988)
PHONE.....................................605 232-4903
EMP: 2
SALES (corp-wide): 37.6B **Privately Held**
WEB: www.interbake.com
SIC: 2052 Cookies; crackers, dry
HQ: Interbake Foods Llc
50 Maplehurst Dr
Brownsburg IN 46112
804 755-7107

(G-11620)
INTERNATIONAL PAPER COMPANY
2811 Cofer Rd (23224-7101)
PHONE.....................................804 230-3100
Vonda Davis, *Controller*
James Buehler, *Manager*
EMP: 108
SALES (corp-wide): 22.3B **Publicly Held**
WEB: www.internationalpaper.com
SIC: 2621 Paper mills
PA: International Paper Company
6400 Poplar Ave
Memphis TN 38197
901 419-9000

(G-11621)
IRIS CO
3925 Park Ave (23221-1117)
PHONE.....................................804 310-1054
EMP: 3
SALES (est): 214.1K **Privately Held**
WEB: www.theirisco.com
SIC: 2992 Lubricating oils & greases

(G-11622)
ITG CIGARS INC
Also Called: Allied Products Division
600 Perdue Ave (23224-5102)
P.O. Box 24508 (23224-0508)
PHONE.....................................804 233-7668
J R Metheny, *Opers-Prdtn-Mfg*
Philip V Mazzone, *Manager*
John Schone, *Manager*
EMP: 43
SALES (corp-wide): 40B **Privately Held**
WEB: www.altadisusa.com
SIC: 2121 3085 Cigars; plastics bottles
HQ: Itg Cigars Inc.
5900 N Andrews Ave Ste 11
Fort Lauderdale FL 33309
954 772-9000

(G-11623)
JADE SUPPLIERS
3304 E Marshall St (23223-7539)
PHONE.....................................804 551-6865
Jaida Cureton, *President*
EMP: 2
SALES (est): 74.4K **Privately Held**
SIC: 2844 Hair preparations, including shampoos

(G-11624)
JAMES E HENSON JR
Also Called: Hdh
422 E Franklin St Ste 104 (23219-2226)
PHONE.....................................804 648-3005
James Henson Jr, *Owner*
EMP: 3
SALES (est): 215.7K **Privately Held**
SIC: 2759 Commercial printing

(G-11625)
JAMES RIVER COAL COMPANY (PA)
901 E Byrd St Fl 2 (23219-4087)
PHONE.....................................804 780-3000
Peter T Socha, *Ch of Bd*
Samuel M Hopkins II, *Vice Pres*
Michael E Weber, *Ch Credit Ofcr*
William B Murphy, *Risk Mgmt Dir*
EMP: 16
SALES (est): 828.9MM **Privately Held**
WEB: www.jamesrivercoal.com
SIC: 1221 Bituminous coal & lignite-surface mining

(G-11626)
JAMES RIVER COAL SERVICE CO (HQ)
901 E Byrd St Fl 2 (23219-4087)
PHONE.....................................606 878-7411
Peter Socha, *CEO*
Talmadge M Mosley, *President*
Dexter Brian Patton III, *President*
Samuel Hopkins, *Treasurer*
Coy K Lane, *Director*
EMP: 25
SQ FT: 10,000
SALES (est): 118.9MM **Privately Held**
SIC: 1222 1221 Underground mining, semibituminous; strip mining, bituminous; coal preparation plant, bituminous or lignite; unit train loading facility, bituminous or lignite

(G-11627)
JAMES RIVER DISTILLERY LLC
2700 Hardy Rd (23220-1131)
PHONE.....................................804 716-5172
Christopher T Craig, *Administration*
EMP: 5
SALES (est): 343.2K **Privately Held**
WEB: www.jrdistillery.com
SIC: 2085 Distilled & blended liquors

(G-11628)
JAMES RIVER ESCROW INC
901 E Byrd St Ste 1600 (23219-4054)
PHONE.....................................804 780-3000

EMP: 2
SALES (est): 157.6K **Privately Held**
SIC: 1241 Coal Mining Services

(G-11629)
JAMES RIVER PRESS
807 Oliver Hill Way (23219-1622)
PHONE.....................................804 230-4515
EMP: 2
SALES (est): 50K **Privately Held**
WEB: www.jamesriverpress.com
SIC: 2752 Commercial printing, offset

(G-11630)
JESTER WOODWORKS LLC VAN
3801 Carolina Ave (23222-2203)
PHONE.....................................804 562-6360
Zachary Jester, *Principal*
EMP: 4
SALES (est): 319.6K **Privately Held**
WEB: www.vanjesterwoodworks.com
SIC: 2431 Millwork

(G-11631)
JEWETT AUTOMATION INC
700 Gordon Ave (23224-7020)
PHONE.....................................804 344-8101
Bryce D Jewett Jr, *President*
Andrew Ferguson, *Engineer*
Matt Reed, *Engineer*
Kevin Welss, *Engineer*
Iggy Castillo, *Info Tech Mgr*
EMP: 40
SALES (est): 8.4MM **Privately Held**
WEB: www.jewettautomation.com
SIC: 3599 Custom machinery

(G-11632)
JEWETT MCH MFG CO INC BRYCE D
2901 Maury St (23224-3553)
PHONE.....................................804 233-9873
Bryce D Jewett Jr, *President*
Gay M Jewett, *Admin Sec*
EMP: 68
SQ FT: 45,000
SALES (est): 12.8MM **Privately Held**
WEB: www.jewettmachine.com
SIC: 3599 Machine shop, jobbing & repair; custom machinery

(G-11633)
JOHN P SCOTT WOODWORKING INC
Also Called: On Display
3400 Formex Rd (23224-6373)
P.O. Box 42007 (23224-9007)
PHONE.....................................804 231-1942
John P Scott, *President*
Beth Scott, *Corp Secy*
EMP: 9
SQ FT: 5,000
SALES (est): 1.2MM **Privately Held**
WEB: www.ondisplayusa.com
SIC: 2541 Cabinets, except refrigerated: show, display, etc.: wood; display fixtures, wood

(G-11634)
JOHNS CREEK ELKHORN COAL CORP
Also Called: James River Coal Company
901 E Byrd St Fl 2 (23219-4087)
PHONE.....................................804 780-3000
EMP: 24
SALES (est): 1.3MM **Privately Held**
SIC: 1241 5989 Coal Mining Services Ret Fuel Dealer
PA: James River Coal Company
901 E Byrd St Fl 2
Richmond VA 23219

(G-11635)
JOI ELEMENT LLC
3010 Lawson St (23224-1946)
PHONE.....................................804 912-8002
Joi Donaldson, *Principal*
EMP: 3
SALES (est): 168K **Privately Held**
SIC: 2819 Industrial inorganic chemicals

(G-11636)
JONES AND JONES AUDIO & VIDEO
3011 Peabody Ln (23223-2107)
PHONE.....................................804 283-3495
Andre M Jones, *Owner*
EMP: 1
SALES (est): 98K **Privately Held**
SIC: 3651 Household audio & video equipment

(G-11637)
JOYEBELLS LLC
Also Called: Joyeblls Sweet Ptato Pies Hnri
695 Trevor Ter (23225-4257)
PHONE.....................................804 304-7695
Joye Berry-Moore, *Mng Member*
EMP: 6
SALES (est): 77K **Privately Held**
SIC: 2053 Pies, bakery: frozen

(G-11638)
JUMPSTART CONSULTANTS INC
4649 Carolina Ave Bldg I (23222-1420)
PHONE.....................................804 321-5867
John Cahill, *President*
Earl Shepherd, *Vice Pres*
Christopher Shepherd, *Treasurer*
Daniel Cahill, *Controller*
▲ EMP: 27
SALES (est): 5.6MM **Privately Held**
WEB: www.jumpstartinc.net
SIC: 2759 Commercial printing

(G-11639)
KAOTIC ENZYMES LLC
3313 W Cary St Ste A (23221-3436)
PHONE.....................................804 519-9479
Jesse Smith, *Administration*
EMP: 3
SALES (est): 202.2K **Privately Held**
WEB: www.jessesmithtattoos.com
SIC: 2869 Enzymes

(G-11640)
KEITH FABRY
1420 Commerce Rd (23224-7512)
PHONE.....................................804 649-7551
EMP: 2
SALES (est): 75.6K **Privately Held**
SIC: 2759 Commercial Printing

(G-11641)
KEMPER PRINTING LLC
3434 Stuart Ave Apt 2 (23221-2313)
PHONE.....................................804 510-8402
Andrea Surface,
EMP: 1
SALES (est): 53.2K **Privately Held**
SIC: 2752 7389 Commercial printing, lithographic;

(G-11642)
KENNETH HILL
1808 Bath St (23220-1706)
PHONE.....................................804 986-8674
Kenneth Hill, *Owner*
EMP: 2
SALES (est): 98.3K **Privately Held**
SIC: 2992 Lubricating oils & greases

(G-11643)
KENWAY EXPRESS
5 Kenway Ave (23223-2709)
PHONE.....................................804 652-1922
Chandrakant Patel, *Principal*
EMP: 4
SALES (est): 296K **Privately Held**
WEB: www.texassportsfishing.com
SIC: 2741 Miscellaneous publishing

(G-11644)
KING OF POPS RICHMOND LLC
2408 W Cary St Apt B (23220-5252)
PHONE.....................................804 475-9026
EMP: 3 EST: 2012
SALES (est): 212.4K **Privately Held**
SIC: 3999 Manufacturing industries

(G-11645)
KINGDOM BLOODLINE APPAREL LLC
1108 E Main St Ste 90656 (23219-3539)
PHONE.....................................866 426-0196

Byron A Boone,
EMP: 2
SALES (est): 100K **Privately Held**
SIC: 2321 Men's & boys' dress shirts

(G-11646)
KISCO SIGNS LLC
3529 Grove Ave (23221-2205)
PHONE.............................804 404-2727
EMP: 2 EST: 2012
SALES (est): 110K **Privately Held**
SIC: 3993 7389 Mfg Signs/Advertising
Specialties

(G-11647)
**LAWTON PUBG & TRANSLATION
LLC**
117 N Crenshaw Ave (23221-2743)
PHONE.............................804 367-4028
EMP: 1 EST: 2015
SALES (est): 40.3K **Privately Held**
SIC: 2741 Misc Publishing

(G-11648)
LAWYERS PRINTING CO
1011 E Main St Ste 50 (23219-3567)
P.O. Box 1654 (23218-1654)
PHONE.............................804 648-3664
EMP: 2
SALES (est): 105.7K **Privately Held**
SIC: 2752 Commercial printing, litho-
graphic

(G-11649)
LBP MANUFACTURING LLC
3001 Cofer Rd (23224-7105)
PHONE.............................804 562-6920
EMP: 3
SALES (est): 334K **Privately Held**
SIC: 3999 Manufacturing industries

(G-11650)
LEE CL TRUCKING LLC
2007 X St (23223-4362)
PHONE.............................804 677-2242
Christen Lee,
EMP: 1
SALES (est): 60K **Privately Held**
SIC: 3537 Trucks: freight, baggage, etc.:
industrial, except mining

(G-11651)
LEGEND BREWING CO
321 W 7th St (23224-2307)
PHONE.............................804 232-8871
Thomas E Martin, *President*
Alen Valencia, *General Mgr*
Allen Valencia, *General Mgr*
Edward G Martin, *Corp Secy*
Alexandria Troupe, *Marketing Staff*
EMP: 50
SQ FT: 20,000
SALES (est): 8MM **Privately Held**
WEB: www.legendbrewing.com
SIC: 2082 5812 Beer (alcoholic bever-
age); eating places

(G-11652)
LEWIS PRINTING COMPANY
Also Called: Conquest Graphics
3900 Carolina Ave (23222-2205)
P.O. Box 27122 (23261-7122)
PHONE.............................804 648-2000
Christopher A Lewis, *President*
Wray Bass, *Vice Pres*
George Lewis, *Vice Pres*
Chrisi Lewis, *Export Mgr*
Jake Bullard, *Opers Staff*
EMP: 40 EST: 1907
SQ FT: 65,000
SALES (est): 12.3MM **Privately Held**
WEB: www.conquestgraphics.com
SIC: 2752 2741 Commercial printing, off-
set; micropublishing

(G-11653)
LEXS OF CARYTOWN LTD
3018 W Cary St (23221-3502)
PHONE.............................804 355-5425
Lisa McSherry, *Principal*
EMP: 1 **Privately Held**
WEB: www.lexsofcarytown.com
SIC: 2335 Ensemble dresses: women's,
misses' & juniors'

PA: Lex's Of Carytown Ltd
3020 W Cary St
Richmond VA 23221

(G-11654)
LIGHTBOX PRINT CO LLC
503 Strawberry St Apt 5 (23220-2659)
PHONE.............................919 608-9520
James Hill, *Principal*
EMP: 2 EST: 2014
SALES (est): 89.6K **Privately Held**
SIC: 2752 Commercial printing, litho-
graphic

(G-11655)
LIGHTING AUTO SERVICES
3611 Hull St (23224-3446)
PHONE.............................804 330-6908
EMP: 2
SALES (est): 125.6K **Privately Held**
SIC: 3647 Automotive lighting fixtures

(G-11656)
LINCOLN PLACE GROUP LLC
700 E Main St Ste 2487 (23219-2619)
PHONE.............................347 363-9721
Kenford Lynch,
EMP: 3
SALES (est): 122K **Privately Held**
SIC: 3589 Commercial cleaning equipment

(G-11657)
LINEAGE LOGISTICS
3100 N Hopkins Rd Ste 202 (23224-6631)
PHONE.............................804 421-6603
Jeff Falls, *Manager*
EMP: 2
SALES (est): 62.3K **Privately Held**
SIC: 2092 Fresh or frozen packaged fish

(G-11658)
LIQUI-BOX CORPORATION (PA)
901 E Byrd St Ste 1105 (23219-4068)
PHONE.............................804 325-1400
Ken Swanson, *President*
Andrew McLeland, *COO*
Lou Marmo, *CFO*
Diana Smith, *Exec Sec*
◆ **EMP:** 65 EST: 1963
SQ FT: 63,000
SALES (est): 370.1MM **Privately Held**
WEB: www.liquibox.com
SIC: 2673 3585 3089 3081 Plastic bags:
made from purchased materials; soda
fountain & beverage dispensing equip-
ment & parts; plastic containers, except
foam; plastic film & sheet; mineral or
spring water bottling

(G-11659)
**LOEHR LIGHTNING
PROTECTION CO**
5268 Hull Street Rd (23224-2424)
PHONE.............................804 231-4236
B K Loehr, *Owner*
Kim Loehr, *Corp Secy*
J J Loehr III, *Vice Pres*
Suzanne Loehr, *Treasurer*
EMP: 15
SQ FT: 4,500
SALES (est): 2.8MM **Privately Held**
WEB: www.loehrlightning.com
SIC: 3643 1731 Lightning protection
equipment; electrical work

(G-11660)
LUMAT YARNS LLC
4590 Vawter Ave (23222-1412)
PHONE.............................804 329-4383
Henk Luykx,
EMP: 1
SALES (est): 46.5K **Privately Held**
WEB: www.lumat.com
SIC: 2282 Beaming yarns, for the trade

(G-11661)
M & M ENTERPRISE LLC
901 Barlen Dr (23225-7305)
PHONE.............................804 499-0087
Joseph Miles Jr, *Mng Member*
EMP: 2
SALES (est): 17K **Privately Held**
SIC: 2741 Miscellaneous publishing

(G-11662)
M1 FABRICATION LLC
4200 Masonic Ln (23223-5553)
PHONE.............................804 222-8885
Chris Liesfeld,
Lew Bryant,
EMP: 3
SALES (est): 256.4K **Privately Held**
SIC: 3441 Fabricated structural metal

(G-11663)
MAMAGREEN LLC
Also Called: Mamagreen Sstnble Otdoor
Lxury
2601 Maury St Bldg 26 (23224-3665)
PHONE.............................312 953-3557
William Kruzel,
EMP: 2
SALES (corp-wide): 2MM **Privately Held**
WEB: www.mamagreen.com
SIC: 2511 Wood household furniture
PA: Mamagreen Llc
222 Merchandise Mart Plz 1519a
Chicago IL 60654
312 953-3557

(G-11664)
MANTELS BY MEUNIER
318 N 24th St (23223-7114)
PHONE.............................804 690-1977
EMP: 1 EST: 2012
SALES (est): 63K **Privately Held**
WEB: www.mantelsbymeunier.com
SIC: 2431 Millwork

(G-11665)
MAPSDIRECT LLC
101 S 15th St Ste 104 (23219-4263)
PHONE.............................804 915-7628
Benjamin Christensen,
EMP: 3
SALES (est): 120.9K **Privately Held**
SIC: 7372 Prepackaged software

(G-11666)
**MARELCO POWER SYSTEMS
INC**
4200 Oakleys Ln (23223-5938)
P.O. Box 440, Howell MI (48844-0440)
PHONE.............................517 546-6330
Peter H Burgher, *Ch of Bd*
Robert Sweaney, *President*
EMP: 53 EST: 1963
SQ FT: 35,000
SALES (est): 5.5MM **Privately Held**
WEB: www.pdicorp.com
SIC: 3677 3699 3679 3612 Transformers
power supply, electronic type; laser weld-
ing, drilling & cutting equipment; power
supplies, all types: static; transformers,
except electric
HQ: Power Distribution, Inc.
4200 Oakleys Ln
Richmond VA 23223
804 737-9880

(G-11667)
**MARELCO POWER SYSTEMS
INC**
4200 Oakleys Ln (23223-5938)
PHONE.............................800 225-4838
EMP: 15
SALES (corp-wide): 4.5B **Privately Held**
SIC: 3677 3612 3674 Mfg Electronic
Coils/Transformers Mfg Transformers Mfg
Semiconductors/Related Devices
HQ: Marelco Power Systems, Inc.
327 Catrell Dr
Howell MI 23223
517 546-6330

(G-11668)
MARTIN PUBLISHING CORP
Also Called: Prepworks
1700 Venable St (23223-6308)
PHONE.............................804 780-1700
J Bryant Martin, *President*
Monica K Lipford, *Corp Secy*
David P Campbell, *Vice Pres*
EMP: 23
SQ FT: 10,000
SALES (est): 2.3MM **Privately Held**
WEB: www.commonwealthmailing.com
SIC: 2752 Commercial printing, offset

(G-11669)
**MARTIN STAR CABINETRY &
DESIGN**
1610 W Main St (23220-4633)
PHONE.............................804 340-1250
EMP: 3
SALES (est): 288.8K **Privately Held**
WEB: www.martinstar.com
SIC: 2434 Wood kitchen cabinets

(G-11670)
MARY ELIZABETH BURRELL
Also Called: Joseph's Designs
1310 Dance St (23220-6117)
P.O. Box 28234, Henrico (23228-0234)
PHONE.............................804 677-2855
Mary Burrell, *Owner*
EMP: 1
SALES (est): 2.5K **Privately Held**
SIC: 2391 5131 5949 2259 Curtains &
draperies; piece goods & other fabrics;
patterns: sewing, knitting & needlework;
curtains & bedding, knit; venetian blinds;
drapery & upholstery stores

(G-11671)
**MASTER MACHINE & ENGRG
CO**
2806 Decatur St (23224-3612)
PHONE.............................804 231-6648
Walter T Fenner Jr, *CEO*
Creg Shornak, *President*
Francis Russ, *Marketing Staff*
EMP: 8
SQ FT: 11,000
SALES (est): 1.2MM **Privately Held**
WEB: www.mastermachinecoinc.com
SIC: 3599 Machine shop, jobbing & repair

(G-11672)
MATCH MY VALUE INC
1115 Althea St (23222-4637)
PHONE.............................301 456-4308
Durnechia Smith, *President*
EMP: 1
SALES (est): 32.7K **Privately Held**
SIC: 7372 7389 Application computer soft-
ware;

(G-11673)
**MATHEMTICS SCNCE CTR
FUNDATION**
2401 Hartman St (23223-2458)
PHONE.............................862 778-8300
Julia Cothron, *President*
EMP: 2
SALES (est): 81.8K **Privately Held**
WEB: www.mymsic.org
SIC: 2834 Pharmaceutical preparations

(G-11674)
MAXUM MACHINE LLC
2809 Decatur St (23224-3611)
PHONE.............................804 523-1490
Mike Benini, *Mng Member*
EMP: 2
SALES (est): 283.7K **Privately Held**
WEB: www.maxummachine.com
SIC: 3599 Machine shop, jobbing & repair

(G-11675)
**MCDONALD WELDING LLC
DOUG**
720 W 25th St (23225-3615)
PHONE.............................804 928-6496
Doug McDonald,
EMP: 1
SALES (est): 66K **Privately Held**
WEB: www.dougmcdonaldwelding.com
SIC: 7692 Welding repair

(G-11676)
**MECHANICAL MACHINE &
REPAIR**
2100 Stockton St (23224-3736)
PHONE.............................804 231-5866
Larry Flora, *President*
Garrett Moss, *Treasurer*
EMP: 3 EST: 1972
SQ FT: 3,600
SALES (est): 265.9K **Privately Held**
SIC: 3599 3441 Machine shop, jobbing &
repair; fabricated structural metal

(G-11677)
MERU BIOTECHNOLOGIES INC
800 E Leigh St (23219-1551)
PHONE.................................804 316-4466
Dan Rodenhaver, *CEO*
EMP: 3
SALES (est): 99K **Privately Held**
WEB: www.vabiotech.com
SIC: 3674 Molecular devices, solid state

(G-11678)
MINDFUL BARBER LLC
1811 W Broad St (23220-2109)
PHONE.................................757 714-6445
Rachel Thweatt,
EMP: 1
SALES (est): 35K **Privately Held**
SIC: 3999 Hair, dressing of, for the trade

(G-11679)
MODERN LIVING LLC
1607 Rhoadmiller St Ste B (23220-1130)
PHONE.................................877 663-2224
Emily Richards, *Director*
Devin Weisleder,
EMP: 9 EST: 2009
SALES (est): 1.1MM **Privately Held**
WEB: www.modernnursery.com
SIC: 2452 3645 1531 Prefabricated wood
buildings; residential lighting fixtures; op-
erative builders

(G-11680)
**MODULAR INTERIORS GROUP
LLC**
2701 E Main St (23223-7900)
PHONE.................................757 550-8910
John Williams, *Principal*
EMP: 1
SALES (est): 92.8K **Privately Held**
SIC: 2521 Wood office furniture

(G-11681)
MOMENTUM USA INC
4605 Carolina Ave (23222-1420)
PHONE.................................804 329-3000
Vicky Poarch, *Finance Dir*
EMP: 125
SALES (est): 5.3MM **Privately Held**
WEB: www.momentumusainc.com
SIC: 3714 5013 Exhaust systems & parts,
motor vehicle; filters: oil, fuel & air, motor
vehicle; motor vehicle brake systems &
parts; automotive supplies & parts

(G-11682)
**MONOLITHIC MUSIC GROUP
LLC**
5216 Media Rd (23225-6234)
PHONE.................................804 233-2322
Marvin Taylor, *Principal*
EMP: 3 EST: 2010
SALES (est): 147.7K **Privately Held**
SIC: 3674 Read-only memory (ROM)

(G-11683)
**MOORELAND SERVICING CO
LLC**
830 E Main St Ste 2100 (23219-2701)
PHONE.................................804 644-2000
John B Levy, *Administration*
EMP: 2
SALES (est): 103.1K **Privately Held**
SIC: 1389 Roustabout service

(G-11684)
MUNDET INC (HQ)
919 E Main St Ste 1130 (23219-4622)
P.O. Box 70, Colonial Heights (23834-
0070)
PHONE.................................804 644-3970
Stephen Young, *President*
Harvey Robert C L, *Vice Pres*
Francine Childress, *Controller*
Rob Harvey, *Officer*
◆ EMP: 60
SALES (est): 45.9MM
SALES (corp-wide): 1B **Privately Held**
WEB: www.delfortgroup.com
SIC: 2621 2952 Cigarette paper; asphalt
felts & coatings
PA: Delfortgroup Ag
FabrikstraBe 20
Traun 4050
722 977-60

(G-11685)
**MUNDYS PRECISION
AUTOMOTIVE**
Also Called: Mundy's Industrial Parts
2710 Hull St (23224-3614)
PHONE.................................804 231-0435
Robert Mundy, *President*
Sharon K Mundy, *Treasurer*
EMP: 4
SQ FT: 2,500
SALES (est): 458.8K **Privately Held**
SIC: 3599 Machine shop, jobbing & repair

(G-11686)
NATIONS
2729 W Broad St (23220-1905)
PHONE.................................804 257-9891
EMP: 2 EST: 2008
SALES (est): 120K **Privately Held**
SIC: 2599 Mfg Furniture/Fixtures

(G-11687)
**NATIONWIDE CONSUMER
PRODUCTS**
514 Mansfield Dr (23223-5831)
PHONE.................................804 226-0876
EMP: 1
SALES (est): 74.8K **Privately Held**
SIC: 3639 Household Appliances, Nec,
Nsk

(G-11688)
**NEW RICHMOND VENTURES
LLC**
1801 E Cary St (23223-6997)
PHONE.................................804 887-2355
Andy Stefanovich, *Principal*
Graham Henshaw, *Director*
Scott Ukrop, *Director*
EMP: 4
SALES (est): 373.6K **Privately Held**
WEB: www.nrv.vc
SIC: 2599 Hospital beds

(G-11689)
**NEWMARKET CORPORATION
(PA)**
330 S 4th St (23219-4350)
PHONE.................................804 788-5000
Thomas E Gottwald, *Ch of Bd*
Dave Cleaver, *Business Mgr*
M Rudolph West, *Vice Pres*
Ryan Pannell, *Plant Mgr*
Mike Meffert, *Research*
◆ EMP: 80
SALES: 2.1B **Publicly Held**
WEB: www.newmarket.com
SIC: 2869 2899 2841 2865 Industrial or-
ganic chemicals; corrosion preventive lu-
bricant; oil treating compounds; soap &
other detergents; cyclic crudes & interme-
diates

(G-11690)
NINE-TEN PRESS LLC
6 N Shields Ave (23220-4441)
PHONE.................................804 727-9135
Kyle Heiser, *Principal*
EMP: 2
SALES (est): 58.6K **Privately Held**
SIC: 2741 Miscellaneous publishing

(G-11691)
NINJA KOMBUCHA LLC
607 Wickham St (23222-4213)
PHONE.................................757 870-6733
Brett Nobile,
EMP: 1 EST: 2015
SALES (est): 47.9K **Privately Held**
WEB: www.ninjakombucha.com
SIC: 2086 Carbonated beverages, nonal-
coholic: bottled & canned

(G-11692)
NOELLEIMANI ELITE LLC
102 N 7th St (23219-2304)
PHONE.................................804 452-6373
Celestia Reid,
EMP: 1
SALES (est): 39.6K **Privately Held**
SIC: 3999 Hair clippers for human use,
hand & electric

(G-11693)
**NOMAD DELI & CATERING CO
LLC**
207 W Brookland Park Blvd (23222-2601)
PHONE.................................804 677-0843
Anthony Tucker,
EMP: 2
SQ FT: 9,520
SALES (est): 139K **Privately Held**
WEB: www.nomaddelicc.com
SIC: 2099 Food preparations

(G-11694)
NORTHLIGHT PUBLISHING CO
Also Called: Cambell, Marilyn
127 W Clay St (23220-3912)
P.O. Box 16025 (23222-0225)
PHONE.................................804 344-8500
Marilyn Campbell, *President*
EMP: 3
SQ FT: 275
SALES (est): 35K **Privately Held**
SIC: 2741 7336 Newsletter publishing;
graphic arts & related design

(G-11695)
**NORTHROP GRUMMAN
CORPORATION**
Also Called: Northrop Grumman It
110 S 7th St Ste 500 (23219-3932)
PHONE.................................804 371-0019
Gina Hodgkins, *QC Mgr*
Laura Knight, *Program Mgr*
Kim Agee, *Administration*
EMP: 100 **Publicly Held**
WEB: www.northropgrumman.com
SIC: 3812 Search & navigation equipment
PA: Northrop Grumman Corporation
2980 Fairview Park Dr
Falls Church VA 22042

(G-11696)
**NORVELL SIGNS
INCORPORATED**
5928 Nine Mile Rd (23223-3536)
PHONE.................................804 737-2189
Danny Norvell, *President*
Norvell John Dwayne, *Vice Pres*
EMP: 9
SQ FT: 14,000
SALES (est): 600K **Privately Held**
WEB: www.norvellsigns.com
SIC: 3993 7389 Neon signs; sign painting
& lettering shop

(G-11697)
NUDGE LLC
3600 Douglasdale Rd (23221-3801)
PHONE.................................423 521-1969
Philip Beene, *Mng Member*
Chris Garson, *CTO*
Mac Gambill,
EMP: 3
SQ FT: 120
SALES (est): 187.8K **Privately Held**
WEB: www.nudgecoach.com
SIC: 7372 Application computer software

(G-11698)
OK FOUNDRY COMPANY INC
1005 Commerce Rd (23224-7007)
PHONE.................................804 233-9674
Fred Walker, *President*
O'Neil IV James N, *Director*
EMP: 20
SQ FT: 30,000
SALES (est): 3.6MM **Privately Held**
WEB: www.okfoundry.com
SIC: 3321 3543 3365 Gray iron castings;
industrial patterns; aluminum foundries

(G-11699)
**OLD BARN RCLMED WD ANTIQ
FLRG**
3801 Carolina Ave (23222-2203)
P.O. Box 27606 (23261-7606)
PHONE.................................804 329-0079
Samuel C Sikes, *CEO*
Mark Every, *President*
William Dages Jr, *CFO*
EMP: 35
SALES (est): 5.5MM **Privately Held**
WEB: www.wellbornwright.com
SIC: 2431 Millwork

(G-11700)
**OLD DOMINION METAL PDTS
INC**
4300 Vawter Ave (23222-1405)
PHONE.................................804 355-7123
Kent Spencer, *President*
Barbara Lockhart, *Manager*
Rene Spencer, *Manager*
Rene' Spencer, *Admin Sec*
EMP: 20
SALES (est): 4.1MM **Privately Held**
WEB: www.olddominionmetal.com
SIC: 3499 1711 Chair frames, metal; venti-
lation & duct work contractor

(G-11701)
OPPOSABLE THUMBS LLC
Also Called: Chris Chase Studio
1515 Hull St (23224-3803)
PHONE.................................804 502-2937
Chris Chase, *Mng Member*
EMP: 1 EST: 2000
SALES (est): 90K **Privately Held**
SIC: 3553 Furniture makers' machinery,
woodworking

(G-11702)
ORBIS RPM LLC
4577 Carolina Ave (23222-1418)
PHONE.................................804 887-2375
Fred Howe, *Branch Mgr*
EMP: 6
SALES (corp-wide): 1.6B **Privately Held**
WEB: www.corbiplastics.com
SIC: 3081 Unsupported plastics film &
sheet
HQ: Orbis Rpm, Llc
1055 Corporate Center Dr
Oconomowoc WI 53066
262 560-5000

(G-11703)
**PACKAGING CORPORATION
AMERICA**
Also Called: Pca/Richmond 370
2000 Jefferson Davis Hwy (23224-7608)
PHONE.................................804 232-1292
Benjamin Valenzuela, *Production*
Sharon Crummett, *Senior Buyer*
Benny Valenzuela, *Engineer*
David Childress, *Sales Staff*
Bob Argabright, *Branch Mgr*
EMP: 135 **Publicly Held**
WEB: www.packagingcorp.com
SIC: 2653 Boxes, corrugated: made from
purchased materials
PA: Packaging Corporation Of America
1 N Field Ct
Lake Forest IL 60045
847 482-3000

(G-11704)
PAGE LETTERPRESS LLC
2600 Decatur St Ste A (23224-3602)
PHONE.................................866 540-7243
Richard W Gregory, *Principal*
EMP: 2 EST: 2018
SALES (est): 59.8K **Privately Held**
SIC: 2741 Miscellaneous publishing

(G-11705)
PALLET SERVICES
1102 Dinwiddie Ave (23224-5424)
PHONE.................................804 233-6584
Don Staley, *Principal*
EMP: 1
SALES (est): 75.8K **Privately Held**
SIC: 2448 Pallets, wood & wood with metal

(G-11706)
**PARADIGM COMMUNICATIONS
INC**
Also Called: Richmond Free Press
422 E Franklin St Fl 2 (23219-2226)
P.O. Box 27709 (23261-7709)
PHONE.................................804 644-0496
Jean Boone, *President*
Tracy Oliver, *Administration*
EMP: 10
SALES (est): 950K **Privately Held**
WEB: www.richmondfreepress.com
SIC: 2711 Newspapers, publishing & print-
ing

(G-11707)
PARKER INDUSTRIES VIRGINIA INC
8 S Plum St (23220-5317)
PHONE..................................804 254-4140
Joseph E Parker III, *Director*
EMP: 2
SALES (est): 129K **Privately Held**
WEB: www.stephanieparkermakeup.com
SIC: 3999 Manufacturing industries

(G-11708)
PATINAD GRACE LLC
106 S Robinson St (23220-5128)
PHONE..................................804 447-4578
EMP: 3
SALES (est): 142.7K **Privately Held**
WEB: www.richmondmagazine.com
SIC: 2721 Magazines: publishing only, not printed on site

(G-11709)
PDQ PRINTING COMPANY
3612 Mechanicsville Tpke (23223-1330)
PHONE..................................804 228-0077
William D Green, *Partner*
James F Smith Jr, *Partner*
EMP: 3
SQ FT: 4,900
SALES (est): 315.2K **Privately Held**
SIC: 2752 Commercial printing, offset

(G-11710)
PDQ PRINTING LLC
3612 Mechanicsville Tpke (23223-1330)
PHONE..................................804 228-0077
William Green,
EMP: 2
SALES (est): 102.4K **Privately Held**
SIC: 2621 Printing paper

(G-11711)
PEAK DEVELOPMENT RESOURCES LLC
5120 Evelyn Byrd Rd (23225-3022)
P.O. Box 13267 (23225-0267)
PHONE..................................804 233-3707
Stephanie Keck, *CEO*
EMP: 2
SALES (est): 110K **Privately Held**
WEB: www.peakdev.com
SIC: 2741 Newsletter publishing

(G-11712)
PFIZER INC
1211 Sherwood Ave (23220-1212)
PHONE..................................804 257-2000
Scott Fresco, *Project Mgr*
CHI Dzienny, *Buyer*
Erica Brown, *QC Mgr*
Nils Ahlgren, *Research*
Hope Bailey, *Research*
EMP: 14
SALES (corp-wide): 51.7B **Publicly Held**
WEB: www.pfizer.com
SIC: 2833 2834 Antibiotics; drugs acting on the cardiovascular system, except diagnostic
PA: Pfizer Inc.
235 E 42nd St Rm 107
New York NY 10017
212 733-2323

(G-11713)
PFIZER INC
1211 Sherwood Ave (23220-1212)
PHONE..................................804 257-2000
Bryan Coleman, *Branch Mgr*
EMP: 125
SALES (corp-wide): 51.7B **Publicly Held**
WEB: www.pfizer.com
SIC: 2834 Cough medicines
PA: Pfizer Inc.
235 E 42nd St Rm 107
New York NY 10017
212 733-2323

(G-11714)
PHILIP MORRIS USA INC
2601 Maury St (23224-3665)
PHONE..................................804 274-2000
Craig G Schwartz, *Senior VP*
EMP: 69 **Publicly Held**
WEB: www.philipmorrisusa.com
SIC: 2111 Cigarettes

HQ: Philip Morris Usa Inc.
6601 W Brd St
Richmond VA 23230
804 274-2000

(G-11715)
PHLOW CORP
1001 Haxall Point 1b (23219-3940)
PHONE..................................804 207-4893
Eric Edwards, *CEO*
Glenn Gerecke, *COO*
Robert J Mooney, *CFO*
Bernard Gupton, *Director*
EMP: 25
SALES (est): 1.6MM **Privately Held**
WEB: www.phlow-usa.com
SIC: 2834 Pharmaceutical preparations

(G-11716)
PILLAR PUBLISHING & CO LLC
4105 Autumn Glen Ct (23223-1691)
PHONE..................................804 640-1963
EMP: 1
SALES (est): 37.5K **Privately Held**
SIC: 2741 Miscellaneous publishing

(G-11717)
PLAYTEX PRODUCTS LLC
Also Called: Playtex Richmond VA
2901 Maury St (23224-3553)
PHONE..................................804 230-1520
Joey Garthaffner, *Engineer*
EMP: 8
SALES (corp-wide): 1.9B **Publicly Held**
WEB: www.ob-tampons.com
SIC: 2676 Tampons, sanitary: made from purchased paper
HQ: Playtex Products, Llc
6 Research Dr Ste 400
Shelton CT 06484
203 944-5500

(G-11718)
POOLHOUSE DIGITAL AGENCY LLC
23 W Broad St Ste 404 (23220-4295)
PHONE..................................804 876-0335
Will Ritter, *Owner*
EMP: 2
SALES (est): 90K **Privately Held**
WEB: www.poolhouse.co
SIC: 3993 Advertising artwork

(G-11719)
POP PRINTING
6707 Greenvale Dr (23225-2209)
PHONE..................................804 248-9093
Joe Manriquez, *Principal*
EMP: 2
SALES (est): 83.9K **Privately Held**
WEB: www.pop-printing.com
SIC: 2752 Commercial printing, lithographic

(G-11720)
POPMOUNT INC
1817 W Broad St (23220-2109)
PHONE..................................804 232-4999
Jocelyn Senn, *President*
Brian Chilton, *CFO*
EMP: 15
SQ FT: 6,500
SALES (est): 1.3MM **Privately Held**
WEB: www.popmount.com
SIC: 2711 Newspapers, publishing & printing; commercial printing & newspaper publishing combined

(G-11721)
POWER DISTRIBUTION INC (DH)
Also Called: Pdi
4200 Oakleys Ln (23223-5938)
PHONE..................................804 737-9880
Craig Arnold, *CEO*
Jennifer Bartlett, *Vice Pres*
David Bull, *Vice Pres*
Chris Kelly, *Vice Pres*
Dave Mulholland, *Vice Pres*
EMP: 150
SQ FT: 80,000

SALES (est): 110.2MM **Privately Held**
WEB: www.pdicorp.com
SIC: 3677 3612 3613 3621 Electronic coils, transformers & other inductors; constant impedance transformers; filtration devices, electronic; transformers, except electric; switchgear & switchboard apparatus; power circuit breakers; panel & distribution boards & other related apparatus; motors & generators; electric motor & generator parts; electric motor & generator auxillary parts; control equipment for electric buses & locomotives; current-carrying wiring devices; electronic generation equipment
HQ: Eaton Corporation
1000 Eaton Blvd
Cleveland OH 44122
440 523-5000

(G-11722)
PRECIOUS TIME LLC
1111 E Main St Fl 16 (23219-3532)
PHONE..................................804 343-4380
Dwight Hopewell, *Principal*
EMP: 2
SALES (est): 159.5K **Privately Held**
SIC: 3339 Precious metals

(G-11723)
PRECISION TOOL & DIE INC
2805 Decatur St (23224-3611)
PHONE..................................804 233-8810
Charles C Oldham, *President*
Mark Oldham, *Corp Secy*
EMP: 5
SQ FT: 10,000
SALES (est): 736.2K **Privately Held**
WEB: www.precisiontoolanddie.com
SIC: 3544 3599 Special dies & tools; machine & other job shop work; custom machinery

(G-11724)
PRESBYTRIAN OUTLOOK FOUNDATION
1 N 5th St Ste 500 (23219-2231)
PHONE..................................804 359-8442
Kelly Adams, *Finance Mgr*
George Whipple, *Adv Mgr*
Patricia B Gresham, *Manager*
Robert Baskins, *Director*
EMP: 7 EST: 1819
SQ FT: 3,400
SALES (est): 779.2K **Privately Held**
WEB: www.pres-outlook.org
SIC: 2721 5942 Periodicals: publishing only; books, religious

(G-11725)
PRINT RAYGE STUDIOS LLC
1200 Semmes Ave Apt 201 (23224-2181)
PHONE..................................757 537-6995
Brittney Royster, *Principal*
EMP: 2
SALES (est): 83.9K **Privately Held**
SIC: 2752 Commercial printing, lithographic

(G-11726)
PRODUCTION METAL FINISHERS
1802 Currie St (23220-1710)
P.O. Box 26307 (23260-6307)
PHONE..................................804 643-8116
Allan Lakner, *President*
Yolanda Lakner, *Vice Pres*
EMP: 15
SQ FT: 8,500
SALES (est): 445.6K **Privately Held**
SIC: 3471 Chromium plating of metals or formed products; electroplating of metals or formed products

(G-11727)
PUDDING PLEASE LLC
2715 E Broad St (23223-7339)
PHONE..................................804 833-4110
Tracy Doherty, *Administration*
EMP: 10 EST: 2014
SALES (est): 507K **Privately Held**
WEB: www.puddingplease.net
SIC: 2032 Puddings, except meat: packaged in cans, jars, etc.

(G-11728)
RAPID BIOSCIENCES INC
4105 Exeter Rd (23221-3221)
PHONE..................................713 899-6177
Maxwell Minch, *Principal*
EMP: 3 EST: 2015
SALES (est): 96.3K **Privately Held**
SIC: 2835 8731 3826 3823 In vitro diagnostics; biological research; analytical instruments; industrial instrmnts msrmnt display/control process variable;

(G-11729)
RAYCO INDUSTRIES INC
1502 Valley Rd (23222-5499)
PHONE..................................804 321-7111
William Bryan Spangler, *President*
Devin McDaniel, *Division Mgr*
Barbara Poston, *Corp Secy*
Blake Ballard, *Engineer*
Dayle Anderson, *Bookkeeper*
▲ EMP: 35
SQ FT: 34,000
SALES (est): 7.7MM **Privately Held**
WEB: www.raycoindustries.com
SIC: 3553 3444 3549 3537 Woodworking machinery; sheet metalwork; metalworking machinery; industrial trucks & tractors

(G-11730)
REBECCA S CERAMICS
7644 Comanche Dr (23225-1144)
PHONE..................................804 560-4477
Stuart Samuel, *Principal*
Donna Burkhardt, *Bookkeeper*
Fran Rudoff, *Exec Dir*
Claire Brassil, *Director*
EMP: 2 EST: 2008
SALES (est): 125.6K **Privately Held**
SIC: 3269 Pottery products

(G-11731)
RECO BIODIESEL LLC
710 Hospital St (23219-1218)
P.O. Box 25069 (23260-5069)
PHONE..................................804 644-2800
Robert Courain, *Sales Mgr*
Dianne Hunt, *Office Mgr*
Bill Shelton, *Manager*
Bob Corien,
Allen C Goolsby,
EMP: 10
SALES (est): 2.2MM **Privately Held**
WEB: www.recobio.com
SIC: 2911 Diesel fuels

(G-11732)
REFILLS INC
Also Called: Cartridge World Downtown
1503 Hanover Ave (23220-3523)
PHONE..................................804 771-5460
EMP: 3 EST: 2007
SALES (est): 190K **Privately Held**
SIC: 3955 Mfg Carbon Paper/Ink Ribbons

(G-11733)
RETARDED MOBILE SOUND & VISION
1505 Oakwood Ave (23223-7763)
PHONE..................................804 437-7633
Leroy Wilson, *Owner*
EMP: 1
SALES (est): 48.8K **Privately Held**
SIC: 3679 Electronic components

(G-11734)
REVOLUTION RISING PRINT
2517 Susten Ln (23224-4545)
PHONE..................................804 276-4789
Sylvia Mallory, *Principal*
EMP: 2 EST: 2017
SALES (est): 83.9K **Privately Held**
SIC: 2752 Commercial printing, lithographic

(G-11735)
REYNOLDS CONSUMER PRODUCTS LLC
Also Called: Reynolds Foil - Richmond Plant
7th & Bainbridge (23219)
P.O. Box 24688 (23224-0688)
PHONE..................................804 230-5200
Dan Devalk, *Sales Mgr*
Doug Mickle, *Advt Staff*
Thomas Degnan, *Manager*

Mary Anne Wince, *Director*
EMP: 440 **Privately Held**
WEB:
www.reynoldsconsumerproducts.com
SIC: 3497 3353 Foil containers for bakery
goods & frozen foods; aluminum sheet,
plate & foil
HQ: Reynolds Consumer Products Llc
1900 W Field Ct
Lake Forest IL 60045

(G-11736)
**RICHMOND PRESSED MET
WORKS INC**
506 Maury St (23224-4120)
PHONE....................804 233-8371
Richard H Westbrook, *President*
Julie Atkins, *General Mgr*
Brenda Broth, *Manager*
EMP: 9 **EST:** 1997
SQ FT: 25,000
SALES (est): 1.5MM
SALES (corp-wide): 1.7MM **Privately
Held**
WEB: www.dwa-inc.com
SIC: 3471 Electroplating of metals or
formed products
PA: Dwa Inc
506 Maury St
Richmond VA

(G-11737)
**RICHMOND SHOPPING CENTER
INC**
210 E Main St (23219-3740)
PHONE....................804 648-9015
Hilton W Goodwyn Jr, *President*
Robert A Goodwyn, *Vice Pres*
Erline H Goodwyn, *Admin Sec*
EMP: 3
SQ FT: 12,236
SALES (est): 145.4K **Privately Held**
WEB: www.richmond.com
SIC: 2711 Newspapers, publishing & print-
ing

(G-11738)
**RICHMOND SUPPLY AND SVC
LLC**
3903 Carolina Ave (23222-2204)
PHONE....................804 622-9435
Salame K Moses,
EMP: 1
SQ FT: 600
SALES (est): 106.6K **Privately Held**
SIC: 3949 Skin diving equipment, scuba
type

(G-11739)
RICHMOND THREAD LAB LLC
2322 Parkwood Ave (23220-5223)
PHONE....................757 344-1886
C H Thompson, *Mng Member*
Christina Hope Thompson, *Mng Member*
EMP: 3 **EST:** 2014
SALES (est): 186K **Privately Held**
WEB: www.richmondthreadlab.com
SIC: 2339 2389 Women's & misses' ac-
cessories; men's miscellaneous acces-
sories

(G-11740)
**RIVER CITY PRINTING
GRAPHICS**
4301 Nine Mile Rd (23223-4920)
PHONE....................804 226-8100
EMP: 2 **EST:** 2014
SALES (est): 159.6K **Privately Held**
SIC: 2752 Commercial printing, offset

(G-11741)
RIVER CITY PUBLISHING INC
11 S 12th St (23219-4053)
PHONE....................804 240-9115
EMP: 1
SALES (est): 57.8K **Privately Held**
SIC: 2741 Miscellaneous publishing

(G-11742)
RIVERSTONE GROUP LLC
800 E Canal St (23219-3956)
PHONE....................804 643-4200
William H Goodwin Jr,
EMP: 300

SALES (est): 8.2MM **Privately Held**
WEB: www.richmond.com
SIC: 2711 Newspapers, publishing & print-
ing

(G-11743)
**RJR PROVISIONS & PACKAGING
LLC**
1706 Floyd Ave Ste C (23220-4626)
PHONE....................804 649-7400
William Kent Ruffin, *Mng Member*
EMP: 4
SALES (est): 250K **Privately Held**
SIC: 2099 Food preparations

(G-11744)
RNI PRINT SERVICES
Also Called: Richman News Paper
300 E Franklin St (23219-2214)
PHONE....................804 649-6670
Tom Silvestri, *Publisher*
Neil Cornish, *Editor*
Symea Fitts, *Editor*
Deborah Jackson, *Editor*
Cheryl Magazine, *Editor*
EMP: 3
SALES (est): 400.9K **Privately Held**
WEB: www.timesdispatch.com
SIC: 2711 Newspapers, publishing & print-
ing

(G-11745)
ROBIN CAGE POTTERY
Also Called: 43rd St Gallery, The
1410 W 43rd St (23225-3333)
PHONE....................804 233-1758
Robin Cage, *Owner*
EMP: 1
SQ FT: 3,000
SALES (est): 96.4K **Privately Held**
WEB: www.43rdstgallery.com
SIC: 3269 5999 5719 Art & ornamental
ware, pottery; art dealers; pottery

(G-11746)
ROCKIN BABY LLC
314 N 32nd St (23223-7514)
PHONE....................866 855-4378
Kathryn Wiley, *Mng Member*
Bob Mooney,
EMP: 8
SQ FT: 2,000
SALES (est): 1.6MM **Privately Held**
WEB: www.rockinbaby.com
SIC: 2369 Girls' & children's outerwear

(G-11747)
ROSWORKS LLC
Also Called: Tests For Higher Standards
2821 Ellwood Ave (23221-3019)
P.O. Box 7417 (23221-0417)
PHONE....................804 282-3111
Adam Balas, *Engineer*
David Mott, *Mng Member*
Stuart Flanagan Ed,
EMP: 5
SQ FT: 2,368
SALES (est): 500K **Privately Held**
WEB: www.rosworks.com
SIC: 2721 4813 Magazines: publishing
only, not printed on site;

(G-11748)
ROXANN ROBINSON DELEGATE
1904 Hull St (23224-3724)
PHONE....................804 308-1534
Roxann Robinson, *Principal*
EMP: 2 **EST:** 2010
SALES (est): 117.6K **Privately Held**
SIC: 3577 Bar code (magnetic ink) printers

(G-11749)
**RUFFIN & PAYNE
INCORPORATED**
4200 Vawter Ave (23222-1426)
P.O. Box 27286 (23261-7286)
PHONE....................804 329-2691
George E Haw III, *CEO*
Joseph M Ruffin Jr, *Ch of Bd*
Julian M Ruffin III, *Exec VP*
EMP: 101 **EST:** 1892
SQ FT: 70,000

SALES (est): 21.7MM **Privately Held**
WEB: www.ruffin-payne.com
SIC: 2431 2439 5033 3444 Millwork;
doors & door parts & trim, wood; staircases, stairs & railings; trusses, wooden
roof; roofing, siding & insulation; sheet
metalwork; lumber: rough, dressed & finished

(G-11750)
RVA COFFEE LLC
1110b E Main St (23219-3545)
PHONE....................804 822-2015
Ian Kelley, *Partner*
EMP: 4 **EST:** 2014
SALES (est): 202.7K **Privately Held**
SIC: 2051 Doughnuts, except frozen

(G-11751)
RVA FIRESTOPPING LLC
408 German School Rd (23225-5940)
PHONE....................804 972-1301
Ruben Lopez, *Principal*
EMP: 2
SALES (est): 148.8K **Privately Held**
WEB: www.rvafirestopping.com
SIC: 1389 Fire fighting, oil & gas field

(G-11752)
RVA MAGAZINE
3512 Floyd Ave (23221-2713)
PHONE....................804 349-5890
Marisa Browne, *Principal*
EMP: 3 **EST:** 2017
SALES (est): 169.7K **Privately Held**
WEB: www.richmondmagazine.com
SIC: 2721 Magazines: publishing only, not
printed on site

(G-11753)
SAUER BRANDS INC (PA)
2000 W Broad St (23220-2006)
PHONE....................804 359-5786
William W Lovette, *CEO*
Ed Rominger, *Exec VP*
Michelle Rader, *Senior VP*
Wayne Puglisi, *Vice Pres*
Ann Farrar, *Project Mgr*
EMP: 8
SALES (est): 111.6MM **Privately Held**
WEB: www.sauerbrands.com
SIC: 2099 2087 Sauces: dry mixes; ex-
tracts, flavoring

(G-11754)
**SE7EN TRNSP LGSTICS
SYSTEMS LL**
5404 Dstr Dr Fl 2 Ste 104 Flr 2 (23225)
PHONE....................804 869-1716
Karen E Maddox,
EMP: 4
SALES (est): 176.5K **Privately Held**
SIC: 3537 Trucks: freight, baggage, etc.:
industrial, except mining

(G-11755)
SECAR AT RICH LLC
6100 Nine Mile Rd (23223-3539)
PHONE....................804 737-0090
EMP: 2 **EST:** 2009
SALES (est): 143.6K **Privately Held**
SIC: 2842 Mfg Polish/Sanitation Goods

(G-11756)
SELECT CLEANING SERVICE
2218 Walcott Pl (23223-4649)
PHONE....................804 397-1176
Eleanor D Scott, *Owner*
EMP: 8
SALES (est): 35K **Privately Held**
SIC: 3443 Fabricated plate work (boiler
shop)

(G-11757)
**SELLERS ADVANTAGE
RICHMOND**
2710 Fendall Ave (23222-3621)
PHONE....................804 338-3800
Sean Craft, *Principal*
EMP: 1 **EST:** 2007
SALES (est): 57.2K **Privately Held**
WEB: www.richmond.com
SIC: 2711 Newspapers, publishing & print-
ing

(G-11758)
SEQL INC
301 Virginia St Unit 1205 (23219-4187)
PHONE....................804 214-5678
Robert De Wolff, *CEO*
EMP: 5
SALES (est): 55.2K **Privately Held**
SIC: 2741

(G-11759)
SHOCKOE DENIM
13 S 15th St Ste A (23219-4264)
PHONE....................804 269-0851
Anthony Lupesco, *Principal*
EMP: 1
SALES (est): 130K **Privately Held**
WEB: www.shockoeatelier.com
SIC: 2211 Denims

(G-11760)
**SILGAN DSPNSING SYSTEMS
HLDNGS (HQ)**
1001 Haxall Point Ste 701 (23219-3942)
PHONE....................804 923-1971
Kevin Clark, *CEO*
EMP: 8
SALES (est): 535.4K **Publicly Held**
WEB: www.silgandispensing.com
SIC: 3586 Measuring & dispensing pumps

(G-11761)
SOFT PLAY
3707 Nine Mile Rd (23223-4813)
PHONE....................804 226-0380
EMP: 3
SALES (est): 150.7K **Privately Held**
SIC: 2448 Pallets, wood

(G-11762)
SOFTCHALK LLC
22 S Auburn Ave (23221-2910)
PHONE....................877 638-2425
Jennifer Montrose, *Corp Comm Staff*
Deihl Susan, *Marketing Staff*
Susan Evans, *Mng Member*
Natalie Saltzberg, *Manager*
Beth Godwin-Jones, *Info Tech Mgr*
EMP: 20
SQ FT: 1,800
SALES (est): 1.7MM **Privately Held**
WEB: www.softchalk.com
SIC: 7372 Educational computer software

(G-11763)
SONOCO PRODUCTS COMPANY
1850 Commerce Rd (23224-7802)
P.O. Box 1155 (23218-1155)
PHONE....................804 233-5411
Jonathan Anderson, *Plant Mgr*
Scott Brown, *Opers-Prdtn-Mfg*
EMP: 97
SALES (corp-wide): 5.3B **Publicly Held**
WEB: www.sonoco.com
SIC: 2631 4953 Paperboard mills; recy-
cling, waste materials
PA: Sonoco Products Company
1 N 2nd St
Hartsville SC 29550
843 383-7000

(G-11764)
**SOUTHERN GRAPHIC SYSTEMS
LLC**
5301 Lewis Rd (23218)
PHONE....................804 226-2490
Dennis Wilcox, *Manager*
EMP: 84
SQ FT: 30,000
SALES (corp-wide): 258.6MM **Privately
Held**
WEB: www.sgsintl.com
SIC: 3555 2754 Printing trades machinery;
commercial printing, gravure
HQ: Southern Graphic Systems, Llc
626 W Main St Ste 500
Louisville KY 40202
502 637-5443

(G-11765)
SOUTHSIDE OIL CO
2200 W Main St (23220-4433)
PHONE....................804 204-1624
EMP: 2
SALES (est): 81.9K **Privately Held**
SIC: 1311 Crude petroleum production

▲ = Import ▼=Export
◆ =Import/Export

(G-11766)
SOUTHSIDE VOICE INC (PA)
Also Called: Voice Newspaper, The
205 E Clay St (23219-1325)
PHONE....................................804 644-9060
Jack Green, *President*
Marlene Jones, *Principal*
EMP: 12
SQ FT: 2,574
SALES (est): 1.1MM **Privately Held**
WEB: www.voicenewspaper.com
SIC: 2711 Newspapers, publishing & printing

(G-11767)
SPECIALITY GROUP LTD
Also Called: Speciality Drapery
1221 Admiral St (23220-1701)
PHONE....................................804 264-3000
Glenn A Lovette, *President*
Edward Dunford, *Vice Pres*
Carey Ferwerda, *Accounting Mgr*
Ned Dunford, *VP Sales*
Omnia Al-Kilany, *Mktg Dir*
EMP: 25
SQ FT: 24,000
SALES (est): 3MM **Privately Held**
WEB: www.specialtydrapery.com
SIC: 2391 5023 Curtains & draperies; window furnishings

(G-11768)
SPECIALTY FINISHES INC
311 Tynick St (23224-3619)
PHONE....................................804 232-5027
Neil Heath, *President*
June Heath, *Admin Sec*
EMP: 11
SQ FT: 6,200
SALES (est): 1.2MM **Privately Held**
SIC: 3471 Anodizing (plating) of metals or formed products; finishing, metals or formed products

(G-11769)
SPHERINGENICS INC
800 E Leigh St Ste 51 (23219-1599)
PHONE....................................770 330-0782
L Franklin Bost, *CEO*
EMP: 4
SALES (est): 285.9K **Privately Held**
SIC: 2836 Biological products, except diagnostic

(G-11770)
SQ LABS LLC
4238 Oakleys Ct Ste D (23223-5971)
PHONE....................................804 938-8123
Parker Conner, *President*
EMP: 1
SALES (est): 74.6K **Privately Held**
SIC: 3651 5099 Household audio & video equipment; video & audio equipment

(G-11771)
SQUARE ONE PRINTING INC
519 N 22nd St (23223-7205)
PHONE....................................904 993-4321
Nicholas Toce, *Principal*
EMP: 1 EST: 2014
SALES (est): 73.4K **Privately Held**
SIC: 2759 7389 Commercial printing;

(G-11772)
ST COVE POINT LLC
1021 E Cary St Fl 1920 (23219-4072)
PHONE....................................713 897-1624
Ayumu Yamazaki, *Principal*
EMP: 14
SALES (est): 569.2K **Privately Held**
SIC: 1311 Coal liquefaction
HQ: Pacific Summit Energy Llc
2010 Main St Ste 1200
Irvine CA 92614
949 777-3200

(G-11773)
STEMCELLLIFE LLC
800 E Leigh St (23219-1551)
PHONE....................................843 410-3067
Ning Zhang, *CEO*
EMP: 2
SALES (est): 202.7K **Privately Held**
WEB: www.stemcelllifellc.com
SIC: 2833 Medicinal chemicals

(G-11774)
STRICKLAND MACHINE COMPANY LLC
2400 Magnolia Ct (23223-2332)
P.O. Box 8826 (23225-0526)
PHONE....................................804 643-7483
Robert Matthew McGee, *President*
Stuart Grattan, *Vice Pres*
◆ EMP: 31
SQ FT: 24,000
SALES (est): 4.7MM **Privately Held**
WEB: www.stricklandmachine.com
SIC: 3599 Machine shop, jobbing & repair

(G-11775)
STYLE LLC
Also Called: Style Weekly Magazine
1313 E Main St Apt 103 (23219-3600)
PHONE....................................757 222-3990
Jim Wark, *President*
Smith Susan D, *Asst Sec*
EMP: 55
SQ FT: 3,000
SALES (est): 2.5MM **Publicly Held**
WEB: www.styleweekly.com
SIC: 2711 Newspapers: publishing only, not printed on site
HQ: Virginian-Pilot Media Companies, Llc
5429 Greenwich Rd
Virginia Beach VA 23462
757 446-9000

(G-11776)
SWEDISH MATCH NORTH AMER LLC (HQ)
1021 E Cary St Ste 1600 (23219-4000)
PHONE....................................804 787-5100
Lars Dahlgren, *President*
Richard Flaherty, *President*
Conny Karlsson, *Chairman*
Joy Everly, *Vice Pres*
Lars Lfman, *Vice Pres*
▲ EMP: 500
SQ FT: 23,000
SALES (est): 561MM
SALES (corp-wide): 1.5B **Privately Held**
WEB: www.swedishmatch.com
SIC: 2131 5199 Chewing tobacco; smoking tobacco; snuff; lighters, cigarette & cigar
PA: Swedish Match Ab
Sveavagen 44
Stockholm 111 3
865 802-00

(G-11777)
SWEET BABY LUXURY HAIR CO LLC
2207 Mandalay Dr Apt C (23224-2652)
PHONE....................................804 904-9227
Takeitha Green,
EMP: 1
SALES (est): 39.6K **Privately Held**
SIC: 3999 Hair & hair-based products

(G-11778)
SWEET CYNTHIAS PIE CO LLC
2814 Hawthorne Ave (23222-3523)
PHONE....................................804 321-8646
Mia Brown, *Mng Member*
EMP: 1 EST: 2007
SALES (est): 61.2K **Privately Held**
SIC: 2051 Cakes, pies & pastries

(G-11779)
SWEETIE PIE DESSERTS
10 E Clay St (23219-1330)
PHONE....................................804 239-6425
Joann Braxton, *Owner*
EMP: 1
SALES (est): 450K **Privately Held**
SIC: 2099 Desserts, ready-to-mix

(G-11780)
TACTICAL NUCLEAR WIZARD LLC
2211 Fairmount Ave (23223-5139)
PHONE....................................804 231-1671
Gary Hartfield,
EMP: 1
SALES (est): 45.3K **Privately Held**
SIC: 2741

(G-11781)
TALLEY SIGN COMPANY
1908 Chamberlayne Ave (23222-4812)
P.O. Box 27386 (23261-7386)
PHONE....................................804 649-0325
Mike Salmon, *President*
Edward C Doyle, *President*
John Yarrington, *Managing Prtnr*
Burt Jarvis, *Vice Pres*
Michael Dudley, *Sales Mgr*
EMP: 18 EST: 1933
SQ FT: 22,000
SALES (est): 2.5MM **Privately Held**
WEB: www.talleysign.com
SIC: 3993 1799 7359 Electric signs; sign installation & maintenance; sign rental

(G-11782)
TARGET COMMUNICATIONS INC
Also Called: Richmond Magazine
2201 W Broad St Ste 105 (23220-2022)
PHONE....................................804 355-0111
Richard Malkman, *President*
EMP: 23
SALES (est): 3.4MM **Privately Held**
WEB: www.richmondmagazine.com
SIC: 2721 2741 Magazines: publishing only, not printed on site; miscellaneous publishing

(G-11783)
TASTE OF CARRIBEAN
3911 W Chatham Dr (23222-1205)
PHONE....................................804 321-2411
Ernest Nixon Jr, *Owner*
EMP: 1
SALES (est): 51.6K **Privately Held**
SIC: 2035 Pickles, sauces & salad dressings

(G-11784)
TASTE OF LOVE LLC
1808 Rose Ave (23222-4929)
PHONE....................................804 714-4991
Floyd Young,
EMP: 2
SALES (est): 90.4K **Privately Held**
SIC: 2599 Food wagons, restaurant

(G-11785)
TEAM EXCEL INC
1717 E Cary St (23223-6935)
PHONE....................................804 677-3694
Johnathan Mayo, *CEO*
EMP: 1
SALES (est): 32.7K **Privately Held**
SIC: 7372 Prepackaged software

(G-11786)
TEKTONICS DESIGN GROUP LLC (PA)
702 E 4th St (23224-5534)
PHONE....................................804 233-5900
Christopher Hildebrand,
Hinmapon Hisler,
EMP: 5
SALES (est): 784.5K **Privately Held**
WEB: www.tektonics.com
SIC: 3549 7389 Wiredrawing & fabricating machinery & equipment, ex. die; design services

(G-11787)
TEMPERPACK TECHNOLOGIES INC
4447 Carolina Ave (23222-1416)
PHONE....................................434 218-2436
James McGoff, *President*
Ronald Batula, *Safety Mgr*
Zack Haefling, *Production*
Brendon Kargl, *Engineer*
Brian Powers, *CFO*
EMP: 90 EST: 2015
SQ FT: 44,000
SALES (est): 15MM **Privately Held**
WEB: www.temperpack.com
SIC: 2631 Container, packaging & boxboard

(G-11788)
THREADCOUNT LLC
209 E Broad St (23219-1960)
PHONE....................................703 929-7033
EMP: 2 EST: 2017
SALES (est): 125.5K **Privately Held**
WEB: www.threadcountshirts.com
SIC: 2759 Screen printing

(G-11789)
TORO-AIRE INC
Also Called: Washington Post
1001 E Main St Ste 203 (23219-3536)
PHONE....................................804 649-7575
Sue Nostfinger, *Manager*
EMP: 1
SALES (corp-wide): 16.3MM **Privately Held**
WEB: www.toroaire.com
SIC: 2711 Newspapers
PA: Toro-Aire, Inc.
434 E Broadway
Long Beach CA 90802
424 672-4000

(G-11790)
TORTILLERIA GUAVALUEANA
3337 Broad Rock Blvd (23224-6095)
PHONE....................................804 233-4141
EMP: 3
SALES (est): 170.9K **Privately Held**
SIC: 2099 Tortillas, fresh or refrigerated

(G-11791)
TRAK HOUSE LLC
3515 Delaware Ave (23222-2914)
PHONE....................................646 617-4418
Von Seymour,
EMP: 2
SALES (est): 85.4K **Privately Held**
SIC: 2396 5699 Fabric printing & stamping; T-shirts, custom printed

(G-11792)
TRANSFORMATION WELLNESS LLC
1801 Moore St (23220-1616)
PHONE....................................804 366-4632
Tiffani Howard, *Mng Member*
EMP: 1
SALES (est): 100K **Privately Held**
SIC: 2033 Fruit juices: packaged in cans, jars, etc.

(G-11793)
TREE NATURALS INC
4204 Riding Place Rd (23223-4952)
PHONE....................................804 514-4423
Latresha Sayles, *CEO*
EMP: 2
SALES (est): 132.8K **Privately Held**
WEB: www.treenaturals.com
SIC: 2844 Toilet preparations

(G-11794)
TREXLO ENTERPRISES LLC
Also Called: Fastsigns
532 E Main St (23219-2408)
PHONE....................................804 644-7446
Susie Meador, *Manager*
EMP: 1
SALES (corp-wide): 2.9MM **Privately Held**
WEB: www.fastsigns.com
SIC: 3993 Signs & advertising specialties
PA: Trexlo Enterprises, Llc
2361a Greystone Ct Ste A
Rockville VA 23146
804 719-5900

(G-11795)
TRIPLE Y PREMIUM YOGURT
3713 Mill Meadow Dr (23221)
PHONE....................................804 212-5413
Faith A Kaplan, *Owner*
EMP: 5
SALES (est): 139K **Privately Held**
SIC: 2053 Frozen bakery products, except bread

(G-11796)
TWELVE INC
5420 Distributor Dr (23225-6106)
PHONE....................................804 232-1300
Michael Moss, *Branch Mgr*
EMP: 1
SALES (corp-wide): 668K **Privately Held**
WEB: www.1212roof.com
SIC: 3993 Electric signs

PA: Twelve, Inc
5331 Distributor Dr
Richmond VA 23225
804 232-1300

(G-11797)
TWELVE INC (PA)
5331 Distributor Dr (23225-6103)
PHONE..............................804 232-1300
Michael Moss, *President*
EMP: 6
SALES (est): 668K Privately Held
WEB: www.1212roof.com
SIC: 2759 Commercial printing

(G-11798)
TWO RIVERS INSTALLATION CO
3414 Monu Ave Unit 103 (23221)
PHONE..............................804 366-6869
EMP: 4
SALES: 15K Privately Held
SIC: 2591 Mfg Drapery Hardware/Blinds

(G-11799)
UNIVERSAL POWERS INC
Also Called: Up
1009 Holly Spring Ave (23224-5040)
PHONE..............................404 997-8732
Drae Journee Watkins, *CEO*
Mohammad Qadirullah, *COO*
Zanthea Demetrius, *Administration*
Fetigue Gbane,
John Watkins,
EMP: 7
SALES (est): 100K
SALES (corp-wide): 1.8MM Privately
Held
WEB: www.upowers.net
SIC: 3699 4931 4911 Electrical equip-
ment & supplies; electric & other ser-
vices combined;
PA: Mfl Group Inc.
1009 Holly Spring Ave
Richmond VA 23224
404 997-3723

(G-11800)
UNIVERSITY OF RICHMOND
Also Called: Collegian, The
421 Westhampton Way (23173-0006)
PHONE..............................804 289-8000
EMP: 2
SALES (est): 65K Privately Held
WEB: www.thecollegianur.com
SIC: 2711 Newspapers, publishing & print-
ing

(G-11801)
UPTOWN NEON
Also Called: Uptown Eon V
2629 W Cary St (23220-5118)
PHONE..............................804 358-6243
Deborah Solyan, *Owner*
EMP: 2
SQ FT: 2,316
SALES (est): 195.4K Privately Held
SIC: 3993 Signs & advertising specialties

(G-11802)
UTZ QUALITY FOODS LLC
5619 Pride Rd (23224-1020)
PHONE..............................804 232-0241
Ken Dehnel, *Regl Sales Mgr*
Ken Dahnel, *Manager*
EMP: 30
SALES (corp-wide): 845MM Privately
Held
WEB: www.utzsnacks.com
SIC: 2096 Potato chips & similar snacks
PA: Utz Quality Foods, Llc
900 High St
Hanover PA 17331
800 367-7629

(G-11803)
VA PROPERTIES INC
919 E Main St (23219-4625)
PHONE..............................804 237-1455
Breen James P, *President*
EMP: 1 EST: 2010
SALES (est): 47.6K Privately Held
SIC: 2741 Miscellaneous publishing

(G-11804)
VA WRITERS CLUB
Also Called: Verbatim Editing
1011 E Main St Ste LI90 (23219-3526)
PHONE..............................804 648-0357
C Finley Jr, *Exec Dir*
Charlie Filney Jr, *Exec Dir*
EMP: 3 EST: 1993
SALES (est): 88.6K Privately Held
SIC: 2621 Writing paper

(G-11805)
VAN JESTER WOODWORKS
1600 Valley Rd (23222-5409)
PHONE..............................804 562-6360
Zachary Jester, *Principal*
EMP: 2 EST: 2016
SALES (est): 93.8K Privately Held
WEB: www.vanjesterwoodworks.com
SIC: 2431 Millwork

(G-11806)
VIKING FABRICATION SERVICES
Also Called: Viking Supplynet
4593 Carolina Ave (23222-1418)
PHONE..............................804 228-1333
Justin Ellis, *Branch Mgr*
EMP: 7
SALES (corp-wide): 177.9K Privately
Held
WEB: www.vikinggroupinc.com
SIC: 3499 Fire- or burglary-resistive prod-
ucts
HQ: Viking Fabrication Services Llc
210 Industrial Park Dr
Hastings MI 49058

(G-11807)
VIRGINIA AMERICAN INDS INC (PA)
710 Hospital St (23219-1218)
P.O. Box 25328 (23260-5328)
PHONE..............................804 644-2611
Robert C Courain Jr, *Ch of Bd*
R Kenneth Heskett, *President*
Les Dixon, *Vice Pres*
John Moss, *Vice Pres*
Johnny Moss, *VP Sales*
EMP: 175
SQ FT: 12,000
SALES (est): 24.9MM Privately Held
WEB: www.recoconstructors.com
SIC: 3443 3479 1799 Industrial vessels,
tanks & containers; hot dip coating of
metals or formed products; galvanizing of
iron, steel or end-formed products; decon-
tamination services

(G-11808)
VIRGINIA BUS PUBLICATIONS LLC
1207 E Main St Ste 100 (23219-3663)
PHONE..............................804 225-9262
Bernard A Niemeier, *Principal*
Robert Powell, *Editor*
Kevin L Dick, *Prdtn Mgr*
EMP: 8
SALES (est): 709.9K Privately Held
WEB: www.virginiabusiness.com
SIC: 2741 Miscellaneous publishing

(G-11809)
VIRGINIA BUSINESS MAGAZINE
333 E Franklin St (23219-2213)
PHONE..............................804 649-6999
EMP: 2 EST: 2019
SALES (est): 102.4K Privately Held
WEB: www.va-business.com
SIC: 2721 Magazines: publishing only, not
printed on site

(G-11810)
VIRGINIA CABINETRY LLC
1221 School St (23220-1712)
P.O. Box 35225, North Chesterfield
(23235-0225)
PHONE..............................804 612-6469
Nijaz Cirkic,
EMP: 4 EST: 2008
SALES (est): 373.3K Privately Held
WEB: www.virginiacabinetry.com
SIC: 2434 Wood kitchen cabinets

(G-11811)
VIRGINIA CONTROLS INC
2513 Mechanicsville Tpke (23223-2329)
PHONE..............................804 225-5530
Fred Kaull Landon Jr, *President*
Jerry Krajnock, *Mfg Mgr*
Tom Reamsnyder, *Engrg Dir*
David Jordan, *Engineer*
Adam Silvernail, *Engineer*
EMP: 25
SQ FT: 10,000
SALES (est): 4.7MM Privately Held
WEB: www.vacontrols.com
SIC: 3679 3613 Electronic circuits;
switchgear & switchboard apparatus

(G-11812)
VIRGINIA CPTOL CONNECTIONS INC
1001 E Broad St Ste 215 (23219-1928)
PHONE..............................804 643-5554
David L Bailey, *President*
Brad Veach, *Principal*
David Bailey, *Manager*
Wanda Judd, *Exec Dir*
EMP: 2
SALES (est): 64.8K Privately Held
WEB: www.capitol-connections.com
SIC: 2741 Miscellaneous publishing

(G-11813)
VIRGINIA PREMIERE PAINT CONTR
501 E Franklin St (23219-2322)
PHONE..............................804 398-1177
EMP: 3
SALES: 4K Privately Held
SIC: 2851 8249 Paints And Allied Prod-
ucts, Nec

(G-11814)
VIRGINN-PLOT MDIA CMPANIES LLC
24 E 3rd St (23224-4246)
PHONE..............................804 358-0825
Scott Elmquist, *Editor*
Lori Waran, *Adv Dir*
EMP: 3 Publicly Held
WEB: www.styleweekly.com
SIC: 2711 Newspapers, publishing & print-
ing
HQ: Virginian-Pilot Media Companies, Llc
5429 Greenwich Rd
Virginia Beach VA 23462
757 446-9000

(G-11815)
VOYAGER SOFTWARE INC
3908 Wythe Ave (23221-1145)
PHONE..............................919 802-3232
Melody Cutler, *Principal*
EMP: 2
SALES (est): 102.8K Privately Held
SIC: 7372 Business oriented computer
software

(G-11816)
VULCAN CONSTRUCTION MTLS LLC
2800 N Hopkins Rd (23224-6602)
PHONE..............................804 233-9669
Gene Sauvager, *Manager*
EMP: 2 Publicly Held
WEB: www.vulcanmaterials.com
SIC: 3273 Ready-mixed concrete
HQ: Vulcan Construction Materials, Llc
1200 Urban Center Dr
Vestavia AL 35242
205 298-3000

(G-11817)
WADE F ANDERSON
204 N Hamilton St Ste A (23221-2662)
PHONE..............................804 358-8204
Wade F Anderson, *Principal*
EMP: 2 EST: 2011
SALES (est): 175.5K Privately Held
SIC: 3843 Enamels, dentists'

(G-11818)
WARREN VENTURES LLC
6822 Old Jahnke Rd (23225-4123)
PHONE..............................804 267-9098
James Warren, *CEO*
EMP: 1 EST: 2014

SALES (est): 60.5K Privately Held
SIC: 2741

(G-11819)
WCBD-TV (NBC 2)
333 E Franklin St (23219-2213)
PHONE..............................804 649-6000
Sam Barclay, *Principal*
EMP: 1
SALES (est): 44.7K Privately Held
SIC: 3999

(G-11820)
WEIL GROUP RESOURCES LLC (PA)
416 W Franklin St (23220-4906)
PHONE..............................804 643-2828
Jeffrey Vogt, *CEO*
Lewis May, *Vice Pres*
Scott Cardozo, *CFO*
Nitin Manawat, *Director*
Katherine Sellery, *Director*
EMP: 5 EST: 2011
SALES (est): 2.7MM Privately Held
WEB: www.weil-group.com
SIC: 1382 Oil & gas exploration services

(G-11821)
WELLBORN + WRIGHT
3801 Carolina Ave (23222-2203)
P.O. Box 27606 (23261-7606)
PHONE..............................804 329-0079
William Morgan, *Design Engr*
Leah Sickinger, *Controller*
Jennifer Temple, *Assistant*
EMP: 1
SALES (est): 181.7K Privately Held
WEB: www.wellbornwright.com
SIC: 2431 Millwork

(G-11822)
WENDELL WELDER LLC
2009 Westover Hills Blvd (23225-3121)
PHONE..............................804 935-6856
Wendell Fine Welder, *Administration*
EMP: 1
SALES (est): 40.4K Privately Held
SIC: 7692 Welding repair

(G-11823)
WEST 30 CANDLES
200 W 30th St (23225-3718)
PHONE..............................804 874-2461
EMP: 1
SALES (est): 39.6K Privately Held
SIC: 3999 Candles

(G-11824)
WESTROCK COMMERCIAL LLC (DH)
501 S 5th St (23219-0501)
PHONE..............................804 444-1000
Steve Voorhees, *CEO*
EMP: 48
SALES (est): 23.4MM
SALES (corp-wide): 17.5B Publicly Held
WEB: www.westrock.com
SIC: 2752 5112 Commercial printing, litho-
graphic; stationery & office supplies
HQ: Wrkco Inc.
1000 Abernathy Rd Ste 12
Atlanta GA 30328
770 448-2193

(G-11825)
WESTROCK MWV LLC (DH)
501 S 5th St (23219-0501)
PHONE..............................804 444-1000
John A Luke Jr, *President*
Robert Beckler, *President*
Ted Lithgow, *President*
Robert A Feeser, *Exec VP*
Raymond W Lane, *Exec VP*
◆ EMP: 741
SALES (est): 4.4B
SALES (corp-wide): 17.5B Publicly Held
WEB: www.westrock.com
SIC: 2671 2678 2677 2861 Packaging
paper & plastics film, coated & laminated;
plastic film, coated or laminated for pack-
aging; stationery products; envelopes;
gum & wood chemicals; pulp mills; liner-
board

HQ: Wrkco Inc.
1000 Abernathy Rd Ste 12
Atlanta GA 30328
770 448-2193

(G-11826)
WESTROCK RKT LLC
Also Called: Westrock Invoice Processing
501 S 5th St (23219-0501)
P.O. Box 100084, Duluth GA (30096-9373)
PHONE....................................804 444-6431
EMP: 161
SALES (corp-wide): 17.5B Publicly Held
WEB: www.westrock.com
SIC: 2653 Partitions, solid fiber: made from
purchased materials
HQ: Westrock Rkt, Llc
1000 Abernathy Rd Ste 125
Atlanta GA 30328
770 448-2193

(G-11827)
**WESTROCK VIRGINIA
CORPORATION**
501 S 5th St (23219-0501)
PHONE....................................804 444-1000
Jim Hutchison, General Mgr
Heidi Graf, Superintendent
Seth Harrison, Business Mgr
Ben Humphrey, Business Mgr
L Mark Lukacs, Senior VP
◆ EMP: 12
SALES (est): 317.5K
SALES (corp-wide): 17.5B Publicly Held
WEB: www.westrock.com
SIC: 2631 Linerboard
HQ: Westrock Mwv, Llc
501 S 5th St
Richmond VA 23219
804 444-1000

(G-11828)
WHISK
2100 E Main St (23223-7051)
PHONE....................................804 728-1576
Morgan Botwinick, Principal
EMP: 7 EST: 2015
SALES (est): 339K Privately Held
WEB: www.whiskrva.com
SIC: 2051 Cakes, bakery: except frozen

(G-11829)
WHITEHALL ROBINS
1405 Cummings Dr (23220-1101)
PHONE....................................804 257-2000
Joseph Ullery, Principal
EMP: 6
SALES (est): 603.3K Privately Held
SIC: 2834 Pharmaceutical preparations

(G-11830)
WHY CANDLE & CO LLC
423 N 18th St Apt 303 (23223-6387)
PHONE....................................804 876-2240
Justin Sellers,
EMP: 2
SALES (est): 10K Privately Held
SIC: 3999 Candles

(G-11831)
WILLIAMS MACHINE CO INC
1901 Hull St (23224-3723)
PHONE....................................804 231-3892
William O Williams Sr, President
Richard Vaden, Vice Pres
William O Williams Jr, Treasurer
EMP: 7 EST: 1981
SQ FT: 15,000
SALES (est): 1MM Privately Held
WEB: www.williams-machine.com
SIC: 3599 Machine shop, jobbing & repair

(G-11832)
WOOD TELEVISION LLC
111 N 4th St (23219-2201)
PHONE....................................804 775-4600
Dan Ryan, Vice Pres
James Zimmerman, Manager
EMP: 35
SALES (corp-wide): 3B Publicly Held
WEB: www.woodtv.com
SIC: 2711 4833 4841 Newspapers, pub-
lishing & printing; television broadcasting
stations; cable & other pay television
services

HQ: Wood Television Llc
120 College Ave Se
Grand Rapids MI 49503
616 456-8888

(G-11833)
WOOD TELEVISION LLC
Also Called: Richmond Newspapers
333 E Grace St (23219-1717)
P.O. Box 85333 (23293-5333)
PHONE....................................804 649-6069
Lee Graves, Principal
Raymond McDowell, Manager
Greg Neal, Manager
EMP: 74
SALES (corp-wide): 3B Publicly Held
WEB: www.woodtv.com
SIC: 2721 Magazines: publishing & printing
HQ: Wood Television Llc
120 College Ave Se
Grand Rapids MI 49503
616 456-8888

(G-11834)
WWT GROUP INC
206 E Cary St (23219-3737)
PHONE....................................804 648-1900
Peter Wong, President
▲ EMP: 6
SQ FT: 7,000
SALES (est): 630K Privately Held
WEB: www.wwtgroup.com
SIC: 3634 Razors, electric

(G-11835)
WYTHKEN LLC
Also Called: Wythken Printing
900 W Leigh St (23220-3138)
PHONE....................................804 353-8282
Ric Withers,
Charles Aiken,
EMP: 5
SQ FT: 2,000
SALES (est): 919.1K Privately Held
WEB: www.wythken.com
SIC: 2752 Commercial printing, offset

(G-11836)
XP MANUFACTURING LLC
1730 Rhoadmiller St (23220-1109)
PHONE....................................804 510-3747
J O'Brien, Principal
EMP: 1
SALES (est): 50.5K Privately Held
SIC: 3999 Manufacturing industries

(G-11837)
YACOE LLC
606 W 28th St (23225-3502)
PHONE....................................973 735-3095
Morgan Yacoe,
EMP: 1
SALES (est): 78.1K Privately Held
SIC: 3842 Models, anatomical

Ridgeway
Henry County

(G-11838)
**ABSOLUTE MACHINE
ENTERPRISES**
212 Pulaski Rd (24148-4978)
PHONE....................................276 956-1171
Mike Harris, President
EMP: 15
SQ FT: 96,000
SALES (est): 1.9MM Privately Held
SIC: 3599 3441 Machine shop, jobbing &
repair; fabricated structural metal

(G-11839)
BI STATE COIL WINDING INC
2214 Phosphorous St (24148)
P.O. Box 317 (24148-0317)
PHONE....................................276 956-3106
James Hilton, President
Charles Beard, Vice Pres
James Moran, Vice Pres
EMP: 4
SQ FT: 2,500
SALES (est): 376.4K Privately Held
SIC: 7694 Electric motor repair

(G-11840)
**CHESAPEAKE CUSTOM CHEM
CORP**
126 Reservoir Rd (24148)
P.O. Box 615 (24148-0615)
PHONE....................................276 956-3145
James Allen French, President
Eldon Thigpen, Vice Pres
EMP: 5
SALES (est): 12MM Privately Held
WEB: www.chesapeakechemical.com
SIC: 2911 2869 Diesel fuels; industrial or-
ganic chemicals

(G-11841)
DRAKE EXTRUSION INC
Also Called: Duron
790 Industrial Park Rd (24148-4449)
P.O. Box 4868, Martinsville (24115-4868)
PHONE....................................276 632-0159
John Parkinson, CEO
G B Schofield, Vice Pres
Jacoby Stanley, Purch Agent
Paula Hoffman, Accounts Mgr
Bobby Hylton, Manager
◆ EMP: 220
SQ FT: 200,000
SALES (est): 52.7MM
SALES (corp-wide): 8MM Privately Held
WEB: www.drakeextrusion.com
SIC: 2281 Polypropylene yarn, spun: made
from purchased staple
PA: International Fibres Group (Holdings)
Limited
Old Mills
Bradford BD11
113 285-9020

(G-11842)
EVERYTHING UNDER SUN LLC
79 New Jerusalem Rd (24148-3652)
PHONE....................................276 252-2376
Herman L Estes Jr, Mng Member
Kia James,
EMP: 5 EST: 2011
SALES (est): 153.8K Privately Held
SIC: 2099 5149 5499 Food preparations;
organic & diet foods; health foods

(G-11843)
GEORGIA-PACIFIC LLC
25 Industrial Park Rd (24148-4440)
P.O. Box 712 (24148-0712)
PHONE....................................276 632-6301
Rod Anderson, Manager
EMP: 200
SALES (corp-wide): 38.9B Privately Held
WEB: www.gp.com
SIC: 2653 Boxes, corrugated: made from
purchased materials
HQ: Georgia-Pacific Llc
133 Peachtree St Nw
Atlanta GA 30303
404 652-4000

(G-11844)
GRACELAND OF MARTINSVILLE
5950 Greensboro Rd (24148-4903)
PHONE....................................434 250-0050
Jennifer Lakey, Principal
EMP: 2
SALES (est): 148.9K Privately Held
SIC: 3448 Buildings, portable: prefabri-
cated metal

(G-11845)
HOMEPLACE DISTILLERY LLC
10 Fall Creek Rd (24148-3190)
PHONE....................................276 957-3310
David Michael Hundley, Principal
EMP: 4
SALES (est): 220.7K Privately Held
SIC: 2085 Distilled & blended liquors

(G-11846)
L PETERS CUSTOM CABINETS
107 Wind Dancer Ln (24148-4467)
PHONE....................................276 340-9580
EMP: 2
SALES (est): 137.6K Privately Held
SIC: 2434 Wood kitchen cabinets

(G-11847)
PACE CUSTOM SAWING LLC
425 Blackfeather Trl (24148-3154)
PHONE....................................276 956-2000
Robert B Pace, Administration
EMP: 9
SQ FT: 1,200
SALES (est): 1MM Privately Held
WEB: www.timberretriever.wordpress.com
SIC: 2421 Sawmills & planing mills, gen-
eral

(G-11848)
PGF ENTERPRISES LLC
Also Called: Humidity Busters Henry Co
457 Mulberry Rd (24148-3129)
PHONE....................................276 956-4308
Joe Terry, Vice Pres
EMP: 3
SALES (est): 224K Privately Held
SIC: 3822 Auto controls regulating residntl
& coml environmt & applncs

(G-11849)
PULLIAM FURNITURE CO
1114 Mica Rd (24148-3512)
PHONE....................................276 956-3615
EMP: 2
SALES (est): 150K Privately Held
SIC: 2511 Mfg Wood Household Furniture

(G-11850)
QLIFTS LLC
Also Called: Quality Lifts & Accessibility
1317 Eggleston Falls Rd (24148-4320)
PHONE....................................276 632-0058
Kevin Nelson, Mng Member
EMP: 1
SQ FT: 20,000
SALES (est): 500K Privately Held
WEB: www.qlifts.com
SIC: 3999 5999 Wheelchair lifts; wheel-
chair lifts

(G-11851)
RICHARD E SHEPPARD JR
Also Called: Sheppard Furniture Co
991 Mica Rd (24148-3508)
PHONE....................................276 956-2322
Richard E Sheppard Jr, Owner
EMP: 10
SQ FT: 11,500
SALES (est): 550K Privately Held
SIC: 2511 Wood household furniture

(G-11852)
ROBERT D GREGORY
235 Wind Dancer Ln (24148-4340)
PHONE....................................276 632-9170
Robert D Gregory, Principal
EMP: 1 EST: 2010
SALES (est): 68.2K Privately Held
SIC: 3443 Fabricated plate work (boiler
shop)

(G-11853)
**SMART MACHINE
TECHNOLOGIES INC**
Also Called: Fmt Food and Beverage Sys-
tems
650 Frith Dr (24148-4652)
P.O. Box 4828, Martinsville (24115-4828)
PHONE....................................276 632-9853
Mark Gibb, President
Richard Gibb, Chairman
Duane Doerle, Vice Pres
Kim Wehrenberg, Vice Pres
Joann Byrd, Purch Agent
▲ EMP: 65
SQ FT: 85,000
SALES (est): 16.2MM Privately Held
WEB: www.smartmachine.com
SIC: 3556 3552 5084 3469 Food prod-
ucts machinery; textile machinery; food
product manufacturing machinery; metal
stampings; belt conveyor systems, gen-
eral industrial use

(G-11854)
SMITH FABRICATION WELDIN
779 Wright Rd (24148-3975)
PHONE....................................276 734-5269
EMP: 1
SALES (est): 48.1K Privately Held
SIC: 7692 Welding repair

G E O G R A P H I C

(G-11855)
STARSPRINGS USA INC
250 Fontaine Dr (24148-3371)
PHONE................................276 403-4500
Johan Dalin, *President*
Jason Farmer, *Production*
Anette Lundblad, *Sales Staff*
Jessica Dunkley, *Manager*
Michal Janas, *Manager*
EMP: 68
SALES (est): 2.2MM **Privately Held**
WEB: www.starsprings.com
SIC: 2514 3493 Frames for box springs or
bedsprings: metal; automobile springs

(G-11856)
VIRGINIA GLASS PRODUCTS CORP
347 Old Sand Rd (24148-4980)
P.O. Box 5431, Martinsville (24115-5431)
PHONE................................276 956-3131
John D Korff, *President*
Wc Beeler Jr, *Chairman*
Benjamin D Beeler, *Exec VP*
L W Deal II, *Vice Pres*
Lw Deal, *Vice Pres*
▼ EMP: 160 EST: 1956
SQ FT: 110,000
SALES (est): 15.8MM
SALES (corp-wide): 27.3MM **Privately Held**
WEB: www.va-glass.com
SIC: 3211 3231 Tempered glass; products
of purchased glass
PA: Virginia Mirror Company, Incorporated
300 Moss St S
Martinsville VA 24112
276 956-3131

(G-11857)
WEST WINDOW CORPORATION
226 Industrial Pk Dr (24148)
P.O. Box 3071, Martinsville (24115-3071)
PHONE................................276 638-2394
Donald R Hodges, *CEO*
William E Giesler, *Chairman*
David Byrd, *Vice Pres*
Davis Orville L, *Vice Pres*
Tracy Lester, *Treasurer*
EMP: 90 EST: 1945
SQ FT: 145,000
SALES (est): 16.3MM **Privately Held**
WEB: www.westwindow.com
SIC: 3089 Windows, plastic

(G-11858)
WESTROCK CONVERTING LLC
Also Called: Alliance Display & Packaging
500 Frith Dr Bldg A (24148-4564)
PHONE................................276 632-7175
Ed Dimmette, *Manager*
EMP: 60
SALES (corp-wide): 17.5B **Publicly Held**
WEB: www.westrock.com
SIC: 2631 2653 Folding boxboard; boxes,
corrugated: made from purchased materi-
als; partitions, solid fiber: made from pur-
chased materials
HQ: Westrock Converting, Llc
1000 Abernathy Rd Ste 125
Atlanta GA 30328
770 448-2193

(G-11859)
WESTROCK CP LLC
Also Called: Smurfit-Stone Container
588 Industrial Park Rd (24148-4857)
PHONE................................276 632-0698
EMP: 2
SALES (corp-wide): 17.5B **Publicly Held**
WEB: www.westrock.com
SIC: 2653 Boxes, corrugated: made from
purchased materials
HQ: Westrock Cp, Llc
1000 Abernathy Rd Ste 125
Atlanta GA 30328

Riner
Montgomery County

(G-11860)
ANGEL WINGS DRONE SERVICES LLC
703 Mount Elbert Rd Nw (24149-3614)
PHONE................................540 763-2630
Jonathan Spence, *Principal*
EMP: 2 EST: 2016
SALES (est): 139.6K **Privately Held**
WEB: www.flywithangelwings.com
SIC: 3721 Motorized aircraft

(G-11861)
BRIAN K BABCOCK
Also Called: Strange Coffee Company
3203 Pilot Rd (24149-3315)
PHONE................................540 251-3003
Brian Babcock, *Owner*
EMP: 1
SALES (est): 77.8K **Privately Held**
WEB: www.strangecoffeecompany.bigcar-
tel.com
SIC: 2095 7389 Coffee roasting (except by
wholesale grocers); business services

(G-11862)
ELLIOTT MANDOLINS SHOP
774 Sowers Mill Dam Rd Ne (24149-3649)
PHONE................................540 763-2327
Ward Elliot, *Owner*
EMP: 2
SALES (est): 93.2K **Privately Held**
SIC: 3931 Musical instruments

(G-11863)
HIGHLAND ENVIRONMENTAL INC
3702 Nolley Rd (24149-2623)
PHONE................................540 392-6067
Jennifer Miller-Mcclellan, *President*
EMP: 2
SALES (est): 203.9K **Privately Held**
SIC: 3822 Auto controls regulating residntl
& coml environmt & applncs

(G-11864)
MENT SOFTWARE INC
4981 Sidney Church Rd (24149-1725)
PHONE................................540 382-4172
EMP: 2
SALES (est): 124K **Privately Held**
SIC: 7372 Prepackaged Software Services

(G-11865)
POPLAR MANOR ENTERPRISES LLC
Also Called: PME Compost
190 Poplar Manor Ln Nw (24149-3707)
PHONE................................540 763-9542
Willard Farley Jr,
EMP: 3
SALES (est): 10K **Privately Held**
WEB: www.poplarmanorenterprises.com
SIC: 2875 Fertilizers, mixing only

(G-11866)
WHITE OAK GROVE WOODWORKS
995 White Oak Grove Rd Ne (24149-3637)
PHONE................................540 763-2723
Kenneth Ray Sowers, *Owner*
Kathleen Moran, *Bookkeeper*
EMP: 2
SQ FT: 3,000
SALES (est): 110K **Privately Held**
SIC: 2431 2421 Millwork; kiln drying of
lumber

Ringgold
Pittsylvania County

(G-11867)
GLENN R WILLIAMS
Also Called: Glenn R Wllams Athrzed
Frnchse
2206 Hillside Rd (24586-4022)
PHONE................................434 251-9383
Glenn R Williams, *Owner*

EMP: 1
SALES (est): 25K **Privately Held**
SIC: 3545 Machine tool accessories

(G-11868)
IKEA INDUSTRY DANVILLE LLC
100 Ikea Dr (24586-1101)
P.O. Box 498, Danville (24543-0498)
PHONE................................434 822-6080
Bengt Danielsson, *Mng Member*
◆ EMP: 275
SQ FT: 940,000
SALES (est): 61MM
SALES (corp-wide): 242.1K **Privately
Held**
WEB: www.about.ikea.com
SIC: 2511 Wood household furniture
HQ: Inter Ikea Holding B.V.
Olof Palmestraat 1
Delft 2616
152 150-750

(G-11869)
L B DAVIS INC
669 Little Creek Rd (24586-3139)
PHONE................................434 792-3281
Laura Davis, *President*
EMP: 3
SQ FT: 1,500
SALES (est): 180K **Privately Held**
SIC: 2752 Commercial printing, litho-
graphic

(G-11870)
MORGAN OLSON LLC
100 Ikea Dr (24586-1101)
PHONE................................269 659-0200
EMP: 2
SALES (corp-wide): 1.2B **Privately Held**
WEB: www.morganolson.com
SIC: 3713 Truck bodies (motor vehicles)
HQ: Morgan Olson, Llc
1801 S Nottawa St
Sturgis MI 49091
269 659-0200

(G-11871)
OWENS-BROCKWAY GLASS CONT INC
29 Glassblower Ln (24586-4502)
PHONE................................434 799-5880
Bob Lachmiller, *Branch Mgr*
EMP: 250 **Publicly Held**
WEB: www.o-i.com
SIC: 3221 Glass containers
HQ: Owens-Brockway Glass Container Inc.
1 Michael Owens Way
Perrysburg OH 43551

(G-11872)
PANACEUTICS NUTRITION INC
2311 Cane Creek Pkwy (24586-3913)
P.O. Box 110263, Durham NC (27709-
5263)
PHONE................................919 797-9623
Adam Monroe, *CEO*
EMP: 11
SALES (est): 773.4K **Privately Held**
WEB: www.panaceutics.com
SIC: 2834 Pharmaceutical preparations

(G-11873)
PAW PRINT PET SERVICES
575 Chaneys Store Rd (24586-2609)
PHONE................................434 822-5020
Randy Sinclair, *Principal*
EMP: 1 EST: 2011
SALES (est): 114.7K **Privately Held**
SIC: 2752 Commercial printing, litho-
graphic

(G-11874)
STEVENS & SONS LUMBER CO
58 Intersection Rr 726 (24586)
P.O. Box 142 (24586-0142)
PHONE................................434 822-7105
Mark Steven, *President*
Nancy Steven, *Admin Sec*
EMP: 18
SALES (est): 500K **Privately Held**
SIC: 2421 Lumber: rough, sawed or planed

(G-11875)
UNISON TUBE LLC
500 Cane Creek Pkwy Rd (24586-1100)
PHONE................................828 633-3190

Alan Pickering, *President*
Dale Coates, *Vice Pres*
Elizabeth Coates, *Vice Pres*
Julian Kidger,
EMP: 2 EST: 2015
SQ FT: 120
SALES (est): 159.7K **Privately Held**
WEB: www.unisonltd.com
SIC: 3542 Bending machines

Ripplemead
Giles County

(G-11876)
LHOIST NORTH AMERICA VA INC
Also Called: Virginia Plant Us80 & Us81
2093 Big Stony Creek Rd (24150-3036)
PHONE................................540 626-7163
Mot Ludwig De, *President*
Jon Passic, *Principal*
Kyle Kolde, *Vice Pres*
Mike Anderson, *Plant Mgr*
Robert Shelor, *Production*
EMP: 119
SQ FT: 2,000
SALES (est): 26.5MM
SALES (corp-wide): 2.6MM **Privately
Held**
WEB: www.lhoist.com
SIC: 3274 1422 Lime; crushed & broken
limestone
HQ: Lhoist North America, Inc.
5600 Clearfork Main St
Fort Worth TX 76109
817 732-8164

Rixeyville
Culpeper County

(G-11877)
BULL RUN PRINTING
11278 Homeland Rd (22737-1803)
PHONE................................540 937-3447
Sharon Williams, *Owner*
EMP: 1
SALES (est): 94K **Privately Held**
SIC: 2752 Commercial printing, offset

(G-11878)
DNJ DIRTWORKS INC
7131 Rixeyville Rd (22737-2948)
PHONE................................540 937-3138
Julie M Higdon, *Principal*
EMP: 4
SALES (est): 395.6K **Privately Held**
SIC: 2851 Removers & cleaners

(G-11879)
DOVE LOGGING INC
8320 Old Stillhouse Rd (22737-2032)
PHONE................................540 937-4917
John Dove, *Owner*
EMP: 2
SALES (est): 147.8K **Privately Held**
SIC: 2411 Logging camps & contractors

(G-11880)
NORTHWOOD CONTRACTING LLC
16010 Hamilton Ln (22737-2963)
PHONE................................703 624-0928
Sergio Edgardo Gomez, *Administration*
EMP: 2
SALES (est): 49.4K **Privately Held**
SIC: 2499 Wood products

Roanoke
Roanoke County

(G-11881)
AJF SIGN PLACEMENT
5833 Plantation Cir (24019-4939)
PHONE................................540 797-5835
Rosalind Fields, *Principal*
EMP: 1 EST: 2017
SALES (est): 50.6K **Privately Held**
WEB: www.ajfsignplacement.com
SIC: 3993 Signs & advertising specialties

(G-11882)
ARKAY PACKAGING CORPORATION
350 Eastpark Dr (24019-8228)
PHONE...................................540 278-2596
William Whiteside, *Principal*
Robin Rivera, *Human Resources*
Heidi Savinovich, *Sales Mgr*
David Clapsaddle, *Manager*
EMP: 90
SALES (corp-wide): 48.3MM **Privately Held**
WEB: www.arkay.com
SIC: 2657 2759 Folding paperboard boxes; commercial printing
PA: Arkay Packaging Corporation
700 Veterans Memorial Hwy # 300
Hauppauge NY 11788
631 273-2000

(G-11883)
BABY SIGNS BY LACEY
8330 Strathmore Ln (24019-2236)
PHONE...................................540 309-2551
EMP: 2
SALES (est): 75.6K **Privately Held**
WEB: www.roanokebaby.com
SIC: 3993 Signs & advertising specialties

(G-11884)
BATTLEFIELD TERRAIN CONCEPTS
754 Ray St (24019-8017)
PHONE...................................540 977-0696
Douglas B Kline, *Owner*
EMP: 1
SALES (est): 57.5K **Privately Held**
WEB: www.battlefieldterrain.com
SIC: 3999 7389 Miniatures; business services

(G-11885)
BCT RECORDATION INC
4024 Norwood St Sw (24018-1904)
PHONE...................................540 772-1754
Karen W Johnson, *Principal*
EMP: 2
SALES (est): 185.3K **Privately Held**
WEB: www.bctrecordation.com
SIC: 2752 Commercial printing, lithographic

(G-11886)
BEEF PRODUCTS INCORPORATED
3308 Aerial Way Dr Sw (24018-1502)
PHONE...................................540 985-5914
R Dana Underwood, *President*
Mark Gwin, *Vice Pres*
William Preston Holbrok, *Vice Pres*
Charlie Drumheller, *Admin Sec*
EMP: 30
SQ FT: 7,500
SALES (est): 4.5MM **Privately Held**
WEB: www.steaksnmore.com
SIC: 2011 Meat packing plants

(G-11887)
BERGER AND BURROW ENTPS INC
Also Called: Dynamic Mobile Imaging
4502 Starkey Rd (24018-8541)
P.O. Box 17588, Richmond (23226-7588)
PHONE...................................866 483-9729
Deborah A Berger, *Branch Mgr*
EMP: 62 **Privately Held**
WEB: www.dynamicmobileimaging.com
SIC: 3829 Medical diagnostic systems, nuclear
PA: Berger And Burrow Enterprises, Inc.
2301 N Parham Rd Ste 4
Henrico VA 23229

(G-11888)
BEVERLEY M JAMES JR
Also Called: Dent Removal Masters
4536 Fontaine Dr (24018-2915)
PHONE...................................540 354-2300
EMP: 1
SALES (est): 100K **Privately Held**
SIC: 3711 Automobile bodies, passenger car, not including engine, etc.

(G-11889)
BIG LICK BOOMERANG
3017 Embassy Dr (24019-3325)
P.O. Box 669, Hadley MA (01035-0669)
PHONE...................................540 761-4611
Diane Rumbolt, *Principal*
EMP: 1
SALES (est): 50.1K **Privately Held**
WEB: www.biglickboomerang.com
SIC: 3949 Boomerangs

(G-11890)
BIG LICK SEASONINGS LLC
5024 Crossbow Cir (24018-8612)
PHONE...................................540 774-8898
David Legault, *Principal*
EMP: 3 EST: 2014
SALES (est): 143.2K **Privately Held**
WEB: www.biglickseasonings.com
SIC: 2099 Food preparations

(G-11891)
BLANCO INC (PA)
3316 Aerial Way Dr Sw (24018-1502)
PHONE...................................540 389-3040
Kurt Webber, *President*
Alice R Webber, *Corp Secy*
Aaron Bunn, *Prdtn Mgr*
Alice Webbe, *CFO*
EMP: 18
SALES (est): 3.6MM **Privately Held**
WEB: www.blancolabels.com
SIC: 2759 Labels & seals: printing

(G-11892)
BLUE RIDGE SIGN & STAMP CO INC
6446 Peters Creek Rd (24019-4022)
PHONE...................................540 777-5456
Marcia Saunders, *CEO*
Karen Gray, *Director*
Tom Whitmire, *Graphic Designe*
EMP: 10
SQ FT: 5,500
SALES (est): 1.2MM **Privately Held**
WEB: www.signandstamp.com
SIC: 3993 5999 Signs, not made in custom sign painting shops; rubber stamps

(G-11893)
BOXLEY MATERIALS COMPANY
Also Called: Roanoke Plant
3830 Blue Ridge Dr Sw (24018-1551)
P.O. Box 13527 (24035-3527)
PHONE...................................540 777-7600
AB Boxley, *CEO*
EMP: 14
SALES (corp-wide): 2.2B **Publicly Held**
WEB: www.boxley.com
SIC: 3273 Ready-mixed concrete
HQ: Boxley Materials Company
15418 W Lynchburg Slem Tp
Blue Ridge VA 24064
540 777-7600

(G-11894)
BRUSH FORK PRESS LLC
3804 Brandon Ave Sw (24018-7007)
PHONE...................................202 841-3625
Thomas Smith, *Principal*
EMP: 2
SALES (est): 59.2K **Privately Held**
SIC: 2741 Miscellaneous publishing

(G-11895)
BSC VENTURES HOLDINGS INC (PA)
7702 Plantation Rd (24019-3225)
PHONE...................................540 265-6296
Brian Sass, *CEO*
Wayne Honeycutt, *Plant Mgr*
Ronald Roberts, *CFO*
Pam Southerland, *Controller*
Mark Jones, *Sales Staff*
EMP: 4
SALES (est): 88MM **Privately Held**
WEB: www.bscventures.com
SIC: 2677 Envelopes

(G-11896)
BSC VENTURES LLC (HQ)
Also Called: Double Envelope
7702 Plantation Rd (24019-3225)
PHONE...................................540 362-3311
Brian Sass, *President*

Becky Maxey, *President*
John Roberts, *VP Bus Dvlpt*
Ronald R Roberts, *CFO*
Pamela Southerland, *Controller*
▲ EMP: 89 EST: 2001
SQ FT: 200,000
SALES (est): 88MM **Privately Held**
WEB: www.bscventures.com
SIC: 2677 7336 2675 Envelopes; graphic arts & related design; die-cut paper & board
PA: Bsc Ventures Holdings, Inc.
7702 Plantation Rd
Roanoke VA 24019
540 265-6296

(G-11897)
BSC VNTRES ACQUISITION SUB LLC
7702 Plantation Rd (24019-3225)
PHONE...................................540 362-3311
Jon Peyton, *Manager*
EMP: 80
SALES (corp-wide): 88MM **Privately Held**
WEB: www.bscventures.com
SIC: 2677 Envelopes
HQ: Bsc Ventures Llc
7702 Plantation Rd
Roanoke VA 24019
540 362-3311

(G-11898)
BSC VNTRES ACQUISITION SUB LLC
Double Envelope Company
7702 Plantation Rd (24019-3225)
PHONE...................................540 563-0888
Brian Sass, *Manager*
EMP: 190
SALES (corp-wide): 88MM **Privately Held**
WEB: www.bscventures.com
SIC: 2677 5963 Envelopes; direct selling establishments
HQ: Bsc Ventures Llc
7702 Plantation Rd
Roanoke VA 24019
540 362-3311

(G-11899)
C GRAPHIC DISTRIBUTION CTR
3455 Windsor Rd Sw (24018-2045)
PHONE...................................414 762-4282
Mike Leonard, *CFO*
EMP: 2
SALES (est): 83.9K **Privately Held**
SIC: 2752 Commercial printing, lithographic

(G-11900)
CABINETRY WITH TLC LLC
4325 Old Cave Spring Rd (24018-3418)
PHONE...................................540 777-0456
Terri Langford, *Principal*
EMP: 8
SALES (est): 1.1MM **Privately Held**
WEB: www.cabinetrywithtlc.com
SIC: 2434 Wood kitchen cabinets

(G-11901)
CAP OIL CHANGE SYSTEMS LLC
6230 Hinchee Ln (24019-1724)
PHONE...................................540 982-1494
Cynthia Shupe, *President*
Joe Shupe, *Sls & Mktg Exec*
Cindy G Shupe, *Marketing Staff*
EMP: 4
SALES (est): 609.3K **Privately Held**
WEB: www.oilchangesystems.com
SIC: 3559 Automotive maintenance equipment

(G-11902)
CAPCO MACHINERY SYSTEMS INC
307 Eastpark Dr (24019-8227)
P.O. Box 11945 (24022-1945)
PHONE...................................540 977-0404
Edward E West III, *President*
Terry Fitzgerald, *Corp Secy*
Randall G Koerber, *Vice Pres*
Amy West, *Vice Pres*
Daniel Goad, *Associate*

▲ EMP: 50
SQ FT: 50,000
SALES (est): 11.6MM **Privately Held**
WEB: www.capcomachinery.com
SIC: 3541 Grinding machines, metalworking

(G-11903)
CARLEN CONTROLS INCORPORATED
6560 Commonwealth Dr (24018-5160)
PHONE...................................540 772-1736
Eric T Carlen, *President*
Shirley B Carlen, *Vice Pres*
EMP: 10
SQ FT: 5,000
SALES (est): 1.8MM **Privately Held**
WEB: www.carlencontrols.com
SIC: 3829 Pressure transducers

(G-11904)
CARLEN CONTROLS INC
2341 Brookfield Dr (24018-6128)
PHONE...................................540 598-0714
Karen Worrell, *Manager*
EMP: 2
SALES (est): 88.3K **Privately Held**
SIC: 3699 Electrical equipment & supplies

(G-11905)
CARRIER CORPORATION
5346 Peters Creek Rd B (24019-3855)
PHONE...................................540 366-2471
Martin Nelson, *Manager*
EMP: 12
SALES (corp-wide): 77B **Publicly Held**
WEB: www.rtx.com
SIC: 3585 1711 Air conditioning units, complete: domestic or industrial; plumbing, heating, air-conditioning contractors
HQ: Carrier Corporation
13995 Pasteur Blvd
Palm Beach Gardens FL 33418
800 379-6484

(G-11906)
CG PLUS LLC
Also Called: Sematco
275 Eastpark Dr (24019-8231)
PHONE...................................540 977-3200
Chip Roberts, *CEO*
EMP: 22 EST: 2015
SQ FT: 34,000
SALES (est): 1.1MM **Privately Held**
SIC: 3599 Machine shop, jobbing & repair

(G-11907)
CHARLES E OVERFELT
Also Called: Overfelt and Son Welding
2042 Timberview Rd (24019-5534)
PHONE...................................540 562-0808
Charles Overfelt, *Owner*
EMP: 2
SALES (est): 55.3K **Privately Held**
SIC: 7692 Welding repair

(G-11908)
CHOCOLATE PAPER INC
3555 Electric Rd Ste C (24018-4437)
PHONE...................................540 989-7025
Matt Burkett, *Vice Pres*
Carly Almarez, *Asst Mgr*
EMP: 3
SALES (est): 375.9K **Privately Held**
WEB: www.chocolatepaperroanoke.com
SIC: 2621 Catalog paper

(G-11909)
CLARIOS
Also Called: Johnson Controls
3826 Thirlane Rd Nw (24019-3005)
PHONE...................................540 362-5500
Gary Hamilton, *Branch Mgr*
Jim Glover, *Manager*
EMP: 94 **Privately Held**
WEB: www.johnsoncontrols.com
SIC: 2531 Seats, automobile
HQ: Johnson Controls, Inc.
5757 N Green Bay Ave
Milwaukee WI 53209
800 382-2804

(G-11910)
CLARIOS
Also Called: Johnson Controls
6701 Peters Creek Rd # 1 (24019-4060)
PHONE...................................540 366-0981
EMP: 2 **Privately Held**
WEB: www.johnsoncontrols.com
SIC: 2531 Seats, automobile
HQ: Johnson Controls, Inc.
   5757 N Green Bay Ave
   Milwaukee WI 53209
   800 382-2804

(G-11911)
CLAY DECOR LLC
105 Buckingham Ct (24019-8442)
PHONE...................................607 654-7428
Anne Marie Foulke, *Administration*
EMP: 2
SALES (est): 148.3K **Privately Held**
WEB: www.clay-decor.com
SIC: 3259 Structural clay products

(G-11912)
COLLEGIATESKYVIEWS LLC
1317 Longview Rd (24018-7618)
PHONE...................................540 520-6394
Ed Mitchell, *Principal*
EMP: 2 EST: 2009
SALES (est): 122.9K **Privately Held**
WEB: www.collegiateskyviews.com
SIC: 3648 Lighting equipment

(G-11913)
COTY CONNECTIONS INC
6658 Sugar Ridge Dr (24018-7632)
P.O. Box 20044 (24018-0005)
PHONE...................................540 588-0117
Leslie Coty, *Principal*
EMP: 3
SALES (est): 215.7K **Privately Held**
WEB: www.cotyconnections.com
SIC: 2836 Culture media

(G-11914)
CUSTOM TOOL & MACHINE INC
7533 Milk A Way Dr (24019-3216)
PHONE...................................540 563-3074
Sandra S Myers, *President*
Wayne Myers, *Vice Pres*
EMP: 30
SQ FT: 11,000
SALES (est): 4.8MM **Privately Held**
WEB: www.customtool.net
SIC: 3599 Machine shop, jobbing & repair

(G-11915)
DIAMOND 7
6322 Greenway Dr (24019-6137)
PHONE...................................540 362-5958
Brian Abbott, *Principal*
EMP: 2
SALES (est): 125.3K **Privately Held**
WEB: www.diamond7.com
SIC: 2759 Screen printing

(G-11916)
DS SMITH PLC
Also Called: Ds Smith Packaging
6405 Commonwealth Dr (24018-5159)
P.O. Box 20369 (24018-0512)
PHONE...................................540 774-0500
EMP: 2
SALES (corp-wide): 7.3B **Privately Held**
WEB: www.dssmith.com
SIC: 2653 8734 3993 3086 Boxes, corrugated: made from purchased materials; testing laboratories; signs & advertising specialties; plastics foam products
PA: Ds Smith Plc
   350 Euston Road
   London NW1 3
   754 542-9001

(G-11917)
DYNAX AMERICA CORPORATION
568 Eastpark Dr (24019-8229)
PHONE...................................540 966-6010
Tatsuo Kuroda, *President*
Koji Akita, *President*
Masamitsu Kubota, *Exec VP*
Masaki Motomura, *Exec VP*
Lewis Green, *Maint Spvr*
▲ EMP: 600

SQ FT: 200,000
SALES (est): 140.9MM **Privately Held**
WEB: www.dxa.dynax-j.com
SIC: 3714 Motor vehicle transmissions, drive assemblies & parts
HQ: Dynax Corporation
   1053-1, Kamiosatsu
   Chitose HKD 066-0

(G-11918)
ECM MARITIME SERVICES
4225 Colonial Ave (24018-4002)
PHONE...................................540 400-6412
EMP: 2
SALES (est): 196.8K **Privately Held**
WEB: www.ecmmaritime.com
SIC: 3731 Shipbuilding & repairing

(G-11919)
ELBIT SYSTEMS AMER - NGHT VSIO
7635 Plantation Rd (24019-3222)
PHONE...................................540 561-0254
Raanan Horowitz, *Mng Member*
Jed Dennison, *Manager*
EMP: 1
SALES (est): 207.9K
SALES (corp-wide): 1.3B **Privately Held**
WEB: www.elbitsystems-us.com
SIC: 3625 3827 Control equipment, electric; optical instruments & apparatus
HQ: Elbit Systems Of America, Llc
   4700 Marine Creek Pkwy
   Fort Worth TX 76179

(G-11920)
EMBROIDERY BY PATTY
393 Winesap Rd (24019-8419)
PHONE...................................540 597-8173
Patricia Truxillo, *Principal*
EMP: 1
SALES (est): 31.2K **Privately Held**
SIC: 2395 Embroidery & art needlework

(G-11921)
EMTECH LABORATORIES INC
7745 Garland Cir (24019-1631)
P.O. Box 12900 (24022-2900)
PHONE...................................540 265-9156
Moses Nakhle, *President*
Louise Vermillion, *Corp Secy*
EMP: 26
SQ FT: 8,000
SALES (est): 6.8MM **Privately Held**
WEB: www.emtechlaboratories.com
SIC: 3842 3296 Noise protectors, personal; hearing aids; mineral wool

(G-11922)
FAMILY INSIGHT PC
3609 Larson Oaks Dr (24018-3139)
PHONE...................................540 818-1687
Sam Gray, *Principal*
EMP: 3 EST: 2011
SALES (est): 204K **Privately Held**
WEB: www.familyinsight.net
SIC: 2834 Drugs acting on the cardiovascular system, except diagnostic

(G-11923)
FRANKLINS WELDING
718 Greenwich Dr (24019-4908)
PHONE...................................540 330-3454
Samuel Franklins, *Owner*
EMP: 1
SALES (est): 20K **Privately Held**
SIC: 7692 Welding repair

(G-11924)
FRIENDS SPRNGWOOD BRIAL PK LLC
4711 Horseman Dr Ne (24019-5610)
PHONE...................................540 366-0996
Robert H Bird, *Principal*
EMP: 3
SALES (est): 165.2K **Privately Held**
SIC: 3272 Burial vaults, concrete or precast terrazzo

(G-11925)
GIANNI ENTERPRISES INC
Also Called: Virginia Plastic Utilities
3453 Aerial Way Dr Sw (24018-1503)
P.O. Box 4575 (24015-0575)
PHONE...................................540 982-0111

Jaime L Gianni, *President*
Angelo R Gianni Jr, *Vice Pres*
Scott Altman, *Treasurer*
Charlene Altman, *Admin Sec*
EMP: 9
SQ FT: 14,000
SALES (est): 1.4MM **Privately Held**
SIC: 3089 Injection molding of plastics

(G-11926)
GLOBAL METAL FINISHING INC
3646 Aerial Way Dr Sw # 2 (24018-1543)
P.O. Box 3046 (24015-1046)
PHONE...................................540 362-1489
Tamea Woodward, *President*
Benjamin Lawhorn, *General Mgr*
Leigh Wojcik, *Accounting Mgr*
EMP: 10
SALES (est): 1.4MM **Privately Held**
WEB: www.globalmetalfinishing.com
SIC: 3479 Coating of metals & formed products

(G-11927)
GLOVES FOR LIFE LLC
1423 Crestmoor Dr Sw (24018-1131)
PHONE...................................540 343-1697
Deborah Riggsby, *General Mgr*
Zane Riggsby,
EMP: 2
SALES (est): 161.3K **Privately Held**
WEB: www.glovesforlife.com
SIC: 3111 Glove leather

(G-11928)
GREENBROOK TMS NEUROHEALTH CTR
Also Called: Tms Neurohealth Centers
2965 Colonnade Dr Ste 307 (24018-3561)
PHONE...................................855 998-4867
EMP: 1
SALES (corp-wide): 2.7MM **Privately Held**
WEB: www.greenbrooktms.com
SIC: 3312 Blast furnaces & steel mills
PA: Greenbrook Tms Neurohealth Center
   8405 Greensboro Dr # 120
   Mc Lean VA 22102
   703 356-1568

(G-11929)
GROUNDHOG POETRY PRESS LLC
6915 Ardmore Dr (24019-4403)
PHONE...................................540 366-8460
EMP: 2
SALES (est): 45.4K **Privately Held**
SIC: 2741 Miscellaneous publishing

(G-11930)
GULF FASTENERS
3214 Electric Rd (24018-6451)
PHONE...................................540 798-1992
EMP: 2
SALES (est): 93.6K **Privately Held**
SIC: 3965 Fasteners

(G-11931)
HALIFAX FINE FURNISHINGS
4525 Brambleton Ave (24018-3433)
PHONE...................................540 774-3060
Jack L Pittman, *Owner*
Valeta S Pittman, *Mng Member*
EMP: 4
SQ FT: 2,100
SALES (est): 403.4K **Privately Held**
WEB: www.halifaxfinefurnishings.com
SIC: 2599 5712 5713 5944 Factory furniture & fixtures; furniture stores; rugs; clocks

(G-11932)
HARKNESS SCREENS (USA) LIMITED
479 Eastpark Dr (24019-8230)
PHONE...................................540 370-1590
EMP: 6 **Privately Held**
WEB: www.harkness-screens.com
SIC: 3861 Photographic equipment & supplies
HQ: Harkness Screens (Uk) Limited
   Unit A
   Stevenage HERTS SG1 2

(G-11933)
HATTER WELDING INC
292 Industrial Dr (24019-8507)
P.O. Box 487, Fincastle (24090-0487)
PHONE...................................540 589-3848
EMP: 2
SALES (est): 134.2K **Privately Held**
SIC: 7692 Welding repair

(G-11934)
HIGH PERFORMANCE OPTICS INC
5241 Valleypark Dr (24019-3004)
PHONE...................................513 258-5978
EMP: 2 EST: 2011
SALES (est): 88K **Privately Held**
SIC: 3229 Mfg Pressed/Blown Glass

(G-11935)
HILLMANS DISTRIBUTORS
3603 Cedar Ln (24018-4407)
PHONE...................................540 774-1896
W M Hillman, *Owner*
EMP: 2
SALES (est): 113.5K **Privately Held**
SIC: 2843 5162 Oils & greases; resins, synthetic

(G-11936)
IAQ TESTING SERVICES LLC
196 Buckingham Ct (24019-8400)
P.O. Box 489, Daleville (24083-0489)
PHONE...................................540 966-3660
Traci McDaniel, *President*
EMP: 1
SALES (est): 75K **Privately Held**
SIC: 1389 Testing, measuring, surveying & analysis services

(G-11937)
INDUSTRIAL APPARATUS REPR INC
6655 Wellington Rd (24018-5618)
PHONE...................................540 343-9240
Richard Davis, *President*
Patricia Davis, *Vice Pres*
Debbie Bratton, *Admin Sec*
EMP: 15
SALES (est): 2.9MM **Privately Held**
WEB: www.industrialapparatusrepair.com
SIC: 7694 Electric motor repair

(G-11938)
INDUSTRIAL FABRICATORS INC
5163 Starkey Rd (24018-9398)
PHONE...................................540 989-0834
Robert Wood, *President*
Melissa Rice, *Corp Secy*
Toby Loritsch, *Vice Pres*
EMP: 15 EST: 1971
SQ FT: 19,500
SALES (est): 800K **Privately Held**
WEB: www.ificonveyor.com
SIC: 3535 3441 3312 Bulk handling conveyor systems; fabricated structural metal; structural shapes & pilings, steel

(G-11939)
INDUSTRY GRAPHICS
3783 Buckingham Dr (24018-2448)
PHONE...................................540 345-6074
James Hoer, *Owner*
EMP: 2
SALES (est): 74.3K **Privately Held**
WEB: www.industrygraphics.com
SIC: 2759 Screen printing

(G-11940)
INDY HEALTH LABS LLC
4521 Brambleton Ave # 205 (24018-3431)
PHONE...................................540 682-2160
Heman A Marshall III, *Mng Member*
EMP: 2
SALES (est): 104.2K **Privately Held**
SIC: 3821 Clinical laboratory instruments, except medical & dental

(G-11941)
INTEL INVESTIGATIONS LLC
5727 Lost View Ln (24018-8063)
P.O. Box 20216 (24018-0022)
PHONE...................................540 521-4111
Christopher Strom, *General Mgr*
Christopher R Strom,
EMP: 2

SALES (est): 50K **Privately Held**
WEB: www.cs-intel.com
SIC: 3531 Aerial work platforms: hy-
draulic/elec. truck/carrier mounted

(G-11942)
INTELLIMAT INC
3959 Elc Rd Sw Ste 330 (24018)
PHONE......................................540 904-5670
James B Currie, *President*
Thomas Douglas, *Treasurer*
EMP: 6 **Privately Held**
WEB: www.namekraft.com
SIC: 3993 Signs & advertising specialties

(G-11943)
INX INTERNATIOL INK CO
350 Eastpark Dr (24019-8228)
PHONE......................................540 977-0079
Lillie Stevens, *Principal*
EMP: 2 EST: 2010
SALES (est): 108.4K **Privately Held**
SIC: 2893 Printing ink

(G-11944)
ITT CORPORATION
7671 Enon Dr (24019-3267)
PHONE......................................540 362-8000
EMP: 58
SALES (corp-wide): 2.4B **Publicly Held**
SIC: 3625 Mfg Relays/Industrial Controls
PA: Itt Corporation
1133 Westchester Ave N-100
White Plains NY 10604
914 641-2000

(G-11945)
IVORY DOG PRESS LLC
5018 S Gala Dr (24019-7594)
PHONE......................................540 353-3939
EMP: 1
SALES (est): 37.5K **Privately Held**
WEB: www.mhbradford.com
SIC: 2741 Miscellaneous publishing

(G-11946)
JB WOOD WORKS LLC
Also Called: JB Wood Works Roanoke Co
3355 View Ave (24018-3734)
PHONE......................................540 589-5281
EMP: 1
SALES (est): 54.1K **Privately Held**
WEB: www.roanokecountyva.gov
SIC: 2431 Millwork

(G-11947)
JQ & G INC COMPANY
3451 Brandon Ave Sw # 12 (24018-1548)
PHONE......................................540 588-7625
Paul Omiyo, *President*
EMP: 3 EST: 2015
SALES (est): 195.3K **Privately Held**
WEB: www.jqginc.com
SIC: 3669 Traffic signals, electric; pedes-
trian traffic control equipment

(G-11948)
KELTRON CORPORATION
1110 Beaumont Rd (24019-5417)
PHONE......................................540 527-3526
Lauren Mason, *Principal*
Doris Mason, *Admin Sec*
EMP: 20
SALES (est): 777.4K **Privately Held**
SIC: 3675 Electronic capacitors

(G-11949)
KINZIE WOODWORK LLC
5636 S Mountain Dr (24018-9025)
P.O. Box 21641 (24018-0166)
PHONE......................................540 397-1637
Ashley Kinzie, *Principal*
EMP: 4
SALES (est): 404.5K **Privately Held**
WEB: www.kinziewoodwork.com
SIC: 2431 Millwork

(G-11950)
L3HARRIS TECHNOLOGIES INC
Exelis
7635 Plantation Rd (24019-3222)
PHONE......................................540 563-0371
Lacy Litzy, *Vice Pres*
Rene Bullock, *Research*
EMP: 58

SALES (corp-wide): 6.8B **Publicly Held**
WEB: www.harris.com
SIC: 3625 Control equipment, electric
PA: L3harris Technologies, Inc.
1025 W Nasa Blvd
Melbourne FL 32919
321 727-9100

(G-11951)
L3HARRIS TECHNOLOGIES INC
7635 Plantation Rd (24019-3222)
PHONE......................................540 563-0371
Greag Fitzpatrick, *Branch Mgr*
EMP: 600
SALES (corp-wide): 6.8B **Publicly Held**
WEB: www.harris.com
SIC: 3823 Industrial instrmnts
msrmnt display/control process variable;
search & navigation equipment
PA: L3harris Technologies, Inc.
1025 W Nasa Blvd
Melbourne FL 32919
321 727-9100

(G-11952)
LASERCAM LLC
Also Called: Lasercam Express
7519 Hitech Rd (24019-3259)
PHONE......................................540 265-2888
Mike Dill, *Plant Mgr*
Greg Orlik, *Sales Staff*
Gordon Bayless, *Manager*
EMP: 13
SALES (corp-wide): 6.1MM **Privately
Held**
WEB: www.lasercam.com
SIC: 3544 Industrial molds
PA: Lasercam L.L.C
1039 Hoyt Ave
Ridgefield NJ 07657
201 941-1262

(G-11953)
LAWRENCE TRNSP SYSTEMS INC
Rusco Window Company Division
872 Lee Hwy Ste 203 (24019-8692)
P.O. Box 7667 (24019-0667)
PHONE......................................540 966-3797
Billy Wills, *Branch Mgr*
EMP: 60
SALES (corp-wide): 83.2MM **Privately
Held**
WEB: www.lawrencecompanies.com
SIC: 3089 3442 Windows, plastic; siding,
plastic; storm doors or windows, metal
PA: Lawrence Transportation Systems, Inc.
872 Lee Hwy Ste 203
Roanoke VA 24019
540 966-4000

(G-11954)
LEATHER WORLD TECHNOLOGIES LLC
5851 Cloverdale Rd (24019-8074)
PHONE......................................540 265-9038
EMP: 1
SALES (est): 70.8K **Privately Held**
WEB: www.leatherworldtech.com
SIC: 3111 Leather tanning & finishing

(G-11955)
LEISURE PUBLISHING INC
3424 Brambleton Ave (24018-6520)
P.O. Box 21535 (24018-0563)
PHONE......................................540 989-6138
Richard Wells, *President*
EMP: 40
SALES (est): 256.8K **Privately Held**
WEB: www.leisuremedia360.com
SIC: 2741 Miscellaneous publishing

(G-11956)
LEISUREMEDIA360 INC
3424 Brambleton Ave (24018-6520)
P.O. Box 21339 (24018-0544)
PHONE......................................540 989-6138
James Richard Wells, *President*
J Richard Wells, *President*
Denise Kofff, *General Mgr*
Kurt Rheinheimer, *Editor*
Kasey Smith, *COO*
EMP: 25
SQ FT: 7,000

SALES (est): 8MM **Privately Held**
WEB: www.leisuremedia360.com
SIC: 2721 Magazines: publishing only, not
printed on site

(G-11957)
LONGBOW HOLDINGS LLC
Also Called: Industrial Expedite
406 Dexter Rd (24019-4251)
PHONE......................................540 404-1185
Christopher Jones, *Principal*
EMP: 2
SQ FT: 3,000
SALES (est): 166.1K **Privately Held**
SIC: 3625 7699 5084 Industrial controls:
push button, selector switches, pilot; in-
dustrial machinery & equipment repair; in-
dustrial machinery & equipment; industrial
machine parts

(G-11958)
LTC ENTERPRISES LLC
Also Called: Lodging Technology
5431 Peters Creek Rd C (24019-3885)
P.O. Box 7919 (24019-0919)
PHONE......................................540 362-7500
John Centeno, *Sales Staff*
Joshua Brown, *Technical Staff*
Joshua N Brown, *Technical Staff*
Jon Griffin, *Technical Staff*
William C Fizer, *Technical Staff*
EMP: 5
SQ FT: 2,200
SALES (est): 500K **Privately Held**
WEB: www.lodgingtechnology.com
SIC: 3822 Thermostats, except built-in;
temperature controls, automatic

(G-11959)
MARTCL INC
4325 Old Cave Spring Rd (24019-3418)
PHONE......................................540 777-0456
Terri Langford, *Administration*
EMP: 2 EST: 2009
SALES (est): 189.9K **Privately Held**
WEB: www.cabinetrywithtlc.com
SIC: 2434 Wood kitchen cabinets

(G-11960)
MAXX PERFORMANCE INC
3621 Aerial Way Dr Sw (24018-1507)
P.O. Box 711, Chester NY (10918-0711)
PHONE......................................845 987-9432
Winston Samuels, *President*
Marilyn Lee, *Corp Secy*
▼ EMP: 14
SQ FT: 45,000
SALES (est): 2.7MM **Privately Held**
WEB: www.maxxperformance.com
SIC: 2899 2099 2048 Chemical prepara-
tions; leavening compounds, prepared;
feed supplements

(G-11961)
MELISSA MOSS
Also Called: Caaj Appare
5410 Orchard Hill Dr 2h (24019-6074)
PHONE......................................540 397-0408
Melissa Moss, *Owner*
EMP: 1
SALES (est): 42.5K **Privately Held**
SIC: 2389 Apparel & accessories

(G-11962)
MESSER LLC
6561 Forest View Rd (24018-7627)
PHONE......................................540 774-1515
Mathew Fitzpatrick, *Manager*
EMP: 1
SALES (corp-wide): 1.1B **Privately Held**
WEB: www.praxair.com
SIC: 2813 Oxygen, compressed or lique-
fied
HQ: Messer Llc
200 Somerset Corp Blvd # 7000
Bridgewater NJ 08807
908 464-8100

(G-11963)
METALIST
210 Updike Ln (24019-8673)
PHONE......................................540 793-0627
EMP: 2
SALES (est): 162.4K **Privately Held**
WEB: www.the-metalist.com
SIC: 3441 Fabricated structural metal

(G-11964)
METALSA STRUCTURAL PDTS INC
184 Vista Dr (24019-8514)
PHONE......................................540 966-5370
EMP: 2 **Privately Held**
WEB: www.metalsa.com
SIC: 3713 Truck & bus bodies
HQ: Metalsa Structural Products, Inc.
29575 Hudson Dr
Novi MI 48377

(G-11965)
METALSA-ROANOKE INC
184 Vista Dr (24019-8514)
PHONE......................................540 966-5300
Steven Helgeson, *President*
Angel Loredo, *Vice Pres*
Nicolas Villarreal, *Vice Pres*
Alan Bagley, *Production*
Richard Bittle, *Production*
▲ EMP: 200
SALES (est): 85.8MM **Privately Held**
WEB: www.metalsa.com
SIC: 3713 Truck & bus bodies
PA: Grupo Proeza, S.A.P.I. De C.V.
Constitucion No. 405 Pte.
Monterrey N.L. 64000

(G-11966)
MILL MOUNTAIN CAPITAL LLC
Also Called: Origo
6536 Commonwealth Dr (24018-5160)
PHONE......................................540 529-7163
Clay Skelton, *Mng Member*
Brady Sheffer,
EMP: 4
SALES (est): 441.5K **Privately Held**
WEB: www.millmountaincapital.com
SIC: 3829 5999 8742 Instrument board
gauges, automotive: computerized; alarm
& safety equipment stores; transportation
consultant; productivity improvement con-
sultant

(G-11967)
MILLEHAN ENTERPRISES INC
Also Called: Custom Shutter and Blind
4319 Fox Croft Cir (24018-8945)
PHONE......................................540 772-3037
Tom Millehan, *President*
EMP: 4 EST: 1998
SALES (est): 300K **Privately Held**
WEB: www.customshutterblinds.com
SIC: 2431 1751 Venetian blind slats,
wood; cabinet building & installation

(G-11968)
MINTEL GROUP LTD
6348 Spring Run Dr (24018-5400)
PHONE......................................540 989-3945
Carla Bream, *CEO*
Michael Bream, *President*
EMP: 5
SALES (est): 310K **Privately Held**
SIC: 2013 Snack sticks, including jerky:
from purchased meat

(G-11969)
MOFAT PUBLISHING LLC
3812 Concord Pl Ste E (24018-3654)
PHONE......................................540 251-1660
EMP: 4
SALES (est): 55K **Privately Held**
SIC: 2741 Miscellaneous publishing

(G-11970)
MOUTHPIECE EXPRESS LLC
5207 Bernard Dr (24018-4372)
P.O. Box 20239 (24018-0508)
PHONE......................................540 989-8848
Bradley D McGraw, *Administration*
EMP: 5 EST: 2009
SALES (est): 374.4K **Privately Held**
WEB: www.mouthpieceexpress.com
SIC: 3069 Mouthpieces for pipes, cigarette
holders, etc.: rubber

(G-11971)
MT CHESTNUT VINEYARDS LLC
6235 Mount Chestnut Rd (24018-8103)
PHONE......................................540 400-6442
Greg Jamison, *Principal*
EMP: 2 EST: 2008

SALES (est): 81.4K **Privately Held**
WEB: www.bestvirginiawines.com
SIC: 2084 Wines

(G-11972)
MTH HOLDINGS CORP
5430 Peters Creek Rd # 108 (24019-3892)
PHONE..............................276 228-7943
Matthew Clark, *President*
EMP: 99
SALES (est): 5.8MM **Privately Held**
SIC: 3612 Transformers, except electric

(G-11973)
MURRAY CIDER CO INC
103 Murray Farm Rd (24019-8102)
PHONE..............................540 977-9000
Robert E Murray, *President*
Joe K Murray, *Vice Pres*
Mark E Murray, *Vice Pres*
Anne M Reid, *Admin Sec*
EMP: 6
SQ FT: 60,000
SALES (est): 1MM **Privately Held**
WEB: www.murraycider.com
SIC: 2099 Cider, nonalcoholic

(G-11974)
NEXT LEVEL BUILDING SOLUTIONS
5205 Starkey Rd (24018-9367)
PHONE..............................540 685-1500
Ashley Rogers, *General Mgr*
EMP: 15
SALES (corp-wide): 330K **Privately Held**
SIC: 3589 Commercial cleaning equipment
PA: Next Level Building Solutions Inc
   5170 Alean Rd
   Boones Mill VA 24065
   540 400-9169

(G-11975)
NORTH GARDEN PUBLISHING
5227 N Garden Ln (24019-2617)
PHONE..............................540 580-2501
Daniel Colston, *Principal*
EMP: 1
SALES (est): 37.5K **Privately Held**
SIC: 2741 Miscellaneous publishing

(G-11976)
NRD LLC
5180 Peters Creek Rd (24019-3810)
PHONE..............................540 362-1097
Paul Kaiser, *Principal*
EMP: 2
SALES (est): 122.3K **Privately Held**
SIC: 3629 Electrical industrial apparatus

(G-11977)
OGDEN DIRECTORIES INC
4502 Starkey Rd Ste 1 (24018-8517)
P.O. Box 1113, Altoona PA (16603-1113)
PHONE..............................540 375-6524
Travis Bogle, *Manager*
EMP: 8 **Privately Held**
WEB: www.tearpages.eztouse.com
SIC: 2741 Telephone & other directory publishing
HQ: Ogden Directories, Inc.
   1500 Main St
   Wheeling WV 26003

(G-11978)
OPTICAL CABLE CORPORATION (PA)
Also Called: OCC
5290 Concourse Dr (24019-3059)
PHONE..............................540 265-0690
Neil D Wilkin Jr, *Ch of Bd*
Bob Booze, *Vice Pres*
Robert Booze, *Vice Pres*
Bill Kloss, *Vice Pres*
Philip Peters, *Vice Pres*
▲ **EMP:** 167
SQ FT: 146,000
SALES (est): 71.3MM **Publicly Held**
WEB: www.occfiber.com
SIC: 3357 3351 Fiber optic cable (insulated); wire, copper & copper alloy

(G-11979)
ORINOCO NATURAL RESOURCES LLC (PA)
192 Summerfield Ct # 203 (24019-4581)
PHONE..............................713 626-9696
David Dean, *President*
Brian Macmillan, *Vice Pres*
Roger Souders, *Manager*
EMP: 2
SALES (est): 40MM **Privately Held**
WEB: www.sanarepartners.com
SIC: 1382 Oil & gas exploration services

(G-11980)
P & G INTERIORS INC
3356 Aerial Way Dr Sw (24018-1502)
PHONE..............................540 985-3064
EMP: 25
SQ FT: 1,250
SALES (est): 3MM **Privately Held**
SIC: 3446 1751 1742 Drywall/Insulation Contr Mfg Architectural Mtlwrk Carpentry Contractor

(G-11981)
P D R INC
6426 Merriman Rd (24018-6602)
PHONE..............................540 772-2780
Paul D Rucker, *President*
Nancy Rucker, *Vice Pres*
EMP: 3
SQ FT: 1,200
SALES (est): 230K **Privately Held**
SIC: 3829 8711 Tensile strength testing equipment; testing equipment: abrasion, shearing strength, etc.; consulting engineer

(G-11982)
PACKAGING CORPORATION AMERICA
Also Called: Pca/Roanoke 371
7500 Shadwell Dr Ste B (24019-5103)
PHONE..............................540 427-3164
Teresa McMillion, *Controller*
Donald Woodward, *Manager*
EMP: 60 **Publicly Held**
WEB: www.packagingcorp.com
SIC: 2653 Boxes, corrugated: made from purchased materials
PA: Packaging Corporation Of America
   1 N Field Ct
   Lake Forest IL 60045
   847 482-3000

(G-11983)
PAUL E STAHL
Also Called: L K & Associates
4339 Kirkwood Dr (24018-3505)
PHONE..............................772 600-8099
Paul E Stahl, *Owner*
EMP: 1
SALES (est): 107.6K **Privately Held**
SIC: 2521 2522 Wood office furniture; office furniture, except wood

(G-11984)
PEPSI-COLA METRO BTLG CO INC
226 Lee Hwy (24019-8513)
PHONE..............................540 966-5200
Mike Dittrich, *Manager*
David Green, *Manager*
Mark Waldeck, *Manager*
Karen Davis, *Director*
EMP: 200
SALES (corp-wide): 67.1B **Publicly Held**
WEB: www.pepsico.com
SIC: 2086 5149 Carbonated soft drinks, bottled & canned; soft drinks
HQ: Pepsi-Cola Metropolitan Bottling Company, Inc.
   1111 Westchester Ave
   White Plains NY 10604
   914 767-6000

(G-11985)
PILKINGTON NORTH AMERICA INC
7703 Enon Dr (24019-3237)
PHONE..............................540 362-5130
Rosalie Goad, *Manager*
EMP: 223 **Privately Held**
WEB: www.pilkington.com
SIC: 3211 Flat glass

HQ: Pilkington North America, Inc.
   811 Madison Ave Fl 3
   Toledo OH 43604
   419 247-3731

(G-11986)
PK INDUSTRIES LLC
5221 Medmont Cir Sw (24018-1118)
PHONE..............................540 589-2341
Paul F Glassbrenner, *Principal*
EMP: 2
SALES (est): 104.2K **Privately Held**
SIC: 3999 Manufacturing industries

(G-11987)
PLASMERA TECHNOLOGIES LLC
6101 Scotford Ct (24018-3888)
PHONE..............................540 353-5438
Stephen Miko, *President*
EMP: 3 **EST:** 2015
SALES (est): 93.7K **Privately Held**
SIC: 3699 High-energy particle physics equipment

(G-11988)
POGOTEC INC
Also Called: Pogo-CAM
4502 Starkey Rd Ste 109 (24018-8538)
PHONE..............................904 501-5309
Ron Blum Od, *CEO*
Richard Clompus, *Vice Pres*
Jack McDougall, *Vice Pres*
Diane J Munn, *Vice Pres*
Bill Kokonaski, *CFO*
EMP: 7 **EST:** 2014
SALES (est): 159.5K **Privately Held**
WEB: www.pogotec.com
SIC: 3679 Electronic loads & power supplies

(G-11989)
POLYCOAT INC
5369 Doe Run Rd (24018-8732)
P.O. Box 21281 (24018-0130)
PHONE..............................540 989-7833
Gerald Rhodes, *Principal*
EMP: 2
SALES (est): 149.6K **Privately Held**
SIC: 3259 Liner brick or plates for sewer/tank lining, vitrified clay

(G-11990)
PUGAL INC
5535 Cynthia Dr (24018-3809)
PHONE..............................540 765-4955
Pugazhenthi Selvaraj, *President*
EMP: 3
SALES (est): 274.5K **Privately Held**
SIC: 3612 Transformers, except electric

(G-11991)
PURE-MECH INC
2014 Wynmere Dr (24018-2440)
PHONE..............................804 363-1297
Gregory Bellamy, *Owner*
EMP: 2
SALES (est): 88K **Privately Held**
WEB: www.pure-mech.com
SIC: 3589 Water treatment equipment, industrial

(G-11992)
Q PROTEIN INC
6210 Chadsworth Ct (24018-3892)
PHONE..............................240 994-6160
Justin Barone, *President*
EMP: 1
SALES (est): 59.3K **Privately Held**
SIC: 2824 7389 Protein fibers;

(G-11993)
RADON SAFE INC
6439 Pendleton Ave (24019-4117)
P.O. Box 21273 (24018-0129)
PHONE..............................540 265-0101
Jane Solcomb, *President*
Dale Solcomb, *Vice Pres*
EMP: 4
SALES (est): 413K **Privately Held**
WEB: www.radonsafe.com
SIC: 3825 1799 Radar testing instruments, electric; gas leakage detection

(G-11994)
REFORMATION HERALD PUBG ASSN
5240 Hollins Rd (24019-5048)
P.O. Box 7240 (24019-0240)
PHONE..............................540 366-9400
Daniel Lee, *President*
Haroald Montrose, *Treasurer*
▲ **EMP:** 10
SALES (est): 500K **Privately Held**
WEB: www.reformationherald.com
SIC: 2731 Books: publishing & printing

(G-11995)
RICHARD EVANS
Also Called: Housing Associates
4443 Cordell Dr Ste 101 (24018-2901)
P.O. Box 20061 (24018-0007)
PHONE..............................540 774-1905
Richard Evans, *Owner*
Richard E Evans, *Owner*
EMP: 2
SALES (est): 135K **Privately Held**
WEB: www.housingassociates.com
SIC: 2439 1751 1742 Trusses, wooden roof; lightweight steel framing (metal stud) installation; drywall

(G-11996)
ROANOKE STARS
6451 Archcrest Dr Apt 102 (24019-1196)
PHONE..............................540 797-8266
Sarah Schwartz, *Principal*
EMP: 2
SALES (est): 86.6K **Privately Held**
SIC: 3842 Wheelchairs

(G-11997)
ROCKYDALE QUARRIES CORPORATION
Also Called: Rockydale Mundy Quarries
5925 Starkey Rd (24018-9049)
PHONE..............................540 896-1441
EMP: 1
SALES (corp-wide): 13.3MM **Privately Held**
WEB: www.rockydalequarries.com
SIC: 1411 5032 5211 Dimension stone; stone, crushed or broken; lime & plaster; sand & gravel
PA: Rockydale Quarries Corporation
   2343 Highland Farm Rd Nw
   Roanoke VA 24017
   540 774-1696

(G-11998)
RWM INC
5540 Arthur St (24018-9002)
PHONE..............................540 774-7214
Rodney W McNeil, *Principal*
EMP: 2 **EST:** 2009
SALES (est): 70.6K **Privately Held**
WEB: www.rwm-inc.com
SIC: 2431 Millwork

(G-11999)
SEPARATION TECHNOLOGIES LLC (DH)
188 Summerfield Ct # 101 (24019-4514)
PHONE..............................540 992-1501
Randy Dunlap, *President*
Thomas Cerullo, *Vice Pres*
Tim Kuebler, *Vice Pres*
▼ **EMP:** 42
SALES (est): 962.1K
SALES (corp-wide): 1.4MM **Privately Held**
WEB: www.proash.com
SIC: 3272 5169 Concrete products; coal tar products, primary & intermediate
HQ: Titan America Llc
   5700 Lake Wright Dr # 300
   Norfolk VA 23502
   757 858-6500

(G-12000)
SIGN FACTORY INC
3804 Brambleton Ave (24018-3641)
PHONE..............................540 772-0400
Kelly Schulz, *CEO*
EMP: 4
SALES (est): 466.3K **Privately Held**
WEB: www.thesignfactoryva.com
SIC: 3993 Signs & advertising specialties

▲ = Import ▼=Export
◆ =Import/Export

(G-12001)
SKYDOG PUBLICATIONS
6511 Deepwoods Dr (24018-7645)
PHONE...................540 989-2167
James Palmieri, *Owner*
EMP: 1 **EST:** 1997
SALES (est): 43K **Privately Held**
WEB: www.skydogsports.com
SIC: 2731 Book publishing

(G-12002)
SLM DISTRUBUTORS INC
6743 Corntassel Ln (24018-5629)
PHONE...................540 774-6817
Sidney A Maupin, *President*
Sidney Maupin, *President*
EMP: 2
SALES (est): 230K **Privately Held**
SIC: 3442 Window & door frames

(G-12003)
STITCH BEAGLE INC
6520 Commonwealth Dr (24018-5160)
PHONE...................540 777-0002
Robert J Sarmanian, *President*
▲ **EMP:** 2
SALES (est): 244.1K **Privately Held**
WEB: www.stitchbeagle.com
SIC: 3552 Embroidery machines

(G-12004)
STITCH DOCTOR
3754 Stratford Park Dr Sw # 4
(24018-1486)
PHONE...................540 330-1234
Amy Henley, *Principal*
EMP: 2
SALES (est): 79.2K **Privately Held**
SIC: 2395 Embroidery & art needlework

(G-12005)
STITCHDOTPRO LLC
6520 Commonwealth Dr (24018-5160)
PHONE...................540 777-0002
Carlton W Beckner, *Administration*
EMP: 1
SALES (est): 47.6K **Privately Held**
SIC: 2395 Embroidery & art needlework

(G-12006)
SWIFT PRINT
3526 Electric Rd (24018-4453)
PHONE...................540 774-1001
Dan Baldwin, *Owner*
Scott Baldwin, *General Mgr*
Pam Rakes, *Prdtn Mgr*
EMP: 6
SALES (est): 491.3K **Privately Held**
WEB: www.swiftprint.net
SIC: 2759 2791 7334 Commercial printing; typesetting; photocopying & duplicating services

(G-12007)
TACSTRIKE LLC
Also Called: Tacstrike Systems
3464 Colonial Ave Apt O93 (24018-4532)
PHONE...................540 751-8221
Robert Tackett, *President*
Yvonne Ford, *Principal*
Yvonne Tackett, *Treasurer*
EMP: 6 **EST:** 2011
SALES (est): 371K **Privately Held**
WEB: www.tacstrike.com
SIC: 3949 Targets, archery & rifle shooting

(G-12008)
THE MENNEL MILLING CO VA INC
5185 Benois Rd (24018-8527)
PHONE...................540 776-6201
M A Hall, *Principal*
▲ **EMP:** 12
SALES (est): 2.1MM **Privately Held**
WEB: www.mennel.com
SIC: 2041 Flour & other grain mill products

(G-12009)
TIGHT LINES HOLDINGS GROUP
Also Called: Fastsigns
3232 Electric Rd Ste 402 (24018-6424)
PHONE...................540 989-7874
Donald Smith, *President*
Crystall Ayers, *Manager*
EMP: 5

SQ FT: 1,400
SALES (est): 525K **Privately Held**
WEB: www.fastsigns.com
SIC: 3993 Signs & advertising specialties

(G-12010)
TREAD CORPORATION
176 Eastpark Dr (24019-8226)
PHONE...................540 982-6881
Barry Russell, *CEO*
Stef Stoltz, *Senior VP*
Ron Bolling, *Vice Pres*
Andrew Cooper, *Vice Pres*
Mark Stanley, *Engineer*
◆ **EMP:** 96 **EST:** 1957
SQ FT: 86,000
SALES (est): 37MM **Privately Held**
WEB: www.treadcorp.com
SIC: 3499 3537 Ammunition boxes, metal; industrial trucks & tractors

(G-12011)
TREE TECHNOLOGIES INC
6633 Sugar Ridge Dr (24018-7633)
PHONE...................540 589-7988
William Samuel Austin, *President*
EMP: 1
SALES (est): 32.7K **Privately Held**
SIC: 7372 Application computer software

(G-12012)
TRODAT USA
4767 Chippenham Dr (24018-3445)
PHONE...................540 815-8160
Charles Kirchne, *Manager*
EMP: 1
SALES (est): 41K **Privately Held**
SIC: 3953 Marking devices

(G-12013)
UPTIME BUSINESS PRODUCTS LLC
3015 Peters Creek Rd Nw B (24019-2771)
P.O. Box 8567 (24014-0567)
PHONE...................540 982-5750
David Tucker, *Vice Pres*
Jeff Rhodes, *Sales Mgr*
Dwayne Linkous, *Sales Staff*
Victor Corchia,
EMP: 5
SALES (est): 274.8K **Privately Held**
WEB: www.uptime4u.com
SIC: 2522 Office desks & tables: except wood

(G-12014)
VALCOM INC (PA)
5614 Hollins Rd (24019-5056)
PHONE...................540 427-3900
John W Mason Sr, *President*
Troy Van, *Regional Mgr*
Doris A Mason, *Corp Secy*
Gordon Bailey, *Engineer*
David Dixon, *Engineer*
▲ **EMP:** 200
SQ FT: 130,000
SALES (est): 33.3MM **Privately Held**
WEB: www.valcom.com
SIC: 3661 3663 3651 Telephone sets, all types except cellular radio; pagers (one-way); household audio & video equipment

(G-12015)
VALCOM SERVICES LLC
5614 Hollins Rd (24019-5056)
PHONE...................540 427-2400
Gordon Bailey, *Engineer*
John Mason,
EMP: 8
SQ FT: 100,000
SALES (est): 1MM **Privately Held**
WEB: www.valcomservicesllc.com
SIC: 3661 3663 Telephone sets, all types except cellular radio; pagers (one-way)

(G-12016)
VALHALLA VINEYARDS
6500 Mount Chestnut Rd (24018-8108)
PHONE...................540 725-9463
James Vaszik, *Principal*
Debra Vaszik,
EMP: 2
SALES (est): 169.2K **Privately Held**
WEB: www.valhallawines.com
SIC: 2084 Wines

(G-12017)
VANGUARD MTGTION RSTRATION LLC
5637 Penguin Dr (24018-4871)
PHONE...................540 769-1881
Erica Jackson,
EMP: 2
SALES (est): 250K **Privately Held**
SIC: 1389 Construction, repair & dismantling services

(G-12018)
VERTEX SIGNS
4005 Electric Rd Ste 201 (24018-8435)
PHONE...................540 904-5776
Kevin Booker, *Principal*
EMP: 2 **EST:** 2009
SALES (est): 158.9K **Privately Held**
WEB: www.vertexsigns.com
SIC: 3993 Electric signs

(G-12019)
VFP INC (PA)
5410 Fallowater Ln (24018-0906)
PHONE...................540 977-0500
Frank G Van Balen, *Ch of Bd*
Jerry D Arnold, *President*
Bryan Cox, *Business Mgr*
Pete File, *Business Mgr*
Scott File, *Vice Pres*
▲ **EMP:** 80
SALES (est): 65MM **Privately Held**
WEB: www.vfpinc.com
SIC: 3448 2452 Prefabricated metal buildings; prefabricated buildings, wood

(G-12020)
VIRGINIA AIR DISTRIBUTORS INC
6905 Walrond Dr (24019-3249)
PHONE...................540 366-2259
Ron Revia, *Manager*
EMP: 10
SALES (corp-wide): 64.6MM **Privately Held**
WEB: www.virginiaair.com
SIC: 3585 Heating & air conditioning combination units
PA: Virginia Air Distributors Inc
2501 Waterford Lake Dr
Midlothian VA 23112
804 608-3600

(G-12021)
VIRGINIA PLASTICS COMPANY INC
3453 Aerial Way Dr Sw (24018-1503)
P.O. Box 4577 (24015-0577)
PHONE...................540 981-9700
Stephen B Bogese II, *President*
Sharon Bogese, *Corp Secy*
Jimmy Kendrick, *Purchasing*
Susan Hartman, *Human Resources*
Bryan Long, *MIS Dir*
EMP: 50 **EST:** 1949
SQ FT: 67,000
SALES (est): 6.8MM **Privately Held**
WEB: www.vaplastics.com
SIC: 3089 Injection molding of plastics

(G-12022)
WATER CHEMISTRY INCORPORATED
3404 Aerial Way Dr Sw (24018-1504)
P.O. Box 4273 (24015-0273)
PHONE...................540 343-3618
Mary A Russow, *President*
Tim Emmons, *Associate*
EMP: 25 **EST:** 1978
SQ FT: 45,000
SALES (est): 4.8MM **Privately Held**
WEB: www.waterchemistry.com
SIC: 2899 8734 Water treating compounds; water testing laboratory

(G-12023)
WATER TECHNOLOGIES INC
7525 Milk A Way Dr (24019-3216)
PHONE...................540 366-9799
Douglas Johnson, *Manager*
EMP: 3
SALES (corp-wide): 5.3MM **Privately Held**
SIC: 2899 Chemical supplies for foundries

HQ: Water Technologies Inc
8287 214th St W
Lakeville MN 55044
952 469-1147

(G-12024)
WOOD DESIGN & FABRICATION INC
Also Called: Architectural Wood
6877 Sugar Rum Ridge Rd (24018-6951)
PHONE...................540 774-8168
Bruce Cody, *President*
EMP: 15
SQ FT: 10,500 **Privately Held**
SIC: 2431 5031 Millwork; millwork

(G-12025)
WOODY GRAPHICS INC
6421 Merriman Rd (24018-6601)
PHONE...................540 774-4749
Robert Alan, *President*
EMP: 8
SALES (est): 1.1MM **Privately Held**
WEB: www.woodygraphics.com
SIC: 2752 7336 Commercial printing, offset; commercial art & graphic design

---

Roanoke
Roanoke City County

(G-12026)
22 CHURCH LLC
22 Church Ave Sw (24011-2002)
PHONE...................540 342-2817
Anna Karbassiyoon,
EMP: 2
SALES (est): 51.8K **Privately Held**
SIC: 3993 8742 Advertising artwork; marketing consulting services

(G-12027)
A & G COAL CORPORATION (PA)
302 S Jefferson St # 500 (24011-1710)
P.O. Box 1010, Wise (24293-1010)
PHONE...................276 328-3421
James C Justice, *President*
Jerry W Wharton, *President*
James T Miller, *Treasurer*
Stephen W Ball, *Admin Sec*
EMP: 40
SALES (est): 30.1MM **Privately Held**
SIC: 1221 1222 Strip mining, bituminous; bituminous coal-underground mining

(G-12028)
ACTION RESOURCES CORPORATION
Also Called: Miscellaneous Concrete Pdts
1910 Chapman Ave Sw (24016-3130)
P.O. Box 6164 (24017-0164)
PHONE...................540 343-5121
John H Turner, *President*
EMP: 15
SALES (est): 900K **Privately Held**
SIC: 3272 Concrete products, precast

(G-12029)
ADVANCED METAL FINISHING OF VA
523 Norfolk Ave Sw (24016-3013)
PHONE...................540 344-3216
Dwayne Robinson, *CEO*
Julia Roninson, *Vice Pres*
EMP: 7
SALES (est): 858.8K **Privately Held**
WEB: www.amfva.com
SIC: 3471 Anodizing (plating) of metals or formed products; plating of metals or formed products; decorative plating & finishing of formed products; finishing, metals or formed products

(G-12030)
AKZO NOBEL COATINGS INC
2837 Roanoke Ave Sw (24015-5407)
P.O. Box 4627 (24015-0627)
PHONE...................540 982-8301
Mark Beckner, *Plant Mgr*
Dan Shervey, *Accounts Mgr*
Jerry Leonard, *Sales Staff*
Tami Swearingin, *Sales Staff*
Doug Gilliam, *Manager*
EMP: 38

GEOGRAPHIC

SALES (corp-wide): 10.2B **Privately Held**
WEB: www.akzonobel.com
SIC: 2851 2861 Paints & allied products; gum & wood chemicals
HQ: Akzo Nobel Coatings Inc.
8220 Mohawk Dr
Strongsville OH 44136
440 297-5100

(G-12031)
ALLIED TOOL AND MACHINE CO VA
3362 Shenandoah Ave Nw (24017-4942)
PHONE....................540 342-6781
Nan B Kollar, *President*
Joseph Kollar, *Vice Pres*
Sharon L Malone, *Asst Sec*
EMP: 20 **EST:** 1976
SQ FT: 19,000
SALES (est): 2.5MM
SALES (corp-wide): 2.6MM **Privately Held**
SIC: 3444 Sheet metal specialties, not stamped
PA: Allied Tool And Machine Company
115 Corum St
Kernersville NC 27284
336 993-2131

(G-12032)
ALPHA PRESSURE WASHING
4402 Oakland Blvd Nw (24012-2529)
PHONE....................540 293-1287
David Nauss, *Principal*
EMP: 2
SALES (est): 144.7K **Privately Held**
SIC: 3589 High pressure cleaning equipment

(G-12033)
APEX TREE INDUSTRIES
1001 Howbert Ave Sw (24015-1713)
PHONE....................540 915-6489
John Gordon, *Principal*
EMP: 2
SALES (est): 89.4K **Privately Held**
SIC: 3999 Manufacturing industries

(G-12034)
APPOMATTOX LIME COMPANY
2343 Highland Farm Rd Nw (24017-1210)
PHONE....................540 774-1696
J Kenneth Randolph, *Principal*
EMP: 5
SALES (est): 576.9K **Privately Held**
WEB: www.rockydalequarries.com
SIC: 1422 Crushed & broken limestone

(G-12035)
ASSOCIATED ASP PARTNERS LLC (PA)
110 Franklin Rd Sw Fl 9 (24011-2310)
P.O. Box 12626 (24027-2626)
PHONE....................540 345-8867
Michael F Pesch, *CEO*
Bill Greehey, *Ch of Bd*
Bradley C Barron, *Senior VP*
Paul W Brattlof, *Senior VP*
◆ **EMP:** 11
SALES (est): 44.4MM **Privately Held**
WEB: www.associatedasphalt.com
SIC: 1311 Crude petroleum & natural gas

(G-12036)
ASSOCIATED ASPHALT INMAN LLC (PA)
110 Franklin Rd Se Fl 9 (24011-2147)
P.O. Box 12626 (24027-2626)
PHONE....................864 472-2816
EMP: 2
SALES (est): 280.3K **Privately Held**
WEB: www.associatedasphalt.com
SIC: 2951 Asphalt & asphaltic paving mixtures (not from refineries)

(G-12037)
ASSOCIATED ASPHALT TF LLC
110 Franklin Rd Se Fl 9 (24011-2147)
PHONE....................540 529-9789
EMP: 2
SALES (est): 81.9K **Privately Held**
SIC: 1311 Crude petroleum & natural gas

(G-12038)
B & B MACHINE & TOOL INC
Also Called: Bentech
3406 Orange Ave Ne (24012-6451)
PHONE....................540 344-6820
James Benton, *President*
EMP: 45
SQ FT: 9,000
SALES (est): 6.6MM **Privately Held**
WEB: www.bentechmfg.com
SIC: 3599 7692 3743 Machine shop, jobbing & repair; welding repair; railroad equipment

(G-12039)
B & B WELDING INC
Also Called: B & B Welding & Crane Service
1427 Norfolk Ave Se (24013-1240)
PHONE....................540 982-2082
Barry Blount, *President*
EMP: 5
SQ FT: 5,000
SALES (est): 500K **Privately Held**
SIC: 3548 7353 Welding & cutting apparatus & accessories; cranes & aerial lift equipment, rental or leasing

(G-12040)
BADEN RECLAMATION COMPANY
302 S Jefferson St (24011-1711)
P.O. Box 125, Clintwood (24228-0125)
PHONE....................540 776-7890
Harry Baden, *Principal*
EMP: 10
SALES (est): 1.4MM
SALES (corp-wide): 173.4MM **Privately Held**
SIC: 1241 Coal mining services
PA: James C. Justice Companies, Inc.
302 S Jefferson St # 400
Roanoke VA 24011
540 776-7890

(G-12041)
BADGER NEON & SIGN
508 Huntington Blvd Ne (24012-3536)
PHONE....................540 761-5779
Thomas West, *Principal*
EMP: 1
SALES (est): 46K **Privately Held**
SIC: 3993 Neon signs

(G-12042)
BECK MEDIA GROUP
806 Wasena Ave Sw Apt 101 (24015-5351)
P.O. Box 107 (24002-0107)
PHONE....................540 904-6800
Joey Beck, *Owner*
EMP: 5
SALES (est): 386.4K **Privately Held**
WEB: www.lovelybella.com
SIC: 2721 Magazines: publishing & printing

(G-12043)
BENTECH
1429 Centre Ave Nw (24017-5632)
PHONE....................540 344-6820
James Benton, *Owner*
EMP: 2
SALES (est): 135.8K **Privately Held**
WEB: www.bentechmfg.com
SIC: 3545 Tools & accessories for machine tools

(G-12044)
BEST PRINTING INC
4225 Plantation Rd Ne (24012-3137)
P.O. Box 155, Cloverdale (24077-0155)
PHONE....................540 563-9004
Gary S Wilson, *President*
William Figart, *Corp Secy*
Rebecca Bradbury, *Graphic Designe*
Shannon K Christley, *Graphic Designe*
EMP: 4
SQ FT: 1,700
SALES (est): 887.4K **Privately Held**
WEB: www.bestprintingofva.com
SIC: 2752 Commercial printing, offset

(G-12045)
BIG LICK SCREEN PRINTING
802 Kerns Ave Sw (24015-1818)
PHONE....................540 632-2695
EMP: 2

SALES (est): 83.9K **Privately Held**
WEB: www.blsp.rocks
SIC: 2752 Commercial printing, lithographic

(G-12046)
BLACK BEAR CORPORATION
2224 Buford Ave Sw (24015-5506)
P.O. Box 12127 (24023-2127)
PHONE....................540 982-1061
Linda O Jones, *President*
EMP: 4
SQ FT: 13,000
SALES (est): 500K **Privately Held**
WEB: www.blackbearusa.com
SIC: 2842 Laundry cleaning preparations

(G-12047)
BLACKSTONE ENERGY LTD
302 S Jefferson St (24011-1711)
PHONE....................540 776-7890
Griffith Wiliams, *President*
EMP: 9
SALES (est): 224.6K **Privately Held**
SIC: 1241 Coal mining services

(G-12048)
BLUE RDG ANTIGRAVITY TREADMLLS
3408 Wellington Dr Se (24014-6469)
PHONE....................540 977-9540
Bernarda Thompson, *Principal*
EMP: 1
SALES (est): 50.1K **Privately Held**
SIC: 3949 Treadmills

(G-12049)
BLUE RIDGE FABRICATORS INC
3 8th St Sw (24016-3003)
P.O. Box 12427 (24025-2427)
PHONE....................540 342-1102
Barry W Hartman, *President*
Michael W Hamilton, *Vice Pres*
Karen Simmons, *Office Mgr*
EMP: 10
SQ FT: 17,000
SALES (est): 750K **Privately Held**
WEB: www.blueridgefabricators.com
SIC: 3441 Fabricated structural metal

(G-12050)
BLUE STONE BLOCK SPRMKT INC (PA)
Also Called: Masonrymart
1510 Wallace Ave Ne (24012-6104)
P.O. Box 12546 (24026-2546)
PHONE....................540 982-3588
Rita B Corbitt, *President*
Wes Bowman, *Vice Pres*
Robert Corbitt, *Vice Pres*
Keith Jennings, *Vice Pres*
William A Corbitt Jr, *CFO*
▲ **EMP:** 24
SALES (est): 2.6MM **Privately Held**
WEB: www.bluestoneblock.com
SIC: 3271 3272 Blocks, concrete or cinder: standard; concrete products, precast

(G-12051)
BLUESTONE INDUSTRIES INC (HQ)
302 S Jefferson St # 500 (24011-1710)
PHONE....................540 776-7890
James C Justice III, *President*
EMP: 25
SALES (corp-wide): 173.4MM **Privately Held**
SIC: 1221 1311 0115 5083 Bituminous coal & lignite-surface mining; crude petroleum & natural gas; corn; agricultural machinery & equipment; farm machinery; architectural supplies; research services, except laboratory
PA: James C. Justice Companies, Inc.
302 S Jefferson St # 400
Roanoke VA 24011
540 776-7890

(G-12052)
BLUESTONE RESOURCES INC
302 S Jefferson St # 500 (24011-1710)
PHONE....................540 776-7890
Jack Lundin, *CEO*
EMP: 250

SALES (est): 4.5MM **Privately Held**
SIC: 1241 Coal mining services

(G-12053)
BOATWORKS & MORE LLC
152 Crittendon Ave Ne (24012-3002)
PHONE....................540 581-5820
Linda J Ramsingh, *Administration*
EMP: 2 **EST:** 2012
SALES (est): 156.9K **Privately Held**
SIC: 3732 Boat building & repairing

(G-12054)
BOBHRON INC
Also Called: Alien Surfwear & Silk Screen
2527 Avenel Ave Sw (24015-3407)
P.O. Box 4161 (24015-0161)
PHONE....................540 389-5699
Robert Jarrett, *President*
Rhonda Jarrett, *Vice Pres*
EMP: 10
SALES (est): 511.2K **Privately Held**
SIC: 2759 Screen printing

(G-12055)
BROOKS SIGN COMPANY
2724 Nicholas Ave Ne (24012-5628)
PHONE....................540 400-6144
Paschal Brooks IV, *Principal*
EMP: 2
SALES (est): 110.4K **Privately Held**
SIC: 3993 Signs & advertising specialties

(G-12056)
BURNETTES CUSTOM WOOD INC
2481 Eastland Rd (24014-4607)
PHONE....................540 577-9687
Leo Burnette, *Principal*
EMP: 2
SALES (est): 72.3K **Privately Held**
SIC: 2499 Wood products

(G-12057)
BUTLER PARACHUTE SYSTEMS INC
1820 Loudon Ave Nw (24017-5514)
P.O. Box 6098 (24017-0098)
PHONE....................540 342-2501
Manley C Butler Jr, *President*
Robin Guthrie, *Program Mgr*
EMP: 19
SQ FT: 22,000
SALES (est): 1.9MM **Privately Held**
WEB: www.butlerparachutes.com
SIC: 2399 Parachutes

(G-12058)
BUTLER UNMANNED PARACHUTE
1820 Loudon Ave Nw (24017-5514)
P.O. Box 6098 (24017-0098)
PHONE....................540 342-2501
Manley C Butler Jr,
EMP: 19
SQ FT: 22,000
SALES (est): 749.9K
SALES (corp-wide): 2.4MM **Privately Held**
WEB: www.butlerparachutes.com
SIC: 2399 Parachutes
PA: Butler Parachute Systems Group Inc
1820 Loudon Ave Nw
Roanoke VA 24017
540 342-2501

(G-12059)
C MEDIA COMPANY
4423 Pheasant Ridge Rd # 203 (24014-5299)
PHONE....................540 339-9626
EMP: 2
SALES (est): 137.6K **Privately Held**
WEB: www.cmediacompany.com
SIC: 3489 Depth charge release pistols & projectors, over 30 mm.

(G-12060)
CCBCC OPERATIONS LLC
Also Called: Coca-Cola
235 Shenandoah Ave Nw (24016-2455)
PHONE....................540 343-8041
Ken Voudren, *Branch Mgr*
EMP: 220

SALES (corp-wide): 4.8B Publicly Held
WEB: www.cokeconsolidated.com
SIC: 2086 Bottled & canned soft drinks
HQ: Ccbcc Operations, Llc
    4100 Coca Cola Plz
    Charlotte NC 28211
    704 364-8728

(G-12061)
CENTURY CONTROL SYSTEMS INC
307 11th St Se (24013-1105)
P.O. Box 7504 (24019-0504)
PHONE..................................540 992-5100
Stephen M Dean, *President*
EMP: 7
SQ FT: 1,500
SALES (est): 1.7MM Privately Held
WEB: www.centurycontrolsystems-inc.com
SIC: 3823 Industrial process control instruments

(G-12062)
CHANDLER CONCRETE INC
Also Called: Chandler Concrete of Virginia
614 Norfolk Ave Sw (24016-3016)
P.O. Box 12462 (24025-2462)
PHONE..................................540 345-3846
Alvin Gillespie, *Plant Mgr*
Frank Caldwell, *Branch Mgr*
EMP: 40 Privately Held
WEB: www.chandlerconcrete.com
SIC: 3273 3272 Ready-mixed concrete; concrete products
PA: Chandler Concrete Inc
    1006 S Church St
    Burlington NC 27215

(G-12063)
CHANGE COLA INC
620 Salem Ave Sw (24016-3026)
PHONE..................................703 674-9830
James Philips, *President*
Dan Cobb, *Vice Pres*
Kevin Conway, *Vice Pres*
EMP: 3 EST: 2009
SALES (est): 92.6K Privately Held
WEB: www.changecola.com
SIC: 2086 Bottled & canned soft drinks

(G-12064)
CHAPARRAL VIRGINIA INC
2580 Broadway Ave Sw (24014-1620)
PHONE..................................540 767-1238
EMP: 4
SALES (est): 324.6K Privately Held
WEB: www.gerdau.com
SIC: 3312 Blast furnaces & steel mills

(G-12065)
CHARLOTTESVILLE STONE COMPANY
2343 Highland Farm Rd Nw (24017-1210)
PHONE..................................434 295-5700
Kenneth Randolph, *President*
David D H Willis, *Vice Pres*
EMP: 1 EST: 2010
SALES (est): 118.8K
SALES (corp-wide): 13.3MM Privately Held
WEB: www.rockydalequarries.com
SIC: 1422 Crushed & broken limestone
PA: Rockydale Quarries Corporation
    2343 Highland Farm Rd Nw
    Roanoke VA 24017
    540 774-1696

(G-12066)
CHOCKLETT PRESS INC
2922 Nicholas Ave Ne (24012-5618)
PHONE..................................540 345-1820
Robert L Chocklett, *Principal*
Bob Chase, *Sales Staff*
EMP: 85 EST: 1938
SQ FT: 60,000
SALES (est): 19.8MM Privately Held
WEB: www.chocklettpress.com
SIC: 2752 2791 2789 2759 Commercial printing, offset; typesetting; bookbinding & related work; commercial printing

(G-12067)
CHORDA PHARMA LLC
709 S Jefferson St Ste 4 (24016-5106)
PHONE..................................251 753-1042
Richard Carliss, *President*

EMP: 1
SALES (est): 63.9K Privately Held
SIC: 2834 Proprietary drug products

(G-12068)
CONCRETE CASTINGS INC
1909 Progress Dr Se (24013-2911)
PHONE..................................540 427-3006
Dean F Bridges, *President*
EMP: 2
SALES (est): 315.1K Privately Held
SIC: 3272 Septic tanks, concrete; burial vaults, concrete or precast terrazzo

(G-12069)
CONCRETE SPECIALTIES INC
Also Called: C.S.i
1420 16th St Se (24014-2650)
PHONE..................................540 982-0777
Stephen C Rossi, *President*
EMP: 9
SQ FT: 1,000
SALES (est): 747.9K Privately Held
WEB:
www.concretespecialtiescompany.com
SIC: 3272 5211 Manhole covers or frames, concrete; masonry materials & supplies

(G-12070)
CONWED CORP
530 Gregory Ave Ne (24016-2129)
PHONE..................................540 981-0362
Michael Woldanski, *Vice Pres*
▲ EMP: 100
SQ FT: 42,000
SALES (est): 11.9MM Privately Held
WEB: www.swmintl.com
SIC: 3089 3083 3082 3052 Netting, plastic; laminated plastics plate & sheet; unsupported plastics profile shapes; rubber & plastics hose & beltings; packaging paper & plastics film, coated & laminated

(G-12071)
CONWET PLASTICS LLC
530 Gregory Ave Ne (24016-2129)
PHONE..................................540 981-0362
Lawrence Ptaschek, *Principal*
Bill Flannagan, *Manager*
EMP: 9
SALES (est): 1.1MM Privately Held
WEB: www.swmintl.com
SIC: 3081 Unsupported plastics film & sheet

(G-12072)
COOPER CROUSE-HINDS LLC
Also Called: Distribution Center
1700 Blue Hills Dr Ne (24012-8601)
PHONE..................................540 983-1300
Judy Simon, *Manager*
EMP: 16 Privately Held
WEB: www.coopercrouse-hinds.com
SIC: 3699 Fire control or bombing equipment, electronic
HQ: Cooper Crouse-Hinds, Llc
    1201 Wolf St
    Syracuse NY 13208
    315 477-7000

(G-12073)
COSMETIC ESSENCE LLC
4411 Plantation Rd Ne (24012-7410)
PHONE..................................540 563-3000
Linda Atakishiyera, *Research*
Domenic Castellane, *Accounts Mgr*
Roy Drilon, *Manager*
EMP: 100
SALES (corp-wide): 30.1MM Privately Held
WEB: www.voyantbeauty.com
SIC: 2844 Cosmetic preparations
HQ: Cosmetic Essence, Llc
    2182 Hwy 35
    Holmdel NJ 07733
    732 888-7788

(G-12074)
CREATIVE INK INC
416 S Jefferson St 808 (24011-2020)
PHONE..................................540 342-2400
Stephanie Rogol, *President*
EMP: 4

SALES (est): 434.5K Privately Held
WEB: www.creativeinkpromotions.com
SIC: 2759 Screen printing

(G-12075)
CURRY COPY CENTER OF ROANOKE
116 Campbell Ave Sw (24011-1224)
PHONE..................................540 345-2865
Mitzi Willingham, *President*
Teresa Barnett, *Corp Secy*
EMP: 3 EST: 1977
SQ FT: 4,000
SALES (est): 381.7K Privately Held
WEB: www.currycopycenterva.com
SIC: 2752 Photo-offset printing; commercial printing, offset

(G-12076)
CUSTOM AUTO GLASS & PLASTICS
340 Fugate Rd Ne (24012-4432)
PHONE..................................540 362-8798
Carl Dehart, *Owner*
EMP: 1
SALES (est): 94.3K Privately Held
SIC: 3089 Windshields, plastic

(G-12077)
CUSTOMIZED LLC
1610 Rugby Blvd Nw (24017-3632)
PHONE..................................540 492-2975
Demetria Brown,
EMP: 1
SALES (est): 31.2K Privately Held
SIC: 2395 Art goods for embroidering, stamped: purchased materials

(G-12078)
DFA DAIRY BRANDS FLUID LLC
540 Mohawk Ave Ne (24012-5732)
PHONE..................................540 777-4091
EMP: 9
SALES (corp-wide): 15.8B Privately Held
SIC: 2026 Fluid milk
HQ: Dfa Dairy Brands Fluid, Llc
    1405 N 98th St
    Kansas City KS 66111
    816 801-6455

(G-12079)
DWS PUBLICITY LLC
3768 Parliament Rd Sw (24014-2262)
PHONE..................................540 330-3763
EMP: 2
SALES (est): 81K Privately Held
SIC: 2741 Miscellaneous publishing

(G-12080)
E L PRINTING CO
4448 Pheasant Ridge Rd (24014-5322)
PHONE..................................540 776-0373
EMP: 2 EST: 2010
SALES (est): 110K Privately Held
SIC: 2752 Lithographic Commercial Printing

(G-12081)
E W STALEY CORPORATION
Also Called: E & W Machine
2113 Salem Ave Sw (24016-2515)
PHONE..................................540 389-1197
E W Staley, *President*
Yvonne Blackwell, *Corp Secy*
EMP: 8
SALES (est): 1.2MM Privately Held
WEB: www.eandwmachine.com
SIC: 3599 Machine shop, jobbing & repair

(G-12082)
EARL WOOD PRINTING CO
Also Called: ABC Rubber Stamps
3415 Whiteside St Ne (24012-3761)
PHONE..................................540 563-8833
Robert E Wood Jr, *Owner*
EMP: 2 EST: 1933
SQ FT: 2,400
SALES (est): 150K Privately Held
SIC: 2759 2752 Letterpress printing; commercial printing, offset

(G-12083)
EXCEL PRSTHETICS ORTHOTICS INC (PA)
115 Albemarle Ave Se (24013-2205)
PHONE..................................540 982-0205
Douglas C Walters, *President*
Sharol Stoneburner, *General Mgr*
Andrea Britt, *Corp Secy*
Lester C Hinshaw, *Vice Pres*
Karen Walters, *Vice Pres*
EMP: 17 EST: 1975
SQ FT: 6,500
SALES (est): 3.8MM Privately Held
WEB: www.excel-prosthetics.com
SIC: 3842 5999 Limbs, artificial; artificial limbs

(G-12084)
FABRICATED WELDING SPECIALITES
525 Caldwell St Nw (24017-4201)
PHONE..................................540 345-3104
Kenneth Hicks III, *President*
EMP: 1
SALES (est): 122.1K Privately Held
SIC: 7692 Welding repair

(G-12085)
FAITH PUBLISHING LLC
805 Brandon Ave Sw (24015-5007)
PHONE..................................540 632-3608
Tina S Buchanan, *Administration*
EMP: 2
SALES (est): 55K Privately Held
SIC: 2741 Miscellaneous publishing

(G-12086)
FEATHER & PEARL CANDLE CO LLC
1430 Maple Ave Sw (24016-4915)
PHONE..................................540 769-9529
EMP: 1
SALES (est): 42.7K Privately Held
SIC: 3999 Candles

(G-12087)
FIRST IMPRSSIONS PRTG GRAPHICS
2615 Orange Ave Ne Ste A (24012-6256)
PHONE..................................540 342-2679
Mark Lawhorn, *President*
EMP: 2
SALES (est): 250K Privately Held
SIC: 2752 Commercial printing, offset

(G-12088)
FLOWERS BAKERIES LLC
523 Shenandoah Ave Nw (24016-2318)
PHONE..................................540 343-8165
EMP: 47
SALES (corp-wide): 3.9B Publicly Held
SIC: 2051 Mfg Bread/Related Products
HQ: Flowers Bakeries, Llc
    1919 Flowers Cir
    Thomasville GA 31757

(G-12089)
FLOWERS BKG CO LYNCHBURG LLC
3527 Melrose Ave Nw (24017-2711)
PHONE..................................434 528-0441
Allen Branscome, *Manager*
EMP: 4
SALES (corp-wide): 4.1B Publicly Held
SIC: 2051 Bread, all types (white, wheat, rye, etc): fresh or frozen
HQ: Flowers Baking Co. Of Lynchburg, Llc
    1905 Hollins Mill Rd
    Lynchburg VA 24503
    434 528-0441

(G-12090)
FLOWERS BKG CO LYNCHBURG LLC
Also Called: D J Thrift Store
2502 Melrose Ave Nw (24017-3910)
PHONE..................................540 344-5919
Marylou Waldon, *Manager*
EMP: 2
SALES (corp-wide): 4.1B Publicly Held
SIC: 2051 Bread, cake & related products

GEOGRAPHIC

HQ: Flowers Baking Co. Of Lynchburg, Llc
1905 Hollins Mill Rd
Lynchburg VA 24503
434 528-0441

(G-12091)
FOOT LEVELERS INC
Also Called: Shoe Mate Orthopedic Arch Co
518 Pocahontas Ave Ne (24012-5725)
P.O. Box 12611 (24027-2611)
PHONE...................................800 553-4860
Monte H Greenawalt, *CEO*
Kent S Greenawalt, *President*
Mickey Maury, *Principal*
Anthony Conversa, *Vice Pres*
Geoff Miller, *Vice Pres*
▲ EMP: 40
SQ FT: 3,000
SALES (est): 11.7MM **Privately Held**
WEB: www.footlevelers.com
SIC: 3842 Supports: abdominal, ankle,
arch, kneecap, etc.

(G-12092)
FOOTMAXX OF VIRGINIA INC
518 Pocahontas Ave Ne (24012-5725)
P.O. Box 13633 (24035-3633)
PHONE...................................540 345-0008
Kent Greenawalt, *President*
Dwayne Bennett, *Vice Pres*
Dawn Galbraith, *Vice Pres*
Marc Cohen, *Manager*
EMP: 2
SALES (est): 244.3K **Privately Held**
WEB: www.3dmaxx.com
SIC: 3842 Surgical appliances & supplies

(G-12093)
FRANK CHERVAN INC
2005 Greenbrier Ave Se (24013-2651)
PHONE...................................540 586-5600
Gregory M Terrill, *President*
Richard A Terrill, *Chairman*
Glen Campbell, *Maintenance Dir*
Renee Austin, *Project Mgr*
Jim St Clair, *Purchasing*
▲ EMP: 200 EST: 1932
SQ FT: 250,000
SALES (est): 32MM **Privately Held**
WEB: www.chervan.com
SIC: 2521 Wood office furniture

(G-12094)
FREIGHTCAR ROANOKE INC
Also Called: Freight Car
830 Campbell Ave Se (24013-1042)
PHONE...................................540 342-2303
Chris Rajot, *President*
Lynn Tatum, *Maintence Staff*
◆ EMP: 100
SQ FT: 10,000
SALES (est): 16MM
SALES (corp-wide): 229.9MM **Publicly Held**
WEB: www.freightcaramerica.com
SIC: 3743 Freight cars & equipment
HQ: Johnstown America, Llc
129 Industrial Park Rd
Johnstown PA 15904

(G-12095)
G & D MANUFACTURING
2810 Belle Ave Ne (24012-6308)
PHONE...................................540 345-7267
Don Cassaras, *Owner*
Ginger Cassaras, *Owner*
EMP: 2 **Privately Held**
SIC: 3199 Equestrian related leather articles

(G-12096)
GENE TAYLOR
1606 Rugby Blvd Nw (24017-3632)
PHONE...................................540 345-9001
EMP: 2
SALES (est): 105.9K **Privately Held**
SIC: 2389 Mfg Apparel/Accessories

(G-12097)
GIANNI ENTPS INC DBA VRGINA PL
824 4th St Se (24013-1704)
PHONE...................................540 314-6566
EMP: 2
SALES (est): 97.8K **Privately Held**
SIC: 3089 Injection molding of plastics

(G-12098)
GREGORY PALLET & LUMBER CO
2005 Greenbrier Ave Se B (24013-2651)
PHONE...................................540 777-1715
Michael Gregory, *Principal*
EMP: 4
SALES (est): 636.7K **Privately Held**
SIC: 2448 Pallets, wood

(G-12099)
GUTTER-STUFF INDUSTRIES VA LLC
3408 W Ridge Cir Sw (24014-4239)
PHONE...................................540 982-1115
Vincent Basile, *Principal*
EMP: 2
SALES (est): 98.8K **Privately Held**
SIC: 3999 Manufacturing industries

(G-12100)
HARRIS KAYLA
Also Called: Taylormade Cakes
2633 Springhill Dr Nw (24017-3325)
PHONE...................................540 285-0495
Kayla Harris, *Owner*
EMP: 7
SALES (est): 34K **Privately Held**
SIC: 2051 Cakes, bakery: except frozen

(G-12101)
HEDRICK MUSIC INC
3601 Dogwood Ln Sw (24015-4503)
PHONE...................................540 354-2139
Teresa A Hedrick, *Admin Sec*
EMP: 2 EST: 2016
SALES (est): 94.5K **Privately Held**
WEB: www.bandfundamentals.com
SIC: 2741 Miscellaneous publishing

(G-12102)
HOLLYS HOMEMADE TREATS
5448 Setter Rd (24012-8548)
PHONE...................................540 977-1373
Holly Wilkenson, *Owner*
John Hull, *Director*
EMP: 1
SALES (est): 57K **Privately Held**
SIC: 2051 Cakes, pies & pastries

(G-12103)
HOWMET AEROSPACE INC
1775 Seibel Dr Ne (24012-5623)
PHONE...................................540 343-1591
EMP: 2 **Publicly Held**
WEB: www.howmet.com
SIC: 3353 Aluminum sheet & strip
PA: Howmet Aerospace Inc.
201 Isabella St Ste 200
Pittsburgh PA 15212
412 992-2500

(G-12104)
HUB PATTERN CORPORATION (HQ)
2113 Salem Ave Sw (24016-2515)
P.O. Box 4067 (24015-0067)
PHONE...................................540 342-3505
Hubert Humphrey, *CEO*
Lane Witte, *COO*
John A Cloeter, *Vice Pres*
Lou Lovati, *Plant Mgr*
Donald L Cloeter, *Engineer*
EMP: 28 EST: 1966
SQ FT: 25,000
SALES (est): 5.2MM
SALES (corp-wide): 234.9K **Privately Held**
WEB: www.hubcorp.net
SIC: 3543 3544 3599 Industrial patterns;
special dies, tools, jigs & fixtures; industrial molds; machine & other job shop work
PA: Hub Capital Group, Llc
2113 Salem Ave Sw
Roanoke VA 24016
540 342-3505

(G-12105)
INCENSE OIL MORE
535 Mcdowell Ave Nw (24016-1223)
PHONE...................................540 793-8642
EMP: 2 EST: 2010
SALES (est): 120K **Privately Held**
SIC: 2899 Mfg Chemical Preparations

(G-12106)
INFOSEAL LLC (PA)
1825 Blue Hills Cir Ne (24012-8661)
PHONE...................................540 981-1140
Andy Harnett, *Partner*
David Harnett, *Partner*
David Yost, *General Mgr*
Kenneth Weirich, *Plant Mgr*
Infoseal Barr, *Manager*
▲ EMP: 63
SALES (est): 20.3MM **Privately Held**
WEB: www.infoseal.com
SIC: 2759 Commercial printing

(G-12107)
INTERACTIVE ACHIEVEMENT LLC
601 Campbell Ave Sw (24016-3531)
P.O. Box 3122 (24015-1122)
PHONE...................................540 206-3649
Jon Hagmaier, *CEO*
Donald Francolino, *Executive*
Lorraine Lange,
EMP: 17 EST: 2007
SALES (est): 177.1K
SALES (corp-wide): 3.7B **Privately Held**
SIC: 7372 Prepackaged software
HQ: Powerschool Group Llc
150 Parkshore Dr
Folsom CA 95630
916 288-1588

(G-12108)
J C ENTERPRISES
526 Rorer Ave Sw (24016-3604)
PHONE...................................540 345-0552
EMP: 2 EST: 2010
SALES (est): 110K **Privately Held**
SIC: 3446 Mfg Architectural Metalwork

(G-12109)
JACKSON & JACKSON INC
4903 Rowe Ridge Rd Nw (24017-4631)
P.O. Box 19542 (24019-1055)
PHONE...................................434 851-1798
Arthur Jackson, *President*
Rebecca Jackson, *Admin Sec*
EMP: 3
SALES (est): 500K **Privately Held**
SIC: 3531 3599 Forestry related equipment; amusement park equipment

(G-12110)
JEANNIE JACKSON GREEN
Also Called: Abasn Promotional Products
1736 Greenwood Rd Sw (24015-2818)
PHONE...................................540 904-6763
Jeannie Green, *Owner*
EMP: 1
SALES (est): 83.3K **Privately Held**
WEB: www.abasnpromo.com
SIC: 3993 7389 Signs & advertising specialties; embroidering of advertising on shirts, etc.

(G-12111)
JIM SIRRINE
2717 Beverly Blvd Sw (24015-4025)
PHONE...................................540 874-7006
EMP: 2
SALES (est): 76.5K **Privately Held**
SIC: 2032 Canned specialties

(G-12112)
JOHN C NORDT CO INC
Also Called: Guertin Bros
1420 Coulter Dr Nw (24012-1132)
PHONE...................................540 362-9717
Paul W Nordt III, *Ch of Bd*
Robert O Nordt Sr, *Exec VP*
William F Nordt, *Vice Pres*
Gary Leatherman, *CFO*
Lois O Nordt, *Admin Sec*
EMP: 130 EST: 1872
SQ FT: 43,000
SALES (est): 19MM **Privately Held**
WEB: www.jcnordt.com
SIC: 3911 3915 Rings, finger: precious metal; jewelers' castings

(G-12113)
JOHN W GRIESSMAYER JR
Also Called: Mighty
400 Salem Ave Sw Unit 1c (24016-3632)
PHONE...................................540 589-8387
John Griessmayer, *Owner*
EMP: 1 EST: 2013
SALES (est): 70.1K **Privately Held**
SIC: 3993 Signs & advertising specialties

(G-12114)
JUSTICE COAL OF ALABAMA LLC
302 S Jefferson St # 400 (24011-1710)
PHONE...................................540 776-7890
James C Justice III, *President*
Stephen Ball, *Admin Sec*
EMP: 7
SALES (est): 728.6K **Privately Held**
SIC: 1221 Strip mining, bituminous

(G-12115)
JUSTICE LOW SEAM MINING INC
302 S Jefferson St # 400 (24011-1711)
P.O. Box 2178, Beaver WV (25813-2178)
PHONE...................................540 776-7890
James C Justice III, *President*
James T Miller, *Treasurer*
Stephen W Ball, *Admin Sec*
EMP: 13
SALES (est): 1.9MM
SALES (corp-wide): 173.4MM **Privately Held**
SIC: 1241 Bituminous coal mining services, contract basis
PA: James C. Justice Companies, Inc.
302 S Jefferson St # 400
Roanoke VA 24011
540 776-7890

(G-12116)
JWB OF ROANOKE INC
Also Called: Sunnyside Awning Co
601 Salem Ave Sw (24016-3025)
P.O. Box 2602 (24010-2602)
PHONE...................................540 344-7726
James H Via, *President*
Evelyn Farrington, *Admin Sec*
EMP: 12 EST: 1908
SQ FT: 7,000
SALES (est): 1.3MM **Privately Held**
SIC: 2591 2394 Drapery hardware & blinds & shades; canvas awnings & canopies

(G-12117)
KEVINS SIGNS
1007 Industry Ave Se (24013-2905)
PHONE...................................540 427-1070
Kevin Ransom, *Owner*
EMP: 1
SQ FT: 6,000
SALES (est): 86.6K **Privately Held**
SIC: 3993 Signs & advertising specialties

(G-12118)
KING SCREEN
1627 Shenandoah Ave Nw (24017-5549)
PHONE...................................540 904-5864
Scott Garnett, *Owner*
EMP: 4 EST: 2015
SALES (est): 357.6K **Privately Held**
WEB: www.kingscreen.com
SIC: 2759 Screen printing

(G-12119)
KINSEY CRANE & SIGN COMPANY
4663 Ferguson Valley Rd (24014-5963)
PHONE...................................540 345-5063
Frank Kinsey, *President*
Byron Brown, *Admin Sec*
EMP: 7
SALES (est): 525K **Privately Held**
WEB: www.kinseysign.com
SIC: 3993 Signs & advertising specialties

(G-12120)
KINSEY NEON & SIGN COMPANY
1516 Cleveland Ave Sw (24016-3235)
PHONE...................................540 345-5063
EMP: 2
SALES (est): 55.7K **Privately Held**
WEB: www.kinseysign.com
SIC: 3993 Neon signs

▲ = Import ▼=Export
◆ =Import/Export

(G-12121)
KINSEY SIGN COMPANY
2727 Mary Linda Ave Ne (24012-5609)
PHONE..................................540 344-5148
EMP: 1
SALES (est): 81.5K Privately Held
SIC: 3993 Mfg Signs/Advertising Special-
ties

(G-12122)
KONECRANES INC
1226 Trapper Cir Nw Ste E (24012-1144)
PHONE..................................540 366-9502
Lora Gibson, Manager
EMP: 4
SALES (corp-wide): 3.6B Privately Held
WEB: www.konecranes.com
SIC: 3536 Hoists, cranes & monorails
HQ: Konecranes, Inc.
4401 Gateway Blvd
Springfield OH 45502

(G-12123)
KOVATCH MOBILE EQUIPMENT CORP
Also Called: K M E Fire Apparatus
1708 Seibel Dr Ne (24012-5624)
PHONE..................................540 982-3573
Greg Agee, Manager
EMP: 41 Publicly Held
WEB: www.kmefire.com
SIC: 3711 Fire department vehicles (motor
vehicles), assembly of
HQ: Kovatch Mobile Equipment Corp.
1 Industrial Complex
Nesquehoning PA 18240
570 669-9461

(G-12124)
LEE TECH HARDWOOD FLOORS
180 Huntington Blvd Ne (24012-3624)
PHONE..................................540 588-6217
EMP: 1
SALES (est): 117.1K Privately Held
WEB: www.leehardwoodfloors.com
SIC: 2426 1771 1752 Flooring, hardwood;
flooring contractor; floor laying & floor
work

(G-12125)
LFM ROANOKE
36 30th St Nw (24017-5206)
PHONE..................................540 342-0542
EMP: 1
SALES (est): 59.4K Privately Held
SIC: 2711 Newspapers

(G-12126)
LITTLEJOHN PRINTING CO
4185 Bonsack Rd (24012-7017)
P.O. Box 186, Vinton (24179-0186)
PHONE..................................540 977-1377
Richard Sink, Owner
EMP: 1
SALES (est): 97.6K Privately Held
SIC: 2752 Commercial printing, offset

(G-12127)
LLOYD ELECTRIC CO INC
605 3rd St Se (24013-1498)
PHONE..................................540 982-0135
Richard D Lloyd, President
Penny K Lloyd, Vice Pres
Ali Platt, Sales Executive
EMP: 11 EST: 1924
SQ FT: 15,000
SALES (est): 2.5MM Privately Held
WEB: www.lloydelectric.net
SIC: 7694 5063 Electric motor repair; mo-
tors, electric

(G-12128)
LOA MALS ON WHELS WLLIAMSON RD
3333 Williamson Rd Nw (24012-4048)
PHONE..................................540 563-0482
Kevin Escue, Principal
EMP: 2
SALES (est): 141.7K Privately Held
SIC: 3312 Wheels

(G-12129)
LOGOS SOFTWARE INC
324 Campbell Ave Sw (24016-3625)
PHONE..................................540 819-6260

EMP: 2 EST: 2010
SALES (est): 85K Privately Held
SIC: 7372 Prepackaged Software Services

(G-12130)
LONZA E KINGERY
6477 Crowell Gap Rd (24014-7111)
PHONE..................................540 774-8728
Lonza E Kingery, Principal
EMP: 2
SQ FT: 1,031,936
SALES (est): 168.6K Privately Held
SIC: 2834 Pharmaceutical preparations

(G-12131)
M5 TECHNOLOGIES LLC
Also Called: Microscope.com
1222 Mcdowell Ave Ne (24012-8019)
PHONE..................................540 904-0880
Elissa Herring,
EMP: 8
SALES (est): 354.7K Privately Held
SIC: 3827 Microscopes, except electron,
proton & corneal

(G-12132)
MARIO INDUSTRIES VIRGINIA INC (PA)
Also Called: Mario Contract Lighting
2490 Patterson Ave Sw (24016-2528)
P.O. Box 3190 (24015-1190)
PHONE..................................540 342-1111
Louis Scutellaro, President
M Dean Martin, Vice Pres
Joseph Semeniro, Vice Pres
Linda Palmer, Sales Staff
Rhonda Allie, Manager
▲ EMP: 50 EST: 1926
SQ FT: 100,000
SALES (est): 20.1MM Privately Held
WEB: www.mariocontractlighting.com
SIC: 3645 Lamp & light shades

(G-12133)
MARTINS FABRICATING & WELDING
1108 Orange Ave Ne (24012-5842)
PHONE..................................540 343-6001
William Martin, President
EMP: 2
SALES (est): 192.1K Privately Held
SIC: 3441 1799 Fabricated structural
metal; athletic & recreation facilities con-
struction

(G-12134)
MAXIM SYSTEMS INC
4142 Melrose Ave Nw # 12 (24017-5800)
P.O. Box 10731 (24022-0731)
PHONE..................................540 265-9050
Lawerence Munger, President
Rob Fox, Vice Pres
▲ EMP: 5
SQ FT: 2,000
SALES (est): 1.7MM Privately Held
WEB: www.maximsystems.net
SIC: 3593 Fluid power cylinders, hydraulic
or pneumatic

(G-12135)
MBH INC
5623 Wild Oak Dr (24014-5920)
PHONE..................................540 427-5471
Michael S Hoal, Principal
EMP: 2
SALES (est): 151.4K Privately Held
SIC: 2399 Fabricated textile products

(G-12136)
MICRO MEDIA COMMUNICATION INC
378 Allison Ave Sw (24016-4604)
PHONE..................................540 345-2197
Jerry L Hartman, President
EMP: 5
SALES (est): 265.8K Privately Held
SIC: 2741 Directories: publishing only, not
printed on site

(G-12137)
MONTYCO LLC
Also Called: Play By Play
2515 Laburnum Ave Sw (24015-3431)
PHONE..................................540 761-6751
John Montgomery, Owner

EMP: 1
SALES (est): 110K Privately Held
WEB: www.playbyplayonline.net
SIC: 2721 Magazines: publishing only, not
printed on site

(G-12138)
MR-MOW-IT-ALL
Also Called: Jmashby
1102 Tazewell Ave Se (24013-1536)
PHONE..................................540 263-2369
John Ashby, CEO
EMP: 6
SALES (est): 100K Privately Held
SIC: 3524 Lawn & garden equipment

(G-12139)
MUNDY STONE COMPANY
4592 Old Rocky Mount Rd S (24014-5109)
PHONE..................................540 774-1696
Robert Mundy, Principal
EMP: 4
SALES (est): 309.2K Privately Held
WEB: www.rockydalequarries.com
SIC: 1422 Crushed & broken limestone

(G-12140)
NEW YORK AIR BRAKE COMPANY
2875 Larkview Cir Sw (24015-3970)
PHONE..................................540 989-5044
Barbara Tarango, Project Mgr
Justin Terpstra, Opers Staff
Aaron Young, Opers Staff
Taylor Boggs, Engineer
John Brand, Engineer
EMP: 2
SALES (est): 187.9K Privately Held
WEB: www.nyab.com
SIC: 3743 Railroad equipment

(G-12141)
NIDAY INC
4349 Bandy Rd (24014-5941)
PHONE..................................540 427-2776
Joe Niday, Owner
Carol Niday, Admin Sec
EMP: 3
SALES (est): 161K Privately Held
SIC: 2542 Partitions & fixtures, except
wood

(G-12142)
NOKE TRUCK LLC
16 Church Ave Sw (24011-2143)
PHONE..................................540 266-0045
Juan Uriea, Principal
EMP: 2 EST: 2011
SALES (est): 195.8K Privately Held
WEB: www.noketruck.com
SIC: 3715 Truck trailers

(G-12143)
NUVIDRILL LLC
2217 Crystl Spg Ave Sw (24014-2433)
PHONE..................................540 353-8787
Joshua Marcus, Mng Member
Kevin Mallin,
◆ EMP: 4
SALES (est): 1.2MM Privately Held
SIC: 3541 3546 Drilling machine tools
(metal cutting); drills & drilling tools

(G-12144)
PACKAGING CORPORATION AMERICA
1005 Industry Cir Se (24013-2929)
PHONE..................................540 427-3164
Don Woodward, Branch Mgr
EMP: 2 Publicly Held
WEB: www.packagingcorp.com
SIC: 2653 Boxes, corrugated: made from
purchased materials
PA: Packaging Corporation Of America
1 N Field Ct
Lake Forest IL 60045
847 482-3000

(G-12145)
PAVEMENT STENCIL COMPANY
4347 Aerospace Rd Ste A (24014-6115)
P.O. Box 18034 (24014-0783)
PHONE..................................540 427-1325
Chuck Smith, Owner
EMP: 12

SALES (est): 1.8MM Privately Held
WEB: www.pavementstencil.com
SIC: 2631 Stencil board

(G-12146)
PEPSI BOTTLING GROUP
Also Called: Pepsi-Cola
2866 Nicholas Ave Ne (24012-5616)
PHONE..................................540 344-8355
Harold Smith, Principal
Joseph Ogle, Admin Sec
EMP: 6
SALES (est): 468.4K Privately Held
SIC: 2086 Carbonated soft drinks, bottled
& canned

(G-12147)
PHILLIPS ENTERPRISES VA INC
Also Called: Advanced Machining Solutions
1755 Seibel Dr Ne (24012-5623)
PHONE..................................540 563-9915
Roger Phillips, President
EMP: 7
SALES (est): 289.9K Privately Held
WEB: www.advmachsol.com
SIC: 3599 Machine shop, jobbing & repair

(G-12148)
PLASTIC FABRICATING INC
2558 Patterson Ave Sw (24016-2530)
P.O. Box 892, Salem (24153-0892)
PHONE..................................540 345-6901
Carl G Stevens, President
Eric Helm, CFO
EMP: 18
SQ FT: 12,000
SALES (est): 5.6MM Privately Held
WEB: www.plasticfabricatinginc.com
SIC: 3443 Plate work for the metalworking
trade; liners, industrial: metal plate; tanks,
standard or custom fabricated: metal
plate

(G-12149)
PPG INDUSTRIES INC
116 Liberty Rd Ne (24012-4816)
PHONE..................................540 563-2118
Henry Jackson, Principal
▲ EMP: 1
SALES (est): 68.5K Privately Held
SIC: 3999 Manufacturing industries

(G-12150)
PRAXAIR WELDING GAS & SUP STR
1757 Granby St Ne Ste A (24012-5603)
PHONE..................................540 342-9700
EMP: 3
SALES (est): 123.2K Privately Held
SIC: 2813 Industrial gases

(G-12151)
PRECISION NUCLEAR OF VIRGINIA
1906 Belleview Ave Se (24014-1838)
PHONE..................................540 389-8333
Steven Chilinski, President
EMP: 5
SALES (est): 229.7K Privately Held
SIC: 2834 Pharmaceutical preparations

(G-12152)
PRECISION STEEL MFG CORP
1723 Seibel Dr Ne (24012-5623)
PHONE..................................540 985-8963
Mike Amos, President
Eric Boyd, Prdtn Mgr
Rob Crigger, Purchasing
Roger Cronise, Engineer
Debbie Honaker, Human Res Mgr
EMP: 60
SQ FT: 60,000
SALES (est): 13.9MM Privately Held
WEB: www.precisionsteelmfg.com
SIC: 3441 3599 Building components,
structural steel; machine shop, jobbing &
repair

(G-12153)
PRESS PRESS MERCH LLC
128 Albemarle Ave Se (24013-2206)
PHONE..................................540 206-3495
Gregory Szechenyi, CEO
Laila Meftah, Sales Staff
Nathan Blankenship, Manager

EMP: 9 **EST:** 2007
SALES (est): 1MM **Privately Held**
WEB: www.presspressmerch.com
SIC: 2759 Screen printing

(G-12154)
PRINTECH INC
2001 Patterson Ave Sw (24016-2509)
P.O. Box 12705 (24027-2705)
PHONE..............................540 343-9200
Albin B Hammond, *President*
Nancy Hammond, *Corp Secy*
EMP: 15
SQ FT: 25,000
SALES: 548.6K **Privately Held**
SIC: 2752 2761 5112 Business forms,
lithographed; computer forms, manifold or
continuous; computer paper

(G-12155)
PRINTING CONCEPTS OF VIRG
1502 Williamson Rd Ne A (24012-5130)
PHONE..............................540 904-5951
Ruby Johnson, *Principal*
Devon Johnson, *Manager*
Michael Draper,
EMP: 4
SALES (est): 433.9K **Privately Held**
WEB: www.printingconceptsva.com
SIC: 2752 Commercial printing, offset

(G-12156)
PROCHEM TECHNOLOGIES INC
4709 Cheraw Lake Rd Nw (24017-1018)
P.O. Box 13944 (24038-3944)
PHONE..............................540 520-8339
Bobby Lavender, *President*
EMP: 2
SALES (est): 850K **Privately Held**
SIC: 2611 Pulp mills, chemical & semi-
chemical processing

(G-12157)
PROGRESS RAIL SERVICES
CORP
1010 Hollins Rd Ne (24012-8011)
PHONE..............................540 345-4039
Cecil Fergunon, *Branch Mgr*
EMP: 5 **Publicly Held**
WEB: www.progressrail.com
SIC: 3743 Railroad equipment
HQ: Progress Rail Services Corporation
1600 Progress Dr
Albertville AL 35950
256 505-6421

(G-12158)
QUALITY MANUFACTURING CO
518 18th St Sw (24016-3118)
P.O. Box 3185 (24015-1185)
PHONE..............................540 982-6699
Larry B Morris, *President*
EMP: 5 **EST:** 1978
SQ FT: 7,400
SALES (est): 895.3K **Privately Held**
SIC: 3823 Industrial instrmnts msrmnt dis-
play/control process variable

(G-12159)
R&R ORNAMENTAL IRON INC
1727 Cleveland Ave Sw (24016-3133)
PHONE..............................540 798-1699
Reggie Gray, *Owner*
Rich Freeman, *Vice Pres*
EMP: 4 **EST:** 2011
SALES (est): 465.3K **Privately Held**
WEB: www.ironworks4u.com
SIC: 3446 Architectural metalwork

(G-12160)
RAPIDSIGN INC
720 Liberty Rd Ne (24012-4504)
PHONE..............................540 362-2025
Lana Atkins, *President*
EMP: 3
SALES (est): 337.1K **Privately Held**
WEB: www.rapidsignroanoke.com
SIC: 3993 Signs & advertising specialties

(G-12161)
REDDY ICE GROUP INC
1512 Patrick Rd Ne (24012-8603)
PHONE..............................540 777-0253
David Mangrum, *Branch Mgr*
EMP: 22 **Privately Held**
WEB: www.reddyice.com

SIC: 2097 Manufactured ice
HQ: Reddy Ice Group, Inc.
5720 Lbj Fwy Ste 200
Dallas TX 75240

(G-12162)
RENAISSNCE CNTRACT LTG
FURN IN
2807 Mary Linda Ave Ne (24012-5611)
PHONE..............................540 342-1548
Troy Cook, *President*
Megan Slusser, *Admin Asst*
Jessica Wood,
▲ **EMP:** 20
SQ FT: 45,000
SALES (est): 3.1MM **Privately Held**
WEB: www.rclfsitefurnishings.com
SIC: 2511 3645 Wood household furniture;
desk lamps

(G-12163)
RNK OUTDOORS
3022 Pioneer Rd Nw (24012-3438)
PHONE..............................540 797-3698
Eric Folks, *President*
EMP: 2
SALES (est): 141.6K **Privately Held**
SIC: 3545 Machine tool accessories

(G-12164)
ROANOKE
1255 Trapper Cir Nw (24012-1123)
PHONE..............................540 362-8404
EMP: 3 **EST:** 2017
SALES (est): 145.4K **Privately Held**
WEB: www.roanoke.com
SIC: 2711 Newspapers: publishing only,
not printed on site

(G-12165)
ROANOKE ELECTRIC STEEL
CORP (HQ)
102 Westside Blvd Nw (24017-6757)
P.O. Box 13948 (24038-3948)
PHONE..............................540 342-1831
T Joe Crawford, *President*
Mark D Millett, *Vice Pres*
Theresa Wagler, *Vice Pres*
Paul Schuler, *Safety Mgr*
Marion Meador, *Accountant*
◆ **EMP:** 416 **EST:** 2006
SQ FT: 408,000
SALES (est): 376.8MM **Publicly Held**
WEB: www.roanokesteel.com
SIC: 3312 Bars, iron: made in steel mills;
billets, steel

(G-12166)
ROANOKE HOSE & FITTINGS
(PA)
625 Salem Ave Sw (24016-3025)
PHONE..............................540 985-4832
Robert Wood, *Co-Owner*
Michael Browman, *Vice Pres*
Bowman Michael D, *Vice Pres*
Jimmy Browman, *Manager*
EMP: 7
SALES (est): 1MM **Privately Held**
SIC: 3494 Pipe fittings

(G-12167)
ROANOKE STAR SENTINEL
2408 Stanley Ave Se (24014-3330)
P.O. Box 8338 (24014-0338)
PHONE..............................540 400-0990
Stuart Revercomb, *President*
EMP: 4
SALES (est): 193.1K **Privately Held**
WEB: www.theroanokestar.com
SIC: 2711 Newspapers, publishing & print-
ing

(G-12168)
ROANOKE TRIBUNE
2318 Melrose Ave Nw (24017-3906)
P.O. Box 6021 (24017-0021)
PHONE..............................540 343-0326
Claudia Whitworth, *Owner*
EMP: 5 **EST:** 1939
SQ FT: 5,000
SALES (est): 217.7K **Privately Held**
WEB: www.theroanoketribune.org
SIC: 2711 Newspapers, publishing & print-
ing

(G-12169)
ROCKYDALE QUARRIES CORP
4248 Welcome Valley Rd Se (24014-5129)
PHONE..............................540 769-8116
Quarries Rockydale, *Owner*
EMP: 3
SALES (est): 182.1K **Privately Held**
WEB: www.rockydalequarries.com
SIC: 1422 Crushed & broken limestone

(G-12170)
ROCKYDALE QUARRIES
CORPORATION (PA)
2343 Highland Farm Rd Nw (24017-1210)
P.O. Box 8425 (24014-0425)
PHONE..............................540 774-1696
Randolph James Kenneth, *President*
Eddie Gupton, *Business Mgr*
Edgar K Baker, *Vice Pres*
Willis David D, *Vice Pres*
David Willis, *Vice Pres*
EMP: 52
SQ FT: 5,000
SALES (est): 13.3MM **Privately Held**
WEB: www.rockydalequarries.com
SIC: 3274 1442 Lime; construction sand &
gravel

(G-12171)
ROCKYDALE QUARRIES
CORPORATION
Also Called: Jacks Mountain Quarry
2343 Highland Farm Rd Nw (24017-1210)
PHONE..............................540 576-2544
Benny Hopkins, *Manager*
EMP: 16
SALES (corp-wide): 13.3MM **Privately
Held**
WEB: www.rockydalequarries.com
SIC: 1422 Crushed & broken limestone
PA: Rockydale Quarries Corporation
2343 Highland Farm Rd Nw
Roanoke VA 24017
540 774-1696

(G-12172)
S E GREER
3225 Deer Path Trl (24014-6300)
PHONE..............................540 400-0155
S Greer, *Owner*
EMP: 1
SALES (est): 62.4K **Privately Held**
SIC: 2399 Horse harnesses & riding crops,
etc.: non-leather

(G-12173)
S HARMAN MACHINE SHOP INC
Also Called: Harmans Automotive Machine
2141 Loudon Ave Nw (24017-6926)
P.O. Box 1506 (24007-1506)
PHONE..............................540 343-9304
Merrell Hopson, *President*
Diane Getman, *Office Mgr*
EMP: 3
SALES (est): 374.8K **Privately Held**
SIC: 3599 Machine shop, jobbing & repair

(G-12174)
SAFEHOUSE SIGNS INC
720 Liberty Rd Ne (24012-4504)
PHONE..............................540 366-2480
Douglas R Irvin, *President*
Pete Hristov, *Opers Mgr*
Waurayne Cooper, *Purch Dir*
Adam Jackson, *VP Sales*
Stuart Perdue, *Sales Mgr*
EMP: 22
SQ FT: 15,000
SALES (est): 3.1MM **Privately Held**
WEB: www.safehousesigns.com
SIC: 3993 2759 2752 2672 Electric
signs; labels & seals: printing; tag, ticket
& schedule printing: lithographic; coated
& laminated paper; packaging paper &
plastics film, coated & laminated

(G-12175)
SALT WHISTLE BAY PARTNERS
LLC
10 S Jefferson St (24011-1331)
PHONE..............................540 983-7118
Daniel Layman Jr, *Principal*
EMP: 2 **EST:** 2009
SALES (est): 82K **Privately Held**
SIC: 3999 Whistles

(G-12176)
SBK INC
1216 Sylvan Rd Se (24014-2510)
PHONE..............................540 427-5029
Sandra B Kelly, *Principal*
EMP: 2
SALES (est): 84.7K **Privately Held**
SIC: 3999 Manufacturing industries

(G-12177)
SCB SALES INC
Also Called: Etcetera
3214 Brightwood Pl Sw (24014-1410)
P.O. Box 8983 (24014-0773)
PHONE..............................540 342-6502
Susan Bucher, *President*
EMP: 2
SALES (est): 128.5K **Privately Held**
SIC: 2396 Fabric printing & stamping

(G-12178)
SCHWEITZER-MAUDUIT INTL
INC
Also Called: Conwed
530 Gregory Ave Ne (24016-2129)
PHONE..............................540 981-0362
EMP: 3 **Publicly Held**
WEB: www.swmintl.com
SIC: 3081 Unsupported plastics film &
sheet
PA: Schweitzer-Mauduit International, Inc.
100 N Point Ctr E Ste 600
Alpharetta GA 30022

(G-12179)
SCRUBS MOBILE CLEANING LC
10 Church Ave Se Ste 201 (24011-2120)
PHONE..............................540 254-0478
Mikaell Mays,
EMP: 2
SALES (est): 150K **Privately Held**
SIC: 3589 Dishwashing machines, com-
mercial

(G-12180)
SEALMASTER-ROANOKE
3131 Baker Ave Nw Ste B (24017-6807)
PHONE..............................540 344-2090
EMP: 4
SALES (est): 276.2K **Privately Held**
SIC: 2951 Asphalt Paving Mixtures And
Blocks, Nsk

(G-12181)
SENCONTROLOGY INC
3129 Davis Ave (24015-4619)
PHONE..............................540 529-7000
Barbara A Tinnell, *Administration*
EMP: 2 **EST:** 2010
SALES (est): 232.8K **Privately Held**
WEB: www.sencontrology.com
SIC: 3829 Measuring & controlling devices

(G-12182)
SEQUOIA ENERGY LLC
302 S Jefferson St Fl 5th (24011-1710)
PHONE..............................540 776-7890
EMP: 13
SALES (est): 1.6MM
SALES (corp-wide): 173.4MM **Privately
Held**
WEB: www.potentiarenewables.com
SIC: 1241 Coal mining services
PA: James C. Justice Companies, Inc.
302 S Jefferson St # 400
Roanoke VA 24011
540 776-7890

(G-12183)
SHENANDOAH MACHINE &
MAINT CO
2141 Loudon Ave Nw (24017-6926)
PHONE..............................540 343-1758
Gary Sledd, *President*
Connie May, *Corp Secy*
▲ **EMP:** 5
SQ FT: 4,000
SALES (est): 719.7K **Privately Held**
SIC: 3469 7699 Machine parts, stamped
or pressed metal; industrial machinery &
equipment repair

(G-12184)
SHENANDOAH ROBE COMPANY INC
3322 Hollins Rd Ne (24012-7511)
PHONE................................540 362-9811
Richard Mc Clure, *President*
EMP: 70
SQ FT: 25,000
SALES (est): 2.5MM **Privately Held**
SIC: 2389 Uniforms & vestments

(G-12185)
SHIMCHOCKS LITHO SERVICE INC
Also Called: Shimchock's Label Service
121 Sycamore Ave Ne (24012-5109)
PHONE................................540 982-3915
Stephen L Shimchock, *President*
Hortense K Shimchock, *Corp Secy*
Marie Conner, *Vice Pres*
Matthew Shimchock, *Manager*
EMP: 7 **EST:** 1955
SQ FT: 7,000
SALES (est): 270K **Privately Held**
WEB: www.shimchockslabel.com
SIC: 2759 Letterpress printing; screen printing; engraving

(G-12186)
SHIRTS UNLIMITED LLC
1207 9th St Se (24013-2443)
PHONE................................540 342-8337
Pat Lynch, *President*
Frederick Knapp,
EMP: 3
SQ FT: 3,750
SALES (est): 170K **Privately Held**
WEB: www.shirtsunlimited.net
SIC: 2759 Screen printing

(G-12187)
SIGN DESIGN OF ROANOKE INC
2351 Carlton Rd Sw (24015-3912)
PHONE................................540 977-3354
R Allen Williamson, *CEO*
EMP: 8
SQ FT: 5,000
SALES (est): 899K **Privately Held**
SIC: 3993 Signs, not made in custom sign painting shops

(G-12188)
SIGNATURE K-9
345 Luck Ave Sw (24016-5013)
PHONE................................866 820-3647
EMP: 1
SALES (est): 53K **Privately Held**
WEB: www.signaturek9.com
SIC: 3131 Footwear cut stock

(G-12189)
SIR MASA INC
2717 Beverly Blvd Sw (24015-4025)
PHONE................................540 725-1982
M Agnes Sirrine, *President*
James Sirrine, *Treasurer*
EMP: 3
SALES (est): 238.3K **Privately Held**
SIC: 2032 Tortillas: packaged in cans, jars etc.

(G-12190)
SLUMLORD MILLIONAIRE LLC
1925 Salem Ave Sw (24016-2603)
PHONE................................540 529-9259
Roland Macher, *Administration*
EMP: 2
SALES (est): 83.1K **Privately Held**
WEB: www.slumlordmillionaire.net
SIC: 2741 Miscellaneous publishing

(G-12191)
SO UNIQUE CANDY APPLES
16 Church Ave Se (24011-2104)
PHONE................................540 915-4899
EMP: 2 **EST:** 2015
SALES (est): 118.5K **Privately Held**
WEB: www.souniquecandyapples.com
SIC: 2064 Candy & other confectionery products

(G-12192)
SPINFINITY
4142 Melrose Ave Nw (24017-5800)
PHONE................................540 283-9370

EMP: 7 **EST:** 2010
SALES (est): 666.9K **Privately Held**
SIC: 3462 Flange, valve & pipe fitting forgings, ferrous

(G-12193)
SPRECO CREAMERY
2507 Memorial Ave Sw (24015-1912)
PHONE................................540 529-1581
Muhamed Spreco, *Principal*
EMP: 3 **EST:** 2011
SALES (est): 128.2K **Privately Held**
SIC: 2021 Creamery butter

(G-12194)
STAGE SOUND INC
2240 Shenandoah Ave Nw (24017-6923)
PHONE................................540 342-2040
Reid C Henion, *President*
Reid Heinon, *Vice Pres*
Jeff Moore, *Vice Pres*
Brian Taylor, *Vice Pres*
Jay Ensor, *Project Mgr*
EMP: 36
SQ FT: 11,000
SALES (est): 9MM **Privately Held**
WEB: www.stagesound.com
SIC: 3651 7359 Audio electronic systems; audio-visual equipment & supply rental

(G-12195)
STAR CITY WELDING LLC
712 Norfolk Ave Sw (24016-3018)
PHONE................................540 343-1428
Noemi Aguilar Curiel, *Administration*
EMP: 1 **EST:** 2015
SALES (est): 44.4K **Privately Held**
SIC: 7692 Welding repair

(G-12196)
STEAMED INK
1212 Penmar Ave Se (24013-2816)
PHONE................................540 904-6211
Jennifer Rauf, *Principal*
EMP: 2
SALES (est): 83.9K **Privately Held**
SIC: 2752 Commercial printing, lithographic

(G-12197)
STEEL DYNAMICS INC
Roanoke Bar Division
102 Westside Blvd Nw (24017-6757)
P.O. Box 13948 (24038-3948)
PHONE................................540 342-1831
Joe Crawford, *General Mgr*
Lynn Akers, *Safety Mgr*
John Mull, *Sales Staff*
Steve Stultz, *Supervisor*
Richard Lester, *Info Tech Mgr*
EMP: 577 **Publicly Held**
WEB: www.steeldynamics.com
SIC: 3316 7389 3312 Cold finishing of steel shapes; scrap steel cutting; plate, sheet & strip, except coated products
PA: Steel Dynamics, Inc.
7575 W Jefferson Blvd
Fort Wayne IN 46804

(G-12198)
STRATA FILM COATINGS INC
2610 Roanoke Ave Sw (24015-5404)
P.O. Box 3129 (24015-1129)
PHONE................................540 343-3456
Brown D Burton, *President*
EMP: 5
SQ FT: 24,000
SALES (est): 748.9K **Privately Held**
WEB: www.stratafilm.com
SIC: 2821 Plastics materials & resins

(G-12199)
SWIFT PRINT INC (PA)
369 Church Ave Sw (24016-5007)
PHONE................................540 362-2200
Dan Baldwin, *President*
EMP: 10
SQ FT: 1,000
SALES (est): 800.2K **Privately Held**
WEB: www.swiftprint.net
SIC: 2752 Commercial printing, offset

(G-12200)
SWIFT PRINT INC
Also Called: Ground Ent
1003 S Jefferson St (24016-4435)
PHONE................................540 343-8300
Dan Baldwin, *President*
Jeff Shumate, *Manager*
EMP: 3
SALES (corp-wide): 800.2K **Privately Held**
WEB: www.swiftprint.net
SIC: 2752 Commercial printing, offset
PA: Swift Print Inc
369 Church Ave Sw
Roanoke VA 24016
540 362-2200

(G-12201)
SWM INTERNATIONAL LLC
Also Called: Conwed Plastics
1713 Plantation Rd Ne (24012-5231)
PHONE................................651 369-1235
EMP: 3
SALES (est): 292.1K **Privately Held**
WEB: www.swmintl.com
SIC: 3081 Unsupported plastics film & sheet

(G-12202)
T & T SOFTWARE LLC
319 Campbell Ave Sw (24016-3600)
PHONE................................540 389-1915
Theodore Woods, *Principal*
EMP: 2
SALES (est): 151.1K **Privately Held**
SIC: 7372 Prepackaged software

(G-12203)
TIM SHEPHERD ARCHIT FABRICATI
1424 5th St Sw (24016-4508)
PHONE................................540 230-1457
EMP: 1
SALES (est): 89.7K **Privately Held**
SIC: 3499 Mfg Misc Fabricated Metal Products

(G-12204)
TIME MACHINE INC (PA)
5493 Franklin Rd Sw (24014-6661)
PHONE................................540 772-0962
Danny Fowler, *President*
Steve Cerrone, *Controller*
Neala Grill, *Manager*
EMP: 9
SQ FT: 3,200
SALES (est): 800.6K **Privately Held**
WEB: www.atimemachine.com
SIC: 3545 Tools & accessories for machine tools

(G-12205)
TIMES-WORLD LLC
Also Called: Roanoke Times, The
201 Campbell Ave Sw 209 (24011-1105)
P.O. Box 2491 (24010-2491)
PHONE................................540 981-3100
Terry Jamerson, *President*
Tonya Hart, *CFO*
Lisa Hart, *Manager*
▲ **EMP:** 303
SQ FT: 185,000
SALES (est): 17.7MM
SALES (corp-wide): 254.6B **Publicly Held**
WEB: www.jobs.roanoke.com
SIC: 2711 Newspapers, publishing & printing
HQ: Bh Media Group, Inc.
1314 Douglas St Ste 1500
Omaha NE 68102
402 444-1000

(G-12206)
TMP INDUSTRIES LLC
113 Sycamore Ave Ne (24012-5109)
PHONE................................540 761-0435
Mathew Donahue, *Principal*
EMP: 1
SALES (est): 39.6K **Privately Held**
SIC: 3999 Manufacturing industries

(G-12207)
TRANE US INC
1308 Plantation Rd Ne (24012-5713)
PHONE................................540 342-3027
Greg McMahan, *Branch Mgr*
Robin Shepherd, *Manager*
EMP: 6 **Privately Held**
WEB: www.trane.com
SIC: 3585 Refrigeration & heating equipment
HQ: Trane U.S. Inc.
3600 Pammel Creek Rd
La Crosse WI 54601
608 787-2000

(G-12208)
TRANE US INC
2303 Trane Dr Nw (24017-1163)
PHONE................................844 805-3895
Jason Bingham, *Vice Pres*
EMP: 7 **Privately Held**
WEB: www.trane.com
SIC: 3585 Refrigeration & heating equipment
HQ: Trane U.S. Inc.
3600 Pammel Creek Rd
La Crosse WI 54601
608 787-2000

(G-12209)
TRI-DIM FILTER CORPORATION
1615 Cleveland Ave Sw (24016-3131)
PHONE................................540 774-9540
Mike McDaniels, *Branch Mgr*
Mike McDaniel, *Manager*
John Buzzy, *Executive*
EMP: 5
SALES (corp-wide): 4.6B **Privately Held**
WEB: www.tridim.com
SIC: 3564 Filters, air: furnaces, air conditioning equipment, etc.
HQ: Tri-Dim Filter Corporation
93 Industrial Dr
Louisa VA 23093
540 967-2600

(G-12210)
TRIBBETTS MEATS
3492 Jae Valley Rd (24014-6102)
PHONE................................540 427-4671
Gerald E Tribbett, *Owner*
EMP: 5
SALES (est): 40K **Privately Held**
SIC: 2011 Beef products from beef slaughtered on site

(G-12211)
TRIOLOGY MACHINE COMPANY INC
1726 Seibel Dr Ne Ste D (24012-5653)
PHONE................................540 343-9508
Ernest H Dooley, *President*
Sandra Dooley, *Treasurer*
EMP: 5
SQ FT: 3,000
SALES (est): 320K **Privately Held**
SIC: 3599 Machine shop, jobbing & repair

(G-12212)
UNITED DAIRY INC
1814 Hollins Rd Ne Ste C (24012-5358)
PHONE................................540 366-2964
Melvin Brammer, *Manager*
EMP: 7
SALES (corp-wide): 218.9MM **Privately Held**
WEB: www.drinkunited.com
SIC: 2026 0241 Milk processing (pasteurizing, homogenizing, bottling); milk production
PA: United Dairy, Inc.
300 N 5th St
Martins Ferry OH 43935
740 633-1451

(G-12213)
VALLEY CONSTRUCTION NEWS (PA)
426 Campbell Ave Sw (24016-3627)
P.O. Box 791 (24004-0791)
PHONE................................540 344-4899
William Churchill Jr, *Owner*
EMP: 5 **EST:** 1979
SQ FT: 5,000

SALES (est): 508.8K **Privately Held**
WEB: www.vcnonline.com
SIC: 2741 Newsletter publishing

(G-12214)
VALLEY REBUILDERS CO INC
2019 Shenandoah Ave Nw (24017-6920)
PHONE....................540 342-2108
Michael Graham, *President*
EMP: 5
SALES (est): 300K **Privately Held**
SIC: 3519 Diesel engine rebuilding

(G-12215)
VALOR PARTNERS INC
1948 Franklin Rd Sw B201 (24014-1154)
PHONE....................540 725-4156
Doug Johnson, *CEO*
Steve Spencer, *Partner*
Donna Rader, *Director*
EMP: 5
SALES (est): 470.3K **Privately Held**
WEB: www.valorpartners.com
SIC: 7372 Business oriented computer
software

(G-12216)
VARNEY SHEET METAL SHOP
2759 Mary Linda Ave Ne (24012-5609)
PHONE....................540 343-4076
Kathy Seymore, *Principal*
EMP: 2
SALES (est): 260.2K **Privately Held**
WEB: www.varneyinc.com
SIC: 3444 Sheet metalwork

(G-12217)
**VASSE VAUGHT
METALCRAFTING INC**
1915 Belleville Rd Sw (24015-2709)
PHONE....................540 808-8939
Margaret Vaught, *President*
EMP: 2
SALES (est): 279.5K **Privately Held**
WEB: www.vassevaught.com
SIC: 3444 Sheet metalwork

(G-12218)
**VIRGINIA PROSTHETICS INC
(PA)**
4338 Williamson Rd Nw (24012-2893)
PHONE....................540 366-8287
Douglas Call, *President*
Martha M Call, *Vice Pres*
Rebecca Furrow, *Purchasing*
Bradley Conner,
Russell Rich, *Technician*
EMP: 23
SQ FT: 14,000
SALES (est): 6.3MM **Privately Held**
WEB: www.virginiaprosthetics.com
SIC: 3842 5047 Prosthetic appliances;
medical & hospital equipment

(G-12219)
**VIRGINIA PRTG CO ROANOKE
INC (PA)**
501a Campbell Ave Sw (24016-3605)
PHONE....................540 483-7433
Virginia B Turpin, *President*
EMP: 5
SQ FT: 1,500
SALES (est): 499.8K **Privately Held**
WEB: www.virginiaprintingcompanyinc.com
SIC: 2752 2759 7334 Commercial print-
ing, offset; letterpress printing; photocopy-
ing & duplicating services

(G-12220)
VIRGINIA TANK SERVICE INC
1719 Norfolk Ave Se (24013-1327)
P.O. Box 11632 (24022-1632)
PHONE....................540 344-9700
James Myers, *President*
Arnold Ray, *Vice Pres*
Carl Mullins, *Sales Engr*
EMP: 8
SQ FT: 12,000
SALES (est): 1.4MM **Privately Held**
WEB: www.virginiatank.com
SIC: 3443 7699 Tanks, lined: metal plate;
tanks, standard or custom fabricated:
metal plate; tank repair & cleaning serv-
ices; tank & boiler cleaning service

(G-12221)
VIRGINIA TRANE AP141
2303 Trane Dr Nw (24017-1163)
PHONE....................540 580-7702
EMP: 7 **EST:** 2013
SALES (est): 938.9K **Privately Held**
SIC: 3585 Refrigeration & heating equip-
ment

(G-12222)
**VIRGINIA TRANSFORMER CORP
(PA)**
220 Glade View Dr Ne (24012-6470)
PHONE....................540 345-9892
Prabhat K Jain, *CEO*
Anoop Nanda, *President*
Matt Gregg, *COO*
Marc Schillebeeckx, *Exec VP*
Ramesh Ramachandran, *Vice Pres*
◆ **EMP:** 500
SQ FT: 130,000
SALES (est): 230.2MM **Privately Held**
WEB: www.vatransformer.com
SIC: 3612 Specialty transformers; reactor
transformers

(G-12223)
VIRTUOUS HEALTH TODAY INC
7a Church Ave Se (24011-2103)
PHONE....................540 339-2855
Onawa Allen, *President*
EMP: 1
SQ FT: 500
SALES (est): 67.9K **Privately Held**
WEB: www.virtuoushealthtoday.com
SIC: 2721 Periodicals: publishing only

(G-12224)
VIVA LA CUPCAKE
2123 Crystal Sprng Ave Sw (24014-2413)
PHONE....................540 400-0806
Pennie Ahuero, *Owner*
EMP: 4
SALES (est): 319.2K **Privately Held**
WEB: www.vivalacupcakes.com
SIC: 2051 Cakes, bakery: except frozen

(G-12225)
VLYNNS
2501 Williamson Rd Ne (24012-4896)
PHONE....................540 904-2844
Nathaniel Lyles, *Principal*
EMP: 2
SALES (est): 87.2K **Privately Held**
SIC: 3961 Costume jewelry

(G-12226)
**WALKER MACHINE AND FNDRY
CORP**
2415 Russell Ave Sw (24015-4821)
P.O. Box 4587 (24015-0587)
PHONE....................540 344-6265
Edward S Moore, *President*
Glenn D Muzzy, *President*
Andy Thornton, *Corp Secy*
James M Mauck, *Exec VP*
Kenneth R Clark, *Vice Pres*
EMP: 85 **EST:** 1920
SQ FT: 2,500
SALES (est): 23.3MM **Privately Held**
WEB: www.walkerfoundry.com
SIC: 3321 3599 3479 Ductile iron cast-
ings; gray iron castings; machine shop,
jobbing & repair; painting, coating & hot
dipping

(G-12227)
WALTERS PRINTING & MFG CO
315 22nd St Nw (24017-6901)
P.O. Box 12905 (24029-2905)
PHONE....................540 345-8161
Esther M Williams, *President*
John O Williams, *Vice Pres*
Marcia Altizer, *Purchasing*
EMP: 15 **EST:** 1919
SQ FT: 9,600
SALES (est): 2.3MM **Privately Held**
SIC: 2759 2791 2789 2752 Letterpress
printing; typesetting; bookbinding & re-
lated work; commercial printing, offset

(G-12228)
**WILLIS WELDING & MACHINE
CO**
1920 9th St Se (24013-2904)
PHONE....................540 427-3038
Michael G Gee, *President*
Colon Gee, *Vice Pres*
Sherry B Gee, *Vice Pres*
Mildred R Gee, *Treasurer*
EMP: 6 **EST:** 1964
SQ FT: 2,250
SALES (est): 748.8K **Privately Held**
WEB: www.williswelding.com
SIC: 3599 7692 Machine shop, jobbing &
repair; welding repair

(G-12229)
WOOD TELEVISION LLC
Also Called: Virginia Business Magazine
1402 Grandin Ave (24015)
PHONE....................540 343-2405
Paige Chichester, *Branch Mgr*
EMP: 1
SALES (corp-wide): 3B **Publicly Held**
WEB: www.woodtv.com
SIC: 2721 Periodicals
HQ: Wood Television Llc
120 College Ave Se
Grand Rapids MI 49503
616 456-8888

(G-12230)
WOOL FELT PRODUCTS INC
Also Called: Collegiate Pacific
532 Luck Ave Sw (24016-5018)
P.O. Box 300 (24002-0300)
PHONE....................540 981-0281
Charles Atkins, *President*
William Webster, *CFO*
Michele Hall, *Manager*
EMP: 35
SALES (est): 2.7MM **Privately Held**
WEB: www.collegiatepacific.com
SIC: 2261 2396 2392 Screen printing of
cotton broadwoven fabrics; automotive &
apparel trimmings; household furnishings

(G-12231)
YOUNIVERCITY LLC
Also Called: Younivercity, The
207 Eugene Dr Nw (24017-4667)
PHONE....................540 529-7621
Brandon Evans,
EMP: 3
SALES (est): 119.3K **Privately Held**
WEB: www.theyounivercity.com
SIC: 2759 2339 Letterpress & screen
printing; service apparel, washable:
women's

Rochelle
Madison County

(G-12232)
CHESAPEAKE & HUDSON INC
27 Jacks Shop Rd (22738-4061)
PHONE....................301 834-7170
William Hoar, *President*
EMP: 12
SALES (est): 977.1K **Privately Held**
WEB: www.cheshudinc.com
SIC: 2741 Miscellaneous publishing

(G-12233)
ESTUDIO DE FERNANDEZ LLC
6093 S Seminole Trl (22738-3879)
PHONE....................540 948-3196
Toms J Fernndez, *Principal*
EMP: 2
SALES (est): 133.3K **Privately Held**
SIC: 2335 Wedding gowns & dresses

(G-12234)
**MODEL RAILROAD CSTM
BENCHWORK**
8038 S Blue Ridge Tpke (22738-4004)
PHONE....................540 948-4948
Vernon Peachey, *Owner*
EMP: 2
SALES (est): 101K **Privately Held**
WEB: www.modelrrlayouts.com
SIC: 3944 Trains & equipment, toy: electric
& mechanical

Rockbridge Baths
Rockbridge County

(G-12235)
JUMP MOUNTAIN VINEYARD
1493 Walkers Creek Rd (24473-2110)
PHONE....................540 348-6730
EMP: 2
SALES (est): 74.5K **Privately Held**
WEB: www.jumpwines.com
SIC: 2084 Wines

(G-12236)
LEXINGTON VALLEY VINEYARD
80 Norton Way (24473-2543)
PHONE....................540 462-2974
Janet Hale, *Principal*
EMP: 4
SALES (est): 271.1K **Privately Held**
WEB: www.lexingtonvalleyvineyard.com
SIC: 2084 Wines

(G-12237)
RADAR MEDIA LLC
204 Jump Mountain Rd (24473-2121)
PHONE....................540 348-8996
Stephen Mayne, *Editor*
Wendy Redfern,
Wendy Lynch,
Mark Redfern,
EMP: 5
SALES (est): 529.4K **Privately Held**
WEB: www.undertheradarmag.com
SIC: 2741 Miscellaneous publishing

Rockingham
Harrisonburg City County

(G-12238)
ADONICA L MILLER
6152 Singers Glen Rd (22802-0236)
PHONE....................540 820-0820
Adonica Miller, *Principal*
EMP: 2
SALES (est): 62.9K **Privately Held**
SIC: 2711 Newspapers, publishing & print-
ing

(G-12239)
ALTOMAS TECHNOLOGIES LLC
845 Sugar Maple Ln (22801-4636)
PHONE....................540 560-2320
Karim Altaii,
EMP: 2
SALES (est): 145.2K **Privately Held**
SIC: 3625 Motor starters & controllers,
electric

(G-12240)
**ARCHER-DANIELS-MIDLAND
COMPANY**
Also Called: ADM
285 Oakwood Dr (22801-3930)
PHONE....................540 433-2761
Jerry Wayne Miller Sr, *Principal*
EMP: 25
SALES (corp-wide): 64.6B **Publicly Held**
WEB: www.adm.com
SIC: 2041 Flour & other grain mill products
PA: Archer-Daniels-Midland Company
77 W Wacker Dr Ste 4600
Chicago IL 60601
312 634-8100

(G-12241)
BARTRACK INC
2374 Newberry Ln (22801-6052)
PHONE....................717 521-4840
Hunter Markle, *Mng Member*
Brett Danielson,
EMP: 8
SALES (est): 250K **Privately Held**
WEB: www.bartrack.beer
SIC: 3432 7374 7389 Faucets & spigots,
metal & plastic; data processing & prepa-
ration; business services

(G-12242)
BURKHOLDER ENTERPRISES INC
Also Called: Burkholder Entp Wldg & Repr S
3579 Mount Clinton Pike (22802-0704)
PHONE....................................540 867-5030
Boyd B Burkholder, *President*
Sharon Burkholder, *Corp Secy*
EMP: 2
SALES (est): 75K **Privately Held**
SIC: 7692 Welding repair

(G-12243)
CAMPBELL COPY CENTER INC
Also Called: Harrisonburg Prtg & Graphics
4564 S Valley Pike A (22801-3938)
PHONE....................................540 434-4171
John Beery, *President*
James Breneman, *Sales Staff*
Emily Martin, *Graphic Designe*
EMP: 11 EST: 1977
SQ FT: 6,000
SALES (est): 998.2K **Privately Held**
WEB: www.campbellcopy.com
SIC: 2752 Commercial printing, offset

(G-12244)
CARROLL J HARPER
Also Called: Gardens Paths & Ponds
2670 N Valley Pike (22802-1101)
PHONE....................................540 434-8978
Carroll J Harper, *Owner*
EMP: 13
SQ FT: 7,500
SALES (est): 275K **Privately Held**
WEB: www.harperslawnornaments.com
SIC: 3272 5947 Precast terrazo or concrete products; gift shop

(G-12245)
CONMAT GROUP INC
1557 Garbers Church Rd (22801-4570)
P.O. Box 1347, Harrisonburg (22803-1347)
PHONE....................................540 433-9128
Roy D Simmons Jr, *President*
Alan Deleeuwerk, *Vice Pres*
EMP: 31
SALES (est): 5.9MM **Privately Held**
WEB: www.concrete4u.com
SIC: 3273 Ready-mixed concrete

(G-12246)
DAVIDSON PLBG & PIPE SVC LLC
3357 Westbrier Dr (22802-0071)
PHONE....................................540 867-0847
EMP: 1
SALES (est): 66.7K **Privately Held**
SIC: 1389 Oil/Gas Field Services

(G-12247)
DEAVERS LIME AND LITTER LLC
1918 Lacey Spring Rd (22802-1467)
PHONE....................................540 833-4144
Mark G Deavers, *Principal*
EMP: 2 EST: 2012
SALES (est): 277.1K **Privately Held**
SIC: 3274 Lime

(G-12248)
DEGUSTABOX USA LLC
801 Friendship Dr (22802-4566)
PHONE....................................203 514-8966
EMP: 1
SALES (est): 68.2K **Privately Held**
WEB: www.degustabox.com
SIC: 3944 Games, toys & children's vehicles

(G-12249)
DIORIO MANUFACTURING CO LLC
32 Silver Lake Rd (22801-4711)
PHONE....................................540 438-1870
Anthony Diorio,
EMP: 3
SQ FT: 1,000
SALES (est): 500K **Privately Held**
WEB: www.dioriomfg.com
SIC: 3599 Machine shop, jobbing & repair

(G-12250)
DOGWOOD MOUNTAIN LOG HOMES LLC
4563 S Valley Pike (22801-3938)
PHONE....................................540 433-1873
Jack Ridder, *President*
Linda Ridder, *Corp Secy*
Drew Ridder, *Vice Pres*
EMP: 5
SQ FT: 2,300
SALES (est): 124.5K **Privately Held**
WEB:
www.dogwoodmountainloghomes.com
SIC: 2452 Log cabins, prefabricated, wood

(G-12251)
FAREHILL PRECISION LLC
4445 Lewis Byrd Rd (22801-3919)
PHONE....................................540 879-2373
Frank Horst,
David Horst,
EMP: 6 **Privately Held**
SIC: 3541 Machine tools, metal cutting type

(G-12252)
FHP LLC
4445 Lewis Byrd Rd (22801-3919)
PHONE....................................540 879-2560
EMP: 4
SALES (est): 406.1K **Privately Held**
SIC: 3541 Machine tools, metal cutting type

(G-12253)
FLIP FLOP FABRICATION LLC
3361 Spaders Church Rd (22801-2510)
PHONE....................................540 820-5959
William Grattan, *Principal*
EMP: 2 EST: 2015
SALES (est): 58.1K **Privately Held**
SIC: 3999 Manufacturing industries

(G-12254)
H H BACKHOE SERVICE
4765 Pleasant Valley Rd (22801-2526)
PHONE....................................540 574-3578
EMP: 2 EST: 2014
SALES (est): 133.8K **Privately Held**
SIC: 3531 Mfg Construction Machinery

(G-12255)
HQC INC
Also Called: High Qulty Cnstr Rockingham Co
2077 Cory Ln (22802-1453)
P.O. Box 863, Broadway (22815-0863)
PHONE....................................540 820-3277
Ken High, *President*
Greg Hoover, *Corp Secy*
EMP: 15
SALES (est): 669.9K **Privately Held**
WEB: www.rockinghamcountyva.gov
SIC: 3089 Injection molding of plastics

(G-12256)
HUMUS COMPOST COMPANY LLC
865 Pike Church Rd (22801-4505)
PHONE....................................540 421-7169
Jordan Rohrer, *Principal*
EMP: 3
SALES (est): 325.4K **Privately Held**
WEB: www.soilhealthtech.com
SIC: 2875 Compost

(G-12257)
KEANE CABINETRY
3050 Mount Clinton Pike (22802-0961)
PHONE....................................540 867-5336
Jeff Keane, *Owner*
EMP: 1 **Privately Held**
SIC: 2514 Kitchen cabinets: metal

(G-12258)
KREIDER MACHINE SHOP INC
1886 Mount Clinton Pike (22802-0906)
PHONE....................................540 434-5351
John H Kreider, *President*
Sara E Kreider, *Vice Pres*
EMP: 8
SALES (est): 1MM **Privately Held**
WEB: www.kfse.biz
SIC: 3599 Machine shop, jobbing & repair

(G-12259)
LSC COMMUNICATIONS US LLC
Harrisonburg Manufacturing Div
2347 Kratzer Rd (22802-1004)
PHONE....................................540 434-8833
Angie Pyles, *Human Resources*
Dunn Henfley, *Branch Mgr*
Andrew Dixon, *Technician*
EMP: 920
SALES (corp-wide): 6.1B **Publicly Held**
WEB: www.lsccom.com
SIC: 2732 2789 2759 2752 Book printing; bookbinding & related work; commercial printing; commercial printing, lithographic
HQ: Lsc Communications Us, Llc
191 N Wacker Dr Ste 1400
Chicago IL 60606
844 572-5720

(G-12260)
MADISONS CLEANING
2636 Keezletown Rd (22802-2710)
PHONE....................................540 421-1074
Tracy Stein, *Owner*
EMP: 10
SALES (est): 596.6K **Privately Held**
SIC: 2842 Specialty cleaning, polishes & sanitation goods

(G-12261)
MARCO METALS LLC
4773 S Valley Pike (22801-3936)
P.O. Box 2245, Harrisonburg (22801-9507)
PHONE....................................540 437-2324
Mark Smucker, *Mng Member*
John Smucker,
EMP: 18
SQ FT: 20,000
SALES (est): 8MM **Privately Held**
WEB: www.marcometals.com
SIC: 2952 Roofing materials

(G-12262)
MK ENVIRONMENTAL LLC
4121 Traveler Rd (22801-8323)
PHONE....................................540 435-9066
Mary Slonaker,
EMP: 2
SALES (est): 130K **Privately Held**
SIC: 2491 Wood preserving

(G-12263)
MORRIS MACHINE SHOP
4336 Port Republic Rd (22801-8009)
PHONE....................................540 434-8038
R J Morris, *Owner*
EMP: 2
SALES (est): 176.4K **Privately Held**
SIC: 3599 Machine shop, jobbing & repair

(G-12264)
NEW RIVER CONCRETE SUPPLY
2565 John Wayland Hwy # 201 (22801-4559)
P.O. Box 1347, Harrisonburg (22803-1347)
PHONE....................................540 433-9043
Roy D Simmons Jr, *President*
EMP: 5 EST: 1989
SALES (est): 423K **Privately Held**
SIC: 3273 Ready-mixed concrete

(G-12265)
NEXAWARE LLC
1595 Boyers Rd (22801-9341)
PHONE....................................703 880-6697
Gerard Eldering, *Principal*
EMP: 2
SALES (est): 94.3K **Privately Held**
SIC: 3596 Scales & balances, except laboratory

(G-12266)
PACKAGING CORPORATION AMERICA
751 Interstate View Dr (22801-9601)
PHONE....................................540 434-2840
EMP: 2
SALES (est): 90.7K
SALES (corp-wide): 6.4B **Publicly Held**
SIC: 2653 Corrugated And Solid Fiber Boxes, Nsk

PA: Packaging Corporation Of America
1955 W Field Ct
Lake Forest IL 60045
847 482-3000

(G-12267)
PERFORMANCE FLY RODS
5798 Singers Glen Rd (22802-0263)
PHONE....................................540 867-0856
Dave Lewis, *Owner*
Mary Lewis, *Owner*
EMP: 2
SALES (est): 50K **Privately Held**
WEB: www.davelewisflyrods.com
SIC: 3949 Rods & rod parts, fishing

(G-12268)
R R DONNELLEY & SONS COMPANY
2063 Kratzer Rd (22802-1001)
PHONE....................................540 432-5453
Tammy Shifflett, *Manager*
EMP: 15
SALES (corp-wide): 6.2B **Publicly Held**
WEB: www.rrd.com
SIC: 2752 Commercial printing, lithographic
PA: R. R. Donnelley & Sons Company
35 W Wacker Dr
Chicago IL 60601
312 326-8000

(G-12269)
R R DONNELLEY & SONS COMPANY
Banta Book Group
1433 Pleasant Valley Rd (22801-9719)
PHONE....................................540 442-1333
Dave Johnson, *Manager*
EMP: 30
SALES (corp-wide): 6.2B **Publicly Held**
WEB: www.rrd.com
SIC: 2759 Commercial printing
PA: R. R. Donnelley & Sons Company
35 W Wacker Dr
Chicago IL 60601
312 326-8000

(G-12270)
REDCOAT SOLUTIONS INC
3060 N Valley Pike (22802-1105)
PHONE....................................540 437-9843
Farmer Cindy, *Treasurer*
EMP: 2
SALES (est): 86.3K **Privately Held**
WEB: www.redcoatsolutions.com
SIC: 2879 Agricultural chemicals

(G-12271)
REPUBLIC TRUSSWERKS LLC
2681 John Wayland Hwy (22801-4554)
P.O. Box 1347, Harrisonburg (22803-1347)
PHONE....................................540 434-9497
Roy Simmons Jr, *Mng Member*
Rusty Simmons,
EMP: 15
SQ FT: 18,000
SALES (est): 2.2MM **Privately Held**
WEB: www.republictrusswerks.com
SIC: 2439 Trusses, wooden roof
PA: Construction Materials Company
9 Memorial Ln
Lexington VA 24450

(G-12272)
ROCKINGHAM PRECAST INC
3330 Kratzer Rd (22802-1015)
P.O. Box 1347, Harrisonburg (22803-1347)
PHONE....................................540 433-8282
Roy D Simmons, *President*
Michael Hatcher, *General Mgr*
Alan J Deleeuwerk, *Treasurer*
EMP: 25
SALES (est): 2.1MM **Privately Held**
WEB: www.rockinghamprecast.com
SIC: 3273 Ready-mixed concrete

(G-12273)
ROCKINGHAM REDI-MIX INC (PA)
1557 Garbers Church Rd (22801-4570)
P.O. Box 1347, Harrisonburg (22803-1347)
PHONE....................................540 433-9128
Roy Simmons Jr, *President*
BJ Buddy Murtaugh, *Vice Pres*

Mike Tingen, *Opers Mgr*
Rj Wolford, *Opers Mgr*
Andrew Cantwell, *QC Mgr*
EMP: 35 EST: 1976
SALES (est): 8.7MM **Privately Held**
WEB: www.rockinghamredimix.com
SIC: 3273 Ready-mixed concrete

(G-12274)
ROCKINGHAM REDI-MIX INC
Also Called: Newriver Concrete
3330 Kratzer Rd (22802-1015)
P.O. Box 520, Harrisonburg (22803-0520)
PHONE...................................540 433-8282
Michael L Budd, *Branch Mgr*
EMP: 25
SQ FT: 1,500
SALES (corp-wide): 8.7MM **Privately Held**
WEB: www.rockinghamredimix.com
SIC: 3271 3273 Blocks, concrete or cinder: standard; ready-mixed concrete
PA: Rockingham Redi-Mix, Inc.
   1557 Garbers Church Rd
   Rockingham VA 22801
   540 433-9128

(G-12275)
ROCKINGHAM REDI-MIX INC
Also Called: Roanoke Concrete Supply Co
1557 Garbers Church Rd (22801)
PHONE...................................540 433-9128
B J Murtaugh, *Principal*
EMP: 25
SALES (corp-wide): 8.7MM **Privately Held**
WEB: www.rockinghamredimix.com
SIC: 3273 Ready-mixed concrete
PA: Rockingham Redi-Mix, Inc.
   1557 Garbers Church Rd
   Rockingham VA 22801
   540 433-9128

(G-12276)
SHENANDOAH VALLEY PRINTIN
4564 S Valley Pike (22801-3938)
PHONE...................................540 208-1808
EMP: 2
SALES (est): 92.3K **Privately Held**
SIC: 2752 Commercial printing, offset

(G-12277)
SHIFFLETT MACHINE SHOP
3061 Osceola Springs Rd (22801-3829)
PHONE...................................540 433-1731
Gary Shifflett, *Owner*
EMP: 1
SALES (est): 105.2K **Privately Held**
SIC: 3599 Machine shop, jobbing & repair

(G-12278)
STANS SIGNS INC
3128 Osceola Springs Rd (22801-3830)
PHONE...................................540 434-1531
Stanley Shifflett, *President*
Joan Shifflett, *Vice Pres*
EMP: 2 **Privately Held**
SIC: 3993 Signs, not made in custom sign painting shops

(G-12279)
SUTER MACHINE & TOOL
494 Liskey Rd (22801-3901)
P.O. Box 4530, Harrisonburg (22801-9546)
PHONE...................................540 434-2718
Frank Suter, *President*
Elizabeth Suter, *Treasurer*
EMP: 10
SQ FT: 4,000
SALES (est): 850K **Privately Held**
WEB: www.sutermachine.com
SIC: 3544 Special dies & tools

(G-12280)
SWORD & TRUMPET OFFICE
6083 Mount Clinton Pike (22802-0150)
P.O. Box 575, Harrisonburg (22803-0575)
PHONE...................................540 867-9419
Paul Emerson, *CEO*
Crit Lapp, *Principal*
Raymond Brunk, *Chairman*
Stanley Good, *Admin Sec*
EMP: 2
SALES (est): 182.3K **Privately Held**
WEB: www.swordandtrumpet.org
SIC: 2721 Periodicals

(G-12281)
TENNECO AUTOMOTIVE OPER CO INC
4500 Early Rd (22801-9792)
PHONE...................................540 432-3752
Chaes Davidson, *Manager*
EMP: 600
SALES (corp-wide): 17.4B **Publicly Held**
SIC: 3714 Shock absorbers, motor vehicle
HQ: Tenneco Automotive Operating Company, Inc.
   500 N Field Dr
   Lake Forest IL 60045
   847 482-5000

(G-12282)
VISTASHARE LLC
1400 Technology Dr (22802-2542)
PHONE...................................540 432-1900
David Smucker, *Owner*
Patrick Ressler, *Sales Staff*
David Clymer, *Prgrmr*
Isaac Witmer, *Software Dev*
EMP: 2
SALES (est): 210.7K **Privately Held**
WEB: www.vistashare.com
SIC: 7372 Prepackaged software

(G-12283)
WENGERS ELECTRICAL SERVICE LLC
134 Muddy Creek Rd (22802-0105)
PHONE...................................540 867-0101
Randall L Wenger, *Mng Member*
EMP: 5
SALES (est): 703.8K **Privately Held**
SIC: 2672 7389 Coated & laminated paper; automobile recovery service

Rockville
Hanover County

(G-12284)
BROAD STREET TRAFFIC JAMS LLC
11317 Annie Laura Ln (23146-1938)
PHONE...................................804 461-1245
Jeremy Humphrey, *President*
EMP: 1
SALES (est): 39.5K **Privately Held**
SIC: 2033 7389 Jams, jellies & preserves: packaged in cans, jars, etc.; business services

(G-12285)
ESSEX CONCRETE CORP
2391 Lanier Rd (23146-2226)
P.O. Box 127, Tappahannock (22560-0127)
PHONE...................................804 749-1950
Billy Cook, *President*
Mary Saunders, *Human Resources*
EMP: 4
SALES (est): 371.3K **Privately Held**
WEB: www.essexconcrete.com
SIC: 3273 Ready-mixed concrete

(G-12286)
HOMESTED MATERIAL HANDLINGS
2416 Lanier Rd (23146-2227)
PHONE...................................804 299-3389
EMP: 2
SALES (est): 218.8K **Privately Held**
SIC: 3537 Forklift trucks

(G-12287)
HY LEE PAVING CORPORATION (PA)
2100 Quarry Hill Rd (23146-2229)
P.O. Box 5036, Glen Allen (23058-5036)
PHONE...................................804 360-9066
Gordon F Penick III, *CEO*
Joseph B Penick, *President*
Brian Conrad, *Vice Pres*
Claude B Daniels, *Vice Pres*
Harold Gatewood, *Vice Pres*
EMP: 40
SQ FT: 4,000

SALES (est): 25.9MM **Privately Held**
WEB: www.leehypaving.com
SIC: 2951 1611 5032 Asphalt paving mixtures & blocks; highway & street paving contractor; asphalt mixture

(G-12288)
LEGACY VULCAN LLC
Mideast Division
4060 Quarry Hill Rd (23146-2231)
PHONE...................................804 360-2014
Jeff Rickey, *Manager*
EMP: 24 **Publicly Held**
WEB: www.vulcanmaterials.com
SIC: 3273 Ready-mixed concrete
HQ: Legacy Vulcan, Llc
   1200 Urban Center Dr
   Vestavia AL 35242
   205 298-3000

(G-12289)
LUCK STONE CORPORATION
2115 Ashland Rd (23146-2205)
PHONE...................................804 749-3233
Scott Seaborn, *Manager*
Amanda Bowers, *Admin Asst*
EMP: 12
SALES (corp-wide): 824.7MM **Privately Held**
WEB: www.luckstone.com
SIC: 1423 Crushed & broken granite
PA: Luck Stone Corporation
   515 Stone Mill Dr
   Manakin Sabot VA 23103
   804 784-6300

(G-12290)
LUCK STONE CORPORATION
Also Called: Luck Stone-Rockville Plant
2115 Ashland Rd (23146-2205)
PHONE...................................804 749-3232
John Buchannon, *Manager*
EMP: 30
SALES (corp-wide): 824.7MM **Privately Held**
WEB: www.luckstone.com
SIC: 1423 Crushed & broken granite
PA: Luck Stone Corporation
   515 Stone Mill Dr
   Manakin Sabot VA 23103
   804 784-6300

(G-12291)
MARK ELECTRIC INC
17238 Pouncey Tract Rd (23146-1752)
PHONE...................................804 749-4151
Mark Mieckowski, *Owner*
EMP: 7
SALES (est): 650.8K **Privately Held**
SIC: 3699 1731 Electrical equipment & supplies; electrical work

(G-12292)
MARTIN MARIETTA MATERIALS INC
Also Called: Anderson Creek Quarry
1940 Ashland Rd (23146-2200)
P.O. Box 309 (23146-0309)
PHONE...................................804 749-4831
Jason Babcock, *Manager*
EMP: 12 **Publicly Held**
WEB: www.martinmarietta.com
SIC: 1422 Crushed & broken limestone
PA: Martin Marietta Materials Inc
   2710 Wycliff Rd
   Raleigh NC 27607

(G-12293)
MERCHANTS METALS LLC
2356 Lanier Rd (23146-2225)
PHONE...................................804 262-9783
Hunter Newton, *Branch Mgr*
EMP: 5
SALES (corp-wide): 6.1B **Publicly Held**
WEB: www.merchantsmetals.com
SIC: 3496 1799 Miscellaneous fabricated wire products; fence construction
HQ: Merchants Metals Llc
   211 Perimeter Center Pkwy
   Atlanta GA 30346
   770 741-0306

(G-12294)
NUCKOLS CABINETRY LLC
17472 Dunns Chapel Rd (23146-1640)
PHONE...................................804 749-3908

Charles Nuckols, *Principal*
EMP: 2 **EST:** 2001
SALES (est): 133.4K **Privately Held**
SIC: 2434 Wood kitchen cabinets

(G-12295)
PRO IMAGE PRINTING & PUBG LLC
12153 Bienvenue Rd (23146-1619)
PHONE...................................804 798-4400
David Graf, *President*
EMP: 5
SALES (est): 53.7K **Privately Held**
SIC: 2759 7389 Commercial printing;

(G-12296)
RVA CUSTOM SIGNS INC
2412 Gran Ridge Rd Ste 2 (23146)
PHONE...................................804 749-4000
EMP: 1
SALES (est): 50.6K **Privately Held**
SIC: 3993 Signs & advertising specialties

(G-12297)
RVA SIGNS & GRAPHIC
2412 Granite Ridge Rd # 2 (23146-2236)
PHONE...................................804 749-4000
Dennis McIlhenny, *President*
Jon Emerson, *General Mgr*
EMP: 3
SALES (est): 296.1K **Privately Held**
WEB: www.toucan-signs.com
SIC: 3993 Signs & advertising specialties

(G-12298)
SAV-MOR MACHINE WORKS INC
2305 Commerce Center Dr G (23146-2248)
PHONE...................................804 356-7582
EMP: 2
SALES (est): 131.9K **Privately Held**
SIC: 3599 Machine shop, jobbing & repair

(G-12299)
SKIRMISH SUPPLIES
18091 Vontay Rd (23146-1637)
PHONE...................................804 749-3458
Jerry Stone, *Owner*
EMP: 1
SALES (est): 58.3K **Privately Held**
SIC: 3949 Sporting & athletic goods

(G-12300)
SOCK SOFTWARE INC
12335 S Anna Dr Bldg B (23146-1832)
PHONE...................................804 749-4137
Jud Cole, *Principal*
EMP: 3
SALES (est): 216.1K **Privately Held**
SIC: 2252 Socks

(G-12301)
TREXLO ENTERPRISES LLC (PA)
Also Called: Fastsigns
2361a Greystone Ct Ste A (23146-2233)
PHONE...................................804 719-5900
John White, *President*
EMP: 19
SALES (est): 2.9MM **Privately Held**
WEB: www.fastsigns.com
SIC: 3993 Signs & advertising specialties

(G-12302)
VIRGINIA TRUCK TRAILER LL
17517 Carrington Glen Ln (23146-1650)
PHONE...................................804 784-3485
EMP: 3
SALES (est): 95.9K **Privately Held**
SIC: 3715 Truck trailers

(G-12303)
WEBB-MASON INC
2418 Gran Ridge Rd Ste D (23146)
PHONE...................................804 897-1990
Beth Tillack, *Manager*
EMP: 3 **Privately Held**
WEB: www.webbmason.com
SIC: 2759 8742 Commercial printing; marketing consulting services
PA: Webb-Mason, Inc.
   10830 Gilroy Rd
   Hunt Valley MD 21031

Rocky Gap
Bland County

(G-12304)
AFFORDABLE CARE INC
Intersection Of Hwy 52 61 (24366)
P.O. Box 150 (24366-0150)
PHONE....................276 928-1427
Rob Rice, *Manager*
EMP: 5
SALES (corp-wide): 311MM **Privately Held**
WEB: www.affordabledentures.com
SIC: 3843 Dental laboratory equipment
PA: Affordable Care, Llc
1400 Industrial Dr
Kinston NC 28504
919 851-3996

(G-12305)
AMERICAN MINE RESEARCH INC (PA)
12187 N Scenic Hwy (24366-5024)
P.O. Box 234 (24366-0234)
PHONE....................276 928-1712
Robert Graf, *President*
Bob Saxton, *General Mgr*
David Graf, *Corp Secy*
Doug Baker, *Engineer*
Logan Martin, *Engineer*
EMP: 59 EST: 1975
SQ FT: 26,000
SALES (est): 31.1MM **Privately Held**
WEB: www.amr-sales.com
SIC: 3532 Mining machinery

(G-12306)
CHANDLER CONCRETE INC
273 Enterprise Ln (24366-6018)
PHONE....................276 928-1357
Davin Lambert, *Branch Mgr*
EMP: 5 **Privately Held**
WEB: www.chandlerconcrete.com
SIC: 3273 Ready-mixed concrete
PA: Chandler Concrete Inc
1006 S Church St
Burlington NC 27215

(G-12307)
EAST RIVER METALS INC
12195 N Scenic Hwy (24366-5024)
P.O. Box 184 (24366-0184)
PHONE....................276 928-1812
Robert G Graf, *President*
David Graf, *Corp Secy*
EMP: 50
SQ FT: 20,000
SALES (est): 3MM **Privately Held**
WEB: www.cmserm.com
SIC: 3444 Sheet metalwork

(G-12308)
W & B FABRICATORS INC
111 Enterprise Ln (24366)
P.O. Box 179 (24366-0179)
PHONE....................276 928-1060
Aaron Boothe, *President*
Robbie Lester, *Opers Mgr*
Wonda Williams, *Treasurer*
Tnica Ratliss, *Admin Sec*
EMP: 16
SQ FT: 32,000
SALES (est): 2.6MM **Privately Held**
WEB: www.wbfabricators.com
SIC: 7692 3441 3599 3444 Welding repair; fabricated structural metal; machine shop, jobbing & repair; sheet metalwork

Rocky Mount
Franklin County

(G-12309)
A & A MACHINE
80 Energy Blvd (24151-2916)
PHONE....................540 482-0480
Adam Bowman, *Owner*
EMP: 2
SALES (est): 60K **Privately Held**
SIC: 3599 Machine shop, jobbing & repair

(G-12310)
ADAM N ROBINSON
85 Diamond Ave (24151-1342)
PHONE....................540 489-1513
Adam Robinson, *Principal*
EMP: 2
SALES (est): 198.2K **Privately Held**
SIC: 3699 Electrical equipment & supplies

(G-12311)
ADDRESSOGRAPH BARTIZAN LLC
450 Weaver St (24151-2200)
PHONE....................800 552-3282
Chris Rawlings, *Sales Staff*
Barbara Pugh, *Manager*
Robert Scott, *President*
◆ EMP: 35
SQ FT: 7,000
SALES (est): 2.5MM **Privately Held**
WEB: www.imprinters.com
SIC: 2754 Cards, except greeting: gravure printing

(G-12312)
ARTISAN WOODWORK COMPANY LLC
447 Blue Ridge Ct (24151-6029)
PHONE....................540 420-4928
Adam Walters, *Mng Member*
EMP: 1
SALES (est): 70.4K **Privately Held**
SIC: 2431 Millwork

(G-12313)
BACOVA GUILD LTD
701 Orchard Ave (24151-1848)
PHONE....................540 484-4640
Jeff Strasser, *Plant Engr*
EMP: 1
SALES (est): 46.5K **Privately Held**
SIC: 2273 Carpets & rugs

(G-12314)
BRIARWOOD PUBLICATIONS
150 W College St (24151-1272)
PHONE....................540 489-4692
Barbara Turner, *President*
EMP: 2
SALES (est): 134.7K **Privately Held**
SIC: 2741 Miscellaneous publishing

(G-12315)
BRONTZ INC
3000 Chestnut Hill Rd (24151-5739)
PHONE....................540 483-0976
John O'Neil, *President*
Tobby Oneil, *Vice Pres*
EMP: 2
SALES (est): 20.5K **Privately Held**
SIC: 3585 1711 Air conditioning equipment, complete; heating & air conditioning contractors

(G-12316)
CHITTENDEN & ASSOCIATES INC
942 Bowles Valley Rd (24151-6912)
P.O. Box 534, Nokesville (20182-0534)
PHONE....................703 930-2769
Florence R Chittenden, *President*
William E Chittenden, *Vice Pres*
EMP: 2
SALES (est): 150K **Privately Held**
SIC: 3829 Polygraph devices

(G-12317)
DONALD KIRBY
345 Ashpone Tavern Rd (24151-4255)
PHONE....................540 493-8698
Donald Kirby, *Principal*
EMP: 2
SALES (est): 107.8K **Privately Held**
SIC: 2411 Logging

(G-12318)
DONNA CANNADAY
Also Called: Cannaday's Signs & Designs
700 Callaway Rd (24151-4969)
P.O. Box 178, Boones Mill (24065-0178)
PHONE....................540 489-7979
Donna Cannaday, *Owner*
EMP: 1
SALES (est): 62K **Privately Held**
SIC: 3993 Signs & advertising specialties

(G-12319)
DRIVELINE FABRICATIONS INC
19868 Virgil H Goode Hwy (24151-6696)
PHONE....................540 483-3590
David I Tenzer, *Administration*
EMP: 8
SALES (est): 1MM **Privately Held**
WEB: www.drivelinefabrication.com
SIC: 3441 Fabricated structural metal

(G-12320)
ELEGANT CABINETS INC
4131 Franklin St (24151-5344)
PHONE....................540 483-5800
Bradley Hodges, *President*
EMP: 35
SALES (est): 950K **Privately Held**
WEB: www.elegantwoodworksinc.com
SIC: 2434 Wood kitchen cabinets

(G-12321)
EXCHANGE MILLING CO INC (PA)
Also Called: Foothills Farm Supply
1380 Franklin St (24151-6548)
PHONE....................540 483-5324
Bruce Layman, *President*
Pamela Layman, *Treasurer*
EMP: 9
SQ FT: 15,000
SALES (est): 1.9MM **Privately Held**
WEB: www.foothillsfarmsupply.com
SIC: 2048 Prepared feeds

(G-12322)
FERGUSON LAND AND LBR CO INC
1040 N Main St (24151-2219)
P.O. Box 828 (24151-0828)
PHONE....................540 483-5090
John H Ferguson Jr, *President*
John H Ferguson III, *Vice Pres*
Tatum Ferguson, *Vice Pres*
▲ EMP: 60 EST: 1961
SQ FT: 79,000
SALES (est): 9.8MM **Privately Held**
SIC: 2421 Planing mills

(G-12323)
FRANKLIN COUNTY INV CO INC
Also Called: Franklin County Newspapers Inc
310 S Main St (24151-1711)
P.O. Box 250 (24151-0250)
PHONE....................540 483-5113
Andrew Haskell, *President*
Robert H Haskell III, *Treasurer*
EMP: 20 EST: 1980
SALES (est): 1MM
SALES (corp-wide): 254.6B **Publicly Held**
WEB: www.thefranklinnewspost.com
SIC: 2711 Newspapers, publishing & printing; job printing & newspaper publishing combined
HQ: Bh Media Group, Inc.
1314 Douglas St Ste 1500
Omaha NE 68102
402 444-1000

(G-12324)
GEORGE W WRAY
3125 Old Franklin Tpke (24151-5805)
PHONE....................540 483-7792
George Wray, *Principal*
EMP: 2
SALES (est): 176K **Privately Held**
SIC: 3531 Automobile wrecker hoists

(G-12325)
GLOBAL DIRECT LLC
3325 Grassy Hill Rd (24151-3911)
P.O. Box 506 (24151-0506)
PHONE....................540 483-5103
Robert M Cooper Jr,
Tony Doss,
▲ EMP: 5
SQ FT: 10,000 **Privately Held**
SIC: 2392 Household furnishings

(G-12326)
GREAT SOUTHERN WOOD PRSV INC
1050 N Main St (24151-2219)
PHONE....................540 483-5264
James W Rane, *President*

Brent Doggett, *Sales Staff*
Bob White, *Manager*
Ryan Blalock, *Director*
EMP: 150
SALES (corp-wide): 337.5MM **Privately Held**
WEB: www.yellawood.com
SIC: 2491 Structural lumber & timber, treated wood
PA: Great Southern Wood Preserving, Incorporated
1100 Us Highway 431 S
Abbeville AL 36310
334 585-2291

(G-12327)
HOMETOWN ICE CO
520 Weaver St (24151-2280)
PHONE....................540 483-7865
Douglas Arrington, *Owner*
Jeff Brock, *Manager*
EMP: 2
SQ FT: 3,700
SALES (est): 200K **Privately Held**
WEB: www.icyconditions.com
SIC: 2097 5999 Ice cubes; ice

(G-12328)
INDIGO SIGNS LLC
1305 Old Franklin Tpke (24151-5661)
PHONE....................540 489-8400
Karen Gray, *Owner*
EMP: 3
SALES (est): 241.9K **Privately Held**
WEB: www.onlyindigo.com
SIC: 3993 Electric signs

(G-12329)
J C INTERNATIONAL LLC
95 E Court St (24151-1741)
PHONE....................540 243-0086
Garry Volk, *Treasurer*
John Conde, *Mng Member*
Evelyn Conde, *Mng Member*
EMP: 3
SALES (est): 329.9K **Privately Held**
WEB: www.jcinternational.net
SIC: 2899 Fire retardant chemicals

(G-12330)
JAMMIN
Also Called: Jammin Apparel
335 Technology Dr (24151-2995)
PHONE....................540 484-4600
Mark Grinde, *Partner*
Brian Grinde, *Partner*
Valerie Duringer, *Marketing Staff*
EMP: 30
SQ FT: 40,000
SALES (est): 2.9MM **Privately Held**
WEB: www.jammin.com
SIC: 2329 2339 Men's & boys' sportswear & athletic clothing; women's & misses' outerwear

(G-12331)
K B INDUSTRIES INC
Also Called: Boone Welding
7191 Old Forge Rd (24151-5251)
PHONE....................540 483-8883
Keith Boone, *President*
Mimi Boone, *Vice Pres*
EMP: 3
SQ FT: 5,000
SALES (est): 250K **Privately Held**
WEB: www.kbindustries.com
SIC: 3446 Gratings, tread: fabricated metal

(G-12332)
LARRY D MARTIN
Also Called: Seal Craft Asphalt Service
949 Robin Ridge Rd (24151-3608)
PHONE....................540 493-0072
Larry D Martin, *Owner*
EMP: 1
SALES (est): 18K **Privately Held**
SIC: 2951 7389 Asphalt paving mixtures & blocks; business services

(G-12333)
LEES WOOD PRODUCTS INC
110 Smithers St (24151-1043)
P.O. Box 159 (24151-0159)
PHONE....................540 483-9728
Jessie L Robertson, *President*
Darren Clay Robertson, *Corp Secy*

EMP: 18
SQ FT: 10,000
SALES (est): 2.5MM **Privately Held**
WEB: www.leeswoodproducts.com
SIC: 2499 Picture & mirror frames, wood; decorative wood & woodwork

(G-12334)
LIBERTY CABINETS
19 Byrd Ln (24151-1177)
P.O. Box 96 (24151-0096)
PHONE..............................540 493-3149
Kelvin D Linkous, *Principal*
EMP: 3
SALES (est): 484.7K **Privately Held**
WEB: www.libertycabinetsusa.com
SIC: 2434 Wood kitchen cabinets

(G-12335)
LINEAL TECHNOLOGIES INC
Also Called: Plygem Industries
350 State St (24151-1178)
PHONE..............................540 484-6783
Kerry Robinet, *CEO*
Earl Dodson, *President*
▲ **EMP:** 90
SQ FT: 52,000
SALES (est): 28.3MM
SALES (corp-wide): 4.8B **Publicly Held**
SIC: 3089 3442 Extruded finished plastic products; window frames & sash, plastic; window screening, plastic; windows, plastic; metal doors, sash & trim
HQ: Mw Manufacturers Inc.
433 N Main St
Rocky Mount VA 24151
540 483-0211

(G-12336)
LIVELY FULCHER ORGAN BUILDERS
240 Energy Blvd (24151-2914)
PHONE..............................540 352-4401
Mark Lively, *President*
Paul Fulcher, *Vice Pres*
▲ **EMP:** 6
SQ FT: 10,000
SALES (est): 972K **Privately Held**
WEB: www.lively-fulcher.com
SIC: 3931 7699 Organs, all types: pipe, reed, hand, electronic, etc.; musical instrument repair services

(G-12337)
LYNCH PRODUCTS
Also Called: Lynch Sign Products
3117 Chestnut Hill Rd (24151-5714)
PHONE..............................540 483-7800
Steve Lynch, *Owner*
EMP: 2
SALES (est): 136.1K **Privately Held**
SIC: 3993 Signs, not made in custom sign painting shops

(G-12338)
MCAIRLAIDS INC
180 Corporate Dr (24151-3899)
PHONE..............................540 352-5050
Peter Gawley, *President*
Maksimow J Alexander, *Chairman*
Andreas Schmidt, *Vice Pres*
Jon Tibbs, *Vice Pres*
Gus Tosoni, *VP Opers*
◆ **EMP:** 165
SQ FT: 150,000
SALES (est): 40.7MM
SALES (corp-wide): 85.8MM **Privately Held**
WEB: www.mcairlaids.net
SIC: 2621 Absorbent paper
PA: Mcairlaid's Vliesstoffe Gmbh
Munsterstr. 61-65
Steinfurt 48565
255 293-340

(G-12339)
MICHAEL R LITTLE
316 Windy Pines Ln (24151-3433)
PHONE..............................540 489-4785
Michael R Little, *Principal*
EMP: 2
SALES (est): 122.5K **Privately Held**
SIC: 3953 Marking devices

(G-12340)
MW MANUFACTURERS INC (DH)
433 N Main St (24151-1165)
P.O. Box 559 (24151-0559)
PHONE..............................540 483-0211
Art Steinhafel, *President*
Lynn Morstad, *Principal*
Shawn K Poe, *Treasurer*
▲ **EMP:** 800
SQ FT: 600,000
SALES (est): 207.4MM
SALES (corp-wide): 4.8B **Publicly Held**
SIC: 2431 Window frames, wood
HQ: Ply Gem Industries, Inc.
5020 Weston Pkwy Ste 400
Cary NC 27513
919 677-3900

(G-12341)
MW MANUFACTURERS INC
350 State St (24151-1178)
PHONE..............................540 484-6780
Earl Dodson, *Branch Mgr*
EMP: 120
SALES (corp-wide): 4.8B **Publicly Held**
SIC: 2431 Window frames, wood
HQ: Mw Manufacturers Inc.
433 N Main St
Rocky Mount VA 24151
540 483-0211

(G-12342)
NEWBOLD CORPORATION (PA)
450 Weaver St (24151-2207)
PHONE..............................540 489-4400
Robert Scott, *President*
Donna Austin, *Exec VP*
Frank Canestari, *Exec VP*
Dan Harrison, *Vice Pres*
Patrick Climer, *Controller*
◆ **EMP:** 106
SQ FT: 100,000
SALES (est): 25.7MM **Privately Held**
WEB: www.newboldcorp.com
SIC: 3579 3578 Mailing, letter handling & addressing machines; cash registers

(G-12343)
NICHOLS WELDING
92 Redbud Hill Rd (24151-4154)
PHONE..............................540 483-5308
Travis Nichols, *Principal*
EMP: 5
SALES (est): 362.5K **Privately Held**
WEB: www.nicholswelding.net
SIC: 7692 Welding repair

(G-12344)
PER LLC
211 Industry Blvd (24151-3004)
P.O. Box 738 (24151-0738)
PHONE..............................540 489-4737
Aaron Long, *Mng Member*
EMP: 8
SALES (est): 400K **Privately Held**
WEB: www.solidrockmp.com
SIC: 3531 Construction machinery

(G-12345)
PINK STREET SIGNS
1455 Franklin St (24151-6387)
PHONE..............................540 489-8400
EMP: 2
SALES (est): 85K **Privately Held**
SIC: 3993 Signs And Advertising Specialties

(G-12346)
PLY GEM INDUSTRIES INC
433 N Main St (24151-1165)
PHONE..............................540 483-0211
Jim Connor, *Transportation*
Brianna Holland, *Production*
Travis Arthur, *Engineer*
Jessica Richardson, *Cust Mgr*
Lynn Morstad, *Branch Mgr*
EMP: 250
SALES (corp-wide): 4.8B **Publicly Held**
WEB: www.plygem.com
SIC: 2431 Windows, wood
HQ: Ply Gem Industries, Inc.
5020 Weston Pkwy Ste 400
Cary NC 27513
919 677-3900

(G-12347)
POSITIVE FEEDBACK SOFTWARE LL
140 Franco Dr (24151-4026)
PHONE..............................540 243-0300
Patrick Michael McGraw, *Administration*
EMP: 2
SALES (est): 135K **Privately Held**
WEB: www.positive-feedback.net
SIC: 7372 Business oriented computer software

(G-12348)
QLF CUSTOM PIPE ORGAN
240 Energy Blvd (24151-2914)
PHONE..............................540 484-1133
Pat Quigley, *Principal*
Irene Quigley, *Principal*
EMP: 7
SQ FT: 10,000
SALES (est): 813.5K **Privately Held**
WEB: www.qlfcomponents.com
SIC: 3931 Pipes, organ

(G-12349)
QUIGLEY DESIGNS
240 Energy Blvd (24151-2914)
PHONE..............................540 484-1133
Patrick Quigley, *Owner*
EMP: 1
SALES (est): 92.3K **Privately Held**
WEB: www.qlfcomponents.com
SIC: 2499 Decorative wood & woodwork

(G-12350)
ROCKY MOUNT READY MIX CONCRETE
110 Old Franklin Tpke (24151-1577)
PHONE..............................540 483-1288
Ronnie Wray, *President*
Bonnie Wray, *Corp Secy*
Wray Donna Lynn, *Vice Pres*
EMP: 8 **EST:** 1967
SQ FT: 900
SALES (est): 1.7MM **Privately Held**
WEB: www.procon-inc.net
SIC: 3273 Ready-mixed concrete

(G-12351)
RUTROUGH CABINETS INC
7101 Six Mile Post Rd (24151-8000)
PHONE..............................540 489-3211
Tony Rutrough, *Owner*
EMP: 8
SALES (est): 605K **Privately Held**
SIC: 2434 1751 1799 Wood kitchen cabinets; cabinet & finish carpentry; counter top installation

(G-12352)
SOLUTION MATRIX INC
60 Commerce Rd (24151-4199)
PHONE..............................540 352-3211
Linda Rader, *Ch of Bd*
Keith Marshall, *President*
Rick Sell, *President*
Jeremy Adkins, *General Mgr*
Cameron Harjung, *Chairman*
EMP: 40
SQ FT: 25,000
SALES (est): 8.3MM **Privately Held**
WEB: www.solutionmatrixinc.com
SIC: 3842 Braces, elastic

(G-12353)
SOUTHERN HERITAGE HOMES INC
275 Corporate Dr (24151-3854)
PHONE..............................540 489-7700
David Peters, *President*
Robert Jarrett, *Sales Mgr*
EMP: 10
SQ FT: 12,000
SALES (est): 2MM **Privately Held**
WEB: www.shhomes.net
SIC: 2452 Prefabricated wood buildings

(G-12354)
SOUTHWSTERN VRGNIA WHEELCO INC
948 Chantilly Rd (24151-3681)
PHONE..............................540 493-6886
John Dillard Cahill, *Principal*
EMP: 5 **EST:** 2011

SALES (est): 352.9K **Privately Held**
SIC: 1221 Bituminous coal & lignite-surface mining

(G-12355)
TURNERS READY MIX INC
150 Cliff St (24151-1802)
PHONE..............................540 483-9150
Ricky Thomason, *President*
Thomason Susan W, *Vice Pres*
EMP: 10 **EST:** 1960
SQ FT: 8,200
SALES (est): 1.5MM **Privately Held**
WEB: www.turnersreadymixinc.com
SIC: 3273 Ready-mixed concrete

(G-12356)
TWIN CREEKS DISTILLERY INC
510 Franklin St (24151-1608)
P.O. Box 2, Ferrum (24088-0002)
PHONE..............................540 483-1266
Anna Prillaman, *Mng Member*
EMP: 5
SALES (est): 136.6K **Privately Held**
WEB: www.twincreeksdistillery.com
SIC: 2085 Distilled & blended liquors

(G-12357)
UNDERWOOD LOGGING LLC
485 Promise Ln (24151-6367)
P.O. Box 711 (24151-0711)
PHONE..............................540 489-1388
Robert Underwood, *Mng Member*
Tammy Underwood, *Mng Member*
EMP: 3
SALES (est): 265.4K **Privately Held**
SIC: 2411 Timber, cut at logging camp

(G-12358)
VERTICAL BLIND PRODUCTIONS
120 Woods Edge Dr (24151-6478)
PHONE..............................540 484-4995
Anthony Woods, *Principal*
EMP: 1
SALES (est): 117.3K **Privately Held**
SIC: 2591 Blinds vertical

(G-12359)
VIRGINIA EMBALMING COMPANY INC
62 Virginia Market Pl Dr (24151-6862)
PHONE..............................540 334-1150
EMP: 3 **EST:** 2011
SALES (est): 194.7K **Privately Held**
SIC: 2869 Mfg Industrial Organic Chemicals

(G-12360)
VIRGINIA PRTG CO ROANOKE INC
Also Called: Charles Trpin Prtrs Lthgrphics
40 High St (24151-1420)
PHONE..............................540 483-7433
Virginia B Turpin, *President*
EMP: 1
SALES (corp-wide): 499.8K **Privately Held**
WEB: www.virginiaprintingcompanyinc.com
SIC: 2752 Commercial printing, offset
PA: Virginia Printing Company Of Roanoke, Inc.
501a Campbell Ave Sw
Roanoke VA 24016
540 483-7433

Rose Hill
Lee County

(G-12361)
LONESOME TRAILS LLC
232 Neosha Dr (24281-8788)
PHONE..............................276 445-5443
Aaron Hensley,
EMP: 1
SALES (est): 49.1K **Privately Held**
SIC: 3861 Toners, prepared photographic (not made in chemical plants)

(G-12362)
ROUSE WHOLESALE
Rr 1 Box 767 (24281)
PHONE..............................276 445-3220

Charles Rouse, *Owner*
EMP: 2
SQ FT: 4,800
SALES (est): 193.4K **Privately Held**
SIC: 2671 Plastic film, coated or laminated for packaging

(G-12363)
TIMBERLINE BARNS LLC
21680 Wilderness Rd (24281-8799)
PHONE..................................276 445-4366
Daniel Vendley,
EMP: 1
SALES (est): 142.5K **Privately Held**
WEB: www.timberlinebarns.com
SIC: 2499 Woodenware, kitchen & household

(G-12364)
WHITE ROCK TRUSS LLC
21437 Wilderness Rd (24281-8859)
PHONE..................................276 445-5990
Josh Eicher, *Principal*
Daniel Esch, *Mng Member*
EMP: 6
SALES (est): 798.1K **Privately Held**
WEB: www.whiterocktruss.com
SIC: 2439 5031 Trusses, wooden roof; building materials, exterior

Rosedale
Russell County

(G-12365)
GAS FIELD SERVICES INC
St 19708 Rr 19 (24280)
P.O. Box 555 (24280-0555)
PHONE..................................276 873-1214
Tom Shrader, *President*
Terry Moore, *Supervisor*
EMP: 58
SALES (est): 15.7MM **Privately Held**
WEB: www.gasfieldsvc.com
SIC: 3533 Gas field machinery & equipment

(G-12366)
GAS FIELD SERVICES LLC
17908 U S Highway 19 (24280-3548)
P.O. Box 555 (24280-0555)
PHONE..................................276 880-2323
Bernie Dearth, *General Mgr*
Roger Shupe, *Technician*
EMP: 5
SALES (est): 552.7K **Privately Held**
WEB: www.gasfieldsvc.com
SIC: 1389 Oil field services

(G-12367)
QUALITY PORTABLE BUILDINGS
300 Mcfarlane Ln (24280-3561)
PHONE..................................276 880-2007
Chris Johnson, *Principal*
EMP: 4
SALES (est): 386.4K **Privately Held**
SIC: 3448 Prefabricated metal buildings

Roseland
Nelson County

(G-12368)
GREENE HORSE LOGGING LLC
704 Emblys Gap Rd (22967-3104)
PHONE..................................434 277-5146
Jonathan C Kinney, *Administration*
EMP: 3
SALES (est): 150.9K **Privately Held**
SIC: 2411 Logging camps & contractors

(G-12369)
HR WELLNESS AND THERMOGRAPHY
1543 Beech Grove Rd (22967-2213)
PHONE..................................434 361-1996
EMP: 2 **EST:** 2016
SALES (est): 73.2K **Privately Held**
SIC: 2759 Commercial Printing

(G-12370)
MASSIES WOOD PRODUCTS LLC
581 Buffalo Mines Rd (22967-3123)
PHONE..................................434 277-8498
T W Massie,
EMP: 5
SALES (est): 586.9K **Privately Held**
SIC: 2426 Hardwood dimension & flooring mills

(G-12371)
PIEDMONT LOGGING INC
1697 Cow Hollow Rd (22967-3027)
PHONE..................................434 989-1698
EMP: 3
SALES (est): 130K **Privately Held**
SIC: 2411 Logging

(G-12372)
RIVER CITY CIDER LLC
Also Called: Bryants Small Batch
3224 E Branch Loop (22967-2600)
PHONE..................................804 420-9683
EMP: 2
SALES (est): 62.3K **Privately Held**
WEB: www.bryantscider.com
SIC: 2099 Cider, nonalcoholic

Round Hill
Loudoun County

(G-12373)
ABOVE GROUND LEVEL
18331 Turnberry Dr (20141-3505)
PHONE..................................540 338-4363
EMP: 2
SALES (est): 62.9K **Privately Held**
WEB: www.aglmediagroup.com
SIC: 2711 Newspapers

(G-12374)
AERASPACE CORPORATION
26b E Loudoun St (20141)
PHONE..................................703 554-2906
Billy M Sprague, *President*
Stella Sprague, *Corp Secy*
EMP: 7 **Privately Held**
SIC: 3761 Guided missiles & space vehicles

(G-12375)
BOGATI BODGEA
35246 Harry Byrd Hwy (20141-3200)
PHONE..................................540 338-1144
Jim Bogaty, *Principal*
EMP: 3
SALES (est): 194K **Privately Held**
WEB: www.bogatibodega.com
SIC: 2084 Wines

(G-12376)
CV WELDING
8 Longstreet Ave (20141-9421)
PHONE..................................540 338-6521
Gloria Vest, *Principal*
EMP: 1
SALES (est): 56.3K **Privately Held**
SIC: 7692 Welding repair

(G-12377)
DEBRA ROSEL
18280 Turnberry Dr (20141-2574)
PHONE..................................703 675-4963
Debra Rosel, *Owner*
EMP: 1
SALES (est): 72.2K **Privately Held**
SIC: 3578 Calculating & accounting equipment

(G-12378)
FROG VALLEY PUBLISHING
36157 Bell Rd (20141-2440)
PHONE..................................540 338-3224
Sharon Wells, *Principal*
EMP: 2
SALES (est): 116.5K **Privately Held**
WEB: www.frogvalleypublishing.com
SIC: 2741 Miscellaneous publishing

(G-12379)
GUIDE TO CAREGIVING LLC
20114 Airmont Rd (20141-1925)
PHONE..................................571 213-3845
Elisabeth Murphy,
EMP: 1
SALES (est): 3K **Privately Held**
SIC: 2731 Book publishing

(G-12380)
JILL C PERLA
Also Called: Perla-Art
17090 Greenwood Dr (20141-4431)
PHONE..................................703 407-5695
Jill Perla, *Owner*
EMP: 1
SALES (est): 49.3K **Privately Held**
WEB: www.jillperlaart.com
SIC: 3952 Canvas board, artists'

(G-12381)
KELLIS CREATIONS LLC
17209 Grand Valley Ct (20141-2293)
PHONE..................................540 554-2878
Kelli Piliere,
EMP: 1 **EST:** 2011
SALES (est): 69.6K **Privately Held**
SIC: 3269 Pottery cooking & kitchen articles

(G-12382)
KIMS KREATIONS LLC
35366 Carnoustie Cir (20141-2508)
PHONE..................................703 431-7978
Kim Trombly, *Mng Member*
EMP: 1
SALES (est): 66.1K **Privately Held**
WEB: www.kimskreations-va.com
SIC: 2335 Bridal & formal gowns

(G-12383)
MUTUAL BOX LEATHER
17569 Whitby Ct (20141-2197)
PHONE..................................703 626-9770
Donald Crum, *Principal*
EMP: 2
SALES (est): 124.2K **Privately Held**
SIC: 3199 Boxes, leather

(G-12384)
NOVA FIRE SUPPLY LLC
35190 Tate Ct (20141-2553)
PHONE..................................703 909-8339
Garrett Grant, *Owner*
EMP: 1
SALES (est): 48.8K **Privately Held**
SIC: 3429 Nozzles, fire fighting

(G-12385)
R2JB ENTERPRISES
Also Called: Cherry Tree Learning
17270 Arrowood Pl (20141-2490)
PHONE..................................703 727-3342
Robert Moskal, *Partner*
EMP: 1
SALES (est): 121.5K **Privately Held**
SIC: 3499 Novelties & giftware, including trophies

(G-12386)
RACK 10 SOLAR LLC
35091 Paxson Rd (20141-2020)
PHONE..................................703 996-4082
EMP: 5
SALES (est): 221.7K **Privately Held**
SIC: 3679 Power supplies, all types: static

(G-12387)
ROBERT R KLINE
Also Called: On Wing
17707 Lakefield Rd (20141-2416)
PHONE..................................540 454-7003
Robert Kline, *Principal*
EMP: 1
SALES (est): 119.6K **Privately Held**
WEB: www.onwing.us
SIC: 3728 Aircraft parts & equipment

(G-12388)
ROYAL ELEMENTS LLC
35461 Sassafras Dr (20141-2571)
PHONE..................................540 338-2591
EMP: 3
SALES (est): 188K **Privately Held**
SIC: 2819 Industrial inorganic chemicals

(G-12389)
SIGNATURE SIGNS
34434 Harry Byrd Hwy (20141-2108)
P.O. Box 466 (20142-0466)
PHONE..................................540 554-2717
EMP: 2
SALES (est): 200K **Privately Held**
SIC: 3993 7389 Mfg Signs/Advertising Specialties

(G-12390)
SOFTWARE INCENTIVES
19300 Ebenezer Church Rd (20141-1903)
PHONE..................................540 554-2319
Gary Breads, *Owner*
EMP: 1
SALES (est): 110K **Privately Held**
SIC: 7372 Prepackaged software

(G-12391)
STONELEIGH GOLF CLUB
Also Called: Sean Duggan Golf Shop
35271 Prestwick Ct (20141-2504)
PHONE..................................540 338-4653
Sean F Duggan, *Principal*
Matthew Allis, *Food Svc Dir*
EMP: 7
SALES (est): 112.7K **Privately Held**
WEB: www.stoneleighgolf.com
SIC: 3949 Shafts, golf club

(G-12392)
UNISON ARMS LLC
20954 Furr Rd (20141-1805)
PHONE..................................571 342-1108
Ronald Blankenship, *Owner*
EMP: 1
SALES (est): 51.2K **Privately Held**
WEB: www.unison.org.uk
SIC: 3484 7389 Guns (firearms) or gun parts, 30 mm. & below;

(G-12393)
UNITED GRAPHICS INC
35135 Cherry Grove Ln (20141-2340)
P.O. Box 499 (20142-0499)
PHONE..................................540 338-7525
David A Remler, *President*
Kevin Stockdale, *Vice Pres*
EMP: 2
SALES (est): 500K **Privately Held**
SIC: 2759 Commercial printing

(G-12394)
VIZINI INCORPORATED
11 New Cut Rd (20141-2424)
P.O. Box 668 (20142-0668)
PHONE..................................703 508-8662
Rita Hockenbury, *President*
EMP: 1
SALES (est): 112.1K **Privately Held**
SIC: 2396 Apparel findings & trimmings

(G-12395)
WATERFORD PAST-THYMES
35862 Camotop Ct (20141-2499)
PHONE..................................703 434-1758
Melissa Franzen, *Partner*
EMP: 2
SALES (est): 82.3K **Privately Held**
WEB: www.flowerspressed.com
SIC: 3999 Flowers, artificial & preserved

Rowe
Buchanan County

(G-12396)
BELCHER LUMBER CO INC
2700 Breeden Branch Rd (24646-9084)
PHONE..................................276 498-3362
Donald Belcher, *President*
EMP: 3
SALES (est): 246.4K **Privately Held**
WEB: www.spidermantreeservices.com
SIC: 2421 Sawmills & planing mills, general

(G-12397)
EXCEL WELL SERVICE INC
3008 Breeden Branch Rd (24646-9246)
P.O. Box 1191, Vansant (24656-1191)
PHONE..................................276 498-4360
Samuel Keith Looney, *President*

GEOGRAPHIC

Kenneth Horne, *General Mgr*
Lawrence Jarvis, *Vice Pres*
EMP: 16
SALES (est): 1MM **Privately Held**
SIC: 1389 Servicing oil & gas wells

Ruckersville
Greene County

(G-12398)
APPALACHIAN RADIO
CORPORATION
151 Goldenrod Rd (22968-2012)
PHONE.................................865 382-9865
Christopher Moore, *CEO*
EMP: 1
SALES (est): 64.3K **Privately Held**
SIC: 3825 Radio frequency measuring
equipment

(G-12399)
ASHBURY INTL GROUP INC
Also Called: Ashbury Precision Ordnance Mfg
84 Business Park Cir (22968-3083)
P.O. Box 8024, Charlottesville (22906-
8024)
PHONE.................................434 296-8600
Morris Peterson, *President*
Joe Snyder, *Exec VP*
Gary Vance, *Engineer*
Troy Perry, *Marketing Staff*
Charles Overbey, *Director*
◆ **EMP:** 18
SQ FT: 45,500
SALES (est): 4.2MM **Privately Held**
WEB: www.ashburyintlgroup.com
SIC: 3827 3826 Binoculars; laser scientific
& engineering instruments

(G-12400)
BRYAN SMITH
143 Mistland Trl (22968-3194)
PHONE.................................434 242-7698
Bryan Smith, *Owner*
EMP: 1
SALES (est): 44.6K **Privately Held**
SIC: 3799 2452 Trailers & trailer equip-
ment; log cabins, prefabricated, wood

(G-12401)
CRABTREE WELDING
49 Hancock Dr (22968-3549)
PHONE.................................434 990-0140
Donald Crabtree, *Principal*
EMP: 2
SALES (est): 152.4K **Privately Held**
SIC: 7692 Welding repair

(G-12402)
FLAWLESS SHOWER
ENCLOSURES
85 Fox Ridge Ln (22968-3687)
PHONE.................................434 466-3845
EMP: 5
SALES (est): 494.3K **Privately Held**
WEB: www.flawless-va.com
SIC: 3088 Plastics plumbing fixtures

(G-12403)
HARTUNG SCREEN PRINTING
LLC
607 Valley View Rd (22968-2626)
PHONE.................................412 979-7847
Matthew Hartung,
EMP: 2
SALES (est): 66.6K **Privately Held**
SIC: 3999 Manufacturing industries

(G-12404)
LOVINGSTON WINERY
1800 Fray Rd (22968-9422)
PHONE.................................925 286-2824
Justin Falco, *Principal*
EMP: 2
SALES (est): 62.3K **Privately Held**
WEB: www.lovingstonwinery.com
SIC: 2084 Wines

(G-12405)
M T STONE AND STUCCO LLC
22 Hillcrest Dr (22968-9573)
PHONE.................................434 806-7226
Miguel Trujillo, *Owner*

EMP: 1
SALES (est): 83K **Privately Held**
SIC: 3299 Stucco

(G-12406)
MONTIFALCO VINEYARD
1800 Fray Rd (22968-9422)
PHONE.................................434 989-9115
EMP: 2
SALES (est): 128K **Privately Held**
SIC: 2084 Wines

(G-12407)
OLDE SOULS PRESS LLC
642 Mistland Trl (22968-6000)
PHONE.................................434 242-7348
Joanne Lattiak, *Principal*
EMP: 2 EST: 2011
SALES (est): 104K **Privately Held**
WEB: www.oldesoulspress.com
SIC: 2741 Miscellaneous publishing

(G-12408)
PERFORMANCE SIGNS LLC
18 Commerce Dr (22968-3430)
PHONE.................................434 985-7446
Katherine Morris, *Owner*
Melissa Liberatore, *Admin Mgr*
EMP: 12
SQ FT: 8,000
SALES (est): 1.4MM **Privately Held**
WEB: www.performancesigns.net
SIC: 3993 2759 1611 Electric signs;
screen printing; highway & street sign in-
stallation

(G-12409)
PRECISION GAS PIPING LLC
68 Branchland Ct (22968-9545)
PHONE.................................434 531-2427
Roger Hill, *Principal*
EMP: 5
SALES (est): 621.7K **Privately Held**
WEB: www.pgp.mfbiz.com
SIC: 2911 Gases & liquefied petroleum
gases

(G-12410)
PUZZLE PIECE LLC
471 Northridge Rd (22968-3647)
PHONE.................................434 985-8074
Timothy Alley, *Principal*
EMP: 1
SALES (est): 41K **Privately Held**
SIC: 3944 Puzzles

(G-12411)
R & R PRINTING
8458 Seminole Trl Ste 2b (22968-3489)
PHONE.................................434 985-9844
Robert Deluca, *Owner*
EMP: 2
SALES (est): 122K **Privately Held**
WEB: www.rnrprintingco.com
SIC: 2759 2754 2396 Commercial print-
ing; business form & card printing,
gravure; fabric printing & stamping

(G-12412)
R W A MACHINING & WELDING
CO
127 Commerce Dr (22968-3431)
PHONE.................................434 985-7362
Joseph K Sudduth, *President*
Charles Sudduth III, *Vice Pres*
Charles Sudduth Jr, *Director*
EMP: 4 EST: 1969
SQ FT: 6,400 **Privately Held**
WEB: www.rwamachining.com
SIC: 3599 7692 Machine shop, jobbing &
repair; welding repair

(G-12413)
SCHORR WOOD WORKS LLC
314 Lake Dr (22968-3193)
PHONE.................................434 990-1897
Matthew John Schorr Jr, *Principal*
EMP: 1
SALES (est): 54.1K **Privately Held**
SIC: 2431 Millwork

(G-12414)
STA-FIT INDUSTRIES LLC
72 Garden Ct (22968-3668)
PHONE.................................540 308-8215

Steven Eugene Ferrell, *Administration*
EMP: 2
SALES (est): 84.3K **Privately Held**
WEB: www.benchblokz.com
SIC: 3999 Manufacturing industries

(G-12415)
VERTICAL PRAISE
403 Southridge Dr (22968-3690)
PHONE.................................434 985-1513
Holly Carden, *Administration*
EMP: 2
SALES (est): 158.6K **Privately Held**
SIC: 2591 Blinds vertical

(G-12416)
WILLIAMS BROTHERS LUMBER
INC
185 Commerce Dr (22968-3431)
P.O. Box 26, Barboursville (22923-0026)
PHONE.................................434 760-2951
Cleveland F Williams, *President*
James A Williams, *Treasurer*
Joseph H Williams, *Admin Sec*
Scott Fisher,
EMP: 10
SALES (est): 1.5MM **Privately Held**
SIC: 2439 Timbers, structural: laminated
lumber

Rural Retreat
Wythe County

(G-12417)
AEROSPACE COMPONENTS
756 Old King Rd 725 (24368-6115)
PHONE.................................276 686-0123
Michele Demetriades,
EMP: 2
SALES (est): 146.2K **Privately Held**
SIC: 3599 Crankshafts & camshafts, ma-
chining

(G-12418)
BREWCO LLC
860 Gap Of Ridge Rd (24368-2990)
PHONE.................................276 686-5448
Terry Brewer, *Principal*
EMP: 2
SALES (est): 70.8K **Privately Held**
SIC: 2082 Malt beverages

(G-12419)
C B R ENGINE SERVICE
526 Knight Rd (24368-2862)
PHONE.................................276 686-5198
Charlie Buck, *Owner*
EMP: 5 EST: 1962
SALES (est): 391.3K **Privately Held**
SIC: 3714 Motor vehicle engines & parts

(G-12420)
CRISP MANUFACTURING CO
INC
732 Milk Plant Rd (24368-3060)
P.O. Box 396 (24368-0396)
PHONE.................................276 686-4131
Paul Crisp III, *CEO*
Paul Crisp Jr, *President*
Maryln Crisp, *Vice Pres*
B J Pettigrew, *Incorporator*
EMP: 12 EST: 1963
SQ FT: 33,000
SALES (est): 2.6MM **Privately Held**
WEB: www.crispmanufacturing.com
SIC: 3532 Mining machinery

(G-12421)
CUSTOM WELDED STEEL ART
INC
723 Country View Rd (24368-6019)
PHONE.................................276 686-4107
Gale Blevins, *Principal*
EMP: 1
SALES (est): 36.1K **Privately Held**
SIC: 7692 Welding repair

(G-12422)
DALTON ENTERPRISES INC
206 Gienow Rd (24368-3070)
PHONE.................................276 686-9178
Roger L Dalton, *President*
Elizabeth Dalton, *President*

Randy Lyall, *Manager*
Sondra Monahan, *Admin Asst*
EMP: 62
SALES (est): 13.6MM **Privately Held**
WEB: www.adamtrailers.com
SIC: 3715 Trailer bodies; trailers or vans
for transporting horses

(G-12423)
ELECTRO FINISHING INC
6817 W Lee Hwy (24368-2584)
PHONE.................................276 686-6687
Timothy Litz, *President*
Keyth Litz, *Vice Pres*
EMP: 10
SALES (est): 1.1MM **Privately Held**
SIC: 3471 Chromium plating of metals or
formed products; plating of metals or
formed products

(G-12424)
FOUR SEASONS CATERING &
BAKERY
965 Four Seasons Rd (24368-2400)
PHONE.................................276 686-5982
Rhonda Cox, *Owner*
EMP: 1
SALES (est): 54.4K **Privately Held**
SIC: 2099 Food preparations

(G-12425)
J Z UTILITY BARNS LLC
572 Milk Plant Rd (24368-3176)
PHONE.................................276 686-1683
Johnathan S Zook,
EMP: 3
SALES (est): 392.1K **Privately Held**
WEB: www.greenleaf-financial.com
SIC: 3448 Farm & utility buildings

(G-12426)
KLOCKNER PENTAPLAST AMER
INC
600 Gienow Rd (24368-3272)
PHONE.................................276 686-6111
Louie Pritchett, *General Mgr*
Andy Patterson, *Opers Mgr*
Louie Tirtchett, *Branch Mgr*
Robin Zachary, *Supervisor*
EMP: 215
SALES (corp-wide): 4.7MM **Privately
Held**
WEB: www.kpfilms.com
SIC: 3081 Plastic film & sheet
HQ: Klockner Pentaplast Of America, Inc.
3585 Kloeckner Rd
Gordonsville VA 22942
540 832-1400

(G-12427)
LARRY W JARVIS LOGGING
988 Pine Glade Rd (24368-6077)
PHONE.................................276 686-5938
Larry Jarvis, *Principal*
EMP: 2
SALES (est): 250.7K **Privately Held**
SIC: 2411 Logging camps & contractors

(G-12428)
MOUNTAIN VALLEY
ENTERPRISES
313 Killinger Creek Rd (24368-2612)
PHONE.................................276 686-6516
Sharon Sollenberger, *Partner*
Clair Sollenberger, *Partner*
EMP: 1
SALES (est): 60K **Privately Held**
SIC: 2394 5092 Liners & covers, fabric:
made from purchased materials; toys

(G-12429)
PICKLE TYSON
Also Called: Old Mount Airy Machine
204 W Railroad Ave (24368-3300)
PHONE.................................276 686-5368
Tyson Pickle, *Owner*
EMP: 2
SALES (est): 120.7K **Privately Held**
WEB: www.oldmountairymachine.com
SIC: 3541 Machine tools, metal cutting
type

▲ = Import ▼=Export
◆ =Import/Export

(G-12430)
PRO IMAGE GRAPHICS
111 W Buck Ave (24368-2513)
PHONE...................................276 686-6174
EMP: 2
SALES (est): 118.3K Privately Held
SIC: 2759 Screen printing

(G-12431)
RURAL RTREAT WNERY VNYARDS LLC
201 Church St (24368-3180)
P.O. Box 428 (24368-0428)
PHONE...................................276 686-8300
Scott Mecimore,
EMP: 3
SALES (est): 100K Privately Held
WEB: www.ruralrtreatwinery.com
SIC: 2084 Wines

(G-12432)
SNIFFALICIOUS CANDLE LLC
865 Pine Glade Rd (24368-6100)
PHONE...................................276 686-2204
Helen Conley, *Principal*
EMP: 1
SALES (est): 72.9K Privately Held
SIC: 3999 Candles

(G-12433)
WOOD-N-STUFF
8161 Lee Hwy (24368-2911)
PHONE...................................276 686-6557
EMP: 1
SALES (est): 40.9K Privately Held
SIC: 2499 Mfg Wood Products

Rustburg
Campbell County

(G-12434)
BC REPAIRS
261 Bunnyhop Ln (24588-3158)
PHONE...................................434 332-5304
Bryan W Carwile, *Owner*
EMP: 1
SALES (est): 99.8K Privately Held
SIC: 3542 Mechanical (pneumatic or hydraulic) metal forming machines

(G-12435)
BROWN MACHINE WORKS INC
8459 Wards Rd (24588-4259)
P.O. Box 600 (24588-0600)
PHONE...................................434 821-5008
Kenneth Ray Brown, *President*
Sharon Brown, *Vice Pres*
EMP: 22
SQ FT: 15,000
SALES (est): 2MM Privately Held
WEB: www.brownmachine.com
SIC: 3599 Machine shop, jobbing & repair

(G-12436)
CAROLYN WEST
Also Called: Cushion Department, The
628 Meeting House Rd (24588-2961)
PHONE...................................434 332-5007
Carolyn West, *Owner*
EMP: 4
SALES (est): 150K Privately Held
SIC: 2393 2392 Cushions, except spring & carpet: purchased materials; household furnishings

(G-12437)
CHALMERS & KUBECK INC
10613 Wards Rd (24588-4407)
PHONE...................................434 851-3613
Leo Neesley, *Manager*
EMP: 1
SALES (corp-wide): 50.7MM Privately Held
WEB: www.candk.com
SIC: 3625 Actuators, industrial
PA: Chalmers & Kubeck, Inc.
150 Commerce Dr
Aston PA 19014
610 494-4300

(G-12438)
CHARLES M FARISS
2599 Colonial Hwy (24588-4010)
PHONE...................................434 660-0606
Charles M Fariss, *Owner*
EMP: 12
SALES (est): 950K Privately Held
SIC: 3531 Construction machinery

(G-12439)
FIRST PAPER CO INC
Also Called: Concrete World
7320 Wards Rd (24588-2629)
P.O. Box 10456, Lynchburg (24506-0456)
PHONE...................................434 821-6884
Robert C Brown, *President*
Overbey W H, *Vice Pres*
William M Overby Jr, *Vice Pres*
Crystal Brown, *Admin Sec*
Crystal Farris, *Admin Sec*
EMP: 15 EST: 1967
SQ FT: 60,000
SALES (est): 990K Privately Held
SIC: 2262 3272 Screen printing: man-made fiber & silk broadwoven fabrics; concrete products, precast

(G-12440)
HUBERT MICHAEL GILLILAND
52 Buttercup Ln (24588-2948)
PHONE...................................434 332-2285
Hubert M Gilliland, *Principal*
EMP: 1
SALES (est): 97.4K Privately Held
SIC: 7692 Welding repair

(G-12441)
INSTANT GRATIFICATION
190 Campbell Hwy (24588-4134)
PHONE...................................434 332-3769
Ron Wilson, *Principal*
EMP: 2
SALES (est): 154.6K Privately Held
SIC: 2752 Commercial printing, lithographic

(G-12442)
MILL ROAD LOGGING LLC
1635 Bethany Rd (24588-3808)
PHONE...................................434 665-7467
EMP: 2
SALES (est): 81.7K Privately Held
SIC: 2411 Logging

(G-12443)
SCOTT TURF EQUIPMENT LLC
12304 Wards Rd (24588-3633)
PHONE...................................434 401-3031
Jeffrey F Scott, *Branch Mgr*
EMP: 2
SALES (corp-wide): 550K Privately Held
WEB: www.scottturfequipment.com
SIC: 3523 Turf equipment, commercial
PA: Scott Turf Equipment, Llc
12304 Wards Rd
Rustburg VA 24588
434 401-3031

(G-12444)
SCOTT TURF EQUIPMENT LLC (PA)
12304 Wards Rd (24588-3633)
P.O. Box 271, Goode (24556-0271)
PHONE...................................434 401-3031
Jeff Scott,
EMP: 3
SQ FT: 5,000
SALES (est): 550K Privately Held
WEB: www.scottturfequipment.com
SIC: 3523 Turf equipment, commercial

(G-12445)
SEMTEK
654 Acorn Dr (24588-4386)
P.O. Box 399 (24588-0399)
PHONE...................................434 942-4728
Dawn Martin, *Owner*
Eddie Martin, *Co-Owner*
EMP: 4
SALES (est): 135K Privately Held
WEB: www.semtekshop.com
SIC: 3599 Machine shop, jobbing & repair

(G-12446)
SHAWN GAINES
340 Watkins Farm Rd (24588-3796)
PHONE...................................434 332-4819
Shawn Gaines, *Owner*
EMP: 3
SALES (est): 305.5K Privately Held
SIC: 3484 5941 7389 Guns (firearms) or gun parts, 30 mm. & below; firearms; business services

(G-12447)
WISECARVER BROTHERS INC
57 Wisecarver Rd (24588-4230)
PHONE...................................434 332-4511
Gary Wisecarver, *President*
Joann Wisecarver, *Corp Secy*
EMP: 1
SQ FT: 2,000
SALES (est): 178.8K Privately Held
SIC: 3711 Automobile bodies, passenger car, not including engine, etc.

Ruther Glen
Caroline County

(G-12448)
ALPACAS OF LAKELAND WOODS
4305 Jericho Rd (22546-2140)
PHONE...................................804 448-8283
Robin Dhall, *Principal*
EMP: 2
SALES (est): 168.1K Privately Held
SIC: 2231 Alpacas, mohair: woven

(G-12449)
AMERICAN STONE INC
8179 Arba Ave (22546-2950)
P.O. Box 25, Ladysmith (22501-0025)
PHONE...................................804 448-9460
Dino Diana, *President*
Silvio Diana, *Chairman*
EMP: 9
SALES (est): 1.1MM Privately Held
WEB: www.asiprecast.com
SIC: 3272 Stone, cast concrete

(G-12450)
BACKWOODS FABRICATIONS LLC
3236 Oates Ln (22546-2134)
PHONE...................................804 448-2901
Anthony McCormick, *Principal*
EMP: 1
SALES (est): 43.6K Privately Held
SIC: 3999 Manufacturing industries

(G-12451)
BELLS CABINET SHOP
4790 Jericho Rd (22546-2143)
PHONE...................................804 448-3111
Charlie J Bell, *Owner*
EMP: 2 EST: 1954
SALES (est): 152.6K Privately Held
SIC: 2434 Vanities, bathroom: wood

(G-12452)
CITHINNING INC
26721 Ruther Glen Rd (22546-3632)
PHONE...................................804 370-4859
Cary Defenbaugh, *President*
EMP: 5
SALES (est): 426.5K Privately Held
SIC: 2411 Logging camps & contractors

(G-12453)
CR NEON
307 Powder Horn Dr (22546-5064)
PHONE...................................804 339-0497
Rob Picard, *Principal*
EMP: 3
SALES (est): 133.7K Privately Held
WEB: www.crneon.com
SIC: 2813 Neon

(G-12454)
DOMINION DOOR AND DRAWER
26768 Ruther Glen Rd (22546-3632)
PHONE...................................804 955-9302
Elyssa Ferguson, *Principal*
EMP: 2
SALES (est): 174.9K Privately Held
SIC: 2434 Wood kitchen cabinets

(G-12455)
EA DESIGN TECH SERVICES
366 Land Or Dr (22546-1238)
PHONE...................................540 220-7203
Kara Taylor, *Principal*
EMP: 1
SALES (est): 92.5K Privately Held
WEB: www.eadesigntech.com
SIC: 3829 7389 Plotting instruments, drafting & map reading;

(G-12456)
INTEGRITY NATIONAL CORP
17213 Doggetts Fork Rd (22546-4532)
P.O. Box 361, Chester MD (21619-0361)
PHONE...................................540 455-2340
Murphy Fountain, *Director*
EMP: 1
SALES (est): 37K Privately Held
SIC: 7694 Motor repair services

(G-12457)
J H KNIGHTON LUMBER CO INC
25227 Jefferson Davis Hwy (22546-2409)
P.O. Box 536 (22546-0536)
PHONE...................................804 448-4681
David Knighton, *President*
Sandra Hynson, *Vice Pres*
EMP: 40
SQ FT: 5,000
SALES (est): 698.2K Privately Held
WEB: www.knightonlumber.com
SIC: 2411 2421 2426 Logging camps & contractors; sawmills & planing mills, general; hardwood dimension & flooring mills

(G-12458)
MOORE AND SON INC LEWIS S
26406 Mt Vernon Church Rd (22546-4404)
PHONE...................................804 366-7170
Wallis S Moore, *Principal*
EMP: 1
SALES (est): 92K Privately Held
SIC: 2421 Sawmills & planing mills, general

(G-12459)
ORANGE SOCK PAY
17444 Center Dr Ste 5c (22546-2886)
PHONE...................................540 246-6368
EMP: 2
SALES (est): 73.4K Privately Held
WEB: www.orangesockpay.com
SIC: 2252 Socks

(G-12460)
PATRIOTIC PUBLICATIONS LLC
23316 Triple Crown Dr (22546-3487)
PHONE...................................804 814-3017
EMP: 2
SALES (est): 74.9K Privately Held
SIC: 2741 Miscellaneous publishing

(G-12461)
SASSAFRAS SHADE VINEYARD LLC
4492 Ladysmith Rd (22546-2714)
PHONE...................................804 337-9446
Dudley Ann Mueller, *Administration*
EMP: 2
SALES (est): 109.3K Privately Held
WEB: www.sassafrasshade.com
SIC: 2084 Wines

(G-12462)
SAWDUST AND SHAVINGS LLC
976 Swan Ln (22546-1211)
PHONE...................................804 205-8074
EMP: 2
SALES (est): 97.8K Privately Held
SIC: 2421 Sawdust & shavings

(G-12463)
W T JONES & SONS INC
17258 Doggetts Fork Rd (22546-4532)
P.O. Box 277, Ashland (23005-0277)
PHONE...................................804 633-9737
Donald Jones, *President*
Samuel Jones, *Vice Pres*
Garland Jones, *Treasurer*
Carolyn Jones, *Admin Sec*
EMP: 37

SQ FT: 17,000
SALES (est): 5.4MM **Privately Held**
SIC: 2411 2421 Logging; planing mills

(G-12464)
WILLIAMSBURG MILLWORK CORP
Also Called: Atlas Pallets
29155 Richmond Tpke (22546-4207)
P.O. Box 427, Bowling Green (22427-0427)
PHONE..................................804 994-2151
M Raymond Piland III, *President*
M Jordan Piland, *Vice Pres*
Patricia Piland, *Treasurer*
Tracy Lyons, *Admin Sec*
Lynn Piland, *Admin Sec*
EMP: 75
SQ FT: 50,000
SALES (est): 10.2MM **Privately Held**
WEB: www.atlaspallets.com
SIC: 2448 Pallets, wood

Saint Paul
Wise County

(G-12465)
CLINCH VALLEY PUBLISHING CO
Also Called: Clinch Valley Times
16541 Russell St (24283-3513)
P.O. Box 817 (24283-0817)
PHONE..................................276 762-7671
Allen Gregory, *President*
Anne Y Gregory, *President*
EMP: 3
SALES (est): 245.5K **Privately Held**
WEB: www.clinchvalleytimes.net
SIC: 2711 Job printing & newspaper publishing combined

(G-12466)
CROSSCUT INC
5821 Creek Hill Rd (24283-2535)
PHONE..................................276 395-5430
Ralph McCowan, *Principal*
Lowell Bailey, *Exec Dir*
EMP: 3 EST: 2012
SALES (est): 229.3K **Privately Held**
SIC: 2411 Logging

(G-12467)
EDWARDS INC
15606 Bill Dean Rd (24283-3302)
P.O. Box 671 (24283-0671)
PHONE..................................276 762-7746
Gerald Edwards, *President*
EMP: 5
SALES (est): 320.3K **Privately Held**
SIC: 2411 Logging camps & contractors

(G-12468)
LAWSON TIMBER COMPANY
5711 Walton Ln (24283)
PHONE..................................276 395-2069
Jeff Lawson, *Principal*
EMP: 3
SALES (est): 186.5K **Privately Held**
SIC: 2411 Logging

(G-12469)
LOU WALLACE
Also Called: Design Printers
16551 Russell St (24283-3513)
P.O. Box 1019 (24283-1019)
PHONE..................................276 762-2303
Lou Wallace, *Owner*
William Wallace, *Co-Owner*
EMP: 3
SQ FT: 1,500
SALES (est): 300K **Privately Held**
SIC: 2759 5199 2396 Screen printing; advertising specialties; automotive & apparel trimmings

(G-12470)
MCCLURE CONCRETE MATERIALS LLC
389 Frosty Rd (24283)
PHONE..................................276 964-9682
EMP: 3

SALES (corp-wide): 635.5K **Privately Held**
WEB: www.mcclureconcrete.com
SIC: 3273 Ready-mixed concrete
PA: Mcclure Concrete Materials Llc
1201 Iron St
Richlands VA 24641
276 964-9682

Salem
Salem City County

(G-12471)
ABECK INC
405 W 4th St (24153-3632)
PHONE..................................540 375-2841
John Wood, *Principal*
EMP: 4
SALES (est): 327.4K **Privately Held**
SIC: 3524 Grass catchers, lawn mower

(G-12472)
ALICE FARLING
Also Called: CT Machining By Cnc
18 Lake Ave (24153-3238)
PHONE..................................757 802-6936
Alice Farling, *Owner*
EMP: 2
SALES (est): 152K **Privately Held**
SIC: 3599 Machine shop, jobbing & repair

(G-12473)
ALIEN SILKSCREEN LLC
29 Hammit Ln (24153-3135)
PHONE..................................540 389-5699
Brooke Saul, *Mng Member*
EMP: 10
SALES (est): 590K **Privately Held**
WEB: www.aliensilkscreen.com
SIC: 2759 Screen printing

(G-12474)
AMWARE LOGISTICS SERVICES INC
Also Called: Amware Pallet Service
1300 Intervale Dr (24153-6446)
PHONE..................................540 389-9737
EMP: 18
SALES (corp-wide): 46.4MM **Privately Held**
SIC: 2448 Mfg Wood Pallets/Skids
PA: Amware Logistics Services, Inc.
4050 Newpoint Pl
Lawrenceville GA 30043
678 377-8585

(G-12475)
ARBON EQUIPMENT CORPORATION
602 Roanoke St (24153-3506)
PHONE..................................540 387-2113
Juan Gonzales, *Sales Staff*
Tom Burrill, *Manager*
EMP: 5
SALES (corp-wide): 767.8MM **Privately Held**
WEB: www.ritehite.com
SIC: 3537 3449 Loading docks: portable, adjustable & hydraulic; miscellaneous metalwork
HQ: Arbon Equipment Corporation
8900 N Arbon Dr
Milwaukee WI 53223
414 355-2600

(G-12476)
ASSA ABLOY HIGH SEC GROUP INC (DH)
Also Called: Medeco
3625 Alleghany Dr (24153-1977)
P.O. Box 3075 (24153-0330)
PHONE..................................540 380-5000
Thomas Kaika, *President*
Bobby Woolwine, *Vice Pres*
Todd King, *Facilities Mgr*
Paul Taylor, *Opers Staff*
Brett Toney, *Opers Staff*
◆ EMP: 250
SQ FT: 130,000
SALES (est): 28.5MM
SALES (corp-wide): 9.7B **Privately Held**
WEB: www.medeco.com
SIC: 3499 Locks, safe & vault: metal

(G-12477)
AUTOMATION CONTROL DIST CO LLC
1329 W Main St Ste 212 (24153-4707)
PHONE..................................540 797-9892
Matthew McBane,
EMP: 2 **Privately Held**
SIC: 3613 Control panels, electric

(G-12478)
AUTONOMOUS FLIGHT TECH INC
345 Hawthorn Rd (24153-2747)
PHONE..................................540 314-8866
Joshua Lowell May, *Administration*
EMP: 2
SALES (est): 129.4K **Privately Held**
WEB: www.autonomousflight.us
SIC: 3721 Aircraft

(G-12479)
B & S LIQUIDATING CORP
Also Called: Oak Hall Industries
840 Union St (24153-5121)
P.O. Box 1078 (24153-1078)
PHONE..................................540 387-0000
Peter Morrison, *President*
▼ EMP: 150 EST: 1975
SALES (est): 5.7MM **Privately Held**
WEB: www.oakhalli.com
SIC: 2389 Academic vestments (caps & gowns)

(G-12480)
BAKER HUGHES A GE COMPANY LLC
1501 Roanoke Blvd (24153-6422)
PHONE..................................540 387-8847
EMP: 2
SALES (est): 73.6K **Privately Held**
SIC: 1389 Oil & gas field services

(G-12481)
BARRY WAYNE GLADDEN
1344 Roanoke Blvd (24153-5202)
PHONE..................................540 389-6645
Barry Gladden, *President*
EMP: 1 EST: 2016
SALES (est): 36.6K **Privately Held**
SIC: 7692 Welding repair

(G-12482)
BLUE RIBBON COAL SALES LTD
1125 Intervale Dr (24153-6417)
P.O. Box 8414, Roanoke (24014-0414)
PHONE..................................540 387-2077
Dale L Rucker, *Principal*
EMP: 2
SALES (est): 193.7K **Privately Held**
SIC: 1221 Bituminous coal & lignite-surface mining

(G-12483)
BLUE RIDGE SERVO MTR REPR LLC
1017 Tennessee St (24153-6301)
PHONE..................................540 375-2990
Michael Loving, *Owner*
EMP: 1
SALES (est): 40K **Privately Held**
WEB: www.blueridgeservomotorrepair.com
SIC: 3549 Assembly machines, including robotic

(G-12484)
BOLLING STEEL CO INC
5933 Garman Rd (24153-8824)
P.O. Box 1082 (24153-1082)
PHONE..................................540 380-4402
James C Bolling, *President*
Maude P Bolling, *Corp Secy*
Reid W Bolling, *Vice Pres*
EMP: 25 EST: 1979
SQ FT: 20,000
SALES (est): 7.6MM **Privately Held**
SIC: 3441 3443 Fabricated structural metal; fabricated plate work (boiler shop)

(G-12485)
BOWERS MACHINE & TOOL INC
4658 Roger Rd (24153-8456)
PHONE..................................540 380-2040
William Bowers, *President*
EMP: 5

SALES (est): 800K **Privately Held**
SIC: 3599 Machine shop, jobbing & repair

(G-12486)
BREWCO CORP (PA)
Also Called: Brewco Sign
335 Roanoke Blvd (24153-5009)
P.O. Box 699 (24153-0699)
PHONE..................................540 389-2554
Beatrice J Brewer, *Ch of Bd*
Jack Brewer, *President*
John Davis, *Vice Pres*
Barry Brewer, *Treasurer*
EMP: 2
SQ FT: 4,400
SALES (est): 1MM **Privately Held**
SIC: 3081 2759 Vinyl film & sheet; letterpress & screen printing

(G-12487)
C&C ASSEMBLY INC
3410 W Main St (24153-2054)
PHONE..................................540 904-6416
Ryan McClusky, *Sales Staff*
Rick Wilson, *Sales Staff*
Michelle Harden, *Office Mgr*
William Martin, *Manager*
EMP: 4
SALES (est): 951.8K **Privately Held**
WEB: www.candcassembly.com
SIC: 3569 General industrial machinery

(G-12488)
CARBONE AMERICA
540 Branch Dr (24153-4119)
PHONE..................................540 389-7535
Chad Huston, *CPA*
EMP: 5
SALES (est): 118.4K **Privately Held**
WEB: www.mersen.us
SIC: 3624 Carbon & graphite products

(G-12489)
CARTER TOOL & MFG CO INC
1400 Southside Dr (24153-4602)
PHONE..................................540 387-1778
Stover Carter, *President*
EMP: 9
SALES (est): 1.1MM **Privately Held**
WEB: www.cartermachinery.com
SIC: 3544 Special dies & tools

(G-12490)
CONCRETE READY MIXED CORP
22 7th St (24153)
PHONE..................................540 345-3846
Alvin Gillespie, *Manager*
EMP: 7
SALES (corp-wide): 744.8K **Privately Held**
SIC: 3273 Ready-mixed concrete
PA: Concrete Ready Mixed Corporation
614 Norfolk Ave Sw
Roanoke VA
540 345-3846

(G-12491)
CREWS OUTDOORS LLC JOHN
2236 River Oaks Dr (24153-7367)
PHONE..................................540 808-2204
John Crews, *Principal*
EMP: 2
SALES (est): 115.3K **Privately Held**
WEB: www.missilebaits.store
SIC: 3949 Sporting & athletic goods

(G-12492)
CUSTOM MACHINING AND TOOL INC
1281 Southside Dr (24153-4605)
PHONE..................................540 389-9102
Mark Carter, *President*
EMP: 4
SQ FT: 5,000
SALES (est): 318.8K **Privately Held**
WEB: www.custommachiningandtool.com
SIC: 3599 Machine shop, jobbing & repair

(G-12493)
DAILY GRIND
640 Joan Cir (24153-6657)
PHONE..................................540 387-2669
David Thompson, *Principal*
EMP: 2

▲ = Import ▼ =Export
◆ =Import/Export

SALES (est): 115.2K Privately Held
SIC: 3599 Grinding castings for the trade

(G-12494)
DAMON COMPANY OF SALEM INC
2117 Salem Industrial Dr (24153-3145)
P.O. Box 995 (24153-0995)
PHONE..................................540 389-8609
Samuel B Newsom, *President*
Wayne Herkness II, *Chairman*
Steve Fejes, *Sales Staff*
Margaret Harris, *Sales Associate*
Randall Houston, *Branch Mgr*
▲ EMP: 33 EST: 1964
SQ FT: 33,000
SALES: 4.3MM Privately Held
WEB: www.damonco.com
SIC: 3469 3544 Metal stampings; industrial molds

(G-12495)
DANDY PRINTING
213 W 4th St (24153-3636)
PHONE..................................540 986-1100
EMP: 2 EST: 2016
SALES (est): 83.9K Privately Held
SIC: 2752 Lithographic Commercial Printing

(G-12496)
DIGITAL PRINTING SOLUTIONS INC
119 E Burwell St (24153-3824)
PHONE..................................540 389-2066
Allen Walker, *President*
EMP: 3
SQ FT: 5,000
SALES (est): 435.9K Privately Held
SIC: 2752 Promotional printing, lithographic

(G-12497)
DRESSER-RAND COMPANY
4655 Technology Dr (24153-8532)
PHONE..................................540 444-4200
EMP: 33
SALES (corp-wide): 67.4B Privately Held
WEB: www.new.siemens.com
SIC: 3563 Air & gas compressors
HQ: Dresser-Rand Company
    500 Paul Clark Dr
    Olean NY 14760
    716 375-3000

(G-12498)
E S I
1221 Southside Dr (24153-4605)
PHONE..................................540 389-5070
Richard Goodwin, *Mng Member*
EMP: 2
SALES (est): 124.2K Privately Held
SIC: 3993 Signs & advertising specialties

(G-12499)
EARMOLD COMPANY LTD
814 E 8th St (24153-5234)
P.O. Box 3320 (24153-0620)
PHONE..................................540 389-1642
H James Gear, *President*
Alton R Coffey, *Vice Pres*
EMP: 10
SQ FT: 2,000
SALES (est): 1.2MM Privately Held
WEB: www.earmoldltd.com
SIC: 3842 Hearing aids

(G-12500)
ECONO SIGNS
1221 Southside Dr (24153-4605)
PHONE..................................540 389-5070
Richard Goodwin, *Principal*
EMP: 1
SALES (est): 71.4K Privately Held
WEB: www.econosignsllc.com
SIC: 3993 Signs & advertising specialties

(G-12501)
EFI LIGHTING INC
421 Hawley Dr (24153-1957)
PHONE..................................540 353-2880
Michael James Boynton, *Principal*
EMP: 7
SALES (est): 1.1MM Privately Held
SIC: 3648 Lighting equipment

(G-12502)
ELIZABETH ARDEN INC
131 Brand Ave (24153-3907)
PHONE..................................540 444-2408
Ava Greenberg, *Surgery Dir*
EMP: 100 Publicly Held
WEB: www.elizabetharden.com
SIC: 2844 Toilet preparations
HQ: Elizabeth Arden, Inc.
    880 Sw 145th Ave Ste 200
    Pembroke Pines FL 33027

(G-12503)
ELIZABETH ARDEN INC
Also Called: Elizabeth Arden Returns
141 Brand Ave (24153-3907)
PHONE..................................540 444-2406
AVI Greenberg, *Director*
EMP: 7 Publicly Held
WEB: www.elizabetharden.com
SIC: 2844 Perfumes, natural or synthetic
HQ: Elizabeth Arden, Inc.
    880 Sw 145th Ave Ste 200
    Pembroke Pines FL 33027

(G-12504)
EMBROIDERY CONCEPTS
146 W 4th St Ste 2 (24153-3620)
PHONE..................................540 387-0517
Michael Merriell, *Principal*
EMP: 2
SALES (est): 161.6K Privately Held
WEB: www.embroideryconceptsva.com
SIC: 2395 Embroidery products, except schiffli machine

(G-12505)
ERGOJECT LLC
1640 Roanoke Blvd (24153-6420)
PHONE..................................540 375-6415
Bob Patane,
EMP: 1
SQ FT: 5,000
SALES (est): 81K Privately Held
WEB: www.hpsrx.com
SIC: 2834 Pharmaceutical preparations

(G-12506)
FAST SIGNS INC
Also Called: Fastsigns
146 W 4th St Ste 3 (24153-3620)
PHONE..................................540 389-6691
William Jones, *Owner*
Ricky Newman, *Manager*
EMP: 16
SQ FT: 3,200
SALES (est): 1.3MM Privately Held
WEB: www.fastsigns.com
SIC: 3993 2542 Signs & advertising specialties; partitions & fixtures, except wood

(G-12507)
FRAMECO INC
305 Apperson Dr (24153-6914)
PHONE..................................540 375-3683
Don Powell, *Vice Pres*
John D Powell, *Administration*
EMP: 6
SALES (est): 990.6K Privately Held
WEB: www.forseyportlandhomes.com
SIC: 3499 Picture frames, metal

(G-12508)
FRITO-LAY NORTH AMERICA INC
3941 W Main St (24153-8503)
PHONE..................................540 380-3020
Bill Blankenship, *Manager*
EMP: 40
SALES (corp-wide): 67.1B Publicly Held
WEB: www.fritolay.com
SIC: 2052 2013 5812 6794 Cookies; snack sticks, including jerky: from purchased meat; fast-food restaurant, chain; chicken restaurant; franchises, selling or licensing; soft drinks: packaged in cans, bottles, etc.; potato chips & other potato-based snacks
HQ: Frito-Lay North America, Inc.
    7701 Legacy Dr
    Plano TX 75024

(G-12509)
G E FUJI DRIVES USA INC
1501 Roanoke Blvd Rm 212 (24153-6422)
PHONE..................................540 387-7000
Daniel Nakano, *President*
EMP: 16
SALES (est): 1.9MM Privately Held
SIC: 3566 Drives, high speed industrial, except hydrostatic

(G-12510)
GE DRIVES & CONTROLS INC
1501 Roanoke Blvd (24153-6422)
PHONE..................................540 387-7000
Steven S Roy, *President*
◆ EMP: 900
SALES (est): 129MM
SALES (corp-wide): 95.2B Publicly Held
SIC: 3612 Power transformers, electric
PA: General Electric Company
    5 Necco St
    Boston MA 02210
    617 443-3000

(G-12511)
GENERAL ELECTRIC COMPANY
1501 Roanoke Blvd (24153-6492)
PHONE..................................540 387-7000
Stephen Spicer, *Mfg Staff*
Bob Oelschlager, *Branch Mgr*
George Matzko, *Manager*
EMP: 10
SALES (corp-wide): 95.2B Publicly Held
WEB: www.ge.com
SIC: 3625 3823 3545 Electric controls & control accessories, industrial; industrial instrmnts msrmnt display/control process variable; machine tool accessories
PA: General Electric Company
    5 Necco St
    Boston MA 02210
    617 443-3000

(G-12512)
GLADDEN WELDING
4444 Harborwood Rd (24153-8582)
PHONE..................................540 387-1489
Ervin Gladden, *Owner*
EMP: 1
SALES (est): 119.4K Privately Held
WEB: www.gladdeninc.org
SIC: 7692 Welding repair

(G-12513)
GRAHAM-WHITE MANUFACTURING CO (HQ)
1242 S Colorado St (24153-6993)
P.O. Box 1099 (24153-1099)
PHONE..................................540 387-5600
Jim Frantz, *President*
Robert G Cassell Jr, *Vice Pres*
Bruce W Stewart, *Vice Pres*
Ronnie Wright, *Inv Control Mgr*
Edna Lutz, *Buyer*
▲ EMP: 255
SQ FT: 300,000
SALES (est): 45.7MM Publicly Held
WEB: www.grahamwhite.com
SIC: 3743 3321 Railroad equipment, except locomotives; gray iron castings

(G-12514)
HANSON AGGREGATES EAST LLC
2000 Salem Industrial Dr (24153-3142)
PHONE..................................540 387-0271
Bobbie Law, *Manager*
EMP: 75
SALES (corp-wide): 20.8B Privately Held
WEB: www.heidelbergcement.com
SIC: 3272 Concrete products
HQ: Hanson Aggregates East Llc
    3131 Rdu Center Dr
    Morrisville NC 27560
    919 380-2500

(G-12515)
HARRELL PRECISION
Also Called: Harrell Marvin L & Carol L
5756 Hickory Dr (24153-8476)
PHONE..................................540 380-2683
Marvin L Harrell, *President*
Carol Harrel, *Vice Pres*
EMP: 1

SALES (est): 155.8K Privately Held
WEB: www.harrellsprec.com
SIC: 3599 Machine shop, jobbing & repair

(G-12516)
HARRELL TOOL CO
5683 Hickory Dr (24153-8475)
PHONE..................................540 380-2666
Henry Harrell, *Owner*
EMP: 1
SALES (est): 62K Privately Held
SIC: 3599 Machine shop, jobbing & repair

(G-12517)
HAWES JOINERY INC
3503 Jensen Pl (24153-9021)
PHONE..................................540 384-6733
EMP: 1
SALES: 50K Privately Held
SIC: 2434 Mfg Wood Kitchen Cabinets

(G-12518)
HUB PATTERN CORPORATION
Also Called: Hub Corporation
1129 Florida St (24153-6333)
PHONE..................................540 342-3505
Hubert Humphrey, *CEO*
Lane Witte, *COO*
John Cloeter, *Opers Staff*
EMP: 24
SALES (corp-wide): 234.9K Privately Held
WEB: www.hubcorp.net
SIC: 3543 Industrial patterns
HQ: Hub Pattern Corporation
    2113 Salem Ave Sw
    Roanoke VA 24016
    540 342-3505

(G-12519)
IDEAL CABINETS INC
2158 Salem Industrial Dr (24153-3144)
PHONE..................................540 366-1748
EMP: 2
SALES (corp-wide): 1.4MM Privately Held
WEB: www.idealcabinets.com
SIC: 2434 Wood kitchen cabinets
PA: Ideal Cabinets Inc
    103 N Franklin St
    Christiansburg VA 24073
    540 382-7088

(G-12520)
INDUSTRIAL BIODYNAMICS LLC
1537 Mill Race Dr (24153-3137)
PHONE..................................540 357-0033
Jon Hager, *President*
James Christian, *Vice Pres*
Christian James,
Michael Abbott,
Jonathan Hager,
EMP: 4
SALES (est): 474K Privately Held
WEB: www.inbiodyn.com
SIC: 3999 8748 3799 5084 Education aids, devices & supplies; safety training service; trailers & trailer equipment; safety equipment

(G-12521)
INTEGER HOLDINGS CORPORATION
200 S Yorkshire St (24153-6902)
PHONE..................................540 389-7860
Eric Dogan, *Program Mgr*
Peter Hall, *Director*
EMP: 450
SALES (corp-wide): 1.2B Publicly Held
WEB: www.integer.net
SIC: 3675 3692 3691 Electronic capacitors; primary batteries, dry & wet; storage batteries
PA: Integer Holdings Corporation
    5830 Gran Pkwy Ste 1150
    Plano TX 75024
    214 618-5243

(G-12522)
INTEGRATED TEX SOLUTIONS INC
865 Cleveland Ave (24153-2920)
PHONE..................................540 389-8113
Joanne B Thornehill, *CEO*
David Thornhill, *President*
Gregg Lisicki, *Business Mgr*

Debby Gibson, *COO*
Lori Huffman, *Controller*
▲ **EMP:** 100 **EST:** 1936
SQ FT: 90,000
SALES (est): 13.3MM **Privately Held**
WEB: www.intextile.com
SIC: 2394 2339 3543 Tents: made from purchased materials; uniforms, athletic: women's, misses' & juniors'; industrial patterns

(G-12523)
INTRICATE METAL FORMING CO
1701 Midland Rd (24153-6424)
PHONE.................................540 345-9233
Scot Maccormack, *President*
Robert Malouf, *Principal*
Robbie Wright, *Production*
Bobby Malouf, *Purch Mgr*
John Rehak, *Engineer*
▲ **EMP:** 37
SALES (est): 7.5MM **Privately Held**
WEB: www.intricate.com
SIC: 3469 5084 Stamping metal for the trade; tool & die makers' equipment

(G-12524)
JETNEY DEVELOPMENT
1516 High St (24153-7728)
PHONE.................................714 262-0759
EMP: 2
SALES (est): 129.8K **Privately Held**
WEB: www.jetney.com
SIC: 7372 Prepackaged software

(G-12525)
JT TOBACCO
910 E Main St (24153-4422)
PHONE.................................540 387-0383
EMP: 2
SALES (est): 100.8K **Privately Held**
SIC: 3911 Mfg Precious Metal Jewelry

(G-12526)
KEY RECOVERY CORPORATION
Also Called: Dominion Controls
1390 Southside Dr (24153-4748)
PHONE.................................540 444-2628
John D Mayhew, *President*
John Mayhew, *Sales Associate*
EMP: 7 **EST:** 2009
SALES (est): 700K **Privately Held**
WEB: www.dominioncontrols.net
SIC: 3491 Water works valves

(G-12527)
KOPPERS INC
Koppers RR & Utility Pdts Div
4020 Koppers Rd (24153-8530)
PHONE.................................540 380-2061
Robert Wombles, *Vice Pres*
Tim Ries, *Branch Mgr*
Rebecca Hartless, *Manager*
Steven Willis, *Manager*
Mark Franck, *Director*
EMP: 30 **Publicly Held**
WEB: www.koppers.com
SIC: 2491 2421 Poles, posts & pilings: treated wood; railroad cross bridges & switch ties, treated wood; railroad cross-ties, treated wood; sawmills & planing mills, general
HQ: Koppers Inc.
    436 7th Ave
    Pittsburgh PA 15219
    412 227-2001

(G-12528)
LAKE REGION MEDICAL INC
200 S Yorkshire St (24153-6902)
PHONE.................................540 389-7860
Pete Hall, *Opers Mgr*
Jerry Kalafut, *Senior Buyer*
Gary Marceau, *Engineer*
Ron Sink, *Engineer*
Kelli Daniels, *Human Res Mgr*
EMP: 174
SALES (corp-wide): 1.2B **Publicly Held**
SIC: 3841 Surgical & medical instruments
HQ: Lake Region Medical, Inc.
    100 Fordham Rd Ste 3
    Wilmington MA 01887

(G-12529)
LAX LOFT LLC
14 S College Ave (24153-3834)
PHONE.................................540 389-4529
EMP: 1
SALES (est): 80K **Privately Held**
SIC: 3949 Mfg Sporting/Athletic Goods

(G-12530)
LEBANON SEABOARD CORPORATION
525 Branch Dr (24153-4118)
PHONE.................................540 375-0300
EMP: 7
SALES (corp-wide): 147.6MM **Privately Held**
WEB: www.lebsea.com
SIC: 3523 Turf equipment, commercial
PA: Lebanon Seaboard Corporation
    1600 E Cumberland St
    Lebanon PA 17042
    717 273-1685

(G-12531)
LIFE SAFER
162 Saint Johns Place Rd (24153-5565)
PHONE.................................540 375-4145
EMP: 1
SALES (est): 145K **Privately Held**
SIC: 3694 Alternators, automotive

(G-12532)
LINE-X OF BLUE RIDGE
504 Roanoke St (24153-3552)
PHONE.................................540 389-8595
Scott Bowles, *President*
EMP: 3 **EST:** 2009
SALES (est): 362.5K **Privately Held**
WEB: www.linexofsalemva.com
SIC: 2821 Plastics materials & resins

(G-12533)
LIZZIE CANDLES & SOAP INC
4144 Catawba Valley Dr (24153-3340)
PHONE.................................540 384-6151
EMP: 2
SALES (est): 120K **Privately Held**
SIC: 3999 Mfg Candles & Soap

(G-12534)
MAT ENTERPRISES INC
707 Red Ln (24153-2711)
PHONE.................................540 389-2528
Mary Ann Taylor, *President*
EMP: 1 **EST:** 1985
SALES (est): 100.4K **Privately Held**
WEB: www.matpuppets.com
SIC: 3999 Puppets & marionettes

(G-12535)
MECHANICAL DEVELOPMENT CO INC
303 Apperson Dr (24153-6914)
P.O. Box 190 (24153-0190)
PHONE.................................540 389-9395
John D Powell, *President*
Margie H Bowles, *Corp Secy*
EMP: 100
SQ FT: 45,000
SALES (est): 16.4MM **Privately Held**
WEB: www.mechanicaldevelopment.com
SIC: 3545 7692 Precision measuring tools; welding repair

(G-12536)
MERSEN USA PTT CORP
540 Branch Dr (24153-4119)
PHONE.................................540 389-7535
Larry Burichin, *Vice Pres*
Wayne Besecker, *Sales Staff*
Gerhard Doerr, *Marketing Staff*
Wally Paige, *Info Tech Mgr*
Lois Moseley,
EMP: 75
SALES (corp-wide): 1.5MM **Privately Held**
WEB: www.mersen.us
SIC: 3443 Heat exchangers, condensers & components
HQ: Mersen Usa Ptt Corp.
    400 Myrtle Ave
    Boonton NJ 07005
    973 334-0700

(G-12537)
MINUTEMAN PRESS
625 Florida St (24153-5042)
PHONE.................................540 774-1820
Bill Kyle, *Owner*
EMP: 3
SALES (est): 202.2K **Privately Held**
WEB: www.minutemanpress.com
SIC: 2752 Commercial printing, lithographic

(G-12538)
MISSILE BAITS LLC
170 Turner Rd (24153-2312)
P.O. Box 1045 (24153-1045)
PHONE.................................855 466-5738
John Crews Jr, *Owner*
EMP: 9
SALES (est): 771.4K **Privately Held**
WEB: www.missilebaits.store
SIC: 3949 Sporting & athletic goods

(G-12539)
MONOGRAM MAJIK
1714 Starview Dr (24153-2402)
PHONE.................................540 389-2269
Charlyn Perfater, *Owner*
EMP: 2 **EST:** 1997
SALES (est): 77.6K **Privately Held**
SIC: 2395 Embroidery products, except schiffli machine

(G-12540)
MONTGOMERY CNTY NEWSPAPERS INC
Also Called: Blue Ridge
1633 W Main St (24153-3115)
P.O. Box 1125 (24153-1125)
PHONE.................................540 389-9355
Connie Vaughn, *Executive*
EMP: 40 **EST:** 2008
SALES (est): 1.9MM **Privately Held**
WEB: www.ourvalley.org
SIC: 2711 Newspapers: publishing only, not printed on site

(G-12541)
MOUNTAIN SKY LLC
Also Called: E & W Machine Salem Ci
1129 Florida St (24153-6333)
PHONE.................................540 389-1197
Alton B Prillaman, *Administration*
EMP: 3 **EST:** 2013
SALES (est): 251.6K **Privately Held**
WEB: www.eandwmachine.com
SIC: 3444 Forming machine work, sheet metal

(G-12542)
MYSTERY WHL & SCREEN PRTG LLC
1908 Kiska Rd (24153-2343)
PHONE.................................540 514-7349
EMP: 2
SALES (est): 83.9K **Privately Held**
SIC: 2752 Commercial printing, lithographic

(G-12543)
NATIONAL PEENING INC
Also Called: National Peening, Roanoke
2167 Salem Industrial Dr (24153-3145)
PHONE.................................540 387-3522
Mike Price, *Branch Mgr*
EMP: 6 **Privately Held**
WEB: www.sintoamerica.com
SIC: 3398 Metal heat treating
HQ: National Peening, Inc.
    1902 Weinig St
    Statesville NC 28677
    704 872-0113

(G-12544)
NEW MLLENNIUM BLDG SYSTEMS LLC
100 Diugids Ln (24153)
P.O. Box 809 (24153-0809)
PHONE.................................540 389-0211
Ricky Fralin, *Engineer*
Chad Bickford, *Branch Mgr*
Jason Cornett, *Supervisor*
EMP: 87 **Publicly Held**
WEB: www.newmill.com
SIC: 3441 Joists, open web steel: long-span series

HQ: New Millennium Building Systems Llc
    7575 W Jefferson Blvd
    Fort Wayne IN 46804
    260 969-3500

(G-12545)
NOBLE-MET LLC
200 S Yorkshire St (24153-6902)
PHONE.................................540 389-7860
John Trinchere, *Director*
EMP: 185
SQ FT: 50,000
SALES (est): 22.3MM
SALES (corp-wide): 1.2B **Publicly Held**
SIC: 3317 3671 Steel pipe & tubes; electron tubes
HQ: Accellent Llc
    100 Fordham Rd Bldg C
    Wilmington MA 01887
    978 570-6900

(G-12546)
NOVA ROAST
7695 Bradshaw Rd (24153-2206)
PHONE.................................540 239-2459
EMP: 1
SALES (est): 47.3K **Privately Held**
SIC: 2095 Roasted Coffee, Nsk

(G-12547)
NOVOZYMES BIOLOGICALS INC (DH)
5400 Corporate Cir (24153-8300)
PHONE.................................540 389-9361
Shawn Semones, *President*
Jonathan Leder, *Vice Pres*
Richard Olofson, *Treasurer*
Paige Donnelly, *Comms Mgr*
Nickie Matthews, *Manager*
▲ **EMP:** 60
SQ FT: 60,000
SALES (est): 24.4MM
SALES (corp-wide): 21B **Privately Held**
WEB: www.bayer.com
SIC: 2834 Pharmaceutical preparations
HQ: Novozymes A/S
    Krogshojvej 36
    BagsvArd 2880
    444 600-00

(G-12548)
NOVOZYMES BIOLOGICALS INC
145 Brand Ave (24153-3907)
PHONE.................................540 389-9361
EMP: 3
SALES (corp-wide): 21B **Privately Held**
WEB: www.bayer.com
SIC: 2834 Pharmaceutical preparations
HQ: Novozymes Biologicals, Inc.
    5400 Corporate Cir
    Salem VA 24153
    540 389-9361

(G-12549)
OAK HALL INDUSTRIES LP (PA)
Also Called: Oak Hall Cap & Gown
840 Union St (24153-5121)
P.O. Box 1078 (24153-1078)
PHONE.................................540 387-0000
Joseph D Angelo, *Partner*
Jennifer Meador, *General Mgr*
Scott Lively, *Vice Pres*
Brian Weese, *Vice Pres*
Julie Griffith, *Purch Mgr*
▲ **EMP:** 140 **EST:** 1888
SQ FT: 120,000
SALES (est): 33MM **Privately Held**
WEB: www.oakhalli.com
SIC: 2389 Men's miscellaneous accessories

(G-12550)
OC PHARMA LLC
1640 Roanoke Blvd (24153-6420)
PHONE.................................540 375-6415
Robert Patane,
Kathi Rinesmith,
▲ **EMP:** 2
SQ FT: 5,000
SALES (est): 121.5K **Privately Held**
SIC: 2834 Druggists' preparations (pharmaceuticals)

▲ = Import ▼=Export
◆ =Import/Export

(G-12551)
ORICA USA INC
Also Called: E.S. Quarry & Construction Svc
6324 Twine Hollow Rd (24153-8278)
PHONE..............................540 380-3146
William Cole, *Manager*
EMP: 7 **Privately Held**
WEB: www.orica.com
SIC: 2892 Explosives
HQ: Orica Usa Inc.
33101 E Quincy Ave
Watkins CO 80137

(G-12552)
OUR HEALTH MAGAZINE INC
305 S Colorado St (24153-4948)
PHONE..............................540 387-6482
Kim Wood, *President*
Stephen McClintic, *Principal*
Laura Bower, *Manager*
Cindy Trujillo, *Consultant*
EMP: 5
SALES (est): 420.2K **Privately Held**
WEB: www.ourhealthvirginia.com
SIC: 2721 Magazines: publishing only, not
printed on site

(G-12553)
PARKS ELECTRIC MOTOR REPAIR
1490 Southside Dr (24153-4602)
PHONE..............................540 389-6911
Calvin C Parks, *President*
EMP: 4 EST: 1975
SQ FT: 1,800
SALES (est): 275K **Privately Held**
SIC: 7694 Electric motor repair

(G-12554)
PATTERN SHOP INC
27 Wells St (24153-4719)
PHONE..............................540 389-5110
Mark Thomas, *President*
Dave Thomas, *Vice Pres*
EMP: 2
SQ FT: 6,400
SALES (est): 225K **Privately Held**
SIC: 3543 Foundry patternmaking

(G-12555)
PATTERSON BUSINESS SYSTEMS
227 Electric Rd (24153-4431)
PHONE..............................540 389-7726
Denny Himmack, *President*
Will Patterson, *CFO*
Kirk Martin, *Manager*
EMP: 15
SALES (est): 750K **Privately Held**
SIC: 3545 3999 Files, machine tool; bar-
ber & beauty shop equipment

(G-12556)
PHARMACIST PHARMACEUTICAL LLC
1640 Roanoke Blvd (24153-6420)
PHONE..............................540 375-6415
Robert Patane,
EMP: 2
SQ FT: 5,000
SALES (est): 90.3K **Privately Held**
WEB: www.hpsrx.com
SIC: 2834 Pharmaceutical preparations

(G-12557)
PM PUMP COMPANY
5032 Stanley Farm Rd (24153-7948)
PHONE..............................540 380-2012
Phillip Argabright, *Owner*
EMP: 1
SALES (est): 88.4K **Privately Held**
SIC: 3463 Pump, compressor, turbine &
engine forgings, except auto

(G-12558)
PRECISION NUCLEAR VIRGINIA LLC
1634 Midland Rd (24153-6427)
PHONE..............................540 389-1346
Allan Arp, *Mng Member*
David Arnold,
EMP: 7
SQ FT: 3,000

SALES (est): 828.9K **Privately Held**
WEB: www.blueridgeisotopes.com
SIC: 2833 Medicinal chemicals

(G-12559)
QUAKER CHEMICAL CORPORATION
Also Called: Isley, Boyd A Jr
18 Niblick Dr (24153-6815)
PHONE..............................540 389-2038
Boyd A Isley Jr, *Branch Mgr*
EMP: 1
SALES (corp-wide): 1.1B **Publicly Held**
WEB: www.quakerchem.com
SIC: 2899 Chemical preparations
PA: Quaker Chemical Corporation
901 E Hector St
Conshohocken PA 19428
610 832-4000

(G-12560)
R R DONNELLEY & SONS COMPANY
Also Called: Roanoke Division
6450 Technology Dr (24153-8644)
PHONE..............................434 846-7371
Philip Archer, *Director*
EMP: 150
SALES (corp-wide): 6.2B **Publicly Held**
WEB: www.rrd.com
SIC: 2759 2752 2732 7331 Letterpress
printing; commercial printing, offset;
books: printing & binding; direct mail ad-
vertising services; graphic arts & related
design; catalogs: gravure printing, not
published on site
PA: R. R. Donnelley & Sons Company
35 W Wacker Dr
Chicago IL 60601
312 326-8000

(G-12561)
RHENUS AUTOMOTIVE SALEM LLC
6450 Technology Dr (24153-8644)
PHONE..............................270 282-2100
Ulrich Schorb,
EMP: 3
SALES (est): 95.9K
SALES (corp-wide): 17.5B **Privately Held**
SIC: 3714 Motor vehicle brake systems &
parts
HQ: Rhenus Automotive Logistics
Swinnenwijerweg 16
Genk 3600
895 187-00

(G-12562)
RICHARDS-WILBERT INC
165 Simms Dr (24153-4408)
PHONE..............................540 389-5240
Richard Ward, *Sales Staff*
Wilbert Richards, *Branch Mgr*
Dave Sprankle, *Manager*
EMP: 2
SALES (corp-wide): 39.9K **Privately Held**
WEB: www.richardswilbert.com
SIC: 3272 Burial vaults, concrete or pre-
cast terrazzo
PA: Richards-Wilbert, Inc.
1481 Salem Ave
Hagerstown MD 21740
301 790-0124

(G-12563)
ROWE FINE FURNITURE INC
1972 Salem Industrial Dr (24153-3148)
PHONE..............................540 389-8661
Robert Holden, *Branch Mgr*
EMP: 118 **Privately Held**
WEB: www.rowefurniture.com
SIC: 2512 2426 Upholstered household
furniture; frames for upholstered furniture,
wood
PA: Rowe Fine Furniture, Inc.
2121 Gardner St
Elliston VA 24087

(G-12564)
SALEM CUSTOM CABINETS INC
2865 Silver Leaf Dr (24153-8105)
PHONE..............................540 380-4441
Greg Puckett, *Principal*
EMP: 4

SALES (est): 386.9K **Privately Held**
WEB: www.salemcustomcabinets.com
SIC: 2434 Wood kitchen cabinets

(G-12565)
SALEM PRCISION MCH FABRICATION
1291 Southside Dr (24153-4605)
P.O. Box 539 (24153-0539)
PHONE..............................434 793-0677
William Gentry Jr, *President*
Watson Walter Steven, *Vice Pres*
EMP: 12
SALES (est): 1MM **Privately Held**
WEB: www.ppmmach.com
SIC: 3599 Machine shop, jobbing & repair

(G-12566)
SALEM PRINTING CO
900 Iowa St (24153-5294)
PHONE..............................540 387-1106
Joseph H Arrington, *President*
Emily Arrington, *Corp Secy*
Jerry M Cole, *Vice Pres*
Randy Seidel, *Sales Staff*
Charles Lukens, *Office Mgr*
EMP: 20 EST: 1973
SQ FT: 9,500
SALES (est): 2.2MM **Privately Held**
WEB: www.salemprinting.com
SIC: 2752 7334 7338 2791 Commercial
printing, offset; photocopying & duplicat-
ing services; secretarial & court reporting;
typesetting; bookbinding & related work;
commercial printing

(G-12567)
SALEM READY MIX CONCRETE INC
2250 Salem Industrial Dr (24153-3100)
PHONE..............................540 387-1171
Horace B Thomas, *President*
Fred W Genheimer III, *Corp Secy*
Lewis P Thomas, *Vice Pres*
W J Thomas, *Vice Pres*
EMP: 14
SALES (est): 1.2MM **Privately Held**
WEB: www.salemreadymix.com
SIC: 3273 Ready-mixed concrete

(G-12568)
SEACRIST MOTOR SPORTS
2806 W Main St (24153-2058)
P.O. Box 2032 (24153-0465)
PHONE..............................540 309-2234
Dustin Seacrist, *President*
Davies Seacrist, *Treasurer*
Gregg Seacrist, *Treasurer*
Todd Blankenship, *Sales Staff*
EMP: 5
SALES (est): 330K **Privately Held**
WEB: www.seacristmotorsports.com
SIC: 3491 Automatic regulating & control
valves

(G-12569)
SECURE INNOVATIONS INC
3815 Travis Trl (24153-8083)
PHONE..............................540 384-6131
Pete Kesler, *CEO*
EMP: 5 EST: 2009
SALES (est): 522.6K **Privately Held**
WEB: www.secure-innovations.com
SIC: 7372 Prepackaged software

(G-12570)
SELENIX LLC
1640 Roanoke Blvd (24153-6420)
PHONE..............................540 375-6415
Bruce Stockburger, *Principal*
EMP: 1 EST: 2017
SALES (est): 47.2K **Privately Held**
SIC: 2834 Pharmaceutical preparations

(G-12571)
STAR TAG & LABEL INC
1535 Mill Race Dr (24153-3137)
P.O. Box 425 (24153-0425)
PHONE..............................540 389-6848
Patrick A Pollifrone, *President*
Sam Casey, *Plant Mgr*
EMP: 10
SQ FT: 12,000
SALES (est): 2.2MM **Privately Held**
WEB: www.startaglabel.com
SIC: 2759 Labels & seals: printing

(G-12572)
TECTON PRODUCTS LLC
5415 Corporate Cir (24153-8301)
PHONE..............................540 380-5819
Robert Plagemann, *Owner*
Scott Johnson, *Engineer*
Ann Baumann, *Marketing Mgr*
Leif Lothe, *CTO*
EMP: 35 **Privately Held**
WEB: www.tectonproducts.com
SIC: 3089 Plastic hardware & building
products
PA: Tecton Products Llc
4401 15th Ave N
Fargo ND 58102

(G-12573)
TIGHT LINES HOLDINGS GROUP INC
Also Called: Fastsigns
146 W 4th St (24153-3620)
PHONE..............................540 389-6691
Donald Smith, *CEO*
EMP: 10
SQ FT: 12,000
SALES (est): 1.2MM **Privately Held**
WEB: www.fastsigns.com
SIC: 3993 Signs & advertising specialties

(G-12574)
TMEIC CORPORATION
2060 Cook Dr (24153-7237)
PHONE..............................540 725-2031
Charles Lemone, *Branch Mgr*
EMP: 3 **Privately Held**
WEB: www.tmeic.com
SIC: 3554 3621 8711 Paper industries
machinery; power generators; engineer-
ing services
HQ: Tmeic Corporation
1325 Electric Rd
Roanoke VA 24018
540 283-2000

(G-12575)
TOBY LORITSCH INC
1902 Stone Mill Dr (24153-4631)
PHONE..............................540 389-1522
Toby Loritsch, *President*
EMP: 1
SALES (est): 56.5K **Privately Held**
SIC: 7692 Welding repair

(G-12576)
TOKYO EXPRESS
1940 W Main St (24153-3110)
PHONE..............................540 389-6303
Maggie Tran, *Principal*
EMP: 4
SALES (est): 284.6K **Privately Held**
SIC: 2741 Miscellaneous publishing

(G-12577)
TRIMBLE INC
1510 Southside Dr (24153-4676)
PHONE..............................540 904-5925
EMP: 78
SALES (corp-wide): 3.2B **Publicly Held**
WEB: www.trimble.com
SIC: 3812 Search & navigation equipment
PA: Trimble Inc.
935 Stewart Dr
Sunnyvale CA 94085
408 481-8000

(G-12578)
VIRGINIA KIK INC (PA)
Also Called: Kik Custom Products
27 Mill Ln (24153-3103)
P.O. Box 660 (24153-0660)
PHONE..............................540 389-5401
Jeffrey M Nodland, *CEO*
David Cynamon, *President*
Ken Golaszewski, *General Mgr*
Humberto Gomez, *General Mgr*
Michael Peterson, *Vice Pres*
EMP: 34
SQ FT: 38,000
SALES (est): 20.7MM **Privately Held**
WEB: www.kikcorp.com
SIC: 2842 7389 3085 2819 Bleaches,
household: dry or liquid; ammonia, house-
hold; fabric softeners; packaging & label-
ing services; plastics bottles; industrial
inorganic chemicals

GEOGRAPHIC

(G-12579)
VIRGINIA MEDIA INC
1633 W Main St (24153-3115)
PHONE................................304 647-5724
EMP: 2
SALES (corp-wide): 3.7MM **Privately Held**
SIC: 2741 Miscellaneous publishing
HQ: Virginia Media, Inc.
   122 N Court St
   Lewisburg WV 24901
   304 647-5724

(G-12580)
WELLS MACHINING LLC
740 Givens Tyler Rd (24153-8162)
PHONE................................540 380-2603
Robert Wells, Owner
Robert W Wells, Manager
EMP: 4
SALES (est): 295.8K **Privately Held**
WEB: www.wells-machining.com
SIC: 3599 Machine shop, jobbing & repair

(G-12581)
WHEELER INDUSTRIES LLC
470 Keesling Ave (24153-2108)
PHONE................................540 387-2204
EMP: 1
SALES (est): 50.5K **Privately Held**
SIC: 3999 Manufacturing industries

(G-12582)
YOKOHAMA CORP NORTH AMERICA (HQ)
Also Called: Yokohama Tire
1500 Indiana St (24153-7058)
PHONE................................540 389-5426
Yasuo Tominaga, CEO
William Francis, Maint Spvr
Mike Dunaway, Production
Randy Peters, Purch Agent
Rebecca Coe, Purchasing
◆ EMP: 250
SQ FT: 450,000
SALES (est): 753.3MM **Privately Held**
WEB: www.yokohamatire.com
SIC: 3011 5014 Tires & inner tubes; tires & tubes

(G-12583)
YOKOHAMA TIRE MNFCTRING VRGNIA (DH)
1500 Indiana St (24153-7058)
P.O. Box 3250 (24153-0648)
PHONE................................540 389-5426
Bob Irvin, Senior Engr
Brian Aguirre, Sales Staff
Joe Robincheck, Manager
Fardad Niknam, Director
Tetsuro Murakami,
▲ EMP: 52
SQ FT: 950,000
SALES (est): 166.7MM **Privately Held**
WEB: www.yokohamatire.com
SIC: 3011 Tire & inner tube materials & related products
HQ: Yokohama Tire Corporation
   1 Macarthur Pl Ste 800
   Santa Ana CA 92707
   714 870-3800

Saltville
Smyth County

(G-12584)
B & J EMBROIDERY INC
501 Campbell Dr (24370-2507)
PHONE................................276 646-5631
Larry Jackson, President
EMP: 2
SQ FT: 2,000
SALES (est): 18.2K **Privately Held**
SIC: 2395 7389 5999 2759 Embroidery & art needlework; lettering & sign painting services; banners, flags, decals & posters; poster & decal printing & engraving

(G-12585)
JOHN E PICKLE
108 Angler Ln (24370-3270)
PHONE................................276 496-5963
John E Pickle, Principal
EMP: 2
SALES (est): 94.7K **Privately Held**
SIC: 2035 Pickled fruits & vegetables

(G-12586)
MITCHELL SAWMILLING
7009 Clinch Mountain Rd (24370-4023)
PHONE................................276 944-2329
Tina Mitchell, Partner
EMP: 2
SALES (est): 115.5K **Privately Held**
SIC: 2421 Sawmills & planing mills, general

(G-12587)
REGION PRESS
591 Ridgeview Rd (24370-2609)
PHONE................................276 706-6798
EMP: 2 EST: 2016
SALES (est): 45.4K **Privately Held**
SIC: 2741 Miscellaneous publishing

(G-12588)
RELINE AMERICA INC
116 Battleground Ave (24370-3387)
PHONE................................276 496-4000
William D Pleasants Jr, CEO
J Michael Burkhard, President
Tim Cook, General Mgr
Jeff Van Huet, Plant Mgr
Paul Minkin, CFO
▲ EMP: 32
SALES (est): 7.6MM **Privately Held**
WEB: www.relineamerica.com
SIC: 3312 Pipes & tubes

(G-12589)
SALTVILLE GAS STORAGE CO LLC
889 Ader Ln (24370)
PHONE................................276 496-7004
Timothy L Ferguson,
EMP: 30
SALES (est): 1.6MM
SALES (corp-wide): 3.7B **Privately Held**
SIC: 1321 Natural gas liquids
HQ: Spectra Energy Corp
   5400 Westheimer Ct
   Houston TX 77056

(G-12590)
SALTVILLE MACHINE & WELDING
282 Allison Gap Rd (24370-3307)
PHONE................................276 496-3555
Mike Wassum, President
Mary B Wassum, Vice Pres
EMP: 4
SQ FT: 2,200
SALES (est): 150K **Privately Held**
SIC: 3599 7692 Machine shop, jobbing & repair; welding repair

(G-12591)
SALTVILLE PROGRESS INC
226 Panther Ln (24370-4408)
P.O. Box Qq (24370-1171)
PHONE................................276 496-5792
Loretta N Hodgson, President
EMP: 4
SALES (est): 175K **Privately Held**
SIC: 2711 Newspapers: publishing only, not printed on site

(G-12592)
SOUTHWEST KETTLE KORN COMPANY
2419 Highway 107 (24370-3370)
PHONE................................352 201-5664
Geoffrey Hall, President
EMP: 1
SALES (est): 83.7K **Privately Held**
WEB: www.kettlebuckwild.com
SIC: 3589 Cooking equipment, commercial

(G-12593)
TECH OF SOUTHWEST VIRGINIA
118 Shaker Ln (24370)
PHONE................................276 496-5393
Sam Brikey, Owner
EMP: 3
SALES (est): 145.7K **Privately Held**
SIC: 3714 Tire valve cores

(G-12594)
TITAN WHEEL CORP VIRGINIA (HQ)
227 Allison Gap Rd (24370-3386)
PHONE................................276 496-5121
Maurice M Taylor Jr, Ch of Bd
David Salen, President
Mark Young, Opers Mgr
Michael Sheffield, Prdtn Mgr
Susan Robbins, Manager
▲ EMP: 80
SQ FT: 14,000
SALES (est): 53.6MM
SALES (corp-wide): 1.4B **Publicly Held**
WEB: www.titan-intl.com
SIC: 3714 3011 Wheel rims, motor vehicle; tires & inner tubes
PA: Titan International, Inc.
   2701 Spruce St
   Quincy IL 62301
   217 228-6011

(G-12595)
UNITED SALT BAYTOWN LLC
864 Ader Ln (24370-4309)
PHONE................................276 496-3363
Ernie Sambs, Branch Mgr
Mitzi Pickle, Manager
EMP: 46
SALES (corp-wide): 274.6MM **Privately Held**
WEB: www.unitedsalt.com
SIC: 1479 Rock salt mining
HQ: United Salt Baytown Llc
   4800 San Felipe St # 100
   Houston TX 77056
   713 877-2600

(G-12596)
UNITED SALT SALTVILLE LLC
864 Ader Ln (24370-4309)
PHONE................................276 496-3363
Ernest Sands,
EMP: 43
SALES (est): 1.7MM **Privately Held**
WEB: www.unitedsalt.com
SIC: 2819 Calcium compounds & salts, inorganic

(G-12597)
UNITED STATES GYPSUM COMPANY
Also Called: Plasterco Plant
6072 S Main St (24370-3131)
PHONE................................276 496-7733
William Castrey, Branch Mgr
EMP: 204
SALES (corp-wide): 8.2B **Privately Held**
WEB: www.usg.com
SIC: 3275 Gypsum products
HQ: United States Gypsum Company
   550 W Adams St Ste 1300
   Chicago IL 60661
   312 606-4000

(G-12598)
VIRGINIA INSULATED PRODUCTS CO (PA)
647 S Main St (24370-2912)
P.O. Box 459 (24370-0459)
PHONE................................276 496-5136
Andrew Kirchner, President
Paul Kirchner, Vice Pres
Riley Proffitt, Treasurer
EMP: 10 EST: 1974
SALES (est): 1.2MM **Privately Held**
WEB: www.vipwire.com
SIC: 3357 Nonferrous wiredrawing & insulating

(G-12599)
VIRGINIA INSULATED PRODUCTS CO
Hwy 91 (24370)
P.O. Box 459 (24370-0459)
PHONE................................276 496-5136
Andrew Kirschner, President
EMP: 12
SALES (corp-wide): 1.2MM **Privately Held**
WEB: www.vipwire.com
SIC: 3357 Magnet wire, nonferrous

PA: Virginia Insulated Products Co Inc
   647 S Main St
   Saltville VA 24370
   276 496-5136

Saluda
Middlesex County

(G-12600)
ASB GREENWORLD INC
11524 Farm Rd (23149-2828)
PHONE................................804 695-2660
EMP: 3 EST: 2016
SALES (est): 320.7K **Privately Held**
SIC: 3524 Lawn & garden equipment

(G-12601)
C AND S PRECISION WEL
4365 Dragon Dr (23149-2509)
PHONE................................804 815-7963
Steve Docherty,
EMP: 1
SALES (est): 27.6K **Privately Held**
SIC: 7692 3317 Automotive welding; conduit: welded, lock joint or heavy riveted

(G-12602)
CARLTON AND EDWARDS INC
3 1/2 Miles North Rt 17 (23149)
P.O. Box 458 (23149-0458)
PHONE................................804 758-5100
W D Edwards Jr, President
W D Edwards III, Vice Pres
James R Edwards, Treasurer
Rachael Edwards, Admin Sec
EMP: 25 EST: 1962
SALES (est): 4MM **Privately Held**
SIC: 2421 Sawmills & planing mills, general

(G-12603)
FRIDAYS MARINE INC
14879 George Wash Mem Hwy (23149-2579)
P.O. Box 1091 (23149-1091)
PHONE................................804 758-4131
Phillip B Friday, President
Louise Friday, Vice Pres
EMP: 3
SQ FT: 6,000
SALES: 615.5K **Privately Held**
WEB: www.fridaysmarine.com
SIC: 3519 7699 Outboard motors; diesel, semi-diesel or duel-fuel engines, including marine; boat repair; marine engine repair

(G-12604)
KING OF DICE
955 Forest Chapel Rd (23149-2695)
PHONE................................804 758-0776
Wayne Mount, President
Elizabeth Mount, Vice Pres
EMP: 1
SALES (est): 146.1K **Privately Held**
WEB: www.kingofdice.com
SIC: 3089 5013 5531 Novelties, plastic; automotive supplies & parts; automotive parts

(G-12605)
MIDDLESEX CABINET CO
382 Urbanna Rd (23149-2556)
PHONE................................804 758-3617
EMP: 1 EST: 2009
SALES (est): 87.4K **Privately Held**
SIC: 3553 Cabinet makers' machinery

(G-12606)
VIRGINIA BRIDE LLC
Also Called: Dbs Publications
820 Gloucester Rd (23149-2596)
P.O. Box 5550, Glen Allen (23058-5550)
PHONE................................804 822-1768
Vanessa A Frame,
▲ EMP: 5
SALES (est): 319.3K **Privately Held**
WEB: www.vabridemagazine.com
SIC: 2721 Magazines: publishing & printing

▲ = Import ▼=Export
◆ =Import/Export

(G-12607)
VULCAN MATERIALS COMPANY
Also Called: Rappahannock Concrete
15128 George Wash Mem Hwy
(23149-2522)
PHONE................................804 758-5000
Scott Finney, *Branch Mgr*
EMP: 5 **Publicly Held**
WEB: www.vulcanmaterials.com
SIC: 3273 Ready-mixed concrete
PA: Vulcan Materials Company
1200 Urban Center Dr
Vestavia AL 35242

Sandston
Henrico County

(G-12608)
ATLANTIC EMB & DESIGN LLC
510 Eastpark Ct Ste 100 (23150-1330)
PHONE................................757 253-1010
Jerry Assessor,
EMP: 2
SALES (est): 180K **Privately Held**
WEB: www.logocompanyapparel.com
SIC: 2395 Embroidery products, except
schiffli machine

(G-12609)
DEAN FOODS COMPANY
1595 Mary St (23150-4016)
PHONE................................804 737-8272
Chuck Saxton, *Manager*
EMP: 100
SALES (corp-wide): 24MM **Privately
Held**
WEB: www.deanfoods.com
SIC: 2026 Fluid milk
PA: Dean Foods Company
2000 W Broad St
Richmond VA 23220
804 359-5786

(G-12610)
DESIGN SOURCE INC
5401 Lewis Rd Ste A (23150-1996)
PHONE................................804 644-3424
Glen Jordan, *Director*
Bonnie Cauthorn, *Director*
Tammy Clements, *Director*
Lynda Jordan, *Director*
Melissa Miller, *Director*
EMP: 25
SALES (est): 2.2MM **Privately Held**
WEB: www.designsourceinteriors.com
SIC: 2599 2531 7373 7389 Hotel furni-
ture; public building & related furniture;
computer-aided design (CAD) systems
service; interior design services; interior
designer; design, commercial & industrial

(G-12611)
**DOMINION COMFORT
SOLUTIONS LLC**
Also Called: DCS Constitution
209 Stuttaford Dr (23150-1438)
PHONE................................804 501-6429
Leslie Ignace, *Manager*
Kimberly Ignace, *Admin Sec*
EMP: 4
SALES (est): 181.2K **Privately Held**
SIC: 3731 7389 Commercial cargo ships,
building & repairing;

(G-12612)
DOMINION PACKAGING INC
5700 Audubon Dr (23150-1300)
PHONE................................804 447-6921
EMP: 200
SALES (corp-wide): 129MM **Privately
Held**
SIC: 2657 Mfg Folding Paperboard Boxes
PA: Dominion Packaging, Inc.
3001 Cofer Rd
Richmond VA 23150
804 230-5900

(G-12613)
DRYTAC CORPORATION (PA)
5401b Eubank Rd (23150-1943)
PHONE................................804 280-6013
Hayden Kelley, *President*
Marc Oosterhuis, *President*

Darren Speizer, *Vice Pres*
Mark Quiroz, *Warehouse Mgr*
Helen Obryant, *Purch Mgr*
▲ **EMP:** 25
SQ FT: 25,000
SALES (est): 11.8MM **Privately Held**
WEB: www.drytac.com
SIC: 2891 3577 Laminating compounds;
graphic displays, except graphic terminals

(G-12614)
F C HOLDINGS INC (PA)
5901 Lewis Rd (23150-2413)
PHONE................................804 222-2821
Willi Fenske, *Ch of Bd*
W B Carper Jr, *Exec VP*
EMP: 120 **EST:** 1947
SQ FT: 160,000
SALES (est): 11.8MM **Privately Held**
SIC: 3555 6512 2796 Printing trades ma-
chinery; commercial & industrial building
operation; gravure printing plates or cylin-
ders, preparation of

(G-12615)
FIDELITY PRINTING INC
12 E Williamsburg Rd (23150-2012)
P.O. Box 245 (23150-0245)
PHONE................................804 737-7907
Patricia Beahr, *President*
E Wayne Beahr, *Vice Pres*
Everett Wayne Beahr, *Vice Pres*
EMP: 10
SALES (est): 990K **Privately Held**
WEB: www.fidelityprintinginc.com
SIC: 2752 Commercial printing, offset

(G-12616)
GH WINERY LLC
6446 Somerton Pl (23150-5446)
PHONE................................804 737-7416
Jay W Smith,
EMP: 14
SALES (est): 700K **Privately Held**
SIC: 2084 Wines

(G-12617)
GLASDON INC
5200 Anthony Rd Ste D (23150-1929)
PHONE................................804 726-3777
Philip Greenwood, *CEO*
Carl Smith, *Vice Pres*
Clay McDevitt, *Warehouse Mgr*
JD Villegas, *VP Sales*
Josediego Villegas, *Sales Mgr*
▲ **EMP:** 7
SALES (est): 1.4MM
SALES (corp-wide): 43.5MM **Privately
Held**
WEB: www.us.glasdon.com
SIC: 3089 Garbage containers, plastic
HQ: Glasdon International Limited
Glasdon Innovation & Export Centre
Blackpool LANCS FY4 4
125 360-0435

(G-12618)
HEAVENLY PAVING LLC
111 Huntsman Rd (23150-2117)
PHONE................................804 980-9523
Kyla B Munford,
Russell Vanwroten,
EMP: 2
SALES (est): 90.7K **Privately Held**
SIC: 2951 Asphalt paving mixtures &
blocks

(G-12619)
**HOFFMANNS CUSTOM DISPLAY
CASES**
218 Algiers Dr (23150-1603)
PHONE................................804 332-4873
EMP: 2
SALES (est): 110K **Privately Held**
SIC: 3523 Mfg Farm Machinery/Equipment

(G-12620)
**INDUSTRIAL CONTROL
SYSTEMS INC**
20 W Williamsburg Rd (23150-2010)
PHONE................................804 737-1700
Mark William Romers, *President*
Steve A Burke, *Vice Pres*
Glen Lockwood, *Project Engr*
Maria Romers, *Treasurer*
Rowee Yadin, *Software Dev*

EMP: 20
SQ FT: 3,900
SALES (est): 4.8MM **Privately Held**
WEB: www.filtermagic.com
SIC: 3679 1731 7629 3823 Electronic circuits; electronic controls installation; electrical measuring instrument repair &
calibration; electrical equipment repair
services; industrial instrmnts msrmnt dis-
play/control process variable

(G-12621)
IR ENGRAVING LLC
5901 Lewis Rd (23150-2413)
PHONE................................804 222-2821
Kenneth Raup, *Vice Pres*
Neil Suffa, *Controller*
Francesca Wyatt, *Sales Mgr*
Kelly Bartlett, *Accounts Mgr*
Mark Richter, *Sales Engr*
EMP: 94
SQ FT: 160,000
SALES (est): 23MM **Privately Held**
WEB: www.irengraving.com
SIC: 3555 Printing trades machinery

(G-12622)
JEAN SAMUELS
6600 Scandia Lake Pl (23150-5473)
PHONE................................804 328-2294
EMP: 1
SALES (est): 75K **Privately Held**
SIC: 3589 Mfg Service Industry Machinery

(G-12623)
LARRY KANIECKI
Also Called: Larrylandcraftsetc.
2200 E Nine Mile Rd (23150-1660)
PHONE................................804 737-7616
Larry Kaniecki, *Owner*
EMP: 1
SALES (est): 55K **Privately Held**
SIC: 3842 3944 Canes, orthopedic; books,
toy: picture & cutout

(G-12624)
MARTIN METALFAB INC
5891 Lewis Rd (23150-2411)
PHONE................................804 226-1431
James Grubbs III, *President*
Bill Robinson, *Vice Pres*
Marsha Grubbs, *Treasurer*
Joe Collins, *Sales Staff*
Chris Cummings, *Sales Staff*
EMP: 22 **EST:** 1978
SQ FT: 9,000
SALES (est): 5.1MM **Privately Held**
WEB: www.martinmetalfab.com
SIC: 3441 3444 Fabricated structural
metal; sheet metalwork

(G-12625)
**NOLTE MACHINE AND WELDING
LLC**
10 W Williamsburg Rd D (23150-2013)
PHONE................................804 357-7271
Michael Nolte Sr, *Mng Member*
Michael Nolte Jr,
EMP: 2
SALES (est): 74.6K **Privately Held**
SIC: 7692 7389 Welding repair;

(G-12626)
**NOTTOWAY RIVER
PUBLICATIONS**
5861 White Oak Rd (23150-5214)
PHONE................................804 737-7395
EMP: 1
SALES (est): 45.3K **Privately Held**
WEB: www.nottowayriversurvey.net
SIC: 2741 Miscellaneous publishing

(G-12627)
**ONDAL MEDICAL SYSTEMS
AMER INC**
540 Eastpark Ct Ste A (23150-1344)
PHONE................................804 279-0320
Christoph Roeer, *President*
Cheryl Turner, *Accountant*
Frank Weitzel, *Manager*
▲ **EMP:** 12

SALES (est): 2.5MM
SALES (corp-wide): 177.9K **Privately
Held**
WEB: www.ondal.com
SIC: 3841 Surgical & medical instruments
HQ: Ondal Medical Systems Gmbh
Wellastr. 6
Hunfeld 36088
665 281-0

(G-12628)
**POLYKON MANUFACTURING
LLC**
6201 Engineered Wood Way (23150-5037)
PHONE................................804 461-9974
Franois Jackow,
EMP: 50
SALES (est): 1.8MM **Privately Held**
SIC: 2834 Pharmaceutical preparations

(G-12629)
**RICHMOND CORRUGATED BOX
CO**
5301 Corrugated Rd (23150-1957)
P.O. Box 7715, Richmond (23231-0215)
PHONE................................804 222-1300
Mark Williams, *President*
Daniel L Williams Jr, *Chairman*
Charles D White, *Vice Pres*
Chuck White, *Vice Pres*
Shawn Ways, *Cust Mgr*
EMP: 26
SQ FT: 50,000
SALES (est): 5.6MM
SALES (corp-wide): 12.2MM **Privately
Held**
WEB: www.hoodcontainer.com
SIC: 2653 3993 Boxes, corrugated: made
from purchased materials; signs & adver-
tising specialties
PA: Richmond Corrugated, Inc.
5301 Corrugated Rd
Sandston VA 23150
804 222-1300

(G-12630)
**SCHMID EMBROIDERY &
DESIGN**
510 Eastpark Ct Ste 100 (23150-1330)
PHONE................................804 737-4141
Vance Tang, *President*
EMP: 3
SALES (est): 209.2K **Privately Held**
WEB: www.logocompanyapparel.com
SIC: 2395 Embroidery products, except
schiffli machine

(G-12631)
**SCHMITT REALTY HOLDINGS
INC**
3900 Technology Ct (23150-5029)
PHONE................................203 453-4334
Steve Cushman, *Manager*
EMP: 25
SALES (corp-wide): 19.2MM **Privately
Held**
WEB: www.georgeschmitt.com
SIC: 2754 Rotogravure printing
PA: Schmitt Realty Holdings, Inc.
251 Boston Post Rd
Guilford CT 06437
203 453-4334

(G-12632)
SHUPES CLEANING SOLUTIONS
5233 Saltwood Pl (23150-5459)
PHONE................................804 737-6799
Ronald Shupe, *Owner*
EMP: 1
SALES (est): 93.4K **Privately Held**
WEB: www.coastalparadiseinc.com
SIC: 3635 Household vacuum cleaners

(G-12633)
SIMPLY SOUTHERN LLC
461 Evanrude Ln (23150-3436)
PHONE................................804 240-7130
Tracey Winslow, *Mng Member*
Mark Winslow,
EMP: 4
SALES (est): 249.2K **Privately Held**
SIC: 2051 Cakes, pies & pastries

(G-12634)
SMRT MOUTH LLC
6000 Technology Blvd (23150-5000)
PHONE......................................804 363-8863
Amish Patel, *CEO*
David Roberts, *Officer*
EMP: 4
SQ FT: 2,000
SALES (est): 150.8K **Privately Held**
WEB: www.smrtmouth.com
SIC: 3571 3829 7374 3949 Electronic computers; measuring & controlling devices; data processing & preparation; guards: football, basketball, soccer, lacrosse, etc.; commercial physical research

(G-12635)
SOUTHEAST FROZEN FOODS INC
5601 Corrugated Rd (23150-1906)
PHONE......................................800 214-6682
EMP: 59
SALES (corp-wide): 150.5MM **Privately Held**
WEB: www.seff.com
SIC: 2038 Ethnic foods, frozen
PA: Southeast Frozen Foods, Inc.
3261 Executive Way
Miramar FL 33025
800 662-4622

(G-12636)
STANDEX ENGRAVING LLC (HQ)
Also Called: Ir International
5901 Lewis Rd (23150-2413)
PHONE......................................804 236-3092
Philip Maniscalchi III, *Vice Pres*
Keith Morris, *Vice Pres*
E James Haggerty, *Treasurer*
Edward J Trainor, *Mng Member*
◆ EMP: 91
SQ FT: 160,000
SALES (est): 16.6MM **Publicly Held**
WEB: www.irengraving.com
SIC: 2796 3555 3599 Gravure printing plates or cylinders, preparation of; plates & cylinders for rotogravure printing; printing trades machinery; machine shop, jobbing & repair
PA: Standex International Corporation
23 Keewaydin Dr Ste 300
Salem NH 03079
603 893-9701

(G-12637)
STATON MJ & ASSOCIATES LTD
438 E Williamsburg Rd (23150-1641)
PHONE......................................804 737-1946
Marshall Staton Jr, *President*
Susan Staton, *Corp Secy*
EMP: 1
SALES (est): 110K **Privately Held**
SIC: 2541 7389 Wood partitions & fixtures; interior design services

(G-12638)
STEVES & SONS INC
5640 Lewis Rd (23150-2405)
PHONE......................................804 226-4034
Gregg Killelea, *General Mgr*
Greg Killelea, *Branch Mgr*
EMP: 50
SALES (corp-wide): 226MM **Privately Held**
WEB: www.stevesdoors.com
SIC: 2431 Doors, wood
PA: Steves & Sons, Inc.
203 Humble Ave
San Antonio TX 78225
210 924-5111

(G-12639)
WELLS MACHINE CO
15 Lumber Dr (23150-4026)
PHONE......................................804 737-2500
Earnest E Wells Jr, *President*
Earnest E Wells III, *Vice Pres*
EMP: 4 EST: 1978
SQ FT: 5,000
SALES (est): 28.6K **Privately Held**
SIC: 3541 7699 Machine tool replacement & repair parts, metal cutting types; tool repair services

(G-12640)
WESTERN ROTO ENGRAVERS INC
5350 Lewis Rd (23150-1932)
PHONE......................................804 236-0902
Thomas Burnett, *Manager*
EMP: 4
SALES (corp-wide): 12.9MM **Privately Held**
WEB: www.wrecolor.com
SIC: 2759 Engraving
PA: Western Roto Engravers, Incorporated
533 Banner Ave
Greensboro NC 27401
336 275-9821

(G-12641)
WESTROCK CP LLC
5640 Lewis Rd (23150-2405)
PHONE......................................804 236-3237
Ed Shipley, *Manager*
EMP: 41
SALES (corp-wide): 17.5B **Publicly Held**
WEB: www.westrock.com
SIC: 2653 Boxes, corrugated: made from purchased materials
HQ: Westrock Cp, Llc
1000 Abernathy Rd Ste 125
Atlanta GA 30328

(G-12642)
WRE/COLORTECH
5350 Lewis Rd Ste B (23150-1932)
PHONE......................................804 236-0902
Mike Regan, *Principal*
EMP: 3
SALES (est): 189.2K **Privately Held**
WEB: www.wrecolor.com
SIC: 2759 Engraving

Sandy Hook
Goochland County

(G-12643)
BARNES INDUSTRIES INC
4294 Whitehall Rd (23153-2114)
P.O. Box 27766, Richmond (23261-7766)
PHONE......................................804 389-1981
Roddy Barnes, *Principal*
EMP: 2 EST: 2008
SALES (est): 132.2K **Privately Held**
SIC: 3999 Manufacturing industries

(G-12644)
BRIGHT ELM LLC
2975 Stone Creek Dr (23153-2245)
PHONE......................................804 519-3331
Aubrey Lindsey, *Owner*
EMP: 1
SALES (est): 47.9K **Privately Held**
SIC: 7372 7389 Application computer software;

(G-12645)
ROADGLOBE LLC
2975 Stone Creek Dr (23153-2245)
PHONE......................................804 519-3331
Lee Lindsey,
EMP: 1
SALES (est): 60.8K **Privately Held**
SIC: 7372 Application computer software

Sandy Level
Pittsylvania County

(G-12646)
E&S WELDING LLC
1696 Yorkshire Dr (24161-3742)
PHONE......................................434 927-5428
Sean Barbour, *Principal*
EMP: 6
SALES (est): 98.2K **Privately Held**
SIC: 7692 Welding repair

(G-12647)
INDIAN CREEK EXPRESS INC
5529 Grassland Dr (24161-3243)
PHONE......................................434 927-5900
EMP: 2 EST: 2005
SALES (est): 110K **Privately Held**
SIC: 2741 Misc Publishing

Saxe
Charlotte County

(G-12648)
SAUNDERS LOGGING INC
1140 Bacon School Rd (23967-5311)
PHONE......................................434 735-8341
George E Saunders, *Principal*
EMP: 6
SALES (est): 396.7K **Privately Held**
SIC: 2411 Logging camps & contractors

Schuyler
Nelson County

(G-12649)
A 1 WELDING SERVICES
4 Rockfish Xing (22969-2166)
P.O. Box 154 (22969-0154)
PHONE......................................434 831-2562
William Walker Jr, *Principal*
EMP: 1 EST: 1995
SALES (est): 121.9K **Privately Held**
SIC: 7692 Welding repair

(G-12650)
ALBERENE SOAPSTONE COMPANY
42 Alberene Loop (22969-2267)
PHONE......................................434 831-1051
William J Russell, *President*
William G Watkins, *Admin Sec*
William Watkins, *Admin Sec*
Linda Fitzgerald, *Administration*
EMP: 6
SALES (est): 686.9K
SALES (corp-wide): 2.1MM **Privately Held**
WEB: www.alberenesoapstone.com
SIC: 3281 Cut stone & stone products
HQ: Polycor Inc
76 Rue Saint-Paul Bureau 100
Quebec QC G1K 3
418 692-4695

(G-12651)
APPLEBERRY MTN TAXIDERMY SVCS
5046 Green Creek Rd (22969-1607)
PHONE......................................434 831-2232
Steven Morgan, *Owner*
EMP: 1
SALES (est): 84.3K **Privately Held**
SIC: 3111 7699 5084 Leather tanning & finishing; taxidermists; food industry machinery

(G-12652)
NEW WORLDS STONE CO INC
Also Called: Alberene Soapstone Company
42 Alberene Loop (22969-2267)
P.O. Box 300 (22969-0300)
PHONE......................................434 831-1051
K A Sorensen, *President*
Doug Argenbright, *Sales Mgr*
EMP: 8 EST: 1998
SQ FT: 10,000
SALES (est): 530.7K **Privately Held**
WEB: www.alberenesoapstone.com
SIC: 3281 Cut stone & stone products

(G-12653)
POLYCOR VIRGINIA INC
Also Called: Alberene Soapstone Co.
42 Alberene Loop (22969-2267)
P.O. Box 300 (22969-0300)
PHONE......................................434 831-1051
Stephan Normand, *President*
Lance McCardle, *Manager*
EMP: 24
SALES (est): 1.5MM **Privately Held**
WEB: www.alberenesoapstone.com
SIC: 1499 Rubbing stone quarrying

Scottsburg
Halifax County

(G-12654)
ASAL TIE & LUMBER CO INC
9025 James D Hagood Hwy (24589-2541)
PHONE......................................434 454-6555
Johnny Asal, *President*
David Asal, *Shareholder*
EMP: 18
SALES (est): 1.2MM **Privately Held**
SIC: 2421 Sawmills & planing mills, general

(G-12655)
EUGENE MARTIN TRUCKING
1053 Hazelwood Mill Trl (24589-3147)
PHONE......................................434 454-7267
Ollie Eugene Martin, *Principal*
EMP: 2 EST: 1998
SALES (est): 179K **Privately Held**
SIC: 3531 Construction machinery

(G-12656)
PRESS 4 TIME TEES LLC
4056 Dryburg Rd (24589-3120)
PHONE......................................434 446-6633
Shawn Barksdale, *CEO*
EMP: 2
SALES (est): 41.3K **Privately Held**
SIC: 2741 Miscellaneous publishing

Scottsville
Albemarle County

(G-12657)
ADVANCED TOOLING CORPORATION (PA)
5199 W River Rd (24590-4665)
PHONE......................................434 286-7781
Randal Taylor, *President*
George Cushnie, *Vice Pres*
EMP: 2
SALES (est): 750K **Privately Held**
WEB: www.adv-tool.com
SIC: 2399 Fabricated textile products

(G-12658)
BRADLEY ENERGY LLC
7548 Totier Creek Farm Rd (24590-3962)
PHONE......................................434 286-7600
Ralph Bradley,
Dave Snyder,
Mark Thompson,
EMP: 3
SALES (est): 230.2K **Privately Held**
WEB: www.bradleyenergy.com
SIC: 1382 Oil & gas exploration services

(G-12659)
CHARLOTTESVILLE FIRE EXTING
1790 Ed Jones Rd (24590-4367)
PHONE......................................434 295-0803
Greg Lowry, *Mng Member*
EMP: 2
SALES (est): 252.4K **Privately Held**
SIC: 3569 Firefighting apparatus & related equipment

(G-12660)
EVER FORWARD WOODWORKS
531 Hummingbird Rd (24590-9410)
PHONE......................................434 882-0727
Travis Lamb, *Principal*
EMP: 1
SALES (est): 54.1K **Privately Held**
SIC: 2431 Millwork

(G-12661)
JAMES RIVER EMBROIDERY
100 Jackson St (24590-4977)
PHONE......................................434 987-9800
James River, *CEO*
EMP: 2 EST: 2014
SALES (est): 103K **Privately Held**
SIC: 2395 Embroidery & art needlework

▲ = Import ▼=Export
◆ =Import/Export

(G-12662)
KEY DISPLAY LLC
1322 James River Rd (24590-3856)
PHONE..................................434 286-4514
John Billies, *President*
Kevin Billies, *Vice Pres*
Denise Davis, *Treasurer*
EMP: 5
SALES (est): 3.5MM **Privately Held**
WEB: www.keydisplayllc.com
SIC: 3993 Signs & advertising specialties

(G-12663)
LINKS CHOICE LLC (PA)
4545 Kidds Dairy Rd (24590-3593)
PHONE..................................434 286-2202
Stephen Smith, *General Mgr*
Jason Luongo, *Managing Dir*
Brian Kingsley, *Plant Mgr*
Ashley Hicks, *Marketing Staff*
Gerald Cason, *Mng Member*
▲ **EMP:** 26
SQ FT: 20,000
SALES (est): 3.9MM **Privately Held**
WEB: www.linkschoice.com
SIC: 3949 5091 Golf equipment; golf equipment

(G-12664)
RAGLAND TRUCKING INC W E
1051 Gough Town Rd (24590-5464)
PHONE..................................434 286-2414
W E Ragland, *Principal*
EMP: 3
SALES (est): 307.8K **Privately Held**
SIC: 2411 Logging

(G-12665)
RALPH JOHNSON
Also Called: Johnson Logging
7753 Blenheim Rd (24590-3986)
P.O. Box 224 (24590-0224)
PHONE..................................434 286-2735
Ralph Johnson, *Owner*
EMP: 1
SALES (est): 81.8K **Privately Held**
SIC: 2411 Logging

(G-12666)
SAND KING
1840 Ruritan Lake Rd (24590-4473)
PHONE..................................434 465-3498
Donald King, *Owner*
EMP: 5 **EST:** 2013
SALES (est): 486.1K **Privately Held**
SIC: 2426 Flooring, hardwood

(G-12667)
STRUCTURAL STEEL MGT LLC
179 James River Rd (24590-3805)
P.O. Box 874 (24590-0874)
PHONE..................................434 286-2373
Michael Milam, *Mng Member*
Joe Werres,
EMP: 5 **EST:** 2009
SQ FT: 7,000
SALES (est): 916.5K **Privately Held**
WEB: www.structuralsteelmanagementllc.com
SIC: 3441 Building components, structural steel

(G-12668)
THISTLE GATE VINEYARD LLC
5199 W River Rd (24590-4665)
PHONE..................................434 286-2428
George Cushnie Jr, *Principal*
EMP: 2
SALES (est): 138.2K **Privately Held**
WEB: www.thistlegatevineyard.com
SIC: 2084 Wines

(G-12669)
VIRGINIAS MUDD HOT SAUCE LLC
1107 Georgia Creek Rd (24590-4791)
PHONE..................................434 953-6582
Jenise McNeal,
EMP: 1
SALES (est): 39.5K **Privately Held**
SIC: 2033 Chili sauce, tomato: packaged in cans, jars, etc.

(G-12670)
W E RAGLAND LOGGING CO
Also Called: Ragland, Gene Timber
1051 Goults Rd (24590)
PHONE..................................434 286-2705
Gene Ragland, *Owner*
EMP: 13
SALES (est): 880K **Privately Held**
SIC: 2411 Logging camps & contractors

Seaford
York County

(G-12671)
ARTISAN MEADS LLC
Also Called: Lion's Head Meadery
117 Whites Ln (23696-2013)
PHONE..................................757 713-4885
Zeb Johnston,
EMP: 3
SALES (est): 100.5K **Privately Held**
SIC: 2084 7389 Wines;

(G-12672)
BACK CREEK TOWING & SALVAGE
131b Landing Rd (23696-2019)
PHONE..................................757 898-5338
Jeff White, *Owner*
Robert White, *Owner*
Bart White, *Co-Owner*
EMP: 3
SALES (est): 284.2K **Privately Held**
SIC: 3731 Towboats, building & repairing

(G-12673)
CREATIONS FROM HEART LLC
119 Lewis Dr (23696-2410)
PHONE..................................757 234-4300
Randy Cook, *Principal*
EMP: 4
SALES (est): 268.9K **Privately Held**
SIC: 2053 Cakes, bakery: frozen

(G-12674)
HELPING HANDS HOME SERVICES
107 Chisman Cir (23696-2627)
PHONE..................................757 898-3255
Janice Seward, *CEO*
EMP: 15
SALES (est): 1.4MM **Privately Held**
SIC: 2842 Specialty cleaning preparations

(G-12675)
HONEYCUTTS MOBILE MARINE
211 Mastin Ave (23696-2332)
PHONE..................................757 898-7793
Samuel D Honeycutt, *Owner*
EMP: 1
SALES (est): 60K **Privately Held**
SIC: 3732 Boat building & repairing

(G-12676)
LM5 VERTICAL INSPECTIONS LLC
111 Finch Ln (23696-2031)
PHONE..................................757 810-9938
Marshall C Adams IV, *Principal*
EMP: 1
SALES (est): 60K **Privately Held**
SIC: 3534 Elevators & moving stairways

(G-12677)
RUTHERFORD BEAN
1504 Back Creek Rd (23696-2032)
PHONE..................................757 898-4363
Darrell Rutherford, *Owner*
EMP: 1
SALES (est): 67K **Privately Held**
SIC: 2426 Carvings, furniture: wood

(G-12678)
WILSONS WOODWORKS
102 Ellerson Ct (23696-2311)
PHONE..................................757 846-6697
Christopher Wilson, *Principal*
EMP: 2
SALES (est): 85.2K **Privately Held**
SIC: 2431 Millwork

Sedley
Southampton County

(G-12679)
DIXIE PRESS CUSTOM SCREEN
31004 Maple Ave (23878-2659)
PHONE..................................757 569-8241
EMP: 4
SQ FT: 1,840
SALES: 80K **Privately Held**
SIC: 2759 2752 5941 Commercial Printing Lithographic Commercial Printing Ret Sporting Goods/Bicycles

(G-12680)
SEDLEY PRINTING
31017 Maple Ave (23878-2659)
PHONE..................................757 562-5738
James Creasey, *Owner*
EMP: 1
SALES (est): 98.8K **Privately Held**
SIC: 2752 Commercial printing, lithographic

(G-12681)
WARREN MASTERY ENTERPRISES INC
12357 Saint Lukes Rd (23878-2109)
PHONE..................................877 207-6370
Sonia Warren, *President*
EMP: 7 **EST:** 2016
SALES (est): 206.3K **Privately Held**
SIC: 3999 Chairs, hydraulic, barber & beauty shop

Shacklefords
King And Queen County

(G-12682)
IMAGES IN ART INC
5610 Lwis B Pller Mem Hwy (23156-3122)
PHONE..................................804 785-1011
Christopher Aiken, *Owner*
EMP: 2
SALES (est): 177.4K **Privately Held**
WEB: www.imagesinart.com
SIC: 3993 Signs & advertising specialties

(G-12683)
M B S EQUIPMENT SALES INC
2200 Royal Oak School Rd (23156-3138)
P.O. Box 206 (23156-0206)
PHONE..................................804 785-4971
Thomas E Wilson III, *Principal*
Deborah Wilson, *Admin Sec*
EMP: 3
SALES (est): 382K **Privately Held**
SIC: 3582 Commercial laundry equipment

(G-12684)
SHEFFORD WOODLANDS LLC
230 Enterprise Rd (23156)
PHONE..................................804 625-5495
Sebastian Salas, *Mng Member*
EMP: 2 **EST:** 2015
SQ FT: 54,000
SALES (est): 500K **Privately Held**
SIC: 2599 Boards: planning, display, notice

Sharps
Richmond County

(G-12685)
SMITH & SONS OYSTER CO INC B G
70 Samsons Rd Fanom 22460 22460
Fanom (22548)
P.O. Box 69 (22548-0069)
PHONE..................................804 394-2721
Ben G Smith Jr, *President*
Tripp Smith, *Vice Pres*
EMP: 10 **EST:** 1970
SQ FT: 2,500
SALES (est): 996.4K **Privately Held**
SIC: 2091 5146 Oysters: packaged in cans, jars, etc.; seafoods

Shawsville
Montgomery County

(G-12686)
SISSON & RYAN INC (PA)
6475 Roanoke Rd (24162-2008)
P.O. Box 128 (24162-0128)
PHONE..................................540 268-2413
Clyde B Sisson, *Ch of Bd*
David Ryan, *Exec VP*
Thomas M Dunkenberger, *Vice Pres*
EMP: 42 **EST:** 1953
SQ FT: 4,800
SALES (est): 6.1MM **Privately Held**
SIC: 1429 1442 1422 Igneous rock, crushed & broken-quarrying; construction sand & gravel; crushed & broken limestone

(G-12687)
SISSON & RYAN INC
5441 Roanoke Rd (24162)
PHONE..................................540 268-5251
Daniel Sisson, *President*
EMP: 27
SALES (corp-wide): 6.1MM **Privately Held**
SIC: 1429 Igneous rock, crushed & broken-quarrying
PA: Sisson & Ryan, Inc
6475 Roanoke Rd
Shawsville VA 24162
540 268-2413

Shenandoah
Page County

(G-12688)
ALPHA INDUSTRIES INC
1284 Rinacas Corner Rd (22849-4233)
PHONE..................................540 298-2155
Richard Atwell, *President*
EMP: 2
SALES (est): 123.3K **Privately Held**
SIC: 3089 Plastic processing

(G-12689)
GEM LOCKER LLC
611 Williams Ave (22849-1144)
PHONE..................................540 298-8906
Thomas Heffernan, *CFO*
EMP: 2
SALES (est): 94.1K
SALES (corp-wide): 1.3MM **Privately Held**
SIC: 2541 Cabinets, lockers & shelving
PA: Theodore Watson Holding Company, Llc
611 Williams Ave
Shenandoah VA 22849
540 298-8906

(G-12690)
GROVE HILL WELDING SERVICES
3082 Grove Hill River Rd (22849-3307)
PHONE..................................540 282-8252
EMP: 1
SALES (est): 25K **Privately Held**
SIC: 7692 Welding repair

(G-12691)
HARDWOOD DEFENSE LLC
Also Called: Force Furnishings
611 Williams Ave (22849-1144)
PHONE..................................540 298-8906
Thomas Heffernan, *CFO*
EMP: 2
SALES (est): 92.2K
SALES (corp-wide): 1.3MM **Privately Held**
SIC: 2541 Cabinets, lockers & shelving
PA: Theodore Watson Holding Company, Llc
611 Williams Ave
Shenandoah VA 22849
540 298-8906

(G-12692)
HENSLEY FAMILY
306 N 3rd St (22849-1221)
PHONE..............................540 652-8206
Ronald L Hensley, *Principal*
EMP: 6
SALES (est): 544.1K **Privately Held**
WEB: www.papabearsrivercabin.com
SIC: 2411 Logging

(G-12693)
KVK PRECISION SPC INC
500 Quincy Ave (22849-1747)
PHONE..............................540 652-6102
EMP: 2 **EST:** 2015
SALES (est): 160.3K **Privately Held**
WEB: www.kvkprecision.com
SIC: 3599 Machine shop, jobbing & repair

(G-12694)
SHENANDOAH MACHINE SHOP INC
323 Pulaski Ave (22849-1731)
PHONE..............................540 652-8593
Randy Good, *President*
Ron Comer, *Vice Pres*
Lyniel Kite, *Treasurer*
EMP: 15 **EST:** 1970
SQ FT: 6,000
SALES (est): 2MM **Privately Held**
WEB: www.shenandoahmachine.com
SIC: 3599 Machine shop, jobbing & repair

(G-12695)
SIGNS R US LLC
704 S 3rd St (22849-1720)
PHONE..............................540 742-3625
Megan Yager, *Principal*
EMP: 2
SQ FT: 20,000
SALES (est): 67.4K **Privately Held**
SIC: 3993 Signs & advertising specialties

(G-12696)
TACTICAL WALLS LLC
611 Williams Ave (22849-1144)
PHONE..............................540 298-8906
Timothy Matter, *CEO*
Chris Wood, *Vice Pres*
Lambert Nathan, *Engineer*
Thomas Heffernan, *CFO*
▼ **EMP:** 24
SALES (est): 3.6MM
SALES (corp-wide): 1.3MM **Privately Held**
WEB: www.tacticalwalls.com
SIC: 2541 Cabinets, lockers & shelving
PA: Theodore Watson Holding Company, Llc
611 Williams Ave
Shenandoah VA 22849
540 298-8906

(G-12697)
WAR FIGHTER SPECIALTIES LLC
155 S Mcdaniel Ln (22849-3613)
PHONE..............................540 742-4187
Leanne Womack, *Owner*
EMP: 1
SALES (est): 46.6K **Privately Held**
SIC: 3484 3761 3769 3842 Machine guns & grenade launchers; ballistic missiles, complete; airframe assemblies, guided missiles; bulletproof vests; cars, armored, assembly of; industrial buildings, new construction

Shipman
Nelson County

(G-12698)
SAM H HUGHES JR
10271 James River Rd (22971-2556)
PHONE..............................434 263-4432
Sam H Hughes, *Owner*
EMP: 1
SALES (est): 75K **Privately Held**
SIC: 2411 Logging

Singers Glen
Rockingham County

(G-12699)
CREATIVE PASSIONS
6225 Mayberry Rd (22850-2319)
PHONE..............................540 908-7549
Tiffni Trobaugh, *Principal*
EMP: 1
SALES (est): 58.9K **Privately Held**
SIC: 2741 Miscellaneous publishing

Skippers
Greensville County

(G-12700)
GEORGIA-PACIFIC LLC
234 Forest Rd (23879)
P.O. Box 309 (23879-0309)
PHONE..............................434 634-6133
Dr Fu Shou Lin, *Manager*
Fu Lin, *Manager*
EMP: 150
SALES (corp-wide): 38.9B **Privately Held**
WEB: www.gp.com
SIC: 2436 2493 Plywood, softwood; reconstituted wood products
HQ: Georgia-Pacific Llc
133 Peachtree St Nw
Atlanta GA 30303
404 652-4000

(G-12701)
LEGACY VULCAN LLC
Mideast Division
1459 Quarry Rd (23879-2120)
P.O. Box 99 (23879-0099)
PHONE..............................434 634-4158
Derick Harris, *Branch Mgr*
EMP: 38 **Publicly Held**
WEB: www.vulcanmaterials.com
SIC: 1442 1423 Construction sand & gravel; crushed & broken granite
HQ: Legacy Vulcan, Llc
1200 Urban Center Dr
Vestavia AL 35242
205 298-3000

Smithfield
Isle Of Wight County

(G-12702)
ALL ABOUT CUPCAKES
103 Kings Point Ave (23430-2956)
PHONE..............................757 619-5931
Sheryl Coble, *Principal*
EMP: 1 **EST:** 2011
SALES (est): 69.7K **Privately Held**
SIC: 3421 Table & food cutlery, including butchers'

(G-12703)
AMERICAN SKIN LLC
1480 Industrial Dr (23431)
P.O. Box 449 (23431-0449)
PHONE..............................910 259-2232
Wes Blake, *Principal*
EMP: 4 **EST:** 2012
SALES (est): 282.6K **Privately Held**
WEB: www.pork-rinds.com
SIC: 2013 Sausages & other prepared meats

(G-12704)
BAY SAND CO INC
349 Main St (23430-1348)
P.O. Box 961 (23431-0961)
PHONE..............................757 357-9477
Henry Layden, *President*
Nancy Layden, *Admin Sec*
EMP: 6 **EST:** 1991
SALES (est): 1.1MM **Privately Held**
WEB: www.baysandco.com
SIC: 1442 Common sand mining

(G-12705)
BLUE SKY DISTILLERY LLC
20042 Isle Of Wght Indus (23430-6366)
PHONE..............................757 746-8342
EMP: 3
SALES (est): 137.1K **Privately Held**
WEB: www.blueskydistillery.com
SIC: 2085 Distilled & blended liquors

(G-12706)
BROWN BROTHERS INC
Also Called: Brown's Automotive
101 Moore Ave (23430-1856)
PHONE..............................757 357-4086
Wesley Brown, *President*
Darlene Brown, *Vice Pres*
Brown Darlene T, *Vice Pres*
EMP: 4
SQ FT: 17,400
SALES (est): 727.8K **Privately Held**
WEB: www.brownsautomotiveva.com
SIC: 7692 Automotive welding

(G-12707)
CABINET CO OF VIRGINIA CORP
19351 Battery Park Rd (23430-5671)
PHONE..............................757 357-5519
William Riddick, *Principal*
EMP: 3 **EST:** 2009
SALES (est): 360.4K **Privately Held**
WEB: www.thecabinetcompany.net
SIC: 2434 Wood kitchen cabinets

(G-12708)
CAROLINA COLD STORAGE INC
Also Called: Richmond Cold Storage
10070 Old Stage Hwy (23430-2828)
P.O. Box 906 (23431-0906)
PHONE..............................757 357-0434
Frank E Laughon Jr, *Branch Mgr*
EMP: 1 **Privately Held**
WEB: www.smithfield.com
SIC: 2011 Meat packing plants
PA: Carolina Cold Storage, Inc.
4808 Radford Ave
Richmond VA 23230

(G-12709)
CHIPS ON BOARD INCORPORATED
Also Called: Virginia Cutting Systems
1011 Magruder Rd (23430-1707)
PHONE..............................757 357-0789
EMP: 2 **EST:** 2006
SALES: 100K **Privately Held**
SIC: 3541 Cnc Shape Cutting Machines Sales/Service

(G-12710)
COOL WAVE LLC
20576 Suthport Landing Pl (23430)
P.O. Box 12161, Newport News (23612-2161)
PHONE..............................757 269-0200
Bobby Willis, *Owner*
EMP: 2
SALES (est): 253.3K **Privately Held**
WEB: www.coolwavecarwash.com
SIC: 3589 Car washing machinery

(G-12711)
DIGGS INDUSTRIES LLC
102 Cypress Ave (23430-2960)
PHONE..............................757 371-3470
EMP: 2
SALES (est): 103.1K **Privately Held**
SIC: 3999 Manufacturing industries

(G-12712)
EAST COAST TRUSS INC
10537 Shore Point Ln (23430-3140)
P.O. Box 504 (23431-0504)
PHONE..............................757 369-0801
Albin Ronstrom, *Principal*
EMP: 8
SALES (est): 848.3K **Privately Held**
WEB: www.eastcoasttruss.com
SIC: 2439 Structural wood members

(G-12713)
FARMLAND FOODS INC
111 Commerce St (23430-1201)
PHONE..............................757 357-4321
Jeff Yedinak, *Telecomm Dir*
Gary Walters, *Director*
EMP: 2
SALES (est): 62.3K **Privately Held**
SIC: 2011 Meat packing plants

(G-12714)
GRAFIK TRENZ
1402b S Church St (23430-1828)
PHONE..............................757 539-0141
Anna Rosa Chapman, *Owner*
EMP: 1
SALES (est): 65K **Privately Held**
SIC: 3993 2396 5941 Signs & advertising specialties; screen printing on fabric articles; team sports equipment

(G-12715)
HALLWOOD ENTERPRISES INC
405 Grace St (23430-1133)
P.O. Box 381 (23431-0381)
PHONE..............................757 357-3113
Franklin E Hall, *CEO*
Mark J Hall, *President*
EMP: 10 **EST:** 1979
SQ FT: 6,000
SALES (est): 10MM **Privately Held**
WEB: www.hallwood-usa.com
SIC: 2448 Pallets, wood

(G-12716)
ISLE OF WIGHT FOREST PRODUCTS (PA)
21158 Lankford Ln (23430-6236)
PHONE..............................757 357-2009
Lee Hooker, *President*
Amy Hooker, *Corp Secy*
EMP: 8
SALES (est): 5.9MM **Privately Held**
WEB: www.nhbclakeland.com
SIC: 2411 Logging

(G-12717)
KEENS AUTOMOTIVE MACHINE SHOP
1802 S Church St (23430-1853)
PHONE..............................757 365-4481
Carroll Edward Keen Jr, *President*
Carroll Edward Keen Sr, *Corp Secy*
EMP: 2 **EST:** 1973
SQ FT: 16,000
SALES (est): 265.4K **Privately Held**
SIC: 3599 Machine shop, jobbing & repair

(G-12718)
OUTLOOK SKATEBOARDS LLC
11294 Magnolia Pl (23430-5749)
PHONE..............................757 713-5665
Vince Hamilton, *Principal*
EMP: 2 **EST:** 2008
SALES (est): 135.8K **Privately Held**
SIC: 3949 Skateboards

(G-12719)
OWENS & JEFFERSON WTR SYSTEMS
5073 Owens Ln (23430-4027)
PHONE..............................757 357-7359
Rudolph Jefferson, *President*
EMP: 1
SALES (est): 105K **Privately Held**
SIC: 3823 Water quality monitoring & control systems

(G-12720)
PAGAN RIVER ASSOCIATES LLC
107 Water Pointe Ln (23430-2301)
PHONE..............................757 357-5364
Mike Smith, *Principal*
EMP: 2 **EST:** 2015
SALES (est): 67.2K **Privately Held**
SIC: 2082 Malt beverages

(G-12721)
PRECISION WOODWORKS LLC
17209 Riddick Rd (23430-6415)
PHONE..............................757 642-1686
Stephen Corcoran, *Principal*
EMP: 1
SALES (est): 103.9K **Privately Held**
SIC: 2431 Millwork

(G-12722)
PREMIUM PET HEALTH LLC
Also Called: Smithfield Pet
501 N Church St (23430-1214)
PHONE..............................757 357-8880
Zach Wiggins, *Branch Mgr*
EMP: 45 **Privately Held**
WEB: www.frozenpetingredients.com
SIC: 2048 Dry pet food (except dog & cat)

▲ = Import ▼=Export
◆ =Import/Export

HQ: Premium Pet Health Llc
1485 E 61st Ave Unit 1
Denver CO 80216
303 595-4440

(G-12723)
PRETTY PETALS
303 Jefferson Dr (23430-1415)
PHONE..................................757 357-9136
Tim Stephenson, *Owner*
Patti Stephenson, *Owner*
EMP: 2 **EST:** 2003
SALES (est): 127.8K **Privately Held**
SIC: 3999 Artificial trees & flowers

(G-12724)
SMITHFELD PCKGED MATS SLS CORP
200 Commerce St (23430-1204)
PHONE..................................816 243-2855
Glenn T Nunziata, *CFO*
EMP: 1
SALES (est): 45.4K **Privately Held**
WEB: www.smithfield.com
SIC: 2011 Meat packing plants

(G-12725)
SMITHFELD PCKGED MATS SLS CORP
200 Commerce St (23430-1204)
PHONE..................................816 243-2855
Glenn Nunziata, *Principal*
Sherry Schulze, *Principal*
Eric Gauthier, *Director*
EMP: 2
SALES (est): 101.1K **Privately Held**
WEB: www.smithfield.com
SIC: 2011 Meat packing plants

(G-12726)
SMITHFIELD DIRECT LLC (DH)
Also Called: Armour-Eckrich Meats LLC
200 Commerce St (23430-1204)
PHONE..................................757 365-3000
Dwight Potter, *General Mgr*
Ken Wright, *Manager*
Joseph B Sebring, *
Annabelle Torres, *Planning*
EMP: 20
SALES (est): 66.4MM **Privately Held**
WEB: www.armourmeats.com
SIC: 2011 Meat packing plants
HQ: Smithfield Packaged Meats Corp.
805 E Kemper Rd
Cincinnati OH 45246
513 782-3800

(G-12727)
SMITHFIELD FOODS INC
1911 S Church St (23430-1852)
P.O. Box 449 (23431-0449)
PHONE..................................910 862-7675
Doug Sutton, *Vice Pres*
Dennis Treacy, *Vice Pres*
Louie Miller, *Buyer*
Raeann Daman, *Purchasing*
Bradley Lowe, *Research*
EMP: 200 **Privately Held**
WEB: www.smithfieldfoods.com
SIC: 2011 Meat packing plants
HQ: Smithfield Foods, Inc.
200 Commerce St
Smithfield VA 23430
757 365-3000

(G-12728)
SMITHFIELD FOODS INC (HQ)
200 Commerce St (23430-1204)
PHONE..................................757 365-3000
Long Wan, *Ch of Bd*
Dennis Organ, *President*
Bill Gill, *President*
Jack Mandato, *President*
Dariusz Nowakowski, *President*
◆ **EMP:** 210
SALES (est): 11.2B **Privately Held**
WEB: www.smithfieldfoods.com
SIC: 2013 2015 2011 Sausages & other prepared meats; poultry slaughtering & processing; poultry slaughtering & processing; boxed beef from meat slaughtered on site

(G-12729)
SMITHFIELD FOODS INC
111 N Church St (23430-1222)
PHONE..................................757 356-6700
Joel Miller, *Engineer*
Jeffrey Jones, *Pub Rel Mgr*
Bill Gill, *Manager*
Warren Kroeker, *Director*
Matt Cummings, *Analyst*
EMP: 19 **Privately Held**
WEB: www.smithfieldfoods.com
SIC: 2011 Meat packing plants
HQ: Smithfield Foods, Inc.
200 Commerce St
Smithfield VA 23430
757 365-3000

(G-12730)
SMITHFIELD FOODS INC
1 Monette Pkwy (23430-2577)
PHONE..................................757 357-1598
W T Guthrie, *Branch Mgr*
Jeffery Winston, *Administration*
EMP: 50 **Privately Held**
WEB: www.smithfieldfoods.com
SIC: 2011 Meat packing plants
HQ: Smithfield Foods, Inc.
200 Commerce St
Smithfield VA 23430
757 365-3000

(G-12731)
SMITHFIELD FOODS MASTER TRUST
200 Commerce St (23430-1204)
PHONE..................................757 365-3000
Brenda Hampton, *Marketing Staff*
Aaron Trub, *Admin Sec*
EMP: 2
SALES (est): 103.5K **Privately Held**
WEB: www.smithfield.com
SIC: 2011 Meat packing plants

(G-12732)
SMITHFIELD FRESH MEATS CORP
200 Commerce St (23430-1204)
PHONE..................................513 782-3800
Scott Saunders, *President*
Michael H Cole, *Vice Pres*
EMP: 2
SALES (est): 112.8K **Privately Held**
SIC: 2011 Meat packing plants; pork products from pork slaughtered on site; bacon, slab & sliced from meat slaughtered on site; hams & picnics from meat slaughtered on site
HQ: Smithfield Packaged Meats Corp.
805 E Kemper Rd
Cincinnati OH 45246
513 782-3800

(G-12733)
SMITHFIELD PACKAGED MEATS CORP
Also Called: Genuine Smithfield Ham Shop
224 Main St (23430-1325)
PHONE..................................757 357-1798
Dedra Berg, *Marketing Staff*
Debbie Huss, *Manager*
EMP: 3 **Privately Held**
WEB: www.johnmorrell.com
SIC: 2011 Meat packing plants
HQ: Smithfield Packaged Meats Corp.
805 E Kemper Rd
Cincinnati OH 45246
513 782-3800

(G-12734)
SMITHFIELD PACKAGED MEATS CORP
112 Commerce St (23430-1202)
PHONE..................................757 365-3541
Jackie Xu, *Manager*
EMP: 6 **Privately Held**
WEB: www.smithfield.com
SIC: 2011 Pork products from pork slaughtered on site
HQ: Smithfield Packaged Meats Corp.
805 E Kemper Rd
Cincinnati OH 45246
513 782-3800

(G-12735)
SMITHFIELD PACKAGED MEATS CORP
Also Called: Smithfield Packaged Foods
601 N Church St (23430-1221)
PHONE..................................757 357-3131
EMP: 2 **Privately Held**
SIC: 2011 2013 Meat Packing Plant Mfg Prepared Meats
HQ: Smithfield Packaged Meats Corp.
805 E Kemper Rd
Cincinnati OH 45246
513 782-3800

(G-12736)
SMITHFIELD PACKAGED MEATS CORP
111 Commerce St (23430-1201)
PHONE..................................513 782-3800
Todd Scott, *Vice Pres*
Paul McLeod, *Plant Mgr*
Cathie Jenkins, *Train & Dev Mgr*
Rich Linkevich, *Sales Staff*
George Sliney, *Sales Staff*
EMP: 2 **Privately Held**
WEB: www.johnmorrell.com
SIC: 2011 Meat packing plants
HQ: Smithfield Packaged Meats Corp.
805 E Kemper Rd
Cincinnati OH 45246
513 782-3800

(G-12737)
SMITHFIELD PACKAGED MEATS CORP
Also Called: Lykes Meat Group Plant
1911 S Church St (23430-1852)
PHONE..................................757 357-1382
Kevin Clauberg, *General Mgr*
Ambrose Anderson, *Superintendent*
Lynn Katzer, *Superintendent*
Nelly Mejia, *Superintendent*
Ronny Pankau, *Superintendent*
EMP: 60 **Privately Held**
WEB: www.johnmorrell.com
SIC: 2011 2013 Hams & picnics from meat slaughtered on site; pork products from pork slaughtered on site; sausages & other prepared meats; bacon, side & sliced: from purchased meat; sausage casings, natural; frankfurters from purchased meat
HQ: Smithfield Packaged Meats Corp.
805 E Kemper Rd
Cincinnati OH 45246
513 782-3800

(G-12738)
SMITHFIELD PACKAGED MEATS CORP
601 N Church St (23430-1221)
PHONE..................................757 357-3131
Diana Souder, *Manager*
Emanuel McCrainey, *Director*
EMP: 2 **Privately Held**
WEB: www.johnmorrell.com
SIC: 2011 Meat packing plants
HQ: Smithfield Packaged Meats Corp.
805 E Kemper Rd
Cincinnati OH 45246
513 782-3800

(G-12739)
SMITHFIELD SUPPORT SVCS CORP
200 Commerce St (23430-1204)
PHONE..................................757 365-3541
Long Wan, *Ch of Bd*
Kenneth M Sullivan, *President*
Dhamu Thamodaran, *Exec VP*
Glenn T Nunziata, *CFO*
Jackie Xu, *Treasurer*
EMP: 210
SALES (est): 7.9MM **Privately Held**
SIC: 2013 2015 2011 Sausages & other prepared meats; poultry slaughtering & processing; poultry slaughtering & processing; boxed beef from meat slaughtered on site
HQ: Smithfield Foods, Inc.
200 Commerce St
Smithfield VA 23430
757 365-3000

(G-12740)
SMITHFIELD TIMES
228 Main St (23430-1325)
P.O. Box 366 (23431-0366)
PHONE..................................757 357-3288
John Edwards, *Principal*
EMP: 2
SALES (est): 141.9K **Privately Held**
WEB: www.smithfieldtimes.com
SIC: 2711 Commercial printing & newspaper publishing combined

(G-12741)
SOUTHERN STRUCTURAL STEEL INC (PA)
Also Called: Richman Steel
20078 I W I P Rd (23430)
PHONE..................................757 623-0862
Timothy Richman, *CEO*
Matthew Richman, *President*
Laurie S Starkey, *Corp Secy*
Mark Jenner, *Vice Pres*
Rick Valente, *Project Mgr*
EMP: 28
SQ FT: 15,000
SALES (est): 5.1MM **Privately Held**
WEB: www.southernstructuralsteel.com
SIC: 3441 Building components, structural steel

(G-12742)
TIMES PUBLISHING COMPANY
228 Main St (23430-1325)
P.O. Box 366 (23431-0366)
PHONE..................................757 357-3288
John Edwards, *President*
EMP: 12 **EST:** 1986
SALES (est): 706.5K **Privately Held**
WEB: www.smithfieldtimes.com
SIC: 2711 Commercial printing & newspaper publishing combined

(G-12743)
VA DISPLAYS LLC
103 Willow Wood Ave (23430-5974)
PHONE..................................757 251-8060
William H Riddick III, *Administration*
EMP: 2
SALES (est): 164.5K **Privately Held**
WEB: www.vadisplays.com
SIC: 3993 Signs & advertising specialties

(G-12744)
WOBSERS WELDING WORKS LLC
16058 Mill Swamp Rd (23430-3120)
PHONE..................................757 570-0440
EMP: 7 **EST:** 2017
SALES (est): 97.6K **Privately Held**
SIC: 7692 Welding repair

South Boston
Halifax County

(G-12745)
ABB ENTERPRISE SOFTWARE INC
2134 Philpott Rd (24592-6872)
PHONE..................................434 575-2169
EMP: 2 **Privately Held**
WEB: www.new.abb.com
SIC: 3568 Pivots, power transmission
HQ: Abb Enterprise Software Inc.
305 Gregson Dr
Cary NC 27511
919 856-2360

(G-12746)
ANNIN & CO
Annin Flagmakers
3011 Philpott Rd (24592-6827)
P.O. Box 464 (24592-0464)
PHONE..................................434 575-7913
Gary Gibson, *Opers Staff*
William Kelehar, *Branch Mgr*
Brenda Kopp, *Manager*
Bill Grainger, *Technology*
EMP: 30
SALES (corp-wide): 153.6MM **Privately Held**
WEB: www.annin.com
SIC: 2399 Aprons, breast (harness)

PA: Annin & Co., Inc.
105 Eisenhower Pkwy # 203
Roseland NJ 07068
973 228-9400

(G-12747)
APPLE TIRE INC
615 N Main St (24592-3352)
P.O. Box 776 (24592-0776)
PHONE..................434 575-5200
EMP: 2
SALES (est): 85.9K Privately Held
SIC: 3571 Personal computers (microcomputers)

(G-12748)
AQUATIC CO
Lasco Bathware
1100 Industrial Park Rd (24592-6885)
PHONE..................434 572-1200
Scott Hartman, Opers-Prdtn-Mfg
Jeni Binner, Purch Mgr
Stacey Watson, Human Res Mgr
EMP: 300
SALES (corp-wide): 463.9MM Privately Held
WEB: www.aquaticbath.com
SIC: 3088 Shower stalls, fiberglass & plastic
HQ: Aquatic Co.
665 Industrial Rd
Savannah TN 38372

(G-12749)
ARCTECH INC
2348 Eastover Dr (24592-2930)
PHONE..................434 575-7200
Daman S Walia, Branch Mgr
Merlin Brougher, Officer
EMP: 1
SALES (corp-wide): 3.3MM Privately Held
WEB: www.arctech.com
SIC: 3523 Fertilizing, spraying, dusting & irrigation machinery
PA: Arctech Inc
14100 Pk Madow Dr Ste 210
Chantilly VA 20151
703 222-0280

(G-12750)
B J HART ENTERPRISES INC
Also Called: B Hunt Enterprises
4019 Halifax Rd (24592-4821)
PHONE..................434 575-7538
F W Hunt, President
Elaine Hunt, Corp Secy
EMP: 2
SALES (est): 192.2K Privately Held
SIC: 2741 Maps: publishing & printing

(G-12751)
BENTON-THOMAS INC (PA)
408 Edmunds St (24592-3010)
P.O. Box 646 (24592-0646)
PHONE..................434 572-3577
Michael Benton, President
Mickey Thomas, Vice Pres
EMP: 10
SQ FT: 6,000
SALES (est): 1.2MM Privately Held
WEB: www.bentonthomas.com
SIC: 2752 5943 5712 Commercial printing, offset; office forms & supplies; office furniture

(G-12752)
BHK OF AMERICA INC
3045 Philpott Rd (24592-6827)
P.O. Box 353, Ramsey NJ (07446-0353)
PHONE..................201 783-8490
Reiner Kamp, President
Monika Kamp, Vice Pres
▲ EMP: 45 EST: 1976
SQ FT: 80,000
SALES (est): 7.9MM Privately Held
WEB: www.bhkofamerica.com
SIC: 2511 Wood household furniture

(G-12753)
BRIDGEVIEW FULL SVC
1000 Wilborn Ave (24592-3130)
PHONE..................434 575-6800
Anthony Welch, Owner
EMP: 2

SALES (est): 87.2K Privately Held
SIC: 3714 Motor vehicle parts & accessories

(G-12754)
BROWN-FOREMAN COOPEAGES
1141 Philpott Rd (24592-6838)
PHONE..................434 575-0770
Eddie Fanning, President
EMP: 2
SALES (est): 105.6K Privately Held
SIC: 2421 Sawmills & planing mills, general

(G-12755)
COVINGTON BARCODING INC
1154 Mount Zion Church Rd (24592-6754)
PHONE..................434 476-1435
EMP: 2 EST: 2015
SALES (est): 97K Privately Held
SIC: 3577 Bar code (magnetic ink) printers

(G-12756)
CRAZY CUSTOMS
602 Greenway Dr (24592-1714)
PHONE..................434 222-8686
David Epps, Principal
EMP: 3
SALES (est): 298.9K Privately Held
SIC: 3993 Signs & advertising specialties

(G-12757)
CREATIVE INK
1100 Wilborn Ave (24592-3132)
PHONE..................434 572-4379
EMP: 2
SALES (est): 83.9K Privately Held
SIC: 2752 Lithographic Commercial Printing

(G-12758)
D & R USA INC
1054 Commerce Ln (24592-6847)
P.O. Box 446 (24592-0446)
PHONE..................434 572-6665
Martien Vandorsser, President
▲ EMP: 5
SALES (est): 1.4MM Privately Held
WEB: www.denr-metal.com
SIC: 3441 Fabricated structural metal

(G-12759)
DAN RIVER WINDOW CO INC
1111 Wall St (24592-4641)
PHONE..................434 517-0111
Toll Free:..................877 -
Avis Sutherland, President
EMP: 10
SQ FT: 6,000
SALES (est): 700K Privately Held
WEB: www.danriverwindow.com
SIC: 2431 Windows & window parts & trim, wood

(G-12760)
DAVID S CREATH
13011 River Rd (24592-6799)
PHONE..................434 753-2210
EMP: 3 EST: 2010
SALES (est): 140K Privately Held
SIC: 2411 Logging

(G-12761)
DFA DAIRY BRANDS FLUID LLC
1170 Fulp Industrial Rd (24592)
PHONE..................336 714-9032
Michael Hardcastle, Branch Mgr
EMP: 2
SALES (corp-wide): 15.8B Privately Held
SIC: 2026 Fluid milk
HQ: Dfa Dairy Brands Fluid, Llc
1405 N 98th St
Kansas City KS 66111
816 801-6455

(G-12762)
DISTINCT IMPRESSIONS
309 Main St (24592-4627)
P.O. Box 791 (24592-0791)
PHONE..................434 572-8144
Harold Green, Owner
Ida Conner, Manager
EMP: 5
SQ FT: 3,000

SALES (est): 487.5K Privately Held
WEB: www.makeitdistinct.com
SIC: 2395 Embroidery & art needlework

(G-12763)
EMERGENCY VEHICLES INC
Also Called: Evi
2181 E Hyco Rd (24592-6527)
PHONE..................434 575-0509
Rob Ford, Regional Mgr
EMP: 1 Privately Held
WEB: www.evi-fl.com
SIC: 3711 Motor vehicles & car bodies
PA: Emergency Vehicles, Inc.
705 13th St
Lake Park FL 33403

(G-12764)
EPPS COLLISION CNTR & SUPERIOR
221 Webster St (24592-2340)
PHONE..................434 572-4721
David Epps, Administration
EMP: 3
SALES (est): 67.4K Privately Held
SIC: 3993 Signs & advertising specialties

(G-12765)
FELTON BROTHERS TRNST MIX INC (PA)
1 Edmunds St (24592-3001)
P.O. Box 463 (24592-0463)
PHONE..................434 572-2665
Dodson H Felton Jr, President
Dodson H Felton Sr, Vice Pres
EMP: 4 EST: 1947
SQ FT: 5,500
SALES (est): 3.3MM Privately Held
WEB: www.feltonbrothers.com
SIC: 3273 Ready-mixed concrete

(G-12766)
FELTON BROTHERS TRNST MIX INC
613 Railroad Ave (24592-3619)
P.O. Box 463 (24592-0463)
PHONE..................434 572-4614
Ronnie Jones, Branch Mgr
EMP: 8
SALES (corp-wide): 3.3MM Privately Held
WEB: www.feltonbrothers.com
SIC: 3273 Ready-mixed concrete
PA: Felton Brothers Transit Mix, Incorporated
1 Edmunds St
South Boston VA 24592
434 572-2665

(G-12767)
FIREBIRD MANUFACTURING LLC
1057 Bill Tuck Hwy (24592-7135)
PHONE..................434 517-0865
Kathryn C Farley,
Charles F Fuller,
EMP: 2
SALES (est): 328.7K Privately Held
SIC: 2111 Cigarettes

(G-12768)
FLOWERS BAKERIES LLC
4198 Halifax Rd (24592-4834)
PHONE..................434 572-6340
Vikki Lowery, Manager
EMP: 2
SALES (corp-wide): 4.1B Publicly Held
WEB: www.flowersfoods.com
SIC: 2051 Bread, cake & related products
HQ: Flowers Bakeries, Llc
1919 Flowers Cir
Thomasville GA 31757

(G-12769)
FORMPLY PRODUCTS INC
200 Webster St (24592-2341)
P.O. Box 193 (24592-0193)
PHONE..................434 572-4040
James Wilson, President
Jim Birgis, Principal
Rachel Wilson, Vice Pres
Lowll Reaves, Manager
James H Wilson III, Admin Sec
EMP: 12
SQ FT: 15,000

SALES (est): 1.2MM
SALES (corp-wide): 1.4MM Privately Held
SIC: 2436 Plywood, softwood
PA: Rankin Brothers Company
658 Southern Ave
Fayetteville NC
910 483-1478

(G-12770)
GARNIER-THIEBAUT INC
1044 Commerce Ln (24592-6847)
PHONE..................434 572-3965
Jean-Philippe Krukowicz, Branch Mgr
EMP: 6 Privately Held
WEB: www.gtlinens.com
SIC: 2511 Club room furniture: wood
HQ: Garnier Thiebaut, Inc.
3000 S Eads St Ste 2000
Arlington VA 22202
703 920-2448

(G-12771)
GAZETTE VIRGINIAN
3201 Halifax Rd (24592-4994)
PHONE..................434 572-3945
Keith Shelton, Principal
Paula Bryant, Editor
Joe Chandler, Editor
Patricia Seat, Adv Mgr
Dolores Cabaniss, Graphic Designe
EMP: 7
SALES (est): 373.9K Privately Held
WEB: www.gazettevirginian.com
SIC: 2711 Newspapers: publishing only, not printed on site

(G-12772)
GERDAU AMERISTEEL US INC
2171 Bill Tuck Hwy (24592-6379)
PHONE..................434 517-0715
Tim Philcott, Branch Mgr
Pat Westfall, Maintence Staff
EMP: 5 Privately Held
WEB: www.gerdau.com
SIC: 3441 Fabricated structural metal
HQ: Gerdau Ameristeel Us Inc.
4221 W Boy Scout Blvd # 600
Tampa FL 33607
813 286-8383

(G-12773)
H & M LOGGING INC
Also Called: Hodges & Miller Logging
1180 Sinai Rd (24592-6189)
PHONE..................434 476-6569
Kenneth Hodges, President
Mary C Hodges, Corp Secy
Kevin Hodges, Vice Pres
Brandee S Lloyd, Director
EMP: 66
SALES (est): 4.8MM Privately Held
WEB: www.halifaxchamber.net
SIC: 2411 Logging camps & contractors

(G-12774)
HALIFAX GAZETTE PUBLISHING CO
Also Called: Gazette-Virginia, The
3201 Halifax Rd 3209 (24592-4907)
P.O. Box 524 (24592-0524)
PHONE..................434 572-3945
Keith A Shelton, President
Phil Rinker, President
Jeff Humber, General Mgr
Dolores Crute, Editor
Linda Shelton, Treasurer
EMP: 20 EST: 1946
SQ FT: 11,000
SALES (est): 1.4MM Privately Held
WEB: www.gazettevirginian.com
SIC: 2711 2791 2752 Newspapers: publishing only, not printed on site; typesetting; commercial printing, lithographic

(G-12775)
HALIFAX SIGN COMPANY
103 Eanes St (24592-4201)
PHONE..................434 579-3304
EMP: 1
SALES (est): 46K Privately Held
SIC: 3993 Signs & advertising specialties

(G-12776)
HILDEN AMERICA INC
1044 Commerce Ln (24592-6847)
P.O. Box 1098 (24592-1098)
PHONE................................434 572-3965
Russell Basch, *President*
Lisa Girardi, *CFO*
▲ EMP: 30
SALES (est): 2.6MM Privately Held
WEB: www.hildenamerica.com
SIC: 2299 Linen fabrics

(G-12777)
LEGACY VULCAN LLC
Mideast Division
Hwy 360 (24592)
P.O. Box 698 (24592-0698)
PHONE................................434 572-3931
Paul Willis, *Manager*
EMP: 25 Publicly Held
WEB: www.vulcanmaterials.com
SIC: 1442 1423 Construction sand &
gravel; crushed & broken granite
HQ: Legacy Vulcan, Llc
1200 Urban Center Dr
Vestavia AL 35242
205 298-3000

(G-12778)
LEGACY VULCAN LLC
3074 James D Hagood Hwy (24592)
PHONE................................434 572-3967
EMP: 3 Publicly Held
WEB: www.vulcanmaterials.com
SIC: 3273 Ready-mixed concrete
HQ: Legacy Vulcan, Llc
1200 Urban Center Dr
Vestavia AL 35242
205 298-3000

(G-12779)
LEWIS METAL WORKS INC
2512 Hougton Ave (24592-2600)
P.O. Box 27 (24592-0027)
PHONE................................434 572-3043
James Addison Lewis, *President*
Mary Ann Lewis, *Corp Secy*
Addison B Lewis, *Vice Pres*
Drew Chandler Lewis, *Vice Pres*
Judy Thompson, *Admin Asst*
EMP: 35
SQ FT: 6,500
SALES (est): 8.5MM Privately Held
WEB: www.lewismetalworks.com
SIC: 3441 3446 3444 3443 Fabricated
structural metal; architectural metalwork;
sheet metalwork; fabricated plate work
(boiler shop); crane & aerial lift service

(G-12780)
**MARSHALL CON PDTS OF
DANVILLE**
1040 Alphonse Dairy Rd (24592-6398)
PHONE................................434 575-5351
David Vanwhye, *Branch Mgr*
EMP: 6
SALES (corp-wide): 4.8MM Privately
Held
WEB: www.chandlerconcrete.com
SIC: 3273 Ready-mixed concrete
PA: Marshall Concrete Products Of Danville
Inc
1088 Industrial Ave
Danville VA 24541
434 792-1233

(G-12781)
MAST BROS LOGGING LLC
2040 Bill Tuck Hwy (24592-6364)
PHONE................................434 446-2401
Ivan Mast,
EMP: 19
SQ FT: 2,000
SALES (est): 2.5MM Privately Held
WEB: www.mastequipment.com
SIC: 2411 Timber, cut at logging camp

(G-12782)
MERLIN BROUGHER
Also Called: Woodcraft Co, The
1051 Fan Park Dr (24592)
P.O. Box 1449, Halifax (24558-1449)
PHONE................................434 572-8750
Merlin Brougher, *Owner*
EMP: 6
SQ FT: 15,000

SALES (est): 763.3K Privately Held
SIC: 2448 Pallets, wood

(G-12783)
MILLER WASTE MILLS INC
1150 Greens Folly Rd (24592-6203)
PHONE................................434 572-3925
Warren Barth, *Vice Pres*
Thomas Ginther, *Plant Mgr*
Ben Jones, *Branch Mgr*
EMP: 4
SALES (corp-wide): 330.2MM Privately
Held
WEB: www.millerwastemills.com
SIC: 2821 Plastics materials & resins
PA: Miller Waste Mills, Incorporated
580 E Front St
Winona MN 55987
507 454-6906

(G-12784)
NATIONAL CAPS
1065 S Peach Orchard Rd (24592-6226)
PHONE................................434 572-4709
Lee Womack, *Owner*
EMP: 1
SALES (est): 53.1K Privately Held
SIC: 2759 Screen printing

(G-12785)
NOVEC ENERGY PRODUCTION
1225 Plywood Trl (24592-6350)
PHONE................................434 471-2840
EMP: 3
SALES (est): 464.3K Privately Held
SIC: 1311 Crude petroleum & natural gas
production

(G-12786)
OVAL ENGINEERING
5 Broad St (24592-4635)
P.O. Box 118 (24592-0118)
PHONE................................434 572-8867
Garland Ricketts, *Principal*
EMP: 3
SQ FT: 3,700
SALES (est): 320.6K Privately Held
SIC: 3599 Machine shop, jobbing & repair

(G-12787)
PRESS ON PRINTING LLC
2124 E Hyco Rd (24592-6526)
PHONE................................434 575-0990
Norvan Yoder, *Principal*
EMP: 2
SALES (est): 101.5K Privately Held
SIC: 2752 Commercial printing, offset

(G-12788)
**REYNOLDS PRESTO PRODUCTS
INC**
Also Called: Presto Products Company
2225 Philpott Rd (24592-6897)
P.O. Box 527 (24592-0527)
PHONE................................434 572-6961
Ronnie Lacks, *Engineer*
Joy Johnson, *Branch Mgr*
EMP: 350 Privately Held
WEB: www.prestoproducts.com
SIC: 2671 2673 Plastic film, coated or
laminated for packaging; food storage &
frozen food bags, plastic
HQ: Reynolds Presto Products Inc.
670 N Perkins St
Appleton WI 54914
800 558-3525

(G-12789)
**SLAGLE LOGGING & CHIPPING
INC**
1081 Slagles Mill Rd (24592-7160)
PHONE................................434 572-6733
A Bruce Slagle, *Principal*
EMP: 6 EST: 2009
SALES (est): 469.9K Privately Held
SIC: 2411 Logging

(G-12790)
SOUTH BOSTON NEWS INC
Also Called: News and Record
511 Broad St (24592-3225)
P.O. Box 100 (24592-0100)
PHONE................................434 572-2928
Sylvia Mc Laughlin, *President*
Tucker Mc Laughlin, *Vice Pres*

EMP: 12 EST: 1962
SQ FT: 2,500
SALES (est): 751.4K Privately Held
WEB: www.thenewsrecord.com
SIC: 2711 Newspapers: publishing
only, not printed on site; records

(G-12791)
SOUTHERN STATES COOP INC
Also Called: S S C South Boston Petro Svc
1067 Philpott Rd (24592-6831)
PHONE................................434 572-6941
Riley Hart, *Manager*
EMP: 14
SQ FT: 3,000
SALES (corp-wide): 2.1B Privately Held
WEB: www.southernstates.com
SIC: 2048 5999 Prepared feeds; farm
equipment & supplies
PA: Southern States Cooperative, Incorpo-
rated
6606 W Broad St Ste B
Richmond VA 23230
804 281-1000

(G-12792)
**VOESTLPINE HIGH PRFMCE
MTLS CO**
Also Called: Teledyne Vasco CK Company
2306 Eastover Dr (24592-2930)
P.O. Box 447 (24592-0447)
PHONE................................434 575-7994
George Kelly, *President*
EMP: 50
SALES (corp-wide): 13.8B Privately Held
WEB: www.bucorp.com
SIC: 3315 3356 3341 3312 Steel wire &
related products; nonferrous rolling &
drawing; secondary nonferrous metals;
blast furnaces & steel mills; miscella-
neous metalwork; cold finishing of steel
shapes
HQ: Voestalpine High Performance Metals
Corporation
2505 Millennium Dr
Elgin IL 60124
877 992-8764

South Chesterfield
*Colonial Heights City
County*

(G-12793)
ADVANSIX INC
15801 Woods Edge Rd (23834-6059)
PHONE................................804 504-0009
EMP: 26
SALES (corp-wide): 1.3B Publicly Held
WEB: www.advansix.com
SIC: 2899 2821 5162 Chemical prepara-
tions; plastics materials & resins; resins
PA: Advansix Inc.
300 Kimball Dr Ste 101
Parsippany NJ 07054
973 526-1800

(G-12794)
**ALWAYS MORNINGSONG
PUBLISHING**
14600 Fox Knoll Dr (23834-5857)
PHONE................................804 530-1392
Cheryl Wolfe, *Owner*
EMP: 1
SALES (est): 62K Privately Held
SIC: 2741 Music books: publishing only,
not printed on site

(G-12795)
**ANDERSONS WOODWORKS
LLC**
14318 Woodland Hill Dr (23834-6806)
PHONE................................804 530-3736
Robert Anderson, *Principal*
EMP: 2 EST: 2008
SALES (est): 138K Privately Held
SIC: 2431 Millwork

(G-12796)
ARM GLOBAL SOLUTIONS INC
1900 Ruffin Mill Rd (23834-5913)
PHONE................................804 431-3746
EMP: 1

SALES (corp-wide): 645K Privately Held
WEB: www.armglobalsolutions.com
SIC: 2671 Plastic film, coated or laminated
for packaging
PA: Arm Global Solutions, Inc.
138 Joseph Ave
Rochester NY 14605
844 276-4525

(G-12797)
BGB TECHNOLOGY INC
1060 Port Walthall Dr (23834-5919)
PHONE................................804 451-5211
David Richard Holt, *CEO*
Antonio Haynes, *Purch Mgr*
Elena Bobkova, *Engineer*
Wood James, *Manager*
Brian Raynor, *Manager*
▲ EMP: 27
SALES (est): 5.2MM Privately Held
WEB: www.bgbinnovation.com
SIC: 3621 Collector rings, for electric mo-
tors or generators; sliprings, for motors or
generators; windmills, electric generating

(G-12798)
**CAMPOFRIO FD GROUP - AMER
INC**
Also Called: Fiorucci Foods Chesterfield Co
1800 Ruffin Mill Rd (23834-5936)
PHONE................................804 520-7775
Claudio Colmignoli, *CEO*
William Gieg, *President*
Christopher R Maze, *President*
Panico Warren, *President*
Keith Amrhein, *Vice Pres*
▲ EMP: 175
SQ FT: 140,000
SALES (est): 44.9MM Privately Held
WEB: www.fioruccifoods.com
SIC: 2011 5147 5421 Meat packing
plants; meats & meat products; meat mar-
kets, including freezer provisioners
HQ: Campofrio Food Group, Sociedad
Anonima
Avenida De Europa (Pq Empresarial
De La Moraleja Edif Torona) 24
Alcobendas 28108
914 842-700

(G-12799)
CHURCH & DWIGHT CO INC
1851 Touchstone Rd (23834-5949)
PHONE................................804 524-8000
Michael Englert, *Opers Staff*
Kaleem Ahmad, *Engineer*
Meredith Marshall, *Human Resources*
Joe English, *Branch Mgr*
Meredith Holland-Marshall, *Supervisor*
EMP: 50
SALES (corp-wide): 4.3B Publicly Held
WEB: www.churchdwight.com
SIC: 2099 Baking soda
PA: Church & Dwight Co., Inc.
500 Charles Ewing Blvd
Ewing NJ 08628
609 806-1200

(G-12800)
DATASSIST
14522 Fox Knoll Dr (23834-5855)
PHONE................................804 530-5008
Caren Friehaber, *President*
Marc Friehaber, *Vice Pres*
EMP: 2
SALES (est): 130K Privately Held
SIC: 7372 Prepackaged software

(G-12801)
DORMAKABA USA INC
16031 Continental Blvd (23834-5900)
PHONE................................804 966-9166
Loren Rakich, *Vice Pres*
Peter Barbosa, *Materials Mgr*
Vijayan Rakkenchath, *Sales Mgr*
Tim Phillips, *Branch Mgr*
Steve Swain, *Manager*
EMP: 15
SALES (corp-wide): 2.7B Privately Held
WEB: www.dormakaba.com
SIC: 3429 Builders' hardware
HQ: Dormakaba Usa Inc.
100 Dorma Dr
Reamstown PA 17567
717 336-3881

(G-12802)
ESSENTRA PACKAGING INC
1625 Ashton Park Dr Ste D (23834-5907)
PHONE....................................804 518-1803
Mickey Voningelheim, *Production*
Jim Coates, *Engineer*
Nathan Ronning, *Engineer*
Ugur Sisman, *Finance Dir*
Minte Dejong,
EMP: 38
SALES (corp-wide): 1.2B **Privately Held**
WEB: www.essentra.com
SIC: 2672 Adhesive papers, labels or
tapes: from purchased material
HQ: Essentra Packaging Inc.
2 Westbrook Corp Ctr # 200
Westchester IL

(G-12803)
**ETERNAL TECHNOLOGY
CORPORATION**
1800 Touchstone Rd (23834-5950)
PHONE....................................804 524-8555
David LI, *President*
Hui Kuan Mao, *Chairman*
Jeff Trimble, *Vice Pres*
Mike McDermott, *Prdtn Mgr*
▲ EMP: 41
SALES (est): 8.9MM **Privately Held**
WEB: www.eternaltechcorp.com
SIC: 3674 Thin film circuits; semiconductor
diodes & rectifiers
PA: Eternal Materials Co., Ltd.
No. 578, Jiangong Rd.
Kaohsiung City 80778

(G-12804)
EXPRESSWAY PALLET INC
14412 Clearcreek Pl (23834-5828)
PHONE....................................804 231-6177
Delores Carter, *President*
Robert Carter, *Vice Pres*
EMP: 11
SQ FT: 30,000
SALES (est): 1MM **Privately Held**
SIC: 2448 Pallets, wood & wood with metal

(G-12805)
HILL PHOENIX INC
Also Called: Display Case, Plant 2
1925 Ruffin Mill Rd (23834-5937)
PHONE....................................804 317-6882
Monica Knight, *Buyer*
Melanie Sandford, *Analyst*
EMP: 160
SALES (corp-wide): 7.1B **Publicly Held**
WEB: www.hillphoenix.com
SIC: 3585 Refrigeration equipment, com-
plete
HQ: Hill Phoenix, Inc.
2016 Gees Mill Rd Ne
Conyers GA 30013

(G-12806)
HILL PHOENIX INC
1925 Ruffin Mill Rd (23834-5937)
PHONE....................................804 317-6882
EMP: 10
SALES (corp-wide): 7.1B **Publicly Held**
WEB: www.hillphoenix.com
SIC: 3585 Refrigeration equipment, com-
plete
HQ: Hill Phoenix, Inc.
2016 Gees Mill Rd Ne
Conyers GA 30013

(G-12807)
HILL PHOENIX INC
Also Called: AMS Group - Audubon
1925 Ruffin Mill Rd (23834-5937)
PHONE....................................712 563-4623
EMP: 2
SALES (corp-wide): 7.7B **Publicly Held**
SIC: 3533 Mfg Oil/Gas Field Machinery
HQ: Hill Phoenix, Inc.
2016 Gees Mill Rd Ne
Conyers GA 30013
770 285-3100

(G-12808)
HILL PHOENIX INC
Also Called: Display Case Main Plant
1925 Ruffin Mill Rd (23834-5937)
PHONE....................................804 526-4455
Tomas Sanchez, *Opers Mgr*
Ariann Hugee, *Sales Staff*

Jerry L Simicsak, *Manager*
Gil Ethridge, *Info Tech Dir*
Chris Woods, *Technology*
EMP: 160
SALES (corp-wide): 7.1B **Publicly Held**
WEB: www.hillphoenix.com
SIC: 3585 Refrigeration & heating equip-
ment
HQ: Hill Phoenix, Inc.
2016 Gees Mill Rd Ne
Conyers GA 30013

(G-12809)
**HONEYWELL INTERNATIONAL
INC**
15801 Woods Edge Rd (23834-6059)
PHONE....................................804 520-3000
Tim Swinger, *Accounts Mgr*
Joseph Lwupold, *Branch Mgr*
Betty Vasquez, *Manager*
EMP: 208
SALES (corp-wide): 36.7B **Publicly Held**
WEB: www.honeywell.com
SIC: 2824 Nylon fibers; polyester fibers
PA: Honeywell International Inc.
300 S Tryon St
Charlotte NC 28202
704 627-6200

(G-12810)
IBM PHILIP MORRIS
16000 Walthall Indus Pkwy (23834-6002)
PHONE....................................405 600-7997
EMP: 2
SALES (est): 85.9K **Privately Held**
SIC: 3571 Electronic computers

(G-12811)
INFOCUS COATINGS INC
16053 Continental Blvd (23834-5900)
P.O. Box 2606, Surf City NC (28445-0029)
PHONE....................................804 520-1573
Kimberly Tutton, *President*
Shay Turron, *Vice Pres*
EMP: 3 EST: 2009
SQ FT: 4,000
SALES (est): 523.1K **Privately Held**
WEB: www.infocuscoatings.com
SIC: 3851 Lens coating, ophthalmic

(G-12812)
LAVISH NICOLE LLC
2609 Amherst Ridge Way (23834-5387)
PHONE....................................804 386-7556
Ashley Nicholas, *Mng Member*
EMP: 1
SALES (est): 24K **Privately Held**
SIC: 3911 5944 Jewelry, precious metal;
jewelry stores

(G-12813)
**MACHINE TOOL TECHNOLOGY
LLC**
Also Called: Richmond Tooling
1830 Ruffin Mill Cir A (23834-5927)
PHONE....................................804 520-4173
EMP: 13
SALES (est): 923.9K **Privately Held**
WEB: www.richmondtooling.com
SIC: 3612 3599 7539 3089 Machine tool
transformers; machine shop, jobbing & re-
pair; machine shop, automotive; injection
molding of plastics

(G-12814)
**MARYLAND AND VIRGINIA MILK
PR**
Marva Maid Dairy Division
1840 Touchstone Rd (23834-5950)
PHONE....................................804 524-0959
J C Hughes, *Manager*
EMP: 50
SALES (corp-wide): 1.3B **Privately Held**
WEB: www.mdvamilk.com
SIC: 2026 5143 5451 0241 Milk process-
ing (pasteurizing, homogenizing, bottling);
dairy products, except dried or canned;
dairy products stores; milk production
PA: Maryland And Virginia Milk Producers
Cooperative Association, Incorporated
1985 Isaac Newton Sq W
Reston VA 20190
703 742-6800

(G-12815)
**MGC ADVANCED POLYMERS
INC**
1100 Port Walthall Dr (23834-5917)
PHONE....................................804 520-7800
Hisashi Shimazaki, *President*
Susanna Chait, *Corp Secy*
Jonathan Blair, *Prdtn Mgr*
Andrew Digrys, *Plant Engr*
Brandon Hagy, *Manager*
◆ EMP: 35
SALES (est): 9.1MM **Privately Held**
WEB: www.mapnylon.com
SIC: 2824 Nylon fibers
PA: Mitsubishi Gas Chemical Company,Inc.
2-5-2, Marunouchi
Chiyoda-Ku TKY 100-0

(G-12816)
MICHAEL A LATHAM
Also Called: Colonial Sign
16462 Jefferson Davis Hwy (23834-5453)
PHONE....................................804 835-3299
Michael A Latham, *Owner*
EMP: 2
SALES (est): 125.7K **Privately Held**
SIC: 3993 Signs & advertising specialties

(G-12817)
NEW ACTON MOBILE INDS LLC
1750 Touchstone Rd (23834-5946)
PHONE....................................804 520-7171
Bill Duval, *Branch Mgr*
EMP: 5
SALES (corp-wide): 1B **Publicly Held**
WEB: www.willscot.com
SIC: 2451 Mobile homes
HQ: New Acton Mobile Industries Llc
809 Gleneagles Ct Ste 300
Baltimore MD 21286
410 931-9100

(G-12818)
OSOJUICEE HAIR LLC
2901 Piedmont Ave (23834-5714)
PHONE....................................757 215-6555
Ahshah Martin,
EMP: 2
SALES (est): 77K **Privately Held**
SIC: 3999 Hair & hair-based products

(G-12819)
**PERFORMANCE ENGRG & MCH
CO**
14518 Fox Knoll Dr (23834-5855)
PHONE....................................804 530-5577
Michael A Minnicino, *Owner*
EMP: 1
SALES (est): 55K **Privately Held**
WEB: www.gwifm.org
SIC: 3541 Machine tools, metal cutting
type

(G-12820)
POREX CORPORATION
1625 Ashton Park Dr (23834-5907)
PHONE....................................804 518-1012
EMP: 2
SALES (corp-wide): 327.7MM **Privately
Held**
WEB: www.porex.com
SIC: 3082 3842 3841 Unsupported plas-
tics profile shapes; implants, surgical; sur-
gical & medical instruments
HQ: Porex Corporation
500 Bohannon Rd
Fairburn GA 30213
800 241-0195

(G-12821)
**POREX TECHNOLOGIES CORP
(HQ)**
Also Called: Porex Filtration Group
1625 Ashton Park Dr Ste A (23834-5907)
PHONE....................................804 524-4983
Rob Carpio, *President*
Jack Nashette, *Controller*
Julie Hill, *Executive*
◆ EMP: 250
SQ FT: 186,000

SALES (est): 115.5MM
SALES (corp-wide): 327.7MM **Privately
Held**
WEB: www.porex.com
SIC: 3081 3951 3082 2823 Unsupported
plastics film & sheet; pens & mechanical
pencils; unsupported plastics profile
shapes; cigarette tow, cellulosic fiber; cigarette filters
PA: Filtration Group Corporation
600 W 22nd St Ste 300
Oak Brook IL 60523
512 593-7999

(G-12822)
PP PAYNE INC
1625 Ashton Park Dr Ste D (23834-5907)
PHONE....................................804 518-1803
Bob Hood, *President*
EMP: 7
SALES (est): 1MM **Privately Held**
WEB: www.payne-worldwide.com
SIC: 2672 Coated & laminated paper

(G-12823)
RICHMOND TIMES DISPATCH
16071 Continental Blvd (23834-5900)
PHONE....................................804 526-7205
Will Jones, *Principal*
Cheryl Magazine, *Editor*
Paige Mudd, *Editor*
EMP: 2
SALES (est): 105.5K **Privately Held**
WEB: www.richmond.com
SIC: 2711 Newspapers, publishing & print-
ing

(G-12824)
RICHMOND TOOLING INC
1830 Ruffin Mill Cir A (23834-5927)
PHONE....................................804 520-4173
Roger Mc Ginnis, *President*
Corey Gilbert, *Prgrmr*
Elizabeth Mc Ginnis, *Admin Sec*
EMP: 13
SQ FT: 7,200
SALES (est): 2.2MM **Privately Held**
WEB: www.richmondtooling.com
SIC: 3544 Special dies & tools

(G-12825)
S P KINNEY ENGINEERS INC
16301 Jefferson Davis Hwy (23834-5311)
PHONE....................................804 520-4700
Larry Schaffer, *Branch Mgr*
Mike Majersky, *Technical Staff*
EMP: 10
SALES (corp-wide): 5.5MM **Privately
Held**
WEB: www.spkinney.com
SIC: 3569 Filters
PA: S. P. Kinney Engineers, Inc.
143 1st Ave
Carnegie PA 15106
412 276-4600

(G-12826)
SABRA DIPPING COMPANY LLC
15900 Sabra Way (23834-5935)
PHONE....................................804 518-2000
Joseph Johnston, *Engineer*
Marcus Rice, *Engineer*
Deborah Wall, *Finance*
Christine Seaman, *Manager*
EMP: 30 **Privately Held**
WEB: www.sabra.com
SIC: 2099 5148 Salads, fresh or refriger-
ated; vegetables
PA: Sabra Dipping Company, Llc
777 Westchester Ave Fl 3
White Plains NY 10604

(G-12827)
SABRA GO MEDITERRANEAN
15881 Sabra Way (23834-5929)
PHONE....................................804 518-2000
Yossi Ciment, *Director*
Allen Tate, *Technician*
EMP: 3
SALES (est): 263.4K **Privately Held**
SIC: 2099 Food preparations

(G-12828)
SUN CHEMICAL CORPORATION
16000 Continental Blvd (23834-5900)
PHONE....................................804 524-3888

▲ = Import ▼=Export
◆ =Import/Export

Dana Mohr, *Research*
Tim Townsend, *Manager*
Kenny Stuckey, *Manager*
EMP: 50 **Privately Held**
WEB: www.sunchemical.com
SIC: 2893 Printing ink
HQ: Sun Chemical Corporation
35 Waterview Blvd Ste 100
Parsippany NJ 07054
973 404-6000

(G-12829)
XYMID LLC
1918 Ruffin Mill Rd (23834-5913)
PHONE.................................804 744-5229
Matt Miller, *Plant Mgr*
EMP: 12
SALES (corp-wide): 4.6MM **Privately Held**
WEB: www.xymidllc.com
SIC: 2394 2732 Cloth, drop (fabric): made from purchased materials; book printing
PA: Xymid, Llc
5141 Craig Rath Blvd
Midlothian VA 23112
804 423-5798

(G-12830)
ZIMA-PACK LLC
2101 Pine Forest Dr (23834-5384)
PHONE.................................804 372-0707
Adriana Zimbardo, *Managing Prtnr*
Mariano Marannano, *Partner*
EMP: 6
SALES (est): 3MM **Privately Held**
WEB: www.zimapack.com
SIC: 3565 Packaging machinery

South Chesterfield
Petersburg City County

(G-12831)
BEATRICE AURTHUR
Also Called: Sweet Bea Naturals
20402 Stonewood Manor Dr (23803-1776)
PHONE.................................347 420-5612
Beatrice Arthur, *Owner*
EMP: 1
SALES (est): 23K **Privately Held**
SIC: 2841 7389 Textile soap;

(G-12832)
BURLEY HOLT LANGFORD III LLC
5754 Fox Maple Ter (23803-2238)
PHONE.................................804 712-7172
Burley Langford III, *Principal*
EMP: 2 EST: 2016
SALES (est): 87.9K **Privately Held**
SIC: 3589 High pressure cleaning equipment

(G-12833)
COUNTER EFFECTS INC
20300 Little Rd (23803-1433)
PHONE.................................804 451-9016
Gregory L Elko, *Principal*
EMP: 3
SALES (est): 299.5K **Privately Held**
SIC: 3131 Counters

(G-12834)
ED WALKERS REPAIR SERVICES
10073 River Rd (23803-1024)
PHONE.................................804 590-1198
Ed Walker, *Owner*
EMP: 1 EST: 1993
SALES (est): 78.4K **Privately Held**
SIC: 3541 Machine tool replacement & repair parts, metal cutting types

(G-12835)
HIPKINS HORTICULTURE CO LLC
10500 Chesdin Ridge Dr (23803-1049)
PHONE.................................804 926-7116
Daniel Hipkins,
EMP: 3
SQ FT: 1,200
SALES (est): 285K **Privately Held**
SIC: 3524 Lawn & garden equipment

(G-12836)
JAMES ASSOCIATES I LLC
8100 Hickory Rd (23803-1361)
PHONE.................................804 590-2620
EMP: 2
SALES (est): 67K **Privately Held**
SIC: 2339 Women's & misses' outerwear

(G-12837)
MATOACA SPECIALTY ARMS INC
21411 Hampton Ave (23803-2267)
PHONE.................................804 590-2749
Donald Kirkland, *Owner*
EMP: 3
SALES (est): 213.4K **Privately Held**
SIC: 3484 Guns (firearms) or gun parts, 30 mm. & below

(G-12838)
MODERN GRAPHIX
16336 Chinook Dr (23803-1102)
PHONE.................................804 590-1303
John Longest, *Principal*
EMP: 2
SALES (est): 120.1K **Privately Held**
WEB: www.modern-graphix.com
SIC: 2752 Commercial printing, lithographic

(G-12839)
SIGNATURE PUBLISHING LLC
20209 Shire Oak Dr (23803-1420)
PHONE.................................757 348-9692
EMP: 1
SALES (est): 54K **Privately Held**
SIC: 2731 7389 Books-Publishing/Printing Business Services At Non-Commercial Site

(G-12840)
SMITH & SMITH COMMERCIAL HOOD
20117 Shire Oak Dr (23803-1418)
PHONE.................................804 605-0311
Veena Sherice Smith, *Administration*
Veena Smith,
EMP: 2
SALES (est): 66.6K **Privately Held**
SIC: 7692 7349 Welding repair; building maintenance services

South Hill
Mecklenburg County

(G-12841)
AEC VIRGINIA LLC
Berger Sfety Txtles Airbag Div
1556 Montgomery St (23970-3919)
PHONE.................................434 447-7629
Earl Crouch, *Senior VP*
EMP: 120
SQ FT: 150,000
SALES (corp-wide): 152.7MM **Privately Held**
WEB: www.aecnarrowfabrics.com
SIC: 2241 Narrow fabric mills
HQ: Aec Virginia, Llc
32056 E Cir
Boykins VA 23827

(G-12842)
ARTISAN CONCRETE DESIGNS INC
825 Marrow St (23970-2807)
PHONE.................................434 321-3423
EMP: 2
SALES (est): 62.6K **Privately Held**
WEB: www.artisanconcreteva.com
SIC: 3241 Cement, hydraulic

(G-12843)
B & E TRANSIT MIX INC
604 Locust St (23970-3024)
P.O. Box 427 (23970-0427)
PHONE.................................434 447-7331
Jamie A Barker, *President*
Eva Bass, *Admin Sec*
EMP: 7
SQ FT: 1,200
SALES (est): 1MM **Privately Held**
SIC: 3273 Ready-mixed concrete

(G-12844)
BGF INDUSTRIES INC
179 Butts St (23970-3322)
PHONE.................................434 447-2210
Dean Marion, *Plant Mgr*
Thomas Mann, *Manager*
EMP: 100
SALES (corp-wide): 2.6MM **Privately Held**
WEB: www.bgf.com
SIC: 2221 2241 Glass broadwoven fabrics; narrow fabric mills
HQ: Bgf Industries, Inc.
230 Slayton Ave 1a
Danville VA 24540
843 537-3172

(G-12845)
C&K CUSTOM EMBROIDERY & A
10826 Highway One (23970-5202)
PHONE.................................434 447-2987
Kenneth Pitts, *Principal*
EMP: 1
SALES (est): 66.8K **Privately Held**
WEB: www.ckemb.com
SIC: 2395 Embroidery & art needlework

(G-12846)
CAPITAL IDEAS PRESS
Also Called: CIP Imprintables
312 Hodges St (23970-3235)
PHONE.................................434 447-6377
Delores Luster, *Owner*
EMP: 1
SALES (est): 18K **Privately Held**
WEB: www.powerhouseenergyrentals.com
SIC: 2759 Commercial printing

(G-12847)
COLEMAN & SONS TRUCKING LLC
121 Quail Springs Ct (23970-1235)
PHONE.................................434 247-1011
Demetrio Coleman,
EMP: 1
SALES (est): 75K **Privately Held**
SIC: 3537 Trucks: freight, baggage, etc.: industrial, except mining

(G-12848)
DOGWOOD GRAPHICS
105 Mccracken St (23970-2717)
PHONE.................................434 447-6004
Brian Santore,
EMP: 4
SQ FT: 3,000
SALES (est): 176.1K **Privately Held**
WEB: www.dogwoodgraphics.com
SIC: 2752 Commercial printing, offset; advertising posters, lithographed

(G-12849)
DOGWOOD GRAPHICS INC
105 Mccracken St (23970-2717)
P.O. Box 746 (23970-0746)
PHONE.................................434 447-6004
Glenn Allen, *President*
Robin Allen, *Vice Pres*
EMP: 5
SQ FT: 800
SALES (est): 484K **Privately Held**
WEB: www.dogwoodgraphics.com
SIC: 2752 Commercial printing, offset

(G-12850)
FELTON BROTHERS TRNST MIX INC
1241 Plank Rd (23970-3507)
P.O. Box 223 (23970-0223)
PHONE.................................434 447-3778
Hill Felton, *Owner*
EMP: 6
SALES (corp-wide): 3.3MM **Privately Held**
WEB: www.feltonbrothers.com
SIC: 3273 Ready-mixed concrete
PA: Felton Brothers Transit Mix, Incorporated
1 Edmunds St
South Boston VA 24592
434 572-2665

(G-12851)
GLOBAL SAFETY TEXTILES LLC (DH)
1556 Montgomery St (23970-3919)
PHONE.................................434 447-7629
Christopher Divine, *CEO*
Frank Goehring, *President*
Michael Ambler, *COO*
Uwe Zimmermann, *COO*
Gustavo Dominguez, *Vice Pres*
▲ **EMP:** 98
SALES (est): 548.1MM **Privately Held**
WEB: www.southhillva.org
SIC: 3714 2211 3496 Motor vehicle parts & accessories; automotive fabrics, cotton; miscellaneous fabricated wire products
HQ: Global Safety Textiles Gmbh
Hollsteiner Str. 25
Maulburg 79689
762 268-8460

(G-12852)
INTERNATIONAL VENEER CO INC (HQ)
Also Called: Ivc
1551 Montgomery St (23970-3920)
PHONE.................................434 447-7100
Sergio Colombo, *Ch of Bd*
Pitt Neukirchner, *President*
Howerton H Tyler, *Corp Secy*
Roberto Palvarini, *Vice Pres*
Don Williams, *Purch Mgr*
◆ **EMP:** 35
SQ FT: 165,000
SALES (est): 25MM **Privately Held**
WEB: www.ivcusa.com
SIC: 2435 Hardwood veneer & plywood

(G-12853)
IVC-USA INC (PA)
1551 Montgomery St (23970-3920)
PHONE.................................434 447-7100
Scott Edwards, *President*
O C Edwards, *President*
Tim Neukirchner, *General Mgr*
Kevin Walker, *General Mgr*
Tyler Howerton, *Corp Secy*
EMP: 2
SQ FT: 165,000
SALES (est): 28.8MM **Privately Held**
WEB: www.ivcusa.com
SIC: 2435 Veneer stock, hardwood

(G-12854)
JKS CREATION
729 Marrow St (23970-2805)
PHONE.................................804 357-5709
Jason Smith,
EMP: 2
SALES (est): 20K **Privately Held**
SIC: 2759 Laser printing

(G-12855)
KD CARTRIDGES
221b Smith St (23970-2907)
PHONE.................................434 865-3328
▲ **EMP:** 1
SALES: 30K **Privately Held**
SIC: 3356 Nonferrous Rolling And Drawing, Nec

(G-12856)
LEGACY VULCAN LLC
Also Called: Mecklenburg Quarry
1261 Skyline Rd (23970-6126)
PHONE.................................434 447-4696
Bill Stevenson, *Manager*
EMP: 4 **Publicly Held**
WEB: www.vulcanmaterials.com
SIC: 3273 Ready-mixed concrete
HQ: Legacy Vulcan, Llc
1200 Urban Center Dr
Vestavia AL 35242
205 298-3000

(G-12857)
NMB METALS
850 Locust St (23970-3751)
PHONE.................................434 584-0027
EMP: 3 EST: 2014
SALES (est): 206.7K **Privately Held**
SIC: 3369 Nonferrous foundries

(G-12858)
REX MATERIALS INC
Also Called: Rex Materials of Verginia
601 Bailey St (23970-3923)
PHONE.................................434 447-7659
Brad Valentine, *Manager*
EMP: 50
SALES (corp-wide): 16.5MM **Privately Held**
WEB: www.rexmaterials.com
SIC: 3297 Nonclay refractories
PA: Rex Materials, Inc.
　1600 Brewer Rd
　Howell MI 48855
　517 223-3787

(G-12859)
REX ROTO CORPORATION
601 Bailey St (23970-3923)
PHONE.................................434 447-6854
Rick Faulconer, *Branch Mgr*
EMP: 50
SALES (corp-wide): 14MM **Privately Held**
WEB: www.rexmaterials.com
SIC: 2899 Chemical preparations
PA: Rex Roto Corporation
　5600 E Grand River Rd
　Fowlerville MI 48836
　517 223-3787

(G-12860)
SIMMONS LOGGING INC
3006 Brickland Rd (23970-7330)
PHONE.................................434 676-1202
Simmons Jr Victor W, *President*
Victor Simmons, *President*
Nicole Simmons, *Manager*
EMP: 8
SALES (est): 863.3K **Privately Held**
SIC: 2411 Logging camps & contractors

(G-12861)
SOUTHERNLY SWEET TEES
120 S Mecklenburg Ave (23970-2623)
PHONE.................................434 447-6572
Tonja Pearce, *Principal*
EMP: 2
SALES (est): 134.2K **Privately Held**
SIC: 2759 Screen printing

(G-12862)
TRUSWOOD INC
813 Hillcrest Rd (23970-3017)
PHONE.................................434 447-6565
Kerry Roberts, *Manager*
Robert Maddox, *Manager*
EMP: 20
SALES (corp-wide): 20.3MM **Privately Held**
WEB: www.truswood.com
SIC: 2439 Trusses, wooden roof; trusses, except roof: laminated lumber
PA: Truswood, Inc.
　8816 Running Oak Dr
　Raleigh NC 27617
　800 473-8787

(G-12863)
VQC INC
1 Northside Indus Park (23970)
P.O. Box 975 (23970-0975)
PHONE.................................434 447-5091
John Mc Aden Jr, *President*
John W Mc Aden Sr, *Chairman*
Stephanie Lewis, *Plant Mgr*
Sybil Mc Farland, *Treasurer*
Donna Adams, *Asst Sec*
▼ EMP: 120
SQ FT: 63,000
SALES (est): 10MM
SALES (corp-wide): 14.9MM **Privately Held**
WEB: www.vqcinc.com
SIC: 2391 2392 Draperies, plastic & textile: from purchased materials; bedspreads & bed sets: made from purchased materials
PA: Virginia Quilting, Inc.
　100 S Main St
　La Crosse VA 23950
　434 757-1809

(G-12864)
WOMACK PUBLISHING CO INC
Also Called: South Hill Enterprise
914 W Danville St (23970-3602)
P.O. Box 60 (23970-0060)
PHONE.................................434 447-3178
Tom Spargur, *Manager*
EMP: 16
SALES (corp-wide): 33.3MM **Privately Held**
WEB: www.womackpublishing.com
SIC: 2711 Newspapers: publishing only, not printed on site
PA: Womack Publishing Co Inc
　28 N Main St
　Chatham VA 24531
　434 432-2791

South Prince George
Petersburg City County

(G-12865)
BRANDON ENTERPRISES
16305 Lanier Rd (23805-8371)
PHONE.................................804 895-3338
Brandon Clementes, *Owner*
EMP: 3 **Privately Held**
SIC: 3715 Semitrailers for missile transportation

(G-12866)
PMC LOGISTICS LLC
2500 Maury Rd (23805-8007)
PHONE.................................804 414-8400
Nathaniel Patrick Crutcher,
EMP: 2
SALES (est): 95.5K **Privately Held**
SIC: 3537 Trucks: freight, baggage, etc.: industrial, except mining

South Riding
Loudoun County

(G-12867)
CATERPILLAR CORNER LLC
43486 Mink Meadows St (20152-2503)
PHONE.................................703 939-1798
EMP: 2
SALES (est): 83.9K **Privately Held**
SIC: 3531 Construction machinery

(G-12868)
INFOBASE PUBLISHERS INC
25050 Riding Plz Ste 13 (20152-5925)
PHONE.................................703 327-8470
Stuart McCutchan, *President*
Monica McCutchan, *Human Res Dir*
Michael McManus, *Marketing Staff*
John Morris, *Software Dev*
David Leary, *Director*
EMP: 12
SQ FT: 1,200
SALES (est): 1.3MM **Privately Held**
WEB: www.dacis.com
SIC: 2741 7389 Newsletter publishing;

(G-12869)
PARADYM INDUSTRIES INC
25388 Whippoorwill Ter (20152-6683)
PHONE.................................703 424-6930
EMP: 2
SALES (est): 91.9K **Privately Held**
SIC: 3999 Manufacturing industries

(G-12870)
ROMA SFTWR SYSTEMS GROUP INC
25227 Bald Eagle Ter (20152-6691)
PHONE.................................703 437-1579
Rajesh A Singh, *Principal*
EMP: 2
SALES (est): 155.3K **Privately Held**
SIC: 7372 Prepackaged software

(G-12871)
VIRTUAL NTWRK CMMNICATIONS INC
25643 South Village Dr (20152-6339)
PHONE.................................571 445-0306
Mohan Tammisetti, *CEO*
EMP: 1

SALES (est): 98.7K **Privately Held**
WEB: www.virtualnetcom.com
SIC: 3663 Airborne radio communications equipment

Spencer
Henry County

(G-12872)
CHARLES W BRINEGAR ENTERPRISE
2197 George Taylor Rd (24165-3307)
PHONE.................................276 634-6934
Stephen Charles W Brinegar, *President*
Charles W Brinegar, *President*
Pamlea Martin Brinegar, *Corp Secy*
Steven Brian Brinegar, *Vice Pres*
EMP: 8
SALES (est): 830K **Privately Held**
SIC: 2421 Sawmills & planing mills, general

(G-12873)
HODGES SHEET METAL LLC
3134 Golf Course Rd (24165-3493)
PHONE.................................276 957-5344
Frank Hodges, *Mng Member*
Tammy Hodges,
EMP: 2
SQ FT: 1,500
SALES (est): 150K **Privately Held**
WEB: www.hism.us
SIC: 3444 Sheet metalwork

(G-12874)
REA BOYS LOGGING & EQUIP
639 Log Manor Rd (24165-3208)
PHONE.................................276 957-4935
Bernard K REA, *Owner*
EMP: 2
SALES (est): 135.2K **Privately Held**
SIC: 2411 Logging camps & contractors

(G-12875)
WILLIAMS LOGGING AND CHIPPING
2737 Vrgnia N Carolina Rd (24165)
PHONE.................................276 694-8077
Frank Williams, *President*
Sean Williams, *Vice Pres*
EMP: 11
SALES (est): 1.5MM **Privately Held**
SIC: 2411 Wood chips, produced in the field

Sperryville
Rappahannock County

(G-12876)
ANTIMICROBIAL THERAPY INC
11771 Lee Hwy (22740-2125)
P.O. Box 276 (22740-0276)
PHONE.................................540 987-9480
Jeb Sanford, *President*
Scott Kelly, *Vice Pres*
Philip A Sanford, *Vice Pres*
Dianne Sanford, *Treasurer*
Jonathan Robinson, *Technology*
EMP: 4
SALES (est): 412.2K **Privately Held**
WEB: www.sanfordguide.com
SIC: 2731 Books: publishing only

(G-12877)
COPPER FOX DIST ENTPS LLC
9 River Ln (22740-2147)
PHONE.................................540 987-8554
Richard D Wasmund Jr, *Partner*
Sean McCaskey, *Manager*
EMP: 11
SALES (est): 1.8MM **Privately Held**
WEB: www.copperfoxdistillery.com
SIC: 2085 5169 5182 Bourbon whiskey; corn whiskey; gin (alcoholic beverage); rye whiskey; detergents & soaps, except specialty cleaning; neutral spirits

(G-12878)
IRON BRICK ASSOCIATES LLC (PA)
Also Called: Ironbrick
362 Old Hollow Rd (22740-2026)
PHONE.................................703 288-3874
Kevin P Murphy, *CEO*
William O Maxwell, *CFO*
Laura Frost, *Accountant*
Chris Maughan, *Manager*
Courtney Ibrahimi, *Executive Asst*
EMP: 30
SQ FT: 6,901
SALES (est): 67.3MM **Privately Held**
WEB: www.ironbrick.com
SIC: 3571 3574 3572 5045 Electronic computers; data processing & preparation; computer storage devices; computers, peripherals & software; engineering services; computer integrated systems design

(G-12879)
RICHARD PRICE
98 Swindler Hollow Rd (22740-2006)
PHONE.................................804 731-7270
Richard Price, *Principal*
EMP: 1
SALES (est): 54.1K **Privately Held**
WEB: www.guernicamag.com
SIC: 2431 Millwork

Spotsylvania
Spotsylvania County

(G-12880)
710 ESSENTIALS LLC
6901 Countryside Ln (22551-5894)
PHONE.................................540 748-4393
Sharon Purdy,
EMP: 2
SALES (est): 108.8K **Privately Held**
WEB: www.710essentials.com
SIC: 3999 2899 5999 Candles; oils & essential oils; candle shops

(G-12881)
ADVANCED CARBIDE TOOL COMPANY
6802 Lismore Ln (22551-8845)
PHONE.................................540 582-3289
Thomas Bornimier, *Branch Mgr*
EMP: 1 **Privately Held**
WEB: www.advancedcarbide.com
SIC: 3599 Machine shop, jobbing & repair
PA: Advanced Carbide Tool Company
　1385 Industrial Blvd
　Southampton PA 18966

(G-12882)
ALEXIS MYA PUBLISHING LLC
119 Broadfield Ln (22553-1816)
PHONE.................................540 479-2727
N Brown, *President*
EMP: 4
SALES (est): 325.9K **Privately Held**
WEB: www.yourmilitary.com
SIC: 2741 Miscellaneous publishing

(G-12883)
ANN J KITE
8303 Hancock Rd (22553-3513)
PHONE.................................540 656-3070
Ann J Kite, *Principal*
EMP: 2 EST: 2012
SALES (est): 107.2K **Privately Held**
SIC: 3944 Kites

(G-12884)
ANNA LAKE WINERY INC
5621 Courthouse Rd (22551-6100)
PHONE.................................540 895-5085
Willard Heidig, *President*
Ann L Heidig, *Corp Secy*
Jeffrey A Heidig, *Vice Pres*
EMP: 4
SQ FT: 5,000
SALES (est): 407K **Privately Held**
WEB: www.lawinery.com
SIC: 2084 5812 Wines; eating places

▲ = Import ▼=Export
◆ =Import/Export

(G-12885)
CHEWNING LUMBER COMPANY (PA)
11252 Post Oak Rd (22551-5043)
PHONE...................................540 895-5158
Fannie Chewning, *Owner*
EMP: 22 EST: 1965
SQ FT: 2,000
SALES (est): 730K **Privately Held**
SIC: 2421 5399 5411 Sawmills & planing mills, general; country general stores; grocery stores

(G-12886)
CUSTOM PERFORMANCE INC
12631 Herndon Rd (22553-4036)
PHONE...................................540 972-3632
Gabriell Picard, *President*
EMP: 3
SALES (est): 255.2K **Privately Held**
SIC: 2389 Apparel & accessories

(G-12887)
DEFENSE DOGS LLC
10411 Mastin Ln (22551-3444)
PHONE...................................540 895-5611
EMP: 3 EST: 2018
SALES (est): 232.6K **Privately Held**
SIC: 3812 Defense systems & equipment

(G-12888)
EMBROIDERY -N- BEYOND LLC
11413 Chivalry Chase Ln (22551-8921)
PHONE...................................540 972-4333
Maria Bretherick, *Principal*
EMP: 1
SALES (est): 43.8K **Privately Held**
SIC: 2395 Embroidery & art needlework

(G-12889)
EVERETT JONES LUMBER CORP
7437 Courthouse Rd (22551-2704)
PHONE...................................540 582-5655
Everett B Jones Jr, *President*
Shirley B Jones, *Corp Secy*
Hunter Jones, *Vice Pres*
EMP: 18
SQ FT: 5,000
SALES (est): 2.4MM **Privately Held**
SIC: 2421 Lumber: rough, sawed or planed

(G-12890)
FINAL TOUCH CABINETRY
11411 Post Oak Rd (22551-5050)
PHONE...................................540 895-5776
Clifford P Keating, *Administration*
EMP: 2
SALES (est): 163.7K **Privately Held**
WEB: www.finaltouchcabinetry.com
SIC: 2434 Wood kitchen cabinets

(G-12891)
GIRLS WITH CRABS LLC
6910 Fox Ridge Rd (22551-2927)
PHONE...................................540 623-9502
Alexandra Cushing,
EMP: 3
SALES (est): 108K **Privately Held**
WEB: www.vancleveseafood.com
SIC: 2741 5149 Miscellaneous publishing; seasonings, sauces & extracts

(G-12892)
H&H HAULING LLC
10610 Mockingbird Ln (22553-7759)
PHONE...................................540 273-9109
Yvonne Estelle Parker,
EMP: 2
SALES (est): 100K **Privately Held**
SIC: 3799 Transportation equipment

(G-12893)
HAIRFIELD LUMBER CORPORATION
Also Called: H & H Industries
4910 Courthouse Rd (22551-6384)
P.O. Box 5, Mineral (23117-0005)
PHONE...................................540 967-2042
Alfred Hairfield, *CEO*
Alfred H Hairfield, *CEO*
Jeffery J Hairfield, *President*
Berta J Hairfield, *Vice Pres*
Hairfield Berta Jane, *Vice Pres*
EMP: 19

SQ FT: 20,000
SALES (est): 1.7MM **Privately Held**
SIC: 2421 Sawmills & planing mills, general

(G-12894)
HIGHWHEEL WOODWORKS
6708 Holladay Ln (22551-2658)
PHONE...................................540 287-8575
EMP: 1
SALES (est): 54.1K **Privately Held**
SIC: 2431 Mfg Millwork

(G-12895)
HOME FX
12709 Plantation Dr (22551-8039)
PHONE...................................540 455-5269
Howard Jerahmi, *Principal*
EMP: 2
SALES (est): 133.5K **Privately Held**
SIC: 3651 Electronic kits for home assembly: radio, TV, phonograph

(G-12896)
I & M WELDING INC
6301 Tree Haven Ln (22551-2916)
PHONE...................................540 907-3775
Lucas E Ridenour, *Administration*
EMP: 1
SALES (est): 52K **Privately Held**
SIC: 7692 Welding repair

(G-12897)
INTEGRATED DESIGN SOLUTIONS
Also Called: IDS Manufacturing
7916 Twin Oaks Dr (22551-2918)
PHONE...................................540 735-5424
Tammy Heflin, *Owner*
EMP: 10
SALES (est): 413.3K **Privately Held**
SIC: 3499 Fabricated metal products

(G-12898)
INTELLGENT PWR A SOLUTIONS INC
Also Called: Ipas
11916 Sawhill Blvd (22553-3650)
PHONE...................................540 429-6177
William John Elliott Jr, *President*
EMP: 3
SALES (est): 1,000K **Privately Held**
WEB: www.intelligentpowerandair.com
SIC: 3564 Blowers & fans

(G-12899)
IRON LADY PRESS LLC
6100 Sunlight Mountain Rd (22553-4499)
PHONE...................................540 898-7310
EMP: 2
SALES (est): 50K **Privately Held**
SIC: 2741 Miscellaneous publishing

(G-12900)
J J E ENTERPRISE HOLDINGS LLC
10313 Litchfield Dr (22553-4483)
PHONE...................................410 703-9241
Joseph Edmondson, *CEO*
EMP: 1
SALES (est): 69.6K **Privately Held**
WEB:
www.takingitpersonallypromotions.com
SIC: 2678 3951 7319 Stationery products; pens & mechanical pencils; poster advertising service, except outdoor; transit advertising services; media buying service

(G-12901)
LESSON PORTAL LLC
10612 Edinburgh Dr (22553-1735)
PHONE...................................540 455-3546
Chris Hoovler,
EMP: 1
SALES (est): 17K **Privately Held**
SIC: 7372 Application computer software

(G-12902)
LITTLE KING PUBLISHING
10703 Heather Greens Ct (22553-1718)
PHONE...................................540 809-0291
EMP: 1
SALES (est): 37.5K **Privately Held**
SIC: 2741 Miscellaneous publishing

(G-12903)
M S RUSSNAK INDUSTRIES LLC
13363 Post Oak Rd (22551-5439)
PHONE...................................540 848-1450
Matthew S Russnak, *Administration*
EMP: 1
SALES (est): 48K **Privately Held**
WEB: www.msrussnak.com
SIC: 3999 Manufacturing industries

(G-12904)
ME-SHOWS LLC
7614 Baileys Rd (22551-5069)
PHONE...................................855 637-4097
Robenius Williams, *CEO*
Larry L Williams, *Administration*
EMP: 3
SALES (est): 148.5K **Privately Held**
SIC: 2392 Scarves: table, dresser, etc., from purchased materials

(G-12905)
MENDEZ CUSTOM WOODWORKING
12531 Wilderness Park Dr (22551-8112)
PHONE...................................540 621-3849
EMP: 1 EST: 2018
SALES (est): 54.1K **Privately Held**
SIC: 2431 Millwork

(G-12906)
NEVER SAY DIE STUDIOS LLC
309 General Dr (22551-2519)
PHONE...................................478 787-1901
Samuel Ellis, *Principal*
EMP: 2 EST: 2012
SALES (est): 131.6K **Privately Held**
WEB: www.nsdstudios.com
SIC: 3544 Special dies & tools

(G-12907)
P H GLATFELTER COMPANY
11018 Cinnamon Teal Dr (22553-3656)
PHONE...................................540 548-1756
EMP: 6
SALES (corp-wide): 1.6B **Publicly Held**
SIC: 2621 Paper Mill
PA: P. H. Glatfelter Company
96 S George St Ste 520
York PA 28209
717 225-4711

(G-12908)
PAW PRINTS
8006 Avocet Way (22553-3660)
PHONE...................................540 220-2825
EMP: 2 EST: 2010
SALES (est): 110K **Privately Held**
SIC: 2752 Lithographic Commercial Printing

(G-12909)
PIGEON CREEK ALPACAS
5937 Haleys Mill Rd (22551-6357)
PHONE...................................540 894-1121
EMP: 2
SALES (est): 106.9K **Privately Held**
SIC: 2231 Alpacas, mohair: woven

(G-12910)
RAWHIDE LLC
11918 Sawhill Blvd (22553-3650)
PHONE...................................540 548-1148
Antoni H Givens, *Administration*
EMP: 2
SALES (est): 106.8K **Privately Held**
SIC: 3111 Rawhide

(G-12911)
RED DOT LASER ENGRAVING LLC
4417 Shannon Meadows Ln (22551-3107)
PHONE...................................540 842-3509
Stephen Mount, *Administration*
EMP: 1
SALES (est): 52.3K **Privately Held**
SIC: 3479 Etching & engraving

(G-12912)
RICHARDS MICHAEL MR MRS
9704 Lawyers Rd (22551-5510)
PHONE...................................540 854-5812
Michael Richards, *Owner*
▲ EMP: 1

SALES (est): 79.3K **Privately Held**
SIC: 3949 Cases, gun & rod (sporting equipment)

(G-12913)
SEAN APPLEGATE
12502 Plantation Dr (22551-8436)
PHONE...................................540 972-4779
Sean Applegate, *Owner*
EMP: 2 EST: 2016
SALES (est): 85.9K **Privately Held**
SIC: 3577 Computer peripheral equipment

(G-12914)
SHADOW DANCE PUBLISHING LTD
11514 Catharpin Rd (22553-3605)
PHONE...................................540 786-3270
Carolyn Rowland, *Owner*
EMP: 1
SALES (est): 52.2K **Privately Held**
SIC: 2741 Miscellaneous publishing

(G-12915)
SIGN CREATIONS
12501 Herndon Rd (22553-4033)
PHONE...................................540 809-2112
EMP: 1
SALES (est): 46K **Privately Held**
SIC: 3993 Signs & advertising specialties

(G-12916)
SIGNS FOR ANYTHING INC
10430 Courthouse Rd (22553-1746)
PHONE...................................540 376-7006
Christopher Frederick, *President*
EMP: 2
SALES (est): 120K **Privately Held**
WEB: www.signsforanything.com
SIC: 3993 Signs & advertising specialties

(G-12917)
STERLING ENVIRONMENTAL INC
7308 Bloomsbury Ln (22553-1945)
P.O. Box 465 (22553-0465)
PHONE...................................540 898-5079
Stephen M Shomberger, *President*
Sterling Austin, *Vice Pres*
▲ EMP: 8
SQ FT: 1,200
SALES (est): 744.8K **Privately Held**
SIC: 3593 Fluid power cylinders & actuators

(G-12918)
TLS TEES LLC
10305 Gordon Rd (22553-3725)
PHONE...................................540 455-5260
EMP: 2
SALES (est): 87.4K **Privately Held**
SIC: 2759 Screen printing

(G-12919)
TRUSS CONSTRUCTION
10411 Courthouse Rd (22553-1798)
PHONE...................................540 710-0673
Anthony Reed, *Principal*
EMP: 4
SALES (est): 189.2K **Privately Held**
SIC: 2439 Structural wood members

(G-12920)
VETERAN CUSTOMS LLC
8307 Catharpin Landing Rd (22553-3822)
PHONE...................................540 786-2157
EMP: 1
SALES: 5K **Privately Held**
SIC: 3999 Mfg Misc Products

(G-12921)
VIDEOGRAPHERS FREDERICKSBURG
9011 Judiciary Dr (22553-2547)
PHONE...................................540 582-6111
EMP: 1
SALES (est): 68.3K **Privately Held**
SIC: 2335 Wedding gowns & dresses

(G-12922)
VIRGINIA CUSTOM BUILDINGS
6329 Jefferson Davis Hwy (22551-2481)
PHONE...................................540 582-5111
EMP: 1 **Privately Held**
WEB: www.shedsandbuildings.com

SIC: 3949 Playground equipment
PA: Virginia Custom Buildings
280 Broad Street Rd
Manakin Sabot VA 23103

(G-12923)
WATSON WOOD YARD
5730 Courthouse Rd (22551-6102)
PHONE....................................540 895-0006
Ronnie Watson, *Branch Mgr*
EMP: 1 **Privately Held**
WEB: www.watsonsmulchtopsoil.com
SIC: 2499 Mulch or sawdust products,
wood
PA: Watson Wood Yard
11237 Dulin Ln
Mine Run VA 22508

(G-12924)
WOODHELVIN INC
8961 Fox Run Dr (22551-5687)
PHONE....................................540 854-6452
Wayne Ayers, *President*
Julie Ayres, *Vice Pres*
EMP: 2
SALES (est): 241.8K **Privately Held**
SIC: 2421 Lumber: rough, sawed or planed

Spout Spring
Appomattox County

(G-12925)
BDMOORE PUBLICATIONS LLC
226 Tonawanda Lake Rd (24593-2804)
PHONE....................................434 352-7581
Brian Moore, *Principal*
EMP: 2 EST: 2015
SALES (est): 69.2K **Privately Held**
SIC: 2711 Newspapers, publishing & print-
ing

(G-12926)
MOORES MACHINE CO INC
4565 Richmond Hwy (24593-9790)
PHONE....................................434 352-0000
Claude A Moore, *President*
Norma H Moore, *Corp Secy*
Norma Moore, *Admin Sec*
EMP: 10 EST: 1974
SQ FT: 9,050
SALES (est): 1.1MM **Privately Held**
WEB: www.mooresmachinecompany.com
SIC: 7692 Welding repair

(G-12927)
SHUTTER FILMS LLC
3850 Salem Rd (24593-9646)
PHONE....................................434 329-0713
Nick Mendoza,
EMP: 1
SALES (est): 56.4K **Privately Held**
SIC: 3442 Shutters, door or window: metal

(G-12928)
TURBO TELLERS
428 Snapps Mill Rd (24593-9507)
PHONE....................................812 250-1837
Daniel Rogers, *Owner*
Matthew Rust,
EMP: 1
SALES (est): 51.7K **Privately Held**
SIC: 3949 7389 Exercise equipment; busi-
ness services

Spring Grove
Surry County

(G-12929)
DEBORAH F SCARBORO
1022 Forest Ln (23881-8506)
PHONE....................................757 866-0108
Deborah Scarboro, *Owner*
EMP: 1
SALES (est): 92.5K **Privately Held**
SIC: 3089 Flower pots, plastic

(G-12930)
GREEN LEAF LOGISTICS LLC
9700 Colonial Trl W (23881-8414)
P.O. Box 174, Surry (23883-0174)
PHONE....................................757 899-0881

Paul Howell Jr, *Co-Owner*
EMP: 3 EST: 2015
SALES (est): 221K **Privately Held**
SIC: 2448 Pallets, wood

(G-12931)
**NATURES CNTRY SOAPS
CANDLE LLC**
6157 Colonial Trl W (23881-8225)
PHONE....................................757 817-9062
Tammy Duncan, *Principal*
EMP: 1 EST: 2016
SALES (est): 39.6K **Privately Held**
SIC: 3999 Candles

(G-12932)
WAYNE GARRETT LOGGING INC
Also Called: Garrett Trucking
2022 Sunken Meadow Rd (23881-8034)
PHONE....................................757 866-8472
EMP: 19
SALES (est): 1.1MM **Privately Held**
SIC: 2411 Logging

Springfield
Fairfax County

(G-12933)
1CLICK LLC
7123 Layton Dr (22150-2014)
PHONE....................................703 307-6026
Khanpheth Keopradit, *Mng Member*
EMP: 1 EST: 2014
SALES (est): 160K **Privately Held**
WEB: www.1clickmedia.us
SIC: 7372 Prepackaged software

(G-12934)
3189 APPLE RD NE LLC
9325 Castle Hill Rd (22153-3929)
PHONE....................................703 455-5989
EMP: 2
SALES (est): 126.8K **Privately Held**
SIC: 3571 Mfg Electronic Computers

(G-12935)
AFFORDABLE COMPANIES
7830 Backlick Rd Ste 404a (22150-2257)
PHONE....................................703 440-9274
Jason Fields, *Owner*
EMP: 4 EST: 2010
SALES (est): 376.9K **Privately Held**
WEB: www.affordabledoor.com
SIC: 3589 High pressure cleaning equip-
ment

(G-12936)
AFLEX PACKAGING LLC
7600 Fullerton Rd Unit C (22153-2814)
PHONE....................................571 208-9938
EMP: 2
SALES (est): 90.7K **Privately Held**
SIC: 2656 Sanitary food containers

(G-12937)
AK MILLWORK INC
7666 Fullerton Rd Ste F (22153-2818)
PHONE....................................703 337-4848
EMP: 1
SALES (est): 54.1K **Privately Held**
SIC: 2431 Millwork

(G-12938)
AL-NAFEA INC
7942 Cluny Ct Ste 0 (22153-2810)
PHONE....................................703 440-8499
▲ EMP: 3
SALES (est): 190K **Privately Held**
SIC: 2044 Rice Milling

(G-12939)
ALBAN CIRE
7244 Boudinot Dr (22150-2219)
P.O. Box 628 (22150-0628)
PHONE....................................703 455-9300
John McMichael, *Owner*
John Parks, *Partner*
EMP: 4
SQ FT: 31,374
SALES (est): 310K **Privately Held**
SIC: 3011 Automobile tires, pneumatic

(G-12940)
**ALEXANDRIA PACKAGING LLC
(PA)**
7396 Ward Park Ln (22153-2824)
PHONE....................................703 644-5550
Joe Ragans, *Mng Member*
Paul Centarian,
Peter Centarian,
EMP: 85 EST: 1972
SQ FT: 85,000
SALES (est): 4.4MM **Privately Held**
SIC: 2448 2653 2441 5113 Wood pallets
& skids; corrugated & solid fiber boxes;
nailed wood boxes & shook; shipping
supplies

(G-12941)
ALLERMORE INDUSTRIES INC
8299 Raindrop Way (22153-3810)
PHONE....................................703 537-1346
Romella Elkarzazi, *President*
EMP: 1 EST: 2013
SALES (est): 76.7K **Privately Held**
SIC: 3999 Manufacturing industries

(G-12942)
ALPHA PRINTING INC
6116 Rolling Rd Ste 301 (22152-1512)
PHONE....................................703 914-2800
EMP: 2
SALES (est): 85.9K **Privately Held**
WEB: www.alphaprintinginc.com
SIC: 3571 Electronic computers

(G-12943)
ALPHA PRINTING INC
5540 Port Royal Rd (22151-2303)
P.O. Box 11458, Alexandria (22312-0458)
PHONE....................................703 321-2071
Joseph Tucker, *President*
Zia Durrani, *Managing Dir*
EMP: 4
SQ FT: 4,000
SALES (est): 400K **Privately Held**
WEB: www.alphaprintinginc.com
SIC: 2752 Commercial printing, offset

(G-12944)
ALPHAGRAPHICS
7426 Alban Station Blvd A (22150-2331)
PHONE....................................703 866-1988
EMP: 2
SALES (est): 83.9K **Privately Held**
WEB: www.agnortheast.com
SIC: 2752 Commercial printing, litho-
graphic

(G-12945)
AMARI PUBLICATIONS
6600 Comet Cir Apt 101 (22150-4534)
PHONE....................................703 313-0174
Stephen Jackson, *Principal*
EMP: 2 EST: 2018
SALES (est): 59.2K **Privately Held**
SIC: 2741 Miscellaneous publishing

(G-12946)
AMBERTONE PRESS INC
7664 Fullerton Rd (22153-2818)
PHONE....................................703 866-7715
William Whitt, *Principal*
EMP: 2
SALES (est): 191.8K **Privately Held**
WEB: www.ambertone.com
SIC: 2741 Miscellaneous publishing

(G-12947)
AMF METAL INC
6625 Iron Pl (22151-4307)
PHONE....................................703 354-1345
Young Woo Kim, *President*
EMP: 1
SALES (est): 130K **Privately Held**
WEB: www.amfmetal.com
SIC: 3441 Fabricated structural metal

(G-12948)
AND DESIGN INC
7000c Brookfield Plz (22150-2914)
PHONE....................................703 913-0799
Andrea Leahy, *President*
EMP: 3
SQ FT: 1,200

SALES (est): 213.9K **Privately Held**
WEB: www.anddesign.com
SIC: 3993 Signs, not made in custom sign
painting shops

(G-12949)
**APPLICATION TECHNOLOGIES
INC**
7707 Tanner Robert Ct (22153-3142)
PHONE....................................703 644-0506
Aster Dawit, *CEO*
Raju Balajapalli, *President*
EMP: 9
SALES (est): 600K **Privately Held**
WEB: www.apptechs.com
SIC: 7372 7373 7371 7375 Application
computer software; systems integration
services; software programming applica-
tions; data base information retrieval

(G-12950)
APPLIED PLASMA TECH LLC
5408 Port Royal Rd Ste S (22151-2300)
PHONE....................................703 340-5545
Igor Matveev, *President*
EMP: 2
SALES (corp-wide): 608.5K **Privately
Held**
WEB: www.plasmacombustion.com
SIC: 3463 Engine or turbine forgings, non-
ferrous
PA: Applied Plasma Technologies, Llc
1729 Court Petit
Mc Lean VA 22101
703 340-5545

(G-12951)
ARTNER CORP
6096 Deer Ridge Trl (22150-1047)
PHONE....................................703 341-6333
Don Juhasz, *President*
Phil Riersgard, *Admin Sec*
EMP: 3
SQ FT: 16,000
SALES (est): 253.1K **Privately Held**
SIC: 3087 Custom compound purchased
resins

(G-12952)
ASHLAWN ENERGY LLC
6564 Loisdale Ct Ste 600 (22150-1829)
PHONE....................................703 461-3600
Gene Byron, *Director*
Norma Powell Byron,
▲ EMP: 26
SALES (est): 1.5MM **Privately Held**
WEB: www.ashlawnenergyllc.com
SIC: 3629 3691 Electronic generation
equipment; batteries, rechargeable

(G-12953)
ATLANTIC FIREPROOFING INC
5532 Hempstead Way (22151-4009)
PHONE....................................703 940-9444
Khalid Mughal, *Vice Pres*
EMP: 36 EST: 2015
SALES (est): 670.7K **Privately Held**
WEB: www.atlanticfireproofing.com
SIC: 2493 1799 1742 Insulation board,
cellular fiber; fireproofing buildings; water-
proofing; acoustical & insulation work

(G-12954)
AUTHENTIC PRODUCTS LLC
7608 Mcweadon Ln (22150-4913)
PHONE....................................703 451-5984
Brenda Turkson, *Principal*
EMP: 4
SALES (est): 136.9K **Privately Held**
WEB: www.myauthenticproducts.com
SIC: 2033 Fruit juices: concentrated, hot
pack

(G-12955)
AUTOGRIP INC
Also Called: Auto-Grip
7411 Alban Station Ct A102 (22150-2333)
PHONE....................................703 372-5520
Donald Heiby, *CEO*
Dan Hine, *Principal*
EMP: 2
SALES (est): 87.7K **Privately Held**
WEB: www.autogrip.com
SIC: 3423 Screw drivers, pliers, chisels,
etc. (hand tools)

▲ = Import ▼=Export
◆ =Import/Export

(G-12956)
AVENGER LLC
5570 Port Royal Rd Ste B (22151-2310)
PHONE.................................703 573-6445
Craig Sampson, *Branch Mgr*
EMP: 6
SALES (corp-wide): 332.1K **Privately Held**
WEB: www.avengerllc.com
SIC: 3728 Aircraft parts & equipment
PA: Avenger, Llc
148 Sportsmen St
Central Islip NY 11722
631 234-8988

(G-12957)
AVIATION TACTICAL LLC
8638 Woodview Dr (22153-1548)
PHONE.................................970 946-7027
Jeremiah Russell, *President*
EMP: 1 EST: 2015
SALES (est): 70.5K **Privately Held**
SIC: 3812 3861 Flight recorders; motion
picture apparatus & equipment; photo re-
connaissance systems; aerial cameras;
stands, camera & projector

(G-12958)
BANGKOK NOODLE
7022 Commerce St (22150-3433)
PHONE.................................703 866-1396
Richard Barthelemy, *Principal*
EMP: 8 EST: 2011
SALES (est): 574K **Privately Held**
WEB: www.bangkoknoodlehouse.com
SIC: 2098 Noodles (e.g. egg, plain &
water), dry

(G-12959)
**BASTION AND ASSOCIATES
LLC**
8801 Victoria Rd (22151-1132)
PHONE.................................703 343-5158
G Paul Jacobsen, *
EMP: 1
SALES (est): 96K **Privately Held**
WEB: www.bastionandassociates.com
SIC: 3272 Concrete products, precast

(G-12960)
BEST GRANITE & MARBLE
7608 Fullerton Rd (22153-2814)
PHONE.................................703 455-0404
Ned Sevil, *Owner*
EMP: 3
SALES (est): 170K **Privately Held**
WEB: www.best-gm.com
SIC: 3281 Granite, cut & shaped

(G-12961)
BEST MEDICAL BELGIUM INC
7643 Fullerton Rd (22153-2815)
PHONE.................................800 336-4970
Krishnan Suthanthiran, *President*
EMP: 4
SALES (est): 285K **Privately Held**
WEB: www.teambest.com
SIC: 2834 3842 Pharmaceutical prepara-
tions; surgical appliances & supplies

(G-12962)
**BEST MEDICAL INTERNATIONAL
INC (HQ)**
7643 Fullerton Rd (22153-2815)
P.O. Box 315 (22150-0315)
PHONE.................................703 451-2378
Krishnan Suthanthiran, *President*
Ruth Bergin, *Vice Pres*
Marion Speranzo, *Finance Mgr*
Rashmi Emim, *Chief Mktg Ofcr*
Craig Reed, *Director*
◆ EMP: 103
SQ FT: 10,400
SALES (est): 43MM **Privately Held**
WEB: www.teambest.com
SIC: 2834 3842 Pharmaceutical prepara-
tions; surgical appliances & supplies
PA: Best Particle Therapy, Inc.
7643 Fullerton Rd
Springfield VA 22153
703 451-2378

(G-12963)
BF MAYES ASSOC INC
7226 Willow Oak Pl (22151-1543)
PHONE.................................703 451-4994
Bryan Mayes, *Principal*
EMP: 2
SALES (est): 244.4K **Privately Held**
SIC: 3011 Tires & inner tubes

(G-12964)
BLAIR INC
7001 Loisdale Rd (22150-1904)
PHONE.................................703 922-0200
Blair Jackson, *President*
Kelly Frazier, *General Mgr*
R Scott Jackson, *Vice Pres*
Keith Hodge, *Traffic Mgr*
Emmalee Maine, *Production*
▲ EMP: 60 EST: 1960
SQ FT: 28,000
SALES (est): 7.8MM **Privately Held**
WEB: www.blairinc.com
SIC: 3993 Signs & advertising specialties

(G-12965)
BLUE RIDGE SOFTWARE
9003 Maritime Ct (22153-1625)
PHONE.................................703 912-3990
EMP: 2
SALES (est): 95.9K **Privately Held**
SIC: 7372 Prepackaged Software Services

(G-12966)
BOEING COMPANY
7700 Boston Blvd (22153-3144)
PHONE.................................703 923-4000
Samet Ayhan, *Engineer*
Charles Hebert, *Engineer*
Brenda Zuzolo, *Engineer*
Mark Anderson, *Manager*
Kellye H Franklin, *Manager*
EMP: 4518
SALES (corp-wide): 76.5B **Publicly Held**
WEB: www.boeing.com
SIC: 3721 Airplanes, fixed or rotary wing
PA: The Boeing Company
100 N Riverside Plz
Chicago IL 60606
312 544-2000

(G-12967)
**BOWHEAD INTEGRATED
SUPPORT SER**
6564 Loisdale Ct Ste 900 (22150-1822)
PHONE.................................703 413-4226
Justin Corrigan, *Principal*
Deana Wilder, *Principal*
Tim Howell, *Mfg Staff*
EMP: 1 EST: 2014
SALES: 65.2MM **Privately Held**
WEB: www.bowheadsupport.com
SIC: 3795 Tanks & tank components

(G-12968)
**BOWHEAD SYSTEMS
MANAGEMENT LLC**
6564 Loisdale Ct Ste 900 (22150-1822)
PHONE.................................703 413-4251
Cary Randolph, *General Mgr*
Christian Gant, *
EMP: 178 **Privately Held**
WEB: www.bowheadsupport.com
SIC: 2721 Periodicals: publishing only

(G-12969)
BRBG LLC
Also Called: U See App
6708 Grey Fox Dr (22152-2611)
PHONE.................................404 200-4857
Senthil Kumar, *
Stephen Travers Foster, *
EMP: 2
SALES (est): 200K **Privately Held**
SIC: 7372 7371 Application computer soft-
ware; computer software development &
applications

(G-12970)
BRIDGE TO BIZ
7406 Alban Station Ct B20 (22150-2329)
PHONE.................................703 942-6441
Christine Stinson, *President*
Christine H Stinson, *
EMP: 1

SALES (est): 41.3K **Privately Held**
SIC: 2741

(G-12971)
**CANADA DRY POTOMAC
CORPORATION**
5330 Port Royal Rd (22151-2105)
PHONE.................................703 321-6100
Richard Wolfe, *President*
EMP: 150
SALES (corp-wide): 79.2MM **Privately
Held**
WEB: www.canadadry.com
SIC: 2086 Bottled & canned soft drinks
PA: Canada Dry Potomac Corporation
3600 Pennsy Dr
Hyattsville MD 20785
301 773-5500

(G-12972)
**CANTRELL/CUTTER PRINTING
INC**
8221 Smithfield Ave (22152-3060)
PHONE.................................301 773-6340
Don Cantrell, *Principal*
EMP: 2
SALES (est): 110.7K **Privately Held**
SIC: 2752 Commercial printing, litho-
graphic

(G-12973)
CAPITAL NOODLE INC
7668 Fullerton Rd (22153-2818)
PHONE.................................703 569-3224
EMP: 10
SQ FT: 10,000
SALES (est): 981K **Privately Held**
SIC: 2098 5149 5147 5146 Mfg And
Whol Noodles

(G-12974)
CDRS LLC
Also Called: Signs By Tomorrow
7956 Twist Ln (22153-2823)
PHONE.................................703 451-7546
Rob Blumel, *
Robert C Blumel, *
Scott W Curtis, *
EMP: 5
SQ FT: 2,200
SALES (est): 725K **Privately Held**
WEB: www.signsbytomorrow.com
SIC: 3993 Signs & advertising specialties

(G-12975)
CELESTIAL CIRCUITS LLC
6105 Tobey Ct (22150-1023)
PHONE.................................703 851-2843
James Dunstan, *
EMP: 2 EST: 2012
SALES (est): 143K **Privately Held**
SIC: 3571 3812 8731 Electronic comput-
ers; aircraft/aerospace flight instruments
& guidance systems; engineering labora-
tory, except testing

(G-12976)
**CENTRAL NATIONAL-
GOTTESMAN INC**
6715b Electronic Dr (22151-4310)
PHONE.................................703 941-0810
EMP: 5
SALES (corp-wide): 3.5B **Privately Held**
WEB: www.cng-inc.com
SIC: 2679 Paper products, converted
PA: Central National Gottesman Inc.
3 Manhattanville Rd # 301
Purchase NY 10577
914 696-9000

(G-12977)
**COLUMBIA MRROR GL
GRGETOWN INC**
7101 Wimsatt Rd (22151-4005)
PHONE.................................703 333-9990
Glenn Goodreau, *President*
EMP: 4
SALES (est): 299.9K **Privately Held**
WEB: www.columbiaglassdc.com
SIC: 2519 3211 Furniture, household:
glass, fiberglass & plastic; flat glass

(G-12978)
**COMMUNICATIONS CONCEPTS
INC**
Also Called: Writings That Works Newsletter
7481 Huntsman Blvd # 720 (22153-1648)
PHONE.................................703 643-2200
John Delellis, *President*
EMP: 10
SALES (est): 568.2K **Privately Held**
WEB: www.apexawards.com
SIC: 2741 8999 Newsletter publishing; ed-
itorial service

(G-12979)
**CONTEMPORARY
WOODCRAFTS INC**
7721 Fullerton Rd (22153-2820)
PHONE.................................703 451-4257
Rob Grant, *Branch Mgr*
EMP: 1
SALES (corp-wide): 654K **Privately Held**
WEB: www.builtincabinet.com
SIC: 2434 Wood kitchen cabinets
PA: Contemporary Woodcrafts Inc
7337 Wayfarer Dr
Fairfax Station VA 22039
703 787-9711

(G-12980)
CORDIALLY YOURS
8801 Newell Ct (22153-1216)
PHONE.................................703 644-1186
Ruth Hoel, *Principal*
EMP: 1
SALES (est): 87K **Privately Held**
SIC: 2678 Stationery products

(G-12981)
CORPORATE ARMS LLC
8511 Wild Spruce Dr (22153-1843)
P.O. Box 523023 (22152-5023)
PHONE.................................800 256-5803
Thomas Walsh, *
EMP: 3
SALES (est): 164.6K **Privately Held**
SIC: 3484 Machine guns & grenade
launchers

(G-12982)
CORRINNE CALLINS
Also Called: Callico Press
7806c Harrowgate Cir (22152-3807)
PHONE.................................202 780-6233
Corrinne Callins, *Owner*
EMP: 1 EST: 2016
SALES (est): 62.3K **Privately Held**
SIC: 2741 Miscellaneous publishing

(G-12983)
COSTACAMPS-NET LLC
5760 Heming Ave (22151-2713)
PHONE.................................571 482-6858
Jose Costacamps, *CEO*
Andrea Costacamps, *
Digeo Costacamps, *
Lourdes Costacamps, *
EMP: 4
SALES (est): 367.6K **Privately Held**
WEB: www.damianifirearms.com
SIC: 3484 Guns (firearms) or gun parts, 30
mm. & below

(G-12984)
CUPCAKES BY LADYBUG LLC
8695 Bent Arrow Ct (22153-3705)
PHONE.................................571 926-9709
Donald Kendall James, *Administration*
EMP: 4 EST: 2013
SALES (est): 148.6K **Privately Held**
SIC: 2051 Bread, cake & related products

(G-12985)
CUSTOM PRINT
6621 Electronic Dr (22151)
PHONE.................................703 256-1279
EMP: 2
SALES (est): 153.6K **Privately Held**
SIC: 2752 Lithographic Commercial Print-
ing

(G-12986)
CYAN LLC
Also Called: Allegra Print & Imaging
5417b Backlick Rd (22151-3915)
PHONE.................................703 455-3000

GEOGRAPHIC

Anahita Kaviani,
EMP: 5
SQ FT: 2,800
SALES (est): 728.8K **Privately Held**
WEB: www.allegramarketingprint.com
SIC: 2752 Commercial printing, offset

(G-12987)
CYBER INTEL SOLUTIONS INC
8460 Great Lake Ln (22153-4004)
PHONE..................................571 970-2689
Carlos Williams, *President*
EMP: 2
SALES (est): 150.6K **Privately Held**
WEB: www.cyberintelsolution.com
SIC: 7372 7379 Business oriented computer software; computer related maintenance services

(G-12988)
DAVID BURNS
Also Called: Fasttrack Teaching Materials
6215 Lavell Ct (22152-1319)
PHONE..................................703 644-4612
David Burns, *Owner*
EMP: 2
SALES (est): 110K **Privately Held**
WEB: www.fasttrackteaching.com
SIC: 2741 Miscellaneous publishing

(G-12989)
DC METRO MAGAZINE
9607 Little Cobbler Ct (22015-4133)
PHONE..................................703 455-9223
EMP: 3 EST: 2015
SALES (est): 174.1K **Privately Held**
WEB: www.dcmetroplus.com
SIC: 2721 Magazines: publishing only, not printed on site

(G-12990)
DEAN INDUSTRIES INTL LLC
8114 Smithfield Ave (22152-3051)
PHONE..................................703 249-5099
Roger Dean, *Principal*
EMP: 2
SALES (est): 110.9K **Privately Held**
SIC: 3999 Manufacturing industries

(G-12991)
DIANA KHOURY & CO
Also Called: Metro Envelope
7653 Fullerton Rd Ste A (22153-2897)
PHONE..................................703 592-9110
Diana Khoury, *Ch of Bd*
Kamil Khoury, *President*
EMP: 6
SALES (est): 500K **Privately Held**
WEB: www.ohioenvelope.com
SIC: 2677 Envelopes

(G-12992)
DIRECTIONAL SIGN SERVICES INC
6419 Wainfleet Ct (22152-2432)
PHONE..................................703 568-5078
EMP: 2 EST: 2019
SALES (est): 72.6K **Privately Held**
SIC: 3993 Signs & advertising specialties

(G-12993)
DISTRICT ORTHOPEDIC APPLIANCES
7702 Backlick Rd Ste D (22150-2230)
PHONE..................................703 698-7373
Richard Guarrasi, *President*
EMP: 4
SALES (est): 478.8K **Privately Held**
SIC: 3842 Limbs, artificial; braces, orthopedic

(G-12994)
DMEDIA PRINTS
7545 Axton St (22151-2602)
PHONE..................................571 297-3287
EMP: 2 EST: 2014
SALES (est): 106.4K **Privately Held**
SIC: 2752 Lithographic Commercial Printing

(G-12995)
DREAM DOG PRODUCTIONS LLC
Also Called: C&R Publishing
9218 Cutting Horse Ct (22153-1018)
P.O. Box 4227, Woodbridge (22194-4227)
PHONE..................................703 980-0908
Colleen Pelar,
EMP: 2
SALES (est): 100K **Privately Held**
WEB: www.colleenpelar.com
SIC: 2741 Miscellaneous publishing

(G-12996)
ECOWOOD USA INC
Also Called: Ecowood Cabinetry
7801b Loisdale Rd (22150-2105)
PHONE..................................703 347-6858
Bilgehan Yalcin, *Director*
EMP: 4
SALES (est): 275.5K **Privately Held**
WEB: www.ecowoodcabinetry.com
SIC: 2434 5712 Wood kitchen cabinets; cabinet work, custom

(G-12997)
EM MILLWORK INC (PA)
7600 Fullerton Rd (22153-2814)
PHONE..................................571 344-9842
Michelle Sujin Cho, *President*
Jonathan Velasquez, *Project Mgr*
EMP: 9
SALES (est): 5.1MM **Privately Held**
SIC: 2431 Millwork

(G-12998)
ENGAGED MAGAZINE LLC
7514 Gresham St (22151-2911)
PHONE..................................703 485-4878
Doreen Tisone, *Principal*
EMP: 3
SALES (est): 181.5K **Privately Held**
WEB: www.engagedmagazine.com
SIC: 2721 Magazines: publishing only, not printed on site

(G-12999)
ENVIRO WATER
Also Called: Pure Water Tech
6141 Roxbury Ave (22152-1625)
PHONE..................................703 569-0971
Andrew Griffith, *Principal*
EMP: 1
SALES (est): 93.7K **Privately Held**
SIC: 2086 Pasteurized & mineral waters, bottled & canned

(G-13000)
EXCHANGE PUBLISHING
9248 Rockefeller Ln (22153-1104)
PHONE..................................703 644-5184
Ed Linz, *Owner*
EMP: 15 EST: 1997
SALES (est): 879K **Privately Held**
WEB: www.obitnow.com
SIC: 2731 Book publishing

(G-13001)
FALCON CONCRETE CORPORATION
6860 Commercial Dr (22151-4201)
PHONE..................................703 354-7100
EMP: 30
SALES (est): 1.7MM
SALES (corp-wide): 3.5B **Publicly Held**
SIC: 3273 Mfg Ready Mixed Concrete
HQ: Florida Rock Industries
4707 Gordon St
Jacksonville FL 32216
904 355-1781

(G-13002)
FASTSIGNS
6715 Backlick Rd Ste B (22150-2708)
PHONE..................................703 913-5300
Randall Belknap, *President*
EMP: 3
SALES (est): 234.4K **Privately Held**
WEB: www.fastsigns.com
SIC: 3993 Signs & advertising specialties

(G-13003)
FILZ BUILT BICYCLES
6117 Dorchester St (22150-2412)
PHONE..................................703 451-5582

Randolph Filz, *Owner*
EMP: 1
SALES (est): 100K **Privately Held**
SIC: 3751 7699 Bicycles & related parts; professional instrument repair services

(G-13004)
FIVE STAR MEDALS
6813 Bluecurl Cir (22152-3114)
P.O. Box 2638 (22152-0638)
PHONE..................................703 644-4974
Clare Mugno, *Owner*
EMP: 1 **Privately Held**
WEB: www.fivestarmedals.com
SIC: 2789 5094 8412 Display mounting; coins, medals & trophies; historical society

(G-13005)
FOUR LEAF PUBLISHING LLC
8550 Groveland Dr (22153-2246)
PHONE..................................703 440-1304
EMP: 1 EST: 2018
SALES (est): 37.5K **Privately Held**
SIC: 2741 Miscellaneous publishing

(G-13006)
FUDGETIME LLC
5213 Dalton Rd (22151-3728)
PHONE..................................703 462-8544
Hashim Nazarei, *Principal*
EMP: 2 EST: 2012
SALES (est): 66K **Privately Held**
SIC: 2064 Fudge (candy)

(G-13007)
GALAXY EQP MAINT SOLUTIONS INC
6807 Gillings Rd (22152-3230)
PHONE..................................703 866-0246
EMP: 2
SALES (corp-wide): 6.2MM **Privately Held**
SIC: 3531 Mfg Construction Machinery
PA: Galaxy Equipment And Maintenance Solutions, Inc.
4466 Oakdle Cres 1138
Fairfax VA

(G-13008)
GARCIA WOOD FINISHING INC
7014 Essex Ave (22150-3203)
PHONE..................................703 980-6559
David Garcia, *General Mgr*
EMP: 4
SALES (est): 233.5K **Privately Held**
SIC: 3471 Decorative plating & finishing of formed products

(G-13009)
GENERAL CRYO CORPORATION
8129 Ridge Creek Way (22153-1934)
PHONE..................................703 405-9442
Jonathan Gibbs, *Principal*
EMP: 1
SALES (est): 76.7K **Privately Held**
SIC: 3721 Aircraft

(G-13010)
GKI AEROSPACE LLC
8492 Summer Breeze Ln (22153-2518)
PHONE..................................703 451-4562
Gary Ikuma, *Principal*
EMP: 3
SALES (est): 164K **Privately Held**
SIC: 3721 Aircraft

(G-13011)
GLOBAL CONCERN INC
5503 Kempton Dr (22151-1405)
PHONE..................................703 425-5861
Gary Schofield, *Principal*
EMP: 2
SALES (est): 91.5K **Privately Held**
WEB: www.garyschofield.com
SIC: 2741 Miscellaneous publishing

(G-13012)
GOETZ PRINTING COMPANY
7939 Angus Ct (22153-2844)
P.O. Box 2130 (22152-0130)
PHONE..................................703 569-8232
Stephen P Smith, *President*
Mike Gallagher, *Vice Pres*
Craig Hendrickson, *Vice Pres*

Scott Patterson, *Vice Pres*
Harvey Loveless, *Plant Mgr*
EMP: 33
SQ FT: 14,000
SALES (est): 9.2MM **Privately Held**
WEB: www.goetzprinting.com
SIC: 2752 2789 Commercial printing, offset; bookbinding & related work

(G-13013)
GRAHAM GRAPHICS LLC
5308 Atlee Pl (22151-3402)
PHONE..................................703 220-4564
Laurie Graham, *Principal*
EMP: 1
SALES (est): 67.1K **Privately Held**
SIC: 3993 7336 Displays & cutouts, window & lobby; commercial art & graphic design; chart & graph design; graphic arts & related design; commercial art & illustration

(G-13014)
GREAT DEALS LLC
7202 Gentian Ct (22152-3845)
PHONE..................................703 915-0332
Rita Y Vargas,
EMP: 1
SALES (est): 57.3K **Privately Held**
SIC: 2541 Store & office display cases & fixtures

(G-13015)
GYROSCOPE DISC GOLF LLC
9144 Rockefeller Ln (22153-1414)
PHONE..................................703 992-3035
Michael Sullivan, *Principal*
EMP: 2
SALES (est): 77.4K **Privately Held**
SIC: 3812 Gyroscopes

(G-13016)
H & A FINE WOODWORKING (PA)
7801 Loisdale Rd (22150-2105)
PHONE..................................703 822-0006
Hasim Kockaya, *Principal*
EMP: 1
SALES (est): 195.4K **Privately Held**
WEB: www.hawoodworking.com
SIC: 2431 Millwork

(G-13017)
HAMILO LLC
7413 Calamo St (22150-4310)
P.O. Box 6182 (22150-6182)
PHONE..................................703 440-1276
Melody Wheatley, *Owner*
EMP: 1
SALES (est): 5K **Privately Held**
SIC: 3269 Figures: pottery, china, earthenware & stoneware

(G-13018)
HAWKNAD MANUFACTURING INDS INC
6193 Deer Ridge Trl (22150-1040)
PHONE..................................703 941-0444
Charles O Dankwah, *President*
Daniel Dankwah, *Director*
▼ **EMP:** 7
SQ FT: 10,106
SALES (est): 1.3MM **Privately Held**
WEB: www.clearandsmooth.com
SIC: 2844 Cosmetic preparations

(G-13019)
ICEWARP INC
6225 Brandon Ave Ste 310 (22150-2524)
PHONE..................................571 481-4611
Christopher Grady, *President*
Dan Hatter, *Sales Engr*
Chris Grady, *Manager*
Jakub Klos, *CTO*
Ladislav Goc, *Director*
EMP: 8
SALES (est): 881.6K **Privately Held**
WEB: www.icewarp.com
SIC: 7372 Prepackaged software

(G-13020)
ICT MONDIAL INC
6412 Brandon Ave (22150-2513)
PHONE..................................703 254-7416
EMP: 2

SALES (est): 118.9K **Privately Held**
WEB: www.ictmondial.com
SIC: **3861** Photographic equipment & supplies

(G-13021)
IMPRENTA PRINTING
7609 Long Pine Dr (22151-2821)
PHONE..................................703 866-0760
Emilio Sejas, *Owner*
EMP: 3
SQ FT: 2,000
SALES (est): 182.1K **Privately Held**
SIC: **2752** Commercial printing, offset

(G-13022)
IN HOUSE PRINTING
6207 Duntley Ct (22152-1906)
PHONE..................................703 913-6338
Robert Briggs, *Partner*
Tracy Briggs, *Partner*
EMP: 2
SALES (est): 130K **Privately Held**
WEB: www.ihprinting.com
SIC: **2752** Commercial printing, lithographic

(G-13023)
INDUSTRIES IN FOCUS INC (PA)
Also Called: Sir Speedy
7401 Fullerton Rd Ste K (22153-2802)
PHONE..................................703 451-5550
Jonathan Kenny, *President*
EMP: 5
SALES (est): 401.6K **Privately Held**
WEB: www.sirspeedy.com
SIC: **2752 3993** Commercial printing, lithographic; signs & advertising specialties

(G-13024)
INTEL PERSPECTIVES LLC
5647 Ravenel Ln (22151-2427)
PHONE..................................703 321-7507
Peter Makowsky, *Principal*
EMP: 3
SALES (est): 155.7K **Privately Held**
SIC: **3674** Semiconductors & related devices

(G-13025)
ITST INC
9211 Paloma Ln (22153-1604)
PHONE..................................703 455-2152
C Cunningham, *Principal*
EMP: 2
SALES (est): 148.5K **Privately Held**
WEB: www.itst-inc.com
SIC: **3571** Electronic computers

(G-13026)
J & J PRINTING INC
5540 Port Royal Rd (22151-2303)
PHONE..................................703 764-0088
Jeff Reniere, *President*
EMP: 8
SQ FT: 4,000
SALES (est): 1MM **Privately Held**
WEB: www.jjprintva.com
SIC: **2752** Commercial printing, offset

(G-13027)
J&J LOGISTICS CONSULTING LLC
6564 Loisdale Ct Ste 600 (22150-1829)
PHONE..................................404 431-3613
Sylvia McBride,
EMP: 1
SALES (est): 137.5K **Privately Held**
WEB: www.jandjlogisticssolutions.com
SIC: **3537 7373** Industrial trucks & tractors; computer integrated systems design

(G-13028)
JOHN I MERCADO
Also Called: 3M Cleaners
7032b Commerce St (22150-3433)
PHONE..................................703 569-3774
EMP: 4
SQ FT: 1,200
SALES (est): 156.7K **Privately Held**
SIC: **2842** Mfg Polish/Sanitation Goods

(G-13029)
JOY OF CUPCAKES LLC
6802 Hampton Creek Way (22150-4615)
PHONE..................................703 440-0204
Joy Ferrara, *Principal*
EMP: 4
SALES (est): 168K **Privately Held**
SIC: **2051** Bread, cake & related products

(G-13030)
JPF INDUSTRIESINC
6019 Queenston St (22152-1746)
PHONE..................................703 451-0203
James P Foye, *Principal*
EMP: 2 EST: 2009
SALES (est): 113.5K **Privately Held**
SIC: **3999** Manufacturing industries

(G-13031)
KAELIN SIGNS LLC
7952 Pebble Brook Ct (22153-2607)
PHONE..................................571 239-9192
Jonathan Kaelin,
EMP: 1
SALES (est): 56.7K **Privately Held**
SIC: **3993** Signs & advertising specialties

(G-13032)
KEN SIGNS
7304d Boudinot Dr (22150-2207)
PHONE..................................703 451-5474
Ken Logsdon, *Owner*
EMP: 2
SQ FT: 1,800
SALES (est): 200K **Privately Held**
WEB: www.kensigns.com
SIC: **3993 7532** Signs & advertising specialties; truck painting & lettering

(G-13033)
KESSLER MARINE SERVICES INC
Also Called: Kessler Sailing Services
6002 Greeley Blvd (22152-1209)
PHONE..................................571 276-1377
Kenneth Kessler, *Principal*
EMP: 2
SALES (est): 90.7K **Privately Held**
WEB: www.kesslermarineservices.com
SIC: **2911** Fuel additives

(G-13034)
KNGRO LLC
8617 Beech Hollow Ln (22153-3440)
PHONE..................................202 390-9126
Shady Bou Akl, *CEO*
EMP: 1 EST: 2017
SALES (est): 32.7K **Privately Held**
SIC: **7372** Application computer software

(G-13035)
L D PUBLICATIONS GROUP
6910 Barnack Dr (22152-3321)
PHONE..................................703 623-6799
Sharon L Elmouhib, *Owner*
EMP: 4
SALES (est): 100.1K **Privately Held**
SIC: **2741** Miscellaneous publishing

(G-13036)
LA-Z-BOY INCORPORATED
7398 Ward Park Ln (22153-2824)
PHONE..................................703 569-6188
Liz Cumberland, *Branch Mgr*
EMP: 2 **Publicly Held**
WEB: www.la-z-boystore.com
SIC: **2512** Upholstered household furniture
PA: La-Z-Boy Incorporated
1 Lazboy Dr
Monroe MI 48162
734 242-1444

(G-13037)
LARSON BAKER PUBLISHING LLC
6604 Wren Dr (22150-4326)
PHONE..................................703 644-4243
Mark Baker, *Principal*
EMP: 2
SALES (est): 72.8K **Privately Held**
SIC: **2741** Miscellaneous publishing

(G-13038)
LAURA BUSHNELL
7485 Huntsman Blvd (22153-1648)
PHONE..................................703 569-4422
Laura Bushnell, *Executive*
EMP: 2
SALES (est): 56.5K **Privately Held**
SIC: **7372** Prepackaged software

(G-13039)
LEGACY SOLUTIONS
Also Called: Mark Crego
8205 Running Creek Ct (22153-2634)
PHONE..................................703 644-9700
Mark Crego, *Owner*
EMP: 1
SALES (est): 85K **Privately Held**
SIC: **7372** Prepackaged software

(G-13040)
LEGACY VULCAN LLC
Mideast Division
5650 Industrial Dr (22151-4409)
PHONE..................................703 354-5783
John Johnson, *Executive*
EMP: 12
SQ FT: 200 **Publicly Held**
WEB: www.vulcanmaterials.com
SIC: **3273** Ready-mixed concrete
HQ: Legacy Vulcan, Llc
1200 Urban Center Dr
Vestavia AL 35242
205 298-3000

(G-13041)
LEGACY VULCAN LLC
6860 Commercial Dr (22151-4201)
PHONE..................................703 713-3100
Sean Murnane, *Technical Mgr*
EMP: 3 **Publicly Held**
WEB: www.vulcanmaterials.com
SIC: **3273** Ready-mixed concrete
HQ: Legacy Vulcan, Llc
1200 Urban Center Dr
Vestavia AL 35242
205 298-3000

(G-13042)
LEITNER-WISE DEFENSE INC
5240 Port Royal Rd # 210 (22151-2123)
PHONE..................................703 209-0009
Robert Clark, *President*
Paul Leitner-Wise, *Vice Pres*
F Martin Potter, *Treasurer*
Suzanne Leitner-Wise, *Admin Sec*
EMP: 5
SQ FT: 2,000
SALES (est): 750K **Privately Held**
SIC: **3484** Small arms

(G-13043)
LETTERCRAFT SIGNS
6210 Lavell Ct (22152-1319)
PHONE..................................571 215-6900
EMP: 2 EST: 2012
SALES (est): 111.8K **Privately Held**
WEB: www.lettercraftsigns.com
SIC: **3993** Signs & advertising specialties

(G-13044)
LORTON STONE LLC
7544 Fullerton Ct (22153-2829)
PHONE..................................703 923-9440
Michael Lizarraga, *Vice Pres*
Ed Seara, *Vice Pres*
Daniel Sennewald, *Vice Pres*
Gabriel Aldao, *Project Mgr*
Mauricio Benavides, *Project Mgr*
▲ EMP: 22
SALES (est): 4.3MM **Privately Held**
WEB: www.lortonstone.com
SIC: **3281** Cut stone & stone products

(G-13045)
LWAG HOLDINGS INC
Also Called: Lwrc
7200 Fullerton Rd Ste G (22150-2200)
PHONE..................................703 455-8650
EMP: 13
SQ FT: 3,000
SALES (est): 20.7K **Privately Held**
SIC: **3484** Mfg Small Arms
PA: Lwrc International, Llc
815 Chesapeake Dr
Cambridge MD 21613

(G-13046)
MARC R STAGGER
Also Called: Paradise Ice Cream
7702 Backlick Rd Ste I (22150-2230)
PHONE..................................703 913-9445
Eric Staggers, *Owner*
Marc Staggers, *Owner*
EMP: 20
SALES (est): 1.1MM **Privately Held**
WEB: www.paradise-catering.com
SIC: **2024** Ice cream, packaged: molded, on sticks, etc.

(G-13047)
MARKTECHNOLOGIC LLC
5800 Hanover Ave (22150-3840)
PHONE..................................703 470-1224
Marcelo Gonzales, *Principal*
EMP: 4 EST: 2017
SALES (est): 307K **Privately Held**
SIC: **3441** Fabricated structural metal

(G-13048)
METRO TECHNOLOGY LLC
8727 Evangel Dr (22153-1259)
PHONE..................................703 579-7771
Soon Sil Chung, *Principal*
EMP: 2
SALES (est): 147.7K **Privately Held**
SIC: **3069** Medical & laboratory rubber sundries & related products

(G-13049)
MEVATEC CORP
7705 Middle Valley Dr (22153-2228)
PHONE..................................631 261-7000
EMP: 2
SALES (est): 90K **Privately Held**
WEB: www.baesystems.com
SIC: **3679** Electronic components

(G-13050)
MID-ATLANTIC PUBLISHING CO
Also Called: Buyers Guide Newspapers
8136 Old Keene Mill Rd A302 (22152-1850)
PHONE..................................703 866-5156
David Vanover, *President*
Robert R Vanover, *Vice Pres*
Julie Moore, *Treasurer*
Ronald O Moore, *Admin Sec*
EMP: 15 EST: 1982
SQ FT: 1,161
SALES (est): 500K **Privately Held**
WEB: www.bgusa.net
SIC: **2711** Newspapers, publishing & printing

(G-13051)
MK INDUSTRIES LLC
7501 Irene Ct (22153-1700)
PHONE..................................949 525-0778
Melanie Knight, *Principal*
EMP: 2
SALES (est): 88.6K **Privately Held**
SIC: **3999** Manufacturing industries

(G-13052)
MKP PRODUCTS LLC
Also Called: Role Tea
8572 Springfield Oaks Dr (22153-3543)
PHONE..................................703 345-0595
Michael Johnson, *CEO*
Koray Benson, *COO*
EMP: 2
SALES (est): 75.4K **Privately Held**
SIC: **2086** Iced tea & fruit drinks, bottled & canned

(G-13053)
MOBILE OBSERVER
6911 Ontario St (22152-3343)
PHONE..................................703 569-9346
EMP: 3
SALES (est): 100.1K **Privately Held**
SIC: **2711** Newspapers-Publishing/Printing

(G-13054)
MOUNIR & COMPANY INCORPORATED
Also Called: Imaging Zone
6788 Commercial Dr (22151-4209)
PHONE..................................703 354-7400
Mounir Murad, *President*
Chris Chambers, *Vice Pres*

G E O G R A P H I C

Ketan Desai, *Prdtn Mgr*
Kenny Naill, *Marketing Staff*
Ron Fike,
EMP: 15
SQ FT: 15,000
SALES (est): 2.8MM **Privately Held**
WEB: www.imagingzone.com
SIC: 2752 Commercial printing, offset

(G-13055)
MULTI-PACK LLC
7668 Fullerton Rd (22153-2818)
PHONE.................................703 372-2303
EMP: 1
SALES (est): 57.5K **Privately Held**
SIC: 2621 Packaging paper

(G-13056)
NATIONAL INTELLIGENCE EDUCTN P
6108 Hanover Ave (22150-4018)
PHONE.................................703 866-0832
Ralph Watson, *Principal*
EMP: 2 **EST:** 2009
SALES (est): 90.5K **Privately Held**
SIC: 2741 Miscellaneous publishing

(G-13057)
NEATPRINTS LLC
6820 Commercial Dr Ste D (22151-4201)
PHONE.................................703 520-1550
Frederick Dankwa, *Mng Member*
Bertha Anku,
EMP: 3
SALES (est): 70K **Privately Held**
WEB: www.neatprintsllc.com
SIC: 3993 2759 Signs & advertising specialties; promotional printing

(G-13058)
NEW ENGLAND SUPPLY INC
Also Called: New England Chimney Supply
7956 Cameron Brown Ct (22153-2808)
PHONE.................................703 372-2689
EMP: 12
SALES (corp-wide): 12.1MM **Privately Held**
WEB: www.newenglandchimneysupply.com
SIC: 3444 1791 1741 Flues & pipes, stove or furnace: sheet metal; smoke stacks, steel: installation & maintenance; chimney construction & maintenance
PA: New England Supply, Inc.
34 Commerce St
Williston VT 05495
802 858-4577

(G-13059)
NINEES GOURMET ICE CREAM
8628 Bristlecone Pl (22153-1524)
PHONE.................................703 451-4124
Trinette Spratley, *Principal*
EMP: 1
SALES (est): 88.6K **Privately Held**
SIC: 3421 Table & food cutlery, including butchers'

(G-13060)
NORTHWEST TERRITORIAL MINT LLC
6564 Loisdale Ct Ste 318 (22150-1812)
PHONE.................................703 922-5545
Don Ruth, *Branch Mgr*
EMP: 10 **Privately Held**
WEB: www.medallic.medalcraft.com
SIC: 3999 Coins & tokens, non-currency
PA: Northwest Territorial Mint Llc
80 Airpark Vista Blvd
Dayton NV 89403

(G-13061)
NOVA LUMBER & MILLWORK LLC
Also Called: Colonial Hardwoods
7953 Cameron Brown Ct (22153-2809)
PHONE.................................703 451-9217
Jean Fitzgerald, *Mng Member*
EMP: 2
SQ FT: 20,000
SALES (est): 1.1MM **Privately Held**
WEB: www.colonialhardwoods.com
SIC: 2491 2431 Millwork, treated wood; moldings, wood: unfinished & prefinished

(G-13062)
OPSEC INDUSTRIES LLC
7412 Layton Dr (22150-2024)
PHONE.................................571 426-0626
Giovani Perez,
EMP: 2 **EST:** 2017
SALES (est): 81.6K **Privately Held**
SIC: 3999 Manufacturing industries

(G-13063)
OTTO INDUSTRIES LLC
7452 Spring Village Dr # 21 (22150-4946)
PHONE.................................703 256-2684
Lloyd Lehn, *Principal*
EMP: 1
SALES (est): 62K **Privately Held**
SIC: 3999 Manufacturing industries

(G-13064)
OUT OF BUBBLE BAKERY
8555 Groveland Dr (22153-2247)
PHONE.................................571 336-2280
Tameisha Norris, *Principal*
EMP: 4
SALES (est): 239.1K **Privately Held**
WEB: www.obubblebakery.com
SIC: 2051 Cakes, pies & pastries; cakes, bakery: except frozen; bakery, for home service delivery

(G-13065)
P M RESOURCES INC
Also Called: Allegra Print & Imaging
5417b Backlick Rd (22151-3915)
PHONE.................................703 556-0155
David Young, *President*
Mary Ann Young, *Corp Secy*
EMP: 5
SQ FT: 2,500
SALES (est): 615.3K **Privately Held**
WEB: www.allegraspringfield.com
SIC: 2752 7338 2789 Commercial printing, offset; secretarial & court reporting; bookbinding & related work

(G-13066)
PD POWER SYSTEMS LLC
6225 Brandon Ave Ste 460 (22150-2530)
PHONE.................................703 778-3515
Mazen Badr, *Senior VP*
Jerry C Mailey, *Vice Pres*
Tim Fleischer, *Mng Member*
EMP: 18
SALES (est): 34MM **Privately Held**
WEB: www.pd-sys.net
SIC: 3612 Power & distribution transformers

(G-13067)
PINDER INDUSTRIES LLC
7629 Webbwood Ct (22151-2834)
PHONE.................................240 200-0703
Robert Pinder, *Principal*
EMP: 1
SALES (est): 44.7K **Privately Held**
SIC: 3999 Manufacturing industries

(G-13068)
PINKIO HOPPERS
7702 Backlick Rd Ste M (22150-2230)
PHONE.................................571 277-4153
EMP: 2
SALES (est): 128K **Privately Held**
SIC: 3949 Sporting & athletic goods

(G-13069)
PIP BOONCHAN
7209 Tanager St (22150-3535)
PHONE.................................571 327-5522
James D Carroll, *Principal*
EMP: 2
SALES (est): 121K **Privately Held**
SIC: 2752 Commercial printing, offset

(G-13070)
PLAYTEX PRODUCTS LLC
7732 Gromwell Ct (22152-3127)
PHONE.................................703 866-7621
Scott Higginson, *Director*
EMP: 1
SALES (corp-wide): 1.9B **Publicly Held**
WEB: www.ob-tampons.net
SIC: 2676 Diapers, paper (disposable): made from purchased paper

HQ: Playtex Products, Llc
6 Research Dr Ste 400
Shelton CT 06484
203 944-5500

(G-13071)
POHICK CREEK LLC
5647 Ravenel Ln (22151-2427)
PHONE.................................202 888-2034
Trevor Lowing,
Mignote Tamra,
EMP: 2
SQ FT: 5,000
SALES (est): 68.6K **Privately Held**
SIC: 2085 8742 7371 Neutral spirits, except fruit; construction project management consultant; computer software systems analysis & design, custom

(G-13072)
POSTAL INSTANT PRESS INC
Also Called: PIP Printing
7426 Alban Station Blvd A101 (22150-2331)
PHONE.................................703 866-1988
Paul De Bruijn, *General Mgr*
Ernie Lederer, *Branch Mgr*
EMP: 6
SALES (corp-wide): 19.9MM **Privately Held**
WEB: www.pip.com
SIC: 2752 Commercial printing, offset
HQ: Postal Instant Press, Inc.
26722 Plaza
Mission Viejo CA 92691
949 348-5000

(G-13073)
PREMIUM PAVING INC
7817 Loisdale Rd Ste J (22150-2100)
PHONE.................................703 339-5371
Martin Spradlin, *President*
EMP: 17
SQ FT: 2,500
SALES (est): 2.3MM **Privately Held**
WEB: www.premiumpavingaol.com
SIC: 2951 1771 Asphalt paving mixtures & blocks; concrete work

(G-13074)
PRO FURNITURE DOCTOR INC
5407 Kempsville St (22151-3111)
PHONE.................................571 379-7058
Dan Kim, *President*
EMP: 2
SALES (est): 100K **Privately Held**
WEB: www.profurnituredoctor.com
SIC: 2599 Factory furniture & fixtures

(G-13075)
PROTESTANT CHURCH-OWNED
6631 Westbury Oaks Ct (22152-2518)
PHONE.................................502 569-5067
EMP: 1 **EST:** 2017
SALES (est): 37.5K **Privately Held**
WEB: www.pcpaonline.org
SIC: 2741 Miscellaneous publishing

(G-13076)
PT ARMOR INC (PA)
7401h Fullerton Rd (22153-2802)
PHONE.................................703 560-1020
Michael Anthony Glaze, *President*
Donna Lee Wilkins, *Vice Pres*
EMP: 26 **EST:** 2001
SQ FT: 10,000
SALES (est): 2.3MM **Privately Held**
WEB: www.ptarmor.com
SIC: 2389 Men's miscellaneous accessories

(G-13077)
PURE ANOINTING OIL
8006 Pohick Rd (22153-3211)
PHONE.................................703 889-7457
EMP: 2 **EST:** 2018
SALES (est): 74.4K **Privately Held**
SIC: 2899 Chemical preparations

(G-13078)
RAYTHEON COMPANY
8320 Alban Rd Ste 100 (22150-2334)
PHONE.................................703 912-1800
John Wellerman, *Engineer*
Charlie McDonald, *Director*
EMP: 250

SALES (corp-wide): 77B **Publicly Held**
WEB: www.rtx.com
SIC: 3812 Sonar systems & equipment
HQ: Raytheon Company
870 Winter St
Waltham MA 02451
781 522-3000

(G-13079)
REXCON METALS LLC
7621 Mendota Pl (22150-4125)
PHONE.................................703 347-2836
EMP: 2
SALES (est): 148.9K **Privately Held**
SIC: 3441 Fabricated structural metal

(G-13080)
ROASTERS PRIDE INC
Also Called: Printing Center, The
7516 Fullerton Rd D (22153-2812)
P.O. Box 312 (22150-0312)
PHONE.................................703 440-0627
Robert McCarthy, *President*
EMP: 7
SQ FT: 23,000
SALES (est): 793K **Privately Held**
SIC: 2752 Commercial printing, offset

(G-13081)
SCOUT MARKETING LLC
Also Called: Miguel and Valentino
7520 Fullerton Rd (22153-2812)
P.O. Box 1552, Lorton (22199-1552)
PHONE.................................301 986-1470
Christine Dibenidno, *Principal*
▲ **EMP:** 2
SALES (est): 131.6K **Privately Held**
SIC: 2079 Olive oil

(G-13082)
SCSI4ME CORPORATION
7411 Alban Station Ct A103 (22150-2317)
PHONE.................................703 372-1195
EMP: 2
SALES (est): 140K **Privately Held**
SIC: 2752 Lithographic Commercial Printing

(G-13083)
SHENANDOAHS PRIDE LLC
5325 Port Royal Rd (22151-2106)
PHONE.................................703 321-9500
John Gillan, *General Mgr*
Tim Balmat,
EMP: 360
SALES (est): 22.5MM **Publicly Held**
SIC: 2024 2026 Ice cream & frozen desserts; fluid milk
HQ: Garelick Farms, Llc
1199 W Central St Ste 1
Franklin MA 02038
508 528-9000

(G-13084)
SICPA SECURINK CORP (HQ)
8000 Research Way (22153-3131)
PHONE.................................703 455-8050
James E Bonhivert, *President*
Greg Montano, *Engineer*
Anthony F Criscuola, *CFO*
Susan Goodman, *Accounting Mgr*
Sherwin Earl, *Cust Mgr*
▲ **EMP:** 100
SQ FT: 50,000
SALES (est): 29.9MM
SALES (corp-wide): 4.3MM **Privately Held**
WEB: www.sicpa.com
SIC: 2893 Printing ink
PA: Sicpa Holding Sa
Avenue De Florissant 41
Prilly VD 1008
216 275-555

(G-13085)
SIGN CY PLUS GRAPHIC & DESIGN
Also Called: Sign Cy Plus Graphic & Design
6513 Backlick Rd (22150-2701)
PHONE.................................703 912-9300
Ray Rajadi, *Owner*
EMP: 2
SALES (est): 136.1K **Privately Held**
SIC: 3993 Signs & advertising specialties

▲ = Import ▼=Export
◆ =Import/Export

(G-13086)
SIGNS UP
6715 Backlick Rd Ste B (22150-2708)
PHONE..................703 798-5210
Denver Madden, *Principal*
EMP: 1
SALES (est): 66.4K **Privately Held**
SIC: 3993 Signs & advertising specialties

(G-13087)
SILVERSMITH AUDIO
7807 Braemar Way (22153-2901)
PHONE..................619 460-1129
Jeffrey Smith, *Owner*
▲ EMP: 1
SALES (est): 107.9K **Privately Held**
SIC: 3651 Household audio & video equipment

(G-13088)
SMARTFIX
6500 Springfield Mall (22150-1706)
PHONE..................571 723-6499
EMP: 2
SALES (est): 90K **Privately Held**
SIC: 7372 Prepackaged software

(G-13089)
SN SIGNS
6611 Iron Pl (22151-4307)
PHONE..................703 354-3000
EMP: 2
SALES (est): 146.2K **Privately Held**
WEB: www.snsigns.org
SIC: 3993 Signs & advertising specialties

(G-13090)
SNYDER CUSTOM SIGN DISPLAY
8695 Young Ct (22153-2253)
PHONE..................703 362-5675
Howard Birmiel, *Principal*
EMP: 1
SALES (est): 53.7K **Privately Held**
SIC: 3993 Signs & advertising specialties

(G-13091)
SOFTWARE FOR MOBILE PHONES LLC
7516 Candytuft Ct (22153-1803)
PHONE..................703 862-1079
John Tigani, *Administration*
EMP: 2 EST: 2009
SALES (est): 118.6K **Privately Held**
WEB: www.software4mobilephones.com
SIC: 7372 Application computer software

(G-13092)
SOUTHERN IRON WORKS INC
6600 Electronic Dr (22151-4300)
P.O. Box 188 (22150-0188)
PHONE..................703 354-5500
Theodore Shaw, *President*
Frank F Everest, *Exec VP*
Barry L Barger, *Senior VP*
J Garry Spitzer, *Senior VP*
Sue E Peters, *Treasurer*
EMP: 6
SQ FT: 85,000
SALES (est): 930.4K **Privately Held**
WEB: www.siwinc.com
SIC: 3441 Fabricated structural metal

(G-13093)
SPRINGFIELD CONNECTION
8634 Hillside Manor Dr (22152-2238)
PHONE..................703 866-1040
Rajiv Chadha, *Principal*
Ramu Singh, *Manager*
EMP: 4
SALES (est): 176.5K **Privately Held**
WEB: www.springfieldconnection.com
SIC: 2711 Newspapers

(G-13094)
SPUNKYSALES LLC
5525 Callander Dr (22151-1403)
PHONE..................727 492-1636
Robert Youngs,
EMP: 1 EST: 2017
SALES (est): 43.6K **Privately Held**
SIC: 3999 Manufacturing industries

(G-13095)
STREAMVIEW SOFTWARE LLC
8008 Dayspring Ct (22153-2940)
PHONE..................703 455-0793
Emon Rahman, *Principal*
EMP: 2
SALES (est): 69.3K **Privately Held**
SIC: 7372 Prepackaged software

(G-13096)
SUN GAZATTE
Also Called: Sun Gazette
6564 Loisdale Ct Ste 610 (22150-1829)
PHONE..................703 738-2520
Henery Benner, *Principal*
EMP: 3 EST: 2001
SALES (est): 152.2K **Privately Held**
WEB: www.insidenova.com
SIC: 2711 Newspapers

(G-13097)
SUPERIOR LAMINATES
7653 Fullerton Rd Unit G (22153-2897)
PHONE..................703 569-6602
Sandy Obrand, *Owner*
Pam Dettelbah, *Office Mgr*
EMP: 5
SQ FT: 3,100
SALES (est): 436.2K **Privately Held**
SIC: 2541 Cabinets, except refrigerated: show, display, etc.: wood

(G-13098)
TASENS ASSOC
8430 Springfield Oaks Dr (22153-3566)
PHONE..................703 455-2424
EMP: 5
SALES (est): 290K **Privately Held**
SIC: 3841 Mfg Surgical/Medical Instruments

(G-13099)
TMC WELDING
8742 Cold Plain Ct (22153-2422)
PHONE..................703 455-9709
H Yang, *Principal*
EMP: 1
SALES (est): 38K **Privately Held**
SIC: 7692 Welding repair

(G-13100)
TOBACCO PLUS
6127 Backlick Rd Ste D (22150-2637)
PHONE..................703 644-5111
John Smith, *Owner*
EMP: 2 EST: 2009
SALES (est): 118.6K **Privately Held**
SIC: 3999 Cigarette & cigar products & accessories

(G-13101)
TOMS CABINETS & DESIGNS
8129 Edmonton Ct (22152-3329)
PHONE..................703 451-2227
Thomas Fowler, *Owner*
EMP: 1
SALES (est): 81.4K **Privately Held**
WEB: www.tomscabinets.com
SIC: 2434 Wood kitchen cabinets

(G-13102)
TRIMARK ASSOCIATES
6412 Brandon Ave (22150-2513)
PHONE..................703 369-9494
EMP: 2 EST: 1994
SALES (est): 121.7K **Privately Held**
SIC: 3429 Mfg Hardware

(G-13103)
U S GENERAL FUEL CELL CORP
7614 Mendota Pl (22150-4124)
PHONE..................703 451-8064
Dick Snaider, *President*
William Richards, *Principal*
Bill Richards, *Senior VP*
EMP: 3
SALES (est): 266.5K **Privately Held**
SIC: 3629 Electrochemical generators (fuel cells)

(G-13104)
USA TODAY
6883 Commercial Dr (22151-4202)
PHONE..................703 750-8702
Linda Spahr, *Principal*

EMP: 7
SALES (est): 392.1K **Privately Held**
SIC: 2711 Newspapers, publishing & printing

(G-13105)
VIDEO CONVERGENT
6800 Versar Ctr (22151-4174)
PHONE..................703 354-9700
Kumar Natarajan, *President*
EMP: 3
SALES (est): 175.9K **Privately Held**
SIC: 3674 Semiconductors & related devices

(G-13106)
VINIFERA DISTRIBUTING VIRGINIA
7668f Fullerton Rd (22153-2818)
PHONE..................804 261-2890
▲ EMP: 4
SALES (est): 301.6K **Privately Held**
SIC: 2084 Mfg Wines/Brandy/Spirits

(G-13107)
VINTAGE STAR LLC
6203 Hibbling Ave (22150-3331)
PHONE..................808 779-9688
Nicole Miller, *Principal*
EMP: 2
SALES (est): 138.5K **Privately Held**
SIC: 2431 Millwork

(G-13108)
VIRGINIA STAINED GLASS CO INC
5250e Port Royal Rd (22151-2117)
PHONE..................703 425-4611
EMP: 15
SALES (est): 1.1MM **Privately Held**
SIC: 3231 5947 5231 Mfg Products-Purchased Glass Ret Gifts/Novelties Ret Paint/Glass/Wallpaper

(G-13109)
WYFI INDUSTRIES LLC
7107 Granberry Way (22151-3325)
PHONE..................703 333-2059
Robert Sweeney, *Principal*
EMP: 2
SALES (est): 108.1K **Privately Held**
SIC: 3999 Manufacturing industries

(G-13110)
ZZ SUPPLY COMPANY LLC
7011 Calamo St Ste 106 (22150-3510)
PHONE..................703 957-5027
Pooya Bahri,
EMP: 2
SALES (est): 500K **Privately Held**
SIC: 3089 Holders: paper towel, grocery bag, etc.: plastic

Stafford
Stafford County

(G-13111)
ACCACEEK PRECAST
119 Jumping Branch Rd (22554-7250)
P.O. Box 1621 (22555-1621)
PHONE..................540 604-7726
EMP: 3
SALES (est): 239K **Privately Held**
SIC: 3272 Precast terrazo or concrete products

(G-13112)
ADGRFX
500 Ridgecrest Ct (22554-1751)
PHONE..................443 600-7562
Robert Raykhelson, *Owner*
EMP: 2
SALES (est): 72.9K **Privately Held**
SIC: 3993 Signs & advertising specialties

(G-13113)
AFFORDABLE SHEDS COMPANY
3209 Jefferson Davis Hwy (22554-4529)
PHONE..................540 657-6770
EMP: 4

SALES (est): 450.2K **Privately Held**
WEB: www.affordableshedscompany.com
SIC: 3448 Buildings, portable: prefabricated metal

(G-13114)
AMBUSH LLC
2028 Coast Guard Dr (22554-2514)
PHONE..................202 740-3602
EMP: 2
SALES (est): 83.9K **Privately Held**
WEB: www.apmanuscripts.com
SIC: 2752 Commercial printing, lithographic

(G-13115)
AMERICAN DIGITAL PRINT LLC
21 Summerwood Dr (22554-5163)
PHONE..................703 328-4796
Nawaz Chughtai,
Mohammad Chughtai,
EMP: 2
SALES (est): 95.8K **Privately Held**
SIC: 2752 Commercial printing, lithographic

(G-13116)
AMERICAN RHNMTALL MUNITION INC
125 Wdstream Blvd Ste 105 (22556)
PHONE..................703 221-9299
Armin Papperger, *President*
Andreas Knackstedt, *President*
Helmut A Binder, *Principal*
John Somich, *Senior VP*
Bernhard Poeltl, *Vice Pres*
EMP: 11
SALES (est): 2.2MM **Privately Held**
WEB: www.rheinmetall-defence.com
SIC: 3482 Small arms ammunition

(G-13117)
AMERICAN SHIRT PRINTING
247 Doc Stone Rd (22556-4520)
PHONE..................703 405-4014
Thomas Kemper, *Mng Member*
EMP: 2
SALES (est): 110K **Privately Held**
WEB: www.americanshirtprinting.com
SIC: 2262 Printing: manmade fiber & silk broadwoven fabrics

(G-13118)
AQUIA CREEK GEMS
1407 Aquia Dr (22554-2117)
PHONE..................540 659-6120
Richard Martin, *Principal*
EMP: 1
SALES (est): 53.9K **Privately Held**
SIC: 3915 Jewelers' materials & lapidary work

(G-13119)
ART & FRAMING CENTER
53 Doc Stone Rd Ste 101 (22556-4574)
PHONE..................540 720-2800
Latif Ahmadyar, *Principal*
EMP: 1
SALES (est): 87.7K **Privately Held**
WEB: www.artframingcenter.com
SIC: 3999 8742 Framed artwork; marketing consulting services

(G-13120)
ARW PRINTING
39 Francis Ct (22554-7681)
PHONE..................540 720-6906
Alice Wilson, *Principal*
Richard Wilson, *Principal*
EMP: 2
SALES (est): 16K **Privately Held**
SIC: 2752 Commercial printing, lithographic

(G-13121)
AVIAN FASHIONS
61 Boulder Dr (22554-8829)
PHONE..................540 288-0200
Mark Moore, *Owner*
Loraine Moore, *Co-Owner*
EMP: 6
SALES (est): 497.1K **Privately Held**
WEB: www.flightquarters.com
SIC: 2211 Bird's-eye diaper cloth, cotton

(G-13122)
B & H WOOD PRODUCTS INC
295 Heflin Rd (22556-5922)
P.O. Box 5314, Fredericksburg (22403-0314)
PHONE.....................540 752-2480
Michael J Berry, *President*
Helms Steven A, *Vice Pres*
EMP: 12
SQ FT: 3,240
SALES (est): 1.8MM Privately Held
WEB: www.bhwoodproducts.com
SIC: 2499 5039 Handles, poles, dowels & stakes: wood; soil erosion control fabrics

(G-13123)
BIG HUBSTER SHORT KNOCKER GOLF
Also Called: Bhsk Golf
1 Columbia Way (22554-1767)
PHONE.....................757 635-5949
Robert Lee, *Vice Pres*
Dale Hubenthal,
EMP: 2
SALES (est): 101.6K Privately Held
SIC: 3949 Driving ranges, golf, electronic

(G-13124)
BOAZ PUBLISHING INC
Also Called: Stafford Printing
2707 Jefferson Davis Hwy (22554-1734)
PHONE.....................540 659-4554
John Owen, *President*
Margaret Owen, *Corp Secy*
Howard Owen, *Vice Pres*
Julie Griffin, *Graphic Designe*
Julie Maida, *Graphic Designe*
EMP: 15
SQ FT: 10,000
SALES (est): 2.5MM Privately Held
WEB: www.staffordprinting.com
SIC: 2752 2791 Commercial printing, offset; typesetting

(G-13125)
BOBBY S WORLD WELDING INC
4 Bertram Blvd (22556-1890)
PHONE.....................540 845-7659
Bobby World, *Principal*
EMP: 2
SALES (est): 100.7K Privately Held
SIC: 7692 Welding repair

(G-13126)
CANDLES FOR EFFECT LLC
3233 Titanic Dr (22554-2629)
PHONE.....................707 591-3986
Daniel Fudge, *Principal*
EMP: 2
SALES (est): 62.5K Privately Held
SIC: 3999 Candles

(G-13127)
CANON PUBLISHING LLC
1031 Aquia Dr (22554-1940)
PHONE.....................540 840-1240
Jason Canon,
EMP: 2
SALES (est): 70K Privately Held
WEB: www.canonpublishing.com
SIC: 2741 Miscellaneous publishing

(G-13128)
CENTRAL ELECTRONICS CO
1621 Garrisonville Rd (22556-1018)
P.O. Box 213 (22555-0213)
PHONE.....................540 659-3235
Reinhart Lovas, *Owner*
EMP: 2
SQ FT: 2,000
SALES (est): 139.6K Privately Held
SIC: 3812 Radar systems & equipment

(G-13129)
CHANEY ENTERPRISES LTD PARTNR
Also Called: Rowe Concrete
169 Wyche Rd (22554-7118)
PHONE.....................540 659-4100
Kendall F Rowe Jr, *Manager*
EMP: 7
SQ FT: 112,384
SALES (corp-wide): 124.2MM Privately Held
WEB: www.chaneyenterprises.com
SIC: 3273 1623 Ready-mixed concrete; sewer line construction
PA: Chaney Enterprises Limited Partnership
2410 Evergreen Rd Ste 201
Gambrills MD 21054
410 451-0197

(G-13130)
CHESAPEAKE MATERIALS LLC (PA)
2951 Jefferson Davis Hwy (22554-1729)
P.O. Box 57, Jersey (22481-0057)
PHONE.....................540 658-0808
Randolph G Blanton, *President*
William Blanton, *Purch Agent*
William J Blanton Jr,
EMP: 30
SQ FT: 2,000
SALES (est): 1.3MM Privately Held
WEB: www.lakeservices.com
SIC: 1422 Crushed & broken limestone

(G-13131)
CIRCLE T CONTROLS INC
36 Bridgeport Cir (22554-1776)
PHONE.....................540 295-0188
Ronald V Steadman, *President*
EMP: 4
SALES (est): 330K Privately Held
SIC: 3822 Building services monitoring controls, automatic

(G-13132)
CLAUDIA OFORI-ADDO
Also Called: Posh Afrique
10 Naples Rd (22554-7773)
PHONE.....................540 840-5388
Claudia Ofori-Addo, *Owner*
EMP: 2
SALES (est): 67K Privately Held
SIC: 2339 Women's & misses' accessories

(G-13133)
CONNECTEDESCAPE LLC
418 Alder Dr (22554-2541)
PHONE.....................443 910-7559
Jason Moore, *Mng Member*
EMP: 1
SALES (est): 56K Privately Held
SIC: 3669 Emergency alarms

(G-13134)
CUSTOM PROCUREMENT SYSTEMS
1 Bullrush Ct (22554-8501)
PHONE.....................540 720-5756
Robert Heck, *Vice Pres*
EMP: 2
SALES (est): 79.3K Privately Held
SIC: 7372 Prepackaged software

(G-13135)
DAL ENTERPRISES INC
233 Garrisonville Rd # 201 (22554-1551)
PHONE.....................540 720-5584
Deb Levy, *Principal*
Andrew Macdonald, *Project Mgr*
Nick Grunert, *Sales Staff*
Gina Jolley, *Supervisor*
EMP: 1
SALES (est): 81.3K Privately Held
WEB: www.glass.com
SIC: 2721 Magazines: publishing only, not printed on site

(G-13136)
DAMOAH & FAMILY FARM LLC
4 Birkenhead Ln (22554-7743)
PHONE.....................703 919-0329
Mike Damoah, *Principal*
EMP: 5
SALES (est): 152K Privately Held
SIC: 2015 7389 Rabbit slaughtering & processing;

(G-13137)
DEADEYE LLC
240 Marlborough Point Rd (22554-5801)
PHONE.....................540 720-6818
EMP: 3 EST: 2004

SALES: 500K Privately Held
SIC: 7372 Prepackaged Software Services

(G-13138)
DRMTEES LLC
49 Orchid Ln (22554-9452)
PHONE.....................540 720-3743
Dexter McKinnon Jr, *Principal*
EMP: 2
SALES (est): 79K Privately Held
SIC: 2759 Screen printing

(G-13139)
DUDENHEFER FOR DELEGATE
2769 Jefferson Davis Hwy (22554-8325)
PHONE.....................540 628-4012
EMP: 3
SALES (est): 111.5K Privately Held
WEB: www.potomaclocal.com
SIC: 2711 Newspapers, publishing & printing

(G-13140)
EASTERN LEAGUE COMMISSIONER
10 Blue Spruce Cir (22554-7872)
PHONE.....................703 307-2080
EMP: 1
SALES (est): 41K Privately Held
SIC: 3944 Kites

(G-13141)
EDDIES REPAIR SHOP INC
Also Called: Triple E Signs
813 Courthouse Rd (22554-7006)
PHONE.....................540 659-4835
Eugene English, *President*
EMP: 12
SQ FT: 9,292
SALES (est): 587.9K Privately Held
WEB: www.eddiesrepairshop.com
SIC: 3993 Signs & advertising specialties

(G-13142)
EDWIN GLENN CAMPBELL
104 Regatta Ln (22554-4500)
PHONE.....................703 203-6516
Edwin Campbell, *Owner*
EMP: 1
SALES (est): 80K Privately Held
SIC: 3663 Radio & TV communications equipment

(G-13143)
ELUCIDSOFT LLC
210 Wakerobin Dr (22556-6753)
PHONE.....................703 679-7688
EMP: 2
SALES (est): 146.6K Privately Held
WEB: www.elucidsoft.com
SIC: 3652 Pre-recorded records & tapes

(G-13144)
EYE ARMOR INCORPORATED
Also Called: Southern Custom Tactical Gear
30 Big Spring Ln (22554-7300)
PHONE.....................571 238-4096
Joseph Mathern, *President*
Eric Martin, *Vice Pres*
EMP: 2 EST: 2009
SALES (est): 134.3K Privately Held
SIC: 3489 3949 Guns or gun parts, over 30 mm.; cases, gun & rod (sporting equipment)

(G-13145)
FUR THE LOVE OF DOGS LLC
58 Larkwood Ct (22554-1587)
PHONE.....................540 850-5540
Natosha K Collins, *Administration*
EMP: 3
SALES (est): 112.2K Privately Held
SIC: 3999 Furs

(G-13146)
GENESIS SIGN
3665 Jeff Davis Hwy # 102 (22554-7748)
PHONE.....................540 288-8820
Lin Young, *Owner*
EMP: 1
SALES (est): 105.5K Privately Held
SIC: 3993 Signs, not made in custom sign painting shops

(G-13147)
GODOSAN PUBLICATIONS INC
3101 Aquia Dr (22554-2604)
P.O. Box 3267 (22555-3267)
PHONE.....................540 720-0861
Sandra Manigault, *President*
Donald Manigault, *Vice Pres*
EMP: 2 EST: 1997
SALES (est): 97K Privately Held
WEB: www.manigaultinstitute.com
SIC: 2731 2741 Book publishing; miscellaneous publishing

(G-13148)
GREENSPRINGS CUSTOM WOODWO
14 Greenridge Dr (22554-5120)
PHONE.....................703 628-8058
EMP: 2
SALES (est): 158.4K Privately Held
SIC: 2431 Millwork

(G-13149)
GREENSTEIN LLC
4 Willow Glen Ct (22554-8208)
PHONE.....................540 408-9877
Jonathan Greenstein, *Principal*
EMP: 2
SALES (est): 73.4K Privately Held
SIC: 3484 Small arms

(G-13150)
HARBOR ENTPS LTD LBLTY CO
800 Corporate Dr Ste 301 (22554-4889)
PHONE.....................229 226-0911
A Lucas Stewart, *President*
EMP: 2
SALES (corp-wide): 9.5MM Privately Held
WEB: www.survive-a-storm.com
SIC: 3312 3448 Structural shapes & pilings, steel; prefabricated metal buildings
PA: Harbor Enterprises, Limited Liability Company
1207 Sunset Dr
Thomasville GA 31792
229 226-0911

(G-13151)
HONEYWELL TECHNOLOGY SOLU
635 Telegraph Rd (22554-4807)
PHONE.....................703 551-1942
Christopher McAfee, *President*
EMP: 3
SALES (est): 269.1K Privately Held
SIC: 3724 Aircraft engines & engine parts

(G-13152)
IMPERIUM
7 Skyview Ct (22554-5232)
PHONE.....................540 220-6785
Marvin Lasser, *Principal*
EMP: 2
SALES (est): 211.6K Privately Held
WEB: www.imperiuminc.com
SIC: 3829 Ultrasonic testing equipment

(G-13153)
IN GOOD COMPANY LLC
117 Fence Post Rd (22556-6227)
PHONE.....................540 752-1328
EMP: 2
SALES (est): 62.7K Privately Held
WEB: www.truthinbooks.com
SIC: 2731 Book publishing

(G-13154)
INSTITUTE FOR COMPLEXITY MGT
14 Hayes St (22556-8603)
PHONE.....................540 645-1050
Bruce Becker, *COO*
John Hnatio, *Exec Dir*
EMP: 2
SALES (est): 120.3K Privately Held
WEB: www.instituteforcomplexitymanagement.org
SIC: 7372 Application computer software

(G-13155)
IUS BELLO DEFENSE LLC
1015 John Paul Jones Dr (22554-2130)
PHONE.....................540 720-2571
Martin Sprick, *Principal*

▲ = Import ▼=Export
◆ =Import/Export

EMP: 2
SALES (est): 81.9K **Privately Held**
SIC: 3812 Defense systems & equipment

(G-13156)
IVIZ LTD
7 Brannigan Dr (22554-8522)
PHONE....................................877 290-4911
Matthew Cameron Humphrey, *Principal*
EMP: 3
SALES (est): 160.2K **Privately Held**
WEB: www.sonosite.com
SIC: 3845 Electromedical equipment

(G-13157)
J & R LOG & WD PROCESSORS LLC
2063 Jefferson Davis Hwy # 23
(22554-7291)
PHONE....................................703 494-6994
EMP: 2
SALES (est): 98K **Privately Held**
SIC: 2411 Logging

(G-13158)
J L V MANAGEMENT INC
Also Called: Sharpshooter Coffee
6 Saint Elizabeths Ct (22556-3672)
PHONE....................................540 446-6359
Libby Vinso, *Principal*
Joseph Vinso, *Director*
EMP: 2
SALES (est): 133.6K **Privately Held**
SIC: 2095 5499 7389 8748 Coffee roasting (except by wholesale grocers); coffee; coffee service; communications consulting

(G-13159)
JA DESIGNS
10 Guy Ln (22554-6649)
PHONE....................................540 659-2592
James Doyle, *Partner*
Roberta Doyle, *Partner*
EMP: 2 **Privately Held**
SIC: 2499 Decorative wood & woodwork

(G-13160)
JOAN FISK
Also Called: Firehouse Embroidery
280 Jefferson Davis Hwy (22554)
PHONE....................................540 288-0050
Fax: 540 288-1045
EMP: 2 EST: 1998
SALES (est): 91K **Privately Held**
SIC: 2395 Pleating/Stitching Services

(G-13161)
KEEN EYES AUTO DETAILING LLC
3 Lotus Ln (22554-6834)
PHONE....................................252 646-3600
Kwisi W Lewis,
EMP: 1
SALES (est): 50K **Privately Held**
SIC: 3589 Car washing machinery

(G-13162)
KEYSTONE METAL PRODUCTS INC
7 Saint Anthonys Ct (22556-3633)
PHONE....................................540 720-5437
EMP: 5
SQ FT: 2,600
SALES (est): 350K **Privately Held**
SIC: 3446 1799 Mfg Architectural Metalwork Trade Contractor

(G-13163)
KING KREATIONS
210 Spyglass Ln (22556-3659)
PHONE....................................703 883-7123
James Frankel, *Administration*
EMP: 2 EST: 2014
SALES (est): 89.6K **Privately Held**
WEB: www.kingkreationsbuilds.com
SIC: 2323 Men's & boys' neckwear

(G-13164)
KIRBY BURBANK LLC
Also Called: Fastsigns
12 Glenview Ct (22554-1609)
PHONE....................................571 330-0261
Francisco Xaviar, *President*
EMP: 4

SALES (est): 55.7K **Privately Held**
WEB: www.fastsigns.com
SIC: 3993 Signs & advertising specialties

(G-13165)
KORDUSA INC
400 Corporate Dr Ste 201 (22554-4898)
PHONE....................................540 242-5210
Peter Moran, *CEO*
Euseekers Williams, *Director*
EMP: 5
SALES (est): 237.6K **Privately Held**
SIC: 3613 3625 3663 3672 Control panels, electric; relays & industrial controls; digital encoders; printed circuit boards; integrated circuits, semiconductor networks, etc.; solid state electronic devices

(G-13166)
KURT USA PROF DOG TNG
28 Big Spring Ln (22554-7300)
PHONE....................................252 509-4211
Gustavo L Corbalan, *Principal*
Gustavo L Corbalan De Martino,
EMP: 3
SALES (est): 900K **Privately Held**
SIC: 3728 Military aircraft equipment & armament

(G-13167)
L3 TECHNOLOGIES INC
L3 Comcept
50 Tech Pkwy Ste 207 (22556-1818)
PHONE....................................540 658-0591
EMP: 5
SALES (corp-wide): 6.8B **Publicly Held**
WEB: www.l3t.com
SIC: 3812 Aircraft control systems, electronic
HQ: L3 Technologies, Inc.
    600 3rd Ave Fl 34
    New York NY 10016
    212 697-1111

(G-13168)
L3HARRIS TECHNOLOGIES INC
65 Barrett Heights Rd # 109 (22556-8043)
PHONE....................................540 658-3350
Al Koes, *Manager*
EMP: 6
SALES (corp-wide): 6.8B **Publicly Held**
WEB: www.harris.com
SIC: 3812 Search & navigation equipment
PA: L3harris Technologies, Inc.
    1025 W Nasa Blvd
    Melbourne FL 32919
    321 727-9100

(G-13169)
LEGACY VULCAN LLC
100 Vulcan Quarry Rd (22556-8621)
PHONE....................................540 659-3003
EMP: 5 **Publicly Held**
WEB: www.vulcanmaterials.com
SIC: 3273 Ready-mixed concrete
HQ: Legacy Vulcan, Llc
    1200 Urban Center Dr
    Vestavia AL 35242
    205 298-3000

(G-13170)
LEGACY VULCAN LLC
32 Wyche Rd (22554-7115)
PHONE....................................800 732-3964
EMP: 4 **Publicly Held**
WEB: www.vulcanmaterials.com
SIC: 3273 Ready-mixed concrete
HQ: Legacy Vulcan, Llc
    1200 Urban Center Dr
    Vestavia AL 35242
    205 298-3000

(G-13171)
LIONS HEAD WOODWORKS LLC
3307 Aquia Dr (22554-2608)
PHONE....................................540 288-9532
Bradley Scott Stepp, *Principal*
EMP: 1
SALES (est): 54.1K **Privately Held**
SIC: 2431 Millwork

(G-13172)
LIZ B QUILTING LLC
21 Woodlot Ct (22554-8540)
PHONE....................................540 602-7850
Elizabeth Bigger, *Mng Member*

EMP: 1 EST: 2012
SALES (est): 10K **Privately Held**
WEB: www.lizbquilting.com
SIC: 2395 7299 Quilted fabrics or cloth; quilting for individuals

(G-13173)
M&S WELDING
195 Wyche Rd (22554-7118)
PHONE....................................540 371-4009
Mauricio D Castillo, *Principal*
EMP: 2
SALES (est): 141.3K **Privately Held**
SIC: 7692 Welding repair

(G-13174)
MARKS GARAGE
17 Sunrise Valley Ct (22554-8211)
PHONE....................................540 498-3458
EMP: 2 EST: 2012
SALES (est): 110K **Privately Held**
SIC: 3728 7389 Mfg Aircraft Parts/Equipment Business Services At Non-Commercial Site

(G-13175)
MARROQUIN WELDING
183 Rock Hill Church Rd (22556-3514)
PHONE....................................571 340-9165
EMP: 1
SALES (est): 39.9K **Privately Held**
WEB: www.marroquinwelding.com
SIC: 7692 Welding repair

(G-13176)
METROPOLE PRODUCTS INC
Also Called: Mpi
2040 Jefferson Davis Hwy (22554-7219)
P.O. Box 309 (22555-0309)
PHONE....................................540 659-2132
Al Leaman, *President*
Barbara Buder, *Corp Secy*
EMP: 25
SQ FT: 17,000
SALES (est): 5.1MM **Privately Held**
WEB: www.metropoleproducts.com
SIC: 3663 Microwave communication equipment

(G-13177)
MOMENSITY LLC
203 Sail Cv (22554-2417)
P.O. Box 961 (22555-0961)
PHONE....................................804 247-2811
Jermon Green,
EMP: 1
SALES (est): 82.4K
SALES (corp-wide): 131.4K **Privately Held**
WEB: www.momensity10.com
SIC: 3993 2741 Signs & advertising specialties;
PA: Be There Smg, Llc
    203 Sail Cv
    Stafford VA 22554
    804 247-2811

(G-13178)
NVA DOCKS LLC
98 Main St (22554-5832)
PHONE....................................619 500-1964
Douglas Schmidtknecht,
EMP: 5
SALES (est): 75K **Privately Held**
SIC: 2499 Floating docks, wood

(G-13179)
POTOMAC CELLARS LLC
Also Called: Potomac Point Winery
275 Decatur Rd (22554-3014)
PHONE....................................540 446-2266
Cecilia Causey, *Mng Member*
EMP: 20
SALES (est): 1.3MM **Privately Held**
WEB: www.potomacpointwinery.com
SIC: 2084 Wines

(G-13180)
POTOMAC GLASS INC
213 Hope Rd (22554-5302)
PHONE....................................540 288-0210
Russell Bohan, *President*
Revenna Bohan, *Treasurer*
EMP: 3

SALES (est): 352.2K **Privately Held**
WEB: www.potomacglass.com
SIC: 3211 Window glass, clear & colored

(G-13181)
POTOMAC LOCAL NEWS
2769 Jefferson Davis Hwy (22554-8325)
PHONE....................................540 659-2020
EMP: 3 EST: 2017
SALES (est): 125.9K **Privately Held**
WEB: www.potomaclocal.com
SIC: 2711 Newspapers, publishing & printing

(G-13182)
PREDICTIVE HEALTH DEVICES INC
1117 Potomac Dr (22554-2101)
PHONE....................................703 507-0627
Patrick Devaney, *President*
EMP: 2
SALES (est): 86.6K **Privately Held**
SIC: 3841 Surgical & medical instruments

(G-13183)
PRESS AND BINDERY REPAIR
18 W Briar Dr (22556-1240)
PHONE....................................703 209-4247
George A Michaud, *Owner*
EMP: 1
SALES (est): 30K **Privately Held**
SIC: 2759 7699 Commercial printing; repair services

(G-13184)
PUBLISHING
52 Larkwood Ct (22554-1586)
PHONE....................................540 659-6694
Michael Johnson, *Principal*
EMP: 1
SALES (est): 59.6K **Privately Held**
SIC: 2741 Miscellaneous publishing

(G-13185)
R ZIMMERMAN AND ASSOCIATES
51 Greenridge Dr (22554-5122)
PHONE....................................540 446-6846
Jimmy Bynum, *CEO*
Edna Bynum, *Principal*
EMP: 2
SALES (est): 77.4K **Privately Held**
SIC: 3812 7378 Light or heat emission operating apparatus; computer & data processing equipment repair/maintenance

(G-13186)
RUSTSTOP USA LLC
5 Garfield St (22556-3758)
PHONE....................................218 391-5389
Christine Marie Wolk, *CEO*
Nick Wolk, *Co-Owner*
EMP: 2
SALES (est): 76.9K **Privately Held**
SIC: 3479 Metal coating & allied service

(G-13187)
SANDRA MAGURA
Also Called: Brave Bracelet
4 Crosswood Pl (22554-7839)
PHONE....................................540 318-6947
EMP: 1
SALES (est): 48.7K **Privately Held**
SIC: 3961 Mfg Costume Jewelry

(G-13188)
SCHLOTTERER LOGGING
108 Wintergreen Ln (22554-6532)
PHONE....................................910 376-1623
Victor J Schlotters Jr, *Principal*
EMP: 3
SALES (est): 248.6K **Privately Held**
SIC: 2411 Logging

(G-13189)
SCORPION MOLD ABATEMENT LLC
202 Bulkhead Cv (22554-2501)
PHONE....................................540 273-9300
Eric Scordino,
Debbie Tone,
EMP: 1
SALES (est): 156.4K **Privately Held**
WEB: www.scorpionmoldabatement.com
SIC: 3544 Industrial molds

(G-13190)
SIGNS AROUND YOU LLC
27 Snow Dr (22554-7297)
PHONE........................919 449-4762
Megan Tucker, *Principal*
EMP: 1
SALES (est): 50.6K **Privately Held**
SIC: 3993 Signs & advertising specialties

(G-13191)
SMC MULCH YARD INC
78 Shelton Shop Rd (22554-3909)
P.O. Box 777, Garrisonville (22463-0777)
PHONE........................540 657-5454
Victor Debord, *CEO*
Patrice Debord, *President*
EMP: 7
SQ FT: 2,232
SALES (est): 986K **Privately Held**
SIC: 2499 Mulch, wood & bark

(G-13192)
**SOFTWARE DFINED DVCS
GROUP LLC**
Also Called: Sddg
1002 Bailey Ct (22556-6420)
PHONE........................540 623-7175
Dan Hicks, *Partner*
Christopher Quigley, *General Mgr*
EMP: 2 EST: 2015
SALES (est): 190.6K **Privately Held**
SIC: 3679 Microwave components

(G-13193)
**SOUTHEASTERN MECHANICAL
INC (PA)**
27 Bertram Blvd (22556-1893)
PHONE........................888 461-7848
Michael Hinson, *President*
Robert Dailey, *CFO*
EMP: 3
SALES (est): 3.7MM **Privately Held**
WEB: www.smiva.com
SIC: 3822 Air conditioning & refrigeration
controls

(G-13194)
SS WINERY LLC
174 White Pine Cir # 301 (22554-9412)
PHONE........................908 548-3016
Steven Shaw, *Principal*
EMP: 2
SALES (est): 81.4K **Privately Held**
SIC: 2084 Wines

(G-13195)
STAFFORD COUNTY SUN
306 Garrisonville Rd # 103 (22554-1575)
PHONE........................540 659-8923
EMP: 3 EST: 2019
SALES (est): 95.7K **Privately Held**
WEB: www.staffordcountysun.com
SIC: 2711 Newspapers, publishing & print-
ing

(G-13196)
STM SNOW REMOVAL LLC
71 Mt Hope Church Rd (22554-7420)
PHONE........................540 604-0112
Catherine Haga, *CEO*
EMP: 2
SALES (est): 129.1K **Privately Held**
SIC: 3537 7349 4213 Trucks, tractors,
loaders, carriers & similar equipment;
building maintenance services; trucking,
except local

(G-13197)
SUN SIGNS
1105 Potomac Dr (22554-2101)
PHONE........................703 867-9831
Tina Mims, *Owner*
Barry Mims, *Co-Owner*
EMP: 2
SALES (est): 20K **Privately Held**
SIC: 3993 5999 7532 4812 Signs, not
made in custom sign painting shops;
alarm signal systems; customizing serv-
ices, non-factory basis; radio telephone
communication; glass tinting, architectural
or automotive; signs, electrical

(G-13198)
**SWEANY TRCKG &
HARDWOODS LLC**
184 Woodstream Blvd (22556-4629)
PHONE........................540 273-9387
Gary Sweany, *Principal*
EMP: 2
SALES (est): 162.3K **Privately Held**
SIC: 2421 4212 Custom sawmill; lumber
(log) trucking, local

(G-13199)
SWITCHDRAW LLC
31 Laurel Haven Dr (22554-5263)
PHONE........................703 402-2820
Christopher Milleson,
EMP: 2
SALES (est): 56.5K **Privately Held**
SIC: 7372 Prepackaged software

(G-13200)
SYRM LLC
74 Deshields Ct (22556-8614)
P.O. Box 547, Occoquan (22125-0547)
PHONE........................571 308-8707
Dustin Savage, *Vice Pres*
Jonathan Yeoman,
EMP: 2
SALES (est): 137.1K **Privately Held**
WEB: www.syrmllc.com
SIC: 7372 8748 Prepackaged software;
systems engineering consultant, ex. com-
puter or professional

(G-13201)
TCHERE LLC
2769 Jefferson Davis Hwy (22554-8325)
PHONE........................800 889-7832
EMP: 5
SALES (est): 439K **Privately Held**
SIC: 3069 Medical sundries, rubber

(G-13202)
TERRAN PRESS LLC
11 Smelters Trace Rd (22554-8532)
PHONE........................540 720-2516
Lance Gentry, *Principal*
EMP: 2
SALES (est): 45.4K **Privately Held**
SIC: 2741 Miscellaneous publishing

(G-13203)
**TOWNSIDE BUILDING AND
REPR INC**
43 Puri Ln (22554-8200)
PHONE........................540 207-3906
Leslie Williamson, *President*
Steven Williamson, *Vice Pres*
EMP: 3 **Privately Held**
WEB: www.townsidebuilding.com
SIC: 1442 Construction sand mining

(G-13204)
TRIJICON INC
39 Tech Pkwy Ste 207 (22556-8618)
PHONE........................703 445-1600
EMP: 3
SALES (est): 148.8K **Privately Held**
WEB: www.trijicon.com
SIC: 3827 Optical instruments & lenses

(G-13205)
TRUSTCOMM SOLUTIONS LLC
800 Corporate Dr Ste 421 (22554-4889)
PHONE........................281 272-7500
Bob Roe, *President*
EMP: 10 EST: 2015
SQ FT: 3,000
SALES (est): 574.4K
SALES (corp-wide): 1MM **Privately Held**
WEB: www.trustcomm.com
SIC: 3663 Satellites, communications
PA: Trustcomm Solutions Holdings Inc
43 Brannigan Dr
Stafford VA 22554
240 401-5516

(G-13206)
TYLER JSUN GLOBAL LLC
37 Daffodil Ln (22554-9449)
PHONE........................407 221-6135
Terrance Jenkins, *Principal*
EMP: 1 EST: 2015

SALES (est): 51.3K **Privately Held**
SIC: 3931 3651 3679 Synthesizers;
music; drums, parts & accessories (musical instruments); amplifiers: radio, public
address or musical instrument; video
camera-audio recorders, household use;
recording heads, speech & musical equipment

(G-13207)
UBIBIRD INCORPORATED
3227 Aquia Dr (22554-2606)
PHONE........................718 490-3746
Alexander Davis, *President*
EMP: 1
SALES (est): 42.6K **Privately Held**
SIC: 2741

(G-13208)
**UPTONS CUSTOM
WOODWORKING LLC**
14 Chestnut Ln (22556-1246)
PHONE........................540 454-3752
Bordon Upton, *President*
Jonathan Upton, *Vice Pres*
EMP: 4
SQ FT: 1,800
SALES (est): 261.8K **Privately Held**
SIC: 2431 Millwork

(G-13209)
**UTAH STATE UNIV SPACE
DYNMICS**
50 Tech Pkwy Ste 303 (22556-1818)
PHONE........................435 713-3060
Jennifer Bettencourt, *President*
Kathleen Hegemann, *President*
Scott Hinton, *President*
Lyndon Loosle, *CFO*
EMP: 99
SALES (est): 3MM **Privately Held**
WEB: www.spacedynamics.org
SIC: 3761 Guided missiles & space vehi-
cles, research & development

(G-13210)
VIKING WOODWORKING
102 Melody Ln (22554-6829)
PHONE........................540 659-3882
EMP: 1
SALES (est): 54.1K **Privately Held**
SIC: 2431 Millwork

(G-13211)
VOCALZMUSIC
118 Spring Lake Dr (22556-6545)
PHONE........................703 798-2587
EMP: 1
SALES (est): 37.5K **Privately Held**
SIC: 2741 Miscellaneous publishing

(G-13212)
VULCAN MATERIALS COMPANY
100 Vulcan Quarry Rd (22556-8621)
P.O. Box 182, Garrisonville (22463-0182)
PHONE........................540 659-3003
D Gray Kimel Jr, *Manager*
EMP: 24 **Publicly Held**
WEB: www.vulcanmaterials.com
SIC: 3273 Ready-mixed concrete
PA: Vulcan Materials Company
1200 Urban Center Dr
Vestavia AL 35242

(G-13213)
ZEIDO LLC
40 Park Rd (22556-1006)
PHONE........................202 549-5757
Robert Damico, *Principal*
EMP: 1
SALES (est): 78.7K **Privately Held**
SIC: 3674 3861 8731 Infrared sensors,
solid state; aerial cameras; electronic re-
search

Staffordsville
Giles County

(G-13214)
**CATTYWAMPUS WOODWORKS
LLC**
173 Moye Rd (24167-3534)
PHONE........................540 599-2358

April Seiple, *Principal*
EMP: 2
SALES (est): 129K **Privately Held**
SIC: 2431 Millwork

Stanardsville
Greene County

(G-13215)
AX GRAPHICS AND SIGN LLC
2143 Amicus Rd (22973-3577)
PHONE........................775 830-6115
Joshua Phalin, *Principal*
EMP: 1
SALES (est): 49.5K **Privately Held**
SIC: 3993 Signs & advertising specialties

(G-13216)
BLUE RIDGE POTTERY
9 Golden Horseshoe Rd (22973-2601)
PHONE........................434 985-6080
Alan D Ward, *Partner*
Norma J Caron, *Partner*
Norma Caron, *Partner*
EMP: 12
SALES (est): 1.6MM **Privately Held**
WEB: www.blueridgepottery.com
SIC: 3269 5719 Art & ornamental ware,
pottery; pottery

(G-13217)
CHAMELEON SILK SCREEN CO
63 Ford Ave (22973-2444)
P.O. Box 369 (22973-0369)
PHONE........................434 985-7456
Joseph Doerr, *President*
Kathryn Doerr, *Vice Pres*
EMP: 3
SQ FT: 2,200
SALES (est): 358.4K **Privately Held**
WEB: www.chameleonsilkscreen.embarq-
space.com
SIC: 2759 Screen printing

(G-13218)
**CVA INDUSTRIAL PRODUCTS
INC**
558 Pasture Ln (22973-3723)
P.O. Box 620, Ruckersville (22968-0620)
PHONE........................434 985-1870
Fred Weiler, *President*
EMP: 2
SALES (est): 500K **Privately Held**
WEB: www.cva-energy-industrial.com
SIC: 3999 Manufacturing industries

(G-13219)
**FREY RANDALL ANTIQUE
FURNITRE**
Also Called: Frey Rndall Antiq Rproductions
2585 South River Rd (22973-2403)
PHONE........................434 985-7631
Randall Frey, *Owner*
EMP: 2
SALES (est): 83K **Privately Held**
WEB: www.18thcenturyreproductions.com
SIC: 2511 5932 Wood household furni-
ture; antiques

(G-13220)
KILAURWEN LTD
1543 Evergreen Church Rd (22973-3429)
PHONE........................434 985-2535
Robert F Steeves, *President*
Bob Steeves, *Manager*
EMP: 4
SALES (est): 308.9K **Privately Held**
WEB: www.kilaurwenwinery.com
SIC: 2084 Wines

(G-13221)
KINVARIN SOFTWARE LLC
364 Skirmish Rd (22973-2340)
PHONE........................434 985-3737
Herb Fickes, *Principal*
EMP: 2
SALES (est): 128K **Privately Held**
SIC: 7372 Prepackaged software

▲ = Import ▼=Export
◆ =Import/Export

(G-13222)
LAWSONS WELDING SERVICE LLC
181 Mutton Hollow Rd (22973-2739)
PHONE................................434 985-2079
Gregory E Lawson, *Principal*
EMP: 3
SALES (est): 62.9K **Privately Held**
SIC: 7692 Welding repair

(G-13223)
MEDIA GENERAL OPERATIONS INC
Also Called: Green County Records
113 Main St (22973-2970)
P.O. Box 66 (22973-0066)
PHONE................................434 985-2315
Fax: 434 985-8356
EMP: 4
SALES (corp-wide): 674.9MM **Publicly Held**
SIC: 2711 Newspapers-Publishing/Printing
HQ: Media General Operations, Inc.
333 E Franklin St
Richmond VA 75062
804 649-6000

(G-13224)
NELSON HILLS COMPANY
989 Chapman Rd (22973-3625)
PHONE................................434 985-7176
Mark Meyer, *President*
▲ **EMP:** 3
SQ FT: 1,700
SALES (est): 250K **Privately Held**
WEB: www.nelsonhills.com
SIC: 2396 Printing & embossing on plastics fabric articles; screen printing on fabric articles

(G-13225)
ONCOR INDUSTRIES INC
3003 South River Rd (22973-2418)
PHONE................................434 985-3434
Cliff Braun, *Principal*
EMP: 2 EST: 2009
SALES (est): 106.5K **Privately Held**
SIC: 3999 Manufacturing industries

(G-13226)
PAD A CHEEK LLC
157 Sunset Dr (22973-3705)
PHONE................................434 985-4003
Karen Moore,
EMP: 3 EST: 2009
SALES (est): 50K **Privately Held**
WEB: www.padacheek.com
SIC: 2676 Facial tissues: made from purchased paper

(G-13227)
PAWPRINT PUBLISHING LLC
246 Skirmish Rd (22973-2346)
P.O. Box 119, Quinque (22965-0119)
PHONE................................434 985-3876
Nan Clarke, *Principal*
EMP: 1 EST: 2014
SALES (est): 42.6K **Privately Held**
SIC: 2741 Miscellaneous publishing

(G-13228)
SVS ENTERPRISES INC
1640 Pea Ridge Rd (22973-3225)
PHONE................................434 985-6642
Philip Stoltdsus, *President*
Ida Stoltdsus, *Admin Sec*
▲ **EMP:** 4 EST: 1994
SALES (est): 180K **Privately Held**
SIC: 2389 Suspenders

(G-13229)
TUMOLO CUSTOM MILL WORK
646 Dogwood Dr (22973-2003)
PHONE................................434 985-1755
Cory Tumolo, *Executive*
EMP: 2 EST: 2007
SALES (est): 306.5K **Privately Held**
WEB: www.tumoloinc.com
SIC: 2431 Millwork

(G-13230)
VERTICAL PATH CREATIVE LLC
386 Fairlane Dr (22973-3739)
PHONE................................434 414-1357
EMP: 1

SALES (est): 57.3K **Privately Held**
SIC: 2591 Blinds vertical

Stanley
Page County

(G-13231)
MASONITE CORPORATION
280 Donovan Dr (22851-3936)
P.O. Box 100 (22851-0100)
PHONE................................540 778-2211
Doris Buracker, *Regional Mgr*
Spencer Stoneberger, *Vice Pres*
Michele Freeze, *Manager*
EMP: 96
SALES (corp-wide): 2.1B **Publicly Held**
WEB: www.masonite.com
SIC: 2431 3469 Doors, wood; stamping metal for the trade
HQ: Masonite Corporation
1242 E 5th Ave
Tampa FL 33605
813 877-2726

(G-13232)
MASONITE INTERNATIONAL CORP
280 Donovan Dr (22851-3936)
P.O. Box 100 (22851-0100)
PHONE................................540 778-2211
Jim Parish, *Branch Mgr*
EMP: 40
SALES (corp-wide): 2.1B **Publicly Held**
WEB: www.masonite.com
SIC: 2431 3499 Doors, wood; fire- or burglary-resistive products
PA: Masonite International Corporation
1242 E 5th Ave
Tampa FL 33605
800 895-2723

(G-13233)
MATTIE S SOFT SERVE LLC
1438 Goodrich Rd (22851-4205)
PHONE................................540 560-4550
Greg Foltz,
EMP: 8
SALES (est): 430.2K **Privately Held**
WEB: www.mattiessoftserve.com
SIC: 2024 Custard, frozen

(G-13234)
MILLCROFT FARMS CO INC
Also Called: Shanando Candy Co
140 Fox Dr (22851-3739)
P.O. Box 138 (22851-0138)
PHONE................................540 778-3369
Bobby Fox, *President*
Deborah Fox, *Vice Pres*
EMP: 2
SALES (est): 199.9K **Privately Held**
WEB: www.applecandy.com
SIC: 2033 Jellies, edible, including imitation: in cans, jars, etc.

Star Tannery
Frederick County

(G-13235)
CEDAR CREEK VALLEY FARM LLC
160 Flickertail Ln (22654-1909)
PHONE................................540 533-2259
Justin D Boyce, *Administration*
EMP: 1 EST: 2014
SALES (est): 61.9K **Privately Held**
WEB: www.cedarcreekvineyard.com
SIC: 2084 Wines

(G-13236)
CEDAR CREEK WINERY LLC
7384 Zepp Rd (22654-3345)
PHONE................................540 436-8357
Ronald Schmidt, *Owner*
Justin Boyce, *Principal*
EMP: 1 EST: 2009
SALES (est): 65.1K **Privately Held**
WEB: www.cedarcreekvineyard.com
SIC: 2084 Wines

(G-13237)
S CONLEY WELDING COMPANY
262 Half Moon Ln (22654-2173)
PHONE................................540 436-3775
Sheldon Conley, *Owner*
EMP: 1
SALES (est): 51.4K **Privately Held**
SIC: 7692 Welding repair

Staunton
Staunton City County

(G-13238)
ABBEY STAUNTON
2217 N Augusta St (24401-2520)
PHONE................................540 580-1271
EMP: 3 EST: 2013
SALES (est): 109.2K **Privately Held**
WEB: www.thestauntonabbey.com
SIC: 2082 Malt beverages

(G-13239)
ACE MACHINING INC
321 Sangers Ln (24401-6600)
PHONE................................540 294-2453
John C Leavell, *President*
EMP: 1
SALES (est): 94K **Privately Held**
WEB: www.acemachining1.com
SIC: 3599 Machine shop, jobbing & repair

(G-13240)
AMERICAN DENSITY MATERIALS
3826 Spring Hill Rd (24401-6318)
PHONE................................540 887-1217
Al Ashton, *President*
EMP: 5
SALES (est): 464.7K **Privately Held**
WEB: www.americandensitymaterials.com
SIC: 3823 Industrial instrmnts msrmnt display/control process variable

(G-13241)
AMERICAN HISTORY PRESS
404 Locust St (24401-3353)
PHONE................................540 487-1202
David Kane, *Principal*
EMP: 1
SALES (est): 37.5K **Privately Held**
WEB: www.americanhistorypress.com
SIC: 2741 Miscellaneous publishing

(G-13242)
APPALACHIAN WOODS LLC
871 Middlebrook Ave (24401-4539)
PHONE................................540 886-5700
Jason Hochstetler, *Principal*
EMP: 3
SALES (corp-wide): 1.2MM **Privately Held**
WEB: www.appalachianwoods.com
SIC: 2421 Sawmills & planing mills, general
PA: Appalachian Woods, Llc
1240 Cold Springs Rd
Stuarts Draft VA 24477
540 337-1801

(G-13243)
BARCODING INC
404 Yount Ave (24401-1689)
PHONE................................540 416-0116
Brenda Mikesell, *Branch Mgr*
EMP: 2
SALES (corp-wide): 18.7MM **Privately Held**
WEB: www.barcoding.com
SIC: 3577 Bar code (magnetic ink) printers
PA: Barcoding, Inc.
3840 Bank St
Baltimore MD 21224
888 412-7226

(G-13244)
BETTERBILT SOLUTIONS LLC
3553 Old Greenville Rd (24401-5755)
PHONE................................540 324-9117
Frank Fenneran, *Principal*
Ralph Kirtland, *Manager*
EMP: 4

SALES (est): 30.1K **Privately Held**
WEB: www.mount-n-lock.com
SIC: 3714 Motor vehicle parts & accessories

(G-13245)
CADENCE INC (PA)
9 Technology Dr (24401-3500)
P.O. Box 3166 (24402-3166)
PHONE................................540 248-2200
Alan Connor, *President*
Peter Harris, *Chairman*
Jack Abato, *Vice Pres*
Mike Bond, *Vice Pres*
Jeff Crist, *Vice Pres*
▲ **EMP:** 189
SQ FT: 92,000
SALES (est): 55MM **Privately Held**
WEB: www.cadenceinc.com
SIC: 3841 3423 Knives, surgical; knives, agricultural or industrial

(G-13246)
CALLISON ELECTRIC
959 Stingy Hollow Rd (24401-5936)
PHONE................................540 294-3189
James E Callison Jr, *Owner*
EMP: 4
SALES (est): 950K **Privately Held**
SIC: 3641 Electric lamps

(G-13247)
CARDED GRAPHICS LLC
2 Industry Way (24401-9051)
PHONE................................540 248-3716
Murry Pitts, *President*
Dennis Chan, *Production*
Melanie Davis, *Production*
Greg Rexrode, *Purchasing*
Mike Bittner, *Engineer*
EMP: 115
SALES (est): 23.4MM **Privately Held**
SIC: 2657 Folding paperboard boxes

(G-13248)
COCA-COLA CONSOLIDATED INC
48 Christians Creek Rd (24401-9699)
PHONE................................540 886-2494
John Iafolla, *Manager*
EMP: 65
SALES (corp-wide): 4.8B **Publicly Held**
WEB: www.cokeconsolidated.com
SIC: 2086 5149 Bottled & canned soft drinks; groceries & related products
PA: Coca-Cola Consolidated, Inc.
4100 Coca Cola Plz # 100
Charlotte NC 28211
704 557-4400

(G-13249)
COMMONWLTH PRMTNL/DCTIONAL LLC
24 Idlewood Blvd (24401-9303)
P.O. Box 1199, Fishersville (22939-1199)
PHONE................................540 887-2321
Brad Thorpe, *Mng Member*
EMP: 10
SQ FT: 8,000
SALES (est): 770K **Privately Held**
WEB: www.commonwealthpromotional.com
SIC: 2759 5999 Screen printing; education aids, devices & supplies

(G-13250)
DESIGN IN COPPER INC
202 S Lewis St (24401-4257)
PHONE................................540 885-8557
Doug Sheridan, *President*
EMP: 16
SQ FT: 15,000
SALES (est): 2.2MM **Privately Held**
SIC: 3499 Fountains (except drinking), metal

(G-13251)
DESIGNER CABINETS
416 Marquis St (24401-4665)
PHONE................................540 569-0469
David Knopp, *Owner*
EMP: 1
SALES (est): 99.4K **Privately Held**
SIC: 2434 Wood kitchen cabinets

(G-13252)
DETAMORE PRINTING CO
327 N Central Ave (24401-3312)
P.O. Box 2501 (24402-2501)
PHONE.................................540 886-4571
Wilber L Detamore, *Owner*
EMP: 5
SQ FT: 3,600
SALES (est): 670.7K **Privately Held**
SIC: 2752 Commercial printing, offset

(G-13253)
DOUGLAS S HUFF
115 S Jefferson St (24401-4157)
PHONE.................................540 886-4751
Douglas S Huff, *Owner*
EMP: 1
SALES (est): 42K **Privately Held**
SIC: 3231 Doors, glass: made from purchased glass

(G-13254)
DRONES CLUB OF VIRGINIA LLC
101 Village Dr Apt 104 (24401-5092)
PHONE.................................540 324-8180
EMP: 2 **EST:** 2016
SALES (est): 91K **Privately Held**
SIC: 3721 Motorized aircraft

(G-13255)
EXPLORATION PARTNERS
1600 N Coalter St Ste 1 (24401-2500)
PHONE.................................540 213-1333
Jake Ford, *Principal*
EMP: 2
SALES (est): 118.8K **Privately Held**
SIC: 1382 Oil & gas exploration services

(G-13256)
FENCO INCORPORATED
10 Croyden Ln (24401-2977)
P.O. Box 538 (24402-0538)
PHONE.................................540 885-7377
Greg M Humphries, *President*
Timothy Humphries, *Vice Pres*
Bryan Humphries, *Treasurer*
EMP: 30
SQ FT: 42,000
SALES (est): 4.7MM **Privately Held**
WEB: www.fencoinc.com
SIC: 2541 Counters or counter display cases, wood

(G-13257)
FIREFLY SIGN LANGUAGE SERVICES
107 Community Way Apt 534 (24401-4993)
PHONE.................................205 405-7043
Alice Moss, *Administration*
EMP: 1
SALES (est): 77.4K **Privately Held**
SIC: 3993 Signs & advertising specialties

(G-13258)
FLINT BROS LOGGING
77 Grower Ln (24401-6131)
PHONE.................................540 886-1509
Robert Flint, *Owner*
Ronald Flint, *Partner*
EMP: 4
SALES (est): 344.3K **Privately Held**
SIC: 2411 Logging camps & contractors

(G-13259)
FLINT BROTHERS
908 Buttermilk Spring Rd (24401-5411)
PHONE.................................540 886-5761
Loggin Flints, *Owner*
EMP: 4
SALES (est): 253.2K **Privately Held**
SIC: 2411 Logging camps & contractors

(G-13260)
FLOWERS BKG CO LYNCHBURG LLC
350 Greenville Ave (24401-4641)
PHONE.................................540 886-1582
Linda Winne, *Manager*
EMP: 2
SALES (corp-wide): 4.1B **Publicly Held**
SIC: 2051 Bread, cake & related products

HQ: Flowers Baking Co. Of Lynchburg, Llc
1905 Hollins Mill Rd
Lynchburg VA 24503
434 528-0441

(G-13261)
FLYNN INCORPORATED
Also Called: Minuteman Press
113 W Beverley St (24401-4204)
PHONE.................................540 885-2600
Dennis Flynn, *President*
Mary Flynn, *Corp Secy*
EMP: 5
SALES (est): 546.5K **Privately Held**
WEB: www.minutemanpress.com
SIC: 2752 2789 Commercial printing, lithographic; bookbinding & related work

(G-13262)
GANNETT MEDIA CORP
Also Called: Daily News Leader
11 N Central Ave (24401-4212)
P.O. Box 1688, Greenville SC (29602-1688)
PHONE.................................540 885-7281
Gary Stoudt, *Branch Mgr*
EMP: 77 **Publicly Held**
WEB: www.gannett.com
SIC: 2711 Newspapers, publishing & printing
HQ: Gannett Media Corp.
7950 Jones Branch Dr
Mc Lean VA 22102
703 854-6000

(G-13263)
HALMOR CORP
Also Called: Dr Pepper of Staunton
103 Industry Way (24401-9052)
P.O. Box 246, Verona (24482-0246)
PHONE.................................540 248-0095
Bo Wilson, *Manager*
EMP: 29 **Privately Held**
WEB: www.drpepper.com
SIC: 2086 Soft drinks: packaged in cans, bottles, etc.
PA: Halmor Corp
1650 State Farm Blvd
Charlottesville VA 22911

(G-13264)
HATCH GRAPHICS
220 Frontier Dr Ste 104 (24401-9153)
PHONE.................................540 886-2114
Matt Mills, *Manager*
EMP: 1
SALES (est): 63.8K **Privately Held**
SIC: 3993 Signs & advertising specialties

(G-13265)
HEINRICH ENTERPRISES INC
Also Called: Welders Supply & Fabricators
1081 New Hope Rd (24401-9264)
PHONE.................................540 248-1592
Richard J Heinrich, *President*
Russel Heinrich, *Corp Secy*
EMP: 4
SALES (est): 426.6K **Privately Held**
SIC: 3443 Tanks, standard or custom fabricated: metal plate

(G-13266)
HELVETICA DESIGNS
212 N Central Ave (24401-3309)
PHONE.................................540 213-2437
Walter Wittmann, *Owner*
Claudia Wittmann, *Owner*
EMP: 2
SQ FT: 10,000
SALES (est): 86K **Privately Held**
WEB: www.helveticadesigns.com
SIC: 2511 Wood household furniture

(G-13267)
HOWDYSHELLS WELDING
505 Statler Blvd (24401-4438)
PHONE.................................540 886-1960
Kermit Howdyshell, *Owner*
EMP: 1
SALES (est): 43.4K **Privately Held**
SIC: 7692 1799 Welding repair; sandblasting of building exteriors

(G-13268)
INCISION TECH
9 Technology Dr (24401-3500)
P.O. Box 3166 (24402-3166)
PHONE.................................727 254-9183
Ken Cleveland, *CFO*
EMP: 2
SALES (est): 95.3K **Privately Held**
WEB: www.cadenceinc.com
SIC: 3841 Surgical & medical instruments

(G-13269)
JERRYS ENGINES LLC
9 Court Sq (24401-4385)
P.O. Box 235 (24402-0235)
PHONE.................................540 885-1205
K Wayne Glass, *Administration*
EMP: 2 **EST:** 2009
SALES (est): 120.6K **Privately Held**
SIC: 3519 Internal combustion engines

(G-13270)
JUST TECH
113 W Beverley St (24401-4204)
PHONE.................................540 662-2400
EMP: 2
SALES (est): 83.9K **Privately Held**
WEB: www.justtech.com
SIC: 2752 Commercial printing, lithographic

(G-13271)
KARL J PROTIL & SONS INC
347 Cedar Green Rd (24401-5426)
P.O. Box 2522 (24402-2522)
PHONE.................................540 885-6664
Karl Protil, *Principal*
EMP: 2
SALES (est): 119.1K **Privately Held**
SIC: 2499 Decorative wood & woodwork

(G-13272)
KATHY DARMOFALSKI
Also Called: Stitch N Time Sewing
51 Woodland Dr (24401-2367)
PHONE.................................540 885-4759
Kathy Darmofalski, *Owner*
EMP: 2
SALES (est): 30K **Privately Held**
WEB: www.stitchntimesewing.com
SIC: 2391 7641 Curtains, window: made from purchased materials; reupholstery & furniture repair

(G-13273)
KITCH N COOK D POTATO CHIP CO
Also Called: Kitch'n Cook'd Potato Chip
1703 W Beverley St (24401-3007)
PHONE.................................540 886-4473
George Raymond Curry, *President*
Margaret Curry, *Corp Secy*
EMP: 18 **EST:** 1963
SALES (est): 2.4MM **Privately Held**
WEB: www.kitchncookd.com
SIC: 2096 Potato chips & other potato-based snacks

(G-13274)
LEADER PUBLISHING COMPANY
Also Called: News Leader , The
2 W Beverley St (24401-4201)
PHONE.................................540 885-7387
Roger Watson, *President*
EMP: 55
SALES (est): 10.1MM **Publicly Held**
WEB: www.newsleader.com
SIC: 2711 Newspapers: publishing only, not printed on site
HQ: Gannett Media Corp.
7950 Jones Branch Dr
Mc Lean VA 22102
703 854-6000

(G-13275)
LEGACY VULCAN LLC
327 Luck Stone Rd (24401-6281)
PHONE.................................540 886-6758
EMP: 2 **Publicly Held**
WEB: www.vulcanmaterials.com
SIC: 3273 Ready-mixed concrete

HQ: Legacy Vulcan, Llc
1200 Urban Center Dr
Vestavia AL 35242
205 298-3000

(G-13276)
LEVEL 7 SIGNS LLC
25 N Central Ave Fl 2 (24401-4272)
PHONE.................................540 885-1517
Thomas Bell, *Principal*
Randall Perdue, *Litigation*
EMP: 2 **EST:** 2010
SALES (est): 98.8K **Privately Held**
WEB: www.timberlakesmith.com
SIC: 3993 Signs & advertising specialties

(G-13277)
LONE FOUNTAIN LDSCP & HDWR CTR
2986 Churchville Ave (24401-6284)
PHONE.................................540 886-7605
Benjamin Gee, *President*
EMP: 7
SQ FT: 2,400
SALES (est): 814.3K **Privately Held**
SIC: 3429 0781 Builders' hardware; landscape counseling services

(G-13278)
MAD HAT ENTERPRISES
806 Spring Hill Rd (24401-2866)
PHONE.................................540 885-9600
Scott Hatter, *Owner*
EMP: 3
SALES (est): 246.3K **Privately Held**
WEB: www.madhatenterprises.com
SIC: 2759 Screen printing

(G-13279)
MESSER LLC
Also Called: Welding Supply Contractors
725 Opie St (24401-2856)
PHONE.................................540 886-1725
John H Lowe, *Branch Mgr*
EMP: 1
SALES (corp-wide): 1.1B **Privately Held**
WEB: www.praxair.com
SIC: 2813 Industrial gases
HQ: Messer Llc
200 Somerset Corp Blvd # 7000
Bridgewater NJ 08807
908 464-8100

(G-13280)
MID VALLEY MACHINE & TOOL INC
10 Van Fossen Ln (24401-8851)
PHONE.................................540 885-6379
Timothy A Decker, *President*
EMP: 7
SQ FT: 4,800
SALES (est): 621.5K **Privately Held**
WEB: www.midvalleymachine.com
SIC: 3599 Machine shop, jobbing & repair

(G-13281)
MILLER METAL FABRICATORS INC
Also Called: Miller Mental Fabricators
345 National Ave (24401-9108)
P.O. Box 3165 (24402-3165)
PHONE.................................540 886-5575
Mary N Thompson, *President*
Hd Thompson, *Vice Pres*
EMP: 21
SALES (est): 50K **Privately Held**
SIC: 3556 3535 3471 3444 Poultry processing machinery; conveyors & conveying equipment; plating & polishing; sheet metalwork; fabricated plate work (boiler shop)

(G-13282)
OAKS
521 Oak Hill Rd (24401-3509)
PHONE.................................540 885-6664
Tim Protil, *Partner*
Mark Protil, *Partner*
EMP: 3
SQ FT: 1,000
SALES (est): 150K **Privately Held**
WEB: www.nineoaksswimclub.com
SIC: 2431 Woodwork, interior & ornamental

(G-13283)
PARKER COMPOUND BOWS INC
3022 Lee Jackson Hwy (24401-5700)
P.O. Box 105, Mint Spring (24463-0105)
PHONE....................................540 337-5426
Robert Errett, *President*
Rob Mason, *President*
Guy Rowzie, *Senior VP*
Marsha Poole, *Opers Mgr*
Sherry Whitesell, *Accountant*
▲ EMP: 25
SALES (est): 2.9MM **Privately Held**
WEB: www.parkerbows.com
SIC: 3949 Sporting & athletic goods

(G-13284)
PRECISION SCREEN PRINTING
112 College Cir (24401-2307)
PHONE....................................540 886-0026
Anita Bourgeois, *Principal*
EMP: 2
SALES (est): 54.4K **Privately Held**
WEB: www.pspegof.com
SIC: 2759 Screen printing

(G-13285)
RICHARD A LANDES
297 Commerce Rd (24401-4435)
PHONE....................................540 885-1454
Richard A Landes, *Principal*
EMP: 2
SALES (est): 138.6K **Privately Held**
SIC: 3589 Shredders, industrial & commercial

(G-13286)
ROCKYDALE QUARRIES CORPORATION
251 National Ave (24401-4405)
PHONE....................................540 886-2111
John Depasquale, *Manager*
EMP: 1
SALES (corp-wide): 13.3MM **Privately Held**
WEB: www.rockydalequarries.com
SIC: 3274 1442 Lime; construction sand & gravel
PA: Rockydale Quarries Corporation
2343 Highland Farm Rd Nw
Roanoke VA 24017
540 774-1696

(G-13287)
RSSHUTTERLEE LLC
3007 Shutterlee Mill Rd (24401-6304)
PHONE....................................540 290-3712
Lisa Shelton, *Principal*
EMP: 6
SALES (est): 679.9K **Privately Held**
WEB: www.lisasheltonlmt.com
SIC: 3442 Shutters, door or window: metal

(G-13288)
RYZING TECHNOLOGIES LLC
600 Hays Ave (24401-3830)
PHONE....................................949 244-0240
Val Gundling, *President*
Ryan Long, *COO*
Ryan Gundling,
EMP: 3 EST: 2015
SALES (est): 161.5K **Privately Held**
WEB: www.ryzingtech.com
SIC: 2394 Canopies, fabric: made from purchased materials

(G-13289)
S N L FINISHING
356 Sangers Ln (24401-6600)
PHONE....................................540 740-3826
Stanley G Laro, *Owner*
Stan N Laro, *Owner*
Nancy Laro, *Co-Owner*
EMP: 2
SALES (est): 124.4K **Privately Held**
SIC: 2426 Flooring, hardwood

(G-13290)
SCHMIDS PRINTING
Also Called: Commercial Printers
124 E Beverley St (24401-4323)
PHONE....................................540 886-9261
Brenda Groah, *Manager*
EMP: 3
SQ FT: 2,230

SALES (est): 150K **Privately Held**
WEB: www.schmidsprinteryinc.com
SIC: 2759 2752 Commercial printing; commercial printing, lithographic

(G-13291)
SEMCO SERVICES INC (PA)
589 Lee Jackson Hwy (24401-5507)
PHONE....................................540 885-7480
James Haltigan, *President*
Greg Elms, *Area Mgr*
EMP: 30
SQ FT: 3,000
SALES (est): 2.2MM **Privately Held**
WEB: www.semcoservices.com
SIC: 3292 1799 Asbestos insulating materials; asbestos removal & encapsulation

(G-13292)
SHENANDOAH CORPORATION (PA)
Also Called: Shenandoah Valley Water Co
4 Industry Way (24401-9051)
P.O. Box 2555 (24402-2555)
PHONE....................................540 248-2123
William Saxman Jr, *President*
Cyndi Hopkins, *Human Res Mgr*
Janeth B Saxman, *Admin Sec*
EMP: 32 EST: 1975
SQ FT: 15,000
SALES (est): 7.9MM **Privately Held**
WEB: www.crystal-springs.com
SIC: 2086 7389 Water, pasteurized: packaged in cans, bottles, etc.; coffee service

(G-13293)
SHENANDOAH SIGNS PROMOTIONS
220 Frontier Dr Ste 99 (24401-9153)
PHONE....................................540 886-2114
Steven Cash, *Partner*
EMP: 2 EST: 2010
SALES (est): 166.6K **Privately Held**
WEB: www.shenandoahsigncompany.com
SIC: 3993 Signs, not made in custom sign painting shops

(G-13294)
SHORT CIRCUIT ELECTRONICS
600 Richmond Ave (24401-4820)
PHONE....................................540 886-8805
Thomas Wright, *Owner*
EMP: 4
SQ FT: 13,000
SALES (est): 190K **Privately Held**
SIC: 3651 Speaker systems

(G-13295)
SIGN LANGUAGE INTERPRETER
3011 Old Greenville Rd (24401-5668)
PHONE....................................540 460-4445
EMP: 1
SALES (est): 45.6K **Privately Held**
SIC: 3993 Signs & advertising specialties

(G-13296)
SPECTACLE & MIRTH
626 W Frederick St (24401-3103)
PHONE....................................619 961-6941
Carmel Clavin, *Principal*
EMP: 2
SALES (est): 77.4K **Privately Held**
WEB: www.spectacleandmirth.com
SIC: 3851 Spectacles

(G-13297)
STANS SKI AND SNOWBOARD LLC
Also Called: Blue Ridge Pools Staunton Ci
702 Richmond Ave (24401-4953)
PHONE....................................540 885-9625
Stanley Shifflett, *Mng Member*
EMP: 8
SALES (est): 452.4K **Privately Held**
WEB: www.blueridgepoolsandspasva.com
SIC: 3949 Snow skis

(G-13298)
STAUNTON MACHINE WORKS INC
608 Richmond Ave (24401-4820)
PHONE....................................540 886-0733
James A Arehart, *President*
Bobbie A Arehart, *Treasurer*
EMP: 17 EST: 1898

SQ FT: 13,000
SALES (est): 2.7MM **Privately Held**
WEB: www.stauntonmachine.com
SIC: 3599 7389 Machine shop, jobbing & repair; crane & aerial lift service

(G-13299)
STAUNTON OLIVE OIL COMPANY LLC
126 W Beverley St (24401-4393)
PHONE....................................540 290-9665
Gary Gallaugher, *Owner*
EMP: 3
SALES (est): 121.6K **Privately Held**
WEB: www.stauntonoliveoilcompany.com
SIC: 2079 Olive oil

(G-13300)
TEES TO GO 2
704 Middlebrook Ave (24401-4647)
PHONE....................................540 569-2268
EMP: 2
SALES (est): 73.2K **Privately Held**
SIC: 2759 Screen printing

(G-13301)
THOMPSON PUBG LLC GEORGE F
217 Oak Ridge Cir (24401-3511)
PHONE....................................540 887-8166
George Thompson, *Principal*
▲ EMP: 2 EST: 2011
SALES (est): 110.5K **Privately Held**
WEB: www.gftbooks.com
SIC: 2741 Miscellaneous publishing

(G-13302)
TRANSIT MIXED CONCRETE CORP
501 Statler Blvd (24401-4438)
P.O. Box 1647, Charlottesville (22902-1647)
PHONE....................................540 885-7224
Nick Collins, *President*
EMP: 20 EST: 1957
SQ FT: 2,000
SALES (est): 1.7MM **Privately Held**
WEB: www.alliedconcrete.com
SIC: 3273 Ready-mixed concrete

(G-13303)
TTG LLC
704 Middlebrook Ave (24401-4647)
PHONE....................................540 280-7389
Garland Eutsler II, *Administration*
EMP: 2 EST: 2013
SALES (est): 84.8K **Privately Held**
SIC: 7372 Application computer software

(G-13304)
TWEEDLE TEES
1782 Shutterlee Mill Rd (24401-1709)
PHONE....................................540 569-6927
Scott Hatter, *Principal*
EMP: 2
SALES (est): 110.1K **Privately Held**
SIC: 2759 Screen printing

(G-13305)
TWEEDLE TEES PRINTING LLC
1782 Shutterlee Mill Rd (24401-1709)
PHONE....................................540 569-6927
Scott Hatter,
EMP: 1 EST: 2017
SALES (est): 43.6K **Privately Held**
WEB: www.tweedletees.com
SIC: 3999 Manufacturing industries

(G-13306)
VALLEY SCENTS
3125 Lee Jackson Hwy (24401-5713)
PHONE....................................540 688-8855
EMP: 3
SALES (est): 167.6K **Privately Held**
SIC: 2844 Toilet preparations

(G-13307)
WINCHESTER WOODS CONDOS LLC
1527 Dogwood Rd (24401-2410)
PHONE....................................540 885-8390
Melvin Sweeney, *Principal*
EMP: 1 EST: 2015
SALES (est): 60.4K **Privately Held**
SIC: 2499 Wood products

(G-13308)
WOOD MARK T A AUGUSTA GLA
8 Highland Ave (24401-3032)
PHONE....................................540 885-5038
Mark Wood, *Owner*
EMP: 1
SALES (est): 98.1K **Privately Held**
SIC: 3714 Windshield wiper systems, motor vehicle

(G-13309)
ZETA METER INC
765 Middlebrook Ave (24401-4648)
P.O. Box 3008 (24402-3008)
PHONE....................................540 886-3503
Louis Ravina, *President*
EMP: 5 EST: 1961
SQ FT: 3,000
SALES (est): 814.8K **Privately Held**
WEB: www.zeta-meter.com
SIC: 3825 Measuring instruments & meters, electric

Steeles Tavern
Augusta County

(G-13310)
AUGUSTA ACTUATION LLC
1105 Old Providence Rd (24476-2140)
PHONE....................................540 480-7619
Peter Carter, *Mng Member*
Jill Carter,
EMP: 2
SALES (est): 68.9K **Privately Held**
SIC: 3625 3491 1629 2621 Actuators, industrial; valves, automatic control; waste water & sewage treatment plant construction; paper mills

Stephens City
Frederick County

(G-13311)
ADME SOLUTIONS LLC
568 Garden Gate Dr (22655-5346)
PHONE....................................540 664-3521
Chris Hild,
EMP: 2
SALES (est): 10K **Privately Held**
SIC: 7372 7389 Application computer software; business services

(G-13312)
AVON PRODUCTS INC
124 Agape Way (22655-2211)
EMP: 4
SALES (corp-wide): 10.7B **Publicly Held**
SIC: 2844 Mfg & Mkts
PA: Avon Products, Inc.
777 3rd Ave Fl 31
New York NY 10901
212 282-5000

(G-13313)
COMMERCIAL PRESS INC
965 Green St (22655-2810)
P.O. Box 308 (22655-0308)
PHONE....................................540 869-3496
William Grim, *President*
Mark Grim, *Treasurer*
Richard H Grim, *Director*
Sue P Grim, *Admin Sec*
EMP: 15
SQ FT: 4,500 **Privately Held**
SIC: 2752 2759 Commercial printing, offset; letterpress printing

(G-13314)
DOMINION ENTERPRISES
100 Brandylion Ct (22655-3706)
PHONE....................................540 869-3837
Rebecca Bryce, *Accountant*
EMP: 3
SALES (est): 170.9K **Privately Held**
SIC: 2721 Periodicals

GEOGRAPHIC

(G-13315)
DRIVING AIDS DEVELOPMENT CORP
Also Called: D A D C
845 Salem Church Rd (22655-5552)
PHONE................................703 938-6435
Lee Perry, *President*
Perry Dorothy M, *Vice Pres*
EMP: 3
SALES (est): 430.7K **Privately Held**
WEB: www.drivingaids.com
SIC: 3714 Motor vehicle parts & accessories

(G-13316)
EDISONS ONE OFF FBRCATIONS LLC
2610 Double Church Rd (22655-5720)
PHONE................................540 869-5703
Edison Gomez, *Principal*
EMP: 2
SALES (est): 219.8K **Privately Held**
WEB: www.edisonsfabrications.com
SIC: 3441 Fabricated structural metal

(G-13317)
GORES CUSTOM SLAUGHTER & PROC (PA)
Also Called: Gore's Processing
1426 Double Church Rd (22655-3379)
PHONE................................540 869-1029
Jeffrey Gore, *President*
Gore Joseph Frederick, *Vice Pres*
Joe Gore, *Vice Pres*
EMP: 27
SQ FT: 5,000
SALES (est): 3.3MM **Privately Held**
WEB: www.goresmeats.com
SIC: 2011 Meat packing plants

(G-13318)
JENNIFER LAVEY
Also Called: A-1 Welding
245 Nightingale Ave (22655-2449)
PHONE................................540 313-0015
Jennifer Lavey, *Owner*
EMP: 3
SALES (est): 124K **Privately Held**
SIC: 7692 Welding repair

(G-13319)
LEGACY VULCAN LLC
339 Estep Rd (22655)
PHONE................................800 732-3964
EMP: 3 **Publicly Held**
WEB: www.vulcanmaterials.com
SIC: 3273 Ready-mixed concrete
HQ: Legacy Vulcan, Llc
　　1200 Urban Center Dr
　　Vestavia AL 35242
　　205 298-3000

(G-13320)
PRACTICAL SOFTWARE LLC
108 Dickenson Ct (22655-4026)
PHONE................................240 505-0936
EMP: 2 EST: 2011
SALES (est): 76K **Privately Held**
SIC: 7372 Prepackaged software

(G-13321)
S3 TACTICAL LLC
221 Refuge Church Rd (22655-5623)
PHONE................................540 667-6947
James Sarver, *Mng Member*
EMP: 1
SALES (est): 30K **Privately Held**
SIC: 2393 Duffle bags, canvas: made from purchased materials; knapsacks, canvas: made from purchased materials

(G-13322)
SHEN-VALLEY LIME CORP
500 Fairfax Pike (22655-2970)
PHONE................................540 869-2700
Beverley B Shoemaker, *President*
EMP: 3
SALES (est): 314.8K **Privately Held**
SIC: 3274 Lime

(G-13323)
SKY SOFTWARE
114 Lariat Ct (22655-4828)
PHONE................................540 869-6581
EMP: 2 EST: 2008

SALES (est): 100K **Privately Held**
SIC: 7372 Prepackaged Software Services

(G-13324)
TRIDENT TOOL INC
105 Boydton Plank Dr (22655-4512)
PHONE................................540 635-7753
Jeff Mullan, *President*
Pam Mullan, *Admin Sec*
EMP: 5
SQ FT: 14,000
SALES (est): 961.5K **Privately Held**
WEB: www.tridenttool.com
SIC: 3533 2298 Water well drilling equipment; wire rope centers

(G-13325)
VALERIE HILL FARM LLC
1687 Marlboro Rd (22655-5127)
PHONE................................540 869-9567
Shawn Steffey, *Principal*
EMP: 1
SALES (est): 127.9K **Privately Held**
WEB: www.valeriehillwinery.com
SIC: 2084 Wines

(G-13326)
VALLEY REDI-MIX COMPANY INC (PA)
Also Called: Valley Redi-Mix Pump Division
333 Marlboro Rd (22655-5241)
P.O. Box 1476 (22655-1476)
PHONE................................540 869-1990
James T Wilson, *President*
John Watson, *Treasurer*
EMP: 7 EST: 1968
SALES (est): 3.1MM **Privately Held**
SIC: 3273 Ready-mixed concrete

(G-13327)
VASTEC USA
1200 W Fairfax Pike (22655)
PHONE................................302 682-8255
EMP: 1
SALES (est): 54.6K **Privately Held**
WEB: www.vastec-usa.com
SIC: 3999 Manufacturing industries

(G-13328)
VICON INDUSTRIES INC
110 Dickenson Ct (22655-4026)
PHONE................................540 868-9530
EMP: 3
SALES (corp-wide): 35.7MM **Publicly Held**
SIC: 3663 Mfg Radio/Tv Communication Equipment
PA: Vicon Industries, Inc.
　　135 Fell Ct
　　Hauppauge NY 11788
　　631 952-2288

(G-13329)
WINERY WOODWORKS LLC
1215 Marlboro Rd (22655-5250)
PHONE................................540 869-1542
Zachery Layman, *Principal*
EMP: 1
SALES (est): 92.6K **Privately Held**
WEB: www.winerywoodworks.com
SIC: 2431 Millwork

(G-13330)
XLUSION CL FULFILLMENT LLC
5209 Pan Tops Dr (22655-2687)
PHONE................................571 316-9391
Brian Tate,
EMP: 1
SALES (est): 39.6K **Privately Held**
SIC: 3999 Manufacturing industries

Stephenson
Frederick County

(G-13331)
BLONDE INDUSTRIES LLC
268 Christmas Tree Ln (22656-1949)
PHONE................................540 667-8192
Carrie Luebcke, *Principal*
EMP: 1
SALES (est): 39.6K **Privately Held**
SIC: 3999 Manufacturing industries

(G-13332)
CLEVENGERS WELDING INC
134 Slate Ln (22656-1834)
PHONE................................540 662-2191
Charles Clevenger, *Partner*
Terry Clevenger, *Vice Pres*
EMP: 2
SALES (est): 86.4K **Privately Held**
SIC: 7692 Welding repair

(G-13333)
GOLF GUIDE INC
Also Called: Golf Guide Golf Getaways
206 Morlyn Dr (22656-2229)
PHONE................................540 431-5034
James Ciattei, *President*
James N Niapttei, *President*
Barry Lupton, *Vice Pres*
EMP: 3
SALES (est): 186K **Privately Held**
WEB: www.midatlanticgolfgetaways.com
SIC: 2731 Book publishing

(G-13334)
IMPRESSED PRINT SOLUTIONS
260 High Banks Rd (22656-2007)
PHONE................................717 816-0522
EMP: 2
SALES (est): 83.9K **Privately Held**
WEB: www.impressedprint.com
SIC: 2752 Commercial printing, lithographic

(G-13335)
SPARKLENSHINECOLLECTION
122 Poinsettia Way (22656-1997)
PHONE................................703 939-7623
Kishia Jeanine, *Owner*
EMP: 3
SALES (est): 83.5K **Privately Held**
SIC: 2339 Women's & misses' accessories

Sterling
Loudoun County

(G-13336)
1ST CHOICE ACCESSORIES LLC
21119 Fireside Ct (20164-6309)
PHONE................................410 615-1578
EMP: 2
SALES (est): 152.5K **Privately Held**
WEB: www.1stchoiceaccessories.com
SIC: 3694 Automotive electrical equipment

(G-13337)
4WAVE INC
22710 Executive Dr # 203 (20166-9589)
PHONE................................703 787-9283
Tony Githinji, *CEO*
Githinji Anthony, *President*
Anthony Githinji, *Principal*
Michael Minnemann, *Vice Pres*
Brian Rollison, *Production*
EMP: 20
SQ FT: 7,500
SALES (est): 4.4MM **Privately Held**
WEB: www.4waveinc.com
SIC: 3674 8711 Semiconductors & related devices; consulting engineer

(G-13338)
ACES EMBROIDERY
28 Lipscomb Ct (20165-5673)
PHONE................................703 738-4784
Tim Frank, *Mng Member*
EMP: 1
SALES (est): 85K **Privately Held**
SIC: 2395 Embroidery & art needlework

(G-13339)
AEC SOFTWARE INC
22611 Markey Ct Ste 113 (20166-6903)
PHONE................................703 450-1980
Dennis D Bilowus, *President*
Kalvin Saccal, *COO*
Carlos L Thy, *Sales Staff*
Deniz Zen, *Sales Staff*
Khaled Saccal, *Software Dev*
EMP: 22
SQ FT: 5,000

SALES (est): 2MM **Privately Held**
WEB: www.aecsoftware.com
SIC: 7372 7371 Prepackaged software; custom computer programming services

(G-13340)
AKA SOFTWARE LLC
46191 Cecil Ter (20165-8729)
PHONE................................703 406-4619
Vikas Sharma, *Administration*
EMP: 2
SALES (est): 101.3K **Privately Held**
SIC: 7372 Prepackaged software

(G-13341)
ALFARO TORRES GERMAN
21786 Canfield Ter (20164-7040)
PHONE................................703 498-6295
German Alfaro Torres, *Owner*
EMP: 2
SALES (est): 89.4K **Privately Held**
SIC: 1481 Overburden removal, nonmetallic minerals

(G-13342)
ALL PRINTS INC
502 Shaw Rd Ste 107 (20166-9435)
PHONE................................703 435-1922
Hepayat Gabib, *President*
EMP: 4
SALES (est): 240K **Privately Held**
WEB: www.allprintsinc.com
SIC: 2752 Commercial printing, offset

(G-13343)
ALLORA USA LLC
22713 Commerce Center Ct # 140 (20166-2087)
PHONE................................571 291-3485
Yukie Sherwood, *Sales Mgr*
Yuksel Acikgoz, *Mng Member*
▲ EMP: 15
SALES (est): 2MM **Privately Held**
WEB: www.allorausa.com
SIC: 3261 Faucet handles, vitreous china & earthenware

(G-13344)
ANNALEES LLC
22648 Glenn Dr Ste 203 (20164-4448)
PHONE................................703 303-1841
Anna Lee, *Principal*
▲ EMP: 2
SALES (est): 139.8K **Privately Held**
SIC: 2311 Tuxedos: made from purchased materials

(G-13345)
ANTENNA TECHNOLOGIES LTD CO
22560 Glenn Dr Ste 114 (20164-4440)
PHONE................................703 450-5517
Marina Burgstahler, *CEO*
EMP: 11
SALES (est): 830.6K **Privately Held**
SIC: 3663 Antennas, transmitting & communications

(G-13346)
APPLIED SIGNALS INTELLIGENCE
45945 Center Oak Plz # 100 (20166-6572)
PHONE................................571 313-0681
John McCorkle, *CEO*
Jerry Lynch, *President*
EMP: 5
SALES (est): 734.9K **Privately Held**
WEB: www.asigint.com
SIC: 3812 Radar systems & equipment

(G-13347)
APPVITY
22636 Glenn Dr Ste 201 (20164-4443)
PHONE................................571 327-0888
Stephen Leahy, *Founder*
EMP: 1
SALES (est): 70.5K **Privately Held**
WEB: www.appvity.com
SIC: 3652 Pre-recorded records & tapes

(G-13348)
ARC SECOND INC
44880 Falcon Pl Ste 100 (20166-9544)
PHONE................................703 435-5400
EMP: 1

SALES (est): 71.9K **Privately Held**
WEB: www.arcsecond.com
SIC: 3861 Photographic equipment & supplies

(G-13349)
ARMS RACE NUTRITION LLC
22370 Davis Dr Ste 100 (20164-5367)
PHONE................................888 978-2332
Douglas Allen Miller,
EMP: 2
SALES (est): 81.4K **Privately Held**
WEB: www.armsracenutrition.com
SIC: 2023 Dietary supplements, dairy & non-dairy based

(G-13350)
AROMATIC SPICE BLENDS LLC
43671 Trade Center Pl # 166 (20166-2120)
PHONE................................703 477-6865
Deepa Patke, *Mng Member*
EMP: 3
SALES (est): 50K **Privately Held**
WEB: www.aromaticspiceblends.com
SIC: 3999 Manufacturing industries

(G-13351)
ART OF WOOD
15 Oldridge Ct (20165)
PHONE................................703 597-9357
EMP: 2
SALES (est): 60.2K **Privately Held**
SIC: 2499 Decorative wood & woodwork

(G-13352)
ASTRON WIRELESS TECH INC
22560 Glenn Dr Ste 114 (20164-4440)
PHONE................................703 450-5517
James L Jalbert, *CEO*
Robert Jonas, *Principal*
EMP: 13
SALES (est): 2.2MM **Privately Held**
WEB: www.astronwireless.com
SIC: 3663 5065 Antennas, transmitting & communications; communication equipment

(G-13353)
ASTRON WIRELESS TECH LLC (PA)
22560 Glenn Dr Ste 114 (20164-4440)
PHONE................................703 450-5517
Thomas Lopez, *CEO*
William Jonas, *President*
Robert Jonas, *Principal*
Stephen Loftus, *Principal*
Marina Burgstahler, *COO*
EMP: 11
SQ FT: 160,900
SALES (est): 1.3MM **Privately Held**
SIC: 3663 Antennas, transmitting & communications

(G-13354)
ATAVUS INC
21100 Midday Ln (20164-4632)
PHONE................................703 404-2796
Kenneth Nelson, *Principal*
EMP: 2
SALES (est): 102.2K **Privately Held**
WEB: www.rootstrust.com
SIC: 7372 Prepackaged software

(G-13355)
ATI DEVELOPMENT LLC
506 Shaw Rd Ste 330 (20166-6767)
PHONE................................571 313-0857
EMP: 2
SALES (est): 90.8K **Privately Held**
WEB: www.atiroofing.com
SIC: 3312 Stainless steel

(G-13356)
AUTOMATED SIGNATURE TECHNOLOGY
Also Called: Sig Tech
112 Oakgrove Rd Ste 107 (20166-9413)
PHONE................................703 397-0910
Robert M Deshazo III, *President*
Dana D Turman, *Corp Secy*
John P Deshazo, *Vice Pres*
Lindsay S Deshazo, *Vice Pres*
Lindsay Deshazo, *Vice Pres*
EMP: 10
SQ FT: 6,000

SALES (est): 1.6MM **Privately Held**
WEB: www.signaturemachine.com
SIC: 3555 3861 Printing trades machinery; reproduction machines & equipment

(G-13357)
BENABAYE POWER LLC
103 Douglas Ct (20166-9410)
PHONE................................703 574-5800
Laura Benabaye, *Principal*
EMP: 1
SQ FT: 10,000
SALES (est): 113.6K **Privately Held**
SIC: 3524 Lawn & garden equipment

(G-13358)
BEST CHECKS INC
100 Executive Dr Unit 1 (20166-9554)
PHONE................................703 467-9300
Thomas Klarner, *President*
Brian Andrews, *Prdtn Mgr*
Amy McCaw, *Cust Mgr*
Jamie Sansom, *Office Mgr*
▲ EMP: 30
SQ FT: 9,200
SALES (est): 2.8MM **Privately Held**
WEB: www.bestchecks.com
SIC: 2782 Checkbooks

(G-13359)
BI COMMUNICATIONS INC
Also Called: Better Impressions
45150 Business Ct Ste 450 (20166-6726)
P.O. Box 125, Waterford (20197-0125)
PHONE................................703 435-9600
Michael L Healy, *President*
EMP: 16
SQ FT: 7,000
SALES (est): 2.8MM **Privately Held**
WEB: www.betterimpressions.com
SIC: 2752 Commercial printing, offset

(G-13360)
BLUE RIDGE BINDING INC
45570 Shepard Dr Ste 2 (20164-4454)
PHONE................................703 771-1676
Charles R Gillespie, *President*
Marilyn Gillespie, *Admin Sec*
EMP: 5
SQ FT: 3,000
SALES (est): 616.9K **Privately Held**
SIC: 2789 Binding only: books, pamphlets, magazines, etc.

(G-13361)
BROWNS STERLING MOTORS INC
21900 Auto World Cir (20166-2518)
PHONE................................571 390-6900
EMP: 4
SALES (est): 156.9K **Privately Held**
SIC: 3568 Drive chains, bicycle or motorcycle

(G-13362)
BURGERS CABINET SHOP INC
45910 Old Ox Rd (20166-9471)
PHONE................................571 262-8001
Richard Burger, *President*
Michael Burger, *Vice Pres*
Cindy Burger, *Accountant*
EMP: 18
SQ FT: 18,700
SALES (est): 2.2MM **Privately Held**
WEB: www.burgerscabinets.com
SIC: 2514 2541 Medicine cabinets & vanities: metal; cabinets, except refrigerated: show, display, etc.: wood

(G-13363)
CABINET ARTS LLC
45945 Trefoil Ln Ste 136 (20166-4343)
PHONE................................571 313-1891
Serhat Solmaz,
EMP: 2
SALES (est): 217.5K **Privately Held**
WEB: www.cabinetarts.com
SIC: 2434 Wood kitchen cabinets

(G-13364)
CABINET MAKERS
22611 Markey Ct Ste 114-H (20166-6931)
PHONE................................703 421-6331
Eric Colby, *President*
EMP: 3 EST: 2011

SALES (est): 253.6K **Privately Held**
WEB: www.cabinetmakerssupply.net
SIC: 3553 Cabinet makers' machinery

(G-13365)
CARDINAL BAKERY INC
22704 Commrce Ctr Ct # 100 (20166-9387)
PHONE................................703 430-1600
Joseph Politano, *President*
Frank Politano, *Vice Pres*
Teresa Vo, *Accounting Mgr*
EMP: 22
SALES (est): 4MM **Privately Held**
WEB: www.cardinalbakery.com
SIC: 2051 Breads, rolls & buns; bagels, fresh or frozen; rolls, bread type: fresh or frozen

(G-13366)
CBD GENIE LLC
20921 Davenport Dr (20165-6156)
PHONE................................571 434-1776
Ahmad Kabir, *Principal*
EMP: 2
SALES (est): 66.1K **Privately Held**
SIC: 3999

(G-13367)
CENTURY STEEL PRODUCTS INC
45034 Underwood Ln # 201 (20166-2338)
P.O. Box 319 (20167-0319)
PHONE................................703 471-7606
Joel Gundersheimer, *President*
Theodore Beck, *Vice Pres*
Theodore L Schwartzbeck, *Vice Pres*
EMP: 25 EST: 1979
SQ FT: 47,000
SALES (est): 7.6MM **Privately Held**
SIC: 3441 5051 3444 Fabricated structural metal; metals service centers & offices; sheet metalwork

(G-13368)
CENTURY TRUCKING LLC
43751 Beaver Meadow Rd (20166-2103)
PHONE................................703 996-8585
Juan Ferreo, *Owner*
EMP: 1
SALES (est): 133.8K **Privately Held**
SIC: 3713 Dump truck bodies

(G-13369)
CHANTILLY CRUSHED STONE INC
Loudoun Quarries
23076 Shaw Rd (20166-4317)
P.O. Box 220005, Chantilly (20153-0005)
PHONE................................703 471-4411
William Hough, *Vice Pres*
EMP: 40
SALES (corp-wide): 17.4MM **Privately Held**
WEB: www.gudelskygroup.com
SIC: 3281 Cut stone & stone products
PA: Chantilly Crushed Stone, Inc.
25000 Tanner Ln
Chantilly VA 20152
703 471-4461

(G-13370)
CJ & ASSOCIATES LLC
Also Called: Craig Thomas Johnson
47025 Bennington Ct (20165-7560)
PHONE................................301 461-2945
Craig T Johnson, *Owner*
Anna Johnson, *Vice Pres*
EMP: 1
SALES (est): 125.7K **Privately Held**
SIC: 3829 7381 8221 Polygraph devices; detective agency; colleges universities & professional schools

(G-13371)
CLAREN
46950 Cmnty Plz Ste 216 (20164)
PHONE................................571 403-0425
EMP: 2
SALES (est): 190.3K **Privately Held**
SIC: 3578 Calculating & accounting equipment

(G-13372)
COLORNET PRTG & GRAPHICS INC
22570 Glenn Dr (20164-4490)
PHONE................................703 406-9301
Kevin Gilboy, *Manager*
EMP: 1
SALES (corp-wide): 19.2MM **Privately Held**
WEB: www.colornetprinting.com
SIC: 2752 Commercial printing, offset
PA: Colornet Printing And Graphics, Inc.
736 Rockville Pike
Rockville MD 20852
301 208-8200

(G-13373)
COMPU DYNAMICS LLC (PA)
22446 Davis Dr Ste 187 (20164-7111)
PHONE................................703 796-6070
Stephen B Altizer, *President*
Lee Piazza, *Vice Pres*
Alex Cifuentes, *Project Mgr*
David Curtis, *Warehouse Mgr*
Will McRae, *Foreman/Supr*
EMP: 44
SQ FT: 6,600
SALES (est): 5.1MM **Privately Held**
WEB: www.compu-dynamics.com
SIC: 3571 Electronic computers

(G-13374)
CONSOLIDATED MAILING SVCS INC
504 Shaw Rd Ste 208 (20166-9437)
PHONE................................703 904-1600
Larry A Patrick Sr, *President*
Belinda M Patrick, *Admin Sec*
EMP: 35
SQ FT: 10,000
SALES (est): 1.6MM **Privately Held**
SIC: 2752 7331 Commercial printing, offset; mailing service

(G-13375)
CORE NUTRITIONALS LLC
22370 Davis Dr Ste 100 (20164-5367)
PHONE................................888 978-2332
Douglas A Miller,
Stephanie Miller,
EMP: 2 EST: 2009
SALES (est): 176.4K **Privately Held**
WEB: www.corenutritionals.com
SIC: 2023 Dietary supplements, dairy & non-dairy based

(G-13376)
CROSSLINE CREATIONS LLC
44258 Mercure Cir 103 (20166-2085)
PHONE................................703 625-4780
Cory Sokolowski,
Clint Wildman, *Master*
EMP: 2
SALES (est): 250K **Privately Held**
WEB: www.crossline-creations.com
SIC: 3443 Tanks, standard or custom fabricated: metal plate

(G-13377)
CRYPTEK USA CORP
1501 Moran Rd (20166-9372)
PHONE................................571 434-2000
Lynn Rossetti, *Manager*
EMP: 40
SALES (est): 950K **Privately Held**
WEB: www.crytek.com
SIC: 3571 Electronic computers

(G-13378)
CS WOODWORKING DESIGN LLC
43670 Trade Center Pl # 160 (20166-2123)
PHONE................................703 996-1122
Chang Sung Chon,
EMP: 1
SALES (est): 134.6K **Privately Held**
SIC: 2431 Millwork

(G-13379)
CTM AUTOMATED SYSTEMS INC
130 Forest Ridge Dr (20164-2113)
P.O. Box 1205 (20167-8411)
PHONE................................703 742-0755
Carol Moseley, *Owner*

James W Moseley, *Vice Pres*
EMP: 1
SALES (est): 100K **Privately Held**
WEB: www.ctmauto.com
SIC: 7372 Prepackaged software

(G-13380)
CUBICLE LOGIC LLC
20533 Mason Oak Ct (20165-3173)
PHONE 571 989-2823
Ayesha Khan, *Managing Prtnr*
Shahab Khan, *Managing Prtnr*
EMP: 5 **EST:** 2011
SALES (est): 247.5K **Privately Held**
WEB: www.cubiclelogic.com
SIC: 7372 7379 7371 Educational computer software; operating systems computer software; ; custom computer programming services

(G-13381)
CUSTOM SIGNS TODAY
43720 Trade Center Pl # 105 (20166-2189)
PHONE 703 661-0611
Glenn Mc Gee, *President*
Bryan McGee, *General Mgr*
Arlene Mc Gee, *Vice Pres*
EMP: 5
SQ FT: 4,000
SALES (est): 559.8K **Privately Held**
WEB: www.customsignstoday.net
SIC: 3993 Signs & advertising specialties

(G-13382)
DATAPATH INC
21251 Ridgetop Cir # 120 (20166-8532)
PHONE 703 476-1826
EMP: 14
SQ FT: 800
SALES (est): 1.2MM
SALES (corp-wide): 71.7MM **Privately Held**
SIC: 3663 Manufactures Radio/Tv Communication Equipment
PA: Dpii Holdings, Llc
5665 New Northside Dr # 500
Atlanta GA 30328
678 909-4660

(G-13383)
DEAN DELAWARE LLC
22980 Indian Creek Dr # 130 (20166-6734)
PHONE 703 802-6231
Joel Bonfiglio, *Principal*
EMP: 3
SALES (est): 300K **Privately Held**
WEB: www.mcdean.com
SIC: 3721 Aircraft

(G-13384)
DESIGNO ENTERPRISES LLC
45891 Woodland Rd Ste 125 (20166-9006)
PHONE 571 437-5452
Abraham Hamrah, *Administration*
EMP: 11
SALES (est): 1.2MM **Privately Held**
WEB: www.designomotoring.com
SIC: 3993 Signs & advertising specialties

(G-13385)
DHK STORAGE LLC
44965 Aviation Dr Ste 205 (20166-7530)
PHONE 703 870-3741
David Klein, *President*
William Foltyn, *Sales Engr*
EMP: 2
SALES (est): 113.2K
SALES (corp-wide): 245.9K **Privately Held**
WEB: www.dhk.com
SIC: 3572 3577 8731 Computer storage devices; computer peripheral equipment; computer (hardware) development
PA: Dhk Enterprises, Inc.
44965 Aviation Dr Ste 205
Sterling VA 20166
703 637-3990

(G-13386)
DIGITAL DELIGHTS INC
22967 Whitehall Ter (20166-4303)
PHONE 703 661-6888
Parminder Gill, *President*
EMP: 1 **EST:** 2012
SALES (est): 76K **Privately Held**
SIC: 3949 Sporting & athletic goods

(G-13387)
DIRAK INCORPORATED
22560 Glenn Dr Ste 105 (20164-4440)
PHONE 703 378-7637
Greogory Breads, *CEO*
Dieter Ramsauer, *President*
Uwe Schuettler, *Area Mgr*
Jignesh Patel, *Controller*
Stefanie Hooper, *Sales Staff*
▲ **EMP:** 19
SQ FT: 11,000
SALES (est): 8MM
SALES (corp-wide): 87.9K **Privately Held**
WEB: www.us.dirak.com
SIC: 3053 Gaskets, packing & sealing devices
HQ: Dirak Dieter Ramsauer Konstruktionselemente Gmbh
Konigsfelder Str. 1
Ennepetal 58256
233 383-70

(G-13388)
DOUGLAS STUART LLC
22712 Commrce Ctr Ct # 1 (20166-2089)
PHONE 571 210-4440
George Christopher, *Principal*
EMP: 175 **EST:** 2017
SALES (est): 142.9K **Privately Held**
WEB: www.douglasstuartllc.com
SIC: 2752 7389 7322 7373 Commercial printing, lithographic; mailbox rental & related service; adjustment & collection services; computer integrated systems design; editing service

(G-13389)
DREAUXN FILMS LLC
20322 Center Brook Sq (20165-5191)
PHONE 504 452-1117
Lee Tilton,
EMP: 1 **EST:** 2017
SALES (est): 10K **Privately Held**
WEB: www.dreauxnfilms.com
SIC: 3861 Aerial cameras

(G-13390)
DRONECHAKRA INC
47253 Middle Bluff Pl (20165-3127)
PHONE 540 420-7394
Valinder Singh Mabagt, *Owner*
EMP: 2
SALES (est): 91K **Privately Held**
SIC: 3721 Motorized aircraft

(G-13391)
DULLES IRON WORKS INC
43751 Beaver Meadow Rd (20166-2103)
P.O. Box 1473 (20167-8449)
PHONE 703 996-8797
Jose A Flores, *President*
EMP: 4
SQ FT: 6,700
SALES (est): 71.9K **Privately Held**
WEB: www.dullesironworks.com
SIC: 3446 Architectural metalwork

(G-13392)
ELECTRONIC MANUFACTURING CORP
Also Called: Emcor
43720 Trade Center Pl # 100 (20166-2189)
PHONE 703 661-8351
EMP: 10
SALES (est): 850K **Privately Held**
SIC: 3679 Mfg Electronic Components

(G-13393)
EMKA TECHNOLOGIES INC
21515 Ridgetop Cir # 220 (20166-6576)
PHONE 703 237-9001
Serge Kaddoura, *President*
David Poldiak, *Sales Staff*
Virginie Brechet, *Office Mgr*
Josh Burton, *Info Tech Mgr*
EMP: 6
SALES (est): 1.1MM **Privately Held**
WEB: www.emka.fr
SIC: 3826 Analytical instruments

(G-13394)
EPIPHANY IDEATION
20541 Warburton Bay Sq (20165-4753)
PHONE 248 396-5828
Andrew Massara, *Owner*

EMP: 1
SALES (est): 61.5K **Privately Held**
SIC: 3629 Electronic generation equipment

(G-13395)
EUCLID SYSTEMS CORPORATION (PA)
45472 Holiday Dr Ste 7 (20166-9457)
PHONE 703 471-7145
Michael Ross, *President*
George Glady, *Exec VP*
Joann Simonsen, *Exec VP*
Michael McFadden, *Vice Pres*
Rahal Patani, *Vice Pres*
EMP: 60
SALES (est): 18.9MM **Privately Held**
WEB: www.euclidsys.com
SIC: 3851 8042 Ophthalmic goods; contact lenses; offices & clinics of optometrists

(G-13396)
EXOTIC VEHICLE WRAPS INC
23590 Overland Dr Ste 160 (20166-4442)
PHONE 240 320-3335
Nathan Vandervliet, *President*
EMP: 3
SALES (est): 206.6K **Privately Held**
WEB: www.exoticvehiclewraps.com
SIC: 2399 Automotive covers, except seat & tire covers

(G-13397)
FAIRFAX PUBLISHING COMPANY (PA)
Also Called: Hampton Rads Snior Lving Guide
14 Pidgeon Hill Dr # 330 (20165-6166)
P.O. Box 1622 (20167-1602)
PHONE 703 421-2003
Robert O'Malley, *President*
Karen Mackechnie, *Sales Staff*
Karen Cassidy, *Director*
Kelly Wilson, *Executive*
Paula Loyola, *Regional*
EMP: 4
SQ FT: 1,000
SALES (est): 2.9MM **Privately Held**
WEB: www.seniorlivingguide.com
SIC: 2721 Magazines: publishing only, not printed on site

(G-13398)
FIVE GRAPES LLC
45180 Business Ct Ste 100 (20166-6706)
PHONE 703 205-2444
Amy Troutmiller, *General Mgr*
▲ **EMP:** 6
SQ FT: 20,000
SALES (est): 1.7MM **Privately Held**
SIC: 2084 Wines

(G-13399)
FIVE STAR PORTABLES INC
45910 Transamerica Plz # 103 (20166-4363)
PHONE 571 839-7884
Patricia Pimenta, *President*
EMP: 5
SALES (est): 675.3K **Privately Held**
WEB: www.fivestarseptic.com
SIC: 2842 Specialty cleaning, polishes & sanitation goods

(G-13400)
FLYNN ENTERPRISES INC (PA)
Also Called: Allegra Print Signs Design
45668 Terminal Dr Ste 100 (20166-4396)
PHONE 703 444-5555
John Flynn, *Owner*
Frank Cecil, *Production*
Jonathan Zellner, *Marketing Staff*
Jim Lash, *Manager*
Matt Gonzalez, *Graphic Designe*
EMP: 28
SQ FT: 11,000
SALES (est): 2.7MM **Privately Held**
WEB: www.allegradulles.com
SIC: 2752 3993 2789 5999 Commercial printing, offset; signs & advertising specialties; bookbinding & related work; banners, flags, decals & posters; printers' services: folding, collating

(G-13401)
FOOD TECHNOLOGY CORPORATION
45921 Maries Rd Ste 120 (20166-9278)
PHONE 703 444-1870
Shirl C Lakeway Jr, *President*
EMP: 5
SQ FT: 3,000
SALES (est): 3MM **Privately Held**
WEB: www.textureanalyzers.com
SIC: 3827 Optical test & inspection equipment

(G-13402)
FRENCH BREAD FACTORY INC
44225 Mercure Cir Ste 170 (20166-2054)
PHONE 703 761-4070
Napolean Maltez, *President*
Raul Morales, *Vice Pres*
Carlos Suanes, *Controller*
EMP: 19
SQ FT: 8,000
SALES (est): 2.4MM **Privately Held**
WEB: www.thefrenchbreadfactory.com
SIC: 2051 Bakery: wholesale or wholesale/retail combined

(G-13403)
G & H LITHO INC
506 Shaw Rd Ste 312 (20166-9444)
P.O. Box 528 (20167-0528)
PHONE 571 267-7148
James D Hensel, *President*
Charles D Green, *Corp Secy*
EMP: 9
SQ FT: 2,800
SALES (est): 1MM **Privately Held**
SIC: 2752 Commercial printing, offset

(G-13404)
G AND H LITHO
506 Shaw Rd Ste 312 (20166-9444)
P.O. Box 528 (20167-0528)
PHONE 571 267-7148
James D Hensel, *President*
EMP: 2
SALES (est): 111.1K **Privately Held**
SIC: 2759 Commercial printing

(G-13405)
GABRO GRAPHICS INC
Also Called: Gabro Printing & Graphics
22800 Executive Dr # 150 (20166-9588)
PHONE 703 464-8588
Antoine Gabro, *President*
Mike Gabro, *Treasurer*
Doha Gabro, *Admin Sec*
EMP: 17
SQ FT: 1,845
SALES (est): 1.2MM **Privately Held**
WEB: www.gabroprinting.com
SIC: 2752 Commercial printing, offset

(G-13406)
GAM PRINTERS INCORPORATED
45969 Nokes Blvd Ste 130 (20166-6606)
P.O. Box 25 (20167-0025)
PHONE 703 450-4121
Nathaniel Grant, *CEO*
Faith A Grant, *Corp Secy*
EMP: 15
SALES (est): 3.7MM **Privately Held**
WEB: www.graphicsandmarketing.com
SIC: 2752 Commercial printing, offset

(G-13407)
GAMMAFLUX CONTROLS INC (HQ)
113 Executive Dr (20166-9508)
PHONE 703 471-5050
Robert W Davies, *President*
Don Nolen, *Opers Mgr*
EMP: 1
SALES (est): 145K
SALES (corp-wide): 1.4B **Publicly Held**
WEB: www.gammaflux.com
SIC: 3823 Temperature instruments: industrial process type
PA: Barnes Group Inc.
123 Main St
Bristol CT 06010
860 583-7070

▲ = Import ▼=Export
◆ =Import/Export

(G-13408)
GATEKEEPER SECURITY INC
22720 Ladbrook Dr Ste 100 (20166)
PHONE......................................703 673-3320
Christopher A Millar, *CEO*
Mazie Barcus, *Director*
▲ EMP: 23
SALES (est): 5.4MM **Privately Held**
WEB: www.gatekeepersecurity.com
SIC: 3669 Intercommunication systems,
electric

(G-13409)
GAUGE WORKS LLC
43671 Trade Center Pl # 156 (20166-2121)
PHONE......................................703 661-1300
Greg Day,
EMP: 6
SALES (est): 759.2K **Privately Held**
SIC: 3829 Gauging instruments, thickness
ultrasonic

(G-13410)
GEMINI SECURITY LLC
21010 Southbank St (20165-7227)
PHONE......................................703 466-0163
Robin Britt Steffler, *President*
Mark Steffler,
EMP: 2
SALES (est): 90K **Privately Held**
SIC: 7372 Business oriented computer
software

(G-13411)
GIFT TERRARIUMS LLC
204 Marcum Ct (20164-1440)
PHONE......................................571 230-5918
EMP: 1 EST: 2014
SALES (est): 77.4K **Privately Held**
SIC: 3499 Novelties & giftware, including
trophies

(G-13412)
GLOBAL COM INC
23465 Rock Hven Way Ste 1 (20166)
PHONE......................................703 532-6425
Bruce Anderson, *President*
Brett Dodson, *Vice Pres*
Fritz Schirmacher, *Project Mgr*
Ash Patel, *Opers Mgr*
Theresa Petti, *Foreman/Supr*
EMP: 20
SALES (est): 5.7MM **Privately Held**
WEB: www.globalcomva.com
SIC: 3357 Coaxial cable, nonferrous; fiber
optic cable (insulated)

(G-13413)
GRANITE PERCH GRAPHICS
47525 Anchorage Cir (20165-4713)
PHONE......................................703 218-5300
Katrina Pinkston, *Executive*
EMP: 2 EST: 2018
SALES (est): 62.3K **Privately Held**
SIC: 2084 Wines, brandy & brandy spirits

(G-13414)
GREENTEC-USA INC
Also Called: Secure Knowledge
22365 Broderick Dr # 220 (20166-9361)
PHONE......................................703 880-8332
Steve Petruzzo, *President*
Billy Stewart, *Vice Pres*
Bob Waligunda, *Vice Pres*
EMP: 22
SALES (est): 4.5MM **Privately Held**
WEB: www.greentec-usa.com
SIC: 3571 Electronic computers

(G-13415)
**GREENTECH AUTOMOTIVE
CORP (HQ)**
Also Called: Gta
21355 Ridgetop Cir # 250 (20166-8517)
PHONE......................................703 666-9001
Charles Wang, *CEO*
Terry McAuliffe, *Ch of Bd*
Richard Xiaoyun LI, *Senior VP*
▲ EMP: 15 EST: 2012
SALES (est): 17.1MM **Privately Held**
SIC: 3711 Automobile assembly, including
specialty automobiles

PA: Wm Industries Corp.
21355 Ridgetop Cir # 250
Sterling VA 20166
703 666-9001

(G-13416)
GSA SERVICE COMPANY
1310 E Maple Ave (20164-2706)
PHONE......................................703 742-6818
Aaron Caplan, *Owner*
EMP: 1
SALES (est): 100K **Privately Held**
WEB: www.gsaservice.com
SIC: 3999 Manufacturing industries

(G-13417)
GSK CORPORATION INC
45915 Maries Rd Unit 104 (20166-8523)
PHONE......................................240 200-5600
Basem Kadry, *President*
EMP: 1
SALES (corp-wide): 456.8K **Privately
Held**
WEB: www.gskcorp.com
SIC: 2869 Laboratory chemicals, organic
PA: Gsk Corporation
10075 Tyler Ct Ste 10
Ijamsville MD 21754
240 200-5600

(G-13418)
HANG UP
22360 S Sterling Blvd D104 (20164-4242)
P.O. Box 474 (20167-0474)
PHONE......................................703 430-0717
Cindy Knowles, *Owner*
EMP: 3
SQ FT: 1,644
SALES (est): 205K **Privately Held**
WEB: www.thehangup.biz
SIC: 2499 7389 8999 Picture & mirror
frames, wood; interior designer; art
restoration

(G-13419)
HIGH SPEED NETWORKS LLC
22959 Rock Hill Rd (20166-9414)
PHONE......................................703 963-4572
John T Marsh, *President*
John Marsh,
EMP: 1 **Privately Held**
SIC: 3825 Network analyzers

(G-13420)
HOGAR CONTROLS
46040 Center Oak Plz # 125 (20166-8539)
PHONE......................................703 844-1160
EMP: 2
SALES (est): 93K **Privately Held**
SIC: 3651 Speaker systems

(G-13421)
HOMELAND CORPORATION
Also Called: Wicker Warehouse
47202 Redbark Pl (20165-7620)
PHONE......................................571 218-6200
M Omar Malikyar, *President*
EMP: 10
SQ FT: 20,000
SALES (est): 780K **Privately Held**
SIC: 2721 5945 5719 Periodicals; hobby,
toy & game shops; wicker, rattan or reed
home furnishings

(G-13422)
**HONEYWELL INTERNATIONAL
INC**
105 Carpenter Dr (20164-7159)
PHONE......................................703 437-7651
Steven Huff, *Branch Mgr*
EMP: 5
SALES (corp-wide): 36.7B **Publicly Held**
WEB: www.honeywell.com
SIC: 3724 Aircraft engines & engine parts
PA: Honeywell International Inc.
300 S Tryon St
Charlotte NC 28202
704 627-6200

(G-13423)
HUMMERSPORT LLC
47605 Woodboro Ter (20165-4737)
P.O. Box 650622 (20165-0622)
PHONE......................................703 433-1887
Crystal Dunn, *Principal*
EMP: 4

SALES (est): 166.8K **Privately Held**
WEB: www.soccerwire.com
SIC: 2711 Newspapers

(G-13424)
HYDRO SYSTEMS USA INC
45080 Old Ox Rd (20166-2357)
PHONE......................................703 429-1024
EMP: 2
SALES (corp-wide): 355.8K **Privately
Held**
WEB: www.hydro.aero
SIC: 3728 Aircraft parts & equipment
HQ: Hydro Systems Usa Inc.
7028 S 204th St
Kent WA 98032

(G-13425)
IAM ENERGY INCORPORATED
46208 Wales Ter (20165-8740)
PHONE......................................703 939-5681
Shaun K Kama, *Principal*
EMP: 2
SALES (est): 147.4K **Privately Held**
WEB: www.iamenergyinc.com
SIC: 3674 Light emitting diodes

(G-13426)
IDVECTOR
46040 Center Oak Plz # 165 (20166-8539)
PHONE......................................571 313-5064
Michael Tanji, *Principal*
EMP: 3
SALES (est): 179.3K **Privately Held**
WEB: www.vector.com
SIC: 3577 5045 7379 Encoders, com-
puter peripheral equipment; computers,
peripherals & software; computer periph-
eral equipment; computer related consult-
ing services;

(G-13427)
INDYNE INC
Also Called: Classified - Space Systems Div
21351 Gentry Dr Ste 205 (20166-8512)
PHONE......................................703 903-6900
Don Bishop, *President*
EMP: 2
SALES (corp-wide): 195.8MM **Privately
Held**
WEB: www.indyneinc.com
SIC: 3842 Prosthetic appliances
PA: Indyne, Inc.
21351 Gentry Dr Ste 205
Sterling VA 20166
703 903-6900

(G-13428)
INSPIRED EMBROIDERY
46908 Foxstone Pl (20165-3521)
PHONE......................................703 409-3375
EMP: 1 EST: 2014
SALES (est): 58.3K **Privately Held**
SIC: 2395 Embroidery & art needlework

(G-13429)
INTELLIGENCE PRESS INC (PA)
22648 Glenn Dr Ste 305 (20164-4448)
PHONE......................................703 318-8848
Ellen Beswick, *President*
Barbara Bolen, *Finance Dir*
Charlie Passut, *Assoc Editor*
Alex Steis, *CTO*
Nathan Harrison, *Director*
EMP: 13
SQ FT: 3,000
SALES (est): 1.3MM **Privately Held**
WEB: www.naturalgasintel.com
SIC: 2711 Newspapers: publishing only,
not printed on site

(G-13430)
**INTERNATIONAL PUBLISHERS
MKTG**
22841 Quicksilver Dr (20166-2019)
PHONE......................................703 661-1586
Azad Ajamian, *President*
Walter Bacak, *Exec Dir*
▲ EMP: 15 EST: 1987
SALES (est): 1MM **Privately Held**
WEB: www.internationalpubmarket.com
SIC: 2731 Book publishing

(G-13431)
**INTRINSIC SEMICONDUCTOR
CORP**
22660 Executive Dr # 101 (20166-9535)
PHONE......................................703 437-4000
EMP: 13
SALES (est): 783.7K **Privately Held**
SIC: 3674 Mfg Semiconductors/Related
Devices

(G-13432)
IRONTEK LLC
21211 Edgewood Ct (20165-7626)
PHONE......................................703 627-0092
Bechara Rizk, *Mng Member*
Nadim Rizk, *Mng Member*
EMP: 2
SALES (est): 10K **Privately Held**
SIC: 7372 7379 7373 7371 Application
computer software; computer related con-
sulting services; local area network (LAN)
systems integrator; computer software
systems analysis & design, custom

(G-13433)
IT SOLUTIONS 4U INC
21010 Southbank St (20165-7227)
P.O. Box 800 (20167-0800)
PHONE......................................703 624-4430
Shawn G Brown, *President*
EMP: 3
SALES (est): 100K **Privately Held**
WEB: www.it-solutions-4u.com
SIC: 3571 Electronic computers

(G-13434)
**JAMES J TOTARO ASSOCIATES
LLC**
22900 Shaw Rd (20166-9462)
PHONE......................................703 326-9525
EMP: 2
SALES (est): 11.5K **Privately Held**
SIC: 3281 Mfg Cut Stone/Products

(G-13435)
**JEFFERSON MLLWK & DESIGN
INC**
44098 Mercure Cir Ste 115 (20166-2016)
PHONE......................................703 260-3370
Jorge A Kfoury, *President*
Michael Corrigan, *Vice Pres*
Mark Howe, *Vice Pres*
Matt Hancock, *Prdtn Mgr*
James Cox, *Purch Mgr*
EMP: 60
SQ FT: 22,560
SALES (est): 11.6MM **Privately Held**
WEB: www.jeffersonmillwork.com
SIC: 2431 Doors, wood

(G-13436)
JR SALES
903 N Sterling Blvd (20164-3730)
PHONE......................................703 450-4753
John Scannell, *Owner*
EMP: 3
SALES (est): 50K **Privately Held**
SIC: 3524 Lawn & garden equipment

(G-13437)
JUSTICE
21100 Dulles Town Cir # 263 (20166-2489)
PHONE......................................703 421-7001
EMP: 2
SALES (est): 67K **Privately Held**
SIC: 2361 Girls' & children's dresses,
blouses & shirts

(G-13438)
KG OLD OX HOLDINGS INC
44886 Old Ox Rd (20166-2328)
PHONE......................................703 471-5321
Gregory McVeigh, *President*
Kenneth Spellman, *Exec VP*
EMP: 37
SQ FT: 21,000
SALES (est): 15.9MM **Privately Held**
WEB: www.trowbridgesteelco.com
SIC: 3441 Fabricated structural metal

(G-13439)
LABEL LABORATORY INC
11 Acacia Ln Ste 4 (20166-9316)
PHONE......................................703 654-0327
John Decanio, *President*

GEOGRAPHIC

EMP: 3
SALES (est): 24.6K **Privately Held**
SIC: 2754 Labels: gravure printing

(G-13440)
LEYLAND OCEANTECH INC
43720 Trade Center Pl (20166-4480)
PHONE.....................................703 661-6097
Joseph Sung, *President*
◆ EMP: 6
SQ FT: 5,174
SALES (est): 2.1MM **Privately Held**
SIC: 3678 Electronic connectors

(G-13441)
LIBERTY MEDICAL INC
22135 Davis Dr Ste 116 (20164-5365)
PHONE.....................................703 636-2269
Robert Wittmer, *President*
◆ EMP: 3
SQ FT: 2,400
SALES (est): 300K **Privately Held**
WEB: www.libertymedicalinc.com
SIC: 3851 Ophthalmic goods

(G-13442)
LINE-X NORTHERN VIRGINIA INC
100 Glenn Dr Ste A7 (20164-4403)
PHONE.....................................703 433-9333
Daniel E Nelson, *Principal*
EMP: 4
SALES (est): 353K **Privately Held**
WEB: www.linexnv.com
SIC: 2821 Plastics materials & resins

(G-13443)
LITTLE CORNERS PETIT FOURS LLC
1 Greencastle Rd (20164-1137)
PHONE.....................................571 215-4255
Kenneth Monroe Smith, *Administration*
EMP: 3 EST: 2012
SALES (est): 168.7K **Privately Held**
WEB: www.little-corners.com
SIC: 2053 Cakes, bakery: frozen

(G-13444)
LOCI LLC
38 Benton Ct (20165-5697)
PHONE.....................................301 613-7111
John Wise,
EMP: 1
SALES (est): 52.7K **Privately Held**
SIC: 7372 Application computer software; business oriented computer software; educational computer software

(G-13445)
LUFFT USA INC
22400 Davis Dr Ste 100 (20164-7128)
PHONE.....................................805 335-8500
Ann Pattison, *CEO*
Collan Marrs, *Finance*
Erik Wright, *Office Mgr*
Michael Corbett, *Branch Mgr*
Laura Goodfellow, *Technical Staff*
EMP: 13 **Privately Held**
WEB: www.lufft.com
SIC: 3829 Weather tracking equipment
PA: Lufft Usa, Inc.
420 Boardwalk Dr
Youngsville NC 27596

(G-13446)
MAHOGANY STYLES BY TEESHA LLC
21000 Suthbank St Ste 196 (20165)
PHONE.....................................703 433-2170
Teesha Jones, *Principal*
EMP: 2
SALES (est): 87.4K **Privately Held**
SIC: 2759 Screen printing

(G-13447)
MAPHOOK INC
23475 Rock Haven Way (20166-4444)
PHONE.....................................703 661-7000
EMP: 2
SALES (est): 83.2K **Privately Held**
WEB: www.maphook.com
SIC: 7372 Prepackaged software

(G-13448)
MARION NICKEL
45800 Jona Dr (20165-5685)
PHONE.....................................703 444-8158
EMP: 2
SALES (est): 142.5K **Privately Held**
SIC: 3356 Nonferrous Rolling/Drawing

(G-13449)
MARK SPACE INC
22611 Markey Ct Ste 110 (20166-6925)
PHONE.....................................703 404-8550
T M Tuck, *President*
EMP: 9
SQ FT: 5,047
SALES (est): 550K **Privately Held**
SIC: 3663 Radio & TV communications equipment

(G-13450)
MCKEAN DEFENSE GROUP LLC
45240 Business Ct Ste 300 (20166-6703)
PHONE.....................................703 848-7928
Joseph L Carlini, *CEO*
EMP: 4 EST: 2017
SALES (est): 336.4K **Privately Held**
SIC: 3812 Defense systems & equipment

(G-13451)
MECMESIN CORPORATION
45921 Maries Rd Ste 120 (20166-9278)
PHONE.....................................703 433-9247
Shirl Lakeway, *Principal*
▲ EMP: 5
SALES (est): 950K **Privately Held**
WEB: www.mecmesin.com
SIC: 3829 Measuring & controlling devices

(G-13452)
MEGAWATT APPS LLC
20445 Chesapeake Sq # 202 (20165-4343)
PHONE.....................................703 870-4082
Megg Gawat,
EMP: 1
SALES (est): 1K **Privately Held**
WEB: www.megawattapps.com
SIC: 7372 Application computer software

(G-13453)
MERICA LABZ LLC
22370 Davis Dr Ste 100 (20164-5367)
PHONE.....................................844 445-5335
Douglas A Miller,
EMP: 1 EST: 2016
SALES (est): 71K **Privately Held**
WEB: www.mericalabz.com
SIC: 2023 Dietary supplements, dairy & non-dairy based

(G-13454)
MICROTEK MEDICAL INC
101 International Dr (20166-9442)
PHONE.....................................703 904-1220
EMP: 24
SALES (corp-wide): 11.8B **Publicly Held**
SIC: 3841 Mfg Surgical/Medical Instruments
HQ: Microtek Medical Inc.
512 N Lehmberg Rd
Columbus MS 39702
662 327-1863

(G-13455)
MOLD REMOVAL LLC
45498 Lakeside Dr (20165-2519)
PHONE.....................................703 421-0000
EMP: 2
SALES (est): 106.4K **Privately Held**
SIC: 3544 Industrial molds

(G-13456)
MONTOYA SERVICES LLC
14 Millard Ct (20165-6017)
PHONE.....................................571 882-3464
Brian Montoya, *Mng Member*
EMP: 7
SALES (est): 450K **Privately Held**
SIC: 2431 Millwork

(G-13457)
MY PRINTING GUYS
22611 Markey Ct Ste 114-Q (20166-6931)
PHONE.....................................703 430-7940
EMP: 2

SALES (est): 83.9K **Privately Held**
SIC: 2752 Commercial printing, lithographic

(G-13458)
MYA SARAY LLC
43671 Trade Center Pl # 114 (20166-2118)
PHONE.....................................703 996-8800
Mahmoud Badawi, *President*
Hussam Badawi, *Vice Pres*
▲ EMP: 8
SQ FT: 7,000
SALES (est): 5.5MM **Privately Held**
WEB: www.myasaray.com
SIC: 3999 5099 3645 5199 Tobacco pipes, pipestems & bits; crystal goods; chandeliers, residential; charcoal

(G-13459)
NATIONAL LITHOGRAPH INC
22800 Executive Dr # 190 (20166-9506)
PHONE.....................................703 709-9000
Abraham Kochba, *President*
Kochba Beth, *Vice Pres*
Dave Kochba, *Vice Pres*
Elizabeth Kochba, *Vice Pres*
EMP: 10
SQ FT: 4,700
SALES (est): 930K **Privately Held**
WEB: www.nationallitho.com
SIC: 2752 Commercial printing, offset

(G-13460)
NATIONAL VACCINE INFO CTR
21525 Ridgetop Cir # 100 (20166-6510)
PHONE.....................................703 938-0342
Kathryn Williams, *Principal*
Paul Arthur, *Opers Staff*
EMP: 3
SALES (est): 1MM **Privately Held**
WEB: www.nvic.org
SIC: 2836 Vaccines

(G-13461)
NEWS CONNECTION
1 Saarinen Cir (20166-7500)
PHONE.....................................703 661-4999
EMP: 3
SALES (est): 116.2K **Privately Held**
SIC: 2711 Newspapers, publishing & printing

(G-13462)
NOVA POWER SOLUTIONS INC
21515 Ridgetop Cir # 210 (20166-6509)
PHONE.....................................703 657-0122
Leo Miller, *President*
Patti Miller, *President*
Karl Hantho, *Vice Pres*
EMP: 5
SQ FT: 6,000
SALES (est): 4.3MM **Privately Held**
WEB: www.novapower.com
SIC: 3679 3613 Electronic loads & power supplies; power supplies, all types: static; power switching equipment
PA: Lti Datacomm, Inc.
21515 Ridgetop Cir # 210
Sterling VA 20166
703 581-6868

(G-13463)
OBERONS FORGE PRESS LLC
20283 Center Brook Sq (20165-5178)
P.O. Box 650368 (20165-0368)
PHONE.....................................703 434-9275
Elaine Simone, *Principal*
EMP: 1
SALES (est): 37.5K **Privately Held**
SIC: 2741 Miscellaneous publishing

(G-13464)
OMNICARDATA LLC
23551 Pebble Run Pl Ste 1 (20166-4474)
PHONE.....................................703 622-6742
Shahidul Islam,
Joshua Bollinger,
EMP: 2
SQ FT: 600
SALES (est): 56.5K **Privately Held**
SIC: 7372 Prepackaged software

(G-13465)
ONE STOP COMPUTER SERVICES LLC
43676 Trade Ctr Plste 135 (20166)
PHONE.....................................571 442-2045
Ali Alam, *CEO*
EMP: 1 EST: 2015
SALES (est): 115.5K **Privately Held**
WEB: www.onestopcomputerservices.com
SIC: 7372 7379 7378 7375 Prepackaged software; computer related consulting services; computer maintenance & repair; information retrieval services

(G-13466)
ORBCOMM LLC
22970 Indian Creek Dr # 300 (20166-6740)
PHONE.....................................703 433-6300
Marc J Eisenberg, *CEO*
Jon Harden, *Vice Pres*
Dana Johnson, *Vice Pres*
Robert Kettlehake, *Accounts Mgr*
Brian Baynes, *Sales Staff*
EMP: 38
SALES (corp-wide): 272MM **Publicly Held**
WEB: www.orbcomm.com
SIC: 3663 Satellites, communications
HQ: Orbcomm Llc
395 W Passaic St Ste 3
Rochelle Park NJ 07662
703 433-6300

(G-13467)
ORBITAL ATK OPERATION GES
45245 Bus Ct Ste 400 (20166)
PHONE.....................................571 437-7870
EMP: 2
SALES (est): 86K **Privately Held**
SIC: 3764 Propulsion units for guided missiles & space vehicles

(G-13468)
OTT HYDROMET CORP (HQ)
22400 Davis Dr Ste 100 (20164-7128)
PHONE.....................................703 406-2800
Anton Felder, *President*
Deepak Gupta, *Managing Dir*
Daniel W Farrell, *Senior VP*
Ashish H Raval, *Senior VP*
Dan Farrell, *Vice Pres*
▲ EMP: 158 EST: 1975
SQ FT: 31,190
SALES (est): 32MM
SALES (corp-wide): 17.9B **Publicly Held**
WEB: www.sutron.com
SIC: 3829 Geophysical & meteorological testing equipment; meteorologic tracking systems; geophysical or meteorological electronic equipment; meteorological instruments
PA: Danaher Corporation
2200 Penn Ave Nw Ste 800w
Washington DC 20037
202 828-0850

(G-13469)
PETREE ENTERPRISES INC
45945 Trefoil Ln Ste 166 (20166-4344)
PHONE.....................................703 318-0008
Noel Petree, *President*
Karen Petree, *Vice Pres*
Barbara Petree, *Admin Sec*
EMP: 10
SQ FT: 4,000
SALES (est): 2MM **Privately Held**
WEB: www.petreepress.com
SIC: 2752 Commercial printing, offset

(G-13470)
PINK DENTAL LABORATORY LLC
43760 Trade Center Pl # 16 (20166-4482)
PHONE.....................................540 728-5987
Erik Niederhauser,
EMP: 2
SALES (est): 500K **Privately Held**
SIC: 3843 Dental materials

(G-13471)
PLEXI WORLDWIDE LLC
22960 Shaw Rd Ste 601 (20166-9447)
PHONE.....................................804 625-2524
Jessica Grano, *CEO*
EMP: 1

SALES (est): 110.9K **Privately Held**
SIC: 2821 Polymethyl methacrylate resins (plexiglass)

(G-13472)
POINTMAN RESOURCES LLC
107 Juneberry Ct (20164-2116)
P.O. Box 324, Monrovia MD (21770-0324)
PHONE..................................240 429-3423
Albert Srebnick, *President*
Emily Malsch, *Vice Pres*
EMP: 2
SALES (est): 79.5K **Privately Held**
SIC: 3949 5091 5099 7699 Cartridge belts, sporting type; firearms, sporting; firearms & ammunition, except sporting; recreational sporting equipment repair services

(G-13473)
POLIMASTER INC
44873 Falcon Pl Ste 128 (20166-9543)
PHONE..................................703 525-5075
Ludmila Antaouskaya, *Ch of Bd*
James Mehalchick, *General Mgr*
Aliona Gorea, *Opers Mgr*
EMP: 12
SQ FT: 6,000
SALES: 4.4MM
SALES (corp-wide): 2.6MM **Privately Held**
WEB: www.polimaster.us
SIC: 3829 Measuring & controlling devices
PA: Polimaster Holdings Corporation
44873 Falcon Pl Ste 128
Sterling VA 20166
703 525-5075

(G-13474)
POLYTRADE INTERNATIONAL CORP
46608 Silhouette Sq (20164-6321)
PHONE..................................703 598-7269
Bahri Aliriza, *President*
EMP: 6
SALES (est): 605K **Privately Held**
SIC: 2911 7389 Fuel additives; business services

(G-13475)
POTOMAC CREEK WOODWORKS LLC
62 Southall Ct (20165-5799)
PHONE..................................703 444-9805
Michael Reuter, *Principal*
EMP: 4
SALES (est): 364K **Privately Held**
SIC: 2431 Millwork

(G-13476)
PRELUDE COMMUNICATIONS INC
7 Vandercastel Rd (20165-5622)
PHONE..................................703 731-9396
Roland L Waddell, *President*
EMP: 1
SALES (est): 131K **Privately Held**
SIC: 3651 4813 7812 Household audio & video equipment; telephone/video communications; motion picture & video production

(G-13477)
PRICE POINT EQUIPMENT
21010 Southbank St 180 (20165-7227)
PHONE..................................239 216-1688
Blazer Smith, *President*
EMP: 3
SALES (est): 286.6K **Privately Held**
SIC: 3842 Gloves, safety

(G-13478)
PRINTER RESOLUTIONS
702 E Dickenson Ct (20164-3412)
PHONE..................................703 850-5336
Philip Willis, *Principal*
EMP: 2 EST: 2014
SALES (est): 171.9K **Privately Held**
SIC: 2752 Commercial printing, lithographic

(G-13479)
PRINTING PRODUCTIONS INC
1333 Shepard Dr Ste E (20164-4427)
PHONE..................................703 406-2400

Randolph Davis, *President*
Joshua Moore, *Prdtn Mgr*
Jim Davis, *Manager*
EMP: 7
SQ FT: 4,000
SALES (est): 965.5K **Privately Held**
WEB: www.ppidigital.com
SIC: 2752 Commercial printing, offset

(G-13480)
PROFICIENT LINK LLC
22375 Broderick Dr # 155 (20166-9371)
PHONE..................................703 391-6330
Mitchell C Chen,
Terrill Andrews,
Jim Condon,
Laura Verscharen,
Steve Weiss,
EMP: 4
SALES (est): 203.2K **Privately Held**
SIC: 3571 Electronic computers

(G-13481)
PWILLZ CUSTOMZ LLC
22854 Bryant Ct Ste 106 (20166-9530)
PHONE..................................571 926-9622
EMP: 2 EST: 2017
SALES (est): 146.4K **Privately Held**
WEB: www.pwillzcustomz.com
SIC: 2752 Commercial printing, lithographic

(G-13482)
QORE PERFORMANCE INC
22311 Shaw Rd Ste A2 (20166-2354)
PHONE..................................703 755-0724
Jared Willcox, *CEO*
Justin LI, *President*
Scott Stern, *Principal*
Doug Burr, *Sales Staff*
EMP: 5
SALES (est): 780.9K **Privately Held**
WEB: www.qoreperformance.com
SIC: 2389 Men's miscellaneous accessories

(G-13483)
QUALITY GRAPHICS & PRTG INC
22831 Silverbrook Center (20166-4385)
PHONE..................................703 661-6060
Joseph Zaccack, *President*
Sam Zaccack, *Vice Pres*
EMP: 12
SALES (est): 1.9MM **Privately Held**
WEB: www.qgprint.com
SIC: 2752 7336 7334 Commercial printing, offset; graphic arts & related design; photocopying & duplicating services

(G-13484)
RADUS SOFTWARE LLC
47395 Halcyon Pl (20165-3149)
P.O. Box 650476 (20165-0476)
PHONE..................................703 623-8471
Sudi Sankavaram, *Director*
EMP: 2 EST: 2014
SALES (est): 70.2K **Privately Held**
SIC: 7372 Prepackaged software

(G-13485)
RAYTHEON COMPANY
22270 Pacific Blvd (20166-6924)
PHONE..................................703 759-1200
Susanna Kimbel, *General Mgr*
Guy Dubois, *Vice Pres*
Glenda Wallace, *Buyer*
Ron Grotheer, *Engineer*
Tim Hagen, *Technical Staff*
EMP: 320
SALES (corp-wide): 77B **Publicly Held**
WEB: www.rtx.com
SIC: 3812 Sonar systems & equipment
HQ: Raytheon Company
870 Winter St
Waltham MA 02451
781 522-3000

(G-13486)
RAYTHEON COMPANY
23010 Ladbrook Dr Ste 105 (20166-2095)
PHONE..................................703 260-3534
EMP: 49
SALES (corp-wide): 77B **Publicly Held**
WEB: www.rtx.com
SIC: 3812 Search & navigation equipment

HQ: Raytheon Company
870 Winter St
Waltham MA 02451
781 522-3000

(G-13487)
RAYTUM PHOTONICS LLC
43671 Trade Center Pl # 104 (20166-2121)
PHONE..................................703 831-7809
WEI Lu, *Director*
EMP: 6
SALES (est): 758.7K **Privately Held**
WEB: www.raytum-photonics.com
SIC: 3674 7389 Semiconductor diodes & rectifiers;

(G-13488)
RED HOT PUBLISHING LLC
20679 Cutwater Pl (20165-7343)
PHONE..................................703 885-5423
Stephanie Weinbracht, *Principal*
EMP: 2
SALES (est): 94.4K **Privately Held**
WEB: www.entangledpublishing.com
SIC: 2741 Miscellaneous publishing

(G-13489)
RELIADEFENSE LLC
229 Silverleaf Dr (20164-2848)
PHONE..................................571 225-4096
Michael Le,
EMP: 4
SALES (est): 208.5K **Privately Held**
SIC: 3812 Defense systems & equipment

(G-13490)
RESTON SHIRT & GRAPHIC CO INC
22800 Indian Creek Dr C (20166-6713)
PHONE..................................703 318-4802
James Joppich, *President*
Kenny Collins, *Manager*
John Mook, *Manager*
Sarah Turner, *Technology*
EMP: 8
SQ FT: 4,000
SALES (est): 1.1MM **Privately Held**
WEB: www.restonshirt.com
SIC: 2759 5199 Screen printing; advertising specialties

(G-13491)
RESTON TECHNOLOGY GROUP INC
22636 Glenn Dr (20164-4494)
PHONE..................................703 810-8800
Inderpal Bakshi, *CEO*
Inder Singh, *President*
EMP: 16
SALES (est): 684.8K **Privately Held**
WEB: www.rtg-usa.com
SIC: 7372 Prepackaged software

(G-13492)
REVERB NETWORKS INC
21515 Ridgetop Cir # 290 (20166-6576)
PHONE..................................703 665-4222
William T Carlin, *President*
EMP: 23 EST: 2007
SALES (est): 4.4MM **Privately Held**
WEB: www.reverbnetworks.com
SIC: 3663 Antennas, transmitting & communications

(G-13493)
REX MULTISERVICES LLC
21818 Goldstone Ter (20164-7032)
PHONE..................................703 400-1739
Marvin Munguia,
EMP: 2
SALES (est): 100K **Privately Held**
SIC: 3645 Garden, patio, walkway & yard lighting fixtures: electric

(G-13494)
RIGHT SIZED TECHNOLOGIES INC
22636 Glenn Dr Ste 302 (20164-4443)
PHONE..................................703 623-9505
John Barrass, *CEO*
EMP: 15
SALES (est): 1.2MM **Privately Held**
WEB: www.rst-i.com
SIC: 3571 Electronic computers

(G-13495)
ROCKWELL COLLINS INC
Also Called: Rockwell Collins Government Sy
22640 Davis Dr (20164-4470)
PHONE..................................703 234-2100
Kenneth Schreder, *Vice Pres*
Dan Huthwaite, *Facilities Mgr*
Ken Barker, *Mfg Staff*
Michelle Engelken, *Buyer*
James Babcock, *Engineer*
EMP: 40
SALES (corp-wide): 77B **Publicly Held**
WEB: www.rockwellcollins.com
SIC: 3812 Search & navigation equipment
HQ: Rockwell Collins, Inc.
400 Collins Rd Ne
Cedar Rapids IA 52498

(G-13496)
ROCKWELL COLLINS SIMULATION
22640 Davis Dr (20164-4470)
PHONE..................................703 234-2100
Hayan Al Fouad, *Engineer*
Greg Whiteside, *Engineer*
Michele Love, *Business Anlyst*
Steven Whalen, *Business Anlyst*
Tony Sime, *Branch Mgr*
EMP: 226
SALES (corp-wide): 77B **Publicly Held**
WEB: www.rockwellcollins.com
SIC: 3812 Search & navigation equipment
HQ: Rockwell Collins Simulation & Training Solutions Llc
400 Collins Rd Ne
Cedar Rapids IA 52498

(G-13497)
RPC TUBES
104 Carpenter Dr (20164-7160)
PHONE..................................703 471-5659
EMP: 3
SALES (est): 359.6K **Privately Held**
WEB: www.rpccompressors.com
SIC: 3585 Refrigeration & heating equipment

(G-13498)
RYCON INC
Also Called: Speedpro Imaging Northern VA
22135 Davis Dr Ste 112 (20164-5365)
PHONE..................................571 313-8334
Roman Blazauskas, *President*
Shawn Flaherty, *Vice Pres*
EMP: 3
SALES (est): 88.6K **Privately Held**
WEB: www.speedpro.com
SIC: 3993 Signs & advertising specialties

(G-13499)
S A HALAC IRON WORKS INC
21675 Ashgrove Ct (20166-9229)
PHONE..................................703 406-4766
Ahmet Halac, *CEO*
Insel Metin, *President*
Serdar Gurleyci, *Exec VP*
Bill Brent, *Vice Pres*
Steve Brewer, *Vice Pres*
EMP: 96
SQ FT: 85,000
SALES (est): 29MM **Privately Held**
WEB: www.sahalac.com
SIC: 3441 1791 Fabricated structural metal; structural steel erection

(G-13500)
SAFRAN CABIN STERLING INC (HQ)
44931 Falcon Pl (20166-9572)
PHONE..................................571 789-1900
Richard Gennaro, *President*
William T Hillman, *CFO*
EMP: 74 EST: 1953
SQ FT: 20,129
SALES (est): 22.5MM
SALES (corp-wide): 799.9MM **Privately Held**
WEB: www.safran-cabin.com
SIC: 3861 Aerial cameras
PA: Safran
2 Bd Du General Martial Valin
Paris 75015
140 608-080

(G-13501)
SDA SOFTWARE LLC
46030 Manekin Plz Ste 120 (20166-6692)
PHONE....................................703 657-0919
Jim Jeans,
Keith Brennan,
EMP: 2
SALES (est): 56.5K **Privately Held**
SIC: 7372 Prepackaged software

(G-13502)
SECRETBOW PUBG
INSTRUCTION LLC
32 Haxall Ct (20165-5750)
PHONE....................................703 404-3401
Adrienn Salazar, *Principal*
EMP: 2 EST: 2011
SALES (est): 106.1K **Privately Held**
SIC: 2741 Miscellaneous publishing

(G-13503)
SECUREDB INC
45499 Baggett Ter (20166-3026)
PHONE....................................703 231-0008
Vasudeva Karthik, *Principal*
EMP: 1
SALES (est): 67.6K **Privately Held**
SIC: 7372 Business oriented computer
software

(G-13504)
SERENDIB TRADITIONAL LLC
22024 Box Car Sq (20166-3041)
PHONE....................................703 408-1561
Amila Abeysekera,
▲ EMP: 1
SALES (est): 175.5K **Privately Held**
SIC: 2076 Vegetable oil mills

(G-13505)
SESTRA SYSTEMS INC
45180 Business Ct Ste 100 (20166-6706)
PHONE....................................703 429-1596
Lev Volftsun, *CEO*
Kim Aubuchon, *COO*
Victor Block, *CFO*
Anju Olson, *Marketing Staff*
Hard Chad, *Manager*
EMP: 40 EST: 2016
SALES (est): 595.9K **Privately Held**
WEB: www.sestrasystems.com
SIC: 3585 Cold drink dispensing equip-
ment (not coin-operated)

(G-13506)
SHELLYS CHACHKIES LLC
21165 Twinridge Sq (20164-6316)
PHONE....................................571 758-1323
Michelle R Bentley, *Mng Member*
EMP: 2
SALES (est): 67K **Privately Held**
SIC: 2339 Women's & misses' accessories

(G-13507)
SIGNS BY TOMORROW
45449 Severn Way Ste 173 (20166-8918)
PHONE....................................703 444-0007
William Lowson, *President*
EMP: 6
SALES (est): 410K **Privately Held**
WEB: www.signsbytomorrow.com
SIC: 3993 Signs & advertising specialties

(G-13508)
SILVER COMMUNICATIONS
CORP
102 Executive Dr Ste A (20166-9555)
PHONE....................................703 471-7339
Sterling Schiffman, *President*
Dirck Holscher, *Corp Secy*
Kenneth B Chaletzky, *Vice Pres*
Ho Pham, *Vice Pres*
Billie Kornegay, *Admin Asst*
EMP: 35
SQ FT: 20,000
SALES (est): 5.2MM **Privately Held**
WEB: www.silver-com.com
SIC: 2759 2791 2789 2752 Publication
printing; typesetting; bookbinding & re-
lated work; commercial printing, litho-
graphic

(G-13509)
SILYNX COMMUNICATIONS INC
45945 Center Oak Plz # 125 (20166-6583)
P.O. Box 16063, Irvine CA (92623-6063)
PHONE....................................301 217-9223
Matthew Hemenez, *CEO*
ADI Nir, *President*
Ruth Nir, *Vice Pres*
Theresa Nguyen, *Opers Mgr*
Kyle Good, *Controller*
▲ EMP: 11
SQ FT: 3,000
SALES (est): 9.9MM **Privately Held**
WEB: www.silynxcom.com
SIC: 3661 Fiber optics communications
equipment

(G-13510)
SKY MARBLE & GRANITE INC
21592 Atl Blvd Ste 120 (20166)
PHONE....................................571 926-8085
Kamill Yozgat, *President*
Hossam Barakat, *Accounting Mgr*
Robin Simmons, *Sales Associate*
▲ EMP: 11
SQ FT: 12,000
SALES (est): 1.8MM **Privately Held**
WEB: www.sky-marble.com
SIC: 3281 1743 Marble, building: cut &
shaped; marble installation, interior

(G-13511)
SMART START
201 Davis Dr (20164-4416)
PHONE....................................571 267-7140
EMP: 2 EST: 2014
SALES (est): 120.8K **Privately Held**
SIC: 3694 Ignition apparatus & distributors

(G-13512)
SMS DATA PRODUCTS GROUP
INC
22930 Shaw Rd Ste 600 (20166-9448)
PHONE....................................703 709-9898
EMP: 2
SALES (est): 85.9K **Privately Held**
SIC: 3579 Mfg Office Machines

(G-13513)
SOFIE CO
100 Executive Dr Ste 4/7 (20166-9507)
PHONE....................................703 787-4075
Nasrin Pourkiani, *Manager*
Todd Bejian,
EMP: 3 **Privately Held**
WEB: www.sofie.com
SIC: 2834 Pharmaceutical preparations
HQ: Sofie Co.
21000 Atl Blvd Ste 730
Dulles VA 20166

(G-13514)
SOFTWARE SOLUTION &
CLOUD
21424 Cliff Haven Ct (20164-2225)
PHONE....................................703 870-7233
Milan Olumee, *President*
EMP: 2
SALES (est): 65.5K **Privately Held**
SIC: 7372 Application computer software

(G-13515)
STEEL TECH LLC
21202 Huntington Sq # 301 (20166-4266)
PHONE....................................571 585-5861
Jose Abuid, *Administration*
EMP: 9 EST: 2015
SALES (est): 662K **Privately Held**
SIC: 3548 Welding wire, bare & coated

(G-13516)
STERLING SHEET METAL INC
36767 Pelham Ct (20164)
PHONE....................................540 338-0144
David O'Brain, *President*
EMP: 1
SALES (est): 163.5K **Privately Held**
WEB: www.sterlingcustomsheetmetal.com
SIC: 3444 Sheet metal specialties, not
stamped

(G-13517)
STITCHING STATION
21100 Dulles Town Cir (20166-2437)
PHONE....................................703 421-4053

Foo Lee, *Owner*
EMP: 3
SALES (est): 190.3K **Privately Held**
WEB: www.shopdullestowncenter.com
SIC: 2395 Embroidery products, except
schiffli machine

(G-13518)
STRIPPING CENTER OF
STERLING
100 Executive Dr (20166-9507)
PHONE....................................703 904-9577
William Allen, *President*
EMP: 4
SALES (est): 206.8K **Privately Held**
WEB: www.restorationsunlimited.com
SIC: 1081 Overburden removal, metal min-
ing

(G-13519)
STUDIO ONE PRINTING
Also Called: Studio One Screen Prtg & EMB
201 Davis Dr Ste D (20164-4417)
PHONE....................................703 430-8884
Geoffrey Mullikin, *Partner*
EMP: 3
SALES (est): 228.3K **Privately Held**
WEB: www.studiooneprinting.com
SIC: 2759 7389 Screen printing; embroi-
dering of advertising on shirts, etc.

(G-13520)
STYLUS PUBLISHING LLC
22841 Quicksilver Dr (20166-2019)
P.O. Box 605, Herndon (20172-0605)
PHONE....................................703 661-1581
John Von Krorring, *Principal*
Andrea Ciecierski, *Vice Pres*
McKenzie Baker, *Production*
Jane Leathem, *Sales Staff*
Jean Westcott, *Sales Staff*
▲ EMP: 7
SALES (est): 339.5K **Privately Held**
WEB: www.styluspub.presswarehouse.com
SIC: 2731 3999 Books: publishing only;
barber & beauty shop equipment

(G-13521)
STYLUS PUBLISHING LLC
22883 Quicksilver Dr (20166-2019)
PHONE....................................703 661-1504
John Von Knorring, *President*
Varton Ajamian, *President*
EMP: 6
SQ FT: 1,000
SALES (est): 261.2K **Privately Held**
WEB: www.styluspub.presswarehouse.com
SIC: 2731 Books: publishing only

(G-13522)
SUBMARINE TELECOMS FORUM
INC
21495 Ridgetop Cir # 201 (20166-8520)
PHONE....................................703 444-0845
Wayne Nielsen, *President*
Kristian Nielsen, *Vice Pres*
EMP: 3 EST: 2011
SALES (est): 250K **Privately Held**
WEB: www.subtelforum.com
SIC: 2721 Magazines: publishing & printing

(G-13523)
SULLIVAN COMPANY INC N J
22725 Duls Smmt Ct Ste 10 (20166)
P.O. Box 438 (20167-0438)
PHONE....................................703 464-5944
Neil J Sullivan II, *President*
James C Sullivan, *Vice Pres*
Chris Denis, *Engineer*
John Hunton, *Engineer*
Judy F Sullivan, *Treasurer*
EMP: 25
SQ FT: 16,000
SALES (est): 5.2MM **Privately Held**
WEB: www.njsullivan.com
SIC: 3599 3644 Machine shop, jobbing &
repair; outlet boxes (electric wiring de-
vices)

(G-13524)
SUPERIOR IRON WORKS INC
(PA)
45034 Underwood Ln # 100 (20166-2338)
PHONE....................................703 471-5500
Michael Kane, *President*

Gary Essex, *Vice Pres*
Melanie Clements, *CFO*
EMP: 75
SQ FT: 2,400
SALES (est): 10MM **Privately Held**
WEB: www.superioironworks.com
SIC: 3441 3446 Fabricated structural
metal; architectural metalwork

(G-13525)
SURFSIDE CANDLE CO
45445 Baggett Ter (20166-3034)
PHONE....................................540 455-4322
Kristen Corbett, *Principal*
EMP: 1
SALES (est): 39.6K **Privately Held**
WEB: www.surfsidecandleco.com
SIC: 3999 Candles

(G-13526)
SWEET RELIEF INC
504 Shaw Rd Ste 220 (20166-9437)
PHONE....................................703 963-4868
Mark Lannes, *President*
Joe Stubblefield, *Shareholder*
EMP: 7
SQ FT: 2,000
SALES (est): 710K **Privately Held**
WEB: www.sweetrelief.com
SIC: 2844 5122 5999 Cosmetic prepara-
tions; cosmetics; cosmetics

(G-13527)
T-SHIRT FACTORY LLC
20936 Sandian Ter (20165-5858)
PHONE....................................703 589-5175
Hamza Saeed, *Administration*
EMP: 2
SALES (est): 54.5K **Privately Held**
SIC: 2399 Emblems, badges & insignia

(G-13528)
TARMAC CORP
22963 Concrete Plz (20166-2325)
PHONE....................................703 471-0044
Bob Odom, *Principal*
EMP: 7
SALES (est): 918.2K **Privately Held**
SIC: 3273 Ready-mixed concrete

(G-13529)
TENEO INC
44330 Mercure Cir Ste 260 (20166-2024)
P.O. Box 349, Middleburg (20118-0349)
PHONE....................................703 212-3220
Piers Carey, *President*
EMP: 9
SQ FT: 1,000
SALES (est): 3MM **Privately Held**
WEB: www.teneo.net
SIC: 7372 7373 Prepackaged software;
computer integrated systems design
HQ: Teneo Limited
Unit 21
Reading BERKS RG7 4
845 125-9433

(G-13530)
TERRAGO TECHNOLOGIES INC
45610 Woodland Rd (20166-4219)
PHONE....................................678 391-9798
David Basil, *CEO*
David Stokely, *CFO*
EMP: 25
SALES (est): 3.6MM **Privately Held**
WEB: www.terragotech.com
SIC: 7372 Business oriented computer
software

(G-13531)
THORLABS INC
44901 Falcon Pl Ste 113 (20166-9531)
PHONE....................................703 300-3000
Jeff Brooker, *General Mgr*
Geetha Abraham, *General Mgr*
Kevin Lascola, *General Mgr*
Belinda Hegarty, *Buyer*
Wayne Blankenship, *Engineer*
EMP: 20
SALES (corp-wide): 207.1MM **Privately**
Held
WEB: www.thorlabs.com
SIC: 3826 Analytical optical instruments

▲ = Import ▼=Export
◆ =Import/Export

PA: Thorlabs, Inc.
56 Sparta Ave
Newton NJ 07860
973 579-7227

(G-13532)
THORLABS IMAGING SYSTEMS
108 Powers Ct Ste 150 (20166-9330)
PHONE.....................703 651-1705
EMP: 17
SALES (est): 2.9MM Privately Held
SIC: 3827 Mfg Optical Instruments/Lenses
Nonclassified Establishment

(G-13533)
TIA-THE RICHARDS CORP
44931 Falcon Pl Ste 1 (20166-9572)
PHONE.....................703 471-8600
Stanley Richards, President
Harold Richards, Vice Pres
EMP: 60
SQ FT: 22,000
SALES (est): 8.7MM Privately Held
SIC: 3728 Aircraft parts & equipment

(G-13534)
TITAN AMERICA LLC
Also Called: Titan Virginia Ready-Mix
22963 Concrete Plz (20166-2325)
PHONE.....................703 471-0044
Brandon Horton, Opers Mgr
Bob Odom, Branch Mgr
EMP: 86
SALES (corp-wide): 1.4MM Privately Held
WEB: www.titanamerica.com
SIC: 1422 3241 3273 Crushed & broken
limestone; cement, hydraulic; ready-
mixed concrete
HQ: Titan America Llc
5700 Lake Wright Dr # 300
Norfolk VA 23502
757 858-6500

(G-13535)
TOMOTRACE INC
13 Crescent Ct (20164-1601)
PHONE.....................202 207-5423
Maxim Kiselev, President
EMP: 1
SALES (est): 95.8K Privately Held
SIC: 3821 Laboratory apparatus & furniture

(G-13536)
TOTAL SPORTS
101 E Holly Ave (20164-5402)
PHONE.....................703 444-3633
EMP: 1
SALES (est): 63.4K Privately Held
SIC: 3949 Sporting & athletic goods

(G-13537)
TRAJECTORY TEES LLC
21725 Indian Summer Ter (20166-9008)
PHONE.....................419 680-6903
Daryl Copley, Principal
EMP: 2 EST: 2016
SALES (est): 122.3K Privately Held
SIC: 2759 Screen printing

(G-13538)
TRIRON DEFENSE SERVICES LLC
325 W Derby Ct (20164-3810)
PHONE.....................703 472-2458
John Moon, Mng Member
EMP: 1
SALES (est): 49.1K Privately Held
SIC: 3812 Defense systems & equipment

(G-13539)
TRITON DEFENSE SERVICES LLC
325 W Derby Ct (20164-3810)
PHONE.....................703 472-2458
John Moon, Mng Member
EMP: 1
SALES (est): 58.6K Privately Held
SIC: 3812 Defense systems & equipment

(G-13540)
TTM TECHNOLOGIES INC
1200 Severn Way (20166-8904)
PHONE.....................703 652-2200
John Chelberg, Vice Pres

John Nelson, Engineer
Hannah Lim, Controller
Seema Bicocchi, Human Res Mgr
Linh Powell, Branch Mgr
EMP: 300
SALES (corp-wide): 2.6B Publicly Held
WEB: www.ttmtech.com
SIC: 3672 Printed circuit boards
PA: Ttm Technologies, Inc.
200 Sandpointe Ave # 400
Santa Ana CA 92707
714 327-3000

(G-13541)
TYSONS AUTOMOTIVE MACHINE
22863 Bryant Ct Ste 103 (20166-9532)
PHONE.....................703 471-1802
Simon Brown, President
EMP: 1
SQ FT: 1,760
SALES (est): 140K Privately Held
SIC: 3599 Machine shop, jobbing & repair

(G-13542)
UNDERSTANDING LATIN LLC
209 E Staunton Ave (20164-4312)
PHONE.....................703 437-9354
Michael Smedberg, Principal
EMP: 2
SALES (est): 120.6K Privately Held
WEB: www.understandinglatin.com
SIC: 2741 Miscellaneous publishing

(G-13543)
UNITED STONES INC
14 Bryant Ct Ste B (20166-9574)
PHONE.....................703 467-0434
Jeffery Jia, President
John Zhang, Vice Pres
EMP: 20
SALES (est): 1.4MM Privately Held
WEB: www.unitedstones.us
SIC: 1411 Granite dimension stone

(G-13544)
UNIVERSAL STORE CORP
14 Bryant Ct Ste C (20166-9574)
PHONE.....................703 467-0434
Jeffery Jai, President
Jessica Diver, Sales Staff
▲ EMP: 9
SALES (est): 830K Privately Held
SIC: 3911 Jewelry mountings & trimmings

(G-13545)
US SOFTWARE & CONSULTING INC
21165 Whitfield Pl # 106 (20165-7280)
PHONE.....................571 281-4496
Shailaja Arkacharya, President
Raghu Satyanarayana, Vice Pres
Umesh Veeraiah, Vice Pres
EMP: 3
SALES (est): 350K Privately Held
WEB: www.ussc-corp.com
SIC: 7372 Prepackaged software

(G-13546)
VENETIAN SPIDER PRESS LLC
203 Amy Ct (20164-1922)
PHONE.....................310 857-4228
William Devault, Principal
EMP: 1
SALES (est): 41.3K Privately Held
SIC: 2741 Miscellaneous publishing

(G-13547)
VENTEX INC
101 Executive Dr Ste H (20166-9557)
P.O. Box 2720, Ashburn (20146-2720)
PHONE.....................703 787-9802
Harrison Murphy, President
Mike Slavik, Vice Pres
Doug Underwood, Natl Sales Mgr
▲ EMP: 3
SALES (est): 595.3K Privately Held
WEB: www.envirorestu.com
SIC: 2393 Textile bags

(G-13548)
VERTEXUSA LLC (PA)
44330 Mercure Cir Ste 309 (20166-2043)
PHONE.....................213 294-3072
Myung Yi, Managing Prtnr

JP Sihvonen, General Mgr
EMP: 3
SALES (est): 500K Privately Held
SIC: 3999 5199 Mannequins; clothes
hangers

(G-13549)
VIASYSTEMS NORTH AMERICA INC
1200 Severn Way (20166-8904)
PHONE.....................703 450-2600
David M Sindelar, CEO
EMP: 1626
SALES (est): 24.8K
SALES (corp-wide): 2.6B Publicly Held
WEB: www.ttmtech.com
SIC: 3672 Printed circuit boards
HQ: Viasystems, Inc.
520 Maryville Centre Dr # 400
Saint Louis MO 63141
314 727-2087

(G-13550)
VIDEO-SCOPE INTERNATIONAL LTD
105 Executive Dr Ste 110 (20166-9558)
PHONE.....................703 437-5534
Thomas F Lynch, President
Anjie Zeng, Vice Pres
EMP: 3
SQ FT: 1,559
SALES (est): 695.7K Privately Held
WEB: www.videoscopeintl.com
SIC: 3861 Cameras & related equipment

(G-13551)
VIENNA PAINT & DCTG CO INC
Also Called: Benjamin Moore Authorized Ret
22135 Davis Dr Ste 101 (20164-5365)
PHONE.....................703 450-0300
Stephanie Roche, Principal
EMP: 2
SALES (corp-wide): 5MM Privately Held
WEB: www.viennapaints.com
SIC: 2851 5231 Paints & allied products;
paint, glass & wallpaper
PA: Vienna Paint & Decorating Company,
Inc.
203 Maple Ave W
Vienna VA 22180
703 281-5252

(G-13552)
VINTAGE VAULT
17 Nicholson Ct (20165-5616)
PHONE.....................703 862-7159
Laura Lacroix, Principal
EMP: 2
SALES (est): 115.9K Privately Held
SIC: 3599 Industrial machinery

(G-13553)
VISION SIGN INC
45945 Trefoil Ln Ste 184 (20166-4344)
PHONE.....................703 707-0858
Jason Alexander, Principal
Francisco Espino, Production
Jose Espino, Manager
EMP: 6
SALES (est): 602.6K Privately Held
WEB: www.visionsign.net
SIC: 3993 Signs & advertising specialties

(G-13554)
VISIONARY VENTURES LLC
2830 Amendale Rd (20164)
PHONE.....................443 718-9777
Stephanie Vo, CEO
EMP: 1
SALES (est): 47K Privately Held
SIC: 3999 7231 Eyelashes, artificial; facial
salons

(G-13555)
VIVAAN METALS LLC
45662 Terminal Dr Ste 105 (20166-7231)
PHONE.....................571 309-3007
Jyotikaben Shah, Mng Member
EMP: 1
SALES (est): 82.6K Privately Held
SIC: 3444 Sheet metalwork

(G-13556)
VULCAN CONSTRUCTION MTLS LLC
22963 Concrete Plz (20166-2325)
PHONE.....................703 471-0044
Robert Odom, Manager
Bob Odom, Manager
EMP: 60 Publicly Held
WEB: www.vulcanmaterials.com
SIC: 3273 Ready-mixed concrete
HQ: Vulcan Construction Materials, Llc
1200 Urban Center Dr
Vestavia AL 35242
205 298-3000

(G-13557)
WALPOLE WOODWORKERS INC
45681 Okbrook Ct Ste 109 (20166)
PHONE.....................703 433-9929
EMP: 2
SALES (est): 85.2K Privately Held
SIC: 2431 Millwork, Nsk

(G-13558)
WARDEN SYSTEMS
101 Executive Dr Ste E (20166-9557)
PHONE.....................703 627-8002
Sohaib Akhter, Manager
EMP: 3
SALES (est): 172.8K Privately Held
WEB: www.accesys.org
SIC: 7372 7371 Application computer soft-
ware; operating systems computer soft-
ware; custom computer programming
services

(G-13559)
WASHINGTON & BALTIMORE SUBURBA
20 Pidgeon Hill Dr # 201 (20165-6154)
PHONE.....................703 904-1004
EMP: 1
SALES (est): 37.5K Privately Held
SIC: 2741 Miscellaneous publishing

(G-13560)
WATTS & WARD INC
Also Called: Allegra Print & Imaging
45668 Terminal Dr Ste 100 (20166-4396)
PHONE.....................703 435-3388
Ken Hargrave, President
EMP: 8
SQ FT: 6,000
SALES (est): 1.2MM Privately Held
WEB: www.allegradulles.com
SIC: 2752 Commercial printing, offset

(G-13561)
WISDOM CLOTHING COMPANY INC
22135 Davis Dr Ste 108 (20164-5365)
PHONE.....................703 433-0056
Sam Chang, CEO
Ingrid Chang, Vice Pres
EMP: 12
SQ FT: 4,000
SALES (est): 1MM Privately Held
WEB: www.wisdomclothing.com
SIC: 2395 Embroidery products, except
schiffli machine

(G-13562)
WM INDUSTRIES CORP (PA)
Also Called: Wmgta
21355 Ridgetop Cir # 250 (20166-8517)
PHONE.....................703 666-9001
Charles Wang, President
EMP: 10 EST: 2009
SALES (est): 17.1MM Privately Held
WEB: www.wmindustriescorp.com
SIC: 3711 Motor vehicles & car bodies

(G-13563)
WOMENS INTUITION WORLDWIDE
116 Hillsdale Dr (20164-1201)
PHONE.....................703 404-4357
Rose Rosetree, Owner
EMP: 1
SALES (est): 50.2K Privately Held
WEB: www.rose-rosetree.com
SIC: 2731 Book publishing

(G-13564)
WOODWORKERS INC
219 N Cameron Ct (20164-1907)
PHONE...............................571 282-5376
Gelber I Lopez, *Administration*
EMP: 2 EST: 2015
SALES (est): 72K **Privately Held**
SIC: 2431 Woodwork, interior & ornamental

(G-13565)
XCALIBUR SOFTWARE INC
20563 Qrterpath Trace Cir (20165-7568)
PHONE...............................703 896-5700
Amy Wood, *Principal*
EMP: 2
SALES (est): 88.7K **Privately Held**
WEB: www.xcaliburscribe.com
SIC: 7372 Prepackaged software

(G-13566)
Y & S TRADING
46766 Graham Cove Sq (20165-7536)
PHONE...............................703 430-6928
Guirong Yuan, *President*
▲ EMP: 2
SALES (est): 127.2K **Privately Held**
SIC: 3944 Craft & hobby kits & sets

Stony Creek
Sussex County

(G-13567)
ILUKA RESOURCES INC (HQ)
12472 St John Church Rd (23882-3239)
PHONE...............................434 348-4300
Daniel McGrath, *General Mgr*
Melissa Roberts, *General Mgr*
Shane Tilka, *General Mgr*
Matthew B Blackwell, *Principal*
Adele Stratton, *CFO*
◆ EMP: 122
SALES (est): 157MM **Privately Held**
WEB: www.iluka.com
SIC: 1481 Nonmetallic mineral services

(G-13568)
SETZER AND SONS VA INC SMITH
Also Called: Smith Setzer Sons Con Pipe Co
12556 Setzer Rd (23882-3243)
PHONE...............................434 246-3791
Neil Setzer, *President*
Cameron Setzer, *Principal*
Michael Setzer, *Principal*
Jerry Setzer, *Corp Secy*
EMP: 25
SQ FT: 2,500
SALES (est): 2.9MM **Privately Held**
SIC: 3272 Pipe, concrete or lined with concrete

(G-13569)
SHORELINE MATERIALS LLC
26004 Troublefield Rd (23882-2542)
PHONE...............................804 469-4042
EMP: 5
SALES (est): 444.7K **Privately Held**
SIC: 3273 Ready-mixed concrete

(G-13570)
VIRGINIA LP TRUCK INC
11486 Blue Star Hwy (23882-3242)
P.O. Box 307 (23882-0307)
PHONE...............................434 246-8257
Jim Matthews, *Manager*
James Matthews, *Manager*
EMP: 11
SQ FT: 11,000
SALES (est): 1.9MM **Privately Held**
SIC: 3713 Tank truck bodies

Strasburg
Shenandoah County

(G-13571)
ALS SIGN SHOP
33484 Old Valley Pike (22657-3702)
PHONE...............................540 465-3103
Al Sonner, *Principal*
EMP: 2

SALES (est): 134.3K **Privately Held**
SIC: 3993 Signs, not made in custom sign painting shops

(G-13572)
ANTIQUATED HEIRLOOMS LLC
256 Lake Ridge Rd (22657-5220)
PHONE...............................540 771-4120
Rachel Bond, *Administration*
EMP: 2
SALES (est): 89.1K **Privately Held**
SIC: 2511 Wood household furniture

(G-13573)
APPLE VALLEY LLC
478 E Washington St (22657-2354)
PHONE...............................540 465-8360
Frederick Cheshire, *Principal*
EMP: 2 EST: 2014
SALES (est): 92K **Privately Held**
SIC: 3571 Electronic computers

(G-13574)
BOTTOM OF BOTTLE CANDLE CO LLC
71 Mountain Rd (22657-4060)
PHONE...............................540 692-9260
EMP: 1
SALES (est): 39.6K **Privately Held**
WEB: www.bottomofthebottlecandle.com
SIC: 3999 Candles

(G-13575)
BOWDENS FIREWOOD & LOGGING LLC
1265 Coal Mine Rd (22657-4914)
PHONE...............................540 465-4362
James Bowden, *Principal*
EMP: 2 EST: 2014
SALES (est): 172.2K **Privately Held**
WEB: www.cbowdensvalleydogschool.com
SIC: 2411 Logging

(G-13576)
CARPERS WOOD CREATIONS INC
407 Aileen Ave (22657-2455)
P.O. Box 389 (22657-0389)
PHONE...............................540 465-2525
William T Carper, *President*
Herbie Lutz, *Plant Mgr*
Bobby Crews, *Sales Staff*
EMP: 40
SQ FT: 45,000
SALES (est): 5.7MM **Privately Held**
WEB: www.carperswood.com
SIC: 2541 2431 2511 Cabinets, except refrigerated: show, display, etc.: wood; counter & sink tops; shelving, office & store, wood; millwork; mantels, wood; wood household furniture; tables, household: wood; desks, household: wood

(G-13577)
CRICKETTS TRUCKING LLC
225 S Charles St Apt 2 (22657-2655)
PHONE...............................540 333-3812
Carlos Ricketts,
EMP: 1
SALES (est): 50K **Privately Held**
SIC: 3537 Trucks, tractors, loaders, carriers & similar equipment

(G-13578)
EVERLASTING LIFE PRODUCTS INC
233 Kanter Dr (22657-1138)
PHONE...............................703 761-4900
Joseph Lee, *Principal*
EMP: 2
SALES (est): 116.6K **Privately Held**
SIC: 2844 Toothpastes or powders, dentifrices

(G-13579)
FORT VALLEY PAVING
19954 Fort Valley Rd (22657-5106)
PHONE...............................540 636-8960
Barry Fincham, *Owner*
EMP: 2
SALES (est): 224K **Privately Held**
SIC: 2951 Asphalt paving mixtures & blocks

(G-13580)
GAVIN BOURJAILY
228 Signal View Rd (22657-5287)
PHONE...............................540 636-1985
EMP: 3
SALES (est): 121.7K **Privately Held**
WEB: www.globesyndicate.com
SIC: 2711 Newspapers, publishing & printing

(G-13581)
HAGSTROM ELECTRONICS INC
1986 Junction Rd (22657-4103)
PHONE...............................540 465-4677
David Hagstrom, *CEO*
▲ EMP: 5
SALES (est): 50K **Privately Held**
WEB: www.hagstromelectronics.com
SIC: 3674 Integrated circuits, semiconductor networks, etc.

(G-13582)
IAC STRASBURG LLC
806 E Queen St (22657-2700)
P.O. Box 8032, Plymouth MI (48170-8032)
PHONE...............................540 465-3741
Melanie Walker, *Finance Mgr*
Jan McPeak, *Manager*
Dennis E Richardville, *Maintence Staff*
Jason Chin, *Maintence Staff*
Janis N Acosta,
▲ EMP: 200
SALES (est): 20.7MM **Privately Held**
WEB: www.iacgroup.com
SIC: 3089 Automotive parts, plastic
HQ: International Automotive Components Group North America, Inc.
28333 Telegraph Rd
Southfield MI 48034

(G-13583)
IMMORTAL PUBLISHING LLC
15 Deaken Cir (22657-5283)
PHONE...............................540 465-3368
Rachel Zarrella, *Principal*
EMP: 1 EST: 2014
SALES (est): 66.9K **Privately Held**
SIC: 2741 Miscellaneous publishing

(G-13584)
INSPIRATION PUBLICATIONS
234 W King St (22657-1933)
PHONE...............................540 465-3878
EMP: 1 EST: 2016
SALES (est): 37.5K **Privately Held**
SIC: 2741 Miscellaneous publishing

(G-13585)
INTERNATIONAL AUTOMOTIVE COMPO
Also Called: Automotive Industries Division
806 E Queen St (22657-2700)
PHONE...............................540 465-3741
Amelia Galloway, *Buyer*
Dustin Landacre, *Engineer*
Gary Troxell, *Supervisor*
EMP: 918 **Privately Held**
WEB: www.iacna.com
SIC: 2531 3429 Seats, automobile; manufactured hardware (general)
HQ: International Automotive Components Group North America, Inc.
28333 Telegraph Rd
Southfield MI 48034

(G-13586)
JOSEPH RICARD ENTERPRISES LLC
262 E King St (22657-2261)
PHONE...............................540 465-5533
EMP: 2
SALES (est): 201.1K **Privately Held**
WEB: www.onestopstudioshop.com
SIC: 2752 Commercial printing, lithographic

(G-13587)
LEAR CORP STRASBURG
806 E Queen St (22657-2700)
PHONE...............................540 465-6244
Ted Rhea, *Principal*
▲ EMP: 2

SALES (est): 204.9K **Privately Held**
WEB: www.lear.com
SIC: 3714 Motor vehicle parts & accessories

(G-13588)
MCDONALD SAWMILL
Also Called: Mc Donald Sawmill
578 Old Grade Rd (22657-4414)
PHONE...............................540 465-5539
Richard A McDonald, *Owner*
EMP: 3
SALES (est): 305K **Privately Held**
SIC: 2421 4212 2411 Custom sawmill; light haulage & cartage, local; logging

(G-13589)
MERCURY PAPER
495 Radio Station Rd (22657-3706)
PHONE...............................540 465-7700
▲ EMP: 8
SALES (est): 1MM **Privately Held**
SIC: 2621 Book, bond & printing papers

(G-13590)
MERCURY PAPER INC (DH)
495 Radio Station Rd (22657-3706)
PHONE...............................540 465-7700
Duncan Chen, *President*
Chrissy Colborn, *Export Mgr*
Kevin Chapman, *Maint Spvr*
Bobbie Coppage, *Production*
Matthew Fox, *Production*
◆ EMP: 100
SALES (est): 23.3MM
SALES (corp-wide): 6.8B **Privately Held**
WEB: www.mercurypaper.com
SIC: 2621 Tissue paper

(G-13591)
MOUNTAIN VIEW VINEYARD
444 Signal Knob Dr (22657-5251)
PHONE...............................540 683-3200
EMP: 2
SALES (est): 89.3K **Privately Held**
SIC: 2084 Wines

(G-13592)
O-N MINERALS CHEMSTONE COMPANY
Also Called: Carmeuse Lime & Stone
1696 Oranda Rd (22657-3731)
P.O. Box 71 (22657-0071)
PHONE...............................540 465-5161
Jeffery Hines, *Opers Staff*
Mark Snyder, *Opers Staff*
Jim Bottom, *Branch Mgr*
Billy Williams, *Supervisor*
EMP: 172
SALES (corp-wide): 177.9K **Privately Held**
WEB: www.carmeuse.com
SIC: 1422 Limestones, ground
HQ: O-N Minerals (Chemstone) Company
11 Stanwix St Fl 21
Pittsburgh PA 15222
412 995-5500

(G-13593)
PALLET RECYCLING LLC
853 Ash St (22657-2034)
PHONE...............................304 749-7451
Verlin Larry Berg,
Janie Marie Berg,
EMP: 35
SQ FT: 2,448
SALES (est): 2MM **Privately Held**
WEB: www.4pallets.com
SIC: 2448 Pallets, wood
PA: Grant County Mulch, Inc.
181 Mulch Dr
Arthur WV 26847

(G-13594)
PERDUE FARMS INC
455 Radio Station Rd (22657-3706)
PHONE...............................540 465-9665
David Mc Cellen, *Branch Mgr*
EMP: 2
SALES (corp-wide): 5.2B **Privately Held**
WEB: www.perduefarms.com
SIC: 2015 Chicken, processed: fresh; turkey, processed: fresh; poultry, processed: fresh

▲ = Import ▼=Export
◆ =Import/Export

PA: Perdue Farms Inc.
31149 Old Ocean City Rd
Salisbury MD 21804
410 543-3000

(G-13595)
ROOSTERS AMISH SHEDS
411 E King St (22657-2430)
PHONE....................................540 263-2415
EMP: 2
SALES (est): 86.7K **Privately Held**
SIC: 2452 Prefabricated wood buildings

(G-13596)
SIBLINGS RIVALRY BREWERY LLC
239 Greenleaf Rd (22657-5608)
PHONE....................................540 671-3893
EMP: 2
SALES (est): 64.5K **Privately Held**
SIC: 2082 Malt beverages

(G-13597)
SIMPLY DIVINE CANDLES
105 Hailey Ln Apt D5 (22657-3744)
PHONE....................................540 479-0045
Debbie Ritenour, *Principal*
EMP: 2
SALES (est): 101.2K **Privately Held**
SIC: 3999 Candles

(G-13598)
SINES FEATHERS AND FURS LLC
79 Lee Rae Ct (22657-3873)
PHONE....................................540 436-8673
Kevin Sine, *Principal*
EMP: 2 EST: 2012
SALES (est): 79.5K **Privately Held**
SIC: 3999 Furs

(G-13599)
STRASBURG CABINET & SUPPLY
2993 Oranda Rd (22657-4717)
PHONE....................................540 465-3031
Dennis Henry, *President*
Monroe Henry, *Assistant VP*
Henry Dennis, *Vice Pres*
EMP: 2
SALES (est): 245.3K **Privately Held**
SIC: 2434 Vanities, bathroom: wood

(G-13600)
STRATEGIC VOICE SOLUTIONS
28814 Old Valley Pike (22657-3305)
PHONE....................................888 975-6130
EMP: 2 EST: 2016
SALES (est): 88.3K **Privately Held**
SIC: 3663 Mfg Radio/Tv Communication Equipment

(G-13601)
UPM KYMMENE INC
278 Valley View Dr (22657-3117)
PHONE....................................540 465-2700
ARI Nikkie, *Manager*
EMP: 2
SALES (est): 147.4K **Privately Held**
SIC: 2752 Publication printing, lithographic

(G-13602)
WILLIAMS WELDING
14703 Back Rd (22657-4001)
PHONE....................................540 465-8818
Brian Williams, *Owner*
EMP: 1 EST: 2001
SALES (est): 53.3K **Privately Held**
SIC: 7692 Welding repair

Stuart

Patrick County

(G-13603)
AERIAL MACHINE & TOOL CORP
649 Wood Brothers Ln (24171)
PHONE....................................276 694-3148
John Marcaccio, *President*
EMP: 6

SALES (corp-wide): 45.4MM **Privately Held**
WEB: www.capewellaerialsystems.com
SIC: 3429 3549 Aircraft & marine hardware, inc. pulleys & similar items; metalworking machinery
HQ: Aerial Machine & Tool Corp
4298 Jeb Stuart Hwy
Meadows Of Dan VA 24120
276 952-2006

(G-13604)
AFFORDABLE FUEL SUBSTITUTE INC
864 Dobyns Church Rd (24171-3925)
PHONE....................................276 694-8080
Theodore L Alt, *Principal*
EMP: 3
SALES (est): 235K **Privately Held**
SIC: 2869 Fuels

(G-13605)
AT LAB OF AMERICA LLC
2818 Salem Hwy (24171-4614)
PHONE....................................681 207-9161
Anthony Trent, *Principal*
EMP: 4
SALES (est): 227.1K **Privately Held**
WEB: www.turbolabofamerica.com
SIC: 3714 Motor vehicle parts & accessories

(G-13606)
BUFFALO RIDGE WOOD PRODUCTS
4868 Woolwine Hwy (24171-4048)
PHONE....................................276 930-2189
William H Pilson, *Owner*
EMP: 1 **Privately Held**
SIC: 2519 Lawn & garden furniture, except wood & metal

(G-13607)
BURGESS WELDING & FABRICATION
100 Timber Creek Rd (24171-5289)
PHONE....................................276 229-6458
James Burgess, *Principal*
EMP: 1
SALES (est): 30.9K **Privately Held**
SIC: 7692 Welding repair

(G-13608)
COLLINS SAWMILL AND LOGGIN LLC
3567 Clark House Farm Rd (24171-2563)
PHONE....................................276 694-7521
Mark Collins,
EMP: 3 EST: 2001
SALES (est): 312K **Privately Held**
SIC: 2421 Sawmills & planing mills, general

(G-13609)
ENTERPRISE INC
129 N Main St (24171-8802)
P.O. Box 348 (24171-0348)
PHONE....................................276 694-3101
Gail Harding, *President*
Linda Hilton, *Vice Pres*
Steven Henderson, *Admin Sec*
EMP: 6
SQ FT: 900
SALES (est): 240K **Privately Held**
WEB: www.theenterprise.net
SIC: 2711 2752 Newspapers: publishing only, not printed on site; commercial printing, lithographic

(G-13610)
EUGENES MACHINE & WELDING
13996 Jeb Stuart Hwy (24171-1512)
PHONE....................................276 694-6275
Elvin Rorrer, *Owner*
EMP: 2
SALES (est): 100.7K **Privately Held**
SIC: 3599 Machine shop, jobbing & repair

(G-13611)
FAIN ARLICE SAWMILL
737 Peters Creek Dr (24171-3552)
PHONE....................................276 694-8211
Arlice Fain, *Owner*
EMP: 5

SALES (est): 335.6K **Privately Held**
SIC: 2421 Sawmills & planing mills, general

(G-13612)
FOLEY MACHINE
108 Clark Loop (24171-3455)
PHONE....................................276 930-1983
Jay Foley, *Owner*
EMP: 1
SALES (est): 81.7K **Privately Held**
SIC: 3519 Gas engine rebuilding

(G-13613)
GLAD PRECISION MACHINE INC
26 Harbour School Ln (24171-4431)
PHONE....................................276 930-9930
Daniel A Glad, *President*
EMP: 3
SALES (est): 376.6K **Privately Held**
SIC: 3599 Machine shop, jobbing & repair

(G-13614)
HANESBRANDS INC
138 Elainesville Rd (24171)
PHONE....................................336 519-5458
Curtis Gillispie, *Vice Pres*
Bobby Mangrum, *Vice Pres*
Joyce Dehart, *Senior Buyer*
Michael Clark, *Branch Mgr*
Jerry Foley, *Manager*
EMP: 280 **Publicly Held**
WEB: www.hanes.com
SIC: 2322 2341 Men's & boys' underwear & nightwear; women's & children's undergarments
PA: Hanesbrands Inc.
1000 E Hanes Mill Rd
Winston Salem NC 27105

(G-13615)
HESCO OF VIRGINIA LLC
25582 Jeb Stuart Hwy (24171-2973)
P.O. Box 280, Patrick Springs (24133-0280)
PHONE....................................276 694-2818
Richard East, *President*
EMP: 2
SALES (est): 240.6K **Privately Held**
WEB: www.hescoofvirginia.com
SIC: 3599 5085 Machine shop, jobbing & repair; industrial supplies

(G-13616)
HIGH PEAKS KNIFE WORKS
976 Carter Mountain Rd (24171-3768)
PHONE....................................276 694-6563
Jon Porter, *Owner*
EMP: 1
SALES (est): 70.9K **Privately Held**
WEB: www.highpeaksknifeworks.com
SIC: 3421 5941 Knives: butchers', hunting, pocket, etc.; hunting equipment

(G-13617)
HONEYWELL INTERNATIONAL INC
636 Commerce St (24171-4909)
PHONE....................................276 694-2408
EMP: 673
SALES (corp-wide): 36.7B **Publicly Held**
WEB: www.honeywell.com
SIC: 3724 Aircraft engines & engine parts
PA: Honeywell International Inc.
300 S Tryon St
Charlotte NC 28202
704 627-6200

(G-13618)
HOPKINS LUMBER CONTRACTORS INC
29673 Jeb Stuart Hwy (24171-5104)
P.O. Box 926 (24171-0926)
PHONE....................................276 694-2166
John Hopkins, *President*
EMP: 25
SALES (corp-wide): 20.2MM **Privately Held**
SIC: 2421 Sawmills & planing mills, general
PA: Hopkins Lumber Contractors, Inc.
680 Old Sand Rd
Ridgeway VA 24148
276 956-3022

(G-13619)
JERRY LEE MARSHALL
Also Called: JM Logging
551 Elk Creek Rd (24171-3567)
PHONE....................................276 952-5486
Jerry L Marshall, *Owner*
Jerry Marshall, *Owner*
EMP: 2 EST: 1995
SALES (est): 100K **Privately Held**
SIC: 2411 Logging

(G-13620)
KENNETH FOLEY
Also Called: K & D Logging
352 Goose Market Loop (24171-3106)
PHONE....................................276 930-1452
Kenneth Foley, *Owner*
EMP: 1
SALES (est): 64.7K **Privately Held**
SIC: 2411 7389 Timber, cut at logging camp; business services

(G-13621)
L K SMITH MACHINE SHOP
174 Dominion Valley Ln (24171-4737)
PHONE....................................276 694-4109
Loray K Smith, *Partner*
Betty Smith, *Co-Owner*
EMP: 4
SQ FT: 25,000
SALES (est): 200K **Privately Held**
SIC: 3599 Machine shop, jobbing & repair

(G-13622)
LAWSON BROTHERS LOGGING LLC
915 Dobyns Church Rd (24171-3904)
PHONE....................................276 694-8905
Garland Lawson, *Principal*
EMP: 3
SALES (est): 150K **Privately Held**
SIC: 2411 Logging camps & contractors

(G-13623)
MARTIN PALLETS & WEDGES LLC
28839 Jeb Stuart Hwy (24171-5211)
P.O. Box 452, Patrick Springs (24133-0452)
PHONE....................................276 694-4276
Randell Martin,
EMP: 12
SALES (est): 1.4MM **Privately Held**
WEB: www.raddoffice.com
SIC: 2448 Pallets, wood

(G-13624)
MAYO RIVER LOGGING CO INC
4949 Ayers Orchard Rd (24171-2617)
PHONE....................................276 694-6305
Jason Harris, *President*
EMP: 1
SALES (est): 140.3K **Privately Held**
SIC: 2411 Logging camps & contractors

(G-13625)
MECHANICAL DESIGNS OF VIRGINIA
25582 Jeb Stuart Hwy (24171-2973)
P.O. Box 280, Patrick Springs (24133-0280)
PHONE....................................276 694-7442
Wayne Gilley, *President*
Patricia O East, *Corp Secy*
C Richard East, *Vice Pres*
Donna Scott, *VP Finance*
EMP: 32
SQ FT: 35,000
SALES (est): 8.9MM **Privately Held**
WEB: www.mechanicaldesigns.com
SIC: 3599 1761 Machine shop, jobbing & repair; sheet metalwork

(G-13626)
NARROFLEX INC
Also Called: United Elastic-A Narroflex Co
201 S Main St (24171-3960)
PHONE....................................276 694-7171
Xavier Joseph, *President*
◆ EMP: 165
SQ FT: 520,000

SALES (est): 24.1MM
SALES (corp-wide): 111.1MM **Privately Held**
SIC: 2241 Elastic narrow fabrics, woven or braided
HQ: Narroflex Inc
590 South Service Rd
Stoney Creek ON L8E 2
905 643-6066

(G-13627)
RAGGEDEDGE GEAR INC
309 Puppy Creek Dr (24171-3483)
PHONE....................................276 226-9439
Meredith M Bailey, *President*
EMP: 2
SALES (est): 114.4K **Privately Held**
WEB: www.raggededgegear.com
SIC: 3069 Fabricated rubber products

(G-13628)
RORRER TIMBER CO INC
4515 Moorefield Store Rd (24171-4741)
PHONE....................................276 694-6304
Ronald Rorrer, *President*
EMP: 3 **EST:** 2001
SALES (est): 276.9K **Privately Held**
SIC: 2411 Timber, cut at logging camp

(G-13629)
SCOTT LOGGING LLC
2225 Pilson Sawmill Rd (24171-4304)
PHONE....................................276 930-2497
James Scott, *Owner*
EMP: 2
SALES (est): 119.3K **Privately Held**
SIC: 2411 Logging camps & contractors

(G-13630)
SIMS CREEK PUBLISHING LLC
138 Bouldin Church Ln (24171-3345)
PHONE....................................276 694-4278
Johnny Joyce, *Principal*
EMP: 1 **EST:** 2017
SALES (est): 41.3K **Privately Held**
SIC: 2741 Miscellaneous publishing

(G-13631)
STANBURN WINERY LLC
158 Conner Dr (24171-5193)
PHONE....................................276 694-7074
David Stanley, *General Mgr*
Elsie Stanley,
Nelson Stanley,
EMP: 3 **EST:** 2011
SALES (est): 268.1K **Privately Held**
WEB: www.stanburn.com
SIC: 2084 Wines

(G-13632)
STOVALL BROTHERS LUMBER LLC
2400 Pleasant View Dr (24171-3039)
PHONE....................................276 694-6684
Jay B Stovall, *Partner*
George Stoval,
Rodney Stovall,
EMP: 10
SALES (est): 922.4K **Privately Held**
SIC: 2421 Sawmills & planing mills, general

(G-13633)
STUART CONCRETE INC
58 West (24171)
P.O. Box 565 (24171-0565)
PHONE....................................276 694-2828
James Bryant, *President*
Lynn Jarard, *Treasurer*
EMP: 13
SALES (est): 2.5MM **Privately Held**
WEB: www.patrickchamber.com
SIC: 3273 Ready-mixed concrete

(G-13634)
STUART FOREST PRODUCTS LLC
120 Commerce St (24171-5297)
P.O. Box 498 (24171-0498)
PHONE....................................276 694-3842
E J Temple Jr,
EMP: 30
SALES (est): 3.3MM **Privately Held**
WEB: www.townofstuartva.com
SIC: 2083 Malt byproducts

(G-13635)
STUART WILDERNESS INC
14747 Jeb Stuart Hwy (24171-1663)
P.O. Box 559 (24171-0559)
PHONE....................................276 694-4432
William Poff, *President*
Ronnie D Bolt, *Vice Pres*
John Michael Turman, *Treasurer*
EMP: 23
SALES (est): 3.7MM **Privately Held**
SIC: 2421 2426 Sawmills & planing mills, general; hardwood dimension & flooring mills

(G-13636)
TEN OAKS LLC
209 Progress Dr (24171-1655)
P.O. Box 619 (24171-0619)
PHONE....................................276 694-3208
Terri Birkett, *President*
Buddy E Williams, *President*
EMP: 140
SALES (est): 17MM
SALES (corp-wide): 83.5MM **Privately Held**
WEB: www.tenoaksflooring.com
SIC: 2426 Furniture stock & parts, hardwood
PA: Boa-Franc Inc
1255 98e Rue
Saint-Georges QC G5Y 8
418 227-1181

(G-13637)
TURBO LAB
31 Helms Ridge Ln (24171-3470)
PHONE....................................276 952-5997
Austin Cole, *Owner*
EMP: 6
SALES (est): 760K **Privately Held**
WEB: www.turbolabofamerica.com
SIC: 3714 Motor vehicle parts & accessories

(G-13638)
VIRGINA-CAROLINA GRAVE VLT LLC
4734 Moorefield Store Rd (24171-4731)
PHONE....................................276 694-6855
Lamar Howell, *Principal*
EMP: 3
SALES (est): 271.6K **Privately Held**
SIC: 3272 Burial vaults, concrete or pre-cast terrazzo

(G-13639)
WEYERHAEUSER COMPANY
Rr 58 Box W (24171)
PHONE....................................276 694-4404
Steve Cox, *Branch Mgr*
EMP: 1
SALES (corp-wide): 6.5B **Publicly Held**
WEB: www.weyerhaeuser.com
SIC: 2611 Pulp mills
PA: Weyerhaeuser Company
220 Occidental Ave S
Seattle WA 98104
206 539-3000

(G-13640)
WHITLOW LUMBER & LOGGING INC
1463 Fairystone Park Hwy (24171-3302)
PHONE....................................276 930-3854
Robert Whitlow, *President*
Sondra Johnson, *Admin Sec*
EMP: 8
SALES (est): 550K **Privately Held**
WEB:
www.whitlowexcavatingandlogging.com
SIC: 2426 2448 Furniture dimension stock, hardwood; pallets, wood

(G-13641)
WILLIAMS PALLET COMPANY
1601 Fairystone Park Hwy (24171-3301)
PHONE....................................276 930-2081
Billy L Williams, *President*
EMP: 4
SALES (est): 352K **Privately Held**
SIC: 2448 Pallets, wood

Stuarts Draft
Augusta County

(G-13642)
AGGREGATE INDUSTRIES MGT INC
1526 Cold Springs Rd (24477-3025)
P.O. Box 218 (24477-0218)
PHONE....................................540 337-4875
Ron Coon, *Branch Mgr*
EMP: 9
SALES (corp-wide): 1.7B **Privately Held**
WEB: www.lafargeholcim.us
SIC: 3273 Ready-mixed concrete
HQ: Aggregate Industries Management, Inc.
8700 W Bryn Mawr Ave # 300
Chicago IL 60631
773 372-1000

(G-13643)
ANNS STAINED GLASS WINDOWS PA
300 Falling Rock Dr (24477-2930)
PHONE....................................540 337-2249
EMP: 2
SALES (est): 124.6K **Privately Held**
SIC: 3231 Mfg Products-Purchased Glass

(G-13644)
APPALACHIAN WOODS LLC (PA)
1240 Cold Springs Rd (24477-3029)
PHONE....................................540 337-1801
Tom Paulus, *Opers Dir*
Jason Hochstetler, *Manager*
Jonas A Hochstetler,
Raymond Hochstetler,
▼ **EMP:** 13
SQ FT: 21,000
SALES (est): 1.2MM **Privately Held**
WEB: www.appalachianwoods.com
SIC: 2421 Sawmills & planing mills, general

(G-13645)
BRYANT LOGGING
724 Howardsville Tpke (24477-2811)
PHONE....................................540 337-0232
Jerry Bryant, *Principal*
EMP: 2
SALES (est): 81.7K **Privately Held**
SIC: 2411 Logging

(G-13646)
DRAFTCO INCORPORATED
80 Johnson Dr (24477-3199)
P.O. Box 950 (24477-0950)
PHONE....................................540 337-1054
Freddie R Roberts, *President*
Kenneth R Rainwater, *President*
Carl W Roberts, *Vice Pres*
EMP: 45
SQ FT: 24,000
SALES (est): 11.9MM **Privately Held**
WEB: www.draftco.us
SIC: 3443 7692 3444 Fabricated plate work (boiler shop); welding repair; sheet metalwork

(G-13647)
FAB JUNIORS WELDING METAL
3229 Stuarts Draft Hwy (24477-2785)
PHONE....................................540 480-1971
EMP: 1
SALES (est): 28.1K **Privately Held**
SIC: 7692 Welding repair

(G-13648)
HEARTSEEKING LLC
98 Sugarcamp Ln (24477-2916)
PHONE....................................305 778-8040
Elijah Veney,
EMP: 2
SALES (est): 82.9K **Privately Held**
SIC: 2741

(G-13649)
HERSHEY COMPANY
120 Harold Cook Dr (24477-9430)
PHONE....................................540 324-0166
Harold Cook, *Principal*
Darrell Sheets, *QC Mgr*

Bill Perdue, *Manager*
EMP: 417
SALES (corp-wide): 7.9B **Publicly Held**
WEB: www.thehersheycompany.com
SIC: 2064 Candy & other confectionery products
PA: Hershey Company
19 E Chocolate Ave
Hershey PA 17033
717 534-4200

(G-13650)
HKD SNOWMAKERS COM
83 Fall Ridge Dr (24477-2969)
PHONE....................................540 451-1779
EMP: 2
SALES (est): 84.6K **Privately Held**
WEB: www.hkdsnowmakers.com
SIC: 3585 Refrigeration & heating equipment

(G-13651)
HOLLISTER INCORPORATED
366 Draft Ave (24477-2941)
P.O. Box 228 (24477-0228)
PHONE....................................540 943-1733
Bill Doran, *Plant Mgr*
Shelley Miller, *Project Mgr*
Mike Berrington, *Opers Staff*
Jorg Buchs, *Engineer*
George Cisko, *Engineer*
EMP: 400
SQ FT: 150,000
SALES (corp-wide): 875.9MM **Privately Held**
WEB: www.dansac.fi
SIC: 3842 Surgical appliances & supplies
PA: Hollister Incorporated
2000 Hollister Dr
Libertyville IL 60048
847 680-1000

(G-13652)
HUNTS FAMILY VINEYARD LLC
57 Hawkins Pond Ln (24477-2547)
PHONE....................................540 942-8689
Sandra H Hunt, *Administration*
EMP: 4
SALES (est): 283.6K **Privately Held**
SIC: 2084 Wines

(G-13653)
JUNIORS WLDG & MET FABRICATION
Rr 4 (24477)
PHONE....................................540 943-7070
Jason C Campbell, *Owner*
EMP: 1
SALES (est): 55K **Privately Held**
SIC: 7692 7539 Welding repair; automotive repair shops

(G-13654)
KHK INC
Also Called: Sports Line
255 Draft Ave (24477-2929)
P.O. Box 1121 (24477-1121)
PHONE....................................540 337-5068
Kelly H King, *President*
John K King, *Vice Pres*
Kevin King, *Admin Sec*
EMP: 5 **EST:** 1997
SQ FT: 2,500
SALES (est): 800K **Privately Held**
SIC: 2395 2396 Embroidery & art needlework; embroidery products, except schiffli machine; automotive & apparel trimmings

(G-13655)
MCKEE FOODS CORPORATION
272 Patton Farm Rd (24477-2610)
P.O. Box 486 (24477-0486)
PHONE....................................540 943-7101
Shelly Maupin, *Purch Agent*
Angel Payne, *Purch Agent*
Eray Murphy, *Manager*
EMP: 1400
SALES (corp-wide): 1.7B **Privately Held**
WEB: www.mckeefoods.com
SIC: 2052 2051 2099 Cookies; cakes, pies & pastries; food preparations
PA: Mckee Foods Corporation
10260 Mckee Rd
Collegedale TN 37315
423 238-7111

(G-13656)
NIBCO INC
131 Johnson Dr (24477-3100)
PHONE................................540 324-0242
EMP: 22
SALES (corp-wide): 704.3MM **Privately Held**
WEB: www.nibco.com
SIC: 3494 Pipe fittings
PA: Nibco Inc.
  1516 Middlebury St
  Elkhart IN 46516
  574 295-3000

(G-13657)
PLY GEM INDUSTRIES INC
185 Johnson Dr (24477-3100)
PHONE................................540 337-3663
Gary Robinette, *President*
Lindsay Thomas, *Engineer*
EMP: 250
SALES (corp-wide): 4.8B **Publicly Held**
WEB: www.plygem.com
SIC: 2431 Windows, wood; doors, wood
HQ: Ply Gem Industries, Inc.
  5020 Weston Pkwy Ste 400
  Cary NC 27513
  919 677-3900

(G-13658)
REXNORD INDUSTRIES LLC
150 Johnson Dr (24477-3100)
PHONE................................540 337-3510
Eric Fontaine, *Branch Mgr*
EMP: 100 **Publicly Held**
WEB: www.rexnordcorporation.com
SIC: 3568 Couplings, shaft: rigid, flexible,
  universal joint, etc.
HQ: Rexnord Industries, Llc
  111 W Michigan St
  Milwaukee WI 53203
  414 643-3000

(G-13659)
REXNORD INDUSTRIES LLC
Gear
150 Johnson Dr (24477-3100)
P.O. Box 993 (24477-0993)
PHONE................................540 337-3510
Todd Adams, *President*
Jeff Helbling, *Principal*
EMP: 120 **Publicly Held**
WEB: www.rexnordcorporation.com
SIC: 3568 Couplings, shaft: rigid, flexible,
  universal joint, etc.; pulleys, power trans-
  mission
HQ: Rexnord Industries, Llc
  111 W Michigan St
  Milwaukee WI 53203
  414 643-3000

(G-13660)
**SHENANDOAH VALLEY
ORCHARD CO**
205 Horseshoe Cir (24477-9014)
P.O. Box 1032 (24477-1032)
PHONE................................540 337-2837
John Hailey, *President*
Alice Camel, *Admin Sec*
EMP: 50
SALES (est): 833K **Privately Held**
SIC: 7692 2099 Welding repair; cider, non-
  alcoholic

(G-13661)
TIGER PAPER COMPANY INC
2480 Tinkling Spring Rd (24477-3223)
PHONE................................540 337-9510
Sharon Coggings, *President*
EMP: 4
SALES (est): 506.5K **Privately Held**
WEB: www.tigerpaperinc.com
SIC: 2671 5111 Paper coated or laminated
  for packaging; printing & writing paper

Suffolk

Suffolk City County

(G-13662)
1 A LIFE SAFER
1926 Wilroy Rd Ste C (23434-2374)
PHONE................................757 809-0406
Scott Nathan, *Director*

EMP: 2 EST: 2014
SALES (est): 142.5K **Privately Held**
SIC: 3829 Breathalyzers

(G-13663)
A & S GLOBAL INDUSTRIES LLC
1545 Steeple Dr (23433-1615)
PHONE................................757 773-0119
Steven G Gillenwaters,
EMP: 2
SALES (est): 90K **Privately Held**
SIC: 3953 Marking devices

(G-13664)
AIRGAS INC
105 Dill Rd (23434-4873)
PHONE................................757 539-7185
Bill Branton, *Manager*
EMP: 3
SALES (corp-wide): 129.8MM **Privately
Held**
WEB: www.airgas.com
SIC: 2873 5169 Anhydrous ammonia; am-
  monia
HQ: Airgas, Inc.
  259 N Radnor Chester Rd # 100
  Radnor PA 19087
  610 687-5253

(G-13665)
ALEXANDER AMIR
503 S 6th St (23434-3605)
PHONE................................757 714-1802
Shanbria Vaughan, *Partner*
EMP: 2
SALES (est): 73.2K **Privately Held**
SIC: 2759 2395 Screen printing; embroi-
  dery & art needlework

(G-13666)
ALL ABOUT SIGNS LLC
232 Barnes Rd (23437-9307)
PHONE................................757 934-3000
EMP: 2 EST: 2009
SALES (est): 111.2K **Privately Held**
SIC: 3993 Signs & advertising specialties

(G-13667)
AMADAS INDUSTRIES INC
302 Kenyon Rd (23434-7453)
PHONE................................757 539-0231
James C Adams, *CEO*
Perry Jones, *Principal*
EMP: 2 **Privately Held**
WEB: www.amadas.com
SIC: 3531 Construction machinery
PA: Amadas Industries, Inc.
  1100 Holland Rd
  Suffolk VA 23434

(G-13668)
AMADAS INDUSTRIES INC (PA)
1100 Holland Rd (23434-6311)
P.O. Box 1833 (23439-1833)
PHONE................................757 539-0231
James C Adams II, *CEO*
Stanley A Brantley, *President*
William J Adams, *Exec VP*
O K Hobbs Jr, *Exec VP*
Jamie Jache, *Plant Mgr*
◆ EMP: 95
SQ FT: 65,000
SALES (est): 22.5MM **Privately Held**
WEB: www.amadas.com
SIC: 3531 3523 Construction machinery;
  farm machinery & equipment

(G-13669)
**AMETHYST FLAME CANDLES
LLC**
301 Hill St (23434-3812)
PHONE................................757 324-0614
Rhonda Newsom,
EMP: 1
SALES (est): 39.6K **Privately Held**
SIC: 3999 Candles

(G-13670)
ANDES PUBLISHING CO INC
8080 Gates Rd (23437-9483)
P.O. Box 7384 (23437-0384)
PHONE................................757 562-5528
Oscar Baptiste, *Principal*
EMP: 2
SALES (est): 62.6K **Privately Held**
SIC: 2741 Miscellaneous publishing

(G-13671)
ARTISTIC IMPRESSIONS
1780 Mill Wood Way (23434-2336)
PHONE................................757 923-4254
Terri Betts, *Owner*
▲ EMP: 3
SALES (est): 200K **Privately Held**
SIC: 2396 2395 2261 7389 Screen printing on fabric articles; embroidery & art
  needlework; embroidery products, except
  schiffli machine; screen printing of cotton
  broadwoven fabrics; embroidering of advertising on shirts, etc.

(G-13672)
ATARFIL USA INC
324 Moore Ave Bldg 3 (23434-3820)
PHONE................................757 386-8676
Emilio C Torres, *Managing Dir*
Alejandro Carreras Torres, *Director*
EMP: 16
SALES (est): 5MM
SALES (corp-wide): 253.1K **Privately
Held**
WEB: www.atarfil.com
SIC: 3822 Auto controls regulating residntl
  & coml environmt & applncs
HQ: Atarfil Sl
  Carretera Cordoba ((Complejo El Rey
  )), Km 429
  Atarfe 18230

(G-13673)
BARLEN CRAFTS
219 Woodrow Ave (23434-5438)
PHONE................................301 537-3491
Barney Taylor, *Owner*
▼ EMP: 1
SALES (est): 50K **Privately Held**
WEB: www.barlencrafts.com
SIC: 2396 Screen printing on fabric articles

(G-13674)
BASF CORPORATION
2301 Wilroy Rd (23434-2021)
PHONE................................757 538-3700
John Cotton, *Branch Mgr*
Ron Michalczyk, *Manager*
EMP: 1
SALES (corp-wide): 65.6B **Privately Held**
WEB: www.basf.com
SIC: 2869 Industrial organic chemicals
HQ: Basf Corporation
  100 Park Ave
  Florham Park NJ 07932
  973 245-6000

(G-13675)
BAY BREEZE LABRADORS
7115 S Quay Rd (23437-9800)
PHONE................................757 408-5227
Laurie Hudgins, *Principal*
EMP: 2
SALES (est): 105.8K **Privately Held**
SIC: 3999 Pet supplies

(G-13676)
**BAY CABINETS &
CONTRACTORS**
428 E Pinner St (23434-3748)
PHONE................................757 934-2236
Michael Thorne, *President*
EMP: 6
SALES (est): 949.8K **Privately Held**
WEB: www.baycabinetsva.com
SIC: 2517 2541 1751 2431 Wood televi-
  sion & radio cabinets; home entertain-
  ment unit cabinets, wood; television
  cabinets, wood; counter & sink tops; cabi-
  net & finish carpentry; brackets, wood

(G-13677)
BEAUTEES
2269 Airport Rd (23434-7866)
PHONE................................757 439-0269
Heather Boswell, *Principal*
EMP: 2
SALES (est): 73.2K **Privately Held**
SIC: 2759 Screen printing

(G-13678)
BERRY GLOBAL INC
1401 Progress Rd (23434-2147)
PHONE................................757 538-2000
EMP: 2 **Publicly Held**

WEB: www.berryplastics.com
SIC: 3089 3081 Bottle caps, molded plas-
  tic; unsupported plastics film & sheet
HQ: Berry Global, Inc.
  101 Oakley St
  Evansville IN 47710

(G-13679)
BERRY PLASTICS DESIGN LLC
Also Called: Virginia Design Packaging
1401 Progress Rd (23434-2147)
PHONE................................757 538-2000
Lee D Goldstein, *President*
Larry Goldstein, *Exec VP*
Kevin Darragh, *Vice Pres*
Tracie Thomas, *Human Res Mgr*
David Kopsick, *Sales Staff*
◆ EMP: 155
SQ FT: 65,000
SALES (est): 23MM **Publicly Held**
WEB: www.berryplastics.com
SIC: 3089 3086 Plastic containers, except
  foam; plastics foam products
HQ: Berry Global, Inc.
  101 Oakley St
  Evansville IN 47710

(G-13680)
**BLANCHARDS WELDING
REPAIR**
645 Turlington Rd (23434-6042)
PHONE................................757 539-6306
EMP: 1 EST: 2008
SALES (est): 54K **Privately Held**
SIC: 7692 Welding Repair

(G-13681)
BOWDENS CANDLE CREATIONS
905 Macarthur Dr (23434-3013)
PHONE................................757 539-0306
EMP: 2
SALES (est): 62.5K **Privately Held**
WEB: www.bowdenscandlecreations.com
SIC: 3999 Candles

(G-13682)
BURIAL BUTLER SERVICES LLC
1452 Manning Rd (23434-9400)
PHONE................................757 934-8227
Joseph Butler, *Principal*
EMP: 1
SALES (est): 125.1K **Privately Held**
SIC: 3272 Burial vaults, concrete or pre-
  cast terrazzo

(G-13683)
**BYRDS CUSTOM WDWRK &
STAIN GL**
5124 Exeter Dr (23434-7003)
PHONE................................757 242-6786
Fred Byrd, *Principal*
EMP: 2
SALES (est): 193.8K **Privately Held**
SIC: 2431 Millwork

(G-13684)
COACH LLC
Also Called: Amadas Coach
1007 Obici Indus Blvd (23434-5475)
PHONE................................757 925-2862
Mike Hutchinson, *General Mgr*
Shannon Adams, *Marketing Mgr*
Jojo Deocampo, *Asst Mgr*
Jimmy Adams,
Chad Winter, *Technician*
▼ EMP: 37
SQ FT: 50,000
SALES (est): 7.2MM **Privately Held**
WEB: www.amadascoach.com
SIC: 3711 5012 Motor homes, self-con-
  tained, assembly of; recreational vehicles,
  motor homes & trailers
PA: Amadas Industries, Inc.
  1100 Holland Rd
  Suffolk VA 23434

(G-13685)
COMBAT BOUND LLC
6400 Sandgate Dr N (23435-3005)
PHONE................................757 343-3399
Emil Reynolds,
EMP: 1
SALES (est): 64.3K **Privately Held**
SIC: 3829 3721 3812 Thermometers, in-
  cluding digital: clinical; aircraft; search &
  navigation equipment

(G-13686)
COMMERCIAL READY MIX PDTS INC
1275 Portsmouth Blvd (23434-2262)
PHONE.....................................757 925-0939
Joe Bradshaw, *Sales Executive*
Danny Smith, *Manager*
EMP: 14
SALES (corp-wide): 38.3MM **Privately Held**
WEB: www.crmpinc.com
SIC: 3273 Ready-mixed concrete
PA: Commercial Ready Mix Products, Inc.
    115 Hwy 158 W
    Winton NC 27986
    252 358-5461

(G-13687)
COXE TIMBER COMPANY
2901 Kings Fork Rd (23434-7494)
PHONE.....................................757 934-1500
Thomas C Coxe IV, *President*
EMP: 3
SALES (est): 152.8K **Privately Held**
SIC: 2411 Timber, cut at logging camp

(G-13688)
CRAFT DESIGNS CUSTOM INTR PDTS
6222 Winthrope Dr (23435-3049)
PHONE.....................................757 630-1565
Augustus Coleman Jr, *Owner*
EMP: 4
SALES (est): 212.5K **Privately Held**
SIC: 2431 Millwork

(G-13689)
CREATIVE WELDING AND DESIGN
2702 Manning Rd (23434-8560)
PHONE.....................................757 334-1416
Tom Shirk, *Owner*
EMP: 1
SALES (est): 50.4K **Privately Held**
SIC: 7692 Automotive welding

(G-13690)
CROWN CORK & SEAL USA INC
1305 Progress Rd (23434-2149)
PHONE.....................................757 538-1318
John Ballance, *Branch Mgr*
EMP: 25
SALES (corp-wide): 11.6B **Publicly Held**
WEB: www.crowncork.com
SIC: 3411 3545 Metal cans; cams (machine tool accessories)
HQ: Crown Cork & Seal Usa, Inc.
    770 Township Line Rd # 100
    Yardley PA 19067
    215 698-5100

(G-13691)
CROWN ME GALORE COLLECTION LLC
205 Justin Ct (23434-9123)
PHONE.....................................864 540-4476
Sharnell Scott,
EMP: 2
SALES (est): 74.4K **Privately Held**
SIC: 2844 Face creams or lotions

(G-13692)
DAN CHAREWICZ
Also Called: Creative Kustom Tool Co
1558 Cherry Grove Rd N (23432-1822)
PHONE.....................................815 338-2582
Dan Charewicz, *Owner*
EMP: 1
SALES (est): 98K **Privately Held**
SIC: 3089 Injection molding of plastics

(G-13693)
DANA AUTO SYSTEMS GROUP LLC
6920 Harbour View Blvd (23435-3283)
PHONE.....................................757 638-2656
Mike Denio, *General Mgr*
EMP: 20 **Publicly Held**
WEB: www.dana.com
SIC: 3714 Motor vehicle parts & accessories
HQ: Dana Automotive Systems Group, Llc
    3939 Technology Dr
    Maumee OH 43537

(G-13694)
DARDEN PRESSURE WASH AND PLST
2204 Arizona Ave (23434-2704)
PHONE.....................................757 934-1466
Soloman Darden Jr, *Owner*
EMP: 1
SALES (est): 60.6K **Privately Held**
SIC: 3449 Plastering accessories, metal

(G-13695)
DART MECHANICAL INC (PA)
1265 Carolina Rd (23434-8729)
PHONE.....................................757 539-2189
James David Gardner, *President*
James Gardner, *President*
Anthony Sanders, *Admin Sec*
EMP: 8
SALES (est): 930.6K **Privately Held**
WEB: www.dartmechanicalinc.com
SIC: 3315 Welded steel wire fabric

(G-13696)
DB WELDING LLC
6985 Respass Beach Rd (23435-2707)
PHONE.....................................757 483-0413
David Barrett, *Principal*
EMP: 1 **EST:** 2017
SALES (est): 29.8K **Privately Held**
SIC: 7692 Welding repair

(G-13697)
DEFENSE EXECUTIVES LLC
5100 W View Ct (23435-3505)
PHONE.....................................757 638-3678
John Iannetta, *Principal*
EMP: 3 **EST:** 2018
SALES (est): 145.3K **Privately Held**
SIC: 3812 Defense systems & equipment

(G-13698)
DIVERSIFIED VACUUM CORP
2408a Pruden Blvd (23434-4227)
PHONE.....................................757 538-1170
Clive Gleed, *President*
David Rezendes, *Treasurer*
EMP: 2 **EST:** 2016
SALES (est): 177.1K **Privately Held**
WEB: www.diversifiedvacuum.com
SIC: 3559 Semiconductor manufacturing machinery

(G-13699)
DIVERSIFIED VACUUM INC
2408a Pruden Blvd (23434-4227)
PHONE.....................................757 538-1170
Clive Gleed, *President*
David Rezendes, *Vice Pres*
▲ **EMP:** 2
SQ FT: 3,500
SALES (est): 437.1K **Privately Held**
WEB: www.diversifiedvacuum.com
SIC: 3563 Vacuum (air extraction) systems, industrial

(G-13700)
DLM ENTERPRISES INC
3020 Bay Shore Ln (23435-3176)
P.O. Box 6604, Portsmouth (23703-0604)
PHONE.....................................757 617-3470
Dennis M McGovern, *Owner*
Lorraine M McGovern, *Co-Owner*
EMP: 2
SALES (est): 10K **Privately Held**
SIC: 3325 Steel foundries

(G-13701)
DRUH-KE LLC
5617 Nathaniel St (23435-2533)
PHONE.....................................757 274-3117
Cornelius Drake, *Principal*
EMP: 2
SALES (est): 70.7K **Privately Held**
SIC: 2741 Miscellaneous publishing

(G-13702)
EASTER VA ORTHTICS PROSTHETICS
3517 Lingfield Cv (23435-2387)
PHONE.....................................757 967-0526
Lisa Paul, *Principal*
EMP: 2 **EST:** 2014
SALES (est): 84K **Privately Held**
SIC: 3842 Orthopedic appliances

(G-13703)
ELEY HOUSE CANDLES
109 Bosley Ave (23434-5704)
PHONE.....................................757 572-9318
Barry Day, *Administration*
EMP: 1 **EST:** 2014
SALES (est): 60K **Privately Held**
SIC: 3999 Candles

(G-13704)
ELM INVESTMENTS INC
Also Called: Southern Sheet Metal
114 Plover Dr (23434-6320)
PHONE.....................................757 934-2709
Danny Maxwell, *President*
Gayle Linkous, *Corp Secy*
EMP: 28
SQ FT: 12,000
SALES (est): 3MM **Privately Held**
SIC: 3444 3564 Sheet metalwork; exhaust fans: industrial or commercial

(G-13705)
EMBROIDERY AND PRINT HOUSE
312 Saint Brie W (23435-1450)
PHONE.....................................757 636-1676
Marshall Miller, *Principal*
EMP: 2
SALES (est): 137.4K **Privately Held**
WEB: www.embroideryandprinthouse.com
SIC: 2752 Commercial printing, lithographic

(G-13706)
FANCY MEDIA CO INC
5131 River Club Dr # 110 (23435-3846)
PHONE.....................................757 638-7101
Christopher Pfrang, *President*
Helena Guarda, *Comp Spec*
EMP: 2 **EST:** 1997
SALES (est): 260.3K **Privately Held**
WEB: www.fancymedia.com
SIC: 3695 Magnetic & optical recording media

(G-13707)
FEATHER CARBON LLC
6940 Corinth Chapel Rd (23437-9290)
PHONE.....................................757 630-6759
Thomas Queen, *President*
EMP: 1
SALES (est): 141.5K **Privately Held**
SIC: 3714 Motor vehicle parts & accessories

(G-13708)
FEATHERLITE COACHES INC (PA)
1007 Obici Indus Blvd (23434-5475)
PHONE.....................................757 923-3374
Conrad D Clement, *CEO*
Mary Shimek, *Purchasing*
Albert Chitwood, *Human Res Dir*
EMP: 50
SQ FT: 19,469
SALES (est): 11MM **Privately Held**
WEB: www.featherlitecoaches.com
SIC: 3716 Motor homes

(G-13709)
FERGUSON MANUFACTURING CO INC
590 Madison Ave (23434-4638)
P.O. Box 1098 (23439-1098)
PHONE.....................................757 539-3409
Emmett Burton, *President*
Nida Burton, *Vice Pres*
EMP: 10 **EST:** 1917
SQ FT: 40,000
SALES (est): 1MM **Privately Held**
WEB: www.fergusonmfgco.com
SIC: 3523 3524 3423 Farm machinery & equipment; lawn & garden equipment; hand & edge tools

(G-13710)
FLEMING WOODWORKING LLC
5061 Bay Cir (23435-2717)
PHONE.....................................559 259-2296
Jerame Fleming, *Administration*
EMP: 1
SALES (est): 59.5K **Privately Held**
SIC: 2431 Millwork

(G-13711)
FLOWERS BAKERIES LLC
1161 Proctor St (23434-3029)
PHONE.....................................757 539-2898
Larry Kilpatrick, *Director*
EMP: 3
SALES (corp-wide): 4.1B **Publicly Held**
WEB: www.flowersfoods.com
SIC: 2051 Bread, cake & related products
HQ: Flowers Bakeries, Llc
    1919 Flowers Cir
    Thomasville GA 31757

(G-13712)
GAILS DREAM LLC
6012 Scuppernong Dr (23435-1917)
PHONE.....................................757 638-3197
Heather Lauver, *Principal*
EMP: 2 **EST:** 2009
SALES (est): 95.4K **Privately Held**
SIC: 2711 Newspapers, publishing & printing

(G-13713)
GARNETT EMBROIDERY
1217 Peachtree Dr (23434-2911)
PHONE.....................................757 925-0569
Brenda E Garnett, *Owner*
EMP: 1
SALES (est): 61.4K **Privately Held**
WEB: www.garnettembroidery.com
SIC: 2395 Embroidery products, except schiffli machine

(G-13714)
GARTMAN LETTER LIMITED COMPANY
9136 River Cres (23433-1112)
P.O. Box 6147 (23433-0147)
PHONE.....................................757 238-9508
Chip Runyon, *Director*
Margaret Gartman,
Dennis Gartman,
EMP: 3
SALES (est): 201.3K **Privately Held**
WEB: www.thegartmanletter.com
SIC: 2741 Newsletter publishing

(G-13715)
GARYS CLASSIC CAR PARTS
205 Sumner Ave (23434-6732)
PHONE.....................................757 925-0546
Gary Taylor, *Owner*
EMP: 3
SALES (est): 22.6K **Privately Held**
SIC: 3714 Motor vehicle parts & accessories

(G-13716)
GRIFFIN MANUFACTURING COMPANY
7704 Whaleyville Blvd (23438-9332)
PHONE.....................................757 986-4541
Horace Griffin, *President*
Lillian Griffin, *Treasurer*
EMP: 3
SALES (est): 180K **Privately Held**
SIC: 3523 Planting machines, agricultural

(G-13717)
HANDS STEEL MOBILE WELDING LLC
405 Nevada St (23434-5829)
PHONE.....................................757 805-0054
EMP: 8 **EST:** 2018
SALES (est): 88.7K **Privately Held**
SIC: 7692 Welding repair

(G-13718)
HD INNOVATIONS
6709 Chambers Ln (23435-3083)
PHONE.....................................757 420-0774
Traune Turner, *Owner*
EMP: 2
SALES (est): 213.7K **Privately Held**
WEB: www.hdinnovationsva.com
SIC: 3699 Electric sound equipment

(G-13719)
HERBSFORHEALTH
6000 Old College Dr # 187 (23435-2063)
PHONE.....................................757 383-1245
Lynnette Gilmore,
EMP: 4

▲ = Import ▼=Export
◆ =Import/Export

SALES (est): 70K **Privately Held**
SIC: 2833 Botanical products, medicinal: ground, graded or milled

(G-13720)
HERITAGE WOODWORKS LLC (PA)
1002 Obici Indus Blvd (23434-5474)
PHONE................................757 934-1440
Daniele Yancey, *Senior VP*
Ariel Anderson, *Vice Pres*
Caitlin Flinn, *Vice Pres*
Tommy Danner, *Project Mgr*
Kevin Sweeney, *CFO*
EMP: 20
SALES (est): 3.9MM **Privately Held**
WEB: www.hwofva.com
SIC: 2434 Wood kitchen cabinets

(G-13721)
HILLS BROS COFFEE INCORPORATED
1370 Progress Rd (23434-2148)
PHONE................................757 538-8083
Massimo Zanetti, *Principal*
Beverly Nedab, *Human Res Dir*
Michael Parham, *Manager*
Bob Ashford, *Info Tech Mgr*
EMP: 1
SALES (est): 67K **Privately Held**
WEB: www.mzb-usa.com
SIC: 2095 Roasted coffee

(G-13722)
HOLIDAY ICE INC
1200 Progress Rd (23434-2144)
P.O. Box 1246 (23439-1246)
PHONE................................757 934-1294
James F Russell Jr, *President*
William C Russell, *Vice Pres*
Chris Smith, *Controller*
EMP: 20 EST: 1972
SQ FT: 52,000
SALES (est): 4.2MM **Privately Held**
WEB: www.holidayiceinc.com
SIC: 2097 Manufactured ice

(G-13723)
HOLLAND SAND PIT LLC
1652 Pine Acres (23432-1700)
PHONE................................757 745-7140
Jeff Paxton, *Mng Member*
EMP: 20 EST: 2014
SALES (est): 1.6MM **Privately Held**
WEB: www.paxtoncontractors.com
SIC: 1442 Sand mining

(G-13724)
IDENTITY MKTG PROMOTIONAL LLC
2465 Pruden Blvd (23434-4235)
PHONE................................757 966-2863
Karen C Dunn, *Owner*
Nicole Pagan, *Marketing Staff*
EMP: 3
SALES (est): 250K **Privately Held**
WEB: www.idmktgpromo.com
SIC: 3993 7336 Signs & advertising specialties; commercial art & graphic design

(G-13725)
INTERNATIONAL PAPER
1069 Centerbrooke Ln (23434-8475)
PHONE................................757 569-4521
EMP: 1
SALES (est): 57.5K **Privately Held**
SIC: 2621 Paper mills

(G-13726)
JUST FOR FUN
6203 Springhill Way (23435-2848)
PHONE................................757 620-3700
Sharon Upright, *Principal*
EMP: 2
SALES (est): 111.9K **Privately Held**
WEB: www.justforfunva.com
SIC: 2771 Greeting cards

(G-13727)
KALIS KREATIONS & DESIGNS LLC
4104 Colbourn Dr (23435-3795)
PHONE................................757 343-4421
Maxine Harris,
EMP: 12

SALES (est): 270.8K **Privately Held**
SIC: 2395 Art goods for embroidering, stamped: purchased materials

(G-13728)
KIDPRINT OF VIRGINIA INC
317 Saint Brie W (23435-1451)
PHONE................................757 287-3324
Hugh Blanchard, *President*
Joan Blanchard, *Vice Pres*
EMP: 3
SALES (est): 30K **Privately Held**
SIC: 3089 Identification cards, plastic

(G-13729)
KIRK LUMBER COMPANY
815 Kirk Rd (23434-6954)
PHONE................................757 255-4521
EMP: 4 EST: 1965
SQ FT: 10,500
SALES: 4.5MM **Privately Held**
SIC: 2421 Sawmill/Planing Mill

(G-13730)
LEGACY VULCAN LLC
Mideast Division
1273 Portsmouth Blvd (23434-2262)
PHONE................................757 539-5670
Jeanie Clay, *Manager*
EMP: 6 **Publicly Held**
WEB: www.vulcanmaterials.com
SIC: 3273 Ready-mixed concrete
HQ: Legacy Vulcan, Llc
1200 Urban Center Dr
Vestavia AL 35242
205 298-3000

(G-13731)
LESLIE E WILLIS
2527b Bridge Rd (23435-1705)
P.O. Box 6063 (23433-0063)
PHONE................................757 484-4484
Leslie E Willis, *Principal*
EMP: 1
SALES (est): 0 **Privately Held**
SIC: 3731 Shipbuilding & repairing

(G-13732)
LOCKHEED MARTIN CORPORATION
7700 Harbour View Blvd (23435-3835)
PHONE................................757 935-9479
Justin Hirsh, *Engineer*
EMP: 458 **Publicly Held**
WEB: www.lockheedmartin.com
SIC: 3761 3663 3764 3812 Space vehicles, complete; guided missiles, complete; ballistic missiles, complete; guided missiles & space vehicles, research & development; satellites, communications; propulsion units for guided missiles & space vehicles; guided missile & space vehicle engines, research & devel.; warfare counter-measure equipment; missile guidance systems & equipment; sonar systems & equipment; radar systems & equipment; aircraft parts & equipment; research & dev by manuf., aircraft parts & auxiliary equip; research & development on aircraft by the manufacturer
PA: Lockheed Martin Corporation
6801 Rockledge Dr
Bethesda MD 20817

(G-13733)
LOCKHEED MARTIN SERVICES LLC
Also Called: Lockheed Mrtin Ctr For Innvtio
8000 Harbour View Blvd (23435-2940)
PHONE................................757 935-9200
Jim McArthur, *Branch Mgr*
EMP: 1 **Publicly Held**
WEB: www.lockheedmartin.com
SIC: 3812 Aircraft/aerospace flight instruments & guidance systems
HQ: Lockheed Martin Services, Llc
700 N Frederick Ave
Gaithersburg MD 20879

(G-13734)
LOCO PARTS
1471 Spring Meadow Ln (23432-1318)
PHONE................................757 255-2815
Don L Orr, *Owner*
EMP: 1

SALES (est): 84.2K **Privately Held**
SIC: 3743 Locomotives & parts

(G-13735)
LVRCSHULL INCORPORATED
Also Called: N2 Publishing
4027 Appaloosa Ct (23434-7293)
PHONE................................757 995-3931
Vicki Shull, *Principal*
EMP: 2 EST: 2016
SALES (est): 83.4K **Privately Held**
SIC: 2741 Miscellaneous publishing

(G-13736)
M M SILK FLOWERS
305 Copeland Rd (23434-8616)
PHONE................................757 334-7096
Margie Manley, *Owner*
EMP: 1
SALES (est): 56.4K **Privately Held**
SIC: 3999 Manufacturing industries

(G-13737)
MACHINING TECHNOLOGY INC
1492 Progress Rd (23434-2146)
PHONE................................757 538-1781
Greg Taylor, *President*
EMP: 4
SALES (est): 590.6K **Privately Held**
WEB: www.machiningtechinc.com
SIC: 3599 Machine shop, jobbing & repair

(G-13738)
MAGCO INC
602 Carolina Rd (23434-4889)
P.O. Box 1837 (23439-1837)
PHONE................................757 934-0042
Ronald M Davis, *President*
EMP: 11
SQ FT: 3,200
SALES (est): 1.8MM **Privately Held**
WEB: www.magcoinc.net
SIC: 3556 3444 Food products machinery; sheet metalwork

(G-13739)
MASKED BY TEE LLC
242 Craftsman Cir (23434-1530)
PHONE................................757 373-9517
Litesah Williams, *Principal*
EMP: 2
SALES (est): 97.9K **Privately Held**
SIC: 2759 Screen printing

(G-13740)
MASSIMO ZANETTI BEV USA INC (DH)
Also Called: Kauai Coffee Co
1370 Progress Rd (23434-2148)
PHONE................................757 215-7300
John Boyle, *CEO*
Massimo Zanetti, *CEO*
Lambert Susan, *Business Mgr*
Larry Quier, *COO*
Bob Ashford, *Vice Pres*
◆ EMP: 200
SQ FT: 150,000
SALES (est): 113.5MM
SALES (corp-wide): 257.5K **Privately Held**
WEB: www.mzb-usa.com
SIC: 2095 Roasted coffee
HQ: Massimo Zanetti Beverage Group Spa
Via Gian Giacomo Felissent 53
Villorba TV 31020
042 231-2611

(G-13741)
MASSIMO ZANETTI BEV USA INC
1370 Progress Rd (23434-2148)
PHONE................................757 538-8083
EMP: 4
SALES (corp-wide): 257.5K **Privately Held**
WEB: www.mzb-usa.com
SIC: 2095 Roasted coffee
HQ: Massimo Zanetti Beverage Usa, Inc.
1370 Progress Rd
Suffolk VA 23434

(G-13742)
MID ATLANTIC MINING LLC
1129 Woods Pkwy (23434-2550)
PHONE................................757 407-6735

Myrick Faircloth,
Michael Eley,
EMP: 8
SALES (est): 505.6K **Privately Held**
SIC: 2411 1794 1442 1795 Logging camps & contractors; excavation & grading, building construction; construction sand & gravel; gravel & pebble mining; demolition, buildings & other structures

(G-13743)
MILLS MARINE & SHIP REPAIR LLC
211 Market St (23434-5209)
PHONE................................757 539-0956
Donald Mills,
EMP: 1
SALES (est): 93.2K **Privately Held**
WEB: www.millsmarineshiprepair.com
SIC: 3731 Military ships, building & repairing

(G-13744)
MILLS MARINE & SHIP REPAIR LLC
211 Market St (23434-5209)
PHONE................................757 539-0956
Donald Mills, *General Mgr*
Jerome Nixon, *VP Bus Dvlpt*
Priscilla Tarr, *Manager*
Ernestine Mills,
EMP: 5
SQ FT: 3,000
SALES (est): 651.8K **Privately Held**
WEB: www.millsmarineshiprepair.com
SIC: 3731 7699 1711 1742 Commercial cargo ships, building & repairing; industrial machinery & equipment repair; plumbing, heating, air-conditioning contractors; plastering, drywall & insulation; painting & paper hanging; primary copper smelter products

(G-13745)
MONDELEZ GLOBAL LLC
Also Called: Nabisco
200 Johnson Ave (23434-4613)
PHONE................................757 925-3011
James Kilts, *CEO*
EMP: 75 **Publicly Held**
WEB: www.mondelezinternational.com
SIC: 2052 2079 2035 2043 Cookies; crackers, dry; margarine & margarine oils; mustard, prepared (wet); seasonings, meat sauces (except tomato & dry); cereal breakfast foods; nuts: dried, dehydrated, salted or roasted; candy & other confectionery products
HQ: Mondelez Global Llc
905 W Fulton Market
Chicago IL 60607
847 943-4000

(G-13746)
MOONLIGHT WELDING LLC
3200 Indian Trl (23434-8346)
PHONE................................757 449-7003
Floyd Jones, *Principal*
EMP: 2
SALES (est): 201.9K **Privately Held**
WEB: www.moonlightwelding.com
SIC: 7692 Welding repair

(G-13747)
MZGOODIEZ LLC
552 2nd Ave (23434-5650)
P.O. Box 854 (23439-0854)
PHONE................................757 535-6929
Tonya L Johnson Jordan,
Tonya Johnson-Jordan,
EMP: 1
SALES (est): 52.2K **Privately Held**
SIC: 2051 2053 7389 Cakes, bakery: except frozen; pies, bakery: except frozen; cakes, bakery: frozen;

(G-13748)
NANSEMOND PRE-CAST CON CO INC
3737 Nansemond Pkwy (23435-1217)
PHONE................................757 538-2761
Douglas W McConnell, *President*
John McConnell, *Exec VP*
Tom Teske, *Vice Pres*
Yvonne Tooley, *Office Mgr*

Kim Wallace, *Admin Sec*
EMP: 35
SQ FT: 5,000
SALES (est): 6.6MM **Privately Held**
WEB: www.nansemondprecast.com
SIC: 3272 Concrete products, precast

(G-13749)
NASONI LLC
5210 Commando Block (23435)
PHONE....................757 358-7475
John Waddell, *Mng Member*
EMP: 1
SALES (est): 81K **Privately Held**
WEB: www.nasoni.com
SIC: 3432 Faucets & spigots, metal & plastic

(G-13750)
NESTLE USA INC
1368 Progress Rd (23434-2148)
PHONE....................757 538-4178
Jeffrey Byrd, *Manager*
EMP: 139
SALES (corp-wide): 93.5B **Privately Held**
WEB: www.nestleusa.com
SIC: 2023 Evaporated milk
HQ: Nestle Usa, Inc.
　　1812 N Moore St Ste 118
　　Rosslyn VA 22209
　　440 264-7249

(G-13751)
PERCISION WOODWORKS
1614 Pitchkettle Rd (23434-8411)
PHONE....................757 642-1686
EMP: 2
SALES (est): 59.5K **Privately Held**
SIC: 2431 Millwork

(G-13752)
PLUTO GONE LLC
103 Ryan Arch (23434-2138)
PHONE....................804 719-3076
Isaiah Dozier-Robinson, *Mng Member*
EMP: 5
SALES (est): 130.5K **Privately Held**
SIC: 2741 Music books: publishing & printing

(G-13753)
PRODUCERS PEANUT COMPANY INC
337 Moore Ave (23434-3819)
P.O. Box 250 (23439-0250)
PHONE....................757 539-7496
James R Pond, *President*
Richard Herto, *COO*
Catherine P Lawson, *Treasurer*
Sandra Young, *Human Resources*
Kathryn T Pond, *Admin Sec*
▼ **EMP:** 15
SQ FT: 18,000
SALES (est): 3.6MM **Privately Held**
WEB: www.producerspeanut.com
SIC: 2099 Peanut butter

(G-13754)
PURE FAITH PUBLISHING LLC
180 Majestic Dr (23434-8146)
PHONE....................757 925-4957
Brenda Stevenson, *Principal*
EMP: 2
SALES (est): 59.2K **Privately Held**
SIC: 2741 Miscellaneous publishing

(G-13755)
PURE SCENTSATIONS LLC
309 Wood Duck Ct (23434-8096)
PHONE....................334 868-9190
EMP: 1
SALES (est): 39.6K **Privately Held**
SIC: 3999 Candles

(G-13756)
RAYMOND HILL CONSULTING
3809 Deer Path Rd (23434-7335)
PHONE....................757 925-0136
Raymond Hill, *Owner*
EMP: 1 **Privately Held**
SIC: 2759 Flexographic printing

(G-13757)
RCL SOFTWARE INC
211 Equinox Lndg (23434-2060)
PHONE....................757 934-0828
Robert C Langer, *Principal*
EMP: 2 EST: 2009
SALES (est): 116.3K **Privately Held**
WEB: www.rclsoftware.com
SIC: 7372 Prepackaged software

(G-13758)
RDJ ENTERPRISES
202 Eagles Nest Trce (23435-3707)
PHONE....................757 538-0466
Richard K Moody, *Owner*
EMP: 1
SALES (est): 48.5K **Privately Held**
SIC: 3581 Automatic vending machines

(G-13759)
RIVER ROCK ENVIRONMENTAL SVCS
536 Wilroy Rd (23434)
PHONE....................757 690-3916
Allen Trombley,
EMP: 1
SALES (est): 53.2K **Privately Held**
SIC: 3589 Water treatment equipment, industrial

(G-13760)
ROCKS TIKI SURFBOARD SIGNS
1161 Nansemond Pkwy (23434-2200)
PHONE....................757 727-3330
Robert Little, *Principal*
EMP: 1 EST: 2015
SALES (est): 46.7K **Privately Held**
SIC: 3993 Signs & advertising specialties

(G-13761)
SEAGUARD INTERNATIONAL LLC
2000 Amedeo Ct (23434-5481)
PHONE....................484 747-0299
Dan Ballew, *COO*
EMP: 1
SQ FT: 10,000
SALES (est): 1.5MM **Privately Held**
WEB: www.seaguard-zinga.com
SIC: 3679 8711 Electronic circuits; marine engineering

(G-13762)
SHEILA RODRIGUEZ
Also Called: Global Welding and Engineering
5025 Riverfront Dr (23434-7188)
PHONE....................425 221-0519
Sheila Rodriguez, *Owner*
EMP: 1 EST: 2017
SALES (est): 27.6K **Privately Held**
SIC: 7692 Welding repair

(G-13763)
SHELFNWOODWORKS
1534 Olde Mill Creek Dr (23434-2319)
PHONE....................757 350-0408
Franklin Padgett, *Principal*
EMP: 1
SALES (est): 41.5K **Privately Held**
SIC: 2499 Wood products

(G-13764)
SIMPLY WOOD POST SIGNS LLC
9057 New Rd (23437-8302)
PHONE....................757 657-9058
EMP: 2
SALES (est): 87.9K **Privately Held**
SIC: 3993 Signs & advertising specialties

(G-13765)
SO WHAT PUBLICATIONS LLC
138 Berkshire Blvd (23434-9119)
PHONE....................757 934-0148
Louis Hollowell, *Administration*
EMP: 2
SALES (est): 74.2K **Privately Held**
SIC: 2741 Miscellaneous publishing

(G-13766)
SONOCO PRODUCTS COMPANY
Sonoco Consumer Products
326 Moore Ave (23434-3820)
PHONE....................757 539-8349
Jeff Hemingway, *Manager*

Jamie Sabol, *Admin Mgr*
EMP: 50
SALES (corp-wide): 5.3B **Publicly Held**
WEB: www.sonoco.com
SIC: 2655 3411 Cans, composite: foil-fiber & other; from purchased fiber; metal cans
PA: Sonoco Products Company
　　1 N 2nd St
　　Hartsville SC 29550
　　843 383-7000

(G-13767)
SRJ BEDLINERS LLC
Also Called: Line-X of Suffolk
2432 Pruden Blvd (23434-4227)
PHONE....................757 539-7710
Steven Jones,
EMP: 1 EST: 2009
SALES (est): 113.5K **Privately Held**
WEB: www.linexofsuffolk.com
SIC: 2851 Polyurethane coatings; epoxy coatings

(G-13768)
STATELINE BUILDERS INC
2017 Holland Rd (23434-6725)
PHONE....................757 934-6836
Darren Cochran, *Opers Staff*
EMP: 4
SALES (corp-wide): 2.1MM **Privately Held**
WEB: www.statelinebuilders.com
SIC: 3448 Prefabricated metal buildings
PA: Stateline Builders, Inc.
　　370 Caratoke Hwy
　　Moyock NC
　　252 435-6828

(G-13769)
SUFFOLK MATERIALS LLC
1130 Audubon Rd (23434-8125)
P.O. Box 2038 (23432-0038)
PHONE....................757 255-4005
Henry Morgan, *Manager*
Richard Turner,
EMP: 13
SALES (est): 1.2MM **Privately Held**
SIC: 1241 Coal mining services

(G-13770)
T & J WLDG & FABRICATION LLC
1204 Baltic St (23434-4138)
PHONE....................757 672-9929
Joshua Lavallais, *Principal*
EMP: 2
SALES (est): 113.4K **Privately Held**
WEB: www.tjwelds.com
SIC: 3548 2899 7692 3496 Electrodes, electric welding; seam welding apparatus, electric; fluxes: brazing, soldering, galvanizing & welding; automotive welding; gas welding rods

(G-13771)
TIDEWATER BLOCK LLC
999 Kenyon Rd (23434-6751)
P.O. Box 1546 (23439-1546)
PHONE....................757 539-1576
William Weissner, *Purch Mgr*
Sam Finney,
EMP: 21
SALES (est): 3.3MM **Privately Held**
WEB: www.tidewaterblock.com
SIC: 3272 Concrete products, precast

(G-13772)
TIDEWATER PROSTHETIC CENTER (HQ)
150 Burnetts Way Ste 300 (23434-8177)
PHONE....................757 925-4844
Rick Stapleton, *President*
EMP: 8
SQ FT: 1,539
SALES (est): 640.7K
SALES (corp-wide): 1.1B **Publicly Held**
WEB: www.hangerclinic.com
SIC: 3842 Limbs, artificial; abdominal supporters, braces & trusses
PA: Hanger, Inc.
　　10910 Domain Dr Ste 300
　　Austin TX 78758
　　512 777-3800

(G-13773)
TIDEWATER REBAR LLC
1013 Obici Indus Blvd (23434-5475)
PHONE....................757 325-9893
Curtis Raven, *President*
Kevin Kelly, *Vice Pres*
Linda Carlton, *Controller*
EMP: 12
SALES (est): 1.8MM **Privately Held**
WEB: www.tidewaterrebar.com
SIC: 3441 3312 Fabricated structural metal; stainless steel

(G-13774)
TOTAL PARACHUTE RIGGING SOLUTI
197 S Main St (23434-4639)
PHONE....................757 777-8288
Lacey M Schlappi, *President*
EMP: 2
SALES (est): 150.2K **Privately Held**
WEB: www.tprsllc.com
SIC: 2399 Parachutes

(G-13775)
V&M INDUSTRIES INC
489 Green Wing Dr (23434-6469)
PHONE....................757 319-9415
Vito F Basile, *Principal*
EMP: 2 EST: 2009
SALES (est): 93.5K **Privately Held**
SIC: 3999 Manufacturing industries

(G-13776)
VANITY PRINT & PRESS LLC
6304 Orkney Ct (23435-3044)
PHONE....................757 553-1602
Corey Kornegay, *Principal*
EMP: 2
SALES (est): 59.2K **Privately Held**
SIC: 2741 Miscellaneous publishing

(G-13777)
VANWIN COATINGS VIRGINIA LLC
324 Moore Ave (23434-3820)
PHONE....................757 925-4450
Billy Berry, *Manager*
EMP: 8
SALES (corp-wide): 4.3MM **Privately Held**
WEB: www.vanwincoatings.com
SIC: 3479 Coating of metals & formed products; coating, rust preventive
PA: Vanwin Coatings Of Virginia, L.L.C.
　　2601 Trade St Ste A
　　Chesapeake VA 23323
　　757 487-5080

(G-13778)
VIRGINIA CULINARY PATHWAYS LLC
Also Called: Coastal Pies
429 N Main St (23434-4424)
PHONE....................757 298-0599
Regina Brayboy, *Principal*
EMP: 2
SALES (est): 113.1K **Privately Held**
SIC: 2051 Cakes, pies & pastries

(G-13779)
VITEX PACKAGING INC
1137 Progress Rd (23434-2301)
PHONE....................757 538-3115
Tim Hare, *President*
Roger W Jacobs, *President*
Michael Moore, *Vice Pres*
Wayne Utley, *Engrg Dir*
Michael Degrandis, *CFO*
◆ **EMP:** 113
SQ FT: 50,000
SALES (est): 18.7MM
SALES (corp-wide): 537.5MM **Privately Held**
WEB: www.vitexpackaging.com
SIC: 2752 Commercial printing, offset
HQ: Vitex Packaging Group, Inc.
　　1137 Progress Rd
　　Suffolk VA 23434
　　757 538-3115

(G-13780)
VITEX PACKAGING GROUP INC (HQ)
Also Called: Extrusion and Lamination Div
1137 Progress Rd (23434-2301)
PHONE...................................757 538-3115
Bela Szigethy, *President*
Jerome F Anderson, *Vice Pres*
John Phifer, *CFO*
Robert Fitzsimmons, *Treasurer*
Lackey Shane, *Technology*
◆ EMP: 10
SALES (est): 48MM
SALES (corp-wide): 537.5MM **Privately Held**
SIC: 2759 3497 2671 2754 Flexographic printing; metal foil & leaf; packaging paper & plastics film, coated & laminated; commercial printing, gravure; bags: plastic, laminated & coated; adhesives & sealants
PA: Proampac Pg Borrower Llc
12025 Tricon Rd
Cincinnati OH 45246
513 671-1777

(G-13781)
W BERG PRESS
1620 Adams Dr W (23436-1029)
PHONE...................................757 238-9663
EMP: 1
SALES (est): 41K **Privately Held**
SIC: 2731 Books-Publishing/Printing

(G-13782)
WEBDMG LLC
392 Collier Cres (23434-4073)
PHONE...................................757 633-5033
Richard Robinson,
EMP: 1
SALES (est): 43.6K **Privately Held**
WEB: www.webdmg.com
SIC: 7372 7379 7371 Application computer software; ; custom computer programming services; computer software development & applications; software programming applications

(G-13783)
WEIGHTS N LIPSTICK
6128 Bradford Dr (23435-2882)
PHONE...................................251 404-8154
Kenya Andrews, *Principal*
EMP: 2
SALES (est): 74.4K **Privately Held**
SIC: 2844 Lipsticks

(G-13784)
WFT PROMOTIONS LLC
3753 Pear Orchard Way (23435-3461)
PHONE...................................757 560-5056
Jesse A Williams, *Principal*
EMP: 4
SALES (est): 231.4K **Privately Held**
WEB: www.wftpromotions.com
SIC: 3993 Signs & advertising specialties

(G-13785)
WGB LLC
Also Called: Lpm Services
3317 Trotman Wharf Dr (23435-1063)
PHONE...................................757 289-5053
Glenn Bertoline,
▲ EMP: 2
SALES (est): 30K **Privately Held**
WEB: www.wgbhomes.com
SIC: 3674 Computer logic modules

(G-13786)
WOOD TELEVISION LLC
Also Called: Suffolk News-Herald
130-132 S Saratoga St (23434)
P.O. Box 1220 (23439-1220)
PHONE...................................757 539-3437
Tracy Agnew, *Editor*
Cathy Daughtrey, *Bookkeeper*
Hope Rose, *Advt Staff*
Gaither Perry, *Branch Mgr*
EMP: 50
SALES (corp-wide): 3B **Publicly Held**
WEB: www.woodtv.com
SIC: 2711 Newspapers, publishing & printing
HQ: Wood Television Llc
120 College Ave Se
Grand Rapids MI 49503
616 456-8888

Sugar Grove
Smyth County

(G-13787)
MAPLE GROVE LOGGING LLC
182 Sand Mines Rd (24375-3314)
PHONE...................................276 677-0152
Noah Martin,
EMP: 2
SALES (est): 111.3K **Privately Held**
SIC: 2411 Logging

(G-13788)
RYE VALLEY OIL INC
5807 Charlie Taylor Rd (24375-3042)
PHONE...................................276 677-3750
EMP: 4
SALES (est): 419.7K **Privately Held**
WEB: www.ryevalleygear.com
SIC: 3714 Motor vehicle parts & accessories

Sumerduck
Fauquier County

(G-13789)
BROCADE CMMNCTIONS SYSTEMS LLC
14052 Silver Hill Rd (22742-2116)
PHONE...................................540 439-9010
Kevin Herrmann, *Accounts Mgr*
Ron Boggio, *Branch Mgr*
Susan Huynh, *Manager*
Mark Hood, *Senior Mgr*
EMP: 5
SALES (corp-wide): 22.6B **Publicly Held**
WEB: www.broadcom.com
SIC: 3674 Semiconductors & related devices
HQ: Brocade Communications Systems Llc
1320 Ridder Park Dr
San Jose CA 95131

(G-13790)
CABLING SYSTEMS INC
4279 Mount Ephraim Rd (22742-2112)
P.O. Box 143 (22742-0143)
PHONE...................................540 439-0101
Glenn Duckworth, *President*
Marie Duckworth, *Treasurer*
EMP: 3
SALES (est): 421.1K **Privately Held**
WEB: www.cablingsystemsonline.com
SIC: 3699 5063 Electronic training devices; alarm systems

(G-13791)
FLOWERS STEEL LLC
14125 Maryann Ln (22742-2009)
PHONE...................................540 424-8377
Doug Flowers, *Mng Member*
Sandra Flowers, *Mng Member*
EMP: 4
SALES (est): 750K **Privately Held**
SIC: 3441 3446 Building components, structural steel; architectural metalwork

(G-13792)
MONTEMORANO LLC
Also Called: Anna Banana Sweets
5102 Gold Crest Dr (22742-1951)
PHONE...................................540 272-6390
Diane Montemorano, *Mng Member*
EMP: 1 EST: 2013
SALES (est): 77K **Privately Held**
SIC: 2052 7389 Bakery products, dry;

(G-13793)
SUMMERDUCK RACEWAY
14027 Royalls Mill Rd (22742-2030)
PHONE...................................540 845-1656
EMP: 2 EST: 2017
SALES (est): 96.4K **Privately Held**
SIC: 3644 Raceways

(G-13794)
SUNSET PAVERS INC
4635 Midhurst Ct (22742-1947)
PHONE...................................703 507-9101
Carlos A Simoes, *Principal*
EMP: 2 EST: 2009
SALES (est): 172K **Privately Held**
SIC: 3531 Pavers

Surry
Surry County

(G-13795)
AMERICAN BIOPROTECTION INC
Also Called: Sting-Em
1272 Pleasant Point Rd (23883-3104)
P.O. Box 142 (23883-0142)
PHONE...................................866 200-1313
Alan Bardwell, *Director*
EMP: 1
SALES (est): 217.9K **Privately Held**
WEB: www.americanbioprotect.com
SIC: 2992 Oils & greases, blending & compounding

(G-13796)
BACONS CASTLE SUPPLY INC
6797 Colonial Trl E (23883-2202)
PHONE...................................757 357-6159
John M Brock Jr, *President*
EMP: 2
SALES (est): 327.5K **Privately Held**
WEB: www.baconscastle.com
SIC: 3523 Peanut combines, diggers, packers & threshers

(G-13797)
JAMES J GRAY
Also Called: Gray Logging Company
974 Mantura Rd (23883-2145)
PHONE...................................757 617-5279
James J Gray, *Owner*
EMP: 3
SALES (est): 200K **Privately Held**
SIC: 2411 Logging

(G-13798)
MIL-SAT LLC (PA)
Also Called: Mil-Sat Global Communication
318 Bank St (23883-2725)
P.O. Box 189 (23883-0189)
PHONE...................................757 294-9393
Ed Woomer, *Senior Engr*
Mary Ann Richardson, *Mng Member*
Monica Holloway, *Web Dvlpr*
Robert Lynn Oldham,
Donald R Richardson,
EMP: 2
SQ FT: 200
SALES: 3.2MM **Privately Held**
WEB: www.mil-sat.com
SIC: 3663 Satellites, communications

(G-13799)
MIL-SPACE LLC
318 Bank St (23883)
P.O. Box 92 (23883-0092)
PHONE...................................954 862-3613
John Beahm, *Administration*
EMP: 1
SALES (est): 63.3K **Privately Held**
SIC: 3663 Space satellite communications equipment

(G-13800)
SALTY SAWYER LLC
2040 Hog Island Rd (23883-2002)
PHONE...................................757 274-1765
Erik Daigle,
EMP: 1
SALES (est): 39.6K **Privately Held**
SIC: 3999 Manufacturing industries

(G-13801)
SEIZE MOMENTS
Also Called: B P Basl
217 Meadowlark Ln (23883-2446)
PHONE...................................804 794-5911
Barbara Basl, *Mng Member*
EMP: 2
SALES (est): 215.6K **Privately Held**
WEB: www.bpbasl.com
SIC: 2782 Scrapbooks, albums & diaries

Susan
Mathews County

(G-13802)
TRUSS INCORPORATED
453 Millers Ln (23163-2142)
PHONE...................................804 556-3611
Kyle Dabney, *Principal*
EMP: 3
SALES (est): 279.7K **Privately Held**
SIC: 2439 Structural wood members

Sutherland
Dinwiddie County

(G-13803)
ELIZABETH BAILEY
3028 Oxford Dr (23885-8838)
PHONE...................................804 265-8764
Elizabeth Bailey, *Principal*
EMP: 2
SALES (est): 105K **Privately Held**
WEB: www.elizabethbailey.co.uk
SIC: 2741 Miscellaneous publishing

(G-13804)
PAGE PUBLICATIONS LLC
20121 Cox Rd (23885-9457)
PHONE...................................804 733-8636
EMP: 1
SALES (est): 38.8K **Privately Held**
SIC: 2741 Miscellaneous publishing

(G-13805)
PARHAM SERVICES LLC
9901 Boisseau Rd (23885-9241)
P.O. Box 511, Dinwiddie (23841-0511)
PHONE...................................804 586-1202
Deonta Parham, *President*
EMP: 1
SALES (est): 150K **Privately Held**
SIC: 7692 4212 Welding repair; local trucking, without storage

Sutherlin
Pittsylvania County

(G-13806)
CLOVERDALE LUMBER CO INC
5863 S Boston Hwy (24594-2141)
PHONE...................................434 822-5017
C B Anderson, *President*
Nancy Anderson, *Corp Secy*
Robert Anderson, *Vice Pres*
EMP: 45
SQ FT: 11,900
SALES (est): 6.4MM **Privately Held**
SIC: 2421 2426 Sawmills & planing mills, general; hardwood dimension & flooring mills

Swords Creek
Russell County

(G-13807)
E DILLON & COMPANY
2522 Swords Creek Rd (24649-3019)
P.O. Box 160 (24649-0160)
PHONE...................................276 873-6816
Otey C Dudley, *President*
Connie S Miller, *Corp Secy*
EMP: 100 EST: 1868
SQ FT: 6,000
SALES (est): 20.8MM **Privately Held**
WEB: www.edillon.com
SIC: 3281 3271 1422 Cut stone & stone products; blocks, concrete or cinder: standard; crushed & broken limestone

(G-13808)
SNT TRUCKING INC
6929 Miller Creek Rd (24649-7495)
P.O. Box 88 (24649-0088)
PHONE...................................276 991-0931
Nina Miller, *President*
EMP: 2

GEOGRAPHIC

SALES (est): 84.4K **Privately Held**
SIC: 3281 7389 Curbing, paving & walkway stone; business services

Tangier
Accomack County

(G-13809)
PRUITTS BOAT YARD
4401 Long Bridge Rd (23440)
P.O. Box 61 (23440-0061)
PHONE...................................757 891-2565
Jerry Pruitt, *Owner*
EMP: 1
SALES (est): 106.5K **Privately Held**
SIC: 3732 0912 Boat building & repairing;
finfish

Tappahannock
Essex County

(G-13810)
ALS MACHINE & WELDING INC
1209 Desha Rd (22560-5430)
PHONE...................................804 443-3193
Shirley Cervera, *President*
Alber T Cervera, *Vice Pres*
EMP: 2
SALES (est): 980K **Privately Held**
WEB: www.lib.fmhi.usf.edu
SIC: 7692 Welding repair

(G-13811)
AYLETT SAND & GRAVEL INC (PA)
1251 Tappahannock Blvd (22560-9368)
P.O. Box 127 (22560-0127)
PHONE...................................804 443-2366
William Cooke, *President*
Betty Anne Cooke, *Corp Secy*
Stephen Kent Cooke, *Vice Pres*
Cooke Stephen Kent, *Vice Pres*
EMP: 3
SQ FT: 8,000
SALES (est): 2.3MM **Privately Held**
WEB: www.essexconcrete.com
SIC: 1442 Sand mining; gravel mining

(G-13812)
BALDWIN CABINET SHOPS INC
3693 Richmond Hwy (22560-5550)
PHONE...................................804 443-5421
James R Baldwin Jr, *President*
Mary Baldwin, *Treasurer*
EMP: 5 EST: 1972
SQ FT: 2,800
SALES (est): 200K **Privately Held**
SIC: 2434 Wood kitchen cabinets

(G-13813)
BARBOURS PRINTING SERVICE
206 Prince St (22560-5152)
P.O. Box 1029 (22560-1029)
PHONE...................................804 443-4505
Joseph Reinhardt, *President*
Ephriam Augustus-Reinhardt, *President*
Ephriam Augustus Reinhardt, *President*
Joseph E Reinhardt, *Corp Secy*
Shirley Reinhardt, *Vice Pres*
EMP: 6
SALES (est): 160K **Privately Held**
WEB: www.barbourprinting.com
SIC: 2759 2752 2791 2789 Letterpress
printing; commercial printing, offset; type-
setting; bookbinding & related work

(G-13814)
ESSEX CONCRETE CORPORATION (PA)
1251 Tappahannock Blvd (22560-9368)
P.O. Box 127 (22560-0127)
PHONE...................................804 443-2366
Cooke William K, *President*
Betty A Cooke, *Corp Secy*
Cooke Stephen K, *Vice Pres*
Todd Vanlandingham, *Opers Staff*
Bill Larochelle, *Sales Staff*
EMP: 60 EST: 1965
SQ FT: 2,000

SALES (est): 16.1MM **Privately Held**
WEB: www.essexconcrete.com
SIC: 3273 3272 Ready-mixed concrete;
concrete products

(G-13815)
ESSEX CONCRETE CORPORATION
And 360 Rr 17 (22560)
P.O. Box 127 (22560-0127)
PHONE...................................804 443-2366
William Cook, *President*
W W Cooke, *President*
EMP: 14
SALES (corp-wide): 16.1MM **Privately Held**
WEB: www.essexconcrete.com
SIC: 3273 Ready-mixed concrete
PA: Essex Concrete Corporation
1251 Tappahannock Blvd
Tappahannock VA 22560
804 443-2366

(G-13816)
FDP VIRGINIA INC
Also Called: Fdp Brakes
1076 Airport Rd (22560-5401)
P.O. Box 1426 (22560-1426)
PHONE...................................804 443-5356
John J Carney, *President*
Bill Carney, *Vice Pres*
John Carney, *Vice Pres*
Tyson Broaddus, *Production*
Michael Janidlo, *QC Mgr*
▲ EMP: 192
SQ FT: 236,432
SALES (est): 56MM **Privately Held**
WEB: www.fdpbrakes.com
SIC: 3714 Motor vehicle brake systems & parts

(G-13817)
HATICOLE WELDING & MECHANICAL
3166 Desha Rd (22560-5425)
PHONE...................................804 443-7808
Benjamin Gathercole, *Principal*
EMP: 1
SALES (est): 44.5K **Privately Held**
SIC: 7692 Welding repair

(G-13818)
JLB PUBLISHING INC
306 Cross St (22560)
P.O. Box 2564 (22560-2564)
PHONE...................................804 443-0330
Blanks James, *President*
EMP: 10
SALES (est): 228.2K **Privately Held**
WEB: www.realestatepointer.com
SIC: 2741 Miscellaneous publishing

(G-13819)
OMALLEY TIMBER PRODUCTS LLC
250 Commerce Rd (22560-5483)
P.O. Box 940 (22560-0940)
PHONE...................................804 445-1118
Michael O'Malley,
EMP: 100
SQ FT: 1,000
SALES (est): 18.1MM **Privately Held**
WEB: www.omalleylumber.com
SIC: 2421 Sawmills & planing mills, general

(G-13820)
PERDUE FARMS INC
1000 Granary Rd (22560)
P.O. Box 928 (22560-0928)
PHONE...................................804 443-4391
Mike Newsome, *Manager*
EMP: 9
SQ FT: 3,800
SALES (corp-wide): 5.2B **Privately Held**
WEB: www.perduefarms.com
SIC: 2015 Poultry slaughtering & processing
PA: Perdue Farms Inc.
31149 Old Ocean City Rd
Salisbury MD 21804
410 543-3000

(G-13821)
RAPA BOAT SERVICES LLC
139360 W Indus Park (22560-6500)
PHONE...................................804 443-4434
EMP: 3 EST: 2010
SALES (est): 392.2K **Privately Held**
SIC: 3732 Boat building & repairing

(G-13822)
STERILE HOME LLC
2146 Cold Cheer Dr (22560-5066)
PHONE...................................804 314-3589
Patricia R Roth,
EMP: 2
SALES (est): 4K **Privately Held**
SIC: 2842 Specialty cleaning, polishes & sanitation goods

(G-13823)
TAGG DESIGN SPECIALTY PRTG LLC
1013 Tanyard Dr Apt 8 (22560-2378)
PHONE...................................804 572-7777
Adel Green,
EMP: 3
SALES (est): 153.2K **Privately Held**
SIC: 2752 Commercial printing, lithographic

(G-13824)
W A CLEATON AND SONS INC
Also Called: Rappahannock Times
622 Charlotte St (22560-2348)
P.O. Box 1025 (22560-1025)
PHONE...................................804 443-2200
Willie A Cleaton, *President*
Scott Cleaton, *Vice Pres*
Donald W Cleaton, *Treasurer*
Cathy H Cleaton, *Admin Sec*
EMP: 14
SQ FT: 5,000
SALES (est): 1MM **Privately Held**
SIC: 2711 Job printing & newspaper publishing combined

(G-13825)
WILKINS WOODWORKING
246 Rappahannock Beach Dr (22560-5261)
PHONE...................................804 761-8081
Gordon Wilkins, *Principal*
EMP: 2
SALES (est): 269.2K **Privately Held**
SIC: 2431 Millwork

(G-13826)
WILLOW STITCH LLC
223 Prince St (22560-5152)
PHONE...................................804 761-5967
Shelley Pierson, *Principal*
EMP: 1
SALES (est): 50K **Privately Held**
SIC: 2395 Embroidery & art needlework

(G-13827)
WILRICH CONSTRUCTION LLC
1449 Latanes Mill Rd (22560-5612)
P.O. Box 24, St Stephns Ch (23148-0024)
PHONE...................................804 654-0238
EMP: 6
SALES: 150K **Privately Held**
SIC: 3531 Construction Machinery, Nsk

Tazewell
Tazewell County

(G-13828)
BRIAN ALLISON
Also Called: Allison's Woodworks
5418 Thompson Valley Rd (24651-9266)
PHONE...................................276 988-9792
Brian Allison,
EMP: 1 EST: 2013
SALES (est): 119.1K **Privately Held**
SIC: 2084 Wines

(G-13829)
CANAAN LAND ASSOCIATES INC
Also Called: Power-Trac
Tazewell Industrial Park (24651)
P.O. Box 539 (24651-0539)
PHONE...................................276 988-6543

Ed Reynolds, *President*
Nadine Moore, *Opers Mgr*
Carolyn B Reynolds, *Treasurer*
EMP: 55
SALES (est): 6.9MM **Privately Held**
WEB: www.power-trac.com
SIC: 3524 3532 Lawn & garden tractors & equipment; mining machinery

(G-13830)
CLINCH RIVER LLC
21405 Gvrnor G C Pery Hwy (24651-9321)
PHONE...................................276 963-5271
Sam Kinder, *President*
▼ EMP: 54
SQ FT: 60,000
SALES (est): 14.9MM
SALES (corp-wide): 1.6B **Privately Held**
WEB: www.elginindustries.com
SIC: 3532 3441 Mineral beneficiation equipment; fabricated structural metal
HQ: Elgin Equipment Group, Llc
2001 Bttrfeld Rd Ste 1020
Downers Grove IL 60515

(G-13831)
DONUT DIVA LLC
203 Fincastle Tpke (24651-6124)
PHONE...................................276 245-5987
Susan Carr,
EMP: 5
SQ FT: 250
SALES (est): 361.2K **Privately Held**
WEB: www.donutdivatazewell.com
SIC: 2051 Cakes, bakery: except frozen; pies, bakery: except frozen

(G-13832)
ELGIN EQUIPMENT GROUP
21405 Gvrnor G C Pery Hwy (24651-9321)
PHONE...................................276 988-8901
EMP: 2
SALES (est): 163.6K **Privately Held**
SIC: 3532 Mining machinery

(G-13833)
L AND M FOODS
254 Rabbit Patch Rd (24651-8467)
PHONE...................................276 979-4110
Charles Looney, *Principal*
EMP: 3
SALES (est): 187.5K **Privately Held**
SIC: 2099 Food preparations

(G-13834)
MCFARLAND WOODWORKS LLC
2011 Clear Fork Rd (24651-8387)
PHONE...................................276 970-5847
John McFarland,
EMP: 1
SALES (est): 54.1K **Privately Held**
SIC: 2431 Millwork

(G-13835)
MELVINS MACHINE & WELDING
159 Melvin Ln (24651-8381)
P.O. Box 949 (24651-0949)
PHONE...................................276 988-3822
Bryan Melvin, *President*
Karen Melville, *Admin Sec*
EMP: 4
SQ FT: 1,200
SALES (est): 330K **Privately Held**
SIC: 3599 Machine & other job shop work

(G-13836)
MELVINS MACHINE AND DIE INC
197 Melvin Ln (24651-8381)
P.O. Box 949 (24651-0949)
PHONE...................................276 988-3822
Brian Melvin, *President*
EMP: 2
SALES (est): 208.6K **Privately Held**
WEB: www.melvinsmachineanddie.com
SIC: 3599 Machine shop, jobbing & repair

(G-13837)
N A K MECHANICS & WELDING INC
206 Goshen Hill Rd (24651-9549)
PHONE...................................276 971-1860
Gary Keen, *Principal*
EMP: 2 EST: 2007

SALES (est): 106.3K **Privately Held**
SIC: 7692 Welding repair

(G-13838)
NORRIS SCREEN AND MFG LLC
21405 Gvrnor G C Pery Hwy (24651-9321)
PHONE..................................276 988-8901
Brian Walker, *Principal*
▲ EMP: 38 EST: 1977
SQ FT: 12,700
SALES (est): 10.3MM
SALES (corp-wide): 1.6B **Privately Held**
WEB: www.elginindustries.com
SIC: 3532 3589 Mining machinery; water
purification equipment, household type
HQ: Elgin Equipment Group, Llc
2001 Bttrfeld Rd Ste 1020
Downers Grove IL 60515

(G-13839)
**SIMMONS EQUIPMENT
COMPANY**
847 Steeles Ln (24651-5381)
P.O. Box 719, Pounding Mill (24637-0719)
PHONE..................................276 991-3345
Jack L Simmons, *President*
James Coe, *Engineer*
Brandon Keen, *Sales Engr*
Monica Simmons, *Office Mgr*
John L Simmons, *Admin Sec*
EMP: 14
SQ FT: 10,000
SALES (est): 2.6MM **Privately Held**
WEB: www.simmonsequip.com
SIC: 3532 Mining machinery

Temperanceville
Accomack County

(G-13840)
TYSON FOODS INC
11224 Lankford Hwy (23442-2445)
P.O. Box 8 (23442-0008)
PHONE..................................757 824-3471
Derek Daucom, *Plant Mgr*
Craig Clark, *Safety Mgr*
Bill Ricken, *Manager*
Rafael Merida, *Manager*
Ian Redmond, *Supervisor*
EMP: 1100
SALES (corp-wide): 43.1B **Publicly Held**
WEB: www.tysonfoods.com
SIC: 2015 Poultry, processed
PA: Tyson Foods, Inc.
2200 W Don Tyson Pkwy
Springdale AR 72762
479 290-4000

Thaxton
Bedford County

(G-13841)
**APPLIED MANUFACTURING
TECH**
1097 Preserve Ln (24174-3472)
PHONE..................................434 942-1047
Brian Smith, *Owner*
Charlene Smith, *Principal*
EMP: 1
SALES (est): 100K **Privately Held**
SIC: 3999 Manufacturing industries

The Plains
Fauquier County

(G-13842)
CHARTER IP PLLC
7147 Kenthurst Ln (20198-2641)
PHONE..................................540 253-5332
Matthew Lattig, *Owner*
EMP: 2
SALES (est): 296K **Privately Held**
WEB: www.charterip.com
SIC: 3444 Awnings & canopies

(G-13843)
LANDMARK LOGWORKS
3489 Landmark Rd (20198-1724)
PHONE..................................540 687-4124

EMP: 2
SALES (est): 113.4K **Privately Held**
WEB: www.popularwoodworking.com
SIC: 2431 Millwork

(G-13844)
UNICORN EDITIONS LTD
8076 Enon Church Rd (20198-9747)
PHONE..................................540 364-0156
Pino Blangiforti, *CEO*
Anna C Blangiforti, *President*
Melanie Anderson, *Admin Asst*
EMP: 4
SQ FT: 1,500
SALES (est): 561.5K **Privately Held**
WEB: www.absorbine.com
SIC: 2843 Leather finishing agents

Timberville
Rockingham County

(G-13845)
**ANDES GLENDON MEAT
PROCESSING**
18317 N Mountain Rd (22853-2126)
PHONE..................................540 896-7798
Glendon Andes, *Owner*
EMP: 2
SALES (est): 114.3K **Privately Held**
SIC: 2011 Meat packing plants

(G-13846)
CARGILL INCORPORATED
480 Co Op Dr (22853)
P.O. Box 699 (22853-0699)
PHONE..................................540 896-7041
Melton McPike, *Manager*
EMP: 50
SALES (corp-wide): 113.4B **Privately
Held**
WEB: www.peterschocolate.com
SIC: 2015 Poultry slaughtering & process-
ing
PA: Cargill, Incorporated
15407 Mcginty Rd W
Wayzata MN 55391
952 742-7575

(G-13847)
DUNROMIN LOGGING LLC
616 N Mountain Rd (22853-9554)
PHONE..................................540 896-3543
Gillian Lee, *Principal*
EMP: 2
SALES (est): 112.6K **Privately Held**
SIC: 2411 Logging

(G-13848)
EMBROIDERY CRIATIONS
3589 Richardson Rd (22853-2612)
PHONE..................................540 421-5608
EMP: 1
SALES (est): 37.8K **Privately Held**
WEB: www.embroiderycriations.com
SIC: 2395 Embroidery & art needlework

(G-13849)
**FRAZIER QUARRY
INCORPORATED**
Rr 42 (22853)
P.O. Box 588, Harrisonburg (22803-0588)
PHONE..................................540 896-7538
Jeff Holsinger, *Branch Mgr*
EMP: 1
SALES (corp-wide): 16.4MM **Privately
Held**
WEB: www.frazierquarry.com
SIC: 3281 Stone, quarrying & processing
of own stone products
PA: The Frazier Quarry Incorporated
75 Waterman Dr
Harrisonburg VA 22802
540 434-6192

(G-13850)
**JAMERRILL PUBLISHING CO
LLC**
19353 N Mountain Rd (22853-2014)
PHONE..................................540 908-5234
Jamerrill Stewart, *Principal*
EMP: 2

SALES (est): 69.5K **Privately Held**
WEB: www.largefamilytable.com
SIC: 2741 Miscellaneous publishing

(G-13851)
**PILGRIMS PRIDE
CORPORATION**
Also Called: Eastern Division
330 Co Op Dr (22853)
P.O. Box 7275, Broadway (22815-7275)
PHONE..................................540 896-7000
Ted Lankford, *General Mgr*
Ronald Matthews, *Manager*
Leon Miller, *Director*
EMP: 1200
SALES (corp-wide): 177.9K **Publicly
Held**
WEB: www.pilgrims.com
SIC: 2015 Poultry slaughtering & process-
ing
HQ: Pilgrim's Pride Corporation
1770 Promontory Cir
Greeley CO 80634
970 506-8000

(G-13852)
**PRICES ELECTRIC MOTOR
REPAIR**
356 3rd Ave (22853-9512)
P.O. Box 193 (22853-0193)
PHONE..................................540 896-9451
Nelson Price, *President*
Sherry Price Knupp, *Vice Pres*
Joann Price Campbell, *Admin Sec*
EMP: 4
SQ FT: 1,800
SALES (est): 503.4K **Privately Held**
SIC: 7694 Electric motor repair

(G-13853)
**PRUITT WELDING &
FABRICATION**
15510 Evergreen Valley Rd (22853-2627)
PHONE..................................540 896-4268
Aaron Pruitt, *Principal*
EMP: 1
SALES (est): 44.8K **Privately Held**
SIC: 7692 Welding repair

(G-13854)
ROBSON WOODWORKING
Also Called: Standing People Woodworking
16912 Evergreen Valley Rd (22853-2811)
PHONE..................................540 896-6711
John Robson, *Owner*
EMP: 1
SALES (est): 108.4K **Privately Held**
WEB: www.standingpeoplewood.com
SIC: 2515 Sleep furniture

Toano
James City County

(G-13855)
AJC WOODWORKS INC
8305 Richmond Rd (23168-9207)
PHONE..................................757 566-0336
Tony Casnave, *President*
Alona Casnave, *Vice Pres*
EMP: 2 EST: 1987
SQ FT: 2,800
SALES (est): 284.9K **Privately Held**
WEB: www.ajcwood.com
SIC: 2434 Wood kitchen cabinets

(G-13856)
**ARMSTRONG AIRPORT
LIGHTING**
8610 Richmond Rd (23168-9213)
PHONE..................................865 856-2723
Wilford Lee Armstrong, *Owner*
EMP: 1
SQ FT: 800
SALES (est): 300K **Privately Held**
SIC: 3648 Lighting equipment

(G-13857)
ATOMIZER FUEL SYSTEMS INC
8105 Richmond Rd Ste 405 (23168-9263)
PHONE..................................757 250-3773
EMP: 2

SALES (est): 92.3K **Privately Held**
WEB: www.atomizerfuelcomponents.com
SIC: 3714 Motor vehicle parts & acces-
sories

(G-13858)
BURDEN BEARER TEES LLC
8424 Sheldon Branch Pl (23168-9266)
PHONE..................................757 337-7324
EMP: 2 EST: 2018
SALES (est): 73.2K **Privately Held**
SIC: 2759 Screen printing

(G-13859)
CARBON & STEEL LLC
3248 Oak Branch Ln (23168-9617)
PHONE..................................757 871-1808
Michael Damian Seal, *Administration*
EMP: 2 EST: 2015
SALES (est): 130.4K **Privately Held**
SIC: 3441 8711 Fabricated structural
metal; engineering services

(G-13860)
CLAIRE E BOSE
9561 Goddin Ct (23168-9548)
PHONE..................................323 898-2912
Claire Bose, *Owner*
EMP: 1
SALES (est): 36.9K **Privately Held**
SIC: 3931 Musical instruments

(G-13861)
**CREATIVE CABINET WORKS
LLC**
201 Industrial Blvd (23168-9276)
PHONE..................................757 566-1000
Douglas W Hogue, *Principal*
Terrah Hogue, *CPA*
Doug Hogue, *Manager*
Jay Taylor, *Manager*
EMP: 2
SALES (est): 357.9K **Privately Held**
WEB: www.cabinetworksva.com
SIC: 2434 Wood kitchen cabinets

(G-13862)
DANIELS WELDING AND TIRES
8005 Hankins Indus Park (23168-9259)
PHONE..................................757 566-8446
Bruce E Daniels, *President*
Jacqueline K Daniels, *Corp Secy*
EMP: 7
SQ FT: 8,000
SALES (est): 849.8K **Privately Held**
WEB: www.dantireandweld.com
SIC: 7692 5531 5014 7538 Automotive
welding; automotive tires; automobile tires
& tubes; general automotive repair shops;
welding on site

(G-13863)
DAVID STEELE
Also Called: Steele Construction
9120 Barnes Rd (23168-8905)
PHONE..................................757 236-3971
David Steele, *President*
Todd Smith, *Vice Pres*
EMP: 3
SALES (est): 207.6K **Privately Held**
SIC: 1389 Construction, repair & disman-
tling services

(G-13864)
**DESIGN MASTER ASSOCIATES
INC**
3005 John Deere Rd (23168-9332)
PHONE..................................757 566-8500
Byron Whitehurst, *CEO*
Richard Hill, *President*
Tony Schoedel, *Vice Pres*
Tony N Schoedel, *Vice Pres*
Marie Lapetina, *Opers Staff*
▲ EMP: 48
SQ FT: 40,000
SALES (est): 8.8MM **Privately Held**
WEB: www.designmasters.com
SIC: 3499 3231 3229 Novelties & gift-
ware, including trophies; products of pur-
chased glass; pressed & blown glass

(G-13865)
GREYSTONE OF VIRGINIA INC
7992 Richmond Rd (23168-9125)
P.O. Box 609 (23168-0609)
PHONE....................757 566-8070
Everett Fernald Jr, *President*
Michael Deffley, *Vice Pres*
Dave Lippy, *Vice Pres*
David Lippy, *Vice Pres*
EMP: 90
SQ FT: 88,000
SALES (est): 11MM
SALES (corp-wide): 25.7MM **Privately Held**
WEB: www.greyst.com
SIC: 3471 Electroplating of metals or formed products
PA: Induplate Inc.
　1 Greystone Ave Ste 1 # 1
　North Providence RI 02911
　401 231-5770

(G-13866)
INDUPLATE OPERATIONS LLC
7992 Richmond Rd (23168-9125)
PHONE....................757 566-8070
EMP: 2
SALES (est): 110.9K **Privately Held**
WEB: www.greyst.com
SIC: 3599 Machine shop, jobbing & repair

(G-13867)
LILYS ALPACAS LLC
8105 Richmond Rd Ste 203 (23168-9261)
PHONE....................757 865-1001
John Walter Ballentine, *Principal*
EMP: 2
SALES (est): 87.6K **Privately Held**
SIC: 2231 Alpacas, mohair: woven

(G-13868)
MADISON COLONIAL LLC
3204 Lytham Ct (23168-9384)
PHONE....................240 997-2376
Luis Betancourt,
EMP: 2
SALES (est): 138.6K **Privately Held**
WEB: www.madisoncolonial.com
SIC: 3489 5112 7389 Guns or gun parts, over 30 mm.; flame throwers (ordnance); stationery & office supplies;

(G-13869)
ME LATIMER FABRICATOR T A
2301 Little Creek Dam Rd (23168-8600)
PHONE....................757 566-8352
Michael E Latimer,
EMP: 2 EST: 1992
SALES (est): 200K **Privately Held**
SIC: 3444 Sheet metalwork

(G-13870)
MEDICAL ACTION INDUSTRIES INC
9000 Westmont Dr (23168-9351)
PHONE....................757 566-3510
Michael Sahady, *CEO*
EMP: 1
SALES (est): 39.6K **Privately Held**
SIC: 3999 Manufacturing industries

(G-13871)
NEXLEVEL TRANSPORTS INC
3436 Frederick Dr (23168-9362)
PHONE....................757 707-6349
Michael Garland, *President*
EMP: 3
SALES (est): 150K **Privately Held**
SIC: 3441 Railroad car racks, for transporting vehicles: steel

(G-13872)
ORTONS SPECIALTY WELDING LLC
8647 Merry Oaks Ln (23168-9449)
PHONE....................804 405-2675
Jason M Orton, *Administration*
EMP: 1
SALES (est): 57.9K **Privately Held**
WEB: www.ortonswelding.com
SIC: 7692 Welding repair

(G-13873)
PADDOCK ENTERPRISES LLC
150 Industrial Blvd (23168-9215)
PHONE....................757 566-3957
Robert Young, *Opers Mgr*
Mike Ayers, *Manager*
EMP: 13 **Publicly Held**
WEB: www.o-i.com
SIC: 3221 Glass containers
HQ: Paddock Enterprises, Llc
　1 Michael Owens Way
　Perrysburg OH 43551
　567 336-5000

(G-13874)
POST & PALLET LLC
3040 Ridge Dr (23168-9602)
PHONE....................757 645-5292
Phillip Poland, *Principal*
EMP: 8
SALES (est): 830.5K **Privately Held**
WEB: www.postandpallet.com
SIC: 2448 Pallets, wood

(G-13875)
PRESTIGE CABINETS
8019 Hankins Indus Park (23168-9259)
PHONE....................757 741-3201
EMP: 1
SALES (est): 59.1K **Privately Held**
SIC: 2434 Wood kitchen cabinets

(G-13876)
RO-WAY INC
201 Norman Davis Dr (23168-9335)
PHONE....................757 566-3569
Robert Wilson, *President*
EMP: 2 EST: 2012
SALES (est): 128.8K **Privately Held**
SIC: 3489 Ordnance & accessories

(G-13877)
SIGNATURE STONE CORPORATION
8009 A Industrial Park Rd (23168)
PHONE....................757 566-9094
Daniel Dauchess, *President*
Helen Dauchess, *CFO*
▲ EMP: 16
SALES (est): 2.2MM **Privately Held**
WEB: www.signature-stone.com
SIC: 3281 Granite, cut & shaped

(G-13878)
SOUTHERN WOODWORKS INC
8630 Merry Oaks Ln (23168-9448)
PHONE....................757 566-8307
James A Johnston III, *Principal*
EMP: 2
SALES (est): 110.2K **Privately Held**
SIC: 2431 Millwork

(G-13879)
TOANA 2 LIMITED
3326 Toano Dr (23168-9257)
PHONE....................757 566-2001
EMP: 3
SALES (est): 184.9K **Privately Held**
SIC: 3661 Mfg Telephone/Telegraph Apparatus

(G-13880)
WILLIAMSBURG DIRECTORY CO INC
8789 Richmond Rd W (23168-8814)
P.O. Box 729 (23168-0729)
PHONE....................757 566-1981
Joseph Palmer, *President*
EMP: 2
SQ FT: 850
SALES (est): 137.5K **Privately Held**
SIC: 2741 Directories: publishing only, not printed on site

(G-13881)
WRIGHT SIGN SERVICE INC
8008 Hankins Indus Park (23168-9259)
PHONE....................757 566-8329
Raymond P Wright Sr, *President*
EMP: 11
SQ FT: 5,000
SALES (est): 1.2MM **Privately Held**
WEB: www.wrightsign.com
SIC: 3993 Signs & advertising specialties

Toms Brook
Shenandoah County

(G-13882)
CRABILL SLAUGHTERHOUSE INC
Also Called: Crabill Meats
3149 Riverview Dr (22660-2113)
PHONE....................540 436-3248
Eugene Crabill, *President*
EMP: 9
SALES (est): 996.7K **Privately Held**
WEB: www.ajc7.com
SIC: 2011 5421 Meat packing plants; meat & fish markets

(G-13883)
DIRECT STAIRS
1056 Harrisville Rd (22660-2318)
PHONE....................540 436-9290
EMP: 2
SALES (est): 172.2K **Privately Held**
SIC: 3446 Stairs, staircases, stair treads: prefabricated metal

(G-13884)
DUCKWORTH COMPANY
103 River Ct (22660-2132)
PHONE....................540 436-8754
Blaine Duckworth, *Owner*
EMP: 1
SALES (est): 103.3K **Privately Held**
SIC: 2434 Wood kitchen cabinets

Topping
Middlesex County

(G-13885)
ATLANTIC METAL PRODUCTS INC (PA)
65 Industrial Way (23169)
P.O. Box 10 (23169-0010)
PHONE....................804 758-4915
Raymond Campbell Jr, *President*
Tom Walsh, *Corp Secy*
Ronald P Campbell, *Vice Pres*
Alan Blake, *Sales Staff*
▲ EMP: 31 EST: 1977
SQ FT: 7,200
SALES (est): 3.3MM **Privately Held**
WEB: www.ampva.com
SIC: 3441 1791 3823 3556 Fabricated structural metal; structural steel erection; industrial instrmnts msrmnt display/control process variable; food products machinery; textile machinery; fabricated plate work (boiler shop)

(G-13886)
CONTEMPORARY KITCHENS LTD
57 Campbell Dr (23169-2191)
P.O. Box 83 (23169-0083)
PHONE....................804 758-2001
Paul Sherwood, *President*
Mary Ellen Sherwood, *Vice Pres*
EMP: 7 EST: 1979
SALES (est): 605K **Privately Held**
WEB: www.conkit.com
SIC: 2434 2541 2511 2431 Wood kitchen cabinets; wood partitions & fixtures; wood household furniture; millwork

(G-13887)
MARINE FABRICATORS INC
27 Industrial Way (23169)
P.O. Box 140 (23169-0140)
PHONE....................804 758-2248
Charles Avera, *President*
EMP: 1
SALES (est): 128.8K **Privately Held**
SIC: 2299 Tops, combing & converting

Triangle
Prince William County

(G-13888)
AJS E COAST HLG & TRNSPT LLC
18460 Lotus Ct Apt 201 (22172-1745)
PHONE....................540 645-2200
Aj Fetherman, *Mng Member*
EMP: 1
SALES (est): 60K **Privately Held**
SIC: 3537 Trucks: freight, baggage, etc.: industrial, except mining

(G-13889)
COY TIGER PUBLISHING LLC
3589 Wharf Ln (22172-1058)
PHONE....................703 221-8064
EMP: 2
SALES (est): 59.2K **Privately Held**
SIC: 2741 Miscellaneous publishing

(G-13890)
DEFENSE THREAT REDUCTIO
18794 Pier Trail Dr (22172-2352)
PHONE....................703 767-4627
Kim Moore, *Principal*
EMP: 3 EST: 2016
SALES (est): 155K **Privately Held**
SIC: 3812 Defense systems & equipment

(G-13891)
DISPLAYMAKERS COMPANY
4236 Inn St (22172-1706)
PHONE....................703 501-2527
Luz Gonzales, *President*
Daniel Gonzales, *Vice Pres*
EMP: 5
SALES (est): 220K **Privately Held**
WEB: www.display-makers.com
SIC: 2541 Store & office display cases & fixtures

(G-13892)
FIVE TALENTS ENTERPRISES LLC
Also Called: Sew Impressive
4028 Sapling Way (22172-2050)
PHONE....................703 986-6721
Betty Harris,
EMP: 1
SALES (est): 20K **Privately Held**
SIC: 2391 7389 Curtains, window: made from purchased materials;

(G-13893)
FRESHSTART COML JANTR SVCS LLC
220 Choptank Rd (22172)
PHONE....................571 645-0060
Helen Velasquez,
EMP: 1
SALES (est): 53.7K **Privately Held**
SIC: 3589 Commercial cleaning equipment

(G-13894)
HEART PRINT EXPRESSIONS LLC
3320 Mccorkle Ct (22172-2327)
PHONE....................703 221-6441
Roslyn Washington, *Principal*
EMP: 2 EST: 2014
SALES (est): 142K **Privately Held**
SIC: 2752 Commercial printing, lithographic

(G-13895)
KODESCRAFT LLC
3486 Logstone Dr (22172-2054)
PHONE....................703 843-3700
Delwar Shams,
EMP: 1 EST: 2016
SALES (est): 46.8K **Privately Held**
SIC: 7372 7389 Application computer software;

(G-13896)
MANY MINIATURES
3546a Melrose Ave (22172-1114)
PHONE....................703 730-1221
EMP: 1

▲ = Import ▼=Export
◆ =Import/Export

SALES (est): 50K **Privately Held**
SIC: 3999 Mfg Misc Products

(G-13897)
OLIVALS CUSTOM WOODWORKING INC
18870 Crossroads Ct (22172-2026)
PHONE................................703 221-2713
Mark S Olival, *President*
EMP: 1
SALES (est): 111K **Privately Held**
WEB: www.olival.com
SIC: 2431 Millwork

(G-13898)
SIGNMEDIC LLC
3207 Shoreview Rd (22172-1515)
PHONE................................703 919-3381
Matthew McAdams, *President*
EMP: 1
SALES (est): 67.4K **Privately Held**
SIC: 3993 7389 Electric signs; letters for signs, metal; design services

(G-13899)
SIGNS BY JAMES LLC
17409 Joplin Rd (22172-1640)
P.O. Box 526 (22172-0526)
PHONE................................703 656-5067
James Byars, *Principal*
EMP: 1
SALES (est): 48.7K **Privately Held**
SIC: 3993 Signs & advertising specialties

(G-13900)
WAY WITH WORDS PUBLISHING LLC
3316 Dondis Creek Dr (22172-2088)
PHONE................................703 583-1825
Eric Kellum, *Principal*
EMP: 1
SALES (est): 37.5K **Privately Held**
SIC: 2741 Miscellaneous publishing

Troutdale
Grayson County

(G-13901)
THREE PEAKS CRAFTS
9399 Troutdale Hwy (24378-2164)
PHONE................................276 677-3724
Terry Clark, *Owner*
EMP: 1
SALES (est): 78.9K **Privately Held**
WEB: www.3peakscrafts.com
SIC: 2499 Carved & turned wood

Troutville
Botetourt County

(G-13902)
AMERICAN GRAPHICS
283 Fairfield Ln (24175-6828)
P.O. Box 1036, Daleville (24083-1036)
PHONE................................540 977-1912
Jeff Baker, *Owner*
EMP: 4
SQ FT: 3,600
SALES (est): 288K **Privately Held**
WEB: www.semperfishirts.com
SIC: 2759 Screen printing

(G-13903)
BOTETOURT SIGNS N STUFF
8833 Cloverdale Rd (24175-6346)
PHONE................................540 992-3839
Helen Etzler, *Owner*
EMP: 1
SALES (est): 74K **Privately Held**
WEB: www.jlcomputers.com
SIC: 3993 Signs & advertising specialties

(G-13904)
C & M SERVICES LLC (PA)
354 Nace Rd (24175-5805)
PHONE................................540 309-5555
Stephanie Boggs, *General Mgr*
Michael Lorentz, *Mayor*
David Crandall, *Treasurer*
Joel Hankins, *Manager*
Mark Boggs,

EMP: 2
SALES (est): 273.4K **Privately Held**
SIC: 2631 Packaging board

(G-13905)
CATAWBA SOUND STUDIO
Also Called: Catawba Records
1376 Lttle Ctwba Creek Rd (24175-6137)
PHONE................................540 992-4738
Wayne Weikel, *Owner*
EMP: 2
SALES (est): 111.8K **Privately Held**
SIC: 3861 Sound recording & reproducing equipment, motion picture

(G-13906)
CATRINA FASHIONS LLC
5995 Lee Hwy (24175-7124)
P.O. Box 1 (24175-0001)
PHONE................................540 992-2127
Genevieve Journell, *Owner*
EMP: 1
SALES (est): 10K **Privately Held**
WEB: www.catrinafashions.com
SIC: 2335 Bridal & formal gowns

(G-13907)
CLOVERDALE COMPANY INC
Also Called: Band-It
2124 Country Club Rd (24175-7059)
PHONE................................540 777-4414
Ron Kessinger, *President*
Bill Eversole, *Vice Pres*
▲ **EMP:** 53
SQ FT: 33,000
SALES (est): 8.5MM **Privately Held**
SIC: 2435 2436 Veneer stock, hardwood; softwood veneer & plywood

(G-13908)
DIVERSIFIED INDUSTRIES
110 Boone Dr (24175)
P.O. Box 398 (24175-0398)
PHONE................................540 992-1900
Doc Granger, *Principal*
EMP: 1
SALES (est): 118.8K **Privately Held**
SIC: 3999 Manufacturing industries

(G-13909)
DRILL SUPPLY OF VIRGINIA LLC
1195 Country Club Rd (24175-7188)
P.O. Box 368 (24175-0368)
PHONE................................540 992-3595
Stephen R Wills, *Administration*
EMP: 3 EST: 2003
SALES (est): 72.6K **Privately Held**
SIC: 3532 Drills & drilling equipment, mining (except oil & gas)

(G-13910)
GRADALL INDUSTRIES INC
177 East Arrowhead Ct (24175-6919)
PHONE................................540 819-6638
Mark Allison, *Executive*
EMP: 1
SALES (est): 60K **Privately Held**
SIC: 3531 Construction machinery

(G-13911)
IRESON INNOVATION
336 Rollingwood Ct (24175-6679)
PHONE................................540 529-1572
Debbie Ireson, *Principal*
EMP: 2
SALES (est): 123.7K **Privately Held**
WEB: www.stepdoctor.com
SIC: 3448 Prefabricated metal buildings

(G-13912)
JAMISON PRINTING INC
346 Jamison Farm Ln (24175-6063)
PHONE................................540 992-3568
Joseph H Jamison, *President*
EMP: 1
SALES (est): 69.7K **Privately Held**
SIC: 2752 Commercial printing, offset

(G-13913)
JJ S CUPCAKES AND MORE
388 Antler Ln (24175-6886)
PHONE................................319 333-8020
Janee Bradshaw, *Administration*
EMP: 4

SALES (est): 272.3K **Privately Held**
SIC: 2051 Bread, cake & related products

(G-13914)
LITESTEEL TECH AMER LLC
100 Smorgon Way (24175-5918)
P.O. Box 577 (24175-0577)
PHONE................................540 992-5129
Scott Morling, *Mng Member*
Jeff Hoffman,
Rick Howard,
Damien Nicks,
EMP: 23
SQ FT: 120,000
SALES (est): 3.8MM **Privately Held**
SIC: 3441 Building components, structural steel
PA: Ac Distribution Company Pty Limited
Level 5 2 Chifley Square
Sydney NSW

(G-13915)
ROANOKE CEMENT COMPANY LLC (DH)
6071 Catawba Rd (24175-4101)
PHONE................................540 992-1501
John Summerbell, *President*
Kevin Baird, *Vice Pres*
J Pat Borders, *Vice Pres*
▲ **EMP:** 175
SQ FT: 7,000
SALES (est): 50MM
SALES (corp-wide): 1.4MM **Privately Held**
WEB: www.titanamerica.com
SIC: 3273 Ready-mixed concrete
HQ: Titan America Llc
5700 Lake Wright Dr # 300
Norfolk VA 23502
757 858-6500

(G-13916)
ROANOKE ELECTRIC WORKS
7466 Lee Hwy (24175-7554)
PHONE................................540 992-3203
Bruce Rayl, *Principal*
EMP: 1
SALES (est): 51.1K **Privately Held**
SIC: 7694 Electric motor repair

(G-13917)
STICK INDUSTRIES LLC
633 Parsons Rd (24175-3401)
PHONE................................757 725-0436
EMP: 1
SALES (est): 47.3K **Privately Held**
SIC: 3999 Manufacturing industries

(G-13918)
STONEY BROOK VNYRDS WINERY LLC
524 Stoney Battery Rd (24175-7530)
PHONE................................703 932-2619
James Joyce, *Principal*
EMP: 2 EST: 2015
SALES (est): 62.3K **Privately Held**
SIC: 2084 Wines

(G-13919)
VIRGINIA TRANSFORMER CORP
100 Smorgon Way (24175-5918)
PHONE................................540 345-9892
EMP: 7
SALES (corp-wide): 230.2MM **Privately Held**
WEB: www.vatransformer.com
SIC: 3612 Specialty transformers; reactor transformers
PA: Virginia Transformer Corp.
220 Glade View Dr Ne
Roanoke VA 24012
540 345-9892

Troy
Fluvanna County

(G-13920)
BROWNELL METAL STUDIO INC
102a Industrial Way (22974-3967)
PHONE................................434 591-0379
Stephen J Brownell, *President*
Suzanne Brownell, *Treasurer*
EMP: 4

SALES (est): 280K **Privately Held**
WEB: www.brownellmetalstudio.com
SIC: 3499 Novelties & specialties, metal

(G-13921)
CABINETS BY DESIGN
31a Conestoga Way (22974-4479)
PHONE................................434 589-2600
Susan McLaughlin, *Owner*
EMP: 2
SALES (est): 206.4K **Privately Held**
WEB: www.cabinetsva.com
SIC: 2434 Wood kitchen cabinets

(G-13922)
CHIPS INC
26 Zion Park Rd (22974-2807)
PHONE................................434 589-2424
Richard Dost, *President*
Clarke Diehl, *Vice Pres*
Ola Gaylor, *Admin Sec*
EMP: 62
SALES (est): 10.4MM **Privately Held**
WEB: www.chipsinc.net
SIC: 2421 2411 Wood chips, produced at mill; logging

(G-13923)
CORE HEALTH THERMOGRAPHY
5574 Richmond Rd Ste A (22974-1185)
PHONE................................434 207-4810
EMP: 2
SALES (est): 79K **Privately Held**
WEB: www.corehealththermography.com
SIC: 2759 Thermography

(G-13924)
DIXONS TRASH DISPOSAL LLC
5498 Richmond Rd (22974-4420)
PHONE................................434 978-2111
Michael Dixon, *Owner*
EMP: 3
SALES (est): 280K **Privately Held**
SIC: 3639 Garbage disposal units, household

(G-13925)
GLANDORE SPICE
1841 Hunters Lodge Rd (22974-4342)
P.O. Box 1036 (22974-1036)
PHONE................................434 589-2492
EMP: 2
SALES (est): 62.3K **Privately Held**
SIC: 2099 Food preparations

(G-13926)
GRAPHIC GARAGE
77 Zion Park Ct (22974-2814)
PHONE................................434 589-3432
Mike Chenail, *President*
EMP: 1
SALES (est): 80.1K **Privately Held**
WEB: www.tggsigns.com
SIC: 3993 Signs & advertising specialties

(G-13927)
HAR-TRU LLC
Also Called: Har Tru Sports
223 Crossroads Ctr (22974-2826)
P.O. Box 1034 (22974-1034)
PHONE................................434 589-1542
Stacy Taylor, *Branch Mgr*
EMP: 28
SALES (corp-wide): 9.3MM **Privately Held**
WEB: www.hartru.com
SIC: 3949 Tennis equipment & supplies
HQ: Har-Tru, Llc
2200 Old Ivy Rd Ste 100
Charlottesville VA 22903
877 442-7878

(G-13928)
HEARTH & HOME TECHNOLOGIES LLC
162 Industrial Way (22974-3967)
PHONE................................434 589-1482
Jeffrey Hall, *Sales Staff*
Gary Walker, *Branch Mgr*
EMP: 4

SALES (corp-wide): 2.2B **Publicly Held**
WEB: www.fireside.com
SIC: 3429 5023 5719 Fireplace equipment, hardware: andirons, grates, screens; fireplace equipment & accessories; fireplaces & wood burning stoves
HQ: Hearth & Home Technologies, Llc
7571 215th St W
Lakeville MN 55044

(G-13929)
HUBBELL INDUSTRIAL CONTRLS INC
8845 Three Notch Rd (22974-2823)
PHONE....................................434 589-8224
EMP: 120
SALES (corp-wide): 4.5B **Publicly Held**
WEB: www.hubbell.com
SIC: 3625 Motor controls, electric
HQ: Hubbell Industrial Controls, Inc.
4301 Cheyenne Dr
Archdale NC 27263
336 434-2800

(G-13930)
KIBBY WELDING
2428 Richmond Rd (22974-3703)
PHONE....................................607 624-9959
Mike Trevorah, *Principal*
EMP: 1 **EST:** 2018
SALES (est): 25K **Privately Held**
WEB: www.kibbyweldingllc-com.webs.com
SIC: 7692 Welding repair

(G-13931)
LEVAIN BAKING STUDIO INC
1716 Union Mills Rd (22974-2100)
PHONE....................................434 249-5875
Sharlene Mendoza McNeish, *Principal*
EMP: 4
SALES (est): 149.6K **Privately Held**
SIC: 2051 Bread, cake & related products

(G-13932)
LIFE MANAGEMENT COMPANY
3802 Snow Hill Ln (22974-3026)
PHONE....................................434 296-9762
Robert Snow, *Owner*
EMP: 5
SALES (est): 260K **Privately Held**
SIC: 2752 8741 5734 Commercial printing, offset; business management; computer peripheral equipment

(G-13933)
LUCK STONE CORPORATION
223 Crossroads Ctr (22974-2826)
P.O. Box 1034 (22974-1034)
PHONE....................................434 589-1542
Chris Hide, *Manager*
EMP: 28
SALES (corp-wide): 824.7MM **Privately Held**
WEB: www.luckstone.com
SIC: 1423 Crushed & broken granite
PA: Luck Stone Corporation
515 Stone Mill Dr
Manakin Sabot VA 23103
804 784-6300

(G-13934)
MARK S CHAPMAN
Also Called: Art Glass Windows
22 Pine Crest Dr (22974-6219)
P.O. Box 954 (22974-0954)
PHONE....................................434 227-6702
Mark S Chapman, *Owner*
EMP: 1
SALES (est): 5.3K **Privately Held**
WEB: www.artglasswindows.biz
SIC: 3231 Products of purchased glass

(G-13935)
METALSTAR SERVICES LLC
379 Pine Forest Ln (22974-4117)
PHONE....................................434 591-0400
Kenneth L Dosier Jr, *Administration*
EMP: 3
SALES (est): 146.2K **Privately Held**
WEB: www.metalstarservices.com
SIC: 7692 Welding repair

(G-13936)
STRUCTURAL SCULPTURE CORP
2306 Richmond Rd (22974-3729)
PHONE....................................434 207-3070
John Rubino, *President*
EMP: 2 **EST:** 1997
SALES (est): 150K **Privately Held**
SIC: 3441 Fabricated structural metal

(G-13937)
WELD PRO LLC
18180 James Madison Hwy (22974-4113)
PHONE....................................434 531-5811
EMP: 1
SALES (est): 25K **Privately Held**
SIC: 7692 Welding repair

(G-13938)
YOWELL METAL FABRICATION LLC
295 Deer Haven Ln (22974-3647)
PHONE....................................434 971-3018
Melinda Yowell, *Principal*
EMP: 2
SALES (est): 169.2K **Privately Held**
SIC: 3499 Fabricated metal products

Tyro
Nelson County

(G-13939)
FITZGERALD JOHN
Also Called: J H Fitzgerald Jr Logging
266 Big Rock Rd (22976-2012)
PHONE....................................434 277-8044
John Fitzgerald Jr, *Owner*
EMP: 9
SALES (est): 1.3MM **Privately Held**
WEB: www.valogging.com
SIC: 2411 Logging

Tysons
Fairfax County

(G-13940)
ACACIA INVESTMENT HOLDINGS LLC (PA)
1850 Towers Crescent Plz # 500 (22182-6228)
PHONE....................................703 554-1600
Gavin Long, *CEO*
William King, *Admin Sec*
EMP: 5
SALES (est): 255.6MM **Privately Held**
SIC: 3571 5045 Personal computers (microcomputers); computer software

(G-13941)
APPIAN CORPORATION
7950 Jones Branch Dr (22102-3302)
PHONE....................................703 442-8844
Elliot Schipper, *Vice Pres*
Achal Augustine, *Engineer*
Ashley Amador, *Hum Res Coord*
Ben Bowles, *Accounts Exec*
Emily Casanova, *Marketing Staff*
EMP: 2 **Publicly Held**
WEB: www.appian.com
SIC: 7372 Prepackaged software
PA: Appian Corporation
7950 Jones Branch Dr
Mc Lean VA 22102

(G-13942)
CLOUDERA GVRNMNT SLUTIONS INC
8281 Greensboro Dr # 450 (22102-5211)
PHONE....................................888 789-1488
Mary Rorabaugh, *Vice Pres*
Jim Frankola, *CFO*
EMP: 15
SQ FT: 1,000
SALES (est): 951.7K **Publicly Held**
WEB: www.cloudera.com
SIC: 7372 Business oriented computer software

PA: Cloudera, Inc.
5470 Great America Pkwy
Santa Clara CA 95054
650 362-0488

(G-13943)
ENTERPRISE SVCS CMMNCTIONS LLC
1775 Tysons Blvd (22102-4284)
PHONE....................................877 858-3855
Michael Lawrie, *President*
EMP: 3
SALES (est): 121.1K **Publicly Held**
SIC: 7372 3572 Prepackaged software; computer storage devices
PA: Dxc Technology Company
1775 Tysons Blvd Fl 8
Tysons VA 22102
703 245-9675

(G-13944)
ENTERPRISE SVCS WRLD TRADE LLC
1775 Tysons Blvd (22102-4284)
PHONE....................................703 245-9675
Michael Lawrie, *Mng Member*
EMP: 4
SALES (est): 25.8MM **Publicly Held**
WEB: www.dxc.technology
SIC: 7372 Prepackaged software
PA: Dxc Technology Company
1775 Tysons Blvd Fl 8
Tysons VA 22102
703 245-9675

(G-13945)
FORESCOUT GVRNMNT SLTIONS LLC
8350 Broad St Ste 1800 (22102-5151)
PHONE....................................408 538-0946
Niels Jensen, *President*
Michael Decesare, *Director*
Darren Milliken, *Director*
Connie Ng, *General Counsel*
EMP: 40
SALES (est): 2.5MM **Privately Held**
SIC: 3577 7372 Encoders, computer peripheral equipment; application computer software

(G-13946)
HUE AI LLC
1775 Tysons Blvd Fl 5 (22102-4285)
PHONE....................................571 766-6943
Justin Fong,
Keenan Valentine,
EMP: 3
SALES (est): 148.9K **Privately Held**
WEB: www.hueai.com
SIC: 3559 Optical lens machinery

(G-13947)
LUX 1 HOLDING COMPANY INC (HQ)
1775 Tysons Blvd Fl 7 (22102-4285)
PHONE....................................703 245-9675
Vineet Saraogi, *Executive*
Jeneth Epley, *Admin Asst*
EMP: 3
SALES (est): 8.7MM **Publicly Held**
WEB: www.dxc.technology
SIC: 7372 Prepackaged software
PA: Dxc Technology Company
1775 Tysons Blvd Fl 8
Tysons VA 22102
703 245-9675

(G-13948)
REBOUND ANALYTICS LLC
1775 Tysons Blvd Fl 5 (22102-4285)
PHONE....................................202 297-1204
Doug McCormack, *CEO*
EMP: 2
SALES (est): 104.2K **Privately Held**
SIC: 3823 3571 8099 Digital displays of process variables; electronic computers; health screening service

(G-13949)
US ELECTRICAL TESTING LLC
1200 Ste 1765 Grnsboro St (22102)
PHONE....................................703 802-6231
EMP: 2

SALES (est): 110.9K **Privately Held**
SIC: 3825 Analyzers for testing electrical characteristics

(G-13950)
WEWORK C/O THE FIRST TEE DC
1775 Tysons Blvd Fl 5 (22102-4285)
PHONE....................................231 632-0334
Katie Blodgett, *Principal*
EMP: 2
SALES (est): 120.1K **Privately Held**
SIC: 2759 Screen printing

Tysons Corner
Fairfax County

(G-13951)
APTIFY CORPORATION (PA)
7900 Wstpk Dr 5th Fl Atrm # 5 (22102)
PHONE....................................202 223-2600
Amith Nagarajan, *CEO*
Krishna Raman, *Vice Pres*
Rebecca Whitworth, *Opers Staff*
Chris Frederick, *CFO*
Karen Dwyer, *Controller*
EMP: 65
SALES (est): 16.1MM **Privately Held**
WEB: www.aptify.com
SIC: 7372 Prepackaged software

(G-13952)
CVENT INC (HQ)
1765 Grnsboro Stn Pl Fl 7 (22102-3468)
PHONE....................................703 226-3500
Rajeev K Aggarwal, *CEO*
Chuck Ghoorah, *President*
Ryan Costa, *Business Mgr*
Molly Moravec, *Business Mgr*
Larry Samuelson, *Senior VP*
EMP: 650
SQ FT: 116,000
SALES (est): 365.8MM
SALES (corp-wide): 359.8MM **Privately Held**
WEB: www.cvent.com
SIC: 7372 Prepackaged software
PA: Papay Holdco, Llc
1765 Grnsboro Stn Pl Fl 7
Tysons Corner VA 22102
703 226-3500

(G-13953)
DIGITAL GLOBAL SYSTEMS INC
7950 Jones Branch Dr 1a (22102-3302)
PHONE....................................240 477-7149
Fernando Murias, *CEO*
Jeremy Levin, *Vice Pres*
EMP: 20
SALES (est): 5.5MM **Privately Held**
WEB: www.digitalglobalsystems.com
SIC: 3825 Radio frequency measuring equipment

(G-13954)
DYSON DIRECT INC
Also Called: Tysons Corner Center
1961 Chain Bridge Rd (22102-4501)
PHONE....................................571 210-4317
EMP: 2 **Privately Held**
WEB: www.dyson.com
SIC: 3635 Household vacuum cleaners
HQ: Dyson Direct, Inc.
1330 W Fulton St Ste 500
Chicago IL 60607
312 469-5950

(G-13955)
MICROSTRATEGY SERVICES CORP
1850 Towers Crescent Plz # 700 (22182-6231)
PHONE....................................703 848-8600
Michael J Saylor, *President*
Thede Douglas, *Vice Pres*
EMP: 99
SALES (est): 8.1MM **Publicly Held**
WEB: www.microstrategy.com
SIC: 7372 7375 Prepackaged software; information retrieval services
PA: Microstrategy Incorporated
1850 Towers Crescent Plz # 700
Tysons Corner VA 22182

▲ = Import ▼=Export
◆ =Import/Export

(G-13956)
USHER INCORPORATED
1850 Towers Crescent Plz (22182-6230)
PHONE..........................703 848-8600
Jonathan Klein, *President*
Emmett Pepe, *Vice Pres*
Jeremy Price, *Vice Pres*
Douglas Thede, *Treasurer*
W Ming Shao, *Admin Sec*
EMP: 78
SALES (est): 3.1MM **Publicly Held**
WEB: www.microstrategy.com
SIC: 7372 Business oriented computer
   software
PA: Microstrategy Incorporated
   1850 Towers Crescent Plz # 700
   Tysons Corner VA 22182

Union Hall
Franklin County

(G-13957)
ALTERNATIVES INC
CORPORATE
125 Sailboat Ln (24176-3787)
PHONE..........................540 576-2265
Peter Brinckerhoff, *Principal*
EMP: 2
SALES (est): 110K **Privately Held**
WEB: www.missionbased.com
SIC: 2731 Book publishing

(G-13958)
ASPHALT READY MIX INC
1376 Jacks Creek Rd (24176)
PHONE..........................540 576-3483
Randy Bailey, *Superintendent*
EMP: 3
SALES (est): 178.9K **Privately Held**
SIC: 2951 Asphalt paving mixtures &
   blocks

(G-13959)
GEORGE H POLLOK JR
48 Tranquility Bay Dr (24176-1400)
PHONE..........................336 540-8870
George H Pollok Jr, *Principal*
EMP: 4
SALES (est): 405.5K **Privately Held**
SIC: 3714 Motor vehicle parts & acces-
   sories

(G-13960)
POWERMARK CORPORATION
42 Patrick Pl (24176-4132)
PHONE..........................301 639-7319
Paul Bender, *Ch of Bd*
John Wohlgemuth, *Exec Dir*
Alexander Mikonowicz, *Exec Dir*
EMP: 1 **Privately Held**
WEB: www.powermark.org
SIC: 3674 Photovoltaic devices, solid state
PA: Powermark Corporation
   1842 Se Beving Ave
   Port St Lucie FL 34952

(G-13961)
SML COMPOSITES LLC
255 Brooks Mill Rd (24176)
P.O. Box 3 (24176-0003)
PHONE..........................540 576-3318
Douglas Holt, *President*
EMP: 1
SALES (est): 96.2K **Privately Held**
WEB: www.smlcomposites.com
SIC: 3089 Spouting, plastic & glass fiber
   reinforced

Unionville
Orange County

(G-13962)
DODSON LOGGING LLC
24259 Colgate Rd (22567-2135)
PHONE..........................540 547-2582
EMP: 2 EST: 2016
SALES (est): 89.8K **Privately Held**
SIC: 2411 Logging

(G-13963)
HERITAGE LOG HOMES
29502 Mine Run Rd (22567-3522)
PHONE..........................540 854-4926
Rixey Almond, *Owner*
EMP: 2
SALES (est): 118.5K **Privately Held**
SIC: 2452 Log cabins, prefabricated, wood

(G-13964)
MAGNET DIRECTORIES INC
Also Called: Magnet 1 Internet Systems
8244 Zachary Taylor Hwy (22567-2036)
P.O. Box 211, Locust Grove (22508-0211)
PHONE..........................281 251-6640
Daniel Elliot, *President*
Norman Wells, *Vice Pres*
EMP: 5
SALES (est): 198.6K **Privately Held**
SIC: 2741 Telephone & other directory
   publishing

(G-13965)
MORRIS & SONS LOGGING
GLEN
23035 Constitution Hwy (22567-2207)
PHONE..........................540 854-5271
Glen Morris, *President*
EMP: 4 EST: 1964
SALES (est): 351.2K **Privately Held**
SIC: 2411 Logging camps & contractors

Upperville
Fauquier County

(G-13966)
COUNTRY BAKING LLC
9036 John S Mosby Hwy (20184-1722)
PHONE..........................540 592-7422
EMP: 4
SALES (est): 190.5K **Privately Held**
SIC: 2051 Mfg Bread/Related Products

(G-13967)
PATRICIA RAMEY
1797 Blue Ridge Farm Rd (20184-1904)
PHONE..........................703 973-1140
Patricia Ramey, *Principal*
EMP: 3
SALES (est): 221.3K **Privately Held**
SIC: 2421 Sawmills & planing mills, gen-
   eral

(G-13968)
SLATER RUN VINEYARDS LLC
7570 Plum Run Ln (20184-1857)
P.O. Box 619 (20185-0619)
PHONE..........................540 878-1476
Robert Slater, *Principal*
Kiernan S Patusky,
EMP: 6
SALES (est): 570K **Privately Held**
WEB: www.slaterrunvineyards.com
SIC: 2084 Wines

(G-13969)
SLATER RUN VNEYARDS
TASTING RM
9030 John S Mosby Hwy (20184-1721)
PHONE..........................540 592-3042
EMP: 2
SALES (est): 80.3K **Privately Held**
WEB: www.slaterrun.com
SIC: 2084 Wines

Urbanna
Middlesex County

(G-13970)
EAST COAST BOAT LIFTS INC
510 Lord Mott Rd (23175)
P.O. Box 473 (23175-0473)
PHONE..........................804 758-1099
Larry Shores, *President*
Lance Shores, *Vice Pres*
Heather Anderson, *Office Mgr*
EMP: 3
SALES (est): 501K **Privately Held**
WEB: www.eastcoastboatlifts.com
SIC: 3536 Boat lifts

(G-13971)
KOOL CHRISTIAN TEES
70 Streets Ln (23175-2483)
PHONE..........................804 201-1646
Charles Cook, *Principal*
EMP: 2 EST: 2016
SALES (est): 83.6K **Privately Held**
SIC: 2759 Screen printing

(G-13972)
NEENAH FOUNDRY CO
703 Swan View Dr (23175-2438)
PHONE..........................804 758-9592
Glen Hockett, *CEO*
EMP: 1
SALES (est): 111.1K **Privately Held**
SIC: 3321 Gray iron castings

(G-13973)
SHIFFLETT AND SON LOG CO
LLC
Also Called: Shifflett & Son Logging
432 Burch Rd (23175-2162)
PHONE..........................757 434-7979
George A Shifflett, *President*
EMP: 6
SALES (est): 200K **Privately Held**
SIC: 2411 7389 Logging;

Valentines
Brunswick County

(G-13974)
C LINE GRAPHICS INC
Also Called: C Line Graphics Printing Co
4446 Christina Hwy (23887)
P.O. Box 7 (23887-0007)
PHONE..........................434 577-9289
Caroline Watkins, *President*
EMP: 3
SQ FT: 2,000
SALES (est): 323.5K **Privately Held**
SIC: 2752 Commercial printing, offset

Vansant
Buchanan County

(G-13975)
BEAR BRANCH LOGGING INC
1049 Viers Branch Rd (24656-7920)
PHONE..........................276 597-7172
Mark Deel, *President*
EMP: 5
SALES (est): 330K **Privately Held**
SIC: 2411 Logging camps & contractors

(G-13976)
DYNO NOBEL INC
Rr 460 (24656)
PHONE..........................276 935-6436
Stuart Brashear, *Project Mgr*
Mike Scarbarry, *Manager*
EMP: 15
SQ FT: 8,000 **Privately Held**
WEB: www.dynonobel.com
SIC: 2892 Explosives
HQ: Dyno Nobel Inc.
   6440 S Millrock Dr # 150
   Salt Lake City UT 84121
   801 364-4800

(G-13977)
L & D WELL SERVICES INC
2314 Leemaster Dr (24656-9401)
P.O. Box 269 (24656-0269)
PHONE..........................276 597-7211
Michael L Boyd, *President*
Virgil Lawson, *Vice Pres*
EMP: 7
SQ FT: 2,000
SALES (est): 10.4MM **Privately Held**
SIC: 1389 Servicing oil & gas wells

(G-13978)
STRONGERHOLD WELDING &
CONTG
2678 Leemaster Dr (24656-8445)
PHONE..........................276 608-9968
EMP: 1
SALES (est): 51.1K **Privately Held**
SIC: 7692 Welding repair

(G-13979)
VEDCO HOLDINGS INC (HQ)
1793 Dry Fork Rd (24656-8611)
P.O. Box 1198 (24656-1198)
PHONE..........................800 258-8583
Virlo Stiltner, *President*
Red Kennedy, *Vice Pres*
Grant Shrader, *Vice Pres*
EMP: 14
SALES (est): 64MM **Privately Held**
WEB: www.vadrillco.com
SIC: 1241 Coal mining services

(G-13980)
VIRGINIA EXPL & DRLG CO INC
(DH)
1793 Dry Fork Rd (24656-8611)
PHONE..........................276 597-4449
Rodney Jackson, *President*
EMP: 3
SALES (est): 8.7MM **Privately Held**
WEB: www.vadrillco.com
SIC: 1381 Drilling oil & gas wells

Vernon Hill
Halifax County

(G-13981)
BENTTREE ENTERPRISES
1100 Mount Tabor Rd (24597-3280)
PHONE..........................434 770-3632
Phil Lohan, *Principal*
EMP: 2
SALES (est): 119.9K **Privately Held**
WEB: www.benttreealpacas.com
SIC: 3999 Pet supplies

Verona
Augusta County

(G-13982)
ACCUTEC BLADES INC (PA)
1 Razor Blade Ln (24482-9451)
PHONE..........................800 336-4061
Richard Gagliano, *President*
Gary Boyd, *Vice Pres*
Mark Meyer, *Purch Mgr*
Joyce Blevins, *Buyer*
Luis Mendez, *Electrical Engi*
◆ EMP: 143 EST: 2015
SQ FT: 400,000
SALES (est): 60MM **Privately Held**
WEB: www.atblades.com
SIC: 3421 Razor blades & razors

(G-13983)
BALL ADVANCED ALUM TECH
CORP
56 Dunsmore Rd (24482-9450)
P.O. Box 160 (24482-0160)
PHONE..........................540 248-2703
Michael Feldser, *President*
J Hayes Kavanagh, *Corp Secy*
◆ EMP: 180
SQ FT: 90,000
SALES (est): 40.5MM
SALES (corp-wide): 11.4B **Publicly Held**
WEB: www.ball.com
SIC: 3353 3354 Flat rolled shapes, alu-
   minum; shapes, extruded aluminum
HQ: Ball Aerosol And Specialty Container
   Inc.
   9308 W 108th Cir
   Westminster CO 80021

(G-13984)
DEMCO MACHINE INC
1401 Laurel Hill Rd (24482-2709)
PHONE..........................540 248-5135
Dennis Zwart, *President*
EMP: 2
SALES (est): 100K **Privately Held**
SIC: 3599 Machine shop, jobbing & repair

(G-13985)
EFCO CORPORATION
44 Sutton Rd Ste 101 (24482-2585)
P.O. Box 584 (24482-0584)
PHONE..........................540 248-8604
Rob Jones, *Principal*
Travis Morris, *Prgrmr*

EMP: 23 **Publicly Held**
WEB: www.efcocorp.com
SIC: 3442 3449 3446 Window & door frames; curtain wall, metal; architectural metalwork
HQ: Efco Corporation
1000 County Rd
Monett MO 65708
417 235-3193

(G-13986)
ENERGIZER PERSONAL CARE LLC
Also Called: American Safety Razor
1 Razor Blade Ln (24482-9451)
PHONE..........................540 248-9734
Fax: 540 248-0522
EMP: 500
SALES (corp-wide): 2.4B **Publicly Held**
SIC: 3421 Mfg Cutlery
HQ: Energizer Personal Care, Llc
240 Cedar Knolls Rd
Cedar Knolls NJ 07927
973 753-3000

(G-13987)
FLOW BEVERAGES INC
33 Lakeview Ct (24482-2668)
PHONE..........................613 680-3569
Nicholas Reichenbach, CEO
David Mock, President
David Bajurny, COO
Matthew Hoar, CFO
Michael Bajurny, Manager
EMP: 39
SALES (est): 9MM
SALES (corp-wide): 6.6MM **Privately Held**
SIC: 2086 Pasteurized & mineral waters, bottled & canned
PA: Flow Water Inc
283 Dalhousie St Suite 300
Ottawa ON K1N 7
613 680-3569

(G-13988)
HAWK HILL CUSTOM LLC
506 Laurel Hill Rd (24482-2615)
PHONE..........................540 248-4295
Shawn Burkholder, Owner
EMP: 4
SALES (est): 381.6K **Privately Held**
WEB: www.hawkhillcustom.com
SIC: 3949 3489 Sporting & athletic goods; rifles, recoiless

(G-13989)
INSTANT KNWLEDGE COM JILL BYRD
341 Lee Hwy (24482-2549)
PHONE..........................540 885-8730
Kim Stowers, CEO
EMP: 7
SALES (est): 246.2K **Privately Held**
WEB: www.etesters.com
SIC: 2752 Commercial printing, lithographic

(G-13990)
LEVEL 7 SIGNS AND GRAPHICS
317 Skyview Cir (24482-2651)
PHONE..........................540 294-6690
EMP: 1
SALES (est): 46K **Privately Held**
WEB: www.level7signs.com
SIC: 3993 Signs & advertising specialties

(G-13991)
LIPHART STEEL COMPANY INC
75 Mid Valley Ln (24482-2827)
P.O. Box 877 (24482-0877)
PHONE..........................540 248-1009
Paul Leonard, Project Mgr
Rob Kerr, VP Sales
R Ned Ruby, Branch Mgr
Susan Nolley, Manager
EMP: 20
SALES (corp-wide): 36.7MM **Privately Held**
WEB: www.liphartsteel.com
SIC: 3441 3444 3354 Fabricated structural metal; sheet metalwork; aluminum extruded products

PA: Liphart Steel Company, Incorporated
3308 Rosedale Ave
Richmond VA 23230
804 355-7481

(G-13992)
MOUNTAIN TOP SIGNS & GIFTS
106 Maple Dr (24482-2607)
PHONE..........................540 430-0532
EMP: 1
SALES (est): 50.6K **Privately Held**
SIC: 3993 Signs & advertising specialties

(G-13993)
PROVIDES US INC
45 Sutton Rd (24482)
P.O. Box 917 (24482-0917)
PHONE..........................540 569-3434
Thomas Coplai, COO
▲ EMP: 53
SQ FT: 40,000
SALES (est): 11.5MM
SALES (corp-wide): 30.9MM **Privately Held**
WEB: www.providesus.com
SIC: 3585 Heating & air conditioning combination units
PA: Provides Metalmeccanica Srl
Via Piave 82
Latina LT 04100
077 344-01

(G-13994)
ROLLING KNOLL FARM INC
Also Called: Rkf Farms
1146 Lee Hwy (24482-2904)
PHONE..........................540 569-6476
James Franklin Vines, President
EMP: 10
SALES (est): 694.6K **Privately Held**
WEB: www.rollingknollfarm.com
SIC: 2011 Meat packing plants

(G-13995)
SCHREIBER INC R G
Also Called: Mid Valley Press
46 Laurel Hill Rd (24482-2658)
P.O. Box 998 (24482-0998)
PHONE..........................540 248-5300
Elizabeth M Schreiber, President
Robert G Schreiber, Vice Pres
Roxanne Moskowitz, Sales Staff
Paige Grimshaw, Graphic Designe
EMP: 20
SQ FT: 15,000
SALES (est): 3MM **Privately Held**
WEB: www.midvalleypress.com
SIC: 2752 7336 2791 Commercial printing, offset; graphic arts & related design; typesetting

(G-13996)
STAUNTON VA
207 Laurel Hill Rd (24482-2601)
PHONE..........................651 765-6778
EMP: 1 EST: 2019
SALES (est): 39.6K **Privately Held**
SIC: 3999 Manufacturing industries

(G-13997)
Z & Z MACHINE INC
23 Old Laurel Hill Rd (24482-2705)
PHONE..........................540 248-2760
Dennis B Zwart, President
Chris K Zwart, Corp Secy
Amanda Estes, Office Mgr
EMP: 3
SQ FT: 6,200
SALES (est): 440K **Privately Held**
WEB: www.zzmachineinc.com
SIC: 3599 Machine shop, jobbing & repair

Vesuvius
Rockbridge County

(G-13998)
SOUTH RIVER FABRICATORS
6746 Irish Creek Rd (24483-2409)
PHONE..........................540 377-9762
Allen E Grant, Owner
EMP: 1
SALES (est): 152.2K **Privately Held**
SIC: 3441 Fabricated structural metal

(G-13999)
TRAVIS LEE KERR
1677 Pedlar River Rd (24483-2845)
PHONE..........................434 922-7005
Travis Kerr, Principal
EMP: 2
SALES (est): 176.6K **Privately Held**
SIC: 2452 1711 1542 1521 Modular homes, prefabricated, wood; plumbing, heating, air-conditioning contractors; non-residential construction; single-family housing construction

Victoria
Lunenburg County

(G-14000)
CHARLETTE PUBLISHING INC
Also Called: Kenbridge-Victoria Dispatch
1404 Nottoway Blvd (23974-9642)
P.O. Box 40 (23974-0040)
PHONE..........................434 696-5550
Dorothy Tucker, President
EMP: 6
SALES (est): 273.1K **Privately Held**
WEB: www.kenbridgevictoriadispatch.com
SIC: 2711 2759 Commercial printing & newspaper publishing combined; commercial printing

Vienna
Fairfax County

(G-14001)
3S GROUP INC
Also Called: 3 S I
125 Church St Ne Ste 204 (22180-4553)
PHONE..........................703 281-5015
Satpal Singh Sahni, President
Sahni Satpal Singh, Director
EMP: 12
SQ FT: 4,500
SALES (est): 1MM **Privately Held**
WEB: www.threesi.com
SIC: 3695 Computer software tape & disks: blank, rigid & floppy

(G-14002)
A FRAME DIGITAL
1934 Old Gallows Rd # 40 (22182-4042)
P.O. Box 746, Lovettsville (20180-0746)
PHONE..........................571 308-0147
Cindy Crump, Owner
EMP: 1
SALES (est): 43.6K **Privately Held**
SIC: 3999 Manufacturing industries

(G-14003)
A MARKUS DESIGN
1709 Burning Tree Dr (22182-2302)
PHONE..........................703 938-6694
Arlene Markus, Owner
EMP: 1
SALES (est): 72K **Privately Held**
SIC: 3961 Costume jewelry

(G-14004)
ABC IMAGING OF WASHINGTON
8603 Westwood Center Dr (22182-2230)
PHONE..........................703 848-2997
David Sammuli, District Mgr
Dean Desantis, Vice Pres
Lamont Siejack, Facilities Mgr
Bisrat Mebrahtu, Purchasing
Justin Kamiyama, Cust Mgr
EMP: 15
SALES (corp-wide): 144.4MM **Privately Held**
WEB: www.abcimaging.com
SIC: 2752 Commercial printing, offset
PA: Abc Imaging Of Washington, Inc
5290 Shawnee Rd Ste 300
Alexandria VA 22312
202 429-8870

(G-14005)
ADRIANA CALDERON ESCALANTE
Also Called: Moda Preview International
1498 Northern Neck Dr (22182-5511)
PHONE..........................703 926-7638

A Escalante Calderon, Owner
Adriana Escalante Calderon, Owner
EMP: 6
SALES (est): 202.1K **Privately Held**
SIC: 2721 Magazines: publishing only, not printed on site

(G-14006)
AIMEX LLC
8500 Leesburg Pike # 310 (22182-2409)
PHONE..........................212 631-4277
M H Bhuiyan,
EMP: 10
SQ FT: 2,000
SALES (est): 1.3MM **Privately Held**
WEB: www.aimex.us
SIC: 2819 3812 Industrial inorganic chemicals; defense systems & equipment

(G-14007)
ALLERGY ASTHMA NTWRK/MTHERS AS
8229 Boone Blvd Ste 260 (22182-2661)
PHONE..........................800 878-4403
Michael Amato, Ch of Bd
Nancy Sander, President
Greg Cunningham, Vice Pres
Marissa Magnetti, Vice Pres
Delores Libera, Admin Sec
EMP: 10
SQ FT: 3,000
SALES: 2.7MM **Privately Held**
WEB: www.allergyasthmanetwork.org
SIC: 2741 Miscellaneous publishing

(G-14008)
ALPHA SAFE & VAULT INC
1656 Gelding Ln (22182-2039)
PHONE..........................703 281-7233
Katherine Levy, President
Marielou Vierling, General Mgr
EMP: 1
SALES (est): 122.8K **Privately Held**
WEB: www.alphasafeinc.com
SIC: 2522 Office furniture, except wood

(G-14009)
ARKCASE LLC
9601 Pembroke Pl (22182-1443)
PHONE..........................703 272-3270
James Bailey,
EMP: 2
SALES (est): 62.1K **Privately Held**
WEB: www.armedia.com
SIC: 7372 Prepackaged software

(G-14010)
ASIAN FORTUNE ENTERPRISES INC
1604 Spring Hill Rd # 300 (22182-7510)
PHONE..........................703 753-8295
Jizeng Cheng, President
Jizeng Chen, President
Lily Chen, Publisher
EMP: 10
SALES (est): 200K **Privately Held**
WEB: www.asianfortunenews.com
SIC: 2711 Newspapers: publishing only, not printed on site

(G-14011)
ATTACHMATE CORPORATION
8609 Wstwd Ctr Dr Ste 5 (22182-7521)
PHONE..........................703 663-5500
EMP: 26 **Privately Held**
WEB: www.microfocus.com
SIC: 7372 Prepackaged software
HQ: Attachmate Corporation
1111 3rd Ave Ste 2300
Seattle WA 98101
206 217-7100

(G-14012)
AUTODOCS LLC
8229 Boone Blvd Ste 801 (22182-2623)
PHONE..........................703 532-9720
Jay Labonte, General Mgr
Merle Mulvaney, CFO
Christine Shipman, Accounting Dir
Walter Walvick, Finance
Michael Klein, Info Tech Mgr
EMP: 17
SALES (est): 1.3MM **Privately Held**
WEB: www.ipdas.com
SIC: 7372 Business oriented computer software

▲ = Import ▼=Export
◆ =Import/Export

(G-14013)
B GLOBAL LLC
Also Called: Dateme Boutiques
8500 Idylwood Valley Pl (22182-5315)
PHONE................................703 628-2826
Modia Betterjee, *Mng Member*
Huda Batterjee,
EMP: 1 EST: 2015
SALES (est): 68.3K **Privately Held**
WEB: www.datemeboutique.com
SIC: 2034 Dates, dried

(G-14014)
BE THERE DO GOOD LLC
1214 Delta Glen Ct (22182-1319)
PHONE................................703 851-5293
Christopher Bennett,
EMP: 2
SALES (est): 56.5K **Privately Held**
SIC: 7372 Application computer software

(G-14015)
BETHANY HOUSE INC
Also Called: Terra Christa
130 Church St Nw (22180-4507)
PHONE................................703 281-9410
Mary Ruth Vanlandingham, *President*
EMP: 4
SALES (est): 365.7K **Privately Held**
WEB: www.terrachrista.com
SIC: 3993 5947 Signs & advertising spe-
cialties; gifts & novelties

(G-14016)
BG SOLUTIONS LLC
1903 Ballycor Dr (22182-1984)
PHONE................................703 623-4846
EMP: 2
SALES (est): 139.1K **Privately Held**
SIC: 3714 Motor vehicle parts & acces-
sories

(G-14017)
BILLS CUSTOM CABINETRY
Also Called: William Baird, Owner
411 Welles St Se (22180-4840)
PHONE................................703 281-1669
William Baird, *Owner*
EMP: 1
SALES (est): 67K **Privately Held**
SIC: 2434 Wood kitchen cabinets

(G-14018)
**BOXD KITCHEN MERRIFIELD
LLC**
2750 Gallows Rd (22180-7137)
PHONE................................703 909-9572
Woo Lee,
EMP: 2
SALES (est): 90.4K **Privately Held**
SIC: 2599 Food wagons, restaurant

(G-14019)
**BUREAU OF NATIONAL AFFAIRS
INC**
Also Called: Bna
1912 Woodford Rd Ste 100 (22182-3795)
PHONE................................703 847-4741
Fax: 703 847-3058
EMP: 1
SALES (corp-wide): 1.4B **Privately Held**
SIC: 2711 Newspapers-Publishing/Printing
HQ: The Bureau Of National Affairs Inc
1801 S Bell St Ste Cn110
Arlington VA 22202
703 341-3000

(G-14020)
CALIGO LLC
2765 Centerboro Dr # 250 (22181-6192)
PHONE................................914 819-8530
Wesley Freeman,
Nicholas Mahon,
EMP: 2
SALES (est): 83.5K **Privately Held**
SIC: 7372 Application computer software

(G-14021)
CANDIDATE METRICS INC
2104 Polo Pointe Dr (22181-2804)
PHONE................................703 539-2331
David Silver, *CEO*
EMP: 2

SALES (est): 145.5K **Privately Held**
SIC: 7372 Business oriented computer
software

(G-14022)
**CAPITOL CLOSET DESIGN INC
(PA)**
1934 Old Gallows Rd # 105 (22182-4043)
PHONE................................703 827-2700
Larry Nordseth, *President*
Larry Norstadeth, *Project Mgr*
EMP: 18
SALES (est): 2MM **Privately Held**
WEB: www.capitolclosetdesign.net
SIC: 2541 2521 2542 2511 Cabinets,
lockers & shelving; wood office chairs,
benches & stools; bookcases: office:
wood; cabinets: show, display or storage:
except wood; wood desks, bookcases &
magazine racks

(G-14023)
CBE PRESS LLC
2750 Gallows Rd Apt 344 (22180-7165)
PHONE................................703 992-6779
Rob Meagher, *Owner*
EMP: 2 EST: 2015
SALES (est): 114K **Privately Held**
WEB:
www.cannabisbusinessexecutive.com
SIC: 2741 Miscellaneous publishing

(G-14024)
CERNER CORPORATION
1953 Gallows Rd Ste 350 (22182-3934)
PHONE................................703 286-0200
EMP: 1
SALES (corp-wide): 5.6B **Publicly Held**
WEB: www.cerner.com
SIC: 7372 Business oriented computer
software
PA: Cerner Corporation
2800 Rock Creek Pkwy
Kansas City MO 64117
816 221-1024

(G-14025)
**CEYLON CINNAMON GROWERS
LLC**
8321 Old Courthouse Rd # 26
(22182-3817)
PHONE................................703 626-1764
Gayle Barnes,
Arjuna Wickramasinghe,
EMP: 6
SALES (est): 500K **Privately Held**
WEB: www.genuinecinnamon.com
SIC: 2099 Spices, including grinding

(G-14026)
CHAMPION HANDWASH
Also Called: Champions Hand Carwash
8218 Leesburg Pike (22182-2612)
PHONE................................703 893-4216
Fernando Losales, *Manager*
EMP: 20
SALES (est): 1.8MM **Privately Held**
WEB: www.championwash.com
SIC: 3589 7542 Car washing machinery;
carwashes

(G-14027)
CHELONIAN PRESS INC
9723 Days Farm Dr (22182-7304)
PHONE................................703 734-1160
EMP: 2
SALES (est): 106.9K **Privately Held**
SIC: 2741 Misc Publishing

(G-14028)
CMI
8130 Boone Blvd Ste 330 (22182-2640)
PHONE................................703 356-2190
Richard Hugh Clark, *Principal*
Ben Wright, *Sales Staff*
EMP: 53 EST: 2011
SALES (est): 5.2MM **Privately Held**
WEB: www.cmicareers.com
SIC: 3273 Ready-mixed concrete

(G-14029)
COGITARI INC
110 Saratoga Waye Ne (22180-3663)
PHONE................................301 237-7777
Leslie Sayres, *CEO*

EMP: 1
SALES (est): 69.7K **Privately Held**
WEB: www.cogitari.us
SIC: 3993 Signs & advertising specialties

(G-14030)
CONCUR TECHNOLOGIES INC
1919 Gallows Rd Ste 800 (22182-4007)
PHONE................................703 403-8764
Lauren Donovan, *Branch Mgr*
EMP: 6
SALES (corp-wide): 30.4B **Privately Held**
WEB: www.concur.com
SIC: 7372 Business oriented computer
software
HQ: Concur Technologies, Inc.
601 108th Ave Ne Ste 1000
Bellevue WA 98004

(G-14031)
CREATIVE WORKSHOPS
2625 Chain Bridge Rd (22181-5430)
PHONE................................703 938-6177
Elaine Oliver, *Owner*
EMP: 1
SALES (est): 73.9K **Privately Held**
WEB: www.enoliver-pottery.com
SIC: 3269 5719 Vases, pottery; pottery

(G-14032)
DALAUN COUTURE LLC
333 Maple Ave E 1025 (22180-4717)
PHONE................................703 594-1413
Paris Henderson,
EMP: 1 EST: 2017
SALES (est): 49.1K **Privately Held**
SIC: 3161 Clothing & apparel carrying
cases

(G-14033)
DALEEL CORPORATION
8300 Old Courthouse Rd # 210
(22182-3822)
PHONE................................703 824-8130
Souliman Bassam, *Principal*
EMP: 3
SALES (est): 190K **Privately Held**
SIC: 2721 Magazines: publishing & printing

(G-14034)
DAMSELWINGS PRESS
2203 Abbotsford Dr (22181-3220)
PHONE................................703 919-4230
Martha Brettschneider, *Principal*
EMP: 4
SALES (est): 55K **Privately Held**
WEB: www.damselwingsphotography.com
SIC: 2741 Miscellaneous publishing

(G-14035)
DAY & NIGHT PRINTING INC
Also Called: D & N Copy Center
8618 Wstwd Ctr Dr Ll100 (22182-2222)
PHONE................................703 734-4940
Margaret A Hillman, *President*
Jonathan Hillman, *Exec VP*
Carrie Jean Wilson, *CFO*
Carlos Vega, *Manager*
EMP: 40
SALES (est): 7.2MM **Privately Held**
WEB: www.dayandnight.com
SIC: 2752 2789 Commercial printing, off-
set; bookbinding & related work

(G-14036)
DE CARLO ENTERPRISES INC
Also Called: Easy Stone Center
420 Mill St Ne (22180-4542)
PHONE................................703 281-1880
Christopher Decarlo, *President*
Michael Kennedy, *Principal*
EMP: 10
SQ FT: 16,803
SALES (est): 791.3K **Privately Held**
WEB: www.easystonecenter.com
SIC: 3281 Cut stone & stone products

(G-14037)
**DEFENSE ARNAUTICAL
SUPPORT LLC**
1508 Victoria Farms Ln (22182-1529)
PHONE................................703 309-9222
Felipe Rodriguez, *Managing Prtnr*
EMP: 1
SALES (est): 98.7K **Privately Held**
SIC: 3728 Aircraft parts & equipment

(G-14038)
DEFENSE NEWS
1919 Gallows Rd Ste 400 (22182-4038)
PHONE................................703 750-9000
Vago Muradian, *Principal*
Seth Frantzman, *Author*
EMP: 10
SALES (est): 518.2K **Privately Held**
WEB: www.defensenews.com
SIC: 2711 Newspapers, publishing & print-
ing

(G-14039)
DILEWAY LLC
903 Fairway Dr Ne (22180-3633)
PHONE................................703 897-6811
Yongchao Wang, *Administration*
EMP: 5
SALES (est): 338.9K **Privately Held**
SIC: 1382 Oil & gas exploration services

(G-14040)
DISASTER AIDE
115 Casmar St Se (22180-6610)
PHONE................................201 892-8898
Venkat R T Sriraman,
EMP: 1
SALES (est): 57.5K **Privately Held**
SIC: 2621 Molded pulp products

(G-14041)
DR JK LONGEVITY LLC
1521 Boyd Pointe Way # 2501
(22182-7535)
PHONE................................202 304-0896
Hetaf Kamal,
EMP: 1
SALES (est): 37.5K **Privately Held**
SIC: 2741

(G-14042)
**DRENGR DEFENSE INDUSTRIES
LLC**
2211 Goldentree Way (22182-5173)
PHONE................................703 552-9987
George McIngvale, *Principal*
EMP: 2
SALES (est): 43.6K **Privately Held**
SIC: 3999 Manufacturing industries

(G-14043)
EFFITHERMIX LLC
10450 Hunter View Rd (22181-2818)
PHONE................................703 860-9703
Michael Vick,
Alison Sebastian,
EMP: 1
SALES (est): 75.3K **Privately Held**
SIC: 3511 8711 8731 Turbines & turbine
generator sets; mechanical engineering;
commercial physical research; energy re-
search

(G-14044)
ELECTRONICS OF FUTURE INC
Also Called: Etf
9433 Van Arsdale Dr (22181-6117)
PHONE................................518 421-8830
Michael Shur, *CEO*
Paulina Shur, *CFO*
EMP: 2 EST: 2017
SALES (est): 119.8K **Privately Held**
SIC: 3674 Semiconductors & related de-
vices

(G-14045)
ELECTROVITA LLC
2310 Trott Ave (22181-3131)
PHONE................................703 447-7290
Scott Wartenberg, *President*
EMP: 1
SALES (est): 200K **Privately Held**
WEB: www.electrovita.com
SIC: 3845 Electromedical equipment

(G-14046)
ELEVATIVE NETWORKS LLC
1577 Spring Hill Rd # 210 (22182-2284)
PHONE................................703 226-3419
David C Cross,
EMP: 1 EST: 2010
SALES (est): 211.1K **Privately Held**
WEB: www.elevative.com
SIC: 3534 Elevators & equipment

(G-14047)
ELOQUA INC (HQ)
1921 Gallows Rd Ste 250　(22182-3994)
PHONE.................................703 584-2750
Joseph P Payne, *CEO*
Alex P Shootman, *President*
Andre Hs Yee, *Senior VP*
Stephen E Holsten, *Vice Pres*
Donald E Clarke, *CFO*
EMP: 27
SALES (est): 28.8MM **Publicly Held**
WEB: www.oracle.com
SIC: 7372 Business oriented computer
　　software
PA: Oracle Corporation
　　500 Oracle Pkwy
　　Redwood City CA 94065
　　650 506-7000

(G-14048)
ENEXDI LLC
8474 Tyco Rd Ste A　(22182-7519)
PHONE.................................703 748-0596
Anne Brothers, *Business Mgr*
Anne Pyne, *Business Mgr*
Aster Endale, *Production*
Chris Turo, *Production*
Andrea Tasker, *Marketing Staff*
EMP: 13
SALES (est): 1.1MM **Privately Held**
WEB: www.enexdi.com
SIC: 2759 Commercial printing

(G-14049)
ERICSSON INC
1595 Spring Hill Rd # 500　(22182-2228)
PHONE.................................571 262-9254
Mike Simmon, *Manager*
EMP: 50
SALES (corp-wide): 23.5B **Privately Held**
WEB: www.ericsson.com
SIC: 3577 Computer peripheral equipment
HQ: Ericsson Inc.
　　6300 Legacy Dr
　　Plano TX 75024
　　972 583-0000

(G-14050)
ESSKAY STRUCTURES INC
2950 Short Ct　(22181-5906)
PHONE.................................571 242-0011
EMP: 2
SALES (est): 117.3K **Privately Held**
WEB: www.esskaystructures.com
SIC: 3441 Fabricated structural metal

(G-14051)
EXCELSIOR ASSOCIATES INC
1832 Clovermeadow Dr　(22182-1804)
PHONE.................................703 255-1596
Qiang Yuan, *Principal*
EMP: 1
SALES (est): 43.6K **Privately Held**
SIC: 3999 Manufacturing industries

(G-14052)
EXPLOSIVE SPORTS COND LLC
9704 Chilcott Manor Way　(22181-5400)
PHONE.................................703 255-7087
Joann Meginley, *Principal*
EMP: 2
SALES (est): 74.4K **Privately Held**
SIC: 2892 Explosives

(G-14053)
FEDERAL TIMES
1919 Gallows Rd Ste 400　(22182-4038)
PHONE.................................703 750-9000
Alan Cozza, *Accounts Exec*
EMP: 2
SALES (est): 73.1K **Privately Held**
WEB: www.federaltimes.com
SIC: 2721 Periodicals

(G-14054)
FIFTH TRIBE LLC
8245 Boone Blvd Ste 250　(22182-3875)
PHONE.................................703 755-0680
EMP: 1
SALES (est): 63.3K **Privately Held**
WEB: www.fifthtribe.com
SIC: 3652 Pre-recorded records & tapes

(G-14055)
FINANCE BUSINESS FORMS COMPANY
713 Park St Se　(22180-5812)
PHONE.................................703 255-2151
Rosemary Griffin, *President*
Tim Griffin, *Principal*
Frances Griffin, *Vice Pres*
EMP: 3 EST: 1947
SALES (est): 323.5K **Privately Held**
WEB: www.financetabbies.com
SIC: 2752 5021 Business form & card
　　printing, lithographic; filing units

(G-14056)
FK LOGISTICS USA LLC
8609 Wstwd Ctr Dr Ste 1　(22182-7521)
PHONE.................................877 811-8772
Adnan Fernan, *Principal*
Syed Zaidi, *CFO*
Michelle Farmer, *Senior Mgr*
EMP: 2
SALES (est): 19.9K **Privately Held**
WEB: www.fklogisticsusa.com
SIC: 3537 4513 4512 Containers (metal);
　　air cargo; parcel delivery, private air; air
　　cargo carrier, scheduled

(G-14057)
FRENCH PRESS PRINTING LLC
9933 Murnane St　(22181-3112)
PHONE.................................703 268-8241
Sarah Bohn, *Principal*
EMP: 2
SALES (est): 96.7K **Privately Held**
SIC: 2752 Commercial printing, offset

(G-14058)
FUEL YOUR LIFE LLC
2255 Richelieu Dr　(22182-5049)
PHONE.................................703 208-4449
Kristin Wood, *Principal*
EMP: 1
SALES (est): 90.4K **Privately Held**
SIC: 2869 Fuels

(G-14059)
G3 SOLUTIONS LLC
10288 Johns Hollow Rd　(22182-1556)
PHONE.................................703 424-4296
John Covert, *Principal*
EMP: 3
SALES (est): 186.8K **Privately Held**
SIC: 3931 Guitars & parts, electric & non-
　　electric

(G-14060)
GD PACKAGING LLC (PA)
1952 Gallows Rd Ste 110　(22182-3823)
PHONE.................................703 946-8100
Chan Moon,
Tae Kim,
Kathryn Lee,
EMP: 3
SQ FT: 3,500
SALES (est): 210K **Privately Held**
SIC: 3089 Bands, plastic

(G-14061)
GOOSE CREEK GAS LLC
8526 Leesburg Pike　(22182-2405)
PHONE.................................703 827-0611
Eric Schmitz, *Administration*
EMP: 3
SALES (est): 173.5K **Privately Held**
WEB: www.schmitzservices.com
SIC: 1311 Crude petroleum & natural gas

(G-14062)
HEIRLOOMS FURNITURE LLC
Also Called: Freedom Display Cases
1728 Creek Crossing Rd　(22182-2126)
PHONE.................................703 652-6094
Firgia Nieves,
EMP: 1
SALES (est): 15.1K **Privately Held**
WEB: www.freedomdisplaycases.com
SIC: 2499 Decorative wood & woodwork

(G-14063)
HENSOLDT INC
8614 Westwood Center Dr # 550
(22182-1881)
PHONE.................................703 827-3976
Gerald Smith, *CEO*

Courtney Togni, *Manager*
EMP: 3 EST: 2017
SALES (est): 380.6K **Privately Held**
WEB: www.hensoldt.net
SIC: 3812 Defense systems & equipment

(G-14064)
HIGHBROW MAGAZINE LLC
9430 Lakeside Dr　(22182-2047)
PHONE.................................571 480-2867
Taghizadeh Tara, *Principal*
EMP: 2
SALES (est): 97.3K **Privately Held**
SIC: 2721 Magazines: publishing & printing

(G-14065)
HISTORYNET LLC
1919 Gallows Rd Ste 400　(22182-4038)
PHONE.................................703 779-8322
Michael Reinstein,
EMP: 8
SALES (est): 324.4K
SALES (corp-wide): 337.6K **Privately
Held**
WEB: www.historynet.com
SIC: 2721 Magazines: publishing only, not
　　printed on site
PA: Regent Companies, Llc
　　9460 Wilshire B Ste 500
　　Beverly Hills CA 90212
　　310 299-3400

(G-14066)
HOLCIM LLC
2316 Cedar Ln　(22182-5228)
PHONE.................................703 622-4616
EMP: 3
SALES (est): 176.1K **Privately Held**
WEB: www.ambujacement.com
SIC: 3272 Concrete products

(G-14067)
HORTON PUBLISHING CO
2200 Trott Ave　(22181-3130)
PHONE.................................703 281-6963
James Horton, *Owner*
EMP: 2
SALES (est): 94.1K **Privately Held**
SIC: 2741 Miscellaneous publishing

(G-14068)
HUNTER EQP SVC & PARTS INC
9618 Percussion Way　(22182-3334)
PHONE.................................703 785-5526
Michael K McGiffin, *President*
Kelly McGiffin, *Admin Sec*
EMP: 2 **Privately Held**
SIC: 3559 Wheel balancing equipment, au-
　　tomotive

(G-14069)
IBFD NORTH AMERICA INC
8300 Boone Blvd Ste 380　(22182-2626)
PHONE.................................703 442-7757
Sam Van Der Feltz, *CEO*
Joey Walker, *Regional Mgr*
Maarten Goudsmit, *COO*
John G Rienstra, *Vice Pres*
Steven Stroschein, *VP Sls/Mktg*
EMP: 6
SALES (est): 812K **Privately Held**
WEB: www.ibfd.org
SIC: 2721 2731 7299 Periodicals; book
　　publishing; birth certificate facilities

(G-14070)
INFOCESS LLC
Also Called: Campus Axess
8300 Boone Blvd Ste 500　(22182-2681)
PHONE.................................571 723-1010
Mehmet Emin Pala, *President*
EMP: 1
SALES (est): 75.4K **Privately Held**
WEB: www.campusaxess.com
SIC: 7372 7371 Educational computer
　　software; computer software development
　　& applications

(G-14071)
INFRAWHITE TECHNOLOGIES LLC
2671 Avenir Pl Apt 2523　(22180-7493)
PHONE.................................662 902-0376
Maya White, *CEO*
EMP: 1 EST: 2015

SALES (est): 47.9K **Privately Held**
SIC: 7372 8243 7373 7382 Application
　　computer software; software training,
　　computer; local area network (LAN) sys-
　　tems integrator; protective devices, secu-
　　rity; computer related maintenance
　　services; custom computer programming
　　services

(G-14072)
INVIRUSTECH USA INC
1952 Gallows Rd Ste 303　(22182-3823)
PHONE.................................703 826-3109
Kibeom Park, *CEO*
Yeon SOO Han, *Director*
Yong Hoon Jo, *Director*
Chaekwang Rim, *Director*
EMP: 4
SALES (est): 200K **Privately Held**
WEB: www.kicdc.org
SIC: 2835 In vitro diagnostics

(G-14073)
IQ GLOBAL TECHNOLOGIES LLC
Also Called: Secure Iq
8609 Westwood Center Dr　(22182-7521)
PHONE.................................800 601-0678
Patrick L Gardner, *President*
Tony Schloss, *Manager*
Bharat Kandanoor, *Director*
EMP: 1
SQ FT: 4,500
SALES (est): 40.9K **Privately Held**
WEB: www.blueally.com
SIC: 7372 Business oriented computer
　　software

(G-14074)
JB INSTALLATIONS INC
8905 Old Courthouse Rd　(22182-2107)
PHONE.................................703 403-2119
Joseph Buchko, *President*
Suzanne Buchko, *Vice Pres*
EMP: 2
SALES (est): 188.7K **Privately Held**
WEB: www.jbinstallations.com
SIC: 2591 Drapery hardware & blinds &
　　shades

(G-14075)
K & E PRINTING AND GRAPHICS
8219 Cottage St　(22180-6940)
PHONE.................................703 560-4701
Amelia Kyker, *CEO*
Stephen Kyker, *President*
EMP: 5
SALES (est): 545.1K **Privately Held**
SIC: 2752 Commercial printing, offset

(G-14076)
KARLA COLLETTO SWIMWEAR INC
319d Mill St Ne　(22180-4525)
PHONE.................................703 281-3262
Karla A Colletto, *President*
Lisa A Rovan, *Vice Pres*
EMP: 30
SQ FT: 4,000
SALES (est): 3.3MM **Privately Held**
WEB: www.karlacolletto.com
SIC: 2339 7389 Bathing suits: women's,
　　misses' & juniors'; apparel designers,
　　commercial

(G-14077)
KELVIN HUGHES LLC
8614 Westwood Center Dr # 550
(22182-1881)
PHONE.................................703 827-3986
Adrian Pilbeam, *Vice Pres*
Russell Gould,
Christopher Easteal,
EMP: 3
SALES (est): 433K
SALES (corp-wide): 177.9K **Privately
Held**
SIC: 3812 Search & navigation equipment
HQ: Kelvin Hughes Limited
　　Voltage Business Centre
　　Enfield MIDDX EN3 7
　　199 280-5200

▲ = Import ▼=Export
◆ =Import/Export

GEOGRAPHIC

(G-14078)
KICS CUPCAKES LLC
1934 Old Gallows Rd # 350 (22182-4042)
PHONE..........................202 630-5727
Thien Tran, *Principal*
EMP: 4
SALES (est): 142.9K Privately Held
SIC: 2051 Bread, cake & related products

(G-14079)
KONICA MNLTA BUS SLTONS USA IN
1595 Spring Hill Rd # 400 (22182-2228)
PHONE..........................703 553-6000
David Burton, *Branch Mgr*
EMP: 40 Privately Held
WEB: www.kmbs.konicaminolta.us
SIC: 3577 5044 7629 3861 Computer peripheral equipment; office equipment; electrical repair shops; photographic equipment & supplies
HQ: Konica Minolta Business Solutions U.S.A., Inc.
100 Williams Dr
Ramsey NJ 07446
201 825-4000

(G-14080)
KOREA ARSPC INDS FORT WRTH INC
8245 Boone Blvd (22182-3828)
PHONE..........................703 883-2012
Kwang Bae Moon, *Principal*
EMP: 7
SALES (est): 655.1K Privately Held
SIC: 3999 Manufacturing industries
PA: Korea Aerospace Industries. Ltd
78 Gongdan 1-Ro, Sanam-Myeon
Sacheon 52529

(G-14081)
LEGION ATHLETICS INC
8045 Leesburg Pike # 240 (22182-2748)
PHONE..........................727 729-1049
Sean Clouden, *President*
Gabriel Vera, *Principal*
Michael Matthews, *Corp Secy*
Jeremy Blumberg, *Vice Pres*
EMP: 10
SALES (est): 9MM Privately Held
WEB: www.legionathletics.com
SIC: 2023 Dietary supplements, dairy & non-dairy based

(G-14082)
LEIDOS INC
1953 Gallows Rd Ste 810 (22182-4002)
PHONE..........................703 610-8900
John Jumper, *CEO*
Al Coffin, *Branch Mgr*
Tony Helou, *Program Mgr*
Shaun Collins, *Manager*
Christopher Hayes, *Program Dir*
EMP: 38 Publicly Held
WEB: www.leidos.com
SIC: 3577 Computer peripheral equipment
HQ: Leidos, Inc.
1750 Presidents St
Reston VA 20190
571 526-6000

(G-14083)
LOCKHEED MARTIN CORPORATION
2650 Park Tower Dr (22180-7300)
PHONE..........................703 280-9983
Ginger Groeber, *Branch Mgr*
EMP: 8 Publicly Held
WEB: www.lockheedmartin.com
SIC: 3812 Search & navigation equipment
PA: Lockheed Martin Corporation
6801 Rockledge Dr
Bethesda MD 20817

(G-14084)
LOCKHEED MARTIN INTEGRTD SYSTM
2650 Park Twr Dr Ste 400 (22180)
PHONE..........................703 682-5719
Ginger Groeber, *Manager*
EMP: 500 Publicly Held
WEB: www.lockheedmartin.com
SIC: 3812 Search & navigation equipment

HQ: Lockheed Martin Integrated Systems, Llc
6801 Rockledge Dr
Bethesda MD 20817

(G-14085)
LONG SOLUTIONS LLC
9612 Podium Dr (22182-3336)
PHONE..........................703 281-2766
Helen Long, *CEO*
EMP: 1
SALES (est): 96K Privately Held
SIC: 3089 Organizers for closets, drawers, etc.: plastic

(G-14086)
LOWER LANE PUBLISHING LLC
2105 Carrhill Rd (22181-2921)
PHONE..........................703 865-5968
William Farrell, *Principal*
EMP: 2
SALES (est): 66.3K Privately Held
WEB: www.lowerlanepublishing.com
SIC: 2741 Miscellaneous publishing

(G-14087)
LT BUSINESS DYNAMICS LLC
1577 Spring Hill Rd # 260 (22182-2223)
PHONE..........................703 738-6599
Timothy Hawkins, *Managing Prtnr*
Lissette Bishins, *COO*
EMP: 8 EST: 2007
SALES (est): 1.1MM Privately Held
WEB: www.ltbd.com
SIC: 3578 Accounting machines & cash registers

(G-14088)
MACRONETICS INC
8300 Boone Blvd Ste 50 (22182-2626)
PHONE..........................703 848-9290
Vinh Nguyen, *President*
Mario Aleixo, *Exec VP*
EMP: 4
SALES (est): 209.7K Privately Held
SIC: 7372 Prepackaged software

(G-14089)
MAXILICIOUS BAKING COMPANY LLC
1510 Snughill Ct (22182-1724)
PHONE..........................703 448-1788
Samuel David Lowenstein, *Administration*
EMP: 8
SALES (est): 563.3K Privately Held
WEB: www.maxiliciousbaking.com
SIC: 2051 Bread, cake & related products

(G-14090)
MENDES DELI INC
Also Called: Vienna Vintner
320 Maple Ave E F (22180-4716)
PHONE..........................703 242-9463
Orland Mendes, *President*
EMP: 2
SALES (est): 116.9K Privately Held
WEB: www.viennavintner.com
SIC: 2084 Wines

(G-14091)
MICRO FOCUS SOFTWARE INC
Also Called: Novell
8609 Westwood Center Dr # 500 (22182-7521)
PHONE..........................703 663-5500
Troy Richardson, *Manager*
John Gassner, *Director*
EMP: 314 Privately Held
WEB: www.microfocus.com
SIC: 7372 Prepackaged software
HQ: Micro Focus Software Inc.
1800 Novell Pl
Provo UT 84606
801 861-7000

(G-14092)
MID-ATLANTIC PRINTERS LTD
8290 Old Courthouse Rd C (22182-3837)
PHONE..........................703 448-1155
Mark Peters, *Manager*
EMP: 4
SALES (corp-wide): 33.7MM Privately Held
WEB: www.mapl.net
SIC: 2752 Commercial printing, offset

PA: Mid-Atlantic Printers, Ltd.
503 3rd St
Altavista VA 24517
434 369-6633

(G-14093)
MILLSTREET SOFTWARE
411 Mill St Se (22180-5730)
PHONE..........................703 281-1015
Barry Smith, *Owner*
EMP: 2
SALES (est): 175K Privately Held
WEB: www.shsclassof1965.org
SIC: 7372 Business oriented computer software

(G-14094)
MIMETRIX TECHNOLOGIES LLC
10212 Brittenford Dr (22182-1865)
PHONE..........................571 306-1234
Elliott Starin, *CTO*
Kevin Fecher,
EMP: 2
SALES (est): 278.3K Privately Held
WEB: www.mimetrix.com
SIC: 3357 3577 Communication wire; fiber optic cable (insulated); input/output equipment, computer

(G-14095)
MINUTEMAN PRESS OF VIENNA
1880 Howard Ave Ste 101 (22182-2611)
PHONE..........................703 992-0420
Vivek Rai, *Principal*
EMP: 3
SALES (est): 304.1K Privately Held
WEB: www.minutemanpress.com
SIC: 2752 Commercial printing, lithographic

(G-14096)
MIRROR MORNING MUSIC
314 Charles St Se (22180-4856)
PHONE..........................703 405-8181
EMP: 2
SALES (est): 165.7K Privately Held
SIC: 2782 Albums

(G-14097)
MISSION INTEGRATED TECH LLC
1934 Old Gallows Rd (22182-4042)
PHONE..........................202 769-9900
Fahmi Alubbad, *President*
EMP: 4
SALES (est): 16.5MM Privately Held
WEB: www.mit.technology
SIC: 3842 8748 7382 Personal safety equipment; safety training service; security systems services

(G-14098)
MOBILE WALLET GIFTING CORP
10303 Yellow Pine Dr (22182-1344)
PHONE..........................301 523-1052
EMP: 1
SALES (est): 49.1K Privately Held
SIC: 3172 Wallets

(G-14099)
MONGODB INC
8614 Westwood Center Dr # 705 (22182-2450)
PHONE..........................866 237-8815
EMP: 2 Publicly Held
WEB: www.mongodb.com
SIC: 7372 Prepackaged software
PA: Mongodb, Inc.
1633 Broadway Fl 38
New York NY 10019
646 727-4092

(G-14100)
MOONLIGHT PUBLISHING GROUP LLC
101 Yeonas Dr Se (22180-6556)
PHONE..........................703 242-0978
Peter Chapin, *Principal*
EMP: 1 EST: 2014
SALES (est): 52.1K Privately Held
SIC: 2741 Miscellaneous publishing

(G-14101)
NANCY LEE ASMAN
208 Courthouse Cir Sw (22180-6205)
PHONE..........................703 242-8530
Nancy L Asman, *Owner*
EMP: 1 EST: 1987
SALES (est): 60.9K Privately Held
SIC: 7372 Home entertainment computer software

(G-14102)
NATIONAL IMPORTS LLC
Also Called: Kintrex
1934 Old Gallows Rd # 350 (22182-4042)
PHONE..........................703 637-0019
Scott Madsen,
Laurel Miller,
◆ EMP: 5
SQ FT: 2,000
SALES (est): 1.6MM Privately Held
WEB: www.nationalimports.com
SIC: 3264 3825 Magnets, permanent: ceramic or ferrite; measuring instruments & meters, electric

(G-14103)
NEON NATION LLC
2875 Sutton Oaks Ln (22181-6149)
PHONE..........................703 255-4996
Kyle James Burris, *Administration*
EMP: 2 EST: 2012
SALES (est): 131.1K Privately Held
WEB: www.aneonnation.com
SIC: 2813 Neon

(G-14104)
NEURO STAT ANLYTCAL SLTONS LLC
Also Called: Neuro Stat Solutions
1934 Old Gallows Rd # 35 (22182-4042)
P.O. Box 17806, San Antonio TX (78217-0806)
PHONE..........................703 224-8984
William T Thompson, *CEO*
Helene Thompson, *General Mgr*
EMP: 22 EST: 2011
SQ FT: 6,000
SALES (est): 2.3MM Privately Held
WEB: www.neurostatsolutions.com
SIC: 2834 8733 Chlorination tablets & kits (water purification); medical research

(G-14105)
NEXXTEK INC
8422 Berea Dr (22180-7103)
PHONE..........................571 356-2921
Lalith Gopavaram, *President*
EMP: 1
SALES (est): 62K Privately Held
SIC: 7372 7371 Application computer software; computer software systems analysis & design, custom

(G-14106)
NOVELSAT USA
9134 Ermantrude Ct (22182-2010)
PHONE..........................703 295-2119
Lincoln Biederbeck, *Sales Staff*
EMP: 2
SALES (est): 138.3K Privately Held
WEB: www.novelsat.com
SIC: 3663 Radio & TV communications equipment

(G-14107)
OLIVE OIL & FRIENDS LLC
512 Woodland Ct Nw (22180-4134)
PHONE..........................703 385-1845
Pericles Konstas, *Principal*
EMP: 3
SALES (est): 237.6K Privately Held
WEB: www.spartan-oil.com
SIC: 2079 Olive oil

(G-14108)
OSMOTHERAPEUTICS INC
8000 Towers Crescent Dr (22182-6207)
PHONE..........................703 627-1934
Salim Shah, *CEO*
EMP: 1
SALES (est): 52.8K Privately Held
WEB: www.osmotherapeutics.com
SIC: 3999 Hair & hair-based products

(G-14109)
PEACH TEA MONOGRAMS
8853 Glenridge Ct (22182-1708)
PHONE...............................703 973-9977
EMP: 1
SALES (est): 42.2K Privately Held
SIC: 2395 Embroidery & art needlework

(G-14110)
PETERS KNIVES
9812 Oak Valley Ct (22181-5365)
PHONE...............................703 255-5353
Mel Peters, Owner
EMP: 2
SALES (est): 143K Privately Held
SIC: 3421 7389 Knife blades & blanks;

(G-14111)
PIROOZ MANUFACTURING LLC
101 Mashie Dr Se (22180-4961)
PHONE...............................703 281-4244
EMP: 2
SALES (est): 72.5K Privately Held
SIC: 3999 Mfg Misc Products

(G-14112)
PITNEY BOWES INC
8245 Boone Blvd Ste 470 (22182-3832)
P.O. Box 8125, South Charleston WV
(25303-0125)
PHONE...............................304 744-1067
EMP: 50
SALES (corp-wide): 3.8B Publicly Held
SIC: 3579 7359 Mfg Office Machines
　Equipment Rental/Leasing
PA: Pitney Bowes Inc.
　3001 Summer St
　Stamford CT 06905
　203 356-5000

(G-14113)
PRESTON SIGNS INC
295 Windover Ave Nw (22180-4413)
PHONE...............................703 534-3777
Jim Preston, President
Marshall Mc Dade, Vice Pres
EMP: 4
SQ FT: 4,000
SALES (est): 457.9K Privately Held
WEB: www.fallschurchsigns.com
SIC: 3993 7336 Displays, paint process;
　silk screen design

(G-14114)
PRINIT CORPORATION
Also Called: Sir Speedy
1945 Old Gallows Rd # 10 (22182-3931)
PHONE...............................703 847-8880
Nick Ruiz, President
Mary Ruiz, Vice Pres
Vivian Gross, Manager
EMP: 12
SQ FT: 3,000
SALES (est): 2.1MM Privately Held
WEB: www.sirspeedyvienna.com
SIC: 2752 Commercial printing, litho-
　graphic

(G-14115)
PUBLISHERS CIRCLTN
8500 Tyco Rd (22182-2251)
PHONE...............................703 394-5293
EMP: 1 EST: 2013
SALES (est): 49K Privately Held
SIC: 2741 Misc Publishing

(G-14116)
PURA VIDA VIENNA INC
9413 Tuba Ct (22182-1647)
PHONE...............................703 281-6050
Della Jarrett, Principal
EMP: 2
SALES (est): 105K Privately Held
SIC: 1081 Metal mining services

(G-14117)
PURE PASTY COMPANY LLC
128c Church St Nw (22180-4507)
PHONE...............................703 255-7147
Michael Edward Burgess,
EMP: 1 EST: 2009
SQ FT: 1,330
SALES (est): 36.2K Privately Held
WEB: www.purepasty.com
SIC: 2051 Bakery products, partially
　cooked (except frozen)

(G-14118)
RSA SECURITY LLC
8230 Leesburg Pike # 620 (22182-2639)
PHONE...............................703 288-9300
John Dues, Branch Mgr
EMP: 2
SALES (corp-wide): 820MM Privately
Held
WEB: www.rsa.com
SIC: 7372 Prepackaged software
PA: Rsa Security Llc
　174 Middlesex Tpke Bldg 4
　Bedford MA 01730
　781 515-5000

(G-14119)
RXHONESTY INC
1279 Cobble Pond Way (22182-6605)
PHONE...............................908 872-2009
Daniel Peterson, CEO
EMP: 1
SALES (est): 32.7K Privately Held
SIC: 7372 Application computer software

(G-14120)
SAK INDUSTRIES LLC
1310 Beulah Rd (22182-1410)
PHONE...............................202 701-0071
Saad Alotaiby, Principal
EMP: 2
SALES (est): 74.1K Privately Held
SIC: 3999 Manufacturing industries

(G-14121)
SAMIN SCIENCE USA INC
1952 Gallows Rd Ste 110 (22182-3823)
PHONE...............................571 403-3678
Ann Masuda, President
▲ EMP: 1 EST: 2014
SQ FT: 1,500
SALES (est): 92K Privately Held
SIC: 3821 Worktables, laboratory; vacuum
　pumps, laboratory

(G-14122)
SARFEZ PHARMACEUTICALS INC
10402 Dunn Meadow Rd (22182-1327)
PHONE...............................703 759-2565
Fatima Khwaja, CEO
Salim Shah, Founder
EMP: 2
SALES (est): 217.6K Privately Held
WEB: www.sarfezpharma.com
SIC: 2834 7389 Druggists' preparations
　(pharmaceuticals);

(G-14123)
SHARED SPECTRUM COMPANY
1593 Spring Hill Rd # 700 (22182-2249)
PHONE...............................703 761-2818
Mark McHenry, CEO
Theresa McHenry, Exec VP
Andrey Bessarabov, Administration
EMP: 33
SALES (est): 5.3MM Privately Held
WEB: www.sharedspectrum.com
SIC: 3663 Radio & TV communications
　equipment

(G-14124)
SHELTERS TO SHUTTERS
1921 Gallows Rd Ste 700 (22182-3994)
PHONE...............................703 634-6130
Kristen Fagley, Vice Pres
EMP: 5 EST: 2017
SALES (est): 878.8K Privately Held
WEB: www.shelterstoshutters.org
SIC: 3442 Shutters, door or window: metal

(G-14125)
SHINE LIKE ME LLC
8000 Crianza Pl Apt 226 (22182-4080)
PHONE...............................210 862-4197
Adrienne Bunn, Manager
EMP: 1
SALES (est): 83.4K Privately Held
SIC: 2339 Women's & misses' accessories

(G-14126)
SIGHTLINE MEDIA GROUP LLC
Also Called: Army Times
1919 Gallows Rd Ste 400 (22182-4038)
PHONE...............................703 750-7400
Peter Lundquist, President
Wendy Hurwitz, Vice Pres
Gordon Crago, Technology
Megan Morrocco, Director
Erin Muro, Executive
EMP: 262
SALES (est): 25.1MM Privately Held
WEB: www.sightlinemediagroup.com
SIC: 2711 Newspapers: publishing only,
　not printed on site

(G-14127)
SIGNS BY TOMORROW
8150 Leesburg Pike # 120 (22182-7715)
PHONE...............................703 356-3383
Michael Behn, President
EMP: 3
SALES (est): 354.5K Privately Held
WEB: www.signsbytomorrow.com
SIC: 3993 Signs & advertising specialties

(G-14128)
SILVERLINE BREWING COMPANY
506 Mashie Dr Se (22180-4926)
PHONE...............................703 281-5816
Michael Mercer, Principal
EMP: 3
SALES (est): 74.8K Privately Held
SIC: 2082 Malt beverages

(G-14129)
SITSCAPE INC
8245 Boone Blvd Ste 330 (22182-3851)
PHONE...............................571 432-8130
Kevin Yin, President
Sean Cease, Vice Pres
EMP: 10 EST: 2010
SALES (est): 823.7K Privately Held
WEB: www.sitscape.com
SIC: 7372 Application computer software

(G-14130)
SKI ZONE INC
10102 Garrett St (22181-3146)
PHONE...............................703 242-3588
R Redman, Principal
EMP: 2 EST: 2008
SALES (est): 107.1K Privately Held
SIC: 3949 Sporting & athletic goods

(G-14131)
SOVEREIGN INTELLIGENCE LLC
118 Moore Ave Se (22180-5842)
PHONE...............................571 455-4016
Mark Johnson, CEO
Joseph Saunders, COO
Jean-Pierre Bolat, CFO
Sarah Kurcina, Director
EMP: 10
SQ FT: 500
SALES (est): 195.5K Privately Held
WEB: www.sovereign.ai
SIC: 7372 7371 Application computer soft-
　ware; computer software development &
　applications

(G-14132)
SPIRITWAY LLC
8813 Skokie Ln (22182-2346)
PHONE...............................831 676-1014
Michael Whitfield, President
EMP: 1
SALES (est): 39.6K Privately Held
SIC: 7372 Application computer software

(G-14133)
SSC INNOVATIONS LLC
1593 Spring Hill Rd # 700 (22182-2245)
PHONE...............................703 761-2818
Mark McHenry, President
Theresa McHenry,
EMP: 3
SALES (est): 145K Privately Held
WEB: www.sharedspectrum.com
SIC: 3663 Radio & TV communications
　equipment

(G-14134)
STEAM VALLEY PUBLISHING
401 Blair Rd Nw (22180-4106)
PHONE...............................703 255-9884
EMP: 2 EST: 2001
SALES (est): 100K Privately Held
SIC: 2741 Misc Publishing

(G-14135)
SUSTAINABILITY INNOVATIONS LLC
1654 Montmorency Dr (22182-2023)
PHONE...............................703 281-1352
Peter Soyka, Administration
EMP: 2
SALES (est): 111.8K Privately Held
WEB: www.thesustainabilityguys.com
SIC: 3825 Instruments to measure electric-
　ity

(G-14136)
SVR INTERNATIONAL LLC
9702 Carnot Way (22182-3012)
PHONE...............................703 759-2953
Sunil Kapoor,
Renu Kapoor,
EMP: 10
SALES (est): 2MM Privately Held
WEB: www.svrconsulting.com
SIC: 3559 5082 Chemical machinery &
　equipment; brick making machinery; oil
　field equipment

(G-14137)
T C G TECHNOLOGIES LLC
8245 Boone Blvd Ste 704 (22182-3846)
PHONE...............................703 847-5057
Gustavo Sapiurka, CEO
EMP: 2 EST: 2017
SALES (est): 93.1K Privately Held
WEB: www.acsoftware.com
SIC: 7372 Prepackaged software

(G-14138)
TAYLOR COMMUNICATIONS INC
8618 Westwood Center Dr # 105
(22182-2222)
PHONE...............................703 790-9700
David Dilucente, Manager
EMP: 26
SQ FT: 3,000
SALES (corp-wide): 2.4B Privately Held
WEB: www.taylorcorp.com
SIC: 2761 Manifold business forms
HQ: Taylor Communications, Inc.
　1725 Roe Crest Dr
　North Mankato MN 56003
　866 541-0937

(G-14139)
TAYLOR MATTHEWS INC
2011 Gallows Tree Ct (22182-3985)
PHONE...............................703 346-7844
Todd Bendus, Owner
EMP: 2
SALES (est): 54.5K Privately Held
SIC: 2273 Carpets & rugs

(G-14140)
TESLA INC
8500 Tyco Rd (22182-2251)
PHONE...............................703 761-4679
EMP: 7
SALES (corp-wide): 24.5B Publicly Held
WEB: www.tesla.com
SIC: 3711 Automobile assembly, including
　specialty automobiles
PA: Tesla, Inc.
　3500 Deer Creek Rd
　Palo Alto CA 94304
　650 681-5000

(G-14141)
TFI WIND DOWN INC
Also Called: Thomasville Furniture
8461 Leesburg Pike (22182-2404)
PHONE...............................703 714-0500
EMP: 6
SALES (corp-wide): 889.7MM Privately
Held
SIC: 2511 2512 Mfg Wood Household Fur-
　niture Mfg Upholstered Household Furni-
　ture
PA: Tfi Wind Down, Inc.
　1925 Eastchester Dr
　High Point NC 27265
　336 472-4000

(G-14142)
THUMBELINAS
1587 Spring Hill Rd (22182-2292)
PHONE...............................703 448-8043
Richard Kibbey, Principal

EMP: 1
SALES (est): 54.2K **Privately Held**
SIC: 3999 Manufacturing industries

(G-14143)
TORODE COMPANY
531 Druid Hill Rd Ne (22180-3519)
PHONE.............................703 242-9387
Robert Torode, *Owner*
R Torode, *Principal*
EMP: 1
SALES (est): 85.6K **Privately Held**
SIC: 2431 Woodwork, interior & ornamental

(G-14144)
TRADINGBELL INC
1934 Old Gallows Rd (22182-4042)
PHONE.............................703 752-6100
Hari Ramamurthy, *President*
Raj Natarajan, *Vice Pres*
Tj Dhillon, *Admin Sec*
EMP: 57
SQ FT: 5,000
SALES (est): 3.3MM **Privately Held**
WEB: www.tradingbell.com
SIC: 2741 Catalogs: publishing only, not printed on site

(G-14145)
TRANSITION PUBLISHING LLC
2255 Richelieu Dr (22182-5049)
PHONE.............................703 208-4449
Randy Wood, *Principal*
EMP: 2
SALES (est): 74.8K **Privately Held**
SIC: 2741 Miscellaneous publishing

(G-14146)
TRI STATE MASTERS INC
9354 Campbell Rd (22182-2036)
PHONE.............................703 255-0222
David D Movafagh, *Principal*
EMP: 3
SALES (est): 329.1K **Privately Held**
WEB: www.tri-statemasters.com
SIC: 2789 Trade binding services

(G-14147)
ULTRATA LLC
1934 Old Gallows Rd # 35 (22182-4042)
PHONE.............................571 226-0347
Larry Reback, *Principal*
EMP: 12
SALES (est): 729.2K **Privately Held**
SIC: 3571 Electronic computers

(G-14148)
UTRUE INC
100 Shepherdson Ln Ne (22180-4532)
PHONE.............................703 577-0309
Michael Meyer, *President*
EMP: 1
SALES (est): 74.1K **Privately Held**
WEB: www.utrue.net
SIC: 3699 Security control equipment & systems

(G-14149)
UWIN SOFTWARE LLC
8512 Idylwood Rd (22182-5039)
PHONE.............................703 876-0490
P Nguyen, *Administration*
EMP: 2
SALES (est): 140.2K **Privately Held**
WEB: www.uwinsoftware.com
SIC: 7372 Prepackaged software

(G-14150)
VEGA PAGES LLC
914 Desale St Sw (22180-5944)
PHONE.............................703 281-2030
EMP: 2
SALES (est): 111.2K **Privately Held**
SIC: 2741 Misc Publishing

(G-14151)
VESTA PROPERTYS LLC
1295 Difficult Run Ct (22182-1400)
PHONE.............................703 579-7979
EMP: 2
SALES (est): 200K **Privately Held**
SIC: 2521 Mfg Wood Office Furniture

(G-14152)
VIENNA CUSTOM EMBROIDERY LLC
9101 Old Courthouse Rd (22182-2115)
PHONE.............................703 887-1254
Susan Manfred, *Principal*
EMP: 1
SALES (est): 43.3K **Privately Held**
SIC: 2395 Embroidery & art needlework

(G-14153)
VIENNA HOT TUBES PATIO IN
8501 Tyco Rd Ste C (22182-7505)
PHONE.............................703 734-0077
EMP: 1
SALES (est): 43.6K **Privately Held**
SIC: 3999 Hot tubs

(G-14154)
VIENNA PAINT & DCTG CO INC (PA)
203 Maple Ave W (22180-5606)
PHONE.............................703 281-5252
Carole Wolfand, *President*
Bill Cramer, *Corp Secy*
EMP: 4
SQ FT: 3,500
SALES (est): 5MM **Privately Held**
WEB: www.viennapaints.com
SIC: 2851 5231 Paints & allied products; paint

(G-14155)
WALL TO WALL SIGNS
8455 Tyco Rd Ste E (22182-2210)
PHONE.............................703 821-2358
EMP: 1 EST: 2019
SALES (est): 50.6K **Privately Held**
SIC: 3993 Signs & advertising specialties

(G-14156)
WARCOLLAR INDUSTRIES LLC
504 Park St Ne (22180-3561)
PHONE.............................703 981-2862
Eugene Bransfield,
EMP: 1 EST: 2014
SALES (est): 160.9K **Privately Held**
WEB: www.warcollar.com
SIC: 3829 7379 Measuring & controlling devices;

(G-14157)
WASHINGTON BLADE
1645 Trap Rd (22182-2064)
PHONE.............................202 747-2077
EMP: 2
SALES (est): 62.9K **Privately Held**
WEB: www.washingtonblade.com
SIC: 2711 Newspapers, publishing & printing

(G-14158)
WEBGEAR INC
Also Called: Usptgear
1934 Old Gallows Rd # 20 (22182-4042)
PHONE.............................703 532-1000
Samia Farouki, *CEO*
Beau Lendman, *President*
▲ EMP: 15
SQ FT: 5,000
SALES (est): 1MM **Privately Held**
SIC: 2311 5621 5611 Men's & boys' suits & coats; women's clothing stores; men's & boys' clothing stores

(G-14159)
WEBLOGIC
2306 Arden St (22027-1126)
PHONE.............................703 645-0263
Brian Murphy, *Principal*
EMP: 2
SALES (est): 140K **Privately Held**
SIC: 7372 Prepackaged software

(G-14160)
WHITWORTH ANALYTICS LLC
435 Orchard St Nw (22180-4144)
PHONE.............................703 319-8018
Carolyn W Brandon, *Administration*
EMP: 3
SALES (est): 180K **Privately Held**
SIC: 3826 Analytical instruments

(G-14161)
WIZARD TECHNOLOGIES
2083 Hunters Crest Way (22181-2841)
PHONE.............................703 625-0900
Paul Farrell, *Principal*
EMP: 5
SALES (est): 424.6K **Privately Held**
SIC: 3577 Computer peripheral equipment

(G-14162)
WORLD HISTORY GROUP LLC
Also Called: Historynet
1919 Gallows Rd Ste 400 (22182-4038)
PHONE.............................703 779-8322
David Steinhafel,
EMP: 27
SALES (est): 814.3K **Privately Held**
WEB: www.historynet.com
SIC: 2721 7389 Magazines: publishing only, not printed on site;

(G-14163)
ZEBA MAGAZINE LLC
8060 Crianza Pl Apt 406 (22182-4071)
PHONE.............................202 705-7006
Aman Feda, *Mng Member*
Samira Safi,
EMP: 5
SALES (est): 4.2MM **Privately Held**
WEB: www.zebamagazine.com
SIC: 2759 Publication printing

Viewtown
Culpeper County

(G-14164)
STRANGE DESIGNS
90n Toad Hill Ln (22746)
P.O. Box 100 (20106-0100)
PHONE.............................540 937-5858
Merrill Strange, *Owner*
EMP: 3
SALES (est): 141.2K **Privately Held**
SIC: 3269 Pottery products

Vinton
Roanoke County

(G-14165)
BANNERS AND MORE
238 W Madison Ave (24179-4506)
PHONE.............................540 400-8485
Susan Shuler, *Principal*
EMP: 1
SALES (est): 77.7K **Privately Held**
SIC: 3993 Signs & advertising specialties

(G-14166)
BEAR COUNTRY WOODWORKS
201 Morning Dove Ln (24179-4003)
PHONE.............................540 890-0928
Jeffrey Fenner, *Principal*
EMP: 1
SALES (est): 74.3K **Privately Held**
SIC: 2431 Millwork

(G-14167)
BULLDOG PRECIOUS METALS
105 Knoll Ct (24179-4433)
PHONE.............................540 312-1234
Patrick Gobble, *Principal*
EMP: 1
SALES (est): 57.6K **Privately Held**
SIC: 3339 Precious metals

(G-14168)
CARDINAL GLASS INDUSTRIES INC
Also Called: Cardinal Ig Company
2132 Cardinal Park Dr (24179-2321)
PHONE.............................540 892-5600
Tom Hicks, *Safety Dir*
Jack Wiek, *Maint Spvr*
Craig Kemmerling, *Engineer*
Thomas Popek, *Engineer*
Jerry Maines, *Business Anlyst*
EMP: 200
SALES (corp-wide): 1B **Privately Held**
WEB: www.cardinalcorp.com
SIC: 3231 3211 Insulating glass: made from purchased glass; tempered glass: made from purchased glass; flat glass
PA: Cardinal Glass Industries Inc
775 Pririe Ctr Dr Ste 200
Eden Prairie MN 55344
952 229-2600

(G-14169)
CELLY SPORTS SHOP LLC
1110 Vinyard Rd (24179-3632)
PHONE.............................540 981-0205
Jason S Reger,
EMP: 5
SALES (est): 50K **Privately Held**
SIC: 3949 Hockey equipment & supplies, general

(G-14170)
CITIZENS UPHOLSTERY & FURN CO
125 E Lee Ave (24179-2517)
PHONE.............................540 345-5060
Ralph C Chumbley, *President*
Clint D Chumbly, *Vice Pres*
EMP: 4
SQ FT: 2,450
SALES (est): 200K **Privately Held**
WEB: www.citizensupholsteryandfurniture.com
SIC: 2299 7641 Hair, curled: for upholstery, pillow & quilt filling; upholstery work

(G-14171)
CUTTING EDGE CARPET BINDING
433 Walnut Ave (24179-3231)
PHONE.............................540 982-1007
Michael Craft, *Owner*
EMP: 1
SALES (est): 55.4K **Privately Held**
SIC: 2273 1752 Carpets & rugs; carpet laying

(G-14172)
CW SECURITY SOLUTIONS LLC
1326 E Washington Ave (24179-1820)
PHONE.............................540 929-8019
Erin McKee, *Principal*
EMP: 2 EST: 2015
SALES (est): 183.1K **Privately Held**
WEB: www.cwarmor.com
SIC: 3711 7219 Universal carriers, military, assembly of; garment alteration & repair shop

(G-14173)
DARRELL A WILSON
Also Called: Wilsons Sealcoating
1130 Cannon Ln (24179-5466)
PHONE.............................540 598-8412
Darrell Wilson, *Owner*
EMP: 2
SALES (est): 74.4K **Privately Held**
SIC: 2851 Paints, asphalt or bituminous

(G-14174)
JOHNSON MACHINERY SALES INC
2300 Stone Creek Path (24179-1149)
PHONE.............................540 890-8893
Russell E Johnson, *President*
EMP: 4
SALES (est): 250K **Privately Held**
SIC: 3553 7389 Woodworking machinery; business services

(G-14175)
K DUDLEY LOGGING INC
13225 Stewartsville Rd (24179-5922)
PHONE.............................540 890-0220
Kendall Dudley, *President*
EMP: 1
SALES (est): 104.7K **Privately Held**
SIC: 2411 Logging camps & contractors

(G-14176)
KNOTTHEAD WOODWORKING INC
555 Aragona Dr (24179-2842)
PHONE.............................540 344-0293
Turner Charles J, *President*
EMP: 1

GEOGRAPHIC

SALES (est): 90.2K **Privately Held**
SIC: 2431 Millwork

(G-14177)
LANIER OUTDOOR ENTERPRISES LLC
1581 Gravel Hill Rd (24179-5565)
PHONE..........................540 892-5945
Michelle Lanier, *Principal*
EMP: 3
SALES (est): 99.1K **Privately Held**
SIC: 1311 Crude petroleum & natural gas

(G-14178)
M T HOLDING COMPANY LLC
102 N Mitchell Rd (24179-1838)
P.O. Box 1153 (24179-8153)
PHONE..........................540 563-8866
EMP: 50
SQ FT: 7,956
SALES (est): 3.1MM **Privately Held**
SIC: 2782 Mfg Blankbooks/Binders

(G-14179)
MINDMETTLE
801 Brookshire Dr (24179-1907)
P.O. Box 524 (24179-0524)
PHONE..........................540 890-5563
Bernard F Dowdy, *Owner*
EMP: 2
SALES (est): 133.4K **Privately Held**
WEB: www.mindmettle.com
SIC: 7372 7371 Prepackaged software; custom computer programming services

(G-14180)
PLUNKETT BUSINESS GROUP INC
Also Called: M & W Fire Apparatus
845 3rd St (24179-3348)
PHONE..........................540 343-3323
Raymond Plunkett, *President*
EMP: 21
SQ FT: 15,000
SALES (est): 3.1MM **Privately Held**
SIC: 3711 7539 Fire department vehicles (motor vehicles), assembly of; automotive repair shops

(G-14181)
PRECISION FABRICS GROUP INC
Also Called: Vinton Plant
323 W Virginia Ave (24179-3211)
P.O. Box 337 (24179-0337)
PHONE..........................540 343-4448
Dick Bayliss, *Senior Buyer*
Ali Khan, *Manager*
EMP: 400
SALES (corp-wide): 198.9MM **Privately Held**
WEB: www.precisionfabricsgroup.com
SIC: 2231 2221 Weaving mill, broadwoven fabrics: wool or similar fabric; broadwoven fabric mills, manmade
PA: Precision Fabrics Group, Inc.
    301 N Elm St Ste 600
    Greensboro NC 27401
    336 281-3049

(G-14182)
SAV ON SIGNS
238 W Madison Ave (24179-4506)
PHONE..........................540 344-8406
Susan Shuler, *Owner*
Keith Martin, *Principal*
EMP: 8
SALES (est): 720.2K **Privately Held**
WEB: www.savonsigns.net
SIC: 3993 Signs, not made in custom sign painting shops

(G-14183)
SCG SPORTS LLC
15778 Stewartsville Rd (24179-5903)
PHONE..........................540 330-7733
EMP: 3 **EST:** 2015
SALES (est): 210.5K **Privately Held**
WEB: www.vectorvortex.com
SIC: 2759 Screen printing

(G-14184)
STICKERS PLUS LTD
Also Called: Magnets USA
720 3rd St (24179-3342)
PHONE..........................540 857-3045
Alan Turner, *President*
Donald Martin, *COO*
Dale Turner, *Vice Pres*
Dave Withers, *Research*
Patty Troth, *Personnel*
▲ **EMP:** 63
SQ FT: 20,000
SALES (est): 14MM **Privately Held**
WEB: www.magnetsusa.com
SIC: 3499 2621 2672 Magnets, permanent: metallic; specialty or chemically treated papers; coated & laminated paper

(G-14185)
SUNAPSYS INC
850 3rd St (24179-3300)
PHONE..........................540 904-6856
Samuel H McGhee IV, *President*
Ronald Davis, *Vice Pres*
Timoth Rumfelt, *Vice Pres*
Mike Hill, *Engineer*
Raymond Crowder, *Project Engr*
EMP: 14
SQ FT: 6,500
SALES (est): 2.5MM **Privately Held**
WEB: www.sunapsys.com
SIC: 3625 Electric controls & control accessories, industrial

(G-14186)
SUPERIOR METAL & MFG INC
926 10th St (24179)
PHONE..........................540 981-1005
David Selfe, *President*
EMP: 11
SALES (est): 691.8K **Privately Held**
SIC: 3441 Fabricated structural metal

(G-14187)
TONY TRAN HARDWOOD FLOORS
997 Hardy Rd (24179-3643)
PHONE..........................540 793-4094
Tony Tran, *Principal*
EMP: 2
SALES (est): 184.4K **Privately Held**
WEB: www.tophadwoodfloorsva.com
SIC: 2426 1771 1752 Flooring, hardwood; flooring contractor; floor laying & floor work

(G-14188)
UTZ QUALITY FOODS LLC
936 3rd St (24179-3350)
PHONE..........................540 981-0351
Tim Duran, *Manager*
EMP: 30
SALES (corp-wide): 845MM **Privately Held**
WEB: www.utzsnacks.com
SIC: 2096 Potato chips & similar snacks
PA: Utz Quality Foods, Llc
    900 High St
    Hanover PA 17331
    800 367-7629

(G-14189)
VAERO INC
111 W Virginia Ave (24179-3315)
P.O. Box 459 (24179-0459)
PHONE..........................540 344-1000
C Richard Cranwell, *Principal*
EMP: 2
SALES (est): 127K **Privately Held**
SIC: 3721 Aircraft

(G-14190)
VECTOR VORTEX LLC
15778 Stewartsville Rd (24179-5903)
PHONE..........................540 330-7733
William Matthew Brown, *Administration*
EMP: 2 **EST:** 2017
SALES (est): 79.8K **Privately Held**
WEB: www.vectorvortex.com
SIC: 2759 Screen printing

(G-14191)
VENTON FAB & WELDING
7 Walnut Ave (24179-2537)
PHONE..........................540 981-1550
Karen Turner, *Owner*
EMP: 2
SALES (est): 66.6K **Privately Held**
SIC: 7692 Welding repair

Virgilina
Halifax County

(G-14192)
GENERAL EQP SLS & SVC LLC
5090 Ramble Rd (24598-3128)
PHONE..........................434 579-7581
Monty Lowery,
EMP: 7
SALES (est): 400K **Privately Held**
SIC: 3713 Truck & bus bodies

(G-14193)
LONE STAR POLISHING INC
1171 Christie Rd (24598-2310)
PHONE..........................434 585-3372
Jessica Whitney, *Principal*
EMP: 2
SALES (est): 91.6K **Privately Held**
SIC: 3471 Polishing, metals or formed products

Virginia Beach
Virginia Beach City County

(G-14194)
1816 POTTERS ROAD LLC
1816 Potters Rd (23454-4453)
PHONE..........................757 428-1170
Todd J Preti, *Administration*
EMP: 2
SALES (est): 96K **Privately Held**
WEB: www.tidewateremblems.com
SIC: 2759 Screen printing

(G-14195)
2050COMMUNITY LLC
300 25th St Apt 323 (23451-3496)
PHONE..........................202 744-6031
Stefanie Mitchell, *Principal*
EMP: 3
SALES (est): 86.5K **Privately Held**
SIC: 2741 Miscellaneous publishing

(G-14196)
757 PRINTS
3506 Remington Ct (23453-1875)
PHONE..........................757 774-6834
Jeron Mitchell, *Principal*
EMP: 2
SALES (est): 83.9K **Privately Held**
WEB: www.757prints.com
SIC: 2752 Commercial printing, lithographic

(G-14197)
757 SURFBOARDS
593 S Birdneck Rd Ste 101 (23451-5875)
PHONE..........................757 348-2030
EMP: 1
SALES (est): 47K **Privately Held**
WEB: www.757surfboards.com
SIC: 3949 Surfboards

(G-14198)
80PROTONS LLC
4445 Corp Ln Ste 264 (23462)
PHONE..........................571 215-5453
Christian Howe, *Mng Member*
James Granger,
EMP: 2
SALES (est): 56.5K **Privately Held**
SIC: 7372 7389 Application computer software;

(G-14199)
8TH-ELEMENT LLC
2076 Thomas Bishop Ln (23454-1143)
PHONE..........................757 481-6146
David Savino, *Principal*
EMP: 3
SALES (est): 207.5K **Privately Held**
SIC: 2819 Industrial inorganic chemicals

(G-14200)
A 1 COATING
1801 River Rock Arch (23456-6116)
PHONE..........................757 351-5544
EMP: 2 **EST:** 2017
SALES (est): 78.9K **Privately Held**
SIC: 3479 Metal coating & allied service

(G-14201)
A STITCH IN TIME LLC
4009 Bakerfield Rd (23453-1735)
PHONE..........................757 478-4878
Lisa G Blankenship, *Administration*
EMP: 1
SALES (est): 43.7K **Privately Held**
SIC: 2395 Embroidery & art needlework

(G-14202)
A1 SERVICE
733 Lord Nelson Dr (23464-2825)
PHONE..........................757 544-0830
Edward Lee Tweedy, *Owner*
EMP: 1
SALES (est): 120K **Privately Held**
SIC: 2741 Patterns, paper: publishing & printing

(G-14203)
ABACUS RACING & MACHINE SVCS
1372 Baker Rd (23455-3316)
PHONE..........................757 363-8878
William H Thumel, *President*
▲ **EMP:** 7
SQ FT: 26,146
SALES (est): 900K **Privately Held**
WEB: www.abacusracing.com
SIC: 3599 Machine shop, jobbing & repair

(G-14204)
ABLAZE INTERIORS INC
4048 Muddy Creek Rd (23457-1570)
PHONE..........................757 427-0075
Rita P Cheche, *President*
EMP: 2
SALES (est): 305K **Privately Held**
SIC: 3253 Floor tile, ceramic

(G-14205)
ABSOLUTELY FABULOUS
Also Called: Absolutely Fabulous At Towne
2937 West Gibbs Rd (23457-1069)
PHONE..........................757 615-5732
Sharon Carr, *Owner*
EMP: 1 **EST:** 2011
SALES (est): 25K **Privately Held**
WEB: www.absolutelyfabspa.com
SIC: 2512 7389 Upholstered household furniture;

(G-14206)
ABWASSER TECHNOLOGIES INC
3091 Brickhouse Ct (23452-6860)
PHONE..........................757 453-7505
Richard Fahs, *CEO*
Phil Taylor, *Director*
Emilio Coppola, *Administration*
EMP: 2
SALES (est): 114.7K **Privately Held**
SIC: 3589 5084 9511 1629 Sewage & water treatment equipment; pollution control equipment, water (environmental); air, water & solid waste management; waste water & sewage treatment plant construction

(G-14207)
ACME INK INC
940 Culver Ln (23454-6774)
PHONE..........................757 373-3614
Steven Bradley, *Administration*
EMP: 2 **EST:** 2010
SALES (est): 118.7K **Privately Held**
SIC: 2893 Printing ink

(G-14208)
ACO CORPORATION (PA)
3500 Virginia Beach Blvd # 200 (23452-4445)
PHONE..........................757 480-2875
Bill Tragert, *President*
Gordiyenko Vladimir, *General Mgr*
Michael Fridland, *Vice Pres*
Vladimir Gordiyenko, *Vice Pres*

Eric Haskins, *Vice Pres*
▲ **EMP:** 4
SQ FT: 6,500
SALES (est): 1MM **Privately Held**
WEB: www.acocorp.com
SIC: 2426 Furniture stock & parts, hardwood

(G-14209)
ACOUSTICAL SHEETMETAL INC
2600 Production Rd (23454-5254)
PHONE......................757 456-9720
Steinhoff Dieter, *CEO*
Petra E Snowden, *President*
Dieter Steinhoff, *Corp Secy*
Michael Ioland, *Vice Pres*
Dr Michael S Ireland, *Vice Pres*
▲ **EMP:** 76
SQ FT: 14,000
SALES (est): 21MM **Privately Held**
WEB: www.acousticalsheetmetal.com
SIC: 3444 Sheet metal specialties, not stamped

(G-14210)
ACTION GRAPHICS SIGNS
4760 Virginia Beach Blvd (23462-6748)
PHONE......................757 995-2200
EMP: 1
SALES (est): 46K **Privately Held**
WEB: www.agwraps.com
SIC: 3993 Signs & advertising specialties

(G-14211)
ADAMS CO LLC
2681 Indian River Rd (23456-3419)
PHONE......................757 721-0427
Kelly Adams, *Mng Member*
Scott Adams,
EMP: 2
SALES (est): 50K **Privately Held**
WEB: www.adamscpas.com
SIC: 7692 Welding repair

(G-14212)
ADVANCED BUSINESS SERVICES LLC
4445 Corporation Ln # 110 (23462-3264)
PHONE......................757 439-0849
Frank Chebalo, *Managing Prtnr*
Robert K Adams,
EMP: 2
SALES (est): 100K **Privately Held**
WEB: www.murphybusiness.com
SIC: 3577 Computer peripheral equipment

(G-14213)
ADVANCED MACHINE & TOOLING
Also Called: A M T
5725 Arrowhead Dr (23462-3218)
PHONE......................757 518-1222
Jack Evelyn, *President*
Deborah Evelyn, *Treasurer*
EMP: 17
SQ FT: 16,000
SALES (est): 3.1MM **Privately Held**
WEB: www.advanced-machine.com
SIC: 3599 7692 3444 Machine shop, jobbing & repair; welding repair; sheet metalwork

(G-14214)
AEROSPACE TECHNIQUES INC
5701 Cleveland St Ste 640 (23462-1788)
PHONE......................860 347-1200
Clyde Ellsworth Warner, *CEO*
Robert Joseph Bosco, *President*
Jack E Lynn, *President*
Anthony Parillo Jr, *CFO*
Richard B Polivy, *Admin Sec*
EMP: 100
SQ FT: 80,000
SALES (est): 21.1MM **Privately Held**
WEB: www.aerospacetechniques.com
SIC: 3724 3599 4581 3841 Aircraft engines & engine parts; machine shop, jobbing & repair; aircraft maintenance & repair services; surgical & medical instruments; aircraft parts & equipment; motor vehicle parts & accessories

(G-14215)
AFD TECHNOLOGIES LLC
214 40th St (23451-2602)
P.O. Box 1101 (23451-0101)
PHONE......................561 271-7000
Terry Craig, *President*
EMP: 2 **Privately Held**
WEB: www.afdt.com
SIC: 2911 Petroleum refining
PA: Afd Technologies, Llc
6303 Blue Lagoon Dr # 40
Miami FL 33126

(G-14216)
AFFORDABLE CANVAS VIRGINIA LLC
4356 Alfriends Trl (23455-6102)
PHONE......................757 718-5330
Alan Ormond, *President*
EMP: 2
SALES (est): 166.4K **Privately Held**
SIC: 2211 Canvas

(G-14217)
AIR & GAS COMPONENTS LLC
5366 Lake Lawson Rd (23455-6806)
PHONE......................757 473-3571
Charles Prietz, *Principal*
EMP: 3
SALES (est): 237.7K **Privately Held**
SIC: 3563 Air & gas compressors

(G-14218)
AIR BRITT TWO LLC
3244 Sugar Creek Dr (23452-4816)
PHONE......................757 470-9364
Vernon Britt,
EMP: 1 **EST:** 2016
SALES (est): 71.3K **Privately Held**
SIC: 3842 Braces, orthopedic

(G-14219)
AJW SURFBOARDS
208 63rd St (23451-2125)
PHONE......................910 617-8750
Adam Warden,
EMP: 1
SALES (est): 200K **Privately Held**
WEB: www.ajwsurfboards.com
SIC: 3949 Surfboards

(G-14220)
ALIEN PISS WORLD ENTRMT LLC
2085 Lynnhven Pkwy Ste 10 (23456)
PHONE......................757 805-1007
Chaz Ellis, *Mng Member*
EMP: 3
SALES (est): 75.6K **Privately Held**
SIC: 2782 Record albums

(G-14221)
ALIOTH TECHNICAL SERVICES INC
2432 Esplanade Dr (23456-6515)
PHONE......................757 630-0337
Pete Bliagous, *Vice Pres*
EMP: 1
SALES (est): 50K **Privately Held**
SIC: 3546 Power-driven handtools

(G-14222)
ALL MARBLE
4801 Beach Cove Pl (23455-1382)
PHONE......................757 460-8099
Joe Galecki, *Owner*
EMP: 1
SALES (est): 85.1K **Privately Held**
SIC: 3272 1731 Art marble, concrete; electrical work

(G-14223)
ALL SPORTS ATHLETIC APPAREL
2957 Holland Rd (23453-2609)
PHONE......................757 427-6772
Marvin Perry, *Owner*
EMP: 1
SALES (est): 30K **Privately Held**
SIC: 2389 Apparel & accessories

(G-14224)
AMERI SIGN DESIGN
508 Central Dr Ste 107 (23454-5237)
PHONE......................252 544-7712
EMP: 1
SALES (est): 46K **Privately Held**
SIC: 3993 Signs & advertising specialties

(G-14225)
AMPURAGE
1716 Moon Valley Dr (23453-3736)
PHONE......................757 632-8232
Sherry Kincheloe, *CEO*
EMP: 2
SALES (est): 88.3K **Privately Held**
SIC: 3629 Electrical industrial apparatus

(G-14226)
AMWAY PRODUCTS & SERVICES
4449 Clemsford Dr (23456-5432)
PHONE......................757 474-2115
Annette Welch, *Owner*
Mitchel Welch, *Co-Owner*
EMP: 2
SALES (est): 139K **Privately Held**
SIC: 2621 Catalog, magazine & newsprint papers

(G-14227)
ANALYZED IMAGES
4445 Corp Ln Ste 264 (23462)
PHONE......................757 905-4500
Lyndon Plant, *Mng Member*
EMP: 2
SALES (est): 250K **Privately Held**
SIC: 3844 X-ray apparatus & tubes

(G-14228)
ANCHOR DEFENSE INC
4221 Battery Rd (23455-1507)
PHONE......................757 460-3830
Billie Keen, *Principal*
EMP: 3
SALES (est): 164K **Privately Held**
SIC: 3812 Defense systems & equipment

(G-14229)
ANIXTER INC
1209 Baker Rd Ste 509 (23455-3651)
PHONE......................757 460-9718
Michelle Hauber, *Branch Mgr*
EMP: 4 **Publicly Held**
WEB: www.anixterlabstesting.com
SIC: 3699 Security devices
HQ: Anixter Inc.
2301 Patriot Blvd
Glenview IL 60026
224 521-8000

(G-14230)
ANTHONY CORPORATION
332 Cleveland Pl (23462-6529)
PHONE......................757 490-3613
Charlotte Fay Jones, *President*
Michael A Jones, *Vice Pres*
Vickie Jones, *CFO*
Michael Jones, *Mktg Dir*
EMP: 20
SQ FT: 7,000
SALES (est): 2.4MM **Privately Held**
WEB: www.anthcorp.com
SIC: 2591 2391 Shade, curtain & drapery hardware; draperies, plastic & textile: from purchased materials

(G-14231)
ANY AND ALL GRAPHICS LLC
3200 Dam Neck Rd Ste 105 (23453-2632)
PHONE......................757 468-9600
Michael Uhler,
EMP: 7
SALES (est): 759.8K **Privately Held**
WEB: www.anyandallgraphics.com
SIC: 3993 Signs & advertising specialties

(G-14232)
APPFORE LLC
413 Biltmore Ct (23454-3459)
PHONE......................757 597-6990
EMP: 2
SALES (est): 56.5K **Privately Held**
SIC: 7372 Application computer software

(G-14233)
APPLE SHINE
3313 Boynton Ct (23452-4828)
PHONE......................757 714-6393
EMP: 2
SALES (est): 123.8K **Privately Held**
SIC: 3571 Mfg Electronic Computers

(G-14234)
APPLIED FILM TECHNOLOGY INC
5312 Vrginia Bch Blvd Ste (23462)
PHONE......................757 351-4241
Jason Zirpoli, *Principal*
EMP: 1
SALES (est): 90.8K **Privately Held**
SIC: 2899 8999 1799 5719 Hydrofluoric acid compound, for etching or polishing glass; stained glass art; glass tinting, architectural or automotive; window shades; window shades

(G-14235)
AQUAWASH PRESSURE WASHING LLC
5912 Appleton Ct (23464-4914)
PHONE......................757 738-9899
Jaquana Branch, *Mng Member*
EMP: 2
SALES (est): 72K **Privately Held**
SIC: 3443 Housings, pressure

(G-14236)
ARCHITECTURAL GRAPHICS INC (PA)
Also Called: AGI
2655 International Pkwy (23452-7802)
P.O. Box 9175 (23450-9175)
PHONE......................800 877-7868
David W Ramsay, *CEO*
Craig C Rohde, *President*
James W Raynor III, *COO*
Chris Quigley, *Exec VP*
Christopher J Quigley, *Exec VP*
◆ **EMP:** 215 **EST:** 1969
SQ FT: 431,000
SALES: 199.3MM **Privately Held**
WEB: www.agi.net
SIC: 3993 Signs, not made in custom sign painting shops

(G-14237)
ARCHITECTURAL GRAPHICS INC
2820 Crusader Cir (23453-3134)
PHONE......................757 427-1900
Brian Hershelman, *Manager*
EMP: 250
SALES (corp-wide): 199.3MM **Privately Held**
WEB: www.agi.net
SIC: 3993 Signs, not made in custom sign painting shops
PA: Architectural Graphics, Inc.
2655 International Pkwy
Virginia Beach VA 23452
800 877-7868

(G-14238)
ARCHITECTURAL GRAPHICS INC
Also Called: Agi
2800 Crusader Cir (23453-3109)
PHONE......................757 301-7008
Scott Ward, *Plant Mgr*
Mike Savage, *Supervisor*
EMP: 106
SALES (corp-wide): 199.3MM **Privately Held**
WEB: www.agi.net
SIC: 3993 Signs, not made in custom sign painting shops
PA: Architectural Graphics, Inc.
2655 International Pkwy
Virginia Beach VA 23452
800 877-7868

(G-14239)
ARDENT CANDLE COMPANY LLC
1616 Fairfax Dr (23453-1839)
PHONE......................347 906-2011
EMP: 1

SALES (est): 43.6K **Privately Held**
SIC: 3999 Candles

(G-14240)
AROMATHERAPY SHOPPE
315 First Colonial Rd (23454-4654)
PHONE.................................757 531-7431
EMP: 2
SALES (est): 121.5K **Privately Held**
WEB: www.thearomatherapyshoppe.com
SIC: 2844 Toilet preparations

(G-14241)
ARROW MFG LLC
1116 Burlington Rd (23464-5916)
PHONE.................................757 635-6889
EMP: 2 EST: 2017
SALES (est): 64.5K **Privately Held**
SIC: 3999 Manufacturing industries

(G-14242)
ARS MANUFACTURING INC
5878 Bayside Rd (23455-3006)
PHONE.................................757 460-2211
Marge Crittenden, *CEO*
Miyo Mori, *Ch of Bd*
Goichi Mori, *President*
EMP: 165
SALES (est): 14.4MM **Privately Held**
SIC: 3069 3053 3471 3714 Rubber automotive products; gaskets, packing & sealing devices; plating of metals or formed products; motor vehicle parts & accessories; mechanical rubber goods
PA: Arai Seisakusho Co., Ltd.
　2-27-6, Higashinihombashi
　Chuo-Ku TKY 103-0

(G-14243)
ART GRAPHICS N DESIGNS INC
1337 Taylor Farm Rd # 106 (23453-3169)
PHONE.................................757 463-9495
John A Belcher, *President*
Shelly G Belcher, *Admin Sec*
EMP: 1 EST: 2000
SALES (est): 195.2K **Privately Held**
WEB: www.artgraphicsndesignsinc.com
SIC: 3993 Signs & advertising specialties

(G-14244)
ARTCRAFT PRINTING LTD
1136 Jensen Dr B (23451-5872)
PHONE.................................757 428-9138
Teresa Hartman, *President*
EMP: 1
SALES (est): 141.8K **Privately Held**
SIC: 2752 Commercial printing, offset

(G-14245)
ASHBURN SAUCE COMPANY
1087 Horn Point Rd (23456-4123)
PHONE.................................757 621-1113
Willard Ashburn, *President*
EMP: 3
SALES (est): 200K **Privately Held**
WEB: www.ashburnsauce.com
SIC: 2033 Apple sauce: packaged in cans, jars, etc.

(G-14246)
ASHMAN DISTRIBUTING COMPANY
Also Called: Ashman Mfg & Distrg Co
1120 Jensen Dr (23451-5872)
P.O. Box 1068 (23451-0068)
PHONE.................................757 428-6734
Timothy E Ashman, *President*
Alan Doherty, *QC Mgr*
Natalie W Ashman, *Treasurer*
▲ EMP: 10
SQ FT: 10,000
SALES (est): 1.3MM **Privately Held**
WEB: www.ashmanco.com
SIC: 2035 Seasonings, meat sauces (except tomato & dry); mustard, prepared (wet); dressings, salad: raw & cooked (except dry mixes)

(G-14247)
ATM BEACH SERVICES LLC
1804 Saranac Ct (23453-3726)
PHONE.................................757 434-4848
James Holda, *Administration*
EMP: 2
SALES (est): 121.5K **Privately Held**
SIC: 3578 Automatic teller machines (ATM)

(G-14248)
AUMIITU COMBS CREATIONS LLC
1276 Christian Ct (23464-6249)
PHONE.................................757 285-5201
Bernard Combs, *Mng Member*
EMP: 1
SALES (est): 40K **Privately Held**
WEB: www.pembrokemall.com
SIC: 3911 5094 Jewelry, precious metal; jewelry & precious stones

(G-14249)
AURORA INDUSTRIES LLC
2693 Reliance Dr Ste 105 (23452-7844)
PHONE.................................757 301-2574
Hector Cruz, *Mng Member*
Holly Poydack,
EMP: 508
SALES (est): 75.3K **Privately Held**
SIC: 2389 Men's miscellaneous accessories

(G-14250)
AVELIS JOHN
5113 Mansards Ct Apt 103 (23455-3821)
PHONE.................................757 363-2001
John Avelis, *Administration*
EMP: 2
SALES (est): 88.3K **Privately Held**
SIC: 3669 Communications equipment

(G-14251)
AVENUE 7 MAGAZINE LLC
1518 Brenland Cir (23464-6759)
PHONE.................................757 214-4914
Crystal Hairston, *President*
EMP: 3
SALES (est): 136.2K **Privately Held**
SIC: 2721 Magazines: publishing only, not printed on site

(G-14252)
AZARS NATURAL FOODS INC (PA)
Also Called: Azar's Cafe & Market
108 Prescott Ave (23452-1769)
PHONE.................................757 486-7778
Tony Saady, *President*
Lina Azar Saady, *Corp Secy*
Tarek Azar, *Vice Pres*
EMP: 50
SQ FT: 7,000
SALES (est): 2MM **Privately Held**
WEB: www.azarfoods.com
SIC: 2099 5812 Ready-to-eat meals, salads & sandwiches; health food restaurant; sandwiches & submarines shop

(G-14253)
B & G PUBLISHING INC
Also Called: For Sell By Owner Services
3320 Virginia Beach Blvd # 4 (23452-5621)
PHONE.................................757 463-1104
Gary Kusturin, *President*
EMP: 3
SQ FT: 1,500
SALES (est): 216.7K **Privately Held**
WEB: www.tidewaterfsbo.com
SIC: 2741 Miscellaneous publishing

(G-14254)
B&B INSULATION LLC
5178 Cleveland St (23462-6502)
PHONE.................................757 904-0884
William Bolean, *Mng Member*
Timithoy Bolean,
Lynda Houck,
EMP: 3
SALES (est): 117.8K **Privately Held**
SIC: 3731 Shipbuilding & repairing

(G-14255)
B&E SHT-METAL FABRICATIONS INC
944 Seahawk Cir Ste 110 (23452-7864)
PHONE.................................757 536-1279
Kathryn P Elehalt, *Principal*
EMP: 2
SALES (est): 94.2K **Privately Held**
SIC: 3499 Fabricated metal products

(G-14256)
B2 HEALTH SOLUTIONS LLC
2133 Upton Dr (23454-1193)
PHONE.................................757 403-8298
Brian Baxter,
EMP: 1
SALES (est): 110K **Privately Held**
WEB: www.b2healthsolutions.com
SIC: 3564 Air purification equipment

(G-14257)
BACK BAY DEFENSE LLC
5745 Grimstead Rd (23457-1339)
PHONE.................................757 285-6883
Jason Russell,
EMP: 2
SALES (est): 126.5K **Privately Held**
SIC: 3812 Defense systems & equipment

(G-14258)
BAILLIO SAND CO INC
560 Oceana Blvd (23454-4985)
P.O. Box 3005 (23454-9105)
PHONE.................................757 428-3302
EMP: 13
SQ FT: 600
SALES (est): 1.4MM **Privately Held**
SIC: 1442 Sand Mining

(G-14259)
BARBOURSVILLE DISTILLERY LLC
1097 Caton Dr (23454-3105)
PHONE.................................757 961-4590
EMP: 3 EST: 2013
SALES (est): 124.5K **Privately Held**
SIC: 2085 Mfg Distilled/Blended Liquor

(G-14260)
BARGAIN BEACHWEAR INC
1714 Atlantic Ave (23451-3425)
PHONE.................................757 313-5440
Ronnie Elbilia, *President*
EMP: 3
SALES (est): 451.7K **Privately Held**
SIC: 2369 2329 Bathing suits & swimwear: girls', children's & infants'; bathing suits & swimwear: men's & boys'

(G-14261)
BARISO LING
Also Called: Feeling Art
604 Oak Grove Ln (23452-3008)
PHONE.................................757 277-5383
Ling Bariso, *Owner*
EMP: 2
SALES (est): 137.6K **Privately Held**
SIC: 3961 Costume jewelry

(G-14262)
BARON GLASS INC
1601 Diamond Springs Rd (23455-3009)
PHONE.................................757 464-1131
Ivan Morris, *Corp Secy*
Michael Capra, *Exec VP*
John Farr, *Exec VP*
Martin Davidson, *Project Mgr*
Andy Perry, *Prdtn Mgr*
◆ EMP: 250 EST: 1973
SQ FT: 82,000
SALES (est): 29.5MM **Privately Held**
WEB: www.glassbaron.com
SIC: 3229 Glassware, art or decorative

(G-14263)
BAY WELDING
5108 Hemlock Ct (23464-2805)
PHONE.................................757 633-7689
Ernest Bertok, *Owner*
EMP: 1 EST: 2015
SALES (est): 47.9K **Privately Held**
SIC: 7692 Welding repair

(G-14264)
BAYFRONT MEDIA GROUP LLC
1206 Laskin Rd Ste 200 (23451-5276)
EMP: 2
SALES: 250K **Privately Held**
SIC: 2741 Media Publishing

(G-14265)
BEACH GLASS DESIGNS INC
1125 Highcliff Ct (23454-5773)
PHONE.................................757 650-7604
David Lutz, *President*

EMP: 2
SALES (est): 140.7K **Privately Held**
SIC: 3229 Glassware, art or decorative

(G-14266)
BEACH HOT RODS MET FABRICATION
1112 Jensen Dr Ste 102 (23451-5884)
PHONE.................................757 227-8191
Scott Ulerick, *President*
EMP: 2
SALES (est): 132.3K **Privately Held**
SIC: 3499 Fabricated metal products

(G-14267)
BEACH IRON SHOP
106 S First Clnl Rd Ste B (23454)
PHONE.................................757 422-3318
EMP: 2
SALES (est): 162.4K **Privately Held**
WEB: www.beachweldingironshop.com
SIC: 3446 Architectural metalwork

(G-14268)
BEACH PALLETS INC
2509 Lemming Ct (23456-8007)
PHONE.................................757 773-1931
Kathy Brumer, *Principal*
EMP: 4
SALES (est): 273.8K **Privately Held**
SIC: 2448 Pallets, wood

(G-14269)
BEACH SIGN AND DESIGN
2424 Castleton Commerce W (23456-5499)
PHONE.................................757 618-8653
EMP: 2 EST: 2017
SALES (est): 163.2K **Privately Held**
WEB: www.vabeachsign.com
SIC: 3993 Signs & advertising specialties

(G-14270)
BEACH WELDING SERVICE
106 S First Clnl Rd Ste B (23454)
PHONE.................................757 422-3318
Bobby Cherry, *Owner*
Robert Cherry Jr, *Owner*
EMP: 2
SALES (est): 188.1K **Privately Held**
WEB: www.beachweldingironshop.com
SIC: 3446 Railings, bannisters, guards, etc.: made from metal pipe

(G-14271)
BEACH WREATHS AND MORE
725 Monmouth Ln (23464-2909)
PHONE.................................757 943-0703
Yvonne Whitelaw, *Principal*
EMP: 2 EST: 2015
SALES (est): 62.5K **Privately Held**
SIC: 3999 Wreaths, artificial

(G-14272)
BEAUTIFUL GRIND
733 Grant Ave (23452-3002)
P.O. Box 1833, Norfolk (23501-1833)
PHONE.................................757 685-6192
EMP: 2 EST: 2011
SALES (est): 115.8K **Privately Held**
SIC: 3599 Grinding castings for the trade

(G-14273)
BEL SOURI LLC
3700 Silina Dr (23452-3213)
PHONE.................................757 685-5583
Amber Davis,
EMP: 2
SALES (est): 74.4K **Privately Held**
SIC: 2844 Toothpastes or powders, dentifrices

(G-14274)
BELLUM DESIGNS LLC
4940 Rutherford Rd # 301 (23455-4000)
PHONE.................................757 343-9556
Trevor Pantone, *Mng Member*
EMP: 4
SQ FT: 1,500
SALES (est): 50K **Privately Held**
SIC: 2394 Canvas & related products

(G-14275)
BEST RECOGNITION
4969 Haygood Rd (23455-5246)
P.O. Box 62226 (23466-2226)
PHONE....................................757 490-3933
Harrell Peterson, *Owner*
EMP: 3
SALES (est): 263.7K **Privately Held**
SIC: 3089 5199 Engraving of plastic; general merchandise, non-durable

(G-14276)
BIG CHIP CLOTHING COMPANY LLC
2085 Lynnhven Pkwy Ste 10 (23456)
PHONE....................................877 572-6525
Brian G Moss Sr,
EMP: 2
SALES (est): 77.4K **Privately Held**
SIC: 3161 Clothing & apparel carrying cases

(G-14277)
BIG TIMBER HARDWOODS LLC
772 Sandbridge Rd (23456-4521)
PHONE....................................724 301-7051
Scott Edwards,
EMP: 1
SALES (est): 104.9K **Privately Held**
SIC: 2439 Timbers, structural: laminated lumber

(G-14278)
BIG TIME CHARTERS INC
2212 Windward Shore Dr (23451-1728)
PHONE....................................757 496-1040
Steve Hollenzer, *Owner*
EMP: 1
SALES (est): 86.6K **Privately Held**
WEB: www.bigtimecharters.net
SIC: 3732 7999 Fishing boats: lobster, crab, oyster, etc.: small; diving instruction, underwater

(G-14279)
BILL FOOTE
Also Called: Foote Designs Maui
536 Virginia Ave (23451-4642)
P.O. Box 1376 (23451-0376)
PHONE....................................808 298-5423
Bill Foote, *Principal*
◆ EMP: 1
SALES (est): 25K **Privately Held**
WEB: www.nelsonfactory.com
SIC: 3949 7389 Surfboards;

(G-14280)
BIOCER CORPORATION
1 Columbus Ctr Ste 624 (23462-6760)
PHONE....................................757 490-7851
Irfan Jameel, *Principal*
EMP: 2
SALES (est): 127.3K **Privately Held**
SIC: 2499 Woodenware, kitchen & household

(G-14281)
BIRD FABRICATION LLC
2593 Quality Ct (23454-5319)
PHONE....................................225 614-0985
Michael Bird, *Co-Owner*
Da'teonia Joyner, *Co-Owner*
EMP: 2
SALES (est): 86K **Privately Held**
SIC: 3731 Commercial cargo ships, building & repairing; tenders, ships: building & repairing; military ships, building & repairing; commercial passenger ships, building & repairing

(G-14282)
BIRD FABRICATION LLC
2593 Quality Ct Ste 215 (23454-5319)
PHONE....................................225 614-0985
Michael Bird,
EMP: 2
SALES (est): 86K **Privately Held**
SIC: 3731 Shipbuilding & repairing

(G-14283)
BIRDCLOUD CREATIONS
839 S Birdneck Rd (23451-5803)
PHONE....................................757 428-6239
Benjamin Dimartino, *Partner*
Frances Dimartino, *Partner*

EMP: 2
SALES (est): 232.6K **Privately Held**
SIC: 2221 Comforters & quilts, manmade fiber & silk

(G-14284)
BIZCARD XPRESS
3780 Virginia Beach Blvd (23452-3414)
PHONE....................................757 340-4525
Chip Cohen, *Principal*
EMP: 2
SALES (est): 112.9K **Privately Held**
WEB: www.bizcardva.com
SIC: 3993 Signs & advertising specialties

(G-14285)
BLAC RAYVEN PUBLICATIONS
1205 Warwick Dr (23453-3020)
PHONE....................................757 512-4617
EMP: 1 EST: 2011
SALES (est): 59K **Privately Held**
SIC: 2741 Misc Publishing

(G-14286)
BLACK MONEY LABEL LLC
3419 Virginia Beach Blvd (23452-4419)
PHONE....................................201 975-5009
Richard Degroat,
EMP: 5
SALES (est): 100K **Privately Held**
SIC: 2782 Record albums

(G-14287)
BLENDED CRE8TIONS LLC
900 Piney Branch Ln # 102 (23451-6774)
PHONE....................................347 323-2982
Jennifer Rivera,
EMP: 1
SALES (est): 39.7K **Privately Held**
SIC: 3231 Decorated glassware: chipped, engraved, etched, etc.

(G-14288)
BLOOD SWEAT & CHEER
1257 Treefern Dr (23451-6612)
PHONE....................................757 620-1515
Hautau Lachance, *Principal*
EMP: 1
SALES (est): 53.8K **Privately Held**
SIC: 2396 Screen printing on fabric articles

(G-14289)
BLUE CASTLE CUPCAKES LLC
2453 Blue Castle Ln (23454-1921)
PHONE....................................757 618-0600
Sara Rabiner, *Principal*
EMP: 4
SALES (est): 229.4K **Privately Held**
SIC: 2051 Bread, cake & related products

(G-14290)
BMZ USA INC
1429 Miller Store Rd (23455-3324)
PHONE....................................757 821-8494
Sven Bauer, *President*
Kai Th Schoffler, *Managing Dir*
Chuck Pokonosky, *Vice Pres*
◆ EMP: 10
SALES (est): 698.9K
SALES (corp-wide): 465.9MM **Privately Held**
WEB: www.bmz-usa.com
SIC: 3691 Lead acid batteries (storage batteries)
PA: Bmz Holding Gmbh
   Zeche Gustav 1
   Karlstein A. Main 63791
   618 899-560

(G-14291)
BOARD ROOM SOFTWARE INC
1488 Sandbridge Rd (23456-4024)
PHONE....................................757 721-3900
Fax: 757 426-0935
EMP: 2 EST: 1997
SALES (est): 160K **Privately Held**
SIC: 7372 Prepackaged Software Services

(G-14292)
BODYZONE L L C
Also Called: Massaged For You
3734 E Stratford Rd (23455-2928)
PHONE....................................770 922-0700
Jennette D Royster,
EMP: 1
SQ FT: 700

SALES (est): 68.1K **Privately Held**
WEB: www.bodyzone.com
SIC: 3999 Massage machines, electric: barber & beauty shops

(G-14293)
BOOKMARKS BY BULGER
1736 Jude Ct (23464-6542)
PHONE....................................757 362-6841
Sharon Bulger, *Owner*
EMP: 1 EST: 2016
SALES (est): 39.6K **Privately Held**
SIC: 3999 Manufacturing industries

(G-14294)
BOOMIN BASS GLOBAL LLC
Also Called: B.B.G.
2324 Kilburton Priory Ct (23456-5254)
PHONE....................................757 776-8668
Talawrence Sims, *CEO*
EMP: 12
SALES (est): 413.8K **Privately Held**
SIC: 3861 7819 3931 5961 Sound recording & reproducing equipment, motion picture; sound (effects & music production), motion picture; musical instruments, electric & electronic; record &/or tape (music or video) club, mail order; recording studio, noncommercial records

(G-14295)
BOSAN LLC
701 Lynnhaven Pkwy (23452-7299)
PHONE....................................757 340-0822
EMP: 1
SALES (est): 67.4K **Privately Held**
SIC: 3171 Womens Handbags And Purses, Nsk

(G-14296)
BOSS LAIDE EXPRESS LLC
4445 Corp Ln Ste 264 (23462)
PHONE....................................804 263-8759
Dominique Alexus Berry,
EMP: 1
SALES (est): 67.8K **Privately Held**
SIC: 3537 Trucks: freight, baggage, etc.: industrial, except mining

(G-14297)
BOW WOW BUNKIES AND OTHER SIGN
887 Bamberg Pl (23453-3201)
PHONE....................................757 650-0158
Joyce J Carol, *Principal*
EMP: 1
SALES (est): 49.5K **Privately Held**
SIC: 3993 Signs & advertising specialties

(G-14298)
BOWWOWMEOW BAKING COMPANY LLC
4308 Lookout Rd (23455-1521)
PHONE....................................757 636-7922
Amy J Jordan, *Administration*
EMP: 5 EST: 2015
SALES (est): 261.4K **Privately Held**
SIC: 2051 Bread, cake & related products

(G-14299)
BROAD BAY COTTON COMPANY
2601 Reliance Dr Ste 101 (23452-7833)
PHONE....................................757 227-4101
James D Marx, *President*
▲ EMP: 7
SQ FT: 27,000
SALES (est): 1.3MM **Privately Held**
WEB: www.broadbaycotton.com
SIC: 2674 2393 Bags: uncoated paper & multiwall; textile bags

(G-14300)
BROOKE PRINTING
4749 Eldon Ct (23462-7229)
PHONE....................................757 617-2188
Gary Johnson, *Owner*
EMP: 1
SALES (est): 82.9K **Privately Held**
SIC: 2759 Commercial printing

(G-14301)
BROTHERS PRINTING
Also Called: Brothers Impressions
3320 Virginia Beach Blvd # 4 (23452-5621)
PHONE....................................757 431-2656
Glenn Jennar, *President*
Richard Jones, *President*
EMP: 10
SQ FT: 2,700
SALES (est): 1.3MM **Privately Held**
WEB: www.brothersprintingusa.com
SIC: 2752 7389 Commercial printing, offset; printing broker

(G-14302)
BROWN & DUNCAN LLC
5960 Jake Sears Cir (23464-5120)
PHONE....................................832 844-6523
Natasha Brown,
EMP: 2
SALES (est): 59.2K **Privately Held**
SIC: 2741 7389 8742 8999 Miscellaneous publishing; design services; marketing consulting services; commercial & literary writings

(G-14303)
BRYANT EMBROIDERY LLC
Also Called: Embroidme Virginia Beach
3018 Virginia Beach Blvd (23452-6904)
PHONE....................................757 498-3453
Stephanie Bryant, *General Mgr*
Jason Bryant, *Office Mgr*
EMP: 2
SQ FT: 2,900
SALES (est): 159.3K **Privately Held**
WEB: www.embroidme.com
SIC: 2759 2396 2261 2395 Screen printing; screen printing on fabric articles; screen printing of cotton broadwoven fabrics; embroidery & art needlework; advertising, promotional & trade show services

(G-14304)
BRYCE K LONG
3685 Muddy Creek Rd (23456-4134)
PHONE....................................757 510-1748
Bryce K Long, *Principal*
EMP: 1
SALES (est): 50.2K **Privately Held**
SIC: 2741 Miscellaneous publishing

(G-14305)
BUDDY D LTD
Also Called: Tops By George
2940 Buccaneer Rd (23451-1510)
PHONE....................................757 481-7619
George F Dashiell, *President*
EMP: 5
SALES (est): 600K **Privately Held**
WEB: www.marinecanvastopsbygeorge.com
SIC: 2394 7699 Convertible tops, canvas or boat: from purchased materials; boat repair

(G-14306)
BURGESS SNYDER INDUSTRIES INC
Also Called: Burgess Snyder Window Co
560 Baker Rd (23462-1699)
PHONE....................................757 490-3131
Linda Sawyer, *President*
Bill Becraft, *Superintendent*
Jed Gunter, *Superintendent*
Charles T Vaughan, *Chairman*
Chris Johnson, *Vice Pres*
EMP: 30 EST: 1948
SQ FT: 25,000
SALES (est): 7.3MM **Privately Held**
WEB: www.burgess-snyder.com
SIC: 2431 5031 5211 1751 Windows & window parts & trim, wood; doors & door parts & trim, wood; doors & windows; door & window products; window & door (prefabricated) installation; products of purchased glass; nonresidential construction

(G-14307)
BURTON TELECOM LLC
1637 Independence Blvd (23455-4038)
PHONE....................................757 230-6520
Stacey Burton, *Principal*
Tracy Jones, *Principal*
EMP: 2

SALES (est): 142.2K **Privately Held**
WEB: www.burtontelecom.com
SIC: 3674 1731 7382 7622 Semiconductors & related devices; safety & security specialization; protective devices, security; intercommunication equipment repair

(G-14308)
C H J DIGITAL REPRO
223 Expressway Ct (23462-6526)
PHONE.............................757 473-0234
Christi Felter, *Owner*
EMP: 9
SALES (est): 686.9K **Privately Held**
SIC: 2752 Commercial printing, offset

(G-14309)
CABINET LIFTS UNLIMITED
2500 Squadron Ct Ste 102 (23453-3161)
PHONE.............................757 641-9431
Sharon Nelson, *Principal*
EMP: 2
SALES (est): 130K **Privately Held**
SIC: 3429 Cabinet hardware

(G-14310)
CABINET SAVER LLC
3212 Inlet Shore Ct (23451-1292)
PHONE.............................757 969-9839
Skyler Thomas,
EMP: 2
SALES (est): 117.7K **Privately Held**
WEB: www.cabinetcondom.com
SIC: 2541 Cabinets, lockers & shelving

(G-14311)
CAMERON CHEMICALS INC (PA)
Also Called: Cameron Micronutrients
4530 Prof Cir Ste 201 (23455)
PHONE.............................757 487-0656
Robert Bowen, *President*
John Bowen, *Vice Pres*
Mark Whitfield, *CFO*
Brandon Williams, *Sales Staff*
James Bowen, *Admin Sec*
◆ EMP: 15
SQ FT: 88,000
SALES (est): 7.6MM **Privately Held**
WEB: www.cameronchemicals.com
SIC: 2875 Fertilizers, mixing only

(G-14312)
CANADA DRY POTOMAC CORPORATION
1400 Air Rail Ave (23455-3002)
PHONE.............................757 464-1771
EMP: 55
SALES (corp-wide): 79.2MM **Privately Held**
WEB: www.cdpotomac.com
SIC: 2086 Bottled & canned soft drinks
PA: Canada Dry Potomac Corporation
3600 Pennsy Dr
Hyattsville MD 20785
301 773-5500

(G-14313)
CANDLESTICK BAKER INC
1804 Saranac Ct (23453-3726)
PHONE.............................757 761-4473
EMP: 2
SALES (est): 26.3K **Privately Held**
SIC: 3999 Manufacturing Industries, Nec, Nsk

(G-14314)
CANVAS & EARTH
508 Aylesbury Dr Apt 103 (23462-7152)
PHONE.............................757 995-6529
Robert Karl, *Principal*
EMP: 2
SALES (est): 52.7K **Privately Held**
SIC: 2394 Canvas & related products

(G-14315)
CAPER HOLDINGS LLC
577 Sandbridge Rd Ste B (23456-4536)
P.O. Box 6331 (23456-0331)
PHONE.............................757 563-3810
John Pietrzak, *Principal*
EMP: 5
SQ FT: 200

SALES (est): 379.7K **Privately Held**
WEB: www.caperholdings.com
SIC: 7372 7371 8731 Application computer software; custom computer programming services; commercial physical research

(G-14316)
CAPITAL CONCRETE INC
400 Stapleton (23456)
P.O. Box 1137, Norfolk (23501-1137)
PHONE.............................757 627-0630
Sarah Beasley, *Vice Pres*
EMP: 2
SALES (corp-wide): 11.7MM **Privately Held**
WEB: www.capitalconcreteinc.com
SIC: 3273 Ready-mixed concrete
PA: Capital Concrete, Inc.
400 Stapleton St
Norfolk VA 23504
757 627-0630

(G-14317)
CAPPS BOATWORKS INC
2102 W Great Neck Rd (23451-1504)
PHONE.............................757 496-0311
Nelva Capps, *President*
EMP: 8
SALES (est): 552.3K **Privately Held**
WEB: www.cappsboatworks.com
SIC: 3731 Shipbuilding & repairing

(G-14318)
CAPSTONE EMB & SCREEN PRTG
Also Called: Capstone E & S
3005 Glastonbury Dr (23453-5526)
PHONE.............................757 619-0457
Charnette Cade, *Owner*
EMP: 3
SALES (est): 40K **Privately Held**
SIC: 2395 Pleating & stitching

(G-14319)
CAPTN JOEYS CUSTOM CANVAS
1081 Old Dam Neck Rd (23454-5715)
PHONE.............................757 270-8772
John Weinbrecht, *Principal*
EMP: 1 EST: 2007
SALES (est): 64.9K **Privately Held**
SIC: 2211 Canvas

(G-14320)
CAROCON
1357 Taylor Farm Rd (23453-3142)
PHONE.............................804 324-2207
EMP: 3
SALES (est): 262.3K **Privately Held**
SIC: 2653 Boxes, corrugated: made from purchased materials

(G-14321)
CAROLINA CONTAINER CO INC
1357 Taylor Farm Rd (23453-3142)
PHONE.............................804 458-4700
EMP: 3
SALES (est): 205.9K **Privately Held**
WEB: www.carolinacontainer.com
SIC: 2653 Boxes, corrugated: made from purchased materials

(G-14322)
CASEY UNIQUE TRANSPORT SVCS
1533 Lone Oak Ct Apt 107 (23454-4793)
PHONE.............................757 354-7626
Nadira Casey, *CEO*
EMP: 1
SALES (est): 100K **Privately Held**
SIC: 3537 Truck trailers, used in plants, docks, terminals, etc.

(G-14323)
CATALDO INDUSTRIES LLC
4314 Virginia Beach Blvd (23452-1238)
PHONE.............................757 422-0518
Anthony Cataldo, *Principal*
EMP: 12
SALES (est): 1.2MM **Privately Held**
SIC: 3999 Manufacturing industries

(G-14324)
CATAPULT VIDEO
4636 Haygood Rd (23455-5436)
PHONE.............................540 642-9947
William Sykes, *Administration*
EMP: 2
SALES (est): 81.4K **Privately Held**
SIC: 3599 Catapults

(G-14325)
CAVALIER VENTURES LLC
300 32nd St Ste 500 (23451-2968)
PHONE.............................757 491-3000
D Brian Carson, *CFO*
Kelly Dasinger, *Admin Sec*
EMP: 15
SQ FT: 6,487
SALES (est): 639.5K **Privately Held**
SIC: 2085 Distilled & blended liquors

(G-14326)
CBD LIVITY
2733 Sandpiper Rd (23456-4516)
PHONE.............................571 215-1938
Savana Griffith, *Principal*
EMP: 2
SALES (est): 112.9K **Privately Held**
SIC: 3999

(G-14327)
CEDAR LANE FARMS LLC
1836 Pittsburg Lndg (23464-8768)
PHONE.............................757 335-0830
Martha Timberlake,
EMP: 1
SALES (est): 92.6K **Privately Held**
SIC: 3999 Candles; Christmas tree ornaments, except electrical & glass; plants, artificial & preserved

(G-14328)
CEF ENTERPRISES INC
121 Tower Dr (23462-3528)
PHONE.............................757 478-4359
Maureen Acosta, *President*
Roy Lim, *Director*
▲ EMP: 2
SALES (est): 172.9K **Privately Held**
SIC: 3589 Cooking equipment, commercial

(G-14329)
CEOTRONICS INC
512 S Lynnhven Rd Ste 104 (23452)
PHONE.............................757 549-6220
Thomas Gunther, *President*
Gina Millett, *Finance*
Laurence G Cohen, *Admin Sec*
EMP: 5
SQ FT: 11,000
SALES (est): 1.1MM
SALES (corp-wide): 26.5MM **Privately Held**
WEB: www.ceotronics.com
SIC: 3661 Communication headgear, telephone
PA: Ceotronics Ag Audio . Video . Data Communication
Adam-Opel-Str. 6
Rodermark 63322
607 487-510

(G-14330)
CERRAHYAN PUBLISHING INC
2404 Virginia Beach Blvd (23454-4059)
PHONE.............................757 589-1462
Alis Cerrahyan, *Principal*
EMP: 1
SALES (est): 37.5K **Privately Held**
SIC: 2741 Miscellaneous publishing

(G-14331)
CHARLES CONTRACTING CO INC (PA)
Also Called: Atlas Concrete
2821 Crusader Cir (23453-3133)
PHONE.............................757 422-9989
Charles R Pitts Jr, *President*
Peggy Pitts, *Corp Secy*
Charles Pitts, *Branch Mgr*
EMP: 4
SALES (est): 4MM **Privately Held**
WEB: www.atlasconcreteva.com
SIC: 3273 Ready-mixed concrete

(G-14332)
CHEF JOSEPHS KICK SAUCE LLC
1728 Virginia Beach Blvd (23454-4533)
PHONE.............................757 525-1744
Darrell Anderson, *CEO*
EMP: 1 EST: 2014
SQ FT: 3,000
SALES (est): 74.8K **Privately Held**
WEB: www.chefjosephskicksauce.com
SIC: 2035 Pickles, sauces & salad dressings

(G-14333)
CHESAPEAKE BAY CONTROLS INC
Also Called: Beach Controls
533 Gleneagle Dr (23462-4552)
PHONE.............................757 228-5537
Chris Hehl, *Owner*
EMP: 10
SALES (est): 1MM **Privately Held**
WEB: www.chesapeakecontrols.com
SIC: 3491 Automatic regulating & control valves

(G-14334)
CHESAPEAKE BAY DISTILLERY LLC
437 Virginia Beach Blvd (23451-3442)
PHONE.............................757 692-4083
Christopher Richeson, *Mng Member*
EMP: 1
SALES (est): 35.4K **Privately Held**
WEB: www.chesapeakebaydistillery.com
SIC: 2085 Distilled & blended liquors

(G-14335)
CHESAPEAKE COATINGS
4109 Cheswick Ln (23455-6560)
PHONE.............................757 945-2812
Michael Popina, *Principal*
EMP: 2
SALES (est): 152.3K **Privately Held**
SIC: 3479 Metal coating & allied service

(G-14336)
CHEW ON THIS GLUTEN FREE FOODS
3813 Coyote Cir (23456-4961)
PHONE.............................757 440-3757
Marlyn Doering, *Principal*
EMP: 3
SALES (est): 182.9K **Privately Held**
WEB: www.chewonthisglutenfreefoods.com
SIC: 2099 Food preparations

(G-14337)
CHICK LIT LLC
1768 Templeton Ln (23454-3059)
PHONE.............................757 496-9019
Wayne Richmon, *Principal*
EMP: 2
SALES (est): 105.4K **Privately Held**
SIC: 3999 Candles

(G-14338)
CHRIS KENNEDY PUBLISHING LLC
2052 Bierce Dr (23454-7216)
PHONE.............................757 689-2021
Kennedy Christopher, *Principal*
EMP: 2
SALES (est): 50K **Privately Held**
SIC: 2741 Miscellaneous publishing

(G-14339)
CHURCH GUIDE
293 Independence Blvd # 516 (23462-5466)
PHONE.............................757 285-2222
Ray Boetcher, *Exec Dir*
EMP: 5 EST: 2015
SALES (est): 145.6K **Privately Held**
SIC: 2711 Newspapers, publishing & printing

(G-14340)
CJC INDUSTRIES INC
3813 Princess Anne Rd (23456-1973)
PHONE.............................757 227-6767
EMP: 2 EST: 2014
SALES (est): 81.7K **Privately Held**
SIC: 3999 Manufacturing industries

(G-14341)
CK SERVICE INC
3966 Seeman Rd (23452-2459)
PHONE..................................757 486-5880
Cho K Lau, *Principal*
EMP: 1
SALES (est): 80K **Privately Held**
SIC: 3585 Heating & air conditioning combination units

(G-14342)
CLARKE B GRAY
Also Called: Advance Graphics
1069 Dam Neck Rd (23454-5116)
PHONE..................................757 426-7227
Gray B Clarke, *President*
EMP: 5
SALES (est): 390K **Privately Held**
SIC: 2759 3993 Screen printing; signs & advertising specialties

(G-14343)
CLYDE D SEELEY SR
5864 Fitztown Rd (23457-1307)
PHONE..................................757 721-6397
Clyde C Seeley, *Owner*
Dedra Seeley, *Senior VP*
EMP: 2
SALES (est): 108.7K **Privately Held**
SIC: 7692 Welding repair

(G-14344)
COASTAL CABINETS BY JENNA LLC
1017 Laskin Rd Ste 101 (23451-6477)
PHONE..................................757 339-0710
Jenna Ross Boseman, *Administration*
EMP: 2 EST: 2016
SALES (est): 142.4K **Privately Held**
SIC: 2434 Wood kitchen cabinets

(G-14345)
COASTAL EDGE
353 Village Rd (23454-4373)
PHONE..................................757 422-5739
EMP: 4 EST: 2012
SALES (est): 184K **Privately Held**
WEB: www.shop.coastaledge.com
SIC: 3949 Skateboards

(G-14346)
COASTAL LEAK DETECTION
2532 Peritan Rd (23454-3319)
PHONE..................................757 486-0180
Nichols Cameron, *Principal*
EMP: 2 EST: 2007
SALES (est): 207K **Privately Held**
WEB: www.coastalleakdetection.com
SIC: 3599 Water leak detectors

(G-14347)
COASTAL SAFETY INC
Also Called: Balco Sign & Safety
5045 Admiral Wright Rd (23462-2523)
PHONE..................................757 499-9415
Greg Brickles, *President*
Renee Brickles, *Admin Sec*
EMP: 2
SQ FT: 2,300
SALES (est): 227.2K **Privately Held**
WEB: www.balcosignandsafety.com
SIC: 3993 Signs, not made in custom sign painting shops

(G-14348)
COASTAL TAGS & SUPPLY LLC
133 Thames Dr (23452-1605)
PHONE..................................757 995-4139
Robert Keenoy, *Principal*
Jennifer Frankenburg, *Administration*
EMP: 1 EST: 2016
SALES (est): 72.6K **Privately Held**
WEB: www.coastalsupplyusa.com
SIC: 3579 Addressing machines, plates & plate embossers

(G-14349)
COASTAL THREADS INC
750 Lord Dunmore Dr # 101 (23464-2627)
PHONE..................................757 495-2677
Karen Savage, *President*
EMP: 8
SQ FT: 2,000

SALES (est): 700.9K **Privately Held**
WEB: www.coastalthreadsembroidery.com
SIC: 2395 2396 Embroidery products, except schiffli machine; automotive & apparel trimmings

(G-14350)
CODE BLUE
5689 Brandon Blvd (23464-6546)
PHONE..................................757 438-1507
Erik Cope, *Principal*
EMP: 2
SALES (est): 78K **Privately Held**
SIC: 7372 Prepackaged software

(G-14351)
COE & CO INC
5008 Cleveland St (23462-2504)
PHONE..................................757 497-7709
Richard N Coe Jr, *President*
Richard N Coe, *President*
EMP: 3
SQ FT: 3,000
SALES (est): 500K **Privately Held**
SIC: 3715 Trailer bodies

(G-14352)
COGO AIRE LLC
5521 Haden Rd (23455-3118)
PHONE..................................757 332-3551
Gerald L Covert Jr,
EMP: 3
SALES (est): 210K **Privately Held**
SIC: 3585 Refrigeration & heating equipment

(G-14353)
COLONIAL BARNS INC
985 S Military Hwy (23464-3511)
PHONE..................................757 420-8653
Frank Travis, *Branch Mgr*
EMP: 2
SALES (corp-wide): 3.1MM **Privately Held**
WEB: www.colonialbarns.com
SIC: 3448 Prefabricated metal buildings
PA: Colonial Barns, Inc.
953 Bedford St
Chesapeake VA 23322
757 482-2234

(G-14354)
COLONIAL EAST DISTRIBUTORS LLC
413 Davis St Ste 107 (23462-5673)
PHONE..................................844 802-4427
Scott Regina,
EMP: 2
SALES (est): 107.8K **Privately Held**
WEB: www.colonialcigar.com
SIC: 3999 Tobacco pipes, pipestems & bits

(G-14355)
COMBAT COATING
851 Seahawk Cir Ste 108 (23452-7828)
PHONE..................................757 468-9020
Jamie Spears, *President*
EMP: 2
SALES (est): 134.5K **Privately Held**
SIC: 3479 Metal coating & allied service

(G-14356)
COMBAT COATINGS LLC
1132 Little Neck Rd (23452-6039)
PHONE..................................757 468-9020
John Kuchta Jr,
EMP: 8 EST: 1997
SALES (est): 734.4K **Privately Held**
WEB: www.combatcoatings.com
SIC: 3999 Sprays, artificial & preserved

(G-14357)
COMMERCIAL COPIES
Also Called: C H J Commercial Copies
223 Expressway Ct (23462-6526)
PHONE..................................757 473-0234
Cristi Felter, *President*
EMP: 9
SQ FT: 1,700
SALES (est): 630K **Privately Held**
SIC: 2759 7389 Commercial printing; printing broker

(G-14358)
COMMERCIAL PRTG DRECT MAIL SVC
208 16th St (23451-3402)
P.O. Box 9211 (23450-9211)
PHONE..................................757 422-0606
W E Vasile, *President*
EMP: 3
SQ FT: 1,400
SALES (est): 315.2K **Privately Held**
SIC: 2752 7331 2759 Commercial printing, offset; direct mail advertising services; commercial printing

(G-14359)
CONCRETE CREATIONS INC
3601 Dam Neck Rd (23453-2618)
PHONE..................................757 427-6226
David Italiano, *President*
EMP: 8
SQ FT: 3,411 **Privately Held**
WEB: www.concretecreationsvabeach.com
SIC: 3281 Monuments, cut stone (not finishing or lettering only)
PA: Concrete Creations, Inc.
1601 Nanneys Creek Rd
Virginia Beach VA 23457

(G-14360)
CONCRETE CREATIONS INC (PA)
1601 Nanneys Creek Rd (23457-1425)
PHONE..................................757 427-1581
David Italiano, *President*
Teressa Italiano, *Admin Sec*
EMP: 2
SALES (est): 1MM **Privately Held**
WEB: www.concretecreationsvabeach.com
SIC: 3281 Monuments, cut stone (not finishing or lettering only)

(G-14361)
CONSURGO GROUP INC
1452 Taylor Farm Rd # 103 (23453-3147)
PHONE..................................757 373-1717
Robert J Richardson, *CEO*
Doris Richardson, *Vice Pres*
EMP: 10
SALES (est): 65.8K **Privately Held**
WEB: www.consurgogroup.com
SIC: 2395 5046 Embroidery products, except schiffli machine; commercial cooking & food service equipment

(G-14362)
CONTOUR HEALER LLC
1117 Ditchley Rd (23451-3758)
PHONE..................................757 288-6671
Allen Trey White, *President*
EMP: 1
SALES (est): 147.4K **Privately Held**
WEB: www.contourhealer.com
SIC: 3843 5047 5999 7389 Teeth, artificial (not made in dental laboratories); dentists' professional supplies; hospital equipment & supplies;

(G-14363)
CONTROLS CORPORATION AMERICA
Also Called: Concoa America
1501 Harpers Rd (23454-5303)
PHONE..................................757 422-8330
Sander G Dukas, *President*
Charlie Brown, *Business Mgr*
John Cannestro, *Business Mgr*
Robert D Devenio, *Corp Secy*
Ryan Johnson, *Vice Pres*
▲ EMP: 130
SQ FT: 110,000
SALES (est): 37.7MM **Privately Held**
WEB: www.concoa.com
SIC: 3823 3491 3625 3548 Pressure measurement instruments, industrial; flow instruments, industrial process type; pressure valves & regulators, industrial; gas valves & parts, industrial; relays & industrial controls; welding apparatus

(G-14364)
COPY THAT PRINT LLC
474 N Witchduck Rd (23462-1943)
PHONE..................................757 642-3301
Crystal Hale, *Principal*
EMP: 2

SALES (est): 83.9K **Privately Held**
SIC: 2752 Commercial printing, lithographic

(G-14365)
CORE BUSINESS TECHNOLOGIES INC
2485 Las Brisas Dr (23456-4281)
PHONE..................................757 426-0344
EMP: 4 EST: 2003
SALES (est): 260K **Privately Held**
SIC: 3571 3357 5045 5734 Whole Sale Of Fiber Optics Computer And Equipment Cables/ Telephone Software

(G-14366)
CORE ENABLE LLC
703 26th St (23451-4027)
PHONE..................................757 375-4434
Bret Eugene Fisher, *Administration*
EMP: 2
SALES (est): 165.3K **Privately Held**
WEB: www.coreenable.com
SIC: 7372 Prepackaged software

(G-14367)
COREY VEREEN
Also Called: Ctv Candles
1311 Riviera Dr (23464-5026)
PHONE..................................609 468-5409
Corey Vereen, *Owner*
EMP: 2
SALES (est): 43.7K **Privately Held**
SIC: 3999 7389 Candles;

(G-14368)
COVERED INC
205 First Clnl Rd Ste 117 (23454)
PHONE..................................757 463-0434
Michael Dabero, *President*
Joseph Igana, *Treasurer*
EMP: 10
SALES (est): 1.4MM **Privately Held**
WEB: www.coveredusa.com
SIC: 3949 Sporting & athletic goods

(G-14369)
COZY CATERPILLARS
5404 Trumpet Vine Ct (23462-7176)
PHONE..................................757 499-3769
Mary Sutherland, *Principal*
EMP: 1
SALES (est): 60K **Privately Held**
SIC: 3531 Construction machinery

(G-14370)
CRAWL SPACE DOOR SYSTEM INC
3700 Shore Dr Ste 101 (23455-2967)
PHONE..................................757 363-0005
William Sykes, *President*
Sykes Frances H, *Vice Pres*
Chris Qualtieri, *Warehouse Mgr*
▲ EMP: 2
SALES (est): 371.8K **Privately Held**
WEB: www.crawlspacedoors.com
SIC: 3089 3826 Doors, folding: plastic or plastic coated fabric; moisture analyzers

(G-14371)
CREATIVE IMPRESSIONS INC
796 Coverdale Ct (23452-3849)
PHONE..................................757 855-2187
Donald Miller, *President*
EMP: 3
SQ FT: 4,500
SALES (est): 250K **Privately Held**
SIC: 2759 3087 Screen printing; custom compound purchased resins

(G-14372)
CROCHET BY PALM LLC
1617 Rollins Ct (23454-6206)
PHONE..................................757 427-0532
Kaitsuda Dickerson, *Principal*
EMP: 2 EST: 2014
SALES (est): 121.8K **Privately Held**
SIC: 2399 Hand woven & crocheted products

(G-14373)
CROUCH PETRA
Also Called: Honor & Pride
6100 Tradewinds Ct (23464-4403)
PHONE..................................757 681-0828

Petra Crouch, *Owner*
EMP: 2
SALES (est): 82K **Privately Held**
SIC: 2395 Embroidery & art needlework

(G-14374)
CROWN ENTERPRISE LLC
1014 Smoke Tree Ln (23452-4862)
PHONE..............................757 277-8837
EMP: 2
SALES (est): 140.4K **Privately Held**
SIC: 3861 Motion picture film

(G-14375)
CRUNCHY HYDRATION LLC
1805 Kempsville Rd (23464-6802)
PHONE..............................757 362-1607
Megan Riggs, *Principal*
EMP: 1
SALES (est): 39.5K **Privately Held**
WEB: www.crunchyhydration.com
SIC: 2086 Bottled & canned soft drinks

(G-14376)
CUSTOM COUNTER FITTERS INC
1901 Thunderbird Dr (23454-2310)
PHONE..............................757 288-4730
Richard Allred, *Principal*
EMP: 4
SALES (est): 554.6K **Privately Held**
SIC: 3131 Counters

(G-14377)
CUSTOM EMBROIDERY & DESIGNS
Also Called: Pecher Enterprises
713 Vanderbilt Ave (23451-3632)
PHONE..............................757 474-1523
Nancy Peche, *President*
Nancy Pecher, *Owner*
EMP: 2
SALES (est): 100K **Privately Held**
SIC: 2395 Embroidery products, except schiffli machine

(G-14378)
CUSTOM TOPS INC
4940 Rutherford Rd # 209 (23455-4000)
PHONE..............................757 460-3084
Robert W Tyer, *President*
EMP: 2
SQ FT: 1,100
SALES (est): 130K **Privately Held**
WEB: www.customtops.net
SIC: 2394 5199 5999 Canvas boat seats; convertible tops, canvas or boat: from purchased materials; awnings, fabric: made from purchased materials; canvas products; canvas products

(G-14379)
D & M WOODWORKS
5720 Attica Ave (23455-4607)
PHONE..............................757 510-3600
David Aurillo, *Principal*
EMP: 1 **EST:** 2019
SALES (est): 54.1K **Privately Held**
SIC: 2431 Millwork

(G-14380)
DACHA
Also Called: Dacha Systems Installation Svc
966 Lord Dunmore Dr (23464-5450)
P.O. Box 5215 (23471-0215)
PHONE..............................757 754-2805
John Paul Tapscott, *Owner*
EMP: 1
SALES (est): 80K **Privately Held**
SIC: 3669 Communications equipment

(G-14381)
DAE PRINT & DESIGN
223 Expressway Ct (23462-6526)
PHONE..............................757 518-1774
EMP: 5
SALES (est): 333.1K **Privately Held**
WEB: www.daeprint.com
SIC: 2752 Commercial printing, offset

(G-14382)
DAE PRINT & DESIGN
Also Called: Chj Digital Repro
223 Expressway Ct (23462-6526)
PHONE..............................757 473-0234

Christy Felter, *President*
Trevor Goins, *Broker*
Dawn Lewandowski,
EMP: 13
SQ FT: 6,000
SALES (est): 2.1MM **Privately Held**
WEB: www.daeprint.com
SIC: 2752 Commercial printing, offset

(G-14383)
DAILY PEPRAH & PARTNERS SERVIC
138 S Rosemont Rd Ste 209 (23452-4366)
PHONE..............................757 581-6452
Dana Peprah, *Principal*
EMP: 3 **EST:** 2008
SALES (est): 137.2K **Privately Held**
SIC: 2711 Newspapers, publishing & printing

(G-14384)
DAL PUBLISHING
948 Bingham St (23451-5944)
PHONE..............................757 422-6577
Debra Livelli, *Owner*
▲ **EMP:** 1
SALES (est): 55K **Privately Held**
WEB: www.myhomekit.net
SIC: 2741 Miscellaneous publishing

(G-14385)
DAN MILES & ASSOCIATES LLC
Also Called: Custom Printing & Vinyl
1303 Lakeside Rd (23455-4107)
PHONE..............................619 508-0430
Daniel Miles,
EMP: 1
SALES (est): 63.5K **Privately Held**
SIC: 2752 Commercial printing, lithographic

(G-14386)
DANNYS TOOLS LLC
2061 White Water Dr (23456-6177)
PHONE..............................757 282-6229
Danny Matthews, *Principal*
EMP: 3 **EST:** 2015
SALES (est): 98.6K **Privately Held**
SIC: 3599 Industrial machinery

(G-14387)
DARR MARITIME SERVICES
3332 Regent Park Walk (23452-6256)
PHONE..............................757 631-0022
EMP: 1
SALES (est): 92.9K **Privately Held**
SIC: 3731 Shipbuilding & repairing

(G-14388)
DATAHAVEN FOR DYNAMICS LLC
4456 Corporation Ln (23462-3151)
PHONE..............................757 222-2000
Wayne Befus, *VP Finance*
EMP: 2 **EST:** 2011
SALES (est): 91K **Privately Held**
WEB: www.datahaven4dynamics.com
SIC: 7372 Prepackaged software

(G-14389)
DATIS LLC
Also Called: First Class Publishing
925 Brasileno Ct (23456-6443)
PHONE..............................757 961-7498
Winifred D Bragg,
EMP: 1
SALES (est): 63.9K **Privately Held**
SIC: 2741 Miscellaneous publishing

(G-14390)
DATSKAPATAL LOGISTICS LLC
424 Lee Highlands Blvd (23452-6649)
PHONE..............................757 814-7325
Aundra Jenkin, *Mng Member*
EMP: 1 **EST:** 2019
SALES (est): 80K **Privately Held**
SIC: 3537 Trucks: freight, baggage, etc.: industrial, except mining

(G-14391)
DAVID C MAPLE
2518 Hartley St (23456-6554)
PHONE..............................757 563-2423
David Maple, *Principal*
EMP: 1

SALES (est): 41K **Privately Held**
SIC: 3944 Games, toys & children's vehicles

(G-14392)
DAVID F WATERBURY JR
Also Called: A D&G Mobile Welding
4987 Cleveland St Ste 108 (23462-5315)
PHONE..............................757 490-5444
David Waterbury, *Owner*
Gina Bradbury, *Manager*
EMP: 2
SALES (est): 400K **Privately Held**
SIC: 7692 Welding repair

(G-14393)
DAVIS & DAVIS INDUSTRIES LLC
5857 Baynebridge Dr (23464-1554)
PHONE..............................757 269-1534
Michael Davis, *Principal*
EMP: 1
SALES (est): 39.6K **Privately Held**
SIC: 3999 Manufacturing industries

(G-14394)
DAYSPRING PENS LLC
Also Called: Dayspring Pens Norfolk Ci
2697 International Pkwy 120-4 (23452-7858)
PHONE..............................888 694-7367
Daniel Whitehouse, *President*
Lora Dinardo, *Mng Member*
EMP: 5
SQ FT: 1,700
SALES (est): 168.4K **Privately Held**
WEB: www.giftpens.com
SIC: 3951 Fountain pens & fountain pen desk sets

(G-14395)
DC DESIGN AND MEDIA INC
5900 Thurston Ave Ste D (23455-3328)
PHONE..............................757 390-2818
Jennifer Meads, *President*
David Brewer, *Opers Mgr*
EMP: 4 **EST:** 2015
SQ FT: 1,200
SALES (est): 348.9K **Privately Held**
WEB: www.dcdesignandmedia.com
SIC: 3993 Signs & advertising specialties

(G-14396)
DCOMPUTERSCOM
5193 Shore Dr Ste 103 (23455-2500)
PHONE..............................757 460-3324
EMP: 2
SALES (est): 85.9K **Privately Held**
SIC: 3571 Mfg Electronic Computers

(G-14397)
DEES NUTS PEANUT BUTTER
2961 Shore Dr (23451-1248)
PHONE..............................607 437-0189
Diana Dyman, *Principal*
EMP: 2 **EST:** 2016
SALES (est): 62.3K **Privately Held**
SIC: 2099 Peanut butter

(G-14398)
DEEZEL SKATEBOARDS VB LLC
5405 Hatteras Rd (23462-3425)
PHONE..............................757 490-6619
EMP: 2 **EST:** 2007
SALES (est): 91K **Privately Held**
SIC: 3949 Mfg Sporting/Athletic Goods

(G-14399)
DELI-FRESH FOODS INC
1253 Jensen Dr Ste 101 (23451-5995)
PHONE..............................757 428-8126
EMP: 34
SALES (est): 3.1MM
SALES (corp-wide): 4.1MM **Privately Held**
SIC: 2099 Wholesale Mfg And Distributor Sandwiches And Salads
PA: Sun Rayz Products, Inc
　　334 S Hyde Park Ave # 100
　　Tampa FL

(G-14400)
DELMARVA CRANE INC
1616 Deere Ct (23457-1457)
P.O. Box 7044 (23457-0044)
PHONE..............................757 426-0862
Charles A Herzog, *President*
EMP: 1
SALES (est): 144.2K **Privately Held**
SIC: 3531 Cranes

(G-14401)
DELRAND CORP
Also Called: Southern Screen & Graphics
5018 Cleveland St (23462-2530)
PHONE..............................757 490-3355
James De Lutis, *President*
Sara Delutis, *Manager*
EMP: 8
SQ FT: 7,990
SALES (est): 1.3MM **Privately Held**
WEB: www.southernscreen.com
SIC: 2759 2396 2395 Screen printing; automotive & apparel trimmings; pleating & stitching

(G-14402)
DETAS FAMOUS POTATOE SALAD LLC
4643 Georgetown Pl (23455-6224)
PHONE..............................757 609-1130
Deta Green,
EMP: 1
SALES (est): 56.3K **Privately Held**
SIC: 2099 7389 Salads, fresh or refrigerated; business services

(G-14403)
DEVANEZDAYPUBLISHING CO
2220 Sleeper Ct (23456-1273)
PHONE..............................757 493-1634
Zanetta Devane, *Principal*
EMP: 2
SALES (est): 73K **Privately Held**
SIC: 2741 Miscellaneous publishing

(G-14404)
DIFFERENTIAL PRESSURE INSTRS
Also Called: Bartenman Sales
1619 Diamond Springs Rd D (23455-3019)
PHONE..............................757 362-0742
Doug Nicholl, *Vice Pres*
EMP: 2
SALES (corp-wide): 2.1MM **Privately Held**
WEB: www.detroitswitch.com
SIC: 3823 Industrial instrmnts msrmnt display/control process variable
PA: Differential Pressure Instruments, Inc
　　1619 Diamond Springs Rd D
　　Virginia Beach VA 23455
　　757 362-0742

(G-14405)
DIMENSIONS VIRGINIA BEACH INC
371 Phyllis Ct (23452-5627)
PHONE..............................757 340-1115
Jean Higginbotham, *President*
Dana Higginbotham, *Admin Sec*
EMP: 2
SALES (est): 122.1K **Privately Held**
SIC: 3961 Costume jewelry

(G-14406)
DIVERSIFIED ATMOSPHERIC WATER
Also Called: Dawger
2700 Avenger Dr Ste 103b (23452-7394)
P.O. Box 9154 (23450-9154)
PHONE..............................757 617-1782
EMP: 2 **EST:** 2011
SALES (est): 100K **Privately Held**
SIC: 3999 Mfg Misc Products

(G-14407)
DML INDUSTRIES LLC
3200 Dam Neck Rd Ste 104 (23453-2632)
PHONE..............................571 348-4332
Thomas Calhoun Jr,
EMP: 3
SALES (est): 113.3K **Privately Held**
SIC: 2389 7336 Apparel & accessories; commercial art & graphic design

(G-14408)
DODSON LITHO PRINTERS INC
1658 Kempsville Rd (23464-7102)
PHONE..................757 479-4814
Gwen Dodson, *President*
Ronald Dodson, *Vice Pres*
EMP: 4
SALES (est): 200K **Privately Held**
SIC: 2752 Commercial printing, offset

(G-14409)
DOMINION COMPUTER SERVICES
5241 Cleveland St Ste 110 (23462-6548)
PHONE..................757 473-8989
EMP: 4
SQ FT: 2,300
SALES (est): 381.3K **Privately Held**
SIC: 7372 5734 Ret Computer Hardware Software And Software Services

(G-14410)
DOMINION WLDG FABRICATION INC
5361 Meadowside Dr (23455-6690)
PHONE..................757 692-2002
Gloria Ortiz, *President*
EMP: 3
SALES (est): 167K **Privately Held**
SIC: 7692 3731 Welding repair; shipbuilding & repairing

(G-14411)
DONNING PUBLISHERS INC
Also Called: Donning Company Publishers
184 Bsineva Pk Dr Ste 206 (23462)
PHONE..................757 497-1789
Steve Mull, *President*
Barbara Buchanan, *Manager*
EMP: 11 EST: 1974
SQ FT: 2,500
SALES (est): 889.4K
SALES (corp-wide): 296.6MM **Privately Held**
WEB: www.donning.com
SIC: 2741 Miscellaneous publishing
PA: Walsworth Publishing Company, Inc.
306 N Kansas Ave
Marceline MO 64658
660 376-3543

(G-14412)
DOORS DONE RIGHT LLC
1652 Laurel Ln (23451-5969)
PHONE..................757 567-3891
Harrison T Horton, *Principal*
EMP: 2
SALES (est): 97.8K **Privately Held**
WEB: www.doorsdonerightva.com
SIC: 3442 Metal doors, sash & trim

(G-14413)
DRIP PRINTING & DESIGN
617 Jack Rabbit Rd Ste A (23451-6128)
PHONE..................757 962-1594
EMP: 2
SALES (est): 80.6K **Privately Held**
WEB: www.dripprint.com
SIC: 2759 Screen printing

(G-14414)
DRONE TIER SYSTEMS INTL LLC
1309 Eagle Ave (23453-1856)
PHONE..................757 450-7825
Mark Drone, *Principal*
EMP: 2
SALES (est): 76.6K **Privately Held**
SIC: 3721 Motorized aircraft

(G-14415)
DTWELVE ENTERPRISE LLC
Also Called: Dayddream Writing
900 Commonwealth Pl # 200 (23464-4517)
PHONE..................757 837-0452
Latoya Debardelaben, *Vice Pres*
EMP: 1
SQ FT: 800 **Privately Held**
SIC: 2741

(G-14416)
DUDLEY DIX YACHT DESIGN
612 Sandy Springs Ln (23452-3012)
PHONE..................757 962-9273
EMP: 1

(G-14417)
DUDLEY DIX YACHT DESIGN INC
3032 Edinburgh Dr (23452-7004)
PHONE..................757 962-9273
Dudley Dix, *President*
EMP: 2
SALES (est): 60K **Privately Held**
WEB: www.dixdesign.com
SIC: 3732 Boat building & repairing

(G-14418)
DUTCH BARNS
Also Called: Dutch Barns & Gazebos
124 Pennsylvania Ave (23462-2512)
PHONE..................757 497-7356
Raymond Kauffman, *Owner*
EMP: 3 EST: 1975
SQ FT: 880
SALES (est): 262.3K **Privately Held**
WEB: www.vadutchbarns.com
SIC: 2452 5999 Prefabricated buildings, wood; coins

(G-14419)
DW GLOBAL LLC
1528 Taylor Farm Rd # 105 (23453-2980)
PHONE..................757 689-4547
William M Somerindyke Jr,
EMP: 2
SALES (est): 180K **Privately Held**
WEB: www.regulusglobal.com
SIC: 3199 Leather garments

(G-14420)
DYEING TO STITCH
5312 Kempsriver Dr # 102 (23464-5300)
PHONE..................757 366-8740
Ann Robbins, *Mng Member*
Belinda Quigley,
Belinsda Quigley,
Pat R Yan,
EMP: 6
SALES (est): 373.6K **Privately Held**
WEB: www.dyeing2stitch.com
SIC: 2395 Embroidery products, except schiffli machine

(G-14421)
DYNAMIC FABWORKS LLC
2584 Aviator Dr Ste 102 (23453-3174)
PHONE..................757 439-1169
Jake Blankenship, *Mng Member*
EMP: 2
SALES (est): 60K **Privately Held**
SIC: 3499 Machine bases, metal

(G-14422)
DYNAMIC TEAM SPORTS INC
Also Called: Cycle Venture
641 Phoenix Dr (23452-7318)
PHONE..................610 518-3300
James D Samter, *President*
Scott A Samter, *Vice Pres*
EMP: 60
SALES (est): 2.7MM **Privately Held**
WEB: www.dynamicteamsports.com
SIC: 2311 Men's & boys' uniforms

(G-14423)
DYNARIC INC
5925 Thurston Ave (23455-3308)
PHONE..................757 460-3725
Chip Bailess, *Sales Staff*
Tammi Consolini, *Sales Staff*
Dennis Fuller, *Manager*
Carlos Laverde, *Info Tech Mgr*
Steve Long, *Maintence Staff*
EMP: 70
SALES (corp-wide): 60MM **Privately Held**
WEB: www.dynaric.com
SIC: 3089 Bands, plastic
PA: Dynaric Inc.
5740 Bayside Rd
Virginia Beach VA 23455
800 526-0827

(G-14424)
E I DESIGNS POTTERY LLC
5157 Holly Farms Dr (23462-1930)
PHONE..................410 459-3337
Sara Hunter, *Owner*

EMP: 1
SALES (est): 60.3K **Privately Held**
WEB: www.bysarahunter.com
SIC: 3269 7359 3229 3253 Pottery cooking & kitchen articles; dishes, silverware, tables & banquet accessories rental; tableware, glass or glass ceramic; mosaic tile, glazed & unglazed: ceramic

(G-14425)
EAGLE INDUSTRIES UNLIMITED INC (HQ)
2645 Intl Pkwy Ste 102 (23452)
PHONE..................888 343-7547
Stephen M Nolan, *CFO*
John W Carver, *Treasurer*
▲ EMP: 25
SQ FT: 22,000
SALES (est): 72.7MM
SALES (corp-wide): 1.7B **Publicly Held**
WEB: www.eagleindustries.com
SIC: 3842 Bulletproof vests
PA: Vista Outdoor Inc.
1 Vista Way
Anoka MN 55303
763 433-1000

(G-14426)
EAGLE PAPER INTERNATIONAL INC
4605 Pembroke Lake Cir # 100 (23455-6435)
PHONE..................757 363-8103
Jacob Geron, *President*
Angela M Godfrey, *Vice Pres*
Angela Godfrey, *Vice Pres*
Raz Geron, *VP Bus Dvlpt*
◆ EMP: 8
SQ FT: 1,500
SALES (est): 2.5MM **Privately Held**
WEB: www.eaglepaper-intl.com
SIC: 2621 Paper mills

(G-14427)
EARTH FRIENDLY CHEMICALS INC
2585 Horse Pasture Rd # 201 (23453-2993)
PHONE..................757 502-8600
Jamie Welch, *President*
Louis A Isakoff, *Admin Sec*
EMP: 2
SQ FT: 5,000
SALES (est): 270K **Privately Held**
WEB: www.earthfriendlychemicals.com
SIC: 2899 Antifreeze compounds

(G-14428)
EAST COAST BRANDING LLC
2398 Bays Edge Ave (23451-1056)
PHONE..................757 754-0771
Steve Stocks, *Administration*
EMP: 1 EST: 2012
SALES (est): 63K **Privately Held**
WEB: www.epic-made.com
SIC: 2395 Embroidery products, except schiffli machine

(G-14429)
EAST WEST VENTURES LLC
5536 Summer Cres (23462-1965)
PHONE..................757 603-8017
EMP: 1
SALES (est): 61.1K **Privately Held**
WEB: www.upwardbizsolutions.com
SIC: 3993 Signs & advertising specialties

(G-14430)
ECO TECHNOLOGIES
3157 Stonewood Dr (23456-1563)
PHONE..................757 513-4870
EMP: 2
SALES (est): 106K **Privately Held**
WEB: www.etipressurewashing.com
SIC: 3559 Special industry machinery

(G-14431)
EDDY CURRENT TECHNOLOGY INC
Also Called: E C T
2133 E Kendall Cir A (23451-1743)
PHONE..................757 490-1814
EMP: 4
SQ FT: 4,000

SALES (est): 507.9K **Privately Held**
SIC: 3663 3829 Mfg Radio/Tv Communication Equipment Mfg Measuring/Controlling Devices

(G-14432)
EDGE MECHANICAL INC
2429 Bowland Pkwy Ste 115 (23454-5230)
PHONE..................757 228-3540
John S Cherkis, *President*
Robertj Whilden, *Vice Pres*
EMP: 19
SALES (est): 5.6MM **Privately Held**
WEB: www.edgemechanical.com
SIC: 3822 Refrigeration/air-conditioning defrost controls

(G-14433)
EDWARD-COUNCILOR CO INC
1427 Baker Rd (23455-3321)
PHONE..................757 460-2401
William M Edwards, *President*
Charlie Edwards, *Vice Pres*
Thomas R Edwards, *Vice Pres*
EMP: 10
SQ FT: 31,000
SALES (est): 4.2MM **Privately Held**
WEB: www.sanitize.com
SIC: 2819 Industrial inorganic chemicals

(G-14434)
EDWARDS OPTICAL CORPORATION
2441 Windward Shore Dr (23451-1752)
PHONE..................757 496-2550
EMP: 3
SALES: 100K **Privately Held**
SIC: 3827 Mfg & Whol Micro-Miniature Telescopes

(G-14435)
EIGER PRESS
1140 Las Cruces Dr (23454-5752)
PHONE..................757 430-1831
Jeff Andrews, *Principal*
EMP: 1
SALES (est): 53.7K **Privately Held**
SIC: 2741 Miscellaneous publishing

(G-14436)
EILEEN CARLSON
Also Called: Prosperity Publishing
944 S Spigel Dr (23454-1823)
PHONE..................757 339-9900
Eileen Carlson, *Owner*
EMP: 1
SALES (est): 35.9K **Privately Held**
WEB: www.nsnbg.com
SIC: 2741 Miscellaneous publishing

(G-14437)
EL TRAN INVESTMENT CORP
Also Called: Lt Global Trading
5449 N Sunland Dr (23464-4040)
PHONE..................757 439-8111
Eric Tran, *Principal*
EMP: 3
SALES (est): 163.1K **Privately Held**
SIC: 2321 5632 5651 5137 Uniform shirts: made from purchased materials; women's accessory & specialty stores; family clothing stores; unisex clothing stores; uniforms, women's & children's; uniform hats & caps

(G-14438)
ELEMENT FITNESS- LLC
2309 Kingbird Ln (23455-1550)
PHONE..................540 820-4200
EMP: 2 EST: 2016
SALES (est): 74.4K **Privately Held**
SIC: 2819 Elements

(G-14439)
ELEMENT WOODWORKS LLC
2004 Hillsboro Ct (23456-5218)
PHONE..................757 650-9556
Scott Bullock, *Principal*
EMP: 2 EST: 2010
SALES (est): 187.6K **Privately Held**
WEB: www.dhwwoodworks.com
SIC: 2431 Millwork

(G-14440)
ELIZABETH CLAIRE INC
Also Called: Eardley Publications
2100 Mccomas Way Ste 607 (23456-7711)
PHONE..............................757 430-4308
Elizabeth Claire, *President*
EMP: 3
SALES (est): 500K **Privately Held**
WEB: www.elizabethclaire.com
SIC: 2721 Magazines: publishing & printing

(G-14441)
ELIZUR INTERNATIONAL INC
851 Seahawk Cir Ste 102 (23452-7828)
PHONE..............................757 648-8502
EMP: 3 **EST:** 2014
SALES (est): 147.2K **Privately Held**
WEB: www.elizurinc.com
SIC: 3999 Manufacturing industries
PA: Triple-R International Glass Co., Ltd.
No.2, Huaijiang Avenue, Chengnan In-
dustrial Park, Baoying County
Yangzhou

(G-14442)
ELLIOTT LESTSELLE
Also Called: Realdeal Jntral/Floortech Svcs
504 Pheasant Run (23452-8015)
PHONE..............................757 944-8152
Lestselle Elliott, *Owner*
Patricia Elliott, *Principal*
EMP: 3
SALES (est): 171.1K **Privately Held**
SIC: 2676 Sanitary paper products

(G-14443)
EMBROIDER BEE
512 Old Mill Ct (23452-2105)
PHONE..............................757 472-4981
Wright Eileen, *Principal*
EMP: 1
SALES (est): 40.3K **Privately Held**
SIC: 2395 Embroidery & art needlework

(G-14444)
EMBROIDERY N BEYOND LLC
1485 General Booth Blvd # 101
(23454-5102)
PHONE..............................757 962-2105
EMP: 1 **EST:** 2013
SALES (est): 68.4K **Privately Held**
WEB: www.embroiderynbeyond.com
SIC: 2395 Embroidery products, except
schiffli machine

(G-14445)
EMBROIDERY N BEYOND LLC
2728 Saint Charles Ave (23456-6541)
PHONE..............................757 409-2782
EMP: 1
SALES (est): 31.2K **Privately Held**
SIC: 2395 Embroidery & art needlework

(G-14446)
**EMPRESS WORLD PUBLISHING
LLC**
1456 Woodbridge Trl (23453-4719)
PHONE..............................757 471-3806
Sirrico Whitfield, *Administration*
EMP: 2
SALES (est): 92.9K **Privately Held**
WEB: www.empressworldpublishing.com
SIC: 2741 Miscellaneous publishing

(G-14447)
ENCORE PRODUCTS INC
4545 Commerce St # 1906 (23462-3273)
PHONE..............................757 493-8358
Ronald Bublick, *President*
Linda Bublick, *Vice Pres*
EMP: 5 **EST:** 2015
SALES (est): 302.3K **Privately Held**
SIC: 3069 5999 Medical sundries, rubber;
medical apparatus & supplies

(G-14448)
END TO END INC
509 Viking Dr Ste D (23452-7323)
P.O. Box 9018 (23450-9018)
PHONE..............................757 216-1938
Larry C Delone, *CEO*
Kelvin Howard, *President*
Royce Anderson, *CFO*
EMP: 46
SQ FT: 20,000

SALES (est): 6.9MM **Privately Held**
WEB: www.eteinc.com
SIC: 3812 8734 Search & navigation
equipment; testing laboratories

(G-14449)
EPIC MFG LLC
Also Called: Epic Manufacturing
2500 Squadron Ct Ste 106 (23453-3161)
PHONE..............................757 689-4373
Jason Jackson, *Partner*
EMP: 8 **EST:** 2011
SQ FT: 1,300
SALES (est): 550K **Privately Held**
WEB: www.epic-mfg.com
SIC: 3599 3841 5091 5099 Machine
shop, jobbing & repair; surgical & medical
instruments; firearms, sporting; firearms,
except sporting; machine guns & grenade
launchers; machine guns or machine gun
parts, 30 mm. & below

(G-14450)
EQUIPMENT REPAIR SERVICES
6404 Drew Dr (23464-4618)
PHONE..............................757 449-5867
Nelson Garcia, *Owner*
EMP: 1 **EST:** 1997
SALES (est): 42K **Privately Held**
SIC: 1389 Construction, repair & disman-
tling services

(G-14451)
ESSENTIAL ESSENCES
3933 Rainbow Dr (23456-1331)
PHONE..............................757 544-0502
Iris Hughes, *Principal*
EMP: 1
SALES (est): 84.1K **Privately Held**
SIC: 2844 Toilet preparations

(G-14452)
ETEGRITY LLC
2301 Woodland Ct (23456-6014)
PHONE..............................757 301-7455
Helene Basham, *Mng Member*
EMP: 3
SALES (est): 163.9K **Privately Held**
SIC: 7372 Operating systems computer
software

(G-14453)
EUPHORIC TREATZ LLC
Also Called: Diamante Clothing
3383 Lakecrest Rd (23452-5213)
PHONE..............................757 504-4174
Alma Hutton,
EMP: 2
SALES (est): 49.6K **Privately Held**
SIC: 2051 Cakes, bakery: except frozen

(G-14454)
EURO CABINETS INC
100 Aragona Blvd Ste 101 (23462-2752)
PHONE..............................757 671-7884
John Bodale, *President*
Ana Bodale, *General Mgr*
EMP: 14
SQ FT: 2,600
SALES (est): 1.2MM **Privately Held**
SIC: 2434 Wood kitchen cabinets

(G-14455)
EVERY CHANGING WOMAN
905 Roundtable Ct (23464-8846)
PHONE..............................757 343-3088
Ernestine Johnson, *Principal*
EMP: 1
SALES (est): 42.8K **Privately Held**
SIC: 3999 Hair & hair-based products

(G-14456)
EXECUTIVE CREATIONS
5998 Providence Rd (23464-3824)
PHONE..............................757 351-1310
EMP: 1
SALES (est): 42.8K **Privately Held**
SIC: 3999 Manufacturing industries

(G-14457)
EXOTIC WOODWORKS
1820 Clifton Bridge Dr (23456-7819)
PHONE..............................352 408-5373
Luke Robinson, *Principal*
EMP: 1 **EST:** 2018

SALES (est): 54.1K **Privately Held**
SIC: 2431 Millwork

(G-14458)
**FABRICTION SPCLIST OF
VIRGINIA**
Also Called: Fabrication Specialist VA
1130 Flobert Dr (23464-5718)
PHONE..............................757 620-2540
Robert Boller, *President*
Lisa Boller, *Corp Secy*
EMP: 2
SALES (est): 225K **Privately Held**
WEB: www.bobboller.com
SIC: 3429 Cabinet hardware

(G-14459)
FAMARCO NEWCO LLC
Also Called: B and K International
1381 Air Rail Ave (23455-3301)
P.O. Box 5152 (23471-0152)
PHONE..............................757 460-3573
Ron Kunzweiler, *Manager*
Don Stock,
◆ **EMP:** 30
SQ FT: 42,000
SALES (est): 9.7MM **Privately Held**
WEB: www.famarco.com
SIC: 2833 2099 Medicinals & botanicals;
spices, including grinding

(G-14460)
FAR FETCH LLC
200 Golden Oak Ct Ste 320 (23452-8502)
PHONE..............................757 493-3572
William Townsend,
EMP: 1 **EST:** 2011
SALES (est): 61.1K **Privately Held**
WEB: www.budgetbuilder.com
SIC: 7372 Prepackaged software

(G-14461)
FESTIVE FOODS
389 Edwin Dr Ste 100 (23462-4548)
PHONE..............................757 490-9186
Bobby Cannon, *Owner*
Rick Zapka, *Prdtn Mgr*
EMP: 1
SALES (est): 84.9K **Privately Held**
WEB: www.festivefoodsllc.com
SIC: 2099 Food preparations

(G-14462)
FIELD AND SONS LLC
1528 Seafarer Ln (23454-1421)
PHONE..............................757 412-0125
Matt Field, *Principal*
EMP: 2
SALES (est): 99.1K **Privately Held**
SIC: 1311 Crude petroleum & natural gas

(G-14463)
FIELDTECH INDUSTRIES LLC
1905 Sunrise Dr (23455-3139)
PHONE..............................757 286-1503
Luke Hopwood, *Principal*
EMP: 2
SALES (est): 91.7K **Privately Held**
SIC: 3999 Manufacturing industries

(G-14464)
FIRST COLONY PRESS
2404 Laurel Cove Dr (23454-2053)
PHONE..............................757 496-0362
Alma Jacobson, *Principal*
EMP: 1 **EST:** 2013
SALES (est): 49.9K **Privately Held**
SIC: 2741 Miscellaneous publishing

(G-14465)
FIRST LANDING WOODWORKS
311 49th St (23451-2414)
PHONE..............................757 428-7537
EMP: 1
SALES (est): 54.1K **Privately Held**
SIC: 2431 Millwork

(G-14466)
FIVE STAR CUSTOM BLINDS INC
3419 Vrginia Bch Blvd 153 (23452)
PHONE..............................757 236-5577
Brian Luke, *President*
EMP: 7

SALES (est): 436.3K **Privately Held**
WEB: www.fivestarcustomblinds.com
SIC: 2591 Window blinds

(G-14467)
FLOWERS BAKERIES LLC
6001 Indian River Rd (23464-3801)
PHONE..............................757 424-4860
Laura Pruitt, *Manager*
EMP: 4
SALES (corp-wide): 4.1B **Publicly Held**
WEB: www.flowersfoods.com
SIC: 2051 Bread, cake & related products
HQ: Flowers Bakeries, Llc
1919 Flowers Cir
Thomasville GA 31757

(G-14468)
FLYNN ENTERPRISES INC
3157 Virginia Beach Blvd (23452-6927)
PHONE..............................804 461-5753
Jan Balderson, *Accounts Mgr*
Jim Lash, *Manager*
Brian Munson, *Graphic Designe*
EMP: 1 **Privately Held**
WEB: www.allegradulles.com
SIC: 2752 Commercial printing, offset
PA: Flynn Enterprises, Inc.
45668 Terminal Dr Ste 100
Sterling VA 20166

(G-14469)
FLYWAY INC
620 Hilltop West Ctr (23451-6139)
PHONE..............................757 422-3215
Charles A Burnett, *Principal*
EMP: 2
SALES (est): 101.6K **Privately Held**
SIC: 2396 Screen printing on fabric articles

(G-14470)
FONTAINE MELINDA
Also Called: Logic Branding
2635 Bracston Rd (23456-6550)
PHONE..............................757 777-2812
Melinda Fontaine, *Owner*
EMP: 1
SALES (est): 66.8K **Privately Held**
SIC: 3993 Signs & advertising specialties

(G-14471)
FORM FABRICATIONS LLC
1037 Ferry Plantation Rd (23455-5432)
PHONE..............................757 309-8717
Kelly D Marvin, *Mng Member*
EMP: 1
SALES (est): 125K **Privately Held**
SIC: 3599 Custom machinery

(G-14472)
**FORTIS SOLUTIONS GROUP
LLC (PA)**
2505 Hawkeye Ct (23452-7845)
PHONE..............................757 340-8893
John O Wynne Jr, *CEO*
Kenneth Hubel, *General Mgr*
Ken Pizzuco, *COO*
Ray Lavare, *Plant Mgr*
Vito Ghiloni, *Mfg Staff*
◆ **EMP:** 209
SQ FT: 37,500
SALES (est): 207.5MM **Privately Held**
WEB: www.fortissolutionsgroup.com
SIC: 2679 2759 Labels, paper: made from
purchased material; flexographic printing

(G-14473)
FOXCREEK TACTICAL LLC
648 Declaration Rd (23462-2253)
PHONE..............................757 615-0474
Chris Williams, *Administration*
EMP: 2
SALES (est): 130.1K **Privately Held**
WEB: www.3dcartstores.com
SIC: 3489 Ordnance & accessories

(G-14474)
FRAMING CONCEPTS INC (PA)
Also Called: Paradigm
2600 Performance Ct (23453-3765)
PHONE..............................757 460-9882
Christopher Jackson, *President*
Peter A Johnson, *Director*
EMP: 5

SALES (est): 2.4MM **Privately Held**
SIC: 2752 7699 Commercial printing, lithographic; picture framing, custom

(G-14475)
FRIERSON DESIGNS LLC
1165 Jensen Dr (23451-5880)
PHONE.............................757 491-7130
William Frierson,
Grace Frierson,
EMP: 2 EST: 1997
SQ FT: 2,500
SALES (est): 200K **Privately Held**
WEB: www.friersondesigns.com
SIC: 3949 5941 Surfboards; surfing equip-
ment & supplies

(G-14476)
FT INDUSTRIES LLC
1041 Radcliff Lndg (23464-5516)
PHONE.............................757 495-0510
Robert H Woodard, *Administration*
EMP: 2
SALES (est): 97.1K **Privately Held**
SIC: 3999 Manufacturing industries

(G-14477)
FUEL IMPURITIES SEPARATOR
3121 Bray Rd (23452-7109)
PHONE.............................757 340-6833
Jack Godfrey, *Principal*
EMP: 3
SALES (est): 198.1K **Privately Held**
WEB: www.etspiritsoccer.org
SIC: 2869 Fuels

(G-14478)
G-13 HAND-BLOWN ART GLASS
4704 Larkspur Ct (23462-6411)
PHONE.............................757 495-8185
EMP: 2
SALES (est): 95.1K **Privately Held**
SIC: 3229 Mfg Pressed/Blown Glass

(G-14479)
GENERAL FOAM PLASTICS CORP
Also Called: Gfp Plastics
4429 Bonney Rd Ste 500 (23462-3881)
P.O. Box 2196 (23450-2196)
PHONE.............................757 857-0153
Jack Hall, *CEO*
George Dieffenbach, *President*
Ascher Chase, *Principal*
Bill Fields, *Chairman*
Wingate Sung, *COO*
◆ **EMP:** 1500
SALES (est): 955.5K **Privately Held**
WEB: www.generalfoamplasticscorp.com
SIC: 3089 Injection molding of plastics;
plastic processing

(G-14480)
GEORGE F DASHELL JR
2905 Cape Henry Dr (23451-1536)
PHONE.............................305 664-2238
EMP: 1
SALES (est): 40.9K **Privately Held**
SIC: 2394 Canvas & related products

(G-14481)
GERONIMO WELDING FABRICATION
1324 Chippokes Ct (23454-6579)
PHONE.............................757 277-6383
Calvin Dixon, *Principal*
EMP: 1
SALES (est): 27.6K **Privately Held**
SIC: 7692 Welding repair

(G-14482)
GHENT LIVING MAGAZINE LLC
1860 Wolfsnare Rd (23454-3541)
PHONE.............................757 425-7333
Sheila Kilpatrick, *Principal*
EMP: 3
SALES (est): 92.2K **Privately Held**
SIC: 2711 Newspapers, publishing & print-
ing

(G-14483)
GIBSON GIRL PUBLISHING CO LLC
3243 Redgrove Ct (23453-3035)
P.O. Box 11203, Newport News (23601-
9203)
PHONE.............................504 261-8107
Rekaya Gibson,
EMP: 1
SALES (est): 51.6K **Privately Held**
WEB:
www.gibsongirlpublishingcompany.com
SIC: 2731 7389 Book publishing;

(G-14484)
GLOBAL MARINE SERVICES LLC
4229 Buckeye Ct (23462-4904)
PHONE.............................757 284-9284
Andrew Smith, *Owner*
Bashaan Hameed, *Owner*
Latisha Smith, *Owner*
EMP: 4
SALES (est): 75K **Privately Held**
SIC: 3731 Shipbuilding & repairing

(G-14485)
GLOBAL SUPPLY SOLUTIONS
5741 Bayside Rd Ste 108 (23455-3014)
PHONE.............................757 392-1733
Bob Banta, *COO*
EMP: 2
SALES (est): 77.4K **Privately Held**
WEB: www.gssgear.com
SIC: 3812 Search & navigation equipment

(G-14486)
GODDESS OF CHOCOLATE LTD
1125 Nipigon Ct (23454-6736)
PHONE.............................757 301-2126
Jane Cogan, *Principal*
EMP: 1
SALES (est): 76K **Privately Held**
SIC: 2066 Chocolate

(G-14487)
GOMATTERS LLC
1600 Virginia Beach Blvd (23454-4631)
PHONE.............................757 819-4950
Tommy Smith, *President*
EMP: 2
SALES (est): 100.4K **Privately Held**
WEB: www.gomatters.com
SIC: 7372 Application computer software

(G-14488)
GORDON PAPER COMPANY INC (PA)
5713 Ward Ave (23455-3310)
PHONE.............................800 457-7366
Gordon Avia F, *President*
Mark Gordon, *Division Mgr*
Steven Gordon, *COO*
Gordon Mark, *Vice Pres*
Gordon Steven, *Vice Pres*
▲ **EMP:** 105
SQ FT: 275,000
SALES (est): 17.9MM **Privately Held**
WEB: www.gordonpaper.com
SIC: 2621 Paper mills

(G-14489)
GRAY SHUNTINA
Also Called: Royalty Luxurious Hair
448 Peregrine St (23462-1859)
PHONE.............................919 273-7979
Shuntina Gray, *Owner*
EMP: 1
SALES (est): 100K **Privately Held**
SIC: 3999 Hair & hair-based products

(G-14490)
GRAY SCALE PRODUCTIONS
1423 Air Rail Ave (23455-3001)
PHONE.............................757 363-1087
Matthew McKenney, *Owner*
EMP: 2
SALES (est): 134.4K **Privately Held**
SIC: 2759 Screen printing

(G-14491)
GREENBROOK TMS NEUROHEALTH CTR
770 Lynnhven Pkwy Ste 150 (23452)
PHONE.............................855 998-4867
EMP: 1
SALES (corp-wide): 2.7MM **Privately Held**
WEB: www.greenbrooktms.com
SIC: 3312 Blast furnaces & steel mills
PA: Greenbrook Tms Neurohealth Center
8405 Greensboro Dr # 120
Mc Lean VA 22102
703 356-1568

(G-14492)
GREGORYS FLEET SUPPLY CORP
4984 Cleveland St (23462-5307)
PHONE.............................757 490-1606
Claude Gregory Jr, *CEO*
Deborah G Foxwell, *President*
Norma T Gregory, *Corp Secy*
EMP: 20
SQ FT: 10,000
SALES (est): 2MM **Privately Held**
WEB: www.gregorysfleetsupply.com
SIC: 3713 7539 Truck bodies & parts; ma-
chine shop, automotive

(G-14493)
GREGORYS MACHINE SHOP CORP
4984 Cleveland St (23462-5307)
PHONE.............................757 490-1606
EMP: 2
SALES (est): 89.6K **Privately Held**
WEB: www.gregorysmachineshop.com
SIC: 3599 Machine shop, jobbing & repair

(G-14494)
GROUND EFFECTS HAULING INC
3905 Charity Neck Rd (23457-1545)
PHONE.............................757 435-1765
Dana Riggs, *President*
Sally Jullian, *Principal*
EMP: 6
SQ FT: 5,000
SALES (est): 1.5MM **Privately Held**
WEB: www.groundeffectshaulingva.com
SIC: 3443 4212 7699 Dumpsters,
garbage; dump truck haulage; waste
cleaning services

(G-14495)
GSTYLE7 TRUCKING LLC
1385 Fordham Dr (23464-5345)
PHONE.............................757 367-2009
Gerald Cowherd,
EMP: 1
SALES (est): 100K **Privately Held**
SIC: 3537 Trucks, tractors, loaders, carri-
ers & similar equipment

(G-14496)
GUNNYS CALL INC
Also Called: Gunny's Call Ink
2669 Highland Dr (23456-8301)
PHONE.............................757 892-0251
Alberto Manfredi, *CEO*
EMP: 1
SALES (est): 96.6K **Privately Held**
SIC: 2759 2299 Screen printing; batting,
wadding, padding & fillings

(G-14497)
GUNZ CUSTOM WOODWORKS LLC
2208 Rock Lake Loop (23456-6111)
PHONE.............................757 739-2842
Brennan Guenzel, *Owner*
EMP: 2
SALES (est): 88K **Privately Held**
SIC: 2431 Millwork

(G-14498)
HAMPTON ROADS CANVAS CO LLC
4413 General Gage Ct (23462-3113)
PHONE.............................757 560-3170
EMP: 1 EST: 2016
SALES (est): 46.5K **Privately Held**
SIC: 2211 Cotton Broadwoven Fabric Mill

(G-14499)
HAMPTON ROADS GAZETI INC
624 Redkirk Ln (23462-5625)
P.O. Box 61968 (23466-1968)
PHONE.............................757 560-9583
Loretta Davis Kahn, *Owner*
EMP: 3
SALES (est): 8.1K **Privately Held**
WEB: www.hamptonroads.gazeti.org
SIC: 2711 Newspapers: publishing only,
not printed on site

(G-14500)
HAMPTON ROADS SHEET METAL INC
5821 Arrowhead Dr Ste 102 (23462-3259)
PHONE.............................757 543-6009
Howell L Matthews Jr, *President*
EMP: 1
SALES (est): 59.5K **Privately Held**
SIC: 3444 3446 1711 3541 Sheet metal-
work; architectural metalwork; mechanical
contractor; machine tools, metal cutting
type

(G-14501)
HAMPTON ROADS WEDDING GUIDE
1116 Glenside Dr (23464-5804)
PHONE.............................757 474-0332
Marcia Jordan, *Owner*
EMP: 1
SALES (est): 73.7K **Privately Held**
WEB: www.hrweddingguide.com
SIC: 2759 Magazines: printing

(G-14502)
HANBAY INC
424 Investors Pl Ste 103 (23452-1168)
PHONE.............................757 333-6375
Mark Clifford, *Engineer*
Robert Nutt, *Administration*
EMP: 7
SALES (est): 344.2K **Privately Held**
WEB: www.hanbayinc.com
SIC: 3491 Industrial valves
HQ: Hanbay Inc
115 Av Gun
Pointe-Claire QC H9R 3
514 426-1989

(G-14503)
HANDMADE POTTERY
612 Fort Raleigh Dr (23451-4870)
PHONE.............................757 425-0116
Rebecca Waller, *Owner*
EMP: 1
SALES (est): 63.9K **Privately Held**
SIC: 3269 Pottery household articles, ex-
cept kitchen articles

(G-14504)
HANWELL INC
4445 Corp Ln Ste 212 (23462)
PHONE.............................757 213-6841
Ian Robinson, *President*
EMP: 1
SALES (est): 0 **Privately Held**
WEB: www.hanwell.com
SIC: 3575 Computer terminals, monitors &
components

(G-14505)
HARBOUR GRAPHICS INC
641 Phoenix Dr (23452-7318)
PHONE.............................757 368-0474
David Carroll, *Partner*
Amy Johnson, *General Mgr*
Marcia Sandler, *Technology*
EMP: 13
SQ FT: 2,400
SALES (est): 968K **Privately Held**
WEB: www.harbour-graphics.com
SIC: 2261 Screen printing of cotton broad-
woven fabrics

(G-14506)
HARDWIRE
Also Called: Hampton Roads Deversified
Wire
3419 Virginia Beach Blvd (23452-4419)
PHONE.............................757 410-5429
Dave Mitchell, *Owner*
EMP: 12

G
E
O
G
R
A
P
H
I
C

SALES (est): 2.5MM **Privately Held**
WEB: www.hardwirellc.com
SIC: 3679 Transducers, electrical

(G-14507)
HARRINGTON GRAPHICS CO INC
1411 Air Rail Ave (23455-3001)
PHONE......................................757 363-1600
Robert Harrington Sr, *President*
Robert A Harrington Sr, *President*
Lori Harrington, *Office Mgr*
Betty Harrington, *Admin Sec*
EMP: 6
SQ FT: 7,000
SALES (est): 960K **Privately Held**
WEB: www.harringtongraphics.com
SIC: 3993 Signs, not made in custom sign painting shops

(G-14508)
HARYGUL IMPORTS INC MARYLAND
1157 Nimmo Pkwy Ste 104 (23456-7756)
PHONE......................................757 427-5665
Deepak Nachnani, *Branch Mgr*
EMP: 25
SALES (corp-wide): 9.2MM **Privately Held**
WEB: www.shop.coastaledge.com
SIC: 3949 Surfboards
PA: Harygul Imports Incorporated Of Mary-
land
1724 Virginia Beach Blvd # 103
Virginia Beach VA 23454
757 491-9011

(G-14509)
HATTERAS SILKSCREEN
324 London Bridge Rd Ctr (23454-5209)
PHONE......................................757 486-2976
Iris W Peele, *Partner*
Robert H Engel, *Partner*
EMP: 2
SALES (est): 175.3K **Privately Held**
WEB: www.hatterasgear.com
SIC: 2262 Screen printing: manmade fiber & silk broadwoven fabrics

(G-14510)
HAWLEYWOOD LLC
1269 Redwood Farm Ct (23452-4615)
PHONE......................................757 463-0910
Jeffrey Hawley, *Principal*
EMP: 2
SALES (est): 48.3K **Privately Held**
SIC: 2499 Wood products

(G-14511)
HB INC
2601 Reliance Dr (23452-7833)
PHONE......................................757 291-5236
Greg Simon, *President*
EMP: 3
SQ FT: 7,000
SALES (est): 233.2K **Privately Held**
SIC: 3281 Granite, cut & shaped

(G-14512)
HEALTHY HOME ENTERPRISE
4501 Delco Rd (23455-2839)
PHONE......................................757 460-2829
Biondo Mary, *Owner*
EMP: 1 EST: 1995
SALES (est): 56.2K **Privately Held**
SIC: 2836 Biological products, except diagnostic

(G-14513)
HEAR QUICK INCORPORATED
Also Called: Connect Hearing
5386 Kempsriver Dr # 112 (23464-5349)
PHONE......................................757 523-0504
Buck James Reid, *President*
Sammie Reid, *Manager*
EMP: 4
SQ FT: 1,800
SALES (est): 280K **Privately Held**
SIC: 3842 5999 7629 Hearing aids; hearing aids; hearing aid repair

(G-14514)
HEATHERS HANDCRAFTED SOAPS
2000 Waymart Ct (23464-8695)
PHONE......................................757 277-8569
Heather Hogan, *President*
EMP: 1
SALES (est): 47.2K **Privately Held**
SIC: 2841 Soap & other detergents

(G-14515)
HEAVENLY HANDS & FEET INC
5296 Bagpipers Ln (23464-8126)
PHONE......................................757 621-3938
EMP: 2 EST: 2006
SALES (est): 110K **Privately Held**
SIC: 2844 Manicure Preparations Mfg

(G-14516)
HENRY BIJAK
Also Called: Alloy Metal Designs
2709 Sandy Valley Rd (23452-7752)
PHONE......................................757 572-1673
Henry Bijak, *Owner*
EMP: 1 EST: 2012
SALES (est): 57.7K **Privately Held**
SIC: 3324 3544 3325 7389 Aerospace investment castings, ferrous; dies & die holders for metal cutting, forming, die casting; alloy steel castings, except investment; business services

(G-14517)
HERFF JONES LLC
Framing Success
2556 Horse Pasture Rd (23453-2963)
PHONE......................................757 689-3000
Peter Molin, *General Mgr*
Carol Willey, *Controller*
EMP: 40
SALES (corp-wide): 1.1B **Privately Held**
WEB: www.yearbookdiscoveries.com
SIC: 2499 Picture & mirror frames, wood
HQ: Herff Jones, Llc
4501 W 62nd St
Indianapolis IN 46268
800 419-5462

(G-14518)
HERITAGE WOODWORKS LLC
512 Pinewood Dr (23451-4425)
PHONE......................................757 417-7337
EMP: 6
SALES (corp-wide): 3.9MM **Privately Held**
WEB: www.hwofva.com
SIC: 2431 Millwork
PA: Heritage Woodworks, Llc
1002 Obici Indus Blvd
Suffolk VA 23434
757 934-1440

(G-14519)
HERMES ABR LTD A LTD PARTNR (PA)
524 Viking Dr (23452-7316)
P.O. Box 2389 (23450-2389)
PHONE......................................800 464-8314
Jan Cord Becker, *CEO*
Ken Lamay, *Partner*
G Randall Stickley, *Partner*
Jerry Will, *Partner*
Johann Unterwieser, *CFO*
◆ EMP: 195
SQ FT: 245,000
SALES (est): 26.8MM **Privately Held**
WEB: www.hermes-schleifwerkzeuge.com
SIC: 3291 Coated abrasive products

(G-14520)
HERMES ABRASIVES INC
524 Viking Dr (23452-7316)
PHONE......................................757 486-6623
Jan Cord Becker, *President*
Kenneth E Lamay, *Senior VP*
Gary Predki, *Vice Pres*
EMP: 2 EST: 1979
SALES (est): 117.4K **Privately Held**
SIC: 3291 Coated abrasive products

(G-14521)
HEXMAG LLC
2697 Intl Pkwy Ste 100-1 (23452)
PHONE......................................970 203-9100
George Brown, *Mng Member*

Aaron Schefter,
EMP: 16 EST: 2013
SQ FT: 3,500
SALES (est): 1.7MM **Privately Held**
WEB: www.hexmag.com
SIC: 3484 Guns (firearms) or gun parts, 30 mm. & below

(G-14522)
HI-TECH CABINETS INC
129 Pennsylvania Ave (23462-2511)
PHONE......................................757 681-0016
Kevin Kennedy, *Administration*
EMP: 2
SALES (est): 138.6K **Privately Held**
SIC: 2434 Wood kitchen cabinets

(G-14523)
HICKMAN SURFBOARDS
2180 General Booth Blvd (23454-5804)
PHONE......................................757 427-2914
Kim Hickman, *Owner*
EMP: 1
SQ FT: 2,200
SALES (est): 20K **Privately Held**
SIC: 3949 Surfboards

(G-14524)
HILLCO DISPOSAL & RECYCL LLC
2129 General Booth Blvd # 10322 (23454-5872)
PHONE......................................757 301-9669
Michael Hill,
EMP: 2
SALES (est): 150K **Privately Held**
SIC: 3443 Dumpsters, garbage

(G-14525)
HOBBS DOOR SERVICE
4953 Providence Rd (23464-5628)
P.O. Box 15013, Chesapeake (23328-5013)
PHONE......................................757 436-6529
Kurt Hobbs, *Owner*
Janice Hobbs, *Co-Owner*
EMP: 3
SALES (est): 450K **Privately Held**
WEB: www.hobbsdoor.com
SIC: 2431 3442 Garage doors, overhead: wood; garage doors, overhead: metal

(G-14526)
HOLLY BEACH WOODWORKER INC
3801 Hearthside Ln (23453-1626)
PHONE......................................757 831-1410
Stiefel Patricia, *Admin Sec*
EMP: 2 EST: 2014
SALES (est): 133.9K **Privately Held**
WEB: www.hollybeachwoodworker.com
SIC: 2431 Millwork

(G-14527)
HORIZON CUSTOM CABINETS CORP
2697 Intl Pkwy Ste 100-3 (23452)
PHONE......................................757 434-8706
EMP: 2
SALES (est): 171.3K **Privately Held**
WEB: www.horizoncustomcabinets.net
SIC: 2434 Wood kitchen cabinets

(G-14528)
HORIZON CUSTOM CABINETS CORP
2697 Intl Pkwy Ste 100-3 (23452)
PHONE......................................757 306-1007
Robert Bouley, *President*
Robert A Bouley, *Owner*
EMP: 6
SALES (est): 457.3K **Privately Held**
WEB: www.horizoncustomcabinets.net
SIC: 2434 Wood kitchen cabinets

(G-14529)
HORMEL FOODS CORPORATION
1681 Wicomico Ln (23464-7866)
PHONE......................................757 467-5396
Barry Boleyn, *Branch Mgr*
EMP: 3 **Publicly Held**
WEB: www.hormelfoods.com
SIC: 2099 Food preparations

PA: Hormel Foods Corporation
1 Hormel Pl
Austin MN 55912
507 437-5611

(G-14530)
HORTON WREATH SOCIETY INC
1401 Trapelo Ct (23456-5474)
PHONE......................................757 617-2093
EMP: 2
SALES (est): 70.5K **Privately Held**
SIC: 3999 Wreaths, artificial

(G-14531)
HR PUBLISHING GROUP LLC
4632 Broad St Apt 204 (23462-2818)
PHONE......................................757 364-0245
Terri R Wetzel,
EMP: 2 EST: 2016
SALES (est): 45.4K **Privately Held**
SIC: 2741 Miscellaneous publishing

(G-14532)
HUDS TEES
2500 Squadron Ct Ste 102 (23453-3161)
PHONE......................................757 650-6190
John Hudnall, *Principal*
EMP: 2
SALES (est): 103.4K **Privately Held**
WEB: www.hudstees.com
SIC: 2759 Screen printing

(G-14533)
HUNTINGTON INGALLS INC
4313 Two Woods Rd E13 (23455-4444)
PHONE......................................757 688-9832
William Eaton, *Branch Mgr*
Page Nowland, *Director*
EMP: 1 **Publicly Held**
WEB: www.huntingtoningalls.com
SIC: 3731 Shipbuilding & repairing
HQ: Huntington Ingalls Incorporated
4101 Washington Ave
Newport News VA 23607
757 380-2000

(G-14534)
HUSH AEROSPACE LLC
2873 Crusader Cir (23453-3133)
PHONE......................................703 629-6907
Zachary Johns, *Principal*
Gerald Brown, *Principal*
EMP: 3
SALES (est): 117.8K **Privately Held**
SIC: 3721 Motorized aircraft

(G-14535)
HYMONS EMBROIDERY LLC
2573 Townfield Ln (23454-6334)
PHONE......................................757 512-6005
Kimberly Jacobs,
EMP: 2
SALES (est): 49.3K **Privately Held**
SIC: 2395 Embroidery & art needlework

(G-14536)
HYPATIA-ROSE PRESS LLC
5624 Susquehanna Dr (23462-4017)
PHONE......................................757 819-2559
Julia Zay, *Principal*
EMP: 1
SALES (est): 62.9K **Privately Held**
SIC: 2741 Miscellaneous publishing

(G-14537)
I & C HUGHES LLC
Also Called: Iris's Essences
3933 Rainbow Dr (23456-1331)
PHONE......................................757 544-0502
Charles Hughes, *Principal*
Iris Hughes, *Principal*
EMP: 1
SALES (est): 81.6K **Privately Held**
SIC: 2844 0782 5311 7389 Face creams or lotions; lawn & garden services; department stores, discount;

(G-14538)
I B R PLASMA CENTER
949 Chimney Hl Shopg Ctr (23452-3052)
PHONE......................................757 498-5160
Alex Dalmas, *Principal*
EMP: 2
SALES (est): 103.1K **Privately Held**
SIC: 2836 Plasmas

▲ = Import ▼=Export
◆ =Import/Export

(G-14539)
ICE TEK LLC
2585 Horse Pasture Rd # 207
(23453-2994)
PHONE................................757 390-8589
Juvylee Monzaga, *Principal*
Kenneth Phelps, *Principal*
Christopher Monzaga,
EMP: 38
SQ FT: 2,500
SALES (est): 3MM **Privately Held**
WEB: www.icetekva.com
SIC: 3731 1731 7389 Military ships, building & repairing; electrical work; electronic controls installation; voice, data & video wiring contractor; closed circuit television installation; air pollution measuring service

(G-14540)
ICEBURRR JEWELRY (PA)
5024 Sullivan Blvd (23455-5225)
PHONE................................757 537-9520
Chaz Ellis, *CEO*
EMP: 1
SALES (est): 100K **Privately Held**
SIC: 3915 Jewelry parts, unassembled

(G-14541)
IGOR CUSTOM SIGN STRIPE
402 Redhead Way (23451-6531)
PHONE................................757 639-2397
Igor Acord, *Principal*
EMP: 1
SALES (est): 77.2K **Privately Held**
WEB: www.igorscustom.com
SIC: 3993 Signs & advertising specialties

(G-14542)
IMS GEAR HOLDING INC
489 Progress Ln (23454-3477)
PHONE................................757 468-8810
Juergen Moller, *Manager*
EMP: 50
SALES (corp-wide): 609.6MM **Privately Held**
WEB: www.imsgear.com
SIC: 3089 3462 3714 Injection molding of plastics; iron & steel forgings; motor vehicle parts & accessories
HQ: Ims Gear Holding, Inc.
1234 Palmour Dr
Gainesville GA 30501

(G-14543)
IMS GEAR VIRGINIA LLC
489 Progress Ln (23454-3477)
PHONE................................757 468-8810
Guenter Weissenseel, *President*
Timothy Corbin, *Manager*
Andreas Steiert, *Manager*
Sarah Kennedy, *Executive*
Hans-Michael Weissenseel, *Admin Sec*
▲ EMP: 260
SQ FT: 25,000
SALES (est): 27MM **Privately Held**
WEB: www.imsgear.com
SIC: 3714 Motor vehicle parts & accessories

(G-14544)
INDIGO PRESS
3445 Waltham Cir (23452-4041)
PHONE................................757 705-2619
EMP: 1
SALES (est): 44.2K **Privately Held**
SIC: 2741 Misc Publishing

(G-14545)
INK BLOT INC
1329 Harpers Rd Ste 105 (23454-5562)
PHONE................................757 644-6958
Robin Harvey, *President*
Charles Harvey, *Admin Sec*
EMP: 3
SQ FT: 2,400
SALES (est): 247.8K **Privately Held**
WEB: www.inkblottees.com
SIC: 2759 Screen printing

(G-14546)
INNOVATIVE KITCHENS INC
2640 Virginia Beach Blvd (23452-7610)
PHONE................................757 425-7753
Martin J Leszczynski, *President*
EMP: 3

SQ FT: 1,500
SALES (est): 175K **Privately Held**
WEB: www.innkitchensvb.com
SIC: 2434 Wood kitchen cabinets

(G-14547)
INNOVATIVE OFFICE DESIGN LLC
700 Earl Of Chstrfield Ct (23454-2907)
PHONE................................757 496-9221
EMP: 4
SALES (est): 392.4K **Privately Held**
SIC: 2541 Mfg Wood Partitions/Fixtures

(G-14548)
INSIDE BUSINESS
2255 Wake Forest St (23451-1420)
PHONE................................757 439-7158
Michael Herron, *Principal*
EMP: 3
SALES (est): 132K **Privately Held**
WEB: www.pilotonline.com
SIC: 2711 Newspapers, publishing & printing

(G-14549)
INSITE PUBLISHING LLC
2781 Einstein Dr (23456-8169)
PHONE................................757 301-9617
Peter Cousin, *Principal*
Jim Bohrer, *Sales Dir*
EMP: 2
SALES (est): 99.9K **Privately Held**
WEB: www.insitepublishing.com
SIC: 2741 Miscellaneous publishing

(G-14550)
INTELLIGENT ILLUMINATIONS INC (PA)
5101 Cleveland St Ste 302 (23462-6561)
PHONE................................888 455-2465
Larry Williams, *President*
EMP: 14
SALES (est): 1.2MM **Privately Held**
WEB: www.ilums.com
SIC: 3648 Public lighting fixtures

(G-14551)
INTERLENO ENTERPRISES LLC
190 Thalia Vlg Shoppes (23452-1608)
PHONE................................757 340-3613
Edwin Marrero, *Administration*
EMP: 3
SALES (est): 150K **Privately Held**
SIC: 2032 Ethnic foods: canned, jarred, etc.; Spanish foods: packaged in cans, jars, etc.; Mexican foods: packaged in cans, jars, etc.; baby foods, including meats: packaged in cans, jars, etc.

(G-14552)
INTERNTNAL PZZLE CLLCTORS ASSN
1323 Glyndon Dr (23464-4434)
PHONE................................757 420-7576
Marti Reis, *Admin Sec*
EMP: 1
SALES (est): 101.1K **Privately Held**
SIC: 3944 Puzzles

(G-14553)
INTO LIGHT
1100 Lethbridge Ct (23454-6739)
PHONE................................757 816-9002
Dawn Lingle, *Owner*
EMP: 1
SALES (est): 52K **Privately Held**
SIC: 3999 Candles

(G-14554)
ISOBARIC STRATEGIES INC
Also Called: Isobarix
1808 Eden Way (23454-3055)
PHONE................................757 277-2858
Leif Hauge, *President*
EMP: 3
SALES (est): 500K **Privately Held**
WEB: www.isobarix.com
SIC: 3999 Manufacturing industries

(G-14555)
J & J POWDER COATING
2424 Castleton Commerce W
(23456-5499)
PHONE................................757 406-2922

James L Walls II, *Administration*
EMP: 4
SALES (est): 519.5K **Privately Held**
WEB: www.sjsindustrial.net
SIC: 3399 Powder, metal

(G-14556)
J & R PARTNERS (PA)
Also Called: Fastsigns
4780 Euclid Rd (23462-3823)
PHONE................................757 499-3344
Roger Noack, *Partner*
Jean Noack, *Partner*
EMP: 5
SQ FT: 1,500
SALES (est): 622.3K **Privately Held**
WEB: www.fastsigns.com
SIC: 3993 Signs & advertising specialties

(G-14557)
J AND J ENERGY HOLDINGS
4772 Euclid Rd Ste B (23462-3800)
PHONE................................757 963-9763
Tony Jacobs, *Partner*
EMP: 24
SALES (est): 869.5K **Privately Held**
SIC: 1311 Crude petroleum production

(G-14558)
J C STEEL DE TECH
5304 Larkins Lair Ct (23464-4086)
PHONE................................757 376-7469
Catherine Stever, *Principal*
EMP: 2
SALES (est): 92.2K **Privately Held**
SIC: 3441 Fabricated structural metal

(G-14559)
J&J POWDER COATING
2401 Bowland Pkwy Ste 103 (23454-5317)
PHONE................................757 390-0237
EMP: 2
SALES (est): 111.4K **Privately Held**
WEB: www.sjsindustrial.net
SIC: 3479 Coating of metals & formed products

(G-14560)
JACK KENNEDY WELDING
413 Old Forge Ct (23452-3223)
PHONE................................757 340-4269
Jack Kennedy, *Principal*
EMP: 1
SALES (est): 106.9K **Privately Held**
SIC: 7692 Welding repair

(G-14561)
JACKITE INC
3612 West Neck Rd (23456-3431)
PHONE................................757 426-5359
Marguerite Stankus, *President*
Christopher J Stankus, *Vice Pres*
Christopher Stankus, *Vice Pres*
EMP: 15
SALES (est): 750K **Privately Held**
WEB: www.jackite.com
SIC: 3944 Kites

(G-14562)
JAKE PUBLISHING INC
2228 Mill Crossing Dr # 308 (23454-1246)
PHONE................................757 377-6771
Richard L Thibault, *Principal*
EMP: 2 EST: 2009
SALES (est): 105.3K **Privately Held**
WEB: www.pettailsonline.com
SIC: 2741 Miscellaneous publishing

(G-14563)
JAMES HINTZKE
Also Called: Archltctral Rnssnce Techniques
1912 Bernstein Dr (23454-6794)
PHONE................................757 374-4827
James Hintzke, *Owner*
EMP: 1
SALES (est): 42.9K **Privately Held**
WEB: www.valhallasforge.com
SIC: 3952 5211 5251 5331 Artists' materials, except pencils & leads; counter tops; builders' hardware; variety stores

(G-14564)
JANSSON & ASSOCIATE MSTR BLDR
Also Called: Swede Built
5039 Euclid Rd (23462-2529)
PHONE................................757 965-7285
Denise Jansson, *President*
Erik Jansson, *Admin Sec*
EMP: 2
SALES (est): 156.3K **Privately Held**
SIC: 3751 Motorcycles & related parts

(G-14565)
JEFCO INC
1449 Mller Str Rd Ste 102 (23455)
PHONE................................757 460-0403
Jeff White, *Branch Mgr*
EMP: 20
SALES (corp-wide): 15.1MM **Privately Held**
WEB: www.jefcoinc.net
SIC: 3211 5013 Plate & sheet glass; automobile glass
PA: Jefco Inc.
11501 N Lkrdge Pkwy Ste 1
Ashland VA 23005
804 798-7823

(G-14566)
JEFFREY M HAUGHNEY ATTORNEY PC
1537 Quail Point Rd (23454-3115)
PHONE................................757 802-6160
Jeffrey Haughney, *Principal*
EMP: 4
SALES (est): 88.8K **Privately Held**
SIC: 2252 Socks

(G-14567)
JERRY A KOTCHKA
2349 Tierra Monte Arch (23456-6762)
PHONE................................757 721-6782
EMP: 3
SALES (est): 130K **Privately Held**
SIC: 3812 Mfg Search/Navigation Equipment

(G-14568)
JES CONSTRUCTION LLC (PA)
Also Called: Jes Foundation Repair
1741 Corp Landing Pkwy # 101
(23454-5929)
PHONE................................757 558-9909
Matt Malone, *CEO*
Jesse Waltz, *President*
Guy Stello, *CFO*
Kim McDonald, *CTO*
EMP: 91
SALES (est): 14.9MM **Privately Held**
WEB: www.jeswork.com
SIC: 1389 1799 Construction, repair & dismantling services; athletic & recreation facilities construction

(G-14569)
JIMMY FRENCH
6605 Pinewood Ct (23464-1627)
PHONE................................757 583-2536
Jimmy French, *Principal*
EMP: 2
SALES (est): 104.1K **Privately Held**
SIC: 1389 Construction, repair & dismantling services

(G-14570)
JM WALKER PUBLISHING LLC
3045 Silver Maple Dr (23452-6771)
PHONE................................757 340-6659
John Mark Ickes, *Principal*
EMP: 1
SALES (est): 37.5K **Privately Held**
SIC: 2741 Miscellaneous publishing

(G-14571)
JO-JE CORPORATION
Also Called: Brothers Printing
3320 Virginia Beach Blvd (23452-5621)
PHONE................................757 431-2656
Glenn Jenner, *President*
EMP: 7
SQ FT: 2,700
SALES (est): 623.2K **Privately Held**
WEB: www.brothersprintingusa.com
SIC: 2752 Commercial printing, offset

GEOGRAPHIC

(G-14572)
JOHN WILLS STUDIOS INC
800 Seahawk Cir Ste 114 (23452-7849)
PHONE....................................757 468-0260
John Wills, *President*
Nancy Loose, *Vice Pres*
Ira G Midgett, *Admin Sec*
EMP: 18
SQ FT: 6,000
SALES (est): 1MM **Privately Held**
WEB: www.johnwillsstudios.com
SIC: 3281 Marble, building: cut & shaped

(G-14573)
JOINT PLANNING SOLUTIONS LLC
Also Called: Old Goat Technologies
4669 South Blvd Ste 107 (23452-1057)
PHONE....................................757 839-5593
Jason Patwell, *CEO*
Jeffery Birkey, *Principal*
Scott Martin, *COO*
EMP: 1
SALES (est): 76.1K **Privately Held**
WEB: www.jointplanningsolutions.com
SIC: 3829 7389 Measuring & controlling devices;

(G-14574)
JOSEPH CARSON
Also Called: Thunderbird Creations
3744 Virginius Dr (23452-3510)
PHONE....................................757 498-4866
Joseph Carson, *Owner*
EMP: 1 EST: 1998
SALES (est): 10K **Privately Held**
SIC: 3172 Personal leather goods

(G-14575)
JPH WOODCRAFT
941 Timberlake Dr (23464-3236)
PHONE....................................757 615-6812
EMP: 2
SALES (est): 123.9K **Privately Held**
WEB: www.jphwoodcraft.com
SIC: 2511 Wood household furniture

(G-14576)
JRJJ PAPER LLC
168 Business Park Dr (23462-6532)
PHONE....................................757 473-3719
John David Strelitz,
EMP: 4
SALES (est): 137.8K **Privately Held**
WEB: www.streco.com
SIC: 2679 Paper products, converted

(G-14577)
JUICE BAR JUICES INCORPORATED
3877 Holland Rd Ste 418 (23452-2860)
PHONE....................................757 227-6822
Jodie Wilson, *CEO*
EMP: 6
SALES (est): 371K **Privately Held**
WEB: www.juicebar8020.com
SIC: 2037 Fruit juices

(G-14578)
K-NATURO LLC
5733 Hampshire Ln Apt 101 (23462-1524)
PHONE....................................757 343-4604
Casey Stallworth,
EMP: 3
SALES (est): 123.2K **Privately Held**
SIC: 2833 Drugs & herbs: grading, grinding & milling

(G-14579)
K2 INDUSTRIES LLC
1417 Veau Ct (23451-6018)
PHONE....................................757 754-5430
EMP: 2
SALES (est): 74.4K **Privately Held**
SIC: 3999 Manufacturing industries

(G-14580)
KATES CREATIONS
6480 Knotts Island Rd (23457-1206)
PHONE....................................757 721-7062
R Powell, *Principal*
EMP: 2
SALES (est): 84.5K **Privately Held**
WEB: www.hiddenvillamotel.com
SIC: 3999 Manufacturing industries

(G-14581)
KAUFFMAN ENGINEERING INC
889 Seahawk Cir (23452-7809)
PHONE....................................757 468-6000
Larry Holleman, *General Mgr*
EMP: 260
SALES (corp-wide): 140.9MM **Privately Held**
WEB: www.kewire.com
SIC: 3679 Harness assemblies for electronic use: wire or cable
PA: Kauffman Engineering, Llc
701 Ransdell Rd
Lebanon IN 46052
765 482-5640

(G-14582)
KED HAULING CO LLC
600 Chapel Lake Dr # 202 (23454-4113)
PHONE....................................757 319-8652
Shameta Judd, *Mng Member*
EMP: 1
SALES (est): 48K **Privately Held**
SIC: 3799 Transportation equipment

(G-14583)
KEY TO HEART SEASONING LLC
3967 Wyckoff Dr (23452-1874)
PHONE....................................757 752-7581
Tahquisha McDaniel,
EMP: 1
SALES (est): 39.5K **Privately Held**
SIC: 2099 Seasonings: dry mixes

(G-14584)
KILN CREEK ASSOCIATES LP
4661 Haygood Rd Ste 110 (23455-5435)
P.O. Box 5592 (23471-0592)
PHONE....................................757 464-6082
EMP: 3
SALES (est): 220K **Privately Held**
SIC: 3559 Kilns

(G-14585)
KINGDOM BLDRS & SHIP REPR INC
3526 Bancroft Dr (23452-4039)
PHONE....................................757 748-1251
Judith Peters, *President*
EMP: 4
SALES (est): 189.4K **Privately Held**
SIC: 3731 Shipbuilding & repairing

(G-14586)
KITCHEN AND BATH COMPANY LLC
5025 Cleveland St (23462-2527)
PHONE....................................757 417-8200
Doug Pauley, *District Mgr*
Steven Dubdanevich,
EMP: 5
SQ FT: 4,800
SALES (est): 830K **Privately Held**
WEB: www.kbideas.net
SIC: 2434 Wood kitchen cabinets

(G-14587)
KITCO FIBER OPTICS INC
5269 Cleveland St Ste 109 (23462-6550)
PHONE....................................757 216-2208
Timothy B Grass, *Ch of Bd*
Marc Steiner, *President*
Daniel S Morris, *Vice Pres*
Holly Andrews, *Manager*
Gregg Kruer, *Director*
EMP: 64
SQ FT: 15,000
SALES (est): 13.7MM **Privately Held**
WEB: www.kitcofiberoptics.com
SIC: 3678 Electronic connectors

(G-14588)
KITCO/KSARIA LLC
5269 Cleveland St (23462-6550)
PHONE....................................757 216-2220
W Sheppard Miller,
EMP: 6
SALES (est): 950K **Privately Held**
WEB: www.kitcofiberoptics.com
SIC: 3678 Electronic connectors

(G-14589)
KITTY HAWKS KITES INC
328 Laskin Rd (23451-3020)
PHONE....................................757 351-3959
EMP: 1
SALES (est): 66.2K **Privately Held**
WEB: www.kittyhawk.com
SIC: 3944 Kites

(G-14590)
KLIMAX CUSTOM SKATEBOARDS
225 N Palmyra Dr (23462-3540)
PHONE....................................757 589-0683
EMP: 2 EST: 2007
SALES (est): 120K **Privately Held**
SIC: 3949 Mfg Sporting/Athletic Goods

(G-14591)
KMW WORKS LLC
4830 Alicia Dr (23462-3868)
PHONE....................................757 776-6765
Kadmiel Nelson,
EMP: 2
SALES (est): 73.4K **Privately Held**
SIC: 3433 Boilers, low-pressure heating: steam or hot water

(G-14592)
KOHLER INDUSTRIES INC
2748 Nestlebrook Trl (23456-8221)
PHONE....................................757 301-3233
Manfred Kohler, *Principal*
Kirt Borer, *Sales Staff*
EMP: 2
SALES (est): 111.6K **Privately Held**
WEB: www.kohlerindustries.com
SIC: 3999 Manufacturing industries

(G-14593)
KRISMARK INC
Also Called: Little Bay Mar Canvas & More
1209 Baker Rd Ste 403 (23455-3650)
PHONE....................................757 533-9182
Marie Kirk, *President*
EMP: 6
SQ FT: 800
SALES (est): 200K **Privately Held**
WEB: www.littlebaycanvas.com
SIC: 2394 7641 Sails: made from purchased materials; reupholstery

(G-14594)
L E F GEAR
1433 Ashburnham Arch (23456-5412)
PHONE....................................757 274-2151
Linda Encinas Fulgha, *CEO*
EMP: 2
SALES (est): 107.4K **Privately Held**
SIC: 3566 Speed changers, drives & gears

(G-14595)
L&L TRADING COMPANY LLC
3707 Virginia Beach Blvd (23452-3412)
PHONE....................................757 995-3608
Eric Leduc,
EMP: 1
SALES (est): 99.9K **Privately Held**
WEB: www.lltradeco.com
SIC: 3484 Guns (firearms) or gun parts, 30 mm. & below

(G-14596)
L3 TECHNOLOGIES INC
140 F Ave (23460)
PHONE....................................757 425-0142
EMP: 2
SALES (corp-wide): 6.8B **Publicly Held**
WEB: www.l3t.com
SIC: 3663 Telemetering equipment, electronic
HQ: L3 Technologies, Inc.
600 3rd Ave Fl 34
New York NY 10016
212 697-1111

(G-14597)
LA LA LAND CANDY KINGDOM VA01
1602 Atlantic Ave (23451-3423)
PHONE....................................305 342-6737
Avshalom Yehezkiel, *Principal*
EMP: 2

SALES (est): 62.3K **Privately Held**
SIC: 2064 Candy & other confectionery products

(G-14598)
LALANDII COATINGS LLC
1023 Laskin Rd (23451-6302)
PHONE....................................757 425-0131
Greg Lanese, *Principal*
EMP: 2
SALES (est): 153.6K **Privately Held**
SIC: 3479 Coating of metals & formed products

(G-14599)
LANDMARK INDUSTRIES LLC
1072 Laskin Rd Ste 104 (23451-6387)
PHONE....................................757 233-7291
William Wright, *Principal*
EMP: 2
SALES (est): 135.5K **Privately Held**
SIC: 3999 Manufacturing industries

(G-14600)
LARRY LEWIS
Also Called: Lpsoftware
2701 Springhaven Dr (23456-3992)
PHONE....................................757 619-7070
Larry Lewis, *Owner*
EMP: 1
SALES (est): 64.1K **Privately Held**
WEB: www.lpsoftware.net
SIC: 7372 Prepackaged software

(G-14601)
LASTMILE LOGISTIX INCORPORATED
138 S Rosemont Rd 201a (23452-4336)
PHONE....................................757 338-0076
EMP: 2
SALES (est): 145.1K **Privately Held**
SIC: 3537 4213 4212 Trucks: freight, baggage, etc.: industrial, except mining; trucking, except local; less-than-truckload (LTL) transport; local trucking, without storage

(G-14602)
LAUNDRY CHEMICAL PRODUCTS INC
2793 Sandpiper Rd (23456-4516)
PHONE....................................757 363-0662
Robert S Hobbs, *President*
EMP: 1
SALES (est): 1MM **Privately Held**
WEB: www.laundryconsultingvirginiabeach.com
SIC: 2841 5169 Soap & other detergents; chemicals & allied products

(G-14603)
LAVISH
4312 Holland Rd Ste 115 (23452-1378)
PHONE....................................757 498-1238
EMP: 1
SALES (est): 51.8K **Privately Held**
SIC: 2389 Costumes

(G-14604)
LAW HAULING LLC
764 De Laura Ln (23455-5721)
PHONE....................................757 774-3055
Ron Williams,
EMP: 2
SALES (est): 87.2K **Privately Held**
SIC: 3713 Car carrier bodies

(G-14605)
LE LOOK LLC
Also Called: Aphropolitan
4545 Commerce St # 2206 (23462-3279)
PHONE....................................301 237-5072
Nneka Chiazor,
Francis Chiazor,
Chinwe Ezenwa,
EMP: 3
SALES (est): 264.7K **Privately Held**
SIC: 2389 Men's miscellaneous accessories

(G-14606)
LEESA SLEEP LLC
Also Called: Leesa Dream Gallery
3200 Pacific Ave Ste 200 (23451-2917)
PHONE....................................844 335-3372

▲ = Import ▼=Export
◆ =Import/Export

David Wolfe, *CEO*
Rainer Agles, *Project Mgr*
Kassandra Ballord, *Accountant*
Steve Bokmiller, *Accountant*
Ian Kilpatrick, *Marketing Staff*
EMP: 2
SALES (est): 646.7K **Privately Held**
WEB: www.leesa.com
SIC: 2515 Mattresses & bedsprings

(G-14607)
LIBELLI LLC
1080 San Marco Rd (23456-4299)
PHONE...................757 373-9845
Jennifer Elizondo, *Administration*
EMP: 2
SALES (est): 82.3K **Privately Held**
WEB: www.alegzander.com
SIC: 2741 Miscellaneous publishing

(G-14608)
LIDL US LLC
6196 Providence Rd (23464-3737)
PHONE...................757 420-1562
EMP: 2
SALES (corp-wide): 125.9B **Privately Held**
WEB: www.careers.lidl.com
SIC: 2051 Bread, cake & related products
HQ: Lidl Us, Llc
3500 S Clark St
Arlington VA 22202
844 747-5435

(G-14609)
LIDL US LLC
3248 Holland Rd (23453-2829)
PHONE...................757 368-0256
EMP: 2
SALES (corp-wide): 125.9B **Privately Held**
WEB: www.careers.lidl.com
SIC: 2051 Bakery: wholesale or wholesale/retail combined
HQ: Lidl Us, Llc
3500 S Clark St
Arlington VA 22202
844 747-5435

(G-14610)
LIFENET HEALTH (PA)
1864 Concert Dr (23453-1903)
PHONE...................757 464-4761
Rony Thomas, *CEO*
Tom Sander, *President*
Mark Cole, *General Mgr*
Rex Nagao, *General Mgr*
Neil Clouser, *Regional Mgr*
EMP: 375
SQ FT: 38,000
SALES: 376.1MM **Privately Held**
WEB: www.lifenethealth.org
SIC: 3829 3842 8099 Thermometers, including digital: clinical; surgical appliances & supplies; blood related health services

(G-14611)
LIFETIME COATING SPECIALTIES
1317 Mozart Dr (23454-6630)
PHONE...................757 559-1011
EMP: 2 **EST:** 2013
SALES (est): 99K **Privately Held**
WEB: www.lifetimecoating.com
SIC: 3479 Metal coating & allied service

(G-14612)
LIGHTRONICS INC
509 Central Dr Ste 101 (23454-5273)
PHONE...................757 486-3588
Kevin Nelson, *President*
Tammy Collins, *Vice Pres*
Dennis Degen, *Sales Staff*
▲ **EMP:** 25
SQ FT: 15,000
SALES (est): 4MM **Privately Held**
WEB: www.lightronics.com
SIC: 3648 3674 3643 3625 Lighting equipment; semiconductors & related devices; current-carrying wiring devices; relays & industrial controls; switchgear & switchboard apparatus

(G-14613)
LIVINGSTON GROUP INC
4768 Hermitage Rd (23455-4030)
PHONE...................757 460-3115
Larry J Livingston, *President*
Sheila Livingston, *Corp Secy*
EMP: 2
SALES (est): 350K **Privately Held**
SIC: 2879 Soil conditioners

(G-14614)
LLC LITTLE BEAN
Also Called: Sweetpea
468 Viking Dr Ste 101 (23452-7469)
PHONE...................757 937-1600
EMP: 2
SALES (est): 151.4K **Privately Held**
SIC: 2499 Decorative wood & woodwork

(G-14615)
LOCKHEED MARTIN
1293 Perimeter Pkwy (23454-5690)
PHONE...................757 578-3377
Kim Vonmosh, *Manager*
EMP: 100 **Publicly Held**
WEB: www.lockheedmartin.com
SIC: 3812 Search & navigation equipment
HQ: Lockheed Martin Integrated Systems, Llc
6801 Rockledge Dr
Bethesda MD 20817

(G-14616)
LOCKHEED MARTIN CORPORATION
489 Sparrow St (23461-1909)
PHONE...................757 491-3501
Richard Dunn, *Principal*
EMP: 439 **Publicly Held**
WEB: www.lockheedmartin.com
SIC: 3812 Search & navigation equipment
PA: Lockheed Martin Corporation
6801 Rockledge Dr
Bethesda MD 20817

(G-14617)
LOCKHEED MARTIN CORPORATION
5813 Ward Ct (23455-3312)
PHONE...................757 464-0877
Marillyn Hewson, *CEO*
EMP: 8 **Publicly Held**
WEB: www.lockheedmartin.com
SIC: 3812 Search & navigation equipment
PA: Lockheed Martin Corporation
6801 Rockledge Dr
Bethesda MD 20817

(G-14618)
LOCKHEED MARTIN CORPORATION
1619 Diamond Springs Rd (23455-3019)
PHONE...................757 685-3132
Brian Hales, *Manager*
EMP: 1261 **Publicly Held**
WEB: www.lockheedmartin.com
SIC: 3812 Search & navigation equipment
PA: Lockheed Martin Corporation
6801 Rockledge Dr
Bethesda MD 20817

(G-14619)
LOCKHEED MARTIN CORPORATION
1293 Perimeter Pkwy (23454-5690)
PHONE...................757 803-3080
Matt Stuebe, *Manager*
Tom Howard, *Info Tech Dir*
EMP: 9 **Publicly Held**
WEB: www.lockheedmartin.com
SIC: 3812 Search & navigation equipment
PA: Lockheed Martin Corporation
6801 Rockledge Dr
Bethesda MD 20817

(G-14620)
LOCKHEED MARTIN CORPORATION
1293 Perimeter Pkwy (23454-5690)
PHONE...................757 430-6500
Doug Kint, *Branch Mgr*
EMP: 1018 **Publicly Held**
WEB: www.lockheedmartin.com
SIC: 3812 Search & navigation equipment

PA: Lockheed Martin Corporation
6801 Rockledge Dr
Bethesda MD 20817

(G-14621)
LOCKLEAR GROUP INC
2228 Ebb Tide Rd (23451-1502)
PHONE...................757 630-9022
Sean Kenneth Locklear, *Principal*
Jason Podd, *Principal*
EMP: 2
SALES (est): 86K **Privately Held**
SIC: 3731 Shipbuilding & repairing

(G-14622)
LOCUS TECHNOLOGY
341 Cleveland Pl Ste 106 (23462-6547)
PHONE...................757 340-1986
Scott Fogg, *Owner*
EMP: 2
SALES (est): 123.2K **Privately Held**
SIC: 2261 Screen printing of cotton broadwoven fabrics

(G-14623)
LONE TREE PRINTING INC
Also Called: Spectrum Printing
4716 Virginia Beach Blvd (23462-6709)
PHONE...................757 473-9977
Nadine R Olenych, *President*
Richard P Olenych, *Vice Pres*
Dick Olenych, *Info Tech Mgr*
EMP: 11
SQ FT: 5,000
SALES (est): 620K **Privately Held**
WEB: www.thehappyprinters.com
SIC: 2752 Commercial printing, offset

(G-14624)
LOST AND FOUND WINERY
2012 Absalom Dr (23451-1602)
PHONE...................707 321-6292
Bartolomeis Two, *Principal*
EMP: 2
SALES (est): 72.6K **Privately Held**
SIC: 2084 Wines

(G-14625)
LOVE THOSE TZ LLC
1417 Lynnhaven Pkwy (23453-2241)
PHONE...................757 897-0238
Sandra N Breslin, *Mng Member*
EMP: 1
SALES (est): 78.7K **Privately Held**
SIC: 2396 2395 2261 Screen printing on fabric articles; emblems, embroidered; printing of cotton broadwoven fabrics

(G-14626)
LOWE-GO EMB & DESIGNS LLC
3113 Ferry Farm Ln (23452-6528)
PHONE...................757 486-0617
Lloyd Lowe, *Principal*
EMP: 1
SALES (est): 82.7K **Privately Held**
WEB: www.lowe-go.com
SIC: 2395 Embroidery & art needlework

(G-14627)
LS LATE EMBROIDERY
4928 Floral St (23462-5540)
PHONE...................757 639-0647
Laura Slate, *Principal*
EMP: 1
SALES (est): 31.2K **Privately Held**
SIC: 2395 Embroidery & art needlework

(G-14628)
LTS SOFTWARE INC
1716 Corp Landing Pkwy (23454-5681)
PHONE...................757 493-8855
Kathleen Reiley Curry, *Administration*
EMP: 1
SALES (est): 151K
SALES (corp-wide): 132.5MM **Publicly Held**
SIC: 7372 Prepackaged software
PA: Franchise Group, Inc.
2387 Liberty Way
Virginia Beach VA 23456
757 493-8855

(G-14629)
LULULEMON
701 Lynnhaven Pkwy (23452-7299)
PHONE...................757 631-3004

EMP: 1
SALES (est): 42.5K **Privately Held**
SIC: 2389 Apparel & accessories

(G-14630)
MACKES WOODWORKING LLC
1909 Dannemora Dr (23453-3649)
PHONE...................570 856-3242
Christopher Mackes, *Principal*
EMP: 1
SALES (est): 54.1K **Privately Held**
SIC: 2431 Millwork

(G-14631)
MACTAGGART SCOTT USA LLC (DH)
920 Verano Ct (23456-6440)
PHONE...................757 288-1405
Steven Halpern, *President*
Richard Prenter, *Vice Pres*
William Marsh, *Treasurer*
George Merritt,
Alistair Plowman,
EMP: 4
SALES (est): 455.4K
SALES (corp-wide): 52.3MM **Privately Held**
WEB: www.mactag.com
SIC: 3519 3561 3594 Internal combustion engines; pumps & pumping equipment; fluid power pumps & motors
HQ: Mactaggart, Scott & Company Limited
Po Box 1
Loanhead EH20
131 440-0311

(G-14632)
MAD-DEN EMBROIDERY & GIFTS
2332 Kilburton Priory Ct (23456-5254)
PHONE...................757 450-4421
Susan Hahn, *Principal*
EMP: 1
SALES (est): 32.2K **Privately Held**
SIC: 2395 Embroidery & art needlework

(G-14633)
MAGNETIC BRACELETS AND MORE
5199 Cypress Point Cir (23455-6851)
PHONE...................757 499-1282
EMP: 1 **EST:** 2017
SALES (est): 50.8K **Privately Held**
WEB: www.magneticbraceletsandmore.com
SIC: 3961 Bracelets, except precious metal

(G-14634)
MAGOOZLE LLC
Also Called: Podium Pro
2493 Piney Bark Dr (23456-3971)
PHONE...................757 581-6936
Sean Evangelista, *Owner*
EMP: 2 **EST:** 2012
SALES (est): 96.7K **Privately Held**
WEB: www.goldwood.com
SIC: 7372 Application computer software

(G-14635)
MAHOGANY LANDSCAPING & DESIGN
1676 Cottenham Ln (23454-5799)
PHONE...................757 846-7947
Ryan Gay, *Principal*
EMP: 2
SALES (est): 67.6K **Privately Held**
SIC: 3949 Surfboards

(G-14636)
MAJIKSOFT
1644 Macgregory St (23464-7123)
PHONE...................757 510-0929
Paige Ake, *Principal*
EMP: 2 **EST:** 2017
SALES (est): 123.2K **Privately Held**
WEB: www.majiksoft.com
SIC: 7372 Prepackaged software

(G-14637)
MARBLE RESTORATION SYSTEMS
757 Oleander Cir (23464-4203)
P.O. Box 64393 (23467-4393)
PHONE...................757 739-7959

Thomas Butler Sr, *Owner*
EMP: 1
SALES (est): 46K **Privately Held**
SIC: 2842 Specialty cleaning, polishes & sanitation goods

(G-14638)
MARTIN MOBILE WLDG & REPR LLC
5329 Morris Neck Rd (23457-1374)
PHONE....................................757 581-3828
William Martin, *Manager*
EMP: 1
SALES (est): 25K **Privately Held**
SIC: 7692 Welding repair

(G-14639)
MATBOCK LLC
1164 Millers Ln Ste D (23451-5716)
PHONE....................................757 828-6659
Sean Matson, *CEO*
Zach Steinbock, *Principal*
Melissa Matson, *Opers Mgr*
EMP: 2
SALES (est): 230.1K **Privately Held**
WEB: www.matbock.com
SIC: 2389 3728 3021 3089 Men's miscellaneous accessories; military aircraft equipment & armament; boots, rubber or rubber soled fabric; injection molding of plastics

(G-14640)
MATHER AMP CABINET
2681 Prod Rd Ste 107 (23454)
PHONE....................................615 636-1743
EMP: 2
SALES (est): 161.1K **Privately Held**
WEB: www.mathercab.com
SIC: 2434 Wood kitchen cabinets

(G-14641)
MATTHEW CRAWFORD SARGENT
2505 Bodnar Ln (23456-7610)
PHONE....................................757 430-9488
Sargent Matthew Crawford, *Principal*
EMP: 3 EST: 2016
SALES (est): 115.3K **Privately Held**
SIC: 2711 Newspapers, publishing & printing

(G-14642)
MATTHEWS SHEET METAL INC
Also Called: Matthews Sheetmetal
5821 Arrowhead Dr Ste 102 (23462-3259)
PHONE....................................757 543-6009
Lee Mattews, *CEO*
EMP: 2
SALES (est): 500K **Privately Held**
SIC: 3444 1711 Sheet metalwork; plumbing, heating, air-conditioning contractors

(G-14643)
MCKEAN DEFENSE GROUP LLC
Also Called: McKean Defense Group Info Tech
477 Viking Dr Ste 400 (23452-7349)
PHONE....................................202 448-5250
Donald Lehner, *Vice Pres*
John Scipione, *Manager*
Opal-Dawn Martin,
William Baxter, *Training Spec*
Stuart Macaleer,
EMP: 99
SALES (est): 6.2MM **Privately Held**
WEB: www.mckean-defense.com
SIC: 3731 8711 Shipbuilding & repairing; engineering services

(G-14644)
MEDIA MAGIC LLC
4544 Bob Jones Dr (23462-4621)
PHONE....................................757 893-0988
Aaron Yarborough,
EMP: 1
SALES (est): 49.1K **Privately Held**
WEB: www.mediamagicfilms.com
SIC: 3861 7389 Motion picture film;

(G-14645)
MEDTRNIC SOFAMOR DANEK USA INC
900 Mary Lou Ct (23464-8311)
PHONE....................................757 355-5100
Trey Schott, *Branch Mgr*
EMP: 17 **Privately Held**
WEB: www.medtronic.com
SIC: 3841 Surgical & medical instruments
HQ: Medtronic Sofamor Danek Usa, Inc.
1800 Pyramid Pl
Memphis TN 38132
901 396-3133

(G-14646)
MEESH MONOGRAMS
1600 Stephens Rd (23454-1510)
PHONE....................................757 672-4276
Michelle Gregory, *Principal*
EMP: 1
SALES (est): 33.1K **Privately Held**
SIC: 2395 Embroidery & art needlework

(G-14647)
MELISSA DAVIS
4313 Enterprise Blvd (23453-1529)
PHONE....................................757 482-3743
EMP: 1
SALES (est): 57K **Privately Held**
SIC: 3821 Dental Hygeine

(G-14648)
MG CORP
889 Seahawk Cir (23452-7809)
P.O. Box 8187 (23450-8187)
PHONE....................................757 468-6000
Mark F Garcea, *President*
▼ EMP: 700 EST: 1976
SQ FT: 140,000
SALES (est): 2.1MM **Privately Held**
SIC: 3613 3694 3699 3643 Panelboards & distribution boards, electric; harness wiring sets, internal combustion engines; electrical equipment & supplies; current-carrying wiring devices; nonferrous wire-drawing & insulating

(G-14649)
MICHAEL KORS
701 Lynnhaven Pkwy # 1088 (23452-7299)
PHONE....................................757 216-0581
EMP: 1
SALES (est): 42.5K **Privately Held**
SIC: 2389 Apparel & accessories

(G-14650)
MID-ATLANTIC BRACING CORP
2917 Chilton Pl (23456-7931)
PHONE....................................757 301-3952
EMP: 2
SALES: 100K **Privately Held**
SIC: 3842 Mfg Surgical Appliances/Supplies

(G-14651)
MIDNIGHT EMBROIDERY
3725 Harton Ct (23452-3748)
PHONE....................................757 463-1692
Stephen H Smith, *Owner*
EMP: 1
SALES (est): 45.8K **Privately Held**
SIC: 2395 Embroidery products, except schiffli machine

(G-14652)
MIDYETTE BROS MFG INC
1702 Southern Blvd (23454-4528)
PHONE....................................757 425-5022
Ronald Midyette, *President*
Anthony Naghiu, *Vice Pres*
EMP: 2
SQ FT: 2,500
SALES (est): 170K **Privately Held**
SIC: 3498 Tube fabricating (contract bending & shaping)

(G-14653)
MIKES MARINE CUSTOM CANVAS
2244 Red Tide Rd (23451-1533)
PHONE....................................757 496-1090
Michael Johnson, *Owner*
EMP: 2
SALES (est): 156.3K **Privately Held**
WEB: www.mikesmarinecanvas.com
SIC: 2394 Canvas & related products

(G-14654)
MILCOM SYSTEMS CORPORATION VOL
532 Viking Dr (23452-7316)
PHONE....................................757 463-2800
Jack Legg, *Manager*
EMP: 17
SALES: 3MM **Privately Held**
SIC: 3669 Communications equipment

(G-14655)
MISCELLANEOUS & ORNA MTLS INC
2961 Shore Dr (23451-1248)
PHONE....................................757 650-5226
Larry Reece, *President*
Nell Reece, *Admin Sec*
EMP: 7 EST: 2013
SALES (est): 524.5K **Privately Held**
WEB: www.momvb.weebly.com
SIC: 3446 Gates, ornamental metal

(G-14656)
MITCHELLS WOODWORK INC
596 Central Dr Ste 107 (23454-5238)
PHONE....................................757 340-4154
James Mitchell, *President*
Anita Faye Mitchell, *Vice Pres*
EMP: 1
SALES (est): 169.1K **Privately Held**
WEB: www.jimmitchellswoodworking.com
SIC: 2431 Woodwork, interior & ornamental

(G-14657)
MIX IT UP MIXERS AND MORE LLC
2973 Shore Dr (23451-1201)
PHONE....................................757 412-1200
Coleman Ferguson, *Principal*
EMP: 4
SALES (est): 162.9K **Privately Held**
SIC: 2084 Wines, brandy & brandy spirits

(G-14658)
MM EXPORT LLC
4940 Rutherford Rd # 400 (23455-4000)
PHONE....................................757 333-0542
Huseyin Ozkan, *Principal*
EMP: 2
SQ FT: 2,000
SALES (est): 209.7K **Privately Held**
WEB: www.mmexport.us
SIC: 3432 5074 3494 Plastic plumbing fixture fittings, assembly; plumbing & hydronic heating supplies; plumbing fittings & supplies; plumbing & heating valves

(G-14659)
MOBILE CUSTOM FRAMING LLC
2628 Landview Cir (23454-1227)
PHONE....................................757 412-4167
Deanna Dugan, *Principal*
EMP: 1 EST: 2009
SALES (est): 52.5K **Privately Held**
SIC: 2499 Picture frame molding, finished

(G-14660)
MOLD FRESH LLC
4004 Atlantic Ave Apt 308 (23451-2624)
PHONE....................................757 696-9288
Perry Michael Kiriakos, *Administration*
EMP: 2
SALES (est): 113.4K **Privately Held**
SIC: 3544 Industrial molds

(G-14661)
MOMMAS BEST HOMEMADE LLC
3133 Barbour Dr (23456-7905)
PHONE....................................805 509-5419
Tammy Mason, *Administration*
EMP: 4
SALES (est): 292.6K **Privately Held**
WEB: www.mommasbesthomemade.com
SIC: 2844 Toilet preparations

(G-14662)
MONIKEV-FISHER LLC
4832 Linshaw Ln (23455-5322)
PHONE....................................757 343-4153
Bettie F Perry,
EMP: 1

SALES (est): 69.6K **Privately Held**
SIC: 3423 Hand & edge tools

(G-14663)
MORPHIX TECHNOLOGIES INC
2557 Production Rd (23454-5286)
PHONE....................................757 431-2260
Bart Heenan, *President*
Paul Di Nardo, *Treasurer*
Karen Brewington, *Accounts Mgr*
Kimberly Chapman, *Admin Sec*
EMP: 35
SALES (est): 7.3MM **Privately Held**
WEB: www.morphtec.com
SIC: 3829 Measuring & controlling devices

(G-14664)
MORRIS DESIGNS INC
277 N Lynnhven Rd Ste 108 (23452)
PHONE....................................757 463-9400
Kathryn Morris, *President*
EMP: 10
SQ FT: 700
SALES (est): 1.1MM **Privately Held**
WEB: www.morrisdesigns.com
SIC: 2389 7389 Hospital gowns; interior designer

(G-14665)
MOTO FARKLE SUPPORT SERVICES
2077 Bierce Dr (23454-7221)
PHONE....................................757 705-2014
Burky Daniel, *Principal*
EMP: 2
SALES (est): 153.7K **Privately Held**
SIC: 3663 Radio & TV communications equipment

(G-14666)
MOVA CORP
Also Called: Specialty Club
2608 Horse Pasture Rd (23453-2997)
PHONE....................................757 598-5577
Mauricio Mova, *President*
EMP: 1
SQ FT: 1,800
SALES (est): 0 **Privately Held**
SIC: 2095 Instant coffee

(G-14667)
MRS BONES
1616 Hilltop W Shopg Ctr (23451)
PHONE....................................757 412-0500
EMP: 3 EST: 2011
SALES (est): 120K **Privately Held**
SIC: 3999 Mfg Misc Products

(G-14668)
MY BEST FRIENDS CUPCAKES LLC
2200 Glenrose Ct (23456-6335)
P.O. Box 544 (23451-0544)
PHONE....................................757 754-1148
Jackie Jacobs, *Mng Member*
Dillon Jacobs, *Mng Member*
EMP: 2
SALES (est): 81.4K **Privately Held**
SIC: 2047 5149 Dog food; dog food

(G-14669)
NANA STITCHES
2901 Cardini Pl (23453-3214)
PHONE....................................757 689-3767
EMP: 1
SALES (est): 35.3K **Privately Held**
SIC: 2395 Pleating/Stitching Services

(G-14670)
NANOARCA INC
4416 Pope Valley Ct (23456-1477)
PHONE....................................757 589-2526
Bo Xiao, *CEO*
EMP: 1
SALES (est): 64.3K **Privately Held**
SIC: 3826 Analytical instruments

(G-14671)
NAVY
937 Avatar Dr (23454-6826)
PHONE....................................757 417-4236
EMP: 2
SALES (est): 88.3K **Privately Held**
WEB: www.navy.mil
SIC: 3625 Relays & industrial controls

(G-14672)
NBC BOATWORKS
3253 Sandpiper Rd (23456-4311)
PHONE..............................757 630-0420
J Parks Atkinson, *Principal*
▲ EMP: 1 EST: 2012
SALES (est): 81.5K **Privately Held**
SIC: 3732 Boat building & repairing

(G-14673)
NCS PEARSON INC
208 Farmington Rd (23454-4040)
PHONE..............................866 673-9034
Susan Aspey, *Vice Pres*
EMP: 5
SALES (corp-wide): 5B **Privately Held**
WEB: www.pearsonassessments.com
SIC: 3825 Test equipment for electronic &
electric measurement
HQ: Ncs Pearson Inc
5601 Green Valley Dr # 220
Bloomington MN 55437
952 681-3000

(G-14674)
NEICEYS
526 Rivers Reach (23452-8014)
PHONE..............................757 500-1021
Melvineice Holloman, *Owner*
EMP: 1
SALES (est): 10K **Privately Held**
SIC: 3999 Hair & hair-based products

(G-14675)
NER INC
Also Called: Pacific
1820 Atlantic Ave (23451-3309)
PHONE..............................757 437-7727
Ezra Bendayan, *President*
EMP: 5
SQ FT: 3,000
SALES (est): 769.5K **Privately Held**
SIC: 2339 Beachwear: women's, misses' &
juniors'

(G-14676)
NET 100 LTD
5257 Cleveland St Ste 102 (23462-6549)
PHONE..............................757 490-0496
Rod Cannon, *President*
EMP: 5 **Privately Held**
WEB: www.net100ltd.com
SIC: 2298 Cable, fiber
PA: Net 100 Ltd.
3675 Concorde Pkwy # 800
Chantilly VA 20151

(G-14677)
NETUNITY SOFTWARE LLC
2201 Bierce Dr (23454-7219)
PHONE..............................757 744-0147
EMP: 10
SALES (est): 620K **Privately Held**
SIC: 3695 7371 Magnetic And Optical
Recording Media

(G-14678)
NETWORK INDUSTRIES
1810 S Woodside Ln (23454-1030)
PHONE..............................757 435-6163
Anina Budig, *Info Tech Mgr*
EMP: 2 EST: 2015
SALES (est): 68.2K **Privately Held**
WEB: www.networkindustries.org
SIC: 3999 Manufacturing industries

(G-14679)
NEW HEMP US
2608 Horse Pasture Rd # 1 (23453-2997)
PHONE..............................757 977-8098
Michael Copon, *Exec Dir*
EMP: 2
SALES (est): 100K **Privately Held**
SIC: 3999

(G-14680)
NEW LIFE CUSTOM CABINETRY
LLC
1512 Hedgerow Dr (23455-3402)
PHONE..............................757 274-7442
EMP: 2
SALES (est): 101.2K **Privately Held**
SIC: 2434 Wood kitchen cabinets

(G-14681)
NGK-LCKE POLYMR
INSULATORS INC
1609 Diamond Springs Rd (23455-3009)
PHONE..............................757 460-3649
Rit Sato, *President*
Kenny Nakano, *Principal*
Koichi Nakano, *Principal*
Yuya Hagiwara, *Corp Secy*
Naoto Saito, *Corp Secy*
◆ EMP: 100
SQ FT: 110,000
SALES (est): 29.4MM **Privately Held**
WEB: www.ngk-locke.com
SIC: 3264 Insulators, electrical: porcelain
HQ: Ngk North America, Inc.
1105 N Market St Ste 1300
Wilmington DE 19801
302 654-1344

(G-14682)
NO LIE BLADES LLC
Also Called: NLB
1728 Prodan Ln (23453-7076)
PHONE..............................610 442-5539
Henry L Hayes, *CEO*
EMP: 2
SALES (est): 140K **Privately Held**
WEB: www.trainingknives.net
SIC: 3421 Knife blades & blanks

(G-14683)
NO SHORT CUT
918 Chimney Hill Pkwy (23462-6938)
PHONE..............................757 696-0249
Ellen Preston, *Owner*
EMP: 1 EST: 2007
SALES (est): 42.4K **Privately Held**
SIC: 2395 Embroidery & art needlework

(G-14684)
NORTH LAKESIDE PUBG HSE
LLC
2245 N Lakeside Dr (23454-2065)
PHONE..............................757 650-3596
Therese Adams, *Principal*
EMP: 2
SALES (est): 86.7K **Privately Held**
SIC: 2741 Miscellaneous publishing

(G-14685)
NORTHROP GRUMMAN
SYSTEMS CORP
Also Called: Mission Systems
2700 Intl Pkwy Ste 700 (23452)
PHONE..............................757 498-5616
Steven Langhi, *Prdtn Mgr*
Eloy Feliciano, *Engineer*
Edward Killinger, *Manager*
EMP: 200 **Publicly Held**
WEB: www.northropgrumman.com
SIC: 3812 Search & navigation equipment
HQ: Northrop Grumman Systems Corpora-
tion
2980 Fairview Park Dr
Falls Church VA 22042
703 280-2900

(G-14686)
NORTHROP GRUMMAN
SYSTEMS CORP
3845 North Landing Rd (23456-2481)
PHONE..............................757 686-4147
EMP: 2 **Publicly Held**
WEB: www.northropgrumman.com
SIC: 3812 Search & navigation equipment
HQ: Northrop Grumman Systems Corpora-
tion
2980 Fairview Park Dr
Falls Church VA 22042
703 280-2900

(G-14687)
NORTHROP GRUMMAN
SYSTEMS CORP
2700 International Pkwy # 300
(23452-7847)
PHONE..............................757 463-5578
EMP: 8 **Publicly Held**
WEB: www.northropgrumman.com
SIC: 3812 Search & navigation equipment

HQ: Northrop Grumman Systems Corporation
2980 Fairview Park Dr
Falls Church VA 22042
703 280-2900

(G-14688)
NULINE
1749 Virginia Beach Blvd (23454-4529)
PHONE..............................757 425-3213
EMP: 2
SALES (est): 96K **Privately Held**
SIC: 3694 Mfg Engine Electrical Equip-
ment

(G-14689)
NUTRIENTS PLUS LLC
2133 Upton Dr Ste 126 (23454-1194)
PHONE..............................757 430-3400
Markovska Natalia, *Director*
John Moriarty,
Gregory R Gill,
EMP: 3
SQ FT: 1,000
SALES (est): 3MM **Privately Held**
WEB: www.claruschoice.com
SIC: 2873 Fertilizers: natural (organic), ex-
cept compost

(G-14690)
OCEAN APPAREL
INCORPORATED
2984 S Lynnhaven Rd # 118 (23452-6723)
PHONE..............................757 422-8262
John Jones, *President*
EMP: 8
SALES (est): 770K **Privately Held**
WEB: www.oavb.com
SIC: 2759 Screen printing

(G-14691)
OCEAN CREEK APPAREL LLC
1368 Baker Rd (23455-3316)
PHONE..............................757 460-6118
John McGovern,
Brian Ryals,
▼ EMP: 14
SQ FT: 9,000
SALES (est): 1.8MM **Privately Held**
WEB: www.oceancreekapparel.com
SIC: 2759 5137 Screen printing; women's
& children's clothing

(G-14692)
OCEAN FOODS INC
5158 Rugby Rd (23464-7954)
P.O. Box 65603 (23467-5603)
PHONE..............................757 474-6314
William Mall, *President*
Josephine Mall, *Vice Pres*
EMP: 2 EST: 1984
SALES (est): 168.4K **Privately Held**
SIC: 2092 Fish, fresh: prepared

(G-14693)
OLIVE SAVOR
1624 Laskin Rd Ste 730 (23451-7501)
PHONE..............................757 425-3866
Frank Lawrence, *Owner*
Bonnie Lawrence, *Co-Owner*
EMP: 2
SALES (est): 350.9K **Privately Held**
WEB: www.savortheolive.com
SIC: 2099 2079 Vinegar; olive oil

(G-14694)
OMNIDEX PRODUCTS INC
504 Leatherwood Ct (23462-5703)
PHONE..............................757 509-4030
Kenneth Bumgarner, *President*
EMP: 2
SALES (corp-wide): 457.8K **Privately
Held**
WEB: www.omnidex.net
SIC: 2821 Plastics materials & resins
PA: Omnidex Products, Inc.
196 Sentinel Pl Se
Marietta GA 30067
770 539-2543

(G-14695)
OMNIIO LLC
2744 Sonic Dr Ste 101 (23453-3183)
PHONE..............................877 842-5478
Heather Adolphi,
EMP: 12

SALES: 153K **Privately Held**
WEB: www.omybathandbody.com
SIC: 2841 Textile soap

(G-14696)
ON IT SMART SNACKS
1817 Riddle Ave (23454-4526)
P.O. Box 7096 (23457-0096)
PHONE..............................757 705-9259
Ellen Aleskowitz, *President*
EMP: 2
SALES (est): 62.3K **Privately Held**
SIC: 2096 Potato chips & similar snacks

(G-14697)
ON THE ROAD TRANSPORT LLC
464 Investors Pl Ste 206e (23452-1384)
PHONE..............................410 207-2592
Toshiba Eason,
EMP: 1
SALES (est): 40K **Privately Held**
SIC: 3711 Personnel carriers (motor vehi-
cles), assembly of

(G-14698)
ON THE WEEKLY LLC
957 Summerside Ct (23456-6307)
PHONE..............................757 839-2640
EMP: 3 EST: 2014
SALES (est): 106.1K **Privately Held**
SIC: 2711 Newspapers, publishing & print-
ing

(G-14699)
ONE FOUR THREE LLC
Also Called: Vintage Virginia Photos
3781 Jefferson Blvd (23455-1637)
PHONE..............................303 594-7151
K Paige Simmons, *Principal*
Grant Simmons, *Principal*
EMP: 1
SALES (est): 53.2K **Privately Held**
SIC: 2752 Commercial printing, litho-
graphic

(G-14700)
ONE PIECE FABRICATION LLC
1393 Air Rail Ave (23455-3301)
PHONE..............................757 460-8637
Patrick Wallace, *Principal*
EMP: 2
SALES (est): 161.2K **Privately Held**
WEB: www.onepiecefab.com
SIC: 7692 Welding repair

(G-14701)
ONGRADE PLLC
2704 Fayette Ct (23456-7600)
PHONE..............................757 448-5635
EMP: 3
SALES (est): 170.8K **Privately Held**
SIC: 3812 Search & navigation equipment

(G-14702)
OPENING PROTECTION SVCS
LLC
973 Sunnyside Dr (23464-2128)
P.O. Box 64337 (23467-4337)
PHONE..............................757 222-0730
James Rodrigue,
Elizabeth Rodrigue,
Jim Rodrigue,
▲ EMP: 2
SALES (est): 63K **Privately Held**
WEB: www.openingprotection.com
SIC: 3442 1799 Shutters, door or window:
metal; window treatment installation

(G-14703)
ORIEN USA LLC
921 General Hill Dr (23454-2633)
PHONE..............................757 486-2099
John Doran, *Managing Prtnr*
▲ EMP: 5
SALES (est): 698.7K **Privately Held**
WEB: www.orienusa.com
SIC: 3585 7389 Ice making machinery;

(G-14704)
OSG PROPULSION LLC
572 Central Dr Ste 104 (23454-5253)
P.O. Box 8851 (23450-8851)
PHONE..............................757 340-0052
Trudy Cartledge,
Jenny Dimokas,

GEOGRAPHIC

EMP: 2
SQ FT: 4,131
SALES (est): 165.4K **Privately Held**
WEB: www.osgpropulsion.com
SIC: 3731 Commercial cargo ships, building & repairing

(G-14705)
OSI LLC
Also Called: District IV Apparel Company
5205 Mile Course Walk (23455-2566)
P.O. Box 5672 (23471-0672)
PHONE..................................757 967-7533
Dwayne Kay,
EMP: 1
SALES (est): 83K **Privately Held**
WEB: www.osidigital.com
SIC: 2353 7389 Uniform hats & caps;

(G-14706)
OSI MARITIME SYSTEMS INC
4445 Corp Ln Ste 264 (23462)
PHONE..................................877 432-7467
Christian Haugen, *President*
Jim Girard, *CFO*
EMP: 1
SQ FT: 2,051
SALES (est): 91K
SALES (corp-wide): 26.1MM **Privately Held**
WEB: www.osimaritime.com
SIC: 3812 7371 7373 7389 Search & navigation equipment; computer software development; computer integrated systems design;
PA: Osi Geospatial Inc
4585 Canada Way Suite 400
Burnaby BC V5G 4
778 373-4600

(G-14707)
P J HENRY INC
Also Called: Jmi
1164 Millers Ln A (23451-5716)
PHONE..................................757 428-0301
George H Metzger, *President*
Ted R Metzger, *Vice Pres*
Shockett Mike, *Vice Pres*
Mike Shocket, *Vice Pres*
Emily Campbell, *Executive*
EMP: 28
SQ FT: 18,000
SALES (est): 1.7MM **Privately Held**
SIC: 2329 Men's & boys' sportswear & athletic clothing

(G-14708)
PACEM PUBLISHING
2111 San Lorenzo Quay (23456-7724)
PHONE..................................757 214-4800
Kenley John Henry III, *Principal*
EMP: 1
SALES (est): 41.3K **Privately Held**
SIC: 2741 Miscellaneous publishing

(G-14709)
PAN AMERICAN SYSTEMS CORP
Also Called: Pasc
1354 London Bridge Rd # 106 .
(23453-3106)
PHONE..................................757 468-1926
Rolando E Timm, *President*
Judyth Timm, *Vice Pres*
EMP: 5
SQ FT: 5,000
SALES (est): 794.3K **Privately Held**
WEB: www.pasc.com
SIC: 3679 8711 3825 3823 Electronic circuits; electrical or electronic engineering; consulting engineer; instruments to measure electricity; industrial instrmnts msrmnt display/control process variable; auto controls regulating residntl & coml environmt & applncs; relays & industrial controls

(G-14710)
PAR TEES VB
1577 General Booth Blvd (23454-5105)
PHONE..................................757 500-7831
EMP: 2
SALES (est): 92.1K **Privately Held**
SIC: 2759 Screen printing

(G-14711)
PASTIME PUBLICATIONS LLC
1303 Waterfront Dr Apt 10 (23451-6456)
PHONE..................................724 961-2922
EMP: 1
SALES (est): 37.5K **Privately Held**
SIC: 2741 Miscellaneous publishing

(G-14712)
PAWSE & PLAY LLC
4445 Corp Ln Ste 264 (23462)
PHONE..................................757 230-9309
Wanda Privott, *Mng Member*
EMP: 1
SALES (est): 40.9K **Privately Held**
SIC: 2399 Pet collars, leashes, etc.: non-leather

(G-14713)
PCC CORPORATION
Also Called: Printmark Commercial Printers
2728 Nestlebrook Trl (23456-8309)
PHONE..................................757 721-2949
Patrick Cunningham, *President*
Colleen Cunningham, *Vice Pres*
EMP: 25
SALES (est): 2.2MM **Privately Held**
WEB: www.pccav.com
SIC: 2759 Commercial printing

(G-14714)
PCC CORPORATION
Also Called: Printmark Comm. Printers
524 Central Dr Ste 102 (23454-5292)
PHONE..................................757 368-5777
Patrick Cunningham, *President*
EMP: 12
SALES (est): 1.2MM **Privately Held**
SIC: 2752 Commercial printing, offset

(G-14715)
PEARSON & ASSOCIATES
3460 Macdonald Rd (23464-1640)
PHONE..................................757 523-1382
Willard Pearson, *Owner*
EMP: 1
SALES (est): 44.3K **Privately Held**
SIC: 2023 Dietary supplements, dairy & non-dairy based

(G-14716)
PENNROSE PUBLISHING LLC
2909 Pinewood Dr (23452-6818)
PHONE..................................757 631-0579
Johnathan Bristol, *Principal*
EMP: 2
SALES (est): 130.9K **Privately Held**
SIC: 2741 Miscellaneous publishing

(G-14717)
PERSONAL PROTECTIO PRINCIPLES
Also Called: P3 Academy
4017 Roebling Ln (23452-1868)
PHONE..................................757 453-3202
Ryan Rico, *President*
EMP: 1
SALES (est): 75.7K **Privately Held**
SIC: 3949 8299 7381 8748 Target shooting equipment; self-defense & athletic instruction; protective services, guard; business consulting

(G-14718)
PERSONAL TOUCH PRINTING SVCS
912 Martingale Ct (23454-6817)
PHONE..................................757 619-7073
EMP: 2
SALES (est): 83.9K **Privately Held**
SIC: 2752 Lithographic Commercial Printing

(G-14719)
PHAZE II PRODUCTS INC
1100 Bay Colony Dr (23451-3804)
PHONE..................................757 353-3901
George Masisak, *President*
Debbie Presto, *Vice Pres*
EMP: 37
SQ FT: 9,500
SALES (est): 8.5MM **Privately Held**
SIC: 3612 Transformers, except electric

(G-14720)
PHOENIX DESIGNS
1953 Winterhaven Dr (23456-7703)
PHONE..................................757 301-9300
Heidi Faith, *Principal*
EMP: 2 EST: 2018
SALES (est): 62.9K **Privately Held**
SIC: 2711 Newspapers

(G-14721)
PHUBLE INC
2552 Nestlebrook Trl (23456-8297)
PHONE..................................443 388-0657
Philemon Viennas, *CEO*
EMP: 10
SALES (est): 282.3K **Privately Held**
SIC: 2741

(G-14722)
PINK SHOE PUBLISHING
3949 Rainbow Dr (23456-1331)
PHONE..................................757 277-1948
EMP: 2
SALES (est): 65.2K **Privately Held**
SIC: 2741 Miscellaneous publishing

(G-14723)
PINSTRIPE CSTM LONGBOARDS LLC
905 Gneral Beauregard Dr (23454)
PHONE..................................757 635-7183
EMP: 2
SALES (est): 120.6K **Privately Held**
WEB: www.pinstripecustoms.com
SIC: 2431 Millwork

(G-14724)
PITTSBURG TANK & TOWER CO INC
521 Bushnell Dr (23451-7115)
PHONE..................................757 422-1882
Mark Buddemeyer, *Vice Pres*
Greg Garber, *Manager*
EMP: 3
SALES (corp-wide): 87.9MM **Privately Held**
WEB: www.pttg.com
SIC: 3443 Water tanks, metal plate
PA: Pittsburg Tank & Tower Co Inc
1 Watertank Pl
Henderson KY 42420
270 826-9000

(G-14725)
PLANTATION SHUTTER & BLIND
1248 Secretariat Run (23454-5529)
PHONE..................................757 241-7026
EMP: 2
SALES (est): 100.4K **Privately Held**
SIC: 3442 Shutters, door or window: metal

(G-14726)
PLOW SHEAR PRESS LLC
2124 Sandalwood Rd (23451-1320)
PHONE..................................757 346-8821
Irmina Stiles, *Principal*
EMP: 1
SALES (est): 37.5K **Privately Held**
SIC: 2741 Miscellaneous publishing

(G-14727)
PM SERVICES LLC
Also Called: Petersburg Grows
2316 Kilburton Priory Ct (23456-5254)
PHONE..................................804 426-9892
Paul Meyer, *Mng Member*
EMP: 1
SALES (est): 111.5K **Privately Held**
SIC: 3537 7299 1521 7363 Trucks, tractors, loaders, carriers & similar equipment; handyman service; single-family home remodeling, additions & repairs; truck driver services; real estate investors, except property operators

(G-14728)
POLARIS GROUP INTL LLC
4445 Corp Ln Ste 150 (23462)
PHONE..................................757 636-8862
Charles Kubic, *President*
Stephanie Jason, *Vice Pres*
EMP: 2
SALES (est): 105K **Privately Held**
SIC: 3711 3713 Cars, armored, assembly of; specialty motor vehicle bodies

(G-14729)
POLO RALPH LAUREN CORP
4804 Gatwick Dr (23462-6436)
PHONE..................................201 531-6000
Shane Arnold, *CTO*
EMP: 2
SALES (est): 67K **Privately Held**
SIC: 2311 Men's & boys' suits & coats

(G-14730)
POSH PIXIE LLC
4445 Corporation Ln 264 (23462-3262)
PHONE..................................757 794-4949
Jazmine McVay, *Mng Member*
EMP: 1
SALES (est): 47.3K **Privately Held**
SIC: 3999 Manufacturing industries

(G-14731)
POWERBILT STEEL BUILDINGS INC
1559 Laskin Rd (23451-6111)
PHONE..................................757 425-6223
Stephan I Michaels, *President*
EMP: 10 EST: 1996
SALES (est): 1.5MM **Privately Held**
WEB: www.powerbiltbuildings.com
SIC: 3448 Prefabricated metal buildings

(G-14732)
PRECISION GENERATORS COMPANY
200 Golden Oak Ct Ste 250 (23452-8501)
PHONE..................................757 498-4809
Joseph McDonnell, *CEO*
Jerry McDonnell, *Chairman*
▼ EMP: 2
SALES (est): 227.1K **Privately Held**
SIC: 3569 Gas generators

(G-14733)
PRECISION POWDER COATING INC
2593 Aviator Dr Ste 101 (23453-3158)
P.O. Box 10400 (23450-0400)
PHONE..................................757 368-2135
Lou Amati, *President*
Stanley Nance, *Vice Pres*
EMP: 5
SALES (est): 400K **Privately Held**
WEB: www.precision-powder-coat.com
SIC: 3479 Coating of metals & formed products

(G-14734)
PRECISION QULTY SHIP REPR LLC
170 Coral Gables Ct Apt 7 (23452-5527)
PHONE..................................757 322-0654
Marcos Freytes, *Principal*
EMP: 1
SALES (est): 61.6K **Privately Held**
SIC: 3731 Shipbuilding & repairing

(G-14735)
PRECISION WELDING LLC
1984 Grandon Loop Rd (23456-3522)
PHONE..................................434 973-2106
Jonathan Blakey, *Principal*
EMP: 1
SALES (est): 27.6K **Privately Held**
SIC: 7692 Welding repair

(G-14736)
PREMIER MILLWORK & LBR CO INC
517 Viking Dr (23452-7306)
PHONE..................................757 463-8870
George R Melnyk, *President*
Phil Lamberty, *Mfg Staff*
Patricia Melnyk, *Treasurer*
Steve Tyson, *Contractor*
EMP: 40 EST: 1950
SQ FT: 33,000
SALES (est): 6.4MM **Privately Held**
WEB: www.premiermillwork.com
SIC: 2431 Millwork

(G-14737)
PRESSWARDTHEMARK MEDIA PUBLISH
5848 Magnolia Chase Way (23464-6878)
PHONE..................................757 807-2232
Chelsea Nicolle Vann, *Administration*

EMP: 1
SALES (est): 41.3K **Privately Held**
SIC: 2741 Miscellaneous publishing

(G-14738)
PRIME SIGNS
2814 Broad Bay Rd (23451-1624)
PHONE..............................757 481-7889
Wayne Rowe, *Owner*
EMP: 3
SQ FT: 2,500
SALES (est): 117.4K **Privately Held**
SIC: 3993 Signs, not made in custom sign painting shops

(G-14739)
PRINT LINK INC
811 S Lynnhaven Rd (23452-6312)
PHONE..............................757 368-5200
John K Cablach, *President*
John Edmonds, *Business Dir*
EMP: 2
SQ FT: 1,200
SALES (est): 576.5K **Privately Held**
WEB: www.earthfriendlyprinter.net
SIC: 2752 Commercial printing, offset

(G-14740)
PRINT REPUBLIC LLC
916 Delaware Ave (23451-4629)
PHONE..............................757 633-9099
Stephen Michael Snellinger, *Principal*
EMP: 2
SALES (est): 92.3K **Privately Held**
SIC: 2752 Commercial printing, lithographic

(G-14741)
PRISSY PICKLE COMPANY LLC
7 Caribbean Ave (23451-4762)
PHONE..............................804 514-8112
Dena Marie Sawyer,
EMP: 2
SALES (est): 62.3K **Privately Held**
WEB: www.theprissypickle.com
SIC: 2035 Pickles, vinegar

(G-14742)
PROBLEM SOLVER
3749 Frazier Ln (23456-5741)
PHONE..............................757 452-0653
Christopher B Tyszkiewicz, *Principal*
EMP: 3 EST: 2015
SALES (est): 151.8K **Privately Held**
SIC: 2522 Office furniture, except wood

(G-14743)
PROGRAPHICS PRINT XPRESS
5312 Virginia Beach Blvd (23462-1890)
PHONE..............................757 606-8303
EMP: 2
SALES (est): 90.5K **Privately Held**
SIC: 2752 Commercial printing, lithographic

(G-14744)
PROGRESSIVE GRAPHICS INC (PA)
2860 Crusader Cir (23453-3134)
PHONE..............................757 368-3321
Norman G Williams, *President*
David Corleto, *Plant Mgr*
Karen Hull, *Accounting Mgr*
Jerry M Williams, *Sales Mgr*
Laura Bolt, *Accounts Exec*
EMP: 23
SQ FT: 15,000
SALES (est): 3.2MM **Privately Held**
WEB: www.progressivegraphics.com
SIC: 2752 2789 2759 Commercial printing, offset; bookbinding & related work; commercial printing

(G-14745)
PROSPERITY PUBLISHING INC
944 S Spigel Dr (23454-1823)
PHONE..............................757 339-9900
Eileen K Carlson, *Principal*
EMP: 4
SALES (est): 291.5K **Privately Held**
WEB: www.nsnbg.com
SIC: 2741 Miscellaneous publishing

(G-14746)
PRUFREX USA INC
2573 Quality Ct (23454-5297)
PHONE..............................757 963-5400
Kurt Mueller, *CEO*
Yvonne Mueller, *President*
▲ **EMP:** 4
SALES (est): 500K
SALES (corp-wide): 26.3MM **Privately Held**
WEB: www.pruefrex.com
SIC: 3679 Electronic circuits
PA: Prufrex Innovative Power Products Gmbh
Egersdorfer Str. 36
Cadolzburg 90556
910 379-530

(G-14747)
PUNGO PUBLISHING CO LLC
1724 Princess Anne Rd (23456-3807)
P.O. Box 7064 (23457-0064)
PHONE..............................757 748-5331
Doucette John-Henry, *Administration*
EMP: 2 EST: 2015
SALES (est): 60.5K **Privately Held**
WEB: www.princessanneindy.com
SIC: 2741 Miscellaneous publishing

(G-14748)
PUNKINS CUPCAKE CONES
5509 Samuelson Ct (23464-5257)
PHONE..............................757 395-0295
EMP: 4
SALES (est): 167.1K **Privately Held**
SIC: 2051 Bread, cake & related products

(G-14749)
PURE PARADISE WATER OF VB
2133 Upton Dr (23454-1193)
PHONE..............................757 318-0522
Shirley Baptiste-Zwahl, *General Mgr*
EMP: 3
SALES (est): 170.2K **Privately Held**
SIC: 2086 Pasteurized & mineral waters, bottled & canned

(G-14750)
PURPLE DIAMOND PUBLISHING
989 Aspen Dr (23464-3938)
PHONE..............................757 525-2422
Harrison Lisa Diggs, *Principal*
EMP: 2
SALES (est): 59.2K **Privately Held**
SIC: 2741 Miscellaneous publishing

(G-14751)
QUAD PROMO LLC
1423 Air Rail Ave (23455-3001)
PHONE..............................757 353-5729
Tricia Reed,
EMP: 4
SALES (est): 310.4K **Privately Held**
SIC: 2389 Costumes

(G-14752)
QUALITY HOME IMPROVEMENT CORP
5333 Westover Ln (23464-2436)
PHONE..............................757 424-5400
James Wilbur De Loatche Jr, *President*
Trudy De Loatche, *Corp Secy*
EMP: 2
SALES (est): 295.4K **Privately Held**
SIC: 3446 Fences or posts, ornamental iron or steel

(G-14753)
R G ENGINEERING INC
429 Sharp St (23452-7124)
PHONE..............................757 463-3045
Robert Galyon, *President*
David Ellingsworth, *Vice Pres*
Jim Rathbun, *Engineer*
Brian Mitchell, *Info Tech Mgr*
EMP: 12
SQ FT: 5,000
SALES (est): 5.2MM **Privately Held**
WEB: www.rgengineering.com
SIC: 3555 Printing presses

(G-14754)
R G WOODWORKS
2432 London Bridge Rd (23456-3943)
PHONE..............................757 427-2743

Robert Goodman, *Owner*
EMP: 1
SALES (est): 63K **Privately Held**
WEB: www.cabinetsflorida.com
SIC: 2499 Wood products

(G-14755)
R J REYNOLDS TOBACCO COMPANY
6200 Pardue Ct (23464-2107)
PHONE..............................757 420-1280
John Merkel, *Manager*
EMP: 12
SALES (corp-wide): 33.4B **Privately Held**
WEB: www.rjrt.com
SIC: 2111 Cigarettes
HQ: R. J. Reynolds Tobacco Company
401 N Main St
Winston Salem NC 27101
336 741-5000

(G-14756)
RACE TRAC PETROLEUM
5549 Virginia Beach Blvd (23462-5628)
PHONE..............................757 557-0076
EMP: 2
SALES (est): 88.3K **Privately Held**
SIC: 3644 Raceways

(G-14757)
RAGAN SHEET METAL INC
Also Called: RSM
1640 Donna Dr Ste 105 (23451-6286)
PHONE..............................757 333-7248
Anna Ragan, *President*
David Ragan, *Vice Pres*
EMP: 20
SQ FT: 1,200
SALES (est): 2MM **Privately Held**
SIC: 3443 Air coolers, metal plate

(G-14758)
RAIN & ASSOCIATES LLC
Also Called: Aireal Apparel
1236 Northvale Dr (23464-8801)
PHONE..............................757 572-3996
Rainfredo Bautista Jr,
EMP: 1
SALES (est): 5K **Privately Held**
SIC: 2759 3993 2396 5131 Letterpress & screen printing; letters for signs, metal; linings, apparel: made from purchased materials; flags & banners; posters: publishing & printing

(G-14759)
RAINBOW RIDGE BOOKS LLC
1056 Commodore Dr (23454-2859)
PHONE..............................757 481-7399
Jonathan Friedman, *Mng Member*
EMP: 2
SALES (est): 105.8K **Privately Held**
WEB: www.rainbowridgebooks.com
SIC: 2741 Miscellaneous publishing

(G-14760)
RAYBAR JEWELRY DESIGN INC
277 N Lynnhven Rd Ste 109 (23452)
PHONE..............................757 486-4562
Jerry Raynor, *President*
Lori Raynor, *Treasurer*
EMP: 2
SQ FT: 1,000
SALES (est): 167.3K **Privately Held**
WEB: www.raybarfinejewelry.com
SIC: 3911 5094 Jewelry apparel; jewelry & precious stones

(G-14761)
RAYCO SERVICES INC
2984 Cadence Way (23456-6952)
PHONE..............................757 689-2156
Wylene Richardson, *President*
Sally Wylene Richardson, *President*
June Walker, *Corp Secy*
Glen Richardson, *Vice Pres*
▲ **EMP:** 1
SALES (est): 24K **Privately Held**
SIC: 2899 Corrosion preventive lubricant

(G-14762)
RAYTHEON COMPANY
5820 Ward Ct (23455-3313)
PHONE..............................757 363-1252
Mike Mundie, *Branch Mgr*
EMP: 3

SALES (corp-wide): 77B **Publicly Held**
WEB: www.rtx.com
SIC: 3812 Defense systems & equipment
HQ: Raytheon Company
870 Winter St
Waltham MA 02451
781 522-3000

(G-14763)
RE CLEAN AUTOMOTIVE PRODUCTS
2717 Sonic Dr Ste 100 (23453-3126)
PHONE..............................757 368-2694
Don Gattshall, *President*
Ciss Wagner, *Admin Sec*
EMP: 5
SQ FT: 4,800
SALES (est): 390K **Privately Held**
WEB: www.recleanwax.com
SIC: 2842 Polishing preparations & related products

(G-14764)
REALTY RESTORATIONS LLC
5512 Haden Rd (23455-3119)
PHONE..............................757 553-6117
George Cifuentes,
EMP: 1
SALES (est): 25K **Privately Held**
SIC: 3842 Cosmetic restorations

(G-14765)
REBECCA LEIGH FRASER
Also Called: Data Werks
4720 Ocean View Ave (23455-1437)
PHONE..............................912 755-3453
Rebecca Leigh Fraser, *Owner*
EMP: 1
SALES (est): 85.3K **Privately Held**
SIC: 3572 7373 Computer auxiliary storage units; systems integration services

(G-14766)
REDCLAY VISIONS LLC
Also Called: Incision Apps
812 9th St (23451-4504)
PHONE..............................804 869-3616
Jake Schools, *CEO*
Mark Lambert, *President*
EMP: 2
SALES (est): 123.1K **Privately Held**
SIC: 7372 Educational computer software

(G-14767)
REJUVINAGE
2232 Virginia Beach Blvd # 104 (23454-4289)
PHONE..............................757 306-4300
Kyle Riley, *Principal*
EMP: 2
SALES (est): 216.9K **Privately Held**
WEB: www.rejuvinage.com
SIC: 2834 Hormone preparations

(G-14768)
RESIDEX LLC
1449 Miller Str Rd Ste A (23455)
PHONE..............................757 363-2080
Dennis Ross, *Manager*
EMP: 2
SALES (corp-wide): 3.5B **Privately Held**
WEB: www.residex.com
SIC: 2879 5191 Pesticides, agricultural or household; herbicides
HQ: Residex, Llc
29380 Beck Rd
Wixom MI 48393

(G-14769)
RESIDUAL KING LLC
4624 Flicka Ct (23455-2043)
PHONE..............................757 474-3080
Gerard Riley, *Principal*
EMP: 3 EST: 2014
SALES (est): 186.8K **Privately Held**
SIC: 2911 Residues

(G-14770)
RESOURCE CONSULTANTS INC
5700 Thurston Ave Ste 120 (23455-3302)
PHONE..............................757 464-5252
Dick Disharoon, *Principal*
EMP: 2
SALES (est): 81.9K **Privately Held**
SIC: 1382 Oil & gas exploration services

(G-14771)
RICH YOUNG
751 Hecate Dr (23454-6834)
PHONE..............................757 472-2057
Thomas Lamont, *Principal*
EMP: 1 EST: 2012
SALES (est): 69.3K **Privately Held**
SIC: 2253 T-shirts & tops, knit

(G-14772)
RICHARD Y LOMBARD JR
Also Called: Vinyl Weld & Color Co
236 Iroquois Rd (23462-4005)
P.O. Box 62171 (23466-2171)
PHONE..............................757 499-1967
Richard Y Lombard Jr, *Owner*
EMP: 3
SALES (est): 160K **Privately Held**
SIC: 3089 Plastic processing

(G-14773)
RIGHT TGHT WLDG FBRICATION LLC
325 Hospital Dr (23452-6733)
PHONE..............................757 553-0661
Laura Conway,
EMP: 1
SALES (est): 52.9K **Privately Held**
SIC: 7692 Welding repair

(G-14774)
RIGHTWAY INDUSTRIES LTD
1236 Hickman Arch (23454-5878)
PHONE..............................757 435-8889
EMP: 2
SALES (est): 69K **Privately Held**
WEB: www.rightwayind.com
SIC: 3999 Manufacturing industries

(G-14775)
RIO GRAPHICS INC
4676 Princess Anne Rd # 180
(23462-6465)
PHONE..............................757 467-9207
Diana Campean, *President*
Deborah Kuhrt, *Vice Pres*
EMP: 5 **Privately Held**
WEB: www.riographics.net
SIC: 2395 Emblems, embroidered

(G-14776)
RIP SHEARS LLC
3432 Archer Ct (23452-5911)
PHONE..............................757 635-9560
Christopher S Smith,
Christopher Freisendruch,
Michaelle E Smith,
EMP: 3
SALES (est): 199.1K **Privately Held**
WEB: www.ripshears.com
SIC: 3841 5047 Surgical & medical instruments; medical equipment & supplies

(G-14777)
RIVER CITY GRAPHICS LLC
501 Progress Ln (23454-3475)
PHONE..............................757 519-9525
Cary Shreve, *President*
EMP: 4 EST: 1970
SQ FT: 3,500
SALES (est): 508.6K **Privately Held**
WEB: www.rivercityva.com
SIC: 2752 7336 Commercial printing, offset; commercial art & graphic design

(G-14778)
ROLLINS OMA SUE
4745 Thoroughgood Dr (23455-4031)
PHONE..............................757 449-6371
Oma Rollins, *Owner*
EMP: 2
SALES (est): 77K **Privately Held**
SIC: 3571 3575 5063 5099 Electronic computers; keyboards, computer, office machine; electrical supplies; video cassettes, accessories & supplies; stationery & office supplies

(G-14779)
ROMANS ENTERPRISES LLC
Also Called: Ashley Valve
220 Pennsylvania Ave (23462-2514)
PHONE..............................757 216-6401
Toni R Davis, *CEO*
Donald W Davis, *President*

Rick Lohnes, *CFO*
EMP: 10
SALES (est): 1.5MM **Privately Held**
WEB: www.ashleyvalve.com
SIC: 3592 Valves

(G-14780)
RONALD CARPENTER
1917 Rock Lake Loop (23456-5826)
PHONE..............................757 471-3805
Ronald Carpenter, *Principal*
EMP: 2 EST: 1997
SALES (est): 98.3K **Privately Held**
SIC: 2752 Commercial printing, lithographic

(G-14781)
ROYAL COURTYARD
329 Birchwood Park Dr (23452-2446)
PHONE..............................757 431-0045
Noel Gonzalez, *Administration*
EMP: 2
SALES (est): 141.2K **Privately Held**
WEB: www.royalcourtyard.com
SIC: 3999 Stage hardware & equipment, except lighting

(G-14782)
RP55 INC (PA)
Also Called: Indigo Red VA Beach Ci
520 Viking Dr (23452-7316)
PHONE..............................757 428-0300
George H Metzger, *President*
Mike Shocket, *Corp Secy*
Lisa Blumenthal, *Vice Pres*
David Hall, *Vice Pres*
Ralph Reynolds, *Vice Pres*
◆ EMP: 61
SALES (est): 8.7MM **Privately Held**
WEB: www.rp55group.com
SIC: 2329 Men's & boys' sportswear & athletic clothing

(G-14783)
RPM 3D PRINTING
1302 Elk Ct (23464-6367)
PHONE..............................757 266-3168
Chase Carlyle, *Principal*
EMP: 2
SALES (est): 83.9K **Privately Held**
SIC: 2752 Commercial printing, lithographic

(G-14784)
RRB INDUSTRIES INC
3848 Chancery Ln (23452-2810)
PHONE..............................804 517-2014
Ramesh Bridgmohan, *Principal*
EMP: 2 EST: 2018
SALES (est): 71.4K **Privately Held**
SIC: 3999 Manufacturing industries

(G-14785)
RUBBER PLASTIC MET ENGRG CORP
Also Called: RPM Engineering
2533 Aviator Dr (23453-3152)
PHONE..............................757 502-5462
Rex Workman, *President*
Ben Yu, *Vice Pres*
Patrick Dixon, *Controller*
Andrew Bountress, *Sales Mgr*
Danielle Dimichele, *Sales Staff*
▲ EMP: 15
SALES (est): 2.3MM **Privately Held**
WEB: www.rpm-engineering.com
SIC: 3069 3089 3469 Hard rubber & molded rubber products; injection molding of plastics; machine parts, stamped or pressed metal

(G-14786)
RUTHERFORD CONTROLS INTL CORP (HQ)
Also Called: Rci Rutherford Controls
2517 Squadron Ct Ste 104 (23453-3179)
PHONE..............................757 427-1230
Vicky Rutherford, *President*
William Best, *Finance Dir*
▲ EMP: 15
SQ FT: 10,000
SALES: 1MM
SALES (corp-wide): 2.7B **Privately Held**
WEB: www.dormakaba.com
SIC: 3429 7389 Manufactured hardware (general); design, commercial & industrial

PA: Dormakaba Holding Ag
Hofwisenstrasse 24
RUmlang ZH 8153
448 189-011

(G-14787)
RYNOH LIVE
397 Little Neck Rd (23452-5765)
PHONE..............................757 333-3760
Richard Martin Reass, *Principal*
Robert Pleasants, *Exec VP*
John Contreras, *Vice Pres*
Katie Hewett, *Mktg Coord*
Handerhan Katie, *Manager*
EMP: 5
SALES (est): 473.7K **Privately Held**
WEB: www.rynoh.com
SIC: 7372 Prepackaged software

(G-14788)
S B AUTO TRANSPORT LLC
1831 Lincolnshire Pl (23464-6950)
PHONE..............................757 775-3884
Shamekia Brown, *CEO*
EMP: 1
SALES (est): 58.1K **Privately Held**
SIC: 3441 Railroad car racks, for transporting vehicles: steel

(G-14789)
SAFE HARBOR PRESS LLC
5045 Cleveland St (23462-2528)
PHONE..............................757 490-1960
Kenneth Staab, *Managing Prtnr*
Gabriel Dyson, *Sales Staff*
EMP: 1
SALES (est): 170K **Privately Held**
WEB: www.safeharborpress.com
SIC: 2752 Commercial printing, offset

(G-14790)
SALMONS DREDGING INC
781 Princess Anne Rd (23457-1329)
P.O. Box 57008 (23457-0308)
PHONE..............................757 426-6824
James H Salmons Jr, *President*
Crystal Salmons, *Corp Secy*
EMP: 1
SALES (est): 147.5K **Privately Held**
SIC: 3531 Dredging machinery

(G-14791)
SALT SOOTHERS LLC
1544 Bunsen Dr (23454-6911)
PHONE..............................757 412-5867
EMP: 3
SALES (corp-wide): 65K **Privately Held**
WEB: www.saltsoothers.net
SIC: 2899 Salt
PA: Salt Soothers Llc
2702 Princeton Ave
Edmond OK 73034
405 201-2020

(G-14792)
SANDCASTLE SCREEN PRINTING LLC
5250 Challedon Dr 101 (23462-6304)
PHONE..............................757 740-0611
Hanse Hill, *Administration*
EMP: 2
SALES (est): 101.5K **Privately Held**
WEB: www.sandcastlescreenprinting.com
SIC: 2752 Commercial printing, lithographic

(G-14793)
SANJO VIRGINIA BEACH INC
465 Progress Ln (23454-3477)
PHONE..............................757 498-0400
Mike Arnold, *President*
EMP: 1
SALES (est): 106.7K **Privately Held**
WEB: www.millergrpva.com
SIC: 3469 3599 3544 3545 Metal stampings; machine & other job shop work; special dies, tools, jigs & fixtures; machine tool accessories; machine tools, metal cutting type; rolling mill machinery

(G-14794)
SANTA INC
Also Called: SSC
101 Malibu Dr (23452-4446)
PHONE..............................757 463-3553
John Williams, *Vice Pres*

Shannell Williams, *Controller*
EMP: 10
SQ FT: 6,000
SALES (est): 626.3K **Privately Held**
WEB: www.satsyscorp.com
SIC: 3663 Satellites, communications

(G-14795)
SASSY CLOTHING BLANKS LLC
609 General Gage Rd (23462-3119)
PHONE..............................757 473-1980
Lee Fisher, *Principal*
EMP: 2 EST: 2011
SALES (est): 130.3K **Privately Held**
SIC: 2759 Screen printing

(G-14796)
SCHUNCK RBCCA WLPR INSTLLATION
Also Called: Schunck, Rebecca Wallpaper
2205 Elmington Cir (23454-6111)
PHONE..............................757 301-9922
Rebecca Schunck, *Owner*
Ron Schunck, *Co-Owner*
EMP: 2
SALES (est): 98K **Privately Held**
WEB: www.wallpaperinstaller.com
SIC: 2621 1799 Wallpaper (hanging paper); paint & wallpaper stripping

(G-14797)
SCOTT FINEART AND FRMNG INC M
3163 Page Ave (23451-1122)
PHONE..............................757 496-0221
Malvin G Scott III, *Principal*
EMP: 1 EST: 2009
SALES (est): 58.7K **Privately Held**
SIC: 2499 Picture frame molding, finished

(G-14798)
SCULPTURE BY GARY STEVENSON
2104 Pallets Ct (23454-4025)
PHONE..............................757 486-5893
Gary Stevenson, *Owner*
EMP: 2
SALES (est): 120.3K **Privately Held**
SIC: 3299 Architectural sculptures: gypsum, clay, papier mache, etc.

(G-14799)
SEASCAPE AUTOMATION LLC
332 Laskin Rd Apt 501 (23451-3061)
PHONE..............................717 512-5981
Brandon S Smith, *Principal*
Brandon Smith, *Principal*
Sean Tipton, *Principal*
EMP: 2
SALES (est): 81.4K **Privately Held**
SIC: 3599 Industrial machinery

(G-14800)
SEASIDE AUDIO
509 Mayfair Ct (23452-5858)
PHONE..............................757 237-5333
Jeffrey J Schmidt, *Owner*
EMP: 1
SALES (est): 5K **Privately Held**
WEB: www.seasideaudio.com
SIC: 3651 Audio electronic systems

(G-14801)
SECUBIT INC
2697 Intl Pkwy Ste 205-1 (23452)
PHONE..............................757 453-6965
Asaf Bar David, *CEO*
Jana Riddel, *Opers Mgr*
EMP: 4
SALES (est): 266.3K **Privately Held**
WEB: www.adsinc.com
SIC: 3572 Computer storage devices

(G-14802)
SECUTOR SYSTEMS LLC
4445 Corporation Ln (23462-3262)
PHONE..............................757 646-9350
Michael Cain, *Principal*
Jack McGinn,
Ed Harvey,
▲ EMP: 3
SALES (est): 323.4K **Privately Held**
WEB: www.secutorsystems.com
SIC: 3429 Manufactured hardware (general)

(G-14803)
SENTRY SLUTIONS PDTS GROUP LLC
2697 Intl Pkwy Ste 4-230 (23452)
PHONE.................................757 689-6064
Terry Neuthton, *Mng Member*
EMP: 5
SQ FT: 3,200
SALES (est): 2MM **Privately Held**
WEB: www.sentryltp.com
SIC: 3949 Protective sporting equipment

(G-14804)
SERVICE LAMP SUPPLY
805 Toledo Pl (23456-6426)
P.O. Box 6284 (23456-0284)
PHONE.................................757 426-0636
Steven Tate, *Principal*
EMP: 1
SALES (est): 104.9K **Privately Held**
SIC: 3641 Electric lamps

(G-14805)
SGM INC
1412 Crystal Pkwy (23451-3739)
PHONE.................................757 572-3299
Gregory Bergethon, *Administration*
EMP: 2
SALES (est): 102K **Privately Held**
SIC: 2253 Knit outerwear mills

(G-14806)
SHAKLEE INDEPENDENT DISTR
1845 Saville Garden Ct (23453-7006)
PHONE.................................757 553-8765
Doran Davis, *Principal*
EMP: 1
SALES (est): 58.4K **Privately Held**
SIC: 2869 Industrial organic chemicals

(G-14807)
SHIPYRDANDCONTRACTORSUP PLY LLC
3732 W Stratford Rd (23455-1630)
PHONE.................................757 333-2148
Marcus Lind, *CEO*
EMP: 1
SALES (est): 49.1K **Privately Held**
SIC: 3052 Rubber hose

(G-14808)
SIGN BUILDERS
Also Called: Sign Technologies
5773 Arrowhead Dr Ste 302 (23462-3250)
PHONE.................................757 499-2654
Tom Polyson, *Owner*
EMP: 5
SALES (est): 150K **Privately Held**
WEB: www.sign-technologies.com
SIC: 3993 Signs, not made in custom sign painting shops

(G-14809)
SIGN MEDIK
159 Greendale Rd (23452-2349)
PHONE.................................757 748-1048
Andrey Yatsula, *Principal*
EMP: 1
SALES (est): 46K **Privately Held**
SIC: 3993 Signs & advertising specialties

(G-14810)
SIGN RIGHT HERE LLC
4759 Old Hickory Rd (23455-4005)
PHONE.................................757 617-0785
EMP: 1
SALES (est): 46K **Privately Held**
SIC: 3993 Signs & advertising specialties

(G-14811)
SIGN TECH
352 Cleveland Pl Ste 101 (23462-6546)
PHONE.................................757 407-3870
Rudy L Kidder, *Principal*
EMP: 2 EST: 2008
SALES (est): 149.8K **Privately Held**
SIC: 3993 Signs & advertising specialties

(G-14812)
SIGN WIZARDS INC
513 Central Dr (23454-5272)
PHONE.................................757 431-8886
Linda Valencia, *President*
Victor Valencia, *Vice Pres*
EMP: 2

SALES (est): 160K **Privately Held**
SIC: 3993 Signs & advertising specialties

(G-14813)
SIGN WORKS INC
1728 Virginia Beach Blvd # 110 (23454-4533)
PHONE.................................757 428-2525
Lisa Terry, *President*
EMP: 3
SQ FT: 1,748
SALES (est): 344.3K **Privately Held**
SIC: 3993 Neon signs

(G-14814)
SIGN WORLD
701 S Military Hwy (23464-1870)
PHONE.................................757 366-9890
Seoung Kim, *Principal*
EMP: 2
SALES (est): 139.2K **Privately Held**
SIC: 3993 Signs & advertising specialties

(G-14815)
SIGNATURE SEASONINGS LLC
2572 Nestlebrook Trl (23456-8217)
PHONE.................................757 572-8995
Chris Anderson, *Owner*
Vic Chiavola, *VP Mfg*
EMP: 5 EST: 2010
SALES (est): 533.7K **Privately Held**
WEB: www.signatureseasonings.com
SIC: 2099 Seasonings & spices

(G-14816)
SIGNMAKERS INC
2209 Baylake Rd (23455-2825)
PHONE.................................757 621-1212
James McGeein, *Vice Pres*
EMP: 3
SALES (est): 235.5K **Privately Held**
SIC: 3993 Signs & advertising specialties

(G-14817)
SIGNS OF LEARNING LLC
328 Office Square Ln 101c (23462-3658)
PHONE.................................757 635-2735
Cynthia B Miller,
EMP: 1
SALES (est): 94.2K **Privately Held**
SIC: 3993 Signs & advertising specialties

(G-14818)
SIGNS OF SUCCESS INC
1800 Seddon Cir (23451-1537)
P.O. Box 4427 (23454-0427)
PHONE.................................757 481-4788
Gina Paulson, *Principal*
EMP: 4
SALES (est): 529.3K **Privately Held**
WEB: www.signsofsuccessonline.com
SIC: 3993 Signs & advertising specialties

(G-14819)
SIGNS ON SCENE
638 Astor Ln (23464-2609)
PHONE.................................757 435-0841
Chad Franklin, *Principal*
EMP: 1
SALES (est): 73K **Privately Held**
SIC: 3993 Signs & advertising specialties

(G-14820)
SINISTER STITCH CUSTOM LEATHER
2433 Pleasure House Rd (23455-1349)
PHONE.................................757 636-9954
Phillips Aaron, *Principal*
EMP: 1
SALES (est): 37.3K **Privately Held**
SIC: 2395 Embroidery & art needlework

(G-14821)
SIX SEAS PRESS LLC
1017 Witch Point Trl (23455-5645)
PHONE.................................757 363-5869
Sylvia Liu, *Principal*
EMP: 2 EST: 2014
SALES (est): 117.3K **Privately Held**
SIC: 2741 Miscellaneous publishing

(G-14822)
SKIN AMNESTY
1817 Republic Rd (23454-4543)
PHONE.................................757 491-9058

Cynthia Galumbeck, *Owner*
Matthew Galumbeck, *Co-Owner*
EMP: 4
SQ FT: 10,000
SALES (est): 221.9K **Privately Held**
WEB: www.skinamnesty.com
SIC: 2657 Paperboard backs for blister or skin packages

(G-14823)
SKIN RANCH AND TRADE COMPANY
3061 Brickhouse Ct # 111 (23452-6855)
PHONE.................................757 486-7546
EMP: 1
SALES (est): 108.9K **Privately Held**
WEB: www.theskinranch.com
SIC: 2834 5199 Dermatologicals; non-durable goods

(G-14824)
SKIPS TOOLS INC
2409 Litchfield Way (23453-5565)
PHONE.................................757 621-4775
Russell S Brashears Jr, *President*
EMP: 1
SALES (est): 110.5K **Privately Held**
SIC: 3423 Hand & edge tools

(G-14825)
SLIM SILHOUETTES LLC
401 N Great Neck Rd Ste 1 (23454-4063)
PHONE.................................757 337-5965
Keith Nichols, *Principal*
EMP: 7
SALES (est): 417.3K **Privately Held**
WEB: www.slimsilhouettes.com
SIC: 3845 Laser systems & equipment, medical

(G-14826)
SM LUMBER INC
900 Commonwealth Pl 200-3 (23464-4517)
PHONE.................................757 797-8353
Rafael Mason, *President*
EMP: 2
SALES (est): 180K **Privately Held**
SIC: 2426 2435 2421 5031 Hardwood dimension & flooring mills; hardwood veneer & plywood; sawmills & planing mills, general; lumber, plywood & millwork

(G-14827)
SMILES ON CANVAS
4011 Francis Lee Dr (23452-1916)
PHONE.................................757 572-2346
Jones Juliette, *Principal*
EMP: 2
SALES (est): 73.4K **Privately Held**
SIC: 2211 Canvas

(G-14828)
SMOKE DETECTOR INSPECTOR
2581 Sandpiper Rd (23456-4512)
PHONE.................................757 870-4772
EMP: 2 EST: 2019
SALES (est): 88.3K **Privately Held**
SIC: 3669 Smoke detectors

(G-14829)
SNC TECHNICAL SERVICES LLC
2696 Reliance Dr (23452-7832)
PHONE.................................787 820-2141
EMP: 2 **Privately Held**
WEB: www.sncts.com
SIC: 2311 Military uniforms, men's & youths': purchased materials
HQ: Snc Technical Services, Llc
    Road 155 Km 31 1 Barrio G St Ro
    Orocovis PR 00720
    787 867-5560

(G-14830)
SOUL SOCKS LLC
1619 Diamond Springs Rd C (23455-3019)
PHONE.................................757 449-5013
EMP: 2 EST: 2016
SALES (est): 131.2K **Privately Held**
SIC: 2252 Socks

(G-14831)
SOUTHSIDE CONTAINERS
500 Central Dr (23454-5236)
PHONE.................................757 422-1111

EMP: 2
SALES (est): 221K **Privately Held**
WEB: www.southsidecontainers.com
SIC: 2449 Wood containers

(G-14832)
SOUTHSIDE WELDING
4613 Player Ln (23462-4640)
PHONE.................................757 270-7006
Brennon Pope, *Principal*
EMP: 1
SALES (est): 56.6K **Privately Held**
WEB: www.toy-tote.com
SIC: 7692 Welding repair

(G-14833)
SPECIAL COMMUNICATIONS LLC
Also Called: Specomm
2838 Croix Ct (23451-1365)
PHONE.................................202 677-1225
Billy Cason, *CEO*
John T Yarborough, *President*
▲ EMP: 4
SALES (est): 1.5MM **Privately Held**
WEB: www.specommllc.com
SIC: 3663 7389 Satellites, communications;

(G-14834)
SPECIAL PROJECTS OPERATIONS
2569 Horse Pasture Rd (23453-2998)
PHONE.................................410 297-6550
David Wheatley, *President*
EMP: 10
SALES (est): 553.9K **Privately Held**
WEB: www.dwe-spo.com
SIC: 3563 9224 Air & gas compressors; fire protection

(G-14835)
SPECIAL TACTICAL SERVICES LLC
Also Called: STS Gun Mounts
5725 Arrowhead Dr (23462-3218)
PHONE.................................757 554-0699
Dale McClellan, *CEO*
Mark Pierson, *Vice Pres*
Tom Kaupas, *CFO*
▲ EMP: 15
SQ FT: 3,600
SALES (est): 1.3MM **Privately Held**
WEB: www.spectacserv.com
SIC: 3812 3795 3489 7381 Defense systems & equipment; tanks & tank components; ordnance & accessories; security guard service; small arms ammunition

(G-14836)
SPECTRUM ENTERTAINMENT INC
Also Called: Spectrum Puppet Productions
101 S 1st Clnl Rd Ste 101 (23454)
PHONE.................................757 491-2873
Regina Marscheider, *President*
Amida Rhinz, *Admin Sec*
▲ EMP: 2
SQ FT: 3,000
SALES (est): 147K **Privately Held**
WEB: www.stopabuse.com
SIC: 3999 Puppets & marionettes

(G-14837)
SPEEDPRO
5305 Cleveland St (23462-6553)
PHONE.................................757 233-9250
EMP: 1
SALES (est): 85.5K **Privately Held**
WEB: www.speedpro.com
SIC: 3993 Signs & advertising specialties

(G-14838)
SPEEDWAY LLC
212a 70th St (23451-2005)
PHONE.................................757 498-4625
Leslie Leccese, *Manager*
EMP: 1 **Publicly Held**
WEB: www.speedway.com
SIC: 1311 Crude petroleum production
HQ: Speedway Llc
    500 Speedway Dr
    Enon OH 45323
    937 864-3000

(G-14839)
SPICY VINEGAR LLC
2225 Indian Hill Rd (23455-2129)
PHONE..................................757 460-3861
Warren Chauncey, *Principal*
EMP: 3
SALES (est): 160.8K **Privately Held**
SIC: 2099 Vinegar

(G-14840)
SPIRIT SOCKS
1537 Quail Point Rd (23454-3115)
PHONE..................................757 802-6160
Jonathan Haughney, *Principal*
EMP: 2 EST: 2016
SALES (est): 76.9K **Privately Held**
SIC: 2252 Socks

(G-14841)
SPORT CREATIONS LLC
210 44th St (23451-2508)
PHONE..................................757 572-2113
Timothy O'Brien,
EMP: 1
SALES (est): 86.5K **Privately Held**
WEB: www.sport-creations.com
SIC: 3949 7389 Carts, caddy;

(G-14842)
STAN GARFIN PUBLICATIONS INC
1216 Heathcliff Dr (23464-5848)
PHONE..................................757 495-3644
Marilyn F Garfin, *President*
EMP: 2 EST: 2010
SALES (est): 104.4K **Privately Held**
SIC: 2741 Miscellaneous publishing

(G-14843)
STATEMENT LLC
1324 Akinburry Rd (23456-6899)
PHONE..................................757 635-6294
Alexander Bonita, *Principal*
EMP: 3
SALES (est): 204.5K **Privately Held**
SIC: 3272 Precast terrazo or concrete products

(G-14844)
STEALTH MFG & SVCS LLC
2512 Aviator Dr (23453-3151)
P.O. Box 6731 (23456-0731)
PHONE..................................787 679-7548
Susana Reid, *Mng Member*
Joseph Reid,
EMP: 3 EST: 2017
SALES (est): 138.6K **Privately Held**
SIC: 3199 3842 2311 Holsters, leather; bulletproof vests; military uniforms, men's & youths': purchased materials

(G-14845)
STEELMASTER BUILDINGS LLC
1023 Laskin Rd Ste 109 (23451-6302)
PHONE..................................757 961-7006
Karen Willis, *Controller*
Donald H Patterson Jr,
EMP: 13
SALES (est): 2.4MM **Privately Held**
WEB: www.steelmasterusa.com
SIC: 3448 Prefabricated metal buildings

(G-14846)
STEPHEN BIALORUCKI
Also Called: Black Line Swim
5165 Stratford Chase Dr (23464-5556)
PHONE..................................757 374-2080
Stephen Bialorucki, *Owner*
EMP: 3
SALES (est): 93.5K **Privately Held**
SIC: 3949 Team sports equipment

(G-14847)
STEVES PALLETS
1637 Hawks Bill Dr (23464-7873)
PHONE..................................757 576-4488
Steve Hurst, *Principal*
EMP: 4
SALES (est): 405.9K **Privately Held**
SIC: 2448 Pallets, wood

(G-14848)
STIHL INCORPORATED
825 London Bridge Rd (23454-5347)
PHONE..................................757 468-4010
Kevin Jones, *Engineer*
Mike Hopstetter, *Manager*
Melinda Green, *Admin Asst*
EMP: 30
SALES (corp-wide): 4B **Privately Held**
WEB: www.stihldealers.com
SIC: 3546 3398 4225 Chain saws, portable; metal heat treating; warehousing, self-storage
HQ: Stihl Incorporated
536 Viking Dr
Virginia Beach VA 23452
757 486-9100

(G-14849)
STIHL INCORPORATED
2600 International Pkwy (23452-7801)
PHONE..................................757 368-2409
EMP: 5
SALES (corp-wide): 4B **Privately Held**
WEB: www.stihldealers.com
SIC: 3546 3398 Chain saws, portable; metal heat treating
HQ: Stihl Incorporated
536 Viking Dr
Virginia Beach VA 23452
757 486-9100

(G-14850)
STITCHED WITH LOVE LLC
5591 Ershire Ct Apt 203 (23462-1152)
PHONE..................................757 285-6980
Som P Basch-Spruill, *Principal*
EMP: 1 EST: 2017
SALES (est): 42.6K **Privately Held**
SIC: 2395 Embroidery & art needlework

(G-14851)
STITCHWORKS INC
809 Dasa Leo Ct (23456-6794)
PHONE..................................757 631-0300
Mechelle Beauchamp, *President*
Gary Beauchamp, *Treasurer*
Randi Chernitzer, *Accounts Exec*
EMP: 6
SQ FT: 5,000
SALES (est): 900K **Privately Held**
WEB: www.stitchworks.org
SIC: 2395 7336 5199 Embroidery products, except schiffli machine; silk screen design; advertising specialties

(G-14852)
STONESHORE PUBLISHING
900 Northwood Dr (23452-7937)
PHONE..................................757 589-7049
Michael Midgett, *Owner*
EMP: 1 EST: 2018
SALES (est): 37.5K **Privately Held**
WEB: www.stoneshorepublishing.com
SIC: 2741 Miscellaneous publishing

(G-14853)
STONY CREEK SAND & GRAVEL LLC (PA)
222 Central Park Ave (23462-3022)
P.O. Box 810, Quinton (23141-0810)
PHONE..................................804 229-0015
Brian C Purcell,
EMP: 4
SALES (est): 1.8MM **Privately Held**
WEB: www.stonycreeksand.com
SIC: 1442 Construction sand & gravel

(G-14854)
STORM PROTECTION SERVICES
1272 N Great Neck Rd (23454-2100)
P.O. Box 1272 (23451-0272)
PHONE..................................757 496-8200
Jason B Cowan, *President*
EMP: 1 EST: 2001
SALES (est): 154.8K **Privately Held**
SIC: 3442 Storm doors or windows, metal

(G-14855)
STRATUSLIVE LLC
6465 College Park Sq # 310 (23464-3624)
PHONE..................................757 273-8219
Jim Funari, *CEO*
Michael Trainor, *President*
Bill Donnelly, *Exec VP*
Debbie Snyder, *Vice Pres*
Jennifer Mitchell, *Project Mgr*
EMP: 26 EST: 2008

SALES (est): 3.1MM **Privately Held**
WEB: www.stratuslive.com
SIC: 7372 Business oriented computer software

(G-14856)
STRECO FIBRES INTL DISC INC
168 Business Park Dr # 200 (23462-6532)
PHONE..................................757 473-3720
John Strelitz, *President*
EMP: 2
SALES (est): 140.9K **Privately Held**
WEB: www.streco.com
SIC: 2952 Roof cement: asphalt, fibrous or plastic

(G-14857)
STRUCTURAL TECHNOLOGIES LLC (HQ)
Also Called: Hanover Fabricators
126 S Lynnhaven Rd (23452-7407)
P.O. Box 250, Doswell (23047-0250)
PHONE..................................757 498-4448
Stephen R Jones,
▲ EMP: 8 EST: 1963
SQ FT: 22,000
SALES (est): 15.1MM
SALES (corp-wide): 16.6MM **Privately Held**
WEB: www.soundstructures.com
SIC: 2439 Trusses, wooden roof
PA: Sound Structures, Inc.
126 S Lynnhaven Rd
Virginia Beach VA 23452
757 498-4448

(G-14858)
SUGAR & SALT LLC
332 Jefferson Dr (23454)
PHONE..................................434 996-2329
David Shockley, *Principal*
EMP: 2
SALES (est): 127.1K **Privately Held**
SIC: 2051 Bakery: wholesale or wholesale/retail combined

(G-14859)
SURFSIDE EAST INC (PA)
Also Called: Sunny Day Guide
800 Seahawk Cir Ste 106 (23452-7818)
PHONE..................................757 468-0606
J William Blue III, *President*
Jill Prescott, *Production*
Edna Mahan, *Finance Mgr*
Terri Blackmore, *Accounts Exec*
David Bundy, *Accounts Exec*
EMP: 35
SQ FT: 15,000
SALES (est): 4.5MM **Privately Held**
WEB: www.sunnydayguide.com
SIC: 2741 7336 2721 Guides: publishing only, not printed on site; graphic arts & related design; periodicals

(G-14860)
SYNERGY BUSINESS SOLUTIONS LLC
2239 Roanoke Ave (23455-1680)
PHONE..................................757 646-1294
Ann Korsak,
Patrick Gordon,
EMP: 2 EST: 2016
SALES (est): 82.7K **Privately Held**
SIC: 7372 7373 Application computer software; business oriented computer software; office computer automation systems integration; turnkey vendors, computer systems

(G-14861)
T&J WOODWORKING
2593 Quality Ct Ste 226 (23454-5325)
PHONE..................................757 567-5530
Wendy Hitchings, *Principal*
EMP: 2 EST: 2015
SALES (est): 72K **Privately Held**
SIC: 2431 Millwork

(G-14862)
T-K-O BUILDING INCORPORATED
6201 Lippizan Cir (23464-4708)
PHONE..................................757 324-2306
Kareem Petty,
EMP: 1

SALES (est): 56K **Privately Held**
SIC: 1389 Construction, repair & dismantling services

(G-14863)
TACTICAL ELEC MILITARY SUP LLC
2844 Crusader Cir Ste 100 (23453-3148)
PHONE..................................757 689-0476
Shirley Place, *Principal*
EMP: 11
SALES (corp-wide): 11MM **Privately Held**
WEB: www.tacticalelectronics.com
SIC: 3699 Fire control or bombing equipment, electronic
PA: Tactical Electronics And Military Supply Llc
2200 N Hemlock Ave
Broken Arrow OK 74012
866 541-7996

(G-14864)
TAG AMERICA INC
5721 Bayside Rd (23455-3015)
PHONE..................................757 227-9831
Jason Sparrow, *General Mgr*
EMP: 5 EST: 2016
SALES (est): 553K **Privately Held**
SIC: 2851 Removers & cleaners

(G-14865)
TDI LLC
Also Called: Martin Screen Prints and EMB
641 Phoenix Dr (23452-7318)
PHONE..................................757 855-5416
Scott Samter, *President*
Tammy Cole, *Sales Mgr*
William P Martin, *Executive*
EMP: 20
SQ FT: 22,500
SALES (est): 2.3MM **Privately Held**
WEB: www.mspdesigngroup.com
SIC: 2759 Screen printing

(G-14866)
TDI PRINTING GROUP LLC (PA)
Also Called: MSP Design Group
641 Phoenix Dr (23452-7318)
PHONE..................................757 855-5416
Jay McCracken, *Art Dir*
Daniel Clarkson,
Christopher Askins,
Michael Gianascoli,
Brian Holland,
EMP: 23
SQ FT: 22,000
SALES (est): 2.4MM **Privately Held**
WEB: www.mspdesigngroup.com
SIC: 2396 Fabric printing & stamping

(G-14867)
TEA SPOT CATERING LLC
2309 Wheatstone Ct (23456-6047)
PHONE..................................757 427-3525
Wendy Speca, *Principal*
EMP: 4
SALES (est): 253.7K **Privately Held**
WEB: www.theteaspotcatering.com
SIC: 2051 5812 Bakery: wholesale or wholesale/retail combined; caterers

(G-14868)
TEENY TEXTILES
824 22nd St (23451-4081)
PHONE..................................703 731-7336
Amber Genung, *Owner*
EMP: 1
SALES (est): 46.5K **Privately Held**
SIC: 2299 Textile goods

(G-14869)
THREDZ EMB SCREEN PRINT GRAPH
815 Admissions Ct (23462-1049)
PHONE..................................757 636-9569
Sunmi Kuku-Jennings, *Principal*
EMP: 2
SALES (est): 83.9K **Privately Held**
SIC: 2752 Commercial printing, lithographic

(G-14870)
THREE POINTS DESIGN INC
Also Called: Oak Grove Folk Art
684 Princess Anne Rd (23457-1326)
PHONE..................................757 426-2149
Jac Johnson, *President*
EMP: 2
SALES (est): 100K **Privately Held**
WEB: www.threepointsdesign.com
SIC: 2431 Woodwork, interior & ornamental

(G-14871)
TIDALWAVE TUMBLER & TEES LLC
580 Summer Lake Ln (23454-6886)
PHONE..................................757 814-1022
Sharron D Kennovin, *Principal*
EMP: 2 EST: 2019
SALES (est): 73.2K **Privately Held**
SIC: 2759 Screen printing

(G-14872)
TIDEWATER AUTO & INDUS MCH INC
Also Called: Blackwater Engines
949 Seahawk Cir (23452-7811)
P.O. Box 8888 (23450-8888)
PHONE..................................757 855-5091
Craig L Talley, *President*
▲ EMP: 7
SQ FT: 35,000
SALES (est): 1.4MM **Privately Held**
WEB: www.blackwaterengines.com
SIC: 3714 Motor vehicle parts & accessories

(G-14873)
TIDEWATER EMBLEMS LTD
1816 Potters Rd (23454-4453)
P.O. Box 3234 (23454-9334)
PHONE..................................757 428-1170
Mark Huenerberg, *President*
John C Huenerberg, *President*
Mark C Huenerberg, *President*
Frances Huenerberg, *Corp Secy*
EMP: 13 EST: 1962
SQ FT: 5,000
SALES (est): 1.6MM **Privately Held**
WEB: www.tidewateremblems.com
SIC: 2759 2399 Screen printing; decals: printing; emblems, badges & insignia: from purchased materials

(G-14874)
TIDEWATER GRAPHICS INC
Also Called: Minuteman Press
1628 Independence Blvd # 1540 (23455-4085)
PHONE..................................757 464-6136
Ernest Hayes, *President*
Judy R Hayes, *Corp Secy*
EMP: 9
SQ FT: 3,200
SALES (est): 950K **Privately Held**
WEB: www.minutemanpress.com
SIC: 2752 7338 2791 2789 Commercial printing, lithographic; secretarial & court reporting; typesetting; bookbinding & related work

(G-14875)
TIDEWATER HISPANIC NEWSPAPER
2005 Silver Lake Dr (23464-8941)
P.O. Box 64128 (23467-4128)
PHONE..................................757 474-1233
Alex Gomez, *Owner*
Regina Fremont-Gomez, *Principal*
EMP: 4 EST: 2012
SALES (est): 130K **Privately Held**
WEB: www.twhispanicnews.com
SIC: 2711 Newspapers, publishing & printing

(G-14876)
TIDEWATER PROF CONTRS LLC
Also Called: Priority Electrical Service
3009 Belle Haven Dr (23452-6905)
PHONE..................................757 605-1040
Brian Christopher Jones,
EMP: 7
SALES (est): 1.1MM **Privately Held**
WEB: www.pesvb.com
SIC: 3679 Electronic circuits

(G-14877)
TIDEWATER STRUCTURES
609 Berkley Pl (23452-4501)
PHONE..................................757 753-1435
Maria Honeycutt, *Principal*
EMP: 2
SALES (est): 98.4K **Privately Held**
SIC: 2499 Decorative wood & woodwork

(G-14878)
TIDEWATER TECHS LLC
2864 Augusta Cir (23453-3306)
PHONE..................................757 301-1789
Michael Cole, *Web Dvlpr*
EMP: 3 EST: 2019
SALES (est): 162K **Privately Held**
WEB: www.tidewatertechs.com
SIC: 3861 Photographic equipment & supplies

(G-14879)
TIDEWATER TREE
1900 Munden Point Rd (23457-1227)
PHONE..................................757 426-6002
Benny Sawyer, *Principal*
EMP: 2 EST: 2012
SALES (est): 206.4K **Privately Held**
WEB: www.tidewatertreeservice.com
SIC: 3523 Transplanters

(G-14880)
TIDEWATER VIRGINIA USBC INC
700 Baker Rd Ste 102 (23462-1077)
PHONE..................................757 456-2497
Arlene Williams, *Principal*
Preston I Carraway, *Exec Dir*
EMP: 4
SALES (est): 57.5K **Privately Held**
WEB: www.tidewatervirginiausbc.org
SIC: 3949 Bowling alleys & accessories

(G-14881)
TIDEWTER ARCHTCTURAL MLLWK INC
614 10th St (23451-4523)
PHONE..................................757 422-1279
James M Sykes, *President*
EMP: 6
SALES (est): 891.5K **Privately Held**
SIC: 2431 Millwork

(G-14882)
TITUS DEVELOPMENT CORP
340 Constitution Dr (23462-3102)
P.O. Box 64293 (23467-4293)
PHONE..................................757 515-7338
Anthony Crump, *President*
EMP: 3
SALES (est): 5K **Privately Held**
SIC: 3949 Golf equipment

(G-14883)
TITUS PUBLICATIONS
5677 Fitztown Rd (23457-1334)
PHONE..................................757 421-4141
Herbert Titus, *Owner*
EMP: 1
SALES (est): 56.9K **Privately Held**
SIC: 2741 Miscellaneous publishing

(G-14884)
TIZZY TECHNOLOGIES INC
4445 Corp Ln Ste 264 (23462)
PHONE..................................703 344-3348
Muhammad Irfan Azam, *Director*
EMP: 1
SALES (est): 32.7K **Privately Held**
SIC: 7372 7389 Application computer software;

(G-14885)
TLJ PRESSURE WASHING
3736 Snowdrift Cir (23462-6970)
PHONE..................................757 235-9096
EMP: 5
SALES: 100K **Privately Held**
SIC: 3589 Service Industry Machinery, Nec, Nsk

(G-14886)
TODD DRUMMOND CONSULTING LLC
3036 Hemingway Rd (23456-8172)
PHONE..................................603 763-8857
EMP: 2

SALES (est): 66K **Privately Held**
SIC: 1221 Bituminous Coal/Lignite Surface Mining

(G-14887)
TOM L CROCKETT
3745 Jefferson Blvd (23455-1636)
PHONE..................................757 460-1382
Tom Crockett, *Owner*
EMP: 1
SALES (est): 55K **Privately Held**
SIC: 2759 Publication printing

(G-14888)
TOMMY ATKINSON SPORTS ENTP
Also Called: Tommy Atkinson's Sports
1612 Virginia Beach Blvd (23454-4628)
PHONE..................................757 428-0824
Tommy Atkinson, *President*
Judy M Atkinson, *Vice Pres*
Carl M Atkinson, *Treasurer*
EMP: 4
SQ FT: 2,000
SALES (est): 474.7K **Privately Held**
SIC: 2759 5941 Screen printing; sporting goods & bicycle shops

(G-14889)
TOTAL TOUCH SOLUTIONS LLC
1465 London Bridge Rd # 112 (23453-3770)
PHONE..................................757 536-1445
Michaek Kelley, *Director*
EMP: 2
SALES (est): 199.6K **Privately Held**
WEB: www.totaltouchsolutions.com
SIC: 3578 Cash registers

(G-14890)
TOWN PRIDE PUBLISHERS
1206 Laskin Rd Ste 201 (23451-5263)
PHONE..................................757 321-8132
EMP: 2
SALES (est): 91.2K **Privately Held**
SIC: 2741 Misc Publishing

(G-14891)
TRADEMARK TEES
3900 Bonney Rd (23452-2465)
PHONE..................................757 232-4866
Thomas Kasmark, *Principal*
EMP: 2 EST: 2015
SALES (est): 97.4K **Privately Held**
SIC: 2759 Screen printing

(G-14892)
TRANE US INC
230 Clearfield Ave # 126 (23462-1832)
PHONE..................................757 490-2390
Kevin Thompson, *Branch Mgr*
EMP: 61 **Privately Held**
WEB: www.trane.com
SIC: 3585 Refrigeration & heating equipment
HQ: Trane U.S. Inc.
3600 Pammel Creek Rd
La Crosse WI 54601
608 787-2000

(G-14893)
TRIDENT SEC & HOLDINGS LLC
Also Called: 215 Gear
2133-126 Upton Dr Ste 151 (23454)
PHONE..................................757 689-4560
Carrieann Zukosky,
EMP: 3
SALES (est): 336.1K **Privately Held**
WEB: www.215gearstore.com
SIC: 2393 Textile bags

(G-14894)
TRIPLE STITCH DESIGNS LLC
1945 Champion Cir (23456-6798)
PHONE..................................757 376-2666
Frank Russo, *Managing Prtnr*
Christine Russo, *Principal*
EMP: 2
SALES (est): 59.6K **Privately Held**
WEB: www.triplestitchdesigns.com
SIC: 2395 Embroidery & art needlework

(G-14895)
TRUE COLORS SCREEN PRTG LLC
637 10th St (23451-4522)
PHONE..................................757 718-9051
Dany Ha, *Mng Member*
EMP: 4
SALES (est): 178.1K **Privately Held**
WEB: www.truecolorsva.com
SIC: 2759 Commercial printing

(G-14896)
TST TACTICAL DEF SOLUTIONS INC
Also Called: TST Roofing
2516 Squadron Ct (23453-3155)
PHONE..................................757 452-6955
Ryan S Turner, *President*
Kristen Smith, *Business Mgr*
Belinda Fowlkes, *Office Mgr*
Rodjer Bourn, *Sr Project Mgr*
EMP: 15
SALES (est): 2.1MM **Privately Held**
WEB: www.tstdefense.com
SIC: 3732 1542 1761 1793 Boat building & repairing; nonresidential construction; commercial & office building, new construction; institutional building construction; roofing, siding & sheet metal work; roofing & gutter work; roof repair; roofing contractor; glass & glazing work

(G-14897)
TSUNAMI CUSTOM CREATIONS LLC
1432 Watercrest Pl (23464-6142)
PHONE..................................757 913-0960
Hermelyne Carrillo,
EMP: 1
SALES (est): 41K **Privately Held**
SIC: 3953 Screens, textile printing

(G-14898)
TUNNEL OF LOVE
477 S Lynnhaven Rd (23452-6600)
PHONE..................................757 961-5783
Patricia Shaw, *Owner*
EMP: 2
SALES (est): 142K **Privately Held**
WEB: www.tolvb.com
SIC: 2389 Costumes

(G-14899)
U PLAY USA LLC
1440 London Bridge Rd (23453-3730)
PHONE..................................757 301-8690
Bruce Huang, *CEO*
EMP: 6
SALES (est): 387.7K **Privately Held**
SIC: 7372 Home entertainment computer software
PA: U-Play Corporation
No.18, Fumin Road, Jiuzi Ave., Jiujiang District
Wuhu 24109

(G-14900)
ULTRALIFE CORPORATION
1457 Mller Str Rd Ste 106 (23455)
PHONE..................................757 419-2430
James Rasmussen, *Vice Pres*
Richard Measel, *QC Mgr*
Pete Dekker, *Engineer*
Ben Potts, *Engineer*
EMP: 50 **Publicly Held**
WEB: www.ultralifecorporation.com
SIC: 3663 Amplifiers, RF power & IF
PA: Ultralife Corporation
2000 Technology Pkwy
Newark NY 14513

(G-14901)
UNCLE HARRYS INC
468 Viking Dr Ste 100 (23452-7469)
PHONE..................................757 426-7056
Harry Tully, *President*
Eric Donaldson, *CFO*
Terrie Tully, *Treasurer*
EMP: 5
SALES (est): 395.7K **Privately Held**
WEB: www.uncleharrysicecream.com
SIC: 2024 Ice cream, bulk

(G-14902)
UNDER PRESSURE SERVICES INC
4878 Princess Anne Rd (23462-4787)
PHONE...................757 254-5996
Paul Carr, *CEO*
EMP: 3
SALES (est): 81.4K **Privately Held**
SIC: 1389 Construction, repair & dismantling services

(G-14903)
US BUILDING SYSTEMS INC
Also Called: Steel Building Pros
3169 Shipps Corner Rd # 101
(23453-2991)
PHONE...................800 991-9251
Rod Hobbs, *President*
EMP: 20
SALES (est): 3.8MM **Privately Held**
WEB: www.steelbuildingpros.com
SIC: 3448 Prefabricated metal buildings

(G-14904)
V B LOCAL FORM COUPON BOOK
916 Earl Of Chatham Ln (23454-2905)
PHONE...................239 745-9649
Michael Jucksch, *CEO*
EMP: 2
SALES (est): 73.2K **Privately Held**
SIC: 2759 Commercial printing

(G-14905)
V-LITE USA LLC
2504 Squadron Ct Ste 110 (23453-3180)
PHONE...................808 264-3785
Johnny Swan, *Principal*
EMP: 2 EST: 2009
SALES (est): 91.7K **Privately Held**
WEB: www.sandsprecision.com
SIC: 3999 Manufacturing industries

(G-14906)
VANMARK LLC
3421 Chanl Creek Rd Ste 1 (23453)
PHONE...................757 689-3850
Markus Tavenner,
EMP: 8
SQ FT: 1,000
SALES (est): 1.2MM **Privately Held**
WEB: www.vanmarkllc.com
SIC: 3993 7539 7389 Signs & advertising specialties; machine shop, automotive; engraving service

(G-14907)
VEL TYE LLC
1619 Diamond Springs Rd (23455-3019)
PHONE...................757 518-5400
Steven J Herring,
Diane Brink,
Sanford Brink,
Ilane Herring,
EMP: 4
SALES (est): 646.8K **Privately Held**
WEB: www.veltye.com
SIC: 2297 5085 3965 2241 Bonded-fiber fabrics, except felt; fasteners, industrial: nuts, bolts, screws, etc.; fasteners, buttons, needles & pins; narrow fabric mills

(G-14908)
VFG ENTERPRISES LLC
3421 Chanl Creek Rd Ste 1 (23453)
PHONE...................757 343-4866
Joseph Dalton,
Robert McDonald,
EMP: 2
SALES (est): 216.8K **Privately Held**
SIC: 3484 5941 3949 Pistols or pistol parts, 30 mm. & below; hunting equipment; shooting equipment & supplies, general

(G-14909)
VICTOR FORWARD LLC
1206 Laskin Rd Ste 201 (23451-5263)
PHONE...................757 374-2642
Deanna Power, *President*
Melissa Richardson, *Accounts Mgr*
EMP: 6 EST: 2010
SALES (est): 1MM **Privately Held**
WEB: www.victorforward.com
SIC: 2389 Burial garments

(G-14910)
VICTORY TROPICAL OIL USA INC
1 Columbus Ctr Ste 903 (23462-7791)
PHONE...................757 687-8171
Tan Boon Chng, *President*
EMP: 5
SALES (est): 59MM
SALES (corp-wide): 3.3MM **Privately Held**
WEB: www.goldenagri.com.sg
SIC: 2076 Palm kernel oil
HQ: Golden Agri-Resources Europe B.V.
Princenhof Park 22
Driebergen-Rijsenburg
202 182-535

(G-14911)
VIRGINIA BEACH PRINTING & STY
3000 Baltic Ave (23451-3016)
PHONE...................757 428-4282
David Matthews, *President*
John D Matthews, *Vice Pres*
Penny Matthews, *Admin Sec*
EMP: 8
SQ FT: 2,900
SALES (est): 1.1MM **Privately Held**
WEB: www.vabeachprinting.com
SIC: 2752 Commercial printing, offset

(G-14912)
VIRGINIA BEACH PRODUCTS LLC (PA)
4304 Saint Martin Ct (23455-6126)
PHONE...................757 847-9338
Noreen Fertig, *Partner*
Christopher Fertig, *Partner*
William Fertig, *Partner*
EMP: 3
SALES (est): 228.5K **Privately Held**
WEB: www.custombeachwheelchair.com
SIC: 3842 Technical aids for the handicapped

(G-14913)
VIRGINIA BEACH PRODUCTS LLC
5320 Hamilton Ln (23462-5909)
PHONE...................757 847-9338
Noreen Fertig, *Branch Mgr*
EMP: 1
SALES (corp-wide): 228.5K **Privately Held**
WEB: www.custombeachwheelchair.com
SIC: 3842 Surgical appliances & supplies
PA: Virginia Beach Products Llc
4304 Saint Martin Ct
Virginia Beach VA 23455
757 847-9338

(G-14914)
VIRGINIA BEACH SKATEBOARDS
2312 Treesong Trl (23456-6721)
PHONE...................757 385-4131
Richard Larson, *Principal*
EMP: 2
SALES (est): 178.3K **Privately Held**
WEB: www.vbgov.com
SIC: 3949 Skateboards

(G-14915)
VIRGINIA BEACH WINERY LLC
152 Newtown Rd Ste 108 (23462-2400)
PHONE...................757 995-4315
EMP: 2
SALES (est): 140.8K **Privately Held**
WEB: www.vbwinery.com
SIC: 2084 Wines

(G-14916)
VIRGINIA BEACHS MAX BLCK MOLD
1581 General Booth Blvd (23454-5106)
PHONE...................757 354-1935
EMP: 2 EST: 2010
SALES (est): 110K **Privately Held**
SIC: 3544 Mfg Dies/Tools/Jigs/Fixtures

(G-14917)
VIRGINIA BUILDING SERVICES INC
4865 Haygood Rd (23455-5319)
P.O. Box 62179 (23466-2179)
PHONE...................757 605-0288
Nate Rubin, *Principal*
EMP: 25
SALES (est): 4.1MM **Privately Held**
WEB: www.vabuilding.net
SIC: 3731 Offshore supply boats, building & repairing

(G-14918)
VIRGINIA CAROLINA PURE WATER
521 Holbrook Rd (23452-2517)
PHONE...................757 282-6487
Donna Naderman, *President*
Rene Johnson, *Office Mgr*
Donna Naderman,
EMP: 5
SALES (est): 388K **Privately Held**
SIC: 3589 Water treatment equipment, industrial

(G-14919)
VIRGINIA SOFTWARE GROUP INC
2108 Blossom Hill Ct (23457-1355)
PHONE...................757 721-0054
Keith Seckan, *CEO*
EMP: 2 EST: 2009
SALES (est): 162.6K **Privately Held**
WEB: www.virginiasoftwaregroup.com
SIC: 7372 Application computer software

(G-14920)
VIRGINIA STAIRS INC (PA)
2277 Haversham Close (23454-1152)
PHONE...................757 425-6681
Gennaro Fiore, *President*
Sysan Fiore, *Corp Secy*
EMP: 1
SALES (est): 210.7K **Privately Held**
SIC: 2431 Staircases & stairs, wood

(G-14921)
VIRGINIA THERMOGRAPHY LLC
361 Southport Cir Ste 202 (23452-1193)
PHONE...................757 705-9968
Lynn Almloff, *Principal*
EMP: 2 EST: 2016
SALES (est): 88.6K **Privately Held**
WEB: www.virginiathermography.com
SIC: 2759 Thermography

(G-14922)
VIRGINIA VETERANS CREATIONS
4768 Euclid Rd Ste 105 (23462-3810)
PHONE...................757 502-4407
Kathleen Owens, *President*
Christine Early, *Vice Pres*
EMP: 4
SQ FT: 2,500
SALES (est): 335.5K **Privately Held**
WEB: www.vaveteranscreations.com
SIC: 3271 3272 Architectural concrete: block, split, fluted, screen, etc.; precast terrazo or concrete products; furniture, garden: concrete; cast stone, concrete; art marble, concrete

(G-14923)
VIRGINN-PLOT MDIA CMPANIES LLC (DH)
5429 Greenwich Rd (23462-6511)
PHONE...................757 446-9000
Patricia Richardson, *President*
Bruce Bradley, *Exec VP*
Charlie W Hill, *Exec VP*
Michele Vernon Chesley, *Manager*
▲ EMP: 650 EST: 1865
SALES (est): 160.9MM **Publicly Held**
WEB: www.pilotonline.com
SIC: 2711 Commercial printing & newspaper publishing combined

(G-14924)
VIRGINN-PLOT MDIA CMPANIES LLC
5429 Greenwich Rd (23462-6511)
PHONE...................757 446-2848
EMP: 1 **Publicly Held**
WEB: www.pilotonline.com
SIC: 2711 4833 4899 5045 Newspapers, publishing & printing; television broadcasting stations; satellite earth stations; computer software
HQ: Virginian-Pilot Media Companies, Llc
5429 Greenwich Rd
Virginia Beach VA 23462
757 446-9000

(G-14925)
VISTA-GRAPHICS INC (PA)
1264 Perimeter Pkwy (23454-5689)
PHONE...................757 422-8979
Randy Thompson, *President*
Laurie Thompson, *Vice Pres*
Chris Murphy, *Director*
EMP: 23
SALES (est): 9MM **Privately Held**
WEB: www.vistagraphicsinc.com
SIC: 2741 7336 Miscellaneous publishing; graphic arts & related design

(G-14926)
VOLOUR PUB
5635 Banbury Ct (23462-1607)
PHONE...................757 547-6483
Mary Dowtin, *Principal*
EMP: 1 EST: 2012
SALES (est): 46K **Privately Held**
SIC: 2732 Books: printing only

(G-14927)
VSD LLC
5700 Ward Ave (23455-3311)
PHONE...................757 498-4766
Ted Rollins, *Manager*
EMP: 3
SALES (corp-wide): 3.3MM **Privately Held**
WEB: www.vsdonline.com
SIC: 3663 Television broadcasting & communications equipment
PA: Vsd, Llc
1064 Ferry Plantation Rd # 100
Virginia Beach VA 23455
757 498-4766

(G-14928)
W & S FORBES INC
Also Called: Fastsigns
2716 Virginia Beach Blvd (23452-7615)
PHONE...................757 498-7446
William Forbes, *President*
Sharon Forbes, *Corp Secy*
EMP: 5
SQ FT: 1,500
SALES (est): 400K **Privately Held**
WEB: www.fastsigns.com
SIC: 3993 Signs & advertising specialties

(G-14929)
WALSWORTH YEARBOOKS VA EAST
5237 Thatcher Way (23456-6358)
PHONE...................757 636-7104
Cosette Livas, *Owner*
EMP: 1
SALES (est): 56.5K **Privately Held**
SIC: 2732 Book printing

(G-14930)
WATERCRAFT LOGISTICS SVCS CO
1981 Stillwood Ln (23456-4954)
PHONE...................757 348-3089
Russell Morgan, *Principal*
EMP: 1 EST: 2013
SALES (est): 76.3K **Privately Held**
WEB: www.watercraftlogisticsservices.com
SIC: 2741 7389 Technical manuals: publishing & printing;

(G-14931)
WEDA WATER INC
1928 Sandee Cres (23454-2308)
PHONE...................757 515-4338
Klas Lange, *President*
Tracy Norrman, *General Mgr*
Anders Norrman, *Principal*
Stephen A Antolich, *COO*
Sharon Kopy, *CFO*
EMP: 5

SALES (est): 500K **Privately Held**
WEB: www.wedawater.com
SIC: **3731 5084** Submersible marine robots, manned or unmanned; robots, industrial

(G-14932)
WEEKLY WEEDER CO
1400 Fancy Ct (23454-6967)
PHONE..............................757 618-9506
Laura Huckins, *Principal*
EMP: 5
SALES (est): 216.8K **Privately Held**
WEB: www.weekly-weeder.com
SIC: **2711** Newspapers

(G-14933)
WENDYS EMBROIDERY
1761 N Muddy Creek Rd (23456-4154)
PHONE..............................757 685-0414
Wendy Moulton, *President*
EMP: 1
SALES (est): 42.1K **Privately Held**
SIC: **2395** Embroidery & art needlework

(G-14934)
WHAT HECK
516 Holbrook Rd (23452-2518)
PHONE..............................757 343-4058
Lori Hays, *Owner*
EMP: 1
SALES (est): 15K **Privately Held**
SIC: **2395** Embroidery & art needlework

(G-14935)
WHAT WOOD ANALISA DO
4736 Deerfield Ln (23455-5425)
PHONE..............................757 642-2991
Analisa Harvey, *Principal*
EMP: 2
SALES (est): 78.1K **Privately Held**
SIC: **2491** Wood preserving

(G-14936)
WILD BILLS CUSTOM SCREEN PRTG
3322 Virginia Beach Blvd # 117
(23452-5608)
PHONE..............................757 961-7576
William Ward, *Owner*
EMP: 1
SQ FT: 1,200
SALES (est): 68K **Privately Held**
SIC: **2759** Screen printing

(G-14937)
WILD THINGS LLC (HQ)
184 Business Park Dr # 205 (23462-6533)
PHONE..............................757 702-8773
Amy Coyne, *CEO*
Mike Kelleher, *Accounting Mgr*
Grady Burrell, *VP Sales*
◆ EMP: 8 EST: 1981
SALES (est): 2.6MM **Privately Held**
WEB: www.wildthingsgear.com
SIC: **3949** Sporting & athletic goods

(G-14938)
WILLIE SLICK INDUSTRIES
1745 Chase Arbor Cmn (23462-7414)
PHONE..............................843 310-4669
EMP: 1 EST: 2018
SALES (est): 39.6K **Privately Held**
SIC: **3999** Manufacturing industries

(G-14939)
WILSON PIPE & FABRICATION LLC
1233 New Land Dr (23453-3120)
PHONE..............................757 468-1374
Brandon Wilson,
EMP: 2 EST: 2016
SALES (est): 48K **Privately Held**
SIC: **3999** Manufacturing industries

(G-14940)
WINDMILL PROMOTIONS
Also Called: Tidewater Women
3065 Mansfield Ln (23457-1181)
PHONE..............................757 204-4688
Peggy Sijswerda, *Publisher*
Margaret Sijswerda, *Principal*
EMP: 5

SALES (est): 240K **Privately Held**
WEB: www.tidewaterwomen.com
SIC: **2711** Newspapers

(G-14941)
WISE CASE TECHNOLOGIES LLC
3369 Litchfield Rd (23452-6282)
PHONE..............................757 646-9080
Charles Kirkpatrick, *Mng Member*
EMP: 2 EST: 2016
SALES (est): 75.2K **Privately Held**
SIC: **7372** Application computer software

(G-14942)
WOLF CABINETRY INC
5801 Arrowhead Dr (23462-3220)
PHONE..............................757 498-0088
WEI Ting Zeng, *President*
▲ EMP: 4
SALES (est): 580.6K **Privately Held**
SIC: **2434** Wood kitchen cabinets

(G-14943)
WOOD CHUX CABINETS LLC
3024 Bowling Green Dr (23452-6513)
PHONE..............................757 409-0095
EMP: 2
SALES (est): 147.6K **Privately Held**
SIC: **2434** Wood kitchen cabinets

(G-14944)
WORTHINGTON PUBLISHING
509 White Oak Dr (23462-4220)
PHONE..............................757 831-4375
Grant Wylie, *Principal*
▲ EMP: 1
SALES (est): 70.1K **Privately Held**
WEB: www.worthingtonpublishing.com
SIC: **2741** Miscellaneous publishing

(G-14945)
WPO 3 INC
809 23rd St (23451-6310)
PHONE..............................757 491-4140
William P Oberndorfer III, *Principal*
EMP: 2
SALES (est): 101.4K **Privately Held**
SIC: **1241** Coal mining services

(G-14946)
WRITE IMPRESSIONS
4977 Cleveland St (23462-5312)
PHONE..............................757 473-1699
John D Dwyer, *Owner*
EMP: 1
SALES (est): 54K **Privately Held**
WEB: www.writeimpressionsresumes.com
SIC: **2741** Miscellaneous publishing

(G-14947)
X-METRIX INC
2513 Early Ct (23454-2601)
PHONE..............................757 450-5978
Thomas Fox, *President*
EMP: 3
SALES (est): 394.5K **Privately Held**
WEB: www.x-metrix.com
SIC: **3569** General industrial machinery

(G-14948)
XSYTECHNOLOGIESCOM
1 Columbus Ctr Ste 600 (23462-6760)
PHONE..............................757 333-7514
Thomas Brooks, *President*
EMP: 5
SALES (est): 367.5K **Privately Held**
WEB: www.ajonesfamily.com
SIC: **3579** Office machines

(G-14949)
XTERIORS PAVERS LLC
553 Central Dr (23454-5228)
PHONE..............................757 708-5904
EMP: 2
SALES (est): 74.7K **Privately Held**
WEB: www.xteriorspavers.com
SIC: **3281** Cut stone & stone products

(G-14950)
XTREME ADVENTURES INC
Also Called: Powrachute
2140 Marina Shores Dr (23451-6800)
PHONE..............................757 615-4602
Dody Nolan, *Principal*

EMP: 2
SALES (est): 142.5K **Privately Held**
SIC: **3721** Aircraft

(G-14951)
Y2K WEB TECHNOLOGIES
3600 Malibu Palms Dr # 202 (23452-3679)
PHONE..............................757 490-7877
Dan Jones, *Principal*
EMP: 2 EST: 2016
SALES (est): 86K **Privately Held**
SIC: **3721** Aircraft

(G-14952)
YAZDAN PUBLISHING COMPANY
2432 Kestrel Ln (23456-3452)
PHONE..............................757 426-6009
Kevin Todeschi, *Principal*
EMP: 2
SALES (est): 102.2K **Privately Held**
SIC: **2741** Miscellaneous publishing

(G-14953)
YNAFFIT MUSIC PUBLISHING
3557 Light Horse Loop (23453-2250)
PHONE..............................757 270-3316
Gary Wilson, *CEO*
EMP: 1
SALES (est): 37.5K **Privately Held**
SIC: **2741** Miscellaneous publishing

(G-14954)
YOU BUY BOOK PAPERBACK EXC
305 Waverly Dr Ste C (23452-4261)
PHONE..............................757 237-6426
Anne Woodson, *Principal*
EMP: 1
SALES (est): 87.9K **Privately Held**
SIC: **2621** Book paper

(G-14955)
YOUR PERSONAL PRINTER
5305 Hickory Rdg (23455-6681)
PHONE..............................757 679-1139
EMP: 2
SALES (est): 203.5K **Privately Held**
SIC: **2752** Commercial printing, lithographic

(G-14956)
ZB 3D PRINTERS LLC
319 34th St (23451-2804)
PHONE..............................757 695-8278
EMP: 4
SALES (est): 147.2K **Privately Held**
SIC: **2752** Commercial printing, lithographic

(G-14957)
ZERO PRODUCTS LLC
2140 Brush Hill Ln (23456-1245)
PHONE..............................757 285-4000
Gene Markland, *Principal*
Martha Markland,
EMP: 2 EST: 1990
SALES (est): 141.6K **Privately Held**
WEB: www.zzzeroproducts.com
SIC: **2842 5169** Specialty cleaning preparations; specialty cleaning & sanitation preparations

(G-14958)
ZEST
312 Sandbridge Rd (23456-4522)
PHONE..............................757 301-8553
Martha Gaione, *Principal*
EMP: 3
SALES (est): 184.4K **Privately Held**
WEB: www.zestinsandbridge.com
SIC: **3537** Cranes, industrial truck

(G-14959)
ZETA CAR WASHES LLC
1449 Tomcat Blvd Bldg 296 (23460-2177)
PHONE..............................757 469-2141
Sean Forsyth, *Principal*
Scott Alperin, *Principal*
James Jolley, *Principal*
EMP: 3
SALES (est): 122K **Privately Held**
SIC: **3589** Car washing machinery

(G-14960)
ZF TECHNICAL LLC
418 Davis St (23462-5694)
PHONE..............................757 575-5625
Cory Zillig,
EMP: 1
SALES (est): 47K **Privately Held**
SIC: **3949** Target shooting equipment

(G-14961)
ZHE INDUSTRIES LLC
817 Gloria Pl (23454-3803)
PHONE..............................757 759-5466
EMP: 1 EST: 2018
SALES (est): 43.6K **Privately Held**
WEB: www.zheindustries.com
SIC: **3999** Manufacturing industries

(G-14962)
ZHE INDUSTRIES LLC
812 Prince Frederick Ct (23454-3425)
PHONE..............................757 759-5466
Brian J P Zhe, *Administration*
EMP: 1
SALES (est): 60.8K **Privately Held**
WEB: www.zheindustries.com
SIC: **3999** Manufacturing industries

Wake
Middlesex County

(G-14963)
PHASE 2 MARINE CANVAS LLC
2271 Wake Rd (23176-2119)
P.O. Box 71 (23176-0071)
PHONE..............................804 694-7561
Sue Golembicki, *Principal*
EMP: 4
SALES (est): 264.3K **Privately Held**
WEB: www.phase2marinecanvas.com
SIC: **2394** Canvas & related products

Wakefield
Sussex County

(G-14964)
BARNEY FAMILY ENTERPRISES LLC
Also Called: Tamco Paint
317 W Main St (23888-2940)
P.O. Box 711 (23888-0711)
PHONE..............................757 438-2064
Tammy Barney, *President*
Robert Barney, *Vice Pres*
EMP: 5
SALES (est): 2.2MM **Privately Held**
WEB: www.tamcopaint.com
SIC: **2851 7389** Paints & allied products;

(G-14965)
DESIGNER SIGNS
38476 Rocky Hock Rd (23888-2899)
PHONE..............................757 879-1153
EMP: 1
SALES (est): 46K **Privately Held**
SIC: **3993** Signs & advertising specialties

(G-14966)
INDMAR COATINGS CORPORATION
317 W Main St (23888-2940)
P.O. Box 456 (23888-0456)
PHONE..............................757 899-3807
Wilmer Rowe, *President*
EMP: 10
SQ FT: 44,000
SALES (est): 1.7MM **Privately Held**
WEB: www.indmarcoatings.com
SIC: **2851** Paints & allied products

(G-14967)
ISLE OF WIGHT FOREST PRODUCTS
10242 General Mahone Hwy (23888-2709)
PHONE..............................757 899-8115
Brad Clontd, *Branch Mgr*
EMP: 10 **Privately Held**
WEB: www.nhbclakeland.com
SIC: **3272** Poles & posts, concrete

PA: Isle Of Wight Forest Products, Inc
21158 Lankford Ln
Smithfield VA 23430

(G-14968)
K & S WELDING
9399 Kellos Mill Rd (23888-2214)
PHONE..................757 859-6313
Kent Edwards, *Principal*
EMP: 1
SALES (est): 40.6K **Privately Held**
SIC: 7692 Welding repair

(G-14969)
PENNY TRAIL PRESS LLC
37219 Old Wakefield Rd (23888-2724)
PHONE..................757 644-5349
Kathryn Braswell, *Owner*
EMP: 2
SALES (est): 119.7K **Privately Held**
SIC: 2741 5088 8999 Miscellaneous publishing; golf carts; ghost writing

(G-14970)
SEW AND TELL EMBROIDERY
9277 Kellos Mill Rd (23888-2219)
PHONE..................757 641-1227
EMP: 1
SALES (est): 31.2K **Privately Held**
SIC: 2395 Embroidery & art needlework

Walkerton
King And Queen County

(G-14971)
GAIAS GOLD
1858 Canterbury Rd (23177-4034)
PHONE..................804 516-8458
Grant Dionne, *Principal*
EMP: 2
SALES (est): 103.5K **Privately Held**
WEB: www.gaiasgold.com
SIC: 2844 Toilet preparations

Wallops Island
Accomack County

(G-14972)
ORBITAL SCIENCES CORPORATION
34200 Fulton St (23337-2307)
PHONE..................757 824-5619
Steve Nelson, *CEO*
EMP: 463 **Publicly Held**
WEB: www.northropgrumman.com
SIC: 3812 Defense systems & equipment
HQ: Orbital Sciences Llc
45101 Warp Dr
Dulles VA 20166
703 406-5524

Warm Springs
Bath County

(G-14973)
MIKE PUFFENDARGER
Also Called: Southern Most Maple
7738 Big Valley Rd (24484-2436)
PHONE..................540 468-2682
Mike Puffendarger, *Owner*
EMP: 4
SALES (est): 245.4K **Privately Held**
WEB: www.testsite4smm.com
SIC: 2099 Maple syrup

(G-14974)
PRITTS LOGGING
103 Gatewood Dr (24484-2184)
PHONE..................304 646-0004
Eli Pritt, *Principal*
EMP: 2
SALES (est): 81.7K **Privately Held**
SIC: 2411 Logging

(G-14975)
RECORDER PUBLISHING VA INC
2663 Mcguffin Rd (24484-2142)
PHONE..................540 839-6646
Preston Lea Campbell, *Administration*

EMP: 2 EST: 2010
SALES (est): 77.7K **Privately Held**
SIC: 2741 Miscellaneous publishing

Warrenton
Fauquier County

(G-14976)
AC ATLAS PUBLISHING
6811 Sholes Ct (20187-3909)
PHONE..................301 980-0711
Curtis Paul, *Principal*
EMP: 1 EST: 2015
SALES (est): 37.5K **Privately Held**
SIC: 2741 Miscellaneous publishing

(G-14977)
ALLEN WAYNE LTD ARLINGTON
Also Called: Allen Wayne Limited
7128 Lineweaver Rd (20187-3949)
PHONE..................703 321-7414
Roland Owens, *CEO*
Robert Pace, *Vice Pres*
Barbara Yudd, *Technology*
EMP: 6
SQ FT: 3,000
SALES: 1MM **Privately Held**
WEB: www.allenwayne.com
SIC: 2791 2741 7375 2752 Typesetting; technical manual & paper publishing; information retrieval services; commercial printing, lithographic; graphic arts & related design

(G-14978)
ARBEN SOLUTIONS CO
403 Holiday Ct (20186-4363)
PHONE..................703 728-0396
Stephanie Armand, *CEO*
Spencer Armand, *Principal*
Stephanie Corbin, *Principal*
EMP: 2
SALES (est): 131.3K **Privately Held**
WEB: www.arbensolutions.com
SIC: 3842 8748 8742 5047 Respiratory protection equipment, personal; business consulting; management consulting services; management information systems consultant; medical equipment & supplies;

(G-14979)
BACUS WOODWORKS LLC
7203 Manor House Dr (20187-9548)
PHONE..................571 762-3314
Susan Bacus, *Principal*
EMP: 2
SALES (est): 105K **Privately Held**
SIC: 2499 Wood products

(G-14980)
BAD WOLF LLC
7161 James Madison Hwy (20187-9536)
PHONE..................540 347-4255
Ronald Borta, *Principal*
EMP: 2
SALES (est): 156.6K **Privately Held**
SIC: 3448 Prefabricated metal components

(G-14981)
BEEF JERKY OUTL NOVA JERKY LLC
6618 Lancaster Dr (20187-4419)
PHONE..................703 868-6297
EMP: 2
SALES (est): 62.3K **Privately Held**
SIC: 2013 Snack sticks, including jerky: from purchased meat

(G-14982)
BLUEGRASS UNLIMITED INC
9514 James Madison Hwy (20186-7817)
P.O. Box 771 (20188-0771)
PHONE..................540 349-8181
Peter Kuykendall, *President*
Sharon Watts, *Corp Secy*
Richard Spottswood, *Vice Pres*
EMP: 9
SQ FT: 4,000

SALES (est): 994K **Privately Held**
WEB: www.bluegrassmusic.com
SIC: 2721 Magazines: publishing only, not printed on site

(G-14983)
BONZE ASSOCIATES LLC
7070 Honeysuckle Ct (20187-9524)
PHONE..................540 497-2964
Scott Freeman, *Principal*
EMP: 1 EST: 2014
SALES (est): 72.1K **Privately Held**
SIC: 3731 Submersible marine robots, manned or unmanned

(G-14984)
BULL RUN METAL INC
5591 Old Auburn Rd (20187-8335)
PHONE..................540 347-2135
EMP: 4
SALES (est): 372.4K **Privately Held**
SIC: 3499 Fabricated metal products

(G-14985)
C-MORE SYSTEMS INC
680d Industrial Rd (20186-3824)
P.O. Box 340 (20188-0340)
PHONE..................540 347-4683
Ira M Kay, *President*
Gayle A Kay, *Corp Secy*
EMP: 8
SQ FT: 3,000
SALES (est): 169.4K **Privately Held**
WEB: www.cmore.com
SIC: 3827 Gun sights, optical

(G-14986)
CATLILLI GAMES LLC
449 Estate Ave (20186-2649)
PHONE..................540 359-6592
Catherine Swanwick, *Principal*
EMP: 3
SALES (est): 215.6K **Privately Held**
WEB: www.catlilli.com
SIC: 3944 Board games, children's & adults'

(G-14987)
CHRISTOPHER K REDDERSEN
5741 Wilshire Dr (20187-9246)
PHONE..................703 232-6691
Christopher Reddersen, *Owner*
EMP: 1 EST: 2015
SALES (est): 62.2K **Privately Held**
SIC: 3721 7389 Aircraft; business services

(G-14988)
CNE MANUFACTURING SERVICES LLC
173 Keith St Ste 3 (20186-3257)
PHONE..................540 216-0884
Catherine C Howard,
EMP: 36
SALES (est): 2.3MM **Privately Held**
WEB: www.cnemfg.com
SIC: 3571 7378 Electronic computers; computer maintenance & repair

(G-14989)
COMMONWALTH POLYGRAPH SVCS LLC
6121 James Madison Hwy (20187-7314)
P.O. Box 3071 (20188-1771)
PHONE..................540 219-9382
Richard Macwelch,
EMP: 1
SALES (est): 162.1K **Privately Held**
SIC: 3829 Polygraph devices

(G-14990)
CONVEX CORPORATION
7226 Mecklenburg Dr (20187-2230)
PHONE..................703 433-9901
James R Ambrose, *President*
David G Nicholson, *Vice Pres*
Suzanne Poisson, *Shareholder*
EMP: 5 EST: 1975
SALES: 614.4K **Privately Held**
WEB: www.convexcorp.com
SIC: 3577 3669 3663 Computer peripheral equipment; emergency alarms; light communications equipment

(G-14991)
CUSTOM PUBG SOLUTIONS LLC
210 Cannon Way (20186-4307)
PHONE..................540 341-0453
Lisa McIntosh,
EMP: 1
SALES (est): 40K **Privately Held**
SIC: 2721 Magazines: publishing & printing

(G-14992)
D & D SIGNS
6418 Old Meetze Rd (20187-4356)
PHONE..................540 428-3144
EMP: 2
SALES (est): 163.2K **Privately Held**
SIC: 3993 Mfg Signs/Advertising Specialties

(G-14993)
D & S CONTROLS
7206 Marr Dr (20187-2225)
PHONE..................703 655-8189
EMP: 3 EST: 2015
SALES (est): 197.3K **Privately Held**
WEB: www.dscontrols247.com
SIC: 3823 Industrial instrmnts msrmnt display/control process variable

(G-14994)
DELCLOS INDUSTRIES LLC
5459 Claire Ct (20187-4502)
PHONE..................540 349-4049
Lawrence Delclos, *Principal*
EMP: 2 EST: 2018
SALES (est): 74.6K **Privately Held**
SIC: 3999 Manufacturing industries

(G-14995)
DESIGN INTEGRATED TECH INC
Also Called: Dit
100 E Franklin St (20186-3313)
PHONE..................540 349-9425
Stephen Andrews, *President*
Jim Cady, *Executive*
EMP: 12
SQ FT: 3,500
SALES (est): 1.4MM **Privately Held**
WEB: www.ditusa.com
SIC: 3443 3829 Fabricated plate work (boiler shop); testing equipment: abrasion, shearing strength, etc.

(G-14996)
DIANES CROCHET DOLLS & THINGS
5548 Eiseley Ct (20187-9206)
PHONE..................703 229-2173
EMP: 2
SALES (est): 107.2K **Privately Held**
SIC: 2399 Hand woven & crocheted products

(G-14997)
DISCOVERY PUBLICATIONS INC
125 W Shirley Ave (20186-3111)
P.O. Box 3501 (20188-8101)
PHONE..................540 349-8060
Kathryn M Harper, *President*
EMP: 2
SALES (est): 174.8K **Privately Held**
WEB: www.discoverypubs.com
SIC: 2731 Book publishing

(G-14998)
DMH COMPLETE WELDING
1431 Welding Ln (20186-5406)
PHONE..................540 347-7550
Douglas M Hayes, *Owner*
EMP: 1
SALES (est): 100K **Privately Held**
SIC: 7692 Welding repair

(G-14999)
DRONESHIELD LLC
7140 Farm Station Rd B (20187-4008)
PHONE..................202 750-4368
Albert Newell, *Officer*
Oleg Vornik,
EMP: 12
SALES (est): 1.2MM **Privately Held**
WEB: www.droneshield.com
SIC: 3812 Defense systems & equipment

▲ = Import ▼=Export
◆ =Import/Export

(G-15000)
E TRUCKING & SERVICES LLC
4263 Aiken Dr (20187-3935)
PHONE..........................571 241-0856
Ivo Jose Pereira Neto, *Vice Pres*
Eliene Pereira, *Vice Pres*
Ivo J Pereira, *Administration*
EMP: 2
SALES (est): 181.1K **Privately Held**
WEB: www.econtractingservices.com
SIC: **1442** 4959 Construction sand &
gravel; snowplowing

(G-15001)
EAGLE DESIGNS
7249 Ridgedale Dr (20186-7831)
PHONE..........................540 428-1916
Jason Yates, *Owner*
EMP: 1
SALES (est): 64K **Privately Held**
SIC: 2759 Commercial printing

(G-15002)
EAHEART EQUIPMENT INC (PA)
8326 Meetze Rd (20187-4339)
PHONE..........................540 347-2880
Edward McCoy, *President*
Candace Allen, *Assistant*
EMP: 19
SALES (est): 3.7MM **Privately Held**
SIC: 3524 Lawn & garden mowers & ac-
cessories

(G-15003)
ECKS CUSTOM WOODWORKING
7140 Meadow Ln (20187-2557)
PHONE..........................571 765-0807
Joshua Eck, *Principal*
EMP: 2
SALES (est): 65.4K **Privately Held**
SIC: 2431 Millwork

(G-15004)
EODRONES LLC
4154 Weeks Dr (20187-3944)
PHONE..........................703 856-8400
Jim Blanchard,
EMP: 1
SALES (est): 60K **Privately Held**
SIC: 3721 Research & development on air-
craft by the manufacturer

(G-15005)
ESSEX HAND CRAFTED WD PDTS LLC
6649 Garland Dr Unit 7 (20187-2714)
PHONE..........................540 445-5928
Tony Dudley, *Owner*
EMP: 5
SALES (est): 89K **Privately Held**
SIC: 2499 Laundry products, wood

(G-15006)
EXLOC INSTRUMENTS
7089 Lineweaver Rd (20187-3948)
P.O. Box 861406, Vint Hill Farms (20187-
1406)
PHONE..........................540 428-3088
Adrianne Jones, *President*
EMP: 4
SALES (est): 274.9K **Privately Held**
WEB: www.exloc.com
SIC: 3823 Industrial instrmnts msrmnt dis-
play/control process variable

(G-15007)
EXTREME STEEL INC
9705 Rider Rd (20187-7805)
PHONE..........................540 868-9150
Kevin Rodney, *President*
Matt Brady, *General Mgr*
Randy Gardner, *Safety Dir*
George McCelvey, *Purch Agent*
Tom Brown, *Technology*
EMP: 58
SALES (est): 2.5MM **Privately Held**
WEB: www.extremesteelinc.com
SIC: **3441** 1791 3446 Fabricated struc-
tural metal; structural steel erection; archi-
tectural metalwork

(G-15008)
FAUQUIER BUILDING GRNDS
100 Manor Ct (20186-3124)
PHONE..........................540 422-8480

EMP: 3 EST: 2017
SALES (est): 137.9K **Privately Held**
SIC: 2711 Newspapers, publishing & print-
ing

(G-15009)
FAUQUIER ENTERPRISE CENTER
4263 Aiken Dr (20187-3935)
PHONE..........................540 680-2652
EMP: 3
SALES (est): 109K **Privately Held**
WEB: www.fauquiernow.com
SIC: 2711 Newspapers, publishing & print-
ing

(G-15010)
FAUQUIER HEARING SERVICES PLLC
Also Called: Listening Loop Technologies
493 Blackwell Rd Ste 315 (20186-2688)
PHONE..........................540 341-7112
Diane Markva,
EMP: 4
SALES (est): 549.6K **Privately Held**
WEB: www.hearingassessment.com
SIC: **3669** 5999 Intercommunication sys-
tems, electric; hearing aids

(G-15011)
FAUQUIER KID LLC
285 Falmouth St (20186-3627)
PHONE..........................540 349-0027
Jannifer Major, *Principal*
EMP: 3 EST: 2010
SALES (est): 125.3K **Privately Held**
WEB: www.fauquierhealth.org
SIC: 2711 Newspapers

(G-15012)
FAUQUIER NOW
50 Culpeper St Ste 3 (20186-3253)
PHONE..........................540 359-6574
Lou Emerson, *Principal*
Lawrence Emerson, *Editor*
EMP: 1
SALES (est): 66.2K **Privately Held**
WEB: www.fauquiernow.com
SIC: 2711 Newspapers, publishing & print-
ing

(G-15013)
FAUQUIER SERVICES INC
8279 Double Poplars Ln (20187-8313)
PHONE..........................540 341-4133
Gregory Harris, *Principal*
EMP: 1
SALES (est): 71.6K **Privately Held**
WEB: www.fauquiernow.com
SIC: 2711 Newspapers, publishing & print-
ing

(G-15014)
FAUQUIER SILHOUETTES INC
247 Amber Cir (20186-4344)
PHONE..........................540 347-3191
Judith Risdon, *Owner*
EMP: 3 EST: 2016
SALES (est): 116.2K **Privately Held**
WEB: www.fauquier.com
SIC: 2711 Newspapers, publishing & print-
ing

(G-15015)
FAUQUIER TIMES DEMOCRAT
Also Called: Times Community Newspaper
39 Culpeper St (20186-3319)
PHONE..........................540 347-7363
EMP: 40
SALES (est): 1.7MM **Privately Held**
SIC: 2711 Newspapers-Publishing/Printing

(G-15016)
FEI-ZYFER INC
8209 Great Run Ln (20186-9644)
PHONE..........................540 349-8330
Phillip Walker, *Sales Staff*
Steve Strang, *Branch Mgr*
EMP: 2 **Publicly Held**
WEB: www.fei-zyfer.com
SIC: 3663 Radio & TV communications
equipment
HQ: Fei-Zyfer, Inc.
7321 Lincoln Way
Garden Grove CA 92841

(G-15017)
FOX GROUP INC
39 Garrett St Ste 226 (20186-3122)
PHONE..........................925 980-5643
Bernard P O'Meara, *President*
EMP: 99
SALES (est): 5.9MM **Privately Held**
WEB: www.thefoxgroupinc.com
SIC: 3674 Semiconductors & related de-
vices

(G-15018)
FREESTATE ELECTRONICS INC
6530 Commerce Ct (20187-2347)
PHONE..........................540 349-4727
Ronald Harris, *President*
EMP: 2
SQ FT: 6,000
SALES (est): 209K **Privately Held**
WEB: www.fse-inc.com
SIC: 3825 Analog-digital converters, elec-
tronic instrumentation type

(G-15019)
GAITHRSBURG CBINETRY MLLWK INC
4338 Aiken Dr (20187-3933)
PHONE..........................540 347-4551
Stephan Smith, *President*
Kirk S Vetter, *Exec VP*
James R Landoll, *Vice Pres*
Jeff P Schrock, *Vice Pres*
Carolyn Fletcher, *Accounting Mgr*
EMP: 65 EST: 1981
SQ FT: 32,000
SALES (est): 17.2MM **Privately Held**
WEB: www.gcabinet.com
SIC: **2521** 2541 2431 Wood office furni-
ture; table or counter tops, plastic lami-
nated; millwork; woodwork, interior &
ornamental

(G-15020)
GASE ENERGY INC
173 Keith St Ste 300 (20186-3231)
PHONE..........................540 347-2212
Timur Khromaev, *CEO*
Michael Doron, *Ch of Bd*
Herve Collet, *COO*
EMP: 42
SALES (est): 348.6K **Privately Held**
WEB: www.greateastenergy.com
SIC: 1311 Crude petroleum & natural gas
PA: Bezerius Holdings Limited
Floor 3, 11 Boumpoulinas
Nicosia

(G-15021)
GOSS132
798 Col Edmonds Ct (20186-2178)
PHONE..........................202 905-2380
Michael Lester, *Principal*
EMP: 2
SALES (est): 80.8K **Privately Held**
SIC: 3711 Motor vehicles & car bodies

(G-15022)
HAMILTON EQUIPMENT SERVICE LLC
25 Broadview Ave (20186-2710)
PHONE..........................540 341-4141
Vicky Noland,
Thomas Noland,
Travis Noland,
EMP: 7 EST: 2000
SQ FT: 4,000
SALES (est): 1.2MM **Privately Held**
WEB: www.hamilton-equip.com
SIC: **3492** 5083 Hose & tube fittings & as-
semblies, hydraulic/pneumatic; farm &
garden machinery

(G-15023)
HANDI-LEIGH CRAFTED
4507 Canter Ln (20187-8914)
PHONE..........................540 349-7775
Dave Leigh, *Owner*
EMP: 2
SALES (est): 106.3K **Privately Held**
SIC: **3496** 5199 7389 Cages, wire; pet
supplies;

(G-15024)
HARRINGTON SOFTWARE ASSOC INC
7431 Wilson Rd (20186-7464)
PHONE..........................540 349-8074
Susan Harrington, *President*
Frank Harrington, *Vice Pres*
EMP: 6
SALES (est): 700K **Privately Held**
WEB: www.hsainc.net
SIC: 7372 Business oriented computer
software

(G-15025)
HOMETOWN IMPRINTS INC
5439 Old Alexandria Tpke (20187-9361)
PHONE..........................540 878-5848
Jennifer Riggleman, *Principal*
Luther Riggleman, *Principal*
Charlotte Smith, *Principal*
Ronald Smith, *Principal*
EMP: 4
SALES (est): 137.2K **Privately Held**
WEB: www.hometownimprints.com
SIC: 2759 Screen printing

(G-15026)
INCIDENT LOGIC LLC
8262 Lees Ridge Rd (20186-8741)
PHONE..........................540 349-8888
James Atkins, *Partner*
Kris Popovski, *Regl Sales Mgr*
EMP: 2 EST: 2012
SALES (est): 168.1K **Privately Held**
WEB: www.incidentlogic.com
SIC: 7372 Application computer software

(G-15027)
INQUISIENT INC
8278 Falcon Glen Rd (20186-9640)
PHONE..........................888 230-2181
Scott Smith, *CEO*
Bruce Randall Dewoolfson, *President*
Mark Schmeets, *Vice Pres*
Jaimie Francois, *Admin Mgr*
EMP: 13
SQ FT: 2,000
SALES (est): 177.1K **Privately Held**
WEB: www.inquisient.com
SIC: 7372 Application computer software

(G-15028)
KNAP SERVICES INC
173 Keith St Ste 3 (20186-3257)
PHONE..........................540 351-5905
Melinda Whetzel, *CEO*
EMP: 7
SALES (est): 1MM **Privately Held**
SIC: 3271 Concrete block & brick

(G-15029)
KRT ARCHITECTURAL SIGNAGE INC
6799 Kennedy Rd Ste C (20187-3982)
PHONE..........................540 428-3801
Richard Trimble, *President*
Tiffany Ferguson, *Office Mgr*
▲ EMP: 5
SQ FT: 2,000
SALES (est): 430K **Privately Held**
WEB: www.krtsignage.net
SIC: 3993 Signs & advertising specialties

(G-15030)
LEADING EDGE SCREEN PRINTING
Also Called: Workwear Distributors
405 Rosedale Ct (20186-4327)
PHONE..........................540 347-5751
Scott Keithley, *President*
Natalie Keithley, *Admin Sec*
EMP: 17
SQ FT: 4,500
SALES (est): 1.3MM **Privately Held**
WEB: www.lespinc.com
SIC: **2396** 7389 2395 Screen printing on
fabric articles; embroidering of advertising
on shirts, etc.; pleating & stitching

(G-15031)
LEGACY VULCAN LLC
Mideast Division
5485 Afton Ln (20187-4310)
P.O. Box 3481 (20188-8081)
PHONE..........................540 347-3641

William W Sanders III, *Principal*
EMP: 32 **Publicly Held**
WEB: www.vulcanmaterials.com
SIC: 3273 Ready-mixed concrete
HQ: Legacy Vulcan, Llc
1200 Urban Center Dr
Vestavia AL 35242
205 298-3000

(G-15032)
MAGIC GENIUS LLC
5463 Camellia Ct (20187-7200)
PHONE..................................540 454-7595
Eric W Parris,
EMP: 1
SALES (est): 12K **Privately Held**
SIC: 7372 7389 Prepackaged software;
business services

(G-15033)
MATHIAS WELDING
9547 James Madison Hwy (20187-7812)
PHONE..................................540 347-1415
Harold Mathias, *Owner*
EMP: 1
SALES (est): 55.1K **Privately Held**
SIC: 7692 Welding repair

(G-15034)
**MEDITERRANEAN CELLARS
LLC**
8295 Falcon Glen Rd (20186-9642)
PHONE..................................540 428-1984
Katherine Papadopoulos, *President*
EMP: 3
SALES (est): 332.7K **Privately Held**
WEB: www.mediterraneancellars.com
SIC: 2084 Wines

(G-15035)
**MOLON LAVE VINEYARDS &
WINERY**
10075 Lees Mill Rd (20186-8425)
PHONE..................................540 439-5460
K Papadopoulos, *Principal*
Katherine Papadopoulos, *Manager*
EMP: 5 **EST:** 2009
SALES (est): 421.5K **Privately Held**
WEB: www.molonlavevineyards.com
SIC: 2084 Wines

(G-15036)
MORNINGS MYST ALPACAS INC
7280 Burke Ln (20186-7801)
PHONE..................................540 428-1002
Kimberly A Pinello, *Administration*
EMP: 2 **EST:** 2010
SALES (est): 163K **Privately Held**
SIC: 2231 Alpacas, mohair: woven

(G-15037)
MYSTERY GOOSE PRESS LLC
4650 Spring Run Rd (20187-5814)
PHONE..................................540 347-3609
EMP: 1
SALES (est): 37.5K **Privately Held**
SIC: 2741 Miscellaneous publishing

(G-15038)
NOVA ROCK CRAFT LLC
7157 Comrie Ct (20187-3978)
PHONE..................................703 217-7072
EMP: 2 **EST:** 2014
SQ FT: 800
SALES (est): 137.9K **Privately Held**
SIC: 3993 5999 Mfg Signs/Advertising
Specialties Ret Misc Merchandise

(G-15039)
**OLD TOWN WOODWORKING
INC**
545 Old Meetze Rd (20186-3835)
PHONE..................................540 347-3993
William S Nieder, *President*
Danny J Mulvena, *Vice Pres*
Danny Mulvena, *CFO*
EMP: 10
SQ FT: 8,000
SALES (est): 700K **Privately Held**
WEB: www.oldtownwoodworking.com
SIC: 2521 2511 Wood office furniture;
wood household furniture

(G-15040)
OOSKA NEWS CORP
37 Main St (20186-3445)
PHONE..................................540 724-1750
David Duncan, *CEO*
Alexnder Duncan, *Shareholder*
Kathleen Morris, *Shareholder*
Bil Pursche, *Shareholder*
EMP: 7
SQ FT: 1,800
SALES (est): 180K **Privately Held**
WEB: www.ooskanews.com
SIC: 2741 Newsletter publishing

(G-15041)
P-AMERICAS LLC
Also Called: Pepsico
5393 Lee Hwy (20187-9355)
PHONE..................................540 347-3112
Tony Brocato, *Manager*
EMP: 70
SALES (corp-wide): 67.1B **Publicly Held**
WEB: www.pepsicva.com
SIC: 2086 Carbonated soft drinks, bottled
& canned
HQ: P-Americas Llc
1 Pepsi Way
Somers NY 10589
336 896-5740

(G-15042)
**PARAMOUNT SPECIALTY
METALS LLC**
1180 Brittle Ridge Rd (20187-2433)
PHONE..................................980 721-3958
Neil Kaufman,
EMP: 1
SALES (est): 42K **Privately Held**
SIC: 3999 Manufacturing industries

(G-15043)
**PEACE JUSTICE PUBLICATIONS
LLC**
7180 Baldwin Ridge Rd (20187-9180)
PHONE..................................540 349-7862
Linda Swanson, *Principal*
EMP: 2 **EST:** 2010
SALES (est): 87.7K **Privately Held**
SIC: 2741 Miscellaneous publishing

(G-15044)
PILINUT PRESS INC
5089 Old Auburn Rd (20187-8340)
PHONE..................................540 347-6295
EMP: 2
SALES (est): 82.6K **Privately Held**
WEB: www.pilinutpress.com
SIC: 2741 Miscellaneous publishing

(G-15045)
PRINTING FOR YOU
205 Keith St (20186-3231)
PHONE..................................540 351-0191
Cathy Dodson, *Principal*
EMP: 2 **EST:** 2013
SALES (est): 170.1K **Privately Held**
SIC: 2752 Commercial printing, offset

(G-15046)
PRO REFINISH
7381 Moccasin Ln (20186-6117)
PHONE..................................703 853-9665
EMP: 1 **EST:** 2018
SALES (est): 53.7K **Privately Held**
WEB: www.prorefinish.com
SIC: 2434 Wood kitchen cabinets

(G-15047)
**RHINOS INK SCREEN PRTG &
EMB**
268 Broadview Ave (20186-2302)
PHONE..................................540 347-3303
EMP: 2
SALES (est): 80.6K **Privately Held**
WEB: www.rhinosink.com
SIC: 2759 Screen printing

(G-15048)
RIDEFAUQUIER
6757 Beach Rd (20187-7718)
PHONE..................................540 270-8247
Karen Corl, *Principal*
EMP: 3 **EST:** 2018

SALES (est): 98.1K **Privately Held**
WEB: www.fauquiernow.com
SIC: 2711 Newspapers, publishing & print-
ing

(G-15049)
SCOTTIES BAVARIAN FOLK ART
7561 Cannoneer Ct (20186-9720)
PHONE..................................540 341-8884
Scottie Foster, *President*
Lyle Jackson Foster Jr, *Treasurer*
EMP: 2
SALES (est): 170.2K **Privately Held**
WEB: www.bavarianfolkart.com
SIC: 2731 8299 Books: publishing only;
art school, except commercial

(G-15050)
SELIMAX INC
4486 Den Haag Rd (20187-2862)
P.O. Box 315, Gainesville (20156-0315)
PHONE..................................540 347-5784
Arthur Miles, *President*
EMP: 1
SALES (est): 300K **Privately Held**
SIC: 3441 Fabricated structural metal for
bridges

(G-15051)
**SHOOTING STARR ALPACAS
LLC**
7158 Spotsylvania St (20187-4433)
PHONE..................................540 347-4721
William N McDonald, *Administration*
EMP: 2
SALES (est): 150.3K **Privately Held**
SIC: 2231 Alpacas, mohair: woven

(G-15052)
SINGLE SOURCE WELDING LLC
5141 Poplar Pl (20187-2686)
PHONE..................................703 919-7791
Michael Brown Jr, *Owner*
EMP: 1 **EST:** 2000
SALES (est): 51K **Privately Held**
SIC: 7692 5084 Welding repair; brewery
products manufacturing machinery, com-
mercial

(G-15053)
**SPOTTED LOPARD-TABULA
RASA LLC**
7442 Lake Willow Ct (20187-5867)
PHONE..................................571 285-8151
Nadine Hollingsworth,
EMP: 1
SALES (est): 284.8K **Privately Held**
WEB: www.thespottedleoparddesigns.com
SIC: 2434 Wood kitchen cabinets

(G-15054)
SWEET PEA CERAMICS LLC
439 Devon Dr (20186-3056)
PHONE..................................571 292-4313
Nanette Johnson, *Principal*
EMP: 2
SALES (est): 78.4K **Privately Held**
WEB: www.sweetpeaceramics.com
SIC: 3269 Pottery products

(G-15055)
TR PRESS INC (PA)
Also Called: Piedmont Press & Graphics
404 Belle Air Ln (20186-4368)
P.O. Box 3021 (20188-1721)
PHONE..................................540 347-4466
Tony Tedeschi, *President*
Holly Tedeschi, *Vice Pres*
Earl Arrington, *Cust Svc Dir*
Cindy Gray, *Graphic Designe*
EMP: 23
SQ FT: 10,000
SALES (est): 3.6MM **Privately Held**
WEB: www.piedmontpress.com
SIC: 2752 2796 2791 2789 Commercial
printing, offset; platemaking services;
typesetting; bookbinding & related work

(G-15056)
**TRIPLE R WELDING & REPAIR
SVC**
5413 Turkey Run Rd (20187-8858)
PHONE..................................540 347-9026
Ron Kines, *Owner*
EMP: 7

SALES (est): 634.5K **Privately Held**
SIC: 3599 1799 Machine shop, jobbing &
repair; welding on site

(G-15057)
TYPE ETC
6419 Tazewell St (20187-2236)
PHONE..................................540 347-2182
Marie Scheerer, *Principal*
EMP: 2
SALES (est): 153.1K **Privately Held**
SIC: 2752 Commercial printing, offset

(G-15058)
VERTU CORP
Also Called: C-More Competition
680c Industrial Rd (20186-3824)
P.O. Box 340 (20188-0340)
PHONE..................................540 341-3006
Gayle Kay, *President*
Ira Kay, *President*
EMP: 14
SALES (est): 1.6MM **Privately Held**
WEB: www.cmorecomp.com
SIC: 3484 Small arms

(G-15059)
WELLS CUSTOM MFG LLC
71 S 5th St (20186-3363)
PHONE..................................703 623-1396
EMP: 1
SALES (est): 39.6K **Privately Held**
SIC: 3999 Manufacturing industries

Warsaw
Richmond County

(G-15060)
APEX INDUSTRIES LLC
Also Called: Apex Truss
1688 Chestnut Hill Rd (22572)
P.O. Box 247 (22572-0247)
PHONE..................................804 313-2295
Larry Dix,
EMP: 10
SALES (est): 2MM **Privately Held**
WEB: www.apextruss.com
SIC: 2439 Trusses, wooden roof

(G-15061)
BSI EXPRESS
7058 Richmond Rd (22572-3516)
P.O. Box 5, Hustle (22476-0005)
PHONE..................................804 443-7134
India Bennett, *Principal*
EMP: 2
SALES (est): 15K **Privately Held**
SIC: 3715 Truck trailers

(G-15062)
DECK WORLD INC
433 Cobham Park Ln (22572-3625)
PHONE..................................804 798-9003
Lynwood Pierson, *President*
Linda Pierson, *Admin Sec*
EMP: 6
SQ FT: 5,400
SALES (est): 750K **Privately Held**
WEB: www.deckworldinc.com
SIC: 3949 1521 2511 5941 Playground
equipment; patio & deck construction &
repair; wood lawn & garden furniture;
playground equipment

(G-15063)
FRANCE LAWNSCPAPE LLC
1649 Scates Rd (22572-2854)
PHONE..................................804 761-6823
Shawn France,
EMP: 4
SALES (est): 170.5K **Privately Held**
SIC: 3271 7389 Blocks, concrete: land-
scape or retaining wall;

(G-15064)
**HALL HFLIN SEPTIC TANK SVC
INC**
408 Kinderhook Pike (22572-2706)
PHONE..................................804 333-3124
James Hall, *President*
EMP: 4 **EST:** 1987

▲ = Import ▼=Export
◆ =Import/Export

SALES (est): 368.1K **Privately Held**
SIC: **1381** 1711 7699 Service well drilling; septic system construction; septic tank cleaning service

(G-15065)
HAROLD DELANO
171 Fox Hunters Hill Rd (22572-3633)
PHONE..............................804 333-3446
Harold Delano, *Owner*
EMP: 1
SALES (est): 91.6K **Privately Held**
WEB: www.delanoheraldjournal.com
SIC: **2711** Newspapers, publishing & printing

(G-15066)
HOME PRINTING
116 Little Creek Rd (22572-3554)
PHONE..............................804 333-4678
Julie Stanley, *Principal*
EMP: 2
SALES (est): 92.3K **Privately Held**
SIC: **2752** Commercial printing, lithographic

(G-15067)
HOSKINS CREEK TABLE COMPANY
3123 Richmond Rd (22572-3223)
PHONE..............................804 333-0032
John Vaughan, *Principal*
EMP: 1
SALES (est): 83.3K **Privately Held**
WEB: www.hoskinscreektable.com
SIC: **2599** 5712 5021 Boards: planning, display, notice; furniture stores; furniture

(G-15068)
INNOVTIVE IMGES CSTM SGNS MORE
3506 Nomini Grove Rd (22572-4420)
PHONE..............................804 472-3882
Dennis Landman, *Owner*
Elaine Landman, *Co-Owner*
EMP: 2
SQ FT: 2,100
SALES (est): 150K **Privately Held**
WEB: www.innovativeimagesonline.com
SIC: **3993** Signs & advertising specialties

(G-15069)
JEWELLS BUILDINGS
13410 Richmond Rd (22572-3310)
PHONE..............................804 333-4483
Roy Jewell, *Owner*
Janet Childs, *Admin Sec*
EMP: 1
SALES (est): 167.7K **Privately Held**
WEB: www.jewellsstoragebuildings.com
SIC: **3448** Buildings, portable: prefabricated metal

(G-15070)
MULQUEEN INC
2767 Menokin Rd (22572-3043)
P.O. Box 1206 (22572-1206)
PHONE..............................804 333-4847
Herbert J Mulqueen Jr, *President*
Julia Mulqueen, *Treasurer*
EMP: 15
SALES (est): 990K **Privately Held**
SIC: **2439** 1542 1521 Trusses, wooden roof; commercial & office building, new construction; single-family houses

(G-15071)
NORTHERN NECK LUMBER CO INC
16056 History Land Hwy (22572-3057)
P.O. Box 395 (22572-0395)
PHONE..............................804 333-4041
John D Morris, *President*
Judith Harting, *Corp Secy*
Richard Kennen, *Vice Pres*
EMP: 45
SQ FT: 1,000
SALES (est): 6.4MM **Privately Held**
WEB: www.woodpreservers.com
SIC: **2426** 2421 Hardwood dimension & flooring mills; planing mills

(G-15072)
PACKETTS SAND PIT
Islington Rd Ste 763 (22572)
PHONE..............................804 761-6975
EMP: 1
SALES (est): 70.2K **Privately Held**
SIC: **1442** Construction Sand And Gravel, Nsk

(G-15073)
WOOD PRESERVERS INCORPORATED
15939 History Land Hwy (22572-3073)
P.O. Box 158 (22572-0158)
PHONE..............................804 333-4022
William M Wright, *CEO*
Morgan W Wright, *President*
Morgan Wright, *General Mgr*
Peyton Motley, *Vice Pres*
Doug Sanders, *Sales Staff*
▲ EMP: 70 EST: 1955
SQ FT: 2,500
SALES (est): 14MM
SALES (corp-wide): 1.6B **Privately Held**
WEB: www.woodpreservers.com
SIC: **2499** 2421 2491 Mulch, wood & bark; sawmills & planing mills, general; preserving (creosoting) of wood
HQ: Mcfarland Cascade Holdings, Inc.
1640 E Marc St
Tacoma WA 98421
253 572-3033

Washington
Rappahannock County

(G-15074)
CHRISTOPHER L BIRD
100 Horseshoe Hollow Ln (22747-2114)
PHONE..............................540 675-3409
Christopher Bird, *Owner*
EMP: 1
SALES (est): 79.4K **Privately Held**
WEB: www.benniesmachineshop.com
SIC: **1389** Excavating slush pits & cellars

(G-15075)
CRESTA GADINO WINERY LLC
92 School House Rd (22747-1907)
PHONE..............................540 987-9292
William Gadino, *Principal*
Derek Pross, *Opers Dir*
EMP: 2
SALES (est): 185.9K **Privately Held**
WEB: www.gadinocellars.com
SIC: **2084** Wines

(G-15076)
OLD RAG GAZETTE
702 Long Mountain Rd (22747-2020)
PHONE..............................540 675-2001
James Blubaugh, *Principal*
EMP: 2
SALES (est): 67.9K **Privately Held**
SIC: **2711** Newspapers

(G-15077)
RAPPAHANNOCK MEDIA LLC
Also Called: Rappahannock News
309 Jett St (22747)
PHONE..............................540 675-3338
Willam Dennis Brack, *Mng Member*
EMP: 6
SALES (est): 196.6K **Privately Held**
WEB: www.rappnews.com
SIC: **2711** Newspapers, publishing & printing

(G-15078)
REMARK DESIGN INCORPORATED
Gay St (22747)
P.O. Box 232 (22747-0232)
PHONE..............................540 675-3625
Peter Kramer, *President*
EMP: 9
SALES (est): 978.6K **Privately Held**
WEB: www.peterkramer.com
SIC: **2511** Wood household furniture

(G-15079)
STILLPOINT SOFTWARE INC
315 Piedmont Ave (22747-1865)
P.O. Box 418 (22747-0418)
PHONE..............................540 905-7932
Brenton Farmer, *Principal*
EMP: 2 EST: 2014
SALES (est): 142.9K **Privately Held**
SIC: **7372** Prepackaged software

Waterford
Loudoun County

(G-15080)
FURNACE MOUNTAIN VINEYARDS LLC
38593 Daymont Ln (20197-1038)
PHONE..............................571 439-2255
Emily Powers, *Manager*
Bennett N Renshaw, *Administration*
EMP: 2
SALES (est): 185.4K **Privately Held**
WEB: www.8chainsnorth.com
SIC: **2084** Wines

(G-15081)
KLAUS COMPOSITES LLC
14890 Wrights Ln (20197-1602)
PHONE..............................443 995-8458
EMP: 3 EST: 2017
SALES (est): 284.7K **Privately Held**
SIC: **3728** Aircraft parts & equipment

(G-15082)
QUARTZ CREEK VINEYARDS LLC
40817 Browns Ln (20197-1207)
PHONE..............................571 239-9120
Michael Fritze, *Administration*
EMP: 2
SALES (est): 85.7K **Privately Held**
SIC: **2084** Wines

(G-15083)
VILLAGE WINERY
40405 Browns Ln (20197-1203)
PHONE..............................540 882-3780
Kent R Marrs, *Principal*
EMP: 4
SALES (est): 293.3K **Privately Held**
WEB: www.villagewineryandvineyards.com
SIC: **2084** Wines

(G-15084)
WATERFORD PASTTHYMES
16039 Hamilton Station Rd (20197-1104)
PHONE..............................703 431-4095
Betty Framzen, *Partner*
Melissa Ramsen, *Partner*
EMP: 2
SALES (est): 114K **Privately Held**
WEB: www.gardencom.com
SIC: **3999** Flowers, artificial & preserved

Waverly
Sussex County

(G-15085)
MURPHY-BROWN LLC
Also Called: Waverly Feed Mill
27404 Cabin Point Rd (23890-3038)
P.O. Box 1240 (23890-1240)
PHONE..............................804 834-3990
Jerry Logue, *Manager*
EMP: 32 **Privately Held**
WEB: www.smithfieldfoods.com
SIC: **2048** Prepared feeds
HQ: Murphy-Brown Llc
2822 W Nc 24 Hwy
Warsaw NC 28398
910 293-3434

(G-15086)
PARHAMS WLDG & FABRICATION INC
402 N County Dr (23890)
P.O. Box 2 (23890-0002)
PHONE..............................804 834-3504
Ronald Parham, *President*
Regina Parham, *Vice Pres*

Teresa Buhls, *Office Mgr*
EMP: 15
SALES (est): 2.4MM **Privately Held**
WEB: www.parhamswelding.com
SIC: **7692** Welding repair

(G-15087)
PINECREST TIMBER CO
121 Industrial Rd (23890-9500)
P.O. Box 32 (23890-0032)
PHONE..............................804 834-2304
O P Higgins III, *Owner*
EMP: 20 EST: 1977
SQ FT: 1,600
SALES (est): 4.8MM **Privately Held**
SIC: **2411** 2421 Logging camps & contractors; sawmills & planing mills, general

(G-15088)
SMITHFIELD FOODS INC
27408 Cabin Point Rd (23890-3038)
PHONE..............................804 834-9941
EMP: 2 **Privately Held**
WEB: www.smithfieldfoods.com
SIC: **2011** Meat packing plants
HQ: Smithfield Foods, Inc.
200 Commerce St
Smithfield VA 23430
757 365-3000

(G-15089)
SUSSEX SERVICE AUTHORITY
4385 Beef Steak Rd (23890-3727)
PHONE..............................804 834-8930
Wade Stancil, *Maint Spvr*
William J Collins Jr, *Exec Dir*
EMP: 3
SALES (est): 100.8K **Privately Held**
WEB: www.ssa-va.org
SIC: **3589** Sewage & water treatment equipment; water treatment equipment, industrial

(G-15090)
WHEELER MAINTENANCE REPAIR
5399 Triple Bridge Rd (23890-3230)
PHONE..............................804 586-9836
Mark Wheeler, *Owner*
EMP: 1 EST: 2010
SALES (est): 73.6K **Privately Held**
SIC: **7694** Motor repair services

Waynesboro
Waynes City County

(G-15091)
A AT LLC
400 Dupont Blvd (22980-5700)
PHONE..............................316 828-1563
EMP: 9 EST: 2018
SALES (est): 1.5MM **Privately Held**
SIC: **2821** Plastics materials & resins

(G-15092)
AMERICAN HARDWOOD INDS LLC (HQ)
Also Called: A H I
567 N Charlotte Ave (22980-2856)
P.O. Box 1528 (22980-1397)
PHONE..............................540 946-9150
John Odea, *Executive*
John O DEA, *Products*
Graham Lumber, *Products*
◆ EMP: 150 EST: 2008
SALES (est): 79.5MM
SALES (corp-wide): 339MM **Privately Held**
WEB: www.ahwood.com
SIC: **2426** Hardwood dimension & flooring mills; lumber, hardwood dimension
PA: Baillie Lumber Co., L.P.
4002 Legion Dr
Hamburg NY 14075
800 950-2850

(G-15093)
ANDREW PAWLICK
Also Called: Quality Machine
784 N Bayard Ave (22980-2817)
PHONE..............................540 949-8805
Andrew Pawlik, *Owner*
Cindy Slusher, *Manager*

EMP: 5
SALES (est): 704.6K **Privately Held**
WEB: www.qualitymachineserviceinc.com
SIC: 3599 Machine shop, jobbing & repair

(G-15094)
ARCHITECTURAL ACCENTS
500 Loudoun Ave (22980-2727)
PHONE..............................540 943-5888
James Donovan, *Owner*
EMP: 1
SALES (est): 65K **Privately Held**
WEB: www.architecturalaccents.com
SIC: 2431 Millwork

(G-15095)
AREY MACHINE SHOP
551 Calf Mountain Rd (22980-8983)
PHONE..............................540 943-7782
Jeffery R Arey, *Owner*
EMP: 2
SALES (est): 85.7K **Privately Held**
SIC: 3599 Machine shop, jobbing & repair

(G-15096)
ATKINS AUTOMOTIVE CORP
Also Called: NAPA
794 E Main St (22980-5718)
PHONE..............................540 942-5157
Robert C Atkins Sr, *CEO*
EMP: 6
SALES (corp-wide): 7.6MM **Privately Held**
WEB: www.atkinsautomotivenapa.com
SIC: 3714 5531 Booster (jump-start) cables, automotive; automotive parts
PA: Atkins Automotive Corp
315 E Hampton St
Staunton VA 24401
540 885-0843

(G-15097)
AUGUSTA FREE PRESS
1511 Chatham Rd (22980-3340)
P.O. Box 1193 (22980-1303)
PHONE..............................540 910-1233
Crystal Graham, *Principal*
Ted Payne, *Pastor*
EMP: 6 **EST:** 2010
SALES (est): 321.7K **Privately Held**
WEB: www.augustafreepress.com
SIC: 2711 Newspapers, publishing & printing

(G-15098)
AUGUSTA PAINT & DECORATING LLC (PA)
Also Called: Benjamin Moore Authorized Ret
425 W Broad St (22980-4505)
PHONE..............................540 942-1800
Timothy Merritt, *Mng Member*
EMP: 3
SALES (est): 447.5K **Privately Held**
WEB: www.augustapaint.com
SIC: 2851 5231 Paints & allied products; paint, glass & wallpaper

(G-15099)
AVINTIV SPECIALTY MTLS INC
Also Called: Poly-Bond
1020 Shanandah Vlg Dr (22980-9292)
PHONE..............................540 946-9250
Brian Kellner, *Mfg Mgr*
Jim Radzville, *Purch Agent*
Chris Maurice, *Engineer*
Roger Surly, *Controller*
Daniel Stubbs, *Train & Dev Mgr*
EMP: 180 **Publicly Held**
WEB: www.pginw.com
SIC: 2297 Nonwoven fabrics
HQ: Avintiv Specialty Materials Inc.
9335 Hrris Crners Pkwy St
Charlotte NC 28269

(G-15100)
BERRY GLOBAL INC
1020 Shenandoah Vlg Dr (22980-9292)
PHONE..............................540 946-9250
Ian Mills, *Plant Mgr*
Shadi Habib, *Engineer*
Chris Maurice, *Engineer*
Lisa Weeks, *Manager*
Brandi Breeden, *Supervisor*
EMP: 2 **Publicly Held**
WEB: www.berryplastics.com
SIC: 3089 Bottle caps, molded plastic

HQ: Berry Global, Inc.
101 Oakley St
Evansville IN 47710

(G-15101)
BOTTOMLINE SOFTWARE INC
600 Oak Ave (22980-4429)
P.O. Box 1121 (22980-0809)
PHONE..............................540 221-4444
Jeffrey A Schwenk, *President*
EMP: 4
SALES (est): 300K **Privately Held**
SIC: 7372 7379 Prepackaged software; computer related consulting services

(G-15102)
BYERS INC
Waynesboro Metal Fabricators
51 E Side Hwy (22980-7011)
P.O. Box 851 (22980-0629)
PHONE..............................540 949-8092
Sterling Long, *Branch Mgr*
EMP: 28
SALES (corp-wide): 3.5MM **Privately Held**
WEB: www.byersincorporated.com
SIC: 3441 3599 Fabricated structural metal; machine shop, jobbing & repair
PA: Byers, Inc.
43 Douglas Way
Natural Bridge Stati VA 24579
540 572-4588

(G-15103)
C R D N OF THE SHENANDOAH
534 W Main St (22980-4527)
PHONE..............................540 943-8242
Dave Barrett, *President*
EMP: 15
SALES (est): 1.4MM **Privately Held**
WEB:
www.augustacleanersandformals.com
SIC: 2842 Drycleaning preparations

(G-15104)
CHESHIRE CAT AND COMPANY LLC
141 E Broad St Ste T (22980-5035)
PHONE..............................540 221-2538
Roxanne Franchis,
EMP: 1
SQ FT: 3,000
SALES (est): 82K **Privately Held**
SIC: 3993 Signs & advertising specialties

(G-15105)
CHICOPEE INC
1020 Shenandoah Vlg Dr (22980-9292)
PHONE..............................540 946-9250
EMP: 6 **Publicly Held**
WEB: www.berryglobal.com
SIC: 2297 Spunbonded fabrics
HQ: Chicopee, Inc.
9335 Hrris Crners Pkwy St
Charlotte NC 28269

(G-15106)
CUSTOM ORNAMENTAL IRON WORKS
640 Highland Ave (22980-6047)
PHONE..............................540 942-2687
Randy Teter, *Partner*
EMP: 2
SALES (est): 196.2K **Privately Held**
SIC: 3446 Fences or posts, ornamental iron or steel

(G-15107)
D & D INC
200 W 12th St (22980-4771)
PHONE..............................540 943-8113
David Daughtry, *President*
EMP: 5
SALES (est): 250K **Privately Held**
SIC: 3089 Injection molding of plastics

(G-15108)
DRUMHELLERS PRACTICAL CHOI
332 Kingsbury Dr (22980-6554)
P.O. Box 5, Fishersville (22939-0005)
PHONE..............................540 949-0462
Ray Drumheller, *Principal*
EMP: 2

SALES (est): 181.2K **Privately Held**
SIC: 3711 Wreckers (tow truck), assembly of

(G-15109)
DUPONT
510 W Broad St Ste D (22980-4548)
P.O. Box 987 (22980-0721)
PHONE..............................540 949-5361
EMP: 2
SALES (est): 90K **Privately Held**
SIC: 2879 Agricultural chemicals

(G-15110)
DUPONT DE NEMOURS E I TEX OFC
400 Dupont Blvd (22980-5700)
PHONE..............................540 949-2000
Ben Melnyczuk, *Principal*
EMP: 2
SALES (est): 143.4K **Privately Held**
SIC: 2819 Industrial inorganic chemicals

(G-15111)
E & E MACHINE SHOP INC
1367 Hopeman Pkwy (22980-1949)
PHONE..............................540 949-6792
Alan Evers, *President*
Janet Evers, *Vice Pres*
EMP: 10
SQ FT: 8,000
SALES (est): 1.3MM **Privately Held**
SIC: 3599 Machine shop, jobbing & repair

(G-15112)
E E MACHINE SHOP
1367 Hopeman Pkwy (22980-1949)
PHONE..............................540 649-2127
Fax: 540 943-3972
EMP: 3
SALES (est): 250K **Privately Held**
SIC: 3599 Mfg Industrial Machinery

(G-15113)
ECONOCOLOR SIGNS & GRAPHICS
211 W 12th St (22980-4772)
PHONE..............................540 946-0000
EMP: 3
SALES (est): 110K **Privately Held**
SIC: 3993 Mfg Signs/Advertising Specialties

(G-15114)
FAMILY CRAFTERS OF VIRGINIA
124 Poland St (22980-3332)
PHONE..............................540 943-3934
Craig Dearing, *Owner*
EMP: 3
SALES (est): 200K **Privately Held**
SIC: 3441 2431 Fabricated structural metal; millwork

(G-15115)
INDEPENDENT STAMPING INC
180 Port Republic Rd (22980-3946)
PHONE..............................540 949-6839
Ronald E Dameron, *President*
Sally Ann Dameron, *Corp Secy*
EMP: 8
SQ FT: 15,000
SALES (est): 1MM **Privately Held**
SIC: 3469 3312 Stamping metal for the trade; tool & die steel

(G-15116)
INDUSTRIAL MACHINE WORKS INC
444 N Bayard Ave (22980-4006)
P.O. Box 1167 (22980-0841)
PHONE..............................540 949-6115
David Wolfe Jr, *President*
O Douglas Bosserman, *Admin Sec*
EMP: 40 **EST:** 1948
SQ FT: 35,000
SALES: 5.3MM **Privately Held**
WEB: www.industrialmachineworks.com
SIC: 3599 3471 7629 3441 Machine shop, jobbing & repair; electroplating & plating; electrical repair shops; fabricated structural metal

(G-15117)
INVISTA CAPITAL MANAGEMENT LLC
400 Dupont Blvd (22980-5700)
PHONE..............................540 949-2000
Bill Bender, *Research*
Michael Laczynski, *Manager*
EMP: 50
SALES (corp-wide): 38.9B **Privately Held**
WEB: www.invista.com
SIC: 2821 Plastics materials & resins
HQ: Invista Capital Management, Llc
2801 Centerville Rd
Wilmington DE 19808
302 683-3000

(G-15118)
JERRYS ANTIQUE PRINTS LTD
366 Dooms Crossing Rd (22980-8953)
PHONE..............................540 949-7114
EMP: 2 **EST:** 2017 **Privately Held**
SIC: 2752 Lithographic Commercial Printing

(G-15119)
KLANN INC
Also Called: Klann Organ Supply
301 4th St (22980-2858)
PHONE..............................540 949-8351
Philip A Klann, *President*
Debbie Meadows, *Vice Pres*
John Estes, *QC Mgr*
John Reidenouer, *CFO*
Kitty Sprouse, *Credit Mgr*
▲ **EMP:** 48 **EST:** 1910
SQ FT: 45,000
SALES (est): 6.3MM **Privately Held**
WEB: www.klann.com
SIC: 3089 3931 Molding primary plastic; organs, all types: pipe, reed, hand, electronic, etc.

(G-15120)
LAI ENTERPRISES LLC
Also Called: Oryx Designs Promotional Pdts
21 Hannah Cir (22980-6586)
PHONE..............................540 946-0000
Lawrence Arntz, *President*
EMP: 5
SALES (est): 225.5K **Privately Held**
WEB: www.oryxdesigns.com
SIC: 3993 7389 Signs & advertising specialties; advertising, promotional & trade show services

(G-15121)
LEHIGH CEMENT COMPANY LLC
500 Delaware Ave (22980-1920)
PHONE..............................540 942-1181
Scott Dale, *Manager*
EMP: 3
SALES (corp-wide): 20.8B **Privately Held**
WEB: www.lehighwhitecement.com
SIC: 3273 Ready-mixed concrete
HQ: Lehigh Cement Company Llc
300 E John Carpenter Fwy
Irving TX 75062
877 534-4442

(G-15122)
MANTEL USA INC
566 Kindig Rd (22980-7300)
PHONE..............................540 946-6529
Josephus A Paternostre, *President*
Lilian Paternostre, *CFO*
▲ **EMP:** 4
SALES (est): 8.5MM **Privately Held**
WEB: www.bloomaker.com
SIC: 3524 Lawn & garden equipment

(G-15123)
MCCLUNG PRINTING INC (PA)
Also Called: McClung Companies, The
550 N Commerce Ave (22980-2832)
PHONE..............................540 949-8139
Miles John L, *CEO*
Gayle S Trevillian, *Corp Secy*
Sheila Southall, *Vice Pres*
Trevillian Gayle S, *Treasurer*
David Schroen, *Controller*
EMP: 67
SQ FT: 23,000
SALES (est): 6MM **Privately Held**
WEB: www.mcclungco.com
SIC: 2752 7336 Commercial printing, offset; graphic arts & related design

(G-15124)
MEDIA X GROUP LLC
463 Dinwiddie Ave (22980-4013)
PHONE..................................866 966-9640
Stephen Heiser, *Editor*
CAM Abernethy,
EMP: 2
SALES (est): 175.5K **Privately Held**
WEB: www.nuclearstreet.com
SIC: 7372 7374 Publishers' computer software; computer graphics service

(G-15125)
MERCK & CO INC
1308 Chatham Rd (22980-3302)
PHONE..................................540 447-0056
Timothy Reed, *Branch Mgr*
EMP: 2 **Publicly Held**
WEB: www.merck.com
SIC: 2834 Pharmaceutical preparations
PA: Merck & Co., Inc.
2000 Galloping Hill Rd
Kenilworth NJ 07033
908 740-4000

(G-15126)
METAL CRAFT BREWING CO LLC (PA)
Also Called: Basic City Beer Co.
900 Oak Ave (22980-4910)
PHONE..................................816 271-3211
Christopher Lanman,
Bart Lanman,
EMP: 2
SALES (est): 599.8K **Privately Held**
SIC: 2082 5181 Ale (alcoholic beverage); ale

(G-15127)
METFAB INTERNATIONAL INC
800 Ivy St (22980-3749)
PHONE..................................540 943-3732
Carol Faust, *President*
Kelly Faust, *Prdtn Mgr*
Fay Wood, *Purchasing*
Mark Faust, *Engineer*
Bob Wood, *Human Resources*
EMP: 34
SQ FT: 33,000
SALES (est): 8.1MM **Privately Held**
WEB: www.metfabint.com
SIC: 3444 Sheet metal specialties, not stamped

(G-15128)
N C TOOL COMPANY INC
1466 E Side Hwy (22980-8316)
P.O. Box 1448 (22980-1358)
PHONE..................................540 943-4011
C Anthony Tabor, *President*
Mary Tabor, *Treasurer*
Richard Tabor, *Admin Sec*
EMP: 12
SQ FT: 8,500
SALES (est): 2.5MM **Privately Held**
WEB: www.nctoolva.com
SIC: 3599 Machine shop, jobbing & repair

(G-15129)
NEUMAN ALMNIUM IMPACT EXTRSION
1418 Genicom Dr (22980-1956)
PHONE..................................540 248-2703
Patrick Carroll, *President*
David Armentrout, *Vice Pres*
Stan Platek, *CFO*
▲ EMP: 1
SQ FT: 110,000
SALES: 15.8MM
SALES (corp-wide): 9.5MM **Privately Held**
WEB: www.neumanusa.com
SIC: 3354 Aluminum extruded products
HQ: Fried. V. Neuman Gesellschaft M.B.H.
WerkstraBe 1
Marktl 3182
276 250-00

(G-15130)
OPENBOX NETWORKS LLC
176 Beagle Gap Run (22980-9347)
PHONE..................................540 607-0149
Shawn E Fitzgerald,
EMP: 2

SALES (est): 115.5K **Privately Held**
WEB: www.openboxnetworks.com
SIC: 3861 Photographic equipment & supplies

(G-15131)
PLECKERS CUSTOMER ENGRAVING
919 High St (22980-3031)
PHONE..................................540 241-5661
Robert Plecker, *Owner*
EMP: 5
SALES (est): 750K **Privately Held**
SIC: 2759 Commercial printing

(G-15132)
POLY-BOND INC
1020 Shenandoah Vlg Dr (22980-9292)
PHONE..................................540 946-9250
Alec J Hay, *President*
Boyd James G, *Exec VP*
Kent Iberg, *Mfg Staff*
Kenneth Doel, *Treasurer*
Marc Levesque, *Admin Sec*
▼ EMP: 260
SALES (est): 28.8MM **Publicly Held**
SIC: 2297 Spunbonded fabrics
HQ: Avintiv Specialty Materials Inc.
9335 Hrris Crners Pkwy St
Charlotte NC 28269

(G-15133)
R C S ENTERPRISES INC
808 Warwick Cir (22980-3433)
PHONE..................................540 363-5979
Richard C Stehlik, *President*
Mary Anne Stehlik, *Vice Pres*
Mary Stehlik, *Vice Pres*
EMP: 8
SALES (est): 661K **Privately Held**
SIC: 2394 Canvas & related products

(G-15134)
REGAL JEWELERS INC
124 Lucy Ln (22980-3200)
PHONE..................................540 949-4455
Earl Sipe, *President*
EMP: 4
SALES (est): 372.9K **Privately Held**
SIC: 3479 5944 7631 Engraving jewelry silverware, or metal; jewelry stores; jewelry repair services

(G-15135)
RIVER ROCK CUSTOM BAITS LLC
547 Cattle Scales Rd (22980-6330)
PHONE..................................540 414-3293
Robert Shue, *Principal*
EMP: 2 EST: 2012
SALES (est): 137.4K **Privately Held**
WEB: www.river-rock-custom-baits.myshopify.com
SIC: 3949 Sporting & athletic goods

(G-15136)
RLS CARTAGE LLC
1504 Mulberry St (22980-2426)
PHONE..................................540 447-0668
Roy L Smith, *Mng Member*
EMP: 1
SALES (est): 250K **Privately Held**
SIC: 3537 Trucks, tractors, loaders, carriers & similar equipment

(G-15137)
ROASTED BEAN COFFEE & REPAIR
19 Pleasant View Dr (22980-7449)
PHONE..................................434 242-8522
Jeffrey M Morris, *Owner*
EMP: 1
SALES (est): 94K **Privately Held**
SIC: 2095 Roasted coffee

(G-15138)
RONNIE D BRYANT HTG COOLG LLC
1266 Hermitage Rd (22980-6452)
P.O. Box 1085 (22980-0785)
PHONE..................................540 221-0988
Ronnie David Bryant, *Mng Member*
EMP: 1

SALES (est): 175.9K **Privately Held**
SIC: 3585 Parts for heating, cooling & refrigerating equipment

(G-15139)
SHENANDOAH VALLEY SOARING INC
249 Aero Dr (22980-6524)
PHONE..................................804 347-6848
G Pitsenberger, *President*
EMP: 2 EST: 2011
SALES (est): 101.8K **Privately Held**
WEB: www.svsoar.org
SIC: 3721 Gliders (aircraft)

(G-15140)
SUPERIOR QUALITY FOODS
100 Buckingham Pl (22980-6108)
PHONE..................................540 447-0552
Hadley Katzenbach, *Principal*
EMP: 2 EST: 2018
SALES (est): 62.3K **Privately Held**
SIC: 2035 Pickles, sauces & salad dressings

(G-15141)
UNIVERSAL IMPACT INC
901 S Delphine Ave (22980-5714)
PHONE..................................540 885-8676
Robert Schulz, *President*
Schulz Troy, *Opers Staff*
EMP: 9
SALES (est): 1.5MM **Privately Held**
WEB: www.universal-impact.com
SIC: 3353 Aluminum sheet & strip

(G-15142)
VALLEY PRECISION INCORPORATED
501 Delaware Ave (22980-1919)
PHONE..................................540 941-8178
Daniel Drumheller, *CEO*
Walter Carter, *President*
EMP: 40
SQ FT: 25,000
SALES (est): 6.9MM **Privately Held**
WEB: www.vprecision.com
SIC: 3599 3441 7692 3444 Machine shop, jobbing & repair; fabricated structural metal; welding repair; sheet metalwork

(G-15143)
VIRGINIA CAST STONE INC
1720 Harding Ave (22980-1936)
PHONE..................................540 943-9808
David Foresman, *President*
EMP: 12
SQ FT: 20,000
SALES (est): 1.7MM **Privately Held**
WEB: www.virginiacaststone.com
SIC: 3281 Cut stone & stone products

(G-15144)
VIRGINIA PANEL CORPORATION
1400 New Hope Rd (22980-2647)
PHONE..................................540 932-3300
Kimball E Stowers, *CEO*
Gloria H Stowers, *Ch of Bd*
Jeffery P Stowers, *President*
Sandra Stowers, *Vice Pres*
Ryan Fauver, *Engineer*
▲ EMP: 160
SQ FT: 42,000
SALES (est): 44.9MM **Privately Held**
WEB: www.vpc.com
SIC: 3678 3825 Electronic connectors; test equipment for electronic & electric measurement; integrated circuit testers

(G-15145)
VITRULAN CORPORATION
201 Rosser Ave Ste 7 (22980-3512)
P.O. Box 758, Fishersville (22939-0758)
PHONE..................................540 949-8206
Friedhelm Schwender, *President*
Eckhardt Rupp, *Vice Pres*
▲ EMP: 4
SALES (est): 355.6K
SALES (corp-wide): 889.5K **Privately Held**
SIC: 2299 Batting, wadding, padding & fillings

HQ: Vitrulan Textile Glass Gmbh
Bernecker Str. 8
Marktschorgast 95509
922 777-0

(G-15146)
WAYNESBORO TOOL & GRINDING SVC
775 N Bayard Ave (22980-2816)
PHONE..................................540 949-7912
Stu Thomas, *President*
EMP: 1
SQ FT: 6,000
SALES (est): 84K **Privately Held**
SIC: 3599 Machine shop, jobbing & repair

(G-15147)
WHISKYWRGHT FINE HNDCRFTED SPR
200 W 12th St H2-21 (22980-4771)
PHONE..................................703 831-2086
EMP: 4
SALES (est): 286.4K **Privately Held**
SIC: 2085 Distilled & blended liquors

(G-15148)
WOOD TELEVISION LLC
Also Called: News Virginian
544 W Main St (22980-4527)
P.O. Box 1027 (22980-0747)
PHONE..................................540 949-8213
James T Stratton, *Publisher*
Brian Carlton, *Manager*
EMP: 60
SALES (corp-wide): 3B **Publicly Held**
WEB: www.woodtv.com
SIC: 2711 Newspapers, publishing & printing
HQ: Wood Television Llc
120 College Ave Se
Grand Rapids MI 49503
616 456-8888

Weber City
Scott County

(G-15149)
MARDON INC
Also Called: Stateline Graphics
2154 Us Highway 23 North (24290-7073)
PHONE..................................276 386-6662
Peters Mark H, *President*
Mark Peters, *President*
Maggie LI, *General Mgr*
William Liu, *Business Mgr*
David Hughes, *Opers Mgr*
EMP: 7
SQ FT: 5,000
SALES (est): 517K **Privately Held**
SIC: 2752 2262 Commercial printing, offset; screen printing: manmade fiber & silk broadwoven fabrics

Weems
Lancaster County

(G-15150)
CHESAPEAKE BAY FISHING CO LLC
Also Called: John Deere
25 Shipyard Ln (22576)
P.O. Box 1 (22576-0001)
PHONE..................................804 438-6050
Robert W Smith, *President*
EMP: 10
SALES (est): 1.2MM **Privately Held**
WEB: www.deere.com
SIC: 3731 5082 Fishing vessels, large: building & repairing; construction & mining machinery

(G-15151)
W ELLERY KELLUM INC
96 Shipyard Ln (22576)
P.O. Box 249 (22576-0249)
PHONE..................................804 438-5476
Joseph A Kellum, *President*
William Kellum, *Vice Pres*
Thomas Ellery Kellum, *Admin Sec*
EMP: 50 EST: 1945
SQ FT: 10,000

SALES (est): 5.8MM **Privately Held**
WEB: www.kellumseafood.com
SIC: **2092** 2091 Shellfish, fresh: shucked
& packed in nonsealed containers;
canned & cured fish & seafoods

West Point
King William County

(G-15152)
ADAMS WELDING SERVICE
2710 King William Ave (23181-9543)
PHONE..................................804 843-4468
M L Adams, *Owner*
EMP: 1
SALES (est): 43K **Privately Held**
SIC: **7692** Welding repair

(G-15153)
APEX PALLETS LLC
33132 King William Rd (23181-3006)
PHONE..................................804 246-1499
Mark Lenz,
EMP: 14
SALES (est): 660K **Privately Held**
WEB: www.apexpallets.net
SIC: **2448** Pallets, wood

(G-15154)
CAPITAL CITY CANDLE
1350 Riverview Dr (23181-9339)
PHONE..................................571 245-4738
Denise Wade, *Principal*
EMP: 1
SALES (est): 39.6K **Privately Held**
SIC: **3999** Candles

(G-15155)
DIRECT WOOD PRODUCTS (PA)
18501 Eltham Rd (23181-9443)
P.O. Box 856 (23181-0856)
PHONE..................................804 843-4642
John B Britt, *President*
John Britt, *President*
EMP: 26
SALES (est): 8.8MM **Privately Held**
WEB: www.dwp-inc.com
SIC: **2448** Pallets, wood

(G-15156)
FAST LANE SPECIALTIES INC
3560 Shoreline Dr (23181-9336)
PHONE..................................757 784-7474
Jay McArdle, *President*
EMP: 1
SALES (est): 52.7K **Privately Held**
SIC: **2395** Embroidery & art needlework

(G-15157)
GEORGE MCCRACKEN
Also Called: G McCracken
813 Main St (23181)
PHONE..................................804 238-4910
George McCracken, *Owner*
EMP: 1
SALES (est): 41K **Privately Held**
SIC: **3931** French horns & parts

(G-15158)
HACKNEY MILLWORKS INC
300 Industrial Pkwy (23181-9387)
PHONE..................................804 843-3312
Gene Hackney, *President*
Mike Dennis, *Project Mgr*
Maria Inge, *Office Mgr*
EMP: 8
SALES (est): 1.1MM **Privately Held**
WEB: www.hackneymillwork.com
SIC: **2431** Millwork

(G-15159)
NEW KENT CHARLES CY CHRONICLE
Also Called: New Kent-Charles Cy Chronicle
18639 Eltham Rd Ste 203 (23181-9442)
PHONE..................................804 843-4181
Alan Chamberlain, *President*
Paula Chamberlain, *Vice Pres*
EMP: 6
SALES (est): 341.9K **Privately Held**
WEB: www.nkccnews.com
SIC: **2711** Newspapers, publishing & printing

(G-15160)
NUTRIEN AG SOLUTIONS INC
270 Pamunkey Ave (23181)
PHONE..................................757 229-9448
Larry Vandeusen, *Plant Mgr*
Larry Van Deufen, *Manager*
EMP: 5
SALES (corp-wide): 20B **Privately Held**
WEB: www.nutrienagsolutions.com
SIC: **2875** 5191 2048 Fertilizers, mixing
only; pesticides; prepared feeds
HQ: Nutrien Ag Solutions, Inc.
3005 Rocky Mountain Ave
Loveland CO 80538
970 685-3300

(G-15161)
PALLET ASSET RECOVERY SYS LLC
18501 Eltham Rd (23181-9443)
PHONE..................................800 727-2136
J Steven Erie, *Administration*
EMP: 4
SALES (est): 223.7K **Privately Held**
SIC: **2448** Pallets, wood

(G-15162)
TRIPLE GOLD WELDING LLC
330 Seatons Ln (23181-3226)
PHONE..................................804 370-0082
Antwon Porter, *Principal*
EMP: 1
SALES (est): 38.9K **Privately Held**
SIC: **7692** Welding repair

(G-15163)
WESTROCK CP LLC
2401 King William Rd (23181-9565)
PHONE..................................804 843-5229
EMP: 75
SALES (corp-wide): 17.5B **Publicly Held**
WEB: www.westrock.com
SIC: **2653** 2621 Boxes, corrugated: made
from purchased materials; paper mills
HQ: Westrock Cp, Llc
1000 Abernathy Rd Ste 125
Atlanta GA 30328

(G-15164)
WESTROCK CP LLC
Also Called: Westrock Shipping Center
2348 King William Ave (23181-9541)
P.O. Box 100 (23181-0100)
PHONE..................................804 843-5416
Larry Price, *Branch Mgr*
EMP: 117
SALES (corp-wide): 17.5B **Publicly Held**
WEB: www.westrock.com
SIC: **2631** 2653 2621 2674 Container
board; corrugated boxes, partitions, dis-
play items, sheets & pad; kraft paper;
shipping & shopping bags or sacks
HQ: Westrock Cp, Llc
1000 Abernathy Rd Ste 125
Atlanta GA 30328

Weyers Cave
Augusta County

(G-15165)
AMBROSIA PRESS INC
3234 Lee Hwy (24486-2210)
PHONE..................................540 432-1801
Craig Patricia, *President*
Robert Crittenden, *Manager*
EMP: 4
SQ FT: 2,000
SALES (est): 100K **Privately Held**
SIC: **2759** Commercial printing

(G-15166)
ASPEN INDUSTRIES LLC
3584 Lee Hwy (24486-2213)
PHONE..................................540 234-0413
EMP: 1 EST: 2018
SALES (est): 49.9K **Privately Held**
SIC: **3999** Manufacturing industries

(G-15167)
BLUE RIDGE PUBLISHING LLC
3150 Lee Hwy (24486-2209)
PHONE..................................540 234-0807
Paul Oakes, *Principal*

EMP: 2
SALES (est): 70.7K **Privately Held**
SIC: **2741** Miscellaneous publishing

(G-15168)
BUTTERCREAM DREAMS LLC
87 Bluestone Dr (24486-2300)
PHONE..................................540 234-0058
Carrie H Ashton, *Administration*
EMP: 1 EST: 2009
SALES (est): 77.4K **Privately Held**
SIC: **3421** Table & food cutlery, including
butchers'

(G-15169)
CARAUSTAR INDUSTRIAL AND CON
Also Called: Weyers Cave Tube Plant
780 Keezletown Rd Ste 108 (24486-2409)
PHONE..................................540 234-0431
Robert Russell, *General Mgr*
Melody Ritchie, *Manager*
EMP: 8
SALES (corp-wide): 4.6B **Publicly Held**
WEB: www.greif.com
SIC: **2655** Fiber cans, drums & similar
products
HQ: Caraustar Industrial And Consumer
Products Group Inc
5000 Austell Powder Ste
Austell GA 30106
803 548-5100

(G-15170)
CEMS INC
Also Called: Comsonics Electronics Mfg Svcs
780 Keezletown Rd Ste 102 (24486-2409)
P.O. Box 1106, Harrisonburg (22803-1106)
PHONE..................................540 434-7500
Jack Bryant, *President*
Dennis Zimmerman, *President*
Bob Hunt, *General Mgr*
Donn E Meyerhoeffer, *Vice Pres*
Donn Meyerhoeffer, *Vice Pres*
◆ EMP: 40
SQ FT: 7,000
SALES (est): 5.7MM
SALES (corp-wide): 37.6MM **Privately
Held**
SIC: **3829** Cable testing machines
PA: Comsonics, Inc.
1350 Port Republic Rd
Harrisonburg VA 22801
540 434-5965

(G-15171)
CERRO FABRICATED PRODUCTS LLC (DH)
300 Triangle Dr (24486-2448)
PHONE..................................540 208-1606
John Tayloe, *President*
Sam Insana, *Vice Pres*
▲ EMP: 61
SALES (est): 41.3MM
SALES (corp-wide): 254.6B **Publicly
Held**
WEB: www.cerrofabricated.com
SIC: **3351** 3463 3462 Copper rolling &
drawing; nonferrous forgings; iron & steel
forgings
HQ: Marmon Holdings, Inc.
181 W Madison St Ste 2600
Chicago IL 60602
312 372-9500

(G-15172)
FLINT CPS INKS NORTH AMER LLC
106 Triangle Dr (24486-2418)
PHONE..................................540 234-9203
EMP: 2
SALES (est): 74.4K **Privately Held**
SIC: **2893** Printing ink

(G-15173)
HOUFF CORPORATION (HQ)
97 Railside Dr (24486-2416)
PHONE..................................540 234-8088
Neil A Houff, *President*
Dennis W Houff, *Vice Pres*
JD Patton, *Treasurer*
Kern L Houff, *Admin Sec*
EMP: 65
SQ FT: 15,000

SALES: 19.4MM
SALES (corp-wide): 30.3MM **Privately
Held**
WEB: www.houffcorp.com
SIC: **2873** 5191 Fertilizers: natural (or-
ganic), except compost; chemicals, agri-
cultural
PA: Railside Enterprises, Inc.
73 Railside Dr
Weyers Cave VA 24486
540 234-9185

(G-15174)
LILBERN DESIGN VIRGINIA LLC
200 Packaging Dr (24486-2343)
P.O. Box 146 (24486-0146)
PHONE..................................540 234-9900
Karl Stoltzfus, *Mng Member*
Charlie Witman,
EMP: 20
SQ FT: 3,000
SALES (est): 1.5MM **Privately Held**
WEB: www.lilberndesign.com
SIC: **3812** Aircraft control systems, elec-
tronic

(G-15175)
PEPSI-COLA BTLG CO CENTL VA
Also Called: Pepsico
100 Triangle Dr (24486-2418)
P.O. Box 127 (24486-0127)
PHONE..................................540 234-9238
Wayne Davis, *Manager*
EMP: 49
SALES (corp-wide): 111.1MM **Privately
Held**
WEB: www.pepsiva.com
SIC: **2086** Carbonated soft drinks, bottled
& canned
PA: Pepsi-Cola Bottling Co Of Central Vir-
ginia
1150 Pepsi Pl
Charlottesville VA 22901
434 978-2140

(G-15176)
SHEAVES FLOORS LLC
Also Called: Sheaves Racing Slots & Drags
3236 Lee Hwy (24486-2210)
P.O. Box 85 (24486-0085)
PHONE..................................540 234-9080
Jeffrey Sheaves, *Owner*
EMP: 8
SALES (est): 264.7K **Privately Held**
WEB: www.sheavesfloors.com
SIC: **2426** 3086 3253 Hardwood dimen-
sion & flooring mills; carpet & rug cush-
ions, foamed plastic; ceramic wall & floor
tile

(G-15177)
STACKER INC A G
30 Packaging Dr Ste 104 (24486)
P.O. Box 237 (24486-0237)
PHONE..................................540 234-6012
Hahns Kanode, *Principal*
Raubenolt Terry, *Vice Pres*
Villegas Rafael, *Project Mgr*
Senger Randy, *Prdtn Mgr*
Russell Armentrout, *Parts Mgr*
EMP: 17 EST: 2000
SALES (est): 3.3MM **Privately Held**
WEB: www.agstacker.com
SIC: **3537** Stacking machines, automatic

(G-15178)
SUNLITE PLASTICS INC
846 Keezletown Rd (24486-2410)
PHONE..................................540 234-9271
Austin Wagner, *Production*
Daniel Sine, *Opers-Prdtn-Mfg*
EMP: 20
SALES (corp-wide): 19.8MM **Privately
Held**
WEB: www.sunliteplastics.com
SIC: **3089** 3087 3082 2821 Extruded fin-
ished plastic products; custom compound
purchased resins; unsupported plastics
profile shapes; plastics materials & resins
PA: Sunlite Plastics, Inc.
W194n11340 Mccormick Dr
Germantown WI 53022
262 253-0600

▲ = Import ▼=Export
◆ =Import/Export

White Plains
Brunswick County

(G-15179)
LAKESIDE WELDING
2250 Dry Bread Rd (23893-2120)
PHONE..................................434 636-1712
Leonard Turner, *Principal*
EMP: 1
SALES (est): 43.8K **Privately Held**
SIC: 7692 Welding repair

White Post
Clarke County

(G-15180)
KINTERS CABINET SHOP INC J
530 Gun Barrel Rd (22663-2504)
PHONE..................................540 837-1663
Judith G Kinter, *President*
John Kinter, *Vice Pres*
EMP: 3
SALES (est): 311.7K **Privately Held**
SIC: 2512 Upholstered household furniture

(G-15181)
PILLAR ENTERPRISE LTD
201 Ridings Ln (22663-1875)
PHONE..................................540 868-8626
Carl A Johnson, *President*
Andruski Charles R, *Vice Pres*
EMP: 130
SALES (est): 18.9MM
SALES (corp-wide): 34.8MM **Privately Held**
SIC: 3441 Fabricated structural metal for bridges
PA: The Berlin Steel Construction Company
76 Depot Rd
Kensington CT 06037
860 828-3531

(G-15182)
ROBEYS WELDING LLC
14280 Lord Fairfax Hwy (22663-2650)
PHONE..................................540 974-3811
Gary Owen Robey, *Mng Member*
EMP: 1
SALES (est): 321.1K **Privately Held**
SIC: 7692 Welding repair

(G-15183)
SHEN-VAL SCREEN PRINTING LLC
313 Knight Dr (22663-1724)
PHONE..................................540 869-2713
EMP: 2
SALES (est): 83.9K **Privately Held**
SIC: 2752 Commercial printing, lithographic

(G-15184)
SHENANDOAH SHEDS
1518 Fairfax Pike (22663-1807)
PHONE..................................540 869-4050
Gary Arghyris, *Principal*
EMP: 4 EST: 2016
SALES (est): 204.7K **Privately Held**
WEB: www.shenandoahsheds.com
SIC: 2452 Prefabricated wood buildings

White Stone
Lancaster County

(G-15185)
ABBOTT BROTHERS INC
60 Simmons Ln (22578-2144)
PHONE..................................804 436-1001
Gerald Abbott, *Principal*
EMP: 1 EST: 2012
SALES (est): 57.4K **Privately Held**
SIC: 2092 Fresh or frozen packaged fish

(G-15186)
BROOK SUMMER MEDIA
1661 James Wharf Rd (22578-2406)
PHONE..................................804 435-0074
Jim Hapch, *CEO*
Steven Horn, *President*
EMP: 8
SALES (est): 412K **Privately Held**
SIC: 2759 Posters, including billboards: printing

(G-15187)
DOUGS WELDING & ORNAMENTAL IR
118 Old Mail Rd (22578-2630)
PHONE..................................804 435-6363
Douglas Broadus, *Principal*
EMP: 1
SALES (est): 42.5K **Privately Held**
SIC: 7692 Welding repair

(G-15188)
MUSIC PUBLISHERS AMERICA LLC
508 Blue Heron Ln (22578-2827)
P.O. Box 696 (22578-0696)
PHONE..................................917 406-4425
EMP: 1
SALES (est): 41.3K **Privately Held**
WEB: www.musicpublishersofamerica.com
SIC: 2741 Miscellaneous publishing

(G-15189)
OCRAN SHAFT MACHINE
113 Windmill Point Rd (22578-3042)
P.O. Box 876, Deltaville (23043-0876)
PHONE..................................804 435-6301
EMP: 3
SALES (est): 241.8K **Privately Held**
SIC: 3089 Plastic boats & other marine equipment

(G-15190)
VIRGINIA SEAFOODS LLC
Also Called: White Stone Oyster Lancaster
202 Antirap Dr (22578-3038)
PHONE..................................301 520-8200
Thomas Waters Perry IV,
EMP: 12
SALES (est): 397.2K **Privately Held**
SIC: 2091 Seafood products: packaged in cans, jars, etc.

Whitewood
Buchanan County

(G-15191)
CHAD COAL CORP
Harrys Br (24657)
PHONE..................................276 498-4952
James Taylor, *President*
EMP: 15
SQ FT: 80
SALES (est): 971K **Privately Held**
SIC: 1221 1222 Bituminous coal & lignite-surface mining; bituminous coal-underground mining

(G-15192)
POLAR BEAR ICE INC
Rr 638 (24657)
P.O. Box 268, Pilgrims Knob (24634-0268)
PHONE..................................276 259-7873
Frederick Tatum, *President*
Angela Tatum, *Admin Sec*
EMP: 5
SALES (est): 321.5K **Privately Held**
SIC: 2097 5199 Manufactured ice; ice, manufactured or natural

(G-15193)
TINE & COMPANY INC
Hc 66 Box 5 (24657)
PHONE..................................276 881-8232
Earl Cole, *President*
EMP: 3
SALES (est): 280.5K **Privately Held**
SIC: 2421 2448 Sawmills & planing mills, general; pallets, wood

Wicomico Church
Northumberland County

(G-15194)
BERT & CLIFFS MACHINE SHOP
Rr 200 (22579)
P.O. Box 183 (22579-0183)
PHONE..................................804 580-3021
Clifton Ketner, *Owner*
Linda Ketner, *Admin Sec*
EMP: 2
SQ FT: 1,500
SALES (est): 253.9K **Privately Held**
SIC: 3599 Machine shop, jobbing & repair

(G-15195)
FISHER A C JR MARINE RLWY SVC
106 Britney Ln (22579)
P.O. Box 24 (22579-0024)
PHONE..................................804 580-4342
Alfred C Fisher Jr, *Owner*
EMP: 2
SALES (est): 180.4K **Privately Held**
SIC: 3621 Railway motors & control equipment, electric

(G-15196)
VINEYARDS
619 Train Ln (22579)
PHONE..................................804 580-4053
Bruce Watson, *Owner*
EMP: 2
SALES (est): 114.1K **Privately Held**
WEB: www.jaceyvineyards.com
SIC: 2084 Wines

(G-15197)
ZIMBRO AERIAL DRONE INTEGRATIO
5273 Jssie Dupont Mem Hwy (22579)
PHONE..................................757 408-6864
David Zimbro, *President*
EMP: 3 EST: 2016
SALES (est): 156.8K **Privately Held**
SIC: 3728 Target drones

Williamsburg
James City County

(G-15198)
8 SHIRES COLONIALE DISTILLERY
7218 Merrimac Trl (23185-5202)
PHONE..................................757 378-2456
EMP: 3
SALES (est): 117.7K **Privately Held**
WEB: www.8shires.com
SIC: 2085 Distilled & blended liquors

(G-15199)
888 BRANDS LLC
1715 Endeavor Dr (23185-6239)
PHONE..................................757 741-2056
Dustin Devore,
EMP: 3
SALES (est): 69.2K **Privately Held**
WEB: www.888brands.com
SIC: 3535 Conveyors & conveying equipment

(G-15200)
ABOUT TIME
3201 Derby Ln (23185-1464)
PHONE..................................757 253-0143
EMP: 1
SALES (est): 64.9K **Privately Held**
SIC: 3555 Mfg Printing Trades Machinery

(G-15201)
ACCESSIBLE ENVIRONMENTS INC (PA)
106 Wingate Dr (23185-2995)
P.O. Box 5073 (23188-5200)
PHONE..................................757 565-3444
Brigette Weis, *President*
Patricia Weis, *Corp Secy*
Earl Weis, *Vice Pres*
▼ **EMP:** 4 EST: 1998
SQ FT: 1,000
SALES (est): 548.5K **Privately Held**
WEB: www.accessibility-inc.com
SIC: 3842 8361 Technical aids for the handicapped; wheelchairs; home for the physically handicapped

(G-15202)
ACE CABINETS & MORE LLC
104 Mid Ocean (23188-8414)
PHONE..................................757 206-1684
David Hess, *Principal*
EMP: 4
SALES (est): 345.5K **Privately Held**
SIC: 2434 Wood kitchen cabinets

(G-15203)
ANHEUSER-BUSCH LLC
7801 Pocahontas Trl (23185-6302)
PHONE..................................757 253-3600
Damola Oshin, *General Mgr*
Daniel Aguirre, *District Mgr*
Shawn Connolly, *District Mgr*
Scott Vandenbusch, *District Mgr*
Brendan Whitworth, *Vice Pres*
EMP: 162
SALES (corp-wide): 1.4B **Privately Held**
WEB: www.budweisertours.com
SIC: 2082 Beer (alcoholic beverage)
HQ: Anheuser-Busch, Llc
1 Busch Pl
Saint Louis MO 63118
800 342-5283

(G-15204)
ANHEUSER-BUSCH COMPANIES LLC
7801 Pocahontas Trl (23185-6302)
PHONE..................................757 253-3660
Kevin Kolda, *Vice Pres*
Brandon Randall, *Train & Dev Mgr*
Wayne Johnston, *Mktg Dir*
Jerry Studdard, *Branch Mgr*
EMP: 8
SALES (corp-wide): 1.4B **Privately Held**
WEB: www.anheuser-busch.com
SIC: 2082 Beer (alcoholic beverage)
HQ: Anheuser-Busch Companies, Llc
1 Busch Pl
Saint Louis MO 63118
314 632-6777

(G-15205)
APG MEDIA OF CHESAPEAKE LLC
Also Called: Tidewater Review
1430 High St Ste 504 (23185-2882)
PHONE..................................804 843-2282
EMP: 8
SALES (corp-wide): 251.7MM **Privately Held**
WEB: www.stardem.com
SIC: 2711 Commercial printing & newspaper publishing combined
HQ: Apg Media Of Chesapeake, Llc
29088 Airpark Dr
Easton MD 21601

(G-15206)
ARDSEN OFFSET
4399 Ironbound Rd (23188-2623)
PHONE..................................757 220-3299
Jim Suter, *President*
EMP: 2
SALES (est): 180K **Privately Held**
SIC: 2752 Commercial printing, offset

(G-15207)
ARMADILLO INDUSTRIES INC
4001 Elizabeth Killebrew (23188-1344)
PHONE..................................757 508-2348
Michael J Hornby, *President*
Michael Hornby, *Marketing Mgr*
EMP: 2
SALES (est): 291.7K **Privately Held**
WEB: www.armadillo-industries.com
SIC: 3559 Automotive related machinery

(G-15208)
BAKERS CRUST INC
5230 Monticello Ave (23188-8212)
PHONE..................................757 253-2787
John Stein, *Branch Mgr*
EMP: 4 **Privately Held**
WEB: www.bakerscrust.com
SIC: 2051 Cakes, bakery: except frozen

GEOGRAPHIC

PA: Baker's Crust, Inc.
549 S Birdneck Rd Ste 101
Virginia Beach VA 23451

(G-15209)
BALL METAL BEVERAGE CONT CORP
Also Called: Ball Metal Beverage Cont Div
8935 Pocahontas Trl (23185-6249)
PHONE..................................757 887-2062
Mark Orkin, *Plant Mgr*
Steve Chando, *Prdtn Mgr*
Marjorie Daniel, *Human Res Dir*
Marjorie Daniels, *Human Res Mgr*
Pattie Swan, *Marketing Staff*
EMP: 220
SALES (corp-wide): 11.4B **Publicly Held**
WEB: www.ball.com
SIC: 3411 Beverage cans, metal: except beer
HQ: Ball Metal Beverage Container Corp.
9300 W 108th Cir
Westminster CO 80021

(G-15210)
BATCHELDER & COLLINS INC
197 Ewell Rd Ste B (23188-2154)
PHONE..................................757 220-2806
Deborah Caton, *Purch Mgr*
Brad Hasty, *Sales Staff*
Joe Darden, *Sales Associate*
EMP: 5
SALES (corp-wide): 8.1MM **Privately Held**
WEB: www.757brick.com
SIC: 2421 3272 Building & structural materials, wood; concrete stuctural support & building material
PA: Batchelder & Collins Inc
2305 Granby St
Norfolk VA 23517
757 625-2506

(G-15211)
BILLSBURG BREWERY LLC
2054 Jamestown Rd (23185-7911)
PHONE..................................757 926-0981
Roderick Shippey,
EMP: 17
SALES (est): 768K **Privately Held**
WEB: www.billsburg.com
SIC: 2082 Beer (alcoholic beverage)

(G-15212)
BOWSER REPORT
Also Called: Bower Report The
404 Idlewood Ln (23185-4029)
P.O. Box 5156 (23188-5202)
PHONE..................................757 877-5979
Thomas Rice, *Publisher*
R Max Bowser, *Editor*
EMP: 4
SALES (est): 249.9K **Privately Held**
WEB: www.thebowserreport.com
SIC: 2711 2721 Newspapers; periodicals

(G-15213)
BRANDY LTD
302 Harrison Ave (23185-3549)
PHONE..................................757 220-0302
Ann Granger, *President*
EMP: 2
SALES (est): 104.9K **Privately Held**
SIC: 1499 Asbestos mining

(G-15214)
BRIAN ENTERPRISES LLC
Also Called: Health Journal, The
4808 Courthouse St # 204 (23188-2684)
PHONE..................................757 645-4475
Brian Freer, *Mng Member*
Rita Kikoen, *Exec Dir*
Page Freer,
EMP: 8
SQ FT: 1,100
SALES (est): 654.5K **Privately Held**
WEB: www.thehealthjournals.com
SIC: 2731 7812 Book publishing; video production

(G-15215)
BRIAN R HESS
Also Called: Williamsburg Welding Company
123 King William Dr (23188-1920)
PHONE..................................757 240-0689
Brian R Hess, *Owner*

EMP: 1
SALES (est): 60K **Privately Held**
SIC: 7692 Welding repair

(G-15216)
BUNNIES HOT TIPS LLC
4779 Regents Park (23188-1798)
PHONE..................................757 259-9453
EMP: 2
SALES (est): 78.7K **Privately Held**
WEB: www.bunnieshottips.com
SIC: 2741 Miscellaneous publishing

(G-15217)
CANVAS INNOVATIONS INC
8405 Beckenham Ct (23188-6634)
PHONE..................................757 218-7271
Philip Doggett, *Owner*
EMP: 1 EST: 2016
SALES (est): 37.7K **Privately Held**
SIC: 2211 Canvas

(G-15218)
CHALISON INC
Also Called: Sign Visions
1592 Penniman Rd Ste C (23185-5853)
PHONE..................................757 258-2520
Cliston Williams, *President*
Chad Williams, *General Mgr*
EMP: 7
SALES (est): 400K **Privately Held**
WEB: www.signvisions.com
SIC: 3993 Signs, not made in custom sign painting shops

(G-15219)
CHRISTOPHERS BELTS & WALLETS
110 Ware Rd (23185-3144)
PHONE..................................757 253-2564
EMP: 1 EST: 2009
SALES (est): 65.2K **Privately Held**
SIC: 3172 Mfg Personal Leather Goods

(G-15220)
COLONIAL AIR FILTER CLG LLC
2783 Lake Powell Rd (23185-3701)
PHONE..................................757 229-1110
L Michael Green, *Principal*
EMP: 2 EST: 2001
SALES (est): 120K **Privately Held**
SIC: 3599 Air intake filters, internal combustion engine, except auto

(G-15221)
COLONIAL READI-MIX CONCRETE
Also Called: Colonial Redi-Mix Concrete
1571 Manufacture Dr (23185-6274)
PHONE..................................757 888-8500
EMP: 7
SALES (est): 360K **Privately Held**
SIC: 3273 Mfg Ready-Mixed Concrete

(G-15222)
COPPER FOX DISTILLERY
901 Capitol Landing Rd (23185-4326)
PHONE..................................757 903-2076
Richard Wasmund Jr, *Partner*
EMP: 11 EST: 2014
SALES (est): 296.1K **Privately Held**
WEB: www.copperfoxdistillery.com
SIC: 2085 2841 5169 Distilled & blended liquors; corn whiskey; gin (alcoholic beverage); rye whiskey; soap & other detergents; detergents & soaps, except specialty cleaning

(G-15223)
CORESIX PRECISION GLASS INC
1737 Endeavor Dr (23185-6239)
PHONE..................................757 888-1361
Alan Graham, *President*
Al Ralston, *Purchasing*
Michael Palmo, *CFO*
Michelle Lawson, *Finance*
Justin Lawson, *Sales Staff*
▲ EMP: 90
SQ FT: 43,000
SALES (est): 13.3MM **Privately Held**
WEB: www.coresix.com
SIC: 3211 Optical glass, flat

(G-15224)
CORMORANT TECHNOLOGIES LLC
2909 Thomas Smith Ln (23185-7517)
PHONE..................................703 871-5060
William K Wells,
EMP: 3
SALES (est): 320K **Privately Held**
WEB: www.cormoranttechnologies.com
SIC: 3648 Lighting equipment

(G-15225)
CR COMMUNICATIONS
4481 Village Park Dr W (23185-2414)
PHONE..................................757 871-4797
Robert Lamphire, *Partner*
EMP: 2
SALES (est): 138.7K **Privately Held**
SIC: 3663 Radio & TV communications equipment

(G-15226)
CROCHET
1636 Skiffes Creek Cir (23185-6263)
PHONE..................................732 446-9644
EMP: 1
SALES (est): 40.9K **Privately Held**
SIC: 2399 Hand woven & crocheted products

(G-15227)
CUSTOM WELDING INC
Also Called: Custom Welding and Fabrication
126 Tewning Rd (23188-2640)
PHONE..................................757 220-1995
Scott Hederer, *President*
Tracy Repley, *Vice Pres*
Tracy Ripley, *Vice Pres*
EMP: 7 EST: 1997
SQ FT: 1,500
SALES (est): 1MM **Privately Held**
WEB:
www.customweldingofwilliamsburg.net
SIC: 3446 3441 Gates, ornamental metal; fabricated structural metal

(G-15228)
CYBERED CORP
4507 Pleasant View Dr (23188-8036)
PHONE..................................757 573-5456
Edward Langhals, *President*
EMP: 2
SALES (est): 145.6K **Privately Held**
WEB: www.cybered-corp.com
SIC: 7372 7371 Prepackaged software; custom computer programming services

(G-15229)
DAP ENTERPRISES INC
109 Sharps Rd (23188-2570)
PHONE..................................757 921-3576
Ricaute Sanchez, *CEO*
EMP: 2
SALES (est): 88K **Privately Held**
WEB: www.performanceunlim.com
SIC: 2396 2741 2796 Fabric printing & stamping; art copy; publishing & printing; business service newsletters: publishing & printing; color separations for printing; embossing plates for printing

(G-15230)
DAWN BROTHERTON
Also Called: Blue Dragon Publishing
301 Back Forty Loop (23188-2256)
P.O. Box 247, Lightfoot (23090-0247)
PHONE..................................757 645-3211
Dawn Brotherton, *Owner*
EMP: 1
SALES (est): 63.5K **Privately Held**
WEB: www.bluedragonpublishing.com
SIC: 2731 7389 Book publishing;

(G-15231)
DEFEE LLC
111 Royal North Devon (23188-7473)
PHONE..................................757 645-4358
Ann Dodson Defee, *Administration*
EMP: 1
SALES (est): 40.8K **Privately Held**
SIC: 2741 Miscellaneous publishing

(G-15232)
DEKDYNE INC
201 Harrison Ave (23185-3504)
PHONE..................................757 221-2542
David Kranbuehl, *President*
Kay Cheves, *Vice Pres*
EMP: 4
SALES (est): 391.6K **Privately Held**
SIC: 3861 Sensitized film, cloth & paper

(G-15233)
DINING WITH DIGNITY INC
101 Deerwood Dr (23188-7502)
PHONE..................................757 565-2452
Robert Bayton, *President*
EMP: 2
SALES (est): 142.7K **Privately Held**
WEB: www.diningwithdignity.com
SIC: 3914 Silverware

(G-15234)
DIRECT TOOLS FACTORY OUTLET
5601 Richmond Rd (23188-1985)
PHONE..................................757 345-6945
EMP: 2 EST: 2015
SALES (est): 81.4K **Privately Held**
SIC: 3599 Mfg Industrial Machinery

(G-15235)
DIVERGING APPROACH INC
6623 Richmond Rd Ste L (23188-7617)
PHONE..................................757 220-2316
Joseph Stanko, *President*
Jon Kristinsson, *Vice Pres*
Joe Stanko, *Opers Staff*
Jami Kupczak, *Director*
John Allan Nicholls, *Admin Sec*
EMP: 18 EST: 2011
SALES (est): 4.4MM **Privately Held**
WEB: www.divappinc.com
SIC: 3669 8999 Railroad signaling devices, electric; artists & artists' studios

(G-15236)
E COMPONENTS INTERNATIONAL
180 Dennis Dr (23185-4935)
PHONE..................................804 462-5679
Fred Edmonds, *President*
Tammy Revere, *Principal*
EMP: 2 EST: 1999
SALES (est): 50K **Privately Held**
WEB: www.e-components.com
SIC: 3714 Motor vehicle body components & frame

(G-15237)
ECLIPSE HOLSTERS LLC
106 Londonderry Ln (23188-1872)
PHONE..................................907 382-6958
Jessica Hazelaar, *CEO*
EMP: 6
SALES (est): 325.3K **Privately Held**
WEB: www.eclipseholsters.com
SIC: 3842 Personal safety equipment

(G-15238)
EILIG SOFTWARE LLC
84 Carlton Ct (23185-2780)
PHONE..................................757 259-0608
James Gildea, *Partner*
Aisha Gildea, *Partner*
EMP: 2
SALES (est): 109.1K **Privately Held**
SIC: 7372 Prepackaged software

(G-15239)
EMBROIDERY CONNECTION
8628 Croaker Rd (23188-1226)
PHONE..................................757 566-8859
Diana Clay, *Administration*
EMP: 1
SALES (est): 26.9K **Privately Held**
WEB: www.theembroideryconnection.com
SIC: 2395 Embroidery products, except schiffli machine

(G-15240)
EVER BE SIGNS
701 Goodwin St (23185-3910)
PHONE..................................912 660-1436
Danielle Oboyle, *Principal*
EMP: 2

▲ = Import ▼=Export
◆ =Import/Export

SALES (est): 72.6K **Privately Held**
SIC: 3993 Signs & advertising specialties

(G-15241)
EXTINCTION PHARMACEUTICALS
124 Country Club Dr (23188-1516)
P.O. Box 6874 (23188-5231)
PHONE.................................757 258-0498
EMP: 3
SALES (est): 196.6K **Privately Held**
SIC: 2834 Mfg Pharmaceutical Preparations

(G-15242)
FAB SERVICES LLC
104 Park Pl (23185-4766)
PHONE.................................757 869-4480
EMP: 2 EST: 2012
SALES (est): 96.8K **Privately Held**
SIC: 3589 High pressure cleaning equipment

(G-15243)
FINE SIGNS
5691 Mooretown Rd (23188-2113)
PHONE.................................757 565-7833
Jason Hill, *President*
EMP: 3
SALES (est): 65K **Privately Held**
WEB: www.finesignsinc.com
SIC: 3993 Electric signs

(G-15244)
FINE SIGNS & GRAPHICS INC
5691 Mooretown Rd (23188-2113)
PHONE.................................757 565-7833
EMP: 2
SALES (est): 140.5K **Privately Held**
WEB: www.finesignsinc.com
SIC: 3993 Signs & advertising specialties

(G-15245)
FLAT HAT
102 Richmond Rd (23185-3616)
PHONE.................................757 221-3283
Mike Crump, *Principal*
EMP: 5
SALES (est): 40.5K **Privately Held**
WEB: www.flathatnews.com
SIC: 2741 Miscellaneous publishing

(G-15246)
GARGONE JOHN
Also Called: Bigmouth Bagger
8810 Pocahontas Trl 66a (23185-6268)
PHONE.................................540 641-1934
John Gargone, *Owner*
EMP: 1
SALES (est): 47.2K **Privately Held**
WEB: www.bigmouthbagger.net
SIC: 2821 Plastics materials & resins

(G-15247)
GLOBAL - AB INBEV
7801 Pocahontas Trl (23185-6302)
PHONE.................................314 577-2000
EMP: 2
SALES (est): 62.3K **Privately Held**
SIC: 2082 Malt beverages

(G-15248)
GLOBUS WORLD PARTNERS INC
190 The Maine (23185-1423)
PHONE.................................757 645-4274
Robert D Brooks, *Principal*
EMP: 5 EST: 2008
SALES (est): 355.9K **Privately Held**
WEB: www.globusworldpartners.com
SIC: 2671 Plastic film, coated or laminated for packaging

(G-15249)
GRAMPIAN GROUP INC
3225 Fowlers Lake Rd (23185-7506)
PHONE.................................757 277-5557
Joseph V Chatigny, *CEO*
EMP: 6
SALES (est): 100K **Privately Held**
SIC: 3841 Surgical & medical instruments

(G-15250)
GRANDADDYS STUMP GRINDING
221 Old Taylor Rd (23188-1781)
PHONE.................................757 565-5870
Henry West, *Owner*
EMP: 2
SALES (est): 230.8K **Privately Held**
SIC: 3599 Grinding castings for the trade

(G-15251)
GUNN MOUNTAIN COMMUNICATIONS
124 N Turnberry (23188-8944)
PHONE.................................303 880-8616
Bruce Sogoloff, *Owner*
EMP: 1
SALES (est): 35K **Privately Held**
SIC: 3669 Intercommunication systems, electric

(G-15252)
H & A SPECIALTY CO
112 Portland (23188-6455)
PHONE.................................757 206-1115
Doug W Arnold, *President*
EMP: 4 EST: 1946
SQ FT: 300
SALES (est): 290K **Privately Held**
SIC: 2448 5113 Pallets, wood; corrugated & solid fiber boxes

(G-15253)
H&H MEDICAL CORPORATION
Also Called: H&H Associates
328 Mclaws Cir (23185-5648)
PHONE.................................800 326-5708
Paul Harder, *President*
Joseph Dacorta, *Vice Pres*
Kevin Dougherty, *Sales Staff*
Eric Harder, *Manager*
Robert HB Harder, *Admin Sec*
▲ EMP: 42
SQ FT: 22,300
SALES (est): 7.8MM **Privately Held**
WEB: www.buyhandh.com
SIC: 3842 Ligatures, medical

(G-15254)
HIGH SPEED TECH VENTR LLC
120 Tutters Neck (23185-5122)
PHONE.................................571 318-0997
Linda Tang, *Vice Pres*
Ming Tang, *Administration*
EMP: 2
SALES (est): 89.1K **Privately Held**
SIC: 3724 Research & development on aircraft engines & parts

(G-15255)
HIGH THREAT CONCEALMENT LLC
309 Mclaws Cir Ste K (23185-5675)
PHONE.................................757 208-0221
Kristen Osiecki, *Mng Member*
Scott Lambin, *Mng Member*
EMP: 8
SQ FT: 9,000
SALES (est): 3.2MM **Privately Held**
WEB: www.highthreatconcealment.com
SIC: 3052 Rubber & plastics hose & beltings

(G-15256)
INDUST LLC
4037 Frances Berkeley (23188-1399)
PHONE.................................757 208-0587
Kirk Roberts, *Marketing Staff*
George Armbruster,
EMP: 1
SALES (est): 109.6K **Privately Held**
WEB: www.industllc.com
SIC: 3564 Purification & dust collection equipment

(G-15257)
INFOMTION TECH APPLCATIONS LLC
5378 Gardner Ct (23188-1981)
PHONE.................................757 603-3551
Kent Ball, *CEO*
EMP: 2

SALES (est): 97.6K **Privately Held**
SIC: 7372 7371 Application computer software; computer software systems analysis & design, custom

(G-15258)
JAMES SLATER
Also Called: Jimmy's Engine Service
145 Marstons Ln (23188-2908)
PHONE.................................757 566-1543
John Goodman, *Partner*
EMP: 3
SQ FT: 1,000
SALES (est): 140K **Privately Held**
WEB: www.jimmysengineservice.weebly.com
SIC: 3599 Machine shop, jobbing & repair

(G-15259)
JAMES-YORK SECURITY LLC
1226 Penniman Rd (23185-5256)
PHONE.................................757 344-1808
Ethel Hill, *Officer*
Willaim Hill,
Tonya Brooks, *Admin Sec*
EMP: 25
SALES (est): 3.1MM **Privately Held**
SIC: 3577 7381 Computer peripheral equipment; security guard service

(G-15260)
JCLFARMS LLC
107 Barn Elm Rd (23188-6611)
PHONE.................................757 291-1401
James Warren,
EMP: 2
SALES (est): 126.8K **Privately Held**
SIC: 3823 7389 Computer interface equipment for industrial process control; business services

(G-15261)
JOKER BREWING LLC
113 Palace Ln Ste D (23185-3034)
PHONE.................................757 814-0882
Lance Zaal,
EMP: 3
SALES (est): 100K **Privately Held**
SIC: 2082 Beer (alcoholic beverage)

(G-15262)
JON ARMSTRONG
3484 Hunters Rdg (23188-2492)
PHONE.................................757 253-3844
Jon Armstrong, *Manager*
Armstrong Jon, *Manager*
EMP: 2
SALES (est): 65.5K **Privately Held**
SIC: 1389 Oil & gas field services

(G-15263)
KARLS CUSTOM WHEELS
152 Skimino Rd (23188-2223)
PHONE.................................757 565-1997
Karl Gayer, *Owner*
Inga A Gayer, *Co-Owner*
EMP: 2
SALES (est): 169.3K **Privately Held**
SIC: 3312 Blast furnaces & steel mills

(G-15264)
KATHERYN WARREN
Also Called: State Fair Popcorn Company
137 Riviera (23188-9207)
PHONE.................................757 813-5396
Katheryn Warren, *Owner*
Robert Warren, *Owner*
EMP: 2
SALES (est): 69.4K **Privately Held**
WEB: www.statefairpopcorn.com
SIC: 2064 Popcorn balls or other treated popcorn products

(G-15265)
KATHLEEN TILLEY
103 N Waller St (23185-4555)
PHONE.................................703 727-5385
Kathleen Tilley, *Owner*
EMP: 1
SALES (est): 59.5K **Privately Held**
SIC: 2311 7389 Men's & boys' uniforms;

(G-15266)
KENNEDY PROJECTS LLC
Also Called: Chronicling Greatness
111 Meadow Rue Ct (23185-4429)
PHONE.................................757 345-0626
Adam Kennedy,
EMP: 2
SALES (est): 76.9K **Privately Held**
SIC: 2731 7389 Book publishing;

(G-15267)
KM SERVICES LLC
Also Called: Affordable Wheelchair Lifts
2884 Hidden Lake Dr (23185-8020)
PHONE.................................757 524-3420
Shae Murphy, *Mng Member*
Kerry Murphy, *Mng Member*
EMP: 8
SALES (est): 552.3K **Privately Held**
SIC: 3999 5084 Wheelchair lifts; industrial machinery & equipment

(G-15268)
LEONI FIBER OPTICS INC (HQ)
209 Bulifants Blvd (23188-5744)
PHONE.................................757 258-4805
Sharon Terry, *General Mgr*
Juan Diaz, *Managing Dir*
Stefan Gropp, *Regional Mgr*
Jun Nakano, *Regional Mgr*
Catherine Spevetz, *Human Res Dir*
EMP: 3
SALES (est): 6.8MM
SALES (corp-wide): 5.3B **Privately Held**
WEB: www.leoni-americas.com
SIC: 3229 Fiber optics strands
PA: Leoni Ag
 Marienstr. 7
 Nurnberg 90402
 911 202-30

(G-15269)
LEONI FIBER OPTICS INC
215 Bulifants Blvd Ste D (23188-5750)
PHONE.................................757 258-4805
Matthew Webb, *Branch Mgr*
EMP: 4
SALES (corp-wide): 5.3B **Privately Held**
WEB: www.leoni-americas.com
SIC: 3229 Fiber optics strands
HQ: Leoni Fiber Optics, Inc.
 209 Bulifants Blvd
 Williamsburg VA 23188
 757 258-4805

(G-15270)
LESLIE NOBLE
114 National Ln (23185-4911)
PHONE.................................757 291-2904
Leslie Noble, *Principal*
EMP: 2
SALES (est): 83.2K **Privately Held**
SIC: 3544 Special dies, tools, jigs & fixtures

(G-15271)
LKM INDUSTRIES LLC
208 Jeffersons Hundred (23185-8908)
PHONE.................................919 601-6661
EMP: 2 EST: 2014
SALES (est): 101.4K **Privately Held**
SIC: 3999 Manufacturing industries

(G-15272)
LLOYDS PEWTER
143 Brookhaven Dr (23188-2503)
PHONE.................................757 503-1110
Lloyd Richardson, *Owner*
EMP: 2
SALES (est): 1K **Privately Held**
SIC: 3499 Fabricated metal products

(G-15273)
LOCAL VOICE
4732 Longhill Rd Ste 2201 (23188-1584)
PHONE.................................757 565-1079
EMP: 1
SALES (est): 56.4K **Privately Held**
WEB: www.localdailymedia.com
SIC: 2741 Miscellaneous publishing

(G-15274)
LOOSELEAF PUBLICATIONS LLC
108 William Allen (23185-5126)
PHONE................................757 221-8250
Donna Lin Pratt, *Principal*
EMP: 1
SALES (est): 37.5K **Privately Held**
SIC: 2741 Miscellaneous publishing

(G-15275)
M&M GREAT ADVENTURES LLC
111 Clements Mill Trce (23185-5435)
PHONE................................937 344-1415
Michael Pennington, *Mng Member*
Mary Ellen Pennington, *Mng Member*
▼ EMP: 3 EST: 2009
SALES (est): 239K **Privately Held**
SIC: 3949 5199 7389 Camping equipment & supplies; general merchandise, non-durable;

(G-15276)
MEYER AND MEYER INDUSTRIES INC
5103 Salisbury Mews (23188-8500)
PHONE................................757 564-6157
Richard Meyer, *Director*
EMP: 1
SALES (est): 51.4K **Privately Held**
SIC: 3999 Manufacturing industries

(G-15277)
MIGHTY OAK ENTERPRISES INC (PA)
Also Called: Candle Maker, The
1 Bush Garden Blvd (23185)
PHONE................................757 422-6353
Angela Sullivan, *President*
Micheal Shawn Sullivan, *Vice Pres*
EMP: 5 EST: 1980
SALES (est): 76K **Privately Held**
SIC: 3999 5199 5999 Candles; candles; candle shops

(G-15278)
MILLER QUALITY WOODWORK INC
102 Rondane Pl (23188-1023)
PHONE................................757 564-7847
Brian Miller, *Principal*
EMP: 2
SALES (est): 129.1K **Privately Held**
SIC: 2431 Millwork

(G-15279)
MINUTEMAN PRESS
4655 Monticello Ave # 106 (23188-8219)
PHONE................................757 903-0978
EMP: 2 EST: 2018
SALES (est): 83.9K **Privately Held**
WEB: www.minutemanpress.com
SIC: 2752 Commercial printing, lithographic

(G-15280)
MODEL DATASHEET PT INSTRUMENTS
102 Bronze Ct (23185-6325)
PHONE................................716 418-4194
EMP: 2
SALES (est): 127K **Privately Held**
SIC: 3829 Measuring & controlling devices

(G-15281)
MODU SYSTEM AMERICA LLC
Also Called: John Douglas
1715 Endeavor Dr (23185-6239)
PHONE................................757 250-3413
Dan Demartine, *Vice Pres*
John Douglas, *Vice Pres*
Daniel Demartine, *Mng Member*
▲ EMP: 6
SALES (est): 2MM **Privately Held**
WEB: www.modusushi.com
SIC: 3535 2599 Belt conveyor systems, general industrial use; robotic conveyors; carts, restaurant equipment

(G-15282)
NATHAN GROUP LLC
2635 Lake Powell Rd (23185-3703)
PHONE................................757 229-8703
Troy H Lapetina,

Helen Lapetina,
EMP: 2 EST: 2009
SALES (est): 146.6K **Privately Held**
SIC: 3423 Hand & edge tools

(G-15283)
NKS LLC
423 N Boundary St Ste 200 (23185-3615)
PHONE................................757 229-3139
Steven A Meade Esq, *Administration*
EMP: 3
SALES (est): 171.6K **Privately Held**
SIC: 3554 Paper industries machinery

(G-15284)
NORTHROP GRUMMAN CORPORATION
4836 Milden Rd (23188-2529)
PHONE................................757 688-5339
Robert Wilson, *Branch Mgr*
EMP: 2 **Publicly Held**
WEB: www.northropgrumman.com
SIC: 3812 Search & navigation equipment
PA: Northrop Grumman Corporation
2980 Fairview Park Dr
Falls Church VA 22042

(G-15285)
OMOHUNDRO INSTITUTE OF EARLY
Swem Library Landrum Dr (23185)
P.O. Box 8781 (23187-8781)
PHONE................................757 221-1114
Ronald Huffman, *Director*
EMP: 20
SALES: 3.4MM **Privately Held**
WEB: www.oieahc.wm.edu
SIC: 2731 Book publishing

(G-15286)
ONE STOP CLEANING LLC
Also Called: One Stop All Clg Solutions
160 Second St Ste 202 (23185-4524)
P.O. Box 403 (23187-0403)
PHONE................................757 561-2952
Rositsa Vodenicharova, *Principal*
EMP: 5
SALES (est): 203.8K **Privately Held**
WEB: www.onestopcleaningllc.com
SIC: 3991 7349 7389 Brushes for vacuum cleaners, carpet sweepers, etc.; building & office cleaning services;

(G-15287)
OREAMNOS BIOFUELS LLC
4008 Thorngate Dr (23188-1426)
PHONE................................651 269-7737
Lawrence D Sullivan, *Principal*
EMP: 2
SALES (est): 90.7K **Privately Held**
SIC: 2911 Petroleum refining

(G-15288)
ORNAMENT COMPANY
315 Archers Mead (23185-6582)
PHONE................................757 585-0729
Peter Hugh Armour, *President*
EMP: 3
SALES (est): 160K **Privately Held**
WEB: www.theornamentcompany.com
SIC: 3231 Christmas tree ornaments: made from purchased glass

(G-15289)
OSMON INDUSTRIES
208 Moodys Run (23185-6558)
PHONE................................757 564-3088
Robert Osmon, *Principal*
EMP: 2 EST: 2010
SALES (est): 145K **Privately Held**
SIC: 3999 Manufacturing industries

(G-15290)
OXFORD INDUSTRIES INC
Also Called: Tommy Bahama
5625 Richmond Rd (23188-2020)
PHONE................................757 220-8660
Aaron Lewee, *Branch Mgr*
EMP: 14
SALES (corp-wide): 1.1B **Publicly Held**
WEB: www.oxfordinc.com
SIC: 2321 Men's & boys' furnishings

PA: Oxford Industries, Inc.
999 Peachtree St Ne # 688
Atlanta GA 30309
404 659-2424

(G-15291)
PARKWAY PRINTSHOP
410 Lightfoot Rd (23188-9000)
PHONE................................757 378-3959
EMP: 2
SALES (est): 83.9K **Privately Held**
WEB: www.parkwayprintshop.com
SIC: 2752 Commercial printing, lithographic

(G-15292)
PAVER DOCTORS LLC
203 Bethune Dr (23185-5608)
PHONE................................757 903-6275
David Barglof, *Principal*
EMP: 2 EST: 2011
SALES (est): 133.1K **Privately Held**
SIC: 3531 Pavers

(G-15293)
PEGEE WLLMSBURG PTTRNS HSTRIES
105 Dogwood Dr (23185-3709)
PHONE................................757 220-2722
Peggy Miller, *Owner*
EMP: 1 EST: 1972
SALES (est): 75.4K **Privately Held**
WEB: www.pegee.com
SIC: 3543 Foundry patternmaking

(G-15294)
PENINSULA CUSTOM COATERS INC
1598 Penniman Rd Ste D (23185-5851)
PHONE................................757 476-6996
Arthur Sparks, *President*
Melvis I Moreno, *Vice Pres*
EMP: 6
SQ FT: 5,000
SALES (est): 245K **Privately Held**
WEB: www.peninsulacustomcoaters.com
SIC: 3479 Coating or wrapping steel pipe; coating of metals & formed products

(G-15295)
PERFORMANCE AVIATION MFG GROUP
106 Sherwood Dr (23185-5026)
PHONE................................757 766-1150
Clement Makowski, *President*
Robert Pegg, *Vice Pres*
EMP: 2
SALES (est): 92.4K **Privately Held**
SIC: 3999 Manufacturing industries

(G-15296)
PLEASANT RUN PUBG SVCS LLC
217 Martins Rdg (23188-7886)
PHONE................................757 229-8510
EMP: 1
SALES (est): 37.5K **Privately Held**
SIC: 2741 Miscellaneous publishing

(G-15297)
POINSETT PUBLICATIONS INC
4669 Yeardley Loop (23185-7948)
PHONE................................757 378-2856
Kim Holmes, *Principal*
EMP: 4
SALES (est): 203.7K **Privately Held**
SIC: 2741 Miscellaneous publishing

(G-15298)
PRESTIGE CABINETS LLC
4705 Eskerhills (23188-8524)
PHONE................................757 741-3201
EMP: 1
SALES (est): 77.7K **Privately Held**
SIC: 2434 Wood kitchen cabinets

(G-15299)
PRETECH SOLUTIONS INCORPORATED
3444 Frances Berkeley (23188-1334)
PHONE................................757 879-3483
Christopher Smith, *President*
EMP: 2

SALES (est): 50K **Privately Held**
SIC: 3625 Relays & industrial controls

(G-15300)
PRINT LIFE LLC
4904 Grand Strand Dr (23188-2720)
PHONE................................609 442-2838
Eileen Ferreira, *Principal*
EMP: 2
SALES (est): 83.9K **Privately Held**
SIC: 2752 Commercial printing, lithographic

(G-15301)
PRINTWELL INC
3407 Poplar Creek Ln (23188-1005)
PHONE................................757 564-3302
Chris E Jones, *President*
Ralph A Swartz, *Admin Sec*
EMP: 10
SQ FT: 3,400
SALES (est): 1MM **Privately Held**
WEB: www.printwellinc.net
SIC: 2752 Commercial printing, offset

(G-15302)
PROTEAN LLC
1769 Jamestown Rd Ste 1b (23185-2394)
P.O. Box 5772 (23185-5212)
PHONE................................757 273-1131
John Cornett, *CEO*
Mark Bohn, *COO*
Jonathan Godfrey, *Marketing Staff*
EMP: 5
SALES (est): 500K **Privately Held**
WEB: www.proteanhub.com
SIC: 7372 7371 Prepackaged software; custom computer programming services; computer software development

(G-15303)
RAYTHEON COMPANY
1100 Executive Dr (23188-4005)
PHONE................................972 638-3173
Christopher Brandt, *IT/INT Sup*
EMP: 3
SALES (est): 113.3K **Privately Held**
SIC: 3812 Defense systems & equipment

(G-15304)
RED GERANIUM INC
8 Prestwick (23188-7437)
PHONE................................757 645-3421
Lisa Brickey, *Principal*
EMP: 3 EST: 2018
SALES (est): 125.7K **Privately Held**
SIC: 3671 Electron tubes

(G-15305)
REWI LLC
302 Ben Franklin Cir (23188-7639)
PHONE................................757 647-8942
Rosemary E Williams,
EMP: 1
SALES (est): 46.2K **Privately Held**
SIC: 2514 Nursery furniture: metal

(G-15306)
ROBERT AGNELLO
2887 Hidden Lake Dr (23185-8022)
PHONE................................757 345-0829
Robert Agnello, *Principal*
EMP: 4
SALES (est): 424.1K **Privately Held**
SIC: 3589 High pressure cleaning equipment

(G-15307)
ROLHEI LLC
901 Capitol Landing Rd # 8 (23185-4326)
PHONE................................202 850-9000
Gerald Tilk, *Mng Member*
EMP: 2
SALES (est): 5MM **Privately Held**
SIC: 2676 Cleansing tissues: made from purchased paper

(G-15308)
RP FINCH INC
201 Stonehouse Rd (23188-1206)
P.O. Box 340, Toano (23168-0340)
PHONE................................757 566-8022
Robert Finch, *President*
EMP: 8 EST: 2001

▲ = Import ▼=Export
◆ =Import/Export

SALES (est): 1.1MM **Privately Held**
SIC: 3823 Water quality monitoring & control systems

(G-15309)
RUSOLF S OLSZYK
Also Called: Cbd Consulting
122 Deal (23188-9191)
PHONE..................................757 565-2970
Rudolf Olszyk, *Owner*
Peggy Olszyk, *Principal*
EMP: 2
SALES (est): 73.9K **Privately Held**
SIC: 3999

(G-15310)
SERVICE METAL FABRICATORS INC
Also Called: Service Metals
1708 Endeavor Dr (23185-6239)
PHONE..................................757 887-3500
Edgar B Roesch Jr, *President*
Thomas Russ, *President*
Miriam Matthews, *Admin Sec*
EMP: 100 EST: 1981
SQ FT: 24,000
SALES (est): 20.4MM **Privately Held**
WEB: www.sermetfab.com
SIC: 3444 2542 Sheet metal specialties, not stamped; partitions & fixtures, except wood

(G-15311)
SILVER HAND WINERY LLC
Also Called: Silver Hand Meadery
224 Monticello Ave (23185-6430)
PHONE..................................757 378-2225
Glenn Lavender, *Mng Member*
EMP: 6
SALES (est): 75.4K **Privately Held**
WEB: www.silverhandmeadery.com
SIC: 2084 Wines

(G-15312)
SKIPS WOODWORKS
114 The Maine (23185-1423)
PHONE..................................757 390-1948
Amber Parlett, *Principal*
EMP: 1 EST: 2019
SALES (est): 54.1K **Privately Held**
SIC: 2431 Millwork

(G-15313)
SMITH AND FLANNERY
Also Called: Virginia Pewtersmith
6592 Richmond Rd (23188-7200)
PHONE..................................804 794-4979
Dorothy Mauro, *President*
Christoher Mauro, *Vice Pres*
Janet Moe, *Vice Pres*
EMP: 6
SALES (est): 576.2K **Privately Held**
WEB: www.virginiapewtersmith.com
SIC: 3914 Silverware & plated ware

(G-15314)
SOLAR LIGHTING VIRGINIA INC
106 Holcomb Dr (23185-4937)
PHONE..................................757 229-3236
Joseph K Moorman, *Administration*
EMP: 2
SALES (est): 115.8K **Privately Held**
WEB: www.vadaylight.com
SIC: 3648 Lighting equipment

(G-15315)
SOUNDSCAPE COMP & PRFMCE EXCH
109 Meadow Rue Ct (23185-4429)
PHONE..................................757 645-4671
EMP: 1
SALES (est): 53K **Privately Held**
SIC: 2791 Typesetting Services

(G-15316)
SOUTHERN EQUIPMENT COMPANY INC
1571 Manufacture Dr (23185-6274)
PHONE..................................757 888-8500
EMP: 5
SALES (corp-wide): 800.4MM **Privately Held**
SIC: 3273 Mfgs Ready-Mixed Concrete

HQ: Argos Ready Mix (Carolinas) Corp.
3610 Bush St
Raleigh NC 27609
919 790-1520

(G-15317)
SPITFIRE MANAGEMENT LLC
1769 Jamestown Rd Ste 113 (23185-2310)
PHONE..................................757 644-4609
John Taffler, *Mng Member*
Steve Powers, *Mng Member*
EMP: 10
SALES (est): 708.1K **Privately Held**
WEB: www.spitfiremanagement.com
SIC: 7372 Prepackaged software

(G-15318)
STAIB INSTRUMENTS INC
101 Stafford Ct (23185-5767)
PHONE..................................757 565-7000
Philippe Staib, *President*
Lillyan Dylla, *Vice Pres*
EMP: 6
SQ FT: 7,000
SALES (est): 1MM **Privately Held**
WEB: www.staibinstruments.com
SIC: 3826 Analytical instruments

(G-15319)
STARRY NIGHTS SCRAPBOOKING LLC
104 Catawba Ct (23185-5488)
PHONE..................................757 784-6163
Jeananna Labranche,
EMP: 1
SALES (est): 94.8K **Privately Held**
SIC: 2679 Converted paper products

(G-15320)
SUTER ENTERPRISES LTD
Also Called: Kwik Kopy Printing
4399 Ironbound Rd (23188-2623)
PHONE..................................757 220-3299
James A Suter, *President*
Jacqueline S Suter, *Admin Sec*
EMP: 11 EST: 1983
SQ FT: 2,400
SALES (est): 2.1MM **Privately Held**
WEB: www.suterprinting.com
SIC: 2752 2791 2789 2672 Commercial printing, offset; typesetting; bookbinding & related work; coated & laminated paper

(G-15321)
SWAROVSKI NORTH AMERICA LTD
Also Called: Swarovski North America Ltd
5711 Richmond Rd (23188-1993)
PHONE..................................757 253-7924
EMP: 4
SALES (corp-wide): 4.7B **Privately Held**
WEB: www.swarovski.com
SIC: 3961 Costume jewelry
HQ: Swarovski North America Limited
1 Kenney Dr
Cranston RI 02920
401 463-6400

(G-15322)
TASKILL TECHNOLOGIES LLC
3225 Fowlers Lake Rd (23185-7506)
PHONE..................................757 277-5557
Vic Chatigny,
EMP: 2
SALES (est): 82.2K **Privately Held**
SIC: 3679 Electronic circuits

(G-15323)
TCS MATERIALS INC (DH)
5423 Airport Rd (23188-2153)
PHONE..................................757 591-9340
Dan Joyner, *President*
Allen Ramer, *Vice Pres*
EMP: 20
SQ FT: 2,500
SALES (est): 7.7MM **Publicly Held**
SIC: 3273 1442 Ready-mixed concrete; construction sand & gravel
HQ: Legacy Vulcan, Llc
1200 Urban Center Dr
Vestavia AL 35242
205 298-3000

(G-15324)
THERMAL GRADIENT INC
118 Peachtree (23188-9123)
PHONE..................................585 425-3338
Joel Grover, *CEO*
Robert D Juncosa, *CEO*
EMP: 4
SQ FT: 1,500
SALES (est): 527K **Privately Held**
SIC: 3845 Electromedical equipment

(G-15325)
TOMO LLC
Also Called: All Outdoors The
125 Shoal Crk (23188-1406)
PHONE..................................407 694-7464
Adam Roberts, *President*
Ken Futamura, *Vice Pres*
EMP: 4
SALES (est): 360K **Privately Held**
SIC: 2599 Factory furniture & fixtures

(G-15326)
TRIANGLE SKATEBOARD ALLIANCE
5103 Melanies Way (23188-2864)
PHONE..................................804 426-3663
Maxwell Pfannebecker, *Principal*
EMP: 1
SALES (est): 47K **Privately Held**
WEB: www.triangleskateboardalliance.org
SIC: 3949 Skateboards

(G-15327)
UAVARUS LLC
4819 Williamsburg Glade (23185-2115)
PHONE..................................757 876-5507
Mark Motter, *Principal*
EMP: 3
SALES (est): 221.8K **Privately Held**
SIC: 3823 Industrial instrmnts msrmnt display/control process variable

(G-15328)
UNITED PROVIDERS OF CARE LLC
9311 Croaker Rd (23188-1241)
PHONE..................................757 775-5075
Desiree Lucas, *President*
EMP: 1
SALES (est): 46.4K **Privately Held**
SIC: 2771 2782 8082 Greeting cards; scrapbooks, albums & diaries; home health care services; oxygen tent service; visiting nurse service

(G-15329)
UP AND RUNNING COMPUTERS INC
5904 Montpelier Dr (23188-8122)
PHONE..................................757 565-3282
EMP: 2
SALES (est): 139K **Privately Held**
SIC: 7372 7378 7377 5734 Prepackaged Software Services Computer Maintenance Computer Rental Ret Computers/Software Hardware Upgrades Networking

(G-15330)
VAULT PRODUCTIONS LLC
107 Marshall Way (23185-2975)
PHONE..................................703 509-2704
EMP: 3
SALES (est): 170K **Privately Held**
SIC: 3272 Mfg Concrete Products

(G-15331)
VICTORIOUS IMAGES LLC
7191 Richmond Rd Ste E (23188-7239)
P.O. Box 638, Norge (23127-0638)
PHONE..................................757 476-7335
Nancy P Lewis, *Mng Member*
Gerry Lewis,
EMP: 1
SQ FT: 800
SALES (est): 70K **Privately Held**
WEB: www.victoriousimages.com
SIC: 3842 Models, anatomical

(G-15332)
VINTAGE BINDERY WILLIAMSBUR
4 Seasons Ct (23188-1697)
PHONE..................................757 220-0203
EMP: 1
SALES (est): 73.3K **Privately Held**
SIC: 2789 Bookbinding & related work

(G-15333)
VIRGINIA BEER COMPANY LLC
401 Second St (23185-4815)
PHONE..................................770 815-8518
Chris Smith, *Managing Prtnr*
Robby Willey, *Partner*
Michael Rhodes, *Sales Staff*
Luci Legaspi, *Manager*
EMP: 11
SALES (est): 1.1MM **Privately Held**
WEB: www.virginiabeerco.com
SIC: 2082 Malt beverages

(G-15334)
VIRGINIA VENOM VOLLEYBALL
8140 Wrenfield Dr (23188-9332)
P.O. Box 669, Toano (23168-0669)
PHONE..................................757 645-4002
Gregory Koon, *Principal*
EMP: 4
SALES (est): 199.3K **Privately Held**
WEB: www.williamsburgvolleyball.com
SIC: 2836 Venoms

(G-15335)
VIRGINIA VNOM SPT ORGANIZATION
3012 South Chase (23185-8732)
PHONE..................................757 592-6790
EMP: 2
SALES (est): 74.4K **Privately Held**
SIC: 2836 Venoms

(G-15336)
W M S B R G GRAFIX
5810 Mooretown Rd Ste B (23188-1794)
PHONE..................................757 565-5200
EMP: 2
SALES (est): 89K **Privately Held**
SIC: 2759 Commercial Printing, Nec

(G-15337)
WAC ENTERPRISES LLC
410 Lightfoot Rd Ste G (23188-9000)
PHONE..................................757 342-7202
William Craig, *Mng Member*
EMP: 4 EST: 2000
SQ FT: 1,400
SALES (est): 270K **Privately Held**
SIC: 3993 Signs & advertising specialties

(G-15338)
WALTRIP RECYCLING INC
11 Marclay Rd (23185-3713)
PHONE..................................757 229-0434
Larry Waltrip, *President*
Don Broady, *Assoc VP*
Jean T Waltrip, *Admin Sec*
Stephanie Crum, *Admin Asst*
EMP: 30
SQ FT: 1,300
SALES (est): 6.3MM **Privately Held**
WEB: www.williamsburg.yardworksva.com
SIC: 2421 Sawdust, shavings & wood chips

(G-15339)
WAYNE HARBIN BUILDER INC
3705 Strawberry Plains Rd D (23188-3423)
PHONE..................................757 220-8860
Scott Maynor, *General Mgr*
Doug Harbin, *Vice Pres*
Brad Harbin, *Vice Pres*
Sharon Thomas, *Manager*
EMP: 2
SALES (corp-wide): 2.7MM **Privately Held**
WEB: www.harbinbuilder.com
SIC: 3272 Building stone, artificial: concrete
PA: Wayne Harbin Builder Inc
3630 G W Mem Hwy Ste C
Yorktown VA 23693
757 867-8279

(G-15340)
WEEKEND DETAILER LLC
4771 Pelegs Way (23185-2119)
PHONE..................................757 345-2023
EMP: 2
SALES (est): 90.1K **Privately Held**
SIC: 2842 Automobile polish

(G-15341)
WILLIAMSBURG DISTILLERY
7218 Merrimac Trl (23185-5202)
PHONE..................................757 378-2456
David Burley, *Administration*
EMP: 3 EST: 2015
SALES (est): 136.4K **Privately Held**
WEB: www.williamsburg-distillery.com
SIC: 2085 Distilled & blended liquors

(G-15342)
WILLIAMSBURG METAL SPECIALTIES
4548 The Foxes (23188-2424)
PHONE..................................757 229-3393
Sidney Wilson, *Owner*
EMP: 1
SALES (est): 61K **Privately Held**
SIC: 3444 Roof deck, sheet metal

(G-15343)
WILLIAMSBURG WINERY LTD
Also Called: Jamestown Cellars
5800 Wessex Hundred (23185-8063)
PHONE..................................757 229-0999
Patrick G Duffeler, *President*
Simon Smith, *Director*
▲ EMP: 50
SQ FT: 45,000
SALES (est): 4.6MM **Privately Held**
WEB: www.williamsburgwinery.com
SIC: 2084 5182 Wines; wine

(G-15344)
WILLIAMSBURG WOOD WORKS LLC
3001 Stanford Pl (23185-8714)
PHONE..................................757 817-5396
Patrick Russell, *Principal*
EMP: 2
SALES (est): 93.8K **Privately Held**
WEB: www.williamsburgwoodworks.com
SIC: 2431 Millwork

(G-15345)
WILLIMSBURG PRCESS SLTIONS LLC
4771 Winterberry Ct (23188-7254)
PHONE..................................703 577-4448
Don Marohl, *Owner*
EMP: 2 EST: 2010
SALES (est): 201.7K **Privately Held**
WEB: www.wpsconsultingllc.com
SIC: 2752 Commercial printing, lithographic

(G-15346)
WINDOW FASHION DESIGN
Also Called: Mark Works
108 Ingram Rd Ste 23 (23188-2431)
PHONE..................................757 253-8813
Mark Urick, *President*
▲ EMP: 3
SALES (est): 201.2K **Privately Held**
WEB: www.windowfashiondesign.net
SIC: 2591 Drapery hardware & blinds & shades

(G-15347)
WIREDUP INC
3307 Poplar Creek Ln (23188-1058)
PHONE..................................757 565-3655
EMP: 3
SQ FT: 650
SALES: 250K **Privately Held**
SIC: 3651 Sales And Installation Of Home Audio/Video Equipment

(G-15348)
WOODS OF WISDOM LLC
113 J Farm Ln (23188-1850)
PHONE..................................757 645-2043
William Bellucci, *Principal*
EMP: 1
SALES (est): 41.5K **Privately Held**
SIC: 2499 Wood products

(G-15349)
ZIG ZAG PRESS LLC
213 Heritage Pointe (23188-8006)
PHONE..................................757 229-1345
EMP: 2
SALES (est): 77.6K **Privately Held**
SIC: 2741 Misc Publishing

(G-15350)
ZUP LLC
1490 Quarterpath Rd 5a (23185-6544)
PHONE..................................843 822-5664
James J Knicely,
▲ EMP: 2
SALES (est): 142.1K **Privately Held**
WEB: www.zup.com
SIC: 3949 5941 Surfboards; water sport equipment; surfing equipment & supplies

Williamsville
Bath County

(G-15351)
NEVTEK
12512 Dry Run Rd (24487-2045)
PHONE..................................540 925-2322
Nevin Davis, *Owner*
EMP: 1
SALES (est): 78.2K **Privately Held**
WEB: www.nevtek.com
SIC: 3821 Incubators, laboratory

Willis
Floyd County

(G-15352)
A B C MANUFACTURING INC
1721 Kyle Weeks Rd Sw (24380-5027)
PHONE..................................540 789-7961
Nanette West, *President*
C Matthew West, *Corp Secy*
EMP: 5
SALES (est): 280K **Privately Held**
SIC: 3299 Ornamental & architectural plaster work

(G-15353)
ADDEM ENTERPRISES INC
1265 Horse Ridge Rd Nw (24380-4373)
PHONE..................................540 789-4412
Danny Phillps, *President*
EMP: 2
SALES (est): 152.4K **Privately Held**
SIC: 2411 Logging

(G-15354)
BLUE RIDGE STAIRS & WDWRK LLC
344 Rivendell Rd Nw (24380-4490)
PHONE..................................540 320-1953
EMP: 2 EST: 2019
SALES (est): 85.2K **Privately Held**
SIC: 2431 Millwork

(G-15355)
BOUNDARY ROCK FRM & VINYRD LLC
414 Riggins Rd Nw (24380-4650)
PHONE..................................540 789-7098
Tony Equale,
Mary Risacher,
EMP: 2
SALES (est): 120K **Privately Held**
SIC: 2084 Wines, brandy & brandy spirits

(G-15356)
BRICO INC
1658 Sawmill Hill Rd Nw (24380-4391)
PHONE..................................540 763-3731
EMP: 3
SALES (est): 69.2K **Privately Held**
WEB: www.brico.com
SIC: 2711 Newspapers

(G-15357)
BUFFALO MOUNTAIN KOMBUCHA LLC
231 Lght Of Fredom Way Sw (24380)
PHONE..................................540 593-2146
Cassie Pierce, *Mng Member*

Scott Pierce, *Mng Member*
EMP: 5
SQ FT: 2,400
SALES (est): 261.2K **Privately Held**
WEB: www.buffalomountainkombucha.com
SIC: 2086 Iced tea & fruit drinks, bottled & canned

(G-15358)
CLEARVIEW INDUSTRIES LLC
2180 Merifield Rd Nw (24380-4214)
PHONE..................................540 312-0899
Leah Shank, *Principal*
EMP: 1
SALES (est): 39.6K **Privately Held**
SIC: 3999 Manufacturing industries

(G-15359)
COSTELLO SCULPTURES
2226 Duncans Chapel Rd Nw (24380-4326)
PHONE..................................540 763-3433
Michael Costello, *Owner*
Tracy Costello, *Co-Owner*
EMP: 2
SALES (est): 38K **Privately Held**
SIC: 3299 Architectural sculptures: gypsum, clay, papier mache, etc.

(G-15360)
DSE OUTDOOR PRODUCT INC
4705 Indian Valley Rd Nw (24380-4173)
PHONE..................................540 789-4800
Dennis Stilwell, *President*
Denise Stilwell, *Vice Pres*
EMP: 5
SALES (est): 30K **Privately Held**
SIC: 3949 Game calls

(G-15361)
INDIAN RIDGE WOODCRAFT INC
635 Shady Grove Rd Nw (24380-4067)
PHONE..................................540 789-4754
Steve Summers, *President*
EMP: 3
SALES (est): 250K **Privately Held**
SIC: 2531 Church furniture

(G-15362)
KC WOOD MFG
470 Rock Church Rd (24380-4847)
PHONE..................................540 789-8300
Bill Cartwright, *Principal*
EMP: 1
SALES (est): 123.9K **Privately Held**
WEB: www.chevywood.com
SIC: 2439 Trusses, wooden roof

(G-15363)
MACS CUSTOM WOODSHOP
2105 Ferney Creek Rd Nw (24380-4630)
PHONE..................................540 789-4201
Mac Traynham, *Owner*
EMP: 2 EST: 1987
SALES (est): 83.6K **Privately Held**
WEB: www.mactraynham.com
SIC: 2434 Wood kitchen cabinets

(G-15364)
OCOTILLAS MNTNSIDE ALPACAS LLC
4388 Buffalo Mtn Rd Sw (24380-4972)
PHONE..................................540 593-2143
Robert W James, *Administration*
EMP: 5 EST: 2012
SALES (est): 393K **Privately Held**
WEB: www.ocotillasmtnalpacas.com
SIC: 2231 Alpacas, mohair: woven

(G-15365)
SUNLIGHT SOFTWARE
892 Deer Valley Rd Nw (24380-4208)
PHONE..................................540 789-7374
Ronald D Schwartz, *Owner*
EMP: 6
SALES (est): 274.6K **Privately Held**
WEB: www.sunlightsoftware.com
SIC: 7372 7371 Prepackaged software; custom computer programming services

(G-15366)
WHISPERING PINE LAWN FURN
974 Duncans Chapel Rd Nw (24380-4531)
PHONE..................................540 789-7361
Floyd Sommers, *Owner*

Floyd A Sommers, *Principal*
EMP: 1
SALES (est): 45.6K **Privately Held**
SIC: 2511 Lawn furniture: wood

Wilsons
Dinwiddie County

(G-15367)
GOODMAN LUMBER CO INC
5001 Grubby Rd (23894-2501)
PHONE..................................804 265-9030
Thomas Goodman Sr, *President*
Lois Goodman, *Corp Secy*
Thomas Goodman Jr, *Exec VP*
Tillett Paul M, *Vice Pres*
EMP: 20 EST: 1950
SQ FT: 5,200
SALES (est): 1.6MM **Privately Held**
SIC: 2421 2611 Sawmills & planing mills, general; pulp mills

Winchester
Frederick County

(G-15368)
A METROMONT COMPANY
219 Stine Ln (22603-5413)
PHONE..................................540 401-0101
EMP: 3
SALES (est): 344K **Privately Held**
WEB: www.metromont.com
SIC: 3272 Concrete products

(G-15369)
ABELL CORPORATION
Also Called: Poly Processing Co
161 Mcghee Rd (22603-4637)
PHONE..................................540 665-3062
Chuck Bias, *District Mgr*
EMP: 30
SALES (corp-wide): 276.8MM **Privately Held**
WEB: www.polyprocessing.com
SIC: 2821 Polyethylene resins
PA: Abell Corporation
    2500 Sterlington Rd
    Monroe LA 71203
    318 343-7565

(G-15370)
ABOUT CHUCK SEIPP
135 Campfield Ln (22602-2307)
PHONE..................................703 517-0670
EMP: 1
SALES (est): 37.5K **Privately Held**
WEB: www.cjseippmusic.com
SIC: 2741 Miscellaneous publishing

(G-15371)
ACTIVE MINERALS INTERNATIONAL
155 Ashland Dr (22603-3289)
PHONE..................................540 771-3865
EMP: 2
SALES (est): 70.6K **Privately Held**
SIC: 3295 Minerals, ground or treated

(G-15372)
ADO INDUSTRIES LLC
140 Theodore Dr (22602-2035)
PHONE..................................540 877-2769
Anthony Overbaugh, *Owner*
EMP: 1
SALES (est): 38K **Privately Held**
SIC: 3999 Christmas trees, artificial

(G-15373)
AIR-CON ASP SLING STRIPING LLC
212 Thwaite Ln (22603-3960)
PHONE..................................540 664-1989
Eric Hoover,
EMP: 1
SALES (est): 134.7K **Privately Held**
SIC: 2951 Asphalt paving mixtures & blocks

▲ = Import ▼=Export
◆ =Import/Export

(G-15374)
ALAN FORNEY JR
Also Called: A & J Welding
143 Armel Rd (22602-4808)
PHONE..................................540 323-1666
Alan Forney Jr, *Owner*
EMP: 1
SALES (est): 120K **Privately Held**
SIC: 3699 Welding machines & equipment, ultrasonic

(G-15375)
ALLIED SYSTEMS CORPORATION (PA)
220 Arbor Ct (22602-4534)
P.O. Box 2600 (22604-1800)
PHONE..................................540 665-9600
Gene L Frogale, *President*
Robert J Frogale, *Vice Pres*
Barbara Hatcher, *Controller*
EMP: 59
SQ FT: 30,000
SALES (est): 23.4MM **Privately Held**
WEB: www.amcasc.com
SIC: 2431 Panel work, wood

(G-15376)
AMAZENGRAVED LLC
130 Obriens Cir (22602-6122)
PHONE..................................540 313-5658
Kathleen Bell,
Jeffrey Bell,
Virginia Deering,
EMP: 2
SALES (est): 167.2K **Privately Held**
WEB: www.amazengraved.com
SIC: 2759 2796 3479 3089 Schedule, ticket & tag printing & engraving; engraving on copper, steel, wood or rubber: printing plates; etching & engraving; engraving of plastic; engraving service

(G-15377)
AMERICAN WOODMARK CORPORATION
561 Shady Elm Rd (22602-2531)
PHONE..................................540 665-9100
Kent B Guichard, *CEO*
EMP: 346 **Publicly Held**
WEB: www.americanwoodmark.com
SIC: 2434 Wood kitchen cabinets
PA: American Woodmark Corporation
561 Shady Elm Rd
Winchester VA 22602
540 665-9100

(G-15378)
AMERICAN WOODMARK CORPORATION (PA)
561 Shady Elm Rd (22602-2531)
P.O. Box 1980 (22604-8090)
PHONE..................................540 665-9100
Vance W Tang, *Ch of Bd*
M Scott Culbreth, *President*
Mark Barnhart, *General Mgr*
Helen Ramey, *District Mgr*
Peggy Timberlake, *Business Mgr*
◆ EMP: 175 **Publicly Held**
WEB: www.americanwoodmark.com
SIC: 2434 Vanities, bathroom: wood

(G-15379)
AMERICAN WOODMARK CORPORATION
561 Shady Elm Rd (22602-2531)
PHONE..................................540 665-9100
Stan Redmon, *Manager*
EMP: 175 **Publicly Held**
WEB: www.americanwoodmark.com
SIC: 2431 2426 Millwork; hardwood dimension & flooring mills
PA: American Woodmark Corporation
561 Shady Elm Rd
Winchester VA 22602
540 665-9100

(G-15380)
ANCHOR
396 Tyson Dr (22603-4619)
PHONE..................................540 327-9391
Kevin Butler, *Principal*
EMP: 4
SALES (est): 365.5K **Privately Held**
SIC: 3271 Concrete block & brick

(G-15381)
ANN GROGG
3641 Apple Pie Ridge Rd (22603-2511)
PHONE..................................540 667-4279
Ann Grogg, *Owner*
EMP: 1
SALES (est): 25.6K **Privately Held**
SIC: 2711 Newspapers, publishing & printing

(G-15382)
ANNANDALE MLLWK ALIED SYSTEMS (PA)
220 Arbor Ct (22602-4534)
PHONE..................................540 665-9600
Robert J Frogale, *President*
Robert Brown, *Exec VP*
Gene L Frogale, *Vice Pres*
Gene Frogale, *Opers Staff*
Jackie Bates, *Buyer*
EMP: 55 EST: 1952
SQ FT: 30,000
SALES (est): 13.3MM **Privately Held**
WEB: www.amcasc.com
SIC: 2431 Millwork

(G-15383)
ARBON EQUIPMENT CORPORATION
130 Imboden Dr Ste 7 (22603-5797)
PHONE..................................540 542-6790
John Salmon, *Manager*
EMP: 5
SALES (corp-wide): 767.8MM **Privately Held**
WEB: www.ritehite.com
SIC: 3537 3449 Loading docks: portable, adjustable & hydraulic; miscellaneous metalwork
HQ: Arbon Equipment Corporation
8900 N Arbon Dr
Milwaukee WI 53223
414 355-2600

(G-15384)
BARRETT INDUSTRIES INC
Also Called: Barrett Machine
399 Mcghee Rd (22603-4632)
P.O. Box 1505 (22604-8005)
PHONE..................................540 678-1625
Michael Barrett, *President*
Kathy Fitzgerald, *Corp Secy*
Stacy Barrett, *Vice Pres*
EMP: 30
SQ FT: 30,000
SALES (est): 6.3MM **Privately Held**
WEB: www.barrettmachine.com
SIC: 3599 Machine shop, jobbing & repair

(G-15385)
BATTAILE DRIVE LLC
151 Windy Hill Ln (22602-4381)
PHONE..................................540 662-4185
Mark D Smith, *Administration*
EMP: 3
SALES (est): 116.9K **Privately Held**
WEB: www.fabritek.com
SIC: 3599 Machine shop, jobbing & repair

(G-15386)
BEARS SPECIALTY WELDING
147 Anderson St (22602-6705)
PHONE..................................540 247-6813
Barie Polhamus, *Principal*
EMP: 1
SALES (est): 47K **Privately Held**
WEB: www.bearsspecialtywelding.com
SIC: 7692 Welding repair

(G-15387)
BLACKBIRD SPIRITS LLC
Also Called: Dr. Stoner's Frederick Co
104 Shockey Cir (22602-6857)
PHONE..................................540 247-9115
Craig C Stoner, *Mng Member*
David Baxter,
EMP: 3
SALES (est): 600K **Privately Held**
WEB: www.drstoners.net
SIC: 2085 Vodka (alcoholic beverage)

(G-15388)
BLUE MONKEY LLC
3500 Cedar Creek Grade (22602-2745)
PHONE..................................540 664-1297

Matthew Hahn,
EMP: 1 EST: 2012
SALES (est): 105K **Privately Held**
SIC: 3944 5945 Automobiles & trucks, toy; toys & games

(G-15389)
BLUE RIDGE INDUSTRIES INC
266 Arbor Ct (22602-4534)
P.O. Box 1847 (22604-8347)
PHONE..................................540 662-3900
James Possehl, *President*
Mary S Sarle, *President*
John P Good Jr, *Corp Secy*
Regina Zielke, *Vice Pres*
Kevin Brill, *Maint Spvr*
◆ EMP: 114
SQ FT: 75,000
SALES (est): 29.7MM **Privately Held**
WEB: www.blueridgeind.com
SIC: 3089 Injection molding of plastics

(G-15390)
BLUE RIDGE MECHANICAL
831 Front Royal Pike (22602-4421)
PHONE..................................540 662-3148
William Lucas, *Owner*
EMP: 6
SALES (est): 220K **Privately Held**
SIC: 7692 Welding repair

(G-15391)
BREEZE RIDGE ENTERPRISES
939 Frog Hollow Rd (22603-2539)
P.O. Box 4097 (22604-4097)
PHONE..................................703 728-4606
James R Owens Sr, *Owner*
EMP: 1
SALES (est): 250K **Privately Held**
SIC: 2441 Nailed wood boxes & shook

(G-15392)
BRIAN FOX DBA FORTIFIED
204 Woodrow Rd (22602-7601)
PHONE..................................540 535-1195
Brian Fox, *Principal*
EMP: 2
SALES (est): 123.2K **Privately Held**
SIC: 7372 Prepackaged software

(G-15393)
BRIEDE FAMILY VINEYARDS LLC
450 Green Spring Rd (22603-2742)
PHONE..................................540 667-2981
Loretta Briede, *Mng Member*
Paul Briede,
EMP: 2 EST: 2013
SALES (est): 61.3K **Privately Held**
WEB: www.thebriedefamilyvineyards.com
SIC: 2084 Wines

(G-15394)
BRYANS TOOLS LLC
178 Thwaite Ln (22603-3958)
PHONE..................................540 667-5675
Bryan Adams, *Principal*
EMP: 2
SALES (est): 98.6K **Privately Held**
SIC: 3599 Industrial machinery

(G-15395)
BUCKSKIN JHNSON BEEF JERKY LLC
210 Burnt Church Rd (22603-4109)
PHONE..................................540 303-0324
EMP: 2
SALES (est): 68.6K **Privately Held**
SIC: 2013 Snack sticks, including jerky: from purchased meat

(G-15396)
BUDS BLUERIDGE
116 Settlers Cir (22602-6920)
PHONE..................................540 323-7030
Ivan Benavides, *Principal*
EMP: 2
SALES (est): 71K **Privately Held**
SIC: 2711 Commercial printing & newspaper publishing combined

(G-15397)
BUILDERS FIRSTSOURCE INC
296 Arbor Ct (22602-4534)
P.O. Box 888 (22604-0888)
PHONE..................................540 665-0078
Gary Judd, *General Mgr*
Steve Sipe, *General Mgr*
Stephen Sipe, *Branch Mgr*
EMP: 70 **Publicly Held**
WEB: www.bldr.com
SIC: 2421 5211 2431 Building & structural materials, wood; lumber & other building materials; silo staves, wood
PA: Builders Firstsource, Inc.
2001 Bryan St Ste 1600
Dallas TX 75201
214 880-3500

(G-15398)
BURGHOLZER MANUFACTURING LC
154 Laurelwood Dr (22602-4435)
PHONE..................................540 667-8612
James Burgholzer, *Principal*
EMP: 2
SALES (est): 154.1K **Privately Held**
SIC: 3999 Manufacturing industries

(G-15399)
CAT TAIL RUN HAND BOOKBINDING
2160 Cedar Grove Rd (22603-2617)
PHONE..................................540 662-2683
Jill Deiss, *Owner*
EMP: 5
SALES (est): 109.8K **Privately Held**
WEB: www.cattailrun.com
SIC: 2789 Binding only: books, pamphlets, magazines, etc.

(G-15400)
CHARLES JAMES WINERY & VINYRD
4063 Middle Rd (22602-2594)
PHONE..................................540 931-4386
James Bogaty, *Administration*
EMP: 2
SALES (est): 96K **Privately Held**
WEB: www.jamescharleswine.com
SIC: 2084 Wines

(G-15401)
CHRISTIAN CREATIONS INC
425 Eckard Cir (22602-6166)
PHONE..................................540 722-2718
Jone Sheffield, *Owner*
EMP: 1
SALES (est): 69.9K **Privately Held**
SIC: 2399 Horse & pet accessories, textile

(G-15402)
CIVES CORPORATION
210 Cives Ln (22603-5405)
P.O. Box 2778 (22604-1978)
PHONE..................................540 667-3480
Mike Keenan, *Plant Mgr*
Johnathan Goode, *QC Dir*
Robert Matthews, *Persnl Mgr*
Betty Gray, *Human Resources*
William Dehaven, *Office Mgr*
EMP: 150 **Privately Held**
WEB: www.civessteel.com
SIC: 3441 Building components, structural steel
PA: Cives Corporation
3700 Mansell Rd Ste 500
Alpharetta GA 30022
770 993-4424

(G-15403)
CM WELDING LLC
523 Bluebird Trl (22602-3579)
PHONE..................................540 539-4723
John McInturff, *Principal*
EMP: 1
SALES (est): 28.2K **Privately Held**
SIC: 7692 Welding repair

(G-15404)
COBEHN INC
Also Called: Cobehn System
640 Airport Rd (22602-4504)
PHONE..................................540 665-0707
George L Henzel, *President*
Victoria L Henzel, *Corp Secy*

EMP: 4
SQ FT: 5,500
SALES (est): 718.1K **Privately Held**
WEB: www.cobehninc.com
SIC: 2911 3699 Solvents; electrical equipment & supplies

(G-15405)
CORRUGATED CONTAINER CORP
100 Development Ln (22602-2572)
PHONE..................................540 869-5353
David D Higginbotham, *President*
Gerald J Higginbotham, *Vice Pres*
John H Higginbotham, *Vice Pres*
Ronald A Higginbotham, *Vice Pres*
Paul R Higginbotham, *Treasurer*
EMP: 36
SALES (est): 9.7MM **Privately Held**
SIC: 2653 Boxes, corrugated: made from purchased materials

(G-15406)
CREATIVE PRINT SOLUTIONS
408 Misty Meadow Dr (22603-2633)
PHONE..................................540 247-9910
EMP: 2
SALES (est): 83.9K **Privately Held**
SIC: 2752 Commercial printing, lithographic

(G-15407)
CREATIVE URETHANES INC
250 Independence Rd (22602-4501)
PHONE..................................540 542-6676
Richard V Heitfield, *President*
Thomas G Heitfield, *Corp Secy*
John E Tiedemann, *Exec VP*
Denise Ohnysty, *Vice Pres*
EMP: 30
SQ FT: 33,000
SALES (est): 4.2MM **Privately Held**
WEB: www.creativeurethanes.com
SIC: 3949 3089 3442 Skates & parts, roller; molding primary plastic; moldings & trim, except automobile: metal

(G-15408)
CROWN CORK & SEAL USA INC
1461 Martinsburg Pike (22603-4611)
PHONE..................................540 662-2591
Frank Babic, *Mfg Staff*
Kevin Price, *QC Mgr*
EMP: 296
SALES (corp-wide): 11.6B **Publicly Held**
WEB: www.crowncork.com
SIC: 3411 3354 Metal cans; aluminum extruded products
HQ: Crown Cork & Seal Usa, Inc.
    770 Township Line Rd # 100
    Yardley PA 19067
    215 698-5100

(G-15409)
DATALUX CORPORATION (PA)
155 Aviation Dr (22602-4589)
PHONE..................................540 662-1500
Robert H Twyford Jr, *Ch of Bd*
David Clark, *Plant Mgr*
Harold Price, *Engineer*
Kevin Wang, *Engineer*
Kenneth Lose, *Accountant*
▲ EMP: 52 EST: 1960
SQ FT: 17,000
SALES (est): 5.4MM **Privately Held**
WEB: www.datalux.com
SIC: 3575 3571 3577 3643 Cathode ray tube (CRT), computer terminal; electronic computers; computer peripheral equipment; current-carrying wiring devices

(G-15410)
DIXON POWHATAN
325 Arbor Ct (22602-4537)
PHONE..................................410 810-7585
EMP: 2 EST: 2017
SALES (est): 112.6K **Privately Held**
SIC: 3429 Clamps, couplings, nozzles & other metal hose fittings

(G-15411)
DIXON VALVE & COUPLING CO LLC
325 Arbor Ct (22602-4537)
PHONE..................................540 535-2181
Bob Grace, *Branch Mgr*

EMP: 3
SALES (corp-wide): 236.3MM **Privately Held**
WEB: www.dixonvalve.com
SIC: 3429 Manufactured hardware (general)
HQ: Dixon Valve & Coupling Company, Llc
    1 Dixon Dr
    Chestertown MD 21620

(G-15412)
DRAGOON TECHNOLOGIES INC
240 Airport Rd 1 (22602-4569)
PHONE..................................937 439-9223
Robert C Appenzeller Jr, *Branch Mgr*
EMP: 2
SALES (corp-wide): 1.8MM **Privately Held**
WEB: www.dragoonitcn.com
SIC: 3812 Radar systems & equipment
PA: Dragoon Technologies, Inc.
    900 Senate Dr
    Dayton OH 45459
    937 439-9223

(G-15413)
DYNAMIC GRAPHIC FINISHING INC
160 Industrial Dr (22602-2584)
PHONE..................................540 869-0500
Tom Parish, *Manager*
EMP: 7
SALES (corp-wide): 147.7MM **Privately Held**
WEB: www.dynamicgraphic.com
SIC: 2759 Commercial printing
HQ: Dynamic Graphic Finishing, Inc.
    945 Horsham Rd
    Horsham PA 19044
    215 441-8880

(G-15414)
EVOLVE CUSTOM LLC
Also Called: Createk
200 Lenoir Dr Ste B (22603-4660)
PHONE..................................703 570-5700
Gregory Fritz,
EMP: 1
SALES (est): 39.6K
SALES (corp-wide): 1.6MM **Privately Held**
WEB: www.createkinc.com
SIC: 3999 Manufacturing industries
HQ: Evolve Manufacturing Llc
    200 Lenoir Dr Ste B
    Winchester VA 22603
    703 570-5700

(G-15415)
EVOLVE MANUFACTURING LLC (HQ)
200 Lenoir Dr Ste B (22603-4660)
PHONE..................................703 570-5700
Gregory Fritz,
EMP: 1
SALES (est): 1.8MM
SALES (corp-wide): 1.6MM **Privately Held**
WEB: www.evolvemanufacturing.com
SIC: 3999 Artificial trees & flowers
PA: Evolve Holdings, Llc
    200 Lenoir Dr Ste B
    Winchester VA 22603
    703 570-5700

(G-15416)
EVOLVE PLAY LLC
200 Lenoir Dr Ste B (22603-4660)
PHONE..................................703 570-5700
Gregory Fritz,
EMP: 1
SALES (est): 65.4K
SALES (corp-wide): 1.6MM **Privately Held**
WEB: www.evolveplay.net
SIC: 3949 Playground equipment
HQ: Evolve Manufacturing Llc
    200 Lenoir Dr Ste B
    Winchester VA 22603
    703 570-5700

(G-15417)
EXTREME STEEL INC
480 Shady Elm Rd (22602-2523)
PHONE..................................540 868-9150
Kevin Rene Rodney, *President*

Melinda Rodney, *Vice Pres*
Democrat Mills, *Opers Staff*
Derek Stiefel, *Manager*
Elaine Kelly, *Admin Asst*
EMP: 1
SALES (est): 360.2K **Privately Held**
WEB: www.extremesteelinc.com
SIC: 3441 1791 3446 Fabricated structural metal; structural steel erection; architectural metalwork

(G-15418)
FURNITURE ART
306 Lenoir Dr (22603-4608)
PHONE..................................540 667-2533
Richard Oram, *Co-Owner*
EMP: 2
SALES (est): 87.9K **Privately Held**
SIC: 2511 Wood household furniture

(G-15419)
GEDORAN AMERICA INC
117 Oak Ridge Ln (22602-7813)
PHONE..................................540 723-6628
▲ EMP: 1
SALES (est): 90K **Privately Held**
SIC: 2731 Publisher

(G-15420)
GENERAL ELECTRIC COMPANY
125 Apple Valley Rd (22602-2427)
PHONE..................................540 667-5990
Wilbert Whitfield, *Opers-Prdtn-Mfg*
EMP: 500
SALES (corp-wide): 95.2B **Publicly Held**
WEB: www.ge.com
SIC: 3641 Electric lamps
PA: General Electric Company
    5 Necco St
    Boston MA 02210
    617 443-3000

(G-15421)
GREEN BAY PACKAGING INC
Coated Products Winchester Div
285 Park Center Dr (22603-5755)
P.O. Box 3568 (22604-2575)
PHONE..................................540 678-2600
Thomas J Schibly, *Principal*
EMP: 26
SALES (corp-wide): 1.7B **Privately Held**
WEB: www.gbpcoated.com
SIC: 2672 2671 Coated & laminated paper; packaging paper & plastics film, coated & laminated
PA: Green Bay Packaging Inc.
    1700 N Webster Ave
    Green Bay WI 54302
    920 433-5111

(G-15422)
GULFSTREAM AEROSPACE CORP
465 Glendobbin Rd (22603-3335)
PHONE..................................540 722-0347
EMP: 3
SALES (corp-wide): 39.3B **Publicly Held**
WEB: www.gulfstream.com
SIC: 3721 Aircraft
HQ: Gulfstream Aerospace Corporation
    500 Gulfstream Rd
    Savannah GA 31408

(G-15423)
HERSHEY COMPANY
300 Park Center Dr (22603-5785)
P.O. Box 2080 (22604-1280)
PHONE..................................540 722-9830
Mark Cahill, *Principal*
EMP: 117
SALES (corp-wide): 7.9B **Publicly Held**
WEB: www.thehersheycompany.com
SIC: 2098 Macaroni products (e.g. alphabets, rings & shells), dry
PA: Hershey Company
    19 E Chocolate Ave
    Hershey PA 17033
    717 534-4200

(G-15424)
HOLTZMAN EXPRESS
1511 Martinsburg Pike (22603-5416)
PHONE..................................305 347-4000
Ella Holtzman, *Principal*
EMP: 1

SALES (est): 84.8K **Privately Held**
WEB: www.alltravelnetwork.com
SIC: 2741 Miscellaneous publishing

(G-15425)
HOT STAMP SUPPLY COMPANY
141 Marcel Dr 2 (22602-4844)
PHONE..................................540 868-7500
J Mitchell Orndorff, *President*
Dee Dee Shiley, *Finance*
Pam Orndorff, *Shareholder*
▼ EMP: 2
SQ FT: 3,200
SALES (est): 831.7K **Privately Held**
WEB: www.hotstampsupply.com
SIC: 3497 Foil, laminated to paper or other materials

(G-15426)
HP HOOD LLC
160 Hood Way (22602-5321)
PHONE..................................540 869-0045
Scott Pugh, *Controller*
Roland Creswell, *Manager*
Pam Smith, *Planning*
Jeff Parrish, *Maintence Staff*
EMP: 321
SALES (corp-wide): 2.5B **Privately Held**
WEB: www.hood.com
SIC: 2026 Fluid milk
PA: Hp Hood Llc
    6 Kimball Ln Ste 400
    Lynnfield MA 01940
    617 887-8441

(G-15427)
IBS
326 Mcghee Rd (22603-4633)
PHONE..................................540 662-0882
Mike Terpak, *Principal*
EMP: 2
SALES (est): 273.3K **Privately Held**
SIC: 3086 Plastics foam products

(G-15428)
INDENHOOFFEN PRODUCTIONS LLC
173 Echo Ln (22603-3900)
PHONE..................................540 327-0898
Talbert Dehaven,
EMP: 6
SQ FT: 10,000
SALES (est): 331.4K **Privately Held**
SIC: 3955 Print cartridges for laser & other computer printers

(G-15429)
INTERSTATE RESCUE LLC
290 Airport Rd Ste 2 (22602-4705)
PHONE..................................571 283-4206
Brian Gallamore, *Mng Member*
EMP: 11
SALES (est): 3.1MM **Privately Held**
WEB: www.interstaterescue.com
SIC: 3569 Firefighting apparatus & related equipment

(G-15430)
K C I KONECRANES INC
230 Airport Rd 12 (22602-4569)
PHONE..................................540 545-8412
Joe Henry, *Principal*
EMP: 9
SALES (est): 1MM **Privately Held**
WEB: www.konecranes.com
SIC: 3536 Hoists, cranes & monorails

(G-15431)
K T DESIGN & PROTOTYPE INC
170 Kenny Ln I (22602-4604)
PHONE..................................540 678-0215
Kenneth Kovach, *President*
Terri Kovach, *Corp Secy*
EMP: 2
SALES (est): 736.6K **Privately Held**
SIC: 3599 Machine shop, jobbing & repair

(G-15432)
KACZENSKIS WELDING SVCS LLC
236 Mason St (22602-6718)
PHONE..................................540 431-8126
Christian Kaczenski, *Principal*
EMP: 1

▲ = Import ▼=Export
◆ =Import/Export

SALES (est): 25K **Privately Held**
SIC: 7692 Welding repair

(G-15433)
KINGSDOWN INCORPORATED
380 W Brooke Rd (22603-5792)
PHONE..................................540 667-0399
Greg Poole, *Principal*
EMP: 100
SALES (corp-wide): 12.2MM **Privately Held**
WEB: www.kingsdown.com
SIC: 2515 Mattresses, innerspring or box spring; box springs, assembled
HQ: Kingsdown, Incorporated
126 W Holt St
Mebane NC 27302
919 563-3531

(G-15434)
KINGSPAN INSULATION LLC
200 Kingspan Way (22603-4664)
PHONE..................................800 336-2240
Jamey Walters, *Branch Mgr*
EMP: 48 **Privately Held**
WEB: www.kingspanplanttours.us
SIC: 2493 Insulation & roofing material, reconstituted wood
HQ: Kingspan Insulation Llc
2100 Riveredge Pkwy # 175
Atlanta GA 30328
678 589-7331

(G-15435)
KONECRANES INC
230 Airport Rd 12 (22602-4569)
PHONE..................................540 545-8412
Kim Jenkins, *Manager*
EMP: 10
SALES (corp-wide): 3.6B **Privately Held**
WEB: www.konecranes.com
SIC: 3536 Hoists, cranes & monorails
HQ: Konecranes, Inc.
4401 Gateway Blvd
Springfield OH 45502

(G-15436)
KRAFT HEINZ FOODS COMPANY
291 Park Center Dr (22603-5755)
PHONE..................................540 545-7563
Gary Genasimowicz, *Branch Mgr*
EMP: 3
SALES (corp-wide): 24.9B **Publicly Held**
WEB: www.kraftheinzcompany.com
SIC: 2033 Canned fruits & specialties
HQ: Kraft Heinz Foods Company
1 Ppg Pl Ste 3400
Pittsburgh PA 15222
412 456-5700

(G-15437)
KRAFT HEINZ FOODS COMPANY
Also Called: Kraft Foods
220 Park Center Dr (22603-5754)
PHONE..................................540 678-0442
Kevin Scott, *Warehouse Mgr*
Gary Genasimowicz, *Branch Mgr*
EMP: 300
SALES (corp-wide): 24.9B **Publicly Held**
WEB: www.kraftheinzcompany.com
SIC: 2086 2011 2099 Bottled & canned soft drinks; meat packing plants; food preparations
HQ: Kraft Heinz Foods Company
1 Ppg Pl Ste 3400
Pittsburgh PA 15222
412 456-5700

(G-15438)
LAWRENCE FABRICATIONS INC
980 Baker Ln (22603-5724)
PHONE..................................540 667-1141
Edward Lawrence, *President*
EMP: 4
SALES (est): 717.8K **Privately Held**
SIC: 3441 Fabricated structural metal

(G-15439)
LAYMAN ENTERPRISES INC
Also Called: Trophy World
340 Spring Valley Dr (22603-2948)
P.O. Box 830 (22604-0830)
PHONE..................................540 662-7142
Elizabeth Layman, *President*
Libby Layman, *Principal*
EMP: 9

SALES (est): 874.2K **Privately Held**
SIC: 3993 Signs & advertising specialties

(G-15440)
LEWIN ASPHALT INC
300 Ebert Rd (22603-4702)
PHONE..................................540 550-9478
Andrew Lewin, *President*
EMP: 3 **EST:** 2015
SALES (est): 184.9K **Privately Held**
WEB: www.lewinasphalt.com
SIC: 3531 Asphalt plant, including gravel-mix type

(G-15441)
M&H PLASTICS INC
485 Brooke Rd (22603-5764)
PHONE..................................540 504-0030
Kurt Nyberg, *CEO*
Edward J Adams Jr, *CFO*
◆ **EMP:** 115
SALES (est): 47.1MM **Publicly Held**
WEB: www.mhplastics.com
SIC: 3085 3089 Plastics bottles; plastic containers, except foam
HQ: Maynard & Harris Plastics
London Road
Beccles NR34
150 271-5518

(G-15442)
MAPLE HILL EMBROIDERY
1833 Chestnut Grove Rd (22603-2328)
PHONE..................................540 336-1967
Justin Dehaven, *Owner*
EMP: 2
SALES (est): 15K **Privately Held**
SIC: 2395 Embroidery products, except schiffli machine

(G-15443)
MASONITE INTERNATIONAL CORP
130 W Brooke Rd (22603-5700)
PHONE..................................540 665-3083
Frederick Lynch, *Branch Mgr*
EMP: 6
SALES (corp-wide): 2.1B **Publicly Held**
WEB: www.masonite.com
SIC: 2431 Doors, wood
PA: Masonite International Corporation
1242 E 5th Ave
Tampa FL 33605
800 895-2723

(G-15444)
MC FARLANDS MILL INC
587 Round Hill Rd (22602-2233)
PHONE..................................540 667-2272
Robert Mc Farland, *President*
Stephanie See, *Corp Secy*
Robert M McFarland, *Manager*
EMP: 16
SQ FT: 18,000
SALES (est): 1MM **Privately Held**
WEB: www.mcfarlandsmill.com
SIC: 2448 5211 Pallets, wood; millwork & lumber

(G-15445)
MCELROY METAL MILL INC
325 Mcghee Rd (22603-4632)
P.O. Box 3503 (22604-2543)
PHONE..................................540 667-2500
Katie Apodaca, *Owner*
EMP: 2
SALES (corp-wide): 362MM **Privately Held**
WEB: www.mcelroymetal.com
SIC: 3448 Prefabricated metal components
PA: Mcelroy Metal Mill, Inc.
1500 Hamilton Rd
Bossier City LA 71111
318 747-8000

(G-15446)
MEDIPAK
270 Tyson Dr 2 (22603-4654)
PHONE..................................540 667-0233
EMP: 1
SALES (est): 117.1K **Privately Held**
WEB: www.medipak.us
SIC: 3841 Surgical & medical instruments

(G-15447)
MELNOR INC
109 Tyson Dr (22603-4658)
P.O. Box 2840 (22604-2040)
PHONE..................................540 722-5600
Juergen Nies, *President*
Richard Boyle, *Vice Pres*
Rachel Naylor, *Human Resources*
George Lai, *Sales Staff*
Eddie Price, *Business Anlyst*
◆ **EMP:** 46
SQ FT: 157,000
SALES (est): 9.5MM **Privately Held**
WEB: www.melnor.com
SIC: 3524 5083 Lawn & garden equipment; lawn & garden machinery & equipment

(G-15448)
MENASHA PACKAGING COMPANY LLC
310 W Brooke Rd (22603-5792)
PHONE..................................540 546-1110
Norberto Bernabeu, *Branch Mgr*
EMP: 150
SALES (corp-wide): 1.6B **Privately Held**
WEB: www.menasha.com
SIC: 2653 Boxes, corrugated: made from purchased materials
HQ: Menasha Packaging Company, Llc
1645 Bergstrom Rd
Neenah WI 54956
920 751-1000

(G-15449)
MILLER MACHINE & TOOL COMPANY
201 Precision Dr (22603-4623)
P.O. Box 2704 (22604-1904)
PHONE..................................540 662-6512
Carl Leach, *President*
Carl Corbin II, *Vice Pres*
EMP: 20
SQ FT: 13,500
SALES (est): 1.6MM **Privately Held**
WEB: www.millermachinetool.com
SIC: 3599 7699 Machine shop, jobbing & repair; farm machinery repair

(G-15450)
MILLER MILLING COMPANY LLC
302 Park Center Dr (22603-5785)
PHONE..................................540 678-0197
Matt Sirbaugh, *Prdtn Mgr*
Cheryl Burcham, *Facilities Mgr*
Hollis South, *Production*
Dave Renner, *Engineer*
Steve Adams, *Manager*
EMP: 39 **Privately Held**
WEB: www.millermilling.com
SIC: 2041 Durum flour
HQ: Miller Milling Company, Llc
7808 Creekridge Cir # 100
Minneapolis MN 55439
952 826-6331

(G-15451)
MONOFLO INTERNATIONAL INC (PA)
882 Baker Ln (22603-5722)
P.O. Box 2797 (22604-1997)
PHONE..................................540 665-1691
Henning Rader, *President*
Teressa Brewer, *Vice Pres*
John Johnson, *Vice Pres*
Jessica Pike, *Facilities Mgr*
Stuart Hutchins, *Purch Agent*
◆ **EMP:** 170
SQ FT: 175,000
SALES (est): 90MM **Privately Held**
WEB: www.miworldwide.com
SIC: 3089 3523 Plastic containers, except foam; plastic hardware & building products; barn, silo, poultry, dairy & livestock machinery

(G-15452)
MORE THAN A SIGN
1724 Martinsburg Pike (22603-4706)
PHONE..................................540 514-3311
Cynthia Richards, *Principal*
EMP: 2
SALES (est): 90.4K **Privately Held**
SIC: 3993 Signs & advertising specialties

(G-15453)
MY THREE SONS INC
Also Called: MTS Equipment Co
580 Airport Rd (22602-4503)
PHONE..................................540 662-5927
Bill Wolfensberger, *President*
William E Wolfensberger, *President*
Diane Wolfensberger, *Vice Pres*
Harry W Wolfensberger, *Treasurer*
Matthew Wolfensberger, *Treasurer*
EMP: 9
SQ FT: 5,000
SALES (est): 2.2MM **Privately Held**
WEB: www.mtsequipment.com
SIC: 3589 7699 5046 Commercial cooking & foodwarming equipment; restaurant equipment repair; scales, except laboratory

(G-15454)
NAILS CABINET SHOP INC
230 Flowers Ln (22603-2202)
PHONE..................................540 888-3268
Gary L Nail, *President*
Polly S Nail, *Corp Secy*
EMP: 2 **EST:** 1968
SALES (est): 277.8K **Privately Held**
SIC: 2434 5031 Wood kitchen cabinets; kitchen cabinets

(G-15455)
NEW IMAGE GRAPHICS INC
172 Imboden Dr Ste 19 (22603-5799)
PHONE..................................540 678-0900
Ivan Delegan, *President*
Dana Peacock, *Admin Sec*
EMP: 4
SQ FT: 15,000
SALES (est): 250K **Privately Held**
SIC: 2752 Commercial printing, offset

(G-15456)
NUFOCUS SOFTWARE LLC
115 Godwin Ct (22602-6787)
PHONE..................................540 722-0282
Christopher Mauck, *Administration*
EMP: 2 **EST:** 2012
SALES (est): 99.4K **Privately Held**
WEB: www.nufocussolutions.com
SIC: 7372 Prepackaged software

(G-15457)
OLDCASTLE APG NORTHEAST INC
1515 Tyson Dr (22603)
PHONE..................................540 667-4600
Sandy Hayden, *Manager*
EMP: 45
SALES (corp-wide): 30.6B **Privately Held**
WEB: www.oldcastlemasonry.com
SIC: 3271 3272 Blocks, concrete or cinder: standard; concrete products
HQ: Oldcastle Apg Northeast, Inc.
13555 Wellington Cntr Cir
Gainesville VA 20155
703 365-7070

(G-15458)
PACKAGING CORPORATION AMERICA
Also Called: PCA/Supply Services 302e
205 Mcghee Rd (22603-4630)
PHONE..................................540 662-5680
Frances Russel, *Branch Mgr*
EMP: 5 **Publicly Held**
WEB: www.packagingcorp.com
SIC: 2653 Boxes, corrugated: made from purchased materials
PA: Packaging Corporation Of America
1 N Field Ct
Lake Forest IL 60045
847 482-3000

(G-15459)
PENNSYLVANIA DRILLING COMPANY
321 Arbor Ct (22602-4537)
PHONE..................................540 665-5207
Nicole Robbins, *Branch Mgr*
EMP: 1
SALES (corp-wide): 14.1MM **Privately Held**
WEB: www.pennsylvaniadrillingco.com
SIC: 3541 Drilling & boring machines

PA: Pennsylvania Drilling Company
281 Route 30
Imperial PA 15126
412 771-2110

(G-15460)
PINNACLE CONTROL SYSTEMS INC
147 Mountain View Ct (22603-2365)
PHONE..................540 888-4200
Brent Miller, *President*
EMP: 3
SALES (est): 265.8K **Privately Held**
SIC: 3625 Electric controls & control accessories, industrial

(G-15461)
PLASTIC SOLUTIONS INCORPORATED
240 Mcghee Rd (22603-4629)
PHONE..................540 722-4694
Tim Martin, *President*
EMP: 3
SQ FT: 22,000
SALES (est): 329.1K **Privately Held**
WEB: www.plastic-solution.com
SIC: 3089 Fittings for pipe, plastic
PA: Eastern Supply, Inc.
240 Mcghee Rd
Winchester VA 22603

(G-15462)
QG LLC
Also Called: Worldcolor Winchester
160 Century Ln (22603-4601)
PHONE..................540 722-6000
Tony Gavello, *Branch Mgr*
EMP: 155
SALES (corp-wide): 3.9B **Publicly Held**
WEB: www.quad.com
SIC: 2759 2752 Commercial printing; commercial printing, lithographic
HQ: Qg, Llc
N61w23044 Harrys Way
Sussex WI 53089

(G-15463)
QG PRINTING II CORP
160 Century Ln (22603-4601)
PHONE..................540 722-6000
EMP: 519
SALES (corp-wide): 3.9B **Publicly Held**
WEB: www.quad.com
SIC: 2752 Commercial printing, offset
HQ: Qg Printing II Llc
N61w23044 Harrys Way
Sussex WI 53089

(G-15464)
QUAKER HOUGHTON PA INC
156 Doe Trl (22602-1515)
PHONE..................540 877-3631
J Houghton, *Principal*
EMP: 4
SALES (corp-wide): 1.1B **Publicly Held**
WEB: www.houghtonintl.com
SIC: 2869 Hydraulic fluids, synthetic base
HQ: Quaker Houghton Pa, Inc.
901 E Hector St
Conshohocken PA 19428
888 459-9844

(G-15465)
RIDGERUNNER CONTAINER LLC
220 Imboden Dr C (22603-5793)
P.O. Box 3183 (22604-2383)
PHONE..................540 662-2005
Steven Waller, *General Mgr*
Ross Hewitt II, *Mng Member*
EMP: 13
SALES (est): 379.1K **Privately Held**
WEB: www.rcswaste.com
SIC: 2631 Container board

(G-15466)
RIVIANA FOODS INC
Also Called: Winchester Pasta
300 Park Center Dr (22603-5785)
PHONE..................540 722-9830
Mark Cahill, *Manager*
EMP: 100 **Privately Held**
WEB: www.riviana.com
SIC: 2099 Food preparations

HQ: Riviana Foods Inc.
2777 Allen Pkwy Fl 15
Houston TX 77019
713 529-3251

(G-15467)
ROBERT GROGG
3641 Apple Pie Ridge Rd (22603-2511)
PHONE..................540 667-4279
Robert Grogg, *Owner*
EMP: 1
SALES (est): 15K **Privately Held**
SIC: 2711 Newspapers

(G-15468)
ROBERT LUMMUS
Also Called: Dog Trotter K-9 Equipment
934 Baker Ln Ste D (22603-5724)
PHONE..................540 313-4393
Robbert Lummus, *Principal*
EMP: 3
SALES (est): 15.7K **Privately Held**
WEB: www.dogtrotter.net
SIC: 3949 Treadmills

(G-15469)
ROBS WELDING
927 Greenwood Rd (22602-6576)
PHONE..................540 722-4151
Robert J Shields, *Principal*
EMP: 1
SALES (est): 56.7K **Privately Held**
SIC: 7692 Welding repair

(G-15470)
RPC SUPERFOS US INC
411 Brooke Rd (22603-5764)
PHONE..................540 504-7176
Terry Sullivan, *President*
Benny Nielsen, *Exec VP*
Johan Bratt, *Site Mgr*
Sam Debarr, *Opers Staff*
Lars H Tindbaek, *CFO*
▲ EMP: 30
SALES (est): 287.2K **Privately Held**
WEB: www.berryglobal.com
SIC: 2656 Sanitary food containers

(G-15471)
RUBBERMAID COMMERCIAL PDTS LLC
125 Apple Valley Rd (22602-2406)
PHONE..................540 542-8195
Tammy Rhinehardt, *Production*
EMP: 1 EST: 2016
SALES (est): 112.8K **Privately Held**
SIC: 3089 2673 Plastic containers, except foam; bags: plastic, laminated & coated

(G-15472)
RUGGER INDUSTRIES LLC
104 Norfolk Ct (22602-7042)
PHONE..................540 450-7281
Jason Shipe, *Principal*
EMP: 2
SALES (est): 110.9K **Privately Held**
WEB: www.ruggerindustries.com
SIC: 3999 Manufacturing industries

(G-15473)
RUSTY BEAR WOODWORKS LLC
827 Fall Run Ln (22602-3468)
PHONE..................540 327-6579
James Yon, *Principal*
EMP: 1
SALES (est): 59.5K **Privately Held**
WEB: www.rustybearwoodworksllc.com
SIC: 2431 Millwork

(G-15474)
SCHMIDT & BENDER INCORPORATED
204 Mcghee Rd (22603-4629)
PHONE..................770 493-9305
Karlheinz Gerlach, *President*
EMP: 5
SALES (est): 3MM
SALES (corp-wide): 385.1K **Privately Held**
WEB: www.schmidtbender.com
SIC: 3827 Gun sights, optical

PA: Schmidt U. Bender Gmbh
Am GroBacker 42
Biebertal
640 981-1513

(G-15475)
SHADOWS RIDGE INC
113 W Brooke Rd (22603-5422)
PHONE..................540 722-0310
Janice Conrad, *President*
Bob Conrad, *Vice Pres*
▲ EMP: 7
SQ FT: 7,000
SALES (est): 1.5MM **Privately Held**
WEB: www.shadowsridge.com
SIC: 3089 7539 Molding primary plastic; machine shop, automotive

(G-15476)
SHELTER2HOME INC
212 Fort Collier Rd # 2 (22603-5738)
PHONE..................540 327-4426
Andrea Stevens, *President*
EMP: 6
SALES (est): 532.4K **Privately Held**
SIC: 2421 Building & structural materials, wood

(G-15477)
SHENANDOAH PRIMITIVES LLC
158 Bryarly Rd (22603-4100)
PHONE..................540 662-4727
Tommy Brill, *Principal*
EMP: 2 EST: 2011
SALES (est): 89.3K **Privately Held**
WEB: www.shenandoahprimitives.com
SIC: 3999 Framed artwork

(G-15478)
SHOCKEY BROS INC (HQ)
Also Called: Shockey Precast Group
219 Stine Ln (22603-5413)
PHONE..................540 401-0101
Rick Pennell, *President*
Tom McCabe, *Vice Pres*
Marshall Sorenson, *Vice Pres*
Eric Humphries, *Project Mgr*
James Lyons, *Project Mgr*
EMP: 200 EST: 1959
SQ FT: 121,326
SALES: 75K
SALES (corp-wide): 130.3MM **Privately Held**
WEB: www.shockeyprecast.com
SIC: 3272 Concrete stuctural support & building material
PA: Metromont Corporation
2802 White Horse Rd
Greenville SC 29611
804 222-6770

(G-15479)
SMALL FOX PRESS
1108 Purcell Ln (22603-4226)
PHONE..................540 877-4054
Lia Mendez, *Principal*
EMP: 1 EST: 2016
SALES (est): 37.5K **Privately Held**
SIC: 2741 Miscellaneous publishing

(G-15480)
SOUTHEASTERN CONTAINER INC
265 W Brooke Rd (22603-5741)
P.O. Box 1880 (22604-8380)
PHONE..................540 722-2600
Tommy Ledford, *Opers Mgr*
Ralph Henderson, *Manager*
EMP: 200
SALES (corp-wide): 319.9MM **Privately Held**
WEB: www.secontainer.com
SIC: 3085 2656 Plastics bottles; sanitary food containers
PA: Southeastern Container, Inc.
1250 Sand Hill Rd
Enka NC 28728
828 350-7200

(G-15481)
SOUTHERN SCRAP COMPANY INC
370 Stine Ln (22603-5414)
P.O. Box 3235 (22604-2435)
PHONE..................540 662-0265
Steven P Williams, *President*

James Washington, *General Mgr*
EMP: 24
SALES (est): 500K **Privately Held**
WEB: www.southernscrap.net
SIC: 2621 5093 3569 Paper mills; scrap & waste materials; baling machines, for scrap metal, paper or similar material

(G-15482)
SPIDER EMBROIDERY INC
126 Mill Race Dr (22602-6904)
PHONE..................540 955-2347
James L Edwards, *Principal*
EMP: 1
SALES (est): 63K **Privately Held**
SIC: 2395 Embroidery products, except schiffli machine

(G-15483)
STUART M PERRY INCORPORATED (PA)
117 Limestone Ln (22602-2272)
PHONE..................540 662-3431
Dennis W Perry, *President*
Garland E Perry, *Vice Pres*
Perry II Maurice W, *Vice Pres*
Mickey Perry, *Vice Pres*
Maurice W Perry, *Treasurer*
EMP: 110 EST: 1919
SQ FT: 5,000
SALES: 25.4MM **Privately Held**
WEB: www.stuartmperry.com
SIC: 1422 2951 1611 Limestones, ground; asphalt & asphaltic paving mixtures (not from refineries); general contractor, highway & street construction

(G-15484)
SUPER SPLASHER ACQUATICS
141 Krnstown Commons Blvd (22602-5364)
PHONE..................540 630-1565
EMP: 1
SALES (est): 58.3K **Privately Held**
SIC: 3599 Amusement park equipment

(G-15485)
T W ENTERPRISES INC
Also Called: Medipak
270 Tyson Dr Ste 2 (22603-4654)
P.O. Box 3248 (22604-2448)
PHONE..................540 667-0233
Erick Bryne, *President*
Eric Byrn, *President*
EMP: 4 EST: 1975
SQ FT: 4,500
SALES (est): 900K **Privately Held**
WEB: www.medipak.com
SIC: 3841 5047 Surgical & medical instruments; medical equipment & supplies

(G-15486)
T-JAR INC
129 Kinross Dr (22602-6736)
PHONE..................540 974-2567
Brian Beaver, *President*
Scott Rodgers, *Opers Staff*
EMP: 2
SALES (est): 264.4K **Privately Held**
WEB: www.t-jar.com
SIC: 3581 Automatic vending machines

(G-15487)
TAMMY HAIRE
Also Called: Serenity Ridge
2751 Hunting Ridge Rd (22603-2438)
PHONE..................540 722-7246
Tammy Haire, *Owner*
EMP: 1 EST: 2012
SALES (est): 56.3K **Privately Held**
WEB: www.serenityridge.biz
SIC: 2051 7389 Cakes, bakery: except frozen; business services

(G-15488)
TEE SPOT RCHING HIGHER HTS LLC
175 Greenwood Rd (22602-7922)
PHONE..................540 877-5961
Tiarra Dawson, *Principal*
EMP: 1
SALES (est): 84.4K **Privately Held**
SIC: 2759 Screen printing

▲ = Import ▼=Export
◆ =Import/Export

(G-15489)
THROX BREW MARKET AND GRILLE
1518 Martinsburg Pike (22603-5417)
PHONE......................540 323-7360
EMP: 3
SALES (est): 75.4K **Privately Held**
WEB: www.throxmarket.com
SIC: 2082 Malt beverages

(G-15490)
TK AIRCRAFT LLC
124 Elmwood Rd (22602-4406)
PHONE......................540 665-8113
Kenneth Doan, *Principal*
EMP: 2
SALES (est): 130.6K **Privately Held**
SIC: 3721 Aircraft

(G-15491)
TOTAL MOLDING CONCEPTS INC
882 Baker Ln (22603-5722)
PHONE......................540 665-8408
Rader Henning, *Ch of Bd*
Gus Nusu, *President*
Theresa Brewer, *Vice Pres*
Juan Hernandez, *CIO*
▲ EMP: 10
SALES (est): 1.5MM **Privately Held**
SIC: 3089 Injection molding of plastics

(G-15492)
TREX CO INC (PA)
160 Exeter Dr (22603-8614)
PHONE......................540 542-6300
Bryan H Fairbanks, *CEO*
James E Cline, *Ch of Bd*
Kevin Hill, *Business Mgr*
William R Gupp, *Senior VP*
Leslie Adkins, *Vice Pres*
◆ EMP: 118
SQ FT: 36,000
SALES: 745.3MM **Publicly Held**
WEB: www.trex.com
SIC: 2421 Outdoor wood structural products

(G-15493)
TREX COMPANY INC
245 Capitol Ln (22602-2441)
PHONE......................540 542-6800
David Heglas, *Principal*
EMP: 224
SALES (corp-wide): 745.3MM **Publicly Held**
WEB: www.trex.com
SIC: 2821 2823 2493 Plastics materials & resins; cellulosic manmade fibers; reconstituted wood products
PA: Trex Co Inc
    160 Exeter Dr
    Winchester VA 22603
    540 542-6300

(G-15494)
TREX COMPANY INC
3229 Shawnee Dr (22602-2435)
PHONE......................540 542-6800
Fax: 540 678-0285
EMP: 24 EST: 2014
SALES (est): 3.7MM **Privately Held**
SIC: 2821 Mfg Plastic Materials/Resins

(G-15495)
TREX COMPANY INC
331 Apple Valley Rd (22602-2408)
PHONE......................540 542-6314
EMP: 81
SALES (corp-wide): 745.3MM **Publicly Held**
WEB: www.trex.com
SIC: 2421 Outdoor wood structural products
PA: Trex Co Inc
    160 Exeter Dr
    Winchester VA 22603
    540 542-6300

(G-15496)
TREX COMPANY INC
3229 Shawnee Dr (22602-2435)
PHONE......................540 542-6800
EMP: 122

SALES (corp-wide): 745.3MM **Publicly Held**
WEB: www.trex.com
SIC: 2421 Sawmills & planing mills, general
PA: Trex Co Inc
    160 Exeter Dr
    Winchester VA 22603
    540 542-6300

(G-15497)
TWIN CS LLC
438 Mountain Falls Blvd (22602-3486)
P.O. Box 3176, Leesburg (20177-8058)
PHONE......................540 664-6072
Vanessa Campbell,
EMP: 5
SALES (est): 446.9K **Privately Held**
WEB: www.twincsllc.com
SIC: 3449 Miscellaneous metalwork

(G-15498)
UTZ QUALITY FOODS LLC
370 Tyson Dr (22603-4619)
PHONE......................540 535-1927
Kal Shahateet, *Branch Mgr*
EMP: 1
SALES (corp-wide): 845MM **Privately Held**
WEB: www.utzsnacks.com
SIC: 2096 Potato chips & similar snacks
PA: Utz Quality Foods, Llc
    900 High St
    Hanover PA 17331
    800 367-7629

(G-15499)
VALLEY BOMEDICAL PDTS SVCS INC
Also Called: Valley Biomedical Pdts Svcs In
121 Industrial Dr (22602-2583)
PHONE......................540 868-0800
Mario J Romano, *President*
Jody Darnell, *QC Mgr*
Brian Gnegy, *Sales Staff*
Leocadia Romano, *Admin Sec*
EMP: 20
SQ FT: 13,000
SALES (est): 3.4MM **Privately Held**
WEB: www.valleybiomedical.com
SIC: 2836 Biological products, except diagnostic

(G-15500)
VALLEY PROTEINS INC (PA)
151 Valpro Dr (22603-3607)
P.O. Box 3588 (22604-2586)
PHONE......................540 877-2590
Gerald Smith Jr, *President*
Michael Smith, *Vice Pres*
▼ EMP: 40
SQ FT: 2,300
SALES (est): 142.4MM **Privately Held**
WEB: www.valleyproteins.com
SIC: 2077 Animal & marine fats & oils

(G-15501)
VALLEY PROTEINS (DE) INC (PA)
151 Valpro Dr (22603-3607)
P.O. Box 3588 (22604-2586)
PHONE......................540 877-2533
Gerald Smith Jr, *President*
Jay Shestokes, *General Mgr*
Cecil Harrell, *Superintendent*
Richard Ballard, *District Mgr*
Andy Kubena, *District Mgr*
◆ EMP: 139 EST: 1956
SQ FT: 16,000
SALES (est): 501.1MM **Privately Held**
WEB: www.valleyproteins.com
SIC: 2077 Animal & marine fats & oils

(G-15502)
VALLEY PROTEINS (DE) INC
Also Called: Carolina By-Products
107 Kavanaugh Rd (22603)
P.O. Box 999, Lynchburg (24505-0999)
PHONE......................540 877-2590
Ernest Hostetter, *Branch Mgr*
Shayla Cary, *Representative*
EMP: 9

SALES (corp-wide): 501.1MM **Privately Held**
WEB: www.valleyproteins.com
SIC: 2077 Grease rendering, inedible; tallow rendering, inedible
PA: Valley Proteins (De), Inc.
    151 Valpro Dr
    Winchester VA 22603
    540 877-2533

(G-15503)
VAMAC INCORPORATED
601 Mcghee Rd (22603-4656)
PHONE......................540 535-1983
Bill Stokes, *Branch Mgr*
EMP: 46
SALES (corp-wide): 62.9MM **Privately Held**
WEB: www.vamac.com
SIC: 3272 3561 5039 5074 Septic tanks, concrete; pumps & pumping equipment; septic tanks; water purification equipment
PA: Vamac, Incorporated
    4201 Jacque St
    Richmond VA 23230
    804 353-7811

(G-15504)
VITA SPECIALTY FOODS INC
255 Tyson Dr (22603-4655)
PHONE......................540 542-0195
Marcia Dixon, *Principal*
EMP: 5
SALES (corp-wide): 43.4MM **Privately Held**
WEB: www.vitafoodproducts.com
SIC: 2099 Food preparations
HQ: Vita Specialty Foods, Inc.
    2222 W Lake St
    Chicago IL 60612
    800 989-8482

(G-15505)
WATER KING CONDITIONERS
929 Front Royal Pike (22602-4422)
PHONE......................540 667-5821
Robert Wallace, *Owner*
Judy Wallace, *Principal*
EMP: 2
SALES (est): 95K **Privately Held**
SIC: 3589 Commercial cooking & food-warming equipment

(G-15506)
WAYLAND CUSTOM CALIBERS LLC
100 Cobble Stone Dr (22602-6870)
PHONE......................540 533-6842
Brian Dolinar,
Winston Torrance,
EMP: 2
SALES (est): 83.8K **Privately Held**
SIC: 3489 Ordnance & accessories

(G-15507)
WESTROCK MWV LLC
117 Creekside Ln (22602-2429)
PHONE......................540 662-6524
EMP: 227
SALES (corp-wide): 17.5B **Publicly Held**
WEB: www.westrock.com
SIC: 2631 Paperboard mills
HQ: Westrock Mwv, Llc
    501 S 5th St
    Richmond VA 23219
    804 444-1000

(G-15508)
WHITE PROPERTIES OF WINCHESTER
Also Called: White Prpts Stor Solutions
141 Rainville Rd (22602-4802)
PHONE......................540 868-0205
Willis White, *President*
EMP: 14
SALES (est): 514.3K **Privately Held**
WEB: www.whiteproperties.net
SIC: 2511 Storage chests, household: wood

(G-15509)
WHITES ORNAMENTAL IRON WORKS
365 Back Mountain Rd (22602-1618)
PHONE......................540 877-1047

Harry S White Jr, *President*
EMP: 3
SALES (est): 200K **Privately Held**
SIC: 3446 Ornamental metalwork

(G-15510)
WINCHESTER BUILDING SUP CO INC
Also Called: Winchester Precast Frederick
2001 Millwood Pike (22602-4642)
PHONE......................540 667-2301
Kathryn M Perry-Werner, *President*
Michael Perry, *Vice Pres*
Ezekiel Merza, *Sales Staff*
Richard Wilson, *Asst Sec*
EMP: 40
SQ FT: 10,000
SALES (est): 7MM **Privately Held**
WEB: www.winprecast.com
SIC: 3272 5169 Septic tanks, concrete; explosives

(G-15511)
WINCHESTER METALS INC (PA)
195 Ebert Rd (22603-4703)
PHONE......................540 667-9000
Donald M Phelps, *CEO*
Josh Phelps, *President*
Jim Snapp, *Safety Mgr*
Mark Younkins, *Sales Staff*
Jean Settle, *Info Tech Mgr*
EMP: 53 EST: 1975
SQ FT: 42,000
SALES (est): 12.2MM **Privately Held**
WEB: www.winchestermetals.com
SIC: 3441 Fabricated structural metal

(G-15512)
WINCHESTER PRINTERS INC
Also Called: Winchester Mailing Services
212 Independence Rd (22602-4501)
PHONE......................540 662-6911
Irving L Hottle, *Ch of Bd*
Ronald E Hottle, *President*
Gary I Hottle, *Vice Pres*
Gary Hottle, *Vice Pres*
Bill Casella, *Production*
EMP: 32 EST: 1890
SQ FT: 25,000
SALES (est): 4.8MM **Privately Held**
WEB: www.winchesterprinters.com
SIC: 2752 2791 2789 2759 Commercial printing, offset; typesetting; bookbinding & related work; commercial printing

(G-15513)
WINCHESTER TOOL LLC
110a Industrial Dr (22602-2580)
PHONE......................540 869-1150
Robert Hahn,
▲ EMP: 20
SQ FT: 20,000
SALES (est): 3.7MM
SALES (corp-wide): 7.9MM **Privately Held**
WEB: www.fabritek.com
SIC: 3599 3549 3544 Machine shop, jobbing & repair; custom machinery; metalworking machinery; special dies, tools, jigs & fixtures
PA: Fabritek Company, Inc.
    416 Battaile Dr
    Winchester VA 22601
    540 662-9095

(G-15514)
WINCHESTER TRUCK REPAIR LLC
259 Tyson Dr Ste 4 (22603-4662)
P.O. Box 3410 (22604-1110)
PHONE......................540 398-7995
Larry Vought Jr, *Mng Member*
Debra Farrish,
Justin Farrish,
EMP: 9 EST: 2015
SQ FT: 15,000
SALES (est): 476.2K **Privately Held**
WEB: www.winchestertruckrepairs.com
SIC: 3715 7694 Truck trailers; motor repair services

(G-15515)
WINCHESTER WOODWORKING CORP (PA)
351 Victory Rd (22602-4566)
PHONE..................................540 667-1700
James R Hamilton, *President*
John M Hamilton Jr, *Vice Pres*
Richard S Bern Jr, *Treasurer*
EMP: 63
SQ FT: 60,000
SALES (est): 6.9MM **Privately Held**
WEB: www.winchesterwoodworks.com
SIC: 2431 Doors, wood

(G-15516)
WINDRYDER INC
Also Called: Agilitytools.com
157 Warm Springs Rd (22603-2724)
PHONE..................................540 545-8851
Fred Lutz, *President*
Roberta Lutz, *Vice Pres*
EMP: 2 EST: 2008
SALES (est): 103K **Privately Held**
WEB: www.agilitytools.com
SIC: 3799 5961 7389 Golf carts, powered; ;

(G-15517)
WITT ASSOCIATES INC
Also Called: Brainstorm Software
118 Old Forest Cir (22602-6626)
PHONE..................................540 667-3146
Thomas Witt, *President*
Sarah Witt, *Corp Secy*
Tom Witt, *COO*
EMP: 8
SQ FT: 3,200
SALES (est): 910K **Privately Held**
WEB: www.tomwittphotos.com
SIC: 7372 4813 Prepackaged software;

(G-15518)
WORLD WIDE AUTOMOTIVE LLC (HQ)
300 W Brooke Rd (22603-5792)
P.O. Box 6068, Edmond OK (73083-6068)
PHONE..................................540 667-9100
Duncan Gillis, *CEO*
◆ EMP: 30 EST: 1976
SQ FT: 175,000
SALES (est): 116.1MM
SALES (corp-wide): 179.5MM **Privately Held**
WEB: www.wwauto.com
SIC: 3694 3714 Automotive electrical equipment; alternators, automotive; motor vehicle parts & accessories
PA: Bbb Industries, Llc
29627 Renaissance Blvd
Daphne AL 36526
800 280-2737

(G-15519)
WYVERN INTERACTIVE LLC
3438 Front Royal Pike (22602-4910)
PHONE..................................540 336-4498
Morgan Frederick, *Administration*
EMP: 10
SALES (est): 483.6K **Privately Held**
SIC: 3944 7372 7371 Electronic games & toys; educational computer software; software programming applications

(G-15520)
X-STAND TREESTAND COMPANY LLC
140 Theodore Dr (22602-2035)
PHONE..................................540 877-2769
Anthony Overbaugh, *Owner*
▲ EMP: 2 EST: 2010
SALES (est): 170.8K **Privately Held**
WEB: www.x-stand.com
SIC: 3999 Manufacturing industries

(G-15521)
XTREME FBRCTION PWDR CTING LLC
3372 Hunting Ridge Rd (22603-2015)
PHONE..................................540 327-3020
Douglas Seal, *Principal*
EMP: 2
SALES (est): 130.7K **Privately Held**
SIC: 3471 1799 Sand blasting of metal parts; welding on site

(G-15522)
ZEUS TECHNOLOGIES
139 Boundary Ave (22602-6847)
PHONE..................................540 247-4623
Paul Hamman, *Principal*
EMP: 2 EST: 2010
SALES (est): 128.5K **Privately Held**
WEB: www.zeuscs.com
SIC: 7372 Business oriented computer software

Winchester
Winchester City County

(G-15523)
1 A LIFESAFER INC
263 Millwood Ave (22601-4559)
PHONE..................................800 634-3077
EMP: 1 **Privately Held**
WEB: www.lifesafer.com
SIC: 3829 Measuring & controlling devices
PA: 1 A Lifesafer, Inc.
3630 Park 42 Dr Ste 170f
Cincinnati OH 45241

(G-15524)
ADVANCED GRAPHICS LLC
801 Cedar Creek Grade (22601-2706)
PHONE..................................540 931-4850
Chuck Atkinson,
EMP: 1
SALES (est): 129.4K **Privately Held**
WEB: www.advanced-graphics.biz
SIC: 3993 Signs & advertising specialties

(G-15525)
ADVANCED MFG RESTRUCTURING LLC
720 Seldon Dr (22601-3235)
PHONE..................................540 667-5010
EMP: 2
SALES (est): 62.5K **Privately Held**
SIC: 3999 Manufacturing industries

(G-15526)
ALL POINTS COUNTERTOP INC
449 N Cameron St (22601-4845)
P.O. Box 3523 (22604-2552)
PHONE..................................540 665-3875
Charles R Huntsberry Jr, *President*
Donna Knight, *Office Mgr*
EMP: 25
SQ FT: 12,000
SALES (est): 4.6MM **Privately Held**
WEB: www.allpointscountertop.com
SIC: 2821 2541 Plastics materials & resins; counter & sink tops

(G-15527)
ANGEETHI WINCHESTER LLC
2644 Valley Ave (22601-2626)
PHONE..................................703 300-7488
EMP: 1 EST: 2010
SALES (est): 61K **Privately Held**
SIC: 3421 Mfg Cutlery

(G-15528)
ANGLE VALLEY PRESS LLC
203 E Boscawen St (22601-5012)
PHONE..................................540 662-1320
Gregory Bowman, *Principal*
EMP: 2
SALES (est): 134.1K **Privately Held**
WEB: www.anglevalleypress.com
SIC: 2741 Miscellaneous publishing

(G-15529)
APLUS SIGNS AND BUS SVCS LLC
Also Called: Winchester Business Services
5 Featherbed Ln (22601-4466)
PHONE..................................540 667-8010
Udaya Adusumalli, *Mng Member*
Martin Price, *Manager*
Lavanya Adusumalli, *Info Tech Mgr*
EMP: 10
SQ FT: 8,000
SALES (est): 1.1MM **Privately Held**
WEB: www.asignplace.com
SIC: 3993 Signs, not made in custom sign painting shops

(G-15530)
ASHWORTH BROS INC
Also Called: Belt Division
450 Armour Dl (22601-3459)
P.O. Box 2780 (22604-1980)
PHONE..................................540 662-3494
Jack Carothers, *General Mgr*
Kenneth King, *District Mgr*
Jim Tumini, *District Mgr*
Paul Nunes, *Vice Pres*
Dexter James, *Mfg Mgr*
EMP: 176
SALES (corp-wide): 65MM **Privately Held**
WEB: www.ashworth.com
SIC: 3496 Conveyor belts
PA: Ashworth Bros., Inc.
222 Milliken Blvd Ste 7
Fall River MA 02721
508 674-4693

(G-15531)
BLACK ALDER TRAIL LLC
731 Berryville Ave (22601-5630)
PHONE..................................812 219-1975
Jason Hatch, *Manager*
EMP: 2
SALES (est): 20K **Privately Held**
SIC: 2052 Bakery products, dry

(G-15532)
BROKEN WINDOW BREWING CO LLC
12 W Boscawen St 14 (22601-4702)
PHONE..................................703 999-7030
Zachary Aufdenberg, *CEO*
EMP: 2
SQ FT: 1,500
SALES (est): 62.3K **Privately Held**
SIC: 2082 Beer (alcoholic beverage)

(G-15533)
CABINET DESIGN PLUS
31 E Jubal Early Dr (22601-5120)
PHONE..................................540 773-4571
Dean Daniels, *President*
EMP: 1
SALES (est): 100.7K **Privately Held**
WEB: www.cabinetdesignplus.com
SIC: 2434 Wood kitchen cabinets

(G-15534)
CALADAN CONSULTING INC
321 N Pleasant Valley Rd (22601-5607)
P.O. Box 87, Strasburg (22657-0087)
PHONE..................................540 931-9581
Robert Moses, *President*
EMP: 1
SALES (est): 100K **Privately Held**
WEB: www.caladanconsulting.net
SIC: 7372 Word processing computer software

(G-15535)
COVIA HOLDINGS CORPORATION
48 W Boscawen St (22601-4739)
P.O. Box 4250 (22604-4250)
PHONE..................................540 678-1490
Ken Vorpahl, *Manager*
EMP: 4
SALES (corp-wide): 125.5MM **Privately Held**
WEB: www.coviacorp.com
SIC: 1446 Industrial sand
HQ: Covia Holdings Corporation
3 Summit Park Dr Ste 700
Independence OH 44131
440 214-3284

(G-15536)
DAILY GRIND HOSPITAL
190 Campus Blvd Ste 130 (22601-2872)
PHONE..................................540 536-2383
Dutch Miller, *President*
EMP: 2
SALES (est): 203.6K **Privately Held**
SIC: 3599 Grinding castings for the trade

(G-15537)
DOUBLE EDGE DEFENSE LLC
25 Battery Dr (22601-3673)
PHONE..................................540 550-0849
James Slack, *Principal*
EMP: 3

SALES (est): 189.3K **Privately Held**
SIC: 3812 Defense systems & equipment

(G-15538)
EHP
34 Peyton St (22601-4838)
PHONE..................................540 667-1815
Shawn Reiser, *Principal*
EMP: 2 EST: 2007
SALES (est): 100.2K **Privately Held**
SIC: 2899

(G-15539)
EMBER SYSTEMS LLC
3052 Valley Ave Ste 200 (22601-2672)
PHONE..................................540 327-1984
Vera Cesnik, *CEO*
EMP: 4
SALES (est): 127.3K **Privately Held**
SIC: 2741 7336 7371 ; graphic arts & related design; computer software development

(G-15540)
FABRIC ACCENTS BY EMILY
679 Berryville Ave (22601-5663)
PHONE..................................540 678-3999
Emily Seiler, *Owner*
EMP: 1
SALES (est): 55K **Privately Held**
WEB: www.emilysumbrellas.com
SIC: 2391 Curtains & draperies

(G-15541)
FABRITEK COMPANY INC (PA)
416 Battaile Dr (22601-4280)
PHONE..................................540 662-9095
Robert Hahn Jr, *President*
John O Hahn, *Vice Pres*
Peggy Hahn, *Treasurer*
Stephanie Vaughan, *Admin Sec*
EMP: 45 EST: 1964
SQ FT: 35,000
SALES (est): 7.9MM **Privately Held**
WEB: www.fabritek.com
SIC: 3599 Machine shop, jobbing & repair

(G-15542)
FEDERAL-MOGUL PRODUCTS INC
2410 Papermill Rd (22601-3621)
PHONE..................................540 662-3871
Howard Schmitt, *Vice Pres*
EMP: 400
SALES (corp-wide): 17.4B **Publicly Held**
WEB: www.federalmogul.com
SIC: 3714 Motor vehicle parts & accessories
HQ: Federal-Mogul Products Us Llc
26555 Northwestern Hwy
Southfield MI 48033
248 354-7700

(G-15543)
FILTER MEDIA
385 Battaile Dr (22601-4262)
PHONE..................................540 667-9074
EMP: 2
SALES (est): 107.4K **Privately Held**
WEB: www.midwescofilter.com
SIC: 3569 General industrial machinery

(G-15544)
FREESTYLE PRINTS LLC
401 Fox Dr (22601-3040)
PHONE..................................571 246-1806
Aaron David Nelson, *Administration*
EMP: 2 EST: 2013
SALES (est): 133.1K **Privately Held**
SIC: 2752 Commercial printing, lithographic

(G-15545)
GENERAL WELDING
316 Highland Ave (22601-5032)
P.O. Box 2655 (22604-1855)
PHONE..................................540 514-0242
Greg Richard, *Principal*
EMP: 1
SALES (est): 50.8K **Privately Held**
SIC: 7692 Welding repair

▲ = Import ▼=Export
◆ =Import/Export

(G-15546)
GRAPHICS NORTH
Also Called: Graphics Nrth-Sgns Outdoor Ltg
706 Fort Collier Rd (22601-5912)
PHONE..................................540 678-4965
Christopher Lockley, *Partner*
Wayne Brandt, *Partner*
EMP: 3
SALES (est): 250K **Privately Held**
SIC: 3993 Signs & advertising specialties

(G-15547)
HENKEL-HARRIS LLC
2983 S Pleasant Valley Rd (22601-4240)
P.O. Box 3201 (22604-2401)
PHONE..................................540 667-4900
David Gum, *Mng Member*
Charlie Murphy, *Manager*
Aubrey Gum,
Brittany Smith,
▲ EMP: 21 EST: 2013
SQ FT: 280,000
SALES (est): 28.9MM **Privately Held**
SIC: 2511 2521 Wood bedroom furniture;
dining room furniture: wood; wood office
furniture

(G-15548)
HS WINCHESTER LLC
621 W Jubal Early Dr D (22601-6510)
PHONE..................................540 771-0079
Lisa Limoges, *Principal*
EMP: 3
SALES (est): 124.3K **Privately Held**
WEB: www.winchesterstar.com
SIC: 2711 Newspapers, publishing & print-
ing

(G-15549)
IMPRESSIONS GROUP INC
Also Called: Impressions Plus Prtg Copying
2063 Cidermill Ln (22601-2777)
PHONE..................................540 667-9227
Kathy Austin, *Manager*
EMP: 3 **Privately Held**
SIC: 2752 Commercial printing, litho-
graphic
PA: Impressions Group, Inc.
111 Featherbed Ln
Winchester VA
540 667-9227

(G-15550)
JAMES KACIAN
Also Called: Red Moon Press
731 Mahone Dr (22601-6742)
P.O. Box 2461 (22604-1661)
PHONE..................................540 722-2156
Jim Kacian, *Owner*
EMP: 12
SALES (est): 544K **Privately Held**
WEB: www.redmoonpress.com
SIC: 2741 Miscellaneous publishing

(G-15551)
JBTM ENTERPRISES INC
Also Called: Signet Screen Prtg Embordiery
127 Harvest Ridge Dr (22601-2883)
PHONE..................................540 665-9651
Thomas Cesnik, *President*
James Michael Cesnik, *Corp Secy*
Bernard Cesnik, *Shareholder*
Mark Cesnik, *Shareholder*
EMP: 12
SQ FT: 10,000
SALES (est): 1.7MM **Privately Held**
WEB: www.signetscreen.com
SIC: 2759 2395 5199 3993 Screen print-
ing; embroidery & art needlework; adver-
tising specialties; signs & advertising
specialties; automotive & apparel trim-
mings

(G-15552)
LIGHTFACTOR LLC
160 N Indian Aly (22601-4710)
PHONE..................................540 723-9600
Jeffrey Thomas Cesnik,
EMP: 5
SALES (est): 287.5K **Privately Held**
SIC: 3699 7371 8731 Security control
equipment & systems; computer software
development & applications; computer
(hardware) development

(G-15553)
**LOUDON STREET ELECTRIC
SVCS**
Also Called: Blue Ridge Electric Service
1604 S Loudoun St (22601-4446)
PHONE..................................540 662-8463
Rod Wilson, *President*
Antonio Minor, *Director*
EMP: 5 EST: 1950
SQ FT: 8,000
SALES (est): 670.8K **Privately Held**
WEB: www.blueridgeai.com
SIC: 7694 5999 Electric motor repair; mo-
tors, electric

(G-15554)
METTLER-TOLEDO LLC
Also Called: Toledo Scales & Systems
112 Bruce Dr (22601-4213)
PHONE..................................540 665-9495
Wendall Nohe, *Branch Mgr*
EMP: 4
SALES (corp-wide): 3B **Publicly Held**
WEB: www.mt.com
SIC: 3596 Scales & balances, except labo-
ratory
HQ: Mettler-Toledo, Llc
1900 Polaris Pkwy Fl 6
Columbus OH 43240
614 438-4511

(G-15555)
MFRI INC
Also Called: Midwesco Filter Resources
400 Battaile Dr (22601-4263)
P.O. Box 2075 (22604-1275)
PHONE..................................540 667-7022
EMP: 185
SALES (corp-wide): 122.7MM **Publicly
Held**
SIC: 2393 3564 2674 Mfg Textile Bags
Mfg Blowers/Fans Mfg Bags-Uncoated
Paper
PA: Mfri, Inc.
7720 N Lehigh Ave
Niles IL 60714
847 966-1000

(G-15556)
MIGLAS LOUPES LLC
2360 Roosevelt Blvd Apt 2 (22601-3690)
PHONE..................................815 721-9133
Neil Stewart, *Owner*
EMP: 2 EST: 2012
SALES (est): 141.8K **Privately Held**
SIC: 2759 Commercial printing

(G-15557)
MIK WOODWORKING INC
341 Sheridan Ave (22601-3133)
PHONE..................................540 878-1197
John Mikulec, *Principal*
EMP: 4
SALES (est): 526.5K **Privately Held**
WEB: www.mikwoodworking.com
SIC: 2431 Millwork

(G-15558)
MOMMERS HOUSE LLC
440 Royal St (22601-4244)
PHONE..................................540 327-8101
Sheila Elliott, *Principal*
EMP: 3
SALES (est): 121.4K **Privately Held**
WEB: www.mommershouse.com
SIC: 2711 Newspapers, publishing & print-
ing

(G-15559)
MR NOODLE & RICE
19 Weems Ln (22601-3601)
PHONE..................................540 662-4213
Young Cho, *Principal*
EMP: 4
SALES (est): 224.1K **Privately Held**
SIC: 2098 Noodles (e.g. egg, plain &
water), dry

(G-15560)
NATIONAL FILTER MEDIA CORP
309 N Braddock St (22601-3919)
PHONE..................................540 773-4780
EMP: 2

SALES (corp-wide): 922.9MM **Privately
Held**
WEB: www.nfm-filter.com
SIC: 3569 Filters, general line: industrial
HQ: The National Filter Media Corporation
691 N 400 W
Salt Lake City UT 84103
801 363-6736

(G-15561)
OSULLIVAN FILMS INC (HQ)
1944 Valley Ave (22601-6306)
PHONE..................................540 667-6666
Denis Belzile, *CEO*
Eric Buchanan, *General Mgr*
Sven Hlywiak, *Exec VP*
Scott Krueger, *Vice Pres*
Rick Till, *Vice Pres*
EMP: 400
SQ FT: 560,000
SALES (est): 106MM
SALES (corp-wide): 49.2B **Privately Held**
WEB: www.continental-industry.com
SIC: 3081 Unsupported plastics film &
sheet
PA: Continental Ag
Vahrenwalder Str. 9
Hannover 30165
511 938-01

(G-15562)
OSULLIVAN FILMS INC
111 W Jubal Early (22601)
PHONE..................................540 667-6666
C Nickerson, *Branch Mgr*
EMP: 20
SALES (corp-wide): 49.2B **Privately Held**
WEB: www.continental-industry.com
SIC: 3081 Vinyl film & sheet
HQ: O'sullivan Films, Inc.
1944 Valley Ave
Winchester VA 22601
540 667-6666

(G-15563)
**OSULLIVAN FILMS MGT LLC
(DH)**
1944 Valley Ave (22601-6306)
PHONE..................................540 667-6666
Denis Belzile, *CEO*
Ewen Campbell, *President*
Eric Buchanan, *General Mgr*
Dennis Ruen, *Vice Pres*
Rick Lineberg, *QA Dir*
◆ EMP: 392
SALES (est): 107.7MM
SALES (corp-wide): 49.2B **Privately Held**
WEB: www.continental-industry.com
SIC: 3081 Vinyl film & sheet
HQ: Konrad Hornschuch International
Gmbh
Salinenstr. 1
WeiBbach 74679
794 781-0

(G-15564)
**PAGE SHENANDOAH
NEWSPAPER**
Also Called: Shenandoah Valley Herald
2 N Kent St (22601-5038)
PHONE..................................540 574-6251
Thomas T Byrd, *CEO*
Harry F Bird III, *Vice Pres*
EMP: 25 EST: 1978
SALES (est): 829.7K **Privately Held**
WEB: www.winchesterstar.com
SIC: 2711 Newspapers, publishing & print-
ing

(G-15565)
PEARCE WOODWORKING
903 Berryville Ave (22601-5915)
PHONE..................................240 377-1278
EMP: 1 EST: 2016
SALES (est): 54.1K **Privately Held**
SIC: 2431 Millwork

(G-15566)
**PICCADILLY PRINTING
COMPANY**
500 W Jubal Early Dr # 120 (22601-6508)
PHONE..................................540 662-3804
John Morrison, *Owner*
Dave Pyne, *Vice Pres*
Kendra Tolley, *Accounts Mgr*

Heidi Jenkins, *Sales Staff*
EMP: 13
SALES (est): 1.3MM **Privately Held**
WEB: www.picprinting.com
SIC: 2752 Commercial printing, offset

(G-15567)
POLYONE
1944 Valley Ave (22601-6306)
PHONE..................................540 667-6666
Michael Arnick, *Principal*
Todd Costello, *Technology*
EMP: 3
SALES (est): 422.4K **Privately Held**
WEB: www.polyone.com
SIC: 2821 Plastics materials & resins

(G-15568)
PREMIER RETICLES LTD
920 Breckinridge Ln (22601-6707)
PHONE..................................540 667-5258
◆ EMP: 9 EST: 1946
SQ FT: 10,000
SALES: 2MM **Privately Held**
SIC: 3827 Mfg Optical Instruments/Lenses

(G-15569)
PRINTSMITH INK
340 N Pleasant Valley Rd (22601-5608)
PHONE..................................540 323-7554
EMP: 2 EST: 2018
SALES (est): 92.3K **Privately Held**
WEB: www.printsmithink.com
SIC: 2752 Commercial printing, offset

(G-15570)
PROTOMOLD
340 N Pleasant Valley Rd (22601-5608)
PHONE..................................540 542-1740
John Parker, *Owner*
Dan Bunker, *Accounts Mgr*
EMP: 1
SALES (est): 82.3K **Privately Held**
WEB: www.protolabs.com
SIC: 3299 Moldings, architectural: plaster
of paris

(G-15571)
PURCELLVILLE GAZETTE LLC
17 W Boscawen St (22601-4701)
P.O. Box 65, Purcellville (20134-0065)
PHONE..................................540 431-8507
R Webster, *Principal*
EMP: 3
SALES (est): 127.9K **Privately Held**
WEB: www.purcellvillegazette.com
SIC: 2711 Newspapers, publishing & print-
ing

(G-15572)
**QUANTUM MEDICAL BUS SVC
INC**
2209 Harrison St (22601-2729)
PHONE..................................703 727-1020
H Gilliam III, *Branch Mgr*
EMP: 1
SALES (corp-wide): 1.7MM **Privately
Held**
WEB: www.qmbs.com
SIC: 3572 Computer storage devices
PA: Quantum Medical Business Service,
Inc.
5461 Fallowater Ln C
Roanoke VA 24018
540 776-9400

(G-15573)
QUICK DESIGNS LLC
Also Called: Fastsigns
1720 Valley Ave (22601-3140)
PHONE..................................540 450-0750
Bryan Quick, *Mng Member*
Tracey Quick,
EMP: 8
SQ FT: 2,500
SALES (est): 1.3MM **Privately Held**
WEB: www.fastsigns.com
SIC: 3993 Signs & advertising specialties

(G-15574)
QUICKIE MANUFACTURING
3124 Valley Ave (22601-2636)
PHONE..................................856 829-8598
Tom Simpson, *CFO*
EMP: 1 EST: 2019

GEOGRAPHIC

SALES (est): 40.9K **Privately Held**
SIC: 2392 Household furnishings

(G-15575)
QUICKIE MANUFACTURING CORP (HQ)
3124 Valley Ave (22601-2636)
PHONE..................856 829-7900
Michael Magerman, *CEO*
Peter S Vosbikian Jr, *Chairman*
◆ EMP: 60 EST: 1977
SQ FT: 68,000
SALES (est): 160.8MM
SALES (corp-wide): 9.7B **Publicly Held**
WEB: www.quickie.com
SIC: 2392 3991 Mops, floor & dust; brooms
PA: Newell Brands Inc.
6655 Pachtree Dunwoody Rd
Atlanta GA 30328
770 418-7000

(G-15576)
QUICKIE MANUFACTURING CORP
3124 Valley Ave (22601-2636)
P.O. Box 156, Cinnaminson NJ (08077-0156)
PHONE..................856 829-7900
EMP: 1
SALES (est): 39.6K **Privately Held**
SIC: 3999 Manufacturing industries

(G-15577)
R C COLA BOTTLING COMPANY DEL
2927 Shawnee Dr (22601-4203)
PHONE..................540 667-1821
William Bridgefoth, *President*
Scott Bridgeforth, *Vice Pres*
EMP: 60
SALES (est): 5MM **Privately Held**
WEB: www.rccolawinchester.com
SIC: 2086 Soft drinks: packaged in cans, bottles, etc.

(G-15578)
RANDOM ACTS OF CUPCAKES
551 N Braddock St (22601-3923)
PHONE..................540 974-3948
Caroline Brown, *Principal*
EMP: 4
SALES (est): 161.7K **Privately Held**
SIC: 2051 Bread, cake & related products

(G-15579)
REHABLTATION PRACTITIONERS INC (PA)
333 W Cork St Unit 30 (22601-3816)
PHONE..................540 722-9025
Michael Cestaro, *President*
Vicky Baker, *Office Mgr*
EMP: 6
SQ FT: 3,200
SALES (est): 1.2MM **Privately Held**
WEB: www.rpionline.us
SIC: 3842 5999 Limbs, artificial; artificial limbs

(G-15580)
ROYAL CROWN BOTTLING COMPANY
2927 Shawnee Dr (22601-4203)
P.O. Box 2300 (22604-1500)
PHONE..................540 667-1821
W Bridgeforth, *President*
EMP: 16
SALES (est): 2.6MM **Privately Held**
WEB: www.rccolawinchester.com
SIC: 2086 Soft drinks: packaged in cans, bottles, etc.

(G-15581)
ROYAL CROWN BTLG WNCHESTER INC (PA)
2927 Shawnee Dr (22601-4203)
P.O. Box 2300 (22604-1500)
PHONE..................540 667-1821
William Bridgeforth III, *President*
James S Bridgeforth, *Treasurer*
EMP: 55 EST: 1928
SQ FT: 95,000

SALES (est): 13.7MM **Privately Held**
WEB: www.rccolawinchester.com
SIC: 2086 Soft drinks: packaged in cans, bottles, etc.

(G-15582)
RUBBERMAID COMMERCIAL PDTS LLC (DH)
3124 Valley Ave (22601-2694)
PHONE..................540 667-8700
Nicole Brown, *Vice Pres*
Christopher Olenski, *Engrg Mgr*
Jay Dennis, *Engineer*
David Avery, *Accounting Mgr*
Marty Baird, *Sales Mgr*
◆ EMP: 1000
SQ FT: 750,000
SALES (est): 361.4MM
SALES (corp-wide): 9.7B **Publicly Held**
WEB: www.rubbermaidcommercial.com
SIC: 3089 2673 Plastic containers, except foam; bags: plastic, laminated & coated
HQ: Rubbermaid Incorporated
3 Glenlake Pkwy
Atlanta GA 30328
770 418-7000

(G-15583)
SECRET SOCIETY PRESS LLC
112 Morgan St (22601-3830)
PHONE..................540 877-6298
EMP: 1
SALES (est): 45.4K **Privately Held**
WEB: www.secretsocietypress.com
SIC: 2741 Miscellaneous publishing

(G-15584)
SHELTER2HOME LLC
22 Clark St (22601-4848)
P.O. Box 3223 (22604-2423)
PHONE..................540 336-5994
Donald Stevens, *President*
Andrea Stevens, *Treasurer*
EMP: 4
SALES (est): 215.5K **Privately Held**
SIC: 3448 Prefabricated metal buildings

(G-15585)
SHELTERED 2 HOME LLC
Also Called: Vanguard
22 Clark St (22601-4848)
P.O. Box 3223 (22604-2423)
PHONE..................540 686-0091
Crosby Wood, *VP Bus Dvlpt*
Donald Stevens,
Chris Rust, *Treasurer*
EMP: 25
SQ FT: 10,000
SALES (est): 650K **Privately Held**
WEB: www.vlgsb.net
SIC: 3441 Building components, structural steel

(G-15586)
SHENANDOAH VLLY STEAM/GAS ENGI
456 Imperial St (22601-4223)
PHONE..................540 662-6923
Rick Custer, *President*
Steve Giles, *Vice Pres*
Wayne Godlobe, *Treasurer*
Jane McDonald, *Admin Sec*
EMP: 5 EST: 1962 **Privately Held**
SIC: 3743 Engines, steam (locomotive)

(G-15587)
SIR SPEEDY PRINT SIGNS MKTG
32 E Piccadilly St (22601-4824)
PHONE..................540 662-3804
EMP: 2
SALES (est): 72.6K **Privately Held**
SIC: 3993 Signs & advertising specialties

(G-15588)
SOUTHERN STTES WNCHSTER COOP I (PA)
Also Called: Southern States Cooperative
447 Amherst St (22601-3856)
PHONE..................540 662-0375
Calvin Coolidge, *President*
EMP: 13

SALES (est): 2.4MM **Privately Held**
SIC: 0781 5999 2048 Farm machinery & equipment; landscape services; feed & farm supply; prepared feeds

(G-15589)
SWEET TOOTH BAKERY INC
3034 Valley Ave Ste 110 (22601-2670)
PHONE..................540 667-6155
Joyce McDaniel, *President*
Roger McDaniel, *Treasurer*
EMP: 6 **Privately Held**
WEB: www.sweettoothbakerycakes.com
SIC: 2051 5461 Bread, cake & related products; bakeries

(G-15590)
T-SHIRT & SCREEN PRINT CO
Also Called: T-Shirt Attic and Screen Print
65 Featherbed Ln (22601-4466)
PHONE..................540 667-2351
Drema Seal, *President*
EMP: 5
SQ FT: 2,400
SALES (est): 470.9K **Privately Held**
SIC: 2759 3993 Screen printing; signs & advertising specialties

(G-15591)
TAURA NATURAL INGREDIENTS
110 S Indian Aly (22601-4714)
PHONE..................540 723-8691
Mike Turne, *President*
Richard Croad, *Principal*
Mary Joe Mills, *Office Mgr*
Trevor Miles, *Director*
▲ EMP: 8
SALES (est): 1.1MM **Privately Held**
WEB: www.tauraurc.com
SIC: 2034 Vegetables, dried or dehydrated (except freeze-dried)
HQ: Champ Ventures Pty Ltd
G Se 2 195 Gloucester Street
The Rocks NSW 2000

(G-15592)
TEABERRY HILL WOODWORKS LLC
103 N Braddock St (22601-3913)
PHONE..................540 667-5489
Jared Truban, *Principal*
Debra Carbaugh, *Assistant*
EMP: 1
SALES (est): 77.7K **Privately Held**
WEB: www.owentruban.com
SIC: 2431 Millwork

(G-15593)
THREE ANGELS PRETZELS
41 S Loudoun St (22601-4719)
PHONE..................540 722-0400
R Fick, *Manager*
EMP: 1 EST: 2018
SALES (est): 37.5K **Privately Held**
SIC: 2741 Miscellaneous publishing

(G-15594)
TIM PRICE INC
Also Called: Contact
1818 Roberts St (22601-6312)
PHONE..................540 722-8716
Tim Price, *CEO*
Scott Sions, *President*
Gary Groah, *Business Dir*
▲ EMP: 12
SALES (est): 10MM **Privately Held**
WEB: www.contactcorp.net
SIC: 3663 Antennas, transmitting & communications

(G-15595)
TRANSEFFECT LLC
10 W Boscawen St Ste 20 (22601-4748)
PHONE..................703 991-1599
Kevin Frey, *Mng Member*
Brandon Jones,
EMP: 2
SALES (est): 138.1K **Privately Held**
WEB: www.transeffect.com
SIC: 7372 Application computer software

(G-15596)
TRI STATE GRADUATE SUPS LLC
914 S Braddock St (22601-3776)
P.O. Box 2198 (22604-1398)
PHONE..................540 665-5292
Gregg Miller, *Mng Member*
EMP: 1
SALES (est): 79.7K **Privately Held**
SIC: 2389 Academic vestments (caps & gowns)

(G-15597)
TSHIRT ZONE
1850 Apple Blossom Dr (22601-5187)
PHONE..................540 431-5068
EMP: 2 EST: 2016
SALES (est): 124.7K **Privately Held**
WEB: www.mytshirtzone.com
SIC: 2759 Screen printing

(G-15598)
VALLEY ORTHTIC SPECIALISTS INC
1726 Amherst St (22601-2807)
PHONE..................540 667-3631
Sarah Lane, *Owner*
EMP: 3
SALES (est): 343.4K **Privately Held**
WEB: www.valleyorthoticsinc.net
SIC: 3842 Orthopedic appliances

(G-15599)
VIRGINIA NEWS GROUP LLC
Also Called: Clarke Times Courier
2 N Kent St (22601-5038)
PHONE..................540 955-1111
Pam Lettie, *Manager*
EMP: 6
SALES (corp-wide): 14.9MM **Privately Held**
WEB: www.loudountimes.com
SIC: 2711 Newspapers, publishing & printing
PA: Virginia News Group, Llc
1602 Village Market Blvd
Leesburg VA 20175
703 777-1111

(G-15600)
WELLSPRING WOODWORKS LLC
435 N Braddock St (22601-3921)
PHONE..................540 722-8641
Christopher Eyre, *Principal*
EMP: 1
SALES (est): 81.4K **Privately Held**
SIC: 2431 Millwork

(G-15601)
WINCHESTER EVENING STAR INC
Also Called: Amherst Nelson Publishing Co
100 N Loudoun St Ste 110 (22601-7400)
PHONE..................540 667-3200
Thomas T Byrd, *President*
Mike Gochenour, *Publisher*
Thomas W Byrd, *General Mgr*
Cynthia Burton, *Editor*
Rob Stocks, *Editor*
EMP: 116
SALES (est): 7.9MM **Privately Held**
WEB: www.winchesterstar.com
SIC: 2711 Newspapers, publishing & printing

(G-15602)
WINCHESTER TOOL LLC
416 Battaile Dr (22601-4263)
PHONE..................540 869-1150
EMP: 2
SALES (est): 137.8K **Privately Held**
SIC: 3489 Ordnance & accessories

Windsor
Isle Of Wight County

(G-15603)
CUSTOM FABRICATORS INC
20309 Longview Dr (23487-6466)
PHONE..................757 724-0305
Richard A Holmes Sr, *Owner*

▲ = Import ▼=Export
◆ =Import/Export

Marsha Holmes, *Admin Sec*
EMP: 2
SALES (est): 195.9K **Privately Held**
SIC: 3441 Fabricated structural metal

(G-15604)
EMBROIDERY EXPRESSONS
18517 Shady Pine Ln (23487-6750)
PHONE..................................757 255-0713
EMP: 1
SALES (est): 42.6K **Privately Held**
SIC: 2395 Embroidery & art needlework

(G-15605)
HORTON WELDING LLC
10454 Sylvia Cir (23487-5338)
PHONE..................................757 346-8405
William Horton, *Principal*
EMP: 1
SALES (est): 39.7K **Privately Held**
SIC: 7692 Welding repair

(G-15606)
MAURICE BYNUM
Also Called: P. D. & J. Envirocon
15 Virginia Ave (23487-9607)
PHONE..................................757 241-0265
Maurice Bynum, *Owner*
Terry Bynum, *Co-Owner*
EMP: 2 **EST:** 2002
SALES (est): 104.6K **Privately Held**
SIC: 3589 7389 Sewage & water treatment equipment; business services

(G-15607)
VIRGINIA RURAL LETTER
73 E Windsor Blvd (23487-9410)
P.O. Box 54 (23487-0054)
PHONE..................................757 242-6865
Thomas E Sifk, *President*
Marion Neighbours, *Corp Secy*
Larry N Cirkle, *Vice Pres*
EMP: 8
SALES (est): 500K **Privately Held**
WEB: www.virginiarlca.org
SIC: 3944 Craft & hobby kits & sets

(G-15608)
WINDSOR WOODWORKING CO INC
13120 Old Suffolk Rd (23487-5800)
PHONE..................................757 242-4141
Jesse R Williams, *President*
Jay Williams, *Corp Secy*
EMP: 5
SQ FT: 5,500
SALES (est): 400K **Privately Held**
SIC: 2431 2434 Millwork; wood kitchen cabinets; vanities, bathroom: wood

Wirtz
Franklin County

(G-15609)
CALVIN MONTGOMERY
2733 Alean Rd (24184-3870)
PHONE..................................540 334-3058
Calvin Montgomery, *Principal*
EMP: 2
SALES (est): 198.2K **Privately Held**
SIC: 2431 Millwork

(G-15610)
E GIUFFRE INC
400 Greystone Dr (24184-2902)
PHONE..................................540 537-4367
EMP: 1
SALES (est): 56.1K **Privately Held**
SIC: 3489 Ordnance & accessories

(G-15611)
GOT IT COVERED LLC
230 Plybon Ln (24184-2503)
PHONE..................................540 353-5167
Patrick Bush, *Principal*
EMP: 2
SALES (est): 170.5K **Privately Held**
WEB: www.gotitcoveredcanvas.com
SIC: 2394 Canvas & related products

(G-15612)
HARRY HALE LOGGING
2195 Bonbrook Mill Rd (24184-4078)
PHONE..................................540 484-1666
Harry Hale, *Owner*
EMP: 2
SALES (est): 152.3K **Privately Held**
SIC: 2411 Logging camps & contractors

(G-15613)
HELEN HEINMILLER
64 Cameron Cir (24184-3767)
PHONE..................................484 459-4425
Helen Heinmiller, *Principal*
EMP: 2
SALES (est): 76.6K **Privately Held**
WEB: www.helenheinmiller.com
SIC: 2741 Miscellaneous publishing

(G-15614)
INDEPENDENT MACHINING SERVICE
1809 Sample Rd (24184-0077)
PHONE..................................540 797-7284
Nathan Wagner, *President*
EMP: 2
SALES (est): 20.3K **Privately Held**
SIC: 3544 Special dies, tools, jigs & fixtures

(G-15615)
J & P MEAT PROCESSING
10 Jamont Ln (24184-4121)
PHONE..................................540 721-2765
E F Jamison, *Partner*
William Peters, *Partner*
EMP: 10
SALES (est): 889.6K **Privately Held**
SIC: 2011 Meat packing plants

(G-15616)
MONTGOMERY CABINETRY
867 Peters Pike Rd (24184-3860)
PHONE..................................540 721-7000
Gary Montgomery, *Owner*
EMP: 5
SALES (est): 700K **Privately Held**
SIC: 2434 1799 5031 1751 Wood kitchen cabinets; kitchen cabinet installation; kitchen cabinets; cabinet & finish carpentry

(G-15617)
MONTGOMERY FARM SUPPLY CO
3220 Wirtz Rd (24184-4097)
PHONE..................................540 483-7072
Norman Montgomery, *President*
Penny Arrington, *Vice Pres*
EMP: 1
SALES (est): 120K **Privately Held**
SIC: 2874 5191 Phosphatic fertilizers; fertilizer & fertilizer materials

(G-15618)
SOUTHEASTERN LOGGING & CHIPPIN
3850 Burnt Chimney Rd (24184-3965)
PHONE..................................540 493-9781
EMP: 3
SALES (est): 108.7K **Privately Held**
SIC: 2411 Logging camps & contractors

(G-15619)
SOUTHERN STATES ROANOKE COOP
Also Called: Franklin Branch
3220 Wirtz Rd (24184-4097)
PHONE..................................540 483-1217
John Eberhardt, *Manager*
EMP: 2
SALES (corp-wide): 2.1B **Privately Held**
SIC: 2874 5191 Phosphatic fertilizers; farm supplies
HQ: Southern States Roanoke Cooperative Inc
79 Mountain Ave
Troutville VA 24175
540 992-5968

Wise
Wise County

(G-15620)
CONWAY WOODWORKING LLC
7138 Hurricane Rd Ne (24293-4722)
P.O. Box 120 (24293-0120)
PHONE..................................276 328-6590
Benjamin Conway, *Principal*
EMP: 4
SALES (est): 475.7K **Privately Held**
SIC: 2431 Millwork

(G-15621)
DAVIS MINDING MANUFACTURE
5957 Windswept Blvd (24293-4764)
PHONE..................................276 321-7137
Deborah K Davis, *Principal*
EMP: 2
SALES (est): 85.1K **Privately Held**
SIC: 3999 Manufacturing industries

(G-15622)
DAVIS MINING & MFG INC (PA)
5957 Windswept Blvd (24293-4764)
PHONE..................................276 395-3354
W Jack Davis, *Ch of Bd*
L Jack Davis, *Vice Pres*
Deborah Karen Davis, *Treasurer*
William H Roj, *Admin Sec*
◆ **EMP:** 10
SALES (est): 509.6MM **Privately Held**
SIC: 2892 5082 2426 1221 Explosives; mining machinery & equipment, except petroleum; turnings, furniture: wood; strip mining, bituminous; bituminous coal-underground mining

(G-15623)
FALCON COAL CORPORATION
5505 Wise Norton Rd (24293-7705)
P.O. Box 1247 (24293-1247)
PHONE..................................276 679-0600
Tommy Skeens, *President*
Eddie Skeens, *Corp Secy*
Jerry Skeens, *Vice Pres*
Robert Skeens, *Vice Pres*
EMP: 20
SQ FT: 3,000
SALES (est): 2.1MM **Privately Held**
SIC: 1221 Bituminous coal & lignite-surface mining

(G-15624)
GIBSON WELDING
7936 Carter Branch Rd (24293-7514)
PHONE..................................276 328-3324
Judy Gibson, *Owner*
EMP: 3 **EST:** 1998
SALES (est): 282.1K **Privately Held**
SIC: 7692 Welding repair

(G-15625)
GREYBOX STRATEGIES LLC
193 Ridgeview Rd Sw (24293-4619)
PHONE..................................276 328-3249
Robert Robbins, *Mng Member*
EMP: 2
SALES (est): 62.1K **Privately Held**
SIC: 7372 Business oriented computer software

(G-15626)
IMPRESSIONS OF NORTON INC
301 Norton Rd (24293-5632)
PHONE..................................276 328-1100
Henrietta Dotson, *Vice Pres*
EMP: 2
SALES (est): 79K **Privately Held**
SIC: 2759 Screen printing

(G-15627)
IN HOME CARE INC (PA)
Also Called: Signs and Designs
201 Nottingham Ave (24293-5612)
PHONE..................................276 328-6462
Mike Whitaker, *President*
Yvonne Whitaker, *Admin Sec*
EMP: 31
SALES: 3.2MM **Privately Held**
WEB: www.elderpagesswv.com
SIC: 3993 Signs & advertising specialties

(G-15628)
JACKIE E CALHOUN SR
8025 Indian Creek Rd (24293)
PHONE..................................276 328-8318
Jackie Calhoun, *Owner*
Jackie E Calhoun Sr, *Principal*
EMP: 1
SALES (est): 27.2K **Privately Held**
SIC: 7692 Welding repair

(G-15629)
LABXPERIOR CORPORATION
517 W Main St (24293-6905)
P.O. Box 616, Norton (24273-0616)
PHONE..................................276 321-7866
Tina Marie Ball, *CEO*
EMP: 8 **EST:** 2014
SALES (est): 458.1K **Privately Held**
WEB: www.labxperior.org
SIC: 3826 Analytical instruments

(G-15630)
LONGWORTH SPORTS GROUP INC
130 W Main St (24293-7123)
P.O. Box 2770 (24293-2770)
PHONE..................................276 328-3300
Kristi Longworth, *CEO*
EMP: 4
SALES (est): 500K **Privately Held**
WEB: www.longworthsports.com
SIC: 3949 Sporting & athletic goods

(G-15631)
LOUISE RICHARDSON
6810 Bates Airfield Rd (24293-7406)
PHONE..................................276 328-4545
Louise Richardson, *Principal*
EMP: 1
SALES (est): 83.6K **Privately Held**
SIC: 3949 Camping equipment & supplies

(G-15632)
MICHAEL FLEMING
Also Called: Eastern Machine
9808b Coeburn Mountain Rd (24293-7324)
PHONE..................................276 337-9202
Michael Fleming, *Owner*
Melissa Fleming, *Principal*
EMP: 3 **EST:** 2003
SALES (est): 45.7K **Privately Held**
SIC: 7692 Welding repair

(G-15633)
R & R MINING INC
6617b W Main St (24293-7115)
P.O. Box 3546 (24293-3546)
PHONE..................................606 837-9321
EMP: 2
SALES (est): 120K **Privately Held**
SIC: 1479 Chemical/Fertilizer Mineral Mining

(G-15634)
TAAL ENTERPRISES LLC
6538 Cherokee Rd (24293)
P.O. Box 2160 (24293-2160)
PHONE..................................276 328-2408
Mark Mullins, *
EMP: 10
SALES (est): 1MM **Privately Held**
SIC: 3531 Construction machinery

(G-15635)
TAVERN ON MAIN LLC
225 Main St (24293-6903)
PHONE..................................276 328-2208
EMP: 35
SALES (est): 2.9MM **Privately Held**
SIC: 3589 Mfg Service Industry Machinery

(G-15636)
TIMBERLAND EXPRESS INC
4848 Thompson Rd (24293-6614)
PHONE..................................276 679-1965
Oscar Neece, *President*
EMP: 7 **EST:** 2007
SALES (est): 600K **Privately Held**
SIC: 2421 Sawmills & planing mills, general

(G-15637)
WISE CUSTOM MACHINING
5549 Rock Bar Rd (24293-5904)
PHONE..................................276 328-8681

GEOGRAPHIC

Charles Osborne, *Owner*
EMP: 2
SALES (est): 116.7K **Privately Held**
SIC: 3599 Industrial machinery

Wolford
Buchanan County

(G-15638)
ENGINES UNLIMITED INC
4389 Hurley Rd (24658)
PHONE......................276 566-7208
Andy K Crockett, *Principal*
EMP: 3
SALES (est): 246K **Privately Held**
SIC: 3519 Internal combustion engines

Woodbridge
Prince William County

(G-15639)
3D DESIGNS DAZZLING DREAM DESI
12759 Cara Dr (22192-2734)
PHONE......................703 231-9540
Dorothy Nelson, *Owner*
EMP: 1
SALES (est): 72.7K **Privately Held**
SIC: 3961 Costume jewelry

(G-15640)
7M GRAPHIX LLC
945 Highams Ct (22191-1436)
PHONE......................703 910-0915
Howard Carrasco, *General Mgr*
EMP: 1
SALES (est): 84.8K **Privately Held**
WEB: www.7mgraphix.com
SIC: 3993 Signs & advertising specialties

(G-15641)
AANDC SALES INC
3388 Bristol Ct (22193-1340)
PHONE......................703 638-8949
Juan Carlos Magana, *Principal*
EMP: 2
SALES (est): 86.6K **Privately Held**
SIC: 3441 Fabricated structural metal

(G-15642)
ADVANCED PACKET SWITCHING INC
13032 Queen Chapel Rd (22193-4947)
PHONE......................703 627-1746
Rodriguez Janice M, *Admin Sec*
EMP: 3
SALES (est): 175.6K **Privately Held**
SIC: 3679 Electronic switches

(G-15643)
AKMAL KHALIQI
14080 Malta St (22193-5934)
PHONE......................202 710-7582
Mohammed Akmal, *Owner*
EMP: 1
SALES (est): 20K **Privately Held**
SIC: 3861 Editing equipment, motion picture: viewers, splicers, etc.

(G-15644)
ALEETA A GARDNER
Also Called: Why Wellness Company, The
5033 Anchorstone Dr (22192-8320)
PHONE......................571 722-2549
Aleeta A Gardner, *Owner*
EMP: 1
SALES (est): 38.9K **Privately Held**
SIC: 2037 Frozen fruits & vegetables

(G-15645)
ALTERNATIVE CANDLE COMPANY
12331 Midsummer Ln Apt B (22192-6702)
PHONE......................804 350-6980
Amanda Shotts, *Principal*
EMP: 1
SALES (est): 39.6K **Privately Held**
SIC: 3999 Candles

(G-15646)
ARBAN & CAROSI INCORPORATED
13800 Dawson Beach Rd (22191-1497)
PHONE......................703 491-5121
Nicholas Carosi III, *President*
Robin Marcoe, *Opers Mgr*
Bimalendu Kundu, *CFO*
Sharon A Winter, *CFO*
Sharon Winters, *CFO*
▲ **EMP:** 150
SQ FT: 50,000
SALES (est): 26.7MM **Privately Held**
WEB: www.arbancarosi.com
SIC: 3272 Concrete products, precast

(G-15647)
ARC VOSACTHREE
2216 Tacketts Mill Dr (22192-3012)
PHONE......................703 910-7721
EMP: 1
SALES (est): 25K **Privately Held**
SIC: 7692 Welding repair

(G-15648)
ARK HOLDINGS GROUP LLC
13944 Greendale Dr (22191-1484)
PHONE......................202 368-5828
Lennie Mitchell, *President*
EMP: 1
SALES (est): 56.6K **Privately Held**
SIC: 3812 Defense systems & equipment

(G-15649)
ARTISTIC THREAD DESIGNS
15201 Warbler Ct (22193-1683)
PHONE......................703 583-3706
John Gaige, *Owner*
Virginia Gaige, *Owner*
EMP: 2
SALES (est): 80K **Privately Held**
SIC: 3999 Sewing kits, novelty

(G-15650)
ATLAS INC
15513 Marsh Overlook Dr (22191-3789)
PHONE......................646 835-9656
Rajiv Roopan, *President*
EMP: 1
SALES (est): 30.3K **Privately Held**
SIC: 7372 Prepackaged software

(G-15651)
AUTOGRIND PRODUCTS
13600 Dabney Rd (22191-1446)
PHONE......................703 490-7061
William Goldfarb, *President*
EMP: 2
SALES (est): 116.6K **Privately Held**
WEB: www.auto-grind.com
SIC: 3559 Special industry machinery

(G-15652)
AUTOMOTORS INDUSTRIES INC
13503 Kerrydale Rd (22193-4706)
PHONE......................703 459-8930
Edwin Alberto Monge, *President*
EMP: 2
SALES (est): 133K **Privately Held**
SIC: 3999 Manufacturing industries

(G-15653)
BALLISTICS CENTER LLC
2601 Woodfern Ct (22192-2007)
PHONE......................703 380-4901
James Lucore, *Manager*
EMP: 1
SQ FT: 5,000
SALES (est): 88.9K **Privately Held**
WEB: www.theballisticscenter.com
SIC: 3484 5091 Pistols or pistol parts, 30 mm. & below; firearms, sporting

(G-15654)
BARET LLC
Also Called: Baret Bat & Glove Company
15408 Weldin Dr (22193-1054)
PHONE......................808 230-9904
Juan Carlos Baret,
EMP: 1
SALES (est): 87.7K **Privately Held**
WEB: www.baretbats.com
SIC: 3151 Leather gloves & mittens

(G-15655)
BELLASH BAKERY INC
13420 Jefferson Davis Hwy (22191-1211)
PHONE......................516 468-2312
Maria Rubio, *Principal*
EMP: 5
SQ FT: 1,500
SALES (est): 318.2K **Privately Held**
WEB: www.bellashbakery.com
SIC: 2051 Cakes, bakery: except frozen

(G-15656)
BELTWAY LEATHERWORKS LLC
2743 King Iron Ct (22192-1210)
PHONE......................703 457-7829
Dennis Camacho, *Principal*
EMP: 2 **EST:** 2017
SALES (est): 107.8K **Privately Held**
WEB: www.beltwayleatherworks.com
SIC: 3199 Leather goods

(G-15657)
BIRDS WITH BACKPACKS LLC
1501 Spoonbill Ct (22191-3783)
PHONE......................703 897-5531
Nanette Mickle, *Principal*
EMP: 2
SALES (est): 103.5K **Privately Held**
SIC: 3911 5944 Jewelry, precious metal; jewelry stores

(G-15658)
BIRTH RIGHT INDUSTRIES LLC
14157 Renegade Ct (22193-3728)
PHONE......................703 590-6971
Frances Hill, *Principal*
EMP: 2
SALES (est): 86.9K **Privately Held**
SIC: 3999 Manufacturing industries

(G-15659)
BLACK MOLD RMVAL GROUP WDBRDGE
14058 Shoppers Best Way (22192-4131)
PHONE......................571 402-8960
EMP: 2 **EST:** 2010
SALES (est): 110K **Privately Held**
SIC: 3544 Mfg Dies/Tools/Jigs/Fixtures

(G-15660)
BLOCK9INE ENTERPRISES LLC
16813 Jed Forest Ln (22191-5126)
PHONE......................240 728-8601
Darren Campbell, *Principal*
EMP: 2
SALES (est): 67K **Privately Held**
SIC: 2323 Men's & boys' neckwear

(G-15661)
BOEING COMPANY
3308 Weymouth Ct (22192-1000)
PHONE......................703 808-2718
John Crigh, *Branch Mgr*
EMP: 2
SALES (corp-wide): 76.5B **Publicly Held**
WEB: www.boeing.com
SIC: 3721 Airplanes, fixed or rotary wing
PA: The Boeing Company
　　100 N Riverside Plz
　　Chicago IL 60606
　　312 544-2000

(G-15662)
BUCKIT O RICE
15265 Lord Culpeper Ct (22191-3997)
PHONE......................703 897-4190
Tangee M Dingle, *Principal*
▲ **EMP:** 1
SALES (est): 50K **Privately Held**
WEB: www.buckitorice.com
SIC: 2099 Food preparations

(G-15663)
C & G WOODWORKING
4517 Hazelton Dr (22193-5110)
PHONE......................703 878-7196
Craig Mc Sorley, *Owner*
EMP: 2
SALES (est): 194.2K **Privately Held**
WEB: www.candgwoodworking.com
SIC: 2431 Millwork

(G-15664)
CANTY LANE CONFECTIONS LLC
2606 Chester Cir (22191-4305)
PHONE......................703 408-3661
Kendra Marshall, *Mng Member*
EMP: 1
SALES (est): 39.5K **Privately Held**
SIC: 2051 Bakery products, partially cooked (except frozen)

(G-15665)
CAPITAL DISCOUNT MDSE LLC
13923 Jefferson Davis Hwy (22191-2010)
PHONE......................703 499-9368
Dorcas Dadzie,
▲ **EMP:** 12
SALES (est): 2MM **Privately Held**
WEB: www.capitaldm.com
SIC: 2273 2521 5713 Carpets & rugs; wood office furniture; carpets

(G-15666)
CAPITAL FLOORS LLC
2525 Luckland Way (22191-6347)
PHONE......................571 451-4044
Irfan Johri, *Principal*
EMP: 5
SALES (est): 317.8K **Privately Held**
SIC: 2299 2273 Carpet lining: felt, except woven; wilton carpets; finishers of tufted carpets & rugs; smyrna carpets & rugs, machine woven

(G-15667)
CAPITOL IDEA TECHNOLOGY INC
14819 Potomac Branch Dr (22191-4047)
PHONE......................571 233-1949
Michelle Sowers, *CEO*
Daniel J Dutch, *President*
Daniel Dutch, *General Mgr*
EMP: 4
SALES (est): 250K **Privately Held**
WEB: www.capitolideatech.com
SIC: 3571 8742 Electronic computers; management information systems consultant

(G-15668)
CARIBBEAN CHANNEL ONE INC
11763 Gascony Pl (22192-7402)
PHONE......................703 447-3773
Richard A Noel, *CEO*
EMP: 1 **EST:** 2010
SALES (est): 75.1K **Privately Held**
WEB: www.caribbeanchannelone.com
SIC: 2869 Fuels

(G-15669)
CARR GROUP LLC
2821 Powell Dr (22191-1475)
PHONE......................571 723-6562
John Sarsah, *Marketing Staff*
Ernestina Carr,
EMP: 4
SALES (est): 270.8K **Privately Held**
SIC: 3578 8742 8721 Accounting machines & cash registers; management consulting services; human resource consulting services; accounting services, except auditing

(G-15670)
CASA DE FIESTAS DINA
14454 Jefferson Davis Hwy (22191-2806)
PHONE......................703 910-6510
Dina Colindres, *Owner*
EMP: 2 **EST:** 2011
SALES (est): 121.1K **Privately Held**
SIC: 2335 Wedding gowns & dresses

(G-15671)
CITIZENS DEFENSE SOLUTIONS LLC
5935 Hunter Crest Rd (22193-4005)
PHONE......................254 423-1612
Stuart R Seal, *Administration*
EMP: 3
SALES (est): 195.6K **Privately Held**
WEB: www.cds2a.com
SIC: 3812 Defense systems & equipment

▲ = Import ▼=Export
◆ =Import/Export

(G-15672)
CITY SPREE OF WOODBRIDGE
3092 Ps Business Ctr Dr (22192-4229)
EMP: 1
SALES (est): 50.6K **Privately Held**
SIC: 2499 Mfg Wood Products

(G-15673)
CONTROLS UNLIMITED INC
2853 Ps Business Ctr Dr (22192-4226)
PHONE..............................703 897-4300
Glenn Glass, *President*
Michael Looney, *Vice Pres*
Mike Looney, *Vice Pres*
EMP: 7
SALES (est): 1.2MM **Privately Held**
WEB: www.cuicontrols.com
SIC: 3829 3823 Measuring & controlling
devices; industrial instrmnts msrmnt dis-
play/control process variable

(G-15674)
CREATIVE DECORATING
14812 Build America Dr (22191-3437)
P.O. Box 4426 (22194-4426)
PHONE..............................703 643-5556
Jamshid Jafari, *Owner*
EMP: 4
SALES (est): 270.9K **Privately Held**
SIC: 2391 7389 Draperies, plastic & tex-
tile: from purchased materials; interior de-
signer

(G-15675)
CREATIVE DOCUMENT IMAGING
INC
2050 Old Bridge Rd B04 (22192-2484)
PHONE..............................703 497-6767
Luis Mendoza, *President*
EMP: 3
SALES (corp-wide): 957.2K **Privately**
Held
WEB: www.creativedoc.net
SIC: 2752 Commercial printing, offset
PA: Creative Document Imaging Inc
8451 Hilltop Rd Ste I
Fairfax VA 22031
703 208-2212

(G-15676)
CROOKED STITCH BAGS LLC
2902 Archer Ct (22193-1222)
PHONE..............................703 680-0118
Harlean Owens, *Principal*
EMP: 2 EST: 2012
SALES (est): 86.8K **Privately Held**
SIC: 3069 7389 Bags, rubber or rubber-
ized fabric; business services

(G-15677)
CROSSING TRAILS
PUBLICATION
4804 Kentwood Ln (22193-5007)
PHONE..............................703 590-4449
William H Nesbitt, *Owner*
EMP: 1
SALES (est): 55.1K **Privately Held**
SIC: 2741 Miscellaneous publishing

(G-15678)
CSM INTERNATIONAL
CORPORATION
16834 Panorama Dr (22191-4426)
P.O. Box 6230, Falls Church (22040-6230)
PHONE..............................800 767-3805
Kenneth Swanson, *President*
EMP: 4
SQ FT: 2,500
SALES (est): 500K **Privately Held**
SIC: 3599 Custom machinery

(G-15679)
CTI OF WOODBRIDGE
14311 Silverdale Dr (22193-3416)
PHONE..............................703 670-4790
Bret Moore, *Principal*
EMP: 2 EST: 2015
SALES (est): 66.8K **Privately Held**
WEB: www.cti-woodbridge.com
SIC: 2499 Wood products

(G-15680)
DAN MATHENY JERR
14716 Industry Ct (22191-3126)
PHONE..............................703 499-9216

Dan Matheny, *Principal*
EMP: 4
SALES (est): 344.2K **Privately Held**
SIC: 3799 Towing bars & systems

(G-15681)
DECONSYSTEMS
CORPORATION
13513 Delaney Rd (22193-4649)
PHONE..............................703 587-3971
Carlos M Byrd, *CEO*
EMP: 1
SALES (est): 55K **Privately Held**
SIC: 3841 Medical instruments & equip-
ment, blood & bone work

(G-15682)
DEP COPY CENTER INC
14816 Build America Dr (22191-3437)
PHONE..............................703 499-9888
James Hicks, *President*
EMP: 4
SQ FT: 1,800
SALES (est): 250K **Privately Held**
WEB: www.depprinting.com
SIC: 2752 7334 Commercial printing, off-
set; photocopying & duplicating services

(G-15683)
DETRON REALTY LLC
4548 Kendall Dr (22193-5260)
PHONE..............................703 884-6741
Evelyn Siomara Vargas,
EMP: 1
SALES (est): 41K **Privately Held**
SIC: 1389 Construction, repair & disman-
tling services

(G-15684)
DOMINION DEFENSE LLC
15347 Blacksmith Ter (22191-3826)
PHONE..............................703 216-7295
Gary Scott Latta, *Administration*
EMP: 4
SALES (est): 382.2K **Privately Held**
SIC: 3812 Defense systems & equipment

(G-15685)
DOOR SYSTEMS INC
1030 Highams Ct (22191-1445)
PHONE..............................703 490-1800
Walter Rock, *President*
Mike Bradt, *Vice Pres*
EMP: 15
SQ FT: 5,000
SALES (est): 2.4MM **Privately Held**
WEB: www.doorsystemsva.com
SIC: 3699 7699 5211 1751 Door opening
& closing devices, electrical; door & win-
dow repair; door & window products; car-
pentry work

(G-15686)
DOUBLE D LLC
15358 Wits End Dr (22193-5889)
PHONE..............................270 307-2786
Sharon Fentress-Bussey, *Mng Member*
EMP: 2
SALES (est): 73.1K **Privately Held**
SIC: 2721 Periodicals

(G-15687)
DULL INC DOLAN & NORMA
Also Called: All Star Sports
2592 Dynasty Loop (22192-4631)
PHONE..............................703 490-0337
Brian Dull, *CEO*
Dolan J Dull, *President*
Norma Dull, *Corp Secy*
Ronald Dull, *Vice Pres*
EMP: 18
SQ FT: 4,000
SALES (est): 800K **Privately Held**
WEB: www.allstarsportsinfo.com
SIC: 2395 2759 5941 2396 Emblems,
embroidered; screen printing; sporting
goods & bicycle shops; automotive & ap-
parel trimmings

(G-15688)
EIW POWDER COATING
14861 Persistence Dr (22191-3560)
PHONE..............................703 586-9392
EMP: 2

SALES (est): 81.5K **Privately Held**
WEB: www.eiwpc.com
SIC: 3479 Metal coating & allied service

(G-15689)
ELIZABETH A GRGE VLIN STDIO
LL
3499 Beaver Ford Rd (22192-4913)
PHONE..............................703 590-8145
EMP: 1
SALES (est): 55.3K **Privately Held**
WEB:
www.elizabethageorgeviolinstudio.com
SIC: 3931 Violins & parts

(G-15690)
ELO INC
Also Called: Elopitch
4262 Pemberley Ct (22193-5764)
PHONE..............................571 435-0129
EMP: 5
SALES (est): 117.2K **Privately Held**
SIC: 7372 Prepackaged Software Services

(G-15691)
EMBROIDERY CROWN INC
15363 Grist Mill Ter (22191-3803)
PHONE..............................703 986-3022
Haris Azhar, *Principal*
EMP: 3
SALES (est): 94.1K **Privately Held**
SIC: 3231 Products of purchased glass

(G-15692)
EMERALD IRONWORKS INC
14861 Persistence Dr (22191-3560)
PHONE..............................703 690-2477
Michael P Pigott, *President*
Natasha Selhi, *Publisher*
Junstin Piggot, *Vice Pres*
Grace Casey, *Prdtn Mgr*
EMP: 29
SQ FT: 13,000
SALES (est): 2.3MM **Privately Held**
WEB: www.emeraldironworks.com
SIC: 3446 3449 5999 Ornamental metal-
work; miscellaneous metalwork; art, pic-
ture frames & decorations

(G-15693)
EMPLOYMENT GUIDE
14065 Crown Ct (22193-1458)
PHONE..............................703 580-7586
Jeff Le Bel, *Manager*
EMP: 1
SALES (est): 37.5K **Privately Held**
SIC: 2741 Miscellaneous publishing

(G-15694)
ENDREOLA SHEET METAL
14912 Daytona Ct (22193-1929)
PHONE..............................703 496-8538
EMP: 4
SALES (est): 400.7K **Privately Held**
WEB: www.endreolasheetmetal.com
SIC: 3444 Sheet metalwork

(G-15695)
EQUIPMENT REPAIR SERVICES
2004 Cumberland Dr (22191-2515)
PHONE..............................703 491-7681
Donald Mombourquette, *President*
EMP: 1
SALES (est): 100.5K **Privately Held**
SIC: 3531 Construction machinery

(G-15696)
ERICK GONZALEZ
Also Called: Digital State Media
13113 Orleans St (22192-3710)
PHONE..............................703 855-2908
Erick Gonzalez, *Owner*
EMP: 2
SALES (est): 100K **Privately Held**
SIC: 7372 Prepackaged software

(G-15697)
ERVINS BATHTUB REFINISHING
15402 Gunsmith Ter (22191-3928)
P.O. Box 4312 (22194-4312)
PHONE..............................703 730-8831
Ervin Lawrence, *Owner*
EMP: 1
SALES (est): 73K **Privately Held**
SIC: 2851 Paints & allied products

(G-15698)
EUROPRO COATINGS INC
Also Called: Euro Pro Coatings
2714 Code Way (22192-4629)
PHONE..............................703 817-1211
Walter F Hansen, *Principal*
EMP: 3
SALES (est): 222.5K **Privately Held**
SIC: 3479 Coating of metals & formed
products

(G-15699)
EVENTDONE LLC (PA)
4391 Ridgewood Center Dr H
(22192-5399)
PHONE..............................703 239-6410
David Beg, *CEO*
Fahima Kadiri Beg, *President*
EMP: 2
SALES (est): 200K **Privately Held**
SIC: 7372 Application computer software

(G-15700)
EXCLUSIVELY YOURS
EMBROIDERY
5603 Nibbs Ct (22193-4121)
PHONE..............................571 285-2196
Lani McMullan, *Principal*
EMP: 1 EST: 2015
SALES (est): 46.4K **Privately Held**
SIC: 2395 Embroidery & art needlework

(G-15701)
EXPERTSINFRAMING LLC
4164 Merchant Plz (22192-5085)
PHONE..............................703 580-9980
Akramjoh Mirzakhalov,
EMP: 1 EST: 2013
SALES (est): 313.3K **Privately Held**
WEB: www.expertsinframing.com
SIC: 2512 Living room furniture: uphol-
stered on wood frames

(G-15702)
FASHION MECHANICS
2700 Potomac Mills Cir # 111 (22192-4651)
PHONE..............................571 398-0894
EMP: 1
SALES (est): 51.1K **Privately Held**
WEB: www.fashion-mechanics.com
SIC: 2299 Jute & flax textile products

(G-15703)
FEDEX OFFICE & PRINT SVCS
INC
13752 Jefferson Davis Hwy (22191-2007)
PHONE..............................703 491-1300
EMP: 3
SALES (corp-wide): 47.4B **Publicly Held**
SIC: 2759 Commercial Printing
HQ: Fedex Office And Print Services, Inc.
7900 Legacy Dr
Dallas TX 75024
214 550-7000

(G-15704)
FLAVORFUL BAKERY & CAFE
LLC
1210 E Longview Dr (22191-2957)
PHONE..............................301 857-2202
Jennell Hartford, *Administration*
EMP: 1
SALES (est): 50.4K **Privately Held**
SIC: 2051 7389 Cakes, bakery: except
frozen;

(G-15705)
FOREL PUBLISHING CO LLC
3999 Peregrine Ridge Ct (22192-6625)
PHONE..............................703 772-8081
David Leblanc, *Principal*
EMP: 4
SALES (est): 231.8K **Privately Held**
WEB: www.forelpublishing.com
SIC: 2741 Miscellaneous publishing

(G-15706)
FOUZ INC
16030 Barn Swallow Pl (22191-5542)
PHONE..............................571 407-4446
Isra Mushtaha, *Principal*
EMP: 2
SALES (est): 62.3K **Privately Held**
SIC: 2099 Food preparations

GEOGRAPHIC

(G-15707)
FREESTYLE KING LLC
13113 Otto Rd (22193-7013)
PHONE..............................703 309-1144
Olatomiwa Ogunsola, *Administration*
Emily Root,
EMP: 2
SALES (est): 83K **Privately Held**
SIC: 7372 Application computer software

(G-15708)
FROSTED MUFFIN - A
CUPCAKERY
2952 American Eagle Blvd (22191-6068)
PHONE..............................571 989-1722
Jacque Pitts,
EMP: 1
SALES (est): 67.3K **Privately Held**
WEB: www.thefrostedmuffin-va.com
SIC: 2051 Cakes, bakery: except frozen

(G-15709)
GENERAL DYNAMICS
CORPORATION
6204 Trident Ln (22193-4130)
PHONE..............................703 221-1009
EMP: 44
SALES (corp-wide): 31.3B **Publicly Held**
SIC: 3731 Mfg Submarines
PA: General Dynamics Corporation
2941 Frview Pk Dr Ste 100
Falls Church VA 20190
703 876-3000

(G-15710)
GOLD STEM
12550 Dillingham Sq (22192-5259)
PHONE..............................703 680-7000
Lori Lowell, *Owner*
EMP: 50
SALES (est): 3.1MM **Privately Held**
SIC: 3446 Architectural metalwork

(G-15711)
GONMF
13025 Carolyn Forest Dr (22192-5619)
PHONE..............................844 763-7250
EMP: 2
SALES (est): 99.5K **Privately Held**
WEB: www.gonmf.com
SIC: 3714 Motor vehicle parts & acces-
sories

(G-15712)
GPC INC
Also Called: Golden Pride Company
745 Vestal St (22191-5438)
PHONE..............................757 345-3991
Valeriy Korcchak, *President*
Roza Korcchak, *Treasurer*
EMP: 5
SALES (est): 855.9K **Privately Held**
WEB: www.golden-pride.com
SIC: 2899 Chemical supplies for foundries

(G-15713)
GRAYER INDUSTRIES LLC
12452 Cavalier Dr (22192-3314)
PHONE..............................703 491-4629
Terry Gray, *Principal*
EMP: 2 EST: 2011
SALES (est): 93.2K **Privately Held**
SIC: 3999 Manufacturing industries

(G-15714)
GREAT AMERCN
WOODCRAFTERS LLC
14498 Telegraph Rd (22192-4620)
PHONE..............................571 572-3150
EMP: 3
SALES (est): 302.7K **Privately Held**
WEB: www.woodcraftersfurniturestore.com
SIC: 2426 Carvings, furniture: wood

(G-15715)
GREAT NEON ART & SIGN CO
Also Called: Ben & Xander's Fudge Co.
12000 Park Shore Ct (22192-2216)
PHONE..............................703 981-4661
Steve Humleker, *Owner*
EMP: 2 EST: 1992
SALES (est): 134K **Privately Held**
WEB: www.benandxandersfudge.com
SIC: 3993 Signs & advertising specialties

(G-15716)
GREEN COAL SOLUTIONS LLC
13001 Summit School Rd # 4
(22192-2903)
PHONE..............................703 910-4022
Ato Andoh, *Principal*
EMP: 1
SALES (est): 105.6K **Privately Held**
WEB: www.greencoalsolutions.com
SIC: 2821 Coal tar resins

(G-15717)
GREENACRE PLUMBING LLC
11681 Bacon Race Rd (22192-5717)
PHONE..............................703 680-2380
Jeffrey Migliaccio,
EMP: 5
SALES (est): 488.9K **Privately Held**
WEB: www.greenacreplumbing.com
SIC: 3432 7389 Plastic plumbing fixture
fittings, assembly;

(G-15718)
GREENBROOK TMS
NEUROHEALTH CTR
Also Called: Tms Neurohealth Centers
13625 Office Pl Ste 101 (22192-4270)
PHONE..............................703 670-5738
EMP: 1
SALES (corp-wide): 2.7MM **Privately
Held**
WEB: www.greenbrooktms.com
SIC: 3312 Blast furnaces & steel mills
PA: Greenbrook Tms Neurohealth Center
8405 Greensboro Dr # 120
Mc Lean VA 22102
703 356-1568

(G-15719)
GUMAX INTERNATIONAL LTD
Also Called: Gumax Accounting Services
2862 Garber Way (22192-4003)
PHONE..............................866 412-3880
Augustine Guma, *CEO*
Dr John Agbi, *Principal*
Fugi Kalisa, *Principal*
Emmanuel Ssensulike, *Principal*
EMP: 30
SALES: 778.5K **Privately Held**
WEB: www.gumaxcpas.com
SIC: 2051 7371 8721 8049 Bakery:
wholesale or wholesale/retail combined;
custom computer programming services;
accounting, auditing & bookkeeping;
nurses, registered & practical; specialty
food items; frozen specialties

(G-15720)
HAMILTON IRON WORKS INC
14103 Telegraph Rd (22192-4613)
PHONE..............................703 497-4766
Isaac Hamilton, *President*
Greg Williams, *Project Mgr*
Baird Calib, *Opers Mgr*
EMP: 42 EST: 1974
SQ FT: 21,300
SALES (est): 11.2MM **Privately Held**
WEB: www.hamiltoniron.com
SIC: 3441 3449 Fabricated structural
metal; miscellaneous metalwork

(G-15721)
HAND AND HAMMER INC
Also Called: Hand and Hammer Silversmiths
2610 Morse Ln (22192-4627)
PHONE..............................703 491-4866
Chip De Matteo, *President*
EMP: 18
SQ FT: 2,300
SALES (est): 2MM **Privately Held**
WEB: www.handandhammer.com
SIC: 3911 3914 Jewelry apparel; silver-
smithing

(G-15722)
HIGHER PRESS LLC
12209 Dapple Gray Ct (22192-6281)
PHONE..............................703 944-1521
Jenifer Elaine Dent, *Administration*
EMP: 1
SALES (est): 39.4K **Privately Held**
SIC: 2741 Miscellaneous publishing

(G-15723)
HONEY TRUE TEAS LLC
2021 Mayflower Dr (22192-2306)
PHONE..............................703 728-8369
Chris Savage, *Mng Member*
EMP: 3
SALES (est): 257.1K **Privately Held**
WEB: www.truehoneyteas.com
SIC: 2393 Tea bags, fabric: made from pur-
chased materials

(G-15724)
HUQA LIVE LLC
2029 Pyxie Way (22192-2947)
PHONE..............................202 527-9342
Raakin Iqbal,
EMP: 1
SALES (est): 81.5K **Privately Held**
SIC: 3861 7359 7922 Projectors, still or
motion picture, silent or sound; sound &
lighting equipment rental; employment
agency: theatrical, radio & television

(G-15725)
IM APPAREL LLC
12195 Cardamom Dr (22192-1448)
PHONE..............................202 905-5696
Stacey Sowemimo,
EMP: 1
SALES (est): 46.5K **Privately Held**
SIC: 2211 Apparel & outerwear fabrics,
cotton

(G-15726)
IMPACT JUNKIE LLC
15461 Marsh Overlook Dr (22191-3778)
PHONE..............................916 541-0317
Philip Harding, *President*
EMP: 1
SALES (est): 32.7K **Privately Held**
SIC: 7372 Application computer software

(G-15727)
J S & A CAKE DECORATION
1309 E Longview Dr (22191-2922)
PHONE..............................703 494-3767
Johnny McReynolds, *Owner*
EMP: 1
SALES (est): 39.5K **Privately Held**
SIC: 2051 Bread, cake & related products

(G-15728)
JAMES WILLIAMS POLSG &
BUFFING
5406 Staples Ln (22193-3562)
PHONE..............................703 690-2247
James E Willims, *Principal*
EMP: 3
SALES (est): 152.7K **Privately Held**
SIC: 3471 Plating of metals or formed
products

(G-15729)
JB PRODUCTIONS
13813 Botts Ave (22191-1941)
PHONE..............................703 494-6075
Jim Borecky, *Owner*
EMP: 1
SALES (est): 93.8K **Privately Held**
SIC: 2752 Business form & card printing,
lithographic

(G-15730)
JEWEL HOLDING LLC
14273 Silverdale Dr (22193-3414)
PHONE..............................202 271-5265
Willie Faconer,
EMP: 1
SALES (est): 41K **Privately Held**
SIC: 1389 Construction, repair & disman-
tling services

(G-15731)
JOZSA WOOD WORKS
14891 Persistence Dr (22191-3560)
PHONE..............................703 492-9405
Patricia Jozsa, *President*
Frank Jozsa, *Vice Pres*
EMP: 10 EST: 1995
SALES (est): 1.4MM **Privately Held**
SIC: 2431 Woodwork, interior & ornamen-
tal

(G-15732)
JTEES PRINTING
12169 Darnley Rd (22192-6615)
PHONE..............................703 590-4145
Jade Tavaglione, *Owner*
EMP: 2
SALES (est): 119.4K **Privately Held**
WEB: www.jteesprinting.com
SIC: 2759 Screen printing

(G-15733)
JUST WREATHS
4788 S Park Ct (22193-3040)
PHONE..............................571 208-4920
EMP: 2
SALES (est): 101.8K **Privately Held**
SIC: 3999 Wreaths, artificial

(G-15734)
JUSTICE
2700 Potomac Mills Cir # 235
(22192-4653)
PHONE..............................703 490-6664
EMP: 2
SALES (est): 67K **Privately Held**
SIC: 2361 Girls' & children's dresses,
blouses & shirts

(G-15735)
K WALTERS AT THE SIGN OF G
12131 Derriford Ct (22192-5128)
PHONE..............................703 986-0448
Kimberly Walters, *Principal*
EMP: 2
SALES (est): 137.2K **Privately Held**
SIC: 3993 Signs & advertising specialties

(G-15736)
KRAFT
5119 Cannon Bluff Dr (22192-5742)
PHONE..............................703 583-8874
Charles Kraft, *Principal*
EMP: 2
SALES (est): 124.4K **Privately Held**
WEB: www.kraftheinzcompany.com
SIC: 2033 Canned fruits & specialties

(G-15737)
KWIK DESIGN AND PRINT LLC
13406 Occoquan Rd (22191-1721)
PHONE..............................703 898-4681
Raja Ihsan, *Principal*
EMP: 2
SALES (est): 140.5K **Privately Held**
SIC: 2752 Commercial printing, litho-
graphic

(G-15738)
LAMAID LLC
11638 Rumford Ct (22192-7476)
PHONE..............................703 541-8011
Ishan Shams,
EMP: 1
SALES (est): 10K **Privately Held**
SIC: 7372 Application computer software

(G-15739)
LAS CREATION DESIGN LLC
15412 Gunsmith Ter (22191-3928)
PHONE..............................757 880-4211
Laantoinette Camm,
EMP: 1
SALES (est): 46.5K **Privately Held**
SIC: 2295 Resin or plastic coated fabrics

(G-15740)
LIGHTED SIGNS DIRECT INC
941 Highams Ct (22191-1436)
PHONE..............................703 965-5188
Ruth A Fisher, *President*
EMP: 5
SALES (est): 504.4K **Privately Held**
WEB: www.thesaenzgroup.com
SIC: 3993 7319 8744 4225 Signs & ad-
vertising specialties; transit advertising
services; facilities support services; gen-
eral warehousing & storage; commercial
art & graphic design

(G-15741)
LONDOO FOODS LLC
13903 Rope Dr (22191-2227)
PHONE..............................571 243-7627
EMP: 3

SALES (est): 78K **Privately Held**
SIC: 2099 Mfg Food Preparations

(G-15742)
LUCY LOVE CANDLES
2511 Luckland Way (22191-6347)
PHONE..................................571 991-4155
EMP: 2
SALES (est): 106.8K **Privately Held**
SIC: 3999 Candles

(G-15743)
MARIE WEBB
16807 Brandy Moor Loop (22191-4770)
PHONE..................................703 291-5359
Marie Webb, *Owner*
EMP: 1
SALES (est): 10K **Privately Held**
WEB: www.mariewebb.com
SIC: 2844 Cosmetic preparations

(G-15744)
METRO POWER PRINT
16909 Cass Brook Ln (22191-5112)
PHONE..................................703 221-3289
Jay Chevalier, *President*
EMP: 3
SALES (est): 244.9K **Privately Held**
SIC: 2759 Commercial printing

(G-15745)
MEVATEC CORP
4606 Moss Point Pl (22192-5343)
PHONE..................................703 583-9287
D Stokes, *Human Resources*
EMP: 2
SALES (est): 108.5K **Privately Held**
SIC: 3679 Electronic components

(G-15746)
MF CAPITAL LLC
Also Called: Berryganics
13595 Castlebridge Ln (22193-5172)
PHONE..................................703 470-8787
Fayyaz Alam,
EMP: 1
SALES (est): 39.5K **Privately Held**
SIC: 2023 Dietary supplements, dairy &
non-dairy based

(G-15747)
**MICHAEL AND THOMAS CONTG
LLC**
15231 Colony Pl Apt 311 (22191-4965)
PHONE..................................919 397-7960
Michael L Graham, *Principal*
EMP: 1
SALES (est): 100K **Privately Held**
SIC: 1389 Construction, repair & disman-
tling services

(G-15748)
MILLIKEN & COMPANY
3915 Triad Ct (22192-6288)
PHONE..................................571 659-0698
Beth Stinnett, *Branch Mgr*
EMP: 207
SALES (corp-wide): 2.9B **Privately Held**
WEB: www.performancesolutionsbymil-
liken.com
SIC: 2231 Broadwoven fabric mills, wool
PA: Milliken & Company
920 Milliken Rd
Spartanburg SC 29303
864 503-2020

(G-15749)
MOON INDUSTRIES LLC
2016 Stargrass Ct (22192-2957)
PHONE..................................703 878-2428
Lincoln Pitcher, *Principal*
EMP: 2
SALES (est): 102.7K **Privately Held**
SIC: 3999 Manufacturing industries

(G-15750)
MOSHREF MIR ABDUL
Also Called: Moshref, Mir Abdul
2902 Madeira Ct (22192-1923)
PHONE..................................502 356-0019
Mir Abdul Moshref, *Owner*
EMP: 1
SALES (est): 38.9K **Privately Held**
SIC: 2711 Newspapers

(G-15751)
**MOUNT CARMEL PUBLISHING
LLC**
4196 Merchant Plz Ste 348 (22192-5085)
PHONE..................................703 838-2109
Annie Ryan, *Principal*
EMP: 1
SALES (est): 37.5K **Privately Held**
SIC: 2741 Miscellaneous publishing

(G-15752)
**MS BETTYS BAD-ASS CANDLES
LLC**
4313 Marquis Pl (22192-6604)
PHONE..................................540 256-7221
Christopher Higdon, *Administration*
EMP: 2
SALES (est): 61.5K **Privately Held**
SIC: 3999 Candles

(G-15753)
NATHANIEL HOFFELDER
13884 Montoclair Ln (22193-4467)
PHONE..................................571 406-2689
Nathaniel Hoffelder, *Owner*
EMP: 1
SALES (est): 42.5K **Privately Held**
WEB: www.the-digital-reader.com
SIC: 2741 Miscellaneous publishing

(G-15754)
NATURALLY ME LLC
5874 Pontiac Dr (22193-3800)
PHONE..................................703 680-3392
Carrie E Tuning, *Administration*
EMP: 2
SALES (est): 61.6K **Privately Held**
SIC: 2844 Toilet preparations

(G-15755)
NAUTICA OF POTOMAC
Also Called: Nautica Factory Store
2700 Potomac Mills Cir # 325
(22192-4625)
PHONE..................................703 494-9915
Fax: 703 494-6640
EMP: 20 EST: 1999
SALES (est): 590K **Privately Held**
SIC: 2326 Mfg Men's/Boy's Work Clothing

(G-15756)
NAVY
15482 Wheatfield Rd (22193-5706)
PHONE..................................202 781-0981
EMP: 2
SALES (est): 88.3K **Privately Held**
SIC: 3625 Relays & industrial controls

(G-15757)
NEDA JEWELERS INC
Also Called: Neda Jewelers of Dale City
4332 Dale Blvd (22193-2402)
PHONE..................................703 670-2177
John Hashemi, *President*
Osra Hashemi, *Treasurer*
Peggy Fairweather, *Admin Sec*
EMP: 2
SQ FT: 1,600
SALES (est): 500K **Privately Held**
SIC: 3911 Jewelry, precious metal

(G-15758)
NGL WOODBRIDGE
13422 Jefferson Davis Hwy (22191-1211)
PHONE..................................703 492-0430
Linh Nguyen, *Owner*
EMP: 2 EST: 2012
SALES (est): 163.3K **Privately Held**
WEB: www.happynailsngl.com
SIC: 3315 Nails, spikes, brads & similar
items

(G-15759)
NIGHTHAWK WELDING LLC
1221 E Longview Dr (22191-2955)
PHONE..................................540 845-9966
William Dingfelder, *Principal*
EMP: 1
SALES (est): 48.1K **Privately Held**
SIC: 7692 Welding repair

(G-15760)
NIKE INC
2700 Potomac Mills Cir # 511
(22192-4656)
PHONE..................................703 497-4513
Shannon McDaniel, *Branch Mgr*
EMP: 25
SALES (corp-wide): 37.4B **Publicly Held**
WEB: www.nike.com
SIC: 3021 Rubber & plastics footwear
PA: Nike, Inc.
1 Sw Bowerman Dr
Beaverton OR 97005
503 671-6453

(G-15761)
**NM MECHANIC ROAD SERVICE
LLC**
1504 Constellation Pl # 204 (22191-5216)
PHONE..................................571 237-4810
Jose Torres,
EMP: 1
SALES (est): 103.9K **Privately Held**
SIC: 7694 7699 8744 Motor repair serv-
ices; industrial truck repair; tractor repair;
engine repair & replacement, non-auto-
motive;

(G-15762)
NOBLE ENDEAVORS LLC
Also Called: Sign-A-Rama
13859 Smoketown Rd (22192-4206)
PHONE..................................571 402-7061
Bill Mustin, *Mng Member*
EMP: 4
SQ FT: 2,900
SALES (est): 339.3K **Privately Held**
WEB: www.signarama.com
SIC: 3993 Signs & advertising specialties

(G-15763)
NOPAREI PROFESSIONALS LLC
Also Called: Eligmaparable
3418 Brahms Dr (22193-5565)
PHONE..................................571 354-9422
Solave Awumee, *Mng Member*
EMP: 1
SALES (est): 46.4K **Privately Held**
SIC: 2771 7389 Greeting cards;

(G-15764)
NORDIC MINING LLC
3811 Corona Ln (22193-1645)
PHONE..................................703 878-0346
Roald Hansen, *Owner*
EMP: 3 EST: 2015
SALES (est): 112.9K **Privately Held**
SIC: 1221 Bituminous coal & lignite-sur-
face mining

(G-15765)
NXVET LLC
11699 Bacon Race Rd (22192-5717)
PHONE..................................571 358-6198
James Combs, *CEO*
EMP: 3 EST: 2012
SALES (est): 247.4K **Privately Held**
WEB: www.govschedule.com
SIC: 2522 Office chairs, benches & stools,
except wood

(G-15766)
ONE WISH PUBLISHING LLC
13926 Andorra Dr (22193-2355)
PHONE..................................571 285-4227
Trina Walcott, *Administration*
EMP: 2
SALES (est): 65.7K **Privately Held**
SIC: 2741 Miscellaneous publishing

(G-15767)
**OS-GIM PHARMACEUTICALS
INC**
4712 Kilbane Rd (22193-4605)
PHONE..................................301 655-5191
Osamah Jameel, *Principal*
EMP: 3 EST: 2016
SALES (est): 218.6K **Privately Held**
SIC: 2834 Pharmaceutical preparations

(G-15768)
OVAL LLC
14700 Bell Tower Rd (22193-3624)
PHONE..................................757 389-3777
Logan Garrigus,

EMP: 1
SALES (est): 37.5K **Privately Held**
SIC: 2741

(G-15769)
PAINTED LADIES LLC
5648 Minnie Ct (22193-3192)
PHONE..................................571 481-6906
Jameelah Johnson, *Partner*
EMP: 2 EST: 2014
SALES (est): 136K **Privately Held**
WEB:
www.thepaintedladiesllc.blogspot.com
SIC: 3231 Decorated glassware: chipped,
engraved, etched, etc.

(G-15770)
PALMYRENE EMPIRE LLC
Also Called: Manufacturing
5405 Tomlinson Dr (22192-6057)
PHONE..................................703 348-6660
Mohamad Assaf,
EMP: 10
SALES (est): 1.1MM **Privately Held**
SIC: 2759 Advertising literature: printing

(G-15771)
PAMBINA IMPEX
2951 Ps Business Ctr Dr (22192-4227)
PHONE..................................703 910-7309
Khalid Muhammad, *Owner*
EMP: 4 EST: 2010
SALES (est): 383.4K **Privately Held**
WEB: www.pambinaimpex.com
SIC: 3479 Coating of metals & formed
products

(G-15772)
PANEL SYSTEMS INC (PA)
14869 Persistence Dr (22191-3560)
PHONE..................................703 910-6285
Unger Barry M, *President*
Patrick F Fenton, *Vice Pres*
Sheri Revis, *Mktg Dir*
Revis Sheri J, *Admin Sec*
EMP: 27
SQ FT: 17,000
SALES (est): 4.8MM **Privately Held**
WEB: www.psiincusa.com
SIC: 3448 3449 1791 3441 Trusses &
framing: prefabricated metal; panels for
prefabricated metal buildings; miscella-
neous metalwork; structural steel erec-
tion; precast concrete structural framing
or panels, placing of; exterior wall system
installation; fabricated structural metal;
aluminum rolling & drawing

(G-15773)
PAPER AIR FORCE COMPANY
5835 Riverside Dr (22193-3751)
P.O. Box 6130 (22195-6130)
PHONE..................................703 730-2150
Will Sutter, *President*
EMP: 1
SALES (est): 94.3K **Privately Held**
SIC: 3721 Aircraft

(G-15774)
PAUL T MARSHALL
Also Called: After Five Oclock Janitoral
4823 Pearson Dr (22193-5423)
PHONE..................................703 580-0245
Paul T Marshall, *Owner*
EMP: 2
SALES (est): 72.9K **Privately Held**
SIC: 2325 Men's & boys' trousers & slacks

(G-15775)
PERCEPTIONS OF VIRGINIA INC
13065 Saint Andrews Ct (22192-4807)
PHONE..................................703 730-5918
Lynn Shepard, *President*
EMP: 7 EST: 1974
SQ FT: 11,000
SALES (est): 300K **Privately Held**
SIC: 2541 Cabinets, except refrigerated:
show, display, etc.: wood; showcases, ex-
cept refrigerated: wood

(G-15776)
POLARIS PRESS LLC
2212 Tacketts Mill Dr (22192-3012)
PHONE..................................703 680-6060
David Edward Byrne, *Mng Member*
David Byrne, *Manager*

EMP: 6
SALES (est): 868.7K **Privately Held**
WEB: www.polarispress.com
SIC: 2741 Miscellaneous publishing

(G-15777)
POLYFAB DISPLAY COMPANY
14906 Persistence Dr (22191-3560)
P.O. Box 4850 (22194-4850)
PHONE.....................703 497-4577
Alvin W Parker, *President*
Marvin E Parker, *Vice Pres*
EMP: 25
SQ FT: 30,000
SALES (est): 4.5MM **Privately Held**
WEB: www.polyfab-display.com
SIC: 3089 5162 2542 2541 Injection
molding of plastics; plastics products; fix-
tures, store: except wood; wood partitions
& fixtures

(G-15778)
PRECISE TECHNOLOGY INC
11023 Bacon Race Rd (22192-5754)
PHONE.....................703 869-4220
Steven Allen, *Principal*
EMP: 1
SALES (est): 46.7K **Privately Held**
SIC: 3089 Plastics products

(G-15779)
PRECISION SCHEMATICS LLC
3504 Emory Ln (22193-5545)
PHONE.....................612 296-2286
Matthew Green, *Mng Member*
EMP: 1
SALES (est): 45.7K **Privately Held**
SIC: 3999 Manufacturing industries

(G-15780)
PREMIUM MILLWORK INSTALLATIONS
14320 Madrigal Dr (22193-5957)
PHONE.....................757 288-9785
Anthony Hayes, *Principal*
EMP: 1
SALES (est): 112.5K **Privately Held**
WEB: www.gr8trim4u.com
SIC: 2431 Millwork

(G-15781)
PRINCE WILLIAM ATHLETIC CENTER
13000 Sport And Health Dr (22192-2826)
PHONE.....................571 572-3365
Aj Sheta, *Principal*
EMP: 1
SALES (est): 81K **Privately Held**
WEB:
www.kidschoicesportandfuncenter.com
SIC: 3949 Soccer equipment & supplies

(G-15782)
PRINT AFRIK LLC
2608 Miranda Ct (22191-5143)
PHONE.....................202 594-0836
Paul Bangura, *Principal*
EMP: 2
SALES (est): 83.9K **Privately Held**
SIC: 2752 Commercial printing, litho-
graphic

(G-15783)
PRO-CORE
2708 Code Way (22192-4629)
PHONE.....................703 490-4905
Michael Chase, *Owner*
William Thorne, *Co-Owner*
EMP: 1
SALES (est): 118K **Privately Held**
SIC: 7692 Automotive welding

(G-15784)
PROFESSIONAL NETWORK SERVICES
2920 Fox Lair Dr (22191-5013)
PHONE.....................571 283-4858
Picasso Brito, *Owner*
EMP: 2
SALES (est): 113.3K **Privately Held**
SIC: 3841 Surgical & medical instruments

(G-15785)
PROOF OF LIFE BAKING LLC
15369 Hearthstone Ter (22191-4122)
PHONE.....................571 721-8031
Regina Grimes,
EMP: 1
SALES (est): 44.8K **Privately Held**
SIC: 2051 Bread, cake & related products

(G-15786)
PUMPED CARDS
16535 Sherwood Pl (22191-4625)
PHONE.....................202 725-6964
Maria Camille Dowling, *Owner*
◆ EMP: 1
SALES (est): 50.4K **Privately Held**
SIC: 2771 7389 Greeting cards;

(G-15787)
QUICK EAGLE NETWORKS INC
3769 Hetten Ln (22193-1048)
PHONE.....................703 583-3500
Vinita Gupta, *President*
EMP: 3
SALES (corp-wide): 6.5MM **Privately Held**
WEB: www.quickeagle.org
SIC: 3661 Telephone & telegraph appara-
tus
PA: Quick Eagle Networks, Inc.
830 Maude Ave
Mountain View CA 94043
650 962-8282

(G-15788)
R F J LTD
Also Called: Walker Iron Works
13731 Dabney Rd (22191-1406)
PHONE.....................703 494-3255
Joseph R Ferrara, *President*
EMP: 40 EST: 1979
SALES (est): 2MM **Privately Held**
SIC: 3441 3446 Fabricated structural
metal; architectural metalwork

(G-15789)
R&B CUSTOM HOLSTERS LLC
15215 Illinois Rd (22191-3624)
PHONE.....................703 586-2616
Ronald Blankenship,
EMP: 1
SALES (est): 10K **Privately Held**
SIC: 3199 Holsters, leather

(G-15790)
RAISED APPS LLC
1830 Cedar Cove Way (22191-6059)
PHONE.....................703 398-8254
Max Ramirez,
EMP: 1
SALES (est): 32.7K **Privately Held**
SIC: 7372 7389 Prepackaged software;

(G-15791)
RASCO EQUIPMENT SERVICES INC (HQ)
Also Called: Rasco Esi
1635 Woodside Dr Ste 2 (22191-3045)
PHONE.....................703 643-2952
Dr Vincent J Ciccone, *President*
Elizabeth J Ciccone, *Corp Secy*
Charles V Ciccone, *Exec VP*
▲ EMP: 6
SALES (est): 3MM **Privately Held**
WEB: www.rascoengineers.com
SIC: 3589 7699 Sewage & water treat-
ment equipment; industrial machinery &
equipment repair

(G-15792)
REALLY GREAT READING
3071 Ps Business Ctr Dr (22192-4228)
PHONE.....................571 659-2826
EMP: 10
SALES (est): 387.6K **Privately Held**
SIC: 2731 Books-Publishing/Printing

(G-15793)
REEBOK INTERNATIONAL LTD
2700 Potomac Mills Cir (22192-4625)
PHONE.....................703 490-5671
Herbert Hainer, *Branch Mgr*
EMP: 205

SALES (corp-wide): 26.1B **Privately Held**
WEB: www.reebok.com
SIC: 3149 5139 Athletic shoes, except
rubber or plastic; footwear
HQ: Reebok International Ltd.
25 Drydock Ave Ste 110e
Boston MA 02210
781 401-5000

(G-15794)
REID INDUSTRIES LLC
1618 Teal Way (22191-3726)
PHONE.....................703 786-6307
EMP: 1 EST: 2018
SALES (est): 39.6K **Privately Held**
SIC: 3999 Manufacturing industries

(G-15795)
RIINA METTAS JEWELRY LLC
11831 Limoux Pl (22192-7443)
PHONE.....................202 368-9819
Riina Mettas, *Mng Member*
EMP: 1
SALES (est): 58.2K **Privately Held**
WEB: www.riinamettas.com
SIC: 3911 Pearl jewelry, natural or cultured

(G-15796)
RIMFIRE GAMES LLC
15205 Spotted Turtle Ct (22193-5876)
PHONE.....................703 580-4495
Gerardo Gonzalez, *Mng Member*
Kimmy Gorden, *Mng Member*
EMP: 2
SALES (est): 124.7K **Privately Held**
SIC: 7372 7389 Home entertainment com-
puter software;

(G-15797)
RITTER WELDING
3804 Claremont Ln (22193-1634)
PHONE.....................703 680-9601
EMP: 1
SALES (est): 43.7K **Privately Held**
SIC: 7692 Welding Repair

(G-15798)
ROCKBRIDGE EAST LLC
14445 Watson Ln Apt 5 (22193-2951)
PHONE.....................202 701-7927
Olaoluwa Okunola,
EMP: 1
SALES (est): 47.2K **Privately Held**
SIC: 2841 Soap & other detergents

(G-15799)
ROGERS SCREEN PRINTING INC
1313 G St (22191-1602)
PHONE.....................703 491-6794
Leonard Rogers, *President*
Bernard Rogers, *Vice Pres*
Diane Rogers, *Admin Sec*
EMP: 2
SQ FT: 1,000
SALES (est): 210.3K **Privately Held**
WEB: www.rogersscreenprinting.com
SIC: 2759 5699 Screen printing; custom
tailor

(G-15800)
RUBYS EMBROIDERY GEMS
11990 San Ysidro Ct (22192-6248)
PHONE.....................703 590-7902
EMP: 1
SALES (est): 46K **Privately Held**
SIC: 2395 Pleating/Stitching Services

(G-15801)
S&M TRUCKING SERVICE LLC
2830 Wakewater Way (22191-6020)
PHONE.....................980 395-6953
Kearis Pinkney,
EMP: 2
SALES (est): 66K **Privately Held**
SIC: 1442 Construction sand & gravel

(G-15802)
SAMCO TEXTILE PRINTS LLC
2525 Luckland Way (22191-6347)
PHONE.....................571 451-4044
Irfan Johri,
Alina Johri,
Marriam Johri,
Samra Johri,
EMP: 2

SALES (est): 132.8K **Privately Held**
SIC: 2389 2393 2396 Disposable garments & accessories; flour bags, fabric:
made from purchased materials; printing
& embossing on plastics fabric articles;
screen printing on fabric articles

(G-15803)
SANJAR MEDIA LLC
16216 Radburn St (22191-1468)
PHONE.....................703 901-7680
Sands Hakimi,
▲ EMP: 3
SALES (est): 150K **Privately Held**
WEB: www.sanjarmedia.com
SIC: 3695 7319 Computer software tape &
disks: blank, rigid & floppy; media buying
service

(G-15804)
SEATRIX PRINT LLC
2263 York Dr Apt 304 (22191-5707)
PHONE.....................571 241-5748
Semiramis Miranda, *Principal*
EMP: 2
SALES (est): 83.9K **Privately Held**
WEB: www.seatrixprint.com
SIC: 2752 Commercial printing, litho-
graphic

(G-15805)
SHAPER GROUP
4765 Hawfinch Ct (22193-3086)
PHONE.....................703 680-5551
EMP: 2
SALES (est): 71.2K **Privately Held**
SIC: 2731 Books-Publishing/Printing

(G-15806)
SHIRT ART INC
2869 Ps Business Ctr Dr (22192-4227)
PHONE.....................703 680-3963
F Whit Evans, *President*
EMP: 8
SQ FT: 1,800
SALES (est): 814.4K **Privately Held**
WEB: www.shirtartinc.com
SIC: 2396 2395 Screen printing on fabric
articles; art goods for embroidering,
stamped: purchased materials

(G-15807)
SHOEPRINT
2700 Potomac Mills Cir # 238
(22192-4652)
PHONE.....................703 499-9136
EMP: 2
SALES (est): 103.3K **Privately Held**
WEB: www.shoeprint.co
SIC: 2752 Commercial printing, litho-
graphic

(G-15808)
SIGN SHOP
2603 Morse Ln (22192-4628)
PHONE.....................703 590-9534
Micheal Diaz,
EMP: 14
SALES (est): 990K **Privately Held**
WEB: www.thesign-shop.com
SIC: 3993 Electric signs

(G-15809)
SIGNATURE DSGNS FBRICATION LLC
953 Highams Ct (22191-1436)
PHONE.....................571 398-2444
Arthur Simental, *Principal*
EMP: 1
SALES (est): 86.2K **Privately Held**
SIC: 3993 Displays & cutouts, window &
lobby

(G-15810)
SIGNREX INC
14511 Jefferson Davis Hwy (22191-2807)
PHONE.....................703 497-7711
Ethan Hacsh, *Principal*
EMP: 2
SALES (est): 204.2K **Privately Held**
WEB: www.signrex.com
SIC: 3993 Signs & advertising specialties

(G-15811)
SIMURG ARTS LLC
4612 Telfair Ct (22193-3005)
PHONE..............................703 670-7230
EMP: 3
SALES (est): 180.6K Privately Held
SIC: 3993 Mfg Signs/Advertising Special-
ties

(G-15812)
SKYSHIP FANTASY PRESS
5421 Loggerhead Pl (22193-5874)
PHONE..............................703 670-5242
Mara Mahan, *Principal*
EMP: 1
SALES (est): 46.3K Privately Held
SIC: 2741 Miscellaneous publishing

(G-15813)
**SLEEPLESS WARRIOR
PUBLISHING**
14989 Grassy Knoll Ct (22193-6004)
PHONE..............................703 408-4035
Cynthia Little, *Principal*
EMP: 1
SALES (est): 68.5K Privately Held
WEB: www.sleeplesswarrior.com
SIC: 2741 Miscellaneous publishing

(G-15814)
SLYS SUCKER PUNCH LLC
2552 Miranda Ct (22191-5175)
P.O. Box 5322 (22194-5322)
PHONE..............................571 989-3538
Sylvester Harriett,
EMP: 1
SALES (est): 54.4K Privately Held
SIC: 2869 7389 Alcohols, non-beverage;

(G-15815)
SO MANY SOCKS
4883 Cavallo Way (22192-5436)
P.O. Box 1914 (22195-1914)
PHONE..............................703 309-8111
EMP: 2 EST: 2017
SALES (est): 73.4K Privately Held
SIC: 2252 Socks

(G-15816)
**SOFTWARE & SYSTEMS
SOLUTIONS L**
14596 Charity Ct (22193-1200)
PHONE..............................703 801-7452
Dennis Biju, *Principal*
EMP: 2
SALES (est): 104.9K Privately Held
SIC: 7372 Prepackaged software

(G-15817)
SSECURITY LLC
4900 Tobacco Way (22193-3212)
PHONE..............................703 590-4240
Michael Spann, *President*
EMP: 1
SALES (est): 32.7K Privately Held
SIC: 7372 Operating systems computer
software

(G-15818)
SUMI ENTERPRISES
15065 Greenmount Dr (22193-1857)
PHONE..............................703 580-8269
Sue Lee Clark, *Owner*
EMP: 1
SALES (est): 64.1K Privately Held
WEB: www.sumi-enterprises.com
SIC: 2741 Miscellaneous publishing

(G-15819)
SUMMIT WATERFALLS LLC
1965 Knoll Top Ln (22191-3450)
PHONE..............................703 688-4558
Mohammad Rahat, *CEO*
EMP: 2
SALES (est): 112.6K Privately Held
SIC: 7372 Prepackaged software

(G-15820)
SUNCOAST POST-TENSION LTD
15041 Farm Creek Dr (22191-3553)
PHONE..............................703 492-4949
Hamid Ahmady, *Manager*
EMP: 20

SALES (corp-wide): 2.9B Privately Held
WEB: www.suncoast-pt.com
SIC: 3272 Concrete products
HQ: Suncoast Post-Tension, Ltd.
509 N Sam Houston Pkwy E # 300
Houston TX 77060
281 445-8886

(G-15821)
TECHSOURCE LLC
2198 Oberlin Dr (22191-5914)
PHONE..............................757 469-3983
Graylen Ellis,
EMP: 1
SALES (est): 64K Privately Held
SIC: 3577 Computer peripheral equipment

(G-15822)
THERMADON ASSOCIATES
13429 Kingsman Rd (22193-4844)
PHONE..............................571 275-6118
Wayne Henry, *Owner*
EMP: 3
SALES (est): 156.9K Privately Held
SIC: 2721 Periodicals: publishing only

(G-15823)
TOMB GEOPHYSICS LLC
14601 Colony Creek Ct (22193-3378)
P.O. Box 891, Tonganoxie KS (66086-
0891)
PHONE..............................571 733-0930
Elizabeth Burniston,
EMP: 1
SALES (est): 98.8K Privately Held
WEB: www.tombgeophysics.com
SIC: 1382 7389 Aerial geophysical explo-
ration oil & gas; photogrammatic mapping

(G-15824)
TSHIRTSRU
15283 Valley Stream Dr (22191-3921)
PHONE..............................301 744-7872
William David Grier, *Administration*
EMP: 2
SALES (est): 108.5K Privately Held
WEB: www.tshirtsru.com
SIC: 2759 Screen printing

(G-15825)
TYPE SIGNS LLC
4603 Dale Blvd (22193-4738)
PHONE..............................202 355-4403
EMP: 1
SALES (est): 46K Privately Held
SIC: 3993 Signs & advertising specialties

(G-15826)
VETERAN ARMS INC
2522 Basin View Ln (22191-6375)
PHONE..............................703 217-7532
EMP: 2
SALES (est): 89.5K Privately Held
SIC: 3489 Ordnance & accessories

(G-15827)
**VIRGINIA CANDLE COMPANY
LLC**
2173 Potomac Club Pkwy (22191-6548)
PHONE..............................301 828-6498
Larry Moore,
EMP: 1 EST: 2016
SALES (est): 81.1K Privately Held
SIC: 3999 Candles

(G-15828)
WALTER L JAMES
Also Called: Phoenix Printing
5176 Tilbury Way (22193-4963)
PHONE..............................703 622-5970
Walter L James, *Owner*
EMP: 1
SALES (est): 60K Privately Held
SIC: 3555 Printing trades machinery

(G-15829)
WAMMOTH SERVICES LLC
3360 Post Office Rd # 2023 (22193-1456)
PHONE..............................571 309-2969
Stacey Watson, *CEO*
Bill Watson, *Mng Member*
EMP: 3
SALES (est): 291.2K Privately Held
WEB: www.gasfireplaceservice.org
SIC: 3433 Logs, gas fireplace

(G-15830)
WEATHERLY LLC
12763 Stone Lined Cir (22192-5583)
PHONE..............................703 593-3192
Matthew Weatherly,
EMP: 1 EST: 2012
SALES (est): 45K Privately Held
SIC: 2519 Lawn & garden furniture, except
wood & metal

(G-15831)
WENGER MANUFACTURING
3509 Mauti Ct (22192-6473)
PHONE..............................703 878-6946
William Jnr, *Executive*
EMP: 1
SALES (est): 39.6K Privately Held
SIC: 3999 Manufacturing industries

(G-15832)
WILLIE LUCAS
Also Called: Rebirth By D Lucas
4348 Granby Rd (22193-2514)
PHONE..............................919 935-8066
Willie Lucas, *Owner*
Alicia Lucas, *Co-Owner*
EMP: 2
SALES (est): 79.8K Privately Held
SIC: 3993 8742 2721 7389 Signs & ad-
vertising specialties; marketing consulting
services; magazines: publishing only, not
printed on site;

(G-15833)
WISEMAN WELD FABRICATION
4418 Berwick Pl (22192-5165)
PHONE..............................571 393-8480
EMP: 1
SALES (est): 35.9K Privately Held
SIC: 7692 Welding repair

(G-15834)
WOODBRIDGE PRINTING CO
14826 Build America Dr (22191-3437)
PHONE..............................703 494-7333
Hugh A Maples, *Owner*
Donnie Nesaw, *Manager*
EMP: 3 EST: 1964
SQ FT: 2,500
SALES (est): 244.8K Privately Held
WEB: www.woodbridge-printing.com
SIC: 2752 Commercial printing, offset

(G-15835)
WRIGHT DISCOUNT ENTPS LLC
3604 Water Birch Ct (22192-4537)
PHONE..............................703 580-5278
Disney Wright,
EMP: 2
SALES (est): 126.5K Privately Held
SIC: 3581 Automatic vending machines

(G-15836)
WYVERN PUBLICATIONS
14703 Dunbar Ln (22193-1730)
PHONE..............................703 670-3527
James A Sawicki, *Owner*
EMP: 1
SALES (est): 33.4K Privately Held
SIC: 2731 Book publishing

(G-15837)
**YELLOW BRIDGE SOFTWARE
INC**
14814 Statler Dr (22193-3128)
PHONE..............................703 909-5533
Melanie Wright, *Principal*
EMP: 2
SALES (est): 147.4K Privately Held
WEB: www.yellow-bridge.com
SIC: 7372 8748 Prepackaged software;
systems analysis & engineering consult-
ing services

(G-15838)
Z FINEST AIRDUCT CLEANING
3075 Ps Business Ctr Dr (22192-4229)
PHONE..............................703 897-1152
Dan Irby, *Owner*
EMP: 23
SALES (est): 1.6MM Privately Held
SIC: 3564 Air cleaning systems

Woodford
Caroline County

(G-15839)
**GBN MACHINE & ENGINEERING
CORP**
17073 Bull Church Rd (22580-2412)
PHONE..............................804 448-2033
Raj Nainani, *President*
Roderick Gray, *Corp Secy*
Willard P Bailey, *Vice Pres*
EMP: 20
SQ FT: 20,000
SALES (est): 4MM Privately Held
WEB: www.nailerman.com
SIC: 3553 3537 Woodworking machinery;
industrial trucks & tractors

(G-15840)
INDIANA FLOOR INC
16517 Bull Church Rd (22580-2411)
PHONE..............................540 373-1915
EMP: 4
SALES (corp-wide): 12.1MM Privately
Held
SIC: 3089 Mfg Plastic Products
PA: Indiana Floor, Inc.
8194 K&L Terminal Rd
Lorton VA 22079
703 550-0020

(G-15841)
MARBLE MAN
6113 Mudville Rd (22580-2124)
PHONE..............................804 448-9100
John C Hahn, *Owner*
EMP: 1
SALES (est): 86K Privately Held
WEB: www.themarbleman.com
SIC: 3944 Board games, children's &
adults'

(G-15842)
REYNOLDS TIMBER INC
Also Called: Reynolds Edward General Contr
12040 Minarchi Rd (22580-2936)
PHONE..............................804 633-6117
Edward Reynolds, *President*
Jean Reynolds, *Admin Sec*
EMP: 2
SALES (est): 186.4K Privately Held
SIC: 2411 Logging camps & contractors

Woodlawn
Carroll County

(G-15843)
A SIMPLE LIFE MAGAZINE
879 Walkers Knob Rd (24381-2835)
PHONE..............................276 238-2403
Jill Peterson, *Principal*
EMP: 1
SALES (est): 41.3K Privately Held
WEB: www.asimplelifemagazine.com
SIC: 2741 Miscellaneous publishing

(G-15844)
**CARPENTERS CBNETS
WODWORKS LLC**
68 Industry Ln (24381-3605)
PHONE..............................276 236-0853
EMP: 1
SALES (est): 58K Privately Held
SIC: 2431 Millwork

(G-15845)
JOSEPH LINEBERRY
68 Indruty Line (24381)
PHONE..............................276 733-8635
Joseph Lineberry, *Owner*
EMP: 2
SALES (est): 151.7K Privately Held
SIC: 2541 Cabinets, lockers & shelving

(G-15846)
**WOODLAWN PRECISION
MACHINE**
3536 Carrollton Pike (24381-3650)
PHONE..............................276 236-7294
Greg Delp, *President*

GEOGRAPHIC

(PA)=Parent Co (HQ)=Headquarters (DH)=Div Headquarters
✪ = New Business established in last 2 years   2021 Virginia
Industrial Directory   525

Donna Delp, *Corp Secy*
EMP: 4
SQ FT: 3,200
SALES (est): 250K **Privately Held**
WEB: www.woodlawnmachine.com
SIC: 3599 Machine shop, jobbing & repair

Woodstock
Shenandoah County

(G-15847)
ARTISTIC AWARDS
Also Called: Artistic Awards Creative Gifts
176 North River Dr (22664-1543)
PHONE.................................540 636-9940
Jim Munden, *Owner*
Birginia Beazers, *Manager*
EMP: 2 **EST:** 1998
SALES (est): 105.1K **Privately Held**
SIC: 3499 7389 5999 Novelties & gift-
ware, including trophies; engraving serv-
ice; trophies & plaques

(G-15848)
BACKROAD PRECAST LLC
2506 Back Rd (22664-3400)
PHONE.................................540 335-5503
April Reedy,
EMP: 4
SALES (est): 230K **Privately Held**
SIC: 3272 Concrete products used to facili-
tate drainage

(G-15849)
BEAGLE LOGGING COMPANY
206 Beagle Run (22664-3357)
P.O. Box 101 (22664-0101)
PHONE.................................540 459-2425
Roger L Estep, *President*
EMP: 1
SALES (est): 164.8K **Privately Held**
SIC: 2421 2411 Sawmills & planing mills,
general; logging

(G-15850)
CABIN HILL TS LLC
923 S Main St (22664-1121)
PHONE.................................540 459-8912
Todd Buracker,
EMP: 5
SALES (est): 300K **Privately Held**
WEB: www.shentel.com
SIC: 3953 5699 Screens, textile printing;
customized clothing & apparel

(G-15851)
DAILY NEWS RECORD
Also Called: Shenandoah Valley-Herald, The
207 N Main St (22664-1418)
PHONE.................................540 459-4078
Cathy John, *Branch Mgr*
EMP: 11
SALES (corp-wide): 13MM **Privately
Held**
WEB: www.dnronline.com
SIC: 2711 Newspapers, publishing & print-
ing
HQ: Daily News Record
231 S Liberty St
Harrisonburg VA 22801
540 574-6200

(G-15852)
**ELLEN FAIRCHILD-FLUGEL ART
LLC**
924 Lupton Rd (22664-1932)
PHONE.................................540 325-2305
E Fairchild-Flugel, *Mng Member*
Ellen Fairchild-Flugel, *Mng Member*
EMP: 1 **EST:** 2016
SALES (est): 54.8K **Privately Held**
SIC: 3911 3999 Jewelry, precious metal;
manufacturing industries

(G-15853)
FINCH WOODWORKS
206 Hollow Ln (22664-3941)
PHONE.................................540 333-0054
EMP: 1
SALES (est): 54.1K **Privately Held**
WEB: www.finchwoodworks.com
SIC: 2431 Moldings, wood: unfinished &
prefinished

(G-15854)
FOUR STAR PRINTING INC
490 N Main St (22664-1802)
PHONE.................................540 459-2247
Cena Simmons, *President*
EMP: 5 **EST:** 1979
SQ FT: 3,000
SALES (est): 736.6K **Privately Held**
WEB: www.fourstarprinting.info
SIC: 2752 5199 Commercial printing, off-
set; advertising specialties

(G-15855)
INFINITY PUBLICATIONS LLC
230 Lora Dr (22664-1564)
P.O. Box 155 (22664-0155)
PHONE.................................540 331-8713
EMP: 1
SALES (est): 37.5K **Privately Held**
SIC: 2741 Miscellaneous publishing

(G-15856)
LEE STREET PUBLISHING LLC
207 S Lee St (22664-1325)
PHONE.................................540 459-8566
EMP: 1 **EST:** 2016
SALES (est): 40.4K **Privately Held**
SIC: 2741 Miscellaneous publishing

(G-15857)
**LOCKHART MANUFACTURING
INC**
750 Spring Pkwy (22664-1606)
PHONE.................................540 459-8774
Dennis Lochart, *Owner*
EMP: 2 **EST:** 2013
SALES (est): 101K **Privately Held**
SIC: 3999 Manufacturing industries

(G-15858)
MUSE VINEYARDS LLC
16 Serendipity Ln (22664-2412)
PHONE.................................540 459-7033
Robert Muse, *Mng Member*
EMP: 7
SALES (est): 862.7K **Privately Held**
WEB: www.musevineyards.com
SIC: 2084 Wines

(G-15859)
SHELF RELIANCE
1726 Stultz Gap Rd (22664-3312)
PHONE.................................540 459-2050
Holly Cooley, *Principal*
EMP: 2
SALES (est): 25K **Privately Held**
SIC: 2013 2037 Frozen meats from pur-
chased meat; frozen fruits & vegetables

(G-15860)
VANDERBILT MEDIA HOUSE LLC
143 Valley Vista Dr # 202 (22664-1612)
PHONE.................................757 515-9242
Winter Giovanni,
EMP: 15
SALES (est): 409.7K **Privately Held**
SIC: 2731 Book publishing

(G-15861)
VEGAN HERITAGE PRESS
219 E Reservoir Rd (22664-1503)
PHONE.................................540 459-2858
Jon Robertson, *Principal*
EMP: 4
SALES (est): 250K **Privately Held**
WEB: www.veganheritagepress.com
SIC: 2741 Miscellaneous publishing

Woodville
Rappahannock County

(G-15862)
TIMOTHY D FALLS
Also Called: Falls Welding Services
477 Rudasill Mill Rd (22749-1813)
PHONE.................................540 987-8142
Timothy Falls, *Owner*
EMP: 1
SALES (est): 60.4K **Privately Held**
SIC: 7692 3443 Welding repair; liners/lin-
ing

Woolwine
Patrick County

(G-15863)
**1ST SIGNAGE AND LIGHTING
LLC**
Also Called: 911 C.A.S.P.E.R. Systems
10086 Woolwine Hwy 5-C (24185-3503)
PHONE.................................276 229-4200
Judith Ann Freels,
Charles J Freels,
EMP: 5
SALES (est): 237.8K **Privately Held**
WEB: www.911casper.com
SIC: 3993 4822 3999 5065 Electric
signs; signs, not made in custom sign
painting shops; nonvocal message com-
munications; advertising display products;
intercommunication equipment, electronic

(G-15864)
BLUERIDGE WOOD
452 Bob White Rd (24185-3735)
PHONE.................................276 930-2274
Carroll Wood, *Owner*
EMP: 1
SALES (est): 104.5K **Privately Held**
SIC: 2431 Woodwork, interior & ornamen-
tal

(G-15865)
HYLTON & HYLTON LOGGING
5999 Belcher Mountain Rd (24185-3709)
P.O. Box 234 (24185-0234)
PHONE.................................276 930-2245
Herbert Hylton, *Owner*
EMP: 2 **Privately Held**
SIC: 2411 Logging camps & contractors

(G-15866)
HYLTON TIMBER HARVESTING
6039 Belcher Mountain Rd (24185-3708)
P.O. Box 1 (24185-0001)
PHONE.................................276 930-2348
Lawrence Hylton, *Owner*
EMP: 2
SALES (est): 127.6K **Privately Held**
SIC: 2411 Timber, cut at logging camp

(G-15867)
SAM BELCHER & SONS INC
6327 Belcher Mountain Rd (24185-3702)
PHONE.................................276 930-2084
Ellis Belcher, *President*
Benton Belcher, *Vice Pres*
EMP: 2
SALES (est): 130K **Privately Held**
SIC: 2411 Logging

(G-15868)
**WORLEY MACHINE
ENTERPRISES INC**
8735 Woolwine Hwy (24185)
PHONE.................................276 930-2695
Donald Worley, *President*
Chris Worley, *Opers Mgr*
EMP: 35
SQ FT: 6,000
SALES (est): 6.6MM **Privately Held**
WEB: www.worleymachine.com
SIC: 3599 Machine shop, jobbing & repair

(G-15869)
XMC FILMS INC
9622 Woolwine Hwy (24185)
P.O. Box 268 (24185-0268)
PHONE.................................276 930-2848
EMP: 4
SALES (est): 150K **Privately Held**
SIC: 3082 Mfg Plastic Profile Shapes

(G-15870)
ZENTA CORPORATION
Also Called: C & J Led Lighting & Signage
10086 Woolwine Hwy (24185-3503)
PHONE.................................276 930-1500
Judie Freels, *President*
Chuck Freels, *Vice Pres*
Brandy Freels, *Marketing Mgr*
EMP: 5 **EST:** 2004
SQ FT: 3,200

SALES (est): 180K **Privately Held**
WEB: www.ourledconnection.com
SIC: 3645 5063 1731 3646 Garden,
patio, walkway & yard lighting fixtures:
electric; lighting fixtures, commercial & industrial; lighting contractor; commercial
indusl & institutional electric lighting fixtures

Wylliesburg
Charlotte County

(G-15871)
CARDINAL HOMES INC
525 Barnesville Hwy (23976-5217)
PHONE.................................434 735-8111
Linda Devin, *Human Res Mgr*
Bret A Berneche, *Branch Mgr*
James Gordon, *Manager*
EMP: 7
SALES (corp-wide): 3.3MM **Privately
Held**
WEB: www.cardinalhomes.com
SIC: 2452 Modular homes, prefabricated,
wood
PA: Cardinal Homes, Inc.
2712 W 3rd St
Odessa TX 79763
432 337-3250

(G-15872)
LW LOGGING LLC
2095 Barnesville Hwy (23976-6011)
PHONE.................................434 735-8598
Lisa Wilinson, *Principal*
EMP: 3
SALES (est): 160.2K **Privately Held**
SIC: 2411 Logging

Wytheville
Wythe County

(G-15873)
12TH TEE LLC
200 Golf Club Ln (24382-1426)
PHONE.................................276 620-7601
John Dowd, *Principal*
EMP: 2
SALES (est): 168.1K **Privately Held**
SIC: 2759 Screen printing

(G-15874)
ACRYLIFE INC
170 E Franklin St (24382-2626)
PHONE.................................276 228-6704
Charles S Johnson, *President*
Louis P Johnson, *Vice Pres*
Lee H Johnson, *Admin Sec*
▲ **EMP:** 12
SALES (est): 1.6MM **Privately Held**
WEB: www.acrylife.com
SIC: 2952 1761 Roofing materials; roofing
contractor

(G-15875)
**AMCOR RIGID PACKAGING USA
LLC**
474 Gator Ln (24382-1393)
PHONE.................................276 625-8000
Monty Andre, *Opers Mgr*
Robert Waller, *Engineer*
Toy Harrison, *Branch Mgr*
David Devine, *Manager*
Nathan Hale, *Manager*
EMP: 120
SALES (corp-wide): 12.4B **Privately Held**
WEB: www.amcor.com
SIC: 3089 Injection molding of plastics
HQ: Amcor Rigid Packaging Usa, Llc
40600 Ann Arbor Rd E
Plymouth MI 48170

(G-15876)
BLUE RIDGE ANALYTICAL LLC
2280 W Ridge Rd (24382-5028)
PHONE.................................276 228-6464
Gary Mychel Johnson,
EMP: 5
SALES (est): 600K **Privately Held**
SIC: 3826 Environmental testing equip-
ment

(G-15877)
BLUE RIDGE FUDGE LADY INC
200 W Main St (24382-2332)
PHONE................................276 335-2229
EMP: 2
SALES (est): 62.3K **Privately Held**
SIC: 2064 Fudge (candy)

(G-15878)
BLUE RIDGE MARKETING & EMB
295 Chapman Rd (24382-3457)
PHONE................................276 223-0337
Tom Lovelace, *Owner*
Kim Conner, *Marketing Staff*
EMP: 8
SALES (est): 447.5K **Privately Held**
WEB: www.blueridgemarketing.net
SIC: 2395 Embroidery products, except schiffli machine

(G-15879)
BOTTLING GROUP LLC
Also Called: Pepsico
200 Pepsi Way (24382-4975)
PHONE................................276 625-2300
Gregory Quesenberry, *Manager*
Michael White, *Maintence Staff*
EMP: 9
SALES (corp-wide): 67.1B **Publicly Held**
WEB: www.pepsico.com
SIC: 2086 Carbonated soft drinks, bottled & canned
HQ: Bottling Group, Llc
1111 Westchester Ave
White Plains NY 10604
914 253-2000

(G-15880)
BOXLEY MATERIALS COMPANY
Also Called: Wytheville Plant
1050 Church St (24382-3514)
P.O. Box 13527, Roanoke (24035-3527)
PHONE................................540 777-7600
AB Boxley, *CEO*
EMP: 7
SALES (corp-wide): 2.2B **Publicly Held**
WEB: www.boxley.com
SIC: 3273 Ready-mixed concrete
HQ: Boxley Materials Company
15418 W Lynchburg Slem Tp
Blue Ridge VA 24064
540 777-7600

(G-15881)
CADBURY SCHWEPPES BOTTLIN
840 Stafford Umberger Dr (24382-4400)
PHONE................................276 228-7990
EMP: 3
SALES (est): 129.5K **Privately Held**
SIC: 2086 Bottled & canned soft drinks

(G-15882)
CLARKE PRECISION MACHINE INC
585 Stafford Umberger Dr (24382-4466)
P.O. Box 1407 (24382-8407)
PHONE................................276 228-5441
Sandra Clarke, *CEO*
Bob Fowlkes, *Sales Mgr*
EMP: 12
SALES (est): 1.7MM **Privately Held**
WEB: www.clarkeprecisionmachine.com
SIC: 3599 Machine shop, jobbing & repair

(G-15883)
COPERION CORPORATION
196 Appalachian Dr (24382-4467)
PHONE................................276 227-7070
Billy Fields, *Purch Agent*
EMP: 8 **Publicly Held**
WEB: www.zsk101.com
SIC: 3559 Plastics working machinery
HQ: Coperion Corporation
590 Woodbury Glassboro Rd
Sewell NJ 08080

(G-15884)
COPERION CORPORATION
285 Stafford Umberger Dr (24382-4489)
P.O. Box 775 (24382-0775)
PHONE................................276 228-7717
Alan Wood, *Branch Mgr*
EMP: 60 **Publicly Held**

WEB: www.zsk101.com
SIC: 3559 8711 3535 8734 Plastics working machinery; rubber working machinery, including tires; structural engineering; bulk handling conveyor systems; testing laboratories; rolling mill machinery
HQ: Coperion Corporation
590 Woodbury Glassboro Rd
Sewell NJ 08080

(G-15885)
DUKES PRINTING INC
435 Tazewell St Ste C (24382-1912)
PHONE................................276 228-6777
Dale Yontz, *President*
EMP: 2
SALES (est): 333.3K **Privately Held**
SIC: 2752 Commercial printing, offset

(G-15886)
DUNFORD G C SEPTIC TANK INSTAL
410 Saint Lukes Rd (24382-4224)
PHONE................................276 228-8590
EMP: 2 EST: 2007
SALES (est): 100K **Privately Held**
SIC: 3272 Mfg Concrete Products

(G-15887)
EMERSON ELECTRIC CO
555 Peppers Ferry Rd (24382-2063)
PHONE................................276 223-2200
Alfred Ezersole, *Systems Mgr*
EMP: 30
SALES (corp-wide): 18.3B **Publicly Held**
WEB: www.emerson.com
SIC: 3823 Industrial instrmnts msrmnt display/control process variable
PA: Emerson Electric Co.
8000 West Florissant Ave
Saint Louis MO 63136
314 553-2000

(G-15888)
FARMERS MILLING & SUPPLY INC
525 W Railroad Ave (24382-2917)
PHONE................................276 228-2971
Leslie Alan Walters, *President*
James Michael Walters, *Vice Pres*
Manley Dean Walters, *Treasurer*
Willie Louise Walters, *Admin Sec*
EMP: 9
SQ FT: 10,000
SALES (est): 902.6K **Privately Held**
SIC: 2048 0723 5999 Prepared feeds; feed milling custom services; feed & farm supply

(G-15889)
G & W MANUFACTURING INC
325 Stafford Umberger Dr (24382-4402)
P.O. Box 858 (24382-0858)
PHONE................................276 228-8491
Todd Jonas, *President*
EMP: 15
SQ FT: 16,730
SALES (est): 1.3MM **Privately Held**
WEB: www.gwmanufacturing.com
SIC: 3599 Machine shop, jobbing & repair

(G-15890)
HUTCHINSON SEALING SYSTEMS INC
455 Industry Rd (24382-3491)
PHONE................................276 228-6150
Jim Fenton, *Principal*
EMP: 10
SALES (corp-wide): 7B **Publicly Held**
WEB: www.hutchinsonsealing-purchasing.com
SIC: 3069 3535 3053 Rubber automotive products; conveyors & conveying equipment; gaskets, packing & sealing devices
HQ: Hutchinson Sealing Systems, Inc.
3201 Cross Creek Pkwy
Auburn Hills MI 48326
248 375-3720

(G-15891)
HUTCHINSON SEALING SYSTEMS INC
1150 S 3rd St (24382-3925)
PHONE................................276 228-4455
Nira Taengsirilak, *General Mgr*

Michael Bell, *Marketing Staff*
Andre Cadet, *Branch Mgr*
Walter Molitar, *Manager*
EMP: 222
SALES (corp-wide): 7B **Publicly Held**
WEB: www.hutchinsonsealing-purchasing.com
SIC: 3069 3061 3053 Weather strip; sponge rubber; mechanical rubber goods; gaskets, packing & sealing devices
HQ: Hutchinson Sealing Systems, Inc.
3201 Cross Creek Pkwy
Auburn Hills MI 48326
248 375-3720

(G-15892)
JAFREE SHIRT CO INC
1200 W Main St (24382-2110)
P.O. Box 500 (24382-0500)
PHONE................................276 228-2116
Charles C Clatterbuck, *President*
Pearl Freezer, *Vice Pres*
EMP: 118 **EST:** 1936
SQ FT: 56,000
SALES (est): 3.6MM **Privately Held**
SIC: 2331 2321 Blouses, women's & juniors': made from purchased material; men's & boys' furnishings

(G-15893)
JOSHMOR PAC
737 Hogback Rd (24382-5823)
PHONE................................276 620-6537
Deborah Crigger, *Owner*
EMP: 6
SALES (est): 443.3K **Privately Held**
SIC: 3993 Signs & advertising specialties

(G-15894)
JR KAUFFMAN INC
Also Called: Wytheville Metals
3040 Peppers Ferry Rd (24382-4948)
PHONE................................276 228-7070
Rick Kauffman, *President*
Joel Zook, *Purchasing*
Hans Lauer, *Sales Staff*
Richard Mast, *Office Mgr*
Alvin Zook, *Manager*
EMP: 16
SQ FT: 32,000
SALES (est): 3.2MM **Privately Held**
WEB: www.wythemet.com
SIC: 3339 Primary nonferrous metals

(G-15895)
LANE ENTERPRISES INC
510 Kents Ln (24382)
P.O. Box 1352 (24382-8352)
PHONE................................276 223-1051
Matthew Clark, *Branch Mgr*
EMP: 10
SALES (corp-wide): 68.7MM **Privately Held**
WEB: www.lane-enterprises.com
SIC: 3444 3479 Pipe, sheet metal; coating of metals & formed products
PA: Lane Enterprises, Inc.
3905 Hartzdale Dr Ste 514
Camp Hill PA 17011
717 761-8175

(G-15896)
LONGWOOD ELASTOMERS INC
365 George James Dr (24382-4464)
PHONE................................276 228-5406
Joe Freeman, *Branch Mgr*
EMP: 30 **Publicly Held**
WEB: www.longwoodindustries.com
SIC: 3069 3081 Rubber automotive products; unsupported plastics film & sheet
HQ: Longwood Elastomers, Inc.
655 Fairview Rd
Wytheville VA 24382

(G-15897)
LONGWOOD ELASTOMERS INC (DH)
Also Called: Longwood Industries
655 Fairview Rd (24382-4503)
PHONE................................336 272-3710
Dana S Waterman, *President*
Kim Thompson, *CFO*
▲ **EMP:** 11
SQ FT: 9,000

SALES (est): 108.7MM **Publicly Held**
WEB: www.longwoodindustries.com
SIC: 3069 3081 Molded rubber products; unsupported plastics film & sheet

(G-15898)
LONGWOOD ELASTOMERS INC
655 Fairview Rd (24382-4503)
P.O. Box 213 (24382-0213)
PHONE................................276 228-5406
EMP: 200
SALES (corp-wide): 4.3B **Publicly Held**
SIC: 3061 3743 3714 2822 Mechanical Rubber Goods, Nsk
HQ: Longwood Elastomers, Inc.
655 Fairview Rd
Wytheville VA 24382

(G-15899)
MAGNETIC TECHNOLOGIES CORP
262 Saint Lukes Rd (24382-4226)
PHONE................................276 228-7943
Patty Houseman, *Principal*
EMP: 3
SALES (est): 378.5K **Privately Held**
SIC: 3612 Transformers, except electric

(G-15900)
MIDWAY TELEMETRY
906 Cinnamon Run (24382-5951)
PHONE................................276 227-0270
EMP: 2
SALES (est): 78.9K **Privately Held**
WEB: www.midwaytelemetry.com
SIC: 3999 Pet supplies

(G-15901)
MITSUBISHI CHEM ADVANCED MTLS
2530 N 4th St (24382-4420)
PHONE................................276 228-0100
EMP: 5
SALES (est): 248.1K **Privately Held**
WEB: www.plasticperspectives.com
SIC: 2821 Plastics materials & resins

(G-15902)
N D M MACHINE INC
670 Slate Spring Br Rd (24382-5335)
PHONE................................276 621-4424
Dennis Scott, *President*
James Scott, *Vice Pres*
Nancy Scott, *Treasurer*
EMP: 7
SALES (est): 660K **Privately Held**
SIC: 3599 Machine shop, jobbing & repair

(G-15903)
PEPSI CO
316 Gator Ln (24382-1391)
PHONE................................276 625-3900
EMP: 10
SALES (est): 1.2MM **Privately Held**
WEB: www.pepsico.com
SIC: 2086 Carbonated soft drinks, bottled & canned

(G-15904)
PERKINS
131 Queens Knob (24382-4659)
PHONE................................276 227-0551
David Perkins, *Owner*
EMP: 10
SALES (est): 520.5K **Privately Held**
SIC: 3799 Transportation equipment

(G-15905)
QUADRANT HOLDING INC
2530 N 4th St (24382-4420)
PHONE................................276 228-0100
Allan Freeman, *Branch Mgr*
EMP: 80 **Privately Held**
WEB: www.mcam.com
SIC: 2824 3082 2821 3052 Nylon fibers; acrylic fibers; unsupported plastics profile shapes; rods, unsupported plastic; tubes, unsupported plastic; nylon resins; plastic hose
HQ: Mitsubishi Chemical Advanced Materials Inc.
2120 Fairmont Ave
Reading PA 19605
610 320-6600

(G-15906)
QUAKER OATS CO
316 Gator Ln (24382-1391)
PHONE....................................276 625-3923
Pam White, *Principal*
David Kause, *Manager*
EMP: 4
SALES (est): 118.3K **Privately Held**
WEB: www.quakeroats.com
SIC: 2099 Food preparations

(G-15907)
R H SHEPPARD CO INC
1400 Stafford Umberger Dr (24382-4483)
P.O. Box 757 (24382-0757)
PHONE....................................276 228-4000
Jack Senseney, *Principal*
Sarah Hughes, *Purchasing*
EMP: 13
SALES (corp-wide): 711.6K **Privately Held**
WEB: www.rhsheppard.com
SIC: 3714 3321 3369 Gears, motor vehicle; gray iron castings; ductile iron castings; lead, zinc & white metal
HQ: R. H. Sheppard Co., Inc.
101 Philadelphia St
Hanover PA 17331
717 637-3751

(G-15908)
SALEM STONE CORPORATION
Also Called: Wythe Stone Co
2377 Atkins Mill Rd (24382)
P.O. Box 629 (24382-0629)
PHONE....................................276 228-3452
James Collins, *Manager*
EMP: 14
SALES (corp-wide): 34MM **Privately Held**
WEB: www.salemstonecorp.com
SIC: 1422 Crushed & broken limestone
PA: Salem Stone Corporation
5764 Wilderness Rd
Dublin VA 24084
540 674-5556

(G-15909)
SALEM STONE CORPORATION
Rr 11 Box 649 (24382)
P.O. Box 629 (24382-0629)
PHONE....................................276 228-3631
Jamie Cones, *Manager*
EMP: 10
SALES (corp-wide): 34MM **Privately Held**
WEB: www.salemstonecorp.com
SIC: 1422 Crushed & broken limestone
PA: Salem Stone Corporation
5764 Wilderness Rd
Dublin VA 24084
540 674-5556

(G-15910)
SALEM STONE CORPORATION
Also Called: Sand Mountain Sand
345 Ready Mix Rd Intersta (24382)
P.O. Box 629 (24382-0629)
PHONE....................................276 228-6767
Jamie Collins, *Manager*
EMP: 5
SALES (corp-wide): 34MM **Privately Held**
WEB: www.salemstonecorp.com
SIC: 1423 1442 Crushed & broken granite; construction sand & gravel
PA: Salem Stone Corporation
5764 Wilderness Rd
Dublin VA 24084
540 674-5556

(G-15911)
SAND MOUNTAIN SAND CO
Also Called: Sand Mountain Sand Co.
Ext 77 Ofc I-81 (24382)
P.O. Box 629 (24382-0629)
PHONE....................................276 228-6767
Jay O'Brian, *CEO*
EMP: 12
SALES (est): 771.1K
SALES (corp-wide): 34MM **Privately Held**
SIC: 1442 Sand mining

PA: Salem Stone Corporation
5764 Wilderness Rd
Dublin VA 24084
540 674-5556

(G-15912)
SCHAFFNER MTC LLC
Also Called: Schaffner Mtc Transformers
823 Fairview Rd (24382-4507)
PHONE....................................276 228-7943
Courtney Harrell, *Purch Mgr*
Matthew Clarke, *Mng Member*
EMP: 90
SALES (est): 30.5MM
SALES (corp-wide): 195.5MM **Privately Held**
WEB: www.mtctransformers.com
SIC: 3612 5063 Power transformers, electric; transformers, electric
HQ: E M C Schaffner Inc
52 Mayfield Ave
Edison NJ 08837
732 225-9533

(G-15913)
SMART START INC
285 W Monroe St (24382-2343)
PHONE....................................276 223-1006
Don Hoena, *President*
EMP: 2
SALES (est): 154K **Privately Held**
SIC: 3694 Ignition apparatus & distributors

(G-15914)
SOMIC AMERICA INC (DH)
343 E Lee Trinkle Dr (24382-3944)
PHONE....................................276 228-4307
David Keane, *President*
Peter Argue, *Vice Pres*
Jim Coe, *Engineer*
Gary Cole, *Engineer*
Brian Hudson, *Engineer*
▲ EMP: 100
SQ FT: 10,000
SALES (est): 65.2MM **Privately Held**
WEB: www.somicamerica.com
SIC: 3714 Motor vehicle parts & accessories

(G-15915)
SOUTH EAST PRECAST CON LLC
1110 Black Lick Rd (24382-6063)
PHONE....................................276 620-1194
Brian Umberger,
EMP: 2
SALES (est): 195.2K **Privately Held**
SIC: 3272 Precast terrazo or concrete products; prestressed concrete products

(G-15916)
SOUTHWEST SPECIALTY HEAT TREAT
255 E Marshall St (24382-3915)
PHONE....................................276 228-7739
David P Carpenter, *President*
EMP: 15
SQ FT: 8,000
SALES (est): 700K **Privately Held**
WEB: www.swhtva.com
SIC: 3398 Metal heat treating

(G-15917)
T & T SPORTING GOODS
185 Lakeview Dr (24382-1443)
PHONE....................................276 228-5286
Carla Cannoy, *Owner*
EMP: 1
SALES (est): 81K **Privately Held**
SIC: 2395 Embroidery & art needlework

(G-15918)
TECTONICS INC
205 E Railroad Ave (24382-3533)
PHONE....................................276 228-5565
Jeff Collins, *President*
EMP: 4
SQ FT: 12,000 **Privately Held**
WEB: www.tectonicsinc.com
SIC: 3599 3589 8711 Custom machinery; sandblasting equipment; designing: ship, boat, machine & product

(G-15919)
TOTAL PTRCHEMICALS REF USA INC
1150 S 3rd St (24382-3925)
PHONE....................................276 228-6150
Lisa Hook, *COO*
Bernard Stern, *Branch Mgr*
EMP: 3
SALES (corp-wide): 7B **Publicly Held**
WEB: www.totalpetrochemicalsrefiningusa.com
SIC: 2821 Plastics materials & resins
HQ: Total Petrochemicals & Refining Usa, Inc.
1201 La St Ste 1800
Houston TX 77002
713 483-5000

(G-15920)
TRANSFORMER ENGINEERING LLC
823 Fairview Rd (24382-4507)
PHONE....................................216 741-5282
Jeff Boyd, *President*
Tim Groff, *Marketing Staff*
▲ EMP: 68
SQ FT: 50,000
SALES (est): 21.2MM
SALES (corp-wide): 195.5MM **Privately Held**
WEB: www.trenco.com
SIC: 3612 3677 3625 Power transformers, electric; electronic coils, transformers & other inductors; relays & industrial controls
PA: Schaffner Holding Ag
Nordstrasse 11e
Luterbach SO 4542
326 816-626

(G-15921)
VIRGINIA DRVELINE DIFFERENTIAL
645 Black Lick Rd (24382-5807)
PHONE....................................276 227-0299
Jamie Martin, *President*
EMP: 2
SALES (est): 172.3K **Privately Held**
WEB: www.virginiadriveline.wordpress.com
SIC: 3714 Motor vehicle parts & accessories

(G-15922)
WEST END PRECAST LLC
2055 W Lee Hwy (24382-1355)
PHONE....................................276 228-5024
Chris Umberger, *Mng Member*
EMP: 2
SALES (est): 80K **Privately Held**
SIC: 3272 3523 Septic tanks, concrete; concrete products, precast; cattle feeding, handling & watering equipment

(G-15923)
WILLIAMS MEAT PROCESSING
3823 Old Stage Rd (24382-3063)
PHONE....................................276 686-4325
Ernest Williams, *Principal*
EMP: 4
SALES (est): 160.9K **Privately Held**
SIC: 2011 Meat packing plants

(G-15924)
WOOD TELEVISION LLC
Also Called: Smyth County News & Messenger
460 W Main St (24382-2207)
PHONE....................................276 228-6611
Sam Cooper, *Manager*
Molly Thompson, *Manager*
EMP: 10
SALES (corp-wide): 3B **Publicly Held**
WEB: www.woodtv.com
SIC: 2711 Newspapers, publishing & printing
HQ: Wood Television Llc
120 College Ave Se
Grand Rapids MI 49503
616 456-8888

(G-15925)
WORDSPRINT INC (PA)
190 W Spring St (24382-2650)
P.O. Box 544 (24382-0544)
PHONE....................................276 228-6608

Steve Lester, *President*
William Gilmer, *Vice Pres*
Chris Diyorio, *Sales Staff*
Heather Alderman, *Creative Dir*
Treva Adams,
EMP: 29
SQ FT: 15,000
SALES (est): 3.8MM **Privately Held**
WEB: www.wordsprint.com
SIC: 2752 7336 Commercial printing, offset; graphic arts & related design

(G-15926)
WYTHE OIL DISTRIBUTORS INC
1185 Church St (24382-3515)
P.O. Box 13 (24382-0013)
PHONE....................................276 228-4512
Coy Bowling, *President*
EMP: 5
SALES (est): 363.5K **Privately Held**
SIC: 2911 Oils, fuel

(G-15927)
WYTHE POWER EQUIPMENT CO INC
Also Called: Wep Co
1005 E Marshall St (24382-3418)
P.O. Box 658 (24382-0658)
PHONE....................................276 228-7371
B J Bradberry, *President*
Nancy Bradberry, *Vice Pres*
EMP: 30
SQ FT: 7,200
SALES (est): 3MM **Privately Held**
SIC: 3625 3699 3532 Industrial controls: push button, selector switches, pilot; electrical equipment & supplies; mining machinery

(G-15928)
WYTHEVILLE CUSTOM COUNTER TOPS
Also Called: Cabinet Designs
495 S 6th St (24382-2514)
PHONE....................................276 228-4137
Philip Tobelmann, *President*
EMP: 8
SALES (est): 1.1MM **Privately Held**
WEB: www.cabinet-designs.net
SIC: 2434 Wood kitchen cabinets

Yale
Sussex County

(G-15929)
MAKIVIN TRUCKING LLC
22049 Gilliam Rd (23897-5418)
PHONE....................................434 637-1359
Melvin M Boone Jr,
EMP: 1
SALES (est): 150K **Privately Held**
SIC: 3537 Trucks: freight, baggage, etc.: industrial, except mining

Yorktown
York County

(G-15930)
ABSOLUTE PRECISION LLC
103 Brigade Dr (23692-2837)
P.O. Box 757 (23692-0757)
PHONE....................................757 968-3005
Chet Szymecki, *Mng Member*
EMP: 2 EST: 2013
SALES (est): 122.4K **Privately Held**
SIC: 3484 Guns (firearms) or gun parts, 30 mm. & below

(G-15931)
AILAN TRADING INC USA
5731 Grge Wash Hwy Ste 4d (23692)
PHONE....................................757 812-7258
Huixia Wang, *Director*
EMP: 4 EST: 2013
SALES (est): 228.1K
SALES (corp-wide): 511.5K **Privately Held**
SIC: 2092 Seafoods, frozen: prepared

▲ = Import ▼=Export
◆ =Import/Export

PA: Tianjin Ailan Technology Development
Co., Ltd.
No.305, Nanjing Road, Heping District
Tianjin 30001
222 445-0189

(G-15932)
AMES & AMES INC
7205 Rte 17 (23692)
P.O. Box 842 (23692-0842)
PHONE.................................757 877-2328
Ames Ray, *Principal*
EMP: 4 **EST:** 2008
SALES (est): 383K **Privately Held**
SIC: 3494 Valves & pipe fittings

(G-15933)
ASH PRESS LLC
128 Seekright Dr (23693-4561)
PHONE.................................757 778-0747
Ashleigh Amburn, *Principal*
EMP: 1
SALES (est): 41.3K **Privately Held**
SIC: 2741 Miscellaneous publishing

(G-15934)
ATLAS NORTH AMERICA LLC
(DH)
120 Newsome Dr Ste H (23692-5011)
P.O. Box 1309 (23692-1309)
PHONE.................................757 463-0670
Sergio Diehl, *President*
Adrian Culbreath, *Principal*
Andy Culbreath, *Vice Pres*
EMP: 2
SQ FT: 6,000
SALES (est): 3.1MM
SALES (corp-wide): 34B **Privately Held**
WEB: www.na.atlas-elektronik.com
SIC: 3679 3812 8711 7373 Electronic cir-
cuits; sonar systems & equipment; de-
signing: ship, boat, machine & product;
systems engineering, computer related
HQ: Atlas Elektronik Gmbh
Sebaldsbrucker Heerstr. 235
Bremen 28309
421 457-02

(G-15935)
BARTON INDUSTRIES INC
Also Called: Taylored Printing
234 Redoubt Rd (23692-4894)
PHONE.................................757 874-5958
Michael Barton, *President*
Easley Johnson, *Sales Mgr*
EMP: 22
SQ FT: 12,000
SALES (est): 3.7MM **Privately Held**
WEB: www.tayloredprinting.com
SIC: 2752 Commercial printing, offset

(G-15936)
BASES OF VIRGINIA LLC (PA)
106 Greene Dr (23692-4800)
PHONE.................................757 690-8482
Nancy Scott, *President*
EMP: 6
SALES (est): 800K **Privately Held**
WEB: www.basesofva.com
SIC: 3821 Chemical laboratory apparatus

(G-15937)
BINGO CITY
5702 George Wash Mem Hwy
(23692-2490)
PHONE.................................757 890-3168
Georgia Griffin, *Principal*
EMP: 1
SALES (est): 87.4K **Privately Held**
SIC: 3944 Games, toys & children's vehi-
cles

(G-15938)
BLACK DOG GALLERY
114 Ballard St (23690-4033)
PHONE.................................757 989-1700
Virginia Lascara, *Branch Mgr*
EMP: 3
SALES (corp-wide): 211.1K **Privately
Held**
WEB: www.blackdoggallery.net
SIC: 3499 5999 Picture frames, metal; pic-
ture frames, ready made

PA: Black Dog Gallery
619 Jack Rabbit Rd # 101
Virginia Beach VA 23451
757 422-6318

(G-15939)
BLANCO INC
125 Prince Arthur Dr (23693-2853)
PHONE.................................757 766-8123
Dale Marn, *Branch Mgr*
EMP: 2 **Privately Held**
WEB: www.blancolabels.com
SIC: 2672 Coated & laminated paper
PA: Blanco, Inc.
3316 Aerial Way Dr Sw
Roanoke VA 24018

(G-15940)
BW DESIGN BUILD LLC
410 Ferguson Bnd (23693-4534)
PHONE.................................757 504-5052
Bridgett Madden,
EMP: 2
SALES (est): 180K **Privately Held**
SIC: 1389 Construction, repair & disman-
tling services

(G-15941)
CAMPBELL DAVID
1214 Dandy Loop Rd (23692-4538)
PHONE.................................757 877-1633
David Campbell, *Principal*
EMP: 2
SALES (est): 171.2K **Privately Held**
SIC: 2679 Wallpaper

(G-15942)
**COASTAL SERVICES & TECH
LLC**
110 Key Cir (23692-3310)
P.O. Box 2051, Williamsburg (23187-2051)
PHONE.................................757 833-0550
EMP: 16
SALES (est): 5.6MM **Privately Held**
SIC: 3589 Commercial cooking & food-
warming equipment

(G-15943)
**COLONIAL KITCHEN &
CABINETS**
Also Called: Colonial Kitchens
7621 G Washington Mem 2 (23692)
P.O. Box 1311 (23692-1311)
PHONE.................................757 898-1332
Carl E Hart, *President*
Shelma Hart, *Vice Pres*
EMP: 37 **EST:** 1970
SQ FT: 30,000
SALES (est): 3.1MM **Privately Held**
WEB: www.colonialkitchens757.com
SIC: 2434 2541 2521 2511 Wood kitchen
cabinets; wood partitions & fixtures; wood
office furniture; wood household furniture;
single-family housing construction

(G-15944)
**COMMONWEALTH RAPID DRY
INC**
501 Old York Hampton Hwy (23692-4825)
PHONE.................................757 592-0203
James Michael Hall Jr, *Administration*
EMP: 6
SALES (est): 756.2K **Privately Held**
WEB: www.commonwealthrapiddry.com
SIC: 3442 Molding, trim & stripping

(G-15945)
**CRANE RESEARCH & ENGRG
CO INC**
109 Boathouse Cv (23692-2986)
PHONE.................................757 826-1707
Dannie Lee Schrum, *President*
Jeanette Schrum, *Treasurer*
John Biggs, *Marketing Staff*
Bob Kerwin, *Technical Staff*
▲ **EMP:** 40 **EST:** 1975
SALES (est): 5.5MM **Privately Held**
WEB: www.craftbearing.com
SIC: 3599 7692 Machine shop, jobbing &
repair; welding repair

(G-15946)
CUSTOM PRECAST INC
144 Freedom Blvd (23692-4885)
PHONE.................................757 833-8989

EMP: 2
SALES (est): 91.3K **Privately Held**
SIC: 3272 Mfg Concrete Products

(G-15947)
CUT CHECK WRITING SERVICES
105 Somerset Cir (23692-2210)
PHONE.................................757 898-9015
Debra Hargis, *Owner*
EMP: 2
SALES (est): 117.6K **Privately Held**
SIC: 3579 7231 Check writing, endorsing
or signing machines; beauty shops

(G-15948)
**DARE INSTRUMENT
CORPORATION**
1207 Dare Rd (23692-3618)
P.O. Box 948 (23692-0948)
PHONE.................................757 898-5131
EMP: 5 **EST:** 1949
SQ FT: 5,000
SALES (est): 242K **Privately Held**
SIC: 3599 Machine Shop Jobbing & Repair

(G-15949)
DEBS PICTURE THIS INC
3301 Hampton Hwy Ste H (23693-2967)
PHONE.................................757 867-9588
Deb Musselman, *President*
EMP: 3
SALES (est): 348.7K **Privately Held**
WEB: www.debspicturethis.com
SIC: 3499 2759 Picture frames, metal; en-
graving

(G-15950)
DISHMAN FABRICATIONS LLC
Also Called: Ben Dishman Fabrication
201 Production Dr Ste D (23693-4033)
PHONE.................................757 478-5070
Benjamin P Dishman, *Owner*
Dana Dishman, *Manager*
EMP: 3
SALES (est): 114.4K **Privately Held**
WEB: www.dishman-fabrications.com
SIC: 7692 3479 Welding repair; coating of
metals & formed products

(G-15951)
DONALD CRISP JR
117 Production Dr Ste B (23693-4039)
PHONE.................................757 903-6743
Donald Crisp Jr, *Owner*
EMP: 1
SALES (est): 20K **Privately Held**
SIC: 3465 Body parts, automobile:
stamped metal

(G-15952)
ELIZABETH URBAN
Also Called: Promotional Imprints
101 Bryon Rd (23692-4723)
PHONE.................................757 879-1815
Elizabeth Urban, *Owner*
EMP: 1
SALES (est): 20K **Privately Held**
SIC: 2395 2759 Embroidery products, ex-
cept schiffli machine; promotional printing

(G-15953)
EMBROIDERY WORKS
105 Fernwood Bnd (23692-6151)
PHONE.................................757 344-8573
Rick Harrison, *Principal*
EMP: 1
SALES (est): 42.6K **Privately Held**
SIC: 2395 Embroidery & art needlework

(G-15954)
EMBROIDERY WORKS INC
5317 George Wash Mem Hwy
(23692-2704)
PHONE.................................757 868-8840
Richard W Harrison, *President*
EMP: 3 **EST:** 1998
SQ FT: 1,000
SALES (est): 200K **Privately Held**
WEB: www.emb-works.com
SIC: 2395 Embroidery products, except
schiffli machine

(G-15955)
ENGILITY LLC
111 Cybernetics Way # 200 (23693-5642)
PHONE.................................703 633-8300
Anthony Smeraglinolo, *CEO*
Edward P Boykin, *Principal*
Darryll J Pines, *Principal*
Anthony Principi, *Principal*
Charles S Ream, *Principal*
EMP: 93
SALES (corp-wide): 6.3B **Publicly Held**
WEB: www.engility.com
SIC: 3663 Radio & TV communications
equipment
HQ: Engility Llc
4803 Stonecroft Blvd
Chantilly VA 20151
703 708-1400

(G-15956)
EXCEL GRAPHICS
2225 George Wash Mem Hwy
(23693-4126)
PHONE.................................757 596-4334
Jack Hunt, *Owner*
EMP: 4
SALES (est): 366.4K **Privately Held**
SIC: 2262 Screen printing: manmade fiber
& silk broadwoven fabrics

(G-15957)
F & B HOLDING CO
406 Honeysuckle Ln (23693-5708)
PHONE.................................757 766-2770
Farah Bhutta, *President*
EMP: 2 **EST:** 1995
SALES (est): 140.3K **Privately Held**
SIC: 3575 Keyboards, computer, office ma-
chine

(G-15958)
**FALCON TOOL AND DESIGN
INC**
100 Redoubt Rd Ste A (23692-4994)
PHONE.................................757 898-9393
Cynthia A Halberg, *President*
Brian J Halberg, *Opers Mgr*
EMP: 5
SQ FT: 2,000
SALES (est): 589.8K **Privately Held**
SIC: 3469 Metal stampings

(G-15959)
FAME ALL STARS
661 Todd Trl (23692)
PHONE.................................757 817-0214
Erica Flanigan, *Principal*
EMP: 10
SALES (est): 489.7K **Privately Held**
WEB: www.fameallstars.com
SIC: 2321 Sport shirts, men's & boys': from
purchased materials

(G-15960)
**FLOWERS BAKING CO
NORFOLK LLC**
Also Called: Flowers Bakery Outlet
1404 George Washington Me (23693)
PHONE.................................757 596-1443
Gale Joiner, *Manager*
EMP: 3
SALES (corp-wide): 4.1B **Publicly Held**
SIC: 2051 Bread, cake & related products
HQ: Flowers Baking Co. Of Norfolk, Llc
1209 Corprew Ave
Norfolk VA 23504
757 622-6317

(G-15961)
FOLDEM GEAR LLC
115 Winders Ln (23692-3042)
PHONE.................................571 289-5051
Stephen Sturm,
EMP: 2
SALES (est): 74.1K **Privately Held**
WEB: www.foldemgear.com
SIC: 3949 Hunting equipment

(G-15962)
GOURMET KITCHEN TOOLS INC
Also Called: Fastsigns
1215 George Wash Mem Hwy
(23693-4316)
PHONE.................................757 595-3278
Patricia Crouch, *President*

F George Crouch, *Vice Pres*
Barbara Crouch, *Admin Sec*
EMP: 5
SALES (est): 509.3K **Privately Held**
WEB: www.fastsigns.com
SIC: 3993 7532 Signs & advertising specialties; truck painting & lettering

(G-15963)
HAMPTON ROADS SIGN INC
118 Production Dr (23693-4024)
PHONE.................................757 871-2307
Kent Flythe, *Principal*
EMP: 3 EST: 2003
SALES (est): 250.5K **Privately Held**
WEB: www.crossfithamptonroads.com
SIC: 3993 Signs & advertising specialties

(G-15964)
HYDRA HOSE & SUPPLY CO
536 Hampton Hwy (23693-3517)
PHONE.................................757 867-9795
Douglas Kirby, *Manager*
EMP: 2
SALES (est): 153.1K **Privately Held**
WEB: www.hydrahose.net
SIC: 3492 5084 Hose & tube fittings & assemblies, hydraulic/pneumatic; hydraulic systems equipment & supplies

(G-15965)
INDUSTRIAL METALCRAFT INC
114 Hollywood Blvd (23692-3311)
PHONE.................................757 898-9350
EMP: 2
SQ FT: 1,200
SALES (est): 120K **Privately Held**
SIC: 3441 Structural Metal Fabrication

(G-15966)
IRON LUNGS INC
100 Lorna Doone Dr (23692-3429)
PHONE.................................757 877-2529
Glenn Devol, *President*
EMP: 1
SALES (est): 89.8K **Privately Held**
SIC: 1011 Iron ores

(G-15967)
J & R GRAPHIC SERVICES INC
124 Production Dr (23693-4024)
PHONE.................................757 595-2602
Fax: 757 595-2611
EMP: 9
SQ FT: 3,900
SALES (est): 1.9MM **Privately Held**
SIC: 2759 7336 Commercial Printing Commercial Art/Graphic Design

(G-15968)
JAMES M ROHRBACH INC
Also Called: J R Precision Machine Service
117 Greene Dr Ste B (23692-4936)
PHONE.................................757 898-6322
James M Rohrbach, *President*
EMP: 4
SQ FT: 10,000
SALES (est): 150K **Privately Held**
WEB: www.amtechmachine.com
SIC: 3599 Machine shop, jobbing & repair

(G-15969)
JASONS AMMO
301 Oak Point Dr (23692-4435)
PHONE.................................757 715-4689
Jason Patch, *Owner*
EMP: 1
SQ FT: 2,000
SALES (est): 1.7MM **Privately Held**
SIC: 3482 5099 Small arms ammunition; ammunition, except sporting

(G-15970)
JIHOON SOLUTION INC
205 Alexia Ln (23690-2101)
PHONE.................................757 344-1751
Ji Hoon Yoo, *CEO*
Young You, *President*
EMP: 2
SALES (est): 100K **Privately Held**
SIC: 3674 Semiconductors & related devices

(G-15971)
JOHN HENRY PRINTING INC
7300 George Washington Me (23692-5014)
PHONE.................................757 369-9549
Jeff Stanaway, *President*
Randy Stanaway, *President*
EMP: 2
SALES (est): 350.4K **Privately Held**
WEB: www.jhprinting.net
SIC: 2752 2759 Commercial printing, offset; letterpress printing

(G-15972)
KILN CREEK PKWY - OLD YORKTOWN
3120 Kiln Creek Pkwy R (23693-5648)
PHONE.................................757 204-7229
EMP: 2
SALES (est): 106K **Privately Held**
SIC: 3559 Kilns

(G-15973)
LAWSON AND SON CNSTR LLC
109 W Wedgwood Dr (23693-5505)
PHONE.................................478 258-2478
Lionel Lawson, *President*
EMP: 1
SALES (est): 49.6K **Privately Held**
SIC: 1389 1799 8711 8742 Construction, repair & dismantling services; construction site cleanup; construction & civil engineering; construction project management consultant

(G-15974)
LEGEND LENSES LLC
204 School Ln (23692-3206)
PHONE.................................757 871-1331
Doug Hockaday, *Principal*
EMP: 2 EST: 2016
SALES (est): 101.3K **Privately Held**
SIC: 3851 Ophthalmic goods

(G-15975)
LIFELINE OF PRINCE WILLIAM
4615 George Wash Mem Hwy (23692-2766)
P.O. Box 596, Gainesville (20156-0596)
PHONE.................................703 753-9000
Marcel Cadieux, *Principal*
EMP: 4
SALES (est): 443.2K **Privately Held**
SIC: 3842 Wheelchairs

(G-15976)
LINDA M BARNES
Also Called: Creative Candles & Gifts
301 Leigh Rd (23690-9704)
PHONE.................................757 240-7327
EMP: 1
SALES (est): 5K **Privately Held**
SIC: 3999 Mfg Misc Products

(G-15977)
LOCKHEED MARTIN CORPORATION
111 Cybernetics Way # 205 (23693-5642)
PHONE.................................757 509-6808
Scott Frazier, *General Mgr*
EMP: 4 **Publicly Held**
WEB: www.lockheedmartin.com
SIC: 3812 Search & navigation equipment
PA: Lockheed Martin Corporation
6801 Rockledge Dr
Bethesda MD 20817

(G-15978)
MARINE SONIC TECHNOLOGY
120 Newsome Dr Ste H (23692-5011)
PHONE.................................804 693-9602
EMP: 5
SALES (est): 551.3K **Privately Held**
WEB: www.marinesonic.com
SIC: 3812 Search & navigation equipment

(G-15979)
MARTHA BENNETT
Also Called: Momo On The Go
121 Locust Ln (23693-4935)
PHONE.................................757 897-6150
Martha Bennett, *Owner*
EMP: 1

SALES (est): 50K **Privately Held**
WEB: www.momoonthego.com
SIC: 2099 Food preparations

(G-15980)
MASTERMIND LLC
105 Professional Pkwy # 152 (23693-4334)
PHONE.................................757 379-5215
Tariq Graham, *President*
EMP: 2
SALES (est): 50K **Privately Held**
SIC: 2741 Music books: publishing & printing

(G-15981)
MATERA JOHN
Also Called: Yorktown Hardwood Floors
6305 Grg Wshngtn Mrl Hwy (23692)
PHONE.................................757 240-0425
EMP: 1
SALES (est): 77.7K **Privately Held**
SIC: 2426 Hardwood Dimension And Flooring Mills,Nsk

(G-15982)
MICHIE SOFTWARE SYSTEMS INC
131 River Point Dr (23693-2110)
PHONE.................................757 868-7771
Frances Michie, *President*
Fred Michie, *Vice Pres*
EMP: 5
SALES (est): 370K **Privately Held**
WEB: www.michiesoftware.com
SIC: 7372 7379 7371 Prepackaged software; computer related consulting services; custom computer programming services

(G-15983)
OBRIEN MACHINE REPAIR
103 Misty Dr (23692-3116)
PHONE.................................757 898-1387
Timothy O'Brien, *Owner*
Timothy Obrien, *Principal*
EMP: 1
SALES (est): 58.7K **Privately Held**
SIC: 7694 Motor repair services

(G-15984)
POWDER METAL FABRICATION
104 Cove Ct (23692-4328)
PHONE.................................757 898-1614
Peter Carlson, *Principal*
EMP: 2
SALES (est): 137.7K **Privately Held**
SIC: 3499 Fabricated metal products

(G-15985)
RACECOM OF VIRGINIA
200 Commerce Cir (23693-4320)
PHONE.................................757 599-8255
Mike Mullins, *President*
EMP: 2
SALES (est): 200K **Privately Held**
SIC: 3663 Airborne radio communications equipment

(G-15986)
RAY VISIONS INC
317 Blacksmith Arch (23693-4511)
PHONE.................................757 865-6442
Randy Wojcik, *CEO*
Stan Majewski, *Vice Pres*
Carl Zorn, *Admin Sec*
EMP: 4 EST: 1995
SALES (est): 500K **Privately Held**
WEB: www.rayvisions.com
SIC: 3229 Fiber optics strands

(G-15987)
RAYTHEON COMPANY
160 Main Rd (23691-5111)
PHONE.................................757 749-9638
Matthew Flom, *Engineer*
EMP: 3
SALES (corp-wide): 77B **Publicly Held**
WEB: www.rtx.com
SIC: 3812 3663 3761 Defense systems & equipment; space satellite communications equipment; airborne radio communications equipment; guided missiles & space vehicles, research & development; rockets, space & military, complete

HQ: Raytheon Company
870 Winter St
Waltham MA 02451
781 522-3000

(G-15988)
RL BYRD PROPERTIES
169 Goodwin Neck Rd (23692-2123)
PHONE.................................757 817-7920
Colleen Martin, *Principal*
EMP: 3
SALES (est): 169.1K **Privately Held**
SIC: 1442 Sand mining

(G-15989)
RYSON INTERNATIONAL INC
300 Newsome Dr (23692-5006)
PHONE.................................757 898-1530
Ole B Rygh, *President*
Ragnhild M Rygh, *Vice Pres*
Dave Wineman, *Vice Pres*
Marty Foray, *VP Mfg*
Jerry Gonzales, *Production*
◆ EMP: 10
SALES (est): 3.1MM **Privately Held**
WEB: www.ryson.com
SIC: 3535 7371 Bulk handling conveyor systems; computer software development

(G-15990)
SIGN DUDE
2100 George Wash Mem Hwy (23693-4223)
PHONE.................................757 303-7770
EMP: 1
SALES (est): 94.5K **Privately Held**
SIC: 3993 Signs & advertising specialties

(G-15991)
SIMS USA INC
739 Charles Rd (23692-3099)
PHONE.................................757 875-7742
Sandra Allard, *President*
Barry Swanson, *President*
Kreis Reynolds, *Sales Mgr*
Sandra Andreoli, *Mktg Dir*
Jennifer Isaksen, *Manager*
EMP: 5
SALES (est): 838.7K **Privately Held**
WEB: www.travaini.com
SIC: 3821 Laboratory apparatus, except heating & measuring

(G-15992)
SPEEDWAY LLC
1724 George Washington Me (23693)
PHONE.................................757 599-6250
Tannette Brooks, *President*
EMP: 3 **Publicly Held**
WEB: www.speedway.com
SIC: 1311 Crude petroleum production
HQ: Speedway Llc
500 Speedway Dr
Enon OH 45323
937 864-3000

(G-15993)
SPORTS PRODUCTS WORLD ENTPS
300 Commerce Cir Ste D (23693-4321)
PHONE.................................888 493-6079
Jackie Herman, *Principal*
EMP: 2 EST: 2011
SALES (est): 141.1K **Privately Held**
SIC: 3949 Sporting & athletic goods

(G-15994)
STEALTH DUMP TRUCKS INC
111 Old Railway Rd (23692-2945)
PHONE.................................757 890-4888
Eric E Thorvaldson, *President*
Joel D Thorvaldson, *Treasurer*
EMP: 2
SQ FT: 20,000
SALES (est): 150K **Privately Held**
WEB: www.stealthdumptrucks.com
SIC: 3714 Motor vehicle parts & accessories

(G-15995)
TAURUS TECHNOLOGIES INC
103 Beach Rd (23692-3072)
PHONE.................................757 873-2700
Dan Baltrus, *Principal*
EMP: 2

▲ = Import ▼=Export
◆ =Import/Export

SALES (est): 99.7K **Privately Held**
SIC: **3699** Electrical equipment & supplies

(G-15996)
TINTED TIMBER SIGN CO
129 Camelot Cres (23693-3217)
PHONE.................................757 869-3231
Tracey Brewer, *Principal*
EMP: 1
SALES (est): 46K **Privately Held**
SIC: **3993** Signs & advertising specialties

(G-15997)
TWO PEPPERS TRANSPORTATION LLC
1510 Showalter Rd (23692-3405)
PHONE.................................757 761-6674
Dennis M Norge, *Principal*
EMP: 5
SALES (est): 600K **Privately Held**
SIC: **3715** Truck trailers

(G-15998)
VINTNERS CLLAR WINERY YORKTOWN
1213 George Wash Mem Hwy (23693-4312)
PHONE.................................757 223-4261
Glenn Parks, *Owner*
EMP: 5
SALES (est): 160K **Privately Held**
WEB: www.vintnerscellaryorktown.com
SIC: **2084** Wines

(G-15999)
VIRGINIAS PENINSULA PUB FCILTY
145 Goodwin Neck Rd (23692-2122)
PHONE.................................757 898-5012
Patricia Brown, *Opers Staff*
Steven Geisler, *Director*
EMP: 7
SALES (est): 472.3K **Privately Held**
WEB: www.vppsa.org
SIC: **2875** Compost

(G-16000)
WANG SIGN HOLDINGS LLC
Also Called: Fastsigns
1215 Grge Wash Mem Hwy St (23693)
PHONE.................................757 595-3278
John Wang, *Mng Member*
EMP: 3
SALES (est): 100.5K **Privately Held**
SIC: **3993** Signs & advertising specialties

(G-16001)
WILLIAMS INDUSTRIAL REPAIR INC
113 Production Dr (23693-4025)
PHONE.................................757 969-5738
Wayne Williams, *President*
Judy Williams, *Vice Pres*
EMP: 4
SALES (est): 529.7K **Privately Held**
SIC: **3594** Pumps, hydraulic power transfer

(G-16002)
WITCHING HOUR PRESS LLC
105 Maurice Ct (23690-3944)
PHONE.................................571 209-0019
Emily H Joyne, *Principal*
EMP: 1
SALES (est): 41.3K **Privately Held**
SIC: **2741** Miscellaneous publishing

(G-16003)
WJM PRINTED PRODUCTS INC
125 Prince Arthur Dr (23693-2853)
PHONE.................................757 870-1043
Dale Marn, *Principal*
Billy Marn, *Sales Mgr*
EMP: 4
SALES (est): 275.1K **Privately Held**
WEB: www.wjmprintedproducts.com
SIC: **2752** Commercial printing, offset

(G-16004)
YORK TOWN CRIER
3526 George Wash Mem Hwy (23693-3371)
PHONE.................................757 766-1776
Beth Meisner, *Principal*
EMP: 5
SALES (est): 277.1K **Privately Held**
WEB: www.yorktowncrier.com
SIC: **2711** Newspapers, publishing & printing

Zion Crossroads
Orange County

(G-16005)
BOSS INSTRUMENTS LTD INC
104 Sommerfield Dr (22942-7009)
PHONE.................................540 832-5000
John Lauer, *CEO*
John Ryall, *Vice Pres*
Nancy Morris, *Accounts Mgr*
David Gonzalez, *Cust Mgr*
Dave Free, *Sales Staff*
EMP: 12
SQ FT: 8,000
SALES (est): 2.1MM **Privately Held**
WEB: www.bossinst.com
SIC: **3841** Ophthalmic instruments & apparatus

(G-16006)
CROSSROADS IRON WORKS INC
10380 James Madison Hwy (22942-6918)
P.O. Box 997, Troy (22974-0997)
PHONE.................................540 832-7800
Michael W Dailey, *President*
Caroline A Dailey, *Corp Secy*
EMP: 12
SQ FT: 15,000
SALES (est): 1.1MM **Privately Held**
WEB: www.crossroadsironworks.com
SIC: **7692** Welding repair

(G-16007)
DEERFIELD GROUP LLC
1988 W Green Springs Rd (22942-6881)
PHONE.................................434 591-0848
Joe Mazzariello, *Vice Pres*
Steve Fawcett,
EMP: 3 EST: 2009
SALES (est): 500K **Privately Held**
WEB: www.deerfield-group.com
SIC: **2621** Printing paper

(G-16008)
KINETECH LABS INC
49 Forest Ct (22942-6991)
PHONE.................................434 284-1073
Xue Feng, *Shareholder*
EMP: 1
SALES (est): 40.7K **Privately Held**
SIC: **7372** Application computer software

(G-16009)
STEALTH SURGICAL LLC
104 Sommerfield Dr (22942-7009)
PHONE.................................540 832-5580
Joe Albrecht, *General Mgr*
John Laeur,
EMP: 4
SALES (est): 392.1K **Privately Held**
WEB: www.stealthsurgical.com
SIC: **3841** Surgical & medical instruments

(G-16010)
WOOLEN MILLS TAVERN LLC
1125 Loving Rd (22942-6846)
PHONE.................................434 296-2816
EMP: 2
SALES (est): 102.8K **Privately Held**
SIC: **2231** Wool Broadwoven Fabric Mill

Zuni
Isle Of Wight County

(G-16011)
A L DUCK JR INC
26532 River Run Trl (23898-3220)
PHONE.................................757 562-2387
Brenda G Reed, *President*
EMP: 10
SQ FT: 3,600
SALES (est): 550K **Privately Held**
SIC: **2013 5147** Sausages from purchased meat; meats, cured or smoked

---

SIC NO	PRODUCT

A

3291 Abrasive Prdts
2891 Adhesives & Sealants
3563 Air & Gas Compressors
3585 Air Conditioning & Heating Eqpt
3721 Aircraft
3724 Aircraft Engines & Engine Parts
3728 Aircraft Parts & Eqpt, NEC
2812 Alkalies & Chlorine
3363 Aluminum Die Castings
3354 Aluminum Extruded Prdts
3365 Aluminum Foundries
3355 Aluminum Rolling & Drawing, NEC
3353 Aluminum Sheet, Plate & Foil
3483 Ammunition, Large
3826 Analytical Instruments
2077 Animal, Marine Fats & Oils
2389 Apparel & Accessories, NEC
3446 Architectural & Ornamental Metal Work
7694 Armature Rewinding Shops
3292 Asbestos products
2952 Asphalt Felts & Coatings
3822 Automatic Temperature Controls
3581 Automatic Vending Machines
3465 Automotive Stampings
2396 Automotive Trimmings, Apparel Findings, Related Prdts

B

2673 Bags: Plastics, Laminated & Coated
2674 Bags: Uncoated Paper & Multiwall
3562 Ball & Roller Bearings
2836 Biological Prdts, Exc Diagnostic Substances
1221 Bituminous Coal & Lignite: Surface Mining
1222 Bituminous Coal: Underground Mining
2782 Blankbooks & Looseleaf Binders
3312 Blast Furnaces, Coke Ovens, Steel & Rolling Mills
3564 Blowers & Fans
3732 Boat Building & Repairing
3452 Bolts, Nuts, Screws, Rivets & Washers
2732 Book Printing, Not Publishing
2789 Bookbinding
2731 Books: Publishing & Printing
3131 Boot & Shoe Cut Stock & Findings
2342 Brassieres, Girdles & Garments
2051 Bread, Bakery Prdts Exc Cookies & Crackers
3251 Brick & Structural Clay Tile
3991 Brooms & Brushes
2021 Butter

C

3578 Calculating & Accounting Eqpt
2064 Candy & Confectionery Prdts
2033 Canned Fruits, Vegetables & Preserves
2032 Canned Specialties
2394 Canvas Prdts
3624 Carbon & Graphite Prdts
3955 Carbon Paper & Inked Ribbons
3592 Carburetors, Pistons, Rings & Valves
2273 Carpets & Rugs
2823 Cellulosic Man-Made Fibers
3241 Cement, Hydraulic
3253 Ceramic Tile
2043 Cereal Breakfast Foods
2022 Cheese
1479 Chemical & Fertilizer Mining
2899 Chemical Preparations, NEC
2361 Children's & Infants' Dresses & Blouses
3261 China Plumbing Fixtures & Fittings
2066 Chocolate & Cocoa Prdts
2111 Cigarettes
2121 Cigars
3255 Clay Refractories
1459 Clay, Ceramic & Refractory Minerals, NEC
1241 Coal Mining Svcs
3479 Coating & Engraving, NEC
2095 Coffee
3316 Cold Rolled Steel Sheet, Strip & Bars
3582 Commercial Laundry, Dry Clean & Pressing Mchs
2759 Commercial Printing
2754 Commercial Printing: Gravure
2752 Commercial Printing: Lithographic
3646 Commercial, Indl & Institutional Lighting Fixtures
3669 Communications Eqpt, NEC

3577 Computer Peripheral Eqpt, NEC
3572 Computer Storage Devices
3575 Computer Terminals
3271 Concrete Block & Brick
3272 Concrete Prdts
3531 Construction Machinery & Eqpt
1442 Construction Sand & Gravel
2679 Converted Paper Prdts, NEC
3535 Conveyors & Eqpt
2052 Cookies & Crackers
3366 Copper Foundries
2298 Cordage & Twine
2653 Corrugated & Solid Fiber Boxes
3961 Costume Jewelry & Novelties
2261 Cotton Fabric Finishers
2211 Cotton, Woven Fabric
3466 Crowns & Closures
1311 Crude Petroleum & Natural Gas
1423 Crushed & Broken Granite
1422 Crushed & Broken Limestone
1429 Crushed & Broken Stone, NEC
3643 Current-Carrying Wiring Devices
2391 Curtains & Draperies
3087 Custom Compounding Of Purchased Plastic Resins
3281 Cut Stone Prdts
3421 Cutlery
2865 Cyclic-Crudes, Intermediates, Dyes & Org Pigments

D

3843 Dental Eqpt & Splys
2835 Diagnostic Substances
2675 Die-Cut Paper & Board
3544 Dies, Tools, Jigs, Fixtures & Indl Molds
1411 Dimension Stone
2047 Dog & Cat Food
3942 Dolls & Stuffed Toys
2591 Drapery Hardware, Window Blinds & Shades
2034 Dried Fruits, Vegetables & Soup
1381 Drilling Oil & Gas Wells

E

3263 Earthenware, Whiteware, Table & Kitchen Articles
3634 Electric Household Appliances
3641 Electric Lamps
3694 Electrical Eqpt For Internal Combustion Engines
3629 Electrical Indl Apparatus, NEC
3699 Electrical Machinery, Eqpt & Splys, NEC
3845 Electromedical & Electrotherapeutic Apparatus
3675 Electronic Capacitors
3677 Electronic Coils & Transformers
3679 Electronic Components, NEC
3571 Electronic Computers
3678 Electronic Connectors
3471 Electroplating, Plating, Polishing, Anodizing & Coloring
3534 Elevators & Moving Stairways
3431 Enameled Iron & Metal Sanitary Ware
2677 Envelopes
2892 Explosives

F

2241 Fabric Mills, Cotton, Wool, Silk & Man-Made
3499 Fabricated Metal Prdts, NEC
3498 Fabricated Pipe & Pipe Fittings
3443 Fabricated Plate Work
3069 Fabricated Rubber Prdts, NEC
3441 Fabricated Structural Steel
2399 Fabricated Textile Prdts, NEC
2295 Fabrics Coated Not Rubberized
2297 Fabrics, Nonwoven
3523 Farm Machinery & Eqpt
3965 Fasteners, Buttons, Needles & Pins
2875 Fertilizers, Mixing Only
2655 Fiber Cans, Tubes & Drums
2091 Fish & Seafoods, Canned & Cured
2092 Fish & Seafoods, Fresh & Frozen
3211 Flat Glass
2087 Flavoring Extracts & Syrups
2045 Flour, Blended & Prepared
2041 Flour, Grain Milling
3824 Fluid Meters & Counters
3593 Fluid Power Cylinders & Actuators
3594 Fluid Power Pumps & Motors
3492 Fluid Power Valves & Hose Fittings
2657 Folding Paperboard Boxes

3556 Food Prdts Machinery
2099 Food Preparations, NEC
3149 Footwear, NEC
2053 Frozen Bakery Prdts
2037 Frozen Fruits, Juices & Vegetables
2038 Frozen Specialties
2371 Fur Goods
2599 Furniture & Fixtures, NEC

G

3944 Games, Toys & Children's Vehicles
3524 Garden, Lawn Tractors & Eqpt
3053 Gaskets, Packing & Sealing Devices
2369 Girls' & Infants' Outerwear, NEC
3221 Glass Containers
3231 Glass Prdts Made Of Purchased Glass
1041 Gold Ores
3321 Gray Iron Foundries
2771 Greeting Card Publishing
3769 Guided Missile/Space Vehicle Parts & Eqpt, NEC
3764 Guided Missile/Space Vehicle Propulsion Units & parts
3761 Guided Missiles & Space Vehicles
2861 Gum & Wood Chemicals
3275 Gypsum Prdts

H

3423 Hand & Edge Tools
3425 Hand Saws & Saw Blades
3171 Handbags & Purses
3429 Hardware, NEC
2426 Hardwood Dimension & Flooring Mills
2435 Hardwood Veneer & Plywood
2353 Hats, Caps & Millinery
3433 Heating Eqpt
3536 Hoists, Cranes & Monorails
2252 Hosiery, Except Women's
2251 Hosiery, Women's Full & Knee Length
2392 House furnishings: Textile
3639 Household Appliances, NEC
3651 Household Audio & Video Eqpt
3631 Household Cooking Eqpt
2519 Household Furniture, NEC
3633 Household Laundry Eqpt
3632 Household Refrigerators & Freezers
3635 Household Vacuum Cleaners

I

2097 Ice
2024 Ice Cream
2819 Indl Inorganic Chemicals, NEC
3823 Indl Instruments For Meas, Display & Control
3569 Indl Machinery & Eqpt, NEC
3567 Indl Process Furnaces & Ovens
3537 Indl Trucks, Tractors, Trailers & Stackers
2813 Industrial Gases
2869 Industrial Organic Chemicals, NEC
3543 Industrial Patterns
1446 Industrial Sand
3491 Industrial Valves
2816 Inorganic Pigments
3825 Instrs For Measuring & Testing Electricity
3519 Internal Combustion Engines, NEC
3462 Iron & Steel Forgings
1011 Iron Ores

J

3915 Jewelers Findings & Lapidary Work
3911 Jewelry: Precious Metal

K

1455 Kaolin & Ball Clay
2253 Knit Outerwear Mills
2254 Knit Underwear Mills
2259 Knitting Mills, NEC

L

3821 Laboratory Apparatus & Furniture
3952 Lead Pencils, Crayons & Artist's Mtrls
2386 Leather & Sheep Lined Clothing
3151 Leather Gloves & Mittens
3199 Leather Goods, NEC
3111 Leather Tanning & Finishing
3648 Lighting Eqpt, NEC
3274 Lime
3996 Linoleum & Hard Surface Floor Coverings, NEC

S
I
C

SIC NO	PRODUCT
2085	Liquors, Distilled, Rectified & Blended
2411	Logging
2992	Lubricating Oils & Greases
3161	Luggage

M

SIC NO	PRODUCT
2098	Macaroni, Spaghetti & Noodles
3545	Machine Tool Access
3541	Machine Tools: Cutting
3542	Machine Tools: Forming
3599	Machinery & Eqpt, Indl & Commercial, NEC
2083	Malt
2082	Malt Beverages
2761	Manifold Business Forms
3999	Manufacturing Industries, NEC
3953	Marking Devices
2515	Mattresses & Bedsprings
3829	Measuring & Controlling Devices, NEC
3586	Measuring & Dispensing Pumps
2011	Meat Packing Plants
3568	Mechanical Power Transmission Eqpt, NEC
2833	Medicinal Chemicals & Botanical Prdts
2329	Men's & Boys' Clothing, NEC
2323	Men's & Boys' Neckwear
2325	Men's & Boys' Separate Trousers & Casual Slacks
2321	Men's & Boys' Shirts
2311	Men's & Boys' Suits, Coats & Overcoats
2322	Men's & Boys' Underwear & Nightwear
2326	Men's & Boys' Work Clothing
3143	Men's Footwear, Exc Athletic
3412	Metal Barrels, Drums, Kegs & Pails
3411	Metal Cans
3442	Metal Doors, Sash, Frames, Molding & Trim
3497	Metal Foil & Leaf
3398	Metal Heat Treating
2514	Metal Household Furniture
1081	Metal Mining Svcs
1099	Metal Ores, NEC
3469	Metal Stampings, NEC
3549	Metalworking Machinery, NEC
2026	Milk
2023	Milk, Condensed & Evaporated
2431	Millwork
3296	Mineral Wool
3295	Minerals & Earths: Ground Or Treated
3532	Mining Machinery & Eqpt
3496	Misc Fabricated Wire Prdts
2741	Misc Publishing
3449	Misc Structural Metal Work
1499	Miscellaneous Nonmetallic Mining
2451	Mobile Homes
3061	Molded, Extruded & Lathe-Cut Rubber Mechanical Goods
3716	Motor Homes
3714	Motor Vehicle Parts & Access
3711	Motor Vehicles & Car Bodies
3751	Motorcycles, Bicycles & Parts
3621	Motors & Generators
3931	Musical Instruments

N

SIC NO	PRODUCT
1321	Natural Gas Liquids
2711	Newspapers: Publishing & Printing
2873	Nitrogenous Fertilizers
3297	Nonclay Refractories
3644	Noncurrent-Carrying Wiring Devices
3364	Nonferrous Die Castings, Exc Aluminum
3463	Nonferrous Forgings
3369	Nonferrous Foundries: Castings, NEC
3357	Nonferrous Wire Drawing
3299	Nonmetallic Mineral Prdts, NEC
1481	Nonmetallic Minerals Svcs, Except Fuels

O

SIC NO	PRODUCT
2522	Office Furniture, Except Wood
3579	Office Machines, NEC
1382	Oil & Gas Field Exploration Svcs
1389	Oil & Gas Field Svcs, NEC
3533	Oil Field Machinery & Eqpt
3851	Ophthalmic Goods
3827	Optical Instruments
3489	Ordnance & Access, NEC
3842	Orthopedic, Prosthetic & Surgical Appliances/Splys

P

SIC NO	PRODUCT
3565	Packaging Machinery
2851	Paints, Varnishes, Lacquers, Enamels
2671	Paper Coating & Laminating for Packaging
2672	Paper Coating & Laminating, Exc for Packaging

SIC NO	PRODUCT
3554	Paper Inds Machinery
2621	Paper Mills
2631	Paperboard Mills
2542	Partitions & Fixtures, Except Wood
2951	Paving Mixtures & Blocks
3951	Pens & Mechanical Pencils
2844	Perfumes, Cosmetics & Toilet Preparations
2721	Periodicals: Publishing & Printing
3172	Personal Leather Goods
2879	Pesticides & Agricultural Chemicals, NEC
2911	Petroleum Refining
2834	Pharmaceuticals
3652	Phonograph Records & Magnetic Tape
2874	Phosphatic Fertilizers
3861	Photographic Eqpt & Splys
2035	Pickled Fruits, Vegetables, Sauces & Dressings
3085	Plastic Bottles
3086	Plastic Foam Prdts
3083	Plastic Laminated Plate & Sheet
3084	Plastic Pipe
3088	Plastic Plumbing Fixtures
3089	Plastic Prdts
3082	Plastic Unsupported Profile Shapes
3081	Plastic Unsupported Sheet & Film
2821	Plastics, Mtrls & Nonvulcanizable Elastomers
2796	Platemaking & Related Svcs
2395	Pleating & Stitching For The Trade
3432	Plumbing Fixture Fittings & Trim, Brass
3264	Porcelain Electrical Splys
2096	Potato Chips & Similar Prdts
3269	Pottery Prdts, NEC
2015	Poultry Slaughtering, Dressing & Processing
3546	Power Hand Tools
3612	Power, Distribution & Specialty Transformers
3448	Prefabricated Metal Buildings & Cmpnts
2452	Prefabricated Wood Buildings & Cmpnts
7372	Prepackaged Software
2048	Prepared Feeds For Animals & Fowls
3229	Pressed & Blown Glassware, NEC
3692	Primary Batteries: Dry & Wet
3399	Primary Metal Prdts, NEC
3339	Primary Nonferrous Metals, NEC
3334	Primary Production Of Aluminum
3331	Primary Smelting & Refining Of Copper
3672	Printed Circuit Boards
2893	Printing Ink
3555	Printing Trades Machinery & Eqpt
2999	Products Of Petroleum & Coal, NEC
2531	Public Building & Related Furniture
2611	Pulp Mills
3561	Pumps & Pumping Eqpt

R

SIC NO	PRODUCT
3663	Radio & T V Communications, Systs & Eqpt, Broadcast/Studio
3671	Radio & T V Receiving Electron Tubes
3743	Railroad Eqpt
3273	Ready-Mixed Concrete
2493	Reconstituted Wood Prdts
3695	Recording Media
3625	Relays & Indl Controls
3645	Residential Lighting Fixtures
2044	Rice Milling
2384	Robes & Dressing Gowns
3547	Rolling Mill Machinery & Eqpt
3351	Rolling, Drawing & Extruding Of Copper
3356	Rolling, Drawing-Extruding Of Nonferrous Metals
3021	Rubber & Plastic Footwear
3052	Rubber & Plastic Hose & Belting

S

SIC NO	PRODUCT
2068	Salted & Roasted Nuts & Seeds
2656	Sanitary Food Containers
2676	Sanitary Paper Prdts
2013	Sausages & Meat Prdts
2421	Saw & Planing Mills
3596	Scales & Balances, Exc Laboratory
2397	Schiffli Machine Embroideries
3451	Screw Machine Prdts
3812	Search, Detection, Navigation & Guidance Systs & Instrs
3341	Secondary Smelting & Refining Of Nonferrous Metals
3674	Semiconductors
3589	Service Ind Machines, NEC
2652	Set-Up Paperboard Boxes
3444	Sheet Metal Work
3731	Shipbuilding & Repairing
2079	Shortening, Oils & Margarine
3993	Signs & Advertising Displays

SIC NO	PRODUCT
2262	Silk & Man-Made Fabric Finishers
2221	Silk & Man-Made Fiber
3914	Silverware, Plated & Stainless Steel Ware
3484	Small Arms
3482	Small Arms Ammunition
2841	Soap & Detergents
2086	Soft Drinks
2436	Softwood Veneer & Plywood
2842	Spec Cleaning, Polishing & Sanitation Preparations
3559	Special Ind Machinery, NEC
2429	Special Prdt Sawmills, NEC
3566	Speed Changers, Drives & Gears
3949	Sporting & Athletic Goods, NEC
2678	Stationery Prdts
3511	Steam, Gas & Hydraulic Turbines & Engines
3325	Steel Foundries, NEC
3324	Steel Investment Foundries
3317	Steel Pipe & Tubes
3493	Steel Springs, Except Wire
3315	Steel Wire Drawing & Nails & Spikes
3691	Storage Batteries
3259	Structural Clay Prdts, NEC
2439	Structural Wood Members, NEC
2843	Surface Active & Finishing Agents, Sulfonated Oils
3841	Surgical & Medical Instrs & Apparatus
3613	Switchgear & Switchboard Apparatus
2824	Synthetic Organic Fibers, Exc Cellulosic
2822	Synthetic Rubber (Vulcanizable Elastomers)

T

SIC NO	PRODUCT
3795	Tanks & Tank Components
3661	Telephone & Telegraph Apparatus
2393	Textile Bags
2269	Textile Finishers, NEC
2299	Textile Goods, NEC
3552	Textile Machinery
2284	Thread Mills
2296	Tire Cord & Fabric
3011	Tires & Inner Tubes
2141	Tobacco Stemming & Redrying
2131	Tobacco, Chewing & Snuff
3799	Transportation Eqpt, NEC
3792	Travel Trailers & Campers
3713	Truck & Bus Bodies
3715	Truck Trailers
2791	Typesetting

U

SIC NO	PRODUCT
1094	Uranium, Radium & Vanadium Ores

V

SIC NO	PRODUCT
3494	Valves & Pipe Fittings, NEC
2076	Vegetable Oil Mills
3647	Vehicular Lighting Eqpt

W

SIC NO	PRODUCT
3873	Watch & Clock Devices & Parts
2385	Waterproof Outerwear
3548	Welding Apparatus
7692	Welding Repair
2046	Wet Corn Milling
2084	Wine & Brandy
3495	Wire Springs
2331	Women's & Misses' Blouses
2335	Women's & Misses' Dresses
2339	Women's & Misses' Outerwear, NEC
2337	Women's & Misses' Suits, Coats & Skirts
3144	Women's Footwear, Exc Athletic
2341	Women's, Misses' & Children's Underwear & Nightwear
2441	Wood Boxes
2449	Wood Containers, NEC
2511	Wood Household Furniture
2512	Wood Household Furniture, Upholstered
2434	Wood Kitchen Cabinets
2521	Wood Office Furniture
2448	Wood Pallets & Skids
2499	Wood Prdts, NEC
2491	Wood Preserving
2517	Wood T V, Radio, Phono & Sewing Cabinets
2541	Wood, Office & Store Fixtures
3553	Woodworking Machinery
2231	Wool, Woven Fabric

X

SIC NO	PRODUCT
3844	X-ray Apparatus & Tubes

Y

SIC NO	PRODUCT
2281	Yarn Spinning Mills
2282	Yarn Texturizing, Throwing, Twisting & Winding Mills

SIC INDEX

SIC NO	PRODUCT

10 metal mining
1011 Iron Ores
1041 Gold Ores
1081 Metal Mining Svcs
1094 Uranium, Radium & Vanadium Ores
1099 Metal Ores, NEC

12 coal mining
1221 Bituminous Coal & Lignite: Surface Mining
1222 Bituminous Coal: Underground Mining
1241 Coal Mining Svcs

13 oil and gas extraction
1311 Crude Petroleum & Natural Gas
1321 Natural Gas Liquids
1381 Drilling Oil & Gas Wells
1382 Oil & Gas Field Exploration Svcs
1389 Oil & Gas Field Svcs, NEC

14 mining and quarrying of nonmetallic minerals, except fuels
1411 Dimension Stone
1422 Crushed & Broken Limestone
1423 Crushed & Broken Granite
1429 Crushed & Broken Stone, NEC
1442 Construction Sand & Gravel
1446 Industrial Sand
1455 Kaolin & Ball Clay
1459 Clay, Ceramic & Refractory Minerals, NEC
1479 Chemical & Fertilizer Mining
1481 Nonmetallic Minerals Svcs, Except Fuels
1499 Miscellaneous Nonmetallic Mining

20 food and kindred products
2011 Meat Packing Plants
2013 Sausages & Meat Prdts
2015 Poultry Slaughtering, Dressing & Processing
2021 Butter
2022 Cheese
2023 Milk, Condensed & Evaporated
2024 Ice Cream
2026 Milk
2032 Canned Specialties
2033 Canned Fruits, Vegetables & Preserves
2034 Dried Fruits, Vegetables & Soup
2035 Pickled Fruits, Vegetables, Sauces & Dressings
2037 Frozen Fruits, Juices & Vegetables
2038 Frozen Specialties
2041 Flour, Grain Milling
2043 Cereal Breakfast Foods
2044 Rice Milling
2045 Flour, Blended & Prepared
2046 Wet Corn Milling
2047 Dog & Cat Food
2048 Prepared Feeds For Animals & Fowls
2051 Bread, Bakery Prdts Exc Cookies & Crackers
2052 Cookies & Crackers
2053 Frozen Bakery Prdts
2064 Candy & Confectionery Prdts
2066 Chocolate & Cocoa Prdts
2068 Salted & Roasted Nuts & Seeds
2076 Vegetable Oil Mills
2077 Animal, Marine Fats & Oils
2079 Shortening, Oils & Margarine
2082 Malt Beverages
2083 Malt
2084 Wine & Brandy
2085 Liquors, Distilled, Rectified & Blended
2086 Soft Drinks
2087 Flavoring Extracts & Syrups
2091 Fish & Seafoods, Canned & Cured
2092 Fish & Seafoods, Fresh & Frozen
2095 Coffee
2096 Potato Chips & Similar Prdts
2097 Ice
2098 Macaroni, Spaghetti & Noodles
2099 Food Preparations, NEC

21 tobacco products
2111 Cigarettes
2121 Cigars
2131 Tobacco, Chewing & Snuff
2141 Tobacco Stemming & Redrying

22 textile mill products
2211 Cotton, Woven Fabric

2221 Silk & Man-Made Fiber
2231 Wool, Woven Fabric
2241 Fabric Mills, Cotton, Wool, Silk & Man-Made
2251 Hosiery, Women's Full & Knee Length
2252 Hosiery, Except Women's
2253 Knit Outerwear Mills
2254 Knit Underwear Mills
2259 Knitting Mills, NEC
2261 Cotton Fabric Finishers
2262 Silk & Man-Made Fabric Finishers
2269 Textile Finishers, NEC
2273 Carpets & Rugs
2281 Yarn Spinning Mills
2282 Yarn Texturizing, Throwing, Twisting & Winding Mills
2284 Thread Mills
2295 Fabrics Coated Not Rubberized
2296 Tire Cord & Fabric
2297 Fabrics, Nonwoven
2298 Cordage & Twine
2299 Textile Goods, NEC

23 apparel and other finished products made from fabrics and similar material
2311 Men's & Boys' Suits, Coats & Overcoats
2321 Men's & Boys' Shirts
2322 Men's & Boys' Underwear & Nightwear
2323 Men's & Boys' Neckwear
2325 Men's & Boys' Separate Trousers & Casual Slacks
2326 Men's & Boys' Work Clothing
2329 Men's & Boys' Clothing, NEC
2331 Women's & Misses' Blouses
2335 Women's & Misses' Dresses
2337 Women's & Misses' Suits, Coats & Skirts
2339 Women's & Misses' Outerwear, NEC
2341 Women's, Misses' & Children's Underwear & Nightwear
2342 Brassieres, Girdles & Garments
2353 Hats, Caps & Millinery
2361 Children's & Infants' Dresses & Blouses
2369 Girls' & Infants' Outerwear, NEC
2371 Fur Goods
2384 Robes & Dressing Gowns
2385 Waterproof Outerwear
2386 Leather & Sheep Lined Clothing
2389 Apparel & Accessories, NEC
2391 Curtains & Draperies
2392 House furnishings: Textile
2393 Textile Bags
2394 Canvas Prdts
2395 Pleating & Stitching For The Trade
2396 Automotive Trimmings, Apparel Findings, Related Prdts
2397 Schiffli Machine Embroideries
2399 Fabricated Textile Prdts, NEC

24 lumber and wood products, except furniture
2411 Logging
2421 Saw & Planing Mills
2426 Hardwood Dimension & Flooring Mills
2429 Special Prdt Sawmills, NEC
2431 Millwork
2434 Wood Kitchen Cabinets
2435 Hardwood Veneer & Plywood
2436 Softwood Veneer & Plywood
2439 Structural Wood Members, NEC
2441 Wood Boxes
2448 Wood Pallets & Skids
2449 Wood Containers, NEC
2451 Mobile Homes
2452 Prefabricated Wood Buildings & Cmpnts
2491 Wood Preserving
2493 Reconstituted Wood Prdts
2499 Wood Prdts, NEC

25 furniture and fixtures
2511 Wood Household Furniture
2512 Wood Household Furniture, Upholstered
2514 Metal Household Furniture
2515 Mattresses & Bedsprings
2517 Wood T V, Radio, Phono & Sewing Cabinets
2519 Household Furniture, NEC
2521 Wood Office Furniture
2522 Office Furniture, Except Wood
2531 Public Building & Related Furniture
2541 Wood, Office & Store Fixtures
2542 Partitions & Fixtures, Except Wood
2591 Drapery Hardware, Window Blinds & Shades

2599 Furniture & Fixtures, NEC

26 paper and allied products
2611 Pulp Mills
2621 Paper Mills
2631 Paperboard Mills
2652 Set-Up Paperboard Boxes
2653 Corrugated & Solid Fiber Boxes
2655 Fiber Cans, Tubes & Drums
2656 Sanitary Food Containers
2657 Folding Paperboard Boxes
2671 Paper Coating & Laminating for Packaging
2672 Paper Coating & Laminating, Exc for Packaging
2673 Bags: Plastics, Laminated & Coated
2674 Bags: Uncoated Paper & Multiwall
2675 Die-Cut Paper & Board
2676 Sanitary Paper Prdts
2677 Envelopes
2678 Stationery Prdts
2679 Converted Paper Prdts, NEC

27 printing, publishing, and allied industries
2711 Newspapers: Publishing & Printing
2721 Periodicals: Publishing & Printing
2731 Books: Publishing & Printing
2732 Book Printing, Not Publishing
2741 Misc Publishing
2752 Commercial Printing: Lithographic
2754 Commercial Printing: Gravure
2759 Commercial Printing
2761 Manifold Business Forms
2771 Greeting Card Publishing
2782 Blankbooks & Looseleaf Binders
2789 Bookbinding
2791 Typesetting
2796 Platemaking & Related Svcs

28 chemicals and allied products
2812 Alkalies & Chlorine
2813 Industrial Gases
2816 Inorganic Pigments
2819 Indl Inorganic Chemicals, NEC
2821 Plastics, Mtrls & Nonvulcanizable Elastomers
2822 Synthetic Rubber (Vulcanizable Elastomers)
2823 Cellulosic Man-Made Fibers
2824 Synthetic Organic Fibers, Exc Cellulosic
2833 Medicinal Chemicals & Botanical Prdts
2834 Pharmaceuticals
2835 Diagnostic Substances
2836 Biological Prdts, Exc Diagnostic Substances
2841 Soap & Detergents
2842 Spec Cleaning, Polishing & Sanitation Preparations
2843 Surface Active & Finishing Agents, Sulfonated Oils
2844 Perfumes, Cosmetics & Toilet Preparations
2851 Paints, Varnishes, Lacquers, Enamels
2861 Gum & Wood Chemicals
2865 Cyclic-Crudes, Intermediates, Dyes & Org Pigments
2869 Industrial Organic Chemicals, NEC
2873 Nitrogenous Fertilizers
2874 Phosphatic Fertilizers
2875 Fertilizers, Mixing Only
2879 Pesticides & Agricultural Chemicals, NEC
2891 Adhesives & Sealants
2892 Explosives
2893 Printing Ink
2899 Chemical Preparations, NEC

29 petroleum refining and related industries
2911 Petroleum Refining
2951 Paving Mixtures & Blocks
2952 Asphalt Felts & Coatings
2992 Lubricating Oils & Greases
2999 Products Of Petroleum & Coal, NEC

30 rubber and miscellaneous plastics products
3011 Tires & Inner Tubes
3021 Rubber & Plastic Footwear
3052 Rubber & Plastic Hose & Belting
3053 Gaskets, Packing & Sealing Devices
3061 Molded, Extruded & Lathe-Cut Rubber Mechanical Goods
3069 Fabricated Rubber Prdts, NEC
3081 Plastic Unsupported Sheet & Film
3082 Plastic Unsupported Profile Shapes
3083 Plastic Laminated Plate & Sheet
3084 Plastic Pipe

S
I
C

SIC NO	PRODUCT

3085 Plastic Bottles
3086 Plastic Foam Prdts
3087 Custom Compounding Of Purchased Plastic Resins
3088 Plastic Plumbing Fixtures
3089 Plastic Prdts

31 leather and leather products

3111 Leather Tanning & Finishing
3131 Boot & Shoe Cut Stock & Findings
3143 Men's Footwear, Exc Athletic
3144 Women's Footwear, Exc Athletic
3149 Footwear, NEC
3151 Leather Gloves & Mittens
3161 Luggage
3171 Handbags & Purses
3172 Personal Leather Goods
3199 Leather Goods, NEC

32 stone, clay, glass, and concrete products

3211 Flat Glass
3221 Glass Containers
3229 Pressed & Blown Glassware, NEC
3231 Glass Prdts Made Of Purchased Glass
3241 Cement, Hydraulic
3251 Brick & Structural Clay Tile
3253 Ceramic Tile
3255 Clay Refractories
3259 Structural Clay Prdts, NEC
3261 China Plumbing Fixtures & Fittings
3263 Earthenware, Whiteware, Table & Kitchen Articles
3264 Porcelain Electrical Splys
3269 Pottery Prdts, NEC
3271 Concrete Block & Brick
3272 Concrete Prdts
3273 Ready-Mixed Concrete
3274 Lime
3275 Gypsum Prdts
3281 Cut Stone Prdts
3291 Abrasive Prdts
3292 Asbestos products
3295 Minerals & Earths: Ground Or Treated
3296 Mineral Wool
3297 Nonclay Refractories
3299 Nonmetallic Mineral Prdts, NEC

33 primary metal industries

3312 Blast Furnaces, Coke Ovens, Steel & Rolling Mills
3315 Steel Wire Drawing & Nails & Spikes
3316 Cold Rolled Steel Sheet, Strip & Bars
3317 Steel Pipe & Tubes
3321 Gray Iron Foundries
3324 Steel Investment Foundries
3325 Steel Foundries, NEC
3331 Primary Smelting & Refining Of Copper
3334 Primary Production Of Aluminum
3339 Primary Nonferrous Metals, NEC
3341 Secondary Smelting & Refining Of Nonferrous Metals
3351 Rolling, Drawing & Extruding Of Copper
3353 Aluminum Sheet, Plate & Foil
3354 Aluminum Extruded Prdts
3355 Aluminum Rolling & Drawing, NEC
3356 Rolling, Drawing-Extruding Of Nonferrous Metals
3357 Nonferrous Wire Drawing
3363 Aluminum Die Castings
3364 Nonferrous Die Castings, Exc Aluminum
3365 Aluminum Foundries
3366 Copper Foundries
3369 Nonferrous Foundries: Castings, NEC
3398 Metal Heat Treating
3399 Primary Metal Prdts, NEC

34 fabricated metal products, except machinery and transportation equipment

3411 Metal Cans
3412 Metal Barrels, Drums, Kegs & Pails
3421 Cutlery
3423 Hand & Edge Tools
3425 Hand Saws & Saw Blades
3429 Hardware, NEC
3431 Enameled Iron & Metal Sanitary Ware
3432 Plumbing Fixture Fittings & Trim, Brass
3433 Heating Eqpt
3441 Fabricated Structural Steel
3442 Metal Doors, Sash, Frames, Molding & Trim
3443 Fabricated Plate Work
3444 Sheet Metal Work
3446 Architectural & Ornamental Metal Work
3448 Prefabricated Metal Buildings & Cmpnts
3449 Misc Structural Metal Work
3451 Screw Machine Prdts
3452 Bolts, Nuts, Screws, Rivets & Washers

3462 Iron & Steel Forgings
3463 Nonferrous Forgings
3465 Automotive Stampings
3466 Crowns & Closures
3469 Metal Stampings, NEC
3471 Electroplating, Plating, Polishing, Anodizing & Coloring
3479 Coating & Engraving, NEC
3482 Small Arms Ammunition
3483 Ammunition, Large
3484 Small Arms
3489 Ordnance & Access, NEC
3491 Industrial Valves
3492 Fluid Power Valves & Hose Fittings
3493 Steel Springs, Except Wire
3494 Valves & Pipe Fittings, NEC
3495 Wire Springs
3496 Misc Fabricated Wire Prdts
3497 Metal Foil & Leaf
3498 Fabricated Pipe & Pipe Fittings
3499 Fabricated Metal Prdts, NEC

35 industrial and commercial machinery and computer equipment

3511 Steam, Gas & Hydraulic Turbines & Engines
3519 Internal Combustion Engines, NEC
3523 Farm Machinery & Eqpt
3524 Garden, Lawn Tractors & Eqpt
3531 Construction Machinery & Eqpt
3532 Mining Machinery & Eqpt
3533 Oil Field Machinery & Eqpt
3534 Elevators & Moving Stairways
3535 Conveyors & Eqpt
3536 Hoists, Cranes & Monorails
3537 Indl Trucks, Tractors, Trailers & Stackers
3541 Machine Tools: Cutting
3542 Machine Tools: Forming
3543 Industrial Patterns
3544 Dies, Tools, Jigs, Fixtures & Indl Molds
3545 Machine Tool Access
3546 Power Hand Tools
3547 Rolling Mill Machinery & Eqpt
3548 Welding Apparatus
3549 Metalworking Machinery, NEC
3552 Textile Machinery
3553 Woodworking Machinery
3554 Paper Inds Machinery
3555 Printing Trades Machinery & Eqpt
3556 Food Prdts Machinery
3559 Special Ind Machinery, NEC
3561 Pumps & Pumping Eqpt
3562 Ball & Roller Bearings
3563 Air & Gas Compressors
3564 Blowers & Fans
3565 Packaging Machinery
3566 Speed Changers, Drives & Gears
3567 Indl Process Furnaces & Ovens
3568 Mechanical Power Transmission Eqpt, NEC
3569 Indl Machinery & Eqpt, NEC
3571 Electronic Computers
3572 Computer Storage Devices
3575 Computer Terminals
3577 Computer Peripheral Eqpt, NEC
3578 Calculating & Accounting Eqpt
3579 Office Machines, NEC
3581 Automatic Vending Machines
3582 Commercial Laundry, Dry Clean & Pressing Mchs
3585 Air Conditioning & Heating Eqpt
3586 Measuring & Dispensing Pumps
3589 Service Ind Machines, NEC
3592 Carburetors, Pistons, Rings & Valves
3593 Fluid Power Cylinders & Actuators
3594 Fluid Power Pumps & Motors
3596 Scales & Balances, Exc Laboratory
3599 Machinery & Eqpt, Indl & Commercial, NEC

36 electronic and other electrical equipment and components, except computer

3612 Power, Distribution & Specialty Transformers
3613 Switchgear & Switchboard Apparatus
3621 Motors & Generators
3624 Carbon & Graphite Prdts
3625 Relays & Indl Controls
3629 Electrical Indl Apparatus, NEC
3631 Household Cooking Eqpt
3632 Household Refrigerators & Freezers
3633 Household Laundry Eqpt
3634 Electric Household Appliances
3635 Household Vacuum Cleaners
3639 Household Appliances, NEC
3641 Electric Lamps

3643 Current-Carrying Wiring Devices
3644 Noncurrent-Carrying Wiring Devices
3645 Residential Lighting Fixtures
3646 Commercial, Indl & Institutional Lighting Fixtures
3647 Vehicular Lighting Eqpt
3648 Lighting Eqpt, NEC
3651 Household Audio & Video Eqpt
3652 Phonograph Records & Magnetic Tape
3661 Telephone & Telegraph Apparatus
3663 Radio & T V Communications, Systs & Eqpt, Broadcast/Studio
3669 Communications Eqpt, NEC
3671 Radio & T V Receiving Electron Tubes
3672 Printed Circuit Boards
3674 Semiconductors
3675 Electronic Capacitors
3677 Electronic Coils & Transformers
3678 Electronic Connectors
3679 Electronic Components, NEC
3691 Storage Batteries
3692 Primary Batteries: Dry & Wet
3694 Electrical Eqpt For Internal Combustion Engines
3695 Recording Media
3699 Electrical Machinery, Eqpt & Splys, NEC

37 transportation equipment

3711 Motor Vehicles & Car Bodies
3713 Truck & Bus Bodies
3714 Motor Vehicle Parts & Access
3715 Truck Trailers
3716 Motor Homes
3721 Aircraft
3724 Aircraft Engines & Engine Parts
3728 Aircraft Parts & Eqpt, NEC
3731 Shipbuilding & Repairing
3732 Boat Building & Repairing
3743 Railroad Eqpt
3751 Motorcycles, Bicycles & Parts
3761 Guided Missiles & Space Vehicles
3764 Guided Missile/Space Vehicle Propulsion Units & parts
3769 Guided Missile/Space Vehicle Parts & Eqpt, NEC
3792 Travel Trailers & Campers
3795 Tanks & Tank Components
3799 Transportation Eqpt, NEC

38 measuring, analyzing and controlling instruments; photographic, medical an

3812 Search, Detection, Navigation & Guidance Systs & Instrs
3821 Laboratory Apparatus & Furniture
3822 Automatic Temperature Controls
3823 Indl Instruments For Meas, Display & Control
3824 Fluid Meters & Counters
3825 Instrs For Measuring & Testing Electricity
3826 Analytical Instruments
3827 Optical Instruments
3829 Measuring & Controlling Devices, NEC
3841 Surgical & Medical Instrs & Apparatus
3842 Orthopedic, Prosthetic & Surgical Appliances/Splys
3843 Dental Eqpt & Splys
3844 X-ray Apparatus & Tubes
3845 Electromedical & Electrotherapeutic Apparatus
3851 Ophthalmic Goods
3861 Photographic Eqpt & Splys
3873 Watch & Clock Devices & Parts

39 miscellaneous manufacturing industries

3911 Jewelry: Precious Metal
3914 Silverware, Plated & Stainless Steel Ware
3915 Jewelers Findings & Lapidary Work
3931 Musical Instruments
3942 Dolls & Stuffed Toys
3944 Games, Toys & Children's Vehicles
3949 Sporting & Athletic Goods, NEC
3951 Pens & Mechanical Pencils
3952 Lead Pencils, Crayons & Artist's Mtrls
3953 Marking Devices
3955 Carbon Paper & Inked Ribbons
3961 Costume Jewelry & Novelties
3965 Fasteners, Buttons, Needles & Pins
3991 Brooms & Brushes
3993 Signs & Advertising Displays
3996 Linoleum & Hard Surface Floor Coverings, NEC
3999 Manufacturing Industries, NEC

73 business services

7372 Prepackaged Software

76 miscellaneous repair services

7692 Welding Repair
7694 Armature Rewinding Shops

SIC SECTION

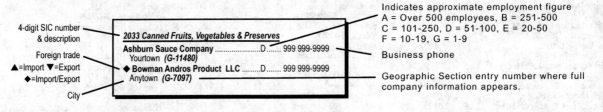

10 METAL MINING

1011 Iron Ores

Iron Dog Metalsmiths ....G...... 703 503-9631
Fairfax *(G-4481)*
Iron Lungs Inc ....G...... 757 877-2529
Yorktown *(G-15966)*
U S Mining Inc ....G...... 804 769-7222
Partlow *(G-10268)*

1041 Gold Ores

Dm Associates LLC ....G...... 571 406-2318
Fairfax *(G-4440)*

1081 Metal Mining Svcs

Adf Unit Trust Inc ....G...... 757 926-5252
Newport News *(G-9157)*
Dynamite Demolition LLC ....G...... 571 241-4658
Alexandria *(G-451)*
East Coast Interiors Inc ....E...... 804 423-2554
North Chesterfield *(G-9867)*
Elixsys Va LLC ....G...... 434 374-2398
Clarksville *(G-3629)*
H & H Mining Company Inc ....G...... 276 566-2105
Grundy *(G-6034)*
Jennmar Corporation ....D...... 540 726-2326
Rich Creek *(G-11007)*
Lambert Metal Services LLC ....G...... 571 261-5811
Manassas *(G-7960)*
Largo Resources USA Inc ....G...... 571 491-7827
Arlington *(G-1025)*
Pura Vida Vienna Inc ....G...... 703 281-6050
Vienna *(G-14116)*
Solite LLC ....E...... 757 494-5200
Chesapeake *(G-3299)*
Stripping Center of Sterling ....G...... 703 904-9577
Sterling *(G-13518)*
William G Sexton ....G...... 276 988-9012
North Tazewell *(G-10111)*

1094 Uranium, Radium & Vanadium Ores

Framatome Inc ....B...... 434 832-3000
Lynchburg *(G-7715)*

1099 Metal Ores, NEC

Metal Magic ....G...... 703 660-9180
Alexandria *(G-530)*
Yue Xu ....G...... 703 503-9451
Fairfax *(G-4586)*

12 COAL MINING

1221 Bituminous Coal & Lignite: Surface Mining

A & G Coal Corporation ....E...... 276 328-3421
Roanoke *(G-12027)*
◆ **Alpha Appalachia Holdings Inc** ....D...... 276 619-4410
Bristol *(G-1964)*
▼ **Appalachia Holding Company** ....F...... 276 619-4410
Bristol *(G-2006)*
Big D Enterprises Inc ....G...... 276 679-1090
Coeburn *(G-3695)*
Blue Ribbon Coal Sales Ltd ....G...... 540 387-2077
Salem *(G-12482)*
Bluestone Industries Inc ....E...... 540 776-7890
Roanoke *(G-12051)*

Chad Coal Corp ....F...... 276 498-4952
Whitewood *(G-15191)*
Coal Energy Resources Inc ....G...... 276 676-3101
Abingdon *(G-24)*
◆ **Coal Fillers Inc** ....G...... 276 322-4675
Bluefield *(G-1860)*
Consolidation Coal Co ....G...... 276 988-3010
Bandy *(G-1558)*
Consolidation Coal Company ....E...... 276 988-3010
Amonate *(G-725)*
◆ **Davis Mining & Mfg Inc** ....F...... 276 395-3354
Wise *(G-15622)*
Dominion Coal Corp ....G...... 276 935-8810
Oakwood *(G-10167)*
Elite Coals Inc ....E...... 276 679-4070
Norton *(G-10118)*
Excello Oil Company Inc ....F...... 276 935-2332
Grundy *(G-6031)*
Fairbanks Coal Co Inc ....G...... 276 395-3354
Coeburn *(G-3698)*
Falcon Coal Corporation ....E...... 276 679-0600
Wise *(G-15623)*
Global Design Contractors Inc ....G...... 703 865-6064
Fairfax *(G-4469)*
Greater Wise Incorporated ....D...... 276 679-1400
Norton *(G-10119)*
Horn Construction Co Inc ....F...... 276 935-4749
Grundy *(G-6035)*
Humphreys Enterprises Inc ....F...... 276 679-1400
Norton *(G-10120)*
Itforesight LLC ....G...... 703 829-7283
Reston *(G-10879)*
James River Coal Company ....F...... 804 780-3000
Richmond *(G-11625)*
James River Coal Service Co ....E...... 606 878-7411
Richmond *(G-11626)*
Justice Coal of Alabama LLC ....G...... 540 776-7890
Roanoke *(G-12114)*
Laurel Run LLC ....G...... 540 364-1238
Hume *(G-6962)*
Mate Creek Energy of West VA ....G...... 276 669-8599
Bristol *(G-2025)*
Nice Wounders Group ....F...... 276 669-6476
Bristol *(G-2028)*
Nordic Mining LLC ....G...... 703 878-0346
Woodbridge *(G-15764)*
Paramont Contura LLC ....G...... 276 679-7020
Norton *(G-10132)*
Pardee Coal Company Inc ....G...... 276 679-1400
Norton *(G-10133)*
Pioneer Group Inc VA ....G...... 276 669-3400
Bristol *(G-2029)*
Pittston Minerals Group Inc ....C...... 804 289-9600
Richmond *(G-11327)*
Rapoca Energy Co ....G...... 423 269-6900
Bristol *(G-2032)*
Riggs Oil Company ....E...... 276 523-2662
Big Stone Gap *(G-1714)*
Southwestern Vrgnia Wheelco Inc ....G...... 540 493-6886
Rocky Mount *(G-12354)*
Standard Banner Coal Corp ....G...... 276 944-5603
Meadowview *(G-8596)*
Stonega Mining & Processing Co ....G...... 276 523-5690
Big Stone Gap *(G-1715)*
Todd Drummond Consulting LLC ....G...... 603 763-8857
Virginia Beach *(G-14886)*
Wellmore Energy Company LLC ....D...... 276 530-7411
Big Rock *(G-1705)*

1222 Bituminous Coal: Underground Mining

A B & J Coal Company Inc ....F...... 276 530-7786
Grundy *(G-6027)*
A & G Coal Corporation ....E...... 276 328-3421
Roanoke *(G-12027)*
Alliance Resource Partners LP ....D...... 276 566-8516
Hurley *(G-6968)*
◆ **Alpha Appalachia Holdings Inc** ....D...... 276 619-4410
Bristol *(G-1964)*
Capital Coal Corporation ....F...... 276 935-7562
Abingdon *(G-20)*
Chad Coal Corp ....F...... 276 498-4952
Whitewood *(G-15191)*
◆ **Davis Mining & Mfg Inc** ....F...... 276 395-3354
Wise *(G-15622)*
Doss Fork Coal Co Inc ....E...... 540 322-4066
Bluefield *(G-1863)*
James River Coal Service Co ....E...... 606 878-7411
Richmond *(G-11626)*
Jewell Smokeless Coal Corp ....E...... 276 935-8810
Oakwood *(G-10170)*
Knox Creek Coal Corporation ....B...... 276 964-4333
Raven *(G-10756)*
Maxxim Shared Services LLC ....G...... 276 679-7020
Norton *(G-10127)*
Pittston Coal Company ....F...... 276 739-3420
Abingdon *(G-53)*
Pittston Minerals Group Inc ....C...... 804 289-9600
Richmond *(G-11327)*
Regent Allied Carbon Energy ....E...... 276 679-4994
Appalachia *(G-800)*
Tennessee Consolidated Coal Co ....G...... 423 658-5115
Bristol *(G-2035)*

1241 Coal Mining Svcs

American Energy LLC ....E...... 276 935-7562
Norton *(G-10112)*
American Highwall Mining LLC ....G...... 276 646-5548
Chilhowie *(G-3544)*
▲ **Asian American Coal Inc** ....G...... 804 648-1611
Richmond *(G-11492)*
Baden Reclamation Company ....F...... 540 776-7890
Roanoke *(G-12040)*
Baystar Coal Company Inc ....F...... 276 322-4900
Bluefield *(G-1858)*
Blackstone Energy Ltd ....G...... 540 776-7890
Roanoke *(G-12047)*
Blueridge Sand Inc ....G...... 276 579-2007
Mouth of Wilson *(G-9091)*
Bluestone Resources Inc ....G...... 540 776-7890
Roanoke *(G-12052)*
Bluff Spur Coal LLC ....E...... 276 679-6962
Norton *(G-10113)*
Bristol Coal Corporation ....F...... 276 935-7562
Grundy *(G-6028)*
C & B Enterprise LLC ....G...... 276 971-4052
Cedar Bluff *(G-2271)*
Coal Extraction Holdings LLC ....G...... 276 466-3322
Bristol *(G-1971)*
Compass Coal Services LLC ....G...... 804 218-8880
Richmond *(G-11164)*
Contura Energy Services LLC ....G...... 276 835-8041
Mc Clure *(G-8373)*
Crown International Inc ....G...... 703 335-0066
Manassas *(G-8053)*
Dacoal Mining Inc ....F...... 276 531-8165
Grundy *(G-6030)*
Dickenson-Russell Coal Co LLC ....B...... 276 889-6100
Cleveland *(G-3655)*

S I C

Erp Environmental Fund Inc ....G...... 304 369-8113
Natural Bridge (G-9105)
Harold Keene Coal Co Inc ....G...... 276 873-5437
Honaker (G-6914)
Hills Coal and Trucking Co ....G...... 276 565-2560
Appalachia (G-797)
Inr Energy LLC ....G...... 804 282-0369
Richmond (G-11249)
Jake Little Construction Inc ....E...... 276 498-7462
Oakwood (G-10169)
James River Escrow Inc ....G...... 804 780-3000
Richmond (G-11628)
Johns Creek Elkhorn Coal Corp ....E...... 804 780-3000
Richmond (G-11634)
Justice Low Seam Mining Inc ....F...... 540 776-7890
Roanoke (G-12115)
Kanawha Eagle Coal LLC ....G...... 304 837-8587
Glen Allen (G-5760)
Lonnie L Sparks ....G...... 276 988-4298
North Tazewell (G-10102)
◆ Maxxim Rebuild Co LLC ....A...... 276 679-7020
Norton (G-10126)
Mountain Energy Resources Inc ....G...... 276 679-3593
Norton (G-10129)
Natural Resources Intl LLC ....G...... 804 282-0369
Richmond (G-11300)
Pardee Coal Company Inc ....G...... 276 679-1400
Norton (G-10133)
Peabody Coaltrade LLC ....G...... 804 378-4655
Midlothian (G-8877)
Ratliff ....G...... 276 794-7377
Lebanon (G-7205)
Regent Allied Carbon Energy ....E...... 276 679-4994
Appalachia (G-800)
Sequoia Energy LLC ....F...... 540 776-7890
Roanoke (G-12182)
Standard Core Drilling Co Inc ....G...... 276 395-3391
Coeburn (G-3703)
Suffolk Materials LLC ....F...... 757 255-4005
Suffolk (G-13769)
Timco Energy Inc ....E...... 276 322-4900
Bluefield (G-1882)
Vedco Holdings Inc ....F...... 800 258-8583
Vansant (G-13979)
Wellmore Energy Company LLC ....D...... 276 530-7411
Big Rock (G-1705)
White Forest Resources Inc ....G...... 804 410-9231
Richmond (G-11449)
William G Sexton ....G...... 276 988-9012
North Tazewell (G-10111)
Wpo 3 Inc ....G...... 757 491-4140
Virginia Beach (G-14945)
Za Contracting LLC ....G...... 703 498-3531
Falls Church (G-4896)

13 OIL AND GAS EXTRACTION

1311 Crude Petroleum & Natural Gas

◆ Associated Asp Partners LLC ....F...... 540 345-8867
Roanoke (G-12035)
Associated Asphalt Tf LLC ....G...... 540 529-9789
Roanoke (G-12037)
Bluestone Industries Inc ....E...... 540 776-7890
Roanoke (G-12051)
Boc Gases ....G...... 540 433-1029
Harrisonburg (G-6297)
BP Investments Ltd ....G...... 580 795-3364
Leesburg (G-7236)
◆ Carpenter Co ....C...... 804 359-0800
Richmond (G-11146)
Carpenter Co ....D...... 804 233-0606
Richmond (G-11032)
Cnx Gas Corporation ....D...... 276 596-5000
Cedar Bluff (G-2273)
Cojax Oil and Gas Corporation ....G...... 703 216-8606
Arlington (G-914)
Colin K Eagen ....G...... 703 716-7505
Reston (G-10822)
Consolidated Natural Gas Co ....B...... 804 819-2000
Richmond (G-11539)
Dominion Energy Inc ....D...... 804 771-3000
Richmond (G-11187)
Emax Oil Company ....G...... 434 295-4111
Charlottesville (G-2624)
Energy 11 LP ....G...... 804 344-8121
Richmond (G-11576)
Energy Resources 12 LP ....G...... 804 344-8121
Richmond (G-11577)
Ernest Beltrami Sr ....G...... 757 516-8581
Franklin (G-5143)

Field and Sons LLC ....G...... 757 412-0125
Virginia Beach (G-14462)
Gase Energy Inc ....E...... 540 347-2212
Warrenton (G-15020)
Goose Creek Gas LLC ....G...... 703 827-0611
Vienna (G-14061)
J and J Energy Holdings ....E...... 757 963-9763
Virginia Beach (G-14557)
Lanier Outdoor Enterprises LLC ....G...... 540 892-5945
Vinton (G-14177)
Masters Energy Inc ....E...... 281 816-9991
Glen Allen (G-5768)
Maury River Oil Company ....G...... 540 463-2233
Lexington (G-7400)
North Ridge ....G...... 540 825-4275
Culpeper (G-3912)
Novec Energy Production ....G...... 434 471-2840
South Boston (G-12785)
Rockhill Resources LLC ....G...... 804 794-6259
Midlothian (G-8893)
Shell ....G...... 276 676-0699
Abingdon (G-60)
Southside Oil ....G...... 804 590-1684
Chesterfield (G-3526)
Southside Oil Co ....G...... 804 204-1624
Richmond (G-11765)
Speedway LLC ....G...... 757 498-4625
Virginia Beach (G-14838)
Speedway LLC ....G...... 757 599-6250
Yorktown (G-15992)
St Cove Point LLC ....F...... 713 897-1624
Richmond (G-11772)
Tiango Field Services LLC ....G...... 804 683-2067
Glen Allen (G-5812)
Tom Wild Petrophysical Svcs ....G...... 434 978-1269
Earlysville (G-4295)
Trident Oil Corp ....G...... 434 974-1401
Free Union (G-5510)
Wooton Consulting ....G...... 804 227-3418
Bumpass (G-2173)

1321 Natural Gas Liquids

Dixie Fuel Company ....G...... 757 249-1264
Newport News (G-9217)
East Tennessee Natural Gas Co ....F...... 276 429-5411
Atkins (G-1516)
Mid-Atlantic Energy LLC ....G...... 804 213-2500
North Chesterfield (G-9931)
Saltville Gas Storage Co LLC ....E...... 276 496-7004
Saltville (G-12589)
Venture Globl Clcsieu Pass LLC ....G...... 202 759-6740
Arlington (G-1209)

1381 Drilling Oil & Gas Wells

Best Value Petroleum Inc ....G...... 703 303-3780
Arlington (G-881)
Bison Inc ....G...... 703 754-4190
Gainesville (G-5572)
Boredacious Inc ....G...... 703 327-5490
Aldie (G-102)
Clarks Directional Boring ....G...... 804 493-7475
Montross (G-9026)
Crudewell Inc ....E...... 540 254-2289
Buchanan (G-2119)
Drilling J ....G...... 804 303-5517
Richmond (G-11191)
Eastcom Directional Drlg Inc ....G...... 757 377-3133
Chesapeake (G-3083)
Exploration Partners LLC ....G...... 434 973-8311
Charlottesville (G-2630)
Glasco Drilling Inc ....G...... 276 964-4117
Cedar Bluff (G-2277)
Hall Hflin Septic Tank Svc Inc ....G...... 804 333-3124
Warsaw (G-15064)
Harrods Natural Resources ....G...... 703 426-7200
Fairfax (G-4475)
Horn Well Drilling Inc Noah ....C...... 276 935-5902
Oakwood (G-10168)
JWT Well Services Inc ....E...... 276 835-8793
Nora (G-9408)
Sands 1b LLC ....G...... 757 673-1140
Chesapeake (G-3283)
Virginia Expl & Drlg Co Inc ....G...... 276 597-4449
Vansant (G-13980)
William G Sexton ....G...... 276 988-9012
North Tazewell (G-10111)

1382 Oil & Gas Field Exploration Svcs

Advanced Resources Intl Inc ....E...... 703 528-8421
Arlington (G-841)

Appalachian Energy Inc ....F...... 276 619-4880
Abingdon (G-13)
Bradley Energy LLC ....G...... 434 286-7600
Scottsville (G-12658)
Catawba Renewable Energy ....G...... 434 426-1390
Catawba (G-2260)
Dileway LLC ....G...... 703 897-6811
Vienna (G-14039)
East End Resources Group LLC ....G...... 804 677-3207
Midlothian (G-8812)
Enervest Operating LLC ....G...... 276 628-1569
Abingdon (G-30)
Exploration Partners ....G...... 540 213-1333
Staunton (G-13255)
Exploration Partners LLC ....G...... 434 973-8311
Charlottesville (G-2630)
Geo Enterprise Inc ....G...... 703 594-3816
Nokesville (G-9393)
Msl Oil & Gas Corp ....G...... 703 971-8805
Alexandria (G-535)
Next Generation MGT Corp ....G...... 703 372-1282
Ashburn (G-1321)
Nomad Geosciences ....G...... 703 390-1147
Reston (G-10909)
Orinoco Natural Resources LLC ....G...... 713 626-9696
Roanoke (G-11979)
Peter Henderson Oil Co ....G...... 434 823-8608
Crozet (G-3846)
Range Resources ....G...... 276 628-1568
Abingdon (G-56)
Resource Consultants Inc ....G...... 757 464-5252
Virginia Beach (G-14770)
Robert K Montgomery II ....G...... 804 730-0361
Mechanicsville (G-8671)
Sam Hurt ....G...... 276 623-1926
Abingdon (G-59)
Sharpe Resources Corp ....G...... 804 580-8107
Heathsville (G-6465)
Spotted Hawk Development LLC ....F...... 703 286-1450
Mc Lean (G-8556)
Summit Appalachia Oper Co LLC ....E...... 276 963-2979
Cedar Bluff (G-2286)
Tomb Geophysics LLC ....G...... 571 733-0930
Woodbridge (G-15823)
Tredegar Petroleum Corporation ....G...... 804 330-1000
North Chesterfield (G-10040)
United Co ....D...... 276 466-0769
Bristol (G-1993)
United Company ....D...... 276 466-3322
Bristol (G-1994)
Valvoline Instant Oil ....G...... 804 823-2104
Chester (G-3465)
Virginia Gas Exploration Co ....G...... 276 676-2380
Abingdon (G-64)
Weil Group Resources LLC ....G...... 804 643-2828
Richmond (G-11820)
William G Sexton ....G...... 276 988-9012
North Tazewell (G-10111)

1389 Oil & Gas Field Svcs, NEC

Acoustcal Drywall Slutions LLC ....G...... 703 722-6637
Ashburn (G-1238)
Air & Beyond LLC ....G...... 804 229-9450
North Chesterfield (G-9808)
Albright Recovery & Cnstr LLC ....G...... 276 835-2026
Clinchco (G-3684)
Anatomy Home Inspection Svc ....G...... 703 771-1568
Leesburg (G-7218)
Appalachian Prod Svcs Inc ....E...... 276 619-4880
Clintwood (G-3687)
Armstrong Family ....G...... 703 737-6188
Leesburg (G-7222)
B & H Excavating ....G...... 540 839-2107
Hot Springs (G-6945)
Baker Hughes A GE Company LLC ....E...... 540 961-9532
Blacksburg (G-1724)
Baker Hughes A GE Company LLC ....G...... 540 387-8847
Salem (G-12480)
Baker Hughes Holdings LLC ....G...... 276 963-0106
Richlands (G-11013)
Bop International Inc ....G...... 571 550-6669
Fairfax (G-4420)
Brecmo LLC ....G...... 276 202-7381
Lebanon (G-7189)
Brightway Inc ....G...... 540 468-2510
Monterey (G-9004)
Browns Services ....G...... 540 295-2047
Catlett (G-2265)
Bw Design Build LLC ....G...... 757 504-5052
Yorktown (G-15940)

SIC SECTION — 14 MINING AND QUARRYING OF NONMETALLIC MINERALS, EXCEPT FUELS

C&J Well Services Inc .... G....... 276 679-5860
Norton (G-10114)

Census Channel .... G....... 757 838-3881
Hampton (G-6111)

Chesapeake Ind Sftwr Testers .... G....... 757 547-1610
Chesapeake (G-3031)

Christopher L Bird .... G....... 540 675-3409
Washington (G-15074)

Construction Solutions Inc .... G....... 757 366-5070
Chesapeake (G-3052)

Creed Apparel .... G....... 804 219-3291
North Chesterfield (G-9853)

D L S & Associates .... G....... 276 796-5275
Pound (G-10511)

David Steele .... G....... 757 236-3971
Toano (G-13863)

Davidson Plbg & Pipe Svc LLC .... G....... 540 867-0847
Rockingham (G-12246)

Davis Brianna .... G....... 703 220-4791
Manassas (G-8054)

Detron Realty LLC .... G....... 703 884-6741
Woodbridge (G-15683)

Didc LLC .... G....... 646 684-5861
Danville (G-3984)

Dw Saltwater Flies LLC .... G....... 757 874-1859
Newport News (G-9218)

Ellington Mechanical Svcs Inc .... G....... 703 220-1651
Alexandria (G-456)

Emezro LLC .... G....... 757 327-2318
Hampton (G-6139)

Equipment Repair Services .... G....... 757 449-5867
Virginia Beach (G-14450)

Excel Well Service Inc .... F....... 276 498-4360
Rowe (G-12397)

Fbgc JV LLC .... G....... 757 727-9442
Hampton (G-6147)

Gas Field Services LLC .... G....... 276 880-2323
Rosedale (G-12366)

H & L Brothers Contractors LLC .... G....... 703 856-1915
Gainesville (G-5588)

Hawkeye Inspection Service .... G....... 804 725-9751
Mathews (G-8355)

Hayes Lumber Inspection Svc .... G....... 804 739-0739
Midlothian (G-8826)

Hickory Hill Consulting LLC .... G....... 804 363-2719
Ashland (G-1433)

Hjk Contracting Inc .... G....... 703 793-8127
Herndon (G-6701)

Iaq Testing Services LLC .... G....... 540 966-3660
Roanoke (G-11936)

Jes Construction LLC .... D....... 757 558-9909
Virginia Beach (G-14568)

Jewel Holding LLC .... G....... 202 271-5265
Woodbridge (G-15730)

Jimmy French .... G....... 757 583-2536
Virginia Beach (G-14569)

Jon Armstrong .... G....... 757 253-3844
Williamsburg (G-15262)

Kidwell Construction LLC .... G....... 540 296-4173
Bedford (G-1642)

Klm Race LLC .... G....... 804 594-6187
North Chesterfield (G-9908)

Klug Servicing LLC .... G....... 804 310-5866
Mechanicsville (G-8649)

L & D Well Services Inc .... G....... 276 597-7211
Vansant (G-13977)

L B Oil Company .... G....... 757 723-8379
Chesapeake (G-3169)

Lawson and Son Cnstr LLC .... G....... 478 258-2478
Yorktown (G-15973)

Litstone Capital LLC .... G....... 703 576-0788
Alexandria (G-262)

Maspaintservice Ltd Lblty Co .... G....... 301 547-1996
Annandale (G-772)

Metropolitan General Contrs .... G....... 703 532-1606
Falls Church (G-4830)

Michael and Thomas Contg LLC ..... G....... 919 397-7960
Woodbridge (G-15747)

Miners Oil Company Inc .... G....... 804 230-5769
Richmond (G-11052)

Mooreland Servicing Co LLC .... G....... 804 644-2000
Richmond (G-11683)

Morris Mountaineer Oil Gas LLC ..... G....... 703 283-9700
Mc Lean (G-8507)

Mr1 Construction LLC .... G....... 301 748-6078
Manassas (G-7977)

Mtf Resources LLC .... G....... 804 240-5335
Midlothian (G-8864)

Oceaneering International Inc .... B....... 757 985-3800
Chesapeake (G-3224)

Ogc Inc .... G....... 703 860-3736
Reston (G-10913)

Ondeck Home Solutions LLC .... G....... 757 535-3771
Portsmouth (G-10464)

Partlow Associates Inc .... G....... 703 863-5695
Arlington (G-1100)

Phil Morgan .... G....... 757 455-9475
Norfolk (G-9686)

Pinnacle Oil Co .... G....... 540 687-6351
Middleburg (G-8732)

Potomac Intl Advisors LLC .... G....... 202 460-9001
Ashburn (G-1328)

Protected By Faith Cnstr LLC .... G....... 804 445-6888
Farnham (G-4963)

Quinn Pumps Inc .... G....... 276 345-9106
Cedar Bluff (G-2284)

Rva Firestopping LLC .... G....... 804 972-1301
Richmond (G-11751)

Sam Home Improvements LLC .... G....... 703 372-6000
Leesburg (G-7341)

Sandhurst-Aec LLC .... G....... 703 533-1413
Falls Church (G-4872)

Schlumberger Technology Corp ...... G....... 757 546-2472
Chesapeake (G-3287)

Schlumberger Technology Corp ...... D....... 540 786-6419
Fredericksburg (G-5359)

Sct Phoenix Oil & Gas LLC .... G....... 702 245-0269
Falls Church (G-4873)

Sej Property Logistics Co .... G....... 516 499-2549
Crewe (G-3816)

Servicing Green Inc .... G....... 540 459-3812
Edinburg (G-4312)

Smith Maintenance Services LLC ..... G....... 252 640-5016
Portsmouth (G-10484)

Special Fleet Services Inc .... D....... 540 434-4488
Harrisonburg (G-6373)

Special Fleet Services Inc .... E....... 540 433-7727
Harrisonburg (G-6374)

T & P Servicing LLC .... G....... 276 945-2040
Bluefield (G-1880)

T-K-O Building Incorporated .... G....... 757 324-2306
Virginia Beach (G-14862)

Take-A-Break Home Imprv LLC .... G....... 434 251-4557
Axton (G-1541)

Tequilla Battle .... G....... 757 769-1595
Hampton (G-6251)

Tim Lacey Builders .... G....... 540 434-3372
Harrisonburg (G-6381)

TT & J Hauling .... G....... 804 647-0375
Richmond (G-11423)

Under Pressure Services Inc .... G....... 757 254-5996
Virginia Beach (G-14902)

VA Designs and Cnstr LLC .... G....... 757 651-8909
Norfolk (G-9777)

Vanguard Mtgtion Rstration LLC ..... G....... 540 769-1881
Roanoke (G-12017)

Vidrio Technologies .... G....... 703 405-4944
Leesburg (G-7371)

Virginia Oil Company .... G....... 540 552-2365
Blacksburg (G-1804)

W P L Incorporated .... G....... 540 298-0999
Elkton (G-4339)

Weston Solutions Inc .... G....... 757 819-5300
Hampton (G-6272)

14 MINING AND QUARRYING OF NONMETALLIC MINERALS, EXCEPT FUELS

1411 Dimension Stone

Barger Son Cnstr Inc Charles W ...... D....... 540 463-2106
Lexington (G-7388)

Blackpearl Soapstone .... G....... 813 909-8400
Madison (G-7849)

Buckingham Slate Company LLC ...... E....... 434 581-1131
Arvonia (G-1232)

Dream Green International LLC .... G....... 814 616-7800
Alexandria (G-194)

Rockydale Quarries Corporation ...... G....... 540 896-1441
Roanoke (G-11997)

Shenandoah Stone Supply Co .... G....... 703 532-0169
Falls Church (G-4925)

United Stones Inc .... E....... 703 467-0434
Sterling (G-13543)

Valley Building Supply Inc .... C....... 540 434-6725
Harrisonburg (G-6383)

▲ **Virginia Mist Granite Corp** .... G....... 540 661-0030
Rapidan (G-10754)

▲ **Virginia Mist Group Inc** .... F....... 540 661-0030
Rapidan (G-10755)

1422 Crushed & Broken Limestone

Appalachian Aggregates LLC .... E....... 276 326-1145
Bluefield (G-1857)

Appomattox Lime Co Inc .... F....... 434 933-8258
Appomattox (G-802)

Appomattox Lime Company .... G....... 540 774-1696
Roanoke (G-12034)

Appomattox Quarry .... G....... 434 295-5700
Appomattox (G-803)

Barger Son Cnstr Inc Charles W ...... D....... 540 463-2106
Lexington (G-7388)

Boxley Materials Company .... E....... 540 777-7600
Blue Ridge (G-1845)

Boxley Materials Company .... E....... 540 777-7600
Blue Ridge (G-1846)

Boxley Materials Company .... F....... 540 777-7600
Arrington (G-1228)

Boxley Materials Company .... E....... 540 777-7600
Lowmoor (G-7598)

Boxley Materials Company .... E....... 540 777-7600
Lynchburg (G-7658)

Boxley Materials Company .... F....... 540 777-7600
Concord (G-3757)

Cardinal Quarries LLC .... F....... 540 674-5556
Dublin (G-4150)

▲ **Cedar Mountain Stone Corp** .... E....... 540 825-3370
Mitchells (G-8954)

Charlottesville Stone Company .... G....... 434 295-5700
Roanoke (G-12065)

Chesapeake Materials LLC .... E....... 540 658-0808
Stafford (G-13130)

Curtis E Harrell .... G....... 540 843-2027
Luray (G-7605)

Dream Green International LLC .... G....... 814 616-7800
Alexandria (G-194)

E Dillon & Company .... D....... 276 873-6816
Swords Creek (G-13807)

F & M Construction Corp .... F....... 276 728-2255
Hillsville (G-6891)

▲ **Frazier Quarry Incorporated** .... E....... 540 434-6192
Harrisonburg (G-6317)

Glade Stone Inc .... G....... 276 429-5241
Glade Spring (G-5676)

Holston River Quarry Inc .... F....... 540 380-5556
Dublin (G-4158)

Jack Stone Quarry .... G....... 804 862-6669
North Dinwiddie (G-10054)

Legacy Vulcan LLC .... F....... 276 679-0880
Big Stone Gap (G-1711)

Lhoist North America VA Inc .... C....... 540 626-7163
Ripplemead (G-11876)

Limestone Dust Corporation .... D....... 276 326-1103
Bluefield (G-1869)

Martin Marietta Materials Inc .... F....... 434 296-5562
North Garden (G-10080)

Martin Marietta Materials Inc .... G....... 804 561-0570
Amelia Court House (G-665)

Martin Marietta Materials Inc .... E....... 804 798-5096
Ashland (G-1459)

Martin Marietta Materials Inc .... E....... 804 744-1130
Midlothian (G-8853)

Martin Marietta Materials Inc .... F....... 804 749-4831
Rockville (G-12292)

Mountain Materials Inc .... G....... 276 762-5563
Castlewood (G-2255)

Mountain Mtls Muth Wlson Plant ..... G....... 276 579-6351
Mouth of Wilson (G-9095)

Mundy Quarries Inc C S .... E....... 540 833-2061
Broadway (G-2090)

Mundy Stone Company .... G....... 540 774-1696
Roanoke (G-12139)

O-N Minerals Chemstone Company ... C....... 540 465-5161
Strasburg (G-13592)

O-N Minerals Chemstone Company ... C....... 540 254-1241
Buchanan (G-2123)

O-N Minerals Chemstone Company ... C....... 540 662-3855
Clear Brook (G-3649)

O-N Minerals Chemstone Company ... C....... 540 869-1066
Middletown (G-8741)

◆ **Pounding Mill Quarry Corp** .... E....... 276 326-1145
Bluefield (G-1875)

Powell Valley Stone Co Inc .... F....... 276 546-2550
Pennington Gap (G-10298)

Redland Quarries NY Inc .... G....... 703 480-3600
Herndon (G-6786)

Rockbridge Stone Products Inc .... G....... 540 258-2841
Glasgow (G-5701)

Rockydale Chrlottesville Quary ....G 434 295-5700
Earlysville (G-4294)
Rockydale Quarries Corp ....G 540 769-8116
Roanoke (G-12169)
Rockydale Quarries Corporation ....F 540 576-2544
Roanoke (G-12171)
Salem Stone Corporation ....F 276 228-3452
Wytheville (G-15908)
Salem Stone Corporation ....G 540 674-5556
Dublin (G-4170)
Salem Stone Corporation ....F 276 228-3631
Wytheville (G-15909)
Salem Stone Corporation ....E 276 766-3449
Hillsville (G-6899)
Sisson & Ryan Inc ....E 540 268-2413
Shawsville (G-12686)
Sisson & Ryan Quarry LLC ....E 540 674-5556
Dublin (G-4171)
Southside Materials LLC ....E 540 674-5556
Dublin (G-4172)
Stuart M Perry Incorporated ....C 540 662-3431
Winchester (G-15483)
Stuart M Perry Incorporated ....E 540 955-1359
Berryville (G-1693)
Titan America LLC ....F 804 236-4122
Richmond (G-11412)
Titan America LLC ....D 703 471-0044
Sterling (G-13534)
Vulcan Construction Mtls LLC ....D 757 545-0980
Chesapeake (G-3367)
Vulcan Construction Mtls LLC ....E 804 862-6660
Prince George (G-10609)
Vulcan Construction Mtls LLC ....G 276 466-5436
Bristol (G-1999)

1423 Crushed & Broken Granite

Boxley Materials Company ....F 540 777-7600
Martinsville (G-8272)
Boxley Materials Company ....E 540 777-7600
Blue Ridge (G-1845)
Cardinal Stone Company Inc ....F 276 236-5457
Galax (G-5630)
Legacy Vulcan LLC ....E 434 634-4158
Skippers (G-12701)
Legacy Vulcan LLC ....E 434 572-3931
South Boston (G-12777)
Legacy Vulcan LLC ....F 804 706-1773
Chester (G-3428)
Legacy Vulcan LLC ....E 540 659-3003
Garrisonville (G-5656)
◆ Luck Stone Corporation ....D 804 784-6300
Manakin Sabot (G-7901)
Luck Stone Corporation ....E 434 767-4043
Burkeville (G-2209)
Luck Stone Corporation ....F 804 749-3233
Rockville (G-12289)
Luck Stone Corporation ....E 804 749-3232
Rockville (G-12290)
Luck Stone Corporation ....E 804 784-4652
Manakin Sabot (G-7902)
Luck Stone Corporation ....E 434 589-1542
Troy (G-13933)
Luck Stone Corporation ....F 757 213-7750
Chesapeake (G-3189)
Luck Stone Corporation ....E 757 545-2020
Norfolk (G-9624)
Martin Marietta Materials Inc ....G 540 894-5952
Fredericksburg (G-5321)
Martinsville Finance & Inv ....G 276 632-9500
Martinsville (G-8309)
Salem Stone Corporation ....E 276 766-3449
Hillsville (G-6899)
Salem Stone Corporation ....E 540 552-9292
Blacksburg (G-1786)
Salem Stone Corporation ....G 276 228-6767
Wytheville (G-15910)

1429 Crushed & Broken Stone, NEC

64 Ways Trucking/Hauling LLC ....F 804 801-5330
Richmond (G-11466)
▲ Frazier Quarry Incorporated ....E 540 434-6192
Harrisonburg (G-6317)
Luck Stone Corporation ....E 703 830-8880
Centreville (G-2316)
Rock Xpress LLC ....G 571 212-6689
Fairfax Station (G-4723)
Salem Stone Corporation ....E 540 552-9292
Blacksburg (G-1786)
Sisson & Ryan Inc ....E 540 268-2413
Shawsville (G-12686)

Sisson & Ryan Inc ....E 540 268-5251
Shawsville (G-12687)

1442 Construction Sand & Gravel

6304 Gravel Avenue LLC ....G 571 287-7544
Chantilly (G-2359)
64 Ways Trucking/Hauling LLC ....F 804 801-5330
Richmond (G-11466)
Aggregate Industries - Mwr Inc ....E 540 775-7600
King George (G-7080)
Aggregate Industries - Mwr Inc ....B 540 379-0765
Falmouth (G-4932)
Aggregate Industries MGT Inc ....F 540 249-5791
Grottoes (G-6013)
Aylett Sand & Gravel Inc ....G 804 443-2366
Tappahannock (G-13811)
Baillio Sand Co Inc ....F 757 428-3302
Virginia Beach (G-14258)
Bar-C Sand Inc ....G 276 701-3888
Cedar Bluff (G-2270)
Bay Sand Co Inc ....G 757 357-9477
Smithfield (G-12704)
Best of Landscaping ....G 804 253-4014
Powhatan (G-10532)
Black Sand Solutions LLC ....G 703 393-1127
Manassas Park (G-8191)
Crossroads Express Inc ....G 434 882-0320
Louisa (G-7552)
Dinkle Enterprises ....G 434 324-8508
Hurt (G-6974)
E Trucking & Services LLC ....G 571 241-0856
Warrenton (G-15000)
Eliene Trucking LLC ....G 571 721-0735
Centreville (G-2304)
▲ Frazier Quarry Incorporated ....E 540 434-6192
Harrisonburg (G-6317)
Gravley Sand Works ....G 434 724-7883
Dry Fork (G-4142)
Hilltop Sand and Gravel Co Inc ....G 571 322-0389
Lorton (G-7493)
Holland Sand Pit LLC ....E 757 745-7140
Suffolk (G-13723)
Legacy Vulcan LLC ....E 434 634-4158
Skippers (G-12701)
Legacy Vulcan LLC ....E 703 690-1172
Lorton (G-7504)
Legacy Vulcan LLC ....E 434 572-3931
South Boston (G-12777)
Legacy Vulcan LLC ....F 804 706-1773
Chester (G-3428)
Legacy Vulcan LLC ....G 804 748-3695
Chester (G-3429)
Legacy Vulcan LLC ....E 540 659-3003
Garrisonville (G-5656)
Legacy Vulcan Corp ....G 757 562-5008
Franklin (G-5148)
Luck Stone Corporation ....E 703 830-8880
Centreville (G-2316)
Mid Atlantic Mining LLC ....G 757 407-6735
Suffolk (G-13742)
Nancy Stephens ....G 540 933-6405
Fort Valley (G-5135)
Packetts Sand Pit ....G 804 761-6975
Warsaw (G-15072)
Percontee Inc ....E 703 471-4411
Chantilly (G-2479)
◆ Pounding Mill Quarry Corp ....E 276 326-1145
Bluefield (G-1875)
RI Byrd Properties ....G 757 817-7920
Yorktown (G-15988)
Rockydale Quarries Corporation ....D 540 774-1696
Roanoke (G-12170)
Rockydale Quarries Corporation ....G 540 886-2111
Staunton (G-13286)
S&M Trucking Service LLC ....G 980 395-6953
Woodbridge (G-15801)
Salem Stone Corporation ....G 276 228-6767
Wytheville (G-15910)
Sand Mountain Sand Co ....F 276 228-6767
Wytheville (G-15911)
Sisson & Ryan Inc ....E 540 268-2413
Shawsville (G-12686)
Stony Creek Sand & Gravel LLC ....G 804 229-0015
Virginia Beach (G-14853)
T&W Block Incorporated ....E 757 787-2646
Onley (G-10201)
Tarmac Mid-Atlantic Inc ....A 757 858-6500
Norfolk (G-9743)
TCS Materials Inc ....G 757 591-9340
Williamsburg (G-15323)

Texture Sand Tresses ....G 757 369-3033
Newport News (G-9354)
Townside Building and Repr Inc ....G 540 207-3906
Stafford (G-13203)
Vulcan Construction Mtls LLC ....E 804 862-6660
Prince George (G-10609)
Vulcan Materials Company ....G 757 622-4110
Norfolk (G-9787)
Walker Sand Stone ....G 540 775-5024
Culpeper (G-3930)

1446 Industrial Sand

Covia Holdings Corporation ....E 540 858-3444
Gore (G-5921)
Covia Holdings Corporation ....G 540 678-1490
Winchester (G-15535)
Dag Blast It Inc ....G 757 237-0735
Chesapeake (G-3061)
Dominion Quikrete Inc ....E 276 957-3235
Martinsville (G-8279)
U S Silica Company ....E 804 883-6700
Montpelier (G-9022)

1455 Kaolin & Ball Clay

Carolinas Solution Group Inc ....G 301 257-6926
Charlottesville (G-2756)

1459 Clay, Ceramic & Refractory Minerals, NEC

City Clay LLC ....G 434 293-0808
Charlottesville (G-2765)

1479 Chemical & Fertilizer Mining

R & R Mining Inc ....G 606 837-9321
Wise (G-15633)
United Salt Baytown LLC ....E 276 496-3363
Saltville (G-12595)

1481 Nonmetallic Minerals Svcs, Except Fuels

Agp Technologies LLC ....G 434 489-6025
Catlett (G-2262)
Alfaro Torres German ....G 703 498-6295
Sterling (G-13341)
▲ Blue Ridge Stone Corp ....G 434 239-9249
Lynchburg (G-7656)
◆ Iluka Resources Inc ....C 434 348-4300
Stony Creek (G-13567)
Ken Musselman & Associates Inc ....G 804 790-0302
Chesterfield (G-3510)
Mines Minerals & Enrgy VA Dept ....D 276 523-8100
Big Stone Gap (G-1713)
Moorman Shickram & Stephen ....G 540 463-3146
Lexington (G-7403)
Peter Adams ....G 540 960-0241
Millboro (G-8938)
Vinnell Corp ....G 703 818-7903
Fairfax (G-4579)

1499 Miscellaneous Nonmetallic Mining

Brandy Ltd ....G 757 220-0302
Williamsburg (G-15213)
Morefield Gem Mine Inc ....G 804 561-3399
Amelia Court House (G-666)
Polycor Virginia Inc ....E 434 831-1051
Schuyler (G-12653)
Royal Standard Minerals Inc ....G 804 580-8107
Heathsville (G-6464)
Soapstone Inc ....G 540 745-3492
Floyd (G-5040)

20 FOOD AND KINDRED PRODUCTS

2011 Meat Packing Plants

Alleghany Highlands AG Ctr LLC ....G 540 474-2422
Monterey (G-9000)
Andes Glendon Meat Processing ....G 540 896-7798
Timberville (G-13845)
Beef Products Incorporated ....E 540 985-5914
Roanoke (G-11886)
Bobbys Meat Processing ....G 276 728-4547
Austinville (G-1528)
Calhouns Ham House ....G 540 825-8319
Culpeper (G-3877)
▲ Campofrio Fd Group - Amer Inc ....C 804 520-7775
South Chesterfield (G-12798)

Cargill Meat Solutions Corp..................G...... 540 437-8000
  Mount Crawford *(G-9052)*

Carolina Cold Storage Inc ....G...... 757 357-0434
  Smithfield *(G-12708)*

Crabill Slaughterhouse Inc ....G...... 540 436-3248
  Toms Brook *(G-13882)*

Crazy Clover Butcher Shop ....G...... 804 370-5291
  Jamaica *(G-7008)*

Donalds Meat Processing LLC ....F...... 540 463-2333
  Lexington *(G-7395)*

Farmland Foods Inc ....G...... 757 357-4321
  Smithfield *(G-12713)*

Foods For Thought Inc ....G...... 434 242-4996
  Orange *(G-10213)*

Gores Custom Slaughter & Proc ....E...... 540 869-1029
  Stephens City *(G-13317)*

Green Valley Meat Processors..................G...... 434 299-5529
  Monroe *(G-8990)*

J & P Meat Processing ....F...... 540 721-2765
  Wirtz *(G-15615)*

Kraft Heinz Foods Company ....B...... 540 678-0442
  Winchester *(G-15437)*

Meat & Wool New Zealand Ltd..............G...... 703 927-4817
  Mc Lean *(G-8497)*

Melrose Bison Farm ....G...... 434 660-6036
  Gladys *(G-5695)*

Rolling Knoll Farm Inc ....F...... 540 569-6476
  Verona *(G-13994)*

Rollins Meat Processing ....G...... 540 672-5177
  Orange *(G-10227)*

Russell Meat Packing Inc ....G...... 276 794-7600
  Castlewood *(G-2256)*

Schrocks Slaughterhouse..................G...... 434 283-5400
  Gladys *(G-5696)*

Smith Valley Meats..................G...... 540 726-3992
  Rich Creek *(G-11008)*

Smithfield Pckgd Mats Sls Corp..........G...... 816 243-2855
  Smithfield *(G-12724)*

Smithfield Pckgd Mats Sls Corp..........G...... 816 243-2855
  Smithfield *(G-12725)*

Smithfield Direct LLC ....E...... 757 365-3000
  Smithfield *(G-12726)*

Smithfield Foods Inc ....A...... 757 933-2977
  Newport News *(G-9343)*

Smithfield Foods Inc..................C...... 910 862-7675
  Smithfield *(G-12727)*

Smithfield Foods Inc ....G...... 804 834-9941
  Waverly *(G-15088)*

Smithfield Foods Inc..................F...... 757 356-6700
  Smithfield *(G-12729)*

Smithfield Foods Inc..................E...... 757 357-1598
  Smithfield *(G-12730)*

◆ Smithfield Foods Inc ....C...... 757 365-3000
  Smithfield *(G-12728)*

Smithfield Foods Master Trust ....G...... 757 365-3000
  Smithfield *(G-12731)*

Smithfield Fresh Meats Corp ....G...... 513 782-3800
  Smithfield *(G-12732)*

Smithfield Packaged Meats Corp ....G...... 757 357-1798
  Smithfield *(G-12733)*

Smithfield Packaged Meats Corp ....G...... 757 365-3541
  Smithfield *(G-12734)*

Smithfield Packaged Meats Corp ....G...... 757 357-3131
  Smithfield *(G-12735)*

Smithfield Packaged Meats Corp ....G...... 513 782-3800
  Smithfield *(G-12736)*

Smithfield Packaged Meats Corp ....D...... 757 357-4321
  Norfolk *(G-9726)*

Smithfield Packaged Meats Corp ....D...... 757 357-1382
  Smithfield *(G-12737)*

Smithfield Packaged Meats Corp ....G...... 757 357-3131
  Smithfield *(G-12738)*

Smithfield Support Svcs Corp ....C...... 757 365-3541
  Smithfield *(G-12739)*

Southern Packing Corporation ....E...... 757 421-2131
  Chesapeake *(G-3303)*

Tribbetts Meats..................G...... 540 427-4671
  Roanoke *(G-12210)*

Tyson Foods Inc..................C...... 434 645-7791
  Jetersville *(G-7017)*

Valley Meat Processors Inc..................G...... 540 879-9041
  Dayton *(G-4069)*

Washington County Meat Packing ....G...... 276 466-3000
  Bristol *(G-2041)*

White Packing Co Inc-VA..................C...... 540 373-9883
  Fredericksburg *(G-5236)*

Williams Meat Processing..................G...... 276 686-4325
  Wytheville *(G-15923)*

Yates Abbattoir..................G...... 540 778-2123
  Luray *(G-7626)*

2013 Sausages & Meat Prdts

A L Duck Jr Inc..................F...... 757 562-2387
  Zuni *(G-16011)*

American Skin LLC..................G...... 910 259-2232
  Smithfield *(G-12703)*

Beef Jerky Outl Nova Jerky LLC ....G...... 703 868-6297
  Warrenton *(G-14981)*

Bobby and Pjs Jerky Shack..................G...... 540 856-2415
  Mount Jackson *(G-9066)*

Buckskin Jhnson Beef Jerky LLC ....G...... 540 303-0324
  Winchester *(G-15395)*

Cha Lua Ngoc Hung..................G...... 703 531-1868
  Falls Church *(G-4773)*

Chinctgue Island Hse Jerky LLC ....G...... 215 353-6393
  Chincoteague *(G-3561)*

Commonwealth Hams Inc ....G...... 434 846-4267
  Lynchburg *(G-7681)*

Elyssa E Strong..................G...... 540 280-3982
  Goshen *(G-5925)*

Ernies Beef Jerky ....G...... 540 460-4341
  Charlottesville *(G-2627)*

Frito-Lay North America Inc ....E...... 540 380-3020
  Salem *(G-12508)*

Hams Down Inc ....G...... 540 374-1405
  Fredericksburg *(G-5193)*

Hams Enterprises LLC ....G...... 703 988-0992
  Clifton *(G-3670)*

Indiana Packers Corporation ....G...... 270 926-2324
  Newport News *(G-9256)*

James A Kennedy & Assoc Inc..........G...... 804 241-6836
  Powhatan *(G-10553)*

Joes Smoked Meat Shack ....G...... 276 644-4001
  Bristol *(G-1980)*

Knauss Snack Food & Co LLC ....G...... 276 656-3500
  Martinsville *(G-8305)*

Logan Food Company ....F...... 703 212-6677
  Alexandria *(G-263)*

Mary Truman..................G...... 469 554-0655
  Freeman *(G-5512)*

Mintel Group Ltd ....G...... 540 989-3945
  Roanoke *(G-11968)*

River Ridge Meats LLC ....G...... 276 773-2191
  Independence *(G-6993)*

Shelf Reliance ....G...... 540 459-2050
  Woodstock *(G-15859)*

Skinny Jerky LLC ....G...... 703 459-8406
  Alexandria *(G-347)*

◆ Smithfield Foods Inc ....C...... 757 365-3000
  Smithfield *(G-12728)*

Smithfield Packaged Meats Corp ....G...... 757 357-3131
  Smithfield *(G-12735)*

Smithfield Packaged Meats Corp ....D...... 757 357-1382
  Smithfield *(G-12737)*

Smithfield Support Svcs Corp ....C...... 757 365-3541
  Smithfield *(G-12739)*

Southern Packing Corporation..........E...... 757 421-2131
  Chesapeake *(G-3303)*

Toms Wild Game Products ....G...... 540 598-3900
  Henrico *(G-6583)*

White Packing Co Inc-VA ....C...... 540 373-9883
  Fredericksburg *(G-5236)*

Williams Incorporated T O ....E...... 757 397-0771
  Portsmouth *(G-10503)*

2015 Poultry Slaughtering, Dressing & Processing

Alleghany Highlands AG Ctr LLC..........G...... 540 474-2422
  Monterey *(G-9000)*

◆ Ariake USA Inc..................D...... 540 432-6550
  Harrisonburg *(G-6293)*

Aura LLC ....G...... 757 965-8400
  Norfolk *(G-9447)*

Cargill Incorporated ....B...... 540 879-2521
  Dayton *(G-4053)*

Cargill Incorporated ....E...... 540 432-5700
  Mount Crawford *(G-9051)*

Cargill Incorporated ....E...... 540 896-7041
  Timberville *(G-13846)*

Damoah & Family Farm LLC ....G...... 703 919-0329
  Stafford *(G-13136)*

Georges Inc ....A...... 540 433-0720
  Harrisonburg *(G-6322)*

▲ Georges Chicken LLC ....G...... 540 984-4121
  Edinburg *(G-4305)*

Georges Chicken LLC ....F...... 540 434-7394
  Harrisonburg *(G-6323)*

New Market Poultry LLC ....G...... 540 740-4260
  New Market *(G-9145)*

Perdue Farms Inc ....B...... 804 722-1276
  Prince George *(G-10604)*

Perdue Farms Inc..................G...... 540 465-9665
  Strasburg *(G-13594)*

Perdue Farms Inc..................G...... 804 443-4391
  Tappahannock *(G-13820)*

Perdue Farms Inc ....D...... 757 494-5564
  Chesapeake *(G-3236)*

Perdue Farms Inc..................C...... 540 828-7700
  Bridgewater *(G-1956)*

Perdue Farms Inc..................G...... 804 453-4656
  Kilmarnock *(G-7074)*

Perdue Farms Inc..................B...... 757 787-5210
  Eastville *(G-4296)*

Pilgrims Pride Corporation ....E...... 540 564-6070
  Harrisonburg *(G-6355)*

Pilgrims Pride Corporation ....A...... 540 896-7000
  Timberville *(G-13851)*

Risser Farms Inc ....G...... 804 387-8584
  New Kent *(G-9138)*

Shortys Breading Company LLC..........G...... 434 390-1772
  Rice *(G-11006)*

◆ Smithfield Foods Inc..................C...... 757 365-3000
  Smithfield *(G-12728)*

Smithfield Support Svcs Corp ....C...... 757 365-3541
  Smithfield *(G-12739)*

Tyson Foods Inc..................A...... 757 824-3471
  Temperanceville *(G-13840)*

Tyson Foods Inc..................A...... 804 798-8357
  Glen Allen *(G-5819)*

Tyson Foods Inc..................C...... 434 645-7791
  Crewe *(G-3819)*

Tyson Foods Inc..................A...... 804 561-2187
  Jetersville *(G-7016)*

Tyson Foods Inc..................G...... 540 740-3118
  New Market *(G-9150)*

Tyson Foods Inc..................C...... 434 645-7791
  Jetersville *(G-7017)*

Virginia Plty Growers Coop Inc ....B...... 540 867-4000
  Hinton *(G-6906)*

Vpgc LLC ....G...... 540 867-4000
  Hinton *(G-6907)*

2021 Butter

Ausome Foods LLC..................G...... 703 478-4866
  Falls Church *(G-4752)*

Buf Creamery LLC ....G...... 434 466-7110
  Manakin Sabot *(G-7896)*

Great Falls Creamery ....G...... 703 272-7609
  Great Falls *(G-5959)*

La Vache Microcreamery ....G...... 434 989-6264
  Charlottesville *(G-2655)*

Spreco Creamery ....G...... 540 529-1581
  Roanoke *(G-12193)*

Tropq Creamery LLC ....G...... 540 680-0916
  Purcellville *(G-10682)*

2022 Cheese

Locksley Estate Frmstead Chese........G...... 703 926-4759
  Middleburg *(G-8726)*

National Bankshares Inc ....G...... 540 552-0890
  Blacksburg *(G-1771)*

2023 Milk, Condensed & Evaporated

Arms Race Nutrition LLC ....G...... 888 978-2332
  Sterling *(G-13349)*

Awesome Wellness..................G...... 540 439-0808
  Bealeton *(G-1596)*

Biomic Sciences LLC ....G...... 434 260-8530
  Charlottesville *(G-2596)*

Core Nutritionals LLC ....G...... 888 978-2332
  Sterling *(G-13375)*

Ganpat Enterprise Inc..................G...... 804 763-2405
  Midlothian *(G-8821)*

Harmony RDS LLC ....G...... 304 433-2188
  Leesburg *(G-7283)*

Hidemand Supplements LLC ....G...... 757 224-3485
  Hampton *(G-6166)*

JPS Consulting LLC ....G...... 571 334-0859
  Fairfax Station *(G-4714)*

Legion Athletics Inc ....F...... 727 729-1049
  Vienna *(G-14081)*

Maryland and Virginia Milk PR..........C...... 757 245-3857
  Newport News *(G-9292)*

merica Labz LLC ....G...... 844 445-5335
  Sterling *(G-13453)*

Mf Capital LLC ....G...... 703 470-8787
  Woodbridge *(G-15746)*

◆ Nestle Holdings Inc ....F...... 703 682-4600
  Arlington *(G-1073)*

Nestle Usa Inc ....C...... 765 778-6000
  Arlington *(G-1074)*

S I C

Nestle Usa Inc ....C 757 538-4178
  Suffolk *(G-13750)*
Nimco Us Inc ....G 314 982-3204
  Arlington *(G-1078)*
Pearson & Associates ....G 757 523-1382
  Virginia Beach *(G-14715)*
Rephidim LLC ....G 312 636-6947
  Charlottesville *(G-2683)*
Revival Labs LLC ....G 949 351-1660
  Alexandria *(G-572)*
Savory Sun VA LLC ....E 540 898-0851
  Fredericksburg *(G-5220)*
Shaklee Authorized Distri ....G 276 744-3546
  Independence *(G-6995)*
Sniffaroo Inc ....G 941 544-3529
  Fredericksburg *(G-5363)*
Sports Supplements South Inc ....G 804 379-6410
  North Chesterfield *(G-9988)*
◆ Timeless Touch LLC ....G 703 986-0096
  Manassas *(G-8167)*
Vitasecrets USA LLC ....G 919 212-1742
  Alexandria *(G-378)*

2024 Ice Cream

7430 Broken Ridge LLC ....G 571 354-0488
  Fredericksburg *(G-5239)*
A & W Masonry Specialists ....G 757 327-3492
  Hampton *(G-6065)*
Cabrera Family Masonry LLC ....G 919 671-7623
  Hampton *(G-6102)*
Cervantes Masonry ....G 804 741-7271
  Henrico *(G-6491)*
Crust & Cream ....G 804 230-5555
  Richmond *(G-11547)*
Epiphany Inc ....G 703 437-3133
  Fairfax *(G-4449)*
Freda Marshall ....G 757 632-1364
  Portsmouth *(G-10433)*
Good Humor Ice Cream LLC ....G 703 898-5516
  Reston *(G-10861)*
Gregs Fun Foods ....G 540 382-6267
  Christiansburg *(G-3592)*
Healthy Snacks Distrs Ltd ....G 703 627-8578
  Fairfax Station *(G-4713)*
Jsc Froyo LLC ....G 571 303-0011
  Arlington *(G-1018)*
Just Desserts ....G 804 310-5958
  Mechanicsville *(G-8647)*
La Michoacana III LLC ....G 804 275-0011
  North Chesterfield *(G-9911)*
Maola Milk and Ice Cream Co ....D 252 638-1131
  Newport News *(G-9289)*
Marc R Stagger ....E 703 913-9445
  Springfield *(G-13046)*
◆ Mars Incorporated ....B 703 821-4900
  Mc Lean *(G-8491)*
Mattie S Soft Serve LLC ....G 540 560-4550
  Stanley *(G-13233)*
Moothru LLC ....G 540 439-6455
  Remington *(G-10770)*
Ms Jos Petite Sweets LLC ....G 571 327-9431
  Alexandria *(G-286)*
Nightingale Inc ....G 804 332-7018
  Henrico *(G-6544)*
Sandy Farnham ....G 804 310-6171
  Moseley *(G-9047)*
Shenandoahs Pride LLC ....B 703 321-9500
  Springfield *(G-13083)*
Splendoras ....F 434 296-8555
  Charlottesville *(G-2880)*
Strongtower Inc ....G 804 723-8050
  Mechanicsville *(G-8683)*
Sweet & Savory By Emily LLC ....G 804 248-8252
  North Chesterfield *(G-9995)*
Sweet Catastrophe LLC ....F 434 296-8555
  Charlottesville *(G-2885)*
Sweet Tooth ....G 434 760-0047
  Charlottesville *(G-2698)*
Trotter Jamil ....G 757 251-8754
  Hampton *(G-6253)*
Tutti Fruitti ....G 703 830-0036
  Centreville *(G-2345)*
Uncle Harrys Inc ....G 757 426-7056
  Virginia Beach *(G-14901)*
We All Scream ....G 804 716-1157
  Richmond *(G-11443)*
Yummy In My Tummy Inc ....G 703 209-1516
  Leesburg *(G-7382)*
Zinga ....G 571 291-2475
  Ashburn *(G-1356)*

2026 Milk

Cocoa Mia Inc ....G 540 493-4341
  Floyd *(G-5020)*
Dean Foods Company ....D 804 737-8272
  Sandston *(G-12609)*
Dfa Dairy Brands Fluid LLC ....G 540 777-4091
  Roanoke *(G-12078)*
Dfa Dairy Brands Fluid LLC ....G 336 714-9032
  Bluefield *(G-1862)*
Dfa Dairy Brands Fluid LLC ....G 336 714-9032
  Forest *(G-5066)*
Dfa Dairy Brands Fluid LLC ....G 336 714-9032
  South Boston *(G-12761)*
HP Hood LLC ....B 540 869-0045
  Winchester *(G-15426)*
Iceberry Inc ....G 703 481-0670
  Reston *(G-10866)*
Maola Milk and Ice Cream Co ....D 252 638-1131
  Newport News *(G-9289)*
Maryland and Virginia Milk PR ....C 757 245-3857
  Newport News *(G-9292)*
Maryland and Virginia Milk PR ....E 804 524-0959
  South Chesterfield *(G-12814)*
◆ Nestle Holdings Inc ....F 703 682-4600
  Arlington *(G-1073)*
Shenandoahs Pride LLC ....B 703 321-9500
  Springfield *(G-13083)*
Trident Seafoods Corp ....F 540 707-0112
  Bedford *(G-1661)*
Tutti Frutti Frozen ....G 703 440-0010
  Burke *(G-2205)*
United Dairy Inc ....G 540 366-2964
  Roanoke *(G-12212)*
Wwf Operating Company ....B 540 434-7328
  Mount Crawford *(G-9063)*

2032 Canned Specialties

Catherine Elliott ....G 276 274-7022
  Bristol *(G-1969)*
▲ Confero Foods LLC ....G 703 334-7516
  Lorton *(G-7476)*
DJS Enterprises ....G 703 973-0977
  Alexandria *(G-191)*
Interleno Enterprises LLC ....G 757 340-3613
  Virginia Beach *(G-14551)*
Jim Sirrine ....G 540 874-7006
  Roanoke *(G-12111)*
Laestrellita ....G 276 650-7099
  Axton *(G-1539)*
◆ Nestle Holdings Inc ....F 703 682-4600
  Arlington *(G-1073)*
Pudding Please LLC ....F 804 833-4110
  Richmond *(G-11727)*
Queen of Amannisa ....G 703 414-7888
  Arlington *(G-1126)*
Rodgers Puddings LLC ....G 757 558-2657
  Chesapeake *(G-3273)*
Sir Masa Inc ....G 540 725-1982
  Roanoke *(G-12189)*
Tindahan ....G 757 243-8207
  Newport News *(G-9356)*
Waterneer USA Inc ....G 703 655-2279
  Chantilly *(G-2520)*

2033 Canned Fruits, Vegetables & Preserves

Acesur North America Inc ....E 757 664-2390
  Norfolk *(G-9419)*
◆ Andros Bowman Products LLC ....D 540 217-4100
  Mount Jackson *(G-9064)*
Ashburn Sauce Company ....G 757 621-1113
  Virginia Beach *(G-14245)*
Authentic Products LLC ....G 703 451-5984
  Springfield *(G-12954)*
Back Pocket Provisions LLC ....G 703 585-3676
  Falls Church *(G-4753)*
Biogeo Genetics ....G 888 448-8376
  Chesapeake *(G-3000)*
Broad Street Traffic Jams LLC ....G 804 461-1245
  Rockville *(G-12284)*
◆ Hunter Company HB ....F 757 664-5200
  Norfolk *(G-9584)*
Jddr Foods Inc ....G 571 356-0165
  Reston *(G-10880)*
Jmy Jams LLC ....G 434 906-0256
  North Garden *(G-10077)*
Juice ....E 202 280-0302
  Falls Church *(G-4812)*
JUIce&i LLC ....G 202 280-0302
  Falls Church *(G-4813)*

Kraft ....G 703 583-8874
  Woodbridge *(G-15736)*
Kraft Heinz Foods Company ....G 540 545-7563
  Winchester *(G-15436)*
Lake Packing Co Inc ....F 804 529-6101
  Lottsburg *(G-7543)*
Littlebird Jams and Jellies ....G 804 586-4420
  North Dinwiddie *(G-10059)*
Lizis Jams ....G 804 837-1904
  Midlothian *(G-8850)*
Lutz Farm & Services ....G 540 477-3574
  Mount Jackson *(G-9075)*
Mad Hatter Foods LLC ....G 434 981-9378
  Charlottesville *(G-2830)*
Maryland and Virginia Milk PR ....C 757 245-3857
  Newport News *(G-9292)*
Millcroft Farms Co Inc ....G 540 778-3369
  Stanley *(G-13234)*
◆ Nestle Holdings Inc ....F 703 682-4600
  Arlington *(G-1073)*
Nestle Prepared Foods Company ....D 434 822-4000
  Danville *(G-4017)*
Nestle Usa Inc ....C 765 778-6000
  Arlington *(G-1074)*
Nobull Burger ....G 434 975-6628
  Charlottesville *(G-2664)*
Old Coots LLC ....G 757 713-2888
  Norfolk *(G-9674)*
Pk Hot Sauce LLc ....G 703 629-0920
  Manassas *(G-7989)*
Pork Barrel Bbq LLC ....G 202 750-7500
  Alexandria *(G-312)*
Shawnee Canning Company Inc ....G 540 888-3429
  Cross Junction *(G-3827)*
Simply Panache Products LLC ....G 757 358-7062
  Hampton *(G-6238)*
Transformation Wellness LLC ....G 804 366-4632
  Richmond *(G-11792)*
Treser Family Foods Inc ....G 540 250-5667
  Blacksburg *(G-1801)*
Virginias Mudd Hot Sauce LLC ....G 434 953-6582
  Scottsville *(G-12669)*
Zo-Zos Jams ....G 804 562-9867
  Glen Allen *(G-5830)*

2034 Dried Fruits, Vegetables & Soup

B Global LLC ....G 703 628-2826
  Vienna *(G-14013)*
Iwoan LLC ....G 347 606-0602
  Falls Church *(G-4809)*
Soleil Foods Ltd Liability Co ....G 201 920-1553
  Fairfax *(G-4679)*
Tabard Corporation ....E 540 477-9664
  Mount Jackson *(G-9081)*
▲ Taura Natural Ingredients ....G 540 723-8691
  Winchester *(G-15591)*

2035 Pickled Fruits, Vegetables, Sauces & Dressings

▲ Ashman Distributing Company ....F 757 428-6734
  Virginia Beach *(G-14246)*
Chef Josephs Kick Sauce LLC ....G 757 525-1744
  Virginia Beach *(G-14332)*
Chilli Richmond LLC ....G 804 329-2262
  Richmond *(G-11530)*
Ferrera Group Usa Inc ....G 703 340-8300
  Leesburg *(G-7273)*
Gallas Foods Inc ....G 703 593-9957
  Reston *(G-10855)*
◆ Hunter Company HB ....F 757 664-5200
  Norfolk *(G-9584)*
John E Pickle ....G 276 496-5963
  Saltville *(G-12585)*
Keswick Gourmet Foods LLC ....G 610 585-2688
  Keswick *(G-7048)*
Kingdom Objectives ....G 434 414-0808
  Farmville *(G-4945)*
Mondelez Global LLC ....D 757 925-3011
  Suffolk *(G-13745)*
Nestle Prepared Foods Company ....D 434 822-4000
  Danville *(G-4017)*
▲ New Silk Road Marketing LLC ....G 434 531-0141
  Charlottesville *(G-2663)*
Pickle Bucket Four LLC ....G 571 259-3726
  Alexandria *(G-308)*
Pickle Bucket Three LLC ....G 571 259-3726
  Alexandria *(G-309)*
Pork Barrel Bbq LLC ....G 202 750-7500
  Alexandria *(G-312)*

Prissy Pickle Company Llc ....G...... 804 514-8112
Virginia Beach *(G-14741)*
◆ San-J International Inc ....E...... 804 226-8333
Henrico *(G-6565)*
Sardana Sushila ....G...... 703 256-5091
Alexandria *(G-577)*
Superior Quality Foods ....G...... 540 447-0552
Waynesboro *(G-15140)*
Taste of Carribean ....G...... 804 321-2411
Richmond *(G-11783)*
Titas Nene Bicol Atchara LLC ....G...... 571 501-8599
Leesburg *(G-7362)*

2037 Frozen Fruits, Juices & Vegetables

Aleeta A Gardner ....G...... 571 722-2549
Woodbridge *(G-15644)*
◆ Andros Bowman Products LLC ....D...... 540 217-4100
Mount Jackson *(G-9064)*
James A Kennedy & Assoc Inc ....G...... 804 241-6836
Powhatan *(G-10553)*
Juice Bar Juices Incorporated...............G...... 757 227-6822
Virginia Beach *(G-14577)*
Shelf Reliance ....G...... 540 459-2050
Woodstock *(G-15859)*
Sp Smoothies Inc ....G...... 757 595-0600
Newport News *(G-9344)*
Swagg Juices LLC ....G...... 757 254-6754
Hampton *(G-6245)*

2038 Frozen Specialties

Cathay Food Corp ....E...... 617 427-1507
Fredericksburg *(G-5408)*
Eastern Shore Seafood Pdts LLC............G...... 757 854-4422
Mappsville *(G-8218)*
Food Portions LLC ....G...... 757 839-3265
Portsmouth *(G-10432)*
Gumax International Ltd ....E...... 866 412-3880
Woodbridge *(G-15719)*
I-Ce-Ny Arlington ....G...... 571 207-6318
Arlington *(G-997)*
James A Kennedy & Assoc Inc ....G...... 804 241-6836
Powhatan *(G-10553)*
Kiddos LLC ....G...... 540 468-2700
Monterey *(G-9008)*
Lily Golden Foods Corporation..............G...... 703 823-8821
Alexandria *(G-260)*
Mom Made Foods LLC...........................F...... 703 740-9241
Alexandria *(G-290)*
Nazret Cultural Foods LLC....................G...... 215 500-9813
Alexandria *(G-290)*
◆ Nestle Holdings Inc ....F...... 703 682-4600
Arlington *(G-1073)*
Nestle Pizza Company Inc ....F...... 757 479-1512
Chesapeake *(G-3217)*
Southeast Frozen Foods Inc ....D...... 800 214-6682
Sandston *(G-12635)*

2041 Flour, Grain Milling

Amherst Milling Co Inc ....G...... 434 946-7601
Amherst *(G-680)*
Archer-Daniels-Midland Company ....E...... 540 433-2761
Rockingham *(G-12240)*
Ardent Mills LLC ....E...... 540 825-1530
Culpeper *(G-3868)*
Ashland Roller Mills Inc ....E...... 804 798-8329
Ashland *(G-1372)*
Big Spring Mill Inc................................E...... 540 268-2267
Elliston *(G-4343)*
Culpeper Farmers Coop Inc ....D...... 540 825-2200
Culpeper *(G-3884)*
Miller Milling Company LLC.................E...... 540 678-0197
Winchester *(G-15450)*
My Mexico Foods & Distrs Inc ....G...... 540 560-3587
Harrisonburg *(G-6350)*
Teds Bulletin ....G...... 571 313-8961
Reston *(G-10970)*
▲ The Mennel Milling Co VA Inc ....F...... 540 776-6201
Roanoke *(G-12008)*
Vaughans Mill Inc ....G...... 540 789-7144
Indian Valley *(G-6998)*
Wades Mill Inc ....G...... 540 348-1400
Raphine *(G-10751)*

2043 Cereal Breakfast Foods

Agee Catering Services ....G...... 434 960-8906
Palmyra *(G-10243)*
Breakfast Lady LLC ....G...... 302 241-7400
Newport News *(G-9185)*

Gaona Granola Co LLC ....G...... 434 996-6653
Charlottesville *(G-2801)*
Gooats LLC ....G...... 267 997-7789
Lorton *(G-7491)*
Mondelez Global LLC ....D...... 757 925-3011
Suffolk *(G-13745)*
Trio Child LLC ....G...... 703 299-0070
Alexandria *(G-368)*
VA Foods LLC..G...... 434 221-1456
Lynch Station *(G-7629)*
Wigglesworth Granola LLC ....G...... 703 443-0130
Leesburg *(G-7378)*

2044 Rice Milling

▲ Al-Nafea Inc ....G...... 703 440-8499
Springfield *(G-12938)*
Clean and Bless ....G...... 434 324-7129
Hurt *(G-6973)*

2045 Flour, Blended & Prepared

Glazed & Twisted LLC ....G...... 703 789-5522
Gainesville *(G-5586)*
Nestle Prepared Foods Company ....D...... 434 822-4000
Danville *(G-4017)*

2046 Wet Corn Milling

Henkel US Operations Corp...................F...... 804 222-6100
Richmond *(G-11236)*
Tapioca LLC ....G...... 703 715-8688
Fairfax *(G-4568)*
Tapioca Go ....G...... 757 410-3836
Chesapeake *(G-3322)*

2047 Dog & Cat Food

Fidough Homemade Dog Treats...........G...... 757 876-4548
Newport News *(G-9227)*
Grace Upon Grace LLC ....G...... 703 999-6678
Leesburg *(G-7282)*
Mars Overseas Holdings Inc ....G...... 703 821-4900
Mc Lean *(G-8493)*
Mars Petcare Us Inc ....D...... 703 821-4900
Mc Lean *(G-8494)*
My Best Friends Cupcakes LLC ....G...... 757 754-1148
Virginia Beach *(G-14668)*
Nestle Purina Petcare Company...........D...... 804 769-1266
King William *(G-7130)*
Nestle Usa Inc ....C...... 765 778-6000
Arlington *(G-1074)*
Spectrum Brands Pet LLC ....F...... 540 951-5481
Blacksburg *(G-1794)*
Sunshine Mills Inc ....D...... 434 476-1451
Halifax *(G-6053)*
Sunshine Mills of Virginia ....D...... 434 476-1451
Halifax *(G-6054)*
Woodys Goodys LLC ....G...... 703 608-8533
Falls Church *(G-4929)*

2048 Prepared Feeds For Animals & Fowls

AG Pack LLC ....G...... 804 514-9080
Disputanta *(G-4103)*
Amherst Milling Co Inc ....G...... 434 946-7601
Amherst *(G-680)*
Big Spring Mill Inc................................E...... 540 268-2267
Elliston *(G-4343)*
Biostar ....G...... 800 686-9544
Gordonsville *(G-5901)*
Charles A Bliss Jr ....G...... 434 685-7311
Danville *(G-3966)*
Crop Production Services Inc ....G...... 804 282-7115
Richmond *(G-11037)*
Culpeper Farmers Coop Inc ....D...... 540 825-2200
Culpeper *(G-3884)*
Dd Pet Products Inc ....G...... 703 532-3983
Arlington *(G-931)*
Exchange Milling Co Inc ....G...... 540 483-5324
Rocky Mount *(G-12321)*
Farmers Milling & Supply Inc ....G...... 276 228-2971
Wytheville *(G-15888)*
Griffin Industries LLC ....F...... 804 876-3415
Doswell *(G-4121)*
Harry Jones Enterprises ....G...... 276 322-5096
North Tazewell *(G-10100)*
Healthy Chef Creations ....E...... 407 339-2433
Mc Lean *(G-8456)*
Horse Sense Balanced ....G...... 540 253-9987
Marshall *(G-8256)*
Limestone Dust Corporation ....D...... 276 326-1103
Bluefield *(G-1869)*

M C Chadwell.......................................G...... 276 445-5495
Ewing *(G-4386)*
▼ Maxx Performance Inc ....F...... 845 987-9432
Roanoke *(G-11960)*
▼ Micron Bio-Systems Inc ....F...... 540 261-2468
Buena Vista *(G-2147)*
Mountain View Rendering Co ....G...... 540 984-4158
Edinburg *(G-4310)*
Murphy-Brown LLC ....F...... 804 834-3990
Waverly *(G-15085)*
Nutrien AG Solutions Inc ....G...... 757 229-9448
West Point *(G-15160)*
Nutrien AG Solutions Inc ....G...... 540 775-2985
Milford *(G-8932)*
Performance Livestock & Feed C ....G...... 888 777-5912
Martinsville *(G-8317)*
Premium Pet Health LLC ....E...... 757 357-8880
Smithfield *(G-12722)*
Pure Blend Organics ....G...... 703 476-1414
Manassas *(G-7991)*
Severn Wharf Custom Rods ....G...... 804 642-0404
Gloucester Point *(G-5876)*
Southern States Coop Inc ....F...... 540 992-1100
Cloverdale *(G-3693)*
▲ Southern States Coop Inc ....B...... 804 281-1000
Richmond *(G-11389)*
Southern States Coop Inc ....E...... 703 378-4865
Chantilly *(G-2495)*
Southern States Coop Inc ....F...... 434 572-6941
South Boston *(G-12791)*
Southern States Coop Inc ....F...... 804 226-2758
Richmond *(G-11390)*
Southern States Coop Inc ....E...... 540 948-5691
Madison *(G-7862)*
Southern Sttes Wnchster Coop I ....F...... 540 662-0375
Winchester *(G-15588)*
Sunshine Mills Inc ....D...... 434 476-1451
Halifax *(G-6053)*
Valley Proteins Inc ....D...... 540 833-6641
Linville *(G-7436)*
Valley Proteins Inc ....D...... 540 833-8322
Linville *(G-7437)*
Valley Proteins (de) Inc ....D...... 434 634-9475
Emporia *(G-4369)*
Vaughans Mill Inc ....G...... 540 789-7144
Indian Valley *(G-6998)*
Wilson Enterprises Inc ....F...... 804 732-6884
North Dinwiddie *(G-10072)*

2051 Bread, Bakery Prdts Exc Cookies & Crackers

A & B Bakery ....G...... 540 965-5500
Covington *(G-3776)*
A Taste of LLC ....G...... 540 848-3186
Fredericksburg *(G-5395)*
Annabs Gluten Free LLC ....G...... 804 491-9288
Mechanicsville *(G-8604)*
Arif Winter ....G...... 757 515-9940
Norfolk *(G-9444)*
Authentic Baking Company LLC ....G...... 803 422-9282
Ashland *(G-1374)*
Bageladies LLC ....G...... 540 248-0908
Charlottesville *(G-2592)*
Bakefully Yours LLC ....G...... 540 229-6232
Marshall *(G-8250)*
Bakefully Yours LLC ....G...... 301 276-4972
Manassas *(G-8034)*
Bakers Crust Inc ....G...... 757 253-2787
Williamsburg *(G-15208)*
Beautifully Made Cupcakes ....G...... 757 287-0024
Chesapeake *(G-2996)*
Bellash Bakery Inc ....G...... 516 468-2312
Woodbridge *(G-15655)*
Bimbo Bakeries ....G...... 804 475-6776
Alexandria *(G-423)*
Bimbo Bakeries USA ....G...... 434 525-2947
Lynchburg *(G-7654)*
Black Rabbit Delights LLC ....G...... 757 453-3359
Norfolk *(G-9465)*
Blue Castle Cupcakes LLC ....G...... 757 618-0600
Virginia Beach *(G-14289)*
Bowwowmeow Baking Company LLC .G...... 757 636-7922
Virginia Beach *(G-14298)*
Cake Passion Custom Cakes LLC.........G...... 757 982-0928
Machipongo *(G-7845)*
Cakebatters LLC ....G...... 276 685-6731
Bristol *(G-1968)*
Canty Lane Confections LLC ....G...... 703 408-3661
Woodbridge *(G-15664)*

SIC

Cardinal Bakery Inc ....E 703 430-1600
  Sterling (G-13365)
Cargotrike Cupcakes ....G...... 804 245-0786
  Midlothian (G-8791)
Carlas Cupcakes LLC ....G...... 703 582-7615
  Herndon (G-6635)
Carriage House Products Inc ....G...... 804 615-2400
  Henrico (G-6488)
▲ Cassandras Grmet Classics Corp ..F 703 590-7900
  Manassas (G-7924)
Charm School LLC ....G...... 415 999-9496
  Richmond (G-11524)
Country Baking LLC ....G...... 540 592-7422
  Upperville (G-13966)
Countryside Bakery ....G...... 540 948-7888
  Aroda (G-1224)
Creggers Cakes & Catering ....G...... 276 646-8739
  Chilhowie (G-3549)
Cupcake Company ....G...... 540 810-0795
  Elkton (G-4324)
Cupcake Cottage LLC ....G...... 540 330-8504
  Daleville (G-3942)
Cupcakes and Lace LLC ....G...... 703 378-1525
  Chantilly (G-2400)
Cupcakes and More LLC ....G...... 804 305-2350
  Richmond (G-11171)
Cupcakes By Cheryl LLC ....G...... 757 592-4185
  Dutton (G-4270)
Cupcakes By Ladybug LLC ....G...... 571 926-9709
  Springfield (G-12984)
Cupcakes On Move LLC ....G...... 804 477-6754
  Richmond (G-11548)
Danville Donuts LLC ....G...... 434 835-4592
  Danville (G-3978)
Dessies Delicious Desserts LLC ....G...... 804 822-7482
  Prince George (G-10591)
Donut Diva LLC ....G...... 276 245-5987
  Tazewell (G-13831)
Elaines Cakes Inc ....G...... 804 748-2461
  Chester (G-3410)
Euphoric Treatz LLC ....G...... 757 504-4174
  Virginia Beach (G-14453)
Faith Mission Home ....F 434 985-7177
  Free Union (G-5506)
Flavorful Bakery & Cafe LLC ....G...... 301 857-2202
  Woodbridge (G-15704)
Flowers Bakeries LLC ....G...... 757 424-4860
  Virginia Beach (G-14467)
Flowers Bakeries LLC ....E 540 343-8165
  Roanoke (G-12088)
Flowers Bakeries LLC ....G...... 434 572-6340
  South Boston (G-12768)
Flowers Bakeries LLC ....G...... 757 539-2898
  Suffolk (G-13711)
Flowers Baking Co Norfolk LLC ....G...... 757 873-0066
  Newport News (G-9231)
Flowers Baking Co Norfolk LLC ....G...... 540 261-1559
  Buena Vista (G-2145)
Flowers Baking Co Norfolk LLC ....G...... 757 596-1443
  Yorktown (G-15960)
Flowers Baking Co Norfolk LLC ....C 757 622-6317
  Norfolk (G-9557)
Flowers Baking Co Oxford Inc ....G...... 610 932-2300
  Chantilly (G-2422)
Flowers Bkg Co Jamestown LLC ....G...... 276 236-5009
  Galax (G-5633)
Flowers Bkg Co Lynchburg LLC ....G...... 434 392-8134
  Farmville (G-4940)
Flowers Bkg Co Lynchburg LLC ....D 434 528-0441
  Lynchburg (G-7710)
Flowers Bkg Co Lynchburg LLC ....G...... 434 528-0441
  Roanoke (G-12089)
Flowers Bkg Co Lynchburg LLC ....E 434 528-0441
  Lynchburg (G-7711)
Flowers Bkg Co Lynchburg LLC ....G...... 434 528-0441
  Ashland (G-1418)
Flowers Bkg Co Lynchburg LLC ....G...... 540 344-5919
  Roanoke (G-12090)
Flowers Bkg Co Lynchburg LLC ....G...... 540 434-4439
  Harrisonburg (G-6316)
Flowers Bkg Co Lynchburg LLC ....G...... 276 647-8767
  Collinsville (G-3711)
Flowers Bkg Co Lynchburg LLC ....G...... 434 978-4104
  Charlottesville (G-2632)
Flowers Bkg Co Lynchburg LLC ....G...... 540 886-1582
  Staunton (G-13260)
Flowers Bkg Co Lynchburg LLC ....G...... 434 385-5044
  Lynchburg (G-7712)
Flowers Bkg Co Lynchburg LLC ....G...... 276 666-2008
  Martinsville (G-8287)

Flowers Bkg Co Lynchburg LLC ....G...... 540 371-1480
  Fredericksburg (G-5289)
Fmp Inc ....G...... 434 392-3222
  Henrico (G-6513)
French Bread Factory Inc ....F 703 761-4070
  Sterling (G-13402)
Frosted Muffin - A Cupcakery ....G...... 571 989-1722
  Woodbridge (G-15708)
Glazed & Twisted LLC ....G...... 703 789-5522
  Gainesville (G-5586)
Goodwin Creek Farm & Bakery ....G...... 434 260-1135
  Afton (G-82)
Gumax International Ltd ....E 866 412-3880
  Woodbridge (G-15719)
Hampton Roads Baking Co LLC ....G...... 757 622-0347
  Norfolk (G-9569)
Harris Kayla ....G...... 540 285-0495
  Roanoke (G-12100)
Heavenly Kakes LLC ....G...... 804 874-3711
  Chester (G-3421)
Heavenly Sent Cupcakes LLC ....G...... 540 219-2162
  Boston (G-1904)
Hollys Homemade Treats ....G...... 540 977-1373
  Roanoke (G-12102)
Its Homeade LLC ....G...... 804 641-8248
  Kinsale (G-7135)
J S & A Cake Decoration ....G...... 703 494-3767
  Woodbridge (G-15727)
Jj S Cupcakes and More ....G...... 319 333-8020
  Troutville (G-13913)
Joy of Cupcakes LLC ....G...... 703 440-0204
  Springfield (G-13029)
Kics Cupcakes LLC ....G...... 202 630-5727
  Vienna (G-14078)
Kim Brj Inc ....G...... 703 642-2367
  Alexandria (G-505)
Kimberlys ....G...... 703 448-7298
  Mc Lean (G-8480)
Kind Cupcakes ....G...... 703 723-6167
  Ashburn (G-1303)
KORA Confections LLC ....G...... 240 478-2222
  King George (G-7098)
Levain Baking Studio Inc ....G...... 434 249-5875
  Troy (G-13931)
Lidl Us LLC ....G...... 757 420-1562
  Virginia Beach (G-14608)
Lidl Us LLC ....G...... 757 368-0256
  Virginia Beach (G-14609)
Lucia Coates ....G...... 434 384-1779
  Lynchburg (G-7759)
Maribeths Bakery Inc ....E 703 739-5839
  Alexandria (G-522)
Marjories Cookie Shop LLC ....G...... 901 205-9055
  Arlington (G-1053)
Martin Tonya ....G...... 804 742-8721
  La Crosse (G-7146)
Maxilicious Baking Company LLC ....G...... 703 448-1788
  Vienna (G-14089)
McKee Foods Corporation ....A 540 943-7101
  Stuarts Draft (G-13655)
Mo Cakes ....G...... 804 349-8634
  Glen Allen (G-5771)
Ms Jos Petite Sweets LLC ....G...... 571 327-9431
  Alexandria (G-286)
Mscbakes LLC ....G...... 434 214-0838
  Farmville (G-4953)
Mzgoodiez LLC ....G...... 757 535-6929
  Suffolk (G-13747)
Out of Bubble Bakery ....G...... 571 336-2280
  Springfield (G-13064)
Panaderia Latina ....F 703 642-5200
  Alexandria (G-548)
Parisian Sweets LLC ....G...... 770 722-8106
  Cape Charles (G-2235)
Pepperidge Farm Distributor ....G...... 540 395-4233
  Charlottesville (G-2845)
Perfect Pink LLC ....G...... 571 969-7465
  Arlington (G-1105)
Pink Cupcake ....G...... 801 349-6301
  Fredericksburg (G-5346)
Proof of Life Baking LLC ....G...... 571 721-8031
  Woodbridge (G-15785)
Proper Pie Co LLC ....G...... 804 343-7437
  Richmond (G-11338)
Punkins Cupcake Cones ....G...... 757 395-0295
  Virginia Beach (G-14748)
Pure Pasty Company LLC ....G...... 703 255-7147
  Vienna (G-14117)
Random Acts of Cupcakes ....G...... 540 974-3948
  Winchester (G-15578)

River City Chocolate LLC ....G...... 804 317-8161
  Midlothian (G-8890)
Robin Stippich ....G...... 757 692-5744
  Newport News (G-9329)
Rockfish Baking Company LLC ....G...... 703 314-7944
  Afton (G-88)
Rva Coffee LLC ....G...... 804 822-2015
  Richmond (G-11750)
Sani LLC ....G...... 703 596-2296
  Lorton (G-7528)
Simply Southern LLC ....G...... 804 240-7130
  Sandston (G-12633)
Solo Per Te Baked Goods Inc ....G...... 804 277-9010
  North Chesterfield (G-9983)
Spotcity Cupcakes LLC ....G...... 703 587-4934
  Fredericksburg (G-5367)
Sub Rosa LLC ....G...... 703 338-3344
  Clifton (G-3676)
Sugar & Salt LLC ....G...... 434 996-2329
  Virginia Beach (G-14858)
Sunbeam Bakeries ....G...... 276 647-8767
  Collinsville (G-3717)
Sweet Cynthias Pie Co LLC ....G...... 804 321-8646
  Richmond (G-11778)
Sweet Success Cupcakes ....G...... 703 674-9442
  Fairfax (G-4565)
Sweet Tooth Bakery Inc ....G...... 540 667-6155
  Winchester (G-15589)
Swurls LLC ....G...... 571 423-9899
  Fairfax Station (G-4725)
Tammy Haire ....G...... 540 722-7246
  Winchester (G-15487)
Tea Spot Catering LLC ....G...... 757 427-3525
  Virginia Beach (G-14867)
Virginia Culinary Pathways LLC ....G...... 757 298-0599
  Suffolk (G-13778)
Viva La Cupcake ....G...... 540 400-0806
  Roanoke (G-12224)
Whisk ....G...... 804 728-1576
  Richmond (G-11828)
Zosaro LLC ....G...... 804 564-9450
  Henrico (G-6593)

2052 Cookies & Crackers

Albemarle Edibles LLC ....G...... 434 242-5567
  Charlottesville (G-2723)
Black Alder Trail LLC ....G...... 812 219-1975
  Winchester (G-15531)
Charm School LLC ....G...... 415 999-9496
  Richmond (G-11524)
Crispery of Virginia LLC ....G...... 757 673-5234
  Portsmouth (G-10413)
Frito-Lay North America Inc ....E 540 380-3020
  Salem (G-12508)
Glamorous Sweet ....G...... 540 903-3683
  Fredericksburg (G-5435)
Hanguk Rice Cake Mark ....G...... 757 874-4150
  Newport News (G-9244)
Interbake Foods LLC ....G...... 605 232-4903
  Richmond (G-11619)
Interbake Foods LLC ....B 540 631-8100
  Front Royal (G-5537)
Kendras Cookies ....G...... 540 660-5645
  Front Royal (G-5539)
Marlor Inc ....F 804 378-5071
  North Chesterfield (G-9923)
McKee Foods Corporation ....A 540 943-7101
  Stuarts Draft (G-13655)
Mondelez Global LLC ....D 757 925-3011
  Suffolk (G-13745)
Montemorano LLC ....G...... 540 272-6390
  Sumerduck (G-13792)
Mothers Macaroons ....G...... 703 532-0104
  Arlington (G-1068)
Murray Biscuit Company LLC ....C 757 547-0249
  Chesapeake (G-3214)
Nightingale Inc ....G...... 804 332-7018
  Henrico (G-6544)
Snyders-Lance Inc ....B 703 339-0541
  Lorton (G-7531)

2053 Frozen Bakery Prdts

Bright Yeast Labs LLC ....G...... 205 790-2544
  Dulles (G-4194)
Creations From Heart LLC ....G...... 757 234-4300
  Seaford (G-12673)
Fat Mltons Sthern Swets Treats ....G...... 804 248-4175
  North Chesterfield (G-9871)
Joyebells LLC ....G...... 804 304-7695
  Richmond (G-11637)

Little Corners Petit Fours LLC ....G....... 571 215-4255
Sterling **(G-13443)**

Mzgoodiez LLC ....G....... 757 535-6929
Suffolk **(G-13747)**

Sugarland Run Pantries ....G....... 571 216-8565
Herndon **(G-6816)**

Triple Y Premium Yogurt ....G....... 804 212-5413
Richmond **(G-11795)**

2064 Candy & Confectionery Prdts

Aunt Nolas Pecan Pralines ....G....... 757 723-1607
Hampton **(G-6086)**

Blue Ridge Fudge Lady Inc ....G....... 276 335-2229
Wytheville **(G-15877)**

Camacho Enterprises LLC ....G....... 757 761-0407
Chesapeake **(G-3023)**

Cecilia M Schultzs ....G....... 301 840-1283
Great Falls **(G-5945)**

Cocoa Mia Inc ....G....... 540 695-0224
Floyd **(G-5019)**

Custom Candyy LLC ....F....... 804 447-8179
Richmond **(G-11549)**

Delicious Dainties LLC ....G....... 240 620-7581
Reston **(G-10838)**

Fudgetime LLC ....G....... 703 462-8544
Springfield **(G-13006)**

Helms Candy Co Inc ....E....... 276 669-2612
Bristol **(G-2019)**

Hershey Company ....B....... 540 324-0166
Stuarts Draft **(G-13649)**

▲ Jhl Inc ....G....... 703 378-0009
Chantilly **(G-2449)**

▼ Jodys Inc ....F....... 757 422-8646
Norfolk **(G-9604)**

Juma Brothers Inc ....G....... 757 312-0544
Portsmouth **(G-10449)**

Kandy Girl Kndy Apples Berries ....G....... 719 200-1662
Newport News **(G-9272)**

Katheryn Warren ....G....... 757 813-5396
Williamsburg **(G-15264)**

La La Land Candy Kingdom Va01 ....G....... 305 342-6737
Virginia Beach **(G-14597)**

Lakota JS Chocolates Corp ....G....... 804 590-0010
Chesterfield **(G-3512)**

Mamas Fudge ....G....... 540 980-8444
Pulaski **(G-10641)**

◆ Mars Incorporated ....B....... 703 821-4900
Mc Lean **(G-8491)**

Mars Logic LLC ....G....... 510 220-7117
Mc Lean **(G-8492)**

Matre Inc ....G....... 703 821-4927
Mc Lean **(G-8495)**

Michael Holt Inc ....G....... 703 597-6999
Arlington **(G-1062)**

Mondelez Global LLC ....D....... 757 925-3011
Suffolk **(G-13745)**

Moretz Candy Co Inc ....E....... 276 669-2533
Bristol **(G-2026)**

My Extra Hands LLC ....G....... 540 847-2063
Fredericksburg **(G-5330)**

◆ Nestle Holdings Inc ....F....... 703 682-4600
Arlington **(G-1073)**

Nestle Usa Inc ....C....... 765 778-6000
Arlington **(G-1074)**

Nicol Candy ....G....... 804 740-2378
Richmond **(G-11305)**

Popcorn Monkey LLC ....G....... 540 687-6539
Middleburg **(G-8733)**

Robin Stippich ....G....... 757 692-5744
Newport News **(G-9329)**

So Unique Candy Apples ....G....... 540 915-4899
Roanoke **(G-12191)**

Southern Tastes LLC ....G....... 757 204-1414
Chesapeake **(G-3304)**

Sugarfina LLC ....G....... 703 844-0049
Mc Lean **(G-8560)**

Sweet Svory Delights By Vickie ....G....... 703 581-8499
Falls Church **(G-4881)**

Tummy-Ymyum Grmet Candy Apples ....G....... 703 368-4756
Bristow **(G-2065)**

Unique Flexique LLC ....G....... 540 439-4465
Bealeton **(G-1607)**

2066 Chocolate & Cocoa Prdts

Barry Enterprises Intl LLC ....G....... 202 812-6822
Leesburg **(G-7227)**

Goddess of Chocolate Ltd ....G....... 757 301-2126
Virginia Beach **(G-14486)**

▲ Jhl Inc ....G....... 703 378-0009
Chantilly **(G-2449)**

◆ Mars Incorporated ....B....... 703 821-4900
Mc Lean **(G-8491)**

RE Max Advantage ....G....... 540 241-2499
Lyndhurst **(G-7844)**

Sweet & Savory By Emily LLC ....G....... 804 248-8252
North Chesterfield **(G-9995)**

2068 Salted & Roasted Nuts & Seeds

Mondelez Global LLC ....D....... 757 925-3011
Suffolk **(G-13745)**

Royal Oak Peanuts LLC ....G....... 434 658-9500
Drewryville **(G-4138)**

2076 Vegetable Oil Mills

▲ Serendib Traditional LLC ....G....... 703 408-1561
Sterling **(G-13504)**

Victory Tropical Oil Usa Inc ....G....... 757 687-8171
Virginia Beach **(G-14910)**

2077 Animal, Marine Fats & Oils

Mountain View Rendering Co ....G....... 540 984-4158
Edinburg **(G-4310)**

◆ Omega Protein Inc ....E....... 804 453-6262
Reedville **(G-10763)**

Omega Protein Inc ....E....... 804 453-4923
Reedville **(G-10764)**

◆ Omega Protein Corporation ....E....... 804 453-6262
Reedville **(G-10765)**

▼ Valley Proteins Inc ....E....... 540 877-2590
Winchester **(G-15500)**

Valley Proteins Inc ....G....... 540 833-6641
Linville **(G-7436)**

◆ Valley Proteins (de) Inc ....C....... 540 877-2533
Winchester **(G-15501)**

Valley Proteins (de) Inc ....G....... 540 877-2590
Winchester **(G-15502)**

Vaport Inc ....G....... 757 397-1397
Portsmouth **(G-10497)**

2079 Shortening, Oils & Margarine

Dean Foods Company ....C....... 804 359-5786
Richmond **(G-11555)**

Global Telecom Group Inc ....G....... 571 291-9631
Mc Lean **(G-8449)**

Global Telecom Group Inc ....G....... 678 896-2468
Chantilly **(G-2428)**

Mediterranean Delight Inc ....G....... 703 751-2656
Alexandria **(G-273)**

Mondelez Global LLC ....D....... 757 925-3011
Suffolk **(G-13745)**

Olive Manassas Oil Co ....G....... 703 543-9206
Manassas **(G-8121)**

Olive Oil & Friends LLC ....G....... 703 385-1845
Vienna **(G-14107)**

Olive Oil Boom ....G....... 703 276-2666
Arlington **(G-1085)**

Olive Oil Boom LLC ....G....... 703 276-2666
Arlington **(G-1086)**

Olive Oil Soap Company ....G....... 540 671-6940
Front Royal **(G-5547)**

Olive Oil Tamproom LLC ....G....... 804 897-6464
Midlothian **(G-8871)**

▲ Olive Oils Abingdon Assoc LLC ....G....... 276 525-1524
Abingdon **(G-52)**

Olive Savor ....G....... 757 425-3866
Virginia Beach **(G-14693)**

▲ Our Familys Olive Oil LLC ....G....... 571 292-1394
Manassas **(G-8124)**

▲ Scout Marketing LLC ....G....... 301 986-1470
Springfield **(G-13081)**

So Olive LLC ....G....... 571 398-2377
Occoquan **(G-10175)**

Staunton Olive Oil Company LLC ....G....... 540 290-9665
Staunton **(G-13299)**

Taste Oil Vinegar Spice ....G....... 540 373-1262
Fredericksburg **(G-5230)**

Vaport Inc ....G....... 757 397-1397
Portsmouth **(G-10497)**

2082 Malt Beverages

Abbey Staunton ....G....... 540 580-1271
Staunton **(G-13238)**

Anheuser-Busch LLC ....C....... 757 253-3600
Williamsburg **(G-15203)**

Anheuser-Busch Companies LLC ....G....... 757 253-3660
Williamsburg **(G-15204)**

Badwolf Brewery LLC ....G....... 571 208-1064
Manassas **(G-7917)**

Bear Chase Brewing Company LLC ....G....... 703 930-7949
Bluemont **(G-1885)**

Billsburg Brewery LLC ....F....... 757 926-0981
Williamsburg **(G-15211)**

Black Hoof Brewing Company LLC ....G....... 571 707-8014
Leesburg **(G-7232)**

Blue Mountain Brewery Inc ....E....... 540 456-8020
Afton **(G-75)**

Blue Mtn Brrel Hse Orgnic Brwr ....E....... 434 263-4002
Arrington **(G-1227)**

Brewco LLC ....G....... 276 686-5448
Rural Retreat **(G-12418)**

Broken Window Brewing Co LLC ....G....... 703 999-7030
Winchester **(G-15532)**

Cape Charles Brewing Company ....G....... 757 678-5699
Cape Charles **(G-2230)**

Colonial Beach Brewing LLC ....G....... 540 760-5661
Colonial Beach **(G-3723)**

Coors Brewing Company ....C....... 540 289-8000
Elkton **(G-4323)**

Craft of Brewing ....G....... 703 687-3932
Ashburn **(G-1259)**

Craftsman Distillery LLC ....G....... 804 454-1514
Chesterfield **(G-3487)**

Crazy Rooster Brewing Co LLC ....G....... 804 464-2958
Powhatan **(G-10541)**

Damascus Brewery ....G....... 276 475-5319
Damascus **(G-3947)**

Dancing Kilt Brewery LLC ....G....... 804 715-0695
Chester **(G-3401)**

Demons Run Brewing LLC ....G....... 703 945-8100
Arlington **(G-936)**

Det Enterprises Inc ....G....... 310 429-3234
Leesburg **(G-7256)**

Dry Fork Fruit Distillery LLC ....G....... 276 952-1222
Martinsville **(G-8281)**

Global - AB Inbev ....G....... 314 577-2000
Williamsburg **(G-15247)**

Isley Brewing Company ....G....... 804 499-0721
Richmond **(G-11252)**

James River Beverage Co LLC ....G....... 434 589-2798
Kents Store **(G-7039)**

Joker Brewing LLC ....G....... 757 814-0882
Williamsburg **(G-15261)**

Kindred Brothers Inc ....G....... 803 318-5097
Richmond **(G-11262)**

Kindred Brothers Inc ....G....... 210 334-7723
Midlothian **(G-8839)**

Kobayashi Winery ....F....... 757 644-4464
Hampton **(G-6181)**

Kombuchick Inc ....G....... 757 818-7703
Norfolk **(G-9613)**

Legend Brewing Co ....E....... 804 232-8871
Richmond **(G-11651)**

Lynx Brewing Company LLC ....G....... 773 819-8748
Portsmouth **(G-10455)**

Metal Craft Brewing Co LLC ....G....... 816 271-3211
Waynesboro **(G-15126)**

▲ Mountain View Brewery LLC ....C....... 540 462-6200
Lexington **(G-7404)**

North Lock LLC ....G....... 703 797-2739
Alexandria **(G-293)**

Old Dominion MBL Canning LLC ....G....... 804 517-1640
Glen Allen **(G-5775)**

Oozlefinch Craft Brewery LLC ....G....... 757 224-7042
Fort Monroe **(G-5133)**

Pagan River Associates LLC ....G....... 757 357-5364
Smithfield **(G-12720)**

Parasitx LLC ....G....... 757 653-6179
Newport News **(G-9310)**

Pretty Ugly Distribution LLC ....G....... 757 672-8958
Chesapeake **(G-3247)**

River Company Rest & Brewry I ....G....... 540 633-6731
Radford **(G-10738)**

Siblings Rivalry Brewery LLC ....G....... 540 671-3893
Strasburg **(G-13596)**

Silverline Brewing Company ....G....... 703 281-5816
Vienna **(G-14128)**

Southpaw Brew Co LLC ....G....... 703 753-5986
Gainesville **(G-5613)**

▲ Starr Hill Brewing Company ....G....... 434 823-5671
Crozet **(G-3851)**

Station 6 Brewing LLC ....G....... 571 510-3532
Ashburn **(G-1336)**

That Damn Mary Brewing LLC ....G....... 804 761-1085
Heathsville **(G-6467)**

Throx Brew Market and Grille ....G....... 540 323-7360
Winchester **(G-15489)**

Trapezium Brewing LLC ....G....... 804 677-5728
Petersburg **(G-10346)**

SIC

Virginia Beer Company LLC ....F 770 815-8518
Williamsburg *(G-15333)*
Virginia Cft Brwing Spport LLC ......G.... 703 960-3230
Alexandria *(G-375)*
Wolffinz LLC ....E 571 292-1427
Manassas *(G-8013)*

2083 Malt

Stuart Forest Products LLC ....E 276 694-3842
Stuart *(G-13634)*

2084 Wine & Brandy

50 West Vineyards ....G.... 571 367-4760
Middleburg *(G-8715)*
Afton Mountain Vineyards Corp ....G.... 540 456-8667
Afton *(G-73)*
Altillo Vineyards & Winery ....G.... 434 324-4160
Hurt *(G-6970)*
Altria Group Inc ....A 804 274-2200
Richmond *(G-11105)*
Ambrosia Vineyards ....G.... 703 237-8717
Falls Church *(G-4746)*
Amrhein Ltd ....G.... 540 929-4632
Bent Mountain *(G-1666)*
Anna Lake Winery Inc ....G.... 540 895-5085
Spotsylvania *(G-12884)*
Arrowine Inc ....F 703 525-0990
Arlington *(G-860)*
Artisan Meads LLC ....G.... 757 713-4885
Seaford *(G-12671)*
Ashton Creek Vineyard LLC ....G.... 804 896-1586
Chester *(G-3388)*
Aspen Dale Winery Barn ....G.... 540 364-1722
Delaplane *(G-4072)*
Attimo Group LLC ....F 540 838-1118
Christiansburg *(G-3570)*
Attimo Winery ....F 540 382-7619
Christiansburg *(G-3571)*
Barns & Vineyards LLC ....G.... 703 801-2719
Ashburn *(G-1245)*
▲ **Barrel Oak Winery LLC** ....E 540 364-6402
Delaplane *(G-4073)*
Barren Ridge Vineyards LLC ....G.... 540 248-3300
Fishersville *(G-5001)*
Beliveau Development Corp ....G.... 540 961-0505
Blacksburg *(G-1725)*
Beliveau Estate Vnyrd Wnery LL ....G.... 540 961-2102
Blacksburg *(G-1726)*
Blue Bee Cider LLC ....F 804 231-0280
Richmond *(G-11128)*
Blue Quartz Winery LLC ....G.... 540 923-4048
Etlan *(G-4372)*
Blue Ridge Vineyard Inc ....G.... 540 798-7642
Eagle Rock *(G-4279)*
Bluemont ....G.... 202 422-6500
Bluemont *(G-1886)*
Bluestone Vineyard Inc ....E 540 828-0099
Bridgewater *(G-1949)*
Blumont Vineyards ....G.... 540 554-8439
Bluemont *(G-1887)*
Bodie Vineyards LLC ....G.... 804 598-2240
Powhatan *(G-10534)*
Bogati Bodgea ....G.... 540 338-1144
Round Hill *(G-12375)*
Boundary Rock Frm & Vinyrd LLC ....G.... 540 789-7098
Willis *(G-15355)*
Boxwood Winery LLC ....G.... 540 687-8778
Middleburg *(G-8718)*
Branches Tasting Room ....G.... 757 620-5393
Chesapeake *(G-3015)*
Breaux Vineyards Ltd ....G.... 540 668-6299
Hillsboro *(G-6860)*
Brent Manor Inn & Vineyards ....G.... 540 226-5958
Faber *(G-4388)*
Brian Allison ....G.... 276 988-9792
Tazewell *(G-13828)*
Briede Family Vineyards LLC ....G.... 540 667-2981
Winchester *(G-15393)*
Bright Meadows Farm ....G.... 434 349-9463
Nathalie *(G-9102)*
Brix 22 Ankida Rdge Tasting Rm ....G.... 434 989-7420
Charlottesville *(G-2750)*
Brix and Columns Vineyards LLC ....G.... 540 810-0566
Mc Gaheysville *(G-8377)*
Brook Hidden Winery LLC ....G.... 703 737-3935
Leesburg *(G-7237)*
Brooke Sterling Co ....G.... 850 650-8080
Great Falls *(G-5941)*
Byrd Cellars LLC ....G.... 804 652-5663
Goochland *(G-5880)*

▲ **Cana Cellars Inc** ....F 540 635-9398
Huntly *(G-6964)*
Cana Vineyards Winery ....G.... 703 348-2458
Middleburg *(G-8717)*
Cardinal Point Vineyard Winery ....G.... 540 456-8400
Afton *(G-76)*
Caret Cellars and Vineyard LLC ....G.... 540 413-6454
Caret *(G-2238)*
Casanel Vineyards ....G.... 540 751-1776
Leesburg *(G-7241)*
Castle Glen Esttes Frm Wnery L ....G.... 804 763-9677
Doswell *(G-4118)*
Castle Gruen Vnyrds Winery LLC ....G.... 540 229-2498
Locust Dale *(G-7440)*
Castle Vineyards LLC ....G.... 571 283-7150
Luray *(G-7604)*
Cedar Creek Valley Farm LLC ....G.... 540 533-2259
Star Tannery *(G-13235)*
Cedar Creek Winery LLC ....G.... 540 436-8357
Star Tannery *(G-13236)*
Charles James Winery & Vinyrd ....G.... 540 931-4386
Winchester *(G-15400)*
Charlottesville Vineyard ....G.... 434 321-8463
Charlottesville *(G-2764)*
Chateau Merrillanne LLC ....G.... 540 656-6177
Orange *(G-10206)*
▲ **Chateau Morrisette Inc** ....E 540 593-2865
Floyd *(G-5018)*
Chateau OBrien At North Point ....G.... 540 364-6441
Markham *(G-8247)*
Chatham Vineyards LLC ....G.... 757 678-5588
Machipongo *(G-7846)*
Chestnut Oak Vineyard LLC ....G.... 434 964-9104
Barboursville *(G-1559)*
Cobbler Mountain Cellars ....G.... 540 364-2802
Delaplane *(G-4074)*
Continental Commercial Corp ....G.... 540 668-6216
Hillsboro *(G-6861)*
Cooper Vineyards LLC ....G.... 540 894-5474
Louisa *(G-7550)*
Courthouse Creek Cider ....G.... 804 543-3157
Maidens *(G-7888)*
Creeks Edge Winery ....G.... 540 822-3825
Lovettsville *(G-7577)*
Cresta Gadino Winery LLC ....G.... 540 987-9292
Washington *(G-15075)*
▲ **Cross Keys Vineyards LLC** ....F 540 234-0505
Mount Crawford *(G-9053)*
Crushed Cellars LLC ....G.... 571 374-9463
Hillsboro *(G-6863)*
Cunningham Creek Winery LLC ....G.... 434 207-3907
Palmyra *(G-10247)*
Delaplane Sellers ....G.... 540 592-7210
Delaplane *(G-4075)*
Delfosse Vineyards Winery LLC ....G.... 434 263-6100
Faber *(G-4389)*
Desert Rose Ranch & Winery LLC ....G.... 540 635-3200
Hume *(G-6960)*
Devault Vineyards LLC ....G.... 434 993-0722
Concord *(G-3759)*
Dombroski Vineyards LLC ....G.... 804 932-8240
New Kent *(G-9130)*
Doukenie Winery ....G.... 540 668-6464
Hillsboro *(G-6864)*
Dragonsrealm Vineyard LLC ....G.... 540 905-9679
Goldvein *(G-5877)*
▲ **DRG Imports LLC** ....G.... 786 246-6548
Richmond *(G-11569)*
Dry Mill Rd LLC ....G.... 703 737-3697
Leesburg *(G-7261)*
Ducard Vineyards Inc ....G.... 434 409-4378
Charlottesville *(G-2620)*
Eagle Sunrise Vineyard LLC ....G.... 703 648-3258
Oakton *(G-10146)*
Effingham Manor LLC ....G.... 703 594-2300
Broad Run *(G-2067)*
Elk Island Winery ....G.... 540 967-0944
Goochland *(G-5882)*
Emerald Lake Vineyard ....G.... 540 270-3399
Hillsboro *(G-6865)*
▲ **Eric Trump Wine Mfg LLC** ....E 434 977-3895
Charlottesville *(G-2791)*
▲ **Exclusive Wine Imports LLC** ....G.... 703 765-9749
Alexandria *(G-458)*
Fabbioli Cellars ....G.... 703 771-1197
Leesburg *(G-7271)*
Faithbrooke Barn Vineyards LLC ....G.... 540 743-1207
Luray *(G-7611)*
Fedor Ventures LLC ....G.... 540 668-6248
Hillsboro *(G-6866)*

Fincastle Vineyard & Winery ....G.... 540 591-9000
Fincastle *(G-4996)*
Firefly Hill Vineyards LLC ....G.... 540 588-0231
Elliston *(G-4345)*
First Colony Winery Ltd ....G.... 434 979-7105
Charlottesville *(G-2795)*
▲ **Five Grapes LLC** ....G.... 703 205-2444
Sterling *(G-13398)*
Fleetwood Farm Winery LLC ....E 703 722-2124
Leesburg *(G-7274)*
Flying Fox Vineyard Lc ....G.... 434 361-1692
Afton *(G-81)*
Foggy Ridge Cider ....G.... 276 398-2337
Dugspur *(G-4188)*
Foster Jackson LLC ....G.... 540 436-9463
Maurertown *(G-8363)*
Fox Meadow Farms LLC ....G.... 540 636-6777
Linden *(G-7428)*
Furnace Mountain Vineyards LLC ....G.... 571 439-2255
Waterford *(G-15080)*
Gallagher Estate Vineyards LLC ....G.... 301 252-3450
Hamilton *(G-6058)*
Gauthier Vineyard LLC ....G.... 703 622-1107
Barhamsville *(G-1571)*
Generals Ridge Vineyard ....G.... 804 472-3172
Hague *(G-6046)*
Gh Winery LLC ....F 804 737-7416
Sandston *(G-12616)*
Glass House Winery LLC ....G.... 434 975-0094
Free Union *(G-5507)*
Glen Manor Vineyards LLC ....G.... 540 635-6324
Front Royal *(G-5533)*
Goodboy LLC ....G.... 540 421-6712
Hillsboro *(G-6869)*
Goose Creek Farms & Winery LLC ....G.... 540 338-2056
Purcellville *(G-10663)*
Grace Estate Winery LLC ....G.... 434 823-1486
Crozet *(G-3833)*
Granite Perch Graphics ....G.... 703 218-5300
Sterling *(G-13413)*
Gray Ghost Vineyards ....G.... 540 937-4869
Amissville *(G-719)*
Grayhaven Winery ....G.... 804 556-3917
Gum Spring *(G-6043)*
Greenhill Winery and Vineyards ....G.... 540 687-6968
Middleburg *(G-8721)*
Hague Winery LLC ....G.... 804 472-9235
Hague *(G-6047)*
Hall White Vineyards ....G.... 434 823-8615
Crozet *(G-3836)*
Hambsch Family Vineyard LLC ....G.... 434 996-1987
Afton *(G-84)*
Hampton Roads Winery LLC ....G.... 757 899-0203
Elberon *(G-4318)*
Harmony Creek Vineyards LLC ....G.... 540 338-7677
Hamilton *(G-6060)*
Hartwood Winery Inc ....G.... 540 752-4893
Fredericksburg *(G-5439)*
Hickory Hill Vineyards LLC ....G.... 540 296-1393
Moneta *(G-8965)*
Hill Top Berry Frm & Winery Lc ....F 434 361-1266
Nellysford *(G-9113)*
Homeplace Vineyard Inc ....G.... 434 432-9463
Chatham *(G-2930)*
Honey Haleys Meadery LLC ....G.... 804 668-5943
Hopewell *(G-6929)*
Hope Crushed Vineyard LLC ....G.... 540 668-6587
Hillsboro *(G-6870)*
Horton Cellars Winery Inc ....F 540 832-7440
Gordonsville *(G-5908)*
Hunters Run Winery LLC ....G.... 703 926-4183
Hamilton *(G-6061)*
Hunting Creek Vineyards Co ....G.... 434 454-9219
Clover *(G-3692)*
Hunts Family Vineyard LLC ....G.... 540 942-8689
Stuarts Draft *(G-13652)*
IL Dolce Winery ....G.... 804 647-0414
Alexandria *(G-234)*
Imperial Revival LLC ....G.... 540 326-8189
Middleburg *(G-8723)*
International Wine Review Hq ....G.... 703 448-5566
Mc Lean *(G-8468)*
◆ **International Wine Spirits Ltd** ....A 804 274-1432
Richmond *(G-11251)*
Iron Heart Winery LLC ....G.... 540 320-0203
Allisonia *(G-618)*
James River Cellars Inc ....G.... 804 550-7516
Glen Allen *(G-5754)*
Jump Mountain Vineyard ....G.... 540 348-6730
Rockbridge Baths *(G-12235)*

Jump Mountain Vineyard LLC ....G....... 434 296-2226
  Charlottesville *(G-2821)*

Kalero Vineyard LLC ....G.......703 216-9036
  Hillsboro *(G-6873)*

Karam Winery ....G.......703 573-3886
  Dunn Loring *(G-4264)*

Keswick Vineyard ....G.......434 295-1834
  Keswick *(G-7049)*

Keswick Vineyards LLC ....F....... 434 244-3341
  Keswick *(G-7050)*

Keswick Winery LLC ....G....... 434 244-3341
  Keswick *(G-7051)*

Kilaurwen Ltd ....G....... 434 985-2535
  Stanardsville *(G-13220)*

Kindred Pointe Stables LLC ....G....... 540 477-3570
  Mount Jackson *(G-9074)*

▲ King Family Vineyards LLC ....G....... 434 823-7800
  Crozet *(G-3840)*

Ko Distilling ....G....... 571 292-1115
  Manassas *(G-7956)*

La ABRA Farm & Winery Inc ....G....... 434 263-5392
  Lovingston *(G-7591)*

Laird & Company ....G....... 434 296-6058
  North Garden *(G-10079)*

Lazy Days Winery ....G....... 804 437-3453
  Midlothian *(G-8845)*

Lee Savoy Inc ....G....... 540 297-9275
  Huddleston *(G-6955)*

Leogrand Vinyards ....G....... 540 586-4066
  Goode *(G-5892)*

Lexington Valley Vineyard ....G....... 540 462-2974
  Rockbridge Baths *(G-12236)*

Lost and Found Winery ....G....... 707 321-6292
  Virginia Beach *(G-14624)*

Lost Creek Vineyard ....F....... 703 443-9836
  Leesburg *(G-7304)*

Lovingston Winery ....G....... 925 286-2824
  Ruckersville *(G-12404)*

Lovington Winery LLC ....G....... 434 263-8467
  Lovingston *(G-7592)*

Madison County Wines LLC ....F....... 540 948-9005
  Madison *(G-7858)*

Maggie Malick Wine Caves LLC ....G....... 540 905-2921
  Hillsboro *(G-6875)*

Marceline Vineyards LLC ....G....... 540 212-9798
  Mount Crawford *(G-9056)*

Martin Lee Enterprises Inc ....G....... 276 623-0125
  Abingdon *(G-49)*

Mediterranean Cellars LLC ....G....... 540 428-1984
  Warrenton *(G-15034)*

Mendes Deli Inc ....G....... 703 242-9463
  Vienna *(G-14090)*

Mermaid Vineyard & Winery LLC ....G....... 757 233-4155
  Norfolk *(G-9639)*

Michael Shaps Winery Managemen ......E....... 434 242-4559
  Charlottesville *(G-2834)*

Mix It Up Mixers and More LLC ....G....... 757 412-1200
  Virginia Beach *(G-14657)*

Molon Lave Vineyards & Winery ....G....... 540 439-5460
  Warrenton *(G-15035)*

Montesquieu Inc ....G....... 703 518-9975
  Alexandria *(G-281)*

Montifalco Vineyard ....G....... 434 989-9115
  Ruckersville *(G-12406)*

Morais Vineyards and Winery ....G....... 540 439-9520
  Bealeton *(G-1601)*

Moss Vineyards LLC ....G....... 434 990-0111
  Dyke *(G-4276)*

Mountain and Vine LLC ....G....... 434 263-6100
  Faber *(G-4390)*

Mountain Run Winery LLC ....G....... 703 638-5559
  Culpeper *(G-3911)*

Mountain View Vineyard ....G....... 540 683-3200
  Strasburg *(G-13591)*

Mountfair Vineyards LLC ....G....... 434 823-7605
  Crozet *(G-3845)*

Mt Chestnut Vineyards LLC ....G....... 540 400-6442
  Roanoke *(G-11971)*

Muse Vineyards LLC ....G....... 540 459-7033
  Woodstock *(G-15858)*

Narmada Winery LLC ....F....... 540 937-8215
  Amissville *(G-720)*

Nectar of Gods Corporation ....G....... 703 582-0856
  Midlothian *(G-8867)*

Nectar of The Gods Corp ....G....... 703 582-0856
  Richmond *(G-11301)*

New River Vineyard & Winery ....G....... 540 392-4870
  Fairlawn *(G-4739)*

Notaviva Vineyards ....G....... 540 668-6756
  Hillsboro *(G-6877)*

Nplainvue LLC ....G....... 434 979-7105
  Charlottesville *(G-2838)*

Oak Crest Vineyard & Winery ....G....... 540 663-2813
  King George *(G-7105)*

Old House Vineyards LLC ....G....... 540 423-1032
  Culpeper *(G-3913)*

Olde Virginia Cidery LLC ....G....... 901 626-0535
  Richmond *(G-11314)*

▲ Pearmund Cellars ....F....... 540 347-3475
  Broad Run *(G-2069)*

Pippin HI Frm & Vineyards LLC ....G....... 434 202-8063
  North Garden *(G-10082)*

Potomac Cellars LLC ....E....... 540 446-2266
  Stafford *(G-13179)*

Potters Craft LLC ....G....... 850 528-6314
  Free Union *(G-5509)*

Preston Rdge Wnery Brewing Inc ....G....... 276 634-8752
  Martinsville *(G-8320)*

▲ PWC Winery LLC ....G....... 703 753-9360
  Haymarket *(G-6438)*

Quartz Creek Vineyards LLC ....G....... 571 239-9120
  Waterford *(G-15082)*

Quattro Goombas Winery ....G....... 703 327-6052
  Aldie *(G-110)*

Rebec Vineyards Inc ....G....... 434 946-5168
  Amherst *(G-707)*

Rewined LLC ....G....... 757 877-3480
  Newport News *(G-9325)*

Rivah Vineyards At Grove LLC ....G....... 804 472-3734
  Kinsale *(G-7137)*

Rockbridge Vineyard Inc ....F....... 540 377-6204
  Raphine *(G-10750)*

Rosa Darby Winery LLC ....G....... 804 561-7492
  Amelia Court House *(G-671)*

Rosemont of Virginia LLC ....G....... 434 636-4372
  La Crosse *(G-7150)*

Rural Rtreat Wnery Vnyards LLC ....G....... 276 686-8300
  Rural Retreat *(G-12431)*

Saga Meadery LLC ....G....... 914 343-0394
  Arlington *(G-1155)*

Sassafras Shade Vineyard LLC ....G....... 804 337-9446
  Ruther Glen *(G-12461)*

Sequoia View Vineyard LLC ....G....... 540 668-6245
  Purcellville *(G-10676)*

Seven Oaks Farm LLC ....G....... 303 653-3299
  Greenwood *(G-6000)*

Shigol Makkoli Winery ....G....... 646 594-7405
  Manassas *(G-8155)*

▲ Silhouette Vineyards LLC ....G....... 540 668-6000
  Hillsboro *(G-6879)*

Silver Hand Winery LLC ....G....... 757 378-2225
  Williamsburg *(G-15311)*

Skippers Creek Vineyard LLC ....G....... 804 598-7291
  Powhatan *(G-10578)*

Slater Run Vineyards LLC ....G....... 540 878-1476
  Upperville *(G-13968)*

Slater Run Vneyards Tasting Rm ....G....... 540 592-3042
  Upperville *(G-13969)*

Spring Run Vineyards LLC ....G....... 804 382-4529
  Chesterfield *(G-3528)*

Ss Winery LLC ....G....... 908 548-3016
  Stafford *(G-13194)*

Stanburn Winery LLC ....G....... 276 694-7074
  Stuart *(G-13631)*

Statice Quo LLC ....G....... 703 646-5411
  Lorton *(G-7534)*

Stillhouse Vineyards LLC ....G....... 434 293-8221
  Hume *(G-6963)*

Stone Mountain Vineyards LLC ....G....... 434 990-9463
  Dyke *(G-4277)*

Stoney Brook Vnyrds Winery LLC ....G....... 703 932-2619
  Troutville *(G-13918)*

Sugarleaf Vineyards ....G....... 434 984-4272
  North Garden *(G-10083)*

Sunset Hills Vineyard LLC ....G....... 540 882-4560
  Purcellville *(G-10681)*

Sweely Estate Winery ....G....... 540 948-7603
  Madison *(G-7863)*

Tarara ....F....... 703 771-7100
  Leesburg *(G-7359)*

▲ Ten Sisters Wine LLC ....G....... 202 577-9774
  Alexandria *(G-595)*

Thibaut-Janisson LLC ....G....... 434 996-3307
  Charlottesville *(G-2889)*

Thistle and Stag Meadery ....G....... 434 842-2200
  Fork Union *(G-5113)*

Thistle Gate Vineyard LLC ....G....... 434 286-2428
  Scottsville *(G-12668)*

Turk Mountain Vineyards ....G....... 540 456-8252
  Afton *(G-93)*

Twin Oaks Tavern Winery ....G....... 540 554-4547
  Bluemont *(G-1892)*

Two Twisted Posts Winery LLC ....G....... 540 668-6587
  Hillsboro *(G-6880)*

Upper Shirley Vineyards ....E....... 804 829-9463
  Charles City *(G-2581)*

Valerie Hill Farm LLC ....G....... 540 869-9567
  Stephens City *(G-13325)*

Valhalla Vineyards ....G....... 540 725-9463
  Roanoke *(G-12016)*

Vanhuss Family Cellars LLC ....G....... 703 737-3930
  Leesburg *(G-7369)*

Vault Field Vineyards LLC ....G....... 804 472-4430
  Kinsale *(G-7138)*

Veramar Vineyard LLC ....G....... 540 955-5510
  Berryville *(G-1699)*

Veritas Works LLC ....F....... 540 456-8000
  Afton *(G-94)*

Vila Pimenta Imports LLC ....G....... 610 533-3278
  Richmond *(G-11437)*

Villa Appalaccia Winery ....G....... 540 593-3100
  Floyd *(G-5045)*

Village Winery ....G....... 540 882-3780
  Waterford *(G-15083)*

Vincents Vineyard Inc ....G....... 276 889-2505
  Lebanon *(G-7210)*

Vineyard Engravers Inc ....G....... 703 941-3700
  Annandale *(G-791)*

Vineyard Services ....G....... 434 964-8270
  Charlottesville *(G-2712)*

Vineyards ....G....... 804 580-4053
  Wicomico Church *(G-15196)*

▲ Vinifera Distributing Virginia ....G....... 804 261-2890
  Springfield *(G-13106)*

Vint Hill Craft Winery LLC ....G....... 540 341-1862
  Broad Run *(G-2071)*

Vintners Cllar Winery Yorktown ....G....... 757 223-4261
  Yorktown *(G-15998)*

Virginia Beach Winery LLC ....G....... 757 995-4315
  Virginia Beach *(G-14915)*

Virginia Mountain Vineyards LL ....G....... 540 473-2979
  Fincastle *(G-4999)*

Virginia Wine Pass LLC ....G....... 540 376-7902
  Fredericksburg *(G-5234)*

▲ Virginia Wineworks LLC ....G....... 434 923-8314
  Charlottesville *(G-2902)*

Welcome To Beaulieu Vineyard ....G....... 707 967-5233
  Arlington *(G-1217)*

Well Hung Vineyard ....G....... 434 245-0182
  Charlottesville *(G-2905)*

West Wind Farm Inc ....G....... 276 699-2020
  Max Meadows *(G-8371)*

Whitebarrel Winery ....G....... 540 382-7619
  Christiansburg *(G-3617)*

Willard Elledge ....G....... 540 984-3375
  Edinburg *(G-4317)*

▲ Williamsburg Winery Ltd ....E....... 757 229-0999
  Williamsburg *(G-15343)*

Willowcroft Farm Vineyards ....G....... 703 777-8161
  Leesburg *(G-7379)*

Windham Winery On Windham Farm ....G....... 540 668-6464
  Hillsboro *(G-6881)*

Winding Road Cellars LLC ....G....... 540 364-1025
  Markham *(G-8248)*

Winebow Inc ....G....... 800 365-9463
  Glen Allen *(G-5829)*

Winebow Group LLC ....G....... 804 752-3670
  Ashland *(G-1512)*

Winery At Bull Run LLC ....G....... 703 815-2233
  Centreville *(G-2353)*

Winery At Kindred Pointe LLC ....G....... 540 481-6016
  Mount Jackson *(G-9083)*

Winery At Lagrange ....G....... 703 753-9360
  Haymarket *(G-6454)*

Winery Inc ....G....... 703 683-1876
  Alexandria *(G-611)*

Wintergreen Winery Ltd ....G....... 434 325-2200
  Nellysford *(G-9114)*

Wisdom Oak Winery ....G....... 434 984-4272
  North Garden *(G-10084)*

Zoll Bros Private Cellars LLC ....F....... 857 498-1665
  Dutton *(G-4275)*

2085 Liquors, Distilled, Rectified & Blended

8 Shires Coloniale Distillery ....G....... 757 378-2456
  Williamsburg *(G-15198)*

Barboursville Distillery LLC ....G....... 757 961-4590
  Virginia Beach *(G-14259)*

Beam Global Spirits and ....G....... 804 763-2823
  Midlothian *(G-8777)*

Belle Isle Craft Spirits Inc................G...... 518 265-7221
Richmond *(G-11503)*

Belmont Farm Distillery....................G...... 540 825-3207
Culpeper *(G-3870)*

Belmont Farms of Virginia Inc.............G...... 540 825-3207
Culpeper *(G-3871)*

Blackbird Spirits LLC.....................G...... 540 247-9115
Winchester *(G-15387)*

Blue Sky Distillery LLC....................G...... 757 746-8342
Smithfield *(G-12705)*

Blue Sky Distillery LLC....................G...... 757 234-3260
Carrollton *(G-2240)*

Bondurant Brothers Dist LLC...............G...... 434 533-3083
Chase City *(G-2910)*

▲ Bowman Distillery Inc A Smith ....F 540 373-4001
Fredericksburg *(G-5255)*

Cape Charles Distillery LLC................F 757 291-8016
Cape Charles *(G-2231)*

Catoctin Creek Custom Rods LLC ....G...... 540 751-1482
Purcellville *(G-10653)*

Catoctin Creek Distlg Co LLC..............G...... 540 751-8404
Purcellville *(G-10654)*

Cavalier Ventures LLC.....................F 757 491-3000
Virginia Beach *(G-14325)*

Chesapeake Bay Distillery LLC ....G...... 757 692-4083
Virginia Beach *(G-14334)*

Copper Fox Dist Entps LLC ....F 540 987-8554
Sperryville *(G-12877)*

Copper Fox Distillery.......................F 757 903-2076
Williamsburg *(G-15222)*

Dead Reckoning Distillery.................G...... 757 535-9864
Norfolk *(G-9519)*

Dead Reckoning Distillery Inc.............G...... 757 620-3182
Chesapeake *(G-3062)*

Deep Creek Distilling Co LLC ....G...... 757 337-0209
Chesapeake *(G-3063)*

Dogged State Distilling Co..................G...... 434 480-0575
Blackstone *(G-1816)*

Dome and Spear Distillery LLC ....G...... 434 851-5477
Evington *(G-4376)*

Falls Church Distillers LLC.................G...... 703 858-9186
Falls Church *(G-4790)*

Falls Church Distillers LLC.................F 703 858-9186
Falls Church *(G-4912)*

Five Mile Mountain Distillery ....G...... 540 588-3158
Floyd *(G-5025)*

Fox River Distilling Company..............G...... 630 402-0027
Glen Allen *(G-5732)*

Hill Top Distillery LLC ....G...... 804 212-8645
Glen Allen *(G-5746)*

Home Brewusa................................G...... 757 459-2739
Norfolk *(G-9582)*

Homeplace Distillery LLC...................G...... 276 957-3310
Ridgeway *(G-11845)*

James River Distillery LLC.................G...... 804 716-5172
Richmond *(G-11627)*

▲ Kdc US Holding Inc........................C...... 434 845-7073
Lynchburg *(G-7750)*

ONeill Distillery LLC Tf.....................G...... 540 822-5812
Lovettsville *(G-7584)*

Pohick Creek LLC.............................G...... 202 888-2034
Springfield *(G-13071)*

Reservoir Distillery LLC ....G...... 804 912-2621
Richmond *(G-11351)*

▲ Silverback Spirits LLC....................G...... 540 456-7070
Afton *(G-89)*

Springfield Distillery LLC ....G...... 434 572-1888
Halifax *(G-6052)*

Squabble State Distlg Co LLC ....G...... 804 393-8380
Bristol *(G-1989)*

▼ Square One Organic Spirits LLC ....G...... 415 612-4151
Charlottesville *(G-2881)*

Stone Mountain Distilling LLC.............G...... 276 970-4081
Lebanon *(G-7208)*

Three Brothers Distillery Inc..............G...... 757 204-1357
Disputanta *(G-4114)*

Three Crosses Distilling Co LL............G...... 804 512-9690
Powhatan *(G-10581)*

Three Crosses Distlg Co LLC ....G...... 804 818-6330
North Chesterfield *(G-10002)*

Tri-Tech Laboratories LLC ....G...... 434 845-7073
Lynchburg *(G-7828)*

Twin Creeks Distillery Inc ....G...... 540 483-1266
Rocky Mount *(G-12356)*

Vanguard Brewpub & Distillery ....G...... 757 224-1807
Hampton *(G-6260)*

Virginia Distillery Co LLC ....G...... 703 869-0083
Arlington *(G-1213)*

▲ Virginia Distillery Co LLC ....G...... 434 285-2900
Lovingston *(G-7593)*

Vitae Spirits Distillery LLC ....G...... 434 242-0350
Charlottesville *(G-2903)*

Whiskywrght Fine Hndcrfted Spr ....G...... 703 831-2086
Waynesboro *(G-15147)*

Whiskywright Fine Handcrafted ....G...... 703 398-0121
Manassas *(G-8011)*

Williamsburg Distillery......................G...... 757 378-2456
Williamsburg *(G-15341)*

Williamsburg Distillery Inc ....G...... 757 676-7950
Gloucester *(G-5869)*

Woods Mill Distillery LLC...................G...... 434 361-2294
Faber *(G-4392)*

2086 Soft Drinks

3300 Artesian Bot Wtr Co LLC ....F 276 928-9903
Bland *(G-1834)*

Bellvue Corp ....G...... 276 806-4418
Portsmouth *(G-10398)*

Bidgood Enterprises.........................G...... 434 489-4952
Danville *(G-3958)*

Black Sphere LLC ....G...... 703 776-0494
Annandale *(G-732)*

Blue Ridge Springs Inc......................F 434 822-0006
Danville *(G-3961)*

Bottling Group LLC..........................F 703 339-5640
Lorton *(G-7468)*

Bottling Group LLC..........................G...... 276 625-2300
Wytheville *(G-15879)*

Bottling Group LLC..........................D...... 434 792-4512
Danville *(G-3962)*

Buffalo Mountain Kombucha LLC ....G...... 540 593-2146
Willis *(G-15357)*

Cadbury Schweppes Bottlin ....G...... 276 228-7990
Wytheville *(G-15881)*

Canada Dry Potomac Corporation ....D...... 757 464-1771
Virginia Beach *(G-14312)*

Canada Dry Potomac Corporation ....E 804 231-7777
Richmond *(G-11517)*

Canada Dry Potomac Corporation ....C...... 703 321-6100
Springfield *(G-12971)*

Ccbcc Operations LLC ....G...... 540 343-8041
Roanoke *(G-12060)*

▲ Central Carolina Btlg Co Inc ....F 434 753-2515
Alton *(G-646)*

Change Cola Inc..............................G...... 703 674-9830
Roanoke *(G-12063)*

Coca Cola Enterprises.......................F 703 578-6447
Alexandria *(G-166)*

Coca-Cola Bottling ....G...... 800 241-2653
Alexandria *(G-167)*

Coca-Cola Consolidated Inc...............D...... 540 886-2494
Staunton *(G-13248)*

Coca-Cola Consolidated Inc...............D...... 540 361-7500
Fredericksburg *(G-5413)*

Coca-Cola Consolidated Inc...............D...... 757 890-8700
Norfolk *(G-9489)*

Coca-Cola Consolidated Inc...............E 703 578-6759
Alexandria *(G-168)*

Coca-Cola Consolidated Inc...............D...... 804 328-5300
Richmond *(G-11160)*

Coca-Cola Consolidated Inc...............C...... 757 446-3000
Norfolk *(G-9490)*

Conscious Cultures LLC ....F 434 227-9297
Afton *(G-78)*

Crunchy Hydration LLC......................G...... 757 362-1607
Virginia Beach *(G-14375)*

Delicious Beverage LLC......................G...... 703 517-0216
Herndon *(G-6654)*

Di Cola Llc Ciro Schiano ....G...... 703 779-0212
Leesburg *(G-7257)*

Dr Pepper Bottlers Lynchburg ....G...... 434 528-5107
Lynchburg *(G-7697)*

Eerkins Inc....................................G...... 703 626-6248
Luray *(G-7608)*

Enviro Water..................................G...... 703 569-0971
Springfield *(G-12999)*

Flow Beverages Inc ....E 613 680-3569
Verona *(G-13987)*

Frito-Lay North America Inc................E 540 380-3020
Salem *(G-12508)*

Halmor Corp ....E 540 248-0095
Staunton *(G-13263)*

Halmor Corp ....G...... 434 295-3177
Charlottesville *(G-2643)*

Iq Energy LLC ....G...... 804 747-8900
Glen Allen *(G-5752)*

Ja-Zan LLC ....G...... 434 978-2140
Charlottesville *(G-2651)*

Kraft Heinz Foods Company ....B...... 540 678-0442
Winchester *(G-15437)*

Living Maka LLC ....G...... 888 690-7058
Arlington *(G-1040)*

Lonesome Pine Beverage Company ......G...... 276 679-2332
Norton *(G-10124)*

Maryland and Virginia Milk PR............C...... 757 245-3857
Newport News *(G-9292)*

Misty Mtn Spring Wtr Co LLC ....E 276 623-5000
Abingdon *(G-50)*

Mj Distribution ....G...... 540 692-0062
Front Royal *(G-5544)*

Mkp Products LLC ....G...... 703 345-0595
Springfield *(G-13052)*

Mojo Fruit Drinks LLC ....G...... 571 278-0755
Alexandria *(G-279)*

Niagara Bottling LLC........................F 804 551-3923
Chester *(G-3440)*

Ninja Kombucha LLC ....G...... 757 870-6733
Richmond *(G-11691)*

P-Americas LLC ....D...... 540 347-3112
Warrenton *(G-15041)*

Pepsi Beverages Company ....G...... 757 857-1251
Norfolk *(G-9683)*

Pepsi Bottling Group ....G...... 540 344-8355
Roanoke *(G-12146)*

Pepsi Co..F 276 625-3900
Wytheville *(G-15903)*

Pepsi Cola Btlg Inc Norton VA ....D...... 276 679-1122
Norton *(G-10134)*

Pepsi Cola Btlg Inc Norton VA ....E 276 963-6606
Cedar Bluff *(G-2283)*

Pepsi-Cola Btlg Co Centl VA ....C...... 434 978-2140
Charlottesville *(G-2674)*

Pepsi-Cola Btlg Co Centl VA ....D...... 434 978-2140
Charlottesville *(G-2675)*

Pepsi-Cola Btlg Co Centl VA ....E 540 234-9238
Weyers Cave *(G-15175)*

Pepsi-Cola General Bottlers ....G...... 276 783-7232
Marion *(G-8239)*

Pepsi-Cola Metro Btlg Co Inc ....C...... 757 857-1251
Norfolk *(G-9684)*

Pepsi-Cola Metro Btlg Co Inc ....D...... 540 361-4467
Fredericksburg *(G-5344)*

Pepsi-Cola Metro Btlg Co Inc ....G...... 434 528-5107
Lynchburg *(G-7785)*

Pepsi-Cola Metro Btlg Co Inc ....C...... 757 887-2310
Newport News *(G-9311)*

Pepsi-Cola Metro Btlg Co Inc ....C...... 540 966-5200
Roanoke *(G-11984)*

Pepsi-Cola Metro Btlg Co Inc ....D...... 434 792-4512
Danville *(G-4024)*

Pepsico Inc ....G...... 276 781-2177
Marion *(G-8240)*

Pepsico Inc ....G...... 804 714-1382
Richmond *(G-11056)*

Pure Paradise Water of Vb ....G...... 757 318-0522
Virginia Beach *(G-14749)*

R C Cola Bottling Company Del ....D...... 540 667-1821
Winchester *(G-15577)*

Royal Crown Bottling Company ....F 540 667-1821
Winchester *(G-15580)*

Royal Crown Btlg Wnchester Inc ....D...... 540 667-1821
Winchester *(G-15581)*

Shenandoah Corporation ....E 540 248-2123
Staunton *(G-13292)*

Tincture Distillers LLC.......................G...... 443 370-2037
Arlington *(G-1192)*

Trinitee Group LLC............................G...... 757 268-9694
Richmond *(G-11420)*

Tru-Ade Company ....G...... 540 662-5484
Clear Brook *(G-3653)*

Winmar Business Group ....G...... 913 908-7413
Gainesville *(G-5622)*

2087 Flavoring Extracts & Syrups

Chef Sous LLC ....G...... 804 938-5477
Glen Allen *(G-5712)*

Gamay Flavors ....G...... 703 751-7430
Alexandria *(G-212)*

Mafco Consolidated Group Inc.............F 804 222-1600
Richmond *(G-11281)*

Sauer Brands Inc ....G...... 804 359-5786
Richmond *(G-11753)*

Southern Flavoring Company Inc ....F 540 586-8565
Bedford *(G-1659)*

2091 Fish & Seafoods, Canned & Cured

Ashton Green Seafood.......................G...... 757 887-3551
Newport News *(G-9172)*

▲ Asian Pacific Seafood LLC..............G...... 251 751-5962
Chesapeake *(G-2984)*

▲ **Bevans Oyster Company** ....D 804 472-2331
Kinsale (G-7133)

Bevans Oyster Company ....G 804 472-2331
Kinsale (G-7134)

Bg Smith & Son Oyster Co ....G 804 394-2721
Farnham (G-4962)

Big Island Oysters ....G 804 389-9589
Hayes (G-6396)

◆ **Chesapeake Bay Packing LLC** ....E 757 244-8440
Newport News (G-9199)

Dockside Seafood ....G 757 357-9298
Battery Park (G-1595)

Eastern Shore Seafood Co Inc ....E 757 787-7539
Onancock (G-10196)

Eastern Shore Seafood Pdts LLC ....G 757 854-4422
Mappsville (G-8218)

Graham and Rollins Inc ....E 757 755-1021
Hampton (G-6160)

Lake Packing Co Inc ....F 804 529-6101
Lottsburg (G-7543)

Ship Point Oyster Company ....G 757 848-3557
Poquoson (G-10376)

Smith & Sons Oyster Co Inc B G ....F 804 394-2721
Sharps (G-12685)

Virginia Seafoods LLC ....F 301 520-8200
White Stone (G-15190)

W Ellery Kellum Inc ....E 804 438-5476
Weems (G-15151)

2092 Fish & Seafoods, Fresh & Frozen

Abbott Brothers Inc ....G 804 436-1001
White Stone (G-15185)

Ailan Trading Inc USA ....G 757 812-7258
Yorktown (G-15931)

Ashton Green Seafood ....G 757 887-3551
Newport News (G-9172)

Bernies Conchs ....G 757 331-3861
Cheriton (G-2946)

Bevans Oyster Company ....G 804 472-2331
Kinsale (G-7134)

▲ **Bevans Oyster Company** ....D 804 472-2331
Kinsale (G-7133)

Captain Faunce Seafood Inc ....E 804 493-8690
Montross (G-9025)

Chesapeake Bay Packing LLC ....E 757 244-8400
Newport News (G-9198)

◆ **Chesapeake Bay Packing LLC** ....E 757 244-8440
Newport News (G-9199)

E J Conrad & Sons Seafood Inc ....E 804 462-7400
Lancaster (G-7160)

Eastern Shore Seafood Co Inc ....E 757 787-7539
Onancock (G-10196)

Eastern Shore Seafood Pdts LLC ....G 757 854-4422
Mappsville (G-8218)

▼ **J H Miles Co Inc** ....E 757 622-9264
Norfolk (G-9598)

Lineage Logistics ....G 804 421-6603
Richmond (G-11657)

Moss Cape LLC ....G 703 234-3890
Chantilly (G-2465)

Ocean Foods Inc ....G 757 474-6314
Virginia Beach (G-14692)

Old Point Packing Inc ....F 757 247-0557
Newport News (G-9308)

Shortys Breading Company LLC ....G 434 390-1772
Rice (G-11006)

Tidewater Foods Inc ....G 757 410-2498
Norfolk (G-9752)

W Ellery Kellum Inc ....E 804 438-5476
Weems (G-15151)

2095 Coffee

Brass Bullet Coffee Co VA LLC ....F 540 373-2432
Fredericksburg (G-5405)

Brian K Babcock ....G 540 251-3003
Riner (G-11861)

Cafes D Afrique LLC ....G 757 725-1050
Hampton (G-6103)

Eastern Shore Cstl Rsting Escr ....G 757 414-0105
Cape Charles (G-2233)

Hills Bros Coffee Incorporated ....G 757 538-8083
Suffolk (G-13721)

Imani M X-Ortiz ....G 540 582-5898
Partlow (G-10266)

J L V Management Inc ....G 540 446-6359
Stafford (G-13158)

Jddr Foods Inc ....G 571 356-0165
Reston (G-10880)

Johnson & Elich Roasters Ltd ....F 540 552-7442
Blacksburg (G-1747)

Kustomcoffee ....G 571 344-9030
Fairfax (G-4644)

Lava Instant Coffee LLC ....G 703 239-0803
Gainesville (G-5595)

Lion Mountain Farms LLC ....G 916 850-9232
Arlington (G-1037)

Loco Beans — Fresh Roasted ....G 703 851-5997
Leesburg (G-7303)

Massimo Zanetti Bev USA Inc ....G 757 215-7409
Portsmouth (G-10458)

◆ **Massimo Zanetti Bev USA Inc** ....C 757 215-7300
Suffolk (G-13740)

Massimo Zanetti Bev USA Inc ....G 757 538-8083
Suffolk (G-13741)

Mova Corp ....G 757 598-5577
Virginia Beach (G-14666)

Nova Roast ....G 540 239-2459
Salem (G-12546)

◆ **Old Mansion Inc** ....E 804 862-9889
Petersburg (G-10331)

Pale Horse LLC ....F 757 576-0656
Chesapeake (G-3232)

Ricks Roasters Coffee Co LLC ....G 540 318-6850
Fredericksburg (G-5479)

Roasted Bean Coffee & Repair ....G 434 242-8522
Waynesboro (G-15137)

Six Pcks Artsan Rasted Cof LLC ....G 757 337-0872
Chesapeake (G-3294)

Virginia Coffee Company LLC ....G 703 566-3037
Alexandria (G-376)

Whinks Coffee Roasters ....G 571 330-6630
Alexandria (G-609)

2096 Potato Chips & Similar Prdts

Frito-Lay North America Inc ....E 540 434-2426
Harrisonburg (G-6318)

Frito-Lay North America Inc ....E 540 380-3020
Salem (G-12508)

▲ **Jhl Inc** ....G 703 378-0009
Chantilly (G-2449)

Kitch N Cook D Potato Chip Co ....F 540 886-4473
Staunton (G-13273)

On It Smart Snacks ....G 757 705-9259
Virginia Beach (G-14696)

Shearers Foods LLC ....G 276 669-6194
Bristol (G-1986)

▼ **Small Fry Inc** ....E 540 477-9664
Mount Jackson (G-9078)

◆ **Snack Alliance Inc** ....C 276 669-6194
Bristol (G-1987)

Sweet T&C Kettle Corn LLC ....G 804 840-0551
Chester (G-3458)

Tabard Corporation ....E 540 477-9664
Mount Jackson (G-9081)

Utz Quality Foods LLC ....G 540 535-1927
Winchester (G-15498)

Utz Quality Foods LLC ....G 757 249-0568
Newport News (G-9370)

Utz Quality Foods LLC ....E 804 232-0241
Richmond (G-11802)

Utz Quality Foods LLC ....E 540 981-0351
Vinton (G-14188)

2097 Ice

Brunswick Ice and Coal Co Inc ....E 434 848-2615
Lawrenceville (G-7178)

Cassco Corporation ....G 540 433-2751
Harrisonburg (G-6299)

Custer Ice Service Inc ....G 434 656-2854
Gretna (G-6007)

Hale Manu Inc ....G 434 973-5850
Crozet (G-3835)

Holiday Ice Inc ....E 757 934-1294
Suffolk (G-13722)

Hometown Ice Co ....G 540 483-7865
Rocky Mount (G-12327)

Manassas Ice & Fuel Co Inc ....G 703 368-3121
Manassas (G-7972)

Polar Bear Ice Inc ....G 276 259-7873
Whitewood (G-15192)

Reddy Ice Corporation ....E 757 855-6065
Norfolk (G-9704)

Reddy Ice Corporation ....G 540 433-2751
Harrisonburg (G-6361)

Reddy Ice Group Inc ....E 540 777-0253
Roanoke (G-12161)

V C Ice and Cold Storage Inc ....G 434 793-1441
Danville (G-4045)

Valley Ice LLC ....F 540 477-4447
Mount Jackson (G-9082)

2098 Macaroni, Spaghetti & Noodles

Bangkok Noodle ....G 703 866-1396
Springfield (G-12958)

Capital Noodle Inc ....F 703 569-3224
Springfield (G-12973)

Fiber Foods Inc ....G 757 853-2888
Norfolk (G-9552)

Hershey Company ....C 540 722-9830
Winchester (G-15423)

Marco and Luca Noodle Str Inc ....G 434 295-3855
Charlottesville (G-2832)

◆ **Maruchan Virginia Inc** ....C 804 275-2800
North Chesterfield (G-9924)

Mr Noodle & Rice ....G 540 662-4213
Winchester (G-15559)

Nestle Prepared Foods Company ....D 434 822-4000
Danville (G-4017)

Noodle Games ....G 757 572-3849
Chesapeake (G-3220)

Pho Ha Vietnamese Noodle ....G 540 438-0999
Harrisonburg (G-6354)

2099 Food Preparations, NEC

A Touch of Elegance LLC ....G 434 634-4592
Emporia (G-4353)

Adopt A Salsa ....G 703 409-9453
Centreville (G-2288)

Ah Love Oil & Vinegar ....G 703 992-7000
Fairfax (G-4402)

Ah Love Oil and Vinegar LLC ....G 703 966-0668
Alexandria (G-123)

Aileen L Brown ....G 757 696-1814
Hampton (G-6079)

Amama Ltd ....G 703 759-9030
Great Falls (G-5935)

◆ **Andros Bowman Products LLC** ....D 540 217-4100
Mount Jackson (G-9064)

Anm Food Services Inc ....G 703 865-4378
Fairfax (G-4592)

Apothecary Spices ....G 703 868-2333
Alexandria (G-138)

◆ **Asmars Mediterranean Food Inc** ....F 703 750-2960
Alexandria (G-418)

Azars Natural Foods Inc ....E 757 486-7778
Virginia Beach (G-14252)

◆ **Barakat Foods Inc** ....F 703 222-9493
Chantilly (G-2374)

Battarbees Catering ....G 540 249-9205
Grottoes (G-6015)

Bent Mt Salsa ....G 803 427-3170
Bent Mountain (G-1667)

Big Fish Cider Co ....G 540 468-2322
Monterey (G-9003)

Big Lick Seasonings LLC ....G 540 774-8898
Roanoke (G-11890)

Bon Vivant Company LLC ....G 703 862-5038
Alexandria (G-151)

Bonumose Biochem LLC ....G 276 206-7337
Charlottesville (G-2598)

Bonumose LLC ....G 276 206-7337
Charlottesville (G-2599)

Boston Spice & Tea Co Inc ....G 540 547-3907
Boston (G-1902)

▲ **Buckit O Rice** ....G 703 897-4190
Woodbridge (G-15662)

Buskey Cider ....G 901 626-0535
Richmond (G-11141)

Bzk Ballston LLC ....F 703 248-0990
Arlington (G-895)

Cake Ballin LLC ....G 540 820-2938
Grottoes (G-6017)

Cargill Turkey Production LLC ....F 540 568-1400
Harrisonburg (G-6298)

Cathay Food Corp ....E 617 427-1507
Fredericksburg (G-5408)

Ceylon Cinnamon Growers LLC ....G 703 626-1764
Vienna (G-14025)

Chefit LLC ....G 202 769-6049
Lorton (G-7471)

Chew On This Gluten Free Foods ....G 757 440-3757
Virginia Beach (G-14336)

Choice Tack ....G 804 314-0787
Goochland (G-5881)

Christian Potier USA Inc ....G 330 815-2202
Lake Frederick (G-7155)

Church & Dwight Co Inc ....E 804 524-8000
South Chesterfield (G-12799)

CNJ Beekeepers Inc ....G 703 378-1629
Chantilly (G-2395)

S I C

Cuisine Solutions Inc ... G ... 303 904-4771
Alexandria *(G-436)*

Damas International LLC ... G ... 469 740-9973
Annandale *(G-739)*

Dees Nuts Peanut Butter ... G ... 607 437-0189
Virginia Beach *(G-14397)*

Deli-Fresh Foods Inc ... E ... 757 428-8126
Virginia Beach *(G-14399)*

Della JS Delectables LLC ... G ... 703 922-4687
Alexandria *(G-444)*

Detas Famous Potatoe Salad LLC ... G ... 757 609-1130
Virginia Beach *(G-14402)*

Dizzy Pig LLC ... G ... 571 379-4884
Manassas *(G-8059)*

Do-Da Innovations LLC ... G ... 804 556-6645
Maidens *(G-7890)*

Dr Ozz Dat Drip Bbq Sauce LLC ... G ... 757 597-4405
Hampton *(G-6133)*

Echo Hill Farm ... G ... 802 586-2239
Arlington *(G-952)*

Evenflow Technologies Inc ... G ... 703 625-2628
Ashburn *(G-1277)*

Everything Under Sun LLC ... G ... 276 252-2376
Ridgeway *(G-11842)*

◆ Famarco Newco LLC ... E ... 757 460-3573
Virginia Beach *(G-14459)*

Farmkart Foods LLC ... G ... 706 461-6395
Alexandria *(G-204)*

Festive Foods ... G ... 757 490-9186
Virginia Beach *(G-14461)*

Fiber Foods Inc ... G ... 757 853-2888
Norfolk *(G-9552)*

Flynns Foods Inc ... G ... 804 779-3205
Mechanicsville *(G-8624)*

Four Seasons Catering & Bakery ... G ... 276 686-5982
Rural Retreat *(G-12424)*

Fouz Inc ... G ... 571 407-4446
Woodbridge *(G-15706)*

Fresh Twist Foods LLC ... G ... 540 904-1291
Christiansburg *(G-3589)*

Frito-Lay North America Inc ... E ... 540 434-2426
Harrisonburg *(G-6318)*

Full Fat Kitchen LLC ... G ... 844 262-6629
Christiansburg *(G-3590)*

Gigis ... G ... 276 608-5737
Abingdon *(G-33)*

Glandore Spice ... G ... 434 589-2492
Troy *(G-13925)*

Health E-Lunch Kids Inc ... G ... 703 402-9064
Falls Church *(G-4804)*

Herbspice LLC ... G ... 240 602-6525
Goochland *(G-5885)*

Honey Gunters ... G ... 540 955-1734
Berryville *(G-1682)*

Hormel Foods Corporation ... G ... 757 467-5396
Virginia Beach *(G-14529)*

J & V Kitchen Inc ... G ... 540 291-2794
Natural Bridge *(G-9107)*

Jacked Up Foods LLC ... G ... 540 623-6313
Fredericksburg *(G-5305)*

▲ Jhl Inc ... G ... 703 378-0009
Chantilly *(G-2449)*

Jjojay LLC ... G ... 240 660-6146
Lovettsville *(G-7580)*

Kashaf Spices ... G ... 571 572-5890
Dumfries *(G-4248)*

Kashaf Spices Inc ... G ... 703 232-3529
Lorton *(G-7501)*

Key To Heart Seasoning LLC ... G ... 757 752-7581
Virginia Beach *(G-14583)*

Kraft Heinz Foods Company ... B ... 540 678-0442
Winchester *(G-15437)*

Kung Fu Tea ... E ... 703 992-8599
Annandale *(G-767)*

L and M Foods ... G ... 276 979-4110
Tazewell *(G-13833)*

Litehouse Inc ... C ... 434 688-3100
Danville *(G-4014)*

Londoo Foods LLC ... G ... 571 243-7627
Woodbridge *(G-15741)*

Lone Wolf Salsa ... G ... 571 445-3499
Gainesville *(G-5597)*

Mafco Consolidated Group Inc ... F ... 804 222-1600
Richmond *(G-11281)*

Marketfare Foods LLC ... C ... 540 371-5110
Fredericksburg *(G-5454)*

Martha Bennett ... G ... 757 897-6150
Yorktown *(G-15979)*

◆ Maruchan Virginia Inc ... C ... 804 275-2800
North Chesterfield *(G-9924)*

▼ Maxx Performance Inc ... F ... 845 987-9432
Roanoke *(G-11960)*

McCormick & Company Inc ... G ... 540 858-2878
Gore *(G-5922)*

McKee Foods Corporation ... A ... 540 943-7101
Stuarts Draft *(G-13655)*

Mezeh - Fair Oaks LLC ... F ... 703 310-9209
Fairfax *(G-4508)*

Mezeh-Reston LLC ... F ... 703 310-9209
Reston *(G-10900)*

Michaels Catering ... G ... 804 815-6985
Hayes *(G-6401)*

Mielata LLC ... G ... 804 245-1227
Midlothian *(G-8860)*

Mighty Meals LLC ... G ... 703 303-1438
Burke *(G-2194)*

Mike Puffendarger ... G ... 540 468-2682
Warm Springs *(G-14973)*

Ms Jos Petite Sweets LLC ... G ... 571 327-9431
Alexandria *(G-286)*

Murray Cider Co Inc ... G ... 540 977-9000
Roanoke *(G-11973)*

Nomad Deli & Catering Co LLC ... G ... 804 677-0843
Richmond *(G-11693)*

Northern Pttsylvnia Cnty Fd CT ... G ... 434 656-6617
Chatham *(G-2932)*

Nutriati Inc ... F ... 804 562-2322
Henrico *(G-6545)*

◆ Old Mansion Inc ... E ... 804 862-9889
Petersburg *(G-10331)*

Olive Savor ... G ... 757 425-3866
Virginia Beach *(G-14693)*

Pasta By Valente Inc ... G ... 434 971-3717
Charlottesville *(G-2841)*

Pb Crave of Nc LLC ... G ... 252 585-1744
Franklin *(G-5153)*

Pops Snacks LLC ... G ... 804 594-7290
North Chesterfield *(G-9950)*

Press Oil & Vinegar LLC ... G ... 434 534-2915
Lynchburg *(G-7787)*

▼ Producers Peanut Company Inc ... F ... 757 539-7496
Suffolk *(G-13753)*

Pruitt Partners LLC ... G ... 703 299-0114
Alexandria *(G-320)*

Quaker Oats Co ... G ... 276 625-3923
Wytheville *(G-15906)*

Quarles Food Stop ... G ... 540 635-1899
Linden *(G-7432)*

Reginalds Homemade LLC ... G ... 804 972-4040
Henrico *(G-6557)*

Reignforest Spices & Tea LLC ... G ... 757 716-5205
Norfolk *(G-9706)*

River City Cider LLC ... G ... 804 420-9683
Roseland *(G-12372)*

Riveras Tortillas ... G ... 703 368-1249
Manassas *(G-8145)*

Riviana Foods Inc ... D ... 540 722-9830
Winchester *(G-15466)*

RJR Provisions & Packaging LLC ... G ... 804 649-7400
Richmond *(G-11743)*

Rocco Specialty Foods Inc ... F ... 540 432-1060
Harrisonburg *(G-6362)*

Rochon & Rochon LLC A Fmly Co ... G ... 571 331-4860
Dumfries *(G-4255)*

Rva Sweets LLC ... G ... 540 748-9298
Henrico *(G-6562)*

S & K Industries Inc ... E ... 703 369-0232
Manassas Park *(G-8209)*

Sabra Dipping Company LLC ... E ... 804 518-2000
South Chesterfield *(G-12826)*

Sabra Dipping Company LLC ... F ... 804 526-5930
Colonial Heights *(G-3745)*

Sabra Go Mediterranean ... G ... 804 518-2000
South Chesterfield *(G-12827)*

Salsa De Los Flores Inc ... G ... 757 450-0796
Chesapeake *(G-3282)*

Salsa Picante Bori ... G ... 256 874-4074
Newport News *(G-9330)*

Salsa Room ... G ... 571 489-8422
Mc Lean *(G-8543)*

Sauer Brands Inc ... G ... 804 359-5786
Richmond *(G-11753)*

Shenandoah Valley Orchard Co ... E ... 540 337-2837
Stuarts Draft *(G-13660)*

Signature Seasonings LLc ... G ... 757 572-8995
Virginia Beach *(G-14815)*

SNC Foods Inc ... G ... 804 726-9907
Glen Allen *(G-5800)*

Spicy Vinegar LLC ... G ... 757 460-3861
Virginia Beach *(G-14839)*

Ssr Foods LLC ... G ... 703 581-7260
Gainesville *(G-5615)*

Stafford Salad Company LLC ... G ... 540 269-2462
Keezletown *(G-7030)*

Sugar Tree Country Store ... G ... 540 396-3469
Mc Dowell *(G-8376)*

Sweetie Pie Desserts ... G ... 804 239-6425
Richmond *(G-11779)*

Taste Oil Vinegar Spice Inc ... G ... 540 825-8415
Culpeper *(G-3923)*

Tincture Distillers LLC ... G ... 443 370-2037
Arlington *(G-1192)*

Tips East LLC ... D ... 757 562-7888
Franklin *(G-5159)*

Tommy V Foods ... G ... 703 254-8764
Falls Church *(G-4884)*

Tortilleria Guavalueana ... G ... 804 233-4141
Richmond *(G-11790)*

Tortilleria San Luis LLC ... G ... 804 901-1501
Richmond *(G-11415)*

Tossd Salad Group LLC ... G ... 703 521-0646
Arlington *(G-1193)*

True Southern Smoke Bbq LLC ... G ... 757 816-0228
Chesapeake *(G-3352)*

VA Foods LLC ... G ... 434 221-1456
Lynch Station *(G-7629)*

Vinegar Hill Acres ... G ... 540 337-6839
Churchville *(G-3622)*

Vita Specialty Foods Inc ... G ... 540 542-0195
Winchester *(G-15504)*

W W Distributors ... G ... 804 301-2308
Richmond *(G-11442)*

Westover Dairy ... G ... 434 528-2560
Lynchburg *(G-7838)*

White Wave ... G ... 540 434-5945
Bridgewater *(G-1960)*

21 TOBACCO PRODUCTS

2111 Cigarettes

Altria Client Services LLC ... F ... 804 274-2000
Richmond *(G-11101)*

Altria Client Services LLC ... G ... 804 274-2000
Richmond *(G-11023)*

Altria Enterprises II LLC ... D ... 804 274-2200
Richmond *(G-11102)*

Altria Group Inc ... F ... 804 274-2000
Richmond *(G-11103)*

Altria Group Inc ... G ... 804 274-2000
Richmond *(G-11104)*

Altria Group Inc ... F ... 804 335-2703
Richmond *(G-11024)*

Altria Group Inc ... A ... 804 274-2200
Richmond *(G-11105)*

Altria Ventures Inc ... G ... 804 274-2000
Richmond *(G-11106)*

Firebird Manufacturing LLC ... G ... 434 517-0865
South Boston *(G-12767)*

Golden Leaf Tobacco Company ... G ... 434 736-2130
Keysville *(G-7057)*

Itg Brands ... G ... 434 792-0521
Danville *(G-4004)*

▲ Philip Morris Duty Free Inc ... D ... 804 274-2000
Richmond *(G-11322)*

◆ Philip Morris USA Inc ... A ... 804 274-2000
Richmond *(G-11323)*

Philip Morris USA Inc ... D ... 804 274-2000
Richmond *(G-11714)*

Philip Morris USA Inc ... E ... 804 274-2000
Richmond *(G-11058)*

Philip Morris USA Inc ... C ... 804 253-8464
North Chesterfield *(G-9949)*

R J Reynolds Tobacco Company ... F ... 757 420-1280
Virginia Beach *(G-14755)*

Richmond Distributors LLC ... G ... 804 497-0713
Richmond *(G-11354)*

2121 Cigars

Altria Client Services LLC ... F ... 804 274-2000
Richmond *(G-11101)*

Civille Smoke Shop ... G ... 434 975-1175
Charlottesville *(G-2766)*

General Cigar Co Inc ... E ... 757 825-7750
Hampton *(G-6157)*

General Cigar Co Inc ... G ... 804 935-2800
Richmond *(G-11599)*

▼ General Cigar Co Inc ... A ... 860 602-3500
Glen Allen *(G-5735)*

Helix Innovations LLC ... G ... 804 274-2000
Richmond *(G-11235)*

Itg Cigars Inc ....E...... 804 233-7668
Richmond *(G-11622)*
◆ John Middleton Co ....G...... 610 792-8000
Richmond *(G-11047)*

2131 Tobacco, Chewing & Snuff

Blakbunni ....G...... 347 239-5139
Mechanicsville *(G-8607)*
◆ John Middleton Co ....G...... 610 792-8000
Richmond *(G-11047)*
◆ Jti Leaf Services (us) LLC ....F...... 434 799-3286
Danville *(G-4007)*
Klds Client Services LLC ....G...... 804 586-7538
Midlothian *(G-8840)*
Philip Morris USA Inc ....A...... 804 274-2000
Chester *(G-3443)*
▲ Swedish Match North Amer LLC ......B...... 804 787-5100
Richmond *(G-11776)*
U S Smokeless Tob Brands Inc ......G...... 804 274-2000
Richmond *(G-11425)*
▼ US Smokeless Tobacco Company ..E...... 804 274-2000
Richmond *(G-11430)*
Virginia Custom Blend LLC ....G...... 804 994-5099
Aylett *(G-1556)*

2141 Tobacco Stemming & Redrying

◆ Danville Leaf Tobacco Co Inc ....C...... 804 359-9311
Richmond *(G-11039)*
Park 500 ....G...... 804 751-2000
Chester *(G-3442)*
◆ Philip Morris USA Inc ....A...... 804 274-2000
Richmond *(G-11323)*
Philip Morris USA Inc ....A...... 804 274-2000
Chester *(G-3443)*
Tobacco Processors Inc ....G...... 804 359-9311
Richmond *(G-11413)*
◆ Universal Leaf Tobacco Co Inc ....D...... 804 359-9311
Richmond *(G-11066)*

22 TEXTILE MILL PRODUCTS

2211 Cotton, Woven Fabric

30+ Denim/Leather Project ....G...... 301 233-0968
Alexandria *(G-395)*
A Toast To Canvas ....G...... 804 363-4395
North Chesterfield *(G-9804)*
Affordable Canvas Virginia LLC ......G...... 757 718-5330
Virginia Beach *(G-14216)*
America Furniture LLC ....G...... 703 939-3678
Manassas *(G-8026)*
American Merchant Inc ....G...... 407 446-9872
Bristol *(G-1966)*
Ankh & Lotus LLC ....G...... 313 333-5138
Petersburg *(G-10304)*
Avian Fashions ....G...... 540 288-0200
Stafford *(G-13121)*
B & C Custom Canvas ....G...... 757 870-0089
Hampton *(G-6087)*
Bleeding Canvas ....G...... 276 623-2345
Glade Spring *(G-5674)*
Canvas Asl LLC ....G...... 804 269-0851
Richmond *(G-11519)*
Canvas Docktors LLC ....G...... 757 759-7108
Hayes *(G-6398)*
Canvas Earth LLC ....G...... 540 522-9373
Culpeper *(G-3878)*
Canvas Innovations Inc ....G...... 757 218-7271
Williamsburg *(G-15217)*
Canvas LLC ....G...... 703 237-6491
Arlington *(G-899)*
Canvas Salon LLC ....G...... 804 926-5518
Richmond *(G-11520)*
Canvas Solutions Inc ....G...... 703 564-8564
Reston *(G-10817)*
Captn Joeys Custom Canvas ....G...... 757 270-8772
Virginia Beach *(G-14319)*
Cold Company LLC ....G...... 757 589-7034
Norfolk *(G-9491)*
▲ Cozy Cloths ....G...... 703 759-2420
Great Falls *(G-5951)*
Custom Canvas Works Inc ....G...... 571 249-6443
Alexandria *(G-437)*
Custom Marine Canvas ....G...... 540 775-6699
King George *(G-7085)*
Cyber-Canvas ....G...... 540 692-9322
Fredericksburg *(G-5418)*
Denim ....G...... 804 918-2361
Richmond *(G-11181)*

Denim Stax Inc ....G...... 434 429-6663
Danville *(G-3981)*
Denim Twist Inc ....G...... 703 273-3009
Fairfax *(G-4612)*
Digital Canvas LLC ....G...... 703 819-3543
Falls Church *(G-4783)*
Dirty Deeds Power Washing ....G...... 804 731-2739
Prince George *(G-10592)*
Docks Canvas & Upholstery ....G...... 540 840-0440
Fredericksburg *(G-5420)*
Fun With Canvas ....G...... 724 689-5821
Manassas *(G-8071)*
Fun With Canvas ....G...... 540 272-2436
Midland *(G-8756)*
Gingham & Grosgrain LLC ....G...... 202 674-2024
Alexandria *(G-216)*
▲ Global Safety Textiles LLC ....D...... 434 447-7629
South Hill *(G-12851)*
Griffin Tapestry Studio ....G...... 434 979-4402
Charlottesville *(G-2641)*
Hampton Roads Canvas Co LLC ......G...... 757 560-3170
Virginia Beach *(G-14498)*
Haverdash ....G...... 804 371-1107
Richmond *(G-11608)*
Herb Dodge Enterprises ....G...... 757 714-4313
Chesapeake *(G-3132)*
Heytex USA Inc ....E...... 540 674-9576
Dublin *(G-4157)*
Hybernations LLC ....G...... 804 744-3580
Midlothian *(G-8831)*
Im Apparel LLC ....G...... 202 905-5696
Woodbridge *(G-15725)*
Imperial Cleaners ....G...... 757 531-1125
Norfolk *(G-9591)*
Integrity Shirts LLC ....G...... 540 577-5544
Blacksburg *(G-1746)*
J&S Marine Canvas LLC ....G...... 757 580-6883
Chesapeake *(G-3147)*
Jean Lee Inc ....G...... 703 630-0276
Quantico *(G-10689)*
Jl Kelley American Apparel LLC ....G...... 434 664-5243
Appomattox *(G-815)*
John S Montgomery ....G...... 757 816-8724
Chesapeake *(G-3152)*
Mach278 LLC ....G...... 716 860-2889
Ashburn *(G-1313)*
Mikes Mobile Canvas ....G...... 804 815-2733
Gloucester *(G-5854)*
Mng Online LLC ....G...... 571 247-8276
Manassas *(G-8109)*
Shockoe Denim ....G...... 804 269-0851
Richmond *(G-11759)*
Smiles On Canvas ....G...... 757 572-2346
Virginia Beach *(G-14827)*
Steffan Lott ....G...... 786 366-9494
Norfolk *(G-9734)*
TI Associates Inc ....D...... 757 857-6266
Norfolk *(G-9750)*
Trotter Jamil ....G...... 757 251-8754
Hampton *(G-6253)*
Uplift Collections ....G...... 804 319-9129
Chesterfield *(G-3536)*
Uplift Collections LLC ....G...... 804 319-9129
Chesterfield *(G-3537)*
Velveteen Videos LLC ....G...... 703 229-3633
Front Royal *(G-5561)*

2221 Silk & Man-Made Fiber

4 Kees Inc ....G...... 757 249-2584
Newport News *(G-9154)*
◆ Bedford Weaving Inc ....C...... 540 586-8235
Bedford *(G-1626)*
BGF Industries Inc ....D...... 434 447-2210
South Hill *(G-12844)*
BGF Industries Inc ....A...... 434 369-4751
Altavista *(G-627)*
◆ BGF Industries Inc ....D...... 843 537-3172
Danville *(G-3957)*
Birdcloud Creations ....G...... 757 428-6239
Virginia Beach *(G-14283)*
Bxi Inc ....G...... 804 282-5434
Richmond *(G-11142)*
▲ Darco Southern LLC ....E...... 276 773-2711
Independence *(G-6981)*
Epic Images ....G...... 540 537-2572
Goodview *(G-5895)*
▲ Griffith Bag Company ....G...... 540 433-2615
Harrisonburg *(G-6326)*
Jose Goncalves Inc ....E...... 703 528-5272
Arlington *(G-1017)*

Mng Online LLC ....G...... 571 247-8276
Manassas *(G-8109)*
Parachuteriggerus LLC ....G...... 703 753-9265
Haymarket *(G-6433)*
Precision Fabrics Group Inc ....B...... 540 343-4448
Vinton *(G-14181)*
Satin Solutions LLC ....G...... 703 218-3481
Fairfax *(G-4673)*
Shore Traders LLC ....G...... 276 632-5073
Martinsville *(G-8328)*
Wave Rider Manufacturing ....G...... 804 654-9427
Deltaville *(G-4089)*

2231 Wool, Woven Fabric

Alpaca + Knitwear ....G...... 703 994-3346
Lorton *(G-7460)*
Alpacas of Lakeland Woods ....G...... 804 448-8283
Ruther Glen *(G-12448)*
Appalachian Alpaca Fibr Co LLC ......G...... 276 728-2349
Hillsville *(G-6883)*
Appalchian Leicester Longwools ......G...... 540 639-3077
Hiwassee *(G-6909)*
Cameron Mountain Alpacas ....G...... 540 832-3025
Gordonsville *(G-5903)*
Crimphaven Alpacas LLC ....G...... 540 463-4063
Lexington *(G-7393)*
Double Jj Alpacas LLC ....G...... 540 286-0992
Midland *(G-8753)*
Hilltop Hideaway Alpacas LLC ....G...... 954 410-7238
Craigsville *(G-3806)*
Lilys Alpacas LLC ....G...... 757 865-1001
Toano *(G-13867)*
Milliken & Company ....C...... 571 659-0698
Woodbridge *(G-15748)*
Mng Online LLC ....G...... 571 247-8276
Manassas *(G-8109)*
Mornings Myst Alpacas Inc ....G...... 540 428-1002
Warrenton *(G-15036)*
Ocotillas Mntnside Alpacas LLC ......G...... 540 593-2143
Willis *(G-15364)*
Olde Woolen Mill LLC ....G...... 571 926-9604
Herndon *(G-6765)*
Perfect Peace Alpacas LLC ....G...... 540 797-1985
Blue Ridge *(G-1854)*
Pigeon Creek Alpacas ....G...... 540 894-1121
Spotsylvania *(G-12909)*
Precision Fabrics Group Inc ....B...... 540 343-4448
Vinton *(G-14181)*
Pyramid Alpacas ....G...... 540 662-5501
Clear Brook *(G-3650)*
Ridge Valley Alpacas ....G...... 540 255-9200
Fairfield *(G-4735)*
Rocky Ridge Alpacas VA LLC ....G...... 540 962-6087
Covington *(G-3795)*
Schmidt Jayme ....G...... 540 961-1792
Blacksburg *(G-1787)*
Shooting Starr Alpacas LLC ....G...... 540 347-4721
Warrenton *(G-15051)*
Sugarloaf Alpaca Company LLC ....G...... 240 500-0007
Lynchburg *(G-7815)*
Thistledown Alpacas Inc ....G...... 804 784-4837
Manakin Sabot *(G-7905)*
Virginia Breeze Alpacas LLC ....G...... 804 641-4811
Midlothian *(G-8918)*
White Pines Alpacas LLC ....G...... 276 475-5831
Abingdon *(G-68)*
Woolen Mills Grill ....G...... 540 323-7552
Clear Brook *(G-3654)*
Woolen Mills Tavern LLC ....G...... 434 296-2816
Zion Crossroads *(G-16010)*

2241 Fabric Mills, Cotton, Wool, Silk & Man-Made

AEC Virginia LLC ....C...... 434 447-7629
South Hill *(G-12841)*
AEC Virginia LLC ....C...... 757 654-6131
Boykins *(G-1918)*
◆ Bedford Weaving Inc ....C...... 540 586-8235
Bedford *(G-1626)*
BGF Industries Inc ....D...... 434 447-2210
South Hill *(G-12844)*
BGF Industries Inc ....A...... 434 369-4751
Altavista *(G-627)*
◆ BGF Industries Inc ....D...... 843 537-3172
Danville *(G-3957)*
Dee K Enterprises Inc ....F...... 540 745-3816
Floyd *(G-5023)*
▲ Franklin Braid Mfg Co ....D...... 434 634-4142
Emporia *(G-4358)*

Jordo Inc ....G... 424 394-2986
Glen Allen (G-5757)
Jordo Inc ....G... 424 394-2986
Glen Allen (G-5758)
◆ Narroflex Inc ....C... 276 694-7171
Stuart (G-13626)
Neighborhood Flags ....G... 804 360-3398
Henrico (G-6539)
Passionate Stitcher ....G... 804 747-7141
Glen Allen (G-5778)
Phenix Engineered Textiles Inc ....C... 757 654-6131
Boykins (G-1919)
▲ Plymkraft Inc ....E... 757 595-0364
Newport News (G-9314)
Rose Winston Designs ....G... 703 717-2264
Fairfax (G-4545)
Vel Tye LLC ....G... 757 518-5400
Virginia Beach (G-14907)

2251 Hosiery, Women's Full & Knee Length

Spanx Inc ....G... 888 806-7311
Martinsville (G-8335)

2252 Hosiery, Except Women's

Alienfeet Sports Socks ....G... 703 864-8892
Alexandria (G-407)
Barry Sock Company ....G... 703 525-1120
Arlington (G-875)
Get Some Socks LLC ....G... 434 466-5054
Culpeper (G-3894)
▲ Gildan Delaware Inc ....F... 276 956-2305
Martinsville (G-8289)
Jeffrey M Haughney Attorney PC ......G... 757 802-6160
Virginia Beach (G-14566)
Orange Sock Pay ....G... 540 246-6368
Ruther Glen (G-12459)
Silly Sport Socks ....G... 703 926-5398
Fairfax (G-4555)
So Many Socks ....G... 703 309-8111
Woodbridge (G-15815)
Sock Software Inc ....G... 804 749-4137
Rockville (G-12300)
Soul Socks LLC ....G... 757 449-5013
Virginia Beach (G-14830)
Spirit Socks ....G... 757 802-6160
Virginia Beach (G-14840)
Toucan Socks ....G... 757 656-9497
Alexandria (G-601)

2253 Knit Outerwear Mills

▲ Claudia & Co ....G... 540 433-1140
Harrisonburg (G-6301)
Fruit For You Inc ....G... 540 668-7750
Hillsboro (G-6868)
H Moss Design ....G... 703 356-7824
Mc Lean (G-8455)
Hanesbrands Inc ....G... 276 236-5174
Galax (G-5638)
Metawear LLC ....G... 561 302-2010
Fairfax (G-4655)
▲ Red Star Consulting LLC ....G... 434 872-0890
Charlottesville (G-2862)
Rich Young ....G... 757 472-2057
Virginia Beach (G-14771)
Sgm Inc ....G... 757 572-3299
Virginia Beach (G-14805)
▲ Vf Imagewear (east) Inc ....A... 276 956-7200
Martinsville (G-8345)
Warriorware LLC ....G... 804 338-9431
North Chesterfield (G-10010)

2254 Knit Underwear Mills

▲ Gildan Delaware Inc ....F... 276 956-2305
Martinsville (G-8289)
▲ Memteks-Usa Inc ....B... 434 973-9800
Earlysville (G-4292)

2259 Knitting Mills, NEC

Mary Elizabeth Burrell ....G... 804 677-2855
Richmond (G-11670)

2261 Cotton Fabric Finishers

▲ Aard-Alltuf Screenprinters ....E... 757 853-7641
Norfolk (G-9415)
▲ Artfx LLC ....C... 757 853-1703
Norfolk (G-9445)
▲ Artistic Impressions ....G... 757 923-4254
Suffolk (G-13671)

Bobs Sports Equipment Sales ....G... 276 669-8066
Bristol (G-2008)
Bryant Embroidery LLC ....G... 757 498-3453
Virginia Beach (G-14303)
Dap Incorporated ....G... 757 921-3576
Newport News (G-9214)
Dews Screen Printer ....F... 757 436-0908
Chesapeake (G-3067)
Dptl Inc ....F... 703 435-2291
Herndon (G-6659)
Emblemax LLC ....E... 703 802-0200
Chantilly (G-2417)
Harbour Graphics Inc ....F... 757 368-0474
Virginia Beach (G-14505)
Jackie Screen Printing ....G... 276 963-0964
Richlands (G-11017)
Krown LLC ....G... 804 307-9722
Midlothian (G-8841)
Locus Technology ....G... 757 340-1986
Virginia Beach (G-14622)
Love Those Tz LLC ....G... 757 897-0238
Virginia Beach (G-14625)
Martin Printwear Inc ....G... 434 352-5660
Appomattox (G-819)
Ocean Impressions Inc....................G... 757 485-3212
Chesapeake (G-3223)
Phoenix Sports and Advg Inc ....G... 276 988-9709
North Tazewell (G-10104)
Pullin Ink ....G... 276 546-2760
Pennington Gap (G-10299)
Snips of Virginia Beach Inc ....F... 888 634-5008
Norfolk (G-9727)
Soforeal Entertainment ....G... 804 442-6850
North Chesterfield (G-9982)
Star Childrens Dress Co Inc ....E... 804 561-5060
Amelia Court House (G-673)
Tee Z Special ....G... 757 488-2435
Chesapeake (G-3328)
Thalhimer Headwear Corporation ......G... 804 355-1200
Richmond (G-11409)
University Pride & Prestige ....G... 757 766-2590
Hampton (G-6256)
Wool Felt Products Inc ....E... 540 981-0281
Roanoke (G-12230)

2262 Silk & Man-Made Fabric Finishers

American Shirt Printing ....G... 703 405-4014
Stafford (G-13117)
Excel Graphics ....G... 757 596-4334
Yorktown (G-15956)
First Paper Co Inc ....F... 434 821-6884
Rustburg (G-12439)
Hatteras Silkscreen ....G... 757 486-2976
Virginia Beach (G-14509)
Ink & More ....G... 804 794-3437
Prince George (G-10596)
Mardon Inc ....G... 276 386-6662
Weber City (G-15149)
T Shirt Unique Inc ....G... 804 557-2989
Providence Forge (G-10629)

2269 Textile Finishers, NEC

Barcroft Associates Ltd Partnr ....G... 786 507-4649
Arlington (G-873)
Product Identification ....G... 804 264-4434
Richmond (G-11336)

2273 Carpets & Rugs

Aeh Designs ....G... 703 860-3204
Reston (G-10779)
Bacova Guild Ltd ....G... 540 484-4640
Rocky Mount (G-12313)
Burlington Industries Inc ....G... 540 258-2811
Glasgow (G-5699)
C & G Flooring LLC ....G... 804 318-0927
Midlothian (G-8785)
▲ Capital Discount Mdse LLC ....F... 703 499-9368
Woodbridge (G-15665)
Capital Floors LLC ....G... 571 451-4044
Woodbridge (G-15666)
Charles City Timber and Mat ....G... 804 829-5850
Charles City (G-2572)
Charles City Timber and Mat ....G... 804 512-8150
Providence Forge (G-10621)
Charles City Timber and Mat ....E... 804 966-8313
Providence Forge (G-10622)
Christine Smith ....G... 703 399-1944
Alexandria (G-429)
Cutting Edge Carpet Binding ....G... 540 982-1007
Vinton (G-14171)

Mohawk Industries Inc ....F... 540 258-2811
Glasgow (G-5700)
Mohawk Industries Inc ....C... 276 728-2141
Hillsville (G-6897)
◆ Nedia Enterprises Inc ....E... 571 223-0200
Ashburn (G-1320)
Regitex Usa LLC ....C... 514 730-1110
Brodnax (G-2104)
Reynolds Container Corporation ....E... 276 647-8451
Collinsville (G-3715)
Tarkett USA Inc ....G... 804 594-0500
North Chesterfield (G-9998)
Taylor Matthews Inc ....G... 703 346-7844
Vienna (G-14139)
Velvet Pile Carpets LLC ....G... 540 920-9473
Gordonsville (G-5918)

2281 Yarn Spinning Mills

Always In Stitches ....G... 804 642-0800
Hayes (G-6394)
▲ Ames Textiles Inc ....E... 540 382-8522
Christiansburg (G-3568)
Celanese Acetate LLC ....E... 540 921-1111
Narrows (G-9096)
Clover Yarns Inc ....C... 434 454-7151
Clover (G-3691)
Cupp Manufacturing Co ....G... 540 249-4011
Grottoes (G-6018)
◆ Drake Extrusion Inc ....C... 276 632-0159
Ridgeway (G-11841)
▲ Fibrxl Performance Inc ....E... 804 329-0491
Richmond (G-11587)
Innovative Yarns Inc ....E... 305 294-7244
Martinsville (G-8300)
▲ Mehler Inc ....D... 276 638-6166
Martinsville (G-8311)
◆ Mehler Engineered Products Inc ....D... 276 638-6166
Martinsville (G-8313)
Parkdale Mills Incorporated ....C... 276 728-1001
Hillsville (G-6898)
Parkdale Mills Incorporated ....G... 276 236-5174
Galax (G-5643)
▲ Texturing Services LLC ....C... 276 632-3130
Martinsville (G-8342)
◆ Universal Fibers Inc ....B... 276 669-1161
Bristol (G-2039)

2282 Yarn Texturizing, Throwing, Twisting & Winding Mills

Apex Clean Energy Inc ....C... 434 220-7595
Charlottesville (G-2729)
Clover Yarns Inc ....C... 434 454-7151
Clover (G-3691)
Lumat Yarns LLC ....G... 804 329-4383
Richmond (G-11660)
Plum Tree Wind LLC ....G... 434 220-7595
Charlottesville (G-2848)
▲ Plymkraft Inc ....E... 757 595-0364
Newport News (G-9314)
▲ Texturing Services LLC ....C... 276 632-3130
Martinsville (G-8342)
US Wrap LLC ....G... 202 441-6072
Centreville (G-2347)

2284 Thread Mills

Home Decor Sewing ....G... 804 364-8750
Glen Allen (G-5747)
Tagstringcom Inc ....G... 954 557-8645
Chantilly (G-2559)

2295 Fabrics Coated Not Rubberized

Advansix Inc ....B... 804 530-6000
Chester (G-3383)
◆ BGF Industries Inc ....D... 843 537-3172
Danville (G-3957)
◆ Bondcote Holdings Inc ....C... 540 980-2640
Pulaski (G-10631)
Dolan Contracting ....G... 703 768-9496
Alexandria (G-192)
Heytex USA Inc ....E... 540 674-9576
Dublin (G-4157)
◆ Heytex USA Inc ....D... 540 980-2640
Pulaski (G-10637)
Intertape Polymer Corp ....C... 434 797-8273
Danville (G-4002)
Las Creation Design LLC ....G... 757 880-4211
Woodbridge (G-15739)
▲ McAllister Mills Inc ....E... 276 773-3114
Independence (G-6989)

Rage Plastics ....G....... 434 309-1718
Altavista (G-638)

Scott Coulter ....G....... 800 775-2925
Fairfax (G-4674)

Tritex LLC ....F....... 276 773-0593
Independence (G-6996)

Worthen Industries ....E....... 804 275-9231
Richmond (G-11068)

2296 Tire Cord & Fabric

Mehler Inc ....D....... 276 638-6166
Martinsville (G-8312)

2297 Fabrics, Nonwoven

Avintiv Specialty Mtls Inc ....C....... 540 946-9250
Waynesboro (G-15099)

◆ Carpenter Co ....C....... 804 359-0800
Richmond (G-11146)

Chicopee Inc ....C....... 540 946-9250
Waynesboro (G-15105)

Heytex USA Inc ....E....... 540 674-9576
Dublin (G-4157)

Johns Manville Corporation ....B....... 540 984-4171
Edinburg (G-4307)

▼ Poly-Bond Inc ....B....... 540 946-9250
Waynesboro (G-15132)

▲ Solid Stone Fabrics Inc ....F....... 276 634-0115
Martinsville (G-8331)

Vel Tye LLC ....G....... 757 518-5400
Virginia Beach (G-14907)

▲ Xymid LLC ....E....... 804 423-5798
Midlothian (G-8925)

2298 Cordage & Twine

Marshall Manufacturing Co ....F....... 757 824-4061
Atlantic (G-1525)

▲ McAllister Mills Inc ....E....... 276 773-3114
Independence (G-6989)

Net 100 Ltd ....G....... 757 490-0496
Virginia Beach (G-14676)

Ocean Products Research Inc .....F....... 804 725-3406
Diggs (G-4093)

Rigging Box Inc ....G....... 703 339-7575
Lorton (G-7526)

Trident Tool Inc ....G....... 540 635-7753
Stephens City (G-13324)

2299 Textile Goods, NEC

Capital Floors LLC ....G....... 571 451-4044
Woodbridge (G-15666)

Capital Linen Services Inc ....F....... 804 744-3334
Midlothian (G-8789)

Citizens Upholstery & Furn Co ....G....... 540 345-5060
Vinton (G-14170)

Clover Yarns Inc ....C....... 434 454-7151
Clover (G-3691)

▲ Cupron Inc ....F....... 804 322-3650
Henrico (G-6495)

Desales Inc ....G....... 804 794-8187
Moseley (G-9038)

Dks Machine Shop Inc ....G....... 540 775-9648
King George (G-7087)

Dutch Lady ....G....... 202 669-0317
Alexandria (G-196)

East Coast Hemp Company LLC ...G....... 540 740-7099
King George (G-7089)

Edignas Fashion ....G....... 757 588-4958
Norfolk (G-9541)

Fashion Mechanics ....G....... 571 398-0894
Woodbridge (G-15702)

Fashion Seoul ....G....... 571 395-8555
Annandale (G-748)

Federal Prison Industries ....G....... 804 733-7881
North Prince George (G-10087)

Gunnys Call Inc ....G....... 757 892-0251
Virginia Beach (G-14496)

▲ Hilden America Inc ....E....... 434 572-3965
South Boston (G-12776)

Marine Fabricators Inc ....G....... 804 758-2248
Topping (G-13887)

◆ Nedia Enterprises Inc ....E....... 571 223-0200
Ashburn (G-1320)

Tea Lady Pillows ....G....... 703 448-0033
Mc Lean (G-8565)

Teeny Textiles ....G....... 703 731-7336
Virginia Beach (G-14868)

▲ Vitrulan Corporation ....G....... 540 949-8206
Waynesboro (G-15145)

▲ Wilner Designs Inc Jane ....F....... 703 998-2551
Falls Church (G-4892)

23 APPAREL AND OTHER FINISHED PRODUCTS MADE FROM FABRICS AND SIMILAR MATERIAL

2311 Men's & Boys' Suits, Coats & Overcoats

▲ Alpha Industries Inc ....B....... 703 378-1420
Chantilly (G-2366)

Ames Cleaners & Formals Inc .....G....... 757 825-3335
Hampton (G-6084)

▲ Annalees LLC ....G....... 703 303-1841
Sterling (G-13344)

Antillian Trading Company LLC .....E....... 703 626-6333
Alexandria (G-414)

Barrons-Hunter Inc ....G....... 434 971-7626
Charlottesville (G-2736)

Billy M Seargeant ....G....... 540 898-6396
Fredericksburg (G-5253)

Cool Comfort By Carson LLC ......G....... 330 348-3149
Alexandria (G-174)

D Carter Inc ....G....... 540 967-1506
Louisa (G-7555)

Dynamic Team Sports Inc ....D....... 610 518-3300
Virginia Beach (G-14422)

Get It Right Enterprise ....G....... 757 869-1736
Newport News (G-9235)

Heroes Apparel LLC ....G....... 804 304-1001
Richmond (G-11611)

Juanita Deshazior ....G....... 703 901-5592
Alexandria (G-248)

Kathleen Tilley ....G....... 703 727-5385
Williamsburg (G-15265)

Polo Ralph Lauren Corp ....G....... 201 531-6000
Virginia Beach (G-14729)

Rbr Tactical Inc ....G....... 804 564-6787
Richmond (G-11347)

Sabatini of London ....G....... 202 277-8227
Alexandria (G-333)

SNC Technical Services LLC ....G....... 787 820-2141
Virginia Beach (G-14829)

Stealth Mfg & Svcs LLC ....G....... 787 679-7548
Virginia Beach (G-14844)

Tiffanys By Sharon Inc ....G....... 804 273-6303
Henrico (G-6582)

Tom James Company ....F....... 703 916-9300
Annandale (G-789)

Tom James Company ....F....... 757 394-3205
Norfolk (G-9760)

▲ Webgear Inc ....F....... 703 532-1000
Vienna (G-14158)

2321 Men's & Boys' Shirts

Coronet Group Inc ....D....... 757 488-4800
Norfolk (G-9507)

Custom Ink ....G....... 571 364-7944
Alexandria (G-178)

El Tran Investment Corp ....G....... 757 439-8111
Virginia Beach (G-14437)

Fame All Stars ....F....... 757 817-0214
Yorktown (G-15959)

◆ Greene Company of Virginia Inc ....G....... 276 638-7101
Martinsville (G-8292)

▲ Hibernate Inc ....G....... 804 513-1777
Glen Allen (G-5744)

▲ International Apparel Ltd ....E....... 571 643-0100
Manassas (G-8084)

Jafree Shirt Co Inc ....C....... 276 228-2116
Wytheville (G-15892)

▲ Jensen Promotional Items Inc ....E....... 757 966-7608
Chesapeake (G-3150)

Kingdom Bloodline Apparel LLC ....G....... 866 426-0196
Richmond (G-11645)

Oxford Industries Inc ....F....... 757 220-8660
Williamsburg (G-15290)

San Pak Inc ....G....... 276 647-5390
Collinsville (G-3716)

▲ Vf Imagewear (east) Inc ....A....... 276 956-7200
Martinsville (G-8345)

2322 Men's & Boys' Underwear & Nightwear

Hanesbrands Inc ....B....... 336 519-5458
Stuart (G-13614)

Hanesbrands Inc ....B....... 276 670-4500
Martinsville (G-8293)

2323 Men's & Boys' Neckwear

Block9ine Enterprises LLC ....G....... 240 728-8601
Woodbridge (G-15660)

Blythe ....G....... 804 364-1717
Richmond (G-11130)

Disse Outdoor Gear LLC ....G....... 804 357-2860
Glen Allen (G-5724)

King Kreations ....G....... 703 883-7123
Stafford (G-13163)

Little Birdy Bags LLC ....G....... 703 757-6565
Great Falls (G-5965)

Thick To Thin LLC ....G....... 607 427-1737
Gainesville (G-5617)

Trademark Branders ....G....... 804 277-4428
Moseley (G-9050)

2325 Men's & Boys' Separate Trousers & Casual Slacks

Larry Hicks ....G....... 276 738-9010
Castlewood (G-2254)

Paul T Marshall ....G....... 703 580-0245
Woodbridge (G-15774)

2326 Men's & Boys' Work Clothing

All Tyed Up ....G....... 804 855-7158
Richmond (G-11482)

Capital Brandworks LLC ....G....... 703 609-7010
Fairfax (G-4423)

Chatham Knitting Mills Inc ....E....... 434 432-4701
Chatham (G-2921)

Cool Comfort By Carson LLC ......G....... 330 348-3149
Alexandria (G-174)

Cowboy Western Wear ....G....... 202 298-8299
Arlington (G-919)

G Gibbs Project LLC ....G....... 804 638-9581
Chester (G-3418)

▲ Lebanon Apparel Corporation ....C....... 276 889-3656
Lebanon (G-7197)

Nautica of Potomac ....E....... 703 494-9915
Woodbridge (G-15755)

No Limits LLC ....G....... 757 729-5612
Norfolk (G-9665)

Palidori LLC ....G....... 757 609-1134
Norfolk (G-9680)

Phillips Medical Manufacturer ....G....... 804 475-9144
Glen Allen (G-5779)

Scrub Exchange LLC ....G....... 434 237-7778
Concord (G-3763)

String Stalker LLC ....G....... 727 430-7545
Glen Allen (G-5802)

Uplift Collections ....G....... 804 319-9129
Chesterfield (G-3536)

Uplift Collections LLC ....G....... 804 319-9129
Chesterfield (G-3537)

2329 Men's & Boys' Clothing, NEC

Adidas North America Inc ....G....... 703 771-6925
Leesburg (G-7214)

Adis America ....G....... 804 794-2848
Midlothian (G-8768)

Artists Innvators Creators LLC ....G....... 757 359-6215
Chesapeake (G-2981)

Aspetto Inc ....G....... 540 547-8487
Fredericksburg (G-5171)

Bajj Usa Inc ....G....... 703 953-1541
Manassas (G-8033)

Bargain Beachwear Inc ....G....... 757 313-5440
Virginia Beach (G-14260)

Battle King Inc ....G....... 757 324-1854
Portsmouth (G-10397)

Chatham Knitting Mills Inc ....E....... 434 432-4701
Chatham (G-2921)

Chesapeake Distributors LLC ......G....... 757 302-1108
Onancock (G-10193)

Christopher Phillip & Moss LLC ....F....... 757 525-0683
Norfolk (G-9484)

Jammin ....E....... 540 484-4600
Rocky Mount (G-12330)

Neu Age Sportswear ....G....... 757 581-8333
Norfolk (G-9658)

▲ New Creation Sourcing Inc ......F....... 703 330-5314
Manassas (G-8117)

P J Henry Inc ....E....... 757 428-0301
Virginia Beach (G-14707)

Psycho Panda ....G....... 540 287-0588
Fredericksburg (G-5473)

Renegade Classics ....G....... 757 336-6611
Chincoteague (G-3565)

S I C

◆ Rp55 Inc ....D..... 757 428-0300
  Virginia Beach *(G-14782)*

Snature LLC ....G..... 571 251-1573
  Alexandria *(G-349)*

Snow Hill Classics Inc ....G..... 703 339-6278
  Lorton *(G-7530)*

Sweetb Designs LLC ....G..... 757 550-0436
  Portsmouth *(G-10490)*

Sweetpeas By Shafer Dobry ....G..... 703 476-6787
  Herndon *(G-6819)*

Tegra LLC ....G..... 470 705-1280
  Norfolk *(G-9746)*

Zyflex LLC ....G..... 804 306-6333
  Midlothian *(G-8927)*

2331 Women's & Misses' Blouses

3mp1re Clothing Co ....G..... 540 892-3484
  Richmond *(G-11073)*

B Queen Nation LLC ....G..... 678 507-4445
  Newport News *(G-9175)*

D Carter Inc ....G..... 540 967-1506
  Louisa *(G-7555)*

Deborah E Ross ....G..... 757 857-6140
  Norfolk *(G-9521)*

▲ Hibernate Inc ....G..... 804 513-1777
  Glen Allen *(G-5744)*

Hybernations LLC ....G..... 804 744-3580
  Midlothian *(G-8831)*

Jafree Shirt Co Inc ....G..... 276 228-2116
  Wytheville *(G-15892)*

Jensen Promotional Items Inc ....G..... 276 521-0143
  Chilhowie *(G-3553)*

Plus Is ME ....G..... 757 693-1505
  Painter *(G-10242)*

Wallpaper Fitted Clothing Co ....G..... 757 639-8531
  Norfolk *(G-9792)*

2335 Women's & Misses' Dresses

A Pinch of Charm ....G..... 757 262-7820
  Newport News *(G-9156)*

A Special Occasion LLC ....G..... 757 868-3160
  Poquoson *(G-10363)*

Andrea Darcell LLC ....G..... 980 533-5128
  Martinsville *(G-8266)*

Ardeens Designs Inc ....G..... 804 562-3840
  Richmond *(G-11117)*

Bcbg Max Azria Group LLC ....G..... 757 497-9575
  Falls Church *(G-4762)*

Casa De Fiestas Dina ....G..... 703 910-6510
  Woodbridge *(G-15670)*

Catrina Fashions LLC ....G..... 540 992-2127
  Troutville *(G-13906)*

Determined LLC ....G..... 804 829-7229
  Hopewell *(G-6923)*

Estudio De Fernandez LLC ....G..... 540 948-3196
  Rochelle *(G-12233)*

First Class Chariots LLC ....G..... 757 334-7298
  Norfolk *(G-9553)*

Formally Yours ....G..... 540 974-3071
  Middletown *(G-8738)*

Kims Kreations LLC ....G..... 703 431-7978
  Round Hill *(G-12382)*

La Princesa ....G..... 703 330-2400
  Manassas *(G-8096)*

Le Reve Bridal Inc ....F..... 703 777-3757
  Leesburg *(G-7297)*

Lexs of Carytown Ltd ....G..... 804 355-5425
  Richmond *(G-11653)*

Life Transformations LLC ....G..... 703 624-0130
  Reston *(G-10887)*

Lilly Lane Incorporated ....G..... 434 792-6387
  Danville *(G-4013)*

Top Shop Onesies & Apparel ....G..... 757 202-3371
  Norfolk *(G-9762)*

Videographers Fredericksburg ....G..... 540 582-6111
  Spotsylvania *(G-12921)*

Zakaa Couture LLC ....G..... 703 554-7506
  Leesburg *(G-7383)*

2337 Women's & Misses' Suits, Coats & Skirts

Differential Brands Group Inc ....G..... 703 448-9985
  Mc Lean *(G-8419)*

▲ Lebanon Apparel Corporation .....C..... 276 889-3656
  Lebanon *(G-7197)*

Nyla LLC ....G..... 800 916-8326
  Herndon *(G-6761)*

Sara Campbell Ltd ....G..... 617 423-3134
  Richmond *(G-11372)*

Sara Campbell Ltd ....G..... 703 996-9074
  Alexandria *(G-338)*

2339 Women's & Misses' Outerwear, NEC

2 Hearts 1 Dress LLC ....G..... 540 300-0655
  Fredericksburg *(G-5166)*

Boho Bae & Company LLC ....G..... 757 344-9197
  Hampton *(G-6098)*

Carousel ....G..... 434 292-7721
  Blackstone *(G-1813)*

Chatham Knitting Mills Inc ....E..... 434 432-4701
  Chatham *(G-2921)*

Claudia Ofori-Addo ....G..... 540 840-5388
  Stafford *(G-13132)*

Dipped In Ice LLC ....G..... 540 845-3567
  Orange *(G-10211)*

Elegance Meets Designs LLC ....G..... 347 567-6348
  Richmond *(G-11199)*

▼ Fannypants LLC ....G..... 703 953-3099
  Chantilly *(G-2420)*

Fit ME By Crystal LLC ....G..... 302 573-1235
  Arlington *(G-967)*

◆ Greene Company of Virginia Inc ..G..... 276 638-7101
  Martinsville *(G-8292)*

Heidi Ho Inc ....E..... 434 736-8763
  Keysville *(G-7059)*

Henry Saint-Denis LLC ....G..... 540 547-6657
  Leesburg *(G-7284)*

▲ Integrated Tex Solutions Inc ....D..... 540 389-8113
  Salem *(G-12522)*

James Associates I LLC ....G..... 804 590-2620
  South Chesterfield *(G-12836)*

Jammin ....E..... 540 484-4600
  Rocky Mount *(G-12330)*

Jennifer Ouk ....G..... 571 232-0991
  Alexandria *(G-497)*

Karla Colletto Swimwear Inc ....E..... 703 281-3262
  Vienna *(G-14076)*

▲ Lebanon Apparel Corporation .....C..... 276 889-3656
  Lebanon *(G-7197)*

▲ Memteks-Usa Inc ....B..... 434 973-9800
  Earlysville *(G-4292)*

Mng Online LLC ....G..... 571 247-8276
  Manassas *(G-8109)*

Mother Teresas Cottage ....G..... 757 850-0350
  Hampton *(G-6204)*

Ner Inc ....G..... 757 437-7727
  Virginia Beach *(G-14675)*

Noir X Jojo LLC ....G..... 757 756-9134
  Hampton *(G-6208)*

Richmond Thread Lab LLC ....G..... 757 344-1886
  Richmond *(G-11739)*

Shellys Chachkies LLC ....G..... 571 758-1323
  Sterling *(G-13506)*

Shine Like Me LLC ....G..... 210 862-4197
  Vienna *(G-14125)*

Sparklenshinecollection ....G..... 703 939-7623
  Stephenson *(G-13335)*

Sport Shack Inc ....G..... 540 372-3719
  Fredericksburg *(G-5487)*

Sweetb Designs LLC ....G..... 757 550-0436
  Portsmouth *(G-10490)*

Worse LLC ....G..... 512 506-0057
  Richmond *(G-11456)*

Younivercity LLC ....G..... 540 529-7621
  Roanoke *(G-12231)*

2341 Women's, Misses' & Children's Underwear & Nightwear

Hanesbrands Inc ....B..... 276 670-4500
  Martinsville *(G-8293)*

Hanesbrands Inc ....G..... 336 519-5458
  Stuart *(G-13614)*

Suzanne Henri Inc ....G..... 434 352-0233
  Appomattox *(G-823)*

2342 Brassieres, Girdles & Garments

Body Creations ....G..... 276 620-9989
  Max Meadows *(G-8366)*

▲ Memteks-Usa Inc ....B..... 434 973-9800
  Earlysville *(G-4292)*

Suzanne Henri Inc ....G..... 434 352-0233
  Appomattox *(G-823)*

2353 Hats, Caps & Millinery

Downunder Hats Virginia LLC ....G..... 804 334-7476
  Moseley *(G-9039)*

El Tran Investment Corp ....G..... 757 439-8111
  Virginia Beach *(G-14437)*

Four Hats Inc ....G..... 571 926-4303
  Marshall *(G-8253)*

Omis Gnome Hats ....G..... 540 230-0258
  Pilot *(G-10357)*

Ophelias Hat & Hair Shop ....G..... 757 331-1713
  Cheriton *(G-2947)*

OSI LLC ....G..... 757 967-7533
  Virginia Beach *(G-14705)*

▲ Pacific View International ....G..... 703 631-8659
  Fairfax *(G-4658)*

▲ R & B Distributing Inc ....D..... 804 794-5848
  North Chesterfield *(G-9955)*

Top It Off Hats ....G..... 703 988-1839
  Herndon *(G-6827)*

Wards Soul Food Kitchen ....G..... 757 865-7069
  Hampton *(G-6270)*

2361 Children's & Infants' Dresses & Blouses

3mp1re Clothing Co ....G..... 540 892-3484
  Richmond *(G-11073)*

Commonwalth Girl Scout Council ....G..... 804 340-2835
  Richmond *(G-11163)*

D Carter Inc ....G..... 540 967-1506
  Louisa *(G-7555)*

Heidi Ho Inc ....E..... 434 736-8763
  Keysville *(G-7059)*

Inch By Inch LLC ....G..... 804 678-8271
  Richmond *(G-11618)*

Justice ....G..... 703 352-8393
  Fairfax *(G-4487)*

Justice ....G..... 703 421-7001
  Sterling *(G-13437)*

Justice ....G..... 703 490-6664
  Woodbridge *(G-15734)*

Star Childrens Dress Co Inc ....E..... 804 561-5060
  Amelia Court House *(G-673)*

2369 Girls' & Infants' Outerwear, NEC

Bargain Beachwear Inc ....G..... 757 313-5440
  Virginia Beach *(G-14260)*

▲ Beadecked Inc ....G..... 703 759-3725
  Great Falls *(G-5939)*

Beadecked Inc ....G..... 703 435-5663
  Herndon *(G-6622)*

Catherine Rachel Braxton ....G..... 757 244-7531
  Newport News *(G-9195)*

Dar Be Dar LLC ....G..... 703 244-1599
  Reston *(G-10832)*

Dream of ME Bowtique ....G..... 804 955-5908
  North Chesterfield *(G-9860)*

Larry Hicks ....G..... 276 738-9010
  Castlewood *(G-2254)*

One of A Kind Kid ....G..... 800 276-0054
  Midlothian *(G-8872)*

Rockin Baby LLC ....G..... 866 855-4378
  Richmond *(G-11746)*

True Religion Apparel Inc ....G..... 323 266-3072
  Arlington *(G-1198)*

2371 Fur Goods

Millers Furs Inc ....G..... 703 772-4593
  Mc Lean *(G-8501)*

2384 Robes & Dressing Gowns

▲ Saffron Fabs Corporation ....G..... 703 544-2791
  Centreville *(G-2334)*

2385 Waterproof Outerwear

Alva Restoration & Waterproof ....G..... 540 785-0805
  Fredericksburg *(G-5243)*

Gloria Barbre ....G..... 703 548-2210
  Alexandria *(G-220)*

Kool-Dri Inc ....F..... 540 997-9241
  Millboro *(G-8936)*

2386 Leather & Sheep Lined Clothing

Cap City Inc ....G..... 757 827-0932
  Hampton *(G-6105)*

Fairway Enterprise LLP ....G..... 434 973-8595
  Charlottesville *(G-2631)*

2389 Apparel & Accessories, NEC

AG Customs Creat & Designs LLC ..G..... 757 927-7339
  Hampton *(G-6078)*

All Sports Athletic Apparel ....G..... 757 427-6772
  Virginia Beach *(G-14223)*

Aurora Industries LLC ....A..... 757 301-2574
  Virginia Beach *(G-14249)*

▼ B & S Liquidating Corp ...C ... 540 387-0000
Salem (G-12479)
Blue Ridge Crest LLC ...E ... 276 236-7149
Galax (G-5629)
Costume Shop ...G ... 804 421-7361
Richmond (G-11168)
Crown On LLC ...G ... 202 427-3042
Emporia (G-4356)
Custom Performance Inc ...G ... 540 972-3632
Spotsylvania (G-12886)
Diversified Solution LLC ...G ... 434 845-5100
Lynchburg (G-7696)
Dml Industries LLC ...G ... 571 348-4332
Virginia Beach (G-14407)
Elks Club 450 ...G ... 540 434-3673
Harrisonburg (G-6313)
Elohim Designs ...G ... 757 292-1890
Chesapeake (G-3087)
Gene Taylor ...G ... 540 345-9001
Roanoke (G-12096)
Go 2 Row Inc ...G ... 804 694-4868
Gloucester (G-5849)
Gracies Gowns Inc ...G ... 540 287-0143
Fredericksburg (G-5292)
Hogue ...G ... 540 374-1144
Fredericksburg (G-5196)
Influences of Zion ...G ... 804 248-4758
Richmond (G-11248)
Jessica Radellant Designs LLC ...G ... 804 301-3994
North Chesterfield (G-9902)
Lavish ...G ... 757 498-1238
Virginia Beach (G-14603)
Le Look LLC ...G ... 301 237-5072
Virginia Beach (G-14605)
Livin Color LLC ...G ... 757 582-6030
Portsmouth (G-10454)
Lou-Voise ...G ... 804 836-5601
Glen Allen (G-5765)
Lululemon ...G ... 434 964-0105
Charlottesville (G-2657)
Lululemon ...G ... 757 631-3004
Virginia Beach (G-14629)
Lululemon Athletica ...G ... 703 787-8327
Reston (G-10891)
▲ Macoy Pubg Masonic Sup Co Inc ...E ... 804 262-6551
Richmond (G-11280)
Matbock LLC ...G ... 757 828-6659
Virginia Beach (G-14639)
McKoon Zaneta ...G ... 410 707-5701
Fredericksburg (G-5456)
Melissa Moss ...G ... 540 397-0408
Roanoke (G-11961)
Michael Kors ...G ... 757 216-0581
Virginia Beach (G-14649)
Morris Designs Inc ...F ... 757 463-9400
Virginia Beach (G-14664)
▲ Oak Hall Industries LP ...C ... 540 387-0000
Salem (G-12549)
Philosophy Worldwide Apparel ...G ... 804 767-0308
Moseley (G-9044)
Premium Med Supply LLC ...G ... 888 506-6367
Richmond (G-11331)
Proknows ...G ... 540 473-2271
Buchanan (G-2125)
PT Armor Inc ...E ... 703 560-1020
Springfield (G-13076)
Qore Performance Inc ...G ... 703 755-0724
Sterling (G-13482)
Quad Promo LLC ...G ... 757 353-5729
Virginia Beach (G-14751)
Reckless Inc ...G ... 757 469-4416
Chesapeake (G-3262)
Red Action Blue Info LLC ...G ... 703 474-2617
Mc Lean (G-8535)
Red Action Blue Info LLC ...G ... 469 224-7673
Fairfax (G-4538)
Richmond Thread Lab LLC ...G ... 757 344-1886
Richmond (G-11739)
Rubins Company Mj Inc ...F ... 571 437-7298
Herndon (G-6797)
Samco Textile Prints LLc ...G ... 571 451-4044
Woodbridge (G-15802)
▲ Sayre Enterprises Inc ...C ... 540 291-3808
Naturl BR STA (G-9112)
Shenandoah Robe Company Inc ...D ... 540 362-9811
Roanoke (G-12184)
Spirit Halloween ...G ... 804 513-2966
Colonial Heights (G-3748)
Stewart David ...G ... 703 431-7233
Alexandria (G-357)
▲ Svs Enterprises Inc ...G ... 434 985-6642
Stanardsville (G-13228)
Tall Toad Costumes ...G ... 276 694-4636
Claudville (G-3641)
Thelma Rethford ...G ... 540 997-9121
Goshen (G-5928)
Tredegar Personal Care LLC ...G ... 804 330-1000
North Chesterfield (G-10039)
Tri State Graduate Sups LLC ...G ... 540 665-5292
Winchester (G-15596)
TS By Extreme LLC ...G ... 804 335-0260
North Chesterfield (G-10005)
Tunnel of Love ...G ... 757 961-5783
Virginia Beach (G-14898)
Valerie Perkins ...G ... 804 279-0011
Chesterfield (G-3538)
Victor Forward LLC ...G ... 757 374-2642
Virginia Beach (G-14909)

2391 Curtains & Draperies

Anthony Corporation ...E ... 757 490-3613
Virginia Beach (G-14230)
Appalachian Manufacturing ...F ... 540 825-3522
Culpeper (G-3866)
Bridgewater Drapery Shop ...G ... 540 828-3312
Bridgewater (G-1950)
Cavan Sales Lo ...G ... 434 757-1680
La Crosse (G-7141)
Creative Decorating ...G ... 703 643-5556
Woodbridge (G-15674)
Custom Windows ...G ... 804 262-1621
Henrico (G-6497)
Drapery House Inc ...G ... 703 669-9622
Leesburg (G-7260)
▲ Elegant Draperies Ltd ...F ... 804 353-4268
Richmond (G-11200)
Endowed Expressions LLC ...G ... 804 638-5459
Richmond (G-11203)
Fabric Accents By Emily ...G ... 540 678-3999
Winchester (G-15540)
Five Talents Enterprises LLC ...G ... 703 986-6721
Triangle (G-13892)
Heidi Yoder ...G ... 540 432-5598
Harrisonburg (G-6327)
Integra Management Group LLC ...F ... 703 791-2007
Manassas (G-8082)
J K Drapery Inc ...F ... 703 941-3788
Alexandria (G-490)
J W Creations ...G ... 276 676-3770
Abingdon (G-43)
Jannie J Jones ...G ... 276 650-3174
Axton (G-1538)
K & Z Inc ...G ... 703 876-1660
Fairfax (G-4488)
Kathy Darmofalski ...G ... 540 885-4759
Staunton (G-13272)
Mary Elizabeth Burrell ...G ... 804 677-2855
Richmond (G-11670)
Mk Interiors Inc ...G ... 804 288-2819
Richmond (G-11294)
Olde Towne Window Works Inc ...E ... 540 371-6987
Fredericksburg (G-5463)
Red River Interiors LLC ...G ... 703 987-1698
Centreville (G-2332)
Shade Mann-Kidwell Corp ...G ... 804 288-2819
Richmond (G-11378)
Speciality Group Ltd ...E ... 804 264-3000
Richmond (G-11767)
Thelmas Interiors Inc ...G ... 757 855-0280
Norfolk (G-9747)
Tl Associates Inc ...D ... 757 857-6266
Norfolk (G-9750)
Virginia Quilting Inc ...C ... 434 757-1809
La Crosse (G-7152)
▼ Vqc Inc ...C ... 434 447-5091
South Hill (G-12863)

2392 House furnishings: Textile

Aquilian LLC ...G ... 703 967-8212
Chantilly (G-2369)
▲ Ashford Court LLC ...D ... 804 743-0700
Richmond (G-11491)
Beaver Creek Wipers ...G ... 276 632-3033
Martinsville (G-8269)
C Cs Linen Plus ...G ... 703 665-0059
Aldie (G-103)
Carolyn West ...G ... 434 332-5007
Rustburg (G-12436)
◆ Carpenter Co ...C ... 804 359-0800
Richmond (G-11146)
▲ Cricket Products Inc ...E ... 804 861-0687
Petersburg (G-10315)
D3companies Inc ...G ... 804 358-2020
Midlothian (G-8807)
▲ Global Direct LLC ...G ... 540 483-5103
Rocky Mount (G-12325)
Hearts Desire ...G ... 804 790-1336
Chesterfield (G-3503)
▲ Hudson Industries Inc ...D ... 804 226-1155
Richmond (G-11244)
Kline Assoc LLC Matt ...G ... 703 780-6466
Alexandria (G-506)
Laura Copenhaver Industries ...G ... 276 783-4663
Marion (G-8230)
Lime & Leaf LLC ...G ... 703 299-2440
Alexandria (G-261)
Magnifazine LLC ...G ... 248 224-1137
Louisa (G-7558)
Market Salamander ...E ... 540 687-8011
Middleburg (G-8728)
Me-Shows LLC ...G ... 855 637-4097
Spotsylvania (G-12904)
Melted Element LLC ...G ... 703 239-7847
Alexandria (G-526)
Poshtique ...G ... 703 404-2825
Great Falls (G-5974)
Quickie Manufacturing ...G ... 856 829-8598
Winchester (G-15574)
◆ Quickie Manufacturing Corp ...D ... 856 829-7900
Winchester (G-15575)
Ryan Studio Inc ...G ... 703 830-6818
Chantilly (G-2488)
Shining Lights LLC ...G ... 703 338-3820
Fairfax (G-4675)
Spartan Shower Shoe LLC ...G ... 540 623-6625
Arlington (G-1173)
Springs Global Us Inc ...E ... 276 670-3440
Martinsville (G-8337)
Stafford Home Products ...G ... 540 337-0068
Fishersville (G-5009)
▲ Tempur-Pedic Technologies LLC ...G ... 276 431-7450
Duffield (G-4186)
Virginia Quilting Inc ...C ... 434 757-1809
La Crosse (G-7152)
▼ Vqc Inc ...C ... 434 447-5091
South Hill (G-12863)
Warrior Luggage Company ...G ... 301 523-9010
Alexandria (G-608)
Windy Hill Collections LLC ...G ... 703 848-8888
Mc Lean (G-8579)
Wool Felt Products Inc ...E ... 540 981-0281
Roanoke (G-12230)

2393 Textile Bags

▲ Broad Bay Cotton Company ...G ... 757 227-4101
Virginia Beach (G-14299)
Carolyn West ...G ... 434 332-5007
Rustburg (G-12436)
CC & More Inc ...G ... 540 786-7052
Fredericksburg (G-5257)
Fabriko Inc ...E ... 434 352-7145
Appomattox (G-810)
Hdt Expeditionary Systems Inc ...G ... 540 373-1435
Fredericksburg (G-5195)
Honey True Teas LLC ...G ... 703 728-8369
Woodbridge (G-15723)
Knp Traders LLC ...G ... 703 376-1955
Chantilly (G-2452)
Lay-N-Go LLC ...G ... 703 799-0799
Alexandria (G-514)
Mfri Inc ...C ... 540 667-7022
Winchester (G-15555)
Philomen Fashion and Designs ...G ... 703 966-5680
Heathsville (G-6463)
Pre Con Inc ...F ... 804 861-0282
Petersburg (G-10337)
S3 Tactical LLC ...G ... 540 667-6947
Stephens City (G-13321)
Samco Textile Prints LLc ...G ... 571 451-4044
Woodbridge (G-15802)
Tent Company of Norfolk LLC ...G ... 757 461-7330
Chesapeake (G-3330)
Trident SEC & Holdings LLC ...G ... 757 689-4560
Virginia Beach (G-14893)
▲ Ventex Inc ...G ... 703 787-9802
Sterling (G-13547)
Warrior Luggage Company ...G ... 301 523-9010
Alexandria (G-608)
▲ Wearmax Inc ...G ... 631 361-7222
Potomac Falls (G-10510)

2394 Canvas Prdts

Aaacm Green Warrior Inc ....G...... 703 865-5991
Fairfax (G-4398)

▼ American Cemetery Supplies Inc .....F...... 757 488-0018
Portsmouth (G-10392)

Bahama Breeze Shutter Awng LLC ....G...... 757 592-0265
Ordinary (G-10236)

Bellum Designs LLC ....G...... 757 343-9556
Virginia Beach (G-14274)

Buddy D Ltd ....G...... 757 481-7619
Virginia Beach (G-14305)

Canvas & Earth ....G...... 757 995-6529
Virginia Beach (G-14314)

Canvas Marine Co ....G...... 703 534-5886
Falls Church (G-4768)

Canvas To Curtains ....G...... 757 665-5406
Bloxom (G-1839)

Cover UPS Marine Canvas ....G...... 757 312-9292
Chesapeake (G-3055)

Crafted Canvas LLC ....G...... 917 426-8377
Dunnsville (G-4268)

Custom Tops Inc ....G...... 757 460-3084
Virginia Beach (G-14378)

Decks Down Under LLC ....G...... 703 758-2572
Reston (G-10836)

Dodd Custom Canvas LLC ....G...... 757 717-4436
Portsmouth (G-10416)

Doyle Sailmakers Virginia ....G...... 757 727-0750
Hampton (G-6132)

Drumsticks Inc ....G...... 804 743-9356
North Chesterfield (G-9861)

George F Dashell Jr ....G...... 305 664-2238
Virginia Beach (G-14480)

Got It Covered LLC ....G...... 540 353-5167
Wirtz (G-15611)

Graham Grham Cnvas Sign Shoppe ......G...... 276 628-8069
Abingdon (G-35)

Hampton Canvas and Rigging ....G...... 757 727-0750
Hampton (G-6162)

Hayes Custom Sails Inc ....G...... 804 642-6496
Hayes (G-6400)

Hdt Expeditionary Systems Inc ....G...... 540 373-1435
Fredericksburg (G-5195)

Husteads Canvas Creations Inc ....E...... 757 627-6912
Norfolk (G-9586)

I Love Art Boutique LLC ....G...... 757 204-1260
Hampton (G-6174)

▲ Integrated Tex Solutions Inc ....D...... 540 389-8113
Salem (G-12522)

JWB of Roanoke Inc ....F...... 540 344-7726
Roanoke (G-12116)

Krismark Inc ....G...... 757 533-9182
Virginia Beach (G-14593)

Latell Sailmakers LLC ....G...... 804 776-6151
Deltaville (G-4082)

Marla Hughes ....G...... 703 309-8267
Alexandria (G-523)

Mikes Marine Custom Canvas ....G...... 757 496-1090
Virginia Beach (G-14653)

Mountain Valley Enterprises ....G...... 276 686-6516
Rural Retreat (G-12428)

▲ Norfolk Tent Company Inc ....F...... 757 461-7330
Norfolk (G-9668)

North Sails Hampton Inc ....G...... 757 723-6280
Hampton (G-6210)

Phase 2 Marine Canvas LLC ....G...... 804 694-7561
Wake (G-14963)

Potomac Sailmakers Inc ....G...... 703 750-2171
Alexandria (G-554)

R C S Enterprises Inc ....G...... 540 363-5979
Waynesboro (G-15133)

Ryzing Technologies LLC ....G...... 949 244-0240
Staunton (G-13288)

Signature Canvasmakers LLC ....G...... 757 788-8890
Hampton (G-6236)

Sunguard Mid Atlantic LLC ....G...... 703 820-8118
Arlington (G-1178)

Virginia Canvas Products Inc ....G...... 757 558-0327
Carrollton (G-2246)

▲ Xymid LLC ....E...... 804 423-5798
Midlothian (G-8925)

Xymid LLC ....F...... 804 744-5229
South Chesterfield (G-12829)

Yeates Mfg Inc ....G...... 757 465-7772
Portsmouth (G-10506)

2395 Pleating & Stitching For The Trade

13 Stitches LLC ....G...... 804 739-8982
Chesterfield (G-3471)

A Hope Skip and A Stitch LLC ....G...... 804 684-5750
Gloucester (G-5834)

A Stitch In Time ....G...... 276 781-2014
Atkins (G-1515)

A Stitch In Time LLC ....G...... 757 478-4878
Virginia Beach (G-14201)

According To Plan LLC ....G...... 703 953-1584
Herndon (G-6603)

Aces Embroidery ....G...... 703 738-4784
Sterling (G-13338)

Advertising Images & EMB ....G...... 703 447-4282
Richmond (G-11088)

Alethia Embroidery ....G...... 540 710-6560
Fredericksburg (G-5242)

Alexander Amir ....G...... 757 714-1802
Suffolk (G-13665)

Alphabet Soup ....G...... 757 569-0110
Franklin (G-5138)

American Eagle EMB Graphics LLC ....G...... 757 673-8337
Chesapeake (G-2966)

American Logo Corp ....G...... 703 356-4709
Falls Church (G-4747)

Ampak Sportswear Inc ....G...... 703 550-1300
Lorton (G-7461)

▲ Artistic Impressions ....G...... 757 923-4254
Suffolk (G-13671)

At The Point Embroidery LLC ....G...... 804 684-9544
Gloucester Point (G-5871)

Atlantic EMB & Design LLC ....G...... 757 253-1010
Sandston (G-12608)

Atlantic Embroidery Works LLC ....G...... 804 282-5027
Henrico (G-6478)

B & J Embroidery Inc ....G...... 276 646-5631
Saltville (G-12584)

Beths Embroidery LLC ....G...... 434 933-8652
Gladstone (G-5681)

BJ Embroidery & Designs ....G...... 804 605-4749
Chesterfield (G-3480)

Blue Ridge Marketing & EMB ....G...... 276 223-0337
Wytheville (G-15878)

Broken Needle Embroidery ....G...... 276 865-4654
Haysi (G-6457)

Brooks Stitch & Fold LLC ....G...... 804 367-7979
Richmond (G-11511)

Bryant Embroidery LLC ....G...... 757 498-3453
Virginia Beach (G-14303)

Busy BS Embroidery ....G...... 757 819-7869
Chesapeake (G-3018)

C&K Custom Embroidery & A ....G...... 434 447-2987
South Hill (G-12845)

Cabin Creations ....G...... 804 529-7245
Callao (G-2215)

Capital Screen Prtg Unlimited ....G...... 703 550-0033
Lorton (G-7470)

Capstone EMB & Screen Prtg ....G...... 757 619-0457
Virginia Beach (G-14318)

Carl G Gilliam Jr ....F...... 276 523-0619
Big Stone Gap (G-1707)

Catberries LLC ....G...... 714 873-8245
Gainesville (G-5575)

Charles R Preston ....G...... 703 757-0495
Great Falls (G-5947)

Coastal Threads Inc ....G...... 757 495-2677
Virginia Beach (G-14349)

Consurgo Group Inc ....F...... 757 373-1717
Virginia Beach (G-14361)

Corporate Designs ....G...... 276 676-9048
Abingdon (G-26)

Crafty Stitcher LLC ....G...... 703 855-2736
Leesburg (G-7248)

Creative Monogramming LLC ....G...... 434 767-4880
Burkeville (G-2208)

▲ Cricket Products Inc ....E...... 804 861-0687
Petersburg (G-10315)

Cross Stitch LLC ....G...... 703 961-1636
Fairfax (G-4434)

Crouch Petra ....G...... 757 681-0828
Virginia Beach (G-14373)

Custom Designs & More ....G...... 540 894-5050
Mineral (G-8946)

Custom EMB & Screen Prtg ....G...... 434 239-2144
Lynchburg (G-7690)

Custom Embroidery & Design ....G...... 804 530-5238
Chester (G-3400)

Custom Embroidery & Designs ....G...... 757 474-1523
Virginia Beach (G-14377)

Custom Logos ....G...... 804 967-0111
Richmond (G-11173)

Customized LLC ....G...... 540 492-2975
Roanoke (G-12077)

D & K Embroidery ....G...... 804 694-4747
Gloucester (G-5844)

D J R Enterprises Inc ....F...... 540 639-9386
Radford (G-10708)

Darlin Monograms LLC ....G...... 757 930-8786
Newport News (G-9215)

Delrand Corp ....G...... 757 490-3355
Virginia Beach (G-14401)

Distinct Impressions ....G...... 434 572-8144
South Boston (G-12762)

Doris Anderson ....G...... 877 869-1543
Poquoson (G-10369)

Dptl Inc ....F...... 703 435-2291
Herndon (G-6659)

Dull Inc Dolan & Norma ....F...... 703 490-0337
Woodbridge (G-15687)

Dyeing To Stitch ....G...... 757 366-8740
Virginia Beach (G-14420)

East Coast Branding LLC ....G...... 757 754-0771
Virginia Beach (G-14428)

East Coast Embroidery ....G...... 804 677-7584
Clarksville (G-3628)

East To West EMB & Design ....G...... 703 335-2397
Manassas (G-7935)

Eleven West Inc ....E...... 540 639-9319
Fairlawn (G-4736)

Elizabeth Ballard-Spitzer ....G...... 757 723-1194
Hampton (G-6138)

Elizabeth Urban ....G...... 757 879-1815
Yorktown (G-15952)

Elletts Embroidery ....G...... 434 392-2290
Farmville (G-4939)

Embellished Embroidery ....G...... 804 926-5785
Chester (G-3411)

Embrace Embroidery LP ....G...... 757 784-3874
Lanexa (G-7166)

Embroider Bee ....G...... 757 472-4981
Virginia Beach (G-14443)

Embroidery -N- Beyond LLC ....G...... 540 972-4333
Spotsylvania (G-12888)

Embroidery Barnyard ....G...... 804 795-1555
Richmond (G-11201)

Embroidery By Patty ....G...... 540 597-8173
Roanoke (G-11920)

Embroidery Concepts ....G...... 540 387-0517
Salem (G-12504)

Embroidery Connection ....G...... 757 566-8859
Williamsburg (G-15239)

Embroidery Criations ....G...... 540 421-5608
Timberville (G-13848)

Embroidery Depot Ltd ....G...... 540 289-5044
Penn Laird (G-10288)

Embroidery Express LLC ....G...... 804 458-5999
Chester (G-3412)

Embroidery Expressons ....G...... 757 255-0713
Windsor (G-15604)

Embroidery N Beyond LLC ....G...... 757 962-2105
Virginia Beach (G-14444)

Embroidery N Beyond LLC ....G...... 757 409-2782
Virginia Beach (G-14445)

Embroidery Works ....G...... 757 344-8573
Yorktown (G-15953)

Embroidery Works Inc ....G...... 757 868-8840
Yorktown (G-15954)

Embroideryville ....G...... 276 768-9727
Independence (G-6982)

Exclusively Yours Embroidery ....G...... 571 285-2196
Woodbridge (G-15700)

Express Yourself Inc ....G...... 434 757-1099
La Crosse (G-7144)

Eye of Needle Embroidery ....G...... 540 837-2089
Boyce (G-1909)

Fancy Stitches ....G...... 804 796-6942
Chesterfield (G-3499)

Fast Lane Specialties Inc ....G...... 757 784-7474
West Point (G-15156)

Fresh Printz LLC ....G...... 540 937-3017
Jeffersonton (G-7012)

Fully Promoted of Alexandria ....G...... 703 575-9003
Alexandria (G-208)

G&M Embroidery Inc ....G...... 757 482-1935
Chesapeake (G-3113)

Garnett Embroidery ....G...... 757 925-0569
Suffolk (G-13713)

Georgette T Hawkins ....G...... 540 825-8928
Culpeper (G-3893)

Global Partners Virginia LLC ....G...... 804 744-8112
Midlothian (G-8822)

Gryphon Threads LLC ....G...... 707 320-7865
Norfolk (G-9567)

H & R Embroidery LLC ....G..... 804 513-8829
  Ashland (G-1424)
Harville Entps of Danville VA ......G... 434 822-2106
  Danville (G-3997)
Heartfelt Stitch Co ....G..... 757 828-6036
  Norfolk (G-9577)
Hickory Embroidery LLC ....G..... 757 482-0873
  Chesapeake (G-3136)
Hickory Ridge Designs Inc...........G..... 888 236-8431
  Martinsville (G-8295)
Hometown Creations ....G..... 434 237-2364
  Lynchburg (G-7736)
Huger Embroidery ....G..... 804 304-8808
  Richmond (G-11245)
Hymons Embroidery LLC ....G..... 757 512-6005
  Virginia Beach (G-14535)
Im Embroidery ....G..... 757 533-5397
  Norfolk (G-9590)
Imagine It Designs LLC ....G..... 703 795-6397
  Falls Church (G-4808)
Impressions of Norton Inc ....G..... 276 679-1560
  Norton (G-10121)
In Stitches ....G..... 434 842-2104
  Fork Union (G-5110)
Inspired Embroidery ....G..... 703 409-3375
  Sterling (G-13428)
It Takes A Stitch Custom ....G..... 703 405-6688
  Arlington (G-1012)
Itty Bitty Stitchings LLC ....G..... 540 829-9197
  Culpeper (G-3896)
Itz ME Creations ....G..... 804 519-6023
  Chesterfield (G-3506)
James River Embroidery ....G..... 434 987-9800
  Scottsville (G-12661)
Janice Martin-Freeman ....G..... 757 234-0056
  Newport News (G-9267)
Jbtm Enterprises Inc ....F..... 540 665-9651
  Winchester (G-15551)
Jean Lee Inc ....G..... 703 630-0276
  Quantico (G-10689)
Joan Fisk ....G..... 540 288-0050
  Stafford (G-13160)
Jonathan Promotions Inc ....G..... 540 891-7700
  Fredericksburg (G-5307)
Jovic Embroidery LLC ....G..... 804 748-2598
  North Chesterfield (G-9903)
Js Monogramming ....G..... 804 862-4324
  Petersburg (G-10328)
Kalis Kreations & Designs LLC ......F..... 757 343-4421
  Suffolk (G-13727)
Kangs Embroidery ....G..... 757 887-5232
  Newport News (G-9273)
Khk Inc ....G..... 540 337-5068
  Stuarts Draft (G-13654)
La Stitchery ....G..... 540 894-9371
  Bumpass (G-2163)
Lakeside Embroidery ....G..... 540 719-2600
  Moneta (G-8970)
Lance Stitcher ....G..... 443 685-4829
  Greenbackville (G-5995)
Leading Edge Screen Printing.........F..... 540 347-5751
  Warrenton (G-15030)
Lifes A Stitch Inc ....G..... 804 672-7079
  Glen Allen (G-5762)
Liz B Quilting LLC ....G..... 540 602-7850
  Stafford (G-13172)
Longs Embroidery ....G..... 540 891-2880
  Fredericksburg (G-5316)
Love Those Tz LLC ....G..... 757 897-0238
  Virginia Beach (G-14625)
Lowe-Go EMB & Designs LLC ....G..... 757 486-0617
  Virginia Beach (G-14626)
Ls Late Embroidery ....G..... 757 639-0647
  Virginia Beach (G-14627)
Mad-Den Embroidery & Gifts ....G..... 757 450-4421
  Virginia Beach (G-14632)
Maple Hill Embroidery ....G..... 540 336-1967
  Winchester (G-15442)
Mc Promotions LLC ....G..... 804 386-7073
  Midlothian (G-8855)
Meesh Monograms ....G..... 757 672-4276
  Virginia Beach (G-14646)
Midnight Embroidery ....G..... 757 463-1692
  Virginia Beach (G-14651)
Minnie ME Monograms ....G..... 423 331-1686
  Chesapeake (G-3206)
Monogram Majik ....G..... 540 389-2269
  Salem (G-12539)
Monogram Shop ....G..... 434 973-1968
  Charlottesville (G-2662)

Mounir E Shaheen ....G..... 757 723-4445
  Hampton (G-6205)
Ms Monogram LLC ....G..... 804 502-3551
  Midlothian (G-8863)
Munchkin Monograms LLC.................G..... 215 970-4375
  Alexandria (G-537)
Nana Stitches ....G..... 757 689-3767
  Virginia Beach (G-14669)
No Short Cut ....G..... 757 696-0249
  Virginia Beach (G-14683)
Norton Embroidery Inc ....G..... 540 550-7331
  Berryville (G-1685)
Nuwave Embroidery ....G..... 540 412-9799
  Fredericksburg (G-5337)
Oaxaca Embroidery LLC ....G..... 540 463-3808
  Lexington (G-7409)
Patty S Pieceworks ....G..... 804 796-3371
  Chesterfield (G-3517)
Peach Tea Monograms ....G..... 703 973-9977
  Vienna (G-14109)
Peggy Sues Advertising Inc ....G..... 276 530-7790
  Conaway (G-3754)
Pegs Embroidery Inc ....G..... 804 378-2053
  Midlothian (G-8878)
Premier Embroidery and Design ....G..... 434 242-2801
  Palmyra (G-10256)
Presto Embroidery LLC ....G..... 571 223-0160
  Broadlands (G-2080)
Q Stitched LLC ....G..... 757 621-6025
  Richmond (G-11342)
Rag Bag Aero Works Inc ....G..... 540 967-5400
  Louisa (G-7564)
Red Eagle Creations ....G..... 804 556-2041
  Maidens (G-7892)
Richs Stitches Inc ....G..... 804 262-3477
  Richmond (G-11364)
Rio Graphics Inc ....G..... 757 467-9207
  Virginia Beach (G-14775)
Rocky Top Embroidery & More...........G..... 540 775-9564
  King George (G-7108)
Rubys Embroidery Gems ....G..... 703 590-7902
  Woodbridge (G-15800)
Sams Monograms ....G..... 703 866-4400
  Annandale (G-781)
Sandy Hobson T/A S H Monograms......G..... 804 730-7211
  Mechanicsville (G-8674)
▲ Sayre Enterprises Inc ....C..... 540 291-3808
  Naturl BR STA (G-9112)
Schmid Embroidery & Design ....G..... 804 737-4141
  Sandston (G-12630)
Schmidt Jayme ....G..... 540 961-1792
  Blacksburg (G-1787)
Scottcraft Monogramming ....G..... 703 971-0309
  Alexandria (G-580)
Sew and Tell Embroidery ....G..... 757 641-1227
  Wakefield (G-14970)
Sew My Monogram LLC ....G..... 804 739-2407
  Midlothian (G-8896)
Sewcial Stitch ....G..... 813 786-2966
  Haymarket (G-6443)
Sherrie & Scott Embroidery ....G..... 804 271-2024
  North Chesterfield (G-9978)
Shirleys Stitches LLC ....G..... 804 370-7182
  Powhatan (G-10574)
Shirleys Unf & Alterations LLC ....G..... 434 985-2042
  Barboursville (G-1566)
Shirt Art Inc ....G..... 703 680-3963
  Woodbridge (G-15806)
Sinister Stitch Custom Leather ....G..... 757 636-9954
  Virginia Beach (G-14820)
Sisters In Stitches LLC ....G..... 757 660-0871
  Hayes (G-6410)
Slopers Stitch House ....G..... 703 368-7197
  Manassas (G-8156)
Snips of Virginia Beach Inc ....F..... 888 634-5008
  Norfolk (G-9727)
Sounds Greek Inc ....G..... 757 548-0062
  Chesapeake (G-3300)
Southern Accent Embroidery ....G..... 843 991-4910
  Midlothian (G-8905)
Spider Embroidery Inc ....G..... 540 955-2347
  Winchester (G-15482)
Sport Shack Inc ....G..... 540 372-3719
  Fredericksburg (G-5487)
Springbrook Craft Works ....G..... 540 896-3404
  Broadway (G-2097)
Stitch Doctor ....G..... 540 330-1234
  Roanoke (G-12004)
Stitch Makers Embroidery ....G..... 804 794-4523
  Midlothian (G-8910)

Stitchdotpro LLC ....G..... 540 777-0002
  Roanoke (G-12005)
Stitched Loop LLC ....G..... 678 467-1973
  Chesapeake (G-3313)
Stitched Mmries By Shannon LLC ......G..... 540 872-9779
  Bumpass (G-2168)
Stitched With Love LLC ....G..... 757 285-6980
  Virginia Beach (G-14850)
Stitches & Bows ....G..... 678 876-1715
  Front Royal (G-5556)
Stitches Corporate & Custom Em ....G..... 434 374-5111
  Clarksville (G-3635)
Stitching Station ....G..... 703 421-4053
  Sterling (G-13517)
Stitchworks Inc ....G..... 757 631-0300
  Virginia Beach (G-14851)
Sunshine Sewing ....G..... 276 628-2478
  Abingdon (G-63)
T & T Sporting Goods ....G..... 276 228-5286
  Wytheville (G-15917)
Taylor Made Custom Embroidery ....G..... 434 636-0660
  La Crosse (G-7151)
Threadlines Inc ....G..... 757 898-8355
  Grafton (G-5932)
Threads Ink LLC ....G..... 703 221-0819
  Dumfries (G-4260)
Timeless Stitches Inc ....G..... 804 798-7677
  Ashland (G-1500)
Tnl Embroidery Inc ....G..... 757 410-2671
  Chesapeake (G-3341)
Total Stitch Embroidery Inc ....G..... 804 275-4853
  North Chesterfield (G-10003)
Track Patch 1 Corporation ....G..... 757 609-2842
  Chesapeake (G-3347)
Triple Stitch Designs LLC ....G..... 757 376-2666
  Virginia Beach (G-14894)
Unlimited Embroidery ....G..... 540 745-3909
  Floyd (G-5044)
Upon A Once Stitch LLC ....G..... 757 562-1900
  Franklin (G-5160)
▲ Vanguard Industries East Inc........C..... 757 665-8405
  Norfolk (G-9778)
Vienna Custom Embroidery LLC ....G..... 703 887-1254
  Vienna (G-14152)
Vienna Quilt Shop ....G..... 703 281-4091
  Mc Lean (G-8576)
Virginia Needle Art Inc ....G..... 540 433-8070
  Harrisonburg (G-6385)
Virginia Quilter ....G..... 540 548-3207
  Fredericksburg (G-5387)
Virginia Quilting Inc ....C..... 434 757-1809
  La Crosse (G-7152)
Wendys Embroidery ....G..... 757 685-0414
  Virginia Beach (G-14933)
What Heck ....G..... 757 343-4058
  Virginia Beach (G-14934)
Willow Stitch LLC ....G..... 804 761-5967
  Tappahannock (G-13826)
Wisdom Clothing Company Inc...........F..... 703 433-0056
  Sterling (G-13561)
Ww Monograms LLC ....G..... 540 687-6510
  Middleburg (G-8735)

2396 Automotive Trimmings, Apparel Findings, Related Prdts

Aardvark Swim and Sport Inc..............E..... 703 631-6045
  Chantilly (G-2361)
Allen Enterprises LLC ....G..... 540 261-2622
  Buena Vista (G-2138)
Anthony Biel ....G..... 703 307-8516
  Dumfries (G-4234)
▲ Artistic Impressions ....G..... 757 923-4254
  Suffolk (G-13671)
Association For Print Tech ....G..... 703 264-7200
  Reston (G-10793)
Atlantic Embroidery Works LLC.........G..... 804 282-5027
  Henrico (G-6478)
Ballyhoo ....G..... 703 294-6075
  Annandale (G-731)
▼ Barlen Crafts ....C..... 301 537-3491
  Suffolk (G-13673)
Bay Etching & Imprinting Inc............E..... 800 925-2877
  Lively (G-7439)
◆ Bedford Weaving Inc ....C..... 540 586-8235
  Bedford (G-1626)
Blood Sweat & Cheer........................G..... 757 620-1515
  Virginia Beach (G-14288)
Bryant Embroidery LLC ....G..... 757 498-3453
  Virginia Beach (G-14303)

S
I
C

Bxi Inc .... G 804 282-5434
Richmond *(G-11142)*

Carl G Gilliam Jr .... F 276 523-0619
Big Stone Gap *(G-1707)*

Coastal Threads Inc .... G 757 495-2677
Virginia Beach *(G-14349)*

Dap Enterprises Inc .... G 757 921-3576
Williamsburg *(G-15229)*

Dap Incorporated .... G 757 921-3576
Newport News *(G-9214)*

Decal Magic .... G 540 984-3786
Edinburg *(G-4302)*

Decosta Enterprises Inc .... G 703 768-4270
Alexandria *(G-443)*

Delrand Corp .... G 757 490-3355
Virginia Beach *(G-14401)*

Dennis W Wiley .... G 540 992-6631
Buchanan *(G-2121)*

Dister Inc .... E 757 857-1946
Norfolk *(G-9525)*

Dister Inc .... E 703 207-0201
Fairfax *(G-4439)*

Dull Inc Dolan & Norma .... F 703 490-0337
Woodbridge *(G-15687)*

Elite Prints .... G 703 780-3403
Alexandria *(G-455)*

Emblemax LLC .... G 703 802-0200
Chantilly *(G-2417)*

Erbosol Printing .... G 757 325-9986
Hampton *(G-6144)*

Flyway Inc .... G 757 422-3215
Virginia Beach *(G-14469)*

Fresh Printz LLC .... G 540 937-3017
Jeffersonton *(G-7012)*

Golden Squeegee Inc .... G 804 355-8018
Richmond *(G-11220)*

Grafik Trenz .... G 757 539-0141
Smithfield *(G-12714)*

Greeks Unlimited .... G 804 368-1611
Hampton *(G-6161)*

Harville Entps of Danville VA .... G 434 822-2106
Danville *(G-3997)*

Hutson Hauling .... G 804 815-2421
Dutton *(G-4273)*

Ideal Printing LLC .... G 434 421-1000
Danville *(G-3999)*

Individual Products & Svcs Inc ... G 757 488-3363
Chesapeake *(G-3141)*

Jackie Screen Printing .... G 276 963-0964
Richlands *(G-11017)*

Jbtm Enterprises Inc .... F 540 665-9651
Winchester *(G-15551)*

Keith Sanders .... G 276 728-0540
Martinsville *(G-8304)*

Khk Inc .... G 540 337-5068
Stuarts Draft *(G-13654)*

Leading Edge Screen Printing ..... F 540 347-5751
Warrenton *(G-15030)*

Lester Enterprises Intl LLC .... G 703 599-3485
Arlington *(G-1032)*

Lou Wallace .... G 276 762-2303
Saint Paul *(G-12469)*

Love Those Tz LLC .... G 757 897-0238
Virginia Beach *(G-14625)*

Martin Printwear Inc .... G 434 352-5660
Appomattox *(G-819)*

Mounir E Shaheen .... G 757 723-4445
Hampton *(G-6205)*

▲ Nelson Hills Company .... G 434 985-7176
Stanardsville *(G-13224)*

Party Headquarters Inc .... G 703 494-5317
Fredericksburg *(G-5467)*

Promocorp Inc .... F 703 942-7100
Alexandria *(G-560)*

R & R Printing .... G 434 985-9844
Ruckersville *(G-12411)*

Rain & Associates LLC .... G 757 572-3996
Virginia Beach *(G-14758)*

▲ Red Star Consulting LLC .... G 434 872-0890
Charlottesville *(G-2862)*

Samco Textile Prints LLc .... G 571 451-4044
Woodbridge *(G-15802)*

Scb Sales Inc .... G 540 342-6502
Roanoke *(G-12177)*

Schmidt Jayme .... G 540 961-1792
Blacksburg *(G-1787)*

Screen Crafts Inc .... E 804 355-4156
Richmond *(G-11374)*

Shirt Art Inc .... G 703 680-3963
Woodbridge *(G-15806)*

Silkscreening Unlimited Inc .... G 703 385-3212
Fairfax *(G-4554)*

Slim Strength Inc .... G 804 715-3080
Richmond *(G-11064)*

Sport Shack Inc .... G 540 372-3719
Fredericksburg *(G-5487)*

Spring Valley Graphics .... G 276 236-4357
Galax *(G-5648)*

Tdi Printing Group LLC .... E 757 855-5416
Virginia Beach *(G-14866)*

Tee Time Threads LLC .... G 757 581-4507
Chesapeake *(G-3327)*

Trak House LLC .... G 646 617-4418
Richmond *(G-11791)*

▲ Vanguard Industries East Inc .. C 757 665-8405
Norfolk *(G-9778)*

Vizini Incorporated .... G 703 508-8662
Round Hill *(G-12394)*

Whats Your Sign .... G 276 632-0576
Martinsville *(G-8353)*

Wool Felt Products Inc .... E 540 981-0281
Roanoke *(G-12230)*

2397 Schiffli Machine Embroideries

Total Stitch Embroidery Inc .... G 804 748-9594
Chester *(G-3462)*

2399 Fabricated Textile Prdts, NEC

ABC Petwear Inc .... G 804 730-3890
Mechanicsville *(G-8599)*

Advanced Tooling Corporation ..... G 434 286-7781
Scottsville *(G-12657)*

Annin & Co .... E 434 575-7913
South Boston *(G-12746)*

Banana Banner Inc .... F 703 823-5933
Alexandria *(G-144)*

Beau-Geste International Inc .... G 434 534-0468
Forest *(G-5053)*

Berkley Latasha .... G 804 572-6394
Henrico *(G-6482)*

Butler Parachute Systems Inc ..... F 540 342-2501
Roanoke *(G-12057)*

Butler Unmanned Parachute .... F 540 342-2501
Roanoke *(G-12058)*

Camco .... G 757 855-5890
Norfolk *(G-9474)*

Chinook & Co LLC .... G 540 463-9556
Lexington *(G-7389)*

Christian Creations Inc .... G 540 722-2718
Winchester *(G-15401)*

Combat V Tactical .... G 540 604-0235
Fredericksburg *(G-5264)*

Creations At Play LLC .... G 757 541-8226
Poquoson *(G-10368)*

Crochet .... G 732 446-9644
Williamsburg *(G-15226)*

Crochet Braids By Twana LLC ...... G 571 201-7190
Fredericksburg *(G-5180)*

Crochet By Grammy .... G 757 637-8416
Hampton *(G-6122)*

Crochet By Palm LLC .... G 757 427-0532
Virginia Beach *(G-14372)*

Danicas S Crochet Club .... G 703 221-8574
Dumfries *(G-4242)*

Dianes Crochet Dolls & Things .... G 703 229-2173
Warrenton *(G-14996)*

Dog Watch of Shenandoah .... G 540 867-5124
Dayton *(G-4054)*

Emergency Traction Device LLC .. G 703 771-1025
Leesburg *(G-7267)*

◆ Evergreen Enterprises Inc .... C 804 231-1800
Richmond *(G-11582)*

Evergreen Enterprises VA LLC ..... G 804 231-1800
Richmond *(G-11583)*

Exotic Vehicle Wraps Inc .... G 240 320-3335
Sterling *(G-13396)*

Festival Design Inc .... G 804 643-5247
Richmond *(G-11586)*

Francis & Murphy .... G 703 256-8644
Annandale *(G-749)*

Freedom Flag Sign & Banner Co .. G 703 359-5353
Fairfax *(G-4627)*

Judy A OBrien .... G 434 568-3148
Drakes Branch *(G-4135)*

Kerry Scott .... G 434 277-9337
Piney River *(G-10361)*

Kiss Krown LLC .... G 757 776-6518
Hampton *(G-6180)*

Mbh Inc .... G 540 427-5471
Roanoke *(G-12135)*

Mumble Wraps LLC .... G 571 358-5388
Manassas *(G-7978)*

Pawse & Play LLC .... G 757 230-9309
Virginia Beach *(G-14712)*

◆ Premier Pet Products LLC .... D 804 594-0613
Glen Allen *(G-5782)*

Qualitycrochetbybarb LLC .... G 202 596-7301
King George *(G-7106)*

R B M Enterprises Inc .... G 804 290-4407
Glen Allen *(G-5786)*

S E Greer .... G 540 400-0155
Roanoke *(G-12172)*

Smbltc Corp .... G 703 596-5218
Manassas *(G-8158)*

Sweetb Designs LLC .... G 757 550-0436
Portsmouth *(G-10490)*

T-Shirt Factory LLC .... G 703 589-5175
Sterling *(G-13527)*

Tamara Smith .... G 910 495-4404
Gore *(G-5923)*

Tidewater Emblems Ltd .... F 757 428-1170
Virginia Beach *(G-14873)*

Total Parachute Rigging Soluti .... G 757 777-8288
Suffolk *(G-13774)*

U S Flag & Signal Company .... E 757 497-8947
Portsmouth *(G-10494)*

▲ Vanguard Industries East Inc .. E 757 665-8405
Norfolk *(G-9778)*

Washington Aed Education Fund .. G 703 739-9513
Alexandria *(G-379)*

Zotz .... G 703 330-2305
Manassas *(G-8015)*

24 LUMBER AND WOOD PRODUCTS, EXCEPT FURNITURE

2411 Logging

A & A Logging LLC .... G 540 229-2830
Culpeper *(G-3861)*

A Cut Above Logging LLC .... G 434 547-5979
Meherrin *(G-8704)*

A Johnson Linwood .... G 804 829-5364
Providence Forge *(G-10617)*

A L Baird Inc .... F 434 848-2129
Lawrenceville *(G-7176)*

Addem Enterprises Inc .... G 540 789-4412
Willis *(G-15353)*

All-N-Logging LLC .... G 434 547-3550
Keysville *(G-7054)*

Allens Logging Inc .... G 434 724-6493
Chatham *(G-2918)*

Andrew Thurston Logging .... G 540 521-6276
Eagle Rock *(G-4278)*

Appalachian Growth Logging LLC G 540 336-2674
Mount Jackson *(G-9065)*

Atkins Clearing & Trucking .... G 540 832-3128
Gordonsville *(G-5898)*

Aubrey L Clary Inc .... E 434 577-2724
Gasburg *(G-5657)*

B H Franklin Logging Inc .... G 434 352-5484
Appomattox *(G-805)*

Bar Logging LLC .... G 757 641-9269
Franklin *(G-5139)*

Barber Logging LLC .... G 276 346-4638
Jonesville *(G-7018)*

Barton Logging Inc .... G 434 390-8504
Green Bay *(G-5987)*

Baur Logging LLC .... G 757 535-5693
Chesapeake *(G-2994)*

Beagle Logging Company .... G 540 459-2425
Woodstock *(G-15849)*

Bear Branch Logging Inc .... G 276 597-7172
Vansant *(G-13975)*

Bennett Logging & Lumber Inc .... E 540 862-7621
Covington *(G-3778)*

Betty P Hicks .... G 540 745-5111
Floyd *(G-5016)*

Billy Bill Logging .... G 804 512-9669
Aylett *(G-1546)*

Bl Nichols Logging Inc .... G 540 875-8690
Huddleston *(G-6952)*

Blue Ridge Logging Co Inc .... G 434 836-5663
Danville *(G-3960)*

Bobby Collins Logging .... G 804 519-0138
Charles City *(G-2570)*

Booth Logging Company .... G 540 334-1075
Boones Mill *(G-1893)*

Bosserman Murry .... G 540 255-7949
Greenville *(G-5997)*

Bowdens Firewood & Logging LLC ......G....... 540 465-4362
Strasburg *(G-13575)*

Brady Jones Logging ....G....... 434 969-4688
Buckingham *(G-2131)*

Branmar Logging Inc ....G....... 540 832-5535
Gordonsville *(G-5902)*

Bryant Brothers Logging L L C ....G....... 434 933-8303
Gladstone *(G-5682)*

Bryant Energy Corp ....G....... 757 887-2181
Newport News *(G-9186)*

Bryant Logging ....G....... 540 337-0232
Stuarts Draft *(G-13645)*

Buck Hall Logging ....G....... 434 696-1244
Green Bay *(G-5988)*

Butler Custom Logging LLC ....G....... 434 634-5658
Emporia *(G-4355)*

Byer Brothers Logging Inc ....G....... 540 962-3071
Covington *(G-3779)*

C H Evelyn Piling Company Inc ....F....... 804 966-2273
Providence Forge *(G-10619)*

C L E Logging Inc ....G....... 276 881-8617
Bandy *(G-1557)*

Calvin Payne ....G....... 276 251-5815
Ararat *(G-830)*

Cardinals Logging ....G....... 804 457-3543
Mineral *(G-8944)*

Carlton Logging LLC ....G....... 804 693-5193
Gloucester *(G-5840)*

Central Virginia Horse Logging ....G....... 434 390-7252
Blackstone *(G-1814)*

CF Smith & Sons ....G....... 540 672-3291
Orange *(G-10205)*

Champion Ventures LLC ....G....... 540 975-0791
New Market *(G-9141)*

Chips Inc ....D....... 434 589-2424
Troy *(G-13922)*

Cithinning Inc ....G....... 804 370-4859
Ruther Glen *(G-12452)*

Clarence D Campbell ....G....... 540 291-2740
Naturl BR STA *(G-9111)*

Clarence Shelton Jr ....G....... 434 710-0448
Chatham *(G-2923)*

Clary Logging Inc Randy J ....G....... 434 636-5268
Brodnax *(G-2100)*

Clary Timber Co Inc ....F....... 434 594-5055
Gasburg *(G-5658)*

Claude David Sanders ....G....... 276 386-6946
Gate City *(G-5661)*

Concord Logging ....G....... 434 660-1889
Concord *(G-3758)*

Connell Log Thnning LLC Knneth ....G....... 434 729-3712
Brodnax *(G-2101)*

Corey Ely Logging LLC ....G....... 423 579-3436
Pennington Gap *(G-10294)*

Coxe Timber Company ....G....... 757 934-1500
Suffolk *(G-13687)*

Crewe Brothers Logging ....G....... 804 829-2288
Charles City *(G-2574)*

Crosscut Inc ....G....... 276 395-5430
Saint Paul *(G-12466)*

CW Houchens and Sons Log LLC ......G....... 804 615-2002
Bumpass *(G-2161)*

Cw Moore & Sons LLC ....F....... 757 653-9011
Courtland *(G-3767)*

Dale Horton Logging ....G....... 276 251-5004
Ararat *(G-831)*

Dan McPherson & Sons Logging ....G....... 540 483-4385
Callaway *(G-2221)*

Danny A Walker ....G....... 434 724-4454
Callands *(G-2213)*

Darden Logging LLC ....G....... 757 647-9432
Franklin *(G-5141)*

David A Bennett ....G....... 540 862-5868
Covington *(G-3786)*

David C Weaver ....F....... 804 561-5929
Amelia Court House *(G-654)*

David S Creath ....G....... 434 753-2210
South Boston *(G-12760)*

David W Slusher ....G....... 540 745-2485
Floyd *(G-5022)*

Davis Logging ....G....... 804 725-7988
North *(G-9802)*

Deane Logging Co Inc ....G....... 540 718-3676
Madison *(G-7850)*

Deeds Brothers Incorporated ....G....... 540 862-7837
Millboro *(G-8935)*

Dillion Logging ....G....... 434 685-1779
Danville *(G-3985)*

Dobyns Family LLC ....G....... 804 462-5554
Lancaster *(G-7159)*

Dodson Logging LLC ....G....... 540 547-2582
Unionville *(G-13962)*

Donald Kirby ....G....... 540 493-8698
Rocky Mount *(G-12317)*

Dove Logging Inc ....G....... 540 937-4917
Rixeyville *(G-11879)*

Dunromin Logging LLC ....G....... 540 896-3543
Timberville *(G-13847)*

Edwards Inc ....G....... 276 762-7746
Saint Paul *(G-12467)*

Eric Tucker ....G....... 540 747-5665
Covington *(G-3788)*

F & P Enterprises Inc ....F....... 804 561-2784
Amelia Court House *(G-657)*

Ferguson Logging Inc ....G....... 540 721-3408
Moneta *(G-8962)*

Fitzgerald John ....G....... 434 277-8044
Tyro *(G-13939)*

Flint Bros Logging ....G....... 540 886-1509
Staunton *(G-13258)*

Flint Brothers ....G....... 540 886-5761
Staunton *(G-13259)*

Foley Logging Inc ....G....... 540 365-3152
Ferrum *(G-4974)*

Foster Logging ....G....... 434 454-7946
Randolph *(G-10748)*

Four Oaks Timber Company ....G....... 434 374-2669
Clarksville *(G-3630)*

Fred B Meadows Sons Loggi ....G....... 434 392-5269
Farmville *(G-4941)*

Fred Fauber ....G....... 434 845-0303
Lynchburg *(G-7718)*

G&O Logging LLC ....G....... 757 653-2181
Courtland *(G-3770)*

Garthrght Land Clearing Inc TW ....G....... 804 370-5408
Providence Forge *(G-10625)*

Gibson Logging Enterprises LLC ....G....... 606 260-1889
Duffield *(G-4178)*

Gibson Logging Inc ....G....... 804 769-1130
King Queen Ch *(G-7126)*

Gibson Logging LLC Rush J ....G....... 540 539-8145
Bluemont *(G-1888)*

Gillespie Inc ....G....... 540 297-4432
Bedford *(G-1639)*

Greene Horse Logging LLC ....G....... 434 277-5146
Roseland *(G-12368)*

H & H Logging Inc ....G....... 434 321-9805
Green Bay *(G-5989)*

H & M Logging Inc ....D....... 434 476-6569
South Boston *(G-12773)*

H & R Logging ....G....... 434 922-7417
Monroe *(G-8991)*

H L Corker & Son Inc ....G....... 804 449-6686
Beaverdam *(G-1609)*

Hal Warner Logging ....G....... 540 474-5533
Blue Grass *(G-1842)*

Hanneman Land Clearing Log LLC .....G....... 804 909-2349
Ashland *(G-1425)*

Harry Hale Logging ....G....... 540 484-1666
Wirtz *(G-15612)*

Harvey Logging Co Inc ....G....... 434 263-5942
Lovingston *(G-7590)*

Hatcher Logging ....G....... 434 352-7975
Appomattox *(G-812)*

Hatcher Logging Corp Virginia ....G....... 434 299-5293
Big Island *(G-1703)*

Hawkins Logging ....G....... 434 577-2114
Brodnax *(G-2102)*

Hensley Family ....G....... 540 652-8206
Shenandoah *(G-12692)*

Hj Shelton Logging Inc ....G....... 434 432-3840
Chatham *(G-2929)*

Hobbs Logging Inc ....G....... 276 628-4952
Abingdon *(G-38)*

Homer Haywood Wheeler II ....G....... 434 946-5126
Amherst *(G-694)*

Honaker & Son Logging LLC ....G....... 434 661-7935
Amherst *(G-695)*

Honaker Son Logging ....G....... 434 933-8251
Gladstone *(G-5684)*

Hoss Excavating & Logging Co L ....G....... 276 628-4068
Abingdon *(G-39)*

Hylton & Hylton Logging ....G....... 276 930-2245
Woolwine *(G-15865)*

Hylton Timber Harvesting ....G....... 276 930-2348
Woolwine *(G-15866)*

Isle of Wight Forest Products ....G....... 757 357-2009
Smithfield *(G-12716)*

J & R Log & WD Processors LLC ....G....... 703 494-6994
Stafford *(G-13157)*

J & W Logging Inc ....G....... 540 474-3531
Blue Grass *(G-1843)*

J D Shelton ....G....... 434 797-4403
Keeling *(G-7025)*

J H Knighton Lumber Co Inc ....E....... 804 448-4681
Ruther Glen *(G-12457)*

J V Ramsey Logging LLC ....G....... 434 610-1844
Appomattox *(G-814)*

James D Crews Logging ....G....... 434 349-1999
Nathalie *(G-9103)*

James J Gray ....G....... 757 617-5279
Surry *(G-13797)*

James River Logging & Excav ....G....... 434 295-8457
Charlottesville *(G-2818)*

Jammerson Logging ....G....... 434 983-7505
Andersonville *(G-726)*

Jeff Britt Logging ....G....... 540 884-2499
Eagle Rock *(G-4281)*

Jenkins Logging ....G....... 540 543-2079
Culpeper *(G-3900)*

Jennings Logging LLC ....G....... 434 248-6876
Prospect *(G-10613)*

Jerry K Wilson Inc ....G....... 434 299-5175
Big Island *(G-1704)*

Jerry Lee Marshall ....G....... 276 952-5486
Stuart *(G-13619)*

Jimmy Dockery Logging ....G....... 276 225-0149
Gate City *(G-5664)*

John P Hines Logging ....G....... 434 392-3861
Rice *(G-11005)*

Johnny Hillman Logging ....G....... 276 467-2406
Fort Blackmore *(G-5122)*

Johnny Sisk & Sons Inc ....F....... 540 547-2202
Culpeper *(G-3902)*

Johnson James Thomas Logging ....G....... 804 966-1552
Charles City *(G-2578)*

Jones Logging ....G....... 276 794-9510
Lebanon *(G-7195)*

K & J Logging Inc ....G....... 540 330-9812
Huddleston *(G-6954)*

K & R Tree Care LLC ....G....... 804 767-0695
Maidens *(G-7891)*

K Dudley Logging Inc ....G....... 540 890-0220
Vinton *(G-14175)*

K H Franklin Logging LLC ....G....... 434 352-9235
Appomattox *(G-817)*

Kenneth Foley ....G....... 276 930-1452
Stuart *(G-13620)*

Knabe Logging LLC ....G....... 434 547-9878
Dillwyn *(G-4096)*

Koppers Utility Indus Pdts Inc ....G....... 434 292-4375
Blackstone *(G-1818)*

L A Bowles Logging Inc ....G....... 804 492-3103
Powhatan *(G-10555)*

L&F Logging Inc ....G....... 276 728-5773
Hillsville *(G-6895)*

Lakeside Logging Inc ....G....... 540 872-2585
Bumpass *(G-2164)*

Larry W Jarvis Logging ....G....... 276 686-5938
Rural Retreat *(G-12427)*

Laurel Fork Logging Inc ....G....... 276 285-3761
Bristol *(G-2024)*

Lawson & Sons Logging LLC ....G....... 434 292-7904
Blackstone *(G-1819)*

Lawson Brothers Logging LLC ....G....... 276 694-8905
Stuart *(G-13622)*

Lawson Timber Company ....G....... 276 395-2069
Saint Paul *(G-12468)*

Layne Logging ....G....... 276 312-1665
Hurley *(G-6969)*

Leonard Logging Inc ....G....... 540 239-6991
Floyd *(G-5031)*

Leroy Woodward ....G....... 540 948-6335
Madison *(G-7857)*

Lester Viar ....G....... 434 277-5504
Lowesville *(G-7596)*

Lester Group ....G....... 276 627-0346
Bassett *(G-1585)*

Lewis Brothers Logging ....G....... 804 478-4243
Mc Kenney *(G-8381)*

Littlefield Logging ....G....... 804 798-5590
Glen Allen *(G-5764)*

Lloyd D Wells Logging Contg ....G....... 434 933-4316
Gladstone *(G-5685)*

Logging Ninja Inc ....G....... 804 569-6054
Mechanicsville *(G-8654)*

Lovell Logging Inc ....G....... 276 632-5191
Martinsville *(G-8306)*

Lw Logging LLC ....G....... 434 735-8598
Wylliesburg *(G-15872)*

S
I
C

M M Wright Inc ....D...... 434 577-2101
  Gasburg *(G-5659)*

Mann Logging ....G...... 434 283-5245
  Gladys *(G-5694)*

Maple Grove Logging LLC ....G...... 276 677-0152
  Sugar Grove *(G-13787)*

Marden Thinning Company Inc ...G...... 540 872-5196
  Bumpass *(G-2165)*

Marion Brothers Logging Inc .....E...... 804 492-3200
  Cumberland *(G-3936)*

Marvin Dudley Logging ....G...... 540 784-3098
  Lexington *(G-7399)*

Mast Bros Logging LLC ....F...... 434 446-2401
  South Boston *(G-12781)*

Mayo River Logging Co Inc ....G...... 276 694-6305
  Stuart *(G-13624)*

McCormick Jr Logging Inc Bd .....G...... 434 238-3593
  Gladstone *(G-5687)*

McDonald Sawmill ....G...... 540 465-5539
  Strasburg *(G-13588)*

McKee Brewer ....G...... 276 579-2048
  Independence *(G-6990)*

Mdj Logging Inc ....G...... 276 889-4658
  Honaker *(G-6915)*

Michael Sanders ....G...... 276 452-2314
  Fort Blackmore *(G-5123)*

Michael W Tuck ....G...... 540 297-1231
  Bedford *(G-1644)*

Mickey Norris Logging ....G...... 276 206-3959
  Marion *(G-8236)*

Mid Atlantic Mining LLC ....G...... 757 407-6735
  Suffolk *(G-13742)*

Mid Atlntic Tree Hrvestors Inc ....E...... 804 769-8826
  Aylett *(G-1550)*

Mighty Oaks Tree Triming & Log ...G...... 585 471-0213
  Lynchburg *(G-7773)*

Mike Gibson & Sons Logging ......G...... 804 769-3510
  King Queen Ch *(G-7127)*

Mill Road Logging LLC ....G...... 434 665-7467
  Rustburg *(G-12442)*

MLS Logging LLC ....G...... 540 223-0394
  Orange *(G-10220)*

Moore C W and Sons LLC ....G...... 757 653-9121
  Courtland *(G-3773)*

Moore Logging Inc ....G...... 276 233-1693
  Dugspur *(G-4189)*

Morris & Sons Logging Glen ....G...... 540 854-5271
  Unionville *(G-13965)*

Mountain Top Logging LLC ....G...... 540 745-6709
  Floyd *(G-5032)*

Mountaintop Logging LLC ....G...... 540 468-3059
  Monterey *(G-9010)*

Moyers Logging ....G...... 540 468-2289
  Monterey *(G-9011)*

Mt Pleasant Log & Excvtg LLC ....G...... 434 922-7326
  Amherst *(G-701)*

Mullican Flooring LP ....D...... 276 565-0220
  Appalachia *(G-798)*

Newell Logging ....G...... 434 636-2743
  La Crosse *(G-7147)*

Nichols Logging Inc ....G...... 540 297-3246
  Huddleston *(G-6956)*

Noel I Hull ....G...... 540 396-6225
  DOE Hill *(G-4115)*

North Fork Inc ....E...... 540 997-5602
  Goshen *(G-5926)*

Parmly Jr Land Logging & Timbe ...G...... 434 842-2900
  Palmyra *(G-10253)*

Pennells Logging ....G...... 434 292-5482
  Blackstone *(G-1823)*

Penningtons Logging LLC ....G...... 276 783-9374
  Chilhowie *(G-3557)*

Peppers Services LLC ....G...... 276 233-6464
  Galax *(G-5645)*

Piedmont Logging Inc ....G...... 434 989-1698
  Roseland *(G-12371)*

Pinecrest Timber Co ....E...... 804 834-2304
  Waverly *(G-15087)*

Poff Logging LLC ....G...... 540 695-0060
  Floyd *(G-5034)*

Polks Logging & Lumber ....G...... 540 477-3376
  Quicksburg *(G-10693)*

Porcupine Logging LLC ....G...... 540 894-1675
  Louisa *(G-7563)*

Pride and Joy Logging Inc ....G...... 540 474-5533
  Blue Grass *(G-1844)*

Pritts Logging ....G...... 304 646-0004
  Warm Springs *(G-14974)*

Pulpwood and Logging Inc ....G...... 434 736-9440
  Keysville *(G-7062)*

▼ Q C Veneer & Logs LLC ....G...... 540 719-4349
  Hardy *(G-6288)*

Quality Logging LLC ....G...... 540 493-7228
  Floyd *(G-5036)*

R David Rosson ....G...... 540 456-8108
  Afton *(G-86)*

R G Logging ....G...... 276 233-9224
  Galax *(G-5646)*

R S Bottoms Logging ....G...... 434 577-3044
  Brodnax *(G-2103)*

Ra Resky Woodsmith LLC ....G...... 757 678-7555
  Machipongo *(G-7848)*

Ragland Trucking Inc W E ....G...... 434 286-2414
  Scottsville *(G-12664)*

Rainbow Hill Farm ....G...... 540 365-7826
  Ferrum *(G-4977)*

Ralph Johnson ....G...... 434 286-2735
  Scottsville *(G-12665)*

Ralph Rice ....G...... 434 385-8614
  Forest *(G-5089)*

Ramsey Brothers Logging Inc .....G...... 540 463-5044
  Lexington *(G-7414)*

Rct Logging LLC ....F...... 434 767-4780
  Green Bay *(G-5991)*

REA Boys Logging & Equip ....G...... 276 957-4935
  Spencer *(G-12874)*

Reaves Timber Corporation ....G...... 434 299-5645
  Coleman Falls *(G-3707)*

Rexrode Timber & Excavation .....G...... 540 474-5892
  Monterey *(G-9013)*

Reynolds Timber Inc ....G...... 804 633-6117
  Woodford *(G-15842)*

Richard C Iroler ....G...... 276 236-3796
  Fries *(G-5517)*

Richardson Logging ....G...... 540 373-5756
  Fredericksburg *(G-5477)*

Robert David Rosson ....G...... 540 456-6173
  Afton *(G-87)*

Robert E Carroll Logging Inc ....E...... 434 636-2168
  Ebony *(G-4298)*

Robert L Penn ....G...... 276 629-2211
  Bassett *(G-1591)*

Roger K Williams ....G...... 540 775-3192
  King George *(G-7110)*

Rorrer Timber Co Inc ....G...... 276 694-6304
  Stuart *(G-13628)*

Rt Logging LLC ....G...... 276 452-2258
  Gate City *(G-5666)*

S & D Adkins Logging LLC ....G...... 434 292-8882
  Crewe *(G-3815)*

S R Jones Jr & Sons Inc ....E...... 434 577-2311
  Gasburg *(G-5660)*

Salyer Logging ....G...... 276 690-0688
  Nickelsville *(G-9385)*

Sam Belcher & Sons Inc ....G...... 276 930-2084
  Woolwine *(G-15867)*

Sam H Hughes Jr ....G...... 434 263-4432
  Shipman *(G-12698)*

Sams Logging Inc ....G...... 434 661-7137
  Monroe *(G-8995)*

Sanders Brothers Logging Inc .....G...... 276 995-2416
  Fort Blackmore *(G-5124)*

Saunders Logging Inc ....G...... 434 735-8341
  Saxe *(G-12648)*

Saw Shop ....G...... 540 365-0745
  Ferrum *(G-4980)*

Sawmill Bottom ....G...... 276 880-2241
  Cleveland *(G-3656)*

Sawyer Logging Inc ....G...... 276 995-2522
  Fort Blackmore *(G-5125)*

Schlotterer Logging ....G...... 910 376-1623
  Stafford *(G-13188)*

Scholl Custom WD & Met Cft LLC ...G...... 804 739-2390
  Chesterfield *(G-3522)*

Scott Logging LLC ....G...... 276 930-2497
  Stuart *(G-13629)*

Seal R L & Sons Logging ....G...... 804 769-3696
  Aylett *(G-1554)*

Sellars Logging ....G...... 757 566-0613
  Barhamsville *(G-1573)*

Shelton Logging Inc ....G...... 434 294-1386
  Crewe *(G-3817)*

Shifflett and Son Log Co LLC ....G...... 757 434-7979
  Urbanna *(G-13973)*

Shumate Inc George C ....E...... 540 463-2244
  Lexington *(G-7417)*

Sickal Logging ....G...... 804 366-1965
  Barhamsville *(G-1574)*

Simmons Logging Inc ....G...... 434 676-1202
  South Hill *(G-12860)*

Slagle Logging & Chipping Inc .....G...... 434 572-6733
  South Boston *(G-12789)*

Slushers Logging & Sawing LLC ...G...... 540 641-1378
  Floyd *(G-5039)*

Southeast Fiber Supply Inc ....G...... 757 653-2318
  Courtland *(G-3774)*

Southeastern Land and Logging ...G...... 540 489-1403
  Ferrum *(G-4982)*

Southeastern Logging & Chippin ...G...... 540 493-9781
  Wirtz *(G-15618)*

Staton & Hauling ....G...... 434 946-7913
  Amherst *(G-709)*

Staton & Son Logging ....G...... 540 570-3614
  Buena Vista *(G-2154)*

Stella-Jones Corporation ....D...... 540 997-9251
  Goshen *(G-5927)*

Steven D Thomas ....G...... 540 254-2964
  Buchanan *(G-2129)*

Sutherlins Logging Inc ....G...... 804 366-3871
  Locust Hill *(G-7455)*

T C Catlett & Sons Lumber Co ......E...... 540 786-2303
  Fredericksburg *(G-5373)*

T W McPherson & Sons ....G...... 540 483-0105
  Callaway *(G-2222)*

Thomas L Alphin Inc ....G...... 540 997-0611
  Goshen *(G-5929)*

Thorpe Logging Inc ....G...... 434 634-6050
  Emporia *(G-4368)*

Three P Logging ....G...... 434 376-9812
  Brookneal *(G-2114)*

Timberline Logging Inc ....G...... 276 393-7239
  Big Stone Gap *(G-1716)*

TNT Bradshaw Logging LLC ....G...... 276 928-1579
  Bland *(G-1837)*

TNT Logging LLC ....G...... 540 997-0611
  Goshen *(G-5930)*

Tomorrows Resources Unlimited ...E...... 434 929-2800
  Madison Heights *(G-7886)*

Underwood Logging LLC ....G...... 540 489-1388
  Rocky Mount *(G-12357)*

Varner Logging LLC ....G...... 540 849-7451
  Churchville *(G-3621)*

Vickie D Blankenship ....G...... 540 977-6377
  Blue Ridge *(G-1856)*

Victor Randall Logging LLC ....G...... 804 241-6630
  Mechanicsville *(G-8693)*

W E Ragland Logging Co ....F...... 434 286-2705
  Scottsville *(G-12670)*

W T Jones & Sons Inc ....E...... 804 633-9737
  Ruther Glen *(G-12463)*

Walter Pillow Logging ....G...... 434 283-5449
  Gladys *(G-5698)*

Waughs Logging ....G...... 540 854-5676
  Culpeper *(G-3931)*

Wayne Garrett Logging Inc ....F...... 757 866-8472
  Spring Grove *(G-12932)*

Wayne Hudson ....G...... 434 568-6361
  Drakes Branch *(G-4136)*

West Midland Timber LLC ....G...... 540 570-5969
  Lexington *(G-7424)*

Wheeler Tember ....G...... 540 672-4186
  Orange *(G-10231)*

Wheeler Thurston E Logging ....G...... 434 946-5265
  Amherst *(G-713)*

William B Gilman ....F...... 804 798-7812
  Ashland *(G-1510)*

▲ William H Scott ....G...... 804 561-5384
  Amelia Court House *(G-677)*

Williams & Son Inc HL ....G...... 540 775-3192
  King George *(G-7123)*

Williams Logging and Chipping .....F...... 276 694-8077
  Spencer *(G-12875)*

Wld Logging & Chipping Inc ....G...... 540 483-1218
  Glade Hill *(G-5671)*

Wood Harvesters ....G...... 276 650-2603
  Axton *(G-1543)*

Woodland Logging Inc ....G...... 276 669-7795
  Bristol *(G-2043)*

Woolfolk Brothers LLC ....G...... 540 967-0664
  Louisa *(G-7575)*

Woolfolk Enterprises ....G...... 540 967-0664
  Louisa *(G-7576)*

Wright Logging LLC ....G...... 434 547-4525
  Keysville *(G-7066)*

Wrights Trucking & Logging ....F...... 434 946-5387
  Amherst *(G-715)*

Wst Products LLC ....G...... 434 736-9100
  Keysville *(G-7067)*

Yoder Logging ....G...... 804 561-3913
  Amelia Court House *(G-679)*

2421 Saw & Planing Mills

Amelia Lumber Company ....E 804 561-2155
  Amelia Court House (G-649)

Anderson Brothers Lumber Co ....E 804 561-2153
  Amelia Court House (G-651)

Anderson Erle P Lumber Company ......E 804 748-0500
  Disputanta (G-4104)

Apex Capital LLC ....G 904 495-6422
  Ashland (G-1370)

▼ Appalachian Woods LLC ....F 540 337-1801
  Stuarts Draft (G-13644)

Appalachian Woods LLC ....G 540 886-5700
  Staunton (G-13242)

Arrington Smith Hunter Lee ....G 540 230-4952
  Christiansburg (G-3569)

Asal Tie & Lumber Co Inc ....F 434 454-6555
  Scottsburg (G-12654)

B & G Bandmill ....G 276 766-4280
  Hillsville (G-6884)

Ball Lumber Co Inc ....D 804 443-5555
  Millers Tavern (G-8939)

▼ Barnes Manufacturing Company ......E 434 676-8210
  Kenbridge (G-7032)

Batchelder & Collins Inc ....G 757 220-2806
  Williamsburg (G-15210)

Beagle Logging Company ....G 540 459-2425
  Woodstock (G-15849)

Belcher Lumber Co Inc ....G 276 498-3362
  Rowe (G-12396)

Beneath The Bark Inc ....E 434 848-3995
  Lawrenceville (G-7177)

Bennett Logging & Lumber Inc ....E 540 862-7621
  Covington (G-3778)

Blue Ridge Portable Sawmill ....G 540 743-2520
  Luray (G-7602)

Bolt Sawmill ....G 434 574-6732
  Farmville (G-4937)

Brodnax Lumber Company ....E 434 729-2852
  Brodnax (G-2099)

Brown-Foreman Coopeages ....G 434 575-0770
  South Boston (G-12754)

Browns Forest Products Inc ....F 434 735-8179
  Drakes Branch (G-4130)

Browns Sawmill Inc ....G 434 542-5776
  Charlotte C H (G-2582)

Builders Firstsource Inc ....D 540 665-0078
  Winchester (G-15397)

Butler Woodcrafters Inc ....G 203 241-9753
  North Chesterfield (G-9836)

C & B Lumber Inc ....E 276 744-3650
  Fries (G-5515)

Campbell Lumber Co Inc ....F 434 293-3021
  North Garden (G-10074)

Carlton and Edwards Inc ....E 804 758-5100
  Saluda (G-12602)

Carlton Orndorff ....G 540 436-3543
  Maurertown (G-8360)

▲ Charles City Forest Products ....E 804 966-2336
  Providence Forge (G-10620)

Charles W Brinegar Enterprise ....G 276 634-6934
  Spencer (G-12872)

Chewning Lumber Company ....E 540 895-5158
  Spotsylvania (G-12885)

Chips Brookneal Inc ....E 434 376-6202
  Brookneal (G-2109)

Chips Inc ....D 434 589-2424
  Troy (G-13922)

Cloverdale Lumber Co Inc ....E 434 822-5017
  Sutherlin (G-13806)

▼ Coleman Lumber Co Inc Robert S ....E 540 854-5711
  Culpeper (G-3879)

Collins Sawmill and Loggin LLC ....G 276 694-7521
  Stuart (G-13608)

Conner Industries Inc ....G 804 706-4229
  Chester (G-3396)

Culbertson Lumber Company Inc ....G 276 679-7620
  Norton (G-10116)

Curtis Russell Lumber Co Inc ....E 276 346-1958
  Jonesville (G-7020)

Dejarnette Lumber Company ....F 804 633-9821
  Milford (G-8930)

Earl D Pierce Sawmill ....G 276 744-7538
  Fries (G-5516)

▲ Enviva Pellets Southampton LLC ......G 301 657-5560
  Franklin (G-5142)

Everett Jones Lumber Corp ....F 540 582-5655
  Spotsylvania (G-12889)

Fain Arlice Sawmill ....G 276 694-8211
  Stuart (G-13611)

Falling Creek Log Yard Inc ....E 804 798-6121
  Ashland (G-1413)

Ferguson Custom Sawmill LLC ....G 540 903-8174
  Fredericksburg (G-5287)

▲ Ferguson Land and Lbr Co Inc ....D 540 483-5090
  Rocky Mount (G-12322)

Fitzgerald Lumber & Log Co Inc ....G 540 348-5199
  Fairfield (G-4730)

▼ Fitzgerald Lumber & Log Co Inc ....E 540 261-3430
  Buena Vista (G-2144)

Gallimore Sawmill Inc ....F 276 236-5064
  Galax (G-5634)

Garrity Custom Sawing LLC ....G 757 488-9324
  Chesapeake (G-3115)

Georgia-Pacific LLC ....B 434 634-5123
  Emporia (G-4359)

Goodman Lumber Co Inc ....G 804 265-9030
  Wilsons (G-15367)

Gregory Lumber Inc ....E 434 432-1000
  Java (G-7011)

Hairfield Lumber Corporation ....E 540 967-2042
  Spotsylvania (G-12893)

Hardwood Mulch Corporation ....G 804 458-7500
  Disputanta (G-4108)

Holland Lumber Co Inc ....E 804 443-4200
  Millers Tavern (G-8940)

Hooke Brothers Lumber Co LLC ....F 540 499-2540
  Monterey (G-9007)

▼ Hopewell Hardwood Sales Inc ....E 804 458-5178
  North Prince George (G-10088)

Hopkins Lumber Contractors Inc ....E 276 694-2166
  Stuart (G-13618)

Independence Lumber Inc ....D 276 773-3744
  Independence (G-6987)

J E Moore Lumber Co Inc ....F 434 634-9740
  Emporia (G-4361)

J H Knighton Lumber Co Inc ....E 804 448-4681
  Ruther Glen (G-12457)

JC Bradley Lumber Co ....G 540 962-4446
  Covington (G-3792)

Jim L Clark ....E 276 393-2359
  Jonesville (G-7022)

Johnny Asal Lumber Co Inc ....G 804 492-4884
  Cumberland (G-3935)

Johnson & Son Lumber Inc ....E 540 752-5557
  Fredericksburg (G-5446)

Jones Lumber Company J E ....E 804 883-6331
  Montpelier (G-9017)

Kirk Lumber Company ....G 757 255-4521
  Suffolk (G-13729)

Koppers Inc ....E 540 380-2061
  Salem (G-12527)

Koppers Industries Inc ....G 540 672-3802
  Orange (G-10218)

Lams Lumber Co ....G 540 832-5173
  Barboursville (G-1563)

Lewis Lumber Mill ....G 276 629-1600
  Bassett (G-1586)

Lindsay Hardwoods Inc ....F 434 392-8615
  Farmville (G-4947)

Mace Lumber Mill ....G 540 249-4458
  Grottoes (G-6021)

Marcus Cox & Sons Inc ....F 540 297-5818
  Moneta (G-8971)

Martin Railroad Tie Co ....G 434 933-4398
  Gladstone (G-5686)

McDonald Sawmill ....G 540 465-5539
  Strasburg (G-13588)

Meadowsend Farm and Sawmill Co .....G 434 975-6598
  Earlysville (G-4291)

Mitchell Sawmilling ....G 276 944-2329
  Saltville (G-12586)

Moore and Son Inc Lewis S ....G 804 366-7170
  Ruther Glen (G-12458)

Morgan Lumber Company Inc ....E 434 735-8151
  Red Oak (G-10759)

Morris Finishing Co ....G 540 674-0079
  Dublin (G-4166)

Mullican Flooring LP ....C 276 679-2924
  Norton (G-10130)

Mullican Flooring LP ....G 276 565-0220
  Appalachia (G-798)

Mumpower Lumber Company ....E 276 669-7491
  Bristol (G-2027)

Neff Lumber Mills Inc ....E 804 896-7031
  Broadway (G-2091)

Nelson Martin ....G 540 879-9016
  Dayton (G-4058)

Next Generation Woods Inc ....G 540 639-3077
  Hiwassee (G-6913)

North Fork Inc ....E 540 997-5602
  Goshen (G-5926)

Northern Neck Lumber Co Inc ....E 804 333-4041
  Warsaw (G-15071)

Northwest Hardwoods ....G 540 631-3245
  Front Royal (G-5546)

Northwest Hardwoods Inc ....G 540 261-2171
  Buena Vista (G-2150)

Northwest Hardwoods Inc ....G 540 261-2171
  Buena Vista (G-2151)

OMalley Timber Products LLC ....D 804 445-1118
  Tappahannock (G-13819)

Ontario Hardwood Company Inc ....E 434 736-9291
  Keysville (G-7061)

Pace Custom Sawing LLC ....G 276 956-2000
  Ridgeway (G-11847)

Patricia Ramey ....G 703 973-1140
  Upperville (G-13967)

Pembelton Forest Products Inc ....E 434 292-7511
  Blackstone (G-1822)

Pierce & Johnson Lumber Co Inc ....E 434 983-2586
  Dillwyn (G-4098)

Pine Products Inc ....E 276 957-2222
  Martinsville (G-8318)

Pine Products LLC ....G 276 957-2222
  Martinsville (G-8319)

Pinecrest Timber Co ....E 804 834-2304
  Waverly (G-15087)

Portable Sawmill Service ....G 276 940-4194
  Gate City (G-5665)

Porters Wood Products Inc ....F 757 654-6430
  Boykins (G-1920)

R A Yancey Lumber Corp ....D 434 823-4107
  Crozet (G-3849)

R D Knighton Sawmill ....G 540 872-3636
  Bumpass (G-2167)

R David Rosson ....G 540 456-8108
  Afton (G-86)

R L Beckley Sawmill Inc ....F 540 872-3621
  Montpelier (G-9019)

Ramsey & Son Lumber Corp ....F 434 946-5429
  Amherst (G-704)

Richard C Iroler ....G 276 236-3796
  Fries (G-5517)

Robertson Lumber Inc ....E 434 369-5603
  Altavista (G-639)

Robertson Lumber Inc ....F 434 335-5100
  Hurt (G-6977)

Rock Hill Lumber Inc ....E 540 547-2889
  Culpeper (G-3918)

Rocky Mount Hardwood Inc ....F 540 483-1428
  Ferrum (G-4979)

▼ Rowe Furniture Inc ....A 540 389-8671
  Elliston (G-4349)

Sawdust and Shavings LLC ....G 804 205-8074
  Ruther Glen (G-12462)

Scott Pallets Inc ....E 804 561-2514
  Amelia Court House (G-672)

Seward Lumber Company Inc ....E 757 866-8911
  Claremont (G-3625)

Shelter2home Inc ....G 540 327-4426
  Winchester (G-15476)

Shumate Inc George C ....E 540 463-2244
  Lexington (G-7417)

SM Lumber Inc ....G 757 797-8353
  Virginia Beach (G-14826)

Smith Mountain Land & Lbr Inc ....F 540 297-1205
  Huddleston (G-6958)

Smythers Daris O Sawmill ....G 540 980-5169
  Allisonia (G-620)

Soga Inc ....G 202 465-7158
  Alexandria (G-587)

Stella-Jones Corporation ....D 540 997-9251
  Goshen (G-5927)

Stevens & Sons Lumber Co ....F 434 822-7105
  Ringgold (G-11874)

Stovall Brothers Lumber LLC ....F 276 694-6684
  Stuart (G-13632)

Stuart Wilderness Inc ....E 276 694-4432
  Stuart (G-13635)

Sweany Trckg & Hardwoods LLC ....G 540 273-9387
  Stafford (G-13198)

T C Catlett & Sons Lumber Co ....E 540 786-2303
  Fredericksburg (G-5373)

Talon Inc ....F 703 777-3600
  Leesburg (G-7358)

Timber Team USA LLC ....G 434 989-1201
  Charlottesville (G-2892)

Timberland Express Inc ....G 276 679-1965
  Wise (G-15636)

Tine & Company Inc ....G...... 276 881-8232
Whitewood (G-15193)
Trent Sawmill Inc ....G...... 434 376-2714
Brookneal (G-2115)
◆ Trex Co Inc ....C...... 540 542-6300
Winchester (G-15492)
Trex Company Inc ....D...... 540 542-6314
Winchester (G-15495)
Trex Company Inc ....C...... 540 542-6800
Winchester (G-15496)
Tucker Timber Products Inc ....F...... 434 736-9661
Keysville (G-7064)
Turman Lumber Company Inc ....E...... 540 639-1250
Christiansburg (G-3614)
▼ Turman Lumber Company Inc ....G...... 540 745-2041
Floyd (G-5043)
▼ Turman Sawmill Inc ....D...... 276 728-3752
Hillsville (G-6901)
▼ Turman-Mercer Sawmills LLC ....F...... 276 728-7974
Hillsville (G-6902)
W R Deacon & Sons Timber Inc ....E...... 540 463-3832
Lexington (G-7422)
W T Jones & Sons Inc ....E...... 804 633-9737
Ruther Glen (G-12463)
Walton Lumber Co Inc ....F...... 540 894-5444
Mineral (G-8952)
Waltrip Recycling Inc ....G...... 757 229-0434
Williamsburg (G-15338)
White Oak Grove Woodworks ....G...... 540 763-2723
Riner (G-11866)
Williams Lumber Supply Inc ....E...... 434 376-3368
Brookneal (G-2116)
Wine Sawmill ....G...... 540 373-8328
Fredericksburg (G-5503)
▲ Wood Preservers Incorporated ....D...... 804 333-4022
Warsaw (G-15073)
Woodberry Farm Inc ....G...... 540 854-6967
Orange (G-10233)
Woodhelvin Inc ....G...... 540 854-6452
Spotsylvania (G-12924)
Woodwrights LLC ....G...... 804 761-0775
Irvington (G-7002)

2426 Hardwood Dimension & Flooring Mills

▲ Aco Corporation ....G...... 757 480-2875
Virginia Beach (G-14208)
Aco Corporation ....G...... 757 480-2875
Norfolk (G-9420)
American Floors ....G...... 804 745-8932
North Chesterfield (G-9815)
American Hands LLC ....G...... 804 349-8974
Powhatan (G-10530)
◆ American Hardwood Inds LLC ....C...... 540 946-9150
Waynesboro (G-15092)
American Woodmark Corporation ....C...... 540 672-3707
Orange (G-10202)
American Woodmark Corporation ....C...... 540 665-9100
Winchester (G-15379)
Anderson Brothers Lumber Co ....E...... 804 561-2153
Amelia Court House (G-651)
Anderson Erle P Lumber Company ....E...... 804 748-0500
Disputanta (G-4104)
Ball Lumber Co Inc ....D...... 804 443-5555
Millers Tavern (G-8939)
Brad Warstler ....G...... 540 745-3595
Floyd (G-5017)
Chantilly Floor Wholesaler Inc ....F...... 703 263-0515
Chantilly (G-2391)
▲ Charles City Forest Products ....E...... 804 966-2336
Providence Forge (G-10620)
Clark Hardwood Flr Refinishing ....G...... 804 350-8871
Powhatan (G-10538)
Cloverdale Lumber Co Inc ....E...... 434 822-5017
Sutherlin (G-13806)
Cochrans Lumber & Millwork Inc ....G...... 540 955-4142
Berryville (G-1675)
Country Corner LLC ....G...... 540 538-3763
Fredericksburg (G-5415)
▲ County Line LLC ....D...... 434 736-8405
Keysville (G-7055)
◆ Davis Mining & Mfg Inc ....F...... 276 395-3354
Wise (G-15622)
Dejarnette Lumber Company ....F...... 804 633-9821
Milford (G-8930)
▼ Fitzgerald Lumber & Log Co Inc ......E...... 540 261-3430
Buena Vista (G-2144)
Fitzgerald Lumber & Log Co Inc ....D...... 540 348-5199
Fairfield (G-4730)
Great Amercn Woodcrafters LLC ....G...... 571 572-3150
Woodbridge (G-15714)

Hickory Frame Corp ....G...... 434 847-8489
Lynchburg (G-7732)
Holland Lumber Co Inc ....E...... 804 443-4200
Millers Tavern (G-8940)
Ignacio C Garcia ....G...... 703 922-9829
Alexandria (G-482)
J H Knighton Lumber Co Inc ....E...... 804 448-4681
Ruther Glen (G-12457)
Johnny Asal Lumber Co Inc ....E...... 804 492-4884
Cumberland (G-3935)
Johnson & Son Lumber Inc ....E...... 540 752-5557
Fredericksburg (G-5446)
Jones Lumber Company J E ....E...... 804 883-6331
Montpelier (G-9017)
Knicely Plaining Mill LLC ....G...... 540 879-2284
Dayton (G-4057)
Kreager Woodworking Inc ....E...... 276 952-2052
Meadows of Dan (G-8592)
Lams Lumber Co ....E...... 540 832-5173
Barboursville (G-1563)
Lee Tech Hardwood Floors ....G...... 540 588-6217
Roanoke (G-12124)
Ludaire Fine Wood Floors Inc ....G...... 276 889-3072
Lebanon (G-7199)
M & P Sawmill Co Inc ....G...... 276 783-5585
Marion (G-8232)
Madera Floors LLC ....G...... 703 855-6847
Reston (G-10892)
Madison Flooring Company LLC ....G...... 540 948-4498
Madison (G-7859)
Massies Wood Products LLC ....G...... 434 277-8498
Roseland (G-12370)
Matera John ....G...... 757 240-0425
Yorktown (G-15981)
Mullican Flooring LP ....D...... 276 565-0220
Appalachia (G-798)
Mullican Flooring LP ....C...... 276 679-2924
Norton (G-10130)
Northern Neck Lumber Co Inc ....E...... 804 333-4041
Warsaw (G-15071)
Ontario Hardwood Company Inc ....E...... 434 736-9291
Keysville (G-7061)
Pembelton Forest Products Inc ....E...... 434 292-7511
Blackstone (G-1822)
Porters Wood Products Inc ....E...... 757 654-6430
Boykins (G-1920)
Portsmouth Lumber Corporation ....F...... 757 397-4646
Portsmouth (G-10471)
▼ Potomac Supply Llc ....D...... 804 472-2527
Kinsale (G-7136)
Rock Hill Lumber Inc ....E...... 540 547-2889
Culpeper (G-3918)
Rowe Fine Furniture Inc ....C...... 540 389-8661
Salem (G-12563)
Rutherford Bean ....G...... 757 898-4363
Seaford (G-12677)
S N L Finishing ....G...... 540 740-3826
Staunton (G-13289)
Sand King ....G...... 434 465-3498
Scottsville (G-12666)
Sheaves Floors LLC ....G...... 540 234-9080
Weyers Cave (G-15176)
Shumate Inc George C ....E...... 540 463-2244
Lexington (G-7417)
SM Lumber Inc ....G...... 757 797-8353
Virginia Beach (G-14826)
▲ Southeastern Wood Products Inc ....F...... 276 632-9025
Martinsville (G-8332)
Stuart Wilderness Inc ....G...... 276 694-4432
Stuart (G-13635)
T C Catlett & Sons Lumber Co ....E...... 540 786-2303
Fredericksburg (G-5373)
Tatums Floor Service ....G...... 804 737-3328
Highland Springs (G-6857)
Ten Oaks LLC ....C...... 276 694-3208
Stuart (G-13636)
Tony Tran Hardwood Floors ....G...... 540 793-4094
Vinton (G-14187)
VA Epoxy Designs LLC ....G...... 757 947-6249
Newport News (G-9371)
Valley Utility Buildings Inc ....G...... 276 679-6736
Big Stone Gap (G-1717)
W R Deacon & Sons Timber Inc ....E...... 540 463-3832
Lexington (G-7422)
Weaber Inc ....G...... 804 876-3588
Doswell (G-4127)
Whitlow Lumber & Logging Inc ....G...... 276 930-3854
Stuart (G-13640)
Wooden Caboose Inc ....G...... 804 748-2101
Chesterfield (G-3543)

2429 Special Prdt Sawmills, NEC

Chesapeake Biofuels ....G...... 804 482-1784
Petersburg (G-10311)
Empc Bio Energy Group LLC ....F...... 757 550-1103
Chesapeake (G-3088)
▼ Ramoneda Brothers LLC ....G...... 540 547-3168
Culpeper (G-3915)
Ramoneda Brothers LLC ....G...... 540 825-9166
Culpeper (G-3916)

2431 Millwork

Abingdon Millwork ....G...... 276 676-2951
Abingdon (G-1)
Adkins Custom Woodworking ....G...... 276 638-8198
Martinsville (G-8263)
Affinity Woodworks LLC ....G...... 330 814-4950
Elkwood (G-4340)
Against Grain Woodworking Inc ....G...... 434 760-2055
Afton (G-74)
Aj Trim LLC ....G...... 703 330-1212
Manassas (G-8021)
AK Millwork Inc ....G...... 703 337-4848
Springfield (G-12937)
All Glass LLC ....G...... 540 288-8111
Fredericksburg (G-5397)
Allied Systems Corporation ....D...... 540 665-9600
Winchester (G-15375)
American Wood Fibers Inc ....E...... 276 646-3075
Marion (G-8222)
American Woodmark Corporation ....C...... 540 672-3707
Orange (G-10202)
American Woodmark Corporation ....C...... 540 665-9100
Winchester (G-15379)
Anchor Woodworks ....G...... 804 458-6443
North Prince George (G-10086)
Andersons Woodworks LLC ....G...... 804 530-3736
South Chesterfield (G-12795)
Annandale Mllwk Alied Systems ....D...... 540 665-9600
Winchester (G-15382)
Apical Woodworks & Nursery LLC ....G...... 434 384-0525
Lynchburg (G-7641)
Architectural Accents ....G...... 540 943-5888
Waynesboro (G-15094)
Architectural Custom Wdwrk Inc ....G...... 804 784-2283
Manakin Sabot (G-7895)
Ark Woodworking LLC ....F...... 540 272-7489
Flint Hill (G-5014)
Arlington Adrndack Wdworks LLC ....G...... 703 964-7700
Arlington (G-857)
Art Creations Company Inc ....G...... 703 257-9510
Manassas (G-7912)
ART&creation Inc ....G...... 571 606-8999
Manassas (G-7913)
Artisan Woodwork Company LLC ....G...... 540 420-4928
Rocky Mount (G-12312)
Arundel Woodworks ....G...... 202 713-8781
Leesburg (G-7223)
Ashland Woodwork Inc ....F...... 804 798-4088
Ashland (G-1373)
Atlantic Staircrafters ....G...... 804 732-3323
Petersburg (G-10307)
Awsi Inc ....F...... 804 798-4088
Ashland (G-1375)
Backwoods Woodworking ....G...... 276 237-2011
Fries (G-5514)
Bahama Breeze Shutter Awng LLC ....G...... 757 592-0265
Ordinary (G-10236)
Banton Custom Woodworking LLC ....G...... 804 334-4766
Chesterfield (G-3477)
Batch Wood Works Inc ....G...... 804 694-5767
Gloucester (G-5837)
Battletown Cstm Woodworks LLC ....G...... 703 618-1548
Berryville (G-1670)
Bay Cabinets & Contractors ....G...... 757 934-2236
Suffolk (G-13676)
Bayside Joinery Co LLC ....G...... 804 551-3951
Dutton (G-4269)
Bayside Woodworking Inc ....G...... 757 337-0380
Chesapeake (G-2995)
Bear Country Woodworks ....G...... 540 890-0928
Vinton (G-14166)
Benchmark Woodworks Inc ....F...... 757 971-3380
Portsmouth (G-10399)
Better Living Inc ....D...... 434 978-1666
Charlottesville (G-2594)
Big D Woodworking ....G...... 757 753-4814
Newport News (G-9180)
Big Dog Woodworking LLC ....G...... 540 359-1056
Richardsville (G-11009)

Blackwater Bldg Cstm Wdwkg LLC ......G....... 540 493-1888
Ferrum *(G-4971)*
Bland Woodworking ......G....... 703 631-6567
Centreville *(G-2295)*
Blue Ridge Millwork ......G....... 434 993-1953
Concord *(G-3756)*
Blue Ridge Stairs & Wdwrk LLC ......G....... 540 320-1953
Willis *(G-15354)*
Blue Ridge Woodworks VA Inc ......G....... 434 477-0313
Monroe *(G-8987)*
Blueridge Wood ......G....... 276 930-2274
Woolwine *(G-15864)*
Bon Air Craftsman LLC ......G....... 804 745-0130
North Chesterfield *(G-9833)*
Bourbon ......G....... 757 371-4710
Chesapeake *(G-3012)*
Bristol Woodworker ......G....... 423 557-4158
Bristol *(G-2011)*
Builders Firstsource Inc ......G....... 434 964-1192
Charlottesville *(G-2601)*
Builders Firstsource Inc ......D....... 540 665-0078
Winchester *(G-15397)*
Burgess Snyder Industries Inc ......E....... 757 490-3131
Virginia Beach *(G-14306)*
Burnette Cabinet Shop Inc ......G....... 540 586-0147
Bedford *(G-1629)*
Byrds Custom Wdwrk & Stain GL ......G....... 757 242-6786
Suffolk *(G-13683)*
C & G Woodworking ......G....... 703 878-7196
Woodbridge *(G-15663)*
Cab-Pool Inc ......F....... 804 218-8294
Henrico *(G-6487)*
Calvin Montgomery ......G....... 540 334-3058
Wirtz *(G-15609)*
Campbell Custom Woodworking ......G....... 757 724-2001
Chesapeake *(G-3024)*
Campostella Builders and Sup ......E....... 757 545-3212
Norfolk *(G-9475)*
Canova Woodworking LLC ......G....... 434 422-0807
Gordonsville *(G-5904)*
Carpenters Cbnets Wodworks LLC ......G....... 276 236-0853
Woodlawn *(G-15844)*
Carpers Wood Creations Inc ......E....... 540 465-2525
Strasburg *(G-13576)*
Cattywampus Woodworks LLC ......G....... 540 599-2358
Staffordsville *(G-13214)*
Cavanaugh Cabinet Inc ......G....... 434 977-7100
Charlottesville *(G-2759)*
Centurion Woodworks LLC ......G....... 703 594-2369
Clifton *(G-3660)*
Century Stair Company ......D....... 703 754-4163
Haymarket *(G-6417)*
Charles H Snead Co ......G....... 540 539-5890
Boyce *(G-1908)*
Charlies Woodworks Inc ......G....... 703 944-0775
Falls Church *(G-4774)*
▼ Chesapeake Outdoor Designs Inc ......F....... 804 632-1900
Midlothian *(G-8794)*
Chris N Chris Woodworking LLC ......G....... 757 810-4672
Hampton *(G-6113)*
Christophers Woodworks LLC ......G....... 757 404-2683
Chesapeake *(G-3035)*
Clarks Lumber & Millwork Inc ......F....... 804 448-9985
Fredericksburg *(G-5412)*
Cline Woodworks LLC ......G....... 540 721-2286
Moneta *(G-8960)*
Closet Pioneers LLC ......G....... 703 844-0400
Lorton *(G-7474)*
Cochrans Lumber & Millwork Inc ......E....... 540 955-4142
Berryville *(G-1675)*
▲ Coffman Stairs LLC ......B....... 276 783-7251
Marion *(G-8225)*
Columbus Woodworks ......G....... 434 528-1052
Lynchburg *(G-7680)*
Conaways Woodworking LLC ......G....... 703 530-8725
Manassas Park *(G-8197)*
Contemporary Kitchens Ltd ......G....... 804 758-2001
Topping *(G-13886)*
Conway Woodworking LLC ......G....... 276 328-6590
Wise *(G-15620)*
Cornerstone Woodworks ......G....... 757 236-2334
Chesapeake *(G-3054)*
Corravoo Woodworks LLC ......G....... 703 966-0929
Ashburn *(G-1258)*
County Line Custom Wdwkg LLC ......G....... 804 338-8436
Moseley *(G-9035)*
Craft Designs Custom Intr Pdts ......G....... 757 630-1565
Suffolk *(G-13688)*
CRC Public Relations ......G....... 703 395-9614
Burke *(G-2187)*
Creative Dimension Group Inc ......D....... 540 891-1953
Fredericksburg *(G-5267)*
Creative Visions Woodworks ......G....... 434 822-0182
Danville *(G-3973)*
Creative Woodworking Specialis ......G....... 804 514-9066
Richmond *(G-11036)*
Criders Finishing Inc ......G....... 703 661-6520
Ashburn *(G-1260)*
Crisman Woodworks ......G....... 804 317-1446
Midlothian *(G-8806)*
Cs Woodworking Design LLC ......G....... 703 996-1122
Sterling *(G-13378)*
Cumberland Millwork ......G....... 757 233-4121
Chesapeake *(G-3058)*
Custom Quality Woodworking ......G....... 703 368-8010
Manassas *(G-7928)*
Custom Woodwork ......G....... 434 489-6991
Danville *(G-3974)*
Cypress Woodworking LLC ......G....... 703 803-6254
Fairfax *(G-4610)*
D & M Woodworks ......G....... 757 510-3600
Virginia Beach *(G-14379)*
Dagnat Woodworks LLC ......G....... 276 627-1039
Bassett *(G-1581)*
Dan River Window Co Inc ......F....... 434 517-0111
South Boston *(G-12759)*
Darbys Build and Design LLC ......G....... 434 989-5493
Gordonsville *(G-5905)*
Darbys Custom Woodworks ......G....... 434 989-5493
Gordonsville *(G-5906)*
David Blanchard Woodworking ......G....... 540 468-3900
Monterey *(G-9005)*
DD&t Custom Woodworking Inc ......G....... 804 360-2714
Richmond *(G-11180)*
Dennington Wdwrk Solutions LLC ......G....... 571 414-6917
Reston *(G-10840)*
DHT Woodworks LLC ......G....... 434 414-2607
Appomattox *(G-809)*
Donald F Rouse ......G....... 276 783-7569
Marion *(G-8226)*
Dover Plank Enterprises LLC ......G....... 757 286-6772
Richmond *(G-11567)*
Dysert Custom Woodwork ......G....... 804 741-4712
Henrico *(G-6505)*
E H Lail Millwork Inc ......F....... 804 271-1111
North Chesterfield *(G-9866)*
E T Moore Jr Co Inc ......F....... 804 231-1823
Richmond *(G-11571)*
Earlyrisers Inc ......G....... 757 566-4199
Barhamsville *(G-1570)*
Ecks Custom Woodworking ......G....... 571 765-0807
Warrenton *(G-15003)*
Eco-Friendly Lumber LLC ......G....... 703 881-1966
Nokesville *(G-9391)*
Element Woodworks LLC ......G....... 757 650-9556
Virginia Beach *(G-14439)*
Em Millwork Inc ......G....... 571 344-9842
Springfield *(G-12997)*
Eric Carr Woodworks ......G....... 202 253-1010
Great Falls *(G-5954)*
Ernies Woodworking ......G....... 540 786-8959
Fredericksburg *(G-5284)*
Essence Woodworks LLC ......G....... 703 945-3108
Fairfax *(G-4450)*
Ever Forward Woodworks ......G....... 434 882-0727
Scottsville *(G-12660)*
Ews Inc ......G....... 757 482-2740
Chesapeake *(G-3095)*
Exotic Woodworks ......G....... 352 408-5373
Virginia Beach *(G-14457)*
Fairfax Woodworking Inc ......G....... 703 339-9578
Chantilly *(G-2419)*
Fairfax Woodworking Inc ......G....... 571 292-2220
Manassas *(G-8068)*
Family Crafters of Virginia ......G....... 540 943-3934
Waynesboro *(G-15114)*
Fancy Gap Woodworks LLC ......G....... 336 816-9881
Fancy Gap *(G-4935)*
Farmstead Finds Salvaging ......G....... 540 845-8200
Fredericksburg *(G-5430)*
Fielside Woodworkig ......G....... 434 203-5530
Hurt *(G-6975)*
Finch Woodworks ......G....... 540 333-0054
Woodstock *(G-15853)*
First Landing Woodworks ......G....... 757 428-7537
Virginia Beach *(G-14465)*
Fleming Woodworking LLC ......G....... 559 259-2296
Suffolk *(G-13710)*
Frederick Enterprises LLC ......E....... 804 405-4976
Richmond *(G-11594)*
Gaithrsburg Cbinetry Mllwk Inc ......D....... 540 347-4551
Warrenton *(G-15019)*
Gaston and Wyatt LLC ......E....... 434 293-7357
Charlottesville *(G-2802)*
Goose Creek Woodworks LLC ......G....... 540 348-4163
Raphine *(G-10749)*
Grayson Ferguson Wdwkg Inc ......G....... 434 528-3405
Lynchburg *(G-7723)*
Grayson Millworks Company Inc ......G....... 276 773-8590
Independence *(G-6984)*
Greensprings Custom Woodwo ......G....... 703 628-8058
Stafford *(G-13148)*
Gunz Custom Woodworks LLC ......G....... 757 739-2842
Virginia Beach *(G-14497)*
H & A Fine Woodworking ......G....... 703 499-0944
Fairfax *(G-4472)*
H & A Fine Woodworking ......G....... 703 822-0006
Springfield *(G-13016)*
Haas Woodworking ......G....... 540 686-5837
Clear Brook *(G-3644)*
Hackney Millworks Inc ......G....... 804 843-3312
West Point *(G-15158)*
Haley Pearsall Inc ......G....... 804 784-3438
Richmond *(G-11230)*
Hampton Woodworks LLC ......G....... 434 989-7556
Charlottesville *(G-2644)*
Hanover Woodworking Studio LLC ......G....... 804 625-5679
Hanover *(G-6281)*
Harper and Taylor Custom ......G....... 804 658-8753
Powhatan *(G-10548)*
Harris Woodworking ......G....... 434 295-4316
North Garden *(G-10076)*
Hayes Stair Co Inc ......E....... 540 751-0201
Purcellville *(G-10664)*
HB Woodworks ......G....... 703 209-4639
Chantilly *(G-2536)*
Heritage Woodworks LLC ......G....... 757 417-7337
Virginia Beach *(G-14518)*
Hernley Woodworks ......G....... 571 419-4889
Ashburn *(G-1290)*
Highwheel Woodworks ......G....... 540 287-8575
Spotsylvania *(G-12894)*
Hobbs Door Service ......G....... 757 436-6529
Virginia Beach *(G-14525)*
Holly Beach Woodworker Inc ......G....... 757 831-1410
Virginia Beach *(G-14526)*
Hoskins Woodworking Llc Jose ......G....... 434 825-2883
Charlottesville *(G-2811)*
Hudson Wdwkg & Restoration LLC ......G....... 703 817-7741
Chantilly *(G-2438)*
Huffs Artisan Woodwork ......G....... 703 399-5493
Fairfax *(G-4477)*
Hypes Custom Wdwkg & HM Improv ......G....... 540 641-7419
Christiansburg *(G-3597)*
Ibs Millwork Corporation ......G....... 703 631-4011
Manassas *(G-8079)*
Innovative Millwork Tech LLC ......G....... 276 646-8336
Chilhowie *(G-3551)*
Interior Building Systems Corp ......D....... 703 335-9655
Manassas *(G-8083)*
Interpretive Wdwrk Design Inc ......G....... 703 330-6105
Manassas *(G-7953)*
J W Creations ......G....... 276 676-3770
Abingdon *(G-43)*
Jaeger & Ernst Inc ......F....... 434 973-7018
Barboursville *(G-1562)*
Jar-Tan Inc ......G....... 757 548-6066
Chesapeake *(G-3148)*
Jarrett Millwork ......G....... 540 377-9173
Fairfield *(G-4731)*
JB Wood Works LLC ......G....... 540 589-5281
Roanoke *(G-11946)*
Jeff Fleisher ......G....... 703 955-6873
New Market *(G-9143)*
Jeff Hoskins ......G....... 804 769-1295
Aylett *(G-1549)*
Jefferson Mllwk & Design Inc ......D....... 703 260-3370
Sterling *(G-13435)*
Jeremiahs Woodwork LLC ......G....... 804 519-0984
Midlothian *(G-8837)*
Jester Woodworks Llc Van ......G....... 804 562-6360
Richmond *(G-11630)*
Jim Champion ......G....... 276 466-9112
Bristol *(G-2022)*
John J Heckford ......G....... 276 889-5646
Lebanon *(G-7194)*
Jon Martin Woodworking LLC ......G....... 540 560-3721
Harrisonburg *(G-6334)*
Jozsa Wood Works ......F....... 703 492-9405
Woodbridge *(G-15731)*

S I C

Jr Woodworks ....G..... 703 577-2663
Alexandria *(G-247)*

Jsd Mill Work LLC ....G..... 703 863-7183
Lignum *(G-7425)*

K & J Woodworking/ Cash ....G..... 703 369-7161
Manassas *(G-8091)*

Kempsville Building Mtls Inc ....G..... 757 875-1850
Newport News *(G-9275)*

Kempsville Building Mtls Inc ....E..... 757 485-0782
Chesapeake *(G-3162)*

Kerschbamer Woodworking LLC ....G..... 434 455-2508
Lynchburg *(G-7751)*

Keystone Vintage Lumber VA LLC .....G..... 804 615-7773
Amelia Court House *(G-661)*

Kingdom Woodworks Virginia LLC ......G..... 757 544-4821
Chesapeake *(G-3164)*

Kinzie Woodwork LLC ....G..... 540 397-1637
Roanoke *(G-11949)*

Knockawe Woodworking LLC ....G..... 804 928-3506
North Chesterfield *(G-9909)*

Knotthead Woodworking Inc ....G..... 540 344-0293
Vinton *(G-14176)*

Labyrinth Woodworks LLC ....G..... 206 235-6272
Lynchburg *(G-7754)*

Landmark Logworks ....G..... 540 687-4124
The Plains *(G-13843)*

Landmark Woodworking Inc ....G..... 703 424-3191
Fairfax Station *(G-4715)*

Legacy Products LLC ....E..... 804 739-9333
Midlothian *(G-8847)*

Legacy Woodworking LLC ....G..... 703 431-8811
Purcellville *(G-10665)*

Lesden Corporation ....G..... 540 373-4940
Fredericksburg *(G-5450)*

Lincoln Woodworking ....G..... 703 297-7512
Purcellville *(G-10666)*

Linden Woodwork LLC ....G..... 540 636-3345
Linden *(G-7431)*

Linetree Woodworks ....G..... 919 619-3013
Powhatan *(G-10556)*

Lions Head Woodworks LLC ....G..... 540 288-9532
Stafford *(G-13171)*

Lm Woodworking LLC ....G..... 703 927-4467
Alexandria *(G-519)*

Local Wood ....G..... 540 955-9522
Berryville *(G-1684)*

Loudoun Stairs Inc ....E..... 703 478-8800
Purcellville *(G-10670)*

M McGuire Woodworks ....G..... 434 841-3702
Lynchburg *(G-7767)*

M S G Custom Wdwrk & Pntg LLC .....G..... 434 977-4752
Charlottesville *(G-2829)*

Mackes Woodworking LLC ....G..... 570 856-3242
Virginia Beach *(G-14630)*

Magnolia Woodworking ....G..... 571 521-9041
Fairfax *(G-4501)*

Mantels By Meunier ....G..... 804 690-1977
Richmond *(G-11664)*

Masco Cabinetry LLC ....C..... 540 727-7859
Culpeper *(G-3907)*

Masonite Corporation ....D..... 540 778-2211
Stanley *(G-13231)*

Masonite International Corp ....G..... 540 665-3083
Winchester *(G-15443)*

Masonite International Corp ....E..... 540 778-2211
Stanley *(G-13232)*

Massey Wood & West Inc ....E..... 804 746-2800
Mechanicsville *(G-8656)*

Maurice Lamb ....G..... 540 962-0903
Covington *(G-3794)*

McFarland Woodworks LLC ....G..... 276 970-5847
Tazewell *(G-13834)*

Mendez Custom Woodworking ....G..... 540 621-3849
Spotsylvania *(G-12905)*

Method Wood Working ....G..... 804 332-3715
Richmond *(G-11288)*

Metrie Inc ....D..... 804 876-3588
Doswell *(G-4123)*

Metro Wood Works Inc ....G..... 757 479-1100
Chesapeake *(G-3203)*

Mid Atlantic Wood Works LLC ....G..... 703 281-4376
Oakton *(G-10158)*

Mik Woodworking Inc ....G..... 540 878-1197
Winchester *(G-15557)*

Millcraft LLC ....G..... 703 225-9860
Chantilly *(G-2463)*

Millcraft LLC ....G..... 703 775-2030
Alexandria *(G-533)*

Millcreek Wood Works ....G..... 804 642-4792
Hayes *(G-6402)*

Millehan Enterprises Inc ....G..... 540 772-3037
Roanoke *(G-11967)*

Miller Cabinets Inc ....G..... 540 434-4835
Harrisonburg *(G-6345)*

Miller Quality Woodwork Inc ....G..... 757 564-7847
Williamsburg *(G-15278)*

Millwork Supply Inc ....F..... 540 552-0201
Blacksburg *(G-1762)*

Mitchells Woodwork Inc ....G..... 757 340-4154
Virginia Beach *(G-14656)*

Mjs Woodworking LLC ....G..... 571 233-4991
Remington *(G-10769)*

Model A Woodworks ....G..... 757 714-1126
Chesapeake *(G-3210)*

Modus Workshop LLC ....G..... 800 376-5735
Harrisonburg *(G-6347)*

Montoya Services LLC ....G..... 571 882-3464
Sterling *(G-13456)*

Morris Woodworks LLC ....G..... 434 392-2285
Farmville *(G-4951)*

Moss Supply Company ....D..... 804 798-8332
Ashland *(G-1466)*

Mount Vernon Woodworks LLC ....G..... 202 222-8387
Alexandria *(G-534)*

▲ Mw Manufacturers Inc ....A..... 540 483-0211
Rocky Mount *(G-12340)*

Mw Manufacturers Inc ....C..... 540 484-6780
Rocky Mount *(G-12341)*

Narrogate Woodworks Inc ....G..... 276 728-3996
Dugspur *(G-4190)*

Natural Woodworking Co ....G..... 540 745-2664
Floyd *(G-5033)*

Noah Paci ....G..... 703 525-5437
Arlington *(G-1079)*

Northampton Custom Milling LLC ......G..... 757 442-4747
Nassawadox *(G-9101)*

Northern Virginia Woodwork Inc ....G..... 540 752-6128
Bealeton *(G-1602)*

Nova Lumber & Millwork LLC ....G..... 703 451-9217
Springfield *(G-13061)*

Oak Hollow Woodworking Inc ....G..... 276 646-2476
Chilhowie *(G-3556)*

Oaks ....G..... 540 885-6664
Staunton *(G-13282)*

Old Barn Rclmed WD Antiq Flrg ....E..... 804 329-0079
Richmond *(G-11699)*

Old South Plantation Shutters ....G..... 703 968-7822
Chantilly *(G-2477)*

Old Virginia Molding & Mllwk ....G..... 757 516-9055
Franklin *(G-5151)*

Olde Virginia Moulding ....G..... 757 516-9055
Franklin *(G-5152)*

Olivals Custom Woodworking Inc ....G..... 703 221-2713
Triangle *(G-13897)*

One Arm Woodworking LLC ....G..... 703 203-9417
Fairfax *(G-4525)*

One Asterisk Woodworks LLC ....G..... 508 332-8151
Fredericksburg *(G-5464)*

Out of Woodwork ....G..... 757 814-8848
Chesapeake *(G-3230)*

Outer Banks Woodworks Inc ....G..... 804 937-4330
North Chesterfield *(G-9944)*

P&L Woodworks ....P..... 240 676-8648
Lovettsville *(G-7585)*

Pan Custom Molding Inc ....G..... 804 787-3821
Mineral *(G-8951)*

Patrick Hawks ....G..... 276 618-2055
Martinsville *(G-8316)*

Paul V Bell ....G..... 703 631-4011
Manassas *(G-8126)*

Pearce Woodworking ....G..... 240 377-1278
Winchester *(G-15565)*

Penguin Woodworking LLC ....G..... 804 502-2656
Powhatan *(G-10562)*

Percision Woodworks ....G..... 757 642-1686
Suffolk *(G-13751)*

Perry Railworks Inc ....G..... 703 794-0507
Manassas *(G-8127)*

Persimmon Woodworking ....G..... 703 618-6909
Hamilton *(G-6063)*

Pettigrew ....G..... 434 979-0018
North Garden *(G-10081)*

Pieces of Wood LLC ....G..... 434 842-3091
Fork Union *(G-5112)*

Piedmont Woodworks LLC ....G..... 540 364-1849
Marshall *(G-8258)*

Pike Woodworks ....G..... 571 329-4377
Haymarket *(G-6436)*

Pinstripe Cstm Longboards LLC ....G..... 757 635-7183
Virginia Beach *(G-14723)*

Plank Road Woodworks ....G..... 617 285-8522
Charlottesville *(G-2847)*

Ply Gem Industries Inc ....C..... 540 337-3663
Stuarts Draft *(G-13657)*

Ply Gem Industries Inc ....C..... 540 483-0211
Rocky Mount *(G-12346)*

Portsmouth Lumber Corporation ....F..... 757 397-4646
Portsmouth *(G-10471)*

Potomac Creek Woodworks LLC ....G..... 703 444-9805
Sterling *(G-13475)*

Precision Doors & Hardware LLC ....F..... 540 373-7300
Fredericksburg *(G-5348)*

Precision Woodworks LLC ....G..... 757 642-1686
Smithfield *(G-12721)*

Premier Millwork & Lbr Co Inc ....E..... 757 463-8870
Virginia Beach *(G-14736)*

Premium Millwork Installations ....G..... 757 288-9785
Woodbridge *(G-15780)*

Progrm For The Archtctrl Wdwrk ....G..... 978 468-5141
Reston *(G-10931)*

Quality Wood Products Inc ....G..... 540 750-1859
Christiansburg *(G-3608)*

R A Onijs Classic Woodwork ....G..... 703 594-3304
Nokesville *(G-9398)*

R Wyatt Inc ....E..... 434 293-7357
Charlottesville *(G-2854)*

Rachael A Peden Originals ....G..... 804 580-8709
Farnham *(G-4964)*

Rainbow Custom Woodworking ....E..... 571 379-5500
Manassas *(G-8138)*

Randolph-Bundy Incorporated ....E..... 757 625-2556
Portsmouth *(G-10474)*

Rappatomac Industries Inc ....G..... 804 529-6440
Callao *(G-2218)*

Rays Woodworks ....G..... 276 251-7297
Claudville *(G-3640)*

RC Tate Woodworks ....G..... 434 822-0035
Danville *(G-4034)*

Red Brook Lumber Co ....G..... 434 293-2077
Charlottesville *(G-2861)*

Rediscover Woodwork ....G..... 757 813-0383
Chesapeake *(G-3263)*

Reierson Woodworking ....G..... 804 541-1945
North Prince George *(G-10091)*

Richard Price ....G..... 804 731-7270
Sperryville *(G-12879)*

River Rock Wood Working ....G..... 540 828-2358
Bridgewater *(G-1957)*

River Valley Custom Millwork ....G..... 540 438-0208
Mount Crawford *(G-9059)*

Riverfarm Woodworks LLC ....G..... 571 721-0988
Alexandria *(G-574)*

Rock Hill Lumber Inc ....E..... 540 547-2889
Culpeper *(G-3918)*

Rogers - Mast-R-Woodwork LLC ....G..... 540 273-1460
King George *(G-7111)*

Ronald Light ....G..... 540 837-2089
Boyce *(G-1911)*

Ronbuilt Corporation ....G..... 276 638-2090
Martinsville *(G-8324)*

Rox Chox & Woodworking LLC ....G..... 703 378-1313
Herndon *(G-6796)*

Rt Door Co LLC ....G..... 540 962-0903
Covington *(G-3796)*

Ruffin & Payne Incorporated ....C..... 804 329-2691
Richmond *(G-11749)*

Rusty Bear Woodworks LLC ....G..... 540 327-6579
Winchester *(G-15473)*

Rva Woodwork LLC ....G..... 804 840-2345
Mechanicsville *(G-8672)*

Rva Woodwork LLC ....G..... 804 840-2345
Henrico *(G-6563)*

Rva Woodworks LLC ....G..... 804 303-3820
Mechanicsville *(G-8673)*

Rwm Inc ....G..... 540 774-7214
Roanoke *(G-11998)*

Rz Woodworks LLC ....G..... 626 833-0628
Colonial Heights *(G-3744)*

S4 Wood Works LLC ....G..... 804 299-0454
Henrico *(G-6564)*

Saunders Custom Woodwork ....G..... 804 520-4090
Colonial Heights *(G-3746)*

Sawmark Woodworks ....G..... 540 657-4814
Fredericksburg *(G-5483)*

Sawmill Creek Wdworkers Forums ......G..... 757 871-8214
Hayes *(G-6407)*

Sb Woodworks ....G..... 804 417-7729
Mechanicsville *(G-8675)*

Scan Industries LLC ....G..... 360 320-8244
Ashburn *(G-1332)*

Schorr Wood Works LLC G 434 990-1897
Ruckersville *(G-12413)*

Sct Woodworks LLC G 804 310-1908
Powhatan *(G-10573)*

Sheffield Woodworking G 571 261-4904
Haymarket *(G-6444)*

Simpson Company Landsca G 703 204-0453
Falls Church *(G-4875)*

Skips Woodworks G 757 390-1948
Williamsburg *(G-15312)*

Snow 39s Woodwork G 540 428-1762
Marshall *(G-8260)*

Southern Woodworks Inc G 757 566-8307
Toano *(G-13878)*

Spec-Trim Mfg Co Inc D 804 739-9333
Midlothian *(G-8906)*

Stair Store Inc F 703 794-0507
Manassas *(G-8161)*

Staircraft G 540 347-7023
Broad Run *(G-2070)*

Stephan Burger Fine Wdwkg G 434 960-5440
Richmond *(G-11398)*

Steve Hollar Wdwkg & Engrv G 703 273-0639
Fairfax *(G-4681)*

Steves & Sons Inc E 804 226-4034
Sandston *(G-12638)*

Stonewall Woodworks LLC G 540 298-1713
Elkton *(G-4335)*

Sugar Maple Ln Woodworker LLC G 434 962-6494
Louisa *(G-7569)*

Symmetrical Wood Works LLC G 703 499-0821
Annandale *(G-786)*

T&J Woodworking G 757 567-5530
Virginia Beach *(G-14861)*

Taylormade Woodworking G 757 288-6256
Chesapeake *(G-3323)*

Teaberry Hill Woodworks LLC G 540 667-5489
Winchester *(G-15592)*

Terrys Custom Woodworks G 703 963-7116
Reston *(G-10972)*

The Millwork Specialist LLC G 804 262-9296
Charlottesville *(G-2703)*

Three Points Design Inc G 757 426-2149
Virginia Beach *(G-14870)*

Tidewter Archtctural Mllwk Inc G 757 422-1279
Virginia Beach *(G-14881)*

Tidewter Exhibits AG Mllwk Mfg G 540 379-1555
Fredericksburg *(G-5493)*

Tim Price Woodworking LLC G 276 794-9405
Lebanon *(G-7209)*

Timothys Custom Woodworking G 540 408-4343
Fredericksburg *(G-5494)*

Tms Corp G 804 262-9296
Charlottesville *(G-2708)*

Torode Company G 703 242-9387
Vienna *(G-14143)*

Touch Class Construction Corp G 757 728-3647
Newport News *(G-9360)*

Towers Custom Woodwork LLC C A G 703 330-7107
Manassas *(G-8169)*

Treo Enterprise Solutions Inc F 804 977-9862
Henrico *(G-6584)*

Triple C Woodworking LLC G 703 779-9966
Leesburg *(G-7365)*

◆ Trm Inc E 920 855-2194
Haymarket *(G-6452)*

True American Woodworkers G 540 748-5805
Bumpass *(G-2169)*

Truly Crafted Woodworking LLC G 571 268-0834
Manassas *(G-8172)*

Tumolo Custom Mill Work G 434 985-1755
Stanardsville *(G-13229)*

Turman Lumber Company Inc E 540 639-1250
Christiansburg *(G-3614)*

Ultimate Woodworks G 804 938-8987
Richmond *(G-11427)*

Union Church Millworks Inc F 540 862-0767
Covington *(G-3801)*

Uptons Custom Woodworking LLC G 540 454-3752
Stafford *(G-13208)*

VA Woodworks LLC G 540 903-6681
Fredericksburg *(G-5385)*

Valley Building Supply Inc C 540 434-6725
Harrisonburg *(G-6383)*

Van Jester Woodworks G 804 562-6360
Richmond *(G-11805)*

Viking Woodworking G 540 659-3882
Stafford *(G-13210)*

Vintage Star LLC G 808 779-9688
Springfield *(G-13107)*

Virginia Railing & Gates LLC F 804 798-8777
Ashland *(G-1506)*

Virginia Stairs Inc G 757 425-6681
Virginia Beach *(G-14920)*

▲ Virginia Woodworking Co Inc E 276 669-3133
Bristol *(G-1997)*

W A Marks Fine Woodworking G 434 973-9785
Barboursville *(G-1569)*

Walker Branch Lumber G 434 676-3199
Kenbridge *(G-7036)*

Walpole Woodworkers Inc G 703 433-9929
Sterling *(G-13557)*

Walrose Woodworks G 276 762-3917
Castlewood *(G-2259)*

Warm Springs Mtn Woodworks G 540 839-9747
Hot Springs *(G-6950)*

Washington Wdwrkrs Guild of NA G 703 222-3460
Chantilly *(G-2519)*

Wellborn + Wright G 804 329-0079
Richmond *(G-11821)*

Wellspring Woodworks LLC G 540 722-8641
Winchester *(G-15600)*

Werrell Woodworks G 757 581-0131
Chesapeake *(G-3375)*

Westmont Woodworking Inc G 757 287-2442
Norfolk *(G-9794)*

White Oak Grove Woodworks G 540 763-2723
Riner *(G-11866)*

Wilkins Woodworking G 804 761-8081
Tappahannock *(G-13825)*

Wilkinson Woodworking G 540 548-2029
Fredericksburg *(G-5391)*

William Mowry Woodworking G 804 282-3831
Richmond *(G-11451)*

Williamsburg Wood Works LLC G 757 817-5396
Williamsburg *(G-15344)*

Wilmas Woodworking G 276 346-3611
Jonesville *(G-7024)*

Wilsons Woodworks G 757 846-6697
Seaford *(G-12678)*

Winchester Woodworking Corp D 540 667-1700
Winchester *(G-15515)*

Windows Direct G 276 755-5187
Cana *(G-2228)*

▲ Windsor Surry Company E 757 294-0853
Dendron *(G-4091)*

Windsor Woodworking Co Inc G 757 242-4141
Windsor *(G-15608)*

Winery Woodworks LLC G 540 869-1542
Stephens City *(G-13329)*

Wisakon Woods G 571 332-9844
Manassas *(G-8179)*

Wonderland Wood Works G 540 636-6158
Front Royal *(G-5564)*

Wood Creations G 571 235-0717
Alexandria *(G-386)*

Wood Creations LLC G 804 553-1862
Richmond *(G-11454)*

Wood Design & Fabrication Inc F 540 774-8168
Roanoke *(G-12024)*

Wood Turns G 904 303-8536
Chesapeake *(G-3380)*

Wood Works By Snyder LLC G 703 203-6952
Gainesville *(G-5623)*

Woodgrain Millwork Inc C 208 452-3801
Marion *(G-8246)*

Woodwork & Cabinets LLC G 703 881-1915
Haymarket *(G-6455)*

Woodwork Career Aliance N Amer G 434 298-4650
Nellysford *(G-9115)*

Woodworkers Inc G 571 282-5376
Sterling *(G-13564)*

Woodworking Wrkshps of The Shn G 540 955-2376
Berryville *(G-1700)*

Woodworks G 434 636-4111
Bracey *(G-1924)*

Woodworks LLC G 804 730-0631
Mechanicsville *(G-8702)*

Woodworks LLC G 757 516-8405
Franklin *(G-5162)*

Worthington Millwork LLC G 540 832-6391
Gordonsville *(G-5919)*

Wrack-It G 434 258-4317
Forest *(G-5106)*

Zeb Woodworks LLC G 703 361-2842
Manassas *(G-8182)*

Zephyr Woodworks LLC G 434 979-4425
North Garden *(G-10085)*

2434 Wood Kitchen Cabinets

A & R Cabinet Co Inc G 804 261-4098
Henrico *(G-6469)*

A&F Ccuston Cabinetry Built G 703 598-7686
Ashburn *(G-1235)*

ACC Cabinetry LLC G 540 333-0189
Berryville *(G-1669)*

Ace Cabinets & More LLC G 757 206-1684
Williamsburg *(G-15202)*

Advanced Cabinets & Tops Inc G 804 355-5541
Richmond *(G-11086)*

Ajc Woodworks Inc G 757 566-0336
Toano *(G-13855)*

Albion Cabinets Stairs Inc G 434 974-4611
Earlysville *(G-4284)*

▲ All Affairs Transportation LLC G 757 342-2474
Newport News *(G-9162)*

American Woodmark Corporation B 540 665-9100
Winchester *(G-15377)*

◆ American Woodmark Corporation C 540 665-9100
Winchester *(G-15378)*

American Woodmark Corporation C 540 672-3707
Orange *(G-10202)*

Arboleda Cabinets Inc F 804 230-0733
Richmond *(G-11487)*

B & J Cabinet Co Inc E 804 271-0192
North Chesterfield *(G-9825)*

Baldwin Cabinet Shops Inc G 804 443-5421
Tappahannock *(G-13812)*

Bells Cabinet Shop G 804 448-3111
Ruther Glen *(G-12451)*

Bernies Furn & Cabinetry Inc G 434 846-6883
Madison Heights *(G-7868)*

Best Cabinets and Closets LLC G 703 830-0542
Centreville *(G-2294)*

Bills Custom Cabinetry G 703 281-1669
Vienna *(G-14017)*

Bishop Custom Cabinets G 804 469-7549
North Dinwiddie *(G-10048)*

Blue Ridge Woodworks VA Inc G 434 477-0313
Monroe *(G-8987)*

Bluebird Cabinetry G 804 937-5429
Richmond *(G-11129)*

Bobby Utt Custom Cabinets G 276 728-9411
Fancy Gap *(G-4933)*

Bowman Woodworking Inc G 540 483-1680
Ferrum *(G-4973)*

Brinkleys Custom Cabinets G 540 525-1780
Buchanan *(G-2117)*

Burnette Cabinet Shop Inc G 540 586-0147
Bedford *(G-1629)*

C&S Custom Cabinets Inc G 540 273-5450
Louisa *(G-7548)*

Cabinet & More G 571 719-5040
Manassas Park *(G-8193)*

Cabinet Arts LLC G 571 313-1891
Sterling *(G-13363)*

Cabinet Arts LLC G 703 870-1456
Arlington *(G-898)*

Cabinet Co of Virginia Corp G 757 357-5519
Smithfield *(G-12707)*

Cabinet Design Plus G 540 773-4571
Winchester *(G-15533)*

Cabinet Discounters Inc F 703 803-7990
Chantilly *(G-2385)*

Cabinet Kingdom LLC G 804 514-9546
Midlothian *(G-8787)*

Cabinet Works of N N G 804 493-8102
Montross *(G-9024)*

Cabinetry & Construction Inc G 804 497-3491
Richmond *(G-11516)*

Cabinetry With TLC LLC G 540 777-0456
Roanoke *(G-11900)*

Cabinets By Design G 434 589-2600
Troy *(G-13921)*

Cabinets By Design Inc G 757 558-9558
Chesapeake *(G-3022)*

Cabinets Direct Inc G 540 884-2329
Eagle Rock *(G-4280)*

Cabinets Ready To Go LLC G 703 665-5620
Chantilly *(G-2386)*

Cabinets To Go LLC G 814 688-7584
Norfolk *(G-9472)*

Cabinets To Go LLC G 804 325-4775
Richmond *(G-11143)*

Carys Mill Woodworking G 804 639-2946
Midlothian *(G-8792)*

Cascade Cabinets & Millwork G 434 685-4000
Cascade *(G-2249)*

S I C

Cedar Forest Cabinetry & Millw.............G...... 703 753-0644
   Nokesville *(G-9390)*

Cherry Hill Cabinetry.............G...... 540 785-4333
   Fredericksburg *(G-5177)*

Cherry Hill Cabinetry.............G...... 703 942-6053
   Mc Lean *(G-8405)*

Chesapeake Cabinet & Finish Co.........G...... 757 787-9422
   Onancock *(G-10192)*

CL Cabinetry Corporation.............G...... 703 586-6766
   Alexandria *(G-430)*

Classic Creations of Tidewater.........G...... 757 548-1442
   Chesapeake *(G-3036)*

Classic Kitchens of Virginia.............F...... 804 784-5075
   Richmond *(G-11158)*

Classic Woodcraft.............G...... 757 631-9354
   Norfolk *(G-9488)*

Closet and Beyond.............G...... 703 962-7894
   Arlington *(G-908)*

Cloud Cabin Arts.............G...... 434 218-3020
   Charlottesville *(G-2768)*

Coastal Cabinets By Jenna LLC.........G...... 757 339-0710
   Virginia Beach *(G-14344)*

Coblentz Custom Cabinets.............G...... 231 362-2728
   Amherst *(G-688)*

Cochrans Lumber & Millwork Inc.........E...... 540 955-4142
   Berryville *(G-1675)*

Colonial Kitchen & Cabinets.............E...... 757 898-1332
   Yorktown *(G-15943)*

Commercial Custom Cabinet Inc.........E...... 804 228-2100
   Richmond *(G-11533)*

Contemporary Kitchens Ltd.............G...... 804 758-2001
   Topping *(G-13886)*

Contemporary Woodcrafts Inc.........G...... 703 451-4257
   Springfield *(G-12979)*

Contemporary Woodcrafts Inc.........F...... 703 787-9711
   Fairfax Station *(G-4703)*

Corner Cabinet Shop Inc.............G...... 540 672-9460
   Orange *(G-10207)*

Cornerstone Cabinets & Design.........G...... 434 239-0976
   Forest *(G-5065)*

Cove Antiques.............G...... 757 787-3881
   Onancock *(G-10194)*

Creative Cabinet Design.............G...... 434 293-4040
   Charlottesville *(G-2774)*

Creative Cabinet Designs LLC.........G...... 703 644-1090
   Pulaski *(G-10633)*

Creative Cabinet Works.............G...... 757 220-1941
   Lanexa *(G-7164)*

Creative Cabinet Works LLC.............G...... 757 566-1000
   Toano *(G-13861)*

Crossroads Cabinets LLC.............G...... 319 431-1588
   Moseley *(G-9037)*

Custom Built Cabinets and.............G...... 812 427-9733
   Jonesville *(G-7021)*

Custom Kraft Inc.............F...... 757 265-2882
   Hampton *(G-6126)*

Daves Cabinet Shop Inc.............G...... 804 861-9275
   North Dinwiddie *(G-10050)*

David Mays Cabinet Maker.............G...... 434 277-8533
   Amherst *(G-689)*

Daylight Cabinetry LLC.............G...... 804 432-4954
   Richmond *(G-11554)*

Deneals Cabinets Inc.............G...... 540 721-8005
   Hardy *(G-6286)*

Designer Cabinets.............G...... 540 569-0469
   Staunton *(G-13251)*

Designs In Wood LLC.............G...... 804 517-1414
   Richmond *(G-11183)*

Dobbs & Assoc.............G...... 804 314-8871
   Ashland *(G-1403)*

Dominion Door and Drawer.............G...... 804 955-9302
   Ruther Glen *(G-12454)*

Duckworth Company.............G...... 540 436-8754
   Toms Brook *(G-13884)*

Dutch Made Cabinets.............G...... 276 728-5700
   Hillsville *(G-6890)*

Ecowood Usa Inc.............G...... 703 347-6858
   Springfield *(G-12996)*

Elegant Cabinets Inc.............E...... 540 483-5800
   Rocky Mount *(G-12320)*

Elite Cabinet LLC.............G...... 703 909-0404
   Alexandria *(G-454)*

Euro Cabinets Inc.............F...... 757 671-7884
   Virginia Beach *(G-14454)*

Expo Cabinetry.............G...... 703 940-3800
   Fairfax *(G-4454)*

Feefees Cabinet LLC.............G...... 804 647-0297
   North Chesterfield *(G-9872)*

Field Inner Prizes LLC.............G...... 540 738-2060
   Brightwood *(G-1961)*

Final Touch Cabinetry.............G...... 540 895-5776
   Spotsylvania *(G-12890)*

First Forest Furniture & Mllwk.........G...... 540 743-2051
   Luray *(G-7612)*

Fitzgeralds Cabinet Shop Inc.............G...... 757 877-2538
   Newport News *(G-9229)*

Francis C James Jr.............G...... 757 442-3630
   Nassawadox *(G-9100)*

Fred Hean Furniture & Wdwrk.........G...... 434 973-5960
   Charlottesville *(G-2634)*

G T Walls Cabinet Shop.............G...... 804 798-6288
   Glen Allen *(G-5734)*

Gary A Watkins Construction.............G...... 703 367-0477
   Manassas Park *(G-8200)*

Gjs Cabinetry Installation.............G...... 540 856-2726
   Edinburg *(G-4306)*

Green Forest Cabinetry.............G...... 757 485-9200
   Chesapeake *(G-3124)*

Greenbrier Custom Cabinets.............G...... 757 438-5475
   Norfolk *(G-9566)*

Greenworks Cstm Cabinetry LLC.........G...... 540 635-5725
   Front Royal *(G-5534)*

Greg Norman and Associates Inc.........F...... 703 205-0031
   Annandale *(G-754)*

Groves Cabinetry Inc.............G...... 540 341-7309
   Jeffersonton *(G-7013)*

H & M Cabinetry.............G...... 804 338-9504
   Midlothian *(G-8824)*

H B Cabinet Refacers.............G...... 571 213-5257
   Centreville *(G-2309)*

Haley Pearsall Inc.............G...... 804 784-3438
   Richmond *(G-11230)*

Hawes Joinery Inc.............G...... 540 384-6733
   Salem *(G-12517)*

Henley Cabinetry Inc.............G...... 804 776-0016
   Hartfield *(G-6390)*

Heritage Cabinets Inc.............G...... 804 861-5251
   North Dinwiddie *(G-10052)*

Heritage Woodworks LLC.............E...... 757 934-1440
   Suffolk *(G-13720)*

Hi-Tech Cabinets Inc.............G...... 757 681-0016
   Virginia Beach *(G-14522)*

Horizon Custom Cabinets Corp.........G...... 757 434-8706
   Virginia Beach *(G-14527)*

Horizon Custom Cabinets Corp.........G...... 757 306-1007
   Virginia Beach *(G-14528)*

Ideal Cabinets Inc.............G...... 540 366-1748
   Salem *(G-12519)*

In Stock Today Cabinets LLC.............F...... 703 972-4030
   Fairfax *(G-4479)*

Innovative Kitchens Inc.............G...... 757 425-7753
   Virginia Beach *(G-14546)*

Interior Building Systems Corp.........D...... 703 335-9655
   Manassas *(G-8083)*

J W Creations.............G...... 276 676-3770
   Abingdon *(G-43)*

Ja Le Custom Crafts.............G...... 804 541-8957
   Disputanta *(G-4109)*

Jaeger & Ernst Inc.............F...... 434 973-7018
   Barboursville *(G-1562)*

Julian Swain Builders Inc.............E...... 757 490-0211
   Norfolk *(G-9608)*

▼ KEC Associates Ltd.............G...... 804 404-2601
   North Chesterfield *(G-9906)*

Kitchen and Bath Company LLC.........G...... 757 417-8200
   Virginia Beach *(G-14586)*

Kitchen Concepts Inc.............G...... 757 547-9238
   Chesapeake *(G-3165)*

Kitchen Krafters Inc.............G...... 540 891-7678
   Fredericksburg *(G-5311)*

Kleppinger Design Group Inc.........F...... 703 208-2208
   Fairfax *(G-4490)*

L Peters Custom Cabinets.............G...... 276 340-9580
   Ridgeway *(G-11846)*

La Prade Enterprises.............G...... 804 271-9899
   North Chesterfield *(G-9912)*

Lantz Custom Woodworking.............G...... 540 438-1819
   Harrisonburg *(G-6336)*

Lawrence Custom Cabinets S.........G...... 757 380-0817
   Newport News *(G-9279)*

Liberty Cabinets.............G...... 540 493-3149
   Rocky Mount *(G-12334)*

Lighthouse Cabinets Inc.............G...... 571 293-1064
   Leesburg *(G-7299)*

Louis G Ball & Son Inc.............G...... 804 725-5202
   Mathews *(G-8356)*

Macs Custom Woodshop.............G...... 540 789-4201
   Willis *(G-15363)*

Mark Debusk Custom Cabinets.........G...... 540 552-3228
   Blacksburg *(G-1759)*

Martcl Inc.............G...... 540 777-0456
   Roanoke *(G-11959)*

Martin Star Cabinetry & Design.........G...... 804 340-1250
   Richmond *(G-11669)*

Marvin Coblentz.............G...... 434 944-1897
   Amherst *(G-699)*

Masco Cabinetry LLC.............B...... 540 477-2961
   Mount Jackson *(G-9076)*

Masco Cabinetry LLC.............C...... 540 727-7859
   Culpeper *(G-3907)*

Masterbrand Cabinets Inc.............C...... 703 396-7804
   Manassas *(G-7973)*

Mather AMP Cabinet.............G...... 615 636-1743
   Virginia Beach *(G-14640)*

McCraw Cabinets.............G...... 434 238-2112
   Forest *(G-5082)*

Mill Cabinet Shop Inc.............E...... 540 828-6763
   Bridgewater *(G-1954)*

Montgomery Cabinetry.............G...... 540 721-7000
   Wirtz *(G-15616)*

Moon Cabinet Inc.............G...... 703 339-8097
   Lorton *(G-7512)*

Nails Cabinet Shop Inc.............G...... 540 888-3268
   Winchester *(G-15454)*

Nelsons Cabinetry.............G...... 804 363-5800
   North Chesterfield *(G-9938)*

Nelsons Cabinetry Inc.............G...... 804 560-4785
   North Chesterfield *(G-9939)*

New Life Custom Cabinetry LLC.........G...... 757 274-7442
   Virginia Beach *(G-14680)*

Nextday Cabinets of Va LLC.............G...... 703 291-8935
   Richmond *(G-11304)*

Nichols Cabinetry LLC.............G...... 540 860-9252
   Luray *(G-7620)*

Norcraft Companies LP.............B...... 434 385-7500
   Lynchburg *(G-7777)*

Norfield-Fogleman Cabinets.............G...... 276 889-1333
   Lebanon *(G-7202)*

Nuckols Cabinetry LLC.............G...... 804 749-3908
   Rockville *(G-12294)*

Panda Kitchen and Bath VA LLC.........G...... 757 889-9888
   Norfolk *(G-9681)*

Peters Melvin Cabinet Shop Inc.........G...... 757 826-7317
   Hampton *(G-6215)*

Phillips Custom Cabinets LLC.............G...... 804 647-1328
   Amelia Court House *(G-667)*

Pinnacle Cabinetry Design LLC.........G...... 804 262-7356
   Richmond *(G-11326)*

Pom Kbf.............G...... 703 992-7877
   Alexandria *(G-552)*

Potomac Shores Cabinetry LLC.........G...... 703 476-5658
   Herndon *(G-6777)*

Precision Millwork & Cabinets.............G...... 434 525-6988
   Evington *(G-4383)*

Premier Cabinets Virginia LLC.........G...... 804 335-7354
   Midlothian *(G-8882)*

Prestige Cabinets.............G...... 757 741-3201
   Toano *(G-13875)*

Prestige Cabinets LLC.............G...... 757 741-3201
   Williamsburg *(G-15298)*

Prestige Inc.............F...... 804 266-1000
   Richmond *(G-11332)*

Pro Refinish.............G...... 703 853-9665
   Warrenton *(G-15046)*

Progressive Designs.............G...... 757 547-9201
   Chesapeake *(G-3251)*

R & B Cabinet Shop.............G...... 540 249-4507
   Grottoes *(G-6023)*

R & K Woodworking Inc.............G...... 540 867-5975
   Dayton *(G-4059)*

Racers Custom Cabinets Inc.............G...... 540 672-4231
   Orange *(G-10225)*

Rader Cabinets.............G...... 434 610-1954
   Lynchburg *(G-7798)*

Ramsey Cabinets Inc.............G...... 434 946-0329
   Amherst *(G-705)*

Rays Custom Cabinets.............G...... 434 528-0189
   Amherst *(G-706)*

Reinhart Custom Cabinets Inc.............G...... 757 303-1438
   Newport News *(G-9323)*

Renaissance Cabinet Shop.............G...... 540 967-0422
   Louisa *(G-7565)*

Richmond Refacing.............G...... 804 739-9222
   Midlothian *(G-8888)*

Rick Boyd Stone Cabinet.............G...... 540 365-2668
   Ferrum *(G-4978)*

Risque Custom Cabinetry.............G...... 703 534-5319
   Falls Church *(G-4867)*

Ritz Refinishing Inc.............G...... 703 378-0462
   Chantilly *(G-2487)*

River City Cabinetry LLC......................G..... 804 397-7950
  Chester *(G-3453)*

Robert Furr Cabinet Shop...................G..... 757 244-1267
  Hampton *(G-6230)*

Rockridge Granite Company LLC ....G..... 434 969-2665
  Buckingham *(G-2136)*

Round Meadows Cabinet Shop ....G..... 276 398-1153
  Laurel Fork *(G-7175)*

Rutrough Cabinets Inc ....G..... 540 489-3211
  Rocky Mount *(G-12351)*

Salem Custom Cabinets Inc ....G..... 540 380-4441
  Salem *(G-12564)*

Sarandi Manufacturing LLC ....F..... 540 705-0205
  Broadway *(G-2095)*

Shively and Carter Cabinets ....G..... 540 483-4149
  Glade Hill *(G-5670)*

Signature Dsigns Cabinetry LLC ....G..... 804 614-0028
  Chesterfield *(G-3524)*

Simply Clssic Cbnets Cnstr LLC ....G..... 804 815-3283
  Locust Hill *(G-7454)*

Southern Pride Cabinets ....G..... 540 365-3227
  Ferrum *(G-4983)*

Spotted Lopard-Tabula Rasa LLC ....G..... 571 285-8151
  Warrenton *(G-15053)*

Starmark Cabinetry..............................F..... 434 385-7500
  Lynchburg *(G-7813)*

Steve K Jones ....G..... 757 930-0217
  Newport News *(G-9347)*

Strasburg Cabinet & Supply ....G..... 540 465-3031
  Strasburg *(G-13599)*

Talmadge Fix ....G..... 540 463-9629
  Lexington *(G-7419)*

Theboxworks ....G..... 434 823-1004
  Crozet *(G-3852)*

Timberlake Cabinet Company ....G..... 540 955-4985
  Berryville *(G-1694)*

Toms Cabinets & Designs ....G..... 703 451-2227
  Springfield *(G-13101)*

Tops of Town Virginia LLC ....G..... 703 242-8100
  Fairfax *(G-4571)*

Trademark Woodworking LLC ....G..... 804 346-5999
  Richmond *(G-11417)*

Triple S Enterprises Inc ....F..... 434 525-8400
  Forest *(G-5102)*

Unique Cabinets Inc ....G..... 434 823-2188
  Crozet *(G-3853)*

US Cabinet & Intr Design LLC ....G..... 202 740-0038
  Falls Church *(G-4887)*

USA Cabinets Store ....G..... 703 204-3444
  Fairfax *(G-4576)*

Vangarde Woodworks Inc ....G..... 804 355-4917
  Richmond *(G-11433)*

Vaughans Custom Cabinets-Home ....G..... 276 398-2440
  Hillsville *(G-6903)*

Village Cabinet Co ....G..... 434 574-6263
  Prospect *(G-10615)*

Virginia Cabinetry LLC ....G..... 804 612-6469
  Richmond *(G-11810)*

Virginia Cabinets LLC...........................G..... 703 793-8307
  Herndon *(G-6840)*

Virginia Cabinetworks Inc ....G..... 540 298-9599
  Elkton *(G-4336)*

Virginia Woodcrafters LLC ....G..... 804 276-2766
  Henrico *(G-6590)*

Voell Custom Kitchens Inc ....G..... 703 528-1776
  Arlington *(G-1215)*

Walkers Creek Cabinet Works ....G..... 540 348-5810
  Middlebrook *(G-8714)*

Walsh Tops Inc ....E..... 757 523-1934
  Chesapeake *(G-3369)*

Washington Cabinetry ....G..... 703 466-5388
  Chantilly *(G-2518)*

Wells Cabinet Shop ....G..... 804 861-8325
  Prince George *(G-10610)*

West Shore Cabinetry ....G..... 804 739-2985
  Midlothian *(G-8920)*

Windsor Woodworking Co Inc ....G..... 757 242-4141
  Windsor *(G-15608)*

▲ Wolf Cabinetry Inc ....G..... 757 498-0088
  Virginia Beach *(G-14942)*

Wood Chux Cabinets LLC.....................G..... 757 409-0095
  Virginia Beach *(G-14943)*

Wood Provision ....G..... 540 456-8522
  Afton *(G-96)*

Woodworking Shop Inc ....G..... 757 872-0890
  Newport News *(G-9381)*

Woodys Woodworking Inc ....G..... 703 525-2030
  Arlington *(G-1221)*

Worthington Millwork LLC ....G..... 540 832-6391
  Gordonsville *(G-5919)*

Wytheville Custom Counter Tops.........G..... 276 228-4137
  Wytheville *(G-15928)*

2435 Hardwood Veneer & Plywood

Advanced Nano Adhesives Inc.............G..... 919 247-6411
  Moneta *(G-8956)*

▲ Charles City Forest Products ....E..... 804 966-2336
  Providence Forge *(G-10620)*

Chips Brookneal Inc.............................E..... 434 376-6202
  Brookneal *(G-2109)*

▲ Cloverdale Company Inc ....D..... 540 777-4414
  Troutville *(G-13907)*

Eastern Panel Manufacturing ....E..... 434 432-3055
  Chatham *(G-2927)*

First Colony Homes Inc ....G..... 540 788-4222
  Calverton *(G-2224)*

Georgia-Pacific LLC..............................B..... 434 634-5123
  Emporia *(G-4359)*

◆ International Veneer Co Inc ....E..... 434 447-7100
  South Hill *(G-12852)*

Ivc-Usa Inc ....G..... 434 447-7100
  South Hill *(G-12853)*

Kennedy Konstruction Kompany ....E..... 540 984-4191
  Edinburg *(G-4308)*

N S Gilbert Lumber LLC ....D..... 276 431-4488
  Duffield *(G-4182)*

SM Lumber Inc ....G..... 757 797-8353
  Virginia Beach *(G-14826)*

◆ Trm Inc ....E..... 920 855-2194
  Haymarket *(G-6452)*

2436 Softwood Veneer & Plywood

▲ Cloverdale Company Inc ....D..... 540 777-4414
  Troutville *(G-13907)*

Formply Products Inc ....F..... 434 572-4040
  South Boston *(G-12769)*

Georgia-Pacific LLC..............................C..... 434 634-6133
  Skippers *(G-12700)*

Georgia-Pacific LLC..............................C..... 434 283-1066
  Gladys *(G-5691)*

Georgia-Pacific LLC..............................B..... 434 634-5123
  Emporia *(G-4359)*

2439 Structural Wood Members, NEC

Apex Industries LLC ....F..... 804 313-2295
  Warsaw *(G-15060)*

Better Living Components Inc...............D..... 434 978-1666
  Charlottesville *(G-2595)*

Big Timber Hardwoods LLC...................G..... 724 301-7051
  Virginia Beach *(G-14277)*

Chesapeake Strl Systems Inc ....E..... 804 966-8340
  Charles City *(G-2573)*

Dominion Bldg Components LLC ....G..... 540 371-2184
  Fredericksburg *(G-5421)*

East Coast Truss Inc ....G..... 757 369-0801
  Smithfield *(G-12712)*

First Colony Homes Inc ....G..... 540 788-4222
  Calverton *(G-2224)*

Hickory Frame Corp ....G..... 434 847-8489
  Lynchburg *(G-7732)*

Kc Wood Mfg ....G..... 540 789-8300
  Willis *(G-15362)*

Kempsville Building Mtls Inc ....E..... 757 485-0782
  Chesapeake *(G-3162)*

Kempsville Building Mtls Inc ....E..... 757 875-1850
  Newport News *(G-9275)*

Kennedy Konstruction Kompany ....E..... 540 984-4191
  Edinburg *(G-4308)*

Lodore Truss Company Inc ....G..... 804 561-4141
  Amelia Court House *(G-664)*

Massaponax Bldg Components Inc ....F..... 540 898-0013
  Fredericksburg *(G-5322)*

Mulqueen Inc ....F..... 804 333-4847
  Warsaw *(G-15070)*

Portsmouth Lumber Corporation ....F..... 757 397-4646
  Portsmouth *(G-10471)*

Quadd Inc ....G..... 540 439-2148
  Remington *(G-10771)*

Quadd Building Systems LLC ....E..... 540 439-2148
  Remington *(G-10772)*

Republic Trusswerks LLC ....F..... 540 434-9497
  Rockingham *(G-12271)*

Richard Evans ....G..... 540 774-1905
  Roanoke *(G-11995)*

Riverside Roof Truss LLC ....D..... 434 793-0217
  Danville *(G-4035)*

Ruffin & Payne Incorporated ....C..... 804 329-2691
  Richmond *(G-11749)*

Shoffner Industries Virginia ....G..... 757 485-1132
  Chesapeake *(G-3292)*

▲ Structural Technologies LLC ....G..... 757 498-4448
  Virginia Beach *(G-14857)*

Structural Technologies LLC ....F..... 888 616-0615
  Doswell *(G-4126)*

Truss Construction ....G..... 540 710-0673
  Spotsylvania *(G-12919)*

Truss Incorporated ....G..... 804 556-3611
  Susan *(G-13802)*

Truss It Inc ....G..... 540 248-2177
  Mount Sidney *(G-9085)*

Truss Systems Inc ....G..... 804 462-5963
  Lancaster *(G-7163)*

Truss-Tech Inc ....E..... 757 787-3014
  Melfa *(G-8712)*

Trussway Manufacturing Inc.................D..... 540 898-3477
  Fredericksburg *(G-5382)*

Truswood Inc ....E..... 434 447-6565
  South Hill *(G-12862)*

Truswood Inc ....D..... 757 833-5300
  Newport News *(G-9365)*

Ufp Mid-Atlantic LLC ....D..... 757 485-3190
  Chesapeake *(G-3355)*

Ufp Mid-Atlantic LLC ....D..... 540 921-1286
  Pearisburg *(G-10278)*

Valley Building Supply Inc ....C..... 540 434-6725
  Harrisonburg *(G-6383)*

White Rock Truss LLC ....G..... 276 445-5990
  Rose Hill *(G-12364)*

Williams Brothers Lumber Inc ....F..... 434 760-2951
  Ruckersville *(G-12416)*

2441 Wood Boxes

Alexandria Packaging LLC ....D..... 703 644-5550
  Springfield *(G-12940)*

Breeze Ridge Enterprises ....D..... 703 728-4606
  Winchester *(G-15391)*

Custom Hope Chests VA LLC ....G..... 703 850-5019
  Herndon *(G-6650)*

Danielson Trading LLC ....G..... 703 764-0450
  Fairfax *(G-4436)*

Don Elthon ....G..... 703 237-2521
  Falls Church *(G-4908)*

Scan Industries LLC ....G..... 360 320-8244
  Ashburn *(G-1332)*

Smalley Package Company Inc ....D..... 540 955-2550
  Berryville *(G-1691)*

Swift Creek Forest Products ....E..... 804 561-1751
  Jetersville *(G-7015)*

2448 Wood Pallets & Skids

Alexandria Packaging LLC ....D..... 703 644-5550
  Springfield *(G-12940)*

Allied Pallet Company ....C..... 804 966-5597
  New Kent *(G-9128)*

Amware Logistics Services Inc ....F..... 540 389-9737
  Salem *(G-12474)*

Andis Pallet Co Inc ....F..... 276 628-9044
  Abingdon *(G-11)*

Andis Wood Products Inc ....G..... 276 628-7764
  Bristol *(G-2005)*

Apex Pallets LLC ....F..... 804 246-1499
  West Point *(G-15153)*

Beach Pallets Inc ....G..... 757 773-1931
  Virginia Beach *(G-14268)*

Bolivia Lumber Company LLC...............E..... 540 862-5228
  Clifton Forge *(G-3678)*

Brown Enterprise Pallets LLC ....G..... 804 447-0485
  Richmond *(G-11512)*

▲ Charles City Forest Products ....E..... 804 966-2336
  Providence Forge *(G-10620)*

Chep (usa) Inc ....D..... 804 226-0229
  Richmond *(G-11527)*

Conglobal Industries LLC ....E..... 757 487-5100
  Chesapeake *(G-3051)*

Curtis Russell Lumber Co Inc...............E..... 276 346-1958
  Jonesville *(G-7020)*

Deep Corporation ....F..... 804 751-1826
  Richmond *(G-11040)*

Direct Wood Products ....E..... 804 843-4642
  West Point *(G-15155)*

Don Elthon ....G..... 703 237-2521
  Falls Church *(G-4908)*

Duck Pallet Co LLC ....G..... 540 477-2771
  Mount Jackson *(G-9069)*

Ellington Wood Products Inc.................F..... 434 922-7545
  Amherst *(G-690)*

Expressway Pallet Inc ....F..... 804 231-6177
  South Chesterfield *(G-12804)*

Green Leaf Logistics LLC ....G..... 757 899-0881
  Spring Grove *(G-12930)*

S I C

Greg & Son Pallets................................G.......757 449-3832
Chesapeake (G-3125)
Gregory Pallet & Lumber Co.............G.......540 777-1715
Roanoke (G-12098)
Grottoes Pallet Co Inc........................G.......540 249-4882
Grottoes (G-6020)
H & A Specialty Co...............................G.......757 206-1115
Williamsburg (G-15252)
Hallwood Enterprises Inc....................F.......757 357-3113
Smithfield (G-12715)
J & D Pallets...E.......540 862-2448
Clifton Forge (G-3680)
JC Pallet Company Inc........................G.......800 754-5050
Barhamsville (G-1572)
Jif Pallets LLC......................................G.......276 963-6107
Doran (G-4117)
Lignetics of Virginia Inc.....................E.......434 676-4800
Kenbridge (G-7034)
Martin Pallets & Wedges LLC............F.......276 694-4276
Stuart (G-13623)
Mc Farlands Mill Inc............................G.......540 667-2272
Winchester (G-15444)
Mechanicsville Pallets Inc.................F.......804 746-4658
Mechanicsville (G-8658)
Merlin Brougher...................................G.......434 572-8750
South Boston (G-12782)
Murdock Acquisition LLC....................G.......804 798-9154
Ashland (G-1467)
P&B Pallet Co.......................................G.......434 309-1028
Lynch Station (G-7628)
Pallet Asset Recovery Sys LLC.........G.......800 727-2136
West Point (G-15161)
Pallet Empire.......................................G.......804 389-3604
Richmond (G-11055)
Pallet Foundation................................G.......703 519-6104
Alexandria (G-304)
Pallet Industries LLC..........................G.......757 238-2912
Carrollton (G-2245)
Pallet Recycling LLC...........................E.......304 749-7451
Strasburg (G-13593)
Pallet Services....................................G.......804 233-6584
Richmond (G-11705)
Palletone of Virginia LLC....................D.......434 372-2101
Chase City (G-2915)
Peters Pallets Inc...............................G.......410 647-8094
Richmond (G-11057)
Piedmont Pallet Corporation.............G.......434 836-6730
Danville (G-4026)
Porters Wood Products Inc................E.......757 654-6430
Boykins (G-1920)
Post & Pallet LLC.................................G.......757 645-5292
Toano (G-13874)
▼ Potomac Supply Llc.........................D.......804 472-2527
Kinsale (G-7136)
Recycled Pallets Inc...........................G.......804 400-9931
Mechanicsville (G-8670)
Scott Pallets Inc..................................E.......804 561-2514
Amelia Court House (G-672)
Smalley Package Company Inc...........D.......540 955-2550
Berryville (G-1691)
Soft Play...G.......804 226-0380
Richmond (G-11761)
Steves Pallets.....................................G.......757 576-4488
Virginia Beach (G-14847)
Swift Creek Forest Products.............E.......804 561-1751
Jetersville (G-7015)
Tidewater Pallets................................G.......757 962-0020
Norfolk (G-9754)
Tine & Company Inc.............................G.......276 881-8232
Whitewood (G-15193)
Triple S Pallets LLC.............................E.......540 810-4581
Mount Crawford (G-9061)
Virginia Pallets & Wood LLC..............G.......434 515-2221
Lawrenceville (G-7187)
Whitlow Lumber & Logging Inc..........G.......276 930-3854
Stuart (G-13640)
Williams Pallet Company....................G.......276 930-2081
Stuart (G-13641)
Williamsburg Millwork Corp..............D.......804 994-2151
Ruther Glen (G-12464)

2449 Wood Containers, NEC

C & L Containers Inc...........................G.......757 398-0447
Chesapeake (G-3020)
Consolidated Wood Products.............G.......540 374-1439
Fredericksburg (G-5266)
Grapevine...G.......540 371-4092
Fredericksburg (G-5436)
Murdock Acquisition LLC....................C.......804 798-9154
Ashland (G-1467)

Smalley Package Company Inc...........D.......540 955-2550
Berryville (G-1691)
Southside Containers..........................G.......757 422-1111
Virginia Beach (G-14831)
▲ Strickland Mfg LLC..........................G.......866 929-3388
Oilville (G-10184)

2451 Mobile Homes

Clayton Homes Inc..............................G.......276 395-7272
Coeburn (G-3696)
Di9 Equity Investors...........................G.......703 860-0901
Reston (G-10841)
Freedom Homes....................................G.......540 382-9015
Christiansburg (G-3588)
Home Pride Inc.....................................F.......276 642-0271
Bristol (G-2020)
Home Pride Inc.....................................E.......276 466-0502
Bristol (G-2021)
Mission Realty Group..........................G.......804 545-6651
Richmond (G-11293)
New Acton Mobile Inds LLC................G.......804 520-7171
South Chesterfield (G-12817)
SMC Holdings & Investment Corp.....G.......703 860-0901
Reston (G-10954)
Tool Wagon LLC...................................G.......434 610-9664
Lynchburg (G-7824)

2452 Prefabricated Wood Buildings & Cmpnts

Alan Mitchell..G.......276 251-5077
Claudville (G-3637)
Aubrey Otis Gunter Jr.........................G.......434 352-8136
Appomattox (G-804)
Blue Ridge Homestead LLC.................G.......540 743-2374
Luray (G-7601)
Bryan Smith..G.......434 242-7698
Ruckersville (G-12400)
Cardinal Homes Inc.............................G.......434 735-8111
Wylliesburg (G-15871)
Chadwick International Inc................F.......703 560-0970
Fairfax (G-4426)
Cherrystone Structures LLC..............F.......434 432-8484
Chatham (G-2922)
Colonial Barns Inc...............................E.......757 482-2234
Chesapeake (G-3046)
Custom Vinyl Products LLC................E.......757 887-3194
Newport News (G-9209)
Devereux Barns LLC............................G.......540 664-1432
Berryville (G-1677)
DFI Systems Inc...................................D.......757 262-1057
Hampton (G-6128)
Dogwood Mountain Log Homes LLC....G.......540 433-1873
Rockingham (G-12250)
Don Elthon...G.......703 237-2521
Falls Church (G-4908)
Dutch Barns..G.......757 497-7356
Virginia Beach (G-14418)
First Colony Homes Inc.......................G.......540 788-4222
Calverton (G-2224)
Heritage Log Homes..............................G.......540 854-4926
Unionville (G-13963)
Highlands Log Structures Inc............G.......276 623-1580
Abingdon (G-37)
Honest Abe Log Homes Inc.................G.......800 231-3695
Martinsville (G-8296)
Kennedy Konstruction Kompany........E.......540 984-4191
Edinburg (G-4308)
Lester Building Systems LLC.............E.......540 665-0182
Clear Brook (G-3646)
Log Home Lovers.................................G.......540 743-7355
Luray (G-7615)
Log Homes By Clore Bros...................G.......540 786-7749
Fredericksburg (G-5315)
McRae of America Inc.........................G.......757 488-6900
Chesapeake (G-3201)
Modern Living LLC...............................G.......877 663-2224
Richmond (G-11679)
Mr Luck Inc...G.......570 766-8734
Norfolk (G-9649)
Old Vrgnia Hand Hewn Log Homes.......F.......276 546-5647
Pennington Gap (G-10296)
Panel Processing Virginia Inc............G.......989 356-9007
Claudville (G-3639)
Pine Glade Buildings LLC....................G.......540 674-5229
Dublin (G-4169)
Pls Installation...................................G.......540 521-1261
Buchanan (G-2124)
Roosters Amish Sheds.........................G.......540 263-2415
Strasburg (G-13595)

Scan Industries LLC............................G.......360 320-8244
Ashburn (G-1332)
Sealants and Coatings Tech..............G.......812 256-3378
Paeonian Springs (G-10239)
Shenandoah Sheds..............................G.......540 869-4050
White Post (G-15184)
Southern Heritage Homes Inc...........F.......540 489-7700
Rocky Mount (G-12353)
Southland Log Homes Inc...................G.......540 268-2243
Christiansburg (G-3610)
Southland Log Homes Inc...................G.......540 548-1617
Fredericksburg (G-5226)
Stella-Jones Corporation...................D.......540 997-9251
Goshen (G-5927)
Travis Lee Kerr....................................G.......434 922-7005
Vesuvius (G-13999)
Valley Structures Inc..........................F.......540 879-9454
Dayton (G-4070)
Valley Utility Buildings Inc...............G.......276 679-6736
Big Stone Gap (G-1717)
Vfp Inc..C.......276 431-4000
Duffield (G-4187)
▲ Vfp Inc...D.......540 977-0500
Roanoke (G-12019)
Virginia Custom Buildings.................F.......804 784-3816
Manakin Sabot (G-7906)
Wilcks Lake Storage Sheds Inc.........F.......434 574-5131
Prospect (G-10616)

2491 Wood Preserving

Alliance Presrvng Hstry Wwii............G.......757 423-1429
Norfolk (G-9434)
Anderson Brothers Lumber Co...........E.......804 561-2153
Amelia Court House (G-651)
Atlantic Wood Industries Inc............E.......757 397-2317
Portsmouth (G-10395)
B H Cobb Lumber Co...........................G.......804 358-3801
Richmond (G-11498)
Blue Ridge Wood Preserving Inc.......F.......540 297-6607
Moneta (G-8957)
C H Evelyn Piling Company Inc..........F.......804 966-2273
Providence Forge (G-10619)
Culpeper Roanoke Rapids LLC...........G.......800 817-6215
Culpeper (G-3886)
Gladys Timber Products Inc..............F.......434 283-4744
Gladys (G-5692)
Great Southern Wood Prsv Inc..........C.......540 483-5264
Rocky Mount (G-12326)
Highland Timber Frame Inc................G.......540 745-7411
Floyd (G-5028)
Jefferson Homebuilders Inc..............G.......540 371-5338
Fredericksburg (G-5306)
Jefferson Homebuilders Inc..............G.......540 727-2240
Culpeper (G-3897)
Jefferson Homebuilders Inc..............C.......540 825-5898
Culpeper (G-3898)
Jefferson Homebuilders Inc..............G.......540 825-5200
Culpeper (G-3899)
Kejaeh Enterprises LLC......................G.......434 476-1300
Halifax (G-6051)
Koppers Inc...E.......540 380-2061
Salem (G-12527)
Koppers Utility Indus Pdts Inc..........G.......434 292-4375
Blackstone (G-1818)
McCready Lumber Company Inc..........G.......540 980-8700
Pulaski (G-10643)
Mk Environmental LLC........................G.......540 435-9066
Rockingham (G-12262)
Nova Lumber & Millwork LLC.............G.......703 451-9217
Springfield (G-13061)
Phytosnitation Vac Systems LLC.......G.......540 641-4170
Blacksburg (G-1779)
▼ Potomac Supply Llc.........................D.......804 472-2527
Kinsale (G-7136)
Rivanna Natural Designs Inc.............G.......434 244-3447
Henrico (G-6560)
Sound Structures Virginia Inc...........G.......804 876-3014
Doswell (G-4125)
Southside Utilities & Maint..............E.......434 735-8853
Red Oak (G-10760)
Stella-Jones Corporation...................D.......540 997-9251
Goshen (G-5927)
▲ Trout River Lumber LLC...................E.......434 645-2600
Crewe (G-3818)
▲ Valley Timber Sales Inc..................F.......540 832-3646
Gordonsville (G-5917)
What Wood Analisa Do........................G.......757 642-2991
Virginia Beach (G-14935)
▲ Wood Preservers Incorporated.......D.......804 333-4022
Warsaw (G-15073)

Woodsong Instruments .... G 540 745-2708
Floyd *(G-5046)*

2493 Reconstituted Wood Prdts

Atlantic Fireproofing Inc .... E 703 940-9444
Springfield *(G-12953)*

Blue Ridge Fiberboard Inc .... D 434 797-1321
Danville *(G-3959)*

▲ Coastal Wood Imports Inc .... F 434 799-1117
Danville *(G-3968)*

Eazy Construction Inc .... G 571 220-8385
Fredericksburg *(G-5424)*

Georgia-Pacific LLC .... B 434 634-5123
Emporia *(G-4359)*

Georgia-Pacific LLC .... C 434 283-1066
Gladys *(G-5691)*

Georgia-Pacific LLC .... C 434 634-6133
Skippers *(G-12700)*

Global Code Usa Inc .... G 908 764-5818
Manassas *(G-7947)*

Huber Engineered Woods LLC .... C 434 476-6628
Crystal Hill *(G-3859)*

Kingspan Insulation LLC .... E 800 336-2240
Winchester *(G-15434)*

Mid-Atlantic Manufacturing Inc .... G 804 798-7462
Oilville *(G-10183)*

Trex Company Inc .... C 540 542-6800
Winchester *(G-15493)*

◆ Webb Furniture Enterprises Inc .... D 276 236-5111
Galax *(G-5654)*

Webb Furniture Enterprises Inc .... D 276 236-6141
Galax *(G-5655)*

2499 Wood Prdts, NEC

Acorn Sales Company Inc .... F 804 359-0505
Richmond *(G-11081)*

Advanced Custom Woodworki .... G 804 310-0511
Charles City *(G-2568)*

All About Frames .... G 703 998-5868
Alexandria *(G-408)*

Amazon Mllwk Installations LLC .... G 703 200-9076
Alexandria *(G-410)*

Amboy Enterprises LLC .... G 804 708-0945
Manakin Sabot *(G-7894)*

American Spirit LLC .... G 703 914-1057
Falls Church *(G-4749)*

Armstrong Green & Embrey Inc .... G 540 898-7434
Fredericksburg *(G-5248)*

Art of Wood .... G 703 597-9357
Sterling *(G-13351)*

Artworks .... G 540 420-3843
Ferrum *(G-4969)*

B & D Trucking of Virginia .... G 540 463-3035
Lexington *(G-7387)*

B & H Wood Products Inc .... F 540 752-2480
Stafford *(G-13122)*

Bacus Woodworks LLC .... G 571 762-3314
Warrenton *(G-14979)*

Batts Woodworking .... G 757 969-5824
Hampton *(G-6088)*

Belchers Woodworking .... G 540 365-7809
Ferrum *(G-4970)*

Benson Fine Woodcrafting LLC .... G 703 372-1871
Lorton *(G-7466)*

Biltco LLC .... G 703 372-5940
Lorton *(G-7467)*

Biocer Corporation .... G 757 490-7851
Virginia Beach *(G-14280)*

Blanc Creatives LLC .... F 434 260-1692
Charlottesville *(G-2741)*

Blue Skys Woodshop .... G 703 567-6220
Alexandria *(G-149)*

◆ Bluegrass Woods Inc .... F 540 997-0174
Millboro *(G-8934)*

Bowld Flavors LLC .... G 757 952-4741
Hampton *(G-6099)*

Buggs Island Dock Service .... G 434 374-8028
Clarksville *(G-3627)*

Burks Fork Log Homes .... G 276 766-0350
Hillsville *(G-6887)*

Burnettes Custom Wood Inc .... G 540 577-9687
Roanoke *(G-12056)*

Burr Fox Specialized Wdwkg .... F 276 666-0127
Martinsville *(G-8273)*

C H Evelyn Piling Company Inc .... F 804 966-2273
Providence Forge *(G-10619)*

Capitol Wood Works .... G 703 237-2071
Falls Church *(G-4772)*

Carris Reels Inc .... E 540 473-2210
Fincastle *(G-4995)*

Casson Art & Frame .... G 276 638-1450
Martinsville *(G-8274)*

Citiwood Urban Forest Products .... G 804 795-9220
Henrico *(G-6493)*

City Spree of Woodbridge .... G ......
Woodbridge *(G-15672)*

Corporate & Museum Frame Inc .... G 804 643-6858
Richmond *(G-11541)*

Country Wood Classics .... G 804 798-1587
Ashland *(G-1396)*

Cove Creek Industries Inc .... G 434 293-6774
Covesville *(G-3775)*

Coyent .... G 804 861-3323
Prince George *(G-10589)*

Creative Crafty Mom LLC .... G 571 206-8570
Dumfries *(G-4241)*

Creative Framing Gallery .... G 703 771-6354
Leesburg *(G-7249)*

Criders Finishing Inc .... G 703 661-6520
Ashburn *(G-1260)*

CTI of Woodbridge .... G 703 670-4790
Woodbridge *(G-15679)*

Custom Moulding & Millwork Inc .... F 540 788-1823
Catlett *(G-2267)*

Cutting Edge Millworks LLC .... G 804 580-7270
Heathsville *(G-6461)*

Dickerson Stump LLC .... G 540 898-9145
Fredericksburg *(G-5273)*

◆ Dimitrios & Co Inc .... G 703 368-1757
Manassas Park *(G-8199)*

Discount Frames Inc .... G 703 550-0000
Lorton *(G-7481)*

Dogwood Montessori &C .... G 540 439-3572
Bealeton *(G-1598)*

Doodadd Shop .... G 276 964-2389
Pounding Mill *(G-10518)*

Driftwood Gallery .... G 804 932-3318
Quinton *(G-10694)*

Edgyash Paddleboards LLC .... G 717 404-6073
Poquoson *(G-10370)*

Ennis Mountain Woods Inc .... G 540 471-9171
Afton *(G-79)*

Erickson & Ripper Framing .... G 703 549-1616
Alexandria *(G-202)*

▼ Erle D Anderson Lbr Pdts Inc .... G 804 748-0500
Disputanta *(G-4107)*

Essex Hand Crafted WD Pdts LLC ...... G 540 445-5928
Warrenton *(G-15005)*

Esteemed Woodcrafts .... G 757 876-5868
Chesapeake *(G-3093)*

Family Tree Care Inc .... G 703 280-1169
Fairfax *(G-4455)*

Fine Arts Framers Inc .... G 703 525-3869
Arlington *(G-965)*

Finest Art & Framing LLC .... G 703 945-9000
Lansdowne *(G-7170)*

Flags of Valor LLC .... E 703 729-8640
Ashburn *(G-1280)*

Forest Carbon Offsets LLC .... G 703 795-4512
Alexandria *(G-206)*

Fred Leach .... G 434 372-5225
Chase City *(G-2911)*

Hang Up .... G 703 430-0717
Sterling *(G-13418)*

Hardwood Mulch Corporation .... G 804 458-7500
Disputanta *(G-4108)*

Hawleywood LLC .... G 757 463-0910
Virginia Beach *(G-14510)*

Healthy By Choice .... G 810 449-5999
Norfolk *(G-9575)*

Heirlooms Furniture LLC .... G 703 652-6094
Vienna *(G-14062)*

Herff Jones LLC .... E 757 689-3000
Virginia Beach *(G-14517)*

Hollybrook Mulch Trucking Inc .... G 540 381-7830
Christiansburg *(G-3593)*

Interpretive Wdwrk Design Inc .... G 703 330-6105
Manassas *(G-7953)*

J K Enterprise Inc .... G 703 352-1858
Fairfax *(G-4483)*

Ja Designs .... G 540 659-2592
Stafford *(G-13159)*

Jerry King .... G 804 550-1243
Glen Allen *(G-5755)*

Jorgensen Woodworking .... G 757 312-9663
Chesapeake *(G-3156)*

Just Handle It LLC .... G 804 285-0786
Richmond *(G-11258)*

Just Woodstuff .... G 540 951-2323
Blacksburg *(G-1748)*

K & W Projects LLC .... G 757 618-9249
Chesapeake *(G-3161)*

Karl J Protil & Sons Inc .... G 540 885-6664
Staunton *(G-13271)*

Kawood LLC .... G 757 488-4658
Portsmouth *(G-10452)*

Kayjae Inc .... G 804 725-9664
Cobbs Creek *(G-3694)*

Keyser Collection .... G 804 740-3237
Richmond *(G-11260)*

Kilpatrick Framing and Art .... G 804 245-6824
Chesterfield *(G-3511)*

Lees Wood Products Inc .... F 540 483-9728
Rocky Mount *(G-12333)*

LLC Little Bean .... G 757 937-1600
Virginia Beach *(G-14614)*

Loudoun Construction LLC .... G 703 895-7242
Middleburg *(G-8727)*

Marathon Millwork Inc .... G 540 743-1721
Luray *(G-7617)*

Maurywood LLC .... G 540 463-6209
Lexington *(G-7401)*

Meissner Cstm Knives Pens LLC .... G 321 693-2392
Hampton *(G-6195)*

Mobile Custom Framing LLC .... G 757 412-4167
Virginia Beach *(G-14659)*

▲ Moslow Wood Products Inc .... D 804 598-5579
Powhatan *(G-10561)*

Museum Framing .... G 703 299-0100
Alexandria *(G-287)*

Mwb Enterprises Inc .... G 434 922-7730
Amherst *(G-702)*

Newcomb Woodworks LLC .... G 804 370-0441
Henrico *(G-6543)*

Norfleet Acquisition Co Inc .... F 540 373-9481
Fredericksburg *(G-5208)*

Norfleet Quality LLC .... G 540 373-9481
Fredericksburg *(G-5209)*

Northwind Associates .... G 757 871-8215
Hayes *(G-6403)*

Northwood Contracting LLC .... G 703 624-0928
Rixeyville *(G-11880)*

Nva Docks LLC .... G 619 500-1964
Stafford *(G-13178)*

Old Dominion Shaker Boxes .... G 703 470-7921
Manassas *(G-7984)*

Pae-Imk International LLC .... E 888 526-5416
Falls Church *(G-4853)*

Paramount Woodworking .... G 804 862-2432
Petersburg *(G-10332)*

Parkside Woods LLC .... G 703 543-6446
Chantilly *(G-2478)*

Prologue .... G 757 871-3708
Newport News *(G-9318)*

Quigley Designs .... G 540 484-1133
Rocky Mount *(G-12349)*

R G Woodworks .... G 757 427-2743
Virginia Beach *(G-14754)*

Recognition Works .... G 804 739-1483
Midlothian *(G-8886)*

Rice S Stake & Wood Products .... G 804 769-3272
Aylett *(G-1552)*

Richmond Woodworks LLC .... G 804 510-3747
Moseley *(G-9046)*

Ron Campbell Art and Framing .... G 540 651-2228
Check *(G-2945)*

Saiflavor .... G 304 520-9464
Harrisonburg *(G-6366)*

Scaffsales International LLC .... G 757 545-5050
Chesapeake *(G-3286)*

Scott Fineart and Frmng Inc M .... G 757 496-0221
Virginia Beach *(G-14797)*

Shahzada Afghan Amrcn Import E .... G 571 245-1345
Alexandria *(G-344)*

Shelfnwoodworks .... G 757 350-0408
Suffolk *(G-13763)*

Skyline Post & Pole LLC .... F 717 949-8170
Broadway *(G-2096)*

SMC Mulch Yard Inc .... G 540 657-5454
Stafford *(G-13191)*

Smyth-Riley .... G 540 477-9652
Mount Jackson *(G-9079)*

Snows Custom Woodwork .... G 540 428-1763
Marshall *(G-8261)*

Southern Finishing Company Inc .... E 276 632-4901
Martinsville *(G-8333)*

St Pierre Inc .... G 540 797-3496
Floyd *(G-5041)*

Strong Oaks Woodshop .... G 540 683-2316
Linden *(G-7433)*

SIC

Three Peaks Crafts ....G...... 276 677-3724
Troutdale *(G-13901)*

Tidewater Structures ....G...... 757 753-1435
Virginia Beach *(G-14877)*

Timberline Barns LLC ....G...... 276 445-4366
Rose Hill *(G-12363)*

Timbertone LLC ....G...... 540 381-9794
Christiansburg *(G-3613)*

Tinkers Treasures ....G...... 708 633-0710
Midlothian *(G-8914)*

Traditional Iron & Woodworking.........G...... 540 439-6911
Remington *(G-10774)*

Virginias Rsurces Recycled LLC.........F...... 804 561-2543
Amelia Court House *(G-676)*

Watson Wood Yard ....G...... 540 895-0006
Spotsylvania *(G-12923)*

Watson Wood Yard ....G...... 540 854-7703
Mine Run *(G-8941)*

Whimsical Expressions ....G...... 804 239-6550
Lanexa *(G-7169)*

Wilbur Frederick - Wood Carver ....G...... 434 263-4827
Lovingston *(G-7594)*

Wilcox Woodworks Inc ....F...... 703 369-3455
Manassas *(G-8012)*

William Keyser ....G...... 703 243-8777
Arlington *(G-1219)*

Winchester Woods Condos LLC ....G...... 540 885-8390
Staunton *(G-13307)*

▲ Wood Preservers Incorporated.......D...... 804 333-4022
Warsaw *(G-15073)*

Wood-N-Stuff ....G...... 276 686-6557
Rural Retreat *(G-12433)*

Woodard LLC ....G...... 540 812-5016
Boston *(G-1905)*

Woodardweb ....G...... 202 337-3730
Alexandria *(G-613)*

Woodducks Odd Jobs Lawn Svc LL ....G...... 804 932-4612
New Kent *(G-9139)*

Woodland Artisans Ltd ....G...... 276 766-3421
Allisonia *(G-621)*

Woodland Group LLC ....G...... 571 312-5951
Alexandria *(G-387)*

Woodmark Designs ....G...... 804 921-9454
Mechanicsville *(G-8701)*

Woods of Wisdom LLC......................G...... 757 645-2043
Williamsburg *(G-15348)*

25 FURNITURE AND FIXTURES

2511 Wood Household Furniture

All A Board Inc ....F...... 804 652-0020
Richmond *(G-11481)*

American Interiors Ltd ....G...... 757 627-0248
Norfolk *(G-9438)*

Amish Heirlooms of Vrgn ....G...... 540 626-8587
Pembroke *(G-10281)*

Antiquated Heirlooms LLC ....G...... 540 771-4120
Strasburg *(G-13572)*

Bassett Direct Sc LLC ....G...... 276 629-6000
Bassett *(G-1577)*

◆ Bassett Furniture Inds Inc ....A...... 276 629-6000
Bassett *(G-1578)*

◆ Bassett Furniture Inds NC LLC ....F...... 276 629-6000
Bassett *(G-1579)*

◆ Bassett Mirror Company Inc ....C...... 276 629-3341
Bassett *(G-1580)*

▲ Becker Designed Inc....................E...... 703 803-6900
Chantilly *(G-2376)*

▲ Bhk of America Inc......................E...... 201 783-8490
South Boston *(G-12752)*

Blaise Gaston Inc ....G...... 434 973-1801
Earlysville *(G-4288)*

Blue Ridge Woodworks VA Inc ....G...... 434 477-0313
Monroe *(G-8987)*

Brass Beds of Virginia Inc ....E...... 804 353-3503
Richmond *(G-11131)*

▲ Butler Woodcrafters Inc ....E...... 877 852-0784
North Chesterfield *(G-9837)*

Capitol Closet Design Inc ....F...... 703 827-2700
Vienna *(G-14022)*

Carpers Wood Creations Inc..............E...... 540 465-2525
Strasburg *(G-13576)*

Central Virginia Hardwood Pdts ....G...... 434 335-5898
Gretna *(G-6006)*

Chesapeake Bay Adirondack LLC........G...... 757 416-4583
Chesapeake *(G-3030)*

Colonial Kitchen & Cabinets ....G...... 757 898-1332
Yorktown *(G-15943)*

Contemporary Kitchens Ltd...............G...... 804 758-2001
Topping *(G-13886)*

Deck World Inc ....G...... 804 798-9003
Warsaw *(G-15062)*

Desantis Design Inc ....G...... 540 751-9014
Purcellville *(G-10659)*

Dixie Woodcraft Inc ....G...... 434 842-3384
Fork Union *(G-5109)*

E A Clore Sons Inc ....D...... 540 948-5821
Madison *(G-7851)*

Frank Chervan ....G...... 540 586-5600
Bedford *(G-1638)*

Frey Randall Antique Furnitre ....G...... 434 985-7631
Stanardsville *(G-13219)*

Furniture Art ....G...... 540 667-2533
Winchester *(G-15418)*

Garnier-Thiebaut Inc ....G...... 434 572-3965
South Boston *(G-12770)*

Helvetica Designs ....G...... 540 213-2437
Staunton *(G-13266)*

▲ Henkel-Harris LLC ....E...... 540 667-4900
Winchester *(G-15547)*

◆ Hermle Uhren GMBH & Co KG ....D...... 434 946-7751
Amherst *(G-693)*

Hooker Furniture Corporation ....C...... 276 632-1763
Martinsville *(G-8298)*

◆ Hooker Furniture Corporation ....C...... 276 632-2133
Martinsville *(G-8297)*

◆ IKEA Industry Danville LLC ....B...... 434 822-6080
Ringgold *(G-11868)*

J W Creations ....G...... 276 676-3770
Abingdon *(G-43)*

Jack Carter Cabinet Maker ....G...... 757 622-9414
Norfolk *(G-9599)*

Jaeger & Ernst Inc ....F...... 434 973-7018
Barboursville *(G-1562)*

▲ Javawood USA LLC ....G...... 703 658-9665
Alexandria *(G-493)*

John J Heckford ....G...... 276 889-5646
Lebanon *(G-7194)*

John Potter Enterprises ....G...... 757 485-2922
Chesapeake *(G-3151)*

Jph Woodcraft ....G...... 757 615-6812
Virginia Beach *(G-14575)*

La Prade Enterprises ....G...... 804 271-9899
North Chesterfield *(G-9912)*

Mamagreen LLC ....G...... 312 953-3557
Richmond *(G-11663)*

Midlothian Custom Workshop LLC ....G...... 804 937-1184
Midlothian *(G-8859)*

Mikrocoze Inc ....G...... 800 542-8715
Chesapeake *(G-3205)*

Mill Cabinet Shop Inc ....E...... 540 828-6763
Bridgewater *(G-1954)*

◆ Old Dominion Wood Products Inc .....E...... 434 845-5511
Lynchburg *(G-7778)*

Old Town Woodworking Inc................F...... 540 347-3993
Warrenton *(G-15039)*

Oregon Woodcraft Inc ....G...... 703 477-4793
Burke *(G-2197)*

Phineas Rose Wood Joinery ....G...... 540 948-4248
Madison *(G-7860)*

Piedmont Station Studio LLC ....G...... 540 364-4427
Delaplane *(G-4077)*

Pine Creek Structures ....G...... 703 791-5700
Manassas *(G-8128)*

Preservation Wood Sales ....G...... 540 553-2023
Floyd *(G-5035)*

Pulliam Furniture Co ....G...... 276 956-3615
Ridgeway *(G-11849)*

Ready To Cover Inc ....G...... 571 379-5766
Manassas *(G-8140)*

Remark Design Incorporated ....G...... 540 675-3625
Washington *(G-15078)*

▲ Renaissnce Cntract Ltg Furn In ......E...... 540 342-1548
Roanoke *(G-12162)*

▼ Richard E Sheppard Jr ....F...... 276 956-2322
Ridgeway *(G-11851)*

Rocky Ridge Furniture ....G...... 419 512-0067
Pearisburg *(G-10276)*

◆ Rowe Fine Furniture Inc ....C...... 540 444-7693
Elliston *(G-4348)*

▼ Rowe Furniture Inc ....A...... 540 389-8671
Elliston *(G-4349)*

Shore Drive Self Storage Corp ....G...... 757 587-6000
Norfolk *(G-9722)*

Smart Buy Kitchen & Bath Plus...........G...... 571 643-1078
Chantilly *(G-2492)*

▲ Southeastern Wood Products Inc .....F...... 276 632-9025
Martinsville *(G-8332)*

Southern Finishing Company Inc.........E...... 276 632-4901
Martinsville *(G-8333)*

Steve M Sheil ....G...... 757 482-2456
Chesapeake *(G-3312)*

Suters Cabinet Shop Inc ....F...... 540 434-2131
Harrisonburg *(G-6378)*

Tfi Wind Down Inc............................G...... 703 714-0500
Vienna *(G-14141)*

▲ Tubular Fabricators Indust Inc.........E...... 804 733-4000
Petersburg *(G-10347)*

Turman Lumber Company Inc ....E...... 540 639-1250
Christiansburg *(G-3614)*

V-B/Williams Furniture Co Inc ....B...... 276 236-6161
Galax *(G-5651)*

Valley Heirlooms LLC ....G...... 540 234-0251
Mount Crawford *(G-9062)*

◆ Vaughan Furniture Company Inc ......F...... 276 236-6111
Galax *(G-5652)*

◆ Vaughan-Bassett Furn Co Inc ....A...... 276 236-6161
Galax *(G-5653)*

Virginia Custom Buildings ....F...... 804 784-3816
Manakin Sabot *(G-7906)*

Whispering Pine Lawn Furn ....G...... 540 789-7361
Willis *(G-15366)*

White Properties of Winchester...........F...... 540 868-0205
Winchester *(G-15508)*

Woodcrafters Inc ....G...... 703 736-2825
Reston *(G-10993)*

Woodcrafters II LLC ....G...... 703 499-5418
Gainesville *(G-5624)*

2512 Wood Household Furniture, Upholstered

Absolutely Fabulous..........................G...... 757 615-5732
Virginia Beach *(G-14205)*

▲ Albany Industries-Galax LLC ....D...... 276 236-0735
Galax *(G-5626)*

◆ Bassett Furniture Inds Inc ....A...... 276 629-6000
Bassett *(G-1578)*

◆ Bassett Furniture Inds NC LLC ....F...... 276 629-6000
Bassett *(G-1579)*

◆ Bassett Mirror Company Inc ....C...... 276 629-3341
Bassett *(G-1580)*

▲ Clayton-Marcus Company Inc ....C...... 540 389-8671
Elliston *(G-4344)*

Creative Seating LLC ....G...... 276 236-3615
Galax *(G-5631)*

◆ Ebi LLC ....D...... 434 797-9701
Danville *(G-3988)*

Expertsinframing LLC ....G...... 703 580-9980
Woodbridge *(G-15701)*

Haltrie LLC ....G...... 703 598-9928
Annandale *(G-755)*

◆ Hooker Furniture Corporation ....C...... 276 632-2133
Martinsville *(G-8297)*

Huddle Furniture Inc.........................E...... 276 647-5129
Collinsville *(G-3714)*

Huddle Furniture Inc.........................D...... 828 874-8888
Martinsville *(G-8299)*

Interlude Home Inc...........................D...... 540 381-7745
Christiansburg *(G-3598)*

Jackson Furniture Company VA...........C...... 540 635-3187
Front Royal *(G-5538)*

Kinters Cabinet Shop Inc J ....G...... 540 837-1663
White Post *(G-15180)*

La-Z-Boy Incorporated ....G...... 703 569-6188
Springfield *(G-13036)*

▲ Riversedge Furniture Co Inc ....E...... 434 847-4155
Lynchburg *(G-7802)*

Ronbuilt Corporation ....G...... 276 638-2090
Martinsville *(G-8324)*

◆ Rowe Fine Furniture Inc ....C...... 540 444-7693
Elliston *(G-4348)*

Rowe Fine Furniture Inc ....C...... 540 389-8661
Salem *(G-12563)*

▼ Rowe Furniture Inc ....A...... 540 389-8671
Elliston *(G-4349)*

▲ Sam Moore Furniture LLC ....B...... 540 586-8253
Bedford *(G-1656)*

Stewart Furniture Design Inc ....E...... 276 744-0186
Fries *(G-5518)*

Tfi Wind Down Inc............................G...... 703 714-0500
Vienna *(G-14141)*

2514 Metal Household Furniture

◆ Bassett Mirror Company Inc ....C...... 276 629-3341
Bassett *(G-1580)*

▲ Becker Designed Inc....................E...... 703 803-6900
Chantilly *(G-2376)*

Brass Beds of Virginia Inc ....E...... 804 353-3503
Richmond *(G-11131)*

Burgers Cabinet Shop Inc......................F...... 571 262-8001
Sterling (G-13362)
Capstone Industries LLC.....................G...... 703 966-6718
Manassas (G-8045)
Demorais International Inc....................G...... 703 369-3326
Manassas (G-7932)
Keane Cabinetry....................................540 867-5336
Rockingham (G-12257)
▲ McKinnon and Harris Inc..................E...... 804 358-2385
Richmond (G-11286)
Rewi LLC..G...... 757 647-8942
Williamsburg (G-15305)
Solgreen Solutions LLC........................G...... 833 765-4733
Alexandria (G-588)
Starsprings USA Inc.............................D...... 276 403-4500
Ridgeway (G-11855)
Summa LLC..G...... 757 254-1000
Newport News (G-9349)

2515 Mattresses & Bedsprings

Brass Beds of Virginia Inc ....E...... 804 353-3503
Richmond (G-11131)
Custom Comfort By Winn Ltd..............F...... 804 452-0929
Hopewell (G-6921)
Direct Buy Mattress LLC.......................G...... 703 346-0323
Midland (G-8752)
Eastern Sleep Products Company ....C...... 804 353-8965
Richmond (G-11195)
Free Union Restaurant Inc ....G...... 434 327-9559
Charlottesville (G-2635)
Kingsdown Incorporated......................D...... 540 667-0399
Winchester (G-15433)
Leesa Sleep LLC..................................G...... 844 335-3372
Virginia Beach (G-14606)
Mattress Deal LLC................................G...... 804 869-3387
Richmond (G-11285)
◆ Paramount Indus Companies Inc .....C...... 757 855-3321
Norfolk (G-9682)
Robson Woodworking............................G...... 540 896-6711
Timberville (G-13854)
Rvmf Inc...G...... 614 921-1223
North Chesterfield (G-9968)
Ssb Manufacturing Company ....G...... 540 891-0236
Fredericksburg (G-5368)
▲ Tempur Production Usa LLC............C...... 276 431-7150
Duffield (G-4185)

2517 Wood T V, Radio, Phono & Sewing Cabinets

Bay Cabinets & Contractors ....G...... 757 934-2236
Suffolk (G-13676)
Hooker Furniture Corporation ....C...... 276 632-1763
Martinsville (G-8298)
◆ Hooker Furniture Corporation...........C...... 276 632-2133
Martinsville (G-8297)
Robert Furr Cabinet Shop ....G...... 757 244-1267
Hampton (G-6230)
Walmer Enterprises ....E...... 703 461-9330
Montross (G-9028)

2519 Household Furniture, NEC

▲ Beckett Corporation ....E...... 757 857-0153
Norfolk (G-9461)
Buffalo Ridge Wood Products ....G...... 276 930-2189
Stuart (G-13606)
Columbia Mrror GL Grgetown Inc ....G...... 703 333-9990
Springfield (G-12977)
Fabrik..G...... 540 651-4169
Copper Hill (G-3764)
Handcrafters of Albemarle Ltd ....G...... 434 823-4649
Crozet (G-3837)
Hockey Stick Builds LLC.......................G...... 617 784-2918
Falls Church (G-4917)
Jr Lamb & Sons.....................................G...... 434 823-2320
Crozet (G-3839)
Natural Woodworking Co ....G...... 540 745-2664
Floyd (G-5033)
Neighborhoods Vi LLC..........................G...... 703 964-5000
Reston (G-10906)
New Wave Thrifty Llc............................G...... 904 400-8539
Norfolk (G-9662)
Poof Inc...G...... 703 298-7516
Haymarket (G-6437)
Summer Interior LLC.............................G...... 540 479-5145
Fredericksburg (G-5371)
Twfutures Inc ....G...... 804 301-6629
Midlothian (G-8915)
Weatherly LLC.......................................G...... 703 593-3192
Woodbridge (G-15830)

2521 Wood Office Furniture

A and H Office Inc ....G...... 703 250-0963
Burke (G-2179)
◆ A C Furniture Company Inc ....C...... 276 650-3356
Axton (G-1531)
Alliance Office Furniture Co ....G .....
Alexandria (G-129)
Aric Lynn LLC..G...... 571 505-7657
Manassas (G-8029)
▲ Capital Discount Mdse LLC ....F...... 703 499-9368
Woodbridge (G-15665)
Capitol Closet Design Inc.....................F...... 703 827-2700
Vienna (G-14022)
CMC Interiors LLC.................................F...... 804 883-5671
Richmond (G-11035)
Colonial Kitchen & Cabinets ....E...... 757 898-1332
Yorktown (G-15943)
▲ Frank Chervan Inc.............................C...... 540 586-5600
Roanoke (G-12093)
Gaithrsburg Cbinetry Mllwk Inc............D...... 540 347-4551
Warrenton (G-15019)
Haltrie LLC..G...... 703 598-9928
Annandale (G-755)
▲ Henkel-Harris LLC...........................E...... 540 667-4900
Winchester (G-15547)
◆ Hooker Furniture Corporation...........C...... 276 632-2133
Martinsville (G-8297)
Interior Building Systems Corp ....D...... 703 335-9655
Manassas (G-8083)
Interpretive Wdwrk Design Inc ....G...... 703 330-6105
Manassas (G-7953)
Its Just Furniture Inc ....G...... 703 357-6405
Fredericksburg (G-5197)
Jack Carter Cabinet Maker ....G...... 757 622-9414
Norfolk (G-9599)
Maurice Lamb ....G...... 540 962-0903
Covington (G-3794)
Modular Interiors Group LLC.................G...... 757 550-8910
Richmond (G-11680)
New Minglewood Mfg Inc ....G...... 276 632-9107
Fieldale (G-4990)
Office Furniture Outlet Inc....................G...... 757 855-5522
Norfolk (G-9673)
Old Town Woodworking Inc ....F...... 540 347-3993
Warrenton (G-15039)
Paul E Stahl ....G...... 772 600-8099
Roanoke (G-11983)
Rockridge Cabinetry LLC.......................G...... 434 969-2665
Buckingham (G-2135)
Russ Fine Woods Inc ....G...... 434 974-6504
Charlottesville (G-2868)
Scan Industries LLC..............................G...... 360 320-8244
Ashburn (G-1332)
Total Millwork LLC................................E...... 571 379-5500
Manassas (G-8168)
Vesta Propertys LLC.............................G...... 703 579-7979
Vienna (G-14151)
Wilcox Woodworks Inc ....G...... 703 369-3455
Manassas (G-8012)
Wood Shop ....G...... 757 824-4055
Atlantic (G-1526)
Woodwrights Cooperative ....G...... 804 358-4800
Richmond (G-11455)
Worthington Millwork LLC ....G...... 540 832-6391
Gordonsville (G-5919)

2522 Office Furniture, Except Wood

AG Lasers Technologies LLC ....F...... 800 255-5515
Front Royal (G-5519)
Alpha Safe & Vault Inc ....G...... 703 281-7233
Vienna (G-14008)
Chuka LLC...G...... 443 837-5522
Leesburg (G-7243)
Corporate Furn Svcs VA LLC................G...... 804 928-1143
Richmond (G-11542)
Corporate Supply Technology ....G...... 703 932-3475
Fairfax (G-4430)
Dextall Inc...G...... 202 701-3208
Fairfax (G-4438)
▼ Duskits LLC.......................................G...... 276 732-3121
Axton (G-1534)
Edwards Consulting ....G...... 804 733-2506
Prince George (G-10593)
Evans Corporate Services LLC ....F...... 703 344-3678
Lorton (G-7485)
▼ Fedsafes LLC.....................................G...... 703 525-1436
Arlington (G-964)
Jh Enterprise Inc...................................G...... 757 639-5049
Norfolk (G-9603)

Modular Design Installations ....G...... 757 871-8885
Newport News (G-9304)
Nxvet LLC..G...... 571 358-6198
Woodbridge (G-15765)
Office Furniture Outlet Inc....................G...... 757 855-5522
Norfolk (G-9673)
Paul E Stahl ....G...... 772 600-8099
Roanoke (G-11983)
Poof Inc...G...... 703 298-7516
Haymarket (G-6437)
Problem Solver ....G...... 757 452-0653
Virginia Beach (G-14742)
Reem Enterprises ....G...... 703 608-2283
Chantilly (G-2486)
Supplies Express Inc ....G...... 703 631-4600
Centreville (G-2343)
Uptime Business Products LLC ....G...... 540 982-5750
Roanoke (G-12013)
Vas of Virginia Inc................................E...... 434 296-5608
Charlottesville (G-2899)
Xact Solutions Inc.................................G...... 703 398-2680
Ashburn (G-1354)

2531 Public Building & Related Furniture

All A Board Inc ....F...... 804 652-0020
Richmond (G-11481)
Clarios..D...... 703 886-3961
Ashburn (G-1255)
Clarios..D...... 540 362-5500
Roanoke (G-11909)
Clarios..G...... 540 366-0981
Roanoke (G-11910)
Design Source Inc.................................E...... 804 644-3424
Sandston (G-12610)
Evans Corporate Services LLC ....F...... 703 344-3678
Lorton (G-7485)
Fitzgeralds Cabinet Shop Inc.................G...... 757 877-2538
Newport News (G-9229)
Funes Project LLC ....G...... 540 364-8054
Marshall (G-8254)
High Bridge Trail State Park..................F...... 434 315-0457
Green Bay (G-5990)
Indian Ridge Woodcraft Inc ....G...... 540 789-4754
Willis (G-15361)
International Automotive Compo ....A...... 540 465-3741
Strasburg (G-13585)
Its Just Furniture Inc ....G...... 703 357-6405
Fredericksburg (G-5197)
Kearney & Associates Inc ....G...... 540 423-9511
Culpeper (G-3905)
Palace Interiors ....G...... 757 592-1509
Hampton (G-6212)
Premier Office Systems LLC.................F...... 804 414-4198
Blackstone (G-1824)
Reflections Light Boxes ....G...... 757 641-3192
Chesapeake (G-3267)
Stephen W Mast ....G...... 804 467-3608
Mechanicsville (G-8681)
Talu LLC...G...... 571 323-5200
Herndon (G-6822)
US Joiner Holding Company ....G...... 434 220-8500
Crozet (G-3854)

2541 Wood, Office & Store Fixtures

All Points Countertop Inc......................E...... 540 665-3875
Winchester (G-15526)
Arboleda Cabinets Inc...........................F...... 804 230-0733
Richmond (G-11487)
B & J Cabinet Co Inc.............................E...... 804 271-0192
North Chesterfield (G-9825)
Bay Cabinets & Contractors ....G...... 757 934-2236
Suffolk (G-13676)
Builders Cabinet Co Inc ....G...... 804 358-7789
Richmond (G-11138)
Burgers Cabinet Shop Inc.....................F...... 571 262-8001
Sterling (G-13362)
Cabinet Saver LLC.................................G...... 757 969-9839
Virginia Beach (G-14310)
Calvins Enterprises ....G...... 540 955-3948
Berryville (G-1672)
Capitol Closet Design Inc......................F...... 703 827-2700
Vienna (G-14022)
Carpers Wood Creations Inc.................E...... 540 465-2525
Strasburg (G-13576)
Cavanaugh Cabinet Inc ....G...... 434 977-7100
Charlottesville (G-2759)
Classic Creations of Tidewater..............G...... 757 548-1442
Chesapeake (G-3036)
Colonial Kitchen & Cabinets ....E...... 757 898-1332
Yorktown (G-15943)

S
I
C

Contemporary Kitchens Ltd ....G...... 804 758-2001
Topping (G-13886)
Creative Dimension Group Inc ....D...... 540 891-1953
Fredericksburg (G-5267)
Custom Woodwork ....G...... 434 489-6991
Danville (G-3974)
Displaymakers Company ....G...... 703 501-2527
Triangle (G-13891)
Ellis Page Company LLC ....E...... 703 464-9404
Manassas (G-7937)
Fenco Incorporated ....E...... 540 885-7377
Staunton (G-13256)
G T Walls Cabinet Shop ....G...... 804 798-6288
Glen Allen (G-5734)
Gaithrsburg Cbinetry Mllwk Inc ....D...... 540 347-4551
Warrenton (G-15019)
Gem Locker LLC ....G...... 540 298-8906
Shenandoah (G-12689)
Great Deals LLC ....G...... 703 915-0332
Springfield (G-13014)
Hardwood Defense LLC ....G...... 540 298-8906
Shenandoah (G-12691)
Heartwood Solid Surfaces Inc ....F...... 703 369-0045
Manassas Park (G-8201)
Huber Engineered Woods LLC ....G...... 434 476-6628
Crystal Hill (G-3859)
Idx Corporation ....C...... 410 551-3600
Fredericksburg (G-5301)
Impact Unlimited Inc ....E...... 702 802-6800
Chantilly (G-2442)
Innovative Office Design LLC ....G...... 757 496-9221
Virginia Beach (G-14547)
Innovative Solid Surfaces LLC ....G...... 540 560-0747
Harrisonburg (G-6331)
John P Scott Woodworking Inc ....G...... 804 231-1942
Richmond (G-11633)
Joseph Lineberry ....G...... 276 733-8635
Woodlawn (G-15845)
Joy-Page Company Inc ....F...... 703 464-9404
Manassas (G-7954)
Julian Industries LLC ....G...... 804 755-6888
Ashland (G-1444)
Kitchen Krafters Inc ....F...... 540 891-7678
Fredericksburg (G-5310)
La Prade Enterprises ....G...... 804 271-9899
North Chesterfield (G-9912)
Marble Max ....G...... 703 723-0071
Ashburn (G-1315)
Mid Atlantic Solid Surface ....G...... 540 972-3050
Locust Grove (G-7449)
Mid-Atlantic Manufacturing Inc ....E...... 804 798-7462
Oilville (G-10183)
Mill Cabinet Shop Inc ....E...... 540 828-6763
Bridgewater (G-1954)
◆ Miller Manufacturing Co Inc ....D...... 804 232-4551
Richmond (G-11051)
Mint Springs Design ....G...... 434 806-7303
Crozet (G-3844)
◆ Modular Wood Systems Inc ....E...... 276 251-5300
Claudville (G-3638)
Natural Stones Inc ....G...... 703 408-8801
Manassas (G-7980)
Perceptions of Virginia Inc ....G...... 703 730-5918
Woodbridge (G-15775)
Polyfab Display Company ....E...... 703 497-4577
Woodbridge (G-15777)
Pro-Tek Inc ....G...... 757 813-9820
Hampton (G-6222)
Richards Building Supply Co ....G...... 540 719-0128
Hardy (G-6289)
Robert Furr Cabinet Shop ....G...... 757 244-1267
Hampton (G-6230)
Rockridge Granite Company LLC ....G...... 434 969-2665
Buckingham (G-2136)
Staton Mj & Associates Ltd ....G...... 804 737-1946
Sandston (G-12637)
Superior Laminates ....G...... 703 569-6602
Springfield (G-13097)
▼ Tactical Walls LLC ....E...... 540 298-8906
Shenandoah (G-12696)
Topcrafters of Virginia Inc ....G...... 804 353-1797
Richmond (G-11414)
V & P Investment LLC ....F...... 703 365-7835
Manassas (G-8009)
Virginia Installations Inc ....G...... 540 298-5300
Elkton (G-4338)
Walmer Enterprises ....E...... 703 461-9330
Montross (G-9028)
Woodmsters Cbnets Str Fixs of ....G...... 434 525-4407
Forest (G-5105)

Woodwright Company ....G...... 540 764-2539
Fredericksburg (G-5504)
Woodwrights Cooperative ....G...... 804 358-4800
Richmond (G-11455)

2542 Partitions & Fixtures, Except Wood

All American Logistic Co ....G...... 571 237-6039
Manassas (G-8022)
▲ Allen Display & Store Eqp Inc ....F...... 804 794-6032
Midlothian (G-8770)
Capitol Closet Design Inc ....F...... 703 827-2700
Vienna (G-14022)
▼ Cazador LLC ....D...... 719 387-7450
Herndon (G-6637)
Champion Billd & Bar Stools ....G...... 703 631-8800
Fairfax (G-4427)
▲ Explus Inc ....D...... 703 260-0780
Dulles (G-4201)
Fast Signs Inc ....F...... 540 389-6691
Salem (G-12506)
Heritage Interiors LLC ....G...... 571 323-5200
Herndon (G-6696)
Idx Corporation ....C...... 410 551-3600
Fredericksburg (G-5301)
Independent Delivery Ex Inc ....G...... 434 660-2389
Forest (G-5075)
Kearney & Associates Inc ....F...... 540 423-9511
Culpeper (G-3905)
Lozier Corp ....G...... 703 742-4098
Reston (G-10890)
◆ Modular Wood Systems Inc ....E...... 276 251-5300
Claudville (G-3638)
Museumrails LLC ....G...... 540 603-2414
Louisa (G-7561)
Niday Inc ....G...... 540 427-2776
Roanoke (G-12141)
Office Furniture Outlet Inc ....G...... 757 855-5522
Norfolk (G-9673)
Polyfab Display Company ....E...... 703 497-4577
Woodbridge (G-15777)
Service Metal Fabricators Inc ....D...... 757 887-3500
Williamsburg (G-15310)
Showall Inc ....G...... 276 646-8779
Chilhowie (G-3560)
▲ Showbest Fixture Corp ....D...... 804 222-5535
Richmond (G-11379)
Showbest Fixture Corp ....E...... 434 298-3925
Blackstone (G-1828)
Sorbilite Inc ....G...... 757 460-7330
Hampton (G-6241)
Tbrsp LLC ....G...... 434 315-5600
Farmville (G-4960)
Thompson Fixture Installation ....F...... 804 378-9352
North Chesterfield (G-10001)
◆ Wegmann Usa Inc ....G...... 434 385-1580
Lynchburg (G-7837)
Wise Manufacturing Inc ....G...... 804 876-3335
Doswell (G-4128)

2591 Drapery Hardware, Window Blinds & Shades

Abington Sunshade & Blinds Co ....F...... 540 435-6450
Penn Laird (G-10287)
Akl Associates Ltd ....G...... 540 269-8228
Keezletown (G-7026)
Anthony Corporation ....E...... 757 490-3613
Virginia Beach (G-14230)
Anything Vertical LLC ....G...... 540 871-6519
Blacksburg (G-1723)
Appalachian Manufacturing ....F...... 540 825-3522
Culpeper (G-3866)
Bath Son and Sons Associates ....G...... 804 722-0687
Petersburg (G-10309)
Demoiselle Vertical LLC ....G...... 202 431-8032
Alexandria (G-446)
First R & R Co Inc ....G...... 804 737-4400
Highland Springs (G-6852)
Five Star Custom Blinds Inc ....G...... 757 236-5577
Virginia Beach (G-14466)
Heidi Yoder ....G...... 540 432-5598
Harrisonburg (G-6327)
Hibiscus Chesecake Elixirs LLC ....G...... 757 932-2539
Chesapeake (G-3135)
Integrated Vertical Tech LLC ....G...... 757 410-7253
Chesapeake (G-3144)
JB Installations Inc ....G...... 703 403-2119
Vienna (G-14074)
Jts Blinds Installation LLC ....G...... 240 682-1009
King George (G-7096)

JWB of Roanoke Inc ....F...... 540 344-7726
Roanoke (G-12116)
Kenney Inc ....G...... 703 731-9208
Herndon (G-6722)
Lutron Electronics Co Inc ....C...... 804 752-3300
Ashland (G-1455)
Macs Construction ....G...... 571 278-5371
Centreville (G-2317)
Maxines Cheesecakes LLC ....G...... 804 586-5135
North Dinwiddie (G-10060)
Perfect Blind ....G...... 703 675-4111
Leesburg (G-7325)
Plum Summer LLC ....G...... 804 519-0009
Reedville (G-10766)
Shade Mann-Kidwell Corp ....G...... 804 288-2819
Richmond (G-11378)
Shadeworks ....G...... 804 642-2618
Hayes (G-6409)
Two Rivers Installation Co ....G...... 804 366-6869
Richmond (G-11798)
Vertical Blind Productions ....G...... 540 484-4995
Rocky Mount (G-12358)
Vertical Innovations LLC ....G...... 540 616-6431
Dublin (G-4173)
Vertical Path Creative LLC ....G...... 434 414-1357
Stanardsville (G-13230)
Vertical Praise ....G...... 434 985-1513
Ruckersville (G-12415)
Vertical Rock Inc ....G...... 855 822-5462
Manassas (G-8010)
Vertical Sunset ....G...... 757 787-7595
Onancock (G-10199)
Vertical Venus LLC ....G...... 571 236-6484
Centreville (G-2351)
▲ Window Fashion Design ....G...... 757 253-8813
Williamsburg (G-15346)

2599 Furniture & Fixtures, NEC

2308 Granby Street Assoc LLC ....G...... 757 627-4844
Norfolk (G-9411)
A C Furniture Company Inc ....B...... 276 650-1802
Axton (G-1532)
A1 Finishing Inc ....F...... 276 632-2121
Martinsville (G-8262)
After Affects Custom Furniture ....G...... 504 510-1792
Hampton (G-6077)
American Assembly LLC ....G...... 757 639-6040
Portsmouth (G-10391)
Arlene Nancys Meals On Wheels ....G...... 404 940-8995
North Dinwiddie (G-10047)
Beach Block Ventures LLC ....G...... 540 848-0921
Colonial Beach (G-3721)
Blue Ridge Shelving Closet LLC ....F...... 540 365-0150
Ferrum (G-4972)
Boxd Kitchen Merrifield Llc ....G...... 703 909-9572
Vienna (G-14018)
Charter of Lynchburg Inc ....D...... 434 239-2671
Lynchburg (G-7677)
Cooking Williams Good ....G...... 804 931-6643
Hopewell (G-6920)
Creative Cabinet Design ....G...... 434 293-4040
Charlottesville (G-2774)
D & T Akers Corporation ....G...... 804 435-2709
Kilmarnock (G-7069)
Design Source Inc ....E...... 804 644-3424
Sandston (G-12610)
El Charro Grill Mexican RES ....G...... 540 745-5303
Floyd (G-5024)
Fitzgeralds Cabinet Shop Inc ....G...... 757 877-2538
Newport News (G-9229)
Genesis Decor LLC ....E...... 804 561-4844
Amelia Court House (G-658)
Gordos Tacos and More LLC ....G...... 757 710-3317
Birdsnest (G-1719)
Halifax Fine Furnishings ....G...... 540 774-3060
Roanoke (G-11931)
Harris Custom Woodworking ....G...... 804 241-9525
Quinton (G-10697)
Hoskins Creek Table Company ....G...... 804 333-0032
Warsaw (G-15067)
▲ Javawood USA LLC ....G...... 703 658-9665
Alexandria (G-493)
Kci Services LLC ....G...... 276 623-7404
Lebanon (G-7196)
Kingmill Enterprises LLC ....G...... 877 895-9453
Charlottesville (G-2822)
▲ Modu System America LLC ....G...... 757 250-3413
Williamsburg (G-15281)
Nations ....G...... 804 257-9891
Richmond (G-11686)

New Richmond Ventures LLC ... G ... 804 887-2355
Richmond (G-11688)
◆ Old Dominion Wood Products Inc ... E ... 434 845-5511
Lynchburg (G-7778)
Pro Furniture Doctor Inc ... G ... 571 379-7058
Springfield (G-13074)
Ronnie and Betty Bridges ... G ... 804 561-4506
Amelia Court House (G-670)
Sauder Manufacturing Co ... G ... 804 897-3400
North Chesterfield (G-9969)
Shefford Woodlands LLC ... G ... 804 625-5495
Shacklefords (G-12684)
Smith Cabinets ... G ... 703 790-9896
Mc Lean (G-8548)
▲ Sorrentino Mariani & Company ... D ... 757 624-9025
Norfolk (G-9730)
South Bay Industries Inc ... G ... 757 489-9344
Norfolk (G-9731)
Swinson Medical LLC ... G ... 540 576-1719
Penhook (G-10285)
Taste of Love LLC ... G ... 804 714-4991
Richmond (G-11784)
Tomo LLC ... G ... 407 694-7464
Williamsburg (G-15325)
Willie Gatling Jr ... G ... 757 236-5206
Newport News (G-9379)

26 PAPER AND ALLIED PRODUCTS

2611 Pulp Mills

Clarence D Campbell ... G ... 540 291-2740
Naturl BR STA (G-9111)
Emerson & Clements Office ... G ... 434 983-5322
Dillwyn (G-4095)
Goodman Lumber Co Inc ... E ... 804 265-9030
Wilsons (G-15367)
Green Waste Organics LLC ... G ... 804 929-8505
Prince George (G-10595)
Greenstone Materials LLC ... G ... 434 973-2113
Charlottesville (G-2640)
L A Bowles Logging Inc ... G ... 804 492-3103
Powhatan (G-10555)
▲ Pre Con Inc ... F ... 804 732-0628
Chester (G-3444)
Prochem Technologies Inc ... G ... 540 520-8339
Roanoke (G-12156)
Pure Earth Recycling Tech Inc ... G ... 434 944-6262
Lynchburg (G-7794)
Theme Queen LLC ... G ... 804 439-0854
Mechanicsville (G-8685)
◆ Westrock Mwv LLC ... A ... 804 444-1000
Richmond (G-11825)
Weyerhaeuser Company ... G ... 276 694-4404
Stuart (G-13639)
Wrkco Inc ... B ... 540 969-5000
Covington (G-3805)

2621 Paper Mills

Amway Products & Services ... G ... 757 474-2115
Virginia Beach (G-14226)
Augusta Actuation LLC ... G ... 540 480-7619
Steeles Tavern (G-13310)
Bear Island Paper Wb LLC ... C ... 804 227-4000
Ashland (G-1379)
Blue Ridge Leader ... G ... 540 338-6200
Purcellville (G-10652)
Brant Industries Inc ... C ... 804 227-3394
Ashland (G-1385)
Breathe Bristol ... G ... 423 254-0323
Bristol (G-1967)
Btbycb Inc ... G ... 703 992-9041
Falls Church (G-4903)
Chocolate Paper Inc ... G ... 540 989-7025
Roanoke (G-11908)
Clipper Magazine LLC ... G ... 888 569-5100
Fairfax (G-4606)
Dap Incorporated ... G ... 757 921-3576
Newport News (G-9214)
Deerfield Group LLC ... G ... 434 591-0848
Zion Crossroads (G-16007)
◆ Delfort USA Inc ... G ... 434 202-7870
Charlottesville (G-2779)
Disaster Aide ... G ... 201 892-8898
Vienna (G-14040)
Dough Pay ME of Bristol LLC ... G ... 276 644-8091
Bristol (G-2017)
◆ Eagle Paper International Inc ... G ... 757 363-8103
Virginia Beach (G-14426)
Frankline Paper ... G ... 757 569-4321
Franklin (G-5144)
Georgia-Pacific LLC ... B ... 434 299-5911
Big Island (G-1702)
▲ Gordon Paper Company Inc ... C ... 800 457-7366
Virginia Beach (G-14488)
Greif Inc ... C ... 434 933-4100
Gladstone (G-5683)
Hitchcock Paper Co ... G ... 571 398-6601
Occoquan (G-10173)
Hollingsworth & Vose Company ... C ... 540 745-7600
Floyd (G-5029)
International Paper ... G ... 757 569-4521
Suffolk (G-13725)
International Paper Company ... C ... 757 569-4321
Franklin (G-5146)
International Paper Company ... C ... 434 845-6071
Lynchburg (G-7745)
International Paper Company ... G ... 804 232-4937
Richmond (G-11046)
International Paper Company ... C ... 804 230-3100
Richmond (G-11620)
International Paper Company ... G ... 757 405-3046
Portsmouth (G-10444)
Linwood L Pope ... G ... 757 654-9397
Courtland (G-3772)
▲ Masa Corporation ... D ... 757 855-3013
Norfolk (G-9633)
◆ McAirlaids Inc ... C ... 540 352-5050
Rocky Mount (G-12338)
▲ Mercury Paper ... G ... 540 465-7700
Strasburg (G-13589)
◆ Mercury Paper Inc ... D ... 540 465-7700
Strasburg (G-13590)
Multi-Pack LLC ... G ... 703 372-2303
Springfield (G-13055)
◆ Mundet Inc ... D ... 804 644-3970
Richmond (G-11684)
◆ Mundet-Hermetite Inc ... D ... 804 748-3319
Colonial Heights (G-3738)
National Junior Tennis League ... G ... 276 669-7540
Bristol (G-1984)
Newport Timber LLC ... F ... 703 243-3355
Arlington (G-1077)
P H Glatfelter Company ... G ... 540 548-1756
Spotsylvania (G-12907)
Paper & Packaging Board ... G ... 703 935-5386
Mc Lean (G-8523)
PDQ Printing LLC ... G ... 804 228-0077
Richmond (G-11710)
▲ Plymkraft Inc ... E ... 757 595-0364
Newport News (G-9314)
Premier Graphics ... G ... 434 432-4070
Chatham (G-2934)
◆ Reynolds Food Packaging LLC ... E ... 800 446-3020
Richmond (G-11352)
▲ Ritemade Paper Converters Inc ... G ... 800 821-5484
Ashland (G-1487)
Schunck Rbcca Wlpr Instllation ... G ... 757 301-9922
Virginia Beach (G-14796)
Signode Industrial Group LLC ... C ... 276 632-2352
Martinsville (G-8329)
Southern Scrap Company Inc ... E ... 540 662-0265
Winchester (G-15481)
St Tissue LLC ... E ... 757 304-5040
Franklin (G-5156)
▲ Stickers Plus Ltd ... D ... 540 857-3045
Vinton (G-14184)
Tranlin Inc ... G ... 866 215-8290
Glen Allen (G-5816)
Tranlin Trading LLC ... G ... 866 215-8290
Charlottesville (G-2894)
VA Writers Club ... G ... 804 648-0357
Richmond (G-11804)
West Rock ... G ... 434 352-2804
Appomattox (G-826)
Westrock Cp LLC ... B ... 804 541-9600
Hopewell (G-6944)
Westrock Cp LLC ... D ... 804 843-5229
West Point (G-15163)
Westrock Cp LLC ... C ... 804 843-5416
West Point (G-15164)
Westrock Mwv LLC ... G ... 434 685-1717
Cascade (G-2253)
Worldwide Papers Inc ... G ... 703 883-8049
Falls Church (G-4893)
Wrkco Inc ... B ... 540 969-5000
Covington (G-3805)
You Buy Book Paperback Exc ... G ... 757 237-6426
Virginia Beach (G-14954)
▲ Yupo Corporation America ... C ... 757 312-9876
Chesapeake (G-3381)

2631 Paperboard Mills

C & M Services LLC ... G ... 540 309-5555
Troutville (G-13904)
Custom Packaging Service ... G ... 804 279-7225
North Chesterfield (G-9856)
Interstate Resources Inc ... G ... 703 243-3355
Arlington (G-1010)
Pavement Stencil Company ... F ... 540 427-1325
Roanoke (G-12145)
◆ Phoenix Packg Operations LLC ... B ... 540 307-4084
Dublin (G-4168)
Ridgerunner Container LLC ... F ... 540 662-2005
Winchester (G-15465)
Signode Industrial Group LLC ... C ... 276 632-2352
Martinsville (G-8329)
Sonoco Products Company ... F ... 434 432-2310
Chatham (G-2936)
Sonoco Products Company ... D ... 804 233-5411
Richmond (G-11763)
Sonoco Products Company ... E ... 540 862-4135
Covington (G-3798)
Temperpack Technologies Inc ... D ... 434 218-2436
Richmond (G-11787)
Westrock Converting LLC ... D ... 276 632-7175
Ridgeway (G-11858)
Westrock Cp LLC ... B ... 804 541-9600
Hopewell (G-6944)
Westrock Cp LLC ... C ... 804 843-5416
West Point (G-15164)
Westrock Mwv LLC ... C ... 540 662-6524
Winchester (G-15507)
Westrock Mwv LLC ... E ... 434 352-7132
Appomattox (G-827)
Westrock Mwv LLC ... G ... 540 474-5811
Monterey (G-9014)
Westrock Mwv LLC ... C ... 540 863-2300
Lowmoor (G-7599)
Westrock Mwv LLC ... D ... 540 377-9745
Raphine (G-10752)
◆ Westrock Mwv LLC ... A ... 804 444-1000
Richmond (G-11825)
◆ Westrock Virginia Corporation ... F ... 804 444-1000
Richmond (G-11827)
Wrkco Inc ... B ... 540 969-5000
Covington (G-3805)

2652 Set-Up Paperboard Boxes

Commonwealth Specialty Packg ... F ... 804 271-0157
Ashland (G-1393)
▲ Old Dominion Box Co Inc ... E ... 434 929-6701
Madison Heights (G-7880)
Old Dominion Box Co Inc ... E ... 434 929-6701
Madison Heights (G-7881)

2653 Corrugated & Solid Fiber Boxes

Alexandria Packaging LLC ... D ... 703 644-5550
Springfield (G-12940)
Atlantic Corrugated Box Co Inc ... E ... 804 231-4050
Richmond (G-11027)
Blue Ridge Packaging Corp ... E ... 276 638-1413
Martinsville (G-8270)
Carocon ... G ... 804 324-2207
Virginia Beach (G-14320)
Carolina Container Co Inc ... G ... 804 458-4700
Virginia Beach (G-14321)
Carolina Container Company ... F ... 804 458-4700
Prince George (G-10588)
Commonwealth Specialty Packg ... F ... 804 271-0157
Ashland (G-1393)
Corrugated Container Corp ... E ... 540 869-5353
Winchester (G-15405)
Custom Packaging Inc ... F ... 804 232-3299
Richmond (G-11551)
Drake Company ... G ... 757 536-1509
Chesapeake (G-3075)
Ds Smith PLC ... G ... 540 774-0500
Roanoke (G-11916)
Georgia-Pacific LLC ... C ... 276 632-6301
Ridgeway (G-11843)
Hollinger Metal Edge Inc ... F ... 540 898-7300
Fredericksburg (G-5298)
▼ Hollinger Metal Edge - VA Inc ... F ... 540 898-7300
Fredericksburg (G-5299)
International Paper Company ... G ... 757 405-3046
Portsmouth (G-10444)
International Paper Company ... D ... 804 861-8164
Petersburg (G-10326)
Interstate Cont Reading LLC ... G ... 703 243-3355
Arlington (G-1009)

SIC

Interstate Resources Inc ....G...... 703 243-3355
Arlington (G-1010)
Menasha Packaging Company LLC .....C 540 546-1110
Winchester (G-15448)
Metal Edge Co ....G...... 800 862-2228
Fredericksburg (G-5325)
▲ Old Dominion Box Co Inc ....E...... 434 929-6701
Madison Heights (G-7880)
Old Dominion Box Co Inc ....E...... 434 929-6701
Madison Heights (G-7881)
Packaging Corporation America ....G...... 540 427-3164
Roanoke (G-12144)
Packaging Corporation America ....B...... 540 434-0785
Harrisonburg (G-6351)
Packaging Corporation America ....G...... 540 432-1353
Harrisonburg (G-6352)
Packaging Corporation America ....G...... 540 434-2840
Rockingham (G-12266)
Packaging Corporation America ....C...... 804 232-1292
Richmond (G-11703)
Packaging Corporation America ....D...... 540 427-3164
Roanoke (G-11982)
Packaging Corporation America ....G...... 540 438-8504
Harrisonburg (G-6353)
Packaging Corporation America ....G...... 540 662-5680
Winchester (G-15458)
Packaging Products Inc ....E...... 276 629-3481
Bassett (G-1588)
Pratt Industries Inc ....E...... 804 412-0245
Ashland (G-1479)
Reynolds Container Corporation ....E...... 276 647-8451
Collinsville (G-3715)
Richmond Corrugated Box Co ....E...... 804 222-1300
Sandston (G-12629)
Sandbox Enterprises ....G...... 410 999-4666
Herndon (G-6800)
Supply One Chesapeake ....G...... 757 485-3570
Chesapeake (G-3317)
Temple-Inland Inc ....G...... 804 861-8164
Petersburg (G-10345)
Westrock Converting LLC ....D...... 276 632-7175
Ridgeway (G-11858)
Westrock Cp LLC ....E...... 804 236-3237
Sandston (G-12641)
Westrock Cp LLC ....G...... 276 632-0698
Ridgeway (G-11859)
Westrock Cp LLC ....C...... 804 222-6380
Richmond (G-11447)
Westrock Cp LLC ....C...... 804 226-5840
Richmond (G-11448)
Westrock Cp LLC ....D...... 804 843-5229
West Point (G-15163)
Westrock Cp LLC ....C...... 276 632-2176
Martinsville (G-8352)
Westrock Cp LLC ....G...... 434 736-8505
Keysville (G-7065)
Westrock Cp LLC ....C...... 804 843-5416
West Point (G-15164)
Westrock Mwv LLC ....C...... 540 969-5230
Covington (G-3803)
Westrock Mwv LLC ....C...... 804 201-2000
Glen Allen (G-5827)
Westrock Rkt LLC ....C...... 804 444-6431
Richmond (G-11826)
York Box & Barrel Mfg Co ....G...... 757 868-9411
Poquoson (G-10379)

2655 Fiber Cans, Tubes & Drums

American Mountain Tech LLC ....G...... 423 646-1864
Abingdon (G-10)
Caraustar Industrial and Con ....G...... 540 234-0431
Weyers Cave (G-15169)
Caraustar Industrial and Con ....F...... 757 562-0345
Franklin (G-5140)
Fibrex Group Inc ....G...... 800 346-4458
Chesapeake (G-3100)
Sonoco Products Company ....E...... 757 539-8349
Suffolk (G-13766)
Sonoco Products Company ....E...... 540 862-4135
Covington (G-3798)

2656 Sanitary Food Containers

Aflex Packaging LLC ....G...... 571 208-9938
Springfield (G-12936)
Ecozenith Usa Inc ....G...... 703 992-6622
Falls Church (G-4786)
International Paper Company ....G...... 757 405-3046
Portsmouth (G-10444)
▲ RPC Superfos Us Inc ....E...... 540 504-7176
Winchester (G-15470)

Southeastern Container Inc ....C...... 540 722-2600
Winchester (G-15480)
Squrl LLC ....G...... 443 481-9941
Charlottesville (G-2882)
Trotter Jamil ....G...... 757 251-8754
Hampton (G-6253)

2657 Folding Paperboard Boxes

Able Mfg LLC ....G...... 804 550-4885
Glen Allen (G-5703)
Arkay Packaging Corporation ....D...... 540 278-2596
Roanoke (G-11882)
Carded Graphics LLC ....C...... 540 248-3716
Staunton (G-13247)
Cauthorne Paper Company Inc ....E...... 804 798-6999
Ashland (G-1388)
Commonwealth Specialty Packg ....F...... 804 271-0157
Ashland (G-1393)
Dominion Packaging Inc ....C...... 804 447-6921
Sandston (G-12612)
▲ Old Dominion Box Co Inc ....E...... 434 929-6701
Madison Heights (G-7880)
Old Dominion Box Co Inc ....E...... 434 929-6701
Madison Heights (G-7881)
Skin Amnesty ....G...... 757 491-9058
Virginia Beach (G-14822)

2671 Paper Coating & Laminating for Packaging

Arm Global Solutions Inc ....G...... 804 431-3746
South Chesterfield (G-12796)
Bunzl Carolinas and Virginia ....G...... 804 236-5000
Henrico (G-6486)
▲ Conwed Corp ....D...... 540 981-0362
Roanoke (G-12070)
Dcp Holdings LLC ....E...... 804 876-3135
Doswell (G-4119)
Glad Products Company ....C...... 434 946-3100
Amherst (G-691)
Globus World Partners Inc ....G...... 757 645-4274
Williamsburg (G-15248)
Green Bay Packaging Inc ....E...... 540 678-2600
Winchester (G-15421)
Mottley Foils Inc ....F...... 434 392-8347
Farmville (G-4952)
Packaging Products Inc ....E...... 276 629-3481
Bassett (G-1588)
▲ Plymkraft Inc ....E...... 757 595-0364
Newport News (G-9314)
Reynolds Presto Products Inc ....B...... 434 572-6961
South Boston (G-12788)
Rouse Wholesale ....G...... 276 445-3220
Rose Hill (G-12362)
Safehouse Signs Inc ....E...... 540 366-2480
Roanoke (G-12174)
Signode Industrial Group LLC ....G...... 276 632-2352
Martinsville (G-8329)
Tiger Paper Company Inc ....G...... 540 337-9510
Stuarts Draft (G-13661)
Tigerseal Products LLC ....G...... 800 899-9389
Beaverdam (G-1614)
Tredegar Corporation ....G...... 804 523-3001
Richmond (G-11418)
◆ Tredegar Corporation ....D...... 804 330-1000
North Chesterfield (G-10029)
◆ Vitex Packaging Group Inc ....F...... 757 538-3115
Suffolk (G-13780)
◆ Westrock Mwv LLC ....A...... 804 444-1000
Richmond (G-11825)

2672 Paper Coating & Laminating, Exc for Packaging

Blanco Inc ....G...... 757 766-8123
Yorktown (G-15939)
Eastern Panel Manufacturing ....E...... 434 432-3055
Chatham (G-2927)
Essentra Packaging Inc ....E...... 804 518-1803
South Chesterfield (G-12802)
Germinal Dimensions Inc ....G...... 540 552-8938
Blacksburg (G-1741)
◆ Giesecke+devrient ....C...... 703 480-2000
Dulles (G-4205)
Green Bay Packaging Inc ....E...... 540 678-2600
Winchester (G-15421)
Greif Inc ....C...... 434 933-4100
Gladstone (G-5683)
▲ Masa Corporation ....D...... 757 855-3013
Norfolk (G-9633)

PP Payne Inc ....G...... 804 518-1803
South Chesterfield (G-12822)
Safehouse Signs Inc ....E...... 540 366-2480
Roanoke (G-12174)
▲ Stickers Plus Ltd ....D...... 540 857-3045
Vinton (G-13766)
Suter Enterprises Ltd ....F...... 757 220-3299
Williamsburg (G-15320)
Tigerseal Products LLC ....G...... 800 899-9389
Beaverdam (G-1614)
Wengers Electrical Service LLC ....G...... 540 867-0101
Rockingham (G-12283)

2673 Bags: Plastics, Laminated & Coated

Built In Style LLC ....G...... 703 753-8518
Haymarket (G-6416)
Extra Space Storage ....G...... 703 719-4354
Alexandria (G-459)
Glad Products Company ....C...... 434 946-3100
Amherst (G-691)
Image Packaging ....G...... 804 730-7358
Mechanicsville (G-8639)
▲ Infinity Global Inc ....E...... 434 793-7570
Danville (G-4000)
Inifinity Global Inc ....G...... 434 793-7570
Danville (G-4001)
◆ Liqui-Box Corporation ....D...... 804 325-1400
Richmond (G-11658)
Monalisa Blakeney ....G...... 703 863-8530
Annandale (G-775)
Nothing But Cake Incorporated ....G...... 540 322-7520
Fredericksburg (G-5336)
▲ Pilgrim International ....G...... 757 989-5045
Newport News (G-9313)
Reynolds Presto Products Inc ....B...... 434 572-6961
South Boston (G-12788)
◆ Rubbermaid Commercial Pdts LLC ..A...... 540 667-8700
Winchester (G-15582)
Rubbermaid Commercial Pdts LLC ....G...... 540 542-8195
Winchester (G-15471)
▲ Tg Polymers Inc ....G...... 585 670-9427
Alexandria (G-597)
Titan Plastics LLC ....G...... 804 339-4464
Glen Allen (G-5813)
Vanguard Plastics ....G...... 804 222-2012
Richmond (G-11434)
◆ Vitex Packaging Group Inc ....F...... 757 538-3115
Suffolk (G-13780)

2674 Bags: Uncoated Paper & Multiwall

▼ Bob Sansone DBA Peggs Co ....G...... 951 360-9170
Ashland (G-1383)
▲ Broad Bay Cotton Company ....G...... 757 227-4101
Virginia Beach (G-14299)
Crosstown Shipg & Sup Co LLC ....G...... 513 252-5370
Alexandria (G-435)
Its All Mx LLC ....G...... 540 785-6295
Chester (G-3425)
Mfri Inc ....C...... 540 667-7022
Winchester (G-15555)
Westrock Cp LLC ....C...... 804 843-5416
West Point (G-15164)

2675 Die-Cut Paper & Board

▲ BSC Ventures LLC ....D...... 540 362-3311
Roanoke (G-11896)
Cauthorne Paper Company Inc ....E...... 804 798-6999
Ashland (G-1388)
Commonwealth Specialty Packg ....F...... 804 271-0157
Ashland (G-1393)
▲ Eska USA BV Inc ....E...... 757 494-7330
Chesapeake (G-3091)
▲ H H Elements Inc ....G...... 434 249-8630
Barboursville (G-1561)
Hollinger Metal Edge Inc ....F...... 540 898-7300
Fredericksburg (G-5298)
Judys Bottle Holder ....G...... 757 606-1093
Chesapeake (G-3160)
Wordsmith Indexing Services ....G...... 540 775-3012
King George (G-7124)

2676 Sanitary Paper Prdts

Dr Finnie Care LLC ....G...... 804 852-7998
Chester (G-3406)
Elliott Lestselle ....G...... 757 944-8152
Virginia Beach (G-14442)
Oralign Baby LLC ....G...... 540 492-0453
Martinsville (G-8315)

Pad A Cheek LLC ....G....... 434 985-4003
Stanardsville *(G-13226)*
Playtex Products LLC ....G....... 804 230-1520
Richmond *(G-11717)*
Playtex Products LLC ....G....... 703 866-7621
Springfield *(G-13070)*
Rolhei LLC ....G....... 202 850-9000
Williamsburg *(G-15307)*
▲ **Sanfacon Virginia Inc** ....E....... 434 376-2301
Brookneal *(G-2112)*

2677 Envelopes

BSC Ventures Holdings Inc ....G....... 540 265-6296
Roanoke *(G-11895)*
▲ **BSC Ventures LLC** ....D....... 540 362-3311
Roanoke *(G-11896)*
BSC Vntres Acquisition Sub LLC ....D....... 540 362-3311
Roanoke *(G-11897)*
BSC Vntres Acquisition Sub LLC ....C....... 540 563-0888
Roanoke *(G-11898)*
Diana Khoury & Co ....G....... 703 592-9110
Springfield *(G-12991)*
Kenmore Envelope Company Inc ....C....... 804 271-2100
Richmond *(G-11259)*
National Envelope Corp ....G....... 703 629-3881
Alexandria *(G-289)*
Reed Envelope Company Inc ....F....... 703 690-2249
Fairfax Station *(G-4722)*
◆ **Westrock Mwv LLC** ....A....... 804 444-1000
Richmond *(G-11825)*

2678 Stationery Prdts

Cordially Yours ....G....... 703 644-1186
Springfield *(G-12980)*
J J E Enterprise Holdings LLC ....G....... 410 703-9241
Spotsylvania *(G-12900)*
▲ **Kaisa Usa Inc** ....G....... 206 228-7711
Mc Kenney *(G-8380)*
◆ **Westrock Mwv LLC** ....A....... 804 444-1000
Richmond *(G-11825)*

2679 Converted Paper Prdts, NEC

Blue Ridge Book Conservation ....G....... 434 295-9373
Charlottesville *(G-2742)*
Bookwrights Press ....G....... 434 263-4818
Lovingston *(G-7589)*
Campbell David ....G....... 757 877-1633
Yorktown *(G-15941)*
Cauthorne Industries Inc ....G....... 804 798-6999
Ashland *(G-1387)*
Cauthorne Paper Company Inc ....E....... 804 798-6999
Ashland *(G-1388)*
Central National-Gottesman Inc ....G....... 703 941-0810
Springfield *(G-12976)*
Conservtion Resources Intl LLC ....E....... 703 321-7730
Lorton *(G-7477)*
Cunningham Entps LLC Daniel ....G....... 804 359-2180
Richmond *(G-11170)*
◆ **Fortis Solutions Group LLC** ....C....... 757 340-8893
Virginia Beach *(G-14472)*
Fritz Ken Tooling & Design ....E....... 804 721-2319
North Chesterfield *(G-9880)*
Indoff Incorporated ....G....... 804 539-2425
Glen Allen *(G-5750)*
Jrjj Paper LLC ....G....... 757 473-3719
Virginia Beach *(G-14576)*
Kapstone ....G....... 804 708-0083
Manakin Sabot *(G-7900)*
Label ....G....... 757 236-8434
Hampton *(G-6275)*
▲ **Manchester Industries Inc VA** ....E....... 804 226-4250
Richmond *(G-11283)*
Pre Con Inc ....E....... 804 414-1560
Chester *(G-3447)*
Product Identification ....G....... 804 264-4434
Richmond *(G-11336)*
▲ **Sanfacon Virginia Inc** ....E....... 434 376-2301
Brookneal *(G-2112)*
Sfi Partners Club ....G....... 757 622-8001
Norfolk *(G-9720)*
▲ **Sihl USA Inc** ....G....... 757 966-7180
Chesapeake *(G-3293)*
Starry Nights Scrapbooking LLC ....G....... 757 784-6163
Williamsburg *(G-15319)*
Unique Industries Inc ....E....... 434 835-0068
Blairs *(G-1833)*
US Greenfiber LLC ....D....... 540 825-8000
Culpeper *(G-3927)*
Wrap Buddies LLC ....G....... 855 644-2783
Jeffersonton *(G-7014)*

27 PRINTING, PUBLISHING, AND ALLIED INDUSTRIES

2711 Newspapers: Publishing & Printing

501 Franklin LLC ....F....... 804 777-9000
Richmond *(G-11465)*
A 1 Painting of Richmond ....G....... 804 237-9939
Midlothian *(G-8766)*
A B M Enterprises Inc ....G....... 804 561-3655
Amelia Court House *(G-648)*
A Proehl ....G....... 540 890-6096
Moneta *(G-8955)*
A Sorted Affiar Richmond LLC ....G....... 804 464-9820
Richmond *(G-11077)*
Above Ground Level ....G....... 540 338-4363
Round Hill *(G-12373)*
Adams Publishing Group LLC ....G....... 276 728-7311
Hillsville *(G-6882)*
Adonica L Miller ....G....... 540 820-0820
Rockingham *(G-12238)*
Advocate-Democrat ....G....... 423 337-7101
Norfolk *(G-9426)*
Agma LLC ....G....... 703 689-3458
Reston *(G-10780)*
Alexandria Fusion ....G....... 703 566-3055
Alexandria *(G-125)*
Alexandria Gazette Packet ....G....... 703 821-5050
Alexandria *(G-126)*
Alexandria Times ....G....... 703 739-0001
Alexandria *(G-127)*
Alter Magazine LLC ....G....... 571 970-3537
Arlington *(G-850)*
Alvarian Press ....G....... 703 864-8018
Reston *(G-10785)*
American City Bus Journals Inc ....F....... 703 258-0800
Arlington *(G-852)*
American Court Comm Newspapers ....G....... 703 237-9806
Falls Church *(G-4900)*
Amissville Alternative ....G....... 540 364-4436
Amissville *(G-716)*
Ann Grogg ....G....... 540 667-4279
Winchester *(G-15381)*
Annandale Times ....G....... 703 437-5400
Reston *(G-10788)*
Apg Media of Chesapeake LLC ....G....... 804 843-2282
Williamsburg *(G-15205)*
Arabesque Media ....G....... 703 745-5395
Fairfax *(G-4410)*
Arlington Boccato LLC ....G....... 703 516-4075
Arlington *(G-858)*
Arlington Community News Lab ....G....... 703 243-7501
Arlington *(G-859)*
Asian Fortune Enterprises Inc ....F....... 703 753-8295
Vienna *(G-14010)*
Augusta Free Press ....G....... 540 910-1233
Waynesboro *(G-15097)*
Babypipscom LLC ....G....... 866 674-9258
Henrico *(G-6480)*
Badd Newz Publications LLC ....G....... 540 479-2848
Fredericksburg *(G-5250)*
Baltimore Business Company LLC ....G....... 301 848-7200
Fairfax *(G-4417)*
Barcroft Center ....G....... 703 228-0701
Arlington *(G-874)*
Barrington Worldwide LLC ....G....... 202 255-4611
Alexandria *(G-145)*
Bay Breeze Publishing LLC ....G....... 757 535-1580
Norfolk *(G-9459)*
Bdmoore Publications LLC ....G....... 434 352-7581
Spout Spring *(G-12925)*
Becke Publishing Incorporated ....G....... 703 225-8742
Arlington *(G-877)*
Beckett Consulting Inc ....G....... 804 580-4164
Heathsville *(G-6459)*
Bedford Bulletin LLC ....G....... 540 586-8612
Bedford *(G-1623)*
Bh Media Group Inc ....G....... 703 241-2608
Falls Church *(G-4764)*
Bingo Tribune Inc ....G....... 804 221-9049
Richmond *(G-11125)*
Bowser Report ....G....... 757 877-5979
Williamsburg *(G-15212)*
Brico Inc ....G....... 540 763-3731
Willis *(G-15356)*
Broken Wing Enterprises Inc ....G....... 804 378-0136
Midlothian *(G-8784)*
Buckingham Beacon ....G....... 434 591-1000
Palmyra *(G-10245)*
Buds Blueridge ....G....... 540 323-7030
Winchester *(G-15396)*
Bulletin News Network Inc ....E....... 703 749-0040
Reston *(G-10813)*
Bureau of National Affairs Inc ....C....... 703 341-3000
Arlington *(G-893)*
Bureau of National Affairs Inc ....G....... 703 847-4741
Vienna *(G-14019)*
C & C Publishing Inc ....G....... 804 598-4035
Powhatan *(G-10536)*
C & C Publishing Inc ....G....... 804 598-4305
Mechanicsville *(G-8610)*
C-Ville Holdings LLC ....E....... 434 817-2749
Charlottesville *(G-2753)*
Camera Club of Richmond ....G....... 804 380-9218
Midlothian *(G-8788)*
Carroll Publishing Corp ....F....... 276 728-7311
Hillsville *(G-6888)*
Catholic Diocese of Arlington ....F....... 703 841-2590
Arlington *(G-903)*
Catholic Virginian Press Inc ....G....... 804 358-3625
Richmond *(G-11152)*
CC Richmond II LP ....G....... 804 213-2706
Richmond *(G-11523)*
Charles Southwell ....G....... 703 892-5469
Arlington *(G-905)*
Charlette Publishing Inc ....G....... 434 696-5550
Victoria *(G-14000)*
Charlie Eco Publishing Inc ....G....... 800 357-0121
Abingdon *(G-22)*
Charlotte Publishing Inc ....F....... 434 568-3341
Drakes Branch *(G-4131)*
Chosun Ilbo Washington Inc ....G....... 703 865-8310
Fairfax *(G-4428)*
Christian News & Comments ....G....... 276 669-6972
Bristol *(G-1970)*
Christian Observer ....G....... 540 464-3570
Lexington *(G-7390)*
Christian Power Weekly News ....G....... 703 658-5272
Annandale *(G-735)*
Church Guide ....G....... 757 285-2222
Virginia Beach *(G-14339)*
Clinch Valley Publishing Co ....G....... 276 762-7671
Saint Paul *(G-12465)*
Coalfield Progress ....D....... 276 679-1101
Norton *(G-10115)*
Coalzoomcom ....G....... 304 920-2588
Chesapeake *(G-3039)*
Cold Press II LLC ....G....... 757 227-0809
Norfolk *(G-9492)*
Commonwealth Times ....G....... 804 828-1058
Richmond *(G-11536)*
Connection Newspapers LLC ....F....... 703 821-5050
Alexandria *(G-172)*
Connection Publishing Inc ....D....... 703 821-5050
Alexandria *(G-173)*
Country Courier ....G....... 804 769-0259
Aylett *(G-1547)*
Covington Virginian Inc ....E....... 540 962-2121
Covington *(G-3784)*
Cox Matthews & Associates Inc ....G....... 703 385-2981
Fairfax *(G-4607)*
Crewe Burkfield Journal ....G....... 434 645-7534
Crewe *(G-3810)*
Crowd Almanac LLC ....G....... 703 385-6989
Fairfax *(G-4609)*
Crozet Gazette LLC ....G....... 434 823-2291
Crozet *(G-3831)*
Cv Corporation of Virginia ....F....... 540 967-0368
Louisa *(G-7554)*
CVille Dream Life ....G....... 434 327-2600
Charlottesville *(G-2776)*
Cville Siren LLC ....G....... 434 987-2008
Charlottesville *(G-2777)*
Daily Deed LLC ....G....... 703 754-0644
Gainesville *(G-5577)*
Daily Distributions Inc ....G....... 703 577-8120
Fairfax *(G-4435)*
Daily Frills LLC ....G....... 540 850-7909
Fredericksburg *(G-5270)*
Daily Grub Hospitality Inc ....G....... 804 221-5323
Richmond *(G-11177)*
Daily Money Matters LLC ....G....... 703 904-9157
Reston *(G-10831)*
Daily News Record ....F....... 540 459-4078
Woodstock *(G-15851)*
Daily News Record ....F....... 540 574-6200
Harrisonburg *(G-6308)*
Daily News Record ....F....... 540 743-5123
Luray *(G-7606)*

S I C

Daily Peprah & Partners Servic ....G...... 757 581-6452
  Virginia Beach (G-14383)
Daily Press Inc ....F...... 757 245-3737
  Newport News (G-9213)
Daily Productions Inc ....G...... 703 477-8444
  Leesburg (G-7252)
Daily Progress ....G...... 540 672-1266
  Orange (G-10210)
Daily Splat LLC ....G...... 703 729-0842
  Ashburn (G-1268)
Daniel Patrick McDermott ....G...... 540 305-3000
  Front Royal (G-5528)
Darklore Publishing LLC ....G...... 703 566-8021
  Alexandria (G-183)
Davis Chetia ....G...... 757 575-9225
  Norfolk (G-9518)
Defense News ....F...... 703 750-9000
  Vienna (G-14038)
Dehardit Press ....G...... 804 693-2795
  Gloucester (G-5845)
Delauri & Associates ....G...... 757 482-9140
  Chesapeake (G-3064)
Doi Nay Newspaper ....G...... 703 748-1239
  Alexandria (G-448)
Dolan LLC ....F...... 804 783-0770
  Richmond (G-11562)
Dorothy Edwards ....G...... 859 608-3539
  Burke (G-2188)
Double T Publishing Inc ....D...... 276 926-8816
  Clintwood (G-3688)
Dudenhefer For Delegate ....G...... 540 628-4012
  Stafford (G-13139)
Eastern Shore Post Inc ....G...... 757 789-7678
  Onley (G-10200)
Economic Dev Auth Cy Richmond ....G...... 804 521-4002
  Richmond (G-11572)
Editorial Prjcts In Edcatn Inc ....F...... 703 292-5111
  Arlington (G-954)
Eir News Service Inc ....D...... 703 777-4494
  Leesburg (G-7264)
El Comercio Newspaper Inc ....G...... 703 859-1554
  Dumfries (G-4244)
Elliott Oil Production LLC ....G...... 434 525-3049
  Forest (G-5071)
Enterprise Inc ....G...... 276 694-3101
  Stuart (G-13609)
Eugene C Hoopes ....G...... 434 293-5852
  Charlottesville (G-2793)
Fairfax Station Times ....G...... 703 437-5400
  Reston (G-10850)
Falls Church News Press ....G...... 703 532-3267
  Falls Church (G-4913)
Fauquier Building Grnds ....G...... 540 422-8480
  Warrenton (G-15008)
Fauquier Enterprise Center ....G...... 540 680-2652
  Warrenton (G-15009)
Fauquier Kid LLC ....G...... 540 349-0027
  Warrenton (G-15011)
Fauquier Now ....G...... 540 359-6574
  Warrenton (G-15012)
Fauquier Services Inc ....G...... 540 341-4133
  Warrenton (G-15013)
Fauquier Silhouettes Inc ....G...... 540 347-3191
  Warrenton (G-15014)
Fauquier Times Democrat ....E...... 540 347-7363
  Warrenton (G-15015)
Feedrva Inc ....G...... 804 513-3100
  Henrico (G-6509)
Flagship Inc ....E...... 757 222-3965
  Norfolk (G-9555)
Floyd Press Inc ....G...... 540 745-2127
  Floyd (G-5026)
Franklin County Inv Co Inc ....E...... 540 483-5113
  Rocky Mount (G-12323)
Fred Good Times LLC ....G...... 540 372-7247
  Fredericksburg (G-5188)
Free Lance-Star Publshng Co of ....B...... 540 374-5000
  Fredericksburg (G-5190)
Freshii ....G...... 804 223-8027
  Richmond (G-11213)
Ft Lee Welcome Center ....G...... 804 734-7488
  Fort Lee (G-5130)
G5 Examiner LLC ....G...... 540 455-9186
  Fredericksburg (G-5291)
Gails Dream LLC ....G...... 757 638-3197
  Suffolk (G-13712)
Gannett Co Inc ....B...... 703 854-6000
  Mc Lean (G-8438)
Gannett GP Media Inc ....G...... 703 854-6000
  Mclean (G-8586)

Gannett Holdings LLC ....G...... 703 854-6000
  Mc Lean (G-8439)
Gannett Media Corp ....D...... 540 885-7281
  Staunton (G-13262)
▲ Gannett Media Corp ....C...... 703 854-6000
  Mc Lean (G-8440)
Gannett Publishing Svcs LLC ....F...... 703 854-6000
  Mc Lean (G-8442)
◆ Gannett River States Pubg Corp ......A...... 703 284-6000
  Mc Lean (G-8443)
◆ Gannett Stllite Info Ntwrk LLC ....A...... 703 854-6000
  Mc Lean (G-8444)
Gatehouse Media LLC ....E...... 804 732-3456
  Petersburg (G-10322)
Gatehuse Media VA Holdings Inc ....G...... 585 598-0030
  Petersburg (G-10323)
Gavin Bourjaily ....G...... 540 636-1985
  Strasburg (G-13580)
Gazette Newspaper ....G...... 276 236-5178
  Galax (G-5635)
Gazette Virginian ....G...... 434 572-3945
  South Boston (G-12771)
Gcoe LLC ....G...... 703 854-6000
  Mc Lean (G-8445)
Ghent Living Magazine LLC ....G...... 757 425-7333
  Virginia Beach (G-14482)
Global Daily ....E...... 703 518-3030
  Alexandria (G-217)
Global X Press ....G...... 202 417-2070
  Mc Lean (G-8450)
Glory Days Press LLC ....G...... 703 443-1964
  Leesburg (G-7280)
Gods Compass Movie LLC ....G...... 434 219-6865
  Lynchburg (G-7722)
Good News Network ....G...... 757 638-3289
  Portsmouth (G-10435)
Grassroots Enterprise Inc ....F...... 703 354-1177
  Herndon (G-6690)
Greater Richmond Dance Project ....F...... 804 302-4338
  Richmond (G-11221)
Halifax Gazette Publishing Co ....E...... 434 572-3945
  South Boston (G-12774)
Hampton Roads Gazeti Inc ....G...... 757 560-9583
  Virginia Beach (G-14499)
Hampton University ....G...... 757 727-5385
  Hampton (G-6164)
Hanover Herald-Progress ....F...... 804 798-9031
  Ashland (G-1427)
Harold Delano ....G...... 804 333-3446
  Warsaw (G-15065)
Haskell Investment Company Inc ....D...... 276 638-8801
  Martinsville (G-8294)
Help Construction Richmond LLC ....G...... 804 320-3220
  Richmond (G-11044)
Henrico ....G...... 434 202-2331
  Henrico (G-6521)
Herald Schlrly Open Access LLC ....G...... 202 412-2272
  Aldie (G-107)
Herald Square LLC ....G...... 540 477-2019
  Mount Jackson (G-9072)
Herndon Publishing Co Inc ....F...... 703 689-0111
  Herndon (G-6697)
Hispanic Newspaper Inc ....G...... 703 478-6806
  Herndon (G-6699)
Hopewell Publishing Company ....G...... 804 452-6127
  Hopewell (G-6934)
Hs Winchester LLC ....G...... 540 771-0079
  Winchester (G-15548)
Hummersport LLC ....G...... 703 433-1887
  Sterling (G-13423)
Infoition News Services Inc ....F...... 703 853-8857
  Reston (G-10871)
Inside Business ....G...... 757 439-7158
  Virginia Beach (G-14548)
Intelligence Press Inc ....F...... 703 318-8848
  Sterling (G-13429)
J & V Publishing LLC ....G...... 571 318-1700
  Herndon (G-6715)
Jack Einreinhof ....G...... 434 239-3072
  Lynchburg (G-7747)
James River Publishing Inc ....G...... 804 740-0729
  Henrico (G-6526)
Joong-Ang Daily News Cal Inc ....E...... 703 281-9660
  Annandale (G-762)
▲ Korea Daily ....F...... 703 281-9660
  Annandale (G-764)
▲ Korea Times Washington DC Inc ......E...... 703 941-8001
  Annandale (G-765)

▲ Korean Weekly Entertainment ....G...... 703 354-7962
  Annandale (G-766)
Krista Hawk LLC ....G...... 703 554-7654
  Lovettsville (G-7581)
Kwe Publishing LLC ....G...... 804 458-4789
  Prince George (G-10598)
Kyung T Jung DBA Krean Entrmt ....G...... 703 658-0000
  Annandale (G-768)
Lai of Richmond LLC ....G...... 804 746-2739
  Mechanicsville (G-8650)
Landmark Cmnty Nwsppers VA LLC .....F...... 276 236-5178
  Galax (G-5640)
Landmark Community Newspapers ......G...... 502 633-4334
  Norfolk (G-9615)
Landmark Media Enterprises LLC ....A...... 757 351-7000
  Norfolk (G-9616)
Landmark Military Newspapers ....G...... 254 690-9000
  Norfolk (G-9617)
Las Americas Newspaper Inc ....G...... 703 256-4200
  Falls Church (G-4821)
Leader Publishing Company ....D...... 540 885-7387
  Staunton (G-13274)
Leadership Perspectives Inc ....G...... 703 629-8977
  Fairfax (G-4645)
Lebanon News Inc ....F...... 276 889-2112
  Lebanon (G-7198)
Leesburg Today Inc ....G...... 703 771-8800
  Lansdowne (G-7171)
Lfm Roanoke ....G...... 540 342-0542
  Roanoke (G-12125)
Lifesitenews Com Inc ....G...... 540 635-3131
  Front Royal (G-5541)
Loudoun Business Inc ....G...... 703 777-2176
  Lansdowne (G-7172)
Loudoun Classical School ....G...... 540 338-6101
  Purcellville (G-10669)
Loudoun Community Band ....G...... 540 882-3838
  Lovettsville (G-7582)
Loudoun Metal & More ....G...... 540 668-5067
  Lovettsville (G-7583)
Loudoun Now ....G...... 703 770-9723
  Leesburg (G-7307)
M & S Publishing Co Inc ....G...... 434 645-7534
  Crewe (G-3814)
Marie Lawson Reporter ....G...... 757 549-2198
  Chesapeake (G-3198)
Mark Toner LLC ....G...... 703 689-0609
  Reston (G-10895)
Matthew Crawford Sargent ....G...... 757 430-9488
  Virginia Beach (G-14641)
McGuffie History Publications ....G...... 540 371-3659
  Fredericksburg (G-5205)
Media General Operations Inc ....G...... 434 985-2315
  Stanardsville (G-13223)
Mella Weekly ....G...... 757 436-2409
  Chesapeake (G-3202)
Mercury Partners Usa LLC ....G...... 757 652-7067
  Franktown (G-5164)
Merrill St Physcians Group Inc ....G...... 804 441-1280
  Chesterfield (G-3514)
Michael S Bond ....G...... 740 971-9157
  Alexandria (G-532)
Mid-Atlantic Publishing Co ....F...... 703 866-5156
  Springfield (G-13050)
Mkrs Corporation ....E...... 203 349-1149
  Herndon (G-6748)
Mobile Observer ....G...... 703 569-9346
  Springfield (G-13053)
Mommers House LLC ....G...... 540 327-8101
  Winchester (G-15558)
Montgomery Cnty Newspapers Inc ......E...... 540 389-9355
  Salem (G-12540)
Moshref Mir Abdul ....G...... 502 356-0019
  Woodbridge (G-15750)
Mountaineer Publishing Co Inc ....G...... 276 935-2123
  Grundy (G-6038)
My Mind On Sports LLC ....G...... 703 261-9629
  Alexandria (G-538)
Nailrod Publications LLC ....G...... 703 351-8130
  Arlington (G-1069)
Neathridge Content Solutions ....G...... 703 979-7170
  Arlington (G-1072)
New Journal and Guide Inc ....F...... 757 543-6531
  Norfolk (G-9660)
New Kent Charles Cy Chronicle ....G...... 804 843-4181
  West Point (G-15159)
New Student Chronicle ....G...... 540 463-4000
  Lexington (G-7407)
News Connection ....G...... 703 661-4999
  Sterling (G-13461)

News-Gazette Corporation.............E 540 463-3116
  Lexington *(G-7408)*

North Arrow Inc.........................G...... 703 250-3215
  Fairfax Station *(G-4720)*

North of James...........................G...... 804 218-5265
  Richmond *(G-11306)*

North Street Enterprise Inc.........E 434 392-4144
  Farmville *(G-4954)*

Nottoway Publishing Co Inc.........F 434 292-3019
  Blackstone *(G-1821)*

Nuevo Milenio Newspaper LLC........G...... 703 501-7180
  Burke *(G-2196)*

Observer Inc..............................G...... 804 545-7500
  Midlothian *(G-8870)*

Old Rag Gazette..........................G...... 540 675-2001
  Washington *(G-15076)*

On The Weekly LLC......................G...... 757 839-2640
  Virginia Beach *(G-14698)*

Page Publications Inc...................G...... 804 733-8636
  North Dinwiddie *(G-10061)*

Page Shenandoah Newspaper.........E 540 574-6251
  Winchester *(G-15564)*

Paradigm Communications Inc........F 804 644-0496
  Richmond *(G-11706)*

Peac LLC..................................G...... 571 261-1527
  Haymarket *(G-6435)*

Penny Saver..............................G...... 434 857-5134
  Danville *(G-4023)*

Perez Armando...........................G...... 202 716-5044
  Arlington *(G-1104)*

Phoenix Designs.........................G...... 757 301-9300
  Virginia Beach *(G-14720)*

Pilot Media...............................G...... 757 446-2000
  Norfolk *(G-9689)*

Platinum Point LLC......................G...... 804 357-3337
  North Chesterfield *(G-10021)*

Politico LLC..............................E 703 647-7999
  Arlington *(G-1114)*

Popmount Inc.............................F 804 232-4999
  Richmond *(G-11720)*

Portico Publications Ltd...............D 434 817-2749
  Charlottesville *(G-2849)*

Posie Press LLC..........................G...... 804 276-0716
  North Chesterfield *(G-9952)*

Potomac Local News....................G...... 540 659-2020
  Stafford *(G-13181)*

Powell Valley Printing Company......F 276 546-1210
  Pennington Gap *(G-10297)*

Press Go Button LLC....................G...... 703 709-5839
  Reston *(G-10930)*

Program Services LLC...................G...... 757 222-3990
  Norfolk *(G-9698)*

Program Services LLC...................G...... 804 526-8656
  Colonial Heights *(G-3742)*

Protocol Media LLC......................F 703 647-8700
  Arlington *(G-1122)*

Publishing Village.......................G...... 804 425-5555
  Chester *(G-3449)*

Purcellville Gazette LLC...............G...... 540 431-8507
  Winchester *(G-15571)*

R A Handy Title Examiner..............G...... 804 739-9520
  Midlothian *(G-8885)*

Randall Publication Inc................F 703 369-0741
  Manassas *(G-7994)*

Randolph-Macon College...............G...... 804 752-7200
  Ashland *(G-1483)*

Randy Edwards...........................G...... 703 591-0545
  Fairfax *(G-4537)*

Rappahannock Media LLC..............G...... 540 675-3338
  Washington *(G-15077)*

Rappahannock Record...................F 804 435-1701
  Kilmarnock *(G-7076)*

Ready For Hillary.......................G...... 703 405-0433
  Arlington *(G-1142)*

Recorder Publishing of VA Inc........F 540 468-2147
  Monterey *(G-9012)*

Renovated Richmond LLC...............G...... 804 467-5470
  Midlothian *(G-8887)*

Republicanpaccom.......................G...... 703 241-8422
  Arlington *(G-1147)*

Richard A Daily Dr......................G...... 540 586-4030
  Goode *(G-5893)*

Richmond Equity Ventures LLC........G...... 804 837-3523
  Richmond *(G-11355)*

Richmond Newspaper Inc................G...... 804 261-1101
  Richmond *(G-11357)*

Richmond Pinball Collective..........G...... 301 652-8000
  North Chesterfield *(G-9963)*

Richmond Publishing.....................G...... 804 229-6267
  Richmond *(G-11359)*

Richmond Schl Hlth & Tech Inc........E 804 751-9191
  Chester *(G-3452)*

Richmond Shopping Center Inc........G...... 804 648-9015
  Richmond *(G-11737)*

Richmond Times Dispatch..............G...... 804 526-7205
  South Chesterfield *(G-12823)*

Richmond Top Moving Co................G...... 804 441-9702
  Richmond *(G-11362)*

Richmond Ventures LLC.................G...... 804 282-5901
  North Chesterfield *(G-9964)*

Richmond1040 LLC.......................G...... 407 538-3624
  Glen Allen *(G-5787)*

Ridefauquier.............................G...... 540 270-8247
  Warrenton *(G-15048)*

Riverstone Group LLC...................B 804 643-4200
  Richmond *(G-11742)*

Rni Print Services.......................G...... 804 649-6670
  Richmond *(G-11744)*

Roanoke..................................G...... 540 362-8404
  Roanoke *(G-12164)*

Roanoke Star Sentinel..................G...... 540 400-0990
  Roanoke *(G-12167)*

Roanoke Tribune.........................G...... 540 343-0326
  Roanoke *(G-12168)*

Robert Deitrich..........................G...... 804 793-8414
  Danville *(G-4036)*

Robert Grogg.............................G...... 540 667-4279
  Winchester *(G-15467)*

Rockingham Publishing Co Inc.........C 540 574-6200
  Harrisonburg *(G-6363)*

Rockingham Publishing Company.......G...... 540 298-9444
  Elkton *(G-4334)*

Rural Life Journal LLC..................G...... 301 774-0305
  Alexandria *(G-332)*

Saltville Progress Inc..................G...... 276 496-5792
  Saltville *(G-12591)*

Sanduja Strategies......................G...... 202 826-9804
  Arlington *(G-1158)*

Saxsmo Publishing LLC..................G...... 804 269-0473
  North Chesterfield *(G-9971)*

Scadco Publishing LLC..................G...... 757 484-4878
  Portsmouth *(G-10478)*

Scott County Herald Virginian.........G...... 276 386-6300
  Gate City *(G-5667)*

Scripps Enterprises Inc................G...... 434 760-3311
  Charlottesville *(G-2690)*

Sellers Advantage Richmond...........G...... 804 338-3800
  Richmond *(G-11757)*

Sentinel Press LLC......................G...... 703 753-5434
  Gainesville *(G-5611)*

Shalom Foundation Inc..................G...... 540 433-5351
  Harrisonburg *(G-6369)*

Shamrock Arlington LLC.................G...... 703 528-7676
  Arlington *(G-1164)*

Shenandoah Publications Inc..........E 540 459-4000
  Edinburg *(G-4314)*

Sightline Media Group LLC.............B 703 750-7400
  Vienna *(G-14126)*

Singh Express Corp......................G...... 202 816-8686
  Reston *(G-10951)*

Smithfield Times........................G...... 757 357-3288
  Smithfield *(G-12740)*

Smyth County News.....................G...... 276 783-5121
  Marion *(G-8243)*

Social Music LLC........................G...... 202 308-3249
  Fredericksburg *(G-5364)*

Sola Richmond LLC......................G...... 804 302-4498
  Midlothian *(G-8904)*

South Boston News Inc..................F 434 572-2928
  South Boston *(G-12790)*

Southside Voice Inc.....................F 804 644-9060
  Richmond *(G-11766)*

Southwest Publisher LLC...............E 540 980-5220
  Pulaski *(G-10647)*

Spacenews Inc...........................F 571 421-2300
  Alexandria *(G-352)*

Springfield Connection.................G...... 703 866-1040
  Springfield *(G-13093)*

Springfield Times.......................G...... 703 437-5400
  Reston *(G-10963)*

Sprouting Star Press....................G...... 703 860-0958
  Reston *(G-10963)*

Stafford County Sun....................G...... 540 659-8923
  Stafford *(G-13195)*

Startup Virginia........................G...... 804 502-3131
  North Chesterfield *(G-9990)*

Style LLC.................................D 757 222-3990
  Richmond *(G-11775)*

Sun Gazette..............................G...... 703 738-2520
  Springfield *(G-13096)*

Sun Publishing Company................E 434 374-8152
  Clarksville *(G-3636)*

T3 Media LLC.............................G...... 804 262-1700
  Richmond *(G-11404)*

Target Advertising Inc.................G...... 757 627-2216
  Norfolk *(G-9741)*

▲ Tide Water Pulication LLC...........E 757 562-3187
  Franklin *(G-5158)*

Tide Water Pulication LLC.............G...... 434 848-2114
  Lawrenceville *(G-7186)*

Tidewater Hispanic Newspaper.........G...... 757 474-1233
  Virginia Beach *(G-14875)*

Tidewater Newspapers Inc..............E 804 693-3101
  Gloucester *(G-5862)*

Tidewater Parent........................G...... 757 222-3900
  Norfolk *(G-9755)*

Times Community Media..................G...... 703 777-1111
  Leesburg *(G-7361)*

Times Publishing Company..............F 757 357-3288
  Smithfield *(G-12742)*

▲ Times-World LLC.....................B 540 981-3100
  Roanoke *(G-12205)*

Toro-Aire Inc............................G...... 804 649-7575
  Richmond *(G-11789)*

Tran Du..................................G...... 512 470-1794
  Arlington *(G-1194)*

University of Richmond.................G...... 804 289-8000
  Richmond *(G-11800)*

Urban Views Weekly LLC................G...... 804 441-6255
  Richmond *(G-11429)*

USA Today.................................G...... 703 267-6964
  Fairfax *(G-4577)*

USA Today.................................G...... 703 750-8702
  Springfield *(G-13104)*

USA Today International Corp..........F 703 854-3400
  Mc Lean *(G-8571)*

USA Today Spt Media Group LLC.......G...... 703 854-6000
  Mc Lean *(G-8572)*

USA Weekend Inc.........................C 703 854-6000
  Mc Lean *(G-8573)*

Valley Publishing Corporation.........G...... 434 591-1000
  Palmyra *(G-10259)*

Valley Trader The Inc..................F 540 869-5132
  Middletown *(G-8747)*

Viet Bao Inc.............................G...... 703 339-9852
  Lorton *(G-7538)*

Village Publishing LLC.................G...... 804 751-0421
  Chester *(G-3466)*

Virginia Gazette Companies LLC.......G...... 757 220-1736
  Newport News *(G-9373)*

Virginia News Group LLC...............G...... 703 777-1111
  Leesburg *(G-7372)*

Virginia News Group LLC...............G...... 540 955-1111
  Winchester *(G-15599)*

Virginia News Group LLC...............G...... 703 777-1111
  Leesburg *(G-7373)*

Virginia News Group LLC...............G...... 703 777-1111
  Ashburn *(G-1350)*

Virginia News Group LLC...............E 703 437-5400
  Reston *(G-10985)*

Virginia Times...........................G...... 804 530-8540
  Chester *(G-3467)*

Virginian Leader Corp..................F 540 921-3434
  Pearisburg *(G-10279)*

▲ Virginn-Plot Mdia Cmpanies LLC....A 757 446-9000
  Virginia Beach *(G-14923)*

Virginn-Plot Mdia Cmpanies LLC.......G...... 804 358-0825
  Richmond *(G-11814)*

Virginn-Plot Mdia Cmpanies LLC.......G...... 757 446-2848
  Virginia Beach *(G-14924)*

W A Cleaton and Sons Inc..............F 804 443-2200
  Tappahannock *(G-13824)*

Warren Sentinel..........................F 540 635-4174
  Front Royal *(G-5563)*

Washingtnpost Nwsweek Intrctiv.......G...... 703 469-2500
  Arlington *(G-1216)*

Washington Blade.......................G...... 202 747-2077
  Vienna *(G-14157)*

Weekly Weeder Co.......................G...... 757 618-9506
  Virginia Beach *(G-14932)*

Whisper Prayers Daily..................G...... 703 690-1184
  Lorton *(G-7542)*

Winchester Evening Star Inc...........C 540 667-3200
  Winchester *(G-15601)*

Windmill Promotions....................G...... 757 204-4688
  Virginia Beach *(G-14940)*

Wise Printing Co Inc....................G...... 276 523-1141
  Big Stone Gap *(G-1718)*

Womack Newspaper Inc..................G...... 434 432-1654
  Chatham *(G-2941)*

S I C

Womack Publishing Co Inc ....F 434 432-2791
Chatham *(G-2942)*

Womack Publishing Co Inc ....G 434 352-8215
Appomattox *(G-828)*

Womack Publishing Co Inc ....F 434 447-3178
South Hill *(G-12864)*

Womack Publishing Co Inc ....G 434 369-6688
Altavista *(G-645)*

Womack Publishing Co Inc ....F 434 432-1654
Emporia *(G-4371)*

Womens Media Watch Azerbaijan ...G 253 381-9667
Brambleton *(G-1936)*

Wood Television LLC ....D 540 825-4416
Culpeper *(G-3932)*

Wood Television LLC ....D 434 793-2311
Danville *(G-4051)*

Wood Television LLC ....F 276 228-6611
Wytheville *(G-15924)*

Wood Television LLC ....G 703 368-9268
Manassas *(G-8014)*

Wood Television LLC ....C 276 669-2181
Bristol *(G-2002)*

Wood Television LLC ....E 540 672-1266
Orange *(G-10232)*

Wood Television LLC ....G 434 385-5400
Lynchburg *(G-7840)*

Wood Television LLC ....E 757 539-3437
Suffolk *(G-13786)*

Wood Television LLC ....C 434 978-7200
Charlottesville *(G-2716)*

Wood Television LLC ....E 804 775-4600
Richmond *(G-11832)*

Wood Television LLC ....G 540 948-5121
Madison *(G-7865)*

Wood Television LLC ....C 804 559-8207
Mechanicsville *(G-8700)*

Wood Television LLC ....D 540 949-8213
Waynesboro *(G-15148)*

World & I ....G 202 636-3334
Annandale *(G-794)*

World Media Enterprises Inc ....F 804 559-8261
Mechanicsville *(G-8703)*

Wp Company LLC ....F 703 518-3000
Alexandria *(G-389)*

Wp Company LLC ....G 703 799-2920
Alexandria *(G-616)*

Wp Company LLC ....G 703 392-1303
Fairfax *(G-4695)*

Wp Company LLC ....G 540 937-4380
Amissville *(G-724)*

Wp Company LLC ....F 703 771-1491
Leesburg *(G-7381)*

York Town Crier ....G 757 766-1776
Yorktown *(G-16004)*

Your Health Magazine ....E 703 288-3130
Annandale *(G-795)*

2721 Periodicals: Publishing & Printing

21st Century Science Assoc Inc ......G 703 777-6943
Leesburg *(G-7212)*

Access Reports Inc ....G 434 384-5334
Lynchburg *(G-7631)*

Adriana Calderon Escalante ....G 703 926-7638
Vienna *(G-14005)*

AGC Information Inc ....E 703 548-3118
Arlington *(G-844)*

▲ Airline Tariff Publishing Co ....B 703 661-7400
Dulles *(G-4191)*

American Assn Nurosurgeons Inc ....E 434 924-5503
Charlottesville *(G-2726)*

American City Bus Journals Inc ....F 703 258-0800
Arlington *(G-852)*

American Spectator ....G 703 807-2011
Alexandria *(G-133)*

Anneker Corp ....F 202 630-3007
Alexandria *(G-136)*

Arabesque Media ....G 703 745-5395
Fairfax *(G-4410)*

Associated Gen Contrs of Amer ......D 703 837-5415
Arlington *(G-862)*

Association For Cmpt McHy Inc ......G 703 528-0726
Arlington *(G-863)*

Audio Mart ....G 434 645-8816
Crewe *(G-3807)*

Autumn Publishing Enterprises ....G 703 978-2132
Fairfax *(G-4414)*

Autumn Publishing Inc ....G 703 368-4857
Manassas *(G-8030)*

Avenue 7 Magazine LLC ....G 757 214-4914
Virginia Beach *(G-14251)*

Barry McVay ....G 703 451-5953
Burke *(G-2182)*

Beck Media Group ....G 540 904-6800
Roanoke *(G-12042)*

Believe Magazine ....G 804 291-7509
Richmond *(G-11029)*

Bluegrass Unlimited Inc ....G 540 349-8181
Warrenton *(G-14982)*

Bowhead Systems Management LLC ...C 703 413-4251
Springfield *(G-12968)*

Bowser Report ....G 757 877-5979
Williamsburg *(G-15212)*

Bureau of National Affairs Inc ....C 703 341-3000
Arlington *(G-893)*

C & C Publishing Inc ....G 804 598-4305
Mechanicsville *(G-8610)*

Cape Fear Publishing Company ....F 804 343-7539
Richmond *(G-11521)*

Capitol Information Group Inc ....D 703 905-8000
Falls Church *(G-4770)*

Carden Jennings Publishing Co ....E 434 817-2000
Charlottesville *(G-2603)*

Career College Central ....G 571 267-3012
Chantilly *(G-2387)*

▼ Cegna Inc ....E 757 632-5000
Hampton *(G-6110)*

Chronicle of The Horse LLC ....E 540 687-6341
Middleburg *(G-8718)*

City Connection Magazine LLC ....G 757 570-9249
Norfolk *(G-9486)*

Collecting Concepts Inc ....E 804 285-0994
Richmond *(G-11162)*

Compass Publications Inc ....G 703 524-3136
Arlington *(G-917)*

Computing With Kids ....G 703 444-9005
Great Falls *(G-5949)*

Custom Pubg Solutions LLC ....G 540 341-0453
Warrenton *(G-14991)*

Dal Enterprises Inc ....G 540 720-5584
Stafford *(G-13135)*

Daleel Corporation ....G 703 824-8130
Vienna *(G-14033)*

DC Metro Magazine ....G 703 455-9223
Springfield *(G-12989)*

Defense Daily ....G 703 522-2012
Arlington *(G-933)*

Discover Sml Magazine ....G 540 719-7881
Hardy *(G-6287)*

Dogwood Ridge Outdoors Inc ....G 540 867-0764
Dayton *(G-4055)*

Dominion Distribution Svcs Inc ....F 757 351-7000
Norfolk *(G-9528)*

Dominion Enterprises ....G 757 226-9440
Norfolk *(G-9530)*

Dominion Enterprises ....G 540 869-3837
Stephens City *(G-13314)*

Dominion Enterprises ....E 757 351-7000
Norfolk *(G-9529)*

Dorsett Publications LLC ....G 540 382-6431
Christiansburg *(G-3584)*

Double D LLC ....G 270 307-2786
Woodbridge *(G-15686)*

Eastern Chrstn Pblications LLC ....G 703 691-8862
Fairfax *(G-4615)*

Editorial Prjcts In Edcatn Inc ....F 703 292-5111
Arlington *(G-954)*

Elizabeth Claire Inc ....G 757 430-4308
Virginia Beach *(G-14440)*

Engaged Magazine LLC ....G 703 485-4878
Springfield *(G-12998)*

Enterprising Women ....G 919 362-1551
Dulles *(G-4199)*

Eutopia Magazine Guelph Press ....G 703 938-6077
Herndon *(G-6670)*

Executive Lifestyle Mag Inc ....G 757 438-5582
Newport News *(G-9222)*

Fairfax Publishing Company ....G 703 421-2003
Sterling *(G-13397)*

Family Magazine Network Inc ....G 703 298-0601
Herndon *(G-6673)*

Fcw Government Tech Group ....D 703 876-5100
Falls Church *(G-4791)*

Fcw Media Group ....D 703 876-5136
Falls Church *(G-4792)*

Federal Times ....G 703 750-9000
Vienna *(G-14053)*

Focus Magazine ....G 434 296-4261
Charlottesville *(G-2796)*

For Rent Magazine ....G 305 305-0494
Henrico *(G-6514)*

Gately John ....G 757 851-3085
Hampton *(G-6156)*

Gja LLC ....G 434 218-0216
Palmyra *(G-10249)*

Global Health Solutions Inc ....G 703 848-2333
Falls Church *(G-4799)*

Highbrow Magazine LLC ....G 571 480-2867
Vienna *(G-14064)*

Historynet LLC ....G 703 779-8322
Vienna *(G-14065)*

Homeland Corporation ....F 571 218-6200
Sterling *(G-13421)*

Homes & Land of Richmond ....G 804 794-8494
Midlothian *(G-8827)*

Homes & Land of Virginia LLC ....G 804 357-7005
Midlothian *(G-8828)*

Ibfd North America Inc ....G 703 442-7757
Vienna *(G-14069)*

Industrial Reporting Inc ....F 804 550-0323
Ashland *(G-1439)*

Inside Air Force ....G 703 416-8528
Arlington *(G-1003)*

Institute of Navigation (dc) ....G 703 366-2723
Manassas *(G-8081)*

Interlocking Con Pavement Inst ....G 703 657-6900
Chantilly *(G-2443)*

Intermission ....G 703 971-7530
Alexandria *(G-488)*

International Publishing Inc ....G 800 377-2838
Chesapeake *(G-3145)*

Interntnal Soc For Cmpttnal Bi ....G 571 293-2113
Leesburg *(G-7288)*

Ivy Creek Media ....G 434 971-1787
Charlottesville *(G-2648)*

Ivy Publication LLC ....F 434 984-4713
Charlottesville *(G-2817)*

JB Pinker Inc ....G 540 943-2760
Afton *(G-85)*

Journal of Orthpdic Spt Physcl ....G 877 766-3450
Alexandria *(G-246)*

Justin Comb ....G 703 783-1082
Alexandria *(G-249)*

K Composite Magazine ....G 703 568-6917
Alexandria *(G-503)*

Kristina Kathleen Mann ....G 703 282-9166
Alexandria *(G-510)*

Landmark Media Enterprises LLC ....A 757 351-7000
Norfolk *(G-9616)*

Last Call Magazine LLC ....G 757 410-0229
Chesapeake *(G-3176)*

Leisuremedia360 Inc ....E 540 989-6138
Roanoke *(G-11956)*

Liberty Media For Women LLC ....F 703 522-4201
Arlington *(G-1034)*

Llama Life II LLC ....G 434 286-4494
Charlottesville *(G-2827)*

Lmr-Inc Com ....G 518 253-9220
Manassas Park *(G-8204)*

Lsc Communications Us LLC ....G 540 564-3900
Harrisonburg *(G-6341)*

Machinery Information Systems ....G 703 836-9700
Alexandria *(G-268)*

Market This LLC ....G 804 382-9220
Glen Allen *(G-5767)*

Mercury Hour ....G 434 237-4011
Lynchburg *(G-7771)*

Mld Publishing ....G 434 535-6008
Lynchburg *(G-7774)*

Montyco LLC ....G 540 761-6751
Roanoke *(G-12137)*

Mystic Empowerment ....G 703 765-0690
Alexandria *(G-539)*

Napolean Magazine ....G 703 641-9062
Falls Church *(G-4834)*

National Geographic Entps ....D 703 528-7868
Arlington *(G-1070)*

Neighborhood Sports LLC ....G 804 282-8033
Richmond *(G-11302)*

Nis Inc ....E 703 323-9170
Fairfax *(G-4519)*

Our Health Magazine Inc ....G 540 387-6482
Salem *(G-12552)*

Palmyra Press Inc ....G 434 589-6634
Palmyra *(G-10252)*

Patinad Grace LLC ....G 804 447-4578
Richmond *(G-11708)*

Personal Selling Power Inc ....E 540 752-7000
Fredericksburg *(G-5469)*

Piedmont Publishing Inc ....F 434 822-1800
Danville *(G-4030)*

Presbytrian Outlook Foundation ....G..... 804 359-8442
Richmond *(G-11724)*

Product Safety Letter ....G..... 703 247-3423
Falls Church *(G-4859)*

Public Utilities Reports Inc ....F..... 703 847-7720
Reston *(G-10934)*

Publishers Press Incorporated ....G..... 540 672-4845
Orange *(G-10223)*

Puryear Group & Associates LLC ....G..... 202 327-3777
Glen Allen *(G-5784)*

Queensmith Communications Corp......F..... 703 370-0606
Alexandria *(G-563)*

Real Estate Weekly ....F..... 434 817-9330
Charlottesville *(G-2681)*

Reason ....G..... 202 256-6197
Charlottesville *(G-2856)*

Rector Visitors of The Univ VA ....G..... 434 924-9136
Charlottesville *(G-2858)*

Rector Visitors of The Univ VA ....G..... 434 924-3124
Charlottesville *(G-2860)*

Richmond Living LLC ....G..... 804 266-5202
Richmond *(G-11356)*

Rosworks LLC ....G..... 804 282-3111
Richmond *(G-11747)*

Rva Magazine ....G..... 804 349-5890
Richmond *(G-11752)*

Senior Publ Free Seniority ....E..... 757 222-3900
Norfolk *(G-9717)*

Shakespeareink Inc ....F..... 804 381-8237
North Chesterfield *(G-9976)*

Shenandoah Specialty Pubg LLC.........G..... 540 463-2319
Lexington *(G-7416)*

Silverchair Scnce + Cmmnctons ....C..... 434 296-6333
Charlottesville *(G-2878)*

Society Nclear Mdcine Mlclar I ....D..... 703 708-9000
Reston *(G-10957)*

Sovereign Media ....G..... 703 964-0361
Mc Lean *(G-8552)*

Spinning In Control LLC ....G..... 703 455-9223
Burke *(G-2203)*

Submarine Telecoms Forum Inc..........G..... 703 444-0845
Sterling *(G-13522)*

Surfside East Inc ....E..... 757 468-0606
Virginia Beach *(G-14859)*

Sword & Trumpet Office ....G..... 540 867-9419
Rockingham *(G-12280)*

Target Communications Inc ....E..... 804 355-0111
Richmond *(G-11782)*

Tax Analysts ....C..... 703 533-4400
Falls Church *(G-4926)*

Thermadon Associates ....G..... 571 275-6118
Woodbridge *(G-15822)*

Tidewater Trading Post Inc ....F..... 757 420-6117
Chesapeake *(G-3339)*

Travel Guide LLC ....E..... 757 351-7000
Norfolk *(G-9766)*

Under Radar LLC ....G..... 540 348-8996
Lexington *(G-7421)*

United States Dept of Army ....G..... 703 614-3727
Fort Belvoir *(G-5119)*

Up-N-Coming Magazine ....G..... 757 343-8829
Norfolk *(G-9775)*

Variance Media Enterprises LLC ....G..... 202 770-1701
Reston *(G-10981)*

Venutec Corporation ....G..... 888 573-8870
Centreville *(G-2350)*

Village Publishing LLC ....G..... 804 751-0421
Chester *(G-3466)*

Virginia Beach Guide Magazine ....G..... 757 627-8712
Norfolk *(G-9782)*

▲ Virginia Bride LLC ....G..... 804 822-1768
Saluda *(G-12606)*

Virginia Business Magazine ....G..... 804 649-6999
Richmond *(G-11809)*

Virginia Real Estate Reviews ....G..... 276 956-5900
Martinsville *(G-8349)*

Virtuous Health Today Inc ....G..... 540 339-2855
Roanoke *(G-12223)*

Vista-Graphics Inc ....G..... 804 559-6140
Mechanicsville *(G-8696)*

Weider History Group Inc ....D..... 703 779-8388
Leesburg *(G-7376)*

West Willow Pubg Group LLC ....G..... 434 386-5667
Forest *(G-5104)*

Willie Lucas ....G..... 919 935-8066
Woodbridge *(G-15832)*

Wood Television LLC ....G..... 540 343-2405
Roanoke *(G-12229)*

Wood Television LLC ....D..... 804 649-6069
Richmond *(G-11833)*

Woods & Waters Publishing Lc............G..... 540 894-9144
Bumpass *(G-2171)*

World History Group LLC ....E..... 703 779-8322
Vienna *(G-14162)*

2731 Books: Publishing & Printing

A V Publication Corp ....G..... 276 251-1760
Ararat *(G-829)*

Acre Media LLC ....G..... 703 314-4465
Alexandria *(G-402)*

▲ Airline Tariff Publishing Co ....B..... 703 661-7400
Dulles *(G-4191)*

Alternatives Inc Corporate ....G..... 540 576-2265
Union Hall *(G-13957)*

AM Tuneshop LLC ....G..... 703 758-9193
Herndon *(G-6611)*

American Inst Arntics Astrntic ....D..... 703 264-7500
Reston *(G-10786)*

American Soc For Hort Science ....F..... 703 836-4606
Alexandria *(G-132)*

Antimicrobial Therapy Inc ....G..... 540 987-9480
Sperryville *(G-12876)*

Apps of All Nations LLC ....G..... 434 851-0651
Lynchburg *(G-7642)*

Autumn Publishing Enterprises ....G..... 703 978-2132
Fairfax *(G-4414)*

Backroads Publications ....G..... 540 949-0329
Lyndhurst *(G-7841)*

Barry McVay ....G..... 703 451-5953
Burke *(G-2182)*

Beatin Path Publications Ltd ....G..... 540 828-6903
Bridgewater *(G-1948)*

Bedford Freeman & Wort ....G..... 651 330-8526
Gordonsville *(G-5900)*

Better Karma LLC ....G..... 703 971-1072
Alexandria *(G-422)*

Bison Printing Inc ....E..... 540 586-3955
Bedford *(G-1627)*

Books International Inc ....G..... 703 661-1500
Dulles *(G-4193)*

Brandylane Publishers Inc ....G..... 804 644-3090
Richmond *(G-11509)*

Brian Enterprises LLC ....G..... 757 645-4475
Williamsburg *(G-15214)*

Broken Column Press LLC ....G..... 703 338-0267
Alexandria *(G-153)*

Capitol City Publishers LLC..................G..... 703 671-5920
Arlington *(G-900)*

Cemark Inc ....F..... 804 763-4100
Midlothian *(G-8793)*

Centennial Books ....G..... 703 751-6162
Alexandria *(G-162)*

Christian Fellowship Publs ....G..... 804 794-5333
North Chesterfield *(G-9843)*

▼ Christian Light Publications ....E..... 540 434-0768
Harrisonburg *(G-6300)*

Citapei Communications Inc.................G..... 703 620-2316
Herndon *(G-6642)*

College Publishing................................G..... 804 364-8410
Glen Allen *(G-5716)*

Colorful Words Media LLC ....G..... 757 268-9690
Hampton *(G-6115)*

Contractors Institute LLC.....................G..... 804 250-6750
Richmond *(G-11165)*

Contractors Institute LLC.....................G..... 804 556-5518
Richmond *(G-11166)*

Csl Enterprises ....G..... 804 695-0400
Gloucester *(G-5842)*

Dawn Brotherton ....G..... 757 645-3211
Williamsburg *(G-15230)*

Dbs Productions ....G..... 434 293-5502
Charlottesville *(G-2778)*

Debra Hewitt ....G..... 540 809-6281
King George *(G-7086)*

Discovery Publications Inc ....G..... 540 349-8060
Warrenton *(G-14997)*

Divine Ntre & Antng Mnsts Inc ....G..... 757 240-8939
Midlothian *(G-8809)*

Dynamic Literacy LLC ....G..... 888 696-8597
Keswick *(G-7046)*

Eastern Chrstn Pblications LLC ....G..... 703 691-8862
Fairfax *(G-4615)*

Egap Enterprises ....G..... 434 374-9089
Buffalo Junction *(G-2159)*

Everette Publishing LLC ....G..... 757 344-9092
Newport News *(G-9221)*

Everyday Education LLC ....G..... 804 752-2517
Ashland *(G-1411)*

Exchange Publishing.............................F..... 703 644-5184
Springfield *(G-13000)*

Fantalife Publishing LLC......................G..... 703 682-2125
Arlington *(G-962)*

Firefall-Literary ....G..... 703 942-6616
Alexandria *(G-462)*

Follett College Store 743 ....G..... 434 961-5317
Charlottesville *(G-2797)*

Forbz House LLC ....G..... 703 216-1491
Gainesville *(G-5584)*

Forstle LLC ....G..... 540 424-6879
Fredericksburg *(G-5186)*

Fox Hill Editorial LLC...........................G..... 434 971-1835
Charlottesville *(G-2798)*

G F I Associates Inc ....G..... 703 533-8555
Fairfax *(G-4460)*

Gadfly LLC ....G..... 703 282-9448
Leesburg *(G-7276)*

▲ Gedoran America Inc ....G..... 540 723-6628
Winchester *(G-15419)*

Gibson Girl Publishing Co LLC ....G..... 504 261-8107
Virginia Beach *(G-14483)*

Global Health Solutions Inc ....G..... 703 848-2333
Falls Church *(G-4799)*

Godosan Publications Inc ....G..... 540 720-0861
Stafford *(G-13147)*

Golf Guide Inc ....G..... 540 431-5034
Stephenson *(G-13333)*

Gooder Group Inc ....F..... 703 698-7750
Fairfax *(G-4470)*

Guardian Publishing House ....G..... 804 321-2139
Richmond *(G-11606)*

Guide To Caregiving LLC ....G..... 571 213-3845
Round Hill *(G-12379)*

Hanks Indexing ....G..... 434 960-6805
North Garden *(G-10075)*

Harbor House Law Press Inc ....G..... 804 776-7605
Deltaville *(G-4080)*

Harris Publications ....G..... 703 764-9279
Clifton *(G-3671)*

Hartenshield Group Inc ....G..... 302 388-4023
Mc Dowell *(G-8374)*

Henderson Publishing ....G..... 276 964-2291
Pounding Mill *(G-10520)*

High Stakes Writing LLC ....G..... 703 819-5490
Annandale *(G-756)*

Holderby & Bierce Inc ....G..... 434 971-8571
Charlottesville *(G-2645)*

Hollis Books LLC ....G..... 703 855-7759
Alexandria *(G-480)*

Holtzbrinck Publishers LLC ....G..... 540 672-7600
Gordonsville *(G-5907)*

Homeactions LLC ....F..... 703 698-7750
Fairfax *(G-4476)*

Homeland Defense Journal ....G..... 703 622-1187
Arlington *(G-992)*

Hope Springs Media ....G..... 434 574-2031
Prospect *(G-10612)*

Houghton Mifflin Harcourt Pubg ....G..... 540 434-0137
Harrisonburg *(G-6329)*

Houghton Mifflin Harcourt Pubg ....C..... 703 243-2602
Arlington *(G-994)*

Huang Shang Jeo ....G..... 703 471-4457
Herndon *(G-6704)*

Ibfd North America Inc ....G..... 703 442-7757
Vienna *(G-14069)*

IDS Publishing Corporation ....G..... 703 821-2323
Mc Lean *(G-8461)*

Ihs Press ....G..... 877 447-7737
Norfolk *(G-9589)*

In Good Company LLC ....G..... 540 752-1328
Stafford *(G-13153)*

Indigo Pen Publishing LLC ....G..... 888 670-4010
Alexandria *(G-484)*

Inevitable Entertainment LLC ....G..... 757 470-1521
Hampton *(G-6175)*

▲ International Publishers Mktg............F..... 703 661-1586
Sterling *(G-13430)*

Ipaatti Inc ....G..... 703 901-7904
Chantilly *(G-2444)*

J & L Communications Inc ....G..... 434 973-1830
Charlottesville *(G-2650)*

Jackson Enterprises Inc ....G..... 703 527-1118
Arlington *(G-1013)*

Kara Keen LLC ....G..... 973 713-1049
Annandale *(G-763)*

Kendall/Hunt Publishing Co..................G..... 804 285-9411
Mechanicsville *(G-8648)*

Kennedy Projects LLC ....G..... 757 345-0626
Williamsburg *(G-15266)*

Knitting Information ....G..... 804 288-4754
Richmond *(G-11263)*

S I C

Komorebi Press LLC .... G 301 910-5041
  Falls Church *(G-4920)*
Kristina Kathleen Mann .... G 703 282-9166
  Alexandria *(G-510)*
Kuykendall LLC David .... G 804 622-2439
  Midlothian *(G-8842)*
L C M B Inc .... G 804 639-1429
  Moseley *(G-9041)*
Lawriter LLC .... E 434 220-4324
  Charlottesville *(G-2656)*
Leigh Ann Carrasco .... G 703 725-4680
  Mc Lean *(G-8486)*
Lexadyne Publishing Inc .... G 703 779-4998
  Leesburg *(G-7298)*
Lift Hill Media LLC .... G 703 408-4145
  Falls Church *(G-4823)*
Lrj Publishing Group LLC .... G 757 788-6163
  Hampton *(G-6186)*
▲ Macoy Pubg Masonic Sup Co Inc ..... E 804 262-6551
  Richmond *(G-11280)*
Marcy Boys Music .... G 757 247-6222
  Newport News *(G-9290)*
▲ Mariner Media Inc .... F 540 264-0021
  Buena Vista *(G-2146)*
Mindful Media LLC .... G 757 627-5151
  Norfolk *(G-9645)*
Missing Lynk Publishing LLC .... G 757 851-1766
  Hampton *(G-6202)*
Mystique Queen Publishing LLC ..... G 484 250-1131
  Norfolk *(G-9652)*
Mythikos Mommy LLC .... G 703 568-7504
  Fairfax Station *(G-4718)*
▲ Napoleon Books .... G 540 463-6804
  Lexington *(G-7406)*
Natasha Matthew .... G 757 407-1897
  Norfolk *(G-9653)*
Nis Inc .... E 703 323-9170
  Fairfax *(G-4519)*
Omohundro Institute of Early .... E 757 221-1114
  Williamsburg *(G-15285)*
Oneidos LLC .... G 703 819-3860
  Manassas *(G-7985)*
Oppiya Learning Company LLC ..... F 804 296-0141
  Glen Allen *(G-5776)*
Our Journey Publishing .... G 571 606-1574
  Dumfries *(G-4254)*
Personal Selling Power Inc .... E 540 752-7000
  Fredericksburg *(G-5469)*
Potomac Books Inc .... F 703 661-1548
  Dulles *(G-4219)*
Public Utilities Reports Inc .... F 703 847-7720
  Reston *(G-10934)*
R B M Enterprises Inc .... G 804 290-4407
  Glen Allen *(G-5786)*
R R Donnelley & Sons Company ..... B 540 564-3900
  Harrisonburg *(G-6359)*
Rainmaker Publishing LLC .... G 703 385-9761
  Fairfax *(G-4536)*
Rbt Center LLC .... G 703 823-8664
  Alexandria *(G-326)*
Really Great Reading .... F 571 659-2826
  Woodbridge *(G-15792)*
Reconciliation Press .... G 703 743-2416
  Gainesville *(G-5610)*
Rector Visitors of The Univ VA ..... G 434 924-3469
  Charlottesville *(G-2857)*
Rector Visitors of The Univ VA ..... E 434 924-3468
  Charlottesville *(G-2859)*
▲ Reformation Herald Pubg Assn ..... F 540 366-9400
  Roanoke *(G-11994)*
Reward Happiness LLC .... G 703 795-0746
  Falls Church *(G-4866)*
Robbworks LLC .... G 571 218-5532
  Fairfax *(G-4669)*
Rookwood Press Inc .... G 434 971-1835
  Charlottesville *(G-2867)*
Room The Wishing Inc .... G 804 746-0375
  Hanover *(G-6284)*
Round House .... G 804 443-4813
  Champlain *(G-2356)*
Salientcontent LLC .... G 571 286-8480
  Fairfax *(G-4672)*
Sashay Communications LLC .... G 703 304-2862
  Arlington *(G-1161)*
Science of Spirituality .... G 804 633-9987
  Bowling Green *(G-1907)*
Scotties Bavarian Folk Art .... G 540 341-8884
  Warrenton *(G-15049)*
Scripps Enterprises Inc .... F 434 973-3345
  Charlottesville *(G-2691)*

Seven Oaks Albemarle LLC .... G 540 984-3829
  Edinburg *(G-4313)*
Shaper Group .... G 703 680-5551
  Woodbridge *(G-15805)*
Signature Publishing LLC .... G 757 348-9692
  South Chesterfield *(G-12839)*
Silverchair Scnce + Cmmnctons ..... C 434 296-6333
  Charlottesville *(G-2878)*
Skydog Publications .... G 540 989-2167
  Roanoke *(G-12001)*
Slate & Shell LLC .... G 804 381-8713
  Richmond *(G-11384)*
Spence Publishing Co Inc .... G 214 939-1700
  Mc Lean *(G-8555)*
Stampers Bay Publishing LLC ...... G 804 776-9122
  Hartfield *(G-6391)*
▲ Stylus Publishing LLC .... G 703 661-1581
  Sterling *(G-13520)*
Stylus Publishing LLC .... G 703 661-1504
  Sterling *(G-13521)*
Tax Analysts .... C 703 533-4400
  Falls Church *(G-4926)*
Thomson Reuters Corporation ..... G 804 346-5135
  Glen Allen *(G-5811)*
Thought & Expression Co LLC ...... E 405 919-0068
  Mc Lean *(G-8567)*
Transforming Daily Lives .... G 916 990-2299
  Clifton *(G-3677)*
Uniformed Services Almanac .... G 703 241-8100
  Fairfax *(G-4574)*
Vanderbilt Media House LLC .... F 757 515-9242
  Woodstock *(G-15860)*
Virginia Engineer .... G 804 779-3527
  Mechanicsville *(G-8695)*
W Berg Press .... G 757 238-9663
  Suffolk *(G-13781)*
Warwick Publishers Inc .... G 434 846-1200
  Lynchburg *(G-7836)*
Wichaar Inc .... G 703 863-3451
  Fairfax Station *(G-4728)*
Winter Giovanni Llc .... G 757 343-9100
  Norfolk *(G-9796)*
Winterloch Publishing LLC .... G 804 571-2782
  North Chesterfield *(G-10013)*
Wolley Segap International .... G 703 426-5164
  Fairfax *(G-4583)*
Womens Intuition Worldwide .... G 703 404-4357
  Sterling *(G-13563)*
Words To Ponder Pubg Co LLC ..... G 803 567-3692
  Hampton *(G-6273)*
Wyvern Publications .... G 703 670-3527
  Woodbridge *(G-15836)*

2732 Book Printing, Not Publishing

Arabesque Media .... G 703 745-5395
  Fairfax *(G-4410)*
▲ Berryville Graphics Inc .... A 540 955-2750
  Berryville *(G-1671)*
Champs Create A Book .... G 757 369-3879
  Newport News *(G-9197)*
▼ Christian Light Publications ...... E 540 434-0768
  Harrisonburg *(G-6300)*
Collinsville Printing Co .... E 276 666-4400
  Martinsville *(G-8276)*
Jeanette Ann Smith .... G 757 622-0182
  Norfolk *(G-9602)*
La Fleur De Lis LLC .... G 703 753-5690
  Gainesville *(G-5594)*
Lsc Communications Us LLC .... A 540 434-8833
  Rockingham *(G-12259)*
R R Donnelley & Sons Company ..... E 703 279-1662
  Fairfax *(G-4535)*
R R Donnelley & Sons Company ..... C 434 846-7371
  Salem *(G-12560)*
Signs of The Times Apostolate ..... G 703 707-0799
  Herndon *(G-6807)*
Volour Pub .... G 757 547-6483
  Virginia Beach *(G-14926)*
Walsworth Yearbooks VA East ..... G 757 636-7104
  Virginia Beach *(G-14929)*
▲ Xymid LLC .... E 804 423-5798
  Midlothian *(G-8925)*
Xymid LLC .... F 804 744-5229
  South Chesterfield *(G-12829)*

2741 Misc Publishing

10 10 LLC .... G 757 627-4311
  Norfolk *(G-9410)*
1trybe Inc .... G 540 270-6043
  Gainesville *(G-5567)*

2 Cities Press LLC .... G 434 249-6043
  Charlottesville *(G-2719)*
2050community LLC .... G 202 744-6031
  Virginia Beach *(G-14195)*
21st Century AMP LLC .... G 571 345-8990
  Arlington *(G-834)*
23o5 Publishing House .... G 757 738-9309
  Chesapeake *(G-2948)*
247 Publishing Inc .... G 757 639-8856
  Chesapeake *(G-2949)*
3 Degrees Publishing LLC .... G 757 634-3164
  Portsmouth *(G-10386)*
3 Donuts Publishing LLC .... G 703 542-7941
  Chantilly *(G-2524)*
A Creative Mind LLC .... G 757 450-2899
  Norfolk *(G-9413)*
A Simple Life Magazine .... G 276 238-2403
  Woodlawn *(G-15843)*
A1 Service .... G 757 544-0830
  Virginia Beach *(G-14202)*
ABC Graphics .... G 804 368-0276
  Ashland *(G-1361)*
About Chuck Seipp .... G 703 517-0670
  Winchester *(G-15370)*
AC Atlas Publishing .... G 301 980-0711
  Warrenton *(G-14976)*
Access Intelligence LLC .... G 202 296-2814
  Arlington *(G-837)*
Access Publishing Co .... G 804 358-0163
  Richmond *(G-11469)*
Access Reports Inc .... G 434 384-5334
  Lynchburg *(G-7631)*
Accuracy Press Institute .... G 804 869-8577
  Alexandria *(G-117)*
Acorn Press LLC .... G 703 760-0920
  Mc Lean *(G-8385)*
ACS Division Polymer Chemistry ..... G 540 231-3029
  Blacksburg *(G-1720)*
Adta & Co Inc .... F 703 930-9280
  Annandale *(G-728)*
Advertech Press LLC .... G 804 404-8560
  Richmond *(G-11087)*
Aether Press LLC .... G 703 409-5684
  Alexandria *(G-122)*
After Curfew Inc .... G 608 214-1289
  Lynchburg *(G-7636)*
Aftershock Advisors LLC .... G 703 787-0139
  Herndon *(G-6604)*
Against All Oddz Publications ...... G 757 300-4645
  Richmond *(G-11480)*
Agile Writer Press .... G 804 986-2985
  Midlothian *(G-8769)*
Ahf Publishing LLC .... G 804 282-6110
  Richmond *(G-11090)*
Alexis Mya Publishing LLC .... G 540 479-2727
  Spotsylvania *(G-12882)*
Allen Sisson Publishers Rep .... G 804 745-0903
  North Chesterfield *(G-9812)*
Allen Wayne Ltd Arlington .... G 703 321-7414
  Warrenton *(G-14977)*
Allende-El Publishing Co LLC .... G 757 528-9997
  Newport News *(G-9163)*
Allergy Asthma Ntwrk/Mthers As ..... F 800 878-4403
  Vienna *(G-14007)*
Allmoods Enterprises LLC .... G 703 241-8748
  Falls Church *(G-4899)*
Altar Ego Publications .... G 540 933-6530
  Fort Valley *(G-5134)*
Always Morningsong Publishing ..... G 804 530-1392
  South Chesterfield *(G-12794)*
Amadi Publishing LLC .... G 703 329-4535
  Alexandria *(G-409)*
Amari Publications .... G 703 313-0174
  Springfield *(G-12945)*
Amarquis Publications LLC .... G 804 464-7203
  North Chesterfield *(G-9814)*
Ambertone Press Inc .... G 703 866-7715
  Springfield *(G-12946)*
American History Press .... G 540 487-1202
  Staunton *(G-13241)*
American Immgrtion Ctrl Fndtio ..... G 540 468-2022
  Monterey *(G-9002)*
American Media Institute .... G 703 872-7840
  Arlington *(G-853)*
Andes Publishing Co Inc .... G 757 562-5528
  Suffolk *(G-13670)*
Andra ONeil Smith .... G 804 436-3764
  Lancaster *(G-7158)*
Andrea Press .... G 434 960-8026
  Earlysville *(G-4285)*

Angle Valley Press LLC G 540 662-1320
Winchester *(G-15528)*
Anointed For Purpose G 804 651-4427
Norfolk *(G-9442)*
Anxious Bench Music Inc G 757 813-4389
Henrico *(G-6474)*
AO Hathaway Publishing LLC G 804 305-9832
Midlothian *(G-8772)*
Apex Publishers G 703 966-1906
Centreville *(G-2290)*
Apostolos Publishing LLC G 703 656-8036
Bristow *(G-2045)*
Apple Ridge Publishers G 703 597-8523
Quicksburg *(G-10692)*
Apprentice Press G 703 352-5005
Fairfax *(G-4594)*
April Press G 804 551-8463
Henrico *(G-6475)*
Arabelle Publishing LLC G 804 298-5082
Chesterfield *(G-3476)*
Arabesque Media G 703 745-5395
Fairfax *(G-4410)*
Arcamax Publishing Inc G 757 596-9730
Newport News *(G-9170)*
Archipelago Publishers Inc G 434 979-5292
Charlottesville *(G-2590)*
Arhat Media Inc G 703 716-5662
Reston *(G-10791)*
Ascension Publishing LLC G 804 212-5347
Midlothian *(G-8775)*
Ash Press LLC G 757 778-0747
Yorktown *(G-15933)*
Asip Publishing Inc G 804 725-4613
Port Haywood *(G-10381)*
Association Publishing Inc G 757 420-2434
Chesapeake *(G-2985)*
Attn Eric Minton G 703 868-4086
Clifton *(G-3657)*
Axios Media Inc E 703 291-3600
Arlington *(G-869)*
B & G Publishing Inc G 757 463-1104
Virginia Beach *(G-14253)*
B & S Xpress LLC G 434 851-2695
Hurt *(G-6971)*
B J Hart Enterprises Inc G 434 575-7538
South Boston *(G-12750)*
B Team Publications LLC G 757 362-3006
Norfolk *(G-9450)*
Badgerdog Literary Publishing G 757 627-2315
Norfolk *(G-9451)*
Bailey & Sons Publishing Co D G 434 990-9291
Orange *(G-10204)*
Balent-Young Publishing Inc G 540 636-2569
Front Royal *(G-5523)*
Ballpark Publications Inc G 757 271-6197
Bracey *(G-1921)*
Bayfront Media Group LLC G
Virginia Beach *(G-14264)*
Bbk Cnsldted Slutions Svcs LLC G 571 229-2276
Manassas *(G-7920)*
Beauty Publications Inc G 434 296-2161
Charlottesville *(G-2737)*
Bible Believers Press G 703 476-0125
Reston *(G-10799)*
Bible Truth Music G 757 365-9956
Newport News *(G-9179)*
Big Mind Publishing Inc G 703 734-8359
Mc Lean *(G-8398)*
Big Paper Records LLC G 804 381-9278
Glen Allen *(G-5708)*
Bill Klinck Publishing G 540 740-3034
New Market *(G-9140)*
Biohouse Publishing Group Inc G 703 858-1738
Ashburn *(G-1246)*
Bishop Montana Ent G 703 777-8248
Leesburg *(G-7231)*
Blac Rayven Publications G 757 512-4617
Virginia Beach *(G-14285)*
Black Pwdr Artificer Press Inc G 804 366-0562
Colonial Beach *(G-3722)*
Black Room Press LLC G 804 929-8040
Glen Allen *(G-5710)*
Blak Tie Publishing Co LLC G 757 839-6727
Chesapeake *(G-3005)*
Blehert G 703 471-7907
Reston *(G-10808)*
Blinkcloud LLC G 484 429-3340
Alexandria *(G-148)*
Blissful Gardenz Inc G 703 360-2191
Alexandria *(G-425)*
Bloom Publication G 757 373-4402
Norfolk *(G-9467)*
Blucloudradio LLC G 757 812-2380
Norfolk *(G-9468)*
Blue Jeans Publishing LLC G 757 277-9428
Chesapeake *(G-3007)*
Blue Ridge Cold Press Company G 276 229-1661
Hillsville *(G-6886)*
Blue Ridge Digital Pubg LLC G 703 785-3970
Falls Church *(G-4902)*
Blue Ridge Publishing LLC G 540 234-0807
Weyers Cave *(G-15167)*
Bluewater Publishing G 804 695-0400
Gloucester *(G-5838)*
Bluf Military Benefits G 402 315-7831
Alexandria *(G-150)*
Book Arts Press Inc G 434 924-8851
Charlottesville *(G-2747)*
Booky Biz LLC G 434 207-3715
Palmyra *(G-10244)*
Borfski Press G 571 439-9093
Newport News *(G-9183)*
Boutique Qulty Bks Pubg Co Inc G 678 316-4150
Christiansburg *(G-3574)*
Braddock Communications G 703 390-5870
Fairfax *(G-4599)*
Branches Publications LLC G 434 525-0432
Forest *(G-5056)*
Briarwood Publications G 540 489-4692
Rocky Mount *(G-12314)*
Bridge To Biz G 703 942-6441
Springfield *(G-12970)*
Bridgeway Professionals Inc G 561 791-1005
Bristow *(G-2048)*
Brightview Press LLC G 703 743-1430
Gainesville *(G-5573)*
Brinkmann Publishing LLC G 703 461-6991
Alexandria *(G-152)*
Brook Vance Publishing LLC G 703 660-1214
Alexandria *(G-154)*
Brown & Duncan LLC G 832 844-6523
Virginia Beach *(G-14302)*
Brush Fork Press LLC G 202 841-3625
Roanoke *(G-11894)*
Bryce K Long G 757 510-1748
Virginia Beach *(G-14304)*
Bull Ridge Corporation G 540 953-1171
Blacksburg *(G-1727)*
Bulletin News Network Inc E 703 749-0040
Reston *(G-10813)*
Bumble Bee Productions Inc G 757 410-9409
Chesapeake *(G-3017)*
Bunnies Hot Tips LLC G 757 259-9453
Williamsburg *(G-15216)*
Burke Publications G 804 321-1756
Richmond *(G-11514)*
Burnsboks Pubg - Pstshirts LLC G 404 354-6082
Norfolk *(G-9470)*
Burwell Group LLC G 703 732-6341
Arlington *(G-894)*
Byd Music Publishing LLC G 305 423-9577
Richmond *(G-11515)*
Byerly Tshawna G 703 359-5598
Fairfax *(G-4602)*
Cameron Aubernon G 540 251-4363
Christiansburg *(G-3577)*
Canon Publishing LLC G 540 840-1240
Stafford *(G-13127)*
Capital Publishing Corp G 571 214-1659
Falls Church *(G-4769)*
Capitol Excellence Pubg LLC G 571 277-9657
Arlington *(G-901)*
Capitol Net G 703 739-3790
Alexandria *(G-159)*
Capitol Publishing Corporation G 703 532-7535
Falls Church *(G-4771)*
Caranus LLC G 703 241-1683
Arlington *(G-902)*
Carden Jennings Publishing Co E 434 817-2000
Charlottesville *(G-2603)*
Carter Jdub Music G 804 329-1815
Richmond *(G-11150)*
Carters Publishing Company LLC G 804 590-4747
Disputanta *(G-4105)*
Cassican Press LLC G 434 392-4832
Rice *(G-11004)*
Cayambis Music Press LLC G 540 951-3504
Blacksburg *(G-1729)*
Cbe Press LLC G 703 992-6779
Vienna *(G-14023)*
CC & C Desktop Publishing & G 757 393-3606
Portsmouth *(G-10406)*
Cerrahyan Publishing Inc G 757 589-1462
Virginia Beach *(G-14330)*
Champion Publications Inc G 757 580-4068
Chesapeake *(G-3029)*
Champion Publishing Inc G 434 817-7222
Charlottesville *(G-2606)*
Chartman Publications LLC G 252 489-0151
Portsmouth *(G-10407)*
Chelonian Press Inc G 703 734-1160
Vienna *(G-14027)*
Chesapeake & Hudson Inc F 301 834-7170
Rochelle *(G-12232)*
Chocolate Dmnds Pblcations LLC G 804 332-5117
Glen Allen *(G-5713)*
Chris Kennedy Publishing LLC G 757 689-2021
Virginia Beach *(G-14338)*
▼ **Christian Light Publications** E 540 434-0768
Harrisonburg *(G-6300)*
Christian Publications G 703 568-4300
Mc Lean *(G-8406)*
Church Hill Gun Club Pubg LLC G 804 236-0802
Richmond *(G-11531)*
Circle of Hope - Asca Fndation G 800 306-4722
Alexandria *(G-165)*
Circlepoint Publishing LLC G 703 339-1580
Lorton *(G-7473)*
City Publications Charlotte G 434 917-5890
Bracey *(G-1923)*
City Publications Richmond G 804 621-0911
Mechanicsville *(G-8611)*
Classico Publishing LLC G 540 310-0067
Fredericksburg *(G-5179)*
Clear Vision Publishing G 757 753-9422
Newport News *(G-9200)*
Clearedjobsnet Inc G 703 871-0037
Falls Church *(G-4905)*
Clifton Creek Press Inc G 703 786-9180
Clifton *(G-3661)*
Cold Front Music LLC G 703 398-6187
Lorton *(G-7475)*
Collecting Concepts Inc E 804 285-0994
Richmond *(G-11162)*
Columbia Books Inc F 800 677-3789
Arlington *(G-915)*
Communications Concepts Inc F 703 643-2200
Springfield *(G-12978)*
Compass Publications Inc G 703 524-3136
Arlington *(G-917)*
Connoisseur Publishing G 303 437-5099
Herndon *(G-6644)*
Conversations Publishing LLC G 804 698-5922
Richmond *(G-11540)*
Coquina Press LLC G 571 577-7550
Purcellville *(G-10657)*
Corrinne Callins G 202 780-6233
Springfield *(G-12982)*
Coy Tiger Publishing LLC G 703 221-8064
Triangle *(G-13889)*
Creative Education & Pubg G 703 856-7005
Falls Church *(G-4778)*
Creative Mnds Publications LLC G 804 740-6010
Richmond *(G-11169)*
Creative Passions G 540 908-7549
Singers Glen *(G-12699)*
Crossing Trails Publication G 703 590-4449
Woodbridge *(G-15677)*
Culpeper Commercial Printers G 540 825-0771
Culpeper *(G-3883)*
Cuthbert Publishing LLC G 540 840-7218
Fredericksburg *(G-5269)*
CWC Publishing Co LLC G 540 439-3851
Midland *(G-8751)*
Dagnewcompany Inc F 703 835-0827
Alexandria *(G-439)*
▲ **Dal Publishing** G 757 422-6577
Virginia Beach *(G-14384)*
Damselwings Press G 703 919-4230
Vienna *(G-14034)*
Dap Enterprises Inc G 757 921-3576
Williamsburg *(G-15229)*
Dap Incorporated G 757 921-3576
Newport News *(G-9214)*
Data-Clear LLC G 703 499-3816
Arlington *(G-929)*
Datis LLC G 757 961-7498
Virginia Beach *(G-14389)*
David A Einhorn G 703 356-6218
Falls Church *(G-4782)*

SIC

David Burns.............................G...... 703 644-4612
Springfield (G-12988)

David Kipps.............................G...... 540 948-4024
Aroda (G-1225)

Davis Publishing Company.............G...... 434 363-2780
Appomattox (G-808)

Decision Point Tech LLC...............G...... 757 286-1065
Norfolk (G-9523)

Defee LLC................................G...... 757 645-4358
Williamsburg (G-15231)

Dementi Milestone Pubg Inc...........G...... 804 784-5151
Manakin Sabot (G-7898)

Destiny 11 Publications LLC...........G...... 804 814-3019
North Chesterfield (G-9858)

Devanezdaypublishing Co..............G...... 757 493-1634
Virginia Beach (G-14403)

Dewey Publications Inc.................G...... 703 524-1355
Arlington (G-939)

Digi Quick Print Inc....................G...... 703 671-9600
Alexandria (G-187)

Discovery Map...........................G...... 703 346-7166
Alexandria (G-190)

Divinely Inspired Press LLC...........G...... 703 763-3790
Manassas (G-8058)

Docdirect Publishing LLC..............G...... 757 237-1106
Chesapeake (G-3069)

Dogwood Logic Inc.....................G...... 540 557-7689
Blacksburg (G-1733)

Doite Media LLC........................G...... 703 594-1322
Broadlands (G-2076)

Dominion Enterprises...................E...... 757 351-7000
Norfolk (G-9529)

Dominion Press Winery LLC............G...... 703 395-5109
Alexandria (G-449)

Dominion Production.....................G...... 804 247-4106
Richmond (G-11564)

Donald N Jensen.........................G...... 202 577-9892
Alexandria (G-193)

Donley Technology.......................G...... 804 224-9427
Colonial Beach (G-3724)

Donning Publishers Inc..................F...... 757 497-1789
Virginia Beach (G-14411)

Doublethink News LLC...................G...... 434 466-2092
Charlottesville (G-2785)

Downtown Writing and Press...........G...... 540 907-9732
Fredericksburg (G-5184)

Dr Jk Longevity LLC.....................G...... 202 304-0896
Vienna (G-14041)

Dream Catcher Enterprises LLC........G...... 540 338-8273
Hamilton (G-6056)

Dream Dog Productions LLC...........G...... 703 980-0908
Springfield (G-12995)

Dreamscape Publishing..................G...... 757 717-2734
Chesapeake (G-3076)

Druh-Ke LLC.............................G...... 757 274-3117
Suffolk (G-13701)

Dtc Press LLC...........................G...... 703 255-9891
Oakton (G-10145)

Dtwelve Enterprise LLC.................G...... 757 837-0452
Virginia Beach (G-14415)

Duck Publishing LLC....................G...... 609 636-8431
Richmond (G-11193)

Dust Gold Publishing LLC...............G...... 540 828-5110
Richmond (G-11570)

DWS Publicity LLC......................G...... 540 330-3763
Roanoke (G-12079)

E H Publishing Company In.............G...... 434 645-1722
Crewe (G-3812)

Editorial Inspirations LLC...............G...... 703 627-0023
Montpelier (G-9016)

Edward Allen Publishing LLC...........G...... 757 768-5544
Hampton (G-6135)

Eiger Press...............................G...... 757 430-1831
Virginia Beach (G-14435)

Eileen Carlson...........................G...... 757 339-9900
Virginia Beach (G-14436)

Elan Publishing Inc......................G...... 434 973-1828
Charlottesville (G-2622)

Elizabeth Bailey.........................G...... 804 265-8764
Sutherland (G-13803)

▲ Elizabeth Neville......................G...... 703 409-4217
Arlington (G-956)

Ember Systems LLC....................G...... 540 327-1984
Winchester (G-15539)

Empire Publishing Corporation.........G...... 804 440-5379
Richmond (G-11575)

Employment Guide.......................G...... 703 580-7586
Woodbridge (G-15693)

Empress Publishing LLC.................G...... 856 630-8198
Petersburg (G-10319)

Empress World Publishing LLC.........G...... 757 471-3806
Virginia Beach (G-14446)

Epic Books Press........................G...... 804 557-3111
Quinton (G-10695)

Faith Publishing LLC....................G...... 540 632-3608
Roanoke (G-12085)

Fast Ra Xpress LLC.....................G...... 804 514-5696
Richmond (G-11585)

Fat Cat Publishings LLC.................G...... 804 368-0378
Ashland (G-1415)

Feat Little Publishing LLC..............G...... 757 594-9265
Newport News (G-9225)

Federated Publications Inc.............D...... 703 854-6000
Mc Lean (G-8428)

Fennec Publishing LLC..................G...... 703 934-6781
Fairfax (G-4622)

Fiction-Atlas Press LLC.................G...... 423 845-0243
Bristol (G-1979)

Financial Press LLC.....................G...... 804 928-6366
Richmond (G-11210)

First Colony Press.......................G...... 757 496-0362
Virginia Beach (G-14464)

First Light Publishing Inc...............G...... 804 639-0659
Chesterfield (G-3500)

Five Ponds Press........................G...... 804 740-5867
Henrico (G-6511)

Flat Hat..................................G...... 757 221-3283
Williamsburg (G-15245)

Forel Publishing Co LLC................G...... 703 772-8081
Woodbridge (G-15705)

Four Leaf Publishing LLC...............G...... 703 440-1304
Springfield (G-13005)

Fowlkes Eagle Publishing LLC.........G...... 757 673-8424
Chesapeake (G-3109)

Freedom Forge Press LLC.............G...... 757 784-1038
Hillsboro (G-6867)

Freedom To Destiny Pubg LLC.........G...... 757 617-8286
Chesapeake (G-3111)

Freeport Press..........................G...... 540 788-9745
Midland (G-8755)

Freshwter Parl Media Group LLC.......G...... 757 785-5483
Norfolk (G-9559)

Frog Valley Publishing..................G...... 540 338-3224
Round Hill (G-12378)

Ft Communications Inc..................G...... 804 739-8555
Midlothian (G-8820)

Gaia Communications LLC.............G...... 703 370-5527
Alexandria (G-210)

Game Day Publications LLC............G...... 804 314-7526
Mechanicsville (G-8626)

Gameplan Press Inc.....................G...... 703 521-1546
Arlington (G-974)

◆ Gannett River States Pubg Corp.....A...... 703 284-6000
Mc Lean (G-8443)

Gartman Letter Limited Company.......G...... 757 238-9508
Suffolk (G-13714)

Gary Burns..............................G...... 703 992-4617
Gainesville (G-5585)

Gay G-Spot LLC........................G...... 650 429-8233
Arlington (G-976)

Genesis Professional Training...........G...... 804 818-3611
Chesterfield (G-3502)

Get It LLC................................F...... 703 625-6844
Alexandria (G-215)

Giant Publishing & Co...................G...... 703 750-6447
Fairfax (G-4467)

Gifted Education Press..................G...... 703 369-5017
Manassas (G-8075)

Gilgit Press LLC.........................G...... 804 359-2524
Richmond (G-11600)

Gilstrap Inc John........................G...... 703 961-9413
Fairfax (G-4468)

Girls With Crabs LLC....................G...... 540 623-9502
Spotsylvania (G-12891)

Give More Media Inc....................G...... 804 762-4500
Richmond (G-11601)

Gjhmotivate.............................G...... 757 487-5486
Chesapeake (G-3120)

GL Hollowell Publishing LLC............G...... 804 796-5968
Chester (G-3419)

Gladstone Media Corporation..........G...... 434 293-8471
Keswick (G-7047)

Glen Allen Press LLC....................G...... 804 747-1776
Glen Allen (G-5737)

Glencourse Press.......................G...... 703 860-2416
Herndon (G-6685)

Global Business Pages..................G...... 855 825-2124
Richmond (G-11603)

Global Concern Inc......................G...... 703 425-5861
Springfield (G-13011)

Global Gospel Publishers...............G...... 434 582-5049
Lynchburg (G-7721)

Gmg Ghostwriting.......................G...... 718 578-8622
Arlington (G-982)

Godosan Publications Inc...............G...... 540 720-0861
Stafford (G-13147)

Golden Quill Editorial Svcs.............G...... 240 838-0464
Arlington (G-984)

Gooder Group Inc.......................F...... 703 698-7750
Fairfax (G-4470)

Goodlion Music & Publishing...........G...... 757 875-0000
Newport News (G-9237)

Gov Panda LLC.........................G...... 571 275-6370
Herndon (G-6688)

Govsearch LLC..........................E...... 703 340-1308
Mclean (G-8587)

Gracenotes..............................G...... 703 825-7922
Fairfax Station (G-4710)

Grateful Press LLC......................G...... 434 202-1161
Charlottesville (G-2806)

Grayson Express........................G...... 276 773-9173
Independence (G-6983)

Gregory McRrae Publishing.............G...... 808 238-9907
Richmond (G-11225)

Groundhog Poetry Press LLC..........G...... 540 366-8460
Roanoke (G-11929)

Guynn Group LLC.......................G...... 804 288-0191
Richmond (G-11228)

Gwen Graber & Associates.............G...... 703 356-9239
Mc Lean (G-8454)

Gwen Nappi.............................G...... 703 329-4836
Alexandria (G-226)

Hamby-Stern Publishing LLC...........G...... 703 425-3719
Burke (G-2190)

Harris Connect LLC......................B...... 757 965-8000
Norfolk (G-9572)

Heart Speaks Publishing LLC..........G...... 803 403-4266
Chesapeake (G-3130)

Heart Star Press LLC....................G...... 540 479-6882
Fredericksburg (G-5440)

Heartseeking LLC.......................G...... 305 778-8040
Stuarts Draft (G-13648)

Heartstrings Press LLC..................G...... 804 462-0884
Lancaster (G-7162)

Hechos Vios Publishing Inc.............G...... 703 496-7019
Manassas (G-7951)

Hedrick Music Inc.......................G...... 540 354-2139
Roanoke (G-12101)

Helen Heinmiller.........................G...... 484 459-4425
Wirtz (G-15613)

Hemlock Design Group Inc.............G...... 703 765-0379
Alexandria (G-477)

Herald Press.............................F...... 540 434-6701
Harrisonburg (G-6328)

Hess Publications.......................G...... 540 771-7515
Berryville (G-1681)

Hey Frase LLC...........................G...... 202 372-5453
Arlington (G-991)

High Impact Music For You LLC........G...... 757 915-8696
Richmond (G-11239)

High Tide Publications Inc..............G...... 804 815-6805
Deltaville (G-4081)

Higher Lving Publications Corp.........G...... 804 789-0592
Mechanicsville (G-8636)

Higher Press LLC........................G...... 703 944-1521
Woodbridge (G-15722)

Hirsch Communication..................G...... 703 960-3649
Alexandria (G-478)

Hmt Publishers LLC.....................G...... 540 839-5628
Hot Springs (G-6946)

Hollawood Publishing LLC..............G...... 804 353-3310
Richmond (G-11240)

Holtzman Express.......................G...... 305 347-4000
Winchester (G-15424)

Homeactions LLC.......................F...... 703 698-7750
Fairfax (G-4476)

Horton Publishing Co....................G...... 703 281-6963
Vienna (G-14067)

How High Publishing LLC...............G...... 703 729-9589
Ashburn (G-1293)

Hr Publishing Group LLC................G...... 757 364-0245
Virginia Beach (G-14531)

Hypatia-Rose Press LLC.................G...... 757 819-2559
Virginia Beach (G-14536)

Ideaphoria Press LLC....................G...... 804 272-6231
North Chesterfield (G-10020)

Ideation Web Studios LLC...............G...... 757 333-3021
Chesapeake (G-3140)

IDS Publishing Corporation.............G...... 703 821-2323
Mc Lean (G-8461)

Immortal Publishing LLC ....G....... 540 465-3368
Strasburg *(G-13583)*

Inamod Group LLC ....G....... 703 626-2453
Alexandria *(G-483)*

Independence Publishing Tlr ....G....... 757 761-8579
Richmond *(G-11246)*

Independent Holiness Publi ....G....... 276 964-2824
Pounding Mill *(G-10521)*

Indian Creek Express Inc ....G....... 434 927-5900
Sandy Level *(G-12647)*

Indigo Press ....G....... 757 705-2619
Virginia Beach *(G-14544)*

Inertia Publishing LLC ....G....... 703 754-9617
Gainesville *(G-5590)*

Infinity Publications LLC ....G....... 540 331-8713
Woodstock *(G-15855)*

Infinity Publishing Group LLC ....G....... 757 874-0135
Newport News *(G-9257)*

Infobase Publishers Inc ....F 703 327-8470
South Riding *(G-12868)*

Infosoft Publishing Co ....G....... 661 288-1414
Chesapeake *(G-3142)*

Inner Peace Warriors LLC ....G....... 703 830-7680
Clifton *(G-3672)*

Inscribe Press LLC ....G....... 707 239-8404
Fredericksburg *(G-5303)*

Inside Washington Publisher ....G....... 703 416-8500
Arlington *(G-1004)*

Insite Publishing LLC ....G....... 757 301-9617
Virginia Beach *(G-14549)*

Inspiration Publications ....G....... 540 465-3878
Strasburg *(G-13584)*

Int Diagnostic Syst ....G....... 414 477-8035
Mc Lean *(G-8465)*

Integra Music Group ....G....... 434 821-3796
Lynchburg *(G-7743)*

Inter-American Group Inc ....G....... 202 255-4528
Mc Lean *(G-8467)*

Ios Press Inc ....G....... 703 830-6300
Clifton *(G-3673)*

Iron Lady Press LLC ....G....... 540 898-7310
Spotsylvania *(G-12899)*

Ivory Dog Press LLC ....G....... 540 353-3939
Roanoke *(G-11945)*

Ivy House Publishing LLC ....G....... 434 295-5015
Charlottesville *(G-2816)*

J-Alm Publishing ....G....... 703 385-9766
Oakton *(G-10152)*

Jake Publishing Inc ....G....... 757 377-6771
Virginia Beach *(G-14562)*

Jamerrill Publishing Co LLC ....G....... 540 908-5234
Timberville *(G-13850)*

James Doctor Press Inc ....G....... 703 476-0579
Herndon *(G-6716)*

James Kacian ....F 540 722-2156
Winchester *(G-15550)*

Jamesgate Press LLC ....G....... 703 892-5621
Arlington *(G-1014)*

Janice Osthus ....G....... 571 212-2247
Fairfax *(G-4485)*

Jlb Publishing Inc ....F 804 443-0330
Tappahannock *(G-13818)*

JM Walker Publishing LLC ....G....... 757 340-6659
Virginia Beach *(G-14570)*

Jmr Gaines ....G....... 540 370-1723
Fredericksburg *(G-5445)*

Kaah Express ....G....... 703 379-0770
Falls Church *(G-4814)*

Kaleidoscope Publishing Ltd ....E 703 821-0571
Mc Lean *(G-8477)*

Kaliopa Publishing LLC ....G....... 703 522-7663
Arlington *(G-1020)*

Kapok Press LLC ....G....... 540 372-2033
Fredericksburg *(G-5198)*

Keane Writers Publishing LLC ....G....... 804 435-2618
Kilmarnock *(G-7071)*

Kenway Express ....G....... 804 652-1922
Richmond *(G-11643)*

Kilmartin Jones Group LLC ....G....... 703 232-1531
Manassas *(G-8094)*

Knights Press LLC ....G....... 703 913-5336
Burke *(G-2191)*

Knowlera Media LLC ....G....... 703 757-5444
Great Falls *(G-5963)*

Knowwho Inc ....G....... 703 619-1544
Alexandria *(G-507)*

▲ Korea Times Washington DC Inc .....E 703 941-8001
Annandale *(G-765)*

Kristina Kathleen Mann ....G....... 703 282-9166
Alexandria *(G-510)*

L D Publications Group ....G....... 703 623-6799
Springfield *(G-13035)*

La Publishing ....G....... 757 650-8364
Moseley *(G-9042)*

Lady Press Creations LLC ....G....... 757 745-7473
Carrollton *(G-2244)*

Lagniappe Publishing LLC ....G....... 804 739-0795
Midlothian *(G-8843)*

Larissa Leclair ....G....... 202 270-8039
Arlington *(G-1026)*

Larson Baker Publishing LLC ....G....... 703 644-4243
Springfield *(G-13037)*

Lauren E Thronson ....G....... 703 536-3625
Mc Lean *(G-8482)*

Lawton Pubg & Translation LLC ....G....... 804 367-4028
Richmond *(G-11647)*

Lee Street Publishing LLC ....G....... 540 459-8566
Woodstock *(G-15856)*

Left Field Media ....G....... 703 980-4710
Fairfax *(G-4646)*

Legacy Word Publishing LLC ....G....... 941 915-4730
Alexandria *(G-515)*

Leisure Publishing Inc ....E 540 989-6138
Roanoke *(G-11955)*

Lennah Press LLC ....G....... 571 235-4809
Ashburn *(G-1306)*

Lewis Printing Company ....E 804 648-2000
Richmond *(G-11652)*

Li Ailin ....G....... 573 808-7280
Arlington *(G-1033)*

Libelli LLC ....G....... 757 373-9845
Virginia Beach *(G-14607)*

Life Sentence Publishing LLC ....G....... 703 300-0474
Alexandria *(G-517)*

Light Designs Publishing Co ....G....... 804 261-6900
Glen Allen *(G-5763)*

Lines Up Inc ....G....... 703 842-3762
Arlington *(G-1036)*

Linley Press LLC ....G....... 561 245-1511
Ashburn *(G-1307)*

Little King Publishing ....G....... 540 809-0291
Spotsylvania *(G-12902)*

LNG Publishing Co Inc ....G....... 703 536-0800
Falls Church *(G-4825)*

Local News Now LLC ....G....... 703 348-0583
Arlington *(G-1041)*

Local Voice ....G....... 757 565-1079
Williamsburg *(G-15273)*

Look Up Publications LLC ....G....... 703 542-2736
Brambleton *(G-1929)*

Loony Moose Publishing LLC ....G....... 703 727-3309
Ashburn *(G-1311)*

Looseleaf Publications LLC ....G....... 757 221-8250
Williamsburg *(G-15274)*

Lost Clipper Enterprises LLC ....G....... 310 386-0972
Purcellville *(G-10668)*

Lower Lane Publishing LLC ....G....... 703 865-5968
Vienna *(G-14086)*

Lvrcshull Incorporated ....G....... 757 995-3931
Suffolk *(G-13735)*

M & M Enterprise LLC ....G....... 804 499-0087
Richmond *(G-11661)*

Macemedia Inc ....F 804 288-5321
Glen Allen *(G-5766)*

Macmillan Holdings LLC ....E 888 330-8477
Gordonsville *(G-5913)*

Madinah Publs & Distrs Inc ....G....... 804 839-8073
North Chesterfield *(G-9918)*

Maggies Rags ....G....... 540 961-1755
Blacksburg *(G-1757)*

Magic and Memories Press LLC ....G....... 703 849-0921
Oakton *(G-10155)*

Magnet Directories Inc ....G....... 281 251-6640
Unionville *(G-13964)*

Magpie Design LLC ....G....... 703 975-5818
Reston *(G-10893)*

Main Gate Publishing Co LLC ....G....... 804 744-2202
Chesterfield *(G-3513)*

Majestic Marketing LLC ....G....... 804 210-7667
Richmond *(G-11282)*

Manassas Consulting Svcs Inc ....G....... 703 346-1358
Manassas *(G-8104)*

Marden Press Printvertise Inc ....G....... 571 295-5322
Ashburn *(G-1316)*

Market This LLC ....G....... 804 382-9220
Glen Allen *(G-5767)*

Masstransit Publishing LLC ....G....... 703 205-2419
Falls Church *(G-4827)*

Mastermind LLC ....G....... 757 379-5215
Yorktown *(G-15980)*

Match Point Press ....G....... 703 548-4202
Alexandria *(G-271)*

Media Africa Inc ....G....... 703 260-6494
Leesburg *(G-7311)*

Media Press ....G....... 703 241-9188
Chantilly *(G-2462)*

Media Relations ....G....... 703 993-8780
Fairfax *(G-4653)*

Megaphone LLC ....E 703 594-7623
Reston *(G-10897)*

Melamedia LLC ....G....... 703 704-5665
Alexandria *(G-525)*

Meltingearth ....G....... 703 395-5855
Herndon *(G-6746)*

▲ Mercury Learning and Info LLC ....G....... 800 232-0223
Dulles *(G-4209)*

Merrill Press ....G....... 571 257-6273
Alexandria *(G-529)*

Merriman Publishing LLC ....G....... 540 370-1852
Fredericksburg *(G-5458)*

Michael Chung MD ....G....... 443 722-5314
Annandale *(G-774)*

Micro Media Communication Inc ....G....... 540 345-2197
Roanoke *(G-12136)*

Mid-Atlantic Printers Ltd ....D 434 369-6633
Altavista *(G-636)*

Mill Creek Press LLC ....G....... 703 638-8395
Alexandria *(G-276)*

Miller Publishing ....G....... 804 901-2315
Highland Springs *(G-6854)*

Miranda Publishing Compan ....G....... 703 207-9499
Falls Church *(G-4832)*

Misra Publishing LLC ....G....... 703 821-2985
Mc Lean *(G-8503)*

Mofat Publishing LLC ....G....... 540 915-5847
Blue Ridge *(G-1852)*

Mofat Publishing LLC ....G....... 540 251-1660
Roanoke *(G-11969)*

Mojo Castle Press LLC ....G....... 703 946-8946
Gainesville *(G-5598)*

Momensity LLC ....G....... 804 247-2811
Stafford *(G-13177)*

Moms Choice LLC ....G....... 757 410-9409
Chesapeake *(G-3211)*

Monday Morning Press LLC ....G....... 804 869-5020
Moseley *(G-9043)*

Monstracity Press ....G....... 703 791-2759
Manassas *(G-8111)*

Mookind Press LLC ....G....... 703 920-1884
Arlington *(G-1067)*

Moon Consortium LLC ....G....... 571 408-9570
Mc Lean *(G-8506)*

Moonlight Publishing Group LLC ....G....... 703 242-0978
Vienna *(G-14100)*

Moss Marketing Company Inc ....G....... 804 794-0654
Midlothian *(G-8862)*

Motley Fool LLC ....G....... 703 838-3665
Alexandria *(G-284)*

Motley Fool Holdings Inc ....G....... 703 838-3665
Alexandria *(G-285)*

Mount Carmel Publishing LLC ....G....... 703 838-2109
Woodbridge *(G-15751)*

MPS Return Center ....G....... 540 672-0792
Orange *(G-10221)*

Mujahid Fnu ....G....... 646 693-2762
Alexandria *(G-536)*

Muse Writers Center ....G....... 757 818-9880
Norfolk *(G-9651)*

Music Publishers America LLC ....G....... 917 406-4425
White Stone *(G-15188)*

Mvmt Inc ....G....... 804 356-6520
Midlothian *(G-8865)*

Mybodymyworship ....G....... 703 669-2901
Leesburg *(G-7317)*

Myboys3 Press ....G....... 804 379-6964
Midlothian *(G-8866)*

Mystery Goose Press LLC ....G....... 540 347-3609
Warrenton *(G-15037)*

Mystic Post Press LLC ....G....... 703 867-3447
Alexandria *(G-540)*

Mythos Publishing LLC ....G....... 703 531-0795
Oakton *(G-10159)*

N A D A Services Corporation ....C 703 821-7000
Mc Lean *(G-8508)*

Namax Music LLC ....G....... 804 271-9535
Richmond *(G-11054)*

Nariad Publishing ....G....... 973 650-8948
Glen Allen *(G-5774)*

Nathaniel Hoffelder ....G....... 571 406-2689
Woodbridge *(G-15753)*

National Institute of Bus Mgt ....G....... 703 394-4921
Falls Church *(G-4835)*

National Intelligence Eductn P ....G....... 703 866-0832
Springfield *(G-13056)*

National Review Institute ....G....... 202 679-7330
Arlington *(G-1071)*

Naylor Cmg.....................G....... 703 934-4714
Mc Lean *(G-8510)*

Neevarpt Productions LLC ....G....... 571 549-1169
Manassas *(G-7982)*

Neighborhood Sports LLC ....G....... 804 282-8033
Richmond *(G-11302)*

Neither Ngex ....G....... 408 676-6439
Chantilly *(G-2467)*

New Look Press LLC ....G....... 804 530-0836
Chester *(G-3439)*

New Paradigm Publishing LLC ....G....... 757 423-3385
Norfolk *(G-9661)*

New Town Holdings Inc ....G....... 703 471-6666
Reston *(G-10907)*

Newswise Inc..................E....... 434 296-9417
Palmyra *(G-10251)*

Niche Publications LLC ....G....... 757 620-2631
Chesapeake *(G-3218)*

Nine-Ten Press LLC ....G....... 804 727-9135
Richmond *(G-11690)*

Ninoska M Marcano ....G....... 202 604-8864
Fairfax *(G-4518)*

Nis Inc ....E....... 703 323-9170
Fairfax *(G-4519)*

North Garden Publishing ....G....... 540 580-2501
Roanoke *(G-11975)*

North Lakeside Pubg Hse LLC ....G....... 757 650-3596
Virginia Beach *(G-14684)*

North South Partners LLC ....E....... 804 213-0600
Richmond *(G-11307)*

North Star Press ....G....... 540 967-5093
Louisa *(G-7562)*

Northampton House Pre ....G....... 201 893-1826
Franktown *(G-5165)*

Northlight Publishing Co ....G....... 804 344-8500
Richmond *(G-11694)*

Nottoway River Publications ....G....... 804 737-7395
Sandston *(G-12626)*

Nova Maris Press ....G....... 434 975-0501
Charlottesville *(G-2667)*

NRC Publishing Virginia LLC ....G....... 703 407-0868
Fairfax *(G-4522)*

Number 6 Publishing LLC ....G....... 703 360-6054
Alexandria *(G-545)*

Oaklea Press Inc ....G....... 804 288-2683
Richmond *(G-11311)*

Oakton Press ....G....... 703 359-6800
Oakton *(G-10161)*

Oberons Forge Press LLC ....G....... 703 434-9275
Sterling *(G-13463)*

ODonnell Susannah Cassedy ....G....... 703 470-8572
Falls Church *(G-4849)*

Ogden Directories Inc..............G....... 540 375-6524
Roanoke *(G-11977)*

Olde Souls Press LLC ....G....... 434 242-7348
Ruckersville *(G-12407)*

One Wish Publishing LLC ....G....... 571 285-4227
Woodbridge *(G-15766)*

Online Biose Inc.................G....... 703 758-6672
Reston *(G-10914)*

Online Publishing & Mktg LLC ....G....... 540 463-2057
Lexington *(G-7410)*

Onthefly Pictures LLC ....G....... 757 339-1520
Portsmouth *(G-10465)*

Ooska News Corp ....G....... 540 724-1750
Warrenton *(G-15040)*

Open Tech Inc ....G....... 703 738-6662
Blacksburg *(G-1777)*

Ostrich Press LLC ....G....... 703 779-7580
Leesburg *(G-7322)*

Outl T Infomarket LLC ....G....... 703 927-1346
Arlington *(G-1092)*

Outthink Corporation ....G....... 434 426-7706
Lynchburg *(G-7779)*

Oval LLC.....................G....... 757 389-3777
Woodbridge *(G-15768)*

Pacem Publishing ....G....... 757 214-4800
Virginia Beach *(G-14708)*

Paddy Publications LLC ....G....... 703 402-2233
Fairfax *(G-4659)*

Page Letterpress LLC ....G....... 866 540-7243
Richmond *(G-11704)*

Page Publications LLC ....G....... 804 733-8636
Sutherland *(G-13804)*

Pages Publishing LLC ....G....... 434 296-0891
Charlottesville *(G-2671)*

Painting Pages Publishing LLC ....G....... 571 266-9529
Leesburg *(G-7323)*

Pandamonk Publishing LLC ....G....... 571 528-1500
Alexandria *(G-305)*

Paperclip Media Inc ....G....... 703 323-9170
Fairfax *(G-4529)*

Paperless Publishing Corp ....G....... 540 552-5882
Blacksburg *(G-1778)*

Paqueteria Express Inc ....G....... 703 330-4580
Manassas *(G-7987)*

Parkgate Press ....G....... 607 280-2364
Falls Church *(G-4854)*

Pastime Publications LLC ....G....... 724 961-2922
Virginia Beach *(G-14711)*

Patriotic Publications LLC ....G....... 804 814-3017
Ruther Glen *(G-12460)*

Pawprint Publishing LLC ....G....... 434 985-3876
Stanardsville *(G-13227)*

Paycock Press LLC ....G....... 703 525-9296
Arlington *(G-1101)*

◆ Payne Publishers Inc ....D....... 703 631-9033
Manassas *(G-7988)*

Pb & J Publishing LLC ....G....... 703 903-9561
Mc Lean *(G-8524)*

Pbp Solutions LLC ....G....... 202 999-8101
Reston *(G-10923)*

Peace Justice Publications LLC ....G....... 540 349-7862
Warrenton *(G-15043)*

Peak Development Resources LLC......G....... 804 233-3707
Richmond *(G-11711)*

Peek—boo Pubg Group Brnd Lcen ......G....... 703 259-8816
Alexandria *(G-307)*

Pennrose Publishing LLC ....G....... 757 631-0579
Virginia Beach *(G-14716)*

Penny Trail Press LLC ....G....... 757 644-5349
Wakefield *(G-14969)*

Perrone Publishing LLC ....G....... 434 962-6694
Palmyra *(G-10254)*

Peterson Idea Consortium Inc ....G....... 804 651-8242
Ashland *(G-1475)*

Pg Games Publishing LLC ....G....... 870 637-4380
Hampton *(G-6216)*

Philip Miles ....G....... 703 760-9832
Mc Lean *(G-8528)*

Phuble Inc....................F....... 443 388-0657
Virginia Beach *(G-14721)*

Pierce Publishing ....G....... 434 386-5667
Lynchburg *(G-7786)*

Pigtale Press LLC ....G....... 703 753-7572
Gainesville *(G-5608)*

Pilinut Press Inc ....G....... 540 347-6295
Warrenton *(G-15044)*

Pillar Publishing & Co LLC ....G....... 804 640-1963
Richmond *(G-11716)*

Pink Press Dior LLC ....G....... 703 781-0345
Fort Belvoir *(G-5117)*

Pink Shoe Publishing ....G....... 757 277-1948
Virginia Beach *(G-14722)*

Pionk Enterprises Intl LLC ....G....... 571 425-8179
Manassas *(G-8129)*

Piper Publishing LLC ....G....... 804 432-9015
Midlothian *(G-8879)*

Piquant Press LLC ....G....... 804 379-3856
Powhatan *(G-10565)*

Pitchstone LLC ....G....... 434 296-2384
Charlottesville *(G-2677)*

Plan B Press ....G....... 215 732-2663
Alexandria *(G-551)*

Pleasant Run Pubg Svcs LLC ....G....... 757 229-8510
Williamsburg *(G-15296)*

Plow Shear Press LLC ....G....... 757 346-8821
Virginia Beach *(G-14726)*

Pluto Gone LLC ....G....... 804 719-3076
Suffolk *(G-13752)*

Poetica Publishing Company ....G....... 757 617-0821
Norfolk *(G-9691)*

Poinsett Publications Inc ....G....... 757 378-2856
Williamsburg *(G-15297)*

Poisoned Publishing ....G....... 540 755-2956
Locust Grove *(G-7450)*

Polaris Press LLC ....G....... 703 680-6060
Woodbridge *(G-15776)*

Polymnia LLC ....G....... 434 422-7842
Charlottesville *(G-2678)*

Portfolio Publication ....G....... 703 802-8676
Chantilly *(G-2481)*

Positive Pasta Publishing LLC ....G....... 804 385-0151
Glen Allen *(G-5780)*

Possibilities Publishing ....G....... 703 585-0934
Burke *(G-2198)*

Postkite LLC ....G....... 202 230-1472
Burke *(G-2199)*

Prepare Him Room Pubg LLC ....G....... 703 909-1147
Purcellville *(G-10674)*

Press 4 Time Tees LLC ....G....... 434 446-6633
Scottsburg *(G-12656)*

Press Enduring ....G....... 540 462-2920
Lexington *(G-7412)*

Press Out Poverty ....G....... 703 691-4329
Fairfax *(G-4531)*

Press Start LLC ....G....... 571 264-1220
Crozet *(G-3848)*

Presswardthemark Media Publish ......G....... 757 807-2232
Virginia Beach *(G-14737)*

Print Store LLC ....G....... 703 821-2201
Falls Church *(G-4858)*

Pro Publishers LLC ....G....... 434 250-6463
Danville *(G-4033)*

Probusiness Publishing LLC ....G....... 571 216-3385
Alexandria *(G-558)*

Profit From Publicity LLC ....G....... 703 409-3630
Fairfax *(G-4534)*

Prolific Purchasing Properties ....G....... 434 329-1476
Lynchburg *(G-7792)*

Prospect Publishing LLC ....G....... 571 435-0241
Alexandria *(G-319)*

Prosperity Publishing Inc ....G....... 757 339-9900
Virginia Beach *(G-14745)*

Protestant Church-Owned ....G....... 502 569-5067
Springfield *(G-13075)*

Prov31 Publishing LLC ....G....... 804 536-0436
Newport News *(G-9319)*

Providence Pubg Group LLC ....G....... 703 352-3152
Fairfax *(G-4663)*

Provisioning Inc ....G....... 571 451-3134
Herndon *(G-6779)*

Prs Towing & Recovery ....G....... 540 838-2388
Radford *(G-10735)*

Psa Publishings LLC ....G....... 703 986-3288
Alexandria *(G-321)*

PSM Publications Inc...............G....... 434 432-8600
Chatham *(G-2935)*

Publication Certified ....G....... 703 259-1936
Fairfax *(G-4666)*

Publications Professionals LLC ....G....... 703 934-4499
Fairfax *(G-4667)*

Publicity Works LLC ....G....... 703 876-0080
Falls Church *(G-4860)*

Publishers Asset LLC ....G....... 540 621-4422
Fredericksburg *(G-5474)*

Publishers Circltn ....G....... 703 394-5293
Vienna *(G-14115)*

Publishers Service Assoc Inc ....G....... 570 322-7848
Herndon *(G-6780)*

Publishers Teaberry Feilds ....G....... 276 783-2546
Marion *(G-8241)*

Publishing.....................G....... 540 659-6694
Stafford *(G-13184)*

Pulp Usa LLC ....G....... 540 907-0093
Fredericksburg *(G-5215)*

Pungo Publishing Co LLC ....G....... 757 748-5331
Virginia Beach *(G-14747)*

Pure Faith Publishing LLC ....G....... 757 925-4957
Suffolk *(G-13754)*

Purple Diamond Publishing ....G....... 757 525-2422
Virginia Beach *(G-14750)*

Purple Ink Press ....G....... 703 753-4638
Gainesville *(G-5609)*

Puzzle Peace Publications LLC ....G....... 973 766-5282
Newport News *(G-9320)*

R B M Enterprises Inc...............G....... 804 290-4407
Glen Allen *(G-5786)*

Racepacket Inc ....G....... 703 486-1466
Arlington *(G-1127)*

Radar Media LLC ....G....... 540 348-8996
Rockbridge Baths *(G-12237)*

Railway Station Press Inc ....G....... 703 683-2335
Alexandria *(G-324)*

Rain & Associates LLC ....G....... 757 572-3996
Virginia Beach *(G-14758)*

Rainbow Ridge Books LLC ....G....... 757 481-7399
Virginia Beach *(G-14759)*

Rambletype LLC ....G....... 540 440-1218
Fredericksburg *(G-5217)*

Raphael Press LLC ....G....... 703 771-7571
Leesburg *(G-7332)*

Real American Revolution ....G....... 703 732-9049
Falls Church *(G-4864)*

Reconciliation Press Inc ....G.... 703 369-6132
Manassas (G-7995)
Recorder Publishing VA Inc ....G.... 540 839-6646
Warm Springs (G-14975)
Red Apple Publications ....G.... 703 430-9272
Great Falls (G-5977)
Red Hot Publishing LLC ....G.... 703 885-5423
Sterling (G-13488)
Redline Productions ....G.... 703 861-8765
Falls Church (G-4865)
Reeses Amazing Printing Svcs ....G.... 804 325-0947
Henrico (G-6556)
Region Press ....G.... 276 706-6798
Saltville (G-12587)
Reign Productions LLC ....G.... 703 317-1393
Alexandria (G-569)
Renegade Publishing LLC ....G.... 703 780-4546
Alexandria (G-570)
Rentury Solutions LLC ....G.... 757 453-5763
Hampton (G-6227)
Restoration Books & Publishing ....G.... 276 224-7244
Martinsville (G-8323)
Retirement Watch LLC ....G.... 571 522-6505
Centreville (G-2333)
Retrospect Publishing ....G.... 703 765-9405
Alexandria (G-571)
Richmond Yellowpages Com ....G.... 804 565-9170
Richmond (G-11363)
Ridan Publishing ....G.... 703 349-2028
Fairfax (G-4542)
Rivanna Pubg Ventures LLC ....G.... 202 549-7940
Charlottesville (G-2685)
River City Publishing Inc ....G.... 804 240-9115
Richmond (G-11741)
Rk Publishing Company LLC ....G.... 434 249-9926
Charlottesville (G-2864)
Road Runner Hold Co LLC ....G.... 703 345-2400
Herndon (G-6793)
Rodders Journal ....G.... 804 496-6906
Ashland (G-1489)
Roll of Honor Foundation ....G.... 703 731-6109
Fairfax (G-4544)
Romac Publishing LLC ....G.... 703 478-9794
Reston (G-10942)
Root Group LLC ....G.... 703 595-7008
Leesburg (G-7339)
Ross Publishing Inc ....G.... 804 674-5004
North Chesterfield (G-9966)
Royal Fern Publishing LLC ....G.... 703 759-0264
Great Falls (G-5978)
S and H Publishing Inc ....G.... 703 915-0913
Hillsboro (G-6878)
S&R Pals Enterprises LLC ....G.... 540 752-1900
Fredericksburg (G-5481)
Saint Marks Publishing ....G.... 540 551-3590
Front Royal (G-5553)
Sajames Publications LLC ....G.... 434 509-5331
Lynchburg (G-7804)
Salt Cedar Publications ....G.... 434 258-5333
Lynchburg (G-7805)
Sambuqcom Inc ....G.... 703 980-8669
Mc Lean (G-8544)
San Francisco Bay Press ....G.... 757 412-5642
Norfolk (G-9714)
San Roderigo Publishing LLC ....G.... 703 968-9502
Fairfax (G-4548)
Sandbox Family Comm Inc ....E.... 910 381-7346
Arlington (G-1157)
Sandra Woodward ....G.... 703 329-7938
Alexandria (G-336)
Sangamon Group LLC ....G.... 571 969-6881
Alexandria (G-337)
Savannah Publications ....G.... 804 674-1937
North Chesterfield (G-9970)
Science Info LLC ....G.... 804 332-5269
Glen Allen (G-5792)
SDC Publishing LLC ....G.... 540 676-3279
Buchanan (G-2127)
Sea Publishing LLC ....G.... 832 744-7049
Aldie (G-111)
Secret Society Press LLC ....G.... 540 877-6298
Winchester (G-15583)
Secretbow Pubg Instruction LLC ....G.... 703 404-3401
Sterling (G-13502)
Selby LLC ....G.... 804 640-4851
Montpelier (G-9021)
Sema Wray ....G.... 804 282-3609
Henrico (G-6566)
Seql Inc ....G.... 804 214-5678
Richmond (G-11758)

Setanta Publishing LLC ....G.... 703 548-3146
Alexandria (G-343)
Seva Publishing LLC ....G.... 757 556-1965
Manassas (G-7999)
Shade Green Publishing ....G.... 540 845-4780
Fredericksburg (G-5360)
Shadow Dance Publishing Ltd ....G.... 540 786-3270
Spotsylvania (G-12914)
Shelton Global Assoc ....G.... 202 841-8463
Reston (G-10949)
Shickel Pubg Co Donna Lou ....G.... 540 879-3568
Dayton (G-4063)
Silverwood Press LLC ....G.... 804 833-0595
Richmond (G-11382)
Simple Scribes Pubg & Dist LLC ....G.... 804 364-3418
Glen Allen (G-5798)
Sims Creek Publishing LLC ....G.... 276 694-4278
Stuart (G-13630)
Six Seas Press LLC ....G.... 757 363-5869
Virginia Beach (G-14821)
Skelly Publishing Inc ....G.... 888 753-5591
Arlington (G-1169)
Skyship Fantasy Press ....G.... 703 670-5242
Woodbridge (G-15812)
Sleepless Warrior Publishing ....G.... 703 408-4035
Woodbridge (G-15813)
Slumlord Millionaire LLC ....G.... 540 529-9259
Roanoke (G-12190)
Small Fox Press ....G.... 540 877-4054
Winchester (G-15479)
Smartech Markets Pubg LLC ....G.... 434 872-9008
Crozet (G-3850)
So Amazing Publications ....G.... 804 412-5224
Petersburg (G-10343)
So What Publications LLC ....G.... 757 934-0148
Suffolk (G-13765)
Solitude Publishers LLC ....G.... 571 970-3918
Alexandria (G-351)
Source Publishing Inc ....G.... 804 747-4080
Richmond (G-11386)
South East Asian Language Publ ....G.... 703 754-6693
Bristow (G-2062)
Sparks Companies Inc ....G.... 703 734-8787
Mc Lean (G-8553)
Splendor Publishing ....G.... 434 665-2339
Lynchburg (G-7811)
Sports Unstoppable LLC ....G.... 571 346-7622
Reston (G-10962)
Spring Hollow Publishing Inc ....G.... 434 984-4718
Charlottesville (G-2695)
Square Penny Publishing LLC ....G.... 757 348-2226
Chesapeake (G-3308)
Stan Garfin Publications Inc ....G.... 757 495-3644
Virginia Beach (G-14842)
Starlight Express LLC ....G.... 434 295-0782
Charlottesville (G-2883)
Steam Valley Publishing ....G.... 703 255-9884
Vienna (G-14134)
Steel Mouse Trap Publications ....G.... 703 542-2327
Chantilly (G-2557)
Steelgate LLC ....G.... 337 263-2490
Brambleton (G-1933)
Steve S 2 Express ....G.... 757 336-7377
Chincoteague (G-3566)
Stillhouse Press ....G.... 530 409-8179
Fairfax (G-4682)
Stockton Creek Press LLC ....G.... 410 490-8863
Charlottesville (G-2884)
Stoneshore Publishing ....G.... 757 589-7049
Virginia Beach (G-14852)
Storey Mill Publishing ....G.... 757 399-4969
Portsmouth (G-10486)
Strive Communications LLC ....G.... 703 925-5900
Reston (G-10967)
Stubborn Press and Company LLC ....G.... 540 394-8412
Forest (G-5098)
Sub Rosa Press Ltd ....G.... 703 777-1157
Leesburg (G-7354)
Sugar Spring Press ....G.... 540 463-4094
Lexington (G-7418)
Sumi Enterprises ....G.... 703 580-8269
Woodbridge (G-15818)
Sunshine Hill Press LLC ....G.... 571 451-8448
Reva (G-11001)
Supa Producer Publishing ....G.... 757 484-2495
Portsmouth (G-10488)
Supermedia LLC ....B.... 703 322-2900
Chantilly (G-2504)
Supracity Publishing LLC ....G.... 804 301-9370
Louisa (G-7570)

Surfside East Inc ....E.... 757 468-0606
Virginia Beach (G-14859)
Sweetbay Publishing LLC ....G.... 703 203-9130
Manassas (G-8164)
Synaptein Solutions Inc ....F.... 703 209-2350
Mc Lean (G-8562)
T2pneuma Publishers LLC ....G.... 703 968-7592
Centreville (G-2344)
Tactical Nuclear Wizard LLC ....G.... 804 231-1671
Richmond (G-11780)
Talk Is Life LLC ....G.... 703 951-3848
Dumfries (G-4258)
Tannhauser Enterprises LLC ....G.... 703 850-1927
Bristow (G-2063)
Target Communications Inc ....E.... 804 355-0111
Richmond (G-11782)
Tax Management Inc ....D.... 703 341-3000
Arlington (G-1181)
Technology News and Literature ....G.... 202 380-5425
Arlington (G-1183)
Teen Ink ....G.... 804 365-8000
Ashland (G-1499)
Terran Press LLC ....G.... 540 720-2516
Stafford (G-13202)
Tertal Publishing LLC ....G.... 571 229-9699
Bristow (G-2064)
▲ Thompson Pubg LLC George F ....G.... 540 887-8166
Staunton (G-13301)
Thomson Reuters Corporation ....B.... 434 973-4396
Charlottesville (G-2704)
Thorn 10 Publishing LLC ....G.... 757 277-9431
Chesapeake (G-3333)
Three Angels Pretzels ....G.... 540 722-0400
Winchester (G-15593)
Thryv Inc ....F.... 434 974-4000
Charlottesville (G-2706)
Tidewater Trading Post Inc ....F.... 757 420-6117
Chesapeake (G-3339)
▲ Tiffany Inc ....G.... 757 622-2915
Norfolk (G-9757)
Timingwallstreet Inc ....G.... 434 489-2380
Danville (G-4041)
Timothy L Hosey ....G.... 270 339-0016
Maurertown (G-8364)
Titus Publications ....G.... 757 421-4141
Virginia Beach (G-14883)
TLC Publishing ....G.... 434 974-6411
Charlottesville (G-2707)
TLC Publishing LLC ....G.... 571 439-0564
Ashburn (G-1341)
Tlpublishing LLC ....G.... 571 992-7972
Ashburn (G-1342)
Tlw Self Publishing Company ....G.... 540 560-2507
Culpeper (G-3925)
Tokyo Express ....G.... 276 632-7599
Martinsville (G-8344)
Tokyo Express ....G.... 540 389-6303
Salem (G-12576)
Topoatlas LLC ....G.... 703 476-5256
Herndon (G-6829)
Touch 3 LLC ....G.... 703 279-8130
Fairfax (G-4572)
Town Pride Publishers ....G.... 757 321-8132
Virginia Beach (G-14890)
Tracy Barrett ....G.... 757 342-3204
Gloucester (G-5863)
Tradingbell Inc ....D.... 703 752-6100
Vienna (G-14144)
Transition Publishing LLC ....G.... 703 208-4449
Vienna (G-14145)
Transport Topics Pubg Group ....G.... 703 838-1770
Arlington (G-1195)
Triad Digital Media Inc ....G.... 336 908-5884
Axton (G-1542)
Trinity Publications LLC ....G.... 804 779-3499
Mechanicsville (G-8688)
Triple OG Publishing LLC ....G.... 804 252-0856
Henrico (G-6586)
Trishs Books ....G.... 804 550-2954
Mechanicsville (G-8690)
Turtle House Press LLC ....G.... 540 268-5487
Elliston (G-4350)
Tvworldwidecom Inc ....G.... 703 961-9250
Chantilly (G-2509)
Twisted Erotica Publishing LLC ....G.... 757 344-7364
Newport News (G-9366)
Twomorrows Yesterdays LLC ....G.... 571 292-2930
Nokesville (G-9402)
Ubibird Incorporated ....G.... 718 490-3746
Stafford (G-13207)

S I C

Ubiquitywave LLC .... G 571 262-1406
  Ashburn *(G-1344)*
Underbite Publishing LLC .... G 703 638-8040
  Alexandria *(G-371)*
Understanding Latin LLC .... G 703 437-9354
  Sterling *(G-13542)*
Urban Works Publicity .... G 703 625-6981
  Arlington *(G-1204)*
US Dept of the Air Force .... G 757 764-5616
  Hampton *(G-6279)*
Usgri/Bitcoin Press Release .... G 202 316-3222
  Arlington *(G-1206)*
Uts Fendrag Publishing Co .... G 804 266-9108
  Richmond *(G-11431)*
VA Properties Inc .... G 804 237-1455
  Richmond *(G-11803)*
Valley Construction News .... G 540 344-4899
  Roanoke *(G-12213)*
Vanity Print & Press LLC .... G 757 553-1602
  Suffolk *(G-13776)*
Variety Press LLC .... G 703 359-0932
  Fairfax *(G-4692)*
Vbk Publishing .... G 757 587-1741
  Norfolk *(G-9779)*
Vega Pages LLC .... G 703 281-2030
  Vienna *(G-14150)*
▼ Vega Productions & Associates ..... G 703 908-9600
  Fairfax *(G-4578)*
Vegan Heritage Press .... G 540 459-2858
  Woodstock *(G-15861)*
Venetian Spider Press LLC .... G 310 857-4228
  Sterling *(G-13546)*
Ventajas Publications LLC .... G 540 825-5337
  Culpeper *(G-3928)*
Venture Publishing LLC .... G 540 570-1908
  Buena Vista *(G-2156)*
Venutec Corporation .... G 888 573-8870
  Centreville *(G-2350)*
Veteran Freelancer .... G 484 772-5931
  Norfolk *(G-9781)*
Victimology Inc .... G 703 528-3387
  Arlington *(G-1210)*
Victory Coachways .... G 434 799-2569
  Danville *(G-4046)*
Vie La Publishing House LLC .... G 804 741-2670
  Henrico *(G-6589)*
Village To Village Press LLC .... G 267 416-0375
  Harrisonburg *(G-6384)*
Viplife Ent Publishing LLC .... G 434 429-6037
  Danville *(G-4047)*
Virginia Academic Press .... G 703 256-1304
  Alexandria *(G-605)*
Virginia Bus Publications LLC .... G 804 225-9262
  Richmond *(G-11808)*
Virginia Cptol Connections Inc ...... G 804 643-5554
  Richmond *(G-11812)*
Virginia Media Inc .... G 304 647-5724
  Salem *(G-12579)*
Virginia Sportsman .... G 434 971-1199
  Charlottesville *(G-2901)*
Vision Academy Publishing LLC .... G 703 753-0710
  Haymarket *(G-6453)*
Vision Publishers LLC .... G 540 867-5302
  Dayton *(G-4071)*
Vision Publishers Inc .... G 540 437-1967
  Harrisonburg *(G-6386)*
Vista-Graphics Inc .... E 757 422-8979
  Virginia Beach *(G-14925)*
Vocalzmusic .... G 703 798-2587
  Stafford *(G-13211)*
Von Holtzbrinck Publishing .... G 540 672-9311
  Orange *(G-10230)*
Walkers Cove Publishing LLC .... G 703 957-4052
  Chantilly *(G-2566)*
Wallace-Caliva Publishing LLC .... G 703 313-4813
  Annandale *(G-792)*
Warren Ventures LLC .... G 804 267-9098
  Richmond *(G-11818)*
Washington & Baltimore Suburba ...... G 703 904-1004
  Sterling *(G-13559)*
Washington Business Info Inc .... E 703 538-7600
  Falls Church *(G-4927)*
Washington International .... G 703 757-5965
  Great Falls *(G-5983)*
Watercraft Logistics Svcs Co .... G 757 348-3089
  Virginia Beach *(G-14930)*
Watertree Press LLC .... G 757 512-5517
  Chesapeake *(G-3371)*
Way With Words Publishing LLC .... G 703 583-1825
  Triangle *(G-13900)*

Wb Fresh Press LLC .... G 757 485-3176
  Chesapeake *(G-3372)*
Wellzone Inc .... G 703 770-2861
  Mc Lean *(G-8578)*
Westend Press LLC .... G 703 992-6939
  Fairfax Station *(G-4727)*
Western Express Inc .... G 434 348-0650
  Emporia *(G-4370)*
White Brick Music .... G 323 821-9449
  Harrisonburg *(G-6387)*
White Knight Press .... G 757 814-7192
  Henrico *(G-6591)*
Wilderwork Pbc .... F 202 285-9455
  Arlington *(G-1218)*
Williamsburg Directory Co Inc .... G 757 566-1981
  Toano *(G-13880)*
Wimabi Press LLC .... G 804 282-3227
  Richmond *(G-11452)*
Windborne Press LLC .... G 804 227-3431
  Beaverdam *(G-1616)*
Wise La Tina Publishing .... G 202 425-1129
  Reston *(G-10992)*
Witching Hour Press LLC .... G 571 209-0019
  Yorktown *(G-16002)*
Wolf Hills Press LLC .... G 276 644-3119
  Bristol *(G-2001)*
Woods & Waters Publishing Lc .... G 540 894-5960
  Bumpass *(G-2172)*
Word College Inc .... G 510 857-3309
  Centreville *(G-2354)*
Work Scene Media LLC .... F 703 910-5959
  Mclean *(G-8589)*
Worldwide Agency LLC .... G 202 888-5895
  Arlington *(G-1222)*
▲ Worthington Publishing .... G 757 831-4375
  Virginia Beach *(G-14944)*
Wright Express .... G 703 467-5738
  Herndon *(G-6845)*
Write Impressions .... G 757 473-1699
  Virginia Beach *(G-14946)*
Write Lab Press LLC .... G 757 390-1030
  Franklin *(G-5163)*
X Press Enterprises LLC .... G 540 587-0100
  Bedford *(G-1665)*
Yardsalesheadquarterscom LLC .... G 757 503-0940
  Newport News *(G-9382)*
Yazdan Publishing Company .... G 757 426-6009
  Virginia Beach *(G-14952)*
Yba Publishing LLC .... G 703 763-2710
  Alexandria *(G-390)*
Ynaffit Music Publishing .... G 757 270-3316
  Virginia Beach *(G-14953)*
Yorgea Inc .... G 704 431-8252
  Norfolk *(G-9799)*
York Publishing Company LLC .... G 571 226-0221
  Manassas *(G-8181)*
Young Movar & Assoc Mrktng .... G 804 320-5860
  North Chesterfield *(G-10046)*
Your Newsy Notes LLC .... G 703 729-3155
  Broadlands *(G-2083)*
Zatara Press LLC .... G 804 754-8682
  Richmond *(G-11462)*
Zebra Press LLC .... G 703 370-6641
  Alexandria *(G-392)*
Zig Zag Press LLC .... G 757 229-1345
  Williamsburg *(G-15349)*
Zinerva Publishing LLC .... G 703 430-7629
  Great Falls *(G-5986)*
Zones LLC .... G 571 244-8206
  Alexandria *(G-617)*
Zook Aviation Inc .... G 540 217-4471
  Harrisonburg *(G-6389)*

2752 Commercial Printing: Lithographic

10 10 LLC .... G 757 627-4311
  Norfolk *(G-9410)*
10 Times Better LLC .... G 850 258-8880
  Carrollton *(G-2239)*
35 Printing LLC .... G 804 926-5737
  Disputanta *(G-4102)*
3d Herndon .... G 202 746-6176
  Herndon *(G-6598)*
757 Prints .... G 757 774-6834
  Virginia Beach *(G-14196)*
A & R Printing .... G 434 829-2030
  Emporia *(G-4352)*
A B Printing LLC .... G 276 783-2837
  Marion *(G-8219)*
A C Graphics Inc .... G 703 246-9466
  Fairfax *(G-4396)*

A Z Printing and Dup Corp .... G 703 549-0949
  Alexandria *(G-116)*
Aaca Embroidery Screen Prtg .... G 703 880-9872
  Herndon *(G-6601)*
ABC Imaging of Washington .... F 703 848-2997
  Vienna *(G-14004)*
ABC Printing .... G 434 847-7468
  Madison Heights *(G-7866)*
Abingdon Printing Inc .... G 276 628-4221
  Abingdon *(G-3)*
Aboriginal Prints LLC .... G 804 994-1987
  Richmond *(G-11468)*
Accelerated Printing Corp Inc .... G 703 437-1084
  Leesburg *(G-7213)*
Advertising Service Agency .... G 757 622-3429
  Norfolk *(G-9425)*
Affordable Printing & Copies .... G 757 728-9770
  Hampton *(G-6076)*
AG Almanac LLC .... G 703 289-1200
  Falls Church *(G-4741)*
Alfa Print LLC .... G 703 754-2433
  Gainesville *(G-5568)*
Alfa Print LLC .... G 703 273-2061
  Fairfax *(G-4591)*
All Prints Inc .... G 703 435-1922
  Sterling *(G-13342)*
Alleghany Printing Co .... G 540 965-4246
  Covington *(G-3777)*
Allegra Network LLC .... G 757 448-8271
  Norfolk *(G-9432)*
Allegra Print & Imaging .... G 703 378-4500
  Chantilly *(G-2365)*
Allen Wayne Ltd Arlington .... G 703 321-7414
  Warrenton *(G-14977)*
Allinder Printing .... G 757 672-4918
  Norfolk *(G-9436)*
Alma Mater LLC .... G 434 248-5465
  Phenix *(G-10354)*
Alpha Printing Inc .... G 703 321-2071
  Springfield *(G-12943)*
AlphaGraphics .... G 703 866-1988
  Springfield *(G-12944)*
AlphaGraphics .... G 703 818-2900
  Chantilly *(G-2367)*
◆ Ambush LLC .... G 480 338-5321
  Dumfries *(G-4233)*
Ambush LLC .... G 202 740-3602
  Stafford *(G-13114)*
American Digital Print LLC .... G 703 328-4796
  Stafford *(G-13115)*
Amh Print Group LLC .... G 804 286-6166
  Mechanicsville *(G-8603)*
Amplify Ventures LLC .... G 571 248-2282
  Gainesville *(G-5570)*
Apollo Press Inc .... E 757 247-9002
  Newport News *(G-9169)*
Ardsen Offset .... G 757 220-3299
  Williamsburg *(G-15206)*
Art Printing Solutions LLC .... G 804 387-3203
  Petersburg *(G-10306)*
Artcraft Printing Ltd .... G 757 428-9138
  Virginia Beach *(G-14244)*
Arw Printing .... G 540 720-6906
  Stafford *(G-13120)*
ASAP Printing & Mailing Co .... G 703 836-2288
  Alexandria *(G-142)*
Ashe Kustomz LLC .... G 804 997-6406
  Richmond *(G-11490)*
Authentic Printing Company LLC ...... G 804 672-6659
  Henrico *(G-6479)*
Avn Prints .... G 703 473-7498
  Alexandria *(G-419)*
B & B Printing .... G 540 586-1020
  Bedford *(G-1622)*
B & B Printing Company Inc .... C 804 794-8273
  North Chesterfield *(G-9824)*
B Franklin Printer .... G 703 845-1583
  Arlington *(G-871)*
B K Printing .... G 703 435-5502
  Herndon *(G-6618)*
Bailey Printing Inc .... F 434 293-5434
  Charlottesville *(G-2734)*
▲ Balmar Inc .... E 703 289-9000
  Falls Church *(G-4761)*
Barbours Printing Service .... G 804 443-4505
  Tappahannock *(G-13813)*
Barg-N-Finders Inc .... G 276 988-4953
  North Tazewell *(G-10094)*
Barry McVay .... G 703 451-5953
  Burke *(G-2182)*

Barton Industries Inc.....E.......757 874-5958
Yorktown *(G-15935)*
Bbj LLC.....G.......757 787-4646
Onancock *(G-10191)*
Bbr Print Inc.....F.......804 230-4515
Richmond *(G-11502)*
BCT Recordation Inc.....G.......540 772-1754
Roanoke *(G-11885)*
Bell Printing Inc.....G.......804 261-1776
Richmond *(G-11123)*
Benjamin Franklin Printing Co.....F.......804 648-6361
Richmond *(G-11504)*
Benton-Thomas Inc.....F.......434 572-3577
South Boston *(G-12751)*
▲ **Berryville Graphics Inc**.....A.......540 955-2750
Berryville *(G-1671)*
Best Image Printers Ltd.....F.......804 272-1006
North Chesterfield *(G-9830)*
Best Impressions Inc.....F.......703 518-1375
Alexandria *(G-421)*
Best Impressions Printing.....G.......804 740-9006
Ashland *(G-1380)*
Best Printing Inc.....G.......540 563-9004
Roanoke *(G-12044)*
Bi Communications Inc.....F.......703 435-9600
Sterling *(G-13359)*
Big EZ Prints.....G.......804 929-3479
Prince George *(G-10587)*
Big Lick Screen Printing.....G.......540 632-2695
Roanoke *(G-12045)*
Bigeye Direct Inc.....D.......703 955-3017
Herndon *(G-6624)*
Bison Printing Inc.....E.......540 586-3955
Bedford *(G-1627)*
Blacktag Screen Printing Inc.....G.......855 423-1680
Hampton *(G-6095)*
Blue Moon Catering Concessions.....G.......276 236-8728
Galax *(G-5628)*
Blueprint Inc.....G.......703 771-9256
Leesburg *(G-7234)*
Boaz Publishing Inc.....F.......540 659-4554
Stafford *(G-13124)*
Bobs Printing Service LLC.....G.......434 352-2680
Appomattox *(G-807)*
Boutique Paw Prints.....G.......434 964-0133
Charlottesville *(G-2748)*
Bowman Teressa.....G.......240 601-9982
Manassas *(G-7921)*
Box Print & Ship - C Bernel.....G.......757 410-7352
Chesapeake *(G-3013)*
Brandy Printing & EMB Inc.....G.......540 825-5583
Brandy Station *(G-1937)*
Branner Printing Service Inc.....E.......540 896-8947
Broadway *(G-2085)*
Brooks Signs Screen Printing.....G.......434 728-3812
Danville *(G-3963)*
Brothers Printing.....F.......757 431-2656
Virginia Beach *(G-14301)*
Brown Printing Company Inc.....G.......703 934-6078
Fairfax *(G-4600)*
Bull Run Printing.....G.......540 937-3447
Rixeyville *(G-11877)*
Burcham Prints Inc.....G.......804 559-7724
Mechanicsville *(G-8608)*
Burke Print Shop.....G.......276 628-3033
Abingdon *(G-19)*
Business Press.....F.......804 282-3150
Richmond *(G-11140)*
Bvm Print VA LLC.....G.......434 845-1153
Lynchburg *(G-7663)*
Bxi Inc.....G.......804 282-5434
Richmond *(G-11142)*
C & B Corp.....G.......434 977-1992
Charlottesville *(G-2752)*
C & R Printing Inc.....G.......703 802-0800
Chantilly *(G-2383)*
C & S Printing Enterprises.....G.......703 385-4495
Fairfax *(G-4603)*
C Graphic Distribution Ctr.....G.......414 762-4282
Roanoke *(G-11899)*
C H J Digital Repro.....G.......757 473-0234
Virginia Beach *(G-14308)*
C Line Graphics Inc.....G.......434 577-9289
Valentines *(G-13974)*
C2-Mask Inc.....G.......703 698-7820
Fairfax *(G-4422)*
Calfee Printing.....G.......304 910-3475
Fincastle *(G-4994)*
Campbell Copy Center Inc.....F.......540 434-4171
Rockingham *(G-12243)*

Campbell Graphics Inc.....G.......804 353-7292
Richmond *(G-11144)*
Campbell Printing Bristol Inc.....G.......276 466-2311
Bristol *(G-2012)*
Canaan Printing Inc.....E.......804 271-4820
North Chesterfield *(G-9839)*
Cantrell/Cutter Printing Inc.....G.......301 773-6340
Springfield *(G-12972)*
Capital Screen Prtg Unlimited.....G.......703 550-0033
Lorton *(G-7470)*
▲ **Carter Composition Corporation**.....C.......804 359-9206
Richmond *(G-11149)*
Cbt Screen Printing LLC.....G.......703 888-8539
Falls Church *(G-4904)*
Century Press Inc.....G.......703 335-5663
Manassas *(G-8048)*
Chanders.....G.......804 752-7678
Ashland *(G-1389)*
Chantilly Prtg & Graphics Inc.....G.......703 471-2800
Herndon *(G-6639)*
Chantilly Services Inc.....G.......703 830-7700
Chantilly *(G-2392)*
Charlotte Printing LLC.....G.......434 738-7155
Randolph *(G-10747)*
Chief Printing Company.....G.......515 480-6577
Richmond *(G-11529)*
Chocklett Press Inc.....D.......540 345-1820
Roanoke *(G-12066)*
Choice Printing Services.....G.......804 690-9064
Glen Allen *(G-5714)*
▼ **Christian Light Publications**.....E.......540 434-0768
Harrisonburg *(G-6300)*
Clarke Inc.....F.......434 847-5561
Moneta *(G-8959)*
Clarks Litho Inc.....F.......703 961-8888
Chantilly *(G-2393)*
Clean Building LLC.....G.......703 589-9544
Alexandria *(G-431)*
Clinch Valley Printing Company.....F.......276 988-5410
North Tazewell *(G-10096)*
CMC Printing and Graphics Inc.....G.......804 744-5821
Midlothian *(G-8798)*
Cmg Impressions Inc.....G.......804 556-2551
Maidens *(G-7887)*
Cnc Printing Inc.....G.......703 378-5222
Chantilly *(G-2394)*
Coalfield Progress.....D.......276 679-1101
Norton *(G-10115)*
Coastal Screen Printing.....G.......541 441-6358
Hampton *(G-6277)*
Coastal Screen Printing.....G.......757 764-1409
Newport News *(G-9202)*
Collinsville Printing Co.....E.......276 666-4400
Martinsville *(G-8276)*
Color Quest LLC.....G.......540 896-8186
Harrisonburg *(G-6304)*
Color Quest LLC.....G.......540 433-4890
Harrisonburg *(G-6303)*
▲ **Color Svc Prtg & Graphics Inc**.....G.......703 321-8100
Falls Church *(G-4776)*
Colornet Prtg & Graphics Inc.....G.......703 406-9301
Sterling *(G-13372)*
Commercial Press Inc.....F.......540 869-3496
Stephens City *(G-13313)*
Commercial Prtg Drect Mail Svc.....G.......757 422-0606
Virginia Beach *(G-14358)*
Commonwealth Reprographics.....F.......434 845-1203
Lynchburg *(G-7682)*
▲ **Composition Systems Inc**.....D.......703 205-0000
Alexandria *(G-171)*
Consolidated Mailing Svcs Inc.....E.......703 904-1600
Sterling *(G-13374)*
Consulting Printing Services.....F.......434 846-6510
Forest *(G-5064)*
Copy Cat Printing LLC.....G.......804 746-0008
Mechanicsville *(G-8615)*
Copy Connection.....G.......757 627-4701
Norfolk *(G-9505)*
Copy Connection LLC.....G.......757 627-4701
Norfolk *(G-9506)*
Copy Dog Printing.....G.......434 528-4134
Lynchburg *(G-7684)*
Copy That Print LLC.....G.......757 642-3301
Virginia Beach *(G-14364)*
Copyland Printing Inc.....F.......703 241-9188
Chantilly *(G-2397)*
Copyright Printing.....G.......804 784-4760
Oilville *(G-10177)*
Coral Graphic Services Inc.....C.......540 869-0500
Berryville *(G-1676)*

Core Prints.....G.......540 356-9195
Fredericksburg *(G-5414)*
Country House Printing.....G.......540 674-4616
Dublin *(G-4153)*
Courtney Press.....G.......804 266-8359
Richmond *(G-11544)*
Crabar/Gbf Inc.....E.......919 732-2101
Chatham *(G-2926)*
Craftsmen Printing Inc.....G.......804 798-7885
Ashland *(G-1398)*
Creative Document Imaging Inc.....G.......703 208-2212
Fairfax *(G-4432)*
Creative Document Imaging Inc.....G.......703 497-6767
Woodbridge *(G-15675)*
Creative Ink.....G.......434 572-4379
South Boston *(G-12757)*
Creative Print Solutions.....G.......540 247-9910
Winchester *(G-15406)*
Creo Industries.....G.......804 385-2035
Christiansburg *(G-3582)*
Crescent Printery Ltd.....G.......276 395-2101
Coeburn *(G-3697)*
Criswell Inc.....F.......434 845-0439
Lynchburg *(G-7687)*
Cross Printing Solutions LLC.....G.......703 208-2214
Fairfax *(G-4433)*
Crosstown Paint.....G.......757 817-7119
Hampton *(G-6123)*
Csl Media LLC.....G.......540 785-3790
Fredericksburg *(G-5268)*
Csl Media LLC.....G.......540 785-3790
Fredericksburg *(G-5181)*
▲ **CSP Productions Inc**.....G.......703 321-8100
Falls Church *(G-4779)*
CTW Printing Concepts.....G.......804 559-5020
Mechanicsville *(G-8616)*
Cunningham Digital Inc.....G.......540 992-2219
Daleville *(G-3941)*
Curry Copy Center of Roanoke.....G.......540 345-2865
Roanoke *(G-12075)*
Custom Dsigns EMB Print Wr LLC.....G.......540 748-5455
Mineral *(G-8947)*
Custom Print.....G.......703 256-1279
Springfield *(G-12985)*
Custom Printing.....G.......540 672-2281
Orange *(G-10208)*
Custom Printing.....G.......804 261-1776
Richmond *(G-11174)*
Custom Prints LLC.....G.......804 839-0749
Richmond *(G-11552)*
Cutie Pies Clay Print Keepskes.....G.......703 533-3313
Leesburg *(G-7251)*
Cwi Marketing & Printing.....G.......540 295-5139
Radford *(G-10706)*
Cyan LLC.....G.......703 455-3000
Springfield *(G-12986)*
D & P Printing & Graphics Inc.....F.......703 941-2114
Alexandria *(G-438)*
Dad13 Inc.....C.......703 550-9555
Newington *(G-9153)*
Dae Print & Design.....G.......757 518-1774
Virginia Beach *(G-14381)*
Dae Print & Design.....F.......757 473-0234
Virginia Beach *(G-14382)*
Dan Miles & Associates LLC.....G.......619 508-0430
Virginia Beach *(G-14385)*
Dandee Printing Co.....G.......540 828-4457
Keezletown *(G-7027)*
Dandy Printing.....G.......540 986-1100
Salem *(G-12495)*
Dap Incorporated.....G.......757 921-3576
Newport News *(G-9214)*
Databrands LLC.....G.......804 282-7890
Richmond *(G-11178)*
Davis Communications Group.....G.......703 548-8892
Alexandria *(G-185)*
Day & Night Printing Inc.....E.......703 734-4940
Vienna *(G-14035)*
DC Custom Print.....G.......301 541-8172
Arlington *(G-930)*
Deem Printing Company Inc.....G.......703 335-5422
Manassas *(G-8055)*
Deem Printing Company Inc.....G.......703 335-2422
Manassas *(G-7930)*
Deer Duplicating Svc Inc.....G.......804 648-6509
Richmond *(G-11557)*
Dehardit Press.....G.......804 693-2795
Gloucester *(G-5845)*
Delong Lithographics Services.....G.......703 550-2110
Lorton *(G-7479)*

DEP Copy Center Inc ....G... 703 499-9888
  Woodbridge (G-15682)
Design Digital Printing LLC ....G... 276 964-9391
  Cedar Bluff (G-2274)
Detamore Printing Co ....G... 540 886-4571
  Staunton (G-13252)
Devin Clark ....G... 276 889-3426
  Lebanon (G-7191)
Digi Quick Print Inc ....G... 703 671-9600
  Alexandria (G-187)
Digital Documents Inc ....G... 571 434-0341
  Herndon (G-6657)
Digital Printing Solutions Inc ....G... 540 389-2066
  Salem (G-12496)
Dister Inc ....E... 757 857-1946
  Norfolk (G-9525)
Dister Inc ....E... 703 207-0201
  Fairfax (G-4439)
Divine Lifestyle Printing LLC ....G... 804 219-3342
  Chester (G-3405)
Dixie Press Custom Screen ....G... 757 569-8241
  Sedley (G-12679)
Dla Document Services ....G... 703 784-2208
  Quantico (G-10688)
Dla Document Services ....G... 804 734-1791
  Fort Lee (G-5128)
Dla Document Services ....F... 757 855-0300
  Norfolk (G-9526)
Dla Document Services ....E... 757 444-7068
  Norfolk (G-9527)
Dmedia Prints ....G... 571 297-3287
  Springfield (G-12994)
Document Automation & Prdtn ....G... 757 878-3389
  Fort Eustis (G-5126)
Dodson Litho Printers Inc ....G... 757 479-4814
  Virginia Beach (G-14408)
Dogwood Graphics ....G... 434 447-6004
  South Hill (G-12848)
Dogwood Graphics Inc ....G... 434 447-6004
  South Hill (G-12849)
Dominion Graphics Inc ....G... 804 353-3755
  Richmond (G-11188)
Dominion Ink LLC ....G... 804 350-7996
  Richmond (G-11563)
Douglas Stuart LLC ....C... 571 210-4440
  Sterling (G-13388)
Dukes Printing Inc ....G... 276 228-6777
  Wytheville (G-15885)
Dupont Printing Service Inc ....G... 703 931-1317
  Falls Church (G-4785)
Dwiggins Corp ....G... 757 366-0066
  Chesapeake (G-3079)
E L Printing Co ....G... 540 776-0373
  Roanoke (G-12080)
Earl Wood Printing Co ....G... 540 563-8833
  Roanoke (G-12082)
East Cast Cstm Screen Prtg LLC ....G... 540 373-7576
  Dutton (G-4272)
Echo Publishing Inc ....G... 757 603-3774
  Norfolk (G-9538)
Economy Printing Inc ....G... 757 485-4445
  Portsmouth (G-10419)
Edible Printing LLC ....G... 212 203-8275
  Luray (G-7607)
Edmonds Prtg / Clor Images Inc ....G... 434 848-2264
  Lawrenceville (G-7179)
Elephant Prints LLC ....G... 703 820-2631
  Alexandria (G-200)
Elite Prints ....G... 703 780-3403
  Alexandria (G-455)
Embroidery and Print House ....G... 757 636-1676
  Suffolk (G-13705)
Engraving and Printing Bureau ....G... 202 997-9580
  Fairfax (G-4446)
Enterprise Inc ....G... 276 694-3101
  Stuart (G-13609)
Ep Computer Service ....G... 804 592-7272
  Madison Heights (G-7872)
Erbosol Printing ....G... 757 325-9986
  Hampton (G-6144)
Ersh-Enterprises Inc ....F... 703 866-1988
  Oakton (G-10147)
Euro Print USA LLC ....G... 703 849-8781
  Annandale (G-747)
Evolution Printing Inc ....G... 571 292-1213
  Manassas (G-8066)
Executive Press Inc ....G... 703 352-1337
  Fairfax (G-4619)
Expo Branders Corporation ....G... 703 865-7581
  Fairfax (G-4453)

Fairfax Printers Inc ....G... 703 273-1220
  Fairfax (G-4621)
Faith First Printing LLC ....G... 757 723-7673
  Hampton (G-6146)
Faith Printing ....G... 804 745-0667
  North Chesterfield (G-9870)
Falcon Lab Inc ....G... 703 442-0124
  Mc Lean (G-8426)
Far West Print Solutions LLC ....G... 757 549-1258
  Chesapeake (G-3097)
Fergusson Printing ....G... 804 355-8621
  Richmond (G-11209)
Fidelity Printing Inc ....F... 804 737-7907
  Sandston (G-12615)
Finance Business Forms Company ......G... 703 255-2151
  Vienna (G-14055)
Fine Prints Designs ....G... 703 560-1519
  Falls Church (G-4914)
First Imprssions Prtg Graphics ....G... 540 342-2679
  Roanoke (G-12087)
Fisher Publications Inc ....G... 804 323-6252
  North Chesterfield (G-9874)
Fleet Services Inc ....F..., 757 625-4214
  Norfolk (G-9556)
Flyermonsterscom ....G... 703 582-5716
  Arlington (G-971)
Flynn Enterprises Inc ....G... 804 461-5753
  Virginia Beach (G-14468)
Flynn Enterprises Inc ....G... 703 444-5555
  Sterling (G-13400)
Flynn Incorporated ....G... 540 885-2600
  Staunton (G-13261)
Fontana Lithograph Inc ....E... 202 296-3276
  Alexandria (G-464)
Forms Unlimited ....G... 757 549-1258
  Chesapeake (G-3107)
Foundry Foundry-A Print ....G... 703 329-3300
  Alexandria (G-207)
Four Star Printing Inc ....G... 540 459-2247
  Woodstock (G-15854)
Framing Concepts Inc ....G... 757 460-9882
  Virginia Beach (G-14474)
Freestyle Prints LLC ....G... 571 246-1806
  Winchester (G-15544)
French Press Printing LLC ....G... 703 268-8241
  Triangle (G-14057)
Full Color Prints ....G... 703 354-9231
  Annandale (G-750)
Full Color Prints ....G... 571 612-8844
  Chantilly (G-2424)
Fuzzyprints ....G... 571 989-3899
  Midland (G-8757)
G & H Litho Inc ....G... 571 267-7148
  Sterling (G-13403)
G I K of Virginia Inc ....G... 804 358-8500
  Richmond (G-11596)
Gabro Graphics Inc ....F... 703 464-8588
  Sterling (G-13405)
Gaia Communications LLC ....G... 703 370-5527
  Alexandria (G-210)
Gam Printers Incorporated ....F... 703 450-4121
  Sterling (G-13406)
Gannett Offset ....G... 781 551-2923
  Mc Lean (G-8441)
Gap Printing ....G... 703 585-1532
  Alexandria (G-466)
Garrison Press Llc ....G... 540 434-2333
  Harrisonburg (G-6319)
Gary D Keys Enterprises Inc ....G... 703 418-1700
  Arlington (G-975)
Gary Gray ....G... 757 238-2135
  Carrollton (G-2242)
Gazette Press Inc ....G... 276 236-4831
  Galax (G-5636)
General Financial Supply Inc ....E... 540 828-3892
  Bridgewater (G-1952)
Genesis Graphics Printing ....G... 703 560-8728
  Falls Church (G-4797)
Georgetown Business Services ....G... 214 708-0249
  Arlington (G-978)
Giant Printing ....G... 703 525-1313
  Fairfax (G-4466)
Giant Printing Inc ....G... 703 645-2292
  Chantilly (G-2426)
GM Printer Experts LLC ....G... 202 250-0569
  Arlington (G-981)
Go Happy Printing ....G... 315 436-1151
  Alexandria (G-221)
Go Happy Printing LLC ....G... 240 423-7397
  Annandale (G-752)

God Spede Printing ....G... 360 359-6458
  Chantilly (G-2429)
Goetz Printing Company ....E... 703 569-8232
  Springfield (G-13012)
Good Guys Printing LLC ....G... 434 942-8229
  Amherst (G-692)
Good Printers Inc ....D... 540 828-4663
  Bridgewater (G-1953)
Graphic Comm Group ....G... 703 818-2700
  Clifton (G-3667)
Graphic Comm Inc ....G... 301 599-9127
  Hillsville (G-6892)
Graphic Communications Inc ....F... 301 599-2020
  Hillsville (G-6893)
Graphic Images Corp ....G... 703 823-6794
  Alexandria (G-225)
Graphic Prints ....G... 757 244-3753
  Newport News (G-9239)
Graphic Prints Inc ....G... 703 787-3880
  Herndon (G-6689)
Grc Enterprises Inc ....G... 540 428-7000
  Manassas (G-8077)
Grubb Printing & Stamp Co Inc ....F... 757 295-8061
  Portsmouth (G-10438)
H&R Printing ....G... 571 277-1454
  Fairfax (G-4473)
Half A Five Enterprise LLC ....G... 703 818-2900
  Chantilly (G-2434)
Halifax Gazette Publishing Co ....E... 434 572-3945
  South Boston (G-12774)
Hammocks Print Shop ....G... 804 453-3265
  Burgess (G-2174)
▲ Hansen Turbine Assemblies Corp ....E... 276 236-7184
  Galax (G-5639)
Harris Printing Company Inc ....G... 540 586-8326
  Bedford (G-1640)
Harrison Management Associates ....G... 703 237-0418
  Arlington (G-989)
Hartman Graphics & Print ....G... 804 720-6549
  Colonial Heights (G-3733)
Harville Entps of Danville VA ....G... 434 822-2106
  Danville (G-3997)
Hatcher Enterprises ....G... 276 673-6077
  Fieldale (G-4988)
Heart Print Expressions LLC ....G... 703 221-6441
  Triangle (G-13894)
Heavenly Gates LLC ....G... 804 790-9840
  Chesterfield (G-3504)
Henrys Color Graphic Design ....G... 703 241-0101
  Falls Church (G-4805)
Herff Jones LLC ....F... 804 598-0971
  Powhatan (G-10549)
Heritage Printing LLC ....G... 804 378-1196
  Richmond (G-11045)
Heritage Printing Service Inc ....F... 804 233-3024
  Richmond (G-11610)
Home Printing ....G... 804 333-4678
  Warsaw (G-15066)
Hooker Printing Inc ....G... 336 339-4802
  Collinsville (G-3713)
Hopewell Publishing Company ....E... 804 452-6127
  Hopewell (G-6934)
House of Stitches & Prints Inc ....G... 276 525-1796
  Abingdon (G-40)
Ibf Group ....G... 703 549-4247
  Alexandria (G-232)
Idezine LLC ....G... 703 946-3490
  Haymarket (G-6426)
Imagenation Design & Prtg LLC ....G... 804 687-3581
  Richmond (G-11613)
Imlay International LLC ....G... 703 914-0526
  Annandale (G-758)
Imprenta Printing ....G... 703 866-0760
  Springfield (G-13021)
Impressed Print Solutions ....G... 717 816-0522
  Stephenson (G-13334)
Impressions Group Inc ....G... 540 667-9227
  Winchester (G-15549)
In House Printing ....G... 703 913-6338
  Springfield (G-13022)
In2 Print ....G... 434 476-7996
  Halifax (G-6050)
Industries In Focus Inc ....G... 703 451-5550
  Springfield (G-13023)
Infinity Printing Inc ....G... 804 378-8656
  North Chesterfield (G-9894)
Inkwell Duck Inc ....G... 703 550-1344
  Lorton (G-7496)
Instant Gratification ....G... 434 332-3769
  Rustburg (G-12441)

Instant Knwledge Com Jill Byrd ....G.... 540 885-8730
Verona *(G-13989)*
Instant Replay ....G.... 434 941-2568
Lynchburg *(G-7742)*
Instant Transactions Corp ....G.... 540 687-3151
Middleburg *(G-8724)*
Interco Print LLC ....G.... 757 351-7000
Norfolk *(G-9594)*
Intl Printers World ....G.... 804 403-3940
Powhatan *(G-10552)*
Iron Pen Web Design & Printing ....G.... 757 645-9945
Portsmouth *(G-10445)*
J & J Printing Inc ....G.... 703 764-0088
Springfield *(G-13026)*
J & L Communications Inc ....G.... 434 973-1830
Charlottesville *(G-2650)*
J & M Printing Inc ....G.... 703 549-2432
Alexandria *(G-241)*
J C Printing Corp ....G.... 703 378-3500
Chantilly *(G-2447)*
James Allen Printing Co ....G.... 540 463-9232
Lexington *(G-7396)*
James Lee Herndon ....G.... 703 549-2585
Manassas Park *(G-8202)*
James River Press ....G.... 804 230-4515
Richmond *(G-11629)*
James River Printing LLC ....G.... 804 520-1000
Colonial Heights *(G-3735)*
Jami Ventures Inc ....G.... 703 352-5679
Fairfax *(G-4484)*
Jamison Printing Inc ....G.... 540 992-3568
Troutville *(G-13912)*
Jammac Corporation ....G.... 757 855-5474
Norfolk *(G-9600)*
Jason Hammond Aldous ....G.... 540 672-5050
Orange *(G-10216)*
JB Productions ....G.... 703 494-6075
Woodbridge *(G-15729)*
Jeanette Ann Smith ....G.... 757 622-0182
Norfolk *(G-9602)*
Jedi Prints LLC ....G.... 757 869-4267
Midlothian *(G-8836)*
Jerrys Antique Prints Ltd ....G.... 540 949-7114
Waynesboro *(G-15118)*
Jo-Je Corporation ....G.... 757 431-2656
Virginia Beach *(G-14571)*
John Henry Printing Inc ....G.... 757 369-9549
Yorktown *(G-15971)*
Johnson Printing Service Inc ....G.... 804 541-3635
Hopewell *(G-6937)*
Johnsons Postcards ....G.... 434 589-7605
Palmyra *(G-10250)*
Joint Lab Systems SEC Svcs LLC ....G.... 443 655-9987
Arlington *(G-1016)*
Jones Direct LLC ....G.... 757 718-3468
Chesapeake *(G-3153)*
Jones Plus LLC ....G.... 757 718-3468
Chesapeake *(G-3154)*
Jones Printing Service Inc ....E.... 757 436-3331
Chesapeake *(G-3155)*
Joseph Ricard Enterprises LLC ....G.... 540 465-5533
Strasburg *(G-13586)*
JT Graphics & Printing Inc ....G.... 703 922-6804
Alexandria *(G-502)*
Judis Heart Prints LLC ....G.... 757 482-9607
Chesapeake *(G-3159)*
Just Print It LLC ....G.... 703 327-2060
Leesburg *(G-7292)*
Just Tech ....G.... 540 662-2400
Staunton *(G-13270)*
K & A Printing ....G.... 716 736-3250
Danville *(G-4008)*
K & E Printing and Graphics ....G.... 703 560-4701
Vienna *(G-14075)*
K & W Printing Services Inc ....G.... 301 868-2141
Arlington *(G-1019)*
Kays Photography and Prints ....G.... 757 344-4817
Lynchburg *(G-7749)*
Kemper Printing LLC ....G.... 804 510-8402
Richmond *(G-11641)*
Kenmore Envelope Company Inc ....C.... 804 271-2100
Richmond *(G-11259)*
Kenneth Lee Woods ....G.... 703 361-7390
Manassas *(G-8093)*
Kibela Print LLC ....G.... 703 436-1646
Lorton *(G-7502)*
Kinkos Copies ....G.... 703 689-0004
Herndon *(G-6724)*
Kpw Ventures Inc ....G.... 703 725-6482
Herndon *(G-6725)*

Kwik Design and Print LLC ....G.... 703 898-4681
Woodbridge *(G-15737)*
L & M Printing Inc ....G.... 703 573-2257
Fairfax *(G-4496)*
L B Davis Inc ....G.... 434 792-3281
Ringgold *(G-11869)*
Labelink Flexibles LLC ....F.... 703 348-4699
Fredericksburg *(G-5448)*
Lake Lithograph Company ....D.... 703 361-8030
Manassas *(G-7959)*
Landmark Printing Co ....G.... 703 226-1000
Annandale *(G-769)*
Lark Printing Inc ....G.... 434 237-4449
Lynchburg *(G-7755)*
Lawyers Printing Co ....G.... 804 648-3664
Richmond *(G-11648)*
Learning To Lean Printing ....G.... 757 718-5586
Chesapeake *(G-3181)*
Legacy Printing Inc ....G.... 804 730-1834
Mechanicsville *(G-8651)*
Lehr Inc ....G.... 703 821-2679
Mc Lean *(G-8484)*
Lewis Printing Company ....E.... 804 648-2000
Richmond *(G-11652)*
Liberty Press Inc ....E.... 540 434-5513
Harrisonburg *(G-6338)*
Liberty Printing House Inc ....G.... 202 664-7702
Lorton *(G-7507)*
Life Management Company ....G.... 434 296-9762
Troy *(G-13932)*
Lightbox Print Co LLC ....G.... 919 608-9520
Richmond *(G-11654)*
Lil Guy Printing ....G.... 757 995-5705
Hampton *(G-6184)*
▲ Liskey & Sons Inc ....F.... 757 627-8712
Norfolk *(G-9620)*
Littlejohn Printing Co ....G.... 540 977-1377
Roanoke *(G-12126)*
Lone Tree Printing Inc ....F.... 757 473-9977
Virginia Beach *(G-14623)*
Louise J Walker ....G.... 540 788-4826
Calverton *(G-2225)*
Love In Print LLC ....G.... 757 739-2416
Chesapeake *(G-3188)*
Lsc Communications Us LLC ....A.... 540 434-8833
Rockingham *(G-12259)*
Luray Copy Services Inc ....G.... 540 743-3433
Luray *(G-7616)*
Lydell Group Incorporated ....G.... 804 627-0500
Richmond *(G-11277)*
M & S Publishing Co Inc ....G.... 434 645-7534
Crewe *(G-3814)*
M&M Printing LLC ....G.... 804 621-4171
Chester *(G-3431)*
M-J Printers Inc ....G.... 540 373-1878
Fredericksburg *(G-5202)*
Maclaren Endeavors LLC ....E.... 804 358-3493
Richmond *(G-11279)*
Macmurray Graphics & Prtg Inc ....G.... 703 680-4847
Montclair *(G-8999)*
Magnified Duplication Prtg Inc ....G.... 276 393-3193
Dryden *(G-4145)*
Marbrooke Printing Inc ....G.... 276 632-7115
Martinsville *(G-8307)*
Mardon Inc ....G.... 276 386-6662
Weber City *(G-15149)*
Mark Four Inc ....G.... 804 330-0765
Powhatan *(G-10557)*
Martin Publishing Corp ....E.... 804 780-1700
Richmond *(G-11668)*
Mary A Thomas ....G.... 434 637-2016
Emporia *(G-4363)*
Matric Kolor ....G.... 757 310-6764
Hampton *(G-6191)*
McCabe Enterprises Inc ....F.... 703 560-7755
Fairfax *(G-4504)*
McClung Printing Inc ....D.... 540 949-8139
Waynesboro *(G-15123)*
McFarland Enterprises Inc ....G.... 703 818-2900
Chantilly *(G-2461)*
Media Services of Richmond ....G.... 804 559-1000
Mechanicsville *(G-8660)*
Meridian Printing & Publishing ....G.... 757 627-8712
Norfolk *(G-9638)*
Metro Printing Center Inc ....G.... 703 620-3532
Reston *(G-10899)*
Michael Beach ....G.... 703 360-7284
Alexandria *(G-531)*
Mid-Atlantic Printers Ltd ....D.... 434 369-6633
Altavista *(G-636)*

Mid-Atlantic Printers Ltd ....G.... 703 448-1155
Vienna *(G-14092)*
Middleburg Printers LLC ....G.... 540 687-5710
Middleburg *(G-8729)*
Mikes Screen Printing ....G.... 276 971-9274
Pounding Mill *(G-10524)*
Minute Man Farms Inc ....G.... 540 423-1028
Culpeper *(G-3909)*
Minute Man Press ....G.... 757 464-6509
Norfolk *(G-9646)*
Minuteman Press ....G.... 757 903-0978
Williamsburg *(G-15279)*
Minuteman Press ....G.... 703 439-2160
Herndon *(G-6747)*
Minuteman Press ....G.... 703 220-7575
Fredericksburg *(G-5459)*
Minuteman Press ....G.... 540 774-1820
Salem *(G-12537)*
Minuteman Press ....G.... 804 441-9761
Richmond *(G-11292)*
Minuteman Press Intl ....G.... 703 299-1150
Alexandria *(G-277)*
Minuteman Press Intl Inc ....G.... 703 522-1944
Arlington *(G-1065)*
Minuteman Press Intl Inc ....G.... 703 787-6506
Reston *(G-10902)*
Minuteman Press of Chester ....G.... 804 898-0050
Chester *(G-3437)*
Minuteman Press of Mc Lean ....G.... 703 356-6612
Mc Lean *(G-8502)*
Minuteman Press of Vienna ....G.... 703 992-0420
Vienna *(G-14095)*
Miracle Prints & More ....G.... 540 656-9645
Fredericksburg *(G-5207)*
Mobile Ink LLC ....F.... 804 218-8384
Midlothian *(G-8861)*
Modern Graphix ....G.... 804 590-1303
South Chesterfield *(G-12838)*
Mogo Inc ....G.... 703 476-8595
Reston *(G-10903)*
Moon River Print Co ....G.... 804 350-2647
Powhatan *(G-10560)*
Mounir & Company Incorporated ....F.... 703 354-7400
Springfield *(G-13054)*
Mountaineer Publishing Co Inc ....G.... 276 935-2123
Grundy *(G-6038)*
Mr Graphics Print Shop LLC ....G.... 703 980-8239
Manassas *(G-8113)*
Mr Print ....G.... 540 338-5900
Purcellville *(G-10671)*
Mvp Press LLC ....F.... 703 661-6877
Dulles *(G-4210)*
My Printing Guys ....G.... 703 430-7940
Sterling *(G-13457)*
Mystery Whl & Screen Prtg LLC ....G.... 540 514-7349
Salem *(G-12542)*
N2n Specialty Printing LLC ....G.... 540 786-5765
Fredericksburg *(G-5331)*
National Lithograph Inc ....F.... 703 709-9000
Sterling *(G-13459)*
New Image Graphics Inc ....G.... 540 678-0900
Winchester *(G-15455)*
Next Level Printing ....G.... 757 288-1399
Norfolk *(G-9664)*
Niblick Inc ....G.... 804 550-1607
Ashland *(G-1470)*
Norfolk Printing Co ....G.... 757 627-1302
Norfolk *(G-9667)*
North Street Enterprise Inc ....E.... 434 392-4144
Farmville *(G-4954)*
Northern Vrgnia Prof Assoc Inc ....G.... 703 525-5218
Falls Church *(G-4837)*
Oasis Global LLC ....F.... 703 560-7755
Fairfax *(G-4524)*
Olde Petersburg Printers ....G.... 804 400-9644
Colonial Heights *(G-3740)*
Oldtown Printing & Copying ....G.... 540 382-6793
Christiansburg *(G-3607)*
Omega Alpha II Inc ....F.... 804 747-7705
Richmond *(G-11315)*
On The Dl Custom Prints LLC ....G.... 757 508-1609
Dumfries *(G-4253)*
One Four Three LLC ....G.... 303 594-7151
Virginia Beach *(G-14699)*
Open Prints LLC ....G.... 866 673-6110
Chesapeake *(G-3229)*
Optimize Print Solutions LLC ....G.... 703 856-7386
Lorton *(G-7519)*
Out of Print LLC ....G.... 919 368-0980
Norfolk *(G-9678)*

P I P Printing 1156 Inc..........G...... 434 792-0020
Danville *(G-4022)*

P M Resources Inc..........G...... 703 556-0155
Springfield *(G-13065)*

Page Printing Connection..........G...... 540 743-7746
Luray *(G-7621)*

Parent Resource Center..........G...... 757 482-5923
Chesapeake *(G-3233)*

Parkland Direct Inc..........D...... 434 385-6225
Forest *(G-5086)*

Parkway Printshop..........G...... 757 378-3959
Williamsburg *(G-15291)*

Party Headquarters Inc..........G...... 703 494-5317
Fredericksburg *(G-5467)*

Pattern and Print LLC..........G...... 540 884-2660
Fincastle *(G-4997)*

Paul Owens..........G...... 804 393-2475
Henrico *(G-6547)*

Paw Print Pet Services..........G...... 434 822-5020
Ringgold *(G-11873)*

Paw Prints..........G...... 540 220-2825
Spotsylvania *(G-12908)*

PCC Corporation..........F...... 757 368-5777
Virginia Beach *(G-14714)*

PDQ Printing Company..........G...... 804 228-0077
Richmond *(G-11709)*

Perfect Image Printing..........G...... 703 824-0010
Falls Church *(G-4856)*

Person Enterprises Inc..........G...... 757 483-6252
Portsmouth *(G-10468)*

Personal Touch Printing Svcs..........G...... 757 619-7073
Virginia Beach *(G-14718)*

Peter Korer..........G...... 702 460-2144
Chesapeake *(G-3237)*

Petree Enterprises Inc..........F...... 703 318-0008
Sterling *(G-13469)*

Pic N Press Custom Prtg LLC..........G...... 571 970-2627
Alexandria *(G-550)*

Piccadilly Printing Company..........F...... 540 662-3804
Winchester *(G-15566)*

PIP Boonchan..........G...... 571 327-5522
Springfield *(G-13069)*

Pixel Designs & Printing..........G...... 571 359-6080
Manassas *(G-8130)*

Pop Printing..........G...... 804 248-9093
Richmond *(G-11719)*

Postal Instant Press Inc..........G...... 703 866-1988
Springfield *(G-13072)*

Potomac Printing Solutions Inc..........D...... 703 723-2511
Leesburg *(G-7326)*

Powell Valley Printing Company..........F...... 276 546-1210
Pennington Gap *(G-10297)*

Powerup Printing Inc..........G...... 804 364-1353
Glen Allen *(G-5781)*

Precision Print & Copy LLC..........G...... 804 740-3514
Richmond *(G-11330)*

Precision Printers..........G...... 703 525-5113
Arlington *(G-1119)*

Press On Printing LLC..........G...... 434 575-0990
South Boston *(G-12787)*

Press-Well Services Inc..........G...... 540 923-4799
Madison *(G-7861)*

Pressed 4 Ink - Custom Apparel..........G...... 540 693-4023
Fredericksburg *(G-5350)*

Prestige Press Inc..........E...... 757 826-5881
Hampton *(G-6220)*

Prinit Corporation..........F...... 703 847-8880
Vienna *(G-14114)*

Print A Promo LLC..........G...... 800 675-6869
Middletown *(G-8742)*

Print Afrik LLC..........G...... 202 594-0836
Woodbridge *(G-15782)*

Print City..........G...... 703 931-1114
Falls Church *(G-4857)*

Print Life LLC..........G...... 609 442-2838
Williamsburg *(G-15300)*

Print Link Inc..........G...... 757 368-5200
Virginia Beach *(G-14739)*

Print LLC..........G...... 757 746-5708
Newport News *(G-9316)*

Print Mail Direct LLC..........G...... 540 899-6451
Fredericksburg *(G-5472)*

Print Plus..........G...... 276 322-2043
Bluefield *(G-1876)*

Print Promotion..........G...... 202 618-8822
Alexandria *(G-316)*

Print Rayge Studios LLC..........G...... 757 537-6995
Richmond *(G-11725)*

Print Republic LLC..........G...... 757 633-9099
Virginia Beach *(G-14740)*

Print Squad LLC..........G...... 434 609-3335
Lynchburg *(G-7788)*

Print Time Inc..........G...... 202 232-0582
Alexandria *(G-555)*

Print World Inc..........F...... 434 237-2200
Alexandria *(G-323)*

Print-N-Paper Inc..........G...... 540 719-7277
Moneta *(G-8974)*

Printcraft Press Incorporated..........E...... 757 397-0759
Portsmouth *(G-10473)*

Printech Inc..........F...... 540 343-9200
Roanoke *(G-12154)*

Printer Fix LLC..........G...... 540 532-4948
Front Royal *(G-5549)*

Printer Gatherer LLC..........G...... 540 420-2426
Henrico *(G-6551)*

Printer Resolutions..........G...... 703 850-5336
Sterling *(G-13478)*

Printers Research Co..........G...... 540 721-9916
Moneta *(G-8975)*

Printersmark Inc..........G...... 804 353-2324
Richmond *(G-11333)*

Printing 4 Kids..........G...... 703 474-1519
Alexandria *(G-556)*

Printing and Sign System Inc..........G...... 703 280-1550
Fairfax *(G-4532)*

Printing Concepts of Virg..........G...... 540 904-5951
Roanoke *(G-12155)*

Printing Department Inc..........G...... 804 282-2739
Richmond *(G-11334)*

Printing Dept Inc..........G...... 804 673-1904
Richmond *(G-11335)*

Printing Dept LLC..........G...... 703 931-5450
Alexandria *(G-317)*

Printing Express Inc..........E...... 540 433-1237
Harrisonburg *(G-6356)*

Printing For You..........G...... 540 351-0191
Warrenton *(G-15045)*

Printing Ideas Inc..........G...... 703 591-1708
Fairfax *(G-4533)*

Printing Plus..........G...... 434 376-3379
Brookneal *(G-2111)*

Printing Productions Inc..........G...... 703 406-2400
Sterling *(G-13479)*

Printing Services..........G...... 540 434-5783
Harrisonburg *(G-6357)*

Printline Graphics LLC..........G...... 757 547-3107
Chesapeake *(G-3248)*

Printpros LLC..........G...... 804 550-1607
Ashland *(G-1480)*

Printpros LLC..........G...... 804 789-8884
Mechanicsville *(G-8668)*

Printsmith Ink..........G...... 540 323-7554
Winchester *(G-15569)*

Printwell Inc..........F...... 757 564-3302
Williamsburg *(G-15301)*

Pritchard Studio..........G...... 276 935-5829
Grundy *(G-6040)*

Pro-Graphx..........G...... 844 777-0288
Martinsville *(G-8321)*

Professional Business Prtg Inc..........G...... 804 423-1355
Richmond *(G-11337)*

Professional Printing Ctr Inc..........E...... 757 547-1990
Chesapeake *(G-3250)*

Professional Services..........G...... 540 953-2223
Blacksburg *(G-1781)*

Program Services LLC..........G...... 757 222-3990
Norfolk *(G-9698)*

Prographics Print Xpress..........G...... 757 606-8303
Virginia Beach *(G-14743)*

Progress Printing Company..........D...... 434 239-9213
Lynchburg *(G-7790)*

Progressive Graphics Inc..........E...... 757 368-3321
Virginia Beach *(G-14744)*

Protoquick Printing LLC..........G...... 202 417-4243
Centreville *(G-2329)*

Pursuit Packaging LLC..........G...... 540 246-4629
Broadway *(G-2094)*

Pwillz Customz LLC..........G...... 571 926-9622
Sterling *(G-13481)*

Qg LLC..........C...... 804 264-3866
Richmond *(G-11343)*

Qg LLC..........C...... 540 722-6000
Winchester *(G-15462)*

Qg Printing II Corp..........A...... 540 722-6000
Winchester *(G-15463)*

Quality Graphics & Prtg Inc..........F...... 703 661-6060
Sterling *(G-13483)*

Quality Printing..........G...... 276 632-1415
Martinsville *(G-8322)*

Quality Stamp Co..........G...... 757 858-0653
Norfolk *(G-9700)*

R & B Communications LLC..........G...... 703 348-7088
Haymarket *(G-6439)*

R & B Impressions Inc..........F...... 703 823-9050
Alexandria *(G-323)*

R B M Enterprises Inc..........G...... 804 290-4407
Glen Allen *(G-5786)*

R R Donnelley & Sons Company..........F...... 540 432-5453
Rockingham *(G-12268)*

R R Donnelley & Sons Company..........B...... 540 564-3900
Harrisonburg *(G-6359)*

R R Donnelley & Sons Company..........C...... 434 846-7371
Salem *(G-12560)*

Rapid Printing Inc..........G...... 540 586-1243
Bedford *(G-1654)*

Rappahannock Entp Assoc Inc..........G...... 703 560-5042
Falls Church *(G-4862)*

Rappahannock Record..........F...... 804 435-1701
Kilmarnock *(G-7076)*

Recorder Publishing of VA Inc..........F...... 540 468-2147
Monterey *(G-9012)*

Redprint Strategy..........G...... 202 656-1002
Alexandria *(G-327)*

Reed Envelope Company Inc..........F...... 703 690-2249
Fairfax Station *(G-4722)*

Reeses Amazing Printing Svcs..........G...... 804 325-0947
Henrico *(G-6556)*

Reston Copy Center..........G...... 703 860-9600
Herndon *(G-6788)*

Reston Copy Center Inc..........G...... 703 860-9600
Reston *(G-10938)*

Revolution Rising Print..........G...... 804 276-4789
Richmond *(G-11734)*

Richmond CLB of Prnt Hse Crfts..........F...... 804 748-3075
Chester *(G-3451)*

Rite Print Shoppe & Supply..........G...... 540 745-3616
Floyd *(G-5038)*

River City Graphics LLC..........G...... 757 519-9525
Virginia Beach *(G-14777)*

River City Printing Graphics..........G...... 804 226-8100
Richmond *(G-11740)*

Rmae Inc..........G...... 804 651-6911
Petersburg *(G-10339)*

Roasters Pride Inc..........G...... 703 440-0627
Springfield *(G-13080)*

Robert Douglas LLC..........G...... 434 284-5111
Charlottesville *(G-2688)*

Rockingham Publishing Co Inc..........C...... 540 574-6200
Harrisonburg *(G-6363)*

Ronald Carpenter..........G...... 757 471-3805
Virginia Beach *(G-14780)*

Rowley Group Inc..........G...... 703 522-1944
Arlington *(G-1153)*

Roxen Incorporated..........G...... 571 208-0782
Manassas *(G-7997)*

Royal Printing Company..........G...... 804 798-8897
Glen Allen *(G-5789)*

Royalcanvascom..........G...... 866 673-6110
Chesapeake *(G-3277)*

Roys Copies..........G...... 804 744-6200
Midlothian *(G-8894)*

Royster Printing Services Inc..........G...... 757 545-3019
Chesapeake *(G-3278)*

RPM 3d Printing..........G...... 757 266-3168
Virginia Beach *(G-14783)*

S J Printing Inc..........G...... 703 378-7142
Manassas Park *(G-8210)*

S&Sprinting..........G...... 434 581-1983
New Canton *(G-9119)*

Safe Harbor Press LLC..........G...... 757 490-1960
Virginia Beach *(G-14789)*

Safeguard Printing Promo..........G...... 804 378-2166
Midlothian *(G-8895)*

Safehouse Signs Inc..........E...... 540 366-2480
Roanoke *(G-12174)*

Salem Printing Co..........E...... 540 387-1106
Salem *(G-12566)*

Sandcastle Screen Printing LLC..........G...... 757 740-0611
Virginia Beach *(G-14792)*

Sb Printing LLC..........G...... 804 247-2404
Richmond *(G-11373)*

Schmids Printing..........G...... 540 886-9261
Staunton *(G-13290)*

Schreiber Inc R G..........E...... 540 248-5300
Verona *(G-13995)*

Scsi4me Corporation..........G...... 703 372-1195
Springfield *(G-13082)*

Seatrix Print LLC..........G...... 571 241-5748
Woodbridge *(G-15804)*

Sedley Printing .... G 757 562-5738
Sedley *(G-12680)*

▲ Sennett Security Products LLC ...... G ... 703 803-8880
Centreville *(G-2338)*

Service Printing of Lynchburg .... G 434 845-3681
Lynchburg *(G-7806)*

Seven Sevens Inc .... G 757 340-1300
Norfolk *(G-9718)*

Shamrock Screen Print LLC .... G 540 219-4337
Culpeper *(G-3919)*

Shelley Imprssons Prtg Copying .... G 540 310-0766
Fredericksburg *(G-5485)*

Shen-Val Screen Printing LLC .... G 540 869-2713
White Post *(G-15183)*

Shenandoah Publications Inc .... E 540 459-4000
Edinburg *(G-4314)*

Shenandoah Valley Printin .... G 540 208-1808
Rockingham *(G-12276)*

Shoeprint .... G 703 499-9136
Woodbridge *(G-15807)*

Sign & Print .... G 703 707-8556
Herndon *(G-6806)*

Signarama Richmond .... G 804 301-9317
North Chesterfield *(G-9979)*

Silver Communications Corp .... E 703 471-7339
Sterling *(G-13508)*

Silverado Printing LLC .... G 703 407-8720
Fairfax *(G-4556)*

Sir Speedy Printing Ctr 7411 .... G 703 821-8781
Mc Lean *(G-8547)*

Smyth Companies LLC .... C 540 586-2311
Bedford *(G-1658)*

Sonya Davis Enterprises LLC .... G 703 264-0533
Forest *(G-5094)*

Southern Printing Co Inc .... E 540 552-8352
Blacksburg *(G-1793)*

Southwest Publisher LLC .... E 540 980-5220
Pulaski *(G-10647)*

Standard Printing Company Inc .... F 540 965-1150
Covington *(G-3799)*

Staples Print & Marketing .... G 434 218-6425
Charlottesville *(G-2696)*

Star Printing Co Inc .... G 757 625-7782
Chesapeake *(G-3311)*

Steamed Ink .... G 540 904-6211
Roanoke *(G-12196)*

Stephenson Lithograph Inc .... G 703 241-0806
Arlington *(G-1176)*

Stephenson Printing Inc. .... D 703 642-9000
Alexandria *(G-589)*

Sterling Flyers Inc .... G 571 830-4476
Reston *(G-10966)*

Stich N Print .... G 276 326-2005
Bluefield *(G-1879)*

Strategic Print Solutions LLC .... G 703 272-3440
Haymarket *(G-6449)*

Suday Promotions Inc .... G 703 376-8640
Chantilly *(G-2503)*

Sumi LLC .... G 571 287-9480
Harrisonburg *(G-6375)*

Sustainable Green Prtg Partnr .... G 703 359-1376
Fairfax *(G-4563)*

Suter Enterprises Ltd .... F 757 220-3299
Williamsburg *(G-15320)*

Sweet and Simple Prints .... G 757 710-1116
Blacksburg *(G-1796)*

Swift Print Inc .... F 540 362-2200
Roanoke *(G-12199)*

Swift Print Inc .... G 540 343-8300
Roanoke *(G-12200)*

Symmetric Systems Inc .... G 804 276-7202
North Chesterfield *(G-9997)*

T Bc .... G 703 969-8221
Manassas *(G-8002)*

Tagg Design Specialty Prtg LLC .... G 804 572-7777
Tappahannock *(G-13823)*

Teagle & Little Incorporated .... D 757 622-5793
Norfolk *(G-9744)*

Tech Express Inc .... G 540 382-9400
Christiansburg *(G-3611)*

Text Art Print .... G 908 619-2809
North Chesterfield *(G-10000)*

Thermo Quick Inc .... G 703 455-0040
Fredericksburg *(G-5377)*

Think Ink Printing .... G 757 315-8565
Chesapeake *(G-3332)*

Thredz EMB Screen Print Graph .... G 757 636-9569
Virginia Beach *(G-14869)*

Thumbprint Events By .... G 703 720-1000
Henrico *(G-6581)*

TI Printing of Virginia LLC .... G 757 315-8565
Chesapeake *(G-3335)*

Tidewater Graphics Inc .... G 757 464-6136
Virginia Beach *(G-14874)*

Tidewater Printers Inc .... F 757 888-0674
Newport News *(G-9355)*

Timothy E Quinn .... G 301 212-9700
Alexandria *(G-365)*

Total Printing Co Inc .... E 804 222-3813
Richmond *(G-11416)*

Touch Honey Dsgn Print Photg .... G 757 606-0411
Chesapeake *(G-3345)*

Tr Press Inc .... E 540 347-4466
Warrenton *(G-15055)*

Trademark Printing LLC .... G 757 410-1800
Portsmouth *(G-10492)*

Trademark Printing LLC .... G 757 803-7612
Chesapeake *(G-3348)*

Tried & True Printing LLC .... G 434 964-8202
Charlottesville *(G-2895)*

Tshirtpod .... G 423 341-8655
Bristol *(G-2037)*

Type Etc .... G 540 347-2182
Warrenton *(G-15057)*

U3 Solutions Inc .... G 703 777-5020
Leesburg *(G-7366)*

United Litho Inc .... G 703 858-4213
Ashburn *(G-1345)*

Universal Printing .... F 276 466-9311
Bristol *(G-1996)*

Upm Kymmene Inc .... G 540 465-2700
Strasburg *(G-13601)*

US Parcel & Copy Center Inc .... G 703 365-7999
Manassas *(G-8007)*

Variety Printing Inc .... G 757 480-1891
Chesapeake *(G-3359)*

Veterans Printing LLC .... G 571 208-0074
Manassas *(G-8175)*

Via Services LLC .... G 703 978-2629
Burke *(G-2206)*

Vibrant Prints LLC .... G 843 425-2506
Reston *(G-10984)*

Victoria Austin .... G 276 632-1742
Martinsville *(G-8346)*

Virginia Beach Printing & Sty .... G 757 428-4282
Virginia Beach *(G-14911)*

Virginia Gazette Companies LLC .... G 757 220-1736
Newport News *(G-9373)*

Virginia Printing Services Inc .... F 757 838-5500
Hampton *(G-6263)*

Virginia Prtg Co Roanoke Inc .... G 540 483-7433
Roanoke *(G-12219)*

Virginia Prtg Co Roanoke Inc .... G 540 483-7433
Rocky Mount *(G-12360)*

Virginia Screen Printing .... G 804 295-7440
North Dinwiddie *(G-10068)*

Vistaprint .... G 757 483-2357
Portsmouth *(G-10498)*

Visual GRAphics&designs .... G 804 221-6983
Mechanicsville *(G-8697)*

◆ Vitex Packaging Inc .... C 757 538-3115
Suffolk *(G-13779)*

Walters Printing & Mfg Co .... F 540 345-8161
Roanoke *(G-12227)*

Walton Industries Inc. .... G 540 898-7888
Fredericksburg *(G-5389)*

Waterford Printing Inc .... G 757 442-5616
Exmore *(G-4387)*

Watts & Ward Inc .... G 703 435-3388
Sterling *(G-13560)*

Wave Printing & Graphics Inc .... G 540 373-1600
Fredericksburg *(G-5390)*

Webb-Mason Inc .... G 703 391-0626
Oakton *(G-10164)*

Webb-Mason Inc .... E 703 242-7278
Reston *(G-10988)*

Welsh Printing Corporation .... G 703 534-0232
Falls Church *(G-4928)*

Western Graphics Inc .... G 575 849-1209
Alexandria *(G-381)*

Westrock Commercial LLC .... E 804 444-1000
Richmond *(G-11824)*

Whats Your Sign .... G 276 632-0576
Martinsville *(G-8353)*

Wilderness Prints .... G 540 309-6803
Moneta *(G-8985)*

Wilkinson Printing Co Inc .... G 804 264-2524
Glen Allen *(G-5828)*

▲ William R Smith Company .... E 804 733-0123
Petersburg *(G-10351)*

Willimsburg Prcess Sltions LLC .... G 703 577-4448
Williamsburg *(G-15345)*

Winchester Printers Inc .... E 540 662-6911
Winchester *(G-15512)*

Wise Printing Co Inc .... G 276 523-1141
Big Stone Gap *(G-1718)*

Wjm Printed Products Inc .... G 757 870-1043
Yorktown *(G-16003)*

Wood Television LLC .... D 540 825-4416
Culpeper *(G-3932)*

Wood Television LLC .... C 434 385-5400
Lynchburg *(G-7840)*

Wood Television LLC .... E 540 672-1266
Orange *(G-10232)*

Woodbridge Printing Co .... G 703 494-7333
Woodbridge *(G-15834)*

Woody Graphics Inc .... G 540 774-4749
Roanoke *(G-12025)*

Wordsprint Inc .... G 540 382-9111
Blacksburg *(G-1807)*

Wordsprint Inc .... E 276 228-6608
Wytheville *(G-15925)*

Workhorse Print Solutions LLC .... G 703 707-1648
Reston *(G-10995)*

Wss Richmond .... G 804 722-0150
Prince George *(G-10611)*

Wythken LLC .... G 804 353-8282
Richmond *(G-11835)*

Xpress Copy & Graphics .... G 540 829-1785
Culpeper *(G-3933)*

Your Personal Printer .... G 757 679-1139
Virginia Beach *(G-14955)*

Zb 3d Printers LLC .... G 757 695-8278
Virginia Beach *(G-14956)*

Zine Graphics Print .... G 703 591-4000
Fairfax *(G-4698)*

Ziva Prints LLC .... G 571 265-9030
Ashburn *(G-1357)*

◆ Zooom Printing LLC .... F 804 343-0009
Richmond *(G-11464)*

Zramics Mtls Science Tech LLC .... G 757 955-0493
Norfolk *(G-9801)*

2754 Commercial Printing: Gravure

◆ Addressograph Bartizan LLC .... E 800 552-3282
Rocky Mount *(G-12311)*

Blue Ridge Buck Saver Inc .... G 434 996-2817
Charlottesville *(G-2743)*

Charlotte Publishing Inc. .... F 434 568-3341
Drakes Branch *(G-4131)*

Clipper Magazine LLC .... G 888 569-5100
Fairfax *(G-4606)*

Grabber Construction Pdts Inc .... G 804 550-9331
Ashland *(G-1423)*

K/R Companies LLC .... G 540 812-2422
Culpeper *(G-3903)*

Knight Owl Graphics .... G 540 955-1744
Berryville *(G-1683)*

Label Laboratory Inc .... G 703 654-0327
Sterling *(G-13439)*

Laura Hooper Calligrathy .... G 213 514-4170
Alexandria *(G-513)*

Lloyd Enterprises Inc .... G 804 266-1185
Richmond *(G-11273)*

Loron Inc .... G 804 780-0000
Henrico *(G-6531)*

Magnolia Graphics .... G 804 550-0012
Ashland *(G-1458)*

R & R Printing .... G 434 985-9844
Ruckersville *(G-12411)*

R R Donnelley & Sons Company .... C 434 846-7371
Salem *(G-12560)*

Reeses Amazing Printing Svcs .... G 804 325-0947
Henrico *(G-6556)*

Schmitt Realty Holdings Inc .... E 203 453-4334
Sandston *(G-12631)*

Southern Graphic Systems LLC .... D 804 226-2490
Richmond *(G-11764)*

Stay In Touch Inc .... F 434 239-7300
Forest *(G-5095)*

Taylor Communications Inc .... G 804 612-7597
Richmond *(G-11407)*

◆ Vitex Packaging Group Inc .... F 757 538-3115
Suffolk *(G-13780)*

Zramics Mtls Science Tech LLC .... G 757 955-0493
Norfolk *(G-9801)*

2759 Commercial Printing

12th Tee LLC .... G 276 620-7601
Wytheville *(G-15873)*

1816 Potters Road LLC....G....757 428-1170
Virginia Beach (G-14194)
3cats Promo....G....540 586-7014
Goode (G-5888)
4l Inc....G....434 792-0020
Danville (G-3951)
A & S Screen Printing....G....540 464-9042
Lexington (G-7386)
A Z Printing and Dup Corp....G....703 549-0949
Alexandria (G-115)
ABC Imaging....G....214 231-1332
Alexandria (G-399)
ABC Imaging....G....571 379-4299
Manassas (G-8017)
ABC Imaging of Washington....F....202 429-8870
Alexandria (G-400)
ABC Imaging of Washington....E....202 429-8870
Chantilly (G-2362)
ABC Imaging of Washington....E....703 396-9081
Manassas (G-7909)
ABC Imaging of Washington....F....571 514-1033
Herndon (G-6602)
Ace Screen Printing Inc....G....540 297-2200
Bedford (G-1617)
Action Tshirts LLC....G....804 359-4645
Richmond (G-11084)
Adoptees....G....571 483-0656
Arlington (G-840)
Alexander Amir....G....757 714-1802
Suffolk (G-13665)
Alien Silkscreen LLC....F....540 389-5699
Salem (G-12473)
Alpha Printing Inc....G....703 914-2800
Fairfax (G-4404)
Amazengraved LLC....G....540 313-5658
Winchester (G-15376)
Ambrosia Press Inc....G....540 432-1801
Weyers Cave (G-15165)
American Graphics....G....540 977-1912
Troutville (G-13902)
American Laser Centers....G....804 200-5000
Richmond (G-11109)
Anthony Biel....G....703 307-8516
Dumfries (G-4234)
Apollo Press Inc....E....757 247-9002
Newport News (G-9169)
Applied Pressures Diamond....G....757 967-7006
Norfolk (G-9443)
Appomattox River Engraving....G....804 561-3565
Amelia Court House (G-652)
ARC Document Solutions Inc....G....703 518-8890
Alexandria (G-139)
Archematerial Inc....G....703 826-6820
Fairfax (G-4411)
Arkay Packaging Corporation....D....540 278-2596
Roanoke (G-11882)
Arrington & Sons Inc....G....703 368-1462
Manassas (G-7911)
Art Guild Inc....F....804 282-5434
Henrico (G-6476)
Arteffects....G....804 266-7691
Henrico (G-6477)
Artisan II Inc....G....703 823-4636
Alexandria (G-141)
Artistees....G....540 373-2888
Fredericksburg (G-5170)
Associate Business Co Inc....G....703 222-4624
Chantilly (G-2371)
Atlantic Textile Group Inc....F....757 249-7777
Newport News (G-9173)
B & J Embroidery Inc....G....276 646-5631
Saltville (G-12584)
Bara Printing Services....G....804 303-8615
Richmond (G-11028)
Barbours Printing Service....G....804 443-4505
Tappahannock (G-13813)
Bayview Engrv Art GL Studio....G....757 331-1595
Cape Charles (G-2229)
Beacon....G....540 408-2560
Fredericksburg (G-5251)
Beautees....G....757 439-0269
Suffolk (G-13677)
Benjamin Franklin Printing Co....F....804 648-6361
Richmond (G-11504)
Best Deal On Shirts LLC....G....757 754-9855
Chesapeake (G-2998)
Big Image Graphics Inc....E....804 379-9910
North Chesterfield (G-9832)
Bigeye Direct Inc....D....703 955-3017
Herndon (G-6624)
Bison Printing Inc....E....540 586-3955
Bedford (G-1627)
Black Eyed Tees....G....276 971-1219
Pounding Mill (G-10515)
Black Magazine LLC....G....804 306-6735
Highland Springs (G-6850)
Blanco Inc....F....540 389-3040
Roanoke (G-11891)
Blue Ridge Embroidery Inc....G....434 296-9746
Charlottesville (G-2744)
Bobhron Inc....F....540 389-5699
Roanoke (G-12054)
Brandito LLC....E....804 747-6721
Richmond (G-11508)
Branner Printing Service Inc....E....540 896-8947
Broadway (G-2085)
Breakaway Holdings LLC....F....703 953-3866
Chantilly (G-2381)
Brewco Corp....G....540 389-2554
Salem (G-12486)
Brook Summer Media....G....804 435-0074
White Stone (G-15186)
Brooke Printing....G....757 617-2188
Virginia Beach (G-14300)
Bruce Moore Printing Co....G....703 361-0369
Manassas (G-7922)
Bryant Embroidery LLC....G....757 498-3453
Virginia Beach (G-14303)
Burden Bearer Tees LLC....G....757 337-7324
Toano (G-13858)
Burruss Signs Inc....G....434 296-6654
Charlottesville (G-2751)
Bxi Inc....G....804 282-5434
Richmond (G-11142)
C2-Mask Inc....G....703 304-9319
Chantilly (G-2384)
Capital Brandworks LLC....G....703 609-7010
Fairfax (G-4423)
Capital Ideas Press....G....434 447-6377
South Hill (G-12846)
Capital Screen Prtg Unlimited....G....703 550-0033
Lorton (G-7470)
Carl G Gilliam Jr....F....276 523-0619
Big Stone Gap (G-1707)
Carla Wilkes....G....434 228-1427
Lynchburg (G-7674)
Cassandras Custom Designs LLC....G....571 229-0389
Manassas (G-8047)
CCI Screenprinting Inc....G....703 978-0257
Fairfax (G-4425)
Chameleon Silk Screen Co....G....434 985-7456
Stanardsville (G-13217)
Charlette Publishing Inc....G....434 696-5550
Victoria (G-14000)
Chocklett Press Inc....D....540 345-1820
Roanoke (G-12066)
CK Graphicwear LLC....G....804 464-1258
Richmond (G-11034)
Clarke B Gray....G....757 426-7227
Virginia Beach (G-14342)
Clarke Inc....F....434 847-5561
Moneta (G-8959)
Classic Creations Screen Prtg....G....276 728-0540
Hillsville (G-6889)
Coalfield Progress....D....276 679-1101
Norton (G-10115)
Collinsville Printing Co....E....276 666-4400
Martinsville (G-8276)
Color Quest LLC....G....540 433-4890
Harrisonburg (G-6303)
Commercial Copies....G....757 473-0234
Virginia Beach (G-14357)
Commercial Press Inc....F....540 869-3496
Stephens City (G-13313)
Commercial Prtg Drect Mail Svc....G....757 422-0606
Virginia Beach (G-14358)
Commonwealth Graphics Inc....G....703 495-0733
Fairfax Station (G-4702)
Commonwlth Prmtnl/Dctional LLC....F....540 887-2321
Staunton (G-13249)
Complex Prints LLC....G....804 274-0266
Richmond (G-11537)
Confetti Advertising Inc....G....276 646-5806
Chilhowie (G-3548)
Core Health Thermography....G....434 207-4810
Troy (G-13923)
Corporate Imprints....G....804 965-9838
Henrico (G-6494)
Cotton Connection....G....434 528-1416
Lynchburg (G-7686)
Courtney Press....G....804 266-8359
Richmond (G-11544)
Creative Designs LLC....G....540 223-0083
Louisa (G-7551)
Creative Impressions Inc....G....757 855-2187
Virginia Beach (G-14371)
Creative Ink Inc....G....540 342-2400
Roanoke (G-12074)
Creative Occasions....G....703 821-3210
Mc Lean (G-8412)
Csl Media LLC....G....540 785-3790
Fredericksburg (G-5181)
Custom Baked Tees....G....703 888-8539
Arlington (G-923)
Custom Ink....G....703 957-1648
Reston (G-10830)
Custom Ink....G....703 884-2678
Gainesville (G-5576)
Custom Ink....G....703 884-2680
Leesburg (G-7250)
Custom Ink....G....434 422-5206
Charlottesville (G-2775)
Custom Ink....G....804 419-5651
Richmond (G-11550)
Custom Logos....G....804 967-0111
Richmond (G-11173)
Customink LLC....C....434 326-1051
Charlottesville (G-2613)
Cut and Bleed LLC....G....804 937-0006
Richmond (G-11176)
Cynthia E Cox....G....276 236-7697
Galax (G-5632)
D J R Enterprises Inc....F....540 639-9386
Radford (G-10708)
Davis Communications Group....G....703 548-8892
Alexandria (G-185)
Deadline Typesetting Inc....G....757 625-5883
Norfolk (G-9520)
Debs Picture This Inc....G....757 867-9588
Yorktown (G-15949)
Decals By Zebra Racing....G....540 439-8883
Bealeton (G-1597)
Delrand Corp....G....757 490-3355
Virginia Beach (G-14401)
Diamond 7....G....540 362-5958
Roanoke (G-11915)
Diamond Screen Graphics Inc....G....804 249-4414
Henrico (G-6500)
Digilink Inc....E....703 340-1800
Alexandria (G-188)
Dister Inc....E....757 857-1946
Norfolk (G-9525)
Dister Inc....E....703 207-0201
Fairfax (G-4439)
Diversity Grphics Slutions LLC....G....757 812-3311
Hampton (G-6129)
Dixie Press Custom Screen....G....757 569-8241
Sedley (G-12679)
Dreambuilders USA LLC....G....908 265-2621
Hampton (G-6134)
Dreams2realitees LLC....G....434 594-6865
Emporia (G-4357)
Drip Printing & Design....G....757 962-1594
Virginia Beach (G-14413)
Drmtees LLC....G....540 720-3743
Stafford (G-13138)
DS Tees LLC....G....540 841-8831
Fredericksburg (G-5278)
Dt Enterprises Inc....G....434 799-3153
Danville (G-3987)
Dull Inc Dolan & Norma....F....703 490-0337
Woodbridge (G-15687)
Dynamic Graphic Finishing Inc....G....540 869-0500
Winchester (G-15413)
Eagle Designs....G....540 428-1916
Warrenton (G-15001)
Earl Wood Printing Co....G....540 563-8833
Roanoke (G-12082)
East Coast Graphics Inc....G....804 798-7100
Ashland (G-1406)
Edgelit Designz & Engrv LLC....G....540 373-8058
Fredericksburg (G-5425)
Eggleston Minor....G....757 819-4958
Norfolk (G-9542)
Ek Screen Prints....G....703 250-2556
Fairfax (G-4445)
El Chamo Printing....G....703 582-5782
Manassas (G-7936)
Eleven West Inc....E....540 639-9319
Fairlawn (G-4736)

Elite Prints ....G...... 703 780-3403
Alexandria **(G-455)**

Elizabeth Urban ....G...... 757 879-1815
Yorktown **(G-15952)**

Enexdi LLC ....F...... 703 748-0596
Vienna **(G-14048)**

Exquisite Invitations Inc ....G...... 276 666-0168
Martinsville **(G-8286)**

Fairway Products Inc ....G...... 804 462-0123
Lancaster **(G-7161)**

Fatim and Sallys Cstm Tees LLC ...G...... 619 884-5864
Chesapeake **(G-3098)**

Fedex Office & Print Svcs Inc ....G...... 703 491-1300
Woodbridge **(G-15703)**

Folder Factory ....G...... 540 984-8852
Edinburg **(G-4304)**

◆ Fortis Solutions Group LLC ....G...... 757 340-8893
Virginia Beach **(G-14472)**

Frederick J Day PC ....G...... 703 820-0110
Falls Church **(G-4794)**

Fso Mission Support LLC ....G...... 571 528-3507
Leesburg **(G-7275)**

G and H Litho ....G...... 571 267-7148
Sterling **(G-13404)**

Gaia Communications LLC ....G...... 703 370-5527
Alexandria **(G-210)**

Garmonte LLC ....G...... 703 575-9003
Alexandria **(G-213)**

Gary D Keys Enterprises Inc ......G...... 703 418-1700
Arlington **(G-975)**

General Financial Supply Inc ......E...... 540 828-3892
Bridgewater **(G-1952)**

Gival Press LLC ....G...... 703 351-0079
Arlington **(G-979)**

Global Promos ....G...... 804 744-8112
Midlothian **(G-8823)**

Golden Squeegee Inc ....G...... 804 355-8018
Richmond **(G-11220)**

Goochland Tees Inc ....G...... 804 708-2041
Oilville **(G-10178)**

Gotham Graphix LLC ....G...... 540 456-6600
Afton **(G-83)**

Gray Scale Productions ....G...... 757 363-1087
Virginia Beach **(G-14490)**

Grubb Printing & Stamp Co Inc ...F...... 757 295-8061
Portsmouth **(G-10438)**

Gunnys Call Inc ....G...... 757 892-0251
Virginia Beach **(G-14496)**

Hampton Roads Bindery Inc ....G...... 757 369-5671
Newport News **(G-9241)**

Hampton Roads Wedding Guide ...G...... 757 474-0332
Virginia Beach **(G-14501)**

Harari Investments ....G...... 703 842-7462
Arlington **(G-988)**

Harrison Management Associates ...G...... 703 237-0418
Arlington **(G-989)**

Harville Entps of Danville VA ......G...... 434 822-2106
Danville **(G-3997)**

Haverline Labels Inc ....G...... 276 647-7785
Collinsville **(G-3712)**

Heritage Treasures LLC ....G...... 571 442-8027
Ashburn **(G-1289)**

High Peak Sportswear Inc ....G...... 540 953-1293
Blacksburg **(G-1743)**

Hometown Imprints Inc ....G...... 540 878-5848
Warrenton **(G-15025)**

Hr Wellness and Thermography ...G...... 434 361-1996
Roseland **(G-12369)**

Huds Tees ....G...... 757 650-6190
Virginia Beach **(G-14532)**

Hughes Posters LLC ....G...... 304 615-3433
Henrico **(G-6523)**

Imagine This Company ....F...... 804 232-1300
Richmond **(G-11614)**

Impressions of Norton Inc ....G...... 276 328-1100
Wise **(G-15626)**

Impressions of Norton Inc ....G...... 276 679-1560
Norton **(G-10121)**

Imprint ID Ltd ....G...... 877 385-7785
Lorton **(G-7495)**

Industry Graphics ....G...... 540 345-6074
Roanoke **(G-11939)**

▲ Infoseal LLC ....D...... 540 981-1140
Roanoke **(G-12106)**

Ink Blot Inc ....G...... 757 644-6958
Virginia Beach **(G-14545)**

Ink It On Anything ....G...... 804 814-5890
Chesterfield **(G-3505)**

Inklings Ink ....G...... 434 842-2200
Fork Union **(G-5111)**

Innovative Graphics & Design .....G...... 276 679-2340
Norton **(G-10122)**

J & D Specialtees ....G...... 804 561-0817
Amelia Court House **(G-659)**

J & R Graphic Services Inc ....G...... 757 595-2602
Yorktown **(G-15967)**

J & W Screen Printing Inc ....G...... 276 963-0862
Cedar Bluff **(G-2279)**

J P R Enterprises ....G...... 757 288-8795
Chesapeake **(G-3146)**

James Allen Printing Co ....G...... 540 463-9232
Lexington **(G-7396)**

James E Henson Jr ....G...... 804 648-3005
Richmond **(G-11624)**

James J Roberts ....G...... 703 330-0448
Manassas **(G-8089)**

Jamie Nicholas ....G...... 703 731-7966
Arlington **(G-1015)**

Jay Malanga ....G...... 703 802-0201
Chantilly **(G-2448)**

Jbtm Enterprises Inc ....F...... 540 665-9651
Winchester **(G-15551)**

Jet Design Graphics Inc ....G...... 804 921-4164
Amelia Court House **(G-660)**

Jjj Inc ....G...... 703 938-0565
Reston **(G-10881)**

JKS Creation ....G...... 804 357-5709
South Hill **(G-12854)**

John Henry Printing Inc ....G...... 757 369-9549
Yorktown **(G-15971)**

Jonathan Promotions Inc ....G...... 540 891-7700
Fredericksburg **(G-5307)**

Jtees Printing ....G...... 703 590-4145
Woodbridge **(G-15732)**

▲ Jumpstart Consultants Inc ......E...... 804 321-5867
Richmond **(G-11638)**

Kalwood Inc ....G...... 540 951-8600
Blacksburg **(G-1749)**

Kash Design ....G...... 540 317-1473
Culpeper **(G-3904)**

Keith Fabry ....G...... 804 649-7551
Richmond **(G-11640)**

Kenmore Envelope Company Inc ...C...... 804 271-2100
Richmond **(G-11259)**

King Screen ....G...... 540 904-5864
Roanoke **(G-12118)**

Kingdom Marketplace Intl LLC .....G...... 757 524-4948
Norfolk **(G-9612)**

Kks Printing & Stationery ....G...... 540 317-5440
Brandy Station **(G-11941)**

Kool Christian Tees ....G...... 804 201-1646
Urbanna **(G-13971)**

Krazy Teesz ....G...... 757 470-4976
Chesapeake **(G-3167)**

Kwik Kopy ....G...... 703 560-5042
Falls Church **(G-4819)**

Labels East Inc ....G...... 757 558-0800
Chesapeake **(G-3171)**

Larry Graves ....G...... 540 972-5320
Locust Grove **(G-7447)**

Larry Ward ....G...... 804 778-7945
Chester **(G-3427)**

Lateeshirt ....G...... 703 532-7329
Arlington **(G-1028)**

Leopard Media LLC ....F...... 703 522-5655
Arlington **(G-1031)**

Leticia E Helleby ....G...... 336 769-7920
Crozet **(G-3842)**

Lettering By Lynne ....G...... 703 548-5427
Alexandria **(G-259)**

Letterpress Direct ....G...... 804 285-8020
Oilville **(G-10182)**

Lighthouse Concepts LLC ....G...... 703 779-9617
Leesburg **(G-7300)**

LL Distributing Inc ....G...... 540 479-2221
Fredericksburg **(G-5313)**

Lou Wallace ....G...... 276 762-2303
Saint Paul **(G-12469)**

Lsc Communications Us LLC ....A...... 540 434-8833
Rockingham **(G-12259)**

Luray Copy Services Inc ....G...... 540 743-3433
Luray **(G-7616)**

Lydell Group Incorporated ....G...... 804 627-0500
Richmond **(G-11277)**

M C Services Inc ....G...... 703 352-1711
Fairfax **(G-4500)**

M&M Engraving Services Inc ....G...... 804 843-3212
Lanexa **(G-7168)**

M-J Printers Inc ....G...... 540 373-1878
Fredericksburg **(G-5202)**

Maclaren Endeavors LLC ....E...... 804 358-3493
Richmond **(G-11279)**

Mad Hat Enterprises ....G...... 540 885-9600
Staunton **(G-13278)**

Mahogany Styles By Teesha LLC ...G...... 703 433-2170
Sterling **(G-13446)**

Mantis Graphics ....G...... 757 482-4186
Chesapeake **(G-3196)**

Marilyn Carter ....G...... 804 901-4757
Henrico **(G-6533)**

Mark-It ....G...... 540 434-4824
Harrisonburg **(G-6343)**

Masked By Tee LLC ....G...... 757 373-9517
Suffolk **(G-13739)**

▲ Max Press Printing ....G...... 757 482-2273
Chesapeake **(G-3199)**

Mendoza Services Inc ....G...... 703 860-9600
Reston **(G-10898)**

Met of Hampton Roads Inc ....G...... 757 249-7777
Newport News **(G-9298)**

Metro Power Print ....G...... 703 221-3289
Woodbridge **(G-15744)**

Miglas Loupes LLC ....G...... 815 721-9133
Winchester **(G-15556)**

Minglewood Trading ....G...... 804 245-6162
North Chesterfield **(G-9932)**

Minuteman Press of Mc Lean ....G...... 703 356-6612
Mc Lean **(G-8502)**

Mobile Tx/Bookkeeping Prtg LLC ...G...... 804 224-8454
Colonial Beach **(G-3725)**

Mojo Custom Sportswear LLC ......G...... 540 632-2116
Daleville **(G-3944)**

Mountaineer Publishing Co Inc ....G...... 276 935-2123
Grundy **(G-6038)**

MSC Imaging Tech LLC ....G...... 804 593-0689
Henrico **(G-6538)**

Multi-Color Corporation ....F...... 757 487-2525
Chesapeake **(G-3213)**

Musicians Publications ....G...... 757 410-3111
Chesapeake **(G-3215)**

Myra J Rudisill ....G...... 540 587-0402
Altavista **(G-637)**

N&J Sales & Services ....G...... 804 559-7172
Mechanicsville **(G-8664)**

Nabina Publications ....G...... 804 276-0454
North Chesterfield **(G-9937)**

National Caps ....G...... 434 572-4709
South Boston **(G-12784)**

▲ National Marking Products Inc ...E...... 804 266-7691
Richmond **(G-11299)**

Neatprints LLC ....G...... 703 520-1550
Springfield **(G-13057)**

Nerd Alert Tees LLC ....G...... 804 938-9375
Midlothian **(G-8868)**

Nets Pix & Things LLC ....G...... 757 466-1337
Norfolk **(G-9657)**

Ocean Apparel Incorporated ....G...... 757 422-8262
Virginia Beach **(G-14690)**

▼ Ocean Creek Apparel LLC ....F...... 757 460-6118
Virginia Beach **(G-14691)**

Off The Press Inc ....G...... 703 533-1199
Falls Church **(G-4850)**

Office Electronics Inc ....G...... 757 622-8001
Norfolk **(G-9672)**

Official Tee Blanco LLC ....G...... 804 418-0218
North Chesterfield **(G-9943)**

Og Pressmore LLC ....G...... 434 218-0304
Bedford **(G-1647)**

Oldtown Printing & Copying ....G...... 540 382-6793
Christiansburg **(G-3607)**

On-Site E Discovery Inc ....A...... 703 683-9710
Alexandria **(G-300)**

Os Ark Group LLC ....G...... 540 261-2622
Buena Vista **(G-2152)**

Over 9000 Media LLC ....G...... 850 210-7114
Norfolk **(G-9679)**

P I P Printing 1156 Inc ....G...... 434 792-0020
Danville **(G-4022)**

Palmyrene Empire LLC ....F...... 703 348-6660
Woodbridge **(G-15770)**

Paper Cover Rock ....G...... 434 979-6366
Charlottesville **(G-2840)**

Paperbuzz ....G...... 434 528-2899
Lynchburg **(G-7781)**

Par Tees Vb ....G...... 757 500-7831
Virginia Beach **(G-14710)**

◆ Payne Publishers Inc ....D...... 703 631-9033
Manassas **(G-7988)**

PCC Corporation ....E...... 757 721-2949
Virginia Beach **(G-14713)**

SIC

Performance Signs LLC ....F 434 985-7446
Ruckersville (G-12408)

Piedmont Prtg & Graphics Inc ....F 434 793-0026
Danville (G-4029)

Pleckers Customer Engraving ....G 540 241-5661
Waynesboro (G-15131)

Precision Screen Printing ....G 540 886-0026
Staunton (G-13284)

Press and Bindery Repair ....G 703 209-4247
Stafford (G-13183)

Press Press Merch LLC ....G 540 206-3495
Roanoke (G-12153)

Pressed 4 Ink LLC ....G 540 834-0125
Fredericksburg (G-5351)

Prestige Press Inc ....E 757 826-5881
Hampton (G-6220)

Print Tent LLC ....G 804 852-9750
Henrico (G-6550)

Printing & Design Services ....G 434 969-1133
Buckingham (G-2134)

Printingwright LLC ....G 757 591-0771
Newport News (G-9317)

Pro Image Graphics ....G 276 686-6174
Rural Retreat (G-12430)

Pro Image Printing & Pubg LLC ....G 804 798-4400
Rockville (G-12295)

Program Services LLC ....G 757 222-3990
Norfolk (G-9698)

Progress Printing Company ....D 434 239-9213
Lynchburg (G-7790)

Progressive Graphics Inc ....E 757 368-3321
Virginia Beach (G-14744)

Qg LLC ....C 540 722-6000
Winchester (G-15462)

Qualatee ....G 434 842-3530
Palmyra (G-10257)

Quality Printing ....G 276 632-1415
Martinsville (G-8322)

R & R Printing ....G 434 985-9844
Ruckersville (G-12411)

R R Donnelley & Sons Company ....G 540 434-8833
Harrisonburg (G-6358)

R R Donnelley & Sons Company ....A 434 846-7371
Lynchburg (G-7797)

R R Donnelley & Sons Company ....E 540 442-1333
Rockingham (G-12269)

R R Donnelley & Sons Company ....E 703 279-1662
Fairfax (G-4535)

R R Donnelley & Sons Company ....C 434 846-7371
Salem (G-12560)

Racer Tees ....G 540 416-1320
Crimora (G-3822)

Rain & Associates LLC ....G 757 572-3996
Virginia Beach (G-14758)

Rappahanock Sports and Graphic ....G 540 891-7662
Fredericksburg (G-5353)

Raymond Hill Consulting ....G 757 925-0136
Suffolk (G-13756)

Reckless Inc ....G 757 469-4416
Chesapeake (G-3262)

Reed Envelope Company Inc ....F 703 690-2249
Fairfax Station (G-4722)

Reeses Amazing Printing Svcs ....G 804 325-0947
Henrico (G-6556)

Reston Shirt & Graphic Co Inc ....G 703 318-4802
Sterling (G-13490)

Rhinos Ink Screen Prtg & EMB ....G 540 347-3303
Warrenton (G-15047)

Ribbons & Sweet Memories ....G 757 874-1871
Newport News (G-9327)

Robert Deluca ....G 540 948-5864
Brightwood (G-1962)

Roberts Screen Printing ....G 757 487-6285
Portsmouth (G-10476)

Roberts Screen Printing ....G 757 487-6285
Chesapeake (G-3272)

Rogers Screen Printing Inc ....G 703 491-6794
Woodbridge (G-15799)

Romaine Printing ....G 804 994-2213
Hanover (G-6283)

Royal Tee LLC ....G 540 892-7694
Richmond (G-11367)

Safehouse Signs Inc ....E 540 366-2480
Roanoke (G-12174)

Salem Printing Co ....E 540 387-1106
Salem (G-12566)

Sans Screenprint Inc ....E 703 368-6700
Manassas (G-8149)

Sanwell Printing Co Inc ....G 276 638-3772
Martinsville (G-8326)

Sassy Clothing Blanks LLC ....G 757 473-1980
Virginia Beach (G-14795)

▲ Sayre Enterprises Inc ....C 540 291-3808
Naturl BR STA (G-9112)

Scg Sports LLC ....G 540 330-7733
Vinton (G-14183)

Schmids Printing ....G 540 886-9261
Staunton (G-13290)

Screen Crafts Inc ....E 804 355-4156
Richmond (G-11374)

Screen Prtg Tchncal Foundation ....G 703 359-1300
Fairfax (G-4552)

Scribbles ....G 703 930-8808
Alexandria (G-581)

Scsi4me Corporation ....G 571 229-9723
Manassas (G-8152)

Separation Unlimited Inc ....F 804 794-4864
North Chesterfield (G-9975)

Shimchocks Litho Service Inc ....G 540 982-3915
Roanoke (G-12185)

Shirts Unlimited LLC ....G 540 342-8337
Roanoke (G-12186)

Shotz From Heart LLC ....G 804 898-5635
Petersburg (G-10342)

Signs Work Inc ....G 804 338-7716
North Chesterfield (G-9981)

Silver Communications Corp ....E 703 471-7339
Sterling (G-13508)

Sina Corp ....G 703 707-8556
Herndon (G-6809)

Sketchz ....G 804 590-1234
Chesterfield (G-3525)

Smartphone Photobooth ....G 757 364-2403
Chesapeake (G-3298)

Southern ATL Screenprint Inc ....F 757 485-7800
Chesapeake (G-3302)

Southernly Sweet Tees ....G 434 447-6572
South Hill (G-12861)

▲ Southprint Inc ....D 276 666-3000
Martinsville (G-8334)

Sports Plus Incorporated ....E 703 222-8255
Chantilly (G-2497)

Sportstitch ....G 804 387-5127
Mechanicsville (G-8680)

Square One Printing Inc ....G 904 993-4321
Richmond (G-11771)

Star Tag & Label Inc ....F 540 389-6848
Salem (G-12571)

Stephenson Printing Inc ....D 703 642-9000
Alexandria (G-589)

Stratgic Trnsp Initiatives Inc ....G 703 647-6564
Alexandria (G-358)

Studio One Printing ....G 703 430-8884
Sterling (G-13519)

Swift Print ....G 540 774-1001
Roanoke (G-12006)

T Shirt Broker ....G 703 362-9297
Herndon (G-6821)

T-Shirt & Screen Print Co ....G 540 667-2351
Winchester (G-15590)

T-Shirt Company LLC ....G 703 669-4619
Leesburg (G-7357)

T3j Enterprises LLC ....G 757 768-0528
Newport News (G-9351)

Taysteesmobilefoodcompany ....G 240 310-6767
Fredericksburg (G-5231)

Tdi LLC ....E 757 855-5416
Virginia Beach (G-14865)

Tee Spot Rching Higher Hts LLC ....G 540 877-5961
Winchester (G-15488)

Tee Zone-VA ....G 434 964-9245
Charlottesville (G-2700)

Tees & Co ....G 757 744-9889
Chesapeake (G-3329)

Tees To Go 2 ....G 540 569-2268
Staunton (G-13300)

Tension Envelope Corp ....G 540 615-5372
Richmond (G-11408)

Tetgraphic Inc ....G 434 845-4450
Lynchburg (G-7821)

Threadcount LLC ....G 703 929-7033
Richmond (G-11788)

Tidalwave Tumbler & Tees LLC ....G 757 814-1022
Virginia Beach (G-14871)

Tidewater Emblems Ltd ....F 757 428-1170
Virginia Beach (G-14873)

Tls Tees LLC ....G 540 455-5260
Spotsylvania (G-12918)

TNT Printing LLC ....G 757 818-5468
Chesapeake (G-3343)

Tom L Crockett ....G 757 460-1382
Virginia Beach (G-14887)

Tommy Atkinson Sports Entp ....G 757 428-0824
Virginia Beach (G-14888)

Total Printing Co Inc ....E 804 222-3813
Richmond (G-11416)

Townsend Screen Printing LLC ....G 804 225-0716
Glen Allen (G-5814)

Trademark Printing LLC ....G 757 465-1736
Portsmouth (G-10493)

Trademark Tees ....G 757 232-4866
Virginia Beach (G-14891)

Trajectory Tees LLC ....G 419 680-6903
Sterling (G-13537)

Triple Images Inc ....G 540 829-1050
Culpeper (G-3926)

Tru Point Design ....G 804 477-0976
Richmond (G-11422)

True Colors Screen Prtg LLC ....G 757 718-9051
Virginia Beach (G-14895)

Tshirt Zone ....G 540 431-5068
Winchester (G-15597)

Tshirtsru ....G 301 744-7872
Woodbridge (G-15824)

Ttg Group LLC ....G 540 454-7235
Arlington (G-1201)

Tweedle Tees ....G 540 569-6927
Staunton (G-13304)

Twelve Inc ....G 804 232-1300
Richmond (G-11797)

Typical Tees LLC ....G 757 641-6514
Newport News (G-9367)

U S Graphics Inc ....G 757 855-2600
Norfolk (G-9772)

U3 Solutions Inc ....G 703 777-5020
Leesburg (G-7366)

Uniformed Services Almanac ....G 703 241-8100
Fairfax (G-4574)

United Graphics Inc ....G 540 338-7525
Round Hill (G-12393)

United Ink Press ....G 703 966-6343
Leesburg (G-7367)

United Screen Design ....G 276 669-4669
Bristol (G-1995)

V B Local Form Coupon Book ....G 239 745-9649
Virginia Beach (G-14904)

Van KY Troung ....G 804 612-6151
Richmond (G-11432)

Vector Vortex LLC ....G 540 330-7733
Vinton (G-14190)

Venutec Corporation ....G 888 573-8870
Centreville (G-2350)

Veridos America Inc ....G 703 480-2025
Dulles (G-4232)

Virginia Gazette Companies LLC ....G 757 220-1736
Newport News (G-9373)

Virginia Prtg Co Roanoke Inc ....G 540 483-7433
Roanoke (G-12219)

Virginia T-Shirt Company LLC ....G 540 752-8141
Fredericksburg (G-5498)

Virginia Tag Service Inc ....G 804 690-7304
King William (G-7132)

Virginia Thermography LLC ....G 757 705-9968
Virginia Beach (G-14921)

Virginian Leader Corp ....F 540 921-3434
Pearisburg (G-10279)

◆ Vitex Packaging Group Inc ....F 757 538-3115
Suffolk (G-13780)

Vk Printing ....G 703 435-5502
Herndon (G-6842)

W M S B R G Grafix ....G 757 565-5200
Williamsburg (G-15336)

Walters Printing & Mfg Co ....F 540 345-8161
Roanoke (G-12227)

▲ Waterway Guide Media LLC ....E 804 776-8999
Deltaville (G-4088)

Wealthy Sistas Media Group ....G 800 917-9435
Dumfries (G-4262)

Webb-Mason Inc ....G 804 897-1990
Rockville (G-12303)

Westend Press LLC ....G 703 992-6939
Fairfax Station (G-4727)

Western Roto Engravers Inc ....G 804 236-0902
Sandston (G-12640)

Wework C/O The First Tee DC ....G 231 632-0334
Tysons (G-13950)

Wild Bills Custom Screen Prtg ....G 757 961-7576
Virginia Beach (G-14936)

Wilkinson Printing Co Inc ....F 804 264-2524
Glen Allen (G-5828)

Willkat Envelopes & Graphics ....G....... 804 798-0243
  Ashland *(G-1511)*
Winchester Printers Inc ....E 540 662-6911
  Winchester *(G-15512)*
Wingspan Publications ....G....... 703 212-0005
  Alexandria *(G-383)*
Winner Made LLC ....G....... 757 828-7623
  Chesapeake *(G-3379)*
Wise Printing Co Inc ....G....... 276 523-1141
  Big Stone Gap *(G-1718)*
Wizard ....G....... 818 988-2283
  Fredericksburg *(G-5392)*
Womack Publishing Co Inc ....G....... 434 352-8215
  Appomattox *(G-828)*
Wood Television LLC ....E 540 672-1266
  Orange *(G-10232)*
Wre/Colortech ....G....... 804 236-0902
  Sandston *(G-12642)*
Younivercity LLC ....G....... 540 529-7621
  Roanoke *(G-12231)*
Zeba Magazine LLC ....G....... 202 705-7006
  Vienna *(G-14163)*
Zramics Mtls Science Tech LLC ....G....... 757 955-0493
  Norfolk *(G-9801)*

2761 Manifold Business Forms

Dad13 Inc ....C 703 550-9555
  Newington *(G-9153)*
▲ Dgi Line Inc ....D 434 797-4114
  Danville *(G-3982)*
Printech Inc ....F 540 343-9200
  Roanoke *(G-12154)*
Standard Register Inc ....F 703 516-4014
  Arlington *(G-1174)*
Taylor Communications Inc ....E 703 790-9700
  Vienna *(G-14138)*
Taylor Communications Inc ....F 937 221-1000
  North Chesterfield *(G-10025)*
Taylor Communications Inc ....G....... 703 904-0133
  Herndon *(G-6823)*
Taylor Communications Inc ....G....... 434 822-1111
  Danville *(G-4040)*
Vas of Virginia Inc ....E 434 296-5608
  Charlottesville *(G-2899)*

2771 Greeting Card Publishing

A Reason To Write ....G....... 703 481-3277
  Fairfax *(G-4397)*
Beau-Geste International Inc ....G....... 434 534-0468
  Forest *(G-5053)*
Caspari Inc ....E 434 817-7880
  Charlottesville *(G-2757)*
DBA Jus Bcuz ....G....... 914 714-9327
  Courtland *(G-3768)*
Just For Fun ....G....... 757 620-3700
  Suffolk *(G-13726)*
Noparei Professionals LLC ....G....... 571 354-9422
  Woodbridge *(G-15763)*
Patricia Gavin ....G....... 703 439-4403
  Middleburg *(G-8731)*
◆ Pumped Cards ....G....... 202 725-6964
  Woodbridge *(G-15786)*
Stay In Touch Inc ....F 434 239-7300
  Forest *(G-5095)*
United Providers of Care LLC ....G....... 757 775-5075
  Williamsburg *(G-15328)*

2782 Blankbooks & Looseleaf Binders

A A Business Forms & Printing ....G....... 703 866-5544
  Fairfax Station *(G-4700)*
Advantage Accnting Bkkping LLC ....G....... 434 989-0443
  North Chesterfield *(G-9806)*
Alien Piss World Entrmt LLC ....G....... 757 805-1007
  Virginia Beach *(G-14220)*
Best Checks Inc ....G....... 703 416-4856
  Arlington *(G-879)*
▲ Best Checks Inc ....E 703 467-9300
  Sterling *(G-13358)*
Big Face Benji Music Group LLC ....G....... 804 229-9450
  North Chesterfield *(G-9831)*
Black Money Label LLC ....G....... 201 975-5009
  Virginia Beach *(G-14286)*
Business Checks of America ....G....... 703 823-1008
  Alexandria *(G-156)*
Deluxe Kitchen and Bath ....G....... 571 594-6363
  Chantilly *(G-2531)*
Ibf Group ....G....... 703 549-4247
  Alexandria *(G-232)*
Little Black Dog Designs ....G....... 757 874-0928
  Newport News *(G-9286)*

M T Holding Company LLC ....E 540 563-8866
  Vinton *(G-14178)*
Metropolitan Accounting & Book ....G....... 703 250-5014
  Burke *(G-2193)*
Mirror Morning Music ....G....... 703 405-8181
  Vienna *(G-14096)*
Photolively LLC ....G....... 804 937-0896
  Powhatan *(G-10564)*
R L Bindery ....G....... 804 625-2609
  Amelia Court House *(G-669)*
Real Is Rare Label LLC ....G....... 757 705-1850
  Norfolk *(G-9702)*
Seize Moments ....G....... 804 794-5911
  Surry *(G-13801)*
Silence In Metropolis LLC ....G....... 571 213-4383
  Chantilly *(G-2556)*
Thompson Media Packaging Inc ....E 804 225-8146
  Glen Allen *(G-5810)*
Tonya Sheridan Crop Organizer ....G....... 540 860-0528
  Luray *(G-7624)*
United Providers of Care LLC ....G....... 757 775-5075
  Williamsburg *(G-15328)*

2789 Bookbinding

5 Plus 7 Bookbinding ....G....... 571 499-0511
  Arlington *(G-836)*
Accelerated Printing Corp Inc ....G....... 703 437-1084
  Leesburg *(G-7213)*
Apollo Press Inc ....E 757 247-9002
  Newport News *(G-9169)*
Arrington & Sons Inc ....G....... 703 368-1462
  Manassas *(G-7911)*
B C R Bookbinding ....G....... 703 534-9181
  Falls Church *(G-4901)*
B K Printing ....G....... 703 435-5502
  Herndon *(G-6618)*
Barbours Printing Service ....G....... 804 443-4505
  Tappahannock *(G-13813)*
▲ Berryville Graphics Inc ....A 540 955-2750
  Berryville *(G-1671)*
Bindery Plus ....G....... 703 357-5002
  Alexandria *(G-147)*
Blue Ridge Binding Inc ....G....... 703 771-1676
  Sterling *(G-13360)*
Branner Printing Service Inc ....E 540 896-8947
  Broadway *(G-2085)*
Brook Brinders Limited ....G....... 434 845-1231
  Lynchburg *(G-7661)*
C & B Corp ....G....... 434 977-1992
  Charlottesville *(G-2752)*
Canaan Printing Inc ....E 804 271-4820
  North Chesterfield *(G-9839)*
Cat Tail Run Hand Bookbinding ....G....... 540 662-2683
  Winchester *(G-15399)*
Chocklett Press Inc ....D 540 345-1820
  Roanoke *(G-12066)*
Clarke Inc ....F 434 847-5561
  Moneta *(G-8959)*
Criswell Inc ....F 434 845-0439
  Lynchburg *(G-7687)*
Custom Book Bindery ....G....... 804 796-9520
  Chester *(G-3399)*
D & P Printing & Graphics Inc ....F 703 941-2114
  Alexandria *(G-438)*
Dad13 Inc ....C 703 550-9555
  Newington *(G-9153)*
Day & Night Printing Inc ....G....... 703 734-4940
  Vienna *(G-14035)*
Ersh-Enterprises Inc ....G....... 703 866-1988
  Oakton *(G-10147)*
Finish Line Die Cutting ....F 804 342-8000
  Richmond *(G-11589)*
Five Star Medals ....G....... 703 644-4974
  Springfield *(G-13004)*
Flynn Enterprises Inc ....E 703 444-5555
  Sterling *(G-13400)*
Flynn Incorporated ....G....... 540 885-2600
  Staunton *(G-13261)*
Gary Gray ....G....... 757 238-2135
  Carrollton *(G-2242)*
Goetz Printing Company ....E 703 569-8232
  Springfield *(G-13012)*
Good Printers Inc ....G....... 540 828-4663
  Bridgewater *(G-1953)*
Graphic Communications Inc ....F 301 599-2020
  Hillsville *(G-6893)*
Hampton Roads Bindery Inc ....G....... 757 369-5671
  Newport News *(G-9241)*
Hopewell Publishing Company ....E 804 452-6127
  Hopewell *(G-6934)*

J & M Printing Inc ....G....... 703 549-2432
  Alexandria *(G-241)*
Jami Ventures Inc ....G....... 703 352-5679
  Fairfax *(G-4484)*
Jennifer Enos ....G....... 571 721-9268
  Alexandria *(G-243)*
Jones Printing Service Inc ....E 757 436-3331
  Chesapeake *(G-3155)*
Lake Lithograph Company ....D 703 361-8030
  Manassas *(G-7959)*
Library Conservation Services ....G....... 540 372-9661
  Fredericksburg *(G-5201)*
Longs-Roullet Bookbinders Inc ....G....... 757 623-4244
  Norfolk *(G-9622)*
Lsc Communications Us LLC ....A 540 434-8833
  Rockingham *(G-12259)*
Lydell Group Incorporated ....G....... 804 627-0500
  Richmond *(G-11277)*
Moonlight Bindery ....G....... 703 549-5261
  Alexandria *(G-282)*
North Street Enterprise Inc ....E 434 392-4144
  Farmville *(G-4954)*
Oldtown Printing & Copying ....G....... 540 382-6793
  Christiansburg *(G-3607)*
One Cut Bindery LLC ....G....... 540 896-7290
  Broadway *(G-2092)*
P I P Printing 1156 Inc ....G....... 434 792-0020
  Danville *(G-4022)*
P M Resources Inc ....G....... 703 556-0155
  Springfield *(G-13065)*
◆ Payne Publishers Inc ....D 703 631-9033
  Manassas *(G-7988)*
Prestige Press Inc ....E 757 826-5881
  Hampton *(G-6220)*
Printcraft Press Incorporated ....E 757 397-0759
  Portsmouth *(G-10473)*
Program Services LLC ....G....... 757 222-3990
  Norfolk *(G-9698)*
Progress Printing Company ....D 434 239-9213
  Lynchburg *(G-7790)*
Progressive Graphics Inc ....E 757 368-3321
  Virginia Beach *(G-14744)*
Rappahannock Entp Assoc Inc ....G....... 703 560-5042
  Falls Church *(G-4862)*
Salem Printing Co ....E 540 387-1106
  Salem *(G-12566)*
Silver Communications Corp ....E 703 471-7339
  Sterling *(G-13508)*
South Winds Bindery LLC ....G....... 540 661-7637
  Locust Grove *(G-7451)*
Southwest Plastic Binding Co ....E 804 226-0400
  Richmond *(G-11391)*
Stephenson Printing Inc ....D 703 642-9000
  Alexandria *(G-589)*
Suter Enterprises Ltd ....F 757 220-3299
  Williamsburg *(G-15320)*
T-Body Promotions LLC ....G....... 757 723-4445
  Hampton *(G-6248)*
Thomas C Albro II ....G....... 703 892-6738
  Arlington *(G-1191)*
Tidewater Graphics Inc ....G....... 757 464-6136
  Virginia Beach *(G-14874)*
Total Printing Co Inc ....E 804 222-3813
  Richmond *(G-11416)*
Tr Press Inc ....E 540 347-4466
  Warrenton *(G-15055)*
Tri State Masters Inc ....G....... 703 255-0222
  Vienna *(G-14146)*
Vintage Bindery Williamsbur ....G....... 757 220-0203
  Williamsburg *(G-15332)*
Walters Printing & Mfg Co ....F 540 345-8161
  Roanoke *(G-12227)*
Wilkinson Printing Co Inc ....F 804 264-2524
  Glen Allen *(G-5828)*
▲ William R Smith Company ....E 804 733-0123
  Petersburg *(G-10351)*
Winchester Printers Inc ....G....... 540 662-6911
  Winchester *(G-15512)*
Wise Printing Co Inc ....G....... 276 523-1141
  Big Stone Gap *(G-1718)*

2791 Typesetting

Adta & Co Inc ....F 703 930-9280
  Annandale *(G-728)*
Allen Wayne Ltd Arlington ....G....... 703 321-7414
  Warrenton *(G-14977)*
Americomm LLC ....D 757 622-2724
  Norfolk *(G-9440)*
Apollo Press Inc ....E 757 247-9002
  Newport News *(G-9169)*

SIC

B K Printing ....G..... 703 435-5502
Herndon *(G-6618)*

Barbours Printing Service ....G..... 804 443-4505
Tappahannock *(G-13813)*

Boaz Publishing Inc ....F..... 540 659-4554
Stafford *(G-13124)*

Business ....G..... 804 559-8770
Mechanicsville *(G-8609)*

C & B Corp ....G..... 434 977-1992
Charlottesville *(G-2752)*

▲ Carter Composition Corporation ....C..... 804 359-9206
Richmond *(G-11149)*

Chocklett Press Inc ....C..... 540 345-1820
Roanoke *(G-12066)*

Coghill Composition Co Inc ....F..... 804 714-1100
Midlothian *(G-8799)*

Criswell Inc ....F..... 434 845-0439
Lynchburg *(G-7687)*

Custom Graphics Inc ....G..... 540 882-3488
Paeonian Springs *(G-10238)*

D & P Printing & Graphics Inc ....F..... 703 941-2114
Alexandria *(G-438)*

Deadline Typesetting Inc ....G..... 757 625-5883
Norfolk *(G-9520)*

E M Communications Inc ....G..... 434 971-4700
Charlottesville *(G-2787)*

Electronic Canvas ....G..... 434 656-3070
Gretna *(G-6008)*

Ern Graphic Design ....G..... 757 281-8801
Hampton *(G-6145)*

Ersh-Enterprises Inc ....F..... 703 866-1988
Oakton *(G-10147)*

Gary D Keys Enterprises Inc ....G..... 703 418-1700
Arlington *(G-975)*

Gary Gray ....G..... 757 238-2135
Carrollton *(G-2242)*

Good Printers Inc ....D..... 540 828-4663
Bridgewater *(G-1953)*

Halifax Gazette Publishing Co ....E..... 434 572-3945
South Boston *(G-12774)*

Hopewell Publishing Company ....E..... 804 452-6127
Hopewell *(G-6934)*

Hto Inc ....G..... 703 533-0440
Falls Church *(G-4806)*

Interntional Scanner Corp Amer ......F..... 703 533-8560
Arlington *(G-1007)*

J & M Printing Inc ....G..... 703 549-2432
Alexandria *(G-241)*

Jami Ventures Inc ....G..... 703 352-5679
Fairfax *(G-4484)*

Jones Printing Service Inc ....E..... 757 436-3331
Chesapeake *(G-3155)*

Lydell Group Incorporated ....G..... 804 627-0500
Richmond *(G-11277)*

Michael Beach ....G..... 703 360-7284
Alexandria *(G-531)*

Mountaineer Publishing Co Inc ....G..... 276 935-2123
Grundy *(G-6038)*

North Street Enterprise Inc ....E..... 434 392-4144
Farmville *(G-4954)*

Oldtown Printing & Copying ....G..... 540 382-6793
Christiansburg *(G-3607)*

Omega Alpha II Inc ....F..... 804 747-7705
Richmond *(G-11315)*

P I P Printing 1156 Inc ....G..... 434 792-0020
Danville *(G-4022)*

Prestige Press Inc ....E..... 757 826-5881
Hampton *(G-6220)*

Printcraft Press Incorporated ....E..... 757 397-0759
Portsmouth *(G-10473)*

Printing and Sign System Inc ....G..... 703 280-1550
Fairfax *(G-4532)*

Program Services LLC ....G..... 757 222-3990
Norfolk *(G-9698)*

Rappahannock Entp Assoc Inc ....G..... 703 560-5042
Falls Church *(G-4862)*

Rappahannock Record ....F..... 804 435-1701
Kilmarnock *(G-7076)*

Salem Printing Co ....E..... 540 387-1106
Salem *(G-12566)*

Schreiber Inc R G ....E..... 540 248-5300
Verona *(G-13995)*

Silver Communications Corp ....E..... 703 471-7339
Sterling *(G-13508)*

Soundscape Comp & Prfmce Exch ...G..... 757 645-4671
Williamsburg *(G-15315)*

Suter Enterprises Ltd ....F..... 757 220-3299
Williamsburg *(G-15320)*

Swift Print ....G..... 540 774-1001
Roanoke *(G-12006)*

Tidewater Graphics Inc ....G..... 757 464-6136
Virginia Beach *(G-14874)*

Total Printing Co Inc ....E..... 804 222-3813
Richmond *(G-11416)*

Tr Press Inc ....E..... 540 347-4466
Warrenton *(G-15055)*

Type & Art ....G..... 804 794-3375
North Chesterfield *(G-10006)*

Type Factory Inc ....G..... 757 826-6055
Hampton *(G-6255)*

Universal Composition Svcs LLC ....G..... 202 255-7995
Leesburg *(G-7368)*

Walters Printing & Mfg Co ....F..... 540 345-8161
Roanoke *(G-12227)*

Wilkinson Printing Co Inc ....F..... 804 264-2524
Glen Allen *(G-5828)*

▲ William R Smith Company ....E..... 804 733-0123
Petersburg *(G-10351)*

Winchester Printers Inc ....E..... 540 662-6911
Winchester *(G-15512)*

Wise Printing Co Inc ....G..... 276 523-1141
Big Stone Gap *(G-1718)*

Wood Television LLC ....E..... 540 672-1266
Orange *(G-10232)*

2796 Platemaking & Related Svcs

Amazengraved LLC ....G..... 540 313-5658
Winchester *(G-15376)*

American Technology Inds Ltd ....E..... 757 436-6465
Chesapeake *(G-2973)*

▲ Carter Composition Corporation ....C..... 804 359-9206
Richmond *(G-11149)*

Criswell Inc ....F..... 434 845-0439
Lynchburg *(G-7687)*

Dap Enterprises Inc ....G..... 757 921-3576
Williamsburg *(G-15229)*

Digilink Inc ....E..... 703 340-1800
Alexandria *(G-188)*

Dorothy Whibley ....G..... 703 892-6612
Montclair *(G-8997)*

F C Holdings Inc ....C..... 804 222-2821
Sandston *(G-12614)*

Grubb Printing & Stamp Co Inc ....F..... 757 295-8061
Portsmouth *(G-10438)*

Hallmark Systems ....G..... 804 744-2694
Midlothian *(G-8825)*

Interntional Scanner Corp Amer ......F..... 703 533-8560
Arlington *(G-1007)*

◆ Kinyo Virginia Inc ....G..... 757 888-2221
Newport News *(G-9276)*

Lotus Engraving LLC ....G..... 703 206-8367
Centreville *(G-2315)*

Neagles Flexo Corporation ....E..... 804 798-1501
Ashland *(G-1469)*

Progress Printing Company ....D..... 434 239-9213
Lynchburg *(G-7790)*

Separation Unlimited Inc ....F..... 804 794-4864
North Chesterfield *(G-9975)*

◆ Standex Engraving LLC ....D..... 804 236-3092
Sandston *(G-12636)*

Stephenson Printing Inc ....D..... 703 642-9000
Alexandria *(G-589)*

Tetra Graphics Inc ....G..... 434 845-4450
Lynchburg *(G-7822)*

Tr Press Inc ....E..... 540 347-4466
Warrenton *(G-15055)*

Visual Communication Co Inc ....G..... 540 427-1060
Boones Mill *(G-1899)*

Visual Communication Co Inc ....G..... 540 427-1060
Boones Mill *(G-1900)*

▲ William R Smith Company ....E..... 804 733-0123
Petersburg *(G-10351)*

Wilson Graphics Incorporated ....G..... 804 748-0646
Chester *(G-3468)*

Wood Television LLC ....E..... 540 672-1266
Orange *(G-10232)*

28 CHEMICALS AND ALLIED PRODUCTS

2812 Alkalies & Chlorine

Albemarle Corporation ....C..... 225 388-8011
Richmond *(G-11092)*

Directed Vapor Tech Intl Inc ....F..... 434 977-1405
Charlottesville *(G-2618)*

Jci Jones Chemicals Inc ....F..... 804 633-5066
Milford *(G-8931)*

T/J One Corp ....G..... 757 548-0093
Chesapeake *(G-3318)*

2813 Industrial Gases

Airgas Usa LLC ....F..... 804 743-0661
North Chesterfield *(G-9809)*

▲ Akaline Cylinders ....G..... 757 896-9100
Hampton *(G-6080)*

Argon ....G..... 804 365-5628
Richmond *(G-11118)*

Boc Group De ....G..... 540 373-1782
Fredericksburg *(G-5404)*

Cr Neon ....G..... 804 339-0497
Ruther Glen *(G-12453)*

H2 As Fuel Corporation ....G..... 703 980-5262
Alexandria *(G-472)*

Linde Gas North America LLC ....G..... 804 752-2744
Ashland *(G-1452)*

Linde Inc ....G..... 804 452-3181
Hopewell *(G-6938)*

Messer LLC ....E..... 804 458-0928
Hopewell *(G-6939)*

Messer LLC ....G..... 540 774-1515
Roanoke *(G-11962)*

Messer LLC ....G..... 804 796-5050
Chester *(G-3435)*

Messer LLC ....G..... 540 886-1725
Staunton *(G-13279)*

Neon Compass Marketing LLC ....G..... 580 330-4699
Alexandria *(G-542)*

Neon District ....G..... 757 663-6970
Norfolk *(G-9654)*

Neon Guitar ....G..... 804 932-3716
New Kent *(G-9136)*

Neon Nation LLC ....G..... 703 255-4996
Vienna *(G-14103)*

Praxair Welding Gas & Sup Str ....G..... 540 342-9700
Roanoke *(G-12150)*

2816 Inorganic Pigments

◆ Hoover Color Corporation ....G..... 540 980-7233
Hiwassee *(G-6912)*

2819 Indl Inorganic Chemicals, NEC

5th Element Co ....G..... 800 684-3144
Lorton *(G-7456)*

8th-Element LLC ....G..... 757 481-6146
Virginia Beach *(G-14199)*

Adaptive Elements LLC ....G..... 571 261-3671
Haymarket *(G-6413)*

Aimex LLC ....F..... 212 631-4277
Vienna *(G-14006)*

Albemarle Corporation ....C..... 225 388-8011
Richmond *(G-11092)*

Arkema Inc ....C..... 800 225-7788
Courtland *(G-3766)*

Arkema Inc ....C..... 434 433-0300
Chatham *(G-2919)*

Black Element LLC ....G..... 757 224-6160
Hampton *(G-6094)*

Bnnt LLC ....G..... 757 369-1939
Newport News *(G-9182)*

Carbide Specialties Inc ....G..... 804 346-3314
Manakin Sabot *(G-7897)*

Celanese Americas LLC ....D..... 540 921-6540
Narrows *(G-9097)*

Chemtrade Chemicals US LLC ....F..... 804 541-0261
Hopewell *(G-6919)*

Chemtrade Chemicals US LLC ....G..... 540 962-6444
Covington *(G-3782)*

Designpure Nanocryst LLC ....G..... 571 458-0951
Arlington *(G-938)*

Dupont De Nemours E I Tex Ofc ....G..... 540 949-2000
Waynesboro *(G-15110)*

Dupont Specialty Pdts USA LLC ....C..... 804 383-2000
North Chesterfield *(G-9865)*

Edward-Councilor Co Inc ....F..... 757 460-2401
Virginia Beach *(G-14433)*

Element Fitness- LLC ....G..... 540 820-4200
Virginia Beach *(G-14438)*

Element One LLC ....G..... 901 292-7721
Leesburg *(G-7266)*

Element Radius LLC ....G..... 540 229-6366
Culpeper *(G-3890)*

Elements of Grace LLC ....G..... 804 526-1482
Colonial Heights *(G-3732)*

Elements of Healing LLC ....G..... 757 951-7155
Portsmouth *(G-10420)*

◆ Evonik Goldschmidt Corporation ....A..... 804 541-8658
Hopewell *(G-6926)*

Framatome Inc ....C..... 434 832-5000
Lynchburg *(G-7714)*

◆ Framatome Inc ....B 434 832-3000
Lynchburg (G-7716)
Fraser Wood Elements LLC ....G 540 373-0853
Fredericksburg (G-5187)
Gilmer Industries Inc ....E 540 434-8877
Harrisonburg (G-6324)
Honeywell International Inc ....G 804 541-5000
Hopewell (G-6931)
◆ Honeywell Resins & Chem LLC ....D 804 541-5000
Hopewell (G-6933)
Human Elements LLC ....G 703 542-7701
Chantilly (G-2537)
Ingevity Virginia Corporation ....C 540 969-3700
Covington (G-3791)
IV Labs Inc ....D 540 585-3030
Christiansburg (G-3599)
JM Huber Corporation ....G 804 357-3698
Glen Allen (G-5756)
JM Huber Corporation ....C 434 476-6628
Crystal Hill (G-3860)
Joi Element LLC ....G 804 912-8002
Richmond (G-11635)
Jr Bernard Hearn ....G 703 821-1373
Mc Lean (G-8476)
Jr Everett Woodson ....G 757 867-3478
Newport News (G-9270)
◆ Mitsubishi Chemical Composites ....C 757 548-7850
Chesapeake (G-3208)
Mitsubshi Chem Hldngs Amer Inc ....E 757 382-5750
Chesapeake (G-3209)
Royal Elements LLC ....G 540 338-2591
Round Hill (G-12388)
STC Catalysts Inc ....G 757 766-5810
Hampton (G-6244)
Tetra Technologies Inc ....E 703 387-2100
Arlington (G-1188)
United Salt Saltville LLC ....E 276 496-3363
Saltville (G-12596)
Urenco USA Inc ....G 575 394-4646
Arlington (G-1205)
▲ US Amines (portsmouth) LLC ....G 757 638-2614
Portsmouth (G-10496)
Virginia Kik Inc ....E 540 389-5401
Salem (G-12578)
Waters Group Inc ....G 703 791-3607
Nokesville (G-9404)

2821 Plastics, Mtrls & Nonvulcanizable Elastomers

A At LLC ....G 316 828-1563
Waynesboro (G-15091)
Abell Corporation ....E 540 665-3062
Winchester (G-15369)
Advansix Inc ....E 804 504-0009
South Chesterfield (G-12793)
Albemarle Corporation ....C 225 388-8011
Richmond (G-11092)
Albemarle County Pub Schools ....G 434 296-3872
Charlottesville (G-2722)
All Points Countertop Inc ....E 540 665-3875
Winchester (G-15526)
BI & Son Enterprises LLC ....G 757 502-7789
Chesapeake (G-3003)
BI & Son Enterprises LLC ....G 757 938-9188
Hampton (G-6093)
Breathe-3dp LLC ....G 276 645-6556
Bristol (G-2009)
◆ Carpenter Co ....C 804 359-0800
Richmond (G-11146)
Celise LLC ....G 757 771-5176
Poquoson (G-10366)
Cht USA Inc ....F 804 271-9010
North Chesterfield (G-9844)
▲ Cht USA Inc ....E 800 852-3147
North Chesterfield (G-9845)
▲ Danchem Technologies Inc ....C 434 797-8120
Danville (G-3975)
Detectamet Inc ....F 804 303-1983
Richmond (G-11184)
Dexco Polymers LP ....G 703 846-2193
Oakton (G-10143)
E I Du Pont De Nemours & Co ....E 804 530-9300
Hopewell (G-6924)
Eastern Bioplastics LLC ....G 540 437-1984
Mount Crawford (G-9054)
Eastman Chemical Company ....D 276 679-1800
Norton (G-10117)
Eastman Chemical Company ....G 276 632-4991
Martinsville (G-8282)

Eastman Chemical Resins Inc ....G 757 562-3121
Courtland (G-3769)
◆ Eastman Performance Films LLC ....A 276 627-3000
Fieldale (G-4984)
Eastman Performance Films LLC ....E 276 762-0242
Fieldale (G-4985)
Eastman Performance Films LLC ....E 276 650-3354
Axton (G-1536)
Eastman Performance Films LLC ....F 276 627-3223
Fieldale (G-4986)
Eastman Performance Films LLC ....G 276 627-3355
Martinsville (G-8284)
Gargone John ....G 540 641-1934
Williamsburg (G-15246)
Green Coal Solutions LLC ....G 703 910-4022
Woodbridge (G-15716)
Henkel US Operations Corp ....F 804 222-6100
Richmond (G-11236)
Honeywell International Inc ....B 804 530-6352
Chester (G-3422)
▲ Hudson Industries Inc ....D 804 226-1155
Richmond (G-11244)
Huntington Foam LLC ....D 540 731-3700
Radford (G-10716)
Invista Capital Management LLC ....E 540 949-2000
Waynesboro (G-15117)
Invista Capital Management LLC ....E 276 656-0500
Martinsville (G-8301)
Line-X Northern Virginia Inc ....G 703 433-9333
Sterling (G-13442)
Line-X of Blue Ridge ....G 540 389-8595
Salem (G-12532)
Line-X of Richmond ....G 804 321-9166
Richmond (G-11270)
Mar-Bal Inc ....G 540 674-5320
Dublin (G-4165)
Miller Waste Mills Inc ....G 434 572-3925
South Boston (G-12783)
Millie B Thompson ....G 276 475-5940
Damascus (G-3949)
Mitsubishi Chem Advanced Mtls ....G 276 228-0100
Wytheville (G-15901)
Mobjack Binnacle Products LLC ....G 804 814-4077
Richmond (G-11295)
Omnidex Products Inc ....G 757 509-4030
Virginia Beach (G-14694)
▲ Plasticlad LLC ....G 757 562-5550
Franklin (G-5154)
Plexi Worldwide LLC ....G 804 625-2524
Sterling (G-13471)
▲ Polibak Plastics America Inc ....G 703 709-3004
Purcellville (G-10673)
Polynt Composites USA Inc ....E 434 432-8836
Chatham (G-2933)
Polyone ....G 540 667-6666
Winchester (G-15567)
Polythane of Virginia Inc ....G 540 586-3511
Bedford (G-1651)
▲ Pre Con Inc ....F 804 732-0628
Chester (G-3444)
Pre Con Inc ....D 804 732-1253
Petersburg (G-10336)
Pre Con Inc ....F 804 861-0282
Petersburg (G-10337)
Pre Con Inc ....D 804 748-5063
Chester (G-3445)
Pre Con Inc ....E 804 414-1560
Chester (G-3446)
Pre Con Inc ....E 804 414-1560
Chester (G-3447)
Quadrant Holding Inc ....D 276 228-0100
Wytheville (G-15905)
◆ SC Medical Overseas Inc ....G 516 935-8500
Norfolk (G-9715)
Ship Sstnability Solutions LLC ....G 757 574-2436
Chesapeake (G-3291)
◆ Sii Inc ....G 540 722-6860
Clear Brook (G-3651)
Solutia Inc ....G 314 674-3150
Fieldale (G-4991)
Strata Film Coatings Inc ....G 540 343-3456
Roanoke (G-12198)
Sunlite Plastics Inc ....G 540 234-9271
Weyers Cave (G-15178)
Teijin-Du Pont Films Inc ....D 804 530-9310
Chester (G-3459)
Toray Plastics (america) Inc ....G 540 636-3887
Front Royal (G-5558)
Total Ptrchemicals Ref USA Inc ....E 434 432-3706
Chatham (G-2939)

Total Ptrchemicals Ref USA Inc ....G 276 228-6150
Wytheville (G-15919)
Transfoam LLC ....G 631 747-0255
Afton (G-92)
Trex Company Inc ....C 540 542-6800
Winchester (G-15493)
Trex Company Inc ....E 540 542-6800
Winchester (G-15494)
Wonders Inc ....G 434 845-0813
Amherst (G-714)
Wynnvision LLC ....G 757 419-1463
Midlothian (G-8924)

2822 Synthetic Rubber (Vulcanizable Elastomers)

Applied Polymer LLC ....G 804 615-5105
Richmond (G-11115)
▲ International Carbide & Engrg ....F 434 568-3311
Drakes Branch (G-4133)
Ko Synthetics Corp ....G 540 580-1760
New Castle (G-9121)
Longwood Elastomers Inc ....C 276 228-5406
Wytheville (G-15898)
Techulon ....G 540 443-9254
Blacksburg (G-1797)
Westland Technologies Inc ....D 703 477-9847
Chantilly (G-2522)

2823 Cellulosic Man-Made Fibers

◆ Porex Technologies Corp ....C 804 524-4983
South Chesterfield (G-12821)
Porex Technologies Corporation ....C 804 275-2631
North Chesterfield (G-9951)
Trex Company Inc ....C 540 542-6800
Winchester (G-15493)
▲ Xymid LLC ....E 804 423-5798
Midlothian (G-8925)

2824 Synthetic Organic Fibers, Exc Cellulosic

Honeywell International Inc ....G 804 541-5000
Hopewell (G-6931)
Honeywell International Inc ....C 804 520-3000
South Chesterfield (G-12809)
◆ Honeywell Resins & Chem LLC ....D 804 541-5000
Hopewell (G-6933)
◆ Mgc Advanced Polymers Inc ....E 804 520-7800
South Chesterfield (G-12815)
Q Protein Inc ....G 240 994-6160
Roanoke (G-11992)
Quadrant Holding Inc ....D 276 228-0100
Wytheville (G-15905)
◆ Universal Fibers Inc ....B 276 669-1161
Bristol (G-2039)

2833 Medicinal Chemicals & Botanical Prdts

Botanica ....G 540 899-5590
Fredericksburg (G-5174)
Commonhealth Botanicals LLC ....G 434 906-2227
Charlottesville (G-2769)
Dalitso LLC ....G 571 385-4927
Alexandria (G-440)
Dreampak LLC ....F 703 751-3511
Mc Lean (G-8421)
◆ Famarco Newco LLC ....E 757 460-3573
Virginia Beach (G-14459)
Hana Tonic LLC ....G 804 993-4262
Oakton (G-10149)
Hempceuticals LLC ....G 757 384-2782
Chesapeake (G-3131)
Herbsforhealth ....G 757 383-1245
Suffolk (G-13719)
James River Enviromental Inc ....G 804 966-7609
Providence Forge (G-10626)
K-Naturo LLC ....G 757 343-4604
Virginia Beach (G-14578)
Next Generation MGT Corp ....G 703 372-1282
Ashburn (G-1321)
Nuna Med LLC ....G 707 373-7171
Richmond (G-11309)
Pfizer Inc ....F 804 257-2000
Richmond (G-11712)
Precision Nuclear Virginia LLC ....G 540 389-1346
Salem (G-12536)
Stemcelllife LLC ....G 843 410-3067
Richmond (G-11773)
Stone Mountain Naturals LLC ....G 276 415-5880
Dryden (G-4146)

SIC

Tearsolutions Inc	G	434 951-0444	
Charlottesville (G-2886)			
Vollara LLC	D	800 704-2378	
Bristol (G-1998)			
Wilson Warehouse	G	804 991-2163	
North Dinwiddie (G-10073)			

2834 Pharmaceuticals

Abbott Laboratories	A	434 369-3100	
Altavista (G-622)			
Abbott Laboratories Inc	G	434 369-3100	
Altavista (G-623)			
Abbott Nutrition Mfg Inc	F	434 369-3100	
Altavista (G-624)			
Adenosine Therapeutics LLC	E	434 979-1902	
Arlington (G-839)			
Adial Corporation	G	434 243-0570	
Keswick (G-7041)			
Adial Pharmaceuticals Inc	G	434 422-9800	
Charlottesville (G-2586)			
▲ Afton Scientific LLC	E	434 979-3737	
Charlottesville (G-2721)			
AG Essence Inc	G	804 915-6650	
Richmond (G-11479)			
Airbase Therapeutics	G	434 825-0074	
Charlottesville (G-2587)			
Albemarle Corporation	C	225 388-8011	
Richmond (G-11092)			
Allergan Sales LLC	G	757 624-5320	
Norfolk (G-9433)			
Allergopharma Usa Inc	G	919 749-6213	
Alexandria (G-128)			
Ampac Fine Chemicals VA LLC	E	804 504-8600	
Petersburg (G-10302)			
Arconic Cbt	G	757 825-6870	
Hampton (G-6085)			
Astellas Pharma Us Inc	G	804 262-3197	
Richmond (G-11120)			
Axon Cells Inc	G	434 987-4460	
Keswick (G-7043)			
Axon Medchem LLC	G	703 650-9359	
Reston (G-10796)			
Axon Sciences Inc	G	434 987-4460	
Charlottesville (G-2732)			
Barr Laboratories Inc	D	434 534-8600	
Forest (G-5052)			
Batonbio LLC	G	347 491-0189	
Moseley (G-9034)			
Bausch Health Americas Inc	G	703 995-2400	
Chantilly (G-2375)			
Best Medical Belgium Inc	G	800 336-4970	
Springfield (G-12961)			
◆ Best Medical International Inc	C	703 451-2378	
Springfield (G-12962)			
Bettera Brands LLC	D	703 222-6340	
Chantilly (G-2377)			
Boehringer Ingelheim Corp	G	703 759-0630	
Reston (G-10810)			
Boehringer Ingelheim Corp	G	800 243-0127	
Ashburn (G-1251)			
Boehringer Ingelheim Corp	G	804 862-8316	
Petersburg (G-10310)			
▼ C B Fleet Company Inc	C	434 528-4000	
Lynchburg (G-7671)			
Careplex Pharmacy	G	757 736-1215	
Hampton (G-6106)			
Cary Pharmaceuticals Inc	G	703 759-7460	
Great Falls (G-5944)			
Cavion Inc	G	434 200-8442	
Charlottesville (G-2760)			
Chantilly Biopharma LLC	F	703 932-3840	
Chantilly (G-2390)			
Chattem Inc	G	540 786-7970	
Fredericksburg (G-5261)			
Chorda Pharma LLC	G	251 753-1042	
Roanoke (G-12067)			
Clinpak Technologies LLC	G	410 357-4454	
Heathsville (G-6460)			
Contraline Inc	G	347 327-3676	
Charlottesville (G-2770)			
Covenant Therapeutics LLC	G	434 296-8668	
Charlottesville (G-2772)			
Daniel Orenzuk	G	410 570-1362	
Purcellville (G-10658)			
Deatrick & Associates Inc	G	703 753-1040	
Haymarket (G-6418)			
Dematology Assoc Virginia P	G	804 549-4030	
Glen Allen (G-5722)			
Diffusion Pharmaceuticals Inc		434 220-0718	
Charlottesville (G-2782)			

Diffusion Pharmaceuticals LLC	F	434 220-0718	
Charlottesville (G-2783)			
DK Pharma Group LLC	G	540 574-4651	
Harrisonburg (G-6309)			
Dova Pharmaceuticals Inc	G	844 506-3682	
Charlottesville (G-2786)			
Dove S Delights LLC	G	540 298-7178	
Elkton (G-4325)			
E Performance Inc	G	703 217-6885	
Mc Lean (G-8422)			
Enginred Bopharmaceuticals Inc	G	860 730-3262	
Danville (G-3991)			
Ergoject LLC	G	540 375-6415	
Salem (G-12505)			
Exponential Biotherapies Inc	G	703 288-3710	
Mc Lean (G-8425)			
Extinction Pharmaceuticals	G	757 258-0498	
Williamsburg (G-15241)			
Family Insight PC	G	540 818-1687	
Roanoke (G-11922)			
Ferrer	G	703 862-4891	
Alexandria (G-461)			
Gee Pharma LLC	G	703 669-8055	
Leesburg (G-7277)			
Genentech Inc	C	703 841-1076	
Arlington (G-977)			
Giant Pharmacy	G	703 723-2161	
Ashburn (G-1286)			
Granules Pharmaceuticals Inc	D	571 325-5950	
Chantilly (G-2431)			
Granules Pharmaceuticals Inc	G	571 325-5950	
Chantilly (G-2432)			
Gs Pharmaceuticals Inc	G	703 789-3344	
Herndon (G-6693)			
Gst Micro LLC	G	203 271-0830	
Henrico (G-6519)			
Helms Candy Co Inc	E	276 669-2612	
Bristol (G-2019)			
Hi-Tech Pharmacal Co Inc	G	804 935-7220	
Richmond (G-11238)			
Hst Global Inc	G	757 766-6100	
Hampton (G-6170)			
IJ Therapeutics LLC	G	804 543-6360	
Richmond (G-11612)			
Infinity Mg Inc	G	703 916-0172	
Annandale (G-759)			
▼ Innocoll Inc	G	703 980-4182	
Broadlands (G-2079)			
Interntnal Phrm Excpnts Adting	G	571 814-3449	
Arlington (G-1008)			
Isothrive LLC	G	855 552-5572	
Manassas (G-8088)			
Kehoe Enterprises LLC	G	540 668-9080	
Hillsboro (G-6874)			
Kerecis LLC	F	703 465-7945	
Arlington (G-1022)			
Landos Biopharma Inc	G	540 218-2262	
Blacksburg (G-1751)			
Lonza E Kingery	G	540 774-8728	
Roanoke (G-12130)			
Loudoun Medical Group PC	E	703 669-6118	
Leesburg (G-7306)			
Ltcpcms Inc	F	888 513-5444	
Ashland (G-1454)			
Macoma Capital	G	434 249-4580	
Gordonsville (G-5914)			
Marah Bitar LLC	G	856 630-4437	
Clintwood (G-3689)			
Mathemtics Scnce Ctr Foundation	G	862 778-8300	
Richmond (G-11673)			
Merck & Co Inc	G	540 447-0056	
Waynesboro (G-15125)			
Merck & Co Inc	G	804 363-0876	
Richmond (G-11287)			
MIND Pharmaceutical LLC	G	434 202-9617	
Charlottesville (G-2835)			
N-Molecular Inc	F	703 547-8161	
Dulles (G-4211)			
Neuro Stat Anlytcal Sltons LLC	E	703 224-8984	
Vienna (G-14104)			
Northern VA Compounders Pllc	G	855 792-5462	
Chantilly (G-2469)			
Northport Research Inc	G	703 508-9773	
Alexandria (G-295)			
Novartis Corporation	G	540 435-1836	
Mc Gaheysville (G-8378)			
▲ Novozymes Biologicals Inc	G	540 389-9361	
Salem (G-12547)			
Novozymes Biologicals Inc	G	540 389-9361	
Salem (G-12548)			

▲ Nutravail Holding Corp	D	703 222-6348	
Chantilly (G-2476)			
▲ Oc Pharma LLC	G	540 375-6415	
Salem (G-12550)			
Os-Gim Pharmaceuticals Inc	G	301 655-5191	
Woodbridge (G-15767)			
Oxystress Therapeutics LLC	G	832 277-0270	
Danville (G-4020)			
Panaceutics Nutrition Inc	F	919 797-9623	
Ringgold (G-11872)			
PBM Foods Inc	B	269 673-8451	
Charlottesville (G-2672)			
PBM International Ltd	G	800 959-2066	
Charlottesville (G-2673)			
PBM Pharmaceuticals Inc	F	434 980-8100	
Charlottesville (G-2842)			
Perrigo Nutritionals	F	434 297-1070	
Charlottesville (G-2676)			
Pfizer Inc	C	804 257-2000	
Richmond (G-11713)			
Pfizer Inc	C	804 652-6782	
Richmond (G-11321)			
Pfizer Inc	F	804 257-2000	
Richmond (G-11712)			
Pharmaceutical RES Assoc Inc	G	703 464-6300	
Reston (G-10924)			
Pharmaceutical Source LLC	G	757 482-3512	
Chesapeake (G-3238)			
Pharmacist Pharmaceutical LLC	G	540 375-6415	
Salem (G-12556)			
Phlow Corp	E	804 207-4893	
Richmond (G-11715)			
Pinnacle Quality Asrn Svcs	G	540 425-4123	
Bedford (G-1650)			
Polykon Manufacturing LLC	E	804 461-9974	
Sandston (G-12628)			
Poms Corporation	C	703 574-9901	
Herndon (G-6776)			
Precision Nuclear of Virginia	G	540 389-8333	
Roanoke (G-12151)			
Precision Pharmacy LLC	F	757 656-6560	
Chesapeake (G-3244)			
Realta Life Sciences Inc	G	757 418-4842	
Norfolk (G-9703)			
Rejuvinage	G	757 306-4300	
Virginia Beach (G-14767)			
Sanofi-Aventis US LLC	G	804 651-1595	
Chesterfield (G-3521)			
Sarfez Pharmaceuticals Inc	G	703 759-2565	
Vienna (G-14122)			
Savory Sun VA LLC	E	540 898-0851	
Fredericksburg (G-5220)			
Scilucent LLC	F	703 435-0033	
Herndon (G-6802)			
Selenix LLC	G	540 375-6415	
Salem (G-12570)			
Serpin Pharma LLC	G	703 343-3258	
Nokesville (G-9399)			
Shenox Pharmaceuticals LLC	G	732 309-2419	
Mc Lean (G-8546)			
Silivhere Technologies Inc	G	434 566-1207	
Charlottesville (G-2875)			
Skin Ranch and Trade Company	G	757 486-7546	
Virginia Beach (G-14823)			
Sofie Co	G	703 787-4075	
Sterling (G-13513)			
Stcube Pharmaceuticals Inc	G	703 815-1446	
Centreville (G-2341)			
Stem Technologies LLC	G	703 787-4654	
Herndon (G-6815)			
Stressa Incorporated	G	540 460-9495	
Buena Vista (G-2155)			
Teva Pharmaceuticals	E	888 838-2872	
Forest (G-5101)			
Third Security Rnr LLC	G	540 633-7900	
Radford (G-10744)			
Topam LLC	G	703 444-4240	
Herndon (G-6828)			
VA Medical Supply Inc	G	757 390-9000	
Chesapeake (G-3357)			
Venkor Specialty Products LLC	G	703 932-3840	
Centreville (G-2349)			
◆ Vidar Systems Corporation	E	703 471-7070	
Herndon (G-6838)			
Virchow Biotech Inc	G	615 549-5999	
Arlington (G-1212)			
Virginia Head and Neck Therape	G	804 837-9594	
North Chesterfield (G-10009)			
Vitaspan Corporation	G	866 459-2773	
Arlington (G-1214)			

Whitehall Robins ....G...... 804 257-2000
Richmond (G-11829)
Wyeth Pharmaceuticals LLC ....C...... 804 652-6000
Richmond (G-11459)

2835 Diagnostic Substances

Alere Inc ....G...... 800 340-4029
Portsmouth (G-10390)
Cardiac Diagnostics LLC ....G...... 703 268-5751
Fairfax (G-4424)
Centaurus Biotech LLC ....G...... 952 210-6881
Chantilly (G-2388)
Contravac Inc ....G...... 434 984-9723
Charlottesville (G-2611)
Global Cell Solutions Inc ....G...... 434 327-3759
Charlottesville (G-2804)
Hamamelis Genomics LLC ....G...... 703 939-3480
Alexandria (G-227)
Immunarray Usa Inc ....G...... 804 212-2975
Richmond (G-11615)
Imol Radiopharmaceuticals LLC ....G...... 434 825-3323
Charlottesville (G-2814)
Invirustech USA Inc ....G...... 703 826-3109
Vienna (G-14072)
Pgenomex Inc ....G...... 703 343-3282
Mc Lean (G-8527)
Provia Biologics Ltd ....G...... 757 305-9263
Norfolk (G-9699)
Rapid Biosciences Inc ....G...... 713 899-6177
Richmond (G-11728)
Smith River Biologicals ....G...... 276 930-2369
Ferrum (G-4981)

2836 Biological Prdts, Exc Diagnostic Substances

Amnion LLC ....G...... 267 255-6700
Leesburg (G-7216)
Appalchian Afrcan Amrcn Cnter ....E...... 276 546-5144
Pennington Gap (G-10293)
Armata Pharmaceuticals Inc ....G...... 804 827-3010
Richmond (G-11488)
Asd Biosystems Inc ....G...... 804 545-3102
Gretna (G-6003)
Atcc Global ....G...... 434 237-6861
Lynchburg (G-7644)
Banvera LLC ....E...... 757 599-9643
Newport News (G-9176)
Coty Connections Inc ....G...... 540 588-0117
Roanoke (G-11913)
Crozet Bopharma Consulting LLC ......G...... 703 598-1940
Crozet (G-3830)
Environmental Dynamics Inc ....G...... 540 261-2008
Buena Vista (G-2142)
Extract Attract Inc ....G...... 757 751-0671
Portsmouth (G-10424)
Famm Project LLC ....G...... 757 975-6492
Newport News (G-9224)
Fishhat Inc ....G...... 703 827-0990
Mc Lean (G-8432)
Food Allergy Lifestyle LLC ....G...... 757 509-3608
Gloucester (G-5847)
Forerunner Federation ....G...... 757 639-6576
Norfolk (G-9558)
Healthsmartvaccines Llc ....G...... 703 961-0734
Chantilly (G-2435)
Healthy Home Enterprise ....G...... 757 460-2829
Virginia Beach (G-14512)
I B R Plasma Center ....G...... 757 498-5160
Virginia Beach (G-14538)
Ked Plasma ....G...... 276 645-6035
Bristol (G-1981)
Mediatech Inc ....E...... 703 471-5955
Manassas (G-8106)
Nanomed Inc ....G...... 540 553-4070
Blacksburg (G-1770)
National Vaccine Info Ctr ....G...... 703 938-0342
Sterling (G-13460)
National Vaccine Informat ....G...... 703 777-3736
Leesburg (G-7319)
North Media LLC ....G...... 202 277-4933
Ashburn (G-1322)
Nutrition Support Services ....G...... 540 626-3081
Pembroke (G-10282)
Omega Black Incorporated ....G...... 240 416-1774
Fredericksburg (G-5340)
Serum Institute India Pvt LLC ....G...... 571 248-0911
Haymarket (G-6442)
Sigarchi Media ....G...... 571 296-5021
Arlington (G-1167)

Solstik ....G...... 571 348-4277
Herndon (G-6812)
Spheringenics Inc ....G...... 770 330-0782
Richmond (G-11769)
▲ Tyton Biosciences LLC ....F...... 434 793-9100
Danville (G-4043)
Valley Bomedical Pdts Svcs Inc ....E...... 540 868-0800
Winchester (G-15499)
Venom Motorsports ....G...... 804 347-7626
Colonial Beach (G-3728)
Virginia Venom Volleyball ....G...... 757 645-4002
Williamsburg (G-15334)
Virginia Vnom Spt Organization ....G...... 757 592-6790
Williamsburg (G-15335)

2841 Soap & Detergents

Aero Clean Technologies LLC ....G...... 434 381-0699
Lynchburg (G-7635)
Aziza Beauty LLC ....G...... 804 525-9989
Richmond (G-11496)
B & B Boutique ....G...... 703 425-8256
Burke (G-2181)
Bahashem Soap Company LLC ....G...... 804 398-0982
Richmond (G-11500)
Bath Sensations LLC ....G...... 804 832-4701
Chesterfield (G-3478)
Beatrice Aurthur ....G...... 347 420-5612
South Chesterfield (G-12831)
Bejoi LLC ....G...... 804 319-7369
Midlothian (G-8779)
Chem Core Inc ....G...... 540 862-2600
Covington (G-3781)
Chem Station of Virginia ....G...... 804 236-0090
Richmond (G-11154)
Chemtron Inc ....G...... 703 550-7772
Lorton (G-7472)
Copper Fox Distillery ....F...... 757 903-2076
Williamsburg (G-15222)
◆ Cumberland Company LP ....G...... 434 392-9911
Farmville (G-4938)
Daily Scrub LLC ....G...... 804 519-3696
Disputanta (G-4106)
Dream It & Do It LLC ....G...... 804 379-5474
Midlothian (G-8811)
◆ Ethyl Corporation ....G...... 804 788-5000
Richmond (G-11580)
Heathers Handcrafted Soaps ....G...... 757 277-8569
Virginia Beach (G-14514)
Julphia Soapworks ....G...... 703 815-8020
Centreville (G-2312)
Laundry Chemical Products Inc ....G...... 757 363-0662
Virginia Beach (G-14602)
Nevins & Moss LLC ....G...... 929 266-3640
Great Falls (G-5968)
◆ Newmarket Corporation ....D...... 804 788-5000
Richmond (G-11689)
Omniio LLC ....F...... 877 842-5478
Virginia Beach (G-14695)
Rebecca Ortizsanchez ....G...... 315 532-4439
Portsmouth (G-10475)
Rockbridge East LLC ....G...... 202 701-7927
Woodbridge (G-15798)
Serene Suds LLC ....G...... 804 433-8032
Richmond (G-11377)
Shantaras Soaps ....G...... 434 221-2382
Brookneal (G-2113)
Simplicity Pure Bath & Bdy LLC ....G...... 540 922-9287
Pearisburg (G-10277)
Soaplight LLC ....G...... 518 898-3441
Hampton (G-6240)
Tamara Smith ....G...... 910 495-4404
Gore (G-5923)
Theodore Turpin ....G...... 434 485-6600
Lynchburg (G-7823)
Todo Blu LLC ....G...... 703 944-9000
Annandale (G-788)
Total Bliss Gourmet Soap LLC ....G...... 540 740-8823
New Market (G-9149)
Valley Green Naturals LLC ....G...... 540 937-4795
Amissville (G-723)

2842 Spec Cleaning, Polishing & Sanitation Preparations

A Better Driving School LLC ....G...... 804 874-5521
Mechanicsville (G-8598)
Albright Recovery & Cnstr LLC ....G...... 276 835-2026
Clinchco (G-3684)
Allgoods Cleaning Service ....G...... 540 434-1511
Harrisonburg (G-6291)

Ascalon International Inc ....G...... 703 926-4343
Reston (G-10792)
Atx Technologies LLC ....G...... 540 586-4100
Bedford (G-1620)
B & B Cleaning Service ....G...... 757 667-9528
Norfolk (G-9448)
Birsch Industries Inc ....G...... 757 622-0355
Norfolk (G-9462)
Black Bear Corporation ....G...... 540 982-1061
Roanoke (G-12046)
Black Jacket LLC ....G...... 425 319-1014
Forest (G-5054)
C R D N Of The Shenandoah ....F...... 540 943-8242
Waynesboro (G-15103)
Cal Syd Inc ....G...... 276 963-3640
Richlands (G-11015)
Chemtron Inc ....G...... 703 550-7772
Lorton (G-7472)
▼ Concept Products Inc ....G...... 434 793-9952
Danville (G-3971)
Dayton Dalice ....G...... 540 233-3657
Front Royal (G-5529)
▲ Ester Yildiz LLC ....G...... 434 202-7790
Charlottesville (G-2628)
Five Star Portables Inc ....G...... 571 839-7884
Sterling (G-13399)
Fragrances Ltd ....G...... 540 636-8099
Front Royal (G-5532)
Global Water Challenge ....G...... 703 379-2713
Arlington (G-980)
Grand Investment LLC ....G...... 804 939-9473
Richmond (G-11604)
Green Air Environmental Svcs ....G...... 757 739-1349
Norfolk (G-9565)
Gregory Briggs ....G...... 804 402-6867
Richmond (G-11224)
Hampton Roads Green Clean LLC ....F...... 757 515-8183
Norfolk (G-9570)
Helping Hands Home Services ....F...... 757 898-3255
Seaford (G-12674)
▼ Hi-Lite Solutions Inc ....F...... 540 450-8375
Clear Brook (G-3645)
Hydrus Usa Inc ....G...... 804 690-8158
Glen Allen (G-5749)
Intense Cleaning Inc ....G...... 703 999-1933
Ashburn (G-1297)
John I Mercado ....G...... 703 569-3774
Springfield (G-13028)
Krystal Clear ....G...... 703 944-2066
Lorton (G-7503)
Leather Luster Inc ....G...... 757 548-0146
Chesapeake (G-3182)
Lubawa Usa Inc ....G...... 703 894-1909
Fredericksburg (G-5317)
Lunano Inc ....G...... 202 594-2959
Mc Lean (G-8490)
Madisons Cleaning ....F...... 540 421-1074
Rockingham (G-12260)
Marble Restoration Systems ....G...... 757 739-7959
Virginia Beach (G-14637)
▼ Nanotouch Materials LLC ....G...... 888 411-6843
Forest (G-5085)
NCH Home Solutions LLC ....G...... 703 723-4077
Ashburn (G-1319)
▲ Newell Industries Intl ....F...... 434 372-0089
Chase City (G-2913)
Polychem Inc ....G...... 540 862-1321
Clifton Forge (G-3682)
RE Clean Automotive Products ....G...... 757 368-2694
Virginia Beach (G-14763)
Rescue ME Cleaning Service ....G...... 540 370-0844
Fredericksburg (G-5219)
Secar At Rich LLC ....G...... 804 737-0090
Richmond (G-11755)
Shakir Waliyyud-Deen ....G...... 706 399-8893
Alexandria (G-583)
Sterile Home LLC ....G...... 804 314-3589
Tappahannock (G-13822)
Superb Cleaning Solutons ....G...... 804 908-9018
Henrico (G-6576)
TLC Cleaners Inc ....F...... 703 425-5577
Fairfax (G-4570)
Triple D Sales Co Inc ....G...... 540 672-5821
Aroda (G-1226)
United Cntry Cllins Assoc Real ....G...... 407 233-4377
Independence (G-6997)
Virginia Kik Inc ....E...... 540 389-5401
Salem (G-12578)
Weekend Detailer LLC ....G...... 757 345-2023
Williamsburg (G-15340)

S I C

Zero Products LLC ....G...... 757 285-4000
Virginia Beach (G-14957)

2843 Surface Active & Finishing Agents, Sulfonated Oils

Finish Agent Inc ....G...... 703 437-7822
Reston (G-10852)
Hillmans Distributors ....G...... 540 774-1896
Roanoke (G-11935)
Unicorn Editions Ltd ....G...... 540 364-0156
The Plains (G-13844)
Uso Path Finder ....G...... 757 395-4270
Norfolk (G-9776)

2844 Perfumes, Cosmetics & Toilet Preparations

A Family Heirloom LLC ....G...... 434 607-1674
Cumberland (G-3934)
Ace Bath Bombs LLC ....G...... 804 839-8639
Hopewell (G-6916)
Adiva Naturals LLC ....G...... 804 683-3738
Richmond (G-11473)
ALC Training Group LLC ....G...... 757 746-0428
Poquoson (G-10364)
All Export Import Usa LLC ....G...... 571 242-2250
Mc Lean (G-8391)
Alpha ....G...... 540 895-5731
Partlow (G-10263)
▲ Amarveda ....E...... 276 782-1819
Marion (G-8221)
Amelia Soap and Herb ....G...... 804 561-5229
Amelia Court House (G-650)
Aromatherapy Shoppe ....G...... 757 531-7431
Virginia Beach (G-14240)
Avon Products Inc ....G......
Stephens City (G-13312)
Beautymania ....G...... 703 300-9042
Alexandria (G-146)
Bel Souri LLC ....G...... 757 685-5583
Virginia Beach (G-14273)
Best Age Today LLC ....G...... 757 618-9181
Chesapeake (G-2997)
Braiding Station Inc ....G...... 804 898-2255
Newport News (G-9184)
Brandimage LLC ....G...... 703 855-5401
Herndon (G-6631)
Bridgetown LLC ....G...... 804 741-0648
Richmond (G-11133)
Brodies Naturals LLC ....G...... 804 507-0542
Richmond (G-11136)
Burroughs Qiana ....G...... 804 218-4031
Richmond (G-11030)
Butter of Life LLC ....G...... 703 507-5298
Falls Church (G-4766)
Chattem Inc ....G...... 540 786-7970
Fredericksburg (G-5261)
Cosmetic Essence LLC ....D...... 540 563-3000
Roanoke (G-12073)
Cosmetics By Makeena ....G...... 757 737-8402
Portsmouth (G-10410)
Covingtons Scrubs With Love ....G...... 804 503-8061
North Chesterfield (G-9852)
Craving Sensations LLC ....G...... 757 609-5038
Portsmouth (G-10412)
Crown ME Galore Collection LLC ....G...... 864 540-4476
Suffolk (G-13691)
Davidson Beauty Systems ....G...... 804 674-4875
Midlothian (G-8808)
Delightful Scents ....G...... 804 245-6999
Richmond (G-11560)
◆ Dorothy Prntice Armtherapy Inc ......G...... 703 657-0160
Fairfax (G-4614)
Dr Kings Little Luxuries LLC ....G...... 434 293-8515
Keswick (G-7045)
East Amber LLC ....G...... 703 414-9409
Occoquan (G-10172)
Ejn LLC ....G...... 646 621-5647
Alexandria (G-452)
Elizabeth Arden Inc ....D...... 540 444-2408
Salem (G-12502)
Elizabeth Arden Inc ....D...... 540 444-2406
Salem (G-12503)
Ellice Darien LLC ....G...... 804 677-9145
Chesterfield (G-3496)
Emge Naturals LLC ....G...... 434 660-6907
Lynchburg (G-7703)
Essential Essences ....G...... 757 544-0502
Virginia Beach (G-14451)

Euvanna Chayanne Cosmetics LLC ......G...... 804 307-4941
Chesterfield (G-3498)
Everlasting Life Product ....G...... 703 761-4900
Mc Lean (G-8424)
Everlasting Life Products Inc ....G...... 703 761-4900
Strasburg (G-13578)
Final Touch II Mfg LLC ....G...... 804 389-3899
North Chesterfield (G-9873)
Fleet International Inc C B ....E...... 866 255-6960
Lynchburg (G-7708)
▲ France Naturals Inc ....G...... 804 694-4777
Gloucester (G-5848)
Fullman Iman ....G...... 908 627-3376
Newport News (G-9233)
Gaias Gold ....G...... 804 516-8458
Walkerton (G-14971)
Getintoforex LLC ....G...... 251 591-2181
Big Stone Gap (G-1710)
Gidgets Beauty Box LLC ....G...... 303 859-5914
Purcellville (G-10662)
Gilbert Idelkhani ....G...... 703 399-1225
Herndon (G-6684)
Gregory Waynette ....G...... 804 239-0230
Richmond (G-11043)
▼ Hawknad Manufacturing Inds Inc ......G...... 703 941-0444
Springfield (G-13018)
Heavenly Hands & Feet Inc ....G...... 757 621-3938
Virginia Beach (G-14515)
Herban House Beauty LLC ....G...... 443 934-9041
Chesapeake (G-3133)
House of Vondrake Lavar LLC ....G...... 804 295-6136
Colonial Heights (G-3734)
I & C Hughes LLC ....G...... 757 544-0502
Virginia Beach (G-14537)
In Your Element Commerce Inc ....G...... 804 426-6914
Richmond (G-11616)
Ivorys Essentials LLC ....G...... 571 201-6147
Gainesville (G-5591)
Jade Suppliers ....G...... 804 551-6865
Richmond (G-11623)
Jan Tana Inc ....G...... 540 586-8266
Goode (G-5891)
Jessica Burdett ....G...... 719 423-0582
Disputanta (G-4110)
▲ Kdc US Holding Inc ....C...... 434 845-7073
Lynchburg (G-7750)
Kemelle Naturals Incorporated ....G...... 850 528-9053
Alexandria (G-251)
Knuude LLC ....G...... 571 298-1746
Charlottesville (G-2654)
Le Splendour LLC ....G...... 703 505-5362
Centreville (G-2314)
Legit Bath Salts Online ....G...... 540 200-8618
Blacksburg (G-1752)
Lovely Reds Creations LLC ....G...... 540 320-2859
Allisonia (G-619)
Marie Webb ....G...... 703 291-5359
Woodbridge (G-15743)
Mommas Best Homemade LLC ....G...... 805 509-5419
Virginia Beach (G-14661)
Natural Balance Concepts LLC ....G...... 804 693-5382
Gloucester (G-5856)
Naturally Me LLC ....G...... 703 680-3392
Woodbridge (G-15754)
Nokyem Naturals LLC ....C...... 757 218-1794
Hampton (G-6209)
OH So Good Organics LLC ....G...... 703 577-9226
Centreville (G-2326)
Pinky & Face Inc ....G...... 703 478-2708
Herndon (G-6773)
Quinns Bath Bombs LLC ....G...... 703 853-5067
Centreville (G-2331)
Rugged Evolution Incorporated ....G...... 757 478-2430
Chesapeake (G-3279)
SAi Beauty LLC ....G...... 703 864-6372
Chantilly (G-2489)
Scents By Scales ....G...... 757 234-3380
Newport News (G-9331)
▲ Securitas Inc ....G...... 800 705-4545
Richmond (G-11063)
Sephora Inside Jcpenney ....G...... 434 973-7851
Charlottesville (G-2692)
Sociiterra International LLC ....G...... 804 461-1876
Mechanicsville (G-8678)
Sun Care Inc ....G...... 703 715-7070
Annandale (G-785)
Sunshine Products Inc ....G...... 703 768-3500
Alexandria (G-592)
Sweet Relief Inc ....G...... 703 963-4868
Sterling (G-13526)

Sweetbriar Scents LLC ....G...... 757 358-6815
Hampton (G-6246)
Techline Mfg LLC ....G...... 804 986-8285
Midlothian (G-8912)
Tree Naturals Inc ....G...... 804 514-4423
Richmond (G-11793)
Tri-Tech Laboratories LLC ....G...... 434 845-7073
Lynchburg (G-7828)
Uh Roh Muh Inc ....G...... 703 725-1684
Centreville (G-2346)
Valley Scents ....G...... 540 688-8855
Staunton (G-13306)
Viloquinne LLC ....G...... 703 493-8864
Lorton (G-7539)
Virginia Aromatics Ltd Company ....G...... 540 672-2847
Orange (G-10229)
Wade M Marcita ....G...... 804 437-2066
Chesterfield (G-3540)
Wear Red Lipstick LLC ....G...... 703 627-2123
Centreville (G-2352)
Weights N Lipstick ....G...... 251 404-8154
Suffolk (G-13783)

2851 Paints, Varnishes, Lacquers, Enamels

Akzo Nobel Coatings Inc ....E...... 540 982-8301
Roanoke (G-12030)
Atomic Armor Inc ....G...... 703 400-3954
Leesburg (G-7225)
Augusta Paint & Decorating LLC ....G...... 540 942-1800
Waynesboro (G-15098)
Axalta Coating Systems LLC ....E...... 540 622-2951
Front Royal (G-5521)
Barney Family Enterprises LLC ....G...... 757 438-2064
Wakefield (G-14964)
Branch House Signature Pdts ....G...... 804 644-3041
Richmond (G-11507)
C & P Inc ....G...... 703 522-2229
Arlington (G-896)
Calloway Enterprises Inc ....G...... 434 525-1147
Forest (G-5058)
Coldens Concepts LLC ....G...... 757 644-9535
Chesapeake (G-3045)
Darrell A Wilson ....G...... 540 598-8412
Vinton (G-14173)
Davis-Frost Inc ....G...... 434 846-2721
Lynchburg (G-7695)
Dispersion Specialties Inc ....F...... 804 798-9137
Ashland (G-1402)
Dnj Dirtworks Inc ....G...... 540 937-3138
Rixeyville (G-11878)
Dual Dynamics Industrail Paint ....G...... 804 543-3216
Aylett (G-1548)
Ennis-Flint Inc ....E...... 804 309-3199
Richmond (G-11579)
Ervins Bathtub Refinishing ....G...... 703 730-8831
Woodbridge (G-15697)
Gateway Green Energy Inc ....G...... 540 280-7475
Fishersville (G-5003)
Gemini Coating of Virginia ....F...... 540 434-4201
Harrisonburg (G-6320)
Gemini Coatings Inc ....F...... 540 434-4201
Harrisonburg (G-6321)
Hanwha Azdel Inc ....D...... 434 385-6359
Forest (G-5073)
Hbh Holdings LLC ....F...... 540 631-9555
Front Royal (G-5536)
HI Caliber Manufacturing LLC ....G...... 804 955-8300
Ashland (G-1432)
Indmar Coatings Corporation ....F...... 757 899-3807
Wakefield (G-14966)
International Paint LLC ....G...... 757 466-0705
Norfolk (G-9595)
K C G Inc ....G...... 703 542-7120
Chantilly (G-2539)
Kwicksilver Systems LLC ....G...... 619 917-1067
Crozet (G-3841)
Lasar Chemicals ....G...... 757 286-9808
Chesapeake (G-3175)
Line X Central Virginia Inc ....G...... 434 525-8878
Evington (G-4378)
M & R Striping LLC ....G...... 703 201-7162
Broad Run (G-2068)
Mkm Coatings LLC ....G...... 804 514-3506
Mechanicsville (G-8663)
Osburn Coatings Inc ....G...... 804 769-3030
Aylett (G-1551)
PPG Industries Inc ....G...... 703 370-5636
Alexandria (G-315)
PPG Industries Inc ....G...... 757 494-5116
Chesapeake (G-3243)

PPG Industries Inc ....G...... 804 794-5331
Richmond *(G-11061)*

Putty LLC ....G...... 434 960-3954
Charlottesville *(G-2851)*

Sampson Coatings Incorporated ....G...... 804 359-5011
Richmond *(G-11371)*

Sherwin-Williams Company ....G...... 804 264-6156
Glen Allen *(G-5795)*

Srj Bedliners LLC ....G...... 757 539-7710
Suffolk *(G-13767)*

Tag America Inc ....G...... 757 227-9831
Virginia Beach *(G-14864)*

Td & D Unlimited LLC ....G...... 703 946-9338
Goldvein *(G-5879)*

Vienna Paint & Dctg Co Inc ....G...... 703 281-5252
Vienna *(G-14154)*

Vienna Paint & Dctg Co Inc ....G...... 703 450-0300
Sterling *(G-13551)*

Vienna Pt Reston/Herndon 04 ....G...... 703 733-3899
Herndon *(G-6839)*

Virginia Premiere Paint Contr ....G...... 804 398-1177
Richmond *(G-11813)*

2861 Gum & Wood Chemicals

Akzo Nobel Coatings Inc ....E...... 540 982-8301
Roanoke *(G-12030)*

Bclf Corporation ....G...... 540 929-1701
Callaway *(G-2219)*

Branch Botanicals Inc ....G...... 703 429-4217
Chantilly *(G-2380)*

◆ Westrock Mwv LLC ....A...... 804 444-1000
Richmond *(G-11825)*

2865 Cyclic-Crudes, Intermediates, Dyes & Org Pigments

Alchemical Hydrogen LLC ....G...... 703 399-9235
Alexandria *(G-124)*

Branch Botanicals Inc ....G...... 703 429-4217
Chantilly *(G-2380)*

◆ Ethyl Corporation ....G...... 804 788-5000
Richmond *(G-11580)*

Lonesome Trails Entps Inc ....G...... 276 445-5443
Ewing *(G-4385)*

National Tars ....G...... 703 368-4220
Manassas *(G-8115)*

◆ Newmarket Corporation ....D...... 804 788-5000
Richmond *(G-11689)*

Synalloy Corporation ....D...... 804 822-3260
Glen Allen *(G-5804)*

Tars Inc ....G...... 434 836-7890
Danville *(G-4039)*

2869 Industrial Organic Chemicals, NEC

83 Gas & Grocery Inc ....G...... 276 926-4388
Clintwood *(G-3685)*

Affordable Fuel Substitute Inc ....G...... 276 694-8080
Stuart *(G-13604)*

Afton Chemical Additives Corp ....F...... 804 788-5000
Richmond *(G-11475)*

Albemarle Corporation ....C...... 225 388-8011
Richmond *(G-11092)*

BASF Corporation ....G...... 757 538-3700
Suffolk *(G-13674)*

Better Fuels of Virginia ....G...... 540 693-4552
Fredericksburg *(G-5252)*

Caribbean Channel One Inc ....G...... 703 447-3773
Woodbridge *(G-15668)*

◆ Carpenter Co ....C...... 804 359-0800
Richmond *(G-11146)*

Carpenter Co ....D...... 804 233-0606
Richmond *(G-11032)*

Chesapeake Custom Chem Corp ....G...... 276 956-3145
Ridgeway *(G-11840)*

Cnv Marine Fuel Specialist LLC ....G...... 757 615-2666
Chesapeake *(G-3038)*

Commercial Fueling 24/7 Inc ....G...... 540 338-6457
Purcellville *(G-10656)*

Dynamic Recycling LLC ....G...... 276 628-6636
Abingdon *(G-29)*

Eco Fuel LLC ....G...... 703 256-6999
Annandale *(G-746)*

◆ Ethyl Corporation ....G...... 804 788-5000
Richmond *(G-11580)*

Evonik Corporation ....C...... 804 541-8658
Hopewell *(G-6925)*

Evonik Corporation ....C...... 804 727-0711
North Chesterfield *(G-9868)*

◆ Evonik Goldschmidt Corporation .....A...... 804 541-8658
Hopewell *(G-6926)*

Freon Doctor Inc ....G...... 877 825-2401
Bumpass *(G-2162)*

Fuel Impurities Separator ....G...... 757 340-6833
Virginia Beach *(G-14477)*

Fuel Your Life LLC ....G...... 703 208-4449
Vienna *(G-14058)*

Global Yacht Fuel LLC ....G...... 954 462-6050
Norfolk *(G-9563)*

Green Fuel of VA ....G...... 804 304-4564
Mechanicsville *(G-8632)*

Green Plains Hopewell LLC ....G...... 804 668-0013
Hopewell *(G-6927)*

Gsk Corporation Inc ....G...... 240 200-5600
Sterling *(G-13417)*

Henkel US Operations Corp ....F...... 804 222-6100
Richmond *(G-11236)*

Hercules Inc ....G...... 804 541-4545
Hopewell *(G-6928)*

Honeywell International Inc ....G...... 804 541-5000
Hopewell *(G-6931)*

◆ Honeywell Resins & Chem LLC ....D...... 804 541-5000
Hopewell *(G-6933)*

Jah Rootz Industries LLC ....G...... 512 925-1109
Harrisonburg *(G-6332)*

Kaotic Enzymes LLC ....G...... 804 519-9479
Richmond *(G-11639)*

Kid Fueled Kco LLC ....G...... 804 720-4091
Prince George *(G-10597)*

Masters Energy Inc ....E...... 281 816-9991
Glen Allen *(G-5768)*

MTI Specialty Silicones Inc ....G...... 540 254-2020
Buchanan *(G-2122)*

◆ Newmarket Corporation ....D...... 804 788-5000
Richmond *(G-11689)*

Osage Bio Energy LLC ....E...... 804 612-8660
Glen Allen *(G-5777)*

Power Fuels LLC ....G...... 276 676-2945
Abingdon *(G-54)*

Qpi ....G...... 434 528-0092
Lynchburg *(G-7796)*

Quaker Houghton Pa Inc ....G...... 540 877-3631
Winchester *(G-15464)*

Real Food For Fuel LLC ....G...... 757 416-4458
Blacksburg *(G-1782)*

S Fuel Co ....G...... 434 220-1044
Charlottesville *(G-2869)*

Shaklee Independent Distr ....G...... 757 553-8765
Virginia Beach *(G-14806)*

Sisko Duel Fuel System ....G...... 804 795-1634
Henrico *(G-6571)*

Slys Sucker Punch LLC ....G...... 571 989-3538
Woodbridge *(G-15814)*

Star Oil LLC ....G...... 757 545-5100
Chesapeake *(G-3310)*

Suganit Bio-Renewables LLC ....G...... 703 736-0634
Reston *(G-10968)*

Suganit Bio-Renewables LLC ....F...... 703 736-0634
Mount Jackson *(G-9080)*

Synalloy Corporation ....D...... 804 822-3260
Glen Allen *(G-5804)*

Taicco Fuel Inc ....G...... 571 405-7700
Richmond *(G-11406)*

Tego Chemie Svc Usadiv of Gold ....G...... 804 541-8658
Hopewell *(G-6941)*

True Energy Fuels ....G...... 276 796-4003
Pound *(G-10514)*

Virginia Embalming Company Inc ....G...... 540 334-1150
Rocky Mount *(G-12359)*

Wholesome Energy LLC ....G...... 540 984-8219
Edinburg *(G-4316)*

2873 Nitrogenous Fertilizers

Agrium US Inc ....G...... 434 738-0515
Boydton *(G-1913)*

Airgas Inc ....G...... 757 539-7185
Suffolk *(G-13664)*

Crop Production Svc ....G...... 804 732-6166
Prince George *(G-10590)*

Houff Corporation ....D...... 540 234-8088
Weyers Cave *(G-15173)*

Houff Corporation ....G...... 540 234-9246
Doswell *(G-4122)*

Hyponex Corporation ....E...... 434 848-2727
Lawrenceville *(G-7181)*

Nutri-Blend Inc ....F...... 804 222-1675
Richmond *(G-11310)*

Nutrients Plus LLC ....G...... 757 430-3400
Virginia Beach *(G-14689)*

Solgreen Solutions LLC ....G...... 833 765-4733
Alexandria *(G-588)*

Southern States Coop Inc ....E...... 703 378-4865
Chantilly *(G-2495)*

Southern States Coop Inc ....F...... 804 226-2758
Richmond *(G-11390)*

▲ Southern States Coop Inc ....B...... 804 281-1000
Richmond *(G-11389)*

Tranlin Inc ....G...... 866 215-8290
Glen Allen *(G-5816)*

Windrush Farm LLC ....G...... 540 589-1878
Copper Hill *(G-3765)*

2874 Phosphatic Fertilizers

Montgomery Farm Supply Co ....G...... 540 483-7072
Wirtz *(G-15617)*

▲ Southern States Coop Inc ....B...... 804 281-1000
Richmond *(G-11389)*

Southern States Coop Inc ....E...... 703 378-4865
Chantilly *(G-2495)*

Southern States Coop Inc ....F...... 804 226-2758
Richmond *(G-11390)*

Southern States Roanoke Coop ....G...... 540 483-1217
Wirtz *(G-15619)*

2875 Fertilizers, Mixing Only

Armstrong Green & Embrey Inc ....G...... 540 898-7434
Fredericksburg *(G-5248)*

▲ Asb Greenworld Inc ....E...... 804 785-9260
Mattaponi *(G-8357)*

◆ Cameron Chemicals Inc ....F...... 757 487-0656
Virginia Beach *(G-14311)*

Castlemans Compost LLC ....G...... 571 283-3030
Herndon *(G-6636)*

Compost Livin LLC ....G...... 703 362-9378
Annandale *(G-736)*

Compost Rva LLC ....G...... 804 639-0363
Midlothian *(G-8802)*

Cow Pie Compost LLC ....G...... 540 272-2854
Midland *(G-8750)*

Crop Production Services Inc ....G...... 804 282-7115
Richmond *(G-11037)*

Enrich Compost LLC ....G...... 518 410-2402
Henrico *(G-6507)*

Humus Compost Company LLC ....G...... 540 421-7169
Rockingham *(G-12256)*

Hyponex Corporation ....E...... 434 848-2727
Lawrenceville *(G-7181)*

Kathezz Compost LLC ....G...... 434 842-9395
Columbia *(G-3752)*

Lesco Inc ....G...... 703 257-9015
Manassas *(G-7962)*

Lesco Inc ....G...... 540 752-1408
Fredericksburg *(G-5449)*

Nutrien AG Solutions Inc ....G...... 757 229-9448
West Point *(G-15160)*

Nutrien AG Solutions Inc ....G...... 540 775-2985
Milford *(G-8932)*

Poplar Manor Enterprises LLC ....G...... 540 763-9542
Riner *(G-11865)*

Synagrow Wwt Inc ....F...... 804 443-2170
Champlain *(G-2358)*

Virginias Peninsula Pub Fcilty ....G...... 757 898-5012
Yorktown *(G-15999)*

2879 Pesticides & Agricultural Chemicals, NEC

Dark Hollow LLC ....G...... 540 355-8218
Lexington *(G-7394)*

Dupont ....G...... 540 949-5361
Waynesboro *(G-15109)*

Dupont Aero LLC ....G...... 540 350-4306
Mount Solon *(G-9086)*

Dupont Circle Solutions ....G...... 202 596-8528
Arlington *(G-946)*

Dupont Credit Union ....G...... 540 868-8714
Harrisonburg *(G-6311)*

▲ Dupont De Nemours Inc ....G...... 804 549-4747
North Chesterfield *(G-9863)*

Dupont James River Gyps Fcilty ....G...... 804 714-3362
North Chesterfield *(G-9864)*

Dupont Threading LLC ....G...... 703 522-1748
Arlington *(G-947)*

Dupont Threading LLC ....G...... 703 734-1425
Ashburn *(G-1274)*

Dupont Ventures LLC ....G...... 574 514-3646
Arlington *(G-948)*

E I Du Pont De Nemours ....G...... 804 550-7560
Ashland *(G-1405)*

E I Du Pont De Nemours & Co ....B...... 804 383-4251
Chesterfield *(G-3494)*

Hayward Trmt & Pest Ctrl LLC ....G 757 263-7858
Norfolk *(G-9574)*

Livingston Group Inc ....G 757 460-3115
Virginia Beach *(G-14613)*

Loudoun Composting ....F 703 327-8428
Chantilly *(G-2544)*

Monsanto Tamantha ....G 434 517-0013
North Prince George *(G-10090)*

Neutra-Green Clg Solutions LLC ....G 804 447-8010
Henrico *(G-6540)*

Redcoat Solutions Inc ....G 540 437-9843
Rockingham *(G-12270)*

Residex LLC ....G 757 363-2080
Virginia Beach *(G-14768)*

Scotts Company LLC ....E 434 848-2727
Lawrenceville *(G-7184)*

South Star Distributers ....F 276 466-4038
Bristol *(G-1988)*

Wright Solutions Inc ....G 703 652-7145
Centreville *(G-2355)*

2891 Adhesives & Sealants

2 P Products ....G 804 273-9822
Richmond *(G-11071)*

◆ Choice Adhesives Corporation ....E 434 847-5671
Lynchburg *(G-7678)*

Coastal Caulking Sealants LLC ....G 757 679-8201
Chesapeake *(G-3040)*

▲ Drytac Corporation ....E 804 280-6013
Sandston *(G-12613)*

Duration Products LLC ....G 804 651-1700
Henrico *(G-6504)*

Graphic Arts Adhesives ....G 804 779-3304
Mechanicsville *(G-8630)*

Henkel US Operations Corp ....F 804 222-6100
Richmond *(G-11236)*

Insul Industries Inc ....F 804 550-1933
Mechanicsville *(G-8641)*

Johns Manville Corporation ....B 804 261-7400
Richmond *(G-11256)*

Lyon Roofing Inc ....G 540 633-0170
Fairlawn *(G-4737)*

Mapei Corp Fredericksburg ....G 540 710-5303
Fredericksburg *(G-5319)*

Mapei Corporation ....D 540 898-5124
Fredericksburg *(G-5320)*

Mapei Corporation ....E 540 361-1085
Fredericksburg *(G-5453)*

Nbe Technologies LLC ....G 540 443-9100
Blacksburg *(G-1772)*

Safety Seal Plastics LLC ....G 703 348-4699
Fredericksburg *(G-5482)*

Stella Stone and Sealant LLC ....G 917 568-6489
Fairfax *(G-4561)*

◆ Vitex Packaging Group Inc ....F 757 538-3115
Suffolk *(G-13780)*

W R Meadows Inc ....G 434 797-1321
Danville *(G-4048)*

Worthen Industries Inc ....E 804 275-9231
Richmond *(G-11067)*

Worthen Industries Inc ....E 804 275-9231
Richmond *(G-11068)*

2892 Explosives

Austin Powder Company ....F 434 842-3589
Fork Union *(G-5107)*

Austin Powder Company ....F 540 992-6097
Daleville *(G-3940)*

C4 Explosive Spt Training LLC ....G 571 379-7955
Manassas *(G-7923)*

C4 Explosive Spt Training LLC ....G 703 881-1481
Bristow *(G-2049)*

◆ Davis Mining & Mfg Inc ....F 276 395-3354
Wise *(G-15622)*

Dyno Nobel Inc ....F 276 935-6436
Vansant *(G-13976)*

Dyno Noble Appalachia Inc ....G 276 940-2201
Duffield *(G-4177)*

Explosive Sports Cond LLC ....G 703 255-7087
Vienna *(G-14052)*

New River Energetics Inc ....G 703 406-5695
Radford *(G-10727)*

New River Ordnance Works Inc ....G 907 888-9615
Blacksburg *(G-1774)*

Orica USA Inc ....G 540 380-3146
Salem *(G-12551)*

Paige Ireco Inc ....G 276 940-2201
Duffield *(G-4183)*

Precision Explosives LLC ....G 833 338-6628
Midland *(G-8761)*

Pyrotechnique By Grucci Inc ....D 540 639-8800
Radford *(G-10736)*

2893 Printing Ink

Acme Ink Inc ....G 757 373-3614
Virginia Beach *(G-14207)*

▲ Cavalier Printing Ink Co Inc ....G 804 271-4214
Richmond *(G-11033)*

Dispersion Specialties Inc ....F 804 798-9137
Ashland *(G-1402)*

Flint CPS Inks North Amer LLC ....G 540 234-9203
Weyers Cave *(G-15172)*

Flint Group US LLC ....G 804 270-1328
Henrico *(G-6512)*

INX Internatiol Ink Co ....G 540 977-0079
Roanoke *(G-11943)*

▼ J M Fry Company ....E 804 236-8100
Henrico *(G-6525)*

Red Tie Group Inc ....G 804 236-4632
Richmond *(G-11349)*

Robert Lewis ....G 917 640-0709
Blackstone *(G-1826)*

▲ Sicpa Securink Corp ....D 703 455-8050
Springfield *(G-13084)*

Sun Chemical Corporation ....E 804 524-3888
South Chesterfield *(G-12828)*

Toner & Ink Warehouse LLC ....G 301 332-2796
Gainesville *(G-5618)*

Wikoff Color Corp ....G 540 586-8111
Bedford *(G-1663)*

▲ Zeller + Gmelin Corporation ....D 800 848-8465
Richmond *(G-11463)*

2899 Chemical Preparations, NEC

141 Repellent Inc ....G 540 421-3956
Lexington *(G-7385)*

710 Essentials LLC ....G 540 748-4393
Spotsylvania *(G-12880)*

A Descal Matic Corp ....G 757 858-5593
Norfolk *(G-9414)*

Advansix Inc ....A 804 541-5000
Hopewell *(G-6917)*

Advansix Inc ....E 804 504-0009
South Chesterfield *(G-12793)*

◆ Afton Chemical Corporation ....B 804 788-5800
Richmond *(G-11476)*

Afton Chemical Corporation ....G 804 788-5250
Richmond *(G-11477)*

Afton Chemical Corporation ....G 804 788-5800
Richmond *(G-11478)*

Afton Chemical Corporation ....F 804 752-8420
Ashland *(G-1364)*

Albemarle Corporation ....C 225 388-8011
Richmond *(G-11092)*

American Concrete Group LLC ....G 276 546-1666
Pennington Gap *(G-10292)*

American Concrete Group LLC ....G 423 323-7566
Bristol *(G-2004)*

Applied Film Technology Inc ....G 757 351-4241
Virginia Beach *(G-14234)*

Aqueous Solutions Global LLC ....G 410 710-7736
Richmond *(G-11486)*

Astro LLC ....G 888 401-1003
Manassas *(G-7915)*

Bishop II Inc ....G 757 855-7137
Norfolk *(G-9464)*

Body Cosmic Skincare ....G 757 701-8232
Chesapeake *(G-3010)*

Brian L Longest ....G 703 759-3847
Great Falls *(G-5940)*

Certified Environmental Drlg ....G 434 979-0123
Charlottesville *(G-2763)*

Chemical Supply Inc ....G 804 353-2971
Richmond *(G-11155)*

Chemtreat Inc ....D 804 513-0756
Ashland *(G-1390)*

Commodore Sales LLC ....E 804 794-1992
North Chesterfield *(G-9850)*

Construction Specialties Group ....G 703 670-5300
Dumfries *(G-4240)*

Den Hertog Frits ....G 540 929-4650
Bent Mountain *(G-1668)*

Earth Friendly Chemicals Inc ....G 757 502-8600
Virginia Beach *(G-14427)*

Ehp ....G 540 667-1815
Winchester *(G-15538)*

Energize Your Size LLC ....G 703 360-1093
Alexandria *(G-457)*

Essential Eats LLC ....G 757 304-2393
Norfolk *(G-9544)*

◆ Ethyl Corporation ....G 804 788-5000
Richmond *(G-11580)*

F & D Manufacturing & Supply ....G 540 586-6111
Bedford *(G-1636)*

Frit Small Dollar Twai ....G 804 697-3968
Richmond *(G-11595)*

Going Forward Imports LLC ....G 301 693-1562
Mount Jackson *(G-9071)*

Gpc Inc ....G 757 345-3991
Woodbridge *(G-15712)*

Grain Free Products Inc ....G 703 418-0000
Alexandria *(G-471)*

▼ Hi-Lite Solutions Inc ....F 540 450-8375
Clear Brook *(G-3645)*

Ice Release Materials LLC ....G 540 239-2438
Ashland *(G-1437)*

Ilma ....G 703 684-5574
Alexandria *(G-235)*

Incense Oil More ....G 540 793-8642
Roanoke *(G-12105)*

▲ Interprome Marketing Inc ....G 804 744-2922
Midlothian *(G-8834)*

ITI Group ....G 703 339-5388
Lorton *(G-7497)*

J C International LLC ....G 540 243-0086
Rocky Mount *(G-12329)*

Kdl Solutions LLC ....G 703 216-2201
Nokesville *(G-9395)*

▲ Kessler Soils Engrg Pdts Inc ....G 571 291-2284
Leesburg *(G-7296)*

◆ Kmx Chemical Corp ....E 757 824-3600
New Church *(G-9125)*

Kmx Chemical Corp. ....F 757 824-3600
New Church *(G-9126)*

◆ Luck Stone Corporation ....D 804 784-6300
Manakin Sabot *(G-7901)*

Mapei Corporation ....E 540 361-1085
Fredericksburg *(G-5453)*

▲ Masa Corporation ....G 757 855-3013
Norfolk *(G-9633)*

▼ Maxx Performance Inc ....F 845 987-9432
Roanoke *(G-11960)*

▲ Morton Salt ....G 757 543-0148
Chesapeake *(G-3212)*

Moth LLC ....G 804 655-8216
North Chesterfield *(G-9933)*

◆ Newmarket Corporation ....D 804 788-5000
Richmond *(G-11689)*

Nova Concrete Products Inc ....G 540 439-2978
Bealeton *(G-1603)*

Otter River Filtration Plant ....G 434 821-8611
Evington *(G-4382)*

Peace Harmony and Love LLC ....G 571 210-5853
Centreville *(G-2328)*

◆ Prochem Inc ....E 540 268-9884
Elliston *(G-4347)*

Pure Anointing Oil ....G 703 889-7457
Springfield *(G-13077)*

Pyrotechnique By Grucci Inc ....D 540 639-8800
Radford *(G-10736)*

Q P I Inc ....G 434 528-0092
Lynchburg *(G-7795)*

Quaker Chemical Corporation ....G 540 389-2038
Salem *(G-12559)*

Quikrete Companies LLC ....E 276 646-8976
Chilhowie *(G-3558)*

Radford Wldg & Fabrication LLC ....G 540 731-4891
Radford *(G-10737)*

▲ Rayco Services Inc ....G 757 689-2156
Virginia Beach *(G-14761)*

Raymond Golden ....G 757 549-1853
Chesapeake *(G-3256)*

Rex Roto Corporation ....E 434 447-6854
South Hill *(G-12859)*

Ruby Salts Oyster Company LLC ....G 757 331-1495
Cape Charles *(G-2236)*

Salt Soothers LLC ....G 757 412-5867
Virginia Beach *(G-14791)*

Sibashi Inc ....G 571 292-6233
Centreville *(G-2340)*

Son1c Wax LLC ....G 703 508-8188
Fairfax Station *(G-4724)*

Suganit Bio-Renewables LLC ....F 703 736-0634
Mount Jackson *(G-9080)*

Synalloy Corporation ....D 804 822-3260
Glen Allen *(G-5804)*

T & J Wldg & Fabrication LLC ....G 757 672-9929
Suffolk *(G-13770)*

Unshrinkit Inc ....G 804 519-7019
Arlington *(G-1202)*

Virginia Fire Protection Svcs ....G...... 276 637-1012
Max Meadows (G-8370)
W R Grace & Co-Conn ....G...... 540 752-6048
Fredericksburg (G-5499)
Water Chemistry Incorporated ....E...... 540 343-3618
Roanoke (G-12022)
Water Technologies Inc ....G...... 540 366-9799
Roanoke (G-12023)
WDFUP LLC ....G...... 757 309-6214
Hampton (G-6271)
Weathertite Industries Inc ....G...... 703 830-8001
Chantilly (G-2521)
▲ Zeller + Gmelin Corporation ....D...... 800 848-8465
Richmond (G-11463)
▲ Zestron Corporation ....E...... 703 393-9880
Manassas (G-8184)

29 PETROLEUM REFINING AND RELATED INDUSTRIES

2911 Petroleum Refining

Advanced Cgnitive Systems Corp ....G...... 804 397-3373
Richmond (G-11474)
Afd Technologies LLC ....G...... 561 271-7000
Virginia Beach (G-14215)
American Biodiesel Corporation ....G...... 703 906-9434
Manassas (G-7910)
C & A and Sons Paving LLC ....G...... 434 209-7357
Forest (G-5057)
Chesapeake Custom Chem Corp ....G...... 276 956-3145
Ridgeway (G-11840)
Cobehn Inc ....G...... 540 665-0707
Winchester (G-15404)
Fuelcor Development LLC ....G...... 703 740-0071
Mc Lean (G-8437)
Gibraltar Energy LLC ....G...... 202 642-2704
Alexandria (G-469)
Kessler Marine Services Inc ....G...... 571 276-1377
Springfield (G-13033)
Mobil Petrochemical Holdings ....G...... 703 846-3000
Fairfax (G-4513)
Oreamnos Biofuels LLC ....G...... 651 269-7737
Williamsburg (G-15287)
Polytrade International Corp ....G...... 703 598-7269
Sterling (G-13474)
Precision Gas Piping LLC ....G...... 434 531-2427
Ruckersville (G-12409)
Quickest Residual Pay ....G...... 703 924-2620
Alexandria (G-564)
Reco Biodiesel LLC ....F...... 804 644-2800
Richmond (G-11731)
Residual King LLC ....G...... 757 474-3080
Virginia Beach (G-14769)
Residual Sense Marketing LLC ....G...... 757 595-0278
Newport News (G-9324)
Riyan Industries ....G...... 703 525-6132
Arlington (G-1148)
Scenter of Town LLC ....G...... 540 372-4145
Fredericksburg (G-5221)
Solevents Floral LLC ....G...... 571 221-5761
Fairfax (G-4557)
Synergy Biofuels LLC ....G...... 276 546-5226
Pennington Gap (G-10300)
Virginia Bodiesel Refinery LLC ....G...... 804 435-1126
Kilmarnock (G-7078)
Viscosity LLC ....G...... 757 343-9071
Chesapeake (G-3363)
Wythe Oil Distributors Inc ....G...... 276 228-4512
Wytheville (G-15926)

2951 Paving Mixtures & Blocks

Air-Con Asp Sling Striping LLC ....G...... 540 664-1989
Winchester (G-15373)
Asphalt Ready Mix Inc ....G...... 540 576-3483
Union Hall (G-13958)
Associated Asphalt Inman LLC ....G...... 864 472-2816
Roanoke (G-12036)
Boxley Materials Company ....F...... 540 777-7600
Lynchburg (G-7659)
Boxley Materials Company ....G...... 540 777-7600
Arrington (G-1229)
Cleanpowerpartners ....G...... 301 651-0690
Alexandria (G-432)
Colony Construction Asp LLC ....G...... 434 767-9930
Burkeville (G-2207)
Colony Construction Asp LLC ....F...... 804 598-1400
Powhatan (G-10540)
Eurovia Atlantic Coast LLC ....G...... 703 230-0850
Chantilly (G-2418)

Fort Valley Paving ....G...... 540 636-8960
Strasburg (G-13579)
Fuller Asphalt Material ....G...... 423 676-4449
Bristol (G-2018)
Goodloe Asphault LLC ....G...... 540 373-5863
Fredericksburg (G-5192)
H&G Decorative Pavers Inc ....G...... 571 338-4949
Bristow (G-2054)
Heavenly Paving LLC ....G...... 804 980-9523
Sandston (G-12618)
Hughie C Rose ....G...... 540 423-5240
North Chesterfield (G-9888)
Hy Lee Paving Corporation ....E...... 804 360-9066
Rockville (G-12287)
Lane Construction Corporation ....F...... 703 471-6883
Chantilly (G-2541)
Larry D Martin ....G...... 540 493-0072
Rocky Mount (G-12332)
Llts Paving ....G...... 276 782-9550
Marion (G-8231)
Loudoun County Asphalt ....G...... 703 669-9001
Leesburg (G-7305)
Powells Paving Sealing LLC ....G...... 540 921-2455
Pembroke (G-10283)
Precision Pavers Inc ....G...... 703 217-4955
Charlottesville (G-2850)
Premium Paving Inc ....F...... 703 339-5371
Springfield (G-13073)
Roubin and Janeiro Inc ....G...... 703 573-9350
Fairfax (G-4546)
Sealmaster-Roanoke ....G...... 540 344-2090
Roanoke (G-12180)
Semmaterials LP ....G...... 757 244-6545
Newport News (G-9334)
Stuart M Perry Incorporated ....C...... 540 662-3431
Winchester (G-15483)
Superior Paving Corporation ....G...... 703 631-5480
Centreville (G-2342)
Wells Belcher Paving Service ....G...... 434 374-5518
Nelson (G-9116)

2952 Asphalt Felts & Coatings

▲ Acrylife Inc ....F...... 276 228-6704
Wytheville (G-15874)
Ennis-Flint Inc ....E...... 804 309-3199
Richmond (G-11579)
Gatorguard LLC ....G...... 434 942-0245
Lynchburg (G-7720)
Johns Manville Corporation ....B...... 804 261-7400
Richmond (G-11256)
Johns Manville Corporation ....B...... 540 984-4171
Edinburg (G-4307)
Marco Metals LLC ....F...... 540 437-2324
Rockingham (G-12261)
◆ Mundet Inc ....D...... 804 644-3970
Richmond (G-11684)
◆ Onduline North America Inc ....D...... 540 898-7000
Fredericksburg (G-5341)
Osburn Coatings Inc ....G...... 804 769-3030
Aylett (G-1551)
Ray Painter Small ....G...... 804 255-7050
Chesterfield (G-3520)
Resurface Incorporated ....F...... 703 335-1950
Manassas (G-8144)
Ridgeline Incorporated ....F...... 540 898-7000
Fredericksburg (G-5355)
Streco Fibres Intl Disc Inc ....G...... 757 473-3720
Virginia Beach (G-14856)
Tallant Industries Inc ....G...... 540 898-7000
Fredericksburg (G-5376)
Tidewater Green ....F...... 757 487-4736
Chesapeake (G-3338)

2992 Lubricating Oils & Greases

American Bioprotection Inc ....G...... 866 200-1313
Surry (G-13795)
Beard Llc Randall ....G...... 434 602-1224
Bremo Bluff (G-1944)
Davids Mobile Service LLC ....G...... 804 481-1647
Hopewell (G-6922)
Due North Ventures LLC ....G...... 540 443-3990
Blacksburg (G-1734)
Iris Co ....G...... 804 310-1054
Richmond (G-11621)
Kenneth Hill ....G...... 804 986-8674
Richmond (G-11642)
Petrostar Global LLC ....G...... 301 919-7879
Chantilly (G-2480)
Wolf Hills Enterprises ....G...... 276 628-8635
Abingdon (G-69)

2999 Products Of Petroleum & Coal, NEC

◆ Afton Chemical Corporation ....B...... 804 788-5800
Richmond (G-11476)
IG Petroleum LLC ....F...... 703 749-1780
Mc Lean (G-8463)
Ultra Petroleum LLC ....G...... 276 964-6118
Richlands (G-11021)

30 RUBBER AND MISCELLANEOUS PLASTICS PRODUCTS

3011 Tires & Inner Tubes

Alban Cire ....G...... 703 455-9300
Springfield (G-12939)
Als Used Tires & Rims ....G...... 703 548-3000
Alexandria (G-130)
BF Mayes Assoc Inc ....G...... 703 451-4994
Springfield (G-12963)
BF Wise & Sons Lc ....G...... 540 547-2918
Reva (G-10999)
Bolvs LLC ....G...... 508 310-8682
Chesterfield (G-3481)
◆ Schrader-Bridgeport Intl Inc ....A...... 434 369-4741
Altavista (G-641)
Tire Kings ....G...... 757 586-5206
Newport News (G-9357)
▲ Titan Wheel Corp Virginia ....D...... 276 496-5121
Saltville (G-12594)
◆ Yokohama Corp North America ....C...... 540 389-5426
Salem (G-12582)
▲ Yokohama Tire Mnfctring Vrgnia .....D...... 540 389-5426
Salem (G-12583)

3021 Rubber & Plastic Footwear

Matbock LLC ....G...... 757 828-6659
Virginia Beach (G-14639)
Nike Inc ....E...... 703 497-4513
Woodbridge (G-15760)
Vans Inc ....F...... 703 442-0161
Mc Lean (G-8574)
Vans Inc ....G...... 757 249-0802
Newport News (G-9372)

3052 Rubber & Plastic Hose & Belting

▲ Conwed Corp ....D...... 540 981-0362
Roanoke (G-12070)
High Threat Concealment LLC ....G...... 757 208-0221
Williamsburg (G-15255)
Mehler Inc ....D...... 276 638-6166
Martinsville (G-8312)
Quadrant Holding Inc ....D...... 276 228-0100
Wytheville (G-15905)
SAI Krishna LLC ....G...... 804 442-7140
Richmond (G-11369)
Shipyrdandcontractorsupply LLC ....G...... 757 333-2148
Virginia Beach (G-14807)

3053 Gaskets, Packing & Sealing Devices

American Gasket & Seal Tech ....F...... 804 271-0020
North Chesterfield (G-9816)
ARS Manufacturing Inc ....C...... 757 460-2211
Virginia Beach (G-14242)
Black Jacket LLC ....G...... 425 319-1014
Forest (G-5054)
▲ Blackhawk Rubber & Gasket Inc .....G...... 888 703-9060
Portsmouth (G-10401)
▲ Darco Southern LLC ....E...... 276 773-2711
Independence (G-6981)
▲ Dirak Incorporated ....G...... 703 378-7637
Sterling (G-13387)
Engineered Enrgy Solutions LLC ....G...... 443 299-2364
Greenbackville (G-5993)
Hitek Sealing Corporation ....G...... 434 944-2404
Appomattox (G-813)
Hollingsworth & Vose Company ....C...... 540 745-7600
Floyd (G-5029)
Hutchinson Sealing Systems Inc ....F...... 276 228-6150
Wytheville (G-15890)
Hutchinson Sealing Systems Inc ....C...... 276 228-4455
Wytheville (G-15891)
▲ Innovatio Sealing Tech Corp ....G...... 434 238-2397
Lynchburg (G-7739)
Macroseal Mechanical LLC ....F...... 804 458-5655
Prince George (G-10599)
Parker-Hannifin Corporation ....B...... 434 846-6541
Lynchburg (G-7782)
Wolverine Advanced Mtls LLC ....E...... 540 552-7674
Blacksburg (G-1806)

SIC

3061 Molded, Extruded & Lathe-Cut Rubber Mechanical Goods

Antmed Corporation ....G...... 703 239-3118
Fairfax *(G-4593)*

ARS Manufacturing Inc ....C...... 757 460-2211
Virginia Beach *(G-14242)*

Briggs Company ....G...... 804 233-0966
Chesterfield *(G-3483)*

Coopers R C Tires ....G...... 434 724-7342
Chatham *(G-2925)*

Fiberglass Customs Inc ....G...... 757 244-0610
Newport News *(G-9226)*

Hutchinson Sealing Systems Inc ....C...... 276 228-4455
Wytheville *(G-15891)*

Longwood Elastomers Inc ....C...... 276 228-5406
Wytheville *(G-15898)*

◆ Morooka America LLC ....F...... 877 667-6652
Ashland *(G-1464)*

Morooka America LLC ....F...... 804 368-0948
Ashland *(G-1465)*

Reiss Manufacturing Inc ....C...... 434 292-1600
Blackstone *(G-1825)*

3069 Fabricated Rubber Prdts, NEC

American Phoenix Inc ....E...... 434 688-0662
Danville *(G-3954)*

Antmed Corporation ....G...... 703 239-3118
Fairfax *(G-4593)*

ARS Manufacturing Inc ....C...... 757 460-2211
Virginia Beach *(G-14242)*

Autombili Lamborghini Amer LLC........F...... 866 681-6276
Herndon *(G-6616)*

Commonwealth Mfg & Dev ....F...... 276 699-2089
Ivanhoe *(G-7003)*

Commonwealth Recycling Svcs..........G...... 931 289-3645
Ivanhoe *(G-7004)*

Creatiate ....G...... 609 703-2378
Midlothian *(G-8805)*

Crooked Stitch Bags LLC ....G...... 703 680-0118
Woodbridge *(G-15676)*

Dandy Point Industries ....G...... 757 851-3280
Hampton *(G-6127)*

▲ Duroline North America Inc ....G...... 757 447-6290
Norfolk *(G-9533)*

Dutch Gap Striping Inc ....G...... 804 594-0069
Powhatan *(G-10543)*

Dx Company LLC ....G...... 703 919-8677
Alexandria *(G-197)*

Encore Products Inc ....G...... 757 493-8358
Virginia Beach *(G-14447)*

▲ Global Trading of Martinsville...........G...... 276 666-0236
Martinsville *(G-8290)*

Hutchinson Sealing Systems Inc ....F...... 276 228-6150
Wytheville *(G-15890)*

Hutchinson Sealing Systems Inc ....C...... 276 228-4455
Wytheville *(G-15891)*

Icarus Medical LLC ....G...... 434 242-0258
Charlottesville *(G-2813)*

Johns Manville Corporation ....B...... 540 984-4171
Edinburg *(G-4307)*

Keystone Rubber Corporation...........G...... 717 235-6863
Greenbackville *(G-5994)*

◆ Kinyo Virginia Inc ....C...... 757 888-2221
Newport News *(G-9276)*

Kokua John LLC ....G...... 509 270-3454
North Garden *(G-10078)*

Lava Flow Yoga LLC ....G...... 703 264-1638
Reston *(G-10885)*

Longwood Elastomers Inc ....E...... 276 228-5406
Wytheville *(G-15896)*

▲ Longwood Elastomers Inc ....F...... 336 272-3710
Wytheville *(G-15897)*

Metro Technology Llc ....G...... 703 579-7771
Springfield *(G-13048)*

Mouthpiece Express LLC ....G...... 540 989-8848
Roanoke *(G-11970)*

Pro Tech Fabrications Inc ....G...... 540 587-5590
Bedford *(G-1653)*

Raggededge Gear Inc ....G...... 276 226-9439
Stuart *(G-13627)*

▲ Rubber Plastic Met Engrg Corp ....F...... 757 502-5462
Virginia Beach *(G-14785)*

Soter Martin of Virginia Inc ....G...... 804 550-2164
Glen Allen *(G-5801)*

Tchere LLC ....G...... 800 889-7832
Stafford *(G-13201)*

Teijin-Du Pont Films Inc ....D...... 804 530-9310
Chester *(G-3459)*

◆ Trelleborg Marine Systems............E...... 540 667-5191
Berryville *(G-1695)*

Trelleborg Marine Systems Usa............E...... 540 667-5191
Berryville *(G-1696)*

Velocity Systems LLC ....F...... 703 707-6280
Dulles *(G-4231)*

Walker Custom Rifles ....G...... 540 399-1632
Culpeper *(G-3929)*

Yama Mountain Gear ....G...... 434 202-9717
Charlottesville *(G-2908)*

▲ Zimar LLC ....G...... 703 688-3339
Falls Church *(G-4897)*

3081 Plastic Unsupported Sheet & Film

Amcor Spclty Crtons Amrcas LLC ....C...... 804 748-3470
Chester *(G-3386)*

Berry Global Inc ....G...... 757 538-2000
Suffolk *(G-13678)*

Brewco Corp ....G...... 540 389-2554
Salem *(G-12486)*

Conwet Plastics LLC ....G...... 540 981-0362
Roanoke *(G-12071)*

◆ Du Pont Tjin Flms US Ltd Prtnr.......E...... 804 530-4076
Chester *(G-3408)*

Du Pont Tjin Flms US Ltd Prtnr ....B...... 804 530-4076
Chester *(G-3409)*

Du Pont Tjin Flms US Ltd Prtnr ....G...... 804 530-9339
North Chesterfield *(G-9862)*

E I Du Pont De Nemours & Co ....E...... 804 530-9300
Hopewell *(G-6924)*

Glad Products Company ....G...... 434 946-3100
Amherst *(G-691)*

Klockner Pentaplast Amer Inc ....B...... 540 832-3600
Gordonsville *(G-5909)*

◆ Klockner Pentaplast Amer Inc..........A...... 540 832-1400
Gordonsville *(G-5910)*

Klockner Pentaplast Amer Inc ....G...... 540 832-7615
Gordonsville *(G-5911)*

Klockner Pentaplast Amer Inc ....G...... 540 832-3600
Charlottesville *(G-2653)*

Klockner Pentaplast Amer Inc ....C...... 276 686-6111
Rural Retreat *(G-12426)*

◆ Liqui-Box Corporation ....D...... 804 325-1400
Richmond *(G-11658)*

Longwood Elastomers Inc ....E...... 276 228-5406
Wytheville *(G-15896)*

▲ Longwood Elastomers Inc ....F...... 336 272-3710
Wytheville *(G-15897)*

Mottley Foils Inc ....G...... 434 392-8347
Farmville *(G-4952)*

Orbis Rpm LLC ....G...... 804 887-2375
Richmond *(G-11702)*

OSullivan Films Inc ....B...... 540 667-6666
Winchester *(G-15561)*

OSullivan Films Inc ....E...... 540 667-6666
Winchester *(G-15562)*

◆ OSullivan Films MGT LLC ....B...... 540 667-6666
Winchester *(G-15563)*

Pallas USA Ltd ....G...... 703 205-0007
Fairfax *(G-4528)*

◆ Porex Technologies Corp ....C...... 804 524-4983
South Chesterfield *(G-12821)*

Raven Ind ....G...... 703 414-3290
Arlington *(G-1130)*

◆ Reynolds Food Packaging LLC ....E...... 800 446-3020
Richmond *(G-11352)*

Schweitzer-Mauduit Intl Inc..............G...... 540 981-0362
Roanoke *(G-12178)*

Swm International LLC ....G...... 651 369-1235
Roanoke *(G-12201)*

Taghleef Industries Inc ....B...... 540 962-1200
Covington *(G-3800)*

▲ Teijin-Du Pont Films Inc ....B...... 804 530-9310
Hopewell *(G-6942)*

Tg Holdings International CV ....G...... 804 330-1000
North Chesterfield *(G-10026)*

Toray Plastics (america) Inc.............G...... 804 636-3887
Front Royal *(G-5558)*

Tredegar Consumer Designs Inc.........G...... 804 330-1000
North Chesterfield *(G-10028)*

◆ Tredegar Corporation ....G...... 804 330-1000
North Chesterfield *(G-10029)*

Tredegar Corporation ....C...... 804 330-1000
North Chesterfield *(G-10030)*

Tredegar Far East Corporation ....G...... 804 330-1000
North Chesterfield *(G-10031)*

Tredegar Film Products Corp ....C...... 847 438-2111
North Chesterfield *(G-10032)*

◆ Tredegar Film Products Corp ....C...... 804 330-1000
North Chesterfield *(G-10033)*

Tredegar Film Products Latin ....G...... 804 330-1000
North Chesterfield *(G-10034)*

Tredegar Film Products US LLC ....B...... 804 330-1000
North Chesterfield *(G-10035)*

Tredegar Films Development Inc ....G...... 804 330-1000
North Chesterfield *(G-10036)*

Tredegar Films Rs Converting ....G...... 804 330-1000
North Chesterfield *(G-10037)*

Tredegar Performance Films Inc ....B...... 804 330-1000
North Chesterfield *(G-10038)*

▲ Virginia Industrial Plas Inc ....F...... 540 298-1515
Elkton *(G-4337)*

3082 Plastic Unsupported Profile Shapes

Aquabean LLC.........................G...... 703 577-0315
Fairfax *(G-4409)*

▲ Arista Tubes Inc ....E...... 434 793-0660
Danville *(G-3956)*

▲ Conwed Corp ....D...... 540 981-0362
Roanoke *(G-12070)*

Ericsons Inc...........................E...... 770 505-6575
Chester *(G-3413)*

Porex Corporation ....G...... 804 518-1012
South Chesterfield *(G-12820)*

◆ Porex Technologies Corp ....C...... 804 524-4983
South Chesterfield *(G-12821)*

Quadrant Holding Inc ....D...... 276 228-0100
Wytheville *(G-15905)*

Sunlite Plastics Inc ....E...... 540 234-9271
Weyers Cave *(G-15178)*

▲ Virginia Industrial Plas Inc ....E...... 540 298-1515
Elkton *(G-4337)*

Xmc Films Inc ....G...... 276 930-2848
Woolwine *(G-15869)*

3083 Plastic Laminated Plate & Sheet

Advanced Drainage Systems Inc ....E...... 540 261-6131
Buena Vista *(G-2137)*

▲ Conwed Corp ....D...... 540 981-0362
Roanoke *(G-12070)*

Eastman Performance Films LLC........D...... 423 224-7768
Martinsville *(G-8283)*

Hanwha Azdel Inc ....D...... 434 385-6359
Forest *(G-5073)*

Hawkins Glass Wholesalers LLC ....E...... 703 372-2990
Lorton *(G-7492)*

◆ Tredegar Corporation ....D...... 804 330-1000
North Chesterfield *(G-10029)*

3084 Plastic Pipe

Advanced Drainage Systems Inc ....E...... 540 261-6131
Buena Vista *(G-2137)*

Lane Enterprises Inc...................F...... 540 439-3201
Bealeton *(G-1600)*

3085 Plastic Bottles

Graham Packg Plastic Pdts Inc ....C...... 540 564-1000
Harrisonburg *(G-6325)*

Itg Cigars Inc ....E...... 804 233-7668
Richmond *(G-11622)*

◆ M&H Plastics Inc ....C...... 540 504-0030
Winchester *(G-15441)*

Southeastern Container Inc ....C...... 540 722-2600
Winchester *(G-15480)*

Virginia Kik Inc ....E...... 540 389-5401
Salem *(G-12578)*

3086 Plastic Foam Prdts

Bedford Storage Investment LLC........D...... 574 284-1000
Bedford *(G-1625)*

◆ Berry Plastics Design LLC ....E...... 757 538-2000
Suffolk *(G-13679)*

Braun & Assoc Inc ....G...... 804 739-8616
Midlothian *(G-8783)*

◆ Carpenter Co........................D...... 804 359-0800
Richmond *(G-11146)*

Carpenter Co ....D...... 804 359-0800
Richmond *(G-11147)*

Carpenter Co ....B...... 804 359-0800
Richmond *(G-11031)*

Carpenter Co ....D...... 804 233-0606
Richmond *(G-11032)*

Carpenter Holdings Inc ....G...... 804 359-0800
Richmond *(G-11148)*

Cellofoam North America Inc............E...... 540 373-1800
Fredericksburg *(G-5259)*

Cellofoam North America Inc............E...... 540 373-4596
Fredericksburg *(G-5258)*

Custom Foam and Cases LLC............G...... 703 201-5908
Culpeper *(G-3887)*

Ds Smith PLC ....G...... 540 774-0500
  Roanoke *(G-11916)*
F & D Manufacturing & Supply ....G...... 540 586-6111
  Bedford *(G-1636)*
Fostek Inc ....D...... 540 587-5870
  Bedford *(G-1637)*
General Display Company LLC ....G...... 703 335-9292
  Manassas *(G-7943)*
▲ Hudson Industries Inc ....D...... 804 226-1155
  Richmond *(G-11244)*
Huntington Foam LLC ....D...... 540 731-3700
  Radford *(G-10716)*
Ibs ....G...... 540 662-0882
  Winchester *(G-15427)*
Instant Systems ....G...... 757 200-5494
  Norfolk *(G-9593)*
Johns Manville Corporation ....B...... 540 984-4171
  Edinburg *(G-4307)*
Magnifoam Delaware Inc ....G...... 804 564-9700
  North Chesterfield *(G-9919)*
NC Foam & Sales ....G...... 540 631-3363
  Front Royal *(G-5545)*
Olan De Mexico SA De CV ....G...... 804 365-8344
  Keswick *(G-7053)*
Polycreteusa LLC ....G...... 804 901-6893
  Charles City *(G-2579)*
Rogers Foam Corporation ....G...... 276 431-2641
  Duffield *(G-4184)*
Sheaves Floors LLC ....G...... 540 234-9080
  Weyers Cave *(G-15176)*
William L Judd Pot & China Co ....G...... 540 743-3294
  Luray *(G-7625)*

3087 Custom Compounding Of Purchased Plastic Resins

Artner Corp ....G...... 703 341-6333
  Springfield *(G-12951)*
Creative Impressions Inc ....G...... 757 855-2187
  Virginia Beach *(G-14371)*
▲ Gs Plastics LLC ....G...... 276 629-7981
  New Castle *(G-9120)*
Sunlite Plastics Inc ....E...... 540 234-9271
  Weyers Cave *(G-15178)*

3088 Plastic Plumbing Fixtures

Aquatic Co ....B...... 434 572-1200
  South Boston *(G-12748)*
Barefoot Spas LLC ....E...... 804 298-3939
  North Chesterfield *(G-9827)*
CPS Contractors Inc ....G...... 804 561-6834
  Moseley *(G-9036)*
E-Z Treat Inc ....F...... 703 753-4770
  Haymarket *(G-6420)*
East Coast Walk In Tubs ....G...... 804 365-8703
  Axton *(G-1535)*
Flawless Shower Enclosures..............G...... 434 466-3845
  Ruckersville *(G-12402)*
Mystical Mirrors & Glass ....G...... 757 399-4682
  Portsmouth *(G-10463)*
Shelton Plumbing & Heating LLC........G...... 804 539-8080
  North Chesterfield *(G-9977)*

3089 Plastic Prdts

Acel LLC ....G...... 888 801-2507
  Burke *(G-2180)*
Advantage Puck Group Inc ....E...... 434 385-9181
  Lynchburg *(G-7634)*
Aldridge Installations LLC ....G...... 804 658-1035
  Richmond *(G-11093)*
Allen Watson ....G...... 703 620-5350
  Reston *(G-10784)*
Alpha Industries ....G...... 540 249-4980
  Grottoes *(G-6014)*
Alpha Industries Inc ....G...... 540 298-2155
  Shenandoah *(G-12688)*
Amazengraved LLC ....G...... 540 313-5658
  Winchester *(G-15376)*
Amcor Rigid Packaging Usa LLC........C...... 276 625-8000
  Wytheville *(G-15875)*
American Manufacturing Co Inc..........E...... 540 825-7234
  Elkwood *(G-4341)*
American Plstic Fbricators Inc ....F...... 434 376-3404
  Brookneal *(G-2107)*
Appalachian Plastics Inc ....E...... 276 429-2581
  Glade Spring *(G-5673)*
Berry Global Inc ....G...... 540 946-9250
  Waynesboro *(G-15100)*
Berry Global Inc ....G...... 757 538-2000
  Suffolk *(G-13678)*

◆ Berry Plastics Design LLC ....C...... 757 538-2000
  Suffolk *(G-13679)*
Best Recognition ....G...... 757 490-3933
  Virginia Beach *(G-14275)*
◆ Blue Ridge Industries Inc ....C...... 540 662-3900
  Winchester *(G-15389)*
Busada Manufacturing Corp ....F...... 540 967-2882
  Louisa *(G-7547)*
Carris Reels Inc ....G...... 540 473-2210
  Fincastle *(G-4995)*
Cbn Secure Technologies Inc ....D...... 434 799-9280
  Danville *(G-3964)*
Cellofoam North America Inc..............E...... 540 373-4596
  Fredericksburg *(G-5258)*
Chilhowie Fence Supply LLC...............F...... 276 780-0452
  Chilhowie *(G-3547)*
Classic Engravers ....G...... 804 748-8717
  Chester *(G-3395)*
▲ Conwed Corp ....G...... 540 981-0362
  Roanoke *(G-8847)*
▲ Crawl Space Door System Inc ....G...... 757 363-0005
  Virginia Beach *(G-14370)*
Creative Corp ....G...... 804 556-4839
  Maidens *(G-7889)*
Creative Urethanes Inc ....E...... 540 542-6676
  Winchester *(G-15407)*
Custom Auto Glass & Plastics ....G...... 540 362-8798
  Roanoke *(G-12076)*
D & D Inc ....G...... 540 943-8113
  Waynesboro *(G-15107)*
Dan Charewicz ....G...... 815 338-2582
  Suffolk *(G-13692)*
Danny Marshall ....G...... 434 797-5861
  Danville *(G-3976)*
Deborah F Scarboro ....G...... 757 866-0108
  Spring Grove *(G-12929)*
Debra Kromer ....G...... 571 248-4070
  Gainesville *(G-5578)*
Decks Down Under LLC ....G...... 703 758-2572
  Reston *(G-10836)*
Degen Enterprises Inc ....G...... 757 853-7651
  Norfolk *(G-9524)*
Delta Circle Industries Inc ....F...... 804 743-3500
  North Chesterfield *(G-9857)*
Dong-A Package USA Corp ....G...... 703 961-1686
  Chantilly *(G-2410)*
Dynaric Inc ....D...... 757 460-3725
  Virginia Beach *(G-14423)*
E-Z Treat Inc ....F...... 703 753-4770
  Haymarket *(G-6420)*
Eagle Contractors ....G...... 703 435-0004
  Gainesville *(G-5581)*
Eastman Performance Films LLC........D...... 423 224-7768
  Martinsville *(G-8283)*
Edmunds Waste Removal Inc..............G...... 804 478-4688
  Mc Kenney *(G-8379)*
Elfinsmith Ltd Inc ....G...... 757 399-4788
  Portsmouth *(G-10421)*
Exterior Systems Inc ....G...... 804 752-2324
  Ashland *(G-1412)*
Fredericksburg Fences LLC ....G...... 540 419-3910
  Fredericksburg *(G-5290)*
Galaxy Plastic Industries Inc ....G...... 434 757-7200
  La Crosse *(G-7145)*
Gauge Works Inc ....G...... 703 661-1300
  Dulles *(G-4203)*
Gd Packaging LLC ....G...... 703 946-8100
  Vienna *(G-14060)*
General Dynamics Mission ....B...... 276 783-3121
  Marion *(G-8227)*
◆ General Foam Plastics Corp ....A...... 757 857-0153
  Virginia Beach *(G-14479)*
Gianni Enterprises Inc ....G...... 540 982-0111
  Roanoke *(G-11925)*
Gianni Entps Inc DBA Vrgina Pl ....G...... 540 314-6566
  Roanoke *(G-12097)*
▲ Glasdon Inc ....G...... 804 726-3777
  Sandston *(G-12617)*
Graham Packg Plastic Pdts Inc ....C...... 540 564-1000
  Harrisonburg *(G-6325)*
▲ Gs Industries Bassett Ltd ....D...... 276 629-5317
  Bassett *(G-1584)*
◆ Harrington Corporation ....C...... 434 845-7094
  Lynchburg *(G-7729)*
Heyco Werk USA Inc ....G...... 434 634-8810
  Emporia *(G-4360)*
Hqc Inc ....F...... 540 820-3277
  Rockingham *(G-12255)*
▲ IAC Strasburg LLC ....C...... 540 465-3741
  Strasburg *(G-13582)*

IMS Gear Holding Inc ....E...... 757 468-8810
  Virginia Beach *(G-14542)*
Indiana Floor Inc ....G...... 540 373-1915
  Woodford *(G-15840)*
Insul Industries Inc ....F...... 804 550-1933
  Mechanicsville *(G-8641)*
◆ Intrapac (harrisonburg) Inc ....B...... 540 434-1703
  Mount Crawford *(G-9055)*
J R Plastics & Machining Inc ....G...... 434 277-8334
  Lowesville *(G-7595)*
Kidprint of Virginia Inc ....G...... 757 287-3324
  Suffolk *(G-13728)*
King of Dice ....G...... 804 758-0776
  Saluda *(G-12604)*
▲ Klann Inc ....E...... 540 949-8351
  Waynesboro *(G-15119)*
Lawrence Trnsp Systems Inc ....D...... 540 966-3797
  Roanoke *(G-11953)*
Legacy Products LLC ....E...... 804 739-9333
  Midlothian *(G-8847)*
Leonard Alum Utlity Bldngs Inc ....G...... 434 792-8202
  Danville *(G-4011)*
Limitless Gear LLC ....G...... 575 921-7475
  Barboursville *(G-1564)*
▲ Lineal Technologies Inc ....D...... 540 484-6783
  Rocky Mount *(G-12335)*
◆ Liqui-Box Corporation ....D...... 804 325-1400
  Richmond *(G-11658)*
Long Solutions LLC ....G...... 703 281-2766
  Vienna *(G-14085)*
◆ M&H Plastics Inc ....C...... 540 504-0030
  Winchester *(G-15441)*
Machine Tool Technology LLC ....F...... 804 520-4173
  South Chesterfield *(G-12813)*
Mar-Bal Inc..................................A...... 440 539-6595
  Blacksburg *(G-1758)*
Mar-Bal Inc..................................C...... 540 674-5320
  Dublin *(G-4165)*
Marion Operations ....G...... 276 783-3121
  Marion *(G-8235)*
Martin Elthon ....G...... 703 853-1801
  Fairfax *(G-4503)*
Matbock LLC ....G...... 757 828-6659
  Virginia Beach *(G-14639)*
Milgard Manufacturing Inc ....G...... 540 834-0340
  Fredericksburg *(G-5328)*
Molding & Traffic ACC LLC ....G...... 540 896-2459
  Broadway *(G-2089)*
Molding Light LLC ....G...... 703 847-0232
  Mc Lean *(G-8505)*
◆ Monoflo International Inc ....C...... 540 665-1691
  Winchester *(G-15451)*
Moubray Company ....G...... 804 435-6334
  Kilmarnock *(G-7073)*
▼ Naj Enterprises LLP ....G...... 202 251-7821
  Mc Lean *(G-8509)*
Nationwide Laminating Inc ....F...... 703 550-8400
  Lorton *(G-7513)*
Norva Plastics Inc ....G...... 757 622-9281
  Norfolk *(G-9670)*
Obsidian Solutions Group LLC ....F...... 540 286-2266
  Fredericksburg *(G-5462)*
Ocran Shaft Machine ....G...... 804 435-6301
  White Stone *(G-15189)*
Office Organizers ....G...... 757 343-6860
  Chesapeake *(G-3226)*
Pan Custom Molding Inc ....G...... 804 787-3820
  Richmond *(G-11318)*
Partnership For Success ....G...... 804 363-3380
  North Chesterfield *(G-9946)*
PC Sands LLC ....G...... 703 534-6107
  Arlington *(G-1102)*
Pelican Products ....F...... 540 636-1624
  Front Royal *(G-5548)*
Pgb Hangers LLC ....G...... 703 851-4221
  Gainesville *(G-5607)*
Plastic Solutions Incorporated ....G...... 540 722-4694
  Winchester *(G-15461)*
Polycap LLC ....G...... 276 883-5700
  Lebanon *(G-7204)*
Polyfab Display Company ....E...... 703 497-4577
  Woodbridge *(G-15777)*
Polythane of Virginia Inc ....G...... 540 586-3511
  Bedford *(G-1651)*
Precise Technology Inc ....G...... 703 869-4220
  Woodbridge *(G-15778)*
Preserve Resources Inc ....E...... 434 710-8131
  Danville *(G-4032)*
Product Dev Mfg & Packg ....G...... 703 777-8400
  Leesburg *(G-7328)*

Employee Codes: A=Over 500 employees, B=251-500
C=101-250, D=51-100, E=20-50, F=10-19, G=1-9

2021 Virginia
Industrial Directory

605

S I C

Project Safe ....G...... 703 505-0440
  Alexandria *(G-318)*

▲ Rehau Automotive LLC ....G...... 703 777-5255
  Leesburg *(G-7333)*

◆ Rehau Construction LLC ....E...... 800 247-9445
  Leesburg *(G-7334)*

▲ Rehau Incorporated ....C...... 703 777-5255
  Leesburg *(G-7335)*

◆ Rehau Industries LLC ....G...... 703 777-5255
  Leesburg *(G-7336)*

Reiss Manufacturing Inc ....C...... 434 292-1600
  Blackstone *(G-1825)*

Richard Y Lombard Jr ....G...... 757 499-1967
  Virginia Beach *(G-14772)*

Rsk Inc ....G...... 703 330-1959
  Manassas *(G-8148)*

▲ Rubber Plastic Met Engrg Corp ...F...... 757 502-5462
  Virginia Beach *(G-14785)*

◆ Rubbermaid Commercial Pdts LLC .A...... 540 667-8700
  Winchester *(G-15582)*

Rubbermaid Commercial Pdts LLC 540 542-8195
  Winchester *(G-15471)*

◆ SC&I of Virginia LLC ....D...... 804 876-3135
  Doswell *(G-4124)*

▲ Shadows Ridge Inc ....G...... 540 722-0310
  Winchester *(G-15475)*

Sheltech Plastics Inc ....G...... 978 794-2160
  Elberon *(G-4319)*

Skycity ....G...... 240 467-6270
  Arlington *(G-1171)*

Sml Composites LLC ....G...... 540 576-3318
  Union Hall *(G-13961)*

▼ South Distributors LLC ....G...... 718 258-0200
  Petersburg *(G-10344)*

◆ Strongwell Corporation ....B...... 276 645-8000
  Bristol *(G-1991)*

Strongwell Corporation ....E...... 276 623-0935
  Abingdon *(G-62)*

Sunlite Plastics Inc ....E...... 540 234-9271
  Weyers Cave *(G-15178)*

Superseal Corp ....G...... 540 645-1408
  Fredericksburg *(G-5229)*

T E L Pak Inc ....G...... 804 794-9529
  Midlothian *(G-8911)*

Tecton Products LLC ....E...... 540 380-5819
  Salem *(G-12572)*

▲ Tessy Plastics LLC ....C...... 434 385-5700
  Lynchburg *(G-7819)*

Tessy Plastics Corp ....C...... 434 385-5700
  Lynchburg *(G-7820)*

Tidewell Marine Inc ....G...... 804 453-6115
  Burgess *(G-2177)*

▲ Total Molding Concepts Inc ....F...... 540 665-8408
  Winchester *(G-15491)*

Tredegar Film Products Corp ....G...... 847 438-2111
  North Chesterfield *(G-10032)*

Trident Plastics Inc ....F...... 804 236-8705
  Richmond *(G-11419)*

Tumbleweed LLC ....G...... 540 261-7404
  Lexington *(G-7420)*

Utilities Products Intl ....G...... 703 725-3150
  Falls Church *(G-4888)*

Utility One Source For Eqp LLC ....D...... 434 525-2929
  Forest *(G-5103)*

Valley Industrial Plastics Inc ....D...... 540 723-8855
  Middletown *(G-8746)*

Veridos America Inc ....G...... 703 480-2025
  Dulles *(G-4232)*

Virginia Plastics Company Inc ....E...... 540 981-9700
  Roanoke *(G-12021)*

West Window Corporation ....D...... 276 638-2394
  Ridgeway *(G-11857)*

Wolverine Advanced Mtls LLC ....E...... 540 552-7674
  Blacksburg *(G-1806)*

ZZ Supply Company LLC ....G...... 703 957-5027
  Springfield *(G-13110)*

31 LEATHER AND LEATHER PRODUCTS

3111 Leather Tanning & Finishing

Appleberry Mtn Taxidermy Svcs .....G...... 434 831-2232
  Schuyler *(G-12651)*

Auslnx LLC ....G...... 571 265-3288
  Arlington *(G-864)*

Embossing Etc ....G...... 540 338-4520
  Hamilton *(G-6057)*

Gloves For Life LLC ....G...... 540 343-1697
  Roanoke *(G-11927)*

Hamilton Perkins Collectn LLC ......G...... 757 544-7161
  Norfolk *(G-9568)*

Hideaway Tannery LLC ....G...... 540 421-2640
  Crimora *(G-3821)*

Journeymen Saddlers Ltd ....F...... 540 687-5888
  Middleburg *(G-8725)*

Leather World Technologies LLC ....G...... 540 265-9038
  Roanoke *(G-11954)*

Middleburg Tack Exchange Ltd ......G...... 540 687-6608
  Middleburg *(G-8730)*

Pauls Shoe Repair & Lea ACC ....G...... 703 759-3735
  Great Falls *(G-5971)*

Rawhide LLC ....G...... 540 548-1148
  Spotsylvania *(G-12910)*

Sierra Tannery LLC ....G...... 804 323-5898
  Midlothian *(G-8898)*

3131 Boot & Shoe Cut Stock & Findings

Avoid Evade Counter LLC ....G...... 703 593-1951
  Reston *(G-10795)*

Baggesen J Rand ....G...... 804 560-0490
  Richmond *(G-11499)*

Bean Counters ....G...... 703 534-1516
  Falls Church *(G-4763)*

CMC Interiors LLC ....F...... 804 883-5671
  Richmond *(G-11035)*

Counter Effects Inc ....G...... 804 451-9016
  South Chesterfield *(G-12833)*

Custom Counter Fitters Inc ....G...... 757 288-4730
  Virginia Beach *(G-14376)*

Fixher Upper LLC ....G...... 804 539-8816
  Hampton *(G-6151)*

No Quarter LLC ....G...... 703 753-0511
  Gainesville *(G-5601)*

Signature K-9 ....G...... 866 820-3647
  Roanoke *(G-12188)*

Tenant Temporary Quarters ....G...... 703 462-8623
  Alexandria *(G-596)*

Upper Decks LLC ....G...... 804 789-0946
  Mechanicsville *(G-8691)*

Upper Weyanoke LLC ....G...... 804 288-7333
  Richmond *(G-11428)*

William K Rand III ....F...... 757 410-7390
  Chesapeake *(G-3377)*

Z & T Sales LLC ....G...... 540 570-9500
  Buena Vista *(G-2157)*

3143 Men's Footwear, Exc Athletic

Barismil LLC ....G...... 703 622-4550
  Herndon *(G-6619)*

Capps Shoe Company ....C...... 434 528-3213
  Gretna *(G-6005)*

▲ Capps Shoe Company ....F...... 434 528-3213
  Lynchburg *(G-7673)*

Jkm Technologies LLC ....G...... 434 979-8600
  Charlottesville *(G-2820)*

3144 Women's Footwear, Exc Athletic

3mp1re Clothing Co ....G...... 540 892-3484
  Richmond *(G-11073)*

Barismil LLC ....G...... 703 622-4550
  Herndon *(G-6619)*

▲ Capps Shoe Company ....F...... 434 528-3213
  Lynchburg *(G-7673)*

Capps Shoe Company ....C...... 434 528-3213
  Gretna *(G-6005)*

Jkm Technologies LLC ....G...... 434 979-8600
  Charlottesville *(G-2820)*

3149 Footwear, NEC

▲ A G S Hanover Incorporated ....F...... 804 798-1891
  Ashland *(G-1360)*

Jkm Technologies LLC ....G...... 434 979-8600
  Charlottesville *(G-2820)*

Reebok International Ltd ....C...... 703 490-5671
  Woodbridge *(G-15793)*

3151 Leather Gloves & Mittens

Baret LLC ....G...... 808 230-9904
  Woodbridge *(G-15654)*

3161 Luggage

Big Chip Clothing Company LLC .....G...... 877 572-6525
  Virginia Beach *(G-14276)*

CC & More Inc ....G...... 540 786-7052
  Fredericksburg *(G-5257)*

Dalaun Couture LLC ....G...... 703 594-1413
  Vienna *(G-14032)*

▲ Gearmaxusa Ltd ....G...... 804 521-4320
  Mechanicsville *(G-8627)*

Interalign LLC ....G...... 804 314-4713
  Richmond *(G-11250)*

Kmarie Krafts Inc ....G...... 804 943-1239
  Chesapeake *(G-3166)*

▲ Koenig Inc ....G...... 804 798-8282
  Ashland *(G-1450)*

Kurvez Galore Boutique LLC ....G...... 336 901-5266
  Ferrum *(G-4975)*

Lexington Papagallo Inc ....G...... 540 463-5988
  Lexington *(G-7398)*

Mercury Luggage Mfg Co ....A...... 804 733-5222
  Petersburg *(G-10330)*

Morose Brand LLC ....G...... 747 346-1550
  Hampton *(G-6203)*

Swrd LLC ....G...... 434 944-2558
  Gladys *(G-5697)*

Thrifty Trunk ....G...... 757 478-7836
  Norfolk *(G-9749)*

▲ Tkl Products Corp ....E...... 804 749-8300
  Oilville *(G-10185)*

Uplift Collections ....G...... 804 319-9129
  Chesterfield *(G-3536)*

Warrior Luggage Company ....G...... 301 523-9010
  Alexandria *(G-608)*

3171 Handbags & Purses

Bosan LLC ....G...... 757 340-0822
  Virginia Beach *(G-14295)*

CC & More Inc ....G...... 540 786-7052
  Fredericksburg *(G-5257)*

Crafted For ME LLC ....G...... 804 412-5273
  Glen Allen *(G-5719)*

Crystal Beach Studio ....G...... 757 787-4605
  Onancock *(G-10195)*

Joshi Rubita ....G...... 571 315-9772
  Alexandria *(G-500)*

3172 Personal Leather Goods

10fold Wallets LLC ....G...... 804 982-0003
  Richmond *(G-11069)*

Christophers Belts & Wallets ....G...... 757 253-2564
  Williamsburg *(G-15219)*

Crystal Beach Studio ....G...... 757 787-4605
  Onancock *(G-10195)*

Joseph Carson ....G...... 757 498-4866
  Virginia Beach *(G-14574)*

Mobile Wallet Gifting Corp ....G...... 301 523-1052
  Vienna *(G-14098)*

Tpp Enterprises LLC ....G...... 757 247-0016
  Newport News *(G-9361)*

3199 Leather Goods, NEC

Barismil LLC ....G...... 703 622-4550
  Herndon *(G-6619)*

Beltway Leatherworks LLC ....G...... 703 457-7829
  Woodbridge *(G-15656)*

Briggs & Riley Travelware LLC ....G...... 703 352-0713
  Fairfax *(G-4421)*

Capitol Leather LLC ....G...... 434 229-8467
  Manassas Park *(G-8195)*

Cedar Industry LLC ....E...... 571 402-4564
  Dumfries *(G-4238)*

Defensor Holsters LLC ....G...... 703 409-4865
  Mc Lean *(G-8417)*

Dw Global LLC ....G...... 757 689-4547
  Virginia Beach *(G-14419)*

Equus Therapeutics Inc ....G...... 540 456-6767
  Afton *(G-80)*

Fine Leather Works LLC ....G...... 703 200-1953
  Mc Lean *(G-8430)*

G & D Manufacturing ....G...... 540 345-7267
  Roanoke *(G-12095)*

Kens Leathercraft ....G...... 540 774-6225
  Boones Mill *(G-1896)*

Leatheroot LLC ....G...... 804 695-1604
  Gloucester *(G-5853)*

LLC Wiley Brothers ....G...... 434 806-9633
  Free Union *(G-5508)*

Mayes Wholesale Tack ....G...... 276 755-3715
  Cana *(G-2227)*

Mutual Box Leather ....G...... 703 626-9770
  Round Hill *(G-12383)*

Pinnell CL Custom Leather ....G...... 434 823-9800
  Crozet *(G-3847)*

PS Its Leather ....G...... 804 762-9489
  Richmond *(G-11339)*

R&B Custom Holsters LLC ....G...... 703 586-2616
  Woodbridge *(G-15789)*

Stealth Mfg & Svcs LLC................G..... 787 679-7548
Virginia Beach *(G-14844)*
Tomlinsons Farrier Service LLC........G..... 540 377-9195
Greenville *(G-5999)*
Valhalla Holsters LLC....................G..... 540 529-4520
Moneta *(G-8983)*
Village Blacksmith LLC.................G..... 804 824-2631
Gloucester *(G-5864)*

32 STONE, CLAY, GLASS, AND CONCRETE PRODUCTS

3211 Flat Glass

All Glass LLC..................................G..... 540 288-8111
Fredericksburg *(G-5397)*
Blackout Tinting LLC.......................G..... 757 416-5658
Norfolk *(G-9466)*
Blake Collection.............................G..... 703 329-1599
Alexandria *(G-424)*
Cardinal Glass Industries Inc..........C..... 540 892-5600
Vinton *(G-14168)*
▲ Coresix Precision Glass Inc.........D..... 757 888-1361
Williamsburg *(G-15223)*
Crafted Glass Inc............................G..... 757 543-5504
Chesapeake *(G-3056)*
Dixie Plate GL & Mirror Co LLC........G..... 540 869-4400
Middletown *(G-8737)*
Dragons Lair Glass Studio..............G..... 540 564-0318
Harrisonburg *(G-6310)*
Glass Fronts Inc.............................F..... 540 672-4410
Orange *(G-10214)*
Hawkins Glass Wholesalers LLC.......E..... 703 372-2990
Lorton *(G-7492)*
Higgins Inc..................................F..... 540 636-3756
Middletown *(G-8740)*
Jefco Inc..E..... 757 460-0403
Virginia Beach *(G-14565)*
Jim Wareheim.................................G..... 804 861-5255
Petersburg *(G-10327)*
Pilkington North America Inc..........C..... 540 362-5130
Roanoke *(G-11985)*
Potomac Glass Inc..........................G..... 540 288-0210
Stafford *(G-13180)*
The Tint...G..... 804 261-4081
Glen Allen *(G-5808)*
▼ Virginia Glass Products Corp.........C..... 276 956-3131
Ridgeway *(G-11856)*
▼ Virginia Mirror Company Inc...........D..... 276 956-3131
Martinsville *(G-8347)*
Virginia Mirror Company Inc............G..... 276 632-9816
Martinsville *(G-8348)*

3221 Glass Containers

Amcor Phrm Packg USA LLC............C..... 434 372-5113
Chase City *(G-2909)*
Nipro Glass Americas Corp..............G..... 434 372-5113
Chase City *(G-2914)*
Owens-Brockway Glass Cont Inc.......C..... 434 799-5880
Ringgold *(G-11871)*
Paddock Enterprises LLC................F..... 757 566-3957
Toano *(G-13873)*

3229 Pressed & Blown Glassware, NEC

Afgd Inc.......................................G..... 804 222-0120
Henrico *(G-6470)*
◆ Baron Glass Inc..........................C..... 757 464-1131
Virginia Beach *(G-14262)*
Beach Glass Designs Inc................G..... 757 650-7604
Virginia Beach *(G-14265)*
Corning Incorporated.......................G..... 703 448-1095
Herndon *(G-6647)*
Corning Incorporated.......................E..... 434 793-9511
Danville *(G-3972)*
Corning Incorporated.......................E..... 540 382-4921
Christiansburg *(G-3580)*
Corning Incorporated.......................D..... 540 382-4921
Christiansburg *(G-3581)*
▲ Design Master Associates Inc.......E..... 757 566-8500
Toano *(G-13864)*
Dixie Plate GL & Mirror Co LLC........G..... 540 869-4400
Middletown *(G-8737)*
E I Designs Pottery LLC.................G..... 410 459-3337
Virginia Beach *(G-14424)*
Eileen Tramonte Design..................G..... 703 241-1996
Arlington *(G-955)*
Fibertech Virginia Inc.....................G..... 540 337-0916
Greenville *(G-5998)*

G-13 Hand-Blown Art Glass.............G..... 757 495-8185
Virginia Beach *(G-14478)*
Gateway Green Energy Inc..............G..... 540 280-7475
Fishersville *(G-5003)*
Global Metro Networks Inc...............G..... 703 837-6030
Alexandria *(G-218)*
High Performance Optics Inc............G..... 513 258-5978
Roanoke *(G-11934)*
Highpoint Glass Works....................G..... 757 442-7155
Pungoteague *(G-10650)*
I T F Circle....................................E..... 276 773-3114
Independence *(G-6986)*
Leoni Fiber Optics Inc....................G..... 757 258-4805
Williamsburg *(G-15268)*
Leoni Fiber Optics Inc....................G..... 757 258-4805
Williamsburg *(G-15269)*
Ray Visions Inc.............................G..... 757 865-6442
Yorktown *(G-15986)*
RH Ceramics..................................G..... 760 880-4088
Norfolk *(G-9707)*
Terrence Smith..............................G..... 703 339-2194
Lorton *(G-7537)*

3231 Glass Prdts Made Of Purchased Glass

AGC Flat Glass North Amer Inc.........G..... 804 222-0120
Henrico *(G-6471)*
Agilent Technologies Inc..................G..... 540 443-9272
Blacksburg *(G-1721)*
All Glass LLC.................................G..... 540 288-8111
Fredericksburg *(G-5397)*
◆ American Mirror Company Inc.........C..... 276 236-5111
Galax *(G-5627)*
Anns Stained Glass Windows PA.......G..... 540 337-2249
Stuarts Draft *(G-13643)*
Architectural Systems Virginia..........G..... 804 270-0477
Richmond *(G-11116)*
◆ Bassett Mirror Company Inc...........C..... 276 629-3341
Bassett *(G-1580)*
Bay Etching & Imprinting Inc...........E..... 800 925-2877
Lively *(G-7439)*
Blended Cre8tions LLC.....................G..... 347 323-2982
Virginia Beach *(G-14287)*
Bottlehood of Virginia Inc................G..... 804 454-0656
Chesterfield *(G-3482)*
Burgess Snyder Industries Inc.........E..... 757 490-3131
Virginia Beach *(G-14306)*
Cain Inc..G..... 434 842-3984
Bremo Bluff *(G-1945)*
Cardinal Glass Industries Inc...........C..... 540 892-5600
Vinton *(G-14168)*
▲ Coffman Stairs LLC.....................B..... 276 783-7251
Marion *(G-8225)*
Crafted Glass Inc............................G..... 757 543-5504
Chesapeake *(G-3056)*
▲ Design Master Associates Inc.......E..... 757 566-8500
Toano *(G-13864)*
Dimension Stone LLC.......................G..... 804 615-7750
Amelia Court House *(G-655)*
Dixie Plate GL & Mirror Co LLC........G..... 540 869-4400
Middletown *(G-8737)*
Douglas S Huff...............................G..... 540 886-4751
Staunton *(G-13253)*
Embroidery Crown Inc......................G..... 703 986-3022
Woodbridge *(G-15691)*
Evs Glass Creations LLC.................G..... 540 412-8242
Fredericksburg *(G-5285)*
Executive Glass Services Inc............G..... 703 689-2178
Herndon *(G-6672)*
Ghti Corporation.............................G..... 703 802-8616
Fairfax *(G-4464)*
Glorias Glass.................................G..... 804 357-0676
New Kent *(G-9133)*
Guardian Fabrication LLC,...............C..... 276 236-5196
Galax *(G-5637)*
Hawkins Glass Wholesalers LLC........E..... 703 372-2990
Lorton *(G-7492)*
Highlands Glass Company LLC.........G..... 276 623-0021
Abingdon *(G-36)*
Interior 2000.................................G..... 804 598-0340
Powhatan *(G-10551)*
Jennings Stained Glass Inc.............F..... 434 283-1301
Gladys *(G-5693)*
Juma Brothers Inc.........................G..... 757 312-0544
Portsmouth *(G-10449)*
Mark S Chapman.............................G..... 434 227-6702
Troy *(G-13934)*
Massey Wood & West Inc................E..... 804 746-2800
Mechanicsville *(G-8656)*
Maureen Melville.............................G..... 703 533-2448
Mc Lean *(G-8496)*

▲ Oran Safety Glass Inc.................F..... 434 336-1620
Emporia *(G-4364)*
Ornament Company...........................G..... 757 585-0729
Williamsburg *(G-15288)*
Painted Ladies LLC.........................G..... 571 481-6906
Woodbridge *(G-15769)*
Raytheon Company...........................F..... 703 872-3400
Arlington *(G-1139)*
Red Star Glass Inc..........................G..... 540 899-5779
Fredericksburg *(G-5218)*
River House Creations LLC...............G..... 757 509-2137
Gloucester *(G-5859)*
Sign Enterprise Inc..........................G..... 540 899-9555
Fredericksburg *(G-5224)*
Stained Glass Creations Inc.............G..... 804 798-8806
Ashland *(G-1496)*
Vinylite Windows Products Inc...........E..... 703 550-7766
Lorton *(G-7540)*
▼ Virginia Glass Products Corp.........C..... 276 956-3131
Ridgeway *(G-11856)*
▼ Virginia Mirror Company Inc...........D..... 276 956-3131
Martinsville *(G-8347)*
Virginia Mirror Company Inc.............G..... 276 632-9816
Martinsville *(G-8348)*
Virginia Stained Glass Co Inc..........F..... 703 425-4611
Springfield *(G-13108)*
▲ Weksler Glass Thermometer Corp...G..... 434 977-4544
Charlottesville *(G-2904)*

3241 Cement, Hydraulic

Artisan Concrete Designs Inc............G..... 434 321-3423
South Hill *(G-12842)*
Dominion Quikrete Inc.....................E..... 757 547-9411
Chesapeake *(G-3071)*
Dominion Quikrete Inc......................E..... 276 957-3235
Martinsville *(G-8279)*
◆ Kerneos Inc................................D..... 757 494-1947
Chesapeake *(G-3163)*
Lafarge Calcium Aluminates Inc........G..... 757 543-8832
Chesapeake *(G-3172)*
Lafarge North America Inc................G..... 505 471-6456
Herndon *(G-6731)*
Lafarge North America Inc................F..... 757 545-2481
Chesapeake *(G-3173)*
R & R Developers Inc......................G..... 276 628-3846
Abingdon *(G-55)*
Titan America LLC...........................C..... 540 622-2350
Front Royal *(G-5557)*
Titan America LLC...........................F..... 804 236-4122
Richmond *(G-11412)*
Titan America LLC...........................D..... 703 471-0044
Sterling *(G-13534)*

3251 Brick & Structural Clay Tile

General Shale Brick Inc....................D..... 276 783-3156
Atkins *(G-1517)*
General Shale Brick Inc...................G..... 800 414-4661
Forest *(G-5072)*
General Shale Brick Inc...................G..... 540 977-5505
Blue Ridge *(G-1849)*
Glen-Gery Corporation......................D..... 703 368-3178
Manassas *(G-7946)*
▲ Lawrenceville Brick Inc................D..... 434 848-3151
Lawrenceville *(G-7182)*
Precision Brick Cutting Ltd................G..... 703 393-2777
Manassas *(G-8132)*
Redland Brick................................G..... 434 848-2397
Lawrenceville *(G-7183)*

3253 Ceramic Tile

Ablaze Interiors Inc.........................G..... 757 427-0075
Virginia Beach *(G-14204)*
Custom Tiles LLC...........................G..... 434 660-7170
Altavista *(G-631)*
E I Designs Pottery LLC..................G..... 410 459-3337
Virginia Beach *(G-14424)*
▲ Elias LLC...................................G..... 703 663-1192
Alexandria *(G-453)*
Evergreen Enterprises Inc...............C..... 804 231-1800
Richmond *(G-11581)*
◆ Evergreen Enterprises Inc............C..... 804 231-1800
Richmond *(G-11582)*
Florida Tile Inc...............................G..... 757 855-9330
Chesapeake *(G-3103)*
▲ General Marble & Granite Co.........C..... 804 353-2761
Richmond *(G-11215)*
Gryphon Tile LLC...........................G..... 540 868-2953
Middletown *(G-8739)*
Krain Building Services LLC...............E..... 703 924-1480
Alexandria *(G-509)*

SIC

Ku Forming Inc..........................G...... 434 946-5934
Amherst (G-697)
Mohawk Industries Inc ....C...... 276 728-2141
Hillsville (G-6897)
Sheaves Floors LLC ....G...... 540 234-9080
Weyers Cave (G-15176)

3255 Clay Refractories

Clinch Valley Repair Service........G...... 276 964-5191
Pounding Mill (G-10517)
Continental Brick Company..........G...... 434 845-5918
Lynchburg (G-7683)
Dominion Quikrete Inc................E...... 276 957-3235
Martinsville (G-8279)
Mapei Corporation....................E...... 540 361-1085
Fredericksburg (G-5453)

3259 Structural Clay Prdts, NEC

Clay Decor LLC ....G...... 607 654-7428
Roanoke (G-11911)
Polycoat Inc.............................G...... 540 989-7833
Roanoke (G-11989)

3261 China Plumbing Fixtures & Fittings

▲ Allora USA LLC ....F...... 571 291-3485
Sterling (G-13343)
CPS Contractors Inc ....G...... 804 561-6834
Moseley (G-9036)

3263 Earthenware, Whiteware, Table & Kitchen Articles

Koolnut LLC ....G...... 213 349-0196
Henrico (G-6528)

3264 Porcelain Electrical Splys

◆ National Imports LLC ....G...... 703 637-0019
Vienna (G-14102)
◆ NGK-Lcke Polymr Insulators Inc..D...... 757 460-3649
Virginia Beach (G-14681)

3269 Pottery Prdts, NEC

April A Phillips Pottery ....G...... 703 464-1283
Herndon (G-6615)
Blue Ridge Pottery.....................F...... 434 985-6080
Stanardsville (G-13216)
Creative Workshops ....G...... 703 938-6177
Vienna (G-14031)
David Ceramics LLC ....G...... 703 430-2692
Great Falls (G-5952)
Diaz Ceramics ....G...... 804 672-7161
Henrico (G-6501)
E I Designs Pottery LLC ....G...... 410 459-3337
Virginia Beach (G-14424)
Emerson Creek Pottery Inc ....E...... 540 297-7524
Bedford (G-1635)
Hamilo LLC ....G...... 703 440-1276
Springfield (G-13017)
Handmade Pottery ....G...... 757 425-0116
Virginia Beach (G-14503)
Hoffman Pottery ....G...... 276 773-3546
Independence (G-6985)
Kellis Creations LLC ....G...... 540 554-2878
Round Hill (G-12381)
Mainly Clay LLC ....G...... 434 390-8138
Farmville (G-4948)
Mdc Camden Clayworks ....G...... 804 798-4971
Glen Allen (G-5769)
Michelle Erickson Pottery ....G...... 757 727-9139
Hampton (G-6198)
Persimmon Street Ceramics That ...G...... 202 256-8238
Arlington (G-1109)
Poddery ....G...... 804 725-5956
Foster (G-5137)
Rebecca S Ceramics ....G...... 804 560-4477
Richmond (G-11730)
Robin Cage Pottery ....G...... 804 233-1758
Richmond (G-11745)
Sophia Street Studio ....G...... 540 372-3459
Fredericksburg (G-5225)
Strange Designs ....G...... 540 937-5858
Viewtown (G-14164)
Sweet Pea Ceramics LLC ....G...... 571 292-4313
Warrenton (G-15054)
Team Ceramic Inc ....G...... 757 572-7725
Chesapeake (G-3325)
Wonderfully Made Ceramics ....G...... 571 261-1633
Nokesville (G-9405)

3271 Concrete Block & Brick

▲ Allied Concrete Company ....E...... 434 296-7181
Charlottesville (G-2724)
▲ Allied Concrete Products LLC.....G...... 757 494-5200
Chesapeake (G-2960)
American Concrete Group LLC ....G...... 276 546-1633
Pennington Gap (G-10291)
Anchor ....G...... 540 327-9391
Winchester (G-15380)
Barron Construction LLC ....G...... 804 400-5569
North Chesterfield (G-9828)
Bills Yard & Lawn Service LLC ....G...... 757 871-4589
Hampton (G-6092)
▲ Blue Stone Block Sprmkt Inc ......E...... 540 982-3588
Roanoke (G-12050)
Bract Rtining Walls Excvtg LLC ......F...... 804 798-5097
Ashland (G-1384)
Chandler Concrete Products of ......D...... 540 382-1734
Christiansburg (G-3578)
Chandler Concrete Products of ......G...... 540 674-4667
Dublin (G-4151)
Cochran Industries Inc - VA ....G...... 276 498-3836
Oakwood (G-10166)
E Dillon & Company ....D...... 276 873-6816
Swords Creek (G-13807)
Edward L Birckhead ....G...... 540 937-4287
Amissville (G-718)
Empire Incorporated ....E...... 757 723-6747
Hampton (G-6140)
France Lawnscpape LLC ....G...... 804 761-6823
Warsaw (G-15063)
General Shale Brick Inc ....G...... 540 977-5505
Blue Ridge (G-1849)
Giant Resource Recovery Inc ....E...... 434 685-7021
Cascade (G-2251)
Hagerstown Block Company ....G...... 540 364-1531
Marshall (G-8255)
Knap Services Inc ....G...... 540 351-5905
Warrenton (G-15028)
Marshall Con Pdts of Danville ....G...... 434 369-4791
Altavista (G-635)
Martinsville Concrete Products ......E...... 276.632-6416
Martinsville (G-8308)
▲ Oldcastle Apg Northeast Inc ......F...... 703 365-7070
Gainesville (G-5605)
Oldcastle Apg Northeast Inc ....G...... 540 667-4600
Winchester (G-15457)
Peoplespace Inc ....G...... 434 825-2168
Charlottesville (G-2844)
Rockingham Redi-Mix Inc ....E...... 540 433-8282
Rockingham (G-12274)
Summit Ldscp & Lawn Care LLC .....G...... 703 856-5353
Falls Church (G-4879)
Supreme Concrete Blocks Inc ....G...... 703 478-1988
Leesburg (G-7355)
T&W Block Incorporated ....E...... 757 787-2646
Onley (G-10201)
Tarmac Florida Inc ....G...... 757 858-6500
Norfolk (G-9742)
Tarmac Mid-Atlantic Inc ....A...... 757 858-6500
Norfolk (G-9743)
Titan America LLC ....G...... 757 533-7152
Norfolk (G-9758)
Triple S Pallets LLC ....E...... 540 810-4581
Mount Crawford (G-9061)
Unicom Technology Park Inc ....G...... 703 502-2850
Chantilly (G-2512)
VA Hardscapes Inc ....G...... 540 955-6245
Berryville (G-1698)
Valley Building Supply Inc ....G...... 540 434-6725
Harrisonburg (G-6383)
Virginia Veterans Creations ....G...... 757 502-4407
Virginia Beach (G-14922)
Xteriors Factory Outlets Inc ....E...... 804 798-6300
Doswell (G-4129)

3272 Concrete Prdts

3314 Monument Ave LLC ....G...... 804 285-9770
Henrico (G-6468)
A Metromont Company ....G...... 540 401-0101
Winchester (G-15368)
Abingdon Pre Cast Products ....G...... 276 628-2472
Abingdon (G-2)
Accaceek Precast ....G...... 540 604-7726
Stafford (G-13111)
Ace Hardwood ....G...... 804 270-4260
Richmond (G-11080)
Action Resources Corporation........F...... 540 343-5121
Roanoke (G-12028)

Alcat Precast Inc ....G...... 804 725-4080
Moon (G-9031)
All Marble ....G...... 757 460-8099
Virginia Beach (G-14222)
Allied Con Co - Suffolk Block ....G...... 757 494-5200
Chesapeake (G-2959)
▲ Allied Concrete Company ....E...... 434 296-7181
Charlottesville (G-2724)
American Stone Inc ....G...... 804 448-9460
Ruther Glen (G-12449)
American Stone Virginia LLC ....G...... 804 448-9460
Ladysmith (G-7154)
Americast Inc ....E...... 757 494-5200
Chesapeake (G-2974)
Americast Inc ....D...... 804 798-6068
Ashland (G-1369)
▲ Americast Inc ....G...... 540 434-6979
Harrisonburg (G-6292)
▲ Arban & Carosi Incorporated .....C...... 703 491-5121
Woodbridge (G-15646)
Arban Precast Stone Ltd ....G...... 703 221-8005
Dumfries (G-4236)
Argos USA LLC ....G...... 804 227-9402
Ashland (G-1371)
Atlantic Wood Industries Inc ....E...... 757 397-2317
Portsmouth (G-10395)
Backroad Precast LLC ....G...... 540 335-5503
Woodstock (G-15848)
Bastion and Associates LLC ....G...... 703 343-5158
Springfield (G-12959)
Batchelder & Collins Inc ....G...... 757 220-2806
Williamsburg (G-15210)
Battle Monument Partners ....G...... 804 644-4924
Richmond (G-11501)
Beasley Concrete Inc ....E...... 804 633-9626
Milford (G-8928)
Blue Ridge Stone Mfg ....G...... 276 676-0040
Abingdon (G-15)
▲ Blue Stone Block Sprmkt Inc ......E...... 540 982-3588
Roanoke (G-12050)
Boggs Water & Sewage Inc ....E...... 757 787-4000
Melfa (G-8708)
Burial Butler Services LLC ....G...... 757 934-8227
Suffolk (G-13682)
C B C Corporation ....G...... 757 868-6571
Poquoson (G-10365)
Carroll J Harper ....F...... 540 434-8978
Rockingham (G-12244)
Chandler Concrete Inc ....E...... 540 345-3846
Roanoke (G-12062)
Chaney Enterprises Ltd Partnr ....F...... 540 710-0075
Fredericksburg (G-5260)
Cme Concrete LLC ....G...... 757 713-0495
Hampton (G-6114)
Coastal Constructors LLC ....G...... 757 545-0080
Chesapeake (G-3041)
Coastal Precast Systems ....G...... 571 442-8648
Leesburg (G-7247)
Coastal Precast Systems LLC ....F...... 757 545-5215
Chesapeake (G-3042)
Concrete Castings Inc ....G...... 540 427-3006
Roanoke (G-12068)
Concrete Pipe & Precast LLC ....C...... 804 798-6068
Ashland (G-1394)
Concrete Pipe & Precast LLC ....E...... 757 485-5228
Chesapeake (G-3049)
Concrete Pipe & Precast LLC ....E...... 804 752-1311
Ashland (G-1395)
Concrete Precast Systems Inc ....G...... 757 545-5215
Cape Charles (G-2232)
◆ Concrete Precast Systems Inc......D...... 757 545-5215
Chesapeake (G-3050)
Concrete Specialties Inc ....G...... 540 982-0777
Roanoke (G-12069)
Cook & Boardman Group LLC.........G...... 757 873-3979
Newport News (G-9205)
Cornerstone Archtectural Stone .....G...... 540 297-3686
Bedford (G-1632)
CT Jamsos Precast Septic Tanks ....G...... 540 483-5944
Callaway (G-2220)
Custom Precast Inc ....G...... 757 833-8989
Yorktown (G-15946)
Custom Vault Corporation ....G...... 804 303-1741
North Chesterfield (G-10017)
Dunford G C Septic Tank Instal ......G...... 276 228-8590
Wytheville (G-15886)
Earthcore Industries LLC ....G...... 757 966-7275
Chesapeake (G-3081)
Empire Incorporated ....E...... 757 723-6747
Hampton (G-6140)

Essex Concrete Corporation ....D.... 804 443-2366
Tappahannock **(G-13814)**

Estate Concrete LLC.........................G.... 703 293-6363
Centreville **(G-2305)**

Finly Corporation ....E.... 434 385-5028
Lynchburg **(G-7707)**

First Paper Co Inc ....F.... 434 821-6884
Rustburg **(G-12439)**

Forterra Pipe & Precast LLC ....F.... 757 485-5228
Chesapeake **(G-3108)**

◆ Framecad America Inc ....F.... 703 615-2451
Fairfax **(G-4626)**

Friends Sprngwood Brial Pk LLC.......G.... 540 366-0996
Roanoke **(G-11924)**

Garrett Corporation ....G.... 276 475-3652
Damascus **(G-3948)**

Hanover Precast Inc ....F.... 804 798-2336
Ashland **(G-1430)**

Hanson Aggregates East LLC ....D.... 540 387-0271
Salem **(G-12514)**

Hearth Pros ....G.... 434 237-5913
Lynchburg **(G-7731)**

Holcim LLC ....G.... 703 622-4616
Vienna **(G-14066)**

Huffman & Huffman Inc ....G.... 276 579-2373
Mouth of Wilson **(G-9093)**

▲ Industrial Welding & Mch Corp .....F.... 276 783-7105
Atkins **(G-1518)**

Isle of Wight Forest Products ....F.... 757 899-8115
Wakefield **(G-14967)**

Jordan Septic Tank Service ....G.... 276 395-3938
Coeburn **(G-3700)**

Joseph L Burruss Burial Vaults.........F.... 804 746-8250
Mechanicsville **(G-8646)**

Juptiers Vault ....G.... 757 404-9535
Norfolk **(G-9609)**

Koppers Industries Inc ....G.... 540 672-3802
Orange **(G-10218)**

Legacy Vulcan LLC ....G.... 703 461-0333
Alexandria **(G-257)**

Lynchburg Ready-Mix Con Co Inc .....E.... 434 846-6563
Lynchburg **(G-7764)**

Markham Burial Vault Service ....E.... 804 271-1441
North Chesterfield **(G-9922)**

Martinsville Concrete Products ....E.... 276 632-6416
Martinsville **(G-8308)**

Mary Jo Kirwan ....G.... 703 421-1919
Herndon **(G-6743)**

Mercer Vault Co ....G.... 540 371-3666
Fredericksburg **(G-5206)**

Metromont Corporation ....D.... 804 222-6770
Richmond **(G-11290)**

Monument32/The Smyers Group.........G.... 804 217-8347
Glen Allen **(G-5773)**

Monumental Pest Control Co.............G.... 571 245-6178
Centreville **(G-2321)**

Monumental Services ....G.... 434 847-6630
Madison Heights **(G-7877)**

Music At Monument ....G.... 202 570-7800
Luray **(G-7619)**

Nansemond Pre-Cast Con Co Inc ......E.... 757 538-2761
Suffolk **(G-13748)**

New River Concrete Supply Co ....F.... 540 639-9679
Radford **(G-10726)**

New River Concrete Supply Inc ....F.... 540 552-1721
Blacksburg **(G-1773)**

Northern Vrgnia Cast Stone LLC ....G.... 703 393-2777
Gainesville **(G-5604)**

Nova Concrete Products Inc ....G.... 540 439-2978
Bealeton **(G-1603)**

Nova Exteriors Inc ....F.... 703 322-1500
Alexandria **(G-544)**

NV Cast Stone ....F.... 703 393-2777
Manassas **(G-8119)**

Oldcastle Apg Northeast Inc ....E.... 540 667-4600
Winchester **(G-15457)**

Oldcastle Infrastructure Inc ....D.... 540 898-6300
Fredericksburg **(G-5339)**

Pre Cast of Virginia ....G.... 540 439-2978
Bealeton **(G-1604)**

Pre Con Inc ....D.... 804 732-1253
Petersburg **(G-10336)**

Quality Culvert ....G.... 434 336-1468
Emporia **(G-4365)**

Quality Precast Stone ....G.... 703 244-4551
Manassas **(G-8136)**

Quikrete Companies LLC ....E.... 276 964-6755
Pounding Mill **(G-10525)**

R R Beasley Inc ....F.... 804 529-6470
Callao **(G-2217)**

R R Beasley Inc ....E.... 804 633-9626
Milford **(G-8933)**

Richards-Wilbert Inc ....G.... 540 477-3842
Mount Jackson **(G-9077)**

Richards-Wilbert Inc ....G.... 540 389-5240
Salem **(G-12562)**

River City Wrap LLC ....G.... 804 914-7325
Midlothian **(G-8892)**

Roland Vault Ltd ....G.... 757 466-8800
Norfolk **(G-9709)**

Royal Group Inc ....E.... 276 783-8161
Marion **(G-8242)**

Seaboard Concrete Products Co.........E.... 804 275-0802
North Chesterfield **(G-9973)**

Seaboard Service of VA Inc..............G.... 804 643-5112
Richmond **(G-11375)**

▼ Separation Technologies LLC.........E.... 540 992-1501
Roanoke **(G-11999)**

Setzer and Sons VA Inc Smith ....E.... 434 246-3791
Stony Creek **(G-13568)**

Shenandoah Castings LLC ....G.... 540 551-5777
Front Royal **(G-5554)**

Shockey Bros Inc ....C.... 540 401-0101
Winchester **(G-15478)**

Shockey Bros Inc ....G.... 540 667-7700
Fredericksburg **(G-5361)**

Smith-Midland Corporation ....D.... 540 439-3266
Midland **(G-8763)**

Smith-Midland Corporation ....C.... 540 439-3266
Midland **(G-8764)**

South East Precast Con LLC ....G.... 276 620-1194
Wytheville **(G-15915)**

Stafford Stone Works LLC ....E.... 540 372-6601
Fredericksburg **(G-5227)**

Statement LLC ....E.... 757 635-6294
Virginia Beach **(G-14843)**

Stevens Burial Vault LLC ....G.... 804 443-5125
Champlain **(G-2357)**

Suncoast Post-Tension Ltd ....E.... 703 492-4949
Woodbridge **(G-15820)**

Tarmac Mid-Atlantic Inc ....A.... 757 858-6500
Norfolk **(G-9743)**

TCS Materials Corp ....F.... 804 863-4525
North Dinwiddie **(G-10064)**

Tidewater Block LLc ....F.... 757 539-1576
Suffolk **(G-13771)**

Tile Optima LLC ....F.... 703 256-5650
Alexandria **(G-598)**

Timberlake Contracting LLC ....G.... 804 449-1517
Beaverdam **(G-1615)**

Tindall Corporation ....C.... 804 861-8447
North Dinwiddie **(G-10065)**

Turlington Sons Sptic Tank Svc ....G.... 804 642-9538
Ordinary **(G-10237)**

United Precast Finisher LLC..............G.... 804 386-6308
Chester **(G-3464)**

Valley Building Supply Inc ....C.... 540 434-6725
Harrisonburg **(G-6383)**

Valley Redi-Mix Company Inc ....E.... 540 631-9050
Front Royal **(G-5560)**

Vamac Incorporated ....E.... 540 535-1983
Winchester **(G-15503)**

Vamaz Inc ....G.... 434 296-8812
Charlottesville **(G-2711)**

Vault ....G.... 540 479-2221
Fredericksburg **(G-5386)**

Vault Productions LLC ....G.... 703 509-2704
Williamsburg **(G-15330)**

Vault Technologies LLC ....G.... 703 283-2550
Fairfax Station **(G-4726)**

Vault44 LLC ....G.... 202 758-6228
Manassas Park **(G-8213)**

Vfp Inc ....C.... 276 431-4000
Duffield **(G-4187)**

Virgina-Carolina Grave Vlt LLC ....G.... 276 694-6855
Stuart **(G-13638)**

Virginia Veterans Creations ....G.... 757 502-4407
Virginia Beach **(G-14922)**

Vulcan Construction Mtls LLC............G.... 276 466-5436
Bristol **(G-1999)**

Wayne Harbin Builder Inc ....G.... 757 220-8860
Williamsburg **(G-15339)**

West End Precast LLC ....G.... 276 228-5024
Wytheville **(G-15922)**

Wimbrough & Sons Inc ....G.... 757 399-1242
Portsmouth **(G-10504)**

Winchester Building Sup Co Inc ....E.... 540 667-2301
Winchester **(G-15510)**

Wright Inc W F ....F.... 804 561-2721
Amelia Court House **(G-678)**

3273 Ready-Mixed Concrete

Aggregate Industries - Mwr Inc.........B.... 540 379-0765
Falmouth **(G-4932)**

Aggregate Industries - Mwr Inc.........E.... 703 361-2276
Manassas **(G-8020)**

Aggregate Industries MGT Inc..........G.... 804 994-5533
Aylett **(G-1544)**

Aggregate Industries MGT Inc..........G.... 540 337-4875
Stuarts Draft **(G-13642)**

Aggregate Industries MGT Inc..........G.... 804 693-2280
Gloucester **(G-5835)**

Aggregate Industries-Wcr Inc............G.... 804 829-9783
Charles City **(G-2569)**

Aggregates Usa LLC ....G.... 276 628-9337
Abingdon **(G-9)**

Allied Concrete Company ....E.... 804 279-7501
North Chesterfield **(G-9813)**

▲ Allied Concrete Company ....E.... 434 296-7181
Charlottesville **(G-2724)**

Allied Concrete Products LLC............G.... 434 634-6571
Emporia **(G-4354)**

American Concrete Group LLC ....G.... 276 546-1633
Pennington Gap **(G-10291)**

Argos USA LLC ....F.... 804 763-6112
Midlothian **(G-8774)**

B & E Transit Mix Inc ....G.... 434 447-7331
South Hill **(G-12843)**

Barger Son Cnstr Inc Charles W ....D.... 540 463-2106
Lexington **(G-7388)**

Beasley Concrete Inc ....E.... 804 633-9626
Milford **(G-8928)**

Bedford Ready-Mix Con Co Inc ....G.... 540 586-8380
Bedford **(G-1624)**

Blue Ridge Concrete Product ....E.... 276 755-2000
Cana **(G-2226)**

Boxley Materials Company ....G.... 540 777-7600
Blue Ridge **(G-1847)**

Boxley Materials Company ....F.... 540 777-7600
Martinsville **(G-8271)**

Boxley Materials Company ....G.... 540 777-7600
Wytheville **(G-15880)**

Boxley Materials Company ....G.... 540 777-7600
Blue Ridge **(G-1848)**

Boxley Materials Company ....F.... 540 777-7600
Roanoke **(G-11893)**

Capital Concrete Inc ....G.... 757 627-0630
Norfolk **(G-9477)**

Capital Concrete Inc ....G.... 757 627-0630
Virginia Beach **(G-14316)**

Cardinal Concrete Company..............C.... 703 550-7650
Herndon **(G-6634)**

Cavalier Concrete Inc ....G.... 434 296-7181
Charlottesville **(G-2758)**

Cemex Cnstr Mtls ATL LLC...............G.... 434 685-7021
Cascade **(G-2250)**

Central Redi-Mix Concrete Inc ....G.... 434 736-0091
Meherrin **(G-8705)**

Chandler Concrete Co Inc ....G.... 434 369-4791
Altavista **(G-629)**

Chandler Concrete Co Inc ....E.... 434 792-1233
Danville **(G-3965)**

Chandler Concrete Inc ....G.... 540 345-3846
Roanoke **(G-12062)**

Chandler Concrete Inc ....G.... 540 297-4369
Moneta **(G-8958)**

Chandler Concrete Inc ....G.... 276 928-1357
Rocky Gap **(G-12306)**

Chandler Concrete of Virginia ....G.... 434 369-4791
Altavista **(G-630)**

Chandler Concrete Products of..........D.... 540 382-1734
Christiansburg **(G-3578)**

Chandler Concrete Products of..........G.... 540 674-4667
Dublin **(G-4151)**

Chandler Concrete Virginia Inc ....G.... 540 382-1734
Christiansburg **(G-3579)**

Chaney Enterprises Ltd Partnr ....F.... 540 710-0075
Fredericksburg **(G-5260)**

Chaney Enterprises Ltd Partnr ....G.... 540 659-4100
Stafford **(G-13129)**

Charles Contracting Co Inc ....G.... 757 422-9989
Virginia Beach **(G-14331)**

Charles County Sand & Grav Co ....G.... 540 775-9550
King George **(G-7083)**

CMI ....D.... 703 356-2190
Vienna **(G-14028)**

Colonial Readi-Mix Concrete ....G.... 757 888-8500
Williamsburg **(G-15221)**

Commercial Ready Mix Pdts Inc.........F.... 757 925-0939
Suffolk **(G-13686)**

S I C

Commercial Ready Mix Pdts Inc............F 757 420-5800
Chesapeake (G-3047)

Concrete Precast Systems Inc............E 703 327-4112
Chantilly (G-2530)

Concrete Ready Mixed Corp............G 540 345-3846
Salem (G-12490)

Conmat Group Inc............E 540 433-9128
Rockingham (G-12245)

Construction Materials Company............G 540 552-5022
Blacksburg (G-1731)

Construction Materials Company............G 540 962-2139
Covington (G-3783)

Construction Materials Company............G 540 463-3441
Lexington (G-7391)

Construction Materials Company............F 540 433-9043
Lexington (G-7392)

Cox Ready Mix Inc SB............E 804 364-0500
Glen Allen (G-5718)

Crh Americas Inc............G 804 633-9841
Milford (G-8929)

Danville Ready Mix............F 434 799-5818
Danville (G-3979)

Dominion Quikrete Inc............E 276 957-3235
Martinsville (G-8279)

Dubrook Concrete Inc............D 703 222-6969
Chantilly (G-2413)

Ennstone............G 703 335-2650
Manassas (G-8065)

Essex Concrete Corp............G 804 749-1950
Rockville (G-12285)

Essex Concrete Corporation............D 804 443-2366
Tappahannock (G-13814)

Essex Concrete Corporation............F 804 443-2366
Tappahannock (G-13815)

Essroc Cement Corp............G 757 545-2481
Chesapeake (G-3092)

Essroc Cement Corporation............G 804 227-4156
Ashland (G-1410)

Etz LLC............G 703 620-3014
Reston (G-10849)

F & M Construction Corp............F 276 728-2255
Hillsville (G-6891)

Falcon Concrete Corporation............E 703 354-7100
Springfield (G-13001)

Felton Brothers Trnst Mix Inc............G 434 572-2665
South Boston (G-12765)

Felton Brothers Trnst Mix Inc............G 434 376-2415
Brookneal (G-2110)

Felton Brothers Trnst Mix Inc............G 434 374-5373
Boydton (G-1915)

Felton Brothers Trnst Mix Inc............G 434 572-4614
South Boston (G-12766)

Felton Brothers Trnst Mix Inc............G 434 848-3966
Lawrenceville (G-7180)

Felton Brothers Trnst Mix Inc............G 434 447-3778
South Hill (G-12850)

Finly Corporation............E 434 385-5028
Lynchburg (G-7707)

Giant Resource Recovery Inc............E 434 685-7021
Cascade (G-2251)

Greenrock Materials LLC............D 804 966-8601
Charles City (G-2576)

Handyman Concrete Inc............E 703 437-7143
Chantilly (G-2535)

Huffman & Huffman Inc............G 276 579-2373
Mouth of Wilson (G-9093)

Lafarge North America Inc............G 703 480-3600
Reston (G-10882)

Legacy Vulcan LLC............E 540 298-1237
Elkton (G-4330)

Legacy Vulcan LLC............D 703 368-2475
Manassas (G-8099)

Legacy Vulcan LLC............F 703 354-5783
Springfield (G-13040)

Legacy Vulcan LLC............E 540 347-3641
Warrenton (G-15031)

Legacy Vulcan LLC............G 540 886-6758
Staunton (G-13275)

Legacy Vulcan LLC............G 540 659-3003
Stafford (G-13169)

Legacy Vulcan LLC............G 800 732-3964
Rapidan (G-10753)

Legacy Vulcan LLC............G 800 732-3964
Dumfries (G-4250)

Legacy Vulcan LLC............G 804 863-4565
North Dinwiddie (G-10056)

Legacy Vulcan LLC............G 800 732-3964
Arlington (G-1030)

Legacy Vulcan LLC............G 800 732-3964
Chantilly (G-2542)

Legacy Vulcan LLC............G 434 572-3967
South Boston (G-12778)

Legacy Vulcan LLC............G 800 732-3964
Stafford (G-13170)

Legacy Vulcan LLC............G 800 732-3964
Stephens City (G-13319)

Legacy Vulcan LLC............G 804 730-1008
Mechanicsville (G-8652)

Legacy Vulcan LLC............G 703 713-3100
Springfield (G-13041)

Legacy Vulcan LLC............G 800 732-3964
Falls Church (G-4822)

Legacy Vulcan LLC............G 800 732-3964
Lorton (G-7505)

Legacy Vulcan LLC............G 800 732-3964
Fredericksburg (G-5312)

Legacy Vulcan LLC............G 800 732-3964
Lorton (G-7506)

Legacy Vulcan LLC............G 276 940-2741
Duffield (G-4181)

Legacy Vulcan LLC............G 757 888-2982
Newport News (G-9280)

Legacy Vulcan LLC............G 804 236-4160
Richmond (G-11268)

Legacy Vulcan LLC............F 804 717-5770
Chester (G-3430)

Legacy Vulcan LLC............G 757 539-5670
Suffolk (G-13730)

Legacy Vulcan LLC............E 804 360-2014
Rockville (G-12288)

Legacy Vulcan LLC............G 434 447-4696
South Hill (G-12856)

Lehigh Cement Company LLC............G 757 928-1559
Newport News (G-9281)

Lehigh Cement Company LLC............G 540 942-1181
Waynesboro (G-15121)

Lorton Enterprises............G 703 725-2933
Lorton (G-7509)

Lynchburg Ready-Mix Con Co Inc............E 434 846-6563
Lynchburg (G-7764)

Lynchburg Ready-Mix Con Co Inc............G 434 946-5562
Amherst (G-847)

Marshall Con Pdts of Danville............D 434 792-1233
Danville (G-4015)

Marshall Con Pdts of Danville............G 434 575-5351
South Boston (G-12780)

Marshall Con Pdts of Danville............G 434 369-4791
Altavista (G-635)

Marshall Concrete Products............F 540 297-4369
Moneta (G-8972)

Martin Marietta Materials Inc............F 804 674-9517
Midlothian (G-8852)

Martinsville Finance & Inv............G 276 632-9500
Martinsville (G-8309)

Marty Corporation............G 276 395-3326
Coeburn (G-3701)

Marty Corporation............G 276 679-3477
Norton (G-10125)

McClure Concrete............G 276 889-2289
Lebanon (G-7201)

McClure Concrete Materials LLC............G 276 964-9682
Richlands (G-11018)

McClure Concrete Materials LLC............G 276 964-9682
Clintwood (G-3690)

McClure Concrete Materials LLC............G 276 679-3477
Norton (G-10128)

McClure Concrete Materials LLC............G 276 964-9682
Saint Paul (G-12470)

McClure Concrete Products Inc............G 276 889-3496
Lebanon (G-7201)

McClure Concrete Products Inc............G 276 964-9682
Richlands (G-11019)

Mix It Up LLC............G 540 434-9868
Harrisonburg (G-6346)

Mountain Materials Inc............E 276 429-5241
Glade Spring (G-5679)

Network 12............G 703 532-2970
Falls Church (G-4923)

New River Concrete Supply............G 540 433-9043
Rockingham (G-12264)

New River Concrete Supply Co............F 540 639-9679
Radford (G-10726)

New River Concrete Supply Inc............F 540 552-1721
Blacksburg (G-1773)

Patton Sand & Concrete............G 276 236-9362
Galax (G-5644)

Quikrete Companies LLC............E 276 646-8976
Chilhowie (G-3558)

R R Beasley Inc............F 804 529-6470
Callao (G-2217)

Ready Set Read LLC............G 804 673-8764
Richmond (G-11348)

Rinker Materials S Centl Inc............F 276 628-9337
Abingdon (G-58)

Roanoke Cement Company LLC............G 540 631-1335
Front Royal (G-5550)

▲ Roanoke Cement Company LLC............C 540 992-1501
Troutville (G-13915)

Rockingham Precast Inc............E 540 433-8282
Rockingham (G-12272)

Rockingham Redi-Mix Inc............E 540 433-9128
Rockingham (G-12273)

Rockingham Redi-Mix Inc............G 540 743-5940
Luray (G-7622)

Rockingham Redi-Mix Inc............G 540 433-9128
Harrisonburg (G-6364)

Rockingham Redi-Mix Inc............G 540 433-9128
Rockingham (G-12275)

Rockingham Redi-Mix Inc............E 540 433-8282
Rockingham (G-12274)

Rocky Mount Ready Mix Concrete............G 540 483-1288
Rocky Mount (G-12350)

Rowe Concrete Supply Store............G 540 710-7693
Fredericksburg (G-5356)

Salem Ready Mix Concrete Inc............F 540 387-1171
Salem (G-12567)

Sb Cox Ready Mix Inc............F 434 292-7300
Blackstone (G-1827)

Sb Cox Ready Mix Inc............F 804 364-0500
Powhatan (G-10572)

Scott Ready............G 703 503-3374
Fairfax (G-4551)

Shoreline Materials LLC............G 804 469-4042
Stony Creek (G-13569)

Southern Equipment Company Inc............G 757 888-8500
Williamsburg (G-15316)

Stuart Concrete Inc............F 276 694-2828
Stuart (G-13633)

Successful Mix LLC............G 540 269-6904
Keezletown (G-7031)

Superior Concrete Inc............E 540 433-2482
Harrisonburg (G-6377)

Superior Concrete Materials............G 703 327-4112
Chantilly (G-2558)

T&W Block Incorporated............E 757 787-2646
Onley (G-10201)

Tamara Ingram............G 434 392-4933
Burkeville (G-2211)

Tarmac Corp............G 703 471-0044
Sterling (G-13528)

Tarmac Florida Inc............C 757 858-6500
Norfolk (G-9742)

Tarmac Mid-Atlantic Inc............A 757 858-6500
Norfolk (G-9743)

TCS Materials Inc............E 757 591-9340
Williamsburg (G-15323)

TCS Materials LLC............D 804 232-1200
Richmond (G-11065)

TCS Materials LLC............F 757 874-5575
Newport News (G-9352)

Titan America LLC............E 703 221-2003
Dumfries (G-4261)

Titan America LLC............G 757 533-7152
Norfolk (G-9758)

Titan America LLC............G 540 372-8717
Fredericksburg (G-5378)

Titan America LLC............F 804 236-4122
Richmond (G-11412)

Titan America LLC............D 703 471-0044
Sterling (G-13534)

Transit Mixed Concrete Corp............E 540 885-7224
Staunton (G-13302)

Turners Ready Mix Inc............F 540 483-9150
Rocky Mount (G-12355)

US Concrete Inc............F 703 471-6969
Chantilly (G-2514)

Valley Redi-Mix Company Inc............G 540 869-1990
Stephens City (G-13326)

Virginia Concrete Company LLC............C 703 354-7100
Herndon (G-6841)

Vulcan Construction Mtls LLC............E 804 862-6665
North Dinwiddie (G-10069)

Vulcan Construction Mtls LLC............G 804 233-9669
Richmond (G-11816)

Vulcan Construction Mtls LLC............G 757 494-3202
Norfolk (G-9785)

Vulcan Construction Mtls LLC............E 757 858-6500
Norfolk (G-9786)

Vulcan Construction Mtls LLC............D 703 471-0044
Sterling (G-13556)

Vulcan Construction Mtls LLC..............G...... 276 466-5436
  Bristol *(G-1999)*
Vulcan Materials Company ....F...... 757 874-5575
  Newport News *(G-9377)*
Vulcan Materials Company ....E...... 540 659-3003
  Stafford *(G-13212)*
Vulcan Materials Company ....G...... 804 270-5385
  Glen Allen *(G-5826)*
Vulcan Materials Company ....F...... 434 848-4775
  Freeman *(G-5513)*
Vulcan Materials Company ....G...... 804 758-5000
  Saluda *(G-12607)*
Vulcan Materials Company ....F...... 540 898-6210
  Fredericksburg *(G-5388)*
Vulcan Materials Company ....E...... 804 693-3606
  Gloucester *(G-5866)*
Vulcan Materials Company ....G...... 804 693-3606
  Gloucester *(G-5867)*
Walker Sand & Stone Inc ....E...... 540 775-5024
  King George *(G-7122)*
Wilson Ready Mix LLC ....G...... 540 324-0555
  Fishersville *(G-5013)*
Wilson Ready Mix LLC ....G...... 434 977-2800
  Charlottesville *(G-2715)*
Wright Inc W F ....F...... 804 561-2721
  Amelia Court House *(G-678)*

3274 Lime

Deavers Lime and Litter LLC ....G...... 540 833-4144
  Rockingham *(G-12247)*
▲ Frazier Quarry Incorporated ....E...... 540 434-6192
  Harrisonburg *(G-6317)*
Lhoist North America VA Inc ....C...... 540 626-7163
  Ripplemead *(G-11876)*
Rockydale Quarries Corporation.........D...... 540 774-1696
  Roanoke *(G-12170)*
Rockydale Quarries Corporation.........G...... 540 886-2111
  Staunton *(G-13286)*
Shen-Valley Lime Corp ....G...... 540 869-2700
  Stephens City *(G-13322)*
Sweet Lime Studios LLC ....G...... 703 312-0034
  Arlington *(G-1180)*

3275 Gypsum Prdts

Stowe Inc A D ....F...... 757 397-1842
  Portsmouth *(G-10487)*
Strober Building Supply ....G...... 540 834-2111
  Fredericksburg *(G-5369)*
United States Gypsum Company ....C...... 757 494-8100
  Norfolk *(G-9773)*
United States Gypsum Company ....C...... 276 496-7733
  Saltville *(G-12597)*

3281 Cut Stone Prdts

▲ Absolute Stone Design LLC..............E...... 804 752-2001
  Glen Allen *(G-5704)*
Alberene Soapstone Company ....G...... 434 831-1051
  Schuyler *(G-12650)*
▲ All Affairs Transportation LLC ....G...... 757 342-2474
  Newport News *(G-9162)*
Anseal Inc ....G...... 571 642-0680
  Lorton *(G-7462)*
Archna & Nazish Inc ....F...... 571 221-6224
  Chantilly *(G-2370)*
Austinville Limestone Co Inc..............E...... 276 699-6262
  Austinville *(G-1527)*
Best Granite & Marble ....G...... 703 455-0404
  Springfield *(G-12960)*
Better Granite Garcia LLC ....F...... 703 624-9912
  Manassas *(G-8038)*
Bishop Stone and Met Arts LLC ....G...... 804 240-1030
  Hanover *(G-6280)*
▲ Brazilian Best Granite Inc ....G...... 804 562-3022
  Richmond *(G-11132)*
Bybee Stone Co Inc ....G...... 812 876-2215
  Fredericksburg *(G-5406)*
Capitol Granite LLC ....E...... 804 379-2641
  Midlothian *(G-8790)*
Cardinal Stone Company Inc ....F...... 276 236-5457
  Galax *(G-5630)*
Chantilly Crushed Stone Inc ....E...... 703 471-4411
  Sterling *(G-13369)*
▲ Classic Granite and Marble Inc........F...... 804 404-8004
  Midlothian *(G-8796)*
Concrete Creations Inc..............G...... 757 427-6226
  Virginia Beach *(G-14359)*
Concrete Creations Inc..............G...... 757 427-1581
  Virginia Beach *(G-14360)*
De Carlo Enterprises Inc ....F...... 703 281-1880
  Vienna *(G-14036)*

E Dillon & Company ....D...... 276 873-6816
  Swords Creek *(G-13807)*
Elkwood Stone & Mulch LLC ....G...... 540 829-9273
  Elkwood *(G-4342)*
Empire Marble & Granite Co ....G...... 804 359-2004
  Richmond *(G-11574)*
Environmental Stoneworks LLC..............E...... 804 553-9560
  Richmond *(G-11204)*
Flagstone ....G...... 815 790-0582
  Alexandria *(G-463)*
Flagstone Oprting Partners LLC ....G...... 703 532-6238
  Mc Lean *(G-8433)*
Fleet Svcs & Installations LLC ....G...... 757 405-1405
  Portsmouth *(G-10431)*
Frazier Quarry Incorporated ....G...... 540 896-7538
  Timberville *(G-13849)*
▲ General Marble & Granite Co ....G...... 804 353-2761
  Richmond *(G-11215)*
Granite Countertop Experts LLC..............G...... 757 826-9316
  Newport News *(G-9238)*
Granite Countertops ....G...... 703 953-3330
  Chantilly *(G-2430)*
Granite Design Inc ....G...... 703 530-1223
  Manassas *(G-8076)*
Granite Top LLC ....G...... 703 257-0714
  Manassas *(G-7948)*
HB Inc ....G...... 757 291-5236
  Virginia Beach *(G-14511)*
Interlock Paving Systems Inc ....G...... 757 722-2591
  Hampton *(G-6176)*
James J Totaro Associates LLC ....G...... 703 326-9525
  Sterling *(G-13434)*
Jnlk Inc ....G...... 434 566-1037
  Louisa *(G-7557)*
John Wills Studios Inc ....F...... 757 468-0260
  Virginia Beach *(G-14572)*
Lakeside Stone & Landscape Sup ....G...... 434 738-3204
  Clarksville *(G-3632)*
Land Venture Two LC ....G...... 703 367-9456
  Manassas *(G-7961)*
Limestone Dust Corporation ....D...... 276 326-1103
  Bluefield *(G-1869)*
▲ Lorton Stone LLC ....E...... 703 923-9440
  Springfield *(G-13044)*
Luck Stone Corporation ....E...... 540 898-6060
  Fredericksburg *(G-5318)*
Luck Stone Corporation ....G...... 757 566-8676
  Newport News *(G-9287)*
◆ Luck Stone Corporation ....D...... 804 784-6300
  Manakin Sabot *(G-7901)*
Modern Exteriors ....F...... 703 978-8602
  Chantilly *(G-2464)*
New Worlds Stone Co Inc ....G...... 434 831-1051
  Schuyler *(G-12652)*
Oakes Memorials & Signs Inc..............G...... 434 836-5888
  Danville *(G-4018)*
Old Dominion Flagstone Inc ....G...... 540 553-0511
  Blacksburg *(G-1776)*
R & S Stone Inc ....G...... 540 745-6788
  Floyd *(G-5037)*
Ray Painter Small ....G...... 804 255-7050
  Chesterfield *(G-3520)*
Rockbridge Stone Products Inc ....G...... 540 258-2841
  Glasgow *(G-5701)*
▲ Signature Stone Corporation ....F...... 757 566-9094
  Toano *(G-13877)*
▲ Sky Marble & Granite Inc..............F...... 571 926-8085
  Sterling *(G-13510)*
Snt Trucking Inc ....G...... 276 991-0931
  Swords Creek *(G-13808)*
Stone Depot Granite ....F...... 703 926-3844
  Lorton *(G-7535)*
▲ Stone Dynamics Inc ....E...... 276 638-7755
  Martinsville *(G-8338)*
Stone Studio LLC ....G...... 703 263-9755
  Chantilly *(G-2500)*
Stone Terroir Usa LLC ....G...... 757 754-2434
  Chesterfield *(G-2591)*
V & P Investment LLC ....F...... 703 365-7835
  Manassas *(G-8009)*
V & P Investment LLC ....G...... 202 631-8596
  Charlottesville *(G-2709)*
Vetsusa II Inc ....E...... 703 300-9874
  Falls Church *(G-4889)*
Virginia Cast Stone Inc ....F...... 540 943-9808
  Waynesboro *(G-15143)*
Winn Stone Products Inc ....G...... 757 465-5363
  Portsmouth *(G-10505)*
Xteriors Manufacturing LLC..............G...... 804 445-3597
  Petersburg *(G-10353)*

Xteriors Pavers LLC ....G...... 757 708-5904
  Virginia Beach *(G-14949)*

3291 Abrasive Prdts

◆ Hermes Abr Ltd A Ltd Partnr ....C...... 800 464-8314
  Virginia Beach *(G-14519)*
Hermes Abrasives Inc ....G...... 757 486-6623
  Virginia Beach *(G-14520)*
Hone Blade LLC ....G...... 804 370-8598
  Mechanicsville *(G-8638)*
▲ International Carbide & Engrg ....F...... 434 568-3311
  Drakes Branch *(G-4133)*
Interntional Abrasive Pdts Inc ....G...... 540 797-7821
  Moneta *(G-8967)*
Mil-Spec Abrasives LLC ....F...... 757 927-6699
  Norfolk *(G-9644)*
◆ Virginia Abrasives Corporation........D...... 804 732-0058
  Petersburg *(G-10349)*
▲ Virginia Materials Inc ....G...... 800 321-2282
  Norfolk *(G-9784)*
◆ Winoa USA Inc ....E...... 540 586-0856
  Bedford *(G-1664)*

3292 Asbestos products

▲ James Hardie Building Pdts Inc ....D...... 540 980-9143
  Pulaski *(G-10639)*
McC Abatement LLC ....G...... 804 731-4238
  North Chesterfield *(G-9927)*
Northern Virginia Insulation ....G...... 703 753-7249
  Haymarket *(G-6431)*
Semco Services Inc ....E...... 540 885-7480
  Staunton *(G-13291)*

3295 Minerals & Earths: Ground Or Treated

Active Minerals International ....G...... 540 771-3865
  Winchester *(G-15371)*
◆ American Borate Corporation ....G...... 800 486-1072
  Chesapeake *(G-2964)*
ARC Dust LLC ....G...... 571 839-0223
  Alexandria *(G-417)*
Giant Resource Recovery Inc ....E...... 434 685-7021
  Cascade *(G-2251)*
◆ Industrial Minerals Inc ....G...... 540 297-8667
  Moneta *(G-8966)*
◆ Kyanite Mining Corporation ....G...... 434 983-2085
  Dillwyn *(G-4097)*
Madidrop Pbc Inc (used In) ....G...... 434 260-3767
  Charlottesville *(G-2831)*
Northeast Solite Corporation ....G...... 804 262-8119
  Richmond *(G-11308)*
Opta (usa) Inc ....G...... 843 296-7074
  Norfolk *(G-9677)*
▼ Virginia Vermiculite LLC ....E...... 540 967-2266
  Louisa *(G-7574)*

3296 Mineral Wool

Emtech Laboratories Inc ....E...... 540 265-9156
  Roanoke *(G-11921)*
Gel Formations LLC ....G...... 704 706-4606
  Richmond *(G-11598)*
Johns Manville Corporation ....B...... 540 984-4171
  Edinburg *(G-4307)*
Johns Manville Corporation ....B...... 804 261-7400
  Richmond *(G-11256)*

3297 Nonclay Refractories

Rex Materials Inc..............E...... 434 447-7659
  South Hill *(G-12858)*

3299 Nonmetallic Mineral Prdts, NEC

A B C Manufacturing Inc ....G...... 540 789-7961
  Willis *(G-15352)*
Central Virginia Stucco Inc ....G...... 434 531-0752
  Charlottesville *(G-2761)*
Cheyenne Autumn Arts ....G...... 804 745-9561
  Chesterfield *(G-3486)*
Costello Sculptures ....G...... 540 763-3433
  Willis *(G-15359)*
M T Stone and Stucco LLC ....G...... 434 806-7226
  Ruckersville *(G-12405)*
Polythane of Virginia Inc ....G...... 540 586-3511
  Bedford *(G-1651)*
Protomold ....G...... 540 542-1740
  Winchester *(G-15570)*
Rd Stucco LLC ....G...... 703 926-2322
  Arlington *(G-1141)*
Sculpture By Gary Stevenson ....G...... 757 486-5893
  Virginia Beach *(G-14798)*

S
I
C

Speed and Accuracy LLC ....G...... 405 375-3432
Herndon *(G-6813)*

▲ Spring Moses Inc ....G...... 804 321-0156
Richmond *(G-11395)*

33 PRIMARY METAL INDUSTRIES

3312 Blast Furnaces, Coke Ovens, Steel & Rolling Mills

ATI Development LLC ....G...... 571 313-0857
Sterling *(G-13355)*

ATI-Endyna Jv LLC ....G...... 410 992-3424
Mc Lean *(G-8397)*

Azz Inc ....E...... 276 466-5558
Bristol *(G-2007)*

Cashmere Handrails Inc ....G...... 757 838-2307
Newport News *(G-9194)*

▲ Chaparral (virginia) Inc ....B...... 972 647-7915
North Dinwiddie *(G-10049)*

Chaparral Virginia Inc ....G...... 540 767-1238
Roanoke *(G-12064)*

◆ Coal Fillers Inc ....G...... 276 322-4675
Bluefield *(G-1860)*

Colonial Rail Systems LLC ....G...... 804 932-5200
New Kent *(G-9129)*

Commercial Metals Company ....E...... 540 775-8501
King George *(G-7084)*

Commercial Metals Company ....F...... 757 625-4201
Norfolk *(G-9499)*

Diamond Source of Virginia ....G...... 804 360-3373
Richmond *(G-11185)*

Donnasatticofcrafts ....G...... 757 855-0559
Norfolk *(G-9531)*

Els Wheels LLC ....G...... 540 370-4397
Fredericksburg *(G-5428)*

Franklin Machine Shop ....G...... 757 241-6744
Hampton *(G-6152)*

General Iron and Steel Co Inc ....F...... 434 676-3975
Alberta *(G-98)*

Gerdau Ameristeel US Inc ....C...... 804 520-0286
North Dinwiddie *(G-10051)*

Greenbrook Tms Neurohealth Ctr ....G...... 804 980-7520
Glen Allen *(G-5738)*

Greenbrook Tms Neurohealth Ctr ....G...... 703 670-5738
Woodbridge *(G-15718)*

Greenbrook Tms Neurohealth Ctr ....G...... 855 998-4867
Roanoke *(G-11928)*

Greenbrook Tms Neurohealth Ctr ....G...... 855 998-4867
Virginia Beach *(G-14491)*

Greenbrook Tms Neurohealth Ctr ....G...... 855 940-4867
Fredericksburg *(G-5293)*

Greenbrook Tms Neurohealth Ctr ....G...... 434 327-1660
Charlottesville *(G-2639)*

Hampton Sheet Metal Inc ....E...... 757 249-1629
Newport News *(G-9242)*

Hanover Iron & Steel Inc ....F...... 804 798-5604
Ashland *(G-1428)*

Harbor Entps Ltd Lblty Co ....G...... 229 226-0911
Stafford *(G-13150)*

▼ Hubs and Wheels Emory Inc ....F...... 276 944-4900
Meadowview *(G-8595)*

Independent Stamping Inc ....G...... 540 949-6839
Waynesboro *(G-15115)*

Industrial Fabricators Inc ....F...... 540 989-0834
Roanoke *(G-11938)*

Innovative Machining Inc ....E...... 804 385-4212
Forest *(G-5077)*

Jeffs Tools Inc ....G...... 804 694-6337
Gloucester *(G-5851)*

K S E ....G...... 571 366-1715
Alexandria *(G-250)*

Karls Custom Wheels ....G...... 757 565-1997
Williamsburg *(G-15263)*

Lane Enterprises Inc ....E...... 540 674-4645
Dublin *(G-4163)*

Linx Industries Inc ....G...... 757 488-1144
Portsmouth *(G-10453)*

Loa Mals On Whels Wliamson Rd ....G...... 540 563-0482
Roanoke *(G-12128)*

Maverick Wheels LLC ....G...... 540 891-2681
Fredericksburg *(G-5323)*

Nucor Corporation ....G...... 804 379-3704
North Chesterfield *(G-9941)*

Old Dominion 4 Whl Drv CLB Inc ....G...... 804 750-2349
Richmond *(G-11312)*

Osborne Welding Inc ....E...... 757 487-0900
Portsmouth *(G-10466)*

Protective Solutions Inc ....D...... 703 435-1115
Dulles *(G-4220)*

▲ Reline America Inc ....E...... 276 496-4000
Saltville *(G-12588)*

◆ Roanoke Electric Steel Corp ....B...... 540 342-1831
Roanoke *(G-12165)*

Sam English of VA ....E...... 804 222-7114
Richmond *(G-11370)*

Steel Dynamics Inc ....A...... 540 342-1831
Roanoke *(G-12197)*

Stoner Steel Products ....G...... 434 973-4812
Charlottesville *(G-2697)*

Tidewater Rebar LLC ....F...... 757 325-9893
Suffolk *(G-13773)*

Tms International LLC ....G...... 804 957-9611
North Dinwiddie *(G-10066)*

Ultimate Wheel Svcs LLC ....G...... 703 237-1044
Falls Church *(G-4886)*

Voestlpine High Prfmce Mtls Co ....E...... 434 575-7994
South Boston *(G-12792)*

Washing On Wheels Inc ....G...... 276 699-6275
Ivanhoe *(G-7006)*

West End Fabricators Inc ....G...... 804 360-2106
Oilville *(G-10187)*

Wheels Tracks & Safety LLC ....G...... 434 846-8975
Lynchburg *(G-7839)*

Workers On Wheels ....G...... 703 549-6287
Alexandria *(G-388)*

Yocums Signature Hot Rods ....G...... 757 393-0700
Portsmouth *(G-10507)*

3315 Steel Wire Drawing & Nails & Spikes

C S Lewis & Sons LLC ....G...... 804 275-6879
North Chesterfield *(G-9838)*

Commercial Metals Company ....E...... 540 775-8501
King George *(G-7084)*

Dart Mechanical Inc ....G...... 757 539-2189
Suffolk *(G-13695)*

Intermet Foundries Inc ....G...... 434 528-8721
Lynchburg *(G-7744)*

Kybo Sales LLC ....G...... 276 431-2563
Duffield *(G-4180)*

NGL Woodbridge ....G...... 703 492-0430
Woodbridge *(G-15758)*

Thomas H Rhea MD PC ....G...... 703 658-0300
Annandale *(G-787)*

Times Fiber Communications Inc ....E...... 434 432-1800
Chatham *(G-2938)*

Touch Class Construction Corp ....G...... 757 728-3647
Newport News *(G-9360)*

Voestlpine High Prfmce Mtls Co ....E...... 434 575-7994
South Boston *(G-12792)*

3316 Cold Rolled Steel Sheet, Strip & Bars

◆ Framecad America Inc ....F...... 703 615-2451
Fairfax *(G-4626)*

Steel Dynamics Inc ....A...... 540 342-1831
Roanoke *(G-12197)*

Technology Hub Inc ....G...... 571 370-5100
Chantilly *(G-2508)*

Voestlpine High Prfmce Mtls Co ....E...... 434 575-7994
South Boston *(G-12792)*

3317 Steel Pipe & Tubes

C and S Precision Wel ....G...... 804 815-7963
Saluda *(G-12601)*

Dawson Enterprises Inc ....G...... 276 964-7245
Abingdon *(G-28)*

Noble-Met LLC ....C...... 540 389-7860
Salem *(G-12545)*

Raymond Dawson ....G...... 276 676-9068
Abingdon *(G-57)*

Skyline Fabricating Inc ....G...... 276 498-3560
Raven *(G-10758)*

Synalloy Corporation ....D...... 804 822-3260
Glen Allen *(G-5804)*

Tidewater Wldg Fabrication LLC ....G...... 757 636-6630
Chesapeake *(G-3340)*

Usui International Corporation ....B...... 757 558-7300
Chesapeake *(G-3356)*

3321 Gray Iron Foundries

Bingham & Taylor Corp ....C...... 540 825-8334
Culpeper *(G-3872)*

Cowden ....G...... 276 744-7120
Elk Creek *(G-4320)*

▲ Graham-White Manufacturing Co ....B...... 540 387-5600
Salem *(G-12513)*

Neenah Foundry Co ....G...... 804 758-9592
Urbanna *(G-13972)*

Nomar Castings Inc ....F...... 540 380-3394
Elliston *(G-4346)*

OK Foundry Company Inc ....G...... 804 233-9674
Richmond *(G-11698)*

R H Sheppard Co Inc ....F...... 276 228-4000
Wytheville *(G-15907)*

Walker Machine and Fndry Corp ....D...... 540 344-6265
Roanoke *(G-12226)*

3324 Steel Investment Foundries

Henry Bijak ....G...... 757 572-1673
Virginia Beach *(G-14516)*

Howmet Castings & Services Inc ....B...... 757 838-4680
Hampton *(G-6168)*

Howmet Corporation ....C...... 757 838-4680
Hampton *(G-6169)*

Nomar Castings Inc ....F...... 540 380-3394
Elliston *(G-4346)*

3325 Steel Foundries, NEC

DLM Enterprises Inc ....G...... 757 617-3470
Suffolk *(G-13700)*

Henry Bijak ....G...... 757 572-1673
Virginia Beach *(G-14516)*

Opta (usa) Inc ....G...... 843 296-7074
Norfolk *(G-9677)*

Thistle Foundry & Mch Co Inc ....F...... 276 326-1196
Bluefield *(G-1881)*

3331 Primary Smelting & Refining Of Copper

Mills Marine & Ship Repair LLC ....G...... 757 539-0956
Suffolk *(G-13744)*

3334 Primary Production Of Aluminum

Howmet Aerospace Inc ....C...... 804 281-2262
Richmond *(G-11243)*

3339 Primary Nonferrous Metals, NEC

Bulldog Precious Metals ....G...... 540 312-1234
Vinton *(G-14167)*

Gold Spot ....G...... 804 708-0275
Goochland *(G-5883)*

Jr Kauffman Inc ....F...... 276 228-7070
Wytheville *(G-15894)*

Precious Time LLC ....G...... 804 343-4380
Richmond *(G-11722)*

Rapid Mat Group LLC ....G...... 703 629-2426
Mc Lean *(G-8532)*

Virginia Semiconductor Inc ....E...... 540 373-2900
Fredericksburg *(G-5233)*

3341 Secondary Smelting & Refining Of Nonferrous Metals

Aleris Rolled Products Inc ....D...... 804 714-2100
North Chesterfield *(G-9810)*

Aow Global LLC ....G...... 757 228-5557
Chesapeake *(G-2976)*

▲ Atomized Products Group Inc ....G...... 434 263-4551
Lovingston *(G-7588)*

Casson Art & Frame ....G...... 276 638-1450
Martinsville *(G-8274)*

Fred Sisson ....G...... 843 641-7155
Prince George *(G-10594)*

Saudi Trade Links ....G...... 703 992-3220
Berryville *(G-1688)*

South Western Services Inc ....G...... 540 947-5407
Montvale *(G-9030)*

▼ Universal Impex LLC ....G...... 202 322-4100
Glen Allen *(G-5820)*

Voestlpine High Prfmce Mtls Co ....E...... 434 575-7994
South Boston *(G-12792)*

3351 Rolling, Drawing & Extruding Of Copper

▲ Cerro Fabricated Products LLC ....D...... 540 208-1606
Weyers Cave *(G-15171)*

▲ Optical Cable Corporation ....C...... 540 265-0690
Roanoke *(G-11978)*

3353 Aluminum Sheet, Plate & Foil

Aleris Rolled Products Inc ....D...... 804 714-2180
North Chesterfield *(G-9811)*

◆ Ball Advanced Alum Tech Corp ....C...... 540 248-2703
Verona *(G-13983)*

Hampton Sheet Metal Inc ....E...... 757 249-1629
Newport News *(G-9242)*

Howmet Aerospace Inc ....G...... 757 461-1360
Norfolk *(G-9583)*

Howmet Aerospace Inc ....G..... 540 343-1591
Roanoke (G-12103)
▲ Manakin Industries LLC ....G... 804 784-5514
Manakin Sabot (G-7903)
Mottley Foils Inc.........................F..... 434 392-8347
Farmville (G-4952)
Reynolds Cnsmr Pdts Hldngs Inc ....C..... 540 249-5711
Grottoes (G-6024)
Reynolds Consumer Products LLC ......F..... 804 743-6000
North Chesterfield (G-9959)
Reynolds Consumer Products LLC ......B..... 804 230-5200
Richmond (G-11735)
Skyline Fabricating Inc................G..... 276 498-3560
Raven (G-10758)
Universal Impact Inc....................G..... 540 885-8676
Waynesboro (G-15141)

3354 Aluminum Extruded Prdts

◆ Ball Advanced Alum Tech Corp ....C..... 540 248-2703
Verona (G-13983)
Crown Cork & Seal Usa Inc ....B..... 540 662-2591
Winchester (G-15408)
◆ Electro-Mechanical Corporation ......B..... 276 669-4084
Bristol (G-1975)
▲ Hanover Foils LLC ....E..... 804 496-5835
Ashland (G-1426)
Hy-Mark Cylinders Inc ....E..... 757 251-6744
Hampton (G-6173)
Kaiser Aluminum Corporation ....B..... 804 743-6405
North Chesterfield (G-9904)
Kaiser Bellwood Corporation ....D..... 804 743-6300
North Chesterfield (G-9905)
Kearney-National Inc ....C..... 276 628-7171
Abingdon (G-47)
Latham Architectural Pdts Inc ....G..... 804 308-2205
Midlothian (G-8844)
Liphart Steel Company Inc............E..... 540 248-1009
Verona (G-13991)
◆ Marion Mold & Tool Inc ....E..... 276 783-6101
Marion (G-8234)
Montebello Packaging Inc..............C..... 540 437-0119
Harrisonburg (G-6348)
Naito America ....E..... 804 550-3305
Ashland (G-1468)
▲ Neuman Almnium Impact Extrsion ....G..... 540 248-2703
Waynesboro (G-15129)
Optikinetics Ltd ....G..... 800 575-6784
Ashland (G-1473)
Penny Plate LLC.........................D..... 540 337-3777
Fishersville (G-5006)
◆ Service Center Metals LLC ....C..... 804 518-1550
Prince George (G-10607)
Tredegar Corporation ....C..... 804 330-1000
North Chesterfield (G-10030)
◆ Tredegar Corporation..................D..... 804 330-1000
North Chesterfield (G-10029)
William L Bonnell Company Inc ....G..... 804 330-1147
North Chesterfield (G-10045)

3355 Aluminum Rolling & Drawing, NEC

Millers Custom Metal Svcs LLC..............G..... 804 712-2588
Deltaville (G-4084)
Mitsubishi Chemical Amer Inc /..............G..... 757 382-5750
Chesapeake (G-3207)
Panel Systems Inc ....E..... 703 910-6285
Woodbridge (G-15772)

3356 Rolling, Drawing-Extruding Of Nonferrous Metals

Fred Sisson ....G..... 843 641-7155
Prince George (G-10594)
Hwte Tin Han ....G..... 757 261-5963
Norfolk (G-9587)
Kcsl ....G..... 276 206-5977
Abingdon (G-46)
▲ Kd Cartridges ....G..... 434 865-3328
South Hill (G-12855)
Lane Enterprises Inc ....E..... 540 674-4645
Dublin (G-4163)
Li DDS Pllc Tin W ....G..... 703 352-2500
Fairfax (G-4647)
Lucas-Milhaupt Inc ....G..... 276 591-3351
Bristol (G-1982)
Magnesium Music ....G..... 703 798-5516
Alexandria (G-520)
Marion Nickel ....G..... 703 444-8158
Sterling (G-13448)
Opta (usa) Inc ....G..... 843 296-7074
Norfolk (G-9677)

Titanium 3 LLC ....G..... 617 417-9288
Mc Lean (G-8568)
Titanium Productions Inc ....G..... 757 351-2526
Norfolk (G-9759)
Voestlpine High Prfmce Mtls Co.........E..... 434 575-7994
South Boston (G-12792)
W & O Supply Inc ....E..... 757 967-9959
Portsmouth (G-10500)

3357 Nonferrous Wire Drawing

AFL Network Services Inc.............G..... 864 433-0333
Chesapeake (G-2955)
Algonquin Industries Inc..............E..... 804 550-5401
Ashland (G-1365)
Cable Systems ....G..... 757 853-6313
Norfolk (G-9473)
Core Business Technologies Inc.........G..... 757 426-0344
Virginia Beach (G-14365)
Corning Incorporated ....G..... 703 471-5955
Manassas (G-8052)
Frank M Churillo ....E..... 434 242-6895
Charlottesville (G-2633)
Global Com Inc ....G..... 703 532-6425
Sterling (G-13412)
Irflex Corporation ....G..... 434 483-4304
Danville (G-4003)
JP Nino Corp ....G..... 775 636-8682
Falls Church (G-4811)
Mantis Networks LLC ....G..... 571 306-1234
Reston (G-10894)
▼ Mg Corp ....A..... 757 468-6000
Virginia Beach (G-14648)
Mimetrix Technologies LLC ....G..... 571 306-1234
Vienna (G-14094)
▲ Optical Cable Corporation ....C..... 540 265-0690
Roanoke (G-11978)
◆ Pyott-Boone Electronics Inc ....C..... 276 988-5505
North Tazewell (G-10105)
Smart Start of Glen Allen ....G..... 804 447-7642
Richmond (G-11385)
Te Connectivity ....F..... 540 812-9126
Culpeper (G-3924)
Times Fiber Communications Inc.........C..... 434 432-1800
Chatham (G-2937)
Times Fiber Communications Inc.........C..... 434 432-1800
Chatham (G-2938)
Virginia Insulated Products Co..........F..... 276 496-5136
Saltville (G-12598)
Virginia Insulated Products Co..........F..... 276 496-5136
Saltville (G-12599)
Walton Wiring Inc ....G..... 804 556-3104
Maidens (G-7893)

3363 Aluminum Die Castings

▲ Appalachian Cast Products Inc ....C..... 276 619-5080
Abingdon (G-12)
Bonrick Molds ....G..... 540 898-1512
Fredericksburg (G-5254)
Limatherm Usa Inc.......................G..... 540 402-4060
Leesburg (G-7301)

3364 Nonferrous Die Castings, Exc Aluminum

Bonrick Molds ....G..... 540 898-1512
Fredericksburg (G-5254)
Wegner Metal Arts Inc ....G..... 540 373-5662
Fredericksburg (G-5235)

3365 Aluminum Foundries

Acp LLC ....G..... 276 619-5080
Abingdon (G-6)
G N H & Associates Inc ....G..... 276 632-7867
Axton (G-1537)
Nomar Castings Inc ....F..... 540 380-3394
Elliston (G-4346)
OK Foundry Company Inc ....E..... 804 233-9674
Richmond (G-11698)
▲ Rolls-Royce Crosspointe LLC ....F..... 877 787-6247
Prince George (G-10606)

3366 Copper Foundries

Anne Chapman Casting ....G..... 804 728-1300
Richmond (G-11114)
Chesapeake Propeller LLC ....G..... 804 421-7991
Richmond (G-11156)
Hanover Brassfoundry ....G..... 804 781-1864
Mechanicsville (G-8634)
Lynchburg Machining LLC ....F..... 434 846-7327
Lynchburg (G-7762)

Nomar Castings Inc ....F..... 540 380-3394
Elliston (G-4346)
Propeller Club of The U S Port ....G..... 703 922-6933
Alexandria (G-561)
Turner Sculpture Ltd ....E..... 757 787-2818
Melfa (G-8713)

3369 Nonferrous Foundries: Castings, NEC

Colonial Commercial Elec Co..........G..... 804 720-2455
King Queen Ch (G-7125)
Cryoscience Technologies.................G..... 516 338-6723
Brandy Station (G-1938)
Equestrian Forge Inc ....G..... 703 777-2110
Leesburg (G-7269)
NMB Metals..................................G..... 434 584-0027
South Hill (G-12857)
R H Sheppard Co Inc ....F..... 276 228-4000
Wytheville (G-15907)
Southern Casting LLC ....G..... 757 233-1700
Norfolk (G-9732)
Tidewater Castings Inc ....G..... 757 399-0679
Portsmouth (G-10491)

3398 Metal Heat Treating

Analytic Stress Relieving Inc..........G..... 804 271-5447
North Chesterfield (G-9817)
East Crlina Metal Treating Inc..........G..... 434 333-4412
Lynchburg (G-7699)
L & R Precision Tooling Inc ....E..... 434 525-4120
Lynchburg (G-7752)
National Peening Inc ....G..... 540 387-3522
Salem (G-12543)
Southwest Specialty Heat Treat ....F..... 276 228-7739
Wytheville (G-15916)
Stihl Incorporated ....E..... 757 468-4010
Virginia Beach (G-14848)
Stihl Incorporated ....G..... 757 368-2409
Virginia Beach (G-14849)

3399 Primary Metal Prdts, NEC

Eastman Performance Films LLC........D..... 423 224-7768
Martinsville (G-8283)
H & B Machine ....G..... 276 546-5307
Keokee (G-7040)
J & J Powder Coating ....G..... 757 406-2922
Virginia Beach (G-14555)
Moore Metal..................................G..... 757 930-0849
Newport News (G-9305)

34 FABRICATED METAL PRODUCTS, EXCEPT MACHINERY AND TRANSPORTATION EQUIPMENT

3411 Metal Cans

Ball Metal Beverage Cont Corp ....C..... 757 887-2062
Williamsburg (G-15209)
Crown Cork & Seal Usa Inc ....B..... 540 662-2591
Winchester (G-15408)
Crown Cork & Seal Usa Inc ....E..... 757 538-1318
Suffolk (G-13690)
Loco Crazy Good Inc ....G..... 703 401-4058
Ashburn (G-1310)
Penny Plate LLC.........................D..... 540 337-3777
Fishersville (G-5006)
Reynolds Cnsmr Pdts Hldngs Inc ....C..... 540 249-5711
Grottoes (G-6024)
Reynolds Metals Company LLC ....G..... 804 746-6723
Richmond (G-11353)
Sonoco Products Company ....E..... 757 539-8349
Suffolk (G-13766)
Stratos LLC ....G..... 800 213-4705
Richmond (G-11399)
Van Addo Dorn LLC ....G..... 703 615-4769
Arlington (G-1207)
Van Dorn Pawn ....G..... 703 924-9800
Alexandria (G-603)

3412 Metal Barrels, Drums, Kegs & Pails

Blue Ridge Packaging Corp..............E..... 276 638-1413
Martinsville (G-8270)
▲ C & A Cutter Head Inc ....G..... 276 646-5548
Chilhowie (G-3546)

3421 Cutlery

A & T Partners Inc ....G..... 703 707-8246
Herndon (G-6600)

S I C

◆ Accutec Blades Inc ....C 800 336-4061
  Verona *(G-13982)*
All About Cupcakes ....G 757 619-5931
  Smithfield *(G-12702)*
Angeethi Winchester LLC ....G 703 300-7488
  Winchester *(G-15527)*
Buttercream Dreams LLC ....G 540 234-0058
  Weyers Cave *(G-15168)*
Catoctin Edges LLC ....G 540 687-1244
  Purcellville *(G-10655)*
Classic Edge LLC ....G 804 794-4256
  Midlothian *(G-8795)*
Edmund Davidson ....G 540 997-5651
  Goshen *(G-5924)*
Energizer Personal Care LLC ....B 540 248-9734
  Verona *(G-13986)*
High Peaks Knife Works ....G 276 694-6563
  Stuart *(G-13616)*
Horsemans Knives LLC ....G 540 854-6975
  Locust Grove *(G-7446)*
▲ Jackson 20 ....G 703 842-2790
  Alexandria *(G-242)*
Lil Divas Mobile Spa LLC ....G 757 386-1455
  Norfolk *(G-9619)*
Marin ....G 703 354-1950
  Annandale *(G-771)*
Mazzika Inc ....G 757 489-0028
  Norfolk *(G-9635)*
Meissner Cstm Knives Pens LLC ....G 321 693-2392
  Hampton *(G-6195)*
Ni PHI Thach ....G 434 386-8852
  Madison Heights *(G-7878)*
Ninees Gourmet Ice Cream ....G 703 451-4124
  Springfield *(G-13059)*
No Lie Blades LLC ....G 610 442-5539
  Virginia Beach *(G-14682)*
Palawan Blade LLC ....G 434 294-2065
  New Market *(G-9147)*
▲ Patrick Pierce ....G 804 833-1800
  Henrico *(G-6546)*
Peters Knives ....G 703 255-5353
  Vienna *(G-14110)*
R3 Blades LLC ....G 571 234-3068
  Manassas *(G-7993)*
Sweet Sprinkles ....G 540 373-4750
  Fredericksburg *(G-5490)*
Sword & Shield Coaching LLC ....G 804 557-3937
  Quinton *(G-10700)*
Turner Bragg ....G 804 752-2244
  Ashland *(G-1504)*
Two Swords Strategies LLC ....G 804 337-3103
  Richmond *(G-11424)*
Virginia Blade Inc ....G 434 384-1282
  Lynchburg *(G-7833)*
Virginia Eagle Distrg Co LLC ....G 434 296-5531
  Charlottesville *(G-2900)*
Watkins Products ....G 757 461-2800
  Norfolk *(G-9793)*

3423 Hand & Edge Tools

All Tools Inc ....G 804 598-1549
  Powhatan *(G-10529)*
Antex Usa Inc ....G 804 693-0831
  Hayes *(G-6395)*
Anthony George Ltd Inc ....G 434 369-1204
  Altavista *(G-625)*
Autogrip Inc ....G 703 372-5520
  Springfield *(G-12955)*
Bargers Custom Cabinets LLC ....G 540 261-7230
  Buena Vista *(G-2139)*
▲ Cadence Inc ....G 540 248-2200
  Staunton *(G-13245)*
Calbico LLC ....G 571 332-3334
  Annandale *(G-733)*
Caspian Inc ....G 434 237-1900
  Lynchburg *(G-7675)*
CLC Enterprises LLC ....G 540 622-3488
  Flint Hill *(G-5015)*
Ferguson Manufacturing Co Inc ....F 757 539-3409
  Suffolk *(G-13709)*
Geralds Tools Inc ....G 276 889-2964
  Lebanon *(G-7192)*
J W Altizer ....G 540 382-2652
  Christiansburg *(G-3600)*
Jaco Manufacturing Inc ....F 276 783-2688
  Atkins *(G-1519)*
James Pirtle ....G 540 477-2647
  Mount Jackson *(G-9073)*
Macklin Consulting LLC ....G 202 423-9923
  Alexandria *(G-269)*

Monikev-Fisher LLC ....G 757 343-4153
  Virginia Beach *(G-14662)*
Nathan Group LLC ....G 757 229-8703
  Williamsburg *(G-15282)*
Poquoson Enterprises ....G 757 876-6655
  Poquoson *(G-10375)*
Proskit Usa LLC ....G 804 240-9355
  Amelia Court House *(G-668)*
Skips Tools Inc ....G 757 621-4775
  Virginia Beach *(G-14824)*
Smartech Inc ....G 804 798-8588
  Ashland *(G-1492)*
Superior Magnetic Product ....G 804 752-7897
  Glen Allen *(G-5803)*

3425 Hand Saws & Saw Blades

Alegria John ....G 703 398-6009
  Manassas Park *(G-8186)*
Formable Grabber Inc ....G 434 298-4722
  Covington *(G-3789)*
▲ International Carbide & Engrg ....F 434 568-3311
  Drakes Branch *(G-4133)*
Reeds Carbide Saw Service ....F 434 846-6436
  Lynchburg *(G-7800)*

3429 Hardware, NEC

▲ A-1 Security Mfg Corp ....F 804 359-9003
  Richmond *(G-11078)*
Accurate Machine Inc ....G 757 853-2136
  Norfolk *(G-9418)*
Advantus Corp ....D 804 324-7169
  Petersburg *(G-10301)*
Aerial Machine & Tool Corp ....G 276 694-3148
  Stuart *(G-13603)*
▲ Aerial Machine & Tool Corp ....D 276 952-2006
  Meadows of Dan *(G-8590)*
◆ American Diesel Corp ....G 804 435-3107
  Kilmarnock *(G-7068)*
Boom Bass Cabinets Inc ....G 301 343-4918
  Dumfries *(G-4237)*
Cabinet Lifts Unlimited ....G 757 641-9431
  Virginia Beach *(G-14309)*
Dixon Powhatan ....G 410 810-7585
  Winchester *(G-15410)*
Dixon Valve & Coupling Co LLC ....G 540 535-2181
  Winchester *(G-15411)*
Dometic Corporation ....C 804 746-1313
  Mechanicsville *(G-8618)*
Dormakaba USA Inc ....F 804 966-9166
  South Chesterfield *(G-12801)*
Fabriction Spclist of Virginia ....G 757 620-2540
  Virginia Beach *(G-14458)*
Fastware Inc ....G 703 680-5050
  Manassas *(G-8070)*
Frank For All Ingnitions Keys ....G 804 663-5222
  Richmond *(G-11212)*
Gibson Good Tools Inc ....G 540 249-5100
  Grottoes *(G-6019)*
Grilletech LLC ....G 434 941-7129
  Lynchburg *(G-7726)*
H & B Machine ....G 276 546-5307
  Keokee *(G-7040)*
Hearth & Home Technologies LLC ....G 434 589-1482
  Troy *(G-13928)*
Hearth & Home Technologies LLC ....G 703 367-9413
  Manassas *(G-7950)*
International Automotive Compo ....A 540 465-3741
  Strasburg *(G-13585)*
Jack Clamp Sales Co Inc ....G 757 827-6704
  Hampton *(G-6177)*
Jones Family Office ....G 305 304-3603
  Bristow *(G-2057)*
Key Made Now ....G 804 663-5192
  Glen Allen *(G-5761)*
▲ Linear Devices Corporation ....G 804 368-8428
  Ashland *(G-1453)*
Lone Fountain Ldscp & Hdwr Ctr ....G 540 886-7605
  Staunton *(G-13277)*
M2m LLC ....G 816 204-0938
  Manassas *(G-8103)*
Malpass Construction Co Inc ....G 757 543-3541
  Chesapeake *(G-3195)*
Maritime Associates Inc ....G 571 212-0655
  Alexandria *(G-270)*
ML Manufacturing ....G 434 581-2000
  New Canton *(G-9118)*
Nova Fire Supply LLC ....G 703 909-8339
  Round Hill *(G-12384)*
Premier Manufacturing Inc ....E 757 967-9959
  Portsmouth *(G-10472)*

▲ Rutherford Controls Intl Corp ....F 757 427-1230
  Virginia Beach *(G-14786)*
▲ Schock Metal America Inc ....F 757 549-8300
  Chesapeake *(G-3288)*
▲ Secutor Systems LLC ....G 757 646-9350
  Virginia Beach *(G-14802)*
▲ Simplicikey LLC ....E 703 904-5010
  Herndon *(G-6808)*
Trimark Associates ....G 703 369-9494
  Springfield *(G-13102)*
Valley Doors Unlimited LLC ....G 540 638-0167
  Penn Laird *(G-10290)*
Weiss Soni ....G 703 264-5848
  Reston *(G-10989)*

3431 Enameled Iron & Metal Sanitary Ware

▲ Allied Brass Inc ....E 540 967-5970
  Louisa *(G-7545)*
Ferguson Portable Toilets LLC ....G 434 610-9988
  Appomattox *(G-811)*
▲ Rain Forest Shower System LLC .....G 804 432-8930
  Henrico *(G-6554)*
Sink of America Inc ....G 804 269-1111
  Glen Allen *(G-5799)*

3432 Plumbing Fixture Fittings & Trim, Brass

▲ Allied Brass Inc ....E 540 967-5970
  Louisa *(G-7545)*
Bartrack Inc ....G 717 521-4840
  Rockingham *(G-12241)*
C & F Plumbing ....G 757 606-3124
  Portsmouth *(G-10402)*
Cardinal Park Unit Owners ....G 703 777-2311
  Leesburg *(G-7240)*
▲ Coyne & Delany Company ....E 434 296-0166
  Charlottesville *(G-2773)*
CPS Contractors Inc ....G 804 561-6834
  Moseley *(G-9036)*
Doherty Plumbng Co ....G 757 842-4221
  Chesapeake *(G-3070)*
Euro Design Builders Group ....G 571 236-6189
  Fairfax *(G-4452)*
Greenacre Plumbing LLC ....G 703 680-2380
  Woodbridge *(G-15717)*
Hunter Industries Incorporated ....G 804 739-8978
  Midlothian *(G-8829)*
Mm Export LLC ....G 757 333-0542
  Virginia Beach *(G-14658)*
Nasoni LLC ....G 757 358-7475
  Suffolk *(G-13749)*
Nibco Inc ....B 540 324-0242
  Buena Vista *(G-2149)*
Pk Plumbing Inc ....G 804 909-4160
  Powhatan *(G-10566)*

3433 Heating Eqpt

◆ Alfa Laval Inc ....C 866 253-2528
  Richmond *(G-11095)*
American Solar Inc ....G 703 346-6053
  Annandale *(G-730)*
▲ Best Green Technologies LLC ....F 888 424-8432
  Glen Allen *(G-5707)*
Des Champs Technologies Inc ....C 540 291-1111
  Buena Vista *(G-2141)*
▲ England Stove Works ....G 434 929-0120
  Madison Heights *(G-7871)*
▲ Englands Stove Works Inc ....C 434 929-0120
  Monroe *(G-8989)*
Fives N Amercn Combustn Inc ....G 540 735-8052
  Fredericksburg *(G-5185)*
Houghtaling Associates Inc ....G 804 740-7098
  Richmond *(G-11242)*
KMW Works LLC ....G 757 776-6765
  Virginia Beach *(G-14591)*
Latimer Julian Manufacturing ....G 804 405-6851
  Richmond *(G-11267)*
Modine Manufacturing Company ....E 540 261-9821
  Buena Vista *(G-2148)*
Nellie Harris ....G 434 277-8511
  Lowesville *(G-7597)*
Nova Green Energy LLC ....G 571 210-0589
  Falls Church *(G-4847)*
Old Mill Mechanical Inc ....G 804 932-5060
  New Kent *(G-9137)*
PSL America Inc ....G 703 279-6426
  Fairfax *(G-4664)*
Solar Electric America LLC ....G 804 332-6358
  North Chesterfield *(G-10024)*
Sun Rnr of Virginia Inc ....G 540 271-3403
  Harrisonburg *(G-6376)*

Super RAD Coils Ltd Partnr ....C 804 794-2887
North Chesterfield *(G-9992)*

Virginia Blower Company ....E 276 647-3804
Collinsville *(G-3718)*

Wammoth Services LLC ....G 571 309-2969
Woodbridge *(G-15829)*

3441 Fabricated Structural Steel

4 Shores Trnsprting Lgstix LLC ....G 804 319-6247
Richmond *(G-11074)*

Aandc Sales Inc ....G 703 638-8949
Woodbridge *(G-15641)*

Abingdon Steel Inc ....E 276 628-9269
Abingdon *(G-5)*

Absolute Machine Enterprises ....F 276 956-1171
Ridgeway *(G-11838)*

Advance Mezzanine Systems LLC ....G 703 595-1460
Fredericksburg *(G-5168)*

Alliance Stl Fabrications Inc ....F 703 631-2355
Manassas Park *(G-8187)*

Am-Corcom Inc ....E 540 349-5895
Culpeper *(G-3865)*

American Mtal Fabrications Inc ....E 804 271-8355
Richmond *(G-11026)*

AMF Metal Inc ....G 703 354-1345
Springfield *(G-12947)*

AMF Metal Art Inc ....G 703 354-1345
Fairfax *(G-4407)*

▲ Appalachian Machine Inc ....F 540 674-1914
Dublin *(G-4148)*

Associated Fabricators LLC ....G 434 293-2333
Charlottesville *(G-2731)*

Astra Design Inc ....G 804 257-5467
Richmond *(G-11493)*

▲ Atlantic Metal Products Inc ....E 804 758-4915
Topping *(G-13885)*

B & L Mch & Fabrication Inc ....F 757 853-1800
Norfolk *(G-9449)*

▲ Banker Steel Co LLC ....C 434 847-4575
Lynchburg *(G-7648)*

Bingham Enterprises LLC ....G 434 645-1731
Crewe *(G-3808)*

Blue Ridge Fabricators Inc ....F 540 342-1102
Roanoke *(G-12049)*

Bobby Burns Nowlin ....F 757 827-1588
Hampton *(G-6097)*

Bohling Steel Inc ....E 434 385-5175
Lynchburg *(G-7657)*

Bolling Steel Co Inc ....E 540 380-4402
Salem *(G-12484)*

Broadway Metal Works Inc ....E 540 896-7027
Broadway *(G-2086)*

Brookneal Machine Shop Inc ....G 434 376-2413
Brookneal *(G-2108)*

Browns Welding & Trailer Repr ....G 276 628-4461
Abingdon *(G-17)*

Bullet Enterprises Inc ....G 757 897-9100
Keswick *(G-7044)*

Byers Inc ....E 540 949-8092
Waynesboro *(G-15102)*

C M C Steel Fabricators Inc ....E 540 898-1111
Fredericksburg *(G-5256)*

C Y J Enterprises Corp ....G 703 367-7722
Manassas *(G-8043)*

Carbon & Steel LLC ....G 757 871-1808
Toano *(G-13859)*

Carico Inc ....E 540 373-5983
Fredericksburg *(G-5176)*

Carter Iron and Steel Co ....E 757 826-4559
Hampton *(G-6107)*

Cave Hill Corporation ....E 540 289-5051
McGaheysville *(G-8584)*

Cave Systems Inc ....G 877 344-2283
Henrico *(G-6489)*

Century Steel Products Inc ....E 703 471-7606
Sterling *(G-13367)*

Champion Iron Works Inc ....E 540 955-3633
Berryville *(G-1673)*

Cives Corporation ....C 540 667-3480
Winchester *(G-15402)*

▼ Clinch River LLC ....D 276 963-5271
Tazewell *(G-13830)*

Colonial Wldg Fabrication Inc ....E 757 459-2680
Norfolk *(G-9494)*

Colonnas Ship Yard Inc ....B 757 545-5311
Norfolk *(G-9496)*

Cooper Steel of Virginia LLC ....E 931 205-6117
Monroe *(G-8988)*

Craft Machine Works Inc ....D 757 310-6011
Hampton *(G-6119)*

Craft Mch Wrks Acquisition LLC ....E 757 310-6011
Hampton *(G-6120)*

Creative Fabrication Inc ....E 540 931-4877
Covington *(G-3785)*

CSC Family Holdings Inc ....D 276 669-6649
Bristol *(G-2015)*

Custom Fabricators Inc ....E 757 724-0305
Windsor *(G-15603)*

Custom Metalsmith Inc ....E 276 988-0330
North Tazewell *(G-10097)*

Custom Welding Inc ....G 757 220-1995
Williamsburg *(G-15227)*

▲ D & R USA Inc ....E 434 572-6665
South Boston *(G-12758)*

Dalmatian Hill Engneering ....G 540 289-5079
Port Republic *(G-10383)*

Danny Coltrane ....F 540 629-3814
Radford *(G-10711)*

Delaware Valley Communications ....G 434 823-2282
Charlottesville *(G-2616)*

Dominion Steel Inc ....F 540 898-1249
Fredericksburg *(G-5276)*

Dove Welding and Fabrication ....F 757 262-0996
Hampton *(G-6131)*

Driveline Fabrications Inc ....G 540 483-3590
Rocky Mount *(G-12319)*

East Cast Repr Fabrication LLC ....C 757 455-9600
Norfolk *(G-9535)*

▲ East Coast Stl Fabrication Inc ....E 757 351-2601
Chesapeake *(G-3082)*

Edisons One Off Fbrcations LLC ....G 540 869-5703
Stephens City *(G-13316)*

Elite Fabrication LLC ....G 434 251-2639
Dry Fork *(G-4141)*

Entwistle Company ....E 434 799-6186
Danville *(G-3992)*

Esskay Structures Inc ....G 571 242-0011
Vienna *(G-14050)*

Excel Tool Inc ....F 276 322-0223
Falls Mills *(G-4931)*

Extreme Steel Inc ....D 540 868-9150
Warrenton *(G-15007)*

Extreme Steel Inc ....G 540 868-9150
Winchester *(G-15417)*

Fairlead Integrated LLC ....C 757 384-1957
Portsmouth *(G-10425)*

Fairlead Intgrted Pwr Cntrls L ....F 757 384-1957
Portsmouth *(G-10427)*

Fairlead Prcsion Mfg Intgrtion ....G 757 384-1957
Portsmouth *(G-10429)*

Family Crafters of Virginia ....G 540 943-3934
Waynesboro *(G-15114)*

Fei Inc ....F 540 291-3398
Natural Bridge Stati *(G-9109)*

Fields Inc Oscar S ....E 804 798-3900
Ashland *(G-1416)*

Firedog Fabricators ....G 540 809-7389
Goldvein *(G-5878)*

Flowers Steel LLC ....G 540 424-8377
Sumerduck *(G-13791)*

Foley Material Handling Co Inc ....D 804 798-1343
Ashland *(G-1419)*

Formex LLC ....F 804 231-1988
Richmond *(G-11593)*

Fredericksburg Mch & Stl LLC ....G 540 373-7957
Fredericksburg *(G-5189)*

Frost Industries Inc ....G 804 724-0330
Heathsville *(G-6462)*

Full Awn Fab LLC ....G 540 439-5173
Bealeton *(G-1599)*

Gerdau Ameristeel US Inc ....E 434 517-0715
South Boston *(G-12772)*

Great White Buffalo Entps LLC ....G 434 329-1150
Lynchburg *(G-7724)*

Hamilton Iron Works Inc ....E 703 497-4766
Woodbridge *(G-15720)*

Hanson Industries Inc ....G 434 845-9091
Lynchburg *(G-7728)*

Hbi Custom Fabrication LLC ....G 305 916-0161
Gloucester *(G-5850)*

Heavy Metal Construction Inc ....G 434 547-8061
Chase City *(G-2912)*

Hercules Steel Company Inc ....G 434 535-8571
Jarratt *(G-7010)*

Hi-Tech Machining LLC ....G 434 993-3256
Concord *(G-3760)*

Hucks & Hucks LLC ....G 276 525-1100
Abingdon *(G-41)*

Industrial Fabricators Inc ....F 540 989-0834
Roanoke *(G-11938)*

Industrial Fabricators VA Inc ....D 540 943-5885
Fishersville *(G-5005)*

Industrial Machine Works Inc ....E 540 949-6115
Waynesboro *(G-15116)*

Industrial Metalcraft Inc ....G 757 898-9350
Yorktown *(G-15965)*

Innovative Tech Intl Inc ....E 434 239-1979
Lynchburg *(G-7740)*

J C Steel De Tech ....G 757 376-7469
Virginia Beach *(G-14558)*

J&T Wlding Fbrication Campbell ....F 434 369-8589
Altavista *(G-632)*

Jarrett Welding and Mch Inc ....E 434 793-3717
Danville *(G-4006)*

Jetts Sheet Metal Inc ....G 540 899-7725
Fredericksburg *(G-5444)*

Joy Global Underground Min LLC ....C 276 623-2000
Abingdon *(G-45)*

Kennedy Konstruction Kompany ....E 540 984-4191
Edinburg *(G-4308)*

Key Bridge Global LLC ....G 703 414-3500
Mc Lean *(G-8479)*

KG Old Ox Holdings Inc ....E 703 471-5321
Sterling *(G-13438)*

Kitchens Welding Inc ....G 757 653-2500
Courtland *(G-3771)*

Lapp Metals LLC ....E 434 392-3505
Farmville *(G-4946)*

Lawrence Fabrications Inc ....G 540 667-1141
Winchester *(G-15438)*

Lelo Fabrication ....G 703 581-7852
Gainesville *(G-5596)*

Lelo Fabrication LLC ....G 703 754-1141
Haymarket *(G-6429)*

Leroy Cary ....G 804 561-3526
Amelia Court House *(G-663)*

Lewis Metal Works Inc ....E 434 572-3043
South Boston *(G-12779)*

Liphart Steel Company Inc ....D 804 355-7481
Richmond *(G-11272)*

Liphart Steel Company Inc ....E 540 248-1009
Verona *(G-13991)*

Litesteel Tech Amer LLC ....E 540 992-5129
Troutville *(G-13914)*

Lynchburg Fabrication LLC ....G 434 660-0935
Lynchburg *(G-7760)*

Lynchburg Fabrication Inc VA ....F 434 473-7291
Lynchburg *(G-7761)*

Lyndon Steel Company LLC ....G 434 660-0829
Lynchburg *(G-7766)*

M & S Fabricators ....G 703 550-3900
Lorton *(G-7510)*

M1 Fabrication LLC ....G 804 222-8885
Richmond *(G-11662)*

Machine & Fabg Specialists Inc ....E 757 244-5693
Hampton *(G-6187)*

Mallory Co Inc ....G 757 803-5596
Chesapeake *(G-3194)*

Marktechnologic LLC ....G 703 470-1224
Springfield *(G-13047)*

Martin Metalfab Inc ....E 804 226-1431
Sandston *(G-12624)*

Martins Fabricating & Welding ....G 540 343-6001
Roanoke *(G-12133)*

Mechanical Machine & Repair ....G 804 231-5866
Richmond *(G-11676)*

Metal Products Specialist Inc ....G 757 398-9214
Portsmouth *(G-10460)*

Metalist ....G 540 793-0627
Roanoke *(G-11963)*

Metwood Inc ....F 540 334-4294
Boones Mill *(G-1897)*

Mid Atlntic Mtal Solutions Inc ....G 757 827-1588
Hampton *(G-6200)*

Naff Welding Inc ....F 276 629-1129
Bassett *(G-1587)*

Ncg LLC ....F 757 838-3224
Hampton *(G-6206)*

New Millennium Bldg Systems LLC ....D 540 389-0211
Salem *(G-12544)*

Nexlevel Transports Inc ....G 757 707-6349
Toano *(G-13871)*

Obaugh Welding LLC ....G 540 396-6151
Mc Dowell *(G-8375)*

Osborne Welding Inc ....E 757 487-0900
Portsmouth *(G-10466)*

Panel Systems Inc ....E 703 910-6285
Woodbridge *(G-15772)*

Parkway Manufacturing Company ....F 757 896-9712
Hampton *(G-6213)*

Peebles Welding & Fabrication ....G...... 757 880-5332
Hampton *(G-6214)*

Pegrams Transporting Svcs LLC ......G...... 804 295-1798
Petersburg *(G-10334)*

Performnce Mtal Fbricators Inc ....G...... 757 465-8622
Portsmouth *(G-10467)*

Personal ....G...... 540 845-8771
Fredericksburg *(G-5345)*

Piedmont Fabrication Inc ....F...... 757 543-5570
Chesapeake *(G-3239)*

Piedmont Metal Products Inc ....E...... 540 586-0674
Bedford *(G-1649)*

Pillar Enterprise Ltd ....C...... 540 868-8626
White Post *(G-15181)*

▲ Plan B Design Fabrication Inc ....F...... 804 271-5200
Richmond *(G-11060)*

Precision Steel Mfg Corp ....D...... 540 985-8963
Roanoke *(G-12152)*

Professional Welding Svc Inc ....G...... 757 853-9371
Norfolk *(G-9697)*

R and L Machine Shop Inc ....G...... 757 487-8879
Chesapeake *(G-3254)*

R F J Ltd..E...... 703 494-3255
Woodbridge *(G-15788)*

R W P Johnson Products Ltd ....F...... 804 453-7705
Burgess *(G-2176)*

Radford Wldg & Fabrication LLC ....G...... 540 731-4891
Radford *(G-10737)*

Red Acres Equipment Inc ....G...... 434 352-5086
Appomattox *(G-821)*

Rexcon Metals LLC ....G...... 703 347-2836
Springfield *(G-13079)*

Richmond Steel Inc ....E...... 804 355-8080
Richmond *(G-11360)*

S & K Welding Inc ....G...... 276 988-5591
North Tazewell *(G-10106)*

S A Halac Iron Works Inc ....D...... 703 406-4766
Sterling *(G-13499)*

S B Auto Transport LLC ....G...... 757 775-3884
Virginia Beach *(G-14788)*

Selimax Inc ....G...... 540 347-5784
Warrenton *(G-15050)*

Sheltered 2 Home LLC ....E...... 540 686-0091
Winchester *(G-15585)*

Shickel Corporation ....D...... 540 828-2536
Bridgewater *(G-1959)*

Ship Sstnability Solutions LLC ....G...... 757 574-2436
Chesapeake *(G-3291)*

Silver Lake Welding Svc Inc ....F...... 540 879-2591
Dayton *(G-4064)*

SMI-Owen Steel Company Inc ....C...... 434 391-3903
Farmville *(G-4958)*

South River Fabricators ....G...... 540 377-9762
Vesuvius *(G-13998)*

Southern Iron Works Inc ....G...... 703 354-5500
Springfield *(G-13092)*

Southern Structural Steel Inc ....E...... 757 623-0862
Smithfield *(G-12741)*

Specialist Manufacture..........................G...... 540 974-0780
Middletown *(G-8743)*

Specialty Enterprises Inc ....G...... 804 781-0314
Mechanicsville *(G-8679)*

Spectrum Metal Services Inc ....G...... 804 744-0387
Midlothian *(G-8908)*

Spigner Structural & Miscellan ....E...... 703 625-7572
Berryville *(G-1692)*

Stamptech Inc ....G...... 804 768-4658
Chester *(G-3456)*

Steel Fab ....G...... 276 628-3843
Lebanon *(G-7207)*

Steelfab Inc ....G...... 703 538-2320
Alexandria *(G-355)*

Steelfab of Virginia Inc ....D...... 434 348-9021
Emporia *(G-4367)*

Structural Sculpture Corp ....G...... 434 207-3070
Troy *(G-13936)*

Structural Steel MGT LLC ....G...... 434 286-2373
Scottsville *(G-12667)*

Superior Fabrication LLC ....F...... 276 865-4000
Haysi *(G-6458)*

Superior Iron Works Inc ....D...... 703 471-5500
Sterling *(G-13524)*

Superior Metal & Mfg Inc ....F...... 540 981-1005
Vinton *(G-14186)*

Tech Dynamism LLC ....G...... 434 227-5324
Charlottesville *(G-2887)*

Technifab of Virginia Inc ....E...... 276 988-7517
North Tazewell *(G-10109)*

Tecnico Corporation ....B...... 757 545-4013
Chesapeake *(G-3326)*

Thermasteel Inc ....G...... 540 633-5000
Radford *(G-10742)*

Tidewater Rebar LLC ....F...... 757 325-9893
Suffolk *(G-13773)*

Tri Com Inc ....G...... 804 561-3582
Amelia Court House *(G-675)*

Trinity Steel Erection Inc ....E...... 804 598-8811
Powhatan *(G-10582)*

TST Fabrications LLC ....G...... 757 627-9101
Norfolk *(G-9769)*

Turbo Sales & Fabrication Inc ....E...... 276 930-2422
Floyd *(G-5042)*

Two N One Fabrication LLC ....G...... 757 642-2613
Chesapeake *(G-3354)*

TYe Custom Metal Fabricators ....G...... 804 863-2551
North Dinwiddie *(G-10067)*

Usr Steel LLC ....G...... 571 480-3497
Centreville *(G-2348)*

Valley Precision Incorporated...............E...... 540 941-8178
Waynesboro *(G-15142)*

Valmont Industries Inc ....E...... 804 733-0808
Petersburg *(G-10348)*

Virginia Carolina Steel Inc ....E...... 757 853-7403
Norfolk *(G-9783)*

Virginia Steel & Building Spc ....F...... 434 528-4302
Lynchburg *(G-7834)*

Virginia Steel & Fabrication ....E...... 276 688-2125
Bastian *(G-1594)*

W & B Fabricators Inc ....F...... 276 928-1060
Rocky Gap *(G-12308)*

W&W-Afco Steel LLC ....E...... 276 669-6649
Bristol *(G-2040)*

Wahoo Industries ....G...... 434 929-2466
Lynchburg *(G-7835)*

Waynesboro Alloy Works Inc ....G...... 540 965-4038
Covington *(G-3802)*

Weldment Dynamics LLC ....G...... 540 840-7866
Mineral *(G-8953)*

Weston Company ....G...... 540 349-1200
Gainesville *(G-5621)*

Williams Bridge Company ....E...... 703 335-7800
Manassas *(G-8178)*

Winchester Metals Inc ....D...... 540 667-9000
Winchester *(G-15511)*

Wolf Hills Fabricators LLC ....F...... 276 466-2743
Abingdon *(G-70)*

York Fabrication ....G...... 804 241-0136
La Crosse *(G-7153)*

York Fabrication LLC ....G...... 804 241-0136
Boydton *(G-1917)*

3442 Metal Doors, Sash, Frames, Molding & Trim

Aaron S Walters ....G...... 804 783-6925
Richmond *(G-11467)*

AG Lasers Technologies LLC ....F...... 800 255-5515
Front Royal *(G-5519)*

Bahama Breeze Shutter Awng LLC ....G...... 757 592-0265
Ordinary *(G-10236)*

Benchmark Doors ....B...... 540 898-5700
Fredericksburg *(G-5173)*

Blessed Hands Cnstr & Maint ....G...... 703 762-6595
Arlington *(G-885)*

Commonwealth Rapid Dry ....G...... 757 592-0203
Yorktown *(G-15944)*

Creative Urethanes Inc ....E...... 540 542-6676
Winchester *(G-15407)*

Doors Done Right LLC ....G...... 757 567-3891
Virginia Beach *(G-14412)*

Efco Corporation ....E...... 540 248-8604
Verona *(G-13985)*

Emco Enterprises Inc ....B...... 540 843-7900
Luray *(G-7609)*

Fusion Pwdr Cating Fabrication ....G...... 757 319-3760
Chesapeake *(G-3112)*

Hankins & Johann Incorporated............G...... 804 266-2421
Richmond *(G-11233)*

Hobbs Door Service ....G...... 757 436-6529
Virginia Beach *(G-14525)*

Jmd Jmd LLC ....G...... 703 945-0099
Ashburn *(G-1299)*

Kawneer Company Inc ....D...... 540 433-2711
Harrisonburg *(G-6335)*

Lawrence Trnsp Systems Inc ....D...... 540 966-3797
Roanoke *(G-11953)*

▲ Lineal Technologies Inc ....D...... 540 484-6783
Rocky Mount *(G-12335)*

Lutron Electronics Co Inc ....C...... 804 752-3300
Ashland *(G-1455)*

McKeon Door of Dc Inc ....G...... 301 807-1006
Alexandria *(G-272)*

Milgard Manufacturing Inc ....G...... 540 834-0340
Fredericksburg *(G-5328)*

▲ Opening Protection Svcs LLC ....G...... 757 222-0730
Virginia Beach *(G-14702)*

Plantation Shutter & Blind ....G...... 757 241-7026
Virginia Beach *(G-14725)*

Rsshutterlee LLC ....G...... 540 290-3712
Staunton *(G-13287)*

Shelters To Shutters ....G...... 703 634-6130
Vienna *(G-14124)*

Shutter Films LLC ....G...... 434 329-0713
Spout Spring *(G-12927)*

Shutterbooth ....G...... 804 662-0471
Powhatan *(G-10575)*

Sjp Consulting LLC ....G...... 804 277-8153
Mechanicsville *(G-8677)*

SLM Distrubutors Inc ....G...... 540 774-6817
Roanoke *(G-12002)*

Storm Protection Services ....G...... 757 496-8200
Virginia Beach *(G-14854)*

Tmac Services Inc ....F...... 804 368-0936
Ashland *(G-1501)*

Vinylite Windows Products Inc ....E...... 703 550-7766
Lorton *(G-7540)*

West Garage Doors Inc ....G...... 434 799-4070
Danville *(G-4050)*

3443 Fabricated Plate Work

Accurate Machine Inc ....G...... 757 853-2136
Norfolk *(G-9418)*

Adamson Global Technology Corp ....G...... 804 748-6453
Chester *(G-3382)*

Aigis Blast Protection..........................G...... 703 871-5173
Reston *(G-10782)*

▲ Air & Liquid Systems Corp ....C...... 434 845-7081
Lynchburg *(G-7637)*

◆ Alfa Laval USA Inc ....E...... 804 222-5300
Richmond *(G-11097)*

▼ Amthor International Inc...................D...... 845 778-5576
Gretna *(G-6002)*

Aquawash Pressure Washing LLC ....G...... 757 738-9899
Virginia Beach *(G-14235)*

▲ Atlantic Metal Products Inc ....E...... 804 758-4915
Topping *(G-13885)*

Biomass English Partners LLC ....G...... 804 226-8227
Richmond *(G-11126)*

Bolling Steel Co Inc ....E...... 540 380-4402
Salem *(G-12484)*

Bwx Technologies Inc ....G...... 434 522-6000
Lynchburg *(G-7666)*

▲ Bwxt Government Group Inc ....C...... 434 522-6000
Lynchburg *(G-7668)*

Bwxt Nclear Oprtions Group Inc ....B...... 434 522-6000
Lynchburg *(G-7669)*

Cardinal Pumps Exchangers Inc ....G...... 757 485-2666
Chesapeake *(G-3026)*

▲ Catalina Cylinders...........................E...... 757 896-9100
Hampton *(G-6108)*

Coil Exchange Inc ....G...... 703 369-7150
Manassas Park *(G-8196)*

▲ Colonnas Ship Yard Inc ....A...... 757 545-2414
Norfolk *(G-9495)*

Colonnas Ship Yard Inc ....G...... 757 545-2414
Norfolk *(G-9497)*

▼ Core Engineered Solutions Inc.........F...... 703 563-0320
Herndon *(G-6646)*

▲ Covan Worldiwde Moving & Stor ......G...... 757 766-2305
Hampton *(G-6117)*

Creative Fabrication Inc ....E...... 540 931-4877
Covington *(G-3785)*

Crossline Creations LLC ....G...... 703 625-4780
Sterling *(G-13376)*

Cryosel LLC ....G...... 757 778-1854
Hampton *(G-6124)*

CSC Family Holdings Inc ....D...... 276 669-6649
Bristol *(G-2015)*

Cushing Metals LLC ....G...... 804 339-1114
King William *(G-7128)*

Davco Fabricating & Welding ....G...... 434 836-0234
Danville *(G-3887)*

Des Champs Technologies Inc ....C...... 540 291-1111
Buena Vista *(G-2141)*

Design Integrated Tech Inc ....F...... 540 349-9425
Warrenton *(G-14995)*

Digital Machining Company ....G...... 540 786-7138
Fredericksburg *(G-5274)*

Draftco Incorporated ....E...... 540 337-1054
Stuarts Draft *(G-13646)*

Entwistle Company ....E ...... 434 799-6186 Danville *(G-3992)*	**Tritech Solutions Virginia Inc** ....G ...... 434 664-2140 Appomattox *(G-824)*	**Cupples Products Inc** ....E ...... 804 717-1971 Chester *(G-3398)*
Falck Schmidt Def Systems Corp ....G ... 805 689-1739 Lorton *(G-7487)*	**Valley Tool & Design Inc** ....G ...... 540 249-5710 Grottoes *(G-6026)*	▲ **Cushing Manufacturing & Eqp Co** ....E ...... 804 231-1161 Richmond *(G-11038)*
Fields Inc Oscar S ....E ...... 804 798-3900 Ashland *(G-1416)*	**Virginia American Inds Inc** ....C ...... 804 644-2611 Richmond *(G-11807)*	**Cushing Metals LLC** ....G ...... 804 339-1114 King William *(G-7128)*
Fusion Pwdr Cating Fabrication ....G ...... 757 319-3760 Chesapeake *(G-3112)*	**Virginia Metals Inc** ....F ...... 276 628-8151 Abingdon *(G-67)*	**Custom Metal Fabricators Inc** ....E ...... 804 271-6094 North Chesterfield *(G-9855)*
Ground Effects Hauling Inc ....G ...... 757 435-1765 Virginia Beach *(G-14494)*	**Virginia Steel & Fabrication** ....E ...... 276 688-2125 Bastian *(G-1594)*	**Custom Ornamental Iron Inc** ....D ...... 804 798-1991 Glen Allen *(G-5720)*
Happy Little Dumpsters LLC ....G ...... 540 422-0272 Elkton *(G-4327)*	**Virginia Tank Service Inc** ....G ...... 540 344-9700 Roanoke *(G-12220)*	**Design Assstnce Cnstr Systems** ....E ...... 757 393-0704 Portsmouth *(G-10415)*
Heinrich Enterprises Inc ....G ...... 540 248-1592 Staunton *(G-13265)*	**Warden Shackle Express** ....G ...... 540 980-2056 Pulaski *(G-10649)*	**Draftco Incorporated** ....E ...... 540 337-1054 Stuarts Draft *(G-13646)*
Hillco Disposal & Recycl LLC ....G ...... 757 301-9669 Virginia Beach *(G-14524)*	**Waterline Nnk LLC** ....G ...... 804 577-4160 Kilmarnock *(G-7079)*	**Duct Shop LLC** ....G ...... 804 368-8543 Ashland *(G-1404)*
Hudsons Welding Shop ....G ...... 434 822-1452 Danville *(G-3998)*	**Weston Company** ....E ...... 540 349-1200 Gainesville *(G-5621)*	**E G D Sheet Metal LLC** ....E ...... 571 577-1647 Manassas *(G-8060)*
Hy-Mark Cylinders Inc ....E ...... 757 251-6744 Hampton *(G-6173)*	**3444 Sheet Metal Work**	**East River Metals Inc** ....E ...... 276 928-1812 Rocky Gap *(G-12307)*
Industrial Fabricators VA Inc ....D ... 540 943-5885 Fishersville *(G-5005)*	**A & J Seamless Gutters Inc** ....G ...... 757 291-6890 Newport News *(G-9155)*	**Elm Investments Inc** ....E ...... 757 934-2709 Suffolk *(G-13704)*
Junk In My Trunk LLC ....G ...... 703 753-7505 Haymarket *(G-6428)*	**Aaacm Green Warrior Inc** ....G ...... 703 865-5991 Fairfax *(G-4398)*	**Endreola Sheet Metal** ....G ...... 703 496-8538 Woodbridge *(G-15694)*
◆ **Kelvin International Corp** ....F ...... 757 833-1011 Newport News *(G-9274)*	**Accurate Machine Inc** ....G ...... 757 853-2136 Norfolk *(G-9418)*	**Entwistle Company** ....E ...... 434 799-6186 Danville *(G-3992)*
Keo-Corp LLC ....G ...... 636 515-5549 New Kent *(G-9135)*	**Accutech Fabrication Inc** ....F ...... 434 528-4858 Lynchburg *(G-7632)*	**Fairfax Metals LLC** ....G ...... 571 594-1937 Ashburn *(G-1278)*
Lane Enterprises Inc ....E ...... 540 674-4645 Dublin *(G-4163)*	▲ **Acoustical Sheetmetal Inc** ....D ...... 757 456-9720 Virginia Beach *(G-14209)*	**Fh Sheet Metal Inc** ....G ...... 703 408-4622 Manassas *(G-7940)*
Lawrence Brothers Inc ....E ...... 276 322-4988 Bluefield *(G-1868)*	**Advanced Machine & Tooling** ....F ...... 757 518-1222 Virginia Beach *(G-14213)*	**Fields Inc Oscar S** ....E ...... 804 798-3900 Ashland *(G-1416)*
Lewis Metal Works Inc ....E ...... 434 572-3043 South Boston *(G-12779)*	**Air Metal Corp** ....G ...... 804 262-1004 Richmond *(G-11091)*	**Figure Engineering LLC** ....E ...... 540 818-5034 Lorton *(G-7489)*
Lori Katz ....G ...... 703 475-1640 Alexandria *(G-264)*	**Air Tight Duct Systems Inc** ....G ...... 540 361-7888 Fredericksburg *(G-5169)*	**Flipclean Corp** ....G ...... 804 233-4845 Richmond *(G-11591)*
Martin Elthon ....G ...... 703 853-1801 Fairfax *(G-4503)*	**Allied Tool and Machine Co VA** ....E ...... 540 342-6781 Roanoke *(G-12031)*	**Flippen & Sons Inc** ....G ...... 804 233-1461 Richmond *(G-11592)*
Mersen USA Ptt Corp ....D ...... 540 389-7535 Salem *(G-12536)*	**American Metal Fabricators LLC** ....G ...... 540 834-2400 Fredericksburg *(G-5244)*	**Fred Kinkead** ....G ...... 540 828-2955 Bridgewater *(G-1951)*
Metro Sign & Design Inc ....E ...... 703 631-1866 Manassas Park *(G-8205)*	**Amherst Technologies** ....G ...... 434 946-0329 Amherst *(G-681)*	**Fusion Pwdr Cating Fabrication** ....G ...... 757 319-3760 Chesapeake *(G-3112)*
Miller Metal Fabricators Inc ....E ...... 540 886-5575 Staunton *(G-13281)*	**Amilcar S Sheet Metal LLC** ....G ...... 571 330-8371 Norfolk *(G-9441)*	**General Sheet Metal Co Inc** ....G ...... 571 221-3270 Manassas *(G-8073)*
Modine Manufacturing Company ....G ... 540 464-3640 Lexington *(G-7402)*	▲ **Appalachian Machine Inc** ....F ...... 540 674-1914 Dublin *(G-4148)*	**Greendale Railing Company** ....E ...... 804 363-7809 Richmond *(G-11223)*
Old Stone Corp ....F ...... 813 731-7600 Cascade *(G-2252)*	**Applied Technology Group Inc** ....E ...... 703 960-5555 Alexandria *(G-416)*	**Halls Mechanical Services LLC** ....G ...... 276 673-3300 Fieldale *(G-4987)*
Pittsburg Tank & Tower Co Inc ....G ... 757 422-1882 Virginia Beach *(G-14724)*	**Atlantic Fabrication & Boiler** ....F ...... 757 494-0597 Portsmouth *(G-10394)*	**Hampton Roads Sheet Metal Inc** ....G ... 757 543-6009 Virginia Beach *(G-14500)*
Plastic Fabricating Inc ....F ...... 540 345-6901 Roanoke *(G-12148)*	**Avm Sheet Metal Inc** ....G ...... 703 975-7715 Manassas *(G-8031)*	▼ **Hmb Inc** ....D ...... 540 967-1060 Louisa *(G-7556)*
Ragan Sheet Metal Inc ....E ...... 757 333-7248 Virginia Beach *(G-14757)*	**B & G Stainless Works Inc** ....G ...... 703 339-6002 Lorton *(G-7464)*	**Hodges Sheet Metal LLC** ....G ...... 276 957-5344 Spencer *(G-12873)*
Red Stitch Tactical LLC ....G ...... 703 798-4385 Manassas *(G-8141)*	**Baker & Hazlewood** ....G ...... 804 798-5199 Ashland *(G-1377)*	**Hughes Mechanical Systems** ....G ...... 757 855-3238 Chesapeake *(G-3138)*
Riggins Company LLC ....D ...... 757 826-0525 Hampton *(G-6228)*	**Baker Sheet Metal Corporation** ....D ... 757 853-4325 Norfolk *(G-9454)*	**I C E** ....G ...... 276 988-0330 North Tazewell *(G-10101)*
Robert D Gregory ....G ...... 276 632-9170 Ridgeway *(G-11852)*	**Benchmark Doors** ....B ...... 540 898-5700 Fredericksburg *(G-5173)*	**Innovative Machining Inc** ....E ...... 804 385-4212 Forest *(G-5077)*
Sam English of VA ....E ...... 804 222-7114 Richmond *(G-11370)*	**Bloxom Sheet Metal Inc** ....G ...... 757 436-4181 Chesapeake *(G-3006)*	**J & M Sheet Metal Inc** ....G ...... 571 722-2805 Centreville *(G-2311)*
Samuel Son & Co (usa) Inc ....C ...... 276 415-9970 Lebanon *(G-7206)*	**Bobby Burns Nowlin** ....F ...... 757 827-1588 Hampton *(G-6097)*	**JD Concrete LLC** ....F ...... 703 331-2155 Manassas Park *(G-8203)*
Select Cleaning Service ....G ...... 804 397-1176 Richmond *(G-11756)*	**Brown Russel** ....G ...... 540 547-3000 Culpeper *(G-3876)*	**Jvh Company Inc** ....E ...... 804 798-0888 Ashland *(G-1446)*
Service Machine & Wldg Co Inc ....D ... 804 798-1381 Ashland *(G-1490)*	**C and J Fabrication Inc** ....G ...... 757 399-3340 Portsmouth *(G-10403)*	**Kearney-National Inc** ....C ...... 276 628-7171 Abingdon *(G-47)*
Shantanu Tank ....G ...... 757 766-3829 Hampton *(G-6233)*	**Callahan Paving Products Inc** ....G ...... 434 589-9000 Crozier *(G-3857)*	**Koit Sheet Metal Inc** ....G ...... 703 625-3981 Chantilly *(G-2540)*
Sheltech Plastics Inc ....G ...... 978 794-2160 Elberon *(G-4319)*	**Capstone Industries LLC** ....G ...... 703 966-6718 Manassas *(G-8045)*	**Lane Enterprises Inc** ....F ...... 276 223-1051 Wytheville *(G-15895)*
Shickel Corporation ....D ...... 540 828-2536 Bridgewater *(G-1959)*	**Carico Inc** ....E ...... 540 373-5983 Fredericksburg *(G-5176)*	**Lane Enterprises Inc** ....F ...... 540 439-3201 Bealeton *(G-1600)*
Suburban Contractors LLC ....G ...... 703 739-5600 Manassas *(G-8001)*	**Centerline Fabricators** ....G ...... 540 318-6769 Fredericksburg *(G-5410)*	**Lane Enterprises Inc** ....E ...... 540 674-4645 Dublin *(G-4163)*
Super RAD Coils Ltd Partnr ....C ...... 804 794-2887 North Chesterfield *(G-9992)*	**Century Steel Products Inc** ....E ...... 703 471-7606 Sterling *(G-13367)*	**Lb Telesystems Inc** ....E ...... 703 919-8991 Chantilly *(G-2456)*
Superior Boiler LLC ....E ...... 804 226-8227 Richmond *(G-11402)*	**Charter Ip Pllc** ....G ...... 540 253-5332 The Plains *(G-13842)*	**Lee High Sheet Metal Inc** ....F ...... 703 698-5168 Fairfax *(G-4498)*
Synalloy Corporation ....D ...... 804 822-3260 Glen Allen *(G-5804)*	**Cladding Facade Solutions LLC** ....G ... 571 748-7698 Fredericksburg *(G-5262)*	**Lewis Metal Works Inc** ....E ...... 434 572-3043 South Boston *(G-12779)*
Technifab of Virginia Inc ....E ...... 276 988-7517 North Tazewell *(G-10109)*	**Colonial Wldg Fabrication Inc** ....E ...... 757 459-2680 Norfolk *(G-9494)*	**Liphart Steel Company Inc** ....E ...... 540 248-1009 Verona *(G-13991)*
Tecnico Corporation ....B ...... 757 545-4013 Chesapeake *(G-3326)*	**Commonwealth Mechanical Inc** ....G ... 757 825-0740 Hampton *(G-6116)*	**Lyon Roofing Inc** ....G ...... 540 633-0170 Fairlawn *(G-4737)*
Thorium Power Inc ....G ...... 703 918-4904 Mc Lean *(G-8566)*	**Contech Engnered Solutions LLC** ....G ... 513 645-7000 Abingdon *(G-25)*	**Mabe Dg & Assoc Inc** ....G ...... 804 530-1406 Chester *(G-3432)*
Timothy D Falls ....G ...... 540 987-8142 Woodville *(G-15862)*	**Continental Auto Systems Inc** ....C ... 540 825-4100 Culpeper *(G-3880)*	**Magco Inc** ....F ...... 757 934-0042 Suffolk *(G-13738)*

SIC

Martin Metalfab Inc ....E...... 804 226-1431
 Sandston *(G-12624)*

Matthews Sheet Metal Inc ....G...... 757 543-6009
 Virginia Beach *(G-14642)*

McGill Airflow LLC ....G...... 804 965-5367
 Ashland *(G-1461)*

ME Latimer Fabricator T A ....G...... 757 566-8352
 Toano *(G-13869)*

Merrifield Metals Inc ....G...... 703 849-9100
 Fairfax *(G-4506)*

Metfab International Inc ....E...... 540 943-3732
 Waynesboro *(G-15127)*

Miller Metal Fabricators Inc ....E...... 540 886-5575
 Staunton *(G-13281)*

Mitsubishi Chemical Amer Inc ......G...... 757 382-5750
 Chesapeake *(G-3207)*

Mobile Sheet Metal LLC ....G...... 540 450-6324
 Boyce *(G-1910)*

Moore Sign Corporation ....E...... 804 748-5836
 Chester *(G-3438)*

Mountain Sky LLC ....G...... 540 389-1197
 Salem *(G-12541)*

Naito America ....E...... 804 550-3305
 Ashland *(G-1468)*

New England Supply Inc ....F...... 703 372-2689
 Springfield *(G-13058)*

Northrop Custom Metal LLC ....G...... 703 751-7042
 Alexandria *(G-296)*

Nzo LLC ....F...... 434 660-7338
 Bedford *(G-1646)*

Paulette Fabricators Inc ....G...... 804 798-3700
 Ashland *(G-1474)*

Precision Sheetmetal Inc ....G...... 757 389-5730
 Norfolk *(G-9694)*

Precision Shtmtl Fbrcation LLC .....G...... 757 865-2508
 Hampton *(G-6217)*

Pro Sheet Metal Inc ....G...... 703 675-7724
 Alexandria *(G-557)*

Production Manufacturing Inc ....G...... 513 892-2331
 Great Falls *(G-5976)*

Professional Welding Svc Inc ....G...... 757 853-9371
 Norfolk *(G-9697)*

Progressive Manufacturing Corp ....E...... 804 717-5353
 Chester *(G-3448)*

PSI Group ....G...... 804 798-3210
 Ashland *(G-1481)*

R Gonzalez Sheetmetal LLC ....G...... 571 316-8241
 Manassas *(G-8137)*

▲ Rayco Industries Inc ....E...... 804 321-7111
 Richmond *(G-11729)*

Riddleberger Brothers Inc ....B...... 540 434-1731
 Mount Crawford *(G-9058)*

Robert Montgomery ....G...... 703 737-0491
 Leesburg *(G-7338)*

Ruffin & Payne Incorporated ....C...... 804 329-2691
 Richmond *(G-11749)*

S Joye & Son Inc ....G...... 804 745-2419
 North Chesterfield *(G-10023)*

Sams Gutter Shop ....G...... 276 632-6522
 Martinsville *(G-8325)*

Santiago Sheet Metal LLC ....G...... 703 870-4581
 Alexandria *(G-576)*

Seher Resources Inc ....G...... 703 771-7170
 Leesburg *(G-7344)*

Service Metal Fabricators Inc ....D...... 757 887-3500
 Williamsburg *(G-15310)*

Sheet Metal Products Inc ....F...... 757 562-1986
 Franklin *(G-5155)*

Shickel Corporation ....D...... 540 828-2536
 Bridgewater *(G-1959)*

Shoprat Metal Works LLC ....G...... 571 499-1534
 Annandale *(G-782)*

Silver Lake Welding Svc Inc ....F...... 540 879-2591
 Dayton *(G-4064)*

Solar Sheet Metal Inc ....G...... 770 256-2618
 Manassas Park *(G-8211)*

Southern Air Sheet Metal ....G...... 434 907-2268
 Lynchburg *(G-7809)*

Spears & Associate ....G...... 540 752-5577
 Hartwood *(G-6392)*

Spencer Stnless Alum Guttering .....G...... 434 277-8359
 Amherst *(G-708)*

Spig Industry LLC ....F...... 276 644-9510
 Bristol *(G-2034)*

Stallworks LLC ....G...... 434 933-8939
 Gladstone *(G-5688)*

Sterling Sheet Metal Inc ....G...... 540 338-0144
 Sterling *(G-13516)*

Structureworks Fabrication ....G...... 877 489-8064
 Fredericksburg *(G-5370)*

Superior Awning Service Inc ....G...... 757 399-8161
 Portsmouth *(G-10489)*

Sweet Briar Sheet Metal Svcs ....G...... 434 946-0403
 Amherst *(G-710)*

Tabet Manufacturing Co Inc ....E...... 757 627-1855
 Norfolk *(G-9739)*

Technifab of Virginia Inc ....E...... 276 988-7517
 North Tazewell *(G-10109)*

Tecnico Corporation ....B...... 757 545-4013
 Chesapeake *(G-3326)*

Tek-AM Corp ....F...... 703 321-9144
 Lorton *(G-7536)*

Thermasteel Rp Ltd ....G...... 540 633-5000
 Radford *(G-10743)*

Tmn LLC ....F...... 703 335-8191
 Manassas *(G-8003)*

Tower Hill Corp ....E...... 703 368-7727
 Manassas *(G-8005)*

TST Fabrications LLC ....F...... 757 627-9101
 Norfolk *(G-9770)*

Valley Precision Incorporated ....E...... 540 941-8178
 Waynesboro *(G-15142)*

Varney Sheet Metal Shop ....G...... 540 343-4076
 Roanoke *(G-12216)*

Vasse Vaught Metalcrafting Inc .....G...... 540 808-8939
 Roanoke *(G-12217)*

Virginia Blower Company ....E...... 276 647-3804
 Collinsville *(G-3718)*

Virginia Steel & Fabrication ....E...... 276 688-2125
 Bastian *(G-1594)*

Vivaan Metals LLC ....G...... 571 309-3007
 Sterling *(G-13555)*

VT Milcom Inc ....D...... 757 548-2956
 Chesapeake *(G-3366)*

W & B Fabricators Inc ....F...... 276 928-1060
 Rocky Gap *(G-12308)*

Waynesboro Alloy Works Inc ....G...... 540 965-4038
 Covington *(G-3802)*

◆ Wegmann Usa Inc ....D...... 434 385-1580
 Lynchburg *(G-7837)*

Western Sheet Metal Inc ....G...... 804 732-0230
 North Dinwiddie *(G-10070)*

Westside Metal Fabricators ....G...... 804 744-0387
 Midlothian *(G-8921)*

Williams Fabrication Inc ....G...... 540 862-4200
 Covington *(G-3804)*

Williamsburg Metal Specialties .....G...... 757 229-3393
 Williamsburg *(G-15342)*

Z & M Sheet Metal Inc ....G...... 703 631-9600
 Chantilly *(G-2523)*

3446 Architectural & Ornamental Metal Work

Alliance Stl Fabrications Inc ....F...... 703 631-2355
 Manassas Park *(G-8187)*

Art-A-Metal LLC ....G...... 757 787-1574
 Onancock *(G-10190)*

Beach Iron Shop ....G...... 757 422-3318
 Virginia Beach *(G-14267)*

Beach Welding Service ....G...... 757 422-3318
 Virginia Beach *(G-14270)*

Bill Kelley Metalsmith ....G...... 804 798-4286
 Ashland *(G-1381)*

Bobby Burns Nowlin ....F...... 757 827-1588
 Hampton *(G-6097)*

Caldwell Industries Inc ....G...... 703 403-3272
 Alexandria *(G-428)*

Carico Inc ....E...... 540 373-5983
 Fredericksburg *(G-5176)*

Century Stair Company ....D...... 703 754-4163
 Haymarket *(G-6417)*

Chase Architectural Metal LLC ......G...... 804 230-1136
 Richmond *(G-11525)*

Colonial Iron Works Inc ....G...... 804 862-4141
 Petersburg *(G-10312)*

Custom Ornamental Iron Inc ....D...... 804 798-1991
 Glen Allen *(G-5720)*

Custom Ornamental Iron Works .....G...... 540 942-2687
 Waynesboro *(G-15106)*

Custom Railing Solutions Inc ....G...... 757 455-8501
 Norfolk *(G-9512)*

Custom Welding Inc ....G...... 757 220-1995
 Williamsburg *(G-15227)*

Direct Stairs ....G...... 540 436-9290
 Toms Brook *(G-13883)*

Dulles Iron Works Inc ....G...... 703 996-8797
 Sterling *(G-13391)*

Eddies Mind Inc ....G...... 540 731-9304
 Radford *(G-10712)*

Efco Corporation ....E...... 540 248-8604
 Verona *(G-13985)*

Emerald Ironworks Inc ....E...... 703 690-2477
 Woodbridge *(G-15692)*

Extreme Steel Inc ....D...... 540 868-9150
 Warrenton *(G-15007)*

Extreme Steel Inc ....G...... 540 868-9150
 Winchester *(G-15417)*

Fields Inc Oscar S ....E...... 804 798-3900
 Ashland *(G-1416)*

Flowers Steel LLC ....G...... 540 424-8377
 Sumerduck *(G-13791)*

Folley Fencing Service ....G...... 276 629-8487
 Patrick Springs *(G-10270)*

Fusion Pwdr Cating Fabrication .....G...... 757 319-3760
 Chesapeake *(G-3112)*

Gold Stem ....E...... 703 680-7000
 Woodbridge *(G-15710)*

Greendale Railing Company ....G...... 804 363-7809
 Richmond *(G-11223)*

Griffins Perch Ironworks ....G...... 434 977-0582
 Charlottesville *(G-2642)*

Hampton Roads Sheet Metal Inc ....G...... 757 543-6009
 Virginia Beach *(G-14500)*

Hlk Custom Stainless Inc ....G...... 571 261-5811
 Manassas *(G-8078)*

J C Enterprises ....G...... 540 345-0552
 Roanoke *(G-12108)*

Josh McDaniel ....G...... 804 748-4330
 Chesterfield *(G-3509)*

K B Industries Inc ....G...... 540 483-8883
 Rocky Mount *(G-12331)*

Kearney-National Inc ....C...... 276 628-7171
 Abingdon *(G-47)*

Keystone Metal Products Inc ....G...... 540 720-5437
 Stafford *(G-13162)*

Lewis Metal Works Inc ....E...... 434 572-3043
 South Boston *(G-12779)*

Meany & Oliver Companies Inc ......G...... 703 851-7131
 Arlington *(G-1058)*

Miscellaneous & Orna Mtls Inc ......G...... 757 650-5226
 Virginia Beach *(G-14655)*

Moore Sign Corporation ....E...... 804 748-5836
 Chester *(G-3438)*

P & G Interiors Inc ....E...... 540 985-3064
 Roanoke *(G-11980)*

Quality Home Improvement Corp ....G...... 757 424-5400
 Virginia Beach *(G-14752)*

R F J Ltd ....E...... 703 494-3255
 Woodbridge *(G-15788)*

R&R Ornamental Iron Inc ....G...... 540 798-1699
 Roanoke *(G-12159)*

Richardson Ornamental Iron ....G...... 757 420-1426
 Chesapeake *(G-3270)*

Shickel Corporation ....D...... 540 828-2536
 Bridgewater *(G-1959)*

Silver City Iron Inc ....G...... 434 566-7644
 Charlottesville *(G-2876)*

Spitzer Machine Shop ....G...... 540 896-5827
 Fulks Run *(G-5566)*

Stuart-Dean Co Inc ....D...... 703 578-1885
 Falls Church *(G-4878)*

Superior Iron Works Inc ....G...... 703 471-5500
 Sterling *(G-13524)*

Technifab of Virginia Inc ....E...... 276 988-7517
 North Tazewell *(G-10109)*

Tecnico Corporation ....B...... 757 545-4013
 Chesapeake *(G-3326)*

Timmons & Kelley Architects ....G...... 804 897-5636
 Midlothian *(G-8913)*

Virginia Archtectural Mtls LLC ....G...... 540 710-7701
 Fredericksburg *(G-5232)*

Virginia Railing & Gates LLC ....F...... 804 798-8777
 Ashland *(G-1506)*

Virginia Stair Company ....G...... 434 823-2587
 Barboursville *(G-1568)*

Whites Ornamental Iron Works ......G...... 540 877-1047
 Winchester *(G-15509)*

Wm Coffman Resources LLC ....G...... 800 810-9204
 Marion *(G-8245)*

3448 Prefabricated Metal Buildings & Cmpnts

Affordable Sheds Company ....G...... 540 657-6770
 Stafford *(G-13113)*

Alans Factory Outlet ....G...... 540 860-1035
 Luray *(G-7600)*

American Buildings Company ....C...... 434 757-2220
 La Crosse *(G-7139)*

Bad Wolf LLC ....G...... 540 347-4255
 Warrenton *(G-14980)*

Christopher Hawkins ....G.... 540 361-1679
  Fredericksburg (G-5178)

Colonial Barns Inc ....G.... 757 420-8653
  Virginia Beach (G-14353)

▲ Cushing Manufacturing & Eqp Co ....E.... 804 231-1161
  Richmond (G-11038)

Faun Trackway (usa) Inc ....G.... 202 459-0802
  Arlington (G-963)

General Dynamics Mission ....B.... 276 783-3121
  Marion (G-8227)

Graceland of Martinsville ....G.... 434 250-0050
  Ridgeway (G-11844)

Harbor Entps Ltd Lblty Co ....G.... 229 226-0911
  Stafford (G-13150)

Hartz Contractors Inc ....G.... 757 870-2978
  Newport News (G-9246)

Ireson Innovation ....G.... 540 529-1572
  Troutville (G-13911)

J Z Utility Barns LLC ....G.... 276 686-1683
  Rural Retreat (G-12425)

Jewells Buildings ....G.... 804 333-4483
  Warsaw (G-15069)

Kennedy Konstruction Kompany ....E.... 540 984-4191
  Edinburg (G-4308)

Leonard Alum Utlity Bldngs Inc ....G.... 540 951-0236
  Blacksburg (G-1753)

Leonard Alum Utlity Bldngs Inc ....G.... 434 237-5301
  Lynchburg (G-7756)

Leonard Alum Utlity Bldngs Inc ....G.... 434 792-8202
  Danville (G-4011)

◆ Matthias Enterprises Inc ....E.... 757 591-9371
  Newport News (G-9296)

McElroy Metal Mill Inc ....G.... 757 485-3100
  Chesapeake (G-3200)

McElroy Metal Mill Inc ....G.... 540 667-2500
  Winchester (G-15445)

Morton Buildings Inc ....G.... 540 366-3705
  Culpeper (G-3910)

Nci Group Inc ....D.... 804 957-6811
  Prince George (G-10603)

Oaks At Timberlake ....G.... 434 525-7107
  Evington (G-4381)

Panel Systems Inc ....E.... 703 910-6285
  Woodbridge (G-15772)

Powerbilt Steel Buildings Inc ....F.... 757 425-6223
  Virginia Beach (G-14731)

Quality Portable Buildings ....G.... 276 880-2007
  Rosedale (G-12367)

Shelter2home LLC ....G.... 540 336-5994
  Winchester (G-15584)

Stateline Builders Inc ....G.... 757 934-6836
  Suffolk (G-13768)

Steelmaster Buildings LLC ....F.... 757 961-7006
  Virginia Beach (G-14845)

True Steel LLC ....G.... 540 680-2906
  Charlottesville (G-2896)

▼ TSC Corporation ....E.... 540 633-5000
  Radford (G-10746)

US Building Systems Inc ....E.... 800 991-9251
  Virginia Beach (G-14903)

▲ Vfp Inc ....D.... 540 977-0500
  Roanoke (G-12019)

Vfp Inc ....C.... 276 431-4000
  Duffield (G-4187)

3449 Misc Structural Metal Work

3d Design and Mfg LLC ....G.... 804 214-3229
  Powhatan (G-10527)

American Buildings Company ....C.... 434 757-2220
  La Crosse (G-7139)

Arbon Equipment Corporation ....G.... 540 542-6790
  Winchester (G-15383)

Arbon Equipment Corporation ....G.... 540 387-2113
  Salem (G-12475)

B & R Rebar ....F.... 800 526-1024
  Richmond (G-11497)

Brady Contracting Service ....G.... 703 864-9207
  Manassas (G-8042)

Brown Russel ....G.... 540 547-3000
  Culpeper (G-3876)

Commercial Metals Company ....E.... 540 775-8501
  King George (G-7084)

Darden Pressure Wash and Plst ....G.... 757 934-1466
  Suffolk (G-13694)

Efco Corporation ....E.... 540 248-8604
  Verona (G-13985)

Emerald Ironworks Inc ....E.... 703 690-2477
  Woodbridge (G-15692)

Fabritech ....G.... 540 825-1544
  Culpeper (G-3891)

Hamilton Iron Works Inc ....E.... 703 497-4766
  Woodbridge (G-15720)

Horse Pasture Mfg LLC ....G.... 276 952-2558
  Meadows of Dan (G-8591)

▲ Industrial Welding & Mch Corp ....F.... 276 783-7105
  Atkins (G-1518)

Jerry King ....G.... 804 550-1243
  Glen Allen (G-5755)

Kevins Welding ....G.... 703 242-8649
  Oakton (G-10153)

L B Foster Company ....G.... 804 722-0398
  Petersburg (G-10329)

Mechanicsville Metal Works Inc ....G.... 804 266-5055
  Mechanicsville (G-8657)

Panel Systems Inc ....E.... 703 910-6285
  Woodbridge (G-15772)

Rebarsolutions ....F.... 540 300-9975
  Dayton (G-4060)

Sextons Incorporated ....G.... 276 783-4212
  Atkins (G-1520)

Steelfab Inc ....G.... 703 538-2320
  Alexandria (G-355)

Twin CS LLC ....G.... 540 664-6072
  Winchester (G-15497)

Voestlpine High Prfmce Mtls Co ....E.... 434 575-7994
  South Boston (G-12792)

Ward Entp Fabrication LLC ....G.... 757 675-5712
  Hampton (G-6269)

3451 Screw Machine Prdts

GM International Ltd Company ....G.... 703 577-0829
  Leesburg (G-7281)

Patriot Solutions Group LLC ....G.... 571 367-4979
  Chantilly (G-2549)

Progressive Manufacturing Corp ....E.... 804 717-5353
  Chester (G-3448)

Ramatech LLC ....G.... 240 449-7435
  Chantilly (G-2553)

▼ Rrb Industries Inc ....G.... 804 396-3270
  North Chesterfield (G-9967)

3452 Bolts, Nuts, Screws, Rivets & Washers

Lt Pressure Washer Services ....G.... 703 626-9010
  Alexandria (G-266)

Merchants Metals LLC ....G.... 877 518-7665
  Fredericksburg (G-5324)

Push Pin Crative Solutions LLC ....G.... 703 313-0619
  Alexandria (G-562)

▲ Vanguard Industries East Inc ....C.... 757 665-8405
  Norfolk (G-9778)

Zipnut Technology LLC ....G.... 703 442-7339
  Falls Church (G-4898)

3462 Iron & Steel Forgings

Babb Railroad Construction ....F.... 276 995-2090
  Fort Blackmore (G-5120)

▲ Cerro Fabricated Products LLC ....D.... 540 208-1606
  Weyers Cave (G-15171)

Coastal Waters Sales & Svc LLC ....G.... 757 893-9040
  Chesapeake (G-3044)

Crossroads Farrier Inc ....G.... 434 589-4501
  Louisa (G-7553)

Double Horseshoe Saloon ....G.... 434 202-8714
  Charlottesville (G-2784)

Full Tilt Performance ....G.... 276 628-0036
  Abingdon (G-31)

Horseshoe Bend Imprvs LLC ....G.... 434 969-1672
  Howardsville (G-6951)

Immco LLC ....F.... 804 271-6979
  North Chesterfield (G-9890)

IMS Gear Holding Inc ....E.... 757 468-8810
  Virginia Beach (G-14542)

Keppick LLC Kim ....G.... 540 364-3668
  Delaplane (G-4076)

Landrum Horse Shoeing Inc ....G.... 434 836-0847
  Blairs (G-1831)

M Gautreaux Horseshoe ....G.... 540 840-3153
  Beaverdam (G-1610)

Polar Traction Inc ....G.... 703 241-1958
  Arlington (G-1113)

Progressive Manufacturing Corp ....E.... 804 717-5353
  Chester (G-3448)

RPI AAR Railroad Tank Car Prj ....G.... 540 822-4800
  Leesburg (G-7340)

Southwest Cmprsr Pmpg Pckges I ....G.... 276 963-6400
  Cedar Bluff (G-2285)

Spinfinity ....G.... 540 283-9370
  Roanoke (G-12192)

Valley Wheel Co Inc ....G.... 276 964-5013
  Richlands (G-11022)

▲ Virginia Forge Company LLC ....G.... 540 254-2236
  Buchanan (G-2130)

◆ Wegmann Usa Inc ....D.... 434 385-1580
  Lynchburg (G-7837)

White Oak Forge Ltd ....G.... 540 636-4545
  Huntly (G-6967)

Yakattack LLC ....G.... 804 561-4274
  Burkeville (G-2212)

Yakattack LLC ....G.... 434 392-3233
  Farmville (G-4961)

3463 Nonferrous Forgings

Applied Plasma Tech LLC ....G.... 703 340-5545
  Springfield (G-12950)

Catalina Cylinders Inc ....D.... 757 896-9100
  Hampton (G-6109)

▲ Cerro Fabricated Products LLC ....D.... 540 208-1606
  Weyers Cave (G-15171)

▲ Craft Bearing Company Inc ....E.... 757 247-6000
  Newport News (G-9208)

Jordan Consulting and Research ....G.... 703 597-7812
  Herndon (G-6719)

PM Pump Company ....G.... 540 380-2012
  Salem (G-12557)

Turner Sculpture Ltd ....E.... 757 787-2818
  Melfa (G-8713)

3465 Automotive Stampings

Aftermarket Parts Solutions ....G.... 757 227-3166
  Norfolk (G-9428)

Davids Mobile Service LLC ....G.... 804 481-1647
  Hopewell (G-6922)

Donald Crisp Jr ....G.... 757 903-6743
  Yorktown (G-15951)

Wheels N Motion ....G.... 804 991-3090
  Petersburg (G-10350)

3466 Crowns & Closures

▲ Saco ....G.... 804 457-3744
  Gum Spring (G-6044)

3469 Metal Stampings, NEC

A K Metal Fabricators Inc ....F.... 703 823-1661
  Alexandria (G-114)

Blanc Creatives LLC ....F.... 434 260-1692
  Charlottesville (G-2741)

▲ County Line LLC ....D.... 434 736-8405
  Keysville (G-7055)

▲ Damon Company of Salem Inc ....E.... 540 389-8609
  Salem (G-12494)

Datacut Precision Machining ....G.... 434 237-8320
  Lynchburg (G-7693)

Elfinsmith Ltd Inc ....G.... 757 399-4788
  Portsmouth (G-10421)

Falcon Tool and Design Inc ....G.... 757 898-9393
  Yorktown (G-15958)

Hanson Industries Inc ....G.... 434 845-9091
  Lynchburg (G-7728)

Independent Stamping Inc ....G.... 540 949-6839
  Waynesboro (G-15115)

International Designs LLC ....G.... 804 275-1044
  North Chesterfield (G-9899)

▲ Intricate Metal Forming Co ....E.... 540 345-9233
  Salem (G-12523)

▼ Kennley Corporation ....G.... 804 275-9088
  North Chesterfield (G-9907)

Macs Smack LLC ....G.... 804 913-9126
  Hanover (G-6282)

Masonite Corporation ....D.... 540 778-2211
  Stanley (G-13231)

Mica Co of Canada Inc ....G.... 757 244-7311
  Newport News (G-9299)

Randy Hawthorne ....G.... 434 547-3460
  Dillwyn (G-4099)

Rick USA Stamping Corporation ....G.... 540 980-1327
  Pulaski (G-10645)

▲ Rubber Plastic Met Engrg Corp ....F.... 757 502-5462
  Virginia Beach (G-14785)

Sanjo Virginia Beach Inc ....G.... 757 498-0400
  Virginia Beach (G-14793)

Savage Transparency LLC ....G.... 760 218-6457
  Chesapeake (G-3284)

▲ Shenandoah Machine & Maint Co .....G.... 540 343-1758
  Roanoke (G-12183)

Short Run Stamping Company Inc ......D.... 804 861-6872
  Petersburg (G-10341)

▲ Smart Machine Technologies Inc .....D.... 276 632-9853
  Ridgeway (G-11853)

S
I
C

Stamptech Inc ....G...... 434 845-9091
Lynchburg (G-7812)

Virginia Metals Inc ....F...... 276 628-8151
Abingdon (G-67)

Wobanc Danforth ....G...... 804 222-7877
Richmond (G-11453)

3471 Electroplating, Plating, Polishing, Anodizing & Coloring

Advanced Finishing Systems ....F...... 804 642-7669
Hayes (G-6393)

Advanced Metal Finishing of VA ....G...... 540 344-3216
Roanoke (G-12029)

Alexandria Coatings LLC ....E...... 703 643-1636
Lorton (G-7459)

American Stripping Company ....E...... 703 368-9922
Manassas Park (G-8188)

ARS Manufacturing Inc ....C...... 757 460-2211
Virginia Beach (G-14242)

Avm Inc ....G...... 703 802-6212
Chantilly (G-2373)

Brass Age Restorations ....G...... 540 743-4674
Luray (G-7603)

Brass Copper Metal Refinishing........G...... 434 636-5531
Bracey (G-1922)

Colonial Plating Shop ....G...... 804 648-6276
Richmond (G-11532)

Custom Restorations Inc ....G...... 804 693-6526
Gloucester (G-5843)

Dave Cleary ....G...... 727 327-5118
Manassas Park (G-8198)

Electro Finishing Inc....................F...... 276 686-6687
Rural Retreat (G-12423)

Electroplate - Rite Corp ....D...... 540 674-9363
Dublin (G-4155)

Garcia Wood Finishing Inc..............G...... 703 980-6559
Springfield (G-13008)

Global Polishing System LLC ....G...... 937 534-1538
Leesburg (G-7279)

Greystone of Virginia Inc ....G...... 757 566-8070
Toano (G-13865)

Gwendolyn H Spear ....G...... 757 725-2747
Portsmouth (G-10439)

Hankins & Johann Incorporated......G...... 804 266-2421
Richmond (G-11233)

Hudgins Plating Inc C R ....D...... 434 847-6647
Goode (G-5890)

Industrial Machine Works Inc ....E...... 540 949-6115
Waynesboro (G-15116)

Industrial Plating Corp ....G...... 434 582-1920
Lynchburg (G-7738)

James Williams Polsg & Buffing.......G...... 703 690-2247
Woodbridge (G-15728)

Lone Star Polishing Inc ....G...... 434 585-3372
Virgilina (G-14193)

Miller Metal Fabricators Inc............E...... 540 886-5575
Staunton (G-13281)

Production Metal Finishers ....F...... 804 643-8116
Richmond (G-11726)

Restortech Inc ....F...... 703 204-0401
Herndon (G-6789)

Richmond Pressed Met Works Inc ......G...... 804 233-8371
Richmond (G-11736)

Royal Silver Mfg Co Inc ....F...... 757 855-6004
Norfolk (G-9711)

Sifco Applied Srfc Cncepts LLC ....G...... 757 855-4305
Norfolk (G-9724)

Specialty Finishes Inc ....F...... 804 232-5027
Richmond (G-11768)

Stuart-Dean Co Inc......................D...... 703 578-1885
Falls Church (G-4878)

US Anodizing Inc ....G...... 540 937-2801
Amissville (G-722)

Valley Coml Indus Svcs LLC ....F...... 540 908-1156
Dayton (G-4068)

Virginia Custom Plating Inc ....G...... 804 789-0719
Mechanicsville (G-8694)

Virginia Silver Plating Inc...............G...... 757 244-3645
Newport News (G-9375)

Xtreme Fbrction Pwdr Cting LLC ....G...... 540 327-3020
Winchester (G-15521)

3479 Coating & Engraving, NEC

A 1 Coating ....G...... 757 351-5544
Virginia Beach (G-14200)

Advanced Coating Solutions LLC ......G...... 540 898-9370
Fredericksburg (G-5241)

Advanced Cstm Coatings VA LLC ....G...... 757 726-2628
Hampton (G-6072)

Amazengraved LLC ....G...... 540 313-5658
Winchester (G-15376)

American Buildings Company............C...... 434 757-2220
La Crosse (G-7139)

American Stripping Company ....E...... 703 368-9922
Manassas Park (G-8188)

B & B Powder Inc ....G...... 540 921-1158
Pearisburg (G-10272)

B and B Powder Coating ....G...... 540 921-1158
Pearisburg (G-10273)

Candies & Chrome Coatings LLC ....G...... 757 812-1490
Chesapeake (G-3025)

Chesapeake Coatings ....G...... 757 945-2812
Virginia Beach (G-14335)

Combat Coating ....G...... 757 468-9020
Virginia Beach (G-14355)

Commonwealth Galvanizing LLC ....F...... 804 368-0025
Ashland (G-1392)

Creative Coatings Inc ....F...... 540 636-7911
Front Royal (G-5527)

Cresset Corporation ....F...... 804 798-2691
Ashland (G-1399)

Custom Restorations Inc ....G...... 804 693-6526
Gloucester (G-5843)

Customer 1 One Inc ....F...... 276 645-9003
Bristol (G-1974)

Defensecoat Industries LLC ....G...... 804 356-5316
Richmond (G-11559)

Detective Coating LLC ....G...... 804 893-3313
North Chesterfield (G-9859)

Dishman Fabrications LLC ....G...... 757 478-5070
Yorktown (G-15950)

Eastman Performance Films LLC ....D...... 423 224-7768
Martinsville (G-8283)

Eiw Powder Coating ....G...... 703 586-9392
Woodbridge (G-15688)

Eric Margry ....G...... 703 548-7808
Alexandria (G-201)

Europro Coatings Inc ....G...... 703 817-1211
Woodbridge (G-15698)

Extreme Powder Coating LLC ....G...... 703 339-8233
Lorton (G-7486)

Extreme Powder Works LLC ....G...... 540 483-2684
Henry (G-6595)

Fusion Pwdr Cating Fabrication.........G...... 757 319-3760
Chesapeake (G-3112)

General Dynamics ....D...... 757 398-0785
Portsmouth (G-10434)

Global Metal Finishing Inc ....F...... 540 362-1489
Roanoke (G-11926)

Hales Painting Inc ....E...... 540 719-1972
Moneta (G-8964)

Hanover Powder Coating LL ....G...... 804 798-5988
Ashland (G-1429)

Hee K Yoon ....G...... 703 322-9208
Centreville (G-2310)

Hitek Powder Coating ....G...... 434 845-7000
Evington (G-4377)

Hudgins Plating Inc C R ....G...... 434 847-6647
Goode (G-5890)

Hydro Prep & Coating Inc ....G...... 804 530-2178
Chester (G-3423)

Industrial Glvanizers Amer Inc ....G...... 804 763-1760
Petersburg (G-10325)

Infocus Coatings Inc.....................G...... 804 530-4645
Chester (G-3424)

◆ Integrated Global Services Inc.........D...... 804 794-1646
North Chesterfield (G-9898)

J&J Powder Coating ....G...... 757 390-0237
Virginia Beach (G-14559)

Ja Engraving Company LLC ....G...... 540 230-8490
Christiansburg (G-3601)

Jacobs Powder Coating LLC ....G...... 540 208-7762
Penn Laird (G-10289)

John A Treese ....G...... 540 731-0250
Radford (G-10718)

K & W Projects LLC ....G...... 757 618-9249
Chesapeake (G-3161)

Kbm Powder Coating LLC ....G...... 804 496-6860
Ashland (G-1448)

Lalandii Coatings LLC ....G...... 757 425-0131
Virginia Beach (G-14598)

Lane Enterprises Inc.....................F...... 276 223-1051
Wytheville (G-15895)

Lifetime Coating Specialties ....G...... 757 559-1011
Virginia Beach (G-14611)

▲ Lohmann Specialty Coatings LLC......G...... 859 334-4900
Orange (G-10219)

Lynchburg Powder Coating ....G...... 434 239-8454
Lynchburg (G-7763)

Margaret Atkins..........................G...... 434 315-3184
Farmville (G-4949)

Merrill Fine Arts Engrv Inc ....E...... 703 339-3900
Lorton (G-7511)

Metalspray International Inc ....D...... 804 794-1646
Midlothian (G-8856)

Metalspray United Inc ....F...... 804 794-1646
Midlothian (G-8857)

Morgan E McKinney ....G...... 804 389-9371
Richmond (G-11296)

Onyx Coating Solutions LLC ....G...... 434 660-4627
Concord (G-3762)

Pambina Impex ....G...... 703 910-7309
Woodbridge (G-15771)

Peninsula Custom Coaters Inc ....G...... 757 476-6996
Williamsburg (G-15294)

Permaguard Coatings LLC ....G...... 929 352-5665
Mechanicsville (G-8667)

Piedmont Powder Coating Inc ....G...... 434 334-8434
Danville (G-4027)

Precision Powder Coating Inc ....G...... 757 368-2135
Virginia Beach (G-14733)

Prince Group of Virginia LLC ....F...... 703 953-0577
Arlington (G-1120)

Red DOT Laser Engraving LLC ....G...... 540 842-3509
Spotsylvania (G-12911)

Regal Jewelers Inc ....G...... 540 949-4455
Waynesboro (G-15134)

Richmond Powder Coating Inc ....G...... 804 226-4111
Highland Springs (G-6856)

Ruststop USA LLC ....G...... 218 391-5389
Stafford (G-13186)

Shiny Stuff ....G...... 540 586-4446
Bedford (G-1657)

Simpsons Express Paintin ....G...... 804 744-8587
Midlothian (G-8902)

Slejs Custom Coating LLC ....G...... 817 975-6274
Chesapeake (G-3295)

South Atlantic LLC ....E...... 804 798-3257
Ashland (G-1494)

Stephen C Marston ....G...... 757 562-0271
Franklin (G-5157)

Suntek Holding Company ....D...... 276 632-4991
Martinsville (G-8339)

Tc Kustoms ....G...... 434 348-3488
Drewryville (G-4139)

Technical Urethanes Inc ....G...... 540 667-1770
Clear Brook (G-3652)

Thermal Spray Solutions Inc ....E...... 757 673-2468
Chesapeake (G-3331)

Thierry Duguet Engraver Inc ....G...... 434 979-3647
Charlottesville (G-2890)

Tidal Corrosion Services LLC............G...... 757 216-4011
Norfolk (G-9751)

Top Shelf Coatings LLC ....G...... 804 241-8644
Aylett (G-1555)

Tz Industries LLC ....G...... 540 903-7210
King George (G-7117)

▼ Uniquecoat Technologies LLC..........G...... 804 784-0997
Oilville (G-10186)

Vanwin Coatings Virginia LLC ....E...... 757 487-5080
Chesapeake (G-3358)

Vanwin Coatings Virginia LLC ....G...... 757 925-4450
Suffolk (G-13777)

Virginia American Inds Inc ....C...... 804 644-2611
Richmond (G-11807)

Walker Machine and Fndry Corp ....D...... 540 344-6265
Roanoke (G-12226)

William Butler Aluminum ....G...... 804 393-1046
Richmond (G-11450)

3482 Small Arms Ammunition

Alacran ....G...... 540 629-6095
Dublin (G-4147)

American Rhnmtall Munition Inc ....F...... 703 221-9299
Stafford (G-13116)

Ammo Company LLC ....G...... 703 304-4210
Catlett (G-2263)

Ballou Enterprises LLC ....G...... 804 496-6620
Ashland (G-1378)

Broadstone Security LLC ....G...... 703 566-2814
Arlington (G-890)

Chesapeake Cartridge Corp ....G...... 703 989-0903
Dublin (G-4152)

Chesapeake Cartridge Corp Inc ....G...... 703 989-0903
Blacksburg (G-1730)

Dsg TEC Usa Inc ....G...... 619 757-5430
Midland (G-8754)

Dunlap Woodcrafts ....G...... 703 631-5147
Chantilly (G-2414)

Jasons Ammo ....G...... 757 715-4689
Yorktown (G-15969)

Johnson Enterprises LLC ....G...... 804 432-0469
New Kent (G-9134)

K2w Enterprises Corporation ....G...... 540 603-0114
Centreville (G-2313)

Leitner-Wise Manufacturing LLC..........G...... 703 209-0009
Alexandria (G-258)

Match Ammo LLC ....G...... 804 266-2666
Richmond (G-11284)

Nantrak Tactical LLC ....G...... 757 517-2226
Franklin (G-5150)

◆ Northrop Grmman Innvtion Syste ....C...... 703 406-5000
Dulles (G-4212)

Orthoinsight LLC ....G...... 703 722-2553
Chantilly (G-2548)

Proofmark Corp ....G...... 804 453-4337
Burgess (G-2175)

▲ Special Tactical Services LLC ....F...... 757 554-0699
Virginia Beach (G-14835)

United Armament LLC ....G...... 804 839-1800
North Chesterfield (G-10007)

3483 Ammunition, Large

Alexander M Robertson.....................G...... 434 299-5221
Big Island (G-1701)

Allegiance Inc ....G...... 276 639-6884
Clintwood (G-3686)

Bethany Warthan ....G...... 434 294-2937
Blackstone (G-1811)

Bwxt Y - 12 LLC.....................G...... 434 316-7633
Lynchburg (G-7670)

Goldbelt Wolf LLC ....D...... 703 584-8889
Alexandria (G-470)

Iaeva Mercantile LLC ....G...... 301 523-6566
Mc Lean (G-8460)

Lig Nex1 Co Ltd.....................G...... 703 888-2501
Arlington (G-1035)

Multinational Defense Svcs LLC ....G...... 727 333-7290
Mclean (G-8588)

◆ Northrop Grmman Innvtion Syste ....C...... 703 406-5000
Dulles (G-4212)

3484 Small Arms

Absolute Precision LLC ....G...... 757 968-3005
Yorktown (G-15930)

Accuracy International N Amer ....G...... 907 440-4024
Fredericksburg (G-5240)

Alexander Industries Inc ....G...... 540 443-9250
Radford (G-10703)

Amherst Arms and Supply LLC ....G...... 434 929-1978
Madison Heights (G-7867)

Backwoods Security LLC ....G...... 804 641-0674
Moseley (G-9033)

Ballistics Center LLC ....G...... 703 380-4901
Woodbridge (G-15653)

Be Ready Enterprises LLC ....G...... 540 422-9210
Fredericksburg (G-5172)

Broadstone Security LLC ....G...... 703 566-2814
Arlington (G-890)

Carotank Road LLC ....G...... 703 951-7790
Alexandria (G-161)

Casey Traxler.......................G...... 703 402-0745
Leesburg (G-7242)

Corporate Arms Llc ....G...... 800 256-5803
Springfield (G-12981)

Costacamps-Net LLC ....G...... 571 482-6858
Springfield (G-12983)

Epic Mfg LLC ....G...... 757 689-4373
Virginia Beach (G-14449)

Fausti USA Service LLC ....G...... 540 371-3287
Fredericksburg (G-5286)

Fjord Defense Inc ....G...... 571 214-2183
Alexandria (G-205)

▲ FN America LLC ....C...... 703 288-3500
Mc Lean (G-8434)

FN America LLC ....G...... 540 288-8002
Fredericksburg (G-5431)

Forging The Warrior Spirit ....G...... 703 851-4789
Marshall (G-8252)

Grayman Usa LLC..................G...... 703 598-6934
Aldie (G-106)

Greenstein LLC ....G...... 540 408-9877
Stafford (G-13149)

Hexmag LLC ....F...... 970 203-9100
Virginia Beach (G-14521)

Kennesaw Holding Company ....G...... 603 866-6944
Fairfax (G-4643)

Kriss Usa Inc ....E...... 714 333-1988
Chesapeake (G-3168)

L&L Trading Company LLC..................G...... 757 995-3608
Virginia Beach (G-14595)

Leitner-Wise Defense Inc ....G...... 703 209-0009
Springfield (G-13042)

Leitner-Wise Manufacturing LLC..........G...... 703 209-0009
Alexandria (G-258)

Lwag Holdings Inc ....F...... 703 455-8650
Springfield (G-13045)

Matoaca Specialty Arms Inc ....G...... 804 590-2749
South Chesterfield (G-12837)

Matthew Mitchell ....G...... 615 454-0787
Fredericksburg (G-5455)

Rifle Building LLC ....G...... 518 879-9195
Norfolk (G-9708)

Shawn Gaines ....G...... 434 332-4819
Rustburg (G-12446)

Small Arms Mfg Solutions LLC ....G...... 757 673-7769
Chesapeake (G-3297)

Tr Partners Lc ....G...... 804 484-4091
Glen Allen (G-5815)

Unison Arms LLC ....G...... 571 342-1108
Round Hill (G-12392)

US Tactical Inc ....G...... 703 217-8781
Oakton (G-10163)

Vertu Corp ....E...... 540 341-3006
Manassas (G-8174)

Vertu Corp ....F...... 540 341-3006
Warrenton (G-15058)

Vfg Enterprises LLC ....G...... 757 343-4866
Virginia Beach (G-14908)

War Fighter Specialties LLC ....G...... 540 742-4187
Shenandoah (G-12697)

Whisper Tactical LLC ....G...... 757 645-5938
Chesapeake (G-3376)

3489 Ordnance & Access, NEC

Axon Enterprise Inc ....G...... 602 459-1278
Arlington (G-870)

Barker Collision Precision LLC ....G...... 716 481-8253
Richmond (G-11121)

C Media Company ....G...... 540 339-9626
Roanoke (G-12059)

Ccf/Swiss Inc ....G...... 804 622-4277
Richmond (G-11153)

Country Wood Crafts ....G...... 540 833-4985
Linville (G-7434)

E Giuffre Inc ....G...... 540 537-4367
Wirtz (G-15610)

Entwistle Company ....E...... 434 799-6186
Danville (G-3992)

Eye Armor Incorporated ....G...... 571 238-4096
Stafford (G-13144)

Foxcreek Tactical LLC ....G...... 757 615-0474
Virginia Beach (G-14473)

H & S Tactical LLC ....G...... 540 710-2715
Fredericksburg (G-5294)

Hawk Hill Custom LLC..............G...... 540 248-4295
Verona (G-13988)

ITT Defense & Electronics...............A...... 703 790-6300
Mc Lean (G-8474)

Kongsberg Defense Systems Inc ....G...... 703 838-8910
Alexandria (G-255)

Kongsberg Prtech Systems USA C ....G...... 703 838-8910
Alexandria (G-256)

Larsco LLC ....G...... 804 400-0667
North Chesterfield (G-9913)

Mabe Tactical LLC..................G...... 276 524-4912
Big Stone Gap (G-1712)

Madison Colonial LLC ....G...... 240 997-2376
Toano (G-13868)

◆ Northrop Grmman Innvtion Syste......C...... 703 406-5000
Dulles (G-4212)

Red Moon Partners LLC ....G...... 757 240-4305
Hampton (G-6226)

Ro-Way Inc ....G...... 757 566-3569
Toano (G-13876)

▲ Special Tactical Services LLC ....F...... 757 554-0699
Virginia Beach (G-14835)

Theos Shotgun Corner ....G...... 434 248-6250
Charlotte C H (G-2584)

Theresa Lucas Setelin ....G...... 804 266-2324
Glen Allen (G-5809)

Veteran Arms Inc ....G...... 703 217-7532
Woodbridge (G-15826)

Wayland Custom Calibers LLC...........G...... 540 533-6842
Winchester (G-15506)

◆ Wegmann Usa Inc ....D...... 434 385-1580
Lynchburg (G-7837)

Winchester Tool LLC ....G...... 540 869-1150
Winchester (G-15602)

3491 Industrial Valves

Alfa Laval Champ LLC ....G...... 866 253-2528
Richmond (G-11094)

◆ Alfa Laval Inc ....C...... 866 253-2528
Richmond (G-11095)

Augusta Actuation LLC ....G...... 540 480-7619
Steeles Tavern (G-13310)

Chesapeake Bay Controls Inc ....F...... 757 228-5537
Virginia Beach (G-14333)

▲ Controls Corporation America.......C...... 757 422-8330
Virginia Beach (G-14363)

Curtiss-Wright Corporation ....F...... 703 779-7800
Ashburn (G-1266)

Firewall LLC ....G...... 804 977-8777
Mechanicsville (G-8623)

Flow Dynamics Inc ....G...... 804 835-9740
Petersburg (G-10320)

Hanbay Inc ....G...... 757 333-6375
Virginia Beach (G-14502)

Key Recovery Corporation ....G...... 540 444-2628
Salem (G-12526)

Schrader-Bridgeport Intl Inc ....C...... 434 369-4741
Altavista (G-642)

◆ Schrader-Bridgeport Intl Inc ....A...... 434 369-4741
Altavista (G-641)

Seacrist Motor Sports ....G...... 540 309-2234
Salem (G-12568)

Seager Valve ....G...... 757 478-0607
Chesapeake (G-3289)

Valve Automation Center ....G...... 804 752-2700
Ashland (G-1505)

3492 Fluid Power Valves & Hose Fittings

Alpha Developement Bureau...............F...... 540 337-4900
Fishersville (G-5000)

Hamilton Equipment Service LLC ....G...... 540 341-4141
Warrenton (G-15022)

Hy-Tech Usa Inc ....G...... 804 647-2048
Midlothian (G-8830)

Hydra Hose & Supply Co ....G...... 757 867-9795
Yorktown (G-15964)

Mid-Atlantic Rubber Inc ....F...... 540 710-5690
Fredericksburg (G-5326)

Moog Inc ....G...... 716 652-2000
Blacksburg (G-1764)

Riverside Hydraulics LLC ....G...... 804 545-6700
Ashland (G-1488)

◆ Schrader-Bridgeport Intl Inc ....A...... 434 369-4741
Altavista (G-641)

Schrader-Bridgeport Intl Inc ....C...... 434 369-4741
Altavista (G-642)

Valley Supply and Services LLC...........G...... 276 979-4547
North Tazewell (G-10110)

3493 Steel Springs, Except Wire

Starsprings USA Inc ....D...... 276 403-4500
Ridgeway (G-11855)

3494 Valves & Pipe Fittings, NEC

American Manufacturing Co Inc...........E...... 540 825-7234
Elkwood (G-4341)

Ames & Ames Inc..................G...... 757 877-2328
Yorktown (G-15932)

Ames & Ames Inc..................G...... 757 851-4723
Hampton (G-6083)

Azz Inc ....E...... 276 466-5558
Bristol (G-2007)

Dante Industries Inc ....G...... 757 605-6100
Norfolk (G-9516)

Fluid Energy ....G...... 757 549-5160
Chesapeake (G-3106)

▲ International Carbide & Engrg ....F...... 434 568-3311
Drakes Branch (G-4133)

◆ Ksb America Corporation ....G...... 804 222-1818
Richmond (G-11265)

Mm Export LLC ....G...... 757 333-0542
Virginia Beach (G-14658)

Nibco Inc ....E...... 540 324-0242
Stuarts Draft (G-13656)

Roanoke Hose & Fittings ....G...... 540 985-4832
Roanoke (G-12166)

3495 Wire Springs

Custom Made Springs Inc ....G...... 757 489-8202
Norfolk (G-9511)

Oxiwear Inc ....G...... 571 212-7526
Arlington (G-1093)

▲ Prototype Productions Inc ....D...... 703 858-0011
Chantilly (G-2483)

SIC

3496 Misc Fabricated Wire Prdts

Ashworth Bros Inc..........C....... 540 662-3494
Winchester *(G-15530)*
C S Lewis & Sons LLC..........G....... 804 275-6879
North Chesterfield *(G-9838)*
Electrnic Cabling Assembly Inc..........E....... 434 293-2593
Charlottesville *(G-2789)*
◆ **Fyne-Wire Specialties Inc**..........E....... 540 825-2701
Brandy Station *(G-1939)*
▲ **Global Safety Textiles LLC**..........D....... 434 447-7629
South Hill *(G-12851)*
Handi-Leigh Crafted..........G....... 540 349-7775
Warrenton *(G-15023)*
Heco Slings Corporation..........F....... 757 855-7139
Norfolk *(G-9578)*
I & I Sling Inc..........G....... 703 550-9405
Lorton *(G-7494)*
Jack Campbell Widner..........G....... 703 646-8841
Chilhowie *(G-3552)*
Marshall Manufacturing Co..........F....... 757 824-4061
Atlantic *(G-1525)*
Maxx Material Systems LLC..........E....... 757 637-4026
Hampton *(G-6192)*
Mazzella Jhh Company Inc..........G....... 757 827-9600
Hampton *(G-6193)*
Merchants Metals LLC..........G....... 804 262-9783
Rockville *(G-12293)*
Merchants Metals LLC..........G....... 877 518-7665
Fredericksburg *(G-5324)*
▼ **Mid Valley Products**..........G....... 757 625-0780
Norfolk *(G-9643)*
Modek Inc..........G....... 804 550-7300
Ashland *(G-1463)*
Northern Virginia Wire Works..........G....... 571 221-1882
Gainesville *(G-5603)*
Pgb Hangers LLC..........G....... 703 851-4221
Gainesville *(G-5607)*
Quiltery LLC..........G....... 540 377-9191
Fairfield *(G-4734)*
R A Pearson Company..........D....... 804 550-7300
Ashland *(G-1482)*
▲ **Silver Spur Conveyors**..........G....... 276 596-9414
Raven *(G-10757)*
Spades & Diamonds Clothing Co..........G....... 804 271-0374
Chesterfield *(G-3527)*
T & J Wldg & Fabrication LLC..........G....... 757 672-9929
Suffolk *(G-13770)*
Unarco Industries LLC..........C....... 434 792-9531
Danville *(G-4044)*

3497 Metal Foil & Leaf

▼ **Hot Stamp Supply Company**..........G....... 540 868-7500
Winchester *(G-15425)*
Mottley Foils Inc..........F....... 434 392-8347
Farmville *(G-4952)*
Reynolds Consumer Products LLC..........B....... 804 230-5200
Richmond *(G-11735)*
◆ **Vitex Packaging Group Inc**..........F....... 757 538-3115
Suffolk *(G-13780)*

3498 Fabricated Pipe & Pipe Fittings

American Mar & Indus Svcs LLC..........F....... 757 573-1209
Chesapeake *(G-2968)*
◆ **Applied Felts Inc**..........D....... 276 656-1904
Martinsville *(G-8267)*
Azz Inc..........E....... 276 466-5558
Bristol *(G-2007)*
C & B Piping (e) Inc..........G....... 434 946-7170
Amherst *(G-686)*
Davco Fabricating & Welding..........G....... 434 836-0234
Danville *(G-3980)*
Green Point..........G....... 703 391-5006
Herndon *(G-6691)*
◆ **Harrington Corporation**..........C....... 434 845-7094
Lynchburg *(G-7729)*
Lane Enterprises Inc..........F....... 540 439-3201
Bealeton *(G-1600)*
Lokring Mid-Atlantic Inc..........G....... 757 423-2784
Norfolk *(G-9621)*
Mica Co of Canada Inc..........G....... 757 244-7311
Newport News *(G-9299)*
Midyette Bros Mfg Inc..........G....... 757 425-5022
Virginia Beach *(G-14652)*
Riggins Company LLC..........D....... 757 826-0525
Hampton *(G-6228)*
RPS Shenandoah Inc..........F....... 540 635-2131
Front Royal *(G-5551)*
Super RAD Coils Ltd Partnr..........C....... 804 794-2887
North Chesterfield *(G-9992)*
U S Pipe Fabrication..........F....... 540 439-7373
Remington *(G-10775)*
▲ **United States Pipe Fndry LLC**..........F....... 540 439-7373
Remington *(G-10776)*

3499 Fabricated Metal Prdts, NEC

Agile Access Control Inc..........G....... 408 213-9555
Chantilly *(G-2363)*
American Mtal Fbrcation VA LLC..........G....... 434 851-1002
Appomattox *(G-801)*
Amfab Inc..........G....... 757 543-1485
Chesapeake *(G-2975)*
Artistic Awards..........G....... 540 636-9940
Woodstock *(G-15847)*
◆ **Assa Abloy High SEC Group Inc**..........C....... 540 380-5000
Salem *(G-12476)*
Atlantic Containment LLC..........E....... 540 289-5051
McGaheysville *(G-8583)*
B&E Sht-Metal Fabrications Inc..........G....... 757 536-1279
Virginia Beach *(G-14255)*
Beach Hot Rods Met Fabrication..........G....... 757 227-8191
Virginia Beach *(G-14266)*
Black Dog Gallery..........G....... 757 989-1700
Yorktown *(G-15938)*
Brownell Metal Studio Inc..........G....... 434 591-0379
Troy *(G-13920)*
Buerlein & Co LLC..........G....... 804 355-1758
Richmond *(G-11513)*
Bull Run Metal Inc..........G....... 540 347-2135
Warrenton *(G-14984)*
Burnopp Metal LLC..........G....... 434 525-4746
Evington *(G-4375)*
C L Towing..........G....... 703 625-7126
Alexandria *(G-157)*
Caldwell Mountain Copper..........G....... 540 473-2167
Fincastle *(G-4993)*
Centrex Fab..........G....... 804 598-6000
Powhatan *(G-10537)*
▲ **Cochrane USA Inc**..........G....... 202 434-8163
Fredericksburg *(G-5263)*
▲ **Colonnas Ship Yard Inc**..........A....... 757 545-2414
Norfolk *(G-9495)*
Colonnas Ship Yard Inc..........A....... 757 545-2414
Norfolk *(G-9497)*
Cushing Metals LLC..........G....... 804 339-1114
King William *(G-7128)*
Custom Fabrication Svcs Inc..........G....... 540 483-8809
Henry *(G-6594)*
Debs Picture This Inc..........G....... 757 867-9588
Yorktown *(G-15949)*
Depco-Dfnse Engneered Pdts LLC..........G....... 804 271-7000
Chesterfield *(G-3493)*
Design In Copper Inc..........F....... 540 885-8557
Staunton *(G-13250)*
▲ **Design Master Associates Inc**..........E....... 757 566-8500
Toano *(G-13864)*
Drs Custom Fabrication LLC..........G....... 703 680-4259
Dumfries *(G-4243)*
Ds & RC Enterprises LLC..........G....... 804 824-5478
Gloucester *(G-5846)*
Dynamic Fabworks LLC..........G....... 757 439-1169
Virginia Beach *(G-14421)*
Electromagnetic Shielding Inc..........G....... 540 286-3780
Fredericksburg *(G-5426)*
▼ **Fedsafes LLC**..........G....... 703 525-1436
Arlington *(G-964)*
Finish Line Shtmtal & Fbrictns..........G....... 757 262-1122
Hampton *(G-6149)*
Flip-N-Haul LLC..........G....... 804 932-4372
New Kent *(G-9132)*
Frameco Inc..........G....... 540 375-3683
Salem *(G-12507)*
Gift Terrariums LLC..........G....... 571 230-5918
Sterling *(G-13411)*
Gyrfalcon Aerial Systems LLC..........G....... 757 724-1861
Mechanicsville *(G-8633)*
Hallmark Fabricators Inc..........G....... 804 230-0880
Richmond *(G-11607)*
HP Metal Fabrication..........G....... 703 466-5551
Bristow *(G-2055)*
HP Metal Fabrication LLC..........G....... 571 499-0298
Nokesville *(G-9394)*
Integrated Design Solutions..........F....... 540 735-5424
Spotsylvania *(G-12897)*
◆ **Intrapac (harrisonburg) Inc**..........B....... 540 434-1703
Mount Crawford *(G-9055)*
◆ **Kool Looks Inc**..........F....... 808 224-1887
Bristow *(G-2058)*
Lloyds Pewter..........G....... 757 503-1110
Williamsburg *(G-15272)*
Masonite International Corp..........E....... 540 778-2211
Stanley *(G-13232)*
Michael W Gillespie..........G....... 540 894-0288
Louisa *(G-7560)*
Mitchell Lock Out..........G....... 276 322-4087
Bluefield *(G-1870)*
New ERA Technology LLC..........G....... 571 308-8525
Fairfax *(G-4517)*
Old Dominion Metal Pdts Inc..........E....... 804 355-7123
Richmond *(G-11700)*
Ora Inc..........G....... 540 368-3012
Fredericksburg *(G-5466)*
Performnce Mtal Fbricators Inc..........G....... 757 465-8622
Portsmouth *(G-10467)*
▼ **Phipps & Bird Inc**..........F....... 804 254-2737
Richmond *(G-11059)*
Powder Metal Fabrication..........G....... 757 898-1614
Yorktown *(G-15984)*
▲ **Prototype Productions Inc**..........D....... 703 858-0011
Chantilly *(G-2483)*
R2jb Enterprises..........G....... 703 727-3342
Round Hill *(G-12385)*
Shickel Corporation..........D....... 540 828-2536
Bridgewater *(G-1959)*
Spraying Systems Co..........G....... 804 364-0095
Richmond *(G-11394)*
Standard Marine Inc..........F....... 757 824-0293
Mears *(G-8597)*
▲ **Stickers Plus Ltd**..........D....... 540 857-3045
Vinton *(G-14184)*
T&M Metal Fabrication LLC..........G....... 703 726-6949
Ashburn *(G-1338)*
Tim Shepherd Archit Fabricati..........G....... 540 230-1457
Roanoke *(G-12203)*
◆ **Tread Corporation**..........D....... 540 982-6881
Roanoke *(G-12010)*
Uav Communications Inc..........E....... 757 271-3428
Newport News *(G-9368)*
US Joiner Holding Company..........G....... 434 220-8500
Crozet *(G-3854)*
Utron Kinetics LLC..........G....... 703 369-5552
Manassas *(G-8008)*
Viking Fabrication Services..........G....... 804 228-1333
Richmond *(G-11806)*
Virginia Mtals Fabrication LLC..........G....... 804 622-2900
North Chesterfield *(G-10043)*
Waller Brothers Trophy Shop..........G....... 434 376-5465
Nathalie *(G-9104)*
Word Play By Deb LLC..........G....... 703 389-5112
Alexandria *(G-614)*
Wrights Iron Inc..........G....... 540 661-1089
Orange *(G-10235)*
Yowell Metal Fabrication LLC..........G....... 434 971-3018
Troy *(G-13938)*

35 INDUSTRIAL AND COMMERCIAL MACHINERY AND COMPUTER EQUIPMENT

3511 Steam, Gas & Hydraulic Turbines & Engines

Alstom Renewable US LLC..........E....... 804 763-2196
Midlothian *(G-8771)*
Atlantic Research Corporation..........C....... 540 854-2000
Culpeper *(G-3869)*
Birge Croft..........G....... 757 547-0838
Chesapeake *(G-3002)*
Continental Auto Systems Inc..........C....... 540 825-4100
Culpeper *(G-3880)*
Coriolis Wind Inc..........F....... 703 969-1257
Great Falls *(G-5950)*
Edge McS LLC..........G....... 804 379-6772
Midlothian *(G-8813)*
Edgeconnex Inc..........G....... 757 855-0351
Norfolk *(G-9540)*
Effithermix LLC..........G....... 703 860-9703
Vienna *(G-14043)*
▲ **Hydropower Turbine Systems**..........G....... 804 360-7992
Powhatan *(G-10550)*
Siemens Industry Inc..........G....... 757 766-4190
Hampton *(G-6234)*
Virginia Electric and Power Co..........F....... 757 558-5459
Chesapeake *(G-3360)*
Zenman Technology LLC..........G....... 757 679-6703
Norfolk *(G-9800)*

3519 Internal Combustion Engines, NEC

◆ **American Diesel Corp** ....G...... 804 435-3107
Kilmarnock *(G-7068)*
American Marine and Engine.................G...... 276 263-1211
Collinsville *(G-3708)*
Avei ....G...... 571 278-0823
Centreville *(G-2292)*
▲ **Barr Marine By E D M** ....G...... 540 291-4180
Natural Bridge Stati *(G-9108)*
Chesapeake Integrated Bioenrgy ....G...... 202 253-5953
Fairfax Station *(G-4701)*
Engines Unlimited Inc ....G...... 276 566-7208
Wolford *(G-15638)*
Fairbanks Morse LLC ....G...... 757 623-2711
Norfolk *(G-9548)*
Foley Machine ....G...... 276 930-1983
Stuart *(G-13612)*
Fridays Marine Inc ....G...... 804 758-4131
Saluda *(G-12603)*
Invista Precision Concepts ....G...... 276 656-0504
Martinsville *(G-8302)*
Jerrys Engines LLC ....G...... 540 885-1205
Staunton *(G-13269)*
M & B Diesel Supply LLC ....G...... 757 903-8146
Newport News *(G-9288)*
Mactaggart Scott Usa LLC ....G...... 757 288-1405
Virginia Beach *(G-14631)*
Man Diesel & Turbo N Amer Inc.................G...... 703 373-0690
Herndon *(G-6741)*
Mays Auto Machine Shop Inc ....G...... 276 646-3752
Chilhowie *(G-3555)*
Mdr Performance Engines LLC ....G...... 540 338-1001
Leesburg *(G-7310)*
Performance Consulting Inc ....G...... 434 724-2904
Dry Fork *(G-4143)*
Periflame LLC ....F...... 888 996-3526
Arlington *(G-1107)*
Valley Rebuilders Co Inc ....G...... 540 342-2108
Roanoke *(G-12214)*
◆ **Volvo Penta Marine Pdts LLC** ....G...... 757 436-2800
Chesapeake *(G-3364)*
Volvo Penta of Americas LLC ....C...... 757 436-2800
Chesapeake *(G-3365)*
Western Branch Diesel Inc ....E...... 703 369-5005
Manassas *(G-8177)*
Wheatley Racing ....G...... 804 276-3670
North Chesterfield *(G-10044)*

3523 Farm Machinery & Eqpt

Afritech LLC ....G...... 703 550-0392
Alexandria *(G-405)*
Alban Tractor Co Inc ....F...... 540 667-4200
Clear Brook *(G-3643)*
◆ **Amadas Industries Inc** ....D...... 757 539-0231
Suffolk *(G-13668)*
Arctech Inc ....G...... 434 575-7200
South Boston *(G-12749)*
Bacons Castle Supply Inc ....G...... 757 357-6159
Surry *(G-13796)*
Bae Systems Tctcal Vhcl System ....E...... 571 461-6000
Falls Church *(G-4759)*
Beery Brothers ....G...... 540 879-2970
Dayton *(G-4052)*
Bh Cooper Farm & Mill Inc ....G...... 276 694-6292
Critz *(G-3823)*
Case Mechanical ....G...... 804 501-0003
Richmond *(G-11151)*
Case Mechanical LLC ....G...... 757 272-6050
Newport News *(G-9193)*
Commercial Water Works Inc ....G...... 434 534-8244
Forest *(G-5061)*
Eric Washington ....G...... 434 249-3567
Charlottesville *(G-2626)*
Ferguson Manufacturing Co Inc ....F...... 757 539-3409
Suffolk *(G-13709)*
Frye Delance ....G...... 540 923-4581
Etlan *(G-4373)*
Gas House Co ....G...... 434 822-1324
Danville *(G-3996)*
Griffin Manufacturing Company ....G...... 757 986-4541
Suffolk *(G-13716)*
Harris Company Inc ....G...... 540 894-4413
Mineral *(G-8949)*
Hartwood Landscape Inc ....G...... 540 379-2650
Fredericksburg *(G-5438)*
Hnh Partners Inc ....G...... 757 539-2353
Annandale *(G-757)*
Hoffmanns Custom Display Cases ....G...... 804 332-4873
Sandston *(G-12619)*

Jerry Cantrell.................G...... 540 379-7689
Fredericksburg *(G-5443)*
Joglex Corporation ....G...... 540 833-2444
Linville *(G-7435)*
L & N Wood Products Inc ....G...... 804 784-4734
Oilville *(G-10181)*
Lebanon Seaboard Corporation ....G...... 540 375-0300
Salem *(G-12530)*
Lesco Inc ....G...... 804 957-5516
Disputanta *(G-4112)*
Live Cases ....G...... 703 627-0994
Oakton *(G-10154)*
Milnesville Enterprises LLC ....G...... 540 487-4073
Bridgewater *(G-1955)*
Modek Inc ....G...... 804 550-7300
Ashland *(G-1463)*
◆ **Monoflo International Inc** ....G...... 540 665-1691
Winchester *(G-15451)*
Norfields Farm Inc ....G...... 540 832-2952
Gordonsville *(G-5916)*
P & P Farm Machinery Inc ....G...... 276 794-7806
Lebanon *(G-7203)*
R A Pearson Company ....D...... 804 550-7300
Ashland *(G-1482)*
Ronald Stephen Rhodes ....G...... 540 435-1441
Keezletown *(G-7029)*
Scott Turf Equipment LLC ....G...... 434 401-3031
Rustburg *(G-12443)*
Scott Turf Equipment LLC ....G...... 434 401-3031
Rustburg *(G-12444)*
Silk Tree Manufacturing Inc ....G...... 434 983-1941
Dillwyn *(G-4100)*
Southern Sttes Wnchster Coop I.........F...... 540 662-0375
Winchester *(G-15588)*
Sustaita Lawn Care ....G...... 434 390-8118
Cumberland *(G-3937)*
Tidewater Tree ....G...... 757 426-6002
Virginia Beach *(G-14879)*
Timothy C Vass ....G...... 276 728-7753
Hillsville *(G-6900)*
Titan Turf LLC ....G...... 276 768-7833
Galax *(G-5650)*
Valley Grounds Inc ....E...... 540 382-6710
Christiansburg *(G-3615)*
Virginia Carolina Buildings.................F...... 434 645-7411
Crewe *(G-3820)*
Vmek Group LLC ....G...... 804 380-1831
Midlothian *(G-8919)*
West End Precast LLC ....G...... 276 228-5024
Wytheville *(G-15922)*
Zipnut Technology LLC ....G...... 703 442-7339
Falls Church *(G-4898)*

3524 Garden, Lawn Tractors & Eqpt

Abeck Inc ....G...... 540 375-2841
Salem *(G-12471)*
Antonio Robinson ....G...... 804 368-9889
Petersburg *(G-10305)*
Asb Greenworld Inc ....G...... 804 695-2660
Saluda *(G-12600)*
Beltsville Construction Supply.................G...... 703 392-8588
Manassas *(G-8037)*
Benabaye Power LLC ....G...... 703 574-5800
Sterling *(G-13357)*
Canaan Land Associates Inc ....D...... 276 988-6543
Tazewell *(G-13829)*
Carters Power Equipment Inc.................G...... 804 796-4895
Chester *(G-3392)*
Cub Cadet Culpeper LLC ....G...... 540 825-8381
Culpeper *(G-3882)*
Direct Cut Lawn Tree Svc LLC ....G...... 804 516-7771
Manakin Sabot *(G-7899)*
Douglas Vince Johner ....G...... 276 780-2369
Chilhowie *(G-3550)*
Eaheart Equipment Inc ....F...... 540 347-2880
Warrenton *(G-15002)*
Eaheart Equipment Inc ....F...... 703 366-3880
Manassas *(G-7934)*
Ferguson Manufacturing Co Inc ....F...... 757 539-3409
Suffolk *(G-13709)*
Hipkins Horticulture Co LLC.................G...... 804 926-7116
South Chesterfield *(G-12835)*
Jr Sales ....G...... 703 450-4753
Sterling *(G-13436)*
▲ **Mantel USA Inc** ....G...... 540 946-6529
Waynesboro *(G-15122)*
Mark T Goodman ....G...... 540 582-2328
Partlow *(G-10267)*
◆ **Melnor Inc** ....E...... 540 722-5600
Winchester *(G-15447)*

Mr-Mow-It-all ....G...... 540 263-2369
Roanoke *(G-12138)*
Quest Expedition Outfitte ....G...... 434 244-7140
Charlottesville *(G-2853)*
Robert C Reed ....G...... 804 493-7297
Montross *(G-9027)*
Silver Lining Assistance Inc ....F...... 540 825-8371
Culpeper *(G-3921)*
Tri-County Ope ....G...... 434 676-4441
Kenbridge *(G-7035)*

3531 Construction Machinery & Eqpt

Altec Industries ....G...... 804 621-4080
Chester *(G-3385)*
Altec Industries Inc ....C...... 540 992-5300
Daleville *(G-3938)*
Amadas Industries Inc ....G...... 757 539-0231
Suffolk *(G-13667)*
◆ **Amadas Industries Inc** ....D...... 757 539-0231
Suffolk *(G-13668)*
Archer Construction ....G...... 276 637-6905
Max Meadows *(G-8365)*
B & T LLC ....G...... 804 720-1758
Chester *(G-3389)*
Bobcat Service of T N C ....G...... 757 482-2773
Chesapeake *(G-3009)*
Breeze-Eastern LLC ....G...... 973 602-1001
Fredericksburg *(G-5175)*
Caterpillar Corner LLC ....G...... 703 939-1798
South Riding *(G-12867)*
Charles M Fariss ....F...... 434 660-0606
Rustburg *(G-12438)*
Chucks Concrete Pumping LLC ....G...... 804 347-3986
Henrico *(G-6492)*
Clean Marine Electronics Inc ....G...... 703 847-5142
Falls Church *(G-4775)*
Clements Backhoe LLC ....G...... 804 598-6230
Powhatan *(G-10539)*
Cody Sterling Hawkins ....G...... 276 477-0238
Bristol *(G-1972)*
Cozy Caterpillars ....G...... 757 499-3769
Virginia Beach *(G-14369)*
Cubbage Crane Maintenance ....G...... 804 739-5459
Chesterfield *(G-3491)*
Cuz To Cuz Trucking ....G...... 757 806-0358
Newport News *(G-9210)*
D K Backhoe Loader Serv ....G...... 434 969-1685
Buckingham *(G-2132)*
David R Powell ....G...... 434 724-2642
Dry Fork *(G-4140)*
Delmarva Crane Inc ....G...... 757 426-0862
Virginia Beach *(G-14400)*
Dewey L Sams ....G...... 540 664-4034
Berryville *(G-1678)*
Dexter W Estes ....G...... 434 996-8068
Lyndhurst *(G-7843)*
Diloreto Partners Inc ....G...... 804 271-2363
Richmond *(G-11041)*
Ditch Witch of Virginia ....G...... 804 798-2590
Glen Allen *(G-5725)*
Drillco National Group Inc ....G...... 703 631-3222
Chantilly *(G-2411)*
Edwards Kretz Lohr & Assoc ....F...... 804 673-9666
Henrico *(G-6506)*
Electronic Devices Inc ....G...... 757 421-2968
Chesapeake *(G-3085)*
Equipment Repair Services ....G...... 703 491-7681
Woodbridge *(G-15695)*
Eugene Martin Trucking ....G...... 434 454-7267
Scottsburg *(G-12655)*
Galaxy Eqp Maint Solutions Inc ....G...... 703 866-0246
Springfield *(G-13007)*
George W Wray ....G...... 540 483-7792
Rocky Mount *(G-12324)*
Giant Gradall and Eqp Rentl ....G...... 703 878-3032
Montclair *(G-8998)*
Gradall Industries Inc ....G...... 540 819-6638
Troutville *(G-13910)*
Graves ....G...... 434 656-2491
Pittsville *(G-10362)*
H D and Company ....G...... 540 651-4354
Check *(G-2944)*
H H Backhoe Service ....G...... 540 574-3578
Rockingham *(G-12254)*
H&L Backhoe Service Inc ....G...... 540 399-5013
Richardsville *(G-11010)*
Haislip Farms LLC ....G...... 801 932-4087
Quinton *(G-10696)*
HM Trucking ....G...... 703 932-7058
Herndon *(G-6702)*

◆ Hotspot Energy Inc ....F 757 410-8640
   Chesapeake (G-3137)

Imco Inc ....E 434 299-5919
   Monroe (G-8992)

Innovative Wireless Tech Inc ....E 434 316-5230
   Lynchburg (G-7741)

Intel Investigations LLC ....G 540 521-4111
   Roanoke (G-11941)

Jackson & Jackson Inc ....G 434 851-1798
   Roanoke (G-12109)

James River Industries BT ....G 702 515-9937
   Lynchburg (G-7748)

Jet Managers International Inc ....G 703 829-0679
   Alexandria (G-244)

John Demasco ....G 434 977-4214
   Charlottesville (G-2652)

Kennedys Excavating LLC ....G 423 383-0143
   Bristol (G-2023)

◆ Lemac Corporation ....E 804 862-8481
   North Dinwiddie (G-10057)

Lewin Asphalt Inc ....G 540 550-9478
   Winchester (G-15440)

MIC Industries Inc ....F 540 678-2900
   Clear Brook (G-3647)

▲ MIC Industries Inc ....E 703 318-1900
   Clear Brook (G-3648)

Mid-Atlantic Backhoe Inc ....G 804 897-3443
   Midlothian (G-8858)

Miguel Soto ....G 571 274-3790
   Leesburg (G-7315)

ML Manufacturing ....G 434 581-2000
   New Canton (G-9118)

Mosena Enterprises Inc ....G 757 562-7033
   Franklin (G-5149)

Moxley Brothers ....G 276 236-6580
   Galax (G-5642)

Moyer Brothers Contracting Inc ......G 540 743-7864
   Luray (G-7618)

▲ Mrp Munufacturing Inc ....E 434 525-1993
   Forest (G-5084)

Paver Doctors LLC ....G 757 903-6275
   Williamsburg (G-15292)

Pearson Equipment Company ....G 434 845-3171
   Lynchburg (G-7784)

Per LLC ....G 540 489-4737
   Rocky Mount (G-12344)

▲ Plasser American Corporation ....C 757 543-3526
   Chesapeake (G-3242)

Platnick Crane and Steel LLC ....F 276 322-5477
   Bluefield (G-1874)

Ralph Matney ....G 276 644-9259
   Bristol (G-2031)

S & S Backhoe & Excvtr Svc LLC .....G 434 656-3184
   Gretna (G-6010)

S & S Equipment Sls & Svc Inc ....G 757 421-3000
   Chesapeake (G-3280)

Salmons Dredging Inc ....G 757 426-6824
   Virginia Beach (G-14790)

Shantell C Young ....G 251 348-7247
   Newport News (G-9335)

Sopko Manufacturing Inc ....F 434 848-3460
   Lawrenceville (G-7185)

Southern Plumbing & Backhoe In ......G 804 598-7470
   Moseley (G-9048)

Spectra Quest Inc ....G 804 261-3300
   Henrico (G-6574)

◆ St Engineering North Amer Inc ....E 703 739-2610
   Alexandria (G-353)

Sunset Pavers Inc ....G 703 507-9101
   Sumerduck (G-13794)

Taal Enterprises LLC ....G 276 328-2408
   Wise (G-15634)

Tadano Mantis Corporation ....E 800 272-3325
   Richlands (G-11020)

Terex Corporation ....G 540 361-7755
   Fredericksburg (G-5492)

Terrabuilt Corp International ....G 540 687-4211
   Middleburg (G-8734)

Treescapes Inc ....G 434 294-0865
   Alberta (G-99)

Tri-City Industrial Builders ....G 276 669-4621
   Bristol (G-2036)

Utiliscope Corp ....G 804 550-5233
   Glen Allen (G-5822)

Virginia Wave Inc ....G 804 693-4278
   Gloucester (G-5865)

Vision Tech Land Systems ....B 703 739-2610
   Alexandria (G-377)

W & M Backhoe Service ....G 540 775-7185
   King George (G-7121)

Wayrick Inc ....G 276 988-8091
   Lebanon (G-7211)

Westmoreland Pallet Compan ....G 804 224-9450
   Colonial Beach (G-3729)

Wilrich Construction LLC ....G 804 654-0238
   Tappahannock (G-13827)

3532 Mining Machinery & Eqpt

American Mine Research Inc ....D 276 928-1712
   Rocky Gap (G-12305)

▲ Bluefield Manufacturing Inc ....E 276 322-3441
   Bluefield (G-1859)

Canaan Land Associates Inc ....D 276 988-6543
   Tazewell (G-13829)

▼ Clinch River LLC ....G 276 963-5271
   Tazewell (G-13830)

Crisp Manufacturing Co Inc ....F 276 686-4131
   Rural Retreat (G-12420)

▼ D L Williams Company ....G 276 326-3338
   Bluefield (G-1861)

Damascus Equipment LLC ....E 276 676-2376
   Abingdon (G-27)

Dane Meades Shop ....G 276 926-4847
   Pound (G-10512)

Drill Supply of Virginia LLC ....G 540 992-3595
   Troutville (G-13909)

Elgin Equipment Group ....G 276 988-8901
   Tazewell (G-13832)

Elswick Inc ....G 276 971-3060
   Cedar Bluff (G-2275)

Frank Calandra Inc ....G 412 963-9071
   Cedar Bluff (G-2276)

Frank Calandra Inc ....G 276 964-7023
   Pounding Mill (G-10519)

▼ GE Fairchild Mining Equipment ....D 540 921-8000
   Glen Lyn (G-5832)

Geebo Inc ....G 888 439-3113
   Mc Lean (G-8446)

◆ Heintzmann Corporation ....D 304 284-8004
   Cedar Bluff (G-2278)

HHh Underground LLC ....F 804 365-6905
   Glen Allen (G-5743)

Innovative Wireless Tech Inc ....E 434 316-5230
   Lynchburg (G-7741)

J and R Manufacturing Inc ....E 276 210-1647
   Bluefield (G-1865)

Jennmar Corporation ....D 540 726-2326
   Rich Creek (G-11007)

Jennmar of Pennsylvania LLC ....F 276 964-2107
   Cedar Bluff (G-2280)

Jennmar of Pennsylvania LLC ....G 276 964-7000
   Cedar Bluff (G-2281)

Joy Global Underground Min LLC ....C 276 623-2000
   Abingdon (G-45)

Joy Global Underground Min LLC ....F 276 679-1082
   Norton (G-10123)

Joy Global Underground Min LLC ....G 276 431-2821
   Duffield (G-4179)

Joy Global Underground Min LLC ....G 276 322-5421
   Bluefield (G-1867)

Komatsu Mining Corp ....G 276 623-2000
   Abingdon (G-48)

Lawrence Brothers Inc ....E 276 322-4988
   Bluefield (G-1868)

◆ Longwall - Associates Inc ....C 276 646-2004
   Chilhowie (G-3554)

Looneys Bit Service Inc ....G 276 531-8767
   Maxie (G-8372)

Mefcor Incorporated ....G 276 322-5021
   North Tazewell (G-10103)

Mescher Manufacturing Co Inc ....F 276 530-7856
   Grundy (G-6037)

▲ Norris Screen and Mfg LLC ....E 276 988-8901
   Tazewell (G-13838)

▲ Pemco Corporation ....D 276 326-2611
   Bluefield (G-1872)

Simmons Equipment Company ....G 276 991-3345
   Tazewell (G-13839)

Stella-Jones Corporation ....D 540 997-9251
   Goshen (G-5927)

Tramline Inc ....G 276 322-3183
   Bluefield (G-1883)

Wolf Hills Fabricators LLC ....F 276 466-2743
   Abingdon (G-70)

Wright Machine & Manufacturing ....G 276 688-2391
   Bland (G-1838)

Wythe Power Equipment Co Inc ....E 276 228-7371
   Wytheville (G-15927)

3533 Oil Field Machinery & Eqpt

Gas Field Services Inc ....D 276 873-1214
   Rosedale (G-12365)

Hill Phoenix Inc ....G 712 563-4623
   South Chesterfield (G-12807)

Mobil Petrochemical Holdings ....G 703 846-3000
   Fairfax (G-4513)

Reamco Inc ....G 703 690-2000
   Lorton (G-7525)

Trident Tool Inc ....G 540 635-7753
   Stephens City (G-13324)

3534 Elevators & Moving Stairways

AB Lighting and Production LLC ....G 703 550-7707
   Lorton (G-7457)

America Heavy Industry ....G 757 858-2000
   Norfolk (G-9437)

▲ Appalachian Machine Inc ....F 540 674-1914
   Dublin (G-4148)

Christopher Hawkins ....G 540 361-1679
   Fredericksburg (G-5178)

Elevating Eqp Insptn Svc LLC ....F 800 346-0287
   Bedford (G-1634)

Elevative Networks LLC ....G 703 226-3419
   Vienna (G-14046)

Lm5 Vertical Inspections LLC ....G 757 810-9938
   Seaford (G-12676)

3535 Conveyors & Eqpt

888 Brands LLC ....G 757 741-2056
   Williamsburg (G-15199)

Advanced Air Systems Inc ....D 276 666-8829
   Martinsville (G-8264)

Alliance Industrial Corp ....E 434 239-2641
   Lynchburg (G-7638)

▲ Automated Conveyor Systems Inc ....C 434 385-6699
   Lynchburg (G-7645)

B R Products ....G 804 693-2639
   Gloucester (G-5836)

Barry-Whmller Cont Systems Inc ....D 434 582-1200
   Lynchburg (G-7649)

Coperion Corporation ....D 276 228-7717
   Wytheville (G-15884)

Cross-Land Conveyors LLC ....G 540 287-9150
   Partlow (G-10265)

Flexible Conveyor Systems Inc ....F 804 897-9572
   North Chesterfield (G-9876)

▼ GE Fairchild Mining Equipment ....D 540 921-8000
   Glen Lyn (G-5832)

Hutchinson Sealing Systems Inc ....E 276 228-6150
   Wytheville (G-15890)

Industrial Fabricators Inc ....E 540 989-0834
   Roanoke (G-11938)

▲ Innoveyor Inc ....G 757 485-0500
   Chesapeake (G-3143)

Joy Global Underground Min LLC ....G 276 322-5454
   Bluefield (G-1866)

Joy Global Underground Min LLC ....C 276 623-2000
   Abingdon (G-45)

Maxx Material Systems LLC ....E 757 637-4026
   Hampton (G-6192)

Miller Metal Fabricators Inc ....E 540 886-5575
   Staunton (G-13281)

▲ Modu System America LLC ....G 757 250-3413
   Williamsburg (G-15281)

Performance Drives Inc ....D 304 327-7725
   Bluefield (G-1873)

Precisncntainertechnologies LL ....G 540 425-4756
   Bedford (G-1652)

Reliable Welding & Fabricators ....F 276 629-2593
   Bassett (G-1589)

◆ Ryson International Inc ....F 757 898-1530
   Yorktown (G-15989)

▲ SE Holdings LLC ....D 434 385-9181
   Forest (G-5091)

Simplimatic Automation LLC ....D 434 385-9181
   Forest (G-5092)

▲ Smart Machine Technologies Inc ......D 276 632-9853
   Ridgeway (G-11853)

▲ Sterling Blower Company ....G 434 316-5310
   Forest (G-5096)

▲ Tazz Conveyor Corporation ....F 276 988-4883
   North Tazewell (G-10108)

West River Conveyors & McHy Co ....E 276 259-5353
   Oakwood (G-10171)

3536 Hoists, Cranes & Monorails

Altec Industries Inc ....C 540 992-5300
   Daleville (G-3938)

Columbus McKinnon Corporation ....C 276 475-3124
  Damascus (G-3946)
East Coast Boat Lifts Inc ....G 804 758-1099
  Urbanna (G-13970)
Excelscion Med Cding Blling LL ....G 561 866-1000
  Martinsville (G-8285)
Foley Material Handling Co Inc ....D 804 798-1343
  Ashland (G-1419)
K C I Konecranes Inc ....G 540 545-8412
  Winchester (G-15430)
Konecranes Inc ....G 540 366-9502
  Roanoke (G-12122)
Konecranes Inc ....F 540 545-8412
  Winchester (G-15435)
ML Manufacturing ....G 434 581-2000
  New Canton (G-9118)
◆ Rex Companies Inc ....E 757 873-5452
  Newport News (G-9326)
Universal Marine Lift Inc ....G 804 829-5838
  Charles City (G-2580)
Wolf Hills Fabricators LLC ....F 276 466-2743
  Abingdon (G-70)

3537 Indl Trucks, Tractors, Trailers & Stackers

A & L Transport LLC ....G 757 735-0047
  Portsmouth (G-10387)
A Williams Transport LLC ....G 804 896-5878
  Midlothian (G-8767)
Ajs E Coast Hlg & Trnspt LLC.............G 540 645-2200
  Triangle (G-13888)
◆ American Track Carrier LLC ....F 804 752-7533
  Ashland (G-1368)
Anthony Lamon Williams ....G 757 927-8141
  Newport News (G-9168)
Arbon Equipment Corporation ....G 540 542-6790
  Winchester (G-15383)
Arbon Equipment Corporation ....G 540 387-2113
  Salem (G-12475)
Armstead Hauling Inc ....G 804 675-8221
  Richmond (G-11489)
Blue Ridge Pallet LLC ....F 540 836-8115
  Lyndhurst (G-7842)
Bookers Transport LLC ....G 757 762-9233
  Chesapeake (G-3011)
Boss Laide Express LLC ....G 804 263-8759
  Virginia Beach (G-14296)
Cannon Enterprises LLC ....G 757 876-3463
  Newport News (G-9191)
Casey Unique Transport Svcs ....G 757 354-7626
  Virginia Beach (G-14322)
Coleman & Sons Trucking LLC ....G 434 247-1011
  South Hill (G-12847)
Cricketts Trucking LLC.........................G 540 333-3812
  Strasburg (G-13577)
Datskapatal Logistics LLC ....G 757 814-7325
  Virginia Beach (G-14390)
Delivery Junkies..................................F 540 329-9060
  Richmond (G-11561)
DER LLC ....G 434 736-9100
  Keysville (G-7056)
▼ East Coast Custom Coaches Inc ......F 571 292-1583
  Manassas (G-8062)
Figure Freight LLC ....G 757 814-3610
  Newport News (G-9228)
Fk Logistics Usa LLC ....G 877 811-8772
  Vienna (G-14056)
Gbn Machine & Engineering Corp.........E 804 448-2033
  Woodford (G-15839)
Golco Logistics LLC ....G 571 234-3466
  Newport News (G-9236)
Greenline Trucking Inc ....G 804 638-1138
  Chester (G-3420)
Gstyle7 Trucking LLC ....G 757 367-2009
  Virginia Beach (G-14495)
Hek Logistics LLC ....G 757 637-8778
  Dumfries (G-4247)
Homested Material Handlings................G 804 299-3389
  Rockville (G-12286)
Innovative Tech Intl Inc ....E 434 239-1979
  Lynchburg (G-7740)
J&J Logistics Consulting LLC..............G 404 431-3613
  Springfield (G-13027)
Kalmar USA Inc ....F 757 465-7995
  Portsmouth (G-10451)
Lastmile Logistix Incorporated.............G 757 338-0076
  Virginia Beach (G-14601)
Lee CL Trucking LLC ....G 804 677-2242
  Richmond (G-11650)

Makivin Trucking LLC...........................G 434 637-1359
  Yale (G-15929)
Mighty Mann Inc ....F 757 945-8056
  Hampton (G-6201)
Mosena Enterprises Inc ....G 757 562-7033
  Franklin (G-5149)
PM Services LLC ....G 804 426-9892
  Virginia Beach (G-14727)
PMC Logistics LLC ....G 804 414-8400
  South Prince George (G-12866)
R&Y Trucking LLC ....G 404 781-1312
  Chesapeake (G-3255)
▲ Rayco Industries Inc ....E 804 321-7111
  Richmond (G-11729)
RI Logistics LLC ....G 703 209-3100
  Arlington (G-1149)
Rls Cartage LLC ....G 540 447-0668
  Waynesboro (G-15136)
Rol-Lift International LLC ....G 757 650-2040
  Chesapeake (G-3274)
Rolling With Class LLC ....G 804 836-9760
  North Chesterfield (G-9965)
S&R Transport LLC ....G 757 344-0251
  Hampton (G-6231)
Samuel L Brown ....G 804 892-5629
  Ford (G-5047)
Se7en Trnsp Lgstics Systems LL ....G 804 869-1716
  Richmond (G-11754)
Shop Guys ....G 804 317-9440
  Midlothian (G-8897)
Silvio Enterprise LLC ....G 703 731-0147
  Falls Church (G-4874)
Southern Virginia Equipment ....G 434 390-0318
  Keysville (G-7063)
Srm Logistics LLC ....G 757 232-9928
  Chesapeake (G-3309)
Stacker Inc A G ....F 540 234-6012
  Weyers Cave (G-15177)
Stephen W Mast ....G 804 467-3608
  Mechanicsville (G-8681)
Stm Snow Removal LLC ....G 540 604-0112
  Stafford (G-13196)
Team 1 Trucking LLC ....G 800 296-9740
  Norfolk (G-9745)
Terex Corporation ....G 540 361-7755
  Fredericksburg (G-5492)
Total Lift Care LLC ....G 540 631-0008
  Front Royal (G-5559)
◆ Tread Corporation ....D 540 982-6881
  Roanoke (G-12010)
Triple Z Transport LLC ....G 804 335-5962
  Mechanicsville (G-8689)
Utility One Source For Eqp LLC ....D 434 525-2929
  Forest (G-5103)
Utility Trailer Mfg Co ....A 276 783-8800
  Atkins (G-1522)
V & S Xpress LLC ....G 804 714-4259
  Highland Springs (G-6858)
Volvo Group North America LLC ....G 336 393-2000
  Dublin (G-4174)
Vrenp LLC ....G 757 510-7770
  Portsmouth (G-10499)
Wilbar Truck Equipment Inc ....G 757 397-3200
  Portsmouth (G-10502)
Zest ....G 757 301-8553
  Virginia Beach (G-14958)

3541 Machine Tools: Cutting

▲ Action Tool Service Inc ....F 757 838-4555
  Hampton (G-6069)
Automated Machine & Tech Inc ....E 757 898-7844
  Grafton (G-5931)
B & M Machinery Inc ....G 434 525-1498
  Lynchburg (G-7647)
Beydler Cnc LLC ....G 760 954-4397
  Amherst (G-683)
▲ Capco Machinery Systems Inc ....E 540 977-0404
  Roanoke (G-11902)
Capstone Industries LLC ....G 703 966-6718
  Manassas (G-8045)
Case-Polytech Inc ....G 804 752-3500
  Ashland (G-1386)
Cbg LLC ....G 757 465-0333
  Portsmouth (G-10405)
Centurion Tools LLC ....G 540 967-5402
  Louisa (G-7549)
Charis Machine LLC ....G 276 546-6675
  Duffield (G-4176)
Chips On Board Incorporated................G 757 357-0789
  Smithfield (G-12709)

Ed Walkers Repair Services ....G 804 590-1198
  South Chesterfield (G-12834)
Elite Fabrication & Machine ....G 540 392-6055
  Christiansburg (G-3587)
Farehill Precision LLC ....G 540 879-2373
  Rockingham (G-12251)
FHP LLC ....G 540 879-2560
  Rockingham (G-12252)
GM International Ltd Company ....G 703 577-0829
  Leesburg (G-7281)
Hampton Roads Sheet Metal Inc ....G 757 543-6009
  Virginia Beach (G-14500)
Its Manufacturing Incorporated.............G 804 397-0504
  Crewe (G-3813)
J & A Tools ....G 434 414-0871
  Amherst (G-696)
Keo-Corp LLC ....G 636 515-5549
  New Kent (G-9135)
Limitorque Corp ....G 804 639-0529
  Midlothian (G-8849)
LLC Link Masters ....G 804 241-3962
  Mechanicsville (G-8653)
Lynchburg Machining LLC ....F 434 846-7327
  Lynchburg (G-7762)
Marco Machine & Design Inc ....G 804 275-5555
  North Chesterfield (G-9921)
Mescher Manufacturing Co Inc ....G 276 530-7856
  Grundy (G-6037)
Mg Enterprise LLC ....G 703 646-2761
  Fairfax (G-4509)
Microfab LLC ....G 276 620-7200
  Max Meadows (G-8369)
◆ Nuvidrill LLC ....G 540 353-8787
  Roanoke (G-12143)
Pennsylvania Drilling Company ....G 540 665-5207
  Winchester (G-15459)
Performance Engrg & Mch Co ....G 804 530-5577
  South Chesterfield (G-12819)
Pickle Tyson ....G 276 686-5368
  Rural Retreat (G-12429)
Ridge Tool Company ....G 540 672-5150
  Orange (G-10226)
Sanjo Virginia Beach Inc ....G 757 498-0400
  Virginia Beach (G-14793)
◆ Sonic Tools LP ....F 804 798-0538
  Ashland (G-1493)
Tants Mch & Fabrication Inc ....G 757 434-9448
  Chesapeake (G-3321)
Thirty Seven Cent Machine ....G 276 673-1400
  Martinsville (G-8343)
Vulcan Machine Co ....G 240 486-2685
  Fort Valley (G-5136)
Wells Machine Co ....G 804 737-2500
  Sandston (G-12639)
Williams Deburring Small Parts.............G 540 726-7485
  Narrows (G-9099)

3542 Machine Tools: Forming

◆ American Gfm Corporation ....C 757 487-2442
  Chesapeake (G-2967)
Bc Repairs ....G 434 332-5304
  Rustburg (G-12434)
Canline USA Corporation ....F 540 380-8585
  Lynchburg (G-7672)
Jeff Shearer ....G 703 313-7670
  Alexandria (G-494)
Unison Tube LLC ....G 828 633-3190
  Ringgold (G-11875)

3543 Industrial Patterns

Culpeper Mdel Barnstormers Inc ....G 540 349-2733
  Broad Run (G-2066)
Dlba Robotics Ltd ....E 757 288-0206
  Hampton (G-6130)
Hub Pattern Corporation ....G 540 342-3505
  Roanoke (G-12104)
Hub Pattern Corporation ....E 540 342-3505
  Salem (G-12518)
▲ Integrated Tex Solutions Inc ....D 540 389-8113
  Salem (G-12522)
Lynchburg Machining LLC ....F 434 846-7327
  Lynchburg (G-7762)
OK Foundry Company Inc.....................G 804 233-9674
  Richmond (G-11698)
Pattern Shop Inc ....G 540 389-5110
  Salem (G-12554)
Pattern Svcs & Fabrication LLC ....G 540 731-4891
  Radford (G-10734)
Pegee Wllmsburg Pttrns Hstries ....G 757 220-2722
  Williamsburg (G-15293)

Precision Patterns Inc ....G...... 434 385-4279
  Forest (G-5088)

3544 Dies, Tools, Jigs, Fixtures & Indl Molds

Black Mold Busters Chesapeake..........G...... 757 606-9608
  Chesapeake (G-3004)
Black Mold Rmval Group Wdbrdge......G...... 571 402-8960
  Woodbridge (G-15659)
Btmc Holdings Inc ....G...... 616 794-0100
  Christiansburg (G-3575)
Carter Tool & Mfg Co Inc ....G...... 540 387-1778
  Salem (G-12489)
Classic Machine Inc ....F...... 804 798-1111
  Ashland (G-1391)
▲ Damon Company of Salem Inc ....E...... 540 389-8609
  Salem (G-12494)
Die Cast Connections Inc ....G...... 276 669-5991
  Bristol (G-2016)
Dimension Tool LLC ....G...... 804 350-9707
  Chester (G-3404)
Electronic Dev Labs Inc ....E...... 434 799-0807
  Danville (G-3990)
GM International Ltd Company..............G...... 703 577-0829
  Leesburg (G-7281)
Henry Bijak ....G...... 757 572-1673
  Virginia Beach (G-14516)
Hub Pattern Corporation ....E...... 540 342-3505
  Roanoke (G-12104)
Independent Machining Service ....G...... 540 797-7284
  Wirtz (G-15614)
Keo-Corp LLC ....G...... 636 515-5549
  New Kent (G-9135)
L & R Precision Tooling Inc ....E...... 434 525-4120
  Lynchburg (G-7752)
Lasercam LLc ....F...... 540 265-2888
  Roanoke (G-11952)
▲ Lenzkes Clamping Tools Inc ....F...... 540 381-1533
  Christiansburg (G-3603)
Leslie Noble ....G...... 757 291-2904
  Williamsburg (G-15270)
Live Trendy or Die LLC ....G...... 856 371-7638
  Lynchburg (G-7758)
Maco Tool Inc ....G...... 989 224-6723
  Christiansburg (G-3604)
◆ Marion Mold & Tool Inc ....E...... 276 783-6101
  Marion (G-8234)
Mold Fresh LLC ....G...... 757 696-9288
  Virginia Beach (G-14660)
Mold Removal LLC ....G...... 703 421-0000
  Sterling (G-13455)
Never Say Die Studios LLC ....G...... 478 787-1901
  Spotsylvania (G-12906)
Newport Cutter Grinding Co Inc ....F...... 757 838-3224
  Hampton (G-6207)
Parkway Stl Rule Ctng Dies Inc ....E...... 540 586-4948
  Bedford (G-1648)
Precision Tool & Die Inc ....G...... 804 233-8810
  Richmond (G-11723)
Redco Machine Inc ....E...... 540 586-3545
  Bedford (G-1655)
Revere Mold & Engineering Inc ....F...... 804 748-5059
  Chester (G-3450)
Richmond Tooling Inc ....F...... 804 520-4173
  South Chesterfield (G-12824)
Roto-Die Company Inc ....B...... 276 952-2026
  Meadows of Dan (G-8593)
Sanjo Virginia Beach Inc ....G...... 757 498-0400
  Virginia Beach (G-14793)
Sanxin Wire Die Inc ....G...... 434 220-0435
  Charlottesville (G-2689)
Scorpion Mold Abatement LLC ....G...... 540 273-9300
  Stafford (G-13189)
▲ Star US Precision Industry Ltd ....G...... 804 747-8948
  Richmond (G-11397)
Suter Machine & Tool ....F...... 540 434-2718
  Rockingham (G-12279)
Triton Industries Inc ....F...... 757 887-1956
  Newport News (G-9364)
Virginia Beachs Max Blck Mold ....G...... 757 354-1935
  Virginia Beach (G-14916)
Wallace Precision Tooling ....G...... 540 456-6437
  Afton (G-95)
▲ Winchester Tool LLC ....E...... 540 869-1150
  Winchester (G-15513)

3545 Machine Tool Access

Balancemaster Inc ....G...... 434 258-5078
  Concord (G-3755)
Bentech ....G...... 540 344-6820
  Roanoke (G-12043)

Brock Enterprises Virginia LLC............G...... 276 971-4549
  Richlands (G-11014)
Crown Cork & Seal Usa Inc ....E...... 757 538-1318
  Suffolk (G-13690)
D & S Tool Inc ....G...... 540 731-1463
  Radford (G-10707)
Diamondback Tool Co ....G...... 800 899-2358
  Charlottesville (G-2781)
Don Elthon ....G...... 703 237-2521
  Falls Church (G-4908)
Excel Tool Inc ....F...... 276 322-0223
  Falls Mills (G-4931)
General Electric Company ....F...... 540 387-7000
  Salem (G-12511)
Glenn R Williams ....G...... 434 251-9383
  Ringgold (G-11867)
Grimsleys House Tools Inc ....G...... 757 399-4438
  Portsmouth (G-10437)
Kennametal Inc ....C...... 540 740-3128
  New Market (G-9144)
Mechanical Development Co Inc ....D...... 540 389-9395
  Salem (G-12535)
Old 97 Choppers ....G...... 434 799-5400
  Danville (G-4019)
Patterson Business Systems ....F...... 540 389-7726
  Salem (G-12555)
Permit Pushers ....G...... 703 237-6461
  Arlington (G-1108)
Reeds Carbide Saw Service ....F...... 434 846-6436
  Lynchburg (G-7800)
Ridge Tool Company ....C...... 540 672-5150
  Orange (G-10226)
Rnk Outdoors ....G...... 540 797-3698
  Roanoke (G-12163)
Sanjo Virginia Beach Inc ....G...... 757 498-0400
  Virginia Beach (G-14793)
Specialty Tooling LLC ....G...... 804 912-1158
  Henrico (G-6573)
Teledyne Instruments Inc ....D...... 757 723-6531
  Hampton (G-6250)
Time Machine Inc ....G...... 540 772-0962
  Roanoke (G-12204)
Trinity Construction Svcs Inc ....G...... 757 455-8660
  Norfolk (G-9768)
Uma Inc ....E...... 540 879-2040
  Dayton (G-4067)
Xtreme Diamond LLC ....G...... 703 753-0567
  Haymarket (G-6456)

3546 Power Hand Tools

Alioth Technical Services Inc ....G...... 757 630-0337
  Virginia Beach (G-14221)
Eclipse Scroll Saw ....G...... 804 779-3549
  New Kent (G-9131)
◆ Microaire Surgical Instrs LLC ....C...... 800 722-0822
  Charlottesville (G-2659)
◆ Monti Tools Inc ....G...... 832 623-7970
  Manassas (G-8112)
◆ Nuvidrill LLC ....G...... 540 353-8787
  Roanoke (G-12143)
Southern States Coop Inc ....F...... 804 226-2758
  Richmond (G-11390)
Stihl Incorporated ....E...... 757 468-4010
  Virginia Beach (G-14848)
Stihl Incorporated ....G...... 757 368-2409
  Virginia Beach (G-14849)

3547 Rolling Mill Machinery & Eqpt

Coperion Corporation............................D...... 276 228-7717
  Wytheville (G-15884)
Sanjo Virginia Beach Inc ....G...... 757 498-0400
  Virginia Beach (G-14793)

3548 Welding Apparatus

B & B Welding Inc ....G...... 540 982-2082
  Roanoke (G-12039)
Brads Wldg & Align Boring LLC ....G...... 276 340-1605
  Patrick Springs (G-10269)
◆ Controls Corporation America..........C...... 757 422-8330
  Virginia Beach (G-14363)
Custom Designers Inc ....G...... 703 830-8582
  Centreville (G-2299)
Jones & Sons Inc ....G...... 434 836-3851
  Blairs (G-1830)
Lewis Welding & Cnstr Works ....G...... 434 696-5527
  Keysville (G-7060)
Maxwell Incorporated ....G...... 804 370-3697
  Ashland (G-1460)
Phillips Welding Service Inc ....G...... 434 989-7236
  Madison Heights (G-7882)

Radford Wldg & Fabrication LLC ....G...... 540 731-4891
  Radford (G-10737)
Skyline Fabricating Inc ....G...... 276 498-3560
  Raven (G-10758)
Steel Tech LLC ....G...... 571 585-5861
  Sterling (G-13515)
T & J Wldg & Fabrication LLC ....G...... 757 672-9929
  Suffolk (G-13770)
Valley Supply and Services LLC..........G...... 276 979-4547
  North Tazewell (G-10110)
William Keyser ....G...... 703 243-8777
  Arlington (G-1219)

3549 Metalworking Machinery, NEC

Advantage Machine & Engrg ....F...... 757 488-5085
  Portsmouth (G-10388)
▲ Aerial Machine & Tool Corp ....D...... 276 952-2006
  Meadows of Dan (G-8590)
Aerial Machine & Tool Corp ....G...... 276 694-3148
  Stuart (G-13603)
Blue Ridge Servo Mtr Repr LLC ....G...... 540 375-2990
  Salem (G-12483)
East Coast Fabricators Inc....................G...... 540 587-7170
  Bedford (G-1633)
Germaine Clark LLC ....G...... 571 309-1724
  Alexandria (G-214)
Hampton Roads Component Assemb...G...... 757 236-8627
  Hampton (G-6163)
Marco Machine & Design Inc ....F...... 804 275-5555
  North Chesterfield (G-9921)
MIC Industries Inc ....F...... 540 678-2900
  Clear Brook (G-3647)
▲ MIC Industries Inc ....G...... 703 318-1900
  Clear Brook (G-3648)
Newport Cutter Grinding Co Inc ....F...... 757 838-3224
  Hampton (G-6207)
Parker Manufacturing LLC ....G...... 804 507-0593
  Richmond (G-11319)
Prototec Inc ....G...... 434 832-7440
  Lynchburg (G-7793)
▲ Rayco Industries Inc ....E...... 804 321-7111
  Richmond (G-11729)
Simplimatic Automation LLC ....D...... 434 385-9181
  Forest (G-5092)
Tektonics Design Group LLC ....G...... 804 233-5900
  Richmond (G-11786)
Tessy Plastics Corp ....G...... 434 385-5700
  Lynchburg (G-7820)
West Engineering Company Inc ....G...... 804 798-3966
  Ashland (G-1508)
▲ Winchester Tool LLC ....E...... 540 869-1150
  Winchester (G-15513)

3552 Textile Machinery

Abstruse Technical Services ....G...... 540 489-8940
  Ferrum (G-4966)
Art Connected ....G...... 540 628-2162
  Fredericksburg (G-5400)
Artgiftsetccom ....G...... 703 772-3587
  Arlington (G-861)
▲ Atlantic Metal Products Inc ....E...... 804 758-4915
  Topping (G-13885)
▲ Authentic Knitting Board LLC..........G...... 434 842-1180
  Fork Union (G-5108)
Dennis W Wiley ....G...... 540 992-6631
  Buchanan (G-2121)
MSP Group LLC ....G...... 757 855-5416
  Norfolk (G-9650)
Rendas ....G...... 804 776-6215
  Deltaville (G-4086)
▲ Smart Machine Technologies Inc ....D...... 276 632-9853
  Ridgeway (G-11853)
▲ Stitch Beagle Inc ....G...... 540 777-0002
  Roanoke (G-12003)
Thermo-Flex Technologies Inc ....G...... 919 247-6411
  Moneta (G-8982)
Traditionl Scrnprntg & Monogrm ....G...... 276 935-7110
  Grundy (G-6042)

3553 Woodworking Machinery

Atelier Fonteneau LLC..........................G...... 540 371-5074
  Fredericksburg (G-5401)
Bargers Custom Cabinets LLC ....G...... 540 261-7230
  Buena Vista (G-2139)
Cabinet Makers ....G...... 703 421-6331
  Sterling (G-13364)
Cabinet Masters ....G...... 703 331-5781
  Manassas Park (G-8194)
Cane Connection ....G...... 804 261-6555
  Richmond (G-11145)

Carrs Floor Services...................G...... 434 525-8420
  Forest *(G-5059)*
Copper Woodworks....................G...... 757 421-7328
  Chesapeake *(G-3053)*
Custom Cabinet Works ....G...... 540 972-1734
  Locust Grove *(G-7442)*
Dobbs & Associates ....G...... 804 769-4266
  King William *(G-7129)*
Eclipse Scroll Saw ....G...... 804 779-3549
  New Kent *(G-9131)*
Elk Creek Woodworking Inc.......G...... 434 258-5142
  Forest *(G-5070)*
Fred Hean Furniture & Wdwrk .....G...... 434 973-5960
  Charlottesville *(G-2634)*
Gathersburg Cabntry ....G...... 703 742-8472
  Herndon *(G-6679)*
Gbn Machine & Engineering Corp ....E 804 448-2033
  Woodford *(G-15839)*
H C Sexton and Associates ....G...... 434 409-1073
  Crozet *(G-3834)*
Johnson Machinery Sales Inc .....G...... 540 890-8893
  Vinton *(G-14174)*
Laurie Grusha Zipf ....G...... 703 794-9497
  Manassas *(G-8098)*
Middlesex Cabinet Co ....G...... 804 758-3617
  Saluda *(G-12605)*
Oaktree Woodworks ....G...... 804 815-4669
  Gloucester *(G-5857)*
Opposable Thumbs LLC ....G...... 804 502-2937
  Richmond *(G-11701)*
R & S Molds Inc ....G...... 434 352-8612
  Appomattox *(G-820)*
▲ Rayco Industries Inc ....E 804 321-7111
  Richmond *(G-11729)*
Vangarde Woodworks Inc ....G...... 804 355-4917
  Richmond *(G-11433)*
Williamson Wood ....G...... 434 823-1882
  Crozet *(G-3856)*

3554 Paper Inds Machinery

Bay West Paper...........................G...... 804 639-3530
  Chesterfield *(G-3479)*
▲ Craft Industrial Incorporated ....E 757 825-1195
  Hampton *(G-6118)*
Genik Incorporated ....G...... 804 226-2907
  Richmond *(G-11218)*
◆ Jud Corporation ....G...... 757 485-4371
  Chesapeake *(G-3158)*
Nks LLC ....G...... 757 229-3139
  Williamsburg *(G-15283)*
Tmeic Corporation ....G...... 540 725-2031
  Salem *(G-12574)*
West Engineering Company Inc ....E 804 798-3966
  Ashland *(G-1508)*

3555 Printing Trades Machinery & Eqpt

About Time ....G...... 757 253-0143
  Williamsburg *(G-15200)*
American Technology Inds Ltd...........E 757 436-6465
  Chesapeake *(G-2973)*
Automated Signature Technology...........F 703 397-0910
  Sterling *(G-13356)*
◆ Canon Virginia Inc ....A 757 881-6000
  Newport News *(G-9192)*
F C Holdings Inc..........................C...... 804 222-2821
  Sandston *(G-12614)*
Genik Incorporated ....G...... 804 226-2907
  Richmond *(G-11218)*
Ir Engraving LLC ....D...... 804 222-2821
  Sandston *(G-12621)*
Karma Group Inc ....G...... 717 253-9379
  Manassas *(G-8092)*
◆ Kinyo Virginia Inc ....C...... 757 888-2221
  Newport News *(G-9276)*
▲ Masa Corporation of Virginia ....G...... 757 855-3013
  Norfolk *(G-9634)*
Melvin Riley ....G...... 240 381-6111
  Falls Church *(G-4829)*
Muller Martini Corp ....G...... 804 282-4802
  Richmond *(G-11297)*
Naito America ....E 804 550-3305
  Ashland *(G-1468)*
Old World Labs LLC ....G...... 800 282-0386
  Norfolk *(G-9675)*
R G Engineering Inc...................F 757 463-3045
  Virginia Beach *(G-14753)*
Southern Graphic Systems LLC...........D...... 804 226-2490
  Richmond *(G-11764)*
Southern Gravure Service Inc .....G...... 804 226-2490
  Richmond *(G-11387)*

◆ Standex Engraving LLC ....D...... 804 236-3092
  Sandston *(G-12636)*
Walter L James ....G...... 703 622-5970
  Woodbridge *(G-15828)*

3556 Food Prdts Machinery

◆ AMF Automation Tech LLC.....C...... 804 355-7961
  Richmond *(G-11110)*
AMF Bakery Systems Corp ....G...... 800 225-3771
  Richmond *(G-11111)*
▲ Atlantic Metal Products Inc ....E 804 758-4915
  Topping *(G-13885)*
Blackstone Herb Cottage ....G...... 434 292-1135
  Blackstone *(G-1812)*
▲ Elvaria LLC ....G...... 703 935-0041
  Gainesville *(G-5582)*
Excalibur Technology Svcs LLC ....G...... 703 853-8307
  Bristow *(G-2051)*
Finco Inc ....G...... 301 645-4538
  Fredericksburg *(G-5288)*
Georges Family Farms LLC ....E 540 477-3181
  Mount Jackson *(G-9070)*
Gulp Juicery LLC ....G...... 804 933-9483
  Goochland *(G-5884)*
◆ Haas Machinery Amer Inc Franz ......F 804 222-6022
  Richmond *(G-11229)*
Jbt Aerotech ....G...... 336 254-4104
  Richmond *(G-11254)*
M & H Paragon Inc ....G...... 540 994-0080
  Pulaski *(G-10640)*
Mactavish Machine Mfg Co........G...... 804 264-6109
  North Chesterfield *(G-9916)*
Magco Inc ....F 757 934-0042
  Suffolk *(G-13738)*
Miller Metal Fabricators Inc.......G...... 540 886-5575
  Staunton *(G-13281)*
Reliance Industries Inc ....G...... 832 788-0108
  Falls Church *(G-4924)*
◆ Ross Industries Inc ....C...... 540 439-3271
  Midland *(G-8762)*
▲ Smart Machine Technologies Inc ......D...... 276 632-9853
  Ridgeway *(G-11853)*
▼ Tetra Pak Tubex Inc ....E 540 967-0733
  Louisa *(G-7571)*
Texacan Beef & Pork Co LLC .....G...... 703 858-5565
  Ashburn *(G-1340)*
Tromp Group Americas LLC ......G...... 800 225-3771
  Richmond *(G-11421)*
Unique Engineering Concepts .....G...... 540 586-6761
  Bedford *(G-1662)*

3559 Special Ind Machinery, NEC

Aai Textron ....G...... 434 292-5805
  Blackstone *(G-1810)*
Acp LLC ....G...... 276 619-5080
  Abingdon *(G-6)*
Alacran ....G...... 540 629-6095
  Dublin *(G-4147)*
Applied Materials Inc ....G...... 540 583-0466
  Dumfries *(G-4235)*
Armadillo Industries Inc ....G...... 757 508-2348
  Williamsburg *(G-15207)*
Autogrind Products ....G...... 703 490-7061
  Woodbridge *(G-15651)*
Barismil LLC ....G...... 703 622-4550
  Herndon *(G-6619)*
Bishop Distributors LLC ....G...... 757 618-6401
  Norfolk *(G-9463)*
Cap Oil Change Systems LLC ....G...... 540 982-1494
  Roanoke *(G-11901)*
Coperion Corporation ....G...... 276 227-7070
  Wytheville *(G-15883)*
Coperion Corporation ....D...... 276 228-7717
  Wytheville *(G-15884)*
Dallas-Katec Incorporated ....G...... 757 428-8822
  Norfolk *(G-9515)*
Discountcryo Co ....G...... 804 733-3229
  Petersburg *(G-10317)*
Diversified Vacuum Corp ....G...... 757 538-1170
  Suffolk *(G-13698)*
Eco Technologies ....G...... 757 513-4870
  Virginia Beach *(G-14430)*
Ecolochem International Inc ......G...... 757 855-9000
  Norfolk *(G-9539)*
Envirnmntal Solutions Intl Inc ....G...... 703 263-7600
  Ashburn *(G-1276)*
Federal-Mogul Powertrain LLC ....G...... 540 953-4676
  Blacksburg *(G-1738)*
▲ Fiber Consulting Services ......G...... 804 746-2357
  Mechanicsville *(G-8622)*

▲ Garbuio Inc ....G...... 804 279-0020
  Richmond *(G-11214)*
Gohring Components Corp ....G...... 757 665-4110
  Parksley *(G-10262)*
▲ Hauni Richmond Inc ....C...... 804 222-5259
  Richmond *(G-11234)*
▼ Hmb Inc ....D...... 540 967-1060
  Louisa *(G-7556)*
Hotrodz Performance & Motor .....G...... 571 337-2988
  Oakton *(G-10150)*
Hue Ai LLC ....G...... 571 766-6943
  Tysons *(G-13946)*
Hunter Eqp Svc & Parts Inc ....G...... 703 785-5526
  Vienna *(G-14068)*
Industrial Machine Mfg Inc.........E 804 271-6979
  North Chesterfield *(G-9892)*
Jae El Incorporated.....................G...... 540 535-5210
  Leesburg *(G-7291)*
Kiln Creek Associates LP ....G...... 757 464-6082
  Virginia Beach *(G-14584)*
Kiln Creek Pkwy - Old Yorktown ....G...... 757 204-7229
  Yorktown *(G-15972)*
Kiln Doctor Inc ....G...... 540 636-6016
  Front Royal *(G-5540)*
Mactavish Machine Mfg Co ....G...... 804 264-6109
  North Chesterfield *(G-9916)*
▲ Maida Development Company ....D...... 757 723-0785
  Hampton *(G-6188)*
Maida Development Company .....E 757 719-3038
  Hampton *(G-6189)*
Milhous Control Company ....G...... 434 946-5302
  Amherst *(G-700)*
▲ Molins Richmond Inc ....D...... 804 887-2525
  Henrico *(G-6536)*
Mr Robot Inc ....G...... 804 426-3394
  North Chesterfield *(G-9934)*
Poly Processing Company LLC...........G...... 804 368-7199
  Ashland *(G-1477)*
Product Engineered Systems ......G...... 804 794-3586
  Midlothian *(G-8883)*
Spring Grove Inc ....G...... 540 721-1502
  Moneta *(G-8981)*
▲ Sterling Blower Company ......D...... 434 316-5310
  Forest *(G-5096)*
Superior Garniture Components ....G...... 804 769-4319
  King William *(G-7131)*
Svr International LLC...................F 703 759-2953
  Vienna *(G-14136)*
Universal Fiber Systems LLC ....E 276 669-1161
  Bristol *(G-2038)*
West Engineering Company Inc ....E 804 798-3966
  Ashland *(G-1508)*
Wigwam Industries ....G...... 434 823-4663
  Crozet *(G-3855)*
Wintek Corporation.....................G...... 973 252-8200
  Goodview *(G-5897)*

3561 Pumps & Pumping Eqpt

American Manufacturing Co Inc...........E 540 825-7234
  Elkwood *(G-4341)*
Bae Systems Tctcal Vhcl System ....E 571 461-6000
  Falls Church *(G-4759)*
▲ Beckett Corporation ....E 757 857-0153
  Norfolk *(G-9461)*
Colfax Corporation ....G...... 757 328-3987
  Glen Allen *(G-5715)*
Curtiss-Wright Corporation ....D...... 757 494-3810
  Chesapeake *(G-3059)*
Envirnmntal Solutions Intl Inc ....F 703 263-7600
  Ashburn *(G-1276)*
Flowserve Corporation ....D...... 757 485-8044
  Chesapeake *(G-3104)*
Flowserve Corporation ....C...... 434 528-4400
  Lynchburg *(G-7713)*
Flowserve Corporation ....G...... 804 271-4031
  North Chesterfield *(G-9877)*
Flowserve Corporation ....B...... 757 485-8000
  Chesapeake *(G-3105)*
◆ Framatome Inc ....B...... 434 832-3000
  Lynchburg *(G-7716)*
Gravittional Systems Engrg Inc ....F 312 224-8152
  Clifton *(G-3668)*
Hasco Sales Inc ....G...... 804 740-1869
  Glen Allen *(G-5741)*
Khem Precision Machining LLC ....G...... 804 915-8922
  Richmond *(G-11261)*
◆ Ksb America Corporation ....G...... 804 222-1818
  Richmond *(G-11265)*
Mactaggart Scott Usa LLC ....G...... 757 288-1405
  Virginia Beach *(G-14631)*

SIC

Mark A Harber..............................G..... 276 546-6051
Pennington Gap *(G-10295)*

Mefcor Incorporated.....................G..... 276 322-5021
North Tazewell *(G-10103)*

Nellie Harris..............................G..... 434 277-8511
Lowesville *(G-7597)*

Shane Harper..............................G..... 540 297-4800
Moneta *(G-8976)*

▲ SKF Lbrication Systems USA Inc....D..... 757 951-0370
Hampton *(G-6239)*

Vamac Incorporated.....................E..... 540 535-1983
Winchester *(G-15503)*

Vamaz Inc.................................G..... 434 296-8812
Charlottesville *(G-2711)*

3562 Ball & Roller Bearings

Linear Rotary Bearings Inc.............G..... 540 261-1375
Richmond *(G-11271)*

P and H Casters Co Inc.................G..... 817 312-1083
Danville *(G-4021)*

3563 Air & Gas Compressors

Air & Gas Components LLC.............G..... 757 473-3571
Virginia Beach *(G-14217)*

▲ Air Systems International Inc.........E..... 757 424-3967
Chesapeake *(G-2957)*

Atlas Copco Compressor Aif VA......G..... 540 226-8655
Fredericksburg *(G-5249)*

Bauer Compressors Inc.................E..... 757 855-6006
Norfolk *(G-9457)*

◆ Bauer Compressors Inc...............C..... 757 855-6006
Norfolk *(G-9458)*

Breeze-Eastern LLC......................G..... 973 602-1001
Fredericksburg *(G-5175)*

David S Welch............................G..... 276 398-4024
Fancy Gap *(G-4934)*

▲ Diversified Vacuum Inc................G..... 757 538-1170
Suffolk *(G-13699)*

Dresser-Rand Company.................E..... 540 444-4200
Salem *(G-12497)*

Gravittional Systems Engrg Inc.........F..... 312 224-8152
Clifton *(G-3668)*

Ingersoll Rand Inc.......................G..... 804 214-7054
North Chesterfield *(G-9896)*

Special Projects Operations............F..... 410 297-6550
Virginia Beach *(G-14834)*

◆ Universal Air Products Corp..........E..... 757 461-0077
Norfolk *(G-9774)*

3564 Blowers & Fans

Agri Ventilation Systems LLC...........E..... 540 879-9864
Bridgewater *(G-1947)*

▲ Air Systems International Inc.........E..... 757 424-3967
Chesapeake *(G-2957)*

Airocare Inc...............................G..... 703 788-1500
Dulles *(G-4192)*

B2 Health Solutions LLC................G..... 757 403-8298
Virginia Beach *(G-14256)*

Best Blower Sales & Svc LLC...........G..... 434 352-1909
Appomattox *(G-806)*

▼ Buffalo Air Handling Company.......C..... 434 946-7455
Amherst *(G-685)*

Bwx Technologies Inc...................E..... 757 595-7982
Newport News *(G-9187)*

Des Champs Technologies Inc.........C..... 540 291-1111
Buena Vista *(G-2141)*

Elm Investments Inc.....................E..... 757 934-2709
Suffolk *(G-13704)*

GE Energy.................................G..... 757 595-7982
Newport News *(G-9234)*

Hayden Enterprises......................G..... 910 791-3132
Chesapeake *(G-3129)*

Indust LLC.................................G..... 757 208-0587
Williamsburg *(G-15256)*

Intellgent Pwr A Solutions Inc.........G..... 540 429-6177
Spotsylvania *(G-12898)*

Jay Douglas Carper.....................G..... 757 595-7660
Newport News *(G-9268)*

Mfri Inc....................................C..... 540 667-7022
Winchester *(G-15555)*

Phoenixaire LLC..........................G..... 703 647-6546
Arlington *(G-1111)*

Purer Air...................................G..... 804 921-8234
Richmond *(G-11341)*

Tri-Dim Filter Corporation..............G..... 540 774-9540
Roanoke *(G-12209)*

◆ Tri-Dim Filter Corporation............C..... 540 967-2600
Louisa *(G-7573)*

◆ Universal Air Products Corp..........E..... 757 461-0077
Norfolk *(G-9774)*

Usui International Corporation..........B..... 757 558-7300
Chesapeake *(G-3356)*

Virginia Blower Company................E..... 276 647-3804
Collinsville *(G-3718)*

Z Finest Airduct Cleaning...............E..... 703 897-1152
Woodbridge *(G-15838)*

Zentox Corporation......................F..... 757 868-0870
Poquoson *(G-10380)*

3565 Packaging Machinery

◆ Belvac Production McHy Inc..........C..... 434 239-0358
Lynchburg *(G-7652)*

▲ Cda Usa Inc.............................G..... 804 918-3707
Henrico *(G-6490)*

◆ Ess Technologies Inc..................E..... 540 961-5716
Blacksburg *(G-1736)*

Flexicell Inc...............................G..... 804 550-7300
Richmond *(G-11211)*

Hartness International A Div............D..... 434 455-0357
Lynchburg *(G-7730)*

▲ Hauni Richmond Inc...................C..... 804 222-5259
Richmond *(G-11234)*

Ilantech Inc................................G..... 571 226-7042
Ashburn *(G-1294)*

Khem Precision Machining LLC........G..... 804 915-8922
Richmond *(G-11261)*

Masa Corporation of Virginia..........G..... 804 271-8102
North Chesterfield *(G-9925)*

Modek Inc..................................G..... 804 550-7300
Ashland *(G-1463)*

R A Pearson Company...................G..... 804 550-7300
Ashland *(G-1482)*

◆ Ross Industries Inc....................G..... 540 439-3271
Midland *(G-8762)*

▲ Sealpac Usa LLC.......................G..... 804 261-0580
North Chesterfield *(G-9974)*

▲ Shibuya Hoppmann Corporation....D..... 540 829-2564
Manassas *(G-8154)*

Sml Packaging LLC.......................F..... 434 528-3640
Lynchburg *(G-7808)*

Summit Beverage Group LLC...........G..... 276 781-0671
Marion *(G-8244)*

Tcg Technologies Inc....................G..... 540 587-8624
Bedford *(G-1660)*

Tigerseal Products LLC..................G..... 800 899-9389
Beaverdam *(G-1614)*

▲ Weightpack Inc.........................E..... 804 598-4512
Powhatan *(G-10584)*

Zima-Pack LLC............................G..... 804 372-0707
South Chesterfield *(G-12830)*

3566 Speed Changers, Drives & Gears

Donovan Pat Racing Enterprise........G..... 540 829-8396
Culpeper *(G-3889)*

G E Fuji Drives Usa Inc.................F..... 540 387-7000
Salem *(G-12509)*

Groovin Gears.............................G..... 804 729-4177
Richmond *(G-11226)*

Heclyn Precision Gear Company........F..... 215 739-7094
Machipongo *(G-7847)*

L E F Gear.................................G..... 757 274-2151
Virginia Beach *(G-14594)*

3567 Indl Process Furnaces & Ovens

Associated Printing Svcs Inc............G..... 804 360-5770
Richmond *(G-11119)*

▼ Buffalo Air Handling Company.......C..... 434 946-7455
Amherst *(G-685)*

▼ Consutech Systems LLC...............E..... 804 746-4120
Mechanicsville *(G-8614)*

▼ Isotemp Research Inc..................G..... 434 295-3101
Charlottesville *(G-2815)*

Kiln Doctor Inc............................G..... 540 636-6016
Front Royal *(G-5540)*

Mac Bone Industries Ltd................G..... 804 264-3603
Richmond *(G-11278)*

Modine Manufacturing Company.......E..... 540 261-9821
Buena Vista *(G-2148)*

Setliff and Company LLC.................G..... 434 793-1173
Danville *(G-4038)*

3568 Mechanical Power Transmission Eqpt, NEC

ABB Enterprise Software Inc............G..... 434 575-2169
South Boston *(G-12209)*

Browns Sterling Motors Inc.............G..... 571 390-6900
Sterling *(G-13361)*

Federal-Mogul Powertrain LLC.........B..... 540 557-3300
Blacksburg *(G-1737)*

Ggb LLC....................................G..... 571 234-9597
Manassas *(G-8074)*

Parsons Corporation....................D..... 703 558-0036
Arlington *(G-1099)*

Parsons Corporation....................C..... 703 988-8500
Centreville *(G-2327)*

Progressive Manufacturing Corp.......E..... 804 717-5353
Chester *(G-3448)*

Rexnord Industries LLC..................G..... 540 337-3510
Stuarts Draft *(G-13658)*

Rexnord Industries LLC..................G..... 540 337-3510
Stuarts Draft *(G-13659)*

Twin Disc Incorporated.................D..... 757 487-3670
Chesapeake *(G-3353)*

3569 Indl Machinery & Eqpt, NEC

◆ Alfa Laval Inc...........................C..... 866 253-2528
Richmond *(G-11095)*

◆ Alfa Laval US Holding Inc............D..... 804 222-5300
Richmond *(G-11096)*

American Spin-A-Batch Co Intl.........G..... 804 798-1349
Ashland *(G-1367)*

C&C Assembly Inc.......................G..... 540 904-6416
Salem *(G-12487)*

Cantel Medical Corp.....................G..... 800 633-3080
Mount Jackson *(G-9067)*

Charlottesville Fire Exting...............G..... 434 295-0803
Scottsville *(G-12659)*

Chase Filters & Components LLC......E..... 757 327-0036
Hampton *(G-6112)*

Commonwealth Rescue Systems.......G..... 540 438-8972
Harrisonburg *(G-6305)*

Envirnmntal Solutions Intl Inc..........F..... 703 263-7600
Ashburn *(G-1276)*

Filter Media................................G..... 540 667-9074
Winchester *(G-15543)*

▲ Filtroil LLC..............................E..... 804 359-9125
Richmond *(G-11588)*

Fire Systems Services Inc...............G..... 757 825-6379
Hampton *(G-6150)*

Interstate Rescue LLC...................F..... 571 283-4206
Winchester *(G-15429)*

Johns Manville Corporation.............B..... 540 984-4171
Edinburg *(G-4307)*

◆ Kelvin International Corp..............F..... 757 833-1011
Newport News *(G-9274)*

Mekatronich Corp........................G..... 954 499-5794
Christianburg *(G-3605)*

Metallum3d LLC...........................G..... 434 409-2401
Crozet *(G-3843)*

National Filter Media Corp..............G..... 540 773-4780
Winchester *(G-15560)*

Omni Filter and Mfg Inc.................E..... 804 550-1600
Ashland *(G-1472)*

▲ Porvair Filtration Group Inc..........D..... 804 550-1600
Ashland *(G-1478)*

▼ Precision Generators Company.......G..... 757 498-4809
Virginia Beach *(G-14732)*

S P Kinney Engineers Inc...............F..... 804 520-4700
South Chesterfield *(G-12825)*

Shop Guys..................................G..... 804 317-9440
Midlothian *(G-8897)*

▲ SKF Lbrication Systems USA Inc....D..... 757 951-0370
Hampton *(G-6239)*

Southern Scrap Company Inc...........E..... 540 662-0265
Winchester *(G-15481)*

Tri-Dim Filter Corporation..............G..... 540 967-2600
Louisa *(G-7572)*

Verdex Technologies Inc.................G..... 804 491-9733
North Chesterfield *(G-10008)*

Vmek Group LLC.........................G..... 804 380-1831
Midlothian *(G-8919)*

Vogel Lubrication.........................F..... 757 380-8585
Hampton *(G-6266)*

World Fashion City Inc..................G..... 703 887-8123
Alexandria *(G-615)*

X-Metrix Inc...............................G..... 757 450-5978
Virginia Beach *(G-14947)*

3571 Electronic Computers

1st Stop Electronics LLC................G..... 804 931-0517
Richmond *(G-11070)*

3189 Apple Rd Ne LLC..................G..... 703 455-5989
Springfield *(G-12934)*

Acacia Acquisitions LLC.................G..... 703 554-1600
Ashburn *(G-1236)*

Acacia Investment Holdings LLC.......G..... 703 554-1600
Tysons *(G-13940)*

Access Prime Techncl Sltns.............G..... 757 651-6523
Hampton *(G-6068)*

Ace Title & Escrow Inc ....G.... 703 629-5768
Alexandria *(G-401)*
Alligatortalez ....G.... 703 791-4238
Manassas *(G-8023)*
Alpha Printing Inc ....G.... 703 914-2800
Springfield *(G-12942)*
Apple Frankies Ent Inc ....G.... 540 845-7372
Fredericksburg *(G-5246)*
Apple Shine ....G.... 757 714-6393
Virginia Beach *(G-14233)*
Apple Tire Inc ....G.... 434 575-5200
South Boston *(G-12747)*
Apple Valley LLC ....G.... 540 465-8360
Strasburg *(G-13573)*
Apple-Polishers LLC ....G.... 571 918-1027
Leesburg *(G-7219)*
Apples & Belles LLC ....G.... 804 530-3180
Chester *(G-3387)*
Apples Closet ....G.... 540 825-9551
Culpeper *(G-3867)*
Augusta Apple LLC ....G.... 540 337-7170
Churchville *(G-3619)*
Auru Technologies Inc ....G.... 434 632-6978
Clarksville *(G-3626)*
Avenger Computer Solutions ....G.... 240 305-7835
Arlington *(G-867)*
Bander Computers ....G.... 757 398-3443
Portsmouth *(G-10396)*
Beets & Apples ....G.... 703 743-4112
Haymarket *(G-6415)*
Bradshaw Viola ....G.... 571 274-5244
Falls Church *(G-4765)*
Candy Apples and Favors LLC ....G.... 804 674-4061
Richmond *(G-11518)*
Capitol Idea Technology Inc ....G.... 571 233-1949
Woodbridge *(G-15667)*
Celestial Circuits LLC ....G.... 703 851-2843
Springfield *(G-12975)*
Centripetal Networks Inc ....E.... 571 252-5080
Herndon *(G-6638)*
CIS Secure Computing Inc ....E.... 703 996-0500
Ashburn *(G-1254)*
CNE Manufacturing Services LLC ....E.... 540 216-0884
Warrenton *(G-14988)*
Compu Dynamics LLC ....E.... 703 796-6070
Sterling *(G-13373)*
Core Business Technologies Inc ....G.... 757 426-0344
Virginia Beach *(G-14365)*
Cryptek USA Corp ....E.... 571 434-2000
Sterling *(G-13377)*
D-Ta Systems Corporation ....G.... 571 775-8924
Arlington *(G-925)*
Dark3 Inc ....G.... 703 398-1101
Alexandria *(G-182)*
Data Management LLC ....G.... 703 222-4246
Centreville *(G-2300)*
▲ **Datalux Corporation** ....D.... 540 662-1500
Winchester *(G-15409)*
Dcomputerscom ....G.... 757 460-3324
Virginia Beach *(G-14396)*
Dell Inc ....A.... 301 581-0513
Fairfax *(G-4437)*
Dimensionu Inc ....E.... 804 447-4220
Henrico *(G-6502)*
Durabook Federal Inc ....G.... 888 414-9844
Glen Allen *(G-5727)*
Embedded Systems LLC ....G.... 860 269-8148
Haymarket *(G-6422)*
Emes LLC ....G.... 703 680-0807
Dumfries *(G-4245)*
Essolutions Inc ....F.... 240 215-6992
Arlington *(G-959)*
Evergreen Design Inc ....G.... 540 984-4653
Edinburg *(G-4303)*
Extreme Computer Services Inc ....G.... 703 730-8821
Dumfries *(G-4246)*
Fat Apple LLC ....G.... 434 823-2481
Crozet *(G-3832)*
Fed Reach Inc ....G.... 703 507-8822
Lorton *(G-7488)*
Finders Keepers Recruiting ....G.... 703 963-0874
Fairfax *(G-4457)*
First Colony Technology LLC ....G.... 434 579-3655
Providence Forge *(G-10624)*
Fta Goverment Services Inc ....G.... 571 612-0413
Chantilly *(G-2423)*
Gdm International Services Inc ....G.... 540 687-6687
Middleburg *(G-8720)*
▲ **General Dynmics Mssion Systems** ..E.... 877 449-0600
Fairfax *(G-4463)*
Gravitonus ....G.... 571 321-2019
Fairfax *(G-4629)*
Green Apple Assoc A Virgin ....G.... 804 551-5040
Richmond *(G-11222)*
Greentec-Usa Inc ....E.... 703 880-8332
Sterling *(G-13414)*
Hadrian Inc ....G.... 703 724-7760
Ashburn *(G-1288)*
Hewlett-Packard Federal LLC ....E.... 800 727-5472
Herndon *(G-6698)*
Hitachi Vantara Federal Corp ....C.... 703 787-2900
Reston *(G-10865)*
Horizon Global Partners LLC ....F.... 703 597-2351
Ashburn *(G-1292)*
Hp Inc ....C.... 703 535-3355
Alexandria *(G-230)*
IBM Philip Morris ....G.... 405 600-7997
South Chesterfield *(G-12810)*
Ice Enterprises Inc ....F.... 703 934-4879
Fairfax *(G-4632)*
Inhand Networks Inc ....G.... 703 348-2988
Fairfax *(G-4634)*
Intellect Computers Inc ....F.... 703 931-5100
Alexandria *(G-239)*
▲ **Interbyte** ....G.... 703 825-8774
Alexandria *(G-486)*
Iron Bow Holdings Inc ....G.... 703 795-1790
Chantilly *(G-2445)*
Iron Bow Holdings Inc ....C.... 703 279-3000
Herndon *(G-6712)*
Iron Brick Associates LLC ....E.... 703 288-3874
Sperryville *(G-12878)*
It Solutions 4u Inc ....G.... 703 624-4430
Sterling *(G-13433)*
Itst Inc ....G.... 703 455-2152
Springfield *(G-13025)*
Junoventure LLC ....G.... 410 247-1908
Ashland *(G-1445)*
Kirkland Holdings Co ....G.... 571 348-1005
Alexandria *(G-254)*
Laserserv Inc ....E.... 804 359-6188
Richmond *(G-11266)*
Lockheed Martin Corporation ....C.... 703 367-2121
Manassas *(G-7966)*
▲ **Mandylion Research Labs LLC** ....E.... 703 628-4284
Oakton *(G-10156)*
Mercury Systems Inc ....G.... 510 252-0870
Fairfax *(G-4654)*
Microtude LLC ....G.... 703 581-7991
Ashburn *(G-1317)*
Mildef Inc ....G.... 703 224-8835
Alexandria *(G-275)*
Montauk Systems Corporation ....G.... 954 695-6819
Ashburn *(G-1318)*
N-Ask Incorporated ....D.... 703 715-7909
Fairfax *(G-4515)*
Ncs Technologies Inc ....G.... 703 743-8500
Manassas *(G-7981)*
▲ **Ncs Technologies Inc** ....C.... 703 743-8500
Gainesville *(G-5600)*
Nvis Inc ....F.... 571 201-8095
Reston *(G-10911)*
Pbp Solutions LLC ....G.... 202 999-8101
Reston *(G-10923)*
Proficient Link LLC ....G.... 703 391-6330
Sterling *(G-13480)*
Rebound Analytics LLC ....G.... 202 297-1204
Tysons *(G-13948)*
Red Apple Productions LLC ....G.... 703 237-1034
Arlington *(G-1145)*
Right Sized Technologies Inc ....F.... 703 623-9505
Sterling *(G-13494)*
Rollins Oma Sue ....G.... 757 449-6371
Virginia Beach *(G-14778)*
Ronald Carter ....G.... 571 278-6659
Burke *(G-2202)*
Sector 5 Inc ....G.... 571 348-1005
Alexandria *(G-341)*
Sector Five Inc ....G.... 571 348-1005
Alexandria *(G-342)*
Sensor Networks LLC ....G.... 703 481-2224
Reston *(G-10947)*
Smith Distributors & Mktg LLC ....G.... 540 760-6833
Fredericksburg *(G-5362)*
Smrt Mouth LLC ....G.... 804 363-8863
Sandston *(G-12634)*
Spur Defense Systems ....G.... 540 742-8394
King George *(G-7114)*
Symbolics - David K Schmidt ....G.... 703 455-0430
Burke *(G-2204)*
Symmple Technologies ....G.... 703 591-7716
Fairfax *(G-4566)*
T3b LLC ....G.... 202 550-4475
Mc Lean *(G-8563)*
Taxlaw20 LLC ....G.... 202 470-3980
Mc Lean *(G-8564)*
Technlogy Advncement Group Inc ....G.... 703 406-3000
Dulles *(G-4228)*
The For American Society ....G.... 703 331-0075
Falls Church *(G-4882)*
Ultrata LLC ....F.... 571 226-0347
Vienna *(G-14147)*
United Federal Systems Inc ....F.... 703 881-7777
Manassas *(G-8173)*
Vps Services Inc ....G.... 202 538-1990
Ashburn *(G-1352)*

3572 Computer Storage Devices

Absolute EMC Llc ....G.... 703 774-7505
Centreville *(G-2287)*
Core Business Technologies Inc ....G.... 757 426-0344
Virginia Beach *(G-14365)*
Dell EMC ....G.... 301 897-1400
Reston *(G-10839)*
Dhk Storage LLC ....G.... 703 870-3741
Sterling *(G-13385)*
▲ **Drs Leonardo Inc** ....C.... 703 416-8000
Arlington *(G-944)*
Electrmchncal Ctrl Systems Inc ....G.... 434 610-5747
Lynchburg *(G-7700)*
Elite Masonry Contractor LLC ....G.... 757 773-9908
Chesapeake *(G-3086)*
EMC Corporation ....E.... 703 749-2260
Mc Lean *(G-8423)*
EMC Corporation ....F.... 703 553-2522
Arlington *(G-958)*
EMC Metal Fabrication ....G.... 804 355-1030
Richmond *(G-11202)*
Emcs Inc ....G.... 443 223-2335
Chesterfield *(G-3497)*
Enterprise Svcs Cmmnctions LLC ....G.... 877 858-3855
Tysons *(G-13943)*
Essolutions Inc ....F.... 240 215-6992
Arlington *(G-959)*
Gratispicks Inc ....G.... 757 739-4143
Portsmouth *(G-10436)*
Hitachi Vantara Federal Corp ....C.... 703 787-2900
Reston *(G-10865)*
Hitachi Vantara LLC ....G.... 405 593-3783
Herndon *(G-6700)*
Iron Brick Associates LLC ....E.... 703 288-3874
Sperryville *(G-12878)*
Meridian Tech Systems Inc ....G.... 301 606-6490
Leesburg *(G-7313)*
Network Storage Corp ....E.... 703 834-7500
Chantilly *(G-2468)*
Pbp Solutions LLC ....G.... 202 999-8101
Reston *(G-10923)*
Quantum Connect LLC ....G.... 703 251-3342
Herndon *(G-6784)*
Quantum Medical Bus Svc Inc ....G.... 703 727-1020
Winchester *(G-15572)*
Quantum Reefs LLC ....G.... 703 560-1448
Annandale *(G-779)*
Quantum Technologies Inc ....G.... 703 214-9756
Falls Church *(G-4861)*
R T Sales Inc ....G.... 703 542-5862
Haymarket *(G-6440)*
Rebecca Leigh Fraser ....G.... 912 755-3453
Virginia Beach *(G-14765)*
Ret Corp ....G.... 703 471-8108
Mc Lean *(G-8537)*
Rising Edge Technologies Inc ....G.... 703 471-8108
Mc Lean *(G-8538)*
Secubit Inc ....G.... 757 453-6965
Virginia Beach *(G-14801)*
Unifiedonline Inc ....G.... 816 679-1893
Fairfax *(G-4690)*
Unifiedonline LLC ....G.... 816 679-1893
Fairfax *(G-4691)*
United States Dept of Army ....G.... 757 878-4831
Fort Eustis *(G-5127)*
Western Digital Corporation ....G.... 434 933-8162
Gladstone *(G-5689)*

3575 Computer Terminals

▲ **Datalux Corporation** ....D.... 540 662-1500
Winchester *(G-15409)*
Essolutions Inc ....F.... 240 215-6992
Arlington *(G-959)*

S I C

F & B Holding Co ....G...... 757 766-2770
Yorktown **(G-15957)**

George Perez ....G...... 757 362-3131
Norfolk **(G-9561)**

Hanwell Inc ....G...... 757 213-6841
Virginia Beach **(G-14504)**

N A D C ....G...... 703 331-5611
Manassas **(G-7979)**

Otsan Technical Service LLC ....G...... 276 696-7163
Bristol **(G-1985)**

Rollins Oma Sue ....G...... 757 449-6371
Virginia Beach **(G-14778)**

Stanford Electronics Mfg & Sls ....G...... 434 676-6630
Brodnax **(G-2105)**

◆ US 21 Inc ....D...... 703 560-0021
Fairfax **(G-4575)**

3577 Computer Peripheral Eqpt, NEC

1st Stop Electronics LLC ....G...... 804 931-0517
Richmond **(G-11070)**

Action Digital Inc ....G...... 804 358-7289
Richmond **(G-11083)**

Advanced Business Services LLC .....G...... 757 439-0849
Virginia Beach **(G-14212)**

Andres R Henriquz ....G...... 703 629-9821
Alexandria **(G-413)**

Atlantic Computing LLC ....G...... 434 293-2022
Charlottesville **(G-2591)**

Audio - Video Solutions ....G...... 240 565-4381
Bristow **(G-2047)**

Barcoding Inc ....G...... 540 416-0116
Staunton **(G-13243)**

Black Box Corporation ....G...... 781 449-1900
Amherst **(G-684)**

Bow Industries of Virginia ....G...... 703 361-7704
Manassas **(G-8041)**

◆ Canon Virginia Inc ....A...... 757 881-6000
Newport News **(G-9192)**

Charlotte County School Board ....E...... 434 542-4933
Charlotte C H **(G-2583)**

Cisco Systems Inc ....D...... 703 484-5500
Herndon **(G-6641)**

Comxi World LLC ....G...... 804 299-5234
Glen Allen **(G-5717)**

Convex Corporation ....G...... 703 433-9901
Warrenton **(G-14990)**

Covington Barcoding Inc ....G...... 434 476-1435
South Boston **(G-12755)**

▲ Datalux Corporation ....D...... 540 662-1500
Winchester **(G-15409)**

Dhk Storage LLC ....G...... 703 870-3741
Sterling **(G-13385)**

▲ Digital Access Control Inc...............F...... 703 463-0113
Chantilly **(G-2408)**

Disrupt6 Inc ....G...... 571 721-1155
Leesburg **(G-7258)**

▲ Drytac Corporation ....E...... 804 280-6013
Sandston **(G-12613)**

Elekon Industries USA Inc ....E...... 757 766-1500
Hampton **(G-6136)**

Ericsson Inc ....E...... 571 262-9254
Vienna **(G-14049)**

Essolutions Inc ....F...... 240 215-6992
Arlington **(G-959)**

Exhibit Design & Prod Svcs LLC ....G...... 804 347-0924
Henrico **(G-6508)**

Fna Jewels ....G...... 703 591-6817
Fairfax **(G-4459)**

Forescout Gvrnment Sltions LLC ......E...... 408 538-0946
Tysons **(G-13945)**

Ganleys ....G...... 703 476-8864
Herndon **(G-6678)**

Global Scnning Americas VA Inc.......G...... 703 717-5631
Chantilly **(G-2427)**

Ice Enterprises Inc ....F...... 703 934-4879
Fairfax **(G-4632)**

Idvector ....G...... 571 313-5064
Sterling **(G-13426)**

Innovative Computer Engrg Inc ....G...... 703 934-4879
Fairfax **(G-4635)**

Innovative Computer Engrg Inc ....G...... 703 934-2782
Fairfax **(G-4636)**

Intel Corporation ....G...... 571 312-2320
Alexandria **(G-238)**

Intex LLC ....G...... 703 899-3336
Reston **(G-10878)**

Iowave Inc ....E...... 703 979-9283
Arlington **(G-1011)**

Isomet Corporation ....E...... 703 321-8301
Manassas **(G-8087)**

James-York Security LLC ....E...... 757 344-1808
Williamsburg **(G-15259)**

Juniper Networks (us) Inc ....C...... 571 203-1700
Herndon **(G-6721)**

Konica Mnlta Bus Sltons USA In ....E...... 703 553-6000
Vienna **(G-14079)**

Laserserv Inc ....E...... 804 359-6188
Richmond **(G-11266)**

Leidos Inc ....E...... 703 610-8900
Vienna **(G-14082)**

Leidos Inc ....E...... 703 734-5315
Mc Lean **(G-8485)**

Local Energy Technologies ....G...... 717 371-0041
Mc Lean **(G-8487)**

Lockheed Martin Corporation ....C...... 703 367-2121
Manassas **(G-7966)**

Mantis Networks LLC 571 306-1234
Reston **(G-10894)**

Materials Development Corp ....G...... 703 257-1500
Manassas **(G-8105)**

Mellanox Federal Systems LLC ....F...... 703 969-5735
Herndon **(G-6745)**

Mercury Solutions LLC......................G...... 703 474-9456
Leesburg **(G-7312)**

Meridian Tech Systems Inc ....G...... 301 606-6490
Leesburg **(G-7313)**

Michael Burnette ....G...... 757 478-8585
Newport News **(G-9300)**

Mimetrix Technologies LLC ....G...... 571 306-1234
Vienna **(G-14094)**

Multimdal Idntfcation Tech LLC ....G...... 818 729-1954
Reston **(G-10905)**

Neosystems Corp ....G...... 571 234-4949
Fairfax **(G-4516)**

Northern Virginia Compute ....G...... 540 479-4455
Fredericksburg **(G-5461)**

Nsgdatacom Inc ....E...... 703 464-0151
Chantilly **(G-2475)**

Old World Labs LLC ....G...... 800 282-0386
Norfolk **(G-9675)**

Palo Alto Ntwrks Pub Sctor LLC ....F...... 240 328-3016
Reston **(G-10918)**

Refurb Factory LLC ....G...... 301 799-8385
Alexandria **(G-328)**

Roxann Robinson Delegate ....G...... 804 308-1534
Richmond **(G-11748)**

Sean Applegate ....G...... 540 972-4779
Spotsylvania **(G-12913)**

SJ Dobert ....G...... 301 847-5000
Reston **(G-10952)**

Spur Defense Systems ....G...... 540 742-8394
King George **(G-7114)**

Storage Technology...........................G...... 703 817-1528
Chantilly **(G-2502)**

Symbol Technologies LLC ....G...... 703 263-2533
Chantilly **(G-2506)**

Teams It ....G...... 757 868-1129
Poquoson **(G-10377)**

Techsource LLC ....G...... 757 469-3983
Woodbridge **(G-15821)**

Tq-Systems USA Inc ....G...... 757 503-3927
Chesapeake **(G-3346)**

▼ Troesen Enterprises LLC ....G...... 571 405-3199
Alexandria **(G-369)**

Troy Patrick ....G...... 703 507-4914
Alexandria **(G-370)**

◆ US 21 Inc ....D...... 703 560-0021
Fairfax **(G-4575)**

Van Rosendale John ....G...... 757 868-8593
Poquoson **(G-10378)**

◆ Vidar Systems Corporation ....E...... 703 471-7070
Herndon **(G-6838)**

Wizard Technologies ....G...... 703 625-0900
Vienna **(G-14161)**

Xerox Alumni Association Inc ....G...... 703 848-0624
Mc Lean **(G-8581)**

3578 Calculating & Accounting Eqpt

Accounting Executive Svcs LLC ....G...... 757 406-1127
Norfolk **(G-9417)**

American Highwall Systems ....F...... 276 646-2004
Chilhowie **(G-3545)**

Atm Beach Services LLC ....G...... 757 434-4848
Virginia Beach **(G-14247)**

Carr Group LLC ....G...... 571 723-6562
Woodbridge **(G-15669)**

Catering Machine Company ....G...... 757 332-0024
Carrollton **(G-2241)**

Claren ....G...... 571 403-0425
Sterling **(G-13371)**

Debra Rosel ....G...... 703 675-4963
Round Hill **(G-12377)**

Enc Enterprises ....G...... 703 578-1924
Falls Church **(G-4788)**

Idemia America Corp ....G...... 703 263-0100
Reston **(G-10867)**

Lt Business Dynamics LLC ....G...... 703 738-6599
Vienna **(G-14087)**

Maysteel Porters LLC ....C...... 434 846-7412
Lynchburg **(G-7769)**

Mgi Fuel Express LLC ....G...... 804 541-0299
North Prince George **(G-10089)**

◆ Newbold Corporation ....C...... 540 489-4400
Rocky Mount **(G-12342)**

Rega Enterprises Inc ....G...... 757 488-8056
Chesapeake **(G-3268)**

Total Touch Solutions LLC ....G...... 757 536-1445
Virginia Beach **(G-14889)**

3579 Office Machines, NEC

Coastal Tags & Supply LLC ....G...... 757 995-4139
Virginia Beach **(G-14348)**

Cut Check Writing Services ....G...... 757 898-9015
Yorktown **(G-15947)**

International Roll-Call Corp ....E...... 804 730-9600
Mechanicsville **(G-8642)**

Jones Direct LLC ....G...... 757 718-3468
Chesapeake **(G-3153)**

Konica Mnlta Bus Sltons USA In ....C...... 703 461-8195
Alexandria **(G-508)**

Kusters Engineering SEC Inc ....G...... 703 967-1449
Falls Church **(G-4818)**

MB Services LLC ....G...... 703 906-8625
Alexandria **(G-524)**

◆ Newbold Corporation ....C...... 540 489-4400
Rocky Mount **(G-12342)**

Pitney Bowes Business Insight ....G...... 540 786-5744
Fredericksburg **(G-5347)**

Pitney Bowes Inc ....G...... 703 658-6900
Alexandria **(G-310)**

Pitney Bowes Inc ....E...... 304 744-1067
Vienna **(G-14112)**

Pitney Bowes Inc ....E...... 757 322-8000
Norfolk **(G-9690)**

Pitney Bowes Inc ....E...... 804 798-3210
Ashland **(G-1476)**

SMS Data Products Group Inc ....G...... 703 709-9898
Sterling **(G-13512)**

Tigerseal Products LLC ....G...... 800 899-9389
Beaverdam **(G-1614)**

Xsytechnologiescom ....G...... 757 333-7514
Virginia Beach **(G-14948)**

3581 Automatic Vending Machines

Chow Time LLC ....G...... 804 934-9305
Richmond **(G-11157)**

Compass Group Usa Inc ....E...... 757 485-4401
Chesapeake **(G-3048)**

Hailey Bug Vending ....G...... 757 665-4402
Bloxom **(G-1841)**

▲ Hampton Roads Vending ....G...... 703 927-6125
Chesapeake **(G-3127)**

Jacatai Vending ....G...... 804 317-2526
North Chesterfield **(G-9901)**

Lorrie Carpenter ....G...... 804 720-6442
Alexandria **(G-265)**

Rdj Enterprises ....G...... 757 538-0466
Suffolk **(G-13758)**

T-Jar Inc ....G...... 540 974-2567
Winchester **(G-15486)**

Wright Discount Entps LLC ....G...... 703 580-5278
Woodbridge **(G-15835)**

3582 Commercial Laundry, Dry Clean & Pressing Mchs

Capital Linen Services Inc ....F...... 804 744-3334
Midlothian **(G-8789)**

M B S Equipment Sales Inc ....G...... 804 785-4971
Shacklefords **(G-12683)**

Mosena Enterprises Inc ....G...... 757 562-7033
Franklin **(G-5149)**

Rodgers Services LLC........................G...... 301 848-6384
King George **(G-7109)**

Ship Shape Cleaning LLC ....G...... 757 769-3845
Portsmouth **(G-10480)**

3585 Air Conditioning & Heating Eqpt

Academy Boys and Girls Soccer ....G...... 804 380-9005
Chesterfield **(G-3472)**

Airpac Inc G 540 635-5011
Front Royal *(G-5520)*
◆ **Alfa Laval Inc** C 866 253-2528
Richmond *(G-11095)*
◆ **Alfa Laval USA Inc** E 804 222-5300
Richmond *(G-11097)*
Berts Inc G 757 865-8040
Newport News *(G-9178)*
Beta Contractors LLC G 703 424-1940
Herndon *(G-6623)*
Brontz Inc G 540 483-0976
Rocky Mount *(G-12315)*
▼ **Buffalo Air Handling Company** C 434 946-7455
Amherst *(G-685)*
C & M Heating & AC LLC G 276 618-0955
Axton *(G-1533)*
Carrier Corporation F 540 366-2471
Roanoke *(G-11905)*
Chappelle Mechanical Svcs LLC G 240 299-3000
Dumfries *(G-4239)*
Chase Group II A/C & Htg Svc G 571 245-7379
Fredericksburg *(G-5411)*
CK Service Inc G 757 486-5880
Virginia Beach *(G-14341)*
Cogo Aire LLC G 757 332-3551
Virginia Beach *(G-14352)*
Commercial Tech Inc G 703 468-1339
Manassas *(G-8051)*
Darwin Marquina G 703 220-2940
Alexandria *(G-441)*
Dometic Corporation C 804 746-1313
Mechanicsville *(G-8618)*
Draft Doctor G 804 986-6588
Richmond *(G-11568)*
Ecoer Inc G 703 348-2538
Fairfax *(G-4617)*
Ensons Inc G 703 644-6694
Burke *(G-2189)*
Griffin Pipe Products Co LLC G 434 845-8021
Lynchburg *(G-7725)*
Hang Men High Heating & Coolg G 804 651-3320
Richmond *(G-11232)*
Hill Phoenix Inc C 804 317-6882
South Chesterfield *(G-12805)*
Hill Phoenix Inc F 804 317-6882
South Chesterfield *(G-12806)*
Hill Phoenix Inc C 804 526-4455
South Chesterfield *(G-12808)*
Hkd Snowmakers Com G 540 451-1779
Stuarts Draft *(G-13650)*
Hussmann Corporation G 540 775-2502
King George *(G-7094)*
JRS Repco Inc G 540 334-3051
Boones Mill *(G-1895)*
◆ **Liqui-Box Corporation** D 804 325-1400
Richmond *(G-11658)*
Mac Bone Industries Ltd G 804 264-3603
Richmond *(G-11278)*
Metropolitan Equipment Group G 804 744-4774
North Chesterfield *(G-9929)*
▲ **Orien Usa LLC** G 757 486-2099
Virginia Beach *(G-14703)*
Power Anywhere LLC G 703 625-4115
Arlington *(G-1118)*
Proto-Technics Inc E 540 672-5193
Orange *(G-10222)*
▲ **Provides US Inc** D 540 569-3434
Verona *(G-13993)*
Quang D Nguyen G 703 715-2244
Herndon *(G-6782)*
Refcon Services Inc F 757 616-0691
Chesapeake *(G-3266)*
Ronnie D Bryant Htg Coolg LLC G 540 221-0988
Waynesboro *(G-15138)*
RPC Tubes G 703 471-5659
Sterling *(G-13497)*
Sestra Systems Inc E 703 429-1596
Sterling *(G-13505)*
Siemens Industry Inc D 757 490-6026
Norfolk *(G-9723)*
Silvas Heat & Air G 757 596-5991
Newport News *(G-9342)*
Spot Coolers Inc G 804 222-5530
Richmond *(G-11392)*
Super RAD Coils Ltd Partnr C 804 794-2887
North Chesterfield *(G-9992)*
Terry Brown G 804 721-6667
Prince George *(G-10608)*
Trane Company G 304 348-2800
Ashland *(G-1502)*
Trane Inc G 540 376-3064
Fredericksburg *(G-5380)*
Trane US Inc D 804 747-4774
Ashland *(G-1503)*
Trane US Inc G 540 342-3027
Roanoke *(G-12207)*
Trane US Inc G 434 793-4822
Danville *(G-4042)*
Trane US Inc D 434 327-1601
Charlottesville *(G-2893)*
Trane US Inc G 844 805-3895
Roanoke *(G-12208)*
Trane US Inc G 757 485-7700
Chesapeake *(G-3350)*
Trane US Inc D 757 490-2390
Virginia Beach *(G-14892)*
Trane US Inc G 540 376-3064
Fredericksburg *(G-5381)*
Tranter Inc G 757 533-9185
Norfolk *(G-9765)*
Universal Dynamics Inc G 703 490-7000
Fredericksburg *(G-5384)*
Utility Trailer Mfg Co A 276 783-8800
Atkins *(G-1522)*
Vertiv Corporation E 703 726-4100
Ashburn *(G-1349)*
Virginia Air Distributors Inc F 540 366-2259
Roanoke *(G-12020)*
Virginia Blower Company E 276 647-3804
Collinsville *(G-3718)*
Virginia Trane Ap141 G 540 580-7702
Roanoke *(G-12221)*
Wilson Mechanical Repair Servi G 804 317-4919
Mechanicsville *(G-8698)*

3586 Measuring & Dispensing Pumps

Silgan Dspnsing Systems Hldngs G 804 923-1971
Richmond *(G-11760)*

3589 Service Ind Machines, NEC

2r2s Inc G 804 262-6922
Richmond *(G-11072)*
A Descal Matic Corp G 757 858-5593
Norfolk *(G-9414)*
▲ **A-1 Security Mfg Corp** F 804 359-9003
Richmond *(G-11078)*
Abwasser Technologies Inc G 757 453-7505
Virginia Beach *(G-14206)*
Advantage Systems G 703 370-4500
Alexandria *(G-119)*
Affordable Companies G 703 440-9274
Springfield *(G-12935)*
Alpha Pressure Washing G 540 293-1287
Roanoke *(G-12032)*
Aquao2 Wastewater Treatment Sy G 540 365-0154
Ferrum *(G-4967)*
▼ **Aquarobic International Inc** G 540 365-0154
Ferrum *(G-4968)*
Bernard Speed G 540 514-9041
Fredericksburg *(G-5403)*
Bissell G 703 827-5769
Mc Lean *(G-8399)*
Broswell Water Systems G 757 436-1871
Chesapeake *(G-3016)*
Burley Holt Langford III LLC G 804 712-7172
South Chesterfield *(G-12832)*
Camelot G 434 978-1049
Charlottesville *(G-2602)*
Car Wash Care Inc G 703 385-9181
Fairfax *(G-4605)*
Caravelle Industries Inc G 434 432-2331
Leesburg *(G-7238)*
Caravelle Industries Inc F 434 432-2331
Chatham *(G-2920)*
▲ **CEF Enterprises Inc** G 757 478-4359
Virginia Beach *(G-14328)*
Champion Handwash E 703 893-4216
Vienna *(G-14026)*
City of Danville E 434 799-5137
Danville *(G-3967)*
Coastal Services & Tech LLC F 757 833-0550
Yorktown *(G-15942)*
Commonwlth H20 Svcs Inc-Blue R F 434 975-4426
Charlottesville *(G-2610)*
Cool Wave LLC G 757 269-0200
Smithfield *(G-12710)*
D Atwood G 703 508-5080
Gwynn *(G-6045)*
Detail Maxx LLC G 703 942-8965
Mc Lean *(G-8418)*
Dominion Water Products Inc E 804 236-9480
Richmond *(G-11189)*
Doswell Water Treatment Plant F 804 876-3557
Doswell *(G-4120)*
Ecolochem Inc D 804 327-6846
North Chesterfield *(G-10019)*
Fab Services LLC G 757 869-4480
Williamsburg *(G-15242)*
Fantabulous Chef Service G 804 245-4492
Richmond *(G-11208)*
Freshstart Coml Jantr Svcs LLC G 571 645-0060
Triangle *(G-13893)*
H20 Pro G 540 785-6811
Fredericksburg *(G-5295)*
Henrico Chubbys G 804 285-4469
Richmond *(G-11237)*
Heyward Inc Virginia Inc G 804 965-0086
Glen Allen *(G-5742)*
Infilco Degremont Inc E 804 756-7600
Richmond *(G-11247)*
Jean Samuels G 804 328-2294
Sandston *(G-12622)*
Keen Eyes Auto Detailing LLC G 252 646-3600
Stafford *(G-13161)*
Lincoln Place Group LLC G 347 363-9721
Richmond *(G-11656)*
Magic Wand Inc E 276 466-3921
Bristol *(G-1983)*
Maurice Bynum G 757 241-0265
Windsor *(G-15606)*
McCoy Water Filter Inc G 804 222-2089
Henrico *(G-6534)*
Metro Water Purification LLC G 804 366-2158
Chester *(G-3436)*
My Three Sons Inc G 540 662-5927
Winchester *(G-15453)*
New Look Pressure Washing LLC G 804 476-2000
Henrico *(G-6542)*
Next Level Building Solutions G 540 400-9169
Boones Mill *(G-1898)*
Next Level Building Solutions F 540 685-1500
Roanoke *(G-11974)*
▲ **Norris Screen and Mfg LLC** E 276 988-8901
Tazewell *(G-13838)*
Old Dominion Brush Company Inc G 800 446-9823
Richmond *(G-11313)*
Outrageous Shine LLC G 804 741-9274
Richmond *(G-11317)*
Parsons Pressure Washing G 757 894-3110
New Church *(G-9127)*
Piedmont Environmental Sys G 434 836-4547
Danville *(G-4025)*
Planet Care Inc G 540 980-2420
Pulaski *(G-10644)*
Pressures On G 757 681-8999
Chesapeake *(G-3246)*
◆ **Prochem Inc** E 540 268-9884
Elliston *(G-4347)*
Pure-Mech Inc G 804 363-1297
Roanoke *(G-11991)*
▲ **Q B Enterprises Inc** G 540 825-2950
Orange *(G-10224)*
▲ **Rasco Equipment Services Inc** G 703 643-2952
Woodbridge *(G-15791)*
Richard A Landes G 540 885-1454
Staunton *(G-13285)*
Rio Take Back LLC G 540 371-3636
Fredericksburg *(G-5480)*
Rivanna Water & Observatory G 434 973-5709
Charlottesville *(G-2687)*
River Rock Environmental Svcs G 757 690-3916
Suffolk *(G-13759)*
Robert Agnello G 757 345-0829
Williamsburg *(G-15306)*
Robert E Horne G 804 920-1847
Disputanta *(G-4113)*
S&H Mobile Cleaning Service G 540 254-1135
Buchanan *(G-2126)*
Sanitech Corp E 703 339-7001
Lorton *(G-7529)*
Scrubs Mobile Cleaning Lc G 540 254-0478
Roanoke *(G-12179)*
Smith Brothers Car Wash Inc G 757 397-7711
Portsmouth *(G-10483)*
Soap N Suds Laudromats G 757 313-0515
Norfolk *(G-9728)*
Solar Sea Water LLC G 215 452-9992
Arlington *(G-1172)*
Southwest Kettle Korn Company G 352 201-5664
Saltville *(G-12592)*

Suez Treatment Solutions Inc............F......804 550-4971
Ashland *(G-1497)*
◆ Suez Wts Services Usa Inc...........C......757 855-9000
Norfolk *(G-9737)*
Sussex Service Authority.............G......804 834-8930
Waverly *(G-15089)*
Tabb Enterprise LLC.................F......434 238-7196
Lynchburg *(G-7818)*
Tavern On Main LLC..................E......276 328-2208
Wise *(G-15635)*
Tectonics Inc.......................G......276 228-5565
Wytheville *(G-15918)*
The City of Radford.................F......540 731-3662
Radford *(G-10741)*
Tlj Pressure Washing................G......757 235-9096
Virginia Beach *(G-14885)*
Two Oaks...........................G......434 352-8181
Appomattox *(G-825)*
Virginia Carolina Pure Water........G......757 282-6487
Virginia Beach *(G-14918)*
Water Filtration Plant..............F......276 656-5137
Martinsville *(G-8351)*
Water King Conditioners.............G......540 667-5821
Winchester *(G-15505)*
Wolf Equipment Inc..................E......757 596-1660
Newport News *(G-9380)*
▲ Zenpure Corporation...............G......703 335-9910
Manassas *(G-8183)*
Zeta Car Washes LLC.................G......757 469-2141
Virginia Beach *(G-14959)*

3592 Carburetors, Pistons, Rings & Valves

Carburetors Unlimited...............G......703 273-0751
Manassas *(G-8046)*
Romans Enterprises LLC..............F......757 216-6401
Virginia Beach *(G-14779)*
Valve Safe Solutions LLC............G......540 721-7808
Moneta *(G-8984)*
▲ Zenith Fuel Systems LLC...........D......276 669-5555
Bristol *(G-2044)*

3593 Fluid Power Cylinders & Actuators

Garvey Precision Machine Inc........E......757 490-0498
Hampton *(G-6155)*
General Engineering Co VA...........D......276 628-6068
Abingdon *(G-32)*
Kollmorgen Corporation..............B......540 633-3536
Radford *(G-10721)*
▲ Maxim Systems Inc.................G......540 265-9050
Roanoke *(G-12134)*
▲ Sterling Environmental Inc........G......540 898-5079
Spotsylvania *(G-12917)*

3594 Fluid Power Pumps & Motors

Gravittional Systems Engrg Inc......F......312 224-8152
Clifton *(G-3668)*
Mac Bone Industries Ltd.............G......804 264-3603
Richmond *(G-11278)*
Mactaggart Scott Usa LLC............G......757 288-1405
Virginia Beach *(G-14631)*
Maersk Oil Trading Inc..............G......757 857-4800
Norfolk *(G-9630)*
Williams Industrial Repair Inc......G......757 969-5738
Yorktown *(G-16001)*

3596 Scales & Balances, Exc Laboratory

Mettler-Toledo LLC..................G......540 665-9495
Winchester *(G-15554)*
Nexaware LLC........................G......703 880-6697
Rockingham *(G-12265)*

3599 Machinery & Eqpt, Indl & Commercial, NEC

1 Hour A 24 Hr Er A VA Bch Lck......G......757 295-8288
Norfolk *(G-9409)*
3dxtremes...........................G......757 741-8671
Norfolk *(G-9412)*
460 Machine Company.................G......804 861-8787
Prince George *(G-10586)*
A & A Machine.......................G......540 482-0480
Rocky Mount *(G-12309)*
A & A Precision Machining LLC.......G......804 493-8416
Montross *(G-9023)*
A & B Machine Co Inc................F......757 482-0505
Chesapeake *(G-2950)*
A & V Precision Machine Inc.........G......804 222-9466
Richmond *(G-11075)*
▲ Abacus Racing & Machine Svcs......G......757 363-8878
Virginia Beach *(G-14203)*

Ablcomp LLC.........................G......434 942-5325
Lynchburg *(G-7630)*
Absolute Machine Enterprises........F......276 956-1171
Ridgeway *(G-11838)*
Accurate Machine Inc................G......757 853-2136
Norfolk *(G-9418)*
Ace Machining Inc...................G......540 294-2453
Staunton *(G-13239)*
Aci-Strickland LLC..................E......804 643-7483
Richmond *(G-11470)*
Action Machining....................G......703 339-7232
Lorton *(G-7458)*
Adamantine Precision Tools..........G......804 354-9118
Richmond *(G-11085)*
Adams Machine Shop Inc..............G......434 656-2905
Gretna *(G-6001)*
Adesso Precision Machine Co.........G......757 857-5544
Norfolk *(G-9421)*
Advance Design & Manufacturing......D......703 256-9550
Alexandria *(G-404)*
Advanced Carbide Tool Company.......G......540 582-3289
Spotsylvania *(G-12881)*
Advanced Machine & Tooling..........F......757 518-1222
Virginia Beach *(G-14213)*
Advex Corporation...................E......757 865-6660
Hampton *(G-6073)*
Aerospace Components................G......276 686-0123
Rural Retreat *(G-12417)*
Aerospace Techniques Inc............D......860 347-1200
Virginia Beach *(G-14214)*
AGF Defcom Inc......................F......757 842-4252
Chesapeake *(G-2956)*
Air Barge Company...................G......310 378-2928
Mc Lean *(G-8390)*
Alice Farling.......................G......757 802-6936
Salem *(G-12472)*
▲ Alliance Machine and Engrv LLC....F......804 798-1199
Ashland *(G-1366)*
American Gen Fabrication Inc........G......757 329-4384
Hampton *(G-6082)*
American Machine Co Richmond........F......804 231-1157
Richmond *(G-11025)*
Amg Inc.............................D......434 385-7525
Lynchburg *(G-7640)*
Andrew Pawlick......................G......540 949-8805
Waynesboro *(G-15093)*
APM Enterprises Inc.................G......540 921-3399
Pearisburg *(G-10271)*
▲ Appalachian Machine Inc...........F......540 674-1914
Dublin *(G-4148)*
Arcola Industries LLC...............G......703 723-0092
Broadlands *(G-2072)*
Arey Machine Shop...................G......540 943-7782
Waynesboro *(G-15095)*
Arlington Mch Fabrication Inc.......G......804 559-2500
Mechanicsville *(G-8605)*
Armes Prcsion McHning Fbrction......G......434 237-4552
Lynchburg *(G-7643)*
Arrow Machine Inc...................G......804 272-0202
North Chesterfield *(G-9820)*
▲ Artcraft Fabricators Inc..........D......757 399-7777
Portsmouth *(G-10393)*
Austins Cycle Company...............G......757 653-0182
Capron *(G-2237)*
Automated Machine & Tech Inc........E......757 898-7844
Grafton *(G-5931)*
Automated Prod Machining Inc........F......540 832-0835
Gordonsville *(G-5899)*
Avf Screw Machine LLC...............G......571 393-3099
Clifton *(G-3658)*
B & B Machine & Tool Inc............E......540 344-6820
Roanoke *(G-12038)*
B & H Machine Works.................G......540 636-3366
Front Royal *(G-5522)*
Baptist Valley Machine Sp LLC.......G......276 988-8284
North Tazewell *(G-10093)*
Barrett Industries Inc..............E......540 678-1625
Winchester *(G-15384)*
Basic Converting Equipment..........G......804 794-2090
Midlothian *(G-8776)*
Battaile Drive LLC..................G......540 662-4185
Winchester *(G-15385)*
Bdl Prototype & Automation LLC......G......540 868-2577
Middletown *(G-8736)*
Beautiful Grind.....................G......757 685-6192
Virginia Beach *(G-14272)*
BEC Welding & Machine Shop..........G......540 984-3793
Edinburg *(G-4300)*
Bert & Cliffs Machine Shop..........G......804 580-3021
Wicomico Church *(G-15194)*

Blue Ridge Machine Works Inc........G......540 249-4640
Grottoes *(G-6016)*
Blue Ridge Marble Mfrs LLC..........G......434 582-6139
Lynchburg *(G-7655)*
Bmg Metals Inc......................G......804 622-9452
Henrico *(G-6483)*
Bowers Machine & Tool Inc...........G......540 380-2040
Salem *(G-12485)*
Brison Industries Inc...............G......434 665-2231
Lynchburg *(G-7660)*
Brookneal Machine Shop Inc..........G......434 376-2413
Brookneal *(G-2108)*
Brown Machine Works Inc.............G......434 821-5008
Rustburg *(G-12435)*
Bryan Tool & Machining Inc..........F......540 896-6758
Broadway *(G-2087)*
Bryans Tools LLC....................G......540 667-5675
Winchester *(G-15394)*
Burns Machine Inc...................G......815 434-3131
Ninde *(G-9387)*
Byers Inc...........................E......540 949-8092
Waynesboro *(G-15102)*
C & B Technology LLC................G......757 545-3112
Chesapeake *(G-3019)*
C & M Auto Machine Shop Inc.........G......703 780-0566
Alexandria *(G-427)*
CA Jones Inc........................G......757 595-0005
Newport News *(G-9188)*
Calavera Tool Works.................G......434 964-6447
Charlottesville *(G-2754)*
Callaghan Machine Shop..............G......540 962-4779
Covington *(G-3780)*
Caravelle Western Inds Inc..........G......703 777-9412
Leesburg *(G-7239)*
Carrythewhatreplications LLC........G......804 254-2933
Richmond *(G-11522)*
Catapult Solutions Inc..............G......434 401-1077
Lynchburg *(G-7676)*
Catapult Video......................G......540 642-9947
Virginia Beach *(G-14324)*
Catron Machine & Welding Inc........G......276 783-6826
Marion *(G-8223)*
Cavitronix Corporation..............G......540 622-6240
Front Royal *(G-5526)*
Central Machine Shop Inc............F......276 669-2816
Abingdon *(G-21)*
Cg Plus LLC.........................E......540 977-3200
Roanoke *(G-11906)*
▲ CH Krammes & Co Inc...............G......434 589-1663
Palmyra *(G-10246)*
Chesapeake Machine Works Inc........F......757 543-1001
Chesapeake *(G-3032)*
Clarke Precision Machine Inc........F......276 228-5441
Wytheville *(G-15882)*
Classic Machine Inc.................F......804 798-1111
Ashland *(G-1391)*
Clays Machine Shop & Welding........G......434 324-4997
Hurt *(G-6972)*
Clays Welding Co Inc................G......540 788-3992
Catlett *(G-2266)*
Clodfelter Machine Inc..............F......804 744-3848
Midlothian *(G-8797)*
Cnc Models LLC......................G......703 669-0709
Leesburg *(G-7246)*
Cnk Machine Manufacturing Inc.......F......804 320-1082
North Chesterfield *(G-9847)*
Coastal Leak Detection..............G......757 486-0180
Virginia Beach *(G-14346)*
Cold Roll Steel Mch & Mfg LLC.......G......804 275-9229
North Chesterfield *(G-9848)*
Cole Tool Inc.......................F......540 942-5174
Fishersville *(G-5002)*
Colonial Air Filter Clg LLC.........G......757 229-1110
Williamsburg *(G-15220)*
Commercial Machine Inc..............F......804 329-5405
Richmond *(G-11534)*
Commercial Machine & Fabg...........G......276 944-3643
Meadowview *(G-8594)*
Commercial Tool & Die Inc...........G......540 364-3922
Marshall *(G-8251)*
Craft Machine Works Inc.............D......757 310-6011
Hampton *(G-6119)*
Craft Mch Wrks Acquisition LLC......E......757 310-6011
Hampton *(G-6120)*
Craft Repair Incorporated...........F......757 838-0721
Hampton *(G-6121)*
▲ Crane Research & Engrg Co Inc.....E......757 826-1707
Yorktown *(G-15945)*
▲ Crossroads Machine Inc............G......757 482-5414
Chesapeake *(G-3057)*

CSM International Corporation	G	800 767-3805	
Woodbridge (G-15678)			
Culpeper Machine & Supply Co	G	540 825-4644	
Culpeper (G-3885)			
Cupp Manufacturing Co	G	540 249-4011	
Grottoes (G-6018)			
Custom Machine Incorporated	G	434 846-8987	
Lynchburg (G-7691)			
Custom Machining and Tool Inc	G	540 389-9102	
Salem (G-12492)			
Custom Metal Fabricators Inc	F	804 271-6094	
North Chesterfield (G-9855)			
Custom Tool & Machine Inc	G	540 563-3074	
Roanoke (G-11914)			
Cycle Machine LLC	G	804 779-0055	
Manquin (G-8215)			
Cycle Specialist	G	757 599-5236	
Newport News (G-9211)			
D & R Pro Tools LLC	G	804 338-1754	
Crewe (G-3811)			
D & S Tool Inc	G	540 731-1463	
Radford (G-10707)			
Daily Grind	G	540 387-2669	
Salem (G-12493)			
Daily Grind Hospital	G	540 536-2383	
Winchester (G-15536)			
Dale Stidham	G	276 523-1428	
Big Stone Gap (G-1708)			
Daltons Automotive	G	804 798-7909	
Ashland (G-1401)			
Daniels Certified Welding	G	434 848-4911	
Freeman (G-5511)			
Dannys Tools LLC	G	757 282-6229	
Virginia Beach (G-14386)			
Dare Instrument Corporation	G	757 898-5131	
Yorktown (G-15948)			
Daves Machine Shop	G	540 903-0172	
Fredericksburg (G-5419)			
Demco Machine Inc	G	540 248-5135	
Verona (G-13984)			
Dempsey & Corcoran	G	434 294-3942	
Blackstone (G-1815)			
Dickerson Machine and Design	G	540 789-7945	
Christiansburg (G-3583)			
Diorio Manufacturing Co LLC	G	540 438-1870	
Rockingham (G-12249)			
Direct Tools Factory Outlet	G	757 345-6945	
Williamsburg (G-15234)			
Dixie Plastics & Machining	G	434 283-3778	
Gladys (G-5690)			
Dks Machine Shop Inc	G	540 775-9648	
King George (G-7087)			
Dublin Machine Inc	G	540 674-9347	
Dublin (G-4154)			
Dyer LLC	G	757 926-9374	
Chesapeake (G-3080)			
E & E Machine Shop Inc	F	540 949-6792	
Waynesboro (G-15111)			
E E Machine Shop	G	540 649-2127	
Waynesboro (G-15112)			
E W Staley Corporation	G	540 389-1197	
Roanoke (G-12081)			
Eagle Aviation Tech LLC	D	757 224-6269	
Newport News (G-9219)			
East Tools Inc	G	703 754-1931	
Haymarket (G-6421)			
Ecp Inc	G	804 222-2460	
Richmond (G-11196)			
Elswick Inc	G	276 971-3060	
Cedar Bluff (G-2275)			
Engine and Frame LLC	G	757 407-0134	
Richmond (G-11578)			
Entwistle Company	E	434 799-6186	
Danville (G-3992)			
Epic Mfg LLC	G	757 689-4373	
Virginia Beach (G-14449)			
Erodex Inc	G	804 525-6609	
Richmond (G-11205)			
Ervin Coppridge Machine Co	G	804 561-1246	
Amelia Court House (G-656)			
Eugenes Machine & Welding	G	276 694-6275	
Stuart (G-13610)			
EZ Tool Rental	G	703 531-4700	
Falls Church (G-4911)			
F & M Tools LLC	G	757 361-9225	
Chesapeake (G-3096)			
Fabritek Company Inc	E	540 662-9095	
Winchester (G-15541)			
Falling Creek Metal Products	G	804 744-1061	
Midlothian (G-8817)			

Farage Precision LLC	G	901 264-2422	
Fairfax (G-4456)			
Farmer Machine Company Inc	E	804 550-7310	
Ashland (G-1414)			
Fields Inc Oscar S	E	804 798-3900	
Ashland (G-1416)			
Fleeton Machine Works Inc	G	804 453-6130	
Reedville (G-10761)			
Form Fabrications LLC	G	757 309-8717	
Virginia Beach (G-14471)			
Fort Chiswell Machine Tl Pdts	G	276 637-3022	
Max Meadows (G-8368)			
Fredericksburg Mch & Stl LLC	G	540 373-7957	
Fredericksburg (G-5189)			
G & W Manufacturing Inc	F	276 228-8491	
Wytheville (G-15889)			
Gale Welding and Mch Co Inc	F	804 732-4521	
Petersburg (G-10321)			
Garvey Prcision Components LLC	E	757 310-6028	
Hampton (G-6154)			
Garvey Precision Machine Inc	E	757 490-0498	
Hampton (G-6155)			
Gates City Machine and Repair	G	276 386-3456	
Gate City (G-5662)			
General Engineering Co VA	D	276 628-6068	
Abingdon (G-32)			
▲ Geoquip Inc	D	757 485-2500	
Chesapeake (G-3118)			
Geoquip Manufacturing Inc	E	757 485-8525	
Chesapeake (G-3119)			
Glad Precision Machine Inc	G	276 930-9930	
Stuart (G-13613)			
Glade Machine Inc	F	276 429-2114	
Glade Spring (G-5675)			
Grandaddys Stump Grinding	G	757 565-5870	
Williamsburg (G-15250)			
Grays Welding LLC	G	434 401-4559	
Coleman Falls (G-3706)			
Green Trophy	G	619 387-6244	
Fort Lee (G-5131)			
Gregorys Machine Shop Corp	G	757 490-1606	
Virginia Beach (G-14493)			
H & H Enterprises Inc	G	804 684-5901	
Hayes (G-6399)			
Halifax Machine & Welding Inc	G	434 572-3856	
Halifax (G-6049)			
Hall Industries Inc	F	540 337-1210	
Fishersville (G-5004)			
Hampton Machine Shop Inc	E	757 245-9243	
Newport News (G-9240)			
Hanover Machine & Tool Co Inc	F	804 746-4156	
Mechanicsville (G-8635)			
Harrell Precision	G	540 380-2683	
Salem (G-12515)			
Harrell Tool Co	G	540 380-2666	
Salem (G-12516)			
Harris Machine Products Inc	G	804 784-4511	
Oilville (G-10179)			
Haywood Machine Inc	G	540 663-2606	
King George (G-7093)			
Henrico Tool & Die Co Inc	G	804 222-5017	
Richmond (G-11609)			
Hesco of Virginia LLC	G	276 694-2818	
Stuart (G-13615)			
Hi-Tech Machining LLC	E	434 993-3256	
Concord (G-3760)			
Hi-Tech Machining LLC	G	434 993-3256	
Concord (G-3761)			
Highstar Industrial Tech	F	757 398-9300	
Portsmouth (G-10442)			
Hillcraft Machine & Welding	G	804 779-2280	
Mechanicsville (G-8637)			
Howards Precision Mch Sp Inc	G	540 890-2342	
Blue Ridge (G-1850)			
Hub Pattern Corporation	E	540 342-3505	
Roanoke (G-12104)			
Huffman Tool Co	G	540 745-3359	
Floyd (G-5030)			
Hurd Machine Shop Inc	G	540 980-6265	
Pulaski (G-10638)			
Imperial Machine Company Inc	G	804 271-6022	
North Chesterfield (G-9891)			
Induplate Operations LLC	G	757 566-8070	
Toano (G-13866)			
Industrial Fabricators VA Inc	D	540 943-5885	
Fishersville (G-5005)			
Industrial Machine Mfg Inc	G	804 271-6979	
North Chesterfield (G-9892)			
Industrial Machine Works Inc	E	540 949-6115	
Waynesboro (G-15116)			

Innovated Machine & Tl Co Inc	E	757 887-2181	
Newport News (G-9260)			
International Designs LLC	G	804 275-1044	
North Chesterfield (G-9899)			
International Machine Service	G	757 868-8487	
Poquoson (G-10373)			
Intuitive Global LLC	G	571 388-6183	
Manassas (G-8085)			
J and E Machine Shop Inc	G	804 966-7180	
Charles City (G-2577)			
Jackson & Jackson Inc	G	434 851-1798	
Roanoke (G-12109)			
James M Rohrbach Inc	G	757 898-6322	
Yorktown (G-15968)			
James Slater	G	757 566-1543	
Williamsburg (G-15258)			
JD Gordon Tool Company LLC	G	804 832-9907	
Locust Hill (G-7453)			
Jerry Johnston	G	540 674-0932	
Dublin (G-4160)			
Jewett Automation Inc	E	804 344-8101	
Richmond (G-11631)			
Jewett Mch Mfg Co Inc Bryce D	D	804 233-9873	
Richmond (G-11632)			
John & Lloyd Horst	G	540 867-5655	
Dayton (G-4056)			
Johnson Welding Service	G	757 787-4429	
Greenbush (G-5996)			
Jvh Company Inc	G	804 798-0888	
Ashland (G-1446)			
K & K Machining Incorporated	F	540 298-1700	
Elkton (G-4328)			
K T Design & Prototype Inc	G	540 678-0215	
Winchester (G-15431)			
Keens Automotive Machine Shop	G	757 365-4481	
Smithfield (G-12717)			
Kelly Swenson	G	434 634-3926	
Emporia (G-4362)			
▼ Kelmar Inc	F	540 439-8952	
Midland (G-8759)			
Khem Precision Machining LLC	G	804 915-8922	
Richmond (G-11261)			
Kirby of VA	G	434 835-4349	
Danville (G-4010)			
Kirintec Inc	G	571 527-1437	
Alexandria (G-253)			
Kishbaugh Enterprises LLC	G	571 375-2042	
Falls Church (G-4816)			
Kreider Machine Shop Inc	G	540 434-5351	
Rockingham (G-12258)			
KVk Precision Spc Inc	G	540 652-6102	
Shenandoah (G-12693)			
L & L Tool and Machine Inc	G	757 224-3445	
Newport News (G-9277)			
L & R Precision Tooling Inc	E	434 525-4120	
Lynchburg (G-7752)			
L H Corporation	F	540 674-8803	
Dublin (G-4162)			
L H Gaither Co Inc	G	703 335-2300	
Manassas (G-7957)			
L Industries	G	540 948-4806	
Madison (G-7855)			
L K Smith Machine Shop	G	276 694-4109	
Stuart (G-13621)			
L S Industries Inc	F	540 948-4806	
Madison (G-7856)			
Lake Manufacturing Inc	F	540 297-2957	
Moneta (G-8969)			
Liberty Park	G	540 832-7680	
Gordonsville (G-5912)			
Little Enterprises LLC	G	804 869-8612	
Purcellville (G-10667)			
Machine & Fabg Specialists Inc	E	757 244-5693	
Hampton (G-6187)			
Machine Services Inc	G	757 487-5566	
Chesapeake (G-3192)			
Machine Specialties Inc	F	804 798-8920	
Ashland (G-1457)			
Machine Tool Technology LLC	F	804 520-4173	
South Chesterfield (G-12813)			
Machining Technology Inc	G	757 538-1781	
Suffolk (G-13737)			
Macs Machine Shop	G	540 269-2222	
Keezletown (G-7028)			
Marco Machine & Design Inc	F	804 275-5555	
North Chesterfield (G-9921)			
Mars Machine Works Inc	G	804 642-4760	
Gloucester Point (G-5873)			
Martinsville Machine Works	G	276 632-6491	
Martinsville (G-8310)			

SIC

Master Machine & Auto LLC ....G....... 757 244-8401
Newport News (G-9293)

Master Machine & Engrg Co ....G....... 804 231-6648
Richmond (G-11671)

▼ Master Machine & Tool Co Inc ....F....... 757 245-6653
Newport News (G-9294)

Master Mold of Virginia LLC ....G....... 757 868-8283
Newport News (G-9295)

Maxum Machine LLC ....G....... 804 523-1490
Richmond (G-11674)

Mechanical Designs of Virginia ....E....... 276 694-7442
Stuart (G-13625)

Mechanical Machine & Repair ....G....... 804 231-5866
Richmond (G-11676)

Melos Manufacturing ....G....... 434 401-9496
Lynchburg (G-7770)

Melvins Machine & Welding ....G....... 276 988-3822
Tazewell (G-13835)

Melvins Machine and Die Inc ....G....... 276 988-3822
Tazewell (G-13836)

▲ Merwins Affordable Grinding ....G....... 757 461-3405
Norfolk (G-9640)

Met Machine Inc ....G....... 540 864-6007
New Castle (G-9122)

▲ Metal Processing Inc ....F....... 540 731-0008
Radford (G-10724)

Mid Valley Machine & Tool Inc ....G....... 540 885-6379
Staunton (G-13280)

Mill Run Specialties ....G....... 703 759-3480
Great Falls (G-5967)

Millennium Services Inc ....G....... 804 733-8505
Prince George (G-10601)

Miller Machine & Tool Company ....E....... 540 662-6512
Winchester (G-15449)

Miller Roll Grinding & Mfg ....G....... 804 559-5745
Mechanicsville (G-8662)

Morris Machine Shop ....G....... 540 434-8038
Rockingham (G-12263)

▼ Mountain Precision Tool Co Inc........F....... 540 552-0178
Blacksburg (G-1769)

Mountain Tech Inc................................G....... 434 710-4896
Blairs (G-1832)

Mundys Precision Automotive ....G....... 804 231-0435
Richmond (G-11685)

N C Tool Company Inc ....F....... 540 943-4011
Waynesboro (G-15128)

N D M Machine Inc ....G....... 276 621-4424
Wytheville (G-15902)

N Rolls-Ryce Amer Holdings Inc ....F....... 703 834-1700
Chantilly (G-2466)

Naff Welding Inc..................................F....... 276 629-1129
Bassett (G-1587)

Neault LLC ....G....... 804 283-5948
Manquin (G-8217)

Newport Cutter Grinding Co Inc ....F....... 757 838-3224
Hampton (G-6207)

Non Stop Enterprise Ltd.......................G....... 276 945-2028
Bluefield (G-1871)

Norfolk Machine and Wldg Inc.............E....... 757 489-0330
Norfolk (G-9666)

Norman Precision Machining LLC ....G....... 540 674-0932
Dublin (G-4167)

North Machine Shop ....G....... 804 725-5443
Dutton (G-4274)

▲ O D B Machine Co ....F....... 434 929-4002
Madison Heights (G-7879)

Omni Repair Company ....G....... 757 853-1220
Norfolk (G-9676)

Oval Engineering ....G....... 434 572-8867
South Boston (G-12786)

Painter Machine Shop Inc ....G....... 540 463-5854
Lexington (G-7411)

Parts Manufacturing Virginia ....G....... 540 845-3289
Fredericksburg (G-5212)

Patriot Tools LLC ....G....... 757 718-4591
Chesapeake (G-3235)

Pete Burr Machine Works Inc ....G....... 540 249-5693
Grottoes (G-6022)

Phil Gunn Machine Co Inc....................G....... 804 271-7059
North Chesterfield (G-9948)

Phillips Enterprises VA Inc...................G....... 540 563-9915
Roanoke (G-12147)

Piedmont Precision Mch Co Inc ....D....... 434 793-0677
Danville (G-4028)

Piedmont Wldg & Maint Svc LLC ....G....... 434 447-6600
La Crosse (G-7149)

Pioneer Machine Co Inc ....F....... 276 699-1500
Austinville (G-1530)

Pitts Auto Parts Inc ....F....... 540 373-3720
Fredericksburg (G-5213)

Precision Grinding Co ....F....... 540 955-3200
Berryville (G-1686)

Precision Machine & Design ....G....... 540 726-8229
Narrows (G-9098)

Precision Machine Co Inc ....G....... 804 359-5758
North Chesterfield (G-9953)

Precision Machine Works Inc ....F....... 540 825-1882
Culpeper (G-3914)

Precision Mch & Firearm Svc ....G....... 540 659-3037
Fredericksburg (G-5471)

Precision Solutions Inc ....G....... 804 452-2217
Prince George (G-10605)

Precision Steel Mfg Corp ....D....... 540 985-8963
Roanoke (G-12152)

Precision Tool & Die Inc ....G....... 804 233-8810
Richmond (G-11723)

Pricewalker Inc....................................G....... 804 359-5758
North Chesterfield (G-9954)

Product Engineered Systems ....G....... 804 794-3586
Midlothian (G-8883)

Profile Machineworks LLC ....G....... 703 361-2959
Manassas Park (G-8207)

Profile Machineworks LLC ....G....... 571 991-6331
Manassas (G-7990)

Progressive Machine Works ....G....... 434 237-5517
Lynchburg (G-7791)

Progressive Manufacturing Corp ....E....... 804 717-5353
Chester (G-3448)

Proton Systems LLC ....G....... 757 224-5685
Hampton (G-6223)

▲ Prototype Productions Inc ....D....... 703 858-0011
Chantilly (G-2483)

Quality Machine Shop ....G....... 757 722-6077
Hampton (G-6224)

R and L Machine Shop Inc ....E....... 757 487-8879
Chesapeake (G-3254)

R W A Machining & Welding Co ....G....... 434 985-7362
Ruckersville (G-12412)

Rapid Manufacturing Inc ....E....... 804 598-7467
Powhatan (G-10570)

Raven Machine ....G....... 804 271-6001
North Chesterfield (G-9957)

Recap LLC ....G....... 703 521-3406
Arlington (G-1144)

Redco Machine Inc ....E....... 540 586-3545
Bedford (G-1655)

Refco Mfg ....G....... 757 487-2222
Chesapeake (G-3265)

Ricks Machine Shop ....G....... 804 518-5266
Petersburg (G-10338)

Rmj Machine Technologies Inc ....F....... 434 582-4719
Lynchburg (G-7803)

Rod & Staff Welding ....G....... 434 392-3090
Farmville (G-4956)

Rst Machine Service Ltd ....G....... 276 236-8623
Galax (G-5647)

S Harman Machine Shop Inc ....G....... 540 343-9304
Roanoke (G-12173)

Salem Prcision Mch Fabrication ....F....... 434 793-0677
Salem (G-12565)

Saltville Machine & Welding ....G....... 276 496-3555
Saltville (G-12590)

Sanjo Virginia Beach Inc ....G....... 757 498-0400
Virginia Beach (G-14793)

Sav-Mor Machine Works Inc ....G....... 804 356-7582
Rockville (G-12298)

Seascape Automation LLC ....G....... 717 512-5981
Virginia Beach (G-14799)

Semtek ....G....... 434 942-4728
Rustburg (G-12445)

Serenity Ridge Machining ....G....... 571 261-2042
Gainesville (G-5612)

Service Machine & Wldg Co Inc ....D....... 804 798-1381
Ashland (G-1490)

Shenandoah Machine Shop Inc..............F....... 540 652-8593
Shenandoah (G-12694)

Shickel Corporation ....D....... 540 828-2536
Bridgewater (G-1959)

Shifflett Machine Shop ....G....... 540 433-1731
Rockingham (G-12277)

Smyth Cnty Mch Fabrication LLC ....E....... 276 783-4582
Atkins (G-1521)

Snider & Sons Inc ....G....... 540 626-5849
Pembroke (G-10284)

Sopko Manufacturing Inc ....F....... 434 848-3460
Lawrenceville (G-7185)

Southern Machining Inc ....G....... 276 628-1072
Abingdon (G-61)

Southern Region Machine Svc ....G....... 276 393-3472
Castlewood (G-2257)

Specialty Machining & Fabg ....G....... 540 984-4265
Edinburg (G-4315)

SRI Seven Fair Lakes LLC ....G....... 703 631-2350
Fairfax (G-4560)

Ssa Fabrication LLC ....G....... 703 479-7377
Manassas Park (G-8212)

◆ Standex Engraving LLC ....D....... 804 236-3092
Sandston (G-12636)

Staunton Machine Works Inc ....F....... 540 886-0733
Staunton (G-13298)

Steelwright Products ....G....... 951 870-6670
Beaverdam (G-1612)

◆ Strickland Machine Company LLC .....E....... 804 643-7483
Richmond (G-11774)

Sudden Service Inc ....G....... 804 266-6200
Richmond (G-11401)

Sullivan Company Inc N J ....E....... 703 464-5944
Sterling (G-13523)

Sullivan Machine Shop ....G....... 540 350-2549
Mount Solon (G-9090)

Super Splasher Acquatics ....G....... 540 630-1565
Winchester (G-15484)

Superior Float Tanks LLC ....G....... 757 966-6350
Norfolk (G-9738)

Superior Metal Fabricators ....F....... 804 236-3266
Richmond (G-11403)

Swissomation Virginia LLC ....G....... 434 944-3322
Amherst (G-671)

▼ Systems Technology VA LLC ....G....... 540 884-1784
Eagle Rock (G-4283)

Tanner Tool & Machine Inc ....G....... 804 561-5141
Amelia Court House (G-674)

Tasco USA Co Inc ....G....... 703 209-0193
Fairfax (G-4685)

Taylor Mfg & Design LLC ....G....... 757 902-1820
Hampton (G-6249)

Technical Machine Service Inc ....G....... 276 638-2105
Martinsville (G-8340)

Tectonics Inc ....G....... 276 228-5565
Wytheville (G-15918)

Tek-AM Corp ....F....... 703 321-9144
Lorton (G-7536)

Thistle Foundry & Mch Co Inc ....F....... 276 326-1196
Bluefield (G-1881)

Thomson Industries Inc ....G....... 540 633-3549
Radford (G-10745)

Total Machine LLC ....G....... 540 775-2375
King George (G-7115)

Triology Machine Company Inc ....G....... 540 343-9508
Roanoke (G-12211)

Triple R Welding & Repair Svc ....G....... 540 347-9026
Warrenton (G-15056)

True Precision Machining Inc ....G....... 703 314-7071
Nokesville (G-9401)

Turning 65 Inc ....G....... 540 289-5768
McGaheysville (G-8585)

Tysons Automotive Machine ....G....... 703 471-1802
Sterling (G-13541)

Valley Outsourcing ....F....... 540 320-0892
Blacksburg (G-1803)

Valley Precision Incorporated ....E....... 540 941-8178
Waynesboro (G-15142)

Valley Restaurant Repair Inc.................G....... 540 294-1118
Fishersville (G-5011)

Vintage Vault ....G....... 703 862-7159
Sterling (G-13552)

Virginia Highlands Machining...............F....... 276 628-8555
Abingdon (G-65)

Virginia Laser Corporation ....G....... 276 628-9284
Abingdon (G-66)

Virginia Machine & Sup Co Inc ....E....... 757 380-8500
Newport News (G-9374)

Virginia Mobile AC Systems Inc ....G....... 757 650-0957
Chesapeake (G-3362)

Vision Machine and Fabrication ....G....... 757 865-1234
Hampton (G-6264)

W & B Fabricators Inc ....F....... 276 928-1060
Rocky Gap (G-12308)

W D Barnette Enterprise Inc ....G....... 757 494-0530
Chesapeake (G-3368)

Walker Machine and Fndry Corp ....D....... 540 344-6265
Roanoke (G-12226)

Walter Hedge ....G....... 757 548-4750
Chesapeake (G-3370)

Waynesboro Alloy Works Inc ....G....... 540 965-4038
Covington (G-3802)

Waynesboro Tool & Grinding Svc ....G....... 540 949-7912
Waynesboro (G-15146)

Wells Machining LLC ....G....... 540 380-2603
Salem (G-12580)

West End Machine & Welding............E 804 266-9631
   Richmond *(G-11446)*

Whats Your Grind LLC ....G 757 447-8506
   Portsmouth *(G-10501)*

Williams Company Incorporated ....F 276 466-3342
   Bristol *(G-2000)*

Williams Fabrication Inc ....E 540 862-4200
   Covington *(G-3804)*

Williams Machine Co Inc ....G 804 231-3892
   Richmond *(G-11831)*

Willis Welding & Machine Co ....G 540 427-3038
   Roanoke *(G-12228)*

▲ Winchester Tool LLC ....G 540 869-1150
   Winchester *(G-15513)*

Winpro LLC ....G 703 450-7904
   Herndon *(G-6844)*

Wise Custom Machining ....G 276 328-8681
   Wise *(G-15637)*

Woodlawn Precision Machine ....G 276 236-7294
   Woodlawn *(G-15846)*

Worley Machine Enterprises Inc.........G 276 930-2695
   Woolwine *(G-15868)*

▲ Wortham Machine and Welding.......F 434 676-8080
   Kenbridge *(G-7037)*

Z & Z Machine Inc ....G 540 248-2760
   Verona *(G-13997)*

36 ELECTRONIC AND OTHER ELECTRICAL EQUIPMENT AND COMPONENTS, EXCEPT COMPUTER

3612 Power, Distribution & Specialty Transformers

AA Renwble Enrgy Hydro Sys Inc........G 804 739-0045
   Moseley *(G-9032)*

ABB Enterprise Software Inc ....B 276 688-3325
   Bland *(G-1835)*

Atlantic Wind Energy LLC ....G 757 401-9604
   Chesapeake *(G-2986)*

Caravels LLC ....C 540 345-9892
   Centreville *(G-2297)*

Clean Power & Service LLC ....G 703 443-1717
   Leesburg *(G-7244)*

Critical Power Group Inc ....G 703 443-1717
   Ashburn *(G-1261)*

Earl Energy LLC ....E 757 606-2034
   Portsmouth *(G-10418)*

◆ Electro-Mechanical Corporation ....B 276 669-4084
   Bristol *(G-1975)*

Electro-Mechanical Corporation.........G 276 645-8232
   Bristol *(G-1976)*

Electro-Mechanical Corporation.........B 276 669-4084
   Bristol *(G-1977)*

Face X LLC ....G 757 624-2121
   Norfolk *(G-9547)*

◆ GE Drives & Controls Inc ....A 540 387-7000
   Salem *(G-12510)*

Machine Tool Technology LLC ....F 804 520-4173
   South Chesterfield *(G-12813)*

Macks Transformer Service ....G 276 935-4366
   Grundy *(G-6036)*

Magnetic Technologies Corp ....G 276 228-7943
   Wytheville *(G-15899)*

Marelco Power Systems Inc ....F 800 225-4838
   Richmond *(G-11667)*

Marelco Power Systems Inc ....D 517 546-6330
   Richmond *(G-11666)*

Mgke Construction LLC ....G 571 282-8415
   Manassas *(G-8108)*

Mth Holdings Corp ....D 276 228-7943
   Roanoke *(G-11972)*

National Technical Svcs Inc ....G 434 713-1528
   Chatham *(G-2931)*

Pd Power Systems LLC ....F 703 778-3515
   Springfield *(G-13066)*

▲ Pemco Corporation ....D 276 326-2611
   Bluefield *(G-1872)*

Phaze II Products Inc ....E 757 353-3901
   Virginia Beach *(G-14719)*

Power Catch Inc ....G 757 962-0999
   Norfolk *(G-9693)*

Power Distribution Inc ....C 804 737-9880
   Richmond *(G-11721)*

◆ Power Distribution Pdts Inc ....E 276 646-3296
   Bristol *(G-2030)*

Power Hub Ventures LLC ....G 540 443-9214
   Blacksburg *(G-1780)*

Pugal Inc ....G 540 765-4955
   Roanoke *(G-11990)*

Schaffner Mtc LLC ....D 276 228-7943
   Wytheville *(G-15912)*

▲ SMC Electrical Products Inc ....E 276 285-3841
   Bristol *(G-2033)*

Solgreen Solutions LLC ....G 833 765-4733
   Alexandria *(G-588)*

▲ Transformer Engineering LLC ....D 216 741-5282
   Wytheville *(G-15920)*

Venus Tech LLC ....G 703 389-5557
   Herndon *(G-6836)*

◆ Virginia Transformer Corp ....B 540 345-9892
   Roanoke *(G-12222)*

Virginia Transformer Corp ....G 540 345-9892
   Troutville *(G-13919)*

3613 Switchgear & Switchboard Apparatus

American Manufacturing Co Inc..........E 540 825-7234
   Elkwood *(G-4341)*

◆ Anord Mardix (usa) Inc ....G 800 228-4689
   Henrico *(G-6473)*

Automation Control Dist Co LLC.........G 540 797-9892
   Salem *(G-12477)*

Azz Inc ....G 276 466-5558
   Bristol *(G-2007)*

Critical Power Group Inc ....G 703 443-1717
   Ashburn *(G-1261)*

▲ Dallas Electrical Company Inc ....G 804 798-0002
   Ashland *(G-1400)*

Edge McS LLC ....G 804 379-6772
   Midlothian *(G-8813)*

◆ Electro-Mechanical Corporation.......B 276 669-4084
   Bristol *(G-1975)*

Instrumentation and Control...............D 804 550-5770
   Ashland *(G-1440)*

Kordusa Inc ....G 540 242-5210
   Stafford *(G-13165)*

▲ Lightronics Inc ....E 757 486-3588
   Virginia Beach *(G-14612)*

▼ Mg Corp ....A 757 468-6000
   Virginia Beach *(G-14648)*

Nova Power Solutions Inc ....G 703 657-0122
   Sterling *(G-13462)*

Pascor Atlantic Corporation ....E 276 688-2220
   Bland *(G-1836)*

Power Distribution Inc ....C 804 737-9880
   Richmond *(G-11721)*

◆ Power Distribution Pdts Inc ....E 276 646-3296
   Bristol *(G-2030)*

Schneider Electric Usa Inc.................G 703 968-0300
   Fairfax *(G-4550)*

Shenandoah Control Systems.............G 540 837-1627
   Boyce *(G-1912)*

▲ SMC Electrical Products Inc ....E 276 285-3841
   Bristol *(G-2033)*

Vertiv Corporation ....F 804 747-6030
   Glen Allen *(G-5825)*

Villalva Inc ....G 703 527-0091
   Arlington *(G-1211)*

Virginia Controls Inc ....G 804 225-5530
   Richmond *(G-11811)*

3621 Motors & Generators

Alberts Associates Inc ....G 757 638-3352
   Portsmouth *(G-10389)*

American Nexus LLC ....G 804 405-5443
   Richmond *(G-11484)*

Andy Meade ....G 276 940-3000
   Duffield *(G-4175)*

▲ Aspen Motion Technologies Inc ....B 540 639-4440
   Radford *(G-10704)*

Avcom of Virginia Inc ....G 804 794-2500
   North Chesterfield *(G-9822)*

▲ BGB Technology Inc ....E 804 451-5211
   South Chesterfield *(G-12797)*

Bwx Technologies Inc ....G 434 385-2535
   Lynchburg *(G-7664)*

Bwx Technologies Inc ....F 434 316-7638
   Lynchburg *(G-7665)*

Bwx Technologies Inc ....C 980 365-4300
   Lynchburg *(G-7666)*

CF Adams Brokerage Co Inc ....G 757 287-9717
   Chesapeake *(G-3028)*

Critical Power Group Inc ....G 703 443-1717
   Ashburn *(G-1261)*

Danaher Corporation ....G 540 639-9046
   Radford *(G-10709)*

Danaher Motion ....G 540 639-9046
   Radford *(G-10710)*

Edge McS LLC ....G 804 379-6772
   Midlothian *(G-8813)*

Electric Motor and Contg Co ....C 757 487-2121
   Chesapeake *(G-3084)*

Electrical Mech Resources Inc ....E 804 226-1600
   Richmond *(G-11197)*

Emotion US LLC ....F 540 639-9045
   Radford *(G-10713)*

Falco Emotors Inc.............................E 571 313-1154
   Dulles *(G-4202)*

Fisher A C Jr Marine Rlwy Svc ....G 804 580-4342
   Wicomico Church *(G-15195)*

GE Energy Manufacturing Inc............G 540 775-6308
   King George *(G-7090)*

▲ Georator Corporation ....F 703 368-2101
   Manassas *(G-7945)*

▲ Hansen Turbine Assemblies Corp .....E 276 236-7184
   Galax *(G-5639)*

Holcomb Rock Company ....G 434 386-6050
   Lynchburg *(G-7735)*

Hydrogen Motors Inc ....G 703 407-9802
   Oakton *(G-10151)*

Industrial Drives ....G 540 639-2495
   Radford *(G-10717)*

Kollmorgen Corporation ....B 540 639-9045
   Radford *(G-10722)*

Kollmorgen Corporation ....E 540 633-3400
   Radford *(G-10723)*

Kollmorgen Corporation ....B 540 633-3536
   Radford *(G-10721)*

▲ Kollmorgen Corporation ....A 540 639-9045
   Radford *(G-10720)*

Man Diesel & Turbo N Amer Inc...........C 703 373-0690
   Herndon *(G-6741)*

Moog Components Group.....................G 540 443-4699
   Blacksburg *(G-1763)*

▲ Nippon Pulse America Inc ....G 540 633-1677
   Radford *(G-10728)*

Nova Synchro of VA Inc ....G 703 241-4136
   Arlington *(G-1084)*

Power Distribution Inc ....C 804 737-9880
   Richmond *(G-11721)*

▲ Safran Usa Inc ....F 703 351-9898
   Alexandria *(G-334)*

Steves Generator Service LLC ....G 540 661-8675
   Barboursville *(G-1567)*

Technical Motor Service LLC...............G 276 638-1135
   Martinsville *(G-8341)*

Tmeic Corporation ....G 540 725-2031
   Salem *(G-12574)*

Tri State Generators LLC ....F 434 660-3851
   Monroe *(G-8996)*

Uriel Wind Inc ....G 804 672-4471
   North Chesterfield *(G-10042)*

Worldgen LLC ....G 434 244-2849
   Charlottesville *(G-2717)*

3624 Carbon & Graphite Prdts

◆ BGF Industries Inc ....D 843 537-3172
   Danville *(G-3957)*

Carbone America ....G 540 389-7535
   Salem *(G-12488)*

Dixon Mediation Group LLC ....F 703 517-3556
   Fairfax Station *(G-4709)*

Wingman Industries LLC.....................G 540 489-3119
   Callaway *(G-2223)*

3625 Relays & Indl Controls

A-Systems Incorporated ....F 434 295-7200
   Charlottesville *(G-2720)*

Action Digital Inc ....G 804 358-7289
   Richmond *(G-11083)*

Altomas Technologies LLC ....G 540 560-2320
   Rockingham *(G-12239)*

Augusta Actuation LLC ....G 540 480-7619
   Steeles Tavern *(G-13310)*

Bwx Technologies Inc ....E 757 595-7982
   Newport News *(G-9187)*

▲ Cardinal Control Systems Inc ....G 703 437-0437
   Reston *(G-10818)*

Chalmers & Kubeck Inc ....G 434 851-3613
   Rustburg *(G-12437)*

Constrained Optimization Inc ....G 434 944-8564
   Forest *(G-5063)*

▲ Controls Corporation America ....G 757 422-8330
   Virginia Beach *(G-14363)*

Eagle Eye Electric ....G 540 672-1673
   Orange *(G-10212)*

Elbit Systems Amer - Nght Vsio ....G 540 561-0254
   Roanoke *(G-11919)*

SIC

Electric Motor and Contg Co ....C 757 487-2121
Chesapeake *(G-3084)*

Electro-Kinetics Inc ....F 845 887-4930
Charlottesville *(G-2623)*

Electromatics Incorporated ....G 804 798-8318
Ashland *(G-1408)*

Electromotive Inc ....E 703 331-0100
Manassas *(G-8063)*

Etheridge Electric Inc ....G 804 372-6428
Powhatan *(G-10544)*

General Electric Company ....F 540 387-7000
Salem *(G-12511)*

Heritage Electrical Corp ....F 804 743-4614
North Chesterfield *(G-9884)*

Hubbell Industrial Contrls Inc ....C 434 589-8224
Troy *(G-13929)*

▲ In Motion Us LLC ....C 540 605-9622
Blacksburg *(G-1745)*

◆ Intelligent Platforms LLC ....A 434 978-5000
Charlottesville *(G-2647)*

ITT Corporation ....D 540 362-8000
Roanoke *(G-11944)*

ITT LLC ....G 703 550-2594
Lorton *(G-7498)*

Javatec Inc ....G 276 621-4572
Crockett *(G-3825)*

Kollmorgen Corporation ....B 540 633-3536
Radford *(G-10721)*

Kordusa Inc ....G 540 242-5210
Stafford *(G-13165)*

◆ Ksb America Corporation ....G 804 222-1818
Richmond *(G-11265)*

L3harris Technologies Inc ....D 540 563-0371
Roanoke *(G-11950)*

▲ Lightronics Inc ....E 757 486-3588
Virginia Beach *(G-14612)*

Longbow Holdings LLC ....G 540 404-1185
Roanoke *(G-11957)*

◆ Lutron Shading Solutions ....G 804 752-3300
Ashland *(G-1456)*

Mefcor Incorporated ....G 276 322-5021
North Tazewell *(G-10103)*

Moog Inc ....G 716 652-2000
Blacksburg *(G-1764)*

Motion Control Systems Inc ....D 540 731-0540
New River *(G-9151)*

Navy ....G 757 417-4236
Virginia Beach *(G-14671)*

Navy ....G 202 781-0981
Woodbridge *(G-15756)*

Nugen Mobility Inc ....G 703 858-0036
Ashburn *(G-1323)*

Pacific Scientific Company ....F 815 226-3100
Radford *(G-10733)*

Pan American Systems Corp ....G 757 468-1926
Virginia Beach *(G-14709)*

Peraton Inc ....D 719 599-1500
Herndon *(G-6770)*

Peraton Inc ....C 703 668-6000
Herndon *(G-6771)*

Pinnacle Control Systems Inc ....G 540 888-4200
Winchester *(G-15460)*

◆ Power Distribution Pdts Inc ....E 276 646-3296
Bristol *(G-2030)*

◆ Power Systems & Controls Inc ......D 804 355-2803
Richmond *(G-11328)*

▲ Precision Fabrication LLC ....G 804 210-1613
Gloucester *(G-5858)*

Pretech Solutions Incorporated ....G 757 879-3483
Williamsburg *(G-15299)*

Production Systems Solutions ....G 434 324-7843
Hurt *(G-6976)*

Rockwell Automation Inc ....D 804 560-6444
Richmond *(G-11062)*

Smartdoor Systems Inc ....G 703 560-8093
Falls Church *(G-4876)*

▲ SMC Electrical Products Inc ....E 276 285-3841
Bristol *(G-2033)*

Sprecher & Schuh Inc ....F 804 379-6065
North Chesterfield *(G-9989)*

Sunapsys Inc ....F 540 904-6856
Vinton *(G-14185)*

▲ Transformer Engineering LLC ....D 216 741-5282
Wytheville *(G-15920)*

White Collar 4 Hire ....G 804 212-4604
Chesterfield *(G-3541)*

Wythe Power Equipment Co Inc ....E 276 228-7371
Wytheville *(G-15927)*

3629 Electrical Indl Apparatus, NEC

A-Systems Incorporated ....F 434 295-7200
Charlottesville *(G-2720)*

▲ ABB Power Protection LLC ....C 804 236-3300
Richmond *(G-11079)*

Alstom Renewable US LLC ....E 804 763-2196
Midlothian *(G-8771)*

Ampurage ....G 757 632-8232
Virginia Beach *(G-14225)*

Apg Electronics ....G 540 672-7252
Orange *(G-10203)*

▲ Ashlawn Energy LLC ....E 703 461-3600
Springfield *(G-12952)*

Comprhnsive Enrgy Slutions Inc ....G 434 989-2547
Barboursville *(G-1560)*

Cozino Enterprise Inc ....G 804 921-1896
Richmond *(G-11545)*

Dometic Corporation ....C 804 746-1313
Mechanicsville *(G-8618)*

Edge McS LLC ....G 804 379-6772
Midlothian *(G-8813)*

Epiphany Ideation ....G 248 396-5828
Sterling *(G-13394)*

Exide Technologies LLC ....E 434 975-6001
Charlottesville *(G-2629)*

L 3 Maritime Systems ....D 703 443-1700
Herndon *(G-6727)*

Management Solutions LC ....G 540 967-9600
Louisa *(G-7559)*

Nrd LLC ....G 540 362-1097
Roanoke *(G-11976)*

Power Distribution Inc ....C 804 737-9880
Richmond *(G-11721)*

U S General Fuel Cell Corp ....G 703 451-8064
Springfield *(G-13103)*

3631 Household Cooking Eqpt

Savage Transparency LLC ....G 760 218-6457
Chesapeake *(G-3284)*

Unitedslickmart LLC ....G 800 714-0532
Reston *(G-10979)*

3632 Household Refrigerators & Freezers

Hill Phoenix Inc ....G 800 283-1109
North Chesterfield *(G-9886)*

3633 Household Laundry Eqpt

Elite Laundry and Car Wash LLC ....G 540 373-6150
Fredericksburg *(G-5427)*

3634 Electric Household Appliances

Absolute Furn Solutions LLC ....G 757 550-5630
Chesapeake *(G-2951)*

Alterntive Energywave Tech LLC ....G 757 897-1312
Newport News *(G-9166)*

Axiom Armor LLC ....G 540 583-6184
Bedford *(G-1621)*

Cleanvent Dryer Exhaust Spclsts ....G 804 730-1754
Mechanicsville *(G-8612)*

◆ Hamilton Beach Brands Inc ....B 804 273-9777
Glen Allen *(G-5739)*

▲ Hamilton Beach Brands Holdg Co ....F 804 273-9777
Glen Allen *(G-5740)*

Intuit Your Life Network LLC ....G 757 588-0533
Norfolk *(G-9596)*

Matthews Home Decor ....G 804 379-2640
Midlothian *(G-8854)*

Track Patch 1 Corporation ....G 757 289-5870
Norfolk *(G-9763)*

TRC Design Inc ....G 804 779-3383
Mechanicsville *(G-8687)*

Vollara LLC ....D 800 704-2378
Bristol *(G-1998)*

▲ Wwt Group Inc ....G 804 648-1900
Richmond *(G-11834)*

3635 Household Vacuum Cleaners

2 Busy Brooms Cleaning Service ....G 540 476-1190
Grottoes *(G-6011)*

Dawn Group Inc ....G 703 750-6767
Annandale *(G-740)*

Dyson Direct Inc ....G 571 210-4317
Tysons Corner *(G-13954)*

Shupes Cleaning Solutions ....G 804 737-6799
Sandston *(G-12632)*

3639 Household Appliances, NEC

Alterations Done Affordably ....G 540 423-2412
Culpeper *(G-3864)*

BFI Waste Services LLC ....E 804 222-1152
Richmond *(G-11124)*

Dixons Trash Disposal LLC ....G 434 978-2111
Troy *(G-13924)*

Jane Hfl Gresham ....G 757 397-2208
Portsmouth *(G-10446)*

Luis A Matos ....G 703 486-0015
Arlington *(G-1049)*

Nationwide Consumer Products ....G 804 226-0876
Richmond *(G-11687)*

Orlando Garzon Cuellar ....G 571 274-6913
Manassas *(G-8123)*

Value America ....G 434 951-4100
Charlottesville *(G-2710)*

3641 Electric Lamps

Callison Electric ....G 540 294-3189
Staunton *(G-13246)*

Extremeht2com ....G 804 665-6304
Richmond *(G-11584)*

General Electric Company ....G 804 965-1020
Glen Allen *(G-5736)*

General Electric Company ....B 540 667-5990
Winchester *(G-15420)*

Green Edge Lighting LLC ....G 804 462-0221
Mechanicsville *(G-8631)*

Natural Lighting LLC ....G 703 347-7004
Alexandria *(G-541)*

▲ Priority Wire & Cable Inc ....G 757 361-0207
Chesapeake *(G-3249)*

Service Lamp Supply ....G 757 426-0636
Virginia Beach *(G-14804)*

3643 Current-Carrying Wiring Devices

Akg Inc ....G 540 574-0760
Harrisonburg *(G-6290)*

Brantner and Associates Inc ....G 540 825-2111
Culpeper *(G-3875)*

▲ Datalux Corporation ....G 540 662-1500
Winchester *(G-15409)*

Ddg Supply Inc ....G 804 730-0118
Mechanicsville *(G-8617)*

Delta Electronics Inc ....F 703 354-3350
Alexandria *(G-445)*

Hubbell Incorporated ....E 540 394-2107
Christiansburg *(G-3595)*

J and R Manufacturing Inc ....E 276 210-1647
Bluefield *(G-1865)*

▲ Lightronics Inc ....E 757 486-3588
Virginia Beach *(G-14612)*

Loehr Lightning Protection Co ....F 804 231-4236
Richmond *(G-11659)*

Mefcor Incorporated ....G 276 322-5021
North Tazewell *(G-10103)*

▼ Mg Corp ....A 757 468-6000
Virginia Beach *(G-14648)*

Pascor Atlantic Corporation ....E 276 688-2220
Bland *(G-1836)*

▲ Pemco Corporation ....D 276 326-2611
Bluefield *(G-1872)*

Plug Electrical ....G 804 873-8688
Henrico *(G-6549)*

Power Distribution Inc ....C 804 737-9880
Richmond *(G-11721)*

▲ Safran Usa Inc ....F 703 351-9898
Alexandria *(G-334)*

Schneider Electric Usa Inc ....G 703 968-0300
Fairfax *(G-4550)*

Shore Holders ....F 434 542-4105
Phenix *(G-10355)*

▲ SMC Electrical Products Inc ....E 276 285-3841
Bristol *(G-2033)*

Thor Systems Inc ....G 804 353-7477
Richmond *(G-11410)*

3644 Noncurrent-Carrying Wiring Devices

Allspark Industrial LLC ....G 804 977-2732
Richmond *(G-11483)*

Chester Raceway ....G 804 717-2330
Chester *(G-3394)*

Fork Mountain Raceway LLC ....G 540 229-1828
Madison *(G-7852)*

L J S Stores Inc ....F 804 561-6999
Amelia Court House *(G-662)*

Mica Co of Canada Inc ....G 757 244-7311
Newport News *(G-9299)*

Race Trac Petroleum ....G.... 804 694-9079
Gloucester Point *(G-5875)*
Race Trac Petroleum ....G.... 757 557-0076
Virginia Beach *(G-14756)*
Rolling Thunder Raceway LLC ....G.... 336 401-2360
Ararat *(G-832)*
Route 58 Raceway Inc ....G.... 434 441-3903
Danville *(G-4037)*
▲ **SMC Electrical Products Inc** ....E.... 276 285-3841
Bristol *(G-2033)*
Sullivan Company Inc N J ....E.... 703 464-5944
Sterling *(G-13523)*
Summerduck Raceway ....G.... 540 845-1656
Sumerduck *(G-13793)*
Vina Express Inc ....G.... 703 237-9398
Falls Church *(G-4890)*

3645 Residential Lighting Fixtures

American Hands LLC ....G.... 804 349-8974
Powhatan *(G-10530)*
▲ **Demorais & Associates Pllc** ....G.... 703 754-7991
Gainesville *(G-5580)*
Dennis H Fredrick ....G.... 804 358-6000
Richmond *(G-11182)*
▲ **Mario Industries Virginia Inc** ....E.... 540 342-1111
Roanoke *(G-12132)*
Modern Living LLC ....G.... 877 663-2224
Richmond *(G-11679)*
▲ **Mya Saray LLC** ....G.... 703 996-8800
Sterling *(G-13458)*
▲ **Renaissnce Cntract Ltg Furn In** ....E.... 540 342-1548
Roanoke *(G-12162)*
Rex Multiservices LLC ....G.... 703 400-1739
Sterling *(G-13493)*
▲ **Spring Moses Inc** ....G.... 804 321-0156
Richmond *(G-11395)*
Zenta Corporation ....G.... 276 930-1500
Woolwine *(G-15870)*

3646 Commercial, Indl & Institutional Lighting Fixtures

1earthmatters LLC ....G.... 202 412-8882
Fairfax *(G-4393)*
Acuity Brands Lighting Inc ....G.... 804 320-3444
Richmond *(G-11472)*
American Orthotic ....G.... 757 548-5296
Chesapeake *(G-2972)*
Century Lighting Solutions LLC ....G.... 202 281-8393
Alexandria *(G-163)*
Crenshaw Lighting Corporation ....G.... 540 745-3900
Floyd *(G-5021)*
Deporter Dominick & Assoc LLC ....G.... 703 530-9255
Manassas *(G-8057)*
▲ **Electro-Luminx Lighting Corp** ....G.... 804 355-1692
Richmond *(G-11198)*
Energy Sherlock LLC ....G.... 703 346-7584
Leesburg *(G-7268)*
Frank Hagerty ....G.... 540 809-0589
Fredericksburg *(G-5432)*
Green Solutions Lighting LLC ....G.... 804 334-2705
Richmond *(G-11605)*
Hickey Electric Co Inc ....F.... 434 384-1896
Madison Heights *(G-7874)*
◆ **Hubbell Entertainment** ....F.... 540 382-6111
Christiansburg *(G-3594)*
Hubbell Lighting Inc ....B.... 540 382-6111
Christiansburg *(G-3596)*
Iba Led ....G.... 434 566-2109
Orange *(G-10215)*
Pacific Technology Inc ....F.... 571 421-7861
Annandale *(G-778)*
Revolution Soultions VA LLC ....G.... 804 539-5058
Fairfax *(G-4540)*
Stack Labs Inc ....E.... 503 453-5172
Haymarket *(G-6448)*
Zenta Corporation ....G.... 276 930-1500
Woolwine *(G-15870)*

3647 Vehicular Lighting Eqpt

Brush 10 ....G.... 540 582-3820
Partlow *(G-10264)*
Emergency Vehicle Outfitters ....G.... 571 228-2837
Lynchburg *(G-7702)*
Fog Light Solutions LLC ....G.... 703 201-0532
Great Falls *(G-5955)*
Lighting Auto Services ....G.... 804 330-6908
Richmond *(G-11655)*
Superior Panel Technology ....G.... 562 776-9494
Chesterfield *(G-3531)*
Supreme Edgelight Devices Inc ....G.... 276 236-3711
Galax *(G-5649)*
Theory3 Inc ....G.... 804 335-1001
Goochland *(G-5886)*
William K Whitaker ....G.... 562 776-9494
Chesterfield *(G-3542)*

3648 Lighting Eqpt, NEC

ARC Lighting LLC ....G.... 757 513-7717
Chesapeake *(G-2979)*
Armstrong Airport Lighting ....G.... 865 856-2723
Toano *(G-13856)*
Audio-Visuals Actions Inc ....G.... 703 751-1010
Alexandria *(G-143)*
Bloombeams LLC ....G.... 804 822-1022
Midlothian *(G-8780)*
Brite Lite Inc ....G.... 540 972-0212
Locust Grove *(G-7441)*
Collegiateskyviews LLC ....G.... 540 520-6394
Roanoke *(G-11912)*
Cormorant Technologies LLC ....G.... 703 871-5060
Williamsburg *(G-15224)*
Dogtown Lights LLC ....G.... 804 334-5088
Richmond *(G-11186)*
Efi Lighting Inc ....G.... 540 353-2880
Salem *(G-12501)*
Eflamelightingcom Inc ....G.... 434 822-0632
Danville *(G-3989)*
▲ **Environmental Ltg Solutions** ....G.... 202 361-2686
Haymarket *(G-6423)*
Force Forge ....G.... 804 454-5191
Fort Lee *(G-5129)*
Frank Hagerty ....G.... 540 809-0589
Fredericksburg *(G-5432)*
Gateway Green Energy Inc ....G.... 540 280-7475
Fishersville *(G-5003)*
Giving Light Inc ....G.... 757 236-2405
Hampton *(G-6159)*
Intelligent Illuminations Inc ....F.... 888 455-2465
Virginia Beach *(G-14550)*
▲ **Led Solar and Light Company** ....G.... 703 201-3250
Herndon *(G-6733)*
▲ **Lightronics Inc** ....E.... 757 486-3588
Virginia Beach *(G-14612)*
Luminaire Technologies Inc ....G.... 276 579-2007
Mouth of Wilson *(G-9094)*
Project Cost Gvrnment Svcs LLC ....G.... 239 334-3371
Alexandria *(G-559)*
Roto Rays Inc ....G.... 703 437-3353
Herndon *(G-6795)*
Rth Innovations LLC ....G.... 804 384-6767
Gloucester *(G-5860)*
Solar Lighting Virginia Inc ....G.... 757 229-3236
Williamsburg *(G-15314)*
Spotlight Dance LLC ....G.... 703 753-9173
Haymarket *(G-6447)*
Spotlight On Sports LLC ....G.... 804 615-3284
Midlothian *(G-8909)*
Spotlight Studio ....G.... 540 338-2690
Purcellville *(G-10679)*
Traffic Systems LLC ....F.... 703 530-9655
Manassas *(G-8170)*
Wright Look ....G.... 540 672-5085
Orange *(G-10234)*

3651 Household Audio & Video Eqpt

1602 Group LLC ....E.... 703 933-0024
Alexandria *(G-394)*
◆ **AC Cetera Inc** ....G.... 724 532-3363
Fairfax *(G-4400)*
Action Digital Inc ....G.... 804 358-7289
Richmond *(G-11083)*
Applied Vsual Cmmnications Inc ....E.... 703 787-6668
Herndon *(G-6614)*
Better Cables LLC ....G.... 872 222-5371
Broadlands *(G-2073)*
Better Cables LLC ....G.... 703 724-0906
Broadlands *(G-2074)*
Collabrtive Tech Cmmnctons Cor ....G.... 804 477-8695
Richmond *(G-11161)*
Digigram Inc ....G.... 330 476-5247
Fairfax *(G-4613)*
Goto Unit USA ....G.... 703 598-6642
Centreville *(G-2307)*
Hill Brenton ....G.... 757 560-9332
Hampton *(G-6167)*
Hipro Call Inc ....G.... 703 397-5155
Reston *(G-10864)*
Hogar Controls ....G.... 703 844-1160
Sterling *(G-13420)*
Home Fx ....G.... 540 455-5269
Spotsylvania *(G-12895)*
▲ **Htdepot LLC** ....G.... 703 830-2818
Chantilly *(G-2437)*
I10cartel Records LLC ....G.... 713 979-8182
Newport News *(G-9255)*
Impression An Everlasting Inc ....F.... 804 363-7185
Mechanicsville *(G-8640)*
Innovative Home Media LLC ....G.... 804 513-4784
Midlothian *(G-8832)*
Jones and Jones Audio & Video ....G.... 804 283-3495
Richmond *(G-11636)*
Kollmorgen Corporation ....B.... 540 633-3536
Radford *(G-10721)*
▼ **Korea Express Washington Inc** ....G.... 703 339-8201
Fairfax *(G-4493)*
Luminous Audio Technology ....G.... 804 741-5826
Richmond *(G-11275)*
Machina Dynamica Inc ....G.... 571 405-0709
Falls Church *(G-4826)*
Mu-Del Electronics LLC ....F.... 703 368-8900
Manassas *(G-8114)*
Prelude Communications Inc ....G.... 703 731-9396
Sterling *(G-13476)*
Rappahannock & Potomac Rep LLC ....G.... 540 373-9545
Fredericksburg *(G-5475)*
Rdk LLC ....G.... 540 446-8327
Mount Sidney *(G-9084)*
Rivercity Communications ....G.... 804 304-9590
Henrico *(G-6561)*
Seaside Audio ....G.... 757 237-5333
Virginia Beach *(G-14800)*
Short Circuit Electronics ....G.... 540 886-8805
Staunton *(G-13294)*
▲ **Silversmith Audio** ....G.... 619 460-1129
Springfield *(G-13087)*
SQ Labs LLC ....G.... 804 938-8123
Richmond *(G-11770)*
Stage Sound Inc ....E.... 540 342-2040
Roanoke *(G-12194)*
Star Home Theater LLC ....G.... 855 978-2748
Leesburg *(G-7351)*
Stone Mountain Ventures Inc ....F.... 888 244-9306
Huddleston *(G-6959)*
Ten Companies LLC ....G.... 703 669-1008
Leesburg *(G-7360)*
Transcedent Integration ....G.... 703 880-3019
Chantilly *(G-2561)*
Tyler JSun Global LLC ....G.... 407 221-6135
Stafford *(G-13206)*
Ultracomm Llc ....G.... 703 622-6397
Purcellville *(G-10683)*
▲ **Valcom Inc** ....C.... 540 427-3900
Roanoke *(G-12014)*
VT Aepco Inc ....G.... 703 658-7500
Alexandria *(G-607)*
Wiredup Inc ....G.... 757 565-3655
Williamsburg *(G-15347)*

3652 Phonograph Records & Magnetic Tape

Appvity ....G.... 571 327-0888
Sterling *(G-13347)*
Cee Corporation ....G.... 571 526-4447
Reston *(G-10820)*
Citadel Studios Inc ....G.... 407 766-6302
Manassas *(G-8050)*
Elucidsoft LLC ....G.... 703 679-7688
Stafford *(G-13143)*
Erp Initiatives LLC ....G.... 703 439-9352
Leesburg *(G-7270)*
Fifth Tribe LLC ....G.... 703 755-0680
Vienna *(G-14054)*
Finite Wisdom ....G.... 804 794-9585
Henrico *(G-6510)*
◆ **Furnace Mfg Inc** ....F.... 703 205-0007
Alexandria *(G-465)*
Genformax LLC ....G.... 703 346-7445
Mc Lean *(G-8447)*
I Sw LLC ....G.... 703 270-1540
Fairfax *(G-4478)*
Innovation Station Music LLC ....G.... 703 405-6727
Annandale *(G-760)*
Itkm Systems LLC ....G.... 502 370-6488
Mechanicsville *(G-8643)*
Memoryblue ....G.... 703 891-3840
Mc Lean *(G-8498)*
Raven Enterprises LLC ....G.... 804 355-6386
Richmond *(G-11346)*
Renmus Technologies Inc ....G.... 703 624-9144
Manassas *(G-8143)*

S I C

Rezgateway ....G....... 703 286-5331
Reston *(G-10940)*

Scenethink Inc ....G....... 434 987-6525
Charlottesville *(G-2872)*

Zojoi LLC ....G....... 804 397-5000
Charlottesville *(G-2718)*

3661 Telephone & Telegraph Apparatus

Ai Metrix Inc ....E....... 703 254-2000
Alexandria *(G-406)*

Avaya Federal Solutions Inc ......E....... 703 390-8333
Fairfax *(G-4415)*

Avaya Federal Solutions Inc ......F....... 703 653-8000
Fairfax *(G-4416)*

Avaya Federal Solutions Inc ......F....... 908 953-6000
Arlington *(G-866)*

C Dcap Modem Line ....G....... 804 561-6267
Mannboro *(G-8214)*

Ceotronics Inc ....G....... 757 549-6220
Virginia Beach *(G-14329)*

G2k Labs Inc ....G....... 703 965-8367
Chantilly *(G-2425)*

General Dynamics Govt Syst ......E....... 703 383-3605
Oakton *(G-10148)*

General Dynamics Info Tech Inc...D....... 703 268-7000
Herndon *(G-6681)*

General Dynmics One Source LLC ......F....... 703 906-6397
Falls Church *(G-4796)*

Greenzone Systems Inc ....G....... 703 567-6039
Arlington *(G-987)*

Iowave Inc ....E....... 703 979-9283
Arlington *(G-1011)*

L3harris Technologies Inc..........D....... 434 455-9390
Forest *(G-5079)*

L3harris Technologies Inc..........E....... 434 455-6600
Forest *(G-5080)*

Luna Innovations Incorporated ......E....... 540 961-5190
Blacksburg *(G-1756)*

Melvin Crutchfield ....G....... 804 440-3547
North Chesterfield *(G-9928)*

Moaz Marwa ....G....... 571 225-4743
Alexandria *(G-278)*

Mobitrum Corporation ....G....... 301 793-4728
Mc Lean *(G-8504)*

Nsgdatacom Inc ....E....... 703 464-0151
Chantilly *(G-2475)*

Photonblue LLC ....G....... 804 747-7412
Richmond *(G-11324)*

Photonvision LLC ....G....... 540 808-6266
Charlottesville *(G-2846)*

◆ Pyott-Boone Electronics Inc .....C....... 276 988-5505
North Tazewell *(G-10105)*

Quick Eagle Networks Inc ....G....... 703 583-3500
Woodbridge *(G-15787)*

Siemens AG ....G....... 757 875-7000
Newport News *(G-9337)*

▲ Silynx Communications Inc ....F....... 301 217-9223
Sterling *(G-13509)*

Softwright LLC ....G....... 434 975-4310
Charlottesville *(G-2694)*

Toana 2 Limited ....G....... 757 566-2001
Toano *(G-13879)*

Torrance Enterprises Inc ....G....... 804 748-5481
Chesterfield *(G-3533)*

US 1 Cable LLC ....G....... 571 224-3955
Gainesville *(G-5620)*

▲ Valcom Inc ....C....... 540 427-3900
Roanoke *(G-12014)*

Valcom Services LLC ....G....... 540 427-2400
Roanoke *(G-12015)*

Voice 1 Communication LLC ....G....... 804 795-7503
Richmond *(G-11441)*

3663 Radio & T V Communications, Systs & Eqpt, Broadcast/Studio

Active Sense Technologies LLC...........G....... 352 226-1479
Abingdon *(G-7)*

Advantech Inc ....G....... 703 402-0590
Alexandria *(G-120)*

Ambervision Technologies ....G....... 571 594-1664
Brambleton *(G-1926)*

Andrew Corp ....G....... 703 726-5900
Ashburn *(G-1241)*

Andrew Corporation ....G....... 434 386-5262
Forest *(G-5050)*

Angerole Mounts LLC ....G....... 434 249-3977
Charlottesville *(G-2588)*

Antenna Technologies Ltd Co ......F....... 703 450-5517
Sterling *(G-13345)*

Antensan Usa Inc ....G....... 703 836-0300
Alexandria *(G-137)*

Apogee Communications ....G....... 703 481-1622
Herndon *(G-6613)*

Applied Technollogy ....G....... 703 660-8422
Alexandria *(G-415)*

Aprize Satellite Inc ....G....... 703 273-7010
Fairfax *(G-4595)*

Are You Wired LLC ....G....... 804 512-3990
North Chesterfield *(G-9819)*

Astrocomm Technologies LLC .....G....... 703 606-2022
Oak Hill *(G-10135)*

Astron Wireless Tech Inc ....F....... 703 450-5517
Sterling *(G-13352)*

Astron Wireless Tech LLC ....F....... 703 450-5517
Sterling *(G-13353)*

Atlas Scntfic Tchncal Svcs LLC ......G....... 540 492-5051
Bowling Green *(G-1906)*

Audio-Visuals Actions Inc ....G....... 703 751-1010
Alexandria *(G-143)*

Avcom of Virginia Inc ....E....... 804 794-2500
North Chesterfield *(G-9823)*

Ballas LLC ....G....... 703 689-9644
Oak Hill *(G-10136)*

Beckley LLC ....G....... 843 822-8091
Leesburg *(G-7228)*

Binge Live Inc ....G....... 757 679-7715
Chesapeake *(G-2999)*

Boeing Company ....G....... 703 467-2534
Herndon *(G-6628)*

C-3 Comm Systems LLC ....G....... 703 829-0588
Arlington *(G-897)*

Caci Nss Inc ....E....... 703 434-4000
Reston *(G-10814)*

CC Wireless Corporation ....G....... 757 802-8140
Norfolk *(G-9479)*

Coleman Microwave Co ....E....... 540 984-8848
Edinburg *(G-4301)*

Comcast Tech Center ....G....... 571 229-9112
Manassas *(G-7925)*

Commscope Technologies LLC ....C....... 703 548-6777
Alexandria *(G-170)*

Commscope Technologies LLC ....C....... 703 726-5500
Ashburn *(G-1257)*

Commscope Technologies LLC ....C....... 434 386-5300
Forest *(G-5062)*

Communications Vehicle Svc LLC ......G....... 703 542-7449
Chantilly *(G-2529)*

▼ Communications-Applied Tech Co...F....... 703 481-0068
Reston *(G-10823)*

▲ Comsonics Inc ....G....... 540 434-5965
Harrisonburg *(G-6306)*

Convex Corporation ....G....... 703 433-9901
Warrenton *(G-14990)*

Cr Communications ....G....... 757 871-4797
Williamsburg *(G-15225)*

Cyviz LLC ....G....... 571 858-3371
Arlington *(G-924)*

Datapath Inc ....F....... 703 476-1826
Sterling *(G-13382)*

Datron Wrld Communications Inc ......G....... 703 647-6235
Alexandria *(G-184)*

Dawnbreaker Communications LLC .....G....... 202 288-0805
Dunn Loring *(G-4263)*

Dbsd North America Inc ....G....... 703 964-1400
Reston *(G-10834)*

Delta Electronics Inc ....F....... 703 354-3350
Alexandria *(G-445)*

Directive Systems and Eng LLC ....G....... 703 754-3876
Haymarket *(G-6419)*

Dtc Communications Inc ....E....... 727 471-6900
Herndon *(G-6663)*

Eagle Mobile Services Inc ....G....... 703 979-1848
Arlington *(G-950)*

Ecko Incorporated ....F....... 276 988-7943
North Tazewell *(G-10098)*

Eddy Current Technology Inc ......G....... 757 490-1814
Virginia Beach *(G-14431)*

Edwin Glenn Campbell ....G....... 703 203-6516
Stafford *(G-13142)*

Electro Techs LLC ....G....... 704 900-1911
Norfolk *(G-9543)*

Engility LLC ....A....... 703 434-4000
Reston *(G-10847)*

Engility LLC ....D....... 703 633-8300
Yorktown *(G-15955)*

Ericsson Inc ....G....... 434 592-5610
Lynchburg *(G-7704)*

Ericsson Inc ....G....... 434 528-7000
Lynchburg *(G-7705)*

Erisys LLC ....G....... 660 864-4474
Herndon *(G-6667)*

Etl Systems Inc ....G....... 703 657-0411
Herndon *(G-6669)*

Fei-Zyfer Inc ....G....... 540 349-8330
Warrenton *(G-15016)*

Finest Productions Inc ....G....... 703 989-2657
Arlington *(G-966)*

First Renaissance Ventures ....G....... 703 408-6961
Mc Lean *(G-8431)*

Gatr Technologies Inc ....D....... 571 258-5020
Ashburn *(G-1284)*

Gcseac Inc ....G....... 276 632-9700
Martinsville *(G-8288)*

◆ General Dynmics Gvrnment Syste ...A....... 703 876-3000
Falls Church *(G-4795)*

General Dynmics One Source LLC ......F....... 703 906-6397
Falls Church *(G-4796)*

Getsat North America Inc ....E....... 571 308-2451
Mc Lean *(G-8448)*

Gomspace North America LLC ......G....... 703 866-8742
Alexandria *(G-222)*

Greenzone Systems Inc ....G....... 703 567-6039
Arlington *(G-987)*

GTS Defense MGT Svcs LLC ....G....... 832 326-7227
Great Falls *(G-5961)*

Idirect Government LLC ....D....... 703 648-8118
Herndon *(G-6705)*

Ils Intrntonal Launch Svcs Inc ....D....... 703 435-5689
Reston *(G-10869)*

Information Systems Group ....G....... 804 526-4220
North Chesterfield *(G-9895)*

Inhand Networks Inc ....G....... 703 348-2988
Fairfax *(G-4634)*

▲ Interbyte ....G....... 703 825-8774
Alexandria *(G-486)*

Iridium Communications Inc ....E....... 703 287-7400
Mc Lean *(G-8469)*

Iridium Holdings LLC ....G....... 703 287-7400
Mc Lean *(G-8470)*

▲ Iridium Satellite LLC ....E....... 703 356-0484
Mc Lean *(G-8471)*

Kajjo Sirwan ....G....... 202 569-1472
Falls Church *(G-4815)*

Key Bridge Global LLC ....G....... 703 414-3500
Mc Lean *(G-8479)*

Kordusa Inc ....G....... 540 242-5210
Stafford *(G-13165)*

L-3 Communications Corp ....G....... 703 375-4911
Manassas *(G-7958)*

L3 Technologies Inc ....C....... 703 889-8640
Ashburn *(G-1305)*

L3 Technologies Inc ....G....... 757 425-0142
Virginia Beach *(G-14596)*

L3harris Technologies Inc..........E....... 703 668-7256
Herndon *(G-6730)*

L3harris Technologies Inc..........G....... 703 344-1000
Chantilly *(G-2454)*

L3harris Technologies Inc..........B....... 434 455-6600
Lynchburg *(G-7753)*

L3harris Technologies Inc..........D....... 434 455-9390
Forest *(G-5079)*

L3harris Technologies Inc..........E....... 434 455-6600
Forest *(G-5080)*

Laser Light Communications Inc ......G....... 571 346-7623
Reston *(G-10883)*

Lb Telesystems Inc ....E....... 703 919-8991
Chantilly *(G-2456)*

Ligado Networks Inc Virginia......B....... 877 678-2920
Reston *(G-10888)*

Little Green Men Inc ....G....... 301 203-8702
Ashburn *(G-1308)*

Lockheed Martin Corporation ......B....... 757 935-9479
Suffolk *(G-13732)*

Lynk Global Inc ....G....... 937 367-8737
Falls Church *(G-4921)*

Mark Space Inc ....G....... 703 404-8550
Sterling *(G-13449)*

Mediasat International Inc ....G....... 703 558-0309
Arlington *(G-1059)*

Metropole Products Inc ....E....... 540 659-2132
Stafford *(G-13176)*

Mil-Sat LLC ....G....... 757 294-9393
Surry *(G-13798)*

Mil-Space LLC ....G....... 954 862-3613
Surry *(G-13799)*

Missionteq LLC ....G....... 703 563-0699
Chantilly *(G-2545)*

Mobile Radio Partners Inc ....F....... 804 525-4013
Henrico *(G-6535)*

Mobile Radio Partners Inc.................G...... 804 364-1553
  Glen Allen (G-5772)
Moto Farkle Support Services ....G...... 757 705-2014
  Virginia Beach (G-14665)
Motorola Solutions Inc ....C...... 703 724-8000
  Leesburg (G-7316)
Mu-Del Electronics LLC ....F...... 703 368-8900
  Manassas (G-8114)
Muhammad Islam ....G...... 631 569-8325
  Reston (G-10904)
Nomad Solutions LLC ....F...... 703 656-9100
  Gainesville (G-5602)
Novelsat USA ....G...... 703 295-2119
  Vienna (G-14106)
Novus Technology Inc ....G...... 703 218-9801
  Fairfax (G-4657)
Oceus Enterprise Solutions LLC ......D...... 703 234-9200
  Reston (G-10912)
Orban ....G...... 804 529-6283
  Lewisetta (G-7384)
Orbcomm LLC ....D...... 703 433-6300
  Dulles (G-4215)
Orbcomm LLC ....E...... 703 433-6300
  Sterling (G-13466)
Orion Applied Science Tech LLC ......G...... 571 393-1942
  Manassas (G-8122)
Pacific and Southern Company ....D...... 703 854-6899
  Mc Lean (G-8522)
Packet Dynamics LLC ....G...... 703 597-1413
  Reston (G-10917)
Peraton Cmmnctons Holdings LLC ...G...... 703 668-6001
  Herndon (G-6769)
Peraton Inc ....E...... 757 857-0099
  Norfolk (G-9685)
Phasor Inc ....G...... 202 256-2075
  Arlington (G-1110)
Product Dev Mfg & Packg ....G...... 703 777-8400
  Leesburg (G-7328)
◆ Pyott-Boone Electronics Inc ....C...... 276 988-5505
  North Tazewell (G-10105)
Racecom of Virginia ....G...... 757 599-8255
  Yorktown (G-15985)
Radio Reconnaissance Tech Inc ......G...... 540 752-7448
  Fredericksburg (G-5352)
Raytheon Company ....G...... 310 647-9438
  Chesapeake (G-3258)
Raytheon Company ....G...... 703 418-0275
  Arlington (G-1135)
Raytheon Company ....G...... 571 250-1101
  Dulles (G-4222)
Raytheon Company ....G...... 757 749-9638
  Yorktown (G-15987)
Raytheon Company ....F...... 703 872-3400
  Arlington (G-1139)
Reverb Networks Inc ....E...... 703 665-4222
  Sterling (G-13492)
Rome Research Corporation ....G...... 757 421-8300
  Chesapeake (G-3275)
Ronald Carter ....G...... 571 278-6659
  Burke (G-2202)
Santa Inc ....F...... 757 463-3553
  Virginia Beach (G-14794)
Satcom-Labs LLC ....G...... 805 427-5556
  Alexandria (G-339)
Selex Communications Inc ....F...... 703 547-6280
  Reston (G-10946)
Shared Spectrum Company ....E...... 703 761-2818
  Vienna (G-14123)
Shoebox Memories ....G...... 703 969-9290
  Fairfax (G-4699)
Signafab LLC ....G...... 703 489-8572
  Louisa (G-7567)
Skymate Inc ....G...... 703 961-5800
  Reston (G-10953)
Smartcell Inc ....G...... 703 989-5887
  Manassas (G-8157)
Softwright LLC ....G...... 434 975-3410
  Charlottesville (G-2694)
Spacequest Ltd ....F...... 703 424-7801
  Fairfax (G-4680)
Speakeasy ....G...... 703 333-5040
  Annandale (G-783)
▲ Special Communications LLC ....G...... 202 677-1225
  Virginia Beach (G-14833)
Spectrarep LLC ....F...... 703 227-9690
  Chantilly (G-2496)
Spectrum ....G...... 757 224-7500
  Newport News (G-9345)
Spicewater Electronic Home Mon ....G...... 276 690-4718
  Gate City (G-5668)

SSC Innovations LLC ....G...... 703 761-2818
  Vienna (G-14133)
◆ St Engineering Idirect Inc ....B...... 703 648-8002
  Herndon (G-6814)
Strategic Voice Solutions ....G...... 888 975-6130
  Strasburg (G-13600)
Sure Site Satellite Inc ....G...... 540 948-5880
  Locust Grove (G-7452)
Tabet Manufacturing Co Inc ....E...... 757 627-1855
  Norfolk (G-9739)
Tekalign Inc ....F...... 703 757-6690
  Reston (G-10971)
Telesat US Services LLC ....G...... 571 559-1500
  Arlington (G-1186)
Thrane Rgonal Workshop- Mackey ...G...... 757 410-3291
  Chesapeake (G-3334)
Tian Corporation ....G...... 703 434-4000
  Reston (G-10973)
▲ Tim Price Inc ....F...... 540 722-8716
  Winchester (G-15594)
Trustcomm Solutions LLC ....F...... 281 272-7500
  Stafford (G-13205)
Ultralife Corporation ....E...... 757 419-2430
  Virginia Beach (G-14900)
Universal Space Network Inc ....G...... 703 488-4150
  Chantilly (G-2513)
US Dept of the Air Force ....G...... 703 808-0492
  Chantilly (G-2515)
V T R International Inc ....G...... 434 385-5300
  Lynchburg (G-7831)
▲ Valcom Inc ....G...... 540 427-3900
  Roanoke (G-12014)
Valcom Services LLC ....G...... 540 427-2400
  Roanoke (G-12015)
Vicon Industries Inc ....G...... 540 868-9530
  Stephens City (G-13328)
Virtual Netcom LLC ....G...... 571 445-0306
  Chantilly (G-2557)
Virtual Ntwrk Cmmnications Inc ......G...... 571 445-0306
  South Riding (G-12871)
Vsd LLC ....G...... 757 498-4766
  Virginia Beach (G-14927)
VT Milcom Inc ....D...... 757 548-2956
  Chesapeake (G-3366)
Wallye LLC ....G...... 631 320-8868
  Chantilly (G-2567)
Wavelab Inc ....G...... 703 860-9321
  Reston (G-10987)
▲ Wireless Ventures USA Inc ....F...... 703 852-1350
  Mc Lean (G-8580)

3669 Communications Eqpt, NEC

▼ All Traffic Solutions Inc ....F...... 814 237-9005
  Herndon (G-6609)
American Safety & Health ....G...... 434 977-2700
  Charlottesville (G-2728)
Annie Lee Traffic Patrol ....G...... 888 682-5882
  Newport News (G-9167)
Applied Vsual Cmmnications Inc ......E...... 703 787-6668
  Herndon (G-6614)
Ats-Sales LLC ....G...... 703 631-6661
  Chantilly (G-2372)
Avelis John ....G...... 757 363-2001
  Virginia Beach (G-14250)
Centripetal Networks Inc ....G...... 571 252-5080
  Herndon (G-6638)
Claritas Creative LLC ....G...... 240 274-5029
  Arlington (G-906)
Connected Intelligence LLC ....G...... 571 241-4540
  Dulles (G-4196)
Connectedescape LLC ....G...... 443 910-7559
  Stafford (G-13133)
Convex Corporation ....G...... 703 433-9901
  Warrenton (G-14990)
Corning Optcal Cmmncations LLC ....G...... 703 848-0200
  Herndon (G-6648)
Dacha ....G...... 757 754-2805
  Virginia Beach (G-14380)
Damsel Detectors ....G...... 757 268-4128
  Portsmouth (G-10414)
▲ Dedicated Micros Inc ....E...... 703 904-7738
  Chantilly (G-2403)
Diverging Approach Inc ....F...... 757 220-2316
  Williamsburg (G-15235)
▲ Drs Leonardo Inc ....C...... 703 416-8000
  Arlington (G-944)
Ecko Incorporated ....F...... 276 988-7943
  North Tazewell (G-10098)
Emergency Alert Solutions Grou ......G...... 703 346-4787
  Great Falls (G-5953)

Emergency Response Tech LLC ....G...... 703 932-1118
  Manassas (G-7938)
Exceletics Inc ....G...... 703 405-5479
  Herndon (G-6671)
▼ Eyegaze Inc ....F...... 703 385-8800
  Fairfax (G-4620)
Fauquier Hearing Services Pllc ....G...... 540 341-7112
  Warrenton (G-15010)
Final Resource Inc ....G...... 703 404-8740
  Herndon (G-6676)
▲ Gatekeeper Security Inc ....E...... 703 673-3320
  Sterling (G-13408)
General Magnetic Sciences Inc ....G...... 571 243-6887
  Manassas (G-7944)
▲ General Magnetic Sciences Inc ......G...... 571 243-6887
  Clifton (G-3666)
Gunn Mountain Communications ......G...... 303 880-8616
  Williamsburg (G-15251)
Industrial Signal LLC ....G...... 703 323-7777
  Arlington (G-1001)
Insignia Technology Svcs LLC ....D...... 757 591-2111
  Ashburn (G-1296)
Iteris Inc ....G...... 949 270-9400
  Fairfax (G-4482)
Johnson Controls ....G...... 804 727-3890
  Richmond (G-11257)
Johnson Controls ....D...... 757 853-6611
  Norfolk (G-9605)
JQ & G Inc Company ....G...... 540 588-7625
  Roanoke (G-11947)
▲ Korman Signs Inc ....E...... 804 262-6050
  Richmond (G-11264)
L3harris Technologies Inc ....C...... 757 594-1607
  Newport News (G-9278)
Life Protect 24/7 Inc ....G...... 888 864-8403
  Norfolk (G-9618)
Mects Services JV ....G...... 248 499-9243
  Fairfax (G-4652)
Milcom Systems Corporation Vol ......F...... 757 463-2800
  Virginia Beach (G-14654)
Mobotrex Inc ....G...... 804 794-1592
  Powhatan (G-10559)
Ms Kathleen B Watkins ....G...... 804 741-0388
  Henrico (G-6537)
Nettalon Inc ....G...... 877 638-8256
  Fredericksburg (G-5332)
Nettalon Security Systems Inc ....F...... 540 368-5290
  Fredericksburg (G-5333)
Noahs Ark Transportation LLC ....G...... 240 476-3381
  Alexandria (G-292)
Northrop Grumman Sperry ....G...... 434 974-2000
  Charlottesville (G-2665)
OHG Science & Technology LLC ....G...... 434 990-0500
  Barboursville (G-1565)
Pacs Inc ....F...... 703 415-4411
  Arlington (G-1094)
▲ Rga LLC ....F...... 804 794-1592
  Powhatan (G-10571)
Senstar Inc ....G...... 703 463-3088
  Herndon (G-6804)
Smoke Detector Inspector ....G...... 757 870-4772
  Virginia Beach (G-14828)
Softwright LLC ....G...... 434 975-4310
  Charlottesville (G-2694)
Sparkzone Inc ....G...... 703 861-0650
  Fairfax (G-4558)
▲ Superior Quality Mfg LLC ....G...... 757 413-9100
  Chesapeake (G-3315)
Tabet Manufacturing Co Inc ....E...... 757 627-1855
  Norfolk (G-9739)
Traffic Systems LLC ....F...... 703 530-9655
  Manassas (G-8170)
Trafficland Inc ....F...... 703 591-1933
  Fairfax (G-4689)
Tri-Ed Distribution Inc ....G...... 757 852-3780
  Norfolk (G-9767)
Trigg Industries LLC ....G...... 757 223-7522
  Newport News (G-9363)
Xamr Corporation ....G...... 703 663-8711
  Fairfax (G-4584)

3671 Radio & T V Receiving Electron Tubes

Cynthia Kriparos ....G...... 757 818-3441
  Chesapeake (G-3060)
Electron Technologies Inc ....G...... 703 818-9400
  Chantilly (G-2416)
Noble-Met LLC ....C...... 540 389-7860
  Salem (G-12545)
Red Geranium Inc ....G...... 757 645-3421
  Williamsburg (G-15304)

3672 Printed Circuit Boards

Advanced Mfg Tech Inc ... D ... 434 385-7197
Lynchburg *(G-7633)*

▲ **An Electronic Instrumentation** ... C ... 703 478-0700
Leesburg *(G-7217)*

Annex Inc ... G ... 703 239-8553
Fairfax *(G-4408)*

Assembly & Design Inc ... F ... 804 379-5432
North Chesterfield *(G-9821)*

Cardinal Mechatronics LLC ... G ... 540 922-2392
Blacksburg *(G-1728)*

Circuit Solutions Intl LLC ... G ... 703 994-6788
Burke *(G-2186)*

Ddi VA ... G ... 571 436-1378
Dulles *(G-4197)*

Dwb Design Inc ... G ... 540 371-0785
Fredericksburg *(G-5422)*

▲ **Electronic Design & Mfg Co** ... D ... 434 385-0046
Lynchburg *(G-7701)*

Ftg Crcuits Fredericksburg Inc ... D ... 540 752-5511
Fredericksburg *(G-5433)*

Kordusa Inc ... G ... 540 242-5210
Stafford *(G-13165)*

Mercury Systems Inc ... G ... 703 243-9538
Arlington *(G-1061)*

Moog Inc ... E ... 276 236-4921
Galax *(G-5641)*

More Technology LLC ... G ... 571 208-9865
Centreville *(G-2322)*

Printed Circuits International ... G ... 804 737-7979
Highland Springs *(G-6855)*

◆ **Pyott-Boone Electronics Inc** ... C ... 276 988-5505
North Tazewell *(G-10105)*

Stanford Electronics Mfg & Sls ... G ... 434 676-6630
Brodnax *(G-2105)*

Ttm Technologies Inc ... B ... 703 652-2200
Sterling *(G-13540)*

Viasystems North America Inc ... A ... 703 450-2600
Sterling *(G-13549)*

W W W Electronics Inc ... F ... 434 973-4702
Charlottesville *(G-2714)*

Zentech Fredericksburg LLC ... E ... 540 372-6500
Fredericksburg *(G-5394)*

3674 Semiconductors

4wave Inc ... E ... 703 787-9283
Sterling *(G-13337)*

Alltek Systems LLC ... G ... 757 438-6905
Charlottesville *(G-2725)*

Applied Materials Inc ... E ... 703 331-1476
Manassas *(G-8028)*

Aquanta Inc ... G ... 703 286-0923
Mc Lean *(G-8395)*

Aware Inc ... G ... 804 598-1016
Powhatan *(G-10531)*

Bluetherm Corporation ... G ... 917 446-8958
Charlottesville *(G-2745)*

Brocade Cmmnctions Systems LLC ... G ... 540 439-9010
Sumerduck *(G-13789)*

Burton Telecom LLC ... G ... 757 230-6520
Virginia Beach *(G-14307)*

Controp USA Inc ... G ... 301 605-4499
Manassas *(G-7926)*

Convergent Bus Solutions LLC ... G ... 804 360-0251
Richmond *(G-11167)*

Convergent Crossfit ... G ... 703 385-5400
Linden *(G-7427)*

Convergent Data Group ... G ... 571 276-0756
Alexandria *(G-433)*

Electronics of Future Inc ... G ... 518 421-8830
Vienna *(G-14044)*

Eopus Innovations LLC ... G ... 703 796-9882
Fairfax *(G-4618)*

▲ **Epic Led** ... G ... 703 499-4485
Manassas *(G-7939)*

▲ **Eternal Technology Corporation** ... E ... 804 524-8555
South Chesterfield *(G-12803)*

Eyl Inc ... G ... 703 682-7018
Arlington *(G-961)*

Fluor Enterprises Inc ... E ... 703 351-1204
Arlington *(G-970)*

Fox Group Inc ... D ... 925 980-5643
Warrenton *(G-15017)*

Genesic Semiconductor Inc ... G ... 703 996-8200
Dulles *(G-4204)*

Global Oled Technology LLC ... F ... 703 870-3282
Herndon *(G-6686)*

Greenerbillcom ... G ... 703 898-5354
Gainesville *(G-5587)*

Greenzone Systems Inc ... G ... 703 567-6039
Arlington *(G-987)*

▲ **Hagstrom Electronics Inc** ... G ... 540 465-4677
Strasburg *(G-13581)*

Iam Energy Incorporated ... G ... 703 939-5681
Sterling *(G-13425)*

Imgen Technologies Lc ... G ... 703 549-2866
Alexandria *(G-236)*

Intel Federal LLC ... E ... 703 633-0953
Fairfax *(G-4637)*

Intel Federal LLC ... G ... 302 644-3756
Reston *(G-10875)*

Intel Perspectives LLC ... G ... 703 321-7507
Springfield *(G-13024)*

◆ **Intelligent Platforms LLC** ... A ... 434 978-5000
Charlottesville *(G-2647)*

Intrinsic Semiconductor Corp ... F ... 703 437-4000
Sterling *(G-13431)*

ITT Defense & Electronics ... A ... 703 790-6300
Mc Lean *(G-8474)*

Jihoon Solution Inc ... G ... 757 344-1751
Yorktown *(G-15970)*

Kihn Solar ... G ... 703 425-2418
Fairfax *(G-4489)*

Kordusa Inc ... G ... 540 242-5210
Stafford *(G-13165)*

L3harris Technologies Inc ... D ... 434 455-9390
Forest *(G-5079)*

L3harris Technologies Inc ... E ... 434 455-6600
Forest *(G-5080)*

Labrador Technology ... G ... 703 791-7660
Manassas *(G-8097)*

Laser Light Federal LLC ... G ... 703 283-0659
Reston *(G-10884)*

Leidos Inc ... C ... 703 676-7451
Fort Belvoir *(G-5116)*

▲ **Lightronics Inc** ... E ... 757 486-3588
Virginia Beach *(G-14612)*

Lightspeed Infrared LLC ... G ... 540 875-6796
Bedford *(G-1643)*

Litesheet Solutions LLC ... G ... 860 213-8311
Forest *(G-5081)*

▼ **Luna Energy LLC** ... G ... 540 553-0500
Blacksburg *(G-1755)*

Marelco Power Systems Inc ... F ... 800 225-4838
Richmond *(G-11667)*

Meru Biotechnologies Inc ... G ... 804 316-4466
Richmond *(G-11677)*

Micron Technology Inc ... D ... 703 396-1000
Manassas *(G-7975)*

Micronergy LLC ... G ... 757 325-6973
Hampton *(G-6199)*

Minequest Inc ... E ... 276 963-6463
Cedar Bluff *(G-2282)*

Monolithic Music Group LLC ... G ... 804 233-2322
Richmond *(G-11682)*

Moog Inc ... F ... 540 552-3011
Blacksburg *(G-1765)*

Moog Inc ... C ... 540 552-3011
Blacksburg *(G-1768)*

Old Dominion Innovations Inc ... F ... 804 477-8712
Ashland *(G-1471)*

Powermark Corporation ... G ... 301 639-7319
Union Hall *(G-13960)*

Qualcomm Inc ... G ... 858 587-1121
Arlington *(G-1125)*

Raytheon Company ... A ... 703 419-1400
Arlington *(G-1138)*

Raytheon Company ... F ... 703 872-3400
Arlington *(G-1139)*

Raytum Photonics LLC ... G ... 703 831-7809
Sterling *(G-13487)*

Semetrol LLC ... G ... 804 536-7005
Chesterfield *(G-3523)*

Semiconductor Technology RES ... G ... 804 304-8092
Richmond *(G-11376)*

Svm Services LLC ... G ... 703 389-5100
Herndon *(G-6818)*

Taylored Information Tech LLC ... G ... 276 479-2122
Nickelsville *(G-9386)*

Tisol ... G ... 703 739-2771
Alexandria *(G-600)*

Tokyo Electron America Inc ... E ... 703 257-2211
Manassas *(G-8004)*

Tq-Systems USA Inc ... G ... 757 503-3927
Chesapeake *(G-3346)*

Transecurity LLC ... G ... 540 443-9231
Blacksburg *(G-1800)*

Trojan Defense LLC ... G ... 703 981-8710
Herndon *(G-6832)*

Troy Patrick ... G ... 703 507-4914
Alexandria *(G-370)*

Ttec LLC ... G ... 540 336-2693
Berryville *(G-1697)*

Video Convergent ... G ... 703 354-9700
Springfield *(G-13105)*

Virginia Semiconductor Inc ... E ... 540 373-2900
Fredericksburg *(G-5233)*

Virtue Solar LLC ... G ... 540 407-8353
Madison *(G-7864)*

▲ **Wgb LLC** ... G ... 757 289-5053
Suffolk *(G-13785)*

Zeido LLC ... G ... 202 549-5757
Stafford *(G-13213)*

3675 Electronic Capacitors

▲ **B Microfarads Inc** ... C ... 276 728-9121
Hillsville *(G-6885)*

Illinois Tool Works Inc ... D ... 434 239-6941
Lynchburg *(G-7737)*

Integer Holdings Corporation ... B ... 540 389-7860
Salem *(G-12521)*

Keltron Corporation ... E ... 540 527-3526
Roanoke *(G-11948)*

3677 Electronic Coils & Transformers

Bobbin Coil Specialists Inc ... G ... 815 385-6205
Forest *(G-5055)*

Chemteq ... F ... 757 622-2223
Norfolk *(G-9481)*

Delta Electronics Inc ... F ... 703 354-3350
Alexandria *(G-445)*

Electro-Mechanical Corporation ... B ... 276 669-4084
Bristol *(G-1977)*

Greenleaf Filtration LLC ... G ... 804 378-7744
Powhatan *(G-10547)*

▼ **Isotemp Research Inc** ... G ... 434 295-3101
Charlottesville *(G-2815)*

Marelco Power Systems Inc ... D ... 517 546-6330
Richmond *(G-11666)*

Marelco Power Systems Inc ... F ... 800 225-4838
Richmond *(G-11667)*

Planet Care Inc ... G ... 540 980-2420
Pulaski *(G-10644)*

Power Distribution Inc ... C ... 804 737-9880
Richmond *(G-11721)*

Quanta Systems LLC ... G ... 703 885-7900
Herndon *(G-6783)*

▲ **SMC Electrical Products Inc** ... E ... 276 285-3841
Bristol *(G-2033)*

Special T Manufacturing Corp ... F ... 276 475-5510
Damascus *(G-3950)*

STS International Incorporated ... E ... 703 575-5180
Arlington *(G-1177)*

▲ **Transformer Engineering LLC** ... D ... 216 741-5282
Wytheville *(G-15920)*

3678 Electronic Connectors

Brantner and Associates Inc ... G ... 540 825-2111
Culpeper *(G-3875)*

Chesapeake Connector & Cable ... G ... 757 855-5504
Norfolk *(G-9482)*

ITT Defense & Electronics ... A ... 703 790-6300
Mc Lean *(G-8474)*

J and R Manufacturing Inc ... E ... 276 210-1647
Bluefield *(G-1865)*

Kitco Fiber Optics Inc ... D ... 757 216-2208
Virginia Beach *(G-14587)*

Kitco/Ksaria LLC ... G ... 757 216-2220
Virginia Beach *(G-14588)*

◆ **Leyland Oceantech Inc** ... G ... 703 661-6097
Sterling *(G-13440)*

Mapp Manufacturing Corporation ... G ... 757 410-0307
Chesapeake *(G-3197)*

▲ **Virginia Panel Corporation** ... C ... 540 932-3300
Waynesboro *(G-15144)*

3679 Electronic Components, NEC

Advanced Packet Switching Inc ... G ... 703 627-1746
Woodbridge *(G-15642)*

Amentum Services Inc ... C ... 703 418-3020
Arlington *(G-851)*

An Electronic Instrumentation ... G ... 434 793-4870
Danville *(G-3955)*

▲ **An Electronic Instrumentation** ... C ... 703 478-0700
Leesburg *(G-7217)*

Atlas North America LLC ... G ... 757 463-0670
Yorktown *(G-15934)*

Benny Babb ....G...... 276 995-2658
  Fort Blackmore *(G-5121)*

Bluewire Prototypes Inc ....G...... 540 200-3200
  Hiwassee *(G-6910)*

Centurylink Switch Room ....G...... 276 646-8000
  Marion *(G-8224)*

Cobham AES Holdings Inc ....F...... 703 414-5300
  Arlington *(G-911)*

Commscope Technologies LLC ....C...... 434 386-5300
  Forest *(G-5062)*

CP Films Inc ....G...... 276 632-4991
  Martinsville *(G-8277)*

Dominion Microprobes Inc ....G...... 434 962-8221
  Charlottesville *(G-2619)*

Dominion Taping & Reeling Inc ....G...... 804 763-2700
  Midlothian *(G-8810)*

▲ Drs Leonardo Inc ....G...... 703 416-8000
  Arlington *(G-944)*

E C A ....G...... 703 234-4142
  Reston *(G-10845)*

E W Systems & Devices Inc ....G...... 540 635-5104
  Front Royal *(G-5531)*

▲ E-Tron Systems Inc ....E...... 703 690-2731
  Lorton *(G-7482)*

Electronic Manufacturing Corp .....F...... 703 661-8351
  Sterling *(G-13392)*

Emsco LLC ....F...... 804 752-1640
  Ashland *(G-1409)*

Face Electronics Lc ....E...... 757 624-2121
  Norfolk *(G-9546)*

Firstguard Technologies Corp ......G...... 703 267-6670
  Fairfax *(G-4624)*

Fleet Waveguides LLC ....G...... 757 337-3311
  Newport News *(G-9230)*

Flip Switch Events LLC ....G...... 703 677-0119
  Ashburn *(G-1281)*

Gemtek Electronic Compone ....G...... 603 218-3902
  Mattaponi *(G-8359)*

▲ Goodrow Holdings Inc ....G...... 804 543-2136
  Mechanicsville *(G-8628)*

Halo Acoustic Wear LLC ....F...... 703 474-6081
  Broadlands *(G-2078)*

Hardwire ....F...... 757 410-5429
  Virginia Beach *(G-14506)*

Illinois Tool Works Inc ....D...... 434 239-6941
  Lynchburg *(G-7737)*

Incandescent Technologies ....G...... 434 385-8825
  Forest *(G-5074)*

Industrial Control Systems Inc ......E...... 804 737-1700
  Sandston *(G-12620)*

▲ Intercon Inc ....D...... 434 525-3390
  Forest *(G-5078)*

ITT Defense & Electronics ....A...... 703 790-6300
  Mc Lean *(G-8474)*

Katz Hadrian ....G...... 202 942-5707
  Mc Lean *(G-8478)*

Kauffman Engineering Inc ....B...... 757 468-6000
  Virginia Beach *(G-14581)*

Leidos Inc ....C...... 703 676-7451
  Fort Belvoir *(G-5116)*

Marelco Power Systems Inc ....D...... 517 546-6330
  Richmond *(G-11666)*

Mary Kay Inc ....G...... 770 497-8800
  Mount Solon *(G-9088)*

Metocean Telematics Inc ....G...... 902 468-2505
  Mc Lean *(G-8499)*

Mevatec Corp ....G...... 703 583-9287
  Woodbridge *(G-15745)*

Mevatec Corp ....G...... 631 261-7000
  Springfield *(G-13049)*

Microwave Circuits Inc ....G...... 434 455-2800
  Lynchburg *(G-7772)*

Moog Components Group ....G...... 540 443-4699
  Blacksburg *(G-1763)*

Nova Power Solutions Inc ....G...... 703 657-0122
  Sterling *(G-13462)*

Odin Scnce Tech Innovation LLC ....G...... 850 582-0799
  Fredericksburg *(G-5338)*

Pan American Systems Corp ....G...... 757 468-1926
  Virginia Beach *(G-14709)*

▲ Pemco Corporation ....D...... 276 326-2611
  Bluefield *(G-1872)*

Piccadilly Circuits ....G...... 703 860-5426
  Reston *(G-10925)*

Pogotec Inc ....G...... 904 501-5309
  Roanoke *(G-11988)*

Printed Circuits International ....G...... 804 737-7979
  Highland Springs *(G-6855)*

▲ Prufrex USA Inc ....G...... 757 963-5400
  Virginia Beach *(G-14746)*

Qinetiq Inc ....E...... 540 658-2720
  Lorton *(G-7523)*

Qinetiq Inc ....G...... 804 436-9000
  Kilmarnock *(G-7075)*

Qinetiq Inc ....E...... 540 658-2720
  Lorton *(G-7524)*

Rack 10 Solar LLC ....G...... 703 996-4082
  Round Hill *(G-12386)*

Radio Reconnaissance Tech Inc ....G...... 540 752-7448
  Fredericksburg *(G-5352)*

Retarded Mobile Sound & Vision ....G...... 804 437-7633
  Richmond *(G-11733)*

Ronart Associates ....G...... 703 362-5373
  Lorton *(G-7527)*

S K Circuits Inc ....G...... 703 376-8718
  Fairfax *(G-4547)*

Seaguard International LLC ....G...... 484 747-0299
  Suffolk *(G-13761)*

Senseware ....G...... 703 975-2919
  Centreville *(G-2339)*

Software Dfined Dvcs Group LLC ....G...... 540 623-7175
  Stafford *(G-13192)*

Steep LLC ....G...... 571 271-5690
  Mc Lean *(G-8559)*

Stevens Switch LLC ....G...... 703 838-0686
  Alexandria *(G-356)*

Sunrise Circuits LLC ....G...... 703 719-9324
  Alexandria *(G-591)*

Tactical Dployment Systems LLC ....G...... 804 672-8426
  Richmond *(G-11405)*

Taskill Technologies LLC ....G...... 757 277-5557
  Williamsburg *(G-15322)*

Techniservices Inc ....G...... 804 275-9207
  North Chesterfield *(G-9999)*

Tidewater Prof Contrs LLC ....G...... 757 605-1040
  Virginia Beach *(G-14876)*

Tyler JSun Global LLC ....G...... 407 221-6135
  Stafford *(G-13206)*

Venomous Scents & Novelties ....G...... 434 660-1164
  Lynchburg *(G-7832)*

Vicious Creations LLC ....G...... 256 479-7689
  Hampton *(G-6262)*

Virginia Controls Inc ....E...... 804 225-5530
  Richmond *(G-11811)*

Virginia Semiconductor Inc ....E...... 540 373-2900
  Fredericksburg *(G-5233)*

Virginia Tek Inc ....F...... 703 391-8877
  Reston *(G-10986)*

Xp Power ....G...... 540 552-0432
  Blacksburg *(G-1808)*

3691 Storage Batteries

▲ Ashlawn Energy LLC ....G...... 703 461-3600
  Springfield *(G-12952)*

Atomized Pdts Group Chspake In ...F...... 757 793-2922
  Chesapeake *(G-2988)*

◆ Bmz Usa Inc ....F...... 757 821-8494
  Virginia Beach *(G-14290)*

East Penn Manufacturing Co ....G...... 540 980-1174
  Pulaski *(G-10635)*

East Penn Manufacturing Co ....E...... 804 798-1771
  Ashland *(G-1407)*

Encell Tech ....G...... 434 202-8370
  Charlottesville *(G-2625)*

First Responder Systems LLC ....G...... 757 410-0353
  Chesapeake *(G-3101)*

Flexel LLC ....F...... 301 314-1004
  Falls Church *(G-4793)*

Integer Holdings Corporation ....B...... 540 389-7860
  Salem *(G-12521)*

Katam Group LLC ....G...... 703 927-6268
  Ashburn *(G-1301)*

Nano Solutions Inc ....G...... 703 481-3321
  Herndon *(G-6749)*

3692 Primary Batteries: Dry & Wet

Integer Holdings Corporation ....B...... 540 389-7860
  Salem *(G-12521)*

3694 Electrical Eqpt For Internal Combustion Engines

1a Smart Start LLC ....G...... 434 336-1202
  Emporia *(G-4351)*

1st Choice Accessories LLC ....G...... 410 615-1578
  Sterling *(G-13336)*

A 1 Smart Start Inc ....G...... 276 644-3045
  Bristol *(G-1963)*

Aavera Engineering LLc ....G...... 434 922-7525
  Monroe *(G-8986)*

Alcolock Va Inc ....G...... 804 515-0022
  Henrico *(G-6472)*

Atlantic Research Corporation ....C...... 540 854-2000
  Culpeper *(G-3869)*

▲ Atlantic Research Corporation ....A...... 703 754-5000
  Gainesville *(G-5571)*

Autoinstruments Corp ....G...... 276 647-5550
  Martinsville *(G-8268)*

Draeger Safety Diagnostics Inc ......G...... 757 819-7471
  Chesapeake *(G-3074)*

Draeger Safety Diagnostics Inc ......G...... 804 768-4294
  Chester *(G-3407)*

Eastern Shore Rebuilders ....G...... 757 709-1250
  Painter *(G-10240)*

Edge McS LLC ....G...... 804 379-6772
  Midlothian *(G-8813)*

Eldor Auto Powertrain USA LLC ......C...... 540 855-1021
  Daleville *(G-3943)*

Electromotive Inc ....E...... 703 331-0100
  Manassas *(G-8063)*

Exide Technologies LLC ....F...... 434 975-6001
  Charlottesville *(G-2629)*

Generator Interlock Tech LLC ....G...... 804 726-2448
  Richmond *(G-11217)*

Grimes French Race Systems ....G...... 540 923-4541
  Madison *(G-7853)*

Infinity Resources Corporation ......G...... 830 822-4962
  Falls Church *(G-4919)*

Life Safer ....G...... 540 375-4145
  Salem *(G-12531)*

Lifesafer ....G...... 571 379-5575
  Manassas *(G-7964)*

Lifesafer Inc ....G...... 757 595-8800
  Newport News *(G-9283)*

Mechanx Corp ....G...... 703 698-7680
  Falls Church *(G-4828)*

▼ Mg Corp ....A...... 757 468-6000
  Virginia Beach *(G-14648)*

Nuline ....G...... 757 425-3213
  Virginia Beach *(G-14688)*

Potomac Altrntor Btry Spclists ....G...... 804 224-2384
  Colonial Beach *(G-3726)*

Research Service Bureau LLC ....G...... 703 593-7507
  Herndon *(G-6787)*

Sanskey LLC ....G...... 703 454-0703
  Ashburn *(G-1331)*

Smart Start ....G...... 571 267-7140
  Sterling *(G-13511)*

Smart Start Inc ....G...... 434 392-3334
  Farmville *(G-4957)*

Smart Start Inc ....G...... 276 223-1006
  Wytheville *(G-15913)*

◆ World Wide Automotive LLC ......E...... 540 667-9100
  Winchester *(G-15518)*

3695 Recording Media

3s Group Inc ....F...... 703 281-5015
  Vienna *(G-14001)*

Atlantic Quality Design Inc ....G...... 540 966-4356
  Fincastle *(G-4992)*

Blockmaster Security Inc ....D...... 703 788-6809
  Herndon *(G-6626)*

Buckeyes Meadow LLC ....G...... 703 535-6868
  Alexandria *(G-155)*

Dsd Laboratories Inc ....F...... 703 904-4384
  Reston *(G-10844)*

Earth Communications Corp ....G...... 434 973-7277
  Charlottesville *(G-2621)*

Education Online ....F...... 571 242-6986
  Leesburg *(G-7263)*

Eiw Group ....G...... 804 677-6214
  Petersburg *(G-10318)*

Fancy Media Co Inc ....G...... 757 638-7101
  Suffolk *(G-13706)*

Frontier Systems LLC ....G...... 314 221-2831
  Great Falls *(G-5956)*

Lightspeed Infrared LLC ....G...... 540 875-6796
  Bedford *(G-1643)*

Mark Pearson ....G...... 703 648-2568
  Oakton *(G-10157)*

Netunity Software LLC ....F...... 757 744-0147
  Virginia Beach *(G-14677)*

One Mile Up Inc ....G...... 703 642-1177
  Annandale *(G-777)*

Preferred Professional Svcs ....G...... 703 803-3563
  Fairfax *(G-4661)*

▲ Sanjar Media LLC ....G...... 703 901-7680
  Woodbridge *(G-15803)*

Sura Solutions Inc ....G...... 703 973-1939
  Leesburg *(G-7356)*

S
I
C

Ta Technical Services LLC ....G...... 540 429-5977
  Fredericksburg *(G-5374)*

Trustedcom LLC ....G...... 440 725-1115
  Herndon *(G-6833)*

Vena Portae Inc ....G...... 703 899-9500
  Ashburn *(G-1348)*

Windrose Media LLC ....G...... 703 464-1274
  Reston *(G-10991)*

3699 Electrical Machinery, Eqpt & Splys, NEC

Adam N Robinson ....G...... 540 489-1513
  Rocky Mount *(G-12310)*

Advanced Graphics Tech Llc ....G...... 804 796-3399
  Chesterfield *(G-3473)*

Advanced Leading Solutions Inc ....G...... 703 447-3876
  Centreville *(G-2289)*

Aero Training Center ....G...... 757 838-6570
  Hampton *(G-6074)*

Affordable Audio Rental ....G...... 804 305-6664
  North Chesterfield *(G-9807)*

Alan Forney Jr ....G...... 540 323-1666
  Winchester *(G-15374)*

All About Security Inc ....G...... 757 887-6700
  Newport News *(G-9161)*

Alliance In-Home Care LLC ....G...... 703 825-1067
  Falls Church *(G-4744)*

Anixter Inc ....G...... 757 460-9718
  Virginia Beach *(G-14229)*

Aretec Inc ....E...... 703 539-8801
  Fairfax *(G-4596)*

Azz Inc ....E...... 276 466-5558
  Bristol *(G-2007)*

◆ Bae Systems Holdings Inc ....B...... 571 461-6000
  Falls Church *(G-4755)*

Bagira Systems USA LLC ....G...... 571 278-1989
  Leesburg *(G-7226)*

Brady Contracting Service ....G...... 703 864-9207
  Manassas *(G-8042)*

Brantley T Jolly Jr ....G...... 703 447-6897
  Mc Lean *(G-8404)*

Bryan Vossekuil ....G...... 540 854-9067
  Mineral *(G-8942)*

C Thompson Enterprises All ....G...... 804 794-3407
  Midlothian *(G-8786)*

Cabling Systems Inc ....G...... 540 439-0101
  Sumerduck *(G-13790)*

Caleigh Systems Inc ....F...... 703 539-5004
  Annandale *(G-734)*

Carlen Controls Inc ....G...... 540 598-0714
  Roanoke *(G-11904)*

Checkpoint Systems Inc ....E...... 804 745-0010
  Richmond *(G-11526)*

Clean Power & Service LLC ....G...... 703 443-1717
  Leesburg *(G-7244)*

Cobehn Inc ....G...... 540 665-0707
  Winchester *(G-15404)*

Comsaco Inc ....E...... 757 466-9188
  Norfolk *(G-9501)*

Cooper Crouse-Hinds LLC ....F...... 540 983-1300
  Roanoke *(G-12072)*

Cornerstone Tech Solutions Inc ....G...... 540 477-2180
  Mount Jackson *(G-9068)*

Dataprivia Inc ....F...... 855 477-4842
  Lynchburg *(G-7694)*

Decor Lighting & Elec Co ....G...... 540 320-8382
  Pulaski *(G-10634)*

Decotec Inc ....G...... 434 589-0881
  Kents Store *(G-7038)*

Design Systems & Services Corp ....E...... 804 722-0396
  Petersburg *(G-10316)*

Door Systems Inc ....F...... 703 490-1800
  Woodbridge *(G-15685)*

Drive Square Inc ....G...... 617 762-4013
  Alexandria *(G-195)*

▲ Drs Leonardo Inc ....C...... 703 416-8000
  Arlington *(G-944)*

E C B Construction Company ....G...... 804 730-2057
  Mechanicsville *(G-8620)*

E L Schneider ....G...... 703 855-1925
  Chantilly *(G-2532)*

Electron Technologies Inc ....G...... 703 818-9400
  Chantilly *(G-2416)*

Exide Technologies ....G...... 678 566-9000
  Midlothian *(G-8816)*

Exide Technologies LLC ....E...... 434 975-6001
  Charlottesville *(G-2629)*

Extremeht2com ....G...... 804 665-6304
  Richmond *(G-11584)*

Federal Equipment Company ....G...... 757 493-0404
  Chesapeake *(G-3099)*

Freeport Technologies Inc ....F...... 571 262-0400
  Herndon *(G-6677)*

Fuelcor Development LLC ....G...... 703 740-0071
  Mc Lean *(G-8437)*

Hd Innovations ....G...... 757 420-0774
  Suffolk *(G-13718)*

I4c Innovations LLC ....E...... 703 488-6100
  Chantilly *(G-2439)*

Icaros Inc ....F...... 301 637-4324
  Chantilly *(G-4631)*

Isomet Corporation ....E...... 703 321-8301
  Manassas *(G-8087)*

Jk Electric Company ....G...... 703 378-7477
  Chantilly *(G-2450)*

K C Supply Corp ....G...... 540 222-2932
  Brandy Station *(G-1940)*

Kennesaw Holding Company ....G...... 603 866-6944
  Fairfax *(G-4643)*

Keo-Corp LLC ....G...... 636 515-5549
  New Kent *(G-9135)*

L & M Electric and Plbg LLC ....F...... 703 768-2222
  Alexandria *(G-512)*

L3harris Technologies Inc ....D...... 434 455-9390
  Forest *(G-5079)*

L3harris Technologies Inc ....G...... 434 455-6600
  Forest *(G-5080)*

Larsen Swen ....G...... 703 754-2592
  Bristow *(G-2059)*

Lightfactor LLC ....G...... 540 723-9600
  Winchester *(G-15552)*

▲ Linear Devices Corporation ....G...... 804 368-8428
  Ashland *(G-1453)*

Lockheed Martin Corporation ....G...... 703 367-2121
  Manassas *(G-7966)*

Mar-Bal Inc ....G...... 540 674-5320
  Dublin *(G-4165)*

Marelco Power Systems Inc ....D...... 517 546-6330
  Richmond *(G-11666)*

Mark Electric Inc ....G...... 804 749-4151
  Rockville *(G-12291)*

Masters Energy Inc ....E...... 281 816-9991
  Glen Allen *(G-5768)*

Medicor Technologies LLC ....G...... 804 616-8895
  Powhatan *(G-10558)*

▼ Mg Corp ....A...... 757 468-6000
  Virginia Beach *(G-14648)*

Moog Inc ....C...... 540 552-3011
  Blacksburg *(G-1768)*

Nettalon Security Systems Inc ....F...... 540 368-5290
  Fredericksburg *(G-5333)*

Nhance Technologies Inc ....F...... 434 582-6110
  Lynchburg *(G-7776)*

North Star Science & Tech LLC ....G...... 410 961-6692
  Oakton *(G-10160)*

Optical Air Data Systems LLC ....E...... 703 393-0754
  Manassas *(G-7986)*

▲ Pemco Corporation ....D...... 276 326-2611
  Bluefield *(G-1872)*

Phoenix Security Group Ltd ....G...... 703 323-4940
  Fairfax Station *(G-4721)*

Plasmera Technologies LLC ....G...... 540 353-5438
  Roanoke *(G-11987)*

Pn Labs ....G...... 804 938-1600
  Moseley *(G-9045)*

Privaris Inc ....G...... 703 592-1180
  Fairfax *(G-4662)*

Qrc LLC ....E...... 540 446-2270
  Fredericksburg *(G-5216)*

Rapiscan Systems Inc ....F...... 703 257-3429
  Manassas *(G-8139)*

Real Estate Consultants ....G...... 949 212-1366
  Fairfax *(G-4668)*

Refibot Inc ....G...... 703 989-2232
  Ashburn *(G-1330)*

Roseann Combs ....G...... 757 228-1795
  Norfolk *(G-9710)*

Safe Guard Security Service ....G...... 276 773-2866
  Independence *(G-6994)*

Schneder Elc It Mssion Crtcal ....B...... 703 968-0300
  Fairfax *(G-4549)*

Schneider Automation Inc ....G...... 804 271-7700
  North Chesterfield *(G-9972)*

Security Evolutions Inc ....G...... 703 953-4739
  Centreville *(G-2337)*

Solgreen Solutions LLC ....G...... 833 765-4733
  Alexandria *(G-588)*

Sparks Electric ....G...... 540 967-0436
  Louisa *(G-7568)*

Spec Ops Inc ....F...... 804 752-4790
  Ashland *(G-1495)*

Stanley Access Tech LLC ....G...... 804 598-0502
  Newport News *(G-9346)*

Stealthpath LLC ....G...... 571 888-6772
  Reston *(G-10965)*

Strdefense LLC ....G...... 703 460-9000
  Fairfax *(G-4562)*

System Innovations Inc ....F...... 540 373-2374
  Fredericksburg *(G-5491)*

Tactical Elec Military Sup LLC ....F...... 757 689-0476
  Virginia Beach *(G-14863)*

Tactical Micro ....G...... 540 907-0091
  Fredericksburg *(G-5375)*

Tag 5 Industries LLC ....G...... 703 647-0325
  Alexandria *(G-361)*

Tangers Electronics LLC ....G...... 757 215-5117
  Norfolk *(G-9740)*

Taurus Technologies Inc ....G...... 757 873-2700
  Yorktown *(G-15995)*

Tidewater Auto Elec Svcs II ....G...... 757 523-5656
  Chesapeake *(G-3337)*

TNT Laser Works LLC ....G...... 571 214-7517
  Leesburg *(G-7363)*

Uma Inc ....E...... 540 879-2040
  Dayton *(G-4067)*

Universal Powers Inc ....G...... 404 997-8732
  Richmond *(G-11799)*

US Dept of the Air Force ....G...... 703 808-0492
  Chantilly *(G-2515)*

Utrue Inc ....G...... 703 577-0309
  Vienna *(G-14148)*

Valley Construction Svcs LLC ....G...... 540 320-8545
  Blacksburg *(G-1802)*

Vigilent Inc ....G...... 202 550-9515
  Alexandria *(G-374)*

Watson Machine Corporation ....G...... 804 598-1500
  Powhatan *(G-10583)*

We Sullivan Co ....G...... 804 273-0905
  Richmond *(G-11444)*

▲ Wiretough Cylinders LLC ....G...... 276 644-9120
  Bristol *(G-2042)*

Woodworth Virginia LLC ....G...... 804 412-0206
  Ashland *(G-1513)*

Wythe Power Equipment Co Inc ....E...... 276 228-7371
  Wytheville *(G-15927)*

37 TRANSPORTATION EQUIPMENT

3711 Motor Vehicles & Car Bodies

Above Rim LLC ....G...... 703 407-9398
  Haymarket *(G-6411)*

Alan Thornhill ....G...... 703 892-5642
  Arlington *(G-848)*

◆ Alpine Armoring Inc ....F...... 703 471-0002
  Chantilly *(G-2368)*

Automotion Inc ....G...... 276 889-3715
  Lebanon *(G-7188)*

Bae Systems Tctcal Vhcl System ....E...... 571 461-6000
  Falls Church *(G-4759)*

◆ Bae Systems Tctcal Vhcl System ....G...... 571 461-6000
  Falls Church *(G-4760)*

Bennett Motorsports Inc ....G...... 434 845-2277
  Evington *(G-4374)*

Beverley M James Jr ....G...... 540 354-2300
  Roanoke *(G-11888)*

Bradley-Morris LLC ....E...... 678 419-4171
  Chesapeake *(G-3014)*

Bret Hamilton Enterprises ....G...... 804 598-8246
  Powhatan *(G-10535)*

Bubbles Wrecker Service ....G...... 434 845-2411
  Lynchburg *(G-7662)*

Buffalo Repair Shop ....G...... 434 374-5915
  Buffalo Junction *(G-2158)*

Charlie Ward ....G...... 276 768-7266
  Independence *(G-6979)*

Chc Transports LLC ....G...... 804 398-8686
  Chesterfield *(G-3485)*

Circle R Carrier Service Inc ....G...... 434 401-5950
  Amherst *(G-687)*

▼ Coach LLC ....E...... 757 925-2862
  Suffolk *(G-13684)*

Cw Security Solutions LLC ....G...... 540 929-8019
  Vinton *(G-14172)*

Daniel Cranford Recovery ....G...... 434 382-8409
  Lynchburg *(G-7692)*

Drumhellers Practical Choi ....G...... 540 949-0462
  Waynesboro *(G-15108)*

Dynamic Towing Eqp & Mfg Inc ....E...... 757 624-1360
  Norfolk *(G-9534)*

Edison 2 LLC ....F...... 434 806-2435
  Charlottesville *(G-2788)*

Emergency Vehicles Inc ....G...... 434 575-0509
South Boston *(G-12763)*

Force Protection Inc ....B...... 703 415-7520
Arlington *(G-973)*

Freedom Lodging LLC ....G...... 757 288-4514
Chesapeake *(G-3110)*

▲ General Dynamics Corporation ....C...... 703 876-3000
Reston *(G-10857)*

Glo 4 Itcom ....G...... 804 527-7608
Richmond *(G-11219)*

Goldbelt Wolf LLC ....D...... 703 584-8889
Alexandria *(G-470)*

Goss132 ....G...... 202 905-2380
Warrenton *(G-15021)*

Grede Radford LLC ....D...... 248 727-1800
Radford *(G-10715)*

▲ Greentech Automotive Corp ....F...... 703 666-9001
Sterling *(G-13415)*

Hamilton Safety Center Inc ....G...... 540 338-0500
Hamilton *(G-6059)*

Hawkins Glass Wholesalers LLC ....E...... 703 372-2990
Lorton *(G-7492)*

Iron Gate Vlntr Fire Dept Inc ....E...... 540 862-5700
Iron Gate *(G-6999)*

Jinks Motor Carriers Inc ....G...... 804 921-3121
Midlothian *(G-8838)*

Joco Transportations LLC ....G...... 804 398-8686
Chesterfield *(G-3508)*

Kovatch Mobile Equipment Corp ....E...... 540 982-3573
Roanoke *(G-12123)*

Life Evac ....E...... 804 652-0171
North Dinwiddie *(G-10058)*

Morgan Race Cars LLC Jeffrey ....G...... 540 907-1205
Fredericksburg *(G-5329)*

On The Road Transport LLC ....G...... 410 207-2592
Virginia Beach *(G-14697)*

Oshkosh Corporation ....G...... 703 525-8400
Arlington *(G-1091)*

Plunkett Business Group Inc ....E...... 540 343-3323
Vinton *(G-14180)*

Polaris Group Intl LLC ....G...... 757 636-8862
Virginia Beach *(G-14728)*

Portsmouth Fire Marshals Ofc ....G...... 757 393-8123
Portsmouth *(G-10470)*

Prfwmpro Fire Fighters ....G...... 703 393-2598
Manassas *(G-8133)*

Protolab Inc ....G...... 703 622-1889
Fredericksburg *(G-5214)*

R and N Express LLC ....G...... 804 909-3761
North Chesterfield *(G-9956)*

Rapid Manufacturing Inc ....E...... 804 598-7467
Powhatan *(G-10570)*

Signature Series - Usa LLC ....G...... 703 201-2543
Aldie *(G-112)*

▼ Specialty Vhcl Solutions LLC ....E...... 609 882-1900
Midlothian *(G-8907)*

TEAM Marketing ....G...... 703 405-0576
Manassas *(G-8165)*

Teen Scott Trucking Inc ....G...... 804 833-9403
Glen Allen *(G-5806)*

Tesla Inc ....G...... 703 761-4679
Vienna *(G-14140)*

Volvo Group North America LLC ....C...... 336 393-2000
Dublin *(G-4174)*

War Fighter Specialties LLC ....G...... 540 742-4187
Shenandoah *(G-12697)*

Wilbar Truck Equipment Inc ....E...... 757 397-3200
Portsmouth *(G-10502)*

Wisecarver Brothers Inc ....G...... 434 332-4511
Rustburg *(G-12447)*

Wm Industries Corp ....F...... 703 666-9001
Sterling *(G-13562)*

York Sportscars Inc ....G...... 804 798-5268
Ashland *(G-1514)*

3713 Truck & Bus Bodies

AMP Sales & Service LLC ....G...... 540 586-1021
Bedford *(G-1619)*

▼ Amthor International Inc ....D...... 845 778-5576
Gretna *(G-6002)*

Bellamy Mfg & Repr Co ....G...... 276 386-7273
Hiltons *(G-6904)*

Century Trucking LLC ....G...... 703 996-8585
Sterling *(G-13368)*

Fontaine Modification Company ....E...... 540 674-4638
Dublin *(G-4156)*

General Eqp Sls & Svc LLC ....G...... 434 579-7581
Virgilina *(G-14192)*

Gregorys Fleet Supply Corp ....E...... 757 490-1606
Virginia Beach *(G-14492)*

H & F Body & Cabinet Shop ....G...... 276 728-9404
Hillsville *(G-6894)*

LAw Hauling LLC ....G...... 757 774-3055
Virginia Beach *(G-14604)*

Leonard Alum Utlity Bldngs Inc ....G...... 434 792-8202
Danville *(G-4011)*

Marvin Ramirez-Aguilar ....G...... 703 241-4092
Arlington *(G-1054)*

Metalsa Structural Pdts Inc ....G...... 540 966-5370
Roanoke *(G-11964)*

▲ Metalsa-Roanoke Inc ....C...... 540 966-5300
Roanoke *(G-11965)*

Morgan Olson LLC ....G...... 269 659-0200
Ringgold *(G-11870)*

Phase II Truck Body Inc ....E...... 276 429-2026
Glade Spring *(G-5680)*

Polaris Group Intl LLC ....G...... 757 636-8862
Virginia Beach *(G-14728)*

Raleigh Mine and Indus Sup Inc ....E...... 276 322-3119
Bluefield *(G-1878)*

S&C Global Products LLC ....G...... 703 499-3635
Manassas *(G-7998)*

Virginia LP Truck Inc ....F...... 434 246-8257
Stony Creek *(G-13570)*

Volvo Group North America LLC ....G...... 336 393-2000
Dublin *(G-4174)*

Wilbar Truck Equipment Inc ....E...... 757 397-3200
Portsmouth *(G-10502)*

3714 Motor Vehicle Parts & Access

1a Smart Start ....G...... 703 330-1372
Manassas *(G-7908)*

Aerospace Techniques Inc ....D...... 860 347-1200
Virginia Beach *(G-14214)*

▼ Amthor International Inc ....D...... 845 778-5576
Gretna *(G-6002)*

ARS Manufacturing Inc ....C...... 757 460-2211
Virginia Beach *(G-14242)*

At Lab of America LLC ....G...... 681 207-9161
Stuart *(G-13605)*

Atkins Automotive Corp ....G...... 540 942-5157
Waynesboro *(G-15096)*

Atlantic Research Corporation ....C...... 540 854-2000
Culpeper *(G-3869)*

Atomizer Fuel Systems Inc ....G...... 757 250-3773
Toano *(G-13857)*

Betterbilt Solutions LLC ....G...... 540 324-9117
Staunton *(G-13244)*

Bg Solutions LLC ....G...... 703 623-4846
Vienna *(G-14016)*

Black Business Today Inc ....G...... 804 528-7407
Richmond *(G-11505)*

Brake Connections ....G...... 540 247-9000
Gore *(G-5920)*

Bridgeview Full Svc ....G...... 434 575-6800
South Boston *(G-12753)*

C B R Engine Service ....G...... 276 686-5198
Rural Retreat *(G-12419)*

▼ Carlisle Indstrl Brke & Frctn ....F...... 814 486-1119
Charlottesville *(G-2605)*

▲ Castello 1935 Inc ....G...... 540 464-5275
Buchanan *(G-2118)*

▲ Cline Automotive Inc ....F...... 804 271-9107
North Chesterfield *(G-9846)*

Colonial Chevrolet Company LP ....B...... 757 455-4500
Norfolk *(G-9493)*

Continental Auto Systems Inc ....D...... 757 890-4900
Newport News *(G-9204)*

Continental Auto Systems Inc ....C...... 540 825-4100
Culpeper *(G-3880)*

Continental Teves ....G...... 540 825-4100
Culpeper *(G-3881)*

Crenshaw of Richmond Inc ....D...... 804 231-6241
Richmond *(G-11546)*

Custom Camshaft Company Inc ....G...... 276 666-6767
Martinsville *(G-8278)*

Dana Auto Systems Group LLC ....E...... 757 638-2656
Suffolk *(G-13693)*

Delphi Inc ....G...... 703 908-0258
Arlington *(G-935)*

Double B Trailers ....G...... 540 586-0651
Goode *(G-5889)*

Driving Aids Development Corp ....G...... 703 938-6435
Stephens City *(G-13315)*

▲ Dynax America Corporation ....A...... 540 966-6010
Roanoke *(G-11917)*

E Components International ....G...... 804 462-5679
Williamsburg *(G-15236)*

▲ East Coast Brake Rbldrs Corp ....F...... 757 466-1308
Norfolk *(G-9537)*

Express Racing & Machine ....G...... 804 521-7891
North Chesterfield *(G-9869)*

F W Baird General Contractor ....C...... 434 724-4499
Chatham *(G-2928)*

▲ Fdp Virginia Inc ....C...... 804 443-5356
Tappahannock *(G-13816)*

Feather Carbon LLC ....G...... 757 630-6759
Suffolk *(G-13707)*

Federal-Mogul Powertrain LLC ....B...... 540 557-3300
Blacksburg *(G-1737)*

Federal-Mogul Products Inc ....B...... 540 662-3871
Winchester *(G-15542)*

Frenchs Auto Parts Inc ....G...... 540 740-3676
New Market *(G-9142)*

Garys Classic Car Parts ....G...... 757 925-0546
Suffolk *(G-13715)*

George H Pollok Jr ....G...... 336 540-8870
Union Hall *(G-13959)*

▲ Global Safety Textiles LLC ....D...... 434 447-7629
South Hill *(G-12851)*

Gonmf ....G...... 844 763-7250
Woodbridge *(G-15711)*

Grede Radford LLC ....D...... 248 727-1800
Radford *(G-10715)*

Grimes French Race Systems ....G...... 540 923-4541
Madison *(G-7853)*

Hampton Roads Processors Inc ....G...... 757 285-8811
Portsmouth *(G-10440)*

Hesss Body Shop ....G...... 276 395-7808
Coeburn *(G-3699)*

High Ground Partners LLC ....G...... 434 944-8254
Lynchburg *(G-7733)*

Hunter Defense Tech Inc ....F...... 540 479-8100
Fredericksburg *(G-5300)*

IMS Gear Holding Inc ....G...... 757 468-8810
Virginia Beach *(G-14542)*

▲ IMS Gear Virginia LLC ....B...... 757 468-8810
Virginia Beach *(G-14543)*

Joe London Training LLC ....G...... 540 272-9205
Culpeper *(G-3901)*

▲ Lear Corp Strasburg ....G...... 540 465-6244
Strasburg *(G-13587)*

Leonard Alum Utlity Bldngs Inc ....G...... 434 792-8202
Danville *(G-4011)*

Lifelineusa ....G...... 540 251-2724
Dublin *(G-4164)*

Longwood Elastomers Inc ....C...... 276 228-5406
Wytheville *(G-15898)*

Miata Realm LLC ....G...... 724 612-1029
Fairfax *(G-4510)*

Momentum Usa Inc ....C...... 804 329-3000
Richmond *(G-11681)*

Muncie Power Products Inc ....C...... 804 275-6724
North Chesterfield *(G-9936)*

Nitto Inc ....G...... 757 436-5540
Chesapeake *(G-3219)*

Performance Counts Automotive ....G...... 434 392-3391
Farmville *(G-4955)*

Performance Cstm Cabinets LLC ....G...... 804 382-3870
Powhatan *(G-10563)*

Precision Components Inc ....G...... 540 297-1853
Huddleston *(G-6957)*

R H Sheppard Co Inc ....F...... 276 228-4000
Wytheville *(G-15907)*

Rector Visitors of The Univ VA ....E...... 434 296-7288
Charlottesville *(G-2682)*

Refuge Golf & Bumper Boats ....G...... 757 336-5420
Chincoteague *(G-3564)*

Rhenus Automotive Salem LLC ....G...... 270 282-2100
Salem *(G-12561)*

Rye Valley Oil Inc ....G...... 276 677-3750
Sugar Grove *(G-13788)*

Schrader-Altavista ....G...... 434 369-8816
Altavista *(G-640)*

◆ Schrader-Bridgeport Intl Inc ....A...... 434 369-4741
Altavista *(G-641)*

▲ SKF Lbrication Systems USA Inc ......D...... 757 951-0370
Hampton *(G-6239)*

▲ Somic America Inc ....D...... 276 228-4307
Wytheville *(G-15914)*

Stealth Dump Trucks Inc ....G...... 757 890-4888
Yorktown *(G-15994)*

Stuart Mathews Engineering ....G...... 804 779-2976
Mechanicsville *(G-8684)*

Tech of Southwest Virginia ....G...... 276 496-5393
Saltville *(G-12593)*

Tele Controls Inc ....G...... 571 490-4500
Arlington *(G-1185)*

Tenneco Automotive Oper Co Inc ....A...... 540 432-3545
Harrisonburg *(G-6379)*

SIC

Tenneco Automotive Oper Co Inc ....A 540 432-3752
Rockingham (G-12281)

Tenneco Automotive Oper Co Inc ....E 540 434-2461
Harrisonburg (G-6380)

Tenneco Inc ....G 540 557-3312
Blacksburg (G-1798)

▲ Tidewater Auto & Indus Mch Inc ....G 757 855-5091
Virginia Beach (G-14872)

▲ Titan Wheel Corp Virginia ....D 276 496-5121
Saltville (G-12594)

Todd Huffman Installs LLC ....G 540 271-4221
Mount Crawford (G-9060)

Turbo Lab ....G 276 952-5997
Stuart (G-13637)

Usui International Corporation ....B 757 558-7300
Chesapeake (G-3356)

Valeo North America Inc ....C 757 827-0310
Hampton (G-6259)

Virginia Drveline Differential ....G 276 227-0299
Wytheville (G-15921)

Virginia Wheel & Rim Inc ....G 804 526-9868
Colonial Heights (G-3751)

Vitesco Technologies Usa LLC ....A 757 875-7000
Newport News (G-9376)

Windshield RPS By Ralph Smiley ....G 804 690-7517
Mechanicsville (G-8699)

Windshield Wizard ....G 757 714-1642
Norfolk (G-9795)

Wolverine Advanced Mtls LLC ....E 540 552-7674
Blacksburg (G-1806)

Wood Mark T A Augusta Gla ....G 540 885-5038
Staunton (G-13308)

◆ World Wide Automotive LLC ....E 540 667-9100
Winchester (G-15518)

York Sportscars Inc ....G 804 798-5268
Ashland (G-1514)

ZF Active Safety & Elec US LLC ....B 276 783-1157
Atkins (G-1523)

ZF Active Safety & Elec US LLC ....C 276 783-1990
Atkins (G-1524)

3715 Truck Trailers

Brandon Enterprises ....G 804 895-3338
South Prince George (G-12865)

BSI Express ....G 804 443-7134
Warsaw (G-15061)

Claude Cofer ....G 540 330-9921
Bedford (G-1631)

Coe & Co Inc ....G 757 497-7709
Virginia Beach (G-14351)

Dalton Enterprises Inc ....D 276 686-9178
Rural Retreat (G-12422)

Hillcrest Transportation Inc ....E 804 861-1100
North Dinwiddie (G-10053)

Holmes Enterprises Inc ....F 804 798-9201
Ashland (G-1434)

Imperial Group Mfg Inc ....C 540 674-1306
Dublin (G-4159)

K O Stith Hauling LLC ....G 804 895-4617
Disputanta (G-4111)

Kandd Transportation Service ....G 434 298-7716
Danville (G-4009)

Lawrence Trlr & Trck Eqp Inc ....F 800 296-6009
Ashland (G-1451)

Miti-Gait LLC ....G 434 738-8632
Clarksville (G-3634)

Mobile Customs LLC ....G 757 903-5092
Manassas (G-8110)

Noke Truck LLC ....G 540 266-0045
Roanoke (G-12142)

Road & Rail Repair Inc ....G 757 558-1920
Chesapeake (G-3271)

S&M Trucking Inc ....G 540 842-1378
Fredericksburg (G-5358)

Trailer Buff Inc ....G 434 361-2500
Afton (G-91)

Two Peppers Transportation LLC ....G 757 761-6674
Yorktown (G-15997)

Utility Trailer Mfg Co ....A 276 783-8800
Atkins (G-1522)

Virginia Truck Trailer LL ....G 804 784-3485
Rockville (G-12302)

Winchester Truck Repair LLC ....G 540 398-7995
Winchester (G-15514)

Wpd Inc ....G 757 859-9498
Ivor (G-7007)

3716 Motor Homes

Featherlite Coaches Inc ....E 757 923-3374
Suffolk (G-13708)

Virginia Custom Coach Builders ....G 540 381-0609
Christiansburg (G-3616)

Virtual Realty ....G 757 718-2633
Quinton (G-10701)

3721 Aircraft

Advanced Aircraft Company LLC ....G 757 325-6712
Hampton (G-6071)

Aerial and Aquatic Robotics ....G 757 932-0909
Norfolk (G-9427)

Aerojet ....G 703 247-2907
Arlington (G-842)

Aerospace & Technology ....G 757 864-7227
Hampton (G-6075)

Aery Aviation LLC ....F 757 271-1600
Newport News (G-9160)

Agustawestland North Amer Inc ....F 703 373-8000
Arlington (G-845)

Agustawestlandbell LLC ....G 703 373-1613
Reston (G-10781)

Air Wisonsin Airlines Corp ....G 757 853-8215
Norfolk (G-9429)

Airbus A300 Leasing Inc ....G 703 834-3400
Herndon (G-6605)

▲ Airbus Americas Inc ....D 703 834-3400
Herndon (G-6606)

▲ Airbus Def Space Holdings Inc ....A 703 466-5600
Herndon (G-6607)

Airbus Group Inc ....E 703 466-5600
Herndon (G-6608)

Airbus Group Supply & Svcs Inc ....F 703 858-2235
Ashburn (G-1240)

Alt Services Inc ....G 757 806-1341
Hampton (G-6081)

Angel Wings Drone Services LLC ....G 540 763-2630
Riner (G-11860)

Autonomous Flight Tech Inc ....G 540 314-8866
Salem (G-12478)

Avigators Incorporated ....G 703 298-6319
Centreville (G-2293)

◆ Bae Systems Land Armaments Inc ....E 571 461-6000
Falls Church (G-4756)

Battlespace Global LLC ....G 703 413-0556
Arlington (G-876)

Bee Systems LLC ....F 760 484-6194
Aldie (G-101)

Bell Textron Inc ....G 817 280-2346
Arlington (G-878)

Big Sky Drone Services LLC ....G 804 378-2970
Powhatan (G-10533)

Blacksky Aerospace LLC ....G 202 500-3743
Arlington (G-884)

Blue Ridge Scientific LLC ....G 540 631-0356
Front Royal (G-5524)

Boeing Company ....B 571 814-4103
Reston (G-10811)

Boeing Company ....G 703 808-2718
Woodbridge (G-15661)

Boeing Company ....A 757 461-5206
Norfolk (G-9469)

Boeing Company ....G 703 413-3407
Arlington (G-889)

Boeing Company ....B 703 961-8174
Chantilly (G-2378)

Boeing Company ....E 703 808-2737
Chantilly (G-2379)

Boeing Company ....A 703 923-4000
Springfield (G-12966)

Calspan Systems Corporation ....C 757 873-1344
Newport News (G-9189)

Cavalry Aerospace LLC ....G 757 995-2029
Chesapeake (G-3027)

Christopher K Reddersen ....G 703 232-6691
Warrenton (G-14987)

Combat Bound LLC ....G 757 343-3399
Suffolk (G-13685)

David Birkenstock ....G 703 343-5718
Herndon (G-6653)

Dean Delaware LLC ....G 703 802-6231
Sterling (G-13383)

Drone Safety LLC ....G 703 589-6738
Alexandria (G-450)

Drone Tier Systems Intl LLC ....G 757 450-7825
Virginia Beach (G-14414)

Dronechakra Inc ....G 540 420-7394
Sterling (G-13390)

Drones Club of Virginia LLC ....G 540 324-8180
Staunton (G-13254)

Eagle Aerospace ....G 540 965-9022
Covington (G-3787)

Eagle Aviation Tech LLC ....D 757 224-6269
Newport News (G-9219)

Electraaero Inc ....G 540 660-2917
Falls Church (G-4910)

Eodrones LLC ....G 703 856-8400
Warrenton (G-15004)

Fredericks Aircraft Company ....G 757 727-3326
Hampton (G-6153)

General Cryo Corporation ....G 703 405-9442
Springfield (G-13009)

▲ General Dynamics Corporation ....C 703 876-3000
Reston (G-10857)

Gibson Sewer Water ....G 540 636-1131
Chester Gap (G-3470)

Gki Aerospace LLC ....G 703 451-4562
Springfield (G-13010)

Golden Section LLC ....G 540 315-4756
Blacksburg (G-1742)

Gulfstream Aerospace Corp ....A 301 967-9767
Falls Church (G-4801)

Gulfstream Aerospace Corp ....G 912 965-3000
Falls Church (G-4802)

Gulfstream Aerospace Corp ....G 540 722-0347
Winchester (G-15422)

Gulfstream Aerospace Corp GA ....G 301 967-9767
Falls Church (G-4803)

Gundlach Aerospace LLC ....G 703 303-0813
Fairfax Station (G-4712)

Hush Aerospace LLC ....G 703 629-6907
Virginia Beach (G-14534)

Hybrid Air Vehicles (us) Inc ....G 703 524-0026
Arlington (G-996)

Jlt Aerospace (north AM ....G 703 459-2380
Herndon (G-6717)

King Aviation ....G 540 439-8621
Midland (G-8760)

Lockheed Martin Corporation ....B 757 484-5789
Chesapeake (G-3185)

Lockheed Martin Corporation ....G 757 935-9479
Suffolk (G-13732)

Magnus Aircraft Incorporated ....G 830 998-7270
Ashburn (G-1314)

Mydrone4hire LLC ....G 540 491-4860
Blue Ridge (G-1853)

Nextflight Jets LLC ....G 703 392-6500
Reston (G-10908)

◆ Northrop Grumman Systems Corp .....B 703 280-2900
Falls Church (G-4845)

Northrop Grumman Systems Corp ....B 703 556-1144
Mc Lean (G-8517)

Northrop Grumman Systems Corp ....B 703 968-1000
Herndon (G-6758)

Pae Avation Technical Svcs LLC ....G 703 717-6000
Arlington (G-1095)

Pae Avation Technical Svcs LLC ....G 864 458-3272
Arlington (G-1096)

Paper Air Force Company ....G 703 730-2150
Woodbridge (G-15773)

Paragon Aviation Services ....G 703 787-8800
Herndon (G-6767)

Pe Crew LLC ....G 540 839-5999
Hot Springs (G-6949)

Pellegrino Aerospace LLC ....G 571 431-7011
Arlington (G-1103)

Preston Aerospace Inc ....G 540 675-3474
Huntly (G-6965)

Raytheon Company ....B 757 421-8319
Chesapeake (G-3259)

Raytheon Technologies Corp ....G 757 838-7980
Hampton (G-6225)

Shenandoah Drones LLC ....G 540 421-3116
New Market (G-9148)

Shenandoah Valley Soaring Inc ....G 804 347-6848
Waynesboro (G-15139)

Silver Wings Inc ....G 703 533-3244
Arlington (G-1168)

Skm Aerospace LLC ....G 703 217-4221
Arlington (G-1170)

Skyboss Drones LLC ....G 434 509-5028
Forest (G-5093)

Springwood Airstrip ....G 540 473-2079
Buchanan (G-2128)

Summit Drones Inc ....G 724 961-9197
Quantico (G-10691)

Sydrus Aerospace LLC ....G 831 402-5286
Gainesville (G-5616)

Textron Inc ....G 757 874-8100
Newport News (G-9353)

◆ Titan II Inc ....D 757 380-2000
Newport News (G-9358)

Tk Aircraft LLC ....G 540 665-8113
  Winchester *(G-15490)*

Top Drone Video ....G 757 288-1774
  Chesapeake *(G-3344)*

Training Services Inc ....F 757 363-1800
  Chesapeake *(G-3349)*

UAS Technologies Inc ....G 703 822-4382
  Mc Lean *(G-8570)*

Unmanned Aerial Prop Systms ....G 757 325-6792
  Hampton *(G-6257)*

Vaero Inc ....G 540 344-1000
  Vinton *(G-14189)*

Vantage Point Drone LLC ....G 703 723-4586
  Ashburn *(G-1346)*

Vh Drones LLC ....G 804 938-9713
  Mechanicsville *(G-8692)*

Walberg Aerospace ....G 321 634-6349
  Hampton *(G-6267)*

Xtreme Adventures Inc ....G 757 615-4602
  Virginia Beach *(G-14950)*

Y2k Web Technologies ....G 757 490-7877
  Virginia Beach *(G-14951)*

Zenith Aerotech Inc ....G 434 202-7790
  Afton *(G-97)*

3724 Aircraft Engines & Engine Parts

Aerospace Techniques Inc ....D 860 347-1200
  Virginia Beach *(G-14214)*

Eagle Aviation Tech LLC ....D 757 224-6269
  Newport News *(G-9219)*

High Speed Tech Ventr LLC ....G 571 318-0997
  Williamsburg *(G-15254)*

Ho-Ho-Kus Incorporated ....D 206 552-4559
  North Chesterfield *(G-9887)*

Honeywell International Inc ....B 804 458-7649
  Hopewell *(G-6930)*

Honeywell International Inc ....A 804 518-2351
  Petersburg *(G-10324)*

Honeywell International Inc ....E 804 515-1500
  Richmond *(G-11241)*

Honeywell International Inc ....A 276 694-2408
  Stuart *(G-13617)*

Honeywell International Inc ....F 703 879-9951
  Herndon *(G-6703)*

Honeywell International Inc ....B 804 530-6352
  Chester *(G-3422)*

Honeywell International Inc ....E 703 626-8363
  Arlington *(G-993)*

Honeywell International Inc ....E 804 541-5618
  Hopewell *(G-6932)*

Honeywell International Inc ....G 703 437-7651
  Sterling *(G-13422)*

Honeywell Technology Solu ....G 703 551-1942
  Stafford *(G-13151)*

Jet Pac LLC ....G 804 334-5216
  Hopewell *(G-6936)*

Mikro Systems Inc ....E 434 244-6480
  Charlottesville *(G-2660)*

Pratt & Whitney Eng Svcs Inc ....G 757 838-7980
  Newport News *(G-9315)*

▲ Safran Usa Inc ....F 703 351-9898
  Alexandria *(G-334)*

Sapentia LLC ....G 703 269-7191
  Mc Lean *(G-8545)*

Uav Communications Inc ....E 757 271-3428
  Newport News *(G-9368)*

3728 Aircraft Parts & Eqpt, NEC

A & A Precision Machining LLC ....G 804 493-8416
  Montross *(G-9023)*

Aai Corporation ....A 410 666-1400
  Blackstone *(G-1809)*

▲ Aerial Machine & Tool Corp ....D 276 952-2006
  Meadows of Dan *(G-8590)*

Aero International LLC ....G 571 203-8360
  Alexandria *(G-121)*

Aerospace Techniques Inc ....D 860 347-1200
  Virginia Beach *(G-14214)*

Allied Aerospace Services LLC ....E 757 873-1344
  Newport News *(G-9164)*

Allied Aerospace Uav LLC ....G 757 873-1344
  Newport News *(G-9165)*

Appalachian Drone Servie LLC ....G 276 346-6350
  Dryden *(G-4144)*

Astronautics Corp of America ....G 571 707-8705
  Ashburn *(G-1244)*

▲ Aurora Flight Sciences Corp ....C 703 369-3633
  Manassas *(G-7916)*

Avenger LLC ....G 703 573-6445
  Springfield *(G-12956)*

Aviation Component Svcs Inc ....G 434 237-7077
  Lynchburg *(G-7646)*

▼ Bae Systems Inc ....C 571 461-6000
  Falls Church *(G-4754)*

◆ Bae Systems Holdings Inc ....B 571 461-6000
  Falls Church *(G-4755)*

Beechhurst Industries Inc ....G 703 334-6703
  Manassas Park *(G-8190)*

Bell Textron Inc ....G 817 280-2346
  Arlington *(G-878)*

Bjd Tel-Comm LLC ....G 703 858-2931
  Ashburn *(G-1247)*

Boeing Company ....C 703 465-3500
  Arlington *(G-888)*

Breeze-Eastern LLC ....G 973 602-1001
  Fredericksburg *(G-5175)*

Charlottesville Flight Center ....G 434 964-1474
  Charlottesville *(G-2607)*

Coastal Aerospace Inc ....G 757 787-3704
  Melfa *(G-8709)*

Combustion Technologies Inc ....G 434 432-1428
  Chatham *(G-2924)*

Curtiss-Wright Controls Inc ....E 703 779-7800
  Ashburn *(G-1265)*

D-Fend Inc ....G 703 728-4283
  Mc Lean *(G-8414)*

D-Star Engineering Corporation ....E 203 925-7630
  Ashburn *(G-1267)*

Defense Arnautical Support LLC ....G 703 309-9222
  Vienna *(G-14037)*

F3 Technologies LLC ....G 804 785-1017
  Mattaponi *(G-8358)*

Firstmark Corp ....F 724 759-2850
  Midlothian *(G-8818)*

General Dynamics Corp ....G 434 964-5301
  Charlottesville *(G-2637)*

General Dynamics Ots Cal Inc ....G 276 783-3121
  Marion *(G-8228)*

Glenmark Group LLC ....G 757 955-6850
  Chesapeake *(G-3121)*

Goodrich Corporation ....F 703 558-8230
  Arlington *(G-985)*

Hydro Systems USA Inc ....G 703 429-1024
  Sterling *(G-13424)*

▲ Interbyte ....G 703 825-8774
  Alexandria *(G-486)*

Interbyte Corp ....E 703 825-8774
  Alexandria *(G-487)*

Klaus Composites LLC ....G 443 995-8458
  Waterford *(G-15081)*

Kurt USA Prof Dog Tng ....G 252 509-4211
  Stafford *(G-13166)*

▲ Laurence Walter Aerospace Solu ....G 757 966-9578
  Chesapeake *(G-3178)*

Lockheed Martin Corporation ....B 757 935-9479
  Suffolk *(G-13732)*

Luminary Air Group LLC ....G 757 655-0705
  Melfa *(G-8711)*

Marks Garage ....G 540 498-3458
  Stafford *(G-13174)*

Matbock LLC ....G 757 828-6659
  Virginia Beach *(G-14639)*

Moog Inc ....G 716 652-2000
  Blacksburg *(G-1764)*

◆ Northrop Grumman Systems Corp ..B 703 280-2900
  Falls Church *(G-4845)*

Octopus Arospc Solutions LLC ....G 866 244-4500
  New Market *(G-9146)*

Orbital Sciences LLC ....B 703 406-5000
  Dulles *(G-4218)*

Potomac Solutions Incorporated ....G 703 888-1762
  Alexandria *(G-313)*

Protective Solutions Inc ....D 703 435-1115
  Dulles *(G-4220)*

Raytheon Company ....G 972 272-0515
  Dulles *(G-4224)*

Robert H Giles Jr ....G 540 808-6334
  Blacksburg *(G-1785)*

Robert R Kline ....G 540 454-7003
  Round Hill *(G-12387)*

▲ Rolls-Royce Crosspointe LLC ....F 877 787-6247
  Prince George *(G-10606)*

Sky Dynamics Corporation ....G 540 297-6754
  Moneta *(G-8978)*

Textron Ground Support Eqp Inc ....G 703 572-5340
  Dulles *(G-4229)*

Tia-The Richards Corp ....D 703 471-8600
  Sterling *(G-13533)*

◆ Titan II Inc ....D 757 380-2000
  Newport News *(G-9358)*

VSE Aviation Inc ....E 703 328-4600
  Alexandria *(G-606)*

Zimbro Aerial Drone Integratio ....G 757 408-6864
  Wicomico Church *(G-15197)*

3731 Shipbuilding & Repairing

Advance Technology Inc ....D 757 223-6566
  Newport News *(G-9158)*

Advanced Integrated Tech LLC ....D 757 416-7407
  Norfolk *(G-9423)*

Alliance Technical Svcs Inc ....D 757 628-9500
  Norfolk *(G-9435)*

Amee Bay LLC ....G 703 365-0450
  Manassas *(G-8024)*

Amee Bay LLC ....D 757 217-2720
  Chesapeake *(G-2963)*

American Maritime Holdings Inc ....G 757 233-9055
  Chesapeake *(G-2969)*

American Maritime Holdings Inc ....G 757 545-4013
  Chesapeake *(G-2970)*

American Maritime Holdings Inc ....E 757 961-9311
  Chesapeake *(G-2971)*

Aviation & Maritime Support SE ....G 757 995-2029
  Chesapeake *(G-2989)*

B&B Insulation LLC ....G 757 904-0884
  Virginia Beach *(G-14254)*

Back Creek Towing & Salvage ....G 757 898-5338
  Seaford *(G-12672)*

◆ Bae Systems Nrfolk Ship Repr I ....A 757 494-4000
  Norfolk *(G-9452)*

Bae Systems Ship Repair Inc ....A 757 494-4000
  Norfolk *(G-9453)*

Bainbridge Recycling Inc ....G 757 472-4142
  Chesapeake *(G-2993)*

Bath Iron Works Corporation ....F 757 855-4182
  Norfolk *(G-9456)*

Bering Sea Environmental LLC ....G 757 223-1446
  Newport News *(G-9177)*

Bird Fabrication LLC ....G 225 614-0985
  Virginia Beach *(G-14281)*

Bird Fabrication LLC ....G 225 614-0985
  Virginia Beach *(G-14282)*

Bonze Associates LLC ....G 540 497-2964
  Warrenton *(G-14983)*

CA Jones Inc ....G 757 595-0005
  Newport News *(G-9188)*

Camber Corporation ....G 540 720-6294
  Fredericksburg *(G-5407)*

Capps Boatworks Inc ....G 757 496-0311
  Virginia Beach *(G-14317)*

CFS-Kbr Mrnas Support Svcs LLC ....E 202 261-1900
  Alexandria *(G-164)*

Chesapeake Bay Fishing Co LLC ....F 804 438-6050
  Weems *(G-15150)*

Clean Way Services LLC ....E 757 606-1840
  Portsmouth *(G-10408)*

▲ Colonnas Ship Yard Inc ....A 757 545-2414
  Norfolk *(G-9495)*

Colonnas Ship Yard Inc ....B 757 545-5311
  Norfolk *(G-9496)*

Colonnas Ship Yard Inc ....A 757 545-2414
  Norfolk *(G-9497)*

Colonnas Shipyard ....G 757 962-0508
  Norfolk *(G-9498)*

Conglobal Industries LLC ....E 757 487-5100
  Chesapeake *(G-3051)*

Cova Ship Repair Inc ....F 757 390-2177
  Norfolk *(G-9508)*

D W Boyd Corporation ....G 757 423-2268
  Norfolk *(G-9514)*

Darr Maritime Services ....G 757 631-0022
  Virginia Beach *(G-14387)*

Dlp Enterprises Inc ....E 757 420-5886
  Chesapeake *(G-3068)*

Dominion Comfort Solutions LLC ....G 804 501-6429
  Sandston *(G-12611)*

Dominion Wldg Fabrication Inc ....G 757 692-2002
  Virginia Beach *(G-14410)*

East Cast Repr Fabrication LLC ....C 757 455-9600
  Norfolk *(G-9535)*

East Cast Repr Fabrication LLC ....D 757 455-9600
  Norfolk *(G-9536)*

Ecm Maritime Services ....G 540 400-6412
  Roanoke *(G-11918)*

Elco Company ....G 703 876-3000
  Falls Church *(G-4787)*

Fairlead Boatworks Inc ....G 757 247-0101
  Newport News *(G-9223)*

Fairlead Integrated LLC ....C 757 384-1957
  Portsmouth *(G-10425)*

SIC

Fairlead Integrated LLC ....D...... 757 606-2034
Portsmouth (G-10426)
Fairlead Intgrted Pwr Cntrls L ....F 757 384-1957
Portsmouth (G-10427)
Fairlead Marine Inc ....G...... 757 606-2034
Portsmouth (G-10428)
Fairlead Prcsion Mfg Intgrtion ....G...... 757 384-1957
Portsmouth (G-10429)
General Dynamics Corporation ....E...... 703 221-1009
Woodbridge (G-15709)
▲ General Dynamics Corporation ....C...... 703 876-3000
Reston (G-10857)
General Dynamics Info Tech Inc ....E...... 540 663-1000
King George (G-7091)
General Dynamics Nassco ....G...... 757 215-2004
Chesapeake (G-3117)
General Dynmics Wrldwide Hldng ......G...... 703 876-3000
Reston (G-10858)
Gillie Boatworks ....G...... 804 370-4825
Deltaville (G-4079)
Global Marine Services LLC ....G...... 757 284-9284
Virginia Beach (G-14484)
Global Services Intl LLC ....G...... 757 535-2394
Chesapeake (G-3122)
Helios Acquisition LLC ....G...... 757 545-6400
Norfolk (G-9579)
Hii Unmnned Mrtime Systems Inc .....E...... 757 688-5672
Newport News (G-9247)
▲ Huntington Ingalls Inc ....B...... 757 380-2000
Newport News (G-9249)
Huntington Ingalls Inc ....A...... 757 380-4982
Hampton (G-6171)
Huntington Ingalls Inc ....G...... 757 688-9832
Virginia Beach (G-14533)
Huntington Ingalls Inc ....G...... 757 380-2000
Newport News (G-9250)
Huntington Ingalls Inc ....F...... 757 440-5390
Norfolk (G-9585)
Huntington Ingalls Inc ....A...... 757 688-1411
Newport News (G-9251)
Huntington Ingalls Inds Inc ....F...... 757 380-2000
Hampton (G-6172)
Huntington Ingalls Inds Inc ....D...... 757 380-7053
Newport News (G-9252)
Huntington Ingalls Inds Inc ....F...... 757 380-2000
Newport News (G-9253)
Huntington Ingalls Inds Inc ....B...... 757 380-2000
Newport News (G-9254)
I Patriot Shipping Corp ....G...... 703 876-3000
Falls Church (G-4807)
ICE Tek LLC ....E...... 757 390-8589
Virginia Beach (G-14539)
Interntional Maritime SEC Corp ....G...... 719 494-6501
Arlington (G-1006)
Jonda Enterprise Inc ....G...... 757 559-5793
Norfolk (G-9606)
K & E Legacy Incorporated ....G...... 757 328-4609
Portsmouth (G-10450)
Kingdom Bldrs & Ship Repr Inc ....G...... 757 748-1251
Virginia Beach (G-14585)
▲ La Playa Incorporated Virginia ....C...... 757 222-1865
Chesapeake (G-3170)
Leslie E Willis ....G...... 757 484-4484
Suffolk (G-13731)
Lifac Inc ....F...... 757 826-6051
Hampton (G-6183)
Locklear Group Inc ....G...... 757 630-9022
Virginia Beach (G-14621)
Lynn Donnell ....G...... 757 685-0263
Chesapeake (G-3191)
Lyon Shipyard Inc ....B...... 757 622-4661
Norfolk (G-9625)
Lyon Shipyard Inc ....E...... 757 622-4661
Norfolk (G-9626)
M & S Marine & Industrial Svcs ....D...... 757 405-9623
Portsmouth (G-10456)
Marcom Services LLC ....G...... 757 963-1851
Portsmouth (G-10457)
Marine Hydraulics Intl LLC ....D...... 757 545-6400
Norfolk (G-9632)
Mathomank Village Tribe ....G...... 757 504-5513
Claremont (G-3624)
McKean Defense Group LLC ....D...... 202 448-5250
Virginia Beach (G-14643)
Metro Machine Corp ....C...... 757 397-1039
Portsmouth (G-10461)
▲ Metro Machine Corp ....B...... 757 543-6801
Norfolk (G-9641)
Metro Machine Corp ....C...... 757 392-3703
Portsmouth (G-10462)

MF&b Mayport Joint Venture ....G...... 757 222-4855
Chesapeake (G-3204)
Mhi Holdings LLC ....B...... 757 545-6400
Norfolk (G-9642)
Mills Marine & Ship Repair LLC ....G...... 757 539-0956
Suffolk (G-13743)
Mills Marine & Ship Repair LLC ....G...... 757 539-0956
Suffolk (G-13744)
MK Industries Inc ....F...... 757 245-0007
Newport News (G-9302)
New Age Repr & Fabrication LLC ....G...... 757 819-3887
Norfolk (G-9659)
Ngc International Inc ....G...... 703 280-2900
Falls Church (G-4836)
◆ Northrop Grumman Newport News ..A...... 757 380-2000
Newport News (G-9306)
Ocean Marine LLC ....G...... 757 222-1306
Norfolk (G-9671)
Oceaneering International Inc ....B...... 757 545-2200
Chesapeake (G-3225)
Offshore Corporation ....G...... 804 526-7665
Colonial Heights (G-3739)
OSG Propulsion LLC ....G...... 757 340-0052
Virginia Beach (G-14704)
Paige Sitta & Associates Inc ....E...... 757 420-5886
Chesapeake (G-3231)
Patriot IV Shipping Corp ....D...... 703 876-3000
Falls Church (G-4855)
▲ Pierside Marine Industries ....E...... 757 852-9571
Norfolk (G-9688)
Pjl Marine Enterprise LLC ....G...... 757 774-1050
Chesapeake (G-3241)
Postal Mechanical Systems ....F...... 757 424-2872
Norfolk (G-9692)
Precision Qulty Ship Repr LLC ....G...... 757 322-0654
Virginia Beach (G-14734)
Quality Coatings Virginia Inc ....E...... 757 494-0801
Chesapeake (G-3252)
Red Eagle Industries LLC ....G...... 434 352-5831
Appomattox (G-822)
Reef Room ....G...... 757 592-0955
Newport News (G-9322)
Sea Technology Ltd ....F...... 804 642-3568
Newport News (G-9333)
Semad Enterprises Inc ....G...... 757 424-6177
Chesapeake (G-3290)
Ship Sstnability Solutions LLC ....G...... 757 574-2436
Chesapeake (G-3291)
▼ Soc LLC ....F...... 757 857-6400
Norfolk (G-9729)
Specialty Marine Inc ....F...... 757 494-1199
Chesapeake (G-3306)
◆ St Engineering North Amer Inc ....E...... 703 739-2610
Alexandria (G-353)
Tactical Marine Repair Inc ....G...... 757 967-8688
Chesapeake (G-3319)
Tecnico Corporation ....B...... 757 545-4013
Chesapeake (G-3326)
Thermcor Inc ....D...... 757 622-7881
Norfolk (G-9748)
Tiffany Yachts Inc ....F...... 804 453-3464
Burgess (G-2178)
United States Dept of Navy ....B...... 757 380-4223
Newport News (G-9369)
United States Dept of Navy ....A...... 757 396-8615
Portsmouth (G-10495)
Virginia Building Services Inc ....E...... 757 605-0288
Virginia Beach (G-14917)
Walashek Holdings Inc ....G...... 757 853-6007
Norfolk (G-9789)
Walashek Industrial & Mar Inc ....E...... 757 853-6007
Norfolk (G-9790)
Walashek Industrial & Mar Inc ....F...... 202 624-2880
Norfolk (G-9791)
Weda Water Inc ....G...... 757 515-4338
Virginia Beach (G-14931)

3732 Boat Building & Repairing

ARC Global Corp ....G...... 757 470-9271
Chesapeake (G-2978)
Atlantic Yacht Basin Inc ....E...... 757 482-2141
Chesapeake (G-2987)
Backwater Inc ....G...... 434 242-5675
Charlottesville (G-2733)
Bae Systems Ship Repair Inc ....A...... 757 494-4000
Norfolk (G-9453)
Bay Custom Inc ....G...... 757 971-4785
Hampton (G-6089)
Bay Custom Mar Fleet Repr Inc ....F...... 757 224-3818
Hampton (G-6090)

BGF Industries Inc ....G...... 434 369-4751
Altavista (G-626)
Big Time Charters Inc ....G...... 757 496-1040
Virginia Beach (G-14278)
Blue Wave Mobile Marine ....G...... 757 831-4810
Chesapeake (G-3008)
Boatworks & More LLC ....G...... 540 581-5820
Roanoke (G-12053)
Brightwork Boat Co ....G...... 804 795-9080
Richmond (G-11134)
Chesapeake Marine Railway ....G...... 804 776-8833
Deltaville (G-4078)
Chesapeake Yachts Inc ....F...... 757 724-1717
Chesapeake (G-3034)
Custom Yacht Service Inc ....F...... 804 438-5563
Dutton (G-4271)
Dudley Dix Yacht Design ....G...... 757 962-9273
Virginia Beach (G-14416)
Dudley Dix Yacht Design Inc ....G...... 757 962-9273
Virginia Beach (G-14417)
East Cast Repr Fabrication LLC ....D...... 757 455-9600
Norfolk (G-9536)
East Cast Repr Fabrication LLC ....G...... 757 455-9600
Norfolk (G-9535)
Erie Boatworks LLC ....G...... 757 204-1815
Chesapeake (G-3090)
Fairlead Boatworks Inc ....D...... 757 247-0101
Newport News (G-9223)
Fiberglass Customs Inc ....G...... 757 244-0610
Newport News (G-9226)
Freedom Hawks Kayaks Inc ....G...... 978 225-1511
Charlottesville (G-2799)
Genesis Boat Works Inc ....G...... 757 869-0345
Hampton (G-6158)
Honeycutts Mobile Marine ....G...... 757 898-7793
Seaford (G-12675)
Indian River Canoe Mfg ....G...... 276 773-3124
Independence (G-6988)
Jennings Boat Yard Inc ....G...... 804 453-7181
Reedville (G-10762)
Jgtsenterprise Inc ....G...... 804 677-4578
Mechanicsville (G-8645)
Keiths Boat Service LLC ....G...... 804 898-1644
Colonial Heights (G-3737)
▲ Linear Devices Corporation ....G...... 804 368-8428
Ashland (G-1453)
M & S Marine & Industrial Svcs ....D...... 757 405-9623
Portsmouth (G-10456)
Mathomank Village Tribe ....G...... 757 504-5513
Claremont (G-3624)
Michael McKittrick ....G...... 804 695-7090
Deltaville (G-4083)
Mtg Enterprises Inc ....G...... 804 269-5218
North Chesterfield (G-9935)
▲ NBC Boatworks ....G...... 757 630-0420
Virginia Beach (G-14672)
Pruitts Boat Yard ....F...... 757 891-2565
Tangier (G-13809)
Rapa Boat Services LLC ....G...... 804 443-4434
Tappahannock (G-13821)
Rappahannock Boat Works Inc ....G...... 540 439-4045
Bealeton (G-1605)
RG Boatworks LLC ....G...... 804 784-1991
Manakin Sabot (G-7904)
Richmond Steel Boat Works Inc ....G...... 804 741-0432
Richmond (G-11361)
Riverine Jet Boats ....G...... 434 258-5874
Madison Heights (G-7883)
Rva Boatworks LLC ....G...... 804 937-7448
Richmond (G-11368)
Severn Yachting LLC ....G...... 804 642-6969
Hayes (G-6408)
Team SSP Ventures Inc ....G...... 804 273-9496
Glen Allen (G-5805)
Tiffany Yachts Inc ....F...... 804 453-3464
Burgess (G-2178)
TST Tactical Def Solutions Inc ....F...... 757 452-6955
Virginia Beach (G-14896)
Tynes Fiberglass Company Inc ....G...... 757 423-0222
Norfolk (G-9771)
Waldens Marina Inc ....G...... 804 776-9440
Deltaville (G-4087)
Zimmerman Marine Incorporated ....F...... 804 776-0367
Deltaville (G-4090)

3743 Railroad Eqpt

Amsted Rail Company Inc ....B...... 804 732-0202
Petersburg (G-10303)
B & B Machine & Tool Inc ....E...... 540 344-6820
Roanoke (G-12038)

Bullet Equipment Sales Inc ....G..... 276 623-5150
  Abingdon (G-18)
Church Trucking LLC ....G..... 757 386-1761
  Norfolk (G-9485)
Clarke County Speed Shop ....G..... 540 955-0479
  Berryville (G-1674)
Crown Motorcar Company LLC ....E..... 434 979-7222
  Charlottesville (G-2612)
◆ Freightcar Roanoke Inc ....D..... 540 342-2303
  Roanoke (G-12094)
▲ Graham-White Manufacturing Co .....B..... 540 387-5600
  Salem (G-12513)
▼ Gregg Company Ltd ....G..... 757 966-1367
  Chesapeake (G-3126)
I AM Express LLC ....G..... 757 535-6944
  Chesapeake (G-3139)
Ie W Railway Supply ....G..... 540 882-3886
  Hillsboro (G-6872)
Loco Parts ....G..... 757 255-2815
  Suffolk (G-13734)
Longwood Elastomers Inc ....C..... 276 228-5406
  Wytheville (G-15898)
New York Air Brake Company ....G..... 540 989-5044
  Roanoke (G-12140)
Precise Freight Solutions ....G..... 703 627-1327
  Manassas (G-8131)
Progress Rail Services Corp ....G..... 540 345-4039
  Roanoke (G-12157)
Shenandoah Vlly Steam/Gas Engi .....G..... 540 662-6923
  Winchester (G-15586)
Wilsons Elite Express LLC ....G..... 804 517-4276
  North Chesterfield (G-10012)

3751 Motorcycles, Bicycles & Parts

Blue Ridge Mch Motorsports LLC ....G..... 540 432-6560
  Harrisonburg (G-6295)
DOT Blue ....G..... 804 564-2563
  Richmond (G-11566)
Filz Built Bicycles ....G..... 703 451-5582
  Springfield (G-13003)
Geza Gear Inc ....E..... 703 327-9844
  Haymarket (G-6425)
Go-Race Inc ....G..... 540 392-0696
  Christiansburg (G-3591)
Jansson & Associate Mstr Bldr ....G..... 757 965-7285
  Virginia Beach (G-14564)
Open Road Grill & Icehouse ....G..... 571 395-4400
  Falls Church (G-4852)
Phat Daddys Polish Shop ....G..... 804 405-5301
  North Chesterfield (G-9947)
Seidle Motorsports ....G..... 276 632-2255
  Martinsville (G-8327)
▲ U S Sidecars Inc ....D..... 434 263-6500
  Arrington (G-1231)
Yum Yum Choppers Inc ....G..... 276 694-6152
  Claudville (G-3642)

3761 Guided Missiles & Space Vehicles

Aeraspace Corporation ....G..... 703 554-2906
  Round Hill (G-12374)
American Tech Sltons Intl Corp ....E..... 540 907-5355
  Fredericksburg (G-5398)
Blacksky Holdings Inc ....E..... 703 935-1930
  Herndon (G-6625)
Bwxt Y - 12 LLC ....G..... 434 316-7633
  Lynchburg (G-7670)
Dallas G Bienhoff ....G..... 571 232-4554
  Annandale (G-738)
Gomspace North America LLC ....G..... 703 866-8742
  Alexandria (G-222)
Lockheed Martin Corporation ....C..... 703 367-2121
  Manassas (G-7966)
Lockheed Martin Corporation ....B..... 757 935-9479
  Suffolk (G-13732)
Lockheed Martin Corporation ....G..... 703 258-2784
  Arlington (G-1047)
Lockheed Martin Corporation ....G..... 703 367-2121
  Manassas (G-7968)
Mbda Incorporated ....G..... 703 351-1230
  Arlington (G-1057)
Nanofactory Cbn Inc ....E..... 434 799-9280
  Danville (G-4016)
◆ Northrop Grmman Gdnce Elec Inc ..E..... 703 280-2900
  Falls Church (G-4839)
◆ Northrop Grumman Systems Corp ..B..... 703 280-2900
  Falls Church (G-4845)
Orbital Sciences LLC ....B..... 703 406-5000
  Dulles (G-4218)
Raytheon Company ....A..... 703 419-1400
  Arlington (G-1138)

Raytheon Company ....G..... 310 647-9438
  Chesapeake (G-3258)
Raytheon Company ....G..... 703 418-0275
  Arlington (G-1135)
Raytheon Company ....G..... 571 250-1101
  Dulles (G-4222)
Raytheon Company ....G..... 757 749-9638
  Yorktown (G-15987)
Raytheon Company ....F..... 703 872-3400
  Arlington (G-1139)
Space Logistics LLC ....G..... 703 406-5474
  Dulles (G-4227)
◆ Titan II Inc ....D..... 757 380-2000
  Newport News (G-9358)
Triquetra Phoenix LLC ....G..... 571 265-6044
  Annandale (G-790)
Utah State Univ Space Dynmics ....D..... 435 713-3060
  Stafford (G-13209)
War Fighter Specialties LLC ....G..... 540 742-4187
  Shenandoah (G-12697)
Yuzhnoye-Us LLC ....G..... 321 537-2720
  Reston (G-10997)

3764 Guided Missile/Space Vehicle Propulsion Units & parts

Aerojet Rocketdyne Inc ....G..... 703 650-0270
  Arlington (G-843)
Aerojet Rocketdyne Inc ....G..... 540 854-2000
  Culpeper (G-3862)
Alliant Tchsystems Oprtons LLC ....G..... 703 412-3223
  Arlington (G-849)
Atk Chan Inc ....G..... 804 266-3428
  Glen Allen (G-5705)
Atlantic Research Corporation ....C..... 540 854-2000
  Culpeper (G-3869)
▲ Atlantic Research Corporation ....A..... 703 754-5000
  Gainesville (G-5571)
Blacksky Holdings Inc ....E..... 703 935-1930
  Herndon (G-6625)
Delta Q Dynamics LLC ....G..... 703 980-9449
  Manassas (G-7931)
Lockheed Martin Corporation ....B..... 757 935-9479
  Suffolk (G-13732)
Northrop Grmman Innvtion Syste ....G..... 540 639-7631
  Radford (G-10729)
◆ Northrop Grmman Innvtion Syste ....C..... 703 406-5000
  Dulles (G-4212)
Orbital Atk Operation Ges ....G..... 571 437-7870
  Sterling (G-13467)
Springfield Custom Auto Mch ....G..... 703 339-0999
  Lorton (G-7532)
Yuzhnoye-Us LLC ....G..... 321 537-2720
  Reston (G-10997)

3769 Guided Missile/Space Vehicle Parts & Eqpt, NEC

A-Tech Corporation ....G..... 703 955-7846
  Chantilly (G-2360)
Calspan Systems Corporation ....C..... 757 873-1344
  Newport News (G-9189)
Deep-Space Intelligent Constru ....G..... 571 247-7376
  Fairfax Station (G-4706)
ITT Defense & Electronics ....A..... 703 790-6300
  Mc Lean (G-8474)
◆ Marion Mold & Tool Inc ....E..... 276 783-6101
  Marion (G-8234)
Moog Inc ....G..... 716 652-2000
  Blacksburg (G-1764)
Orbital Sciences LLC ....B..... 703 406-5000
  Dulles (G-4218)
▲ Prototype Productions Inc ....D..... 703 858-0011
  Chantilly (G-2483)
War Fighter Specialties LLC ....G..... 540 742-4187
  Shenandoah (G-12697)
Wiglance LLC ....G..... 866 301-3662
  North Chesterfield (G-10011)

3792 Travel Trailers & Campers

Custom Concessions Inc ....G..... 800 910-8533
  Lynchburg (G-7689)
Hibbard Iron Works of Hampton ....F..... 757 826-5611
  Hampton (G-6165)
Hillwood Park Inc ....G..... 703 754-6105
  Gainesville (G-5589)

3795 Tanks & Tank Components

◆ Bae Systems Land Armaments Inc ..E..... 571 461-6000
  Falls Church (G-4756)

◆ Bae Systems Land Armaments LP ...D..... 571 461-6000
  Falls Church (G-4757)
Bae Systems Land Armmnts Hldng .....D..... 571 461-6000
  Falls Church (G-4758)
Bowhead Integrated Support Ser ....G..... 703 413-4226
  Springfield (G-12967)
▲ General Dynamics Corporation ....C..... 703 876-3000
  Reston (G-10857)
▲ Special Tactical Services LLC ....F..... 757 554-0699
  Virginia Beach (G-14835)
Threat Prot Wrd Wide Svcs LLC ....G..... 703 795-2445
  Remington (G-10773)
United Defense ....G..... 540 663-9291
  King George (G-7118)

3799 Transportation Eqpt, NEC

Bryan Smith ....G..... 434 242-7698
  Ruckersville (G-12400)
Contra Surplus LLC ....G..... 757 337-9971
  Norfolk (G-9504)
Dan Matheny Jerr ....G..... 703 499-9216
  Woodbridge (G-15680)
Db Enterprises of VA LLC ....G..... 804 931-7667
  Chester (G-3403)
Electrify America LLC ....D..... 703 364-7000
  Herndon (G-6666)
H&H Hauling LLC ....G..... 540 273-9109
  Spotsylvania (G-12892)
Hibbard Iron Works of Hampton ....F..... 757 826-5611
  Hampton (G-6165)
▲ Holmes Enterprises Intl Inc ....E..... 804 798-9201
  Ashland (G-1435)
Industrial Biodynamics LLC ....G..... 540 357-0033
  Salem (G-12520)
Ked Hauling Co LLC ....G..... 757 319-8652
  Virginia Beach (G-14582)
Lee Talbot Associates Inc ....G..... 703 734-8576
  Mc Lean (G-8483)
Perkins ....F..... 276 227-0551
  Wytheville (G-15904)
Racing For Veterans ....G..... 434 822-4201
  Alton (G-647)
Samuel Ross ....G..... 434 531-9219
  Bremo Bluff (G-1946)
SHD Logistics LLC ....G..... 804 405-4943
  Chester (G-3454)
Taylor Boyz LLC ....G..... 540 347-2443
  Midland (G-8765)
Tcts Trucking LLC ....G..... 757 406-6323
  Chesapeake (G-3324)
Twp Transport LLC ....G..... 540 383-7995
  Grottoes (G-6025)
Up and Go Transportation LLC ....G..... 443 859-0193
  Glen Allen (G-5821)
Vlh Transportation Inc ....G..... 757 880-5772
  Hampton (G-6265)
Walter Winget ....G..... 757 339-0303
  Carrollton (G-2247)
Windryder Inc ....G..... 540 545-8851
  Winchester (G-15516)

38 MEASURING, ANALYZING AND CONTROLLING INSTRUMENTS; PHOTOGRAPHIC, MEDICAL AN

3812 Search, Detection, Navigation & Guidance Systs & Instrs

A & A Precision Machining LLC ....G..... 804 493-8416
  Montross (G-9023)
A-Tech Corporation ....G..... 703 955-7846
  Chantilly (G-2360)
Aero Corporation ....G..... 703 896-7721
  Fairfax (G-4401)
Aerojet ....G..... 703 247-2907
  Arlington (G-842)
Aimex LLC ....F..... 212 631-4277
  Vienna (G-14006)
Air Route Optimizer Inc ....G..... 540 364-3470
  Marshall (G-8249)
Alliant Tchsystems Oprtons LLC ....E..... 703 254-2454
  Newington (G-9152)
Anchor Defense Inc ....G..... 757 460-3830
  Virginia Beach (G-14228)
Anra Technologies Inc ....E..... 703 239-3206
  Chantilly (G-2525)
Applied Signals Intelligence ....G..... 571 313-0681
  Sterling (G-13346)

SIC

Applied Video Imaging LLC .... G 434 974-6310
Charlottesville *(G-2589)*
Ares Self Defense Inc .... G 757 561-3538
Providence Forge *(G-10618)*
▼ **Argon St Inc** .... A 703 322-0881
Fairfax *(G-4412)*
Ark Holdings Group Llc .... G 202 368-5828
Woodbridge *(G-15648)*
Ashley Clark Defense LLC .... G 703 867-6665
Ashburn *(G-1243)*
Atlas Defense Platform LLC .... G 703 737-6112
Leesburg *(G-7224)*
Atlas North America LLC .... G 757 463-0670
Yorktown *(G-15934)*
Ats-Sales LLC .... G 703 631-6661
Chantilly *(G-2372)*
Aviation Tactical LLC .... G 970 946-7027
Springfield *(G-12957)*
Axell Wireless Inc .... G 703 414-5300
Arlington *(G-868)*
Back Bay Defense LLC .... G 757 285-6883
Virginia Beach *(G-14257)*
▼ **Bae Systems Inc** .... C 571 461-6000
Falls Church *(G-4754)*
◆ **Bae Systems Holdings Inc** .... B 571 461-6000
Falls Church *(G-4755)*
Bae Systems Info & Elec Sys .... C 703 668-4000
Reston *(G-10797)*
Bae Systems Info & Elec Sys .... B 703 361-1471
Manassas *(G-7918)*
Bae Systems Info & Elec Sys .... G 202 223-8808
Arlington *(G-872)*
◆ **Bae Systems Land Armaments LP** .... D 571 461-6000
Falls Church *(G-4757)*
Barnett Consulting LLC .... G 703 655-1635
Lorton *(G-7465)*
Black Tree LLC .... G 703 669-0178
Mc Lean *(G-8400)*
Blackstone Defense Svcs Corp .... F 571 598-2714
Ashburn *(G-1248)*
Buoya LLC .... G 703 248-9100
Arlington *(G-892)*
Celestial Circuits LLC .... G 703 851-2843
Springfield *(G-12975)*
Central Electronics Co .... G 540 659-3235
Stafford *(G-13128)*
Chaosworks Inc .... G 703 727-0772
Great Falls *(G-5946)*
Chemring Sensors and Electr .... F 434 964-4800
Charlottesville *(G-2608)*
Chemring Snsors Elctrnic Syste .... C 703 661-0283
Dulles *(G-4195)*
Citizens Defense Solutions LLC .... G 254 423-1612
Woodbridge *(G-15671)*
Cobham AES Holdings Inc .... F 703 414-5300
Arlington *(G-911)*
▲ **Cobham Defense Products Inc** .... G 703 414-5300
Arlington *(G-912)*
Cobham Management Services Inc .... F 703 414-5300
Arlington *(G-913)*
Coleman Microwave Co .... E 540 984-8848
Edinburg *(G-4301)*
Combat Bound LLC .... G 757 343-3399
Suffolk *(G-13685)*
Crespo Urban Defense LLC .... G 804 562-7566
North Chesterfield *(G-9854)*
Cronin Defense Strategies LLC .... G 810 625-7060
Arlington *(G-920)*
Defense Dogs LLC .... G 540 895-5611
Spotsylvania *(G-12887)*
Defense Executives LLC .... G 757 638-3678
Suffolk *(G-13697)*
Defense Group .... G 703 633-8300
Chantilly *(G-2404)*
Defense Information Sys .... G 855 401-8554
Arlington *(G-934)*
Defense Information Tech Inc .... G 703 628-0999
Gainesville *(G-5579)*
Defense Insights LLC .... G 703 455-7880
Fairfax Station *(G-4707)*
Defense Threat .... G 703 767-2798
Fort Belvoir *(G-5114)*
Defense Threat Reductio .... G 703 767-4627
Triangle *(G-13890)*
Defense Threat Reductio .... G 703 767-5870
Annandale *(G-742)*
Defense United States Dept .... G 804 292-5642
Richmond *(G-11558)*
Defenseworx LLC .... G 703 568-3295
Centreville *(G-2302)*
Dirt Removal Services LLC .... G 703 499-1299
Catharpin *(G-2261)*
Dmt LLC .... G 434 455-2460
Forest *(G-5067)*
Dominion Defense LLC .... G 703 216-7295
Woodbridge *(G-15684)*
Double Edge Defense LLC .... G 540 550-0849
Winchester *(G-15537)*
Dragoon Technologies Inc .... G 937 439-9223
Winchester *(G-15412)*
Droneshield LLC .... F 202 750-4368
Warrenton *(G-14999)*
Drs C3 & Aviation Company .... G 571 346-7700
Herndon *(G-6661)*
Drs Global Entp Solutions Inc .... E 703 898-9233
Dulles *(G-4198)*
Drs Homeland SEC Solutions Inc .... G 703 682-1801
Arlington *(G-942)*
Drs Leonardo Inc .... F 703 416-7600
Arlington *(G-943)*
Drs Leonardo Inc .... F 757 819-0700
Chesapeake *(G-3077)*
▲ **Drs Leonardo Inc** .... C 703 416-8000
Arlington *(G-944)*
Drs Leonardo Inc .... G 571 383-0152
Chantilly *(G-2412)*
Drs Leonardo Inc .... G 703 260-7979
Herndon *(G-6662)*
Drs Leonardo Inc .... D 703 416-8000
Arlington *(G-945)*
Elite Defense Inc .... G 703 339-0749
Lorton *(G-7484)*
End To End Inc .... E 757 216-1938
Virginia Beach *(G-14448)*
Eurest Raytheon Dulles .... G 571 250-1024
Dulles *(G-4200)*
Falcon Defense Service LLC .... G 703 395-2007
Alexandria *(G-203)*
Firstmark Corp .... F 724 759-2850
Midlothian *(G-8818)*
Flexprotect LLC .... G 703 957-8648
Reston *(G-10853)*
Flight Product Center Inc .... G 703 361-2915
Manassas *(G-7941)*
Form III Defense Solutions LLC .... G 703 542-7372
Brambleton *(G-1928)*
Freeman Aerotech LLC .... G 703 303-0102
Ashburn *(G-1282)*
General Dynamics Corporation .... G 703 925-8636
Herndon *(G-6680)*
General Dynamics Corporation .... E 757 523-2738
Chesapeake *(G-3116)*
General Dynamics Corporation .... G 703 263-2835
Fairfax *(G-4462)*
▲ **General Dynamics Corporation** .... C 703 876-3000
Reston *(G-10857)*
Ghodousi LLC .... G 480 544-3192
Alexandria *(G-468)*
Global Supply Solutions .... G 757 392-1733
Virginia Beach *(G-14485)*
Gradient Dynamics LLC .... G 865 207-9052
Mc Lean *(G-8453)*
Gyroscope Disc Golf LLC .... G 703 992-3035
Springfield *(G-13015)*
Hansen Defense Systems LLC .... G 757 389-1683
Chesapeake *(G-3128)*
Harris Communications and In .... E 703 668-7256
Herndon *(G-6694)*
Harris Corporation .... G 571 203-7605
Herndon *(G-6695)*
Hellen Systems LLC .... G 571 276-7730
Middleburg *(G-8722)*
Hensoldt Inc .... G 703 827-3976
Vienna *(G-14063)*
Iis Raytheon .... G 561 212-2954
Potomac Falls *(G-10509)*
Interad Limited LLC .... F 757 787-7610
Melfa *(G-8710)*
International Cmmnctns Strtgc .... G 703 820-1669
Arlington *(G-1005)*
International Trade & Tech Inc .... G 703 929-0595
Midland *(G-8758)*
ITT Exelis .... G 757 594-1600
Newport News *(G-9261)*
Ius Bello Defense LLC .... G 540 720-2571
Stafford *(G-13155)*
Janes Cyber Defense LLC .... G 703 489-1872
Alexandria *(G-491)*
Janice Research Group .... G 703 971-8901
Alexandria *(G-492)*
Jerry A Kotchka .... G 757 721-6782
Virginia Beach *(G-14567)*
Jnr Defense LLC .... G 541 220-6089
Alexandria *(G-245)*
Kelvin Hughes LLC .... G 703 827-3986
Vienna *(G-14077)*
Kollmorgen Corporation .... B 540 633-3536
Radford *(G-10721)*
L-3 Unmanned Systems Inc .... D 703 889-8640
Ashburn *(G-1304)*
L3 Technologies Inc .... G 540 658-0591
Stafford *(G-13167)*
L3harris Technologies Inc .... G 540 658-3350
Stafford *(G-13168)*
L3harris Technologies Inc .... C 703 790-6300
Mc Lean *(G-8481)*
L3harris Technologies Inc .... C 757 594-1607
Newport News *(G-9278)*
L3harris Technologies Inc .... D 434 455-9390
Forest *(G-5079)*
L3harris Technologies Inc .... E 434 455-6600
Forest *(G-5080)*
L3harris Technologies Inc .... G 703 668-6000
Herndon *(G-6729)*
L3harris Technologies Inc .... D 703 828-1520
Chantilly *(G-2455)*
L3harris Technologies Inc .... G 434 941-5441
Appomattox *(G-818)*
L3harris Technologies Inc .... B 703 668-6239
Herndon *(G-6728)*
L3harris Technologies Inc .... A 540 563-0371
Roanoke *(G-11951)*
Lammasu Defense LLC .... G 540 229-7027
Culpeper *(G-3906)*
Laurel Technologies Partnr .... G 814 534-2027
Arlington *(G-1029)*
Laurel Technologies Partnr .... E 757 819-0700
Chesapeake *(G-3177)*
Lilbern Design Virginia LLC .... E 540 234-9900
Weyers Cave *(G-15174)*
Lockheed Martin .... C 703 588-0670
Arlington *(G-1043)*
Lockheed Martin .... D 202 863-3297
Arlington *(G-1044)*
Lockheed Martin .... D 757 578-3377
Virginia Beach *(G-14615)*
Lockheed Martin .... D 703 272-6061
Fairfax *(G-4648)*
Lockheed Martin .... D 703 982-9008
Lorton *(G-7508)*
Lockheed Martin Corporation .... G 703 280-9983
Vienna *(G-14083)*
Lockheed Martin Corporation .... G 703 771-3515
Leesburg *(G-7302)*
Lockheed Martin Corporation .... B 270 319-4600
Fairfax *(G-4649)*
Lockheed Martin Corporation .... A 703 367-2121
Manassas *(G-7965)*
Lockheed Martin Corporation .... B 757 491-3501
Virginia Beach *(G-14616)*
Lockheed Martin Corporation .... B 540 644-2830
King George *(G-7100)*
Lockheed Martin Corporation .... G 540 891-5882
Fredericksburg *(G-5314)*
Lockheed Martin Corporation .... B 703 724-7552
Ashburn *(G-1309)*
Lockheed Martin Corporation .... B 703 357-7095
Arlington *(G-1045)*
Lockheed Martin Corporation .... A 703 403-9829
Herndon *(G-6735)*
Lockheed Martin Corporation .... B 813 855-5711
Manassas *(G-7967)*
Lockheed Martin Corporation .... A 703 466-3000
Herndon *(G-6736)*
Lockheed Martin Corporation .... G 757 766-3282
Hampton *(G-6278)*
Lockheed Martin Corporation .... A 757 896-4860
Hampton *(G-6185)*
Lockheed Martin Corporation .... G 757 509-6808
Yorktown *(G-15977)*
Lockheed Martin Corporation .... G 757 464-0877
Virginia Beach *(G-14617)*
Lockheed Martin Corporation .... G 703 367-2121
Manassas *(G-7968)*
Lockheed Martin Corporation .... A 757 685-3132
Virginia Beach *(G-14618)*
Lockheed Martin Corporation .... G 757 803-3080
Virginia Beach *(G-14619)*
Lockheed Martin Corporation .... A 757 430-6500
Virginia Beach *(G-14620)*

Company	Code	Phone
Lockheed Martin Corporation Arlington (G-1046)	F	703 418-4900
Lockheed Martin Corporation Chantilly (G-2458)	B	703 378-1880
Lockheed Martin Corporation Chesapeake (G-3184)	C	757 769-7251
Lockheed Martin Corporation King George (G-7101)	D	540 663-3337
Lockheed Martin Corporation Herndon (G-6737)	B	703 787-4027
Lockheed Martin Corporation Chesapeake (G-3186)	D	757 390-7520
Lockheed Martin Corporation Manassas (G-7966)	C	703 367-2121
Lockheed Martin Corporation Suffolk (G-13732)	B	757 935-9479
Lockheed Martin Integrtd Systm Manassas (G-7969)	E	703 367-2121
Lockheed Martin Integrtd Systm Arlington (G-1048)	D	866 562-2363
Lockheed Martin Integrtd Systm Vienna (G-14084)	B	703 682-5719
Lockheed Martin Services LLC Chesapeake (G-3187)	F	757 366-3300
Lockheed Martin Services LLC Suffolk (G-13733)	G	757 935-9200
Marine Sonic Technology Yorktown (G-15978)	G	804 693-9602
Mav6 LLC Herndon (G-6744)	E	601 619-7722
Maverick Cyber-Defense LLC Centreville (G-2319)	G	202 725-7663
▼ Mbda Incorporated Arlington (G-1056)	E	703 387-7170
McKean Defense Group LLC King George (G-7102)	G	540 413-1202
McKean Defense Group LLC Sterling (G-13450)	G	703 848-7928
Meridian Tech Systems Inc Leesburg (G-7313)	G	301 606-6490
Moog Inc Blacksburg (G-1764)	G	716 652-2000
Moog Inc Blacksburg (G-1766)	A	828 837-5115
Moog Inc Blacksburg (G-1767)	B	540 552-3011
Northern Defense Inds LLC Alexandria (G-294)	G	703 836-8346
Northrop Grmman / Hnlulu - US Falls Church (G-4838)	G	808 529-9500
◆ Northrop Grmman Gdnce Elec Inc Falls Church (G-4839)	E	703 280-2900
Northrop Grmman Innvtion Syste Arlington (G-1080)	G	763 744-5219
◆ Northrop Grmman Innvtion Syste Dulles (G-4212)	C	703 406-5000
Northrop Grmman Ovrseas Hldg I Falls Church (G-4840)	G	703 280-4069
Northrop Grmman Worldwide Entp Herndon (G-6756)	G	703 713-4096
Northrop Grumman Corporation North Chesterfield (G-9940)	A	804 272-1321
Northrop Grumman Corporation Chester (G-3441)	G	804 416-6500
Northrop Grumman Corporation Hampton (G-6211)	A	757 838-7221
Northrop Grumman Corporation Chesapeake (G-3221)	G	757 688-6850
Northrop Grumman Corporation King George (G-7104)	A	540 469-9647
Northrop Grumman Corporation Herndon (G-6757)	F	703 713-4096
Northrop Grumman Corporation Williamsburg (G-15284)	G	757 688-5339
Northrop Grumman Corporation Radford (G-10730)	G	703 406-5695
Northrop Grumman Corporation Richmond (G-11695)	D	804 371-0019
Northrop Grumman Corporation Chantilly (G-2470)	F	703 556-5960
Northrop Grumman Corporation Arlington (G-1081)	G	212 978-2800
Northrop Grumman Corporation Chantilly (G-2471)	B	703 449-7120
Northrop Grumman Corporation Mc Lean (G-8511)	G	703 556-1144
Northrop Grumman Corporation Falls Church (G-4841)	B	703 280-2900
Northrop Grumman Global Svcs Falls Church (G-4842)	G	703 280-2900
Northrop Grumman Info Tech Fairfax (G-4520)	E	703 968-1000
Northrop Grumman Innovation Radford (G-10731)	F	540 831-4788
Northrop Grumman Intl Inc Mc Lean (G-8512)	G	703 556-1144
Northrop Grumman Intl Inc Falls Church (G-4843)	E	703 280-2900
Northrop Grumman Intl Trdg Inc Falls Church (G-4844)	G	703 280-2900
Northrop Grumman Systems Corp Arlington (G-1082)	G	703 875-8463
Northrop Grumman Systems Corp Centreville (G-2324)	G	703 808-0961
Northrop Grumman Systems Corp Chesapeake (G-3222)	G	757 312-8375
Northrop Grumman Systems Corp Mc Lean (G-8513)	D	703 556-1144
Northrop Grumman Systems Corp Mc Lean (G-8514)	B	703 556-1144
Northrop Grumman Systems Corp Mc Lean (G-8515)	C	703 556-1144
Northrop Grumman Systems Corp Falls Church (G-4846)	D	703 280-1220
Northrop Grumman Systems Corp Mc Lean (G-8516)	E	703 556-1144
Northrop Grumman Systems Corp Newport News (G-9307)	G	757 380-2612
Northrop Grumman Systems Corp Virginia Beach (G-14685)	G	757 498-5616
Northrop Grumman Systems Corp Charlottesville (G-2666)	A	434 974-2000
Northrop Grumman Systems Corp Virginia Beach (G-14686)	G	757 686-4147
Northrop Grumman Systems Corp Radford (G-10732)	G	304 726-5030
Northrop Grumman Systems Corp Dulles (G-4213)	G	703 406-5474
Northrop Grumman Systems Corp Virginia Beach (G-14687)	G	757 463-5578
Northrop Grumman Systems Corp Chantilly (G-2472)	F	703 633-8300
Northrop Grumman Systems Corp Herndon (G-6759)	C	703 968-1000
Northrop Grumman Systems Corp Herndon (G-6760)	C	703 968-1100
Northrop Grumman Systems Corp Mc Lean (G-8518)	C	703 556-1144
◆ Northrop Grumman Systems Corp Falls Church (G-4845)	B	703 280-2900
Northrop Grumman. Centreville (G-2325)	G	305 466-4655
Nova Defense & Arospc Intl LLC Alexandria (G-297)	G	703 864-6929
Ongrade Pllc Virginia Beach (G-14701)	G	757 448-5635
Orbital Sciences Corporation Wallops Island (G-14972)	B	757 824-5619
Orbital Sciences Corporation Dulles (G-4216)	B	703 405-5012
◆ Orbital Sciences LLC Dulles (G-4217)	A	703 406-5524
Orbital Sciences LLC Dulles (G-4218)	B	703 406-5000
OSI Maritime Systems Inc Virginia Beach (G-14706)	G	877 432-7467
Pae Avation Technical Svcs LLC Arlington (G-1096)	G	864 458-3272
Parry Labs LLC Alexandria (G-306)	E	585 746-8335
◆ Patriot3 Inc Fredericksburg (G-5343)	E	540 891-7353
Peraton Inc Newport News (G-9312)	G	315 838-7009
Perspecta Svcs & Solutions Inc Ashburn (G-1326)	B	781 684-4000
Pons Corp Reston (G-10927)	G	786 270-7774
Potomac Defense LLC Reston (G-10928)	G	703 253-3441
Proxy Technologies Inc Reston (G-10933)	F	703 665-5152
Qinetiq US Holdings Inc Centreville (G-2330)	E	202 429-6630
R F Tech Solutions Inc Powhatan (G-10569)	G	804 241-5250
R Zimmerman and Associates Stafford (G-13185)	G	540 446-6846
Radio Reconnaissance Tech Inc Fredericksburg (G-5352)	G	540 752-7448
Raytheon Applied Sgnal Tech In Mc Lean (G-8533)	G	571 484-9373
Raytheon Company Arlington (G-1131)	F	703 416-5800
Raytheon Company Sterling (G-13485)	B	703 759-1200
Raytheon Company Chantilly (G-2485)	F	703 830-4087
Raytheon Company Dulles (G-4221)	G	571 250-2260
Raytheon Company Arlington (G-1132)	C	703 841-5700
Raytheon Company Chesapeake (G-3257)	C	757 855-4394
Raytheon Company Virginia Beach (G-14762)	G	757 363-1252
Raytheon Company Arlington (G-1133)	E	703 413-1220
Raytheon Company Williamsburg (G-15303)	G	972 638-3173
Raytheon Company Falls Church (G-4863)	E	703 661-7252
Raytheon Company Chesapeake (G-3258)	G	310 647-9438
Raytheon Company Arlington (G-1134)	G	703 418-0275
Raytheon Company Arlington (G-1135)	G	703 418-0275
Raytheon Company Dulles (G-4222)	G	571 250-1101
Raytheon Company Sterling (G-13486)	G	703 260-3534
Raytheon Company Yorktown (G-15987)	G	757 749-9638
Raytheon Company Arlington (G-1136)	G	706 569-6600
Raytheon Company Dulles (G-4223)	D	571 250-3421
Raytheon Company Arlington (G-1137)	F	703 412-3742
Raytheon Company Springfield (G-13078)	C	703 912-1800
Raytheon Company Alexandria (G-567)	G	703 768-4172
Raytheon Company Chesapeake (G-3259)	B	757 421-8319
Raytheon Company Arlington (G-1139)	F	703 872-3400
Raytheon Company Dulles (G-4225)	G	310 647-9438
Raytheon Company Arlington (G-1140)	C	540 658-3172
Reliadefense LLC Sterling (G-13489)	G	571 225-4096
Reyco Global LLC Fairfax (G-4541)	G	719 321-6747
Richmond Defense Firm Henrico (G-6558)	G	804 977-0764
Rockwell Collins Inc Sterling (G-13495)	E	703 234-2100
Rockwell Collins Simulation Sterling (G-13496)	C	703 234-2100
Sage Defense LLC Falls Church (G-4871)	G	703 485-5995
Sailplan Inc Reston (G-10943)	G	703 217-9658
Schiebel Aircraft Inc Manassas (G-8151)	F	540 351-1731
Senstar Inc Herndon (G-6804)	G	703 463-3088
Sentinel Self-Defense LLC Hampton (G-6232)	G	757 234-2501
Sextant Solutions Group LLC Norfolk (G-9719)	G	757 797-4353
Sierra Nevada Corporation Arlington (G-1166)	B	703 412-1502
Skydweller Aero Inc Alexandria (G-348)	G	585 746-8335
Smiths Detection Inc Reston (G-10955)	C	571 346-3400
Spartan Village LLC Gainesville (G-5614)	G	661 724-6438
▲ Special Tactical Services LLC Virginia Beach (G-14835)	F	757 554-0699
Sugpiat Defense LLC Fredericksburg (G-5228)	G	540 623-3626
Thales USA Defense & SEC Inc Arlington (G-1190)	G	571 255-4600
Thermo-Optical Group LLC Lovettsville (G-7587)	G	540 822-9481

◆ Titan II Inc ....D 757 380-2000
Newport News *(G-9358)*

Torrent Loading Systems LLC ......G. 434 509-7307
Lynchburg *(G-7825)*

Trimble Inc ....D 540 904-5925
Salem *(G-12577)*

Triron Defense Services LLC ......G. 703 472-2458
Sterling *(G-13538)*

Triton Defense Services LLC ......G. 703 472-2458
Sterling *(G-13539)*

Ultra Electronics 3phoenix Inc ......G. 703 956-6480
Chantilly *(G-2510)*

Uma Inc ....E 540 879-2040
Dayton *(G-4067)*

United Defense Systems Inc ......G. 401 304-9100
Reston *(G-10978)*

United Technologies I LLC ......G. 804 553-3116
Henrico *(G-6588)*

Utiliscope Corp ....F 804 550-5233
Glen Allen *(G-5822)*

Ventura Defense US Corp ......G. 571 527-1360
Arlington *(G-1208)*

▲ Video Aerial Systems LLC ......G. 434 221-3089
Amherst *(G-712)*

Virginia Citizens Defense ......G. 703 944-4845
Middletown *(G-8748)*

W T Brownley Co Inc ......G. 757 622-7589
Norfolk *(G-9788)*

Weapons Analysis LLC ......G. 540 371-9134
Fredericksburg *(G-5501)*

Weibel Equipment Inc ......G. 571 278-1989
Leesburg *(G-7375)*

Where Good Grows LLC ......G. 240 506-0011
Alexandria *(G-382)*

William B Clark ......G. 804 695-9950
Gloucester *(G-5868)*

▼ X-Com Systems LLC ......E. 703 390-1087
Reston *(G-10996)*

Zombie Defense ......G. 804 972-3991
Glen Allen *(G-5831)*

3821 Laboratory Apparatus & Furniture

◆ Alfa Laval Inc ....C 866 253-2528
Richmond *(G-11095)*

Bases of Virginia LLC ......G. 757 690-8482
Yorktown *(G-15936)*

Biologics Inc ....F 703 367-9020
Manassas *(G-8039)*

Chantil Technology LLC ......G. 703 955-7867
Chantilly *(G-2389)*

Diversified Eductl Systems ......E. 540 687-7060
Middleburg *(G-8719)*

Gallagher-Stone Incorporated ......G. 434 528-5181
Lynchburg *(G-7719)*

Indy Health Labs LLC ......G. 540 682-2160
Roanoke *(G-11940)*

▲ Jackson Pointe LLC ......G. 757 269-7100
Newport News *(G-9264)*

Laser Alignment Systems LLC ......G. 410 507-6820
Gloucester *(G-5852)*

Melissa Davis ......G. 757 482-3743
Virginia Beach *(G-14647)*

Nevtek ......G. 540 925-2322
Williamsville *(G-15351)*

▼ Phipps & Bird Inc ....F 804 254-2737
Richmond *(G-11059)*

Pipet Repair Service Inc ......G. 804 739-3720
Midlothian *(G-8880)*

▲ Samin Science Usa Inc ......G. 571 403-3678
Vienna *(G-14121)*

Sims USA Inc ......G. 757 875-7742
Yorktown *(G-15991)*

Techlab Inc ....D 540 953-1664
Radford *(G-10740)*

Tomotrace Inc ......G. 202 207-5423
Sterling *(G-13535)*

3822 Automatic Temperature Controls

Ark Commercial Services LLC ......F. 202 807-6211
Mc Lean *(G-8396)*

Atarfil Usa Inc ....F 757 386-8676
Suffolk *(G-13672)*

Bas Control Systems LLC ......G. 804 569-2473
Mechanicsville *(G-8606)*

Bwx Technologies Inc ......F. 757 595-7982
Newport News *(G-9187)*

Circle T Controls Inc ......G. 540 295-0188
Stafford *(G-13131)*

Ddc Connections Inc ......G. 703 858-0326
Reston *(G-10835)*

Edge Mechanical Inc ....F 757 228-3540
Virginia Beach *(G-14432)*

◆ Electro-Mechanical Corporation ......B 276 669-4084
Bristol *(G-1975)*

Energytech Solutions LLC ......G. 703 269-8172
Reston *(G-10846)*

Guardit Technologies LLC ......G. 703 232-1132
Fairfax Station *(G-4711)*

Highland Environmental Inc ......G. 540 392-6067
Riner *(G-11863)*

In10m LLC ......G. 202 779-7977
Richmond *(G-11617)*

▲ Intus Windows LLC ....F 202 450-4211
Fairfax *(G-4480)*

Ltc Enterprises LLC ......G. 540 362-7500
Roanoke *(G-11958)*

Pan American Systems Corp ......G. 757 468-1926
Virginia Beach *(G-14709)*

Parker Hannifen Sporlan Div ......G. 804 379-8551
North Chesterfield *(G-9945)*

Pgf Enterprises LLC ......G. 276 956-4308
Ridgeway *(G-11848)*

Sacyr Environment USA LLC ......G. 202 361-4568
Arlington *(G-1154)*

Siemens Industry Inc ....D 804 222-6680
Richmond *(G-11380)*

Siemens Industry Inc ....D 757 490-6026
Norfolk *(G-9723)*

Southeastern Mechanical Inc ......G. 888 461-7848
Stafford *(G-13193)*

State Line Controls Inc ......G. 757 969-8527
Portsmouth *(G-10485)*

Stuarts AC & Refrigeration ......G. 804 405-0960
Richmond *(G-11400)*

Systems Research and Mfg Corp ......G. 703 765-5827
Alexandria *(G-594)*

Uhr Corporation ......G. 703 534-1250
Falls Church *(G-4885)*

3823 Indl Instruments For Meas, Display & Control

A-Tech Corporation ......G. 703 955-7846
Chantilly *(G-2360)*

Activu Corporation ......G. 703 527-4440
Arlington *(G-838)*

American Density Materials ......G. 540 887-1217
Staunton *(G-13240)*

▲ American Hofmann Corporation ......D 434 522-0300
Lynchburg *(G-7639)*

▲ An Electronic Instrumentation ......C 703 478-0700
Leesburg *(G-7217)*

▲ Atlantic Metal Products Inc ......E. 804 758-4915
Topping *(G-13885)*

Automated Precision Inc ....F 757 223-4157
Newport News *(G-9174)*

Benzaco Scientific Inc ......G. 540 371-5560
Fredericksburg *(G-5402)*

◆ Borgwaldt Kc Incorporated ......E. 804 271-6471
Henrico *(G-6485)*

C E C Controls Company Inc ......G. 757 392-0415
Chesapeake *(G-3021)*

Century Control Systems Inc ......G. 540 992-5100
Roanoke *(G-12061)*

▲ Chemetrics Inc ....D 540 788-9026
Midland *(G-8749)*

Computational Systems Inc ......G. 804 858-5800
Midlothian *(G-8803)*

▲ Controls Corporation America ......C 757 422-8330
Virginia Beach *(G-14363)*

Controls Unlimited Inc ......G. 703 897-4300
Woodbridge *(G-15673)*

CP Instruments LLC ......G. 540 558-8596
Harrisonburg *(G-6307)*

▲ Cryopak Verification Tech Inc ......F. 888 827-3393
Buchanan *(G-2120)*

D & S Controls ......G. 703 655-8189
Warrenton *(G-14993)*

Danaher Family LLC ......G. 703 751-9712
Alexandria *(G-181)*

Delta Electronics Inc ....F 703 354-3350
Alexandria *(G-445)*

Differential Pressure Instrs ......G. 757 362-0742
Virginia Beach *(G-14404)*

Earl Energy LLC ......E. 757 606-2034
Portsmouth *(G-10418)*

Electromotive Inc ......G. 703 331-0100
Manassas *(G-8063)*

Electronic Dev Labs Inc ......E. 434 799-0807
Danville *(G-3990)*

Emerson Electric Co ....E 276 223-2200
Wytheville *(G-15887)*

Envirnmntal Solutions Intl Inc ......F. 703 263-7600
Ashburn *(G-1276)*

Environmental Equipment Inc ......G. 804 730-1280
Mechanicsville *(G-8621)*

Exloc Instruments ......G. 540 428-3088
Warrenton *(G-15006)*

Fisher-Rosemount Systems Inc ......G. 804 714-1400
North Chesterfield *(G-9875)*

Fluxteq LLC ......G. 540 951-0933
Blacksburg *(G-1739)*

◆ Framatome Inc ......B. 434 832-3000
Lynchburg *(G-7716)*

Gammaflux Controls Inc ......G. 703 471-5050
Sterling *(G-13407)*

Gas Sentinel LLC ......G. 703 962-7151
Fairfax *(G-4628)*

General Electric Company ......F. 540 387-7000
Salem *(G-12511)*

Harris Corporation ......G. 571 203-7605
Herndon *(G-6695)*

Industrial Control Systems Inc ......E. 804 737-1700
Sandston *(G-12620)*

Isomet Corporation ......E. 703 321-8301
Manassas *(G-8087)*

Jclfarms LLC ......G. 757 291-1401
Williamsburg *(G-15260)*

L3harris Technologies Inc ......B. 847 952-6120
Dulles *(G-4207)*

L3harris Technologies Inc ......B. 703 668-6239
Herndon *(G-6728)*

L3harris Technologies Inc ......A. 540 563-0371
Roanoke *(G-11951)*

L3harris Technologies Inc ......G. 757 594-1607
Newport News *(G-9278)*

Laser Thermal Analysis LLC ......G. 703 300-3403
Charlottesville *(G-2823)*

▼ Lighthouse Instruments LLC ......E. 434 293-3081
Charlottesville *(G-2825)*

Lutron Electronics Co Inc ....C 804 752-3300
Ashland *(G-1455)*

Mefcor Incorporated ......G. 276 322-5021
North Tazewell *(G-10103)*

Omron Scientific Tech Inc ......G. 703 536-6070
Arlington *(G-1087)*

Online Biose Inc ......G. 703 758-6672
Reston *(G-10914)*

Owens & Jefferson Wtr Systems ......G. 757 357-7359
Smithfield *(G-12719)*

Pacific Scientific Company ......F. 815 226-3100
Radford *(G-10733)*

Pan American Systems Corp ......G. 757 468-1926
Virginia Beach *(G-14709)*

Pressure Systems Inc ....C 757 766-4464
Hampton *(G-6219)*

Quality Manufacturing Co ......G. 540 982-6699
Roanoke *(G-12158)*

Rapid Biosciences Inc ......G. 713 899-6177
Richmond *(G-11728)*

Rebound Analytics LLC ......G. 202 297-1204
Tysons *(G-13948)*

Resource Color Control Tech ......G. 540 548-1855
Fredericksburg *(G-5354)*

Reverse Ionizer LLC ......G. 703 403-7256
Herndon *(G-6791)*

Rotondo Envmtl Solutions LLC ......G. 703 212-4830
Alexandria *(G-329)*

RP Finch Inc ......G. 757 566-8022
Williamsburg *(G-15308)*

Sync Optics LLC ......G. 571 203-0580
Fairfax *(G-4567)*

Teledyne Instruments Inc ....D 757 723-6531
Hampton *(G-6250)*

Thintherm LLC ......G. 434 243-5328
Charlottesville *(G-2891)*

Uavarus LLC ......G. 757 876-5507
Williamsburg *(G-15327)*

Uma Inc ......E. 540 879-2040
Dayton *(G-4067)*

Wise County Psa ......G. 276 762-0159
Coeburn *(G-3705)*

3824 Fluid Meters & Counters

Aae Inc ......G. 804 427-1111
Powhatan *(G-10528)*

Engility LLC ......G. 757 366-4422
Chesapeake *(G-3089)*

Speedmter Clbrtion Specialists ......G. 434 821-5374
Evington *(G-4384)*

Teledyne Instruments Inc ....D...... 757 723-6531
Hampton (G-6250)

Trigg Industries LLC ....G...... 757 223-7522
Newport News (G-9363)

3825 Instrs For Measuring & Testing Electricity

Accuamp Incorporated ....G...... 540 908-4079
Grottoes (G-6012)

Acuity Tech Holdg Co LLC ....G...... 410 290-1411
Fredericksburg (G-5167)

▲ American Hofmann Corporation ......D...... 434 522-0300
Lynchburg (G-7639)

Appalachian Radio Corporation ....G...... 865 382-9865
Ruckersville (G-12398)

Avcom of Virginia Inc ....E...... 804 794-2500
North Chesterfield (G-9823)

Battino Contg Solutions LLC ....G...... 703 408-9162
Edinburg (G-4299)

Bee Measure LLC ....G...... 434 234-4630
Charlottesville (G-2738)

Brandervisions ....G...... 804 744-1705
Midlothian (G-8782)

Brandon Jenkins ....G...... 434 294-0917
Crewe (G-3809)

Clifton Laboratories ....G...... 703 830-0368
Clifton (G-3662)

▲ Climet Instruments ....G...... 434 984-5634
Charlottesville (G-2767)

Crfs Inc ....G...... 571 321-5470
Chantilly (G-2398)

Digital Global Systems Inc ....E...... 240 477-7149
Tysons Corner (G-13953)

▼ Dkl International Inc ....G...... 703 938-6700
Reston (G-10842)

Exeye LLC ....G...... 703 319-0976
Bristow (G-2052)

Fluke Networks ....G...... 804 530-1826
Chester (G-3417)

Freestate Electronics Inc ....G...... 540 349-4727
Warrenton (G-15018)

Grid2020 Inc ....F...... 804 918-1982
North Chesterfield (G-9882)

Hermetic Networks Inc ....G...... 804 545-3173
North Chesterfield (G-9885)

High Speed Networks LLC ....G...... 703 963-4572
Sterling (G-13419)

Infoblox Federal Inc ....E...... 703 672-2607
Herndon (G-6708)

▲ Interbyte ....G...... 703 825-8774
Alexandria (G-486)

Isomet Corporation ....E...... 703 321-8301
Manassas (G-8087)

▼ Isotemp Research Inc ....G...... 434 295-3101
Charlottesville (G-2815)

IV Labs Inc ....D...... 540 585-3030
Christiansburg (G-3599)

Kirintec Inc ....G...... 571 527-1437
Alexandria (G-253)

▲ Kollmorgen Corporation ....A...... 540 639-9045
Radford (G-10720)

Langvan ....G...... 703 532-0466
Falls Church (G-4820)

Local Energy Technologies ....G...... 717 371-0041
Mc Lean (G-8487)

Microxact Inc ....G...... 540 394-4040
Radford (G-10725)

Milhous Control Company ....E...... 434 946-5302
Amherst (G-700)

National Affl Mktg Co Inc ....E...... 703 297-7316
Leesburg (G-7318)

◆ National Imports LLC ....G...... 703 637-0019
Vienna (G-14102)

Ncs Pearson Inc ....G...... 866 673-9034
Virginia Beach (G-14673)

Nergysense LLC ....G...... 434 282-2656
Charlottesville (G-2837)

Nexgrid LLC ....E...... 833 639-4743
Fredericksburg (G-5335)

◆ Northrop Grumman Systems Corp ....B...... 703 280-2900
Falls Church (G-4845)

Nusource LLC ....G...... 571 482-7404
Alexandria (G-298)

◆ Okos Solutions LLC ....E...... 703 880-3039
Manassas (G-8120)

Pacific Scientific Company ....F...... 815 226-3100
Radford (G-10733)

Pan American Systems Corp ....G...... 757 468-1926
Virginia Beach (G-14709)

Pipet Repair Service Inc ....G...... 804 739-3720
Midlothian (G-8880)

Radon Safe Inc ....G...... 540 265-0101
Roanoke (G-11993)

Rinehart Technology Svcs LLC ....G...... 804 744-7891
Midlothian (G-8889)

Robert Denton ....G...... 703 435-6960
Herndon (G-6794)

Sawarmor LLC ....G...... 703 779-7719
Leesburg (G-7342)

Semetrol LLC ....G...... 804 536-7005
Chesterfield (G-3523)

Sentientrf ....G...... 503 467-8026
Leesburg (G-7346)

Silicon Equipment Cons LLC ....G...... 804 357-8926
Midlothian (G-8901)

Six3 Advanced Systems Inc ....G...... 703 742-7660
Dulles (G-4226)

Softlogistics LLC ....G...... 703 865-7965
Great Falls (G-5980)

Spectra Lab LLC ....G...... 703 634-5290
Dumfries (G-4257)

Sustainability Innovations LLC ....G...... 703 281-1352
Vienna (G-14135)

Teledyne Lecroy Inc ....G...... 434 984-4500
Charlottesville (G-2701)

Teledyne Lecroy Frontline Inc ....D...... 434 984-4500
Charlottesville (G-2702)

Thermohalt Technology LLC ....G...... 703 880-6697
Oak Hill (G-10139)

US Electrical Testing LLC ....G...... 703 802-6231
Tysons (G-13949)

▲ Virginia Panel Corporation ....C...... 540 932-3300
Waynesboro (G-15144)

Vtech Solution Inc ....F...... 571 257-0913
Chantilly (G-2565)

Xceedium Inc ....E...... 703 539-5410
Herndon (G-6846)

Zeta Meter Inc ....G...... 540 886-3503
Staunton (G-13309)

3826 Analytical Instruments

3d Imging Smltion Corp Amricas ....G...... 800 570-0363
Herndon (G-6599)

Amscien Instrument ....G...... 804 301-0797
Richmond (G-11113)

◆ Ashbury Intl Group Inc ....F...... 434 296-8600
Ruckersville (G-12399)

Axondx LLC ....G...... 540 239-0668
Earlysville (G-4287)

Blue Ridge Analytical LLC ....G...... 276 228-6464
Wytheville (G-15876)

Cerillo LLC ....G...... 434 218-3151
Charlottesville (G-2762)

▲ Chemetrics Inc ....D...... 540 788-9026
Midland (G-8749)

▲ Crawl Space Door System Inc ....G...... 757 363-0005
Virginia Beach (G-14370)

Crown International Inc ....F...... 703 335-0066
Manassas (G-8053)

D-Star Instruments ....G...... 703 335-0770
Manassas (G-7929)

▲ Dynex Technologies Inc ....D...... 703 631-7800
Chantilly (G-2415)

Electronic Dev Labs Inc ....E...... 434 799-0807
Danville (G-3990)

Emka Technologies Inc ....G...... 703 237-9001
Sterling (G-13393)

Flir Detection Inc ....G...... 877 692-2120
Arlington (G-968)

Flir Systems Inc ....G...... 703 416-6666
Arlington (G-969)

Global Cell Solutions Inc ....G...... 434 327-3759
Charlottesville (G-2804)

Greenvision Systems Inc ....G...... 703 467-8784
Reston (G-10863)

Isomet Corporation ....E...... 703 321-8301
Manassas (G-8087)

Jha LLC ....G...... 757 535-2724
Portsmouth (G-10447)

Labxperior Corporation ....G...... 276 321-7866
Wise (G-15629)

Lighthouse Land LLC ....G...... 434 293-3081
Charlottesville (G-2826)

Lumacyte LLC ....F...... 888 472-9295
Keswick (G-7052)

Medical Laboratory Solutions ....G...... 414 425-8605
Norfolk (G-9636)

Meso Scale Discovery LLC ....G...... 571 318-5521
Fairfax (G-4507)

Mid Atlantic Imaging Centers ....G...... 757 223-5059
Newport News (G-9301)

Nanoarca Inc ....G...... 757 589-2526
Virginia Beach (G-14670)

Notalvision Inc ....D...... 703 953-3339
Manassas (G-8118)

▼ Phipps & Bird Inc ....F...... 804 254-2737
Richmond (G-11059)

Rapid Biosciences Inc ....G...... 713 899-6177
Richmond (G-11728)

Regula Forensics Inc ....G...... 703 473-2625
Reston (G-10936)

Rki Instruments Inc ....G...... 703 753-3333
Haymarket (G-6441)

Sciecom LLC ....G...... 703 994-2635
Chantilly (G-2555)

Scinteck Instruments LLC ....G...... 571 426-3598
Centreville (G-2336)

SES ....G...... 540 428-3919
Manassas (G-8153)

Staib Instruments Inc ....G...... 757 565-7000
Williamsburg (G-15318)

Thermo Fisher Scientific Inc ....B...... 540 869-3200
Middletown (G-8744)

Thorlabs Inc ....E...... 703 300-3000
Sterling (G-13531)

Virginia Spectral LLC ....G...... 434 987-2036
Charlottesville (G-2713)

Whitworth Analytics LLC ....G...... 703 319-8018
Vienna (G-14160)

3827 Optical Instruments

A-Tech Corporation ....G...... 703 955-7846
Chantilly (G-2360)

American Rheinmetall Def Inc ....G...... 571 867-0047
Reston (G-10787)

Armstar Corporation ....G...... 703 241-8888
Falls Church (G-4750)

◆ Ashbury Intl Group Inc ....F...... 434 296-8600
Ruckersville (G-12399)

Automated Precision Inc ....F...... 757 223-4157
Newport News (G-9174)

Avcom of Virginia Inc ....E...... 804 794-2500
North Chesterfield (G-9823)

▲ Blue Ridge Optics LLC ....E...... 540 586-8526
Bedford (G-1628)

C-More Systems Inc ....G...... 540 347-4683
Warrenton (G-14985)

Carl Zeiss Optical Inc ....G...... 804 530-8300
Chester (G-3390)

Carl Zeiss Vision Inc ....D...... 800 456-0088
Chester (G-3391)

Cedar Bluff VA Office ....G...... 276 964-4171
Cedar Bluff (G-2272)

Conforma Laboratories Inc ....E...... 757 321-0200
Norfolk (G-9502)

Dg Optics LLC ....G...... 434 227-1017
Charlottesville (G-2617)

Edwards Optical Corporation ....G...... 757 496-2550
Virginia Beach (G-14434)

Elbit Systems Amer - Nght Vsio ....G...... 540 561-0254
Roanoke (G-11919)

Food Technology Corporation ....G...... 703 444-1870
Sterling (G-13401)

Idu Optics LLC ....G...... 707 845-4996
Quinton (G-10698)

International Trade & Tech Inc ....G...... 703 929-0595
Midland (G-8758)

Isomet Corporation ....E...... 703 321-8301
Manassas (G-8087)

▲ Kollmorgen Corporation ....A...... 540 639-9045
Radford (G-10720)

Leica Microsystems Inc ....E...... 812 333-5416
Chantilly (G-2457)

M5 Technologies LLC ....G...... 540 904-0880
Roanoke (G-12131)

Optometrics LLC ....G...... 540 840-5802
Fredericksburg (G-5465)

Optx Imaging Systems LLC ....F...... 703 398-1432
Lorton (G-7520)

◆ Premier Reticles Ltd ....G...... 540 667-5258
Winchester (G-15568)

Qbeam Inc ....G...... 703 574-5330
Leesburg (G-7329)

Rigel Systems Inc ....G...... 215 715-8950
Herndon (G-6792)

Schmidt & Bender Incorporated ....G...... 770 493-9305
Winchester (G-15474)

Spectrum Optometric ....G...... 804 457-8733
North Chesterfield (G-9986)

S
I
C

Thorlabs Imaging Systems ....F 703 651-1705
  Sterling *(G-13532)*
Tredegar Surfc Protection LLC ....G 804 330-1000
  North Chesterfield *(G-10041)*
Trijicon Inc ....G 703 445-1600
  Stafford *(G-13204)*
Venturewise LLC ....G 804 277-9564
  Richmond *(G-11435)*

3829 Measuring & Controlling Devices, NEC

1 A Life Safer ....G 757 809-0406
  Suffolk *(G-13662)*
1 A Lifesafer Inc ....G 800 634-3077
  Christiansburg *(G-3567)*
1 A Lifesafer Inc ....G 800 634-3077
  Winchester *(G-15523)*
1 A Lifesafer Inc ....G 800 634-3077
  Alexandria *(G-393)*
1 A Lifesafer Inc ....G 800 634-3077
  Manassas Park *(G-8185)*
A & A Precision Machining LLC ......G 804 493-8416
  Montross *(G-9023)*
Accurate Machine Inc ....G 757 853-2136
  Norfolk *(G-9418)*
Advanced Technologies Inc ....D 757 873-3017
  Newport News *(G-9159)*
▲ American Hofmann Corporation ...D 434 522-0300
  Lynchburg *(G-7639)*
▲ An Electronic Instrumentation ....C 703 478-0700
  Leesburg *(G-7217)*
Arktis Detection Systems Inc ....G 610 724-9748
  Arlington *(G-856)*
Avcom of Virginia Inc ....E 804 794-2500
  North Chesterfield *(G-9823)*
Axcelis Technologies Inc ....B 571 921-1493
  Manassas *(G-8032)*
Berger and Burrow Entps Inc ....D 866 483-9729
  Roanoke *(G-11887)*
Bwx Technologies Inc ....C 980 365-4300
  Lynchburg *(G-7667)*
Carlen Controls Incorporated ....F 540 772-1736
  Roanoke *(G-11903)*
◆ Cems Inc ....E 540 434-7500
  Weyers Cave *(G-15170)*
Chittenden & Associates Inc ....G 703 930-2769
  Rocky Mount *(G-12316)*
CJ & Associates LLC ....G 301 461-2945
  Sterling *(G-13370)*
Combat Bound LLC ....G 757 343-3399
  Suffolk *(G-13685)*
Commonwealth Polygraph Svcs LLC ..G 540 219-9382
  Warrenton *(G-14989)*
Controls Unlimited Inc ....G 703 897-4300
  Woodbridge *(G-15673)*
David Gaskill ....G 703 768-2172
  Alexandria *(G-442)*
Design Integrated Tech Inc ....F 540 349-9425
  Warrenton *(G-14995)*
Draeger Safety Diagnostics Inc ....G 434 770-5594
  Martinsville *(G-8280)*
Draeger Safety Diagnostics Inc ....G 434 822-0820
  Danville *(G-3986)*
Draeger Safety Diagnostics Inc ....G 703 517-0974
  Purcellville *(G-10660)*
Ea Design Tech Services ....G 540 220-7203
  Ruther Glen *(G-12455)*
Earth Science Technology LLC ....G 703 584-8533
  Lorton *(G-7483)*
Eddy Current Technology Inc ....G 757 490-1814
  Virginia Beach *(G-14431)*
◆ Electro-Mechanical Corporation ...B 276 669-4084
  Bristol *(G-1975)*
Embassy ....G 703 403-3996
  Arlington *(G-957)*
Entan Devices LLC ....G 757 766-1500
  Hampton *(G-6141)*
Face Construction Technologies .....G 757 624-2121
  Norfolk *(G-9545)*
Fgp Sensors Inc ....G 757 766-1500
  Hampton *(G-6148)*
Flow-Tech Inc ....G 804 752-3450
  Ashland *(G-1417)*
◆ Framatome Inc ....B 434 832-3000
  Lynchburg *(G-7716)*
Gauge Works LLC ....G 703 661-1300
  Sterling *(G-13409)*
Imperium ....G 540 220-6785
  Stafford *(G-13152)*
Innerspec Technologies Inc ....E 434 948-1301
  Forest *(G-5076)*

Ixthos Inc ....G 703 779-7800
  Leesburg *(G-7289)*
Jeffrey O Holdren ....G 703 360-9739
  Alexandria *(G-495)*
Joint Planning Solutions LLC ....G 757 839-5593
  Virginia Beach *(G-14573)*
L-1 Standards and Tech Inc ....G 571 428-2227
  Manassas *(G-8095)*
Lexington Measurement Tech ....G 540 261-3966
  Lexington *(G-7397)*
Lifenet Health ....B 757 464-4761
  Virginia Beach *(G-14610)*
▼ Logis-Tech Inc ....C 703 393-4840
  Manassas *(G-7970)*
Lufft Usa Inc ....F 805 335-8500
  Sterling *(G-13445)*
McQ Inc ....G 540 361-4219
  Fredericksburg *(G-5457)*
◆ Measurement Specialties Inc ....C 757 766-1500
  Hampton *(G-6194)*
▲ Mecmesin Corporation ....G 703 433-9247
  Sterling *(G-13451)*
Medias LLC ....G 540 230-7023
  Blacksburg *(G-1761)*
Mill Mountain Capital LLC ....G 540 529-7163
  Roanoke *(G-11966)*
Model Datasheet Pt Instruments .....G 716 418-4194
  Williamsburg *(G-15280)*
Modern Machine and Tool Co Inc ...D 757 873-1212
  Newport News *(G-9303)*
▲ Moog USA Inc ....G 540 586-6700
  Bedford *(G-1645)*
Morphix Technologies Inc ....E 757 431-2260
  Virginia Beach *(G-14663)*
One Volt Associates ....F 301 565-3930
  Mechanicsville *(G-8666)*
▲ Ott Hydromet Corp ....C 703 406-2800
  Sterling *(G-13468)*
P D R Inc ....G 540 772-2780
  Roanoke *(G-11981)*
Polimaster Inc ....F 703 525-5075
  Sterling *(G-13473)*
Power Monitors Inc ....E 540 432-3077
  Mount Crawford *(G-9057)*
Pressure Systems Inc ....C 757 766-4464
  Hampton *(G-6219)*
Race Technology USA LLC ....G 804 358-7289
  Richmond *(G-11344)*
Rapiscan Systems - An O ....G 703 535-7848
  Arlington *(G-1129)*
Refrigeration Solutions Inc ....G 804 752-3188
  Ashland *(G-1484)*
Regula Forensics Inc ....G 703 473-2625
  Reston *(G-10936)*
Reliant Cem Services Inc ....G 717 459-4990
  Lynchburg *(G-7801)*
Scintilex LLC ....G 240 593-7906
  Alexandria *(G-579)*
Sematron LLC ....G 919 360-5806
  Leesburg *(G-7345)*
Sencontrology Inc ....G 540 529-7000
  Roanoke *(G-12181)*
Senstar Inc ....G 703 463-3088
  Herndon *(G-6804)*
Sentek Instrument LLC ....G 540 831-9693
  Blacksburg *(G-1788)*
Sentek Instrument LLC ....G 540 250-2116
  Blacksburg *(G-1789)*
Smrt Mouth LLC ....G 804 363-8863
  Sandston *(G-12634)*
Spectra Quest Inc ....F 804 261-3300
  Henrico *(G-6574)*
System Innovations Inc ....F 540 373-2374
  Fredericksburg *(G-5491)*
Terminus Products Inc ....G 585 546-4990
  Christiansburg *(G-3612)*
TMI Usa Inc ....G 703 668-0114
  Reston *(G-10975)*
Virginia Electronic Monitoring ....G 757 513-0942
  Chesapeake *(G-3361)*
Warcollar Industries LLC ....G 703 981-2862
  Vienna *(G-14156)*

3841 Surgical & Medical Instrs & Apparatus

Absolute Anesthesia ....G 434 277-9360
  Piney River *(G-10360)*
Adult Medical Predictive Devic ....G 434 996-1203
  Keswick *(G-7042)*
Advanced Bioip LLC ....G 301 646-3040
  Leesburg *(G-7215)*

Advancing Eyecare ....E 757 853-8888
  Norfolk *(G-9424)*
Aerospace Techniques Inc ....D 860 347-1200
  Virginia Beach *(G-14214)*
Agent Medical LLC ....G 804 562-9469
  Richmond *(G-11089)*
▲ Alr Technologies Inc ....G 804 554-3500
  North Chesterfield *(G-10016)*
American Medical Devices Inc ....F 276 642-0463
  Bristol *(G-1965)*
▲ Atc Inc ....G 703 267-6898
  Bristow *(G-2046)*
▲ Autopartsource LLC ....G 804 329-3000
  Richmond *(G-11495)*
Baxter Healthcare Corporation ....G 804 226-1962
  Richmond *(G-11122)*
Becton Dickinson and Company ......G 804 744-4495
  Midlothian *(G-8778)*
Bellair Biomedical LLC ....G 276 206-7337
  Charlottesville *(G-2739)*
Biotraces Inc ....F 703 793-1550
  Burke *(G-2185)*
Boss Instruments Ltd Inc ....F 540 832-5000
  Zion Crossroads *(G-16005)*
C R Bard Inc ....G 703 754-2848
  Gainesville *(G-5574)*
▲ Cadence Inc ....C 540 248-2200
  Staunton *(G-13245)*
Carefusion Solutions LLC ....E 571 521-8900
  Reston *(G-10819)*
Caretaker Medical LLC ....G 434 978-7000
  Charlottesville *(G-2604)*
Chemteq ....F 757 622-2223
  Norfolk *(G-9481)*
Computerized Imaging Reference ....E 757 855-1127
  Norfolk *(G-9500)*
Deconsystems Corporation ....G 703 587-3971
  Woodbridge *(G-15681)*
Elcare Innovations Inc ....G 434 525-7685
  Forest *(G-5069)*
Epic Mfg LLC ....G 757 689-4373
  Virginia Beach *(G-14449)*
Epiep Inc ....G 864 423-2526
  Charlottesville *(G-2790)*
Fli USA Inc ....G 571 261-4174
  Gainesville *(G-5583)*
Fmd LLC ....G 703 339-8881
  Lorton *(G-7490)*
Freedom Respiratory ....G 804 266-2002
  Henrico *(G-6515)*
G-Holdings LLC ....G 202 255-9698
  Alexandria *(G-209)*
Gogo Band Inc ....G 804 869-8253
  Ashland *(G-1421)*
Grampian Group Inc ....G 757 277-5557
  Williamsburg *(G-15249)*
Healthy Labradors ....G 757 740-0681
  Norfolk *(G-9576)*
Human Design Medical LLC ....G 434 980-8100
  Charlottesville *(G-2812)*
Hy-Mark Cylinders Inc ....E 757 251-6744
  Hampton *(G-6173)*
Icare Clinical Tech LLC ....G 301 646-3640
  Leesburg *(G-7285)*
Incision Tech ....G 727 254-9183
  Staunton *(G-13268)*
▲ Interbyte ....G 703 825-8774
  Alexandria *(G-486)*
Itl (virginia) Inc ....G 804 381-0905
  Ashland *(G-1441)*
Itl NA Inc ....G 703 435-6700
  Herndon *(G-6713)*
J M H Diagnostic Center ....G 276 628-1439
  Abingdon *(G-42)*
Lake Region Medical Inc ....C 540 389-7860
  Salem *(G-12528)*
Maroon Assistive Tech LLC ....G 703 239-3113
  Blacksburg *(G-1760)*
Medipak ....G 540 667-0233
  Winchester *(G-15446)*
Medmarc ....G 703 652-1305
  Fairfax *(G-4505)*
Medtrnic Sofamor Danek USA Inc ....F 757 355-5100
  Virginia Beach *(G-14645)*
Merit Medical Systems Inc ....D 804 416-1030
  Chester *(G-3433)*
Merit Medical Systems Inc ....G 804 416-1069
  Chester *(G-3434)*
Microaire Surgical Instrs LLC ....F 434 975-8300
  Charlottesville *(G-2658)*

◆ **Microaire Surgical Instrs LLC** ....C 800 722-0822
Charlottesville *(G-2659)*

Microtek Medical Inc ....E 703 904-1220
Sterling *(G-13454)*

Moog Components Group ....G 540 443-4699
Blacksburg *(G-1763)*

Moog Inc ....G 716 652-2000
Blacksburg *(G-1764)*

Neurotech Na Inc ....G 888 980-1197
Manassas *(G-8116)*

Northfield Medical Mfg LLC ....E 800 270-0153
Norfolk *(G-9669)*

Notalvision Inc ....F 888 910-2020
Chantilly *(G-2473)*

▲ **Ondal Medical Systems Amer Inc** ....F 804 279-0320
Sandston *(G-12627)*

Origio Inc ....E 434 979-4000
Charlottesville *(G-2670)*

Owl Peak Technologies Inc ....G 847 612-0609
Charlottesville *(G-2839)*

▲ **Pari Respiratory Equipment Inc** ....F 804 897-3311
Midlothian *(G-8876)*

Peer Technologies Pllc ....G 603 727-8692
Fairfax *(G-4660)*

▼ **Phipps & Bird Inc** ....F 804 254-2737
Richmond *(G-11059)*

Plexus Inc ....G 703 474-0383
Herndon *(G-6775)*

Poamax LLC ....G 757 871-7196
Poquoson *(G-10374)*

Porex Corporation ....G 804 518-1012
South Chesterfield *(G-12820)*

▲ **Pre Holdings Inc** ....G 804 253-7274
Midlothian *(G-8881)*

Predictive Health Devices Inc ....G 703 507-0627
Stafford *(G-13182)*

Product Dev Mfg & Packg ....G 703 777-8400
Leesburg *(G-7328)*

Professional Network Services ....G 571 283-4858
Woodbridge *(G-15784)*

Pulmoflow Inc ....G 831 206-8659
Richmond *(G-11340)*

Quality Equipment Repair ....G 804 815-2268
Deltaville *(G-4085)*

Ramsey Manufacturing LLC ....G 757 232-9034
Norfolk *(G-9701)*

Richmond Light Co ....G 804 276-0559
North Chesterfield *(G-9961)*

Richmond Light Co ....G 804 276-0559
North Chesterfield *(G-9962)*

Rip Shears LLC ....G 757 635-9560
Virginia Beach *(G-14776)*

Riverside Healthcare Assn Inc ....G 757 594-3900
Newport News *(G-9328)*

Rocamed Inc ....G 703 503-3616
Mc Lean *(G-8540)*

Stealth Surgical LLC ....G 540 832-5580
Zion Crossroads *(G-16009)*

Stryker Corporation ....G 571 919-2345
Leesburg *(G-7353)*

Surgical Instr Sharpening Inc ....G 804 883-6010
Beaverdam *(G-1613)*

Sweet Sounds Music Therapy LLC ....G 703 965-3624
Alexandria *(G-360)*

Swinson Medical LLC ....G 540 576-1719
Penhook *(G-10285)*

T W Enterprises Inc ....G 540 667-0233
Winchester *(G-15485)*

Tasens Assoc ....G 703 455-2424
Springfield *(G-13098)*

Tegrex Technologies LLC ....G 805 500-8479
Charlottesville *(G-2888)*

Timberville Drug Store ....G 540 434-2379
Harrisonburg *(G-6382)*

Truefit Dme LLC ....G 434 980-8100
Charlottesville *(G-2897)*

Turner Public Affairs Inc ....G 703 489-7104
Gainesville *(G-5619)*

Tycosys LLC ....G 571 278-5300
Manassas *(G-8006)*

Uma Inc ....E 540 879-2040
Dayton *(G-4067)*

Urologics LLC ....G 757 419-1463
Midlothian *(G-8917)*

Varian Medical Systems Inc ....E 434 977-8495
Charlottesville *(G-2898)*

Veterans Choice Med Sup LLC ....G 571 244-4358
Purcellville *(G-10685)*

Voltmed Inc ....G 443 799-3072
Blacksburg *(G-1805)*

Wal-Star Inc ....F 434 685-1094
Danville *(G-4049)*

Wright Medical Technology Inc ....G 703 729-0643
Ashburn *(G-1353)*

3842 Orthopedic, Prosthetic & Surgical Appliances/Splys

▼ **Accessible Environments Inc** ....G 757 565-3444
Williamsburg *(G-15201)*

Air Britt Two LLC ....G 757 470-9364
Virginia Beach *(G-14218)*

Allcare Non-Medical Wheelchair ....G 757 291-2500
Chesapeake *(G-2958)*

American Cmg Services Inc ....G 804 353-9077
Richmond *(G-11107)*

American Cmg Services Inc ....G 757 548-5656
Chesapeake *(G-2965)*

Anderson Audiology Hearing Aid ....G 540 616-7990
Blacksburg *(G-1722)*

Angel Rides Inc ....G 540 373-5540
Fredericksburg *(G-5245)*

Arben Solutions Co ....G 703 728-0396
Warrenton *(G-14978)*

Ascp Solutions LLC ....F 410 782-1122
Manassas *(G-7914)*

Best Medical Belgium Inc ....G 800 336-4970
Springfield *(G-12961)*

◆ **Best Medical International Inc** ....C 703 451-2378
Springfield *(G-12962)*

Bio-Prosthetic Orthotic Lab ....G 703 527-3123
Arlington *(G-883)*

Biomaterials USA LLC ....G 843 442-4789
Richmond *(G-11127)*

Blue Ridge Chorale of Culpeper ....G 540 717-5888
Culpeper *(G-3874)*

Blue Ridge Prosthetics & Ortho ....G 540 242-4499
Harrisonburg *(G-6296)*

Bristol Orthotic & Prosthetic ....G 276 963-1186
Abingdon *(G-16)*

Byrd Assistive Tech Inc ....G 571 512-6069
Chantilly *(G-2382)*

Coastal Prsttics Orthotics LLC ....G 757 892-5300
Chesapeake *(G-3043)*

Coastal Prsttics Orthotics LLC ....G 757 240-4228
Newport News *(G-9201)*

Comfortrac Inc ....G 703 891-0455
Mc Lean *(G-8407)*

Commonwealth Orthotics & Prost ....G 434 836-4736
Danville *(G-3969)*

Commonwealth Surgical Solution ....G 804 330-0988
North Chesterfield *(G-9851)*

Commonwlth Orthtics Prosthetic ....G 434 836-4736
Danville *(G-3970)*

District Orthopedic Appliances ....G 703 698-7373
Springfield *(G-12993)*

Draeger Safety Diagnostics Inc ....G 540 382-6650
Christiansburg *(G-3585)*

Drake Hearing Aid Centers ....G 703 521-1404
Arlington *(G-941)*

▲ **Eagle Industries Unlimited Inc** ....E 888 343-7547
Virginia Beach *(G-14425)*

Earmold Company Ltd ....F 540 389-1642
Salem *(G-12499)*

Easter VA Orthtics Prosthetics ....G 757 967-0526
Suffolk *(G-13702)*

Eastern Cranial Affiliates LLC ....G 703 807-5899
Arlington *(G-951)*

Eastern Cranial Affiliates LLC ....G 703 807-5899
Fairfax *(G-4616)*

Eclipse Holsters LLC ....G 907 382-6958
Williamsburg *(G-15237)*

Elevate Hearing Aid Center ....G 540 785-4676
Fredericksburg *(G-5281)*

Emtech Laboratories Inc ....E 540 265-9156
Roanoke *(G-11921)*

Excel Prsthetics Orthotics Inc ....F 540 982-0205
Roanoke *(G-12083)*

Excel Prsthetics Orthotics Inc ....G 434 528-3695
Lynchburg *(G-7706)*

Excel Prsthetics Orthotics Inc ....G 434 797-1191
Danville *(G-3993)*

Firemans Shield LLC ....G 804 231-1800
Richmond *(G-11590)*

▲ **Foot Levelers Inc** ....E 800 553-4860
Roanoke *(G-12091)*

Footmaxx of Virginia Inc ....G 540 345-0008
Roanoke *(G-12092)*

▲ **H&H Medical Corporation** ....E 800 326-5708
Williamsburg *(G-15253)*

Hairbotics LLC ....G 703 496-6083
Alexandria *(G-473)*

Hanger Prosthetics Orthotics ....G 703 719-0143
Alexandria *(G-474)*

Hanger Prsthetcs & Ortho Inc ....G 434 846-1803
Lynchburg *(G-7727)*

Hanger Prsthetcs & Ortho Inc ....G 757 873-1984
Newport News *(G-9243)*

Have Happyfeet ....G 757 339-0833
Norfolk *(G-9573)*

Hear Quick Incorporated ....G 757 523-0504
Virginia Beach *(G-14513)*

Hollister Incorporated ....B 540 943-1733
Stuarts Draft *(G-13651)*

Howmedica Osteonics Corp ....G 804 737-9426
Glen Allen *(G-5748)*

Imagine Milling Tech LLC ....G 571 313-1269
Chantilly *(G-2441)*

Indyne Inc ....G 703 903-6900
Sterling *(G-13427)*

K2m Group Holdings Inc ....B 703 777-3155
Leesburg *(G-7295)*

Kay Kare LLC ....G 614 309-8462
Arlington *(G-1021)*

Keystone Supply Co Inc ....G 610 525-3654
Elkton *(G-4329)*

Lane Custom Hearing ....G 540 775-5999
King George *(G-7099)*

Larry Kaniecki ....G 804 737-7616
Sandston *(G-12623)*

Lifeline of Prince William ....G 703 753-9000
Yorktown *(G-15975)*

Lifenet Health ....B 757 464-4761
Virginia Beach *(G-14610)*

Mach278 LLC ....G 716 860-2889
Ashburn *(G-1313)*

▲ **Manakin Industries LLC** ....G 804 784-5514
Manakin Sabot *(G-7903)*

Medical Sports Inc ....G 703 241-9720
Arlington *(G-1060)*

◆ **Microaire Surgical Instrs LLC** ....C 800 722-0822
Charlottesville *(G-2659)*

Mid-Atlantic Bracing Corp ....G 757 301-3952
Virginia Beach *(G-14650)*

Mission Integrated Tech LLC ....G 202 769-9900
Vienna *(G-14097)*

Mitchell Medical LLC ....G 804 640-4851
Montpelier *(G-9018)*

Ms Wheelchair Virginia Inc ....G 540 838-5022
Fairlawn *(G-4738)*

Neuropro Spinal Jaxx Inc ....G 571 334-7424
Burke *(G-2195)*

Northfield Medical Mfg LLC ....E 800 270-0153
Norfolk *(G-9669)*

O Depuy ....G 804 330-0988
North Chesterfield *(G-9942)*

Orthotic Prosthetic Center ....G 703 698-5007
Fairfax *(G-4526)*

Orthotic Solutions L L C ....G 703 849-9200
Fairfax *(G-4527)*

Out On A Limb Quiltworks ....G 804 739-7901
Midlothian *(G-8873)*

Paul Valentine Orthotics ....G 804 355-0283
Richmond *(G-11320)*

Porex Corporation ....G 804 518-1012
South Chesterfield *(G-12820)*

Precept Medical Products Inc ....G 804 236-1010
Richmond *(G-11329)*

Premier Resources Express LLC ....G 717 887-4003
Chesapeake *(G-3245)*

Price Point Equipment ....G 239 216-1688
Sterling *(G-13477)*

Prince William Orthotics & Prs ....G 703 368-7967
Manassas *(G-8134)*

Prostride Orthotics LLC ....G 804 310-3894
Henrico *(G-6552)*

Reach Orthotic Prosthetic Svcs ....G 757 930-0139
Newport News *(G-9321)*

Reach Orthtic Prsthetic Svcs S ....G 757 673-2000
Chesapeake *(G-3261)*

Realty Restorations LLC ....G 757 553-6117
Virginia Beach *(G-14764)*

Regula Forensics Inc ....G 703 473-2625
Reston *(G-10936)*

Rehabltation Practitioners Inc ....G 540 722-9025
Winchester *(G-15579)*

Rescue Systems Inc ....G 276 629-2900
Bassett *(G-1590)*

Rescue Systems Intl Inc ....G 276 629-2900
Fincastle *(G-4998)*

S I C

Roanoke Stars ....G.... 540 797-8266
　Roanoke *(G-11996)*

Sama Artfl Intelligence LLC ....G.... 347 223-2437
　Alexandria *(G-335)*

Senior Mobility LLC ....G.... 540 574-0215
　Harrisonburg *(G-6368)*

Shh Stmlting Healthy Hair LLC ....G.... 973 607-7138
　Fredericksburg *(G-5222)*

Silver Ring Splint Co ....G.... 434 971-4052
　Charlottesville *(G-2877)*

Solution Matrix Inc ....E.... 540 352-3211
　Rocky Mount *(G-12352)*

Southside Youth Festival ....G.... 434 767-2584
　Burkeville *(G-2210)*

Stealth Mfg & Svcs LLC ....G.... 787 679-7548
　Virginia Beach *(G-14844)*

Stryker Corporation ....G.... 571 919-2000
　Leesburg *(G-7352)*

Surefire Auto Detailing ....G.... 703 361-2369
　Manassas *(G-8163)*

Sweetpeas By Shafer Dobry ....G.... 703 476-6787
　Herndon *(G-6819)*

Synergy Orthtics Prsthtics LLC ....G.... 410 788-8901
　Broadlands *(G-2082)*

Tape-Tab LP ....G.... 804 404-6855
　Henrico *(G-6578)*

Thomas Hegens ....F.... 703 205-9000
　Fairfax *(G-4569)*

Tidewater Prosthetic Center ....G.... 757 925-4844
　Norfolk *(G-9756)*

Tidewater Prosthetic Center ....G.... 757 925-4844
　Suffolk *(G-13772)*

▲ Tubular Fabricators Indust Inc.........E.... 804 733-4000
　Petersburg *(G-10347)*

Urologics LLC ....G.... 757 419-1463
　Midlothian *(G-8917)*

Valley Orthtic Specialists Inc ....G.... 540 667-3631
　Winchester *(G-15598)*

Victorious Images LLC ....G.... 757 476-7335
　Williamsburg *(G-15331)*

Virginia Beach Products LLC ....G.... 757 847-9338
　Virginia Beach *(G-14912)*

Virginia Beach Products LLC ....G.... 757 847-9338
　Virginia Beach *(G-14913)*

Virginia Prosthetics Inc ....E.... 540 366-8287
　Roanoke *(G-12218)*

Virginia Prosthetics Orthotics ....G.... 540 949-4248
　Fishersville *(G-5012)*

War Fighter Specialties LLC ....G.... 540 742-4187
　Shenandoah *(G-12697)*

Yacoe LLC ....G.... 973 735-3095
　Richmond *(G-11837)*

3843 Dental Eqpt & Splys

Affordable Care Inc ....G.... 276 928-1427
　Rocky Gap *(G-12304)*

Contour Healer LLC ....G.... 757 288-6671
　Virginia Beach *(G-14362)*

Danville Dental Laboratory ....G.... 434 793-2225
　Danville *(G-3977)*

Denis Britto Dr ....G.... 703 230-6784
　Chantilly *(G-2405)*

Dental Equipment Services LLC ....G.... 703 927-1837
　Leesburg *(G-7253)*

Dentcore Inc ....E.... 844 292-8023
　Chantilly *(G-2406)*

Dof USA Inc ....G.... 888 635-4999
　Chantilly *(G-2409)*

Dr Banaji Girish DDS PC ....G.... 703 849-1300
　Fairfax *(G-4441)*

Flexi-Dent Inc ....G.... 804 897-2455
　Midlothian *(G-8819)*

Frogue ....F.... 703 679-7003
　Reston *(G-10854)*

Henry Schein ....G.... 703 883-8031
　Mc Lean *(G-8457)*

Ilumi Sciences Inc ....G.... 703 894-7576
　Chantilly *(G-2440)*

John E Hilton ....G.... 540 639-1674
　Radford *(G-10719)*

Pink Dental Laboratory LLC ....G.... 540 728-5987
　Sterling *(G-13470)*

Steven Alsahi ....G.... 703 369-0099
　Manassas *(G-8162)*

Timothy Breeden ....G.... 804 748-6433
　Chester *(G-3461)*

Vandent Dental Inc ....G.... 757 678-7973
　Eastville *(G-4297)*

Virginia Dental Sc Inc ....G.... 804 422-1888
　Richmond *(G-11440)*

Wade F Anderson ....G.... 804 358-8204
　Richmond *(G-11817)*

3844 X-ray Apparatus & Tubes

Adani Systems Inc ....G.... 703 528-0035
　Alexandria *(G-118)*

Analyzed Images ....G.... 757 905-4500
　Virginia Beach *(G-14227)*

Berger and Burrow Entps Inc ....E.... 804 282-9729
　Henrico *(G-6481)*

Brachyfoam LLC ....G.... 434 249-9554
　Charlottesville *(G-2749)*

Dilon Technologies Inc ....E.... 757 269-4910
　Newport News *(G-9216)*

Electron Technologies Inc ....G.... 703 818-9400
　Chantilly *(G-2416)*

Locker LLC ....G.... 310 978-1457
　Arlington *(G-1042)*

◆ Mosaic Distribution LLC ....G.... 978 328-7001
　Chantilly *(G-2547)*

▼ Rapiscan Government Svcs Inc ....G.... 571 227-6767
　Arlington *(G-1128)*

River Technologies LLC ....F.... 434 525-4734
　Forest *(G-5090)*

Sim Net Inc ....G.... 804 752-2776
　Beaverdam *(G-1611)*

◆ Vidar Systems Corporation ....E.... 703 471-7070
　Herndon *(G-6838)*

3845 Electromedical & Electrotherapeutic Apparatus

▲ Alr Technologies Inc ....G.... 804 554-3500
　North Chesterfield *(G-10016)*

Aretech LLC ....G.... 571 292-8889
　Ashburn *(G-1242)*

Biosensor Tech LLC ....G.... 318 843-4479
　Glen Allen *(G-5709)*

Bonde Innovation LLC ....G.... 434 951-0444
　Charlottesville *(G-2746)*

Closed Loop LLC ....G.... 804 648-4802
　Richmond *(G-11159)*

E-Kare Inc ....G.... 844 443-5273
　Fairfax *(G-4442)*

Electrovita LLC ....G.... 703 447-7290
　Vienna *(G-14045)*

Farbes LLC ....G.... 240 426-9680
　Alexandria *(G-460)*

Iheartrhythm LLC ....G.... 757 810-5902
　Arlington *(G-999)*

Inspire Living Inc ....G.... 703 991-0451
　Haymarket *(G-6427)*

Iviz Ltd ....G.... 877 290-4911
　Stafford *(G-13156)*

Ivwatch LLC ....E.... 855 489-2824
　Newport News *(G-9262)*

Rivanna Medical LLC ....G.... 828 612-8191
　Charlottesville *(G-2863)*

Sak Consulting ....G.... 703 220-2020
　Lake Ridge *(G-7157)*

Slim Silhouettes LLC ....G.... 757 337-5965
　Virginia Beach *(G-14825)*

Soundpipe LLC ....G.... 434 218-3394
　Charlottesville *(G-2879)*

Thermal Gradient Inc ....G.... 585 425-3338
　Williamsburg *(G-15324)*

Uma Inc ....E.... 540 879-2040
　Dayton *(G-4067)*

Voltmed Inc ....G.... 443 799-3072
　Blacksburg *(G-1805)*

Wood Burn Endoscopy Center ....G.... 703 752-2557
　Annandale *(G-793)*

Xyken LLC ....G.... 703 288-1601
　Mc Lean *(G-8582)*

3851 Ophthalmic Goods

Bausch & Lomb Incorporated ....C.... 434 385-0407
　Lynchburg *(G-7650)*

Better Vision Eyeglass Center ....G.... 757 397-2020
　Portsmouth *(G-10400)*

Conforma Laboratories Inc ....E.... 757 321-0200
　Norfolk *(G-9502)*

Darwins LLC ....G.... 610 256-3716
　Arlington *(G-928)*

Euclid Systems Corporation ....D.... 703 471-7145
　Sterling *(G-13395)*

Eyeglass Repair Shoppe ....G.... 903 509-1517
　Mount Solon *(G-9087)*

House of Vondrake Lavar LLC ....G.... 804 295-6136
　Colonial Heights *(G-3734)*

Infocus Coatings Inc ....G.... 804 520-1573
　South Chesterfield *(G-12811)*

Kasinof & Associates ....G.... 757 827-6530
　Hampton *(G-6179)*

Le Grand Assoc of Pittsburgh ....G.... 757 484-4900
　Chesapeake *(G-3180)*

Legend Lenses LLC ....G.... 757 871-1331
　Yorktown *(G-15974)*

◆ Liberty Medical Inc ....G.... 703 636-2269
　Sterling *(G-13441)*

Medlens Innovations LLC ....G.... 540 636-7976
　Front Royal *(G-5542)*

Northfield Medical Mfg LLC ....E.... 800 270-0153
　Norfolk *(G-9669)*

Northwestern PA Opt Clinic ....G.... 540 721-6017
　Moneta *(G-8973)*

Retivue LLC ....G.... 434 260-2836
　Charlottesville *(G-2684)*

Spectacle & Mirth ....G.... 619 961-6941
　Staunton *(G-13296)*

Spectacular Spectacles Inc ....G.... 540 636-2020
　Front Royal *(G-5555)*

William O Wills Od ....F.... 540 371-9191
　Fredericksburg *(G-5237)*

3861 Photographic Eqpt & Splys

A Better Image ....G.... 804 358-9912
　Richmond *(G-11076)*

Akmal Khaliqi ....G.... 202 710-7582
　Woodbridge *(G-15643)*

▼ Allegheny Instruments Inc ....G.... 540 468-3740
　Monterey *(G-9001)*

ARC Second Inc ....G.... 703 435-5400
　Sterling *(G-13348)*

Ashen Writ LLC ....G.... 757 818-8271
　Chesapeake *(G-2983)*

Automated Signature Technology ....F.... 703 397-0910
　Sterling *(G-13356)*

Aviation Tactical LLC ....G.... 970 946-7027
　Springfield *(G-12957)*

Boomin Bass Global LLC ....F.... 757 776-8668
　Virginia Beach *(G-14294)*

C I T C Imaging ....G.... 540 382-6557
　Christiansburg *(G-3576)*

▲ Canon Environmental Tech Inc.........B.... 804 695-7000
　Gloucester *(G-5839)*

◆ Canon Virginia Inc ....A.... 757 881-6000
　Newport News *(G-9192)*

Catawba Sound Studio ....G.... 540 992-4738
　Troutville *(G-13905)*

Creativexposure LLC ....G.... 540 668-9070
　Hillsboro *(G-6862)*

Crossroad Data Solutions LLC ....G.... 804 302-4312
　Chesterfield *(G-3490)*

Crown Enterprise LLC ....G.... 757 277-8837
　Virginia Beach *(G-14374)*

Cybersquire LLC ....G.... 703 472-0283
　Falls Church *(G-4906)*

Dekdyne Inc ....G.... 757 221-2542
　Williamsburg *(G-15232)*

Digital Design Imaging Svc Inc ....G.... 703 534-7500
　Falls Church *(G-4907)*

Dream Reels Inc ....E.... 540 891-9886
　Fredericksburg *(G-5277)*

Dreauxn Films LLC ....G.... 504 452-1117
　Sterling *(G-13389)*

Dun Inc ....G.... 804 240-4183
　Palmyra *(G-10248)*

Extreme Exposure Media LLC ....F.... 540 434-0811
　Harrisonburg *(G-6315)*

Falcon Screens LLC ....G.... 703 789-3274
　Bristow *(G-2053)*

George Leica Systems ....G.... 804 299-3911
　Ashland *(G-1420)*

Graphus Inc ....G.... 703 481-8861
　Reston *(G-10862)*

Harkness Hall Ltd ....G.... 540 370-1590
　Fredericksburg *(G-5194)*

Harkness Screens (usa) Limited ....G.... 540 370-1590
　Roanoke *(G-11932)*

▲ Harkness Screens (usa) Limited .....E.... 540 370-1590
　Fredericksburg *(G-5437)*

Huqa Live LLC ....G.... 202 527-9342
　Woodbridge *(G-15724)*

Ict Mondial Inc ....G.... 703 254-7416
　Springfield *(G-13020)*

▲ Kollmorgen Corporation ....A.... 540 639-9045
　Radford *(G-10720)*

Konica Mnlta Bus Sltons USA In ....E.... 703 553-6000
　Vienna *(G-14079)*

Lonesome Trails LLC.....G..... 276 445-5443
Rose Hill *(G-12361)*
Media Magic LLC.....G..... 757 893-0988
Virginia Beach *(G-14644)*
Openbox Networks LLC.....G..... 540 607-0149
Waynesboro *(G-15130)*
Pics By Kels Photography LLC.....G..... 540 958-4944
Clifton Forge *(G-3681)*
Q Star Technology LLC.....G..... 703 578-1495
Alexandria *(G-322)*
Rhoades Enterprise.....G..... 804 347-2051
Emporia *(G-4366)*
Ronald Paul Gardner.....G..... 804 815-6529
Hayes *(G-6405)*
Safran Cabin Sterling Inc.....D..... 571 789-1900
Sterling *(G-13500)*
Spider Support Systems.....G..... 703 758-0699
Reston *(G-10961)*
Tidewater Techs LLC.....G..... 757 301-1789
Virginia Beach *(G-14878)*
Tienda Herndon Inc.....G..... 703 478-0478
Herndon *(G-6826)*
Video-Scope International Ltd.....G..... 703 437-5534
Sterling *(G-13550)*
Wimberley Inc.....G..... 703 242-9633
Charlottesville *(G-2907)*
Xerox.....G..... 703 330-4044
Manassas *(G-8180)*
Zeido LLC.....G..... 202 549-5757
Stafford *(G-13213)*

3873 Watch & Clock Devices & Parts

◆ **Hermle Uhren GMBH & Co KG**.....D..... 434 946-7751
Amherst *(G-693)*
Hodges Watch Company LLC.....G..... 703 651-6440
Falls Church *(G-4918)*
Hr Kids LLC.....G..... 210 341-7783
Newport News *(G-9248)*

39 MISCELLANEOUS MANUFACTURING INDUSTRIES

3911 Jewelry: Precious Metal

Ali Baba Handwrought Jewelry.....G..... 757 622-5007
Norfolk *(G-9430)*
Amanda Grace Handcrafted.....G..... 703 539-2151
Fairfax *(G-4405)*
Amelia Lawrence LLC.....G..... 703 493-9095
Manassas *(G-8025)*
Aumiitu Combs Creations LLC.....G..... 757 285-5201
Virginia Beach *(G-14248)*
Birds With Backpacks LLC.....G..... 703 897-5531
Woodbridge *(G-15657)*
Clark & Clark LLC.....G..... 757 264-9000
Norfolk *(G-9487)*
Crystals of Hope.....G..... 434 525-7279
Lynchburg *(G-7688)*
Cynthia Coriopoli Design.....G..... 703 548-2086
Alexandria *(G-180)*
Delmer-Va Inc.....G..... 571 447-1413
Manassas *(G-8056)*
Dmkp Inc.....G..... 703 941-1436
Mc Lean *(G-8420)*
Ellen Fairchild-Flugel Art LLC.....G..... 540 325-2305
Woodstock *(G-15852)*
Eminence Jewelers.....G..... 703 815-1384
Clifton *(G-3664)*
Frangipani Inc.....G..... 703 903-0099
Mc Lean *(G-8436)*
Gabriel D Ofiesh II Inc.....G..... 434 295-9038
Charlottesville *(G-2800)*
Hand and Hammer Inc.....F..... 703 491-4866
Woodbridge *(G-15721)*
Herff Jones LLC.....G..... 703 368-9550
Manassas *(G-7952)*
High Concepts.....G..... 804 683-2226
Glen Allen *(G-5745)*
Hudson Jewelry Co Inc.....G..... 276 646-5565
Marion *(G-8229)*
Hugo Kohl LLC.....G..... 540 564-2755
Harrisonburg *(G-6330)*
Hunt Country Jewelers Inc.....G..... 540 338-8050
Hillsboro *(G-6871)*
Jewelers Services Inc.....F..... 804 353-9612
Chesterfield *(G-3507)*
John C Nordt Co Inc.....C..... 540 362-9717
Roanoke *(G-12112)*
Jones Tonja.....G..... 757 773-9475
Portsmouth *(G-10448)*
Jt Tobacco.....G..... 540 387-0383
Salem *(G-12525)*
Jwlbook LLC.....G..... 571 287-0121
Fairfax *(G-4641)*
Kirk Burkett Manufacturing.....G..... 276 699-6856
Austinville *(G-1529)*
Kweens Essentials LLC.....G..... 703 861-6764
Alexandria *(G-511)*
Lavish Nicole LLC.....G..... 804 386-7556
South Chesterfield *(G-12812)*
Lucia Richie.....G..... 804 878-8969
Midlothian *(G-8851)*
M Shields Studio Inc.....G..... 757 340-1670
Norfolk *(G-9627)*
Metallum.....G..... 703 549-4551
Alexandria *(G-274)*
Neda Jewelers Inc.....G..... 703 670-2177
Woodbridge *(G-15757)*
Patrick Marrietta.....G..... 804 479-9791
Petersburg *(G-10333)*
Price Goldsmith Co.....G..... 757 722-3210
Hampton *(G-6221)*
Raybar Jewelry Design Inc.....G..... 757 486-4562
Virginia Beach *(G-14760)*
Riina Mettas Jewelry LLC.....G..... 202 368-9819
Woodbridge *(G-15795)*
Rng LLC.....G..... 540 825-5322
Culpeper *(G-3917)*
Romancing Stone.....G..... 804 769-7888
Aylett *(G-1553)*
Ronald Steven Hamm.....G..... 434 295-8878
Charlottesville *(G-2866)*
Rubinas Adornments Inc.....G..... 757 623-4246
Norfolk *(G-9712)*
Savy Designs By Sylvia.....G..... 757 547-7525
Chesapeake *(G-3285)*
Studio 29.....G..... 757 624-1445
Norfolk *(G-9736)*
Sue Dille.....G..... 540 951-4100
Blacksburg *(G-1795)*
Susannah Wagner Jewelers Inc.....G..... 804 798-5864
Ashland *(G-1498)*
Sweet Serenity Gifts.....G..... 540 903-1964
Fredericksburg *(G-5489)*
Sylvan Spirit.....G..... 804 330-5454
North Chesterfield *(G-9996)*
Thesia Inc.....G..... 703 726-8845
Aldie *(G-113)*
▲ **Universal Store Corp**.....G..... 703 467-0434
Sterling *(G-13544)*
Wolf Zsuzsi of Budapest.....G..... 703 548-3319
Alexandria *(G-385)*
Yesterdays Treasures.....G..... 757 877-5153
Grafton *(G-5933)*

3914 Silverware, Plated & Stainless Steel Ware

AMG International Inc.....G..... 703 988-4741
Alexandria *(G-412)*
Central Virginia Hardwood Pdts.....G..... 434 335-5898
Gretna *(G-6006)*
Collinsville Engraving LLC.....G..... 276 647-8596
Collinsville *(G-3710)*
Cresset Corporation.....F..... 804 798-2691
Ashland *(G-1399)*
Dining With Dignity Inc.....G..... 757 565-2452
Williamsburg *(G-15233)*
Hand and Hammer Inc.....F..... 703 491-4866
Woodbridge *(G-15721)*
K & S Pewter Inc.....G..... 540 751-0505
Leesburg *(G-7294)*
Lauret Company.....G..... 540 635-1670
Linden *(G-7430)*
Otero Kucbel Enterprises Inc.....G..... 703 734-0209
Mc Lean *(G-8521)*
Regal Products Co.....G..... 804 798-2691
Ashland *(G-1485)*
Royal Silver Mfg Co Inc.....F..... 757 855-6004
Norfolk *(G-9711)*
Smith and Flannery.....G..... 804 794-4979
Williamsburg *(G-15313)*

3915 Jewelers Findings & Lapidary Work

Aquia Creek Gems.....G..... 540 659-6120
Stafford *(G-13118)*
Candlelight Jewels.....G..... 305 301-2536
Fairfax *(G-4604)*
Goyal Gadgets LLC.....G..... 703 757-8294
Great Falls *(G-5957)*
Iceburrr Jewelry.....G..... 757 537-9520
Virginia Beach *(G-14540)*
John C Nordt Co Inc.....C..... 540 362-9717
Roanoke *(G-12112)*
Sapna Creations.....G..... 571 276-1480
Centreville *(G-2335)*
Treasures of African Artists.....G..... 571 263-2152
Alexandria *(G-367)*
Upscale Time LLC.....G..... 434 832-0101
Lynchburg *(G-7830)*

3931 Musical Instruments

Altamont Recorders LLC.....G..... 804 814-2310
Richmond *(G-11099)*
Ambassador Religious Supply.....G..... 757 686-8314
Chesapeake *(G-2962)*
▲ **American Drum Inc**.....G..... 804 226-1778
Richmond *(G-11108)*
Antonio Puducay.....G..... 703 927-2953
Lorton *(G-7463)*
Axeamps LLC.....G..... 540 484-0882
Glade Hill *(G-5669)*
Boomin Bass Global LLC.....F..... 757 776-8668
Virginia Beach *(G-14294)*
Buy Chimes.....G..... 703 293-6395
Fairfax *(G-4601)*
Cabin Creek Musical Instrs.....G..... 276 388-3202
Mouth of Wilson *(G-9092)*
Centellax Inc.....G..... 540 980-2905
Pulaski *(G-10632)*
Claire E Bose.....G..... 323 898-2912
Toano *(G-13860)*
David Bennett.....G..... 703 858-4669
Ashburn *(G-1270)*
Debeer Piano Service LLC.....G..... 703 727-4601
Fairfax *(G-4611)*
El Morgan Company LLC.....G..... 540 623-7086
Fredericksburg *(G-5280)*
Elizabeth A Grge Vlin Stdio LL.....G..... 703 590-8145
Woodbridge *(G-15689)*
Elliott Mandolins Shop.....G..... 540 763-2327
Riner *(G-11862)*
G3 Solutions LLC.....G..... 703 424-4296
Vienna *(G-14059)*
George McCracken.....G..... 804 238-4910
West Point *(G-15157)*
Glory Violin Co LLC.....G..... 703 439-1700
Annandale *(G-751)*
Kimberly Gilbert.....G..... 804 201-6591
Henrico *(G-6527)*
▲ **Klann Inc**.....E..... 540 949-8351
Waynesboro *(G-15119)*
Larry Hicks.....G..... 276 738-9010
Castlewood *(G-2254)*
Litton Guitar Works LLC.....G..... 703 966-0571
Manassas *(G-8101)*
▲ **Lively Fulcher Organ Builders**.....G..... 540 352-4401
Rocky Mount *(G-12336)*
Mack Mimsey.....G..... 757 777-6333
Norfolk *(G-9628)*
Maleys Music.....G..... 571 335-4289
Arlington *(G-1052)*
Michael Reiss LLC.....G..... 757 826-4277
Hampton *(G-6197)*
Mountain Marimba Inc.....G..... 276 773-3899
Independence *(G-6991)*
Potomac Fine Violins LLC.....G..... 239 961-0398
Arlington *(G-1117)*
Power Wrist Bldrs By Tlose Grp.....G..... 800 645-6673
Charlottesville *(G-2679)*
Qlf Custom Pipe Organ.....G..... 540 484-1133
Rocky Mount *(G-12348)*
Queens Guitar Shop.....G..... 703 754-4330
Nokesville *(G-9397)*
Richmond Philharmonic Inc.....G..... 804 673-7400
Richmond *(G-11358)*
Riegger Marin.....G..... 646 896-4739
Blacksburg *(G-1784)*
Rodriguez Guitars.....G..... 804 358-6324
Richmond *(G-11366)*
Stelling Banjo Works Ltd.....G..... 434 295-1917
Afton *(G-90)*
Taloose Group.....G..... 408 221-3277
Charlottesville *(G-2699)*
Tyler JSun Global LLC.....G..... 407 221-6135
Stafford *(G-13206)*
Wm L Mason Fine String Instrs.....G..... 540 645-7499
Fredericksburg *(G-5238)*

S I C

3942 Dolls & Stuffed Toys

Birdies Dolls ....G...... 757 421-7788
 Chesapeake **(G-3001)**
Highland Bears and More ....G...... 757 480-1125
 Norfolk **(G-9581)**
James Lassiter ....G...... 757 595-4242
 Newport News **(G-9265)**
Mondays Child ....G...... 703 754-9048
 Nokesville **(G-9396)**

3944 Games, Toys & Children's Vehicles

▲ Alforas Company ....G...... 703 342-6910
 Annandale **(G-729)**
All That Jaz LLC ....G...... 800 224-8152
 Chesterfield **(G-3474)**
Ann J Kite ....G...... 540 656-3070
 Spotsylvania **(G-12883)**
Ann Kite ....G...... 434 989-4841
 Earlysville **(G-4286)**
Big Stone Gap Corporation ....G...... 276 523-7337
 Big Stone Gap **(G-1706)**
Bingo City ....G...... 757 890-3168
 Yorktown **(G-15937)**
Blue Monkey LLC ....G...... 540 664-1297
 Winchester **(G-15388)**
Catlilli Games LLC ....G...... 540 359-6592
 Warrenton **(G-14986)**
Charlie Moseley ....G...... 571 235-3206
 Reston **(G-10821)**
Christian Family Games LLC ....G...... 703 863-6403
 Great Falls **(G-5948)**
David C Maple ....G...... 757 563-2423
 Virginia Beach **(G-14391)**
Ddk Group LLC ....G...... 201 726-2535
 Lorton **(G-7478)**
▲ Decipher Inc ....D...... 757 664-1111
 Norfolk **(G-9522)**
Decorative Arts Workshop ....G...... 703 321-8373
 Annandale **(G-741)**
Degustabox USA LLC ....G...... 203 514-8966
 Rockingham **(G-12248)**
Douglas Manning ....G...... 703 631-9064
 Centreville **(G-2303)**
Dwight Kite ....G...... 540 564-8858
 Elkton **(G-4326)**
Dynamic Motion LLC ....G...... 804 433-2294
 Richmond **(G-11194)**
Eastern League Commissioner ....G...... 703 307-2080
 Stafford **(G-13140)**
Effective Comm Strategies LLC ....G...... 703 403-5345
 Clifton **(G-3663)**
Epic ....G...... 757 896-8464
 Hampton **(G-6143)**
Game Quest Inc ....G...... 540 639-6547
 Radford **(G-10714)**
Geek Keep LLC ....G...... 703 867-9867
 Manassas **(G-8072)**
Geraldine Browns Child Car ....G...... 757 665-1466
 Bloxom **(G-1840)**
Ghost Wind LLC ....G...... 561 624-1141
 Powhatan **(G-10546)**
Glenn F Kite ....G...... 540 743-6124
 Luray **(G-7613)**
Improbable LLC ....E...... 571 418-6999
 Arlington **(G-1000)**
Interntnl Pzzle Cllctors Assn ....G...... 757 420-7576
 Virginia Beach **(G-14552)**
Iron Horse Co ....G...... 703 256-2853
 Alexandria **(G-489)**
Jackite Inc ....F...... 757 426-5359
 Virginia Beach **(G-14561)**
Jkt Inc ....G...... 804 272-2862
 Chantilly **(G-2451)**
John M Russell ....G...... 540 622-6281
 Linden **(G-7429)**
Kitty Hawks Kites Inc ....G...... 757 351-3959
 Virginia Beach **(G-14589)**
Lana Juarez ....G...... 540 951-3566
 Blacksburg **(G-1750)**
Larry Kaniecki ....G...... 804 737-7616
 Sandston **(G-12623)**
Little Wars Inc ....G...... 703 533-7942
 Falls Church **(G-4824)**
Lyniel W Kite ....G...... 540 298-9657
 Elkton **(G-4332)**
Made By Sandy ....G...... 757 588-1123
 Norfolk **(G-9629)**
Magss Ideas & Concepts ....G...... 804 304-6324
 North Chesterfield **(G-9920)**

Marble Man ....G...... 804 448-9100
 Woodford **(G-15841)**
Miller Kite House ....G...... 540 298-5390
 Elkton **(G-4333)**
Model Railroad Cstm Benchwork ......G...... 540 948-4948
 Rochelle **(G-12234)**
▲ Monkey Puzzle Productions LLC ....G...... 703 919-0182
 Chantilly **(G-2546)**
Monster Fight Club LLC ....G...... 434 284-7258
 Earlysville **(G-4293)**
Motrak Models ....G...... 813 476-4784
 Martinsville **(G-8314)**
Mystical Creations ....G...... 804 943-8386
 Hopewell **(G-6940)**
Newell Brands Inc ....G...... 800 241-1848
 Richmond **(G-11303)**
Pal Enterprises ....G...... 804 763-1769
 Midlothian **(G-8874)**
Premonition Games LLC ....G...... 586 404-7070
 Fredericksburg **(G-5349)**
Putting Tgther Pzzle Peces LLC ......G...... 703 391-1754
 Oak Hill **(G-10138)**
Puzzle Cuts LLC ....G...... 703 470-9333
 Lorton **(G-7522)**
Puzzle Homes LLC ....G...... 804 247-7256
 Henrico **(G-6553)**
Puzzle Palooza Ect ....G...... 703 494-0579
 Occoquan **(G-10174)**
Puzzle Palooza Etc Inc ....G...... 703 368-3619
 Manassas **(G-8135)**
Puzzle Piece LLC ....G...... 434 985-8074
 Ruckersville **(G-12410)**
Quisenberry Stn Live Stm LLC ....G...... 703 799-9643
 Alexandria **(G-565)**
Rocking Horse Ventures Inc ....G...... 804 784-5830
 Richmond **(G-11365)**
Shyanne Branch ....G...... 757 532-4951
 Portsmouth **(G-10481)**
Stylewire LLC ....G...... 770 841-1300
 Lynchburg **(G-7814)**
▲ Theorem Painting ....G...... 703 670-4330
 Dumfries **(G-4259)**
Toy Ray Gun ....G...... 703 662-3348
 Herndon **(G-6830)**
Virginia Rural Letter ....G...... 757 242-6865
 Windsor **(G-15607)**
Walmer Enterprises ....E...... 703 461-9330
 Montross **(G-9028)**
▲ Wilson & Wilson International ....G...... 804 733-3180
 North Dinwiddie **(G-10071)**
◆ Worth Baby Products LLC ....F...... 804 644-4707
 Henrico **(G-6592)**
Wyvern Interactive LLC ....F...... 540 336-4498
 Winchester **(G-15519)**
▲ Y & S Trading ....G...... 703 430-6928
 Sterling **(G-13566)**
Yaya Learning LLC ....G...... 540 230-5051
 Falls Church **(G-4895)**
Your Puzzle Source LLC ....G...... 703 461-7788
 Alexandria **(G-391)**

3949 Sporting & Athletic Goods, NEC

757 Surfboards ....G...... 757 348-2030
 Virginia Beach **(G-14197)**
Abbadon Skateboards LLC ....G...... 703 280-4818
 Annandale **(G-727)**
AJW Surfboards ....G...... 910 617-8750
 Virginia Beach **(G-14219)**
AMF Bowling Worldwide Inc ....G...... 804 730-4000
 Mechanicsville **(G-8601)**
◆ AMF Bowling Worldwide Inc ....F...... 804 730-4000
 Mechanicsville **(G-8602)**
Amherst Arms and Supply LLC ....G...... 434 929-1978
 Madison Heights **(G-7867)**
Aok Quality Solutions ....G...... 757 710-9844
 Onancock **(G-10189)**
Basketball Products Intl LLC ....G...... 757 626-3865
 Norfolk **(G-9455)**
Beltway Bat Company LLC ....G...... 609 760-7243
 Burke **(G-2184)**
Big Daddys Sports Products ....G...... 757 310-8565
 Hampton **(G-6091)**
Big Hubster Short Knocker Golf ......G...... 757 635-5949
 Stafford **(G-13123)**
Big Lick Boomerang ....G...... 540 761-4611
 Roanoke **(G-11889)**
◆ Bill Foote ....G...... 808 298-5423
 Virginia Beach **(G-14279)**
Blue RDG Antigravity Treadmlls ....G...... 540 977-9540
 Roanoke **(G-12048)**

Boomerang Air Sports ....G...... 804 360-0320
 Henrico **(G-6484)**
Buc-DOE Tector Outdoors LLC ....G...... 276 971-1383
 Pounding Mill **(G-10516)**
Bum Pass Water Ski Club Inc ....G...... 240 498-7033
 Bumpass **(G-2160)**
Bush River Corporation ....G...... 804 730-4000
 Richmond **(G-11139)**
C & M Lures LLC ....G...... 703 369-3060
 Manassas Park **(G-8192)**
Canam Uwh ....G...... 906 399-7857
 Remington **(G-10767)**
Catch Surfboard Co LLC ....G...... 949 218-0428
 Norfolk **(G-9478)**
Cave Mma LLC ....G...... 540 455-7623
 Fredericksburg **(G-5409)**
Celly Sports Shop LLC ....G...... 540 981-0205
 Vinton **(G-14169)**
Cerberus Skateboard Co LLC ....G...... 757 715-2225
 Norfolk **(G-9480)**
Champs ....G...... 800 991-6813
 Newport News **(G-9196)**
Christina Bennett ....G...... 703 489-9018
 Norfolk **(G-9483)**
Cj9 Ltd ....G...... 817 946-7421
 Buena Vista **(G-2140)**
Coastal Edge ....G...... 757 422-5739
 Virginia Beach **(G-14345)**
Coastal Hmpton Rads Vllyball C ......G...... 757 759-0204
 Poquoson **(G-10367)**
Commonwlth Soccer Programs LLC ...G...... 804 794-2092
 Midlothian **(G-8801)**
Convoy Skateboards Ltd ....G...... 571 216-2740
 Alexandria **(G-434)**
Core Health & Fitness LLC ....E...... 714 669-1660
 Independence **(G-6980)**
Covered Inc ....F...... 757 463-0434
 Virginia Beach **(G-14368)**
Creative Urethanes Inc ....E...... 540 542-6676
 Winchester **(G-15407)**
Crews Outdoors Llc John ....G...... 540 808-2204
 Salem **(G-12491)**
Crossbow Strategies Inc ....G...... 703 864-7576
 Alexandria **(G-177)**
Custom Fly Grips LLC ....G...... 703 532-1189
 Falls Church **(G-4780)**
Custom Rods & Such ....G...... 434 736-9758
 Drakes Branch **(G-4132)**
Daq Bats LLC ....G...... 202 365-3246
 Mc Lean **(G-8415)**
Davida ....G...... 571 278-4287
 Chantilly **(G-2402)**
Dcsports87 Sport Cards ....G...... 571 334-3314
 Glen Allen **(G-5721)**
Deck World Inc ....G...... 804 798-9003
 Warsaw **(G-15062)**
Deezel Skateboards Vb LLC ....G...... 757 490-6619
 Virginia Beach **(G-14398)**
Dg2 Teler Sales ....G...... 540 955-1996
 Berryville **(G-1679)**
Diamondback Sport ....G...... 434 964-6447
 Charlottesville **(G-2780)**
Digital Delights Inc ....G...... 703 661-6888
 Sterling **(G-13386)**
Discus N More LLC ....G...... 609 678-6102
 Fredericksburg **(G-5275)**
DK Consulting LLC ....G...... 224 402-3333
 Remington **(G-10768)**
Double Eagle Golf Works Inc ....G...... 757 436-4459
 Chesapeake **(G-3072)**
Dse Outdoor Product Inc ....G...... 540 789-4800
 Willis **(G-15360)**
Evans Custom Playsites ....G...... 804 615-3397
 Chester **(G-3414)**
Evergreen Outfitters LLC ....G...... 540 843-2576
 Luray **(G-7610)**
Everything Gos LLC ....G...... 804 290-3870
 Richmond **(G-11206)**
Evolve Play LLC ....G...... 703 570-5700
 Winchester **(G-15416)**
Eye Armor Incorporated ....G...... 571 238-4096
 Stafford **(G-13144)**
Fize Wordsmithing LLC ....G...... 804 756-8243
 Glen Allen **(G-5731)**
Fletchers Hardware & Spt Ctr ....G...... 276 935-8332
 Grundy **(G-6032)**
Foldem Gear LLC ....G...... 571 289-5051
 Yorktown **(G-15961)**
Frierson Designs LLC ....G...... 757 491-7130
 Virginia Beach **(G-14475)**

Git R Done Inc ....G..... 703 843-8697
Reston *(G-10859)*

Glovestix LLC ....G..... 703 909-5146
Ashburn *(G-1287)*

Good Tymes Enterprises Inc ....G..... 276 628-2335
Abingdon *(G-34)*

Goodpasture Knives ....G..... 804 752-8363
Ashland *(G-1422)*

Grit Pack Calls LLC/GP Calls L ....G..... 540 735-5391
Locust Grove *(G-7445)*

Har-Tru LLC ....E..... 434 589-1542
Troy *(G-13927)*

◆ Har-Tru LLC ....E..... 877 442-7878
Charlottesville *(G-2807)*

Harygul Imports Inc Maryland ....E..... 757 427-5665
Virginia Beach *(G-14508)*

Hawk Hill Custom LLC ....G..... 540 248-4295
Verona *(G-13988)*

Hickman Surfboards ....G..... 757 427-2914
Virginia Beach *(G-14523)*

Insights Intl Holdings LLC ....G..... 757 333-1291
Franklin *(G-5145)*

Island Decoys ....G..... 757 336-5319
Chincoteague *(G-3562)*

Its About Golf ....G..... 703 437-1527
Herndon *(G-6714)*

J W Bibb Shooting Bags ....G..... 434 384-9431
Monroe *(G-8993)*

J&A Innovations LLC ....G..... 804 387-6466
Midlothian *(G-8835)*

Jonathan Chandler ....G..... 804 526-1148
Colonial Heights *(G-3736)*

Jovanovich Inc ....G..... 301 653-1739
Alexandria *(G-501)*

Kennesaw Holding Company ....G..... 603 866-6944
Fairfax *(G-4643)*

KG Sports ....G..... 540 538-7216
King George *(G-7097)*

Klimax Custom Skateboards ....G..... 757 589-0683
Virginia Beach *(G-14590)*

Laporte America LLC ....G..... 800 335-8727
Pounding Mill *(G-10522)*

▲ Laporte USA ....G..... 276 964-5566
Pounding Mill *(G-10523)*

▲ Lasermarx Inc ....G..... 434 528-1044
Madison Heights *(G-7876)*

Lax Loft LLC ....G..... 540 389-4529
Salem *(G-12529)*

▲ Links Choice LLC ....E..... 434 286-2202
Scottsville *(G-12663)*

Linsey Echowater System ....G..... 540 434-0212
Harrisonburg *(G-6339)*

Livingston Resources Inc ....G..... 704 892-1989
Richardsville *(G-11011)*

Longworth Sports Group Inc ....G..... 276 328-3300
Wise *(G-15630)*

Louise Richardson ....G..... 276 328-4545
Wise *(G-15631)*

Lovells Replay Sportstop LLC ....G..... 804 507-0271
Richmond *(G-11274)*

Lure LLC ....G..... 434 374-8559
Clarksville *(G-3633)*

Lyons Share LLC ....G..... 443 370-9514
Dumfries *(G-4251)*

▼ M&M Great Adventures LLC ....G..... 937 344-1415
Williamsburg *(G-15275)*

Magic Bullet Skateboards LLC ....G..... 703 371-0363
Fredericksburg *(G-5452)*

Mahogany Landscaping & Design ....G..... 757 846-7947
Virginia Beach *(G-14635)*

Mechanicsville United Futbol ....G..... 804 647-6557
Mechanicsville *(G-8659)*

Missile Baits LLC ....G..... 855 466-5738
Salem *(G-12538)*

Mobile Link Virgina LLC ....G..... 757 583-8300
Norfolk *(G-9647)*

Mountain Plains Industries ....G..... 434 386-0100
Lynchburg *(G-7775)*

Mud Puppy Custom Lures LLC ....G..... 804 895-1489
Prince George *(G-10602)*

Mustang Sports Retail ....G..... 757 679-2814
Chesapeake *(G-3216)*

N Zone Sports ....G..... 703 743-2848
Haymarket *(G-6430)*

▲ Nautilus International Inc ....C..... 276 773-2881
Independence *(G-6992)*

Neuro Tennis Inc ....G..... 240 481-7640
Arlington *(G-1076)*

Nhsa ....G..... 508 420-1902
Alexandria *(G-291)*

Nu-TEC Outdoor Innovations LLC ....G..... 540 365-0551
Ferrum *(G-4976)*

Obdrillers Proshop ....G..... 804 897-3708
Midlothian *(G-8869)*

Offroadarrowcom LLC ....G..... 804 920-2529
Providence Forge *(G-10627)*

Outlook Skateboards LLC ....G..... 757 713-5665
Smithfield *(G-12718)*

▲ Parker Compound Bows Inc ....E..... 540 337-5426
Staunton *(G-13283)*

Performance Fly Rods ....G..... 540 867-0856
Rockingham *(G-12267)*

Personal Protectio Principles ....G..... 757 453-3202
Virginia Beach *(G-14717)*

Pickers Grip LLC ....G..... 434 260-3366
Palmyra *(G-10255)*

Pinkio Hoppers ....G..... 571 277-4153
Springfield *(G-13068)*

Pivotal Gear LLC ....G..... 804 726-1328
Henrico *(G-6548)*

Pointman Resources LLC ....G..... 240 429-3423
Sterling *(G-13472)*

Potomac Health Solutions Inc ....G..... 703 774-8278
Reston *(G-10929)*

Presidium Athletics LLC ....G..... 800 618-9661
Powhatan *(G-10568)*

Prince William Athletic Center ....G..... 571 572-3365
Woodbridge *(G-15781)*

◆ Qubicaamf Worldwide LLC ....B..... 804 569-1000
Mechanicsville *(G-8669)*

▲ Richards Michael Mr Mrs ....G..... 540 854-5812
Spotsylvania *(G-12912)*

Richmond Supply and Svc LLC ....G..... 804 622-9435
Richmond *(G-11738)*

Rick Robbins Bamboo Fly Rods ....G..... 540 463-2864
Lexington *(G-7415)*

River Rock Custom Baits LLC ....G..... 540 414-3293
Waynesboro *(G-15135)*

Robert Lummus ....G..... 540 313-4393
Winchester *(G-15468)*

Rod Fishinfiddler Co ....G..... 703 517-0496
Arlington *(G-1150)*

Round House LLC ....G..... 757 504-3142
Alexandria *(G-331)*

Royal Silver Mfg Co Inc ....F..... 757 855-6004
Norfolk *(G-9711)*

Sara Yannuzzi ....G..... 703 955-2505
Edinburg *(G-4311)*

Sentry Slutions Pdts Group LLC ....G..... 757 689-6064
Virginia Beach *(G-14803)*

Ski Zone Inc ....G..... 703 242-3588
Vienna *(G-14130)*

Skirmish Supplies ....G..... 804 749-3458
Rockville *(G-12299)*

Sml Water Ski Club Inc ....G..... 540 328-0425
Moneta *(G-8980)*

Smrt Mouth LLC ....G..... 804 363-8863
Sandston *(G-12634)*

Snowshoe Retreats LLC ....G..... 540 442-6144
Harrisonburg *(G-6372)*

Soccer Bridge ....G..... 703 356-0462
Mc Lean *(G-8549)*

▼ Spa Guy LLC ....G..... 757 855-0381
Chesapeake *(G-3305)*

Sport Creations LLC ....G..... 757 572-2113
Virginia Beach *(G-14841)*

Sports Products World Entps ....G..... 888 493-6079
Yorktown *(G-15993)*

Stans Ski and Snowboard LLC ....G..... 540 885-9625
Staunton *(G-13297)*

Staunton River Outdoors LLC ....G..... 434 608-2601
Altavista *(G-644)*

Stephen Bialorucki ....G..... 757 374-2080
Virginia Beach *(G-14846)*

Stoneleigh Golf Club ....G..... 540 338-4653
Round Hill *(G-12391)*

Strong Industries LLC ....G..... 757 533-9100
Norfolk *(G-9735)*

Stubby Steves ....G..... 276 988-2915
North Tazewell *(G-10107)*

Surfstroke LLC ....G..... 804 437-2032
Providence Forge *(G-10628)*

Tacstrike LLC ....G..... 540 751-8221
Roanoke *(G-12007)*

Techni Comm ....G..... 703 231-6475
Nokesville *(G-9400)*

Terrapin Sports Supply Inc ....G..... 540 672-9370
Orange *(G-10228)*

Tidewater Virginia Usbc Inc ....G..... 757 456-2497
Virginia Beach *(G-14880)*

Titus Development Corp ....G..... 757 515-7338
Virginia Beach *(G-14882)*

Total Sports ....G..... 703 444-3633
Sterling *(G-13536)*

Triangle Skateboard Alliance ....G..... 804 426-3663
Williamsburg *(G-15326)*

Tru Sports LLC ....G..... 571 266-5059
Manassas *(G-8171)*

Trueway Inc ....G..... 703 527-9248
Arlington *(G-1199)*

Turbo Tellers ....G..... 812 250-1837
Spout Spring *(G-12928)*

Uniques LLC ....G..... 804 307-0902
Midlothian *(G-8916)*

Vfg Enterprises LLC ....G..... 757 343-4866
Virginia Beach *(G-14908)*

Vinci Co LLC ....G..... 888 529-6864
Richmond *(G-11438)*

Virginia Beach Skateboards ....G..... 757 385-4131
Virginia Beach *(G-14914)*

Virginia Custom Buildings ....G..... 540 582-5111
Spotsylvania *(G-12922)*

Virginia Guide Bait Co ....G..... 804 590-2991
Chesterfield *(G-3539)*

Warbird Turkey Calls LLC ....G..... 540 968-0415
Clifton Forge *(G-3683)*

Warrior Trail Consulting LLC ....G..... 703 349-1967
Fairfax *(G-4580)*

Whataseat ....G..... 276 395-7887
Coeburn *(G-3704)*

◆ Wild Things LLC ....G..... 757 702-8773
Virginia Beach *(G-14937)*

Xvd Board Sports LLC ....G..... 757 504-0006
Norfolk *(G-9797)*

Zen Sports Products LLC ....G..... 703 925-0118
Herndon *(G-6847)*

ZF Technical LLC ....G..... 757 575-5625
Virginia Beach *(G-14960)*

▲ Zup LLC ....G..... 843 822-5664
Williamsburg *(G-15350)*

3951 Pens & Mechanical Pencils

Dayspring Pens LLC ....G..... 888 694-7367
Virginia Beach *(G-14394)*

Goulet Pen Company LLC ....E..... 804 368-0482
Henrico *(G-6518)*

J J E Enterprise Holdings LLC ....G..... 410 703-9241
Spotsylvania *(G-12900)*

◆ Porex Technologies Corp ....C..... 804 524-4983
South Chesterfield *(G-12821)*

Porex Technologies Corporation ....C..... 804 275-2631
North Chesterfield *(G-9951)*

▲ Securitas Inc ....G..... 800 705-4545
Richmond *(G-11063)*

3952 Lead Pencils, Crayons & Artist's Mtrls

AW Art LLC ....G..... 540 320-4565
Dublin *(G-4149)*

Clearly-You Inc ....G..... 757 351-0346
Chesapeake *(G-3037)*

Colonial Tailors Chalk ....G..... 850 622-2270
Petersburg *(G-10313)*

Colonial Tailors Chalk Inc ....G..... 757 291-2445
Petersburg *(G-10314)*

Dark Warrior Group LLC ....G..... 757 289-6451
Ashburn *(G-1269)*

Framery and Arts Corp ....G..... 434 525-0444
Lynchburg *(G-7717)*

Ixidor LLC ....G..... 571 332-3888
Falls Church *(G-4810)*

James Hintzke ....G..... 757 374-4827
Virginia Beach *(G-14563)*

Jill C Perla ....G..... 703 407-5695
Round Hill *(G-12380)*

Justinian Posters & Prints ....G..... 703 273-8049
Fairfax *(G-4640)*

▲ Securitas Inc ....G..... 800 705-4545
Richmond *(G-11063)*

Southern Airbrushes ....G..... 434 324-4049
Hurt *(G-6978)*

World of Color Expo LLC ....G..... 703 754-3191
Gainesville *(G-5625)*

3953 Marking Devices

A & S Global Industries LLC ....G..... 757 773-0119
Suffolk *(G-13663)*

Acorn Sales Company Inc ....F..... 804 359-0505
Richmond *(G-11081)*

Bynum ....G..... 757 224-1860
Hampton *(G-6100)*

S I C

Cabin Hill TS LLC ....G...... 540 459-8912
Woodstock *(G-15850)*

Cordial Cricket ....G...... 804 931-8027
Chester *(G-3397)*

County of Hanover ....E...... 804 798-9402
Ashland *(G-1397)*

Dister Inc ....E...... 757 857-1946
Norfolk *(G-9525)*

Dister Inc ....E...... 703 207-0201
Fairfax *(G-4439)*

Impression Obsession ....G...... 804 749-3580
Oilville *(G-10180)*

Jonette D Meade ....G...... 804 247-0639
Richmond *(G-11048)*

Kimyaeasonwood ....G...... 757 502-5001
Franklin *(G-5147)*

M & R Striping LLC ....G...... 703 201-7162
Broad Run *(G-2068)*

▲ Masa Corporation ....D...... 757 855-3013
Norfolk *(G-9633)*

Michael R Little ....G...... 540 489-4785
Rocky Mount *(G-12339)*

▲ National Marking Products Inc ....E...... 804 266-7691
Richmond *(G-11299)*

Quality Stamp Co ....G...... 757 858-0653
Norfolk *(G-9700)*

Southern Stamp Incorporated ....G...... 804 359-0531
Richmond *(G-11388)*

Trodat USA ....G...... 540 815-8160
Roanoke *(G-12012)*

Tsunami Custom Creations LLC ....G...... 757 913-0960
Virginia Beach *(G-14897)*

Wanda Eubanks ....G...... 804 615-7095
Fredericksburg *(G-5500)*

3955 Carbon Paper & Inked Ribbons

Hugo Miranda ....G...... 703 898-3956
Bristow *(G-2056)*

Indenhooffen Productions LLC ....G...... 540 327-0898
Winchester *(G-15428)*

Ink2work LLC ....G...... 605 202-9079
Glen Allen *(G-5751)*

Jennifer Omohundro ....G...... 804 937-9308
Richmond *(G-11255)*

MB Services LLC ....G...... 703 906-8625
Alexandria *(G-524)*

Potomac Laser Recharge ....G...... 703 430-0166
Great Falls *(G-5975)*

Refills Inc ....G...... 804 771-5460
Richmond *(G-11732)*

3961 Costume Jewelry & Novelties

3d Designs Dazzling Dream Desi ....G...... 703 231-9540
Woodbridge *(G-15639)*

A Markus Design ....G...... 703 938-6694
Vienna *(G-14003)*

Bariso Ling ....G...... 757 277-5383
Virginia Beach *(G-14261)*

Bracelets By G Jaffe Inc ....G...... 434 409-3500
Charlottesville *(G-2600)*

◆ Darlene Group Inc ....D...... 401 728-3300
Arlington *(G-927)*

Designer Goldsmith Inc ....G...... 703 777-7661
Leesburg *(G-7254)*

Designer Goldsmith Inc ....G...... 703 777-7661
Leesburg *(G-7255)*

Dimensions Virginia Beach Inc ....G...... 757 340-1115
Virginia Beach *(G-14405)*

Eileen C Johnson ....G...... 855 533-7753
Berryville *(G-1680)*

Highland Bears and More ....G...... 757 480-1125
Norfolk *(G-9581)*

Ileen Shefferman Designs ....G...... 703 821-3261
Mc Lean *(G-8464)*

J&S Fisher LLC ....G...... 540 921-3197
Pearisburg *(G-10275)*

Jeffrey Gill ....G...... 703 309-7061
Charlottesville *(G-2819)*

Klassic Kreatures ....G...... 703 560-4409
Falls Church *(G-4817)*

Lux Costume Jewelry ....G...... 703 665-0674
Arlington *(G-1051)*

Magnetic Bracelets and More ....G...... 757 499-1282
Virginia Beach *(G-14633)*

Pandoras Box ....G...... 757 719-6669
Newport News *(G-9309)*

Sandra Magura ....G...... 540 318-6947
Stafford *(G-13187)*

Swarovski North America Ltd ....G...... 703 267-2332
Fairfax *(G-4564)*

Swarovski North America Ltd ....G...... 571 633-1800
Mc Lean *(G-8561)*

Swarovski North America Ltd ....G...... 703 418-6665
Arlington *(G-1179)*

Swarovski North America Ltd ....G...... 757 253-7924
Williamsburg *(G-15321)*

Vlynns ....G...... 540 904-2844
Roanoke *(G-12225)*

▲ Zoil Jewelry LLC ....G...... 571 340-2256
(G-6849)

3965 Fasteners, Buttons, Needles & Pins

Attic Zipper ....G...... 804 518-5094
Petersburg *(G-10308)*

E Z Mount Bracket Co Inc ....F...... 540 947-5500
Montvale *(G-9029)*

Gulf Fasteners ....G...... 540 798-1992
Roanoke *(G-11930)*

Premier Pins ....G...... 703 631-6660
Chantilly *(G-2482)*

Taylynn Manufacturing LLC ....G...... 804 727-0103
Henrico *(G-6579)*

Vel Tye LLC ....G...... 757 518-5400
Virginia Beach *(G-14907)*

3991 Brooms & Brushes

◆ Brush Holdings Inc ....D...... 804 226-4433
Richmond *(G-11137)*

Old Dominion Brush Company Inc ....G...... 800 446-9823
Richmond *(G-11313)*

One Stop Cleaning LLC ....G...... 757 561-2952
Williamsburg *(G-15286)*

◆ Quickie Manufacturing Corp ....D...... 856 829-7900
Winchester *(G-15575)*

3993 Signs & Advertising Displays

1st Signage and Lighting LLC ....G...... 276 229-4200
Woolwine *(G-15863)*

22 Church LLC ....G...... 540 342-2817
Roanoke *(G-12026)*

7m Graphix Inc ....G...... 703 751-6971
Fairfax *(G-4395)*

7m Graphix LLC ....G...... 703 910-0915
Woodbridge *(G-15640)*

804 Signs LLC ....G...... 804 277-4272
Ashland *(G-1359)*

A Place Called There With Sign ....G...... 434 594-5576
Jarratt *(G-7009)*

Abe Lincoln Flags & Banners ....G...... 703 204-1116
Fairfax *(G-4399)*

Abingdon Sign Co Inc ....G...... 276 628-2594
Abingdon *(G-4)*

Absolute Signs Inc ....G...... 703 229-9436
Manassas *(G-8018)*

Absolute Signs Inc ....G...... 540 668-6807
Hillsboro *(G-6859)*

Accent Signing Company ....G...... 757 857-8800
Norfolk *(G-9416)*

Acorn Sign Graphics Inc ....E...... 804 726-6999
Richmond *(G-11082)*

Action Graphics and Signs Inc ....G...... 757 548-5255
Chesapeake *(G-2953)*

Action Graphics Signs ....G...... 757 995-2200
Virginia Beach *(G-14210)*

Acutech Signs & Graphics Inc ....G...... 757 766-2627
Hampton *(G-6070)*

Ad Vice Inc ....G...... 804 730-0503
Mechanicsville *(G-8600)*

Adco Signs Inc ....G...... 757 787-1393
Onancock *(G-10188)*

Adgrfx ....G...... 443 600-7562
Stafford *(G-13112)*

Admiral Signworks Corp ....F...... 757 422-6700
Norfolk *(G-9422)*

Advance Signs & Graphics Co ....G...... 703 359-8005
Fairfax *(G-4589)*

Advanced Design Fabrication ....F...... 757 484-4486
Chesapeake *(G-2954)*

Advanced Graphics LLC ....G...... 540 931-4850
Winchester *(G-15524)*

Advantage Sign Supply Inc ....E...... 804 798-5784
Ashland *(G-1363)*

Advertising Spc & Promotions ....G...... 540 537-4121
Hardy *(G-6285)*

Ajf Sign Placement ....G...... 540 797-5835
Roanoke *(G-11881)*

Albemarle Signs ....G...... 434 823-1024
Crozet *(G-3828)*

All About Signs LLC ....G...... 757 934-3000
Suffolk *(G-13666)*

All Kinds of Signs ....G...... 434 842-1877
Bremo Bluff *(G-1943)*

All Kinds of Signs Inc ....G...... 703 321-6542
Falls Church *(G-4743)*

▼ All Traffic Solutions Inc ....F...... 814 237-9005
Herndon *(G-6609)*

All-Signs ....G...... 276 632-6733
Martinsville *(G-8265)*

Allen Management Company Inc ....G...... 703 481-8858
Herndon *(G-6610)*

Allgood Promotional Cons ....G...... 434 793-6178
Danville *(G-3953)*

Alliance Signs Virginia LLC ....G...... 804 530-1451
Chester *(G-3384)*

Als Custom Signs ....G...... 804 224-7105
Colonial Beach *(G-3720)*

Als Sign Shop ....G...... 540 465-3103
Strasburg *(G-13571)*

Ameri Sign Design ....G...... 252 544-7712
Virginia Beach *(G-14224)*

American Light Works LLC ....G...... 804 332-3229
Alexandria *(G-131)*

American Made Signs LLC ....G...... 434 971-7446
Charlottesville *(G-2727)*

American Sign Lnguage Svcs LLC ....G...... 571 969-2751
Alexandria *(G-411)*

Amplify Ventures LLC ....G...... 571 248-2282
Gainesville *(G-5570)*

and Design Inc ....G...... 703 913-0799
Springfield *(G-12948)*

Any and All Graphics LLC ....G...... 757 468-9600
Virginia Beach *(G-14231)*

Aplus Signs and Bus Svcs LLC ....F...... 540 667-8010
Winchester *(G-15529)*

Arcade Signs LLC ....G...... 703 815-5440
Centreville *(G-2291)*

◆ Architectural Graphics Inc ....C...... 800 877-7868
Virginia Beach *(G-14236)*

Architectural Graphics Inc ....C...... 757 427-1900
Virginia Beach *(G-14237)*

Architectural Graphics Inc ....C...... 757 301-7008
Virginia Beach *(G-14238)*

Art Graphics N Designs Inc ....G...... 757 463-9495
Virginia Beach *(G-14243)*

Artistic Design ....G...... 540 980-1598
Pulaski *(G-10630)*

Artwolf Signs & Graphics ....G...... 757 567-8122
Norfolk *(G-9446)*

At Sign LLC ....G...... 703 895-7035
Haymarket *(G-6414)*

Awning & Sign Company Inc ....G...... 276 628-8069
Abingdon *(G-14)*

Ax Graphics and Sign LLC ....G...... 775 830-6115
Stanardsville *(G-13215)*

Baby Signs By Lacey ....G...... 540 309-2551
Roanoke *(G-11883)*

Badger Neon & Sign ....G...... 540 761-5779
Roanoke *(G-12041)*

Baker Builders LLC ....G...... 703 753-4904
Nokesville *(G-9389)*

Ball Peen Productions LLC ....G...... 434 293-4392
Charlottesville *(G-2735)*

Ballous Signs and Designs Inc ....G...... 804 986-6635
North Chesterfield *(G-9826)*

Ballpark Signs Inc ....G...... 540 239-7677
Radford *(G-10705)*

▲ Bam Bams LLC ....E...... 703 372-1940
Manassas *(G-7919)*

Banana Banner Inc ....F...... 703 823-5933
Alexandria *(G-144)*

Banner Sings Etc ....G...... 703 698-5466
Fairfax *(G-4418)*

Banners and More ....G...... 540 400-8485
Vinton *(G-14165)*

Bannerworks Signs & Graphics ....G...... 571 292-2567
Manassas *(G-8035)*

Be Bold Sign Studio ....G...... 678 520-1029
Herndon *(G-6621)*

Beach Sign and Design ....G...... 757 618-8653
Virginia Beach *(G-14269)*

Best Printing & Design LLC ....G...... 703 593-9874
Arlington *(G-880)*

Bethany House Inc ....G...... 703 281-9410
Vienna *(G-14015)*

Better Signs ....G...... 540 382-7446
Christiansburg *(G-3573)*

Big Fred Promotions Inc ....G...... 804 832-5510
Gloucester Point *(G-5872)*

Birckhead Signs & Graphics ....G...... 434 295-5962
Charlottesville *(G-2740)*

Bizcard Xpress ....G...... 757 340-4525
Virginia Beach *(G-14284)*

Black Forest Sign Inc ....F...... 540 825-0017
Culpeper *(G-3873)*

▲ Blair Inc ....D...... 703 922-0200
Springfield *(G-12964)*

Blue Ridge Sign & Stamp Co Inc ....F...... 540 777-5456
Roanoke *(G-11892)*

Botetourt Signs N Stuff ....G...... 540 992-3839
Troutville *(G-13903)*

Bow Wow Bunkies and Other Sign ....G... 757 650-0158
Virginia Beach *(G-14297)*

Bristol Sign Co Walden LLC ....G...... 276 669-0811
Bristol *(G-2010)*

Britemoves LLC ....F...... 703 629-6391
Reston *(G-10812)*

Broad Street Signs Inc ....G...... 804 262-1007
Richmond *(G-11135)*

Brooks Gray Sign Company ....F...... 804 233-4343
Richmond *(G-11510)*

Brooks Sign Company ....G...... 540 400-6144
Roanoke *(G-12055)*

Bubba Enterprises Inc ....G...... 703 524-0019
Arlington *(G-891)*

Burruss Signs Inc ....G...... 434 296-6654
Charlottesville *(G-2751)*

Bxi Inc ....G...... 804 282-5434
Richmond *(G-11142)*

C A S Signs ....G...... 804 271-7580
Chesterfield *(G-3484)*

C and F Promotions Inc ....G...... 757 912-5161
Hampton *(G-6101)*

Capital Designs LLC ....G...... 703 444-2728
Great Falls *(G-5943)*

▲ Capitol Exhibit Services Inc ....E...... 703 330-9000
Manassas *(G-8044)*

Capitol Signs Inc ....G...... 804 749-3737
Glen Allen *(G-5711)*

Cdrs LLC ....G...... 703 451-7546
Springfield *(G-12974)*

Chalison Inc ....G...... 757 258-2520
Williamsburg *(G-15218)*

Charlie Watts Signs ....G...... 540 291-3211
Naturl BR STA *(G-9110)*

Chesapeake Signs ....G...... 757 482-6989
Chesapeake *(G-3033)*

Cheshire Cat and Company Llc ....G...... 540 221-2538
Waynesboro *(G-15104)*

Chris Ellis Signs & Airbrush ....G...... 434 447-8013
La Crosse *(G-7142)*

Christopher A Dixon ....G...... 276 644-4222
Abingdon *(G-23)*

Christopher Aiken ....G...... 804 693-6003
Gloucester *(G-5841)*

Clarke B Gray ....G...... 757 426-7227
Virginia Beach *(G-14342)*

Clearimage Creations ....G...... 804 883-0199
Montpelier *(G-9015)*

Coastal Safety Inc ....G...... 757 499-9415
Virginia Beach *(G-14347)*

Cogitari Inc ....G...... 301 237-7777
Vienna *(G-14029)*

Commonwealth Sign & Design ....G...... 804 358-5507
Richmond *(G-11535)*

Complete Sign Inc ....G...... 571 276-8407
Fairfax *(G-4429)*

Cottle Multi Media Inc ....G...... 434 263-5447
Lynch Station *(G-7627)*

Cr8tive Sign Works ....G...... 804 608-8698
Midlothian *(G-8804)*

Craze Signs & Graphics ....G...... 804 748-9233
Chesterfield *(G-3488)*

Crazy Customs ....G...... 434 222-8686
South Boston *(G-12756)*

Create-A-Print and Signs LLC ....G...... 804 920-8055
Chesterfield *(G-3489)*

Creation Sign LLC ....G...... 703 622-5958
Annandale *(G-737)*

Creations At Play LLC ....G...... 757 541-8226
Poquoson *(G-10368)*

Creative Designs of Virginia ....G...... 804 435-2382
Irvington *(G-7000)*

Creative Sign Builders LLC ....G...... 757 622-5591
Norfolk *(G-9509)*

Creative Signs Ltd ....G...... 540 899-0032
Fredericksburg *(G-5416)*

Custom Design Graphics ....G...... 276 466-6270
Bristol *(G-1973)*

Custom Engraving & Signs LLC ....G...... 804 545-3961
Richmond *(G-11172)*

Custom Engraving and Signs LLC ....G...... 804 270-1272
Henrico *(G-6496)*

Custom Sculpture & Sign Co ....G...... 860 876-7529
Nickelsville *(G-9384)*

Custom Sign Shop LLC ....G...... 804 353-2768
Richmond *(G-11175)*

Custom Signs Today ....G...... 703 661-0611
Sterling *(G-13381)*

Customtaylor33 ....G...... 703 785-7919
Aldie *(G-105)*

D & D Signs ....G...... 540 428-3144
Warrenton *(G-14992)*

D & G Signs Inc ....G...... 757 858-2140
Norfolk *(G-9513)*

D & S Construction ....G...... 540 718-5303
Orange *(G-10209)*

D & V Enterprises Inc ....G...... 757 665-5202
Parksley *(G-10261)*

D and L Signs and Services LLC ....G...... 434 265-4115
Boydton *(G-1914)*

Daniel Rollins ....G...... 276 219-3988
Big Stone Gap *(G-1709)*

Danzo LLC ....G...... 703 532-8602
Arlington *(G-926)*

David M Tench Fine Crafte ....G...... 804 261-3628
Richmond *(G-11179)*

Dawgbone Banners & Signs ....G...... 804 526-5734
Chester *(G-3402)*

DC Design and Media Inc ....G...... 757 390-2818
Virginia Beach *(G-14395)*

Defense Holdings Inc ....G...... 703 334-2858
Front Royal *(G-5530)*

Demsign ....G...... 202 787-1518
Arlington *(G-937)*

Designer Signs ....G...... 757 879-1153
Wakefield *(G-14965)*

Designo Enterprises LLC ....F...... 571 437-5452
Sterling *(G-13384)*

Designs Inc ....G...... 757 547-5478
Chesapeake *(G-3065)*

Designs Inc ....G...... 757 410-1600
Chesapeake *(G-3066)*

Di-Mac Outdoors Inc ....G...... 434 489-3211
Danville *(G-3983)*

Directional Sign Services Inc ....G...... 703 568-5078
Springfield *(G-12992)*

Display & Banner Inc ....G...... 703 503-4447
Annandale *(G-744)*

Dmmt Glisan Inc ....G...... 276 620-0298
Max Meadows *(G-8367)*

Donna Cannaday ....G...... 540 489-7979
Rocky Mount *(G-12318)*

Dowling Signs Inc ....E...... 540 373-6675
Fredericksburg *(G-5183)*

Ds Smith PLC ....G...... 540 774-0500
Roanoke *(G-11916)*

Dsh Signs LLC ....F...... 804 270-4003
Richmond *(G-11192)*

Dsigns ....G...... 804 559-5884
Mechanicsville *(G-8619)*

Dwiggins Corp ....G...... 757 366-0066
Chesapeake *(G-3079)*

Dynamic Designs ....G...... 540 371-7173
Fredericksburg *(G-5423)*

E N S Graphics LLC ....G...... 540 830-1776
Broadway *(G-2088)*

E S I ....G...... 540 389-5070
Salem *(G-12498)*

E-Z Auto Specialties ....G...... 540 786-8111
Fredericksburg *(G-5279)*

East West Ventures LLC ....G...... 757 603-8017
Virginia Beach *(G-14429)*

Eastern Shore Signs LLC ....G...... 757 331-4432
Cape Charles *(G-2234)*

Eco-Signs and Graphics ....G...... 336 891-1334
Bassett *(G-1582)*

Econo Signs ....G...... 540 389-5070
Salem *(G-12500)*

Econocolor Signs & Graphics ....G...... 540 946-0000
Waynesboro *(G-15113)*

Economy Signs ....G...... 757 877-5082
Newport News *(G-9220)*

Eddies Repair Shop Inc ....F...... 540 659-4835
Stafford *(G-13141)*

Edwards Eddie Signs Inc ....G...... 540 434-8589
Harrisonburg *(G-6312)*

Eggleston Minor ....G...... 757 819-4958
Norfolk *(G-9542)*

Elfinsmith Ltd Inc ....G...... 757 399-4788
Portsmouth *(G-10421)*

Ellis Signs and Custom Pntg ....G...... 434 584-0032
La Crosse *(G-7143)*

Enterprise Signs & Svc ....G...... 757 338-0027
Hampton *(G-6142)*

Epic Led ....G...... 540 376-7183
Fredericksburg *(G-5282)*

Epps Collision Cntr & Superior ....G...... 434 572-4721
South Boston *(G-12764)*

Eric Walker ....G...... 804 439-2880
Midlothian *(G-8814)*

Eure Custom Signs Inc ....G...... 757 523-0000
Chesapeake *(G-3094)*

Ever Be Signs ....G...... 912 660-1436
Williamsburg *(G-15240)*

Everbrite LLC ....C...... 540 261-2121
Buena Vista *(G-2143)*

Exhibit Foundry ....G...... 540 705-0055
Harrisonburg *(G-6314)*

▲ Explus Inc ....D...... 703 260-0780
Dulles *(G-4201)*

Expo Branders Corporation ....G...... 703 865-7581
Fairfax *(G-4453)*

Express Signs Inc ....G...... 804 796-5197
Chester *(G-3415)*

Falcon Lab Inc ....G...... 703 442-0124
Mc Lean *(G-8426)*

Fast Signs Inc ....F...... 540 389-6691
Salem *(G-12506)*

Fast Signs of Herndon ....G...... 703 713-0743
Herndon *(G-6674)*

Fastsigns ....G...... 703 913-5300
Springfield *(G-13002)*

Fastsigns ....G...... 703 392-7446
Manassas *(G-8069)*

Fastsigns ....G...... 571 510-0400
Leesburg *(G-7272)*

Fastsigns Norfolk ....G...... 757 274-3344
Norfolk *(G-9550)*

Fellers Inc ....G...... 757 853-1363
Norfolk *(G-9551)*

Felts Sign Co ....G...... 804 262-1441
Glen Allen *(G-5730)*

Fiber Sign ....G...... 276 669-9115
Bristol *(G-1978)*

Fincham Signs ....G...... 540 937-4634
Culpeper *(G-3892)*

Fine Line Inc ....G...... 540 436-3626
Maurertown *(G-8361)*

Fine Line LLC ....G...... 540 436-3626
Maurertown *(G-8362)*

Fine Signs ....G...... 757 565-7833
Williamsburg *(G-15243)*

Fine Signs & Graphics Inc ....G...... 757 565-7833
Williamsburg *(G-15244)*

Firefly Sign Language Services ....G...... 205 405-7043
Staunton *(G-13257)*

Flips Graphix Design ....G...... 434 237-3547
Lynchburg *(G-7709)*

Flynn Enterprises Inc ....E...... 703 444-5555
Sterling *(G-13400)*

Fobbs Quality Signs LLC ....G...... 804 714-0102
North Chesterfield *(G-9878)*

Fontaine Melinda ....G...... 757 777-2812
Virginia Beach *(G-14470)*

Forrlace Inc ....G...... 757 873-5777
Newport News *(G-9232)*

Frf Inc ....E...... 434 974-7900
Charlottesville *(G-2636)*

G&M Signs LLC ....G...... 540 405-3232
Nokesville *(G-9392)*

Garris Signs Inc ....G...... 804 598-1127
Powhatan *(G-10545)*

Garys Sign Service ....G...... 434 836-0248
Danville *(G-3995)*

Gemini Incorporated ....D...... 434 315-0312
Farmville *(G-4942)*

General Display Company LLC ....G...... 703 335-9292
Manassas *(G-7943)*

Genesis Sign ....G...... 540 288-8820
Stafford *(G-13146)*

George Thomas Garten ....G...... 540 962-3633
Covington *(G-3790)*

Global Signs & Graphics ....G...... 703 543-1046
Centreville *(G-2306)*

Gourmet Kitchen Tools Inc ....G...... 757 595-3278
Yorktown *(G-15962)*

Grafik Trenz ....G...... 757 539-0141
Smithfield *(G-12714)*

Graham Graphics LLC ....G...... 703 220-4564
Springfield *(G-13013)*

Grand Designs LLC ....G...... 412 295-7730
Centreville *(G-2308)*

Grandesign ....G...... 434 294-0665
Blackstone *(G-1817)*

Graphic Garage ....G...... 434 589-3432
Troy *(G-13926)*

Graphic Sign Worx LLC ....G...... 703 503-3286
Annandale *(G-753)*

Graphics North ....G...... 540 678-4965
Winchester *(G-15546)*

Graphics Shop LLC ....F...... 757 485-7800
Chesapeake *(G-3123)*

Graphtone Signs ....G...... 434 989-9740
Charlottesville *(G-2638)*

Great Neon Art & Sign Co ....G...... 703 981-4661
Woodbridge *(G-15715)*

Green Graphic Signs LLC ....G...... 804 229-3351
North Chesterfield *(G-9881)*

Gtp Ventures Incorporated ....G...... 804 346-8922
Richmond *(G-11227)*

Halifax Sign Company ....G...... 434 579-3304
South Boston *(G-12775)*

Hampton Roads Sign Inc ....G...... 757 871-2307
Yorktown *(G-15963)*

Hand Signs LLC ....G...... 804 482-3568
Richmond *(G-11231)*

Hanna Sign Co ....G...... 540 636-4877
Front Royal *(G-5535)*

Happy Yard Signs ....G...... 757 599-5171
Newport News *(G-9245)*

Harrington Graphics Co Inc ....G...... 757 363-1600
Virginia Beach *(G-14507)*

Harville Entps of Danville VA ....G...... 434 822-2106
Danville *(G-3997)*

Hatch Graphics ....G...... 540 886-2114
Staunton *(G-13264)*

Hereisursign LLC ....G...... 757 277-8487
Norfolk *(G-9580)*

High Hat Inc ....G...... 703 212-7446
Alexandria *(G-229)*

Hip-Hop Spot 24/7 LLC ....G...... 434 660-3166
Lynchburg *(G-7734)*

His Sign LLC ....G...... 877 886-8879
Ashburn *(G-1291)*

Hjs Qwik Signs ....G...... 276 386-2696
Gate City *(G-5663)*

Hollywood Graphics and Signs .....G...... 804 382-2199
Moseley *(G-9040)*

Houser Sign Works ....G...... 804 539-1315
Ashland *(G-1436)*

Howards Signs LLC ....G...... 804 815-8333
North *(G-9803)*

Hunts Creek Slate Signs LLC ....G...... 434 581-1687
Arvonia *(G-1233)*

I H McBride Sign Company Inc ......F...... 434 847-4151
Madison Heights *(G-7875)*

I3 Ingenuity Inc ....G...... 703 524-0019
Arlington *(G-998)*

Ice Scraper Card Inc ....G...... 703 327-4622
Leesburg *(G-7286)*

Identity America Inc ....G...... 276 322-2616
Bluefield *(G-1864)*

Identity Mktg Promotional LLC ......G...... 757 966-2863
Suffolk *(G-13724)*

Idx Corporation ....C...... 410 551-3600
Fredericksburg *(G-5301)*

Igor Custom Sign Stripe ....G...... 757 639-2397
Virginia Beach *(G-14541)*

Illusions Wrap LLC ....G...... 540 710-9727
Fredericksburg *(G-5302)*

Ilmarnock Lettering Co LLC ....G...... 804 435-6956
Kilmarnock *(G-7070)*

Image 360 ....G...... 804 897-8500
North Chesterfield *(G-9889)*

Image Works Inc ....E...... 804 798-5533
Ashland *(G-1438)*

Images In Art Inc ....G...... 804 785-1011
Shacklefords *(G-12682)*

Imagine This Company ....F...... 804 232-1300
Richmond *(G-11614)*

Imperial Sign Co ....G...... 804 541-8545
Hopewell *(G-6935)*

Improvements By Bill LLC ....G...... 571 246-7257
Bluemont *(G-1889)*

In Home Care Inc ....E...... 276 328-6462
Wise *(G-15627)*

Indigo Sign Co ....G...... 804 469-3233
Dewitt *(G-4092)*

Indigo Signs LLC ....G...... 540 489-8400
Rocky Mount *(G-12328)*

Industries In Focus Inc ....G...... 703 451-5550
Springfield *(G-13023)*

Inkd Out Electrical Svc LLC ....F...... 757 369-9827
Newport News *(G-9258)*

Inkd Out LLC ....G...... 757 369-9827
Newport News *(G-9259)*

Innovtive Imges Cstm Sgns More ....G...... 804 472-3882
Warsaw *(G-15068)*

Intellimat Inc ....G...... 540 904-5670
Roanoke *(G-11942)*

J & R Partners ....G...... 757 274-3344
Norfolk *(G-9597)*

J & R Partners ....G...... 757 499-3344
Virginia Beach *(G-14556)*

J B Worsham ....G...... 434 836-9313
Danville *(G-4005)*

J Eubank Signs & Designs ....G...... 434 374-2364
Clarksville *(G-3631)*

J Fred Dowis ....G...... 757 874-7446
Newport News *(G-9263)*

Jackie Screen Printing ....G...... 276 963-0964
Richlands *(G-11017)*

James River Signs Inc ....G...... 757 870-3368
Newport News *(G-9266)*

Jarvis Sign Company ....G...... 804 514-9879
Richmond *(G-11253)*

Jbtm Enterprises Inc ....F...... 540 665-9651
Winchester *(G-15551)*

Jeannie Jackson Green ....G...... 540 904-6763
Roanoke *(G-12110)*

Jerrys Signs Inc ....F...... 276 676-2304
Abingdon *(G-44)*

Joe Giles Signs Inc ....G...... 434 391-9040
Farmville *(G-4944)*

Joeys Sign & Letter Inc ....G...... 757 868-7166
Hampton *(G-6276)*

John W Griessmayer Jr ....G...... 540 589-8387
Roanoke *(G-12113)*

Jones Sign Co Inc ....E...... 804 798-5533
Ashland *(G-1442)*

Joseph Randolph Pike ....G...... 804 798-7188
Ashland *(G-1443)*

Joshmor Pac ....G...... 276 620-6537
Wytheville *(G-15893)*

Justice Signs LLC ....G...... 304 898-2783
Glen Lyn *(G-5833)*

Jv-Rm Holdings Inc ....G...... 703 669-3333
Leesburg *(G-7293)*

K & K Signs ....G...... 540 586-0542
Bedford *(G-1641)*

K Hart Holding Inc ....G...... 800 294-5348
Norfolk *(G-9610)*

K L A Enterprises LLC ....G...... 540 382-9444
Christiansburg *(G-3602)*

K Walters At The Sign of G ....G...... 703 986-0448
Woodbridge *(G-15735)*

Kace Square LLC ....G...... 703 723-3679
Ashburn *(G-1300)*

Kaelin Signs LLC ....G...... 571 239-9192
Springfield *(G-13031)*

Ken Signs ....G...... 703 451-5474
Springfield *(G-13032)*

Kevins Signs ....G...... 540 427-1070
Roanoke *(G-12117)*

Key Display LLC ....G...... 434 286-4514
Scottsville *(G-12662)*

Kin Art Studios LLC ....G...... 804 368-7298
Ashland *(G-1449)*

King Signs and Graphics ....G...... 540 468-2932
Monterey *(G-9009)*

Kinsey Crane & Sign Company ....G...... 540 345-5063
Roanoke *(G-12119)*

Kinsey Neon & Sign Company ....G...... 540 345-5063
Roanoke *(G-12120)*

Kinsey Sign Company ....G...... 540 344-5148
Roanoke *(G-12121)*

Kirby Burbank LLC ....G...... 571 330-0261
Stafford *(G-13164)*

Kisco Signs LLC ....G...... 804 404-2727
Richmond *(G-11646)*

▲ Korman Signs Inc ....E...... 804 262-6050
Richmond *(G-11264)*

Korman Signs Inc ....G...... 804 262-6050
Henrico *(G-6529)*

Krimm Signs LLC ....G...... 571 599-2199
Chantilly *(G-2453)*

▲ Krt Architectural Signage Inc ....G...... 540 428-3801
Warrenton *(G-15029)*

Kwik Signs Inc. ....G...... 804 897-5945
North Chesterfield *(G-9910)*

Lai Enterprises LLC ....G...... 540 946-0000
Waynesboro *(G-15120)*

Larry Rosenbaum ....G...... 703 567-4052
Arlington *(G-1027)*

Layman Enterprises Inc ....G...... 540 662-7142
Winchester *(G-15439)*

Letter Perfect Incorporated ....F...... 540 652-2022
Elkton *(G-4331)*

Lettercraft Signs ....G...... 571 215-6900
Springfield *(G-13043)*

Level 7 Signs LLC ....G...... 540 885-1517
Staunton *(G-13276)*

Level 7 Signs and Graphics ....G...... 540 294-6690
Verona *(G-13990)*

Lfg Group Inc ....G...... 571 512-7446
Fairfax *(G-4499)*

Lighted Signs Direct Inc ....G...... 703 965-5188
Woodbridge *(G-15740)*

Lord Sign ....G...... 301 316-7446
Fairfax Station *(G-4716)*

Loudoun Signs Inc ....G...... 703 669-3333
Leesburg *(G-7308)*

Lynch Products ....G...... 540 483-7800
Rocky Mount *(G-12337)*

Lynchburg Wraps ....G...... 434 385-1370
Lynchburg *(G-7765)*

M&M Signs and Graphics LLC ....G...... 703 803-1043
Chantilly *(G-2460)*

Manny Exhibits & Woodcraft ....G...... 703 354-9231
Annandale *(G-770)*

Martins Custom Designs Inc ....G...... 804 642-0235
Gloucester Point *(G-5874)*

Martins Custom Designs Inc ....F...... 757 245-7129
Newport News *(G-9291)*

McMj Enterprises LLC ....G...... 434 298-0117
Blackstone *(G-1820)*

MCS Design & Production Inc ....G...... 804 550-1000
Ashland *(G-1462)*

Mekelexx Management Services ....G...... 561 644-8621
Fairfax Station *(G-4717)*

Metro Sign & Design Inc ....E...... 703 631-1866
Manassas Park *(G-8205)*

Metro Signs & Graphics Inc ....G...... 804 747-1918
Richmond *(G-11289)*

Michael A Latham ....G...... 804 835-3299
South Chesterfield *(G-12816)*

Michael Neely ....G...... 540 972-3265
Locust Grove *(G-7448)*

Mikes Signs4less ....G...... 540 548-2940
Fredericksburg *(G-5327)*

Miller Creative Solutions LLC ....G...... 202 560-3718
Falls Church *(G-4831)*

Model Sign & Graphics ....G...... 703 527-2121
Fairfax *(G-4514)*

Modern Engravings LLC ....G...... 757 876-3001
Gloucester *(G-5855)*

Momensity LLC ....G...... 804 247-2811
Stafford *(G-13177)*

Moore Sign Corporation ....E...... 804 748-5836
Chester *(G-3438)*

More Than A Sign ....G...... 540 514-3311
Winchester *(G-15452)*

Mountain Top Signs & Gifts ....G...... 540 430-0532
Verona *(G-13992)*

Muddy Feet LLC ....G...... 540 830-0342
Harrisonburg *(G-6349)*

Neatprints LLC ....G...... 703 520-1550
Springfield *(G-13057)*

Neon Nights ....G...... 757 857-6366
Norfolk *(G-9655)*

Neon Nights Inc. ....G...... 757 248-5676
Norfolk *(G-9656)*

New Home Media ....C...... 703 550-2233
Lorton *(G-7515)*

New Homes Media ....G...... 540 654-5350
Fredericksburg *(G-5334)*

New River Sign and Vinyl LLC ....G...... 703 793-0730
Blacksburg *(G-1775)*

Nhm Inc ....G...... 703 550-2233
Lorton *(G-7517)*

Nik Graphix LLC ....G...... 703 863-1075
Alexandria *(G-543)*

Noble Endeavors LLC ....G...... 571 402-7061
Woodbridge *(G-15762)*

Nomadic Display LLC ....G...... 800 336-5019
Lorton *(G-7518)*

Norvell Signs Incorporated ....G...... 804 737-2189
Richmond *(G-11696)*

Nothing But Neon ....G...... 434 842-9395
Columbia *(G-3753)*

Nova Retail LLC .....G..... 703 507-5220 Fairfax (G-4521)	Sandra Signs LLC .....G..... 757 397-4321 Portsmouth (G-10477)	Sign Solutions .....G..... 804 691-1824 Church Road (G-3618)
Nova Rock Craft LLC .....G..... 703 217-7072 Warrenton (G-15038)	Sav On Signs .....G..... 540 344-8406 Vinton (G-14182)	Sign Source .....G..... 804 270-3252 Henrico (G-6569)
Novelty Sign Works LLC .....G..... 804 559-2009 Mechanicsville (G-8665)	Scottys Sign Inc .....F..... 757 245-7129 Newport News (G-9332)	Sign Studio .....G..... 540 789-4200 Moneta (G-8977)
Nva Signs & Striping LLC .....G..... 703 263-1940 Manassas (G-7983)	Scoutco LLC .....G..... 540 433-5136 Harrisonburg (G-6367)	Sign Systems Inc .....G..... 540 639-0669 Fairlawn (G-4740)
Old Soul Signs LLC .....G..... 757 256-5669 Chesapeake (G-3227)	Scoutco LLC .....G..... 540 828-0928 Bridgewater (G-1958)	Sign Tech .....G..... 757 407-3870 Virginia Beach (G-14811)
Old Town Sign Co Inc .....G..... 703 836-7000 Alexandria (G-299)	Scripted Gate Sign Co LLC .....G..... 276 219-3850 Coeburn (G-3702)	Sign Wise LLC .....G..... 540 382-8343 Pilot (G-10358)
Oliver Princess .....G..... 804 683-5779 Chesterfield (G-3515)	Sgx Graphix .....G..... 703 330-3550 Chantilly (G-2490)	Sign With ME VA .....G..... 757 969-9876 Hampton (G-6235)
On Our Way Inc .....G..... 703 444-0007 Dulles (G-4214)	She Signs .....G..... 434 509-3173 Madison Heights (G-7884)	Sign Wizards Inc .....G..... 757 431-8886 Virginia Beach (G-14812)
Pac Bridge LLC .....G..... 434 385-8070 Lynchburg (G-7780)	Shenandoah Signs Promotions .....G..... 540 886-2114 Staunton (G-13293)	Sign Works Inc .....G..... 757 428-2525 Virginia Beach (G-14813)
Patricia Moore .....G..... 757 485-7414 Chesapeake (G-3234)	Sign & Engraving Technology .....F..... 804 744-7749 Midlothian (G-8899)	Sign World .....G..... 757 366-9890 Virginia Beach (G-14814)
◆ Payne Publishers Inc .....D..... 703 631-9033 Manassas (G-7988)	Sign and Seal .....G..... 540 955-2422 Berryville (G-1690)	Sign-N-Date Mobile Notary LLC .....G..... 757 285-9619 Newport News (G-9341)
Performance Signs LLC .....F..... 434 985-7446 Ruckersville (G-12408)	Sign and Seal Associates LLC .....G..... 804 266-0410 Glen Allen (G-5796)	Signarama .....G..... 804 967-3768 Henrico (G-6570)
Phase II Inc .....G..... 434 333-0808 Forest (G-5087)	Sign Biz LLC .....G..... 804 741-7446 Henrico (G-6567)	Signarama .....G..... 703 743-9424 Purcellville (G-10678)
Pink Street Signs .....G..... 540 489-8400 Rocky Mount (G-12345)	Sign Broker LLC .....G..... 703 263-7227 Chantilly (G-2491)	Signature Dsgns Fbrication LLC .....G..... 571 398-2444 Woodbridge (G-15809)
Poolhouse Digital Agency LLC .....G..... 804 876-0335 Richmond (G-11718)	Sign Builders .....G..... 757 499-2654 Virginia Beach (G-14808)	Signature Signs .....G..... 540 554-2717 Round Hill (G-12389)
Positive Signs LLC .....G..... 703 768-7446 Alexandria (G-553)	Sign Crafters Inc .....G..... 804 379-2004 Midlothian (G-8900)	Signd and Seald .....G..... 814 460-2547 Prospect (G-10614)
Potomac Signs Inc .....G..... 703 425-7000 Manassas Park (G-8206)	Sign Creations .....G..... 540 809-2112 Spotsylvania (G-12915)	Signfield Inc .....G..... 540 574-3032 Harrisonburg (G-6370)
Powers Signs Incorporated .....F..... 434 793-6351 Danville (G-4031)	Sign Creations LLC .....G..... 540 899-9555 Fredericksburg (G-5223)	Signmakers Inc .....G..... 757 621-1212 Virginia Beach (G-14816)
Preston Signs Inc .....G..... 703 534-3777 Vienna (G-14113)	Sign Cy Plus Graphic & Design .....G..... 703 912-9300 Springfield (G-13085)	Signmedia Inc .....E..... 757 826-7128 Hampton (G-6237)
Prime Signs .....G..... 757 481-7889 Virginia Beach (G-14738)	Sign Design Inc .....G..... 239 478-8315 Bluemont (G-1891)	Signmedic LLC .....G..... 703 919-3381 Triangle (G-13898)
Printing and Sign System Inc .....G..... 703 280-1550 Fairfax (G-4532)	Sign Design Inc .....G..... 540 338-5614 Purcellville (G-10677)	Signrex Inc .....G..... 703 497-7711 Woodbridge (G-15810)
Promocorp Inc .....F..... 703 942-7100 Alexandria (G-560)	Sign Design of Roanoke Inc .....G..... 540 977-3354 Roanoke (G-12187)	Signs Around You LLC .....G..... 919 449-4762 Stafford (G-13190)
Propst Lettering and Engraving .....G..... 540 896-5368 Broadway (G-2093)	Sign Design of Va LLC .....G..... 804 794-1689 Powhatan (G-10576)	Signs At Work .....G..... 804 338-7716 North Chesterfield (G-9980)
Pure Media Sign Studio LLC .....G..... 703 822-5468 Arlington (G-1123)	Sign Designs .....G..... 804 580-7446 Heathsville (G-6466)	Signs By Clay Downing .....G..... 703 371-6828 Broadlands (G-2081)
Quail Run Signs .....G..... 540 338-8412 Hamilton (G-6064)	Sign Designs of Powhatan Inc .....G..... 804 794-1689 Powhatan (G-10577)	Signs By Dave .....G..... 703 777-2870 Leesburg (G-7348)
Quick Designs LLC .....G..... 540 450-0750 Winchester (G-15573)	Sign Doctor Sales & Service .....G..... 540 743-5200 Luray (G-7623)	Signs By James LLC .....G..... 703 656-5067 Triangle (G-13899)
Quick Signs Inc .....G..... 703 606-3008 Manassas (G-7992)	Sign Dude .....G..... 757 303-7770 Yorktown (G-15990)	Signs By Randy .....G..... 434 328-8872 Charlottesville (G-2693)
R & S Namebadge Inc .....G..... 804 673-2842 Glen Allen (G-5785)	Sign Enterprise Inc .....G..... 540 899-9555 Fredericksburg (G-5224)	Signs By Tomorrow .....G..... 703 356-3383 Vienna (G-14127)
Rabbit Creek Partners LLC .....D..... 877 779-9977 Bluefield (G-1877)	Sign Express Inc .....G..... 757 686-3010 Portsmouth (G-10482)	Signs By Tomorrow .....G..... 703 591-2444 Fairfax (G-4676)
Rain & Associates LLC .....G..... 757 572-3996 Virginia Beach (G-14758)	Sign Factory Inc .....G..... 540 772-0400 Roanoke (G-12000)	Signs By Tomorrow .....G..... 703 444-0007 Sterling (G-13507)
Rapidsign Inc .....G..... 540 362-2025 Roanoke (G-12160)	Sign Graphx Inc .....F..... 703 335-7446 Manassas (G-8000)	Signs Designs & More LLC .....G..... 434 292-4555 Blackstone (G-1829)
Rebecca Burton .....G..... 804 526-3423 Colonial Heights (G-3743)	Sign Gypsies Richmondva LLC .....G..... 804 754-7345 Glen Allen (G-5797)	Signs For Anything Inc .....G..... 540 376-7006 Spotsylvania (G-12916)
Reed Sign Co .....G..... 757 336-5505 Chincoteague (G-3563)	Sign Ink LLC .....F..... 804 250-3700 Ashland (G-1491)	Signs For You LLC .....G..... 703 653-4353 Haymarket (G-6445)
Richardson Enterprises Inc .....G..... 804 733-8956 North Dinwiddie (G-10063)	Sign Language Interpreter .....G..... 540 460-4445 Staunton (G-13295)	Signs of Learning LLC .....G..... 757 635-2735 Virginia Beach (G-14817)
Richmond Corrugated Box Co .....E..... 804 222-1300 Sandston (G-12629)	Sign Managers .....G..... 804 878-0555 Colonial Heights (G-3747)	Signs of Success Inc .....G..... 757 481-4788 Virginia Beach (G-14818)
River City Sign Company .....G..... 804 687-1466 Midlothian (G-8891)	Sign Managers LLC .....G..... 804 381-5198 Richmond (G-11381)	Signs On Scene .....G..... 757 435-0841 Virginia Beach (G-14819)
Riverland Inc .....G..... 703 760-9300 Mc Lean (G-8539)	Sign Master .....G..... 540 886-6900 Fishersville (G-5008)	Signs R US LLC .....G..... 540 742-3625 Shenandoah (G-12695)
Rocks Tiki Surfboard Signs .....G..... 757 727-3330 Suffolk (G-13760)	Sign Medik .....G..... 757 748-1048 Virginia Beach (G-14809)	Signs To Go .....G..... 757 622-7446 Norfolk (G-9725)
Rockstar Wraps LLC .....G..... 703 392-7625 Manassas (G-8146)	Sign of Goldfish .....G..... 540 727-0008 Culpeper (G-3920)	Signs Unlimited Inc .....F..... 703 799-8840 Alexandria (G-585)
Rva Custom Signs Inc .....G..... 804 749-4000 Rockville (G-12296)	Sign On Line LLC .....G..... 571 246-7776 Alexandria (G-584)	Signs Up .....G..... 703 798-5210 Springfield (G-13086)
Rva Signs & Graphic .....G..... 804 749-4000 Rockville (G-12297)	Sign Right Here LLC .....G..... 757 617-0785 Virginia Beach (G-14810)	Signs USA Inc .....G..... 540 432-6366 Harrisonburg (G-6371)
Rycon Inc .....G..... 571 313-8334 Sterling (G-13498)	Sign Scapes Inc .....G..... 804 980-7111 Henrico (G-6568)	Signs Work .....G..... 276 655-4047 Elk Creek (G-4321)
S & S Mixed Signs Inc .....G..... 804 642-2641 Hayes (G-6406)	Sign Shop .....F..... 703 590-9534 Woodbridge (G-15808)	Signsations LLC .....G..... 571 340-3330 Fairfax (G-4677)
Saeam Graphics & Sign Inc .....G..... 703 203-3233 Annandale (G-780)	Sign Shop of Newport News .....G..... 757 873-1157 Newport News (G-9339)	Signspot LLC .....G..... 540 961-7768 Blacksburg (G-1791)
Safehouse Signs Inc .....E..... 540 366-2480 Roanoke (G-12174)	Sign Solutions .....G..... 757 594-9688 Newport News (G-9340)	Signworks of King George .....G..... 540 709-7483 King George (G-7113)

S
I
C

Simms Sign Co/Cash .... G 804 746-0595
  Mechanicsville (G-8676)
Simply Wood Post Signs LLC .... G 757 657-9058
  Suffolk (G-13764)
Simpson Signs .... G 434 369-7389
  Altavista (G-643)
Simurg Arts LLC .... G 703 670-7230
  Woodbridge (G-15811)
Sir Speedy Print Signs Mktg .... G 540 662-3804
  Winchester (G-15587)
Sjm Agency Inc .... G 703 754-3073
  Midlothian (G-8903)
Skyway Outdoor Inc .... F 276 688-0248
  Bastian (G-1593)
Sml Signs & More LLC .... G 540 719-7446
  Moneta (G-8979)
Sn Signs .... G 703 354-3000
  Springfield (G-13089)
Snyder Custom Sign Display .... G 703 362-5675
  Springfield (G-13090)
Speedpro .... G 757 233-9250
  Virginia Beach (G-14837)
Speedpro Imaging - Centreville .... G 571 719-3161
  Manassas (G-8160)
Speedy Sign-A-Rama USA Inc .... G 757 838-7446
  Hampton (G-6242)
Sprint Signs .... G 804 741-7446
  Richmond (G-11396)
St Clair Signs Inc .... G 540 258-2191
  Glasgow (G-5702)
Staab Sign Language Svcs LLC .... G 301 775-2279
  Alexandria (G-354)
Stacey A Peets .... G 847 707-3112
  Henrico (G-6575)
Stahmer Inc .... G 757 838-4200
  Hampton (G-6243)
Stans Signs Inc .... G 540 434-1531
  Rockingham (G-12278)
Stefanik Sign Service .... G 540 295-7248
  Fredericksburg (G-5488)
Steve D Gilnett .... G 804 746-5497
  Mechanicsville (G-8682)
Steves Signworx LLC .... G 434 385-1000
  Forest (G-5097)
Studio B Graphics .... G 703 777-8755
  Purcellville (G-10680)
Suday Promotions Inc .... G 703 376-8640
  Chantilly (G-2503)
Sumners Scoreboards .... G 804 526-7152
  Colonial Heights (G-3750)
Sun Signs .... G 703 867-9831
  Stafford (G-13197)
Superior Signs LLC .... E 804 271-5685
  North Chesterfield (G-9993)
Sykes Signs Inc .... G 276 935-2772
  Grundy (G-6041)
T-Shirt & Screen Print Co .... G 540 667-2351
  Winchester (G-15590)
Talley Sign Company .... F 804 649-0325
  Richmond (G-11781)
Thore Signs .... G 804 513-5621
  Powhatan (G-10580)
Thurston Sign & Graphic .... G 804 285-4617
  Richmond (G-11411)
Tidal Wave Graphics .... G 757 842-6269
  Chesapeake (G-3336)
Tidewater Graphics and Signs .... G 757 622-7446
  Norfolk (G-9753)
Tight Lines Holdings Group .... G 540 989-7874
  Roanoke (G-12009)
Tight Lines Holdings Group Inc .... F 540 389-6691
  Salem (G-12573)
Tinted Timber Sign Co .... G 757 869-3231
  Yorktown (G-15996)
Titan Sign Corporation .... G 540 899-5334
  Fredericksburg (G-5379)
Tko Promos .... G 804 564-1683
  Moseley (G-9049)
TNT GRAphics&signs .... G 757 615-5936
  Chesapeake (G-3342)
Todays Signs Inc .... G 703 352-6200
  Fairfax (G-4688)
Todd & Gloria Price .... G 276 655-4047
  Elk Creek (G-4322)
Torres Graphics and Signs Inc .... G 757 873-5777
  Newport News (G-9359)
Trexlo Enterprises LLC .... F 804 719-5900
  Rockville (G-12301)
Trexlo Enterprises LLC .... G 804 272-7446
  North Chesterfield (G-10004)

Trexlo Enterprises LLC .... G 804 644-7446
  Richmond (G-11794)
Trexlo Enterprises LLC .... G 804 270-7446
  Glen Allen (G-5817)
Trexlo Enterprises LLC .... G 804 624-1977
  Chesterfield (G-3534)
Tsg Concepts Inc 877 777-5734
  Arlington (G-1200)
Twelve Inc .... G 804 232-1300
  Richmond (G-11796)
Type Signs LLC .... G 202 355-4403
  Woodbridge (G-15825)
Uptown Neon .... G 804 358-6243
  Richmond (G-11801)
VA Displays LLC .... G 757 251-8060
  Smithfield (G-12743)
Vance Graphics LLC .... G 276 964-2822
  Pounding Mill (G-10526)
Vanmark LLC .... G 757 689-3850
  Virginia Beach (G-14906)
Vertex Signs .... G 540 904-5776
  Roanoke (G-12018)
Vics Signs & Engraving .... G 757 562-2243
  Franklin (G-5161)
Vinyl Visions LLC .... G 540 369-5244
  King George (G-7119)
Virginia Custom Signs Corp .... G 804 278-8788
  Richmond (G-11439)
Virginia Sign and Lighting Co .... G 703 222-5670
  Manassas (G-8176)
Vision Sign Inc .... G 703 707-0858
  Sterling (G-13553)
Vital Signs & Displays LLC .... G 540 656-8303
  King George (G-7120)
W & S Forbes Inc .... G 757 498-7446
  Virginia Beach (G-14928)
W W Burton .... G 540 547-4668
  Reva (G-11003)
Wac Enterprises LLC .... G 757 342-7202
  Williamsburg (G-15337)
Walker Virginia .... G 757 652-0430
  Newport News (G-9378)
Wall To Wall Signs .... G 703 821-2358
  Vienna (G-14155)
Wang Sign Holdings LLC .... G 757 595-3278
  Yorktown (G-14160)
Washburn Sign Services Inc .... G 540 483-5784
  Martinsville (G-8350)
Wft Promotions LLC .... G 757 560-5056
  Suffolk (G-13784)
Whats Your Sign .... G 276 632-0576
  Martinsville (G-8353)
Whats Your Sign LLC .... G 703 860-2075
  Fairfax (G-4581)
Willie Lucas .... G 919 935-8066
  Woodbridge (G-15832)
Words On Wood Signs Inc .... G 540 493-9353
  Glade Hill (G-5672)
Worth Higgins & Associates Inc ...... E 804 353-0607
  Richmond (G-11457)
Worth Higgins & Associates Inc ...... E 804 353-0607
  Richmond (G-11458)
Worthington Millwork LLC .... G 540 832-6391
  Gordonsville (G-5919)
Wright Sign Service Inc .... F 757 566-8329
  Toano (G-13881)
Wyatt Sign & Painting Company ...... G 804 733-5251
  Petersburg (G-10352)
Xtreme Signs .... G 434 447-5738
  Brodnax (G-2106)
Yesco of Richmond .... G 804 302-4391
  Midlothian (G-8926)
Yesco Sign & Lighting Service .... G 757 369-9827
  Newport News (G-9383)
Your Life Uncorked .... G 757 218-8495
  Hampton (G-6274)
Youve Got It Made LLC .... G 410 840-8744
  Harrisonburg (G-6388)
Zingify LLC .... G 703 689-3636
  Herndon (G-6848)

3996 Linoleum & Hard Surface Floor Coverings, NEC

Advanta Flooring Inc .... G 804 530-5004
  North Chesterfield (G-9805)
▼ Flooring Adventures LLC .... G 804 530-5004
  Chester (G-3416)
Knowles Flooring .... G 571 224-3694
  Fairfax (G-4491)

Pave DMV LLC .... G 703 798-1087
  Alexandria (G-549)

3999 Manufacturing Industries, NEC

1st Signage and Lighting LLC .... G 276 229-4200
  Woolwine (G-15863)
1st Stop Electronics LLC .... G 804 931-0517
  Richmond (G-11070)
20-X Industries LLC .... G 540 922-0005
  Pembroke (G-10280)
3 Gypsies Candle Company LLC ...... G 703 300-2307
  Manassas (G-8016)
6th Floor Candle Company LLC .... G 917 580-2251
  Alexandria (G-397)
710 Essentials LLC .... G 540 748-4393
  Spotsylvania (G-12880)
A and J HM Imprv Angela Towler ..... G 434 429-5087
  Danville (G-3952)
A Frame Digital .... G 571 308-0147
  Vienna (G-14002)
A J Industries .... G 757 871-4109
  Hampton (G-6066)
Academics In A Box Inc .... G 757 286-0673
  Chesapeake (G-2952)
Accuracy Gear LLC .... G 540 230-0257
  Hiwassee (G-6908)
Ace Industries Virginia LLC .... G 757 292-3321
  Radford (G-10702)
Aci Partners LLC .... F 703 818-0500
  Manassas (G-8019)
Adco Signs Inc .... G 757 787-1393
  Onancock (G-10188)
Additive Mfg Exch Amex LLC .... G 703 971-3174
  Alexandria (G-403)
Ado Industries LLC .... G 540 877-2769
  Winchester (G-15372)
Advanced Mfg Restructuring LLC ..... G 540 667-5010
  Winchester (G-15525)
Aero Design & Mfg Co In .... G 218 722-1927
  Mc Lean (G-8389)
Aeroart International Inc .... G 703 406-4376
  Great Falls (G-5934)
▲ Afg Industries - VA .... G 276 619-6000
  Abingdon (G-8)
◆ Afton Chemical Corporation .... B 804 788-5800
  Richmond (G-11476)
▲ Agility Inc .... E 423 383-0962
  Bristol (G-2003)
▼ Ahmed Industries Inc .... G 703 828-7180
  Arlington (G-846)
Al Rayanah USA .... G 703 941-1200
  Falls Church (G-4742)
Alans Apary Hney Bees Svcs LL ..... G 540 881-0405
  Culpeper (G-3863)
Alicesa Foster Graves LLC .... G 804 658-0092
  Richmond (G-11098)
All Care Training & Services .... G 757 346-2703
  Norfolk (G-9431)
Allen Industries Intl LLC .... G 540 797-5230
  Bedford (G-1618)
Allermore Industries Inc .... G 703 537-1346
  Springfield (G-12941)
Alta Industries LLC .... G 703 969-0999
  Brambleton (G-1925)
Alternative Candle Company .... G 804 350-6980
  Woodbridge (G-15645)
Altria .... B 804 274-2100
  Richmond (G-11100)
Amana U S A Incorporated .... G 703 821-7501
  Falls Church (G-4745)
Amato Industries .... G 703 534-1400
  Fairfax (G-4406)
AMC Industries Inc .... G 410 320-5037
  Great Falls (G-5936)
American Knine .... G 757 304-9600
  Carrsville (G-2248)
American Manufacturing Co Inc ...... G 703 361-2210
  Gainesville (G-5569)
Amethyst Flame Candles LLC .... G 757 324-0614
  Suffolk (G-13669)
Andrea Lewis .... G 804 933-4161
  North Chesterfield (G-9818)
Anthony Amusements .... G 703 670-2681
  Manassas (G-8027)
AP Candles LLC .... G 804 276-8681
  Chesterfield (G-3475)
Apex Industries Inc .... G 540 992-5300
  Daleville (G-3939)
Apex Tree Industries .... G 540 915-6489
  Roanoke (G-12033)

Apogee Power Usa LLC ....F 318 572-8967
  Fredericksburg (G-5399)

Appalachian Mineral Services ......G 276 345-4610
  Richlands (G-11012)

Applied Manufacturing Tech ....G 434 942-1047
  Thaxton (G-13841)

Ardent Candle Company LLC ....G 347 906-2011
  Virginia Beach (G-14239)

Aroma Kandles LLC ....G 202 525-1550
  Manassas Park (G-8189)

Aromatic Spice Blends LLC ....G 703 477-6865
  Sterling (G-13350)

Arroman Industries Corp ....G 804 317-4737
  Hopewell (G-6918)

Arrow Mfg LLC ....G 757 635-6889
  Virginia Beach (G-14241)

Art & Framing Center ....G 540 720-2800
  Stafford (G-13119)

Artistic Thread Designs ....G 703 583-3706
  Woodbridge (G-15649)

As Clean As A Whistle ....G 757 753-0600
  Newport News (G-9171)

Aspen Industries LLC ....G 540 234-0413
  Weyers Cave (G-15166)

Aspire Marketing Corporation ....G 434 525-6191
  Forest (G-5051)

Asw Aluminum ....G 434 476-7557
  Halifax (G-6048)

Automotors Industries Inc ....G 703 459-8930
  Woodbridge (G-15652)

Avila Herbals LLC ....G 540 838-1118
  Christiansburg (G-3572)

Awn Candle Company ....G 618 560-6355
  Chesapeake (G-2991)

B&B Industries LLC ....G 703 855-2142
  Alexandria (G-420)

Backwoods Fabrications LLC ....G 804 448-2901
  Ruther Glen (G-12450)

Bally Technologies Inc ....G 917 415-5649
  Chantilly (G-2526)

Barnes Industries Inc ....G 804 389-1981
  Sandy Hook (G-12643)

Battlefield Industries LLC ....G 703 995-4822
  Burke (G-2183)

Battlefield Terrain Concepts ....G 540 977-0696
  Roanoke (G-11884)

Batts Industries LLC ....G 202 669-6015
  Herndon (G-6620)

Bay Breeze Labradors ....G 757 408-5227
  Suffolk (G-13675)

Bea Maurer ....G 540 377-5025
  Fairfield (G-4729)

Beach Wreaths and More ....G 757 943-0703
  Virginia Beach (G-14271)

Bear-Kat Manufacturing LLC ....G 800 442-9700
  Manassas (G-8036)

Beauty Pop LLC ....G 757 416-5858
  Norfolk (G-9460)

BEC ....G 804 330-2500
  North Chesterfield (G-9829)

Beeswax Candle Company LLC .....G 434 528-9885
  Lynchburg (G-7651)

Bellvue Corp ....G 276 806-4418
  Portsmouth (G-10398)

Benttree Enterprises ....G 434 770-3632
  Vernon Hill (G-13981)

Bespokery LLC ....G 703 624-5024
  Fairfax (G-4598)

Bethune Industries LLC ....G 407 579-1308
  Arlington (G-882)

Bg Industries Inc ....G 434 369-2128
  Lynchburg (G-7653)

Birth Right Industries LLC ....G 703 590-6971
  Woodbridge (G-15658)

Bkc Industries Inc ....G 856 694-9400
  Manassas (G-8040)

Black Gold Industries LLC ....G 757 768-4674
  Newport News (G-9181)

Blackwater Manufacturing LLC ......G 804 299-3975
  Ashland (G-1382)

Blind Industries ....G 703 390-9221
  Reston (G-10809)

Blonde Industries LLC ....G 540 667-8192
  Stephenson (G-13331)

Blue Ridge Yurts LLC ....G 540 651-8422
  Pilot (G-10356)

Bobblehouse LLC ....G 703 582-6797
  Ashburn (G-1250)

Bodyzone L L C ....G 770 922-0700
  Virginia Beach (G-14292)

Bookmarks By Bulger ....G 757 362-6841
  Virginia Beach (G-14293)

Bosco Industries ....G 540 671-8053
  Front Royal (G-5525)

Bottom of Bottle Candle Co LLC ....G 540 692-9260
  Strasburg (G-13574)

Bowdens Candle Creations ....G 757 539-0306
  Suffolk (G-13681)

Bowman Nakia ....G 804 263-2181
  Highland Springs (G-6851)

Brad & Moo Merchants LLC ....G 434 738-1130
  Herndon (G-6630)

Brickhouse Industries LLC ....G 757 880-7249
  Hayes (G-6397)

Brights Antique Slot Machine ....G 703 906-8389
  Alexandria (G-426)

Burgholzer Manufacturing Lc ....G 540 667-8612
  Winchester (G-15398)

Burning Brite Candle ....G 540 904-6544
  Goodview (G-5894)

C&M Industries Inc ....G 757 626-1141
  Norfolk (G-9471)

Cajo Industries Inc ....G 804 829-6854
  Charles City (G-2571)

Candle Euphoria ....G 757 327-8567
  Hampton (G-6104)

Candle Fetish ....G 757 535-3105
  Portsmouth (G-10404)

Candle Utopia Incorporated ....G 757 274-2406
  Norfolk (G-9476)

Candles For Effect LLC ....G 707 591-3986
  Stafford (G-13126)

Candles Make Scents LLC ....G 540 223-3972
  Mineral (G-8943)

Candlestick Baker Inc ....G 757 761-4473
  Virginia Beach (G-14313)

Candylicious Crafts LLC ....G 757 915-5542
  Newport News (G-9190)

Capital City Candle ....G 571 245-4738
  West Point (G-15154)

Cardinal Mfg ....G 540 779-7790
  Bedford (G-1630)

Cardinal Tool Inc ....G 804 561-2560
  Amelia Court House (G-653)

Carmel Tctcal Sltons Group LLC ...G 804 943-6121
  Colonial Heights (G-3731)

Cataldo Industries LLC ....F 757 422-0518
  Virginia Beach (G-14323)

Cathay Industries Inc ....G 224 629-4210
  Hiwassee (G-6911)

Cbd Genie LLC ....G 571 434-1776
  Sterling (G-13366)

Cbd Livity ....G 571 215-1938
  Virginia Beach (G-14326)

Cbd Solutions LLC ....G 757 286-8733
  King George (G-7082)

CDK Industries LLC ....G 804 551-3085
  North Chesterfield (G-9841)

Cedar Lane Farms LLC ....G 757 335-0830
  Virginia Beach (G-14327)

Cephas Industries Inc ....G 804 641-1824
  Chester (G-3393)

Chaz & Reetas Creations ....G 804 248-4933
  North Chesterfield (G-9842)

Chesapeake Manufacturing Inc .....G 804 716-2035
  Richmond (G-11528)

Chick Lit LLC ....G 757 496-9019
  Virginia Beach (G-14337)

Christopher Hawkins ....G 540 361-1679
  Fredericksburg (G-5178)

Cjc Industries Inc ....G 757 227-6767
  Virginia Beach (G-14340)

Clarity Candles LLC ....G 703 278-3760
  Arlington (G-907)

Clear Water Manufacturing ....G 434 582-9511
  Madison Heights (G-7869)

Clearview Industries LLC ....G 540 312-0899
  Willis (G-15358)

Clifford Aeroworks LLC ....G 703 304-3675
  Potomac Falls (G-10508)

CM Harris Industries LLC ....G 276 632-8438
  Martinsville (G-8275)

Cobweb Industries LLC ....G 703 834-1000
  Herndon (G-6643)

Cochran Inds Inc - Wytheville ....G 276 498-3836
  Oakwood (G-10165)

Colonial East Distributors LLC ......G 844 802-4427
  Virginia Beach (G-14354)

Combat Coatings LLC ....G 757 468-9020
  Virginia Beach (G-14356)

Commonwealth Provisions LLC .....G 540 699-0222
  Fredericksburg (G-5265)

Copper and Oak Cft Spirits LLC ....G 309 255-2001
  Portsmouth (G-10409)

Corey Vereen ....G 609 468-5409
  Virginia Beach (G-14367)

Cottage Grove Candles ....G 757 751-8333
  Newport News (G-9206)

Cottage Industries Exposition ....G 703 834-0055
  Herndon (G-6649)

Cottage Still Room/Bees Wax CN ..G 434 846-4398
  Lynchburg (G-7685)

Country Scents Candles ....G 757 359-8730
  Portsmouth (G-10411)

Couture Intuition LLC ....G 757 570-8126
  Newport News (G-9207)

Creative Permutations LLC ....G 703 628-3799
  Fairfax Station (G-4704)

Creature Comfort Custom Concie ...G 703 609-7098
  Fairfax (G-4608)

Cresset Corporation ....F 804 798-2691
  Ashland (G-1399)

Cross Match Technologies Inc ....G 703 841-6280
  Arlington (G-921)

Cross Restorations ....G 276 466-8436
  Bristol (G-2014)

Crown Supreme Industries LLC .....G 703 729-1482
  Ashburn (G-1263)

Crypto Industries LLC ....G 703 729-5059
  Ashburn (G-1264)

Crypto Reserve Inc ....G 571 229-0826
  Manassas (G-7927)

CSM Industries Inc ....G 410 818-3262
  Arlington (G-922)

Curry Industries LLC ....G 757 251-7559
  Hampton (G-6125)

Custom Stage Curtain Fbrctrs ....G 804 264-3700
  Richmond (G-11553)

Cva Industrial Products Inc ....G 434 985-1870
  Stanardsville (G-13218)

Cyntherapy Scented Candles LLC ..G 804 901-2681
  Henrico (G-6498)

Cyril Edward Gropen ....G 434 227-9039
  Charlottesville (G-2614)

Davis & Davis Industries LLC ....G 757 269-1534
  Virginia Beach (G-14393)

Davis Minding Manufacture ....G 276 321-7137
  Wise (G-15621)

Dean Industries Intl LLC ....G 703 249-5099
  Springfield (G-12990)

Debbie Belt ....G 912 856-9476
  Richmond (G-11556)

Defazio Industries LLC ....G 703 399-1494
  Henrico (G-6499)

Delclos Industries LLC ....G 540 349-4049
  Warrenton (G-14994)

Diggs Industries LLC ....G 757 371-3470
  Smithfield (G-12711)

Diversified Atmospheric Water ....G 757 617-1782
  Virginia Beach (G-14406)

Diversified Industries ....G 540 992-1900
  Troutville (G-13908)

Dominion Ammunition Mfg Inc ....G 804 276-2851
  North Chesterfield (G-10018)

Dose Guardian LLC ....G 804 726-5448
  Richmond (G-11565)

Doskocil Mfg Co Inc ....G 218 766-2558
  Reston (G-10843)

Draculas Tokens LLC ....G 717 818-5687
  Leesburg (G-7259)

Draeger Safety Diagnostics Inc ......G 703 517-0974
  Purcellville (G-10660)

Dragon Defense Mfg ....G 804 986-6635
  Richmond (G-11190)

Drengr Defense Industries LLC ......G 703 552-9987
  Vienna (G-14042)

Duke Industries LLC ....G 252 404-2344
  Chesapeake (G-3078)

Dulcet Industries LLC ....G 571 758-3191
  Ashburn (G-1273)

Dundee Miniatures LLC ....G 703 669-5591
  Leesburg (G-7262)

E4 Beauty Supply LLC ....G 804 307-4941
  Chesterfield (G-3495)

Earthen Candle Works LLC ....G 540 270-5938
  Ashburn (G-1277)

◆ Earthwalk Communications Inc ..D 703 393-1940
  Manassas (G-8061)

East Coast Candle Co ....G 781 718-9466
  Lynchburg (G-7698)

Employee Codes: A=Over 500 employees, B=251-500
C=101-250, D=51-100, E=20-50, F=10-19, G=1-9   2021 Virginia
Industrial Directory   663

Easyloader Manufacturing LLC ....G...... 540 297-2601
Huddleston **(G-6953)**

Eleven Eleven Candles More LLC ...G... 757 766-0687
Hampton **(G-6137)**

Eley House Candles...........................G...... 757 572-9318
Suffolk **(G-13703)**

Elizur International Inc ....G...... 757 648-8502
Virginia Beach **(G-14441)**

Ellen Fairchild-Flugel Art LLC ....G...... 540 325-2305
Woodstock **(G-15852)**

Elliott Mfg ....G...... 804 737-1475
Richmond **(G-11573)**

Enabled Manufacturing LLC ....G...... 704 491-9414
Blacksburg **(G-1735)**

Endeavor Consulting Group LLC......G...... 202 599-7437
Manassas **(G-8064)**

Erikson Diversified Industries ....G...... 703 216-5482
Fredericksburg **(G-5283)**

Every Changing Woman ....G...... 757 343-3088
Virginia Beach **(G-14455)**

Evolve Custom LLC ....G...... 703 570-5700
Winchester **(G-15414)**

Evolve Manufacturing LLC ....G...... 703 570-5700
Winchester **(G-15415)**

Excelsia Industries LLC ....G...... 804 347-7626
Midlothian **(G-8815)**

Excelsior Associates Inc ....G...... 703 255-1596
Vienna **(G-14051)**

Executive Creations........................G...... 757 351-1310
Virginia Beach **(G-14456)**

▲ Explus Inc ....D...... 703 260-0780
Dulles **(G-4201)**

Express Contract Fullmen ....G...... 540 719-2100
Moneta **(G-8961)**

Eye Dollz Lashes Buty Bar LLC ......G...... 703 480-7899
Manassas **(G-8067)**

EZ Cut Bandmills ....G...... 540 931-2410
Pearisburg **(G-10274)**

Fairlead Precision Mfg....................G...... 757 606-2033
Portsmouth **(G-10430)**

Fairview Place LLC ....G...... 330 257-1138
Norfolk **(G-9549)**

Farlow Industries ....G...... 434 836-4596
Danville **(G-3994)**

Feather & Pearl Candle Co LLC ....G...... 540 769-9529
Roanoke **(G-12086)**

Febrocom LLC ....G...... 703 349-6316
Ashburn **(G-1279)**

Fiddlehand Inc ....G...... 703 340-9806
Herndon **(G-6675)**

Fieldtech Industries LLC ....G...... 757 286-1503
Virginia Beach **(G-14463)**

Fisher Knives Inc ....G...... 434 242-3866
Earlysville **(G-4290)**

Flip Flop Fabrication LLC ....G...... 540 820-5959
Rockingham **(G-12253)**

Flying Fur ....G...... 540 552-1351
Blacksburg **(G-1740)**

Flzhi Technologies LLC ....G...... 214 616-7756
Arlington **(G-972)**

Fortune Nails LLC ....G...... 703 330-1306
Manassas **(G-7942)**

Four Calling Birds Ltd ....G...... 540 317-5761
Hume **(G-6961)**

Fourty4industries LLC ....G...... 703 266-0525
Clifton **(G-3665)**

Fredrick Allen Murphey ....G...... 804 385-1650
Highland Springs **(G-6853)**

Frog Industries LLC ....G...... 757 995-2359
Norfolk **(G-9560)**

Ft Industries LLC ....G...... 757 495-0510
Virginia Beach **(G-14476)**

Fuhgiddabowdit Industries ....G...... 757 598-0331
Poquoson **(G-10371)**

Fur Persons Rescue Fund ....G...... 703 754-7474
Haymarket **(G-6424)**

Fur The Love of Dogs LLC ....G...... 540 850-5540
Stafford **(G-13145)**

G-Force Events Inc ....G...... 804 228-0188
Richmond **(G-11597)**

Garret Industries LLC ....G...... 804 795-1650
Henrico **(G-6516)**

Gavial Engineering and Mfg............G...... 804 627-1437
Charles City **(G-2575)**

General Medical Mfg Co ....G...... 804 254-2737
Richmond **(G-11216)**

Germfreak Inc ....G...... 443 254-0805
Alexandria **(G-467)**

Ghek Industries LLC ....G...... 804 955-0710
Henrico **(G-6517)**

Glanville Industries LLC ....G...... 757 513-2700
Carrollton **(G-2243)**

Glenna Jean Mfg Co ....G...... 804 783-1490
Richmond **(G-11602)**

GMA Industries ....G...... 703 538-5100
Falls Church **(G-4915)**

Go4it LLC ....G...... 703 531-0586
Falls Church **(G-4916)**

Gogo Industries Inc ....G...... 925 708-7804
Charlottesville **(G-2805)**

Gold Canyon Candles ....G...... 540 972-1266
Locust Grove **(G-7444)**

Goodlife Theatre ....G...... 540 547-9873
Boston **(G-1903)**

Gormanlee Industries LLC ....G...... 703 448-1948
Mc Lean **(G-8452)**

Got Scents & Sova Candles ....G...... 434 736-9394
Keysville **(G-7058)**

Gourmet Manufacturing Inc ....G...... 276 638-2367
Martinsville **(G-8291)**

Gray Shuntina ....G...... 919 273-7979
Virginia Beach **(G-14489)**

Grayer Industries LLC ....G...... 703 491-4629
Woodbridge **(G-15713)**

Graymatter Industries LLC ....G...... 276 429-2396
Glade Spring **(G-5677)**

Great Dogs Great Falls LLC ....G...... 703 759-3601
Great Falls **(G-5958)**

Great Falls Tea Garden LLC ....G...... 703 757-6209
Great Falls **(G-5960)**

Green Prana Industries Inc ....G...... 410 790-3011
Buckingham **(G-2133)**

Gsa Service Company ....G...... 703 742-6818
Sterling **(G-13416)**

GSE Industries LLC ....G...... 832 633-9864
Moneta **(G-8963)**

Gutter-Stuff Industries VA LLC ....G...... 540 982-1115
Roanoke **(G-12099)**

Hair Studio Orie Inc ....G...... 703 282-5390
Fairfax **(G-4474)**

Hammond United Industries LLC ....G...... 571 306-9003
Fredericksburg **(G-5296)**

Hanke Industries LLC ....G...... 601 665-2147
Alexandria **(G-475)**

Harmony Lights Candle ....G...... 434 384-5549
Madison Heights **(G-7873)**

Hartung Screen Printing LLC ....G...... 412 979-7847
Ruckersville **(G-12403)**

Hcg Industries LLC ....G...... 540 291-2674
Natural Bridge **(G-9106)**

Heavenly Aromas LLC ....F...... 804 651-6250
Henrico **(G-6520)**

Heavyn & Hopes Candle Co ....G...... 301 980-8299
Alexandria **(G-476)**

Heirloom Candle Company LLC ....G...... 276 889-2505
Lebanon **(G-7193)**

Helltown Industries LLC ....G...... 571 312-4073
Arlington **(G-990)**

Herbal Origins LLC ....G...... 804 715-0015
North Chesterfield **(G-9883)**

Hermitage Industries Co Inc ....G...... 757 638-4551
Chesapeake **(G-3134)**

Hip Occasions LLC ....G...... 540 695-8896
Fredericksburg **(G-5297)**

Hocl Inc ....G...... 877 435-4625
Chantilly **(G-2436)**

Hol Industries LLC ....G...... 703 835-5476
Alexandria **(G-479)**

Horton Wreath Society Inc ....G...... 757 617-2093
Virginia Beach **(G-14530)**

Iconix Industries Inc ....G...... 703 489-0278
Chantilly **(G-2538)**

Ideagirl Industries LLC ....G...... 240 672-8333
Alexandria **(G-233)**

◆ Identification Intl Inc ....F...... 540 953-3343
Blacksburg **(G-1744)**

Indigenous Industries LLC ....G...... 540 847-9851
Fredericksburg **(G-5441)**

Industrial Biodynamics LLC ....G...... 540 357-0033
Salem **(G-12520)**

Industries 247 LLC ....G...... 703 741-0151
Arlington **(G-1002)**

Industries Massive ....G...... 703 347-6074
Alexandria **(G-485)**

Innovative Industries LLC ....G...... 540 317-1733
Culpeper **(G-3895)**

Integrated Global Services Inc ....G...... 804 897-0326
Midlothian **(G-8833)**

Into Light ....G...... 757 816-9002
Virginia Beach **(G-14553)**

Ipac Industries LLC ....G...... 703 362-9090
Fairfax **(G-4639)**

Isobaric Strategies Inc ....G...... 757 277-2858
Virginia Beach **(G-14554)**

Ivy Manufacturing LLC ....G...... 434 249-0134
Charlottesville **(G-2649)**

J Lynette Buty & Bundles LLC ....G...... 276 790-9510
Martinsville **(G-8303)**

James R Napier ....G...... 434 547-5511
Drakes Branch **(G-4134)**

Jember LLC ....G...... 202 631-8521
Alexandria **(G-496)**

Jkm Industries LLC ....G...... 703 599-3112
Alexandria **(G-498)**

Joe Products Inc ....G...... 314 409-4477
Mc Lean **(G-8475)**

Johnny Porter Candle Co ....G...... 540 406-1608
Orange **(G-10217)**

Joint Manufacturing Force LLC ....G...... 910 364-8580
Alexandria **(G-499)**

JPF Industriesinc ....G...... 703 451-0203
Springfield **(G-13030)**

Juggernaut Industries ....G...... 703 686-0191
Manassas **(G-8090)**

Just Wreaths ....G...... 571 208-4920
Woodbridge **(G-15733)**

K and M Industries LLC ....G...... 757 328-0227
Newport News **(G-9271)**

K2 Industries LLC ....G...... 757 754-5430
Virginia Beach **(G-14579)**

Karolina De Los Santos ....G...... 757 597-4315
Hampton **(G-6178)**

Kates Creations ....G...... 757 721-7062
Virginia Beach **(G-14580)**

Katherine Chain ....G...... 804 796-2762
Chester **(G-3426)**

Kay Kollections LLC ....G...... 757 901-7710
Norfolk **(G-9611)**

Kaydee Puppets ....G...... 804 347-6636
Fredericksburg **(G-5199)**

Kd Puppets ....G...... 703 385-4543
Fairfax **(G-4642)**

Kelkase Inc ....G...... 703 670-9443
Fredericksburg **(G-5447)**

Keller Industries LLC ....G...... 573 452-4932
Fredericksburg **(G-5308)**

Kerris Kandles ....G...... 908 698-3968
Dumfries **(G-4249)**

Khan Qaism ....G...... 703 212-8670
Alexandria **(G-252)**

Kii Industries LLC ....G...... 804 232-5791
Richmond **(G-11049)**

King of Pops Richmond LLC ....G...... 804 475-9026
Richmond **(G-11644)**

Klearwall Industries ....G...... 203 689-5404
Moneta **(G-8968)**

Km Services LLC ....G...... 757 524-3420
Williamsburg **(G-15267)**

Kohler Industries Inc ....G...... 757 301-3233
Virginia Beach **(G-14592)**

Korea Arspc Inds Fort Wrth Inc ....G...... 703 883-2012
Vienna **(G-14080)**

▼ Korona Candles Inc ....C...... 540 208-2440
Dublin **(G-4161)**

Kram Industries Inc ....G...... 571 220-9769
Gainesville **(G-5593)**

Krug Industries Inc ....G...... 714 656-5316
Arlington **(G-1024)**

L C Pembroke Manufacturing ....G...... 757 723-3435
Hampton **(G-6182)**

Landmark Industries LLC ....G...... 757 233-7291
Virginia Beach **(G-14599)**

Lanzara Industries LLC ....G...... 703 759-6959
Great Falls **(G-5964)**

Lash and Glow By Tess Llc ....G...... 571 732-1080
Herndon **(G-6732)**

Lashme By Leslie LLC ....G...... 703 595-8628
Fairfax **(G-4497)**

Lavenmoon ....G...... 540 297-3274
Goodview **(G-5896)**

Lbp Manufacturing LLC ....G...... 804 562-6920
Richmond **(G-11649)**

Legacy Mfg LLC ....G...... 434 841-5331
Altavista **(G-634)**

Les Petales Inc ....G...... 804 254-7863
Richmond **(G-11269)**

Less Than Ladylike Candle LLC ....G...... 757 817-0616
Newport News **(G-9282)**

Leviton Manufacturing C ....G...... 804 461-8293
Midlothian **(G-8848)**

Lewis Industries LLC G 434 203-7920
Danville *(G-4012)*

Lexington Pet World G 540 464-4141
Fairfield *(G-4732)*

Light Grey Industries G 703 330-1339
Manassas *(G-8100)*

Lightsmokechill Candle Co LLC G 347 720-2596
Newport News *(G-9284)*

Liht Candles & Oils LLC G 757 776-9005
Chesapeake *(G-3183)*

Lincoln Industries LLC G 434 509-7191
Lynchburg *(G-7757)*

Linda M Barnes G 757 240-7327
Yorktown *(G-15976)*

Lion-Valley Industries G 703 630-3123
Quantico *(G-10690)*

Lisa A McLain G 757 788-1781
Newport News *(G-9285)*

Lisas Candles G 703 940-6733
Herndon *(G-6734)*

Lizzie Candles & Soap Inc G 540 384-6151
Salem *(G-12533)*

LKM Industries LLC G 919 601-6661
Williamsburg *(G-15271)*

Lockhart Manufacturing Inc G 540 459-8774
Woodstock *(G-15857)*

Lost Industries LLC G 434 221-5698
Arrington *(G-1230)*

Loyal Service Systems G 703 361-7888
Manassas *(G-7971)*

Lucy Love Candles G 571 991-4155
Woodbridge *(G-15742)*

Luscious Lovezz LLC G 804 538-4151
Richmond *(G-11276)*

Lux Living Candle Co LLC G 757 462-6470
Chesapeake *(G-3190)*

Luxemanes LLC F 804 922-1410
North Chesterfield *(G-9914)*

M M Silk Flowers G 757 334-7096
Suffolk *(G-13736)*

M S Russnak Industries LLC G 540 848-1450
Spotsylvania *(G-12903)*

Mada Vemi Alpacas G 434 770-1972
Axton *(G-1540)*

Madeline Candle Company LLC G 703 503-9181
Burke *(G-2192)*

Magnes Industries LLC G 540 246-6088
Harrisonburg *(G-6342)*

Mahawara LLC G 443 949-2602
Dulles *(G-4208)*

Maker Industries G 757 560-1692
Chesapeake *(G-3193)*

Manny Weber G 703 819-3338
Leesburg *(G-7309)*

Manufacturing Mystique Inc G 703 719-0943
Alexandria *(G-521)*

Manufacturing Techniques G 804 436-9000
Kilmarnock *(G-7072)*

Many Miniatures G 703 730-1221
Triangle *(G-13896)*

Marcell Sgnture Scnted Candles G 757 502-5236
Norfolk *(G-9631)*

▲ **Mark Bric Display Corp** E 800 742-6275
Prince George *(G-10600)*

Marvelous Green LLC G 540 577-6967
Pulaski *(G-10642)*

Massone Industries Inc G 540 825-7339
Culpeper *(G-3908)*

Mat Enterprises Inc G 540 389-2528
Salem *(G-12534)*

Matt and Molly Trades LLC G 703 585-1858
Gordonsville *(G-5915)*

Maverick Fabrication G 321 210-9004
Newport News *(G-9297)*

Mech Warrior Industries LLC G 703 670-5788
Dumfries *(G-4252)*

Medical Action Industries Inc G 757 566-3510
Toano *(G-13870)*

Meld Manufacturing Corporation G 540 951-3980
Christiansburg *(G-3606)*

Melted Element LLC G 703 239-7847
Alexandria *(G-526)*

Merica Tactical Industries LLC G 804 516-0435
Mechanicsville *(G-8661)*

Meyer and Meyer Industries Inc G 757 564-6157
Williamsburg *(G-15276)*

Mfgs Inc G 844 267-9266
Mc Lean *(G-8500)*

Mg Industries G 804 743-0661
North Chesterfield *(G-9930)*

Micro Tech Industries Inc G 703 674-9647
Leesburg *(G-7314)*

Micron Manufacturing G 703 853-1801
Fairfax *(G-4511)*

Midway Telemetry G 276 378-5933
Marion *(G-8237)*

Midway Telemetry G 276 227-0270
Wytheville *(G-15900)*

Mighty Oak Enterprises Inc G 757 422-6353
Williamsburg *(G-15277)*

Mighty Oak Industries G 434 426-7249
Forest *(G-5083)*

Mindful Barber LLC G 757 714-6445
Richmond *(G-11678)*

Miss Lizzies Loot G 804 484-4212
Richmond *(G-11053)*

Mk Industries LLC G 949 525-0778
Springfield *(G-13051)*

Monarch Manufacturing Works G 757 640-3727
Norfolk *(G-9648)*

Moon Industries LLC G 703 878-2428
Woodbridge *(G-15749)*

Morphotrak LLC F 703 797-2600
Alexandria *(G-283)*

Mountain Creek Industries LLC G 804 432-1601
Meherrin *(G-8706)*

Mr Industries LLC G 484 838-9154
King George *(G-7103)*

Mrs Bones G 757 412-0500
Virginia Beach *(G-14667)*

Ms Bettys Bad-Ass Candles LLC G 540 256-7221
Woodbridge *(G-15752)*

▲ **Mya Saray LLC** G 703 996-8800
Sterling *(G-13458)*

Myrmidon Industries Inc G 540 273-6414
Fredericksburg *(G-5460)*

Nails Hurricane Too G 703 370-5551
Alexandria *(G-288)*

Nannas Cndles Unique Gifts LLC G 276 780-2513
Marion *(G-8238)*

Natures Cntry Soaps Candle LLC G 757 817-9062
Spring Grove *(G-12931)*

Neiceys G 757 500-1021
Virginia Beach *(G-14674)*

▲ **Netstyle Corp** G 703 717-9706
Lorton *(G-7514)*

Network Industries G 757 435-6163
Virginia Beach *(G-14678)*

New Hemp US G 757 977-8098
Virginia Beach *(G-14679)*

Newport Industries Ltd G 440 208-3322
Norfolk *(G-9663)*

Noelleimani Elite LLC G 804 452-6373
Richmond *(G-11692)*

Northwest Territorial Mint LLC F 703 922-5545
Springfield *(G-13060)*

NRJ Industries LLC G 703 707-0368
Chantilly *(G-2474)*

Nutter Candle Company LLC G 703 627-2561
Fairfax *(G-4523)*

OH My Goshyum LLC G 434 975-6628
Charlottesville *(G-2669)*

Old Dominion Pipe Company LLC G 757 710-2681
Painter *(G-10241)*

Old Hickory Candle Company G 804 400-8602
Mc Kenney *(G-8382)*

Omni Technology and Mfg LLC G 703 929-8000
Hamilton *(G-6062)*

Oncor Industries Inc G 434 985-3434
Stanardsville *(G-13225)*

Oneso Inc G 704 560-6354
Arlington *(G-1088)*

Onyx Industries LLC G 425 269-7181
Gainesville *(G-5606)*

Opsec Industries LLC G 571 426-0626
Springfield *(G-13062)*

Osmon Industries G 757 564-3088
Williamsburg *(G-15289)*

Osmotherapeutics Inc G 703 627-1934
Vienna *(G-14108)*

Osojuicee Hair LLC G 757 215-6555
South Chesterfield *(G-12818)*

Otto Industries LLC G 703 256-2684
Springfield *(G-13063)*

Outdoor Leisure G 703 349-1965
Manassas *(G-8125)*

PA Industries Inc G 434 845-0813
Amherst *(G-703)*

Packed Head LLC G 804 677-3603
Chesterfield *(G-3516)*

Pamela J Luttrell Co G 540 837-1525
Bluemont *(G-1890)*

Pandy Co Inc G 804 744-1563
Midlothian *(G-8875)*

Paradym Industries Inc G 703 424-6930
South Riding *(G-12869)*

Paramount Specialty Metals LLC G 980 721-3958
Warrenton *(G-15042)*

Parker Industries Virginia Inc G 804 254-4140
Richmond *(G-11707)*

Patterson Business Systems F 540 389-7726
Salem *(G-12555)*

Pauls Fan Company D 276 530-7311
Grundy *(G-6039)*

Peggy Hank Industries LLC G 434 825-4802
Charlottesville *(G-2843)*

Performance Aviation Mfg Group G 757 766-1150
Williamsburg *(G-15295)*

Pif Industries LLC G 804 677-2945
Richmond *(G-11325)*

Pinder Industries LLC G 240 200-0703
Springfield *(G-13067)*

Pioneer Industries LLC G 757 432-8412
Chesapeake *(G-3240)*

Pirooz Manufacturing LLC G 703 281-4244
Vienna *(G-14111)*

Pk Industries LLC G 540 589-2341
Roanoke *(G-11986)*

Polyiscynurate Insul Mfrs Assn G 703 224-2289
Arlington *(G-1115)*

Pondeca Industries Inc G 703 599-4375
Lorton *(G-7521)*

Pool Hot Tub Allia G 703 838-0083
Alexandria *(G-311)*

◆ **Porex Technologies Corp** C 804 524-4983
South Chesterfield *(G-12821)*

Porex Technologies Corporation C 804 275-2631
North Chesterfield *(G-9951)*

Posh Pixie LLC G 757 794-4949
Virginia Beach *(G-14730)*

Potomac Industries G 540 940-7288
Fredericksburg *(G-5470)*

Powell Manufacturing Co LLC G 804 677-5728
Petersburg *(G-10335)*

Power Clean Industries LLC G 804 372-6838
Powhatan *(G-10567)*

▲ **PPG Industries Inc** G 540 563-2118
Roanoke *(G-12149)*

Precision Schematics LLC G 612 296-2286
Woodbridge *(G-15779)*

Presidential Coin & Antique Co G 703 354-5454
Clifton *(G-3675)*

Pretty Petals G 757 357-9136
Smithfield *(G-12723)*

Primrose Essentials LLC G 703 503-7210
Burke *(G-2200)*

Prism Industries LLC G 804 916-0074
Chesterfield *(G-3518)*

Privateer Industries LLC G 757 857-7273
Norfolk *(G-9696)*

Ptc Enterprises LLC G 703 352-9274
Fairfax *(G-4665)*

Puppet Neighborhood G 804 794-2899
Midlothian *(G-8884)*

Pure Scentsations LLC G 334 868-9190
Suffolk *(G-13755)*

Putt Arund Town Miniature Golf G 804 317-6751
Chesterfield *(G-3519)*

Qlifts LLC G 276 632-0058
Ridgeway *(G-11850)*

Qmt Associates Inc C 703 368-4920
Manassas Park *(G-8208)*

◆ **Quest Industries LLC** G 804 862-8481
North Dinwiddie *(G-10062)*

Quickie Manufacturing Corp G 856 829-7900
Winchester *(G-15576)*

Radavert Industries Inc G 703 425-6777
Burke *(G-2201)*

Rave On Industries LLC G 804 308-0898
Henrico *(G-6555)*

Raw Goods LLC G 862 812-1520
Alexandria *(G-325)*

RC Industries LLC G 757 839-5577
Chesapeake *(G-3260)*

Ready Set Sign LLC G 703 820-0022
Arlington *(G-1143)*

Reaper Precision LLC G 540 841-0028
King George *(G-7107)*

Reddzway LLC G 434 515-0791
Lynchburg *(G-7799)*

Reese Kyndal ....G...... 757 718-0525	Shine Beauty Company ....G...... 757 509-7338	Tetelestai Industries LLC ....G...... 804 596-5232
Norfolk *(G-9705)*	Newport News *(G-9336)*	Henrico *(G-6580)*
Reid Industries LLC ....G...... 703 920-6199	Shooting Star Gallery LLC ....G...... 757 787-4536	Thayer Design Inc ....G...... 434 528-3850
Arlington *(G-1146)*	Onancock *(G-10197)*	Madison Heights *(G-7885)*
Reid Industries LLC ....G...... 703 786-6307	Simply Candles & Gifts ....G...... 315 806-4204	Thomas E Lewis ....G...... 804 529-7526
Woodbridge *(G-15794)*	Lynchburg *(G-7807)*	Lottsburg *(G-7544)*
Requisites Gallery ....G...... 757 376-2754	Simply Divine Candles ....G...... 540 479-0045	Three Hens ....G...... 804 787-3400
Chesapeake *(G-3269)*	Strasburg *(G-13597)*	Goochland *(G-5887)*
Richard Rhea Industries LLC ...G...... 804 320-6575	Sines Feathers and Furs LLC ..G...... 540 436-8673	Thumbelinas ....G...... 703 448-8043
North Chesterfield *(G-9960)*	Strasburg *(G-13598)*	Vienna *(G-14142)*
Richmond Ramps Inc ....G...... 804 932-8507	SM Industries LLC ....G...... 757 966-2343	Tiera Averett ....G...... 804 888-3721
Quinton *(G-10699)*	Chesapeake *(G-3296)*	Chesterfield *(G-3532)*
Ride-Away Inc ....F...... 804 233-8267	Smith Mountain Industries Ltd ...G...... 540 576-3117	Tighty Whitey Soap Candle LLC ...G...... 202 818-9169
North Chesterfield *(G-10022)*	Martinsville *(G-8330)*	Alexandria *(G-364)*
Rightway Industries Ltd ....G...... 757 435-8889	▲ Snakeclamp Products LLC ....G...... 903 265-8001	Tippers LLC ....G...... 703 391-7232
Virginia Beach *(G-14774)*	Christiansburg *(G-3609)*	Reston *(G-10974)*
Ring Fire Manufacturing LLC ...G...... 804 617-9288	Sniffalicious Candle LLC ....G...... 276 686-2204	Tmp Industries LLC ....G...... 540 761-0435
Henrico *(G-6559)*	Rural Retreat *(G-12432)*	Roanoke *(G-12206)*
Rock Industries LLC ....G...... 703 637-8500	Social Dynamics Industries ......G...... 703 441-2869	TN Cor Industries Incorporated ...G...... 703 682-2001
Falls Church *(G-4868)*	Dumfries *(G-4256)*	Alexandria *(G-366)*
Rockin Rack LLC ....G...... 540 359-2264	Sol Shining ....G...... 571 719-3957	Tobacco Plus ....G...... 703 644-5111
Bealeton *(G-1606)*	Manassas *(G-8159)*	Springfield *(G-13100)*
Rogue Cltivation Solutions LLC ...G...... 540 955-8641	Solvent Industries Inc ....G...... 540 760-8611	Todd Industries ....G...... 571 275-2782
Berryville *(G-1687)*	Fredericksburg *(G-5365)*	Leesburg *(G-7364)*
Rose Welding Inc ....G...... 540 312-0138	Sophie Gs Candles LLC ....G...... 202 253-7798	Tonys Unisex Barber ....G...... 757 237-7049
New Castle *(G-9123)*	Haymarket *(G-6446)*	Norfolk *(G-9761)*
Rough Industries LLC ....G...... 215 514-4144	Southcoast Welding & Mfg LLC ...G...... 757 574-0090	Torishima Pump Mfg Co Ltd .....G...... 866 374-1130
Alexandria *(G-330)*	Chesapeake *(G-3301)*	North Chesterfield *(G-10027)*
Roxannas Candles ....G...... 804 243-9697	Southern Fire & Safety Co ....G...... 434 546-6774	Tradition Candle LLC ....G...... 630 881-7194
Chesapeake *(G-3276)*	Lynchburg *(G-7810)*	Norfolk *(G-9764)*
Royal Courtyard ....G...... 757 431-0045	Southerns M&P LLC ....G...... 804 330-2407	Trial Exhibits Inc ....G...... 804 672-0880
Virginia Beach *(G-14781)*	North Chesterfield *(G-9985)*	Henrico *(G-6585)*
Rrb Industries Inc ....G...... 804 517-2014	Southpaw Mechanical LLC ....G...... 540 577-6967	Triax Music Industries ....G...... 757 839-1215
Virginia Beach *(G-14784)*	Pulaski *(G-10646)*	Chesapeake *(G-3351)*
Rsi ....G...... 908 752-1496	Soywick Candles LLC ....G...... 571 333-4750	Triple Threat Industries LLC ....G...... 703 413-7919
Falls Church *(G-4869)*	Lansdowne *(G-7173)*	Arlington *(G-1197)*
RSR Industries LLC ....G...... 703 408-8048	Spartan Inds Martinsville ....G...... 276 632-3033	Tut & Titi LLC ....G...... 757 761-1921
Alexandria *(G-575)*	Martinsville *(G-8336)*	Hampton *(G-6254)*
Rugger Industries LLC ....G...... 540 450-7281	Spartancore Industries ....G...... 540 322-7563	Tweedle Tees Printing LLC ......G...... 540 569-6927
Winchester *(G-15472)*	Fredericksburg *(G-5486)*	Staunton *(G-13305)*
Rural Squirrel LLC ....G...... 540 364-2281	▲ Spectrum Entertainment Inc ...G...... 757 491-2873	Two Blue Candle Co LLC ....G...... 786 301-3371
Marshall *(G-8259)*	Virginia Beach *(G-14836)*	Herndon *(G-6834)*
Rusolf S Olszyk ....G...... 757 565-2970	Sphinx Industries Inc ....G...... 804 279-8894	Unique Wreaths ....G...... 540 322-9301
Williamsburg *(G-15309)*	North Chesterfield *(G-9987)*	Fredericksburg *(G-5383)*
Russell Frye LLC ....G...... 276 646-1293	Spunkysales LLC ....G...... 727 492-1636	V&M Industries Inc ....G...... 757 319-9415
Chilhowie *(G-3559)*	Springfield *(G-13094)*	Suffolk *(G-13775)*
Rwh Industries Inc ....G...... 540 736-8007	STA-Fit Industries LLC ....G...... 540 308-8215	V-Lite USA LLC ....G...... 808 264-3785
Fredericksburg *(G-5357)*	Ruckersville *(G-12414)*	Virginia Beach *(G-14905)*
S & J Industries LLC ....G...... 757 810-8399	Stately Dogs ....G...... 276 644-4098	Valentinecherry Creations ....G...... 757 848-6137
Gloucester *(G-5861)*	Bristol *(G-1990)*	Hampton *(G-6258)*
S&D Industries LLC ....G...... 901 208-5036	Staunton VA ....G...... 651 765-6778	Valley Bee Supply Inc ....G...... 540 941-8127
Norfolk *(G-9713)*	Verona *(G-13996)*	Fishersville *(G-5010)*
S&T Industries LLC ....G...... 276 686-4842	Stick Industries LLC ....G...... 757 725-0436	Vastec USA ....G...... 302 682-8255
Crockett *(G-3826)*	Troutville *(G-13917)*	Stephens City *(G-13327)*
Safety 1 Industries LLC ....G...... 540 635-4673	Stone Quarry ....G...... 757 722-9653	Vella Mac Industries Inc ....F...... 757 724-0026
Front Royal *(G-5552)*	Newport News *(G-9348)*	Norfolk *(G-9780)*
Sak Industries LLC ....G...... 202 701-0071	Storge Industries LLC ....G...... 571 414-1413	Velocity LLC ....G...... 703 304-6152
Vienna *(G-14120)*	Fort Belvoir *(G-5118)*	Reston *(G-10982)*
Sallmae LLC ....G...... 931 472-9467	Strauch Fiber Equipment C ......G...... 540 864-8869	Verde Candles ....G...... 804 338-1350
Fort Lee *(G-5132)*	New Castle *(G-9124)*	Glen Allen *(G-5824)*
Salt Whistle Bay Partners LLC ...G...... 540 983-7118	Strike Force Manufacturing Inc ...G...... 804 731-0831	Vertexusa LLC ....G...... 213 294-3072
Roanoke *(G-12175)*	North Prince George *(G-10092)*	Sterling *(G-13548)*
Salty Sawyer LLC ....G...... 757 274-1765	Styles By Jaimonique LLC ....G...... 804 255-8581	Vertexusa LLC ....G...... 213 294-9072
Surry *(G-13800)*	Colonial Heights *(G-3749)*	Herndon *(G-6837)*
Sauder Manufacturing Co ....G...... 434 372-4151	▲ Stylus Publishing LLC ....G...... 703 661-1581	Veteran Customs LLC ....G...... 540 786-2157
Chase City *(G-2916)*	Sterling *(G-13520)*	Spotsylvania *(G-12920)*
Savage Thrust Industries LLC ...G...... 702 405-1045	Sun Manufacturing LLC ....G...... 434 942-4626	Veteran Force Industries LLC ...G...... 912 492-5800
Manassas *(G-8150)*	Forest *(G-5099)*	Alexandria *(G-373)*
Sayre Enterprises Inc ....G...... 540 291-3800	Sundigger Industries LLC ....G...... 703 360-4139	Veteran Made LLC ....G...... 703 328-2570
Buena Vista *(G-2153)*	Alexandria *(G-590)*	Leesburg *(G-7370)*
Sbk Inc ....G...... 540 427-5029	Sunglow Industries Inc ....G...... 703 870-9918	Vibe Candle Co LLC ....G...... 757 589-3274
Roanoke *(G-12176)*	Newport News *(G-9350)*	Hampton *(G-6261)*
Scrub Skinz LLC ....G...... 804 338-1350	Sunny Slope LLC ....G...... 434 384-8994	Vienna Hot Tubes Patio In ....G...... 703 734-0077
Glen Allen *(G-5793)*	Lynchburg *(G-7816)*	Vienna *(G-14153)*
SDS Industries ....G...... 207 266-9448	Supernal Industries LLC ....G...... 804 380-1742	Virginia Candle Company LLC ...G...... 301 828-6498
Alexandria *(G-340)*	Chesapeake *(G-3316)*	Woodbridge *(G-15827)*
Second Chance Dog Rescue .....G...... 540 752-1741	Supernova Industries Inc ....G...... 703 731-2987	Virginia Fire Protection Svcs ....G...... 276 637-1012
Fredericksburg *(G-5484)*	Chantilly *(G-2505)*	Max Meadows *(G-8370)*
Second Samuel Industries Inc ...G...... 703 715-2295	Surfside Candle Co ....G...... 540 455-4322	Visionary Ventures LLC ....G...... 443 718-9777
Fairfax *(G-4553)*	Sterling *(G-13525)*	Sterling *(G-13554)*
Seven Bends LLC ....G...... 540 392-0553	Suzies Zoo Inc ....G...... 434 547-4161	Vortex Industries LLC ....G...... 703 732-5458
Blacksburg *(G-1790)*	Farmville *(G-4959)*	Fairfax *(G-4694)*
Sharon Solomon ....G...... 757 515-2325	Sweet Baby Luxury Hair Co LLC ...G...... 804 904-9227	Walker Virginia ....G...... 757 652-0430
Norfolk *(G-9721)*	Richmond *(G-11777)*	Newport News *(G-9378)*
Shenandoah Primitives LLC ......G...... 540 662-4727	Sweet Heat Candles ....G...... 804 921-8233	Warren Mastery Enterprises Inc ...G...... 877 207-6370
Winchester *(G-15477)*	Henrico *(G-6577)*	Sedley *(G-12681)*
Shepherd Enterprises Anchor Rm ...G...... 757 641-7829	Tamco Enterprises Inc ....G...... 757 627-9551	Waterford Past-Thymes ....G...... 703 434-1758
Portsmouth *(G-10479)*	Chesapeake *(G-3320)*	Round Hill *(G-12395)*
Sherman Industries LLC ....G...... 240 888-1134	Teresa Blount ....G...... 804 402-1349	Waterford Pastthymes ....G...... 703 431-4095
Alexandria *(G-345)*	Chester *(G-3460)*	Waterford *(G-15084)*

Watkins Industries LLC..........G......540 371-5007
Manakin Sabot (G-7907)

Wcbd-TV (nbc 2)..........G......804 649-6000
Richmond (G-11819)

Wells Custom Mfg LLC..........G......703 623-1396
Warrenton (G-15059)

Wenger Manufacturing..........G......703 878-6946
Woodbridge (G-15831)

West 30 Candles..........G......804 874-2461
Richmond (G-11823)

Wf Med..........G......703 339-5388
Lorton (G-7541)

Wheeler Industries LLC..........G......540 387-2204
Salem (G-12581)

Whicker Home Industries LLC..........G......703 675-7642
Colonial Beach (G-3730)

Why Candle & Co LLC..........G......804 876-2240
Richmond (G-11830)

Willie Slick Industries..........G......843 310-4669
Virginia Beach (G-14938)

Wilson Industries & Svcs Un..........G......703 472-6392
Fairfax (G-4582)

Wilson Pipe & Fabrication LLC..........G......757 468-1374
Virginia Beach (G-14939)

Winding Creek Candle Co LLC..........G......757 410-1991
Chesapeake (G-3378)

Wine With Everything LLC..........G......703 777-4899
Leesburg (G-7380)

Winn Industries LLC..........G......571 334-2676
Lignum (G-7426)

Wise Feline Inc..........G......703 609-2686
Alexandria (G-384)

Wolfsbane Industries LLC..........G......703 972-5072
Purcellville (G-10687)

Wop Hair LLC..........G......804 277-4666
North Chesterfield (G-10014)

Wrap Pack Industries Inc..........G......804 897-1351
Midlothian (G-8923)

Wreaths Bows & Blessings..........G......276 340-2380
Martinsville (G-8354)

Wreaths Galore and More LLC..........G......804 312-6947
Chester (G-3469)

Wright Machine & Manufacturing..........G......276 688-2391
Bland (G-1838)

Wyfi Industries LLC..........G......703 333-2059
Springfield (G-13109)

Wylie Wagg of Tysons LLC..........G......703 748-0022
Falls Church (G-4894)

▲ X-Stand Treestand Company LLC...G......540 877-2769
Winchester (G-15520)

Xlusion CL Fulfillment LLC..........G......571 316-9391
Stephens City (G-13330)

Xp Manufacturing LLC..........G......804 510-3747
Richmond (G-11836)

Xp Manufacturing LLC..........G......804 833-1411
North Chesterfield (G-10015)

Xplor Industries..........G......804 306-6621
Richmond (G-11460)

Yobnug LLC..........G......703 385-1880
Fairfax (G-4696)

York River Glassworks LLC..........G......804 815-0492
Gloucester (G-5870)

Yup Candles LLC..........G......571 248-6772
Nokesville (G-9406)

Zakufdm LLC..........G......330 338-0930
Fredericksburg (G-5393)

Zhe Industries LLC..........G......757 759-5466
Virginia Beach (G-14961)

Zhe Industries LLC..........G......757 759-5466
Virginia Beach (G-14962)

73 BUSINESS SERVICES

7372 Prepackaged Software

01 Communique Laboratory Inc..........G......703 224-8262
Arlington (G-833)

1click LLC..........G......703 307-6026
Springfield (G-12933)

300 Qubits LLC..........G......202 320-0196
Arlington (G-835)

3r Behavioral Solutions Inc..........G......571 332-6232
Alexandria (G-396)

4c North America Inc..........G......540 850-8470
Mc Lean (G-8383)

4gurus LLC..........G......703 520-5084
Fairfax (G-4587)

4gurus LLC..........G......703 520-5084
Fairfax (G-4588)

5gl Software Inc..........G......703 861-3644
Fairfax (G-4394)

8020 Software LLC..........G......434 466-8020
Charlottesville (G-2585)

80protons LLC..........G......571 215-5453
Virginia Beach (G-14198)

Accounting Technology LLC..........F......434 316-6000
Forest (G-5049)

Acharya Brothers Computing..........G......703 729-3035
Ashburn (G-1237)

Acintyo Inc..........G......703 349-3400
Mc Lean (G-8384)

Acro Software Inc..........G......703 753-7508
Haymarket (G-6412)

Actionstep Inc..........G......540 809-9326
Richmond (G-11471)

Active Navigation Inc..........F......571 346-7607
Reston (G-10777)

Adme Solutions LLC..........G......540 664-3521
Stephens City (G-13311)

Adnet Systems Inc..........F......571 313-1356
Reston (G-10778)

Adobe Inc..........D......571 765-5400
Mc Lean (G-8386)

Adobe Systems Federal LLC..........E......571 765-5523
Mc Lean (G-8387)

Adv3ntus Software LLC..........G......703 288-3380
Mc Lean (G-8388)

Advanced Rsponse Concepts Corp......G......703 246-8560
Fairfax (G-4590)

AEC Software Inc..........E......703 450-1980
Sterling (G-13339)

Aetas Mobile LLC..........G......704 258-9159
Oakton (G-10140)

Agaram Technologies Inc..........D......703 297-8591
Ashburn (G-1239)

Agora Data Services LLC..........G......703 328-7758
Fredericksburg (G-5396)

Ai Machines Inc..........G......973 204-9772
Fairfax (G-4403)

Aida Health Inc..........G......202 739-1345
Arlington (G-847)

Ailsa Software LLC..........G......703 407-6470
Chantilly (G-2364)

Aka Software LLC..........G......703 406-4619
Sterling (G-13340)

Akamai Technologies Inc..........E......877 425-2624
Reston (G-10783)

▼ All Traffic Solutions Inc..........F......814 237-9005
Herndon (G-6609)

Alpine Method Technologies LLC..........G......716 310-4935
Aldie (G-100)

American Institute RES Inc..........G......703 470-1037
Mc Lean (G-8392)

American Quality Software Inc..........G......571 730-4532
Falls Church (G-4748)

American Soc For Engrg Educatn........G......804 742-5611
Port Royal (G-10385)

Amity Software Inc..........G......571 312-0880
Arlington (G-854)

Amogh Consultants Inc..........G......469 867-1583
Herndon (G-6612)

AMS Services LLC..........G......804 869-4777
Richmond (G-11112)

Analystsoft Inc..........G......844 782-8758
Alexandria (G-134)

Andromeda3 Inc..........G......240 246-5816
Great Falls (G-5937)

Animate Systems Inc..........G......804 233-8085
Richmond (G-11485)

Annoai Inc..........G......571 490-5316
Reston (G-10789)

Antheon Solutions Inc..........G......703 298-1891
Reston (G-10790)

Any Job Software Inc..........G......540 347-4347
Catlett (G-2264)

Apex Mobile App LLC..........G......804 245-0471
Midlothian (G-8773)

Appfore LLC..........G......757 597-6990
Virginia Beach (G-14232)

Appian Corporation..........G......703 442-8844
Tysons (G-13941)

Appian Corporation..........C......703 442-8844
Mc Lean (G-8393)

Application Technologies Inc..........G......703 644-0506
Springfield (G-12949)

Applied Visual Sciences Inc..........G......703 539-6190
Leesburg (G-7220)

Aptify Corporation..........G......202 223-2600
Mc Lean (G-8394)

Aptify Corporation..........D......202 223-2600
Tysons Corner (G-13951)

Arctan Inc..........G......202 379-4723
Arlington (G-855)

Aretec Inc..........E......703 539-8801
Fairfax (G-4596)

Argent Line LLC..........G......703 519-1209
Alexandria (G-140)

Arkcase LLC..........G......703 272-3270
Vienna (G-14009)

▲ Arqball LLC..........G......434 260-1890
Charlottesville (G-2730)

Artusmode Software LLC..........G......703 794-6100
Great Falls (G-5938)

Atavus Inc..........G......703 404-2796
Sterling (G-13354)

Athena Services LLC..........G......201 232-9114
Falls Church (G-4751)

Athenas Workshop Inc..........G......703 615-4429
Reston (G-10794)

Atlas Inc..........G......646 835-9656
Woodbridge (G-15650)

Ats Corporation..........E......571 766-2400
Fairfax (G-4413)

Attachmate Corporation..........E......703 663-5500
Vienna (G-14011)

▲ Auralog Inc..........B......602 470-0300
Harrisonburg (G-6294)

Ausome Ones LLC..........G......703 637-7105
Arlington (G-865)

Autodocs LLC..........G......703 532-9720
Vienna (G-14012)

Averia Health Solutions LLC..........G......703 716-0791
Oakton (G-10141)

Avitech Consulting LLC..........G......757 810-2716
Chesapeake (G-2990)

Axios Systems Inc..........E......703 326-1357
Herndon (G-6617)

B & L Biotech Usa Inc..........G......703 272-7507
Fairfax (G-4597)

B&B Consulting Services Inc..........G......804 550-1517
Ashland (G-1376)

B3sk Software LLC..........G......757 484-4516
Chesapeake (G-2992)

Bap LLC..........G......800 507-9728
Purcellville (G-10651)

Basvin Software LLC..........G......703 537-0888
Fairfax (G-4419)

Bayonet..........G......804 323-3204
Glen Allen (G-5706)

Be There Do Good LLC..........G......703 851-5293
Vienna (G-14014)

Beetlebug Software LLC..........G......571 223-5041
Leesburg (G-7229)

Behealth Solutions LLC..........G......434 422-9090
Charlottesville (G-2593)

Best Software Inc..........G......949 753-1222
Reston (G-10798)

Bigbrassband LLC..........E......571 223-7137
Leesburg (G-7230)

Bizwhazee LLC..........G......703 889-8499
Reston (G-10800)

Blackboard Connect Inc..........G......919 841-0175
Reston (G-10801)

Blackboard Holdings Inc..........A......202 463-4860
Reston (G-10802)

Blackboard Inc..........C......202 463-4860
Reston (G-10803)

Blackboard Inc..........G......512 474-8363
Reston (G-10804)

Blackboard Inc..........G......254 251-3203
Reston (G-10805)

Blackboard Inc..........G......202 463-4860
Reston (G-10806)

Blackboard Super Holdco Inc..........G......202 463-4860
Reston (G-10807)

Blackfish Software LLC..........G......703 779-9649
Leesburg (G-7233)

Blackwolf Software..........G......434 978-4903
Charlottesville (G-2597)

Bloomforth Corp..........G......703 408-8993
Centreville (G-2296)

Blue Beacon LLC..........G......202 643-9043
Ashburn (G-1249)

Blue Ridge Software..........G......703 912-3990
Springfield (G-12965)

Blulogix LLC..........E......443 333-4100
Mc Lean (G-8401)

Bluvector Inc..........G......571 565-2100
Arlington (G-886)

BMC Software Inc..........F......713 918-8800
Mc Lean (G-8402)

BMC Software Inc ....E... 703 404-0230 Herndon (G-6627)	Cobalt Co ....G... 888 426-2258 Arlington (G-909)	Cvent Inc ....G... 571 830-2301 Mc Lean (G-8413)
Bnd Software ....G... 202 997-1070 Leesburg (G-7235)	Cobalt Company ....G... 888 426-2258 Arlington (G-910)	Cvent Inc ....A... 703 226-3500 Tysons Corner (G-13952)
Board Room Software Inc ....G... 757 721-3900 Virginia Beach (G-14291)	Code Blue ....G... 757 438-1507 Virginia Beach (G-14350)	Cyber Intel Solutions Inc ....G... 571 970-2689 Springfield (G-12987)
Boardeffect LLC ....E... 866 672-2666 Arlington (G-887)	Codeworx Lc ....G... 571 306-3859 Alexandria (G-169)	Cybered Corp ....G... 757 573-5456 Williamsburg (G-15228)
Bond International Sftwr Inc ....G... 804 601-4640 Midlothian (G-8781)	Cognition Point Inc ....G... 703 402-8945 Aldie (G-104)	▲ Cyberex Corporation ....G... 703 904-0980 Herndon (G-6651)
Boshkins Software Corporation ....G... 703 318-7785 Herndon (G-6629)	Cole Software LLC ....G... 540 456-8210 Afton (G-77)	Cynosure Services Inc ....G... 410 209-0796 Alexandria (G-179)
Bottomline Software Inc ....G... 540 221-4444 Waynesboro (G-15101)	Coleman and Coleman Software ....G... 804 276-5372 North Chesterfield (G-9849)	Cynthia Gray ....G... 703 860-5711 Herndon (G-6652)
Boxwood Technology Inc ....F... 703 707-8686 Mc Lean (G-8403)	College and University Educati ....G... 540 820-7384 Harrisonburg (G-6302)	D-Orbit Inc ....G... 703 533-5661 Falls Church (G-4781)
Brain Based Learning Inc ....G... 804 320-0158 North Chesterfield (G-9834)	▼ Collier Research and Dev Corp ....F... 757 825-0000 Newport News (G-9203)	Daghigh Software Co Inc ....G... 703 323-7475 Fairfax Station (G-4705)
Bravatek Solutions Inc ....G... 866 490-8590 Chantilly (G-2527)	Colonial Apps LLC ....G... 804 744-8535 Midlothian (G-8800)	Data Fusion Solutions Inc ....G... 877 326-0034 Fredericksburg (G-5271)
Brbg LLC ....G... 404 200-4857 Springfield (G-12969)	Commonlook ....G... 202 902-0986 Arlington (G-916)	Data Research Group Corp ....G... 571 350-9590 Culpeper (G-3888)
Brian Fox DBA Fortified ....G... 540 535-1195 Winchester (G-15392)	Compu Management Corp ....G... 276 669-3822 Bristol (G-2013)	Databasics Inc ....E... 703 262-0097 Reston (G-10833)
Bright Elm LLC ....G... 804 519-3331 Sandy Hook (G-12644)	Computer Corp of America ....G... 703 241-7830 Arlington (G-918)	Datablink Inc ....G... 703 639-0600 Mc Lean (G-8416)
Bright Solutions Inc ....G... 703 926-7451 Ashburn (G-1252)	Computer Solution Co of VA Inc ....E... 804 794-3491 Richmond (G-11538)	Datahaven For Dynamics LLC ....G... 757 222-2000 Virginia Beach (G-14388)
Build Software LLC ....G... 703 629-2549 Clifton (G-3659)	Computing Technologies Inc ....G... 703 280-8800 Mechanicsville (G-8613)	Dataone Software ....G... 877 438-8467 Norfolk (G-9517)
C2c Smart Compliance LLC ....F... 703 872-7340 Alexandria (G-158)	Comscore Inc ....G... 703 438-2000 Reston (G-10824)	Datassist ....G... 804 530-5008 South Chesterfield (G-12800)
Ca Inc ....B... 800 225-5224 Herndon (G-6632)	Concilio Labs Inc ....G... 571 282-4248 Mc Lean (G-8408)	Deadeye LLC ....G... 540 720-6818 Stafford (G-13137)
Cabaide LLC ....G... 571 262-2710 Ashburn (G-1253)	Concur Technologies Inc ....G... 703 403-8764 Vienna (G-14030)	Deca Software LLC ....G... 202 607-5707 Alexandria (G-186)
Caci Products Company ....G... 973 437-9800 Reston (G-10815)	Congero Technology Group Inc ....E... 434 266-4376 Reston (G-10825)	Decade Five LLC ....G... 434 984-3065 Charlottesville (G-2615)
Cae Software Solutions LLC ....G... 734 417-6991 Oakton (G-10142)	Connect Software LLC ....G... 706 974-8300 Reston (G-10826)	Decisonq Infrmtion Oprtons Inc ....G... 703 938-7153 Arlington (G-932)
Caerus LLC ....G... 703 772-7688 Great Falls (G-5942)	Connectus Inc ....G... 703 560-7777 Falls Church (G-4777)	Deep Prose Software LLC ....G... 703 815-0715 Centreville (G-2301)
Caladan Consulting Inc ....G... 540 931-9581 Winchester (G-15534)	Contactengine Inc ....G... 571 348-3220 Mc Lean (G-8409)	Defensative LLC ....F... 202 557-6937 Reston (G-10837)
Caligo LLC ....G... 914 819-8530 Vienna (G-14020)	Coolr Group Inc ....G... 571 933-3762 Chantilly (G-2396)	Deltek Systems Inc ....G... 703 734-8606 Herndon (G-6655)
Cambis LLC ....G... 202 746-6124 Falls Church (G-4767)	Coop Systems Inc ....E... 703 581-6364 Herndon (G-6645)	Deltek Systems Inc ....G... 800 456-2009 Herndon (G-6656)
Cambrio Studios LLC ....G... 540 908-5129 Charlottesville (G-2755)	Corascloud Inc ....E... 703 797-1881 Mc Lean (G-8410)	Delullo Software LLC ....G... 570 419-6736 Lorton (G-7480)
Candidate Metrics Inc ....G... 703 539-2331 Vienna (G-14021)	Corce Collec Business System ....E... 703 790-7272 Mc Lean (G-8411)	Department Info Tech Inc ....G... 703 868-6691 Chantilly (G-2407)
Canvas Solutions Inc ....G... 703 436-8069 Reston (G-10816)	Core Enable LLC ....G... 757 375-4434 Virginia Beach (G-14366)	Designer Software Inc ....G... 540 842-8425 Fredericksburg (G-5272)
Caper Holdings LLC ....G... 757 563-3810 Virginia Beach (G-14315)	Corillian Payment Solutions ....E... 703 259-3000 Reston (G-10827)	Diamondefense LLC ....F... 571 321-2012 Annandale (G-743)
Capital Software Corporation ....G... 703 404-3000 Chantilly (G-2528)	Cosaic ....G... 800 821-8147 Charlottesville (G-2771)	Diehappy LLC ....G... 804 283-6025 Glen Allen (G-5723)
Capo Software ....G... 571 205-8695 Herndon (G-6633)	Cougaar Software Inc ....E... 703 506-1700 Fairfax (G-4431)	Digital Beans Inc ....G... 703 775-2225 Alexandria (G-189)
Cardinal Applications LLC ....G... 540 270-4369 Amissville (G-717)	Cougarbearbobcat LLC ....G... 804 690-8006 Richmond (G-11543)	Digital Synergy Inc ....G... 540 951-5900 Blacksburg (G-1732)
Carla Bedard ....G... 212 773-1851 Alexandria (G-160)	Covata Usa Inc ....G... 703 657-5260 Reston (G-10828)	Digitized Risk LLC ....G... 703 662-3510 Ashburn (G-1271)
Cerberus LLC ....G... 703 372-9750 Arlington (G-904)	CPA Global North America LLC ....D... 703 739-2234 Alexandria (G-175)	Dino Software Corporation ....E... 703 768-2610 Alexandria (G-447)
Cerner Corporation ....G... 703 286-0200 Vienna (G-14024)	CPA Global Services US Inc ....F... 703 739-2234 Alexandria (G-176)	Diskcopy Inc ....G... 703 658-3539 Falls Church (G-4784)
Chiru Software Inc ....G... 703 201-1914 Broadlands (G-2075)	Crafter Software ....G... 703 955-3480 Reston (G-10829)	Dispersive Technologies Inc ....G... 252 725-0874 Herndon (G-6658)
CIO Controls Inc ....G... 703 365-2227 Manassas (G-8049)	Cross Cloud Solutions Inc ....G... 703 724-7526 Ashburn (G-1262)	Divergence Software Inc ....G... 703 690-9870 Fairfax Station (G-4708)
Ciphercloud Inc ....G... 703 659-0533 Herndon (G-6640)	Crystal Technology Inc ....F... 703 968-2590 Chantilly (G-2399)	Divvy Cloud Corporation ....F... 571 290-5077 Arlington (G-940)
Circinus Software LLC ....G... 571 522-1724 Centreville (G-2298)	Ctm Automated Systems Inc ....G... 703 742-0755 Sterling (G-13379)	Dominion Computer Services ....G... 757 473-8989 Virginia Beach (G-14409)
Clarivate Analytics (us) LLC ....D... 434 817-2000 Charlottesville (G-2609)	Ctrl-Pad Inc ....G... 757 216-9170 Norfolk (G-9510)	Dominion Leasing Software ....G... 804 378-2204 Powhatan (G-10542)
Clearview Software Corporation ....G... 804 381-6300 Lynchburg (G-7679)	Cubicle Logic LLC ....G... 571 989-2823 Sterling (G-13380)	Donaty Software Inc ....G... 540 822-5496 Lovettsville (G-7578)
Cloud Ridge Labs LLC ....G... 434 477-5060 Forest (G-5060)	Cunning Running Software Inc ....G... 703 926-5864 Mineral (G-8945)	Doucraft Services ....G... 703 620-4965 Oakton (G-10144)
Cloudera Gvrnment Slutions Inc ....F... 888 789-1488 Tysons (G-13942)	Curious Compass LLC ....G... 540 735-5013 Fredericksburg (G-5182)	DP Facilities Inc ....E... 866 589-6125 Ashburn (G-1272)
Clover LLC ....G... 703 771-4286 Leesburg (G-7245)	Custom Computer Software ....G... 540 972-3027 Locust Grove (G-7443)	Dp Technology ....G... 703 835-6157 Broadlands (G-2077)
Cnl Software Inc ....G... 317 522-0313 Ashburn (G-1256)	Custom Procurement Systems ....G... 540 720-5756 Stafford (G-13134)	Dreamvision Software LLC ....G... 703 378-7191 Herndon (G-6660)
Co Construct LLC ....G... 434 326-0500 Crozet (G-3829)	Custom Sftwr Dsign Sltions LLC ....G... 888 423-4049 Fredericksburg (G-5417)	Driving 4 Dollars ....G... 757 609-1298 Henrico (G-6503)

Dutch Duck Software	G	703 525-6564	
Arlington *(G-949)*			
Dynamic Literacy LLC	G	888 696-8597	
Keswick *(G-7046)*			
E Primera Enable Corp	F	703 476-2270	
Herndon *(G-6664)*			
E Z Data Inc	G	540 775-2961	
King George *(G-7088)*			
E-Agree LLC	F	571 358-8012	
Manassas *(G-7933)*			
Eastern Shore VA Mstr Grdners	G	757 678-7688	
Accomac *(G-71)*			
Eastwind Software LLC	G	434 525-9241	
Forest *(G-5068)*			
Ecometrix	G	703 525-0524	
Arlington *(G-953)*			
Editek Inc	G	703 652-9495	
Fairfax *(G-4443)*			
Educational Options Inc	G	480 777-7720	
Falls Church *(G-4909)*			
Educren Inc	G	804 410-4305	
Glen Allen *(G-5728)*			
Edulinked LLC	G	703 869-2228	
Herndon *(G-6665)*			
Efftex Development Inc	G	800 708-8894	
Alexandria *(G-198)*			
Eilig Software LLC	G	757 259-0608	
Williamsburg *(G-15238)*			
Einstitute Inc	F	571 255-0530	
Fairfax *(G-4444)*			
Ekagra Partners LLC	F	571 421-1100	
Leesburg *(G-7265)*			
Electric Elders Inc	G	703 213-9327	
Alexandria *(G-199)*			
Elo Inc	G	571 435-0129	
Woodbridge *(G-15690)*			
Eloqua Inc	E	703 584-2750	
Vienna *(G-14047)*			
Enterprise Hive LLC	G	804 438-9393	
Irvington *(G-7001)*			
Enterprise Itech Corp	G	703 731-7881	
Fairfax *(G-4447)*			
Enterprise Svcs Cmmnctions LLC	G	877 858-3855	
Tysons *(G-13943)*			
Enterprise Svcs Wrld Trade LLC	G	703 245-9675	
Tysons *(G-13944)*			
Enterprize Software LLC	G	571 271-5862	
Brambleton *(G-1927)*			
Entertainment Software Assoc	G	703 383-3976	
Fairfax *(G-4448)*			
Envitia Inc	G	703 871-5255	
Reston *(G-10848)*			
Epicidentity Inc	F	833 723-3437	
Chantilly *(G-2533)*			
Erick Gonzalez	G	703 855-2908	
Woodbridge *(G-15696)*			
Erp Cloud Technologies LLC	G	727 723-0801	
Herndon *(G-6668)*			
Erp Software Services Inc	G	703 957-3073	
Chantilly *(G-2534)*			
Essential Software Dev LLC	G	540 222-1254	
Fairfax *(G-4451)*			
Etegrity LLC	G	757 301-7455	
Virginia Beach *(G-14452)*			
Euclidian Systems Inc	G	703 963-7209	
Arlington *(G-960)*			
Evaluation Tech For Dev LLC	G	434 851-0651	
Charlottesville *(G-2794)*			
Eventdone LLC	G	703 239-6410	
Woodbridge *(G-15699)*			
Execware LLC	G	202 607-8904	
Falls Church *(G-4789)*			
Ezara Inc	G	434 409-4232	
Earlysville *(G-4289)*			
Ezl Software LLC	G	804 288-0748	
Richmond *(G-11207)*			
Fair Value Games LLC	G	804 307-9110	
Glen Allen *(G-5729)*			
Far Fetch LLC	G	757 493-3572	
Virginia Beach *(G-14460)*			
Federal Data Corporation	G	703 734-3773	
Mc Lean *(G-8427)*			
Filenet Corporation	F	703 312-1500	
Mc Lean *(G-8429)*			
Finch Computing	G	571 599-7480	
Reston *(G-10851)*			
Fintech Sys Inc	G	703 278-0606	
Fairfax *(G-4623)*			
First Objective Software Inc	G	757 855-0191	
Norfolk *(G-9554)*			
Five Sixteen Solutions	G	703 435-4247	
Fairfax *(G-4625)*			
Fixmee LLC	G	703 731-1444	
Fairfax *(G-4458)*			
Flexprotect LLC	G	703 957-8648	
Reston *(G-10853)*			
Flockdata LLC	G	703 870-6916	
Chantilly *(G-2421)*			
Forescout Gvrnment Sltions LLC	E	408 538-0946	
Tysons *(G-13945)*			
Fortify Software	G	571 286-6320	
Mc Lean *(G-8435)*			
Fountainhead Systems Ltd	G	804 320-0527	
North Chesterfield *(G-9879)*			
Fourth Corporation	G	703 229-6222	
Mineral *(G-8948)*			
Freestyle King LLC	G	703 309-1144	
Woodbridge *(G-15707)*			
Frost Property Solutions LLC	G	804 571-2147	
Mechanicsville *(G-8625)*			
Fta Goverment Services Inc	G	571 612-0413	
Chantilly *(G-2423)*			
Future Tense LLC	G	703 994-7814	
Ashburn *(G-1283)*			
Fyllo LLC	G	540 846-6441	
Fredericksburg *(G-5191)*			
Gainsafe Inc	G	703 598-2583	
Alexandria *(G-211)*			
Gannett Media Tech Intl	G	757 547-7274	
Chesapeake *(G-3114)*			
Gary Smith	G	703 218-1801	
Fairfax *(G-4461)*			
Gbp Software LLC	G	703 967-3896	
Reston *(G-10856)*			
Gemini Security LLC	G	703 466-0163	
Sterling *(G-13410)*			
General Dynamics Corporation	G	703 729-3106	
Ashburn *(G-1285)*			
Genesis Infosolutions Inc	G	703 835-4469	
Herndon *(G-6682)*			
Geopliant LLC	G	888 273-7658	
Falls Church *(G-4798)*			
George Perez	G	757 362-3131	
Norfolk *(G-9561)*			
Get Aura Inc	G	703 801-4382	
Herndon *(G-6683)*			
Giant Lion Software LLC	G	703 764-8060	
Fairfax *(G-4465)*			
Giant Software LLC	G	540 292-6232	
Charlottesville *(G-2803)*			
Gigasheet Inc	G	703 231-8758	
Leesburg *(G-7278)*			
Global Info Netwrk Systems Inc	G	703 409-4204	
Fort Belvoir *(G-5115)*			
Glonet Incorporated	G	571 499-5000	
Alexandria *(G-219)*			
Go Vivace Inc	G	703 869-9463	
Mc Lean *(G-8451)*			
Goda Software Inc	G	703 373-7568	
Arlington *(G-983)*			
Gold Brand Software LLC	G	703 450-1321	
Herndon *(G-6687)*			
Gollygee Software Inc	G	703 437-3751	
Reston *(G-10860)*			
Gomatters LLC	G	757 819-4950	
Virginia Beach *(G-14487)*			
Goon Squad Apps LLC	G	706 410-6139	
Norfolk *(G-9564)*			
Govhawk LLC	G	703 439-1349	
Alexandria *(G-223)*			
Govready Pbc	G	917 304-3488	
Alexandria *(G-224)*			
Govtribe Inc	G	202 505-4681	
Arlington *(G-986)*			
Green Physics Corporation	G	703 989-6706	
Manassas *(G-7949)*			
Greenestep LLC	E	703 546-4236	
Clifton *(G-3669)*			
Grektek LLC	G	202 607-4734	
Herndon *(G-6692)*			
Grey Market Labs Pbc	G	929 274-4465	
Falls Church *(G-4800)*			
Greybox Strategies LLC	G	276 328-3249	
Wise *(G-15625)*			
Gryphon Software Corporat	G	814 486-3753	
Floyd *(G-5027)*			
Gtras Inc	D	703 342-4282	
Chantilly *(G-2433)*			
Guidance Software Inc	G	703 433-5400	
Dulles *(G-4206)*			
Guppy Group Inc	G	917 544-9749	
Fairfax *(G-4471)*			
Harbinger Tech Solutions LLC	F	757 962-6130	
Norfolk *(G-9571)*			
Harlequin Custom Databases	G	434 823-6466	
Crozet *(G-3838)*			
Harrington Software Assoc Inc	G	540 349-8074	
Warrenton *(G-15024)*			
Health Data Services Inc	G	434 817-9000	
Charlottesville *(G-2808)*			
Healthcare Simulations LLC	G	757 399-4502	
Portsmouth *(G-10441)*			
Healthrx Corporation	G	703 352-1760	
Fairfax *(G-4630)*			
Henry Shaw	E	844 621-2158	
Alexandria *(G-228)*			
Heytopia LLC	G	703 794-3082	
Mc Lean *(G-8458)*			
Hitachi Vantara Federal Corp	C	703 787-2900	
Reston *(G-10865)*			
Hkl Research Inc	G	434 979-6382	
Charlottesville *(G-2809)*			
Hkl Research Inc	G	434 979-5569	
Charlottesville *(G-2810)*			
Hotbed Technologies Inc	F	703 462-2350	
Mc Lean *(G-8459)*			
Hp Inc	G	703 535-3355	
Alexandria *(G-230)*			
Hr Software LLC	G	703 665-5134	
Great Falls *(G-5962)*			
Hss Inc	G	610 444-7409	
Henrico *(G-6522)*			
Huespace Inc	G	540 406-0496	
Arlington *(G-995)*			
Hygistics LLC	G	804 297-1504	
Crozier *(G-3858)*			
I Bit-Lab	G	703 568-4035	
Alexandria *(G-231)*			
Icewarp Inc	G	571 481-4611	
Springfield *(G-13019)*			
Iconicloud Inc	G	703 864-1203	
Alexandria *(G-481)*			
IDS Publishing Corporation	G	703 821-2323	
Mc Lean *(G-8461)*			
Ifexo LLC	G	443 856-7705	
Mc Lean *(G-8462)*			
Ihs Computer Service Inc	G	540 249-4833	
Port Republic *(G-10384)*			
Ikanow LLC	E	619 884-4434	
Reston *(G-10868)*			
Impact Junkie LLC	G	916 541-0317	
Woodbridge *(G-15726)*			
Impact Software Soutions Inc	G	703 615-5212	
Reston *(G-10870)*			
Improbable LLC	E	571 418-6999	
Arlington *(G-1000)*			
Improvebuild LLC	G	703 372-2646	
Ashburn *(G-1295)*			
Incident Logic LLC	G	540 349-8888	
Warrenton *(G-15026)*			
Index Systems Inc	G	571 420-4600	
Herndon *(G-6706)*			
Induko Inc	G	703 217-4262	
Manassas *(G-8080)*			
Infinite Studio LLC	G	864 293-4522	
Charlottesville *(G-2646)*			
Infocess LLC	G	571 723-1010	
Vienna *(G-14070)*			
Infomtion Tech Applcations LLC	G	757 603-3551	
Williamsburg *(G-15257)*			
Inforce Group LLC	G	703 788-6835	
Herndon *(G-6709)*			
Informatica Corp	G	703 234-8500	
Reston *(G-10872)*			
Informatica LLC	G	650 385-7000	
Alexandria *(G-237)*			
Information Analysis Inc	E	703 383-3000	
Fairfax *(G-4633)*			
Infrascale Inc	G	703 520-7072	
Reston *(G-10873)*			
Infrawhite Technologies LLC	G	662 902-0376	
Vienna *(G-14070)*			
Innovative Dynamic Solutions	G	703 234-5282	
Herndon *(G-6710)*			
Inovitech LLC	G	877 429-0377	
Leesburg *(G-7287)*			
Inquisient Inc	F	888 230-2181	
Warrenton *(G-15027)*			
Insource Sftwr Solutions Inc	E	804 378-8981	
North Chesterfield *(G-9897)*			

Institute For Complexity MGT..............G...... 540 645-1050
Stafford (G-13154)

Integrated Software Solutions..............G...... 703 255-1130
Reston (G-10874)

Intelligent Bus Platforms LLC..............E...... 202 640-8868
Reston (G-10876)

Intelligent Software Design..............G...... 703 731-9091
Mc Lean (G-8466)

Intelligize Incorporated..............G...... 888 925-8627
Reston (G-10877)

Interactive Achievement LLC..............F...... 540 206-3649
Roanoke (G-12107)

Interntional Registration Plan..............G...... 502 845-0398
Lake Ridge (G-7156)

Intor Inc..............G...... 757 296-2175
Alexandria (G-240)

Intouch For Inmates LLC..............G...... 862 246-6283
Lynchburg (G-7746)

Intuit Inc..............C...... 540 752-6100
Fredericksburg (G-5442)

Invelos Software Inc..............G...... 540 786-8560
Fredericksburg (G-5304)

Invincea Inc..............C...... 703 352-7680
Fairfax (G-4638)

Invision Inc..............F...... 703 774-3881
Manassas (G-8086)

Invizer LLC..............G...... 410 903-2507
Herndon (G-6711)

Iq Global Technologies LLC..............G...... 800 601-0678
Vienna (G-14073)

Iron Forge Software LLC..............G...... 571 263-6540
Oak Hill (G-10137)

Irontek LLC..............G...... 703 627-0092
Sterling (G-13432)

Iselfschooling..............G...... 703 821-3282
Mc Lean (G-8472)

Iskoyisal Inc..............G...... 703 992-6629
Mc Lean (G-8473)

Itechnologies Inc..............G...... 703 723-5141
Ashburn (G-1298)

Itegrity Systems..............G...... 703 968-6300
Chantilly (G-2446)

Itek Software LLC..............G...... 312 404-3086
Glen Allen (G-5753)

Itek Software LLC..............G...... 804 505-4835
Henrico (G-6524)

Ivans Inc..............G...... 804 271-0477
North Chesterfield (G-9900)

Ivy Software Inc..............G...... 804 769-7193
Manquin (G-8216)

Jarcam Sports..............G...... 678 995-4607
Norfolk (G-9601)

Jay Blue Pos Inc..............G...... 703 672-2869
Annandale (G-761)

Jenzabar Inc..............C...... 540 432-5200
Harrisonburg (G-6333)

Jetney Development..............G...... 714 262-0759
Salem (G-12524)

Jkm Software LLC..............G...... 703 754-9175
Gainesville (G-5592)

Jnet Direct Inc..............G...... 703 629-6406
Herndon (G-6718)

Joint Knowledge Software I..............G...... 703 803-7470
Fairfax (G-4486)

Joint Lab Systems SEC Svcs LLC........G...... 443 655-9987
Arlington (G-1016)

Jpg Software..............G...... 757 546-8416
Chesapeake (G-3157)

Js Software Inc..............G...... 214 924-3179
Herndon (G-6720)

K12excellence Inc..............G...... 804 270-9600
Glen Allen (G-5759)

KCS Inc..............G...... 703 981-0523
Alexandria (G-504)

Keeva LLC..............G...... 240 766-5382
Ashburn (G-1302)

Keystone Software Inc..............G...... 703 866-1593
Manassas (G-7955)

Keystone Technology LLC..............G...... 540 361-8318
Fredericksburg (G-5309)

Kimball Consulting Inc..............G...... 703 516-6000
Arlington (G-1023)

Kindred Brothers Inc..............G...... 803 318-5097
Richmond (G-11262)

Kinemetrx Incorporated..............G...... 703 596-5095
Herndon (G-6723)

Kinetech Labs Inc..............G...... 434 284-1073
Zion Crossroads (G-16008)

Kinvarin Software LLC..............G...... 434 985-3737
Stanardsville (G-13221)

Kling Research and Sftwr Inc..............G...... 540 364-2524
Marshall (G-8257)

Km Data Strategists LLC..............G...... 703 689-1087
Aldie (G-108)

Kngro LLC..............G...... 202 390-9126
Springfield (G-13034)

Kodescraft LLC..............G...... 703 843-3700
Triangle (G-13895)

Koloza LLC..............G...... 301 204-9864
Fairfax (G-4492)

Kratos Tech Trning Sltions Inc..............G...... 757 466-3660
Norfolk (G-9614)

Kryptowire LLC..............G...... 571 314-0153
Fairfax (G-4494)

Kuary LLC..............G...... 703 980-3804
Fairfax (G-4495)

Kwick Help LLC..............G...... 703 499-7223
Herndon (G-6726)

Lamaid LLC..............G...... 703 541-8011
Woodbridge (G-15738)

Larry Lewis..............G...... 757 619-7070
Virginia Beach (G-14600)

Laura Bushnell..............G...... 703 569-4422
Springfield (G-13038)

Leapfrog Software LLC..............G...... 804 677-7051
Midlothian (G-8846)

Leaseaccelerator Inc..............F...... 866 446-0980
Reston (G-10886)

Legacy Solutions..............G...... 703 644-9700
Springfield (G-13039)

Lesson Portal LLC..............G...... 540 455-3546
Spotsylvania (G-12901)

Level Up Fun Corporation..............G...... 703 365-8071
Manassas (G-7963)

Lexia Learning Systems Inc..............G...... 978 405-6242
Harrisonburg (G-6337)

LI Hing Software LLC..............G...... 703 677-7773
Alexandria (G-516)

Light Music LLC..............G...... 914 316-7948
Charlottesville (G-2824)

Lighthouse Software Inc..............G...... 703 327-7650
Chantilly (G-2543)

Lintronics Software Publishing..............G...... 540 552-7204
Blacksburg (G-1754)

Littleshot Apps LLC..............G...... 908 433-5727
Arlington (G-1038)

Livesafe Inc..............E...... 571 312-4645
Arlington (G-1039)

Living Solutions Mid Atlantic..............G...... 202 460-9919
Alexandria (G-518)

Location Bsed Svcs Content LLC..............G...... 703 622-1490
Mc Lean (G-8488)

Loci LLC..............G...... 301 613-7111
Sterling (G-13444)

Lockheed Martin Corporation..............C...... 703 367-2121
Manassas (G-7966)

Lockwood Software Engrg Inc..............F...... 202 494-7886
Mc Lean (G-8489)

Logos Software Inc..............G...... 540 819-6260
Roanoke (G-12129)

Lookingglass Cyber Slution Inc..............D...... 703 351-1000
Reston (G-10889)

Loosely Coupled Software LLC..............G...... 703 707-9235
Herndon (G-6738)

Loyalty Doctors LLC..............G...... 757 675-8283
Norfolk (G-9623)

LTS Software Inc..............G...... 757 493-8855
Virginia Beach (G-14628)

Luckyfoots Software..............G...... 434 296-9358
Charlottesville (G-2828)

Luluverse LLC..............G...... 202 821-9726
Ashburn (G-1312)

Lumos LLC..............G...... 571 294-4290
Arlington (G-1050)

Lux 1 Holding Company Inc..............G...... 703 245-9675
Tysons (G-13947)

Macar International LLC..............G...... 202 842-1818
Alexandria (G-267)

Macro Systems LLC..............G...... 703 359-9211
Fairfax (G-4650)

Macronetics Inc..............G...... 703 848-9290
Vienna (G-14088)

Madgar Enterprises LLC..............G...... 540 760-6946
North Chesterfield (G-9917)

Madison Edgecnnex Holdings LLC..............G...... 703 880-5404
Herndon (G-6739)

Magic Genius LLC..............G...... 540 454-7595
Warrenton (G-15032)

Magnet Forensics Usa Inc..............G...... 519 342-0195
Herndon (G-6740)

Magnigen LLC..............G...... 434 420-1435
Lynchburg (G-7768)

Magoozle LLC..............G...... 757 581-6936
Virginia Beach (G-14634)

Majiksoft..............G...... 757 510-0929
Virginia Beach (G-14636)

Makes Sense To ME Software LLC........G...... 757 771-5289
Hampton (G-6190)

Manan LLC..............F...... 804 320-1414
Henrico (G-6532)

Mantas..............G...... 703 322-4917
Herndon (G-6742)

Mantech Advanced Dev Group Inc..............D...... 703 218-6000
Fairfax (G-4502)

Manufacturing System Svcs Inc..............G...... 800 428-8643
Fairfax (G-4651)

Maphook Inc..............G...... 703 661-7000
Sterling (G-13447)

Mapsdirect LLC..............G...... 804 915-7628
Richmond (G-11665)

Mark Software LLC..............G...... 703 409-4605
Hillsboro (G-6876)

Marketspace Solutions Inc..............G...... 703 989-3509
Centreville (G-2318)

Master Business Solutions Inc..............G...... 804 378-5470
North Chesterfield (G-9926)

Match My Value Inc..............G...... 301 456-4308
Richmond (G-11672)

Materna..............G...... 703 875-8616
Arlington (G-1055)

Maverick Bus Solutions LLC..............G...... 757 870-8489
Portsmouth (G-10459)

Maxpci LLC..............G...... 703 565-3400
Fredericksburg (G-5203)

MCA Systems Inc..............G...... 540 684-1617
Fredericksburg (G-5204)

McAfee LLC..............G...... 571 449-4600
Reston (G-10896)

Media X Group LLC..............G...... 866 966-9640
Waynesboro (G-15124)

Medliminal LLC..............F...... 571 719-6837
Manassas (G-7974)

Meetingsphere Inc..............E...... 703 348-0725
Norfolk (G-9637)

Mega-Tech Inc..............E...... 703 534-1629
Falls Church (G-4922)

Megawatt Apps LLC..............G...... 703 870-4082
Sterling (G-13452)

Ment Software Inc..............G...... 540 382-4172
Riner (G-11864)

Mentoradvisor Inc..............G...... 571 435-7222
Alexandria (G-527)

Meritful Inc..............G...... 703 651-6338
Alexandria (G-528)

Method Innovation Corporation..............G...... 703 266-1115
Clifton (G-3674)

Methodhead Software LLC..............G...... 703 338-1588
Annandale (G-773)

Metis Machine LLC..............F...... 434 483-5692
Charlottesville (G-2833)

Michie Software Systems Inc..............G...... 757 868-7771
Yorktown (G-15982)

Micro Analytics of Virginia..............F...... 703 536-6424
Arlington (G-1063)

Micro Focus Software Inc..............B...... 703 663-5500
Vienna (G-14091)

Micro Services Company..............G...... 804 741-5000
Richmond (G-11291)

Microbanx Systems LLC..............G...... 703 757-1760
Great Falls (G-5966)

Microsoft Corporation..............E...... 434 738-0103
Boydton (G-1916)

Microsoft Corporation..............A...... 703 236-9140
Arlington (G-1064)

Microsoft Corporation..............D...... 571 222-8110
Bristow (G-2060)

Microsoft Corporation..............A...... 703 673-7600
Reston (G-10901)

Microsoft Corporation..............D...... 804 270-0146
Glen Allen (G-5770)

Microstrategy Services Corp..............D...... 703 848-8600
Tysons Corner (G-13955)

Milestone Software Inc..............G...... 703 217-4262
Manassas (G-7976)

Millennium Sftwr Cnsulting LLC..............G...... 434 245-0741
Charlottesville (G-2661)

Millstreet Software..............G...... 703 281-1015
Vienna (G-14093)

Mindmettle..............G...... 540 890-5563
Vinton (G-14179)

Mintmesh Inc....G....703 222-0322
Fairfax *(G-4512)*
Miracle Systems LLC....C....571 431-6397
Arlington *(G-1066)*
Mission Data LLC....F....513 298-1865
Dunn Loring *(G-4265)*
Mission It LLC....G....443 534-0130
Brambleton *(G-1930)*
Mission Secure Inc....G....434 284-8071
Charlottesville *(G-2836)*
Missionteq LLC....G....703 563-0699
Chantilly *(G-2545)*
Molloy Software Assoc Inc....G....703 825-7290
Centreville *(G-2320)*
Mongodb Inc....G....866 237-8815
Vienna *(G-14099)*
Monte Carlo Software LLC....G....703 642-0289
Annandale *(G-776)*
Monticello Software Inc....G....540 854-4200
Mineral *(G-8950)*
Montuno Software Inc....G....703 554-7505
Brambleton *(G-1931)*
MPH Development LLC....G....703 303-4838
Gainesville *(G-5599)*
Multimodal ID....G....703 944-9008
Falls Church *(G-4833)*
My Arch Inc....G....703 375-9302
Centreville *(G-2323)*
Nabiday LLC....G....703 625-8679
Fairfax *(G-4656)*
Nancy Lee Asman....G....703 242-8530
Vienna *(G-14101)*
Nasotech LLC....G....703 493-0436
Herndon *(G-6750)*
Nemesys Software....G....703 435-0508
Herndon *(G-6751)*
Neopath Systems LLC....G....571 238-1333
Herndon *(G-6752)*
Nervve Technologies Inc....G....703 334-1488
Herndon *(G-6753)*
Net6degrees LLC....G....703 201-4480
Purcellville *(G-10672)*
Netcentric Technologies Inc....G....202 661-2180
Arlington *(G-1075)*
Netqos Inc....C....703 708-3699
Herndon *(G-6754)*
New Century Software....G....704 984-3135
Fairfax Station *(G-4719)*
New Health Analytics LLC....F....804 245-8240
Henrico *(G-6541)*
New Tech Innovations....G....703 731-8160
Leesburg *(G-7320)*
Next Screen Media....G....571 295-6398
Aldie *(G-109)*
Nexxtek Inc....G....571 356-2921
Vienna *(G-14105)*
Nguyen & Phan LLC....G....571 730-9948
Lorton *(G-7516)*
Nika Software Inc....G....703 992-5318
Herndon *(G-6755)*
North Star Software Consulting....G....703 628-8564
Leesburg *(G-7321)*
Nortonlifelock Inc....G....703 414-4444
Arlington *(G-1083)*
Nortonlifelock Inc....G....703 883-0180
Mc Lean *(G-8519)*
Ntelos Inc....G....540 992-2211
Daleville *(G-3945)*
Ntelos Inc....G....434 760-0141
Charlottesville *(G-2668)*
Ntt America Solutions Inc....E....571 203-4032
Reston *(G-10910)*
Nuasis Corp....G....571 230-8126
Great Falls *(G-5969)*
Nudge LLC....G....423 521-1969
Richmond *(G-11697)*
Nufocus Software LLC....G....540 722-0282
Winchester *(G-15456)*
Nyx Technologies LLC....G....703 914-8956
Alexandria *(G-546)*
O2o Software Inc....G....571 234-3243
Herndon *(G-6762)*
▼ Objective Intrface Systems Inc....D....703 295-6500
Herndon *(G-6763)*
Objectvideo Labs LLC....E....571 327-3673
Mc Lean *(G-8520)*
Ocean Software Us LLC....G....703 796-1300
Herndon *(G-6764)*
Octoleaf LLC....G....202 579-7279
Ashburn *(G-1324)*
Octopus Software Systems Inc....G....571 224-5283
Falls Church *(G-4848)*
Old World Labs LLC....G....800 282-0386
Norfolk *(G-9675)*
Omnicardata LLC....G....703 622-6742
Sterling *(G-13464)*
One Aperture LLC....G....202 415-0416
Falls Church *(G-4851)*
One One Too LLC....G....505 500-4749
Fredericksburg *(G-5342)*
One Stop Computer Services LLC....G....571 442-2045
Sterling *(G-13465)*
Openwater Software Inc....E....202 765-0247
Arlington *(G-1089)*
Opsense Inc....G....844 757-7578
Dunn Loring *(G-4266)*
Optime Software LLC....G....415 894-0314
Great Falls *(G-5970)*
Oracle America Inc....G....703 310-3600
Arlington *(G-1090)*
Oracle America Inc....F....804 672-0998
Richmond *(G-11316)*
Oracle America Inc....D....703 478-9000
Reston *(G-10915)*
Oracle Heart & Vascular Inc....G....855 739-9953
Fredericksburg *(G-5210)*
Oracle Systems Corporation....A....703 478-9000
Reston *(G-10916)*
Oracle Systems Corporation....B....703 364-2221
Alexandria *(G-547)*
Oracle Worldwide LLC....G....703 224-8806
Alexandria *(G-301)*
◆ Orbital Sciences LLC....A....703 406-5524
Dulles *(G-4217)*
Orbysol Inc....G....703 398-1092
Brambleton *(G-1932)*
Osgoode Media Inc....G....866 573-0754
Herndon *(G-6766)*
P&B Systems LLC....G....717 566-0608
Alexandria *(G-302)*
Packet Stash Inc....G....202 649-0676
Alexandria *(G-303)*
Palladion Software....G....540 429-0999
Fredericksburg *(G-5211)*
Pantheon Integration LLC....G....571 732-1570
Reston *(G-10919)*
Pantheon Software Inc....F....703 387-4000
Arlington *(G-1097)*
Papay Holdco LLC....E....703 226-3544
Arlington *(G-1098)*
Parabon Computation Inc....F....703 689-9689
Reston *(G-10920)*
Parabon Nanolabs Inc....E....703 689-9689
Reston *(G-10921)*
Partfiniti Inc....F....703 679-7278
Haymarket *(G-6434)*
Patron Id Inc....G....954 282-6636
Lynchburg *(G-7783)*
Paya Inc....F....800 261-0240
Reston *(G-10922)*
PC Shareware Inc....G....540 371-5746
Fredericksburg *(G-5468)*
Pcpursuit Inc....G....425 890-5495
Herndon *(G-6768)*
Pdh Mobile Inc....G....703 475-8223
Great Falls *(G-5972)*
People Interact LLC....G....571 223-5888
Leesburg *(G-7324)*
Pep Labs LLC....G....202 669-2562
Ashburn *(G-1325)*
Performance Support Systems....G....757 873-3700
Hayes *(G-6404)*
Performyard Inc....G....703 870-3710
Arlington *(G-1106)*
Permissionbit Inc....G....703 278-3832
Mc Lean *(G-8525)*
Personam Inc....G....571 297-9371
Mc Lean *(G-8526)*
Pexip Inc....G....703 480-3181
Herndon *(G-6772)*
Philadelphia Riverboat LLC....G....757 640-9205
Norfolk *(G-9687)*
Photo Finale Inc....F....703 564-3400
Mc Lean *(G-8529)*
Pl Square Technologies Inc....G....571 255-6253
Chantilly *(G-2550)*
Pivit....G....301 395-0895
Chantilly *(G-2551)*
Pixia Corp....E....571 203-9665
Herndon *(G-6774)*
Plateau Software Inc....G....703 385-8300
Fairfax *(G-4530)*
Playcall Inc....G....571 385-6203
Great Falls *(G-5973)*
Player Pursuits LLC....G....202 207-6000
Mc Lean *(G-8530)*
Pleasant Vly Bus Solutions LLC....E....703 391-0977
Reston *(G-10926)*
Pleasy LLC....G....774 234-4299
Arlington *(G-1112)*
Pma It Solutions Inc....G....571 336-2408
Portsmouth *(G-10469)*
Pointerra Us Inc....E....571 528-8799
Ashburn *(G-1327)*
Poplicus Incorporated....E....866 209-9100
Arlington *(G-1116)*
Positive Feedback Software LL....G....540 243-0300
Rocky Mount *(G-12347)*
Pouchmouse Studios Inc....G....310 462-0599
Alexandria *(G-314)*
Practical Software LLC....G....240 505-0936
Stephens City *(G-13320)*
Prager University Foundation....G....323 577-2437
Herndon *(G-6778)*
Prall Software Consulting LLC....G....703 777-8423
Leesburg *(G-7327)*
Pramaan Inc....G....703 327-6750
Chantilly *(G-2552)*
Primatics Financial LLC....D....703 342-0040
Mc Lean *(G-8531)*
Prime 3 Software Inc....G....757 763-8560
Norfolk *(G-9695)*
Profitoptics Inc....G....804 360-2776
Glen Allen *(G-5783)*
Prop LLC....G....571 970-5031
Arlington *(G-1121)*
Protean LLC....G....757 273-1131
Williamsburg *(G-15302)*
Protectedbyai Inc....G....571 489-6906
Reston *(G-10932)*
Qmulos Products Inc....G....202 557-5162
Arlington *(G-1124)*
Quadramed Corporation....C....703 709-2300
Herndon *(G-6781)*
Quantum Computing Inc....G....703 436-2161
Leesburg *(G-7330)*
Quest Software Inc....F....703 234-3000
Reston *(G-10935)*
Raastech Software LLC....G....888 565-3397
Herndon *(G-6785)*
Rabbit Software LLC....G....703 939-1708
Ashburn *(G-1329)*
Radus Software LLC....G....703 623-8471
Sterling *(G-13484)*
Raimist Software LLC....G....703 568-7638
Chantilly *(G-2484)*
Raincrow Studios LLC....G....540 746-8696
Harrisonburg *(G-6360)*
Raised Apps LLC....G....703 398-8254
Woodbridge *(G-15790)*
Rand Worldwide Inc....G....804 290-8850
Richmond *(G-11345)*
Rcl Software Inc....G....757 934-0828
Suffolk *(G-13757)*
RDS Control Systems Inc....G....888 578-9428
Fishersville *(G-5007)*
RE Discovery Software Inc....F....434 975-3256
Charlottesville *(G-2680)*
RE Innovative Sftwr Solutions....F....434 989-8558
Charlottesville *(G-2855)*
Readspeaker LLC....G....703 462-8738
Mc Lean *(G-8534)*
Reconart Inc....G....855 732-6627
Alexandria *(G-568)*
Red Hat Inc....F....703 748-2201
Mc Lean *(G-8536)*
Redclay Visions LLC....G....804 869-3616
Virginia Beach *(G-14766)*
Redono LLC....G....757 553-2305
Chesapeake *(G-3264)*
Reger Research....G....703 328-6465
Chantilly *(G-2554)*
Relational Data Solutions Inc....G....703 369-3580
Manassas *(G-8142)*
Relational Systems Design Ltd....G....703 385-7073
Fairfax *(G-4539)*
Rentbot LLC....G....844 473-6826
Richmond *(G-11350)*
Reservation Gateway Inc....G....703 286-5331
Reston *(G-10937)*

S I C

Employee Codes: A=Over 500 employees, B=251-500
C=101-250, D=51-100, E=20-50, F=10-19, G=1-9

2021 Virginia
Industrial Directory

671

Resounding LLC ....G..... 804 677-0947	**Scratcherguru LLC** ....G..... 804 239-8629	**Solarwinds North America Inc** ....G..... 877 946-3751
North Chesterfield *(G-9958)*	Montpelier *(G-9020)*	Herndon *(G-6811)*
Reston Software LLC ....G..... 703 234-2932	**Scriyb LLC** ....F..... 202 549-7070	**Solutions Wise Group** ....G..... 804 748-0205
Reston *(G-10939)*	Leesburg *(G-7343)*	North Chesterfield *(G-9984)*
Reston Technology Group Inc ....F..... 703 810-8800	**Scw Software Inc** ....G..... 540 937-5332	**Sonawane Webdynamics Inc** ....G..... 703 629-7254
Sterling *(G-13491)*	Amissville *(G-721)*	Ashburn *(G-1335)*
Results Software ....G..... 703 713-9100	**SDA Software LLC** ....G..... 703 657-0919	**Source Consulting Inc** ....G..... 540 785-0268
Herndon *(G-6790)*	Sterling *(G-13501)*	Fredericksburg *(G-5366)*
Reuseit Software Inc ....G..... 703 365-8071	**Secure Elements Incorporated** ....E..... 703 234-7840	**Source360 LLC** ....G..... 703 232-1563
Manassas *(G-7996)*	Herndon *(G-6803)*	Chantilly *(G-2494)*
Rgolf Inc ....G..... 540 443-9296	**Secure Innovations Inc** ....G..... 540 384-6131	**South Anna Inc** ....G..... 804 316-9660
Blacksburg *(G-1783)*	Salem *(G-12569)*	Henrico *(G-6572)*
RI Software Corp ....G..... 301 537-1593	**Securedb Inc** ....G..... 703 231-0008	**Southpark Hi LLC** ....G..... 804 777-9000
Purcellville *(G-10675)*	Sterling *(G-13503)*	Chester *(G-3455)*
Richlynd Federal LLC ....G..... 703 354-1500	**Self Solutions LLC** ....E..... 202 725-0866	**Sovereign Intelligence LLC** ....F..... 571 455-4016
Alexandria *(G-573)*	Alexandria *(G-582)*	Vienna *(G-14131)*
Ridge Business Solutions LLC ....E..... 571 241-8714	**Semanticsolutions LLC** ....G..... 703 980-7395	**Spectrum Center Inc** ....F..... 703 848-4750
Reston *(G-10941)*	Ashburn *(G-1333)*	Mc Lean *(G-8554)*
Rimfire Games LLC ....G..... 703 580-4495	**Sentient Vision Systems Inc** ....G..... 703 531-8564	**Spedapps LLC** ....G..... 757 541-2663
Woodbridge *(G-15796)*	Glen Allen *(G-5794)*	Chesapeake *(G-3307)*
Rivanna Software LLC ....G..... 434 806-6105	**Serendipitme LLC** ....G..... 301 370-2466	**Spiritway LLC** ....G..... 831 676-1014
Charlottesville *(G-2686)*	Leesburg *(G-7347)*	Vienna *(G-14132)*
Riverland Solutions Corp ....G..... 571 247-2382	**Serious Games Interactive Inc** ....E..... 703 624-0842	**Spitfire Management LLC** ....F..... 757 644-4609
Leesburg *(G-7337)*	Arlington *(G-1163)*	Williamsburg *(G-15317)*
Rjm Technologies Inc ....G..... 703 323-6677	**Servhawk LLC** ....G..... 703 447-1456	**Spotspot Co** ....G..... 804 909-7353
Fairfax *(G-4543)*	Great Falls *(G-5979)*	Richmond *(G-11393)*
Roadglobe LLC ....G..... 804 519-3331	**Sgv Software Automtn RES Corp** ....E..... 703 904-0678	**Springboard Retail Inc** ....E..... 888 347-2191
Sandy Hook *(G-12645)*	Herndon *(G-6805)*	Falls Church *(G-4877)*
Rodyn Vibration Analysis Inc ....G..... 434 326-6797	**Sharestream Edcatn Rsurces LLC** ....F..... 301 208-8000	**Spritelogic LLC** ....G..... 703 568-0468
Charlottesville *(G-2865)*	Reston *(G-10948)*	Mc Lean *(G-8557)*
Rogue Software LLC ....G..... 703 945-9175	**Shield Technology Corporation** ....G..... 540 882-3254	**Spydrsafe Mobile Security Inc** ....G..... 703 286-0750
Fairfax *(G-4670)*	Lovettsville *(G-7586)*	Mc Lean *(G-8558)*
Rollstream Inc ....G..... 703 277-2150	**Shiftone** ....G..... 415 806-5006	**Sqlexec LLC** ....G..... 703 600-9343
Fairfax *(G-4671)*	Arlington *(G-1165)*	Annandale *(G-784)*
Roma Sftwr Systems Group Inc ....G..... 703 437-1579	**Siemens Industry Software Inc** ....G..... 757 591-6633	**Sra Companies Inc** ....A..... 703 803-1500
South Riding *(G-12870)*	Newport News *(G-9338)*	Chantilly *(G-2498)*
Rosetta Stone Inc ....E..... 703 387-5800	**Signal Vine Inc** ....F..... 703 480-0278	**Srg Government Solutions Inc** ....G..... 703 609-7027
Arlington *(G-1151)*	Alexandria *(G-346)*	Fairfax *(G-4559)*
◆ **Rosetta Stone Ltd.** ....B..... 540 432-6166	**Silent Circle Americas LLC** ....G..... 202 499-6427	**Srn Software LLC** ....G..... 703 646-5186
Harrisonburg *(G-6365)*	Fairfax *(G-4678)*	Lorton *(G-7533)*
Routemarket Inc ....G..... 703 829-7087	**Simulyze Inc** ....F..... 703 391-7001	**Ssecurity LLC** ....G..... 703 590-4240
Arlington *(G-1152)*	Reston *(G-10950)*	Woodbridge *(G-15817)*
Rowing Team LLC ....E..... 855 462-7238	**Singlecomm LLC** ....G..... 203 559-5486	**Stardog Union** ....E..... 202 408-8770
Glen Allen *(G-5788)*	Richmond *(G-11383)*	Arlington *(G-1175)*
Rsa Security LLC ....G..... 703 288-9300	**Sip-Tone** ....G..... 703 480-0228	**Stellar Day Products Corp** ....G..... 804 748-8086
Vienna *(G-14118)*	Herndon *(G-6810)*	North Chesterfield *(G-9991)*
Rufina Inc ....G..... 703 577-2333	**Sitscape Inc** ....F..... 571 432-8130	**Stellosphere Inc** ....G..... 631 897-4678
Falls Church *(G-4870)*	Vienna *(G-14129)*	Ashburn *(G-1337)*
Rxhonesty Inc ....G..... 908 872-2009	**Sky Software** ....G..... 540 869-6581	**Stillpoint Software Inc** ....G..... 540 905-7932
Vienna *(G-14119)*	Stephens City *(G-13323)*	Washington *(G-15079)*
Rynoh Live ....G..... 757 333-3760	**Slipstream Aviation Sftwr Inc** ....G..... 703 729-6535	**Stratuslive LLC** ....E..... 757 273-8219
Virginia Beach *(G-14787)*	Leesburg *(G-7349)*	Virginia Beach *(G-14855)*
S Software Development System ....G..... 571 633-0554	**Smartfix** ....G..... 571 723-6499	**Streamview Software LLC** ....G..... 703 455-0793
Mc Lean *(G-8541)*	Springfield *(G-13088)*	Springfield *(G-13095)*
Safety Software Inc ....F..... 434 296-8789	**Snowbird Holdings Inc** ....G..... 703 796-0445	**Structured Software Inc** ....G..... 703 266-0588
Charlottesville *(G-2870)*	Reston *(G-10956)*	Fairfax *(G-4683)*
Sage Software Inc ....G..... 503 439-5271	**Soft Edge Inc** ....G..... 703 442-8353	**Summit Waterfalls LLC** ....G..... 703 688-4558
Mc Lean *(G-8542)*	Mc Lean *(G-8550)*	Woodbridge *(G-15819)*
Saicomp LLC ....G..... 714 421-8967	**Softchalk LLC** ....E..... 877 638-2425	**Sunlight Software** ....G..... 540 789-7374
Petersburg *(G-10340)*	Richmond *(G-11762)*	Willis *(G-15365)*
Sailfish LLC ....G..... 203 570-3553	**Softchoice Corporation** ....G..... 703 480-1952	**Sunmicro Software Incorporated** ....G..... 703 587-9362
Arlington *(G-1156)*	Mc Lean *(G-8551)*	Herndon *(G-6817)*
Salem Infotech Inc ....F..... 703 731-9711	**Software & Systems Solutions L** ....G..... 703 801-7452	**Sunny Day Fund Solutions Inc** ....G..... 703 622-1005
Herndon *(G-6798)*	Woodbridge *(G-15816)*	Falls Church *(G-4880)*
Salesforce Maps ....G..... 571 388-4990	**Software Ag Inc** ....F..... 703 480-1860	**Superior Global Solutions Inc** ....G..... 804 794-3507
Charlottesville *(G-2871)*	Reston *(G-10958)*	Chesterfield *(G-3530)*
Salus LLC ....G..... 475 222-3784	**Software Ag Inc** ....C..... 703 860-5050	**Supplier Solutions Inc** ....F..... 703 791-7720
Herndon *(G-6799)*	Reston *(G-10959)*	Fairfax *(G-4684)*
Samvit Solutions LLC ....G..... 703 481-1274	**Software Engineering Solutions** ....G..... 703 842-1823	**Supravista Medical Dss LLC** ....G..... 740 339-0080
Reston *(G-10944)*	Ashburn *(G-1334)*	Farnham *(G-4965)*
Sapr3 Associates Inc ....G..... 501 256-8645	**Software Flow Corporation** ....G..... 301 717-0331	**Survivalware Inc** ....G..... 703 780-2044
Herndon *(G-6801)*	Great Falls *(G-5981)*	Alexandria *(G-593)*
Sas Federal LLC ....G..... 571 227-7000	**Software For Mobile Phones LLC** ....G..... 703 862-1079	**Svanaco Inc** ....G..... 571 312-3790
Arlington *(G-1159)*	Springfield *(G-13091)*	Alexandria *(G-359)*
Sas Institute Inc ....G..... 804 217-8352	**Software Incentives** ....G..... 540 554-2319	**Swami Shriji LLC** ....G..... 804 322-9644
Glen Allen *(G-5790)*	Round Hill *(G-12390)*	North Chesterfield *(G-9994)*
Sas Institute Inc ....E..... 571 227-7000	**Software Insight** ....G..... 703 549-8554	**Switchdraw LLC** ....G..... 703 402-2820
Arlington *(G-1160)*	Alexandria *(G-350)*	Stafford *(G-13199)*
Savi Technology Inc ....E..... 571 227-7950	**Software Quality Experts LLC** ....G..... 703 291-4641	**Syftkog** ....G..... 540 693-5875
Alexandria *(G-578)*	Reston *(G-10960)*	Fredericksburg *(G-5372)*
Schafer Government Svcs LLC ....G..... 202 594-4124	**Software Quality Institute** ....G..... 703 313-8404	**Synaptein Solutions Inc** ....F..... 703 209-2350
Arlington *(G-1162)*	Alexandria *(G-586)*	Mc Lean *(G-8562)*
Schribble Inc ....G..... 804 869-6878	**Software Security Cons LLC** ....G..... 571 234-3663	**Syncdog LLC** ....G..... 800 430-1268
Glen Allen *(G-5791)*	Leesburg *(G-7350)*	Reston *(G-10969)*
Sciencelogic Inc ....C..... 703 354-1010	**Software Solution & Cloud** ....G..... 703 870-7233	**Synergy Business Solutions LLC** ....G..... 757 646-1294
Reston *(G-10945)*	Sterling *(G-13514)*	Virginia Beach *(G-14860)*
Scientific Software Solutions ....F..... 434 293-7661	**Software Specialists Inc** ....G..... 540 449-2805	**Syntec Business Systems Inc** ....G..... 804 303-2864
Charlottesville *(G-2873)*	Blacksburg *(G-1792)*	Forest *(G-5100)*
Scivera LLC ....G..... 434 974-1301	**Software To Fit LLC** ....G..... 703 378-7239	**Synteras LLC** ....G..... 703 766-6222
Charlottesville *(G-2874)*	Chantilly *(G-2493)*	Herndon *(G-6820)*

Syrm LLC ....G...... 571 308-8707
  Stafford (G-13200)

Systems America Inc ....G...... 703 203-8421
  Chantilly (G-2507)

T & T Software LLC ....G...... 540 389-1915
  Roanoke (G-12202)

T C G Technologies LLC ....G...... 703 847-5057
  Vienna (G-14137)

T5 Group LLC ....G...... 704 575-7721
  Lynchburg (G-7817)

Tate Global LLC ....G...... 703 282-0737
  Alexandria (G-362)

Tconnex Inc ....G...... 703 910-3400
  Herndon (G-6824)

Team Excel Inc ....G...... 804 677-3694
  Richmond (G-11785)

Tech Enterprises Inc ....G...... 703 352-0001
  Fairfax (G-4686)

Technica Software LLC ....G...... 703 371-7134
  Arlington (G-1182)

Technology Destiny LLC ....G...... 703 400-8929
  Brambleton (G-1934)

Teendrivingstickercom LLC ....G...... 571 643-6956
  Manassas (G-8166)

Tekadventure LLC ....G...... 646 580-2511
  Chantilly (G-2560)

Teknostrata Inc ....G...... 877 983-5667
  Arlington (G-1184)

Telos Idntity MGT Slutions LLC ....D...... 703 724-3800
  Ashburn (G-1339)

Tenant Turner ....G...... 804 241-8810
  Glen Allen (G-5807)

Teneo Inc ....G...... 703 212-3220
  Sterling (G-13529)

Teresa C Shankman ....G...... 703 533-9322
  Arlington (G-1187)

Terrago Technologies Inc ....E...... 678 391-9798
  Sterling (G-13530)

Terralign Group Inc ....G...... 571 388-4990
  Herndon (G-6825)

Tetravista LLC ....G...... 703 606-6509
  Arlington (G-1189)

Textore Inc ....F...... 571 321-2013
  Fairfax (G-4687)

Third Eye Development Intl Inc ....G...... 631 682-1848
  Alexandria (G-363)

Thomas Brothers Software Corp ...G...... 540 320-3505
  Pulaski (G-10648)

Thoughtweb USA Inc ....G...... 575 639-1726
  Oakton (G-10162)

Three Foot Software LLC ....G...... 434 202-0217
  Charlottesville (G-2705)

Tibco Software Federal Inc ....E...... 703 208-3900
  Falls Church (G-4883)

Tiome Inc ....G...... 703 531-8963
  Alexandria (G-599)

Tizzy Technologies Inc ....G...... 703 344-3348
  Virginia Beach (G-14884)

Tobacco Quitter LLC ....G...... 540 818-3396
  Blacksburg (G-1799)

Transeffect LLC ....G...... 703 991-1599
  Winchester (G-15595)

Travelserver Software Inc ....G...... 571 209-5907
  Lansdowne (G-7174)

Travelserver Software Inc ....G...... 703 406-7664
  Great Falls (G-5982)

Trax International Corporation .....G...... 434 485-7100
  Lynchburg (G-7826)

Tree Technologies Inc ....G...... 540 589-7988
  Roanoke (G-12011)

Tremolo Security Inc ....G...... 703 844-2727
  Arlington (G-1196)

Tri Corp ....G...... 703 780-8753
  Alexandria (G-602)

Triblio Inc ....F...... 703 942-9557
  Reston (G-10976)

Trimech Solutions LLC ....E...... 804 257-9965
  Glen Allen (G-5818)

Tringapps Inc ....G...... 703 698-6910
  Fairfax (G-4573)

Triple Yolk LLC ....G...... 540 923-4040
  Reva (G-11002)

Trisec Assoc Inc ....G...... 703 471-6564
  Herndon (G-6831)

Trk Systems Inc ....G...... 804 777-9445
  Chesterfield (G-3535)

Troopmaster Software Inc ....G...... 434 589-6788
  Palmyra (G-10258)

Ttg LLC ....G...... 540 280-7389
  Staunton (G-13303)

▲ Tumalow Inc ....G...... 847 644-9009
  Bumpass (G-2170)

Tumorpix LLC ....G...... 804 754-3961
  Henrico (G-6587)

Turning Point Software Inc ....G...... 703 448-6672
  Mc Lean (G-8569)

Tympic Software Inc ....G...... 703 858-0996
  Ashburn (G-1343)

U Play Usa LLC ....G...... 757 301-8690
  Virginia Beach (G-14899)

Ub-04 Software Inc ....G...... 804 754-2708
  Richmond (G-11426)

Ubicabus LLC ....F...... 804 512-5324
  Colonial Beach (G-3727)

Unboxed ....G...... 336 253-4085
  Chantilly (G-2511)

Unifiedonline Inc ....G...... 816 679-1893
  Fairfax (G-4690)

Unifiedonline LLC ....G...... 816 679-1893
  Fairfax (G-4691)

Unifyia Inc ....F...... 703 344-6758
  Reston (G-10977)

Unison Vrtual Acqstion Off LLC ...G...... 571 449-4188
  Dulles (G-4230)

Unisoncare Corporation ....G...... 804 721-3702
  Chester (G-3463)

Unseen Technologies Inc ....G...... 704 207-7391
  Lynchburg (G-7829)

Up and Running Computers Inc ....G...... 757 565-3282
  Williamsburg (G-15329)

Upkeepr Corp ....G...... 703 718-6304
  Arlington (G-1203)

US Software & Consulting Inc .....G...... 571 281-4496
  Sterling (G-13545)

▲ USA Security Solution Corp ......G...... 804 435-9999
  Kilmarnock (G-7077)

Usher Incorporated ....D...... 703 848-8600
  Tysons Corner (G-13956)

Uvsity Corporation ....G...... 571 308-3241
  Brambleton (G-1935)

Uwin Software LLC ....G...... 703 876-0490
  Vienna (G-14149)

Uzio Inc ....C...... 800 984-7952
  Reston (G-10980)

Valor Partners Inc ....G...... 540 725-4156
  Roanoke (G-12215)

Van Vierssen Marcel ....G...... 703 471-0393
  Herndon (G-6835)

Vartender LLC ....G...... 703 376-7751
  Chantilly (G-2562)

Veamea Inc ....G...... 703 382-2288
  Mc Lean (G-8575)

Vegnos Corporation ....G...... 571 721-1685
  Alexandria (G-604)

Velocity Services Corporation .....E...... 540 368-2708
  Fredericksburg (G-5497)

Velocity Software Inc ....G...... 703 338-0909
  Ashburn (G-1347)

Venture Apps LLC ....G...... 804 747-3405
  Glen Allen (G-5823)

Verint Systems Inc ....G...... 703 481-9326
  Reston (G-10983)

Verisma Systems Inc ....F...... 866 390-7404
  Alexandria (G-372)

Vermark Global Systems Inc ....G...... 703 629-1571
  Fairfax (G-4693)

Virginia Software Group Inc ....G...... 757 721-0054
  Virginia Beach (G-14919)

Virtual Ea Inc ....G...... 703 855-9593
  Nokesville (G-9403)

Vision Business Solutions ....G...... 540 622-6383
  Front Royal (G-5562)

Vision Software Technologies .....G...... 703 722-4480
  Chantilly (G-2563)

Vistashare LLC ....G...... 540 432-1900
  Rockingham (G-12282)

Vitalcode Inc ....G...... 703 622-1154
  Ashburn (G-1351)

Vitara LLC ....G...... 972 200-3680
  Chantilly (G-2564)

Voice Software LLC ....G...... 571 331-2861
  Leesburg (G-7374)

Volarre Inc ....G...... 202 258-2640
  Mc Lean (G-8577)

Voyager Software Inc ....G...... 919 802-3232
  Richmond (G-11815)

Wanderers Hideaway ....G...... 904 480-6117
  Hampton (G-6268)

Warden Systems ....G...... 703 627-8002
  Sterling (G-13558)

Waveset ....G...... 703 904-7411
  Herndon (G-6843)

Web Transitions Inc ....G...... 540 334-1707
  Boones Mill (G-1901)

Webdmg LLC ....G...... 757 633-5033
  Suffolk (G-13782)

Weblogic ....G...... 703 645-0263
  Vienna (G-14159)

Websauce Software LLC ....G...... 540 319-4002
  Lexington (G-7423)

Welcomepoint LLC ....G...... 703 371-0499
  Falls Church (G-4891)

Wellsky Humn Social Svcs Corp ...D...... 703 674-5100
  Reston (G-10990)

While Software LLC ....G...... 202 290-6705
  Great Falls (G-5984)

Whispering Woods Software LLC ...G...... 434 282-1275
  Charlottesville (G-2906)

Whiteboard Applications Inc ....G...... 703 297-2835
  Leesburg (G-7377)

Whooley Inc ....G...... 703 307-4963
  Great Falls (G-5985)

Whos Up Games LLC ....G...... 804 248-2270
  Ashland (G-1509)

Willu LLC ....F...... 844 809-4558
  Arlington (G-1220)

Winchendon Group Inc ....G...... 703 960-0978
  Alexandria (G-610)

Wise Case Technologies LLC ......G...... 757 646-9080
  Virginia Beach (G-14941)

Witt Associates Inc ....G...... 540 667-3146
  Winchester (G-15517)

Workdynamics Technologies Inc ...E...... 703 481-9874
  Reston (G-10994)

Working Software LLC ....G...... 703 992-6280
  Falls Church (G-4930)

Writlab LLC ....G...... 703 996-9162
  Arlington (G-1223)

Wyvern Interactive LLC ....F...... 540 336-4498
  Winchester (G-15519)

Xcalibur Software Inc ....G...... 703 896-5700
  Sterling (G-13565)

Xlnt Solutions Inc ....G...... 703 819-9265
  Fairfax (G-4585)

Yamco LLC ....G...... 804 749-0480
  Richmond (G-11461)

Yellow Bridge Software Inc ....G...... 703 909-5533
  Woodbridge (G-15837)

Yellow Dog Software LLC ....G...... 757 818-9360
  Norfolk (G-9798)

Young and Healthy Mktg LLC ......G...... 214 945-5816
  Meherrin (G-8707)

Your Way Software ....G...... 703 591-2064
  Fairfax (G-4697)

Zachary Systems Inc ....G...... 703 286-7267
  Ashburn (G-1355)

Zachary Systems Incorporated ....G...... 703 723-8965
  Broadlands (G-2084)

Zeurix LLC ....G...... 571 297-9460
  Reston (G-10998)

Zeus Technologies ....G...... 540 247-4623
  Winchester (G-15522)

Zynga Inc ....G...... 901 683-8310
  Ashburn (G-1358)

76 MISCELLANEOUS REPAIR SERVICES

7692 Welding Repair

A 1 Welding Services ....G...... 434 831-2562
  Schuyler (G-12649)

A A J Welding Inc ....G...... 276 688-0191
  Bastian (G-1592)

A&H Welding Inc ....G...... 703 628-4817
  Alexandria (G-398)

Aaron D Crouse ....G...... 757 827-6123
  Hampton (G-6067)

Absolute Welding LLC ....G...... 434 569-5351
  Farmville (G-4936)

Action Iron LLC ....G...... 703 594-2909
  Nokesville (G-9388)

Adams Co LLC ....G...... 757 721-0427
  Virginia Beach (G-14211)

Adams Welding Service ....G...... 804 843-4468
  West Point (G-15152)

Advanced Machine & Tooling ....F...... 757 518-1222
  Virginia Beach (G-14213)

All Things Welded ....G...... 423 492-0880
  Marion (G-8220)

Als Machine & Welding Inc ....G....... 804 443-3193
Tappahannock *(G-13810)*

Alston Welding Svc ....G....... 757 547-7351
Chesapeake *(G-2961)*

American Sheet Metal & Welding ....G....... 757 627-9203
Norfolk *(G-9439)*

Amg Inc ....D....... 434 385-7525
Lynchburg *(G-7640)*

Apex Welding Service LLC ....G....... 757 773-1151
Chesapeake *(G-2977)*

ARC Vosacthree ....G....... 703 910-7721
Woodbridge *(G-15647)*

Arco Welding Inc ....F....... 540 710-6944
Fredericksburg *(G-5247)*

Arcworx Welding LLC ....G....... 540 394-1494
Leesburg *(G-7221)*

Armstrong Gordan ....G....... 757 547-1090
Chesapeake *(G-2980)*

Ascwelding ....G....... 757 274-4486
Chesapeake *(G-2982)*

Automated Machine & Tech Inc ....E....... 757 898-7844
Grafton *(G-5931)*

B & B Machine & Tool Inc ....E....... 540 344-6820
Roanoke *(G-12038)*

B & B Welding & Fabrication ....G....... 540 663-5949
King George *(G-7081)*

B & G Stainless Works Inc ....G....... 703 339-6002
Lorton *(G-7464)*

B and B Welding Service LLC ....G....... 804 994-2797
Aylett *(G-1545)*

Barry Wayne Gladden ....G....... 540 389-6645
Salem *(G-12481)*

Bay Welding ....G....... 757 633-7689
Virginia Beach *(G-14263)*

Bearkers Welding ....G....... 434 324-7616
Gretna *(G-6004)*

Bears Specialty Welding ....G....... 540 247-6813
Winchester *(G-15386)*

Berkle Welding & Fabrication ....F....... 804 708-0662
Oilville *(G-10176)*

Bethels Welding ....G....... 434 946-7160
Amherst *(G-682)*

Blanchards Welding Repair ....G....... 757 539-6306
Suffolk *(G-13680)*

Blands Welding & Fabg Co ....G....... 276 495-8132
Nora *(G-9407)*

Blue Ridge Mechanical ....G....... 540 662-3148
Winchester *(G-15390)*

BNC Welding ....G....... 757 706-2361
Hampton *(G-6096)*

Bobby S World Welding Inc ....G....... 540 845-7659
Stafford *(G-13125)*

Boldens Welding & Trailor Sls ....G....... 276 647-8357
Collinsville *(G-3709)*

Boroughbridge Metal & Wldg LLC ....G....... 804 387-3510
Richmond *(G-11506)*

Boyters Welding & Fabrication ....G....... 434 636-5974
La Crosse *(G-7140)*

Bradley Adkins ....G....... 304 910-6553
North Tazewell *(G-10095)*

Brian R Hess ....G....... 757 240-0689
Williamsburg *(G-15215)*

Brizendine Welding & Repr Inc ....G....... 804 443-1903
Dunnsville *(G-4267)*

Broadway Metal Works Inc ....E....... 540 896-7027
Broadway *(G-2086)*

Brocks Welding Service ....G....... 540 967-3258
Louisa *(G-7546)*

Brown Brothers Inc ....G....... 757 357-4086
Smithfield *(G-12706)*

Brown Welding Inc ....G....... 804 240-3094
North Chesterfield *(G-9835)*

Browns Welding & Trailer Repr ....G....... 276 628-4461
Abingdon *(G-17)*

Burgess Welding & Fabrication ....G....... 276 229-6458
Stuart *(G-13607)*

Burkholder Enterprises Inc ....G....... 540 867-5030
Rockingham *(G-12242)*

Bursey Machine & Welding ....G....... 540 862-5033
Clifton Forge *(G-3679)*

C & C Piping & Fabrication LLC ....F....... 434 369-9353
Altavista *(G-628)*

C and S Precision Wel ....G....... 804 815-7963
Saluda *(G-12601)*

Caldwell Industries Inc ....G....... 703 403-3272
Alexandria *(G-428)*

Canaan Welding LLC ....G....... 703 339-7799
Lorton *(G-7469)*

Carter Welding LLC ....G....... 276 346-1873
Jonesville *(G-7019)*

Caseys Welding Service ....G....... 804 275-7960
North Chesterfield *(G-9840)*

Chambers Welding Inc Carl ....G....... 276 794-7170
Lebanon *(G-7190)*

Charles E Overfelt ....G....... 540 562-0808
Roanoke *(G-11907)*

Chesapeake Thermite Wldg LLC ....G....... 804 725-1111
Port Haywood *(G-10382)*

Clark Welding Service ....G....... 276 565-3607
Appalachia *(G-796)*

Clays Welding Co Inc ....G....... 540 788-3992
Catlett *(G-2266)*

Clevengers Welding Inc ....G....... 540 662-2191
Stephenson *(G-13332)*

Clyde D Seeley Sr ....G....... 757 721-6397
Virginia Beach *(G-14343)*

CM Welding LLC ....G....... 540 539-4723
Winchester *(G-15403)*

Collins Wldg & Fabrication LLC ....G....... 540 392-8171
Check *(G-2943)*

Commercial Machine Inc ....F....... 804 329-5405
Richmond *(G-11534)*

Consolidated Welding LLC ....G....... 757 348-6304
Norfolk *(G-9503)*

Countryside Machining Inc ....G....... 434 929-0065
Madison Heights *(G-7870)*

Crabtree Welding ....G....... 434 990-0140
Ruckersville *(G-12401)*

▲ **Crane Research & Engrg Co Inc** ....E....... 757 826-1707
Yorktown *(G-15945)*

Creative Welding and Design ....G....... 757 334-1416
Suffolk *(G-13689)*

Cross Machine Welding ....G....... 276 699-1974
Ivanhoe *(G-7005)*

Crossroads Iron Works Inc ....F....... 540 832-7800
Zion Crossroads *(G-16006)*

Culpepper ....G....... 804 276-1478
Chesterfield *(G-3492)*

Curtis Wharam ....G....... 434 983-3904
Dillwyn *(G-4094)*

Custom Welded Steel Art Inc ....G....... 276 686-4107
Rural Retreat *(G-12421)*

Cv Welding ....G....... 540 338-6521
Round Hill *(G-12376)*

D P Welding Inc ....G....... 757 232-0460
Newport News *(G-9212)*

Dale Stidham ....G....... 276 523-1428
Big Stone Gap *(G-1708)*

Daniels Certified Welding ....G....... 434 848-4911
Freeman *(G-5511)*

Daniels Welding and Tires ....G....... 757 566-8446
Toano *(G-13862)*

David F Waterbury Jr ....G....... 757 490-5444
Virginia Beach *(G-14392)*

Db Welding LLC ....G....... 757 483-0413
Suffolk *(G-13696)*

Dishman Fabrications LLC ....G....... 757 478-5070
Yorktown *(G-15950)*

Diversfied Wldg Fbrication LLC ....G....... 804 449-6699
Beaverdam *(G-1608)*

Dmh Complete Welding ....G....... 540 347-7550
Warrenton *(G-14998)*

Dna Welding LLC ....G....... 703 256-2976
Annandale *(G-745)*

Dominion Wldg Fabrication Inc ....G....... 757 692-2002
Virginia Beach *(G-14410)*

Dons Welding ....G....... 540 896-3445
Fulks Run *(G-5565)*

Doors & More Welding ....G....... 804 798-4833
Glen Allen *(G-5726)*

Double B Trailers ....G....... 540 586-0651
Goode *(G-5889)*

Double D S Wldg & Fabrication ....G....... 757 566-0019
Lanexa *(G-7165)*

Dougs Welding & Ornamental Ir ....G....... 804 435-6363
White Stone *(G-15187)*

Dozier Tank & Welding Company ....G....... 757 543-5759
Chesapeake *(G-3073)*

Dozier Tank and Welding Co ....G....... 804 232-0092
Richmond *(G-11042)*

Draftco Incorporated ....E....... 540 337-1054
Stuarts Draft *(G-13646)*

Drake Welding Services Inc ....G....... 757 399-7705
Portsmouth *(G-10417)*

E&S Welding LLC ....G....... 434 927-5428
Sandy Level *(G-12646)*

Eastern Shore Wldg Fabrication ....G....... 443 944-3451
Greenbackville *(G-5992)*

Easton Welding LLC ....G....... 703 368-9727
Bristow *(G-2050)*

Elite Welders LLC ....G....... 757 613-1345
Portsmouth *(G-10422)*

Emergency Welding Inc ....G....... 804 829-2976
Providence Forge *(G-10623)*

Entwistle Company ....E....... 434 799-6186
Danville *(G-3992)*

Eric S Welding Service ....G....... 540 717-3256
Reva *(G-11000)*

Erics Welding ....G....... 434 996-6502
Charlottesville *(G-2792)*

Erin Welding Service Inc ....G....... 540 899-3970
Fredericksburg *(G-5429)*

Fab Juniors Welding Metal ....G....... 540 480-1971
Stuarts Draft *(G-13647)*

Fabricated Welding Specialites ....G....... 540 345-3104
Roanoke *(G-12084)*

Falls Stamping & Welding Co ....E....... 330 928-1191
Pulaski *(G-10636)*

Fitzgerald Welding & Repair ....G....... 757 543-7312
Chesapeake *(G-3102)*

Franklins Welding ....G....... 540 330-3454
Roanoke *(G-11923)*

Franks Welding Inc ....G....... 540 668-6185
Purcellville *(G-10661)*

Frayser Welding Co ....G....... 804 798-8764
Glen Allen *(G-5733)*

Fridleys Welding Service Inc ....G....... 804 674-1949
Chesterfield *(G-3501)*

G&G Welding & Fabricating ....G....... 276 202-3815
Richlands *(G-11016)*

Gale Welding and Mch Co Inc ....F....... 804 732-4521
Petersburg *(G-10321)*

Gammons Welding & Fabrication ....G....... 276 627-0664
Bassett *(G-1583)*

Gary Clark ....G....... 540 373-4598
Fredericksburg *(G-5434)*

Gary L Lawson ....G....... 757 848-7003
Poquoson *(G-10372)*

General Welding ....G....... 540 514-0242
Winchester *(G-15545)*

Genesis Welding Inc ....G....... 276 935-2482
Grundy *(G-6033)*

George King Welding Inc ....G....... 540 379-3407
King George *(G-7092)*

Gerloff Inc Charles W ....G....... 757 853-5232
Norfolk *(G-9562)*

Geronimo Welding Fabrication ....G....... 757 277-6383
Virginia Beach *(G-14481)*

Gibson Welding ....G....... 276 328-3324
Wise *(G-15624)*

Gladden Welding ....G....... 540 387-1489
Salem *(G-12512)*

Glr Welding & Fabrication ....G....... 276 337-1401
Pound *(G-10513)*

Grammers Welding ....G....... 804 730-7296
Mechanicsville *(G-8629)*

Grove Hill Welding Services ....G....... 540 282-8252
Shenandoah *(G-12690)*

H&W Welding Co Inc ....G....... 540 334-1431
Boones Mill *(G-1894)*

Hands Steel Mobile Welding LLC ....G....... 757 805-0054
Suffolk *(G-13717)*

Hanover Wldg & Met Fabrication ....G....... 804 550-2272
Ashland *(G-1431)*

Harts Welding & Fabrication L ....G....... 804 785-3030
Cologne *(G-3719)*

Haticole Welding & Mechanical ....G....... 804 443-7808
Tappahannock *(G-13817)*

Hatter Welding Inc ....G....... 540 589-3848
Roanoke *(G-11933)*

Hicks Welding LLC Richard L ....G....... 434 392-9824
Farmville *(G-4943)*

Highland Wldg Fabrication LLC ....G....... 540 474-3105
Monterey *(G-9006)*

Highlands Welding and Fabr ....G....... 276 429-4438
Glade Spring *(G-5678)*

Hill Welding Services Corp ....G....... 540 923-4474
Madison *(G-7854)*

Hinkle Welding & Fabrication ....G....... 434 447-2770
Kenbridge *(G-7033)*

Horton Welding LLC ....G....... 757 346-8405
Windsor *(G-15605)*

Hot Worx Inc ....G....... 757 967-9809
Portsmouth *(G-10443)*

Howdyshells Welding ....G....... 540 886-1960
Staunton *(G-13267)*

Hubert Michael Gilliland ....G....... 434 332-2285
Rustburg *(G-12440)*

Hudsons Welding Shop ....G....... 434 822-1452
Danville *(G-3998)*

I & M Welding Inc ....G...... 540 907-3775
Spotsylvania *(G-12896)*

I A Welding LLC ....G...... 757 455-8500
Norfolk *(G-9588)*

Industrial Alloy Welding LLC ....G...... 757 573-8496
Norfolk *(G-9592)*

Industrial Commercial Wldg LLC ....G...... 703 707-6347
Herndon *(G-6707)*

Industrial Welding & Mech Inc ....F...... 804 744-8812
North Chesterfield *(G-9893)*

Innovative Machining Inc ....E...... 804 385-4212
Forest *(G-5077)*

J & J Welding LLC ....G...... 571 271-3337
Lovettsville *(G-7579)*

J & J Welding LLC ....G...... 703 431-1044
Leesburg *(G-7290)*

J&T Wlding Fbrication Campbell ....F...... 434 369-8589
Altavista *(G-632)*

Jack Kennedy Welding ....G...... 757 340-4269
Virginia Beach *(G-14560)*

Jackie E Calhoun Sr ....G...... 276 328-8318
Wise *(G-15628)*

Jarrett Welding and Mch Inc ....F...... 434 793-3717
Danville *(G-4006)*

Jay Dees Welding Services ....G...... 757 675-8368
Chesapeake *(G-3149)*

JD Goodman Welding ....G...... 804 598-1070
Powhatan *(G-10554)*

Jeffs Mobile Welding Inc ....G...... 757 870-7049
Newport News *(G-9269)*

Jennifer Lavey ....G...... 540 313-0015
Stephens City *(G-13318)*

Jennifer Reynolds ....G...... 804 229-1697
Mechanicsville *(G-8644)*

Jesse Dudley Jr ....G...... 540 663-3773
King George *(G-7095)*

Jet Weld Inc ....G...... 540 836-0163
Churchville *(G-3620)*

Jims Orna Fabrication & Wldg ....G...... 434 581-1420
New Canton *(G-9117)*

Johnson Welding Service ....G...... 757 787-4429
Greenbush *(G-5996)*

Jones Welding Construction ....G...... 434 369-1069
Altavista *(G-633)*

Joshs Welding & Fabrication ....G...... 540 244-9950
Luray *(G-7614)*

Js Welding ....G...... 434 352-0576
Appomattox *(G-816)*

Juniors Wldg & Met Fabrication ....G...... 540 943-7070
Stuarts Draft *(G-13653)*

Jws Welding & Repair ....G...... 804 720-2523
North Dinwiddie *(G-10055)*

K & S Welding ....G...... 757 859-6313
Wakefield *(G-14968)*

K & T Machine and Welding Inc ....F...... 804 296-8625
Ashland *(G-1447)*

Kaczenskis Welding Svcs LLC ....G...... 540 431-8126
Winchester *(G-15432)*

Kanan Welding ....G...... 703 339-7799
Lorton *(G-7500)*

Keens Welding & Aluminum Works ....G...... 540 958-9600
Covington *(G-3793)*

Kens Welding ....G...... 540 788-3556
Catlett *(G-2268)*

Kibby Welding ....G...... 607 624-9959
Troy *(G-13930)*

Kings Mobile Welding & Fabric ....G...... 571 620-4665
Fredericksburg *(G-5200)*

Lakeside Welding ....G...... 434 636-1712
White Plains *(G-15179)*

Lawless Wldg & Fabrication Inc ....G...... 276 806-8077
Fieldale *(G-4989)*

Lawsons Welding Service LLC ....G...... 434 985-2079
Stanardsville *(G-13222)*

Ld Welding & Fabrication Co ....F...... 757 553-2471
Chesapeake *(G-3179)*

Lewis A Dudley ....G...... 540 884-2454
Eagle Rock *(G-4282)*

Lewis Earl Mills ....G...... 540 295-2061
Fredericksburg *(G-5451)*

Lindas Welding & Mech LLC ....G...... 757 719-1567
Lanexa *(G-7167)*

Long Metalwork & Machine Inc ....G...... 804 529-6233
Callao *(G-2216)*

Louie Dufour ....G...... 540 839-5232
Hot Springs *(G-6947)*

Louies Welding and Fabrication ....G...... 540 839-5232
Hot Springs *(G-6948)*

Lovings Welding & Fabricating ....G...... 804 370-3084
Mechanicsville *(G-8655)*

Lv Iron Works & Wldg Svcs Inc ....G...... 703 499-2270
Chantilly *(G-2459)*

M L Welding ....G...... 540 984-4883
Edinburg *(G-4309)*

M&M Welding LLC ....G...... 703 201-4066
Manassas *(G-8102)*

M&Q Welding LLC ....G...... 804 564-8864
North Chesterfield *(G-9915)*

M&S Welding ....G...... 540 371-4009
Stafford *(G-13173)*

Machine & Fabg Specialists Inc ....E...... 757 244-5693
Hampton *(G-6187)*

Machine Welding Pritchett Inc ....G...... 434 949-7239
Dolphin *(G-4116)*

Marroquin Welding ....G...... 571 340-9165
Stafford *(G-13175)*

Martin Mobile Wldg & Repr LLC ....G...... 757 581-3828
Virginia Beach *(G-14638)*

Mathias Welding ....G...... 540 347-1415
Warrenton *(G-15033)*

MB Weld LLC ....G...... 540 434-4042
Harrisonburg *(G-6344)*

McDonald Welding LLC Doug ....G...... 804 928-6496
Richmond *(G-11675)*

McMillan Welding Inc ....G...... 276 728-1031
Hillsville *(G-6896)*

Meadows Welding ....G...... 434 603-0000
Farmville *(G-4950)*

Mealers Welding Repairs ....G...... 251 363-4640
Bumpass *(G-2166)*

Mechanical Development Co Inc ....D...... 540 389-9395
Salem *(G-12535)*

Memorial Welding LLC ....G...... 703 369-2428
Manassas *(G-8107)*

Merciers Welding ....G...... 540 635-4175
Front Royal *(G-5543)*

Metals of Distinction Inc ....G...... 757 727-0773
Hampton *(G-6196)*

Metalstar Services LLC ....G...... 434 591-0400
Troy *(G-13935)*

Michael Fleming ....G...... 276 337-9202
Wise *(G-15632)*

Michaels Welding ....G...... 434 238-5302
Evington *(G-4379)*

Mid Atlantic Welding Tech ....G...... 804 330-8191
Richmond *(G-11050)*

Mikes Wrecker Service & Bdy Sp ....G...... 540 996-4152
Millboro *(G-8937)*

Millers Custom Metal Svcs LLC ....G...... 804 712-2588
Deltaville *(G-4084)*

Monks Welding LLC ....G...... 276 206-8051
Abingdon *(G-51)*

Moonlight Welding LLC ....G...... 757 449-7003
Suffolk *(G-13746)*

Moores Machine Co Inc ....F...... 434 352-0000
Spout Spring *(G-12926)*

Mos Welding Shop ....G...... 434 525-1137
Evington *(G-4380)*

Mount Slon Wldg Fbrication LLC ....G...... 540 350-2733
Mount Solon *(G-9089)*

Mtn Man Welding ....G...... 540 463-9352
Lexington *(G-7405)*

Myers Repair Company ....G...... 804 222-3674
Richmond *(G-11298)*

N A K Mechanics & Welding Inc ....G...... 276 971-1860
Tazewell *(G-13837)*

Naff Welding & Mach Works ....G...... 276 629-1129
Henry *(G-6596)*

New Age Repr & Fabrication LLC ....G...... 757 819-3887
Norfolk *(G-9659)*

Nichols Welding ....G...... 540 483-5308
Rocky Mount *(G-12343)*

Nicks Wldg & Fabrication LLC ....G...... 434 251-2696
Callands *(G-2214)*

Nighthawk Welding LLC ....G...... 540 845-9966
Woodbridge *(G-15759)*

Nolte Machine and Welding LLC ....G...... 804 357-7271
Sandston *(G-12625)*

Norfolk Machine and Wldg Inc ....E...... 757 489-0330
Norfolk *(G-9666)*

Norrisbilt Fbrction MBL Wldg L ....E...... 276 325-0269
Norton *(G-10131)*

One Piece Fabrication LLC ....G...... 757 460-8637
Virginia Beach *(G-14700)*

ONeals Welding & Repair LLC ....G...... 757 421-0702
Chesapeake *(G-3228)*

Ortons Specialty Welding LLC ....G...... 804 405-2675
Toano *(G-13872)*

Outlaw Welding LLC ....G...... 434 929-4734
Monroe *(G-8994)*

Owen Co LLC ....G...... 571 261-1316
Haymarket *(G-6432)*

P & C Heavy Truck Repair ....G...... 804 520-7619
Colonial Heights *(G-3741)*

Parham Services LLC ....G...... 804 586-1202
Sutherland *(G-13805)*

Parhams Wldg & Fabrication Inc ....F...... 804 834-3504
Waverly *(G-15086)*

Philip Back ....G...... 540 570-9353
Fairfield *(G-4733)*

Piedmont Welding & Maintenance ....G...... 434 447-6600
La Crosse *(G-7148)*

Porter Welding ....G...... 276 565-2694
Appalachia *(G-799)*

Precision Machine Co Inc ....G...... 804 359-5758
North Chesterfield *(G-9953)*

Precision Welding LLC ....G...... 434 973-2106
Virginia Beach *(G-14735)*

Premo Welding ....G...... 757 880-6951
Hampton *(G-6218)*

Pro-Core ....G...... 703 490-4905
Woodbridge *(G-15783)*

Professional Welding Svc Inc ....G...... 757 853-9371
Norfolk *(G-9697)*

Progressive Manufacturing Corp ....E...... 804 717-5353
Chester *(G-3448)*

Pruitt Welding & Fabrication ....G...... 540 896-4268
Timberville *(G-13853)*

▲ Quality Welding Inc ....E...... 434 296-1402
Charlottesville *(G-2852)*

R & D Welding Services ....G...... 757 761-3499
Chesapeake *(G-3253)*

R W A Machining & Welding Co ....G...... 434 985-7362
Ruckersville *(G-12412)*

Radford Wldg & Fabrication LLC ....G...... 540 731-4891
Radford *(G-10737)*

Raffy Welding LLC ....G...... 703 945-0554
Leesburg *(G-7331)*

Rails End Wood & Met Crafters ....G...... 540 463-9565
Lexington *(G-7413)*

Randolph Scotts Welding ....G...... 434 656-1471
Gretna *(G-6009)*

Raven Machine ....G...... 804 271-6001
North Chesterfield *(G-9957)*

Rawley Pike Welding LLC ....G...... 540 867-5335
Hinton *(G-6905)*

Ray Gorham ....G...... 703 971-1807
Alexandria *(G-566)*

Rectors Repair & Welding LLC ....G...... 540 809-5683
Fredericksburg *(G-5476)*

Richmond Steel Inc ....G...... 804 798-4766
Ashland *(G-1486)*

Rick A Debernard Welding Inc ....G...... 540 834-8348
Fredericksburg *(G-5478)*

Ricks Custom Welding Inc ....G...... 540 675-1888
Huntly *(G-6966)*

Ridge Top Welding ....G...... 540 947-5118
Blue Ridge *(G-1855)*

Right Tght Wldg Fbrication LLC ....G...... 757 553-0661
Virginia Beach *(G-14773)*

Ritter Welding ....G...... 703 680-9601
Woodbridge *(G-15797)*

Road Rnner MBL Wldg Fbrction L ....G...... 757 915-2077
Hampton *(G-6229)*

Robeys Welding LLC ....G...... 540 974-3811
White Post *(G-15182)*

Robs Welding ....G...... 540 722-4151
Winchester *(G-15469)*

Rockingham Welding Svc LLC ....G...... 540 879-9500
Dayton *(G-4061)*

Rod & Staff Welding ....G...... 434 392-3090
Farmville *(G-4956)*

Rodeo Welding LLC ....G...... 571 379-4179
Manassas *(G-8147)*

Roop Welding & General Repair ....G...... 276 346-3338
Jonesville *(G-7023)*

Rt 100 Welding Fab Machin ....G...... 276 766-0100
Barren Springs *(G-1575)*

Ry Fabricating LLC ....G...... 571 835-0567
King George *(G-7112)*

S Conley Welding Company ....G...... 540 436-3775
Star Tannery *(G-13237)*

S3 Mobile Welding & Cutting ....G...... 757 647-0322
Chesapeake *(G-3281)*

Saltville Machine & Welding ....G...... 276 496-3555
Saltville *(G-12590)*

Sb Welding and Fab LLC ....G...... 540 955-0797
Berryville *(G-1689)*

Schrocks Repair ....G...... 540 879-2406
Dayton *(G-4062)*

SD Davis Welding & Equipment ....G...... 804 691-2112
Ford *(G-5048)*

Sea Marine LLC ....F...... 757 528-9869
Norfolk *(G-9716)*

Shaw LLC ....G...... 540 967-9783
Louisa *(G-7566)*

Sheila Rodriguez ....G...... 425 221-0519
Suffolk *(G-13762)*

Shenandoah Valley Orchard Co ....E...... 540 337-2837
Stuarts Draft *(G-13660)*

Shrews Welding and Fabrica ....G...... 703 785-8035
Bristow *(G-2061)*

Single Source Welding LLC ....G...... 703 919-7791
Warrenton *(G-15052)*

Skyline Fabricating Inc ....G...... 276 498-3560
Raven *(G-10758)*

Smith & Smith Commercial Hood ....G...... 804 605-0311
South Chesterfield *(G-12840)*

Smith Fabrication Weldin ....G...... 276 734-5269
Ridgeway *(G-11854)*

Smiths Welding ....G...... 540 651-2382
Pilot *(G-10359)*

Smittys Welding ....G...... 540 962-7550
Covington *(G-3797)*

Snider & Sons Inc ....G...... 540 626-5849
Pembroke *(G-10284)*

Sopko Manufacturing Inc ....F...... 434 848-3460
Lawrenceville *(G-7185)*

Southfork Enterprises ....G...... 540 879-4372
Dayton *(G-4065)*

Southside Welding ....G...... 757 270-7006
Virginia Beach *(G-14832)*

Standard Welding Corp ....G...... 757 423-0470
Norfolk *(G-9733)*

Star City Welding LLC ....G...... 540 343-1428
Roanoke *(G-12195)*

Steel Mates ....G...... 540 825-7333
Culpeper *(G-3922)*

Stephen Dunnavant ....G...... 804 337-3629
Chesterfield *(G-3529)*

Stern Welding LLC ....G...... 571 283-1355
Chantilly *(G-2499)*

Steve Stone ....G...... 276 956-8451
Henry *(G-6597)*

Stick It Welding & Fabrication ....G...... 757 710-5774
Hallwood *(G-6055)*

Stickmans Welding Service LLC ....G...... 434 547-9774
Dillwyn *(G-4101)*

Straight Line Welding LLC ....G...... 804 837-0363
Chester *(G-3457)*

Streetwerkz Customs ....G...... 804 921-6483
Powhatan *(G-10579)*

Strongerhold Welding & Contg ....G...... 276 608-9968
Vansant *(G-13978)*

Structures Unlimited ....G...... 434 361-2294
Faber *(G-4391)*

▲ Swaby Group ....G...... 540 788-6051
Catlett *(G-2269)*

Swift Mobile Welding LLC ....G...... 757 367-9060
Hampton *(G-6247)*

Sycamore Hollow Welding ....G...... 540 879-2266
Dayton *(G-4066)*

▼ Systems Technology VA LLC ....G...... 540 884-1784
Eagle Rock *(G-4283)*

T & J Wldg & Fabrication LLC ....G...... 757 672-9929
Suffolk *(G-13770)*

Terry Plymouth ....G...... 757 838-2718
Hampton *(G-6252)*

Tidewater Wldg Fabrication LLC ....G...... 757 636-6630
Chesapeake *(G-3340)*

Timothy D Falls ....G...... 540 987-8142
Woodville *(G-15862)*

TMC Welding ....G...... 703 455-9709
Springfield *(G-13099)*

TNT Piping and Welding ....G...... 804 224-1634
Fredericksburg *(G-5495)*

Toby Loritsch Inc ....G...... 540 389-1522
Salem *(G-12575)*

Toms Welding ....G...... 434 989-1553
Arvonia *(G-1234)*

Top Bead Welding Service Inc ....E...... 540 901-8730
Broadway *(G-2098)*

Torchs Mobile Welding ....G...... 804 216-0412
Mechanicsville *(G-8686)*

Total Welding Solutions LLC ....G...... 703 898-8720
Haymarket *(G-6450)*

Tribe 9 LLC ....G...... 757 542-5348
Newport News *(G-9362)*

Triple Gold Welding LLC ....G...... 804 370-0082
West Point *(G-15162)*

Tritech Solutions Virginia Inc ....G...... 434 664-2140
Appomattox *(G-824)*

Trl Inc ....G...... 276 794-7196
Castlewood *(G-2258)*

Truitts Welding Service ....G...... 757 787-7290
Onancock *(G-10198)*

Turners Welding ....G...... 540 373-1107
King George *(G-7116)*

Tweedies Repair Service ....G...... 540 576-2617
Penhook *(G-10286)*

Twin City Welding Company ....F...... 276 669-9322
Bristol *(G-1992)*

United Welding Inc ....G...... 540 628-2286
Fredericksburg *(G-5496)*

Unlimited Welding LLC ....G...... 540 683-4776
Middletown *(G-8745)*

Valley Precision Incorporated ....E...... 540 941-8178
Waynesboro *(G-15142)*

Valley Welding ....G...... 276 733-7942
Barren Springs *(G-1576)*

Valley Welding ....G...... 276 733-7943
Draper *(G-4137)*

Valley Welding Inc ....G...... 540 338-5323
Purcellville *(G-10684)*

Van Der Hyde Dan ....G...... 434 250-7389
Chatham *(G-2940)*

Venton Fab & Welding ....G...... 540 981-1550
Vinton *(G-14191)*

Veterans Welding LLC ....G...... 804 904-7951
Richmond *(G-11436)*

Virginia Mtal Fabrications LLC ....G...... 540 292-0562
Churchville *(G-3623)*

Virginia Welding LLC ....G...... 703 263-1964
Chantilly *(G-2516)*

W & B Fabricators Inc ....F...... 276 928-1060
Rocky Gap *(G-12308)*

Walkers Certified Welding Inc ....G...... 804 541-2612
Hopewell *(G-6943)*

Walkers Welding ....G...... 214 779-0089
Purcellville *(G-10686)*

Wards Wldg & Fabrication LLC ....G...... 540 219-1460
Brandy Station *(G-1942)*

Watts Fabrication & Welding ....G...... 804 798-5988
Ashland *(G-1507)*

WEB Welding LLC ....G...... 703 212-4840
Alexandria *(G-380)*

Weld Pro LLC ....G...... 434 531-5811
Troy *(G-13937)*

Welding & Fabrication LLC ....G...... 540 907-7461
Fredericksburg *(G-5502)*

Welding Fabrication & Design ....G...... 757 739-0025
Chesapeake *(G-3373)*

Welding Unlimited ....G...... 540 833-4146
Linville *(G-7438)*

Weldment Dynamics LLC ....G...... 540 840-7866
Mineral *(G-8953)*

Weldone Inc ....G...... 804 784-8860
Richmond *(G-11445)*

Weldprotech Inc ....G...... 757 485-3293
Chesapeake *(G-3374)*

Wendell Welder LLC ....G...... 804 935-6856
Richmond *(G-11822)*

West End Machine & Welding ....E...... 804 266-9631
Richmond *(G-11446)*

West Engineering Company Inc ....E...... 804 798-3966
Ashland *(G-1508)*

Whispering Pines Weld & Iron ....G...... 434 465-0704
Palmyra *(G-10260)*

Whitleys Welding Inc ....G...... 804 350-6203
Powhatan *(G-10585)*

Williams Fabrication Inc ....E...... 540 862-4200
Covington *(G-3804)*

Williams Welding ....G...... 540 465-8818
Strasburg *(G-13602)*

Willis Welding & Machine Co ....G...... 540 427-3038
Roanoke *(G-12228)*

Wiseman Weld Fabrication ....G...... 571 393-8480
Woodbridge *(G-15833)*

Wobsers Welding Works LLC ....G...... 757 570-0440
Smithfield *(G-12744)*

Woerner Welding & Fabrication ....G...... 804 349-6563
Midlothian *(G-8922)*

Wonder Bug Welding ....G...... 703 354-9499
Alexandria *(G-612)*

▲ Wortham Machine and Welding ....F...... 434 676-8080
Kenbridge *(G-7037)*

Wrights Iron Inc ....G...... 540 661-1089
Orange *(G-10235)*

7694 Armature Rewinding Shops

Ace Rebuilders Inc ....F...... 804 798-3838
Ashland *(G-1362)*

Anlac LLC ....G...... 703 370-3500
Alexandria *(G-135)*

Austin Industrial Services LLC ....F...... 804 232-8940
Richmond *(G-11494)*

Bi State Coil Winding Inc ....G...... 276 956-3106
Ridgeway *(G-11839)*

Cole Electric of Virginia Inc ....G...... 276 935-7562
Grundy *(G-6029)*

Cuton Power Inc ....G...... 703 996-9350
Chantilly *(G-2401)*

Dougs Mobile Electric ....G...... 757 438-6045
Norfolk *(G-9532)*

Electric Motor and Contg Co ....C...... 757 487-2121
Chesapeake *(G-3084)*

Electric Works ....G...... 540 381-2917
Christiansburg *(G-3586)*

Engine Scout Professionals LLC ....G...... 757 621-8526
Portsmouth *(G-10423)*

F & R Electric Inc ....F...... 276 979-8480
North Tazewell *(G-10099)*

Industrial Apparatus Repr Inc ....F...... 540 343-9240
Roanoke *(G-11937)*

Integrity National Corp ....G...... 540 455-2340
Ruther Glen *(G-12456)*

Jims Electric Motor Co Inc ....F...... 703 550-8624
Lorton *(G-7499)*

K E Marine ....G...... 757 787-1313
Accomac *(G-72)*

Land Electric Company ....G...... 757 625-0444
Chesapeake *(G-3174)*

Lineage Mechanical LLC ....G...... 804 687-5649
Henrico *(G-6530)*

Lloyd Elc Co Harrisonburg Inc ....G...... 540 433-5335
Harrisonburg *(G-6340)*

Lloyd Electric Co Inc ....F...... 540 982-0135
Roanoke *(G-12127)*

Loudon Street Electric Svcs ....G...... 540 662-8463
Winchester *(G-15553)*

Mahoy Electric Service Co Inc ....G...... 540 977-0035
Blue Ridge *(G-1851)*

Marion Electric Company ....G...... 276 783-4765
Marion *(G-8233)*

NM Mechanic Road Service LLC ....G...... 571 237-4810
Woodbridge *(G-15761)*

Obrien Machine Repair ....G...... 757 898-1387
Yorktown *(G-15983)*

Parks Electric Motor Repair ....G...... 540 389-6911
Salem *(G-12553)*

Prices Electric Motor Repair ....G...... 540 896-9451
Timberville *(G-13852)*

Roanoke Electric Works ....G...... 540 992-3203
Troutville *(G-13916)*

S&S Electric Motor Service Inc ....G...... 540 577-7366
Radford *(G-10739)*

Tatums Cstm Exhaust & Met Repr ....G...... 276 692-4884
Critz *(G-3824)*

Thompson Electric Motor Svc ....G...... 434 372-3814
Chase City *(G-2917)*

Transonic Power Controls & Svc ....G...... 703 754-8943
Haymarket *(G-6451)*

▲ Trevor LLC ....G...... 434 528-3884
Lynchburg *(G-7827)*

Twin City Motor Exchange Inc ....G...... 276 326-3606
Bluefield *(G-1884)*

Wheeler Maintenance Repair ....G...... 804 586-9836
Waverly *(G-15090)*

Winchester Truck Repair LLC ....G...... 540 398-7995
Winchester *(G-15514)*

Zerk Motors LLC ....G...... 540 322-2003
Fredericksburg *(G-5505)*

ALPHABETIC SECTION

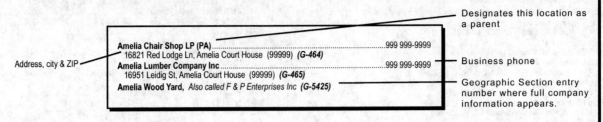

Designates this location as a parent

Address, city & ZIP

Amelia Chair Shop LP (PA)
16821 Red Lodge Ln, Amelia Court House (99999) *(G-464)* 999 999-9999
Amelia Lumber Company Inc
16951 Leidig St, Amelia Court House (99999) *(G-465)* 999 999-9999
Amelia Wood Yard, *Also called F & P Enterprises Inc (G-5425)*

Business phone

Geographic Section entry number where full company information appears.

See footnotes for symbols and codes identification.

* Companies listed alphabetically.

* Complete physical or mailing address.

---

01 Communique Laboratory Inc 703 224-8262
1100 N Glebe Rd Ste 1010 Arlington (22201) *(G-833)*
1 A Life Safer 757 809-0406
1926 Wilroy Rd Ste C Suffolk (23434) *(G-13662)*
1 A Lifesafer Inc 800 634-3077
175 Independence Blvd Christiansburg (24073) *(G-3567)*
1 A Lifesafer Inc 800 634-3077
263 Millwood Ave Winchester (22601) *(G-15523)*
1 A Lifesafer Inc 800 634-3077
5712 General Wash Dr Alexandria (22312) *(G-393)*
1 A Lifesafer Inc 800 634-3077
9108 Manassas Dr Ste A Manassas Park (20111) *(G-8185)*
1 Agrocare, Fairfax *Also called J K Enterprise Inc (G-4483)*
1 Hour A 24 Hr Er A VA Bch Lck 757 295-8288
313 W Bute St Norfolk (23510) *(G-9409)*
10 10 LLC 757 627-4311
259 W York St Norfolk (23510) *(G-9410)*
10 Times Better LLC 850 258-8880
13249 Woodlake Dr Carrollton (23314) *(G-2239)*
10fold Wallets LLC 804 982-0003
1329 Amherst Ave Richmond (23227) *(G-11069)*
123945495max Gun Shop, Harrisonburg *Also called Elks Club 450 (G-6313)*
12th Tee LLC 276 620-7601
200 Golf Club Ln Wytheville (24382) *(G-15873)*
13 Stitches LLC 804 739-8982
13810 Brandy Oaks Pl Chesterfield (23832) *(G-3471)*
141 Repellent Inc 540 421-3956
1 High Meadow Dr Lexington (24450) *(G-7385)*
1602 Group LLC 703 933-0024
5600 General Wash Dr Alexandria (22312) *(G-394)*
1816 Potters Road LLC 757 428-1170
1816 Potters Rd Virginia Beach (23454) *(G-14194)*
1a Smart Start 703 330-1372
10400 Morias Ct Unit A Manassas (20110) *(G-7908)*
1a Smart Start LLC 434 336-1202
705 N Main St Emporia (23847) *(G-4351)*
1click LLC 703 307-6026
7123 Layton Dr Springfield (22150) *(G-12933)*
1earthmatters LLC 202 412-8882
12404b Liberty Bridge Rd Fairfax (22033) *(G-4393)*
1st Choice Accessories LLC 410 615-1578
21119 Fireside Ct Sterling (20164) *(G-13336)*
1st Signage and Lighting LLC 276 229-4200
10086 Woolwine Hwy 5-C Woolwine (24185) *(G-15863)*
1st Stop Electronics LLC 804 931-0517
1209 Garber St Richmond (23231) *(G-11070)*
1trybe Inc 540 270-6043
15112 Windy Hollow Cir Gainesville (20155) *(G-5567)*
2 Busy Brooms Cleaning Service 540 476-1190
779 Paine Run Rd Grottoes (24441) *(G-6011)*
2 Cities Press LLC 434 249-6043
1957 Ridgetop Dr Charlottesville (22903) *(G-2719)*
2 Hearts 1 Dress LLC 540 300-0655
614 Caroline St Fredericksburg (22401) *(G-5166)*
2 P Products 804 273-9822
8205 Costin Dr Richmond (23229) *(G-11071)*
20-X Industries LLC 540 922-0005
186 Doe Creek Rd Pembroke (24136) *(G-10280)*
2050community LLC 202 744-6031
300 25th St Apt 323 Virginia Beach (23451) *(G-14195)*
215 Gear, Virginia Beach *Also called Trident SEC & Holdings LLC (G-14893)*
21st Century AMP LLC 571 345-8990
5128 25th Pl N Arlington (22207) *(G-834)*
21st Century Science Assoc Inc 703 777-6943
60 Sycolin Rd Se Ste 203 Leesburg (20175) *(G-7212)*
22 Church LLC 540 342-2817
22 Church Ave Sw Roanoke (24011) *(G-12026)*
2308 Granby Street Assoc LLC 757 627-4844
2308 Granby St Norfolk (23517) *(G-9411)*

23o5 Publishing House 757 738-9309
109 Gainsborough Sq Chesapeake (23320) *(G-2948)*
247 Publishing Inc 757 639-8856
905 Poquoson Xing Chesapeake (23320) *(G-2949)*
2r2s Inc 804 262-6922
1421 Greycourt Ave Richmond (23227) *(G-11072)*
3 Degrees Publishing LLC 757 634-3164
3806 Banstr Rvr Rch Apt D Portsmouth (23703) *(G-10386)*
3 Donuts Publishing LLC 703 542-7941
43868 Paramount Pl Chantilly (20152) *(G-2524)*
3 Gypsies Candle Company LLC 703 300-2307
9663 Janet Rose Ct Manassas (20111) *(G-8016)*
3 S I, Vienna *Also called 3s Group Inc (G-14001)*
30+ Denim/Leather Project 301 233-0968
5800 Quantrell Ave # 716 Alexandria (22312) *(G-395)*
300 Qubits LLC 202 320-0196
425 N Jackson St Arlington (22201) *(G-835)*
3189 Apple Rd Ne LLC 703 455-5989
9325 Castle Hill Rd Springfield (22153) *(G-12934)*
3300 Artesian Bot Wtr Co LLC 276 928-9903
1593 Wilderness Rd Bland (24315) *(G-1834)*
3314 Monument Ave LLC 804 285-9770
607 Baldwin Rd Henrico (23229) *(G-6468)*
35 Printing LLC 804 926-5737
7069 Gregory Ln Disputanta (23842) *(G-4102)*
3cats Promo 540 586-7014
320 Hunting Ln Goode (24556) *(G-5888)*
3d Central, Richmond *Also called Carrythewhatreplications LLC (G-11522)*
3d Design and Mfg LLC 804 214-3229
2620 Farmington Ln Powhatan (23139) *(G-10527)*
3d Designs Dazzling Dream Desi 703 231-9540
12759 Cara Dr Woodbridge (22192) *(G-15639)*
3d Herndon 202 746-6176
761a Monroe St Herndon (20170) *(G-6598)*
3d Imging Smltion Corp Amricas 800 570-0363
365 Herndon Pkwy Ste 18 Herndon (20170) *(G-6599)*
3d Systems, Herndon *Also called Vidar Systems Corporation (G-6838)*
3disc, Herndon *Also called 3d Imging Smltion Corp Amricas (G-6599)*
3dxtremes 757 741-8671
501 Boush St Ste B Norfolk (23510) *(G-9412)*
3M Cleaners, Springfield *Also called John I Mercado (G-13028)*
3mp1re Clothing Co 540 892-3484
5642 Trafalgar Park Richmond (23228) *(G-11073)*
3r Behavioral Solutions Inc 571 332-6232
4203 Kimbrelee Ct Alexandria (22309) *(G-396)*
3s Group Inc 703 281-5015
125 Church St Ne Ste 204 Vienna (22180) *(G-14001)*
4 Kees Inc 757 249-2584
744 Village Green Pkwy Newport News (23602) *(G-9154)*
4 Shores Trnsprting Lgstix LLC 804 319-6247
1304 Elmshadow Dr Richmond (23231) *(G-11074)*
43rd St Gallery, The, Richmond *Also called Robin Cage Pottery (G-11745)*
460 Machine Company 804 861-8787
6104 Hardware Dr Prince George (23875) *(G-10586)*
4c North America Inc 540 850-8470
1765 Greensboro Stn Pl 90 Mc Lean (22102) *(G-8383)*
4gurus LLC (PA) **703 520-5084**
4169 Lower Park Dr Fairfax (22030) *(G-4587)*
4gurus LLC 703 520-5084
4181 Lower Park Dr Fairfax (22030) *(G-4588)*
4l Inc 434 792-0020
329 Riverview Dr Danville (24541) *(G-3951)*
4wave Inc 703 787-9283
22710 Executive Dr # 203 Sterling (20166) *(G-13337)*
5 Plus 7 Bookbinding 571 499-0511
5509 5th St S Arlington (22204) *(G-836)*
50 West Vineyards 571 367-4760
39060 John Mosby Hwy Middleburg (20117) *(G-8715)*

A

**A
L
P
H
A
B
E
T
I
C**

501 Franklin LLC..804 777-9000
  501 E Franklin St Richmond (23219) *(G-11465)*

5654 VI Byway, Bedford *Also called Polythane of Virginia Inc (G-1651)*

5gl Software Inc...703 861-3644
  4117 Marble Ln Fairfax (22033) *(G-4394)*

5th Element Co...800 684-3144
  8534 Terminal Rd Lorton (22079) *(G-7456)*

6304 Gravel Avenue LLC................................571 287-7544
  14000 Thunderbolt Pl K Chantilly (20151) *(G-2359)*

64 Ways Trucking/Hauling LLC........................804 801-5330
  2101 Decatur St Richmond (23224) *(G-11466)*

6th Floor Candle Company LLC......................917 580-2251
  6410 Castlefin Way Alexandria (22315) *(G-397)*

7 Up Bottling, Richmond *Also called Canada Dry Potomac Corporation (G-11517)*

710 Essentials LLC.....................................540 748-4393
  6901 Countryside Ln Spotsylvania (22551) *(G-12880)*

7430 Broken Ridge LLC................................571 354-0488
  11212 Carriage House Ct Fredericksburg (22408) *(G-5239)*

757 Prints..757 774-6834
  3506 Remington Ct Virginia Beach (23453) *(G-14196)*

757 Surfboards...757 348-2030
  593 S Birdneck Rd Ste 101 Virginia Beach (23451) *(G-14197)*

7m Graphix Inc...703 751-6971
  3160 Spring St Ste B Fairfax (22031) *(G-4395)*

7m Graphix LLC...703 910-0915
  945 Highams Ct Woodbridge (22191) *(G-15640)*

8 Shires Coloniale Distillery..........................757 378-2456
  7218 Merrimac Trl Williamsburg (23185) *(G-15198)*

8020 Software LLC....................................434 466-8020
  1015 Glenwood Station Ln Charlottesville (22901) *(G-2585)*

804 Signs LLC...804 277-4272
  10978 Richardson Rd Ashland (23005) *(G-1359)*

80protons LLC...571 215-5453
  4445 Corp Ln Ste 264 Virginia Beach (23462) *(G-14198)*

83 Gas & Grocery Inc.................................276 926-4388
  Rr 83 Clintwood (24228) *(G-3685)*

868 Estate Vineyards, Hillsboro *Also called Silhouette Vineyards LLC (G-6879)*

888 Brands LLC.......................................757 741-2056
  1715 Endeavor Dr Williamsburg (23185) *(G-15199)*

8th-Element LLC.......................................757 481-6146
  2076 Thomas Bishop Ln Virginia Beach (23454) *(G-14199)*

911 C.A.S.P.E.R. Systems, Woolwine *Also called 1st Signage and Lighting LLC (G-15863)*

A B & J Coal Company Inc..........................276 530-7786
  237 Main St Grundy (24614) *(G-6027)*

A & A, Newport News *Also called Anthony Lamon Williams (G-9168)*

A & A Logging LLC....................................540 229-2830
  2041 Leon Rd Culpeper (22701) *(G-3861)*

A & A Machine...540 482-0480
  80 Energy Blvd Rocky Mount (24151) *(G-12309)*

A & A Precision Machining LLC........................804 493-8416
  80 Industrial Park Rd Montross (22520) *(G-9023)*

A & B Bakery...540 965-5500
  4420 Johnson Creek Rd Covington (24426) *(G-3776)*

A & B Machine Co Inc.................................757 482-0505
  633 Water Oak Ct Chesapeake (23322) *(G-2950)*

A & G Coal Corporation (PA).........................276 328-3421
  302 S Jefferson St # 500 Roanoke (24011) *(G-12027)*

A & J Seamless Gutters Inc..........................757 291-6890
  122 Tazewell Rd Newport News (23608) *(G-9155)*

A & J Welding, Winchester *Also called Alan Forney Jr (G-15374)*

A & L Transport LLC..................................757 735-0047
  509 Delham Rd Portsmouth (23701) *(G-10387)*

A & R Cabinet Co Inc.................................804 261-4098
  10190 Purcell Rd Henrico (23228) *(G-6469)*

A & R Printing...434 829-2030
  500 N Main St Emporia (23847) *(G-4352)*

A & S Global Industries LLC..........................757 773-0119
  1545 Steeple Dr Suffolk (23433) *(G-13663)*

A & S Screen Printing.................................540 464-9042
  176 W Midland Trl Lexington (24450) *(G-7386)*

A & S Screen Printing and EMB, Lexington *Also called A & S Screen Printing (G-7386)*

A & T Partners Inc....................................703 707-8246
  298 Sunset Park Dr Herndon (20170) *(G-6600)*

A & V Precision Machine Inc..........................804 222-9466
  5710 Charles City Cir Richmond (23231) *(G-11075)*

A & W Masonry Specialists............................757 327-3492
  2147 Cunningham Dr # 104 Hampton (23666) *(G-6065)*

A 1 Coating...757 351-5544
  1801 River Rock Arch Virginia Beach (23456) *(G-14200)*

A 1 Painting of Richmond.............................804 237-9939
  13817 Barnes Spring Rd Midlothian (23112) *(G-8766)*

A 1 Smart Start Inc...................................276 644-3045
  108 Vance St Bristol (24201) *(G-1963)*

A 1 Welding Services..................................434 831-2562
  4 Rockfish Xing Schuyler (22969) *(G-12649)*

A A Business Forms & Printing........................703 866-5544
  6007 Captain Marr Ct Fairfax Station (22039) *(G-4700)*

A A J Welding Inc.....................................276 688-0191
  3531 Grapefield Rd Bastian (24314) *(G-1592)*

A and H Office Inc.....................................703 250-0963
  5804 Wood Poppy Ct Burke (22015) *(G-2179)*

A and J HM Imprv Angela Towler.....................434 429-5087
  208 Gatewood Ave Danville (24541) *(G-3952)*

A At LLC..316 828-1563
  400 Dupont Blvd Waynesboro (22980) *(G-15091)*

A B B Electric Systems, Bland *Also called ABB Enterprise Software Inc (G-1835)*

A B C Manufacturing Inc..............................540 789-7961
  1721 Kyle Weeks Rd Sw Willis (24380) *(G-15352)*

A B M Enterprises Inc.................................804 561-3655
  16310 Goodes Bridge Rd Amelia Court House (23002) *(G-648)*

A B Printing LLC......................................276 783-2837
  425 S Main St Marion (24354) *(G-8219)*

A Better Ceaning Service, Mechanicsville *Also called A Better Driving School LLC (G-8598)*

A Better Driving School LLC...........................804 874-5521
  9011 Brigadier Rd Mechanicsville (23116) *(G-8598)*

A Better Image...804 358-9912
  2317 Westwood Ave Ste 213 Richmond (23230) *(G-11076)*

A C Furniture, Axton *Also called A C Furniture Company Inc (G-1532)*

A C Furniture Company Inc (PA).......................276 650-3356
  3872 Martin Dr Axton (24054) *(G-1531)*

A C Furniture Company Inc..........................276 650-1802
  3872 Martin Dr Axton (24054) *(G-1532)*

A C Graphics Inc......................................703 246-9466
  2800 Dorr Ave Ste H Fairfax (22031) *(G-4396)*

A C W, Manakin Sabot *Also called Architectural Custom Wdwrk Inc (G-7895)*

A Cab-Pool, Henrico *Also called Cab-Pool Inc (G-6487)*

A Creative Mind LLC...................................757 450-2899
  1939 Kingston Ave Norfolk (23503) *(G-9413)*

A Cut Above Logging LLC............................434 547-5979
  3608 Crymes Rd Meherrin (23954) *(G-8704)*

A D& G Mobile Welding, Virginia Beach *Also called David F Waterbury Jr (G-14392)*

A Descal Matic Corp..................................757 858-5593
  1518 Springmeadow Blvd Norfolk (23518) *(G-9414)*

A E T, Covington *Also called Taghleef Industries Inc (G-3800)*

A Family Heirloom LLC................................434 607-1674
  17 Booker Rd Cumberland (23040) *(G-3934)*

A Frame Digital..571 308-0147
  1934 Old Gallows Rd # 40 Vienna (22182) *(G-14002)*

A G C, Arlington *Also called Associated Gen Contrs of Amer (G-862)*

A G S Hanover Incorporated..........................804 798-1891
  11234 Air Park Rd Ashland (23005) *(G-1360)*

A H I, Waynesboro *Also called American Hardwood Inds LLC (G-15092)*

A Hope Skip and A Stitch LLC.........................804 684-5750
  7914 Snow Haven Ln Gloucester (23061) *(G-5834)*

A J Industries..757 871-4109
  307 Clay St Hampton (23663) *(G-6066)*

A Johnson Linwood...................................804 829-5364
  7141 S Lott Cary Rd Providence Forge (23140) *(G-10617)*

A K Metal Fabricators Inc...........................703 823-1661
  4401 Wheeler Ave Alexandria (22304) *(G-114)*

A L Baird Inc...434 848-2129
  12679 Christanna Hwy Lawrenceville (23868) *(G-7176)*

A L Baird Trucking, Lawrenceville *Also called A L Baird Inc (G-7176)*

A L Duck Jr Inc.......................................757 562-2387
  26532 River Run Trl Zuni (23898) *(G-16011)*

A M H, Chesapeake *Also called American Maritime Holdings Inc (G-2971)*

A M I S, Chesapeake *Also called American Mar & Indus Svcs LLC (G-2968)*

A M T, Virginia Beach *Also called Advanced Machine & Tooling (G-14213)*

A Markus Design......................................703 938-6694
  1709 Burning Tree Dr Vienna (22182) *(G-14003)*

A Metromont Company.................................540 401-0101
  219 Stine Ln Winchester (22603) *(G-15368)*

A Pinch of Charm.....................................757 262-7820
  805 Ashley Pl Newport News (23608) *(G-9156)*

A Place Called There With Sign......................434 594-5576
  2050 Aberdour Rd Jarratt (23867) *(G-7009)*

A Proehl...540 890-6096
  9505 Stewartsville Rd Moneta (24121) *(G-8955)*

A Reason To Write...................................703 481-3277
  3611 Deerberry Ct Fairfax (22033) *(G-4397)*

A Simple Life Magazine...............................276 238-2403
  879 Walkers Knob Rd Woodlawn (24381) *(G-15843)*

A Smith Bowman Distillery, Fredericksburg *Also called Bowman Distillery Inc A Smith (G-5255)*

A Sorted Affiar Richmond LLC.......................804 464-9820
  8605 Seldondale Ln Richmond (23229) *(G-11077)*

A Special Occasion LLC.............................757 868-3160
  110 Lee Ave Poquoson (23662) *(G-10363)*

A Stitch In Time.....................................276 781-2014
  6620 Lee Hwy Atkins (24311) *(G-1515)*

A Stitch In Time LLC.................................757 478-4878
  4009 Bakerfield Rd Virginia Beach (23453) *(G-14201)*

A Taste of LLC.......................................540 848-3186
  33 Wellspring Dr Fredericksburg (22405) *(G-5395)*

A To Z Lettering, Mechanicsville *Also called Steve D Gilnett (G-8682)*

A Toast To Canvas...................................804 363-4395
  10272 Cherylann Rd North Chesterfield (23236) *(G-9804)*

A Touch of Elegance LLC 434 634-4592
339 Halifax St Emporia (23847) ***(G-4353)***
A V Publication Corp 276 251-1760
386 Hainted Rock Ln Ararat (24053) ***(G-829)***
A Williams Transport LLC 804 896-5878
13926 Hull Street Rd # 1083 Midlothian (23112) ***(G-8767)***
A Z Printing and Dup Corp (PA) **703 549-0949**
421 Clifford Ave Alexandria (22305) ***(G-115)***
A Z Printing and Dup Corp 703 549-0949
2000a Jffrson Davis Hwy F Alexandria (22301) ***(G-116)***
A&D Distributors, Chesapeake *Also called Ambassador Religious Supply* ***(G-2962)***
A&F Ccuston Cabinetry Built 703 598-7686
21806 Petworth Ct Ashburn (20147) ***(G-1235)***
A&H Welding Inc 703 628-4817
6236 Indian Run Pkwy Alexandria (22312) ***(G-398)***
A&M Designs, Dumfries *Also called Anthony Biel* ***(G-4234)***
A- Systems, Charlottesville *Also called A-Systems Incorporated* ***(G-2720)***
A-1 Security Mfg Corp 804 359-9003
3001 Moore St Richmond (23230) ***(G-11078)***
A-1 Welding, Stephens City *Also called Jennifer Lavey* ***(G-13318)***
A-Systems Incorporated 434 295-7200
2030 Avon Ct Ste 8 Charlottesville (22902) ***(G-2720)***
A-Tech Corporation 703 955-7846
14800 Conference Cntr Dr Chantilly (20151) ***(G-2360)***
A1 Finishing Inc 276 632-2121
100a Tensbury Dr Martinsville (24112) ***(G-8262)***
A1 Service 757 544-0830
733 Lord Nelson Dr Virginia Beach (23464) ***(G-14202)***
AA Renwble Enrgy Hydro Sys Inc 804 739-0045
4101 Hobblebush Ter Moseley (23120) ***(G-9032)***
AAA Iron Works, Alexandria *Also called Caldwell Industries Inc* ***(G-428)***
AAA-Bar Printing & Forms Co, Richmond *Also called Lloyd Enterprises Inc* ***(G-11273)***
Aaacm Green Warrior Inc 703 865-5991
5215 Mornington Ct Fairfax (22032) ***(G-4398)***
Aab Coal Mining Company, Big Stone Gap *Also called Riggs Oil Company* ***(G-1714)***
Aaca Embroidery Screen Prtg 703 880-9872
13200 Lazy Glen Ln Herndon (20171) ***(G-6601)***
Aae Inc 804 427-1111
1352 Anderson Hwy Ste G Powhatan (23139) ***(G-10528)***
Aai Corporation 410 666-1400
277 Dominy Corner Rd Blackstone (23824) ***(G-1809)***
Aai Textron 434 292-5805
1279 W 10th St Ste B Blackstone (23824) ***(G-1810)***
Aandc Sales Inc 703 638-8949
3388 Bristol Ct Woodbridge (22193) ***(G-15641)***
Aard-Alltuf Screenprinters 757 853-7641
4625 E Princess Anne Rd Norfolk (23502) ***(G-9415)***
Aard/Altuf Screen Printers, Norfolk *Also called Aard-Alltuf Screenprinters* ***(G-9415)***
Aardvark Screen Print, Chantilly *Also called Aardvark Swim and Sport Inc* ***(G-2361)***
Aardvark Swim and Sport Inc (PA) **703 631-6045**
14221a Willard Rd # 1050 Chantilly (20151) ***(G-2361)***
Aaron D Crouse 757 827-6123
3308 W Lewis Rd Hampton (23666) ***(G-6067)***
Aaron S Walters 804 783-6925
1021 E Cary St Richmond (23219) ***(G-11467)***
Aavera Engineering LLc 434 922-7525
596 Ashby Woods Rd Monroe (24574) ***(G-8986)***
AB, Locust Grove *Also called Larry Graves* ***(G-7447)***
AB Lighting and Production LLC 703 550-7707
8249 Backlick Rd Ste F Lorton (22079) ***(G-7457)***
Abacus Racing & Machine Svcs 757 363-8878
1372 Baker Rd Virginia Beach (23455) ***(G-14203)***
Abasn Promotional Products, Roanoke *Also called Jeannie Jackson Green* ***(G-12110)***
ABB Enterprise Software Inc 434 575-2169
2134 Philpott Rd South Boston (24592) ***(G-12745)***
ABB Enterprise Software Inc 276 688-3325
171 Industry Dr Bland (24315) ***(G-1835)***
ABB Power Protection LLC (HQ) **804 236-3300**
5900 Eastport Blvd Ste V Richmond (23231) ***(G-11079)***
Abbadon Skateboards LLC 703 280-4818
4006 Winterset Dr Annandale (22003) ***(G-727)***
Abbey Staunton 540 580-1271
2217 N Augusta St Staunton (24401) ***(G-13238)***
Abbott Brothers Inc 804 436-1001
60 Simmons Ln White Stone (22578) ***(G-15185)***
Abbott Crtcal Care Systems Div, Altavista *Also called Abbott Laboratories* ***(G-622)***
Abbott Laboratories 434 369-3100
1518 Main St Altavista (24517) ***(G-622)***
Abbott Laboratories Inc 434 369-3100
215 Clarion Rd Altavista (24517) ***(G-623)***
Abbott Nutrition, Altavista *Also called Abbott Laboratories Inc* ***(G-623)***
Abbott Nutrition Mfg Inc 434 369-3100
1518 Main St Altavista (24517) ***(G-624)***
ABC Graphics 804 368-0276
11435 Mount Hermon Rd Ashland (23005) ***(G-1361)***
ABC Imaging 214 231-1332
5290 Shawnee Rd Lbby Alexandria (22312) ***(G-399)***
ABC Imaging 571 379-4299
8480 Virginia Meadows Dr Manassas (20109) ***(G-8017)***
ABC Imaging of Washington (PA) **202 429-8870**
5290 Shawnee Rd Ste 300 Alexandria (22312) ***(G-400)***
ABC Imaging of Washington 703 848-2997
8603 Westwood Center Dr Vienna (22182) ***(G-14004)***
ABC Imaging of Washington 202 429-8870
14101 Parke Long Ct Chantilly (20151) ***(G-2362)***
ABC Imaging of Washington 703 396-9081
10498 Colonel Ct Manassas (20110) ***(G-7909)***
ABC Imaging of Washington 571 514-1033
601 Carlisle Dr Herndon (20170) ***(G-6602)***
ABC Petwear Inc 804 730-3890
8005 Strawhorn Dr Mechanicsville (23116) ***(G-8599)***
ABC Printing 434 847-7468
184 Scottsmill Rd Madison Heights (24572) ***(G-7866)***
ABC Rubber Stamps, Roanoke *Also called Earl Wood Printing Co* ***(G-12082)***
Abe Lincoln Flags & Banners 703 204-1116
8634 Lee Hwy Fairfax (22031) ***(G-4399)***
Abeck Inc 540 375-2841
405 W 4th St Salem (24153) ***(G-12471)***
Abell Corporation 540 665-3062
161 Mcghee Rd Winchester (22603) ***(G-15369)***
Abingdon Millwork 276 676-2951
550 Lowry Dr Sw Abingdon (24210) ***(G-1)***
Abingdon Olive Oil Company, Abingdon *Also called Olive Oils Abingdon Assoc LLC* ***(G-52)***
Abingdon Pre Cast Products 276 628-2472
15455 Steinman Rd Abingdon (24210) ***(G-2)***
Abingdon Printing Inc 276 628-4221
1272 Hill St Abingdon (24210) ***(G-3)***
Abingdon Sign Co Inc 276 628-2594
17156 Lee Hwy Abingdon (24210) ***(G-4)***
Abingdon Steel Inc 276 628-9269
25479 Hillman Hwy Abingdon (24210) ***(G-5)***
Abington Sunshade & Blinds Co 540 435-6450
7680 Kathleen Ct Penn Laird (22846) ***(G-10287)***
Ablaze Interiors Inc 757 427-0075
4048 Muddy Creek Rd Virginia Beach (23457) ***(G-14204)***
Ablcomp LLC 434 942-5325
147 Mill Ridge Rd Ste 138 Lynchburg (24502) ***(G-7630)***
Able Mfg LLC 804 550-4885
10487 Washington Hwy Glen Allen (23059) ***(G-5703)***
Aboriginal Prints LLC 804 994-1987
4248 Oakleys Ct Ste C Richmond (23223) ***(G-11468)***
About Chuck Seipp 703 517-0670
135 Campfield Ln Winchester (22602) ***(G-15370)***
About Time 757 253-0143
3201 Derby Ln Williamsburg (23185) ***(G-15200)***
Above Ground Level 540 338-4363
18331 Turnberry Dr Round Hill (20141) ***(G-12373)***
Above Rim LLC 703 407-9398
14505 Holshire Way Haymarket (20169) ***(G-6411)***
Absolute Anesthesia 434 277-9360
3818 Patrick Henry Hwy Piney River (22964) ***(G-10360)***
Absolute EMC Llc 703 774-7505
14126 Wood Rock Way Centreville (20121) ***(G-2287)***
Absolute Furn Solutions LLC 757 550-5630
3739 Holland Blvd Chesapeake (23323) ***(G-2951)***
Absolute Machine Enterprises 276 956-1171
212 Pulaski Rd Ridgeway (24148) ***(G-11838)***
Absolute Perfection, Appomattox *Also called Suzanne Henri Inc* ***(G-823)***
Absolute Precision LLC 757 968-3005
103 Brigade Dr Yorktown (23692) ***(G-15930)***
Absolute Signs Inc 703 229-9436
11900 Livingston Rd # 161 Manassas (20109) ***(G-8018)***
Absolute Signs Inc 540 668-6807
15573 Woodgrove Rd Hillsboro (20132) ***(G-6859)***
Absolute Stone Design LLC 804 752-2001
11200 Washington Hwy Glen Allen (23059) ***(G-5704)***
Absolute Welding LLC 434 569-5351
586 Hardtimes Rd Farmville (23901) ***(G-4936)***
Absolutely Fabulous 757 615-5732
2937 West Gibbs Rd Virginia Beach (23457) ***(G-14205)***
Absolutely Fabulous At Towne, Virginia Beach *Also called Absolutely Fabulous* ***(G-14205)***
Abstruse Technical Services 540 489-8940
635 Thompson Ridge Cir Ferrum (24088) ***(G-4966)***
Abuelita Mexican Foods, Manassas Park *Also called S & K Industries Inc* ***(G-8209)***
Abwasser Technologies Inc 757 453-7505
3091 Brickhouse Ct Virginia Beach (23452) ***(G-14206)***
AC Atlas Publishing 301 980-0711
6811 Sholes Ct Warrenton (20187) ***(G-14976)***
AC Cetera Inc 724 532-3363
9812 Bacon Ct Fairfax (22032) ***(G-4400)***
Acacia Acquisitions LLC (HQ) **703 554-1600**
21445 Beaumeade Cir Ashburn (20147) ***(G-1236)***
Acacia Investment Holdings LLC (PA) **703 554-1600**
1850 Towers Crescent Plz # 500 Tysons (22182) ***(G-13940)***
Academics In A Box Inc 757 286-0673
1508 Sams Cir Chesapeake (23320) ***(G-2952)***

ALPHABETIC

Academy Boys and Girls Soccer 804 380-9005
6400 Belmont Rd Chesterfield (23832) *(G-3472)*

ACC Cabinetry LLC 540 333-0189
409 Jack Enders Blvd # 4 Berryville (22611) *(G-1669)*

Accaceek Precast 540 604-7726
119 Jumping Branch Rd Stafford (22554) *(G-13111)*

Accelerated Printing Corp Inc 703 437-1084
41636 Carter Ridge Ln Leesburg (20176) *(G-7213)*

Accent Signing Company 757 857-8800
2704 Arkansas Ave Norfolk (23513) *(G-9416)*

Access Intelligence LLC 202 296-2814
1911 Fort Myer Dr Ste 310 Arlington (22209) *(G-837)*

Access Prime Techncl Sltns 757 651-6523
616 Pelham Dr Hampton (23669) *(G-6068)*

Access Publishing Co 804 358-0163
413 Stuart Cir Unit 3d Richmond (23220) *(G-11469)*

Access Reports Inc 434 384-5334
1624 Dogwood Ln Lynchburg (24503) *(G-7631)*

Accessible Environments Inc (PA) **757 565-3444**
106 Wingate Dr Williamsburg (23185) *(G-15201)*

Acco Stone, Blacksburg *Also called Salem Stone Corporation* *(G-1786)*

According To Plan LLC 703 953-1584
2503 James Madison Cir Herndon (20171) *(G-6603)*

Accounting Executive Svcs LLC 757 406-1127
1813 While Ln Norfolk (23518) *(G-9417)*

Accounting Technology LLC 434 316-6000
106 Vista Centre Dr Forest (24551) *(G-5049)*

Accuamp Incorporated 540 908-4079
37 Auburn Dr Grottoes (24441) *(G-6012)*

Accuracy Gear LLC 540 230-0257
4988 Lead Mine Rd Hiwassee (24347) *(G-6908)*

Accuracy International N Amer 907 440-4024
3410 Shannon Park Dr # 100 Fredericksburg (22408) *(G-5240)*

Accuracy Press Institute 804 869-8577
5270 Duke St Apt 328 Alexandria (22304) *(G-117)*

Accurate Machine Inc 757 853-2136
3317 Tait Ter Norfolk (23513) *(G-9418)*

Accutec Blades Inc (PA) **800 336-4061**
1 Razor Blade Ln Verona (24482) *(G-13982)*

Accutech Fabrication Inc 434 528-4858
910 Orchard St Lynchburg (24501) *(G-7632)*

Ace Bath Bombs LLC 804 839-8639
207 S 9th Ave Hopewell (23860) *(G-6916)*

Ace Cabinets & More LLC 757 206-1684
104 Mid Ocean Williamsburg (23188) *(G-15202)*

Ace Hardwood 804 270-4260
11105 Woodbaron Ct Richmond (23233) *(G-11080)*

Ace Industries Virginia LLC 757 292-3321
609 E Main St Apt C Radford (24141) *(G-10702)*

Ace Machining Inc 540 294-2453
321 Sangers Ln Staunton (24401) *(G-13239)*

Ace Rebuilders Inc 804 798-3838
517 S Washington Hwy Ashland (23005) *(G-1362)*

Ace Screen Printing Inc 540 297-2200
1379 Pecks Rd Bedford (24523) *(G-1617)*

Ace Title & Escrow Inc 703 629-5768
5820 Tilbury Rd Alexandria (22310) *(G-401)*

Acel LLC 888 801-2507
9518 Claychin Ct Burke (22015) *(G-2180)*

Aces Embroidery 703 738-4784
28 Lipscomb Ct Sterling (20165) *(G-13338)*

Acesur North America Inc 757 664-2390
981 Scott St Ste 100 Norfolk (23502) *(G-9419)*

Acf, Axton *Also called A C Furniture Company Inc* *(G-1531)*

Acf Environmental, Richmond *Also called Diloreto Partners Inc* *(G-11041)*

Acharya Brothers Computing 703 729-3035
43611 Picketts Corner Ter Ashburn (20148) *(G-1237)*

Aci Partners LLC 703 818-0500
8854 Rixlew Ln Manassas (20109) *(G-8019)*

Aci-Strickland LLC 804 643-7483
2400 Magnolia Ct Richmond (23223) *(G-11470)*

Acintyo Inc 703 349-3400
7423 Old Maple Sq Mc Lean (22102) *(G-8384)*

Acken Signs, Bluefield *Also called Rabbit Creek Partners LLC* *(G-1877)*

Acme Ink Inc 757 373-3614
940 Culver Ln Virginia Beach (23454) *(G-14207)*

Aco Corporation (PA) **757 480-2875**
3500 Virginia Beach Blvd # 200 Virginia Beach (23452) *(G-14208)*

Aco Corporation 757 480-2875
1430 Ballentine Blvd Norfolk (23504) *(G-9420)*

Acorn Press LLC 703 760-0920
1110 Brook Valley Ln Mc Lean (22102) *(G-8385)*

Acorn Sales Company Inc 804 359-0505
1506 Tomlynn St Richmond (23230) *(G-11081)*

Acorn Sign Graphics Inc 804 726-6999
4109 W Clay St Richmond (23230) *(G-11082)*

Acorn Sign Manufacturing, Richmond *Also called Acorn Sales Company Inc* *(G-11081)*

Acoustcal Drywall Slutions LLC 703 722-6637
43730 Piedmont Hunt Ter Ashburn (20148) *(G-1238)*

Acoustical Sheetmetal Inc 757 456-9720
2600 Production Rd Virginia Beach (23454) *(G-14209)*

Acp LLC 276 619-5080
26372 Hillman Hwy Abingdon (24210) *(G-6)*

Acre Media LLC 703 314-4465
6214 Roudsby Ln Alexandria (22315) *(G-402)*

Acro Software Inc 703 753-7508
5331 Chaffins Farm Ct Haymarket (20169) *(G-6412)*

Acrylife Inc 276 228-6704
170 E Franklin St Wytheville (24382) *(G-15874)*

ACS, Lynchburg *Also called Automated Conveyor Systems Inc* *(G-7645)*

ACS, Richmond *Also called Advanced Cgnitive Systems Corp* *(G-11474)*

ACS Division Polymer Chemistry 540 231-3029
Virginia Tech 410 Dvidson Blacksburg (24061) *(G-1720)*

Action Digital Inc 804 358-7289
2317 Westwood Ave Ste 101 Richmond (23230) *(G-11083)*

Action Graphics and Signs Inc (PA) **757 548-5255**
112 Wayne Ave Chesapeake (23320) *(G-2953)*

Action Graphics Signs 757 995-2200
4760 Virginia Beach Blvd Virginia Beach (23462) *(G-14210)*

Action Iron LLC 703 594-2909
14250 Fitzwater Dr Nokesville (20181) *(G-9388)*

Action Machining 703 339-7232
7240 Telegraph Square Dr Lorton (22079) *(G-7458)*

Action Resources Corporation 540 343-5121
1910 Chapman Ave Sw Roanoke (24016) *(G-12028)*

Action Tool Service Inc 757 838-4555
2202 Mingee Dr Hampton (23661) *(G-6069)*

Action Tshirts LLC 804 359-4645
2926 W Marshall St Lowr Richmond (23230) *(G-11084)*

Actionstep Inc 540 809-9326
919 E Main St Ste 1155 Richmond (23219) *(G-11471)*

Active Minerals International 540 771-3865
155 Ashland Dr Winchester (22603) *(G-15371)*

Active Navigation Inc 571 346-7607
11720 Plaza America Dr # 150 Reston (20190) *(G-10777)*

Active Sense Technologies LLC 352 226-1479
165 Park St Se Abingdon (24210) *(G-7)*

Activu Corporation 703 527-4440
1100 Wilson Blvd Arlington (22209) *(G-838)*

Acuity Brands Lighting Inc 804 320-3444
7311 Riverside Dr Richmond (23225) *(G-11472)*

ACUITY BRANDS LIGHTING, INC., Richmond *Also called Acuity Brands Lighting
Inc (G-11472)*

Acuity Tech Holdg Co LLC (PA) **410 290-1411**
1191 Central Park Blvd Fredericksburg (22401) *(G-5167)*

Acutech Signs & Graphics Inc 757 766-2627
26 Research Dr Hampton (23666) *(G-6070)*

Ad Vice Inc 804 730-0503
6400 Mechanicsville Tpke Trpk2 Mechanicsville (23111) *(G-8600)*

Adam N Robinson 540 489-1513
85 Diamond Ave Rocky Mount (24151) *(G-12310)*

Adamantine Precision Tools 804 354-9118
3117 Aspen Ave Richmond (23228) *(G-11085)*

Adams Co LLC 757 721-0427
2681 Indian River Rd Virginia Beach (23456) *(G-14211)*

Adams Machine Shop Inc 434 656-2905
672 E Gretna Rd Gretna (24557) *(G-6001)*

Adams Publishing Group LLC 276 728-7311
804 N Main St Hillsville (24343) *(G-6882)*

Adams Trucking, Millboro *Also called Peter Adams* *(G-8938)*

Adams Welding Service 804 843-4468
2710 King William Ave West Point (23181) *(G-15152)*

Adamson Global Technology Corp 804 748-6453
13101 N Enon Church Rd # 15 Chester (23836) *(G-3382)*

Adani Systems Inc (PA) **703 528-0035**
901 N Pitt St Ste 325 Alexandria (22314) *(G-118)*

Adaptive Elements LLC 571 261-3671
15143 La Jolla Ct Haymarket (20169) *(G-6413)*

Adco Signs Inc 757 787-1393
165 Market St Ste 1 Onancock (23417) *(G-10188)*

Addem Enterprises Inc 540 789-4412
1265 Horse Ridge Rd Nw Willis (24380) *(G-15353)*

Additive Mfg Exch Amex LLC 703 971-3174
5316 Jesmond St Alexandria (22315) *(G-403)*

Addressograph Bartizan LLC 800 552-3282
450 Weaver St Rocky Mount (24151) *(G-12311)*

Adenosine Therapeutics LLC 434 979-1902
1881 N Nash St Unit 301 Arlington (22209) *(G-839)*

Adesso Precision Machine Co 757 857-5544
3517 Argonne Ave Norfolk (23509) *(G-9421)*

Adf Unit Trust Inc 757 926-5252
11815 Ftn Way Ste 300 Newport News (23606) *(G-9157)*

Adgrfx 443 600-7562
500 Ridgecrest Ct Stafford (22554) *(G-13112)*

Adial Corporation 434 243-0570
4098 Wood Ln Keswick (22947) *(G-7041)*

Adial Pharmaceuticals Inc 434 422-9800
1001 Res Pk Blvd Ste 100 Charlottesville (22911) *(G-2586)*

Adidas North America Inc....703 771-6925
241 Fort Evans Rd Ne # 897 Leesburg (20176) *(G-7214)*
Adidas Outlet Store Leesburg, Leesburg *Also called Adidas North America Inc (G-7214)*
Adis America....804 794-2848
1309 Walton Creek Dr Midlothian (23114) *(G-8768)*
Adiva Naturals LLC....804 683-3738
1802 E Franklin St Us Richmond (23223) *(G-11473)*
Adkins Custom Woodworking....276 638-8198
928 Foxfire Rd Martinsville (24112) *(G-8263)*
Adlers Art & Frame, Lorton *Also called Discount Frames Inc (G-7481)*
ADM, Rockingham *Also called Archer-Daniels-Midland Company (G-12240)*
Adme Solutions LLC....540 664-3521
568 Garden Gate Dr Stephens City (22655) *(G-13311)*
Admiral Signworks Corp....757 422-6700
1531 Early St Norfolk (23502) *(G-9422)*
Adnet Systems Inc....571 313-1356
11260 Roger Bacon Dr # 403 Reston (20190) *(G-10778)*
Ado Industries LLC....540 877-2769
140 Theodore Dr Winchester (22602) *(G-15372)*
Adobe Inc....571 765-5400
7930 Jones Branch Dr Fl 5 Mc Lean (22102) *(G-8386)*
Adobe Systems Federal LLC....571 765-5523
7930 Jones Branch Dr # 500 Mc Lean (22102) *(G-8387)*
Adonica L Miller....540 820-0820
6152 Singers Glen Rd Rockingham (22802) *(G-12238)*
Adoorable Ideas, Chester *Also called Teresa Blount (G-3460)*
Adopt A Salsa....703 409-9453
14135 Asher Vw Centreville (20121) *(G-2288)*
Adoptees....571 483-0656
4631 28th Rd S Arlington (22206) *(G-840)*
Adriana Calderon Escalante....703 926-7638
1498 Northern Neck Dr Vienna (22182) *(G-14005)*
Adta & Co Inc....703 930-9280
7039 Columbia Pike Annandale (22003) *(G-728)*
Adult Medical Predictive Devic....434 996-1203
1406 Sandown Ln Keswick (22947) *(G-7042)*
Adv3ntus Software LLC....703 288-3380
8201 Greensboro Dr Ste 71 Mc Lean (22102) *(G-8388)*
Advance Design & Manufacturing....703 256-9550
6460a General Green Way Alexandria (22312) *(G-404)*
Advance Engine Design, North Chesterfield *Also called Cline Automotive Inc (G-9846)*
Advance Graphics, Virginia Beach *Also called Clarke B Gray (G-14342)*
Advance Mezzanine Systems LLC....703 595-1460
1320 Alum Spring Rd Fredericksburg (22401) *(G-5168)*
Advance Signs & Graphics Co....703 359-8005
10608 Orchard St Fairfax (22030) *(G-4589)*
Advance Technology Inc....757 223-6566
316 49th St Newport News (23607) *(G-9158)*
Advanced Air Systems Inc....276 666-8829
113 E Main St Martinsville (24112) *(G-8264)*
Advanced Aircraft Company LLC....757 325-6712
1100 Exploration Way Hampton (23666) *(G-6071)*
Advanced Bioip LLC....301 646-3640
41655 Catoctin Springs Ct Leesburg (20176) *(G-7215)*
Advanced Business Services LLC....757 439-0849
4445 Corporation Ln # 110 Virginia Beach (23462) *(G-14212)*
Advanced Cabinets & Tops Inc....804 355-5541
1726 Arlington Rd Richmond (23230) *(G-11086)*
Advanced Carbide Tool Company....540 582-3289
6802 Lismore Ln Spotsylvania (22551) *(G-12881)*
Advanced Cgnitive Systems Corp....804 397-3373
2601 The Terrace Richmond (23222) *(G-11474)*
Advanced Coating Solutions LLC....540 898-9370
4915 Trade Center Dr Fredericksburg (22408) *(G-5241)*
Advanced Cstm Coatings VA LLC....757 726-2628
39 Leicester Ter Hampton (23666) *(G-6072)*
Advanced Custom Woodworki....804 310-0511
609 Roxbury Indus Ctr Charles City (23030) *(G-2568)*
Advanced Design Fabrication....757 484-4486
1220 Fleetway Dr Ste B Chesapeake (23323) *(G-2954)*
Advanced Drainage Systems Inc....540 261-6131
510 Factory St Buena Vista (24416) *(G-2137)*
Advanced Finishing Systems....804 642-7669
2954 George Wash Mem Hwy Hayes (23072) *(G-6393)*
Advanced Graphics LLC....540 931-4850
801 Cedar Creek Grade Winchester (22601) *(G-15524)*
Advanced Graphics Tech Llc....804 796-3399
11120 Nash Rd Chesterfield (23838) *(G-3473)*
Advanced Integrated Tech LLC....757 416-7407
2427 Ingleside Rd Norfolk (23513) *(G-9423)*
Advanced Leading Solutions Inc....703 447-3876
14641 Lee Hwy Ste D9 Centreville (20121) *(G-2289)*
Advanced Machine & Tooling....757 518-1222
5725 Arrowhead Dr Virginia Beach (23462) *(G-14213)*
Advanced Machining Solutions, Roanoke *Also called Phillips Enterprises VA Inc (G-12147)*
Advanced Metal Finishing of VA....540 344-3216
523 Norfolk Ave Sw Roanoke (24016) *(G-12029)*
Advanced Mfg Restructuring LLC....540 667-5010
720 Seldon Dr Winchester (22601) *(G-15525)*
Advanced Mfg Tech Inc....434 385-7197
28 Millrace Dr Lynchburg (24502) *(G-7633)*
Advanced Nano Adhesives Inc....919 247-6411
360 Firstwatch Dr Moneta (24121) *(G-8956)*
Advanced Packet Switching Inc....703 627-1746
13032 Queen Chapel Rd Woodbridge (22193) *(G-15642)*
Advanced Printing & Graphics, Richmond *Also called Omega Alpha II Inc (G-11315)*
Advanced Resources Intl Inc (PA)....**703 528-8421**
4501 Fairfax Dr Ste 910 Arlington (22203) *(G-841)*
Advanced Rsponse Concepts Corp (HQ)....**703 246-8560**
11250 Waples Mill Rd Fairfax (22030) *(G-4590)*
Advanced Technologies Inc....757 873-3017
875 City Center Blvd Newport News (23606) *(G-9159)*
Advanced Tooling Corporation (PA)....**434 286-7781**
5199 W River Rd Scottsville (24590) *(G-12657)*
Advancing Eyecare (HQ)....**757 853-8888**
5358 Robin Hood Rd Norfolk (23513) *(G-9424)*
Advansix Inc....804 541-5000
905 E Randolph Rd Hopewell (23860) *(G-6917)*
Advansix Inc....804 530-6000
4101 Bermuda Hundred Rd Chester (23836) *(G-3383)*
Advansix Inc....804 504-0009
15801 Woods Edge Rd South Chesterfield (23834) *(G-12793)*
Advanta Flooring Inc....804 530-5004
7518 Whitepine Rd North Chesterfield (23237) *(G-9805)*
Advantage Accnting Bkkping LLC....434 989-0443
8121 Virginia Pine Ct North Chesterfield (23237) *(G-9806)*
Advantage Machine & Engrg....757 488-5085
2043 Ponderosa St Portsmouth (23701) *(G-10388)*
Advantage Puck Group Inc....434 385-9181
109 Ramsey Pl Lynchburg (24501) *(G-7634)*
Advantage Puck Technologies, Lynchburg *Also called Advantage Puck Group Inc (G-7634)*
Advantage Sign Supply Inc....804 798-5784
303 Ashcake Rd Ste J Ashland (23005) *(G-1363)*
Advantage Systems....703 370-4500
3917 Wheeler Ave Alexandria (22304) *(G-119)*
Advantech Inc....703 402-0590
3213 Duke St Alexandria (22314) *(G-120)*
Advantus Corp....804 324-7169
1818 Dock St Petersburg (23803) *(G-10301)*
Advertech Press LLC....804 404-8560
701 Erin Crescent St Richmond (23231) *(G-11087)*
Advertising Images & EMB....703 447-4282
5608 W Marshall St Richmond (23230) *(G-11088)*
Advertising Service Agency....757 622-3429
807 Granby St Norfolk (23510) *(G-9425)*
Advertising Spc & Promotions....540 537-4121
41 Turtleback Path Rd Hardy (24101) *(G-6285)*
Advex Corporation....757 865-6660
41 Research Dr Hampton (23666) *(G-6073)*
Advice Sign Consultants, Mechanicsville *Also called Ad Vice Inc (G-8600)*
Advision Sign Co., Nokesville *Also called Baker Builders LLC (G-9389)*
Advocate-Democrat....423 337-7101
440 Bank St Norfolk (23510) *(G-9426)*
AEC Software Inc....703 450-1980
22611 Markey Ct Ste 113 Sterling (20166) *(G-13339)*
AEC Virginia LLC....434 447-7629
1556 Montgomery St South Hill (23970) *(G-12841)*
AEC Virginia LLC....757 654-6131
3205 6th E Cir Boykins (23827) *(G-1918)*
Aeh Designs....703 860-3204
10721 Oldfield Dr Reston (20191) *(G-10779)*
Aeraspace Corporation....703 554-2906
26b E Loudoun St Round Hill (20141) *(G-12374)*
Aerial and Aquatic Robotics....757 932-0909
1138 Bolling Ave Apt 221a Norfolk (23508) *(G-9427)*
Aerial Machine & Tool Corp (HQ)....**276 952-2006**
4298 Jeb Stuart Hwy Meadows of Dan (24120) *(G-8590)*
Aerial Machine & Tool Corp....276 694-3148
649 Wood Brothers Ln Stuart (24171) *(G-13603)*
Aero Clean Technologies LLC....434 381-0699
1320 Stephenson Ave Lynchburg (24501) *(G-7635)*
Aero Corporation....703 896-7721
4000 Legato Rd Ste 1100 Fairfax (22033) *(G-4401)*
Aero Design & Mfg Co In....218 722-1927
7930 Jones Branch Dr # 900 Mc Lean (22102) *(G-8389)*
Aero International LLC (HQ)....**571 203-8360**
641 S Washington St Alexandria (22314) *(G-121)*
Aero Training Center....757 838-6570
220 Hankins Dr Hampton (23669) *(G-6074)*
Aeroart International Inc....703 406-4376
11797 Hollyview Dr Great Falls (22066) *(G-5934)*
Aerofin, Lynchburg *Also called Air & Liquid Systems Corp (G-7637)*
Aerojet, Culpeper *Also called Atlantic Research Corporation (G-3869)*
Aerojet....703 247-2907
1300 Wilson Blvd Ste 1000 Arlington (22209) *(G-842)*
Aerojet Rocketdyne Inc....703 650-0270
1300 Wilson Blvd Ste 1000 Arlington (22209) *(G-843)*
Aerojet Rocketdyne Inc....540 854-2000
7499 Pine Stake Rd Bldg 5 Culpeper (22701) *(G-3862)*

ALPHABETIC

Aerospace & Technology..757 864-7227
1 E Durand St Hampton (23681) *(G-6075)*
Aerospace Components...276 686-0123
756 Old King Rd 725 Rural Retreat (24368) *(G-12417)*
Aerospace Systems, Falls Church *Also called Northrop Grumman Systems Corp* *(G-4845)*
Aerospace Techniques Inc...860 347-1200
5701 Cleveland St Ste 640 Virginia Beach (23462) *(G-14214)*
Aery Aviation LLC...757 271-1600
305 Cherokee Dr Newport News (23602) *(G-9160)*
Aetas Mobile LLC..704 258-9159
11002 Vale Rd Oakton (22124) *(G-10140)*
Aether Press LLC..703 409-5684
3201 Landover St Apt 803 Alexandria (22305) *(G-122)*
Afd Technologies LLC...561 271-7000
214 40th St Virginia Beach (23451) *(G-14215)*
Affinity Woodworks LLC...330 814-4950
21457 Business Ct Elkwood (22718) *(G-4340)*
Affordable Audio Rental...804 305-6664
5624 Gilling Rd North Chesterfield (23234) *(G-9807)*
Affordable Canvas Virginia LLC.......................................757 718-5330
4356 Alfriends Trl Virginia Beach (23455) *(G-14216)*
Affordable Care Inc...276 928-1427
Intersection Of Hwy 52 61 Rocky Gap (24366) *(G-12304)*
Affordable Companies...703 440-9274
7830 Backlick Rd Ste 404a Springfield (22150) *(G-12935)*
Affordable Fuel Substitute Inc..276 694-8080
864 Dobyns Church Rd Stuart (24171) *(G-13604)*
Affordable Printing & Copies...757 728-9770
1926 E Pembroke Ave Hampton (23663) *(G-6076)*
Affordable Sheds Company...540 657-6770
3209 Jefferson Davis Hwy Stafford (22554) *(G-13113)*
Affordable Wheelchair Lifts, Williamsburg *Also called Km Services LLC* *(G-15267)*
Afg Industries - VA..276 619-6000
18370 Oak Park Dr Abingdon (24210) *(G-8)*
Afgd Inc..804 222-0120
6200 Gorman Rd Henrico (23231) *(G-6470)*
AFL Network Services Inc...864 433-0333
825 Greenbrier Cir Ste C Chesapeake (23320) *(G-2955)*
Aflex Packaging LLC...571 208-9938
7600 Fullerton Rd Unit C Springfield (22153) *(G-12936)*
Afritech LLC..703 550-0392
7912 Morning Ride Ct Alexandria (22315) *(G-405)*
After Affects Custom Furniture.......................................504 510-1792
32 Scotland Rd Hampton (23663) *(G-6077)*
After Curfew Inc...608 214-1289
97 Mesena Dr Apt 302 Lynchburg (24502) *(G-7636)*
After Five Oclock Janitoral, Woodbridge *Also called Paul T Marshall* *(G-15774)*
Aftermarket Parts Solutions..757 227-3166
6336 E Virginia Bch Blvd Norfolk (23502) *(G-9428)*
Aftershock Advisors LLC..703 787-0139
560 Herndon Pkwy Ste 130 Herndon (20170) *(G-6604)*
Afton Chemical Additives Corp (HQ)................................**804 788-5000**
330 S 4th St Richmond (23219) *(G-11475)*
Afton Chemical Corporation (HQ)...................................**804 788-5800**
500 Spring St Richmond (23219) *(G-11476)*
Afton Chemical Corporation..804 788-5250
101 E Byrd St Richmond (23219) *(G-11477)*
Afton Chemical Corporation..804 788-5800
330 S 4th St Richmond (23219) *(G-11478)*
Afton Chemical Corporation..804 752-8420
11289 Central Dr C Ashland (23005) *(G-1364)*
Afton Mountain Vineyards Corp.......................................540 456-8667
234 Vineyard Ln Afton (22920) *(G-73)*
Afton Scientific LLC..434 979-3737
2020 Avon Ct Ste 1 Charlottesville (22902) *(G-2721)*
AG Almanac LLC..703 289-1200
2735 Hartland Rd Ste 101 Falls Church (22043) *(G-4741)*
AG Customs Creat & Designs LLC...................................757 927-7339
21 E Big Sky Dr Hampton (23666) *(G-6078)*
AG Essence Inc...804 915-6650
1601 Overbrook Rd Ste C Richmond (23220) *(G-11479)*
AG Lasers Technologies LLC...800 255-5515
1330 Progress Dr Front Royal (22630) *(G-5519)*
AG Pack LLC..804 514-9080
9700 Robin Rd Disputanta (23842) *(G-4103)*
AG Wraps, Chesapeake *Also called Action Graphics and Signs Inc* *(G-2953)*
Against All Oddz Publications...757 300-4645
2500 Chamberlayne Ave Richmond (23222) *(G-11480)*
Against Grain Woodworking Inc.......................................434 760-2055
101 Woodpecker Way Afton (22920) *(G-74)*
Agaram Technologies Inc...703 297-8591
20130 Lakeview Center Plz Ashburn (20147) *(G-1239)*
AGC Flat Glass North Amer Inc.......................................804 222-0120
6200 Gorman Rd Henrico (23231) *(G-6471)*
AGC Information Inc...703 548-3118
2300 Olston Blvd Ste 400 Arlington (22201) *(G-844)*
Agee Catering Services...434 960-8906
56 Agee Ln Palmyra (22963) *(G-10243)*
Agent Medical LLC..804 562-9469
1145 Gaskins Rd Ste 102 Richmond (23238) *(G-11089)*

AGF Defcom Inc..757 842-4252
604 Green Tree Rd Ste C Chesapeake (23320) *(G-2956)*
Agfm, Chesapeake *Also called American Gfm Corporation* *(G-2967)*
Aggregate Industries - Mwr Inc......................................540 775-7600
15141 Cleve Dr King George (22485) *(G-7080)*
Aggregate Industries - Mwr Inc......................................540 379-0765
301 Warrenton Rd Falmouth (22405) *(G-4932)*
Aggregate Industries - Mwr Inc......................................703 361-2276
9321 Developers Dr Manassas (20109) *(G-8020)*
Aggregate Industries MGT Inc..540 249-5791
Rr 340 Grottoes (24441) *(G-6013)*
Aggregate Industries MGT Inc..804 994-5533
1566 Mckendree Ln Aylett (23009) *(G-1544)*
Aggregate Industries MGT Inc..540 337-4875
1526 Cold Springs Rd Stuarts Draft (24477) *(G-13642)*
Aggregate Industries MGT Inc..804 693-2280
Rr 17 Gloucester (23061) *(G-5835)*
Aggregate Industries-Wcr Inc..804 829-9783
7420 Two Mile Trl Charles City (23030) *(G-2569)*
Aggregates - Eden Quarry, Cascade *Also called Cemex Cnstr Mtls ATL LLC* *(G-2250)*
Aggregates Usa LLC..276 628-9337
21339 Gravel Lake Rd Abingdon (24211) *(G-9)*
Aggressive Audio, Ashburn *Also called Little Green Men Inc* *(G-1308)*
AGI, Virginia Beach *Also called Architectural Graphics Inc* *(G-14236)*
Agi, Virginia Beach *Also called Architectural Graphics Inc* *(G-14238)*
Agile Access Control Inc..408 213-9555
14101 Willard Rd Ste A Chantilly (20151) *(G-2363)*
Agile Writer Press...804 986-2985
13620 Cradle Hill Rd Midlothian (23112) *(G-8769)*
Agilent Technologies Inc..540 443-9272
2000 Kraft Dr Ste 1103 Blacksburg (24060) *(G-1721)*
Agility Inc..423 383-0962
7761 Cunningham Rd Bristol (24202) *(G-2003)*
Agilitytools.com, Winchester *Also called Windryder Inc* *(G-15516)*
Agma LLC...703 689-3458
12158 Chancery Stn Cir Reston (20190) *(G-10780)*
Agora Data Services LLC...703 328-7758
16 Ridge Pointe Ln Fredericksburg (22405) *(G-5396)*
Agp Technologies LLC...434 489-6025
4368 Dumfries Rd Catlett (20119) *(G-2262)*
Agri Ventilation Systems LLC...540 879-9864
221 Old River Rd Bridgewater (22812) *(G-1947)*
Agrium US Inc...434 738-0515
449 A Washington St Boydton (23917) *(G-1913)*
AGS, Ashland *Also called A G S Hanover Incorporated* *(G-1360)*
AGS, North Chesterfield *Also called American Gasket & Seal Tech* *(G-9816)*
Agustawestland NA, Arlington *Also called Agustawestland North Amer Inc* *(G-845)*
Agustawestland North Amer Inc (HQ)...............................**703 373-8000**
2345 Crystal Dr Ste 906 Arlington (22202) *(G-845)*
Agustawestlandbell LLC..703 373-1613
11700 Plaza America Dr # 900 Reston (20190) *(G-10781)*
Agway, Richmond *Also called Southern States Coop Inc* *(G-11389)*
Ah Love Oil & Vinegar...703 992-7000
2910 District Ave Ste 165 Fairfax (22031) *(G-4402)*
Ah Love Oil and Vinegar LLC...703 966-0668
601 S View Ter Alexandria (22314) *(G-123)*
Ahf Publishing LLC...804 282-6170
411 Libbie Ave Richmond (23226) *(G-11090)*
Ahh Products, Haymarket *Also called Poof Inc* *(G-6437)*
Ahmed Industries Inc...703 828-7180
3611 18th St S Arlington (22204) *(G-846)*
Ai Machines Inc...973 204-9772
8225 Adenlee Ave Apt 101 Fairfax (22031) *(G-4403)*
Ai Metrix Inc (HQ)..**703 254-2000**
5971 Kingstowne Vlg Alexandria (22315) *(G-406)*
AIAA, Reston *Also called American Inst Arntics Astrntic* *(G-10786)*
Aida Health Inc...202 739-1345
1901 N Moore St Ste 1004 Arlington (22209) *(G-847)*
Aigis Blast Protection..703 871-5173
11710 Plaza America Dr # 2000 Reston (20190) *(G-10782)*
Ailan Trading Inc USA...757 812-7258
5731 Grge Wash Hwy Ste 4d Yorktown (23692) *(G-15931)*
Aileen L Brown..757 696-1814
2018 Laguard Dr Hampton (23661) *(G-6079)*
Ailsa Software LLC...703 407-6470
4314 General Kearny Ct Chantilly (20151) *(G-2364)*
Aimex LLC...212 631-4277
8500 Leesburg Pike # 310 Vienna (22182) *(G-14006)*
Aina Holdings, Herndon *Also called Airbus Americas Inc* *(G-6606)*
Air & Beyond LLC...804 229-9450
2100 Breezy Point Cir # 204 North Chesterfield (23235) *(G-9808)*
Air & Gas Components LLC...757 473-3571
5366 Lake Lawson Rd Virginia Beach (23455) *(G-14217)*
Air & Liquid Systems Corp..434 845-7081
4621 Murray Pl Lynchburg (24502) *(G-7637)*
Air Barge Company...310 378-2928
5840 Bermuda Ct Mc Lean (22101) *(G-8390)*

Air Britt Two LLC 757 470-9364
3244 Sugar Creek Dr Virginia Beach (23452) ***(G-14218)***
Air Liquid America, North Chesterfield *Also called Airgas Usa LLC* ***(G-9809)***
Air Metal Corp 804 262-1004
7608 Compton Rd Richmond (23228) ***(G-11091)***
Air Route Optimizer Inc 540 364-3470
5649 John Barton Payne Rd Marshall (20115) ***(G-8249)***
Air Systems International Inc 757 424-3967
829 Juniper Cres Chesapeake (23320) ***(G-2957)***
Air Tight Duct Systems Inc 540 361-7888
451 Central Rd Ste C Fredericksburg (22401) ***(G-5169)***
Air Wisonsin Airlines Corp 757 853-8215
6170 Miller Store Rd Norfolk (23502) ***(G-9429)***
Air-Con Asp Sling Striping LLC 540 664-1989
212 Thwaite Ln Winchester (22603) ***(G-15373)***
Airaware, Altavista *Also called Schrader-Bridgeport Intl Inc* ***(G-641)***
Airbase Therapeutics 434 825-0074
1167 Raintree Dr Charlottesville (22901) ***(G-2587)***
Airbus A300 Leasing Inc 703 834-3400
198 Van Buren St Ste 300 Herndon (20170) ***(G-6605)***
Airbus Americas Inc (HQ) **703 834-3400**
2550 Wasser Ter Ste 9100 Herndon (20171) ***(G-6606)***
Airbus Def Space Holdings Inc 703 466-5600
2550 Wasser Ter Ste 9000 Herndon (20171) ***(G-6607)***
Airbus Group Inc (HQ) **703 466-5600**
2550 Wasser Ter Ste 9000 Herndon (20171) ***(G-6608)***
Airbus Group Supply & Svcs Inc 703 858-2235
21780 Filigree Ct Ashburn (20147) ***(G-1240)***
Aireal Apparel, Virginia Beach *Also called Rain & Associates LLC* ***(G-14758)***
Airgas Inc 757 539-7185
105 Dill Rd Suffolk (23434) ***(G-13664)***
Airgas Usa LLC 804 743-0661
5901 Jefferson Davis Hwy North Chesterfield (23234) ***(G-9809)***
Airline Tariff Publishing Co (PA) **703 661-7400**
45005 Aviation Dr Ste 400 Dulles (20166) ***(G-4191)***
Airocare Inc 703 788-1500
44330 Mercure Cir Ste 150 Dulles (20166) ***(G-4192)***
Airpac Inc 540 635-5011
888 Shenandoah Shores Rd Front Royal (22630) ***(G-5520)***
Airphx, Arlington *Also called Phoenixaire LLC* ***(G-1111)***
Airsource Filterless Tech, Chesapeake *Also called Hayden Enterprises* ***(G-3129)***
Ais Industrial Services, Richmond *Also called Austin Industrial Services LLC* ***(G-11494)***
Aj Trim LLC 703 330-1212
7750 Wellingford Dr Manassas (20109) ***(G-8021)***
Ajc Woodworks Inc 757 566-0336
8305 Richmond Rd Toano (23168) ***(G-13855)***
Ajf Sign Placement 540 797-5835
5833 Plantation Cir Roanoke (24019) ***(G-11881)***
Ajs E Coast Hlg & Trnspt LLC 540 645-2200
18460 Lotus Ct Apt 201 Triangle (22172) ***(G-13888)***
AJW Surfboards 910 617-8750
208 63rd St Virginia Beach (23451) ***(G-14219)***
AK Millwork Inc 703 337-4848
7666 Fullerton Rd Ste F Springfield (22153) ***(G-12937)***
Aka Software LLC 703 406-4619
46191 Cecil Ter Sterling (20165) ***(G-13340)***
Akaline Cylinders 757 896-9100
2400 Aluminum Ave Hampton (23661) ***(G-6080)***
Akamai Technologies Inc 877 425-2624
11111 Sunset Hills Rd # 250 Reston (20190) ***(G-10783)***
Akg Inc 540 574-0760
1730 Dealton Ave Harrisonburg (22801) ***(G-6290)***
Akina Pharamacy, Chantilly *Also called Northern VA Compounders Pllc* ***(G-2469)***
Akl Associates Ltd 540 269-8228
1213 Indian Trail Rd Keezletown (22832) ***(G-7026)***
Akmal Khaliqi 202 710-7582
14080 Malta St Woodbridge (22193) ***(G-15643)***
Akzo Nobel, Norfolk *Also called International Paint LLC* ***(G-9595)***
Akzo Nobel Coatings Inc 540 982-8301
2837 Roanoke Ave Sw Roanoke (24015) ***(G-12030)***
Al Rayanah USA 703 941-1200
3708 Sleepy Hollow Rd Falls Church (22041) ***(G-4742)***
Al-Nafea Inc 703 440-8499
7942 Cluny Ct Ste 0 Springfield (22153) ***(G-12938)***
Alacran 540 629-6095
5590 Bagging Plant Rd Dublin (24084) ***(G-4147)***
Alacrity Services, Clifton *Also called Gravittional Systems Engrg Inc* ***(G-3668)***
Alan Forney Jr 540 323-1666
143 Armel Rd Winchester (22602) ***(G-15374)***
Alan Mitchell 276 251-5077
57 Dan Valley Farm Rd Claudville (24076) ***(G-3637)***
Alan Thornhill 703 892-5642
2600 S Veitch St Apt 401 Arlington (22206) ***(G-848)***
Alans Apary Hney Bees Svcs LL 540 881-0405
205 S Main St 161 Culpeper (22701) ***(G-3863)***
Alans Factory Outlet 540 860-1035
128 Hill House Ln Luray (22835) ***(G-7600)***
Alban Cire 703 455-9300
7244 Boudinot Dr Springfield (22150) ***(G-12939)***
Alban Tractor Co Inc 540 667-4200
351 Zachary Ann Ln Clear Brook (22624) ***(G-3643)***
Albany Industries-Galax LLC 276 236-0735
626 Creekview Dr Galax (24333) ***(G-5626)***
Albemarle Corporation 225 388-8011
5721 Gulfstream Rd Richmond (23250) ***(G-11092)***
Albemarle County Pub Schools 434 296-3872
907 Henry Ave Charlottesville (22903) ***(G-2722)***
Albemarle Edibles LLC 434 242-5567
1738 Allied St Charlottesville (22903) ***(G-2723)***
Albemarle Signs 434 823-1024
3921 Browns Gap Tpke Crozet (22932) ***(G-3828)***
Alberene Soapstone Co., Schuyler *Also called Polycor Virginia Inc* ***(G-12653)***
Alberene Soapstone Company, Schuyler *Also called New Worlds Stone Co Inc* ***(G-12652)***
Alberene Soapstone Company 434 831-1051
42 Alberene Loop Schuyler (22969) ***(G-12650)***
Alberts Associates Inc 757 638-3352
5220 Cobble Hill Rd Portsmouth (23703) ***(G-10389)***
Albion Cabinets Stairs Inc 434 974-4611
395 Reas Ford Rd Ste 150 Earlysville (22936) ***(G-4284)***
Albright Recovery & Cnstr LLC 276 835-2026
138 Dunrobin Rd Clinchco (24226) ***(G-3684)***
ALC Training Group LLC 757 746-0428
8 Valasia Rd Poquoson (23662) ***(G-10364)***
Alcat Precast Inc 804 725-4080
125 Blue Crab Dr Moon (23119) ***(G-9031)***
Alchemical Hydrogen LLC 703 399-9235
1776 Potomac Greens Dr Alexandria (22314) ***(G-124)***
Alcoa Howmet, Hampton, Hampton *Also called Howmet Castings & Services Inc* ***(G-6168)***
Alcolock Va Inc 804 515-0022
8143 Staples Mill Rd Henrico (23228) ***(G-6472)***
Aldridge Installations LLC 804 658-1035
2142 Tomlynn St Richmond (23230) ***(G-11093)***
Aleeta A Gardner 571 722-2549
5033 Anchorstone Dr Woodbridge (22192) ***(G-15644)***
Alegria John 703 398-6009
8395 Euclid Ave Ste S Manassas Park (20111) ***(G-8186)***
Alegria Furniture Restoration, Manassas Park *Also called Alegria John* ***(G-8186)***
Alere Inc 800 340-4029
1342 Court St Portsmouth (23704) ***(G-10390)***
Aleris Rolled Products Inc 804 714-2100
1801 Reymet Rd North Chesterfield (23237) ***(G-9810)***
Aleris Rolled Products Inc 804 714-2180
1701 Reymet Rd North Chesterfield (23237) ***(G-9811)***
Alethia Embroidery 540 710-6560
6109 Fox Point Rd Fredericksburg (22407) ***(G-5242)***
Alexander Amir 757 714-1802
503 S 6th St Suffolk (23434) ***(G-13665)***
Alexander Arms, Radford *Also called Alexander Industries Inc* ***(G-10703)***
Alexander Industries Inc (PA) **540 443-9250**
Us Army Rdford Arsnal 104 Radford (24141) ***(G-10703)***
Alexander M Robertson 434 299-5221
10327 Big Island Hwy Big Island (24526) ***(G-1701)***
Alexandria Arlington Bureau, Alexandria *Also called Wp Company LLC* ***(G-389)***
Alexandria Armature Works, Alexandria *Also called Anlac LLC* ***(G-135)***
Alexandria Coatings LLC 703 643-1636
9418 Gunston Cove Rd Lorton (22079) ***(G-7459)***
Alexandria Fusion 703 566-3055
1900 Duke St Alexandria (22314) ***(G-125)***
Alexandria Gazette Packet 703 821-5050
1606 King St Alexandria (22314) ***(G-126)***
Alexandria Metal Finishers, Lorton *Also called Alexandria Coatings LLC* ***(G-7459)***
Alexandria Packaging LLC (PA) **703 644-5550**
7396 Ward Park Ln Springfield (22153) ***(G-12940)***
Alexandria Times 703 739-0001
300 S Washington St Alexandria (22314) ***(G-127)***
Alexis Mya Publishing LLC 540 479-2727
119 Broadfield Ln Spotsylvania (22553) ***(G-12882)***
Alfa Laval Champ LLC 866 253-2528
5400 Intl Trade Dr Richmond (23231) ***(G-11094)***
Alfa Laval Inc (HQ) **866 253-2528**
5400 Intl Trade Dr Richmond (23231) ***(G-11095)***
Alfa Laval US Holding Inc (HQ) **804 222-5300**
5400 Intl Trade Dr Richmond (23231) ***(G-11096)***
Alfa Laval USA Inc (HQ) **804 222-5300**
5400 Intl Trade Dr Richmond (23231) ***(G-11097)***
Alfa Print LLC 703 754-2433
8419 Holstein Pony Ct Gainesville (20155) ***(G-5568)***
Alfa Print LLC 703 273-2061
10370 Main St Fairfax (22030) ***(G-4591)***
Alfaro Torres German 703 498-6295
21786 Canfield Ter Sterling (20164) ***(G-13341)***
Alforas Company 703 342-6910
7138 Little River Tpke Annandale (22003) ***(G-729)***
Algonquin Industries Inc 804 550-5401
10117 Leadbetter Pl Ashland (23005) ***(G-1365)***
Ali Baba Handwrought Jewelry 757 622-5007
333 Waterside Dr 312 Norfolk (23510) ***(G-9430)***

ALPHABETIC

Alice Farling...757 802-6936
18 Lake Ave Salem (24153) *(G-12472)*

Alicesa Foster Graves LLC......................................804 658-0092
7414 Griffin Ave Richmond (23227) *(G-11098)*

Alien Piss World Entrmt LLC.................................757 805-1007
2085 Lynnhven Pkwy Ste 10 Virginia Beach (23456) *(G-14220)*

Alien Silkscreen LLC..540 389-5699
29 Hammit Ln Salem (24153) *(G-12473)*

Alien Surfwear & Silk Screen, Roanoke *Also called Bobhron Inc (G-12054)*

Alienfeet Sports Socks...703 864-8892
6510 Cottonwood Dr Alexandria (22310) *(G-407)*

Alioth Technical Services Inc.................................757 630-0337
2432 Esplanade Dr Virginia Beach (23456) *(G-14221)*

All A Board Inc...804 652-0020
395 Dabbs House Rd Richmond (23223) *(G-11481)*

All About Cupcakes...757 619-5931
103 Kings Point Ave Smithfield (23430) *(G-12702)*

All About Frames..703 998-5868
6641 Wakefield Dr Ste 115 Alexandria (22307) *(G-408)*

All About Security Inc..757 887-6700
229 Gate House Rd Newport News (23608) *(G-9161)*

All About Signs LLC...757 934-3000
232 Barnes Rd Suffolk (23437) *(G-13666)*

All Affairs Transportation LLC...............................757 342-2474
724 City Center Blvd C Newport News (23606) *(G-9162)*

All American Logistic Co..571 237-6039
9110 Forestview Dr Manassas (20112) *(G-8022)*

All American Mobility, Fredericksburg *Also called Christopher Hawkins (G-5178)*

All Care Training & Services...................................757 346-2703
801 E 26th St Norfolk (23504) *(G-9431)*

All Export Import Usa LLC....................................571 242-2250
1350 Beverly Rd 115-334 Mc Lean (22101) *(G-8391)*

All Glass LLC..540 288-8111
27 Utah Pl Ste 101 Fredericksburg (22405) *(G-5397)*

All Kinds of Signs..434 842-1877
2878 James Madison Hwy Bremo Bluff (23022) *(G-1943)*

All Kinds of Signs Inc..703 321-6542
1938 Pimmit Dr Falls Church (22043) *(G-4743)*

All Marble...757 460-8099
4801 Beach Cove Pl Virginia Beach (23455) *(G-14222)*

All Outdoors The, Williamsburg *Also called Tomo LLC (G-15325)*

All Points Countertop Inc......................................540 665-3875
449 N Cameron St Winchester (22601) *(G-15526)*

All Prints Inc..703 435-1922
502 Shaw Rd Ste 107 Sterling (20166) *(G-13342)*

All Sports Athletic Apparel....................................757 427-6772
2957 Holland Rd Virginia Beach (23453) *(G-14223)*

All Star Sports, Woodbridge *Also called Dull Inc Dolan & Norma (G-15687)*

All That Jaz LLC..800 224-8152
6000 Centralia Rd Chesterfield (23832) *(G-3474)*

All Things Welded..423 492-0880
1341 Matson Dr Marion (24354) *(G-8220)*

All Tools Inc...804 598-1549
1885 Hope Meadow Way Powhatan (23139) *(G-10529)*

All Traffic Solutions Inc (PA).................................**814 237-9005**
12950 Worldgate Dr # 310 Herndon (20170) *(G-6609)*

All Tyed Up...804 855-7158
516 S Pine St Apt 2 Richmond (23220) *(G-11482)*

All-N-Logging LLC...434 547-3550
450 Walton Rd Keysville (23947) *(G-7054)*

All-Signs...276 632-6733
140 Rosenwall Dr Martinsville (24112) *(G-8265)*

Allcare Non-Medical Wheelchair............................757 291-2500
405 Honey Locust Way Chesapeake (23320) *(G-2958)*

Alleghany Graphic Design Prtg, Covington *Also called Alleghany Printing Co (G-3777)*

Alleghany Highlands AG Ctr LLC...........................540 474-2422
6095 Potomac River Rd Monterey (24465) *(G-9000)*

Alleghany Meats, Monterey *Also called Alleghany Highlands AG Ctr LLC (G-9000)*

Alleghany Printing Co...540 965-4246
261 W Main St Covington (24426) *(G-3777)*

Allegheny Instruments Inc......................................540 468-3740
1509 Jackson River Rd Monterey (24465) *(G-9001)*

Allegiance Inc...276 639-6884
182 Camp Jacob Rd Clintwood (24228) *(G-3686)*

Allegra Network LLC..757 448-8271
879 Poplar Hall Dr Norfolk (23502) *(G-9432)*

Allegra Print & Imaging, Fairfax *Also called C2-Mask Inc (G-4422)*

Allegra Print & Imaging, Springfield *Also called Cyan LLC (G-12986)*

Allegra Print & Imaging, Sterling *Also called Watts & Ward Inc (G-13560)*

Allegra Print & Imaging, Springfield *Also called P M Resources Inc (G-13065)*

Allegra Print & Imaging...703 378-4500
14158 Willard Rd Chantilly (20151) *(G-2365)*

Allegra Print Signs Design, Sterling *Also called Flynn Enterprises Inc (G-13400)*

Allegra Richmond Henrico Co, Richmond *Also called Fergusson Printing (G-11209)*

Allen Display & Store Eqp Inc................................804 794-6032
14301 Sommerville Ct Midlothian (23113) *(G-8770)*

Allen Enterprises LLC...540 261-2622
2271 Sycamore Ave Ste A Buena Vista (24416) *(G-2138)*

Allen Industries Intl LLC..540 797-5230
414 Jackson St Bedford (24523) *(G-1618)*

Allen Management Company Inc.............................703 481-8858
316 Victory Dr Herndon (20170) *(G-6610)*

Allen Sisson Publishers Rep...................................804 745-0903
2102 Ramsgate Sq North Chesterfield (23236) *(G-9812)*

Allen Watson..703 620-5350
11017 Howland Dr Reston (20191) *(G-10784)*

Allen Wayne Ltd Arlington.....................................703 321-7414
7128 Lineweaver Rd Warrenton (20187) *(G-14977)*

Allen Wayne Limited, Warrenton *Also called Allen Wayne Ltd Arlington (G-14977)*

Allende-El Publishing Co LLC.................................757 528-9997
304 Windy Ridge Ln Newport News (23602) *(G-9163)*

Allens Logging Inc..434 724-6493
11400 Franklin Tpke Chatham (24531) *(G-2918)*

Allergan Sales LLC...757 624-5320
999 Waterside Dr Ste 2000 Norfolk (23510) *(G-9433)*

Allergopharma Usa Inc...919 749-6213
1940 Duke St Ste 200 Alexandria (22314) *(G-128)*

Allergy Asthma Ntwrk/Mthers As...........................800 878-4403
8229 Boone Blvd Ste 260 Vienna (22182) *(G-14007)*

Allermore Industries Inc...703 537-1346
8299 Raindrop Way Springfield (22153) *(G-12941)*

Allgood Promotional Cons......................................434 793-6178
2323 Riverside Dr Ste K Danville (24540) *(G-3953)*

Allgoods Cleaning Service......................................540 434-1511
429 Eastover Dr Harrisonburg (22801) *(G-6291)*

Alliance Display & Packaging, Ridgeway *Also called Westrock Converting LLC (G-11858)*

Alliance In-Home Care LLC.....................................703 825-1067
6201 Leesburg Pike Ste 6 Falls Church (22044) *(G-4744)*

Alliance Industrial Corp..434 239-2641
208 Tomahawk Indus Park Lynchburg (24502) *(G-7638)*

Alliance Machine and Engrv LLC.............................804 798-1199
10190 Maple Leaf Ct Ashland (23005) *(G-1366)*

Alliance Office Furniture Co....................................
307 Yoakum Pkwy Apt 922 Alexandria (22304) *(G-129)*

Alliance Presrvng Hstry Wwii.................................757 423-1429
5922 Powhatan Ave Norfolk (23508) *(G-9434)*

Alliance Resource Partners LP...............................276 566-8516
Hwy 643 Hurley (24620) *(G-6968)*

Alliance Signs Virginia LLC....................................804 530-1451
12603 Green Garden Ter Chester (23836) *(G-3384)*

Alliance Stl Fabrications Inc...................................703 631-2355
9106 Manassas Dr Manassas Park (20111) *(G-8187)*

Alliance Technical Svcs Inc (PA).............................**757 628-9500**
900 Granby St Ste 228 Norfolk (23510) *(G-9435)*

Alliant Tchsystems Oprtons LLC.............................703 412-3223
1300 Wilson Blvd Ste 400 Arlington (22209) *(G-849)*

Alliant Tchsystems Oprtons LLC.............................703 254-2454
8560 Cinderbed Rd Ste 700 Newington (22122) *(G-9152)*

Allied Aerospace, Newport News *Also called Calspan Systems Corporation (G-9189)*

Allied Aerospace Indutries, Newport News *Also called Allied Aerospace Uav LLC (G-9165)*

Allied Aerospace Services LLC...............................757 873-1344
703 City Center Blvd Newport News (23606) *(G-9164)*

Allied Aerospace Uav LLC......................................757 873-1344
703 City Center Blvd Newport News (23606) *(G-9165)*

Allied Brass Inc...540 967-5970
195 Duke St Louisa (23093) *(G-7545)*

Allied Con Co - Suffolk Block.................................757 494-5200
3900 Shannon St Chesapeake (23324) *(G-2959)*

Allied Concrete Company (HQ)................................**434 296-7181**
1000 Harris St Charlottesville (22903) *(G-2724)*

Allied Concrete Company..804 279-7501
1231 Willis Rd North Chesterfield (23237) *(G-9813)*

Allied Concrete Products, North Chesterfield *Also called Allied Concrete Company (G-9813)*

Allied Concrete Products LLC.................................434 634-6571
120 Courtland Rd Emporia (23847) *(G-4354)*

Allied Concrete Products LLC (HQ).........................**757 494-5200**
3900 Shannon St Chesapeake (23324) *(G-2960)*

Allied Pallet Company (PA)......................................**804 966-5597**
7151 Poindexter Rd New Kent (23124) *(G-9128)*

Allied Products Division, Richmond *Also called Itg Cigars Inc (G-11622)*

Allied Systems Corporation (PA).............................**540 665-9600**
220 Arbor Ct Winchester (22602) *(G-15375)*

Allied Tool and Machine Co VA...............................540 342-6781
3362 Shenandoah Ave Nw Roanoke (24017) *(G-12031)*

Alligatortalez..703 791-4238
7892 English St Manassas (20112) *(G-8023)*

Allinder Printing...757 672-4918
7565 Buttercup Cir Norfolk (23518) *(G-9436)*

Allison's Woodworks, Tazewell *Also called Brian Allison (G-13828)*

Allmetal Manufacturing, Chantilly *Also called Communications Vehicle Svc LLC (G-2529)*

Allmoods Enterprises LLC......................................703 241-8748
314 N Van Buren St Falls Church (22046) *(G-4899)*

Allora USA LLC...571 291-3485
22713 Commerce Center Ct # 140 Sterling (20166) *(G-13343)*

Alloy Metal Designs, Virginia Beach *Also called Henry Bijak (G-14516)*

Allspark Industrial LLC...804 977-2732
2605 W Main St Richmond (23220) *(G-11483)*

(G-0000) Company's Geographic Section entry number

Alltek Systems LLC 757 438-6905
1350 Villaverde Ln Charlottesville (22902) **(G-2725)**
Alma Mater LLC 434 248-5465
6655 Red House Rd Phenix (23959) **(G-10354)**
Alpaca + Knitwear 703 994-3346
8257 Singleleaf Ln Lorton (22079) **(G-7460)**
Alpacas of Lakeland Woods 804 448-8283
4305 Jericho Rd Ruther Glen (22546) **(G-12448)**
Alpha 540 895-5731
10700 Edenton Rd Partlow (22534) **(G-10263)**
Alpha & Omega Towel Washing Co, Richmond *Also called Gregory Briggs* **(G-11224)**
Alpha Appalachia Holdings Inc (HQ) **276 619-4410**
1 Alpha Pl Bristol (24209) **(G-1964)**
Alpha Developement Bureau 540 337-4900
167 Expo Rd Fishersville (22939) **(G-5000)**
Alpha Graphics US 635, Alexandria *Also called J & M Printing Inc* **(G-241)**
Alpha Industries 540 249-4980
901 Dogwood Ave Grottoes (24441) **(G-6014)**
Alpha Industries Inc (PA) **703 378-1420**
14200 Pk Madow Dr Ste 110 Chantilly (20151) **(G-2366)**
Alpha Industries Inc 540 298-2155
1284 Rinacas Corner Rd Shenandoah (22849) **(G-12688)**
Alpha Pressure Washing 540 293-1287
4402 Oakland Blvd Nw Roanoke (24012) **(G-12032)**
Alpha Printing Inc 703 914-2800
6116 Rolling Rd Ste 301 Springfield (22152) **(G-12942)**
Alpha Printing Inc 703 321-2071
5540 Port Royal Rd Springfield (22151) **(G-12943)**
Alpha Printing Inc 703 914-2800
8451 Hilltop Rd Ste A Fairfax (22031) **(G-4404)**
Alpha Safe & Vault Inc 703 281-7233
1656 Gelding Ln Vienna (22182) **(G-14008)**
Alphabet Soup 757 569-0110
111 E 2nd Ave Franklin (23851) **(G-5138)**
AlphaGraphics, Richmond *Also called Campbell Graphics Inc* **(G-11144)**
AlphaGraphics, Falls Church *Also called AG Almanac LLC* **(G-4741)**
AlphaGraphics, Richmond *Also called Lydell Group Incorporated* **(G-11277)**
AlphaGraphics 703 866-1988
7426 Alban Station Blvd A Springfield (22150) **(G-12944)**
AlphaGraphics 703 818-2900
4515 Daly Dr Chantilly (20151) **(G-2367)**
AlphaGraphics 584, Reston *Also called Mogo Inc* **(G-10903)**
AlphaGraphics Loudoun, Leesburg *Also called U3 Solutions Inc* **(G-7366)**
Alphin Logging, Goshen *Also called Thomas L Alphin Inc* **(G-5929)**
Alpine Armoring Inc (PA) **703 471-0002**
4170 Lafayette Center Dr # 100 Chantilly (20151) **(G-2368)**
Alpine Method Technologies LLC 716 310-4935
41144 Hickory Hedge Pl Aldie (20105) **(G-100)**
Alpine Mthod Tchnlges/ Alpine, Aldie *Also called Alpine Method Technologies LLC* **(G-100)**
Alpolic Metal Composite Mtls, Chesapeake *Also called Mitsubishi Chemical Composites* **(G-3208)**
Alr Technologies Inc 804 554-3500
7400 Beaufont Spring Dr # 3 North Chesterfield (23225) **(G-10016)**
Als Custom Signs 804 224-7105
2376 Longfield Rd Colonial Beach (22443) **(G-3720)**
Als Machine & Welding Inc 804 443-3193
1209 Desha Rd Tappahannock (22560) **(G-13810)**
Als Sign Shop 540 465-3103
33484 Old Valley Pike Strasburg (22657) **(G-13571)**
Als Used Tires & Rims 703 548-3000
1108 Queen St Alexandria (22314) **(G-130)**
Alsi, Centreville *Also called Advanced Leading Solutions Inc* **(G-2289)**
Alstom Renewable US LLC 804 763-2196
2800 Waterford Lake Dr Midlothian (23112) **(G-8771)**
Alston Welding Svc 757 547-7351
213 Thrasher Rd Chesapeake (23320) **(G-2961)**
Alt Services Inc 757 806-1341
807 Sheffield St Hampton (23666) **(G-6081)**
Alta Industries LLC 703 969-0999
23394 Virginia Rose Pl Brambleton (20148) **(G-1925)**
Altamont Recorders LLC 804 814-2310
1710 Altamont Ave Richmond (23230) **(G-11099)**
Altar Ego Publications 540 933-6530
928 Camp Roosevelt Rd Fort Valley (22652) **(G-5134)**
Altavista Journal, The, Altavista *Also called Womack Publishing Co Inc* **(G-645)**
Altec Industries 804 621-4080
13301 Great Coastal Dr Chester (23836) **(G-3385)**
Altec Industries Inc 540 992-5300
325 S Center Dr Daleville (24083) **(G-3938)**
Alter Magazine LLC 571 970-3537
2659 S Walter Reed Dr Arlington (22206) **(G-850)**
Alterations Done Affordably 540 423-2412
10150 Alum Springs Rd Culpeper (22701) **(G-3864)**
Alternative Candle Company 804 350-6980
12331 Midsummer Ln Apt B Woodbridge (22192) **(G-15645)**
Alternatives Inc Corporate 540 576-2265
125 Sailboat Ln Union Hall (24176) **(G-13957)**
Alterntive Energywave Tech LLC 757 897-1312
16 Bosch Ln Newport News (23606) **(G-9166)**
Altillo Vineyards & Winery 434 324-4160
620 Level Run Rd Hurt (24563) **(G-6970)**
Altist Welding & Fabrication, Poquoson *Also called Gary L Lawson* **(G-10372)**
Altomas Technologies LLC 540 560-2320
845 Sugar Maple Ln Rockingham (22801) **(G-12239)**
Altria 804 274-2100
6601 W Broad St Richmond (23230) **(G-11100)**
Altria Client Services LLC 804 274-2000
6601 W Broad St Richmond (23230) **(G-11101)**
Altria Client Services LLC 804 274-2000
2325 Bells Rd Richmond (23234) **(G-11023)**
Altria Enterprises II LLC (HQ) **804 274-2200**
6601 W Broad St Richmond (23230) **(G-11102)**
Altria Group, Richmond *Also called Altria Client Services LLC* **(G-11023)**
Altria Group Inc 804 274-2000
6603 W Broad St Richmond (23230) **(G-11103)**
Altria Group Inc 804 274-2000
5720 Gulfstream Rd Richmond (23250) **(G-11104)**
Altria Group Inc 804 335-2703
4201 Commerce Rd Richmond (23234) **(G-11024)**
Altria Group Inc (PA) **804 274-2200**
6601 W Broad St Richmond (23230) **(G-11105)**
Altria Ventures, Richmond *Also called Altria Client Services LLC* **(G-11101)**
Altria Ventures Inc (HQ) **804 274-2000**
6601 W Broad St Richmond (23230) **(G-11106)**
Alva Restoration & Waterproof 540 785-0805
12209 Mcclain St Fredericksburg (22407) **(G-5243)**
Alvarian Press 703 864-8018
11517 Olde Tiverton Cir Reston (20194) **(G-10785)**
Always In Stitches 804 642-0800
6622 Powhatan Dr Hayes (23072) **(G-6394)**
Always Morningsong Publishing 804 530-1392
14600 Fox Knoll Dr South Chesterfield (23834) **(G-12794)**
AM Services, Richlands *Also called Appalachian Mineral Services* **(G-11012)**
AM Tuneshop LLC 703 758-9193
12481 Manderley Way Herndon (20171) **(G-6611)**
Am-Corcom Inc 540 349-5895
14115 Lovers Ln Ste 157a Culpeper (22701) **(G-3865)**
Amadas Coach, Suffolk *Also called Coach LLC* **(G-13684)**
Amadas Industries Inc 757 539-0231
302 Kenyon Rd Suffolk (23434) **(G-13667)**
Amadas Industries Inc (PA) **757 539-0231**
1100 Holland Rd Suffolk (23434) **(G-13668)**
Amadi Publishing LLC 703 329-4535
4020 Javins Dr Alexandria (22310) **(G-409)**
Amama Ltd (PA) **703 759-9030**
9505 Arnon Chapel Rd Great Falls (22066) **(G-5935)**
Amana U S A Incorporated 703 821-7501
6669 Avignon Blvd Falls Church (22043) **(G-4745)**
Amanda Grace Handcrafted 703 539-2151
12461 Hayes Ct Unit 101 Fairfax (22033) **(G-4405)**
Amanda Grace Jewelry, Fairfax *Also called Amanda Grace Handcrafted* **(G-4405)**
Amari Publications 703 313-0174
6600 Comet Cir Apt 101 Springfield (22150) **(G-12945)**
Amarquis Publications LLC 804 464-7203
3915 Berrybrook Dr North Chesterfield (23234) **(G-9814)**
Amarveda 276 782-1819
221 W Main St Marion (24354) **(G-8221)**
Amato Industries 703 534-1400
2801 Juniper St Ste 1 Fairfax (22031) **(G-4406)**
Amazengraved LLC 540 313-5658
130 Obriens Cir Winchester (22602) **(G-15376)**
Amazon Mllwk Installations LLC 703 200-9076
5505 Sheldon Dr Alexandria (22312) **(G-410)**
Ambassador Religious Supply 757 686-8314
3305b Taylor Ct Chesapeake (23321) **(G-2962)**
Ambertone Press Inc 703 866-7715
7664 Fullerton Rd Springfield (22153) **(G-12946)**
Ambervision Technologies 571 594-1664
42771 Chatelain Cir Brambleton (20148) **(G-1926)**
Amboy Enterprises LLC 804 708-0945
561 Hill Grove Rd Manakin Sabot (23103) **(G-7894)**
Ambrosia Press Inc 540 432-1801
3234 Lee Hwy Weyers Cave (24486) **(G-15165)**
Ambrosia Vineyards 703 237-8717
2825 Rosemary Ln Falls Church (22042) **(G-4746)**
Ambush LLC 480 338-5321
15702 Brandywine Rd Dumfries (22025) **(G-4233)**
Ambush LLC 202 740-3602
2028 Coast Guard Dr Stafford (22554) **(G-13114)**
AMC Industries Inc 410 320-5037
1108 Marlene Ln Great Falls (22066) **(G-5936)**
Amcor Phrm Packg USA LLC 434 372-5113
194 Duckworth Dr Chase City (23924) **(G-2909)**
Amcor Rigid Packaging Usa LLC 276 625-8000
474 Gator Ln Wytheville (24382) **(G-15875)**
Amcor Spclty Crtons Amrcas LLC 804 748-3470
701 Algroup Way Chester (23836) **(G-3386)**

ALPHABETIC

AMD, Bristol *Also called American Medical Devices Inc* ***(G-1965)***
Amdrop, Leesburg *Also called Amnion LLC* ***(G-7216)***
Amee Bay LLC 703 365-0450
10440 Balls Ford Rd Manassas (20109) ***(G-8024)***
Amee Bay LLC 757 217-2720
540 Woodlake Cir Ste B Chesapeake (23320) ***(G-2963)***
Amelia Bulletin-Monitor, Amelia Court House *Also called A B M Enterprises Inc* ***(G-648)***
Amelia Lawrence LLC 703 493-9095
12837 Mill Race Ct Manassas (20112) ***(G-8025)***
Amelia Lumber Company 804 561-2155
16951 Leidig St Amelia Court House (23002) ***(G-649)***
Amelia Soap and Herb 804 561-5229
6840 Sparks Ln Amelia Court House (23002) ***(G-650)***
Amelia Woodworks, Amelia Court House *Also called Ronnie and Betty Bridges* ***(G-670)***
Amentum Services Inc 703 418-3020
2341 Richmond Hwy Arlington (22202) ***(G-851)***
Ameri Sign Design 252 544-7712
508 Central Dr Ste 107 Virginia Beach (23454) ***(G-14224)***
America Furniture LLC 703 939-3678
8328 Shoppers Sq Manassas (20111) ***(G-8026)***
America Heavy Industry 757 858-2000
2635 Nevada Ave Norfolk (23513) ***(G-9437)***
Americam Mulch, Christiansburg *Also called Hollybrook Mulch Trucking Inc* ***(G-3593)***
American Assembly LLC 757 639-6040
2746 Greenwood Dr Portsmouth (23702) ***(G-10391)***
American Assn Nurosurgeons Inc 434 924-5503
1224 Jefferson Park Ave Charlottesville (22903) ***(G-2726)***
American Biodiesel Corporation 703 906-9434
9562 Oakenshaw Dr Manassas (20110) ***(G-7910)***
American Bioprotection Inc 866 200-1313
1272 Pleasant Point Rd Surry (23883) ***(G-13795)***
American Borate Corporation 800 486-1072
4100 Buell St Chesapeake (23324) ***(G-2964)***
American Buildings Company 434 757-2220
501 Golden Eagle Dr La Crosse (23950) ***(G-7139)***
American Cartridge Charge, Norfolk *Also called Jammac Corporation* ***(G-9600)***
American Cemetery Supplies Inc 757 488-0018
2001 Laigh Rd Portsmouth (23701) ***(G-10392)***
American City Bus Journals Inc 703 258-0800
1100 Wilson Blvd Ste 800 Arlington (22209) ***(G-852)***
American Cmg Services Inc 804 353-9077
2000 Bremo Rd Ste 205 Richmond (23226) ***(G-11107)***
American Cmg Services Inc (PA) **757 548-5656**
1521 Technology Dr Chesapeake (23320) ***(G-2965)***
American Concrete Group LLC 276 546-1633
515 Industrial Dr Pennington Gap (24277) ***(G-10291)***
American Concrete Group LLC (PA) **276 546-1666**
R-2 Woodway Pennington Gap (24277) ***(G-10292)***
American Concrete Group LLC 423 323-7566
618 Lime State Rd Bristol (24202) ***(G-2004)***
American Court Comm Newspapers 703 237-9806
200 Little Falls St Falls Church (22046) ***(G-4900)***
American Density Materials 540 887-1217
3826 Spring Hill Rd Staunton (24401) ***(G-13240)***
American Diesel Corp 804 435-3107
101 American Dr Kilmarnock (22482) ***(G-7068)***
American Digital Print LLC 703 328-4796
21 Summerwood Dr Stafford (22554) ***(G-13115)***
American Drum Inc 804 226-1778
2800 Seven Hills Blvd Richmond (23231) ***(G-11108)***
American Egle EMB Graphics LLC 757 673-8337
3108 Woodbaugh Dr Chesapeake (23321) ***(G-2966)***
American Electric Motors, Lynchburg *Also called Trevor LLC* ***(G-7827)***
American Energy LLC 276 935-7562
Phillips Crk Norton (24273) ***(G-10112)***
American Floors 804 745-8932
1249 Raynor Dr North Chesterfield (23235) ***(G-9815)***
American Gasket & Seal Tech 804 271-0020
7400 Whitepine Rd North Chesterfield (23237) ***(G-9816)***
American Gen Fabrication Inc 757 329-4384
915 Laredo Ct Hampton (23669) ***(G-6082)***
American Gfm Corporation (PA) **757 487-2442**
1200 Cavalier Blvd Chesapeake (23323) ***(G-2967)***
American Graphics 540 977-1912
283 Fairfield Ln Troutville (24175) ***(G-13902)***
American Hands LLC 804 349-8974
3611 Maidens Rd Powhatan (23139) ***(G-10530)***
American Hardwood Inds LLC (HQ) **540 946-9150**
567 N Charlotte Ave Waynesboro (22980) ***(G-15092)***
American Highwall Mining LLC 276 646-5548
215 Kendall Ave Chilhowie (24319) ***(G-3544)***
American Highwall Systems 276 646-2004
212 Kendall Ave Chilhowie (24319) ***(G-3545)***
American History Press 540 487-1202
404 Locust St Staunton (24401) ***(G-13241)***
American Hofmann Corporation (HQ) **434 522-0300**
3700 Cohen Pl Lynchburg (24501) ***(G-7639)***
American Immgrtion Ctrl Fndtio 540 468-2022
224 W Main St Monterey (24465) ***(G-9002)***
American Inst Arntics Astrntic (PA) **703 264-7500**
12700 Sunrise Valley Dr # 2 Reston (20191) ***(G-10786)***
American Institute RES Inc 703 470-1037
6825 Redmond Dr Ste I Mc Lean (22101) ***(G-8392)***
American Interiors Ltd 757 627-0248
833 W 21st St Norfolk (23517) ***(G-9438)***
American Knine 757 304-9600
4007 Burdette Rd Carrsville (23315) ***(G-2248)***
American Laser Centers 804 200-5000
2004 Bremo Rd Richmond (23226) ***(G-11109)***
American Light Works LLC 804 332-3229
907 W Glebe Rd Alexandria (22305) ***(G-131)***
American Logo Corp 703 356-4709
2190 Pimmit Dr Ste H Falls Church (22043) ***(G-4747)***
American Machine Co Richmond 804 231-1157
2200 Commerce Rd Richmond (23234) ***(G-11025)***
American Made Signs LLC 434 971-7446
407 Earhart St B Charlottesville (22903) ***(G-2727)***
American Manufacturing Co Inc 703 361-2210
5517 Wellington Rd Gainesville (20155) ***(G-5569)***
American Manufacturing Co Inc (PA) **540 825-7234**
22011 Greenhouse Rd Elkwood (22718) ***(G-4341)***
American Mar & Indus Svcs LLC 757 573-1209
912 Executive Ct Chesapeake (23320) ***(G-2968)***
American Marine and Engine 276 263-1211
216 Ridge Rd Collinsville (24078) ***(G-3708)***
American Maritime Holdings Inc 757 233-9055
816 Industrial Ave Chesapeake (23324) ***(G-2969)***
American Maritime Holdings Inc 757 545-4013
800 Seaboard Ave Chesapeake (23324) ***(G-2970)***
American Maritime Holdings Inc (PA) **757 961-9311**
813 Industrial Ave Chesapeake (23324) ***(G-2971)***
American Media Institute 703 872-7840
2420 S Queen St Arlington (22202) ***(G-853)***
American Medical Devices Inc 276 642-0463
1788 Island Rd Bristol (24201) ***(G-1965)***
American Merchant Inc 407 446-9872
750 Old Abingdon Hwy Bristol (24201) ***(G-1966)***
American Metal Fabricators LLC 540 834-2400
4932 Trade Center Dr Fredericksburg (22408) ***(G-5244)***
American Mine Research Inc (PA) **276 928-1712**
12187 N Scenic Hwy Rocky Gap (24366) ***(G-12305)***
American Mirror, Galax *Also called Webb Furniture Enterprises Inc* ***(G-5654)***
American Mirror Company Inc 276 236-5111
300 E Grayson St Galax (24333) ***(G-5627)***
American Mountain Tech LLC 423 646-1864
19182 Sterling Dr Abingdon (24211) ***(G-10)***
American Mtal Fabrications Inc 804 271-8355
2512 Sisco Ave Richmond (23234) ***(G-11026)***
American Mtal Fbrcation VA LLC 434 851-1002
3061 Holiday Lake Rd Appomattox (24522) ***(G-801)***
American Nexus LLC 804 405-5443
1700 E Marshall St # 114 Richmond (23223) ***(G-11484)***
American Orthotic 757 548-5296
1521 Technology Dr Chesapeake (23320) ***(G-2972)***
American Orthtic Prsthetic Ctr, Richmond *Also called American Cmg Services Inc* ***(G-11107)***
American Pallet, Richmond *Also called Deep Corporation* ***(G-11040)***
American Phoenix Inc 434 688-0662
121 Martha St Danville (24541) ***(G-3954)***
American Plstic Fbricators Inc 434 376-3404
536 Cook Ave Brookneal (24528) ***(G-2107)***
American Quality Software Inc 571 730-4532
2740 Pioneer Ln Falls Church (22043) ***(G-4748)***
American Rheinmetall Def Inc (PA) **571 867-0047**
11180 Sunrise Valley Dr Reston (20191) ***(G-10787)***
American Rhnmtall Munition Inc 703 221-9299
125 Wdstream Blvd Ste 105 Stafford (22556) ***(G-13116)***
American Safety & Health (PA) **434 977-2700**
513 Stewart St Ste G Charlottesville (22902) ***(G-2728)***
American Safety Razor, Verona *Also called Energizer Personal Care LLC* ***(G-13986)***
American Sheet Metal & Welding 757 627-9203
2713 Colley Ave Norfolk (23517) ***(G-9439)***
American Shirt Printing 703 405-4014
247 Doc Stone Rd Stafford (22556) ***(G-13117)***
American Sign Lnguage Svcs LLC 571 969-2751
8707 Bradgate Rd Alexandria (22308) ***(G-411)***
American Skin LLC 910 259-2232
1480 Industrial Dr Smithfield (23431) ***(G-12703)***
American Soc For Engrg Educatn 804 742-5611
68 Port Royal Sq Unit 68 Port Royal (22535) ***(G-10385)***
American Soc For Hort Science 703 836-4606
1018 Duke St Alexandria (22314) ***(G-132)***
American Solar Inc 703 346-6053
8703 Chippendale Ct Annandale (22003) ***(G-730)***
American Spectator 703 807-2011
122 S Royal St Alexandria (22314) ***(G-133)***
American Spin-A-Batch Co Intl 804 798-1349
14523 Augusta Ln Ashland (23005) ***(G-1367)***
American Spirit LLC 703 914-1057
6302 Crosswoods Cir Falls Church (22044) ***(G-4749)***

American Stone Inc 804 448-9460
8179 Arba Ave Ruther Glen (22546) ***(G-12449)***
American Stone Virginia LLC 804 448-9460
8179 Arba Ave Ladysmith (22501) ***(G-7154)***
American Stripping Company 703 368-9922
9205 Vassau Ct Manassas Park (20111) ***(G-8188)***
American Tech Sltons Intl Corp (PA) **540 907-5355**
49 Bethany Way Fredericksburg (22406) ***(G-5398)***
American Technology Inds Ltd 757 436-6465
826 Professional Pl W Chesapeake (23320) ***(G-2973)***
American Track Carrier LLC 804 752-7533
11191 Air Park Rd Ashland (23005) ***(G-1368)***
American Wood Fibers Inc 276 646-3075
514 Lee Hwy Marion (24354) ***(G-8222)***
American Woodmark Corporation 540 665-9100
561 Shady Elm Rd Winchester (22602) ***(G-15377)***
American Woodmark Corporation (PA) **540 665-9100**
561 Shady Elm Rd Winchester (22602) ***(G-15378)***
American Woodmark Corporation 540 672-3707
281 Kentucky Rd Orange (22960) ***(G-10202)***
American Woodmark Corporation 540 665-9100
561 Shady Elm Rd Winchester (22602) ***(G-15379)***
Americaneagle.com, Alexandria *Also called Svanaco Inc* ***(G-359)***
Americast Inc 757 494-5200
3900 Shannon St Chesapeake (23324) ***(G-2974)***
Americast Inc 804 798-6068
11352 Virginia Precast Rd Ashland (23005) ***(G-1369)***
Americast Inc (HQ) **540 434-6979**
210 Stone Spring Rd Harrisonburg (22801) ***(G-6292)***
Americomm LLC (PA) **757 622-2724**
1048 W 27th St Norfolk (23517) ***(G-9440)***
Americomm Direct Marketing, Norfolk *Also called Americomm LLC* ***(G-9440)***
Ameridarts, Richardsville *Also called Livingston Resources Inc* ***(G-11011)***
Ameridisc, Fredericksburg *Also called Designer Software Inc* ***(G-5272)***
Ames & Ames Inc 757 877-2328
7205 Rte 17 Yorktown (23692) ***(G-15932)***
Ames & Ames Inc 757 851-4723
95 Apollo Dr Hampton (23669) ***(G-6083)***
Ames Cleaners & Formals Inc 757 825-3335
10 Town Center Way Hampton (23666) ***(G-6084)***
Ames Textiles Inc 540 382-8522
200 Industrial Dr Christiansburg (24073) ***(G-3568)***
Ames Textiles Synt Yarns Div, Christiansburg *Also called Ames Textiles Inc* ***(G-3568)***
Ames Tuxedo, Hampton *Also called Ames Cleaners & Formals Inc* ***(G-6084)***
Amethyst Flame Candles LLC 757 324-0614
301 Hill St Suffolk (23434) ***(G-13669)***
AMF, Richmond *Also called Bush River Corporation* ***(G-11139)***
AMF Automation Tech LLC (PA) **804 355-7961**
2115 W Laburnum Ave Richmond (23227) ***(G-11110)***
AMF Bakery Systems Corp 800 225-3771
2115 W Laburnum Ave Richmond (23227) ***(G-11111)***
AMF Bowling Worldwide Inc 804 730-4000
8100 Amf Dr Mechanicsville (23111) ***(G-8601)***
AMF Bowling Worldwide Inc (HQ) **804 730-4000**
7313 Bell Creek Rd Mechanicsville (23111) ***(G-8602)***
AMF Metal Inc 703 354-1345
6625 Iron Pl Springfield (22151) ***(G-12947)***
AMF Metal Art Inc 703 354-1345
4315 Argonne Dr Fairfax (22032) ***(G-4407)***
Amfab Inc 757 543-1485
1424 Campostella Rd Chesapeake (23320) ***(G-2975)***
Amg Inc 434 385-7525
301 Jefferson Ridge Pkwy Lynchburg (24501) ***(G-7640)***
AMG International Inc 703 988-4741
6731 Applemint Ln Alexandria (22310) ***(G-412)***
Amh Print Group LLC 804 286-6166
7286 Hanover Green Dr C Mechanicsville (23111) ***(G-8603)***
Amherst Arms and Supply LLC 434 929-1978
4811 S Amherst Hwy Madison Heights (24572) ***(G-7867)***
Amherst Milling Co Inc 434 946-7601
140 Union Hill Rd Amherst (24521) ***(G-680)***
Amherst Nelson Publishing Co, Winchester *Also called Winchester Evening Star Inc* ***(G-15601)***
Amherst Technologies 434 946-0329
126 Sardis Rd Amherst (24521) ***(G-681)***
Amilcar S Sheet Metal LLC 571 330-8371
1548 Chela Ave Norfolk (23503) ***(G-9441)***
Amish Heirlooms of Vrgn 540 626-8587
619 Snidow St Pembroke (24136) ***(G-10281)***
Amissville Alternative 540 364-4436
7564 Tapps Ford Rd Amissville (20106) ***(G-716)***
Amity Software Inc 571 312-0880
1111 Army Navy Dr Arlington (22202) ***(G-854)***
Ammo Company LLC 703 304-4210
16022 Fleetwood Dr Catlett (20119) ***(G-2263)***
Amnion LLC 267 255-6700
14980 Limestone School Rd Leesburg (20176) ***(G-7216)***
Amogh Consultants Inc 469 867-1583
2440 Dakota Lakes Dr Herndon (20171) ***(G-6612)***
Amonate Mine, Amonate *Also called Consolidation Coal Company* ***(G-725)***
Amor De Beauty, Hampton *Also called Karolina De Los Santos* ***(G-6178)***
AMP Sales & Service LLC 540 586-1021
740 Industrial Ave Bedford (24523) ***(G-1619)***
Ampac Fine Chemicals VA LLC 804 504-8600
2820 Normandy Dr Petersburg (23805) ***(G-10302)***
Ampak Sportswear Inc 703 550-1300
8253 Backlick Rd Ste B Lorton (22079) ***(G-7461)***
Amplify Ventures LLC 571 248-2282
14305 Northbrook Ln Gainesville (20155) ***(G-5570)***
Ampurage 757 632-8232
1716 Moon Valley Dr Virginia Beach (23453) ***(G-14225)***
Amrhein Ltd 540 929-4632
9243 Patterson Dr Bent Mountain (24059) ***(G-1666)***
AMS, Fredericksburg *Also called Advance Mezzanine Systems LLC* ***(G-5168)***
AMS Group - Audubon, South Chesterfield *Also called Hill Phoenix Inc* ***(G-12807)***
AMS Services LLC 804 869-4777
2014 Skipwith Rd Richmond (23294) ***(G-11112)***
Amscien Instrument 804 301-0797
4408 Hungary Glen Ter Richmond (23294) ***(G-11113)***
Amsted Rail Company Inc 804 732-0202
2580 Frontage Rd Petersburg (23805) ***(G-10303)***
Amtech, Grafton *Also called Automated Machine & Tech Inc* ***(G-5931)***
Amthor International Inc 845 778-5576
237 Indl Dr Gretna (24557) ***(G-6002)***
Amti, Lynchburg *Also called Advanced Mfg Tech Inc* ***(G-7633)***
Amware Logistics Services Inc 540 389-9737
1300 Intervale Dr Salem (24153) ***(G-12474)***
Amware Pallet Service, Salem *Also called Amware Logistics Services Inc* ***(G-12474)***
Amway Products & Services 757 474-2115
4449 Clemsford Dr Virginia Beach (23456) ***(G-14226)***
An Electronic Instrumentation 434 793-4870
350 Slayton Ave Danville (24540) ***(G-3955)***
An Electronic Instrumentation (PA) **703 478-0700**
309 Kellys Ford Plz Se Leesburg (20175) ***(G-7217)***
Ana's House Braids and Styles, Richmond *Also called Burroughs Qiana* ***(G-11030)***
Analystsoft Inc 844 782-8758
901 N Pitt St Ste 325 Alexandria (22314) ***(G-134)***
Analytic Stress Relieving Inc 804 271-5447
7523 Whitepine Rd North Chesterfield (23237) ***(G-9817)***
Analyzed Images 757 905-4500
4445 Corp Ln Ste 264 Virginia Beach (23462) ***(G-14227)***
Anatomy Home Inspection Svc 703 771-1568
15200 James Monroe Hwy Leesburg (20176) ***(G-7218)***
Anchor, Gainesville *Also called Oldcastle Apg Northeast Inc* ***(G-5605)***
Anchor 540 327-9391
396 Tyson Dr Winchester (22603) ***(G-15380)***
Anchor Canteen, Chesapeake *Also called Compass Group Usa Inc* ***(G-3048)***
Anchor Defense Inc 757 460-3830
4221 Battery Rd Virginia Beach (23455) ***(G-14228)***
Anchor Woodworks 804 458-6443
2607 Douglas Ln North Prince George (23860) ***(G-10086)***
and Design Inc 703 913-0799
7000c Brookfield Plz Springfield (22150) ***(G-12948)***
Andersen, Luray *Also called Emco Enterprises Inc* ***(G-7609)***
Anderson Audiology Hearing Aid 540 616-7990
3607 S Main St Blacksburg (24060) ***(G-1722)***
Anderson Brothers Lumber Co 804 561-2153
8700 Otterburn Rd Amelia Court House (23002) ***(G-651)***
Anderson Creek Quarry, Rockville *Also called Martin Marietta Materials Inc* ***(G-12292)***
Anderson Erle P Lumber Company 804 748-0500
15610 James River Dr Disputanta (23842) ***(G-4104)***
Andersons Woodworks LLC 804 530-3736
14318 Woodland Hill Dr South Chesterfield (23834) ***(G-12795)***
Andes Glendon Meat Processing 540 896-7798
18317 N Mountain Rd Timberville (22853) ***(G-13845)***
Andes Publishing Co Inc 757 562-5528
8080 Gates Rd Suffolk (23437) ***(G-13670)***
Andis Pallet Co Inc 276 628-9044
25058 Regal Dr Abingdon (24211) ***(G-11)***
Andis Wood Products Inc 276 628-7764
13455 Smith Creek Rd Bristol (24202) ***(G-2005)***
Andra ONeil Smith 804 436-3764
2561 Morattico Rd Lancaster (22503) ***(G-7158)***
Andrea Darcell LLC 980 533-5128
712 3rd St Martinsville (24112) ***(G-8266)***
Andrea Lewis 804 933-4161
6526 Iron Bridge Rd North Chesterfield (23234) ***(G-9818)***
Andrea Press 434 960-8026
3558 Loftland Dr Earlysville (22936) ***(G-4285)***
Andres R Henriquz 703 629-9821
8625 Village Way Alexandria (22309) ***(G-413)***
Andrew Corp 703 726-5900
19700 Janelia Farm Blvd Ashburn (20147) ***(G-1241)***
Andrew Corporation 434 386-5262
140 Vista Centre Dr Forest (24551) ***(G-5050)***
Andrew Pawlick 540 949-8805
784 N Bayard Ave Waynesboro (22980) ***(G-15093)***

A L P H A B E T I C

Andrew Thurston Logging 540 521-6276
561 Elburnell Dr Eagle Rock (24085) *(G-4278)*

Andromeda3 Inc 240 246-5816
938 Leigh Mill Rd Great Falls (22066) *(G-5937)*

Andros Bowman Products LLC (HQ) **540 217-4100**
10119 Old Valley Pike Mount Jackson (22842) *(G-9064)*

Andros Foods North America, Mount Jackson *Also called Andros Bowman Products LLC (G-9064)*

Andy Meade 276 940-3000
119 Mullins Dr Duffield (24244) *(G-4175)*

Andy's Small Engine Repairs, Duffield *Also called Andy Meade (G-4175)*

Angeethi Winchester LLC 703 300-7488
2644 Valley Ave Winchester (22601) *(G-15527)*

Angel Rides Inc 540 373-5540
11929 Gardenia Dr Fredericksburg (22407) *(G-5245)*

Angel Wings Drone Services LLC 540 763-2630
703 Mount Elbert Rd Nw Riner (24149) *(G-11860)*

Angerole Mounts LLC 434 249-3977
100 Aviation Dr Ste 116 Charlottesville (22911) *(G-2588)*

Angle Valley Press LLC 540 662-1320
203 E Boscawen St Winchester (22601) *(G-15528)*

Anheuser-Busch LLC 757 253-3600
7801 Pocahontas Trl Williamsburg (23185) *(G-15203)*

Anheuser-Busch Companies LLC 757 253-3660
7801 Pocahontas Trl Williamsburg (23185) *(G-15204)*

Animate Systems Inc 804 233-8085
4700 Devonshire Rd Richmond (23225) *(G-11485)*

Anixter Inc 757 460-9718
1209 Baker Rd Ste 509 Virginia Beach (23455) *(G-14229)*

Ankh & Lotus LLC 313 333-5138
704 High St Petersburg (23803) *(G-10304)*

Anlac LLC 703 370-3500
3025 Colvin St Alexandria (22314) *(G-135)*

Anm Food Services Inc 703 865-4378
11211 Lee Hwy Ste G Fairfax (22030) *(G-4592)*

Ann Grogg 540 667-4279
3641 Apple Pie Ridge Rd Winchester (22603) *(G-15381)*

Ann J Kite 540 656-3070
8303 Hancock Rd Spotsylvania (22553) *(G-12883)*

Ann Kite 434 989-4841
900 Reas Ford Rd Earlysville (22936) *(G-4286)*

Anna Banana Sweets, Sumerduck *Also called Montemorano LLC (G-13792)*

Anna Lake Winery Inc 540 895-5085
5621 Courthouse Rd Spotsylvania (22551) *(G-12884)*

Annabs Gluten Free LLC 804 491-9288
10198 Summer Hill Rd Mechanicsville (23116) *(G-8604)*

Annalees LLC 703 303-1841
22648 Glenn Dr Ste 203 Sterling (20164) *(G-13344)*

Annandale Mllwk Alied Systems (PA) **540 665-9600**
220 Arbor Ct Winchester (22602) *(G-15382)*

Annandale Times 703 437-5400
1760 Reston Pkwy Reston (20190) *(G-10788)*

Anne Chapman Casting 804 728-1300
2939 W Marshall St Richmond (23230) *(G-11114)*

Anneker Corp 202 630-3007
514 E Glendale Ave Alexandria (22301) *(G-136)*

Annex Inc 703 239-8553
10131 Zion Dr Fairfax (22032) *(G-4408)*

Annie Lee Traffic Patrol 888 682-5882
1187 Old Denbigh Blvd Newport News (23602) *(G-9167)*

Annin & Co 434 575-7913
3011 Philpott Rd South Boston (24592) *(G-12746)*

Annoai Inc 571 490-5316
11951 Freedom Dr Fl 15 Reston (20190) *(G-10789)*

Anns Stained Glass Windows PA 540 337-2249
300 Falling Rock Dr Stuarts Draft (24477) *(G-13643)*

Anointed For Purpose 804 651-4427
328 E Ingram Ct Norfolk (23505) *(G-9442)*

Anord Mardix (usa) Inc 800 228-4689
2704 Seven Hills Blvd Henrico (23231) *(G-6473)*

Anra Aviation, Chantilly *Also called Anra Technologies Inc (G-2525)*

Anra Technologies Inc 703 239-3206
25050 Riding Plz Chantilly (20152) *(G-2525)*

Anseal Inc 571 642-0680
8532u Terminal Rd Lorton (22079) *(G-7462)*

Antenna Technologies Ltd Co 703 450-5517
22560 Glenn Dr Ste 114 Sterling (20164) *(G-13345)*

Antennamast Systems, Cascade *Also called Old Stone Corp (G-2252)*

Antensan Usa Inc 703 836-0300
637 S Washington St Alexandria (22314) *(G-137)*

Antex Usa Inc 804 693-0831
4914 Ste B Grge Wshngtn M Hayes (23072) *(G-6395)*

Antheon Solutions Inc 703 298-1891
1712 Clubhouse Rd Ste 122 Reston (20190) *(G-10790)*

Anthony Amusements 703 670-2681
5973 Twin Rivers Dr Manassas (20112) *(G-8027)*

Anthony Biel 703 307-8516
15049 Holleyside Dr Dumfries (22025) *(G-4234)*

Anthony Corporation 757 490-3613
332 Cleveland Pl Virginia Beach (23462) *(G-14230)*

Anthony George Ltd Inc 434 369-1204
1806 Elizabeth St Altavista (24517) *(G-625)*

Anthony Lamon Williams 757 927-8141
231 Lochaven Dr Newport News (23602) *(G-9168)*

Antillian Trading Company LLC 703 626-6333
7204 Spring Faire Ct C Alexandria (22315) *(G-414)*

Antimicrobial Therapy Inc 540 987-9480
11771 Lee Hwy Sperryville (22740) *(G-12876)*

Antiquated Heirlooms LLC 540 771-4120
256 Lake Ridge Rd Strasburg (22657) *(G-13572)*

Antmed Corporation 703 239-3118
11092b Lee Hwy 104 Fairfax (22030) *(G-4593)*

Antonio Puducay 703 927-2953
8179 Douglas Fir Dr Lorton (22079) *(G-7463)*

Antonio Robinson 804 368-9889
2773 Meadowbrook St Petersburg (23803) *(G-10305)*

Anxious Bench Music Inc 757 813-4389
2207 Fon Du Lac Rd Henrico (23229) *(G-6474)*

Any and All Graphics LLC 757 468-9600
3200 Dam Neck Rd Ste 105 Virginia Beach (23453) *(G-14231)*

Any Job Software Inc 540 347-4347
7801 Overbrook Dr Catlett (20119) *(G-2264)*

Anything Vertical LLC 540 871-6519
1410 Ashford Ct Blacksburg (24060) *(G-1723)*

AO Hathaway Publishing LLC 804 305-9832
14241 Midlothian Tpke Midlothian (23113) *(G-8772)*

AOC Metal Works, Chester *Also called Stamptech Inc (G-3456)*

Aok Quality Solutions 757 710-9844
25137 Serenity Ln Onancock (23417) *(G-10189)*

Aow Global LLC 757 228-5557
814 Greenbrier Cir Ste B Chesapeake (23320) *(G-2976)*

AP Candles LLC 804 276-8681
4902 Ventura Rd Chesterfield (23832) *(G-3475)*

Apex Capital LLC 904 495-6422
11129 Air Park Rd Ashland (23005) *(G-1370)*

Apex Clean Energy Inc (PA) **434 220-7595**
310 4th St Ne Ste 300 Charlottesville (22902) *(G-2729)*

Apex Industries LLC 804 313-2295
1688 Chestnut Hill Rd Warsaw (22572) *(G-15060)*

Apex Industries Inc 540 992-5300
325 S Center Dr Daleville (24083) *(G-3939)*

Apex Mobile App LLC 804 245-0471
8834 Buffalo Nickel Turn Midlothian (23112) *(G-8773)*

Apex Pallets LLC 804 246-1499
33132 King William Rd West Point (23181) *(G-15153)*

Apex Publishers 703 966-1906
6002 Rockton Ct Centreville (20121) *(G-2290)*

Apex Tree Industries 540 915-6489
1001 Howbert Ave Sw Roanoke (24015) *(G-12033)*

Apex Truss, Warsaw *Also called Apex Industries LLC (G-15060)*

Apex Welding Service LLC 757 773-1151
662 Lacy Oak Dr Chesapeake (23320) *(G-2977)*

Apg Electronics 540 672-7252
15339 Kerby Dr Orange (22960) *(G-10203)*

Apg Media of Chesapeake LLC 804 843-2282
1430 High St Ste 504 Williamsburg (23185) *(G-15205)*

Aphropolitan, Virginia Beach *Also called Le Look LLC (G-14605)*

API Services, Newport News *Also called Automated Precision Inc (G-9174)*

Apical Woodworks & Nursery LLC 434 384-0525
1010 Pioneer Ct Lynchburg (24503) *(G-7641)*

Aplus Networking, Crewe *Also called Brandon Jenkins (G-3809)*

Aplus Signs and Bus Svcs LLC 540 667-8010
5 Featherbed Ln Winchester (22601) *(G-15529)*

APM Enterprises Inc 540 921-3399
205 N Main St Pearisburg (24134) *(G-10271)*

Apogee Communications 703 481-1622
900 Mcdaniel Ct Herndon (20170) *(G-6613)*

Apogee Power Usa LLC 318 572-8967
14 Little Field Dr Fredericksburg (22405) *(G-5399)*

Apollo Press Inc 757 247-9002
708 Thimble Shoals Blvd # 1 Newport News (23606) *(G-9169)*

Apostolos Publishing LLC 703 656-8036
9648 Laurencekirk Pl Bristow (20136) *(G-2045)*

Apothecary Spices 703 868-2333
1200 N Quaker Ln Alexandria (22302) *(G-138)*

Appalachia Holding Company (HQ) **276 619-4410**
1 Alpha Pl Bristol (24202) *(G-2006)*

Appalachian Aggregates LLC 276 326-1145
171 Saint Clair Xing Bluefield (24605) *(G-1857)*

Appalachian Alpaca Fibr Co LLC 276 728-2349
5197 Snake Creek Rd Hillsville (24343) *(G-6883)*

Appalachian Cast Products, Abingdon *Also called Acp LLC (G-6)*

Appalachian Cast Products Inc (PA) **276 619-5080**
26372 Hillman Hwy Abingdon (24210) *(G-12)*

Appalachian Drone Servie LLC 276 346-6350
422 Murphy Hobbs Rd Dryden (24243) *(G-4144)*

Appalachian Energy Inc (PA) **276 619-4880**
230 Charwood Dr Abingdon (24210) *(G-13)*

Appalachian Growth Logging LLC 540 336-2674
2782 Supinlick Ridge Rd Mount Jackson (22842) *(G-9065)*

Appalachian Machine Inc 540 674-1914
  5304 Laboratory St Dublin (24084) *(G-4148)*

Appalachian Manufacturing 540 825-3522
  16184 Brandy Rd Culpeper (22701) *(G-3866)*

Appalachian Mineral Services 276 345-4610
  113 Augusta Ave Richlands (24641) *(G-11012)*

Appalachian Plastics Inc 276 429-2581
  34001 Glove Dr Glade Spring (24340) *(G-5673)*

Appalachian Prod Svcs Inc (HQ) **276 619-4880**
  2487 Rose Rdg Clintwood (24228) *(G-3687)*

Appalachian Production Svcs, Clintwood *Also called Appalachian Prod Svcs Inc* *(G-3687)*

Appalachian Radio Corporation 865 382-9865
  151 Goldenrod Rd Ruckersville (22968) *(G-12398)*

Appalachian Woods LLC (PA) **540 337-1801**
  1240 Cold Springs Rd Stuarts Draft (24477) *(G-13644)*

Appalachian Woods LLC 540 886-5700
  871 Middlebrook Ave Staunton (24401) *(G-13242)*

Appalchian Afrcan Amrcn Cltral, Pennington Gap *Also called Appalchian Afrcan Amrcn Cnter* *(G-10293)*

Appalachian Afrcan Amrcn Cnter 276 546-5144
  265 Leona St Pennington Gap (24277) *(G-10293)*

Appalchian Leicester Longwools 540 639-3077
  4615 Mountain Pride Rd Hiwassee (24347) *(G-6909)*

Appfore LLC 757 597-6990
  413 Biltmore Ct Virginia Beach (23454) *(G-14232)*

Appian Corporation 703 442-8844
  7950 Jones Branch Dr Tysons (22102) *(G-13941)*

Appian Corporation (PA) **703 442-8844**
  7950 Jones Branch Dr Mc Lean (22102) *(G-8393)*

Apple Frankies Ent Inc 540 845-7372
  3217 Lancaster Ring Rd Fredericksburg (22408) *(G-5246)*

Apple Ridge Publishers 703 597-8523
  217 Bob White Ln Quicksburg (22847) *(G-10692)*

Apple Shine 757 714-6393
  3313 Boynton Ct Virginia Beach (23452) *(G-14233)*

Apple Tire Inc 434 575-5200
  615 N Main St South Boston (24592) *(G-12747)*

Apple Valley LLC 540 465-8360
  478 E Washington St Strasburg (22657) *(G-13573)*

Apple-Polishers LLC 571 918-1027
  1212 Cannon Ct Ne Leesburg (20176) *(G-7219)*

Appleberry Mtn Taxidermy Svcs 434 831-2232
  5046 Green Creek Rd Schuyler (22969) *(G-12651)*

Apples & Belles LLC 804 530-3180
  1425 Chaplin Bay Dr Chester (23836) *(G-3387)*

Apples Closet 540 825-9551
  203 N Main St Culpeper (22701) *(G-3867)*

Application Technologies Inc 703 644-0506
  7707 Tanner Robert Ct Springfield (22153) *(G-12949)*

Applied Electronics, Newport News *Also called Matthias Enterprises Inc* *(G-9296)*

Applied Felts Inc 276 656-1904
  450 College Dr Martinsville (24112) *(G-8267)*

Applied Film Technology Inc 757 351-4241
  5312 Vrgnia Bch Blvd Ste Virginia Beach (23462) *(G-14234)*

Applied Manufacturing Tech 434 942-1047
  1097 Preserve Ln Thaxton (24174) *(G-13841)*

Applied Materials Inc 703 331-1476
  7900 Sudley Rd Ste 303 Manassas (20109) *(G-8028)*

Applied Materials Inc 540 583-0466
  17539 Jefferson Davis Hwy Dumfries (22026) *(G-4235)*

Applied Plasma Tech LLC 703 340-5545
  5408 Port Royal Rd Ste S Springfield (22151) *(G-12950)*

Applied Polymer LLC 804 615-5105
  12840 River Rd Richmond (23238) *(G-11115)*

Applied Pressures Diamond 757 967-7006
  7425 Sewells Point Rd Norfolk (23513) *(G-9443)*

Applied Signals Intelligence 571 313-0681
  45945 Center Oak Plz # 100 Sterling (20166) *(G-13346)*

Applied Technollogy 703 660-8422
  6917 Tulsa Ct Alexandria (22307) *(G-415)*

Applied Technology Associates, Chantilly *Also called A-Tech Corporation* *(G-2360)*

Applied Technology Group Inc 703 960-5555
  2401 Huntington Ave Alexandria (22303) *(G-416)*

Applied Video Imaging LLC 434 974-6310
  355 Rio Road West Ste 101 Charlottesville (22901) *(G-2589)*

Applied Visual Sciences Inc (PA) **703 539-6190**
  525 E Market St 116k Leesburg (20176) *(G-7220)*

Applied Vsual Cmmnications Inc 703 787-6668
  450 Springpark Pl # 1200 Herndon (20170) *(G-6614)*

Appomattox Lime Co Inc (HQ) **434 933-8258**
  143 Quarry Rd Appomattox (24522) *(G-802)*

Appomattox Lime Company 540 774-1696
  2343 Highland Farm Rd Nw Roanoke (24017) *(G-12034)*

Appomattox Quarry 434 295-5700
  143 Quarry Rd Appomattox (24522) *(G-803)*

Appomattox River Engraving 804 561-3565
  10050 Mattoax Ln Amelia Court House (23002) *(G-652)*

Apprentice Press 703 352-5005
  10605 Center St Fairfax (22030) *(G-4594)*

Apprentice School-Newport News, Newport News *Also called Huntington Ingalls Inc* *(G-9250)*

Apps of All Nations LLC 434 851-0651
  1506 Hamilton Dr Lynchburg (24503) *(G-7642)*

Appvity 571 327-0888
  22636 Glenn Dr Ste 201 Sterling (20164) *(G-13347)*

April A Phillips Pottery 703 464-1283
  11296 Fairwind Way Herndon (20190) *(G-6615)*

April Press 804 551-8463
  2507 Waldo Ln Henrico (23228) *(G-6475)*

Aprize Satellite Inc 703 273-7010
  3554 Chain Bridge Rd # 103 Fairfax (22030) *(G-4595)*

APT Finders Free Locaters Svc, Midlothian *Also called Ft Communications Inc* *(G-8820)*

Aptify Corporation 202 223-2600
  7901 Jones Branch Dr Fl 5 Mc Lean (22102) *(G-8394)*

Aptify Corporation (PA) **202 223-2600**
  7900 Wstpk Dr 5th Fl Atrm # 5 Tysons Corner (22102) *(G-13951)*

Aquabean LLC 703 577-0315
  8913 Glade Hill Rd Fairfax (22031) *(G-4409)*

Aquanta Inc 703 286-0923
  1775 Tysons Blvd Fl 5 Mc Lean (22102) *(G-8395)*

Aquao2 Wastewater Treatment Sy 540 365-0154
  5800 Prillaman Switch Rd Ferrum (24088) *(G-4967)*

Aquarobic International Inc 540 365-0154
  5800 Prillaman Switch Rd Ferrum (24088) *(G-4968)*

Aquatic Co 434 572-1200
  1100 Industrial Park Rd South Boston (24592) *(G-12748)*

Aquawash Pressure Washing LLC 757 738-9899
  5912 Appleton Ct Virginia Beach (23464) *(G-14235)*

Aqueous Solutions Global LLC 410 710-7736
  2828 Cofer Rd Richmond (23224) *(G-11486)*

Aquia Creek Gems 540 659-6120
  1407 Aquia Dr Stafford (22554) *(G-13118)*

Aquilian LLC 703 967-8212
  4800 Leighfield Valley Dr Chantilly (20151) *(G-2369)*

Arabelle Publishing LLC 804 298-5082
  10106 Krause Rd Ste 102 Chesterfield (23832) *(G-3476)*

Arabesque Media 703 745-5395
  4000 Legato Rd Fairfax (22033) *(G-4410)*

Arban & Carosi Incorporated 703 491-5121
  13800 Dawson Beach Rd Woodbridge (22191) *(G-15646)*

Arban Precast Stone Ltd 703 221-8005
  19000 Colonial Port Rd Dumfries (22026) *(G-4236)*

Arben Solutions Co 703 728-0396
  403 Holiday Ct Warrenton (20186) *(G-14978)*

Arboleda Cabinets Inc 804 230-0733
  5421 Distributor Dr Richmond (23225) *(G-11487)*

Arboleda Counter Tops, Richmond *Also called Arboleda Cabinets Inc* *(G-11487)*

Arbon Equipment Corporation 540 542-6790
  130 Imboden Dr Ste 7 Winchester (22603) *(G-15383)*

Arbon Equipment Corporation 540 387-2113
  602 Roanoke St Salem (24153) *(G-12475)*

ARC Document Solutions Inc 703 518-8890
  300 N Henry St Alexandria (22314) *(G-139)*

ARC Dust LLC 571 839-0223
  6148 Old Telegraph Rd Alexandria (22310) *(G-417)*

ARC Global Corp 757 470-9271
  2119 Brennhaven Trl Chesapeake (23323) *(G-2978)*

ARC Lighting LLC 757 513-7717
  2001 Dewald Rd Chesapeake (23322) *(G-2979)*

ARC Second Inc 703 435-5400
  44880 Falcon Pl Ste 100 Sterling (20166) *(G-13348)*

ARC Vosacthree 703 910-7721
  2216 Tacketts Mill Dr Woodbridge (22192) *(G-15647)*

Arcade Signs LLC 703 815-5440
  14641 Lee Hwy Ste D7 Centreville (20121) *(G-2291)*

Arcamax Publishing Inc 757 596-9730
  11830 Canon Blvd Ste A Newport News (23606) *(G-9170)*

Archematerial Inc 703 826-6820
  9848b Main St Fairfax (22031) *(G-4411)*

Archer Construction 276 637-6905
  156 Rome Rd Max Meadows (24360) *(G-8365)*

Archer-Daniels-Midland Company 540 433-2761
  285 Oakwood Dr Rockingham (22801) *(G-12240)*

Archipelago Publishers Inc 434 979-5292
  925 Marshall St Charlottesville (22901) *(G-2590)*

Architctral Rnssnce Techniques, Virginia Beach *Also called James Hintzke* *(G-14563)*

Architectural Accents 540 943-5888
  500 Loudoun Ave Waynesboro (22980) *(G-15094)*

Architectural Custom Wdwrk Inc 804 784-2283
  44 Plaza Dr Manakin Sabot (23103) *(G-7895)*

Architectural Graphics Inc (PA) **800 877-7868**
  2655 International Pkwy Virginia Beach (23452) *(G-14236)*

Architectural Graphics Inc. 757 427-1900
  2820 Crusader Cir Virginia Beach (23453) *(G-14237)*

Architectural Graphics Inc. 757 301-7008
  2800 Crusader Cir Virginia Beach (23453) *(G-14238)*

Architectural Systems Virginia (PA) **804 270-0477**
  9522 Downing St Richmond (23238) *(G-11116)*

Architectural Wood, Roanoke *Also called Wood Design & Fabrication Inc* *(G-12024)*

Archna & Nazish Inc....571 221-6224
14000 Willard Rd Chantilly (20151) ***(G-2370)***
Arco Welding Inc....540 710-6944
329 Wallace Ln Ste A Fredericksburg (22408) ***(G-5247)***
Arcola Industries LLC....703 723-0092
21364 Chickacoan Trail Dr Broadlands (20148) ***(G-2072)***
Arconic Cbt....757 825-6870
1 Howmet Dr Hampton (23661) ***(G-6085)***
Arcsys, Norfolk *Also called Harbinger Tech Solutions LLC* ***(G-9571)***
Arctan Inc....202 379-4723
2200 Wilson Blvd 102-150 Arlington (22201) ***(G-855)***
Arctech Inc....434 575-7200
2348 Eastover Dr South Boston (24592) ***(G-12749)***
Arcworx Welding LLC....540 394-1494
40949 Pearce Cir Leesburg (20176) ***(G-7221)***
Ardeens Designs Inc....804 562-3840
4610 Lkfeld Mews Pl Apt G Richmond (23231) ***(G-11117)***
Ardent Candle Company LLC....347 906-2011
1616 Fairfax Dr Virginia Beach (23453) ***(G-14239)***
Ardent Mills LLC....540 825-1530
1900 Industry Dr Culpeper (22701) ***(G-3868)***
Ardsen Offset....757 220-3299
4399 Ironbound Rd Williamsburg (23188) ***(G-15206)***
Are You Wired LLC....804 512-3990
2737 Perlock Rd North Chesterfield (23237) ***(G-9819)***
Ares Self Defense Inc....757 561-3538
11537 Winding River Rd Providence Forge (23140) ***(G-10618)***
Aretec Inc....703 539-8801
10201 Fairfax Blvd # 223 Fairfax (22030) ***(G-4596)***
Aretech LLC (PA)....**571 292-8889**
21720 Red Rum Dr Ste 187 Ashburn (20147) ***(G-1242)***
Arey Machine Shop....540 943-7782
551 Calf Mountain Rd Waynesboro (22980) ***(G-15095)***
Argent Line LLC....703 519-1209
211 N Union St Alexandria (22314) ***(G-140)***
Argon....804 365-5628
3805 Cutshaw Ave Richmond (23230) ***(G-11118)***
Argon St Inc (HQ)....**703 322-0881**
12701 Fair Lakes Cir # 800 Fairfax (22033) ***(G-4412)***
Argos USA LLC....804 227-9402
9680 Old Ridge Rd Ashland (23005) ***(G-1371)***
Argos USA LLC....804 763-6112
3636 Warbro Rd Midlothian (23112) ***(G-8774)***
Arhat Media Inc....703 716-5662
11901 Escalante Ct Reston (20191) ***(G-10791)***
Ariake USA Inc (HQ)....**540 432-6550**
1711 N Liberty St Harrisonburg (22802) ***(G-6293)***
Arias Windchimes, Manassas Park *Also called Qmt Associates Inc* ***(G-8208)***
Aric Lynn Co, Manassas *Also called Aric Lynn LLC* ***(G-8029)***
Aric Lynn LLC....571 505-7657
11033 Wooldridge Dr Manassas (20111) ***(G-8029)***
Arif Winter....757 515-9940
1455 Mellwood Ct Ste B Norfolk (23513) ***(G-9444)***
Arista Tubes Inc....434 793-0660
187 Cane Creek Blvd Danville (24540) ***(G-3956)***
Ark Commercial Services LLC....202 807-6211
1775 Tysons Blvd Mc Lean (22102) ***(G-8396)***
Ark Holdings Group Llc....202 368-5828
13944 Greendale Dr Woodbridge (22191) ***(G-15648)***
Ark Woodworking LLC....540 272-7489
694 Zachary Taylor Hwy Flint Hill (22627) ***(G-5014)***
Arkansas Gazette, The, Mc Lean *Also called Gannett River States Pubg Corp* ***(G-8443)***
Arkay Packaging Corporation....540 278-2596
350 Eastpark Dr Roanoke (24019) ***(G-11882)***
Arkcase LLC....703 272-3270
9601 Pembroke Pl Vienna (22182) ***(G-14009)***
Arkema Inc....800 225-7788
27123 Shady Brook Trl Courtland (23837) ***(G-3766)***
Arkema Inc....434 433-0300
601 Tightsqueeze Indus Rd Chatham (24531) ***(G-2919)***
Arktis Detection Systems Inc....610 724-9748
2011 Crystal Dr Ste 400 Arlington (22202) ***(G-856)***
Arlene Nancys Meals On Wheels....404 940-8995
8709 Squirrel Level Rd North Dinwiddie (23803) ***(G-10047)***
Arlington Adrndack Wdworks LLC....703 964-7700
5010 23rd St S Arlington (22206) ***(G-857)***
Arlington Boccato LLC....703 516-4075
1011 Arlington Blvd # 30 Arlington (22209) ***(G-858)***
Arlington Community News Lab....703 243-7501
149 N Abingdon St Arlington (22203) ***(G-859)***
Arlington Cthlic Hrald Newsppr, Arlington *Also called Catholic Diocese of Arlington* ***(G-903)***
Arlington Mch Fabrication Inc....804 559-2500
8444 Erle Rd Mechanicsville (23116) ***(G-8605)***
Arm Global Solutions Inc....804 431-3746
1900 Ruffin Mill Rd South Chesterfield (23834) ***(G-12796)***
Armadillo Industries Inc....757 508-2348
4001 Elizabeth Killebrew Williamsburg (23188) ***(G-15207)***
Armata Pharmaceuticals Inc....804 827-3010
800 E Leigh St Ste 54 Richmond (23219) ***(G-11488)***
Armes Prcsion McHning Fbrction....434 237-4552
173 Fastener Dr Lynchburg (24502) ***(G-7643)***
Armour-Eckrich Meats LLC, Smithfield *Also called Smithfield Direct LLC* ***(G-12726)***
Arms Race Nutrition LLC....888 978-2332
22370 Davis Dr Ste 100 Sterling (20164) ***(G-13349)***
Armstar Corporation....703 241-8888
3122 Patrick Henry Dr Falls Church (22044) ***(G-4750)***
Armstead Hauling Inc....804 675-8221
2906 Stockton St Richmond (23224) ***(G-11489)***
Armstrong Gordan....757 547-1090
505 San Pedro Dr Chesapeake (23322) ***(G-2980)***
Armstrong Airport Lighting....865 856-2723
8610 Richmond Rd Toano (23168) ***(G-13856)***
Armstrong Family....703 737-6188
43271 Meadowood Ct Leesburg (20176) ***(G-7222)***
Armstrong Green & Embrey Inc....540 898-7434
4821 Massaponax Church Rd Fredericksburg (22407) ***(G-5248)***
Armstrong Welding & Repair, Chesapeake *Also called Armstrong Gordan* ***(G-2980)***
Army Pubg Directorate-Apd, Fort Belvoir *Also called United States Dept of Army* ***(G-5119)***
Army Times, Vienna *Also called Sightline Media Group LLC* ***(G-14126)***
Aroma Kandles LLC....202 525-1550
9407 Silver Meteor Ct Manassas Park (20111) ***(G-8189)***
Aromatherapy Shoppe....757 531-7431
315 First Colonial Rd Virginia Beach (23454) ***(G-14240)***
Aromatic Spice Blends LLC....703 477-6865
43671 Trade Center Pl # 166 Sterling (20166) ***(G-13350)***
Arqball LLC....434 260-1890
1030 Linden Ave Charlottesville (22902) ***(G-2730)***
Arrington & Sons Inc....703 368-1462
10500 Dumfries Rd Manassas (20110) ***(G-7911)***
Arrington Smith Hunter Lee....540 230-4952
789 Talon Ln Christiansburg (24073) ***(G-3569)***
Arroman Industries Corp....804 317-4737
609 Elm Ct Hopewell (23860) ***(G-6918)***
Arrow Machine Inc....804 272-0202
309 Ruthers Rd North Chesterfield (23235) ***(G-9820)***
Arrow Mfg LLC....757 635-6889
1116 Burlington Rd Virginia Beach (23464) ***(G-14241)***
Arrowine Inc (PA)....**703 525-0990**
4508 Lee Hwy Arlington (22207) ***(G-860)***
ARS Manufacturing Inc....757 460-2211
5878 Bayside Rd Virginia Beach (23455) ***(G-14242)***
Art & Framing Center....540 720-2800
53 Doc Stone Rd Ste 101 Stafford (22556) ***(G-13119)***
Art Connected....540 628-2162
181 Kings Hwy Ste 205 Fredericksburg (22405) ***(G-5400)***
Art Creations Company Inc....703 257-9510
8492b Signal Hill Rd Manassas (20110) ***(G-7912)***
Art Glass Windows, Troy *Also called Mark S Chapman* ***(G-13934)***
Art Graphics N Designs Inc....757 463-9495
1337 Taylor Farm Rd # 106 Virginia Beach (23453) ***(G-14243)***
Art Guild Inc....804 282-5434
8433 Glazebrook Ave Henrico (23228) ***(G-6476)***
Art Guild Signs & Graphics, Richmond *Also called Bxi Inc* ***(G-11142)***
Art of Wood....703 597-9357
15 Oldridge Ct Sterling (20165) ***(G-13351)***
Art Printing Solutions LLC....804 387-3203
219 Nansemond St Petersburg (23803) ***(G-10306)***
ART&creation Inc....571 606-8999
8492b Signal Hill Rd Manassas (20110) ***(G-7913)***
Art-A-Metal LLC....757 787-1574
20485 Market St Onancock (23417) ***(G-10190)***
Artcraft Fabricators Inc (PA)....**757 399-7777**
2707 Syer Rd Portsmouth (23707) ***(G-10393)***
Artcraft Printing Ltd....757 428-9138
1136 Jensen Dr B Virginia Beach (23451) ***(G-14244)***
Arteffects....804 266-7691
5606 Greendale Rd Henrico (23228) ***(G-6477)***
Artfx LLC (HQ)....**757 853-1703**
1125 Azalea Garden Rd Norfolk (23502) ***(G-9445)***
Artfx, Inc., Norfolk *Also called Artfx LLC* ***(G-9445)***
Artgiftsetccom....703 772-3587
3519 13th St N Arlington (22201) ***(G-861)***
Artisan Concrete Designs Inc....434 321-3423
825 Marrow St South Hill (23970) ***(G-12842)***
Artisan Group, The, Arlington *Also called Buoya LLC* ***(G-892)***
Artisan II Inc....703 823-4636
4311 Wheeler Ave Alexandria (22304) ***(G-141)***
Artisan Meads LLC....757 713-4885
117 Whites Ln Seaford (23696) ***(G-12671)***
Artisan Woodwork Company LLC....540 420-4928
447 Blue Ridge Ct Rocky Mount (24151) ***(G-12312)***
Artistees....540 373-2888
513 Jackson St Fredericksburg (22401) ***(G-5170)***
Artistic Awards....540 636-9940
176 North River Dr Woodstock (22664) ***(G-15847)***
Artistic Awards Creative Gifts, Woodstock *Also called Artistic Awards* ***(G-15847)***
Artistic Design....540 980-1598
4616 Newbern Heights Dr Pulaski (24301) ***(G-10630)***

Artistic Impressions 757 923-4254
1780 Mill Wood Way Suffolk (23434) *(G-13671)*

Artistic Thread Designs 703 583-3706
15201 Warbler Ct Woodbridge (22193) *(G-15649)*

Artists Innvators Creators LLC 757 359-6215
2716 Spinners Way Chesapeake (23323) *(G-2981)*

Artner Corp 703 341-6333
6096 Deer Ridge Trl Springfield (22150) *(G-12951)*

Arton Glass & Crmic Decorators, Lively *Also called Bay Etching & Imprinting Inc* *(G-7439)*

Artusmode Software LLC 703 794-6100
11529 Seneca Farm Way Great Falls (22066) *(G-5938)*

Artwolf Signs & Graphics 757 567-8122
1131 Smith St Norfolk (23510) *(G-9446)*

Artworks 540 420-3843
544 Running Brook Rd Ferrum (24088) *(G-4969)*

Arundel Woodworks 202 713-8781
525 E Market St Leesburg (20176) *(G-7223)*

Arw Printing 540 720-6906
39 Francis Ct Stafford (22554) *(G-13120)*

As Clean As A Whistle 757 753-0600
304 Belray Dr Newport News (23601) *(G-9171)*

Asal Tie & Lumber Co Inc 434 454-6555
9025 James D Hagood Hwy Scottsburg (24589) *(G-12654)*

ASAP Printing & Graphics, Alexandria *Also called ASAP Printing & Mailing Co* *(G-142)*

ASAP Printing & Mailing Co 703 836-2288
2805 Mount Vernon Ave Alexandria (22301) *(G-142)*

Asb Greenworld Inc 804 785-9260
496 Airport Rd Mattaponi (23110) *(G-8357)*

Asb Greenworld Inc 804 695-2660
11524 Farm Rd Saluda (23149) *(G-12600)*

Ascalon International Inc 703 926-4343
11951 Freedom Dr Fl 13 Reston (20190) *(G-10792)*

Ascension Publishing LLC 804 212-5347
13330 Thornridge Ln Midlothian (23112) *(G-8775)*

Ascp Solutions LLC 410 782-1122
8629 Mathis Ave Manassas (20110) *(G-7914)*

Ascwelding 757 274-4486
420 Forest Rd Chesapeake (23322) *(G-2982)*

Asd Biosystems Inc 804 545-3102
440 Johnson Farm Rd Gretna (24557) *(G-6003)*

Ash Press LLC 757 778-0747
128 Seekright Dr Yorktown (23693) *(G-15933)*

Ashburn Sauce Company 757 621-1113
1087 Horn Point Rd Virginia Beach (23456) *(G-14245)*

Ashbury Intl Group Inc 434 296-8600
84 Business Park Cir Ruckersville (22968) *(G-12399)*

Ashbury Precision Ordnance Mfg, Ruckersville *Also called Ashbury Intl Group Inc* *(G-12399)*

Ashe Kustomz LLC 804 997-6406
3806 Alma Ave Richmond (23222) *(G-11490)*

Ashen Writ LLC 757 818-8271
2701 Derry Dr Chesapeake (23323) *(G-2983)*

Ashford Court LLC 804 743-0700
5915 Midlothian Tpke Richmond (23225) *(G-11491)*

Ashford Court Richmond Ci, Richmond *Also called Evergreen Enterprises Inc* *(G-11582)*

Ashland Milling Co, Ashland *Also called Ashland Roller Mills Inc* *(G-1372)*

Ashland Roller Mills Inc 804 798-8329
14471 Washington Hwy Ashland (23005) *(G-1372)*

Ashland Woodwork Inc 804 798-4088
101 Henry Clay Rd Ashland (23005) *(G-1373)*

Ashland Woodwork & Supply, Ashland *Also called Awsi Inc* *(G-1375)*

Ashlawn Energy LLC 703 461-3600
6564 Loisdale Ct Ste 600 Springfield (22150) *(G-12952)*

Ashley Clark Defense LLC 703 867-6665
43732 Clemens Ter Ashburn (20147) *(G-1243)*

Ashley Valve, Virginia Beach *Also called Romans Enterprises LLC* *(G-14779)*

Ashman Distributing Company 757 428-6734
1120 Jensen Dr Virginia Beach (23451) *(G-14246)*

Ashman Mfg & Distrg Co, Virginia Beach *Also called Ashman Distributing Company (G-14246)*

Ashp, Charlottesville *Also called American Safety & Health* *(G-2728)*

Ashs, Alexandria *Also called American Soc For Hort Science* *(G-132)*

Ashton Creek Vineyard LLC 804 896-1586
14501 Jefferson Davis Hwy Chester (23831) *(G-3388)*

Ashton Green Seafood 757 887-3551
203 Sunrise Ct Newport News (23608) *(G-9172)*

Ashworth Bros Inc 540 662-3494
450 Armour Dl Winchester (22601) *(G-15530)*

Asian American Coal Inc 804 648-1611
4 N 4th St Apt 100 Richmond (23219) *(G-11492)*

Asian Fortune Enterprises Inc 703 753-8295
1604 Spring Hill Rd # 300 Vienna (22182) *(G-14010)*

Asian Pacific Seafood LLC 251 751-5962
152 Greengable Way Chesapeake (23322) *(G-2984)*

Asip Publishing Inc 804 725-4613
1275 Lighthouse Rd Port Haywood (23138) *(G-10381)*

Asmars Mediterranean Food Inc 703 750-2960
6460 Gen Green Way Ste F Alexandria (22312) *(G-418)*

Aspen Dale Winery Barn 540 364-1722
3180 Aspen Dale Ln Delaplane (20144) *(G-4072)*

Aspen Industries LLC 540 234-0413
3584 Lee Hwy Weyers Cave (24486) *(G-15166)*

Aspen Motion Technologies Inc 540 639-4440
1120 W Rock Rd Radford (24141) *(G-10704)*

Aspetto Inc 540 547-8487
1691 Jefferson Davis Hwy Fredericksburg (22401) *(G-5171)*

Asphalt Ready Mix Inc 540 576-3483
1376 Jacks Creek Rd Union Hall (24176) *(G-13958)*

Aspire Marketing Corporation (PA) 434 525-6191
1168 Everett Rd Forest (24551) *(G-5051)*

Assa Abloy High SEC Group Inc (HQ) 540 380-5000
3625 Alleghany Dr Salem (24153) *(G-12476)*

Assembly & Design Inc 804 379-5432
425 Southlake Blvd Ste 1b North Chesterfield (23236) *(G-9821)*

Associate Business Co Inc 703 222-4624
4300 Chntly Shp Ctr Dr # 2 Chantilly (20151) *(G-2371)*

Associated Asp Partners LLC (PA) 540 345-8867
110 Franklin Rd Sw Fl 9 Roanoke (24011) *(G-12035)*

Associated Asphalt Inman LLC (PA) 864 472-2816
110 Franklin Rd Se Fl 9 Roanoke (24011) *(G-12036)*

Associated Asphalt Tf LLC 540 529-9789
110 Franklin Rd Se Fl 9 Roanoke (24011) *(G-12037)*

Associated Fabricators LLC 434 293-2333
1229 Harris St Charlottesville (22903) *(G-2731)*

Associated Gen Contrs of Amer (PA) 703 837-5415
2300 Wilson Blvd Ste 300 Arlington (22201) *(G-862)*

Associated Printing Svcs Inc 804 360-5770
2504 Brookstone Ln Richmond (23233) *(G-11119)*

Association For Cmpt McHy Inc 703 528-0726
2315 N Burlington St Arlington (22207) *(G-863)*

Association For Print Tech 703 264-7200
1899 Preston White Dr Reston (20191) *(G-10793)*

Association Publishing Inc 757 420-2434
2117 Smith Ave Chesapeake (23320) *(G-2985)*

Astellas Pharma Us Inc 804 262-3197
9701 Electra Ln Richmond (23228) *(G-11120)*

Astra Design Inc 804 257-5467
16 S Allen Ave Richmond (23220) *(G-11493)*

Astro LLC 888 401-1003
9705 Liberia Ave Ste 299 Manassas (20110) *(G-7915)*

Astrocomm Technologies LLC 703 606-2022
2702 Copper Creek Rd Oak Hill (20171) *(G-10135)*

Astron Wireless Tech Inc 703 450-5517
22560 Glenn Dr Ste 114 Sterling (20164) *(G-13352)*

Astron Wireless Tech LLC (PA) 703 450-5517
22560 Glenn Dr Ste 114 Sterling (20164) *(G-13353)*

Astronautics Corp of America 571 707-8705
44735 Audubon Sq Apt 522 Ashburn (20147) *(G-1244)*

Asw Aluminum 434 476-7557
1105 Chaffin Trl Halifax (24558) *(G-6048)*

At Lab of America LLC 681 207-9161
2818 Salem Hwy Stuart (24171) *(G-13605)*

At Sign LLC 703 895-7035
5008 Warwick Hills Ct Haymarket (20169) *(G-6414)*

At The Point Embroidery LLC 804 684-9544
1758 Hoven Rd Gloucester Point (23062) *(G-5871)*

Atarfil Usa Inc 757 386-8676
324 Moore Ave Bldg 3 Suffolk (23434) *(G-13672)*

Atavus Inc 703 404-2796
21100 Midday Ln Sterling (20164) *(G-13354)*

Atc Inc 703 267-6898
8962 Edmonston Dr Bristow (20136) *(G-2046)*

Atcc Global (PA) 434 237-6861
6015 Fort Ave Ste 23 Lynchburg (24502) *(G-7644)*

Atdi, Mc Lean *Also called Spectrum Center Inc* *(G-8554)*

Atelier Fonteneau LLC 540 371-5074
304 Interstate Bus Park Fredericksburg (22405) *(G-5401)*

Athena Services LLC 201 232-9114
7000 Falls Reach Dr # 312 Falls Church (22043) *(G-4751)*

Athenas Workshop Inc 703 615-4429
11115 Glade Dr Reston (20191) *(G-10794)*

ATI, Chesapeake *Also called American Technology Inds Ltd* *(G-2973)*

ATI Development LLC 571 313-0857
506 Shaw Rd Ste 330 Sterling (20166) *(G-13355)*

ATI-Endyna Jv LLC 410 992-3424
7926 Jones Branch Dr # 620 Mc Lean (22102) *(G-8397)*

Atk Chan Inc 804 266-3428
10444 Mountain Glen Pkwy Glen Allen (23060) *(G-5705)*

Atkins Automotive Corp 540 942-5157
794 E Main St Waynesboro (22980) *(G-15096)*

Atkins Clearing & Trucking 540 832-3128
1856 Hanback Rd Gordonsville (22942) *(G-5898)*

Atlantic Computing LLC 434 293-2022
1155 Inglecress Dr Charlottesville (22901) *(G-2591)*

Atlantic Containment LLC 540 289-5051
806 Island Ford Rd McGaheysville (22840) *(G-8583)*

Atlantic Corrugated Box Co Inc 804 231-4050
1701 Ruffin Rd Richmond (23234) *(G-11027)*

Atlantic EMB & Design LLC 757 253-1010
510 Eastpark Ct Ste 100 Sandston (23150) *(G-12608)*

A
L
P
H
A
B
E
T
I
C

Atlantic Embroidery Works LLC 804 282-5027
1507 N Parham Rd Henrico (23229) *(G-6478)*

Atlantic Fabrication & Boiler 757 494-0597
1 Beechwood Ct Portsmouth (23702) *(G-10394)*

Atlantic Fireproofing Inc 703 940-9444
5532 Hempstead Way Springfield (22151) *(G-12953)*

Atlantic Metal Products Inc (PA) **804 758-4915**
65 Industrial Way Topping (23169) *(G-13885)*

Atlantic Metrocast, Portsmouth *Also called Atlantic Wood Industries Inc (G-10395)*

Atlantic Quality Design Inc 540 966-4356
5815 Lee Ln Fincastle (24090) *(G-4992)*

Atlantic Research Corporation 540 854-2000
7499 Pine Stake Rd Culpeper (22701) *(G-3869)*

Atlantic Research Corporation (HQ) **703 754-5000**
5945 Wellington Rd Gainesville (20155) *(G-5571)*

Atlantic Staircrafters 804 732-3323
1133 Triad Pkwy Petersburg (23803) *(G-10307)*

Atlantic Textile Group Inc 757 249-7777
499 Muller Ln Newport News (23606) *(G-9173)*

Atlantic Vent, Newport News *Also called Jay Douglas Carper (G-9268)*

Atlantic Wind Energy LLC 757 401-9604
305 Stonewood Ct Chesapeake (23320) *(G-2986)*

Atlantic Wood Industries Inc 757 397-2317
3904 Burtons Point Rd Portsmouth (23704) *(G-10395)*

Atlantic Yacht Basin Inc 757 482-2141
2615 Basin Rd Chesapeake (23322) *(G-2987)*

Atlas Inc 646 835-9656
15513 Marsh Overlook Dr Woodbridge (22191) *(G-15650)*

Atlas Concrete, Virginia Beach *Also called Charles Contracting Co Inc (G-14331)*

Atlas Copco Compressor Aif VA 540 226-8655
3905 Lancaster Ring Rd Fredericksburg (22408) *(G-5249)*

Atlas Defense Platform LLC 703 737-6112
19186 Charandy Dr Leesburg (20175) *(G-7224)*

Atlas North America LLC (HQ) **757 463-0670**
120 Newsome Dr Ste H Yorktown (23692) *(G-15934)*

Atlas Pallets, Ruther Glen *Also called Williamsburg Millwork Corp (G-12464)*

Atlas Scntfc Tchncal Svcs LLC 540 492-5051
18149 Harding Dr Bowling Green (22427) *(G-1906)*

Atm Beach Services LLC 757 434-4848
1804 Saranac Ct Virginia Beach (23453) *(G-14247)*

Atomic Armor Inc 703 400-3954
202 Church St Se Ste 524 Leesburg (20175) *(G-7225)*

Atomic Dog Mobile Catering, Newport News *Also called Willie Gatling Jr (G-9379)*

Atomized Pdts Group Chspake In 757 793-2922
808 Curtis Saunders Ct Chesapeake (23321) *(G-2988)*

Atomized Products Group Inc (PA) **434 263-4551**
885 Freshwater Cove Ln Lovingston (22949) *(G-7588)*

Atomizer Fuel Systems Inc 757 250-3773
8105 Richmond Rd Ste 405 Toano (23168) *(G-13857)*

Atpco, Dulles *Also called Airline Tariff Publishing Co (G-4191)*

Ats, Ferrum *Also called Abstruse Technical Services (G-4966)*

Ats Corporation (HQ) **571 766-2400**
4000 Legato Rd Ste 600 Fairfax (22033) *(G-4413)*

Ats Corporation of Virginia, Fairfax *Also called Ats Corporation (G-4413)*

Ats-Sales LLC 703 631-6661
14522k Lee Rd Chantilly (20151) *(G-2372)*

Attachmate Corporation 703 663-5500
8609 Wstwd Ctr Dr Ste 5 Vienna (22182) *(G-14011)*

Attic Zipper 804 518-5094
2214 W Washington St Petersburg (23803) *(G-10308)*

Attimo Group LLC 540 838-1118
4071 Childress Rd Christiansburg (24073) *(G-3570)*

Attimo Studio, Christiansburg *Also called Attimo Group LLC (G-3570)*

Attimo Winery 540 382-7619
4025 Childress Rd Christiansburg (24073) *(G-3571)*

Attn Eric Minton 703 868-4086
13708 Springstone Ct Clifton (20124) *(G-3657)*

Atx Technologies LLC 540 586-4100
414 Jackson St Bedford (24523) *(G-1620)*

Aubrey L Clary Inc 434 577-2724
2763 Ankum Rd Gasburg (23857) *(G-5657)*

Aubrey Otis Gunter Jr 434 352-8136
1316 Skyline Rd Appomattox (24522) *(G-804)*

Audio - Video Solutions 240 565-4381
8802 Grantham Ct Bristow (20136) *(G-2047)*

Audio Mart 434 645-8816
436 Whitmore Town Rd Crewe (23930) *(G-3807)*

Audio-Visuals Actions Inc 703 751-1010
3919 Wheeler Ave Alexandria (22304) *(G-143)*

Auggie Company, Reston *Also called Weiss Soni (G-10989)*

Augusta Actuation LLC 540 480-7619
1105 Old Providence Rd Steeles Tavern (24476) *(G-13310)*

Augusta Apple LLC 540 337-7170
196 Wildwood Dr Churchville (24421) *(G-3619)*

Augusta Free Press 540 910-1233
1511 Chatham Rd Waynesboro (22980) *(G-15097)*

Augusta Paint & Decorating LLC (PA) **540 942-1800**
425 W Broad St Waynesboro (22980) *(G-15098)*

Aumiitu Combs Creations LLC 757 285-5201
1276 Christian Ct Virginia Beach (23464) *(G-14248)*

Aunt Becky's Candle Shoppe, Leesburg *Also called Manny Weber (G-7309)*

Aunt Nolas Pecan Pralines 757 723-1607
7 Whipple Dr Hampton (23663) *(G-6086)*

Auntie Anne's Hand Rolled Pret, North Chesterfield *Also called Marlor Inc (G-9923)*

Aura LLC 757 965-8400
5018 E Princess Anne Rd Norfolk (23502) *(G-9447)*

Auralog Inc 602 470-0300
135 W Market St Harrisonburg (22801) *(G-6294)*

Aurora Flight Sciences Corp (HQ) **703 369-3633**
9950 Wakeman Dr Manassas (20110) *(G-7916)*

Aurora Industries LLC 757 301-2574
2693 Reliance Dr Ste 105 Virginia Beach (23452) *(G-14249)*

Auru Technologies Inc 434 632-6978
101 Crescent Dr Clarksville (23927) *(G-3626)*

AusInx LLC 571 265-3288
2201 Wilson Blvd Apt 904 Arlington (22201) *(G-864)*

Ausome Foods LLC 703 478-4866
2251 Pimmit Dr Apt 214 Falls Church (22043) *(G-4752)*

Ausome Ones LLC 703 637-7105
5929 5th St N Arlington (22203) *(G-865)*

Austin Industrial Services LLC 804 232-8940
1001 E 4th St Richmond (23224) *(G-11494)*

Austin Powder Company 434 842-3589
Rr 6 Fork Union (23055) *(G-5107)*

Austin Powder Company 540 992-6097
1432 Roanoke Rd Daleville (24083) *(G-3940)*

Austins Cycle Company 757 653-0182
22419 Barrow Rd Capron (23829) *(G-2237)*

Austinville Limestone Co Inc 276 699-6262
223 Newtown Church Rd Austinville (24312) *(G-1527)*

Authentic Baking Company LLC 803 422-9282
203 N Washington Hwy Ashland (23005) *(G-1374)*

Authentic Knitting Board LLC 434 842-1180
60 Carysbrook Rd Fork Union (23055) *(G-5108)*

Authentic Printing Company LLC 804 672-6659
9020 Shewalt Dr Henrico (23228) *(G-6479)*

Authentic Products LLC 703 451-5984
7608 Mcweadon Ln Springfield (22150) *(G-12954)*

Auto Clinic, Falls Church *Also called Mechanx Corp (G-4828)*

Auto-Grip, Springfield *Also called Autogrip Inc (G-12955)*

Autodocs LLC 703 532-9720
8229 Boone Blvd Ste 801 Vienna (22182) *(G-14012)*

Autogrind Products 703 490-7061
13600 Dabney Rd Woodbridge (22191) *(G-15651)*

Autogrip Inc 703 372-5520
7411 Alban Station Ct A102 Springfield (22150) *(G-12955)*

Autoinstruments Corp 276 647-5550
47 Ford St Martinsville (24112) *(G-8268)*

Automated Conveyor Systems Inc 434 385-6699
6 Millrace Dr Lynchburg (24502) *(G-7645)*

Automated Machine & Tech Inc 757 898-7844
125 Greene Dr Grafton (23692) *(G-5931)*

Automated Panels, Maurertown *Also called Timothy L Hosey (G-8364)*

Automated Precision Inc 757 223-4157
750 City Center Blvd Newport News (23606) *(G-9174)*

Automated Prod Machining Inc 540 832-0835
300 Taylor St Gordonsville (22942) *(G-5899)*

Automated Signature Technology 703 397-0910
112 Oakgrove Rd Ste 107 Sterling (20166) *(G-13356)*

Automation Control Dist Co LLC 540 797-9892
1329 W Main St Ste 212 Salem (24153) *(G-12477)*

Autombili Lamborghini Amer LLC (HQ) **866 681-6276**
2200 Ferdinand Porsche Dr Herndon (20171) *(G-6616)*

Automotion Inc 276 889-3715
942 E Main St Lebanon (24266) *(G-7188)*

Automotive Industries Division, Strasburg *Also called International Automotive Compo (G-13585)*

Automotors Industries Inc 703 459-8930
13503 Kerrydale Rd Woodbridge (22193) *(G-15652)*

Autonomous Flight Tech Inc 540 314-8866
345 Hawthorn Rd Salem (24153) *(G-12478)*

Autopartsource LLC (HQ) **804 329-3000**
4605 Carolina Ave Richmond (23222) *(G-11495)*

Autumn Publishing Enterprises 703 978-2132
4289 Country Squire Ln Fairfax (22032) *(G-4414)*

Autumn Publishing Inc 703 368-4857
7219 Nathan Ct Manassas (20109) *(G-8030)*

Avaya Federal Solutions Inc 703 390-8333
12730 Fair Lakes Cir Fairfax (22033) *(G-4415)*

Avaya Federal Solutions Inc (HQ) **703 653-8000**
12730 Fair Lakes Cir Fairfax (22033) *(G-4416)*

Avaya Federal Solutions Inc 908 953-6000
4250 Fairfax Dr Fl 10 Arlington (22203) *(G-866)*

Avcom of Virginia Inc 804 794-2500
500 Southlake Blvd North Chesterfield (23236) *(G-9822)*

Avcom of Virginia Inc (PA) **804 794-2500**
7729 Pocoshock Way North Chesterfield (23235) *(G-9823)*

(G-0000) Company's Geographic Section entry number

Avei 571 278-0823
5584 Sequoia Farms Dr Centreville (20120) *(G-2292)*
Avelis John 757 363-2001
5113 Mansards Ct Apt 103 Virginia Beach (23455) *(G-14250)*
Avenger LLC 703 573-6445
5570 Port Royal Rd Ste B Springfield (22151) *(G-12956)*
Avenger Computer Solutions 240 305-7835
4729 Washington Blvd Arlington (22205) *(G-867)*
Avenue 7 Magazine LLC 757 214-4914
1518 Brenland Cir Virginia Beach (23464) *(G-14251)*
Averia Health Solutions LLC 703 716-0791
3401 Waples Glen Ct Oakton (22124) *(G-10141)*
Avf Screw Machine LLC 571 393-3099
5754 Old Clifton Rd Clifton (20124) *(G-3658)*
Avian Fashions 540 288-0200
61 Boulder Dr Stafford (22554) *(G-13121)*
Aviation & Maritime Support SE 757 995-2029
516 Innovation Dr Ste 201 Chesapeake (23320) *(G-2989)*
Aviation Component Svcs Inc 434 237-7077
18245 Forest Rd Lynchburg (24502) *(G-7646)*
Aviation Tactical LLC 970 946-7027
8638 Woodview Dr Springfield (22153) *(G-12957)*
Avigators Incorporated 703 298-6319
6331 Fairfax National Way Centreville (20120) *(G-2293)*
Avila Herbals LLC 540 838-1118
4025 Childress Rd Christiansburg (24073) *(G-3572)*
Avintiv Specialty Mtls Inc 540 946-9250
1020 Shanandoah Vlg Dr Waynesboro (22980) *(G-15099)*
Avitech Consulting LLC 757 810-2716
721 River Strand Chesapeake (23320) *(G-2990)*
Avm Inc 703 802-6212
14630 Flint Lee Rd Unit D Chantilly (20151) *(G-2373)*
Avm Sheet Metal Inc 703 975-7715
12041 Coloriver Rd Manassas (20112) *(G-8031)*
Avn Prints 703 473-7498
4003 Javins Dr Alexandria (22310) *(G-419)*
Avoid Evade Counter LLC 703 593-1951
2332 Archdale Rd Reston (20191) *(G-10795)*
Avon Products Inc ....
124 Agape Way Stephens City (22655) *(G-13312)*
AW Art LLC 540 320-4565
208 Dunbar Ave Apt A Dublin (24084) *(G-4149)*
Award Crafters, Manassas *Also called Aci Partners LLC (G-8019)*
Aware Inc 804 598-1016
4300 Spoonbill Ct Powhatan (23139) *(G-10531)*
Awesome Wellness 540 439-0808
12602 Lake Coventry Dr Bealeton (22712) *(G-1596)*
Awn Candle Company 618 560-6355
228 Crosswinds Dr Apt 303 Chesapeake (23320) *(G-2991)*
Awning & Sign Company Inc 276 628-8069
17311 Lee Hwy Abingdon (24210) *(G-14)*
Awsi Inc 804 798-4088
101 Henry Clay Rd Ashland (23005) *(G-1375)*
Ax Graphics and Sign LLC 775 830-6115
2143 Amicus Rd Stanardsville (22973) *(G-13215)*
Axalta Coating Systems LLC 540 622-2951
7961 Winchester Rd Front Royal (22630) *(G-5521)*
Axcelis Technologies Inc 571 921-1493
8140 Flannery Ct Manassas (20109) *(G-8032)*
Axeamps LLC 540 484-0882
330 Housman Dr Glade Hill (24092) *(G-5669)*
Axell Wireless Inc 703 414-5300
2121 Crystal Dr Ste 625 Arlington (22202) *(G-868)*
Axiom Armor LLC 540 583-6184
115 S Bridge St Bedford (24523) *(G-1621)*
Axios Media Inc 703 291-3600
3100 Clarendon Blvd # 1300 Arlington (22201) *(G-869)*
Axios Systems Inc 703 326-1357
2411 Dulles Corner Park # 475 Herndon (20171) *(G-6617)*
Axon Cells Inc 434 987-4460
756 Club Dr Keswick (22947) *(G-7043)*
Axon Dx, Earlysville *Also called Axondx LLC (G-4287)*
Axon Enterprise Inc 602 459-1278
1100 Wilson Blvd Ste 1210 Arlington (22209) *(G-870)*
Axon Medchem LLC 703 650-9359
12020 Sunrise Valley Dr Reston (20191) *(G-10796)*
Axon Sciences Inc 434 987-4460
200 Garrett St Ste H Charlottesville (22902) *(G-2732)*
Axondx LLC 540 239-0668
379 Reas Ford Rd Ste 1 Earlysville (22936) *(G-4287)*
Aylett Sand & Gravel Inc (PA) **804 443-2366**
1251 Tappahannock Blvd Tappahannock (22560) *(G-13811)*
Azar's Cafe & Market, Virginia Beach *Also called Azars Natural Foods Inc (G-14252)*
Azars Natural Foods Inc (PA) 757 486-7778
108 Prescott Ave Virginia Beach (23452) *(G-14252)*
Aziza Beauty LLC 804 525-9989
3406 Wellington St Richmond (23222) *(G-11496)*
Aziza Beauty Supply, Richmond *Also called Aziza Beauty LLC (G-11496)*
Azz Glvnizing Services-Bristol, Bristol *Also called Azz Inc (G-2007)*

Azz Inc 276 466-5558
14781 Industrial Park Rd Bristol (24202) *(G-2007)*
B & B Boutique 703 425-8256
10700 Dundas Oak Ct Burke (22015) *(G-2181)*
B & B Cleaning Service 757 667-9528
301 Naval Base Rd # 702 Norfolk (23505) *(G-9448)*
B & B Machine & Tool Inc 540 344-6820
3406 Orange Ave Ne Roanoke (24012) *(G-12038)*
B & B Powder Inc 540 921-1158
212 Sugar Run Rd Pearisburg (24134) *(G-10272)*
B & B Printing 540 586-1020
402 E Main St Bedford (24523) *(G-1622)*
B & B Printing Company Inc 804 794-8273
521 Research Rd North Chesterfield (23236) *(G-9824)*
B & B Welding & Crane Service, Roanoke *Also called B & B Welding Inc (G-12039)*
B & B Welding & Fabrication 540 663-5949
6261 Saint Pauls Rd King George (22485) *(G-7081)*
B & B Welding Inc 540 982-2082
1427 Norfolk Ave Se Roanoke (24013) *(G-12039)*
B & C Custom Canvas 757 870-0089
16 Hampshire Dr Hampton (23669) *(G-6087)*
B & D Trucking of Virginia 540 463-3035
2970 W Midland Trl Lexington (24450) *(G-7387)*
B & E Transit Mix Inc 434 447-7331
604 Locust St South Hill (23970) *(G-12843)*
B & G Bandmill 276 766-4280
931 Deerfield Rd Hillsville (24343) *(G-6884)*
B & G Publishing Inc 757 463-1104
3320 Virginia Beach Blvd # 4 Virginia Beach (23452) *(G-14253)*
B & G Stainless Works Inc 703 339-6002
8538 Terminal Rd Ste Hjk Lorton (22079) *(G-7464)*
B & H Excavating 540 839-2107
1266 Shady Ln Hot Springs (24445) *(G-6945)*
B & H Machine Works 540 636-3366
201b E 4th St Front Royal (22630) *(G-5522)*
B & H Wood Products Inc 540 752-2480
295 Heflin Rd Stafford (22556) *(G-13122)*
B & J Cabinet Co Inc 804 271-0192
7600 Dalebrook Dr North Chesterfield (23237) *(G-9825)*
B & J Embroidery Inc 276 646-5631
501 Campbell Dr Saltville (24370) *(G-12584)*
B & L Biotech Usa Inc 703 272-7507
3959 Pender Dr Ste 350 Fairfax (22030) *(G-4597)*
B & L Mch & Fabrication Inc 757 853-1800
3411 Amherst St Norfolk (23513) *(G-9449)*
B & M Machinery Inc 434 525-1498
449 Old Plantation Dr Lynchburg (24502) *(G-7647)*
B & R Rebar 800 526-1024
950 Masonic Ln Richmond (23223) *(G-11497)*
B & S Liquidating Corp 540 387-0000
840 Union St Salem (24153) *(G-12479)*
B & S Xpress LLC 434 851-2695
14241 Rockford School Rd Hurt (24563) *(G-6971)*
B & T Excavating, Chester *Also called B & T LLC (G-3389)*
B & T LLC 804 720-1758
13701 Vance Dr Chester (23836) *(G-3389)*
B and B Powder Coating 540 921-1158
212 Sugar Run Rd Pearisburg (24134) *(G-10273)*
B and B Welding Service LLC 804 994-2797
552 Hazelwood Rd Aylett (23009) *(G-1545)*
B and D Welding & Fabrication, North Tazewell *Also called Bradley Adkins (G-10095)*
B and K International, Virginia Beach *Also called Famarco Newco LLC (G-14459)*
B C R Bookbinding 703 534-9181
707 W Broad St Falls Church (22046) *(G-4901)*
B C Wood Products, Ashland *Also called Murdock Acquisition LLC (G-1467)*
B D I, Chantilly *Also called Becker Designed Inc (G-2376)*
B Franklin Printer 703 845-1583
501 S Lexington St Arlington (22204) *(G-871)*
B Global LLC 703 628-2826
8500 Idylwood Valley Pl Vienna (22182) *(G-14013)*
B H Cobb Lumber Co 804 358-3801
2300 Hermitage Rd Ste B Richmond (23220) *(G-11498)*
B H Franklin Logging Inc 434 352-5484
462 Woodlawn Trl Appomattox (24522) *(G-805)*
B Hunt Enterprises, South Boston *Also called B J Hart Enterprises Inc (G-12750)*
B J Hart Enterprises Inc 434 575-7538
4019 Halifax Rd South Boston (24592) *(G-12750)*
B K Printing 703 435-5502
605 Carlisle Dr Herndon (20170) *(G-6618)*
B Microfarads Inc 276 728-9121
205 Mill St Hillsville (24343) *(G-6885)*
B P Basl, Surry *Also called Seize Moments (G-13801)*
B Queen Nation LLC 678 507-4445
169 Colony Rd Newport News (23602) *(G-9175)*
B R M M, Harrisonburg *Also called Blue Ridge Mch Motorsports LLC (G-6295)*
B R Products 804 693-2639
6910 Tracey Ct Gloucester (23061) *(G-5836)*
B T & M, Christiansburg *Also called Btmc Holdings Inc (G-3575)*

A
L
P
H
A
B
E
T
I
C

B Team Publications LLC 757 362-3006
9516 26th Bay St Norfolk (23518) *(G-9450)*

B&B, North Chesterfield *Also called B & B Printing Company Inc (G-9824)*

B&B Consulting Services Inc 804 550-1517
9317 Totopotomoy Trl Ashland (23005) *(G-1376)*

B&B Industries LLC 703 855-2142
7923 San Leandro Pl Alexandria (22309) *(G-420)*

B&B Insulation LLC 757 904-0884
5178 Cleveland St Virginia Beach (23462) *(G-14254)*

B&E Sht-Metal Fabrications Inc 757 536-1279
944 Seahawk Cir Ste 110 Virginia Beach (23452) *(G-14255)*

B&T, Culpeper *Also called Bingham & Taylor Corp (G-3872)*

B.B.G., Virginia Beach *Also called Boomin Bass Global LLC (G-14294)*

B2 Health Solutions LLC 757 403-8298
2133 Upton Dr Virginia Beach (23454) *(G-14256)*

B3sk Software LLC 757 484-4516
3220 Meadowbrook Ln Chesapeake (23321) *(G-2992)*

Babb Railroad Construction 276 995-2090
334 Taylor Town Rd Fort Blackmore (24250) *(G-5120)*

Baby Fanatic, Henrico *Also called Worth Baby Products LLC (G-6592)*

Baby Signs By Lacey 540 309-2551
8330 Strathmore Ln Roanoke (24019) *(G-11883)*

Babypipscom LLC 866 674-9258
3900 Westerre Pkwy # 300 Henrico (23233) *(G-6480)*

Back Bay Defense LLC 757 285-6883
5745 Grimstead Rd Virginia Beach (23457) *(G-14257)*

Back Creek Towing & Salvage 757 898-5338
131b Landing Rd Seaford (23696) *(G-12672)*

Back Pocket Provisions LLC 703 585-3676
2908 Marshall St Falls Church (22042) *(G-4753)*

Back's Welding Service, Fairfield *Also called Philip Back (G-4733)*

Backroad Precast LLC 540 335-5503
2506 Back Rd Woodstock (22664) *(G-15848)*

Backroads Publications 540 949-0329
1461 Love Rd Lyndhurst (22952) *(G-7841)*

Backwater Inc 434 242-5675
633 W Main St Charlottesville (22903) *(G-2733)*

Backwoods Fabrications LLC 804 448-2901
3236 Oates Ln Ruther Glen (22546) *(G-12450)*

Backwoods Security LLC 804 641-0674
5300 Otterdale Rd Moseley (23120) *(G-9033)*

Backwoods Woodworking 276 237-2011
144 Backwoods Farm Ln Fries (24330) *(G-5514)*

Bacons Castle Supply Inc 757 357-6159
6797 Colonial Trl E Surry (23883) *(G-13796)*

Bacova Guild Ltd 540 484-4640
701 Orchard Ave Rocky Mount (24151) *(G-12313)*

Bacus Woodworks LLC 571 762-3314
7203 Manor House Dr Warrenton (20187) *(G-14979)*

Bad Wolf LLC 540 347-4255
7161 James Madison Hwy Warrenton (20187) *(G-14980)*

Badd Newz Publications LLC 540 479-2848
4515 Kay Ct Fredericksburg (22408) *(G-5250)*

Baden Reclamation Company 540 776-7890
302 S Jefferson St Roanoke (24011) *(G-12040)*

Badger Neon & Sign 540 761-5779
508 Huntington Blvd Ne Roanoke (24012) *(G-12041)*

Badgerdog Literary Publishing 757 627-2315
500 E Main St Ste 1300 Norfolk (23510) *(G-9451)*

Badwolf Brewery LLC 571 208-1064
9776 Center St Manassas (20110) *(G-7917)*

Bae Systems Inc (HQ) **571 461-6000**
2941 Frview Pk Dr Ste 100 Falls Church (22042) *(G-4754)*

Bae Systems Holdings Inc (HQ) **571 461-6000**
2941 Frview Pk Dr Ste 100 Falls Church (22042) *(G-4755)*

Bae Systems Info & Elec Sys 703 668-4000
11487 Sunset Hills Rd Reston (20190) *(G-10797)*

Bae Systems Info & Elec Sys 703 361-1471
9300 Wellington Rd 110 Manassas (20110) *(G-7918)*

Bae Systems Info & Elec Sys 202 223-8808
4301 Fairfax Dr Ste 800 Arlington (22203) *(G-872)*

Bae Systems Land Armaments Inc (HQ) **571 461-6000**
2941 Frview Pk Dr Ste 100 Falls Church (22042) *(G-4756)*

Bae Systems Land Armaments LP (HQ) **571 461-6000**
2941 Frview Pk Dr Ste 100 Falls Church (22042) *(G-4757)*

Bae Systems Land Armmnts Hldng 571 461-6000
2941 Frview Pk Dr Ste 100 Falls Church (22042) *(G-4758)*

Bae Systems Nrfolk Ship Repr I 757 494-4000
750 W Berkley Ave Norfolk (23523) *(G-9452)*

Bae Systems Ship Repair Inc (HQ) **757 494-4000**
750 W Berkley Ave Norfolk (23523) *(G-9453)*

Bae Systems Srvvbility Systems, Falls Church *Also called Bae Systems Tctcal Vhcl System (G-4759)*

Bae Systems Tctcal Vhcl System 571 461-6000
2941 Frview Pk Dr Ste 100 Falls Church (22042) *(G-4759)*

Bae Systems Tctcal Vhcl System (HQ) **571 461-6000**
2941 Frview Pk Dr Ste 100 Falls Church (22042) *(G-4760)*

Bag Plant Warehouse & Maint, Petersburg *Also called Pre Con Inc (G-10337)*

Bageladies LLC 540 248-0908
732 Merion Greene Charlottesville (22901) *(G-2592)*

Baggesen J Rand 804 560-0490
7101 Jahnke Rd Richmond (23225) *(G-11499)*

Bagira Systems USA LLC 571 278-1989
44001 Indian Fields Ct Leesburg (20176) *(G-7226)*

Bagzoo.com, Appomattox *Also called Fabriko Inc (G-810)*

Bahama Breeze Shutter Awng LLC 757 592-0265
3759 George Wash Mem Hwy Ordinary (23131) *(G-10236)*

Bahashem Soap Company LLC 804 398-0982
1221a Hull St Richmond (23224) *(G-11500)*

Bailey & Sons Publishing Co D 434 990-9291
197 E Main St Orange (22960) *(G-10204)*

Bailey Printing Inc 434 293-5434
914 Harris St Charlottesville (22903) *(G-2734)*

Baillio Sand Co Inc 757 428-3302
560 Oceana Blvd Virginia Beach (23454) *(G-14258)*

Bainbridge Recycling Inc 757 472-4142
5360 Bainbridge Blvd Chesapeake (23320) *(G-2993)*

Bajj Usa Inc 703 953-1541
8025 Towering Oak Way Manassas (20111) *(G-8033)*

Bakefully Yours LLC 540 229-6232
10398 Brenna Ct Marshall (20115) *(G-8250)*

Bakefully Yours LLC 301 276-4972
8136 Flannery Ct Manassas (20109) *(G-8034)*

Baker & Hazlewood 804 798-5199
11242 Hopson Rd Ashland (23005) *(G-1377)*

Baker Builders LLC 703 753-4904
7329 Foster Ln Nokesville (20181) *(G-9389)*

Baker Hughes A GE Company LLC 540 961-9532
2851 Commerce St Blacksburg (24060) *(G-1724)*

Baker Hughes A GE Company LLC 540 387-8847
1501 Roanoke Blvd Salem (24153) *(G-12480)*

Baker Hughes Holdings LLC 276 963-0106
2652 Chestnut St Richlands (24641) *(G-11013)*

Baker Sheet Metal Corporation 757 853-4325
3541 Argonne Ave Norfolk (23509) *(G-9454)*

Bakers Crust Inc 757 253-2787
5230 Monticello Ave Williamsburg (23188) *(G-15208)*

Bakery Feeds, Doswell *Also called Griffin Industries LLC (G-4121)*

Balancemaster Inc 434 258-5078
2246 Toll Gate Rd Concord (24538) *(G-3755)*

Balco Sign & Safety, Virginia Beach *Also called Coastal Safety Inc (G-14347)*

Baldwin Cabinet Shops Inc 804 443-5421
3693 Richmond Hwy Tappahannock (22560) *(G-13812)*

Balent-Young Publishing Inc 540 636-2569
951 Poca Bella Dr Front Royal (22630) *(G-5523)*

Balfour of Northern VA, Mc Lean *Also called Dmkp Inc (G-8420)*

Ball Advanced Alum Tech Corp 540 248-2703
56 Dunsmore Rd Verona (24482) *(G-13983)*

Ball Lumber Co Inc 804 443-5555
7343 Rchmond Tpphnnock Hw Millers Tavern (23115) *(G-8939)*

Ball Metal Beverage Cont Corp 757 887-2062
8935 Pocahontas Trl Williamsburg (23185) *(G-15209)*

Ball Metal Beverage Cont Div, Williamsburg *Also called Ball Metal Beverage Cont Corp (G-15209)*

Ball Peen Productions LLC 434 293-4392
1304 East Market St Ste O Charlottesville (22902) *(G-2735)*

Ballas LLC 703 689-9644
13610 Old Dairy Rd Oak Hill (20171) *(G-10136)*

Ballistics Center LLC 703 380-4901
2601 Woodfern Ct Woodbridge (22192) *(G-15653)*

Ballou Enterprises LLC 804 496-6620
11034 Air Park Rd Ste 1 Ashland (23005) *(G-1378)*

Ballous Signs and Designs Inc 804 986-6635
2501 Foxberry Cir North Chesterfield (23235) *(G-9826)*

Ballpark Publications Inc 757 271-6197
169 Happy Trl Bracey (23919) *(G-1921)*

Ballpark Signs Inc 540 239-7677
105 Harrison St Radford (24141) *(G-10705)*

Bally Technologies Inc 917 415-5649
24847 Myers Glen Pl Chantilly (20152) *(G-2526)*

Ballyhoo 703 294-6075
7138 Little River Tpke Annandale (22003) *(G-731)*

Balmar Inc (HQ) **703 289-9000**
2818 Fallfax Dr Falls Church (22042) *(G-4761)*

Baltimore Business Company LLC 301 848-7200
12836 Point Pleasant Dr Fairfax (22033) *(G-4417)*

Bam Bams LLC 703 372-1940
10498 Colonel Ct Ste 104 Manassas (20110) *(G-7919)*

Bambooink, Richmond *Also called Bbr Print Inc (G-11502)*

Banana Banner Inc 703 823-5933
3148 Duke St Alexandria (22314) *(G-144)*

Banana Banner Signs, Alexandria *Also called Banana Banner Inc (G-144)*

Band-It, Troutville *Also called Cloverdale Company Inc (G-13907)*

Bander Computers 757 398-3443
722 County St Portsmouth (23704) *(G-10396)*

Bangkok Noodle 703 866-1396
7022 Commerce St Springfield (22150) *(G-12958)*

(G-0000) Company's Geographic Section entry number

Banker Steel Co LLC (HQ).....434 847-4575
1619 Wythe Rd Ste B Lynchburg (24501) ***(G-7648)***
Banner Sings Etc.....703 698-5466
7252 Arlington Blvd Fairfax (20151) ***(G-4418)***
Banners and More.....540 400-8485
238 W Madison Ave Vinton (24179) ***(G-14165)***
Bannerworks Signs & Graphics.....571 292-2567
11900 Livingston Rd # 139 Manassas (20109) ***(G-8035)***
Banton Custom Woodworking LLC.....804 334-4766
13712 Brandy Oaks Rd Chesterfield (23832) ***(G-3477)***
Banvera LLC.....757 599-9643
956 J Clyde Morris Blvd Newport News (23601) ***(G-9176)***
Bap LLC.....800 507-9728
425 Crosman Ct Purcellville (20132) ***(G-10651)***
Baptist Valley Machine Sp LLC.....276 988-8284
4958 Baptist Valley Rd North Tazewell (24630) ***(G-10093)***
Bar Logging LLC.....757 641-9269
22373 Sedley Rd Franklin (23851) ***(G-5139)***
Bar-C Sand Inc.....276 701-3888
3353 Mountain Rd Cedar Bluff (24609) ***(G-2270)***
Bara Printing Services.....804 303-8615
2944 Bells Rd Richmond (23234) ***(G-11028)***
Barakat Foods Inc.....703 222-9493
13893j Willard Rd Chantilly (20151) ***(G-2374)***
Barber Logging LLC.....276 346-4638
444 Henry Gibbons Rd Jonesville (24263) ***(G-7018)***
Barbours Printing Service.....804 443-4505
206 Prince St Tappahannock (22560) ***(G-13813)***
Barboursville Distillery LLC.....757 961-4590
1097 Caton Dr Virginia Beach (23454) ***(G-14259)***
Barcoderental.com, Fairfax *Also called Manufacturing System Svcs Inc* ***(G-4651)***
Barcoding Inc.....540 416-0116
404 Yount Ave Staunton (24401) ***(G-13243)***
Barcroft Associates Ltd Partnr.....786 507-4649
1120 S George Mason Dr Arlington (22204) ***(G-873)***
Barcroft Center.....703 228-0701
4200 S Four Mile Run Dr Arlington (22206) ***(G-874)***
Barefoot Bucha, Afton *Also called Conscious Cultures LLC* ***(G-78)***
Barefoot Spas LLC.....804 298-3939
8401 Fort Darling Rd North Chesterfield (23237) ***(G-9827)***
Baret LLC.....808 230-9904
15408 Weldin Dr Woodbridge (22193) ***(G-15654)***
Baret Bat & Glove Company, Woodbridge *Also called Baret LLC* ***(G-15654)***
Barg-N-Finders Inc.....276 988-4953
30672 Gvrnor G C Pery Hwy North Tazewell (24630) ***(G-10094)***
Bargain Beachwear Inc.....757 313-5440
1714 Atlantic Ave Virginia Beach (23451) ***(G-14260)***
Bargain Finders Marketplace, North Tazewell *Also called Barg-N-Finders Inc* ***(G-10094)***
Barger Son Cnstr Inc Charles W.....540 463-2106
Hwy 60 E Lexington (24450) ***(G-7388)***
Bargers Custom Cabinets LLC.....540 261-7230
982 Linden Ave Buena Vista (24416) ***(G-2139)***
Barismil LLC.....703 622-4550
2517 James Maury Dr Herndon (20171) ***(G-6619)***
Bariso Ling.....757 277-5383
604 Oak Grove Ln Virginia Beach (23452) ***(G-14261)***
Barker Collision Precision LLC.....716 481-8253
1123 Penobscot Rd Richmond (23227) ***(G-11121)***
Barker Microfarads, Hillsville *Also called B Microfarads Inc* ***(G-6885)***
Barlen Crafts.....301 537-3491
219 Woodrow Ave Suffolk (23434) ***(G-13673)***
Barnes Industries Inc.....804 389-1981
4294 Whitehall Rd Sandy Hook (23153) ***(G-12643)***
Barnes Manufacturing Company.....434 676-8210
621 Main St Kenbridge (23944) ***(G-7032)***
Barnett Consulting LLC.....703 655-1635
9253 Plaskett Ln Lorton (22079) ***(G-7465)***
Barnette's Machine Shop, Chesapeake *Also called W D Barnette Enterprise Inc* ***(G-3368)***
Barney Family Enterprises LLC.....757 438-2064
317 W Main St Wakefield (23888) ***(G-14964)***
Barns & Vineyards LLC.....703 801-2719
43257 Preston Ct Ashburn (20147) ***(G-1245)***
Baron Glass Inc.....757 464-1131
1601 Diamond Springs Rd Virginia Beach (23455) ***(G-14262)***
Barr Laboratories Inc.....434 534-8600
2150 Perrowville Rd Forest (24551) ***(G-5052)***
Barr Marine By E D M.....540 291-4180
100 Douglas Way Natural Bridge Stati (24579) ***(G-9108)***
Barrel Oak Winery LLC.....540 364-6402
3623 Grove Ln Delaplane (20144) ***(G-4073)***
Barren Ridge Vineyards LLC.....540 248-3300
984 Barrenridge Rd Fishersville (22939) ***(G-5001)***
Barrett Industries Inc.....540 678-1625
399 Mcghee Rd Winchester (22603) ***(G-15384)***
Barrett Machine, Winchester *Also called Barrett Industries Inc* ***(G-15384)***
Barricade Building Products, Doswell *Also called SC&I of Virginia LLC* ***(G-4124)***
Barrington Worldwide LLC.....202 255-4611
526 King St Ste 211 Alexandria (22314) ***(G-145)***
Barron Construction LLC.....804 400-5569
6209 Tandem Ct North Chesterfield (23234) ***(G-9828)***
Barrons-Hunter Inc.....434 971-7626
556 Dettor Rd Ste 101 Charlottesville (22903) ***(G-2736)***
Barry Enterprises Intl LLC.....202 812-6822
18256 Oak Lake Ct Leesburg (20176) ***(G-7227)***
Barry McVay.....703 451-5953
6055 Ridge Ford Dr Burke (22015) ***(G-2182)***
Barry Sock Company.....703 525-1120
201 N Barton St Arlington (22201) ***(G-875)***
Barry Wayne Gladden.....540 389-6645
1344 Roanoke Blvd Salem (24153) ***(G-12481)***
Barry-Whmller Cont Systems Inc.....434 582-1200
1320 Wards Ferry Rd Lynchburg (24502) ***(G-7649)***
Bartenman Sales, Virginia Beach *Also called Differential Pressure Instrs* ***(G-14404)***
Barton Industries Inc.....757 874-5958
234 Redoubt Rd Yorktown (23692) ***(G-15935)***
Barton Logging Inc.....434 390-8504
2503 Old Peach Tree Rd Green Bay (23942) ***(G-5987)***
Bartrack Inc.....717 521-4840
2374 Newberry Ln Rockingham (22801) ***(G-12241)***
Bas Control Systems LLC.....804 569-2473
8420 Meadowbridge Rd C Mechanicsville (23116) ***(G-8606)***
Bases of Virginia LLC (PA).....**757 690-8482**
106 Greene Dr Yorktown (23692) ***(G-15936)***
BASF Corporation.....757 538-3700
2301 Wilroy Rd Suffolk (23434) ***(G-13674)***
Basic City Beer Co., Waynesboro *Also called Metal Craft Brewing Co LLC* ***(G-15126)***
Basic Converting Equipment.....804 794-2090
2310 Conte Dr Midlothian (23113) ***(G-8776)***
Basketball Products Intl LLC.....757 626-3865
2406 Colley Ave B Norfolk (23517) ***(G-9455)***
Bassett Direct Sc LLC.....276 629-6000
3525 Fairystone Park Hwy Bassett (24055) ***(G-1577)***
Bassett Furniture Inds Inc (PA).....**276 629-6000**
3525 Fairystone Park Hwy Bassett (24055) ***(G-1578)***
Bassett Furniture Inds NC LLC (HQ).....**276 629-6000**
3525 Fairystone Park Hwy Bassett (24055) ***(G-1579)***
Bassett Mirror Company Inc.....276 629-3341
1290 Philpott Dr Bassett (24055) ***(G-1580)***
Bastion and Associates LLC.....703 343-5158
8801 Victoria Rd Springfield (22151) ***(G-12959)***
Basvin Software LLC.....703 537-0888
5531 Starboard Ct Fairfax (22032) ***(G-4419)***
Batch Wood Works Inc.....804 694-5767
7336 Wellford Ln Gloucester (23061) ***(G-5837)***
Batchelder & Collins Inc.....757 220-2806
197 Ewell Rd Ste B Williamsburg (23188) ***(G-15210)***
Bath Iron Works Corporation.....757 855-4182
9727 Avionics Loop Norfolk (23511) ***(G-9456)***
Bath Sensations LLC.....804 832-4701
8207 Hampton Bluff Ter Chesterfield (23832) ***(G-3478)***
Bath Son and Sons Associates.....804 722-0687
2016 W Washington St Petersburg (23803) ***(G-10309)***
Batonbio LLC.....347 491-0189
7055 Golden Aster Dr Moseley (23120) ***(G-9034)***
Battaile Drive LLC.....540 662-4185
151 Windy Hill Ln Winchester (22602) ***(G-15385)***
Battarbees Catering.....540 249-9205
701b Elm Ave Grottoes (24441) ***(G-6015)***
Battino Contg Solutions LLC.....703 408-9162
43674 Leesmill Sq Edinburg (22824) ***(G-4299)***
Battle King Inc.....757 324-1854
309 Ansell Ave Apt F Portsmouth (23702) ***(G-10397)***
Battle Monument Partners.....804 644-4924
530 E Main St Ste 1000 Richmond (23219) ***(G-11501)***
Battlefield Industries LLC.....703 995-4822
6371 Birch Leaf Ct Burke (22015) ***(G-2183)***
Battlefield Screen Printing, Chantilly *Also called Sports Plus Incorporated* ***(G-2497)***
Battlefield Terrain Concepts.....540 977-0696
754 Ray St Roanoke (24019) ***(G-11884)***
Battlespace Global LLC (PA).....**703 413-0556**
1215 S Clark St Ste 301 Arlington (22202) ***(G-876)***
Battletown Cstm Woodworks LLC.....703 618-1548
10 Farmers Ln Berryville (22611) ***(G-1670)***
Batts Industries LLC.....202 669-6015
715 Alabama Dr Herndon (20170) ***(G-6620)***
Batts Woodworking.....757 969-5824
246 Bannon Ct Hampton (23666) ***(G-6088)***
Bauer Compressors Inc.....757 855-6006
1340 Azalea Garden Rd Norfolk (23502) ***(G-9457)***
Bauer Compressors Inc (PA).....**757 855-6006**
1328 Azalea Garden Rd Norfolk (23502) ***(G-9458)***
Baur Logging LLC.....757 535-5693
3036 Falmouth Dr Chesapeake (23321) ***(G-2994)***
Bausch & Lomb Incorporated.....434 385-0407
1501 Graves Mill Rd Lynchburg (24502) ***(G-7650)***
Bausch Health Americas Inc.....703 995-2400
3701 Concorde Pkwy # 800 Chantilly (20151) ***(G-2375)***

ALPHABETIC

Baxter Healthcare Corporation 804 226-1962
5800 S Laburnum Ave Richmond (23231) *(G-11122)*

Bay Breeze Labradors 757 408-5227
7115 S Quay Rd Suffolk (23437) *(G-13675)*

Bay Breeze Publishing LLC 757 535-1580
4839 Coventry Ln Norfolk (23518) *(G-9459)*

Bay Cabinets & Contractors 757 934-2236
428 E Pinner St Suffolk (23434) *(G-13676)*

Bay Custom Inc 757 971-4785
407 Rotary St Hampton (23661) *(G-6089)*

Bay Custom Mar Fleet Repr Inc 757 224-3818
407 Rotary St Hampton (23661) *(G-6090)*

Bay Etching & Imprinting Inc 800 925-2877
43 Lively Oaks Rd Lively (22507) *(G-7439)*

Bay Sand Co Inc 757 357-9477
349 Main St Smithfield (23430) *(G-12704)*

Bay Welding 757 633-7689
5108 Hemlock Ct Virginia Beach (23464) *(G-14263)*

Bay West Paper 804 639-3530
11401 Carters Crossing Rd Chesterfield (23838) *(G-3479)*

Bayfront Media Group LLC 757 935-3530
1206 Laskin Rd Ste 200 Virginia Beach (23451) *(G-14264)*

Bayonet 804 323-3204
5219 Hickory Park Dr B Glen Allen (23059) *(G-5706)*

Bayside Joinery Co LLC 804 551-3951
51 Willow Oak Dr Dutton (23050) *(G-4269)*

Bayside Woodworking Inc 757 337-0380
548 Winwood Dr Chesapeake (23323) *(G-2995)*

Baystar Coal Company Inc 276 322-4900
356 S College Ave Bluefield (24605) *(G-1858)*

Bayview Engrv Art GL Studio 757 331-1595
309 Mason Ave Cape Charles (23310) *(G-2229)*

Bbg, Richmond *Also called Brazilian Best Granite Inc (G-11132)*

Bbj LLC 757 787-4646
152 Market St Onancock (23417) *(G-10191)*

Bbk Cnsldted Slutions Svcs LLC 571 229-2276
8688 Carlton Dr Manassas (20110) *(G-7920)*

Bbr Print Inc 804 230-4515
807 Oliver Hill Way Richmond (23219) *(G-11502)*

Bc Repairs 434 332-5304
261 Bunnyhop Ln Rustburg (24588) *(G-12434)*

Bcbg Max Azria Group LLC 757 497-9575
7907 Powers Blvd Falls Church (22042) *(G-4762)*

Bclf Corporation 540 929-1701
266 Sunflower Ln Callaway (24067) *(G-2219)*

BCT Recordation Inc 540 772-1754
4024 Norwood St Sw Roanoke (24018) *(G-11885)*

BCT Virginia, Norfolk *Also called Dister Inc (G-9525)*

BCT Virginia, Fairfax *Also called Dister Inc (G-4439)*

Bdl Prototype & Automation LLC 540 868-2577
621 Klines Mill Rd Bldg B Middletown (22645) *(G-8736)*

Bdmoore Publications LLC 434 352-7581
226 Tonawanda Lake Rd Spout Spring (24593) *(G-12925)*

Bdrc USA LLC, Norfolk *Also called Steffan Lott (G-9734)*

Be Bold Sign Studio 678 520-1029
1204 Sunrise Ct Herndon (20170) *(G-6621)*

Be Ready Enterprises LLC 540 422-9210
612 Lafayette Blvd # 200 Fredericksburg (22401) *(G-5172)*

Be Ready Tactical, Fredericksburg *Also called Be Ready Enterprises LLC (G-5172)*

Be There Do Good LLC 703 851-5293
1214 Delta Glen Ct Vienna (22182) *(G-14014)*

Bea Maurer 540 377-5025
6051 N Lee Hwy Fairfield (24435) *(G-4729)*

Beach Block Ventures LLC 540 848-0921
215 Irving Ave N Colonial Beach (22443) *(G-3721)*

Beach Controls, Virginia Beach *Also called Chesapeake Bay Controls Inc (G-14333)*

Beach Glass Designs Inc 757 650-7604
1125 Highcliff Ct Virginia Beach (23454) *(G-14265)*

Beach Hot Rods Met Fabrication 757 227-8191
1112 Jensen Dr Ste 102 Virginia Beach (23451) *(G-14266)*

Beach Iron Shop 757 422-3318
106 S First Clnl Rd Ste B Virginia Beach (23454) *(G-14267)*

Beach Pallets Inc 757 773-1931
2509 Lemming Ct Virginia Beach (23456) *(G-14268)*

Beach Sign and Design 757 618-8653
2424 Castleton Commerce W Virginia Beach (23456) *(G-14269)*

Beach Welding Service 757 422-3318
106 S First Clnl Rd Ste B Virginia Beach (23454) *(G-14270)*

Beach Wreaths and More 757 943-0703
725 Monmouth Ln Virginia Beach (23464) *(G-14271)*

Beacon 540 408-2560
212 Freedom Ct Ste G Fredericksburg (22408) *(G-5251)*

Beadecked Inc (PA) 703 759-3725
10201 Brennanhill Ct Great Falls (22066) *(G-5939)*

Beadecked Inc 703 435-5663
342 Victory Dr Herndon (20170) *(G-6622)*

Beagle Logging Company 540 459-2425
206 Beagle Run Woodstock (22664) *(G-15849)*

Beam Global Spirits and 804 763-2823
5309 Commonwealth Ctr Midlothian (23112) *(G-8777)*

Bean Counters 703 534-1516
2833 Woodlawn Ave Apt 402 Falls Church (22042) *(G-4763)*

Bear Branch Logging Inc 276 597-7172
1049 Viers Branch Rd Vansant (24656) *(G-13975)*

Bear Chase Brewing Company LLC 703 930-7949
18288 Blueridge Mtn Rd Bluemont (20135) *(G-1885)*

Bear Country Woodworks 540 890-0928
201 Morning Dove Ln Vinton (24179) *(G-14166)*

Bear Island Paper Wb LLC 804 227-4000
10026 Old Ridge Rd Ashland (23005) *(G-1379)*

Bear-Kat Manufacturing LLC 800 442-9700
12351 Randolph Ridge Ln Manassas (20109) *(G-8036)*

Beard Llc Randall 434 602-1224
2614 Cloverdale Rd Bremo Bluff (23022) *(G-1944)*

Bearkers Welding 434 324-7616
771 Mercury Rd Gretna (24557) *(G-6004)*

Bears Specialty Welding 540 247-6813
147 Anderson St Winchester (22602) *(G-15386)*

Beasley Concrete Inc 804 633-9626
16090 Aspen Rd Milford (22514) *(G-8928)*

Beatin Path Publications Ltd 540 828-6903
302 E College St Bridgewater (22812) *(G-1948)*

Beatley Custom Cabinets, Kilmarnock *Also called D & T Akers Corporation (G-7069)*

Beatrice Aurthur 347 420-5612
20402 Stonewood Manor Dr South Chesterfield (23803) *(G-12831)*

Beau-Geste International Inc (PA) **434 534-0468**
1835 Rocky Branch Dr Forest (24551) *(G-5053)*

Beautees 757 439-0269
2269 Airport Rd Suffolk (23434) *(G-13677)*

Beautiful Grind 757 685-6192
733 Grant Ave Virginia Beach (23452) *(G-14272)*

Beautifully Made Cupcakes 757 287-0024
1121 Railroad Ave Chesapeake (23324) *(G-2996)*

Beauty & Beyond Salon, Newport News *Also called Braiding Station Inc (G-9184)*

Beauty Pop LLC 757 416-5858
313 Dixie Dr Norfolk (23505) *(G-9460)*

Beauty Publications Inc 434 296-2161
418 E Water St Charlottesville (22902) *(G-2737)*

Beautymania 703 300-9042
5801 Duke St Alexandria (22304) *(G-146)*

Beaver Creek Wipers 276 632-3033
2201 Appalachian Dr Martinsville (24112) *(G-8269)*

BEC 804 330-2500
8012 Midlothian Tpke # 200 North Chesterfield (23235) *(G-9829)*

BEC Welding & Machine Shop 540 984-3793
16842 Senedo Rd Edinburg (22824) *(G-4300)*

Beck Media Group 540 904-6800
806 Wasena Ave Sw Apt 101 Roanoke (24015) *(G-12042)*

Becke Publishing Incorporated 703 225-8742
5101 1st St N Arlington (22203) *(G-877)*

Becker Designed Inc 703 803-6900
14954 Bogle Dr Chantilly (20151) *(G-2376)*

Becker SMC, Bristol *Also called SMC Electrical Products Inc (G-2033)*

Beckett Consulting Inc 804 580-4164
129 Bowsprit Ln Heathsville (22473) *(G-6459)*

Beckett Corporation (PA) **757 857-0153**
3321 E Princess Anne Rd Norfolk (23502) *(G-9461)*

Beckley LLC 843 822-8091
18313 Buccaneer Ter Leesburg (20176) *(G-7228)*

Beckley & Company, Leesburg *Also called Beckley LLC (G-7228)*

Becky Burton, Interpreter, Colonial Heights *Also called Rebecca Burton (G-3743)*

Becton Dickinson and Company 804 744-4495
11300 Longtown Dr Midlothian (23112) *(G-8778)*

Bedford Freeman & Wort 651 330-8526
16365 James Madison Hwy Gordonsville (22942) *(G-5900)*

Bedford Bulletin LLC 540 586-8612
402 E Main St Bedford (24523) *(G-1623)*

Bedford Ready-Mix Con Co Inc 540 586-8380
805 Railroad Ave Bedford (24523) *(G-1624)*

Bedford Storage, Bedford *Also called Fostek Inc (G-1637)*

Bedford Storage Investment LLC 574 284-1000
1001 Broad St Bedford (24523) *(G-1625)*

Bedford Weaving Inc 540 586-8235
1211 Monroe St Bedford (24523) *(G-1626)*

Bee Measure LLC 434 234-4630
2319 Highland Ave Charlottesville (22903) *(G-2738)*

Bee Systems LLC 760 484-6194
39367 Saddleridge Ln Aldie (20105) *(G-101)*

Beechhurst Industries Inc 703 334-6703
9203 Enterprise Ct Ste J Manassas Park (20111) *(G-8190)*

Beef Jerky Outl Nova Jerky LLC 703 868-6297
6618 Lancaster Dr Warrenton (20187) *(G-14981)*

Beef Products Incorporated 540 985-5914
3308 Aerial Way Dr Sw Roanoke (24018) *(G-11886)*

Beery Brothers 540 879-2970
4840 Witmer Ln Dayton (22821) *(G-4052)*

Beeswax Candle Company LLC 434 528-9885
109 13th St Lynchburg (24504) *(G-7651)*

Beetlebug Software LLC 571 223-5041
43103 Nrthlake Ovrlook Te Leesburg (20176) *(G-7229)*

(G-0000) Company's Geographic Section entry number

Beets & Apples 703 743-4112
  5049 Burnside Farm Pl Haymarket (20169) *(G-6415)*

Beez Nuts Balms, Mechanicsville Also called Sociiterra International LLC *(G-8678)*

Behealth Solutions LLC 434 422-9090
  1165 Tennis Rd Charlottesville (22901) *(G-2593)*

Bejoi LLC 804 319-7369
  12613 Village School Ln Midlothian (23112) *(G-8779)*

Bel Souri LLC 757 685-5583
  3700 Silina Dr Virginia Beach (23452) *(G-14273)*

Belcher Lumber Co Inc 276 498-3362
  2700 Breeden Branch Rd Rowe (24646) *(G-12396)*

Belcher Wells Paving, Nelson Also called Wells Belcher Paving Service *(G-9116)*

Belchers Woodworking 540 365-7809
  1544 King Richard Rd Ferrum (24088) *(G-4970)*

Believe Magazine 804 291-7509
  4131 Dorset Rd Richmond (23234) *(G-11029)*

Beliveau Development Corp 540 961-0505
  104 Roanoke St W Blacksburg (24060) *(G-1725)*

Beliveau Estate Vnyrd Wnery LL 540 961-2102
  3899 Eakin Farm Rd Blacksburg (24060) *(G-1726)*

Bell Printing Inc 804 261-1776
  1720 E Parham Rd Richmond (23228) *(G-11123)*

Bell Textron Inc 817 280-2346
  2231 Crystal Dr Ste 1010 Arlington (22202) *(G-878)*

Bellair Biomedical LLC 276 206-7337
  34 Canterbury Rd Charlottesville (22903) *(G-2739)*

Bellamy Manufacturing & Repair, Hiltons Also called Bellamy Mfg & Repr Co *(G-6904)*

Bellamy Mfg & Repr Co 276 386-7273
  170 Academy Rd Ste 101 Hiltons (24258) *(G-6904)*

Bellash Bakery Inc 516 468-2312
  13420 Jefferson Davis Hwy Woodbridge (22191) *(G-15655)*

Belle Isle Cft Sprits Rchmond, Richmond Also called Belle Isle Craft Spirits Inc *(G-11503)*

Belle Isle Craft Spirits Inc 518 265-7221
  615 Maury St Richmond (23224) *(G-11503)*

Bells Cabinet Shop 804 448-3111
  4790 Jericho Rd Ruther Glen (22546) *(G-12451)*

Bellum Designs LLC 757 343-9556
  4940 Rutherford Rd # 301 Virginia Beach (23455) *(G-14274)*

Bellvue Corp 276 806-4418
  3810 George Wash Hwy Portsmouth (23702) *(G-10398)*

Belmont Farm Distillery 540 825-3207
  13490 Cedar Run Rd Culpeper (22701) *(G-3870)*

Belmont Farms of Virginia Inc 540 825-3207
  13490 Cedar Run Rd Culpeper (22701) *(G-3871)*

Belt Division, Winchester Also called Ashworth Bros Inc *(G-15530)*

Beltsville Construction Supply 703 392-8588
  10337 Balls Ford Rd Manassas (20109) *(G-8037)*

Beltway Bat Company LLC 609 760-7243
  5942 Heritage Square Dr Burke (22015) *(G-2184)*

Beltway Leatherworks LLC 703 457-7829
  2743 King Iron Ct Woodbridge (22192) *(G-15656)*

Belusa Chocolates, Arlington Also called Michael Holt Inc *(G-1062)*

Belvac Production McHy Inc 434 239-0358
  237 Graves Mill Rd Lynchburg (24502) *(G-7652)*

Ben & Xander's Fudge Co., Woodbridge Also called Great Neon Art & Sign Co *(G-15715)*

Ben Dishman Fabrication, Yorktown Also called Dishman Fabrications LLC *(G-15950)*

Benabaye Power LLC 703 574-5800
  103 Douglas Ct Sterling (20166) *(G-13357)*

Benchmark Doors 540 898-5700
  310 Central Rd Ste 1 Fredericksburg (22401) *(G-5173)*

Benchmark Woodworks Inc 757 971-3380
  2517 Turnpike Rd Portsmouth (23707) *(G-10399)*

Bend The Bare Vents, North Chesterfield Also called Madgar Enterprises LLC *(G-9917)*

Beneath The Bark Inc 434 848-3995
  3711 Planters Rd Lawrenceville (23868) *(G-7177)*

Benjamin Franklin Printing Co 804 648-6361
  1528 High St Richmond (23220) *(G-11504)*

Benjamin Moore Authorized Ret, Herndon Also called Vienna Pt Reston/Herndon 04 *(G-6839)*

Benjamin Moore Authorized Ret, Sterling Also called Vienna Paint & Dctg Co Inc *(G-13551)*

Benjamin Moore Authorized Ret, Waynesboro Also called Augusta Paint & Decorating LLC *(G-15098)*

Bennett Logging & Lumber Inc 540 862-7621
  6800 Rich Patch Rd Covington (24426) *(G-3778)*

Bennett Motorsports Inc 434 845-2277
  314 Miles Ln Evington (24550) *(G-4374)*

Benny Babb 276 995-2658
  7585 Rye Cove Memorial Rd Fort Blackmore (24250) *(G-5121)*

Benson Fine Woodcrafting LLC 703 372-1871
  10842 Greene Dr Lorton (22079) *(G-7466)*

Bent Mt Salsa 803 427-3170
  671 Glendale Rd Bent Mountain (24059) *(G-1667)*

Bentech, Roanoke Also called B & B Machine & Tool Inc *(G-12038)*

Bentech 540 344-6820
  1429 Centre Ave Nw Roanoke (24017) *(G-12043)*

Benton-Thomas Inc (PA) **434 572-3577**
  408 Edmunds St South Boston (24592) *(G-12751)*

Benttree Enterprises 434 770-3632
  1100 Mount Tabor Rd Vernon Hill (24597) *(G-13981)*

Benzaco Scientific Inc (PA) **540 371-5560**
  1406 Interstate Bus Park Fredericksburg (22405) *(G-5402)*

Berger and Burrow Entps Inc 866 483-9729
  4502 Starkey Rd Roanoke (24018) *(G-11887)*

Berger and Burrow Entps Inc (PA) **804 282-9729**
  2301 N Parham Rd Ste 4 Henrico (23229) *(G-6481)*

Bering Sea Environmental LLC 757 223-1446
  606 Thimble Shoals Blvd B2 Newport News (23606) *(G-9177)*

Berkle Welding & Fabrication 804 708-0662
  1146 Tricounty Dr Ste B Oilville (23129) *(G-10176)*

Berkley Latasha 804 572-6394
  4530 Kings Hill Rd Henrico (23231) *(G-6482)*

Berkley Yard, Norfolk Also called Luck Stone Corporation *(G-9624)*

Bernard Speed 540 514-9041
  126 Cranes Corner Rd Fredericksburg (22405) *(G-5403)*

Bernies Conchs 757 331-3861
  20400 Mill St Cheriton (23316) *(G-2946)*

Bernies Furn & Cabinetry Inc 434 846-6883
  186 Meadowview Ln Madison Heights (24572) *(G-7868)*

Berry Global Inc 540 946-9250
  1020 Shenandoah Vlg Dr Waynesboro (22980) *(G-15100)*

Berry Global Inc 757 538-2000
  1401 Progress Rd Suffolk (23434) *(G-13678)*

Berry Plastics Design LLC 757 538-2000
  1401 Progress Rd Suffolk (23434) *(G-13679)*

Berryganics, Woodbridge Also called Mf Capital LLC *(G-15746)*

Berryville Graphics Inc (HQ) **540 955-2750**
  25 Jack Enders Blvd Berryville (22611) *(G-1671)*

Bert & Cliffs Machine Shop 804 580-3021
  Rr 200 Wicomico Church (22579) *(G-15194)*

Berts Inc 757 865-8040
  108 Nicewood Dr Newport News (23602) *(G-9178)*

Bespokery LLC 703 624-5024
  4126 Leonard Dr Fairfax (22030) *(G-4598)*

Best Age Today LLC 757 618-9181
  109 Gainsborough Sq Chesapeake (23320) *(G-2997)*

Best Blower Sales & Svc LLC 434 352-1909
  208 Autumn Ln Appomattox (24522) *(G-806)*

Best Cabinets and Closets LLC 703 830-0542
  14600 Jovet Ct Centreville (20120) *(G-2294)*

Best Checks Inc 703 416-4856
  1300 Crystal Dr Arlington (22202) *(G-879)*

Best Checks Inc 703 467-9300
  100 Executive Dr Unit 1 Sterling (20166) *(G-13358)*

Best Deal On Shirts LLC 757 754-9855
  3315 S Military Hwy Chesapeake (23323) *(G-2998)*

Best Granite & Marble 703 455-0404
  7608 Fullerton Rd Springfield (22153) *(G-12960)*

Best Green Technologies LLC 888 424-8432
  5208 Brockton Ct Glen Allen (23059) *(G-5707)*

Best Image Printers Ltd 804 272-1006
  2735 Buford Rd North Chesterfield (23235) *(G-9830)*

Best Impressions Inc 703 518-1375
  5701t General Wash Dr Alexandria (22312) *(G-421)*

Best Impressions Printing 804 740-9006
  11034 Air Park Rd Ste 17 Ashland (23005) *(G-1380)*

Best Medical Belgium Inc 800 336-4970
  7643 Fullerton Rd Springfield (22153) *(G-12961)*

Best Medical International Inc (HQ) **703 451-2378**
  7643 Fullerton Rd Springfield (22153) *(G-12962)*

Best of Landscaping 804 253-4014
  4662 Bell Rd Powhatan (23139) *(G-10532)*

Best Printing, Norfolk Also called Seven Sevens Inc *(G-9718)*

Best Printing & Design LLC 703 593-9874
  3842 Columbia Pike # 102 Arlington (22204) *(G-880)*

Best Printing Inc 540 563-9004
  4225 Plantation Rd Ne Roanoke (24012) *(G-12044)*

Best Recognition 757 490-3933
  4969 Haygood Rd Virginia Beach (23455) *(G-14275)*

Best Software Inc 949 753-1222
  11413 Isaac Newton Sq S Reston (20190) *(G-10798)*

Best Value Petroleum Inc 703 303-3780
  5630 Lee Hwy Arlington (22207) *(G-881)*

Beta Contractors LLC 703 424-1940
  3304 Applegrove Ct Herndon (20171) *(G-6623)*

Bethany House Inc 703 281-9410
  130 Church St Nw Vienna (22180) *(G-14015)*

Bethany Warthan 434 294-2937
  957 N Main St Blackstone (23824) *(G-1811)*

Bethels Welding 434 946-7160
  2347 S Amherst Hwy Amherst (24521) *(G-682)*

Beths Embroidery LLC 434 933-8652
  589 Allens Creek Rd Gladstone (24553) *(G-5681)*

Bethune Industries LLC 407 579-1308
  2139 N Pierce Ct Arlington (22209) *(G-882)*

Better Cables LLC 872 222-5371
  43300 Southern Walk Plz Broadlands (20148) *(G-2073)*

(PA)=Parent Co (HQ)=Headquarters (DH)=Div Headquarters

Better Cables LLC (PA) 703 724-0906
43150 Arundell Ct Broadlands (20148) *(G-2074)*

Better Fuels of Virginia 540 693-4552
12301 Dell Way Fredericksburg (22407) *(G-5252)*

Better Granite Garcia LLC 703 624-9912
6954 Wellington Rd 3 Manassas (20109) *(G-8038)*

Better Impressions, Sterling *Also called Bi Communications Inc (G-13359)*

Better Karma LLC 703 971-1072
6018 Goldenrod Ct Alexandria (22310) *(G-422)*

Better Living Inc 434 978-1666
2553 Proffit Rd Charlottesville (22911) *(G-2594)*

Better Living Components Inc 434 978-1666
2553 Proffit Rd Charlottesville (22911) *(G-2595)*

Better Signs 540 382-7446
1035 Cambria St Ne Ste C Christiansburg (24073) *(G-3573)*

Better Vision Eyeglass Center 757 397-2020
3235 Academy Ave Ste 200 Portsmouth (23703) *(G-10400)*

Bettera Brands LLC 703 222-6340
14790 Flint Lee Rd Chantilly (20151) *(G-2377)*

Betterbilt Solutions LLC 540 324-9117
3553 Old Greenville Rd Staunton (24401) *(G-13244)*

Betty P Hicks 540 745-5111
4427 Floyd Hwy N Floyd (24091) *(G-5016)*

Bevans Oyster Company (PA) 804 472-2331
1090 Skipjack Rd Kinsale (22488) *(G-7133)*

Bevans Oyster Company 804 472-2331
1090 Skipjack Rd 610 Kinsale (22488) *(G-7134)*

Beverley M James Jr 540 354-2300
4536 Fontaine Dr Roanoke (24018) *(G-11888)*

Beydler Cnc LLC 760 954-4397
1328 N Amherst Hwy Amherst (24521) *(G-683)*

Beydler's Manibolt Driller, Amherst *Also called Beydler Cnc LLC (G-683)*

BF Mayes Assoc Inc 703 451-4994
7226 Willow Oak Pl Springfield (22153) *(G-12963)*

BF Wise & Sons Lc 540 547-2918
3890 Ridgeview Rd Reva (22735) *(G-10999)*

BFI Waste Services LLC 804 222-1152
2490 Charles City Rd Richmond (23231) *(G-11124)*

BFI Waste Services of Richmond, Richmond *Also called BFI Waste Services LLC (G-11124)*

Bg Industries Inc 434 369-2128
107 Woodberry Ln Lynchburg (24502) *(G-7653)*

Bg Smith & Son Oyster Co 804 394-2721
70 Simonson Rd Farnham (22460) *(G-4962)*

Bg Solutions LLC 703 623-4846
1903 Ballycor Dr Vienna (22182) *(G-14016)*

BGB Technology Inc 804 451-5211
1060 Port Walthall Dr South Chesterfield (23834) *(G-12797)*

BGF Industries Inc 434 447-2210
179 Butts St South Hill (23970) *(G-12844)*

BGF Industries Inc 434 369-4751
1523 Main St Altavista (24517) *(G-626)*

BGF Industries Inc 434 369-4751
401 Amherst Ave Altavista (24517) *(G-627)*

BGF Industries Inc (HQ) 843 537-3172
230 Slayton Ave 1a Danville (24540) *(G-3957)*

Bh Cooper Farm & Mill Inc 276 694-6292
1268 Abram Penn Hwy Critz (24082) *(G-3823)*

Bh Media Group Inc 703 241-2608
3236 Spring Ln Falls Church (22041) *(G-4764)*

Bhk of America Inc 201 783-8490
3045 Philpott Rd South Boston (24592) *(G-12752)*

Bhsk Golf, Stafford *Also called Big Hubster Short Knocker Golf (G-13123)*

Bi Communications Inc 703 435-9600
45150 Business Ct Ste 450 Sterling (20166) *(G-13359)*

Bi State Coil Winding Inc 276 956-3106
2214 Phosphorous St Ridgeway (24148) *(G-11839)*

Bible Believers Press 703 476-0125
11692 Generation Ct Reston (20191) *(G-10799)*

Bible Truth Music 757 365-9956
709 Willow Dr Newport News (23605) *(G-9179)*

Bickford Broadcast Vehicles, Chantilly *Also called Lb Telesystems Inc (G-2456)*

Bidgood Enterprises 434 489-4952
845 River Ridge Rd Danville (24541) *(G-3958)*

Big Chip Clothing Company LLC 877 572-6525
2085 Lynnhven Pkwy Ste 10 Virginia Beach (23456) *(G-14276)*

Big D Enterprises Inc 276 679-1090
195 Marigold Ln Coeburn (24230) *(G-3695)*

Big D Woodworking 757 753-4814
314 Mona Dr Newport News (23608) *(G-9180)*

Big Daddys Sports Products 757 310-8565
1 Cortez Ct Hampton (23666) *(G-6091)*

Big Dog Woodworking LLC 540 359-1056
21066 White Rock Dr Richardsville (22736) *(G-11009)*

Big EZ Prints 804 929-3479
4550 Jefferson Pointe Ln Prince George (23875) *(G-10587)*

Big Face Benji Music Group LLC 804 229-9450
2100 Breezy Point Cir # 204 North Chesterfield (23235) *(G-9831)*

Big Fish Cider Co 540 468-2322
59 Spruce St Monterey (24465) *(G-9003)*

Big Fred Promotions Inc 804 832-5510
7554 Bellehaven Dr Gloucester Point (23062) *(G-5872)*

Big Hubster Short Knocker Golf 757 635-5949
1 Columbia Way Stafford (22554) *(G-13123)*

Big Image Graphics Inc 804 379-9910
800 Gordon School Pl North Chesterfield (23236) *(G-9832)*

Big Island Oysters 804 389-9589
9817 Misty Ln Hayes (23072) *(G-6396)*

Big Lick Boomerang 540 761-4611
3017 Embassy Dr Roanoke (24019) *(G-11889)*

Big Lick Screen Printing 540 632-2695
802 Kerns Ave Sw Roanoke (24015) *(G-12045)*

Big Lick Seasonings LLC 540 774-8898
5024 Crossbow Cir Roanoke (24018) *(G-11890)*

Big Mind Publishing Inc 703 734-8359
940 Swinks Mill Rd Mc Lean (22102) *(G-8398)*

Big Paper Records LLC 804 381-9278
11318 Old Scotland Rd Glen Allen (23059) *(G-5708)*

Big Sky Drone Services LLC 804 378-2970
1730 Calais Trl Powhatan (23139) *(G-10533)*

Big Spring Mill Inc 540 268-2267
1931 Big Spring Dr Elliston (24087) *(G-4343)*

Big Stone Gap Corporation 276 523-7337
1942 Neeley Rd Big Stone Gap (24219) *(G-1706)*

Big Stone Machine Shop, Big Stone Gap *Also called Dale Stidham (G-1708)*

Big Timber Hardwoods LLC 724 301-7051
772 Sandbridge Rd Virginia Beach (23456) *(G-14277)*

Big Time Charters Inc 757 496-1040
2212 Windward Shore Dr Virginia Beach (23451) *(G-14278)*

Bigbrassband LLC 571 223-7137
15 N King St Fl 3 Leesburg (20176) *(G-7230)*

Bigeye Direct Inc 703 955-3017
13860 Redskin Dr Herndon (20171) *(G-6624)*

Bigmouth Bagger, Williamsburg *Also called Gargone John (G-15246)*

Bill Foote 808 298-5423
536 Virginia Ave Virginia Beach (23451) *(G-14279)*

Bill Kelley Metalsmith 804 798-4286
10423 Dow Gil Rd Ashland (23005) *(G-1381)*

Bill Klinck Publishing 540 740-3034
140 Rocky Mountain Ln New Market (22844) *(G-9140)*

Bills Custom Cabinetry 703 281-1669
411 Welles St Se Vienna (22180) *(G-14017)*

Bills Yard & Lawn Service LLC 757 871-4589
308 Brightwood Ave Hampton (23661) *(G-6092)*

Billsburg Brewery LLC 757 926-0981
2054 Jamestown Rd Williamsburg (23185) *(G-15211)*

Billy Bill Logging 804 512-9669
95 Mitchells Mill Rd Aylett (23009) *(G-1546)*

Billy M Seargeant 540 898-6396
4312 Mine Rd Fredericksburg (22408) *(G-5253)*

Biltco LLC 703 372-5940
7402 Lockport Pl Ste C Lorton (22079) *(G-7467)*

Bimbo Bakeries 804 475-6776
6636 Fleet Dr Alexandria (22310) *(G-423)*

Bimbo Bakeries USA 434 525-2947
20446 Lynchburg Hwy Lynchburg (24502) *(G-7654)*

Bindery Plus 703 357-5002
3221 Colvin St Alexandria (22314) *(G-147)*

Binge Live Inc 757 679-7715
2329 Sanderson Rd Chesapeake (23322) *(G-2999)*

Bingham & Taylor Corp 540 825-8334
601 Nalle Pl Culpeper (22701) *(G-3872)*

Bingham Enterprises LLC 434 645-1731
610 W Virginia Ave Crewe (23930) *(G-3808)*

Bingo Bugle Newspaper, Lynchburg *Also called Jack Einreinhof (G-7747)*

Bingo City 757 890-3168
5702 George Wash Mem Hwy Yorktown (23692) *(G-15937)*

Bingo Tribune Inc 804 221-9049
6500 Barcroft Ln Richmond (23226) *(G-11125)*

Bio-Prosthetic Orthotic Lab 703 527-3123
5275 Lee Hwy Ste G3 Arlington (22207) *(G-883)*

Biocer Corporation 757 490-7851
1 Columbus Ctr Ste 624 Virginia Beach (23462) *(G-14280)*

Biocide USA, Norfolk *Also called Green Air Environmental Svcs (G-9565)*

Biogeo Genetics 888 448-8376
228 Suth Mltary Hwy Ste B Chesapeake (23323) *(G-3000)*

Biohouse Publishing Group Inc 703 858-1738
42783 Macauley Pl Ashburn (20148) *(G-1246)*

Biologics Inc 703 367-9020
8761 Virginia Meadows Dr Manassas (20109) *(G-8039)*

Biomass English Partners LLC 804 226-8227
2890 Seven Hills Blvd Richmond (23231) *(G-11126)*

Biomaterials USA LLC 843 442-4789
2405 Westwood Ave Ste 203 Richmond (23230) *(G-11127)*

Biomic Sciences LLC 434 260-8530
4351 Seminole Trl Charlottesville (22911) *(G-2596)*

Biosensor Tech LLC 318 843-4479
4810 Garden Spring Ln # 206 Glen Allen (23059) *(G-5709)*

Biostar 800 686-9544
1 Cleveland St Ste 800 Gordonsville (22942) *(G-5901)*

Biotivia Arlington Co, Arlington *Also called Vitaspan Corporation* **(G-1214)**

Biotraces Inc (PA) **703 793-1550**
5660 Oak Tanager Ct Burke (22015) **(G-2185)**

Birckhead Signs & Graphics 434 295-5962
823 Monticello Rd A Charlottesville (22902) **(G-2740)**

Bird Fabrication LLC 225 614-0985
2593 Quality Ct Virginia Beach (23454) **(G-14281)**

Bird Fabrication LLC 225 614-0985
2593 Quality Ct Ste 215 Virginia Beach (23454) **(G-14282)**

Birdcloud Creations 757 428-6239
839 S Birdneck Rd Virginia Beach (23451) **(G-14283)**

Birdies Dolls 757 421-7788
1904 Battlefield Blvd S B Chesapeake (23322) **(G-3001)**

Birds With Backpacks LLC 703 897-5531
1501 Spoonbill Ct Woodbridge (22191) **(G-15657)**

Birge Croft 757 547-0838
1337 Lindale Dr Ste G Chesapeake (23320) **(G-3002)**

Birkenstock Aerospace, Herndon *Also called David Birkenstock* **(G-6653)**

Birsch Industries Inc 757 622-0355
3412 Strathmore Ave Norfolk (23504) **(G-9462)**

Birth Right Industries LLC 703 590-6971
14157 Renegade Ct Woodbridge (22193) **(G-15658)**

Bishop Custom Cabinets 804 469-7549
10500 Duncan Rd North Dinwiddie (23803) **(G-10048)**

Bishop Distributors LLC 757 618-6401
150 S Military Hwy Norfolk (23502) **(G-9463)**

Bishop II Inc 757 855-7137
2325 Palmyra St Norfolk (23513) **(G-9464)**

Bishop Montana Ent 703 777-8248
706 Amber Ct Ne Leesburg (20176) **(G-7231)**

Bishop Stone and Met Arts LLC 804 240-1030
8001 Cadys Mill Rd Hanover (23069) **(G-6280)**

Bison Inc 703 754-4190
5571 Pageland Ln Gainesville (20155) **(G-5572)**

Bison Printing Inc 540 586-3955
1342 On Time Rd Bedford (24523) **(G-1627)**

Bissell 703 827-5769
6125 Long Meadow Rd Mc Lean (22101) **(G-8399)**

Bizcard Xpress 757 340-4525
3780 Virginia Beach Blvd Virginia Beach (23452) **(G-14284)**

Bizwhazee LLC 703 889-8499
11600 Sunrise Valley Dr # 300 Reston (20191) **(G-10800)**

BJ Embroidery & Designs 804 605-4749
5304 Ridgerun Pl Chesterfield (23832) **(G-3480)**

Bjd Tel-Comm LLC 703 858-2931
20610 Crescent Pointe Pl Ashburn (20147) **(G-1247)**

Bkc Industries Inc 856 694-9400
11220 Assett Loop Ste 210 Manassas (20109) **(G-8040)**

Bl & Son Enterprises LLC 757 502-7789
1720 S Park Ct Chesapeake (23320) **(G-3003)**

Bl & Son Enterprises LLC 757 938-9188
4 Pirates Cv Hampton (23669) **(G-6093)**

Bl Nichols Logging Inc 540 875-8690
1895 Preston Mill Rd Huddleston (24104) **(G-6952)**

Blac Rayven Publications 757 512-4617
1205 Warwick Dr Virginia Beach (23453) **(G-14285)**

Black Alder Trail LLC 812 219-1975
731 Berryville Ave Winchester (22601) **(G-15531)**

Black Ark Art & Design Studio, Norfolk *Also called Eggleston Minor* **(G-9542)**

Black Bear Corporation 540 982-1061
2224 Buford Ave Sw Roanoke (24015) **(G-12046)**

Black Box Corporation 781 449-1900
E Commerce St Amherst (24521) **(G-684)**

Black Business Today Inc 804 528-7407
201 W Marshall St Apt 204 Richmond (23220) **(G-11505)**

Black Diamond Gold Fuel, Chesapeake *Also called Raymond Golden* **(G-3256)**

Black Dog Gallery 757 989-1700
114 Ballard St Yorktown (23690) **(G-15938)**

Black Element LLC 757 224-6160
1123 West Ave Hampton (23669) **(G-6094)**

Black Eyed Tees 276 971-1219
772 Thru Dr Pounding Mill (24637) **(G-10515)**

Black Forest Sign Inc 540 825-0017
15373 Rocky Ridge Ln # 2 Culpeper (22701) **(G-3873)**

Black Gold Industries LLC 757 768-4674
12844 Daybreak Cir Newport News (23602) **(G-9181)**

Black Hoof Brewing Company LLC 571 707-8014
11 S King St Leesburg (20175) **(G-7232)**

Black Jacket LLC 425 319-1014
1237 Smoketree Dr Forest (24551) **(G-5054)**

Black Line Swim, Virginia Beach *Also called Stephen Bialorucki* **(G-14846)**

Black Magazine LLC 804 306-6735
828 Wales Dr Highland Springs (23075) **(G-6850)**

Black Mold Busters Chesapeake 757 606-9608
4416 Portsmouth Blvd E Chesapeake (23321) **(G-3004)**

Black Mold Rmval Group Wdbrdge 571 402-8960
14058 Shoppers Best Way Woodbridge (22192) **(G-15659)**

Black Money Label LLC 201 975-5009
3419 Virginia Beach Blvd Virginia Beach (23452) **(G-14286)**

Black Oak Processing & Smoking, Goshen *Also called Elyssa E Strong* **(G-5925)**

Black Pwdr Artificer Press Inc 804 366-0562
1212 Monroe Bay Ave Colonial Beach (22443) **(G-3722)**

Black Rabbit Delights LLC 757 453-3359
1702 Bellevue Ave Norfolk (23509) **(G-9465)**

Black Room Press LLC 804 929-8040
4901 Olde Mill Pond Ln Glen Allen (23060) **(G-5710)**

Black Sand Solutions LLC 703 393-1127
9323 Brandon St Manassas Park (20111) **(G-8191)**

Black Sphere LLC 703 776-0494
4541 Garbo Ct Annandale (22003) **(G-732)**

Black Tree LLC 703 669-0178
8200 Greensboro Dr # 404 Mc Lean (22102) **(G-8400)**

Blackbird Spirits LLC 540 247-9115
104 Shockey Cir Winchester (22602) **(G-15387)**

Blackboard Connect Inc 919 841-0175
11720 Plaza America Dr # 11 Reston (20190) **(G-10801)**

Blackboard Holdings Inc 202 463-4860
11720 Plaza America Dr # 6 Reston (20190) **(G-10802)**

Blackboard Inc (HQ) **202 463-4860**
11720 Plaza America Dr # 11 Reston (20190) **(G-10803)**

Blackboard Inc 512 474-8363
11720 Plaza America Dr # 11 Reston (20190) **(G-10804)**

Blackboard Inc 254 251-3203
11720 Plaza America Dr # 11 Reston (20190) **(G-10805)**

Blackboard Inc 202 463-4860
1807 Michael Faraday Ct Reston (20190) **(G-10806)**

Blackboard Super Holdco Inc (HQ) **202 463-4860**
11720 Plaza America Dr # 11 Reston (20190) **(G-10807)**

Blackfish Software LLC (PA) **703 779-9649**
335 Whipp Dr Se Leesburg (20175) **(G-7233)**

Blackhawk Rubber & Gasket Inc 888 703-9060
4105 Kalona Rd Portsmouth (23703) **(G-10401)**

Blackout Tinting LLC 757 416-5658
1533 Azalea Garden Rd Norfolk (23502) **(G-9466)**

Blackpearl Soapstone 813 909-8400
2858 N Seminole Trl Madison (22727) **(G-7849)**

Blacksky Aerospace LLC 202 500-3743
623 19th St S Arlington (22202) **(G-884)**

Blacksky Holdings Inc (PA) **703 935-1930**
13241 Wdlnd Pk Rd Ste 300 Herndon (20171) **(G-6625)**

Blackstone Defense Svcs Corp 571 598-2714
20254 Northpark Dr Ashburn (20147) **(G-1248)**

Blackstone Energy Ltd 540 776-7890
302 S Jefferson St Roanoke (24011) **(G-12047)**

Blackstone Herb Cottage 434 292-1135
101 S Main St Blackstone (23824) **(G-1812)**

Blacktag Screen Printing Inc 855 423-1680
307 Ireland St Hampton (23663) **(G-6095)**

Blackwater Bldg Cstm Wdwkg LLC 540 493-1888
50 Nelson St Ferrum (24088) **(G-4971)**

Blackwater Engines, Virginia Beach *Also called Tidewater Auto & Indus Mch Inc* **(G-14872)**

Blackwater Manufacturing LLC 804 299-3975
116 Sylvia Rd Ashland (23005) **(G-1382)**

Blackwolf Software 434 978-4903
4300 Sylvan Ln Charlottesville (22911) **(G-2597)**

Blair Inc 703 922-0200
7001 Loisdale Rd Springfield (22150) **(G-12964)**

Blaise Gaston Inc 434 973-1801
686 Fairhope Ave Earlysville (22936) **(G-4288)**

Blak Tie Publishing Co LLC 757 839-6727
1106 Lands End Dr Chesapeake (23322) **(G-3005)**

Blakbunni 347 239-5139
6012 Saber Ct Mechanicsville (23111) **(G-8607)**

Blake Collection 703 329-1599
6222 Tally Ho Ln Alexandria (22307) **(G-424)**

Blake James L, Alexandria *Also called Blake Collection* **(G-424)**

Blakeney United Disposal, Annandale *Also called Monalisa Blakeney* **(G-775)**

Blanc Creatives LLC 434 260-1692
735b Walnut St Charlottesville (22902) **(G-2741)**

Blanchards Welding Repair 757 539-6306
645 Turlington Rd Suffolk (23434) **(G-13680)**

Blanco Inc 757 766-8123
125 Prince Arthur Dr Yorktown (23693) **(G-15939)**

Blanco Inc (PA) **540 389-3040**
3316 Aerial Way Dr Sw Roanoke (24018) **(G-11891)**

Bland Woodworking 703 631-6567
5309 Caliper Ct Centreville (20120) **(G-2295)**

Blands Welding & Fabg Co 276 495-8132
5880 Brushy Ridge Rd Nora (24272) **(G-9407)**

Bleeding Canvas 276 623-2345
31208 Lee Hwy Glade Spring (24340) **(G-5674)**

Blehert 703 471-7907
11919 Moss Point Ln Reston (20194) **(G-10808)**

Blended Cre8tions LLC 347 323-2982
900 Piney Branch Ln # 102 Virginia Beach (23451) **(G-14287)**

Blessed Hands Cnstr & Maint 703 762-6595
1918 S Glebe Rd Arlington (22204) **(G-885)**

Blind Industries 703 390-9221
12310 Sunrise Valley Dr Reston (20191) **(G-10809)**

A L P H A B E T I C

Blinkcloud LLC 484 429-3340
65 N Wash St Ste 425 Alexandria (22314) ***(G-148)***
Blissful Gardenz Inc 703 360-2191
5119 Rosemont Ave Alexandria (22309) ***(G-425)***
Block9ine Enterprises LLC 240 728-8601
16813 Jed Forest Ln Woodbridge (22191) ***(G-15660)***
Blockmaster Security Inc 703 788-6809
2325 Dulles Corn Herndon (20171) ***(G-6626)***
Blonde Industries LLC 540 667-8192
268 Christmas Tree Ln Stephenson (22656) ***(G-13331)***
Blood Sweat & Cheer 757 620-1515
1257 Treefern Dr Virginia Beach (23451) ***(G-14288)***
Bloom Publication 757 373-4402
417 W 20th St Norfolk (23517) ***(G-9467)***
Bloombeams LLC 804 822-1022
5316 Clipper Cove Rd Midlothian (23112) ***(G-8780)***
Bloomberg Industry Group, Arlington *Also called Bureau of National Affairs Inc* ***(G-893)***
Bloomforth Corp 703 408-8993
6419 Mccoy Rd Centreville (20121) ***(G-2296)***
Bloxom Sheet Metal Inc 757 436-4181
813 Prfvnal Pl W Ste B101 Chesapeake (23320) ***(G-3006)***
Blucloudradio LLC 757 812-2380
259 Granby St Norfolk (23510) ***(G-9468)***
Blue Beacon LLC 202 643-9043
44214 Bristow Cir Ashburn (20147) ***(G-1249)***
Blue Bee Cider LLC 804 231-0280
1320 Summit Ave Richmond (23230) ***(G-11128)***
Blue Castle Cupcakes LLC 757 618-0600
2453 Blue Castle Ln Virginia Beach (23454) ***(G-14289)***
Blue Dragon Publishing, Williamsburg *Also called Dawn Brotherton* ***(G-15230)***
Blue Jeans Publishing LLC 757 277-9428
617 Stoneleigh Ct Chesapeake (23322) ***(G-3007)***
Blue Line Yoga Virginia, Poquoson *Also called ALC Training Group LLC* ***(G-10364)***
Blue Monkey LLC 540 664-1297
3500 Cedar Creek Grade Winchester (22602) ***(G-15388)***
Blue Moon Catering Concessions 276 236-8728
101 E Oldtown St Galax (24333) ***(G-5628)***
Blue Mountain Brewery Inc 540 456-8020
9519 Critzers Shop Rd Afton (22920) ***(G-75)***
Blue Mtn Brrel Hse Orgnic Brwr 434 263-4002
495 Cooperative Way Arrington (22922) ***(G-1227)***
Blue Quartz Winery LLC 540 923-4048
2861 S F T Valley Rd Etlan (22719) ***(G-4372)***
Blue RDG Antigravity Treadmlls 540 977-9540
3408 Wellington Dr Se Roanoke (24014) ***(G-12048)***
Blue Rdge Leader Loudoun Today, Purcellville *Also called Blue Ridge Leader* ***(G-10652)***
Blue Ribbon Coal Sales Ltd 540 387-2077
1125 Intervale Dr Salem (24153) ***(G-12482)***
Blue Ridge, Salem *Also called Montgomery Cnty Newspapers Inc* ***(G-12540)***
Blue Ridge Analytical LLC 276 228-6464
2280 W Ridge Rd Wytheville (24382) ***(G-15876)***
Blue Ridge Binding Inc 703 771-1676
45570 Shepard Dr Ste 2 Sterling (20164) ***(G-13360)***
Blue Ridge Book Conservation 434 295-9373
634 Big Oak Rd Charlottesville (22903) ***(G-2742)***
Blue Ridge Buck Saver Inc 434 996-2817
225 Heather Crest Pl Charlottesville (22903) ***(G-2743)***
Blue Ridge Chorale of Culpeper 540 717-5888
754 Germanna Hwy Culpeper (22701) ***(G-3874)***
Blue Ridge Cold Press Company 276 229-1661
4373 Greenberry Rd Hillsville (24343) ***(G-6886)***
Blue Ridge Concrete Product 276 755-2000
14950 Fancy Gap Hwy Cana (24317) ***(G-2226)***
Blue Ridge Crest LLC 276 236-7149
301 Shaw St Galax (24333) ***(G-5629)***
Blue Ridge Digital Pubg LLC 703 785-3970
426 E Columbia St Falls Church (22046) ***(G-4902)***
Blue Ridge Electric Service, Winchester *Also called Loudon Street Electric Svcs* ***(G-15553)***
Blue Ridge Embroidery Inc 434 296-9746
550 Meade Ave Charlottesville (22902) ***(G-2744)***
Blue Ridge Fabricators Inc 540 342-1102
3 8th St Sw Roanoke (24016) ***(G-12049)***
Blue Ridge Fiberboard Inc 434 797-1321
250 Celotex Dr Danville (24541) ***(G-3959)***
Blue Ridge Flutes, Blacksburg *Also called Riegger Marin* ***(G-1784)***
Blue Ridge Fudge Lady Inc 276 335-2229
200 W Main St Wytheville (24382) ***(G-15877)***
Blue Ridge Hearts Pine Floors, Hillsville *Also called B & G Bandmill* ***(G-6884)***
Blue Ridge Homestead LLC 540 743-2374
1773 E Rocky Branch Rd Luray (22835) ***(G-7601)***
Blue Ridge Industries Inc 540 662-3900
266 Arbor Ct Winchester (22602) ***(G-15389)***
Blue Ridge Leader 540 338-6200
128 S 20th St Purcellville (20132) ***(G-10652)***
Blue Ridge Logging Co Inc 434 836-5663
408 Vicar Rd Danville (24540) ***(G-3960)***
Blue Ridge Machine Works Inc 540 249-4640
103 6th St Grottoes (24441) ***(G-6016)***
Blue Ridge Marble Mfrs LLC 434 582-6139
147 Mill Ridge Rd 234b Lynchburg (24502) ***(G-7655)***
Blue Ridge Marketing & EMB 276 223-0337
295 Chapman Rd Wytheville (24382) ***(G-15878)***
Blue Ridge Mch Motorsports LLC 540 432-6560
971 Acorn Dr Harrisonburg (22802) ***(G-6295)***
Blue Ridge Mechanical 540 662-3148
831 Front Royal Pike Winchester (22602) ***(G-15390)***
Blue Ridge Millwork 434 993-1953
116 S And S Ln Concord (24538) ***(G-3756)***
Blue Ridge Optics LLC 540 586-8526
1617 Longwood Ave Bedford (24523) ***(G-1628)***
Blue Ridge Packaging Corp 276 638-1413
355 Industrial Park Dr Martinsville (24115) ***(G-8270)***
Blue Ridge Pallet LLC 540 836-8115
17 Commonwealth Dr Lyndhurst (22952) ***(G-7842)***
Blue Ridge Plant, Blue Ridge *Also called Boxley Materials Company* ***(G-1848)***
Blue Ridge Pools Staunton Ci, Staunton *Also called Stans Ski and Snowboard LLC* ***(G-13297)***
Blue Ridge Portable Sawmill 540 743-2520
3729 Ida Rd Luray (22835) ***(G-7602)***
Blue Ridge Pottery 434 985-6080
9 Golden Horseshoe Rd Stanardsville (22973) ***(G-13216)***
Blue Ridge Prestain, Front Royal *Also called Hbh Holdings LLC* ***(G-5536)***
Blue Ridge Prosthetics & Ortho 540 242-4499
1951 Evelyn Byrd Ave E Harrisonburg (22801) ***(G-6296)***
Blue Ridge Publishing LLC 540 234-0807
3150 Lee Hwy Weyers Cave (24486) ***(G-15167)***
Blue Ridge Quarry, Blue Ridge *Also called Boxley Materials Company* ***(G-1846)***
Blue Ridge Scientific LLC 540 631-0356
2392 Catlett Mountain Rd Front Royal (22630) ***(G-5524)***
Blue Ridge Servo Mtr Repr LLC 540 375-2990
1017 Tennessee St Salem (24153) ***(G-12483)***
Blue Ridge Shelving Closet LLC 540 365-0150
5800 Prillaman Switch Rd Ferrum (24088) ***(G-4972)***
Blue Ridge Sign & Stamp Co Inc 540 777-5456
6446 Peters Creek Rd Roanoke (24019) ***(G-11892)***
Blue Ridge Software 703 912-3990
9003 Maritime Ct Springfield (22153) ***(G-12965)***
Blue Ridge Springs Inc 434 822-0006
223 Riverview Dr Ste F Danville (24541) ***(G-3961)***
Blue Ridge Stairs & Wdwrk LLC 540 320-1953
344 Rivendell Rd Nw Willis (24380) ***(G-15354)***
Blue Ridge Stone Corp 434 239-9249
762 Lawyers Rd Lynchburg (24501) ***(G-7656)***
Blue Ridge Stone Mfg 276 676-0040
26053 Harrison Rd Abingdon (24210) ***(G-15)***
Blue Ridge Vineyard Inc 540 798-7642
1027 Shiloh Dr Eagle Rock (24085) ***(G-4279)***
Blue Ridge Wood Preserving Inc 540 297-6607
1220 Hendricks Store Rd Moneta (24121) ***(G-8957)***
Blue Ridge Woodworks VA Inc 434 477-0313
130 Oakview Dr Monroe (24574) ***(G-8987)***
Blue Ridge Yurts LLC 540 651-8422
369 Parkway Ln S Pilot (24138) ***(G-10356)***
Blue Sky Distillery LLC 757 746-8342
20042 Isle Of Wght Indus Smithfield (23430) ***(G-12705)***
Blue Sky Distillery LLC 757 234-3260
15104 S Brading Ct Carrollton (23314) ***(G-2240)***
Blue Skys Woodshop 703 567-6220
1502 Mount Vernon Ave Alexandria (22301) ***(G-149)***
Blue Stone Block Sprmkt Inc (PA) **540 982-3588**
1510 Wallace Ave Ne Roanoke (24012) ***(G-12050)***
Blue Wave Mobile Marine 757 831-4810
4108 Neptune Ct Chesapeake (23325) ***(G-3008)***
Bluebird Cabinetry 804 937-5429
7333 Strath Rd Richmond (23231) ***(G-11129)***
Bluefield Manufacturing Inc 276 322-3441
215 Suppliers Rd Bluefield (24605) ***(G-1859)***
Bluegrass Unlimited Inc 540 349-8181
9514 James Madison Hwy Warrenton (20186) ***(G-14982)***
Bluegrass Woods Inc 540 997-0174
223 Millboro Indus Rd Millboro (24460) ***(G-8934)***
Bluemont 202 422-6500
18035 Raven Rocks Rd Bluemont (20135) ***(G-1886)***
Blueprint Inc 703 771-9256
503 Meade Dr Sw Leesburg (20175) ***(G-7234)***
Blueridge Sand Inc 276 579-2007
9916 Wilson Hwy Mouth of Wilson (24363) ***(G-9091)***
Blueridge Wood 276 930-2274
452 Bob White Rd Woolwine (24185) ***(G-15864)***
Bluestone Industries Inc (HQ) **540 776-7890**
302 S Jefferson St # 500 Roanoke (24011) ***(G-12051)***
Bluestone Resources Inc 540 776-7890
302 S Jefferson St # 500 Roanoke (24011) ***(G-12052)***
Bluestone Vineyard Inc 540 828-0099
4702 Spring Creek Rd Bridgewater (22812) ***(G-1949)***
Bluetherm Corporation 917 446-8958
416 E Main St Ste 301e Charlottesville (22902) ***(G-2745)***

Bluewater Publishing 804 695-0400
7348 Main St Gloucester (23061) ***(G-5838)***
Bluewire Prototypes Inc 540 200-3200
6309 Old Ferry Rd Hiwassee (24347) ***(G-6910)***
Bluf Military Benefits 402 315-7831
3023 King St Alexandria (22302) ***(G-150)***
Bluff Spur Coal LLC 276 679-6962
5703 Crutchfield Dr Norton (24273) ***(G-10113)***
Blulogix LLC 443 333-4100
1356 Beverly Rd Ste 300 Mc Lean (22101) ***(G-8401)***
Blumont Vineyards 540 554-8439
18755 Foggy Bottom Rd Bluemont (20135) ***(G-1887)***
Bluvector Inc 571 565-2100
4501 Fairfax Dr Ste 750 Arlington (22203) ***(G-886)***
Blythe, Chantilly *Also called Eurovia Atlantic Coast LLC* ***(G-2418)***
Blythe 804 364-1717
11713 W Broad St Richmond (23233) ***(G-11130)***
BMC, Bassett *Also called Bassett Mirror Company Inc* ***(G-1580)***
BMC Software Inc 713 918-8800
8401 Greensboro Dr # 100 Mc Lean (22102) ***(G-8402)***
BMC Software Inc 703 404-0230
2201 Coop Way Ste 200 Herndon (20171) ***(G-6627)***
Bmg Metals Inc 804 622-9452
6301 Gorman Rd Henrico (23231) ***(G-6483)***
BMW, Charlottesville *Also called Crown Motorcar Company LLC* ***(G-2612)***
Bmz Usa Inc 757 821-8494
1429 Miller Store Rd Virginia Beach (23455) ***(G-14290)***
Bna, Vienna *Also called Bureau of National Affairs Inc* ***(G-14019)***
BNC Welding 757 706-2361
125 Semple Farm Rd Hampton (23666) ***(G-6096)***
Bnd Software 202 997-1070
17190 Silver Charm Pl Leesburg (20176) ***(G-7235)***
Bnnt LLC 757 369-1939
300 Ed Wright Ln Ste A Newport News (23606) ***(G-9182)***
Board Room Software Inc 757 721-3900
1488 Sandbridge Rd Virginia Beach (23456) ***(G-14291)***
Boardeffect LLC 866 672-2666
1515 N Courthouse Rd # 210 Arlington (22201) ***(G-887)***
Boatworks & More LLC 540 581-5820
152 Crittendon Ave Ne Roanoke (24012) ***(G-12053)***
Boaz Publishing Inc 540 659-4554
2707 Jefferson Davis Hwy Stafford (22554) ***(G-13124)***
Bob Sansone DBA Peggs Co 951 360-9170
100 Haley Rd Ashland (23005) ***(G-1383)***
Bob's Printing, Alexandria *Also called Michael Beach* ***(G-531)***
Bobbin Coil Specialists Inc 815 385-6205
1185 Spring Creek Dr Forest (24551) ***(G-5055)***
Bobblehouse LLC 703 582-6797
20341 Bowfonds St Ashburn (20147) ***(G-1250)***
Bobby and Pjs Jerky Shack 540 856-2415
1849 Kelly Rd Mount Jackson (22842) ***(G-9066)***
Bobby Burns Nowlin 757 827-1588
502 Copeland Dr Hampton (23661) ***(G-6097)***
Bobby Collins Logging 804 519-0138
9601 Little Elam Rd Charles City (23030) ***(G-2570)***
Bobby S World Welding Inc 540 845-7659
4 Bertram Blvd Stafford (22556) ***(G-13125)***
Bobby Utt Custom Cabinets 276 728-9411
2437 Greenberry Rd Fancy Gap (24328) ***(G-4933)***
Bobbys Meat Processing 276 728-4547
1247 Ridge Rd Austinville (24312) ***(G-1528)***
Bobcat of Lynchburg, Lynchburg *Also called Pearson Equipment Company* ***(G-7784)***
Bobcat Service of T N C 757 482-2773
936 Mount Pleasant Rd Chesapeake (23322) ***(G-3009)***
Bobhron Inc 540 389-5699
2527 Avenel Ave Sw Roanoke (24015) ***(G-12054)***
Bobs Printing Service LLC 434 352-2680
Hwy 460 W Appomattox (24522) ***(G-807)***
Bobs Sports Equipment Sales 276 669-8066
11192 Goose Creek Rd Bristol (24202) ***(G-2008)***
Boc Gases 540 433-1029
940 S High St Harrisonburg (22801) ***(G-6297)***
Boc Group De 540 373-1782
5 Rodney Ln Fredericksburg (22405) ***(G-5404)***
Bodie Vineyards LLC 804 598-2240
1809 May Way Dr Powhatan (23139) ***(G-10534)***
Body Cosmic Skincare 757 701-8232
1301 Canal Dr Apt 11d Chesapeake (23323) ***(G-3010)***
Body Creations 276 620-9989
162 Acorn Ln Max Meadows (24360) ***(G-8366)***
Bodyzone L L C 770 922-0700
3734 E Stratford Rd Virginia Beach (23455) ***(G-14292)***
Boehringer Ingelheim Corp 703 759-0630
1780 Business Center Dr Reston (20190) ***(G-10810)***
Boehringer Ingelheim Corp 800 243-0127
44521 Hastings Dr Ashburn (20147) ***(G-1251)***
Boehringer Ingelheim Corp 804 862-8316
2820 Normandy Dr Petersburg (23805) ***(G-10310)***
Boeing Company 703 465-3500
929 Long Bridge Dr Arlington (22202) ***(G-888)***
Boeing Company 703 467-2534
460 Herndon Pkwy Ste 300 Herndon (20170) ***(G-6628)***
Boeing Company 571 814-4103
11720 Sunrise Valley Dr Reston (20191) ***(G-10811)***
Boeing Company 703 808-2718
3308 Weymouth Ct Woodbridge (22192) ***(G-15661)***
Boeing Company 757 461-5206
5700 Lake Wright Dr # 204 Norfolk (23502) ***(G-9469)***
Boeing Company 703 413-3407
1215 S Clark St Ste 100 Arlington (22202) ***(G-889)***
Boeing Company 703 961-8174
15059 Confrnce Ctr Dr # 500 Chantilly (20151) ***(G-2378)***
Boeing Company 703 808-2737
15059 Confrnce Ctr Dr # 500 Chantilly (20151) ***(G-2379)***
Boeing Company 703 923-4000
7700 Boston Blvd Springfield (22153) ***(G-12966)***
Bogati Bodgea 540 338-1144
35246 Harry Byrd Hwy Round Hill (20141) ***(G-12375)***
Boggs Water & Sewage Inc 757 787-4000
28367 Railroad Ave Melfa (23410) ***(G-8708)***
Bohling Steel Inc 434 385-5175
3410 Forest Brook Rd Lynchburg (24501) ***(G-7657)***
Boho Bae & Company LLC 757 344-9197
1585 Briarfield Rd # 142 Hampton (23666) ***(G-6098)***
Bolden's Welding Shop, Collinsville *Also called Boldens Welding & Trailor Sls* ***(G-3709)***
Boldens Welding & Trailor Sls 276 647-8357
37 Turner Rd Collinsville (24078) ***(G-3709)***
Bolivia Lumber Company LLC 540 862-5228
101 Matthews Ln Clifton Forge (24422) ***(G-3678)***
Bolling Steel Co Inc 540 380-4402
5933 Garman Rd Salem (24153) ***(G-12484)***
Bolt Sawmill 434 574-6732
2524 Deer Run Rd Farmville (23901) ***(G-4937)***
Bolvs LLC 508 310-8682
9218 Scotts Bluff Ln Chesterfield (23832) ***(G-3481)***
Bon Air Craftsman LLC 804 745-0130
1806 Buford Rd North Chesterfield (23235) ***(G-9833)***
Bon Vivant Company LLC 703 862-5038
107 S West St Alexandria (22314) ***(G-151)***
Bond Cote, Pulaski *Also called Heytex USA Inc* ***(G-10637)***
Bond International Sftwr Inc 804 601-4640
15871 City View Dr Midlothian (23113) ***(G-8781)***
Bondcote Holdings Inc 540 980-2640
509 Burgis Ave Pulaski (24301) ***(G-10631)***
Bonde Innovation LLC 434 951-0444
315 Old Ivy Way Ste 301 Charlottesville (22903) ***(G-2746)***
Bondurant Brothers Dist LLC 434 533-3083
9 E 3rd St Chase City (23924) ***(G-2910)***
Bonrick Molds 540 898-1512
10701 Stoner Dr Ste 3 Fredericksburg (22408) ***(G-5254)***
Bonumose Biochem LLC 276 206-7337
1725 Discovery Dr 220 Charlottesville (22911) ***(G-2598)***
Bonumose LLC 276 206-7337
1725 Discovery Dr Ste 220 Charlottesville (22911) ***(G-2599)***
Bonze Associates LLC 540 497-2964
7070 Honeysuckle Ct Warrenton (20187) ***(G-14983)***
Book Arts Press Inc 434 924-8851
2023 Ivy Rd Charlottesville (22903) ***(G-2747)***
Bookers Transport LLC 757 762-9233
2728 Whitestone Ave Chesapeake (23323) ***(G-3011)***
Bookmarks By Bulger 757 362-6841
1736 Jude Ct Virginia Beach (23464) ***(G-14293)***
Books International Inc 703 661-1500
22841 Quicksilver Dr Dulles (20166) ***(G-4193)***
Bookwrights Press 434 263-4818
1060 Old Ridge Rd Lovingston (22949) ***(G-7589)***
Booky Biz LLC 434 207-3715
37 Burns Plz Palmyra (22963) ***(G-10244)***
Boom Bass Cabinets Inc 301 343-4918
17698d Main St Dumfries (22026) ***(G-4237)***
Boom Media Services, North Chesterfield *Also called Symmetric Systems Inc* ***(G-9997)***
Boomerang Air Sports 804 360-0320
11512 Bridgetender Dr Henrico (23233) ***(G-6484)***
Boomin Bass Global LLC 757 776-8668
2324 Kilburton Priory Ct Virginia Beach (23456) ***(G-14294)***
Boone Welding, Rocky Mount *Also called K B Industries Inc* ***(G-12331)***
Booth Logging Company 540 334-1075
664 Cascade Ln Boones Mill (24065) ***(G-1893)***
Bop International Inc 571 550-6669
12128 Monument Dr # 236 Fairfax (22033) ***(G-4420)***
Boredacious Inc 703 327-5490
24660 James Monroe Hwy Aldie (20105) ***(G-102)***
Borfski Press 571 439-9093
1000 University Pl Newport News (23606) ***(G-9183)***
Borgwaldt Kc Incorporated 804 271-6471
2800 Charles City Rd Henrico (23231) ***(G-6485)***
Boroughbridge Metal & Wldg LLC 804 387-3510
903 Boroughbridge Rd Richmond (23225) ***(G-11506)***
Bosan LLC 757 340-0822
701 Lynnhaven Pkwy Virginia Beach (23452) ***(G-14295)***

ALPHABETIC

Bosco Industries 540 671-8053
234 Cloud St Front Royal (22630) *(G-5525)*

Boshkins Software Corporation 703 318-7785
2507 Branding Iron Ct Herndon (20171) *(G-6629)*

Boss Instruments Ltd Inc 540 832-5000
104 Sommerfield Dr Zion Crossroads (22942) *(G-16005)*

Boss Laide Express LLC 804 263-8759
4445 Corp Ln Ste 264 Virginia Beach (23462) *(G-14296)*

Bosserman Murry 540 255-7949
2613 Cold Springs Rd Greenville (24440) *(G-5997)*

Boston Spice & Tea Co Inc 540 547-3907
12207 Obannons Mill Rd Boston (22713) *(G-1902)*

Botanica 540 899-5590
811 Lafayette Blvd Fredericksburg (22401) *(G-5174)*

Botetourt Signs N Stuff 540 992-3839
8833 Cloverdale Rd Troutville (24175) *(G-13903)*

Bottlehood of Virginia Inc 804 454-0656
8301 Macandrew Ter Chesterfield (23838) *(G-3482)*

Bottling Group LLC 703 339-5640
8550 Terminal Rd Lorton (22079) *(G-7468)*

Bottling Group LLC 276 625-2300
200 Pepsi Way Wytheville (24382) *(G-15879)*

Bottling Group LLC 434 792-4512
1001 Riverside Dr Danville (24540) *(G-3962)*

Bottom of Bottle Candle Co LLC 540 692-9260
71 Mountain Rd Strasburg (22657) *(G-13574)*

Bottomline Software Inc 540 221-4444
600 Oak Ave Waynesboro (22980) *(G-15101)*

Boudreaux's Butt Paste, Lynchburg *Also called C B Fleet Company Inc (G-7671)*

Boundary Rock Frm & Vinyrd LLC 540 789-7098
414 Riggins Rd Nw Willis (24380) *(G-15355)*

Bourbon 757 371-4710
1105 Murray Dr Chesapeake (23322) *(G-3012)*

Boutique Paw Prints 434 964-0133
201 E Main St Charlottesville (22902) *(G-2748)*

Boutique Qulty Bks Pubg Co Inc 678 316-4150
960 Oaktree Blvd Christiansburg (24073) *(G-3574)*

Bow Hunting Lifestyle Apparel, Glen Allen *Also called String Stalker LLC (G-5802)*

Bow Industries of Virginia 703 361-7704
10349 Balls Ford Rd Manassas (20109) *(G-8041)*

Bow Wow Bunkies and Other Sign 757 650-0158
887 Bamberg Pl Virginia Beach (23453) *(G-14297)*

Bowdens Candle Creations 757 539-0306
905 Macarthur Dr Suffolk (23434) *(G-13681)*

Bowdens Firewood & Logging LLC 540 465-4362
1265 Coal Mine Rd Strasburg (22657) *(G-13575)*

Bower Report The, Williamsburg *Also called Bowser Report (G-15212)*

Bowers Machine & Tool Inc 540 380-2040
4658 Roger Rd Salem (24153) *(G-12485)*

Bowhead Integrated Support Ser 703 413-4226
6564 Loisdale Ct Ste 900 Springfield (22150) *(G-12967)*

Bowhead Systems Management LLC 703 413-4251
6564 Loisdale Ct Ste 900 Springfield (22150) *(G-12968)*

Bowld Flavors LLC 757 952-4741
1516 Denton Dr Hampton (23664) *(G-6099)*

Bowman Nakia 804 263-2181
1415 Renee Ln Highland Springs (23075) *(G-6851)*

Bowman Teressa 240 601-9982
8464 Georgian Ct Manassas (20110) *(G-7921)*

Bowman Distillery Inc A Smith 540 373-4555
1 Bowman Dr Ste 100 Fredericksburg (22408) *(G-5255)*

Bowman Woodworking Inc 540 483-1680
6829 Providence Church Rd Ferrum (24088) *(G-4973)*

Bowser Report 757 877-5979
404 Idlewood Ln Williamsburg (23185) *(G-15212)*

Bowwowmeow Baking Company LLC 757 636-7922
4308 Lookout Rd Virginia Beach (23455) *(G-14298)*

Box Print & Ship - C Bernel 757 410-7352
480 Kempsville Rd Ste 105 Chesapeake (23320) *(G-3013)*

Boxd Kitchen Merrifield Llc 703 909-9572
2750 Gallows Rd Vienna (22180) *(G-14018)*

Boxley Materials Company (HQ) **540 777-7600**
15418 W Lynchburg Slem Tp Blue Ridge (24064) *(G-1845)*

Boxley Materials Company 540 777-7600
15415 W Lynchburg Salem T Blue Ridge (24064) *(G-1846)*

Boxley Materials Company 540 777-7600
739 Warrick Barn Rd Arrington (22922) *(G-1228)*

Boxley Materials Company 540 777-7600
7612 Rich Patch Rd Lowmoor (24457) *(G-7598)*

Boxley Materials Company 540 777-7600
762 Lawyers Rd Lynchburg (24501) *(G-7658)*

Boxley Materials Company 540 777-7600
15418 W Lynchburg Blue Ridge (24064) *(G-1847)*

Boxley Materials Company 540 777-7600
201 Koehler Rd Martinsville (24112) *(G-8271)*

Boxley Materials Company 540 777-7600
1299 Stage Rd Concord (24538) *(G-3757)*

Boxley Materials Company 540 777-7600
1050 Church St Wytheville (24382) *(G-15880)*

Boxley Materials Company 540 777-7600
139 Healing Springs Rd Blue Ridge (24064) *(G-1848)*

Boxley Materials Company 540 777-7600
3830 Blue Ridge Dr Sw Roanoke (24018) *(G-11893)*

Boxley Materials Company 540 777-7600
3785 Carver Rd Martinsville (24112) *(G-8272)*

Boxley Materials Company 540 777-7600
3535 John Capron Rd Lynchburg (24501) *(G-7659)*

Boxley Materials Company 540 777-7600
739 Warrick Barn Rd Arrington (22922) *(G-1229)*

Boxwood Technology Inc 703 707-8686
1430 Spring Hill Rd Fl 6 Mc Lean (22102) *(G-8403)*

Boxwood Winery LLC 540 687-8778
2042 Burrland Rd Middleburg (20118) *(G-8716)*

Boyters Welding & Fabrication 434 636-5974
1695 Reed Rd La Crosse (23950) *(G-7140)*

BP Investments Ltd 580 795-3364
43531 Firestone Pl Leesburg (20176) *(G-7236)*

Bracelets By G Jaffe Inc 434 409-3500
3015 Colonial Dr Charlottesville (22911) *(G-2600)*

Brachyfoam LLC 434 249-9554
722 Preston Ave Ste 108 Charlottesville (22903) *(G-2749)*

Bract Rtining Walls Excvtg LLC 804 798-5097
10423 Dow Gil Rd Ashland (23005) *(G-1384)*

Brad & Moo Merchants LLC 434 738-1130
2703 Robaleed Way Herndon (20171) *(G-6630)*

Brad Warstler 540 745-3595
297 Sumner Ln Ne Floyd (24091) *(G-5017)*

Braddock Communications 703 390-5870
4211 Ridge Top Rd # 3413 Fairfax (22030) *(G-4599)*

Bradley Adkins 304 910-6553
205 Walnut St Ste D North Tazewell (24630) *(G-10095)*

Bradley Energy LLC 434 286-7600
7548 Totier Creek Farm Rd Scottsville (24590) *(G-12658)*

Bradley-Morris LLC 678 419-4171
1545 Crossways Blvd # 200 Chesapeake (23320) *(G-3014)*

Brads Wldg & Align Boring LLC 276 340-1605
74 Holt Valley Ln Trlr 4 Patrick Springs (24133) *(G-10269)*

Bradshaw Viola 571 274-5244
5501 Seminary Rd Apt 807s Falls Church (22041) *(G-4765)*

Brady Contracting Service 703 864-9207
10920 Peninsula Ct Manassas (20111) *(G-8042)*

Brady Jones Logging 434 969-4688
Rr 1 Buckingham (23921) *(G-2131)*

Braiding Station Inc 804 898-2255
1386 Washington Blvd Newport News (23604) *(G-9184)*

Brain Based Learning Inc 804 320-0158
725 Twinridge Ln North Chesterfield (23235) *(G-9834)*

Brainstorm Software, Winchester *Also called Witt Associates Inc (G-15517)*

Brake Connections 540 247-9000
135 Fletcher Rd Gore (22637) *(G-5920)*

Branch Botanicals Inc 703 429-4217
14800 Conference Ctr Chantilly (20151) *(G-2380)*

Branch House Signature Pdts 804 644-3041
2501 Monument Ave Richmond (23220) *(G-11507)*

Branches Publications LLC 434 525-0432
1985 Colby Dr Forest (24551) *(G-5056)*

Branches Tasting Room 757 620-5393
2125 Starmount Pkwy # 105 Chesapeake (23321) *(G-3015)*

Brandervisions 804 744-1705
13507 E Boundary Rd Ste A Midlothian (23112) *(G-8782)*

Brandimage LLC 703 855-5401
1156 Cypress Tree Pl Herndon (20170) *(G-6631)*

Brandito LLC 804 747-6721
2601 Mury St Whse 28 Spac 28 Whse Richmond (23224) *(G-11508)*

Brandon Enterprises 804 895-3338
16305 Lanier Rd South Prince George (23805) *(G-12865)*

Brandon Jenkins 434 294-0917
512 E Georgia Ave Crewe (23930) *(G-3809)*

Brandy Ltd 757 220-0302
302 Harrison Ave Williamsburg (23185) *(G-15213)*

Brandy Printing & EMB Inc 540 825-5583
19638 Church Rd Brandy Station (22714) *(G-1937)*

Brandylane Publishers Inc 804 644-3090
5 S 1st St Richmond (23219) *(G-11509)*

Branmar Logging Inc 540 832-5535
8164 S Spotswood Trl Gordonsville (22942) *(G-5902)*

Branner Printing Service Inc 540 896-8947
13963 Timber Way Broadway (22815) *(G-2085)*

Brant Industries Inc 804 227-3394
10026 Old Ridge Rd Ashland (23005) *(G-1385)*

Brantley T Jolly Jr 703 447-6897
1539 Brookhaven Dr Mc Lean (22101) *(G-8404)*

Brantner and Associates Inc 540 825-2111
751 Old Brandy Rd Culpeper (22701) *(G-3875)*

Brass Age Restorations 540 743-4674
1631 Stonyman Rd Luray (22835) *(G-7603)*

Brass Beds of Virginia Inc 804 353-3503
3210 W Marshall St Ste B Richmond (23230) *(G-11131)*

Brass Bullet Coffee Co VA LLC 540 373-2432
500 Interstate Bus Park Fredericksburg (22405) *(G-5405)*

Brass Copper Metal Refinishing 434 636-5531
803 Holly Grove Ln Bracey (23919) *(G-1922)*

Braun & Assoc Inc 804 739-8616
5904 Eastbluff Ct Midlothian (23112) *(G-8783)*

Bravatek Solutions Inc (PA) **866 490-8590**
42757 Cedar Ridge Blvd Chantilly (20152) *(G-2527)*

Brave Bracelet, Stafford *Also called Sandra Magura* *(G-13187)*

Brazilian Best Granite Inc (PA) **804 562-3022**
6512 W Broad St Richmond (23230) *(G-11132)*

Brbg LLC 404 200-4857
6708 Grey Fox Dr Springfield (22152) *(G-12969)*

Breakaway Holdings LLC (HQ) **703 953-3866**
14100 Parke Long Ct Ste G Chantilly (20151) *(G-2381)*

Breakfast Lady LLC 302 241-7400
833 41st St Newport News (23607) *(G-9185)*

Breathe Bristol 423 254-0323
39 Piedmont Ave Bristol (24201) *(G-1967)*

Breathe-3dp LLC 276 645-6556
14401 Industrial Park Rd Bristol (24202) *(G-2009)*

Breaux Vineyards Ltd 540 668-6299
36888 Breaux Vineyards Ln Hillsboro (20132) *(G-6860)*

Brecmo LLC 276 202-7381
12262 U S Highway 19 Lebanon (24266) *(G-7189)*

Breek Media, Fairfax *Also called Arabesque Media* *(G-4410)*

Breeze Auto, Culpeper *Also called K/R Companies LLC* *(G-3903)*

Breeze Ridge Enterprises 703 728-4606
939 Frog Hollow Rd Winchester (22603) *(G-15391)*

Breeze-Eastern LLC 973 602-1001
1671 Jefferson Davis Hwy # 107 Fredericksburg (22401) *(G-5175)*

Brent Manor Inn & Vineyards 540 226-5958
100 Brent Manor Ln Faber (22938) *(G-4388)*

Bret Hamilton Enterprises 804 598-8246
2025 New Dorset Rd Powhatan (23139) *(G-10535)*

Brewco Corp (PA) **540 389-2554**
335 Roanoke Blvd Salem (24153) *(G-12486)*

Brewco LLC 276 686-5448
860 Gap Of Ridge Rd Rural Retreat (24368) *(G-12418)*

Brewco Sign, Salem *Also called Brewco Corp* *(G-12486)*

Brian Allison 276 988-9792
5418 Thompson Valley Rd Tazewell (24651) *(G-13828)*

Brian Enterprises LLC 757 645-4475
4808 Courthouse St # 204 Williamsburg (23188) *(G-15214)*

Brian Fox DBA Fortified 540 535-1195
204 Woodrow Rd Winchester (22602) *(G-15392)*

Brian K Babcock 540 251-3003
3203 Pilot Rd Riner (24149) *(G-11861)*

Brian L Longest 703 759-3847
10006 Minburn St Great Falls (22066) *(G-5940)*

Brian R Hess 757 240-0689
123 King William Dr Williamsburg (23188) *(G-15215)*

Briarwood Publications 540 489-4692
150 W College St Rocky Mount (24151) *(G-12314)*

Brickhouse Industries LLC 757 880-7249
8465 Little England Rd Hayes (23072) *(G-6397)*

Brico Inc 540 763-3731
1658 Sawmill Hill Rd Nw Willis (24380) *(G-15356)*

Bridge To Biz 703 942-6441
7406 Alban Station Ct B20 Springfield (22150) *(G-12970)*

Bridgetown LLC 804 741-0648
9020 Michaux Ln Richmond (23229) *(G-11133)*

Bridgeview Full Svc 434 575-6800
1000 Wilborn Ave South Boston (24592) *(G-12753)*

Bridgewater Drapery Shop 540 828-3312
203 N Main St Bridgewater (22812) *(G-1950)*

Bridgeway Professionals Inc 561 791-1005
9979 Broadsword Dr Bristow (20136) *(G-2048)*

Briede Family Vineyards LLC 540 667-2981
450 Green Spring Rd Winchester (22603) *(G-15393)*

Briggs & Riley Travelware LLC 703 352-0713
11703 Lee Jackson Mem Hwy Fairfax (22033) *(G-4421)*

Briggs Company 804 233-0966
5501 Fairpines Ct Chesterfield (23832) *(G-3483)*

Bright Elm LLC 804 519-3331
2975 Stone Creek Dr Sandy Hook (23153) *(G-12644)*

Bright Meadows Farm 434 349-9463
1181 Nathalie Rd Nathalie (24577) *(G-9102)*

Bright Solutions Inc 703 926-7451
44260 Marchand Ln Ashburn (20147) *(G-1252)*

Bright Yeast Labs LLC 205 790-2544
23600 Overland Dr Ste 150 Dulles (20166) *(G-4194)*

Brights Antique Slot Machine 703 906-8389
3406 Burgundy Rd Alexandria (22303) *(G-426)*

Brightview Press LLC 703 743-1430
13459 Brightview Way Gainesville (20155) *(G-5573)*

Brightway Inc 540 468-2510
80 Potomac River Rd Monterey (24465) *(G-9004)*

Brightwork Boat Co 804 795-9080
7601 Fourdale Ln Richmond (23231) *(G-11134)*

Brinkleys Custom Cabinets 540 525-1780
1462 Bobletts Gap Rd Buchanan (24066) *(G-2117)*

Brinkmann Publishing LLC 703 461-6991
5233 Bessley Pl Alexandria (22304) *(G-152)*

Brison Industries Inc 434 665-2231
512 Ivanhoe Trl Lynchburg (24504) *(G-7660)*

Bristol Coal Corporation 276 935-7562
1021 Walnut St Grundy (24614) *(G-6028)*

Bristol Herald Courier, Bristol *Also called Wood Television LLC* *(G-2002)*

Bristol Orthotic & Prosthetic 276 963-1186
445 Prtrfeld Hwy Sw Ste C Abingdon (24210) *(G-16)*

Bristol Sign Co Walden LLC 276 669-0811
6870 Gate City Hwy Bristol (24202) *(G-2010)*

Bristol Woodworker 423 557-4158
24396 Briscoe Dr Bristol (24202) *(G-2011)*

Brite Lite Inc 540 972-0212
205 Monticello Cir Locust Grove (22508) *(G-7441)*

Britemoves LLC 703 629-6391
1900 Campus Commons Dr Reston (20191) *(G-10812)*

Britto Orthodontics, Chantilly *Also called Denis Britto Dr* *(G-2405)*

Brix 22 Ankida Rdge Tasting Rm 434 989-7420
209 2nd St Sw Charlottesville (22902) *(G-2750)*

Brix and Columns Vineyards LLC 540 810-0566
1501 Dave Berry Rd Mc Gaheysville (22840) *(G-8377)*

Brizendine Welding & Repr Inc 804 443-1903
1790 Howerton Rd Dunnsville (22454) *(G-4267)*

Broad Bay Cotton Company 757 227-4101
2601 Reliance Dr Ste 101 Virginia Beach (23452) *(G-14299)*

Broad Street Signs Inc 804 262-1007
3000 Impala Pl Richmond (23228) *(G-11135)*

Broad Street Traffic Jams 804 461-1245
11317 Annie Laura Ln Rockville (23146) *(G-12284)*

Broadstone Security LLC 703 566-2814
2300 N Pershing Dr Ste 2b Arlington (22201) *(G-890)*

Broadway Metal Works Inc 540 896-7027
621 S Main St Broadway (22815) *(G-2086)*

Brocade Cmmnctions Systems LLC 540 439-9010
14052 Silver Hill Rd Sumerduck (22742) *(G-13789)*

Brock Enterprises Virginia LLC 276 971-4549
1400 Iron St Richlands (24641) *(G-11014)*

Brocks Welding Service 540 967-3258
321 Lakeside Dr Louisa (23093) *(G-7546)*

Brodies Naturals LLC 804 507-0542
8037 Stonemeade Dr Richmond (23231) *(G-11136)*

Brodnax Lumber Company 434 729-2852
2661 Gvrnor Harrison Pkwy Brodnax (23920) *(G-2099)*

Broken Column Press LLC 703 338-0267
244 S Reynolds St Apt 409 Alexandria (22304) *(G-153)*

Broken Needle Embroidery 276 865-4654
252 Pressley Br Haysi (24256) *(G-6457)*

Broken Window Brewing Co LLC 703 999-7030
12 W Boscawen St 14 Winchester (22601) *(G-15532)*

Broken Wing Enterprises Inc 804 378-0136
3632 Derby Ridge Way Midlothian (23113) *(G-8784)*

Brontz Inc 540 483-0976
3000 Chestnut Hill Rd Rocky Mount (24151) *(G-12315)*

Brook Brinders Limited 434 845-1231
311 Rivermont Ave Ste A Lynchburg (24504) *(G-7661)*

Brook Hidden Winery LLC 703 737-3935
43301 Spinks Ferry Rd Leesburg (20176) *(G-7237)*

Brook Summer Media 804 435-0074
1661 James Wharf Rd White Stone (22578) *(G-15186)*

Brook Vance Publishing LLC 703 660-1214
127 S Fairfax St Ste 326 Alexandria (22314) *(G-154)*

Brooke Printing 757 617-2188
4749 Eldon Ct Virginia Beach (23462) *(G-14300)*

Brooke Sterling Co 850 650-8080
9102 White Chimney Ln Great Falls (22066) *(G-5941)*

Brookneal Machine Shop Inc 434 376-2413
102 Todd St Brookneal (24528) *(G-2108)*

Brooks Gray Sign Company 804 233-4343
2661 Hull St Richmond (23224) *(G-11510)*

Brooks Sign Company 540 400-6144
2724 Nicholas Ave Ne Roanoke (24012) *(G-12055)*

Brooks Signs Screen Printing 434 728-3812
101 Ripley Pl Danville (24540) *(G-3963)*

Brooks Stitch & Fold LLC 804 367-7979
711 N Sheppard St Richmond (23221) *(G-11511)*

Brooks-Gray Sign Company, Richmond *Also called Brooks Gray Sign Company* *(G-11510)*

Broswell Water Systems 757 436-1871
824 Hidden Harbor Ct Chesapeake (23322) *(G-3016)*

Brothers Impressions, Virginia Beach *Also called Brothers Printing* *(G-14301)*

Brothers Printing, Virginia Beach *Also called Jo-Je Corporation* *(G-14571)*

Brothers Printing 757 431-2656
3320 Virginia Beach Blvd # 4 Virginia Beach (23452) *(G-14301)*

Brown Russel 540 547-3000
20381 Dove Hill Rd Culpeper (22701) *(G-3876)*

Brown & Duncan LLC 832 844-6523
5960 Jake Sears Cir Virginia Beach (23464) *(G-14302)*

Brown Brothers Inc 757 357-4086
101 Moore Ave Smithfield (23430) *(G-12706)*

A
L
P
H
A
B
E
T
I
C

Brown Enterprise Pallets LLC 804 447-0485
2601 Maury St Richmond (23224) *(G-11512)*
Brown Machine Works Inc 434 821-5008
8459 Wards Rd Rustburg (24588) *(G-12435)*
Brown Printing Company Inc 703 934-6078
11350 Random Hills Rd # 800 Fairfax (22030) *(G-4600)*
Brown Street Plant, Petersburg *Also called Pre Con Inc (G-10336)*
Brown Welding Inc 804 240-3094
3206 Old Courthouse Rd North Chesterfield (23236) *(G-9835)*
Brown's Automotive, Smithfield *Also called Brown Brothers Inc (G-12706)*
Brown's Heating & Air, Prince George *Also called Terry Brown (G-10608)*
Brown-Foreman Coopeages 434 575-0770
1141 Philpott Rd South Boston (24592) *(G-12754)*
Brownell Metal Studio Inc 434 591-0379
102a Industrial Way Troy (22974) *(G-13920)*
Browns Forest Products Inc 434 735-8179
360 Craftons Gate Hwy Drakes Branch (23937) *(G-4130)*
Browns Sawmill Inc 434 542-5776
445 Sawmill Rd Charlotte C H (23923) *(G-2582)*
Browns Services 540 295-2047
10767 Brent Town Rd Catlett (20119) *(G-2265)*
Browns Sterling Motors Inc 571 390-6900
21900 Auto World Cir Sterling (20166) *(G-13361)*
Browns Welding & Trailer Repr 276 628-4461
24487 Regal Dr Abingdon (24211) *(G-17)*
Bruce Moore Printing Co 703 361-0369
9239 Bayberry Ave Manassas (20110) *(G-7922)*
Brunswick Ice and Coal Co Inc 434 848-2615
514 New St Lawrenceville (23868) *(G-7178)*
Brunswick Times Gazette, Lawrenceville *Also called Tide Water Pulication LLC (G-7186)*
Brush 10 ....540 582-3820
9200 Thurston Ln Partlow (22534) *(G-10264)*
Brush Fork Press LLC 202 841-3625
3804 Brandon Ave Sw Roanoke (24018) *(G-11894)*
Brush Holdings Inc (PA) **804 226-4433**
110 Tuckahoe Blvd Richmond (23226) *(G-11137)*
Brw, Ashland *Also called Bract Rtining Walls Excvtg LLC (G-1384)*
Bryan Smith 434 242-7698
143 Mistland Trl Ruckersville (22968) *(G-12400)*
Bryan Tool & Machining Inc 540 896-6758
2970 Mayland Rd Broadway (22815) *(G-2087)*
Bryan Vossekuil 540 854-9067
5501 Hickory Tree Ln Mineral (23117) *(G-8942)*
Bryans Tools LLC 540 667-5675
178 Thwaite Ln Winchester (22603) *(G-15394)*
Bryant Brothers Logging L L C 434 933-8303
2711 W James Anderson Hwy Gladstone (24553) *(G-5682)*
Bryant Embroidery LLC 757 498-3453
3018 Virginia Beach Blvd Virginia Beach (23452) *(G-14303)*
Bryant Energy Corp 757 887-2181
250 Picketts Line Newport News (23603) *(G-9186)*
Bryant Logging 540 337-0232
724 Howardsville Tpke Stuarts Draft (24477) *(G-13645)*
Bryants Small Batch, Roseland *Also called River City Cider LLC (G-12372)*
Bryce K Long 757 510-1748
3685 Muddy Creek Rd Virginia Beach (23456) *(G-14304)*
BSC Ventures Holdings Inc (PA) **540 265-6296**
7702 Plantation Rd Roanoke (24019) *(G-11895)*
BSC Ventures LLC (HQ) **540 362-3311**
7702 Plantation Rd Roanoke (24019) *(G-11896)*
BSC Vntres Acquisition Sub LLC 540 362-3311
7702 Plantation Rd Roanoke (24019) *(G-11897)*
BSC Vntres Acquisition Sub LLC 540 563-0888
7702 Plantation Rd Roanoke (24019) *(G-11898)*
BSI Express 804 443-7134
7058 Richmond Rd Warsaw (22572) *(G-15061)*
Btbycb Inc 703 992-9041
2301 Brilyn Pl Falls Church (22046) *(G-4903)*
Btmc Holdings Inc 616 794-0100
795 Roanoke St Christiansburg (24073) *(G-3575)*
Bubba Enterprises Inc 703 524-0019
3300 Fairfax Dr Ste 302 Arlington (22201) *(G-891)*
Bubbles Wrecker Service 434 845-2411
903 Buchanan St Lynchburg (24501) *(G-7662)*
Buc-DOE Tector Outdoors LLC 276 971-1383
126 Sunshine Ln Pounding Mill (24637) *(G-10516)*
Buck Hall Logging 434 696-1244
864 Blankenship Pond Rd Green Bay (23942) *(G-5988)*
Buckeyes Meadow LLC 703 535-6868
424 N West St Alexandria (22314) *(G-155)*
Buckingham Beacon 434 591-1000
2987 Lake Monticello Rd Palmyra (22963) *(G-10245)*
Buckingham Slate Company LLC 434 581-1131
715 Arvon Rd Arvonia (23004) *(G-1232)*
Buckit O Rice 703 897-4190
15265 Lord Culpeper Ct Woodbridge (22191) *(G-15662)*
Buckskin Jhnson Beef Jerky LLC 540 303-0324
210 Burnt Church Rd Winchester (22603) *(G-15395)*
Buddy D Ltd 757 481-7619
2940 Buccaneer Rd Virginia Beach (23451) *(G-14305)*
Budget Printing Services Ng, Henrico *Also called Paul Owens (G-6547)*
Buds Blueridge 540 323-7030
116 Settlers Cir Winchester (22602) *(G-15396)*
Buerlein & Co LLC 804 355-1758
6767 Frest Hl Ave Ste 315 Richmond (23225) *(G-11513)*
Buf Creamery LLC 434 466-7110
931 Dover Farm Rd Manakin Sabot (23103) *(G-7896)*
Buffalo Air Handling Company 434 946-7455
467 Zane Snead Dr Amherst (24521) *(G-685)*
Buffalo Mountain Kombucha LLC 540 593-2146
231 Lght Of Fredom Way Sw Willis (24380) *(G-15357)*
Buffalo Repair Shop 434 374-5915
1406 Cow Rd Buffalo Junction (24529) *(G-2158)*
Buffalo Ridge Wood Products 276 930-2189
4868 Woolwine Hwy Stuart (24171) *(G-13606)*
Buffalo Wood Products Div, Dillwyn *Also called Kyanite Mining Corporation (G-4097)*
Buggs Island Dock Service 434 374-8028
413 Virginia Ave Clarksville (23927) *(G-3627)*
Build Software LLC 703 629-2549
11501 Henderson Rd Clifton (20124) *(G-3659)*
Builders Cabinet Co Inc 804 358-7789
959 Myers St Ste C Richmond (23230) *(G-11138)*
Builders Firstsource Inc 434 964-1192
4257 Seminole Trl Charlottesville (22911) *(G-2601)*
Builders Firstsource Inc 540 665-0078
296 Arbor Ct Winchester (22602) *(G-15397)*
Built In Style LLC 703 753-8518
6021 Empire Lakes Ct Haymarket (20169) *(G-6416)*
Bull Ridge Corporation 540 953-1171
2628 Mount Tabor Rd Blacksburg (24060) *(G-1727)*
Bull Run Metal Inc 540 347-2135
5591 Old Auburn Rd Warrenton (20187) *(G-14984)*
Bull Run Printing 540 937-3447
11278 Homeland Rd Rixeyville (22737) *(G-11877)*
Bulldog Precious Metals 540 312-1234
105 Knoll Ct Vinton (24179) *(G-14167)*
Bullet Enterprises Inc 757 897-9100
4985 Richmond Rd Keswick (22947) *(G-7044)*
Bullet Equipment Sales Inc 276 623-5150
15696 Porterfield Hwy Abingdon (24210) *(G-18)*
Bulletin News Network Inc 703 749-0040
11190 Sunrise Valley Dr # 20 Reston (20191) *(G-10813)*
Bulletinnews, Reston *Also called Bulletin News Network Inc (G-10813)*
Bum Pass Water Ski Club Inc 240 498-7033
3654 Buckner Rd Bumpass (23024) *(G-2160)*
Bumble Bee Productions Inc 757 410-9409
1049 Shoal Creek Trl Chesapeake (23320) *(G-3017)*
Bunnies Hot Tips LLC 757 259-9453
4779 Regents Park Williamsburg (23188) *(G-15216)*
Bunzl Carolinas and Virginia 804 236-5000
2400 Distribution Dr Henrico (23231) *(G-6486)*
Buoya LLC 703 248-9100
1825 N Bryan St Arlington (22201) *(G-892)*
Burcham Prints Inc 804 559-7724
8340 Sherton Ct Mechanicsville (23116) *(G-8608)*
Burden Bearer Tees LLC 757 337-7324
8424 Sheldon Branch Pl Toano (23168) *(G-13858)*
Bureau of National Affairs Inc (HQ) **703 341-3000**
1801 S Bell St Ste Cn110 Arlington (22202) *(G-893)*
Bureau of National Affairs Inc 703 847-4741
1912 Woodford Rd Ste 100 Vienna (22182) *(G-14019)*
Burgers Cabinet Shop Inc 571 262-8001
45910 Old Ox Rd Sterling (20166) *(G-13362)*
Burgess Snyder Industries Inc 757 490-3131
560 Baker Rd Virginia Beach (23462) *(G-14306)*
Burgess Snyder Window Co, Virginia Beach *Also called Burgess Snyder Industries Inc (G-14306)*
Burgess Welding & Fabrication 276 229-6458
100 Timber Creek Rd Stuart (24171) *(G-13607)*
Burgholzer Manufacturing Lc 540 667-8612
154 Laurelwood Dr Winchester (22602) *(G-15398)*
Burial Butler Services LLC 757 934-8227
1452 Manning Rd Suffolk (23434) *(G-13682)*
Burke Print Shop 276 628-3033
370 Trigg St Abingdon (24210) *(G-19)*
Burke Publications 804 321-1756
2822 Griffin Ave Richmond (23222) *(G-11514)*
Burkholder Enterprises Inc 540 867-5030
3579 Mount Clinton Pike Rockingham (22802) *(G-12242)*
Burkholder Entp Wldg & Repr S, Rockingham *Also called Burkholder Enterprises Inc (G-12242)*
Burks Fork Log Homes 276 766-0350
5058 Sylvatus Hwy Hillsville (24343) *(G-6887)*
Burley Holt Langford III LLC 804 712-7172
5754 Fox Maple Ter South Chesterfield (23803) *(G-12832)*
Burlington Industries Inc 540 258-2811
404 Anderson St Glasgow (24555) *(G-5699)*
Burnette Cabinet Shop Inc 540 586-0147
5106 Falling Creek Rd Bedford (24523) *(G-1629)*

704
2021 Virginia
Industrial Directory
(G-0000) Company's Geographic Section entry number

Burnettes Custom Wood Inc 540 577-9687
2481 Eastland Rd Roanoke (24014) *(G-12056)*
Burning Brite Candle 540 904-6544
502 Pleasure Point Dr Goodview (24095) *(G-5894)*
Burnopp Metal LLC 434 525-4746
189 Buffalo Ln Evington (24550) *(G-4375)*
Burns Machine Inc 815 434-3131
16475 Ridge Rd Ninde (22526) *(G-9387)*
Burnsboks Pubg - Pstshirts LLC 404 354-6082
7409 W Kenmore Dr Apt 4 Norfolk (23505) *(G-9470)*
Burr Fox Specialized Wdwkg 276 666-0127
373 Old Liberty Dr Martinsville (24112) *(G-8273)*
Burroughs Qiana 804 218-4031
8842 Proctors Run Dr Richmond (23237) *(G-11030)*
Burruss Signs Inc 434 296-6654
704 Altavista Ave Charlottesville (22902) *(G-2751)*
Bursey Machine & Welding 540 862-5033
1225 Grace Ave Clifton Forge (24422) *(G-3679)*
Burton Telecom LLC 757 230-6520
1637 Independence Blvd Virginia Beach (23455) *(G-14307)*
Burwell Group LLC 703 732-6341
1404 N Sycamore St Arlington (22205) *(G-894)*
Busada Manufacturing Corp 540 967-2882
78 Rescue Ln Louisa (23093) *(G-7547)*
Bush River Corporation 804 730-4000
8100 Amf Dr Richmond (23227) *(G-11139)*
Business 804 559-8770
7481 Tangle Ridge Dr Mechanicsville (23111) *(G-8609)*
Business Center, Richmond *Also called Business Press* *(G-11140)*
Business Checks of America 703 823-1008
3221 Colvin St Alexandria (22314) *(G-156)*
Business Press 804 282-3150
2112 Spencer Rd Richmond (23230) *(G-11140)*
Buskey Cider 901 626-0535
2910 W Leigh St Richmond (23230) *(G-11141)*
Busy BS Embroidery 757 819-7869
712 Colony Dr Chesapeake (23322) *(G-3018)*
Butler Custom Logging LLC 434 634-5658
775 Mitchell Rd Emporia (23847) *(G-4355)*
Butler Parachute Systems Inc 540 342-2501
1820 Loudon Ave Nw Roanoke (24017) *(G-12057)*
Butler Unmanned Parachute 540 342-2501
1820 Loudon Ave Nw Roanoke (24017) *(G-12058)*
Butler Virginia C R Orange Co, Charlottesville *Also called Allied Concrete Company* *(G-2724)*
Butler Woodcrafters Inc 203 241-9753
569 Southlake Blvd Ste B North Chesterfield (23236) *(G-9836)*
Butler Woodcrafters Inc (HQ) **877 852-0784**
413 Branchway Rd Ste A North Chesterfield (23236) *(G-9837)*
Butter of Life LLC 703 507-5298
6166 Leesburg Pike B215 Falls Church (22044) *(G-4766)*
Buttercream Dreams LLC 540 234-0058
87 Bluestone Dr Weyers Cave (24486) *(G-15168)*
Buy Chimes 703 293-6395
3827 Jancie Rd Fairfax (22030) *(G-4601)*
Buyers Guide Newspapers, Springfield *Also called Mid-Atlantic Publishing Co* *(G-13050)*
Bvm Print VA LLC 434 845-1153
1709 Memorial Ave Lynchburg (24501) *(G-7663)*
Bvs, Midlothian *Also called Brandervisions* *(G-8782)*
Bw Container Systems, Lynchburg *Also called Barry-Whmller Cont Systems Inc* *(G-7649)*
Bw Design Build LLC 757 504-5052
410 Ferguson Bnd Yorktown (23693) *(G-15940)*
Bwx Technologies Inc 434 385-2535
109 Ramsey Pl Lynchburg (24501) *(G-7664)*
Bwx Technologies Inc 434 316-7638
110 Ramsey Pl Lynchburg (24501) *(G-7665)*
Bwx Technologies Inc 434 522-6000
800 Main St Lynchburg (24504) *(G-7666)*
Bwx Technologies Inc 757 595-7982
11864 Canon Blvd Ste 105 Newport News (23606) *(G-9187)*
Bwx Technologies Inc (PA) **980 365-4300**
800 Main St Ste 4 Lynchburg (24504) *(G-7667)*
Bwxt, Lynchburg *Also called Bwx Technologies Inc* *(G-7667)*
Bwxt Government Group Inc (HQ) **434 522-6000**
2016 Mount Athos Rd Lynchburg (24504) *(G-7668)*
Bwxt Nclear Oprtions Group Inc (HQ) **434 522-6000**
2016 Mount Athos Rd Lynchburg (24504) *(G-7669)*
Bwxt Y - 12 LLC (HQ) **434 316-7633**
109 Ramsey Pl Lynchburg (24501) *(G-7670)*
Bxi Inc 804 282-5434
2111 Lake Ave Richmond (23230) *(G-11142)*
Bybee Stone Co Inc 812 876-2215
210 England Pointe Dr Fredericksburg (22406) *(G-5406)*
Byd Music Publishing LLC 305 423-9577
1504 Bowen St Richmond (23224) *(G-11515)*
Byer Bros Excvtg Alleghany Co, Covington *Also called Byer Brothers Logging Inc* *(G-3779)*
Byer Brothers Logging Inc 540 962-3071
620 E Morris Hill Rd Covington (24426) *(G-3779)*
Byerly Tshawna 703 359-5598
4116 Lamarre Dr Fairfax (22030) *(G-4602)*
Byers Inc 540 949-8092
51 E Side Hwy Waynesboro (22980) *(G-15102)*
Bynum 757 224-1860
13 Neff Dr Hampton (23669) *(G-6100)*
Byrd Assistive Tech Inc 571 512-6069
13893 Willard Rd Ste A Chantilly (20151) *(G-2382)*
Byrd Cellars LLC 804 652-5663
2442 Davis Mill Rd Goochland (23063) *(G-5880)*
Byrds Custom Wdwrk & Stain GL 757 242-6786
5124 Exeter Dr Suffolk (23434) *(G-13683)*
Bzk Ballston LLC 703 248-0990
933 N Quincy St Arlington (22203) *(G-895)*
C & A and Sons Paving LLC 434 209-7357
105 Dinlake Ct Forest (24551) *(G-5057)*
C & A Cutter Head Inc 276 646-5548
212 Kendall Ave Chilhowie (24319) *(G-3546)*
C & B Corp 434 977-1992
750 Harris St Ste 208 Charlottesville (22903) *(G-2752)*
C & B Enterprise LLC 276 971-4052
2677 Steelsburg Hwy Ste 1 Cedar Bluff (24609) *(G-2271)*
C & B Lumber Inc 276 744-3650
3594 Turkey Knob Rd Fries (24330) *(G-5515)*
C & B Piping (e) Inc 434 946-7170
390 Lexington Tpke Amherst (24521) *(G-686)*
C & B Technology LLC 757 545-3112
804 Industrial Ave Ste H Chesapeake (23324) *(G-3019)*
C & C Piping & Fabrication LLC 434 369-9353
853 Lynch Mill Rd Altavista (24517) *(G-628)*
C & C Publishing Inc 804 598-4035
725 Petersburg Rd Powhatan (23139) *(G-10536)*
C & C Publishing Inc (PA) **804 598-4305**
8460 Times Dispatch Blvd Mechanicsville (23116) *(G-8610)*
C & F Plumbing 757 606-3124
5816 Brookmere Ln Portsmouth (23703) *(G-10402)*
C & G Flooring LLC 804 318-0927
5141 Craig Rath Blvd Midlothian (23112) *(G-8785)*
C & G Woodworking 703 878-7196
4517 Hazelton Dr Woodbridge (22193) *(G-15663)*
C & J Led Lighting & Signage, Woolwine *Also called Zenta Corporation* *(G-15870)*
C & L Containers Inc 757 398-0447
911 Live Oak Dr Ste 108 Chesapeake (23320) *(G-3020)*
C & M Auto Machine Shop Inc 703 780-0566
8804 Badger Dr Alexandria (22309) *(G-427)*
C & M Heating & AC LLC 276 618-0955
5087 Irisburg Rd Axton (24054) *(G-1533)*
C & M Lures LLC 703 369-3060
9428 Wilcoxen Dr Manassas Park (20111) *(G-8192)*
C & M Services LLC (PA) **540 309-5555**
354 Nace Rd Troutville (24175) *(G-13904)*
C & P Inc 703 522-2229
3332 Lee Hwy Arlington (22207) *(G-896)*
C & R Printing Inc 703 802-0800
4447b Brkfld Crprt Dr Chantilly (20151) *(G-2383)*
C & S Printing Enterprises 703 385-4495
10408 Lee Hwy Fairfax (22030) *(G-4603)*
C A S Signs 804 271-7580
6424 Mill River Trce Chesterfield (23832) *(G-3484)*
C and F Promotions Inc 757 912-5161
83 W Mercury Blvd Hampton (23669) *(G-6101)*
C and J Fabrication Inc 757 399-3340
1023 Virginia Ave Portsmouth (23707) *(G-10403)*
C and M Auto Machine Shop Svc, Alexandria *Also called C & M Auto Machine Shop Inc* *(G-427)*
C and S Precision Wel 804 815-7963
4365 Dragon Dr Saluda (23149) *(G-12601)*
C B C Corporation 757 868-6571
657 Poquoson Ave Poquoson (23662) *(G-10365)*
C B Fleet Company Inc (HQ) **434 528-4000**
4615 Murray Pl Lynchburg (24502) *(G-7671)*
C B R Engine Service 276 686-5198
526 Knight Rd Rural Retreat (24368) *(G-12419)*
C C Wireless, Norfolk *Also called CC Wireless Corporation* *(G-9479)*
C Cs Linen Plus 703 665-0059
41568 Tring Ln Aldie (20105) *(G-103)*
C D Campbell Logging, Naturl BR STA *Also called Clarence D Campbell* *(G-9111)*
C Dcap Modem Line 804 561-6267
3800 Richmond Rd Mannboro (23105) *(G-8214)*
C E C Controls Company Inc 757 392-0415
315 Great Bridge Blvd C Chesapeake (23320) *(G-3021)*
C Graphic Distribution Ctr 414 762-4282
3455 Windsor Rd Sw Roanoke (24018) *(G-11899)*
C H Evelyn Piling Company Inc 804 966-2273
2200 Barnetts Rd Providence Forge (23140) *(G-10619)*
C H J Commercial Copies, Virginia Beach *Also called Commercial Copies* *(G-14357)*
C H J Digital Repro 757 473-0234
223 Expressway Ct Virginia Beach (23462) *(G-14308)*
C I T C Imaging 540 382-6557
405 N Franklin St Christiansburg (24073) *(G-3576)*

A L P H A B E T I C

C J Shelton Logging, Chatham *Also called Clarence Shelton Jr* ***(G-2923)***
C J Steel, Manassas *Also called C Y J Enterprises Corp* ***(G-8043)***
C L E Logging Inc......276 881-8617
380 Reynolds Ridge Rd Bandy (24602) ***(G-1557)***
C L Towing......703 625-7126
624 Notabene Dr Alexandria (22305) ***(G-157)***
C Line Graphics Inc......434 577-9289
4446 Christina Hwy Valentines (23887) ***(G-13974)***
C Line Graphics Printing Co, Valentines *Also called C Line Graphics Inc* ***(G-13974)***
C M C Steel Fabricators Inc......540 898-1111
9434 Crossroads Pkwy Fredericksburg (22408) ***(G-5256)***
C M D S, Harrisonburg *Also called Jenzabar Inc* ***(G-6333)***
C Media Company......540 339-9626
4423 Pheasant Ridge Rd # 203 Roanoke (24014) ***(G-12059)***
C P S, Chesapeake *Also called Concrete Precast Systems Inc* ***(G-3050)***
C R Bard Inc......703 754-2848
14241 Clubhouse Rd Gainesville (20155) ***(G-5574)***
C R D N of The Shenandoah......540 943-8242
534 W Main St Waynesboro (22980) ***(G-15103)***
C R I, Gloucester *Also called Custom Restorations Inc* ***(G-5843)***
C S Lewis & Sons LLC......804 275-6879
3940 Evelake Rd North Chesterfield (23237) ***(G-9838)***
C S P Printing & Graphics, Falls Church *Also called CSP Productions Inc* ***(G-4779)***
C Thompson Enterprises All......804 794-3407
1701 Winterfield Rd Midlothian (23113) ***(G-8786)***
C Y J Enterprises Corp......703 367-7722
7121 Gary Rd Manassas (20109) ***(G-8043)***
C&C Assembly Inc......540 904-6416
3410 W Main St Salem (24153) ***(G-12487)***
C&J Well Services Inc......276 679-5860
580 Hawthorne Dr Ne Norton (24273) ***(G-10114)***
C&K Custom Embroidery & A......434 447-2987
10826 Highway One South Hill (23970) ***(G-12845)***
C&M Industries Inc......757 626-1141
3425 Westminster Ave Norfolk (23504) ***(G-9471)***
C&R Publishing, Springfield *Also called Dream Dog Productions LLC* ***(G-12995)***
C&S Custom Cabinets Inc......540 273-5450
215 Cedar Creek Rd Louisa (23093) ***(G-7548)***
C-3 Comm Systems LLC......703 829-0588
3100 Clarendon Blvd # 200 Arlington (22201) ***(G-897)***
C-More Competition, Manassas *Also called Vertu Corp* ***(G-8174)***
C-More Competition, Warrenton *Also called Vertu Corp* ***(G-15058)***
C-More Systems Inc......540 347-4683
680d Industrial Rd Warrenton (20186) ***(G-14985)***
C-Sol, Oakton *Also called Cae Software Solutions LLC* ***(G-10142)***
C-Ville Holdings LLC......434 817-2749
308 E Main St Charlottesville (22902) ***(G-2753)***
C-Ville Weekly, Charlottesville *Also called Portico Publications Ltd* ***(G-2849)***
C-Ville Weekly, Charlottesville *Also called C-Ville Holdings LLC* ***(G-2753)***
C.L.m, Fredericksburg *Also called Clarks Lumber & Millwork Inc* ***(G-5412)***
C.S.i, Roanoke *Also called Concrete Specialties Inc* ***(G-12069)***
C2-Mask Inc......703 698-7820
2812 Merrilee Dr Ste E Fairfax (22031) ***(G-4422)***
C2-Mask Inc......703 304-9319
14100 Parke Long Ct Ste H Chantilly (20151) ***(G-2384)***
C2c Smart Compliance LLC......703 872-7340
110 N Royal St Ste 525 Alexandria (22314) ***(G-158)***
C4 Explosive Spt Training LLC......571 379-7955
10219 Nokesville Rd Manassas (20110) ***(G-7923)***
C4 Explosive Spt Training LLC......703 881-1481
7981 Sequoia Park Way Bristow (20136) ***(G-2049)***
CA, Herndon *Also called Netqos Inc* ***(G-6754)***
Ca Inc......800 225-5224
2291 Wood Oak Dr Ste 200 Herndon (20171) ***(G-6632)***
CA Jones Inc......757 595-0005
11832 Fishing Point Dr # 100 Newport News (23606) ***(G-9188)***
CA Technologies A Broadcom Co, Herndon *Also called Ca Inc* ***(G-6632)***
Caaj Appare, Roanoke *Also called Melissa Moss* ***(G-11961)***
Cab-Pool Inc......804 218-8294
11838 Chase Wellesley Dr # 416 Henrico (23233) ***(G-6487)***
Cabaide LLC......571 262-2710
19775 Belmont Executive P Ashburn (20147) ***(G-1253)***
Cabin Creations......804 529-7245
14921 Richmond Rd Callao (22435) ***(G-2215)***
Cabin Creek Musical Instrs......276 388-3202
290 Bakers Branch Rd Mouth of Wilson (24363) ***(G-9092)***
Cabin Hill TS LLC......540 459-8912
923 S Main St Woodstock (22664) ***(G-15850)***
Cabinet & More......571 719-5040
9207 Enterprise Ct Manassas Park (20111) ***(G-8193)***
Cabinet Arts LLC......571 313-1891
45945 Trefoil Ln Ste 136 Sterling (20166) ***(G-13363)***
Cabinet Arts LLC......703 870-1456
1510 Clarendon Blvd Arlington (22209) ***(G-898)***
Cabinet Co of Virginia Corp......757 357-5519
19351 Battery Park Rd Smithfield (23430) ***(G-12707)***
Cabinet Design Plus......540 773-4571
31 E Jubal Early Dr Winchester (22601) ***(G-15533)***
Cabinet Designs, Wytheville *Also called Wytheville Custom Counter Tops* ***(G-15928)***
Cabinet Discounters Inc......703 803-7990
14501 Lee Jackson Memoria Chantilly (20151) ***(G-2385)***
Cabinet Gallery, The, Hardy *Also called Richards Building Supply Co* ***(G-6289)***
Cabinet Kingdom LLC......804 514-9546
9025 Hidden Nest Dr Midlothian (23112) ***(G-8787)***
Cabinet Lifts Unlimited......757 641-9431
2500 Squadron Ct Ste 102 Virginia Beach (23453) ***(G-14309)***
Cabinet Makers......703 421-6331
22611 Markey Ct Ste 114-H Sterling (20166) ***(G-13364)***
Cabinet Masters......703 331-5781
9107 Industry Dr Manassas Park (20111) ***(G-8194)***
Cabinet Saver LLC......757 969-9839
3212 Inlet Shore Ct Virginia Beach (23451) ***(G-14310)***
Cabinet Works of N N......804 493-8102
17503 Kings Hwy Montross (22520) ***(G-9024)***
Cabinetry & Construction Inc......804 497-3491
18 S Thompson St Ste 162 Richmond (23221) ***(G-11516)***
Cabinetry With TLC LLC......540 777-0456
4325 Old Cave Spring Rd Roanoke (24018) ***(G-11900)***
Cabinets By Design......434 589-2600
31a Conestoga Way Troy (22974) ***(G-13921)***
Cabinets By Design Inc......757 558-9558
1220 Scholastic Way Ste B Chesapeake (23323) ***(G-3022)***
Cabinets Direct Inc......540 884-2329
907 Prices Bluff Rd Eagle Rock (24085) ***(G-4280)***
Cabinets Ready To Go LLC......703 665-5620
14801 Murdock St Ste 150 Chantilly (20151) ***(G-2386)***
Cabinets To Go LLC......814 688-7584
416 Campostella Rd Norfolk (23523) ***(G-9472)***
Cabinets To Go LLC......804 325-4775
2305 Westwood Ave Richmond (23230) ***(G-11143)***
Cable Systems......757 853-6313
3411 Progress Rd Norfolk (23502) ***(G-9473)***
Cabling Systems Inc......540 439-0101
4279 Mount Ephraim Rd Sumerduck (22742) ***(G-13790)***
Cabrera Family Masonry LLC......919 671-7623
201 Courtney Dr Hampton (23669) ***(G-6102)***
Caci Nss Inc......703 434-4000
11955 Fredom Dr Ste 12000 Reston (20190) ***(G-10814)***
Caci Products Company......973 437-9800
2100 Reston Pkwy Ste 500 Reston (20191) ***(G-10815)***
Cadbury Schweppes Bottlin......276 228-7990
840 Stafford Umberger Dr Wytheville (24382) ***(G-15881)***
Cadence Inc (PA)......**540 248-2200**
9 Technology Dr Staunton (24401) ***(G-13245)***
Cae Software Solutions LLC......734 417-6991
11313 Lapham Dr Oakton (22124) ***(G-10142)***
Caerus LLC......703 772-7688
204 Falcon Ridge Rd Great Falls (22066) ***(G-5942)***
Cafes D Afrique LLC......757 725-1050
81 Joynes Rd Hampton (23666) ***(G-6103)***
Cain Inc......434 842-3984
765 Bremo Bluff Rd Bremo Bluff (23022) ***(G-1945)***
Cajo Industries Inc......804 829-6854
21642 Old Neck Rd Charles City (23030) ***(G-2571)***
Cake Ballin LLC......540 820-2938
382 Trayfoot Rd Grottoes (24441) ***(G-6017)***
Cake Passion Custom Cakes LLC......757 982-0928
14093 Jordan Rd Machipongo (23405) ***(G-7845)***
Cakebatters LLC......276 685-6731
1110 Glenway Ave Bristol (24201) ***(G-1968)***
Cal Syd Inc......276 963-3640
2111 3rd St Richlands (24641) ***(G-11015)***
Caladan Consulting Inc......540 931-9581
321 N Pleasant Valley Rd Winchester (22601) ***(G-15534)***
Calavera Tool Works......434 964-6447
1229 Harris St Ste 11 Charlottesville (22903) ***(G-2754)***
Calbico LLC......571 332-3334
3845 Whitman Rd Annandale (22003) ***(G-733)***
Caldwell Industries Inc......703 403-3272
4406 Longworthe Sq Alexandria (22309) ***(G-428)***
Caldwell Mountain Copper......540 473-2167
2391 Lees Gap Rd Fincastle (24090) ***(G-4993)***
Caleigh Systems Inc......703 539-5004
7515 Little River Tpke Annandale (22003) ***(G-734)***
Calfee Printing......304 910-3475
92 Camp Eagle Rd Fincastle (24090) ***(G-4994)***
Calhouns Ham House......540 825-8319
211 S East St Culpeper (22701) ***(G-3877)***
California Sidecar, Arrington *Also called U S Sidecars Inc* ***(G-1231)***
Caligo LLC......914 819-8530
2765 Centerboro Dr # 250 Vienna (22181) ***(G-14020)***
Callaghan Machine Shop......540 962-4779
4256 Callaghan Cir Covington (24426) ***(G-3780)***
Callahan Paving Products Inc......434 589-9000
1850 Covington Rd Crozier (23039) ***(G-3857)***
Callico Press, Springfield *Also called Corrinne Callins* ***(G-12982)***

Callison Electric..540 294-3189
959 Stingy Hollow Rd Staunton (24401) *(G-13246)*

Calloway Enterprises Inc.................................434 525-1147
200 Britt Pl Forest (24551) *(G-5058)*

Calspan Systems Corporation (HQ)..............**757 873-1344**
703 City Center Blvd Newport News (23606) *(G-9189)*

Calverton Press, Calverton *Also called Louise J Walker (G-2225)*

Calvin G. Hall, Radford *Also called Radford Wldg & Fabrication LLC (G-10737)*

Calvin Montgomery..540 334-3058
2733 Alean Rd Wirtz (24184) *(G-15609)*

Calvin Payne...276 251-5815
4037 Ararat Hwy Ararat (24053) *(G-830)*

Calvins Enterprises...540 955-3948
213 Josephine St Berryville (22611) *(G-1672)*

Calypso Labs, Ashburn *Also called Future Tense LLC (G-1283)*

Camacho Enterprises LLC................................757 761-0407
1403 Greenbrier Pkwy # 220 Chesapeake (23320) *(G-3023)*

Camber Corporation..540 720-6294
30 Blackjack Rd Fredericksburg (22405) *(G-5407)*

Cambis LLC..202 746-6124
5575 Seminary Rd Apt 306 Falls Church (22041) *(G-4767)*

Cambrio Studios LLC..540 908-5129
227 Monte Vista Ave Charlottesville (22903) *(G-2755)*

Camco..757 855-5890
3424 Azalea Garden Rd Norfolk (23513) *(G-9474)*

Camelot..434 978-1049
4285 Seminole Trl Charlottesville (22911) *(G-2602)*

Camera Club of Richmond................................804 380-9218
16301 Midlothian Tpke Midlothian (23113) *(G-8788)*

Cameron Aubernon..540 251-4363
405 Turpin Walk Christiansburg (24073) *(G-3577)*

Cameron Chemicals Inc (PA)........................**757 487-0656**
4530 Prof Cir Ste 201 Virginia Beach (23455) *(G-14311)*

Cameron Micronutrients, Virginia Beach *Also called Cameron Chemicals Inc (G-14311)*

Cameron Mountain Alpacas..............................540 832-3025
18453 Cameron Rd Gordonsville (22942) *(G-5903)*

Campbell Copy Center Inc................................540 434-4171
4564 S Valley Pike A Rockingham (22801) *(G-12243)*

Campbell Custom Woodworking.........................757 724-2001
1040 Vanderploeg Dr Chesapeake (23320) *(G-3024)*

Campbell David..757 877-1633
1214 Dandy Loop Rd Yorktown (23692) *(G-15941)*

Campbell Graphics Inc.....................................804 353-7292
2904 W Clay St Richmond (23230) *(G-11144)*

Campbell Lumber Co Inc (PA).......................**434 293-3021**
4195 Plank Rd North Garden (22959) *(G-10074)*

Campbell Printing Bristol Inc............................276 466-2311
22220 Stevens Private Dr Bristol (24202) *(G-2012)*

Campofrio Fd Group - Amer Inc........................804 520-7775
1800 Ruffin Mill Rd South Chesterfield (23834) *(G-12798)*

Campostella Builders and Sup..........................757 545-3212
1109 Poppleton St Norfolk (23523) *(G-9475)*

Campus Axess, Vienna *Also called Infocess LLC (G-14070)*

Cana Cellars LLC...540 635-9398
14437 Hume Rd Huntly (22640) *(G-6964)*

Cana Vineyards Winery.....................................703 348-2458
38600 John Mosby Hwy Middleburg (20117) *(G-8717)*

Canaan Land Associates Inc.............................276 988-6543
Tazewell Industrial Park Tazewell (24651) *(G-13829)*

Canaan Printing Inc...804 271-4820
4820 Jefferson Davis Hwy North Chesterfield (23234) *(G-9839)*

Canaan Welding LLC..703 339-7799
7002 Newington Rd Ste A Lorton (22079) *(G-7469)*

Canada Bread, Martinsville *Also called Hanesbrands Inc (G-8293)*

Canada Dry Potomac Corporation......................757 464-1771
1400 Air Rail Ave Virginia Beach (23455) *(G-14312)*

Canada Dry Potomac Corporation......................804 231-7777
3100 N Hopkins Rd Ste 102 Richmond (23224) *(G-11517)*

Canada Dry Potomac Corporation......................703 321-6100
5330 Port Royal Rd Springfield (22151) *(G-12971)*

Canam Underwater Hockey Gear, Remington *Also called DK Consulting LLC (G-10768)*

Canam Uwh..906 399-7857
23231 Hubbards Rd Remington (22734) *(G-10767)*

Candidate Metrics Inc......................................703 539-2331
2104 Polo Pointe Dr Vienna (22181) *(G-14021)*

Candies & Chrome Coatings LLC.......................757 812-1490
908 Marble Arch Chesapeake (23322) *(G-3025)*

Candle Euphoria..757 327-8567
10 Westminister Dr Hampton (23666) *(G-6104)*

Candle Fetish..757 535-3105
1025 City Park Ave Portsmouth (23701) *(G-10404)*

Candle Maker, The, Williamsburg *Also called Mighty Oak Enterprises Inc (G-15277)*

Candle Utopia Incorporated..............................757 274-2406
2400 Myrtle Ave Norfolk (23504) *(G-9476)*

Candlelight Jewels...305 301-2536
12101 Elm Forest Way Fairfax (22030) *(G-4604)*

Candles For Effect LLC....................................707 591-3986
3233 Titanic Dr Stafford (22554) *(G-13126)*

Candles Make Scents LLC................................540 223-3972
36 Derby Ridge Rd Mineral (23117) *(G-8943)*

Candlestick Baker Inc......................................757 761-4473
1804 Saranac Ct Virginia Beach (23453) *(G-14313)*

Candy Apples and Favors LLC..........................804 674-4061
2907 Matisse Ln Richmond (23224) *(G-11518)*

Candylicious Crafts LLC...................................757 915-5542
442 Winterhaven Dr Newport News (23606) *(G-9190)*

Cane Connection...804 261-6555
6941 Lakeside Ave Richmond (23228) *(G-11145)*

Canline USA Corporation..................................540 380-8585
1030 Mcconville Rd Ste 1 Lynchburg (24502) *(G-7672)*

Cannaday's Signs & Designs, Rocky Mount *Also called Donna Cannaday (G-12318)*

Cannon Enterprises LLC...................................757 876-3463
459 Old Colonial Way # 104 Newport News (23608) *(G-9191)*

Canon Environmental Tech Inc..........................804 695-7000
6000 Industrial Dr Gloucester (23061) *(G-5839)*

Canon Publishing LLC......................................540 840-1240
1031 Aquia Dr Stafford (22554) *(G-13127)*

Canon Virginia Inc (HQ)................................**757 881-6000**
12000 Canon Blvd Newport News (23606) *(G-9192)*

Canova Woodworking LLC................................434 422-0807
758 Lightwood Rd Gordonsville (22942) *(G-5904)*

Cantel Medical Corp...800 633-3080
5569 Main St Mount Jackson (22842) *(G-9067)*

Cantrell/Cutter Printing Inc..............................301 773-6340
8221 Smithfield Ave Springfield (22152) *(G-12972)*

Canty Lane Confections LLC.............................703 408-3661
2606 Chester Cir Woodbridge (22191) *(G-15664)*

Canvas & Earth...757 995-6529
508 Aylesbury Dr Apt 103 Virginia Beach (23462) *(G-14314)*

Canvas Asl LLC...804 269-0851
13 S 15th St Ste A Richmond (23219) *(G-11519)*

Canvas Docktors LLC.......................................757 759-7108
2784 Pigeon Hill Rd Hayes (23072) *(G-6398)*

Canvas Earth LLC..540 522-9373
403 Lesco Blvd Apt B Culpeper (22701) *(G-3878)*

Canvas Innovations Inc....................................757 218-7271
8405 Beckenham Ct Williamsburg (23188) *(G-15217)*

Canvas LLC...703 237-6491
6039 27th St N Arlington (22207) *(G-899)*

Canvas Marine Co..703 534-5886
2756 Cameron Rd Falls Church (22042) *(G-4768)*

Canvas Salon LLC..804 926-5518
212 E Clay St Richmond (23219) *(G-11520)*

Canvas Solutions Inc (PA)............................**703 436-8069**
11911 Freedom Dr Ste 850 Reston (20190) *(G-10816)*

Canvas Solutions Inc..703 564-8564
1801 Old Reston Ave Reston (20190) *(G-10817)*

Canvas To Curtains..757 665-5406
14609 Bethel Church Rd Bloxom (23308) *(G-1839)*

Cap City Inc..757 827-0932
4809 W Mercury Blvd Hampton (23666) *(G-6105)*

Cap Oil Change Systems LLC...........................540 982-1494
6230 Hinchee Ln Roanoke (24019) *(G-11901)*

Capco Machinery Systems Inc..........................540 977-0404
307 Eastpark Dr Roanoke (24019) *(G-11902)*

Cape Charles Brewing Company........................757 678-5699
2198 Stone Rd Cape Charles (23310) *(G-2230)*

Cape Charles Distillery LLC..............................757 291-8016
240 Monroe Ave Cape Charles (23310) *(G-2231)*

Cape Fear Publishing Company.........................804 343-7539
109 E Cary St Richmond (23219) *(G-11521)*

Caper Holdings LLC...757 563-3810
577 Sandbridge Rd Ste B Virginia Beach (23456) *(G-14315)*

Capewell Aerial Systems, Meadows of Dan *Also called Aerial Machine & Tool Corp (G-8590)*

Capital Brandworks LLC...................................703 609-7010
3833 Pickett Rd Fairfax (22031) *(G-4423)*

Capital City Candle..571 245-4738
1350 Riverview Dr West Point (23181) *(G-15154)*

Capital Coal Corporation...................................276 935-7562
23377 Harbor Light Cir Abingdon (24211) *(G-20)*

Capital Concrete Inc (PA).............................**757 627-0630**
400 Stapleton St Norfolk (23504) *(G-9477)*

Capital Concrete Inc..757 627-0630
400 Stapleton Virginia Beach (23456) *(G-14316)*

Capital Designs LLC...703 444-2728
442 Seneca Rd Great Falls (22066) *(G-5943)*

Capital Discount Mdse LLC...............................703 499-9368
13923 Jefferson Davis Hwy Woodbridge (22191) *(G-15665)*

Capital Floors LLC...571 451-4044
2525 Luckland Way Woodbridge (22191) *(G-15666)*

Capital Ideas Press..434 447-6377
312 Hodges St South Hill (23970) *(G-12846)*

Capital Linen Services Inc................................804 744-3334
2430 Oak Lake Blvd Midlothian (23112) *(G-8789)*

Capital Noodle Inc...703 569-3224
7668 Fullerton Rd Springfield (22153) *(G-12973)*

Capital Publishing Corp....................................571 214-1659
3140 Graham Rd Falls Church (22042) *(G-4769)*

A
L
P
H
A
B
E
T
I
C

Capital Screen Prtg Unlimited 703 550-0033
  8382 Terminal Rd Ste A Lorton (22079) *(G-7470)*

Capital Software Corporation 703 404-3000
  25669 Pleasant Woods Ct Chantilly (20152) *(G-2528)*

Capitol City Publishers LLC 703 671-5920
  3485 S Wakefield St Arlington (22206) *(G-900)*

Capitol Closet Design Inc (PA) **703 827-2700**
  1934 Old Gallows Rd # 105 Vienna (22182) *(G-14022)*

Capitol Excellence Pubg LLC 571 277-9657
  1050 N Taylor St Apt 607 Arlington (22201) *(G-901)*

Capitol Exhibit Services Inc 703 330-9000
  12299 Livingston Rd Manassas (20109) *(G-8044)*

Capitol Granite LLC 804 379-2641
  1700 Oak Lake Blvd E Midlothian (23112) *(G-8790)*

Capitol Idea Technology Inc 571 233-1949
  14819 Potomac Branch Dr Woodbridge (22191) *(G-15667)*

Capitol Imaging, Alexandria *Also called Timothy E Quinn* *(G-365)*

Capitol Information Group Inc 703 905-8000
  7600 A Lsburg Pike Ste 30 Falls Church (22043) *(G-4770)*

Capitol Leather LLC 434 229-8467
  125 Market St Manassas Park (20111) *(G-8195)*

Capitol Net 703 739-3790
  4 Herbert St Alexandria (22305) *(G-159)*

Capitol Publishing Corporation 703 532-7535
  7290 Highland Estates Pl Falls Church (22043) *(G-4771)*

Capitol Signs Inc 804 749-3737
  11214 Howards Mill Rd Glen Allen (23059) *(G-5711)*

Capitol Trade Show Services, Manassas *Also called Capitol Exhibit Services Inc (G-8044)*

Capitol Wood Works 703 237-2071
  6008 Kelsey Ct Falls Church (22044) *(G-4772)*

Capo Software 571 205-8695
  13064 Monterey Estates Dr Herndon (20171) *(G-6633)*

Capps Boatworks Inc 757 496-0311
  2102 W Great Neck Rd Virginia Beach (23451) *(G-14317)*

Capps Shoe Company (PA) **434 528-3213**
  260 Fastener Dr Lynchburg (24502) *(G-7673)*

Capps Shoe Company 434 528-3213
  224 Industrial Dr Gretna (24557) *(G-6005)*

Capstone E & S, Virginia Beach *Also called Capstone EMB & Screen Prtg (G-14318)*

Capstone EMB & Screen Prtg 757 619-0457
  3005 Glastonbury Dr Virginia Beach (23453) *(G-14318)*

Capstone Industries LLC 703 966-6718
  7728 Beckham Ct Manassas (20111) *(G-8045)*

Captain Faunce Seafood Inc 804 493-8690
  2811 Cople Hwy Montross (22520) *(G-9025)*

Captn Joeys Custom Canvas 757 270-8772
  1081 Old Dam Neck Rd Virginia Beach (23454) *(G-14319)*

Car Wash Care Inc 703 385-9181
  3809 Keith Ave Fairfax (22030) *(G-4605)*

Caranus LLC 703 241-1683
  1027 N Livingston St Arlington (22205) *(G-902)*

Caraustar Industrial and Con 540 234-0431
  780 Keezletown Rd Ste 108 Weyers Cave (24486) *(G-15169)*

Caraustar Industrial and Con 757 562-0345
  1601 Carrsville Hwy Franklin (23851) *(G-5140)*

Caravelle Industries Inc 434 432-2331
  60 Sycolin Rd Se Leesburg (20175) *(G-7238)*

Caravelle Industries Inc (PA) **434 432-2331**
  2045 U S Hwy 29 N Chatham (24531) *(G-2920)*

Caravelle Vehicle Wshg Systems, Chatham *Also called Caravelle Industries Inc (G-2920)*

Caravelle Western Inds Inc 703 777-9412
  60a Sycolin Rd Se Leesburg (20175) *(G-7239)*

Caravels LLC 540 345-9892
  5870 Trinity Pkwy Ste 600 Centreville (20120) *(G-2297)*

Carbide Specialties Inc 804 346-3314
  573 Fords Rd Manakin Sabot (23103) *(G-7897)*

Carbon & Steel LLC 757 871-1808
  3248 Oak Branch Ln Toano (23168) *(G-13859)*

Carbone America 540 389-7535
  540 Branch Dr Salem (24153) *(G-12488)*

Carburetors Unlimited 703 273-0751
  10369 Balls Ford Rd Manassas (20109) *(G-8046)*

Cardboard Safari, Charlottesville *Also called Kingmill Enterprises LLC (G-2822)*

Carded Graphics LLC 540 248-3716
  2 Industry Way Staunton (24401) *(G-13247)*

Carden Jennings Publishing Co 434 817-2000
  375 Greenbrier Dr Ste 100 Charlottesville (22901) *(G-2603)*

Cardiac Diagnostics LLC 703 268-5751
  9103 Vosger Ct Fairfax (22031) *(G-4424)*

Cardinal Applications LLC 540 270-4369
  154 Battle Mountain Rd Amissville (20106) *(G-717)*

Cardinal Bakery Inc 703 430-1600
  22704 Commrce Ctr Ct # 100 Sterling (20166) *(G-13365)*

Cardinal Concrete, Fredericksburg *Also called Vulcan Materials Company (G-5388)*

Cardinal Concrete Company 703 550-7650
  13880 Dulles Corner Ln Herndon (20171) *(G-6634)*

Cardinal Control Systems Inc 703 437-0437
  1529 Park Glen Ct Reston (20190) *(G-10818)*

Cardinal Glass Industries Inc 540 892-5600
  2132 Cardinal Park Dr Vinton (24179) *(G-14168)*

Cardinal Homes Inc 434 735-8111
  525 Barnesville Hwy Wylliesburg (23976) *(G-15871)*

Cardinal Ig Company, Vinton *Also called Cardinal Glass Industries Inc (G-14168)*

Cardinal Mechatronics LLC 540 922-2392
  207 Wharton St Se Apt 12 Blacksburg (24060) *(G-1728)*

Cardinal Mfg 540 779-7790
  940 Orange St Bedford (24523) *(G-1630)*

Cardinal Park Unit Owners 703 777-2311
  12 Cardinal Park Dr Se # 107 Leesburg (20175) *(G-7240)*

Cardinal Point Vineyard Winery 540 456-8400
  9423 Batesville Rd Afton (22920) *(G-76)*

Cardinal Pumps Exchangers Inc 757 485-2666
  1403 Greenbrier Pkwy # 12 Chesapeake (23320) *(G-3026)*

Cardinal Quarries LLC 540 674-5556
  5764 Wilderness Rd Dublin (24084) *(G-4150)*

Cardinal Stone Company Inc 276 236-5457
  2650 Fishers Gap Rd Galax (24333) *(G-5630)*

Cardinal Tool Inc 804 561-2560
  8020 S Amelia Ave Amelia Court House (23002) *(G-653)*

Cardinals Logging 804 457-3543
  4617 Old Frdericksburg Rd Mineral (23117) *(G-8944)*

Cardwell Printing & Advg, Newport News *Also called Tidewater Printers Inc (G-9355)*

Care & Surface Specialties, North Chesterfield *Also called Evonik Corporation (G-9868)*

Career College Central 571 267-3012
  14200 Park Meadow Dr 117s Chantilly (20151) *(G-2387)*

Carefusion Solutions LLC 571 521-8900
  12120 Sunset Hills Rd # 300 Reston (20190) *(G-10819)*

Careplex Pharmacy 757 736-1215
  3000 Coliseum Dr Fl 2 Hampton (23666) *(G-6106)*

Caret Cellars and Vineyard LLC 540 413-6454
  495 Meadow Landing Ln Caret (22436) *(G-2238)*

Caretaker Medical LLC 434 978-7000
  941 Glenwood Station Ln # 301 Charlottesville (22901) *(G-2604)*

Cargill Incorporated 540 879-2521
  135 Huffman Dr Dayton (22821) *(G-4053)*

Cargill Incorporated 540 432-5700
  5688 S Valley Pike Mount Crawford (22841) *(G-9051)*

Cargill Incorporated 540 896-7041
  480 Co Op Dr Timberville (22853) *(G-13846)*

Cargill Meat Solutions Corp 540 437-8000
  5688 S Valley Pike Mount Crawford (22841) *(G-9052)*

Cargill Turkey Production LLC (HQ) **540 568-1400**
  1 Kratzer Ave Harrisonburg (22802) *(G-6298)*

Cargotrike Cupcakes 804 245-0786
  713 Colony Oak Ln Midlothian (23114) *(G-8791)*

Caribbean Channel One Inc 703 447-3773
  11763 Gascony Pl Woodbridge (22192) *(G-15668)*

Carico Inc 540 373-5983
  1300 Belman Rd Fredericksburg (22401) *(G-5176)*

Carl G Gilliam Jr 276 523-0619
  618 Wood Ave W Ste 100 Big Stone Gap (24219) *(G-1707)*

Carl Zeiss Optical Inc 804 530-8300
  13017 N Kingston Ave Chester (23836) *(G-3390)*

Carl Zeiss Vision Inc 800 456-0088
  13017 N Kingston Ave Chester (23836) *(G-3391)*

Carla Bedard 212 773-1851
  5273 Colonel Johnson Ln Alexandria (22304) *(G-160)*

Carla Wilkes 434 228-1427
  1010 9th St Lynchburg (24504) *(G-7674)*

Carlas Cupcakes LLC 703 582-7615
  13229 Pleasant Glen Ct Herndon (20171) *(G-6635)*

Carlen Controls Incorporated 540 772-1736
  6560 Commonwealth Dr Roanoke (24018) *(G-11903)*

Carlen Controls Inc 540 598-0714
  2341 Brookfield Dr Roanoke (24018) *(G-11904)*

Carlisle Indstrl Brke & Frctn 814 486-1119
  4040 Lewis And Clark Dr Charlottesville (22911) *(G-2605)*

Carlton and Edwards Inc 804 758-5100
  3 1/2 Miles North Rt 17 Saluda (23149) *(G-12602)*

Carlton Logging LLC 804 693-5193
  5106 Chestnut Fork Rd Gloucester (23061) *(G-5840)*

Carlton Orndorff 540 436-3543
  5271 Zepp Rd Maurertown (22644) *(G-8360)*

Carmel Tctcal Sltons Group LLC 804 943-6121
  200 Lakeview Ave Ste B Colonial Heights (23834) *(G-3731)*

Carmeuse Lime & Stone, Strasburg *Also called O-N Minerals Chemstone Company (G-13592)*

Carmeuse Lime & Stone, Buchanan *Also called O-N Minerals Chemstone Company (G-2123)*

Carmeuse Lime & Stone, Clear Brook *Also called O-N Minerals Chemstone Company (G-3649)*

Carmeuse Lime & Stone, Middletown *Also called O-N Minerals Chemstone Company (G-8741)*

Carocon 804 324-2207
  1357 Taylor Farm Rd Virginia Beach (23453) *(G-14320)*

Carolina By-Products, Winchester *Also called Valley Proteins (de) Inc (G-15502)*

Carolina Cold Storage Inc 757 357-0434
  10070 Old Stage Hwy Smithfield (23430) *(G-12708)*

Carolina Container Co Inc 804 458-4700
  1357 Taylor Farm Rd Virginia Beach (23453) *(G-14321)*

Carolina Container Company..............804 458-4700
5701 Quality Way Prince George (23875) ***(G-10588)***
Carolina Steel Fabrication, Bristol *Also called CSC Family Holdings Inc* ***(G-2015)***
Carolinas Solution Group Inc..............301 257-6926
476 Cleveland Ave Charlottesville (22903) ***(G-2756)***
Carolyn West..............434 332-5007
628 Meeting House Rd Rustburg (24588) ***(G-12436)***
Carotank Road LLC..............703 951-7790
1800 Diagonal Rd Ste 600 Alexandria (22314) ***(G-161)***
Carousel..............434 292-7721
104 N Main St Blackstone (23824) ***(G-1813)***
Carpenter Co (PA)..............**804 359-0800**
5016 Monument Ave Richmond (23230) ***(G-11146)***
Carpenter Co..............804 359-0800
5016 Monument Ave Richmond (23230) ***(G-11147)***
Carpenter Co..............804 359-0800
2400 Jefferson Davis Hwy Richmond (23234) ***(G-11031)***
Carpenter Co..............804 233-0606
2600 Jefferson Davis Hwy Richmond (23234) ***(G-11032)***
Carpenter Holdings Inc (HQ)..............**804 359-0800**
5016 Monument Ave Richmond (23230) ***(G-11148)***
Carpenters Cbnets Wodworks LLC..............276 236-0853
68 Industry Ln Woodlawn (24381) ***(G-15844)***
Carpers Wood Creations Inc..............540 465-2525
407 Aileen Ave Strasburg (22657) ***(G-13576)***
Carr Group LLC..............571 723-6562
2821 Powell Dr Woodbridge (22191) ***(G-15669)***
Carriage House Products Inc..............804 615-2400
5511 Lakeside Ave Henrico (23228) ***(G-6488)***
Carrier Corporation..............540 366-2471
5346 Peters Creek Rd B Roanoke (24019) ***(G-11905)***
Carris Reels Inc..............540 473-2210
64 W Wind Rd Fincastle (24090) ***(G-4995)***
Carroll J Harper..............540 434-8978
2670 N Valley Pike Rockingham (22802) ***(G-12244)***
Carroll News, Hillsville *Also called Carroll Publishing Corp* ***(G-6888)***
Carroll News, The, Hillsville *Also called Adams Publishing Group LLC* ***(G-6882)***
Carroll Publishing Corp..............276 728-7311
1192 W Stuart Dr Hillsville (24343) ***(G-6888)***
Carrs Floor Services..............434 525-8420
220 London Downs Dr Forest (24551) ***(G-5059)***
Carrythewhatreplications LLC..............804 254-2933
1308 W Main St Richmond (23220) ***(G-11522)***
Carter Composition Corporation..............804 359-9206
2007 N Hamilton St Richmond (23230) ***(G-11149)***
Carter Iron and Steel Co..............757 826-4559
408 Industry Dr Hampton (23661) ***(G-6107)***
Carter Jdub Music..............804 329-1815
315 Flicker Dr Richmond (23227) ***(G-11150)***
Carter Printing Co, Richmond *Also called Carter Composition Corporation* ***(G-11149)***
Carter Tool & Mfg Co Inc..............540 387-1778
1400 Southside Dr Salem (24153) ***(G-12489)***
Carter Welding LLC..............276 346-1873
365 Cowboy Ln Jonesville (24263) ***(G-7019)***
Carters Power Equipment Inc..............804 796-4895
4807 W Hundred Rd Ste A Chester (23831) ***(G-3392)***
Carters Publishing Company LLC..............804 590-4747
10300 Lamore Dr Disputanta (23842) ***(G-4105)***
Cartridge World Downtown, Richmond *Also called Refills Inc* ***(G-11732)***
Cary Pharmaceuticals Inc..............703 759-7460
9903 Windy Hollow Rd Great Falls (22066) ***(G-5944)***
Cary's Fabricating Service, Amelia Court House *Also called Leroy Cary* ***(G-663)***
Carys Mill Woodworking..............804 639-2946
12742 Spectrim Ln Midlothian (23112) ***(G-8792)***
Casa De Fiestas Dina..............703 910-6510
14454 Jefferson Davis Hwy Woodbridge (22191) ***(G-15670)***
Casanel Vineyards..............540 751-1776
17956 Canby Rd Leesburg (20175) ***(G-7241)***
Cascade Cabinets & Millwork..............434 685-4000
3464 Huntington Trl Cascade (24069) ***(G-2249)***
Case Mechanical..............804 501-0003
2512 Grenoble Rd Richmond (23294) ***(G-11151)***
Case Mechanical LLC..............757 272-6050
110 Stonewall Pl Newport News (23606) ***(G-9193)***
Case-Polytech Inc..............804 752-3500
11100 Air Park Rd Ashland (23005) ***(G-1386)***
Casey Traxler..............703 402-0745
15600 Malvosin Pl Leesburg (20176) ***(G-7242)***
Casey Unique Transport Svcs..............757 354-7626
1533 Lone Oak Ct Apt 107 Virginia Beach (23454) ***(G-14322)***
Caseys Welding Service..............804 275-7960
6429 Iron Bridge Rd North Chesterfield (23234) ***(G-9840)***
Cashmere Handrails Inc..............757 838-2307
27 Milford Rd Newport News (23601) ***(G-9194)***
Caspari Inc..............434 817-7880
100 W Main St Charlottesville (22902) ***(G-2757)***
Caspian Inc..............434 237-1900
3813 Wards Rd Ste B Lynchburg (24502) ***(G-7675)***
Cassandras Custom Designs LLC..............571 229-0389
7856 Rebel Walk Dr Manassas (20109) ***(G-8047)***
Cassandras Grmet Classics Corp..............703 590-7900
10681 Wakeman Ct Manassas (20110) ***(G-7924)***
Cassco Corporation..............540 433-2751
125 W Bruce St Harrisonburg (22801) ***(G-6299)***
Cassican Press LLC..............434 392-4832
746 Gates Bass Rd Rice (23966) ***(G-11004)***
Casson Art, Martinsville *Also called Casson Art & Frame* ***(G-8274)***
Casson Art & Frame..............276 638-1450
2000 N Fork Rd Martinsville (24112) ***(G-8274)***
Castello 1935 Inc..............540 464-5275
18145 Main St Buchanan (24066) ***(G-2118)***
Castle Glen Esttes Frm Wnery L..............804 763-9677
18185 Narrow Path Trl Doswell (23047) ***(G-4118)***
Castle Gruen Vnyrds Winery LLC..............540 229-2498
1272 Meander Run Rd Locust Dale (22948) ***(G-7440)***
Castle Vineyards LLC..............571 283-7150
2150 Mims Rd Luray (22835) ***(G-7604)***
Castlemans Compost LLC..............571 283-3030
12421 Rock Ridge Rd Herndon (20170) ***(G-6636)***
Cat Tail Run Hand Bookbinding..............540 662-2683
2160 Cedar Grove Rd Winchester (22603) ***(G-15399)***
Cataldo Industries LLC..............757 422-0518
4314 Virginia Beach Blvd Virginia Beach (23452) ***(G-14323)***
Catalina Cylinders..............757 896-9100
2400 Aluminum Ave Hampton (23661) ***(G-6108)***
Catalina Cylinders Inc..............757 896-9100
2400 Aluminum Ave Hampton (23661) ***(G-6109)***
Catapult Solutions Inc..............434 401-1077
104 Cupola St Lynchburg (24502) ***(G-7676)***
Catapult Video..............540 642-9947
4636 Haygood Rd Virginia Beach (23455) ***(G-14324)***
Catawba Records, Troutville *Also called Catawba Sound Studio* ***(G-13905)***
Catawba Renewable Energy..............434 426-1390
7625 Miller Cove Rd Catawba (24070) ***(G-2260)***
Catawba Sound Studio..............540 992-4738
1376 Lttle Ctwba Creek Rd Troutville (24175) ***(G-13905)***
Catberries LLC..............714 873-8245
15529 Tuxedo Ln Gainesville (20155) ***(G-5575)***
Catch Surf Norfolk, Norfolk *Also called Catch Surfboard Co LLC* ***(G-9478)***
Catch Surfboard Co LLC..............949 218-0428
1416 Ballentine Blvd Norfolk (23504) ***(G-9478)***
Catering By Catherine, Bristol *Also called Catherine Elliott* ***(G-1969)***
Catering Machine Company..............757 332-0024
10068 Rainbow Rd Carrollton (23314) ***(G-2241)***
Caterpillar Authorized Dealer, Clear Brook *Also called Alban Tractor Co Inc* ***(G-3643)***
Caterpillar Corner LLC..............703 939-1798
43486 Mink Meadows St South Riding (20152) ***(G-12867)***
Cathay Food Corp..............617 427-1507
148 Basalt Dr Fredericksburg (22406) ***(G-5408)***
Cathay Industries Inc..............224 629-4210
2170 Julia Simpkins Rd Hiwassee (24347) ***(G-6911)***
Catherine Elliott..............276 274-7022
921 Lawrence Ave Bristol (24201) ***(G-1969)***
Catherine Rachel Braxton..............757 244-7531
818 26th St Newport News (23607) ***(G-9195)***
Catholic Diocese of Arlington..............703 841-2590
200 N Glebe Rd Ste 614 Arlington (22203) ***(G-903)***
Catholic Virginian Press Inc..............804 358-3625
7800 Carousel Ln Richmond (23294) ***(G-11152)***
Cathy's Specialty, Newport News *Also called Catherine Rachel Braxton* ***(G-9195)***
Catlilli Games LLC..............540 359-6592
449 Estate Ave Warrenton (20186) ***(G-14986)***
Catoctin Creek Custom Rods LLC..............540 751-1482
201 N 18th St Purcellville (20132) ***(G-10653)***
Catoctin Creek Distlg Co LLC..............540 751-8404
120 W Main St Purcellville (20132) ***(G-10654)***
Catoctin Edges LLC..............540 687-1244
901 W Main St Purcellville (20132) ***(G-10655)***
Catrina Fashions LLC..............540 992-2127
5995 Lee Hwy Troutville (24175) ***(G-13906)***
Catron Machine & Welding Inc..............276 783-6826
138 Harris Ln Marion (24354) ***(G-8223)***
Cattywampus Woodworks LLC..............540 599-2358
173 Moye Rd Staffordsville (24167) ***(G-13214)***
Cauthorne Industries Inc..............804 798-6999
12124 Washington Hwy Ashland (23005) ***(G-1387)***
Cauthorne Paper Company Inc..............804 798-6999
12124 Washington Hwy Ashland (23005) ***(G-1388)***
Cavalier Concrete Inc..............434 296-7181
1000 Harris St Charlottesville (22903) ***(G-2758)***
Cavalier Ink & Coatings, Richmond *Also called Cavalier Printing Ink Co Inc* ***(G-11033)***
Cavalier Mirror, Galax *Also called American Mirror Company Inc* ***(G-5627)***
Cavalier Printing Ink Co Inc (PA)..............**804 271-4214**
2807 Transport St Richmond (23234) ***(G-11033)***
Cavalier Steel, Lynchburg *Also called Bohling Steel Inc* ***(G-7657)***
Cavalier Ventures LLC..............757 491-3000
300 32nd St Ste 500 Virginia Beach (23451) ***(G-14325)***
Cavalry Aerospace LLC..............757 995-2029
516 Innovation Dr Ste 201 Chesapeake (23320) ***(G-3027)***

ALPHABETIC

Cavan Sales Lo...434 757-1680
3334 Country Club Rd La Crosse (23950) ***(G-7141)***
Cavanaugh Cabinet Inc (PA)...**434 977-7100**
1329 E High St Charlottesville (22902) ***(G-2759)***
Cave Hill Corporation...540 289-5051
806 Island Ford Rd McGaheysville (22840) ***(G-8584)***
Cave Hill Mech & Maint Svc, McGaheysville *Also called Cave Hill Corporation* ***(G-8584)***
Cave Mma LLC...540 455-7623
1504 Interstate Bus Park Fredericksburg (22405) ***(G-5409)***
Cave Systems Inc...877 344-2283
113 Williamson Ct Henrico (23229) ***(G-6489)***
Cavion Inc...434 200-8442
310 2nd St Se Ste B Charlottesville (22902) ***(G-2760)***
Cavitronix Corporation...540 622-6240
830 John Marshall Hwy Front Royal (22630) ***(G-5526)***
Cayambis Music Press LLC...540 951-3504
1718 Honeysuckle Dr Blacksburg (24060) ***(G-1729)***
Cazador LLC...719 387-7450
2553 Dulles View Dr Herndon (20171) ***(G-6637)***
CB Suppliers, Burke *Also called Ronald Carter* ***(G-2202)***
Cbd Consulting, Williamsburg *Also called Rusolf S Olszyk* ***(G-15309)***
Cbd Genie LLC...571 434-1776
20921 Davenport Dr Sterling (20165) ***(G-13366)***
Cbd Livity...571 215-1938
2733 Sandpiper Rd Virginia Beach (23456) ***(G-14326)***
Cbd Solutions LLC...757 286-8733
9052 Mullen Rd King George (22485) ***(G-7082)***
Cbe Press LLC...703 992-6779
2750 Gallows Rd Apt 344 Vienna (22180) ***(G-14023)***
Cbg LLC...757 465-0333
4013 Seaboard Ct Ste A3 Portsmouth (23701) ***(G-10405)***
Cbn Secure Technologies Inc...434 799-9280
350 Stinson Dr Danville (24540) ***(G-3964)***
Cbp, Newport News *Also called Chesapeake Bay Packing LLC* ***(G-9199)***
Cbt Screen Printing LLC...703 888-8539
310a S Washington St Falls Church (22046) ***(G-4904)***
CC & C Desktop Publishing &...757 393-3606
25 Beacon Rd Portsmouth (23702) ***(G-10406)***
CC & More Inc...540 786-7052
3509 Shannon Park Dr # 117 Fredericksburg (22408) ***(G-5257)***
CC Richmond II LP...804 213-2706
11 S 12th St Ste 115 Richmond (23219) ***(G-11523)***
CC Wireless Corporation...757 802-8140
956 E Little Creek Rd Norfolk (23518) ***(G-9479)***
Ccbcc Operations LLC...540 343-8041
235 Shenandoah Ave Nw Roanoke (24016) ***(G-12060)***
Ccf/Swiss Inc...804 622-4277
313 Berwickshire Dr Richmond (23229) ***(G-11153)***
CCI Screenprinting Inc...703 978-0257
5003 Gadsen Dr Fairfax (22032) ***(G-4425)***
Cda Usa Inc...804 918-3707
4310 Eubank Rd Henrico (23231) ***(G-6490)***
Cdc Lofton Warehouse, Raphine *Also called Westrock Mwv LLC* ***(G-10752)***
CDI, Fairfax *Also called Creative Document Imaging Inc* ***(G-4432)***
CDK Industries LLC...804 551-3085
11318 W Providence Rd North Chesterfield (23236) ***(G-9841)***
Cdrs LLC...703 451-7546
7956 Twist Ln Springfield (22153) ***(G-12974)***
Cecilia M Schultzs...301 840-1283
929 Hickory Run Ln Great Falls (22066) ***(G-5945)***
Cedar Bluff VA Office...276 964-4171
2308 Cedar Valley Dr Cedar Bluff (24609) ***(G-2272)***
Cedar Creek Valley Farm LLC...540 533-2259
160 Flickertail Ln Star Tannery (22654) ***(G-13235)***
Cedar Creek Winery LLC...540 436-8357
7384 Zepp Rd Star Tannery (22654) ***(G-13236)***
Cedar Forest Cabinetry & Millw...703 753-0644
4224 Ringwood Rd Nokesville (20181) ***(G-9390)***
Cedar Industry LLC...571 402-4564
3042 Clancy Dr Dumfries (22026) ***(G-4238)***
Cedar Lane Farms LLC...757 335-0830
1836 Pittsburg Lndg Virginia Beach (23464) ***(G-14327)***
Cedar Mountain Stone Corp...540 825-3370
10496 Quarry Dr Mitchells (22729) ***(G-8954)***
Cee Corporation...571 526-4447
11250 Roger Bacon Dr 2a Reston (20190) ***(G-10820)***
CEF Enterprises Inc...757 478-4359
121 Tower Dr Virginia Beach (23462) ***(G-14328)***
Cegna Inc...757 632-5000
110 Clseum Crssing Ste 50 Hampton (23666) ***(G-6110)***
Celanese Acetate LLC...540 921-1111
3520 Virginia Ave Narrows (24124) ***(G-9096)***
Celanese Americas LLC...540 921-6540
3520 Virginia Ave Narrows (24124) ***(G-9097)***
Celestial Circuits LLC...703 851-2843
6105 Tobey Ct Springfield (22150) ***(G-12975)***
Celise LLC...757 771-5176
8 Freeman Dr Poquoson (23662) ***(G-10366)***
Cellofoam North America Inc...540 373-4596
57 Joseph Mills Dr Fredericksburg (22408) ***(G-5258)***
Cellofoam North America Inc...540 373-1800
57 Joseph Mills Dr Fredericksburg (22408) ***(G-5259)***
Celly Sports Shop LLC...540 981-0205
1110 Vinyard Rd Vinton (24179) ***(G-14169)***
Celotex, Danville *Also called Blue Ridge Fiberboard Inc* ***(G-3959)***
Cemark Inc...804 763-4100
13531 E Boundary Rd Ste A Midlothian (23112) ***(G-8793)***
Cemex Cnstr Mtls ATL LLC...434 685-7021
101 Solite Dr Cascade (24069) ***(G-2250)***
Cems Inc...540 434-7500
780 Keezletown Rd Ste 102 Weyers Cave (24486) ***(G-15170)***
Census Channel...757 838-3881
4410 Claiborne Sq E # 334 Hampton (23666) ***(G-6111)***
Centaurus Biotech LLC...952 210-6881
4229 Lafayette Center Dr Chantilly (20151) ***(G-2388)***
Centellax Inc...540 980-2905
1740 Smith Ln Pulaski (24301) ***(G-10632)***
Centennial Books...703 751-6162
1591 Chapel Hill Dr Alexandria (22304) ***(G-162)***
Centerline Fabricators...540 318-6769
199 Tyler Von Way Fredericksburg (22405) ***(G-5410)***
Centerville Concrete, Manassas *Also called Aggregate Industries - Mwr Inc* ***(G-8020)***
Central Belting Hose & Rbr Co, Chesterfield *Also called Briggs Company* ***(G-3483)***
Central Carolina Btlg Co Inc...434 753-2515
2140 Mount Carmel Rd Alton (24520) ***(G-646)***
Central Electronics Co...540 659-3235
1621 Garrisonville Rd Stafford (22556) ***(G-13128)***
Central Machine Shop Inc...276 669-2816
14773 Wallace Pike Abingdon (24210) ***(G-21)***
Central National-Gottesman Inc...703 941-0810
6715b Electronic Dr Springfield (22151) ***(G-12976)***
Central Redi-Mix Concrete Inc...434 736-0091
3907 Patrick Henry Hwy Meherrin (23954) ***(G-8705)***
Central Virginia Hardwood Pdts...434 335-5898
3217 Renan Rd Gretna (24557) ***(G-6006)***
Central Virginia Home Magazine, Forest *Also called West Willow Pubg Group LLC* ***(G-5104)***
Central Virginia Horse Logging...434 390-7252
400 7th St Blackstone (23824) ***(G-1814)***
Central Virginia Manufacturing, Bedford *Also called Nzo LLC* ***(G-1646)***
Central Virginia Stucco Inc...434 531-0752
2725 Thmas Jefferson Pkwy Charlottesville (22902) ***(G-2761)***
Central Virginian, The, Louisa *Also called Cv Corporation of Virginia* ***(G-7554)***
Centrex Fab...804 598-6000
4010 Jefferson Woods Dr Powhatan (23139) ***(G-10537)***
Centripetal Networks Inc (PA)...**571 252-5080**
2251 Corp Park Dr Ste 150 Herndon (20171) ***(G-6638)***
Centurion Tools LLC...540 967-5402
637 Industrial Dr Louisa (23093) ***(G-7549)***
Centurion Woodworks LLC...703 594-2369
13414 Cavalier Woods Dr Clifton (20124) ***(G-3660)***
Century Control Systems Inc...540 992-5100
307 11th St Se Roanoke (24013) ***(G-12061)***
Century Lighting Solutions LLC...202 281-8393
311 N Washington St 3l Alexandria (22314) ***(G-163)***
Century Press Inc...703 335-5663
10443 Balls Ford Rd Manassas (20109) ***(G-8048)***
Century Stair Company...703 754-4163
15175 Washington St Haymarket (20169) ***(G-6417)***
Century Steel Products Inc...703 471-7606
45034 Underwood Ln # 201 Sterling (20166) ***(G-13367)***
Century Trucking LLC...703 996-8585
43751 Beaver Meadow Rd Sterling (20166) ***(G-13368)***
Centurylink Switch Room...276 646-8000
132 W Main St Marion (24354) ***(G-8224)***
Ceotronics Inc...757 549-6220
512 S Lynnhven Rd Ste 104 Virginia Beach (23452) ***(G-14329)***
Cephas Industries Inc...804 641-1824
13701 Allied Rd Chester (23836) ***(G-3393)***
Cerberus LLC...703 372-9750
3145 17th St N Arlington (22201) ***(G-904)***
Cerberus Skateboard Co LLC...757 715-2225
241 Granby St Norfolk (23510) ***(G-9480)***
Cerillo LLC...434 218-3151
1516 Cherry Ave Charlottesville (22903) ***(G-2762)***
Cerner Corporation...703 286-0200
1953 Gallows Rd Ste 350 Vienna (22182) ***(G-14024)***
Cerrahyan Publishing Inc...757 589-1462
2404 Virginia Beach Blvd Virginia Beach (23454) ***(G-14330)***
Cerro Fabricated Products LLC (HQ)...**540 208-1606**
300 Triangle Dr Weyers Cave (24486) ***(G-15171)***
Certified Environmental Drlg...434 979-0123
2471 Poplar Dr Charlottesville (22903) ***(G-2763)***
Cervantes Masonry...804 741-7271
8408 Spalding Dr Henrico (23229) ***(G-6491)***
Ceva Awards, Gretna *Also called Central Virginia Hardwood Pdts* ***(G-6006)***
Ceylon Cinnamon Growers LLC...703 626-1764
8321 Old Courthouse Rd # 26 Vienna (22182) ***(G-14025)***
CF Adams Brokerage Co Inc...757 287-9717
1507 Mulligan Ct Chesapeake (23322) ***(G-3028)***

CF Smith & Sons 540 672-3291
12243 Mayhurst Ln Orange (22960) *(G-10205)*
CFC Farm & Home Center, Culpeper *Also called Culpeper Farmers Coop Inc (G-3884)*
CFS-Kbr Mrnas Support Svcs LLC 202 261-1900
1725 Duke St Ste 400 Alexandria (22314) *(G-164)*
Cg Plus LLC 540 977-3200
275 Eastpark Dr Roanoke (24019) *(G-11906)*
CH Krammes & Co Inc 434 589-1663
3794 Haden Martin Rd Palmyra (22963) *(G-10246)*
Cha Lua Ngoc Hung 703 531-1868
6799 Wilson Blvd Unit 2 Falls Church (22044) *(G-4773)*
Chad Coal Corp 276 498-4952
Harrys Br Whitewood (24657) *(G-15191)*
Chadwick International Inc (PA) 703 560-0970
8300 Arlington Blvd B2 Fairfax (22031) *(G-4426)*
Chalison Inc 757 258-2520
1592 Penniman Rd Ste C Williamsburg (23185) *(G-15218)*
Chalmers & Kubeck Inc 434 851-3613
10613 Wards Rd Rustburg (24588) *(G-12437)*
Chambers Welding Inc Carl 276 794-7170
4353 N 71 Lebanon (24266) *(G-7190)*
Chameleon Silk Screen Co 434 985-7456
63 Ford Ave Stanardsville (22973) *(G-13217)*
Champion Billd & Bar Stools 703 631-8800
13041 Fair Lk Shpg Ctr Fairfax (22033) *(G-4427)*
Champion Handwash 703 893-4216
8218 Leesburg Pike Vienna (22182) *(G-14026)*
Champion Iron Works Inc 540 955-3633
509 Jack Enders Blvd Berryville (22611) *(G-1673)*
Champion Publications Inc 757 580-4068
1018 New Mill Dr Chesapeake (23322) *(G-3029)*
Champion Publishing Inc 434 817-7222
516 Brookway Dr Charlottesville (22901) *(G-2606)*
Champion Ventures LLC 540 975-0791
358 Jackson Ave New Market (22844) *(G-9141)*
Champions Hand Carwash, Vienna *Also called Champion Handwash (G-14026)*
Champs 800 991-6813
12300 Jefferson Ave # 415 Newport News (23602) *(G-9196)*
Champs Create A Book 757 369-3879
960 Willbrook Rd Newport News (23602) *(G-9197)*
Chanders 804 752-7678
13223 Cedar Ln Ashland (23005) *(G-1389)*
Chandler Concrete Co Inc 434 369-4791
1503 Main St Altavista (24517) *(G-629)*
Chandler Concrete Co Inc 434 792-1233
1088 Industrial Ave Danville (24541) *(G-3965)*
Chandler Concrete Inc 540 345-3846
614 Norfolk Ave Sw Roanoke (24016) *(G-12062)*
Chandler Concrete Inc 540 297-4369
14418 Moneta Rd Moneta (24121) *(G-8958)*
Chandler Concrete Inc 276 928-1357
273 Enterprise Ln Rocky Gap (24366) *(G-12306)*
Chandler Concrete of Virginia, Roanoke *Also called Chandler Concrete Inc (G-12062)*
Chandler Concrete of Virginia 434 369-4791
1503 Main St Altavista (24517) *(G-630)*
Chandler Concrete Products of (PA) 540 382-1734
700 Block Ln Christiansburg (24073) *(G-3578)*
Chandler Concrete Products of 540 674-4667
5488 Bagging Plant Rd Dublin (24084) *(G-4151)*
Chandler Concrete Virginia Inc 540 382-1734
700 Block Ln Christiansburg (24073) *(G-3579)*
Chaney Ent. Concrete, Fredericksburg *Also called Chaney Enterprises Ltd Partnr (G-5260)*
Chaney Enterprises, King George *Also called Charles County Sand & Grav Co (G-7083)*
Chaney Enterprises Ltd Partnr 540 710-0075
8520 Indian Hills Ct Fredericksburg (22407) *(G-5260)*
Chaney Enterprises Ltd Partnr 540 659-4100
169 Wyche Rd Stafford (22554) *(G-13129)*
Change Cola Inc 703 674-9830
620 Salem Ave Sw Roanoke (24016) *(G-12063)*
Chantil Technology LLC 703 955-7867
13528 Tabscott Dr Chantilly (20151) *(G-2389)*
Chantilly Biopharma LLC 703 932-3840
3701 Concorde Pkwy # 500 Chantilly (20151) *(G-2390)*
Chantilly Crushed Stone Inc 703 471-4411
23076 Shaw Rd Sterling (20166) *(G-13369)*
Chantilly Floor Wholesaler Inc 703 263-0515
14516 Lee Rd Unit K Chantilly (20151) *(G-2391)*
Chantilly Prtg & Graphics Inc 703 471-2800
13808 Redskin Dr Herndon (20171) *(G-6639)*
Chantilly Services Inc 703 830-7700
14240 Sullyfield Cir A Chantilly (20151) *(G-2392)*
Chaosworks Inc 703 727-0772
9844 Beach Mill Rd Great Falls (22066) *(G-5946)*
Chaparral (virginia) Inc 972 647-7915
25801 Hofheimer Way North Dinwiddie (23803) *(G-10049)*
Chaparral Virginia Inc 540 767-1238
2580 Broadway Ave Sw Roanoke (24014) *(G-12064)*
Chappelle Mechanical Svcs LLC 240 299-3000
3701 Dalebrook Dr Dumfries (22025) *(G-4239)*
Charge-It Toner Co., Christiansburg *Also called C I T C Imaging (G-3576)*
Charis Machine LLC 276 546-6675
301 Dry Creek Rd Duffield (24244) *(G-4176)*
Charles A Bliss Jr 434 685-7311
1653 Stony Mill Rd Danville (24540) *(G-3966)*
Charles City Forest Products 804 966-2336
2200 Roxbury Rd Providence Forge (23140) *(G-10620)*
Charles City Timber and Mat 804 829-5850
5900 Chambers Rd Charles City (23030) *(G-2572)*
Charles City Timber and Mat 804 512-8150
2200 Barnetts Rd Providence Forge (23140) *(G-10621)*
Charles City Timber and Mat (PA) 804 966-8313
2221 Barnetts Rd Providence Forge (23140) *(G-10622)*
Charles Contracting Co Inc (PA) 757 422-9989
2821 Crusader Cir Virginia Beach (23453) *(G-14331)*
Charles County Sand & Grav Co 540 775-9550
13250 James Madison Pkwy King George (22485) *(G-7083)*
Charles E Overfelt 540 562-0808
2042 Timberview Rd Roanoke (24019) *(G-11907)*
Charles H Snead Co 540 539-5890
118 E Main St Boyce (22620) *(G-1908)*
Charles James Winery & Vinyrd 540 931-4386
4063 Middle Rd Winchester (22602) *(G-15400)*
Charles M Fariss 434 660-0606
2599 Colonial Hwy Rustburg (24588) *(G-12438)*
Charles R Preston 703 757-0495
9801 Georgetown Pike Great Falls (22066) *(G-5947)*
Charles Southwell 703 892-5469
4401 1st Rd S Arlington (22204) *(G-905)*
Charles Trpin Prtrs Lthgrphics, Rocky Mount *Also called Virginia Prtg Co Roanoke Inc (G-12360)*
Charles W Brinegar Enterprise 276 634-6934
2197 George Taylor Rd Spencer (24165) *(G-12872)*
Charlette Publishing Inc 434 696-5550
1404 Nottoway Blvd Victoria (23974) *(G-14000)*
Charlie Eco Publishing Inc 800 357-0121
19410 Rich Valley Rd Abingdon (24210) *(G-22)*
Charlie Moseley 571 235-3206
11400 Washington Plz W # 102 Reston (20190) *(G-10821)*
Charlie Ward 276 768-7266
2267 Riverside Dr Independence (24348) *(G-6979)*
Charlie Watts Signs 540 291-3211
856 Petites Gap Rd Naturl BR STA (24579) *(G-9110)*
Charlies Woodworks Inc 703 944-0775
7109 Carol Ln Falls Church (22042) *(G-4774)*
Charlotte County School Board 434 542-4933
200 Evergreen Rd Charlotte C H (23923) *(G-2583)*
Charlotte Gazette, Drakes Branch *Also called Charlotte Publishing Inc (G-4131)*
Charlotte Printing LLC 434 738-7155
22950 Kings Hwy Randolph (23962) *(G-10747)*
Charlotte Publishing Inc 434 568-3341
4789 Drakes Main St Drakes Branch (23937) *(G-4131)*
Charlottesville Fire Exting 434 295-0803
1790 Ed Jones Rd Scottsville (24590) *(G-12659)*
Charlottesville Flight Center 434 964-1474
200 Aviation Dr Ste 140 Charlottesville (22911) *(G-2607)*
Charlottesville Guide, Charlottesville *Also called Carden Jennings Publishing Co (G-2603)*
Charlottesville Stone Company 434 295-5700
2343 Highland Farm Rd Nw Roanoke (24017) *(G-12065)*
Charlottesville Vineyard 434 321-8463
508 Harris Rd Charlottesville (22903) *(G-2764)*
Charm School LLC 415 999-9496
311 W Broad St Richmond (23220) *(G-11524)*
Charter Ip Pllc 540 253-5332
7147 Kenthurst Ln The Plains (20198) *(G-13842)*
Charter of Lynchburg Inc 434 239-2671
139 Winebarger Cir Lynchburg (24501) *(G-7677)*
Charter Time Furniture, Lynchburg *Also called Charter of Lynchburg Inc (G-7677)*
Chartman Publications LLC 252 489-0151
3908 Clifford St Portsmouth (23707) *(G-10407)*
Chase Architectural Metal LLC 804 230-1136
500 Albany Ave Richmond (23224) *(G-11525)*
Chase Filters & Components LLC 757 327-0036
307 E St Hampton (23661) *(G-6112)*
Chase Group II A/C & Htg Svc 571 245-7379
109 Ringgold Rd Fredericksburg (22405) *(G-5411)*
Chase II, Raymond C, Fredericksburg *Also called Chase Group II A/C & Htg Svc (G-5411)*
Chateau Merrillanne LLC 540 656-6177
16234 Marquis Rd Orange (22960) *(G-10206)*
Chateau Morrisette Inc (PA) 540 593-2865
287 Winery Rd Sw Floyd (24091) *(G-5018)*
Chateau OBrien At North Point 540 364-6441
3238 Railstop Rd Markham (22643) *(G-8247)*
Chatham Knitting Mills Inc 434 432-4701
119 S Main St Chatham (24531) *(G-2921)*
Chatham Vineyards LLC 757 678-5588
9232 Chatham Rd Machipongo (23405) *(G-7846)*
Chattem Inc 540 786-7970
11906 Rutherford Dr Fredericksburg (22407) *(G-5261)*
Chattem Consumer Products, Fredericksburg *Also called Chattem Inc (G-5261)*

ALPHABETIC

Chaz & Reetas Creations 804 248-4933
8642 Pine Glade Ln North Chesterfield (23237) *(G-9842)*

Chc Transports LLC 804 398-8686
7719 Centerbrook Ln Chesterfield (23832) *(G-3485)*

Checkered Flag Sports, Martinsville *Also called Southprint Inc (G-8334)*

Checkpoint Systems Inc 804 745-0010
6829 Atmore Dr Ste A Richmond (23225) *(G-11526)*

Chef Josephs Kick Sauce LLC 757 525-1744
1728 Virginia Beach Blvd Virginia Beach (23454) *(G-14332)*

Chef Sous LLC 804 938-5477
4860 Cox Rd Ste 200 Glen Allen (23060) *(G-5712)*

Chefit LLC 202 769-6049
9151 Furey Rd Lorton (22079) *(G-7471)*

Chelonian Press Inc 703 734-1160
9723 Days Farm Dr Vienna (22182) *(G-14027)*

Chem Core Inc 540 862-2600
9300 Winterberry Ave Covington (24426) *(G-3781)*

Chem Station of Virginia 804 236-0090
5745 Charles City Cir Richmond (23231) *(G-11154)*

Chemetrics Inc 540 788-9026
4295 Catlett Rd Midland (22728) *(G-8749)*

Chemical Supply Inc 804 353-2971
1600 Roseneath Rd Ste B Richmond (23230) *(G-11155)*

Chemring Sensors and Electr 434 964-4800
4010 Hunterstand Ct Charlottesville (22911) *(G-2608)*

Chemring Snsors Elctrnic Syste (HQ) **703 661-0283**
23031 Ladbrook Dr Dulles (20166) *(G-4195)*

Chemteq 757 622-2223
600 W 24th St Ste B Norfolk (23517) *(G-9481)*

Chemtrade Chemicals US LLC 804 541-0261
511 Plant St Hopewell (23860) *(G-6919)*

Chemtrade Chemicals US LLC 540 962-6444
714 N Mill Rd Covington (24426) *(G-3782)*

Chemtreat Inc 804 513-0756
10040 Lickinghole Rd Ashland (23005) *(G-1390)*

Chemtron Inc (PA) **703 550-7772**
7350 Lockport Pl Ste C Lorton (22079) *(G-7472)*

Chep (usa) Inc 804 226-0229
3707 Nine Mile Rd Richmond (23223) *(G-11527)*

Cherry Hill Cabinetry (PA) **540 785-4333**
1320 Cntl Pk Blvd Ste 108 Fredericksburg (22401) *(G-5177)*

Cherry Hill Cabinetry 703 942-6053
6232 Old Dominion Dr Mc Lean (22101) *(G-8405)*

Cherry Tree Learning, Round Hill *Also called R2jb Enterprises (G-12385)*

Cherrystone Structures LLC 434 432-8484
2180 Walkers Well Rd Chatham (24531) *(G-2922)*

Cherrywood, Lexington *Also called Talmadge Fix (G-7419)*

Chesapeake & Hudson Inc 301 834-7170
27 Jacks Shop Rd Rochelle (22738) *(G-12232)*

Chesapeake Bay Adirondack LLC 757 416-4583
732 Keeling Dr Chesapeake (23322) *(G-3030)*

Chesapeake Bay Controls Inc 757 228-5537
533 Gleneagle Dr Virginia Beach (23462) *(G-14333)*

Chesapeake Bay Distillery LLC 757 692-4083
437 Virginia Beach Blvd Virginia Beach (23451) *(G-14334)*

Chesapeake Bay Fishing Co LLC 804 438-6050
25 Shipyard Ln Weems (22576) *(G-15150)*

Chesapeake Bay Packing LLC 757 244-8400
703 Jefferson Ave Newport News (23607) *(G-9198)*

Chesapeake Bay Packing LLC (PA) **757 244-8440**
800 Terminal Ave Newport News (23607) *(G-9199)*

Chesapeake Biofuels 804 482-1784
1925 Puddledock Rd Petersburg (23803) *(G-10311)*

Chesapeake Cabinet & Finish Co 757 787-9422
25110 Nottingham Ln Onancock (23417) *(G-10192)*

Chesapeake Cartridge Corp 703 989-0903
5366 Wilderness Rd Dublin (24084) *(G-4152)*

Chesapeake Cartridge Corp Inc 703 989-0903
2020 Kraft Dr Ste 2100 Blacksburg (24060) *(G-1730)*

Chesapeake Coatings 757 945-2812
4109 Cheswick Ln Virginia Beach (23455) *(G-14335)*

Chesapeake Connector & Cable 757 855-5504
5248 Cape Henry Ave Norfolk (23513) *(G-9482)*

Chesapeake Custom Chem Corp 276 956-3145
126 Reservoir Rd Ridgeway (24148) *(G-11840)*

Chesapeake Distributors LLC 757 302-1108
15068 Holly St Onancock (23417) *(G-10193)*

Chesapeake Ind Sftwr Testers 757 547-1610
1541 Shillelagh Rd Chesapeake (23323) *(G-3031)*

Chesapeake Integrated Bioenrgy 202 253-5953
7742 Clifton Rd Fairfax Station (22039) *(G-4701)*

Chesapeake Machine Works Inc 757 543-1001
550 Freeman Ave Chesapeake (23324) *(G-3032)*

Chesapeake Manufacturing Inc 804 716-2035
506 Maury St Richmond (23224) *(G-11528)*

Chesapeake Marine Railway 804 776-8833
548 Deagles Rd Deltaville (23043) *(G-4078)*

Chesapeake Materials LLC (PA) **540 658-0808**
2951 Jefferson Davis Hwy Stafford (22554) *(G-13130)*

Chesapeake Outdoor Designs Inc 804 632-1900
1600 Sville Chase Turn Ln Midlothian (23112) *(G-8794)*

Chesapeake Propeller LLC 804 421-7991
6331 River Rd Richmond (23229) *(G-11156)*

Chesapeake Signs 757 482-6989
824 Sycamore Ln Chesapeake (23322) *(G-3033)*

Chesapeake Strl Systems Inc 804 966-8340
2401 Roxbury Rd Charles City (23030) *(G-2573)*

Chesapeake Thermite Wldg LLC 804 725-1111
1065 Possum Point Rd Port Haywood (23138) *(G-10382)*

Chesapeake Yachts Inc 757 724-1717
1700 Shipyard Rd Chesapeake (23323) *(G-3034)*

Cheshire Cat and Company Llc 540 221-2538
141 E Broad St Ste T Waynesboro (22980) *(G-15104)*

Chester Raceway 804 717-2330
1900 W Hundred Rd Chester (23836) *(G-3394)*

Chesterfield Observer, Midlothian *Also called Observer Inc (G-8870)*

Chestnut Oak Vineyard LLC 434 964-9104
5050 Stony Point Rd Barboursville (22923) *(G-1559)*

Chetia Plugg Publication, Norfolk *Also called Davis Chetia (G-9518)*

Chew On This Gluten Free Foods 757 440-3757
3813 Coyote Cir Virginia Beach (23456) *(G-14336)*

Chewning Lumber Company (PA) **540 895-5158**
11252 Post Oak Rd Spotsylvania (22551) *(G-12885)*

Cheyenne Autumn Arts 804 745-9561
7500 Hadley Ln Chesterfield (23832) *(G-3486)*

Chicago Tribune, Newport News *Also called Virginia Gazette Companies LLC (G-9373)*

Chick Lit LLC 757 496-9019
1768 Templeton Ln Virginia Beach (23454) *(G-14337)*

Chicken Farms Division, Harrisonburg *Also called Georges Chicken LLC (G-6323)*

Chicopee Inc 540 946-9250
1020 Shenandoah Vlg Dr Waynesboro (22980) *(G-15105)*

Chief Printing Company 515 480-6577
11 S 21st St Richmond (23223) *(G-11529)*

Chilhowie Fence Supply LLC 276 780-0452
1517 Hwy 107 Chilhowie (24319) *(G-3547)*

Chilli Richmond LLC 804 329-2262
109 W Lancaster Rd Richmond (23222) *(G-11530)*

Chinctgue Island Hse Jerky LLC 215 353-6393
6339 Maddox Blvd Chincoteague (23336) *(G-3561)*

Chinook & Co LLC 540 463-9556
151 Pullen Rd Lexington (24450) *(G-7389)*

Chips Brookneal Inc 434 376-6202
24 Price Ave Hwy 501 N Brookneal (24528) *(G-2109)*

Chips Inc 434 589-2424
26 Zion Park Rd Troy (22974) *(G-13922)*

Chips On Board Incorporated 757 357-0789
1011 Magruder Rd Smithfield (23430) *(G-12709)*

Chiru Software Inc 703 201-1914
21525 Glebe View Dr Broadlands (20148) *(G-2075)*

Chittenden & Associates Inc 703 930-2769
942 Bowles Valley Rd Rocky Mount (24151) *(G-12316)*

Chj Digital Repro, Virginia Beach *Also called Dae Print & Design (G-14382)*

Chocklett Press Inc 540 345-1820
2922 Nicholas Ave Ne Roanoke (24012) *(G-12066)*

Chocolate Dmnds Pblcations LLC 804 332-5117
708 Francis Rd Glen Allen (23059) *(G-5713)*

Chocolate Paper Inc 540 989-7025
3555 Electric Rd Ste C Roanoke (24018) *(G-11908)*

Choice Adhesives Corporation 434 847-5671
2500 Carroll Ave Lynchburg (24501) *(G-7678)*

Choice Printing Services 804 690-9064
5504 Barnsley Ter Glen Allen (23059) *(G-5714)*

Choice Tack 804 314-0787
1680 Ragland Rd Goochland (23063) *(G-5881)*

Chorda Pharma LLC 251 753-1042
709 S Jefferson St Ste 4 Roanoke (24016) *(G-12067)*

Chosun Ilbo Washington Inc 703 865-8310
9840 Main St Ste 100 Fairfax (22031) *(G-4428)*

Chow Time LLC 804 934-9305
2117 Tuckaway Ln Richmond (23229) *(G-11157)*

Chris Chase Studio, Richmond *Also called Opposable Thumbs LLC (G-11701)*

Chris Ellis Signs & Airbrush 434 447-8013
1399 N Mecklenburg Ave La Crosse (23950) *(G-7142)*

Chris Kennedy Publishing LLC 757 689-2021
2052 Bierce Dr Virginia Beach (23454) *(G-14338)*

Chris N Chris Woodworking LLC 757 810-4672
5 Ashe Meadows Dr Hampton (23664) *(G-6113)*

Christian Creations 540 722-2718
425 Eckard Cir Winchester (22602) *(G-15401)*

Christian Family Games LLC 703 863-6403
422 River Bend Rd Great Falls (22066) *(G-5948)*

Christian Fellowship Publs 804 794-5333
11515 Allecingie Pkwy North Chesterfield (23235) *(G-9843)*

Christian Light Publications (PA) **540 434-0768**
1051 Mount Clinton Pike Harrisonburg (22802) *(G-6300)*

Christian News & Comments 276 669-6972
44 New York St Bristol (24201) *(G-1970)*

Christian Observer 540 464-3570
56 Robinson Ln Lexington (24450) *(G-7390)*

(G-0000) Company's Geographic Section entry number

Christian Potier USA Inc	330 815-2202
113 Flycatcher Way Lake Frederick (22630) *(G-7155)*	
Christian Power Weekly News	703 658-5272
7218 Poplar St Annandale (22003) *(G-735)*	
Christian Publications	703 568-4300
1504 Lincoln Way Unit 305 Mc Lean (22102) *(G-8406)*	
Christina Bennett	703 489-9018
122 E Randall Ave Norfolk (23503) *(G-9483)*	
Christine Smith	703 399-1944
7509 Ashby Ln Unit D Alexandria (22315) *(G-429)*	
Christopher A Dixon	276 644-4222
25218 Lee Hwy Abingdon (24211) *(G-23)*	
Christopher Aiken	804 693-6003
8209 Spring Hill Frm Rd W Gloucester (23061) *(G-5841)*	
Christopher Hawkins	540 361-1679
1273 Central Park Blvd Fredericksburg (22401) *(G-5178)*	
Christopher K Reddersen	703 232-6691
5741 Wilshire Dr Warrenton (20187) *(G-14987)*	
Christopher L Bird	540 675-3409
100 Horseshoe Hollow Ln Washington (22747) *(G-15074)*	
Christopher Phillip & Moss LLC	757 525-0683
532 W 35th St Ste C Norfolk (23508) *(G-9484)*	
Christophers Belts & Wallets	757 253-2564
110 Ware Rd Williamsburg (23185) *(G-15219)*	
Christophers Woodworks LLC	757 404-2683
1900 Ballahack Rd Chesapeake (23322) *(G-3035)*	
Chronicle of The Horse LLC	540 687-6341
108 The Plains Rd Middleburg (20117) *(G-8718)*	
Chronicle of The Horse, The, Middleburg Also called Chronicle of The Horse LLC *(G-8718)*	
Chronicling Greatness, Williamsburg Also called Kennedy Projects LLC *(G-15266)*	
Cht USA Inc	804 271-9010
8021 Reycan Rd North Chesterfield (23237) *(G-9844)*	
Cht USA Inc	800 852-3147
7820 Whitepine Rd North Chesterfield (23237) *(G-9845)*	
Chucks Concrete Pumping LLC	804 347-3986
6717 Whitelake Dr Henrico (23231) *(G-6492)*	
Chuka LLC	443 837-5522
1501 Balch Dr S Apt 310 Leesburg (20175) *(G-7243)*	
Chula Junction, Amelia Court House Also called L J S Stores Inc *(G-662)*	
Church & Dwight Co Inc	804 524-8000
1851 Touchstone Rd South Chesterfield (23834) *(G-12799)*	
Church Guide	757 285-2222
293 Independence Blvd # 516 Virginia Beach (23462) *(G-14339)*	
Church Hill Gun Club Pubg LLC	804 236-0802
500 N 29th St Richmond (23223) *(G-11531)*	
Church Trucking LLC	757 386-1761
5328 Bellefield Rd Norfolk (23502) *(G-9485)*	
Cigs and Sodas, Portsmouth Also called Bellvue Corp *(G-10398)*	
CIO Controls Inc	703 365-2227
8140 Ashton Ave Ste 210 Manassas (20109) *(G-8049)*	
CIP Imprintables, South Hill Also called Capital Ideas Press *(G-12846)*	
Ciphercloud Inc	703 659-0533
560 Herndon Pkwy Ste 100 Herndon (20170) *(G-6640)*	
Circinus Software LLC	571 522-1724
6552 Palisades Dr Centreville (20121) *(G-2298)*	
Circle of Hope - Asca Fndation	800 306-4722
1101 King St Ste 625 Alexandria (22314) *(G-165)*	
Circle R Carrier Service Inc	434 401-5950
915 Lexington Tpke Amherst (24521) *(G-687)*	
Circle T Controls Inc	540 295-0188
36 Bridgeport Cir Stafford (22554) *(G-13131)*	
Circlepoint Publishing LLC	703 339-1580
10824 Anita Dr Lorton (22079) *(G-7473)*	
Circuit Solutions Intl LLC	703 994-6788
6111 Wilmington Dr Burke (22015) *(G-2186)*	
CIS Secure Computing Inc	703 996-0500
21050 Ashburn Crossing Dr Ashburn (20147) *(G-1254)*	
Cisco Systems Inc	703 484-5500
13600 Dulles Tech Dr Herndon (20171) *(G-6641)*	
Cislunar Space Development, Annandale Also called Dallas G Bienhoff *(G-738)*	
Citadel Studios Inc	407 766-6302
11571 Purse Dr Manassas (20112) *(G-8050)*	
Citapei Communications Inc	703 620-2316
2755 Viking Dr Herndon (20171) *(G-6642)*	
Cithinning Inc	804 370-4859
26721 Ruther Glen Rd Ruther Glen (22546) *(G-12452)*	
Citiwood Urban Forest Products	804 795-9220
5454 Charles City Rd Henrico (23231) *(G-6493)*	
Citizens Defense Solutions LLC	254 423-1612
5935 Hunter Crest Rd Woodbridge (22193) *(G-15671)*	
Citizens Upholstery & Furn Co	540 345-5060
125 E Lee Ave Vinton (24179) *(G-14170)*	
City Clay LLC	434 293-0808
700 Harris St Ste 104 Charlottesville (22903) *(G-2765)*	
City Connection Magazine LLC	757 570-9249
900 Granby St Ste 249 Norfolk (23510) *(G-9486)*	
City of Danville	434 799-5137
229 Northside Dr Danville (24540) *(G-3967)*	
City Publications Charlotte	434 917-5890
2883 Highway Nine O Three Bracey (23919) *(G-1923)*	

City Publications Richmond	804 621-0911
8106 S Mayfield Ln Mechanicsville (23111) *(G-8611)*	
City Spree of Woodbridge	
3092 Ps Business Ctr Dr Woodbridge (22192) *(G-15672)*	
Cives Corporation	540 667-3480
210 Cives Ln Winchester (22603) *(G-15402)*	
Civilian Agencies, Mc Lean Also called Northrop Grumman Systems Corp *(G-8515)*	
Civille Smoke Shop (PA)	**434 975-1175**
108 4th St Ne Charlottesville (22902) *(G-2766)*	
CJ & Associates LLC	301 461-2945
47025 Bennington Ct Sterling (20165) *(G-13370)*	
Cj9 Ltd	817 946-7421
101 Hillside Dr Buena Vista (24416) *(G-2140)*	
Cjc Industries Inc	757 227-6767
3813 Princess Anne Rd Virginia Beach (23456) *(G-14340)*	
CK Graphicwear LLC	804 464-1258
4001 Garden Rd Richmond (23235) *(G-11034)*	
CK Service Inc	757 486-5880
3966 Seeman Rd Virginia Beach (23452) *(G-14341)*	
CL Cabinetry Corporation	703 586-6766
6531 Little River Tpke A1 Alexandria (22312) *(G-430)*	
Cladding Facade Solutions LLC	571 748-7698
5109 Commonwealth Dr Fredericksburg (22407) *(G-5262)*	
Claire E Bose	323 898-2912
9561 Goddin Ct Toano (23168) *(G-13860)*	
Claren	571 403-0425
46950 Cmnty Plz Ste 216 Sterling (20164) *(G-13371)*	
Clarence D Campbell	540 291-2740
33 Cedar Bottom Rd Naturl BR STA (24579) *(G-9111)*	
Clarence Shelton Jr	434 710-0448
2328 Fairview Rd Chatham (24531) *(G-2923)*	
Clarios	703 886-3961
22001 Loudoun County Pkwy Ashburn (20147) *(G-1255)*	
Clarios	540 362-5500
3826 Thirlane Rd Nw Roanoke (24019) *(G-11909)*	
Clarios	540 366-0981
6701 Peters Creek Rd # 1 Roanoke (24019) *(G-11910)*	
Claritas Creative LLC	240 274-5029
1010 20th St S Arlington (22202) *(G-906)*	
Clarity Candles LLC	703 278-3760
1001 N Fillmore St Arlington (22201) *(G-907)*	
Clarivate Analytics (us) LLC	434 817-2000
375 Greenbrier Dr Ste 200 Charlottesville (22901) *(G-2609)*	
Clark & Clark LLC	757 264-9000
7474 N Shore Rd Norfolk (23505) *(G-9487)*	
Clark Hardwood Flr Refinishing	804 350-8871
2340 Mosby Rd Powhatan (23139) *(G-10538)*	
Clark Print Shop, Lebanon Also called Devin Clark *(G-7191)*	
Clark Welding Service	276 565-3607
369 Callahan Ave Appalachia (24216) *(G-796)*	
Clark's Custom Cut Sawmill, Jonesville Also called Jim L Clark *(G-7022)*	
Clarke B Gray	757 426-7227
1069 Dam Neck Rd Virginia Beach (23454) *(G-14342)*	
Clarke County Speed Shop	540 955-0479
607 E Main St Berryville (22611) *(G-1674)*	
Clarke Inc	434 847-5561
1110 Benni Ct Moneta (24121) *(G-8959)*	
Clarke Precision Machine Inc	276 228-5441
585 Stafford Umberger Dr Wytheville (24382) *(G-15882)*	
Clarke Times Courier, Winchester Also called Virginia News Group LLC *(G-15599)*	
Clarks Directional Boring	804 493-7475
47 Glenn St Montross (22520) *(G-9026)*	
Clarks Litho Inc	703 961-8888
14700 Avion Pkwy Ste 300 Chantilly (20151) *(G-2393)*	
Clarks Lumber & Millwork Inc	804 448-9985
1195 Intl Pkwy Ste 101 Fredericksburg (22406) *(G-5412)*	
Clary Logging Inc Randy J	434 636-5268
1192 Gasburg Rd Brodnax (23920) *(G-2100)*	
Clary Timber Co Inc	434 594-5055
3290 Ankum Rd Gasburg (23857) *(G-5658)*	
Classic Creations, Martinsville Also called Keith Sanders *(G-8304)*	
Classic Creations of Tidewater	757 548-1442
1335 Lindale Dr Ste B Chesapeake (23320) *(G-3036)*	
Classic Creations Screen Prtg	276 728-0540
358 Industrial Park Dr Hillsville (24343) *(G-6889)*	
Classic Edge LLC	804 794-4256
14300 Midlothian Tpke E Midlothian (23113) *(G-8795)*	
Classic Engravers	804 748-8717
12821 Percival St Chester (23831) *(G-3395)*	
Classic Granite and Marble Inc	804 404-8004
14301 Justice Rd Midlothian (23113) *(G-8796)*	
Classic Kitchens of Virginia	804 784-5075
12535 Patterson Ave Richmond (23238) *(G-11158)*	
Classic Machine Inc	804 798-1111
10989 Richardson Rd Ashland (23005) *(G-1391)*	
Classic Machine & Engineering, Ashland Also called Classic Machine Inc *(G-1391)*	
Classic Woodcraft	757 631-9354
884 E Little Creek Rd Norfolk (23518) *(G-9488)*	
Classico Publishing LLC	540 310-0067
119 Huntington Hills Ln Fredericksburg (22401) *(G-5179)*	

A
L
P
H
A
B
E
T
I
C

Classified - Space Systems Div, Sterling *Also called Indyne Inc* **(G-13427)**

Claude Cofer 540 330-9921
2488 Teass Ter Bedford (24523) *(G-1631)*

Claude David Sanders 276 386-6946
977 Nickelsville Hwy Gate City (24251) *(G-5661)*

Claudia & Co 540 433-1140
40 W Washington St Harrisonburg (22802) *(G-6301)*

Claudia Hand Painted, Harrisonburg *Also called Claudia & Co* **(G-6301)**

Claudia Ofori-Addo 540 840-5388
10 Naples Rd Stafford (22554) *(G-13132)*

Clay Decor LLC 607 654-7428
105 Buckingham Ct Roanoke (24019) *(G-11911)*

Clays Machine Shop & Welding 434 324-4997
2357 Pocket Rd Hurt (24563) *(G-6972)*

Clays Welding Co Inc 540 788-3992
10541 Bristersburg Rd Catlett (20119) *(G-2266)*

Clayton Homes Inc 276 395-7272
11416 Norton Coeburn Rd Coeburn (24230) *(G-3696)*

Clayton-Marcus Company Inc (HQ) **540 389-8671**
2121 Gardner St Elliston (24087) *(G-4344)*

CLC Enterprises LLC 540 622-3488
32 Mountain View Rd Flint Hill (22627) *(G-5015)*

Clean and Bless 434 324-7129
2044 Shula Dr Hurt (24563) *(G-6973)*

Clean Building LLC 703 589-9544
4104 Sunburst Ct Alexandria (22303) *(G-431)*

Clean Marine Electronics Inc 703 847-5142
1918 Anderson Rd Falls Church (22043) *(G-4775)*

Clean Power & Service LLC 703 443-1717
20413 Crimson Pl Leesburg (20175) *(G-7244)*

Clean Way Services LLC 757 606-1840
1121 High St Portsmouth (23704) *(G-10408)*

Cleaning Up, Mc Lean *Also called Frangipani Inc* **(G-8436)**

Cleanpowerpartners 301 651-0690
6614 The Pkwy Alexandria (22310) *(G-432)*

Cleanvent Dryer Exhust Spclsts 804 730-1754
6115 Silverbell Ln Mechanicsville (23111) *(G-8612)*

Clear Vision Publishing 757 753-9422
103 Wreck Shoal Dr Newport News (23606) *(G-9200)*

Clear Water Manufacturing 434 582-9511
161 Crennel Dr Madison Heights (24572) *(G-7869)*

Clearedjobsnet Inc 703 871-0037
1069 W Broad St Ste 775 Falls Church (22046) *(G-4905)*

Clearimage Creations 804 883-0199
16253 Wild Cherry Ln Montpelier (23192) *(G-9015)*

Clearly-You Inc 757 351-0346
1700 S Park Ct Unit B Chesapeake (23320) *(G-3037)*

Clearview Industries LLC 540 312-0899
2180 Merifield Rd Nw Willis (24380) *(G-15358)*

Clearview Software Corporation 804 381-6300
1607a Enterprise Dr Lynchburg (24502) *(G-7679)*

Clements Backhoe LLC 804 598-6230
1886 Nichols Rd Powhatan (23139) *(G-10539)*

Clevengers Welding Inc 540 662-2191
134 Slate Ln Stephenson (22656) *(G-13332)*

Clifford Aeroworks LLC 703 304-3675
42 Whittingham Cir Potomac Falls (20165) *(G-10508)*

Clifton Creek Press Inc 703 786-9180
7500 Weymouth Hill Rd Clifton (20124) *(G-3661)*

Clifton Laboratories 703 830-0368
7236 Clifton Rd. Clifton (20124) *(G-3662)*

Climet Instruments 434 984-5634
1932 Arlington Blvd Ste 6 Charlottesville (22903) *(G-2767)*

Clinch River LLC 276 963-5271
21405 Gvrnor G C Pery Hwy Tazewell (24651) *(G-13830)*

Clinch Valley Printing Company 276 988-5410
205 Walnut St North Tazewell (24630) *(G-10096)*

Clinch Valley Publishing Co 276 762-7671
16541 Russell St Saint Paul (24283) *(G-12465)*

Clinch Valley Repair Service 276 964-5191
2737 Pounding Mill Br Rd Pounding Mill (24637) *(G-10517)*

Clinch Valley Times, Saint Paul *Also called Clinch Valley Publishing Co* **(G-12465)**

Cline Automotive Inc 804 271-9107
2530 Willis Rd North Chesterfield (23237) *(G-9846)*

Cline Chemicals, Richlands *Also called Cal Syd Inc* **(G-11015)**

Cline Woodworks LLC 540 721-2286
5137 Scruggs Rd Moneta (24121) *(G-8960)*

Clinpak Technologies LLC 410 357-4454
358 Sandy Beach Rd Heathsville (22473) *(G-6460)*

Clipper Magazine LLC 888 569-5100
5709 Hampton Forest Way Fairfax (22030) *(G-4606)*

Clodfelter Machine Inc 804 744-3848
3017 Warbro Rd Midlothian (23112) *(G-8797)*

Closed Loop LLC 804 648-4802
1801 Libbie Ave Richmond (23226) *(G-11159)*

Closet and Beyond 703 962-7894
2300 24th Rd S Apt 927 Arlington (22206) *(G-908)*

Closet Pioneers LLC 703 844-0400
7300 Lockport Pl Ste 11 Lorton (22079) *(G-7474)*

Cloud Cabin Arts 434 218-3020
1719b Allied St Charlottesville (22903) *(G-2768)*

Cloud Ridge Labs LLC 434 477-5060
1173 Research Way Forest (24551) *(G-5060)*

Cloudera Gvrnment Slutions Inc 888 789-1488
8281 Greensboro Dr # 450 Tysons (22102) *(G-13942)*

Cloudridge, Forest *Also called Cloud Ridge Labs LLC* **(G-5060)**

Clover LLC 703 771-4286
202 Church St Se Ste 210 Leesburg (20175) *(G-7245)*

Clover Yarns Inc 434 454-7151
1030 Tanyard Branch Rd Clover (24534) *(G-3691)*

Cloverdale Company Inc 540 777-4414
2124 Country Club Rd Troutville (24175) *(G-13907)*

Cloverdale Lumber Co Inc 434 822-5017
5863 S Boston Hwy Sutherlin (24594) *(G-13806)*

Cluetrust, Reston *Also called Gbp Software LLC* **(G-10856)**

Clyde D Seeley Sr 757 721-6397
5864 Fitztown Rd Virginia Beach (23457) *(G-14343)*

CM Harris Industries LLC 276 632-8438
2191 Greenhill Dr Martinsville (24112) *(G-8275)*

CM Welding LLC 540 539-4723
523 Bluebird Trl Winchester (22602) *(G-15403)*

CMC Interiors LLC 804 883-5671
2110 Ruffin Rd Richmond (23234) *(G-11035)*

CMC King George, King George *Also called Commercial Metals Company* **(G-7084)**

CMC Printing and Graphics Inc 804 744-5821
13513 E Boundary Rd Ste A Midlothian (23112) *(G-8798)*

CMC Rebar Virginia, Fredericksburg *Also called C M C Steel Fabricators Inc* **(G-5256)**

CMC Rebar Virginia, Norfolk *Also called Commercial Metals Company* **(G-9499)**

CMC Steel Products, Farmville *Also called SMI-Owen Steel Company Inc* **(G-4958)**

Cme Concrete LLC 757 713-0495
245 Loch Cir Hampton (23669) *(G-6114)*

Cmg Contracting, Chesapeake *Also called American Orthotic* **(G-2972)**

Cmg Impressions Inc 804 556-2551
2746 Maidens Loop Ste F Maidens (23102) *(G-7887)*

CMI 703 356-2190
8130 Boone Blvd Ste 330 Vienna (22182) *(G-14028)*

Cnc Metal Design, Manassas *Also called Capstone Industries LLC* **(G-8045)**

Cnc Models LLC 703 669-0709
620 Marshall Dr Ne Leesburg (20176) *(G-7246)*

Cnc Printing Inc 703 378-5222
14220 Sullyfield Cir J Chantilly (20151) *(G-2394)*

CNE Manufacturing Services LLC 540 216-0884
173 Keith St Ste 3 Warrenton (20186) *(G-14988)*

Cnir, Reston *Also called Bae Systems Info & Elec Sys* **(G-10797)**

CNJ Beekeepers Inc 703 378-1629
4719 Lewis Woods Ct Chantilly (20151) *(G-2395)*

Cnk Machine Manufacturing Inc 804 320-1082
615 Moorefield Park Dr A North Chesterfield (23236) *(G-9847)*

Cnl Software Inc 317 522-0313
19775 Belmont Executive P # 420 Ashburn (20147) *(G-1256)*

Cnv Marine Fuel Specialist LLC 757 615-2666
1509 Taft Rd Chesapeake (23322) *(G-3038)*

Cnx Gas Corporation 276 596-5000
627 Claypool Hill Mall Rd Cedar Bluff (24609) *(G-2273)*

Co Construct LLC 434 326-0500
1814 Clay Dr Crozet (22932) *(G-3829)*

Coach LLC 757 925-2862
1007 Obici Indus Blvd Suffolk (23434) *(G-13684)*

Coal Energy Resources Inc 276 676-3101
966 W Main St Ste C Abingdon (24210) *(G-24)*

Coal Extraction Holdings LLC (HQ) **276 466-3322**
1005 Glenway Ave Bristol (24201) *(G-1971)*

Coal Fillers Inc (PA) **276 322-4675**
Hc 640 Bluefield (24605) *(G-1860)*

Coalfield Progress (PA) **276 679-1101**
725 Park Ave Sw Norton (24273) *(G-10115)*

Coalzoomcom 304 920-2588
1448 Carrolton Way Chesapeake (23320) *(G-3039)*

Coastal Aerospace Inc 757 787-3704
21419 Fair Oaks Rd Melfa (23410) *(G-8709)*

Coastal Cabinets By Jenna LLC 757 339-0710
1017 Laskin Rd Ste 101 Virginia Beach (23451) *(G-14344)*

Coastal Caulking Sealants LLC 757 679-8201
109 Duffield Pl Chesapeake (23320) *(G-3040)*

Coastal Constructors LLC 757 545-0080
1316 Yacht Dr Ste 307 Chesapeake (23320) *(G-3041)*

Coastal Edge 757 422-5739
353 Village Rd Virginia Beach (23454) *(G-14345)*

Coastal Hmpton Rads Vllyball C 757 759-0204
102 Ct Deayllon Poquoson (23662) *(G-10367)*

Coastal Leak Detection 757 486-0180
2532 Peritan Rd Virginia Beach (23454) *(G-14346)*

Coastal Pies, Suffolk *Also called Virginia Culinary Pathways LLC* **(G-13778)**

Coastal Precast Systems 571 442-8648
227 Town Branch Ter Sw Leesburg (20175) *(G-7247)*

Coastal Precast Systems LLC (PA) **757 545-5215**
1316 Yacht Dr Ste 307 Chesapeake (23320) *(G-3042)*

Coastal Prsttics Orthotics LLC (PA) 757 892-5300
433 Network Sta Chesapeake (23320) *(G-3043)*

Coastal Prsttics Orthotics LLC 757 240-4228
11818 Rock Landing Dr # 104 Newport News (23606) *(G-9201)*

Coastal Safety Inc 757 499-9415
5045 Admiral Wright Rd Virginia Beach (23462) *(G-14347)*

Coastal Screen Printing 541 441-6358
12 Provider Ct Hampton (23665) *(G-6277)*

Coastal Screen Printing 757 764-1409
909 Bickerton Ct Newport News (23608) *(G-9202)*

Coastal Services & Tech LLC 757 833-0550
110 Key Cir Yorktown (23692) *(G-15942)*

Coastal Tags & Supply LLC 757 995-4139
133 Thames Dr Virginia Beach (23452) *(G-14348)*

Coastal Threads Inc 757 495-2677
750 Lord Dunmore Dr # 101 Virginia Beach (23464) *(G-14349)*

Coastal Waters Sales & Svc LLC 757 893-9040
801 Butler St Ste 17 Chesapeake (23323) *(G-3044)*

Coastal Wood Imports Inc 434 799-1117
116 Walden Ct Danville (24541) *(G-3968)*

Cobalt Co 888 426-2258
2550 S Clark St Ste 850 Arlington (22202) *(G-909)*

Cobalt Company 888 426-2258
2511 Richmond Hwy Ste 850 Arlington (22202) *(G-910)*

Cobbler Mountain Cellars 540 364-2802
5909 Long Fall Ln Delaplane (20144) *(G-4074)*

Cobehn Inc 540 665-0707
640 Airport Rd Winchester (22602) *(G-15404)*

Cobehn System, Winchester Also called Cobehn Inc *(G-15404)*

Cobham AES Holdings Inc (HQ) **703 414-5300**
2121 Crystal Dr Ste 625 Arlington (22202) *(G-911)*

Cobham Analytical Solutions, Centreville Also called Parsons Corporation *(G-2327)*

Cobham Corp N Amer Arlington, Arlington Also called Cobham Management Services Inc *(G-913)*

Cobham Defense Products Inc 703 414-5300
2121 Crystal Dr Ste 625 Arlington (22202) *(G-912)*

Cobham Management Services Inc 703 414-5300
2121 Crystal Dr Ste 625 Arlington (22202) *(G-913)*

Coblentz Custom Cabinets 231 362-2728
121 Blue Ledge Loop Rd Amherst (24521) *(G-688)*

Cobweb Industries LLC 703 834-1000
1506 Coat Ridge Rd Herndon (20170) *(G-6643)*

Coca Cola Enterprises 703 578-6447
5401 Seminary Rd Alexandria (22311) *(G-166)*

Coca-Cola, Roanoke Also called Ccbcc Operations LLC *(G-12060)*

Coca-Cola, Alexandria Also called Coca Cola Enterprises *(G-166)*

Coca-Cola Bottling 800 241-2653
5349 Seminary Rd Alexandria (22311) *(G-167)*

Coca-Cola Consolidated Inc 540 886-2494
48 Christians Creek Rd Staunton (24401) *(G-13248)*

Coca-Cola Consolidated Inc 540 361-7500
57 Commerce Pkwy Fredericksburg (22406) *(G-5413)*

Coca-Cola Consolidated Inc 757 890-8700
2000 Monticello Ave Norfolk (23517) *(G-9489)*

Coca-Cola Consolidated Inc 703 578-6759
5401 Seminary Rd Alexandria (22311) *(G-168)*

Coca-Cola Consolidated Inc 804 328-5300
4530 Oakleys Ln Richmond (23231) *(G-11160)*

Coca-Cola Consolidated Inc 757 446-3000
2000 Monticello Ave Norfolk (23517) *(G-9490)*

Cochran Inds Inc - Wytheville 276 498-3836
8112 Riverside Dr Oakwood (24631) *(G-10165)*

Cochran Industries Inc - VA (PA) **276 498-3836**
8112 Riverside Dr Oakwood (24631) *(G-10166)*

Cochrane USA Inc (PA) **202 434-8163**
3551 Lee Hill Dr Fredericksburg (22408) *(G-5263)*

Cochrans Lumber & Millwork Inc 540 955-4142
523 Jack Enders Blvd Berryville (22611) *(G-1675)*

Cocoa Mia Inc 540 695-0224
109 E Main St Floyd (24091) *(G-5019)*

Cocoa Mia Inc 540 493-4341
537 Needmore Ln Ne Floyd (24091) *(G-5020)*

Code Blue 757 438-1507
5689 Brandon Blvd Virginia Beach (23464) *(G-14350)*

Codehero, Fredericksburg Also called MCA Systems Inc *(G-5204)*

Codeworx Lc 571 306-3859
2256 N Beauregard St # 1 Alexandria (22311) *(G-169)*

Cody Sterling Hawkins 276 477-0238
110 Terrance Cir Bristol (24201) *(G-1972)*

Coe & Co Inc 757 497-7709
5008 Cleveland St Virginia Beach (23462) *(G-14351)*

Coffman Stairs LLC (PA) **276 783-7251**
138 E Main St 1 Marion (24354) *(G-8225)*

Coghill Composition Co Inc 804 714-1100
10801 Tealby Ct Midlothian (23112) *(G-8799)*

Cogitari Inc 301 237-7777
110 Saratoga Waye Ne Vienna (22180) *(G-14029)*

Cognition Point Inc 703 402-8945
25492 Tomey Ct Aldie (20105) *(G-104)*

Cogo Aire LLC 757 332-3551
5521 Haden Rd Virginia Beach (23455) *(G-14352)*

Coil Exchange Inc 703 369-7150
9203 Enterprise Ct Ste B Manassas Park (20111) *(G-8196)*

Cojax Oil and Gas Corporation 703 216-8606
3033 Wilson Blvd E-605 Arlington (22201) *(G-914)*

Cold Company LLC 757 589-7034
2804 Colchester Cres Norfolk (23504) *(G-9491)*

Cold Front Music LLC 703 398-6187
7317 Ardglass Dr Lorton (22079) *(G-7475)*

Cold Press II LLC 757 227-0809
1902 Colley Ave Norfolk (23517) *(G-9492)*

Cold Roll Steel Mch & Mfg LLC 804 275-9229
8808c Metro Ct North Chesterfield (23237) *(G-9848)*

Coldens Concepts LLC 757 644-9535
3613 Ahoy Dr Chesapeake (23321) *(G-3045)*

Cole Electric of Virginia Inc 276 935-7562
20104 Riverside Dr Grundy (24614) *(G-6029)*

Cole Software LLC 540 456-8210
736 Fox Hollow Rd Afton (22920) *(G-77)*

Cole Tool Inc 540 942-5174
124 Hickory Hill Ln Fishersville (22939) *(G-5002)*

Coleman & Sons Trucking LLC 434 247-1011
121 Quail Springs Ct South Hill (23970) *(G-12847)*

Coleman and Coleman Software 804 276-5372
8108 Surreywood Dr North Chesterfield (23235) *(G-9849)*

Coleman Lumber Co Inc Robert S 540 854-5711
7019 Everona Rd Culpeper (22701) *(G-3879)*

Coleman Microwave Co 540 984-8848
109 Molineau Rd Edinburg (22824) *(G-4301)*

Colfax Corporation 757 328-3987
10571 Telg Rd Ste 201 Glen Allen (23059) *(G-5715)*

Colin K Eagen 703 716-7505
1893 Preston White Dr Reston (20191) *(G-10822)*

Collaborative AV, Richmond Also called Collabrtive Tech Cmmnctons Cor *(G-11161)*

Collabrtive Tech Cmmnctons Cor 804 477-8695
12830 West Creek Pkwy F Richmond (23238) *(G-11161)*

Collecting Concepts Inc 804 285-0994
8100 Three Chopt Rd # 226 Richmond (23229) *(G-11162)*

College and University Educati 540 820-7384
343 W Bruce St Harrisonburg (22801) *(G-6302)*

College Publishing 804 364-8410
12309 Lynwood Dr Glen Allen (23059) *(G-5716)*

Collegian, The, Richmond Also called University of Richmond *(G-11800)*

Collegiate Pacific, Roanoke Also called Wool Felt Products Inc *(G-12230)*

Collegiateskyviews LLC 540 520-6394
1317 Longview Rd Roanoke (24018) *(G-11912)*

Collier Research and Dev Corp (PA) **757 825-0000**
760 Pilot House Dr Ste A Newport News (23606) *(G-9203)*

Collins Machine Works, Portsmouth Also called Artcraft Fabricators Inc *(G-10393)*

Collins Sawmill and Loggin LLC 276 694-7521
3567 Clark House Farm Rd Stuart (24171) *(G-13608)*

Collins Wldg & Fabrication LLC 540 392-8171
833 Hale Rd Ne Check (24072) *(G-2943)*

Collinsville Engraving LLC 276 647-8596
3410 Virginia Ave Collinsville (24078) *(G-3710)*

Collinsville Printing Co 276 666-4400
79 Beaver Creek Dr Martinsville (24112) *(G-8276)*

Colonial Air Filter Clg LLC 757 229-1110
2783 Lake Powell Rd Williamsburg (23185) *(G-15220)*

Colonial Apps LLC 804 744-8535
4438 Old Fox Trl Midlothian (23112) *(G-8800)*

Colonial Awards, Gloucester Also called Ds & RC Enterprises LLC *(G-5846)*

Colonial Barns Inc (PA) **757 482-2234**
953 Bedford St Chesapeake (23322) *(G-3046)*

Colonial Barns Inc 757 420-8653
985 S Military Hwy Virginia Beach (23464) *(G-14353)*

Colonial Beach Brewing LLC 540 760-5661
215 Washington Ave Ste C Colonial Beach (22443) *(G-3723)*

Colonial Brass, Richmond Also called Colonial Plating Shop *(G-11532)*

Colonial Chevrolet Company LP 757 455-4500
6252 E Virginia Bch Blvd Norfolk (23502) *(G-9493)*

Colonial Commercial Elec Co 804 720-2455
832 Court Hse Landing Rd King Queen Ch (23085) *(G-7125)*

Colonial East Distributors LLC 844 802-4427
413 Davis St Ste 107 Virginia Beach (23462) *(G-14354)*

Colonial Hardwoods, Springfield Also called Nova Lumber & Millwork LLC *(G-13061)*

Colonial Iron Works Inc 804 862-4141
215 N South St Petersburg (23803) *(G-10312)*

Colonial Kitchen & Cabinets 757 898-1332
7621 G Washington Mem 2 Yorktown (23692) *(G-15943)*

Colonial Kitchens, Yorktown Also called Colonial Kitchen & Cabinets *(G-15943)*

Colonial Metal Crafts, Richmond Also called Dennis H Fredrick *(G-11182)*

Colonial Plating Shop 804 648-6276
9 S 1st St Richmond (23219) *(G-11532)*

Colonial Rail Systems LLC 804 932-5200
9000 Deer Trace Ln New Kent (23124) *(G-9129)*

Colonial Readi-Mix Concrete 757 888-8500
1571 Manufacture Dr Williamsburg (23185) *(G-15221)*

A
L
P
H
A
B
E
T
I
C

Colonial Redi-Mix Concrete, Williamsburg *Also called Colonial Readi-Mix Concrete* ***(G-15221)***
Colonial Sign, South Chesterfield *Also called Michael A Latham* ***(G-12816)***
Colonial Tailors Chalk...850 622-2270
2041 Midway Ave Petersburg (23803) ***(G-10313)***
Colonial Tailors Chalk Inc...757 291-2445
2041 Midway Ave Petersburg (23803) ***(G-10314)***
Colonial Wldg Fabrication Inc...757 459-2680
5801 Curlew Dr Norfolk (23502) ***(G-9494)***
Colonnas Ship Yard Inc (PA)...**757 545-2414**
400 E Indian River Rd Norfolk (23523) ***(G-9495)***
Colonnas Ship Yard Inc...757 545-5311
400 E Indian River Rd Norfolk (23523) ***(G-9496)***
Colonnas Ship Yard Inc...757 545-2414
400 E Indian River Rd Norfolk (23523) ***(G-9497)***
Colonnas Shipyard...757 962-0508
150 S Main St Norfolk (23523) ***(G-9498)***
Colony Construction Asp LLC...434 767-9930
920 Dutchtown Rd Burkeville (23922) ***(G-2207)***
Colony Construction Asp LLC (PA)...**804 598-1400**
2333 Anderson Hwy Powhatan (23139) ***(G-10540)***
Color Quest LLC...540 433-4890
105 Newman Ave Harrisonburg (22801) ***(G-6303)***
Color Quest LLC...540 896-8186
300 Waterman Dr Ste 100 Harrisonburg (22802) ***(G-6304)***
Color Svc Prtg & Graphics Inc...703 321-8100
2927 Gallows Rd Ste 101 Falls Church (22042) ***(G-4776)***
Colorful Words Media LLC...757 268-9690
2104 Newton Rd Hampton (23663) ***(G-6115)***
Colornet Prtg & Graphics Inc...703 406-9301
22570 Glenn Dr Sterling (20164) ***(G-13372)***
Coltrane Welding & Fabrication, Radford *Also called Danny Coltrane* ***(G-10711)***
Columbia Books Inc (PA)...**800 677-3789**
1560 Wilson Blvd Ste 825 Arlington (22209) ***(G-915)***
Columbia Mrror GL Grgetown Inc...703 333-9990
7101 Wimsatt Rd Springfield (22151) ***(G-12977)***
Columbus McKinnon Corporation...276 475-3124
22364 Jeb Stuart Hwy Damascus (24236) ***(G-3946)***
Columbus Woodworks...434 528-1052
905a Graves Mill Rd Lynchburg (24502) ***(G-7680)***
Combat Bound LLC...757 343-3399
6400 Sandgate Dr N Suffolk (23435) ***(G-13685)***
Combat Coating...757 468-9020
851 Seahawk Cir Ste 108 Virginia Beach (23452) ***(G-14355)***
Combat Coatings LLC...757 468-9020
1132 Little Neck Rd Virginia Beach (23452) ***(G-14356)***
Combat V Tactical...540 604-0235
304 Laurel Ave Fredericksburg (22408) ***(G-5264)***
Combustion Technologies Inc...434 432-1428
1804 Slatesville Rd Chatham (24531) ***(G-2924)***
Comcast Tech Center...571 229-9112
9450 Innovation Dr Manassas (20110) ***(G-7925)***
Comfort & Support, Fairfax *Also called Thomas Hegens* ***(G-4569)***
Comfortrac Inc...703 891-0455
7901 Jones Branch Dr 6th Mc Lean (22102) ***(G-8407)***
Command & Control Systems, Reston *Also called Engility LLC* ***(G-10847)***
Command & Control Systems, Chesapeake *Also called Engility LLC* ***(G-3089)***
Commercial Copies...757 473-0234
223 Expressway Ct Virginia Beach (23462) ***(G-14357)***
Commercial Custom Cabinet Inc...804 228-2100
1606 Magnolia St Richmond (23222) ***(G-11533)***
Commercial Fueling 24/7 Inc...540 338-6457
115 E Main St Purcellville (20132) ***(G-10656)***
Commercial Hvacr, Manassas *Also called Commercial Tech Inc* ***(G-8051)***
Commercial Machine Inc...804 329-5405
2706 Rady St Richmond (23222) ***(G-11534)***
Commercial Machine & Fabg...276 944-3643
28219 Robindale Rd Meadowview (24361) ***(G-8594)***
Commercial Metals Company...540 775-8501
10924 Dennis W Kerns Pkwy King George (22485) ***(G-7084)***
Commercial Metals Company...757 625-4201
1344 Ballentine Blvd Norfolk (23504) ***(G-9499)***
Commercial Press Inc...540 869-3496
965 Green St Stephens City (22655) ***(G-13313)***
Commercial Printers, Staunton *Also called Schmids Printing* ***(G-13290)***
Commercial Prtg Drect Mail Svc...757 422-0606
208 16th St Virginia Beach (23451) ***(G-14358)***
Commercial Ready Mix Pdts Inc...757 925-0939
1275 Portsmouth Blvd Suffolk (23434) ***(G-13686)***
Commercial Ready Mix Pdts Inc...757 420-5800
1888 S Military Hwy Chesapeake (23320) ***(G-3047)***
Commercial Tech Inc...703 468-1339
8986 Mike Garcia Dr Manassas (20109) ***(G-8051)***
Commercial Tool & Die Inc...540 364-3922
7591 E Main St Marshall (20115) ***(G-8251)***
Commercial Water Works Inc...434 534-8244
1167 Greenbrook Ct Forest (24551) ***(G-5061)***
Commodore Sales LLC...804 794-1992
11002 Trade Rd North Chesterfield (23236) ***(G-9850)***

Common Health H2o-Blue Ridge, Charlottesville *Also called Commonwlth H20 Svcs Inc-Blue R* ***(G-2610)***
Commonhealth Botanicals LLC...434 906-2227
604 Bleeker St Charlottesville (22903) ***(G-2769)***
Commonlook...202 902-0986
1600 Wilson Blvd Arlington (22209) ***(G-916)***
Commonwealth Girl Scout Council...804 340-2835
4900 Augusta Ave Richmond (23230) ***(G-11163)***
Commonwealth Laminating Coating, Martinsville *Also called Suntek Holding Company* ***(G-8339)***
Commonwealth Polygraph Svcs LLC...540 219-9382
6121 James Madison Hwy Warrenton (20187) ***(G-14989)***
Commonwealth Dimensional, Ashland *Also called Commonwealth Specialty Packg* ***(G-1393)***
Commonwealth Galvanizing LLC...804 368-0025
10988 Leadbetter Rd Ashland (23005) ***(G-1392)***
Commonwealth Graphics Inc...703 495-0733
8613 Mallard Vw Fairfax Station (22039) ***(G-4702)***
Commonwealth Hams Inc...434 846-4267
3700 Candlers Mountain Rd Lynchburg (24502) ***(G-7681)***
Commonwealth Mechanical Inc...757 825-0740
504 Rotary St Hampton (23661) ***(G-6116)***
Commonwealth Mfg & Dev...276 699-2089
5226 Ivanhoe Rd Ivanhoe (24350) ***(G-7003)***
Commonwealth Orthotics & Prost...434 836-4736
413 Munt Cross Rd Ste 107 Danville (24540) ***(G-3969)***
Commonwealth Printing, Norfolk *Also called Senior Publ Free Seniority* ***(G-9717)***
Commonwealth Provisions LLC...540 699-0222
11720 Main St Ste 128 Fredericksburg (22408) ***(G-5265)***
Commonwealth Rapid Dry Inc...757 592-0203
501 Old York Hampton Hwy Yorktown (23692) ***(G-15944)***
Commonwealth Recycling Svcs...931 289-3645
5226 Ivanhoe Rd Ivanhoe (24350) ***(G-7004)***
Commonwealth Reprographics...434 845-1203
58 9th St Lynchburg (24504) ***(G-7682)***
Commonwealth Rescue Systems...540 438-8972
615 Pleasant Valley Rd Harrisonburg (22801) ***(G-6305)***
Commonwealth Sign & Design...804 358-5507
2025 W Broad St Richmond (23220) ***(G-11535)***
Commonwealth Specialty Packg...804 271-0157
12124 Washington Hwy Ashland (23005) ***(G-1393)***
Commonwealth Surgical Solution...804 330-0988
720 Mrfield Pk Dr Ste 105 North Chesterfield (23236) ***(G-9851)***
Commonwealth Times...804 828-1058
817 W Broad St Richmond (23284) ***(G-11536)***
Commonwealth Toner and Ink, Richmond *Also called Jennifer Omohundro* ***(G-11255)***
Commonwlth H20 Svcs Inc-Blue R...434 975-4426
325 Greenbrier Dr Charlottesville (22901) ***(G-2610)***
Commonwlth Orthtics Prosthetic...434 836-4736
949 Piney Forest Rd Ste 1 Danville (24540) ***(G-3970)***
Commonwlth Prmtnl/Dctional LLC...540 887-2321
24 Idlewood Blvd Staunton (24401) ***(G-13249)***
Commonwlth Soccer Programs LLC...804 794-2092
1153 Huguenot Trl Midlothian (23113) ***(G-8801)***
Commscope Technologies LLC...703 548-6777
422 N Alfred St Alexandria (22314) ***(G-170)***
Commscope Technologies LLC...703 726-5500
19700 Janelia Farm Blvd Ashburn (20147) ***(G-1257)***
Commscope Technologies LLC...434 386-5300
140 Vista Centre Dr Forest (24551) ***(G-5062)***
Communications Concepts Inc...703 643-2200
7481 Huntsman Blvd # 720 Springfield (22153) ***(G-12978)***
Communications Vehicle Svc LLC...703 542-7449
25395 Pleasant Valley Rd Chantilly (20152) ***(G-2529)***
Communications-Applied Tech Co (PA)...**703 481-0068**
11250 Roger Bacon Dr # 14 Reston (20190) ***(G-10823)***
Compass Coal Services LLC...804 218-8880
9 Stonehurst Grn Richmond (23226) ***(G-11164)***
Compass Group Usa Inc...757 485-4401
914 Cavalier Blvd Chesapeake (23323) ***(G-3048)***
Compass Publications Inc (PA)...**703 524-3136**
4600 Fairfax Dr Ste 304 Arlington (22203) ***(G-917)***
Complete Sign Inc...571 276-8407
2832 Dorr Ave Ste B Fairfax (22031) ***(G-4429)***
Complex Prints LLC...804 274-0266
12 W Broad St Richmond (23220) ***(G-11537)***
Complexible, Arlington *Also called Stardog Union* ***(G-1175)***
Composition Systems Inc...703 205-0000
840 S Pickett St Alexandria (22304) ***(G-171)***
Compost Livin LLC...703 362-9378
3719 Rose Ln Annandale (22003) ***(G-736)***
Compost Rva LLC...804 639-0363
6607 Southshore Dr Midlothian (23112) ***(G-8802)***
Comprhnsive Enrgy Slutions Inc...434 989-2547
6243 Flintstone Dr Barboursville (22923) ***(G-1560)***
Compu Dynamics LLC (PA)...**703 796-6070**
22446 Davis Dr Ste 187 Sterling (20164) ***(G-13373)***
Compu Management Corp...276 669-3822
3127 Lee Hwy Ste B Bristol (24202) ***(G-2013)***

Computational Systems Inc 804 858-5800
  201 Wylderose Dr Midlothian (23113) *(G-8803)*

Computer Corp America Federal, Arlington *Also called Computer Corp of America* *(G-918)*

Computer Corp of America 703 241-7830
  4025 38th Pl N Arlington (22207) *(G-918)*

Computer Solution Co of VA Inc 804 794-3491
  200 S 10th St Ste 900 Richmond (23219) *(G-11538)*

Computerized Imaging Reference 757 855-1127
  900 Asbury Ave Norfolk (23513) *(G-9500)*

Computing Technologies Inc (PA) 703 280-8800
  6372 Mechanicsville Tpke # 112 Mechanicsville (23111) *(G-8613)*

Computing With Kids 703 444-9005
  903 Falls Bridge Ln Great Falls (22066) *(G-5949)*

Comsaco Inc 757 466-9188
  3737 E Virginia Bch Blvd Norfolk (23502) *(G-9501)*

Comscore Inc (PA) 703 438-2000
  11950 Democracy Dr # 600 Reston (20190) *(G-10824)*

Comsonics Inc (PA) 540 434-5965
  1350 Port Republic Rd Harrisonburg (22801) *(G-6306)*

Comsonics Electronics Mfg Svcs, Weyers Cave *Also called Cems Inc (G-15170)*

Comxi World LLC 804 299-5234
  5231 Hickory Park Dr B Glen Allen (23059) *(G-5717)*

Conaways Woodworking LLC 703 530-8725
  9201 Fairway Ct Manassas Park (20111) *(G-8197)*

Concept Products Inc 434 793-9952
  338 Winston Cir Danville (24540) *(G-3971)*

Concilio Labs Inc 571 282-4248
  1640 Boro Pl 400 Mc Lean (22102) *(G-8408)*

Concoa America, Virginia Beach *Also called Controls Corporation America (G-14363)*

Concord Logging 434 660-1889
  465 Toll Gate Rd Concord (24538) *(G-3758)*

Concrete Castings Inc 540 427-3006
  1909 Progress Dr Se Roanoke (24013) *(G-12068)*

Concrete Creations Inc 757 427-6226
  3601 Dam Neck Rd Virginia Beach (23453) *(G-14359)*

Concrete Creations Inc (PA) 757 427-1581
  1601 Nanneys Creek Rd Virginia Beach (23457) *(G-14360)*

Concrete Pipe & Precast LLC (PA) 804 798-6068
  11352 Virginia Precast Rd Ashland (23005) *(G-1394)*

Concrete Pipe & Precast LLC 757 485-5228
  3801 Cook Blvd Chesapeake (23323) *(G-3049)*

Concrete Pipe & Precast LLC 804 752-1311
  10364 Design Rd Ashland (23005) *(G-1395)*

Concrete Pipe & Products Co, Chesapeake *Also called Forterra Pipe & Precast
LLC (G-3108)*

Concrete Precast Systems, Chesapeake *Also called Coastal Constructors LLC (G-3041)*

Concrete Precast Systems Inc 757 545-5215
  1134 Bayshore Rd Cape Charles (23310) *(G-2232)*

Concrete Precast Systems Inc (PA) 757 545-5215
  1316 Yacht Dr Chesapeake (23320) *(G-3050)*

Concrete Precast Systems Inc 703 327-4112
  44146 Wade Dr Chantilly (20152) *(G-2530)*

Concrete Ready Mixed Corp 540 345-3846
  22 7th St Salem (24153) *(G-12490)*

Concrete Sales Office, Blue Ridge *Also called Boxley Materials Company (G-1847)*

Concrete Specialties Inc 540 982-0777
  1420 16th St Se Roanoke (24014) *(G-12069)*

Concrete World, Rustburg *Also called First Paper Co Inc (G-12439)*

Concur Technologies Inc 703 403-8764
  1919 Gallows Rd Ste 800 Vienna (22182) *(G-14030)*

Confero Foods LLC 703 334-7516
  8176 Mccauley Way Lorton (22079) *(G-7476)*

Confetti Advertising Inc 276 646-5806
  1207 Horseshoe Bend Rd Chilhowie (24319) *(G-3548)*

Conforma Contact Lenses, Norfolk *Also called Conforma Laboratories Inc (G-9502)*

Conforma Laboratories Inc 757 321-0200
  4707 Colley Ave Norfolk (23508) *(G-9502)*

Congero Technology Group Inc 434 266-4376
  12110 Sunset Hills Rd Reston (20190) *(G-10825)*

Conglobal Industries LLC 757 487-5100
  806 Meads Ct Chesapeake (23323) *(G-3051)*

Conicville Ostrich, Mount Jackson *Also called Lutz Farm & Services (G-9075)*

Conmat Group Inc 540 433-9128
  1557 Garbers Church Rd Rockingham (22801) *(G-12245)*

Connect Hearing, Virginia Beach *Also called Hear Quick Incorporated (G-14513)*

Connect Software LLC 706 974-8300
  11654 Plaza America Dr Reston (20190) *(G-10826)*

Connected Intelligence LLC 571 241-4540
  43403 Stukely Dr Dulles (20166) *(G-4196)*

Connectedescape LLC 443 910-7559
  418 Alder Dr Stafford (22554) *(G-13133)*

Connection Newspapers, Alexandria *Also called Connection Publishing Inc (G-173)*

Connection Newspapers LLC 703 821-5050
  1606 King St Alexandria (22314) *(G-172)*

Connection Publishing Inc 703 821-5050
  1606 King St Alexandria (22314) *(G-173)*

Connectus Inc 703 560-7777
  3419 Arnold Ln Falls Church (22042) *(G-4777)*

Connell Log Thnning LLC Knneth 434 729-3712
  3401 Gvrnor Harrison Pkwy Brodnax (23920) *(G-2101)*

Conner Industries Inc 804 706-4229
  12110 Old Stage Rd Chester (23836) *(G-3396)*

Connoisseur Publishing 303 437-5099
  12905 Centre Park Cir Herndon (20171) *(G-6644)*

Conquest Graphics, Richmond *Also called Lewis Printing Company (G-11652)*

Conrock, Covington *Also called Construction Materials Company (G-3783)*

Conrock, Lexington *Also called Construction Materials Company (G-7391)*

Conrock, Lexington *Also called Construction Materials Company (G-7392)*

Conrock, Radford *Also called New River Concrete Supply Co (G-10726)*

Conscious Cultures LLC 434 227-9297
  615 Pauls Creek Rd Afton (22920) *(G-78)*

Conservtion Resources Intl LLC 703 321-7730
  7350 Lockport Pl Ste A Lorton (22079) *(G-7477)*

Consolidated Mailing Svcs Inc 703 904-1600
  504 Shaw Rd Ste 208 Sterling (20166) *(G-13374)*

Consolidated Natural Gas Co (HQ) 804 819-2000
  120 Tredegar St Richmond (23219) *(G-11539)*

Consolidated Welding LLC 757 348-6304
  5948 Jerry Rd Norfolk (23502) *(G-9503)*

Consolidated Wood Products 540 374-1439
  11901 Bowman Dr Ste 101 Fredericksburg (22408) *(G-5266)*

Consolidation Coal Co 276 988-3010
  700 Dry Fork Rd Bandy (24602) *(G-1558)*

Consolidation Coal Company 276 988-3010
  Rr 637 Amonate (24601) *(G-725)*

Consopt, Forest *Also called Constrained Optimization Inc (G-5063)*

Constrained Optimization Inc 434 944-8564
  1033 S Oak Lawn Dr Forest (24551) *(G-5063)*

Construction Materials Company 540 552-5022
  801 Industrial Park Rd Blacksburg (24060) *(G-1731)*

Construction Materials Company 540 962-2139
  820 W Chestnut St Covington (24426) *(G-3783)*

Construction Materials Company 540 463-3441
  9 Memorial Ln Lexington (24450) *(G-7391)*

Construction Materials Company (PA) 540 433-9043
  9 Memorial Ln Lexington (24450) *(G-7392)*

Construction Solutions Inc 757 366-5070
  1733 S Park Ct Chesapeake (23320) *(G-3052)*

Construction Specialties Group 703 670-5300
  15783 Crocus Ln Dumfries (22025) *(G-4240)*

Consultant Contractors, Danville *Also called V C Ice and Cold Storage Inc (G-4045)*

Consulting Printing Services 434 846-6510
  1085 Vista Park Dr Ste A Forest (24551) *(G-5064)*

Consurgo Group Inc 757 373-1717
  1452 Taylor Farm Rd # 103 Virginia Beach (23453) *(G-14361)*

Consutech Systems LLC 804 746-4120
  8407 Erle Rd Mechanicsville (23116) *(G-8614)*

Contact, Winchester *Also called Tim Price Inc (G-15594)*

Contactengine Inc 571 348-3220
  6849 Old Dominion Dr # 315 Mc Lean (22101) *(G-8409)*

Container-Care Virginia, Chesapeake *Also called Conglobal Industries LLC (G-3051)*

Contech Engnered Solutions LLC 513 645-7000
  25581 Hillman Hwy Abingdon (24210) *(G-25)*

Contemporary Kitchens Ltd 804 758-2001
  57 Campbell Dr Topping (23169) *(G-13886)*

Contemporary Woodcrafts Inc 703 451-4257
  7721 Fullerton Rd Springfield (22153) *(G-12979)*

Contemporary Woodcrafts Inc (PA) 703 787-9711
  7337 Wayfarer Dr Fairfax Station (22039) *(G-4703)*

Continental Auto Systems Inc 757 890-4900
  615 Bland Blvd Newport News (23602) *(G-9204)*

Continental Auto Systems Inc 540 825-4100
  13456 Lovers Ln Culpeper (22701) *(G-3880)*

Continental Brick Company (PA) 434 845-5918
  1000 Church St Lynchburg (24504) *(G-7683)*

Continental Commercial Corp 540 668-6216
  36716 Charles Town Pike Hillsboro (20132) *(G-6861)*

Continental Teves 540 825-4100
  13456 Lovers Ln Culpeper (22701) *(G-3881)*

Contour Healer LLC 757 288-6671
  1117 Ditchley Rd Virginia Beach (23451) *(G-14362)*

Contra Surplus LLC 757 337-9971
  222 W 21st St Ste F621 Norfolk (23517) *(G-9504)*

Contractors Institute LLC 804 250-6750
  1100 Welborne Dr Ste 103 Richmond (23229) *(G-11165)*

Contractors Institute LLC 804 556-5518
  1100 Welborne Dr Ste 103 Richmond (23229) *(G-11166)*

Contraline Inc 347 327-3676
  1216 Harris St Charlottesville (22903) *(G-2770)*

Contravac Inc 434 984-9723
  1000 Research Park Blvd # 103 Charlottesville (22911) *(G-2611)*

Controls Corporation America 757 422-8330
  1501 Harpers Rd Virginia Beach (23454) *(G-14363)*

Controls Unlimited Inc 703 897-4300
  2853 Ps Business Ctr Dr Woodbridge (22192) *(G-15673)*

Controp USA Inc 301 605-4499
  9720 Capital Ct Ste 301 Manassas (20110) *(G-7926)*

ALPHABETIC

Contura Energy Services LLC...276 835-8041
1465 Herndon Rd Mc Clure (24269) ***(G-8373)***
Convergent Bus Solutions LLC...804 360-0251
13316 College Valley Ln Richmond (23233) ***(G-11167)***
Convergent Crossfit...703 385-5400
698 Jonathan Rd Linden (22642) ***(G-7427)***
Convergent Data Group...571 276-0756
6421 Willowood Ln Alexandria (22310) ***(G-433)***
Conversations Publishing LLC...804 698-5922
100 Shockoe Slip Richmond (23219) ***(G-11540)***
Converting Division, Ashland *Also called Pratt Industries Inc* ***(G-1479)***
Convex Corporation...703 433-9901
7226 Mecklenburg Dr Warrenton (20187) ***(G-14990)***
Convoy Skateboards Ltd...571 216-2740
3544 Huntley Manor Ln Alexandria (22306) ***(G-434)***
Conway Woodworking LLC...276 328-6590
7138 Hurricane Rd Ne Wise (24293) ***(G-15620)***
Conwed, Roanoke *Also called Schweitzer-Mauduit Intl Inc* ***(G-12178)***
Conwed Corp...540 981-0362
530 Gregory Ave Ne Roanoke (24016) ***(G-12070)***
Conwed Plastics, Roanoke *Also called Swm International LLC* ***(G-12201)***
Conwet Plastics LLC...540 981-0362
530 Gregory Ave Ne Roanoke (24016) ***(G-12071)***
Cook & Boardman Group LLC...757 873-3979
700 Flag Stone Way Ste C Newport News (23608) ***(G-9205)***
Cook Composites, Chatham *Also called Polynt Composites USA Inc* ***(G-2933)***
Cooking Williams Good...804 931-6643
3102 Sussex Dr Hopewell (23860) ***(G-6920)***
Cool Comfort By Carson LLC...330 348-3149
5006 Barbour Dr Ste B Alexandria (22304) ***(G-174)***
Cool Wave LLC...757 269-0200
20576 Suthport Landing Pl Smithfield (23430) ***(G-12710)***
Coolr Group Inc...571 933-3762
14100 Parke Long Ct Ste I Chantilly (20151) ***(G-2396)***
Coop Systems Inc...703 581-6364
2201 Coop Way Ste 600 Herndon (20171) ***(G-6645)***
Cooper Crouse-Hinds LLC...540 983-1300
1700 Blue Hills Dr Ne Roanoke (24012) ***(G-12072)***
Cooper Steel of Virginia LLC...931 205-6117
275 Francis Ave Monroe (24574) ***(G-8988)***
Cooper Vineyards LLC...540 894-5474
13372 Shannon Hill Rd Louisa (23093) ***(G-7550)***
Cooper's Cookie Company, Leesburg *Also called Grace Upon Grace LLC* ***(G-7282)***
Cooper's R C Racing Products, Chatham *Also called Coopers R C Tires* ***(G-2925)***
Coopers R C Tires...434 724-7342
1020 Cooper Rd Chatham (24531) ***(G-2925)***
Coors Brewing Company...540 289-8000
Rr 340 Box South Elkton (22827) ***(G-4323)***
Coperion Corporation...276 227-7070
196 Appalachian Dr Wytheville (24382) ***(G-15883)***
Coperion Corporation...276 228-7717
285 Stafford Umberger Dr Wytheville (24382) ***(G-15884)***
Copper and Oak Cft Spirits LLC...309 255-2001
739a High St Portsmouth (23704) ***(G-10409)***
Copper Fox Dist Entps LLC...540 987-8554
9 River Ln Sperryville (22740) ***(G-12877)***
Copper Fox Distillery...757 903-2076
901 Capitol Landing Rd Williamsburg (23185) ***(G-15222)***
Copper Woodworks...757 421-7328
2248 Shillelagh Rd Chesapeake (23323) ***(G-3053)***
Copy Cat Printing LLC...804 746-0008
5516 Mechanicsville Tpke Mechanicsville (23111) ***(G-8615)***
Copy Connection...757 627-4701
236 E Main St Norfolk (23510) ***(G-9505)***
Copy Connection LLC...757 627-4701
236 E Main St Norfolk (23510) ***(G-9506)***
Copy Dog Printing...434 528-4134
3022 Memorial Ave Lynchburg (24501) ***(G-7684)***
Copy That Print LLC...757 642-3301
474 N Witchduck Rd Virginia Beach (23462) ***(G-14364)***
Copyland Printing Inc...703 241-9188
14101 Sllyfeld Cir Ste 11 Chantilly (20151) ***(G-2397)***
Copyright Printing...804 784-4760
1393 Broad Street Rd Oilville (23129) ***(G-10177)***
Coquina Press LLC...571 577-7550
19682 Telegraph Sprng Rd Purcellville (20132) ***(G-10657)***
Coral Graphic Services Inc...540 869-0500
25 Jack Enders Blvd Berryville (22611) ***(G-1676)***
Corascloud Inc...703 797-1881
7918 Jones Branch Dr # 800 Mc Lean (22102) ***(G-8410)***
Corce Collec Business System (HQ)...**703 790-7272**
7927 Jones Branch Dr # 3200 Mc Lean (22102) ***(G-8411)***
Cordial Cricket...804 931-8027
3524 Festival Park Plz Chester (23831) ***(G-3397)***
Cordially Yours...703 644-1186
8801 Newell Ct Springfield (22153) ***(G-12980)***
Core Business Technologies Inc...757 426-0344
2485 Las Brisas Dr Virginia Beach (23456) ***(G-14365)***
Core Enable LLC...757 375-4434
703 26th St Virginia Beach (23451) ***(G-14366)***
Core Engineered Solutions Inc...703 563-0320
620 Herndon Pkwy Ste 120 Herndon (20170) ***(G-6646)***
Core Health & Fitness LLC...714 669-1660
709 Powerhouse Rd Independence (24348) ***(G-6980)***
Core Health Thermography...434 207-4810
5574 Richmond Rd Ste A Troy (22974) ***(G-13923)***
Core Nutritionals LLC...888 978-2332
22370 Davis Dr Ste 100 Sterling (20164) ***(G-13375)***
Core Prints...540 356-9195
1130 International Pkwy # 119 Fredericksburg (22406) ***(G-5414)***
Coresix Precision Glass Inc...757 888-1361
1737 Endeavor Dr Williamsburg (23185) ***(G-15223)***
Corey Ely Logging LLC...423 579-3436
370 Ely Pucketts Creek Rd Pennington Gap (24277) ***(G-10294)***
Corey Vereen...609 468-5409
1311 Riviera Dr Virginia Beach (23464) ***(G-14367)***
Corillian Payment Solutions (HQ)...**703 259-3000**
11600 Sunrise Valley Dr # 100 Reston (20191) ***(G-10827)***
Corio-Poli, Cynthia, Alexandria *Also called Cynthia Coriopoli Design* ***(G-180)***
Coriolis Wind Inc...703 969-1257
1211 Trotting Horse Ln Great Falls (22066) ***(G-5950)***
Cormorant Technologies LLC...703 871-5060
2909 Thomas Smith Ln Williamsburg (23185) ***(G-15224)***
Corner Cabinet Shop Inc...540 672-9460
315 Caroline St Orange (22960) ***(G-10207)***
Cornerstone Archtectural Stone...540 297-3686
705 Industrial Ave Bedford (24523) ***(G-1632)***
Cornerstone Cabinets & Design...434 239-0976
171 Vista Centre Dr Forest (24551) ***(G-5065)***
Cornerstone Protection Svcs, Mount Jackson *Also called Cornerstone Tech Solutions Inc* ***(G-9068)***
Cornerstone Tech Solutions Inc...540 477-2180
5421 Main St Ste 400 Mount Jackson (22842) ***(G-9068)***
Cornerstone Woodworks...757 236-2334
2043 Lockard Ave Chesapeake (23320) ***(G-3054)***
Corning, Manassas *Also called Mediatech Inc* ***(G-8106)***
Corning Incorporated...703 448-1095
13221 Wdlnd Pk Rd Ste 400 Herndon (20171) ***(G-6647)***
Corning Incorporated...703 471-5955
9345 Discovery Blvd Manassas (20109) ***(G-8052)***
Corning Incorporated...434 793-9511
265 Corning Dr Danville (24541) ***(G-3972)***
Corning Incorporated...540 382-4921
3050 N Frank Christiansburg (24073) ***(G-3580)***
Corning Incorporated...540 382-4921
3050 N Franklin St Christiansburg (24073) ***(G-3581)***
Corning Optcal Cmmncations LLC...703 848-0200
13221 Woodland Park Rd Herndon (20171) ***(G-6648)***
Coronet Group Inc...757 488-4800
809 Brandon Ave Ste 302 Norfolk (23517) ***(G-9507)***
Corporate & Museum Frame Inc...804 643-6858
301 W Broad St Richmond (23220) ***(G-11541)***
Corporate Arms Llc...800 256-5803
8511 Wild Spruce Dr Springfield (22153) ***(G-12981)***
Corporate Designs...276 676-9048
25177 Watauga Rd Abingdon (24211) ***(G-26)***
Corporate Furn Svcs VA LLC...804 928-1143
5717 Oakleys Pl Richmond (23223) ***(G-11542)***
Corporate Identity, Manassas *Also called International Apparel Ltd* ***(G-8084)***
Corporate Imprints...804 965-9838
6920 Lakeside Ave Ste C Henrico (23228) ***(G-6494)***
Corporate Supply Technology...703 932-3475
3908 Plum Run Ct Fairfax (22033) ***(G-4430)***
Corporation Trust Co, The, Lorton *Also called Falck Schmidt Def Systems Corp* ***(G-7487)***
Corravoo Woodworks LLC...703 966-0929
20273 Rosedale Ct Ashburn (20147) ***(G-1258)***
Corrinne Callins...202 780-6233
7806c Harrowgate Cir Springfield (22152) ***(G-12982)***
Corrugated Container Corp...540 869-5353
100 Development Ln Winchester (22602) ***(G-15405)***
Cosaic...800 821-8147
609 East Market St Charlottesville (22902) ***(G-2771)***
Cosmetic Essence LLC...540 563-3000
4411 Plantation Rd Ne Roanoke (24012) ***(G-12073)***
Cosmetics By Makeena...757 737-8402
17 Rodgers Pl Portsmouth (23702) ***(G-10410)***
Costacamps-Net LLC...571 482-6858
5760 Heming Ave Springfield (22151) ***(G-12983)***
Costello Sculptures...540 763-3433
2226 Duncans Chapel Rd Nw Willis (24380) ***(G-15359)***
Costume Shop...804 421-7361
1503 Bellevue Ave Richmond (23227) ***(G-11168)***
COTS, Mechanicsville *Also called Computing Technologies Inc* ***(G-8613)***
Cottage Grove Candles...757 751-8333
639 Nansemond Dr Newport News (23605) ***(G-9206)***
Cottage Industries Exposition...703 834-0055
2831 Mustang Dr Herndon (20171) ***(G-6649)***
Cottage Still Room/Bees Wax CN...434 846-4398
31 Cabell St Lynchburg (24504) ***(G-7685)***

Cottle Multi Media Inc 434 263-5447
3390 Mount Airy Rd Lynch Station (24571) *(G-7627)*
Cotton Connection 434 528-1416
416 Main St Lynchburg (24504) *(G-7686)*
Cotton Kids, Great Falls *Also called Beadecked Inc (G-5939)*
Coty Connections Inc 540 588-0117
6658 Sugar Ridge Dr Roanoke (24018) *(G-11913)*
Cougaar Software Inc 703 506-1700
8260 Willow Oaks Corporat Fairfax (22031) *(G-4431)*
Cougarbearbobcat LLC 804 690-8006
3400 Ellwood Ave Richmond (23221) *(G-11543)*
Counter Effects Inc 804 451-9016
20300 Little Rd South Chesterfield (23803) *(G-12833)*
Country Baking LLC 540 592-7422
9036 John S Mosby Hwy Upperville (20184) *(G-13966)*
Country Corner LLC 540 538-3763
155 Enon Rd Fredericksburg (22405) *(G-5415)*
Country Courier 804 769-0259
8127 Richmnd Tapahnock Hw Aylett (23009) *(G-1547)*
Country House Printing 540 674-4616
525 Church St Dublin (24084) *(G-4153)*
Country Scents Candles 757 359-8730
925 Martin Ave Portsmouth (23701) *(G-10411)*
Country Vintner, The, Ashland *Also called Winebow Group LLC (G-1512)*
Country Wood Classics 804 798-1587
12625 Mount Hermon Rd Ashland (23005) *(G-1396)*
Country Wood Crafts 540 833-4985
8997 Mount Zion Rd Linville (22834) *(G-7434)*
Country Woodcrafts, Linville *Also called Country Wood Crafts (G-7434)*
Countryside Bakery 540 948-7888
3615 Elly Rd Aroda (22709) *(G-1224)*
Countryside Machining Inc 434 929-0065
494 Possum Island Rd Madison Heights (24572) *(G-7870)*
County Line LLC 434 736-8405
8818 Church St Keysville (23947) *(G-7055)*
County Line Custom Wdwkg LLC 804 338-8436
21311 Genito Rd Moseley (23120) *(G-9035)*
County of Hanover 804 798-9402
10417 Dow Gil Rd Ashland (23005) *(G-1397)*
Courier Record, Blackstone *Also called Nottoway Publishing Co Inc (G-1821)*
Courthouse Creek Cider 804 543-3157
1581 Maidens Rd Maidens (23102) *(G-7888)*
Courtney Press 804 266-8359
19 E Main St Richmond (23219) *(G-11544)*
Couture Intuition LLC 757 570-8126
909 Forest Lake Ct # 303 Newport News (23605) *(G-9207)*
Cova Ship Repair Inc 757 390-2177
2131 Cromwell Rd Norfolk (23504) *(G-9508)*
Covan Worldiwde Moving & Stor 757 766-2305
61 Basil Sawyer Dr Hampton (23666) *(G-6117)*
Covata Usa Inc 703 657-5260
11190 Sunrise Valley Dr # 140 Reston (20191) *(G-10828)*
Cove Antiques 757 787-3881
18368 Hermitage Rd Onancock (23417) *(G-10194)*
Cove Creek Industries Inc 434 293-6774
15 Mi S Of C Vll On Us 29 Covesville (22931) *(G-3775)*
Covenant Therapeutics LLC 434 296-8668
1229 Harris St Ste 11 Charlottesville (22903) *(G-2772)*
Cover UPS Marine Canvas 757 312-9292
228 Hall Dr Chesapeake (23322) *(G-3055)*
Covered Inc 757 463-0434
205 First Clnl Rd Ste 117 Virginia Beach (23454) *(G-14368)*
Covia Holdings Corporation 540 858-3444
334 Sand Mine Rd Gore (22637) *(G-5921)*
Covia Holdings Corporation 540 678-1490
48 W Boscawen St Winchester (22601) *(G-15535)*
Covington Barcoding Inc 434 476-1435
1154 Mount Zion Church Rd South Boston (24592) *(G-12755)*
Covington Paperboard Mill, Covington *Also called Wrkco Inc (G-3805)*
Covington Virginian Inc 540 962-2121
128 N Maple Ave Covington (24426) *(G-3784)*
Covingtons Scrubs With Love 804 503-8061
4912 Burnt Oak Dr North Chesterfield (23234) *(G-9852)*
Cow Pie Compost LLC 540 272-2854
10337 Messick Rd Midland (22728) *(G-8750)*
Cowboy Western Wear 202 298-8299
1708 14th St S Arlington (22204) *(G-919)*
Cowden 276 744-7120
2294 Elk View Rd Elk Creek (24326) *(G-4320)*
Cox Matthews & Associates Inc (PA) **703 385-2981**
10520 Warwick Ave Ste B8 Fairfax (22030) *(G-4607)*
Cox Printing, Galax *Also called Cynthia E Cox (G-5632)*
Cox Ready Mix Inc SB (HQ) **804 364-0500**
12554 W Broad St Glen Allen (23058) *(G-5718)*
Coxe Timber Company 757 934-1500
2901 Kings Fork Rd Suffolk (23434) *(G-13687)*
Coy Tiger Publishing LLC 703 221-8064
3589 Wharf Ln Triangle (22172) *(G-13889)*
Coyent 804 861-3323
5117 Courthouse Rd Prince George (23875) *(G-10589)*
Coyne & Delany Company (PA) **434 296-0166**
1565 Avon Street Ext Charlottesville (22902) *(G-2773)*
Cozino Enterprise Inc 804 921-1896
2402 Decatur St Richmond (23224) *(G-11545)*
Cozy Caterpillars 757 499-3769
5404 Trumpet Vine Ct Virginia Beach (23462) *(G-14369)*
Cozy Cloths 703 759-2420
626 Philip Digges Dr Great Falls (22066) *(G-5951)*
CP Films Inc 276 632-4991
1450 Beaver Creek Dr Martinsville (24112) *(G-8277)*
CP Instruments LLC 540 558-8596
2322 Blue Stone Hills Dr Harrisonburg (22801) *(G-6307)*
CPA Global North America LLC (HQ) **703 739-2234**
2318 Mill Rd Fl 12 Alexandria (22314) *(G-175)*
CPA Global Services US Inc 703 739-2234
2318 Mill Rd Fl 12 Alexandria (22314) *(G-176)*
Cpfilms, Axton *Also called Eastman Performance Films LLC (G-1536)*
CPS, Richmond *Also called Crop Production Services Inc (G-11037)*
CPS, Chesapeake *Also called Coastal Precast Systems LLC (G-3042)*
CPS Contractors Inc 804 561-6834
17707 Hull Street Rd Moseley (23120) *(G-9036)*
Cr Communications 757 871-4797
4481 Village Park Dr W Williamsburg (23185) *(G-15225)*
Cr Neon 804 339-0497
307 Powder Horn Dr Ruther Glen (22546) *(G-12453)*
Cr8tive Sign Works 804 608-8698
5613 Promontory Pointe Rd Midlothian (23112) *(G-8804)*
Crabar/Gbf Inc 919 732-2101
1 Ennis Dr Chatham (24531) *(G-2926)*
Crabill Meats, Toms Brook *Also called Crabill Slaughterhouse Inc (G-13882)*
Crabill Slaughterhouse Inc 540 436-3248
3149 Riverview Dr Toms Brook (22660) *(G-13882)*
Crabtree Welding 434 990-0140
49 Hancock Dr Ruckersville (22968) *(G-12401)*
Craft Bearing Company Inc 757 247-6000
5000 Chestnut Ave Newport News (23605) *(G-9208)*
Craft Designs Custom Intr Pdts 757 630-1565
6222 Winthrope Dr Suffolk (23435) *(G-13688)*
Craft Industrial Incorporated 757 825-1195
2300 58th St Hampton (23661) *(G-6118)*
Craft Machine Works Inc 757 310-6011
2102 48th St Hampton (23661) *(G-6119)*
Craft Mch Wrks Acquisition LLC (HQ) **757 310-6011**
2102 48th St Hampton (23661) *(G-6120)*
Craft of Brewing 703 687-3932
21140 Ashburn Crossing Dr Ashburn (20147) *(G-1259)*
Craft Repair Incorporated 757 838-0721
550 Rotary St Hampton (23661) *(G-6121)*
Crafted Canvas LLC 917 426-8377
4097 Essex Mill Rd Dunnsville (22454) *(G-4268)*
Crafted For ME LLC 804 412-5273
9412 Broad Meadows Rd Glen Allen (23060) *(G-5719)*
Crafted Glass Inc 757 543-5504
1338 Atlantic Ave Chesapeake (23324) *(G-3056)*
Crafter Software 703 955-3480
1800 Alexander Bell Dr Reston (20191) *(G-10829)*
Craftsman Distillery LLC 804 454-1514
8325 Regalia Pl Chesterfield (23838) *(G-3487)*
Craftsmen Printing Inc 804 798-7885
305 England St Ashland (23005) *(G-1398)*
Crafty Stitcher LLC 703 855-2736
18943 Canoe Landing Ct Leesburg (20176) *(G-7248)*
Craig Thomas Johnson, Sterling *Also called CJ & Associates LLC (G-13370)*
Crane Research & Engrg Co Inc 757 826-1707
109 Boathouse Cv Yorktown (23692) *(G-15945)*
Craving Sensations LLC 757 609-5038
2606 Gothic St Portsmouth (23707) *(G-10412)*
Crawl Space Door System Inc 757 363-0005
3700 Shore Dr Ste 101 Virginia Beach (23455) *(G-14370)*
Craze Signs & Graphics 804 748-9233
8106 Gates Bluff Ct Chesterfield (23832) *(G-3488)*
Crazy Clover Butcher Shop 804 370-5291
1176 Briery Swamp Rd Jamaica (23079) *(G-7008)*
Crazy Customs 434 222-8686
602 Greenway Dr South Boston (24592) *(G-12756)*
Crazy Rooster Brewing Co LLC 804 464-2958
1560 Oakbridge Dr Powhatan (23139) *(G-10541)*
Crazy Tees, North Chesterfield *Also called Soforeal Entertainment (G-9982)*
CRC Public Relations 703 395-9614
6307 Buffie Ct Burke (22015) *(G-2187)*
Create-A-Print and Signs LLC 804 920-8055
10406 Beachcrest Pl Chesterfield (23832) *(G-3489)*
Createk, Winchester *Also called Evolve Custom LLC (G-15414)*
Creatiate 609 703-2378
14007 Shadow Ridge Rd Midlothian (23112) *(G-8805)*
Creation Sign LLC 703 622-5958
7364 Mcwhorter Pl Annandale (22003) *(G-737)*
Creations At Play LLC 757 541-8226
129 Bennett Rd Poquoson (23662) *(G-10368)*

ALPHABETIC

Creations By Clark & Clark, Norfolk *Also called Clark & Clark LLC* ***(G-9487)***
Creations From Heart LLC.....757 234-4300
119 Lewis Dr Seaford (23696) ***(G-12673)***
Creative Cabinet Design.....434 293-4040
1109 Harris St Charlottesville (22903) ***(G-2774)***
Creative Cabinet Designs LLC.....703 644-1090
5295 Crossbow Dr Pulaski (24301) ***(G-10633)***
Creative Cabinet Works.....757 220-1941
15980 Kentflatts Ln Lanexa (23089) ***(G-7164)***
Creative Cabinet Works LLC.....757 566-1000
201 Industrial Blvd Toano (23168) ***(G-13861)***
Creative Candles & Gifts, Yorktown *Also called Linda M Barnes* ***(G-15976)***
Creative Coatings Inc.....540 636-7911
116 Success Rd Front Royal (22630) ***(G-5527)***
Creative Corp.....804 556-4839
2353 Country Ln Maidens (23102) ***(G-7889)***
Creative Crafty Mom LLC.....571 206-8570
17410 Glennville Dr Dumfries (22026) ***(G-4241)***
Creative Decorating.....703 643-5556
14812 Build America Dr Woodbridge (22191) ***(G-15674)***
Creative Designs LLC.....540 223-0083
1134 Kents Mill Rd Louisa (23093) ***(G-7551)***
Creative Designs of Virginia.....804 435-2382
63 Rappahannock Rd Irvington (22480) ***(G-7000)***
Creative Dimension Group Inc.....540 891-1953
11700 Shannon Dr Fredericksburg (22408) ***(G-5267)***
Creative Document Imaging Inc (PA).....**703 208-2212**
8451 Hilltop Rd Ste I Fairfax (22031) ***(G-4432)***
Creative Document Imaging Inc.....703 497-6767
2050 Old Bridge Rd B04 Woodbridge (22192) ***(G-15675)***
Creative Education & Pubg.....703 856-7005
3339 Ardley Ct Falls Church (22041) ***(G-4778)***
Creative Fabrication Inc.....540 931-4877
200 Industrial Ln Covington (24426) ***(G-3785)***
Creative Framing Gallery.....703 771-6354
525 E Market St Ste M Leesburg (20176) ***(G-7249)***
Creative Impressions Inc.....757 855-2187
796 Coverdale Ct Virginia Beach (23452) ***(G-14371)***
Creative Ink.....434 572-4379
1100 Wilborn Ave South Boston (24592) ***(G-12757)***
Creative Ink Inc.....540 342-2400
416 S Jefferson St 808 Roanoke (24011) ***(G-12074)***
Creative Kustom Tool Co, Suffolk *Also called Dan Charewicz* ***(G-13692)***
Creative Mnds Publications LLC.....804 740-6010
2325 Crowncrest Dr Richmond (23233) ***(G-11169)***
Creative Monogramming LLC.....434 767-4880
629 Harper Rd Burkeville (23922) ***(G-2208)***
Creative Monogrim, Farmville *Also called Elletts Embroidery* ***(G-4939)***
Creative Occasions.....703 821-3210
1312 Chain Bridge Rd # 3 Mc Lean (22101) ***(G-8412)***
Creative Passions.....540 908-7549
6225 Mayberry Rd Singers Glen (22850) ***(G-12699)***
Creative Permutations LLC.....703 628-3799
9412 Englefield Ct Fairfax Station (22039) ***(G-4704)***
Creative Print Solutions.....540 247-9910
408 Misty Meadow Dr Winchester (22603) ***(G-15406)***
Creative Seating LLC.....276 236-3615
1080 Grouse Hollow Ln Galax (24333) ***(G-5631)***
Creative Sign Builders LLC.....757 622-5591
2401 Fawn St Norfolk (23504) ***(G-9509)***
Creative Signs Ltd.....540 899-0032
1231 Kings Hwy Fredericksburg (22405) ***(G-5416)***
Creative Urethanes Inc.....540 542-6676
250 Independence Rd Winchester (22602) ***(G-15407)***
Creative Visions Woodworks.....434 822-0182
146 Hayes Ct Danville (24541) ***(G-3973)***
Creative Welding and Design.....757 334-1416
2702 Manning Rd Suffolk (23434) ***(G-13689)***
Creative Woodworking Specialis.....804 514-9066
10501 Hobby Hill Rd Richmond (23235) ***(G-11036)***
Creative Workshops.....703 938-6177
2625 Chain Bridge Rd Vienna (22181) ***(G-14031)***
Creativexposure LLC.....540 668-9070
36388 Charles Town Pike Hillsboro (20132) ***(G-6862)***
Creature Comfort Custom Concie.....703 609-7098
3713 Burrows Ave Fairfax (22030) ***(G-4608)***
Creed Apparel.....804 219-3291
4902 Whetstone Rd North Chesterfield (23234) ***(G-9853)***
Creeks Edge Winery.....540 822-3825
41255 Annas Ln Lovettsville (20180) ***(G-7577)***
Creggers Cakes & Catering.....276 646-8739
1043 St Clairs Creek Rd Chilhowie (24319) ***(G-3549)***
Crenshaw Equipment, Richmond *Also called Crenshaw of Richmond Inc* ***(G-11546)***
Crenshaw Lighting Corporation.....540 745-3900
115 Lighting Way Floyd (24091) ***(G-5021)***
Crenshaw of Richmond Inc.....804 231-6241
1700 Commerce Rd Richmond (23224) ***(G-11546)***
Creo Industries.....804 385-2035
525 Silver Leaf Dr Christiansburg (24073) ***(G-3582)***
Crescent Communications, Falls Church *Also called Kajjo Sirwan* ***(G-4815)***
Crescent Printery Ltd.....276 395-2101
307 2nd St Sw Coeburn (24230) ***(G-3697)***
Crespo Urban Defense LLC.....804 562-7566
1725 Creek Bottom Way North Chesterfield (23236) ***(G-9854)***
Cresset Corporation.....804 798-2691
11232 Hopson Rd Ste 1 Ashland (23005) ***(G-1399)***
Cresta Gadino Winery LLC.....540 987-9292
92 School House Rd Washington (22747) ***(G-15075)***
Crewe Brothers Logging.....804 829-2288
8821 Stagg Run Rd Charles City (23030) ***(G-2574)***
Crewe Burkfield Journal.....434 645-7534
107 W Carolina Ave Crewe (23930) ***(G-3810)***
Crewe Burkville Jounal, Crewe *Also called M & S Publishing Co Inc* ***(G-3814)***
Crewe Chronicle, Crewe *Also called Crewe Burkfield Journal* ***(G-3810)***
Crews James D, Nathalie *Also called James D Crews Logging* ***(G-9103)***
Crews Outdoors Llc John.....540 808-2204
2236 River Oaks Dr Salem (24153) ***(G-12491)***
Crfs Inc.....571 321-5470
4230 Lafayette Center Dr D Chantilly (20151) ***(G-2398)***
Crh Americas Inc.....804 633-9841
16326 Industrial Dr Milford (22514) ***(G-8929)***
Cri Mutual Press, Lynchburg *Also called Commonwealth Reprographics* ***(G-7682)***
Cricket Products Inc.....804 861-0687
1921 Anchor Ave Petersburg (23803) ***(G-10315)***
Cricketts Trucking LLC.....540 333-3812
225 S Charles St Apt 2 Strasburg (22657) ***(G-13577)***
Criders Finishing Inc.....703 661-6520
21641 Beaumeade Cir # 317 Ashburn (20147) ***(G-1260)***
Crimphaven Alpacas LLC.....540 463-4063
4165 W Midland Trl Lexington (24450) ***(G-7393)***
Crisman Woodworks.....804 317-1446
5509 Chestnut Bluff Rd Midlothian (23112) ***(G-8806)***
Crisp Manufacturing Co Inc.....276 686-4131
732 Milk Plant Rd Rural Retreat (24368) ***(G-12420)***
Crispery of Virginia LLC.....757 673-5234
2728 Sterling Point Dr Portsmouth (23703) ***(G-10413)***
Crispery, The, Portsmouth *Also called Crispery of Virginia LLC* ***(G-10413)***
Criswell Inc.....434 845-0439
1709 Memorial Ave Lynchburg (24501) ***(G-7687)***
Critical Power Group Inc.....703 443-1717
21760 Beaumeade Cir # 190 Ashburn (20147) ***(G-1261)***
Crochet.....732 446-9644
1636 Skiffes Creek Cir Williamsburg (23185) ***(G-15226)***
Crochet Braids By Twana LLC.....571 201-7190
1313 Walker Dr Fredericksburg (22401) ***(G-5180)***
Crochet By Grammy.....757 637-8416
502 Marshall St Hampton (23669) ***(G-6122)***
Crochet By Palm LLC.....757 427-0532
1617 Rollins Ct Virginia Beach (23454) ***(G-14372)***
Cronin Defense Strategies LLC.....810 625-7060
4659 28th Rd S Arlington (22206) ***(G-920)***
Crooked Stitch Bags LLC.....703 680-0118
2902 Archer Ct Woodbridge (22193) ***(G-15676)***
Crop Production Services Inc.....804 282-7115
804 Mrfield Pk Dr Ste 210 Richmond (23236) ***(G-11037)***
Crop Production Svc.....804 732-6166
5025 E Whitehill Ct Prince George (23875) ***(G-10590)***
Cross Cloud Solutions Inc.....703 724-7526
21769 Oakville Ter Ashburn (20147) ***(G-1262)***
Cross Keys Vineyards LLC.....540 234-0505
6011 E Timber Ridge Rd Mount Crawford (22841) ***(G-9053)***
Cross Machine Welding.....276 699-1974
137 Rakestown Rd Ivanhoe (24350) ***(G-7005)***
Cross Match Technologies Inc.....703 841-6280
1550 Crystal Dr Ste 505 Arlington (22202) ***(G-921)***
Cross Printing Solutions LLC.....703 208-2214
8451 Hilltop Rd Ste B Fairfax (22031) ***(G-4433)***
Cross Restorations.....276 466-8436
11136 Goose Creek Rd Bristol (24202) ***(G-2014)***
Cross Stitch LLC.....703 961-1636
4018 Royal Lytham Dr Fairfax (22033) ***(G-4434)***
Cross Tie Equine, Greenville *Also called Tomlinsons Farrier Service LLC* ***(G-5999)***
Cross-Land Conveyors LLC.....540 287-9150
10909 Astarita Ave Partlow (22534) ***(G-10265)***
Crossbow Strategies Inc.....703 864-7576
1 W Alexandria Ave Alexandria (22301) ***(G-177)***
Crosscut Inc.....276 395-5430
5821 Creek Hill Rd Saint Paul (24283) ***(G-12466)***
Crossing Trails Publication.....703 590-4449
4804 Kentwood Ln Woodbridge (22193) ***(G-15677)***
Crossline Creations LLC.....703 625-4780
44258 Mercure Cir 103 Sterling (20166) ***(G-13376)***
Crossroad Data Solutions LLC.....804 302-4312
7305 Hancock Village Dr # 13 Chesterfield (23832) ***(G-3490)***
Crossroads Cabinets LLC.....319 431-1588
7607 Rock Cress Dr Moseley (23120) ***(G-9037)***
Crossroads Express Inc.....434 882-0320
358 Bybee Rd Louisa (23093) ***(G-7552)***
Crossroads Farrier Inc.....434 589-4501
67 Rollins Ln Louisa (23093) ***(G-7553)***

Crossroads Iron Works Inc......540 832-7800
10380 James Madison Hwy Zion Crossroads (22942) ***(G-16006)***
Crossroads Machine Inc......757 482-5414
815 Bedford St Chesapeake (23322) ***(G-3057)***
Crosstown Paint......757 817-7119
125 Claremont Ave Hampton (23661) ***(G-6123)***
Crosstown Shipg & Sup Co LLC......513 252-5370
2639 Arlington Dr Apt 303 Alexandria (22306) ***(G-435)***
Crouch Petra......757 681-0828
6100 Tradewinds Ct Virginia Beach (23464) ***(G-14373)***
Crowd Almanac LLC......703 385-6989
10605 Cedar Ave Fairfax (22030) ***(G-4609)***
Crown Cork & Seal Usa Inc......540 662-2591
1461 Martinsburg Pike Winchester (22603) ***(G-15408)***
Crown Cork & Seal Usa Inc......757 538-1318
1305 Progress Rd Suffolk (23434) ***(G-13690)***
Crown Enterprise LLC......757 277-8837
1014 Smoke Tree Ln Virginia Beach (23452) ***(G-14374)***
Crown International Inc......703 335-0066
8508 Virginia Meadows Dr Manassas (20109) ***(G-8053)***
Crown ME Galore Collection LLC......864 540-4476
205 Justin Ct Suffolk (23434) ***(G-13691)***
Crown Motorcar Company LLC......434 979-7222
1295 Richmond Rd Charlottesville (22911) ***(G-2612)***
Crown On LLC......202 427-3042
3001 Sussex Dr Emporia (23847) ***(G-4356)***
Crown Supreme Industries LLC......703 729-1482
43240 Baltusrol Ter Ashburn (20147) ***(G-1263)***
Crozet Bopharma Consulting LLC......703 598-1940
1041 Half Mile Branch Rd Crozet (22932) ***(G-3830)***
Crozet Gazette LLC......434 823-2291
1335 Pleasant Green St Crozet (22932) ***(G-3831)***
Crsi, Mineral *Also called Cunning Running Software Inc* ***(G-8945)***
Crudewell Drilling, Buchanan *Also called Crudewell Inc* ***(G-2119)***
Crudewell Inc......540 254-2289
60 Drill Rig Dr Buchanan (24066) ***(G-2119)***
Crunchy Hydration LLC......757 362-1607
1805 Kempsville Rd Virginia Beach (23464) ***(G-14375)***
Crushed Cellars LLC......571 374-9463
37938 Charles Town Pike Hillsboro (20132) ***(G-6863)***
Crust & Cream......804 230-5555
4610 Forest Hill Ave Richmond (23225) ***(G-11547)***
Cryopak Verification Tech Inc......888 827-3393
120 Parkway Dr Buchanan (24066) ***(G-2120)***
Cryoscience Technologies......516 338-6723
13487 Landons Ln Brandy Station (22714) ***(G-1938)***
Cryosel LLC......757 778-1854
224 Salters Creek Rd Hampton (23661) ***(G-6124)***
Cryptek USA Corp......571 434-2000
1501 Moran Rd Sterling (20166) ***(G-13377)***
Crypto Industries LLC......703 729-5059
23507 Bentley Grove Pl Ashburn (20148) ***(G-1264)***
Crypto Reserve Inc......571 229-0826
9809 Cockrell Rd Manassas (20110) ***(G-7927)***
Crystal Beach Studio......757 787-4605
16383 Crystal Beach Rd Onancock (23417) ***(G-10195)***
Crystal Technology Inc......703 968-2590
13558 Smallwood Ln Chantilly (20151) ***(G-2399)***
Crystals of Hope......434 525-7279
527 Capstone Dr Lynchburg (24502) ***(G-7688)***
Cs Woodworking Design LLC......703 996-1122
43670 Trade Center Pl # 160 Sterling (20166) ***(G-13378)***
CSC Family Holdings Inc......276 669-6649
15083 Industrial Park Rd Bristol (24202) ***(G-2015)***
Csd Solutions, Fredericksburg *Also called Custom Sftwr Dsign Sltions LLC* ***(G-5417)***
Cses, Dulles *Also called Chemring Snsors Elctrnic Syste* ***(G-4195)***
Cses Niitek Production Fcilty, Charlottesville *Also called Chemring Sensors and Electr* ***(G-2608)***
Csi, Alexandria *Also called Composition Systems Inc* ***(G-171)***
Csl Enterprises......804 695-0400
7348 Main St Gloucester (23061) ***(G-5842)***
Csl Media LLC......540 785-3790
220 Industrial Dr Fredericksburg (22408) ***(G-5268)***
Csl Media LLC......540 785-3790
2366 Plank Rd Fredericksburg (22401) ***(G-5181)***
CSM Industries Inc......410 818-3262
850 N Randolph St Ste 170 Arlington (22203) ***(G-922)***
CSM International Corporation......800 767-3805
16834 Panorama Dr Woodbridge (22191) ***(G-15678)***
CSP Productions Inc......703 321-8100
2927 Gallows Rd Ste 101 Falls Church (22042) ***(G-4779)***
CSP Unlimited, Lorton *Also called Capital Screen Prtg Unlimited* ***(G-7470)***
CT Jamsos Precast Septic Tanks......540 483-5944
865 Algoma Rd Callaway (24067) ***(G-2220)***
CT Machining By Cnc, Salem *Also called Alice Farling* ***(G-12472)***
Ctc FL, Petersburg *Also called Colonial Tailors Chalk Inc* ***(G-10314)***
CTI of Woodbridge......703 670-4790
14311 Silverdale Dr Woodbridge (22193) ***(G-15679)***
Ctm Automated Systems Inc......703 742-0755
130 Forest Ridge Dr Sterling (20164) ***(G-13379)***
Ctrl-Pad Inc......757 216-9170
1543 Bolling Ave Norfolk (23508) ***(G-9510)***
Ctv Candles, Virginia Beach *Also called Corey Vereen* ***(G-14367)***
CTW, Port Haywood *Also called Chesapeake Thermite Wldg LLC* ***(G-10382)***
CTW Printing Concepts......804 559-5020
8388 Shady Grove Rd Mechanicsville (23116) ***(G-8616)***
Cub Cadet Culpeper LLC......540 825-8381
11332 James Monroe Hwy Culpeper (22701) ***(G-3882)***
Cubbage Crane Maintenance......804 739-5459
12500 Second Branch Rd Chesterfield (23838) ***(G-3491)***
Cubicle Logic LLC......571 989-2823
20533 Mason Oak Ct Sterling (20165) ***(G-13380)***
Cued-In, Harrisonburg *Also called College and University Educati* ***(G-6302)***
Cuisine Solutions Inc......303 904-4771
85 S Bragg St Ste 600 Alexandria (22312) ***(G-436)***
Culbertson Lumber Company Inc......276 679-7620
4637 Overlook Rd Norton (24273) ***(G-10116)***
Culpeper Commercial Printers......540 825-0771
122 W Spencer St Culpeper (22701) ***(G-3883)***
Culpeper Farmers Coop Inc (PA)......**540 825-2200**
15172 Brandy Rd Culpeper (22701) ***(G-3884)***
Culpeper Machine & Supply Co......540 825-4644
105 N Commerce St Culpeper (22701) ***(G-3885)***
Culpeper Mdel Barnstormers Inc......540 349-2733
6061 Captains Walk Broad Run (20137) ***(G-2066)***
Culpeper Roanoke Rapids LLC......800 817-6215
15487 Braggs Corner Rd Culpeper (22701) ***(G-3886)***
Culpeper Star Exponent, Culpeper *Also called Wood Television LLC* ***(G-3932)***
Culpeper Wood Preservers, Fredericksburg *Also called Jefferson Homebuilders Inc* ***(G-5306)***
Culpeper Wood Preservers, Culpeper *Also called Jefferson Homebuilders Inc* ***(G-3898)***
Culpeper Wood Preservers, Culpeper *Also called Jefferson Homebuilders Inc* ***(G-3899)***
Culpepper......804 276-1478
9107 Berry Patch Dr Chesterfield (23832) ***(G-3492)***
Cumberland Company LP (PA)......**434 392-9911**
113 E 2nd St Ste A Farmville (23901) ***(G-4938)***
Cumberland Millwork......757 233-4121
1821 Engle Ave Chesapeake (23320) ***(G-3058)***
Cumberland Resources, Norton *Also called Bluff Spur Coal LLC* ***(G-10113)***
Cunning Running Software Inc......703 926-5864
668 Windway Ln Mineral (23117) ***(G-8945)***
Cunningham Creek Winery LLC......434 207-3907
3304 Ruritan Lake Rd Palmyra (22963) ***(G-10247)***
Cunningham Digital Inc......540 992-2219
1615 Roanoke Rd Daleville (24083) ***(G-3941)***
Cunningham Entps LLC Daniel......804 359-2180
2211 Dickens Rd Ste A Richmond (23230) ***(G-11170)***
Cupcake Company......540 810-0795
3391 Barbershop Ln Elkton (22827) ***(G-4324)***
Cupcake Cottage LLC......540 330-8504
175 Cambridge Dr Daleville (24083) ***(G-3942)***
Cupcakes and Lace LLC......703 378-1525
4405 Cub Run Rd Chantilly (20151) ***(G-2400)***
Cupcakes and More LLC......804 305-2350
1504 Southbury Ave Richmond (23231) ***(G-11171)***
Cupcakes By Cheryl LLC......757 592-4185
1937 Windsor Rd Dutton (23050) ***(G-4270)***
Cupcakes By Ladybug LLC......571 926-9709
8695 Bent Arrow Ct Springfield (22153) ***(G-12984)***
Cupcakes On Move LLC......804 477-6754
4212 Seamore St Richmond (23223) ***(G-11548)***
Cupp Manufacturing Co......540 249-4011
73 Stonewall Ln Grottoes (24441) ***(G-6018)***
Cupples Products Inc......804 717-1971
2001 Ware Btm Spring Rd Chester (23836) ***(G-3398)***
Cupron Inc......804 322-3650
4329 November Ave Henrico (23231) ***(G-6495)***
Curious Compass LLC......540 735-5013
1009 Hotchkiss Pl Fredericksburg (22401) ***(G-5182)***
Curry Copy Center of Roanoke......540 345-2865
116 Campbell Ave Sw Roanoke (24011) ***(G-12075)***
Curry Industries LLC......757 251-7559
1707 Neptune Dr Hampton (23669) ***(G-6125)***
Curtis E Harrell......540 843-2027
223 Wilson Ave Luray (22835) ***(G-7605)***
Curtis Russell Lumber Co Inc......276 346-1958
Rr 2 Box 2312 Jonesville (24263) ***(G-7020)***
Curtis Wharam......434 983-3904
273 Allens Lake Rd Dillwyn (23936) ***(G-4094)***
Curtiss Wright Control, Ashburn *Also called Curtiss-Wright Corporation* ***(G-1266)***
Curtiss-Wright Controls Inc......703 779-7800
20130 Lakeview Center Plz # 200 Ashburn (20147) ***(G-1265)***
Curtiss-Wright Corporation......703 779-7800
20130 Lakeview Center Plz # 200 Ashburn (20147) ***(G-1266)***
Curtiss-Wright Corporation......757 494-3810
1101 Cavalier Blvd Chesapeake (23323) ***(G-3059)***

ALPHABETIC

Cushing Manufacturing & Eqp Co 804 231-1161
2901 Commerce Rd Richmond (23234) *(G-11038)*

Cushing Manufacturing Company, Richmond *Also called Cushing Manufacturing & Eqp Co (G-11038)*

Cushing Metals LLC 804 339-1114
733 Kelley Ln King William (23086) *(G-7128)*

Cushion Department, The, Rustburg *Also called Carolyn West (G-12436)*

Custer Ice Service Inc 434 656-2854
202 Coffey St Gretna (24557) *(G-6007)*

Custom Auto Glass & Plastics 540 362-8798
340 Fugate Rd Ne Roanoke (24012) *(G-12076)*

Custom Baked Tees 703 888-8539
5918 3rd St S Arlington (22204) *(G-923)*

Custom Bars & Entrmt Systems, Norfolk *Also called Greenbrier Custom Cabinets (G-9566)*

Custom Book Bindery 804 796-9520
4441 Treely Rd Chester (23831) *(G-3399)*

Custom Built Cabinets and 812 427-9733
598 Living Waters Dr Jonesville (24263) *(G-7021)*

Custom Cabinet Works 540 972-1734
223 Battlefield Rd Locust Grove (22508) *(G-7442)*

Custom Camshaft Company Inc 276 666-6767
67 Motorsports Dr Martinsville (24112) *(G-8278)*

Custom Candyy LLC 804 447-8179
120 E Roanoke St Richmond (23224) *(G-11549)*

Custom Canvas Works Inc 571 249-6443
4555 Interlachen Ct G Alexandria (22312) *(G-437)*

Custom Comfort By Winn Ltd 804 452-0929
15 Rev Cw Harris St Hopewell (23860) *(G-6921)*

Custom Computer Software 540 972-3027
135 Green St Locust Grove (22508) *(G-7443)*

Custom Concessions Inc 800 910-8533
115 Rowse Dr Lynchburg (24502) *(G-7689)*

Custom Counter Fitters Inc 757 288-4730
1901 Thunderbird Dr Virginia Beach (23454) *(G-14376)*

Custom Design Graphics 276 466-6778
130 Marshall Rd Bristol (24201) *(G-1973)*

Custom Design Products, Maidens *Also called Creative Corp (G-7889)*

Custom Designers Inc 703 830-8582
5866 Old Centreville Rd Centreville (20121) *(G-2299)*

Custom Designs & More 540 894-5050
121b Mineral Ave Mineral (23117) *(G-8946)*

Custom Dsigns EMB Print Wr LLC 540 748-5455
5600 Dogwood Tree Ln Mineral (23117) *(G-8947)*

Custom EMB & Screen Prtg 434 239-2144
528a Crowell Ln Lynchburg (24502) *(G-7690)*

Custom Embroidery & Design 804 530-5238
732 Okuma Dr Chester (23836) *(G-3400)*

Custom Embroidery & Designs 757 474-1523
713 Vanderbilt Ave Virginia Beach (23451) *(G-14377)*

Custom Engraving & Signs LLC 804 545-3961
8427 Glazebrook Ave Richmond (23228) *(G-11172)*

Custom Engraving and Signs LLC 804 270-1272
9120 Crystalwood Ln Henrico (23294) *(G-6496)*

Custom Fab & Finish, Radford *Also called John A Treese (G-10718)*

Custom Fabrication Svcs Inc 540 483-8809
3399 Providence Church Rd Henry (24102) *(G-6594)*

Custom Fabricators Inc 757 724-0305
20309 Longview Dr Windsor (23487) *(G-15603)*

Custom Fly Grips LLC 703 532-1189
2231 Van Buren Ct Falls Church (22043) *(G-4780)*

Custom Foam and Cases LLC 703 201-5908
2565 Beahm Town Rd Culpeper (22701) *(G-3887)*

Custom Graphics Inc 540 882-3488
16552 Clarkes Gap Rd Paeonian Springs (20129) *(G-10238)*

Custom Hope Chests VA LLC 703 850-5019
1521 Powells Tavern Pl Herndon (20170) *(G-6650)*

Custom Ink 703 957-1648
11130i South Lakes Dr Reston (20191) *(G-10830)*

Custom Ink 571 364-7944
419 King St Alexandria (22314) *(G-178)*

Custom Ink 703 884-2678
8171 Stonewall Shops Sq Gainesville (20155) *(G-5576)*

Custom Ink 703 884-2680
1019a Edwards Ferry Rd Ne Leesburg (20176) *(G-7250)*

Custom Ink 434 422-5206
2118 Barracks Rd Charlottesville (22903) *(G-2775)*

Custom Ink 804 419-5651
3401 W Cary St Richmond (23221) *(G-11550)*

Custom Kraft Inc 757 265-2882
213 Salters Creek Rd Hampton (23661) *(G-6126)*

Custom Logos 804 967-0111
3108 N Parham Rd Ste 600a Richmond (23294) *(G-11173)*

Custom Machine Incorporated 434 846-8987
7249 Richmond Hwy Lynchburg (24504) *(G-7691)*

Custom Machining and Tool Inc 540 389-9102
1281 Southside Dr Salem (24153) *(G-12492)*

Custom Made Springs Inc 757 489-8202
822 W 40th St Norfolk (23508) *(G-9511)*

Custom Marine Canvas 540 775-6699
6099 Marineview Rd King George (22485) *(G-7085)*

Custom Metal Fabricators Inc 804 271-6094
7601 Whitepine Rd North Chesterfield (23237) *(G-9855)*

Custom Metalsmith Inc 276 988-0330
205 Walnut St North Tazewell (24630) *(G-10097)*

Custom Moulding & Millwork Inc 540 788-1823
3131 Gaskins Ln Catlett (20119) *(G-2267)*

Custom Ornamental Iron Inc 804 798-1991
10412 Knotty Pine Ln Glen Allen (23059) *(G-5720)*

Custom Ornamental Iron Works 540 942-2687
640 Highland Ave Waynesboro (22980) *(G-15106)*

Custom Packaging Inc 804 232-3299
1003 Commerce Rd Richmond (23224) *(G-11551)*

Custom Packaging Service 804 279-7225
2220 Station Rd North Chesterfield (23234) *(G-9856)*

Custom Performance Inc 540 972-3632
12631 Herndon Rd Spotsylvania (22553) *(G-12886)*

Custom Plantation Shutters, Chesapeake *Also called Jar-Tan Inc (G-3148)*

Custom Power Solutions, Chesapeake *Also called Cynthia Kriparos (G-3060)*

Custom Precast Inc 757 833-8989
144 Freedom Blvd Yorktown (23692) *(G-15946)*

Custom Print 703 256-1279
6621 Electronic Dr Springfield (22151) *(G-12985)*

Custom Printing 540 672-2281
124 Chapman St Orange (22960) *(G-10208)*

Custom Printing 804 261-1776
1720 E Parham Rd Richmond (23228) *(G-11174)*

Custom Printing & Vinyl, Virginia Beach *Also called Dan Miles & Associates LLC (G-14385)*

Custom Prints LLC 804 839-0749
3505 Austin Ave Richmond (23222) *(G-11552)*

Custom Procurement Systems 540 720-5756
1 Bullrush Ct Stafford (22554) *(G-13134)*

Custom Pubg Solutions LLC 540 341-0453
210 Cannon Way Warrenton (20186) *(G-14991)*

Custom Quality Woodworking 703 368-8010
9603 Clover Hill Rd Manassas (20110) *(G-7928)*

Custom Railing Solutions Inc 757 455-8501
5875 Adderley St Norfolk (23502) *(G-9512)*

Custom Restorations Inc 804 693-6526
7264 Belroi Rd Gloucester (23061) *(G-5843)*

Custom Rods & Such 434 736-9758
4140 Westpoint Stevens Rd Drakes Branch (23937) *(G-4132)*

Custom Screens Shds & Shutters, Ashland *Also called Tmac Services Inc (G-1501)*

Custom Sculpture & Sign Co 860 876-7529
127 Wampler St Nickelsville (24271) *(G-9384)*

Custom Sftwr Dsign Sltions LLC 888 423-4049
3 Gallagher Ln Fredericksburg (22405) *(G-5417)*

Custom Shutter and Blind, Roanoke *Also called Millehan Enterprises Inc (G-11967)*

Custom Sign Shop LLC 804 353-2768
1016 Nth Blvd Richmond (23230) *(G-11175)*

Custom Signs Today 703 661-0611
43720 Trade Center Pl # 105 Sterling (20166) *(G-13381)*

Custom Stage Curtain Fbrctrs 804 264-3700
9 W Cary St Richmond (23220) *(G-11553)*

Custom Tiles LLC 434 660-7170
1701 Avondale Dr Altavista (24517) *(G-631)*

Custom Tool & Machine Inc 540 563-3074
7533 Milk A Way Dr Roanoke (24019) *(G-11914)*

Custom Tops Inc 757 460-3084
4940 Rutherford Rd # 209 Virginia Beach (23455) *(G-14378)*

Custom Vault Corporation 804 303-1741
1011 Boulder Springs Dr North Chesterfield (23225) *(G-10017)*

Custom Vinyl Products LLC 757 887-3194
260 Enterprise Dr Newport News (23603) *(G-9209)*

Custom Welded Steel Art Inc 276 686-4107
723 Country View Rd Rural Retreat (24368) *(G-12421)*

Custom Welding and Fabrication, Williamsburg *Also called Custom Welding Inc (G-15227)*

Custom Welding Inc 757 220-1995
126 Tewning Rd Williamsburg (23188) *(G-15227)*

Custom Windows 804 262-1621
2238 Cresthaven Ct Henrico (23238) *(G-6497)*

Custom Woodwork 434 489-6991
1603 Halifax Rd Danville (24540) *(G-3974)*

Custom Yacht Service Inc. 804 438-5563
561 Wading Creek Rd Dutton (23050) *(G-4271)*

Custom-Tiles.com, Altavista *Also called Custom Tiles LLC (G-631)*

Customer 1 One Inc 276 645-9003
138 Bob Morrison Blvd Bristol (24201) *(G-1974)*

Customink LLC 434 326-1051
1180 Seminole Trl Charlottesville (22901) *(G-2613)*

Customized 540 492-2975
1610 Rugby Blvd Nw Roanoke (24017) *(G-12077)*

Customscoop, Alexandria *Also called Macar International LLC (G-267)*

Customtaylor33 ....703 785-7919
26077 Blackberry Knoll Ct Aldie (20105) *(G-105)*

Cut and Bleed LLC 804 937-0006
1600 Roseneath Rd Richmond (23230) *(G-11176)*

Cut Check Writing Services 757 898-9015
105 Somerset Cir Yorktown (23692) *(G-15947)*

Cuthbert Publishing LLC 540 840-7218
7416 N Katie Dr Fredericksburg (22407) *(G-5269)*
Cutie Pies Clay Print Keepskes 703 533-3313
18420 Mill Run Ct Leesburg (20176) *(G-7251)*
Cuton Power Inc 703 996-9350
3725 Concorde Pkwy Chantilly (20151) *(G-2401)*
Cutting Edge Carpet Binding 540 982-1007
433 Walnut Ave Vinton (24179) *(G-14171)*
Cutting Edge Millworks LLC 804 580-7270
1334 Sampsons Wharf Rd Heathsville (22473) *(G-6461)*
Cuz To Cuz Trucking 757 806-0358
1211 73rd St Newport News (23605) *(G-9210)*
Cv Corporation of Virginia (PA) **540 967-0368**
89 Rescue Ln Louisa (23093) *(G-7554)*
Cv Welding 540 338-6521
8 Longstreet Ave Round Hill (20141) *(G-12376)*
Cva Industrial Products Inc 434 985-1870
558 Pasture Ln Stanardsville (22973) *(G-13218)*
Cvent Inc 571 830-2301
8180 Greensboro Dr # 900 Mc Lean (22102) *(G-8413)*
Cvent Inc (HQ) **703 226-3500**
1765 Grnsboro Stn Pl Fl 7 Tysons Corner (22102) *(G-13952)*
CVille Dream Life 434 327-2600
901 Montrose Ave Charlottesville (22902) *(G-2776)*
Cville Siren LLC 434 987-2008
1117 Leonard St Charlottesville (22902) *(G-2777)*
CW Houchens and Sons Log LLC 804 615-2002
3022 Holly Grove Dr Bumpass (23024) *(G-2161)*
Cw Moore & Sons LLC 757 653-9011
23388 Lee St Courtland (23837) *(G-3767)*
Cw Security Solutions LLC 540 929-8019
1326 E Washington Ave Vinton (24179) *(G-14172)*
CWC Publishing Co LLC 540 439-3851
10466 Old Carolina Rd Midland (22728) *(G-8751)*
Cwi Marketing & Printing 540 295-5139
800 Wadsworth St Radford (24141) *(G-10706)*
Cyan LLC 703 455-3000
5417b Backlick Rd Springfield (22151) *(G-12986)*
Cyber Intel Solutions Inc 571 970-2689
8460 Great Lake Ln Springfield (22153) *(G-12987)*
Cyber-Canvas 540 692-9322
19 Sanford Ferry Ct Fredericksburg (22406) *(G-5418)*
Cybered Corp 757 573-5456
4507 Pleasant View Dr Williamsburg (23188) *(G-15228)*
Cyberex Corporation 703 904-0980
520 Herndon Pkwy Ste H Herndon (20170) *(G-6651)*
Cybersquire LLC 703 472-0283
511 Great Falls St Falls Church (22046) *(G-4906)*
Cycle Machine LLC 804 779-0055
116d Commerce Park Dr Manquin (23106) *(G-8215)*
Cycle Specialist 757 599-5236
11115 Jefferson Ave Newport News (23601) *(G-9211)*
Cycle Venture, Virginia Beach *Also called Dynamic Team Sports Inc* *(G-14422)*
Cynosure Services Inc 410 209-0796
1615 Duke St Alexandria (22314) *(G-179)*
Cyntherapy Scented Candles LLC 804 901-2681
3312 Hawkins Rd Henrico (23228) *(G-6498)*
Cynthia Coriopoli Design 703 548-2086
105 N Union St Alexandria (22314) *(G-180)*
Cynthia E Cox 276 236-7697
2867 Glendale Rd Galax (24333) *(G-5632)*
Cynthia Gray 703 860-5711
12313 Delevan Dr Herndon (20171) *(G-6652)*
Cynthia Kriparos 757 818-3441
1201 Gillette Ct Chesapeake (23323) *(G-3060)*
Cypress Home, Richmond *Also called Evergreen Enterprises Inc* *(G-11581)*
Cypress Woodworking LLC 703 803-6254
12221 Colchester Hunt Dr Fairfax (22030) *(G-4610)*
Cyril Edward Gropen 434 227-9039
1020 Locust Ave Charlottesville (22901) *(G-2614)*
Cyviz LLC 571 858-3371
900 N Glebe Rd Ste 2 Arlington (22203) *(G-924)*
D & D Inc 540 943-8113
200 W 12th St Waynesboro (22980) *(G-15107)*
D & D Signs 540 428-3144
6418 Old Meetze Rd Warrenton (20187) *(G-14992)*
D & G Signs Inc 757 858-2140
2640 Arkansas Ave Norfolk (23513) *(G-9513)*
D & K Embroidery 804 694-4747
2212 Hickory Fork Rd Gloucester (23061) *(G-5844)*
D & M Woodworks 757 510-3600
5720 Attica Ave Virginia Beach (23455) *(G-14379)*
D & N Copy Center, Vienna *Also called Day & Night Printing Inc* *(G-14035)*
D & P Printing & Graphics Inc 703 941-2114
5641i General Wash Dr Alexandria (22312) *(G-438)*
D & R Pro Tools LLC 804 338-1754
683 Namozine Rd Crewe (23930) *(G-3811)*
D & R USA Inc 434 572-6665
1054 Commerce Ln South Boston (24592) *(G-12758)*
D & S Construction 540 718-5303
15187 Buena Vista Dr Orange (22960) *(G-10209)*
D & S Controls 703 655-8189
7206 Marr Dr Warrenton (20187) *(G-14993)*
D & S Tool Inc 540 731-1463
1303 W Main St Radford (24141) *(G-10707)*
D & T Akers Corporation 804 435-2709
1281 Goodluck Rd Kilmarnock (22482) *(G-7069)*
D & V Enterprises Inc 757 665-5202
18475 Dunne Ave Parksley (23421) *(G-10261)*
D A D C, Stephens City *Also called Driving Aids Development Corp* *(G-13315)*
D and L Signs and Services LLC 434 265-4115
3482 Antlers Rd Boydton (23917) *(G-1914)*
D Atwood 703 508-5080
35 Gwynnville Rd Gwynn (23066) *(G-6045)*
D Carter Inc 540 967-1506
5159 W Old Mountain Rd Louisa (23093) *(G-7555)*
D J R Enterprises Inc 540 639-9386
1012 W Main St Radford (24141) *(G-10708)*
D J Thrift Store, Roanoke *Also called Flowers Bkg Co Lynchburg LLC* *(G-12090)*
D K Backhoe Loader Serv 434 969-1685
26 Manteo Rd Buckingham (23921) *(G-2132)*
D L S & Associates 276 796-5275
8205 S Mountain Rd Pound (24279) *(G-10511)*
D L Williams Company 276 326-3338
412 Ridgeway Dr Bluefield (24605) *(G-1861)*
D M T, Forest *Also called Dmt LLC* *(G-5067)*
D P Welding Inc 757 232-0460
834 Wyemouth Dr Newport News (23602) *(G-9212)*
D S I, Ashland *Also called Dispersion Specialties Inc* *(G-1402)*
D W Boyd Corporation 757 423-2268
4003 Colley Ave Norfolk (23508) *(G-9514)*
D-Fend Inc 703 728-4283
1640 Boro Pl Mc Lean (22102) *(G-8414)*
D-Orbit Inc 703 533-5661
6864 Frase Dr Falls Church (22043) *(G-4781)*
D-Star Aerospace, Ashburn *Also called D-Star Engineering Corporation* *(G-1267)*
D-Star Engineering Corporation (PA) **203 925-7630**
22805 Watson Heights Cir Ashburn (20148) *(G-1267)*
D-Star Instruments 703 335-0770
8424 Quarry Rd Ste 203 Manassas (20110) *(G-7929)*
D-Ta Systems Corporation 571 775-8924
2611 Richmond Hwy Ste 600 Arlington (22202) *(G-925)*
D3companies Inc 804 358-2020
201 Wylderose Dr Midlothian (23113) *(G-8807)*
Dacha 757 754-2805
966 Lord Dunmore Dr Virginia Beach (23464) *(G-14380)*
Dacha Systems Installation Svc, Virginia Beach *Also called Dacha* *(G-14380)*
Dacoal Mining Inc 276 531-8165
4014 Starbranch Rd Grundy (24614) *(G-6030)*
Dacs, Portsmouth *Also called Design Assstnce Cnstr Systems* *(G-10415)*
Dad13 Inc 703 550-9555
8401 Terminal Rd Newington (22122) *(G-9153)*
Dae Print & Design 757 518-1774
223 Expressway Ct Virginia Beach (23462) *(G-14381)*
Dae Print & Design 757 473-0234
223 Expressway Ct Virginia Beach (23462) *(G-14382)*
Dag Blast It Inc 757 237-0735
315 Hanbury Rd W B Chesapeake (23322) *(G-3061)*
Daghigh Software Co Inc 703 323-7475
10622 Timberidge Rd Fairfax Station (22039) *(G-4705)*
Dagnat Woodworks LLC 276 627-1039
1089 Flamingo Rd Bassett (24055) *(G-1581)*
Dagnewcompany Inc 703 835-0827
5934 Woodfield Estates Dr Alexandria (22310) *(G-439)*
Daily Deed LLC 703 754-0644
4256 Lawnvale Dr Gainesville (20155) *(G-5577)*
Daily Distributions Inc 703 577-8120
10464 Malone Ct Fairfax (22032) *(G-4435)*
Daily Frills LLC 540 850-7909
8121 Twelfth Corps Dr Fredericksburg (22407) *(G-5270)*
Daily Grind 540 387-2669
640 Joan Cir Salem (24153) *(G-12493)*
Daily Grind Hospital 540 536-2383
190 Campus Blvd Ste 130 Winchester (22601) *(G-15536)*
Daily Grub Hospitality Inc 804 221-5323
4912 W Marshall St Ste C Richmond (23230) *(G-11177)*
Daily Money Matters LLC 703 904-9157
1935 Crescent Park Dr Reston (20190) *(G-10831)*
Daily News Leader, Staunton *Also called Gannett Media Corp* *(G-13262)*
Daily News Record, Harrisonburg *Also called Rockingham Publishing Co Inc* *(G-6363)*
Daily News Record 540 459-4078
207 N Main St Woodstock (22664) *(G-15851)*
Daily News Record (HQ) **540 574-6200**
231 S Liberty St Harrisonburg (22801) *(G-6308)*
Daily News Record 540 743-5123
1113 E Main St Luray (22835) *(G-7606)*
Daily Peprah & Partners Servic 757 581-6452
138 S Rosemont Rd Ste 209 Virginia Beach (23452) *(G-14383)*

ALPHABETIC

Daily Press Inc (HQ) 757 245-3737
703 Mariners Row Newport News (23606) ***(G-9213)***
Daily Productions Inc 703 477-8444
18592 Colston Ct Leesburg (20176) ***(G-7252)***
Daily Progress 540 672-1266
146 Byrd St Orange (22960) ***(G-10210)***
Daily Scrub LLC 804 519-3696
12090 Foxwood Dr Disputanta (23842) ***(G-4106)***
Daily Splat LLC 703 729-0842
20310 Mustoe Pl Ashburn (20147) ***(G-1268)***
Dal Enterprises Inc 540 720-5584
233 Garrisonville Rd # 201 Stafford (22554) ***(G-13135)***
Dal Publishing 757 422-6577
948 Bingham St Virginia Beach (23451) ***(G-14384)***
Dalaun Couture LLC 703 594-1413
333 Maple Ave E 1025 Vienna (22180) ***(G-14032)***
Dale Horton Logging 276 251-5004
804 Kibler Valley Rd Ararat (24053) ***(G-831)***
Dale Quarry, Chester *Also called Legacy Vulcan LLC* ***(G-3428)***
Dale Stidham 276 523-1428
219 E 5th St S Big Stone Gap (24219) ***(G-1708)***
Daleel Corporation 703 824-8130
8300 Old Courthouse Rd # 210 Vienna (22182) ***(G-14033)***
Dalitso LLC 571 385-4927
1602 Belle View Blvd # 321 Alexandria (22307) ***(G-440)***
Dallas Electrical Company Inc 804 798-0002
11038 Air Park Rd Ste 1 Ashland (23005) ***(G-1400)***
Dallas G Bienhoff 571 232-4554
8455 Chapelwood Ct Annandale (22003) ***(G-738)***
Dallas-Katec Incorporated (PA) 757 428-8822
4511 Maiden Ln Norfolk (23518) ***(G-9515)***
Dalmatian Hill Engneering 540 289-5079
7190 Charlie Town Rd Port Republic (24471) ***(G-10383)***
Dalton Enterprises Inc 276 686-9178
206 Gienow Rd Rural Retreat (24368) ***(G-12422)***
Daltons Automotive 804 798-7909
11006 Air Park Rd Ashland (23005) ***(G-1401)***
Damas International LLC 469 740-9973
4327 Ravensworth Rd Annandale (22003) ***(G-739)***
Damascus Brewery 276 475-5319
32173 Government Rd Damascus (24236) ***(G-3947)***
Damascus Equipment LLC 276 676-2376
26161 Old Trail Rd 2 Abingdon (24210) ***(G-27)***
Damoah & Family Farm LLC 703 919-0329
4 Birkenhead Ln Stafford (22554) ***(G-13136)***
Damon Company of Salem Inc 540 389-8609
2117 Salem Industrial Dr Salem (24153) ***(G-12494)***
Damsel Detectors 757 268-4128
4417 Faigle Rd Portsmouth (23703) ***(G-10414)***
Damselwings Press 703 919-4230
2203 Abbotsford Dr Vienna (22181) ***(G-14034)***
Dan Charewicz 815 338-2582
1558 Cherry Grove Rd N Suffolk (23432) ***(G-13692)***
Dan Matheny Jerr 703 499-9216
14716 Industry Ct Woodbridge (22191) ***(G-15680)***
Dan McPherson & Sons Logging 540 483-4385
705 Pine Spur Rd Callaway (24067) ***(G-2221)***
Dan Miles & Associates LLC 619 508-0430
1303 Lakeside Rd Virginia Beach (23455) ***(G-14385)***
Dan River Window Co Inc 434 517-0111
1111 Wall St South Boston (24592) ***(G-12759)***
Dan Vally Farm, Claudville *Also called Alan Mitchell* ***(G-3637)***
Dan Van Der Hyde Repair Wldg, Chatham *Also called Van Der Hyde Dan* ***(G-2940)***
Dana Auto Systems Group LLC 757 638-2656
6920 Harbour View Blvd Suffolk (23435) ***(G-13693)***
Dana Thayer Design, Madison Heights *Also called Thayer Design Inc* ***(G-7885)***
Danaher Corporation 540 639-9046
501 W Main St Radford (24141) ***(G-10709)***
Danaher Family LLC 703 751-9712
503 N Quaker Ln Alexandria (22304) ***(G-181)***
Danaher Motion, Radford *Also called Kollmorgen Corporation* ***(G-10722)***
Danaher Motion 540 639-9046
501 W Main St Radford (24141) ***(G-10710)***
Danchem Technologies Inc 434 797-8120
1975 Old Richmond Rd Danville (24540) ***(G-3975)***
Dancing Kilt Brewery LLC 804 715-0695
12912 Old Stage Rd Chester (23836) ***(G-3401)***
Dandee Printing Co 540 828-4457
1881 Mountain Valley Rd Keezletown (22832) ***(G-7027)***
Dandy Point Industries 757 851-3280
326 Dandy Point Rd Hampton (23664) ***(G-6127)***
Dandy Printing 540 986-1100
213 W 4th St Salem (24153) ***(G-12495)***
Dane Meades Shop 276 926-4847
9334 Clintwood Hwy Pound (24279) ***(G-10512)***
Danicas S Crochet Club 703 221-8574
17432 Terri Ct Dumfries (22026) ***(G-4242)***
Daniel Cranford Recovery 434 382-8409
132 Fredonia Ave Lynchburg (24503) ***(G-7692)***
Daniel Orenzuk 410 570-1362
37519 Oak Green Ln Purcellville (20132) ***(G-10658)***
Daniel Patrick McDermott 540 305-3000
214 E Jackson St Front Royal (22630) ***(G-5528)***
Daniel Rollins 276 219-3988
4210 Powell Valley Rd Big Stone Gap (24219) ***(G-1709)***
Daniels Certified Welding 434 848-4911
290 Powell Ln Freeman (23856) ***(G-5511)***
Daniels Welding and Tires 757 566-8446
8005 Hankins Indus Park Toano (23168) ***(G-13862)***
Danielson Trading LLC 703 764-0450
3992 White Clover Ct Fairfax (22031) ***(G-4436)***
Danny A Walker 434 724-4454
657 Mountain Dr Callands (24530) ***(G-2213)***
Danny Coltrane 540 629-3814
8259 Sawgrass Way Radford (24141) ***(G-10711)***
Danny Marshall 434 797-5861
1088 Industrial Ave Danville (24541) ***(G-3976)***
Dannys Tools LLC 757 282-6229
2061 White Water Dr Virginia Beach (23456) ***(G-14386)***
Dante Industries Inc 757 605-6100
1324 Ballentine Blvd Norfolk (23504) ***(G-9516)***
Danville Dental Laboratory 434 793-2225
747 Main St Danville (24541) ***(G-3977)***
Danville Donuts LLC 434 835-4592
111 Sandy Ct Ste C Danville (24541) ***(G-3978)***
Danville Leaf Tobacco Co Inc (HQ) 804 359-9311
9201 Forest Hill Ave Fl 1 Richmond (23235) ***(G-11039)***
Danville Ready Mix 434 799-5818
503 Wilkerson Rd Danville (24540) ***(G-3979)***
Danville Register & Bee, Danville *Also called Wood Television LLC* ***(G-4051)***
Danville Sign Service, Danville *Also called J B Worsham* ***(G-4005)***
Danville Wtr Pltion Ctrl Plant, Danville *Also called City of Danville* ***(G-3967)***
Danzo LLC 703 532-8602
5852 Washington Blvd # 4 Arlington (22205) ***(G-926)***
Dap Enterprises Inc 757 921-3576
109 Sharps Rd Williamsburg (23188) ***(G-15229)***
Dap Incorporated 757 921-3576
11015 Warwick Blvd Newport News (23601) ***(G-9214)***
Daq Bats LLC 202 365-3246
6147 Tompkins Dr Mc Lean (22101) ***(G-8415)***
Dar Be Dar LLC 703 244-1599
11058 Aldbury Ct Reston (20194) ***(G-10832)***
Darbys Build and Design LLC 434 989-5493
18147 Springer Ln Gordonsville (22942) ***(G-5905)***
Darbys Custom Woodworks 434 989-5493
18147 Springer Ln Gordonsville (22942) ***(G-5906)***
Darco Southern LLC 276 773-2711
253 Darco Dr Independence (24348) ***(G-6981)***
Darden Logging LLC 757 647-9432
19483 Drake Rd Franklin (23851) ***(G-5141)***
Darden Pressure Wash and Plst 757 934-1466
2204 Arizona Ave Suffolk (23434) ***(G-13694)***
Dare Instrument Corporation 757 898-5131
1207 Dare Rd Yorktown (23692) ***(G-15948)***
Dark Cubed, Alexandria *Also called Dark3 Inc* ***(G-182)***
Dark Hollow LLC 540 355-8218
513 Beatty Holw Lexington (24450) ***(G-7394)***
Dark Warrior Group LLC 757 289-6451
21888 Brickshire Cir Ashburn (20148) ***(G-1269)***
Dark3 Inc (PA) 703 398-1101
202 Birch St Alexandria (22305) ***(G-182)***
Darklore Publishing LLC 703 566-8021
5375 Duke St Alexandria (22304) ***(G-183)***
Darlene Group Inc 401 728-3300
2775 N Quincy St Arlington (22207) ***(G-927)***
Darlin Monograms LLC 757 930-8786
241 Petersburg Ct Newport News (23606) ***(G-9215)***
Darr Maritime Services 757 631-0022
3332 Regent Park Walk Virginia Beach (23452) ***(G-14387)***
Darrell A Wilson 540 598-8412
1130 Cannon Ln Vinton (24179) ***(G-14173)***
Dart Mechanical Inc (PA) 757 539-2189
1265 Carolina Rd Suffolk (23434) ***(G-13695)***
Darwin Hvac, Alexandria *Also called Darwin Marquina* ***(G-441)***
Darwin Marquina 703 220-2940
4713 Perch Pl Alexandria (22309) ***(G-441)***
Darwins LLC 610 256-3716
3416 3rd St N Arlington (22201) ***(G-928)***
Data Fusion Solutions Inc 877 326-0034
7218 River Rd Fredericksburg (22407) ***(G-5271)***
Data Management LLC 703 222-4246
14704 Vrginia Infantry Rd Centreville (20121) ***(G-2300)***
Data Research Group Corp 571 350-9590
233 E Davis St Ste 400 Culpeper (22701) ***(G-3888)***
Data Science, Fairfax *Also called Aretec Inc* ***(G-4596)***
Data Visible, Charlottesville *Also called Vas of Virginia Inc* ***(G-2899)***
Data Werks, Virginia Beach *Also called Rebecca Leigh Fraser* ***(G-14765)***

Data-Clear LLC 703 499-3816
  513 N Frederick St Arlington (22203) *(G-929)*

Databasics Inc 703 262-0097
  12700 Sunrise Valley Dr # 102 Reston (20191) *(G-10833)*

Datablink Inc (HQ) **703 639-0600**
  7921 Jones Branch Dr # 101 Mc Lean (22102) *(G-8416)*

Databrands LLC 804 282-7890
  1910 Byrd Ave Ste 131 Richmond (23230) *(G-11178)*

Datacut Precision Machining 434 237-8320
  200 Airpark Dr Lynchburg (24502) *(G-7693)*

Datahaven For Dynamics LLC 757 222-2000
  4456 Corporation Ln Virginia Beach (23462) *(G-14388)*

Datalux Corporation (PA) **540 662-1500**
  155 Aviation Dr Winchester (22602) *(G-15409)*

Dataone Software 877 438-8467
  150 Granby St Norfolk (23510) *(G-9517)*

Datapath Inc 703 476-1826
  21251 Ridgetop Cir # 120 Sterling (20166) *(G-13382)*

Dataprivia Inc 855 477-4842
  1942 Thmson Dr Lwer Level Lower Level Lynchburg (24501) *(G-7694)*

Datassist 804 530-5008
  14522 Fox Knoll Dr South Chesterfield (23834) *(G-12800)*

Dateme Boutiques, Vienna Also called B Global LLC *(G-14013)*

Datis LLC 757 961-7498
  925 Brasileno Ct Virginia Beach (23456) *(G-14389)*

DATRON WORLD COMMUNICATIONS, INC., Alexandria Also called Datron Wrld
Communications Inc *(G-184)*

Datron Wrld Communications Inc 703 647-6235
  500 Montgomery St Ste 400 Alexandria (22314) *(G-184)*

Datskapatal Logistics LLC 757 814-7325
  424 Lee Highlands Blvd Virginia Beach (23452) *(G-14390)*

Davco Fabricating & Welding 434 836-0234
  2035 Woodlake Dr Danville (24540) *(G-3980)*

Dave Cleary 727 327-5118
  9313 Cougar Ct Manassas Park (20111) *(G-8198)*

Daves Cabinet Shop Inc 804 861-9275
  22418 Cox Rd North Dinwiddie (23803) *(G-10050)*

Daves Machine Shop 540 903-0172
  34 New Hope Church Rd Fredericksburg (22405) *(G-5419)*

Davic Drapery Company, Fairfax Also called K & Z Inc *(G-4488)*

David A Bennett 540 862-5868
  6415 Rich Patch Rd Covington (24426) *(G-3786)*

David A Einhorn 703 356-6218
  1944 Storm Dr Falls Church (22043) *(G-4782)*

David Aponte Sr, Henrico Also called Rivercity Communications *(G-6561)*

David Bennett 703 858-4669
  43730 Partlow Rd Ashburn (20147) *(G-1270)*

David Birkenstock 703 343-5718
  13577 Big Boulder Rd Herndon (20171) *(G-6653)*

David Blanchard Woodworking 540 468-3900
  132 W Main St Monterey (24465) *(G-9005)*

David Burns 703 644-4612
  6215 Lavell Ct Springfield (22152) *(G-12988)*

David C Maple 757 563-2423
  2518 Hartley St Virginia Beach (23456) *(G-14391)*

David C Weaver 804 561-5929
  14851 N Lodore Rd Amelia Court House (23002) *(G-654)*

David Ceramics LLC 703 430-2692
  641 Kentland Dr Great Falls (22066) *(G-5952)*

David F Waterbury Jr 757 490-5444
  4987 Cleveland St Ste 108 Virginia Beach (23462) *(G-14392)*

David Gaskill 703 768-2172
  4101 Komes Ct Alexandria (22306) *(G-442)*

David Hicks Logging, Floyd Also called Betty P Hicks *(G-5016)*

David Jr Press, Fairfax Also called Fairfax Printers Inc *(G-4621)*

David Kipps 540 948-4024
  2022 Repton Mill Rd Aroda (22709) *(G-1225)*

David M Tench Fine Crafte 804 261-3628
  6218 Ellis Ave Richmond (23228) *(G-11179)*

David Mays Cabinet Maker 434 277-8533
  1063 Lowesville Rd Amherst (24521) *(G-689)*

David R Powell 434 724-2642
  584 Primitive Baptst Rd W Dry Fork (24549) *(G-4140)*

David S Creath 434 753-2210
  13011 River Rd South Boston (24592) *(G-12760)*

David S Welch 276 398-4024
  162 Golden Leaves Dr Fancy Gap (24328) *(G-4934)*

David Steele 757 236-3971
  9120 Barnes Rd Toano (23168) *(G-13863)*

David W Slusher 540 745-2485
  717 Black Ridge Rd Sw Floyd (24091) *(G-5022)*

Davida 571 278-4287
  3015 Virginia Dare Ct Chantilly (20151) *(G-2402)*

Davids Mobile Service LLC 804 481-1647
  3213 Clay St Hopewell (23860) *(G-6922)*

Davidson Beauty Systems 804 674-4875
  10917 Hull Street Rd Midlothian (23112) *(G-8808)*

Davidson Plbg & Pipe Svc LLC 540 867-0847
  3357 Westbrier Dr Rockingham (22802) *(G-12246)*

Davis Brianna 703 220-4791
  7105 Signal Hill Rd Manassas (20111) *(G-8054)*

Davis & Davis Industries LLC 757 269-1534
  5857 Baynebridge Dr Virginia Beach (23464) *(G-14393)*

Davis Chetia 757 575-9225
  8426 Tidewater Dr Apt 7 Norfolk (23518) *(G-9518)*

Davis Communications Group 703 548-8892
  901 N Washington St # 603 Alexandria (22314) *(G-185)*

Davis Logging 804 725-7988
  827 Bookers Ln North (23128) *(G-9802)*

Davis Minding Manufacture 276 321-7137
  5957 Windswept Blvd Wise (24293) *(G-15621)*

Davis Mining & Mfg Inc (PA) **276 395-3354**
  5957 Windswept Blvd Wise (24293) *(G-15622)*

Davis Publishing Company 434 363-2780
  677 Eldon Rd Appomattox (24522) *(G-808)*

Davis-Frost Inc (PA) **434 846-2721**
  3416 Candlers Mountain Rd Lynchburg (24502) *(G-7695)*

Dawgbone Banners & Signs 804 526-5734
  3900 Lanyard Ct Chester (23831) *(G-3402)*

Dawger, Virginia Beach Also called Diversified Atmospheric Water *(G-14406)*

Dawn Brotherton 757 645-3211
  301 Back Forty Loop Williamsburg (23188) *(G-15230)*

Dawn Group Inc 703 750-6767
  4021 Woodland Rd Annandale (22003) *(G-740)*

Dawnbreaker Communications LLC 202 288-0805
  2178 Harithy Dr Dunn Loring (22027) *(G-4263)*

Dawson Enterprises Inc 276 964-7245
  21306 Crosswinds Dr Abingdon (24211) *(G-28)*

Day & Night Printing Inc 703 734-4940
  8618 Wstwd Ctr Dr Ll100 Vienna (22182) *(G-14035)*

Dayddream Writing, Virginia Beach Also called Dtwelve Enterprise LLC *(G-14415)*

Daydream Writing, Hampton Also called Lrj Publishing Group LLC *(G-6186)*

Daylight Cabinetry LLC 804 432-4954
  5203 New Kent Rd Richmond (23225) *(G-11554)*

Dayspring Pens LLC 888 694-7367
  2697 International Pkwy 120-4 Virginia Beach (23452) *(G-14394)*

Dayspring Pens Norfolk Ci, Virginia Beach Also called Dayspring Pens LLC *(G-14394)*

Dayton Dalice 540 233-3657
  218 E 4th St Front Royal (22630) *(G-5529)*

DAYTON LUMBER MILL, Dayton Also called Nelson Martin *(G-4058)*

Db Enterprises of VA LLC 804 931-7667
  14213 Delamere Dr Chester (23831) *(G-3403)*

Db Welding LLC 757 483-0413
  6985 Respass Beach Rd Suffolk (23435) *(G-13696)*

DBA Jus Bcuz 914 714-9327
  24291 Otter Dr Courtland (23837) *(G-3768)*

Dbs Productions LLC 434 293-5502
  1808 Rugby Pl Charlottesville (22903) *(G-2778)*

Dbs Publications, Saluda Also called Virginia Bride LLC *(G-12606)*

Dbsd North America Inc 703 964-1400
  11700 Plaza America Dr Reston (20190) *(G-10834)*

Dbt Publications, Mechanicsville Also called Trishs Books *(G-8690)*

DC Custom Print 301 541-8172
  4213 S Four Mile Run Dr Arlington (22204) *(G-930)*

DC Design and Media Inc 757 390-2818
  5900 Thurston Ave Ste D Virginia Beach (23455) *(G-14395)*

DC Metro Magazine 703 455-9223
  9607 Little Cobbler Ct Springfield (22015) *(G-12989)*

DC Recovery, Lynchburg Also called Daniel Cranford Recovery *(G-7692)*

Dcomputerscom 757 460-3324
  5193 Shore Dr Ste 103 Virginia Beach (23455) *(G-14396)*

Dcp Holdings LLC 804 876-3135
  10351 Verdon Rd Doswell (23047) *(G-4119)*

DCS Constitution, Sandston Also called Dominion Comfort Solutions LLC *(G-12611)*

Dcsports87 Sport Cards 571 334-3314
  9201 Dolmen Ct Glen Allen (23060) *(G-5721)*

Dd Pet Products Inc 703 532-3983
  2906 N Kensington St Arlington (22207) *(G-931)*

DD&t Custom Woodworking Inc 804 360-2714
  12109 Glastonbury Pl Richmond (23233) *(G-11180)*

Ddc Connections Inc 703 858-0326
  2434 Brussels Ct Reston (20191) *(G-10835)*

Ddg Supply Inc 804 730-0118
  9480 Shelley Dr Mechanicsville (23116) *(G-8617)*

Ddi VA 571 436-1378
  1200 Severn Way Dulles (20166) *(G-4197)*

Ddk Group LLC 201 726-2535
  8115 Bluebonnet Dr Lorton (22079) *(G-7478)*

De Carlo Enterprises Inc 703 281-1880
  420 Mill St Ne Vienna (22180) *(G-14036)*

De Costa's Silkscreening, Alexandria Also called Decosta Enterprises Inc *(G-443)*

De-Tech Solutions, Chesapeake Also called Lynn Donnell *(G-3191)*

Dead Reckoning Distillery 757 535-9864
  312 W 24th St Norfolk (23517) *(G-9519)*

Dead Reckoning Distillery Inc 757 620-3182
  100 Columbus Ave Chesapeake (23321) *(G-3062)*

Deadeye LLC 540 720-6818
  240 Marlborough Point Rd Stafford (22554) *(G-13137)*

ALPHABETIC

Deadline Digital Printing, Norfolk *Also called Deadline Typesetting Inc* *(G-9520)*
Deadline Typesetting Inc 757 625-5883
1048b W 27th St Norfolk (23517) *(G-9520)*
Deal Products, Prince George *Also called Fred Sisson* *(G-10594)*
Dean Delaware LLC 703 802-6231
22980 Indian Creek Dr # 130 Sterling (20166) *(G-13383)*
Dean Foods Company (PA) **804 359-5786**
2000 W Broad St Richmond (23220) *(G-11555)*
Dean Foods Company 804 737-8272
1595 Mary St Sandston (23150) *(G-12609)*
Dean Industries Intl LLC 703 249-5099
8114 Smithfield Ave Springfield (22152) *(G-12990)*
Deane Logging Co Inc 540 718-3676
4771 S Seminole Trl Madison (22727) *(G-7850)*
Deatrick & Associates Inc 703 753-1040
5618 Swift Creek Ct Haymarket (20169) *(G-6418)*
Deavers Lime and Litter LLC 540 833-4144
1918 Lacey Spring Rd Rockingham (22802) *(G-12247)*
Debbie Belt 912 856-9476
5302 Caledonia Rd Richmond (23225) *(G-11556)*
Debeer Piano Service LLC 703 727-4601
4907 Bentonbrook Dr Fairfax (22030) *(G-4611)*
Deborah E Ross 757 857-6140
6830 Orangewood Ave Norfolk (23513) *(G-9521)*
Deborah F Scarboro 757 866-0108
1022 Forest Ln Spring Grove (23881) *(G-12929)*
Debra Hewitt 540 809-6281
7147 Peppermill Rd King George (22485) *(G-7086)*
Debra Kromer 571 248-4070
8053 Crimson Leaf Ct Gainesville (20155) *(G-5578)*
Debra Rosel 703 675-4963
18280 Turnberry Dr Round Hill (20141) *(G-12377)*
Debs Picture This Inc 757 867-9588
3301 Hampton Hwy Ste H Yorktown (23693) *(G-15949)*
Deca Software LLC 202 607-5707
211 N Union St Alexandria (22314) *(G-186)*
Decade Five LLC 434 984-3065
400 Ivy Farm Dr Charlottesville (22901) *(G-2615)*
Decal Magic 540 984-3786
2549 Palmyra Church Rd Edinburg (22824) *(G-4302)*
Decals By Zebra Racing 540 439-8883
11672 Marsh Rd Bealeton (22712) *(G-1597)*
Decipher Inc 757 664-1111
259 Granby St Ste 100 Norfolk (23510) *(G-9522)*
Decision Point Tech LLC 757 286-1065
7407 Muirfield Rd Norfolk (23505) *(G-9523)*
Decisonq Infrmtion Oprtons Inc 703 938-7153
1776 Wilson Blvd Fl 5 Arlington (22209) *(G-932)*
Deck World Inc 804 798-9003
433 Cobham Park Ln Warsaw (22572) *(G-15062)*
Decks Down Under LLC 703 758-2572
2054 Chadds Ford Dr Reston (20191) *(G-10836)*
Deconsystems Corporation 703 587-3971
13513 Delaney Rd Woodbridge (22193) *(G-15681)*
Decor Lighting & Elec Co 540 320-8382
620 Jefferson Ave N Pulaski (24301) *(G-10634)*
Decorative Arts Workshop 703 321-8373
8912 Burbank Rd Annandale (22003) *(G-741)*
Decosta Enterprises Inc 703 768-4270
1116 Collingwood Rd Alexandria (22308) *(G-443)*
Decotec Inc 434 589-0881
1172 Perkins Rd Kents Store (23084) *(G-7038)*
Dedicated Micros Inc (HQ) **703 904-7738**
3855 Centerview Dr # 400 Chantilly (20151) *(G-2403)*
Dee K Enterprises Inc 540 745-3816
220 Appalachian Rd Floyd (24091) *(G-5023)*
Deeds Brothers Incorporated 540 862-7837
8286 Douthat State Pk Rd Millboro (24460) *(G-8935)*
Deeds Thrift Stores, Charlottesville *Also called Flowers Bkg Co Lynchburg LLC* *(G-2632)*
Deem Printing Company Inc 703 335-5422
7519 Presidential Ln Manassas (20109) *(G-8055)*
Deem Printing Company Inc 703 335-2422
9052 Euclid Ave Manassas (20110) *(G-7930)*
Deep Clean Carpet & Upholstery, Newport News *Also called Jr Everett Woodson* *(G-9270)*
Deep Corporation 804 751-1826
2500 Deepwater Trml Rd Richmond (23234) *(G-11040)*
Deep Creek Distilling Co LLC 757 337-0209
801 Butler St Ste 12 Chesapeake (23323) *(G-3063)*
Deep Prose Software LLC 703 815-0715
15004 Tarleton Dr Centreville (20120) *(G-2301)*
Deep-Space Intelligent Constru 571 247-7376
11314 Robert Carter Rd Fairfax Station (22039) *(G-4706)*
Deer Duplicating Svc Inc 804 648-6509
15 N 3rd St Richmond (23219) *(G-11557)*
Deerfield Group LLC 434 591-0848
1988 W Green Springs Rd Zion Crossroads (22942) *(G-16007)*
Dees Nuts Peanut Butter 607 437-0189
2961 Shore Dr Virginia Beach (23451) *(G-14397)*
Deezel Skateboards Vb LLC 757 490-6619
5405 Hatteras Rd Virginia Beach (23462) *(G-14398)*

Defazio Industries LLC 703 399-1494
3900 Westerre Pkwy # 300 Henrico (23233) *(G-6499)*
Defee LLC 757 645-4358
111 Royal North Devon Williamsburg (23188) *(G-15231)*
Defensative LLC 202 557-6937
1861 Wiehle Ave Ste 250 Reston (20190) *(G-10837)*
Defense Arnautical Support LLC 703 309-9222
1508 Victoria Farms Ln Vienna (22182) *(G-14037)*
Defense Daily, Arlington *Also called Leopard Media LLC* *(G-1031)*
Defense Daily 703 522-2012
1911 Fort Myer Dr Ste 310 Arlington (22209) *(G-933)*
Defense Dogs LLC 540 895-5611
10411 Mastin Ln Spotsylvania (22551) *(G-12887)*
Defense Executives LLC 757 638-3678
5100 W View Ct Suffolk (23435) *(G-13697)*
Defense Group, Mc Lean *Also called Northrop Grumman Systems Corp* *(G-8513)*
Defense Group 703 633-8300
4803 Stonecroft Blvd Chantilly (20151) *(G-2404)*
Defense Holdings Inc 703 334-2858
999d Shenandoah Shores Rd Front Royal (22630) *(G-5530)*
Defense Information Sys 855 401-8554
4601 Fairfax Dr Ste 1200 Arlington (22203) *(G-934)*
Defense Information Tech Inc (PA) **703 628-0999**
8355 Roxborough Loop Gainesville (20155) *(G-5579)*
Defense Insights LLC 703 455-7880
9915 Evenstar Ln Fairfax Station (22039) *(G-4707)*
Defense News 703 750-9000
1919 Gallows Rd Ste 400 Vienna (22182) *(G-14038)*
Defense Systems Sector, Mc Lean *Also called Northrop Grumman Systems Corp* *(G-8516)*
Defense Threat 703 767-2798
6200 Meade Rd Fort Belvoir (22060) *(G-5114)*
Defense Threat Reductio 703 767-4627
18794 Pier Trail Dr Triangle (22172) *(G-13890)*
Defense Threat Reductio 703 767-5870
7444 Fountain Head Dr Annandale (22003) *(G-742)*
Defense United States Dept 804 292-5642
400 N 8th St Ste 584 Richmond (23219) *(G-11558)*
Defensecoat Industries LLC 804 356-5316
5511a Biggs Rd Richmond (23224) *(G-11559)*
Defenseworx LLC 703 568-3295
14110 Sorrel Chase Ct Centreville (20121) *(G-2302)*
Defensor Holsters LLC 703 409-4865
6205 Long Meadow Rd Mc Lean (22101) *(G-8417)*
Degen Enterprises Inc 757 853-7651
2532 Ingleside Rd Norfolk (23513) *(G-9524)*
Degustabox USA LLC 203 514-8966
801 Friendship Dr Rockingham (22802) *(G-12248)*
Dehardit Press 804 693-2795
7339 Lewis Ave Gloucester (23061) *(G-5845)*
Dejarnette Lumber Company 804 633-9821
17186 Alliance Dr Milford (22514) *(G-8930)*
Deka Batteries & Cables, Ashland *Also called East Penn Manufacturing Co* *(G-1407)*
Dekdyne Inc 757 221-2542
201 Harrison Ave Williamsburg (23185) *(G-15232)*
Delany Products, Charlottesville *Also called Coyne & Delany Company* *(G-2773)*
Delaplane Sellers 540 592-7210
2187 Winchester Rd Delaplane (20144) *(G-4075)*
Delauri & Associates 757 482-9140
505 Hatteras Cres Chesapeake (23322) *(G-3064)*
Delaware Valley Communications 434 823-2282
1716 Browns Gap Tpke Charlottesville (22901) *(G-2616)*
Delclos Industries LLC 540 349-4049
5459 Claire Ct Warrenton (20187) *(G-14994)*
Delfort USA Inc 434 202-7870
216 3rd St Ne Ste C Charlottesville (22902) *(G-2779)*
Delfosse Vineyards Winery LLC 434 263-6100
500 Del Fosse Winery Ln Faber (22938) *(G-4389)*
Delfosse Vinyrd Winery Nelson, Faber *Also called Mountain and Vine LLC* *(G-4390)*
Deli-Fresh Foods Inc 757 428-8126
1253 Jensen Dr Ste 101 Virginia Beach (23451) *(G-14399)*
Delicious Beverage LLC 703 517-0216
760 Palmer Dr Herndon (20170) *(G-6654)*
Delicious Dainties LLC 240 620-7581
2351 Millennium Ln Reston (20191) *(G-10838)*
Delightful Scents 804 245-6999
6823 W Carnation St Apt E Richmond (23225) *(G-11560)*
Delivery Junkies 540 329-9060
5710 Dendron Dr Richmond (23223) *(G-11561)*
Dell EMC 301 897-1400
10700 Parkridge Blvd Reston (20191) *(G-10839)*
Dell Inc 301 581-0513
8270 Wllw Oaks Crprte 3 Fairfax (22031) *(G-4437)*
Della JS Delectables LLC 703 922-4687
6605 Schurtz St Alexandria (22310) *(G-444)*
Delmarva Air Compressor, Greenbackville *Also called Engineered Enrgy Solutions LLC* *(G-5993)*
Delmarva Crane Inc 757 426-0862
1616 Deere Ct Virginia Beach (23457) *(G-14400)*

(G-0000) Company's Geographic Section entry number

Delmer-Va Inc 571 447-1413
11149 Wortham Crest Cir Manassas (20109) *(G-8056)*
Delong Lithographics Services 703 550-2110
7205 Lockport Pl Ste D Lorton (22079) *(G-7479)*
Delphi Inc 703 908-0258
2530 N Randolph St Arlington (22207) *(G-935)*
Delrand Corp 757 490-3355
5018 Cleveland St Virginia Beach (23462) *(G-14401)*
Delta Circle Industries Inc 804 743-3500
8001 Reycan Rd North Chesterfield (23237) *(G-9857)*
Delta Electronics Inc 703 354-3350
5730 General Wash Dr Alexandria (22312) *(G-445)*
Delta Q Dynamics LLC 703 980-9449
8347 Tillett Loop Manassas (20110) *(G-7931)*
Deltek Systems Inc 703 734-8606
13880 Dulles Corner Ln # 400 Herndon (20171) *(G-6655)*
Deltek Systems Inc 800 456-2009
2291 Wood Oak Dr Herndon (20171) *(G-6656)*
Delullo Software LLC 570 419-6736
8528 Blue Rock Ln Lorton (22079) *(G-7480)*
Deluxe Kitchen and Bath 571 594-6363
42713 Latrobe St Chantilly (20152) *(G-2531)*
Dematology Assoc Virginia P 804 549-4030
301 Cncourse Blvd Ste 190 Glen Allen (23059) *(G-5722)*
Demco Machine Inc 540 248-5135
1401 Laurel Hill Rd Verona (24482) *(G-13984)*
Dementi Milestone Pubg Inc 804 784-5151
1530 Oak Grove Dr Manakin Sabot (23103) *(G-7898)*
Demoiselle Vertical LLC 202 431-8032
5800 Quantrell Ave # 1620 Alexandria (22312) *(G-446)*
Demons Run Brewing LLC 703 945-8100
4020 41st St N Arlington (22207) *(G-936)*
Demorais & Associates Pllc 703 754-7991
8028 Montour Heights Dr Gainesville (20155) *(G-5580)*
Demorais International Inc 703 369-3326
9255 Center St Ste 200 Manassas (20110) *(G-7932)*
Dempsey & Corcoran 434 294-3942
926 Church St Blackstone (23824) *(G-1815)*
Demsign 202 787-1518
4401 Lee Hwy Apt 77 Arlington (22207) *(G-937)*
Den Hertog Frits 540 929-4650
10063 Fortune Ridge Rd Bent Mountain (24059) *(G-1668)*
Deneals Cabinets Inc (PA) **540 721-8005**
2650 Edwardsville Rd Hardy (24101) *(G-6286)*
Denim 804 918-2361
4748 Finlay St Richmond (23231) *(G-11181)*
Denim Stax Inc 434 429-6663
234 N Union St Danville (24541) *(G-3981)*
Denim Twist Inc 703 273-3009
4800 Braddock Knoll Way Fairfax (22030) *(G-4612)*
Denis Britto Dr 703 230-6784
4080 Lafayette Center Dr # 160 Chantilly (20151) *(G-2405)*
Dennington Wdwrk Solutions LLC 571 414-6917
2211 Lofty Heights Pl Reston (20191) *(G-10840)*
Dennis H Fredrick 804 358-6000
7940 Blueberry Hill Ct Richmond (23229) *(G-11182)*
Dennis W Wiley 540 992-6631
43 Wheatland Rd Buchanan (24066) *(G-2121)*
Dent Removal Masters, Roanoke *Also called Beverley M James Jr (G-11888)*
Dental Equipment Services LLC 703 927-1837
18111 Gore Ln Leesburg (20175) *(G-7253)*
Dentalpartshaus, Richmond *Also called Virginia Dental Sc Inc (G-11440)*
Dentcore Inc 844 292-8023
14100 Pk Madow Dr Ste 100 Chantilly (20151) *(G-2406)*
DEP Copy Center Inc 703 499-9888
14816 Build America Dr Woodbridge (22191) *(G-15682)*
Department Info Tech Inc 703 868-6691
13551 Tabscott Dr Chantilly (20151) *(G-2407)*
Depco-Dfnse Engineered Pdts LLC 804 271-7000
7925 Cogbill Rd Chesterfield (23832) *(G-3493)*
Deporter Dominick & Assoc LLC 703 530-9255
7853 Coppermine Dr Ste C Manassas (20109) *(G-8057)*
Dept of Economics, Ashland *Also called Randolph-Macon College (G-1483)*
DER LLC 434 736-9100
161 Kings Hwy Keysville (23947) *(G-7056)*
Des Champs Technologies Inc 540 291-1111
225 S Magnolia Ave Buena Vista (24416) *(G-2141)*
Desales Inc 804 794-8187
21411 Genito Rd Moseley (23120) *(G-9038)*
Desantis Design Inc 540 751-9014
105 E Cornwell Ln Purcellville (20132) *(G-10659)*
Desert Rose Ranch & Winery LLC 540 635-3200
13726 Hume Rd Hume (22639) *(G-6960)*
Design Assstnce Cnstr Systems 757 393-0704
900 Port Centre Pkwy Portsmouth (23704) *(G-10415)*
Design Digital Printing LLC 276 964-9391
337 Laurelwood Acres Rd Cedar Bluff (24609) *(G-2274)*
Design In Copper Inc 540 885-8557
202 S Lewis St Staunton (24401) *(G-13250)*
Design Integrated Tech Inc 540 349-9425
100 E Franklin St Warrenton (20186) *(G-14995)*
Design Master Associates Inc 757 566-8500
3005 John Deere Rd Toano (23168) *(G-13864)*
Design Printers, Saint Paul *Also called Lou Wallace (G-12469)*
Design Source Inc 804 644-3424
5401 Lewis Rd Ste A Sandston (23150) *(G-12610)*
Design Systems & Services Corp 804 722-0396
318 E Wythe St Petersburg (23803) *(G-10316)*
Designer Cabinets 540 569-0469
416 Marquis St Staunton (24401) *(G-13251)*
Designer Goldsmith Inc 703 777-7661
39272 Mount Gilead Rd Leesburg (20175) *(G-7254)*
Designer Goldsmith Inc 703 777-7661
203 Harrison St Se Ste A Leesburg (20175) *(G-7255)*
Designer Signs 757 879-1153
38476 Rocky Hock Rd Wakefield (23888) *(G-14965)*
Designer Software Inc 540 842-8425
4605 Carr Dr Fredericksburg (22408) *(G-5272)*
Designo Enterprises LLC 571 437-5452
45891 Woodland Rd Ste 125 Sterling (20166) *(G-13384)*
Designpure Nanocryst LLC 571 458-0951
5990 Rchmond Hwy Apt 1104 Arlington (22203) *(G-938)*
Designs Inc 757 547-5478
110 Battlefield Blvd N Chesapeake (23320) *(G-3065)*
Designs Inc (PA) **757 410-1600**
110 Battlefield Blvd N Chesapeake (23320) *(G-3066)*
Designs By Ms. Rita, Petersburg *Also called Patrick Marrietta (G-10333)*
Designs In Wood LLC 804 517-1414
3410 W Leigh St Richmond (23230) *(G-11183)*
Dessies Delicious Desserts LLC 804 822-7482
213 Wren St Prince George (23875) *(G-10591)*
Destiny 11 Publications LLC 804 814-3019
10401 Crooked Branch Ter North Chesterfield (23237) *(G-9858)*
Det Enterprises Inc 310 429-3234
40742 Greyhouse Pl Leesburg (20175) *(G-7256)*
Detail Maxx LLC 703 942-8965
1544 Spring Hill Rd Mc Lean (22102) *(G-8418)*
Detamore Printing Co 540 886-4571
327 N Central Ave Staunton (24401) *(G-13252)*
Detas Famous Potatoe Salad LLC 757 609-1130
4643 Georgetown Pl Virginia Beach (23455) *(G-14402)*
Detectamet Inc 804 303-1983
5111 Glen Alden Dr Richmond (23231) *(G-11184)*
Detective Coating LLC 804 893-3313
10910 Southlake Ct Ste H North Chesterfield (23236) *(G-9859)*
Determined LLC 804 829-7229
105 S Mesa Dr Hopewell (23860) *(G-6923)*
Detron Realty LLC 703 884-6741
4548 Kendall Dr Woodbridge (22193) *(G-15683)*
Devanezdaypublishing Co 757 493-1634
2220 Sleeper Ct Virginia Beach (23456) *(G-14403)*
Devault Vineyards LLC 434 993-0722
247 Station Ln Concord (24538) *(G-3759)*
Development News Service, Alexandria *Also called Hemlock Design Group Inc (G-477)*
Devereux Barns LLC 540 664-1432
1671 Lockes Mill Rd Berryville (22611) *(G-1677)*
Devils Backbone Brewing Co, Lexington *Also called Mountain View Brewery LLC (G-7404)*
Devin Clark 276 889-3426
63 Old Fincastle Rd Lebanon (24266) *(G-7191)*
Dewey L Sams 540 664-4034
212 1st St Berryville (22611) *(G-1678)*
Dewey Publications Inc 703 524-1355
1840 Wilson Blvd Ste 203 Arlington (22201) *(G-939)*
Dews Screen Printer 757 436-0908
809 Prof Pl W Ste A104 Chesapeake (23320) *(G-3067)*
Dews Screen Printers, Chesapeake *Also called Dews Screen Printer (G-3067)*
Dexco Polymers LP 703 846-2193
3438 Valewood Dr Oakton (22124) *(G-10143)*
Dextall Inc 202 701-3208
2720 Prosperity Ave # 400 Fairfax (22031) *(G-4438)*
Dexter W Estes 434 996-8068
70 Blackwell Ln Lyndhurst (22952) *(G-7843)*
Dfa Dairy Brands Fluid LLC 540 777-4091
540 Mohawk Ave Ne Roanoke (24012) *(G-12078)*
Dfa Dairy Brands Fluid LLC 336 714-9032
37306 Gov G C Peery Hwy Bluefield (24605) *(G-1862)*
Dfa Dairy Brands Fluid LLC 336 714-9032
12572 E Lynchburg Slem Tp Forest (24551) *(G-5066)*
Dfa Dairy Brands Fluid LLC 336 714-9032
1170 Fulp Industrial Rd South Boston (24592) *(G-12761)*
DFI Systems Inc 757 262-1057
2513 58th St Hampton (23661) *(G-6128)*
Dg Optics LLC 434 227-1017
2330 Walnut Ridge Ln Charlottesville (22911) *(G-2617)*
Dg2 Teler Sales 540 955-1996
11 W Main St Berryville (22611) *(G-1679)*
Dgi Line Inc (PA) **434 797-4114**
306 Updike Pl Danville (24541) *(G-3982)*

A L P H A B E T I C

Dhk Storage LLC 703 870-3741
44965 Aviation Dr Ste 205 Sterling (20166) *(G-13385)*
DHT Woodworks LLC 434 414-2607
388 Charles Dr Appomattox (24522) *(G-809)*
Di Cola Llc Ciro Schiano 703 779-0212
19537 Emerald Park Dr Leesburg (20175) *(G-7257)*
Di-Mac Outdoors Inc 434 489-3211
166 Meadowbrook Cir Danville (24541) *(G-3983)*
Di9 Equity Investors 703 860-0901
11710 Plaza America Dr Reston (20190) *(G-10841)*
Diamante Clothing, Virginia Beach *Also called Euphoric Treatz LLC (G-14453)*
Diamond 7 .... 540 362-5958
6322 Greenway Dr Roanoke (24019) *(G-11915)*
Diamond Screen Graphics Inc 804 249-4414
4305 Sarellen Rd Henrico (23231) *(G-6500)*
Diamond Source of Virginia 804 360-3373
12813 Fox Meadow Dr Richmond (23233) *(G-11185)*
Diamondback Sport 434 964-6447
1229 Harris St Ste 11 Charlottesville (22903) *(G-2780)*
Diamondback Tool Co 800 899-2358
1229 Harris St Ste 11 Charlottesville (22903) *(G-2781)*
Diamondefense LLC 571 321-2012
3436 Holly Rd Annandale (22003) *(G-743)*
Diana Khoury & Co 703 592-9110
7653 Fullerton Rd Ste A Springfield (22153) *(G-12991)*
Dianes Crochet Dolls & Things 703 229-2173
5548 Eiseley Ct Warrenton (20187) *(G-14996)*
Diaz Ceramics 804 672-7161
2406 Skeet St Henrico (23294) *(G-6501)*
Dickenson Star/Cmbrlnd Times, Clintwood *Also called Double T Publishing Inc (G-3688)*
Dickenson-Russell Coal Co LLC 276 889-6100
7546 Gravel Lick Rd Cleveland (24225) *(G-3655)*
Dickerson Machine and Design 540 789-7945
3371 Zimmerman Ln Christiansburg (24073) *(G-3583)*
Dickerson Stump LLC 540 898-9145
5618 Massaponax Church Rd Fredericksburg (22407) *(G-5273)*
Didc LLC 646 684-5861
106 Willoughby Pl Apt B Danville (24541) *(G-3984)*
Die Cast Connections Inc 276 669-5991
14660 Industrial Park Rd Bristol (24202) *(G-2016)*
Diehappy LLC 804 283-6025
14854 Elliot Ridge Way Glen Allen (23059) *(G-5723)*
Dietz Press, Petersburg *Also called William R Smith Company (G-10351)*
Differential Brands Group Inc 703 448-9985
2001 International Dr Mc Lean (22102) *(G-8419)*
Differential Pressure Instrs 757 362-0742
1619 Diamond Springs Rd D Virginia Beach (23455) *(G-14404)*
Diffusion Pharmaceuticals Inc (PA) **434 220-0718**
1317 Carlton Ave Ste 400 Charlottesville (22902) *(G-2782)*
Diffusion Pharmaceuticals LLC 434 220-0718
1317 Carlton Ave Ste 400 Charlottesville (22902) *(G-2783)*
Diggs Industries LLC 757 371-3470
102 Cypress Ave Smithfield (23430) *(G-12711)*
Digi Quick Print Inc 703 671-9600
5100 Leesburg Pike Ste B Alexandria (22302) *(G-187)*
Digigram Inc 330 476-5247
4035 Ridge Top Rd Ste 700 Fairfax (22030) *(G-4613)*
Digilink Inc 703 340-1800
840 S Pickett St Alexandria (22304) *(G-188)*
Digital Access Control Inc 703 463-0113
14163 Robert Paris Ct B Chantilly (20151) *(G-2408)*
Digital Beans Inc 703 775-2225
104 Stewart Ave Apt 1 Alexandria (22301) *(G-189)*
Digital Canvas LLC 703 819-3543
3218 Dashiell Rd Falls Church (22042) *(G-4783)*
Digital Delights Inc 703 661-6888
22967 Whitehall Ter Sterling (20166) *(G-13386)*
Digital Design Imaging Svc Inc 703 534-7500
100 W Jefferson St # 102 Falls Church (22046) *(G-4907)*
Digital Documents Inc 571 434-0341
12529 Misty Water Dr Herndon (20170) *(G-6657)*
Digital Global Systems Inc 240 477-7149
7950 Jones Branch Dr 1a Tysons Corner (22102) *(G-13953)*
Digital High Point, Prince George *Also called Carolina Container Company (G-10588)*
Digital Image Printing, Daleville *Also called Cunningham Digital Inc (G-3941)*
Digital Machining Company 540 786-7138
9200 Rapidan Dr Fredericksburg (22407) *(G-5274)*
Digital Printing Solutions Inc 540 389-2066
119 E Burwell St Salem (24153) *(G-12496)*
Digital State Media, Woodbridge *Also called Erick Gonzalez (G-15696)*
Digital Synergy LLC 540 951-5900
2020 Kraft Dr Ste 2300 Blacksburg (24060) *(G-1732)*
Digitized Risk LLC 703 662-3510
21786 Findon Ct Ashburn (20147) *(G-1271)*
Dileway LLC 703 897-6811
903 Fairway Dr Ne Vienna (22180) *(G-14039)*
Dillion Logging 434 685-1779
169 Whitmore Dr Danville (24540) *(G-3985)*
Dilon Technologies Inc 757 269-4910
12050 Jefferson Ave # 340 Newport News (23606) *(G-9216)*
Diloreto Partners Inc 804 271-2363
5005 Castlewood Rd Richmond (23234) *(G-11041)*
Dimension Stone LLC 804 615-7750
9860 Knobs Hill Ln Amelia Court House (23002) *(G-655)*
Dimension Tool LLC 804 350-9707
4001 Centralia Rd Chester (23831) *(G-3404)*
Dimensional Communications, Alexandria *Also called Print Promotion (G-316)*
Dimensions Virginia Beach Inc 757 340-1115
371 Phyllis Ct Virginia Beach (23452) *(G-14405)*
Dimensionu Inc 804 447-4220
1895 Billingsgate Cir B Henrico (23238) *(G-6502)*
Dimitrios & Co Inc 703 368-1757
9203 Enterprise Ct Ste U Manassas Park (20111) *(G-8199)*
Dining With Dignity Inc 757 565-2452
101 Deerwood Dr Williamsburg (23188) *(G-15233)*
Dinkle Enterprises 434 324-8508
2440 Roark Mill Rd Hurt (24563) *(G-6974)*
Dinkle, C W Enterprises, Hurt *Also called Dinkle Enterprises (G-6974)*
Dino Software Corporation 703 768-2610
1912 Earldale Ct Ste 200 Alexandria (22306) *(G-447)*
Diorio Manufacturing Co LLC 540 438-1870
32 Silver Lake Rd Rockingham (22801) *(G-12249)*
Dipped In Ice LLC 540 845-3567
18539 Brick Church Rd Orange (22960) *(G-10211)*
Dirak Incorporated 703 378-7637
22560 Glenn Dr Ste 105 Sterling (20164) *(G-13387)*
Direct Buy Mattress LLC 703 346-0323
8819 Commerce St Midland (22728) *(G-8752)*
Direct Cut Lawn Tree Svc LLC 804 516-7771
1657 Manakin Rd Manakin Sabot (23103) *(G-7899)*
Direct Stairs 540 436-9290
1056 Harrisville Rd Toms Brook (22660) *(G-13883)*
Direct Tools Factory Outlet 757 345-6945
5601 Richmond Rd Williamsburg (23188) *(G-15234)*
Direct Wood Products (PA) **804 843-4642**
18501 Eltham Rd West Point (23181) *(G-15155)*
Directed Vapor Tech Intl Inc 434 977-1405
4006 Hunterstand Ct # 101 Charlottesville (22911) *(G-2618)*
Directional Sign Services Inc 703 568-5078
6419 Wainfleet Ct Springfield (22152) *(G-12992)*
Directive Systems and Eng LLC 703 754-3876
2702 Rodgers Ter Haymarket (20169) *(G-6419)*
Dirt Removal Services LLC 703 499-1299
11921 Bluebird Ln Catharpin (20143) *(G-2261)*
Dirty Deeds Power Washing 804 731-2739
7355 Trailing Rock Rd Prince George (23875) *(G-10592)*
Disaster Aide 201 892-8898
115 Casmar St Se Vienna (22180) *(G-14040)*
Discopy, Falls Church *Also called Diskcopy Inc (G-4784)*
Discount Frames Inc (PA) **703 550-0000**
7200 Telegraph Square Dr Lorton (22079) *(G-7481)*
Discountcryo Co 804 733-3229
2200 E Washington St Petersburg (23803) *(G-10317)*
Discover Granite & Marble, Manassas *Also called V & P Investment LLC (G-8009)*
Discover Sml Magazine (PA) **540 719-7881**
40 Village Springs Dr Hardy (24101) *(G-6287)*
Discovery Map 703 346-7166
3110 Mount Vernon Ave # 220 Alexandria (22305) *(G-190)*
Discovery Publications Inc 540 349-8060
125 W Shirley Ave Warrenton (20186) *(G-14997)*
Discus N More LLC 609 678-6102
6308 Sweetbriar Dr Fredericksburg (22407) *(G-5275)*
Dishman Fabrications LLC 757 478-5070
201 Production Dr Ste D Yorktown (23693) *(G-15950)*
Diskcopy Inc 703 658-3539
6228 Lakeview Dr Falls Church (22041) *(G-4784)*
Dispersion Specialties Inc 804 798-9137
11237 Leadbetter Rd Ashland (23005) *(G-1402)*
Dispersive Technologies Inc 252 725-0874
3076 Centreville Rd # 114 Herndon (20171) *(G-6658)*
Display & Banner Inc 703 503-4447
8125 Briar Creek Dr Annandale (22003) *(G-744)*
Display Case Main Plant, South Chesterfield *Also called Hill Phoenix Inc (G-12808)*
Display Case, Plant 2, South Chesterfield *Also called Hill Phoenix Inc (G-12805)*
Displaymakers Company 703 501-2527
4236 Inn St Triangle (22172) *(G-13891)*
Disrupt6 Inc 571 721-1155
18625 Darden Ct Leesburg (20176) *(G-7258)*
Disse Outdoor Gear LLC 804 357-2860
5901 Herrick Pl Glen Allen (23059) *(G-5724)*
Dister Inc (PA) **757 857-1946**
925 Denison Ave Norfolk (23513) *(G-9525)*
Dister Inc 703 207-0201
2800 Juniper St Ste 5 Fairfax (22031) *(G-4439)*
Distinct Impressions 434 572-8144
309 Main St South Boston (24592) *(G-12762)*
Distribution Center, Roanoke *Also called Cooper Crouse-Hinds LLC (G-12072)*
District IV Apparel Company, Virginia Beach *Also called OSI LLC (G-14705)*

District Orthopedic Appliances 703 698-7373
7702 Backlick Rd Ste D Springfield (22150) *(G-12993)*

Dit, Warrenton *Also called Design Integrated Tech Inc (G-14995)*

Ditch Witch of Virginia 804 798-2590
11053 Washington Hwy Glen Allen (23059) *(G-5725)*

Divergence Software Inc 703 690-9870
8519 Oak Pointe Way Fairfax Station (22039) *(G-4708)*

Diverging Approach Inc 757 220-2316
6623 Richmond Rd Ste L Williamsburg (23188) *(G-15235)*

Diversfied Wldg Fbrication LLC 804 449-6699
19212 Woodsons Mill Rd Beaverdam (23015) *(G-1608)*

Diversified Atmospheric Water 757 617-1782
2700 Avenger Dr Ste 103b Virginia Beach (23452) *(G-14406)*

Diversified Eductl Systems 540 687-7060
205 E Washington St Middleburg (20118) *(G-8719)*

Diversified Industries 540 992-1900
110 Boone Dr Troutville (24175) *(G-13908)*

Diversified Solution LLC 434 845-5100
101 Duncraig Dr Unit 209 Lynchburg (24502) *(G-7696)*

Diversified Vacuum Corp 757 538-1170
2408a Pruden Blvd Suffolk (23434) *(G-13698)*

Diversified Vacuum Inc 757 538-1170
2408a Pruden Blvd Suffolk (23434) *(G-13699)*

Diversity Grphics Slutions LLC 757 812-3311
1 Bounty Cir Hampton (23669) *(G-6129)*

Divine Creations, Portsmouth *Also called Shyanne Branch (G-10481)*

Divine Lifestyle Printing LLC 804 219-3342
3307 Greenham Dr Chester (23831) *(G-3405)*

Divine Ntre & Antng Mnsts Inc 757 240-8939
14301 Trophy Buck Ct Midlothian (23112) *(G-8809)*

Divinely Inspired Press LLC 703 763-3790
5764 Laurel Glen Ct Manassas (20112) *(G-8058)*

Divvy Cloud Corporation 571 290-5077
2111 Wilson Blvd Ste 450 Arlington (22201) *(G-940)*

Divvycloud, Arlington *Also called Divvy Cloud Corporation (G-940)*

Dixie Fuel Company 757 249-1264
512 Muller Ln Ste B Newport News (23606) *(G-9217)*

Dixie Plastics & Machining 434 283-3778
1802 Long Island Rd Gladys (24554) *(G-5690)*

Dixie Plate GL & Mirror Co LLC 540 869-4400
6773 Valley Pike Middletown (22645) *(G-8737)*

Dixie Press Custom Screen 757 569-8241
31004 Maple Ave Sedley (23878) *(G-12679)*

Dixie Sign Company, Ashland *Also called Joseph Randolph Pike (G-1443)*

Dixie Woodcraft Inc 434 842-3384
154 Red Bank Ln Fork Union (23055) *(G-5109)*

Dixon Mediation Group LLC 703 517-3556
10107 View Point Ct Fairfax Station (22039) *(G-4709)*

Dixon Powhatan 410 810-7585
325 Arbor Ct Winchester (22602) *(G-15410)*

Dixon Valve & Coupling Co LLC 540 535-2181
325 Arbor Ct Winchester (22602) *(G-15411)*

Dixons Trash Disposal LLC 434 978-2111
5498 Richmond Rd Troy (22974) *(G-13924)*

Dizzy Pig LLC 571 379-4884
8763 Virginia Meadows Dr Manassas (20109) *(G-8059)*

DJS Enterprises 703 973-0977
515 Prince St Alexandria (22314) *(G-191)*

DK Consulting LLC 224 402-3333
23231 Hubbards Rd Remington (22734) *(G-10768)*

DK Pharma Group LLC 540 574-4651
947 Summit Ave Harrisonburg (22802) *(G-6309)*

Dkl International Inc 703 938-6700
11921 Freedom Dr Ste 550 Reston (20190) *(G-10842)*

Dks Machine Shop Inc 540 775-9648
15079 Sunset Ln King George (22485) *(G-7087)*

Dla Document Services 703 784-2208
1001 Barnett Ave Code40 Quantico (22134) *(G-10688)*

Dla Document Services 804 734-1791
2900 41st St Fort Lee (23801) *(G-5128)*

Dla Document Services 757 855-0300
1279 Franklin St Rm 129 Norfolk (23511) *(G-9526)*

Dla Document Services 757 444-7068
1641 Morris St Bldg Kbb Norfolk (23511) *(G-9527)*

Dlba Robotics Ltd 757 288-0206
506 Industry Dr Hampton (23661) *(G-6130)*

DLM Enterprises Inc 757 617-3470
3020 Bay Shore Ln Suffolk (23435) *(G-13700)*

Dlp Enterprises Inc (PA) **757 420-5886**
820 Greenbrier Cir Ste 10 Chesapeake (23320) *(G-3068)*

Dm Associates LLC 571 406-2318
4110 Whitacre Rd Fairfax (22032) *(G-4440)*

Dmedia Prints 571 297-3287
7545 Axton St Springfield (22151) *(G-12994)*

Dmh Complete Welding 540 347-7550
1431 Welding Ln Warrenton (20186) *(G-14998)*

Dmkp Inc 703 941-1436
1340 Old Chain Bridge Rd Mc Lean (22101) *(G-8420)*

Dml Industries LLC 571 348-4332
3200 Dam Neck Rd Ste 104 Virginia Beach (23453) *(G-14407)*

Dmmt Glisan Inc 276 620-0298
4450 E Lee Hwy Max Meadows (24360) *(G-8367)*

Dmprobes, Charlottesville *Also called Dominion Microprobes Inc (G-2619)*

Dmt LLC (PA) **434 455-2460**
1019 Dillard Dr Forest (24551) *(G-5067)*

Dna Welding LLC 703 256-2976
7471 Little River Tpke Annandale (22003) *(G-745)*

Dnj Dirtworks Inc 540 937-3138
7131 Rixeyville Rd Rixeyville (22737) *(G-11878)*

Do-Da Innovations LLC 804 556-6645
2415 Two Turtles Rd Maidens (23102) *(G-7890)*

Dobbs & Assoc 804 314-8871
9988 Lickinghole Rd Ste 2 Ashland (23005) *(G-1403)*

Dobbs & Associates 804 769-4266
191 Powhatan Trl King William (23086) *(G-7129)*

Dobyns Family LLC 804 462-5554
525 Colinbrook Way 1 Lancaster (22503) *(G-7159)*

Docdirect Publishing LLC 757 237-1106
1017 Timber Neck Mall Chesapeake (23320) *(G-3069)*

Docks Canvas & Upholstery 540 840-0440
371 Greenbank Rd Fredericksburg (22406) *(G-5420)*

Dockside Seafood 757 357-9298
1002 Newport St Battery Park (23304) *(G-1595)*

Document Automation & Prdtn 757 878-3389
655 Williamson Ave Fort Eustis (23604) *(G-5126)*

Dodd Custom Canvas LLC 757 717-4436
828 Pacific Ave Portsmouth (23707) *(G-10416)*

Dodson Litho Printers Inc 757 479-4814
1658 Kempsville Rd Virginia Beach (23464) *(G-14408)*

Dodson Logging LLC 540 547-2582
24259 Colgate Rd Unionville (22567) *(G-13962)*

Dof USA Inc 888 635-4999
14225 Sullyfield Cir E Chantilly (20151) *(G-2409)*

Dog Trotter K-9 Equipment, Winchester *Also called Robert Lummus (G-15468)*

Dog Watch of Shenandoah 540 867-5124
153 Clover Hill Rd Dayton (22821) *(G-4054)*

Dogged State Distilling Co 434 480-0575
3181 Hungarytown Rd Blackstone (23824) *(G-1816)*

Dogtown Lights LLC 804 334-5088
1600 Roseneath Rd Ste I Richmond (23230) *(G-11186)*

Dogwood Graphics 434 447-6004
105 Mccracken St South Hill (23970) *(G-12848)*

Dogwood Graphics Inc 434 447-6004
105 Mccracken St South Hill (23970) *(G-12849)*

Dogwood Logic Inc 540 557-7689
203 Roanoke St W Blacksburg (24060) *(G-1733)*

Dogwood Montessori &C 540 439-3572
10741 James Madison Hwy Bealeton (22712) *(G-1598)*

Dogwood Mountain Log Homes LLC 540 433-1873
4563 S Valley Pike Rockingham (22801) *(G-12250)*

Dogwood Ridge Outdoors Inc 540 867-0764
4253 Woodcock Ln Dayton (22821) *(G-4055)*

Doherty Plumbng Co 757 842-4221
600 Oxbow Ct Chesapeake (23322) *(G-3070)*

Doi Nay Newspaper 703 748-1239
6515 Gretna Green Way Alexandria (22312) *(G-448)*

Doit, Chantilly *Also called Department Info Tech Inc (G-2407)*

Doite Media LLC 703 594-1322
43135 Dry Ridge Ter Broadlands (20148) *(G-2076)*

Dolan Contracting 703 768-9496
5508 Bradley Blvd Alexandria (22311) *(G-192)*

Dolan LLC 804 783-0770
801 E Main St Ste 302 Richmond (23219) *(G-11562)*

Dombroski Vineyards LLC 804 932-8240
8400 Old Church Rd New Kent (23124) *(G-9130)*

Dome and Spear Distillery LLC 434 851-5477
4529 Dearborn Rd Evington (24550) *(G-4376)*

Dometic Corporation 804 746-1313
8433 Erle Rd Mechanicsville (23116) *(G-8618)*

Dometic Environmental Systems, Mechanicsville *Also called Dometic Corporation (G-8618)*

Dominion Ammunition Mfg Inc 804 276-2851
106 Turner Rd North Chesterfield (23225) *(G-10018)*

Dominion Bldg Components LLC 540 371-2184
68 Cool Spring Rd Ste B Fredericksburg (22405) *(G-5421)*

Dominion Coal Corp 276 935-8810
15498 Riverside Dr Oakwood (24631) *(G-10167)*

Dominion Comfort Solutions LLC 804 501-6429
209 Stuttaford Dr Sandston (23150) *(G-12611)*

Dominion Computer Services 757 473-8989
5241 Cleveland St Ste 110 Virginia Beach (23462) *(G-14409)*

Dominion Controls, Salem *Also called Key Recovery Corporation (G-12526)*

Dominion Defense LLC 703 216-7295
15347 Blacksmith Ter Woodbridge (22191) *(G-15684)*

Dominion Distribution Svcs Inc (HQ) **757 351-7000**
150 Granby St Norfolk (23510) *(G-9528)*

Dominion Door and Drawer 804 955-9302
26768 Ruther Glen Rd Ruther Glen (22546) *(G-12454)*

Dominion Energy Inc 804 771-3000
2901 Charles City Rd Richmond (23231) *(G-11187)*

Dominion Energy Virginia, Chesapeake *Also called Virginia Electric and Power Co (G-3360)*

Dominion Enterprises 757 351-7000
150 Granby St Ste 150 Norfolk (23510) ***(G-9529)***

Dominion Enterprises 757 226-9440
413 W York St Norfolk (23510) ***(G-9530)***

Dominion Enterprises 540 869-3837
100 Brandylion Ct Stephens City (22655) ***(G-13314)***

Dominion Graphics Inc 804 353-3755
3110 W Leigh St Richmond (23230) ***(G-11188)***

Dominion Ink LLC 804 350-7996
1111 Carrolton St Richmond (23221) ***(G-11563)***

Dominion Leasing Software 804 378-2204
1545 Standing Ridge Dr B Powhatan (23139) ***(G-10542)***

Dominion Microprobes Inc 434 962-8221
1027 Stonewood Dr Charlottesville (22911) ***(G-2619)***

Dominion Packaging Inc 804 447-6921
5700 Audubon Dr Sandston (23150) ***(G-12612)***

Dominion Press Winery LLC 703 395-5109
8733b Cooper Rd Alexandria (22309) ***(G-449)***

Dominion Production 804 247-4106
1421 Rogers St Richmond (23223) ***(G-11564)***

Dominion Quikrete Inc (PA) **757 547-9411**
932 Professional Pl Chesapeake (23320) ***(G-3071)***

Dominion Quikrete Inc 276 957-3235
930 Meadowood Trl Martinsville (24112) ***(G-8279)***

Dominion Sign Company, Richmond *Also called Gtp Ventures Incorporated* ***(G-11227)***

Dominion Steel Inc 540 898-1249
4920 Quality Dr Fredericksburg (22408) ***(G-5276)***

Dominion Taping & Reeling Inc 804 763-2700
3930 Castle Rock Rd Ste D Midlothian (23112) ***(G-8810)***

Dominion Water Products Inc (PA) **804 236-9480**
5707 S Laburnum Ave Richmond (23231) ***(G-11189)***

Dominion Wldg Fabrication Inc 757 692-2002
5361 Meadowside Dr Virginia Beach (23455) ***(G-14410)***

Domino's, Franklin *Also called Tips East LLC* ***(G-5159)***

Don Elthon 703 237-2521
404 E Broad St Falls Church (22046) ***(G-4908)***

Donald Crisp Jr 757 903-6743
117 Production Dr Ste B Yorktown (23693) ***(G-15951)***

Donald F Rouse 276 783-7569
219 Autumn Ln 21 Marion (24354) ***(G-8226)***

Donald Kirby 540 493-8698
345 Ashpone Tavern Rd Rocky Mount (24151) ***(G-12317)***

Donald N Jensen 202 577-9892
3301 Coryell Ln Alexandria (22302) ***(G-193)***

Donalds Meat Processing LLC 540 463-2333
194 Mccorkle Dr Lexington (24450) ***(G-7395)***

Donaty Software Inc 540 822-5496
39891 Honeysuckle Ct Lovettsville (20180) ***(G-7578)***

Dong-A Package USA Corp 703 961-1686
4115 Pleasant Valley Rd Chantilly (20151) ***(G-2410)***

Donley Technology 804 224-9427
220 Garfield Ave Colonial Beach (22443) ***(G-3724)***

Donna Cannaday 540 489-7979
700 Callaway Rd Rocky Mount (24151) ***(G-12318)***

Donnasatticofcrafts 757 855-0559
4566 Kennebeck Ave Norfolk (23513) ***(G-9531)***

Donnelly's Printing & Graphics, Reston *Also called Jjj Inc* ***(G-10881)***

Donning Company Publishers, Virginia Beach *Also called Donning Publishers Inc* ***(G-14411)***

Donning Publishers Inc 757 497-1789
184 Bsineva Pk Dr Ste 206 Virginia Beach (23462) ***(G-14411)***

Donovan Pat Racing Enterprise 540 829-8396
17525 Kibler Rd Culpeper (22701) ***(G-3889)***

Dons Welding 540 896-3445
14238 Pine Crest Ln Fulks Run (22830) ***(G-5565)***

Donut Diva LLC 276 245-5987
203 Fincastle Tpke Tazewell (24651) ***(G-13831)***

Doodadd Shop 276 964-2389
155 Legend St Pounding Mill (24637) ***(G-10518)***

Door Systems Inc 703 490-1800
1030 Highams Ct Woodbridge (22191) ***(G-15685)***

Doors & More Welding 804 798-4833
11196 Woodstock Hts Dr Glen Allen (23059) ***(G-5726)***

Doors Done Right LLC 757 567-3891
1652 Laurel Ln Virginia Beach (23451) ***(G-14412)***

Dorcas Electric Services, Herndon *Also called Beta Contractors LLC* ***(G-6623)***

Doris Anderson 877 869-1543
17 Emmaus Rd Poquoson (23662) ***(G-10369)***

Dormakaba USA Inc 804 966-9166
16031 Continental Blvd South Chesterfield (23834) ***(G-12801)***

Dorothy Edwards 859 608-3539
6040 Heathwick Ct Burke (22015) ***(G-2188)***

Dorothy Prntice Armtherapy Inc (PA) **703 657-0160**
11851 Monument Dr Apt 412 Fairfax (22030) ***(G-4614)***

Dorothy Whibley 703 892-6612
15443 Beachview Dr Montclair (22025) ***(G-8997)***

Dorsett Publications LLC 540 382-6431
630 Depot St Ne Christiansburg (24073) ***(G-3584)***

Dose Guardian LLC (PA) **804 726-5448**
6130 Midlothian Tpke Richmond (23225) ***(G-11565)***

Doskocil Mfg Co Inc 218 766-2558
11801 Riders Ln Reston (20191) ***(G-10843)***

Doss Fork Coal Co Inc 540 322-4066
111 1/2 S College Ave Bluefield (24605) ***(G-1863)***

Doswell Quarry, Ashland *Also called Martin Marietta Materials Inc* ***(G-1459)***

Doswell Water Treatment Plant 804 876-3557
10076 Kings Dominion Blvd Doswell (23047) ***(G-4120)***

DOT Blue 804 564-2563
303 W 30th St Richmond (23225) ***(G-11566)***

Double B Trailers 540 586-0651
9145 Forest Rd Goode (24556) ***(G-5889)***

Double D LLC 270 307-2786
15358 Wits End Dr Woodbridge (22193) ***(G-15686)***

Double D S Wldg & Fabrication 757 566-0019
3931 Ropers Church Rd Lanexa (23089) ***(G-7165)***

Double Ds Welding & Fabricati, Lanexa *Also called Double D S Wldg & Fabrication* ***(G-7165)***

Double Eagle Golf Works Inc 757 436-4459
434 Las Gaviotas Blvd Chesapeake (23322) ***(G-3072)***

Double Edge Defense LLC 540 550-0849
25 Battery Dr Winchester (22601) ***(G-15537)***

Double Envelope, Roanoke *Also called BSC Ventures LLC* ***(G-11896)***

Double Horseshoe Saloon 434 202-8714
1522 E High St Charlottesville (22902) ***(G-2784)***

Double Jj Alpacas LLC 540 286-0992
12480 Tower Hill Rd Midland (22728) ***(G-8753)***

Double T Publishing Inc 276 926-8816
Main St Ste 202 Clintwood (24228) ***(G-3688)***

Doublethink News LLC 434 466-2092
121 Washington Ave Charlottesville (22903) ***(G-2785)***

Doucraft Services 703 620-4965
3603 Twilight Ct Oakton (22124) ***(G-10144)***

Doug, Ford *Also called SD Davis Welding & Equipment* ***(G-5048)***

Dough Pay ME of Bristol LLC 276 644-8091
15290 Turnberry Ct Bristol (24202) ***(G-2017)***

Dough-Licious, Chesapeake *Also called Camacho Enterprises LLC* ***(G-3023)***

Douglas Manning 703 631-9064
5101 Doyle Ln Centreville (20120) ***(G-2303)***

Douglas S Huff 540 886-4751
115 S Jefferson St Staunton (24401) ***(G-13253)***

Douglas Stuart LLC 571 210-4440
22712 Commrce Ctr Ct # 1 Sterling (20166) ***(G-13388)***

Douglas Vince Johner 276 780-2369
1639 Whitetop Rd Chilhowie (24319) ***(G-3550)***

Dougs Mobile Electric 757 438-6045
1062 W 37th St Norfolk (23508) ***(G-9532)***

Dougs Welding & Ornamental Ir 804 435-6363
118 Old Mail Rd White Stone (22578) ***(G-15187)***

Doukenie Winery 540 668-6464
14727 Mountain Rd Hillsboro (20132) ***(G-6864)***

Dova Pharmaceuticals Inc 844 506-3682
200 Garrett St Ste P Charlottesville (22902) ***(G-2786)***

Dove Logging Inc 540 937-4917
8320 Old Stillhouse Rd Rixeyville (22737) ***(G-11879)***

Dove S Delights LLC 540 298-7178
308 Hill Ave Elkton (22827) ***(G-4325)***

Dove Welding and Fabrication 757 262-0996
2353 52nd St Hampton (23661) ***(G-6131)***

Dover Plank Enterprises LLC 757 286-6772
2315 Rosewood Ave Richmond (23220) ***(G-11567)***

Dowling Signs Inc 540 373-6675
1801 Princess Anne St Fredericksburg (22401) ***(G-5183)***

Downtown Writing and Press 540 907-9732
1102 Prince Edward St Fredericksburg (22401) ***(G-5184)***

Downunder Hats Virginia LLC 804 334-7476
6600 Glen Falls Xing Moseley (23120) ***(G-9039)***

Doyle Sailmakers Virginia 757 727-0750
4111 Kecoughtan Rd Hampton (23669) ***(G-6132)***

Dozier Tank & Welding Company 757 543-5759
801 Industrial Ave Chesapeake (23324) ***(G-3073)***

Dozier Tank and Welding Co 804 232-0092
2212 Deepwater Trml Rd Richmond (23234) ***(G-11042)***

DP Facilities Inc 866 589-6125
19775 Belmont Executive P Ashburn (20147) ***(G-1272)***

Dp Technology 703 835-6157
21411 Deepwood Ter Broadlands (20148) ***(G-2077)***

Dptl Inc 703 435-2291
623 Carlisle Dr Herndon (20170) ***(G-6659)***

Dr Banaji Girish DDS PC 703 849-1300
8505 Arlington Blvd # 370 Fairfax (22031) ***(G-4441)***

Dr Finnie Care LLC 804 852-7998
1601 Carty Bay Dr Chester (23836) ***(G-3406)***

Dr Jk Longevity LLC 202 304-0896
1521 Boyd Pointe Way # 2501 Vienna (22182) ***(G-14041)***

Dr Kings Little Luxuries LLC 434 293-8515
640 Bunker Hill Ln Keswick (22947) ***(G-7045)***

Dr Ozz Dat Drip Bbq Sauce LLC 757 597-4405
1585 Briarfield Rd # 112 Hampton (23666) ***(G-6133)***

Dr Pepper Bottlers Lynchburg 434 528-5107
121 Bradley Dr Lynchburg (24501) ***(G-7697)***

Dr Pepper of Staunton, Staunton *Also called Halmor Corp* ***(G-13263)***

ALPHABETIC SECTION
Duck Publishing LLC

Dr Pepper of Staunton, Va., Charlottesville *Also called Halmor Corp* ***(G-2643)***
Dr. Stoner's Frederick Co, Winchester *Also called Blackbird Spirits LLC* ***(G-15387)***
Draculas Tokens LLC...717 818-5687
19449 Xerox Dr Leesburg (20176) ***(G-7259)***
Draeger Ignition Interlock, Chesapeake *Also called Draeger Safety Diagnostics Inc* ***(G-3074)***
Draeger Ignition Interlock, Purcellville *Also called Draeger Safety Diagnostics Inc* ***(G-10660)***
Draeger Safety Diagnostics Inc...757 819-7471
215 Research Dr Ste 105 Chesapeake (23320) ***(G-3074)***
Draeger Safety Diagnostics Inc...804 768-4294
12530 Iron Bridge Rd Chester (23831) ***(G-3407)***
Draeger Safety Diagnostics Inc...540 382-6650
415 N Franklin St Christiansburg (24073) ***(G-3585)***
Draeger Safety Diagnostics Inc...434 770-5594
176 Tensbury Dr Martinsville (24112) ***(G-8280)***
Draeger Safety Diagnostics Inc...434 822-0820
3401 Westover Dr Danville (24541) ***(G-3986)***
Draeger Safety Diagnostics Inc...703 517-0974
37251 E Richardson Ln Purcellville (20132) ***(G-10660)***
Draft Doctor...804 986-6588
1901 Cedarhurst Dr Richmond (23225) ***(G-11568)***
Draftco Incorporated...540 337-1054
80 Johnson Dr Stuarts Draft (24477) ***(G-13646)***
Dragon Defense Mfg...804 986-6635
8526 Sanford Dr Richmond (23228) ***(G-11190)***
Dragons Lair Glass Studio...540 564-0318
814 Spotswood Dr Harrisonburg (22802) ***(G-6310)***
Dragonsrealm Vineyard LLC...540 905-9679
3061 Heavenly Ln Goldvein (22720) ***(G-5877)***
Dragoon Technologies Inc...937 439-9223
240 Airport Rd 1 Winchester (22602) ***(G-15412)***
Drake Company...757 536-1509
800 Twin Peak Ct Chesapeake (23320) ***(G-3075)***
Drake Extrusion Inc...276 632-0159
790 Industrial Park Rd Ridgeway (24148) ***(G-11841)***
Drake Hearing Aid Centers (PA)...**703 521-1404**
403 S Cleve Rd Arlington (22204) ***(G-941)***
Drake Welding Services Inc...757 399-7705
202 Monitor Rd Portsmouth (23707) ***(G-10417)***
Drapery House Inc...703 669-9622
18 Sycolin Rd Se Leesburg (20175) ***(G-7260)***
Dream Catcher Enterprises LLC...540 338-8273
38409 Stone Eden Dr Hamilton (20158) ***(G-6056)***
Dream Dog Productions LLC...703 980-0908
9218 Cutting Horse Ct Springfield (22153) ***(G-12995)***
Dream Green International LLC...814 616-7800
2800 Eisenhower Ave # 220 Alexandria (22314) ***(G-194)***
Dream It & Do It LLC...804 379-5474
14451 W Salisbury Rd Midlothian (23113) ***(G-8811)***
Dream of ME Bowtique...804 955-5908
9411 Kennesaw Rd North Chesterfield (23236) ***(G-9860)***
Dream Reels Inc...540 891-9886
6014 N Cranston Ln Fredericksburg (22407) ***(G-5277)***
Dreambuilders USA LLC...908 265-2621
603 Marcella Rd Apt 5 Hampton (23666) ***(G-6134)***
Dreampak LLC...703 751-3511
7901 Jones Branch Dr # 420 Mc Lean (22102) ***(G-8421)***
Dreams2realitees LLC...434 594-6865
408 Wolfe St Emporia (23847) ***(G-4357)***
Dreamscape Publishing...757 717-2734
805 Dunwood Ct Chesapeake (23322) ***(G-3076)***
Dreamvision Software LLC...703 378-7191
13800 Coppermine Rd # 305 Herndon (20171) ***(G-6660)***
Dreauxn Films LLC...504 452-1117
20322 Center Brook Sq Sterling (20165) ***(G-13389)***
Drengr Defense Industries LLC...703 552-9987
2211 Goldentree Way Vienna (22182) ***(G-14042)***
Dresser-Rand Company...540 444-4200
4655 Technology Dr Salem (24153) ***(G-12497)***
DRG Imports LLC...786 246-6548
1535 West Ave Richmond (23220) ***(G-11569)***
Driftwood Gallery...804 932-3318
2800 Brianwood Ct Quinton (23141) ***(G-10694)***
Drill Supply of Virginia LLC...540 992-3595
1195 Country Club Rd Troutville (24175) ***(G-13909)***
Drillco National Group Inc...703 631-3222
14620 Flint Lee Rd Unit E Chantilly (20151) ***(G-2411)***
Drilling J...804 303-5517
2610 Pine Grove Dr Richmond (23294) ***(G-11191)***
Drip Printing & Design...757 962-1594
617 Jack Rabbit Rd Ste A Virginia Beach (23451) ***(G-14413)***
Drive Square Inc (PA)...**617 762-4013**
3213 Duke St Ste 656 Alexandria (22314) ***(G-195)***
Driveline Fabrications Inc...540 483-3590
19868 Virgil H Goode Hwy Rocky Mount (24151) ***(G-12319)***
Driving 4 Dollars...757 609-1298
1300 Oakland Rd Henrico (23231) ***(G-6503)***
Driving Aids Development Corp...703 938-6435
845 Salem Church Rd Stephens City (22655) ***(G-13315)***
Drmtees LLC...540 720-3743
49 Orchid Ln Stafford (22554) ***(G-13138)***
Drone Safety LLC...703 589-6738
3602 Old Vernon Ct Alexandria (22309) ***(G-450)***
Drone Tier Systems Intl LLC...757 450-7825
1309 Eagle Ave Virginia Beach (23453) ***(G-14414)***
Dronechakra Inc...540 420-7394
47253 Middle Bluff Pl Sterling (20165) ***(G-13390)***
Drones Club of Virginia LLC...540 324-8180
101 Village Dr Apt 104 Staunton (24401) ***(G-13254)***
Droneshield LLC...202 750-4368
7140 Farm Station Rd B Warrenton (20187) ***(G-14999)***
Drs C3 & Aviation Company...571 346-7700
12930 Worldgate Dr # 700 Herndon (20170) ***(G-6661)***
Drs C3 Aviation Company, Chesapeake *Also called Drs Leonardo Inc* ***(G-3077)***
Drs Custom Fabrication LLC...703 680-4259
15017 Huntgate Ln Dumfries (22025) ***(G-4243)***
Drs Global Entp Solutions Inc...703 898-9233
45975 Nokes Blvd Ste 145 Dulles (20166) ***(G-4198)***
Drs Homeland SEC Solutions Inc...703 682-1801
2345 Crystal Dr Ste 915 Arlington (22202) ***(G-942)***
Drs Leonardo Inc...703 416-7600
1235 S Clark St Ste 700 Arlington (22202) ***(G-943)***
Drs Leonardo Inc...757 819-0700
825 Greenbrier Cir Chesapeake (23320) ***(G-3077)***
Drs Leonardo Inc (HQ)...**703 416-8000**
2345 Crystal Dr Ste 1000 Arlington (22202) ***(G-944)***
Drs Leonardo Inc...571 383-0152
3859 Centerview Dr # 200 Chantilly (20151) ***(G-2412)***
Drs Leonardo Inc...703 260-7979
1033 Sterling Rd Ste 104 Herndon (20170) ***(G-6662)***
Drs Leonardo Inc...703 416-8000
2345 Crystal Dr Ste 1000 Arlington (22202) ***(G-945)***
Druh-Ke LLC...757 274-3117
5617 Nathaniel St Suffolk (23435) ***(G-13701)***
Drumhellers Practical Choi...540 949-0462
332 Kingsbury Dr Waynesboro (22980) ***(G-15108)***
Drumsticks Inc...804 743-9356
6042 Jessup Rd North Chesterfield (23234) ***(G-9861)***
Dry Fork Fruit Distillery LLC...276 952-1222
1355 Mount Olivet Rd Martinsville (24112) ***(G-8281)***
Dry Mill Rd LLC...703 737-3697
102 Dry Mill Rd Sw # 101 Leesburg (20175) ***(G-7261)***
Dry Mill Vineyards and Winery, Leesburg *Also called Vanhuss Family Cellars LLC* ***(G-7369)***
Dryfork Mine Supply, North Tazewell *Also called Lonnie L Sparks* ***(G-10102)***
Drytac Corporation (PA)...**804 280-6013**
5401b Eubank Rd Sandston (23150) ***(G-12613)***
Ds & RC Enterprises LLC...804 824-5478
7576 South Shore Dr Gloucester (23061) ***(G-5846)***
Ds Smith Packaging, Roanoke *Also called Ds Smith PLC* ***(G-11916)***
Ds Smith PLC...540 774-0500
6405 Commonwealth Dr Roanoke (24018) ***(G-11916)***
DS Tees LLC...540 841-8831
6927 Versaille Dr Fredericksburg (22407) ***(G-5278)***
Dsd Laboratories Inc...703 904-4384
11921 Freedom Dr Ste 550 Reston (20190) ***(G-10844)***
Dse Outdoor Product Inc...540 789-4800
4705 Indian Valley Rd Nw Willis (24380) ***(G-15360)***
Dsg TEC Usa Inc...619 757-5430
4818 Midland Rd Midland (22728) ***(G-8754)***
Dsh Signs LLC...804 270-4003
2036 Dabney Rd Richmond (23230) ***(G-11192)***
Dsigns...804 559-5884
8529 Meadowbridge Rd Mechanicsville (23116) ***(G-8619)***
Dt Enterprises Inc...434 799-3153
418 Trade St Danville (24541) ***(G-3987)***
Dtc Communications Inc (HQ)...**727 471-6900**
2303 Dulles Station Blvd # 205 Herndon (20171) ***(G-6663)***
Dtc Press LLC...703 255-9891
2979 Westhurst Ln Oakton (22124) ***(G-10145)***
Dtwelve Enterprise LLC...757 837-0452
900 Commonwealth Pl # 200 Virginia Beach (23464) ***(G-14415)***
Du Pont Tjin Flms US Ltd Prtnr (PA)...**804 530-4076**
3600 Discovery Dr Chester (23836) ***(G-3408)***
Du Pont Tjin Flms US Ltd Prtnr...804 530-4076
3600 Discovery Dr Chester (23836) ***(G-3409)***
Du Pont Tjin Flms US Ltd Prtnr...804 530-9339
5401 Jefferson Davis Hwy North Chesterfield (23234) ***(G-9862)***
Dual Dynamics Industrail Paint...804 543-3216
3156 Smokey Rd Aylett (23009) ***(G-1548)***
Dublin Machine Inc...540 674-9347
98 Dublin Park Rd Dublin (24084) ***(G-4154)***
Dublin Machine Enterprises, Dublin *Also called Jerry Johnston* ***(G-4160)***
Dubrook Concrete Inc...703 222-6969
4215 Lafayette Center Dr # 1 Chantilly (20151) ***(G-2413)***
Ducard Vineyards Inc...434 409-4378
1885 Kernwood Pl Charlottesville (22911) ***(G-2620)***
Duck Pallet Co LLC...540 477-2771
738 Conicville Rd Mount Jackson (22842) ***(G-9069)***
Duck Publishing LLC...609 636-8431
13129 Middle Ridge Way Richmond (23233) ***(G-11193)***

A L P H A B E T I C

Duckworth Company..........................540 436-8754
103 River Ct Toms Brook (22660) *(G-13884)*

Duct Shop LLC..........................804 368-8543
105 Sylvia Rd Ashland (23005) *(G-1404)*

Dudenhefer For Delegate..........................540 628-4012
2769 Jefferson Davis Hwy Stafford (22554) *(G-13139)*

Dudley Dix Yacht Design..........................757 962-9273
612 Sandy Springs Ln Virginia Beach (23452) *(G-14416)*

Dudley Dix Yacht Design Inc..........................757 962-9273
3032 Edinburgh Dr Virginia Beach (23452) *(G-14417)*

Due North Ventures LLC..........................540 443-3990
3809 S Main St Blacksburg (24060) *(G-1734)*

Duke Industries LLC..........................252 404-2344
813 Shipton Ct Chesapeake (23320) *(G-3078)*

Dukes Printing Inc..........................276 228-6777
435 Tazewell St Ste C Wytheville (24382) *(G-15885)*

Dulcet Industries LLC..........................571 758-3191
43367 Chokeberry Sq Ashburn (20147) *(G-1273)*

Dull Inc Dolan & Norma..........................703 490-0337
2592 Dynasty Loop Woodbridge (22192) *(G-15687)*

Dulles Iron Works Inc..........................703 996-8797
43751 Beaver Meadow Rd Sterling (20166) *(G-13391)*

Dun Inc..........................804 240-4183
374 White Oak Dr Palmyra (22963) *(G-10248)*

Dundee Miniatures LLC..........................703 669-5591
40371 Foxfield Ln Leesburg (20175) *(G-7262)*

Dunford G C Septic Tank Instal..........................276 228-8590
410 Saint Lukes Rd Wytheville (24382) *(G-15886)*

Dunkum's Machine Shop, Newport News *Also called Master Machine & Auto LLC* *(G-9293)*

Dunlap Woodcrafts..........................703 631-5147
14600 Flint Lee Rd Whseg Chantilly (20151) *(G-2414)*

Dunromin Logging LLC..........................540 896-3543
616 N Mountain Rd Timberville (22853) *(G-13847)*

Dupont, Hopewell *Also called E I Du Pont De Nemours & Co* *(G-6924)*

Dupont..........................540 949-5361
510 W Broad St Ste D Waynesboro (22980) *(G-15109)*

Dupont Aero LLC..........................540 350-4306
205 Lookout Mountain Ln Mount Solon (22843) *(G-9086)*

Dupont Circle Solutions..........................202 596-8528
3100 Clarendon Blvd # 200 Arlington (22201) *(G-946)*

Dupont Credit Union..........................540 868-8714
1820 S High St Harrisonburg (22801) *(G-6311)*

Dupont De Nemours Inc..........................804 549-4747
3905 Beulah Rd North Chesterfield (23237) *(G-9863)*

Dupont De Nemours E I Tex Ofc..........................540 949-2000
400 Dupont Blvd Waynesboro (22980) *(G-15110)*

Dupont James River Gyps Fcilty..........................804 714-3362
1202 Bellwood Rd North Chesterfield (23237) *(G-9864)*

Dupont Printing Service Inc..........................703 931-1317
3425 Payne St Side Falls Church (22041) *(G-4785)*

Dupont Specialty Pdts USA LLC..........................804 383-2000
5401 Jefferson Davis Hwy North Chesterfield (23234) *(G-9865)*

Dupont Threading LLC..........................703 522-1748
2250 Clarendon Blvd Arlington (22201) *(G-947)*

Dupont Threading LLC..........................703 734-1425
43149 Laughing Quail Ct Ashburn (20148) *(G-1274)*

Dupont Ventures LLC..........................574 514-3646
6034 21st St N Arlington (22205) *(G-948)*

Durabook Federal Inc..........................888 414-9844
4860 Cox Rd Ste 200 Glen Allen (23060) *(G-5727)*

Duration Products LLC..........................804 651-1700
8568 Sanford Dr Henrico (23228) *(G-6504)*

Duroline North America Inc..........................757 447-6290
4414 Killam Ave Unit A Norfolk (23508) *(G-9533)*

Duron, Ridgeway *Also called Drake Extrusion Inc* *(G-11841)*

Duskits LLC..........................276 732-3121
514 Country Place Rd Axton (24054) *(G-1534)*

Dust Gold Publishing LLC..........................540 828-5110
3126 W Cary St Richmond (23221) *(G-11570)*

Dutch Barns..........................757 497-7356
124 Pennsylvania Ave Virginia Beach (23462) *(G-14418)*

Dutch Barns & Gazebos, Virginia Beach *Also called Dutch Barns* *(G-14418)*

Dutch Duck Software..........................703 525-6564
2606 23rd Rd N Arlington (22207) *(G-949)*

Dutch Gap Striping Inc..........................804 594-0069
1939a Woodberry Mill Rd Powhatan (23139) *(G-10543)*

Dutch Lady..........................202 669-0317
1003 King St Alexandria (22314) *(G-196)*

Dutch Made Cabinets..........................276 728-5700
620 Island Creek Dr Hillsville (24343) *(G-6890)*

Dvti, Charlottesville *Also called Directed Vapor Tech Intl Inc* *(G-2618)*

Dw Global LLC..........................757 689-4547
1528 Taylor Farm Rd # 105 Virginia Beach (23453) *(G-14419)*

Dw Saltwater Flies LLC..........................757 874-1859
928 Lacon Dr Newport News (23608) *(G-9218)*

Dwb Design Inc..........................540 371-0785
91 Sandy Ridge Rd Fredericksburg (22405) *(G-5422)*

Dwiggins Corp..........................757 366-0066
1424 Battlefield Blvd N Chesapeake (23320) *(G-3079)*

Dwight Kite..........................540 564-8858
337 W Spring Ave Elkton (22827) *(G-4326)*

DWS Publicity LLC..........................540 330-3763
3768 Parliament Rd Sw Roanoke (24014) *(G-12079)*

Dx Company LLC..........................703 919-8677
5445 Richenbacher Ave Alexandria (22304) *(G-197)*

Dyeing To Stitch..........................757 366-8740
5312 Kempsriver Dr # 102 Virginia Beach (23464) *(G-14420)*

Dyer LLC..........................757 926-9374
605 Treemont Ct Chesapeake (23323) *(G-3080)*

Dynamic Designs..........................540 371-7173
40 Cool Spring Rd Ste 101 Fredericksburg (22405) *(G-5423)*

Dynamic Fabworks LLC..........................757 439-1169
2584 Aviator Dr Ste 102 Virginia Beach (23453) *(G-14421)*

Dynamic Graphic Finishing Inc..........................540 869-0500
160 Industrial Dr Winchester (22602) *(G-15413)*

Dynamic Literacy LLC..........................888 696-8597
265 Campbell Rd Keswick (22947) *(G-7046)*

Dynamic Mobile Imaging, Roanoke *Also called Berger and Burrow Entps Inc* *(G-11887)*

Dynamic Mobile Imaging, Henrico *Also called Berger and Burrow Entps Inc* *(G-6481)*

Dynamic Motion LLC..........................804 433-2294
2701 Emerywood Pkwy # 10 Richmond (23294) *(G-11194)*

Dynamic Recycling LLC..........................276 628-6636
26319 Old Trail Rd Abingdon (24210) *(G-29)*

Dynamic Team Sports Inc..........................610 518-3300
641 Phoenix Dr Virginia Beach (23452) *(G-14422)*

Dynamic Towing Eqp & Mfg Inc..........................757 624-1360
1120 E Brambleton Ave Norfolk (23504) *(G-9534)*

Dynamite Demolition LLC..........................571 241-4658
8020 Ashboro Dr Alexandria (22309) *(G-451)*

Dynaric Inc..........................757 460-3725
5925 Thurston Ave Virginia Beach (23455) *(G-14423)*

Dynax America Corporation..........................540 966-6010
568 Eastpark Dr Roanoke (24019) *(G-11917)*

Dynex Technologies Inc (HQ)..........................**703 631-7800**
14340 Sullyfield Cir Chantilly (20151) *(G-2415)*

Dyno Nobel Inc..........................276 935-6436
Rr 460 Vansant (24656) *(G-13976)*

Dyno Noble Appalachia Inc (HQ)..........................**276 940-2201**
Hwy 23 N Duffield (24244) *(G-4177)*

Dysert Custom Woodwork..........................804 741-4712
11201 Pinewood Ct Henrico (23238) *(G-6505)*

Dyson Direct Inc..........................571 210-4317
1961 Chain Bridge Rd Tysons Corner (22102) *(G-13954)*

E & E Machine Shop Inc..........................540 949-6792
1367 Hopeman Pkwy Waynesboro (22980) *(G-15111)*

E & W Machine, Roanoke *Also called E W Staley Corporation* *(G-12081)*

E & W Machine Salem Ci, Salem *Also called Mountain Sky LLC* *(G-12541)*

E A Clore Sons Inc..........................540 948-5821
303 Clore Pl Madison (22727) *(G-7851)*

E C A..........................703 234-4142
12100 Sunset Hills Rd Reston (20190) *(G-10845)*

E C B Construction Company..........................804 730-2057
8390 Brittewood Cir Mechanicsville (23116) *(G-8620)*

E C L, Charlottesville *Also called Electrnic Cabling Assembly Inc* *(G-2789)*

E C T, Virginia Beach *Also called Eddy Current Technology Inc* *(G-14431)*

E Components International..........................804 462-5679
180 Dennis Dr Williamsburg (23185) *(G-15236)*

E D I, Chesapeake *Also called Electronic Devices Inc* *(G-3085)*

E D L, Danville *Also called Electronic Dev Labs Inc* *(G-3990)*

E D M, Lynchburg *Also called Electronic Design & Mfg Co* *(G-7701)*

E Dillon & Company..........................276 873-6816
2522 Swords Creek Rd Swords Creek (24649) *(G-13807)*

E E Machine Shop..........................540 649-2127
1367 Hopeman Pkwy Waynesboro (22980) *(G-15112)*

E G D Sheet Metal LLC..........................571 577-1647
10262 Cub Run Ct Manassas (20109) *(G-8060)*

E Giuffre Inc..........................540 537-4367
400 Greystone Dr Wirtz (24184) *(G-15610)*

E H Lail Millwork Inc..........................804 271-1111
3040 Goolsby Ave North Chesterfield (23234) *(G-9866)*

E H Publishing Company In..........................434 645-1722
105 Guy Ave Crewe (23930) *(G-3812)*

E I Designs Pottery LLC..........................410 459-3337
5157 Holly Farms Dr Virginia Beach (23462) *(G-14424)*

E I Du Pont De Nemours..........................804 550-7560
10431 Old Telegraph Rd Ashland (23005) *(G-1405)*

E I Du Pont De Nemours & Co..........................804 383-4251
13300 Carters Way Rd Chesterfield (23838) *(G-3494)*

E I Du Pont De Nemours & Co..........................804 530-9300
1 Discovery Dr Hopewell (23860) *(G-6924)*

E I T, Leesburg *Also called An Electronic Instrumentation* *(G-7217)*

E J Conrad & Sons Seafood Inc..........................804 462-7400
1947 Rocky Neck Rd Lancaster (22503) *(G-7160)*

E L Printing Co..........................540 776-0373
4448 Pheasant Ridge Rd Roanoke (24014) *(G-12080)*

E L Schneider..........................703 855-1925
42727 Iron Bit Pl Chantilly (20152) *(G-2532)*

E M Communications Inc 434 971-4700
1201 East Market St Charlottesville (22902) *(G-2787)*

E N S Graphics LLC 540 830-1776
230 Eisenhower Dr Broadway (22815) *(G-2088)*

E Performance Inc 703 217-6885
6657 Chilton Ct Mc Lean (22101) *(G-8422)*

E Primera Enable Corp 703 476-2270
12358 Marionwood Ct Herndon (20171) *(G-6664)*

E S I 540 389-5070
1221 Southside Dr Salem (24153) *(G-12498)*

E T Moore Jr Co Inc 804 231-1823
3100 N Hopkins Rd Ste 101 Richmond (23224) *(G-11571)*

E Trucking & Services LLC 571 241-0856
4263 Aiken Dr Warrenton (20187) *(G-15000)*

E W Staley Corporation 540 389-1197
2113 Salem Ave Sw Roanoke (24016) *(G-12081)*

E W Systems & Devices Inc 540 635-5104
100 Lakewood Dr Front Royal (22630) *(G-5531)*

E Z Data Inc 540 775-2961
7981 Caledon Rd King George (22485) *(G-7088)*

E Z Mount Bracket Co Inc 540 947-5500
1307 Price St Montvale (24122) *(G-9029)*

E&E Home Inprovements, Cana *Also called Windows Direct* *(G-2228)*

E&S Welding LLC 434 927-5428
1696 Yorkshire Dr Sandy Level (24161) *(G-12646)*

E-Agree LLC (PA) **571 358-8012**
8577 Sudley Rd Ste D Manassas (20110) *(G-7933)*

E-Kare Inc 844 443-5273
3040 Williams Dr Ste 610 Fairfax (22031) *(G-4442)*

E-Tron Systems Inc 703 690-2731
9406 Gunston Cove Rd F Lorton (22079) *(G-7482)*

E-Z Auto Specialties 540 786-8111
7102 River Rd Fredericksburg (22407) *(G-5279)*

E-Z Fasteners, Montvale *Also called E Z Mount Bracket Co Inc (G-9029)*

E-Z Treat Inc 703 753-4770
16211 Thoroughfare Rd Haymarket (20168) *(G-6420)*

E.S. Quarry & Construction Svc, Salem *Also called Orica USA Inc (G-12551)*

E4 Beauty Supply LLC 804 307-4941
14431 Old Bond St Chesterfield (23832) *(G-3495)*

Ea Design Tech Services 540 220-7203
366 Land Or Dr Ruther Glen (22546) *(G-12455)*

Eagle Aerospace 540 965-9022
713 Rose Ave Covington (24426) *(G-3787)*

Eagle Aviation Tech LLC 757 224-6269
7505 Warwick Blvd Newport News (23607) *(G-9219)*

Eagle Contractors 703 435-0004
12814 Lee Hwy Gainesville (20155) *(G-5581)*

Eagle Designs 540 428-1916
7249 Ridgedale Dr Warrenton (20186) *(G-15001)*

Eagle Eye Electric 540 672-1673
11281 Rapidan Rd Orange (22960) *(G-10212)*

Eagle Industries Unlimited Inc (HQ) **888 343-7547**
2645 Intl Pkwy Ste 102 Virginia Beach (23452) *(G-14425)*

Eagle Mobile Services Inc 703 979-1848
3233 Columbia Pike Ste B Arlington (22204) *(G-950)*

Eagle Paper International Inc 757 363-8103
4605 Pembroke Lake Cir # 100 Virginia Beach (23455) *(G-14426)*

Eagle Sunrise Vineyard LLC 703 648-3258
11214 Country Pl Oakton (22124) *(G-10146)*

Eaheart Equipment Inc (PA) **540 347-2880**
8326 Meetze Rd Warrenton (20187) *(G-15002)*

Eaheart Equipment LLC 703 366-3880
10413 Dumfries Rd Manassas (20110) *(G-7934)*

Eardley Publications, Virginia Beach *Also called Elizabeth Claire Inc (G-14440)*

Earl D Pierce Sawmill 276 744-7538
5611 Ivanhoe Rd Fries (24330) *(G-5516)*

Earl Energy LLC 757 606-2034
650 Chautauqua Ave Portsmouth (23707) *(G-10418)*

Earl Wood Printing Co 540 563-8833
3415 Whiteside St Ne Roanoke (24012) *(G-12082)*

Early Mountain Vineyards, Madison *Also called Madison County Wines LLC (G-7858)*

Earlyrisers Inc 757 566-4199
18423 Heath Industrial Rd Barhamsville (23011) *(G-1570)*

Earmold Company Ltd 540 389-1642
814 E 8th St Salem (24153) *(G-12499)*

Earth Communications Corp 434 973-7277
2370 Proffit Rd Charlottesville (22911) *(G-2621)*

Earth Friendly Chemicals Inc 757 502-8600
2585 Horse Pasture Rd # 201 Virginia Beach (23453) *(G-14427)*

Earth Science Technology LLC 703 584-8533
6747 Newington Rd Lorton (22079) *(G-7483)*

Earthcore Industries LLC 757 966-7275
4000 Holland Blvd Chesapeake (23323) *(G-3081)*

Earthen Candle Works LLC 540 270-5938
23490 Bluemont Chapel Ter Ashburn (20148) *(G-1275)*

Earthwalk Communications Inc 703 393-1940
10511 Battleview Pkwy Manassas (20109) *(G-8061)*

East Amber LLC 703 414-9409
1435 Occoquan Heights Ct Occoquan (22125) *(G-10172)*

East Cast Cstm Screen Prtg LLC 540 373-7576
156 Ewellville Ln Dutton (23050) *(G-4272)*

East Cast Repr Fabrication LLC (PA) **757 455-9600**
5803 Curlew Dr Norfolk (23502) *(G-9535)*

East Cast Repr Fabrication LLC 757 455-9600
5803 Curlew Dr Ste D Norfolk (23502) *(G-9536)*

East Coast Boat Lifts Inc 804 758-1099
510 Lord Mott Rd Urbanna (23175) *(G-13970)*

East Coast Brake & Rebuilders, Norfolk *Also called East Coast Brake Rbldrs Corp (G-9537)*

East Coast Brake Rbldrs Corp 757 466-1308
5812 Curlew Dr Norfolk (23502) *(G-9537)*

East Coast Branding LLC 757 754-0771
2398 Bays Edge Ave Virginia Beach (23451) *(G-14428)*

East Coast Candle Co 781 718-9466
220 Mcconville Rd Apt 58 Lynchburg (24502) *(G-7698)*

East Coast Custom Coaches Inc 571 292-1583
11900 Livingston Rd # 119 Manassas (20109) *(G-8062)*

East Coast Embroidery 804 677-7584
43 Duskany Point Dr Clarksville (23927) *(G-3628)*

East Coast Fabricators Inc 540 587-7170
1635 Venture Blvd Bedford (24523) *(G-1633)*

East Coast Graphics Inc 804 798-7100
11046 Air Park Rd Ste 1 Ashland (23005) *(G-1406)*

East Coast Hemp Company LLC 540 740-7099
2259 Kings Hwy Ste 102 King George (22485) *(G-7089)*

East Coast Interiors Inc 804 423-2554
11000 Trade Rd North Chesterfield (23236) *(G-9867)*

East Coast MBL Bus Launchpad, Manassas *Also called East Coast Custom Coaches Inc (G-8062)*

East Coast Stl Fabrication Inc 757 351-2601
1401 Precon Dr Ste 102 Chesapeake (23320) *(G-3082)*

East Coast Truss Inc 757 369-0801
10537 Shore Point Ln Smithfield (23430) *(G-12712)*

East Coast Walk In Tubs 804 365-8703
1855 Irisburg Rd Axton (24054) *(G-1535)*

East Crlina Metal Treating Inc 434 333-4412
3117 Odd Fellows Rd Lynchburg (24501) *(G-7699)*

East End Resources Group LLC 804 677-3207
2920 Polo Pkwy Midlothian (23113) *(G-8812)*

East Penn Manufacturing Co 540 980-1174
4769 Wurno Rd Pulaski (24301) *(G-10635)*

East Penn Manufacturing Co 804 798-1771
10001 Whitesel Rd Ashland (23005) *(G-1407)*

East River Metals Inc 276 928-1812
12195 N Scenic Hwy Rocky Gap (24366) *(G-12307)*

East Tennessee Natural Gas Co 276 429-5411
127 Shortly Stone Rd Atkins (24311) *(G-1516)*

East To West EMB & Design 703 335-2397
9153 Key Commons Ct Manassas (20110) *(G-7935)*

East Tools Inc 703 754-1931
4187 Benvenue Rd Haymarket (20169) *(G-6421)*

East West Ventures LLC 757 603-8017
5536 Summer Cres Virginia Beach (23462) *(G-14429)*

Eastcom Directional Drlg Inc 757 377-3133
509 Giles Dr Chesapeake (23322) *(G-3083)*

Easter VA Orthtics Prosthetics 757 967-0526
3517 Lingfield Cv Suffolk (23435) *(G-13702)*

Eastern Bioplastics LLC 540 437-1984
100 White Picket Trl Mount Crawford (22841) *(G-9054)*

Eastern Chrstn Pblications LLC 703 691-8862
3574 University Dr Fairfax (22030) *(G-4615)*

Eastern Cranial Affiliates LLC 703 807-5899
5275 Lee Hwy Ste 102 Arlington (22207) *(G-951)*

Eastern Cranial Affiliates LLC (PA) **703 807-5899**
10523 Main St Fairfax (22030) *(G-4616)*

Eastern Division, Timberville *Also called Pilgrims Pride Corporation (G-13851)*

Eastern League Commissioner 703 307-2080
10 Blue Spruce Cir Stafford (22554) *(G-13140)*

Eastern Machine, Wise *Also called Michael Fleming (G-15632)*

Eastern Panel Manufacturing 434 432-3055
235 Woodlawn Hts Chatham (24531) *(G-2927)*

Eastern Shore Cstl Rsting Escr 757 414-0105
17366 Lankford Hwy Cape Charles (23310) *(G-2233)*

Eastern Shore Post Inc 757 789-7678
24391 Lankford Hwy Onley (23418) *(G-10200)*

Eastern Shore Rebuilders 757 709-1250
31378 Pennyville Rd Painter (23420) *(G-10240)*

Eastern Shore Seafood Co Inc 757 787-7539
21325 Bayside Rd Onancock (23417) *(G-10196)*

Eastern Shore Seafood Pdts LLC 757 854-4422
13249 Lankford Hwy Mappsville (23407) *(G-8218)*

Eastern Shore Signs LLC 757 331-4432
22156 S Bayside Rd Cape Charles (23310) *(G-2234)*

Eastern Shore VA Mstr Grdners 757 678-7688
23203 Front St Accomac (23301) *(G-71)*

Eastern Shore Wldg Fabrication 443 944-3451
2497 Captains Corridor Greenbackville (23356) *(G-5992)*

Eastern Sleep Products Company 804 353-8965
4901 Fitzhugh Ave Ste 300 Richmond (23230) *(G-11195)*

ALPHABETIC

Eastman Chemical Company 276 679-1800
500 Hawthorne Ave Norton (24273) *(G-10117)*

Eastman Chemical Company 276 632-4991
345 Beaver Creek Dr Martinsville (24112) *(G-8282)*

Eastman Chemical Resins Inc 757 562-3121
27123 Shady Brook Trl Courtland (23837) *(G-3769)*

Eastman Performance Films LLC (HQ) **276 627-3000**
4210 The Great Rd Fieldale (24089) *(G-4984)*

Eastman Performance Films LLC 276 762-0242
4210 The Great Rd Fieldale (24089) *(G-4985)*

Eastman Performance Films LLC 276 650-3354
47 Brenda Dr Axton (24054) *(G-1536)*

Eastman Performance Films LLC 423 224-7768
1450 Beaver Creek Dr Martinsville (24112) *(G-8283)*

Eastman Performance Films LLC 276 627-3223
4129 The Great Rd Fieldale (24089) *(G-4986)*

Eastman Performance Films LLC 276 627-3355
140 Hollie Dr Martinsville (24112) *(G-8284)*

Easton Welding LLC 703 368-9727
12615 Izaak Walton Dr Bristow (20136) *(G-2050)*

Eastville Farm 23/24, Eastville *Also called Perdue Farms Inc* *(G-4296)*

Eastwind Software LLC 434 525-9241
201 Eastwind Dr Forest (24551) *(G-5068)*

Easy Stone Center, Vienna *Also called De Carlo Enterprises Inc (G-14036)*

Easyloader Manufacturing LLC 540 297-2601
207 Byway Rd Huddleston (24104) *(G-6953)*

Eazy Construction Inc 571 220-8385
56 Antler Trl Fredericksburg (22406) *(G-5424)*

Ebi LLC 434 797-9701
745 Kentuck Rd Danville (24540) *(G-3988)*

ECB Security Co, Mechanicsville *Also called E C B Construction Company (G-8620)*

Echo Hill Farm 802 586-2239
1320 Fort Myer Dr Apt 812 Arlington (22209) *(G-952)*

Echo Publishing Inc 757 603-3774
2910 Church St Norfolk (23504) *(G-9538)*

Ecko Incorporated 276 988-7943
Tazewell Industrial Park North Tazewell (24630) *(G-10098)*

Ecko Fire Protections, North Tazewell *Also called Ecko Incorporated (G-10098)*

Ecks Custom Woodworking 571 765-0807
7140 Meadow Ln Warrenton (20187) *(G-15003)*

Eclipse Holsters LLC 907 382-6958
106 Londonderry Ln Williamsburg (23188) *(G-15237)*

Eclipse Scroll Saw 804 779-3549
11700 Lock Ln New Kent (23124) *(G-9131)*

Ecm Maritime Services 540 400-6412
4225 Colonial Ave Roanoke (24018) *(G-11918)*

Ecm Universe, Chantilly *Also called Raimist Software LLC (G-2484)*

Eco Fuel LLC 703 256-6999
7413 Little River Tpke Annandale (22003) *(G-746)*

Eco Technologies 757 513-4870
3157 Stonewood Dr Virginia Beach (23456) *(G-14430)*

Eco-Friendly Lumber LLC 703 881-1966
13413 Vint Hill Rd Nokesville (20181) *(G-9391)*

Eco-Signs and Graphics 336 891-1334
6520 Virginia Ave Bassett (24055) *(G-1582)*

Ecoer Inc 703 348-2538
3900 Jermantown Rd # 150 Fairfax (22030) *(G-4617)*

Ecolochem Inc 804 327-6846
7400 Beaufont Spring Dr # 3 North Chesterfield (23225) *(G-10019)*

Ecolochem International Inc 757 855-9000
4545 Patent Rd Norfolk (23502) *(G-9539)*

Ecometrix 703 525-0524
1510 N George Mason Dr Arlington (22205) *(G-953)*

Econo Signs 540 389-5070
1221 Southside Dr Salem (24153) *(G-12500)*

Econocolor Signs & Graphics 540 946-0000
211 W 12th St Waynesboro (22980) *(G-15113)*

Economic Dev Auth Cy Richmond 804 521-4002
501 E Franklin St Richmond (23219) *(G-11572)*

Economy Printing Inc 757 485-4445
4519 George Wash Hwy Portsmouth (23702) *(G-10419)*

Economy Signs 757 877-5082
168 Little John Pl Newport News (23602) *(G-9220)*

Ecowood Cabinetry, Springfield *Also called Ecowood Usa Inc (G-12996)*

Ecowood Usa Inc 703 347-6858
7801b Loisdale Rd Springfield (22150) *(G-12996)*

Ecozenith Usa Inc 703 992-6622
2230 George C Marshall Dr # 122 Falls Church (22043) *(G-4786)*

Ecp Inc 804 222-2460
5725 Charles City Cir Richmond (23231) *(G-11196)*

Ed Walkers Repair Services 804 590-1198
10073 River Rd South Chesterfield (23803) *(G-12834)*

Ed's Apparel, Chesapeake *Also called Elohim Designs (G-3087)*

Eddie's Citrus Kicker, Farmville *Also called Kingdom Objectives (G-4945)*

Eddies Mind Inc 540 731-9304
1000 Stockton St Radford (24141) *(G-10712)*

Eddies Repair Shop Inc 540 659-4835
813 Courthouse Rd Stafford (22554) *(G-13141)*

Eddy Current Technology Inc 757 490-1814
2133 E Kendall Cir A Virginia Beach (23451) *(G-14431)*

Edge McS LLC 804 379-6772
14321 Sommerville Ct Midlothian (23113) *(G-8813)*

Edge Mechanical Inc 757 228-3540
2429 Bowland Pkwy Ste 115 Virginia Beach (23454) *(G-14432)*

Edgeconnex Inc 757 855-0351
3800 Village Ave Norfolk (23502) *(G-9540)*

Edgelit Designz & Engrv LLC 540 373-8058
52 Colemans Mill Dr Fredericksburg (22405) *(G-5425)*

Edgyash Paddleboards LLC 717 404-6073
4 Roberts Landing Dr Poquoson (23662) *(G-10370)*

Edible Printing LLC 212 203-8275
329 Mechanic St Luray (22835) *(G-7607)*

Edignas Fashion 757 588-4958
547 E Little Creek Rd Norfolk (23505) *(G-9541)*

Edison 2 LLC 434 806-2435
108 2nd St Sw Ste 2 Charlottesville (22902) *(G-2788)*

Edisons One Off Fbrcations LLC 540 869-5703
2610 Double Church Rd Stephens City (22655) *(G-13316)*

Editek Inc 703 652-9495
10907 Mddlgate Dr Fairfax Fairfax (22032) *(G-4443)*

Editorial Inspirations LLC 703 627-0023
15086 Brown Pleasants Rd Montpelier (23192) *(G-9016)*

Editorial Prjcts In Edcatn Inc 703 292-5111
4201 Wilson Blvd Arlington (22230) *(G-954)*

Edmonds Prtg / Clor Images Inc 434 848-2264
13770 Christanna Hwy Lawrenceville (23868) *(G-7179)*

Edmund Davidson 540 997-5651
3345 Virginia Ave Goshen (24439) *(G-5924)*

Edmunds Waste Removal Inc 804 478-4688
8507 Mckenney Hwy Mc Kenney (23872) *(G-8379)*

Education Online 571 242-6986
205 Colleen Ct Ne Leesburg (20176) *(G-7263)*

Education Week, Arlington *Also called Editorial Prjcts In Edcatn Inc (G-954)*

Educational Options Inc 480 777-7720
500 W Annandale Rd # 400 Falls Church (22046) *(G-4909)*

Educren Inc 804 410-4305
11535 Nuckols Rd Ste E Glen Allen (23059) *(G-5728)*

Edulinked LLC 703 869-2228
13390 Spofford Rd Apt 303 Herndon (20171) *(G-6665)*

Edward Allen Publishing LLC 757 768-5544
73 Terri Sue Ct Hampton (23666) *(G-6135)*

Edward L Birckhead 540 937-4287
82 Viewtown Rd Amissville (20106) *(G-718)*

Edward-Councilor Co Inc 757 460-2401
1427 Baker Rd Virginia Beach (23455) *(G-14433)*

Edwards Consulting 804 733-2506
2801 Irwin Rd Prince George (23875) *(G-10593)*

Edwards Eddie Signs Inc 540 434-8589
119 Pleasant Hill Rd Harrisonburg (22801) *(G-6312)*

Edwards Inc 276 762-7746
15606 Bill Dean Rd Saint Paul (24283) *(G-12467)*

Edwards Kretz Lohr & Assoc 804 673-9666
2215 Cox Rd Henrico (23233) *(G-6506)*

Edwards Optical Corporation 757 496-2550
2441 Windward Shore Dr Virginia Beach (23451) *(G-14434)*

Edwin Glenn Campbell 703 203-6516
104 Regatta Ln Stafford (22554) *(G-13142)*

Eeis, Bedford *Also called Elevating Eqp Insptn Svc LLC (G-1634)*

Eerkins Inc 703 626-6248
1134 E Main St Luray (22835) *(G-7608)*

Efco Corporation 540 248-8604
44 Sutton Rd Ste 101 Verona (24482) *(G-13985)*

Effective Comm Strategies LLC 703 403-5345
6608 Ladyslipper Ln Clifton (20124) *(G-3663)*

Effem Food, Mc Lean *Also called Mars Overseas Holdings Inc (G-8493)*

Effingham Manor LLC 703 594-2300
6190 Georgetown Rd Broad Run (20137) *(G-2067)*

Effithermix LLC 703 860-9703
10450 Hunter View Rd Vienna (22181) *(G-14043)*

Efftex Development Inc 800 708-8894
901 N Pitt St Ste 325 Alexandria (22314) *(G-198)*

Efi Lighting Inc 540 353-2880
421 Hawley Dr Salem (24153) *(G-12501)*

Eflamelightingcom Inc 434 822-0632
215 Wyndover Dr Danville (24541) *(G-3989)*

Egap Enterprises 434 374-9089
678 Cherry Hill Church Rd Buffalo Junction (24529) *(G-2159)*

Eggleston Minor 757 819-4958
616 Naval Base Rd Ste 1 Norfolk (23505) *(G-9542)*

Ehp 540 667-1815
34 Peyton St Winchester (22601) *(G-15538)*

Eiger Press 757 430-1831
1140 Las Cruces Dr Virginia Beach (23454) *(G-14435)*

Eileen C Johnson 855 533-7753
340 Elmington Ln Berryville (22611) *(G-1680)*

Eileen Carlson 757 339-9900
944 S Spigel Dr Virginia Beach (23454) *(G-14436)*

2021 Virginia
Industrial Directory

(G-0000) Company's Geographic Section entry number

Eileen Tramonte Design 703 241-1996
  4504 32nd Rd N Arlington (22207) *(G-955)*

Eilig Software LLC 757 259-0608
  84 Carlton Ct Williamsburg (23185) *(G-15238)*

Einstitute Inc 571 255-0530
  3929 Starters Ct Fairfax (22033) *(G-4444)*

Eir News Service Inc 703 777-4494
  62 Sycolin Rd Se Leesburg (20175) *(G-7264)*

Eiw Group 804 677-6214
  203 N Davis St Petersburg (23803) *(G-10318)*

Eiw Powder Coating 703 586-9392
  14861 Persistence Dr Woodbridge (22191) *(G-15688)*

Ejn LLC 646 621-5647
  5509 Vine St Alexandria (22310) *(G-452)*

Ek Screen Prints 703 250-2556
  3833 Pickett Rd Fairfax (22031) *(G-4445)*

Ekagra Partners LLC 571 421-1100
  161 Fort Evans Rd Ne # 200 Leesburg (20176) *(G-7265)*

Ekare, Fairfax *Also called E-Kare Inc (G-4442)*

El Chamo Printing 703 582-5782
  8501 Bucyrus Ct Ste 104 Manassas (20110) *(G-7936)*

El Charro Grill Mexican RES 540 745-5303
  302 S Locust St Floyd (24091) *(G-5024)*

El Comercio Newspaper Inc 703 859-1554
  17216 Larkin Dr Dumfries (22026) *(G-4244)*

El Morgan Company LLC 540 623-7086
  209 Green Arbor Dr Fredericksburg (22407) *(G-5280)*

El Tran Investment Corp 757 439-8111
  5449 N Sunland Dr Virginia Beach (23464) *(G-14437)*

Elaines Cakes Inc 804 748-2461
  12921 Harrowgate Rd Chester (23831) *(G-3410)*

Elan Publishing Inc 434 973-1828
  3172 Autumn Woods Dr Charlottesville (22911) *(G-2622)*

Elbit Systems Amer - Nght Vsio 540 561-0254
  7635 Plantation Rd Roanoke (24019) *(G-11919)*

Elcare Innovations Inc 434 525-7685
  1208 Rocky Branch Dr Forest (24551) *(G-5069)*

Elco Company 703 876-3000
  3190 Fairview Park Dr Falls Church (22042) *(G-4787)*

Eldor Auto Powertrain USA LLC 540 855-1021
  888 International Pkwy Daleville (24083) *(G-3943)*

Electraaero Inc 540 660-2917
  218 N Cherry St Falls Church (22046) *(G-4910)*

Electric Elders Inc 703 213-9327
  701 Seaton Ave Unit 520 Alexandria (22305) *(G-199)*

Electric Motor and Contg Co (PA)....................757 487-2121
  3703 Cook Blvd Chesapeake (23323) *(G-3084)*

Electric Motor Repair & Sls Co, Bristol *Also called Electro-Mechanical Corporation (G-1975)*

Electric Works 540 381-2917
  593 Smith Creek Rd Christiansburg (24073) *(G-3586)*

Electrical & Mech Resources, Richmond *Also called Electrical Mech Resources Inc (G-11197)*

Electrical Mech Resources Inc 804 226-1600
  4640 Intl Trade Ct Richmond (23231) *(G-11197)*

Electrify America LLC 703 364-7000
  2200 Ferdinand Porsche Dr Herndon (20171) *(G-6666)*

Electrmchncal Ctrl Systems Inc 434 610-5747
  1409 Waterlick Rd Unit B Lynchburg (24501) *(G-7700)*

Electrnic Cabling Assembly Inc 434 293-2593
  711 Charlton Ave Charlottesville (22903) *(G-2789)*

Electro Finishing Inc 276 686-6687
  6817 W Lee Hwy Rural Retreat (24368) *(G-12423)*

Electro Techs LLC 704 900-1911
  9524 Sherwood Pl Norfolk (23503) *(G-9543)*

Electro-Kinetics Inc 845 887-4930
  4942 Mahonia Dr Charlottesville (22911) *(G-2623)*

Electro-Luminx Lighting Corp 804 355-1692
  1320 N Arthur Ashe Blvd Richmond (23230) *(G-11198)*

Electro-Mechanical Corporation (PA)..............276 669-4084
  1 Goodson St Bristol (24201) *(G-1975)*

Electro-Mechanical Corporation 276 645-8232
  100 Goodson St Bristol (24201) *(G-1976)*

Electro-Mechanical Corporation 276 669-4084
  601 Old Airport Rd Bristol (24201) *(G-1977)*

Electromagnetic Shielding Inc 540 286-3780
  115 Juliad Ct Ste 103 Fredericksburg (22406) *(G-5426)*

Electromatics Incorporated 804 798-8318
  11080 Leadbetter Rd Ashland (23005) *(G-1408)*

Electromotive Inc 703 331-0100
  8754 Virginia Meadows Dr Manassas (20109) *(G-8063)*

Electron Technologies Inc 703 818-9400
  4431h Brkfld Crprt Dr Chantilly (20151) *(G-2416)*

Electronic Canvas 434 656-3070
  403 N Main St Gretna (24557) *(G-6008)*

Electronic Design & Mfg Co 434 385-0046
  31 Millrace Dr Lynchburg (24502) *(G-7701)*

Electronic Dev Labs Inc 434 799-0807
  244 Oakland Dr Danville (24540) *(G-3990)*

Electronic Devices Inc 757 421-2968
  3140 Bunch Walnuts Rd Chesapeake (23322) *(G-3085)*

Electronic Manufacturing Corp 703 661-8351
  43720 Trade Center Pl # 100 Sterling (20166) *(G-13392)*

Electronics of Future Inc 518 421-8830
  9433 Van Arsdale Dr Vienna (22181) *(G-14044)*

Electroplate - Rite Corp 540 674-9363
  5529 Lee Hwy Dublin (24084) *(G-4155)*

Electrovita LLC 703 447-7290
  2310 Trott Ave Vienna (22181) *(G-14045)*

Elegance Meets Designs LLC 347 567-6348
  9300 Golden Way Ct Apt P Richmond (23294) *(G-11199)*

Elegant Cabinets Inc 540 483-5800
  4131 Franklin St Rocky Mount (24151) *(G-12320)*

Elegant Draperies Ltd (PA).............................804 353-4268
  1831 Boulevard W Richmond (23230) *(G-11200)*

Elekon Industries USA Inc 757 766-1500
  1000 Lucas Way Hampton (23666) *(G-6136)*

Element Fitness- LLC 540 820-4200
  2309 Kingbird Ln Virginia Beach (23455) *(G-14438)*

Element One LLC 901 292-7721
  105 Courier Ct Ne Leesburg (20176) *(G-7266)*

Element Radius LLC 540 229-6366
  15191 Montanus Dr Culpeper (22701) *(G-3890)*

Element Woodworks LLC 757 650-9556
  2004 Hillsboro Ct Virginia Beach (23456) *(G-14439)*

Elements of Grace LLC 804 526-1482
  220 Suffolk Ave Colonial Heights (23834) *(G-3732)*

Elements of Healing LLC 757 951-7155
  3706 Princeton Pl Apt I3 Portsmouth (23707) *(G-10420)*

Elephant Prints LLC 703 820-2631
  5400 Bradford Ct Apt 32 Alexandria (22311) *(G-200)*

Elevate Hearing Aid Center 540 785-4676
  4903 Plank Rd Ste 101b Fredericksburg (22407) *(G-5281)*

Elevating Eqp Insptn Svc LLC 800 346-0287
  208 W Depot St Bedford (24523) *(G-1634)*

Elevative Networks LLC 703 226-3419
  1577 Spring Hill Rd # 210 Vienna (22182) *(G-14046)*

Eleven Eleven Candles More LLC 757 766-0687
  4 Clydesdale Ct Hampton (23666) *(G-6137)*

Eleven West Inc 540 639-9319
  6598 New River Rd Fairlawn (24141) *(G-4736)*

Eley House Candles 757 572-9318
  109 Bosley Ave Suffolk (23434) *(G-13703)*

Elfinsmith Ltd Inc 757 399-4788
  610 Virginia Ave Portsmouth (23707) *(G-10421)*

Elfinsmith's, Portsmouth *Also called Elfinsmith Ltd Inc (G-10421)*

Elgin Equipment Group 276 988-8901
  21405 Gvrnor G C Pery Hwy Tazewell (24651) *(G-13832)*

Elias LLC 703 663-1192
  5650 General Wash Dr Alexandria (22312) *(G-453)*

Elias Tile, Alexandria *Also called Elias LLC (G-453)*

Eliene Trucking LLC 571 721-0735
  14555 Lock Dr Centreville (20120) *(G-2304)*

Eligmaparable, Woodbridge *Also called Noparei Professionals LLC (G-15763)*

Elite Cabinet LLC 703 909-0404
  5608 General Wash Dr Alexandria (22312) *(G-454)*

Elite Coals Inc 276 679-4070
  5465 Kent Junction Rd Norton (24273) *(G-10118)*

Elite Defense Inc 703 339-0749
  6823 Silver Ann Dr Lorton (22079) *(G-7484)*

Elite Fabrication & Machine 540 392-6055
  942 Radford St Christiansburg (24073) *(G-3587)*

Elite Fabrication LLC 434 251-2639
  8380 Franklin Tpke Dry Fork (24549) *(G-4141)*

Elite Laundry and Car Wash LLC 540 373-6150
  312 Chatham Heights Rd Fredericksburg (22405) *(G-5427)*

Elite Masonry Contractor LLC 757 773-9908
  1226 Priscilla Ln Chesapeake (23322) *(G-3086)*

Elite Prints 703 780-3403
  8121 Richmond Hwy Alexandria (22309) *(G-455)*

Elite Welders LLC 757 613-1345
  900 Broad St Portsmouth (23707) *(G-10422)*

Elixsys Va LLC 434 374-2398
  356 Ulysses Way Clarksville (23927) *(G-3629)*

Elizabeth A Grge Vlin Stdio LL 703 590-8145
  3499 Beaver Ford Rd Woodbridge (22192) *(G-15689)*

Elizabeth Arden Inc 540 444-2408
  131 Brand Ave Salem (24153) *(G-12502)*

Elizabeth Arden Inc 540 444-2406
  141 Brand Ave Salem (24153) *(G-12503)*

Elizabeth Arden Returns, Salem *Also called Elizabeth Arden Inc (G-12503)*

Elizabeth Bailey 804 265-8764
  3028 Oxford Dr Sutherland (23885) *(G-13803)*

Elizabeth Ballard-Spitzer 757 723-1194
  165 Wilderness Rd Hampton (23669) *(G-6138)*

Elizabeth Claire Inc 757 430-4308
  2100 Mccomas Way Ste 607 Virginia Beach (23456) *(G-14440)*

Elizabeth Neville 703 409-4217
  5521 23rd St N Arlington (22205) *(G-956)*

Elizabeth Urban 757 879-1815
  101 Bryon Rd Yorktown (23692) *(G-15952)*

A
L
P
H
A
B
E
T
I
C

Elizur International Inc 757 648-8502
851 Seahawk Cir Ste 102 Virginia Beach (23452) *(G-14441)*

Elk Creek Woodworking Inc 434 258-5142
4785 Bellevue Rd Forest (24551) *(G-5070)*

Elk Island Winery 540 967-0944
5759 River Rd W Goochland (23063) *(G-5882)*

Elks Club 450 .... 540 434-3673
482 S Main St Harrisonburg (22801) *(G-6313)*

Elkwood Stone & Mulch LLC 540 829-9273
13715 Berry Hill Rd Elkwood (22718) *(G-4342)*

Ellen Fairchild-Flugel Art LLC 540 325-2305
924 Lupton Rd Woodstock (22664) *(G-15852)*

Elletts Embroidery 434 392-2290
1437 S Main St Farmville (23901) *(G-4939)*

Ellice Darien LLC 804 677-9145
10300 Sandy Ridge Dr Chesterfield (23832) *(G-3496)*

Ellington Mechanical Svcs Inc 703 220-1651
1602 Belle View Blvd # 3170 Alexandria (22307) *(G-456)*

Ellington Wood Products Inc 434 922-7545
145 Mill Ridge Ln Amherst (24521) *(G-690)*

Elliott Lestselle 757 944-8152
504 Pheasant Run Virginia Beach (23452) *(G-14442)*

Elliott Mandolins Shop 540 763-2327
774 Sowers Mill Dam Rd Ne Riner (24149) *(G-11862)*

Elliott Mfg 804 737-1475
4232 Oakleys Ct Richmond (23223) *(G-11573)*

Elliott Oil Production LLC 434 525-3049
519 Carriage Hill Dr Forest (24551) *(G-5071)*

Ellis Page Company LLC 703 464-9404
10481 Colonel Ct Manassas (20110) *(G-7937)*

Ellis Signs and Custom Pntg 434 584-0032
105 Clover Rd La Crosse (23950) *(G-7143)*

Elm Investments Inc 757 934-2709
114 Plover Dr Suffolk (23434) *(G-13704)*

Elo Inc 571 435-0129
4262 Pemberley Ct Woodbridge (22193) *(G-15690)*

Elohim Designs 757 292-1890
1508 Prospect Dr Chesapeake (23322) *(G-3087)*

Elopitch, Woodbridge *Also called Elo Inc (G-15690)*

Eloqua Inc (HQ) **703 584-2750**
1921 Gallows Rd Ste 250 Vienna (22182) *(G-14047)*

Els Wheels LLC 540 370-4397
30 Castlewood Dr Fredericksburg (22406) *(G-5428)*

Elswick Inc 276 971-3060
Hickory Dr Rr 609 Cedar Bluff (24609) *(G-2275)*

Elswick Machine, Cedar Bluff *Also called Elswick Inc (G-2275)*

Elthon Enterprises, Falls Church *Also called Don Elthon (G-4908)*

Elucidsoft LLC 703 679-7688
210 Wakerobin Dr Stafford (22556) *(G-13143)*

Elvaria LLC 703 935-0041
7689 Limestone Dr Ste 125 Gainesville (20155) *(G-5582)*

Elyssa E Strong 540 280-3982
802 Railroad Ave Goshen (24439) *(G-5925)*

Em Millwork Inc (PA) **571 344-9842**
7600 Fullerton Rd Springfield (22153) *(G-12997)*

Emax Oil Company (PA) **434 295-4111**
1410 Incarnation Dr 205b Charlottesville (22901) *(G-2624)*

Embassy 703 403-3996
6 N Montague St Arlington (22203) *(G-957)*

Embedded Systems LLC 860 269-8148
15714 Victorias Crest Pl Haymarket (20169) *(G-6422)*

Embellished Embroidery 804 926-5785
14620 Gimbel Dr Chester (23836) *(G-3411)*

Ember Systems LLC 540 327-1984
3052 Valley Ave Ste 200 Winchester (22601) *(G-15539)*

Emblemax LLC 703 802-0200
14504f Lee Rd Ste F Chantilly (20151) *(G-2417)*

Embossing Etc 540 338-4520
16919 Ivandale Rd Hamilton (20158) *(G-6057)*

Embrace Embroidery LP 757 784-3874
16101 Diascund Shores Ln Lanexa (23089) *(G-7166)*

Embroid ME Alexandria, Alexandria *Also called Garmonte LLC (G-213)*

Embroider Bee 757 472-4981
512 Old Mill Ct Virginia Beach (23452) *(G-14443)*

Embroidery -N- Beyond LLC 540 972-4333
11413 Chivalry Chase Ln Spotsylvania (22551) *(G-12888)*

Embroidery and Print House 757 636-1676
312 Saint Brie W Suffolk (23435) *(G-13705)*

Embroidery Barnyard 804 795-1555
7704 Lampworth Ter Richmond (23231) *(G-11201)*

Embroidery By Design, Poquoson *Also called Doris Anderson (G-10369)*

Embroidery By Jan, Altavista *Also called Myra J Rudisill (G-637)*

Embroidery By Patty 540 597-8173
393 Winesap Rd Roanoke (24019) *(G-11920)*

Embroidery Concepts 540 387-0517
146 W 4th St Ste 2 Salem (24153) *(G-12504)*

Embroidery Connection 757 566-8859
8628 Croaker Rd Williamsburg (23188) *(G-15239)*

Embroidery Criations 540 421-5608
3589 Richardson Rd Timberville (22853) *(G-13848)*

Embroidery Crown Inc 703 986-3022
15363 Grist Mill Ter Woodbridge (22191) *(G-15691)*

Embroidery Depot Ltd 540 289-5044
7372 Mountain Grove Rd Penn Laird (22846) *(G-10288)*

Embroidery Express LLC 804 458-5999
2600 Bermuda Ave Chester (23836) *(G-3412)*

Embroidery Expressons 757 255-0713
18517 Shady Pine Ln Windsor (23487) *(G-15604)*

Embroidery N Beyond LLC 757 962-2105
1485 General Booth Blvd # 101 Virginia Beach (23454) *(G-14444)*

Embroidery N Beyond LLC 757 409-2782
2728 Saint Charles Ave Virginia Beach (23456) *(G-14445)*

Embroidery Works 757 344-8573
105 Fernwood Bnd Yorktown (23692) *(G-15953)*

Embroidery Works Inc 757 868-8840
5317 George Wash Mem Hwy Yorktown (23692) *(G-15954)*

Embroideryville 276 768-9727
229 Black Rock Mtn Ln Independence (24348) *(G-6982)*

Embroidme Virginia Beach, Virginia Beach *Also called Bryant Embroidery LLC (G-14303)*

EMC Corporation 703 749-2260
8444 Westpark Dr Ste 100 Mc Lean (22102) *(G-8423)*

EMC Corporation 703 553-2522
2011 Crystal Dr Ste 907 Arlington (22202) *(G-958)*

EMC Metal Fabrication 804 355-1030
1855 Boulevard W Richmond (23230) *(G-11202)*

Emco Enterprises Inc 540 843-7900
31 Stoney Brook Ln Luray (22835) *(G-7609)*

Emcor, Sterling *Also called Electronic Manufacturing Corp (G-13392)*

Emcs, Lynchburg *Also called Electrmchncal Ctrl Systems Inc (G-7700)*

Emcs Inc 443 223-2335
14413 Old Bond St Chesterfield (23832) *(G-3497)*

Emerald Ironworks Inc 703 690-2477
14861 Persistence Dr Woodbridge (22191) *(G-15692)*

Emerald Lake Vineyard 540 270-3399
12138 Harpers Ferry Rd Hillsboro (20132) *(G-6865)*

Emergency Alert Solutions Grou 703 346-4787
10002 Park Royal Dr Great Falls (22066) *(G-5953)*

Emergency Lockdown Experts, Great Falls *Also called Emergency Alert Solutions Grou (G-5953)*

Emergency Response Tech LLC 703 932-1118
9532 Liberia Ave Ste 716 Manassas (20110) *(G-7938)*

Emergency Traction Device LLC 703 771-1025
40002 Thomas Mill Rd Leesburg (20175) *(G-7267)*

Emergency Vehicle Outfitters 571 228-2837
448 Crowell Ln Lynchburg (24502) *(G-7702)*

Emergency Vehicles Inc 434 575-0509
2181 E Hyco Rd South Boston (24592) *(G-12763)*

Emergency Welding Inc 804 829-2976
8231 Courthouse Rd Providence Forge (23140) *(G-10623)*

Emerson, Charlottesville *Also called Intelligent Platforms LLC (G-2647)*

Emerson & Clements Office 434 983-5322
1097 Main St Dillwyn (23936) *(G-4095)*

Emerson Creek Pottery Inc 540 297-7524
1068 Pottery Ln Bedford (24523) *(G-1635)*

Emerson Electric Co 276 223-2200
555 Peppers Ferry Rd Wytheville (24382) *(G-15887)*

Emerson Process Management, Midlothian *Also called Computational Systems Inc (G-8803)*

Emes LLC 703 680-0807
15903 Cranberry Ct Dumfries (22025) *(G-4245)*

Emezro LLC 757 327-2318
203 Clay St Hampton (23663) *(G-6139)*

Emge Naturals LLC 434 660-6907
109 Chadwick Dr Lynchburg (24502) *(G-7703)*

Eminence Jewelers 703 815-1384
5756 Union Mill Rd Clifton (20124) *(G-3664)*

Emka Technologies Inc 703 237-9001
21515 Ridgetop Cir # 220 Sterling (20166) *(G-13393)*

Emotion US LLC 540 639-9045
201 W Rock Rd Radford (24141) *(G-10713)*

Empc Bio Energy Group LLC 757 550-1103
2036 Atlantic Ave Chesapeake (23324) *(G-3088)*

Empire Incorporated (PA) 757 723-6747
615 N Back River Rd Hampton (23669) *(G-6140)*

Empire Marble & Granite Co 804 359-2004
1717 Rhoadmiller St Richmond (23220) *(G-11574)*

Empire Publishing Corporation 804 440-5379
5 E Clay St Richmond (23219) *(G-11575)*

Employment Guide 703 580-7586
14065 Crown Ct Woodbridge (22193) *(G-15693)*

Empress Publishing LLC 856 630-8198
300 Addison Way Apt 13-2i Petersburg (23805) *(G-10319)*

Empress World Publishing LLC 757 471-3806
1456 Woodbridge Trl Virginia Beach (23453) *(G-14446)*

Emsco LLC 804 752-1640
10181 Cedar Ridge Dr Ashland (23005) *(G-1409)*

Emtech Laboratories Inc 540 265-9156
7745 Garland Cir Roanoke (24019) *(G-11921)*

Enabled Engineering, Blacksburg *Also called Enabled Manufacturing LLC (G-1735)*

(G-0000) Company's Geographic Section entry number

Enabled Manufacturing LLC 704 491-9414
1412 Honeysuckle Dr Blacksburg (24060) *(G-1735)*
Enc Enterprises 703 578-1924
6014 Leesburg Pike Falls Church (22041) *(G-4788)*
Encell Tech 434 202-8370
1412 Sachem Pl Charlottesville (22901) *(G-2625)*
Encore Products Inc 757 493-8358
4545 Commerce St # 1906 Virginia Beach (23462) *(G-14447)*
End To End Inc 757 216-1938
509 Viking Dr Ste D Virginia Beach (23452) *(G-14448)*
Endeavor Consulting Group LLC 202 599-7437
10632 Tattersall Dr Manassas (20112) *(G-8064)*
Endowed Expressions LLC 804 638-5459
2801 Goldeneye Ct Richmond (23231) *(G-11203)*
Endreola Sheet Metal 703 496-8538
14912 Daytona Ct Woodbridge (22193) *(G-15694)*
Energize Your Size LLC 703 360-1093
8237 Chancery Ct Alexandria (22308) *(G-457)*
Energizer Personal Care LLC 540 248-9734
1 Razor Blade Ln Verona (24482) *(G-13986)*
Energy 11 LP 804 344-8121
814 E Main St Richmond (23219) *(G-11576)*
Energy Resources 12 LP 804 344-8121
814 E Main St Richmond (23219) *(G-11577)*
Energy Sherlock LLC 703 346-7584
40692 Manor House Rd Leesburg (20175) *(G-7268)*
Energysherlock, Leesburg *Also called Energy Sherlock LLC* *(G-7268)*
Energytech Solutions LLC 703 269-8172
10877 Hunter Gate Way Reston (20194) *(G-10846)*
Enervest Operating LLC 276 628-1569
408 W Main St Abingdon (24210) *(G-30)*
Enexdi LLC 703 748-0596
8474 Tyco Rd Ste A Vienna (22182) *(G-14048)*
Engaged Magazine LLC 703 485-4878
7514 Gresham St Springfield (22151) *(G-12998)*
Engility LLC 703 434-4000
11955 Freedom Dr Ste 2000 Reston (20190) *(G-10847)*
Engility LLC 757 366-4422
825 Greenbrier Cir Ste M Chesapeake (23320) *(G-3089)*
Engility LLC 703 633-8300
111 Cybernetics Way # 200 Yorktown (23693) *(G-15955)*
Engine and Frame LLC 757 407-0134
608 Commerce Rd Richmond (23224) *(G-11578)*
Engine Scout Professionals LLC 757 621-8526
3009 Ballard Ave Ste B Portsmouth (23701) *(G-10423)*
Engineered Enrgy Solutions LLC 443 299-2364
37434 Bayside Dr Greenbackville (23356) *(G-5993)*
Engineering Design Mfg, Dulles *Also called Gauge Works Inc (G-4203)*
Engines Unlimited Inc 276 566-7208
4389 Hurley Rd Wolford (24658) *(G-15638)*
Enginred Bopharmaceuticals Inc 860 730-3262
300 Ringgold Indus Pkwy Danville (24540) *(G-3991)*
England Stove Works 434 929-0120
100 W Progress Ln Madison Heights (24572) *(G-7871)*
Englander, Monroe *Also called Englands Stove Works Inc (G-8989)*
Englands Stove Works Inc 434 929-0120
589 S Five Forks Rd Monroe (24574) *(G-8989)*
Engraving and Printing Bureau 202 997-9580
12116 Monu Dr Unit 310 Fairfax (22033) *(G-4446)*
Ennis Mountain Woods Inc 540 471-9171
292 Woodpecker Way Afton (22920) *(G-79)*
Ennis-Flint Inc 804 309-3199
4400 Vawter Ave Richmond (23222) *(G-11579)*
Ennstone 703 335-2650
9321 Developers Dr Manassas (20109) *(G-8065)*
Enrich Compost LLC 518 410-2402
2509 Burnley Ave Henrico (23228) *(G-6507)*
Ensons Inc 703 644-6694
9508 Ironmaster Dr Burke (22015) *(G-2189)*
Entan Devices LLC 757 766-1500
1000 Lucas Way Hampton (23666) *(G-6141)*
Enterprise Hive LLC 804 438-9393
4507 Irvington Rd Ste 200 Irvington (22480) *(G-7001)*
Enterprise Inc 276 694-3101
129 N Main St Stuart (24171) *(G-13609)*
Enterprise Itech Corp 703 731-7881
10014 Manor Pl Fairfax (22032) *(G-4447)*
Enterprise Multimedia Center, Fort Eustis *Also called United States Dept of Army (G-5127)*
Enterprise Signs & Svc 757 338-0027
86 Tide Mill Ln Hampton (23666) *(G-6142)*
Enterprise Svcs Cmmnctions LLC 877 858-3855
1775 Tysons Blvd Tysons (22102) *(G-13943)*
Enterprise Svcs Wrld Trade LLC 703 245-9675
1775 Tysons Blvd Tysons (22102) *(G-13944)*
Enterprising Women 919 362-1551
45685 Elmwood Ct Dulles (20166) *(G-4199)*
Enterprize Software LLC 571 271-5862
23082 Sullivans Cove Sq Brambleton (20148) *(G-1927)*
Entertainment Software Assoc 703 383-3976
4025 Fair Ridge Dr # 250 Fairfax (22033) *(G-4448)*

Entwistle Company 434 799-6186
1940 Halifax Rd Danville (24540) *(G-3992)*
Envirnmntal Solutions Intl Inc 703 263-7600
20099 Ashbrook Pl Ste 170 Ashburn (20147) *(G-1276)*
Enviro Water 703 569-0971
6141 Roxbury Ave Springfield (22152) *(G-12999)*
Environmental Dynamics Inc 540 261-2008
2455 Hawthorne Ave Buena Vista (24416) *(G-2142)*
Environmental Equipment Engrg, Mechanicsville *Also called Environmental Equipment Inc (G-8621)*
Environmental Equipment Inc 804 730-1280
8418 Erle Rd Mechanicsville (23116) *(G-8621)*
Environmental Ltg Solutions 202 361-2686
6312 Cullen Pl Haymarket (20169) *(G-6423)*
Environmental Stoneworks LLC 804 553-9560
9051 Hermitage Rd Richmond (23228) *(G-11204)*
Envitia Inc 703 871-5255
11710 Plaza America Dr # 2000 Reston (20190) *(G-10848)*
Enviva Pellets Southampton LLC 301 657-5560
26570 Rose Valley Rd Franklin (23851) *(G-5142)*
Eodrones LLC 703 856-8400
4154 Weeks Dr Warrenton (20187) *(G-15004)*
Eopus Innovations LLC 703 796-9882
3949 Pender Dr Ste 350 Fairfax (22030) *(G-4618)*
Ep Computer Service 804 592-7272
121 Penn Ln Madison Heights (24572) *(G-7872)*
Epic 757 896-8464
2520 58th St Hampton (23661) *(G-6143)*
Epic Band, Lorton *Also called Antonio Puducay (G-7463)*
Epic Books Press 804 557-3111
1921 Ellyson Ct Quinton (23141) *(G-10695)*
Epic Images 540 537-2572
1750 Morris Rd Goodview (24095) *(G-5895)*
Epic Led 540 376-7183
4513 Jefferson Davis Hwy Fredericksburg (22408) *(G-5282)*
Epic Led 703 499-4485
9314 Witch Hazel Way Manassas (20110) *(G-7939)*
Epic Manufacturing, Virginia Beach *Also called Epic Mfg LLC (G-14449)*
Epic Mfg LLC 757 689-4373
2500 Squadron Ct Ste 106 Virginia Beach (23453) *(G-14449)*
Epicidentity Inc 833 723-3437
24941 Castleton Dr Chantilly (20152) *(G-2533)*
Epiep Inc 864 423-2526
315 Old Ivy Way Ste 301 Charlottesville (22903) *(G-2790)*
Epiphany Inc 703 437-3133
3501 Stringfellow Ct Fairfax (22033) *(G-4449)*
Epiphany Ideation 248 396-5828
20541 Warburton Bay Sq Sterling (20165) *(G-13394)*
Epps Collision Cntr & Superior 434 572-4721
221 Webster St South Boston (24592) *(G-12764)*
Equestrian Forge Inc 703 777-2110
222 S King St Ste 4 Leesburg (20175) *(G-7269)*
Equipment Repair Services 757 449-5867
6404 Drew Dr Virginia Beach (23464) *(G-14450)*
Equipment Repair Services 703 491-7681
2004 Cumberland Dr Woodbridge (22191) *(G-15695)*
Equus Therapeutics Inc 540 456-6767
1874 Castle Rock Rd Afton (22920) *(G-80)*
Erbosol Printing 757 325-9986
17 Briarwood Dr Hampton (23666) *(G-6144)*
Ergoject LLC 540 375-6415
1640 Roanoke Blvd Salem (24153) *(G-12505)*
Eric Carr Woodworks 202 253-1010
934 Jaysmith St Great Falls (22066) *(G-5954)*
Eric Margry 703 548-7808
105 N Union St Ste 229 Alexandria (22314) *(G-201)*
Eric Margry Engraving, Alexandria *Also called Eric Margry (G-201)*
Eric S Welding Service 540 717-3256
6121 Duncan Trl Reva (22735) *(G-11000)*
Eric Trump Wine Mfg LLC 434 977-3895
100 Grand Cru Dr Charlottesville (22902) *(G-2791)*
Eric Tucker 540 747-5665
2021 Rich Patch Rd Covington (24426) *(G-3788)*
Eric Walker 804 439-2880
2931 Polo Pkwy Midlothian (23113) *(G-8814)*
Eric Washington 434 249-3567
1416 Decatur Dr Charlottesville (22911) *(G-2626)*
Erick Gonzalez 703 855-2908
13113 Orleans St Woodbridge (22192) *(G-15696)*
Erickson & Ripper Framing 703 549-1616
628 N Washington St Alexandria (22314) *(G-202)*
Erickson & Ripper Gallery, Alexandria *Also called Erickson & Ripper Framing (G-202)*
Erics Welding 434 996-6502
107 Sundrops Ct Charlottesville (22902) *(G-2792)*
Ericsons Inc 770 505-6575
13300 Ramblewood Dr Chester (23836) *(G-3413)*
Ericsson Inc 434 592-5610
314 Jefferson Ridge Pkwy Lynchburg (24501) *(G-7704)*
Ericsson Inc 434 528-7000
5061d Fort Ave Lynchburg (24502) *(G-7705)*

Ericsson Inc 571 262-9254
1595 Spring Hill Rd # 500 Vienna (22182) *(G-14049)*

Erie Boatworks LLC 757 204-1815
1020 Redstart Ave Chesapeake (23324) *(G-3090)*

Erikson Diversified Industries 703 216-5482
5825 Plank Rd Ste 113 Fredericksburg (22407) *(G-5283)*

Erin Welding Service Inc 540 899-3970
1112 James Madison Cir Fredericksburg (22405) *(G-5429)*

Erisys LLC 660 864-4474
13800 Coppermine Rd Herndon (20171) *(G-6667)*

Erle D Anderson Lbr Pdts Inc 804 748-0500
15610 James River Dr Disputanta (23842) *(G-4107)*

Ern Graphic Design 757 281-8801
203 Brooke Dr Hampton (23669) *(G-6145)*

Ernest Beltrami Sr 757 516-8581
31163 Beltrami Dr Franklin (23851) *(G-5143)*

Ernies Beef Jerky 540 460-4341
4696 Three Notch D Rd Charlottesville (22901) *(G-2627)*

Ernies Woodworking 540 786-8959
800 Galway Ln Fredericksburg (22407) *(G-5284)*

Erodex Inc 804 525-6609
5727 S Laburnum Ave Richmond (23231) *(G-11205)*

Erp Cloud Technologies LLC 727 723-0801
2551 Dulles View Dr Herndon (20171) *(G-6668)*

Erp Environmental Fund Inc 304 369-8113
15 Appledore Ln Natural Bridge (24578) *(G-9105)*

Erp Initiatives LLC 703 439-9352
21868 Foxden Ln Leesburg (20175) *(G-7270)*

Erp Software Services Inc 703 957-3073
25878 Rawley Springs Dr Chantilly (20152) *(G-2534)*

Ersh-Enterprises Inc 703 866-1988
3003 Westhurst Ct A101 Oakton (22124) *(G-10147)*

Ervin Coppridge Machine Co 804 561-1246
9500 S Amelia Ave Amelia Court House (23002) *(G-656)*

Ervins Bathtub Refinishing 703 730-8831
15402 Gunsmith Ter Woodbridge (22191) *(G-15697)*

Escr Coffee, Cape Charles *Also called Eastern Shore Cstl Rsting Escr* *(G-2233)*

Esi Total Fuel Management, Ashburn *Also called Envirmmntal Solutions Intl Inc* *(G-1276)*

Eska USA BV Inc 757 494-7330
1910 Campostella Rd Chesapeake (23324) *(G-3091)*

Ess Technologies Inc 540 961-5716
3160 State St Blacksburg (24060) *(G-1736)*

Essence Woodworks LLC 703 945-3108
13200 Goose Pond Ln Fairfax (22033) *(G-4450)*

Essential Eats LLC 757 304-2393
1031 Quail St Norfolk (23513) *(G-9544)*

Essential Essences 757 544-0502
3933 Rainbow Dr Virginia Beach (23456) *(G-14451)*

Essential Software Dev LLC 540 222-1254
9430 Silver King Ct # 302 Fairfax (22031) *(G-4451)*

Essentra Packaging Inc 804 518-1803
1625 Ashton Park Dr Ste D South Chesterfield (23834) *(G-12802)*

Essex Concrete Corp 804 749-1950
2391 Lanier Rd Rockville (23146) *(G-12285)*

Essex Concrete Corporation (PA) **804 443-2366**
1251 Tappahannock Blvd Tappahannock (22560) *(G-13814)*

Essex Concrete Corporation 804 443-2366
And 360 Rr 17 Tappahannock (22560) *(G-13815)*

Essex Hand Crafted WD Pdts LLC 540 445-5928
6649 Garland Dr Unit 7 Warrenton (20187) *(G-15005)*

Esskay Structures Inc 571 242-0011
2950 Short Ct Vienna (22181) *(G-14050)*

Essolutions Inc (HQ) **240 215-6992**
1401 S Clark St Ste 200 Arlington (22202) *(G-959)*

Essroc Cement Corp 757 545-2481
100 Pratt St Chesapeake (23324) *(G-3092)*

Essroc Cement Corporation 804 227-4156
9680 Old Ridge Rd Ashland (23005) *(G-1410)*

Esstech Engineering, Louisa *Also called Management Solutions LC* *(G-7559)*

Estate Concrete LLC 703 293-6363
15900 Lee Hwy Centreville (20120) *(G-2305)*

Estate of J E Currell The, Kilmarnock *Also called Rappahannock Record* *(G-7076)*

Esteemed Woodcrafts 757 876-5868
425 Butterfly Dr Chesapeake (23322) *(G-3093)*

Ester Yildiz LLC 434 202-7790
675 Peter Jefferson Pkwy Charlottesville (22911) *(G-2628)*

Estes Construction, Lyndhurst *Also called Dexter W Estes* *(G-7843)*

Estudio De Fernandez LLC 540 948-3196
6093 S Seminole Trl Rochelle (22738) *(G-12233)*

Etcetera, Roanoke *Also called Scb Sales Inc* *(G-12177)*

Etegrity LLC 757 301-7455
2301 Woodland Ct Virginia Beach (23456) *(G-14452)*

Eternal Technology Corporation 804 524-8555
1800 Touchstone Rd South Chesterfield (23834) *(G-12803)*

Etf, Vienna *Also called Electronics of Future Inc* *(G-14044)*

Etheridge Automation, Powhatan *Also called Etheridge Electric Inc* *(G-10544)*

Etheridge Electric Inc 804 372-6428
2430 New Dorset Ter Powhatan (23139) *(G-10544)*

Ethyl Corporation (HQ) **804 788-5000**
330 S 4th St Richmond (23219) *(G-11580)*

Etl Systems Inc 703 657-0411
297 Herndon Pkwy Ste 303 Herndon (20170) *(G-6669)*

Etz LLC 703 620-3014
1938 Upper Lake Dr Reston (20191) *(G-10849)*

Euclid Systems Corporation (PA) **703 471-7145**
45472 Holiday Dr Ste 7 Sterling (20166) *(G-13395)*

Euclidian Systems Inc (PA) **703 963-7209**
1100 Wilson Blvd Ste 1008 Arlington (22209) *(G-960)*

Eugene C Hoopes 434 293-5852
710 Park St Charlottesville (22902) *(G-2793)*

Eugene Martin Trucking 434 454-7267
1053 Hazelwood Mill Trl Scottsburg (24589) *(G-12655)*

Eugenes Machine & Welding 276 694-6275
13996 Jeb Stuart Hwy Stuart (24171) *(G-13610)*

Euphoric Treatz LLC 757 504-4174
3383 Lakecrest Rd Virginia Beach (23452) *(G-14453)*

Eure Custom Signs Inc 757 523-0000
1228 S Military Hwy Ste D Chesapeake (23320) *(G-3094)*

Eurest Raytheon Dulles 571 250-1024
22260 Pacific Blvd Dulles (20166) *(G-4200)*

Euro Cabinets Inc 757 671-7884
100 Aragona Blvd Ste 101 Virginia Beach (23462) *(G-14454)*

Euro Design Builders Group 571 236-6189
12400 Stewarts Ford Ct Fairfax (22033) *(G-4452)*

Euro Print USA LLC 703 849-8781
3728 Hummer Rd Annandale (22003) *(G-747)*

Euro Pro Coatings, Woodbridge *Also called Europro Coatings Inc* *(G-15698)*

Europro Coatings Inc 703 817-1211
2714 Code Way Woodbridge (22192) *(G-15698)*

Eurovia Atlantic Coast LLC (HQ) **703 230-0850**
14500 Avion Pkwy Ste 310 Chantilly (20151) *(G-2418)*

Eutopia Magazine Guelph Press 703 938-6077
2579 John Milton Dr # 105 Herndon (20171) *(G-6670)*

Euvanna Chayanne Cosmetics LLC 804 307-4941
14431 Old Bond St Chesterfield (23832) *(G-3498)*

Evaluation Tech For Dev LLC 434 851-0651
708 Montrose Ave Charlottesville (22902) *(G-2794)*

Evans Corporate Services LLC 703 344-3678
7985 Almeda Ct Lorton (22079) *(G-7485)*

Evans Custom Playsites 804 615-3397
14609 Gimbel Dr Chester (23836) *(G-3414)*

Evans Mactavis Agregrats, North Chesterfield *Also called Mactavish Machine Mfg Co* *(G-9916)*

Evenflow Technologies Inc 703 625-2628
43895 Camellia St Ashburn (20147) *(G-1277)*

Event Guru Software, Fairfax *Also called 4gurus LLC* *(G-4587)*

Event Guru Software, Fairfax *Also called 4gurus LLC* *(G-4588)*

Eventdone LLC (PA) **703 239-6410**
4391 Ridgewood Center Dr H Woodbridge (22192) *(G-15699)*

Ever Be Signs 912 660-1436
701 Goodwin St Williamsburg (23185) *(G-15240)*

Ever Forward Woodworks 434 882-0727
531 Hummingbird Rd Scottsville (24590) *(G-12660)*

Everbrite LLC 540 261-2121
627 E 30th St Buena Vista (24416) *(G-2143)*

Everett Jones Lumber Corp 540 582-5655
7437 Courthouse Rd Spotsylvania (22551) *(G-12889)*

Everette Publishing LLC 757 344-9092
106 Tillerson Dr Newport News (23602) *(G-9221)*

Evergreen Design Inc 540 984-4653
520 Stoney Creek Blvd Edinburg (22824) *(G-4303)*

Evergreen Enterprises Inc 804 231-1800
5915 Midlothian Tpke Richmond (23225) *(G-11581)*

Evergreen Enterprises Inc (PA) **804 231-1800**
5915 Midlothian Tpke Richmond (23225) *(G-11582)*

Evergreen Enterprises VA LLC 804 231-1800
5915 Midlothian Tpke Richmond (23225) *(G-11583)*

Evergreen Outfitters LLC 540 843-2576
18 E Main St Luray (22835) *(G-7610)*

Everlasting Life Product 703 761-4900
6812 Dean Dr Mc Lean (22101) *(G-8424)*

Everlasting Life Products Inc 703 761-4900
233 Kanter Dr Strasburg (22657) *(G-13578)*

Every Changing Woman 757 343-3088
905 Roundtable Ct Virginia Beach (23464) *(G-14455)*

Everyday Education LLC 804 752-2517
13041 Hill Club Ln Ashland (23005) *(G-1411)*

Everything Gos LLC 804 290-3870
801 Windomere Ave Richmond (23227) *(G-11206)*

Everything Under Sun LLC 276 252-2376
79 New Jerusalem Rd Ridgeway (24148) *(G-11842)*

Evi, South Boston *Also called Emergency Vehicles Inc* *(G-12763)*

Evi Technology, Dulles *Also called L3harris Technologies Inc* *(G-4207)*

Evo, Lynchburg *Also called Emergency Vehicle Outfitters* *(G-7702)*

Evolution Printing Inc 571 292-1213
7200 S Hill Dr Manassas (20109) *(G-8066)*

Evolve Custom LLC...703 570-5700
200 Lenoir Dr Ste B Winchester (22603) ***(G-15414)***
Evolve Manufacturing LLC (HQ)...**703 570-5700**
200 Lenoir Dr Ste B Winchester (22603) ***(G-15415)***
Evolve Play LLC...703 570-5700
200 Lenoir Dr Ste B Winchester (22603) ***(G-15416)***
Evolve Solutions Group, Herndon *Also called E Primera Enable Corp* ***(G-6664)***
Evonik Corporation...804 541-8658
914 E Randolph Rd Hopewell (23860) ***(G-6925)***
Evonik Corporation...804 727-0711
7801 Whitepine Rd North Chesterfield (23237) ***(G-9868)***
Evonik Goldschmidt Corporation...804 541-8658
914 E Randolph Rd Hopewell (23860) ***(G-6926)***
Evs Glass Creations LLC...540 412-8242
4 Kendale Ln Fredericksburg (22407) ***(G-5285)***
Ews Inc...757 482-2740
909 Hanbury Ct Chesapeake (23322) ***(G-3095)***
Excalibur Technology Svcs LLC...703 853-8307
8854 Stable Forest Pl Bristow (20136) ***(G-2051)***
Excel Graphics...757 596-4334
2225 George Wash Mem Hwy Yorktown (23693) ***(G-15956)***
Excel Prsthetics Orthotics Inc (PA)...**540 982-0205**
115 Albemarle Ave Se Roanoke (24013) ***(G-12083)***
Excel Prsthetics Orthotics Inc...434 528-3695
2201 Langhorne Rd Ste A Lynchburg (24501) ***(G-7706)***
Excel Prsthetics Orthotics Inc...434 797-1191
312 S Main St Danville (24541) ***(G-3993)***
Excel Tool Inc...276 322-0223
162 Tabor Ave Falls Mills (24613) ***(G-4931)***
Excel Well Service Inc...276 498-4360
3008 Breeden Branch Rd Rowe (24646) ***(G-12397)***
Exceletics Inc...703 405-5479
2707 Floris Ln Herndon (20171) ***(G-6671)***
Excello Oil Company Inc (PA)...**276 935-2332**
20813 Riverside Dr Grundy (24614) ***(G-6031)***
Excelscion Med Cding Blling LL...561 866-1000
314 Fairy Street Ext B Martinsville (24112) ***(G-8285)***
Excelsia Industries LLC...804 347-7626
14218 Chimney House Rd Midlothian (23112) ***(G-8815)***
Excelsior Associates Inc...703 255-1596
1832 Clovermeadow Dr Vienna (22182) ***(G-14051)***
Exchange Milling Co Inc (PA)...**540 483-5324**
1380 Franklin St Rocky Mount (24151) ***(G-12321)***
Exchange Mntor Pblctons Forums, Arlington *Also called Access Intelligence LLC* ***(G-837)***
Exchange Publishing...703 644-5184
9248 Rockefeller Ln Springfield (22153) ***(G-13000)***
Exclusive Wine Imports LLC...703 765-9749
7210 Marlan Dr Alexandria (22307) ***(G-458)***
Exclusively Yours Embroidery...571 285-2196
5603 Nibbs Ct Woodbridge (22193) ***(G-15700)***
Executive Creations...757 351-1310
5998 Providence Rd Virginia Beach (23464) ***(G-14456)***
Executive Glass Services Inc...703 689-2178
3305 Wellhouse Ct Herndon (20171) ***(G-6672)***
Executive Lifestyle Mag Inc...757 438-5582
703 Juniper Dr Newport News (23601) ***(G-9222)***
Executive Press Inc...703 352-1337
10412 Main St Ste 1 Fairfax (22030) ***(G-4619)***
Execware LLC...202 607-8904
3440 S Jefferson St # 1125 Falls Church (22041) ***(G-4789)***
Exelis, Mc Lean *Also called L3harris Technologies Inc* ***(G-8481)***
Exelis C4i, Herndon *Also called Harris Corporation* ***(G-6695)***
Exelis Systems Corp - Folbos, Newport News *Also called L3harris Technologies Inc* ***(G-9278)***
Exeye LLC...703 319-0976
10224 Broadsword Dr Bristow (20136) ***(G-2052)***
Exhibit Design & Prod Svcs LLC...804 347-0924
4300 Eubank Rd Henrico (23231) ***(G-6508)***
Exhibit Foundry...540 705-0055
794 N Main St Harrisonburg (22802) ***(G-6314)***
Exide Technologies...678 566-9000
14231 Riverdowns South Dr Midlothian (23113) ***(G-8816)***
Exide Technologies LLC...434 975-6001
4035 Hunterstand Ct Charlottesville (22911) ***(G-2629)***
Exide Transportation Group, Midlothian *Also called Exide Technologies* ***(G-8816)***
Exloc Instruments...540 428-3088
7089 Lineweaver Rd Warrenton (20187) ***(G-15006)***
Exotic Vehicle Wraps Inc...240 320-3335
23590 Overland Dr Ste 160 Sterling (20166) ***(G-13396)***
Exotic Woodworks...352 408-5373
1820 Clifton Bridge Dr Virginia Beach (23456) ***(G-14457)***
Exper T'S, Blacksburg *Also called Schmidt Jayme* ***(G-1787)***
Expertsinframing LLC...703 580-9980
4164 Merchant Plz Woodbridge (22192) ***(G-15701)***
Exploration Partners...540 213-1333
1600 N Coalter St Ste 1 Staunton (24401) ***(G-13255)***
Exploration Partners LLC (PA)...**434 973-8311**
1414 Sachem Pl Ste 1 Charlottesville (22901) ***(G-2630)***
Explorations Partners, Charlottesville *Also called Exploration Partners LLC* ***(G-2630)***
Explosive Sports Cond LLC...703 255-7087
9704 Chilcott Manor Way Vienna (22181) ***(G-14052)***
Explus Inc...703 260-0780
44156 Mercure Cir Dulles (20166) ***(G-4201)***
Expo Branders Corporation...703 865-7581
9667 Main St Ste D Fairfax (22031) ***(G-4453)***
Expo Cabinetry...703 940-3800
2940 Prosperity Ave B Fairfax (22031) ***(G-4454)***
Exponential Biotherapies Inc...703 288-3710
7921 Jones Branch Dr # 133 Mc Lean (22102) ***(G-8425)***
Express Cmputers Alexandria Ci, Alexandria *Also called Refurb Factory LLC* ***(G-328)***
Express Contract Fullmen...540 719-2100
477 Backnine Dr Moneta (24121) ***(G-8961)***
Express Printing, Herndon *Also called Digital Documents Inc* ***(G-6657)***
Express Racing & Machine...804 521-7891
9740 Jefferson Davis Hwy North Chesterfield (23237) ***(G-9869)***
Express Signs Inc...804 796-5197
11932 Centre St Chester (23831) ***(G-3415)***
Express Yourself Inc (PA)...**434 757-1099**
223 Moseley St La Crosse (23950) ***(G-7144)***
Expressway Pallet Inc...804 231-6177
14412 Clearcreek Pl South Chesterfield (23834) ***(G-12804)***
Exquisite Invitations Inc...276 666-0168
1010 Foxfire Rd Martinsville (24112) ***(G-8286)***
Exterior Systems Inc...804 752-2324
11505 N Lakeridge Pkwy Ashland (23005) ***(G-1412)***
Extinction Pharmaceuticals...757 258-0498
124 Country Club Dr Williamsburg (23188) ***(G-15241)***
Extra Space Storage...703 719-4354
5321 Shawnee Rd Alexandria (22312) ***(G-459)***
Extract Attract Inc...757 751-0671
201 Edison Ave Portsmouth (23702) ***(G-10424)***
Extrema Cables, Charlottesville *Also called Frank M Churillo* ***(G-2633)***
Extreme Computer Services Inc...703 730-8821
15712 Cranberry Ct Dumfries (22025) ***(G-4246)***
Extreme Exposure Media LLC...540 434-0811
847 Martin Luther King Jr Harrisonburg (22801) ***(G-6315)***
Extreme Powder Coating LLC...703 339-8233
8384b Terminal Rd Lorton (22079) ***(G-7486)***
Extreme Powder Works LLC...540 483-2684
24102 Providence Ch Rd Henry (24102) ***(G-6595)***
Extreme Signs and Graphics, Max Meadows *Also called Dmmt Glisan Inc* ***(G-8367)***
Extreme Steel Inc...540 868-9150
9705 Rider Rd Warrenton (20187) ***(G-15007)***
Extreme Steel Inc...540 868-9150
480 Shady Elm Rd Winchester (22602) ***(G-15417)***
Extremeht2com...804 665-6304
522 Rossmore Rd Richmond (23225) ***(G-11584)***
Extrusion and Lamination Div, Suffolk *Also called Vitex Packaging Group Inc* ***(G-13780)***
Eye Armor Incorporated...571 238-4096
30 Big Spring Ln Stafford (22554) ***(G-13144)***
Eye Dollz Lashes Buty Bar LLC...703 480-7899
10432 Balls Ford Rd Manassas (20109) ***(G-8067)***
Eye of Needle Embroidery...540 837-2089
146 Morning Star Ln Boyce (22620) ***(G-1909)***
Eyegaze Inc...703 385-8800
10363 Democracy Ln Fairfax (22030) ***(G-4620)***
Eyeglass Repair Shoppe...903 509-1517
141 Bear Trap Farm Rd Mount Solon (22843) ***(G-9087)***
Eyl Inc...703 682-7018
2011 Crystal Dr Ste 400 Arlington (22202) ***(G-961)***
EZ Cut Bandmills...540 931-2410
175 Rose Bush Ln Pearisburg (24134) ***(G-10274)***
EZ Tool Rental...703 531-4700
1103 W Broad St Falls Church (22046) ***(G-4911)***
Ezara Inc...434 409-4232
1112 Frays Mountain Rd Earlysville (22936) ***(G-4289)***
Ezgo, Gainesville *Also called Kram Industries Inc* ***(G-5593)***
Ezl Software LLC...804 288-0748
110 Countryside Ln Richmond (23229) ***(G-11207)***
F & B Holding Co...757 766-2770
406 Honeysuckle Ln Yorktown (23693) ***(G-15957)***
F & D Manufacturing & Supply...540 586-6111
1023 Pearsall Dr Bedford (24523) ***(G-1636)***
F & M Construction Corp...276 728-2255
927 Training Center Rd Hillsville (24343) ***(G-6891)***
F & M Tools LLC...757 361-9225
1500 Linden Ave Chesapeake (23325) ***(G-3096)***
F & P Enterprises Inc (PA)...**804 561-2784**
15961 Goodes Bridge Rd Amelia Court House (23002) ***(G-657)***
F & R Electric Inc...276 979-8480
29835 Gvrnor G C Pery Hwy North Tazewell (24630) ***(G-10099)***
F C Holdings Inc (PA)...**804 222-2821**
5901 Lewis Rd Sandston (23150) ***(G-12614)***
F C James Company, Nassawadox *Also called Francis C James Jr* ***(G-9100)***
F W Baird General Contractor...434 724-4499
581 Smith Rd Chatham (24531) ***(G-2928)***
F3 Technologies LLC...804 785-1017
1776 Patriot Way Mattaponi (23110) ***(G-8358)***

ALPHABETIC

Fab Juniors Welding Metal..540 480-1971
3229 Stuarts Draft Hwy Stuarts Draft (24477) *(G-13647)*

Fab Services LLC...757 869-4480
104 Park Pl Williamsburg (23185) *(G-15242)*

Fabbioli Cellars...703 771-1197
15669 Limestone School Rd Leesburg (20176) *(G-7271)*

Fabric Accents By Emily...540 678-3999
679 Berryville Ave Winchester (22601) *(G-15540)*

Fabricated Welding Specialites....................................540 345-3104
525 Caldwell St Nw Roanoke (24017) *(G-12084)*

Fabrication Division, Chesapeake *Also called VT Milcom Inc* *(G-3366)*

Fabrication Specialist VA, Virginia Beach *Also called Fabriction Spclist of Virginia* *(G-14458)*

Fabricraft Metal Works, Culpeper *Also called Brown Russel* *(G-3876)*

Fabriction Spclist of Virginia....................................757 620-2540
1130 Flobert Dr Virginia Beach (23464) *(G-14458)*

Fabrik..540 651-4169
210 Daniels Run Rd Ne Copper Hill (24079) *(G-3764)*

Fabriko Inc...434 352-7145
1065 Confederate Blvd Appomattox (24522) *(G-810)*

Fabritech..540 825-1544
20381 Dove Hill Rd Culpeper (22701) *(G-3891)*

Fabritek Company Inc (PA)..................................**540 662-9095**
416 Battaile Dr Winchester (22601) *(G-15541)*

Face Companies, The, Norfolk *Also called Face Construction Technologies* *(G-9545)*

Face Construction Technologies...................................757 624-2121
427 W 35th St Norfolk (23508) *(G-9545)*

Face Electronics Lc..757 624-2121
427 W 35th St Norfolk (23508) *(G-9546)*

Face X LLC...757 624-2121
427 W 35th St Norfolk (23508) *(G-9547)*

Fain Arlice Sawmill...276 694-8211
737 Peters Creek Dr Stuart (24171) *(G-13611)*

Fair Value Games LLC...804 307-9110
11608 Norwich Pkwy Glen Allen (23059) *(G-5729)*

Fairbanks Coal Co Inc...276 395-3354
450 Front St W Coeburn (24230) *(G-3698)*

Fairbanks Morse LLC..757 623-2711
981 Scott St Ste A Norfolk (23502) *(G-9548)*

Fairfax Metals LLC..571 594-1937
22795 Milltown Farm Ct Ashburn (20148) *(G-1278)*

Fairfax Plastics, Fairfax *Also called Martin Elthon* *(G-4503)*

Fairfax Printers Inc..703 273-1220
10608 Oliver St Fairfax (22030) *(G-4621)*

Fairfax Publishing Company (PA)..............................**703 421-2003**
14 Pidgeon Hill Dr # 330 Sterling (20165) *(G-13397)*

Fairfax Screen Printing, Herndon *Also called Dptl Inc* *(G-6659)*

Fairfax Station Times...703 437-5400
1920 Assn Dr Ste 500 Reston (20191) *(G-10850)*

Fairfax Woodworking Inc..703 339-9578
14714 Old Lee Rd Chantilly (20151) *(G-2419)*

Fairfax Woodworking Inc...571 292-2220
12042 Cadet Ct Manassas (20109) *(G-8068)*

Fairlead Boatworks Inc...757 247-0101
99 Jefferson Ave Newport News (23607) *(G-9223)*

Fairlead Integrated LLC (PA)................................**757 384-1957**
650 Chautauqua Ave Portsmouth (23707) *(G-10425)*

Fairlead Integrated LLC..757 606-2034
176 Lincoln St Portsmouth (23704) *(G-10426)*

Fairlead Intgrted Pwr Cntrls L.....................................757 384-1957
650 Chautauqua Ave Portsmouth (23707) *(G-10427)*

Fairlead IPC, Portsmouth *Also called Fairlead Intgrted Pwr Cntrls L* *(G-10427)*

Fairlead Marine Inc..757 606-2034
650 Chautauqua Ave Portsmouth (23707) *(G-10428)*

Fairlead PMI, Portsmouth *Also called Fairlead Prcsion Mfg Intgrtion* *(G-10429)*

Fairlead Prcsion Mfg Intgrtion.....................................757 384-1957
750 Chautauqua Ave Portsmouth (23707) *(G-10429)*

Fairlead Precision Mfg..757 606-2033
933 Broad St Unit 7008 Portsmouth (23707) *(G-10430)*

Fairview Place LLC..330 257-1138
1232 Westover Ave Norfolk (23507) *(G-9549)*

Fairway Enterprise LLP..434 973-8595
977 Seminole Trl Charlottesville (22901) *(G-2631)*

Fairway Products Inc..804 462-0123
5459 Mary Ball Rd Lancaster (22503) *(G-7161)*

Faith First Printing LLC..757 723-7673
5 Allison Sutton Dr Hampton (23669) *(G-6146)*

Faith Mission Home..434 985-7177
8239 Mission Home Rd Free Union (22940) *(G-5506)*

Faith Printing..804 745-0667
7814 Midlothian Tpke North Chesterfield (23235) *(G-9870)*

Faith Publishing LLC...540 632-3608
805 Brandon Ave Sw Roanoke (24015) *(G-12085)*

Faithbrooke Barn Vineyards LLC....................................540 743-1207
4468 Us Highway 340 N Luray (22835) *(G-7611)*

Falck Schmidt Def Systems Corp....................................805 689-1739
8534f Terminal Rd Lorton (22079) *(G-7487)*

Falco Emotors Inc...571 313-1154
100 Executive Dr Ste C Dulles (20166) *(G-4202)*

Falcon Coal Corporation...276 679-0600
5505 Wise Norton Rd Wise (24293) *(G-15623)*

Falcon Concrete Corporation..703 354-7100
6860 Commercial Dr Springfield (22151) *(G-13001)*

Falcon Defense Service LLC...703 395-2007
5813 Colfax Ave Alexandria (22311) *(G-203)*

Falcon Lab Inc..703 442-0124
1765 Greensboro Station P Mc Lean (22102) *(G-8426)*

Falcon Screens LLC..703 789-3274
9518 Merrimont Trace Cir Bristow (20136) *(G-2053)*

Falcon Tool and Design Inc...757 898-9393
100 Redoubt Rd Ste A Yorktown (23692) *(G-15958)*

Falling Creek Log Yard Inc..804 798-6121
14281 Washington Hwy Ashland (23005) *(G-1413)*

Falling Creek Metal Products..804 744-1061
3909 Bellson Park Dr Midlothian (23112) *(G-8817)*

Falls Church Distillers LLC...703 858-9186
6230 Cheryl Dr Falls Church (22044) *(G-4790)*

Falls Church Distillers LLC...703 858-9186
442 S Washington St Ste A Falls Church (22046) *(G-4912)*

Falls Church News Press...703 532-3267
200 Little Falls St # 508 Falls Church (22046) *(G-4913)*

Falls Stamping & Welding Co...330 928-1191
28 Jefferson Ave S Pulaski (24301) *(G-10636)*

Falls Welding Services, Woodville *Also called Timothy D Falls* *(G-15862)*

Famarco Newco LLC..757 460-3573
1381 Air Rail Ave Virginia Beach (23455) *(G-14459)*

Fame All Stars..757 817-0214
661 Todd Trl Yorktown (23692) *(G-15959)*

Family Crafters of Virginia...540 943-3934
124 Poland St Waynesboro (22980) *(G-15114)*

Family Insight PC..540 818-1687
3609 Larson Oaks Dr Roanoke (24018) *(G-11922)*

Family Magazine Network Inc..703 298-0601
485 Springpark Pl Herndon (20170) *(G-6673)*

Family Power Washing, Fredericksburg *Also called Bernard Speed* *(G-5403)*

Family Tree Care Inc...703 280-1169
2913 Hideaway Rd Fairfax (22031) *(G-4455)*

Famm Project LLC...757 975-6492
9601 Warwick Blvd Newport News (23601) *(G-9224)*

Fancy Gap Woodworks LLC...336 816-9881
347 Forest Haven Dr Fancy Gap (24328) *(G-4935)*

Fancy Hill Jams and Jellies, Natural Bridge *Also called J & V Kitchen Inc* *(G-9107)*

Fancy Media Co Inc..757 638-7101
5131 River Club Dr # 110 Suffolk (23435) *(G-13706)*

Fancy Stitches..804 796-6942
6201 Chstrfeld Meadows Dr Chesterfield (23832) *(G-3499)*

Fannypants LLC..703 953-3099
4229 Lafayette Center Dr # 1150 Chantilly (20151) *(G-2420)*

Fantabulous Chef Service..804 245-4492
1719 Winesap Dr Richmond (23231) *(G-11208)*

Fantalife Publishing LLC...703 682-2125
1405 S Fern St 502 Arlington (22202) *(G-962)*

Fantasy Factory, Buchanan *Also called Proknows* *(G-2125)*

Far Fetch LLC...757 493-3572
200 Golden Oak Ct Ste 320 Virginia Beach (23452) *(G-14460)*

Far West Print Solutions LLC..757 549-1258
722 Montebello Cir Chesapeake (23322) *(G-3097)*

Farage Precision LLC...901 264-2422
10202 Aspen Willow Dr Fairfax (22032) *(G-4456)*

Farbes LLC..240 426-9680
6590 Irvin Ct Alexandria (22312) *(G-460)*

Farehill Precision LLC..540 879-2373
4445 Lewis Byrd Rd Rockingham (22801) *(G-12251)*

Farlow Industries...434 836-4596
1201 Piney Forest Rd Danville (24540) *(G-3994)*

Farmer Machine Company Inc...804 550-7310
10395 Sliding Ridge Rd Ashland (23005) *(G-1414)*

Farmers Milling & Supply Inc..276 228-2971
525 W Railroad Ave Wytheville (24382) *(G-15888)*

Farmkart Foods LLC..706 461-6395
2500 N Van Dorn St Apt 12 Alexandria (22302) *(G-204)*

Farmland Foods Inc..757 357-4321
111 Commerce St Smithfield (23430) *(G-12713)*

Farmstead Finds Salvaging...540 845-8200
550 Long Meadow Dr Fredericksburg (22406) *(G-5430)*

Farmville Printing, Farmville *Also called North Street Enterprise Inc* *(G-4954)*

Fashion Mechanics...571 398-0894
2700 Potomac Mills Cir # 111 Woodbridge (22192) *(G-15702)*

Fashion Seoul...571 395-8555
4305 Markham St Annandale (22003) *(G-748)*

Fast Lane Specialties Inc...757 784-7474
3560 Shoreline Dr West Point (23181) *(G-15156)*

Fast Ra Xpress LLC..804 514-5696
5003 Colwyck Dr Richmond (23223) *(G-11585)*

Fast Signs Inc..540 389-6691
146 W 4th St Ste 3 Salem (24153) *(G-12506)*

Fast Signs of Herndon...703 713-0743
2465 Centreville Rd J20 Herndon (20171) *(G-6674)*

Fastsigns, Winchester *Also called Quick Designs LLC* *(G-15573)*

(G-0000) Company's Geographic Section entry number

Fastsigns, Stafford *Also called Kirby Burbank LLC* ***(G-13164)***
Fastsigns, Herndon *Also called Fast Signs of Herndon* ***(G-6674)***
Fastsigns, Salem *Also called Tight Lines Holdings Group Inc* ***(G-12573)***
Fastsigns, Forest *Also called Phase II Inc* ***(G-5087)***
Fastsigns, Yorktown *Also called Wang Sign Holdings LLC* ***(G-16000)***
Fastsigns, Salem *Also called Fast Signs Inc* ***(G-12506)***
Fastsigns, Rockville *Also called Trexlo Enterprises LLC* ***(G-12301)***
Fastsigns, Arlington *Also called Danzo LLC* ***(G-926)***
Fastsigns, North Chesterfield *Also called Trexlo Enterprises LLC* ***(G-10004)***
Fastsigns, Virginia Beach *Also called J & R Partners* ***(G-14556)***
Fastsigns, Roanoke *Also called Tight Lines Holdings Group* ***(G-12009)***
Fastsigns, Mc Lean *Also called Riverland Inc* ***(G-8539)***
Fastsigns, Virginia Beach *Also called W & S Forbes Inc* ***(G-14928)***
Fastsigns, Yorktown *Also called Gourmet Kitchen Tools Inc* ***(G-15962)***
Fastsigns, Richmond *Also called Trexlo Enterprises LLC* ***(G-11794)***
Fastsigns, Alexandria *Also called Positive Signs LLC* ***(G-553)***
Fastsigns, Glen Allen *Also called Trexlo Enterprises LLC* ***(G-5817)***
Fastsigns, Chesapeake *Also called Dwiggins Corp* ***(G-3079)***
Fastsigns 703 913-5300
6715 Backlick Rd Ste B Springfield (22150) ***(G-13002)***
Fastsigns 703 392-7446
7612 Stream Walk Ln Manassas (20109) ***(G-8069)***
Fastsigns 571 510-0400
934 Edwards Ferry Rd Ne Leesburg (20176) ***(G-7272)***
Fastsigns Fairfax, Fairfax *Also called Todays Signs Inc* ***(G-4688)***
Fastsigns Norfolk 757 274-3344
2000 Colonial Ave Norfolk (23517) ***(G-9550)***
Fasttrack Teaching Materials, Springfield *Also called David Burns* ***(G-12988)***
Fastware Inc 703 680-5050
8474 Virginia Meadows Dr Manassas (20109) ***(G-8070)***
Fat Apple LLC 434 823-2481
387 Grayrock Dr Crozet (22932) ***(G-3832)***
Fat Cat Publishings LLC 804 368-0378
406 Carter Forest Dr Ashland (23005) ***(G-1415)***
Fat Mltons Sthern Swets Treats 804 248-4175
8908 Talon Ln North Chesterfield (23237) ***(G-9871)***
Fatim and Sallys Cstm Tees LLC 619 884-5864
920 Green Sea Trl Chesapeake (23323) ***(G-3098)***
Faun Trackway (usa) Inc 202 459-0802
1655 Fort Myer Dr Ste 950 Arlington (22209) ***(G-963)***
Fauquier Building Grnds 540 422-8480
100 Manor Ct Warrenton (20186) ***(G-15008)***
Fauquier Enterprise Center 540 680-2652
4263 Aiken Dr Warrenton (20187) ***(G-15009)***
Fauquier Hearing Services Pllc 540 341-7112
493 Blackwell Rd Ste 315 Warrenton (20186) ***(G-15010)***
Fauquier Kid LLC 540 349-0027
285 Falmouth St Warrenton (20186) ***(G-15011)***
Fauquier Now 540 359-6574
50 Culpeper St Ste 3 Warrenton (20186) ***(G-15012)***
Fauquier Services Inc 540 341-4133
8279 Double Poplars Ln Warrenton (20187) ***(G-15013)***
Fauquier Silhouettes Inc 540 347-3191
247 Amber Cir Warrenton (20186) ***(G-15014)***
Fauquier Times Democrat 540 347-7363
39 Culpeper St Warrenton (20186) ***(G-15015)***
Fausti USA Service LLC 540 371-3287
3509 Shannon Park Dr # 113 Fredericksburg (22408) ***(G-5286)***
Fbgc JV LLC 757 727-9442
135 Kings Way Hampton (23669) ***(G-6147)***
Fcw Government Tech Group 703 876-5100
3110 Frview Pk Dr Ste 777 Falls Church (22042) ***(G-4791)***
Fcw Media Group 703 876-5136
3141 Frview Pk Dr Ste 777 Falls Church (22042) ***(G-4792)***
Fdp Brakes, Tappahannock *Also called Fdp Virginia Inc* ***(G-13816)***
Fdp Virginia Inc 804 443-5356
1076 Airport Rd Tappahannock (22560) ***(G-13816)***
Feat Little Publishing LLC 757 594-9265
46 Hopkins St Newport News (23601) ***(G-9225)***
Feather & Pearl Candle Co LLC 540 769-9529
1430 Maple Ave Sw Roanoke (24016) ***(G-12086)***
Feather Carbon LLC 757 630-6759
6940 Corinth Chapel Rd Suffolk (23437) ***(G-13707)***
Featherlite Coaches Inc (PA) **757 923-3374**
1007 Obici Indus Blvd Suffolk (23434) ***(G-13708)***
Febrocom LLC 703 349-6316
22457 Terra Rosa Pl Ashburn (20148) ***(G-1279)***
Fed Reach Inc 703 507-8822
9024 Haywood Ave Lorton (22079) ***(G-7488)***
Federal Data Corporation 703 734-3773
7575 Colshire Dr Mc Lean (22102) ***(G-8427)***
Federal Equipment Company 757 493-0404
650 Woodlake Dr Chesapeake (23320) ***(G-3099)***
Federal Prison Industries 804 733-7881
1100 River Rd North Prince George (23860) ***(G-10087)***
Federal Times 703 750-9000
1919 Gallows Rd Ste 400 Vienna (22182) ***(G-14053)***
Federal-Mogul Powertrain LLC 540 557-3300
300 Industrial Park Rd Se Blacksburg (24060) ***(G-1737)***
Federal-Mogul Powertrain LLC 540 953-4676
2901 Prosperity Rd Blacksburg (24060) ***(G-1738)***
Federal-Mogul Products Inc 540 662-3871
2410 Papermill Rd Winchester (22601) ***(G-15542)***
Federated Publications Inc 703 854-6000
7950 Jones Branch Dr Mc Lean (22102) ***(G-8428)***
Fedex Office & Print Svcs Inc 703 491-1300
13752 Jefferson Davis Hwy Woodbridge (22191) ***(G-15703)***
Fedor Ventures LLC 540 668-6248
16110 Mountain Ridge Ln Hillsboro (20132) ***(G-6866)***
Fedsafes LLC 703 525-1436
5130 Wilson Blvd Arlington (22205) ***(G-964)***
Fedweek, Glen Allen *Also called Macemedia Inc* ***(G-5766)***
Feedrva Inc 804 513-3100
2601 Lafayette Ave Henrico (23228) ***(G-6509)***
Feefees Cabinet LLC 804 647-0297
2530 Noel St North Chesterfield (23237) ***(G-9872)***
Feeling Art, Virginia Beach *Also called Bariso Ling* ***(G-14261)***
Fei Ltd 540 291-3398
37 Rock Bridge Indus Park Natural Bridge Stati (24579) ***(G-9109)***
Fei-Zyfer Inc 540 349-8330
8209 Great Run Ln Warrenton (20186) ***(G-15016)***
Fellers Inc 757 853-1363
930 Denison Ave Norfolk (23513) ***(G-9551)***
Felton Brothers Trnst Mix Inc (PA) **434 572-2665**
1 Edmunds St South Boston (24592) ***(G-12765)***
Felton Brothers Trnst Mix Inc 434 376-2415
813b Lynchburg Ave Brookneal (24528) ***(G-2110)***
Felton Brothers Trnst Mix Inc 434 374-5373
703 Puryear Rd Boydton (23917) ***(G-1915)***
Felton Brothers Trnst Mix Inc 434 572-4614
613 Railroad Ave South Boston (24592) ***(G-12766)***
Felton Brothers Trnst Mix Inc 434 848-3966
301 South St Lawrenceville (23868) ***(G-7180)***
Felton Brothers Trnst Mix Inc 434 447-3778
1241 Plank Rd South Hill (23970) ***(G-12850)***
Felts Sign Co 804 262-1441
1501 Fauver Ave Glen Allen (23060) ***(G-5730)***
Femme Promo, Chantilly *Also called Suday Promotions Inc* ***(G-2503)***
Fenco Incorporated 540 885-7377
10 Croyden Ln Staunton (24401) ***(G-13256)***
Fennec Publishing LLC 703 934-6781
9906 Great Oaks Way Fairfax (22030) ***(G-4622)***
Ferguson Custom Sawmill LLC 540 903-8174
1709 Nottingham Dr Fredericksburg (22408) ***(G-5287)***
Ferguson Land and Lbr Co Inc 540 483-5090
1040 N Main St Rocky Mount (24151) ***(G-12322)***
Ferguson Logging Inc 540 721-3408
289 Shoreline Marina Cir # 110 Moneta (24121) ***(G-8962)***
Ferguson Manufacturing Co Inc 757 539-3409
590 Madison Ave Suffolk (23434) ***(G-13709)***
Ferguson Portable Toilets LLC 434 610-9988
2556 Hancock Rd Appomattox (24522) ***(G-811)***
Fergusson Printing 804 355-8621
4109 Jacque St Richmond (23230) ***(G-11209)***
Ferrer 703 862-4891
3096 Madison Hill Ct Alexandria (22310) ***(G-461)***
Ferrera Group Usa Inc 703 340-8300
673 Potomac Station Dr Ne # 141 Leesburg (20176) ***(G-7273)***
Festival Design Inc 804 643-5247
309 N Monroe St Richmond (23220) ***(G-11586)***
Festival Flags, Richmond *Also called Festival Design Inc* ***(G-11586)***
Festive Foods 757 490-9186
389 Edwin Dr Ste 100 Virginia Beach (23462) ***(G-14461)***
Fetti Bear Apparel and ACC, North Chesterfield *Also called TS By Extreme LLC* ***(G-10005)***
Fgp Sensors Inc 757 766-1500
1000 Lucas Way Hampton (23666) ***(G-6148)***
Fgt, Fairfax *Also called Firstguard Technologies Corp* ***(G-4624)***
Fh Sheet Metal Inc 703 408-4622
9011 Centreville Rd # 56 Manassas (20110) ***(G-7940)***
FHP LLC 540 879-2560
4445 Lewis Byrd Rd Rockingham (22801) ***(G-12252)***
Fiber Consulting Services 804 746-2357
8134 Ashty Pl Mechanicsville (23116) ***(G-8622)***
Fiber Foods Inc 757 853-2888
2400 Florida Ave Norfolk (23513) ***(G-9552)***
Fiber Sign 276 669-9115
314 Goodson St Bristol (24201) ***(G-1978)***
Fiberglass Customs Inc 757 244-0610
7826 Warwick Blvd Newport News (23607) ***(G-9226)***
Fibertech Virginia Inc 540 337-0916
340 Old Quarry Ln Greenville (24440) ***(G-5998)***
Fibrex Environmental Products, Chesapeake *Also called Fibrex Group Inc* ***(G-3100)***
Fibrex Group Inc 800 346-4458
738 Burrow Ave Chesapeake (23324) ***(G-3100)***
Fibrxl Performance Inc 804 329-0491
4590 Vawter Ave Richmond (23222) ***(G-11587)***

ALPHABETIC

Fiction-Atlas Press LLC...........423 845-0243
348 Magnolia Dr Bristol (24201) **(G-1979)**
Fiddlehand Inc...........703 340-9806
2620 Viking Dr Herndon (20171) **(G-6675)**
Fidelity Contracting Company, Manassas *Also called Interior Building Systems Corp* **(G-8083)**
Fidelity Printing Inc...........804 737-7907
12 E Williamsburg Rd Sandston (23150) **(G-12615)**
Fidough Homemade Dog Treats...........757 876-4548
767 Terrace Dr Newport News (23601) **(G-9227)**
Field and Sons LLC...........757 412-0125
1528 Seafarer Ln Virginia Beach (23454) **(G-14462)**
Field Inner Prizes LLC...........540 738-2060
116 Dodson Ln Brightwood (22715) **(G-1961)**
Fieldale Quarry, Martinsville *Also called Boxley Materials Company* **(G-8272)**
Fields Inc Oscar S...........804 798-3900
10412 Design Rd Ashland (23005) **(G-1416)**
Fieldtech Industries LLC...........757 286-1503
1905 Sunrise Dr Virginia Beach (23455) **(G-14463)**
Fielside Woodworkig...........434 203-5530
1657 Spring Rd Hurt (24563) **(G-6975)**
Fifth Tribe LLC...........703 755-0680
8245 Boone Blvd Ste 250 Vienna (22182) **(G-14054)**
Figure Engineering LLC...........540 818-5034
8580 Cinder Bed Rd # 1000 Lorton (22079) **(G-7489)**
Figure Freight LLC...........757 814-3610
550 Pavilion Pl Apt 8b Newport News (23606) **(G-9228)**
Filenet Corporation...........703 312-1500
8401 Greensboro Dr # 400 Mc Lean (22102) **(G-8429)**
Filter Media...........540 667-9074
385 Battaile Dr Winchester (22601) **(G-15543)**
Filtroil LLC...........804 359-9125
2600 E Cary St Apt 5102 Richmond (23223) **(G-11588)**
Filz Built Bicycles...........703 451-5582
6117 Dorchester St Springfield (22150) **(G-13003)**
Final Resource Inc...........703 404-8740
12103 Courtney Ct Herndon (20170) **(G-6676)**
Final Touch Cabinetry...........540 895-5776
11411 Post Oak Rd Spotsylvania (22551) **(G-12890)**
Final Touch II Mfg LLC...........804 389-3899
2545 Bellwood Rd Ste 305 North Chesterfield (23237) **(G-9873)**
Finance Business Forms Company...........703 255-2151
713 Park St Se Vienna (22180) **(G-14055)**
Financial Press LLC...........804 928-6366
9702 Gayton Rd Richmond (23238) **(G-11210)**
Fincastle Vineyard & Winery...........540 591-9000
203 Maple Ridge Ln Fincastle (24090) **(G-4996)**
Finch Computing...........571 599-7480
12018 Sunrise Valley Dr Reston (20191) **(G-10851)**
Finch Woodworks...........540 333-0054
206 Hollow Ln Woodstock (22664) **(G-15853)**
Fincham Signs...........540 937-4634
10255 Rixeyville Rd Culpeper (22701) **(G-3892)**
Finco Inc...........301 645-4538
3401 Plank Rd Fredericksburg (22407) **(G-5288)**
Finders Keepers Recruiting...........703 963-0874
4405 Fair Stone Dr # 301 Fairfax (22033) **(G-4457)**
Fine Arts Engraving Company, Lorton *Also called Merrill Fine Arts Engrv Inc* **(G-7511)**
Fine Arts Framers Inc...........703 525-3869
4022 18th Rd N Arlington (22207) **(G-965)**
Fine Leather Works LLC...........703 200-1953
8201 Greensboro Dr # 300 Mc Lean (22102) **(G-8430)**
Fine Line Inc...........540 436-3626
25118 Old Valley Pike Maurertown (22644) **(G-8361)**
Fine Line LLC...........540 436-3626
25118 Old Valley Pike Maurertown (22644) **(G-8362)**
Fine Prints Designs...........703 560-1519
7326 Ronald St Falls Church (22046) **(G-4914)**
Fine Signs...........757 565-7833
5691 Mooretown Rd Williamsburg (23188) **(G-15243)**
Fine Signs & Graphics Inc...........757 565-7833
5691 Mooretown Rd Williamsburg (23188) **(G-15244)**
Finest Art & Framing LLC...........703 945-9000
19358 Diamond Lake Dr Lansdowne (20176) **(G-7170)**
Finest Productions Inc...........703 989-2657
901 N Pollard St Apt 2408 Arlington (22203) **(G-966)**
Finish Agent Inc...........703 437-7822
1318 Sundial Dr Reston (20194) **(G-10852)**
Finish Line Die Cutting...........804 342-8000
800 W Leigh St Richmond (23220) **(G-11589)**
Finish Line Shtmtal & Fbrictns...........757 262-1122
600 Copeland Dr Hampton (23661) **(G-6149)**
Finite Wisdom...........804 794-9585
8212 Cobbler Ct Henrico (23228) **(G-6510)**
Finly Corporation...........434 385-5028
3401 Forest Brook Rd Lynchburg (24501) **(G-7707)**
Fintech Sys Inc...........703 278-0606
4095 River Forth Dr Fairfax (22030) **(G-4623)**
Fiorucci Foods Chesterfield Co, South Chesterfield *Also called Campofrio Fd Group - Amer Inc* **(G-12798)**
Fip Cabinet, Brightwood *Also called Field Inner Prizes LLC* **(G-1961)**
Fire Systems Services Inc...........757 825-6379
110 Coliseum Xing Hampton (23666) **(G-6150)**
Firebird Manufacturing LLC...........434 517-0865
1057 Bill Tuck Hwy South Boston (24592) **(G-12767)**
Firedog Fabricators...........540 809-7389
13732 Blackwells Mill Rd Goldvein (22720) **(G-5878)**
Firefall-Literary...........703 942-6616
4905 Tunlaw St Alexandria (22312) **(G-462)**
Firefly Hill Vineyards LLC...........540 588-0231
4289 Northfork Rd Elliston (24087) **(G-4345)**
Firefly Sign Language Services...........205 405-7043
107 Community Way Apt 534 Staunton (24401) **(G-13257)**
Firehouse Embroidery, Stafford *Also called Joan Fisk* **(G-13160)**
Firemans Shield LLC...........804 231-1800
5915 Midlothian Tpke Richmond (23225) **(G-11590)**
Firewall LLC (PA)...........**804 977-8777**
7045 Mechanicsville Tpke Mechanicsville (23111) **(G-8623)**
First Class Chariots LLC...........757 334-7298
6352 E Virginia Bch Blvd Norfolk (23502) **(G-9553)**
First Class Publishing, Virginia Beach *Also called Datis LLC* **(G-14389)**
First Colony Homes Inc...........540 788-4222
4163 Old Calverton Rd Calverton (20138) **(G-2224)**
First Colony Press...........757 496-0362
2404 Laurel Cove Dr Virginia Beach (23454) **(G-14464)**
First Colony Technology LLC...........434 579-3655
4603 Black Rail Ct Providence Forge (23140) **(G-10624)**
First Colony Winery Ltd...........434 979-7105
1650 Harris Creek Rd Charlottesville (22902) **(G-2795)**
First Forest Furniture & Mllwk...........540 743-2051
1079 Us Highway 211 W Luray (22835) **(G-7612)**
First Impressions, Powhatan *Also called Mark Four Inc* **(G-10557)**
First Imprssions Prtg Graphics...........540 342-2679
2615 Orange Ave Ne Ste A Roanoke (24012) **(G-12087)**
First Landing Woodworks...........757 428-7537
311 49th St Virginia Beach (23451) **(G-14465)**
First Light Publishing Inc...........804 639-0659
14402 Twickenham Pl Chesterfield (23832) **(G-3500)**
First Objective Software Inc...........757 855-0191
1185 Pineridge Rd Norfolk (23502) **(G-9554)**
First Paper Co Inc...........434 821-6884
7320 Wards Rd Rustburg (24588) **(G-12439)**
First R & R Co Inc...........804 737-4400
125 S Cedar Ave Highland Springs (23075) **(G-6852)**
First Renaissance Ventures...........703 408-6961
1915 Chain Bridge Rd 500b Mc Lean (22102) **(G-8431)**
First Responder Systems LLC...........757 410-0353
901 Cedarwood Trce Chesapeake (23322) **(G-3101)**
Firstguard Technologies Corp...........703 267-6670
4031 University Dr # 100 Fairfax (22030) **(G-4624)**
Firstmark Corp (HQ)...........**724 759-2850**
2742 Live Oak Ln Midlothian (23113) **(G-8818)**
Fisher A C Jr Marine Rlwy Svc...........804 580-4342
106 Britney Ln Wicomico Church (22579) **(G-15195)**
Fisher Knives Inc...........434 242-3866
825 Norwood Ln Earlysville (22936) **(G-4290)**
Fisher Publications Inc...........804 323-6252
9918 Midlothian Tpke North Chesterfield (23235) **(G-9874)**
Fisher-Rosemount Systems Inc...........804 714-1400
8130 Virginia Pine Ct North Chesterfield (23237) **(G-9875)**
Fishhat Inc...........703 827-0990
6823 Old Dominion Dr Mc Lean (22101) **(G-8432)**
Fit ME By Crystal LLC...........302 573-1235
3535 S Ball St Apt 108 Arlington (22202) **(G-967)**
Fitcon Graphics, Big Stone Gap *Also called Carl G Gilliam Jr* **(G-1707)**
Fitzgerald John...........434 277-8044
266 Big Rock Rd Tyro (22976) **(G-13939)**
Fitzgerald Lumber & Log Co Inc (PA)...........**540 261-3430**
403 E 29th St Buena Vista (24416) **(G-2144)**
Fitzgerald Lumber & Log Co Inc...........540 348-5199
5459 Northley Hwy Fairfield (24435) **(G-4730)**
Fitzgerald Welding & Repair...........757 543-7312
4906 Bainbridge Blvd Chesapeake (23320) **(G-3102)**
Fitzgeralds Cabinet Shop Inc...........757 877-2538
13191 Warwick Blvd Newport News (23602) **(G-9229)**
Five Grapes LLC...........703 205-2444
45180 Business Ct Ste 100 Sterling (20166) **(G-13398)**
Five Mile Mountain Distillery...........540 588-3158
489 Floyd Hwy S Floyd (24091) **(G-5025)**
Five Ponds Press...........804 740-5867
10210 Windbluff Dr Henrico (23238) **(G-6511)**
Five Sixteen Solutions...........703 435-4247
5510 Hampton Forest Way Fairfax (22030) **(G-4625)**
Five Star Custom Blinds Inc...........757 236-5577
3419 Vrginia Bch Blvd 153 Virginia Beach (23452) **(G-14466)**
Five Star Medals...........703 644-4974
6813 Bluecurl Cir Springfield (22152) **(G-13004)**
Five Star Portables Inc...........571 839-7884
45910 Transamerica Plz # 103 Sterling (20166) **(G-13399)**

Five Talents Enterprises LLC 703 986-6721
4028 Sapling Way Triangle (22172) *(G-13892)*

Fives N Amercn Combustn Inc 540 735-8052
2217 Princess Anne St 329-1 Fredericksburg (22401) *(G-5185)*

Fixher Upper LLC 804 539-8816
145 Lasalle Ave Hampton (23661) *(G-6151)*

Fixmee LLC 703 731-1444
4609 Luxberry Dr Fairfax (22032) *(G-4458)*

Fize Wordsmithing LLC 804 756-8243
10001 Christiano Dr Glen Allen (23060) *(G-5731)*

Fjord Defense Inc 571 214-2183
1725 Duke St Alexandria (22314) *(G-205)*

Fk Logistics Usa LLC 877 811-8772
8609 Wstwd Ctr Dr Ste 1 Vienna (22182) *(G-14056)*

Flags of Valor LLC 703 729-8640
44200 Waxpool Rd Ste 137 Ashburn (20147) *(G-1280)*

Flagship Inc 757 222-3965
150 W Brambleton Ave Norfolk (23510) *(G-9555)*

Flagship, The, Norfolk *Also called Flagship Inc (G-9555)*

Flagstone 815 790-0582
5000 Treetop Ln Alexandria (22310) *(G-463)*

Flagstone Oprting Partners LLC 703 532-6238
8448 Holly Leaf Dr Mc Lean (22102) *(G-8433)*

Flat Hat 757 221-3283
102 Richmond Rd Williamsburg (23185) *(G-15245)*

Flavorful Bakery & Cafe LLC 301 857-2202
1210 E Longview Dr Woodbridge (22191) *(G-15704)*

Flawless Shower Enclosures 434 466-3845
85 Fox Ridge Ln Ruckersville (22968) *(G-12402)*

Fleet International Inc C B (HQ) **866 255-6960**
4615 Murray Pl Lynchburg (24502) *(G-7708)*

Fleet Printing, Norfolk *Also called Fleet Services Inc (G-9556)*

Fleet Services Inc 757 625-4214
712 W 20th St Norfolk (23517) *(G-9556)*

Fleet Svcs & Installations LLC (PA) **757 405-1405**
3535 Elmhurst Ln Portsmouth (23701) *(G-10431)*

Fleet Waveguides LLC 757 337-3311
700 Tech Center Pkwy # 200 Newport News (23606) *(G-9230)*

Fleeton Machine Works Inc 804 453-6130
890 Main St Reedville (22539) *(G-10761)*

Fleetwood Farm Winery LLC 703 722-2124
23075 Evergreen Mills Rd Leesburg (20175) *(G-7274)*

Fleming Woodworking LLC 559 259-2296
5061 Bay Cir Suffolk (23435) *(G-13710)*

Fletchers Hardware & Spt Ctr 276 935-8332
100 Walnut St Grundy (24614) *(G-6032)*

Flexel LLC 301 314-1004
3225 Sherry Ct Falls Church (22042) *(G-4793)*

Flexi-Dent Inc 804 897-2455
1256 Sycamore Sq Ste 201 Midlothian (23113) *(G-8819)*

Flexible Conveyor Systems Inc 804 897-9572
11310 Business Center Dr North Chesterfield (23236) *(G-9876)*

Flexicell Inc 804 550-7300
4329 November Ave Richmond (23231) *(G-11211)*

Flexicell, Div of, Ashland *Also called R A Pearson Company (G-1482)*

Flexprotect LLC 703 957-8648
11911 Freedom Dr Ste 850 Reston (20190) *(G-10853)*

Fli USA Inc 571 261-4174
15810 Spyglass Hill Loop Gainesville (20155) *(G-5583)*

Flight Product Center Inc 703 361-2915
9998 Wakeman Dr Manassas (20110) *(G-7941)*

Flint Bros Logging 540 886-1509
77 Grower Ln Staunton (24401) *(G-13258)*

Flint Brothers 540 886-5761
908 Buttermilk Spring Rd Staunton (24401) *(G-13259)*

Flint CPS Inks North Amer LLC 540 234-9203
106 Triangle Dr Weyers Cave (24486) *(G-15172)*

Flint Group US LLC 804 270-1328
8000 Villa Park Dr Henrico (23228) *(G-6512)*

Flip Flop Fabrication LLC 540 820-5959
3361 Spaders Church Rd Rockingham (22801) *(G-12253)*

Flip Switch Events LLC 703 677-0119
23294 Virginia Rae Ct Ashburn (20148) *(G-1281)*

Flip-N-Haul LLC 804 932-4372
5627 Gentry Dr New Kent (23124) *(G-9132)*

Flipclean Corp 804 233-4845
2102 Decatur St Richmond (23224) *(G-11591)*

Flippen & Sons Inc 804 233-1461
2100 Porter St Richmond (23225) *(G-11592)*

Flips Graphix Design 434 237-3547
14413 Wards Rd Lynchburg (24502) *(G-7709)*

Flir Detection Inc 877 692-2120
1201 S Joyce St Ste C6 Arlington (22202) *(G-968)*

Flir Systems, Arlington *Also called Flir Detection Inc (G-968)*

Flir Systems Inc 703 416-6666
900 S Walter Reed Dr Arlington (22204) *(G-969)*

Flockdata LLC 703 870-6916
4501 Lees Corner Rd Chantilly (20151) *(G-2421)*

Flooring Adventures LLC 804 530-5004
670 Hp Way Chester (23836) *(G-3416)*

Florida Tile Inc 757 855-9330
500 Woodlake Cir Ste B Chesapeake (23320) *(G-3103)*

Florida Tile 89, Chesapeake *Also called Florida Tile Inc (G-3103)*

Flow Beverages Inc 613 680-3569
33 Lakeview Ct Verona (24482) *(G-13987)*

Flow Dynamics Inc 804 835-9740
1620 Berkeley Ave Petersburg (23805) *(G-10320)*

Flow-Tech Inc 804 752-3450
10993 Richardson Rd Ashland (23005) *(G-1417)*

Flowers Bakeries LLC 757 424-4860
6001 Indian River Rd Virginia Beach (23464) *(G-14467)*

Flowers Bakeries LLC 540 343-8165
523 Shenandoah Ave Nw Roanoke (24016) *(G-12088)*

Flowers Bakeries LLC 434 572-6340
4198 Halifax Rd South Boston (24592) *(G-12768)*

Flowers Bakeries LLC 757 539-2898
1161 Proctor St Suffolk (23434) *(G-13711)*

Flowers Bakery, Norfolk *Also called Flowers Baking Co Norfolk LLC (G-9557)*

Flowers Bakery, Lynchburg *Also called Flowers Bkg Co Lynchburg LLC (G-7710)*

Flowers Bakery Outlet, Yorktown *Also called Flowers Baking Co Norfolk LLC (G-15960)*

Flowers Bakery Outlet, Harrisonburg *Also called Flowers Bkg Co Lynchburg LLC (G-6316)*

Flowers Baking Co Norfolk LLC 757 873-0066
808 City Center Blvd Newport News (23606) *(G-9231)*

Flowers Baking Co Norfolk LLC 540 261-1559
527 E 29th St Buena Vista (24416) *(G-2145)*

Flowers Baking Co Norfolk LLC 757 596-1443
1404 George Washington Me Yorktown (23693) *(G-15960)*

Flowers Baking Co Norfolk LLC (HQ) **757 622-6317**
1209 Corprew Ave Norfolk (23504) *(G-9557)*

Flowers Baking Co Norfolk Whse, Newport News *Also called Flowers Baking Co Norfolk LLC (G-9231)*

Flowers Baking Co Oxford Inc 610 932-2300
4144 Pepsi Pl Chantilly (20151) *(G-2422)*

Flowers Bkg Co Jamestown LLC 276 236-5009
7599 Carrollton Pike A Galax (24333) *(G-5633)*

Flowers Bkg Co Lynchburg LLC 434 392-8134
2799 W 3rd St Farmville (23901) *(G-4940)*

Flowers Bkg Co Lynchburg LLC (HQ) **434 528-0441**
1905 Hollins Mill Rd Lynchburg (24503) *(G-7710)*

Flowers Bkg Co Lynchburg LLC 434 528-0441
3527 Melrose Ave Nw Roanoke (24017) *(G-12089)*

Flowers Bkg Co Lynchburg LLC 434 528-0441
3301 Odd Fellows Rd Lynchburg (24501) *(G-7711)*

Flowers Bkg Co Lynchburg LLC 434 528-0441
9474 Totopotomoy Trl Ashland (23005) *(G-1418)*

Flowers Bkg Co Lynchburg LLC 540 344-5919
2502 Melrose Ave Nw Roanoke (24017) *(G-12090)*

Flowers Bkg Co Lynchburg LLC 540 434-4439
60 Charles St Harrisonburg (22802) *(G-6316)*

Flowers Bkg Co Lynchburg LLC 276 647-8767
3416 Virginia Ave Ste 1 Collinsville (24078) *(G-3711)*

Flowers Bkg Co Lynchburg LLC 434 978-4104
360 Greenbrier Dr Charlottesville (22901) *(G-2632)*

Flowers Bkg Co Lynchburg LLC 540 886-1582
350 Greenville Ave Staunton (24401) *(G-13260)*

Flowers Bkg Co Lynchburg LLC 434 385-5044
2120 Lakeside Dr Lynchburg (24501) *(G-7712)*

Flowers Bkg Co Lynchburg LLC 276 666-2008
309 Lavinder St Martinsville (24112) *(G-8287)*

Flowers Bkg Co Lynchburg LLC 540 371-1480
230 Industrial Dr Fredericksburg (22408) *(G-5289)*

Flowers Steel LLC 540 424-8377
14125 Maryann Ln Sumerduck (22742) *(G-13791)*

Flowserve Corporation 757 485-8044
3732 Cook Blvd Ste 101 Chesapeake (23323) *(G-3104)*

Flowserve Corporation 434 528-4400
5114 Woodall Rd Lynchburg (24502) *(G-7713)*

Flowserve Corporation 804 271-4031
7445 Whitepine Rd North Chesterfield (23237) *(G-9877)*

Flowserve Corporation 757 485-8000
3900 Cook Blvd Chesapeake (23323) *(G-3105)*

Floyd Press Inc 540 745-2127
710 E Main St Floyd (24091) *(G-5026)*

Fluid Energy 757 549-5160
404 Penhook Ct Chesapeake (23322) *(G-3106)*

Fluke Networks 804 530-1826
524 Fairway Woods Dr Chester (23836) *(G-3417)*

Fluor Enterprises Inc 703 351-1204
2300 Clarendon Blvd # 1110 Arlington (22201) *(G-970)*

Fluvanna Review The, Palmyra *Also called Valley Publishing Corporation (G-10259)*

Fluxteq LLC 540 951-0933
1800 Kraft Dr Ste 109 Blacksburg (24060) *(G-1739)*

Flyermonsterscom 703 582-5716
3140 Washington Blvd Arlington (22201) *(G-971)*

Flying Fox Vineyard Lc 434 361-1692
845 Elk Mountain Rd Afton (22920) *(G-81)*

Flying Fur 540 552-1351
301 Cork Dr Blacksburg (24060) *(G-1740)*

A
L
P
H
A
B
E
T
I
C

Flynn Enterprises Inc............804 461-5753
3157 Virginia Beach Blvd Virginia Beach (23452) ***(G-14468)***
Flynn Enterprises Inc (PA)............**703 444-5555**
45668 Terminal Dr Ste 100 Sterling (20166) ***(G-13400)***
Flynn Incorporated............540 885-2600
113 W Beverley St Staunton (24401) ***(G-13261)***
Flynns Foods Inc............804 779-3205
4152 Peppertown Rd Mechanicsville (23111) ***(G-8624)***
Flyway Inc............757 422-3215
620 Hilltop West Ctr Virginia Beach (23451) ***(G-14469)***
Flzhi Technologies LLC............214 616-7756
3737 27th St N Arlington (22207) ***(G-972)***
Fmd LLC............703 339-8881
7200 Telegraph Square Dr Lorton (22079) ***(G-7490)***
Fmp Inc............434 392-3222
11217 Eastborough Ct Henrico (23233) ***(G-6513)***
Fmt Food and Beverage Systems, Ridgeway *Also called Smart Machine Technologies Inc* ***(G-11853)***
FN America LLC (HQ)............**703 288-3500**
7950 Jones Branch Dr Mc Lean (22102) ***(G-8434)***
FN America LLC............540 288-8002
14 Hazel Park Ln Fredericksburg (22405) ***(G-5431)***
Fna Jewels............703 591-6817
12309 Fox Lake Ct Fairfax (22033) ***(G-4459)***
Fnh USA, Mc Lean *Also called FN America LLC* ***(G-8434)***
Fobbs Quality Signs LLC............804 714-0102
7013 Irongate Dr North Chesterfield (23234) ***(G-9878)***
Focus Magazine............434 296-4261
34 University Cir Charlottesville (22903) ***(G-2796)***
Fog Light Solutions LLC............703 201-0532
912 Jaysmith St Great Falls (22066) ***(G-5955)***
Foggy Ridge Cider............276 398-2337
53 Chisholm Creek Rd Dugspur (24325) ***(G-4188)***
Foh Sounds, Hayes *Also called Ronald Paul Gardner* ***(G-6405)***
Foldem Gear LLC............571 289-5051
115 Winders Ln Yorktown (23692) ***(G-15961)***
Folder Factory............540 984-8852
116 N High St Edinburg (22824) ***(G-4304)***
Foley Logging Inc............540 365-3152
1849 Henry Rd Ferrum (24088) ***(G-4974)***
Foley Machine............276 930-1983
108 Clark Loop Stuart (24171) ***(G-13612)***
Foley Material Handling Co Inc............804 798-1343
11327 Virginia Crane Dr Ashland (23005) ***(G-1419)***
Follett College Store 743............434 961-5317
501 College Dr Charlottesville (22902) ***(G-2797)***
Folley Fencing Service............276 629-8487
1542 Koger Mill Rd Patrick Springs (24133) ***(G-10270)***
Fontaine Melinda............757 777-2812
2635 Bracston Rd Virginia Beach (23456) ***(G-14470)***
Fontaine Modification Company............540 674-4638
5135 Cougar Trail Rd Dublin (24084) ***(G-4156)***
Fontana Lithograph Inc............202 296-3276
1207 Alden Rd Alexandria (22308) ***(G-464)***
Food Allergy Lifestyle LLC............757 509-3608
3608 Morris Farm Ln Gloucester (23061) ***(G-5847)***
Food Portions LLC............757 839-3265
1805 High St Portsmouth (23704) ***(G-10432)***
Food Technology Corporation............703 444-1870
45921 Maries Rd Ste 120 Sterling (20166) ***(G-13401)***
Foods For Thought Inc............434 242-4996
13418 Old Gordonsville Rd Orange (22960) ***(G-10213)***
Foot Levelers Inc............800 553-4860
518 Pocahontas Ave Ne Roanoke (24012) ***(G-12091)***
Foote Designs Maui, Virginia Beach *Also called Bill Foote* ***(G-14279)***
Foothills Farm Supply, Rocky Mount *Also called Exchange Milling Co Inc* ***(G-12321)***
Footmaxx of Virginia Inc............540 345-0008
518 Pocahontas Ave Ne Roanoke (24012) ***(G-12092)***
For Rent Magazine............305 305-0494
3923 Deep Rock Rd Henrico (23233) ***(G-6514)***
For Sell By Owner Services, Virginia Beach *Also called B & G Publishing Inc* ***(G-14253)***
Forbidden City Foods, Charlottesville *Also called New Silk Road Marketing LLC* ***(G-2663)***
Forbz House LLC............703 216-1491
7371 Atlas Walk Way Ste 1 Gainesville (20155) ***(G-5584)***
Force Forge............804 454-5191
1803 Harrison Ct Fort Lee (23801) ***(G-5129)***
Force Furnishings, Shenandoah *Also called Hardwood Defense LLC* ***(G-12691)***
Force Protection Inc............703 415-7520
2450 Crystal Dr Ste 1060 Arlington (22202) ***(G-973)***
Forel Publishing Co LLC............703 772-8081
3999 Peregrine Ridge Ct Woodbridge (22192) ***(G-15705)***
Forerunner Federation............757 639-6576
520 W 21st St Norfolk (23517) ***(G-9558)***
Forescout Gvrnment Sltions LLC............408 538-0946
8350 Broad St Ste 1800 Tysons (22102) ***(G-13945)***
Forest Carbon Offsets LLC............703 795-4512
2121 Eisenhower Ave Alexandria (22314) ***(G-206)***
Forestry Equipment of VA, Forest *Also called Utility One Source For Eqp LLC* ***(G-5103)***

Forging The Warrior Spirit............703 851-4789
6566 Chimney Oaks Ct Marshall (20115) ***(G-8252)***
Fork Mountain Raceway LLC............540 229-1828
3943 Hebron Valley Rd Madison (22727) ***(G-7852)***
Form Fabrications LLC............757 309-8717
1037 Ferry Plantation Rd Virginia Beach (23455) ***(G-14471)***
Form III Defense Solutions LLC............703 542-7372
42878 Chatelain Cir Brambleton (20148) ***(G-1928)***
Formable Grabber Inc............434 298-4722
4425 Midland Trl Covington (24426) ***(G-3789)***
Formally Yours............540 974-3071
160 Headley Rd Middletown (22645) ***(G-8738)***
Formex LLC............804 231-1988
2800 Cofer Rd Richmond (23224) ***(G-11593)***
Formply Products Inc............434 572-4040
200 Webster St South Boston (24592) ***(G-12769)***
Forms Unlimited............757 549-1258
1220 Executive Blvd # 105 Chesapeake (23320) ***(G-3107)***
Formymate, Charlottesville *Also called Jeffrey Gill* ***(G-2819)***
Forrlace Inc (PA)............**757 873-5777**
11712 Jefferson Ave Ste A Newport News (23606) ***(G-9232)***
Forstle LLC............540 424-6879
1210 Walker Dr Fredericksburg (22401) ***(G-5186)***
Fort Chiswell Machine Tl Pdts............276 637-3022
324 Apache Run Max Meadows (24360) ***(G-8368)***
Fort Valley Paving............540 636-8960
19954 Fort Valley Rd Strasburg (22657) ***(G-13579)***
Forterra Pipe & Precast LLC............757 485-5228
3801 Cook Blvd Chesapeake (23323) ***(G-3108)***
Fortify Software............571 286-6320
9004 Old Dominion Dr Mc Lean (22102) ***(G-8435)***
Fortis Solutions Group LLC (PA)............**757 340-8893**
2505 Hawkeye Ct Virginia Beach (23452) ***(G-14472)***
Fortune Nails LLC............703 330-1306
9401 Liberia Ave Manassas (20110) ***(G-7942)***
Fostek, Bedford *Also called Bedford Storage Investment LLC* ***(G-1625)***
Fostek Inc............540 587-5870
1001 Broad St Bedford (24523) ***(G-1637)***
Foster Jackson LLC............540 436-9463
4374 Swartz Rd Maurertown (22644) ***(G-8363)***
Foster Logging............434 454-7946
6121 Clover Rd Randolph (23962) ***(G-10748)***
Foundry Foundry-A Print............703 329-3300
1420 Prince St Ste 200 Alexandria (22314) ***(G-207)***
Fountainhead Systems Ltd............804 320-0527
8950 Cardiff Rd North Chesterfield (23236) ***(G-9879)***
Four Calling Birds Ltd............540 317-5761
6160 Keyser Rd Hume (22639) ***(G-6961)***
Four Hats Inc............571 926-4303
5967 Moore Rd Marshall (20115) ***(G-8253)***
Four Leaf Publishing LLC............703 440-1304
8550 Groveland Dr Springfield (22153) ***(G-13005)***
Four Oaks Timber Company............434 374-2669
126 Wilbourne Rd Clarksville (23927) ***(G-3630)***
Four Seasons Catering & Bakery............276 686-5982
965 Four Seasons Rd Rural Retreat (24368) ***(G-12424)***
Four Star Printing Inc............540 459-2247
490 N Main St Woodstock (22664) ***(G-15854)***
Four Wheel Supply, Richlands *Also called Brock Enterprises Virginia LLC* ***(G-11014)***
Fourth Corporation............703 229-6222
6018 Stubbs Bridge Rd Mineral (23117) ***(G-8948)***
Fourty4industries LLC............703 266-0525
14002 Marleigh Ln Clifton (20124) ***(G-3665)***
Fouz Inc............571 407-4446
16030 Barn Swallow Pl Woodbridge (22191) ***(G-15706)***
Fowlkes Eagle Publishing LLC............757 673-8424
2003 Fern Mill Ct Chesapeake (23323) ***(G-3109)***
Fox Group Inc............925 980-5643
39 Garrett St Ste 226 Warrenton (20186) ***(G-15017)***
Fox Hill Editorial LLC............434 971-1835
520 Rookwood Pl Charlottesville (22903) ***(G-2798)***
Fox Meadow Farms LLC............540 636-6777
3310 Freezeland Rd Linden (22642) ***(G-7428)***
Fox River Distilling Company............630 402-0027
2114 Liesfeld Pkwy Glen Allen (23060) ***(G-5732)***
Fox Screen Print, Newport News *Also called Atlantic Textile Group Inc* ***(G-9173)***
Fox Screen Print & Embrodiery, Newport News *Also called Met of Hampton Roads Inc* ***(G-9298)***
Foxcreek Tactical LLC............757 615-0474
648 Declaration Rd Virginia Beach (23462) ***(G-14473)***
Fragrances Ltd............540 636-8099
1724 N Shenandoah Ave Front Royal (22630) ***(G-5532)***
Framatome Inc............434 832-5000
1724 Mount Athos Rd Lynchburg (24504) ***(G-7714)***
Framatome Inc............434 832-3000
7207 Ibm Dr Lynchburg (24501) ***(G-7715)***
Framatome Inc (HQ)............**434 832-3000**
3315 Old Forest Rd Lynchburg (24501) ***(G-7716)***
Framecad America Inc............703 615-2451
3603 Mclean Ave Fairfax (22030) ***(G-4626)***

Frameco Inc 540 375-3683
  305 Apperson Dr Salem (24153) *(G-12507)*

Framery and Arts Corp. 434 525-0444
  2703 Memorial Ave Lynchburg (24501) *(G-7717)*

Framing Concepts Inc (PA)............................**757 460-9882**
  2600 Performance Ct Virginia Beach (23453) *(G-14474)*

France Lawnscpape LLC 804 761-6823
  1649 Scates Rd Warsaw (22572) *(G-15063)*

France Naturals Inc 804 694-4777
  7546 John Clayton Mem Hwy Gloucester (23061) *(G-5848)*

Francis & Murphy 703 256-8644
  4305 Backlick Rd Annandale (22003) *(G-749)*

Francis C James Jr. 757 442-3630
  10198 Shell St Nassawadox (23413) *(G-9100)*

Frangipani Inc 703 903-0099
  1155 Daleview Dr Mc Lean (22102) *(G-8436)*

Frank Calandra Inc 412 963-9071
  147 Champion St Cedar Bluff (24609) *(G-2276)*

Frank Calandra Inc 276 964-7023
  258 Kappa Dr Pounding Mill (24637) *(G-10519)*

Frank Chervan 540 586-5600
  1576 Dawn Dr Bedford (24523) *(G-1638)*

Frank Chervan Inc 540 586-5600
  2005 Greenbrier Ave Se Roanoke (24013) *(G-12093)*

Frank For All Ingnitions Keys 804 663-5222
  8001 W Broad St Richmond (23294) *(G-11212)*

Frank Hagerty 540 809-0589
  6 Westmoreland Pl Fredericksburg (22405) *(G-5432)*

Frank M Churillo 434 242-6895
  104 Lupine Ln Charlottesville (22911) *(G-2633)*

Frank's Engraving Service, Montclair *Also called Dorothy Whibley* *(G-8997)*

Franklin Braid Mfg Co 434 634-4142
  620 Davis St Emporia (23847) *(G-4358)*

Franklin Branch, Wirtz *Also called Southern States Roanoke Coop* *(G-15619)*

Franklin County Inv Co Inc 540 483-5113
  310 S Main St Rocky Mount (24151) *(G-12323)*

Franklin County Newspapers Inc, Rocky Mount *Also called Franklin County Inv Co Inc (G-12323)*

Franklin Machine Shop 757 241-6744
  530 Aberdeen Rd Ste A Hampton (23661) *(G-6152)*

Franklin Yard, Franklin *Also called Legacy Vulcan Corp (G-5148)*

Franklin's Printing, Chantilly *Also called McFarland Enterprises Inc (G-2461)*

Franklin's Printing, Chantilly *Also called Half A Five Enterprise LLC (G-2434)*

Franklin, VA Tube Plant, Franklin *Also called Caraustar Industrial and Con (G-5140)*

Frankline Paper 757 569-4321
  34040 Union Camp Dr Franklin (23851) *(G-5144)*

Franklins Welding 540 330-3454
  718 Greenwich Dr Roanoke (24019) *(G-11923)*

Franks Welding Inc. 540 668-6185
  14181 Paris Breeze Pl Purcellville (20132) *(G-10661)*

Fraser Wood Elements LLC 540 373-0853
  1023 Caroline St Fredericksburg (22401) *(G-5187)*

Frayser Welding Co 804 798-8764
  11281 Cobbs Rd Glen Allen (23059) *(G-5733)*

Frazier Quarry Incorporated (PA)................**540 434-6192**
  75 Waterman Dr Harrisonburg (22802) *(G-6317)*

Frazier Quarry Incorporated 540 896-7538
  Rr 42 Timberville (22853) *(G-13849)*

Fred B Meadows Sons Loggi 434 392-5269
  1604 Briery Rd Farmville (23901) *(G-4941)*

Fred Fauber... 434 845-0303
  258 Whispering Stream Ln Lynchburg (24501) *(G-7718)*

Fred Good Times LLC 540 372-7247
  2011 Princess Anne St # 103 Fredericksburg (22401) *(G-5188)*

Fred Hean Furniture & Wdwrk 434 973-5960
  3226 Lonesome Mountain Rd Charlottesville (22911) *(G-2634)*

Fred Kinkead 540 828-2955
  2727 N River Rd Bridgewater (22812) *(G-1951)*

Fred Leach 434 372-5225
  290 Boondock Rd Chase City (23924) *(G-2911)*

Fred Sisson 843 641-7155
  5497 Snow Creek Ct Prince George (23875) *(G-10594)*

Freda Marshall 757 632-1364
  5210 Forestdale Dr Portsmouth (23703) *(G-10433)*

Frederick Enterprises LLC 804 405-4976
  1505 Cummings Dr Richmond (23220) *(G-11594)*

Frederick J Day PC 703 820-0110
  5673 Columbia Pike # 100 Falls Church (22041) *(G-4794)*

Fredericks Aircraft Company (PA).................**757 727-3326**
  1100 Exploration Way Hampton (23666) *(G-6153)*

Fredericksburg Fences LLC 540 419-3910
  4617 Mine Rd Fredericksburg (22408) *(G-5290)*

Fredericksburg Mch & Stl LLC 540 373-7957
  2202 Airport Ave Fredericksburg (22401) *(G-5189)*

Fredericksburg Plant, Falmouth *Also called Aggregate Industries - Mwr Inc (G-4932)*

Fredrick Allen Murphey 804 385-1650
  319 S Kalmia Ave Highland Springs (23075) *(G-6853)*

Free Lance-Star Publshng Co of 540 374-5000
  1340 Cntl Pk Blvd Ste 100 Fredericksburg (22401) *(G-5190)*

Free Union Restaurant Inc 434 327-9559
  3618 Free Union Rd Charlottesville (22901) *(G-2635)*

Free-Lance Star, Fredericksburg *Also called Free Lance-Star Publshng Co of (G-5190)*

Freedom Display Cases, Vienna *Also called Heirlooms Furniture LLC (G-14062)*

Freedom Flag Sign & Banner Co 703 359-5353
  10608 Orchard St Fairfax (22030) *(G-4627)*

Freedom Forge Press LLC 757 784-1038
  35700 Bowen Pl Hillsboro (20132) *(G-6867)*

Freedom Hawks Kayaks Inc 978 225-1511
  200 Garrett St Ste H Charlottesville (22902) *(G-2799)*

Freedom Homes 540 382-9015
  1340 W Main St Christiansburg (24073) *(G-3588)*

Freedom Lodging LLC 757 288-4514
  601 Montebello Cir Chesapeake (23322) *(G-3110)*

Freedom Respiratory 804 266-2002
  2852 E Parham Rd Henrico (23228) *(G-6515)*

Freedom To Destiny Pubg LLC 757 617-8286
  427 Gardenia Cir Chesapeake (23325) *(G-3111)*

Freeman Aerotech LLC 703 303-0102
  43975 Lords Valley Ter Ashburn (20147) *(G-1282)*

Freeport Press 540 788-9745
  5206 Hunt Crossing Ln Midland (22728) *(G-8755)*

Freeport Technologies Inc 571 262-0400
  470 Springpark Pl Ste 100 Herndon (20170) *(G-6677)*

Freestate Electronics Inc 540 349-4727
  6530 Commerce Ct Warrenton (20187) *(G-15018)*

Freestyle King LLC 703 309-1144
  13113 Otto Rd Woodbridge (22193) *(G-15707)*

Freestyle Prints LLC 571 246-1806
  401 Fox Dr Winchester (22601) *(G-15544)*

Freight Car, Roanoke *Also called Freightcar Roanoke Inc (G-12094)*

Freightcar Roanoke Inc 540 342-2303
  830 Campbell Ave Se Roanoke (24013) *(G-12094)*

French Bread Factory Inc 703 761-4070
  44225 Mercure Cir Ste 170 Sterling (20166) *(G-13402)*

French Press Printing LLC 703 268-8241
  9933 Murnane St Vienna (22181) *(G-14057)*

Frenchs Auto Parts Inc 540 740-3676
  Rr 11 New Market (22844) *(G-9142)*

Freon Doctor Inc 877 825-2401
  4021 Lewiston Rd Bumpass (23024) *(G-2162)*

Fresh Printz LLC 540 937-3017
  19248 Walnut Hills Rd Jeffersonton (22724) *(G-7012)*

Fresh Twist Foods LLC 540 904-1291
  3145 N Franklin St Christiansburg (24073) *(G-3589)*

Freshii 804 223-8027
  1700 Willow Lawn Dr Richmond (23230) *(G-11213)*

Freshstart Coml Jantr Svcs LLC 571 645-0060
  220 Choptank Rd Triangle (22172) *(G-13893)*

Freshwter Parl Media Group LLC 757 785-5483
  3577 Norland Ct Norfolk (23513) *(G-9559)*

Frey Randall Antique Furnitre 434 985-7631
  2585 South River Rd Stanardsville (22973) *(G-13219)*

Frey Rndall Antiq Rproductions, Stanardsville *Also called Frey Randall Antique Furnitre (G-13219)*

Frf Inc 434 974-7900
  2165 Seminole Trl Charlottesville (22901) *(G-2636)*

Fridays Marine Inc 804 758-4131
  14879 George Wash Mem Hwy Saluda (23149) *(G-12603)*

Fridleys Welding Service Inc 804 674-1949
  5550 Quail Ridge Ter Chesterfield (23832) *(G-3501)*

Friends Sprngwood Brial Pk LLC 540 366-0996
  4711 Horseman Dr Ne Roanoke (24019) *(G-11924)*

Frierson Designs LLC 757 491-7130
  1165 Jensen Dr Virginia Beach (23451) *(G-14475)*

Frit Small Dollar Twai 804 697-3968
  701 E Byrd St Richmond (23219) *(G-11595)*

Frito-Lay, Marion *Also called Pepsico Inc (G-8240)*

Frito-Lay North America Inc 540 434-2426
  455 Pleasant Valley Rd Harrisonburg (22801) *(G-6318)*

Frito-Lay North America Inc 540 380-3020
  3941 W Main St Salem (24153) *(G-12508)*

Fritz Ken Tooling & Design 804 721-2319
  1324 Hybla Rd North Chesterfield (23236) *(G-9880)*

Frog Industries LLC 757 995-2359
  3905 Granby St Norfolk (23504) *(G-9560)*

Frog Valley Publishing 540 338-3224
  36157 Bell Rd Round Hill (20141) *(G-12378)*

Frogue 703 679-7003
  11303 Geddys Ct Ste F Reston (20191) *(G-10854)*

Front Royal Warren Sentinel, Front Royal *Also called Warren Sentinel (G-5563)*

Frontier Systems LLC 314 221-2831
  805 Lake Windermere Ct Great Falls (22066) *(G-5956)*

Frost Industries Inc 804 724-0330
  157 Miskimon Rd Heathsville (22473) *(G-6462)*

Frost Property Solutions LLC (PA)...............**804 571-2147**
  11137 Countryside Ln Mechanicsville (23116) *(G-8625)*

Frosted Muffin - A Cupcakery 571 989-1722
  2952 American Eagle Blvd Woodbridge (22191) *(G-15708)*

A
L
P
H
A
B
E
T
I
C

Fruit For You Inc 540 668-7750
37488 Chartwell Ln Hillsboro (20132) *(G-6868)*
Frye Delance 540 923-4581
103 Champe Plain Rd Etlan (22719) *(G-4373)*
Fso Mission Support LLC 571 528-3507
43830 Lost Corner Rd Leesburg (20176) *(G-7275)*
Ft Communications Inc 804 739-8555
15431 Houndmaster Ter Midlothian (23112) *(G-8820)*
Ft Industries LLC 757 495-0510
1041 Radcliff Lndg Virginia Beach (23464) *(G-14476)*
Ft Lee Welcome Center 804 734-7488
500 Lee Ave Fort Lee (23801) *(G-5130)*
Fta Goverment Services Inc 571 612-0413
5175 Parkstone Dr Ste 170 Chantilly (20151) *(G-2423)*
Ftg Crcuits Fredericksburg Inc 540 752-5511
1026 Warrenton Rd Fredericksburg (22406) *(G-5433)*
Ftwsa, Marshall *Also called Forging The Warrior Spirit (G-8252)*
Fudgetime LLC 703 462-8544
5213 Dalton Rd Springfield (22151) *(G-13006)*
Fuel Impurities Separator 757 340-6833
3121 Bray Rd Virginia Beach (23452) *(G-14477)*
Fuel Your Life LLC 703 208-4449
2255 Richelieu Dr Vienna (22182) *(G-14058)*
Fuelcor Development LLC 703 740-0071
906 Ridge Dr Mc Lean (22101) *(G-8437)*
Fuhgiddabowdit Industries 757 598-0331
547 Wythe Creek Rd Poquoson (23662) *(G-10371)*
Full Awn Fab LLC 540 439-5173
10251 Fayettesville Rd Bealeton (22712) *(G-1599)*
Full Color Prints 703 354-9231
6400 Holyoke Dr Annandale (22003) *(G-750)*
Full Color Prints 571 612-8844
4280 Henninger Ct Chantilly (20151) *(G-2424)*
Full Fat Kitchen LLC 844 262-6629
3145 N Franklin St Christiansburg (24073) *(G-3590)*
Full Tilt Performance 276 628-0036
1099 Cummings St Abingdon (24211) *(G-31)*
Fuller Asphalt Material 423 676-4449
828 Tri State Lime Rd Bristol (24202) *(G-2018)*
Fullman Iman 908 627-3376
13224 Margaux Cir Apt 4 Newport News (23608) *(G-9233)*
Fully Promoted of Alexandria 703 575-9003
108 S Early St Alexandria (22304) *(G-208)*
Fun With Canvas 724 689-5821
7008 Tech Cir Manassas (20109) *(G-8071)*
Fun With Canvas 540 272-2436
4522 Catlett Rd Midland (22728) *(G-8756)*
Funace Media, Alexandria *Also called Furnace Mfg Inc (G-465)*
Funes Project LLC 540 364-8054
8302 E Main St Marshall (20115) *(G-8254)*
Fur Persons Rescue Fund 703 754-7474
3097 James Madison Hwy Haymarket (20169) *(G-6424)*
Fur The Love of Dogs LLC 540 850-5540
58 Larkwood Ct Stafford (22554) *(G-13145)*
Furnace Mfg Inc 703 205-0007
6315 Bren Mar Dr Ste 195 Alexandria (22312) *(G-465)*
Furnace Mountain Vineyards LLC 571 439-2255
38593 Daymont Ln Waterford (20197) *(G-15080)*
Furniture Art 540 667-2533
306 Lenoir Dr Winchester (22603) *(G-15418)*
Furseller, Mc Lean *Also called Millers Furs Inc (G-8501)*
Fusion Pwdr Cating Fabrication 757 319-3760
1220 Fleetway Dr Ste F Chesapeake (23323) *(G-3112)*
Future Tense LLC 703 994-7814
42582 Glass Ln Ashburn (20148) *(G-1283)*
Fuzzyprints 571 989-3899
4681 Midland Rd Midland (22728) *(G-8757)*
Fyllo LLC 540 846-6441
402 Hanover St Fredericksburg (22401) *(G-5191)*
Fyne-Wire Specialties Inc 540 825-2701
19633 Church Rd Brandy Station (22714) *(G-1939)*
G & D Manufacturing 540 345-7267
2810 Belle Ave Ne Roanoke (24012) *(G-12095)*
G & H Litho Inc 571 267-7148
506 Shaw Rd Ste 312 Sterling (20166) *(G-13403)*
G & L Printing, Carrollton *Also called Gary Gray (G-2242)*
G & W Manufacturing Inc 276 228-8491
325 Stafford Umberger Dr Wytheville (24382) *(G-15889)*
G and H Litho 571 267-7148
506 Shaw Rd Ste 312 Sterling (20166) *(G-13404)*
G E Fuji Drives Usa Inc 540 387-7000
1501 Roanoke Blvd Rm 212 Salem (24153) *(G-12509)*
G F I Associates Inc (HQ) **703 533-8555**
8280 Willow Oaks Corp Dr Fairfax (22031) *(G-4460)*
G Gibbs Project LLC 804 638-9581
3701 Mineola Dr Chester (23831) *(G-3418)*
G I K of Virginia Inc 804 358-8500
1638 Ownby Ln Richmond (23220) *(G-11596)*
G M S, Manassas *Also called General Magnetic Sciences Inc (G-7944)*
G M S, Clifton *Also called General Magnetic Sciences Inc (G-3666)*
G McCracken, West Point *Also called George McCracken (G-15157)*
G N H & Associates Inc 276 632-7867
1219 Irisburg Rd Axton (24054) *(G-1537)*
G T Walls Cabinet Shop 804 798-6288
13527 Mountain Rd Glen Allen (23059) *(G-5734)*
G&D America, Dulles *Also called Giesecke+devrient (G-4205)*
G&G Welding & Fabricating 276 202-3815
113 Augusta Ave Richlands (24641) *(G-11016)*
G&M Embroidery Inc 757 482-1935
205 Ashley Rd Chesapeake (23322) *(G-3113)*
G&M Signs LLC 540 405-3232
13760 Vint Hill Rd Nokesville (20181) *(G-9392)*
G&O Logging LLC 757 653-2181
23191 Hanging Tree Rd Courtland (23837) *(G-3770)*
G&R Metals, Hampton *Also called Machine & Fabg Specialists Inc (G-6187)*
G-13 Hand-Blown Art Glass 757 495-8185
4704 Larkspur Ct Virginia Beach (23462) *(G-14478)*
G-Force Events Inc 804 228-0188
4245 Carolina Ave Richmond (23222) *(G-11597)*
G-Holdings LLC 202 255-9698
2121 Eisenhower Ave # 600 Alexandria (22314) *(G-209)*
G-Technology Group, Alexandria *Also called Ghodousi LLC (G-468)*
G2k Labs Inc 703 965-8367
4506 Daly Dr Ste 200 Chantilly (20151) *(G-2425)*
G3 Solutions LLC 703 424-4296
10288 Johns Hollow Rd Vienna (22182) *(G-14059)*
G5 Examiner LLC 540 455-9186
10716 Lotus Ct Fredericksburg (22407) *(G-5291)*
Gabriel D Ofiesh II Inc 434 295-9038
908 E High St Charlottesville (22902) *(G-2800)*
Gabro Graphics Inc 703 464-8588
22800 Executive Dr # 150 Sterling (20166) *(G-13405)*
Gabro Printing & Graphics, Sterling *Also called Gabro Graphics Inc (G-13405)*
Gadfly LLC 703 282-9448
288 Wood Trestle Ter Se Leesburg (20175) *(G-7276)*
Gaia Communications LLC 703 370-5527
35 E Linden St Ste 3a Alexandria (22301) *(G-210)*
Gaias Gold 804 516-8458
1858 Canterbury Rd Walkerton (23177) *(G-14971)*
Gails Dream LLC 757 638-3197
6012 Scuppernong Dr Suffolk (23435) *(G-13712)*
Gainsafe Inc 703 598-2583
427 S Fairfax St Alexandria (22314) *(G-211)*
Gaithrsburg Cbinetry Mllwk Inc 540 347-4551
4338 Aiken Dr Warrenton (20187) *(G-15019)*
Galax Office Supply, Galax *Also called Gazette Press Inc (G-5636)*
Galaxy Eqp Maint Solutions Inc 703 866-0246
6807 Gillings Rd Springfield (22152) *(G-13007)*
Galaxy Plastic Industries Inc 434 757-7200
539 Golden Eagle Dr La Crosse (23950) *(G-7145)*
Gale Welding and Mch Co Inc 804 732-4521
415 E Bank St Petersburg (23803) *(G-10321)*
Gallagher Estate Vineyards LLC 301 252-3450
38547 Piggott Bottom Rd Hamilton (20158) *(G-6058)*
Gallagher-Stone Incorporated (PA) **434 528-5181**
2103 Wiggington Rd Lynchburg (24502) *(G-7719)*
Gallas Foods Inc 703 593-9957
12051 Summer Meadow Ln Reston (20194) *(G-10855)*
Gallimore Sawmill Inc 276 236-5064
3965 Coal Creek Rd Galax (24333) *(G-5634)*
Gam Printers Incorporated 703 450-4121
45969 Nokes Blvd Ste 130 Sterling (20166) *(G-13406)*
Gamay Flavors 703 751-7430
4717 Eisenhower Ave Ste B Alexandria (22304) *(G-212)*
Game Day Publications LLC 804 314-7526
9073 Winter Spring Dr Mechanicsville (23116) *(G-8626)*
Game Institute, The, Fairfax *Also called Einstitute Inc (G-4444)*
Game Quest Inc 540 639-6547
1085 E Main St Radford (24141) *(G-10714)*
Gameplan Press Inc 703 521-1546
910 S George Mason Dr Arlington (22204) *(G-974)*
Gammaflux Controls Inc (HQ) **703 471-5050**
113 Executive Dr Sterling (20166) *(G-13407)*
Gammons Welding & Fabrication 276 627-0664
151 Northview Cir Bassett (24055) *(G-1583)*
Ganleys 703 476-8864
2615 John Milton Dr Herndon (20171) *(G-6678)*
Gannett Co Inc (PA) **703 854-6000**
7950 Jones Branch Dr Mc Lean (22102) *(G-8438)*
Gannett GP Media Inc 703 854-6000
7950 Jones Branch Dr Mclean (22101) *(G-8586)*
Gannett Holdings LLC (HQ) **703 854-6000**
7950 Jones Branch Dr Mc Lean (22102) *(G-8439)*
Gannett Media Corp 540 885-7281
11 N Central Ave Staunton (24401) *(G-13262)*
Gannett Media Corp (HQ) **703 854-6000**
7950 Jones Branch Dr Mc Lean (22102) *(G-8440)*
Gannett Media Tech Intl 757 547-7274
1317 Executive Blvd # 300 Chesapeake (23320) *(G-3114)*

Gannett Offset 781 551-2923
7950 Jones Branch Dr Mc Lean (22107) *(G-8441)*

Gannett Publishing Svcs LLC (HQ) **703 854-6000**
7950 Jones Branch Dr Mc Lean (22102) *(G-8442)*

Gannett River States Pubg Corp (HQ) **703 284-6000**
7950 Jones Branch Dr Mc Lean (22102) *(G-8443)*

Gannett Stllite Info Ntwrk LLC (HQ) **703 854-6000**
7950 Jones Branch Dr Mc Lean (22102) *(G-8444)*

Ganpat Enterprise Inc 804 763-2405
13623 Genito Rd Midlothian (23112) *(G-8821)*

Gaona Granola Co LLC 434 996-6653
120 Yellowstone Dr # 303 Charlottesville (22903) *(G-2801)*

Gap Printing 703 585-1532
5413a Vine St Alexandria (22310) *(G-466)*

Garbuio Inc 804 279-0020
2800 Charles City Rd Richmond (23231) *(G-11214)*

Garcia Wood Finishing Inc 703 980-6559
7014 Essex Ave Springfield (22150) *(G-13008)*

Garden Weddings By Clore Bros, Fredericksburg *Also called Log Homes By Clore Bros* *(G-5315)*

Gardens Paths & Ponds, Rockingham *Also called Carroll J Harper* *(G-12244)*

Gargone John 540 641-1934
8810 Pocahontas Trl 66a Williamsburg (23185) *(G-15246)*

Garmonte LLC 703 575-9003
4656 King St Ste A Alexandria (22302) *(G-213)*

Garnett Embroidery 757 925-0569
1217 Peachtree Dr Suffolk (23434) *(G-13713)*

Garnier-Thiebaut Inc 434 572-3965
1044 Commerce Ln South Boston (24592) *(G-12770)*

Garret Industries LLC 804 795-1650
7453 Willson Rd Henrico (23231) *(G-6516)*

Garrett Corporation 276 475-3652
23215 Fisher Hollow Rd Damascus (24236) *(G-3948)*

Garrett Trucking, Spring Grove *Also called Wayne Garrett Logging Inc* *(G-12932)*

Garris Sign Company, Powhatan *Also called Garris Signs Inc* *(G-10545)*

Garris Signs Inc 804 598-1127
4250 Pierce Rd Powhatan (23139) *(G-10545)*

Garrison Press Llc 540 434-2333
164 Waterman Dr Harrisonburg (22802) *(G-6319)*

Garrity Custom Sawing LLC 757 488-9324
4121 Sorrento Dr Chesapeake (23321) *(G-3115)*

Garthright Land Clearing Inc TW 804 370-5408
4665 Bailey Rd Providence Forge (23140) *(G-10625)*

Gartman Letter Limited Company 757 238-9508
9136 River Cres Suffolk (23433) *(G-13714)*

Garvey Prcision Components LLC 757 310-6028
2102 48th St Hampton (23661) *(G-6154)*

Garvey Precision Machine Inc 757 490-0498
2102 48th St Hampton (23661) *(G-6155)*

Gary A Watkins Construction 703 367-0477
9204 Vassau Ct Ste C Manassas Park (20111) *(G-8200)*

Gary Burns 703 992-4617
15164 Windy Hollow Cir Gainesville (20155) *(G-5585)*

Gary Clark 540 373-4598
61 Trails End Ln Fredericksburg (22405) *(G-5434)*

Gary Clark's Welding, Fredericksburg *Also called Gary Clark* *(G-5434)*

Gary D Keys Enterprises Inc 703 418-1700
2117 Crystal Plaza Arc Arlington (22202) *(G-975)*

Gary Gray 757 238-2135
15205 Carrollton Blvd Carrollton (23314) *(G-2242)*

Gary L Lawson 757 848-7003
1026 Poquoson Ave Poquoson (23662) *(G-10372)*

Gary Smith 703 218-1801
9206 Saint Marks Pl Fairfax (22031) *(G-4461)*

Garys Classic Car Parts 757 925-0546
205 Sumner Ave Suffolk (23434) *(G-13715)*

Garys Sign Service 434 836-0248
221 Franklin Tpke Danville (24540) *(G-3995)*

Gas Field Services Inc 276 873-1214
St 19708 Rr 19 Rosedale (24280) *(G-12365)*

Gas Field Services LLC 276 880-2323
17908 U S Highway 19 Rosedale (24280) *(G-12366)*

Gas House Co 434 822-1324
1414 Westover Dr Danville (24541) *(G-3996)*

Gas Sentinel LLC 703 962-7151
10340 Democracy Ln # 101 Fairfax (22030) *(G-4628)*

Gase Energy Inc 540 347-2212
173 Keith St Ste 300 Warrenton (20186) *(G-15020)*

Gaston and Wyatt LLC 434 293-7357
1317 Carlton Ave Ste 110 Charlottesville (22902) *(G-2802)*

Gatehouse Media LLC 804 732-3456
15 Franklin St Petersburg (23803) *(G-10322)*

Gatehuse Media VA Holdings Inc 585 598-0030
15 Franklin St Petersburg (23803) *(G-10323)*

Gatekeeper Security Inc 703 673-3320
22720 Ladbrook Dr Ste 100 Sterling (20166) *(G-13408)*

Gately John 757 851-3085
1 Sugarberry Run Hampton (23669) *(G-6156)*

Gates City Machine and Repair 276 386-3456
111 Valleyview St Gate City (24251) *(G-5662)*

Gateway Green Energy Inc 540 280-7475
65 Adin Cir Fishersville (22939) *(G-5003)*

Gathersburg Cabntry 703 742-8472
1130 Elden St Herndon (20170) *(G-6679)*

Gatorguard LLC 434 942-0245
3604 Montridge Pl Lynchburg (24501) *(G-7720)*

Gatr Technologies Inc 571 258-5020
21580 Beaumeade Cir # 220 Ashburn (20147) *(G-1284)*

Gauge Works Inc 703 661-1300
43671 Trade Center Pl # 156 Dulles (20166) *(G-4203)*

Gauge Works LLC 703 661-1300
43671 Trade Center Pl # 156 Sterling (20166) *(G-13409)*

Gauthier Vineyard LLC 703 622-1107
19665 High Bluff Ln Barhamsville (23011) *(G-1571)*

Gavial Engineering and Mfg 804 627-1437
7000 Westover Rd Charles City (23030) *(G-2575)*

Gavin Bourjaily 540 636-1985
228 Signal View Rd Strasburg (22657) *(G-13580)*

Gay G-Spot LLC 650 429-8233
1300 S Arlington Ridge Rd # 516 Arlington (22202) *(G-976)*

Gazette Journal, Gloucester *Also called Tidewater Newspapers Inc* *(G-5862)*

Gazette Newspaper 276 236-5178
108 W Stuart Dr Galax (24333) *(G-5635)*

Gazette Press Inc 276 236-4831
510 S Main St Galax (24333) *(G-5636)*

Gazette Virginian 434 572-3945
3201 Halifax Rd South Boston (24592) *(G-12771)*

Gazette, The, Galax *Also called Landmark Cmnty Nwsppers VA LLC* *(G-5640)*

Gazette-Virginia, The, South Boston *Also called Halifax Gazette Publishing Co* *(G-12774)*

Gbn Machine & Engineering Corp 804 448-2033
17073 Bull Church Rd Woodford (22580) *(G-15839)*

Gbp Software LLC 703 967-3896
11654 Plaza America Dr # 214 Reston (20190) *(G-10856)*

Gcoe LLC 703 854-6000
7950 Jones Branch Dr Mc Lean (22102) *(G-8445)*

Gcseac Inc 276 632-9700
200 Sellers St Martinsville (24112) *(G-8288)*

Gd Packaging LLC (PA) **703 946-8100**
1952 Gallows Rd Ste 110 Vienna (22182) *(G-14060)*

Gdm International Services Inc (PA) **540 687-6687**
22456 Sam Fred Rd Middleburg (20117) *(G-8720)*

GE Drives & Controls Inc 540 387-7000
1501 Roanoke Blvd Salem (24153) *(G-12510)*

GE Energy 757 595-7982
11864 Canon Blvd Ste 105 Newport News (23606) *(G-9234)*

GE Energy Manufacturing Inc 540 775-6308
10900 Birchwood Dr King George (22485) *(G-7090)*

GE Fairchild Mining Equipment (PA) **540 921-8000**
200 Fairchild Ln Glen Lyn (24093) *(G-5832)*

Gearmaxusa Ltd 804 521-4320
10137 Spring Ivy Ln Mechanicsville (23116) *(G-8627)*

Gedoran America Inc 540 723-6628
117 Oak Ridge Ln Winchester (22602) *(G-15419)*

Gee Pharma LLC 703 669-8055
200 Lawson Rd Se Leesburg (20175) *(G-7277)*

Geebo Inc 888 439-3113
1350 Beverly Rd Apt 218 Mc Lean (22101) *(G-8446)*

Geek Keep LLC 703 867-9867
11560 Temple Loop Manassas (20112) *(G-8072)*

Gel Formations LLC 704 706-4606
800 E Leigh St Richmond (23219) *(G-11598)*

Gem Locker LLC 540 298-8906
611 Williams Ave Shenandoah (22849) *(G-12689)*

Gemini Incorporated 434 315-0312
102 Hauschild Rd Farmville (23901) *(G-4942)*

Gemini Coating of Virginia 540 434-4201
3333 Willow Spring Rd Harrisonburg (22801) *(G-6320)*

Gemini Coatings Inc 540 434-4201
3333 Willow Spring Rd Harrisonburg (22801) *(G-6321)*

Gemini Security LLC 703 466-0163
21010 Southbank St Sterling (20165) *(G-13410)*

Gemtek Electronic Compone 603 218-3902
30 Rundlith Hill Rd Mattaponi (23110) *(G-8359)*

Gemtek Electronic Component, Mattaponi *Also called Gemtek Electronic Compone* *(G-8359)*

Gene Taylor 540 345-9001
1606 Rugby Blvd Nw Roanoke (24017) *(G-12096)*

Genentech Inc 703 841-1076
2435 13th Ct N Arlington (22201) *(G-977)*

General Cigar Co Inc 757 825-7750
2105 Aluminum Ave Hampton (23661) *(G-6157)*

General Cigar Co Inc 804 935-2800
2100 E Cary St Fl 2 Richmond (23223) *(G-11599)*

General Cigar Co Inc (HQ) **860 602-3500**
10900 Nuckols Rd Ste 100 Glen Allen (23060) *(G-5735)*

General Cryo Corporation 703 405-9442
8129 Ridge Creek Way Springfield (22153) *(G-13009)*

General Display Company LLC 703 335-9292
10390 Central Park Dr Manassas (20110) *(G-7943)*

General Dynamics 757 398-0785
650 Chautauqua Ave Portsmouth (23707) *(G-10434)*

A
L
P
H
A
B
E
T
I
C

General Dynamics Advanced Info, Oakton *Also called General Dynamics Govt Syst* **(G-10148)**
General Dynamics Corp...434 964-5301
321 Hillsdale Dr Ste 100 Charlottesville (22901) **(G-2637)**
General Dynamics Corporation (PA)...**703 876-3000**
11011 Sunset Hills Rd Reston (20190) **(G-10857)**
General Dynamics Corporation...703 925-8636
540 Huntmar Park Dr Ste E Herndon (20170) **(G-6680)**
General Dynamics Corporation...757 523-2738
700 Independence Pkwy # 100 Chesapeake (23320) **(G-3116)**
General Dynamics Corporation...703 729-3106
20766 Silverthistle Ct Ashburn (20147) **(G-1285)**
General Dynamics Corporation...703 221-1009
6204 Trident Ln Woodbridge (22193) **(G-15709)**
General Dynamics Corporation...703 263-2835
12450 Fair Lkes Cir 200 Fairfax (22033) **(G-4462)**
General Dynamics Govt Syst...703 383-3605
10455 White Granite Dr Oakton (22124) **(G-10148)**
General Dynamics Info Tech Inc...540 663-1000
16501 Commerce Dr Ste 300 King George (22485) **(G-7091)**
General Dynamics Info Tech Inc...703 268-7000
13857 Mclearen Rd Herndon (20171) **(G-6681)**
General Dynamics Mission...276 783-3121
150 Johnston Rd Marion (24354) **(G-8227)**
General Dynamics Nassco...757 215-2004
2620 Indian River Rd Chesapeake (23325) **(G-3117)**
General Dynamics Ots Cal Inc...276 783-3121
325 Brunswick Ln Marion (24354) **(G-8228)**
General Dynmics Gvrnment Syste (HQ)...**703 876-3000**
2941 Fairview Park Dr Falls Church (22042) **(G-4795)**
General Dynmics Mssion Systems (HQ)...**877 449-0600**
12450 Fair Lakes Cir Fairfax (22033) **(G-4463)**
General Dynmics Nassco-Norfolk, Norfolk *Also called Metro Machine Corp* **(G-9641)**
General Dynmics One Source LLC...703 906-6397
3150 Frview Pk Dr Ste 100 Falls Church (22042) **(G-4796)**
General Dynmics Wrldwide Hldng (HQ)...**703 876-3000**
11011 Sunset Hills Rd Reston (20190) **(G-10858)**
General Electric Company...540 387-7000
1501 Roanoke Blvd Salem (24153) **(G-12511)**
General Electric Company...804 965-1020
4521 Highwoods Pkwy # 200 Glen Allen (23060) **(G-5736)**
General Electric Company...540 667-5990
125 Apple Valley Rd Winchester (22602) **(G-15420)**
General Engineering Co VA...276 628-6068
26485 Hillman Hwy Abingdon (24210) **(G-32)**
General Eqp Sls & Svc LLC...434 579-7581
5090 Ramble Rd Virgilina (24598) **(G-14192)**
General Financial Supply Inc...540 828-3892
213b Dry River Rd Bridgewater (22812) **(G-1952)**
General Foam Plastics Corp...757 857-0153
4429 Bonney Rd Ste 500 Virginia Beach (23462) **(G-14479)**
General Iron and Steel Co Inc...434 676-3975
400 Virginia Ave Alberta (23821) **(G-98)**
General Magnetic Sciences Inc...571 243-6887
9518 Technology Dr Manassas (20110) **(G-7944)**
General Magnetic Sciences Inc (PA)...**571 243-6887**
6420 Stonehaven Ct Clifton (20124) **(G-3666)**
General Marble & Granite Co...804 353-2761
2118 Lake Ave Richmond (23230) **(G-11215)**
General Medical Mfg Co...804 254-2737
1601 Willow Lawn Dr Richmond (23230) **(G-11216)**
General Products, Fredericksburg *Also called Benchmark Doors* **(G-5173)**
General Shale Brick Inc...276 783-3156
7164 Lee Hwy Atkins (24311) **(G-1517)**
General Shale Brick Inc...800 414-4661
1085 Venture Dr Forest (24551) **(G-5072)**
General Shale Brick Inc...540 977-5505
770 Webster Rd Blue Ridge (24064) **(G-1849)**
General Sheet Metal Co Inc...571 221-3270
10814 Valley Falls Ct Manassas (20112) **(G-8073)**
General Welding...540 514-0242
316 Highland Ave Winchester (22601) **(G-15545)**
Generals Ridge Vineyard...804 472-3172
1618 Weldons Dr Hague (22469) **(G-6046)**
Generator Interlock Tech LLC...804 726-2448
1735 Arlington Rd Richmond (23230) **(G-11217)**
Genesic Semiconductor Inc...703 996-8200
43670 Trade Center Pl # 15 Dulles (20166) **(G-4204)**
Genesis Boat Works Inc...757 869-0345
8 Blackwater Ln Hampton (23669) **(G-6158)**
Genesis Decor LLC...804 561-4844
15401 Goodes Bridge Rd Amelia Court House (23002) **(G-658)**
Genesis Graphics Printing...703 560-8728
7635 Holmes Run Dr Falls Church (22042) **(G-4797)**
Genesis Infosolutions Inc...703 835-4469
2613 Tarleton Corner Dr Herndon (20171) **(G-6682)**
Genesis Professional Training...804 818-3611
14503 Houghton St Chesterfield (23832) **(G-3502)**
Genesis Sign...540 288-8820
3665 Jeff Davis Hwy # 102 Stafford (22554) **(G-13146)**
Genesis Welding Inc...276 935-2482
1062 Alleghany Rd Grundy (24614) **(G-6033)**
Genformax LLC...703 346-7445
7918 Jones Branch Dr # 540 Mc Lean (22102) **(G-8447)**
Genik Incorporated...804 226-2907
6119 Miller Rd Richmond (23231) **(G-11218)**
Genuine Smithfield Ham Shop, Smithfield *Also called Smithfield Packaged Meats Corp* **(G-12733)**
Genx Pharmacy, Chesapeake *Also called Precision Pharmacy LLC* **(G-3244)**
Geo Enterprise Inc...703 594-3816
10456 Lonesome Rd Nokesville (20181) **(G-9393)**
Geopliant LLC...888 273-7658
2831 Summerfield Rd Falls Church (22042) **(G-4798)**
Geoquip Inc...757 485-2500
1111 Cavalier Blvd Chesapeake (23323) **(G-3118)**
Geoquip Manufacturing Inc...757 485-8525
1111 Cavalier Blvd Chesapeake (23323) **(G-3119)**
Georator Corporation...703 368-2101
9617 Center St Manassas (20110) **(G-7945)**
George F Dashell Jr...305 664-2238
2905 Cape Henry Dr Virginia Beach (23451) **(G-14480)**
George H Pollok Jr...336 540-8870
48 Tranquility Bay Dr Union Hall (24176) **(G-13959)**
George King Welding Inc...540 379-3407
13417 Poplar Neck Rd King George (22485) **(G-7092)**
George Leica Systems...804 299-3911
9415 Atlee Commerce Blvd A Ashland (23005) **(G-1420)**
George McCracken...804 238-4910
813 Main St West Point (23181) **(G-15157)**
George Perez...757 362-3131
9609 Dolphin Run Norfolk (23518) **(G-9561)**
George Thomas Garten...540 962-3633
201 W Locust St Covington (24426) **(G-3790)**
George W Wray...540 483-7792
3125 Old Franklin Tpke Rocky Mount (24151) **(G-12324)**
George's Chicken, Edinburg *Also called Georges Chicken LLC* **(G-4305)**
Georges Inc...540 433-0720
501 N Liberty St Harrisonburg (22802) **(G-6322)**
Georges Chicken LLC (HQ)...**540 984-4121**
19992 Senedo Rd Edinburg (22824) **(G-4305)**
Georges Chicken LLC...540 434-7394
1620 S Main St Harrisonburg (22801) **(G-6323)**
Georges Family Farms LLC...540 477-3181
560 Caverns Rd Mount Jackson (22842) **(G-9070)**
Georgetown Business Services...214 708-0249
554 23rd St S Arlington (22202) **(G-978)**
Georgette T Hawkins...540 825-8928
12244 Hawkins Ln Culpeper (22701) **(G-3893)**
Georgia-Pacific LLC...434 299-5911
9363 Lee Jackson Hwy Big Island (24526) **(G-1702)**
Georgia-Pacific LLC...276 632-6301
25 Industrial Park Rd Ridgeway (24148) **(G-11843)**
Georgia-Pacific LLC...434 634-5123
634 Davis St Emporia (23847) **(G-4359)**
Georgia-Pacific LLC...434 634-6133
234 Forest Rd Skippers (23879) **(G-12700)**
Georgia-Pacific LLC...434 283-1066
Hwy 501 S Gladys (24554) **(G-5691)**
Geraldine Browns Child Car...757 665-1466
15132 Bethel Church Rd Bloxom (23308) **(G-1840)**
Geralds Tools Inc...276 889-2964
3304 N 71 Lebanon (24266) **(G-7192)**
Gerdau Ameristeel Dinwiddie Co, North Dinwiddie *Also called Chaparral (virginia) Inc* **(G-10049)**
Gerdau Ameristeel US Inc...434 517-0715
2171 Bill Tuck Hwy South Boston (24592) **(G-12772)**
Gerdau Ameristeel US Inc...804 520-0286
25801 Hofheimer Way North Dinwiddie (23803) **(G-10051)**
Gerloff Inc Charles W...757 853-5232
2622 Cromwell Rd Norfolk (23509) **(G-9562)**
Germaine Clark LLC...571 309-1724
124 Dale St Alexandria (22305) **(G-214)**
Germfreak Inc...443 254-0805
6310 Olmi Landrith Dr Alexandria (22307) **(G-467)**
Germinal Dimensions Inc...540 552-8938
915 Allendale Ct Blacksburg (24060) **(G-1741)**
Geroge's, Harrisonburg *Also called Georges Inc* **(G-6322)**
Geronimo Welding Fabrication...757 277-6383
1324 Chippokes Ct Virginia Beach (23454) **(G-14481)**
Get Aura Inc...703 801-4382
2553 Dulles View Dr Fl 4 Herndon (20171) **(G-6683)**
Get It LLC...703 625-6844
1620 Fitzgerald Ln Alexandria (22302) **(G-215)**
Get It Right Enterprise...757 869-1736
213 Piez Ave Newport News (23601) **(G-9235)**
Get Some Socks LLC...434 466-5054
2180 Cottonwood Ln Culpeper (22701) **(G-3894)**
Getintoforex LLC...251 591-2181
106 Wood Ave W Big Stone Gap (24219) **(G-1710)**

Getsat North America Inc...571 308-2451
1750 Tysons Blvd Ste 1500 Mc Lean (22102) ***(G-8448)***
Getxlaced, Norfolk *Also called Reese Kyndal* ***(G-9705)***
Geza Gear Inc...703 327-9844
5501 Merchants View Sq # 211 Haymarket (20169) ***(G-6425)***
Gfp Plastics, Virginia Beach *Also called General Foam Plastics Corp* ***(G-14479)***
Ggb LLC...571 234-9597
7516 Aruba Ct Manassas (20109) ***(G-8074)***
Gh Winery LLC...804 737-7416
6446 Somerton Pl Sandston (23150) ***(G-12616)***
Ghek Industries LLC...804 955-0710
1204 Middleberry Dr Henrico (23231) ***(G-6517)***
Ghent Living Magazine LLC...757 425-7333
1860 Wolfsnare Rd Virginia Beach (23454) ***(G-14482)***
Ghodousi LLC...480 544-3192
5700 Gen Wshngtn Dr Ste H Alexandria (22312) ***(G-468)***
Ghost Wind LLC...561 624-1141
1545 Meade Point Dr Powhatan (23139) ***(G-10546)***
Ghti Corporation...703 802-8616
4100 Meadow Hill Ln Fairfax (22033) ***(G-4464)***
Gianni Enterprises Inc...540 982-0111
3453 Aerial Way Dr Sw Roanoke (24018) ***(G-11925)***
Gianni Entps Inc DBA Vrgina Pl...540 314-6566
824 4th St Se Roanoke (24013) ***(G-12097)***
Giant Gradall and Eqp Rentl...703 878-3032
16006 Prestwick Ct Montclair (22025) ***(G-8998)***
Giant Lion Software LLC...703 764-8060
5075 Coleridge Dr Fairfax (22032) ***(G-4465)***
Giant Pharmacy...703 723-2161
43330 Junction Plz Ashburn (20147) ***(G-1286)***
Giant Printing...703 525-1313
8400 Hilltop Rd Fairfax (22031) ***(G-4466)***
Giant Printing Inc...703 645-2292
4116 Walney Rd Ste F Chantilly (20151) ***(G-2426)***
Giant Publishing & Co...703 750-6447
4107 Oak Village Ldg Fairfax (22033) ***(G-4467)***
Giant Resource Recovery Inc...434 685-7021
Rr 1 Cascade (24069) ***(G-2251)***
Giant Software LLC...540 292-6232
115 Roades Ct Charlottesville (22902) ***(G-2803)***
Gibraltar Energy LLC...202 642-2704
6524 Langleigh Way Alexandria (22315) ***(G-469)***
Gibson Girl Publishing Co LLC...504 261-8107
3243 Redgrove Ct Virginia Beach (23453) ***(G-14483)***
Gibson Good Tools Inc...540 249-5100
402 5th St Grottoes (24441) ***(G-6019)***
Gibson Logging Enterprises LLC...606 260-1889
185 Colfax Dr Duffield (24244) ***(G-4178)***
Gibson Logging Inc...804 769-1130
12853 The Trail King Queen Ch (23085) ***(G-7126)***
Gibson Logging LLC Rush J...540 539-8145
4447 River Rd Bluemont (20135) ***(G-1888)***
Gibson Sewer Water...540 636-1131
8 Avery Dr Chester Gap (22623) ***(G-3470)***
Gibson Welding...276 328-3324
7936 Carter Branch Rd Wise (24293) ***(G-15624)***
Gidgets Beauty Box LLC...303 859-5914
550 E Main St Purcellville (20132) ***(G-10662)***
Giesecke+devrient (HQ)...**703 480-2000**
45925 Horseshoe Dr # 100 Dulles (20166) ***(G-4205)***
Gift Terrariums LLC...571 230-5918
204 Marcum Ct Sterling (20164) ***(G-13411)***
Gifted Education Press...703 369-5017
10201 Yuma Ct Manassas (20109) ***(G-8075)***
Gigasheet Inc...703 231-8758
17359 Cannonade Dr Leesburg (20176) ***(G-7278)***
Gigis...276 608-5737
8436 Hidden Valley Rd Abingdon (24210) ***(G-33)***
Gilbert Idelkhani...703 399-1225
862 Dogwood Ct Herndon (20170) ***(G-6684)***
Gildan Delaware Inc (HQ)...**276 956-2305**
3375 Joseph Martin Hwy Martinsville (24112) ***(G-8289)***
Gilgit Press LLC...804 359-2524
2309 Monument Ave Richmond (23220) ***(G-11600)***
Gillespie Inc...540 297-4432
3117 Glenwood Dr Bedford (24523) ***(G-1639)***
Gilliam Welding, Hampton *Also called Metals of Distinction Inc* ***(G-6196)***
Gillie Boatworks...804 370-4825
467 North End Rd Deltaville (23043) ***(G-4079)***
Gilman Trucking, Ashland *Also called William B Gilman* ***(G-1510)***
Gilmer Industries Inc...540 434-8877
560 Stone Spring Rd Harrisonburg (22801) ***(G-6324)***
Gilmerton, Chesapeake *Also called Luck Stone Corporation* ***(G-3189)***
Gilstrap Inc John...703 961-9413
12758 Lavender Keep Cir Fairfax (22033) ***(G-4468)***
Gingham & Grosgrain LLC...202 674-2024
206 Adams Ave Alexandria (22301) ***(G-216)***
Ginnys Ink, Newport News *Also called Walker Virginia* ***(G-9378)***
Girls With Crabs LLC...540 623-9502
6910 Fox Ridge Rd Spotsylvania (22551) ***(G-12891)***
Git R Done Inc...703 843-8697
11710 Plaza America Dr # 2000 Reston (20190) ***(G-10859)***
Gival Press LLC...703 351-0079
5200 1st St N Arlington (22203) ***(G-979)***
Give More Media Inc...804 762-4500
115 S 15th St Ste 502 Richmond (23219) ***(G-11601)***
Giving Light Inc...757 236-2405
15 Stephanies Rd Hampton (23666) ***(G-6159)***
Gja LLC...434 218-0216
2 Putt Cir Palmyra (22963) ***(G-10249)***
Gjhmotivate...757 487-5486
3005 Camelot Blvd Chesapeake (23323) ***(G-3120)***
Gjs Cabinetry Installation...540 856-2726
2164 Dellinger Gap Rd Edinburg (22824) ***(G-4306)***
Gki Aerospace LLC...703 451-4562
8492 Summer Breeze Ln Springfield (22153) ***(G-13010)***
GL Hollowell Publishing LLC...804 796-5968
4336 Milsmith Rd Chester (23831) ***(G-3419)***
Glad Precision Machine Inc...276 930-9930
26 Harbour School Ln Stuart (24171) ***(G-13613)***
Glad Products Company...434 946-3100
317 Zane Snead Dr Amherst (24521) ***(G-691)***
Gladden Welding...540 387-1489
4444 Harborwood Rd Salem (24153) ***(G-12512)***
Glade Machine Inc...276 429-2114
13092 Old Monroe Rd Glade Spring (24340) ***(G-5675)***
Glade Stone Inc...276 429-5241
14196 Monroe Rd Glade Spring (24340) ***(G-5676)***
Gladstone Media Corporation...434 293-8471
214 Clarks Tract Keswick (22947) ***(G-7047)***
Gladys Timber Products Inc...434 283-4744
8759 Brookneal Hwy Gladys (24554) ***(G-5692)***
Glamorous Sweet...540 903-3683
210 Hartlake Dr Fredericksburg (22406) ***(G-5435)***
Glandore Spice...434 589-2492
1841 Hunters Lodge Rd Troy (22974) ***(G-13925)***
Glanville Industries LLC...757 513-2700
12210 Waterview Trl Carrollton (23314) ***(G-2243)***
Glasco Drilling Inc...276 964-4117
3095 Steelsburg Hwy Cedar Bluff (24609) ***(G-2277)***
Glasdon Inc...804 726-3777
5200 Anthony Rd Ste D Sandston (23150) ***(G-12617)***
Glass Fronts Inc...540 672-4410
215 Red Hill Rd Orange (22960) ***(G-10214)***
Glass House Winery LLC...434 975-0094
5898 Free Union Rd Free Union (22940) ***(G-5507)***
Glazed & Twisted LLC...703 789-5522
5664 Shoal Creek Dr Gainesville (20155) ***(G-5586)***
Glen Allen Press LLC...804 747-1776
4036 Cox Rd Ste D Glen Allen (23060) ***(G-5737)***
Glen Manor Vineyards LLC...540 635-6324
2244 Browntown Rd Front Royal (22630) ***(G-5533)***
Glen-Gery Capital Plant, Manassas *Also called Glen-Gery Corporation* ***(G-7946)***
Glen-Gery Corporation...703 368-3178
9905 Godwin Dr Manassas (20110) ***(G-7946)***
Glencourse Press...703 860-2416
2170 Glencourse Ln Herndon (20191) ***(G-6685)***
Glenmark Group LLC...757 955-6850
1105a International Plz Chesapeake (23323) ***(G-3121)***
Glenmore Life, Palmyra *Also called Gja LLC* ***(G-10249)***
Glenn F Kite...540 743-6124
11 Meadow Ln Luray (22835) ***(G-7613)***
Glenn R Williams...434 251-9383
2206 Hillside Rd Ringgold (24586) ***(G-11867)***
Glenn R Wllams Athrzed Frnchse, Ringgold *Also called Glenn R Williams* ***(G-11867)***
Glenna Jean Manufacturing, Petersburg *Also called Cricket Products Inc* ***(G-10315)***
Glenna Jean Mfg Co...804 783-1490
119 Shockoe Slip Richmond (23219) ***(G-11602)***
Glo 4 Itcom...804 527-7608
5104 Wythe Ave Richmond (23226) ***(G-11219)***
Glo Quips, Gloucester *Also called Dehardit Press* ***(G-5845)***
Global - AB Inbev...314 577-2000
7801 Pocahontas Trl Williamsburg (23185) ***(G-15247)***
Global Business Pages...855 825-2124
6820 Atmore Dr Richmond (23225) ***(G-11603)***
Global Cell Solutions Inc...434 327-3759
770 Harris St Ste 104 Charlottesville (22903) ***(G-2804)***
Global Code Usa Inc...908 764-5818
8620 Rolling Rd Manassas (20110) ***(G-7947)***
Global Com Inc...703 532-6425
23465 Rock Hven Way Ste 1 Sterling (20166) ***(G-13412)***
Global Concern Inc...703 425-5861
5503 Kempton Dr Springfield (22151) ***(G-13011)***
Global Daily...703 518-3030
5 Cameron St Ste 5 # 5 Alexandria (22314) ***(G-217)***
Global Design Contractors Inc...703 865-6064
9253 Eljames Dr Fairfax (22032) ***(G-4469)***
Global Direct LLC...540 483-5103
3325 Grassy Hill Rd Rocky Mount (24151) ***(G-12325)***
Global Embroidery, Midlothian *Also called Global Partners Virginia LLC* ***(G-8822)***

ALPHABETIC

Global Gospel Publishers..434 582-5049
221 Farley Branch Dr Lynchburg (24502) *(G-7721)*

Global Health Solutions Inc..................................703 848-2333
2146 Kings Garden Way Falls Church (22043) *(G-4799)*

Global Info Netwrk Systems Inc............................703 409-4204
6906 Inlet Cove Dr Fort Belvoir (22060) *(G-5115)*

Global Marine Services LLC..................................757 284-9284
4229 Buckeye Ct Virginia Beach (23462) *(G-14484)*

Global Metal Finishing Inc....................................540 362-1489
3646 Aerial Way Dr Sw # 2 Roanoke (24018) *(G-11926)*

Global Metro Networks Inc....................................703 837-6030
201 N Union St Ste 300 Alexandria (22314) *(G-218)*

Global Oled Technology LLC..................................703 870-3282
13873 Park Center Rd # 330 Herndon (20171) *(G-6686)*

Global Partners Virginia LLC.................................804 744-8112
3005 E Boundary Ter Ste G Midlothian (23112) *(G-8822)*

Global Polishing System LLC................................937 534-1538
28 W Market St Leesburg (20176) *(G-7279)*

Global Promos..804 744-8112
3005 E Boundary Ter Ste G Midlothian (23112) *(G-8823)*

Global Safety Textiles LLC (HQ)............................**434 447-7629**
1556 Montgomery St South Hill (23970) *(G-12851)*

Global Scnning Americas VA Inc............................703 717-5631
14155 Sullyfield Cir C Chantilly (20151) *(G-2427)*

Global Services Intl LLC..757 535-2394
623 Sedgefield Ct Chesapeake (23322) *(G-3122)*

Global Signs & Graphics.......................................703 543-1046
5875 Trinity Pkwy Ste 110 Centreville (20120) *(G-2306)*

Global Supply Solutions..757 392-1733
5741 Bayside Rd Ste 108 Virginia Beach (23455) *(G-14485)*

Global Telecom Group Inc (PA)..............................**571 291-9631**
8220 Crestwood Heights Dr # 1401 Mc Lean (22102) *(G-8449)*

Global Telecom Group Inc......................................678 896-2468
4080 Lafayette Center Dr # 25 Chantilly (20151) *(G-2428)*

Global Trading of Martinsville................................276 666-0236
240 Stonewall Jackson Trl Martinsville (24112) *(G-8290)*

Global Water Challenge...703 379-2713
2900 S Quincy St Ste 375 Arlington (22206) *(G-980)*

Global Welding and Engineering, Suffolk *Also called Sheila Rodriguez (G-13762)*

Global X Press...202 417-2070
660 Chain Bridge Rd Mc Lean (22101) *(G-8450)*

Global Yacht Fuel LLC...954 462-6050
5353 E Princess Anne Rd F Norfolk (23502) *(G-9563)*

Globus World Partners Inc.....................................757 645-4274
190 The Maine Williamsburg (23185) *(G-15248)*

Glonet Incorporated..571 499-5000
277 S Washington St # 300 Alexandria (22314) *(G-219)*

Gloria Barbre..703 548-2210
105 N Union St Alexandria (22314) *(G-220)*

Glorias Glass..804 357-0676
9500 New Kent Hwy New Kent (23124) *(G-9133)*

Glory Days Press LLC..703 443-1964
19875 Evergreen Mills Rd Leesburg (20175) *(G-7280)*

Glory Violin Co LLC...703 439-1700
7601 Little River Tpke Annandale (22003) *(G-751)*

Gloves For Life LLC...540 343-1697
1423 Crestmoor Dr Sw Roanoke (24018) *(G-11927)*

Glovestix LLC...703 909-5146
21861 Parsells Ridge Ct Ashburn (20148) *(G-1287)*

Glr Welding & Fabrication......................................276 337-1401
5831 Luray Ln Pound (24279) *(G-10513)*

GM International Ltd Company................................703 577-0829
43194 Parkers Ridge Dr Leesburg (20176) *(G-7281)*

GM Printer Experts LLC...202 250-0569
4600 S Four Mile Run Dr A Arlington (22204) *(G-981)*

GMA Industries...703 538-5100
313 Hillwood Ave Falls Church (22046) *(G-4915)*

GMAC, Bedford *Also called Bedford Weaving Inc (G-1626)*

Gmg Ghostwriting...718 578-8622
4220 Campbell Ave # 607 Arlington (22206) *(G-982)*

GNB Industrial Power, Charlottesville *Also called Exide Technologies LLC (G-2629)*

Go 2 Row Inc..804 694-4868
6494 Jenkins Ln Gloucester (23061) *(G-5849)*

Go Happy Printing...315 436-1151
2350 Duke St Ste D Alexandria (22314) *(G-221)*

Go Happy Printing LLC..240 423-7397
8422 Frost Way Annandale (22003) *(G-752)*

Go Vivace Inc..703 869-9463
1616 Anderson Rd Ste 303 Mc Lean (22102) *(G-8451)*

Go-Race Inc..540 392-0696
1265 Moose Dr Christiansburg (24073) *(G-3591)*

Go4it LLC...703 531-0586
107 Hillier St Falls Church (22046) *(G-4916)*

God Spede Printing...360 359-6458
4177 Meadowland Ct Chantilly (20151) *(G-2429)*

Goda Software Inc...703 373-7568
2011 Crystal Dr Arlington (22202) *(G-983)*

Goddess of Chocolate Ltd......................................757 301-2126
1125 Nipigon Ct Virginia Beach (23454) *(G-14486)*

Godosan Publications Inc......................................540 720-0861
3101 Aquia Dr Stafford (22554) *(G-13147)*

Gods Compass Movie LLC.....................................434 219-6865
1608 Linden Ave Lynchburg (24503) *(G-7722)*

Goetz Printing Company..703 569-8232
7939 Angus Ct Springfield (22153) *(G-13012)*

Gogo Band Inc..804 869-8253
201 Duncan St Ashland (23005) *(G-1421)*

Gogo Industries Inc..925 708-7804
318 4th St Se Apt 33 Charlottesville (22902) *(G-2805)*

Gohring Components Corp.....................................757 665-4110
24013 Bennett St Parksley (23421) *(G-10262)*

Going Forward Imports LLC...................................301 693-1562
266 Wunder St Mount Jackson (22842) *(G-9071)*

Golco Logistics LLC..571 234-3466
300 Continental Pkwy # 315 Newport News (23602) *(G-9236)*

Gold Brand Software LLC.......................................703 450-1321
1282 Mason Mill Ct Herndon (20170) *(G-6687)*

Gold Canyon Candles...540 972-1266
104 Hillside Dr Locust Grove (22508) *(G-7444)*

Gold Smith Designer, Alexandria *Also called Metallum (G-274)*

Gold Spot...804 708-0275
1940 Sandy Hook Rd # 101 Goochland (23063) *(G-5883)*

Gold Stem...703 680-7000
12550 Dillingham Sq Woodbridge (22192) *(G-15710)*

Gold-Micro, Edinburg *Also called Evergreen Design Inc (G-4303)*

Goldbelt Wolf LLC...703 584-8889
5500 Cherokee Ave Ste 200 Alexandria (22312) *(G-470)*

Golden Leaf Tobacco Company..............................434 736-2130
3662 Ontario Rd Ste B Keysville (23947) *(G-7057)*

Golden Pride Company, Woodbridge *Also called Gpc Inc (G-15712)*

Golden Quill Editorial Svcs....................................240 838-0464
4301 Columbia Pike # 235 Arlington (22204) *(G-984)*

Golden Section LLC...540 315-4756
1810 New London Ct Blacksburg (24060) *(G-1742)*

Golden Squeegee Inc..804 355-8018
1508 Belleville St Richmond (23230) *(G-11220)*

Goldensqueegee, Richmond *Also called Golden Squeegee Inc (G-11220)*

Golf Guide Golf Getaways, Stephenson *Also called Golf Guide Inc (G-13333)*

Golf Guide Inc...540 431-5034
206 Morlyn Dr Stephenson (22656) *(G-13333)*

Gollygee Software Inc...703 437-3751
1474 Northpoint Vlg Ctr Reston (20194) *(G-10860)*

Gomatters LLC..757 819-4950
1600 Virginia Beach Blvd Virginia Beach (23454) *(G-14487)*

Gomspace NA, Alexandria *Also called Gomspace North America LLC (G-222)*

Gomspace North America LLC................................703 866-8742
211 N Union St Ste 100 Alexandria (22314) *(G-222)*

Gonmf..844 763-7250
13025 Carolyn Forest Dr Woodbridge (22192) *(G-15711)*

Gooats LLC...267 997-7789
8538 Terminal Rd Ste O Lorton (22079) *(G-7491)*

Goochland Tees Inc...804 708-2041
1390 Broad Street Rd C Oilville (23129) *(G-10178)*

Good Guys Printing LLC...434 942-8229
450 Maple Run Rd Amherst (24521) *(G-692)*

Good Humor Ice Cream LLC...................................703 898-5516
1612 Becontree Ln Apt 3a Reston (20190) *(G-10861)*

Good News Network..757 638-3289
3850 Broadway St Portsmouth (23703) *(G-10435)*

Good Printers Inc..540 828-4663
213 Dry River Rd Bridgewater (22812) *(G-1953)*

Good Tymes Enterprises Inc...................................276 628-2335
228 Preston St Sw Abingdon (24210) *(G-34)*

Goodboy LLC..540 421-6712
36559 Vineyard View Pl Hillsboro (20132) *(G-6869)*

Gooder Group, Fairfax *Also called Homeactions LLC (G-4476)*

Gooder Group Inc..703 698-7750
2724 Dorr Ave Ste 103 Fairfax (22031) *(G-4470)*

Goodlife Theatre...540 547-9873
3753 Slate Mills Rd Boston (22713) *(G-1903)*

Goodlion Music & Publishing.................................757 875-0000
701 Industrial Park Dr B Newport News (23608) *(G-9237)*

Goodloe Asphault LLC...540 373-5863
102 Fauquier St Fredericksburg (22401) *(G-5192)*

Goodman Lumber Co Inc.......................................804 265-9030
5001 Grubby Rd Wilsons (23894) *(G-15367)*

Goodnight Jewelers, Culpeper *Also called Rng LLC (G-3917)*

Goodpasture Knives..804 752-8363
13432 Farrington Rd Ashland (23005) *(G-1422)*

Goodrich Corporation..703 558-8230
1000 Wilson Blvd Ste 2300 Arlington (22209) *(G-985)*

Goodrow Holdings Inc...804 543-2136
9431 Studley Plntn Dr Mechanicsville (23116) *(G-8628)*

Goodwin Creek Farm & Bakery...............................434 260-1135
151 Goodwin Creek Trl Afton (22920) *(G-82)*

Goon Squad Apps LLC..706 410-6139
3218a Pretty Lake Ave Norfolk (23518) *(G-9564)*

2021 Virginia
Industrial Directory

(G-0000) Company's Geographic Section entry number

Goose Creek Farms & Winery LLC 540 338-2056
18050 Tranquility Rd Purcellville (20132) *(G-10663)*

Goose Creek Gas LLC 703 827-0611
8526 Leesburg Pike Vienna (22182) *(G-14061)*

Goose Creek Woodworks LLC 540 348-4163
579 Davis Rd Raphine (24472) *(G-10749)*

Gordon Paper Company Inc (PA) **800 457-7366**
5713 Ward Ave Virginia Beach (23455) *(G-14488)*

Gordos Tacos and More LLC 757 710-3317
11363 Seaside Rd Birdsnest (23307) *(G-1719)*

Gore's Processing, Stephens City *Also called Gores Custom Slaughter & Proc (G-13317)*

Gores Custom Slaughter & Proc (PA) **540 869-1029**
1426 Double Church Rd Stephens City (22655) *(G-13317)*

Gormanlee Industries LLC 703 448-1948
1021 Savile Ln Mc Lean (22101) *(G-8452)*

Goss132 .... 202 905-2380
798 Col Edmonds Ct Warrenton (20186) *(G-15021)*

Got It Covered LLC 540 353-5167
230 Plybon Ln Wirtz (24184) *(G-15611)*

Got Scents & Sova Candles 434 736-9394
245 Tech Ln Keysville (23947) *(G-7058)*

Gotham Graphix LLC 540 456-6600
8125 Batesville Rd Afton (22920) *(G-83)*

Goto Unit USA 703 598-6642
4707 Cochran Pl Centreville (20120) *(G-2307)*

Gouchland Custom Buildings, Manakin Sabot *Also called Virginia Custom Buildings (G-7906)*

Goulet Pen Company LLC 804 368-0482
1590 E Parham Rd Henrico (23228) *(G-6518)*

Gourmet Kitchen Tools Inc 757 595-3278
1215 George Wash Mem Hwy Yorktown (23693) *(G-15962)*

Gourmet Manufacturing Inc 276 638-2367
400 Starling Ave Martinsville (24112) *(G-8291)*

Gourmet Royol, Harrisonburg *Also called Ariake USA Inc (G-6293)*

Gov Panda LLC 571 275-6370
409 Spring St Herndon (20170) *(G-6688)*

Government Sign Solution, Henrico *Also called Stacey A Peets (G-6575)*

Govhawk LLC 703 439-1349
3201 Landover St Apt 1706 Alexandria (22305) *(G-223)*

Govini, Arlington *Also called Poplicus Incorporated (G-1116)*

Govready Pbc 917 304-3488
4324 Raleigh Ave Apt 204 Alexandria (22304) *(G-224)*

Govready Public Benefit, Alexandria *Also called Govready Pbc (G-224)*

Govsearch LLC 703 340-1308
1861 Intl Dr Ste 270 Mclean (22102) *(G-8587)*

Govtribe Inc 202 505-4681
2311 Wilson Blvd Fl 3 Arlington (22201) *(G-986)*

Goyal Gadgets LLC 703 757-8294
1193 Lees Meadow Ct Great Falls (22066) *(G-5957)*

Gpc Inc 757 345-3991
745 Vestal St Woodbridge (22191) *(G-15712)*

Grabber Construction Pdts Inc 804 550-9331
9424 Atlee Commerce Blvd C Ashland (23005) *(G-1423)*

Grace Estate Winery LLC 434 823-1486
5281 Mount Juliet Farm Crozet (22932) *(G-3833)*

Grace Upon Grace LLC 703 999-6678
775 Gteway Dr Se Apt 1111 Leesburg (20175) *(G-7282)*

Graceland of Martinsville 434 250-0050
5950 Greensboro Rd Ridgeway (24148) *(G-11844)*

Gracenotes 703 825-7922
6309 Pohick Station Dr Fairfax Station (22039) *(G-4710)*

Gracies Gowns Inc 540 287-0143
1919 Captain Dr Fredericksburg (22408) *(G-5292)*

Gradall Industries Inc 540 819-6638
177 East Arrowhead Ct Troutville (24175) *(G-13910)*

Gradient Dynamics LLC 865 207-9052
604 Boyle Ln Mc Lean (22102) *(G-8453)*

Grafik Trenz 757 539-0141
1402b S Church St Smithfield (23430) *(G-12714)*

Graham Alliance, Hampton *Also called Cegna Inc (G-6110)*

Graham and Rollins Inc 757 755-1021
509 Bassette St Hampton (23669) *(G-6160)*

Graham Graphics LLC 703 220-4564
5308 Atlee Pl Springfield (22151) *(G-13013)*

Graham Grham Cnvas Sign Shoppe 276 628-8069
1002 W Main St Abingdon (24210) *(G-35)*

Graham Packg Plastic Pdts Inc 540 564-1000
291 W Wolfe St Harrisonburg (22802) *(G-6325)*

Graham-White Manufacturing Co (HQ) **540 387-5600**
1242 S Colorado St Salem (24153) *(G-12513)*

Grain Free Products Inc 703 418-0000
7503 Calderon Ct Unit F Alexandria (22306) *(G-471)*

Grammers Welding 804 730-7296
6269 Fieldshire Ct Mechanicsville (23111) *(G-8629)*

Grampian Group Inc 757 277-5557
3225 Fowlers Lake Rd Williamsburg (23185) *(G-15249)*

Grand Designs LLC 412 295-7730
14787 Green Park Way Centreville (20120) *(G-2308)*

Grand Investment LLC 804 939-9473
3823 Creighton Rd Richmond (23223) *(G-11604)*

Grand Pop's Best, North Chesterfield *Also called Pops Snacks LLC (G-9950)*

Grand Springs Distribution, Alton *Also called Central Carolina Btlg Co Inc (G-646)*

Grandaddys Stump Grinding 757 565-5870
221 Old Taylor Rd Williamsburg (23188) *(G-15250)*

Grandesign 434 294-0665
606 S Main St Blackstone (23824) *(G-1817)*

Grandloving, Lancaster *Also called Heartstrings Press LLC (G-7162)*

Granite Countertop Experts LLC 757 826-9316
5875 Jefferson Ave Bldg B Newport News (23605) *(G-9238)*

Granite Countertops 703 953-3330
4080 Walney Rd Ste F Chantilly (20151) *(G-2430)*

Granite Design Inc 703 530-1223
6954 Wellingford Dr Manassas (20109) *(G-8076)*

Granite Perch Graphics 703 218-5300
47525 Anchorage Cir Sterling (20165) *(G-13413)*

Granite Top LLC 703 257-0714
10498 Business Center Ct Manassas (20110) *(G-7948)*

Granules Pharmaceuticals Inc (HQ) **571 325-5950**
3701 Concorde Pkwy # 800 Chantilly (20151) *(G-2431)*

Granules Pharmaceuticals Inc 571 325-5950
3725 Concorde Pkwy Chantilly (20151) *(G-2432)*

Grapevine 540 371-4092
607 Payton Dr Fredericksburg (22405) *(G-5436)*

Graphic Arts Adhesives 804 779-3304
9102 Knight Dr Mechanicsville (23116) *(G-8630)*

Graphic Comm Group 703 818-2700
6738 Bunkers Ct Clifton (20124) *(G-3667)*

Graphic Comm Inc 301 599-9127
2340 Island Creek Dr Hillsville (24343) *(G-6892)*

Graphic Communications Inc 301 599-2020
2340 Island Creek Dr Hillsville (24343) *(G-6893)*

Graphic Garage 434 589-3432
77 Zion Park Ct Troy (22974) *(G-13926)*

Graphic Images Corp 703 823-6794
3660 Wheeler Ave Alexandria (22304) *(G-225)*

Graphic Prints 757 244-3753
311 Poplar Ave Newport News (23607) *(G-9239)*

Graphic Prints Inc 703 787-3880
12707 Fantasia Dr Herndon (20170) *(G-6689)*

Graphic Sign Worx LLC 703 503-3286
5025 Linette Ln Annandale (22003) *(G-753)*

Graphics North 540 678-4965
706 Fort Collier Rd Winchester (22601) *(G-15546)*

Graphics Nrth-Sgns Outdoor Ltg, Winchester *Also called Graphics North (G-15546)*

Graphics Shop LLC 757 485-7800
1700 Liberty St Chesapeake (23324) *(G-3123)*

Graphtone Signs 434 989-9740
1803 Solomon Rd Apt 4 Charlottesville (22901) *(G-2638)*

Graphus Inc 703 481-8861
11111 Chessington Pl Reston (20194) *(G-10862)*

Grassroots Enterprise Inc (HQ) **703 354-1177**
13005 Bankfoot Ct Herndon (20171) *(G-6690)*

Grateful Press LLC 434 202-1161
593 Rosemont Dr Charlottesville (22903) *(G-2806)*

Gratispicks Inc 757 739-4143
50 Beechdale Rd Portsmouth (23702) *(G-10436)*

Graves 434 656-2491
973 Court Rd Pittsville (24139) *(G-10362)*

Gravitonus 571 321-2019
4031 University Dr Fairfax (22030) *(G-4629)*

Gravittional Systems Engrg Inc 312 224-8152
6400 Newman Rd Clifton (20124) *(G-3668)*

Gravley Sand Works 434 724-7883
648 Flamingo Rd Fl 2 Dry Fork (24549) *(G-4142)*

Gray Shuntina 919 273-7979
448 Peregrine St Virginia Beach (23462) *(G-14489)*

Gray Ghost Vineyards 540 937-4869
14706 Lee Hwy Amissville (20106) *(G-719)*

Gray Logging Company, Surry *Also called James J Gray (G-13797)*

Gray Scale Productions 757 363-1087
1423 Air Rail Ave Virginia Beach (23455) *(G-14490)*

Grayer Industries LLC 703 491-4629
12452 Cavalier Dr Woodbridge (22192) *(G-15713)*

Grayhaven Winery 804 556-3917
4675 E Grey Fox Rd Gum Spring (23065) *(G-6043)*

Grayman Usa LLC 703 598-6934
40487 Aspen Highlands Ct Aldie (20105) *(G-106)*

Graymatter Industries LLC 276 429-2396
13088 Prices Bridge Rd Glade Spring (24340) *(G-5677)*

Grays Welding LLC 434 401-4559
1478 Fontella Rd Coleman Falls (24536) *(G-3706)*

Grayson Express 276 773-9173
2686 Graystone Rd Independence (24348) *(G-6983)*

Grayson Ferguson Wdwkg Inc 434 528-3405
2920 Sackett St Lynchburg (24501) *(G-7723)*

Grayson Millworks Company Inc 276 773-8590
315 W Main St Independence (24348) *(G-6984)*

Grc Direct, Manassas *Also called Grc Enterprises Inc (G-8077)*

Grc Enterprises Inc 540 428-7000
9203 Mike Garcia Dr Manassas (20109) ***(G-8077)***
Great Amercn Woodcrafters LLC 571 572-3150
14498 Telegraph Rd Woodbridge (22192) ***(G-15714)***
Great Deals LLC 703 915-0332
7202 Gentian Ct Springfield (22152) ***(G-13014)***
Great Dogs Great Falls LLC 703 759-3601
9859 Georgetown Pike Great Falls (22066) ***(G-5958)***
Great Falls Creamery 703 272-7609
766 Walker Rd Great Falls (22066) ***(G-5959)***
Great Falls Tea Garden LLC 703 757-6209
901 Winstead St Great Falls (22066) ***(G-5960)***
Great Neon Art & Sign Co 703 981-4661
12000 Park Shore Ct Woodbridge (22192) ***(G-15715)***
Great Source Education Group, Harrisonburg *Also called Houghton Mifflin Harcourt Pubg* ***(G-6329)***
Great Southern Wood Prsv Inc 540 483-5264
1050 N Main St Rocky Mount (24151) ***(G-12326)***
Great White Buffalo Entps LLC 434 329-1150
107 Jordan Dr Lynchburg (24502) ***(G-7724)***
Greater Richmond Dance Project 804 302-4338
5470 W Broad St Richmond (23230) ***(G-11221)***
Greater Wise Incorporated 276 679-1400
State Rte 610 Norton (24273) ***(G-10119)***
Grede Radford LLC 248 727-1800
1701 W Main St Radford (24141) ***(G-10715)***
Greeks Unlimited 804 368-1611
428 Greenbriar Ave Hampton (23661) ***(G-6161)***
Green Air Environmental Svcs 757 739-1349
8508 Benjamin Ave Norfolk (23518) ***(G-9565)***
Green Apple Assoc A Virgin 804 551-5040
2238 John Rolfe Pkwy Richmond (23233) ***(G-11222)***
Green Bay Packaging Inc 540 678-2600
285 Park Center Dr Winchester (22603) ***(G-15421)***
Green Coal Solutions LLC 703 910-4022
13001 Summit School Rd # 4 Woodbridge (22192) ***(G-15716)***
Green County Records, Stanardsville *Also called Media General Operations Inc* ***(G-13223)***
Green Edge Lighting LLC 804 462-0221
8436 Erle Rd Mechanicsville (23116) ***(G-8631)***
Green Forest Cabinetry 757 485-9200
723 Fenway Ave Chesapeake (23323) ***(G-3124)***
Green Fuel of VA 804 304-4564
8104 Cypresstree Ln Mechanicsville (23111) ***(G-8632)***
Green Graphic Signs LLC 804 229-3351
8807 Elkview Ct North Chesterfield (23236) ***(G-9881)***
Green Leaf Logistics LLC 757 899-0881
9700 Colonial Trl W Spring Grove (23881) ***(G-12930)***
Green Physics Corporation 703 989-6706
9411 Main St Ste 204a Manassas (20110) ***(G-7949)***
Green Plains Hopewell LLC 804 668-0013
701 S 6th St Hopewell (23860) ***(G-6927)***
Green Point 703 391-5006
12155 Eddyspark Dr Herndon (20170) ***(G-6691)***
Green Prana Industries Inc 410 790-3011
76 The Way Apt A Buckingham (23921) ***(G-2133)***
Green Solutions Lighting LLC 804 334-2705
206 Oxford Cir W Richmond (23221) ***(G-11605)***
Green Trophy 619 387-6244
373a Coral Sea Dr Fort Lee (23801) ***(G-5131)***
Green Valley Meat Processors 434 299-5529
2494 W Perch Rd Monroe (24574) ***(G-8990)***
Green Waste Organics LLC 804 929-8505
5333 Hall Farm Rd Prince George (23875) ***(G-10595)***
Greenacre Plumbing LLC 703 680-2380
11681 Bacon Race Rd Woodbridge (22192) ***(G-15717)***
Greenbrier Custom Cabinets 757 438-5475
535 W 25th St Ste B Norfolk (23517) ***(G-9566)***
Greenbrook Tms Neurohealth Ctr 804 980-7520
100 Eastshore Dr Ste 110 Glen Allen (23059) ***(G-5738)***
Greenbrook Tms Neurohealth Ctr 703 670-5738
13625 Office Pl Ste 101 Woodbridge (22192) ***(G-15718)***
Greenbrook Tms Neurohealth Ctr 855 998-4867
2965 Colonnade Dr Ste 307 Roanoke (24018) ***(G-11928)***
Greenbrook Tms Neurohealth Ctr 855 998-4867
770 Lynnhven Pkwy Ste 150 Virginia Beach (23452) ***(G-14491)***
Greenbrook Tms Neurohealth Ctr 855 940-4867
10304 Spotsylvania Ave # 106 Fredericksburg (22408) ***(G-5293)***
Greenbrook Tms Neurohealth Ctr 434 327-1660
630 Peter Jefferson Pkwy Charlottesville (22911) ***(G-2639)***
Greendale Railing Company 804 363-7809
2031a Westwood Ave Richmond (23230) ***(G-11223)***
Greene Company of Virginia Inc 276 638-7101
2075 Stultz Rd Martinsville (24112) ***(G-8292)***
Greene Horse Logging LLC 434 277-5146
704 Emblys Gap Rd Roseland (22967) ***(G-12368)***
Greenerbillcom 703 898-5354
7371 Atlas Way Ste 337 Gainesville (20155) ***(G-5587)***
Greenestep LLC 703 546-4236
5665 Lonesome Dove Ct Clifton (20124) ***(G-3669)***
Greenhill Winery and Vineyards 540 687-6968
23595 Winery Ln Middleburg (20117) ***(G-8721)***
Greenleaf Filtration LLC 804 378-7744
1500 Oakbridge Ter Ste D Powhatan (23139) ***(G-10547)***
Greenline Trucking Inc 804 638-1138
611 Green Orchard Dr Chester (23836) ***(G-3420)***
Greenrock Materials LLC 804 966-8601
2271 Roxbury Rd Charles City (23030) ***(G-2576)***
Greensprings Custom Woodwo 703 628-8058
14 Greenridge Dr Stafford (22554) ***(G-13148)***
Greenstein LLC 540 408-9877
4 Willow Glen Ct Stafford (22554) ***(G-13149)***
Greenstone Materials LLC 434 973-2113
1949 Northside Dr Charlottesville (22911) ***(G-2640)***
Greentec-Usa Inc 703 880-8332
22365 Broderick Dr # 220 Sterling (20166) ***(G-13414)***
Greentech Automotive Corp (HQ) **703 666-9001**
21355 Ridgetop Cir # 250 Sterling (20166) ***(G-13415)***
Greentree Toner, Blackstone *Also called Robert Lewis* ***(G-1826)***
Greenvision Systems Inc 703 467-8784
11710 Plaza America Dr # 2000 Reston (20190) ***(G-10863)***
Greenworks Cstm Cabinetry LLC 540 635-5725
135 Morrison Ln Front Royal (22630) ***(G-5534)***
Greenzone Systems Inc 703 567-6039
901 N Stuart St Ste 1200 Arlington (22203) ***(G-987)***
Greg & Son Pallets 757 449-3832
1500 Liberty St Chesapeake (23324) ***(G-3125)***
Greg Norman and Associates Inc (PA) **703 205-0031**
4115 Annandale Rd Ste 102 Annandale (22003) ***(G-754)***
Gregg Company Ltd 757 966-1367
1600 Dockyard Lndg Chesapeake (23321) ***(G-3126)***
Gregory Waynette 804 239-0230
62221 Leopold Cir Richmond (23234) ***(G-11043)***
Gregory Briggs 804 402-6867
6006 Westbourne Dr Richmond (23230) ***(G-11224)***
Gregory Lumber Inc 434 432-1000
12121 Halifax Rd Java (24565) ***(G-7011)***
Gregory McRrae Publishing 808 238-9907
3600 W Broad St Unit 537 Richmond (23230) ***(G-11225)***
Gregory Pallet & Lumber Co 540 777-1715
2005 Greenbrier Ave Se B Roanoke (24013) ***(G-12098)***
Gregory Wood Products, Ferrum *Also called Blue Ridge Shelving Closet LLC* ***(G-4972)***
Gregorys Fleet Supply Corp 757 490-1606
4984 Cleveland St Virginia Beach (23462) ***(G-14492)***
Gregorys Machine Shop Corp 757 490-1606
4984 Cleveland St Virginia Beach (23462) ***(G-14493)***
Gregs Fun Foods 540 382-6267
1731 Hazelnut Rd Christiansburg (24073) ***(G-3592)***
Greif Inc 434 933-4100
861 Fiber Plant Rd Gladstone (24553) ***(G-5683)***
Grektek LLC 202 607-4734
13520 Mclearen Rd Herndon (20171) ***(G-6692)***
Grey Market Labs Pbc 929 274-4465
6446 Overbrook St Falls Church (22043) ***(G-4800)***
Grey Wolf Machine Co., Dublin *Also called Dublin Machine Inc* ***(G-4154)***
Greybox Strategies LLC 276 328-3249
193 Ridgeview Rd Sw Wise (24293) ***(G-15625)***
Greystone of Virginia Inc 757 566-8070
7992 Richmond Rd Toano (23168) ***(G-13865)***
Grid2020 Inc (PA) **804 918-1982**
7405 Whitepine Rd North Chesterfield (23237) ***(G-9882)***
Griffin Industries LLC 804 876-3415
16375 Doswell Park Rd Doswell (23047) ***(G-4121)***
Griffin Manufacturing Company 757 986-4541
7704 Whaleyville Blvd Suffolk (23438) ***(G-13716)***
Griffin Pipe Products Co LLC 434 845-8021
10 Adams St Lynchburg (24504) ***(G-7725)***
Griffin Tapestry Studio 434 979-4402
1800 Yorktown Dr Charlottesville (22901) ***(G-2641)***
Griffins Perch Ironworks 434 977-0582
2259 Stony Point Rd Charlottesville (22911) ***(G-2642)***
Griffith Bag Company 540 433-2615
510 Waterman Dr Harrisonburg (22802) ***(G-6326)***
Grilletech LLC 434 941-7129
3022 Memorial Ave Lynchburg (24501) ***(G-7726)***
Grimes French Race Systems 540 923-4541
3943 Hebron Valley Rd Madison (22727) ***(G-7853)***
Grimsleys House Tools Inc 757 399-4438
355 Crawford St Ste 620 Portsmouth (23704) ***(G-10437)***
Grit Pack Calls LLC/GP Calls L 540 735-5391
34435 Parker Rd Locust Grove (22508) ***(G-7445)***
Groovin Gears 804 729-4177
1600 Roseneath Rd Ste H Richmond (23230) ***(G-11226)***
Grottoes Pallet Co Inc 540 249-4882
802 Edgewood St Grottoes (24441) ***(G-6020)***
Ground Effects Hauling Inc 757 435-1765
3905 Charity Neck Rd Virginia Beach (23457) ***(G-14494)***
Ground Ent, Roanoke *Also called Swift Print Inc* ***(G-12200)***
Groundhog Poetry Press LLC 540 366-8460
6915 Ardmore Dr Roanoke (24019) ***(G-11929)***

Grove Hill Welding Services 540 282-8252
3082 Grove Hill River Rd Shenandoah (22849) *(G-12690)*

Groves Cabinetry Inc 540 341-7309
19253 Hillcrest Ln Jeffersonton (22724) *(G-7013)*

Grubb Printing & Stamp Co Inc 757 295-8061
3303 Airline Blvd Ste 1g Portsmouth (23701) *(G-10438)*

Grupo Phoenix, Dublin *Also called Phoenix Packg Operations LLC (G-4168)*

Gryphon Software Corporat 814 486-3753
120 W Main St Floyd (24091) *(G-5027)*

Gryphon Threads LLC 707 320-7865
2232 Corbett Ave Norfolk (23518) *(G-9567)*

Gryphon Tile LLC 540 868-2953
106 Crest River Dr Middletown (22645) *(G-8739)*

Gs Industries Bassett Ltd 276 629-5317
85 Rosemont Rd Bassett (24055) *(G-1584)*

Gs Pharmaceuticals Inc (PA) **703 789-3344**
2301 Woodland Crossing Dr Herndon (20171) *(G-6693)*

Gs Plastics LLC 276 629-7981
23580 Craigs Creek Rd New Castle (24127) *(G-9120)*

Gsa Service Company 703 742-6818
1310 E Maple Ave Sterling (20164) *(G-13416)*

GSE Industries LLC 832 633-9864
321 Spinnaker Sail Ct Moneta (24121) *(G-8963)*

Gsk Corporation Inc 240 200-5600
45915 Maries Rd Unit 104 Sterling (20166) *(G-13417)*

Gst Micro LLC 203 271-0830
8356 Town Hall Ct Henrico (23231) *(G-6519)*

Gstyle7 Trucking LLC 757 367-2009
1385 Fordham Dr Virginia Beach (23464) *(G-14495)*

Gta, Sterling *Also called Greentech Automotive Corp (G-13415)*

Gtp Ventures Incorporated 804 346-8922
3825 Gaskins Rd Richmond (23233) *(G-11227)*

Gtras Inc 703 342-4282
4229 Lafayette Center Dr # 1750 Chantilly (20151) *(G-2433)*

GTS Defense MGT Svcs LLC 832 326-7227
1129 Edward Dr Ste 100 Great Falls (22066) *(G-5961)*

Guardian Fabrication LLC 276 236-5196
110 Jack Guynn Dr Galax (24333) *(G-5637)*

Guardian Galax, Galax *Also called Guardian Fabrication LLC (G-5637)*

Guardian Publishing House 804 321-2139
3319 Hanes Ave Richmond (23222) *(G-11606)*

Guardit Technologies LLC 703 232-1132
9407 Braymore Cir Fairfax Station (22039) *(G-4711)*

Guertin Bros, Roanoke *Also called John C Nordt Co Inc (G-12112)*

Guidance Software Inc 703 433-5400
21000 Atl Blvd Ste 750 Dulles (20166) *(G-4206)*

Guide To Caregiving LLC 571 213-3845
20114 Airmont Rd Round Hill (20141) *(G-12379)*

Gulf Fasteners 540 798-1992
3214 Electric Rd Roanoke (24018) *(G-11930)*

Gulfstream Aerospace Corp 301 967-9767
3150 Fairview Park Dr Falls Church (22042) *(G-4801)*

Gulfstream Aerospace Corp 912 965-3000
2941 Fairview Park Dr Falls Church (22042) *(G-4802)*

Gulfstream Aerospace Corp 540 722-0347
465 Glendobbin Rd Winchester (22603) *(G-15422)*

Gulfstream Aerospace Corp GA 301 967-9767
3150 Fairview Park Dr Falls Church (22042) *(G-4803)*

Gulp Juicery LLC 804 933-9483
2753 Dogtown Rd Goochland (23063) *(G-5884)*

Gumax Accounting Services, Woodbridge *Also called Gumax International Ltd (G-15719)*

Gumax International Ltd 866 412-3880
2862 Garber Way Woodbridge (22192) *(G-15719)*

Gundlach Aerospace LLC 703 303-0813
11480 Robert Stephens Dr Fairfax Station (22039) *(G-4712)*

Gunn Mountain Communications 303 880-8616
124 N Turnberry Williamsburg (23188) *(G-15251)*

Gunny's Call Ink, Virginia Beach *Also called Gunnys Call Inc (G-14496)*

Gunnys Call Inc 757 892-0251
2669 Highland Dr Virginia Beach (23456) *(G-14496)*

Gunz Custom Woodworks LLC 757 739-2842
2208 Rock Lake Loop Virginia Beach (23456) *(G-14497)*

Guppy Group Inc 917 544-9749
3609 Prosperity Ave Fairfax (22031) *(G-4471)*

Gutter-Stuff Industries VA LLC 540 982-1115
3408 W Ridge Cir Sw Roanoke (24014) *(G-12099)*

Guynn Group LLC 804 288-0191
8140 Greystone East Cir Richmond (23229) *(G-11228)*

Gwen Graber & Associates 703 356-9239
1617 Bryan Branch Rd Mc Lean (22101) *(G-8454)*

Gwen Nappi 703 329-4836
3309 Russell Rd Alexandria (22305) *(G-226)*

Gwendolyn H Spear 757 725-2747
2508 Oakleaf Pl Apt 201 Portsmouth (23707) *(G-10439)*

Gyrfalcon Aerial Systems LLC 757 724-1861
9211 Trumpet Ct Mechanicsville (23116) *(G-8633)*

Gyrfalcon Arial Systems Hnover, Mechanicsville *Also called Gyrfalcon Aerial Systems LLC (G-8633)*

Gyroscope Disc Golf LLC 703 992-3035
9144 Rockefeller Ln Springfield (22153) *(G-13015)*

Gyrus Systems, Henrico *Also called Manan LLC (G-6532)*

H & A Fine Woodworking 703 499-0944
10304 Nantucket Ct Fairfax (22032) *(G-4472)*

H & A Fine Woodworking (PA) **703 822-0006**
7801 Loisdale Rd Springfield (22150) *(G-13016)*

H & A Specialty Co 757 206-1115
112 Portland Williamsburg (23188) *(G-15252)*

H & B Machine 276 546-5307
1289 Rocklick Rd Keokee (24265) *(G-7040)*

H & F Body & Cabinet Shop 276 728-9404
4191 Fancy Gap Hwy Hillsville (24343) *(G-6894)*

H & H Enterprises Inc 804 684-5901
2950 George Wash Mem Hwy Hayes (23072) *(G-6399)*

H & H Industries, Spotsylvania *Also called Hairfield Lumber Corporation (G-12893)*

H & H Logging Inc 434 321-9805
864 Blankenship Pond Rd Green Bay (23942) *(G-5989)*

H & H Mining Company Inc 276 566-2105
1074 Stacy Hollow Rd Grundy (24614) *(G-6034)*

H & L Brothers Contractors LLC 703 856-1915
12250 Scarlet Maple Dr Gainesville (20155) *(G-5588)*

H & M Cabinetry 804 338-9504
2940 Queenswood Rd Midlothian (23113) *(G-8824)*

H & M Logging Inc 434 476-6569
1180 Sinai Rd South Boston (24592) *(G-12773)*

H & R Embroidery LLC 804 513-8829
12390 Goddins Hill Rd Ashland (23005) *(G-1424)*

H & R Logging 434 922-7417
111 Dancing Creek Rd Monroe (24574) *(G-8991)*

H & S Tactical LLC 540 710-2715
4920 Trade Center Dr Fredericksburg (22408) *(G-5294)*

H and R Logging, Monroe *Also called H & R Logging (G-8991)*

H B Cabinet Refacers 571 213-5257
5307 Sammie Kay Ln Centreville (20120) *(G-2309)*

H C Sexton and Associates 434 409-1073
6635 Highlander Way Crozet (22932) *(G-3834)*

H D and Company 540 651-4354
3291 Daniels Run Rd Ne Check (24072) *(G-2944)*

H H Backhoe Service 540 574-3578
4765 Pleasant Valley Rd Rockingham (22801) *(G-12254)*

H H Elements Inc 434 249-8630
4005 Gilbert Station Rd Barboursville (22923) *(G-1561)*

H L Corker & Son Inc 804 449-6686
18310 Teman Rd Beaverdam (23015) *(G-1609)*

H Moss Design 703 356-7824
1208 Old Stable Rd Mc Lean (22102) *(G-8455)*

H&G Decorative Pavers Inc 571 338-4949
8721 Linton Hall Rd Bristow (20136) *(G-2054)*

H&H Associates, Williamsburg *Also called H&H Medical Corporation (G-15253)*

H&H Hauling LLC 540 273-9109
10610 Mockingbird Ln Spotsylvania (22553) *(G-12892)*

H&H Medical Corporation 800 326-5708
328 Mclaws Cir Williamsburg (23185) *(G-15253)*

H&J, Richmond *Also called Hankins & Johann Incorporated (G-11233)*

H&L Backhoe Service Inc 540 399-5013
21025 White Rock Dr Richardsville (22736) *(G-11010)*

H&R Printing 571 277-1454
4801 Great Heron Ter Fairfax (22033) *(G-4473)*

H&W Welding Co Inc 540 334-1431
592 Harmony Rd Boones Mill (24065) *(G-1894)*

H2 As Fuel Corporation 703 980-5262
6131 Lincolnia Rd Ste 104 Alexandria (22312) *(G-472)*

H20 Pro 540 785-6811
12021 Dogwood Ave Fredericksburg (22407) *(G-5295)*

Haas Franz Machinery America, Richmond *Also called Haas Machinery Amer Inc Franz (G-11229)*

Haas Machinery Amer Inc Franz 804 222-6022
6207 Settler Rd Richmond (23231) *(G-11229)*

Haas Woodworking 540 686-5837
430 Hopewell Rd Clear Brook (22624) *(G-3644)*

Habesha View, Alexandria *Also called Dagnewcompany Inc (G-439)*

Hackney Millworks Inc 804 843-3312
300 Industrial Pkwy West Point (23181) *(G-15158)*

Hadrian Inc 703 724-7760
43849 Tattinger Ter Ashburn (20148) *(G-1288)*

Hagerstown Block Company 540 364-1531
8244 E Main St Marshall (20115) *(G-8255)*

Hagstrom Electronics Inc 540 465-4677
1986 Junction Rd Strasburg (22657) *(G-13581)*

Hague Winery LLC 804 472-9235
8268 Cople Hwy Hague (22469) *(G-6047)*

Hailey Bug Vending 757 665-4402
16501 Kegotank Rd Bloxom (23308) *(G-1841)*

Hair Studio Orie Inc 703 282-5390
12154 Penderview Ter # 1233 Fairfax (22033) *(G-4474)*

Hairbotics LLC 703 496-6083
5400 Shawnee Rd Ste 110 Alexandria (22312) *(G-473)*

Hairfield Lumber Corporation 540 967-2042
4910 Courthouse Rd Spotsylvania (22551) *(G-12893)*
Haislip Farms LLC 801 932-4087
2831 New Kent Hwy Quinton (23141) *(G-10696)*
Hal Warner Logging 540 474-5533
1118 Blue Grass Valley Rd Blue Grass (24413) *(G-1842)*
Hale Manu Inc 434 973-5850
1510 Seminole Trl Crozet (22932) *(G-3835)*
Hales Painting Inc. 540 719-1972
74 Scruggs Rd Moneta (24121) *(G-8964)*
Haley Pearsall Cabinet Makers, Richmond *Also called Haley Pearsall Inc* *(G-11230)*
Haley Pearsall Inc 804 784-3438
12601 River Rd Richmond (23238) *(G-11230)*
Half A Five Enterprise LLC 703 818-2900
4515 Daly Dr Ste J Chantilly (20151) *(G-2434)*
Halifax Fine Furnishings 540 774-3060
4525 Brambleton Ave Roanoke (24018) *(G-11931)*
Halifax Gazette Publishing Co 434 572-3945
3201 Halifax Rd 3209 South Boston (24592) *(G-12774)*
Halifax Machine & Welding Inc 434 572-3856
5043 Halifax Rd Halifax (24558) *(G-6049)*
Halifax Sign Company 434 579-3304
103 Eanes St South Boston (24592) *(G-12775)*
Hall Hflin Septic Tank Svc Inc 804 333-3124
408 Kinderhook Pike Warsaw (22572) *(G-15064)*
Hall Industries Inc 540 337-1210
162 Expo Rd Fishersville (22939) *(G-5004)*
Hall White Vineyards 434 823-8615
5190 Sugar Ridge Rd Crozet (22932) *(G-3836)*
Hallmark Fabricators Inc 804 230-0880
601 Gordon Ave Richmond (23224) *(G-11607)*
Hallmark Systems 804 744-2694
13600 Winterberry Ridge Midlothian (23112) *(G-8825)*
Halls Mechanical Services LLC 276 673-3300
2216 John Baker Rd Fieldale (24089) *(G-4987)*
Hallwood Enterprises Inc 757 357-3113
405 Grace St Smithfield (23430) *(G-12715)*
Halmor Corp 540 248-0095
103 Industry Way Staunton (24401) *(G-13263)*
Halmor Corp (PA) **434 295-3177**
1650 State Farm Blvd Charlottesville (22911) *(G-2643)*
Halo Acoustic Wear LLC 703 474-6081
42770 Hollowind Ct Broadlands (20148) *(G-2078)*
Haltrie LLC 703 598-9928
4209 Americana Dr Apt 103 Annandale (22003) *(G-755)*
Hamamelis Genomics LLC 703 939-3480
105 E Windsor Ave Alexandria (22301) *(G-227)*
Hambsch Family Vineyard LLC 434 996-1987
2559 Craigs Store Rd Afton (22920) *(G-84)*
Hamby-Stern Publishing LLC 703 425-3719
5200 Dalby Ln Burke (22015) *(G-2190)*
Hamilo LLC 703 440-1276
7413 Calamo St Springfield (22150) *(G-13017)*
Hamilton Beach Brands Inc (HQ) **804 273-9777**
4421 Waterfront Dr Glen Allen (23060) *(G-5739)*
Hamilton Beach Brands Holdg Co (PA) **804 273-9777**
4421 Waterfront Dr Glen Allen (23060) *(G-5740)*
Hamilton Equipment Service LLC 540 341-4141
25 Broadview Ave Warrenton (20186) *(G-15022)*
Hamilton Iron Works Inc 703 497-4766
14103 Telegraph Rd Woodbridge (22192) *(G-15720)*
Hamilton Perkins Collectn LLC 757 544-7161
201 W Tazewell St Apt 312 Norfolk (23510) *(G-9568)*
Hamilton Safety Center Inc 540 338-0500
39071 E Colonial Hwy Hamilton (20158) *(G-6059)*
Hammocks Print Shop 804 453-3265
14537 N Cumberland Hwy Burgess (22432) *(G-2174)*
Hammond Printing Company, Orange *Also called Jason Hammond Aldous* *(G-10216)*
Hammond United Industries LLC 571 306-9003
21 Noel Dr Fredericksburg (22408) *(G-5296)*
Hampton Canvas and Rigging 757 727-0750
4111 Kecoughtan Rd Hampton (23669) *(G-6162)*
Hampton Machine Shop Inc 757 245-9243
900 39th St Newport News (23607) *(G-9240)*
Hampton Rads Snior Lving Guide, Sterling *Also called Fairfax Publishing Company* *(G-13397)*
Hampton Roads Baking Co LLC 757 622-0347
1209 Corprew Ave Norfolk (23504) *(G-9569)*
Hampton Roads Bindery Inc 757 369-5671
15466 Warwick Blvd Newport News (23608) *(G-9241)*
Hampton Roads Canvas Co LLC 757 560-3170
4413 General Gage Ct Virginia Beach (23462) *(G-14498)*
Hampton Roads Component Assemb 757 236-8627
58 Rotherham Ln Hampton (23666) *(G-6163)*
Hampton Roads Deversified Wire, Virginia Beach *Also called Hardwire* *(G-14506)*
Hampton Roads Gazeti Inc 757 560-9583
624 Redkirk Ln Virginia Beach (23462) *(G-14499)*
Hampton Roads Green Clean LLC 757 515-8183
1328 Bolton St Norfolk (23504) *(G-9570)*

Hampton Roads Processors Inc 757 285-8811
4500 Norman Rd Portsmouth (23703) *(G-10440)*
Hampton Roads Services, Chesapeake *Also called Hampton Roads Vending* *(G-3127)*
Hampton Roads Sheet Metal Inc 757 543-6009
5821 Arrowhead Dr Ste 102 Virginia Beach (23462) *(G-14500)*
Hampton Roads Sign Inc 757 871-2307
118 Production Dr Yorktown (23693) *(G-15963)*
Hampton Roads Vending 703 927-6125
1508 Sams Cir Ste B130 Chesapeake (23320) *(G-3127)*
Hampton Roads Wedding Guide 757 474-0332
1116 Glenside Dr Virginia Beach (23464) *(G-14501)*
Hampton Roads Winery LLC 757 899-0203
6074 New Design Rd Elberon (23846) *(G-4318)*
Hampton Script, Hampton *Also called Hampton University* *(G-6164)*
Hampton Seafood Market, Hampton *Also called Graham and Rollins Inc* *(G-6160)*
Hampton Sheet Metal Inc 757 249-1629
509 Muller Ln Newport News (23606) *(G-9242)*
Hampton University 757 727-5385
203 Stone Manor Hampton (23668) *(G-6164)*
Hampton Woodworks LLC 434 989-7556
1235 Chatham Rdg Charlottesville (22901) *(G-2644)*
Hams Down Inc 540 374-1405
2007 Plank Rd Fredericksburg (22401) *(G-5193)*
Hams Enterprises LLC 703 988-0992
7421 Beckwith Ln Clifton (20124) *(G-3670)*
Hana Tonic LLC 804 993-4262
11232 Sorrel Ridge Ln Oakton (22124) *(G-10149)*
Hanbay Inc 757 333-6375
424 Investors Pl Ste 103 Virginia Beach (23452) *(G-14502)*
Hand and Hammer Inc 703 491-4866
2610 Morse Ln Woodbridge (22192) *(G-15721)*
Hand and Hammer Silversmiths, Woodbridge *Also called Hand and Hammer Inc* *(G-15721)*
Hand Signs LLC 804 482-3568
2002 National St Richmond (23231) *(G-11231)*
Handcrafters of Albemarle Ltd 434 823-4649
5786 Three Notch D Rd C Crozet (22932) *(G-3837)*
Handi-Leigh Crafted 540 349-7775
4507 Canter Ln Warrenton (20187) *(G-15023)*
Handmade Pottery 757 425-0116
612 Fort Raleigh Dr Virginia Beach (23451) *(G-14503)*
Hands Steel Mobile Welding LLC 757 805-0054
405 Nevada St Suffolk (23434) *(G-13717)*
Handy Bus Shipg & Prtg Svc, Norfolk *Also called Jeanette Ann Smith* *(G-9602)*
Handyman Concrete Inc 703 437-7143
25232 Willard Rd Chantilly (20152) *(G-2535)*
Hanesbrands Inc 276 670-4500
380 Beaver Creek Dr Martinsville (24112) *(G-8293)*
Hanesbrands Inc. 276 236-5174
1012 Glendale Rd Galax (24333) *(G-5638)*
Hanesbrands Inc. 336 519-5458
138 Elainesville Rd Stuart (24171) *(G-13614)*
Hang Men High Heating & Coolg 804 651-3320
109 Norman Dr Richmond (23227) *(G-11232)*
Hang Up 703 430-0717
22360 S Sterling Blvd D104 Sterling (20164) *(G-13418)*
Hanger Prosthetics Orthotics 703 719-0143
7011c Manchester Blvd Alexandria (22310) *(G-474)*
Hanger Prsthetcs & Ortho Inc 434 846-1803
2015 Tate Springs Rd # 1 Lynchburg (24501) *(G-7727)*
Hanger Prsthetcs & Ortho Inc 757 873-1984
704 Thmble Shls Blvd 400b Newport News (23606) *(G-9243)*
Hanguk Rice Cake Mark 757 874-4150
15320 Warwick Blvd Newport News (23608) *(G-9244)*
Hanke Industries LLC 601 665-2147
7221 Barry Rd Alexandria (22315) *(G-475)*
Hankins & Johann Incorporated 804 266-2421
7609 Compton Rd Richmond (23228) *(G-11233)*
Hanks Indexing 434 960-6805
2049 Middlebranch Dr North Garden (22959) *(G-10075)*
Hanna Sign Co 540 636-4877
20 Water St Ste 1 Front Royal (22630) *(G-5535)*
Hanneman Land Clearing Log LLC 804 909-2349
12314 Wildwood Blvd Ashland (23005) *(G-1425)*
Hanover Brassfoundry 804 781-1864
5155 Cold Harbor Rd Mechanicsville (23111) *(G-8634)*
Hanover Fabricators, Virginia Beach *Also called Structural Technologies LLC* *(G-14857)*
Hanover Foils LLC 804 496-5835
301 Hill Carter Pkwy Ashland (23005) *(G-1426)*
Hanover Herald-Progress 804 798-9031
112 Thompson St Ste B Ashland (23005) *(G-1427)*
Hanover Iron & Steel Inc 804 798-5604
11149 Leadbetter Rd Ashland (23005) *(G-1428)*
Hanover Machine & Tool Co Inc 804 746-4156
8059 Elm Dr Mechanicsville (23111) *(G-8635)*
Hanover Manufacturing Plant, Ashland *Also called Algonquin Industries Inc* *(G-1365)*
Hanover Powder Coating LL 804 798-5988
11535 Fox Cross Rd Ashland (23005) *(G-1429)*
Hanover Precast Inc 804 798-2336
12351 Maple St Ashland (23005) *(G-1430)*

(G-0000) Company's Geographic Section entry number

Hanover Wldg & Met Fabrication 804 550-2272
10998 Leadbetter Rd Ashland (23005) *(G-1431)*

Hanover Woodworking Studio LLC 804 625-5679
8032 Cadys Mill Rd Hanover (23069) *(G-6281)*

Hansen Defense Systems LLC 757 389-1683
3037 Curling Ct Chesapeake (23322) *(G-3128)*

Hansen Turbine Assemblies Corp 276 236-7184
1056 Edmonds Rd Galax (24333) *(G-5639)*

Hanson Aggregates East LLC 540 387-0271
2000 Salem Industrial Dr Salem (24153) *(G-12514)*

Hanson Industries Inc 434 845-9091
19 Millrace Dr Lynchburg (24502) *(G-7728)*

Hanwell Inc 757 213-6841
4445 Corp Ln Ste 212 Virginia Beach (23462) *(G-14504)*

Hanwha Azdel Inc 434 385-6359
2000 Enterprise Dr Forest (24551) *(G-5073)*

Hapco Division, Abingdon *Also called Kearney-National Inc* *(G-47)*

Happy Little Dumpsters LLC 540 422-0272
507 Mount Olivet Ch Rd Elkton (22827) *(G-4327)*

Happy Yard Signs 757 599-5171
813 Olive Dr Newport News (23601) *(G-9245)*

Har Tru Sports, Troy *Also called Har-Tru LLC (G-13927)*

Har-Tru LLC 434 589-1542
223 Crossroads Ctr Troy (22974) *(G-13927)*

Har-Tru LLC (HQ) 877 442-7878
2200 Old Ivy Rd Ste 100 Charlottesville (22903) *(G-2807)*

Harari Investments 703 842-7462
4600 S Four Mile Run Dr # 503 Arlington (22204) *(G-988)*

Harbinger Tech Solutions LLC 757 962-6130
2014 Granby St Ste 200 Norfolk (23517) *(G-9571)*

Harbor Entps Ltd Lblty Co 229 226-0911
800 Corporate Dr Ste 301 Stafford (22554) *(G-13150)*

Harbor House Law Press Inc 804 776-7605
17456 General Puller Hwy Deltaville (23043) *(G-4080)*

Harbour Graphics Inc 757 368-0474
641 Phoenix Dr Virginia Beach (23452) *(G-14505)*

Harco, Lynchburg *Also called Harrington Corporation (G-7729)*

Hard Wind Farm, Etlan *Also called Frye Delance (G-4373)*

Hardwire 757 410-5429
3419 Virginia Beach Blvd Virginia Beach (23452) *(G-14506)*

Hardwood Defense LLC 540 298-8906
611 Williams Ave Shenandoah (22849) *(G-12691)*

Hardwood Mulch Corporation 804 458-7500
15610 James River Dr Disputanta (23842) *(G-4108)*

Harkness Hall Ltd 540 370-1590
10 Harkness Blvd Fredericksburg (22401) *(G-5194)*

Harkness Screens (usa) Limited 540 370-1590
479 Eastpark Dr Roanoke (24019) *(G-11932)*

Harkness Screens (usa) Limited 540 370-1590
100 Rverside Pkwy Ste 209 Fredericksburg (22406) *(G-5437)*

Harlequin Custom Databases 434 823-6466
5193 Three Notch D Rd Crozet (22932) *(G-3838)*

Harmans Automotive Machine, Roanoke *Also called S Harman Machine Shop Inc (G-12173)*

Harmony Creek Vineyards LLC 540 338-7677
18548 Harmony Church Rd Hamilton (20158) *(G-6060)*

Harmony Lights Candle 434 384-5549
1088 Monacan Park Rd Madison Heights (24572) *(G-7873)*

Harmony RDS LLC 304 433-2188
44050 Woodridge Pkwy Leesburg (20176) *(G-7283)*

Harold Delano 804 333-3446
171 Fox Hunters Hill Rd Warsaw (22572) *(G-15065)*

Harold Keene Coal Co Inc 276 873-5437
Rr 67 Honaker (24260) *(G-6914)*

Harper and Taylor Custom 804 658-8753
1408 Stavemill Rd Powhatan (23139) *(G-10548)*

Harrell Marvin L & Carol L, Salem *Also called Harrell Precision (G-12515)*

Harrell Precision 540 380-2683
5756 Hickory Dr Salem (24153) *(G-12515)*

Harrell Tool Co 540 380-2666
5683 Hickory Dr Salem (24153) *(G-12516)*

Harriet Craft, Oakton *Also called Doucraft Services (G-10144)*

Harrington Corporation (PA) 434 845-7094
3721 Cohen Pl Lynchburg (24501) *(G-7729)*

Harrington Graphics Co Inc 757 363-1600
1411 Air Rail Ave Virginia Beach (23455) *(G-14507)*

Harrington Software Assoc Inc 540 349-8074
7431 Wilson Rd Warrenton (20186) *(G-15024)*

Harris Kayla 540 285-0495
2633 Springhill Dr Nw Roanoke (24017) *(G-12100)*

Harris Communications and In 703 668-7256
2235 Monroe St Herndon (20171) *(G-6694)*

Harris Company Inc 540 894-4413
252 Poplar Ave Mineral (23117) *(G-8949)*

Harris Connect LLC 757 965-8000
6315 N Center Dr Norfolk (23502) *(G-9572)*

Harris Corporation, Lynchburg *Also called L3harris Technologies Inc (G-7753)*

Harris Corporation 571 203-7605
2235 Monroe St Herndon (20171) *(G-6695)*

Harris Custom Woodworking 804 241-9525
1637 Arrowhead Rd Quinton (23141) *(G-10697)*

Harris Govt Comm Sys, Chantilly *Also called L3harris Technologies Inc (G-2455)*

Harris Healthcare, Herndon *Also called Quadramed Corporation (G-6781)*

Harris Machine Products Inc 804 784-4511
1075 Merchants Ln Oilville (23129) *(G-10179)*

Harris Printing Company Inc 540 586-8326
401 W Franklin St Bedford (24523) *(G-1640)*

Harris Publications 703 764-9279
11403 Henderson Rd Clifton (20124) *(G-3671)*

Harris Woodworking 434 295-4316
2857 Southern Hills Dr North Garden (22959) *(G-10076)*

Harrison Management Associates 703 237-0418
1000 N Kensington St Arlington (22205) *(G-989)*

Harrisonburg Feed Mill, Harrisonburg *Also called Pilgrims Pride Corporation (G-6355)*

Harrisonburg Prtg & Graphics, Rockingham *Also called Campbell Copy Center Inc (G-12243)*

Harrods Natural Resources (PA) 703 426-7200
9675 Main St Ste C Fairfax (22031) *(G-4475)*

Harry Hale Logging 540 484-1666
2195 Bonbrook Mill Rd Wirtz (24184) *(G-15612)*

Harry Jones Enterprises 276 322-5096
35240 Gvrnor G C Pery Hwy North Tazewell (24630) *(G-10100)*

Hartenshield Group Inc 302 388-4023
321 Davis Run Rd Mc Dowell (24458) *(G-8374)*

Hartman Graphics & Print 804 720-6549
3204 Glenview Ave Colonial Heights (23834) *(G-3733)*

Hartness International A Div 434 455-0357
2250 Murrell Rd Lynchburg (24501) *(G-7730)*

Harts Welding & Fabrication L 804 785-3030
1358 Buena Vista Rd Cologne (23181) *(G-3719)*

Hartung Screen Printing LLC 412 979-7847
607 Valley View Rd Ruckersville (22968) *(G-12403)*

Hartwood Landscape Inc 540 379-2650
43 Debbie Dr Fredericksburg (22406) *(G-5438)*

Hartwood Winery Inc 540 752-4893
345 Hartwood Rd Fredericksburg (22406) *(G-5439)*

Hartz Contractors Inc 757 870-2978
424 Skipjack Rd Newport News (23602) *(G-9246)*

Harvey Logging Co Inc 434 263-5942
116 Cannery Loop Lovingston (22949) *(G-7590)*

Harville Entps of Danville VA 434 822-2106
260 Gilliland Dr Danville (24541) *(G-3997)*

Harygul Imports Inc Maryland 757 427-5665
1157 Nimmo Pkwy Ste 104 Virginia Beach (23456) *(G-14508)*

Hasco Sales Inc 804 740-1869
11725 Lincolnshire Ct Glen Allen (23059) *(G-5741)*

Haskell Investment Company Inc (HQ) 276 638-8801
204 Broad St Martinsville (24112) *(G-8294)*

Hatch Graphics 540 886-2114
220 Frontier Dr Ste 104 Staunton (24401) *(G-13264)*

Hatcher Enterprises 276 673-6077
67 Duke St Fieldale (24089) *(G-4988)*

Hatcher Logging 434 352-7975
14547 Richmond Hwy Appomattox (24522) *(G-812)*

Hatcher Logging Corp Virginia 434 299-5293
14437 Big Island Hwy Big Island (24526) *(G-1703)*

Haticole Welding & Mechanical 804 443-7808
3166 Desha Rd Tappahannock (22560) *(G-13817)*

Hatter Welding Inc 540 589-3848
292 Industrial Dr Roanoke (24019) *(G-11933)*

Hatteras Silkscreen 757 486-2976
324 London Bridge Rd Ctr Virginia Beach (23454) *(G-14509)*

Hauni Richmond Inc 804 222-5259
2800 Charles City Rd Richmond (23231) *(G-11234)*

Have Happyfeet 757 339-0833
609 Obendorfer Rd Norfolk (23523) *(G-9573)*

Haverdash 804 371-1107
2100 Decatur St Richmond (23224) *(G-11608)*

Haverline Labels Inc 276 647-7785
11 Printers Ln Collinsville (24078) *(G-3712)*

Havus, Arlington *Also called Hybrid Air Vehicles (us) Inc (G-996)*

Hawes Joinery Inc 540 384-6733
3503 Jensen Pl Salem (24153) *(G-12517)*

Hawk Hill Custom LLC 540 248-4295
506 Laurel Hill Rd Verona (24482) *(G-13988)*

Hawkeye Inspection Service 804 725-9751
116 Williamsdale Ln Mathews (23109) *(G-8355)*

Hawkins Glass Wholesalers LLC 703 372-2990
9712 Gunston Cove Rd J Lorton (22079) *(G-7492)*

Hawkins Logging 434 577-2114
1394 Connell Rd Brodnax (23920) *(G-2102)*

Hawknad Manufacturing Inds Inc 703 941-0444
6193 Deer Ridge Trl Springfield (22150) *(G-13018)*

Hawleywood LLC 757 463-0910
1269 Redwood Farm Ct Virginia Beach (23452) *(G-14510)*

Hayden Enterprises 910 791-3132
1151 Eagle Pointe Way Chesapeake (23322) *(G-3129)*

Hayes Custom Sails Inc 804 642-6496
4104 George Wash Mem Hwy Hayes (23072) *(G-6400)*

A
L
P
H
A
B
E
T
I
C

Hayes Lumber Inspection Svc 804 739-0739
5414 Meadow Chase Rd Midlothian (23112) *(G-8826)*

Hayes Stair Co Inc 540 751-0201
121 N Bailey Ln Purcellville (20132) *(G-10664)*

Hayward Trmt & Pest Ctrl LLC 757 263-7858
8422 Tidewater Dr Ste B Norfolk (23518) *(G-9574)*

Haywood Machine Inc 540 663-2606
6484 Landing Rd King George (22485) *(G-7093)*

HB Inc 757 291-5236
2601 Reliance Dr Virginia Beach (23452) *(G-14511)*

HB Woodworks 703 209-4639
25921 Kimberly Rose Dr Chantilly (20152) *(G-2536)*

Hbh Holdings LLC 540 631-9555
999 Shenandoah Shores Rd Front Royal (22630) *(G-5536)*

Hbi Custom Fabrication LLC 305 916-0161
4613 Pampa Rd Gloucester (23061) *(G-5850)*

Hbp, Falls Church *Also called Balmar Inc (G-4761)*

Hcg Industries LLC 540 291-2674
1575 Wert Faulkner Hwy Natural Bridge (24578) *(G-9106)*

Hd Innovations 757 420-0774
6709 Chambers Ln Suffolk (23435) *(G-13718)*

Hdh, Richmond *Also called James E Henson Jr (G-11624)*

Hdt Engineering Services, Fredericksburg *Also called Hunter Defense Tech Inc (G-5300)*

Hdt Expeditionary Systems Inc 540 373-1435
415 Wolfe St Fredericksburg (22401) *(G-5195)*

Health Data Services Inc 434 817-9000
503 Faulconer Dr Ste 1 Charlottesville (22903) *(G-2808)*

Health E-Lunch Kids Inc 703 402-9064
7722 Willow Point Dr Falls Church (22042) *(G-4804)*

Health Journal, The, Williamsburg *Also called Brian Enterprises LLC (G-15214)*

Healthcare Simulations LLC 757 399-4502
200 High St Ste 405 Portsmouth (23704) *(G-10441)*

Healthrx Corporation (PA) **703 352-1760**
4031 University Dr # 100 Fairfax (22030) *(G-4630)*

Healthsmartvaccines LLc 703 961-0734
4437 Brkfld Crprt Dr 2 Chantilly (20151) *(G-2435)*

Healthy By Choice 810 449-5999
3534 Humboldt St Norfolk (23513) *(G-9575)*

Healthy Chef Creations 407 339-2433
5922 Autumn Dr Mc Lean (22101) *(G-8456)*

Healthy Home Enterprise 757 460-2829
4501 Delco Rd Virginia Beach (23455) *(G-14512)*

Healthy Labradors 757 740-0681
440 Monticello Ave # 1900 Norfolk (23510) *(G-9576)*

Healthy Snacks Distrs Ltd 703 627-8578
7103 Woodrise Ct Fairfax Station (22039) *(G-4713)*

Hean, Fred Furniture and Wdwrk, Charlottesville *Also called Fred Hean Furniture & Wdwrk (G-2634)*

Hear Quick Incorporated 757 523-0504
5386 Kempsriver Dr # 112 Virginia Beach (23464) *(G-14513)*

Heart Print Expressions LLC 703 221-6441
3320 Mccorkle Ct Triangle (22172) *(G-13894)*

Heart Speaks Publishing LLC 803 403-4266
1912 Starling St Apt 302 Chesapeake (23322) *(G-3130)*

Heart Star Press LLC 540 479-6882
8 Yorktown Dr Fredericksburg (22405) *(G-5440)*

Heartfelt Stitch Co 757 828-6036
3568 Ladd Ave Norfolk (23502) *(G-9577)*

Hearth & Home Technologies LLC 434 589-1482
162 Industrial Way Troy (22974) *(G-13928)*

Hearth & Home Technologies LLC 703 367-9413
10126 Hrry J Parrish Blvd Manassas (20110) *(G-7950)*

Hearth Pros 434 237-5913
20451 Timberlake Rd Lynchburg (24502) *(G-7731)*

Hearts Desire 804 790-1336
11700 Beechwood Forest Dr Chesterfield (23838) *(G-3503)*

Heartseeking LLC 305 778-8040
98 Sugarcamp Ln Stuarts Draft (24477) *(G-13648)*

Heartstrings Press LLC 804 462-0884
49 Starview Pl Lancaster (22503) *(G-7162)*

Heartwood Solid Surfaces Inc 703 369-0045
8198 Euclid Ct Manassas Park (20111) *(G-8201)*

Heathers Handcrafted Soaps 757 277-8569
2000 Waymart Ct Virginia Beach (23464) *(G-14514)*

Heavenly Aromas LLC 804 651-6250
118 N Cedar Ave Henrico (23075) *(G-6520)*

Heavenly Gates LLC 804 790-9840
10200 Christina Rd Chesterfield (23832) *(G-3504)*

Heavenly Ham, Lynchburg *Also called Commonwealth Hams Inc (G-7681)*

Heavenly Hands & Feet Inc 757 621-3938
5296 Bagpipers Ln Virginia Beach (23464) *(G-14515)*

Heavenly Kakes LLC 804 874-3711
12417 Branner Way Apt 304 Chester (23836) *(G-3421)*

Heavenly Paving LLC 804 980-9523
111 Huntsman Rd Sandston (23150) *(G-12618)*

Heavenly Sent Cupcakes LLC 540 219-2162
6401 Griffinsburg Rd Boston (22713) *(G-1904)*

Heavy Metal Construction Inc 434 547-8061
501 Greenhouse Rd Chase City (23924) *(G-2912)*

Heavyn & Hopes Candle Co 301 980-8299
6503 Grange Ln Unit 202 Alexandria (22315) *(G-476)*

Hechos Vios Publishing Inc 703 496-7019
8711 Plntn Ln Ste 301 Manassas (20110) *(G-7951)*

Heckford, Artisan of Wood, Lebanon *Also called John J Heckford (G-7194)*

Heclyn Precision Gear Company 215 739-7094
3350 Vaucluse Ln Machipongo (23405) *(G-7847)*

Heco Slings Corporation 757 855-7139
4570 Progress Rd Norfolk (23502) *(G-9578)*

Hedrick Music Inc 540 354-2139
3601 Dogwood Ln Sw Roanoke (24015) *(G-12101)*

Hee K Yoon (PA) **703 322-9208**
6408 Brass Button Ct Centreville (20121) *(G-2310)*

Heidi Ho Inc 434 736-8763
8322 George Wash Hwy Keysville (23947) *(G-7059)*

Heidi Yoder 540 432-5598
920 Smithland Rd Harrisonburg (22802) *(G-6327)*

Heinrich Enterprises Inc 540 248-1592
1081 New Hope Rd Staunton (24401) *(G-13265)*

Heintzmann Corporation (HQ) **304 284-8004**
147 Champion St Cedar Bluff (24609) *(G-2278)*

Heirloom Candle Company LLC 276 889-2505
2313 E Main St Lebanon (24266) *(G-7193)*

Heirlooms Furniture LLC 703 652-6094
1728 Creek Crossing Rd Vienna (22182) *(G-14062)*

Hek Logistics LLC 757 637-8778
17615 Harpers Ferry Dr Dumfries (22025) *(G-4247)*

Helen Heinmiller 484 459-4425
64 Cameron Cir Wirtz (24184) *(G-15613)*

Helios Acquisition LLC 757 545-6400
543 E Indian River Rd Norfolk (23523) *(G-9579)*

Helix Innovations LLC 804 274-2000
6603 W Broad St Richmond (23230) *(G-11235)*

Hellen Systems LLC 571 276-7730
9 N Liberty St Middleburg (20117) *(G-8722)*

Helltown Industries LLC 571 312-4073
1812 S Oakland St Arlington (22204) *(G-990)*

Helms Candy Co Inc 276 669-2612
3001 Lee Hwy Bristol (24202) *(G-2019)*

Help Construction Richmond LLC 804 320-3220
2520 Prof Rd Ste A Richmond (23235) *(G-11044)*

Helping Hands Home Services 757 898-3255
107 Chisman Cir Seaford (23696) *(G-12674)*

Helvetica Designs 540 213-2437
212 N Central Ave Staunton (24401) *(G-13266)*

Hemlock Design Group Inc 703 765-0379
2804 Boswell Ave Alexandria (22306) *(G-477)*

Hempceuticals LLC 757 384-2782
2150 Old Greenbrier Rd Chesapeake (23320) *(G-3131)*

Henderson Petroleum, Crozet *Also called Peter Henderson Oil Co (G-3846)*

Henderson Publishing 276 964-2291
811 Evas Walk Pounding Mill (24637) *(G-10520)*

Henkel US Operations Corp 804 222-6100
4414 Sarellen Rd Richmond (23231) *(G-11236)*

Henkel-Harris LLC 540 667-4900
2983 S Pleasant Valley Rd Winchester (22601) *(G-15547)*

Henley Cabinetry Inc 804 776-0016
10880 General Puller Hwy I Hartfield (23071) *(G-6390)*

Henrico 434 202-2331
3426 Pump Rd Henrico (23233) *(G-6521)*

Henrico Chubbys 804 285-4469
6016 W Broad St Richmond (23230) *(G-11237)*

Henrico Citizen, Richmond *Also called T3 Media LLC (G-11404)*

Henrico Tool & Die Co Inc 804 222-5017
405 Dabbs House Rd Richmond (23223) *(G-11609)*

Henry Bijak 757 572-1673
2709 Sandy Valley Rd Virginia Beach (23452) *(G-14516)*

Henry Saint-Denis LLC 540 547-6657
404 Ayrlee Ave Nw Leesburg (20176) *(G-7284)*

Henry Schein 703 883-8031
1420 Beverly Rd Ste 350 Mc Lean (22101) *(G-8457)*

Henry Shaw 844 621-2158
2800 Eisenhower Ave # 220 Alexandria (22314) *(G-228)*

Henrys Color Graphic Design 703 241-0101
6269 Leesburg Pike Falls Church (22044) *(G-4805)*

Hensley Family 540 652-8206
306 N 3rd St Shenandoah (22849) *(G-12692)*

Hensoldt Inc 703 827-3976
8614 Westwood Center Dr # 550 Vienna (22182) *(G-14063)*

Herald Press 540 434-6701
1251 Virginia Ave Harrisonburg (22802) *(G-6328)*

Herald Schlrly Open Access LLC 202 412-2272
41891 Fraser Downs Ter Aldie (20105) *(G-107)*

Herald Square LLC 540 477-2019
3691 Conicville Rd Mount Jackson (22842) *(G-9072)*

Herald-Progress-Hano, Ashland *Also called Hanover Herald-Progress (G-1427)*

Herb Dodge Enterprises 757 714-4313
1601 Rokeby Ave Chesapeake (23325) *(G-3132)*

Herbal Origins LLC 804 715-0015
11650 Belvdr Vista Ln # 103 North Chesterfield (23235) *(G-9883)*

(G-0000) Company's Geographic Section entry number

Herban House Beauty LLC 443 934-9041
  3612 Dock Point Arch Chesapeake (23321) *(G-3133)*

Herbs of Happy Hill, Chester *Also called Katherine Chain (G-3426)*

Herbsforhealth 757 383-1245
  6000 Old College Dr # 187 Suffolk (23435) *(G-13719)*

Herbspice LLC 240 602-6525
  2753 Dogtown Rd Goochland (23063) *(G-5885)*

Hercules Inc 804 541-4545
  1111 Hercules Rd Hopewell (23860) *(G-6928)*

Hercules Steel Company Inc 434 535-8571
  305 Jarratt Ave Jarratt (23867) *(G-7010)*

Hereisursign LLC 757 277-8487
  169 W Ocean Ave Norfolk (23503) *(G-9580)*

Herff Jones LLC 804 598-0971
  2020 New Dorset Rd Powhatan (23139) *(G-10549)*

Herff Jones LLC 757 689-3000
  2556 Horse Pasture Rd Virginia Beach (23453) *(G-14517)*

Herff Jones LLC 703 368-9550
  9426 Robnel Ave Manassas (20110) *(G-7952)*

Heritage Cabinets Inc 804 861-5251
  23024 Airpark Dr North Dinwiddie (23803) *(G-10052)*

Heritage Electrical Corp 804 743-4614
  7725 Whitepine Rd North Chesterfield (23237) *(G-9884)*

Heritage Interiors LLC 571 323-5200
  2553 Dulles View Dr Herndon (20171) *(G-6696)*

Heritage Log Homes 540 854-4926
  29502 Mine Run Rd Unionville (22567) *(G-13963)*

Heritage Printing LLC 804 378-1196
  11331 Bsneva Ctr Dr Ste C Richmond (23236) *(G-11045)*

Heritage Printing Service Inc 804 233-3024
  2611 Decatur St Richmond (23224) *(G-11610)*

Heritage Treasures LLC 571 442-8027
  44710 Cape Ct Ste 120 Ashburn (20147) *(G-1289)*

Heritage Woodworks LLC (PA) **757 934-1440**
  1002 Obici Indus Blvd Suffolk (23434) *(G-13720)*

Heritage Woodworks LLC 757 417-7337
  512 Pinewood Dr Virginia Beach (23451) *(G-14518)*

Hermes Abr Ltd A Ltd Partnr (PA) **800 464-8314**
  524 Viking Dr Virginia Beach (23452) *(G-14519)*

Hermes Abrasives Inc 757 486-6623
  524 Viking Dr Virginia Beach (23452) *(G-14520)*

Hermetic Networks Inc 804 545-3173
  7637 Hull Street Rd # 201 North Chesterfield (23235) *(G-9885)*

Hermitage Industries Co Inc 757 638-4551
  3008 Trappers Run Chesapeake (23321) *(G-3134)*

Hermle North America, Amherst *Also called Hermle Uhren GMBH & Co KG (G-693)*

Hermle Uhren GMBH & Co KG 434 946-7751
  340 Industrial Park Dr Amherst (24521) *(G-693)*

Herndon Publishing Co Inc 703 689-0111
  1043 Sterling Rd Ste 104 Herndon (20170) *(G-6697)*

Hernley Woodworks 571 419-4889
  42649 Cochrans Lock Dr Ashburn (20148) *(G-1290)*

Heroes Apparel LLC 804 304-1001
  1614 Ownby Ln Richmond (23220) *(G-11611)*

Heroes Bottled Water, Gainesville *Also called Winmar Business Group (G-5622)*

Hershey Company 540 324-0166
  120 Harold Cook Dr Stuarts Draft (24477) *(G-13649)*

Hershey Company 540 722-9830
  300 Park Center Dr Winchester (22603) *(G-15423)*

Hesco of Virginia LLC 276 694-2818
  25582 Jeb Stuart Hwy Stuart (24171) *(G-13615)*

Hess Publications 540 771-7515
  1983 Lockes Mill Rd Berryville (22611) *(G-1681)*

Hesss Body Shop 276 395-7808
  303 2nd St Sw Coeburn (24230) *(G-3699)*

Hewlett-Packard Federal LLC 800 727-5472
  13600 Eds Dr Herndon (20171) *(G-6698)*

Hexmag LLC 970 203-9100
  2697 Intl Pkwy Ste 100-1 Virginia Beach (23452) *(G-14521)*

Hey Frase LLC 202 372-5453
  919 N Lincoln St Apt 653 Arlington (22201) *(G-991)*

Heyco Werk USA Inc 434 634-8810
  300 Industrial Park Way Emporia (23847) *(G-4360)*

Heytex USA Inc 540 674-9576
  4090 Pepperell Way Dublin (24084) *(G-4157)*

Heytex USA Inc (HQ) **540 980-2640**
  509 Burgis Ave Pulaski (24301) *(G-10637)*

Heytopia LLC 703 794-3082
  8421 Broad St Unit 1516 Mc Lean (22102) *(G-8458)*

Heyward Inc Virginia Inc 804 965-0086
  10146 W Broad St Glen Allen (23060) *(G-5742)*

HHh Underground LLC 804 365-6905
  10353 Cedar Ln Glen Allen (23059) *(G-5743)*

HI Caliber Manufacturing LLC 804 955-8300
  11263 Air Park Rd Ste B-4 Ashland (23005) *(G-1432)*

Hi-Lite Solutions Inc 540 450-8375
  1285 Brucetown Rd Clear Brook (22624) *(G-3645)*

Hi-Tech Cabinets Inc 757 681-0016
  129 Pennsylvania Ave Virginia Beach (23462) *(G-14522)*

Hi-Tech Machining LLC 434 993-3256
  1481 Doss Rd Concord (24538) *(G-3760)*

Hi-Tech Machining LLC 434 993-3256
  1481 Doss Rd Concord (24538) *(G-3761)*

Hi-Tech Pharmacal Co Inc 804 935-7220
  9878 Maryland Dr Richmond (23233) *(G-11238)*

Hibbard Iron Works of Hampton 757 826-5611
  514 Aberdeen Rd Hampton (23661) *(G-6165)*

Hibbard's Iron Works, Hampton *Also called Hibbard Iron Works of Hampton (G-6165)*

Hibernate Inc 804 513-1777
  14249 Big Apple Rd Glen Allen (23059) *(G-5744)*

Hibiscus Chesecake Elixirs LLC 757 932-2539
  4131 Williamson St Chesapeake (23324) *(G-3135)*

Hickey Electric Co Inc 434 384-1896
  4262 S Amherst Hwy # 100 Madison Heights (24572) *(G-7874)*

Hickey Electric Heating and A, Madison Heights *Also called Hickey Electric Co Inc (G-7874)*

Hickman Surfboards 757 427-2914
  2180 General Booth Blvd Virginia Beach (23454) *(G-14523)*

Hickory Embroidery LLC 757 482-0873
  1805 Sanderson Rd Chesapeake (23322) *(G-3136)*

Hickory Frame Corp 434 847-8489
  1400 Thurman Ave Lynchburg (24501) *(G-7732)*

Hickory Hill Consulting LLC 804 363-2719
  9174 Hickory Hill Rd Ashland (23005) *(G-1433)*

Hickory Hill Vineyards LLC 540 296-1393
  1722 Hickory Cove Ln Moneta (24121) *(G-8965)*

Hickory Ridge Designs Inc 888 236-8431
  1103 Brookdale St Ste A Martinsville (24112) *(G-8295)*

Hicks Welding LLC Richard L 434 392-9824
  23 Raines Rd Farmville (23901) *(G-4943)*

Hidden Treasures, Alexandria *Also called Word Play By Deb LLC (G-614)*

Hideaway Tannery LLC 540 421-2640
  153 Thorofare Rd Crimora (24431) *(G-3821)*

Hidemand Supplements LLC 757 224-3485
  299 Floyd Thompson Blvd Hampton (23666) *(G-6166)*

Higgins Inc 540 636-3756
  2091 Guard Hill Rd Middletown (22645) *(G-8740)*

Higgins & Associates, Middletown *Also called Higgins Inc (G-8740)*

High Bridge Trail State Park 434 315-0457
  6888 Green Bay Rd Green Bay (23942) *(G-5990)*

High Concepts 804 683-2226
  9509 Brant Ln Glen Allen (23060) *(G-5745)*

High Ground Partners LLC 434 944-8254
  1423 Robin Hood Pl Lynchburg (24503) *(G-7733)*

High Hat Inc 703 212-7446
  380 S Pickett St Alexandria (22304) *(G-229)*

High Impact Music For You LLC 757 915-8696
  630 Windomere Ave Richmond (23227) *(G-11239)*

High Peak Sportswear Inc 540 953-1293
  209 College Ave Blacksburg (24060) *(G-1743)*

High Peak Teeshirt Factory, Blacksburg *Also called High Peak Sportswear Inc (G-1743)*

High Peaks Knife Works 276 694-6563
  976 Carter Mountain Rd Stuart (24171) *(G-13616)*

High Performance Optics Inc 513 258-5978
  5241 Valleypark Dr Roanoke (24019) *(G-11934)*

High Qulty Cnstr Rockingham Co, Rockingham *Also called Hqc Inc (G-12255)*

High Speed Networks LLC 703 963-4572
  22959 Rock Hill Rd Sterling (20166) *(G-13419)*

High Speed Tech Ventr LLC 571 318-0997
  120 Tutters Neck Williamsburg (23185) *(G-15254)*

High Stakes Writing LLC 703 819-5490
  6920 Braddock Rd B-614 Annandale (22003) *(G-756)*

High Threat Concealment LLC 757 208-0221
  309 Mclaws Cir Ste K Williamsburg (23185) *(G-15255)*

High Tide Publications Inc 804 815-6805
  1000 Bland Point Rd Deltaville (23043) *(G-4081)*

Highbrow Magazine LLC 571 480-2867
  9430 Lakeside Dr Vienna (22182) *(G-14064)*

Higher Lving Publications Corp 804 789-0592
  8290 Carrolton Ridge Pl Mechanicsville (23111) *(G-8636)*

Higher Press LLC 703 944-1521
  12209 Dapple Gray Ct Woodbridge (22192) *(G-15722)*

Highland Bears and More 757 480-1125
  8263 Simons Dr Norfolk (23505) *(G-9581)*

Highland Environmental Inc 540 392-6067
  3702 Nolley Rd Riner (24149) *(G-11863)*

Highland Sign, Abingdon *Also called Christopher A Dixon (G-23)*

Highland Timber Frame Inc 540 745-7411
  1019 Thunderstruck Rd Ne Floyd (24091) *(G-5028)*

Highland Wldg Fabrication LLC 540 474-3105
  5221 Potomac River Rd Monterey (24465) *(G-9006)*

Highlands Glass Company LLC 276 623-0021
  918 E Main St Abingdon (24210) *(G-36)*

Highlands Log Structures Inc 276 623-1580
  26289 Harrison Rd Abingdon (24210) *(G-37)*

Highlands Welding and Fabr 276 429-4438
  33438 Seven Springs Rd R Glade Spring (24340) *(G-5678)*

Highpoint Glass Works 757 442-7155
  30389 Bobtown Rd Pungoteague (23422) *(G-10650)*

Highstar Industrial Tech................................757 398-9300
  1410 Court St Portsmouth (23704) *(G-10442)*

Hightech Signs, Charlottesville *Also called Frf Inc (G-2636)*

Highwheel Woodworks................................540 287-8575
  6708 Holladay Ln Spotsylvania (22551) *(G-12894)*

Hii Unmnned Mrtime Systems Inc (HQ)..........**757 688-5672**
  4101 Washington Ave Newport News (23607) *(G-9247)*

Hilden America Inc................................434 572-3965
  1044 Commerce Ln South Boston (24592) *(G-12776)*

Hill Brenton................................757 560-9332
  37 Kenilworth Dr Hampton (23666) *(G-6167)*

Hill Phoenix Inc................................804 317-6882
  1925 Ruffin Mill Rd South Chesterfield (23834) *(G-12805)*

Hill Phoenix Inc................................804 317-6882
  1925 Ruffin Mill Rd South Chesterfield (23834) *(G-12806)*

Hill Phoenix Inc................................712 563-4623
  1925 Ruffin Mill Rd South Chesterfield (23834) *(G-12807)*

Hill Phoenix Inc................................800 283-1109
  1301 Battery Brooke Pkwy North Chesterfield (23237) *(G-9886)*

Hill Phoenix Inc................................804 526-4455
  1925 Ruffin Mill Rd South Chesterfield (23834) *(G-12808)*

Hill Top Berry Frm & Winery Lc................................434 361-1266
  2800 Berry Hill Rd Nellysford (22958) *(G-9113)*

Hill Top Distillery LLC................................804 212-8645
  6020 Stonewick Ct Glen Allen (23059) *(G-5746)*

Hill Welding Services Corp................................540 923-4474
  162 Duet Rd Madison (22727) *(G-7854)*

Hillco Disposal & Recycl LLC................................757 301-9669
  2129 General Booth Blvd # 10322 Virginia Beach (23454) *(G-14524)*

Hillcraft Machine & Welding................................804 779-2280
  1069 Old Church Rd Mechanicsville (23111) *(G-8637)*

Hillcraft Machine Company, Mechanicsville *Also called Hillcraft Machine & Welding (G-8637)*

Hillcrest Transportation Inc (PA)................................**804 861-1100**
  25452 Hofheimer Way North Dinwiddie (23803) *(G-10053)*

Hillmans Distributors................................540 774-1896
  3603 Cedar Ln Roanoke (24018) *(G-11935)*

Hills Bros Coffee Incorporated................................757 538-8083
  1370 Progress Rd Suffolk (23434) *(G-13721)*

Hills Coal and Trucking Co................................276 565-2560
  4719 Callahan Ave Appalachia (24216) *(G-797)*

Hillsborough Vineyards, Hillsboro *Also called Continental Commercial Corp (G-6861)*

Hilltop Hideaway Alpacas LLC................................954 410-7238
  511 Bennetts Springs Ln Craigsville (24430) *(G-3806)*

Hilltop Sand and Gravel Co Inc................................571 322-0389
  8245 Backlick Rd Ste D2 Lorton (22079) *(G-7493)*

Hillwood Park Inc................................703 754-6105
  14280 Gardner Manor Pl Gainesville (20155) *(G-5589)*

Hinkle Welding & Fabrication................................434 447-2770
  1415 Hinkle Rd Kenbridge (23944) *(G-7033)*

Hip Occasions LLC................................540 695-8896
  9504 Moores Creek Dr Fredericksburg (22408) *(G-5297)*

Hip-Hop Spot 24/7 LLC................................434 660-3166
  100 Holmes Cir Apt 4 Lynchburg (24501) *(G-7734)*

Hipkins Horticulture Co LLC................................804 926-7116
  10500 Chesdin Ridge Dr South Chesterfield (23803) *(G-12835)*

Hipro Call Inc................................703 397-5155
  11921 Freedom Dr Reston (20190) *(G-10864)*

Hirsch Communication................................703 960-3649
  5904 Mount Eagle Dr Alexandria (22303) *(G-478)*

Hirschfeld Steel, Bristol *Also called W&W-Afco Steel LLC (G-2040)*

His Sign LLC................................877 886-8879
  44050 Ashbrn Shpg Plz Ashburn (20147) *(G-1291)*

Hispanic Newspaper Inc................................703 478-6806
  761c Monroe St Ste 200 Herndon (20170) *(G-6699)*

Hispanic Yellow Pages, Fairfax *Also called Vega Productions & Associates (G-4578)*

Historic Organ Study Tours, Richmond *Also called Raven Enterprises LLC (G-11346)*

Historynet, Vienna *Also called World History Group LLC (G-14162)*

Historynet LLC................................703 779-8322
  1919 Gallows Rd Ste 400 Vienna (22182) *(G-14065)*

Hitachi Vantara Federal Corp................................703 787-2900
  11950 Democracy Dr # 200 Reston (20190) *(G-10865)*

Hitachi Vantara LLC................................405 593-3783
  2201 Coop Way Ste 300 Herndon (20171) *(G-6700)*

Hitchcock Paper Co................................571 398-6601
  125 Mill St Occoquan (22125) *(G-10173)*

Hitek Powder Coating................................434 845-7000
  314 Miles Ln Evington (24550) *(G-4377)*

Hitek Sealing Corporation................................434 944-2404
  191 Police Tower Rd Appomattox (24522) *(G-813)*

Hj Shelton Logging Inc................................434 432-3840
  1565 Transco Rd Chatham (24531) *(G-2929)*

Hjk Contracting Inc................................703 793-8127
  12504 Nathaniel Oaks Dr Herndon (20171) *(G-6701)*

Hjs Qwik Signs................................276 386-2696
  772 Filter Plant Frd Gate City (24251) *(G-5663)*

Hkd Snowmakers Com................................540 451-1779
  83 Fall Ridge Dr Stuarts Draft (24477) *(G-13650)*

Hkl Research Inc (PA)................................**434 979-6382**
  310 Old Ivy Way Ste 301 Charlottesville (22903) *(G-2809)*

Hkl Research Inc................................434 979-5569
  455 Rookwood Dr Charlottesville (22903) *(G-2810)*

Hlk Custom Stainless Inc................................571 261-5811
  10476 Godwin Dr Manassas (20112) *(G-8078)*

HM Trucking................................703 932-7058
  1358 Rock Chapel Rd Herndon (20170) *(G-6702)*

Hmb Inc................................540 967-1060
  119 Jefferson Hwy Louisa (23093) *(G-7556)*

Hmt Publishers LLC................................540 839-5628
  11328 Sam Snead Hwy Hot Springs (24445) *(G-6946)*

Hnh Partners LLC................................757 539-2353
  7535 Little River Tpke Annandale (22003) *(G-757)*

Ho-Ho-Kus Incorporated................................206 552-4559
  10911 Southlake Ct North Chesterfield (23236) *(G-9887)*

Hobbs Door Service................................757 436-6529
  4953 Providence Rd Virginia Beach (23464) *(G-14525)*

Hobbs Logging Inc................................276 628-4952
  22505 Breezy Point Rd Abingdon (24211) *(G-38)*

Hockey Stick Builds LLC................................617 784-2918
  2345 Highland Ave Falls Church (22046) *(G-4917)*

Hocl Inc................................877 435-4625
  3656 Centerview Dr Ste 6 Chantilly (20151) *(G-2436)*

Hodges & Miller Logging, South Boston *Also called H & M Logging Inc (G-12773)*

Hodges Sheet Metal LLC................................276 957-5344
  3134 Golf Course Rd Spencer (24165) *(G-12873)*

Hodges Typographers, Falls Church *Also called Hto Inc (G-4806)*

Hodges Watch Company LLC................................703 651-6440
  204 Pennsylvania Ave Falls Church (22046) *(G-4918)*

Hoffman Pottery................................276 773-3546
  100 Driftwood Ln Independence (24348) *(G-6985)*

Hoffmanns Custom Display Cases................................804 332-4873
  218 Algiers Dr Sandston (23150) *(G-12619)*

Hogar Controls................................703 844-1160
  46040 Center Oak Plz # 125 Sterling (20166) *(G-13420)*

Hogue................................540 374-1144
  210 Amaret St Fredericksburg (22401) *(G-5196)*

Hol Industries LLC................................703 835-5476
  8588 Richmond Hwy Alexandria (22309) *(G-479)*

Holcim LLC................................703 622-4616
  2316 Cedar Ln Vienna (22182) *(G-14066)*

Holcomb Rock Company................................434 386-6050
  4839 Holcomb Rock Rd Lynchburg (24503) *(G-7735)*

Holderby & Bierce Inc................................434 971-8571
  180 Walnut Ln Charlottesville (22911) *(G-2645)*

Holiday Ice Inc................................757 934-1294
  1200 Progress Rd Suffolk (23434) *(G-13722)*

Holland Lumber Co Inc................................804 443-4200
  Hwy 360 Millers Tavern (23115) *(G-8940)*

Holland Sand Pit LLC................................757 745-7140
  1652 Pine Acres Suffolk (23432) *(G-13723)*

Hollawood Publishing LLC................................804 353-3310
  2317 Westwood Ave 201a Richmond (23230) *(G-11240)*

Hollinger Metal Edge Inc................................540 898-7300
  9401 Northeast Dr Fredericksburg (22408) *(G-5298)*

Hollinger Metal Edge - VA Inc (PA)................................**540 898-7300**
  9401 Northeast Dr Fredericksburg (22408) *(G-5299)*

Hollingsworth & Vose Company................................540 745-7600
  289 Parkview Rd Ne Floyd (24091) *(G-5029)*

Hollis Books LLC................................703 855-7759
  5904 Mount Eagle Dr # 1009 Alexandria (22303) *(G-480)*

Hollister Incorporated................................540 943-1733
  366 Draft Ave Stuarts Draft (24477) *(G-13651)*

Holly Beach Woodworker Inc................................757 831-1410
  3801 Hearthside Ln Virginia Beach (23453) *(G-14526)*

Hollybrook Mulch Trucking Inc................................540 381-7830
  505 College St Christiansburg (24073) *(G-3593)*

Hollys Homemade Treats................................540 977-1373
  5448 Setter Rd Roanoke (24012) *(G-12102)*

Hollywood Graphics and Signs................................804 382-2199
  1135 Bradbury Rd Moseley (23120) *(G-9040)*

Hollywood Signs, North Dinwiddie *Also called Richardson Enterprises Inc (G-10063)*

Holmes Enterprises Inc................................804 798-9201
  11114 Leadbetter Rd Ashland (23005) *(G-1434)*

Holmes Enterprises Intl Inc................................804 798-9201
  11114 Leadbetter Rd Ashland (23005) *(G-1435)*

Holston River Quarry Inc (PA)................................**540 380-5556**
  5764 Wilderness Rd Dublin (24084) *(G-4158)*

Holtzbrinck Publishers LLC................................540 672-7600
  16365 James Madison Hwy Gordonsville (22942) *(G-5907)*

Holtzman Express................................305 347-4000
  1511 Martinsburg Pike Winchester (22603) *(G-15424)*

Home Brewusa (PA)................................**757 459-2739**
  5802 E Virginia Bch Blvd Norfolk (23502) *(G-9582)*

Home Decor Sewing................................804 364-8750
  5814 Shady Hills Way Glen Allen (23059) *(G-5747)*

Home Fx................................540 455-5269
  12709 Plantation Dr Spotsylvania (22551) *(G-12895)*

Home Pride Inc................................276 642-0271
  21528 Travalite Dr Ste 2 Bristol (24202) *(G-2020)*

Home Pride Inc (PA) 276 466-0502
  15100 Indl Pk Rd Bristol (24202) *(G-2021)*

Home Printing 804 333-4678
  116 Little Creek Rd Warsaw (22572) *(G-15066)*

Home Search Magazine, Norfolk *Also called Pilot Media* *(G-9689)*

Home Town Computers, Portsmouth *Also called Bander Computers* *(G-10396)*

Homeactions LLC 703 698-7750
  2724 Dorr Ave Ste 103 Fairfax (22031) *(G-4476)*

Homeland Corporation 571 218-6200
  47202 Redbark Pl Sterling (20165) *(G-13421)*

Homeland Defense Journal 703 622-1187
  4301 Wilson Blvd Ste 1003 Arlington (22203) *(G-992)*

Homeplace Distillery LLC 276 957-3310
  10 Fall Creek Rd Ridgeway (24148) *(G-11845)*

Homeplace Vineyard Inc 434 432-9463
  880 Climax Rd Chatham (24531) *(G-2930)*

Homer Haywood Wheeler II 434 946-5126
  836 Campbells Mill Rd Amherst (24521) *(G-694)*

Homes & Land of Richmond 804 794-8494
  1811 Huguenot Rd Ste 201 Midlothian (23113) *(G-8827)*

Homes & Land of Virginia LLC 804 357-7005
  15764 Wc Main St Midlothian (23113) *(G-8828)*

Homested Material Handlings 804 299-3389
  2416 Lanier Rd Rockville (23146) *(G-12286)*

Hometown Creations 434 237-2364
  1059 Coronado Ln Lynchburg (24502) *(G-7736)*

Hometown Ice Co 540 483-7865
  520 Weaver St Rocky Mount (24151) *(G-12327)*

Hometown Imprints Inc 540 878-5848
  5439 Old Alexandria Tpke Warrenton (20187) *(G-15025)*

Honaker & Son Logging LLC 434 661-7935
  262 Bryant Hollow Rd Amherst (24521) *(G-695)*

Honaker Son Logging 434 933-8251
  62 Old Thirteen Ln Gladstone (24553) *(G-5684)*

Hone Blade LLC 804 370-8598
  9014 Brigadier Rd Mechanicsville (23116) *(G-8638)*

Honest Abe Log Homes Inc 800 231-3695
  200 Meadowood Trl Martinsville (24112) *(G-8296)*

Honey Gunters 540 955-1734
  100 Bee Line Ln Berryville (22611) *(G-1682)*

Honey Haleys Meadery LLC 804 668-5943
  235 E Broadway Hopewell (23860) *(G-6929)*

Honey True Teas LLC 703 728-8369
  2021 Mayflower Dr Woodbridge (22192) *(G-15723)*

Honeycutts Mobile Marine 757 898-7793
  211 Mastin Ave Seaford (23696) *(G-12675)*

Honeywell Authorized Dealer, Mount Crawford *Also called Riddleberger Brothers Inc* *(G-9058)*

Honeywell International Inc 804 458-7649
  105 Winston Churchill Dr Hopewell (23860) *(G-6930)*

Honeywell International Inc 804 518-2351
  220 Perry St Petersburg (23803) *(G-10324)*

Honeywell International Inc 804 541-5000
  905 E Randolph Rd Hopewell (23860) *(G-6931)*

Honeywell International Inc 804 515-1500
  7870 Villa Park Dr # 900 Richmond (23228) *(G-11241)*

Honeywell International Inc 276 694-2408
  636 Commerce St Stuart (24171) *(G-13617)*

Honeywell International Inc 703 879-9951
  400 Herndon Pkwy Ste 100 Herndon (20170) *(G-6703)*

Honeywell International Inc 804 520-3000
  15801 Woods Edge Rd South Chesterfield (23834) *(G-12809)*

Honeywell International Inc 804 530-6352
  4101 Bermuda Hundred Rd Chester (23836) *(G-3422)*

Honeywell International Inc 703 626-8363
  1530 Wilson Blvd Ste 1000 Arlington (22209) *(G-993)*

Honeywell International Inc 804 541-5618
  7006 Laprade St Hopewell (23860) *(G-6932)*

Honeywell International Inc 703 437-7651
  105 Carpenter Dr Sterling (20164) *(G-13422)*

Honeywell Resins & Chem LLC (HQ) 804 541-5000
  905 E Randolph Rd Bldg 97 Hopewell (23860) *(G-6933)*

Honeywell Technology Solu 703 551-1942
  635 Telegraph Rd Stafford (22554) *(G-13151)*

Honor & Pride, Virginia Beach *Also called Crouch Petra* *(G-14373)*

Hooke Brothers Lumber Co LLC 540 499-2540
  Hwy 84 17 Miles W Monterey (24465) *(G-9007)*

Hooker Furniture Corporation (PA) 276 632-2133
  440 Commonwealth Blvd E Martinsville (24112) *(G-8297)*

Hooker Furniture Corporation 276 632-1763
  850 Hooker St Martinsville (24112) *(G-8298)*

Hooker Printing Inc 336 339-4802
  11 Printers Ln Collinsville (24078) *(G-3713)*

Hoover Color Corporation 540 980-7233
  2170 Julia Simpkins Rd Hiwassee (24347) *(G-6912)*

Hope Crushed Vineyard LLC 540 668-6587
  12970 Harpers Ferry Rd Hillsboro (20132) *(G-6870)*

Hope Springs Media 434 574-2031
  988 Sulphur Spring Rd Prospect (23960) *(G-10612)*

Hopewell Hardwood Sales Inc 804 458-5178
  13513 Old Stage Rd North Prince George (23860) *(G-10088)*

Hopewell Publishing Company 804 452-6127
  516 E Randolph Rd Hopewell (23860) *(G-6934)*

Hopkins Lumber Contractors Inc 276 694-2166
  29673 Jeb Stuart Hwy Stuart (24171) *(G-13618)*

Horizon Custom Cabinets Corp 757 434-8706
  2697 Intl Pkwy Ste 100-3 Virginia Beach (23452) *(G-14527)*

Horizon Custom Cabinets Corp 757 306-1007
  2697 Intl Pkwy Ste 100-3 Virginia Beach (23452) *(G-14528)*

Horizon Global Partners LLC 703 597-2351
  20097 Old Line Ter Ashburn (20147) *(G-1292)*

Hormel Foods Corporation 757 467-5396
  1681 Wicomico Ln Virginia Beach (23464) *(G-14529)*

Horn Construction Co Inc 276 935-4749
  Rr 83 Grundy (24614) *(G-6035)*

Horn Well Drilling Inc Noah 276 935-5902
  1070 Sandy Valley Ln Oakwood (24631) *(G-10168)*

Horse Pasture Mfg LLC 276 952-2558
  1202 Luke Helms Rd Meadows of Dan (24120) *(G-8591)*

Horse Sense Balanced 540 253-9987
  4292 Belvoir Rd Marshall (20115) *(G-8256)*

Horsemans Knives LLC 540 854-6975
  6317 Louisianna Rd Locust Grove (22508) *(G-7446)*

Horseshoe Bend Imprvs LLC 434 969-1672
  1253 Axtell Rd Howardsville (24562) *(G-6951)*

Horton Cellars Winery Inc 540 832-7440
  6399 Spotswood Trl Gordonsville (22942) *(G-5908)*

Horton Publishing Co 703 281-6963
  2200 Trott Ave Vienna (22181) *(G-14067)*

Horton Vineyards, Gordonsville *Also called Horton Cellars Winery Inc* *(G-5908)*

Horton Welding LLC 757 346-8405
  10454 Sylvia Cir Windsor (23487) *(G-15605)*

Horton Wreath Society Inc 757 617-2093
  1401 Trapelo Ct Virginia Beach (23456) *(G-14530)*

Hoskins Creek Table Company 804 333-0032
  3123 Richmond Rd Warsaw (22572) *(G-15067)*

Hoskins Woodworking Llc Jose 434 825-2883
  537 2nd St Ne Charlottesville (22902) *(G-2811)*

Hospice Gowns By Lou-Voise, Glen Allen *Also called Lou-Voise* *(G-5765)*

Hoss Excavating & Logging Co L 276 628-4068
  15402 Providence Rd Abingdon (24210) *(G-39)*

Hot Stamp Supply Company 540 868-7500
  141 Marcel Dr 2 Winchester (22602) *(G-15425)*

Hot Worx Inc 757 967-9809
  230 Sandpiper Dr Portsmouth (23704) *(G-10443)*

Hotbed Technologies Inc 703 462-2350
  6718 Whittier Ave Ste 100 Mc Lean (22101) *(G-8459)*

Hotrodz Performance & Motor 571 337-2988
  2961a Hunter Mill Rd # 106 Oakton (22124) *(G-10150)*

Hotspot Energy Inc 757 410-8640
  4021 Holland Blvd Chesapeake (23323) *(G-3137)*

Houff Corporation (HQ) **540 234-8088**
  97 Railside Dr Weyers Cave (24486) *(G-15173)*

Houff Corporation 540 234-9246
  10394 Doswell Rd Doswell (23047) *(G-4122)*

Houghtaling Associates Inc 804 740-7098
  2830 Ackley Ave Ste 101 Richmond (23228) *(G-11242)*

Houghton Mifflin Harcourt Pubg 540 434-0137
  1170 S Dogwood Dr Harrisonburg (22801) *(G-6329)*

Houghton Mifflin Harcourt Pubg 703 243-2602
  1600 Wilson Blvd Ste 710 Arlington (22209) *(G-994)*

House of Stitches & Prints Inc 276 525-1796
  1271 W Main St Abingdon (24210) *(G-40)*

House of Vondrake Lavar LLC 804 295-6136
  207 Archer Ave Colonial Heights (23834) *(G-3734)*

Household 6, Gore *Also called Tamara Smith* *(G-5923)*

Houser Sign Works 804 539-1315
  11242 Hopson Rd Ste 13 Ashland (23005) *(G-1436)*

Housing Associates, Roanoke *Also called Richard Evans* *(G-11995)*

How High Publishing LLC 703 729-9589
  44383 Oakmont Manor Sq Ashburn (20147) *(G-1293)*

Howards Precision Mch Sp Inc 540 890-2342
  2035 Blue Ridge Sprng Rd Blue Ridge (24064) *(G-1850)*

Howards Signs LLC 804 815-8333
  14296 John Clyton Mem Hwy North (23128) *(G-9803)*

Howdyshells Welding 540 886-1960
  505 Statler Blvd Staunton (24401) *(G-13267)*

Howmedica Osteonics Corp 804 737-9426
  5500 Cox Rd Ste K Glen Allen (23060) *(G-5748)*

Howmet Aerospace Inc 804 281-2262
  6603 W Broad St Richmond (23230) *(G-11243)*

Howmet Aerospace Inc 757 461-1360
  5610 E Virginia Bch Blvd Norfolk (23502) *(G-9583)*

Howmet Aerospace Inc 540 343-1591
  1775 Seibel Dr Ne Roanoke (24012) *(G-12103)*

Howmet Castings & Services Inc 757 838-4680
  1 Howmet Dr Hampton (23661) *(G-6168)*

Howmet Corporation 757 838-4680
  1 Howmet Dr Hampton (23661) *(G-6169)*

Hp Inc 703 535-3355
1316 Mount Vernon Ave Alexandria (22301) *(G-230)*
HP Hood LLC 540 869-0045
160 Hood Way Winchester (22602) *(G-15426)*
HP Metal Fabrication 703 466-5551
10302 Bristow Center Dr Bristow (20136) *(G-2055)*
HP Metal Fabrication LLC 571 499-0298
13615 Carriage Ford Rd Nokesville (20181) *(G-9394)*
Hqc Inc 540 820-3277
2077 Cory Ln Rockingham (22802) *(G-12255)*
Hr Kids LLC 210 341-7783
188 Arthur Way Newport News (23602) *(G-9248)*
Hr Publishing Group LLC 757 364-0245
4632 Broad St Apt 204 Virginia Beach (23462) *(G-14531)*
Hr Software LLC 703 665-5134
752 Kentland Dr Great Falls (22066) *(G-5962)*
Hr Wellness and Thermography 434 361-1996
1543 Beech Grove Rd Roseland (22967) *(G-12369)*
Hrgc LLC, Norfolk *Also called Hampton Roads Green Clean LLC* *(G-9570)*
Hs Winchester LLC 540 771-0079
621 W Jubal Early Dr D Winchester (22601) *(G-15548)*
Hss Inc 610 444-7409
10514 Gayton Rd Henrico (23238) *(G-6522)*
Hst Global Inc 757 766-6100
150 Research Dr Hampton (23666) *(G-6170)*
Htdepot LLC 703 830-2818
4124 Walney Rd Ste C Chantilly (20151) *(G-2437)*
Hto Inc 703 533-0440
7603 Fisher Dr Falls Church (22043) *(G-4806)*
Hts, Powhatan *Also called Hydropower Turbine Systems* *(G-10550)*
Huang Shang Jeo 703 471-4457
13025 Rose Petal Cir Herndon (20171) *(G-6704)*
Hub Corporation, Salem *Also called Hub Pattern Corporation* *(G-12518)*
Hub Pattern Corporation (HQ) **540 342-3505**
2113 Salem Ave Sw Roanoke (24016) *(G-12104)*
Hub Pattern Corporation 540 342-3505
1129 Florida St Salem (24153) *(G-12518)*
Hubbell Entertainment 540 382-6111
2000 Electric Way Christiansburg (24073) *(G-3594)*
Hubbell Incorporated 540 394-2107
2000 Electric Way Christiansburg (24073) *(G-3595)*
Hubbell Industrial Contrls Inc 434 589-8224
8845 Three Notch Rd Troy (22974) *(G-13929)*
Hubbell Lighting Inc 540 382-6111
2000 Electric Way Christiansburg (24073) *(G-3596)*
Huber Engineered Woods LLC 434 476-6628
1000 Chaney Ln Crystal Hill (24539) *(G-3859)*
Hubert Michael Gilliland 434 332-2285
52 Buttercup Ln Rustburg (24588) *(G-12440)*
Hubs and Wheels Emory Inc 276 944-4900
28435 Blaine St Meadowview (24361) *(G-8595)*
Hucks & Hucks LLC 276 525-1100
26669 Newbanks Rd Abingdon (24210) *(G-41)*
Huddle Furniture Inc 276 647-5129
3483 Virginia Ave Collinsville (24078) *(G-3714)*
Huddle Furniture Inc 828 874-8888
225 Beaver Creek Dr Martinsville (24112) *(G-8299)*
Hudgins Plating Inc C R 434 847-6647
6756 E Lynchburg Slem Tpk Goode (24556) *(G-5890)*
Huds Tees 757 650-6190
2500 Squadron Ct Ste 102 Virginia Beach (23453) *(G-14532)*
Hudson Industries Inc 804 226-1155
5250 Klockner Dr Richmond (23231) *(G-11244)*
Hudson Jewelry Co Inc 276 646-5565
570 Lee Hwy Marion (24354) *(G-8229)*
Hudson Logging, Drakes Branch *Also called Wayne Hudson* *(G-4136)*
Hudson Medical, Richmond *Also called Hudson Industries Inc* *(G-11244)*
Hudson Wdwkg & Restoration LLC 703 817-7741
14620 Flint Lee Rd Chantilly (20151) *(G-2438)*
Hudsons Welding Shop 434 822-1452
1757 Westover Dr Danville (24541) *(G-3998)*
Hue Ai LLC 571 766-6943
1775 Tysons Blvd Fl 5 Tysons (22102) *(G-13946)*
Huespace Inc 540 406-0496
801 15th St S Apt 210 Arlington (22202) *(G-995)*
Huffman & Huffman Inc 276 579-2373
4621 Potato Creek Rd Mouth of Wilson (24363) *(G-9093)*
Huffman Tool Co 540 745-3359
1367 Hcklbrry Ridge Rd Ne Floyd (24091) *(G-5030)*
Huffs Artisan Woodwork 703 399-5493
3308 Sydenham St Apt 40 Fairfax (22031) *(G-4477)*
Huger Embroidery 804 304-8808
11 1/2 Tapoan Rd Richmond (23226) *(G-11245)*
Hughes Mechanical Systems 757 855-3238
2652 Indian River Rd Chesapeake (23325) *(G-3138)*
Hughes Posters LLC 304 615-3433
1704 Tunbridge Dr Henrico (23238) *(G-6523)*
Hughie C Rose 540 423-5240
6919 Jefferson Davis Hwy North Chesterfield (23237) *(G-9888)*

Hugo Kohl LLC 540 564-2755
217 S Liberty St Ste 103 Harrisonburg (22801) *(G-6330)*
Hugo Miranda 703 898-3956
8730 Diamond Hill Dr Bristow (20136) *(G-2056)*
Human Design Medical LLC 434 980-8100
200 Garrett St Ste P Charlottesville (22902) *(G-2812)*
Human Elements LLC 703 542-7701
25071 Kingscote Ct Chantilly (20152) *(G-2537)*
Humidity Busters Henry Co, Ridgeway *Also called Pgf Enterprises LLC* *(G-11848)*
Hummersport LLC 703 433-1887
47605 Woodboro Ter Sterling (20165) *(G-13423)*
Humphreys Enterprises Inc 276 679-1400
6999 Polk Rd Norton (24273) *(G-10120)*
Humus Compost Company LLC 540 421-7169
865 Pike Church Rd Rockingham (22801) *(G-12256)*
Hunt Country Jewelers Inc 540 338-8050
36955 Charles Town Pike Hillsboro (20132) *(G-6871)*
Hunter Company HB (HQ) **757 664-5200**
981 Scott St Ste 100 Norfolk (23502) *(G-9584)*
Hunter Defense Tech Inc 540 479-8100
10300 Spotsylvania Ave # 100 Fredericksburg (22408) *(G-5300)*
Hunter Eqp Svc & Parts Inc 703 785-5526
9618 Percussion Way Vienna (22182) *(G-14068)*
Hunter Industries Incorporated 804 739-8978
13808 Cannonade Ln Midlothian (23112) *(G-8829)*
Hunters Run Winery LLC 703 926-4183
40325 Charles Town Pike Hamilton (20158) *(G-6061)*
Hunting Creek Vineyards Co 434 454-9219
2000 Addie Williams Trl Clover (24534) *(G-3692)*
Huntington Foam LLC 540 731-3700
604 17th St Radford (24141) *(G-10716)*
Huntington Ingalls Inc (HQ) **757 380-2000**
4101 Washington Ave Newport News (23607) *(G-9249)*
Huntington Ingalls Inc 757 380-4982
100 E St Hampton (23661) *(G-6171)*
Huntington Ingalls Inc 757 688-9832
4313 Two Woods Rd E13 Virginia Beach (23455) *(G-14533)*
Huntington Ingalls Inc 757 380-2000
4101 Washington Ave Newport News (23607) *(G-9250)*
Huntington Ingalls Inc 757 440-5390
9727 Avionics Loop Ste M Norfolk (23511) *(G-9585)*
Huntington Ingalls Inc 757 688-1411
4101 Washington Ave Newport News (23607) *(G-9251)*
Huntington Ingalls Inds Inc 757 380-2000
2175 Aluminum Ave Hampton (23661) *(G-6172)*
Huntington Ingalls Inds Inc 757 380-7053
230 41st St Fl 2521 Newport News (23607) *(G-9252)*
Huntington Ingalls Inds Inc 757 380-2000
3100 Washington Ave Newport News (23607) *(G-9253)*
Huntington Ingalls Inds Inc (PA) **757 380-2000**
4101 Washington Ave Newport News (23607) *(G-9254)*
Huntington Solutions Radva Div, Radford *Also called Huntington Foam LLC* *(G-10716)*
Hunts Creek Slate Signs LLC 434 581-1687
247 Boxwood Dr Arvonia (23004) *(G-1233)*
Hunts Family Vineyard LLC 540 942-8689
57 Hawkins Pond Ln Stuarts Draft (24477) *(G-13652)*
Huqa Live LLC 202 527-9342
2029 Pyxie Way Woodbridge (22192) *(G-15724)*
Hurd Machine Shop Inc 540 980-6265
224 12th St Nw Pulaski (24301) *(G-10638)*
Hush Aerospace LLC 703 629-6907
2873 Crusader Cir Virginia Beach (23453) *(G-14534)*
Hussmann Corporation 540 775-2502
6095 Marineview Rd King George (22485) *(G-7094)*
Husteads Canvas Creations Inc 757 627-6912
628 W 24th St Norfolk (23517) *(G-9586)*
Hutchinson Sealing Systems Inc 276 228-6150
455 Industry Rd Wytheville (24382) *(G-15890)*
Hutchinson Sealing Systems Inc 276 228-4455
1150 S 3rd St Wytheville (24382) *(G-15891)*
Hutson Hauling 804 815-2421
1795 Windsor Rd Dutton (23050) *(G-4273)*
Hw Logging, Amherst *Also called Homer Haywood Wheeler II* *(G-694)*
Hwte Tin Han 757 261-5963
850 Kempsville Rd Norfolk (23502) *(G-9587)*
Hy Lee Paving Corporation (PA) **804 360-9066**
2100 Quarry Hill Rd Rockville (23146) *(G-12287)*
Hy-Mark Cylinders Inc 757 251-6744
530 Aberdeen Rd Ste C Hampton (23661) *(G-6173)*
Hy-Tech Usa Inc 804 647-2048
14501 Charter Walk Ln Midlothian (23114) *(G-8830)*
Hybernations LLC 804 744-3580
2801 Sagecreek Ct Midlothian (23112) *(G-8831)*
Hybrid Air Vehicles (us) Inc 703 524-0026
2300 Wilson Blvd Ste 205a Arlington (22201) *(G-996)*
Hydra Hose & Supply Co 757 867-9795
536 Hampton Hwy Yorktown (23693) *(G-15964)*
Hydro Prep & Coating Inc 804 530-2178
2401 Bermuda Ave Chester (23836) *(G-3423)*

Hydro Systems USA Inc..703 429-1024
  45080 Old Ox Rd Sterling (20166) *(G-13424)*
Hydrogen Motors Inc..703 407-9802
  3600 Twilight Ct Oakton (22124) *(G-10151)*
Hydropower Turbine Systems.....................................804 360-7992
  1940 Flint Lock Ct Powhatan (23139) *(G-10550)*
Hydrus Usa Inc..804 690-8158
  5323 Stone Horse Rd Glen Allen (23059) *(G-5749)*
Hygenic Solutions, Falls Church *Also called American Spirit LLC (G-4749)*
Hygistics LLC..804 297-1504
  1025 Hunters Woods Crozier (23039) *(G-3858)*
Hylton & Hylton Logging...276 930-2245
  5999 Belcher Mountain Rd Woolwine (24185) *(G-15865)*
Hylton Timber Harvesting...276 930-2348
  6039 Belcher Mountain Rd Woolwine (24185) *(G-15866)*
Hymons Embroidery LLC..757 512-6005
  2573 Townfield Ln Virginia Beach (23454) *(G-14535)*
Hypatia-Rose Press LLC...757 819-2559
  5624 Susquehanna Dr Virginia Beach (23462) *(G-14536)*
Hypes Custom Wdwkg & HM Improv.............................540 641-7419
  465 School Ln Christiansburg (24073) *(G-3597)*
Hyponex Corporation...434 848-2727
  3175 Bright Leaf Rd Lawrenceville (23868) *(G-7181)*
I & C Hughes LLC...757 544-0502
  3933 Rainbow Dr Virginia Beach (23456) *(G-14537)*
I & I Sling Inc...703 550-9405
  7403 Lockport Pl Ste A Lorton (22079) *(G-7494)*
I & M Welding Inc...540 907-3775
  6301 Tree Haven Ln Spotsylvania (22551) *(G-12896)*
I A Welding LLC..757 455-8500
  5875 Adderley St Norfolk (23502) *(G-9588)*
I AM Express LLC..757 535-6944
  3216 Hector Ln Chesapeake (23323) *(G-3139)*
I B R Plasma Center..757 498-5160
  949 Chimney Hl Shopg Ctr Virginia Beach (23452) *(G-14538)*
I Bit-Lab..703 568-4035
  704a Little St Alexandria (22301) *(G-231)*
I C E..276 988-0330
  205 Walnut St North Tazewell (24630) *(G-10101)*
I C S E, Ashland *Also called Instrumentation and Control (G-1440)*
I H McBride Sign Company Inc..................................434 847-4151
  5493 S Amherst Hwy Madison Heights (24572) *(G-7875)*
I Love Art Boutique LLC..757 204-1260
  110 Coliseum Xing # 6092 Hampton (23666) *(G-6174)*
I Patriot Shipping Corp...703 876-3000
  3190 Fairview Park Dr Falls Church (22042) *(G-4807)*
I Sw LLC...703 270-1540
  2750 Prosperity Ave # 600 Fairfax (22031) *(G-4478)*
I T F Circle...276 773-3114
  173 Rainbow Cir Independence (24348) *(G-6986)*
I W T, Lynchburg *Also called Innovative Wireless Tech Inc (G-7741)*
I-Ce-Ny Arlington...571 207-6318
  4150 Campbell Ave Ste 101 Arlington (22206) *(G-997)*
I10cartel Records LLC..713 979-8182
  3802 Woodbridge Dr Newport News (23608) *(G-9255)*
I3, Blacksburg *Also called Identification Intl Inc (G-1744)*
I3 Ingenuity Inc..703 524-0019
  3300 Fairfax Dr Ste 302 Arlington (22201) *(G-998)*
I4c Innovations LLC..703 488-6100
  3800 Concorde Pkwy # 400 Chantilly (20151) *(G-2439)*
IAC Strasburg LLC..540 465-3741
  806 E Queen St Strasburg (22657) *(G-13582)*
Iaeva Mercantile LLC..301 523-6566
  6611 Denny Pl Mc Lean (22101) *(G-8460)*
Iam Energy Incorporated...703 939-5681
  46208 Wales Ter Sterling (20165) *(G-13425)*
Iaq Testing Services LLC..540 966-3660
  196 Buckingham Ct Roanoke (24019) *(G-11936)*
Iastv & Magazine, Alexandria *Also called Justin Comb (G-249)*
Iba Led...434 566-2109
  12046 Spicers Mill Rd Orange (22960) *(G-10215)*
Ibf Group...703 549-4247
  3844 Brighton Ct Alexandria (22305) *(G-232)*
Ibfd North America Inc..703 442-7757
  8300 Boone Blvd Ste 380 Vienna (22182) *(G-14069)*
IBM Philip Morris..405 600-7997
  16000 Walthall Indus Pkwy South Chesterfield (23834) *(G-12810)*
Ibs..540 662-0882
  326 Mcghee Rd Winchester (22603) *(G-15427)*
Ibs Millwork Corporation...703 631-4011
  8501 Buckeye Timber Dr Manassas (20109) *(G-8079)*
Icare Clinical Tech LLC...301 646-3640
  41655 Catoctin Springs Ct Leesburg (20176) *(G-7285)*
Icaros Inc (PA)..**301 637-4324**
  4100 Monu Crnr Dr Ste 520 Fairfax (22030) *(G-4631)*
Icarus Medical LLC..434 242-0258
  105 E Main St Charlottesville (22902) *(G-2813)*
Icarus Medical Innovation, Charlottesville *Also called Icarus Medical LLC (G-2813)*
Ice, Fairfax *Also called Innovative Computer Engrg Inc (G-4635)*

Ice Enterprises Inc..703 934-4879
  10302 Eaton Pl Ste 100 Fairfax (22030) *(G-4632)*
Ice Release Materials LLC...540 239-2438
  10338 Stony Run Ln Ashland (23005) *(G-1437)*
Ice Scraper Card Inc...703 327-4622
  40503 Dogwood Run Ln Leesburg (20175) *(G-7286)*
ICE Tek LLC..757 390-8589
  2585 Horse Pasture Rd # 207 Virginia Beach (23453) *(G-14539)*
Iceberry Inc (PA)..**703 481-0670**
  11990 Market St Ste C Reston (20190) *(G-10866)*
Iceburrr Jewelry (PA)..**757 537-9520**
  5024 Sullivan Blvd Virginia Beach (23455) *(G-14540)*
Icewarp Inc..571 481-4611
  6225 Brandon Ave Ste 310 Springfield (22150) *(G-13019)*
Iconicloud Inc...703 864-1203
  6220 Quander Rd Alexandria (22307) *(G-481)*
Iconix Industries Inc..703 489-0278
  43567 Mink Meadows St Chantilly (20152) *(G-2538)*
Ict Mondial Inc...703 254-7416
  6412 Brandon Ave Springfield (22150) *(G-13020)*
ID Web Studios, Chesapeake *Also called Ideation Web Studios LLC (G-3140)*
Ideagirl Industries LLC...240 672-8333
  307 Clifford Ave Alexandria (22305) *(G-233)*
Ideal Cabinets Inc..540 366-1748
  2158 Salem Industrial Dr Salem (24153) *(G-12519)*
Ideal Printing LLC..434 421-1000
  180 Confederate Ave Danville (24541) *(G-3999)*
Ideaphoria Press LLC...804 272-6231
  7758 Yarmouth Dr North Chesterfield (23225) *(G-10020)*
Ideation Web Studios LLC..757 333-3021
  660 Independence Pkwy # 310 Chesapeake (23320) *(G-3140)*
Idemia America Corp..703 263-0100
  11951 Freedom Dr Ste 1800 Reston (20190) *(G-10867)*
Identification Intl Inc..540 953-3343
  3120 Commerce St Blacksburg (24060) *(G-1744)*
Identity America Inc..276 322-2616
  112 Spruce St Ste 4 Bluefield (24605) *(G-1864)*
Identity Mktg Promotional LLC....................................757 966-2863
  2465 Pruden Blvd Suffolk (23434) *(G-13724)*
Idezine LLC..703 946-3490
  15755 Cool Spring Dr Haymarket (20169) *(G-6426)*
Idiq Pmo, Mc Lean *Also called Northrop Grumman Systems Corp (G-8514)*
Idirect Government LLC (HQ).....................................**703 648-8118**
  13921 Park Center Rd # 600 Herndon (20171) *(G-6705)*
IDS Manufacturing, Spotsylvania *Also called Integrated Design Solutions (G-12897)*
IDS Publishing Corporation..703 821-2323
  7730 Bridle Path Ln Mc Lean (22102) *(G-8461)*
Idu Optics LLC...707 845-4996
  7012 N Hairpin Dr Quinton (23141) *(G-10698)*
Idvector...571 313-5064
  46040 Center Oak Plz # 165 Sterling (20166) *(G-13426)*
Idx Baltimore, Fredericksburg *Also called Idx Corporation (G-5301)*
Idx Corporation..410 551-3600
  11032 Tidewater Trl Fredericksburg (22408) *(G-5301)*
Ie W Railway Supply..540 882-3886
  38200 Charles Town Pike Hillsboro (20132) *(G-6872)*
Ifco Systems, Richmond *Also called Chep (usa) Inc (G-11527)*
Ifexo LLC..443 856-7705
  7902 Tysons One Pl Mc Lean (22102) *(G-8462)*
Ig Flooring, Alexandria *Also called Ignacio C Garcia (G-482)*
IG Petroleum LLC..703 749-1780
  1420 Spring Hill Rd # 600 Mc Lean (22102) *(G-8463)*
Ignacio C Garcia...703 922-9829
  6310 Windsor Ave Alexandria (22315) *(G-482)*
Igor Custom Sign Stripe..757 639-2397
  402 Redhead Way Virginia Beach (23451) *(G-14541)*
Igt, Herndon *Also called Idirect Government LLC (G-6705)*
Iheartrhythm LLC...757 810-5902
  2550 Washington Blvd Arlington (22201) *(G-999)*
Ihs Computer Service Inc...540 249-4833
  7991 Port Republic Rd Port Republic (24471) *(G-10384)*
Ihs Press..877 447-7737
  222 W 21st St Ste F122 Norfolk (23517) *(G-9589)*
Iis Raytheon..561 212-2954
  47737 League Ct Potomac Falls (20165) *(G-10509)*
IJ Therapeutics LLC...804 543-6360
  111 Virginia St Ste 300 Richmond (23219) *(G-11612)*
Ikanow LLC...619 884-4434
  11921 Freedom Dr Ste 550 Reston (20190) *(G-10868)*
IKEA Industry Danville LLC......................................434 822-6080
  100 Ikea Dr Ringgold (24586) *(G-11868)*
IL Dolce Winery..804 647-0414
  2601 Park Center Dr C1407 Alexandria (22302) *(G-234)*
Ilantech LLC...571 226-7042
  43413 Wheatlands Chase Ct Ashburn (20148) *(G-1294)*
Ileen Shefferman Designs...703 821-3261
  6460 Madison Ct Mc Lean (22101) *(G-8464)*
Illinois Tool Works Inc...434 239-6941
  1205 Mcconville Rd Lynchburg (24502) *(G-7737)*

A
L
P
H
A
B
E
T
I
C

Illusions Wrap LLC ... 540 710-9727
3719 Lafayette Blvd Fredericksburg (22408) ***(G-5302)***
Ilma ... 703 684-5574
651 S Washington St Alexandria (22314) ***(G-235)***
Ilmarnock Lettering Co LLC ... 804 435-6956
31 Tartan Village Dr Kilmarnock (22482) ***(G-7070)***
Ils Intrntonal Launch Svcs Inc ... 703 435-5689
12110 Sunset Hills Rd # 4 Reston (20190) ***(G-10869)***
Iluka Resources Inc (HQ) ... **434 348-4300**
12472 St John Church Rd Stony Creek (23882) ***(G-13567)***
Ilumi Sciences Inc ... 703 894-7576
4150 Lafayette Center Dr # 500 Chantilly (20151) ***(G-2440)***
Im Apparel LLC ... 202 905-5696
12195 Cardamom Dr Woodbridge (22192) ***(G-15725)***
Im Embroidery ... 757 533-5397
415 W York St Norfolk (23510) ***(G-9590)***
Image 360 ... 804 897-8500
11605 Busy St North Chesterfield (23236) ***(G-9889)***
Image Packaging ... 804 730-7358
7204 History Ln Mechanicsville (23111) ***(G-8639)***
Image Works Inc ... 804 798-5533
11046 Leadbetter Rd Ashland (23005) ***(G-1438)***
Imagenation Design & Prtg LLC ... 804 687-3581
4226 Riding Place Rd Richmond (23223) ***(G-11613)***
Images In Art Inc ... 804 785-1011
5610 Lwis B Pller Mem Hwy Shacklefords (23156) ***(G-12682)***
Images In Art Signs & Graphic, Gloucester *Also called Christopher Aiken* ***(G-5841)***
Imagine It Designs LLC ... 703 795-6397
6547 Orland St Falls Church (22043) ***(G-4808)***
Imagine Milling Tech LLC ... 571 313-1269
14220 Sullyfield Cir B Chantilly (20151) ***(G-2441)***
Imagine This Company ... 804 232-1300
5331 Distributor Dr Richmond (23225) ***(G-11614)***
Imaging Zone, Springfield *Also called Mounir & Company Incorporated* ***(G-13054)***
Iman Fullman Mua, Newport News *Also called Fullman Iman* ***(G-9233)***
Imani M X-Ortiz ... 540 582-5898
5405 Partlow Rd Partlow (22534) ***(G-10266)***
Imani M X-Ortiz Og Distributor, Partlow *Also called Imani M X-Ortiz* ***(G-10266)***
Imco Inc ... 434 299-5919
767 Wilderness Creek Rd Monroe (24574) ***(G-8992)***
Imgen Technologies Lc ... 703 549-2866
602 Virginia Ave Alexandria (22302) ***(G-236)***
Imlay International LLC ... 703 914-0526
5023 Backlick Rd Ste A Annandale (22003) ***(G-758)***
Immco LLC ... 804 271-6979
7516 Whitepine Rd North Chesterfield (23237) ***(G-9890)***
Immortal Publishing LLC ... 540 465-3368
15 Deaken Cir Strasburg (22657) ***(G-13583)***
Immunarray Usa Inc (HQ) ... **804 212-2975**
737 N 5th St Ste 304 Richmond (23219) ***(G-11615)***
Imol Radiopharmaceuticals LLC ... 434 825-3323
1200 Five Springs Rd Charlottesville (22902) ***(G-2814)***
Impact East, Ashland *Also called Grabber Construction Pdts Inc* ***(G-1423)***
Impact Junkie LLC ... 916 541-0317
15461 Marsh Overlook Dr Woodbridge (22191) ***(G-15726)***
Impact Software Soutions Inc ... 703 615-5212
12001 Creekbend Dr Reston (20194) ***(G-10870)***
Impact Unlimited Inc ... 702 802-6800
14291 Park Meadow Dr Chantilly (20151) ***(G-2442)***
Imperial Cleaners ... 757 531-1125
9311 Sloane St Norfolk (23503) ***(G-9591)***
Imperial Group Mfg Inc ... 540 674-1306
4969 Stepp Pl Dublin (24084) ***(G-4159)***
Imperial Machine Company Inc ... 804 271-6022
7631 Whitepine Rd North Chesterfield (23237) ***(G-9891)***
Imperial Revival LLC ... 540 326-8189
8 Orange Dr Middleburg (20117) ***(G-8723)***
Imperial Sign Co ... 804 541-8545
111 S Main St Hopewell (23860) ***(G-6935)***
Imperium ... 540 220-6785
7 Skyview Ct Stafford (22554) ***(G-13152)***
Imprenta Printing ... 703 866-0760
7609 Long Pine Dr Springfield (22151) ***(G-13021)***
Impressed Print Solutions ... 717 816-0522
260 High Banks Rd Stephenson (22656) ***(G-13334)***
Impression An Everlasting Inc ... 804 363-7185
6274 Banshire Dr Mechanicsville (23111) ***(G-8640)***
Impression Obsession ... 804 749-3580
2546 Turkey Creek Rd Oilville (23129) ***(G-10180)***
Impressions Group Inc ... 540 667-9227
2063 Cidermill Ln Winchester (22601) ***(G-15549)***
Impressions of Norton Inc ... 276 328-1100
301 Norton Rd Wise (24293) ***(G-15626)***
Impressions of Norton Inc ... 276 679-1560
832 Park Ave Nw Norton (24273) ***(G-10121)***
Impressions Plus Prtg Copying, Winchester *Also called Impressions Group Inc* ***(G-15549)***
Imprint ID Ltd ... 877 385-7785
7960 Conell Ct Lorton (22079) ***(G-7495)***
Improbable LLC ... 571 418-6999
3033 Wilson Blvd Ste 260 Arlington (22201) ***(G-1000)***
Improvebuild LLC ... 703 372-2646
20672 Meadowthrash Ct Ashburn (20147) ***(G-1295)***
Improvements By Bill LLC ... 571 246-7257
732 Beechwood Ln Bluemont (20135) ***(G-1889)***
IMS Gear Holding Inc ... 757 468-8810
489 Progress Ln Virginia Beach (23454) ***(G-14542)***
IMS Gear Virginia LLC ... 757 468-8810
489 Progress Ln Virginia Beach (23454) ***(G-14543)***
Imsc, Arlington *Also called Interntional Maritime SEC Corp* ***(G-1006)***
In Good Company LLC ... 540 752-1328
117 Fence Post Rd Stafford (22556) ***(G-13153)***
In Home Care Inc (PA) ... **276 328-6462**
201 Nottingham Ave Wise (24293) ***(G-15627)***
In House Printing ... 703 913-6338
6207 Duntley Ct Springfield (22152) ***(G-13022)***
In Motion Us LLC ... 540 605-9622
3157 State St Blacksburg (24060) ***(G-1745)***
In Stitches ... 434 842-2104
Rr 671 Fork Union (23055) ***(G-5110)***
In Stock Today Cabinets LLC ... 703 972-4030
2817 Dorr Ave Fairfax (22031) ***(G-4479)***
In Your Element Commerce Inc ... 804 426-6914
3425 W Cary St Richmond (23221) ***(G-11616)***
In10m LLC ... 202 779-7977
700 E Main St 2487 Richmond (23219) ***(G-11617)***
In2 Print ... 434 476-7996
3151 Chatham Rd Halifax (24558) ***(G-6050)***
Inamod Group LLC ... 703 626-2453
6387 Strawbridge Sq Dr Alexandria (22312) ***(G-483)***
Incandescent Technologies ... 434 385-8825
107 Cygnet Cir Forest (24551) ***(G-5074)***
Incense Oil More ... 540 793-8642
535 Mcdowell Ave Nw Roanoke (24016) ***(G-12105)***
Inch By Inch LLC ... 804 678-8271
200 N 21st St Richmond (23223) ***(G-11618)***
Incident Logic LLC ... 540 349-8888
8262 Lees Ridge Rd Warrenton (20186) ***(G-15026)***
Incision Apps, Virginia Beach *Also called Redclay Visions LLC* ***(G-14766)***
Incision Tech ... 727 254-9183
9 Technology Dr Staunton (24401) ***(G-13268)***
Incode, Herndon *Also called Poms Corporation* ***(G-6776)***
Incubatize, Ashburn *Also called Acharya Brothers Computing* ***(G-1237)***
Incuhub, The, Portsmouth *Also called Pma It Solutions Inc* ***(G-10469)***
Indenhooffen Productions LLC ... 540 327-0898
173 Echo Ln Winchester (22603) ***(G-15428)***
Independence Lumber Inc ... 276 773-3744
407 Lumber Ln Independence (24348) ***(G-6987)***
Independence Publishing Tlr ... 757 761-8579
10011 Palace Ct Apt A Richmond (23238) ***(G-11246)***
Independent Delivery Ex Inc ... 434 660-2389
1436 Jefferson Dr W Forest (24551) ***(G-5075)***
Independent Holiness Publi ... 276 964-2824
175 Green Mountain Rd Pounding Mill (24637) ***(G-10521)***
Independent Machining Service ... 540 797-7284
1809 Sample Rd Wirtz (24184) ***(G-15614)***
Independent Speedy Printing, Fairfax *Also called C & S Printing Enterprises* ***(G-4603)***
Independent Stamping Inc ... 540 949-6839
180 Port Republic Rd Waynesboro (22980) ***(G-15115)***
Index Systems Inc ... 571 420-4600
13503 Copper Bed Rd Herndon (20171) ***(G-6706)***
Indian Creek Express Inc ... 434 927-5900
5529 Grassland Dr Sandy Level (24161) ***(G-12647)***
Indian Ridge Woodcraft Inc ... 540 789-4754
635 Shady Grove Rd Nw Willis (24380) ***(G-15361)***
Indian River Canoe Mfg ... 276 773-3124
832 E Main St Independence (24348) ***(G-6988)***
Indiana Floor Inc ... 540 373-1915
16517 Bull Church Rd Woodford (22580) ***(G-15840)***
Indiana Packers Corporation ... 270 926-2324
603 Pilot House Dr Fl 4th Newport News (23606) ***(G-9256)***
Indigenous Industries LLC ... 540 847-9851
110 Kellogg Mill Rd Fredericksburg (22406) ***(G-5441)***
Indigo Pen Publishing LLC ... 888 670-4010
7102 Snug Harbor Ct Alexandria (22315) ***(G-484)***
Indigo Press ... 757 705-2619
3445 Waltham Cir Virginia Beach (23452) ***(G-14544)***
Indigo Red VA Beach Ci, Virginia Beach *Also called Rp55 Inc* ***(G-14782)***
Indigo Sign Co ... 804 469-3233
16189 Glebe Rd Dewitt (23840) ***(G-4092)***
Indigo Signs LLC ... 540 489-8400
1305 Old Franklin Tpke Rocky Mount (24151) ***(G-12328)***
Individual Products & Svcs Inc ... 757 488-3363
4720 Elizabeth Harbor Dr Chesapeake (23321) ***(G-3141)***
Indmar Coatings Corporation ... 757 899-3807
317 W Main St Wakefield (23888) ***(G-14966)***
Indoff Incorporated ... 804 539-2425
12021 Wheat Ridge Ct Glen Allen (23059) ***(G-5750)***
Induko Inc ... 703 217-4262
7012 Trappers Ct Manassas (20111) ***(G-8080)***

Induplate Operations LLC 757 566-8070
7992 Richmond Rd Toano (23168) ***(G-13866)***
Indust LLC 757 208-0587
4037 Frances Berkeley Williamsburg (23188) ***(G-15256)***
Industrial Alloy Welding LLC 757 573-8496
5875 Adderley St Norfolk (23502) ***(G-9592)***
Industrial Apparatus Repr Inc 540 343-9240
6655 Wellington Rd Roanoke (24018) ***(G-11937)***
Industrial Biodynamics LLC 540 357-0033
1537 Mill Race Dr Salem (24153) ***(G-12520)***
Industrial Commercial Wldg LLC 703 707-6347
1456 Winterberry Ct Herndon (20170) ***(G-6707)***
Industrial Control Systems Inc 804 737-1700
20 W Williamsburg Rd Sandston (23150) ***(G-12620)***
Industrial Drives 540 639-2495
201 W Rock Rd Radford (24141) ***(G-10717)***
Industrial Engraving Co, Boones Mill *Also called Visual Communication Co Inc* ***(G-1900)***
Industrial Expedite, Roanoke *Also called Longbow Holdings LLC* ***(G-11957)***
Industrial Fabricators Inc 540 989-0834
5163 Starkey Rd Roanoke (24018) ***(G-11938)***
Industrial Fabricators VA Inc 540 943-5885
48 Mule Academy Rd Fishersville (22939) ***(G-5005)***
Industrial Galvanizers VA, Petersburg *Also called Valmont Industries Inc* ***(G-10348)***
Industrial Glvanizers Amer Inc (HQ) **804 763-1760**
3535 Halifax Rd Ste A Petersburg (23805) ***(G-10325)***
Industrial Machine Mfg, North Chesterfield *Also called Immco LLC* ***(G-9890)***
Industrial Machine Mfg Inc 804 271-6979
8140 Virginia Pine Ct North Chesterfield (23237) ***(G-9892)***
Industrial Machine Works Inc 540 949-6115
444 N Bayard Ave Waynesboro (22980) ***(G-15116)***
Industrial Metalcraft Inc 757 898-9350
114 Hollywood Blvd Yorktown (23692) ***(G-15965)***
Industrial Minerals Inc 540 297-8667
208 Red Oak Rd Moneta (24121) ***(G-8966)***
Industrial Plating Corp 434 582-1920
318 Crowell Ln Lynchburg (24502) ***(G-7738)***
Industrial Reporting Inc 804 550-0323
10244 Timber Ridge Dr Ashland (23005) ***(G-1439)***
Industrial Signal LLC 703 323-7777
3835 9th St N Apt 808w Arlington (22203) ***(G-1001)***
Industrial Welding & Mch Corp 276 783-7105
5723 Atkins Tank Rd Atkins (24311) ***(G-1518)***
Industrial Welding & Mech Inc 804 744-8812
2401 Bellwood Rd North Chesterfield (23237) ***(G-9893)***
Industries 247 LLC 703 741-0151
4238 Wilson Blvd Ste 3136 Arlington (22203) ***(G-1002)***
Industries In Focus Inc (PA) **703 451-5550**
7401 Fullerton Rd Ste K Springfield (22153) ***(G-13023)***
Industries Massive 703 347-6074
7129 Rock Ridge Ln Alexandria (22315) ***(G-485)***
Industry Graphics 540 345-6074
3783 Buckingham Dr Roanoke (24018) ***(G-11939)***
Indy Health Labs LLC 540 682-2160
4521 Brambleton Ave # 205 Roanoke (24018) ***(G-11940)***
Indyne Inc 703 903-6900
21351 Gentry Dr Ste 205 Sterling (20166) ***(G-13427)***
Inertia Publishing LLC 703 754-9617
8405 Churchside Dr Gainesville (20155) ***(G-5590)***
Inevitable Entertainment LLC 757 470-1521
221 Bryson Cir Hampton (23666) ***(G-6175)***
Infilco Degremont Inc 804 756-7600
8007 Discovery Dr Richmond (23229) ***(G-11247)***
Infinite Studio LLC 864 293-4522
2174 Whispering Hollow Ln Charlottesville (22911) ***(G-2646)***
Infinite Technologies O&P, Fairfax *Also called Eastern Cranial Affiliates LLC* ***(G-4616)***
Infinity Global Inc (PA) **434 793-7570**
501 Bridge St Danville (24541) ***(G-4000)***
Infinity Mg Inc 703 916-0172
7700 Little River Tpke Annandale (22003) ***(G-759)***
Infinity Printing Inc 804 378-8656
11025 Research Ct North Chesterfield (23236) ***(G-9894)***
Infinity Publications LLC 540 331-8713
230 Lora Dr Woodstock (22664) ***(G-15855)***
Infinity Publishing Group LLC 757 874-0135
394 Deputy Ln Newport News (23608) ***(G-9257)***
Infinity Resources Corporation 830 822-4962
900 S Washington St B104 Falls Church (22046) ***(G-4919)***
Influences of Zion 804 248-4758
8114 Presquile Rd Richmond (23231) ***(G-11248)***
Infobase Publishers Inc 703 327-8470
25050 Riding Plz Ste 13 South Riding (20152) ***(G-12868)***
Infoblox Federal Inc 703 672-2607
13454 Snrs Vly Dr Ste 570 Herndon (20171) ***(G-6708)***
Infocess LLC 571 723-1010
8300 Boone Blvd Ste 500 Vienna (22182) ***(G-14070)***
Infocus Coatings Inc 804 520-1573
16053 Continental Blvd South Chesterfield (23834) ***(G-12811)***
Infocus Coatings Inc 804 530-4645
107 Crystal Downs Ct Chester (23836) ***(G-3424)***
Infoition News Services Inc 703 853-8857
1900 Cmpus Cmmons Dr Ste Reston (20191) ***(G-10871)***
Infomtion Tech Applcations LLC 757 603-3551
5378 Gardner Ct Williamsburg (23188) ***(G-15257)***
Inforce Group LLC 703 788-6835
6601 Coop Way Set 600 600 Set Herndon (20171) ***(G-6709)***
Informatica Corp 703 234-8500
11710 Plaza America Dr # 2000 Reston (20190) ***(G-10872)***
Informatica Federal Sales Div, Reston *Also called Informatica Corp* ***(G-10872)***
Informatica LLC 650 385-7000
428 Hume Ave Alexandria (22301) ***(G-237)***
Information Analysis Inc 703 383-3000
11240 Waples Mill Rd # 201 Fairfax (22030) ***(G-4633)***
Information Systems Globl Svcs, Chesapeake *Also called Lockheed Martin Corporation* ***(G-3184)***
Information Systems Group 804 526-4220
605 N Courthouse Rd # 201 North Chesterfield (23236) ***(G-9895)***
Infoseal LLC (PA) **540 981-1140**
1825 Blue Hills Cir Ne Roanoke (24012) ***(G-12106)***
Infosoft Publishing Co 661 288-1414
521 San Pedro Dr Chesapeake (23322) ***(G-3142)***
Infrascale Inc (PA) **703 520-7072**
12110 Sunset Hills Rd # 600 Reston (20190) ***(G-10873)***
Infrawhite Technologies LLC 662 902-0376
2671 Avenir Pl Apt 2523 Vienna (22180) ***(G-14071)***
Ingersoll Rand Inc 804 214-7054
540 Southlake Blvd North Chesterfield (23236) ***(G-9896)***
Ingevity Virginia Corporation 540 969-3700
958 E Riverside St Covington (24426) ***(G-3791)***
Ingram's Concrete Finishing, Burkeville *Also called Tamara Ingram* ***(G-2211)***
Inhand Networks Inc (PA) **703 348-2988**
3900 Jermantown Rd # 150 Fairfax (22030) ***(G-4634)***
Inifinity Global Inc 434 793-7570
1750 S Main St Danville (24541) ***(G-4001)***
Ink & More 804 794-3437
7106 Courthouse Rd Prince George (23875) ***(G-10596)***
Ink Blot Inc 757 644-6958
1329 Harpers Rd Ste 105 Virginia Beach (23454) ***(G-14545)***
Ink It On Anything 804 814-5890
4141 Round Hill Dr Chesterfield (23832) ***(G-3505)***
Ink Mart of Nova, Centreville *Also called Sibashi Inc* ***(G-2340)***
Ink2work LLC 605 202-9079
10307 W Broad St Ste 255 Glen Allen (23060) ***(G-5751)***
Inkd Out Electrical Svc LLC 757 369-9827
719 Industrial Park Dr C Newport News (23608) ***(G-9258)***
Inkd Out LLC 757 369-9827
719 Industrial Park Dr C Newport News (23608) ***(G-9259)***
Inklings Ink 434 842-2200
2053 East River Rd Fork Union (23055) ***(G-5111)***
Inklings Ink Screen Printing A, Fork Union *Also called Inklings Ink* ***(G-5111)***
Inkwell Duck Inc 703 550-1344
7607 Surry Grove Ct Lorton (22079) ***(G-7496)***
Inner Peace Warriors LLC 703 830-7680
12101 Beaver Creek Rd Clifton (20124) ***(G-3672)***
Innerspec Technologies Inc (PA) **434 948-1301**
2940 Perrowville Rd Forest (24551) ***(G-5076)***
Innocoll Inc 703 980-4182
42662 Kitchen Prim Ct Broadlands (20148) ***(G-2079)***
Innovated Machine & Tl Co Inc 757 887-2181
250 Picketts Line Newport News (23603) ***(G-9260)***
Innovatio Sealing Tech Corp 434 238-2397
4925 Boonsboro Rd Pmb 212 Lynchburg (24503) ***(G-7739)***
Innovation Station Music LLC 703 405-6727
6612 Jessamine Ln Annandale (22003) ***(G-760)***
Innovative Computer Engrg Inc 703 934-4879
10302 Eaton Pl Ste 200 Fairfax (22030) ***(G-4635)***
Innovative Computer Engrg Inc 703 934-2782
10302 Eaton Pl Ste 200 Fairfax (22030) ***(G-4636)***
Innovative Dynamic Solutions 703 234-5282
12808 Pinecrest Rd Herndon (20171) ***(G-6710)***
Innovative Graphics & Design 276 679-2340
55 15th St Nw Norton (24273) ***(G-10122)***
Innovative Home Media LLC 804 513-4784
12319 Swift Crossing Dr Midlothian (23112) ***(G-8832)***
Innovative Industries, Reston *Also called Allen Watson* ***(G-10784)***
Innovative Industries LLC 540 317-1733
214 N East St Culpeper (22701) ***(G-3895)***
Innovative Kitchens Inc 757 425-7753
2640 Virginia Beach Blvd Virginia Beach (23452) ***(G-14546)***
Innovative Machining Inc 804 385-4212
2104 Graves Mill Rd Forest (24551) ***(G-5077)***
Innovative Millwork Tech LLC 276 646-8336
370 Deer Valley Rd Chilhowie (24319) ***(G-3551)***
Innovative Office Design LLC 757 496-9221
700 Earl Of.Chstrfield Ct Virginia Beach (23454) ***(G-14547)***
Innovative Solid Surfaces LLC 540 560-0747
1021 W Market St Harrisonburg (22801) ***(G-6331)***
Innovative Tech Intl Inc 434 239-1979
220 Jefferson Ridge Pkwy Lynchburg (24501) ***(G-7740)***

A L P H A B E T I C

Innovative Wireless Tech Inc.................................434 316-5230
1100 Main St Ste 202 Lynchburg (24504) *(G-7741)*

Innovative Yarns Inc..305 294-7244
820 Roy St Martinsville (24112) *(G-8300)*

Innoveyor Inc..757 485-0500
3712 Profit Way Ste B Chesapeake (23323) *(G-3143)*

Innovtive Imges Cstm Sgns More.......................804 472-3882
3506 Nomini Grove Rd Warsaw (22572) *(G-15068)*

Inorganic Ventures, Christiansburg Also called IV Labs Inc *(G-3599)*

Inovitech LLC...877 429-0377
205 Wildman St Ne Leesburg (20176) *(G-7287)*

Inquisient Inc..888 230-2181
8278 Falcon Glen Rd Warrenton (20186) *(G-15027)*

Inr Energy LLC...804 282-0369
7275 Glen Forest Dr # 206 Richmond (23226) *(G-11249)*

Inscribe Press LLC...707 239-8404
12400 Regiment Ln Fredericksburg (22407) *(G-5303)*

Inside Air Force...703 416-8528
1919 S Eads St Ste 201 Arlington (22202) *(G-1003)*

Inside Business...757 439-7158
2255 Wake Forest St Virginia Beach (23451) *(G-14548)*

Inside Washington Publisher...........................703 416-8500
1225 S Clark St Ste 1400 Arlington (22202) *(G-1004)*

Insights Intl Holdings LLC..............................757 333-1291
601 N Mechanic St Ste 414 Franklin (23851) *(G-5145)*

Insignia Technology Svcs LLC.........................757 591-2111
45150 Russell Branch Pkwy # 300 Ashburn (20147) *(G-1296)*

Insite Publishing LLC......................................757 301-9617
2781 Einstein Dr Virginia Beach (23456) *(G-14549)*

Insource Sftwr Solutions Inc (PA)..................804 378-8981
11321 Business Center Dr North Chesterfield (23236) *(G-9897)*

Insource Solutions, North Chesterfield Also called Insource Sftwr Solutions Inc *(G-9897)*

Inspiration Publications..................................540 465-3878
234 W King St Strasburg (22657) *(G-13584)*

Inspire Living Inc...703 991-0451
13815 Piedmont Vista Dr Haymarket (20169) *(G-6427)*

Inspired Embroidery.......................................703 409-3375
46908 Foxstone Pl Sterling (20165) *(G-13428)*

Inspireyourpeople.com, Richmond Also called Give More Media Inc *(G-11601)*

Installers, Norfolk Also called Phil Morgan *(G-9686)*

Instant Gratification.......................................434 332-3769
190 Campbell Hwy Rustburg (24588) *(G-12441)*

Instant Knwledge Com Jill Byrd.......................540 885-8730
341 Lee Hwy Verona (24482) *(G-13989)*

Instant Replay..434 941-2568
2052 Garfield Ave Lynchburg (24501) *(G-7742)*

Instant Systems...757 200-5494
5505 Robin Hood Rd Ste A Norfolk (23513) *(G-9593)*

Instant Transactions Corp...............................540 687-3151
35396 Millville Rd Middleburg (20117) *(G-8724)*

Institute For Complexity MGT..........................540 645-1050
14 Hayes St Stafford (22556) *(G-13154)*

Institute of Navigation (dc)............................703 366-2723
8551 Rixlew Ln Ste 360 Manassas (20109) *(G-8081)*

Instrumentation and Control............................804 550-5770
10991 Leadbetter Rd Ashland (23005) *(G-1440)*

Insul Industries Inc..804 550-1933
10287 Still Spring Ct Mechanicsville (23116) *(G-8641)*

Int Diagnostic Syst...414 477-8035
7730 Bridle Path Ln Mc Lean (22102) *(G-8465)*

Integer Holdings Corporation...........................540 389-7860
200 S Yorkshire St Salem (24153) *(G-12521)*

Integra Drapes, Manassas Also called Integra Management Group LLC *(G-8082)*

Integra Management Group LLC.......................703 791-2007
7819 Abbey Oaks Ct Manassas (20112) *(G-8082)*

Integra Music Group.......................................434 821-3796
105 Cupola St Lynchburg (24502) *(G-7743)*

Integrated Design Solutions............................540 735-5424
7916 Twin Oaks Dr Spotsylvania (22551) *(G-12897)*

Integrated Global Services Inc.........................804 897-0326
2713 Oak Lake Blvd Midlothian (23112) *(G-8833)*

Integrated Global Services Inc (PA)................804 794-1646
7600 Whitepine Rd North Chesterfield (23237) *(G-9898)*

Integrated Software Solutions.........................703 255-1130
1800 Alexander Bell Dr Reston (20191) *(G-10874)*

Integrated Tex Solutions Inc...........................540 389-8113
865 Cleveland Ave Salem (24153) *(G-12522)*

Integrated Vertical Tech LLC...........................757 410-7253
401 S Monterey Dr Chesapeake (23320) *(G-3144)*

Integrity National Corp...................................540 455-2340
17213 Doggetts Fork Rd Ruther Glen (22546) *(G-12456)*

Integrity Shirts LLC..540 577-5544
3130 Commerce St Blacksburg (24060) *(G-1746)*

Intel Corporation...571 312-2320
201 N Union St Alexandria (22314) *(G-238)*

Intel Federal LLC..703 633-0953
4100 Monu Crnr Dr Ste 540 Fairfax (22030) *(G-4637)*

Intel Federal LLC..302 644-3756
11911 Freedom Dr Reston (20190) *(G-10875)*

Intel Investigations LLC..................................540 521-4111
5727 Lost View Ln Roanoke (24018) *(G-11941)*

Intel Perspectives LLC....................................703 321-7507
5647 Ravenel Ln Springfield (22151) *(G-13024)*

Intellect Computers Inc (PA).........................703 931-5100
5100 Leesburg Pike # 100 Alexandria (22302) *(G-239)*

Intellgent Pwr A Solutions Inc.........................540 429-6177
11916 Sawhill Blvd Spotsylvania (22553) *(G-12898)*

Intelligence Press Inc (PA)............................703 318-8848
22648 Glenn Dr Ste 305 Sterling (20164) *(G-13429)*

Intelligent Bus Platforms LLC..........................202 640-8868
12020 Sunrise Valley Dr Reston (20191) *(G-10876)*

Intelligent Illuminations Inc (PA)...................888 455-2465
5101 Cleveland St Ste 302 Virginia Beach (23462) *(G-14550)*

Intelligent Platforms LLC (HQ)......................434 978-5000
2500 Austin Dr Charlottesville (22911) *(G-2647)*

Intelligent Software Design.............................703 731-9091
6728 Pine Creek Ct Mc Lean (22101) *(G-8466)*

Intelligize Incorporated (HQ)........................888 925-8627
1920 Assn Dr Ste 200 Reston (20191) *(G-10877)*

Intellimat Inc...540 904-5670
3959 Elc Rd Sw Ste 330 Roanoke (24018) *(G-11942)*

Intellirf Systems, Leesburg Also called National Affl Mktg Co Inc *(G-7318)*

Intense Cleaning Inc.......................................703 999-1933
43264 Gatwick Sq Ashburn (20147) *(G-1297)*

Inter-American Group Inc...............................202 255-4528
1800 Old Meadow Rd # 1002 Mc Lean (22102) *(G-8467)*

Interactive Achievement LLC...........................540 206-3649
601 Campbell Ave Sw Roanoke (24016) *(G-12107)*

Interad Limited LLC..757 787-7610
18321 Parkway Rd Melfa (23410) *(G-8710)*

Interalign LLC..804 314-4713
1711 Charles St Richmond (23226) *(G-11250)*

Interbake Foods LLC.......................................605 232-4903
900 Terminal Pl Richmond (23220) *(G-11619)*

Interbake Foods LLC.......................................540 631-8100
100 Baker Plz Front Royal (22630) *(G-5537)*

Interbyte..703 825-8774
7041 Kings Manor Dr Alexandria (22315) *(G-486)*

Interbyte Corp..703 825-8774
7041 Kings Manor Dr Alexandria (22315) *(G-487)*

Interco Print LLC..757 351-7000
150 Granby St Norfolk (23510) *(G-9594)*

Intercon Inc...434 525-3390
1222 Corporate Park Dr Forest (24551) *(G-5078)*

Interior 2000..804 598-0340
2434 New Dorset Cir Powhatan (23139) *(G-10551)*

Interior Building Systems Corp.........................703 335-9655
8501 Buckeye Timber Dr Manassas (20109) *(G-8083)*

Interleno Enterprises LLC................................757 340-3613
190 Thalia Vlg Shoppes Virginia Beach (23452) *(G-14551)*

Interlock Paving Systems Inc...........................757 722-2591
802 W Pembroke Ave Hampton (23669) *(G-6176)*

Interlocking Con Pavement Inst........................703 657-6900
14801 Murdock St Ste 230 Chantilly (20151) *(G-2443)*

Interlude Home Inc...540 381-7745
135 Warren St Christiansburg (24073) *(G-3598)*

Intermedia.aero, Fairfax Also called Aero Corporation *(G-4401)*

Intermet Foundries Inc....................................434 528-8721
1132 Mount Athos Rd Lynchburg (24504) *(G-7744)*

Intermission...703 971-7530
6205 Redwood Ln Alexandria (22310) *(G-488)*

Intermission Magazine, Alexandria Also called Intermission *(G-488)*

International Apparel Ltd.................................571 643-0100
13711 Dumfries Rd Manassas (20112) *(G-8084)*

International Automotive Compo.......................540 465-3741
806 E Queen St Strasburg (22657) *(G-13585)*

International Carbide & Engrg...........................434 568-3311
5000 Drakes Main St Drakes Branch (23937) *(G-4133)*

International Cmmnctns Strtgc..........................703 820-1669
1916 Wilson Blvd Ste 3 Arlington (22201) *(G-1005)*

International Designs LLC.................................804 275-1044
8310 Shell Rd Ste 102 North Chesterfield (23237) *(G-9899)*

International Machine Service...........................757 868-8487
19 Phillips Rd Poquoson (23662) *(G-10373)*

International Paint LLC.....................................757 466-0705
981 Scott St Ste 100 Norfolk (23502) *(G-9595)*

International Paper..757 569-4521
1069 Centerbrooke Ln Suffolk (23434) *(G-13725)*

International Paper Company............................757 569-4321
34040 Union Camp Dr Franklin (23851) *(G-5146)*

International Paper Company............................434 845-6071
3491 Mayflower Dr Lynchburg (24501) *(G-7745)*

International Paper Company............................757 405-3046
3100 Elmhurst Ln Portsmouth (23701) *(G-10444)*

International Paper Company............................804 861-8164
2333 Wells Rd Petersburg (23805) *(G-10326)*

International Paper Company............................804 232-4937
3100 Hopkins Rd Richmond (23234) *(G-11046)*

(G-0000) Company's Geographic Section entry number

ALPHABETIC SECTION
Itegrity Systems

International Paper Company 804 230-3100
2811 Cofer Rd Richmond (23224) ***(G-11620)***
International Publishers Mktg 703 661-1586
22841 Quicksilver Dr Sterling (20166) ***(G-13430)***
International Publishing Inc (PA) **800 377-2838**
1208 Centerville Tpke N Chesapeake (23320) ***(G-3145)***
International Replica Arms Co, Hampton *Also called Red Moon Partners LLC* ***(G-6226)***
International Roll-Call Corp 804 730-9600
8346 Old Richfood Rd C Mechanicsville (23116) ***(G-8642)***
International Trade & Tech Inc (PA) **703 929-0595**
4818 Midland Rd Midland (22728) ***(G-8758)***
International Veneer Co Inc (HQ) **434 447-7100**
1551 Montgomery St South Hill (23970) ***(G-12852)***
International Wine Review Hq 703 448-5566
6625 Old Chesterbrook Rd Mc Lean (22101) ***(G-8468)***
International Wine Spirits Ltd 804 274-1432
6603 W Broad St Richmond (23230) ***(G-11251)***
Interntional Abrasive Pdts Inc 540 797-7821
413 Hillcrest Heights Dr Moneta (24121) ***(G-8967)***
Interntional Maritime SEC Corp 719 494-6501
2400 Clarendon Blvd Arlington (22201) ***(G-1006)***
Interntional Registration Plan 502 845-0398
4196 Merchant Plz Lake Ridge (22192) ***(G-7156)***
Interntional Scanner Corp Amer (PA) **703 533-8560**
5901 Lee Hwy Arlington (22207) ***(G-1007)***
Interntnal Phrm Excpnts Adting 571 814-3449
3138 10th St N Ste 500 Arlington (22201) ***(G-1008)***
Interntnal Pzzle Cllctors Assn 757 420-7576
1323 Glyndon Dr Virginia Beach (23464) ***(G-14552)***
Interntnal Soc For Cmpttnal Bi 571 293-2113
525k E Market St Rm 330 Leesburg (20176) ***(G-7288)***
Interpretive Wdwrk Design Inc 703 330-6105
8513 Phoenix Dr Manassas (20110) ***(G-7953)***
Interprome Marketing Inc 804 744-2922
3005 E Boundary Ter Ste J Midlothian (23112) ***(G-8834)***
Interstate Cont Reading LLC 703 243-3355
1800 N Kent St Ste 1200 Arlington (22209) ***(G-1009)***
Interstate Rescue LLC 571 283-4206
290 Airport Rd Ste 2 Winchester (22602) ***(G-15429)***
Interstate Resources Inc 703 243-3355
1800 N Kent St Arlington (22209) ***(G-1010)***
Intertape Polymer Corp 434 797-8273
1101 Eagle Springs Rd Danville (24540) ***(G-4002)***
Interview Angel, Ashland *Also called Peterson Idea Consortium Inc* ***(G-1475)***
Intex LLC 703 899-3336
11409 Fieldstone Ln Reston (20191) ***(G-10878)***
Intl Printers World 804 403-3940
3887 Old Buckingham Rd Powhatan (23139) ***(G-10552)***
Into Light 757 816-9002
1100 Lethbridge Ct Virginia Beach (23454) ***(G-14553)***
Intor Inc 757 296-2175
901 N Pitt St Ste 325 Alexandria (22314) ***(G-240)***
Intouch For Inmates LLC 862 246-6283
212 Mountain Laurel Dr Lynchburg (24503) ***(G-7746)***
Intrapac (harrisonburg) Inc 540 434-1703
4850 Crowe Dr Mount Crawford (22841) ***(G-9055)***
Intricate Metal Forming Co 540 345-9233
1701 Midland Rd Salem (24153) ***(G-12523)***
Intrinsic Semiconductor Corp 703 437-4000
22660 Executive Dr # 101 Sterling (20166) ***(G-13431)***
Intuit Inc 540 752-6100
110 Juliad Ct Ste 107 Fredericksburg (22406) ***(G-5442)***
Intuit Your Life Network LLC 757 588-0533
8100 Simons Dr Ste 100 Norfolk (23505) ***(G-9596)***
Intuitive Global LLC 571 388-6183
12701 Crystal Lake Ct Manassas (20112) ***(G-8085)***
Intus Windows LLC 202 450-4211
2720 Prosperity Ave # 400 Fairfax (22031) ***(G-4480)***
Invelos Software Inc 540 786-8560
12830 Mill Rd Fredericksburg (22407) ***(G-5304)***
Invincea Inc 703 352-7680
3975 University Dr # 460 Fairfax (22030) ***(G-4638)***
Invirustech USA Inc 703 826-3109
1952 Gallows Rd Ste 303 Vienna (22182) ***(G-14072)***
Invision Inc 703 774-3881
10432 Balls Ford Rd # 300 Manassas (20109) ***(G-8086)***
Invista Capital Management LLC 540 949-2000
400 Dupont Blvd Waynesboro (22980) ***(G-15117)***
Invista Capital Management LLC 276 656-0500
1008 Dupont Rd Martinsville (24112) ***(G-8301)***
Invista Precision Concepts 276 656-0504
1008 Dupont Rd Martinsville (24112) ***(G-8302)***
Invizer LLC 410 903-2507
2552 James Maury Dr Herndon (20171) ***(G-6711)***
INX Internatiol Ink Co 540 977-0079
350 Eastpark Dr Roanoke (24019) ***(G-11943)***
Ios Press Inc 703 830-6300
6751 Tepper Dr Clifton (20124) ***(G-3673)***
Iowave Inc 703 979-9283
2100 Washington Blvd # 1001 Arlington (22204) ***(G-1011)***

Ipaatti Inc 703 901-7904
14074 Eagle Chase Cir Chantilly (20151) ***(G-2444)***
Ipac Industries LLC 703 362-9090
11943 Goodwood Dr Fairfax (22030) ***(G-4639)***
Ipas, Spotsylvania *Also called Intellgent Pwr A Solutions Inc* ***(G-12898)***
Ipea, Arlington *Also called Interntnal Phrm Excpnts Adting* ***(G-1008)***
Ips, Chesapeake *Also called Individual Products & Svcs Inc* ***(G-3141)***
Iq Energy LLC 804 747-8900
4860 Cox Rd Ste 300 Glen Allen (23060) ***(G-5752)***
Iq Global Technologies LLC 800 601-0678
8609 Westwood Center Dr Vienna (22182) ***(G-14073)***
Ir Engraving LLC 804 222-2821
5901 Lewis Rd Sandston (23150) ***(G-12621)***
Ir International, Sandston *Also called Standex Engraving LLC* ***(G-12636)***
Ireson Innovation 540 529-1572
336 Rollingwood Ct Troutville (24175) ***(G-13911)***
Irflex Corporation 434 483-4304
300 Ringgold Indus Pkwy Danville (24540) ***(G-4003)***
Iridium Communications Inc (PA) **703 287-7400**
1750 Tysons Blvd Ste 1400 Mc Lean (22102) ***(G-8469)***
Iridium Holdings LLC (HQ) **703 287-7400**
1750 Tysons Blvd Ste 1400 Mc Lean (22102) ***(G-8470)***
Iridium Satellite LLC (HQ) **703 356-0484**
1750 Tysons Blvd Ste 1400 Mc Lean (22102) ***(G-8471)***
Iris Co 804 310-1054
3925 Park Ave Richmond (23221) ***(G-11621)***
Iris's Essences, Virginia Beach *Also called I & C Hughes LLC* ***(G-14537)***
Iron Bow Holdings Inc 703 795-1790
3635 Concorde Pkwy # 700 Chantilly (20151) ***(G-2445)***
Iron Bow Holdings Inc (PA) **703 279-3000**
2303 Dulles Station Blvd # 400 Herndon (20171) ***(G-6712)***
Iron Brick Associates LLC (PA) **703 288-3874**
362 Old Hollow Rd Sperryville (22740) ***(G-12878)***
Iron Dog Metalsmiths 703 503-9631
9238 Kristin Ln Fairfax (22032) ***(G-4481)***
Iron Forge Software LLC 571 263-6540
2608 Iron Forge Rd Oak Hill (20171) ***(G-10137)***
Iron Gate Vlntr Fire Dept Inc 540 862-5700
300 Third St Iron Gate (24448) ***(G-6999)***
Iron Heart Winery LLC 540 320-0203
3742 Boone Furnace Rd Allisonia (24347) ***(G-618)***
Iron Horse Co 703 256-2853
6209 Berlee Dr Alexandria (22312) ***(G-489)***
Iron Lady Press LLC 540 898-7310
6100 Sunlight Mountain Rd Spotsylvania (22553) ***(G-12899)***
Iron Lungs Inc 757 877-2529
100 Lorna Doone Dr Yorktown (23692) ***(G-15966)***
Iron Pen Web Design & Printing 757 645-9945
707 North St Portsmouth (23704) ***(G-10445)***
Ironbrick, Sperryville *Also called Iron Brick Associates LLC* ***(G-12878)***
Irontek LLC 703 627-0092
21211 Edgewood Ct Sterling (20165) ***(G-13432)***
Iscb, Leesburg *Also called Interntnal Soc For Cmpttnal Bi* ***(G-7288)***
Iscoa, Arlington *Also called Interntional Scanner Corp Amer* ***(G-1007)***
Iselfschooling 703 821-3282
1202 Buchanan St Mc Lean (22101) ***(G-8472)***
Iskoyisal Inc 703 992-6629
1648 Westwind Way Mc Lean (22102) ***(G-8473)***
Island Decoys 757 336-5319
6136 Maddox Blvd Chincoteague (23336) ***(G-3562)***
Island Treasure's Gourmet, Manassas *Also called Cassandras Grmet Classics Corp* ***(G-7924)***
Isle of Wight Forest Products 757 899-8115
10242 General Mahone Hwy Wakefield (23888) ***(G-14967)***
Isle of Wight Forest Products (PA) **757 357-2009**
21158 Lankford Ln Smithfield (23430) ***(G-12716)***
Isley Brewing Company 804 499-0721
1715 Summit Ave Richmond (23230) ***(G-11252)***
Isley, Boyd A Jr, Salem *Also called Quaker Chemical Corporation* ***(G-12559)***
Isobaric Strategies Inc 757 277-2858
1808 Eden Way Virginia Beach (23454) ***(G-14554)***
Isobarix, Virginia Beach *Also called Isobaric Strategies Inc* ***(G-14554)***
Isomet Corporation (PA) **703 321-8301**
10342 Battleview Pkwy Manassas (20109) ***(G-8087)***
Isotemp Research Inc 434 295-3101
1801 Broadway St Charlottesville (22902) ***(G-2815)***
Isothrive LLC 855 552-5572
9385 Discovery Blvd Manassas (20109) ***(G-8088)***
Issues In Higher Education, Fairfax *Also called Cox Matthews & Associates Inc* ***(G-4607)***
It Solutions 4u Inc 703 624-4430
21010 Southbank St Sterling (20165) ***(G-13433)***
It Takes A Stitch Custom 703 405-6688
2700 25th St N Arlington (22207) ***(G-1012)***
IT&t, Midland *Also called International Trade & Tech Inc* ***(G-8758)***
Italica Imports, Norfolk *Also called Acesur North America Inc* ***(G-9419)***
Itechnologies Inc 703 723-5141
44037 Lords Valley Ter Ashburn (20147) ***(G-1298)***
Itegrity Systems 703 968-6300
13990 Parkeast Cir Chantilly (20151) ***(G-2446)***

ALPHABETIC

Itek Software LLC 312 404-3086
11604 Peavey St Glen Allen (23059) *(G-5753)*

Itek Software LLC 804 505-4835
5402 Glenside Dr Ste D Henrico (23228) *(G-6524)*

Iteris Inc 949 270-9400
11781 Lee Jackson Memoria Fairfax (22033) *(G-4482)*

Itforesight LLC 703 829-7283
11561 North Shore Dr # 21 Reston (20190) *(G-10879)*

Itg Brands 434 792-0521
200 Kentuck Rd Danville (24540) *(G-4004)*

Itg Cigars Inc 804 233-7668
600 Perdue Ave Richmond (23224) *(G-11622)*

ITI Group 703 339-5388
8245 Backlick Rd Ste D Lorton (22079) *(G-7497)*

Itkm Systems LLC 502 370-6488
9220 Stephens Manor Dr Mechanicsville (23116) *(G-8643)*

Itl (virginia) Inc 804 381-0905
305 Ashcake Rd Ste L Ashland (23005) *(G-1441)*

Itl NA Inc 703 435-6700
1175 Herndon Pkwy Ste 350 Herndon (20170) *(G-6713)*

Its About Golf 703 437-1527
649 Alabama Dr Herndon (20170) *(G-6714)*

Its All Mx LLC 540 785-6295
2400 Burgess Rd Chester (23836) *(G-3425)*

Its Homeade LLC 804 641-8248
Rr 203 Box 309 Kinsale (22488) *(G-7135)*

Its Just Furniture Inc 703 357-6405
1285 Central Park Blvd Fredericksburg (22401) *(G-5197)*

Its Manufacturing Incorporated 804 397-0504
1918 W Virginia Ave Crewe (23930) *(G-3813)*

Itst Inc 703 455-2152
9211 Paloma Ln Springfield (22153) *(G-13025)*

ITT Corporation 540 362-8000
7671 Enon Dr Roanoke (24019) *(G-11944)*

ITT Defense & Electronics 703 790-6300
1650 Tysons Blvd Ste 1700 Mc Lean (22102) *(G-8474)*

ITT Exelis 757 594-1600
11830 Canon Blvd Ste J Newport News (23606) *(G-9261)*

ITT LLC 703 550-2594
6012 Chapman Rd Lorton (22079) *(G-7498)*

Itty Bitty Stitchings LLC 540 829-9197
13396 Chestnut Fork Rd Culpeper (22701) *(G-3896)*

Itz ME Creations 804 519-6023
7607 Rolling Fields Pl Chesterfield (23832) *(G-3506)*

Ius Bello Defense LLC 540 720-2571
1015 John Paul Jones Dr Stafford (22554) *(G-13155)*

IV Labs Inc 540 585-3030
300 Technology Dr Christiansburg (24073) *(G-3599)*

Ivans Inc 804 271-0477
9740 Jefferson Davis Hwy North Chesterfield (23237) *(G-9900)*

Ivc, South Hill *Also called International Veneer Co Inc* *(G-12852)*

Ivc-Usa Inc (PA) **434 447-7100**
1551 Montgomery St South Hill (23970) *(G-12853)*

Iviz Ltd 877 290-4911
7 Brannigan Dr Stafford (22554) *(G-13156)*

Ivory Dog Press LLC 540 353-3939
5018 S Gala Dr Roanoke (24019) *(G-11945)*

Ivorys Essentials LLC 571 201-6147
14100 Estate Manor Dr Gainesville (20155) *(G-5591)*

Ivwatch LLC 855 489-2824
700 Tech Center Pkwy # 300 Newport News (23606) *(G-9262)*

Ivy Creek Media 434 971-1787
2465 Williston Dr Charlottesville (22901) *(G-2648)*

Ivy House Publishing LLC 434 295-5015
3738 Morgantown Rd Charlottesville (22903) *(G-2816)*

Ivy Manufacturing LLC 434 249-0134
1615 W Pines Dr Charlottesville (22901) *(G-2649)*

Ivy Publication LLC 434 984-4713
4282 Ivy Rd Charlottesville (22903) *(G-2817)*

Ivy Software Inc 804 769-7193
1146 Richmond Tapp Hwy Manquin (23106) *(G-8216)*

Iwoan LLC 347 606-0602
3709 S George Mason Dr # 713 Falls Church (22041) *(G-4809)*

Ixidor LLC 571 332-3888
3705 S Grge Msn Dr 2315 Falls Church (22041) *(G-4810)*

Ixthos Inc 703 779-7800
741 Miller Dr Se Ste D1 Leesburg (20175) *(G-7289)*

J & A Tools 434 414-0871
407 Hartless Rd Amherst (24521) *(G-696)*

J & D Pallets 540 862-2448
2050 State Ave Clifton Forge (24422) *(G-3680)*

J & D Specialtees 804 561-0817
12421 Loblolly Dr Amelia Court House (23002) *(G-659)*

J & J Enterprises, Clarksville *Also called Lakeside Stone & Landscape Sup* *(G-3632)*

J & J Powder Coating 757 406-2922
2424 Castleton Commerce W Virginia Beach (23456) *(G-14555)*

J & J Printing Inc 703 764-0088
5540 Port Royal Rd Springfield (22151) *(G-13026)*

J & J Welding LLC 571 271-3337
11760 Armistead Filler Ln Lovettsville (20180) *(G-7579)*

J & J Welding LLC 703 431-1044
15770 Temple Hall Ln Leesburg (20176) *(G-7290)*

J & K Screen Printing Company, Danville *Also called Harville Entps of Danville VA* *(G-3997)*

J & L Communications Inc 434 973-1830
909 Gardens Blvd Charlottesville (22901) *(G-2650)*

J & M Printing Inc 703 549-2432
1001 N Fairfax St Ste 100 Alexandria (22314) *(G-241)*

J & M Sheet Metal Inc 571 722-2805
14141 Asher Vw Centreville (20121) *(G-2311)*

J & P Meat Processing 540 721-2765
10 Jamont Ln Wirtz (24184) *(G-15615)*

J & R Graphic Services Inc 757 595-2602
124 Production Dr Yorktown (23693) *(G-15967)*

J & R Log & WD Processors LLC 703 494-6994
2063 Jefferson Davis Hwy # 23 Stafford (22554) *(G-13157)*

J & R Partners 757 274-3344
2000 Colonial Ave Norfolk (23517) *(G-9597)*

J & R Partners (PA) **757 499-3344**
4780 Euclid Rd Virginia Beach (23462) *(G-14556)*

J & V Kitchen Inc 540 291-2794
9 Surrey Ln Natural Bridge (24578) *(G-9107)*

J & V Publishing LLC 571 318-1700
2427 Little Current Dr # 2722 Herndon (20171) *(G-6715)*

J & W Logging Inc 540 474-3531
1353 Wimer Mountain Rd Blue Grass (24413) *(G-1843)*

J & W Screen Printing Inc 276 963-0862
Rr 460 Cedar Bluff (24609) *(G-2279)*

J and E Machine Shop Inc 804 966-7180
106 Rxbury Indus Ctr Ste Charles City (23030) *(G-2577)*

J and J Energy Holdings 757 963-9763
4772 Euclid Rd Ste B Virginia Beach (23462) *(G-14557)*

J and R Manufacturing Inc 276 210-1647
351 Industrial Park Rd Bluefield (24605) *(G-1865)*

J B Worsham 434 836-9313
202 Nelson Ave Danville (24540) *(G-4005)*

J C Enterprises 540 345-0552
526 Rorer Ave Sw Roanoke (24016) *(G-12108)*

J C International LLC 540 243-0086
95 E Court St Rocky Mount (24151) *(G-12329)*

J C Printing Corp 703 378-3500
14508c Lee Rd Chantilly (20151) *(G-2447)*

J C Steel De Tech 757 376-7469
5304 Larkins Lair Ct Virginia Beach (23464) *(G-14558)*

J D Shelton 434 797-4403
18465 Old Richmond Rd Keeling (24566) *(G-7025)*

J D Welding, King George *Also called Jesse Dudley Jr* *(G-7095)*

J E Moore Lumber Co Inc 434 634-9740
1275 Brink Rd Emporia (23847) *(G-4361)*

J Eubank Signs & Designs 434 374-2364
598 Buffalo Rd Clarksville (23927) *(G-3631)*

J Fred Dowis 757 874-7446
15454 Warwick Blvd Newport News (23608) *(G-9263)*

J H Fitzgerald Jr Logging, Tyro *Also called Fitzgerald John* *(G-13939)*

J H Knighton Lumber Co Inc 804 448-4681
25227 Jefferson Davis Hwy Ruther Glen (22546) *(G-12457)*

J H Miles Co Inc (PA) **757 622-9264**
902 Southampton Ave Norfolk (23510) *(G-9598)*

J Henry Holland, Hampton *Also called Mazzella Jhh Company Inc* *(G-6193)*

J J E Enterprise Holdings LLC 410 703-9241
10313 Litchfield Dr Spotsylvania (22553) *(G-12900)*

J K Drapery Inc 703 941-3788
5641I General Wash Dr Alexandria (22312) *(G-490)*

J K Enterprise Inc 703 352-1858
3600 Ox Ridge Ct Fairfax (22033) *(G-4483)*

J L Sexton & Son, North Tazewell *Also called William G Sexton* *(G-10111)*

J L V Management Inc 540 446-6359
6 Saint Elizabeths Ct Stafford (22556) *(G-13158)*

J Lynette Buty & Bundles LLC 276 790-9510
707 Berkshire Pl Martinsville (24112) *(G-8303)*

J M Fry Company (PA) **804 236-8100**
4329 Eubank Rd Henrico (23231) *(G-6525)*

J M H Diagnostic Center 276 628-1439
605 Campus Dr Abingdon (24210) *(G-42)*

J P R Enterprises 757 288-8795
1011 Annette St Chesapeake (23324) *(G-3146)*

J R Plastics & Machining Inc 434 277-8334
2820 Lowesville Rd Lowesville (22922) *(G-7595)*

J R Precision Machine Service, Yorktown *Also called James M Rohrbach Inc* *(G-15968)*

J Reynolds Welding & Repair, Mechanicsville *Also called Jennifer Reynolds* *(G-8644)*

J S & A Cake Decoration 703 494-3767
1309 E Longview Dr Woodbridge (22191) *(G-15727)*

J T Packard, Richmond *Also called ABB Power Protection LLC* *(G-11079)*

J V Ramsey Logging LLC 434 610-1844
220 Oak Ln Appomattox (24522) *(G-814)*

J W Altizer 540 382-2652
2255 Mud Pike Christiansburg (24073) *(G-3600)*

J W Bibb Shooting Bags 434 384-9431
923 Ambrose Rucker Rd Monroe (24574) *(G-8993)*

(G-0000) Company's Geographic Section entry number

J W Creations..276 676-3770
  22530 Aven Ln Abingdon (24211) *(G-43)*

J Z Utility Barns LLC..276 686-1683
  572 Milk Plant Rd Rural Retreat (24368) *(G-12425)*

J&A Innovations LLC.......................................804 387-6466
  1925 Regiment Ter Midlothian (23113) *(G-8835)*

J&J Logistics Consulting LLC.......................404 431-3613
  6564 Loisdale Ct Ste 600 Springfield (22150) *(G-13027)*

J&J Powder Coating..757 390-0237
  2401 Bowland Pkwy Ste 103 Virginia Beach (23454) *(G-14559)*

J&S Creations, Pearisburg *Also called J&S Fisher LLC (G-10275)*

J&S Fisher LLC..540 921-3197
  301 Forest Hill Dr Pearisburg (24134) *(G-10275)*

J&S Marine Canvas LLC..................................757 580-6883
  1629 Falls Brook Run Chesapeake (23322) *(G-3147)*

J&T Wlding Fbrication Campbell...................434 369-8589
  569 Riverbend Rd Altavista (24517) *(G-632)*

J-Alm Publishing..703 385-9766
  3403 Miller Heights Rd Oakton (22124) *(G-10152)*

J.M. Fry Printing Inks, Henrico *Also called J M Fry Company (G-6525)*

Ja Designs...540 659-2592
  10 Guy Ln Stafford (22554) *(G-13159)*

Ja Engraving Company LLC..............................540 230-8490
  100 Ash Dr Christiansburg (24073) *(G-3601)*

Ja Le Custom Crafts..804 541-8957
  8900 Teakwood Dr Disputanta (23842) *(G-4109)*

Ja-Zan LLC..434 978-2140
  1150 Pepsi Pl Ste 100 Charlottesville (22901) *(G-2651)*

Jacatai Vending...804 317-2526
  9643 Ransom Hills Ter North Chesterfield (23237) *(G-9901)*

Jack Campbell Widner.....................................703 646-8841
  3479 Whitetop Rd Chilhowie (24319) *(G-3552)*

Jack Carter Cabinet Maker.............................757 622-9414
  125 E Severn Rd Norfolk (23505) *(G-9599)*

Jack Clamp Sales Co Inc................................757 827-6704
  4116 W Mercury Blvd Hampton (23666) *(G-6177)*

Jack Einreinhof...434 239-3072
  136 Yorkshire Cir Lynchburg (24502) *(G-7747)*

Jack Kennedy Welding......................................757 340-4269
  413 Old Forge Ct Virginia Beach (23452) *(G-14560)*

Jack Stone Quarry..804 862-6669
  23308 Cox Rd North Dinwiddie (23803) *(G-10054)*

Jacked Up Foods LLC......................................540 623-6313
  11403 Meadow Wood Ave Fredericksburg (22407) *(G-5305)*

Jackie E Calhoun Sr...276 328-8318
  8025 Indian Creek Rd Wise (24293) *(G-15628)*

Jackie Screen Printing.....................................276 963-0964
  2401 Front St Richlands (24641) *(G-11017)*

Jackite Inc...757 426-5359
  3612 West Neck Rd Virginia Beach (23456) *(G-14561)*

Jacks Mountain Quarry, Roanoke *Also called Rockydale Quarries Corporation (G-12171)*

Jackson & Jackson Inc...................................434 851-1798
  4903 Rowe Ridge Rd Nw Roanoke (24017) *(G-12109)*

Jackson 20...703 842-2790
  480 King St Alexandria (22314) *(G-242)*

Jackson Enterprises Inc...................................703 527-1118
  4908 Washington Blvd Arlington (22205) *(G-1013)*

Jackson Furniture Company VA.......................540 635-3187
  239 E 6th St Front Royal (22630) *(G-5538)*

Jackson Pointe LLC..757 269-7100
  628 Hofstadter Rd Ste 6 Newport News (23606) *(G-9264)*

Jaco Manufacturing Inc...................................276 783-2688
  263 Nicks Creek Rd Atkins (24311) *(G-1519)*

Jacobs Powder Coating LLC..........................540 208-7762
  8253 Spotswood Trl Penn Laird (22846) *(G-10289)*

Jade Suppliers..804 551-6865
  3304 E Marshall St Richmond (23223) *(G-11623)*

Jae El Incorporated..540 535-5210
  42305 Green Meadow Ln Leesburg (20176) *(G-7291)*

Jaeger & Ernst Inc...434 973-7018
  4785 Burnley Station Rd Barboursville (22923) *(G-1562)*

Jaeger & Ernst Cabinetmakers, Barboursville *Also called Jaeger & Ernst Inc (G-1562)*

Jafree Shirt Co Inc...276 228-2116
  1200 W Main St Wytheville (24382) *(G-15892)*

Jah Rootz Industries LLC................................512 925-1109
  26 Pleasant Hill Rd Harrisonburg (22801) *(G-6332)*

Jake Little Construction Inc.............................276 498-7462
  2862 Wilderness Rd Oakwood (24631) *(G-10169)*

Jake Publishing Inc...757 377-6771
  2228 Mill Crossing Dr # 308 Virginia Beach (23454) *(G-14562)*

Jamerrill Publishing Co LLC...........................540 908-5234
  19353 N Mountain Rd Timberville (22853) *(G-13850)*

James A Kennedy & Assoc Inc........................804 241-6836
  4529 Mattox Crossing Ct Powhatan (23139) *(G-10553)*

James Allen Printing Co...................................540 463-9232
  145 E Midland Trl Lexington (24450) *(G-7396)*

James Associates I LLC..................................804 590-2620
  8100 Hickory Rd South Chesterfield (23803) *(G-12836)*

James D Crews Logging...................................434 349-1999
  3030 Armistead Rd Nathalie (24577) *(G-9103)*

James Doctor Press Inc....................................703 476-0579
  3311 Bywater Ct Herndon (20171) *(G-6716)*

James E Henson Jr...804 648-3005
  422 E Franklin St Ste 104 Richmond (23219) *(G-11624)*

James Hardie Building Pdts Inc.......................540 980-9143
  1000 James Hardy Way Pulaski (24301) *(G-10639)*

James Hintzke...757 374-4827
  1912 Bernstein Dr Virginia Beach (23454) *(G-14563)*

James J Gray...757 617-5279
  974 Mantura Rd Surry (23883) *(G-13797)*

James J Roberts...703 330-0448
  7808 Lake Dr Manassas (20111) *(G-8089)*

James J Totaro Associates LLC......................703 326-9525
  22900 Shaw Rd Sterling (20166) *(G-13434)*

James Kacian...540 722-2156
  731 Mahone Dr Winchester (22601) *(G-15550)*

James Lassiter..757 595-4242
  725 Arrowhead Dr Newport News (23601) *(G-9265)*

James Lee Herndon..703 549-2585
  164 Colburn Dr Manassas Park (20111) *(G-8202)*

James M Rohrbach Inc......................................757 898-6322
  117 Greene Dr Ste B Yorktown (23692) *(G-15968)*

James Pirtle...540 477-2647
  10817 Senedo Rd Mount Jackson (22842) *(G-9073)*

James R Napier...434 547-5511
  2299 Westpoint Stevens Rd Drakes Branch (23937) *(G-4134)*

James River Beverage Co LLC........................434 589-2798
  1111 Dogwood Dr Kents Store (23084) *(G-7039)*

James River Cellars Inc....................................804 550-7516
  11008 Washington Hwy Glen Allen (23059) *(G-5754)*

James River Cellars Winery, Glen Allen *Also called James River Cellars Inc (G-5754)*

James River Coal Company, Richmond *Also called Johns Creek Elkhorn Coal Corp (G-11634)*

James River Coal Company (PA)......................**804 780-3000**
  901 E Byrd St Fl 2 Richmond (23219) *(G-11625)*

James River Coal Service Co (HQ)..................**606 878-7411**
  901 E Byrd St Fl 2 Richmond (23219) *(G-11626)*

James River Distillery LLC..............................804 716-5172
  2700 Hardy Rd Richmond (23220) *(G-11627)*

James River Embroidery...................................434 987-9800
  100 Jackson St Scottsville (24590) *(G-12661)*

James River Enviromental Inc..........................804 966-7609
  8075 Long Reach Rd Providence Forge (23140) *(G-10626)*

James River Escrow Inc....................................804 780-3000
  901 E Byrd St Ste 1600 Richmond (23219) *(G-11628)*

James River Industries BT..............................702 515-9937
  300 Lucado Pl Lynchburg (24504) *(G-7748)*

James River Logging & Excav.........................434 295-8457
  3462 Scottsville Rd Charlottesville (22902) *(G-2818)*

James River Press..804 230-4515
  807 Oliver Hill Way Richmond (23219) *(G-11629)*

James River Printing LLC.................................804 520-1000
  2900 Cedar Ln Ste A Colonial Heights (23834) *(G-3735)*

James River Publishing Inc..............................804 740-0729
  11202 Pinewood Ct Henrico (23238) *(G-6526)*

James River Signs Inc......................................757 870-3368
  724 City Center Blvd A Newport News (23606) *(G-9266)*

James Slater..757 566-1543
  145 Marstons Ln Williamsburg (23188) *(G-15258)*

James T Davis, Lynchburg *Also called Davis-Frost Inc (G-7695)*

James Williams Polsg & Buffing.....................703 690-2247
  5406 Staples Ln Woodbridge (22193) *(G-15728)*

James-York Security LLC.................................757 344-1808
  1226 Penniman Rd Williamsburg (23185) *(G-15259)*

Jamesgate Press LLC.......................................703 892-5621
  2312 S Pierce St Arlington (22202) *(G-1014)*

Jamestown Cellars, Williamsburg *Also called Williamsburg Winery Ltd (G-15343)*

Jami Ventures Inc...703 352-5679
  9653 Fairfax Blvd Ste 205 Fairfax (22031) *(G-4484)*

Jamie Nicholas..703 731-7966
  4812 20th Pl N Arlington (22207) *(G-1015)*

Jamie Nicholas Prtg & Graphics, Arlington *Also called Jamie Nicholas (G-1015)*

Jamison Printing Inc...540 992-3568
  346 Jamison Farm Ln Troutville (24175) *(G-13912)*

Jammac Corporation...757 855-5474
  6610 E Virginia Bch Blvd Norfolk (23502) *(G-9600)*

Jammerson Logging..434 983-7505
  Rr 632 Andersonville (23936) *(G-726)*

Jammin..540 484-4600
  335 Technology Dr Rocky Mount (24151) *(G-12330)*

Jammin Apparel, Rocky Mount *Also called Jammin (G-12330)*

Jan Tana Inc...540 586-8266
  1208 Hideaway Rd Goode (24556) *(G-5891)*

Janao, Fairfax *Also called Janice Osthus (G-4485)*

Jane Hfl Gresham..757 397-2208
  212 Chautauqua Ave Portsmouth (23707) *(G-10446)*

Janes Cyber Defense LLC...............................703 489-1872
  4220 Shannon Hill Rd Alexandria (22310) *(G-491)*

Janice Martin-Freeman 757 234-0056
30 Holloway Rd Newport News (23602) ***(G-9267)***
Janice Osthus 571 212-2247
2862 Glenvale Dr Fairfax (22031) ***(G-4485)***
Janice Research Group 703 971-8901
6363 Walker Ln Ste 110 Alexandria (22310) ***(G-492)***
Janie Draperies Shop, Axton *Also called Jannie J Jones* ***(G-1538)***
Jannie J Jones 276 650-3174
994 Birchwood Rd Axton (24054) ***(G-1538)***
Jansson & Associate Mstr Bldr 757 965-7285
5039 Euclid Rd Virginia Beach (23462) ***(G-14564)***
Jar-Tan Inc 757 548-6066
936 Professional Pl C1 Chesapeake (23320) ***(G-3148)***
Jarcam Sports 678 995-4607
3174 E Ocean View Ave Norfolk (23518) ***(G-9601)***
Jarrett Millwork 540 377-9173
5987 N Lee Hwy Fairfield (24435) ***(G-4731)***
Jarrett Millwork & Moldings, Fairfield *Also called Jarrett Millwork* ***(G-4731)***
Jarrett Welding and Mch Inc (PA) **434 793-3717**
1212 Goodyear Blvd Danville (24541) ***(G-4006)***
Jarvis Sign Company 804 514-9879
109 Maple Ave Richmond (23226) ***(G-11253)***
Jason Hammond Aldous 540 672-5050
127 Berry Hill Rd Orange (22960) ***(G-10216)***
Jasons Ammo 757 715-4689
301 Oak Point Dr Yorktown (23692) ***(G-15969)***
Javatec Inc 276 621-4572
300 Chaney Branch Rd Crockett (24323) ***(G-3825)***
Javawood USA LLC 703 658-9665
5641 General Wash Dr Alexandria (22312) ***(G-493)***
Jay Blue Pos Inc 703 672-2869
5105m Backlick Rd Annandale (22003) ***(G-761)***
Jay Dees Welding Services 757 675-8368
3023 Elbyrne Dr Chesapeake (23325) ***(G-3149)***
Jay Douglas Carper 757 595-7660
200 Old Marina Ln Newport News (23602) ***(G-9268)***
Jay Malanga 703 802-0201
14504 Lee Rd Chantilly (20151) ***(G-2448)***
JB Installations Inc 703 403-2119
8905 Old Courthouse Rd Vienna (22182) ***(G-14074)***
JB Pinker Inc 540 943-2760
179 Azalea Dr Afton (22920) ***(G-85)***
JB Productions 703 494-6075
13813 Botts Ave Woodbridge (22191) ***(G-15729)***
JB Wood Works LLC 540 589-5281
3355 View Ave Roanoke (24018) ***(G-11946)***
JB Wood Works Roanoke Co, Roanoke *Also called JB Wood Works LLC* ***(G-11946)***
Jbt Aerotech 336 254-4104
5300 Federal Rd Richmond (23250) ***(G-11254)***
Jbtm Enterprises Inc 540 665-9651
127 Harvest Ridge Dr Winchester (22601) ***(G-15551)***
JC Bradley Lumber Co 540 962-4446
4500 Indian Draft Rd Covington (24426) ***(G-3792)***
JC Pallet Company Inc (PA) **800 754-5050**
18427 New Kent Hwy Barhamsville (23011) ***(G-1572)***
Jcd, Alexandria *Also called Janes Cyber Defense LLC* ***(G-491)***
Jci Jones Chemicals Inc 804 633-5066
16248 Industrial Dr Milford (22514) ***(G-8931)***
Jclfarms LLC 757 291-1401
107 Barn Elm Rd Williamsburg (23188) ***(G-15260)***
JD Concrete LLC 703 331-2155
9207 Enterprise Ct Manassas Park (20111) ***(G-8203)***
JD Goodman Welding 804 598-1070
2559 Walkers Ridge Cir Powhatan (23139) ***(G-10554)***
JD Gordon Tool Company LLC 804 832-9907
139 Bennett Crest Dr Locust Hill (23092) ***(G-7453)***
Jddr Foods Inc 571 356-0165
12255 Angel Wing Ct Reston (20191) ***(G-10880)***
Jean Lee Inc 703 630-0276
334 Potomac Ave Quantico (22134) ***(G-10689)***
Jean Samuels 804 328-2294
6600 Scandia Lake Pl Sandston (23150) ***(G-12622)***
Jeanette Ann Smith 757 622-0182
3535 Tidewater Dr Norfolk (23509) ***(G-9602)***
Jeannie Jackson Green 540 904-6763
1736 Greenwood Rd Sw Roanoke (24015) ***(G-12110)***
Jedi Prints LLC 757 869-4267
13905 Deer Thicket Ln Midlothian (23112) ***(G-8836)***
Jefco Inc 757 460-0403
1449 Mller Str Rd Ste 102 Virginia Beach (23455) ***(G-14565)***
Jeff Britt Logging 540 884-2499
1063 Allen Branch Rd Eagle Rock (24085) ***(G-4281)***
Jeff Fleisher 703 955-6873
645 Highview Rd New Market (22844) ***(G-9143)***
Jeff Hoskins 804 769-1295
11414 W River Rd Aylett (23009) ***(G-1549)***
Jeff Shearer 703 313-7670
6150 Manchester Park Cir Alexandria (22310) ***(G-494)***
Jefferson Homebuilders Inc 540 371-5338
10229 Tidewater Trl Fredericksburg (22408) ***(G-5306)***
Jefferson Homebuilders Inc 540 727-2240
15487 Braggs Corner Rd Culpeper (22701) ***(G-3897)***
Jefferson Homebuilders Inc (PA) **540 825-5898**
501 N Main St Culpeper (22701) ***(G-3898)***
Jefferson Homebuilders Inc 540 825-5200
15487 Braggs Corner Rd Culpeper (22701) ***(G-3899)***
Jefferson Labs, Newport News *Also called Jackson Pointe LLC* ***(G-9264)***
Jefferson Mllwk & Design Inc 703 260-3370
44098 Mercure Cir Ste 115 Sterling (20166) ***(G-13435)***
Jeffrey Gill 703 309-7061
2508 Buck Island Rd Charlottesville (22902) ***(G-2819)***
Jeffrey M Haughney Attorney PC 757 802-6160
1537 Quail Point Rd Virginia Beach (23454) ***(G-14566)***
Jeffrey O Holdren 703 360-9739
9440 Mount Vernon Cir Alexandria (22309) ***(G-495)***
Jeffs Mobile Welding Inc 757 870-7049
415 Oakwood Pl Newport News (23608) ***(G-9269)***
Jeffs Tools Inc 804 694-6337
6317 Ark Rd Gloucester (23061) ***(G-5851)***
Jember LLC 202 631-8521
7421 Fordson Rd Apt A11 Alexandria (22306) ***(G-496)***
Jenfab, Covington *Also called Williams Fabrication Inc* ***(G-3804)***
Jenkins Logging 540 543-2079
3183 Meander Run Rd Culpeper (22701) ***(G-3900)***
Jennifer Enos 571 721-9268
3311 Commwl Ave Apt F Alexandria (22305) ***(G-243)***
Jennifer Lavey 540 313-0015
245 Nightingale Ave Stephens City (22655) ***(G-13318)***
Jennifer Omohundro 804 937-9308
10309 Wilkes Ridge Pl Richmond (23233) ***(G-11255)***
Jennifer Ouk 571 232-0991
3901 Fairfax Pkwy Alexandria (22312) ***(G-497)***
Jennifer Reynolds 804 229-1697
9234 Fair Hill Ct Mechanicsville (23116) ***(G-8644)***
Jennings Boat Yard Inc 804 453-7181
169 Boatyard Rd Reedville (22539) ***(G-10762)***
Jennings Logging LLC 434 248-6876
178 Jennings Farm Ln Prospect (23960) ***(G-10613)***
Jennings Stained Glass Inc 434 283-1301
1802 Long Island Rd Gladys (24554) ***(G-5693)***
Jennmar Corporation 540 726-2326
101 Powell Mountain Rd Rich Creek (24147) ***(G-11007)***
Jennmar of Pennsylvania LLC 276 964-2107
470 Wardell Indus Pk Rd Cedar Bluff (24609) ***(G-2280)***
Jennmar of Pennsylvania LLC 276 964-7000
559 Wardell Ind Park Rd Cedar Bluff (24609) ***(G-2281)***
Jensen Apparel, Chesapeake *Also called Jensen Promotional Items Inc* ***(G-3150)***
Jensen Promotional Items Inc (PA) **757 966-7608**
315 Great Bridge Blvd A Chesapeake (23320) ***(G-3150)***
Jensen Promotional Items Inc 276 521-0143
1201 E Lee Hwy Chilhowie (24319) ***(G-3553)***
Jenzabar Inc 540 432-5200
181 S Liberty St Harrisonburg (22801) ***(G-6333)***
Jeremiahs Woodwork LLC 804 519-0984
3003 Cove Ridge Rd Midlothian (23112) ***(G-8837)***
Jerry A Kotchka 757 721-6782
2349 Tierra Monte Arch Virginia Beach (23456) ***(G-14567)***
Jerry Cantrell 540 379-7689
1090 Truslow Rd Fredericksburg (22406) ***(G-5443)***
Jerry Johnston 540 674-0932
5015 Woodlyn St Dublin (24084) ***(G-4160)***
Jerry K Wilson Inc 434 299-5175
1810 Hunting Creek Rd Big Island (24526) ***(G-1704)***
Jerry King 804 550-1243
10477c Cobbs Rd Glen Allen (23059) ***(G-5755)***
Jerry Lee Marshall 276 952-5486
551 Elk Creek Rd Stuart (24171) ***(G-13619)***
Jerry's Signs & Awnings, Abingdon *Also called Jerrys Signs Inc* ***(G-44)***
Jerrys Antique Prints Ltd 540 949-7114
366 Dooms Crossing Rd Waynesboro (22980) ***(G-15118)***
Jerrys Engines LLC 540 885-1205
9 Court Sq Staunton (24401) ***(G-13269)***
Jerrys Signs Inc 276 676-2304
15775 Porterfield Hwy Abingdon (24210) ***(G-44)***
Jes Construction LLC (PA) **757 558-9909**
1741 Corp Landing Pkwy # 101 Virginia Beach (23454) ***(G-14568)***
Jes Foundation Repair, Virginia Beach *Also called Jes Construction LLC* ***(G-14568)***
Jesse Dudley Jr 540 663-3773
16084 Dudley Dr King George (22485) ***(G-7095)***
Jesse Nails and Spa, Madison Heights *Also called Ni PHI Thach* ***(G-7878)***
Jessica Burdett 719 423-0582
12232 Prince George Dr Disputanta (23842) ***(G-4110)***
Jessica Burdett Ind Conslt, Disputanta *Also called Jessica Burdett* ***(G-4110)***
Jessica Radellant Designs LLC 804 301-3994
735 Hartford Ln North Chesterfield (23236) ***(G-9902)***
Jester Woodworks Llc Van 804 562-6360
3801 Carolina Ave Richmond (23222) ***(G-11630)***
Jet Design Graphics Inc 804 921-4164
8925 Dunnston Dr Amelia Court House (23002) ***(G-660)***

Jet Managers International Inc 703 829-0679
  211 N Union St Ste 100 Alexandria (22314) *(G-244)*

Jet Pac LLC 804 334-5216
  215 E Randolph Rd Hopewell (23860) *(G-6936)*

Jet Weld Inc 540 836-0163
  217 Union Church Rd Churchville (24421) *(G-3620)*

Jetney Development 714 262-0759
  1516 High St Salem (24153) *(G-12524)*

Jetts Sheet Metal Inc 540 899-7725
  211 Newton Rd Fredericksburg (22405) *(G-5444)*

Jewel Holding LLC 202 271-5265
  14273 Silverdale Dr Woodbridge (22193) *(G-15730)*

Jewelers Services Inc 804 353-9612
  6523 Centralia Rd Chesterfield (23832) *(G-3507)*

Jewell Smokeless Coal Corp (HQ) **276 935-8810**
  1029 Miners Rd Oakwood (24631) *(G-10170)*

Jewells Buildings 804 333-4483
  13410 Richmond Rd Warsaw (22572) *(G-15069)*

Jewett Automation Inc 804 344-8101
  700 Gordon Ave Richmond (23224) *(G-11631)*

Jewett Mch Mfg Co Inc Bryce D 804 233-9873
  2901 Maury St Richmond (23224) *(G-11632)*

Jewl's N' Gems By Tonja, Portsmouth *Also called Jones Tonja (G-10448)*

Jgtsenterprise Inc 804 677-4578
  9073 Brevet Ln Mechanicsville (23116) *(G-8645)*

Jh Enterprise Inc 757 639-5049
  233 W 30th St Norfolk (23504) *(G-9603)*

Jha LLC 757 535-2724
  151 Florida Ave Portsmouth (23707) *(G-10447)*

Jhl Inc 703 378-0009
  14516c Lee Rd Chantilly (20151) *(G-2449)*

Jif Pallets LLC 276 963-6107
  3242 Kents Ridge Rd Doran (24612) *(G-4117)*

Jihoon Solution Inc 757 344-1751
  205 Alexia Ln Yorktown (23690) *(G-15970)*

Jill C Perla 703 407-5695
  17090 Greenwood Dr Round Hill (20141) *(G-12380)*

Jim Champion 276 466-9112
  23531 Young Dr Bristol (24202) *(G-2022)*

Jim L Clark 276 393-2359
  1220 Cox Rd Jonesville (24263) *(G-7022)*

Jim Sirrine 540 874-7006
  2717 Beverly Blvd Sw Roanoke (24015) *(G-12111)*

Jim Warehime 804 861-5255
  214a Grove Ave Petersburg (23803) *(G-10327)*

Jimmy Dockery Logging 276 225-0149
  206 Misty Morning Cir Gate City (24251) *(G-5664)*

Jimmy French 757 583-2536
  6605 Pinewood Ct Virginia Beach (23464) *(G-14569)*

Jimmy's Engine Service, Williamsburg *Also called James Slater (G-15258)*

Jims Electric Motor Co Inc 703 550-8624
  8811 Telegraph Rd Lorton (22079) *(G-7499)*

Jims Orna Fabrication & Wldg 434 581-1420
  2553 Cartersville Rd New Canton (23123) *(G-9117)*

Jinks Motor Carriers Inc 804 921-3121
  12220 Chattanooga Plz Midlothian (23112) *(G-8838)*

Jj S Cupcakes and More 319 333-8020
  388 Antler Ln Troutville (24175) *(G-13913)*

Jjj Inc 703 938-0565
  11250 Roger Bacon Dr Reston (20190) *(G-10881)*

Jjojay LLC 240 660-6146
  11 Stocks St Lovettsville (20180) *(G-7580)*

Jk Electric Company 703 378-7477
  14720 Flint Lee Rd Chantilly (20151) *(G-2450)*

Jkm Industries LLC 703 599-3112
  2413 Culpeper Rd Alexandria (22308) *(G-498)*

Jkm Software LLC 703 754-9175
  5446 Lick River Ln Gainesville (20155) *(G-5592)*

Jkm Technologies LLC 434 979-8600
  525 Rookwood Pl Charlottesville (22903) *(G-2820)*

JKS Creation 804 357-5709
  729 Marrow St South Hill (23970) *(G-12854)*

Jkt Inc 804 272-2862
  4429 Brkfld Crprt Dr # 800 Chantilly (20151) *(G-2451)*

Jl Kelley American Apparel LLC 434 664-5243
  386 Cub Creek Rd Appomattox (24522) *(G-815)*

Jlb Publishing Inc 804 443-0330
  306 Cross St Tappahannock (22560) *(G-13818)*

Jls3, Arlington *Also called Joint Lab Systems SEC Svcs LLC (G-1016)*

Jlt Aerospace (north AM 703 459-2380
  13873 Park Center Rd # 201 Herndon (20171) *(G-6717)*

JM Huber Corporation 804 357-3698
  5108 Old Forester Ln Glen Allen (23060) *(G-5756)*

JM Huber Corporation 434 476-6628
  1000 Chaney Ln Crystal Hill (24539) *(G-3860)*

JM Logging, Stuart *Also called Jerry Lee Marshall (G-13619)*

JM USA, Rich Creek *Also called Jennmar Corporation (G-11007)*

JM Walker Publishing LLC 757 340-6659
  3045 Silver Maple Dr Virginia Beach (23452) *(G-14570)*

Jmashby, Roanoke *Also called Mr-Mow-It-all (G-12138)*

Jmd Fairfax Co, Ashburn *Also called Jmd Jmd LLC (G-1299)*

Jmd Jmd LLC 703 945-0099
  44697 Malden Pl Ashburn (20147) *(G-1299)*

Jmi, Virginia Beach *Also called P J Henry Inc (G-14707)*

Jmr Gaines 540 370-1723
  17 N Pointe Dr Fredericksburg (22405) *(G-5445)*

Jmy Jams LLC 434 906-0256
  4410 Monacan Trail Rd North Garden (22959) *(G-10077)*

Jnet Direct Inc 703 629-6406
  1555 Coomber Ct Herndon (20170) *(G-6718)*

Jnlk Inc 434 566-1037
  358 Bybee Rd Louisa (23093) *(G-7557)*

Jnr Defense LLC 541 220-6089
  1463 N Highview Ln # 101 Alexandria (22311) *(G-245)*

Jo-Je Corporation 757 431-2656
  3320 Virginia Beach Blvd Virginia Beach (23452) *(G-14571)*

Joan Fisk 540 288-0050
  280 Jefferson Davis Hwy Stafford (22554) *(G-13160)*

Joco Transportations LLC 804 398-8686
  7719 Centerbrook Ln Chesterfield (23832) *(G-3508)*

Jody's Popcorn, Norfolk *Also called Jodys Inc (G-9604)*

Jodys Inc (PA) **757 422-8646**
  2842 Cromwell Rd Norfolk (23509) *(G-9604)*

Joe Giles Signs Inc 434 391-9040
  1006 E 3rd St Farmville (23901) *(G-4944)*

Joe London Training LLC 540 272-9205
  8021 Olympic Way Culpeper (22701) *(G-3901)*

Joe Products Inc 314 409-4477
  1350 Beverly Rd 115-416 Mc Lean (22101) *(G-8475)*

Joes Smoked Meat Shack 276 644-4001
  1609 Euclid Ave Bristol (24201) *(G-1980)*

Joeys Sign & Letter Inc 757 868-7166
  128 Church St Hampton (23662) *(G-6276)*

Joglex Corporation 540 833-2444
  5239 Williamsburg Rd Linville (22834) *(G-7435)*

John & Lloyd Horst 540 867-5655
  2667 W Dry River Rd Dayton (22821) *(G-4056)*

John A Treese 540 731-0250
  4805 Shelburne Rd Radford (24141) *(G-10718)*

John C Nordt Co Inc 540 362-9717
  1420 Coulter Dr Nw Roanoke (24012) *(G-12112)*

John Deere, Weems *Also called Chesapeake Bay Fishing Co LLC (G-15150)*

John Deere Authorized Dealer, Manassas *Also called Western Branch Diesel Inc (G-8177)*

John Deere Authorized Dealer, Chesapeake *Also called Twin Disc Incorporated (G-3353)*

John Deere Authorized Dealer, Deltaville *Also called Zimmerman Marine Incorporated (G-4090)*

John Demasco 434 977-4214
  1520 Garth Gate Ln Charlottesville (22901) *(G-2652)*

John Douglas, Williamsburg *Also called Modu System America LLC (G-15281)*

John E Hilton 540 639-1674
  1151 E Main St Ste A Radford (24141) *(G-10719)*

John E Pickle 276 496-5963
  108 Angler Ln Saltville (24370) *(G-12585)*

John Henry Printing Inc 757 369-9549
  7300 George Washington Me Yorktown (23692) *(G-15971)*

John I Mercado 703 569-3774
  7032b Commerce St Springfield (22150) *(G-13028)*

John J Heckford 276 889-5646
  Rr 1 Box Creekside Lebanon (24266) *(G-7194)*

John M Russell 540 622-6281
  139 Henry Way Linden (22642) *(G-7429)*

John Middleton Co (HQ) **610 792-8000**
  2325 Bells Rd Richmond (23234) *(G-11047)*

John P Hines Logging 434 392-3861
  Rr 460 Rice (23966) *(G-11005)*

John P Scott Woodworking Inc 804 231-1942
  3400 Formex Rd Richmond (23224) *(G-11633)*

John Potter Enterprises 757 485-2922
  764 Shell Rd Chesapeake (23323) *(G-3151)*

John S Montgomery 757 816-8724
  1253 Kingsway Dr Chesapeake (23320) *(G-3152)*

John W Griessmayer Jr 540 589-8387
  400 Salem Ave Sw Unit 1c Roanoke (24016) *(G-12113)*

John Wills Studios Inc 757 468-0260
  800 Seahawk Cir Ste 114 Virginia Beach (23452) *(G-14572)*

Johner's Contracting, Chilhowie *Also called Douglas Vince Johner (G-3550)*

Johnny Asal Lumber Co Inc 804 492-4884
  118 Salem Church Rd Cumberland (23040) *(G-3935)*

Johnny Hillman Logging 276 467-2406
  Rr 1 Fort Blackmore (24250) *(G-5122)*

Johnny Porter Candle Co 540 406-1608
  211 Morton St Orange (22960) *(G-10217)*

Johnny Sisk & Sons Inc 540 547-2202
  1097 Leon Rd Culpeper (22701) *(G-3902)*

Johns Creek Elkhorn Coal Corp 804 780-3000
  901 E Byrd St Fl 2 Richmond (23219) *(G-11634)*

Johns Manville Corporation 540 984-4171
  182 Johns Manville Dr Edinburg (22824) *(G-4307)*

Johns Manville Corporation 804 261-7400
7400 Ranco Rd Richmond (23228) *(G-11256)*

Johnson & Elich Roasters Ltd 540 552-7442
700 N Main St Ste C Blacksburg (24060) *(G-1747)*

Johnson & Son Lumber Inc 540 752-5557
88 Storck Rd Fredericksburg (22406) *(G-5446)*

Johnson Controls, Ashburn *Also called Clarios (G-1255)*

Johnson Controls, Roanoke *Also called Clarios (G-11909)*

Johnson Controls, Roanoke *Also called Clarios (G-11910)*

Johnson Controls 804 727-3890
8555 Magellan Pkwy # 1000 Richmond (23227) *(G-11257)*

Johnson Controls 757 853-6611
3750 Progress Rd Norfolk (23502) *(G-9605)*

Johnson Enterprises LLC 804 432-0469
5752 Mako Rd New Kent (23124) *(G-9134)*

Johnson James Thomas Logging 804 966-1552
2421 C C Rd Charles City (23030) *(G-2578)*

Johnson Logging, Scottsville *Also called Ralph Johnson (G-12665)*

Johnson Machinery Sales Inc 540 890-8893
2300 Stone Creek Path Vinton (24179) *(G-14174)*

Johnson Printing Service Inc 804 541-3635
404 E Poythress St Hopewell (23860) *(G-6937)*

Johnson Welding Service 757 787-4429
21736 Parsons Rd Greenbush (23357) *(G-5996)*

Johnson's Logging, Providence Forge *Also called A Johnson Linwood (G-10617)*

Johnsons Postcards 434 589-7605
9 Corn Pone Ln Palmyra (22963) *(G-10250)*

Joi Element LLC 804 912-8002
3010 Lawson St Richmond (23224) *(G-11635)*

Joint Knowledge Software I 703 803-7470
3996 Alcoa Dr Fairfax (22033) *(G-4486)*

Joint Lab Systems SEC Svcs LLC 443 655-9987
1515 Richmond Hwy # 1623 Arlington (22202) *(G-1016)*

Joint Manufacturing Force LLC 910 364-8580
6010 Good Lion Ct Alexandria (22315) *(G-499)*

Joint Planning Solutions LLC 757 839-5593
4669 South Blvd Ste 107 Virginia Beach (23452) *(G-14573)*

Joker Brewing LLC 757 814-0882
113 Palace Ln Ste D Williamsburg (23185) *(G-15261)*

Jon Armstrong 757 253-3844
3484 Hunters Rdg Williamsburg (23188) *(G-15262)*

Jon Martin Woodworking LLC 540 560-3721
1230 Harmony Dr Apt A Harrisonburg (22802) *(G-6334)*

Jonathan & Co Unlimited, Fredericksburg *Also called Jonathan Promotions Inc (G-5307)*

Jonathan Chandler 804 526-1148
1208 Covington Rd Colonial Heights (23834) *(G-3736)*

Jonathan Promotions Inc 540 891-7700
4808 Jefferson Davis Hwy Fredericksburg (22408) *(G-5307)*

Jonda Enterprise Inc 757 559-5793
1725 Canton Ave Norfolk (23523) *(G-9606)*

Jones Tonja 757 773-9475
5809 Dunkirk St Portsmouth (23703) *(G-10448)*

Jones & Sons Inc 434 836-3851
7521 U S Highway 29 Blairs (24527) *(G-1830)*

Jones and Jones Audio & Video 804 283-3495
3011 Peabody Ln Richmond (23223) *(G-11636)*

Jones Direct LLC 757 718-3468
931 Ventures Way Chesapeake (23320) *(G-3153)*

Jones Family Office 305 304-3603
8000 Gainsford Ct Bristow (20136) *(G-2057)*

Jones Logging 276 794-9510
Rr 3 Lebanon (24266) *(G-7195)*

Jones Lumber Company J E 804 883-6331
17055 Mountain Rd Montpelier (23192) *(G-9017)*

Jones Plus LLC 757 718-3468
931 Ventures Way Chesapeake (23320) *(G-3154)*

Jones Printing Service Inc (PA) **757 436-3331**
931 Ventures Way Chesapeake (23320) *(G-3155)*

Jones Sign Co Inc 804 798-5533
11046 Leadbetter Rd Ashland (23005) *(G-1442)*

Jones Welding Construction 434 369-1069
4361 Bedford Hwy Altavista (24517) *(G-633)*

Jonette D Meade 804 247-0639
2917 Monteith Rd Richmond (23235) *(G-11048)*

Joong-Ang Daily News Cal Inc 703 281-9660
7023 Little River Tpke # 101 Annandale (22003) *(G-762)*

Joong-Ang Daily News Wash, Annandale *Also called Joong-Ang Daily News Cal Inc (G-762)*

Jordan Consulting and Research 703 597-7812
13230 Pleasant Glen Ct Herndon (20171) *(G-6719)*

Jordan Septic Tank Service 276 395-3938
Old Coeburn Norton Hwy Coeburn (24230) *(G-3700)*

Jordo Inc (PA) **424 394-2986**
4020 Gaelic Ln Apt Q Glen Allen (23060) *(G-5757)*

Jordo Inc 424 394-2986
4990 Sadler Pl 30204 Glen Allen (23060) *(G-5758)*

Jorgensen Woodworking 757 312-9663
1213 Vail Ct Chesapeake (23320) *(G-3156)*

Jose Goncalves Inc 703 528-5272
4808 Lee Hwy Arlington (22207) *(G-1017)*

Joseph Carson 757 498-4866
3744 Virginius Dr Virginia Beach (23452) *(G-14574)*

Joseph L Burruss Burial Vaults 804 746-8250
8171 Elm Dr Mechanicsville (23111) *(G-8646)*

Joseph Lineberry 276 733-8635
68 Indutry Line Woodlawn (24381) *(G-15845)*

Joseph Randolph Pike 804 798-7188
646 N Washington Hwy Ashland (23005) *(G-1443)*

Joseph Ricard Enterprises LLC 540 465-5533
262 E King St Strasburg (22657) *(G-13586)*

Joseph's Designs, Richmond *Also called Mary Elizabeth Burrell (G-11670)*

Josh McDaniel 804 748-4330
7701 Rhodes Ln Chesterfield (23838) *(G-3509)*

Joshi Rubita 571 315-9772
8654 Venoy Ct Alexandria (22309) *(G-500)*

Joshmor Pac 276 620-6537
737 Hogback Rd Wytheville (24382) *(G-15893)*

Joshs Welding & Fabrication 540 244-9950
2532 Stonyman Rd Luray (22835) *(G-7614)*

Journal of Neurosurgery DC, Charlottesville *Also called American Assn Nurosurgeons Inc (G-2726)*

Journal of Orthpdic Spt Physcl 877 766-3450
1111 N Fairfax St Ste 100 Alexandria (22314) *(G-246)*

Journal Orthopaedic Spt Physcl, Alexandria *Also called Journal of Orthpdic Spt Physcl (G-246)*

Journeymen Saddlers Ltd 540 687-5888
2 W Federal St Middleburg (20117) *(G-8725)*

Jovanovich Inc 301 653-1739
5750 Governors Pond Cir Alexandria (22310) *(G-501)*

Jovic Embroidery LLC 804 748-2598
9517 Chipping Dr North Chesterfield (23237) *(G-9903)*

Joy Global Underground Min LLC 276 623-2000
26161 Old Trail Rd Ste 1 Abingdon (24210) *(G-45)*

Joy Global Underground Min LLC 276 679-1082
722 Kentucky Ave Sw Norton (24273) *(G-10123)*

Joy Global Underground Min LLC 276 431-2821
811 Boone Trail Rd Duffield (24244) *(G-4179)*

Joy Global Underground Min LLC 276 322-5454
1081 Hockman Pike Bluefield (24605) *(G-1866)*

Joy Global Underground Min LLC 276 322-5421
1081 Hockman Pike Bluefield (24605) *(G-1867)*

Joy of Cupcakes LLC 703 440-0204
6802 Hampton Creek Way Springfield (22150) *(G-13029)*

Joy Virginn-Plot Fund Fndation 757 446-2000
150 W Brambleton Ave Norfolk (23510) *(G-9607)*

Joy-Page Company Inc 703 464-9404
10481 Colonel Ct Manassas (20110) *(G-7954)*

Joyebells LLC 804 304-7695
695 Trevor Ter Richmond (23225) *(G-11637)*

Joyeblls Sweet Ptato Pies Hnri, Richmond *Also called Joyebells LLC (G-11637)*

Jozsa Wood Works 703 492-9405
14891 Persistence Dr Woodbridge (22191) *(G-15731)*

JP Nino Corp 775 636-8682
8116 Arlington Blvd 178 Falls Church (22042) *(G-4811)*

JPF Industriesinc 703 451-0203
6019 Queenston St Springfield (22152) *(G-13030)*

Jpg Software 757 546-8416
636 Broadwinsor Cres Chesapeake (23322) *(G-3157)*

Jph Woodcraft 757 615-6812
941 Timberlake Dr Virginia Beach (23464) *(G-14575)*

JPS Consulting LLC 571 334-0859
8311 Ivy Green Rd Fairfax Station (22039) *(G-4714)*

JQ & G Inc Company 540 588-7625
3451 Brandon Ave Sw # 12 Roanoke (24018) *(G-11947)*

Jr Bernard Hearn 703 821-1373
958 Saigon Rd Mc Lean (22102) *(G-8476)*

Jr Everett Woodson 757 867-3478
213 Picard Dr Newport News (23602) *(G-9270)*

Jr Kauffman Inc 276 228-7070
3040 Peppers Ferry Rd Wytheville (24382) *(G-15894)*

Jr Lamb & Sons 434 823-2320
5725 Locust Ln Crozet (22932) *(G-3839)*

Jr Sales 703 450-4753
903 N Sterling Blvd Sterling (20164) *(G-13436)*

Jr Woodworks 703 577-2663
2918 Bryan St Alexandria (22302) *(G-247)*

Jrjj Paper LLC 757 473-3719
168 Business Park Dr Virginia Beach (23462) *(G-14576)*

JRS Repco Inc 540 334-3051
125 Autumn Chase Ln Boones Mill (24065) *(G-1895)*

Js Monogramming 804 862-4324
1781 Anchor Ave Petersburg (23803) *(G-10328)*

Js Software Inc 214 924-3179
1158 Millwood Pond Dr Herndon (20170) *(G-6720)*

Js Welding 434 352-0576
Hwy 460 Appomattox (24522) *(G-816)*

Jsc Froyo LLC 571 303-0011
4014 Campbell Ave Arlington (22206) *(G-1018)*

Jsd Mill Work LLC 703 863-7183
24022 Batna Rd Lignum (22726) *(G-7425)*

JT Graphics & Printing Inc 703 922-6804
5409a Vine St Alexandria (22310) *(G-502)*

Jt Tobacco 540 387-0383
910 E Main St Salem (24153) *(G-12525)*

Jtees Printing 703 590-4145
12169 Darnley Rd Woodbridge (22192) *(G-15732)*

Jti Leaf Services (us) LLC (HQ) **434 799-3286**
202 Stinson Dr Danville (24540) *(G-4007)*

Jts Blinds Installation LLC 240 682-1009
4385 Navigator Ln King George (22485) *(G-7096)*

Juanita Deshazior 703 901-5592
5300 Holmes Run Pkwy Alexandria (22304) *(G-248)*

Jud Corporation 757 485-4371
3732 Profit Way Chesapeake (23323) *(G-3158)*

Judis Heart Prints LLC 757 482-9607
501 Natchez Trce Chesapeake (23322) *(G-3159)*

Judy A OBrien 434 568-3148
104 Bedford St Drakes Branch (23937) *(G-4135)*

Judys Bottle Holder 757 606-1093
2222 Ships Xing Chesapeake (23323) *(G-3160)*

Juggernaut Industries 703 686-0191
8700 Virginia Meadows Dr Manassas (20109) *(G-8090)*

Juice 202 280-0302
2824 Fallfax Dr Falls Church (22042) *(G-4812)*

Juice Bar Juices Incorporated 757 227-6822
3877 Holland Rd Ste 418 Virginia Beach (23452) *(G-14577)*

JUIce&i LLC 202 280-0302
2824 Fallfax Dr Falls Church (22042) *(G-4813)*

Julian Industries LLC 804 755-6888
10984 Leadbetter Rd Ashland (23005) *(G-1444)*

Julian Swain Builders Inc 757 490-0211
5618 E Virginia Bch Blvd Norfolk (23502) *(G-9608)*

Julies Datery, Alexandria *Also called Pruitt Partners LLC* *(G-320)*

Julphia Soapworks 703 815-8020
13718 Eastcliff Cir Centreville (20120) *(G-2312)*

Juma Brothers Inc 757 312-0544
3325 Victory Blvd Portsmouth (23701) *(G-10449)*

Jump Mountain Vineyard 540 348-6730
1493 Walkers Creek Rd Rockbridge Baths (24473) *(G-12235)*

Jump Mountain Vineyard LLC 434 296-2226
310 Hedge St Charlottesville (22902) *(G-2821)*

Jumping Jacks, Chesapeake *Also called American Egle EMB Graphics LLC* *(G-2966)*

Jumpstart Consultants Inc 804 321-5867
4649 Carolina Ave Bldg I Richmond (23222) *(G-11638)*

Juniors Wldg & Met Fabrication 540 943-7070
Rr 4 Stuarts Draft (24477) *(G-13653)*

Juniper Networks (us) Inc 571 203-1700
2251 Corp Park Dr Ste 200 Herndon (20171) *(G-6721)*

Junk In My Trunk LLC 703 753-7505
6864 Jockey Club Ln Haymarket (20169) *(G-6428)*

Junoventure LLC 410 247-1908
14140 Washington Hwy Ashland (23005) *(G-1445)*

Juptiers Vault 757 404-9535
5920 Adderley St Norfolk (23502) *(G-9609)*

Just Braids By Sharon Solomon, Norfolk *Also called Sharon Solomon* *(G-9721)*

Just Desserts 804 310-5958
9468 Crescent View Dr Mechanicsville (23116) *(G-8647)*

Just For Fun 757 620-3700
6203 Springhill Way Suffolk (23435) *(G-13726)*

Just Handle It LLC 804 285-0786
1903 West Club Ln Richmond (23226) *(G-11258)*

Just Print It LLC 703 327-2060
41250 Stone School Ln Leesburg (20175) *(G-7292)*

Just Tech 540 662-2400
113 W Beverley St Staunton (24401) *(G-13270)*

Just Woodstuff 540 951-2323
3829 Catawba Rd Blacksburg (24060) *(G-1748)*

Just Wreaths 571 208-4920
4788 S Park Ct Woodbridge (22193) *(G-15733)*

Justice 703 352-8393
11759l Fair Oaks Mall Fairfax (22033) *(G-4487)*

Justice 703 421-7001
21100 Dulles Town Cir # 263 Sterling (20166) *(G-13437)*

Justice 703 490-6664
2700 Potomac Mills Cir # 235 Woodbridge (22192) *(G-15734)*

Justice Coal of Alabama LLC 540 776-7890
302 S Jefferson St # 400 Roanoke (24011) *(G-12114)*

Justice Low Seam Mining Inc 540 776-7890
302 S Jefferson St # 400 Roanoke (24011) *(G-12115)*

Justice Signs LLC 304 898-2783
205 Houston Ln Glen Lyn (24093) *(G-5833)*

Justin Comb 703 783-1082
5145 Duke St Ste D-107 Alexandria (22304) *(G-249)*

Justinian Posters & Prints 703 273-8049
3977 Chain Bridge Rd # 202 Fairfax (22030) *(G-4640)*

Jv-Rm Holdings Inc 703 669-3333
525 E Market St Ste D Leesburg (20176) *(G-7293)*

Jvh Company Inc (PA) **804 798-0888**
11206 Hopson Rd Ashland (23005) *(G-1446)*

JWB of Roanoke Inc 540 344-7726
601 Salem Ave Sw Roanoke (24016) *(G-12116)*

Jwlbook LLC 571 287-0121
11619 Fairfax Commons Dr Fairfax (22030) *(G-4641)*

Jws Welding & Repair 804 720-2523
11735 Old Stage Rd North Dinwiddie (23805) *(G-10055)*

JWT Well Services Inc 276 835-8793
3992 Dante Mountain Rd Nora (24272) *(G-9408)*

K & A Printing 716 736-3250
480 Peacock Acres Trl Danville (24541) *(G-4008)*

K & D Logging, Stuart *Also called Kenneth Foley* *(G-13620)*

K & E Legacy Incorporated 757 328-4609
3303 Airline Blvd Ste 3g Portsmouth (23701) *(G-10450)*

K & E Printing and Graphics 703 560-4701
8219 Cottage St Vienna (22180) *(G-14075)*

K & J Logging Inc 540 330-9812
4468 Dundee Rd Huddleston (24104) *(G-6954)*

K & J Woodworking/ Cash 703 369-7161
7230 Yates Ford Rd Manassas (20111) *(G-8091)*

K & K Machining Incorporated 540 298-1700
709 Shenandoah Ave Elkton (22827) *(G-4328)*

K & K Signs 540 586-0542
5337 E Lynchburg Salem Bedford (24523) *(G-1641)*

K & R Tree Care LLC 804 767-0695
2750 River Rd W Maidens (23102) *(G-7891)*

K & S Pewter Inc 540 751-0505
42403 Stumptown Rd Leesburg (20176) *(G-7294)*

K & S Welding 757 859-6313
9399 Kellos Mill Rd Wakefield (23888) *(G-14968)*

K & T Machine and Welding Inc 804 296-8625
15100 Washington Hwy Ashland (23005) *(G-1447)*

K & W Printing Services Inc 301 868-2141
4001 9th St N Ste 102 Arlington (22203) *(G-1019)*

K & W Projects LLC 757 618-9249
3304 Dietz Dr Chesapeake (23323) *(G-3161)*

K & Z Inc 703 876-1660
2807 Merrilee Dr Ste D Fairfax (22031) *(G-4488)*

K and M Industries LLC 757 328-0227
471 Dunmore Dr Newport News (23602) *(G-9271)*

K B Industries Inc 540 483-8883
7191 Old Forge Rd Rocky Mount (24151) *(G-12331)*

K C G Inc 703 542-7120
25793 Phar Lap Ct Chantilly (20152) *(G-2539)*

K C I Konecranes Inc 540 545-8412
230 Airport Rd 12 Winchester (22602) *(G-15430)*

K C Supply Corp 540 222-2932
11453 Verga Ln Brandy Station (22714) *(G-1940)*

K Composite Magazine 703 568-6917
7011 Green Spring Ln Alexandria (22306) *(G-503)*

K Dudley Logging Inc 540 890-0220
13225 Stewartsville Rd Vinton (24179) *(G-14175)*

K E Marine 757 787-1313
24263 Baylys Neck Rd Accomac (23301) *(G-72)*

K H Franklin Logging LLC 434 352-9235
812 Woodlawn Trl Appomattox (24522) *(G-817)*

K Hart Holding Inc 800 294-5348
938 Sutton St Norfolk (23504) *(G-9610)*

K L A Enterprises LLC 540 382-9444
424 Peppers Fry Rd Nw Christiansburg (24073) *(G-3602)*

K M E Fire Apparatus, Roanoke *Also called Kovatch Mobile Equipment Corp* *(G-12123)*

K O Stith Hauling LLC 804 895-4617
6204 Oak Shades Park Dr Disputanta (23842) *(G-4111)*

K S E 571 366-1715
1800 Diagonal Rd Ste 600 Alexandria (22314) *(G-250)*

K T Design & Prototype Inc 540 678-0215
170 Kenny Ln I Winchester (22602) *(G-15431)*

K Tonyale The Brand, Highland Springs *Also called Bowman Nakia* *(G-6851)*

K Walters At The Sign of G 703 986-0448
12131 Derriford Ct Woodbridge (22192) *(G-15735)*

K&M Lawn Grdn & Arborist Sups, Culpeper *Also called Silver Lining Assistance Inc* *(G-3921)*

K-Naturo LLC 757 343-4604
5733 Hampshire Ln Apt 101 Virginia Beach (23462) *(G-14578)*

K.O. Components, Amelia Court House *Also called Cardinal Tool Inc* *(G-653)*

K/R Companies LLC 540 812-2422
19221 Rolling Hills Dr Culpeper (22701) *(G-3903)*

K12excellence Inc 804 270-9600
5318 Twin Hickory Rd Glen Allen (23059) *(G-5759)*

K2 Industries LLC 757 754-5430
1417 Veau Ct Virginia Beach (23451) *(G-14579)*

K2m Group Holdings Inc 703 777-3155
600 Hope Pkwy Se Leesburg (20175) *(G-7295)*

K2w Enterprises Corporation 540 603-0114
14227 Canteen Ct Centreville (20121) *(G-2313)*

Kaah Express 703 379-0770
5613 Leesburg Pike Ste 26 Falls Church (22041) *(G-4814)*

Kace Square LLC 703 723-3679
43352 Old Ryan Rd Ashburn (20148) *(G-1300)*

Kaczenskis Welding Svcs LLC 540 431-8126
236 Mason St Winchester (22602) *(G-15432)*

A
L
P
H
A
B
E
T
I
C

Kaelin Signs LLC 571 239-9192
7952 Pebble Brook Ct Springfield (22153) ***(G-13031)***
Kaisa Usa Inc 206 228-7711
20520 Unico Rd Mc Kenney (23872) ***(G-8380)***
Kaiser Aluminum & Chemical, North Chesterfield *Also called Kaiser Bellwood Corporation* ***(G-9905)***
Kaiser Aluminum Corporation 804 743-6405
1901 Reymet Rd North Chesterfield (23237) ***(G-9904)***
Kaiser Bellwood Corporation 804 743-6300
1901 Reymet Rd North Chesterfield (23237) ***(G-9905)***
Kajjo Sirwan 202 569-1472
5597 Seminary Rd Apt 218 Falls Church (22041) ***(G-4815)***
Kaleidoscope Publishing Ltd 703 821-0571
1420 Spring Hill Rd # 490 Mc Lean (22102) ***(G-8477)***
Kalero Vineyard LLC 703 216-9036
13141 Sagle Rd Hillsboro (20132) ***(G-6873)***
Kaliopa Publishing LLC 703 522-7663
1050 N Taylor St Apt 504 Arlington (22201) ***(G-1020)***
Kalis Kreations & Designs LLC 757 343-4421
4104 Colbourn Dr Suffolk (23435) ***(G-13727)***
Kalmar USA Inc 757 465-7995
3115 Watson St Portsmouth (23707) ***(G-10451)***
Kalwood Inc 540 951-8600
101 Mcdonald St Blacksburg (24060) ***(G-1749)***
Kanan Welding 703 339-7799
8538 Terminal Rd Lorton (22079) ***(G-7500)***
Kanawha Eagle Coal LLC (PA) **304 837-8587**
4701 Cox Rd Ste 285 Glen Allen (23060) ***(G-5760)***
Kandd Transportation Service 434 298-7716
3304 U S Highway 29 Ste C Danville (24540) ***(G-4009)***
Kandy Girl Kndy Apples Berries 719 200-1662
57 Otsego Dr Newport News (23602) ***(G-9272)***
Kangs Embroidery 757 887-5232
15525 Warwick Blvd Newport News (23608) ***(G-9273)***
Kaotic Enzymes LLC 804 519-9479
3313 W Cary St Ste A Richmond (23221) ***(G-11639)***
Kapok Press LLC 540 372-2033
1712 Augustine Ave Fredericksburg (22401) ***(G-5198)***
Kapstone 804 708-0083
1900 Manakin Rd Ste H Manakin Sabot (23103) ***(G-7900)***
Kara Keen LLC 973 713-1049
3430 Ethel Ct Annandale (22003) ***(G-763)***
Karam Winery 703 573-3886
2139 Tysons Executive Ct Dunn Loring (22027) ***(G-4264)***
Karl J Protil & Sons Inc 540 885-6664
347 Cedar Green Rd Staunton (24401) ***(G-13271)***
Karla Colletto Swimwear Inc 703 281-3262
319d Mill St Ne Vienna (22180) ***(G-14076)***
Karls Custom Wheels 757 565-1997
152 Skimino Rd Williamsburg (23188) ***(G-15263)***
Karma Group Inc 717 253-9379
10497 Labrador Loop Manassas (20112) ***(G-8092)***
Karolina De Los Santos 757 597-4315
339 Kinsmen Way Hampton (23666) ***(G-6178)***
Karselis Arts, Chesterfield *Also called Cheyenne Autumn Arts* ***(G-3486)***
Kash Design 540 317-1473
509 S Main St Ste 121 Culpeper (22701) ***(G-3904)***
Kashaf Spices 571 572-5890
15407 Windsong Ln Dumfries (22025) ***(G-4248)***
Kashaf Spices Inc 703 232-3529
10595 Furnace Rd Lorton (22079) ***(G-7501)***
Kasinof & Associates 757 827-6530
2040 Coliseum Dr Ste 33 Hampton (23666) ***(G-6179)***
Katam Group LLC 703 927-6268
41783 Prairie Aster Ct Ashburn (20148) ***(G-1301)***
Kates Creations 757 721-7062
6480 Knotts Island Rd Virginia Beach (23457) ***(G-14580)***
Katherine Chain 804 796-2762
14705 Happy Hill Rd Chester (23831) ***(G-3426)***
Katheryn Warren 757 813-5396
137 Riviera Williamsburg (23188) ***(G-15264)***
Kathezz Compost LLC 434 842-9395
351 Scenic River Dr Columbia (23038) ***(G-3752)***
Kathleen Tilley 703 727-5385
103 N Waller St Williamsburg (23185) ***(G-15265)***
Kathy Darmofalski 540 885-4759
51 Woodland Dr Staunton (24401) ***(G-13272)***
Katz Hadrian 202 942-5707
1324 Lancia Dr Mc Lean (22102) ***(G-8478)***
Kauai Coffee Co, Suffolk *Also called Massimo Zanetti Bev USA Inc* ***(G-13740)***
Kauffman Engineering Inc 757 468-6000
889 Seahawk Cir Virginia Beach (23452) ***(G-14581)***
Kawneer Company Inc 540 433-2711
2031 Deyerle Ave Harrisonburg (22801) ***(G-6335)***
Kawood LLC 757 488-4658
300 Saunders Dr Portsmouth (23701) ***(G-10452)***
Kay Gee Plastics, Norfolk *Also called Degen Enterprises Inc* ***(G-9524)***
Kay Kare LLC 614 309-8462
3800 Fairfax Dr Arlington (22203) ***(G-1021)***
Kay Kollections LLC 757 901-7710
311 Walker Ave Norfolk (23523) ***(G-9611)***
Kaydee Puppets 804 347-6636
620 Wolfe St Fredericksburg (22401) ***(G-5199)***
Kayjae Inc 804 725-9664
323 Creek Ln Cobbs Creek (23035) ***(G-3694)***
Kays Photography and Prints 757 344-4817
1560 Caroline St Lynchburg (24501) ***(G-7749)***
Kbm Powder Coating LLC 804 496-6860
11042 Air Park Rd Ste 7 Ashland (23005) ***(G-1448)***
Kc Wood Mfg 540 789-8300
470 Rock Church Rd Willis (24380) ***(G-15362)***
Kci Comminications, Falls Church *Also called Capitol Information Group Inc* ***(G-4770)***
Kci Services LLC 276 623-7404
1731 Pioneer Dr Lebanon (24266) ***(G-7196)***
KCS Inc 703 981-0523
6917 Columbia Dr Alexandria (22307) ***(G-504)***
Kcsl 276 206-5977
22619 Montego Bay Rd Abingdon (24211) ***(G-46)***
Kd Cartridges 434 865-3328
221b Smith St South Hill (23970) ***(G-12855)***
Kd Puppets 703 385-4543
4212 Sideburn Rd Fairfax (22030) ***(G-4642)***
Kdc Lynchburg, Lynchburg *Also called Kdc US Holding Inc* ***(G-7750)***
Kdc US Holding Inc (HQ) **434 845-7073**
1000 Robins Rd Lynchburg (24504) ***(G-7750)***
Kdl Solutions LLC 703 216-2201
10845 Crockett Rd Nokesville (20181) ***(G-9395)***
Keane Cabinetry 540 867-5336
3050 Mount Clinton Pike Rockingham (22802) ***(G-12257)***
Keane Writers Publishing LLC 804 435-2618
87 Mariners Watch Ln Kilmarnock (22482) ***(G-7071)***
Kearney & Associates Inc 540 423-9511
17477 Stevensburg Rd Culpeper (22701) ***(G-3905)***
Kearney-National Inc 276 628-7171
26252 Hillman Hwy Abingdon (24210) ***(G-47)***
KEC Associates Ltd 804 404-2601
467 Southlake Blvd North Chesterfield (23236) ***(G-9906)***
Ked Hauling Co LLC 757 319-8652
600 Chapel Lake Dr # 202 Virginia Beach (23454) ***(G-14582)***
Ked Plasma 276 645-6035
1315 Euclid Ave Bristol (24201) ***(G-1981)***
Keen Eyes Auto Detailing LLC 252 646-3600
3 Lotus Ln Stafford (22554) ***(G-13161)***
Keene Carpet, Honaker *Also called Harold Keene Coal Co Inc* ***(G-6914)***
Keens Automotive Machine Shop 757 365-4481
1802 S Church St Smithfield (23430) ***(G-12717)***
Keens Welding & Aluminum Works 540 958-9600
1507 Mountain View Dr Covington (24426) ***(G-3793)***
Keep It Simple Syrup, Glen Allen *Also called Chef Sous LLC* ***(G-5712)***
Keeva LLC 240 766-5382
20258 Ordinary Pl Ashburn (20147) ***(G-1302)***
Kehoe Enterprises LLC 540 668-9080
15971 Charter House Ln Hillsboro (20132) ***(G-6874)***
Keith Fabry 804 649-7551
1420 Commerce Rd Richmond (23224) ***(G-11640)***
Keith Sanders 276 728-0540
1216 Mulberry Rd Martinsville (24112) ***(G-8304)***
Keiths Boat Service LLC 804 898-1644
1147 Cumberland Dr Colonial Heights (23834) ***(G-3737)***
Kejaeh Enterprises LLC 434 476-1300
2121 Grubby Rd Halifax (24558) ***(G-6051)***
Kelkase Inc 703 670-9443
30 Kinsley Ln Fredericksburg (22406) ***(G-5447)***
Keller Industries LLC 573 452-4932
9321 Blue Pine Ln Fredericksburg (22407) ***(G-5308)***
Kellis Creations LLC 540 554-2878
17209 Grand Valley Ct Round Hill (20141) ***(G-12381)***
Kelly Swenson 434 634-3926
552 N Main St Emporia (23847) ***(G-4362)***
Kelmar Inc 540 439-8952
5212 Midland Rd Midland (22728) ***(G-8759)***
Keltron Corporation 540 527-3526
1110 Beaumont Rd Roanoke (24019) ***(G-11948)***
Kelvin Hughes LLC 703 827-3986
8614 Westwood Center Dr # 550 Vienna (22182) ***(G-14077)***
Kelvin International Corp 757 833-1011
742 Bluecrab Rd Newport News (23606) ***(G-9274)***
Kemelle Naturals Incorporated 850 528-9053
35 W Reed Ave Alexandria (22305) ***(G-251)***
Kemper Printing LLC 804 510-8402
3434 Stuart Ave Apt 2 Richmond (23221) ***(G-11641)***
Kempsville Building Mtls Inc (HQ) **757 485-0782**
3300 Business Center Dr Chesapeake (23323) ***(G-3162)***
Kempsville Building Mtls Inc 757 875-1850
814 Chapman Way Newport News (23608) ***(G-9275)***
Ken Musselman & Associates Inc 804 790-0302
12025 Trailbrook Dr Chesterfield (23838) ***(G-3510)***
Ken Signs 703 451-5474
7304d Boudinot Dr Springfield (22150) ***(G-13032)***

Kenbridge-Victoria Dispatch, Victoria *Also called Charlette Publishing Inc* ***(G-14000)***
Kendall/Hunt Publishing Co 804 285-9411
9037 Gold Ridge Ln Mechanicsville (23116) ***(G-8648)***
Kendras Cookies 540 660-5645
116 Nottingham Ct Front Royal (22630) ***(G-5539)***
Kenkashi, Copper Hill *Also called Windrush Farm LLC* ***(G-3765)***
Kenmore Envelope Company Inc 804 271-2100
4641 Intl Trade Ct Richmond (23231) ***(G-11259)***
Kennametal Inc 540 740-3128
450 New Market Depot Rd New Market (22844) ***(G-9144)***
Kennedy Konstruction Kompany (PA) **540 984-4191**
1634 Chapman Landing Rd Edinburg (22824) ***(G-4308)***
Kennedy Projects LLC 757 345-0626
111 Meadow Rue Ct Williamsburg (23185) ***(G-15266)***
Kennedys Excavating LLC 423 383-0143
18455 Lavender Ln Bristol (24202) ***(G-2023)***
Kennesaw Holding Company 603 866-6944
4231 Monu Wall Way 313 Fairfax (22030) ***(G-4643)***
Kenneth Foley 276 930-1452
352 Goose Market Loop Stuart (24171) ***(G-13620)***
Kenneth Hill 804 986-8674
1808 Bath St Richmond (23220) ***(G-11642)***
Kenneth Lee Woods 703 361-7390
8216 Birch St Manassas (20111) ***(G-8093)***
Kenney Inc 703 731-9208
916 Barker Hill Rd Herndon (20170) ***(G-6722)***
Kennley Corporation 804 275-9088
8808b Metro Ct North Chesterfield (23237) ***(G-9907)***
Kens Leathercraft 540 774-6225
6760 S Indian Grave Rd Boones Mill (24065) ***(G-1896)***
Kens Welding 540 788-3556
8534 Burwell Rd Catlett (20119) ***(G-2268)***
Kenway Express 804 652-1922
5 Kenway Ave Richmond (23223) ***(G-11643)***
Keo-Corp LLC 636 515-5549
8535 Red Juniper Ln New Kent (23124) ***(G-9135)***
Keppick LLC Kim 540 364-3668
3064 Lost Corner Rd Delaplane (20144) ***(G-4076)***
Kerecis LLC 703 465-7945
2200 Clarendon Blvd # 140 Arlington (22201) ***(G-1022)***
Kerneos Inc 757 494-1947
1316 Priority Ln Chesapeake (23324) ***(G-3163)***
Kerris Kandles 908 698-3968
15087 Lindenberry Ln Dumfries (22025) ***(G-4249)***
Kerry Scott 434 277-9337
3136 Patrick Henry Hwy Piney River (22964) ***(G-10361)***
Kerschbamer Woodworking LLC 434 455-2508
1701 12th St Lynchburg (24501) ***(G-7751)***
Kessler Marine Services Inc 571 276-1377
6002 Greeley Blvd Springfield (22152) ***(G-13033)***
Kessler Sailing Services, Springfield *Also called Kessler Marine Services Inc* ***(G-13033)***
Kessler Soils Engrg Pdts Inc (PA) **571 291-2284**
17775 Running Colt Pl Leesburg (20175) ***(G-7296)***
Keswick Gourmet Foods LLC 610 585-2688
1726 Downing Ct Keswick (22947) ***(G-7048)***
Keswick Vineyard 434 295-1834
6131 Gordonsville Rd Keswick (22947) ***(G-7049)***
Keswick Vineyards LLC 434 244-3341
1575 Winery Dr Keswick (22947) ***(G-7050)***
Keswick Winery LLC 434 244-3341
1575 Keswick Winery Dr Keswick (22947) ***(G-7051)***
Kevins Signs 540 427-1070
1007 Industry Ave Se Roanoke (24013) ***(G-12117)***
Kevins Welding 703 242-8649
10218 Bushman Dr Apt 103 Oakton (22124) ***(G-10153)***
Key Bridge Global LLC 703 414-3500
8416 Holly Leaf Dr Mc Lean (22102) ***(G-8479)***
Key Display LLC 434 286-4514
1322 James River Rd Scottsville (24590) ***(G-12662)***
Key Made Now 804 663-5192
9811 Brook Rd Glen Allen (23059) ***(G-5761)***
Key Recovery Corporation 540 444-2628
1390 Southside Dr Salem (24153) ***(G-12526)***
Key To Heart Seasoning LLC 757 752-7581
3967 Wyckoff Dr Virginia Beach (23452) ***(G-14583)***
Keyser Collection 804 740-3237
509 N Gaskins Rd Richmond (23238) ***(G-11260)***
Keystone Metal Products Inc 540 720-5437
7 Saint Anthonys Ct Stafford (22556) ***(G-13162)***
Keystone Rubber Corporation 717 235-6863
1539 Stockton Ave Greenbackville (23356) ***(G-5994)***
Keystone Software Inc 703 866-1593
10707 Dabshire Way Manassas (20110) ***(G-7955)***
Keystone Supply Co Inc 610 525-3654
2547 Waterloo Mill Ln Elkton (22827) ***(G-4329)***
Keystone Technology LLC 540 361-8318
6709 Willcher Ct Fredericksburg (22407) ***(G-5309)***
Keystone Vintage Lumber VA LLC 804 615-7773
12700 Coverly Rd Amelia Court House (23002) ***(G-661)***
KG Old Ox Holdings Inc 703 471-5321
44886 Old Ox Rd Sterling (20166) ***(G-13438)***
KG Sports 540 538-7216
14130 Ryan Ln King George (22485) ***(G-7097)***
Kg-Sports, King George *Also called KG Sports* ***(G-7097)***
Khan Qaism 703 212-8670
678 S Pickett St Alexandria (22304) ***(G-252)***
Khazana, Alexandria *Also called Christine Smith* ***(G-429)***
Khem Precision Machining LLC 804 915-8922
3007 W Clay St Ste D Richmond (23230) ***(G-11261)***
Khk Inc 540 337-5068
255 Draft Ave Stuarts Draft (24477) ***(G-13654)***
Kibby Welding 607 624-9959
2428 Richmond Rd Troy (22974) ***(G-13930)***
Kibela Print LLC 703 436-1646
7464 Wounded Knee Rd Lorton (22079) ***(G-7502)***
Kics Cupcakes LLC 202 630-5727
1934 Old Gallows Rd # 350 Vienna (22182) ***(G-14078)***
Kid Fueled Kco LLC 804 720-4091
7100 Whispering Winds Dr Prince George (23875) ***(G-10597)***
Kiddos LLC 540 468-2700
27 W Main St Monterey (24465) ***(G-9008)***
Kidprint of Virginia Inc 757 287-3324
317 Saint Brie W Suffolk (23435) ***(G-13728)***
Kidwell Construction LLC 540 296-4173
507 South St Bedford (24523) ***(G-1642)***
Kihn Solar 703 425-2418
10012 Manor Pl Fairfax (22032) ***(G-4489)***
Kii Industries LLC 804 232-5791
2916 Glenan Dr Richmond (23234) ***(G-11049)***
Kik Custom Products, Salem *Also called Virginia Kik Inc* ***(G-12578)***
Kilaurwen Ltd 434 985-2535
1543 Evergreen Church Rd Stanardsville (22973) ***(G-13220)***
Kilmartin Jones Group LLC 703 232-1531
5555 Old Farm Ln Manassas (20109) ***(G-8094)***
Kiln Creek Associates LP 757 464-6082
4661 Haygood Rd Ste 110 Virginia Beach (23455) ***(G-14584)***
Kiln Creek Pkwy - Old Yorktown 757 204-7229
3120 Kiln Creek Pkwy R Yorktown (23693) ***(G-15972)***
Kiln Doctor Inc 540 636-6016
100 E 8th St Front Royal (22630) ***(G-5540)***
Kilpatrick Framing and Art 804 245-6824
10607 Poachers Run Chesterfield (23832) ***(G-3511)***
Kim Brj Inc 703 642-2367
6251 Little River Tpke Alexandria (22312) ***(G-505)***
Kimball Consulting Inc 703 516-6000
3811 Fairfax Dr Ste 400 Arlington (22203) ***(G-1023)***
Kimberly Gilbert 804 201-6591
11312 Halbrooke Ct Henrico (23233) ***(G-6527)***
Kimberlys 703 448-7298
7022 Old Dominion Dr Mc Lean (22101) ***(G-8480)***
Kims Kreations LLC 703 431-7978
35366 Carnoustie Cir Round Hill (20141) ***(G-12382)***
Kimyaeasonwood 757 502-5001
31030 Walters Hwy Franklin (23851) ***(G-5147)***
Kin Art Studios LLC 804 368-7298
11028 Leadbetter Rd Ashland (23005) ***(G-1449)***
Kin Art Wraps, Ashland *Also called Kin Art Studios LLC* ***(G-1449)***
Kind Cupcakes 703 723-6167
22070 Auction Barn Dr Ashburn (20148) ***(G-1303)***
Kindred Brothers Inc 803 318-5097
12830 West Creek Pkwy Richmond (23238) ***(G-11262)***
Kindred Brothers Inc 210 334-7723
3124 Queens Grant Dr Midlothian (23113) ***(G-8839)***
Kindred Pointe Stables LLC 540 477-3570
3575 Conicville Rd Mount Jackson (22842) ***(G-9074)***
Kindred Spirit Brewing, Richmond *Also called Kindred Brothers Inc* ***(G-11262)***
Kinemetrx Incorporated 703 596-5095
309 Senate Ct Herndon (20170) ***(G-6723)***
Kinetech Labs Inc 434 284-1073
49 Forest Ct Zion Crossroads (22942) ***(G-16008)***
King Aviation 540 439-8621
6555 Stoney Rd Midland (22728) ***(G-8760)***
King Family Vineyards LLC 434 823-7800
6550 Roseland Farm Crozet (22932) ***(G-3840)***
King Kong Kases, Ashland *Also called Koenig Inc* ***(G-1450)***
King Kreations 703 883-7123
210 Spyglass Ln Stafford (22556) ***(G-13163)***
King of Dice 804 758-0776
955 Forest Chapel Rd Saluda (23149) ***(G-12604)***
King of Pops Richmond LLC 804 475-9026
2408 W Cary St Apt B Richmond (23220) ***(G-11644)***
King Screen 540 904-5864
1627 Shenandoah Ave Nw Roanoke (24017) ***(G-12118)***
King Signs and Graphics 540 468-2932
3858 Jackson River Rd Monterey (24465) ***(G-9009)***
Kingdom Bldrs & Ship Repr Inc 757 748-1251
3526 Bancroft Dr Virginia Beach (23452) ***(G-14585)***
Kingdom Bloodline Apparel LLC 866 426-0196
1108 E Main St Ste 90656 Richmond (23219) ***(G-11645)***

ALPHABETIC

Kingdom Jewelry, The, Henrico *Also called Berkley Latasha* **(G-6482)**

Kingdom Marketplace Intl LLC (PA) **757 524-4948**
  999 Waterside Dr Ste 2525 Norfolk (23510) *(G-9612)*

Kingdom Objectives 434 414-0808
  39 Bear Branch Rd Farmville (23901) *(G-4945)*

Kingdom Woodworks Virginia LLC 757 544-4821
  1213 Fentress Airfield Rd Chesapeake (23322) *(G-3164)*

Kingmill Enterprises LLC 877 895-9453
  203 Camellia Dr Charlottesville (22903) *(G-2822)*

Kings Mobile Welding & Fabric 571 620-4665
  446 Hanson Ave Fredericksburg (22401) *(G-5200)*

Kingsdown Incorporated 540 667-0399
  380 W Brooke Rd Winchester (22603) *(G-15433)*

Kingspan Insulation LLC 800 336-2240
  200 Kingspan Way Winchester (22603) *(G-15434)*

Kinko's, Herndon *Also called Kinkos Copies* **(G-6724)**

Kinkos Copies 703 689-0004
  13085 Worldgate Dr Herndon (20170) *(G-6724)*

Kinsey Crane & Sign Company 540 345-5063
  4663 Ferguson Valley Rd Roanoke (24014) *(G-12119)*

Kinsey Neon & Sign Company 540 345-5063
  1516 Cleveland Ave Sw Roanoke (24016) *(G-12120)*

Kinsey Sign Company 540 344-5148
  2727 Mary Linda Ave Ne Roanoke (24012) *(G-12121)*

Kinters Cabinet Shop Inc J 540 837-1663
  530 Gun Barrel Rd White Post (22663) *(G-15180)*

Kintrex, Vienna *Also called National Imports LLC* **(G-14102)**

Kinvarin Software LLC 434 985-3737
  364 Skirmish Rd Stanardsville (22973) *(G-13221)*

Kinyo Virginia Inc 757 888-2221
  290 Enterprise Dr Newport News (23603) *(G-9276)*

Kinzie Woodwork LLC 540 397-1637
  5636 S Mountain Dr Roanoke (24018) *(G-11949)*

Kirby Burbank LLC 571 330-0261
  12 Glenview Ct Stafford (22554) *(G-13164)*

Kirby of VA 434 835-4349
  547 Arnett Blvd Danville (24540) *(G-4010)*

Kirintec Inc 571 527-1437
  400 Madison St Apt 2208 Alexandria (22314) *(G-253)*

Kirk Burkett Manufacturing 276 699-6856
  107 C St Austinville (24312) *(G-1529)*

Kirk Lumber Company 757 255-4521
  815 Kirk Rd Suffolk (23434) *(G-13729)*

Kirkland Holdings Co (PA) **571 348-1005**
  2000 Duke St Ste 110 Alexandria (22314) *(G-254)*

Kisco Signs LLC 804 404-2727
  3529 Grove Ave Richmond (23221) *(G-11646)*

Kishbaugh Enterprises LLC 571 375-2042
  6316 Castle Pl Ste 301 Falls Church (22044) *(G-4816)*

Kiss Krown LLC 757 776-6518
  102 Doolittle Rd Hampton (23669) *(G-6180)*

Kitch N Cook D Potato Chip Co 540 886-4473
  1703 W Beverley St Staunton (24401) *(G-13273)*

Kitch'n Cook'd Potato Chip, Staunton *Also called Kitch N Cook D Potato Chip Co* **(G-13273)**

Kitchen & Bath Ideas, Lynchburg *Also called Norcraft Companies LP* **(G-7777)**

Kitchen and Bath Company LLC 757 417-8200
  5025 Cleveland St Virginia Beach (23462) *(G-14586)*

Kitchen and Bath Design, Chantilly *Also called Smart Buy Kitchen & Bath Plus* **(G-2492)**

Kitchen and Bath Design Studio, Annandale *Also called Greg Norman and Associates Inc* **(G-754)**

Kitchen Concepts Inc 757 547-9238
  1220 Executive Blvd # 102 Chesapeake (23320) *(G-3165)*

Kitchen Krafters Inc 540 891-7678
  198 Wilcox St Fredericksburg (22408) *(G-5310)*

Kitchen Krafters Inc (PA) **540 891-7678**
  4134 Lafayette Blvd Fredericksburg (22408) *(G-5311)*

Kitchens Welding Inc 757 653-2500
  22311 Southampton Pkwy Courtland (23837) *(G-3771)*

Kitco Fiber Optics Inc 757 216-2208
  5269 Cleveland St Ste 109 Virginia Beach (23462) *(G-14587)*

Kitco/Ksaria LLC 757 216-2220
  5269 Cleveland St Virginia Beach (23462) *(G-14588)*

Kitty Hawks Kites Inc 757 351-3959
  328 Laskin Rd Virginia Beach (23451) *(G-14589)*

Kks Printing & Stationery 540 317-5440
  15051 Jats Dr Brandy Station (22714) *(G-1941)*

Klann Inc 540 949-8351
  301 4th St Waynesboro (22980) *(G-15119)*

Klann Organ Supply, Waynesboro *Also called Klann Inc* **(G-15119)**

Klassic Kreatures 703 560-4409
  3105 Manor Rd Falls Church (22042) *(G-4817)*

Klassic Tee's, Chester *Also called Larry Ward* **(G-3427)**

Klaus Composites LLC 443 995-8458
  14890 Wrights Ln Waterford (20197) *(G-15081)*

Klds Client Services LLC 804 586-7538
  2118 Tomahawk Ridge Pl Midlothian (23112) *(G-8840)*

Klearwall Industries 203 689-5404
  530 Anchor Dr Moneta (24121) *(G-8968)*

Kleppinger Design Group Inc 703 208-2208
  2809 Merrilee Dr Fairfax (22031) *(G-4490)*

Klimax Custom Skateboards 757 589-0683
  225 N Palmyra Dr Virginia Beach (23462) *(G-14590)*

Kline Assoc LLC Matt 703 780-6466
  1109 Waynewood Blvd Alexandria (22308) *(G-506)*

Kling Research and Sftwr Inc 540 364-2524
  3233 Fortune Mountain Rd Marshall (20115) *(G-8257)*

Klm Race LLC 804 594-6187
  10910 Southlake Ct North Chesterfield (23236) *(G-9908)*

Klockner Pentaplast Amer Inc 540 832-3600
  3585 Kloeckner Rd Gordonsville (22942) *(G-5909)*

Klockner Pentaplast Amer Inc (HQ) **540 832-1400**
  3585 Kloeckner Rd Gordonsville (22942) *(G-5910)*

Klockner Pentaplast Amer Inc 540 832-7615
  3758 Kloeckner Rd Gordonsville (22942) *(G-5911)*

Klockner Pentaplast Amer Inc 540 832-3600
  1670 Discovery Dr Charlottesville (22911) *(G-2653)*

Klockner Pentaplast Amer Inc 276 686-6111
  600 Gienow Rd Rural Retreat (24368) *(G-12426)*

Klug Servicing LLC 804 310-5866
  4372 River Rd. Mechanicsville (23116) *(G-8649)*

Km Data Strategists LLC 703 689-1087
  24310 Wrens Landing Ct Aldie (20105) *(G-108)*

Km Services LLC 757 524-3420
  2884 Hidden Lake Dr Williamsburg (23185) *(G-15267)*

Kmarie Krafts Inc 804 943-1239
  3107 Kemet Rd Apt 202 Chesapeake (23325) *(G-3166)*

KMW Works LLC 757 776-6765
  4830 Alicia Dr Virginia Beach (23462) *(G-14591)*

Kmx Chemical Corp (PA) **757 824-3600**
  30474 Energy Dr New Church (23415) *(G-9125)*

Kmx Chemical Corp 757 824-3600
  30474 Energy Dr New Church (23415) *(G-9126)*

Knabe Logging LLC 434 547-9878
  2072 Gravel Hill Rd Dillwyn (23936) *(G-4096)*

Knap Services Inc 540 351-5905
  173 Keith St Ste 3 Warrenton (20186) *(G-15028)*

Knauss Snack Food & Co LLC 276 656-3500
  200 Knauss Dr Martinsville (24112) *(G-8305)*

Kngro LLC 202 390-9126
  8617 Beech Hollow Ln Springfield (22153) *(G-13034)*

Knicely Plaining Mill LLC 540 879-2284
  2015 Harness Shop Rd Dayton (22821) *(G-4057)*

Knight Owl Graphics 540 955-1744
  900 Swimley Rd Berryville (22611) *(G-1683)*

Knights Press LLC 703 913-5336
  9005 Brook Ford Rd Burke (22015) *(G-2191)*

Knitting Information 804 288-4754
  7809 Wanymala Rd Richmond (23229) *(G-11263)*

Knockawe Woodworking LLC 804 928-3506
  301 Brighton Dr North Chesterfield (23235) *(G-9909)*

Knotthead Woodworking Inc 540 344-0293
  555 Aragona Dr Vinton (24179) *(G-14176)*

Knowlera Media LLC 703 757-5444
  774 Walker Rd Ste H Great Falls (22066) *(G-5963)*

Knowles Flooring 571 224-3694
  3891 Fairfax Sq Fairfax (22031) *(G-4491)*

Knowlton Packaging, Lynchburg *Also called Tri-Tech Laboratories LLC* **(G-7828)**

Knowwho Inc 703 619-1544
  3201 Cunningham Dr Alexandria (22309) *(G-507)*

Knox Creek Coal Corporation 276 964-4333
  2295 Gvrnor G C Pery Hwy Raven (24639) *(G-10756)*

Knp Traders LLC 703 376-1955
  4211 Pleasant Valley Rd # 230 Chantilly (20151) *(G-2452)*

Knuude LLC 571 298-1746
  770 Old Brook Rd Charlottesville (22901) *(G-2654)*

Knuude Organics Skin Care, Charlottesville *Also called Knuude LLC* **(G-2654)**

Ko Distilling 571 292-1115
  10381 Central Park Dr Manassas (20110) *(G-7956)*

Ko Synthetics Corp 540 580-1760
  96 12th St New Castle (24127) *(G-9121)*

Kobayashi Winery 757 644-4464
  660 Pennsylvania Ave Hampton (23661) *(G-6181)*

Kodescraft LLC 703 843-3700
  3486 Logstone Dr Triangle (22172) *(G-13895)*

Koenig Inc 804 798-8282
  11040 Patterson Park Rd Ashland (23005) *(G-1450)*

Kohler Industries Inc 757 301-3233
  2748 Nestlebrook Trl Virginia Beach (23456) *(G-14592)*

Koit Sheet Metal Inc 703 625-3981
  25446 Stallion Branch Ter Chantilly (20152) *(G-2540)*

Koket, Gainesville *Also called Demorais & Associates Pllc* **(G-5580)**

Kokua John LLC 509 270-3454
  2833 Southern Hills Dr North Garden (22959) *(G-10078)*

Kollmorgen Corporation (HQ) **540 639-9045**
  203a W Rock Rd Radford (24141) *(G-10720)*

Kollmorgen Corporation 540 633-3536
  501 W Main St Radford (24141) *(G-10721)*

ALPHABETIC SECTION L B Davis Inc

Kollmorgen Corporation 540 639-9045
201 W Rock Rd Radford (24141) ***(G-10722)***
Kollmorgen Corporation 540 633-3400
203a W Rock Rd Radford (24141) ***(G-10723)***
Koloza LLC 301 204-9864
10345 Latney Rd Fairfax (22032) ***(G-4492)***
Komatsu Mining Corp 276 623-2000
26161 Old Trail Rd Abingdon (24210) ***(G-48)***
Kombuchick Inc 757 818-7703
2500 Church St Norfolk (23504) ***(G-9613)***
Komorebi Press LLC 301 910-5041
1069 W Broad St Ste 804 Falls Church (22046) ***(G-4920)***
Konecranes Inc 540 366-9502
1226 Trapper Cir Nw Ste E Roanoke (24012) ***(G-12122)***
Konecranes Inc 540 545-8412
230 Airport Rd 12 Winchester (22602) ***(G-15435)***
Kongsberg Defense Systems Inc 703 838-8910
1725 Duke St Ste 600 Alexandria (22314) ***(G-255)***
Kongsberg Prtech Systems USA C 703 838-8910
1725 Duke St Ste 600 Alexandria (22314) ***(G-256)***
Konica Mnlta Bus Sltons USA In 703 461-8195
5775 General Wash Dr Alexandria (22312) ***(G-508)***
Konica Mnlta Bus Sltons USA In 703 553-6000
1595 Spring Hill Rd # 400 Vienna (22182) ***(G-14079)***
Kool Christian Tees 804 201-1646
70 Streets Ln Urbanna (23175) ***(G-13971)***
Kool Looks Inc 808 224-1887
12620 Crabtree Falls Dr Bristow (20136) ***(G-2058)***
Kool-Dri Inc 540 997-9241
33640 Mountain Valley Rd Millboro (24460) ***(G-8936)***
Koolnut LLC 213 349-0196
2115 Clarke St Henrico (23228) ***(G-6528)***
Koppee Shoppe, Chester *Also called Custom Book Bindery* ***(G-3399)***
Koppers Inc 540 380-2061
4020 Koppers Rd Salem (24153) ***(G-12527)***
Koppers Industries Inc 540 672-3802
110 Walker St Orange (22960) ***(G-10218)***
Koppers Utility Indus Pdts Inc 434 292-4375
2960 Cox Rd Blackstone (23824) ***(G-1818)***
Kopy Korner, Blacksburg *Also called Kalwood Inc* ***(G-1749)***
Kora Confections, King George *Also called KORA Confections LLC* ***(G-7098)***
KORA Confections LLC 240 478-2222
6193 Curtis Cir King George (22485) ***(G-7098)***
Kordusa Inc 540 242-5210
400 Corporate Dr Ste 201 Stafford (22554) ***(G-13165)***
Korea Arspc Inds Fort Wrth Inc 703 883-2012
8245 Boone Blvd Vienna (22182) ***(G-14080)***
Korea Daily 703 281-9660
7023 Little River Tpke # 300 Annandale (22003) ***(G-764)***
Korea Express Washington Inc 703 339-8201
10944 Keys Ct Fairfax (22032) ***(G-4493)***
Korea Times Washington DC Inc 703 941-8001
7601 Little River Tpke Annandale (22003) ***(G-765)***
Korean Express, Fairfax *Also called Korea Express Washington Inc* ***(G-4493)***
Korean Weekly Entertainment 703 354-7962
7353 Mcwhorter Pl Ste 210 Annandale (22003) ***(G-766)***
Korman Signs Inc 804 262-6050
3029 Lincoln Ave Richmond (23228) ***(G-11264)***
Korman Signs Inc 804 262-6050
3029 Lincoln Ave Henrico (23228) ***(G-6529)***
Kornfections & Treasures Too, Chantilly *Also called Jhl Inc* ***(G-2449)***
Korona Candles Inc 540 208-2440
3994 Pepperell Way Dublin (24084) ***(G-4161)***
Kovatch Mobile Equipment Corp 540 982-3573
1708 Seibel Dr Ne Roanoke (24012) ***(G-12123)***
Kpw Ventures Inc 703 725-6482
1116 Clinch Rd Herndon (20170) ***(G-6725)***
Kraft 703 583-8874
5119 Cannon Bluff Dr Woodbridge (22192) ***(G-15736)***
Kraft Foods, Chesapeake *Also called Nestle Pizza Company Inc* ***(G-3217)***
Kraft Foods, Winchester *Also called Kraft Heinz Foods Company* ***(G-15437)***
Kraft Heinz Foods Company 540 545-7563
291 Park Center Dr Winchester (22603) ***(G-15436)***
Kraft Heinz Foods Company 540 678-0442
220 Park Center Dr Winchester (22603) ***(G-15437)***
Krain Building Services LLC 703 924-1480
6698 Fleet Dr Alexandria (22310) ***(G-509)***
Kram Industries Inc 571 220-9769
4710 Angus Dr Gainesville (20155) ***(G-5593)***
Kratos Tech Trning Sltions Inc 757 466-3660
5700 Lake Wright Dr # 103 Norfolk (23502) ***(G-9614)***
Krazy Teesz 757 470-4976
820 Live Oak Dr Ste D Chesapeake (23320) ***(G-3167)***
Kreager Woodworking Inc 276 952-2052
9412 Jeb Stuart Hwy Meadows of Dan (24120) ***(G-8592)***
Kreider Machine Shop Inc 540 434-5351
1886 Mount Clinton Pike Rockingham (22802) ***(G-12258)***
Krimm Signs LLC 571 599-2199
4429 Brkfeld Corp Dr Ste Chantilly (20151) ***(G-2453)***
Krismark Inc 757 533-9182
1209 Baker Rd Ste 403 Virginia Beach (23455) ***(G-14593)***
Kriss Systems, SA, Chesapeake *Also called Kriss Usa Inc* ***(G-3168)***
Kriss Usa Inc (HQ) **714 333-1988**
912 Corporate Ln Chesapeake (23320) ***(G-3168)***
Krista Hawk LLC 703 554-7654
22 Mills Ct Lovettsville (20180) ***(G-7581)***
Kristina Kathleen Mann 703 282-9166
2709 Farnsworth Dr Alexandria (22303) ***(G-510)***
Krown LLC 804 307-9722
5131 Morning Dove Mews Midlothian (23112) ***(G-8841)***
Krt Architectural Signage Inc 540 428-3801
6799 Kennedy Rd Ste C Warrenton (20187) ***(G-15029)***
Krug Industries Inc 714 656-5316
5292 Old Dominion Dr Arlington (22207) ***(G-1024)***
Kryptowire LLC 571 314-0153
5352 Brandon Ridge Way Fairfax (22032) ***(G-4494)***
Krystal Clear 703 944-2066
8865 Cherokee Rose Way Lorton (22079) ***(G-7503)***
Ksb America Corporation (HQ) **804 222-1818**
4415 Sarellen Rd Richmond (23231) ***(G-11265)***
Kse, Leesburg *Also called Kessler Soils Engrg Pdts Inc* ***(G-7296)***
Ksquared Cupcakes, Norfolk *Also called Arif Winter* ***(G-9444)***
Ku Forming Inc 434 946-5934
414 Rosecliff Farms Rd Amherst (24521) ***(G-697)***
Kuary LLC 703 980-3804
8901 Garden Gate Dr Fairfax (22031) ***(G-4495)***
Kung Fu Tea 703 992-8599
7895 Heritage Dr Annandale (22003) ***(G-767)***
Kurt USA Prof Dog Tng 252 509-4211
28 Big Spring Ln Stafford (22554) ***(G-13166)***
Kurvez Galore Boutique LLC 336 901-5266
8394 Franklin St Ferrum (24088) ***(G-4975)***
Kusters Engineering SEC Inc 703 967-1449
3190 Fairview Park Dr Falls Church (22042) ***(G-4818)***
Kustomcoffee 571 344-9030
10631 West Dr Fairfax (22030) ***(G-4644)***
Kustomcoffee.com, Fairfax *Also called Kustomcoffee* ***(G-4644)***
Kuykendall LLC David 804 622-2439
2511 Whispering Oaks Ct Midlothian (23112) ***(G-8842)***
KVk Precision Spc Inc 540 652-6102
500 Quincy Ave Shenandoah (22849) ***(G-12693)***
Kwe Publishing LLC 804 458-4789
5015 Takach Rd Prince George (23875) ***(G-10598)***
Kweens Essentials LLC 703 861-6764
3823 Monte Vista Pl Alexandria (22309) ***(G-511)***
Kwick Help LLC 703 499-7223
1043 Sterling Rd Ste 102 Herndon (20170) ***(G-6726)***
Kwicksilver Systems LLC 619 917-1067
5303 Ashlar Ave Crozet (22932) ***(G-3841)***
Kwik Design and Print LLC 703 898-4681
13406 Occoquan Rd Woodbridge (22191) ***(G-15737)***
Kwik Kopy 703 560-5042
3406 Casilear Rd Falls Church (22042) ***(G-4819)***
Kwik Kopy Printing, Falls Church *Also called Kwik Kopy* ***(G-4819)***
Kwik Kopy Printing, Williamsburg *Also called Suter Enterprises Ltd* ***(G-15320)***
Kwik Kopy Printing, Fairfax *Also called Jami Ventures Inc* ***(G-4484)***
Kwik Kopy Printing, Herndon *Also called B K Printing* ***(G-6618)***
Kwik Signs Inc 804 897-5945
611 Research Rd Ste B North Chesterfield (23236) ***(G-9910)***
Kwikpoint, Alexandria *Also called Gaia Communications LLC* ***(G-210)***
Kyanite Mining Corporation (PA) **434 983-2085**
30 Willis Mtn Plant Ln Dillwyn (23936) ***(G-4097)***
Kybo Sales LLC 276 431-2563
4812 Boone Trail Rd Duffield (24244) ***(G-4180)***
Kyung T Jung DBA Krean Entrmt 703 658-0000
7353 Mcwhorter Pl Annandale (22003) ***(G-768)***
L & D Well Services Inc 276 597-7211
2314 Leemaster Dr Vansant (24656) ***(G-13977)***
L & L Tool and Machine Inc 757 224-3445
505 Edwards Ct Newport News (23608) ***(G-9277)***
L & M Contracting, Alexandria *Also called L & M Electric and Plbg LLC* ***(G-512)***
L & M Electric and Plbg LLC 703 768-2222
2601 Beacon Hill Rd Alexandria (22306) ***(G-512)***
L & M Printing Inc 703 573-2257
2810 Dorr Ave Ste D Fairfax (22031) ***(G-4496)***
L & N Wood Products Inc 804 784-4734
2055 Valpark Dr Oilville (23129) ***(G-10181)***
L & R Precision Tooling Inc 434 525-4120
3720 Cohen Pl Lynchburg (24501) ***(G-7752)***
L 3 Maritime Systems 703 443-1700
2235 Monroe St Herndon (20171) ***(G-6727)***
L A Bowles Logging Inc 804 492-3103
2120 Ballsville Rd Powhatan (23139) ***(G-10555)***
L and M Foods 276 979-4110
254 Rabbit Patch Rd Tazewell (24651) ***(G-13833)***
L B Davis Inc 434 792-3281
669 Little Creek Rd Ringgold (24586) ***(G-11869)***

ALPHABETIC

L B Foster Company 804 722-0398
　26401 Hofheimer Way Petersburg (23804) *(G-10329)*

L B Oil Company 757 723-8379
　305 Bartell Dr Chesapeake (23322) *(G-3169)*

L C M B Inc 804 639-1429
　16801 Starlee Ct Moseley (23120) *(G-9041)*

L C Pembroke Manufacturing 757 723-3435
　756 N First St Hampton (23664) *(G-6182)*

L D Publications Group 703 623-6799
　6910 Barnack Dr Springfield (22152) *(G-13035)*

L E F Gear...757 274-2151
　1433 Ashburnham Arch Virginia Beach (23456) *(G-14594)*

L H Corporation 540 674-8803
　4945 Stepp Pl Dublin (24084) *(G-4162)*

L H Gaither Co Inc 703 335-2300
　10402 Johnson Dr Manassas (20110) *(G-7957)*

L Industries 540 948-4806
　140 Fairground Rd Madison (22727) *(G-7855)*

L J S Stores Inc 804 561-6999
　12850 Patrick Henry Hwy Amelia Court House (23002) *(G-662)*

L K & Associates, Roanoke *Also called Paul E Stahl (G-11983)*

L K Smith Machine Shop 276 694-4109
　174 Dominion Valley Ln Stuart (24171) *(G-13621)*

L Peters Custom Cabinets 276 340-9580
　107 Wind Dancer Ln Ridgeway (24148) *(G-11846)*

L S Industries Inc 540 948-4806
　140 Fairground Rd Madison (22727) *(G-7856)*

L T I, Mouth of Wilson *Also called Luminaire Technologies Inc (G-9094)*

L&D Healthy Foods & Snacks, Alexandria *Also called Lorrie Carpenter (G-265)*

L&F Logging Inc 276 728-5773
　395 Hardscuffle Rd Hillsville (24343) *(G-6895)*

L&L Trading Company LLC 757 995-3608
　3707 Virginia Beach Blvd Virginia Beach (23452) *(G-14595)*

L-1 Standards and Tech Inc 571 428-2227
　10364 Battleview Pkwy Manassas (20109) *(G-8095)*

L-3 Communications Corp 703 375-4911
　9507 Oakenshaw Dr Manassas (20110) *(G-7958)*

L-3 Mustang Technology, Ashburn *Also called L3 Technologies Inc (G-1305)*

L-3 Unmanned Systems Inc 703 889-8640
　44611 Guilford Dr Ste 125 Ashburn (20147) *(G-1304)*

L.A. Dudley Welding, Eagle Rock *Also called Lewis A Dudley (G-4282)*

L3 Technologies Inc 703 889-8640
　44611 Guilford Dr Ste 125 Ashburn (20147) *(G-1305)*

L3 Technologies Inc 757 425-0142
　140 F Ave Virginia Beach (23460) *(G-14596)*

L3 Technologies Inc 540 658-0591
　50 Tech Pkwy Ste 207 Stafford (22556) *(G-13167)*

L3harris Technologies Inc 540 563-0371
　7635 Plantation Rd Roanoke (24019) *(G-11950)*

L3harris Technologies Inc 540 658-3350
　65 Barrett Heights Rd # 109 Stafford (22556) *(G-13168)*

L3harris Technologies Inc 847 952-6120
　44965 Aviation Dr Ste 400 Dulles (20166) *(G-4207)*

L3harris Technologies Inc 703 668-6239
　12975 Worldgate Dr Herndon (20170) *(G-6728)*

L3harris Technologies Inc 540 563-0371
　7635 Plantation Rd Roanoke (24019) *(G-11951)*

L3harris Technologies Inc 703 790-6300
　1650 Tysons Blvd Mc Lean (22102) *(G-8481)*

L3harris Technologies Inc 757 594-1607
　11830 Canon Blvd Newport News (23606) *(G-9278)*

L3harris Technologies Inc 434 455-9390
　12860 E Lynchburg Salem Forest (24551) *(G-5079)*

L3harris Technologies Inc 434 455-6600
　110 Vista Centre Dr Ste 4 Forest (24551) *(G-5080)*

L3harris Technologies Inc 703 668-6000
　12975 Worldgate Dr Herndon (20170) *(G-6729)*

L3harris Technologies Inc 703 668-7256
　2235 Monroe St Herndon (20171) *(G-6730)*

L3harris Technologies Inc 703 344-1000
　15049 Confrnce Ctr Dr # 600 Chantilly (20151) *(G-2454)*

L3harris Technologies Inc 434 455-6600
　221 Jefferson Ridge Pkwy Lynchburg (24501) *(G-7753)*

L3harris Technologies Inc 703 828-1520
　4125 Lafayette Center Dr # 700 Chantilly (20151) *(G-2455)*

L3harris Technologies Inc 434 941-5441
　5155 Old Evergreen Rd Appomattox (24522) *(G-818)*

La ABRA Farm & Winery Inc 434 263-5392
　1362 Fortunes Cove Ln Lovingston (22949) *(G-7591)*

La Fleur De Lis LLC 703 753-5690
　5600 Artemus Rd Gainesville (20155) *(G-5594)*

La La Land Candy Kingdom Va01 ....305 342-6737
　1602 Atlantic Ave Virginia Beach (23451) *(G-14597)*

La Michoacana III LLC 804 275-0011
　9110 Jefferson Davis Hwy North Chesterfield (23237) *(G-9911)*

La Playa Incorporated Virginia 757 222-1865
　550 Woodlake Cir Chesapeake (23320) *(G-3170)*

La Prade Enterprises 804 271-9899
　5260 Ronson Rd North Chesterfield (23234) *(G-9912)*

La Princesa 703 330-2400
　8388 Centreville Rd Manassas (20111) *(G-8096)*

La Publishing 757 650-8364
　6100 Otterdale Rd Moseley (23120) *(G-9042)*

La Stitchery 540 894-9371
　115 Old Burruss Mill Rd Bumpass (23024) *(G-2163)*

La Vache Microcreamery 434 989-6264
　2324 Glenn Ct Charlottesville (22901) *(G-2655)*

La-Z-Boy Incorporated 703 569-6188
　7398 Ward Park Ln Springfield (22153) *(G-13036)*

Label 757 236-8434
　56 Newmarket Sq Hampton (23605) *(G-6275)*

Label Laboratory Inc 703 654-0327
　11 Acacia Ln Ste 4 Sterling (20166) *(G-13439)*

Label Systems, North Chesterfield *Also called Masa Corporation of Virginia (G-9925)*

Labelink Flexibles LLC 703 348-4699
　18 Blackjack Rd Fredericksburg (22405) *(G-5448)*

Labels East Inc 757 558-0800
　817 Butler St Chesapeake (23323) *(G-3171)*

Labrador Technology 703 791-7660
　12219 Vista Brooke Dr Manassas (20112) *(G-8097)*

Labxperior Corporation 276 321-7866
　517 W Main St Wise (24293) *(G-15629)*

Labyrinth Woodworks LLC 206 235-6272
　66 North Princeton Cir Lynchburg (24503) *(G-7754)*

Laconiko, Manassas *Also called Our Familys Olive Oil LLC (G-8124)*

Lady Press Creations LLC 757 745-7473
　13408 Southwind Ct Carrollton (23314) *(G-2244)*

Laestrellita 276 650-7099
　140 Axton Rd Axton (24054) *(G-1539)*

Lafarge Calcium Aluminates Inc 757 543-8832
　1316 Priority Ln Chesapeake (23324) *(G-3172)*

Lafarge North America Inc 505 471-6456
　12950 Worldgate Dr # 500 Herndon (20170) *(G-6731)*

Lafarge North America Inc 703 480-3600
　12018 Sunrise Valley Dr # 5 Reston (20191) *(G-10882)*

Lafarge North America Inc 757 545-2481
　100 Pratt St Chesapeake (23324) *(G-3173)*

Lagniappe Publishing LLC 804 739-0795
　5624 Beacon Hill Dr Midlothian (23112) *(G-8843)*

Lai Enterprises LLC 540 946-0000
　21 Hannah Cir Waynesboro (22980) *(G-15120)*

Lai of Richmond LLC 804 746-2739
　8106 Academy Dr Mechanicsville (23116) *(G-8650)*

Laird & Company 434 296-6058
　3638 Laird Ln North Garden (22959) *(G-10079)*

Lake Lithograph Company 703 361-8030
　10371 Central Park Dr Manassas (20110) *(G-7959)*

Lake Machine, Moneta *Also called Lake Manufacturing Inc (G-8969)*

Lake Manufacturing Inc 540 297-2957
　2586 Tuck Rd Moneta (24121) *(G-8969)*

Lake Packing Co Inc 804 529-6101
　755 Lake Landing Dr Lottsburg (22511) *(G-7543)*

Lake Region Medical Inc 540 389-7860
　200 S Yorkshire St Salem (24153) *(G-12528)*

Lakeside Embroidery 540 719-2600
　70 Scruggs Rd Ste 103 Moneta (24121) *(G-8970)*

Lakeside Logging Inc 540 872-2585
　2165 Bumpass Rd Bumpass (23024) *(G-2164)*

Lakeside Stone & Landscape Sup 434 738-3204
　300 Pamunkey Dr Clarksville (23927) *(G-3632)*

Lakeside Welding 434 636-1712
　2250 Dry Bread Rd White Plains (23893) *(G-15179)*

Lakota JS Chocolates Corp 804 590-0010
　15600 Chesdin Landing Ter Chesterfield (23838) *(G-3512)*

Lalandii Coatings LLC 757 425-0131
　1023 Laskin Rd Virginia Beach (23451) *(G-14598)*

Lamaid LLC 703 541-8011
　11638 Rumford Ct Woodbridge (22192) *(G-15738)*

Lambert Metal Services LLC 571 261-5811
　10476 Godwin Ct Manassas (20110) *(G-7960)*

Lammasu Defense LLC 540 229-7027
　17476 Safe Haven Way Culpeper (22701) *(G-3906)*

Lams Lumber Co 540 832-5173
　Rr 20 Barboursville (22923) *(G-1563)*

Lana Juarez 540 951-3566
　115 N Main St Blacksburg (24060) *(G-1750)*

Lance Stitcher 443 685-4829
　3640 Captains Corridor Greenbackville (23356) *(G-5995)*

Land Electric Company 757 625-0444
　1525 Boxwood Dr Chesapeake (23323) *(G-3174)*

Land Venture Two LC 703 367-9456
　8303 Quarry Rd Manassas (20110) *(G-7961)*

Landmark Cmnty Nwsppers VA LLC (HQ)...........**276 236-5178**
　108 W Stuart Dr Galax (24333) *(G-5640)*

Landmark Community Newspapers 502 633-4334
　150 Granby St Fl 19 Norfolk (23510) *(G-9615)*

Landmark Industries LLC 757 233-7291
　1072 Laskin Rd Ste 104 Virginia Beach (23451) *(G-14599)*

Landmark Logworks 540 687-4124
  3489 Landmark Rd The Plains (20198) (G-13843)
Landmark Media Enterprises LLC (PA) 757 351-7000
  150 Granby St Norfolk (23510) (G-9616)
Landmark Military Newspapers 254 690-9000
  150 W Brambleton Ave Norfolk (23510) (G-9617)
Landmark Printing Co 703 226-1000
  7535 Little River Tpke 120c Annandale (22003) (G-769)
Landmark Woodworking Inc 703 424-3191
  8304 Greenside Dr Fairfax Station (22039) (G-4715)
Landos Biopharma Inc 540 218-2262
  1800 Kraft Dr Ste 216 Blacksburg (24060) (G-1751)
Landrum Horse Shoeing Inc 434 836-0847
  324 Landrum Rd Blairs (24527) (G-1831)
Lane Auto Parts, Fredericksburg Also called Pitts Auto Parts Inc (G-5213)
Lane Construction Corporation 703 471-6883
  25094 Tanner Ln Chantilly (20152) (G-2541)
Lane Custom Hearing 540 775-5999
  10988 Laforce Ln King George (22485) (G-7099)
Lane Enterprises Inc 540 439-3201
  6369 Schoolhouse Rd Bealeton (22712) (G-1600)
Lane Enterprises Inc 540 674-4645
  Rr 103 Dublin (24084) (G-4163)
Lane Enterprises Inc 276 223-1051
  510 Kents Ln Wytheville (24382) (G-15895)
Lane Metal Products, Bealeton Also called Lane Enterprises Inc (G-1600)
Lane-Dublin Division, Dublin Also called Lane Enterprises Inc (G-4163)
Langley Afb, Hampton Also called US Dept of the Air Force (G-6279)
Langvan 703 532-0466
  6787 Wilson Blvd Falls Church (22044) (G-4820)
Lanier Outdoor Enterprises LLC 540 892-5945
  1581 Gravel Hill Rd Vinton (24179) (G-14177)
Lantz Custom Woodworking 540 438-1819
  641 Acorn Dr Harrisonburg (22802) (G-6336)
Lanzara Industries LLC 703 759-6959
  544 Springvale Rd Great Falls (22066) (G-5964)
Laporte America LLC 800 335-8727
  129 Post St Pounding Mill (24637) (G-10522)
Laporte USA 276 964-5566
  14463 Gvrnor G C Pery Hwy Pounding Mill (24637) (G-10523)
Lapp Metals LLC 434 392-3505
  304 Industrial Park Rd Farmville (23901) (G-4946)
Largo Resources USA Inc 571 491-7827
  4250 Fairfax Dr Ste 600 Arlington (22203) (G-1025)
Larissa Leclair 202 270-8039
  6138 12th St N Arlington (22205) (G-1026)
Lark Printing Inc 434 237-4449
  485 Hopkins Rd Lynchburg (24502) (G-7755)
Larktale, Richmond Also called Dynamic Motion LLC (G-11194)
Larry D Martin 540 493-0072
  949 Robin Ridge Rd Rocky Mount (24151) (G-12332)
Larry Graves 540 972-5320
  1514 Lakeview Pkwy Locust Grove (22508) (G-7447)
Larry Hicks 276 738-9010
  595 Copper Ridge Rd Castlewood (24224) (G-2254)
Larry Kaniecki 804 737-7616
  2200 E Nine Mile Rd Sandston (23150) (G-12623)
Larry Lewis 757 619-7070
  2701 Springhaven Dr Virginia Beach (23456) (G-14600)
Larry Rosenbaum 703 567-4052
  5500 Columbia Pike # 422 Arlington (22204) (G-1027)
Larry W Jarvis Logging 276 686-5938
  988 Pine Glade Rd Rural Retreat (24368) (G-12427)
Larry Ward 804 778-7945
  13907 Old Hampstead Ln Chester (23831) (G-3427)
Larrylandcraftsetc., Sandston Also called Larry Kaniecki (G-12623)
Larsco LLC 804 400-0667
  830 Montour Dr North Chesterfield (23236) (G-9913)
Larsen Swen 703 754-2592
  9244 Bowers Brook Pl Bristow (20136) (G-2059)
Larson Baker Publishing LLC 703 644-4243
  6604 Wren Dr Springfield (22150) (G-13037)
Las Americas Newspaper Inc 703 256-4200
  3809 Bell Manor Ct Falls Church (22041) (G-4821)
Las Americas Yellow Pages, Falls Church Also called Las Americas Newspaper Inc (G-4821)
Las Creation Design LLC 757 880-4211
  15412 Gunsmith Ter Woodbridge (22191) (G-15739)
Lasar Chemicals 757 286-9808
  704 Fordsmere Ct Chesapeake (23322) (G-3175)
Laser Alignment Systems LLC 410 507-6820
  6718 Main St Gloucester (23061) (G-5852)
Laser Light Communications Inc 571 346-7623
  1818 Library St Ste 500 Reston (20190) (G-10883)
Laser Light Federal LLC 703 283-0659
  1818 Library St Ste 500 Reston (20190) (G-10884)
Laser Thermal Analysis LLC 703 300-3403
  1009 Cottage Green Way Charlottesville (22903) (G-2823)
Lasercam Express, Roanoke Also called Lasercam LLc (G-11952)

Lasercam LLc 540 265-2888
  7519 Hitech Rd Roanoke (24019) (G-11952)
Lasermarx Inc 434 528-1044
  301 E Progress Ln Madison Heights (24572) (G-7876)
Laserserv Inc 804 359-6188
  2317 Westwood Ave Ste 114 Richmond (23230) (G-11266)
Lash and Glow By Tess Llc 571 732-1080
  384 Elden St Herndon (20170) (G-6732)
Lashme By Leslie LLC 703 595-8628
  13281c Leafcrest Ln # 304 Fairfax (22033) (G-4497)
Lassosmart.com, Charlottesville Also called Spring Hollow Publishing Inc (G-2695)
Last Call Magazine LLC 757 410-0229
  1013 Saint Andrews Way C Chesapeake (23320) (G-3176)
Lastmile Logistix Incorporated 757 338-0076
  138 S Rosemont Rd 201a Virginia Beach (23452) (G-14601)
Lateeshirt 703 532-7329
  5131 Lee Hwy Arlington (22207) (G-1028)
Latell Sailmakers LLC 804 776-6151
  17467 General Puller Hwy Deltaville (23043) (G-4082)
Latham Architectural Pdts Inc 804 308-2205
  13912 Two Notch Pl Midlothian (23112) (G-8844)
Latimer Julian Manufacturing 804 405-6851
  101 Eisenhower Dr Richmond (23227) (G-11267)
Latin Tempo Distributors, Arlington Also called Villalva Inc (G-1211)
Laundry Chemical Products Inc 757 363-0662
  2793 Sandpiper Rd Virginia Beach (23456) (G-14602)
Laura Bushnell 703 569-4422
  7485 Huntsman Blvd Springfield (22153) (G-13038)
Laura Copenhaver Industries 276 783-4663
  114 W Main St Marion (24354) (G-8230)
Laura Hooper Calligrathy 213 514-4170
  4605 Dolphin Ln Alexandria (22309) (G-513)
Laurel Fork Logging Inc 276 285-3761
  7139 Pembroke Cir Bristol (24202) (G-2024)
Laurel Run LLC 540 364-1238
  11171 Hume Rd Hume (22639) (G-6962)
Laurel Technologies Partnr 814 534-2027
  2345 Crystal Dr Arlington (22202) (G-1029)
Laurel Technologies Partnr 757 819-0700
  825 Greenbrier Cir Ste M Chesapeake (23320) (G-3177)
Lauren E Thronson 703 536-3625
  1944 Valleywood Rd Mc Lean (22101) (G-8482)
Laurence Walter Aerospace Solu 757 966-9578
  1105a International Plz Chesapeake (23323) (G-3178)
Lauret Company 540 635-1670
  13386 John Marshall Hwy Linden (22642) (G-7430)
Laurie Grusha Zipf 703 794-9497
  7030 Gray Fox Trl Manassas (20112) (G-8098)
Lava Flow Yoga LLC 703 264-1638
  1970 Winterport Cluster Reston (20191) (G-10885)
Lava Instant Coffee LLC 703 239-0803
  14764 Soapstone Dr # 403 Gainesville (20155) (G-5595)
Lavenmoon 540 297-3274
  1148 Red Horse Dr Goodview (24095) (G-5896)
Lavish 757 498-1238
  4312 Holland Rd Ste 115 Virginia Beach (23452) (G-14603)
Lavish Nicole LLC 804 386-7556
  2609 Amherst Ridge Way South Chesterfield (23834) (G-12812)
LAw Hauling LLC 757 774-3055
  764 De Laura Ln Virginia Beach (23455) (G-14604)
Lawless Wldg & Fabrication Inc 276 806-8077
  3372 River Rd Fieldale (24089) (G-4989)
Lawrence Brothers Inc 276 322-4988
  203 Lawrence Rd Bluefield (24605) (G-1868)
Lawrence Custom Cabinets S 757 380-0817
  53 Buxton Ave Newport News (23607) (G-9279)
Lawrence Fabrications Inc 540 667-1141
  980 Baker Ln Winchester (22603) (G-15438)
Lawrence Trlr & Trck Eqp Inc 800 296-6009
  11362 Washington Hwy Ashland (23005) (G-1451)
Lawrence Trnsp Systems Inc 540 966-3797
  872 Lee Hwy Ste 203 Roanoke (24019) (G-11953)
Lawrenceville Brick Inc 434 848-3151
  16144 Gvrnor Hrrison Pkwy Lawrenceville (23868) (G-7182)
Lawrenceville Machine Shop, Lawrenceville Also called Sopko Manufacturing Inc (G-7185)
Lawriter LLC 434 220-4324
  1467 Greenbrier Pl 6 Charlottesville (22901) (G-2656)
Lawson & Sons Logging LLC 434 292-7904
  3543 Rocky Hill Rd Blackstone (23824) (G-1819)
Lawson and Son Cnstr LLC 478 258-2478
  109 W Wedgwood Dr Yorktown (23693) (G-15973)
Lawson Brothers Logging LLC 276 694-8905
  915 Dobyns Church Rd Stuart (24171) (G-13622)
Lawson Timber Company 276 395-2069
  5711 Walton Ln Saint Paul (24283) (G-12468)
Lawsons Welding Service LLC 434 985-2079
  181 Mutton Hollow Rd Stanardsville (22973) (G-13222)
Lawton Pubg & Translation LLC 804 367-4028
  117 N Crenshaw Ave Richmond (23221) (G-11647)

A
L
P
H
A
B
E
T
I
C

Lawyers Printing Co.......804 648-3664
1011 E Main St Ste 50 Richmond (23219) ***(G-11648)***
Lawyers Road Quarry, Lynchburg *Also called Boxley Materials Company* ***(G-7658)***
Lax Loft LLC.......540 389-4529
14 S College Ave Salem (24153) ***(G-12529)***
Lay-N-Go LLC.......703 799-0799
8418 Stable Dr Alexandria (22308) ***(G-514)***
Layman Enterprises Inc.......540 662-7142
340 Spring Valley Dr Winchester (22603) ***(G-15439)***
Layne Logging.......276 312-1665
8287 Hurley Rd Hurley (24620) ***(G-6969)***
Lazy Days Winery.......804 437-3453
3816 Old Gun Rd W Midlothian (23113) ***(G-8845)***
Lb Telesystems Inc.......703 919-8991
4001 Westfax Dr Ste 100 Chantilly (20151) ***(G-2456)***
Lbp Manufacturing LLC.......804 562-6920
3001 Cofer Rd Richmond (23224) ***(G-11649)***
Ld Welding & Fabrication Co.......757 553-2471
801 Butler St Ste 6 Chesapeake (23323) ***(G-3179)***
Le Grand Assoc of Pittsburgh.......757 484-4900
3800 Poplar Hill Rd Ste E Chesapeake (23321) ***(G-3180)***
LE GRAND ASSOCIATES OF PITTSBURGH INC, Chesapeake *Also called Le Grand Assoc of Pittsburgh* ***(G-3180)***
Le Look LLC.......301 237-5072
4545 Commerce St # 2206 Virginia Beach (23462) ***(G-14605)***
Le Reve Bridal & Tuxedo Wear, Leesburg *Also called Le Reve Bridal Inc* ***(G-7297)***
Le Reve Bridal Inc.......703 777-3757
213 Loudoun St Se Leesburg (20175) ***(G-7297)***
Le Splendour LLC.......703 505-5362
14060 Darkwood Cir Centreville (20121) ***(G-2314)***
Leadconnector LLC, Mclean *Also called Govsearch LLC* ***(G-8587)***
Leader Publishing Company.......540 885-7387
2 W Beverley St Staunton (24401) ***(G-13274)***
Leadership Perspectives Inc.......703 629-8977
5701 Windsor Gate Ln Fairfax (22030) ***(G-4645)***
Leading Edge Screen Printing.......540 347-5751
405 Rosedale Ct Warrenton (20186) ***(G-15030)***
Leapfrog Software LLC.......804 677-7051
1611 Oakengate Ln Midlothian (23113) ***(G-8846)***
Lear Corp Strasburg.......540 465-6244
806 E Queen St Strasburg (22657) ***(G-13587)***
Learning To Lean Printing.......757 718-5586
2501 Cedar Rd Chesapeake (23323) ***(G-3181)***
Leaseaccelerator Inc (PA).......**866 446-0980**
10740 Parkridge Blvd # 70 Reston (20191) ***(G-10886)***
Leather Luster Inc.......757 548-0146
908 Executive Ct Ste 103 Chesapeake (23320) ***(G-3182)***
Leather World Technologies LLC.......540 265-9038
5851 Cloverdale Rd Roanoke (24019) ***(G-11954)***
Leatheroot LLC.......804 695-1604
6988 Indian Springs Ln Gloucester (23061) ***(G-5853)***
Lebanon Apparel Corporation.......276 889-3656
70 Thornhill Dr Lebanon (24266) ***(G-7197)***
Lebanon News Inc.......276 889-2112
308 Clinch Mountain Ave Lebanon (24266) ***(G-7198)***
Lebanon Seaboard Corporation.......540 375-0300
525 Branch Dr Salem (24153) ***(G-12530)***
Lectrotab, Ashland *Also called Linear Devices Corporation* ***(G-1453)***
Led Solar and Light Company.......703 201-3250
1312 Yellow Tavern Ct Herndon (20170) ***(G-6733)***
Lee CL Trucking LLC.......804 677-2242
2007 X St Richmond (23223) ***(G-11650)***
Lee High Sheet Metal Inc.......703 698-5168
8441 Lee Hwy Fairfax (22031) ***(G-4498)***
Lee Savoy Inc.......540 297-9275
1822 Echo Forest Way Huddleston (24104) ***(G-6955)***
Lee Street Publishing LLC.......540 459-8566
207 S Lee St Woodstock (22664) ***(G-15856)***
Lee Talbot Associates Inc.......703 734-8576
6656 Chilton Ct Mc Lean (22101) ***(G-8483)***
Lee Tech Hardwood Floors.......540 588-6217
180 Huntington Blvd Ne Roanoke (24012) ***(G-12124)***
Lees Wood Products Inc.......540 483-9728
110 Smithers St Rocky Mount (24151) ***(G-12333)***
Leesa Dream Gallery, Virginia Beach *Also called Leesa Sleep LLC* ***(G-14606)***
Leesa Sleep LLC.......844 335-3372
3200 Pacific Ave Ste 200 Virginia Beach (23451) ***(G-14606)***
Leesburg Today Inc.......703 771-8800
19301 Winmeade Dr Ste 224 Lansdowne (20176) ***(G-7171)***
Left Field Media.......703 980-4710
10815 Charles Dr Fairfax (22030) ***(G-4646)***
Legacy A Ryan Company, Chantilly *Also called Ryan Studio Inc* ***(G-2488)***
Legacy Mfg LLC.......434 841-5331
110 Tracie Dr Altavista (24517) ***(G-634)***
Legacy Printing Inc.......804 730-1834
8051 Ellerson Station Dr Mechanicsville (23111) ***(G-8651)***
Legacy Products LLC.......804 739-9333
12727 Spectrim Ln Midlothian (23112) ***(G-8847)***
Legacy Solutions.......703 644-9700
8205 Running Creek Ct Springfield (22153) ***(G-13039)***
Legacy Vulcan LLC.......540 298-1237
5967 Humes Run Rd Elkton (22827) ***(G-4330)***
Legacy Vulcan LLC.......434 634-4158
1459 Quarry Rd Skippers (23879) ***(G-12701)***
Legacy Vulcan LLC.......703 368-2475
8537 Vulcan Ln Manassas (20109) ***(G-8099)***
Legacy Vulcan LLC.......703 690-1172
10000 Ox Rd Lorton (22079) ***(G-7504)***
Legacy Vulcan LLC.......434 572-3931
Hwy 360 South Boston (24592) ***(G-12777)***
Legacy Vulcan LLC.......703 354-5783
5650 Industrial Dr Springfield (22151) ***(G-13040)***
Legacy Vulcan LLC.......540 347-3641
5485 Afton Ln Warrenton (20187) ***(G-15031)***
Legacy Vulcan LLC.......540 886-6758
327 Luck Stone Rd Staunton (24401) ***(G-13275)***
Legacy Vulcan LLC.......804 706-1773
11520 Iron Bridge Rd Chester (23831) ***(G-3428)***
Legacy Vulcan LLC.......540 659-3003
100 Vulcan Quarry Rd Stafford (22556) ***(G-13169)***
Legacy Vulcan LLC.......800 732-3964
11454 Quarry Dr Rapidan (22733) ***(G-10753)***
Legacy Vulcan LLC.......804 748-3695
12020 Old Stage Rd Chester (23831) ***(G-3429)***
Legacy Vulcan LLC.......800 732-3964
217 Canal Rd Dumfries (22026) ***(G-4250)***
Legacy Vulcan LLC.......804 863-4565
26505 Simpson Rd North Dinwiddie (23803) ***(G-10056)***
Legacy Vulcan LLC.......800 732-3964
2651 S Shirlington Rd Arlington (22206) ***(G-1030)***
Legacy Vulcan LLC.......800 732-3964
25086 Tanner Ln Chantilly (20152) ***(G-2542)***
Legacy Vulcan LLC.......434 572-3967
3074 James D Hagood Hwy South Boston (24592) ***(G-12778)***
Legacy Vulcan LLC.......800 732-3964
32 Wyche Rd Stafford (22554) ***(G-13170)***
Legacy Vulcan LLC.......800 732-3964
339 Estep Rd Stephens City (22655) ***(G-13319)***
Legacy Vulcan LLC.......804 730-1008
6385 Power Rd Mechanicsville (23111) ***(G-8652)***
Legacy Vulcan LLC.......703 713-3100
6860 Commercial Dr Springfield (22151) ***(G-13041)***
Legacy Vulcan LLC.......800 732-3964
7103 Gordons Rd Falls Church (22043) ***(G-4822)***
Legacy Vulcan LLC.......800 732-3964
8402 Terminal Rd Lorton (22079) ***(G-7505)***
Legacy Vulcan LLC.......800 732-3964
9151 Luck Stone Ln Fredericksburg (22407) ***(G-5312)***
Legacy Vulcan LLC.......800 732-3964
8413 Terminal Rd Q Lorton (22079) ***(G-7506)***
Legacy Vulcan LLC.......276 940-2741
Dffield Va 24244 Rr 23 Duffield (24244) ***(G-4181)***
Legacy Vulcan LLC.......757 888-2982
313 O Hara Ln Newport News (23602) ***(G-9280)***
Legacy Vulcan LLC.......804 236-4160
5600 Old Osborne Tpke Richmond (23231) ***(G-11268)***
Legacy Vulcan LLC.......540 659-3003
1012 Garrisonville Rd Garrisonville (22463) ***(G-5656)***
Legacy Vulcan LLC.......804 717-5770
5601 Ironbridge Pkwy Chester (23831) ***(G-3430)***
Legacy Vulcan LLC.......757 539-5670
1273 Portsmouth Blvd Suffolk (23434) ***(G-13730)***
Legacy Vulcan LLC.......804 360-2014
4060 Quarry Hill Rd Rockville (23146) ***(G-12288)***
Legacy Vulcan LLC.......434 447-4696
1261 Skyline Rd South Hill (23970) ***(G-12856)***
Legacy Vulcan LLC.......703 461-0333
701 S Van Dorn St Alexandria (22304) ***(G-257)***
Legacy Vulcan LLC.......276 679-0880
6420 Powell Valley Rd Big Stone Gap (24219) ***(G-1711)***
Legacy Vulcan Corp.......757 562-5008
2001 Whitley Ln Ste B Franklin (23851) ***(G-5148)***
Legacy Woodworking LLC.......703 431-8811
205 Ken Culbert Ln Purcellville (20132) ***(G-10665)***
Legacy Word Publishing LLC.......941 915-4730
5906 Westchester St Alexandria (22310) ***(G-515)***
Legend Brewing Co.......804 232-8871
321 W 7th St Richmond (23224) ***(G-11651)***
Legend Lenses LLC.......757 871-1331
204 School Ln Yorktown (23692) ***(G-15974)***
Legion Athletics Inc.......727 729-1049
8045 Leesburg Pike # 240 Vienna (22182) ***(G-14081)***
Legit Bath Salts Online.......540 200-8618
1338 S Main St Blacksburg (24060) ***(G-1752)***
Lehigh Cement Company LLC.......757 928-1559
21 Stanley Dr Newport News (23608) ***(G-9281)***
Lehigh Cement Company LLC.......540 942-1181
500 Delaware Ave Waynesboro (22980) ***(G-15121)***

Lehr Inc (PA) 703 821-2679
1356 Beverly Rd Ste 180 Mc Lean (22101) *(G-8484)*

Leica Microsystems Inc 812 333-5416
14280 Pk Madow Dr Ste 100 Chantilly (20151) *(G-2457)*

Leidos Inc 703 610-8900
1953 Gallows Rd Ste 810 Vienna (22182) *(G-14082)*

Leidos Inc 703 734-5315
7927 Jones Branch Dr # 200 Mc Lean (22102) *(G-8485)*

Leidos Inc 703 676-7451
8725 John J Kingman Rd # 6201 Fort Belvoir (22060) *(G-5116)*

Leigh Ann Carrasco 703 725-4680
7107 Sea Cliff Rd Mc Lean (22101) *(G-8486)*

Leisure Publishing Inc 540 989-6138
3424 Brambleton Ave Roanoke (24018) *(G-11955)*

Leisuremedia360 Inc 540 989-6138
3424 Brambleton Ave Roanoke (24018) *(G-11956)*

Leitner-Wise Defense Inc 703 209-0009
5240 Port Royal Rd # 210 Springfield (22151) *(G-13042)*

Leitner-Wise Manufacturing LLC 703 209-0009
108 S Early St Alexandria (22304) *(G-258)*

Lelo Fabrication 703 581-7852
5626 Lick River Ln Gainesville (20155) *(G-5596)*

Lelo Fabrication LLC 703 754-1141
1518 Duffey Dr Haymarket (20169) *(G-6429)*

Lemac Corporation 804 862-8481
22909 Airpark Dr North Dinwiddie (23803) *(G-10057)*

Lennah Press LLC 571 235-4809
20103 Prairie Dunes Ter Ashburn (20147) *(G-1306)*

Lenzkes Clamping Tools Inc 540 381-1533
825 Radford St Christiansburg (24073) *(G-3603)*

Leo Paul & Associates, Manquin *Also called Neault LLC (G-8217)*

Leogrand Vinyards 540 586-4066
1343 Wingfield Dr Goode (24556) *(G-5892)*

Leonard Alum Utlity Bldngs Inc 540 951-0236
3930 S Main St Blacksburg (24060) *(G-1753)*

Leonard Alum Utlity Bldngs Inc 434 237-5301
20530 Timberlake Rd Lynchburg (24502) *(G-7756)*

Leonard Alum Utlity Bldngs Inc 434 792-8202
1080 Riverside Dr Danville (24540) *(G-4011)*

Leonard Buildings & Truck ACC, Blacksburg *Also called Leonard Alum Utlity Bldngs Inc (G-1753)*

Leonard Logging Inc 540 239-6991
3172 Floyd Hwy S Floyd (24091) *(G-5031)*

Leoni Fiber Optics Inc (HQ) **757 258-4805**
209 Bulifants Blvd Williamsburg (23188) *(G-15268)*

Leoni Fiber Optics Inc 757 258-4805
215 Bulifants Blvd Ste D Williamsburg (23188) *(G-15269)*

Leopard Media LLC 703 522-5655
1011 Arlington Blvd # 131 Arlington (22209) *(G-1031)*

Leroy Cary 804 561-3526
5270 Dennisville Rd Amelia Court House (23002) *(G-663)*

Leroy Woodward 540 948-6335
168 Garth Run Rd Madison (22727) *(G-7857)*

Les Petales Inc 804 254-7863
401 Old Locke Ln Richmond (23226) *(G-11269)*

Lesco Inc 804 957-5516
5045 County Dr Disputanta (23842) *(G-4112)*

Lesco Inc 703 257-9015
8420 Kao Cir Manassas (20110) *(G-7962)*

Lesco Inc 540 752-1408
115 Juliad Ct Ste 107 Fredericksburg (22406) *(G-5449)*

Lesden Corporation 540 373-4940
802 Interstate Bus Park Fredericksburg (22405) *(G-5450)*

Leslie E Willis 757 484-4484
2527b Bridge Rd Suffolk (23435) *(G-13731)*

Leslie Noble 757 291-2904
114 National Ln Williamsburg (23185) *(G-15270)*

Less Than Ladylike Candle LLC 757 817-0616
80 Meredith Way Newport News (23606) *(G-9282)*

Lesson Portal LLC 540 455-3546
10612 Edinburgh Dr Spotsylvania (22553) *(G-12901)*

Lester Viar 434 277-5504
261 Gunter Hollow Ln Lowesville (22967) *(G-7596)*

Lester Building Systems LLC 540 665-0182
276 Woodbine Rd Clear Brook (22624) *(G-3646)*

Lester Enterprises Intl LLC 703 599-3485
4500 S Four Mile Run Dr Arlington (22204) *(G-1032)*

Lester Group 276 627-0346
1230 Oak Level Rd Bassett (24055) *(G-1585)*

Let Global, Mc Lean *Also called Local Energy Technologies (G-8487)*

Leticia E Helleby 336 769-7920
1088 Old Trail Dr Crozet (22932) *(G-3842)*

Letter Perfect Incorporated 540 652-2022
2454 North East Side Hwy # 8 Elkton (22827) *(G-4331)*

Lettercraft Signs 571 215-6900
6210 Lavell Ct Springfield (22152) *(G-13043)*

Lettering By Lynne 703 548-5427
3315 Carolina Pl Alexandria (22305) *(G-259)*

Letterpress Direct 804 285-8020
1146 Tricounty Dr Oilville (23129) *(G-10182)*

Levain Baking Studio Inc 434 249-5875
1716 Union Mills Rd Troy (22974) *(G-13931)*

Level 7 Signs LLC 540 885-1517
25 N Central Ave Fl 2 Staunton (24401) *(G-13276)*

Level 7 Signs and Graphics 540 294-6690
317 Skyview Cir Verona (24482) *(G-13990)*

Level Up Fun Corporation 703 365-8071
10512 Coral Berry Dr Manassas (20110) *(G-7963)*

Leviton Manufacturing C 804 461-8293
1607 Upperbury Dr Midlothian (23114) *(G-8848)*

Lewin Asphalt Inc 540 550-9478
300 Ebert Rd Winchester (22603) *(G-15440)*

Lewis A Dudley 540 884-2454
10115 Narrow Passage Rd Eagle Rock (24085) *(G-4282)*

Lewis Brothers Logging 804 478-4243
21108 Westover Dr Mc Kenney (23872) *(G-8381)*

Lewis Earl Mills 540 295-2061
1385 Truslow Rd Fredericksburg (22406) *(G-5451)*

Lewis Industries LLC 434 203-7920
4587 Horseshoe Rd Danville (24541) *(G-4012)*

Lewis Lumber Mill 276 629-1600
63 Healms Rd Bassett (24055) *(G-1586)*

Lewis Metal Works Inc 434 572-3043
2512 Hougton Ave South Boston (24592) *(G-12779)*

Lewis Printing Company 804 648-2000
3900 Carolina Ave Richmond (23222) *(G-11652)*

Lewis Welding & Cnstr Works 434 696-5527
523 Lunenburg County Rd Keysville (23947) *(G-7060)*

Lexacom, North Chesterfield *Also called Master Business Solutions Inc (G-9926)*

Lexadyne Publishing Inc 703 779-4998
525k E Market St Ste 240 Leesburg (20176) *(G-7298)*

Lexia Learning Systems Inc 978 405-6242
135 W Market St Harrisonburg (22801) *(G-6337)*

Lexington Measurement Tech 540 261-3966
25 Meadow Heights Ln Lexington (24450) *(G-7397)*

Lexington Papagallo Inc 540 463-5988
23 N Main St Lexington (24450) *(G-7398)*

Lexington Pet World 540 464-4141
3920 N Lee Hwy Fairfield (24435) *(G-4732)*

Lexington Valley Vineyard 540 462-2974
80 Norton Way Rockbridge Baths (24473) *(G-12236)*

Lexs of Carytown Ltd 804 355-5425
3018 W Cary St Richmond (23221) *(G-11653)*

Leyland Oceantech Inc 703 661-6097
43720 Trade Center Pl Sterling (20166) *(G-13440)*

Lfg Group Inc 571 512-7446
9320 Branch Side Ln Fairfax (22031) *(G-4499)*

Lfm Roanoke 540 342-0542
36 30th St Nw Roanoke (24017) *(G-12125)*

Lhoist North America VA Inc 540 626-7163
2093 Big Stony Creek Rd Ripplemead (24150) *(G-11876)*

Li Ailin 573 808-7280
520 12th St S Apt 721 Arlington (22202) *(G-1033)*

Li DDS Pllc Tin W 703 352-2500
12289 Engelmann Oak Ln Fairfax (22030) *(G-4647)*

LI Hing Software LLC 703 677-7773
2059 Huntington Ave # 912 Alexandria (22303) *(G-516)*

Libelli LLC 757 373-9845
1080 San Marco Rd Virginia Beach (23456) *(G-14607)*

Liberty Cabinets 540 493-3149
19 Byrd Ln Rocky Mount (24151) *(G-12334)*

Liberty Media For Women LLC (PA) **703 522-4201**
1600 Wilson Blvd Ste 801 Arlington (22209) *(G-1034)*

Liberty Medical Inc 703 636-2269
22135 Davis Dr Ste 116 Sterling (20164) *(G-13441)*

Liberty Park 540 832-7680
1 Cleveland St Ste 13 Gordonsville (22942) *(G-5912)*

Liberty Press Inc 540 434-5513
300 Waterman Dr Harrisonburg (22802) *(G-6338)*

Liberty Printing House Inc 202 664-7702
7300 Lockport Pl Ste 2 Lorton (22079) *(G-7507)*

Library Conservation Services 540 372-9661
1431 Franklin St Fredericksburg (22401) *(G-5201)*

Lidl Us LLC 757 420-1562
6196 Providence Rd Virginia Beach (23464) *(G-14608)*

Lidl Us LLC 757 368-0256
3248 Holland Rd Virginia Beach (23453) *(G-14609)*

Lifac Inc 757 826-6051
505 Howmet Dr Hampton (23661) *(G-6183)*

Life Evac 804 652-0171
23301 Airport Rd North Dinwiddie (23803) *(G-10058)*

Life Management Company 434 296-9762
3802 Snow Hill Ln Troy (22974) *(G-13932)*

Life Protect 24/7 Inc 888 864-8403
6160 Commander Pkwy Norfolk (23502) *(G-9618)*

Life Safer 540 375-4145
162 Saint Johns Place Rd Salem (24153) *(G-12531)*

Life Sentence Publishing LLC 703 300-0474
5706 Evergreen Knoll Ct Alexandria (22303) *(G-517)*

Life Transformations LLC 703 624-0130
11490 Waterhaven Ct Reston (20190) *(G-10887)*

A
L
P
H
A
B
E
T
I
C

Lifegas, Ashland *Also called Linde Gas North America LLC* **(G-1452)**
Lifeline of Prince William 703 753-9000
  4615 George Wash Mem Hwy Yorktown (23692) **(G-15975)**
Lifelineusa 540 251-2724
  4085 Pepperell Way Dublin (24084) **(G-4164)**
Lifenet Health (PA) **757 464-4761**
  1864 Concert Dr Virginia Beach (23453) **(G-14610)**
Lifes A Stitch Inc 804 672-7079
  3213 Forest Lodge Ct Glen Allen (23060) **(G-5762)**
Lifesafer 571 379-5575
  8512 Bucyrus Ct Manassas (20110) **(G-7964)**
Lifesafer Inc 757 595-8800
  11849 Tug Boat Ln Newport News (23606) **(G-9283)**
Lifesitenews Com Inc 540 635-3131
  4 Family Life Ln Front Royal (22630) **(G-5541)**
Lifetime Coating Specialties 757 559-1011
  1317 Mozart Dr Virginia Beach (23454) **(G-14611)**
Lift Hill Media LLC 703 408-4145
  3320 Arnold Ln Falls Church (22042) **(G-4823)**
Lig Nex1 Co Ltd 703 888-2501
  1101 Wilson Blvd Ste 1600 Arlington (22209) **(G-1035)**
Ligado Networks Inc Virginia 877 678-2920
  10802 Parkridge Blvd Reston (20191) **(G-10888)**
Light Designs Publishing Co 804 261-6900
  9915 Greenwood Rd Ste B Glen Allen (23060) **(G-5763)**
Light Grey Industries 703 330-1339
  10346 Portsmouth Rd Manassas (20109) **(G-8100)**
Light Music LLC 914 316-7948
  1050 Druid Ave Apt 204 Charlottesville (22902) **(G-2824)**
Light Tape, Richmond *Also called Electro-Luminx Lighting Corp* **(G-11198)**
Lightbox Print Co LLC 919 608-9520
  503 Strawberry St Apt 5 Richmond (23220) **(G-11654)**
Lighted Signs Direct Inc 703 965-5188
  941 Highams Ct Woodbridge (22191) **(G-15740)**
Lightfactor LLC 540 723-9600
  160 N Indian Aly Winchester (22601) **(G-15552)**
Lighthouse Cabinets Inc 571 293-1064
  110 Richard Dr Se Leesburg (20175) **(G-7299)**
Lighthouse Concepts LLC 703 779-9617
  114 Courier Ct Ne Leesburg (20176) **(G-7300)**
Lighthouse Instruments LLC (PA) **434 293-3081**
  2020 Avon Ct Ste 4 Charlottesville (22902) **(G-2825)**
Lighthouse Land LLC 434 293-3081
  2020 Avon Ct Charlottesville (22902) **(G-2826)**
Lighthouse Software Inc 703 327-7650
  43643 Mink Meadows St Chantilly (20152) **(G-2543)**
Lighthouse Woodworking, Boyce *Also called Ronald Light* **(G-1911)**
Lighting Auto Services 804 330-6908
  3611 Hull St Richmond (23224) **(G-11655)**
Lightronics Inc 757 486-3588
  509 Central Dr Ste 101 Virginia Beach (23454) **(G-14612)**
Lightsmokechill Candle Co LLC 347 720-2596
  109 Jefferson Point Ln 2d Newport News (23602) **(G-9284)**
Lightspeed Infrared LLC 540 875-6796
  302 W Washington St Bedford (24523) **(G-1643)**
Lightsquared Inc of Virginia, Reston *Also called Ligado Networks Inc Virginia* **(G-10888)**
Lightwav, Richmond *Also called Tactical Dployment Systems LLC* **(G-11405)**
Lignetics of Virginia Inc 434 676-4800
  11068 South Hill Rd Kenbridge (23944) **(G-7034)**
Liht Candles & Oils LLC 757 776-9005
  1100 S Bttlfeld Blvd 15 # 15734 Chesapeake (23322) **(G-3183)**
Liisu Yarns, Meadows of Dan *Also called Horse Pasture Mfg LLC* **(G-8591)**
Lil Divas Mobile Spa LLC 757 386-1455
  229 W 30th St Apt D Norfolk (23504) **(G-9619)**
Lil Guy Printing 757 995-5705
  7 Camellia Ln Hampton (23663) **(G-6184)**
Lilbern Design Virginia LLC 540 234-9900
  200 Packaging Dr Weyers Cave (24486) **(G-15174)**
Lillie's, Hampton *Also called Aileen L Brown* **(G-6079)**
Lilly Lane Incorporated 434 792-6387
  119 Mall Dr Danville (24540) **(G-4013)**
Lily Golden Foods Corporation 703 823-8821
  820 S Pickett St Alexandria (22304) **(G-260)**
Lilys Alpacas LLC 757 865-1001
  8105 Richmond Rd Ste 203 Toano (23168) **(G-13867)**
Limatherm Usa Inc 540 402-4060
  960 Sycolin Rd Se Ste 155 Leesburg (20175) **(G-7301)**
Lime & Leaf LLC 703 299-2440
  311 Cameron St Alexandria (22314) **(G-261)**
Limestone Dust Corporation 276 326-1103
  230 Saint Clair Xing Bluefield (24605) **(G-1869)**
Limitless Gear LLC 575 921-7475
  63 White Cedar Rd Barboursville (22923) **(G-1564)**
Limitorque Corp 804 639-0529
  15407 Fox Crest Ln Midlothian (23112) **(G-8849)**
Lincoln Industries LLC 434 509-7191
  2925 Rivermont Ave Lynchburg (24503) **(G-7757)**
Lincoln Place Group LLC 347 363-9721
  700 E Main St Ste 2487 Richmond (23219) **(G-11656)**

Lincoln Woodworking 703 297-7512
  37612 Chappelle Hill Rd Purcellville (20132) **(G-10666)**
Linda M Barnes 757 240-7327
  301 Leigh Rd Yorktown (23690) **(G-15976)**
Lindas Welding & Mech LLC 757 719-1567
  7251 Otey Dr Lanexa (23089) **(G-7167)**
Linde Gas North America LLC 804 752-2744
  11132 Progress Rd Ashland (23005) **(G-1452)**
Linde Inc 804 452-3181
  107 Industrial St Hopewell (23860) **(G-6938)**
Linden Woodwork LLC 540 636-3345
  60 Redmile Ct Linden (22642) **(G-7431)**
Lindsay Hardwoods Inc 434 392-8615
  124 Sheppards Rd Farmville (23901) **(G-4947)**
Line Riders Custom Lures, Midlothian *Also called Uniques LLC* **(G-8916)**
Line X Central Virginia Inc 434 525-8878
  1077 Sunburst Rd Evington (24550) **(G-4378)**
Line-X Northern Virginia Inc 703 433-9333
  100 Glenn Dr Ste A7 Sterling (20164) **(G-13442)**
Line-X of Blue Ridge 540 389-8595
  504 Roanoke St Salem (24153) **(G-12532)**
Line-X of Chesapeake, Hampton *Also called Bl & Son Enterprises LLC* **(G-6093)**
Line-X of Richmond 804 321-9166
  6405 Dickens Pl Ste F Richmond (23230) **(G-11270)**
Line-X of Suffolk, Suffolk *Also called Srj Bedliners LLC* **(G-13767)**
Lineage Logistics 804 421-6603
  3100 N Hopkins Rd Ste 202 Richmond (23224) **(G-11657)**
Lineage Mechanical LLC 804 687-5649
  113 N Kalmia Ave Henrico (23075) **(G-6530)**
Lineal Technologies Inc 540 484-6783
  350 State St Rocky Mount (24151) **(G-12335)**
Linear Devices Corporation 804 368-8428
  11126 Air Park Rd Ste G Ashland (23005) **(G-1453)**
Linear Rotary Bearings Inc 540 261-1375
  6417 Rigsby Rd Richmond (23226) **(G-11271)**
Lines Up Inc 703 842-3762
  3033 Wilson Blvd Ste 700 Arlington (22201) **(G-1036)**
Linetree Woodworks 919 619-3013
  1870 Lower Mill Rd Powhatan (23139) **(G-10556)**
Links Choice LLC (PA) **434 286-2202**
  4545 Kidds Dairy Rd Scottsville (24590) **(G-12663)**
Linley Press LLC 561 245-1511
  43799 Michener Dr Ashburn (20147) **(G-1307)**
Linsey Echowater System 540 434-0212
  105 Newman Ave Harrisonburg (22801) **(G-6339)**
Lintronics Publishing Group, Blacksburg *Also called Lintronics Software Publishing* **(G-1754)**
Lintronics Software Publishing 540 552-7204
  1991 Mountainside Dr Blacksburg (24060) **(G-1754)**
Linwood L Pope 757 654-9397
  23120 Bryant Church Rd Courtland (23837) **(G-3772)**
Linx Industries Inc 757 488-1144
  2600 Airline Blvd Portsmouth (23701) **(G-10453)**
Lion Mountain Farms LLC 916 850-9232
  2400 S Glebe Rd Apt 603 Arlington (22206) **(G-1037)**
Lion's Head Meadery, Seaford *Also called Artisan Meads LLC* **(G-12671)**
Lion-Valley Industries 703 630-3123
  1999 Hill Ave Quantico (22134) **(G-10690)**
Lions Head Woodworks LLC 540 288-9532
  3307 Aquia Dr Stafford (22554) **(G-13171)**
Liphart Steel Company Inc (PA) **804 355-7481**
  3308 Rosedale Ave Richmond (23230) **(G-11272)**
Liphart Steel Company Inc 540 248-1009
  75 Mid Valley Ln Verona (24482) **(G-13991)**
Liqui-Box Corporation (PA) **804 325-1400**
  901 E Byrd St Ste 1105 Richmond (23219) **(G-11658)**
Lisa A McLain 757 788-1781
  905 Pine Mill Ct Newport News (23602) **(G-9285)**
Lisas Candles 703 940-6733
  13395 Coppermine Rd # 204 Herndon (20171) **(G-6734)**
Liskey & Sons Inc 757 627-8712
  1228 Ballentine Blvd Norfolk (23504) **(G-9620)**
Liskey and Sons Printing, Norfolk *Also called Liskey & Sons Inc* **(G-9620)**
Listening Loop Technologies, Warrenton *Also called Fauquier Hearing Services Pllc* **(G-15010)**
Litehouse Inc 434 688-3100
  145 Cane Creek Blvd Danville (24540) **(G-4014)**
Litesheet Solutions LLC 860 213-8311
  1191 Venture Dr Ste A Forest (24551) **(G-5081)**
Litesteel Tech Amer LLC 540 992-5129
  100 Smorgon Way Troutville (24175) **(G-13914)**
Litstone Capital LLC 703 576-0788
  2800 Eisenhower Ave Alexandria (22314) **(G-262)**
Little Bay Mar Canvas & More, Virginia Beach *Also called Krismark Inc* **(G-14593)**
Little Birdy Bags LLC 703 757-6565
  10106 Nedra Dr Great Falls (22066) **(G-5965)**
Little Black Dog Designs 757 874-0928
  910 Healey Dr Newport News (23608) **(G-9286)**

(G-0000) Company's Geographic Section entry number

Little Corners Petit Fours LLC 571 215-4255
1 Greencastle Rd Sterling (20164) ***(G-13443)***
Little Enterprises LLC 804 869-8612
18600 Telegraph Sprng Rd Purcellville (20132) ***(G-10667)***
Little Green Men Inc 301 203-8702
20675 Exchange St Ashburn (20147) ***(G-1308)***
Little King Publishing 540 809-0291
10703 Heather Greens Ct Spotsylvania (22553) ***(G-12902)***
Little Wars Inc 703 533-7942
3033 Crane Dr Falls Church (22042) ***(G-4824)***
Littlebird Jams and Jellies 804 586-4420
25321 Cox Rd North Dinwiddie (23803) ***(G-10059)***
Littlefield Logging 804 798-5590
13534 Greenwood Rd Glen Allen (23059) ***(G-5764)***
Littlejohn Printing Co 540 977-1377
4185 Bonsack Rd Roanoke (24012) ***(G-12126)***
Littleshot Apps LLC 908 433-5727
4639 5th St S Arlington (22204) ***(G-1038)***
Litton Guitar Works LLC 703 966-0571
9716 Manassas Forge Dr Manassas (20111) ***(G-8101)***
Live Cases 703 627-0994
3102 Borge St Oakton (22124) ***(G-10154)***
Live Trendy or Die LLC 856 371-7638
1615 Spottswood Pl Lynchburg (24503) ***(G-7758)***
Lively Fulcher Organ Builders 540 352-4401
240 Energy Blvd Rocky Mount (24151) ***(G-12336)***
Livesafe Inc 571 312-4645
1400 Key Blvd Ste 100 Arlington (22209) ***(G-1039)***
Livesafe.ly, Arlington *Also called Livesafe Inc* ***(G-1039)***
Livin Color LLC 757 582-6030
215 Chautauqua Ave Portsmouth (23707) ***(G-10454)***
Living Maka LLC 888 690-7058
3100 Clarendon Blvd # 200 Arlington (22201) ***(G-1040)***
Living Solutions Mid Atlantic 202 460-9919
6402 15th St Alexandria (22307) ***(G-518)***
Livingston Group Inc 757 460-3115
4768 Hermitage Rd Virginia Beach (23455) ***(G-14613)***
Livingston Resources Inc 704 892-1989
21009 Walkers Ln Richardsville (22736) ***(G-11011)***
Liz B Quilting LLC 540 602-7850
21 Woodlot Ct Stafford (22554) ***(G-13172)***
Lizis Jams 804 837-1904
13717 Cannonade Ln Midlothian (23112) ***(G-8850)***
Lizzie Candles & Soap Inc 540 384-6151
4144 Catawba Valley Dr Salem (24153) ***(G-12533)***
LKM Industries LLC 919 601-6661
208 Jeffersons Hundred Williamsburg (23185) ***(G-15271)***
LL Distributing Inc 540 479-2221
11417 Scott Dr Fredericksburg (22407) ***(G-5313)***
Llama Life II LLC 434 286-4494
5232 Blenheim Rd Charlottesville (22902) ***(G-2827)***
LLC Link Masters 804 241-3962
7201 Trench Trl Mechanicsville (23111) ***(G-8653)***
LLC Little Bean 757 937-1600
468 Viking Dr Ste 101 Virginia Beach (23452) ***(G-14614)***
LLC Wiley Brothers 434 806-9633
4289 Free Union Rd Free Union (22940) ***(G-5508)***
Lloyd D Wells Logging Contg 434 933-4316
12789 Anderson Hwy Gladstone (24553) ***(G-5685)***
Lloyd Elc Co Harrisonburg Inc 540 433-5335
870 N Liberty St Harrisonburg (22802) ***(G-6340)***
Lloyd Electric Co Inc 540 982-0135
605 3rd St Se Roanoke (24013) ***(G-12127)***
Lloyd Enterprises Inc 804 266-1185
5407 Lakeside Ave Ste 3 Richmond (23228) ***(G-11273)***
Lloyds Pewter 757 503-1110
143 Brookhaven Dr Williamsburg (23188) ***(G-15272)***
Llts Paving 276 782-9550
506 Horne Ave Marion (24354) ***(G-8231)***
Lm Woodworking LLC 703 927-4467
8516 Stable Dr Alexandria (22308) ***(G-519)***
Lm5 Vertical Inspections LLC 757 810-9938
111 Finch Ln Seaford (23696) ***(G-12676)***
Lmr-Inc Com 518 253-9220
9104 Manassas Dr Ste N Manassas Park (20111) ***(G-8204)***
LNG Publishing Co Inc (PA) **703 536-0800**
7389 Lee Hwy Ste 300 Falls Church (22042) ***(G-4825)***
Loa Mals On Whels Wlliamson Rd 540 563-0482
3333 Williamson Rd Nw Roanoke (24012) ***(G-12128)***
Local Energy Technologies 717 371-0041
1111 Wimbledon Dr Mc Lean (22101) ***(G-8487)***
Local News Now LLC 703 348-0583
4075 Wilson Blvd Fl 8 Arlington (22203) ***(G-1041)***
Local Voice 757 565-1079
4732 Longhill Rd Ste 2201 Williamsburg (23188) ***(G-15273)***
Local Wood 540 955-9522
40 Kimble Rd Berryville (22611) ***(G-1684)***
Location Bsed Svcs Content LLC 703 622-1490
1419 Mayhurst Blvd Mc Lean (22102) ***(G-8488)***
Locator Services, Alexandria *Also called Machinery Information Systems* ***(G-268)***
Loci LLC 301 613-7111
38 Benton Ct Sterling (20165) ***(G-13444)***
Locker LLC (HQ) **310 978-1457**
2900 Crystal Dr Ste 910 Arlington (22202) ***(G-1042)***
Lockhart Manufacturing Inc 540 459-8774
750 Spring Pkwy Woodstock (22664) ***(G-15857)***
Lockheed Martin 703 588-0670
850 N Randolph St Arlington (22203) ***(G-1043)***
Lockheed Martin 202 863-3297
2711 Richmond Hwy # 916 Arlington (22202) ***(G-1044)***
Lockheed Martin 757 578-3377
1293 Perimeter Pkwy Virginia Beach (23454) ***(G-14615)***
Lockheed Martin 703 272-6061
10530 Rosehaven St # 300 Fairfax (22030) ***(G-4648)***
Lockheed Martin 703 982-9008
10505 Furnace Rd Ste 101 Lorton (22079) ***(G-7508)***
Lockheed Martin Corporation 703 280-9983
2650 Park Tower Dr Vienna (22180) ***(G-14083)***
Lockheed Martin Corporation 703 771-3515
825 E Market St Leesburg (20176) ***(G-7302)***
Lockheed Martin Corporation 270 319-4600
10530 Rosehaven St # 500 Fairfax (22030) ***(G-4649)***
Lockheed Martin Corporation 703 367-2121
9500 Godwin Dr Manassas (20110) ***(G-7965)***
Lockheed Martin Corporation 703 367-2121
9500 Godwin Dr Manassas (20110) ***(G-7966)***
Lockheed Martin Corporation 757 491-3501
489 Sparrow St Virginia Beach (23461) ***(G-14616)***
Lockheed Martin Corporation 540 644-2830
16539 Commerce Dr Ste 10 King George (22485) ***(G-7100)***
Lockheed Martin Corporation 540 891-5882
4545 Empire Ct Fredericksburg (22408) ***(G-5314)***
Lockheed Martin Corporation 703 724-7552
43881 Devin Shafron Dr # 150 Ashburn (20147) ***(G-1309)***
Lockheed Martin Corporation 703 357-7095
1711 26th St S Arlington (22206) ***(G-1045)***
Lockheed Martin Corporation 703 403-9829
13530 Dulles Tech Dr # 300 Herndon (20171) ***(G-6735)***
Lockheed Martin Corporation 813 855-5711
9500 Godwin Dr Manassas (20110) ***(G-7967)***
Lockheed Martin Corporation 703 466-3000
13560 Dulles Tech Dr Herndon (20171) ***(G-6736)***
Lockheed Martin Corporation 757 766-3282
87 Oak St Hampton (23665) ***(G-6278)***
Lockheed Martin Corporation 757 896-4860
22 Enterprise Pkwy # 120 Hampton (23666) ***(G-6185)***
Lockheed Martin Corporation 757 509-6808
111 Cybernetics Way # 205 Yorktown (23693) ***(G-15977)***
Lockheed Martin Corporation 757 464-0877
5813 Ward Ct Virginia Beach (23455) ***(G-14617)***
Lockheed Martin Corporation 703 367-2121
9500 Godwin Dr Manassas (20110) ***(G-7968)***
Lockheed Martin Corporation 757 685-3132
1619 Diamond Springs Rd Virginia Beach (23455) ***(G-14618)***
Lockheed Martin Corporation 757 803-3080
1293 Perimeter Pkwy Virginia Beach (23454) ***(G-14619)***
Lockheed Martin Corporation 757 935-9479
7700 Harbour View Blvd Suffolk (23435) ***(G-13732)***
Lockheed Martin Corporation 757 430-6500
1293 Perimeter Pkwy Virginia Beach (23454) ***(G-14620)***
Lockheed Martin Corporation 703 418-4900
2461 S Clark St Ste 125 Arlington (22202) ***(G-1046)***
Lockheed Martin Corporation 703 378-1880
4262 Entre Ct Chantilly (20151) ***(G-2458)***
Lockheed Martin Corporation 757 769-7251
1408 Stephanie Way Chesapeake (23320) ***(G-3184)***
Lockheed Martin Corporation 703 258-2784
2461 S Clark St Ste 720 Arlington (22202) ***(G-1047)***
Lockheed Martin Corporation 540 663-3337
5323 Windsor Dr King George (22485) ***(G-7101)***
Lockheed Martin Corporation 703 787-4027
2245 Monroe St Herndon (20171) ***(G-6737)***
Lockheed Martin Corporation 757 484-5789
3416 Maori Dr Chesapeake (23321) ***(G-3185)***
Lockheed Martin Corporation 757 390-7520
1801 Sara Dr Ste L Chesapeake (23320) ***(G-3186)***
Lockheed Martin Integrtd Systm 703 367-2121
9500 Godwin Dr Manassas (20110) ***(G-7969)***
Lockheed Martin Integrtd Systm 866 562-2363
2001 Richmond Hwy # 900 Arlington (22202) ***(G-1048)***
Lockheed Martin Integrtd Systm 703 682-5719
2650 Park Twr Dr Ste 400 Vienna (22180) ***(G-14084)***
Lockheed Martin Services LLC 757 366-3300
500 Woodlake Dr Ste 2 Chesapeake (23320) ***(G-3187)***
Lockheed Martin Services LLC 757 935-9200
8000 Harbour View Blvd Suffolk (23435) ***(G-13733)***
Lockheed Mrtin Ctr For Innvtio, Suffolk *Also called Lockheed Martin Services LLC* ***(G-13733)***
Locklear Group Inc 757 630-9022
2228 Ebb Tide Rd Virginia Beach (23451) ***(G-14621)***

ALPHABETIC

Locksley Estate Frmstead Chese 703 926-4759
23876 Champe Ford Rd Middleburg (20117) *(G-8726)*

Lockwood Software Engrg Inc 202 494-7886
1409 Mayhurst Blvd Mc Lean (22102) *(G-8489)*

Loco Beans — Fresh Roasted 703 851-5997
1003 Rollins Dr Sw Leesburg (20175) *(G-7303)*

Loco Crazy Good Inc 703 401-4058
21108 Stonecrop Pl Ashburn (20147) *(G-1310)*

Loco Parts 757 255-2815
1471 Spring Meadow Ln Suffolk (23432) *(G-13734)*

Locus Technology 757 340-1986
341 Cleveland Pl Ste 106 Virginia Beach (23462) *(G-14622)*

Lodging Technology, Roanoke *Also called Ltc Enterprises LLC (G-11958)*

Lodore Truss Company Inc 804 561-4141
18101 Genito Rd Amelia Court House (23002) *(G-664)*

Loehr Lightning Protection Co 804 231-4236
5268 Hull Street Rd Richmond (23224) *(G-11659)*

Log Home Lovers 540 743-7355
903 E Main St Luray (22835) *(G-7615)*

Log Homes By Clore Bros 540 786-7749
5927 River Rd Fredericksburg (22407) *(G-5315)*

Logan Food Company 703 212-6677
4300 Wheeler Ave Alexandria (22304) *(G-263)*

Logan Sausage Company, Alexandria *Also called Logan Food Company (G-263)*

Logging, Covington *Also called Eric Tucker (G-3788)*

Logging Ninja Inc 804 569-6054
6088 Green Haven Dr Mechanicsville (23111) *(G-8654)*

Logic Branding, Virginia Beach *Also called Fontaine Melinda (G-14470)*

Logical Decisions, Fairfax *Also called Gary Smith (G-4461)*

Logicon Tactical Systems Div, Arlington *Also called Northrop Grumman Systems Corp (G-1082)*

Logis-Tech Inc 703 393-4840
9450 Innovation Dr Ste 1 Manassas (20110) *(G-7970)*

Logo In 50 Minutes, Alexandria *Also called Henry Shaw (G-228)*

Logomotion, Ashland *Also called County of Hanover (G-1397)*

Logos Software Inc 540 819-6260
324 Campbell Ave Sw Roanoke (24016) *(G-12129)*

Lohmann Specialty Coatings LLC 859 334-4900
14218 Litchfield Dr Orange (22960) *(G-10219)*

Lokring Mid-Atlantic Inc 757 423-2784
2715 Monticello Ave Ste C Norfolk (23517) *(G-9621)*

Londoo Foods LLC 571 243-7627
13903 Rope Dr Woodbridge (22191) *(G-15741)*

Lone Fountain Ldscp & Hdwr Ctr 540 886-7605
2986 Churchville Ave Staunton (24401) *(G-13277)*

Lone Star Polishing Inc 434 585-3372
1171 Christie Rd Virgilina (24598) *(G-14193)*

Lone Tree Printing Inc 757 473-9977
4716 Virginia Beach Blvd Virginia Beach (23462) *(G-14623)*

Lone Wolf Salsa 571 445-3499
15070 Danehurst Cir Gainesville (20155) *(G-5597)*

Lonesome Pine Beverage Company 276 679-2332
213 6th St Nw Norton (24273) *(G-10124)*

Lonesome Trails LLC 276 445-5443
232 Neosha Dr Rose Hill (24281) *(G-12361)*

Lonesome Trails Entps Inc 276 445-5443
227 Vrlin Hnsley Dr Ewing Ewing (24248) *(G-4385)*

Long Metalwork & Machine Inc 804 529-6233
16686 Richmond Rd Callao (22435) *(G-2216)*

Long Solutions LLC 703 281-2766
9612 Podium Dr Vienna (22182) *(G-14085)*

Longbow Holdings LLC 540 404-1185
406 Dexter Rd Roanoke (24019) *(G-11957)*

Longs Embroidery 540 891-2880
120 Falcon Dr Ste 8 Fredericksburg (22408) *(G-5316)*

Longs Repair & Welding, Castlewood *Also called Trl Inc (G-2258)*

Longs-Roullet Bookbinders Inc 757 623-4244
2800 Monticello Ave Norfolk (23504) *(G-9622)*

Longwall - Associates Inc 276 646-2004
212 Kendall Ave Chilhowie (24319) *(G-3554)*

Longwood Elastomers Inc 276 228-5406
365 George James Dr Wytheville (24382) *(G-15896)*

Longwood Elastomers Inc (HQ) **336 272-3710**
655 Fairview Rd Wytheville (24382) *(G-15897)*

Longwood Elastomers Inc 276 228-5406
655 Fairview Rd Wytheville (24382) *(G-15898)*

Longwood Industries, Wytheville *Also called Longwood Elastomers Inc (G-15897)*

Longworth Sports Group Inc 276 328-3300
130 W Main St Wise (24293) *(G-15630)*

Lonnie L Sparks 276 988-4298
135 Sparks Hollow Rd North Tazewell (24630) *(G-10102)*

Lonza E Kingery 540 774-8728
6477 Crowell Gap Rd Roanoke (24014) *(G-12130)*

Look Up Publications LLC 703 542-2736
42533 Magellan Sq Brambleton (20148) *(G-1929)*

Lookingglass Cyber Slution Inc (PA) **703 351-1000**
10740 Parkridge Blvd # 200 Reston (20191) *(G-10889)*

Looney's Clean Tile and Grout, Ashburn *Also called Intense Cleaning Inc (G-1297)*

Looneys Bit Service Inc 276 531-8767
Rr 609 Maxie (24628) *(G-8372)*

Loony Moose Publishing LLC 703 727-3309
42993 Nashua St Ashburn (20147) *(G-1311)*

Looseleaf Publications LLC 757 221-8250
108 William Allen Williamsburg (23185) *(G-15274)*

Loosely Coupled Software LLC 703 707-9235
13218 Lazy Glen Ln Herndon (20171) *(G-6738)*

Lord Sign 301 316-7446
10993 Centrepointe Way Fairfax Station (22039) *(G-4716)*

Lori Katz 703 475-1640
105 N Union St Ste 8 Alexandria (22314) *(G-264)*

Loron Inc 804 780-0000
3 Alexis Dr Henrico (23231) *(G-6531)*

Lorrie Carpenter 804 720-6442
2714 Williamsburg St Alexandria (22314) *(G-265)*

Lorton Enterprises 703 725-2933
8254 Laurel Heights Loop Lorton (22079) *(G-7509)*

Lorton Stone LLC 703 923-9440
7544 Fullerton Ct Springfield (22153) *(G-13044)*

Los Angeles Tee-Shirt, Arlington *Also called Lateeshirt (G-1028)*

Lost and Found Winery 707 321-6292
2012 Absalom Dr Virginia Beach (23451) *(G-14624)*

Lost Clipper Enterprises LLC 310 386-0972
18113 Linden Grove Ct Purcellville (20132) *(G-10668)*

Lost Creek Vineyard 703 443-9836
43277 Spinks Ferry Rd Leesburg (20176) *(G-7304)*

Lost Industries LLC 434 221-5698
170 Lost Ln Arrington (22922) *(G-1230)*

Lotus Engraving LLC 703 206-8367
13673 Bent Tree Cir # 103 Centreville (20121) *(G-2315)*

Lou Wallace 276 762-2303
16551 Russell St Saint Paul (24283) *(G-12469)*

Lou-Voise 804 836-5601
5417 Woolshire Dr Glen Allen (23059) *(G-5765)*

Loudon Street Electric Svcs 540 662-8463
1604 S Loudoun St Winchester (22601) *(G-15553)*

Loudoun Business Inc 703 777-2176
19301 Winmeade Dr Ste 21 Lansdowne (20176) *(G-7172)*

Loudoun Classical School 540 338-6101
441 E Main St Purcellville (20132) *(G-10669)*

Loudoun Community Band 540 882-3838
39604 Rickard Rd Lovettsville (20180) *(G-7582)*

Loudoun Composting 703 327-8428
44150 Wade Dr Chantilly (20152) *(G-2544)*

Loudoun Construction LLC 703 895-7242
37256 Mountville Rd Middleburg (20117) *(G-8727)*

Loudoun County Asphalt 703 669-9001
42050 Cochran Mill Rd Leesburg (20175) *(G-7305)*

Loudoun Medical Group PC 703 669-6118
116 Edwards Ferry Rd Ne Leesburg (20176) *(G-7306)*

Loudoun Metal & More 540 668-5067
11811 Berlin Tpke Lovettsville (20180) *(G-7583)*

Loudoun Now 703 770-9723
. 15 N King St Ste 101 Leesburg (20176) *(G-7307)*

Loudoun Signs Inc 703 669-3333
525 E Market St Ste D Leesburg (20176) *(G-7308)*

Loudoun Stairs Inc 703 478-8800
341 N Maple Ave Purcellville (20132) *(G-10670)*

Louie Dufour 540 839-5232
5456 Sam Snead Hwy Hot Springs (24445) *(G-6947)*

Louies Welding and Fabrication 540 839-5232
5456 Sam Snead Hwy Hot Springs (24445) *(G-6948)*

Louis G Ball & Son Inc 804 725-5202
1203 Callis Field Ln Mathews (23109) *(G-8356)*

Louise J Walker 540 788-4826
4007 Old Calverton Rd Calverton (20138) *(G-2225)*

Louise Richardson 276 328-4545
6810 Bates Airfield Rd Wise (24293) *(G-15631)*

Love In Print LLC 757 739-2416
718 Sutherland Dr Chesapeake (23320) *(G-3188)*

Love Rugby Company, Norfolk *Also called Christina Bennett (G-9483)*

Love Those Tz LLC 757 897-0238
1417 Lynnhaven Pkwy Virginia Beach (23453) *(G-14625)*

Lovell Logging Inc 276 632-5191
1124 Windy Ridge Rd Martinsville (24112) *(G-8306)*

Lovells Replay Sportstop LLC 804 507-0271
2550 New Market Rd Richmond (23231) *(G-11274)*

Lovely Reds Creations LLC 540 320-2859
4169 Boone Furnace Rd Allisonia (24347) *(G-619)*

Lovings Welding & Fabricating 804 370-3084
8175 Newman Dr Mechanicsville (23116) *(G-8655)*

Lovingston Winery 925 286-2824
1800 Fray Rd Ruckersville (22968) *(G-12404)*

Lovington Winery LLC 434 263-8467
885 Freshwater Cove Ln Lovingston (22949) *(G-7592)*

Lowe-Go EMB & Designs LLC 757 486-0617
3113 Ferry Farm Ln Virginia Beach (23452) *(G-14626)*

Lower Dock Yard, Richmond *Also called Legacy Vulcan LLC (G-11268)*

(G-0000) Company's Geographic Section entry number

Lower Lane Publishing LLC 703 865-5968
2105 Carrhill Rd Vienna (22181) *(G-14086)*

Loyal Service Systems 703 361-7888
8709 Quarry Rd Manassas (20110) *(G-7971)*

Loyalty Doctors LLC 757 675-8283
182 Blades St Norfolk (23503) *(G-9623)*

Lozier Corp 703 742-4098
11961 Grey Squirrel Ln Reston (20194) *(G-10890)*

LPI Technical Services, Chesapeake Also called La Playa Incorporated Virginia *(G-3170)*

Lpm Services, Suffolk Also called Wgb LLC *(G-13785)*

Lpsoftware, Virginia Beach Also called Larry Lewis *(G-14600)*

Lrj Publishing Group LLC 757 788-6163
2104 Newton Rd Hampton (23663) *(G-6186)*

Ls Late Embroidery 757 639-0647
4928 Floral St Virginia Beach (23462) *(G-14627)*

Lsc Communications Us LLC 540 564-3900
1025 Willow Spring Rd Harrisonburg (22801) *(G-6341)*

Lsc Communications Us LLC 540 434-8833
2347 Kratzer Rd Rockingham (22802) *(G-12259)*

Lt Business Dynamics LLC 703 738-6599
1577 Spring Hill Rd # 260 Vienna (22182) *(G-14087)*

Lt Global Trading, Virginia Beach Also called El Tran Investment Corp *(G-14437)*

Lt Pressure Washer Services 703 626-9010
5341 Taney Ave Apt 202 Alexandria (22304) *(G-266)*

Ltc Enterprises LLC 540 362-7500
5431 Peters Creek Rd C Roanoke (24019) *(G-11958)*

Ltcpcms Inc 888 513-5444
9555 Kings Charter Dr G Ashland (23005) *(G-1454)*

LTS Software Inc 757 493-8855
1716 Corp Landing Pkwy Virginia Beach (23454) *(G-14628)*

Lubawa Usa Inc 703 894-1909
10300 Ste 100 Fredericksburg (22408) *(G-5317)*

Lucas-Milhaupt Inc 276 591-3351
23 Colony Cir Bristol (24201) *(G-1982)*

Lucia Coates 434 384-1779
4925 Boonsboro Rd Lynchburg (24503) *(G-7759)*

Lucia Richie 804 878-8969
13000 E Coal Hopper Ln Midlothian (23113) *(G-8851)*

Luck Stone - Spttsylvnia Plant, Fredericksburg Also called Luck Stone Corporation *(G-5318)*

Luck Stone Corporation (PA) **804 784-6300**
515 Stone Mill Dr Manakin Sabot (23103) *(G-7901)*

Luck Stone Corporation 703 830-8880
15717 Lee Hwy Centreville (20121) *(G-2316)*

Luck Stone Corporation 434 767-4043
Off Hwy 360 460 Byp Burkeville (23922) *(G-2209)*

Luck Stone Corporation 540 898-6060
9100 Luck Stone Ln Fredericksburg (22407) *(G-5318)*

Luck Stone Corporation 804 749-3233
2115 Ashland Rd Rockville (23146) *(G-12289)*

Luck Stone Corporation 804 749-3232
2115 Ashland Rd Rockville (23146) *(G-12290)*

Luck Stone Corporation 804 784-4652
485 Boscobel Rd Manakin Sabot (23103) *(G-7902)*

Luck Stone Corporation 757 566-8676
538 Oyster Point Rd Newport News (23602) *(G-9287)*

Luck Stone Corporation 434 589-1542
223 Crossroads Ctr Troy (22974) *(G-13933)*

Luck Stone Corporation 757 213-7750
4606 Bainbridge Blvd Chesapeake (23320) *(G-3189)*

Luck Stone Corporation 757 545-2020
508 E Indian River Rd Norfolk (23523) *(G-9624)*

Luck Stone Luck Stone Cmpanies, Manakin Sabot Also called Luck Stone Corporation *(G-7901)*

Luck Stone-Boscobel Plant, Manakin Sabot Also called Luck Stone Corporation *(G-7902)*

Luck Stone-Burkeville Plant, Burkeville Also called Luck Stone Corporation *(G-2209)*

Luck Stone-Fairfax Plant, Centreville Also called Luck Stone Corporation *(G-2316)*

Luck Stone-Rockville Plant, Rockville Also called Luck Stone Corporation *(G-12290)*

Luckyfoots Software 434 296-9358
1160 Foxchase Rdg Charlottesville (22902) *(G-2828)*

Lucy Love Candles 571 991-4155
2511 Luckland Way Woodbridge (22191) *(G-15742)*

Ludaire Fine Wood Floors Inc 276 889-3072
644 Clydes Way Dr Lebanon (24266) *(G-7199)*

Lufft Usa Inc 805 335-8500
22400 Davis Dr Ste 100 Sterling (20164) *(G-13445)*

Luggage Plus, Fairfax Also called Briggs & Riley Travelware LLC *(G-4421)*

Luis A Matos 703 486-0015
3833 9th St S Arlington (22204) *(G-1049)*

Lululemon 434 964-0105
2050 Bond St Ste 120 Charlottesville (22901) *(G-2657)*

Lululemon 757 631-3004
701 Lynnhaven Pkwy Virginia Beach (23452) *(G-14629)*

Lululemon Athletica 703 787-8327
11957 Market St Reston (20190) *(G-10891)*

Luluverse 202 821-9726
43353 Greyswallow Ter Ashburn (20147) *(G-1312)*

Luluverse Media, Ashburn Also called Luluverse *(G-1312)*

Lumacyte LLC 888 472-9295
1145 River Rd Ste 16 Keswick (22947) *(G-7052)*

Lumat Yarns LLC 804 329-4383
4590 Vawter Ave Richmond (23222) *(G-11660)*

Luminaire Technologies Inc 276 579-2007
9932 Wilson Hwy Mouth of Wilson (24363) *(G-9094)*

Luminary Air Group LLC 757 655-0705
18321 Parkway Melfa (23410) *(G-8711)*

Luminous Audio Technology 804 741-5826
8705 W Broad St Richmond (23294) *(G-11275)*

Lumos LLC 571 294-4290
3601 Fairfax Dr Apt 1006 Arlington (22201) *(G-1050)*

Luna Energy LLC (HQ) **540 553-0500**
2851 Commerce St Blacksburg (24060) *(G-1755)*

Luna Innovations Incorporated 540 961-5190
3155 State St Blacksburg (24060) *(G-1756)*

Lunano Inc 202 594-2959
6602 Mclean Ct Mc Lean (22101) *(G-8490)*

Luray Copy Services Inc 540 743-3433
27 E Main St Luray (22835) *(G-7616)*

Lure LLC 434 374-8559
171 Long Meadow Dr Clarksville (23927) *(G-3633)*

Luscious Lovezz LLC 804 538-4151
1806 Smmit Ave Ste 30010 Richmond (23230) *(G-11276)*

Lutron Electronics Co Inc 804 752-3300
11520 Sunshade Ln Ashland (23005) *(G-1455)*

Lutron Shading Solutions 804 752-3300
11520 Sunshade Ln Ashland (23005) *(G-1456)*

Lutz Farm & Services 540 477-3574
14144 Senedo Rd Mount Jackson (22842) *(G-9075)*

Lux 1 Holding Company Inc (HQ) **703 245-9675**
1775 Tysons Blvd Fl 7 Tysons (22102) *(G-13947)*

Lux Costume Jewelry 703 665-0674
4238 Wilson Blvd Arlington (22203) *(G-1051)*

Lux Living Candle Co LLC 757 462-6470
812 Evelyn Way Chesapeake (23322) *(G-3190)*

Luxemanes LLC 804 922-1410
10819 Trade Rd North Chesterfield (23236) *(G-9914)*

Lv Iron Works & Wldg Svcs Inc 703 499-2270
14004 Willard Rd Unit M Chantilly (20151) *(G-2459)*

Lvrcshull Incorporated 757 995-3931
4027 Appaloosa Ct Suffolk (23434) *(G-13735)*

Lw Aerospace, Chesapeake Also called Glenmark Group LLC *(G-3121)*

Lw Logging LLC 434 735-8598
2095 Barnesville Hwy Wylliesburg (23976) *(G-15872)*

Lwag Holdings Inc 703 455-8650
7200 Fullerton Rd Ste G Springfield (22150) *(G-13045)*

Lwrc, Springfield Also called Lwag Holdings Inc *(G-13045)*

Lydell Group Incorporated 804 627-0500
3007 Lincoln Ave Richmond (23228) *(G-11277)*

Lykes Meat Group Plant, Smithfield Also called Smithfield Packaged Meats Corp *(G-12737)*

Lynch Products 540 483-7800
3117 Chestnut Hill Rd Rocky Mount (24151) *(G-12337)*

Lynch Sign Products, Rocky Mount Also called Lynch Products *(G-12337)*

Lynchburg Fabrication LLC 434 660-0935
503 Old Plantation Dr Lynchburg (24502) *(G-7760)*

Lynchburg Fabrication Inc VA 434 473-7291
2824 Carroll Ave Lynchburg (24501) *(G-7761)*

Lynchburg Machining LLC 434 846-7327
120 Bradley Dr Lynchburg (24501) *(G-7762)*

Lynchburg Orthopedic Lab, Lynchburg Also called Hanger Prsthetcs & Ortho Inc *(G-7727)*

Lynchburg Plant, Lynchburg Also called Boxley Materials Company *(G-7659)*

Lynchburg Powder Coating 434 239-8454
317 Crowell Ln Lynchburg (24502) *(G-7763)*

Lynchburg Pwdr Cting Mdia Blst, Lynchburg Also called Lynchburg Powder Coating *(G-7763)*

Lynchburg Ready-Mix Con Co Inc (PA) **434 846-6563**
100 Halsey Rd Lynchburg (24501) *(G-7764)*

Lynchburg Ready-Mix Con Co Inc 434 946-5562
Hwy Ste 29n Amherst (24521) *(G-698)*

Lynchburg Wraps 434 385-1370
1053 Cottontown Rd Lynchburg (24503) *(G-7765)*

Lyndon Steel Company LLC 434 660-0829
99 Woodberry Ln Ste E Lynchburg (24502) *(G-7766)*

Lyniel W Kite 540 298-9657
3099 Carrier Ln Elkton (22827) *(G-4332)*

Lynk Global Inc (PA) **937 367-8737**
510 N Washington St # 200 Falls Church (22046) *(G-4921)*

Lynn Donnell 757 685-0263
952 Saint Andrews Reach B Chesapeake (23320) *(G-3191)*

Lynx Brewing Company LLC 773 819-8748
33 Aylwin Rd Portsmouth (23702) *(G-10455)*

Lyon Roofing Inc 540 633-0170
7822 Peppers Ferry Blvd Fairlawn (24141) *(G-4737)*

Lyon Shipyard Inc 757 622-4661
1818 Brown Ave Norfolk (23504) *(G-9625)*

Lyon Shipyard Inc 757 622-4661
1818 Brown Ave Norfolk (23504) *(G-9626)*

A L P H A B E T I C

Lyons Share LLC 443 370-9514
4297 Mulcaster Ter Dumfries (22025) ***(G-4251)***
M & B Diesel Supply LLC 757 903-8146
725 Industrial Park Dr Newport News (23608) ***(G-9288)***
M & H Paragon Inc 540 994-0080
64 1st St Ne Pulaski (24301) ***(G-10640)***
M & M Enterprise LLC 804 499-0087
901 Barlen Dr Richmond (23225) ***(G-11661)***
M & P Sawmill Co Inc 276 783-5585
1762 Stoney Battery Rd Marion (24354) ***(G-8232)***
M & R Striping LLC 703 201-7162
6040 Fieldcrest Ln Broad Run (20137) ***(G-2068)***
M & S Fabricators 703 550-3900
8249 Backlick Rd Ste G Lorton (22079) ***(G-7510)***
M & S Marine & Industrial Svcs 757 405-9623
702 Fifth St Portsmouth (23704) ***(G-10456)***
M & S Publishing Co Inc 434 645-7534
107 W Carolina Ave Crewe (23930) ***(G-3814)***
M & W Fire Apparatus, Vinton *Also called Plunkett Business Group Inc* ***(G-14180)***
M B S Equipment Sales Inc 804 785-4971
2200 Royal Oak School Rd Shacklefords (23156) ***(G-12683)***
M C Chadwell 276 445-5495
323 Old Bailey Dr Ewing (24248) ***(G-4386)***
M C Services Inc 703 352-1711
4922 Princess Anne Ct Fairfax (22032) ***(G-4500)***
M Co Marine, Chesapeake *Also called Mallory Co Inc* ***(G-3194)***
M Gautreaux Horseshoe 540 840-3153
15444 Beaver Den Ln Beaverdam (23015) ***(G-1610)***
M H Reinhart Technical Center, Richmond *Also called Carpenter Co* ***(G-11032)***
M L Welding 540 984-4883
525 Swover Creek Rd Edinburg (22824) ***(G-4309)***
M M Silk Flowers 757 334-7096
305 Copeland Rd Suffolk (23434) ***(G-13736)***
M M Wright Inc (PA) **434 577-2101**
6894 Christanna Hwy Gasburg (23857) ***(G-5659)***
M McGuire Woodworks 434 841-3702
407 Howard Dr Lynchburg (24503) ***(G-7767)***
M S G Custom Wdwrk & Pntg LLC 434 977-4752
1122 Daniel Morris Ln Charlottesville (22902) ***(G-2829)***
M S Russnak Industries LLC 540 848-1450
13363 Post Oak Rd Spotsylvania (22551) ***(G-12903)***
M Shields Studio Inc 757 340-1670
9628 18th Bay St Norfolk (23518) ***(G-9627)***
M T Holding Company LLC 540 563-8866
102 N Mitchell Rd Vinton (24179) ***(G-14178)***
M T Stone and Stucco LLC 434 806-7226
22 Hillcrest Dr Ruckersville (22968) ***(G-12405)***
M&H Plastics Inc 540 504-0030
485 Brooke Rd Winchester (22603) ***(G-15441)***
M&M Engraving Services Inc 804 843-3212
16601 Cooks Mill Rd Lanexa (23089) ***(G-7168)***
M&M Great Adventures LLC 937 344-1415
111 Clements Mill Trce Williamsburg (23185) ***(G-15275)***
M&M Printing LLC 804 621-4171
3185 Poplar View Pl Chester (23831) ***(G-3431)***
M&M Signs and Graphics LLC 703 803-1043
14512 Lee Rd Ste A Chantilly (20151) ***(G-2460)***
M&M Welding LLC 703 201-4066
8010 Ashland Ave Apt 3 Manassas (20109) ***(G-8102)***
M&Q Welding LLC 804 564-8864
2306 Ives Ln North Chesterfield (23235) ***(G-9915)***
M&S Welding 540 371-4009
195 Wyche Rd Stafford (22554) ***(G-13173)***
M-J Printers Inc 540 373-1878
502 Kenmore Ave Fredericksburg (22401) ***(G-5202)***
M1 Fabrication LLC 804 222-8885
4200 Masonic Ln Richmond (23223) ***(G-11662)***
M2m LLC 816 204-0938
10262 Battleview Pkwy Manassas (20109) ***(G-8103)***
M5 Technologies LLC 540 904-0880
1222 Mcdowell Ave Ne Roanoke (24012) ***(G-12131)***
Mabe Dg & Assoc Inc 804 530-1406
2140 E Hundred Rd Chester (23836) ***(G-3432)***
Mabe Tactical LLC 276 524-4912
4820 Back Valley Rd Big Stone Gap (24219) ***(G-1712)***
Mac Bone Industries Ltd 804 264-3603
9301 Old Staples Mill Rd Richmond (23228) ***(G-11278)***
Macabes Printing Group, Fairfax *Also called Oasis Global LLC* ***(G-4524)***
Macar International LLC 202 842-1818
4900 Leesburg Pike # 209 Alexandria (22302) ***(G-267)***
Mace Lumber Mill 540 249-4458
13189 Port Republic Rd Grottoes (24441) ***(G-6021)***
Macemedia Inc 804 288-5321
11551 Nuckols Rd Ste L Glen Allen (23059) ***(G-5766)***
Mach278 LLC 716 860-2889
44715 Prentice Dr # 792 Ashburn (20146) ***(G-1313)***
Machina Dynamica Inc 571 405-0709
8003 Chanute Pl Apt 10 Falls Church (22042) ***(G-4826)***
Machine & Fabg Specialists Inc 757 244-5693
810 Kiwanis St Hampton (23661) ***(G-6187)***
Machine Services Inc 757 487-5566
3825 Holland Blvd Chesapeake (23323) ***(G-3192)***
Machine Specialties Inc 804 798-8920
9989 Lickinghole Rd Ashland (23005) ***(G-1457)***
Machine Tool Technology LLC 804 520-4173
1830 Ruffin Mill Cir A South Chesterfield (23834) ***(G-12813)***
Machine Welding Pritchett Inc 434 949-7239
3659 Liberty Rd Dolphin (23843) ***(G-4116)***
Machinery Information Systems 703 836-9700
315 S Patrick St Fl 3 Alexandria (22314) ***(G-268)***
Machining Technology Inc 757 538-1781
1492 Progress Rd Suffolk (23434) ***(G-13737)***
Mack Mimsey 757 777-6333
1319 Melrose Pkwy Norfolk (23508) ***(G-9628)***
Mackes Woodworking LLC 570 856-3242
1909 Dannemora Dr Virginia Beach (23453) ***(G-14630)***
Macklin Consulting LLC 202 423-9923
2702 King St Alexandria (22302) ***(G-269)***
Macks Transformer Service 276 935-4366
Rr 460 Box E Grundy (24614) ***(G-6036)***
Maclaren Endeavors LLC 804 358-3493
8000 Villa Park Dr Richmond (23228) ***(G-11279)***
Macmillan Holdings LLC 888 330-8477
16365 James Madison Hwy Gordonsville (22942) ***(G-5913)***
Macmurray Graphics & Prtg Inc 703 680-4847
4177 Waterway Dr Montclair (22025) ***(G-8999)***
Maco Tool Inc 989 224-6723
1015 Radford St Christiansburg (24073) ***(G-3604)***
Macoma Capital 434 249-4580
204 N Main St Gordonsville (22942) ***(G-5914)***
Macoy Pubg & Masonic Sup Co, Richmond *Also called Macoy Pubg Masonic Sup Co Inc* ***(G-11280)***
Macoy Pubg Masonic Sup Co Inc 804 262-6551
3011 Dumbarton Rd Richmond (23228) ***(G-11280)***
Macro Systems LLC 703 359-9211
3867 Plaza Dr Fairfax (22030) ***(G-4650)***
Macronetics Inc 703 848-9290
8300 Boone Blvd Ste 50 Vienna (22182) ***(G-14088)***
Macroseal Mechanical LLC 804 458-5655
2122 E Whitehill Rd Prince George (23875) ***(G-10599)***
Macs Construction 571 278-5371
14508 Smithwood Dr Centreville (20120) ***(G-2317)***
Macs Custom Woodshop 540 789-4201
2105 Ferney Creek Rd Nw Willis (24380) ***(G-15363)***
Macs Machine Shop 540 269-2222
3420 Rush Ln Keezletown (22832) ***(G-7028)***
Macs Smack LLC 804 913-9126
13278 Depot Rd Hanover (23069) ***(G-6282)***
Mactaggart Scott Usa LLC (HQ) **757 288-1405**
920 Verano Ct Virginia Beach (23456) ***(G-14631)***
Mactavish Machine Mfg Co 804 264-6109
7429 Whitepine Rd North Chesterfield (23237) ***(G-9916)***
Mad Hat Enterprises 540 885-9600
806 Spring Hill Rd Staunton (24401) ***(G-13278)***
Mad Hatter Foods LLC 434 981-9378
1305 Belmont Park Charlottesville (22902) ***(G-2830)***
Mad-Den Embroidery & Gifts 757 450-4421
2332 Kilburton Priory Ct Virginia Beach (23456) ***(G-14632)***
Mada Vemi Alpacas 434 770-1972
125 Tommy Carter Rd Axton (24054) ***(G-1540)***
Made By Sandy 757 588-1123
1865 Branchwood St Norfolk (23518) ***(G-9629)***
Madeline Candle Company LLC 703 503-9181
6440 Lake Meadow Dr Burke (22015) ***(G-2192)***
Madera Floors LLC 703 855-6847
1908 Reston Metro Plz # 1119 Reston (20190) ***(G-10892)***
Madgar Enterprises LLC 540 760-6946
4673 Melody Rd North Chesterfield (23234) ***(G-9917)***
Madidrop Pbc Inc (used In) 434 260-3767
1985 Snow Point Ln Charlottesville (22902) ***(G-2831)***
Madinah Publs & Distrs Inc 804 839-8073
2308 Lancashire Dr North Chesterfield (23235) ***(G-9918)***
Madison Colonial LLC 240 997-2376
3204 Lytham Ct Toano (23168) ***(G-13868)***
Madison County Eagle, Madison *Also called Wood Television LLC* ***(G-7865)***
Madison County Wines LLC 540 948-9005
6109 Wolftown Hood Rd Madison (22727) ***(G-7858)***
Madison Edgecnnex Holdings LLC 703 880-5404
2201 Coop Way Ste 200 Herndon (20171) ***(G-6739)***
Madison Flooring Company Inc 540 948-4498
333 Oak Park Rd Madison (22727) ***(G-7859)***
Madisons Cleaning 540 421-1074
2636 Keezletown Rd Rockingham (22802) ***(G-12260)***
Maersk Fluid Technology, Inc., Norfolk *Also called Maersk Oil Trading Inc* ***(G-9630)***
Maersk Oil Trading Inc 757 857-4800
1 Commercial Pl Norfolk (23510) ***(G-9630)***
Mafco Consolidated Group Inc 804 222-1600
4400 Williamsburg Ave Richmond (23231) ***(G-11281)***
Mafco Natural Products, Richmond *Also called Mafco Consolidated Group Inc* ***(G-11281)***
Mag Aerospace, Newport News *Also called Uav Communications Inc* ***(G-9368)***

Magco Inc 757 934-0042
602 Carolina Rd Suffolk (23434) *(G-13738)*

Maggie Malick Wine Caves LLC 540 905-2921
12138 Harpers Ferry Rd Hillsboro (20132) *(G-6875)*

Maggies Rags 540 961-1755
507 Rose Ave Blacksburg (24060) *(G-1757)*

Magic and Memories Press LLC 703 849-0921
11300 Hunt Farm Ln Oakton (22124) *(G-10155)*

Magic Bullet Skateboards LLC 703 371-0363
17 Argyle Hills Dr Fredericksburg (22405) *(G-5452)*

Magic Genius LLC 540 454-7595
5463 Camellia Ct Warrenton (20187) *(G-15032)*

Magic Wand Inc 276 466-3921
1100 Page St Bristol (24201) *(G-1983)*

Magnes Industries LLC 540 246-6088
1034 Betsy Ross Ct Harrisonburg (22802) *(G-6342)*

Magnesium Music 703 798-5516
6609 10th St Unit B1 Alexandria (22307) *(G-520)*

Magnet 1 Internet Systems, Unionville *Also called Magnet Directories Inc* *(G-13964)*

Magnet Directories Inc 281 251-6640
8244 Zachary Taylor Hwy Unionville (22567) *(G-13964)*

Magnet Forensics Usa Inc (PA) **519 342-0195**
2250 Corp Park Dr Ste 130 Herndon (20171) *(G-6740)*

Magnetic Bracelets and More 757 499-1282
5199 Cypress Point Cir Virginia Beach (23455) *(G-14633)*

Magnetic Technologies Corp 276 228-7943
262 Saint Lukes Rd Wytheville (24382) *(G-15899)*

Magnets USA, Vinton *Also called Stickers Plus Ltd* *(G-14184)*

Magnifazine LLC 248 224-1137
730 Carter Ln Louisa (23093) *(G-7558)*

Magnified Duplication Prtg Inc 276 393-3193
6345 Cave Springs Rd Dryden (24243) *(G-4145)*

Magnifoam Delaware Inc 804 564-9700
8020 Whitepine Rd North Chesterfield (23237) *(G-9919)*

Magnigen LLC 434 420-1435
1318 Eyrie View Dr Lynchburg (24503) *(G-7768)*

Magnolia Graphics 804 550-0012
10421 Rapidan Way Ashland (23005) *(G-1458)*

Magnolia Woodworking 571 521-9041
8610 Crestview Dr Fairfax (22031) *(G-4501)*

Magnus Aircraft Incorporated 830 998-7270
20130 Lkview Ctr Plz Ste Ashburn (20147) *(G-1314)*

Magoozle LLC 757 581-6936
2493 Piney Bark Dr Virginia Beach (23456) *(G-14634)*

Magpie Design LLC 703 975-5818
2312 Toddsbury Pl Reston (20191) *(G-10893)*

Magss Ideas & Concepts 804 304-6324
8959 Cardiff Rd North Chesterfield (23236) *(G-9920)*

Mahawara LLC 443 949-2602
44330 Mercure Cir 100j Dulles (20166) *(G-4208)*

Mahogany Landscaping & Design 757 846-7947
1676 Cottenham Ln Virginia Beach (23454) *(G-14635)*

Mahogany Styles By Teesha LLC 703 433-2170
21000 Suthbank St Ste 196 Sterling (20165) *(G-13446)*

Mahoy Electric Service Co Inc 540 977-0035
175 Macgregor Dr Blue Ridge (24064) *(G-1851)*

Maida Development Company (PA) **757 723-0785**
201 S Mallory St Hampton (23663) *(G-6188)*

Maida Development Company 757 719-3038
9 Williams St Hampton (23663) *(G-6189)*

Mailing Resources, Richmond *Also called Printing Department Inc* *(G-11334)*

Main Gate Publishing Co LLC 804 744-2202
10410 Genito Ln Chesterfield (23832) *(G-3513)*

Mainly Clay LLC 434 390-8138
217 N Main St Farmville (23901) *(G-4948)*

Majestic Marketing LLC 804 210-7667
1806 Smmit Ave Ste 30010 Richmond (23230) *(G-11282)*

Majiksoft 757 510-0929
1644 Macgregory St Virginia Beach (23464) *(G-14636)*

Major Business Systems, Chatham *Also called Crabar/Gbf Inc* *(G-2926)*

Maker Industries 757 560-1692
635 Mile Creek Ln Chesapeake (23322) *(G-3193)*

Makes Sense To ME Software LLC 757 771-5289
303 Gaines Mill Ln Hampton (23669) *(G-6190)*

Makivin Trucking LLC 434 637-1359
22049 Gilliam Rd Yale (23897) *(G-15929)*

Maleys Music 571 335-4289
2499 N Harrison St Arlington (22207) *(G-1052)*

Mallory Co Inc 757 803-5596
509 Downing Dr Chesapeake (23322) *(G-3194)*

Malpass Construction Co Inc 757 543-3541
2650 Indian River Rd Chesapeake (23325) *(G-3195)*

Mamagreen LLC 312 953-3557
2601 Maury St Bldg 26 Richmond (23224) *(G-11663)*

Mamagreen Sstnble Otdoor Lxury, Richmond *Also called Mamagreen LLC* *(G-11663)*

Mamas Fudge 540 980-8444
5344 Thornspring Rd Pulaski (24301) *(G-10641)*

Man Diesel & Turbo N Amer Inc 703 373-0690
2200 Ferdinand Porsche Dr Herndon (20171) *(G-6741)*

Management Solutions LC 540 967-9600
348 Industrial Dr Louisa (23093) *(G-7559)*

Manakin Industries LLC 804 784-5514
758 Double Oak Ln Manakin Sabot (23103) *(G-7903)*

Manan LLC 804 320-1414
5400 Glenside Dr Ste B Henrico (23228) *(G-6532)*

Manassas Consulting Svcs Inc 703 346-1358
12788 Lost Creek Ct Manassas (20112) *(G-8104)*

Manassas Ice & Fuel Co Inc (PA) **703 368-3121**
9009 Center St Ste 1 Manassas (20110) *(G-7972)*

Manchester Industries Inc VA (HQ) **804 226-4250**
200 Orleans St Richmond (23231) *(G-11283)*

Mandylion Research Labs LLC 703 628-4284
10611 Hannah Farm Rd Oakton (22124) *(G-10156)*

Mann Logging 434 283-5245
611 County Airport Rd Gladys (24554) *(G-5694)*

Mann-Kdwell Intr Win Tratments, Richmond *Also called Shade Mann-Kidwell Corp* *(G-11378)*

Manny Exhibits & Woodcraft 703 354-9231
6400 Holyoke Dr Annandale (22003) *(G-770)*

Manny Weber 703 819-3338
207 Rosemeade Pl Sw Leesburg (20175) *(G-7309)*

Mantas 703 322-4917
13650 Dulles Tech Dr Herndon (20171) *(G-6742)*

Mantech Advanced Dev Group Inc (HQ) **703 218-6000**
12015 Lee Jackson Mem Hwy Fairfax (22033) *(G-4502)*

Mantel USA Inc 540 946-6529
566 Kindig Rd Waynesboro (22980) *(G-15122)*

Mantels By Meunier 804 690-1977
318 N 24th St Richmond (23223) *(G-11664)*

Mantis Graphics 757 482-4186
613 Blackthorne Dr Chesapeake (23322) *(G-3196)*

Mantis Networks LLC 571 306-1234
11160 South Lakes Dr # 190 Reston (20191) *(G-10894)*

Manufacturing, Woodbridge *Also called Palmyrene Empire LLC* *(G-15770)*

Manufacturing, Midlothian *Also called Specialty Vhcl Solutions LLC* *(G-8907)*

Manufacturing Mystique Inc 703 719-0943
5713 Habersham Way Alexandria (22310) *(G-521)*

Manufacturing Plant, Lynchburg *Also called Framatome Inc* *(G-7714)*

Manufacturing System Svcs Inc 800 428-8643
10394 Democracy Ln Fairfax (22030) *(G-4651)*

Manufacturing Techniques 804 436-9000
180 Technology Park Dr Kilmarnock (22482) *(G-7072)*

Many Miniatures 703 730-1221
3546a Melrose Ave Triangle (22172) *(G-13896)*

Maola Milk and Ice Cream Co (HQ) **252 638-1131**
5500 Chestnut Ave Newport News (23605) *(G-9289)*

Mapei Corp Fredericksburg 540 710-5303
9420 Cosner Dr Fredericksburg (22408) *(G-5319)*

Mapei Corporation 540 898-5124
9420 Cosner Dr Fredericksburg (22408) *(G-5320)*

Mapei Corporation 540 361-1085
300 Nelms Cir Fredericksburg (22406) *(G-5453)*

Maphook Inc 703 661-7000
23475 Rock Haven Way Sterling (20166) *(G-13447)*

Maple Grove Logging LLC 276 677-0152
182 Sand Mines Rd Sugar Grove (24375) *(G-13787)*

Maple Hill Embroidery 540 336-1967
1833 Chestnut Grove Rd Winchester (22603) *(G-15442)*

Mapp Manufacturing Corporation 757 410-0307
3712 Profit Way Ste F Chesapeake (23323) *(G-3197)*

Mapsdirect LLC 804 915-7628
101 S 15th St Ste 104 Richmond (23219) *(G-11665)*

Mar, Fredericksburg *Also called Mid-Atlantic Rubber Inc* *(G-5326)*

Mar-Bal Inc 440 539-6595
2020 Kraft Dr Ste 3003 Blacksburg (24060) *(G-1758)*

Mar-Bal Inc 540 674-5320
5400 Reserve Way Dublin (24084) *(G-4165)*

Marah Bitar LLC (PA) **856 630-4437**
419 Commanders Ln Clintwood (24228) *(G-3689)*

Marathon Millwork Inc 540 743-1721
119 Planning Mill Rd Luray (22835) *(G-7617)*

Marble Man 804 448-9100
6113 Mudville Rd Woodford (22580) *(G-15841)*

Marble Max 703 723-0071
21760 Beaumeade Cir # 135 Ashburn (20147) *(G-1315)*

Marble Restoration Systems 757 739-7959
757 Oleander Cir Virginia Beach (23464) *(G-14637)*

Marbrooke Printing Inc 276 632-7115
20 Bridge St S Martinsville (24112) *(G-8307)*

Marc R Stagger 703 913-9445
7702 Backlick Rd Ste I Springfield (22150) *(G-13046)*

Marceline Vineyards LLC 540 212-9798
5887 Cross Keys Rd Mount Crawford (22841) *(G-9056)*

Marcell Sgnture Scnted Candles 757 502-5236
9642 Sherwood Pl Apt 1 Norfolk (23503) *(G-9631)*

Marco and Luca Noodle Str Inc 434 295-3855
809 Park St Charlottesville (22902) *(G-2832)*

Marco Machine & Design Inc 804 275-5555
7740 Whitepine Rd North Chesterfield (23237) *(G-9921)*

Marco Metals LLC...540 437-2324
4773 S Valley Pike Rockingham (22801) ***(G-12261)***
Marcom Services LLC...757 963-1851
620 Lincoln St Portsmouth (23704) ***(G-10457)***
Marcus Cox & Sons Inc...540 297-5818
3743 White House Rd Moneta (24121) ***(G-8971)***
Marcy Boys Music...757 247-6222
3013 Williams St Newport News (23607) ***(G-9290)***
Marden Press Printvertise Inc...571 295-5322
21662 Steatite Ct Ashburn (20147) ***(G-1316)***
Marden Thinning Company Inc...540 872-5196
610 Diggstown Rd Bumpass (23024) ***(G-2165)***
Mardon Inc...276 386-6662
2154 Us Highway 23 North Weber City (24290) ***(G-15149)***
Marelco Power Systems Inc...517 546-6330
4200 Oakleys Ln Richmond (23223) ***(G-11666)***
Marelco Power Systems Inc...800 225-4838
4200 Oakleys Ln Richmond (23223) ***(G-11667)***
Margaret Atkins...434 315-3184
1547 Cumberland Rd Farmville (23901) ***(G-4949)***
Maribeths Bakery Inc...703 739-5839
6441a Gen Green Way Alexandria (22312) ***(G-522)***
Marie Lawson Reporter...757 549-2198
301 Esplanade Pl Chesapeake (23320) ***(G-3198)***
Marie Webb...703 291-5359
16807 Brandy Moor Loop Woodbridge (22191) ***(G-15743)***
Marilyn Carter...804 901-4757
2531 Lkfeld Mews Ct Apt G Henrico (23231) ***(G-6533)***
Marin...703 354-1950
4210 John Marr Dr Annandale (22003) ***(G-771)***
Marine Fabricators Inc...804 758-2248
27 Industrial Way Topping (23169) ***(G-13887)***
Marine Hydraulics Intl LLC (HQ)...**757 545-6400**
543 E Indian River Rd Norfolk (23523) ***(G-9632)***
Marine Sonic Technology...804 693-9602
120 Newsome Dr Ste H Yorktown (23692) ***(G-15978)***
Marineland, Blacksburg *Also called Spectrum Brands Pet LLC* ***(G-1794)***
Mariner Co, Buena Vista *Also called Mariner Media Inc* ***(G-2146)***
Mariner Media Inc...540 264-0021
131 W 21st St Buena Vista (24416) ***(G-2146)***
Mario Contract Lighting, Roanoke *Also called Mario Industries Virginia Inc* ***(G-12132)***
Mario Industries Virginia Inc (PA)...**540 342-1111**
2490 Patterson Ave Sw Roanoke (24016) ***(G-12132)***
Marion Brothers Logging Inc...804 492-3200
656 Anderson Hwy Cumberland (23040) ***(G-3936)***
Marion Electric Company...276 783-4765
440 1/2 N Main St Marion (24354) ***(G-8233)***
Marion Mold & Tool Inc...276 783-6101
176 Rifton Dr Marion (24354) ***(G-8234)***
Marion Nickel...703 444-8158
45800 Jona Dr Sterling (20165) ***(G-13448)***
Marion Operations...276 783-3121
150 Johnston Rd Marion (24354) ***(G-8235)***
Maritime Associates Inc...571 212-0655
148 N Early St Alexandria (22304) ***(G-270)***
Marjories Cookie Shop LLC...901 205-9055
4071 S Four Mile Run Dr Arlington (22204) ***(G-1053)***
Mark A Harber...276 546-6051
2097 Ward Hill Rd Pennington Gap (24277) ***(G-10295)***
Mark Bric Display Corp...800 742-6275
4740 Chudoba Pkwy Prince George (23875) ***(G-10600)***
Mark Crego, Springfield *Also called Legacy Solutions* ***(G-13039)***
Mark Debusk Custom Cabinets...540 552-3228
1001 Palmer Dr Blacksburg (24060) ***(G-1759)***
Mark Electric Inc...804 749-4151
17238 Pouncey Tract Rd Rockville (23146) ***(G-12291)***
Mark Four Inc...804 330-0765
1837 High Hill Dr Powhatan (23139) ***(G-10557)***
Mark It Plus, Richmond *Also called Cunningham Entps LLC Daniel* ***(G-11170)***
Mark Pearson...703 648-2568
3104 Bandol Ln Oakton (22124) ***(G-10157)***
Mark S Chapman...434 227-6702
22 Pine Crest Dr Troy (22974) ***(G-13934)***
Mark Software LLC...703 409-4605
37433 Hidden Springs Ln Hillsboro (20132) ***(G-6876)***
Mark Space Inc...703 404-8550
22611 Markey Ct Ste 110 Sterling (20166) ***(G-13449)***
Mark T Goodman...540 582-2328
4300 Partlow Rd Partlow (22534) ***(G-10267)***
Mark Toner LLC...703 689-0609
1507 Inlet Ct Reston (20190) ***(G-10895)***
Mark Works, Williamsburg *Also called Window Fashion Design* ***(G-15346)***
Mark-It...540 434-4824
125 W Water St Harrisonburg (22801) ***(G-6343)***
Market Salamander...540 687-8011
200 W Washington St Middleburg (20117) ***(G-8728)***
Market This LLC...804 382-9220
10808 Kittery Pl Glen Allen (23060) ***(G-5767)***
Marketfare Foods LLC...540 371-5110
37 Mclane Dr Fredericksburg (22406) ***(G-5454)***
Marketspace Solutions Inc...703 989-3509
5210 Honeysuckle Ct Centreville (20120) ***(G-2318)***
Markham Burial Vault Service (PA)...**804 271-1441**
8400 Jefferson Davis Hwy North Chesterfield (23237) ***(G-9922)***
Markham Wilbert, North Chesterfield *Also called Markham Burial Vault Service* ***(G-9922)***
Marks Garage...540 498-3458
17 Sunrise Valley Ct Stafford (22554) ***(G-13174)***
Marktechnologic LLC...703 470-1224
5800 Hanover Ave Springfield (22150) ***(G-13047)***
Marla Hughes...703 309-8267
6102 Bayliss Knoll Ct Alexandria (22310) ***(G-523)***
Marlor Inc...804 378-5071
11500 Mdlthn Tpke 470 North Chesterfield (23235) ***(G-9923)***
Maroon Assistive Tech LLC...703 239-3113
214 Woods Edge Ct Blacksburg (24060) ***(G-1760)***
Marroquin Welding...571 340-9165
183 Rock Hill Church Rd Stafford (22556) ***(G-13175)***
Mars Incorporated (PA)...**703 821-4900**
6885 Elm St Ste 1 Mc Lean (22101) ***(G-8491)***
Mars Logic LLC...510 220-7117
6507 Smoot Dr Mc Lean (22101) ***(G-8492)***
Mars Machine Works Inc...804 642-4760
Hwy 17s Gloucester Point (23062) ***(G-5873)***
Mars Overseas Holdings Inc (HQ)...**703 821-4900**
6885 Elm St Ste 1 Mc Lean (22101) ***(G-8493)***
Mars Petcare Us Inc...703 821-4900
6885 Elm St Mc Lean (22101) ***(G-8494)***
Marshal Concrete Products, Christiansburg *Also called Chandler Concrete Products of* ***(G-3578)***
Marshall Con Pdts of Danville (PA)...**434 792-1233**
1088 Industrial Ave Danville (24541) ***(G-4015)***
Marshall Con Pdts of Danville...434 369-4791
1503 Main St Altavista (24517) ***(G-635)***
Marshall Con Pdts of Danville...434 575-5351
1040 Alphonse Dairy Rd South Boston (24592) ***(G-12780)***
Marshall Concrete Products, Christiansburg *Also called Chandler Concrete Virginia Inc* ***(G-3579)***
Marshall Concrete Products...540 297-4369
14418 Moneta Rd Moneta (24121) ***(G-8972)***
Marshall Division, Marshall *Also called Hagerstown Block Company* ***(G-8255)***
Marshall Manufacturing Co...757 824-4061
32489 Nocks Landing Rd Atlantic (23303) ***(G-1525)***
Martcl Inc...540 777-0456
4325 Old Cave Spring Rd Roanoke (24018) ***(G-11959)***
Martha Bennett...757 897-6150
121 Locust Ln Yorktown (23693) ***(G-15979)***
Martin Tonya...804 742-8721
1432 Wray Rd La Crosse (23950) ***(G-7146)***
Martin Elthon...703 853-1801
2983 Prosperity Ave Fairfax (22031) ***(G-4503)***
Martin Lee Enterprises Inc...276 623-0125
20308 Alvarado Rd Abingdon (24211) ***(G-49)***
Martin Marietta Aggregates, North Garden *Also called Martin Marietta Materials Inc* ***(G-10080)***
Martin Marietta Materials Inc...804 674-9517
1 Parkwest Cir Midlothian (23114) ***(G-8852)***
Martin Marietta Materials Inc...540 894-5952
9100 Luck Stone Ln Fredericksburg (22407) ***(G-5321)***
Martin Marietta Materials Inc...434 296-5562
2625 Red Hill Rd North Garden (22959) ***(G-10080)***
Martin Marietta Materials Inc...804 561-0570
12301 Patrick Henry Hwy Amelia Court House (23002) ***(G-665)***
Martin Marietta Materials Inc...804 798-5096
12068 Stone Quarry Dr Ashland (23005) ***(G-1459)***
Martin Marietta Materials Inc...804 744-1130
3636 Warbro Rd Midlothian (23112) ***(G-8853)***
Martin Marietta Materials Inc...804 749-4831
1940 Ashland Rd Rockville (23146) ***(G-12292)***
Martin Metalfab Inc...804 226-1431
5891 Lewis Rd Sandston (23150) ***(G-12624)***
Martin Mobile Wldg & Repr LLC...757 581-3828
5329 Morris Neck Rd Virginia Beach (23457) ***(G-14638)***
Martin Pallets & Wedges LLC...276 694-4276
28839 Jeb Stuart Hwy Stuart (24171) ***(G-13623)***
Martin Printwear Inc...434 352-5660
200 Industrial Park Appomattox (24522) ***(G-819)***
Martin Publishing Corp...804 780-1700
1700 Venable St Richmond (23223) ***(G-11668)***
Martin Railroad Tie Co...434 933-4398
220 Tye Yard Rd Gladstone (24553) ***(G-5686)***
Martin Screen Prints and EMB, Virginia Beach *Also called Tdi LLC* ***(G-14865)***
Martin Star Cabinetry & Design...804 340-1250
1610 W Main St Richmond (23220) ***(G-11669)***
Martins Custom Designs Inc (PA)...**804 642-0235**
1707 Shane Rd Gloucester Point (23062) ***(G-5874)***
Martins Custom Designs Inc...757 245-7129
340 Ed Wright Ln Newport News (23606) ***(G-9291)***
Martins Fabricating & Welding...540 343-6001
1108 Orange Ave Ne Roanoke (24012) ***(G-12133)***

Martinsville Concrete Products..................................276 632-6416
530 Hairston St Martinsville (24112) *(G-8308)*

Martinsville Finance & Inv (PA)..............................**276 632-9500**
184 Tensbury Dr Martinsville (24112) *(G-8309)*

Martinsville Machine Works......................................276 632-6491
1106 Memorial Blvd S Martinsville (24112) *(G-8310)*

Martinsville Plant, Martinsville *Also called Boxley Materials Company (G-8271)*

Martinsville Plant, Martinsville *Also called Hooker Furniture Corporation (G-8298)*

Marty Corporation (PA)..**276 395-3326**
502a Front St W Coeburn (24230) *(G-3701)*

Marty Corporation..276 679-3477
465 Industrial Way Norton (24273) *(G-10125)*

Marty Materials, Coeburn *Also called Marty Corporation (G-3701)*

Marty Materials, Norton *Also called Marty Corporation (G-10125)*

Maruchan Virginia Inc...804 275-2800
8101 Whitepine Rd North Chesterfield (23237) *(G-9924)*

Marvelous Green LLC...540 577-6967
4250 Mcfall Hollow Rd Pulaski (24301) *(G-10642)*

Marvin Coblentz...434 944-1897
121 Blue Ledge Loop Rd Amherst (24521) *(G-699)*

Marvin Dudley Logging...540 784-3098
785 Bunker Hill Mill Rd Lexington (24450) *(G-7399)*

Marvin Ramirez-Aguilar..703 241-4092
2150 Patrick Henry Dr Arlington (22205) *(G-1054)*

Mary A Thomas..434 637-2016
195 Concord Ln Emporia (23847) *(G-4363)*

Mary Ann's Trucking, Amelia Court House *Also called Virginias Rsurces Recycled LLC (G-676)*

Mary Elizabeth Burrell...804 677-2855
1310 Dance St Richmond (23220) *(G-11670)*

Mary Jo Kirwan..703 421-1919
2616 Stone Mountain Ct Herndon (20170) *(G-6743)*

Mary Kay Inc..770 497-8800
69 Reeves Rd Mount Solon (22843) *(G-9088)*

Mary Truman..469 554-0655
18021 Gvrnor Hrrison Pkwy Freeman (23856) *(G-5512)*

Maryland and Virginia Milk PR..................................757 245-3857
5500 Chestnut Ave Newport News (23605) *(G-9292)*

Maryland and Virginia Milk PR..................................804 524-0959
1840 Touchstone Rd South Chesterfield (23834) *(G-12814)*

Masa Corporation (PA)..**757 855-3013**
5445 Henneman Dr Ste 200 Norfolk (23513) *(G-9633)*

Masa Corporation of Virginia (HQ)...........................**757 855-3013**
5445 Henneman Dr Ste 200 Norfolk (23513) *(G-9634)*

Masa Corporation of Virginia...................................804 271-8102
2203 Station Rd North Chesterfield (23234) *(G-9925)*

Masco Cabinetry LLC...540 727-7859
641 Maddox Dr Culpeper (22701) *(G-3907)*

Masco Cabinetry LLC...540 477-2961
1325 Industrial Park Rd Mount Jackson (22842) *(G-9076)*

Mascotcandy.com, Richmond *Also called Debbie Belt (G-11556)*

Masked By Tee LLC..757 373-9517
242 Craftsman Cir Suffolk (23434) *(G-13739)*

Masonite Corporation..540 778-2211
280 Donovan Dr Stanley (22851) *(G-13231)*

Masonite International Corp......................................540 665-3083
130 W Brooke Rd Winchester (22603) *(G-15443)*

Masonite International Corp......................................540 778-2211
280 Donovan Dr Stanley (22851) *(G-13232)*

Masonrymart, Roanoke *Also called Blue Stone Block Sprmkt Inc (G-12050)*

Maspaintservice Ltd Lblty Co....................................301 547-1996
4415 Forest Glen Ct Annandale (22003) *(G-772)*

Massaged For You, Virginia Beach *Also called Bodyzone L L C (G-14292)*

Massaponax Bldg Components Inc.............................540 898-0013
8737 Jefferson Davis Hwy Fredericksburg (22407) *(G-5322)*

Massey Coal Export Company, Bristol *Also called Appalachia Holding Company (G-2006)*

Massey Wood & West Inc...804 746-2800
8404 Erle Rd Mechanicsville (23116) *(G-8656)*

Massies Wood Products LLC.....................................434 277-8498
581 Buffalo Mines Rd Roseland (22967) *(G-12370)*

Massimo Zanetti Bev USA Inc...................................757 215-7409
1200 Court St Portsmouth (23704) *(G-10458)*

Massimo Zanetti Bev USA Inc (HQ)...........................**757 215-7300**
1370 Progress Rd Suffolk (23434) *(G-13740)*

Massimo Zanetti Bev USA Inc...................................757 538-8083
1370 Progress Rd Suffolk (23434) *(G-13741)*

Massone Industries Inc..540 825-7339
14131 Inlet Rd Culpeper (22701) *(G-3908)*

Masstransit Publishing LLC.......................................703 205-2419
2260 Cartbridge Rd Falls Church (22043) *(G-4827)*

Mast Bros Logging LLC...434 446-2401
2040 Bill Tuck Hwy South Boston (24592) *(G-12781)*

Master Business Solutions Inc..................................804 378-5470
400 Southlake Blvd Ste C North Chesterfield (23236) *(G-9926)*

Master Machine & Auto LLC......................................757 244-8401
5823 Jefferson Ave Newport News (23605) *(G-9293)*

Master Machine & Engrg Co......................................804 231-6648
2806 Decatur St Richmond (23224) *(G-11671)*

Master Machine & Tool Co Inc...................................757 245-6653
5857 Jefferson Ave Newport News (23605) *(G-9294)*

Master Mold of Virginia LLC....................................757 868-8283
5857 Jefferson Ave Newport News (23605) *(G-9295)*

Masterbrand Cabinets Inc..703 396-7804
8424 Kao Cir Manassas (20110) *(G-7973)*

Mastermind LLC...757 379-5215
105 Professional Pkwy # 152 Yorktown (23693) *(G-15980)*

Masters Energy Inc..281 816-9991
9601 Hastings Mill Dr Glen Allen (23060) *(G-5768)*

Mat Enterprises Inc...540 389-2528
707 Red Ln Salem (24153) *(G-12534)*

Matbock LLC...757 828-6659
1164 Millers Ln Ste D Virginia Beach (23451) *(G-14639)*

Match Ammo LLC..804 266-2666
6020 W Broad St Richmond (23230) *(G-11284)*

Match My Value Inc..301 456-4308
1115 Althea St Richmond (23222) *(G-11672)*

Match Point Press..703 548-4202
909 N Overlook Dr Alexandria (22305) *(G-271)*

Mate Creek Energy of West VA (PA).........................**276 669-8599**
148 Bristol East Rd Bristol (24202) *(G-2025)*

Matera John...757 240-0425
6305 Grg Wshngtn Mrl Hwy Yorktown (23692) *(G-15981)*

Materials Development Corp......................................703 257-1500
12169 Balls Ford Rd Manassas (20109) *(G-8105)*

Materna..703 875-8616
2111 Wilson Blvd Arlington (22201) *(G-1055)*

Mathemtics Scnce Ctr Foundation.............................862 778-8300
2401 Hartman St Richmond (23223) *(G-11673)*

Mather AMP Cabinet...615 636-1743
2681 Prod Rd Ste 107 Virginia Beach (23454) *(G-14640)*

Mathias Welding..540 347-1415
9547 James Madison Hwy Warrenton (20187) *(G-15033)*

Mathomank Village Tribe..757 504-5513
68 Mancha Ave Claremont (23899) *(G-3624)*

Matoaca Specialty Arms Inc......................................804 590-2749
21411 Hampton Ave South Chesterfield (23803) *(G-12837)*

Matre Inc (HQ)...**703 821-4927**
6885 Elm St Mc Lean (22101) *(G-8495)*

Matric Kolor..757 310-6764
905 G St Hampton (23661) *(G-6191)*

Matrix Gallery, Blacksburg *Also called Lana Juarez (G-1750)*

Matt and Molly Trades LLC......................................703 585-1858
101 Mt View Farm Rd Gordonsville (22942) *(G-5915)*

Matthew Crawford Sargent.......................................757 430-9488
2505 Bodnar Ln Virginia Beach (23456) *(G-14641)*

Matthew Mitchell..615 454-0787
93 Cedar Grove Rd Fredericksburg (22406) *(G-5455)*

Matthews Home Decor..804 379-2640
13102 Dawnwood Ter Midlothian (23114) *(G-8854)*

Matthews Sheet Metal Inc..757 543-6009
5821 Arrowhead Dr Ste 102 Virginia Beach (23462) *(G-14642)*

Matthews Sheetmetal, Virginia Beach *Also called Matthews Sheet Metal Inc (G-14642)*

Matthias Enterprises Inc..757 591-9371
722 Bluecrab Rd Ste A Newport News (23606) *(G-9296)*

Mattie S Soft Serve LLC...540 560-4550
1438 Goodrich Rd Stanley (22851) *(G-13233)*

Mattress Deal LLC..804 869-3387
7601 W Broad St Richmond (23294) *(G-11285)*

Maureen Melville...703 533-2448
1909 Massachusetts Ave Mc Lean (22101) *(G-8496)*

Maurice Bynum..757 241-0265
15 Virginia Ave Windsor (23487) *(G-15606)*

Maurice Lamb..540 962-0903
222 E Parrish St Covington (24426) *(G-3794)*

Maury River Oil Company..540 463-2233
172 Old Buena Vista Rd Lexington (24450) *(G-7400)*

Maurywood LLC...540 463-6209
317 Jackson Ave Lexington (24450) *(G-7401)*

Mav6 LLC (PA)..**601 619-7722**
1071 Cedar Chase Ct Herndon (20170) *(G-6744)*

Maverick Bus Solutions LLC......................................757 870-8489
46 Candlelight Ln Portsmouth (23703) *(G-10459)*

Maverick Cyber-Defense LLC....................................202 725-7663
14001c Saint Germain Dr # 6 Centreville (20121) *(G-2319)*

Maverick Fabrication...321 210-9004
5931 Marshall Ave Newport News (23605) *(G-9297)*

Maverick Wheels LLC...540 891-2681
301 Butternut Dr Fredericksburg (22408) *(G-5323)*

Max Press Printing...757 482-2273
517 Kempsville Rd Ste I Chesapeake (23320) *(G-3199)*

Maxgen U.S. Company, Alexandria *Also called World Fashion City Inc (G-615)*

Maxilicious Baking Company LLC...............................703 448-1788
1510 Snughill Ct Vienna (22182) *(G-14089)*

Maxim Systems Inc..540 265-9050
4142 Melrose Ave Nw # 12 Roanoke (24017) *(G-12134)*

Maximilian Press Publishers, Chesapeake *Also called Max Press Printing (G-3199)*

Maxines Cheesecakes LLC..804 586-5135
8771 Lake Jordan Way North Dinwiddie (23803) *(G-10060)*

A
L
P
H
A
B
E
T
I
C

Maxpci LLC 703 565-3400
  1107 Walker Dr Fredericksburg (22401) *(G-5203)*
Maxum Machine LLC 804 523-1490
  2809 Decatur St Richmond (23224) *(G-11674)*
Maxwell Incorporated 804 370-3697
  10997 Richardson Rd # 10 Ashland (23005) *(G-1460)*
Maxwell Welding, Ashland *Also called Maxwell Incorporated (G-1460)*
Maxx Material Systems LLC 757 637-4026
  315 E St Hampton (23661) *(G-6192)*
Maxx Performance Inc 845 987-9432
  3621 Aerial Way Dr Sw Roanoke (24018) *(G-11960)*
Maxxim Rebuild Co LLC (HQ) **276 679-7020**
  5703 Crutchfield Dr Norton (24273) *(G-10126)*
Maxxim Shared Services LLC 276 679-7020
  5703 Crutchfield Dr Norton (24273) *(G-10127)*
Mayes Wholesale Tack 276 755-3715
  86 Lacys Ln Cana (24317) *(G-2227)*
Mayo River Logging Co Inc 276 694-6305
  4949 Ayers Orchard Rd Stuart (24171) *(G-13624)*
Mays Auto Machine Shop Inc 276 646-3752
  714 Belle Hollow Rd Chilhowie (24319) *(G-3555)*
Maysteel Porters LLC 434 846-7412
  3726 Cohen Pl Lynchburg (24501) *(G-7769)*
Mazzella Jhh Company Inc 757 827-9600
  402 Aberdeen Rd Hampton (23661) *(G-6193)*
Mazzika LLC 757 489-0028
  4800 Colley Ave Ste D Norfolk (23508) *(G-9635)*
MB Services LLC 703 906-8625
  5236 Winter View Dr Alexandria (22312) *(G-524)*
MB Weld LLC 540 434-4042
  815 Grant St Harrisonburg (22802) *(G-6344)*
Mbda Incorporated (HQ) **703 387-7170**
  1300 Wilson Blvd Ste 550 Arlington (22209) *(G-1056)*
Mbda Incorporated 703 351-1230
  1300 Wilson Blvd Ste 550 Arlington (22209) *(G-1057)*
Mbh Inc 540 427-5471
  5623 Wild Oak Dr Roanoke (24014) *(G-12135)*
Mc Donald Sawmill, Strasburg *Also called McDonald Sawmill (G-13588)*
Mc Farlands Mill Inc 540 667-2272
  587 Round Hill Rd Winchester (22602) *(G-15444)*
Mc Promotions LLC 804 386-7073
  14419 Michaux Wood Way Midlothian (23113) *(G-8855)*
MCA Systems Inc 540 684-1617
  810 Caroline St Ste 202 Fredericksburg (22401) *(G-5204)*
McAfee LLC 571 449-4600
  11911 Freedom Dr Ste 400 Reston (20190) *(G-10896)*
McAirlaids Inc 540 352-5050
  180 Corporate Dr Rocky Mount (24151) *(G-12338)*
McAllister Mills Inc 276 773-3114
  173 Rainbow Cir Independence (24348) *(G-6989)*
McC Abatement LLC 804 731-4238
  7511 Troycott Rd North Chesterfield (23237) *(G-9927)*
McCabe Enterprises Inc 703 560-7755
  8451 Hilltop Rd Ste B Fairfax (22031) *(G-4504)*
McCabes Printing Group, Fairfax *Also called McCabe Enterprises Inc (G-4504)*
McClung Companies, The, Waynesboro *Also called McClung Printing Inc (G-15123)*
McClung Printing Inc (PA) **540 949-8139**
  550 N Commerce Ave Waynesboro (22980) *(G-15123)*
McClure Concrete 276 889-2289
  13761 U S Highway 19 Lebanon (24266) *(G-7200)*
McClure Concrete Materials LLC (PA) **276 964-9682**
  1201 Iron St Richlands (24641) *(G-11018)*
McClure Concrete Materials LLC 276 964-9682
  569 Happy Valley Dr Clintwood (24228) *(G-3690)*
McClure Concrete Materials LLC 276 679-3477
  465 Industrial Park Rd Norton (24273) *(G-10128)*
McClure Concrete Materials LLC 276 964-9682
  389 Frosty Rd Saint Paul (24283) *(G-12470)*
McClure Concrete Products Inc 276 889-3496
  Hwy Rte 19 Lebanon (24266) *(G-7201)*
McClure Concrete Products Inc (PA) **276 964-9682**
  1201 Iron St Richlands (24641) *(G-11019)*
McCormick & Company Inc 540 858-2878
  563 Fletcher Rd Gore (22637) *(G-5922)*
McCormick Jr Logging Inc Bd 434 238-3593
  424 Riverside Dr Gladstone (24553) *(G-5687)*
McCoy Water Filter Inc 804 222-2089
  8441 Varina Rd Henrico (23231) *(G-6534)*
McCraw Cabinets 434 238-2112
  1075 London Dr Forest (24551) *(G-5082)*
McCready Lumber Company Inc 540 980-8700
  4801 Wurno Rd Pulaski (24301) *(G-10643)*
McDonald Sawmill 540 465-5539
  578 Old Grade Rd Strasburg (22657) *(G-13588)*
McDonald Welding LLC Doug 804 928-6496
  720 W 25th St Richmond (23225) *(G-11675)*
McElroy Metal Mill Inc 757 485-3100
  3052 Yadkin Rd Chesapeake (23323) *(G-3200)*
McElroy Metal Mill Inc 540 667-2500
  325 Mcghee Rd Winchester (22603) *(G-15445)*

McElroy Metal Service Center, Chesapeake *Also called McElroy Metal Mill Inc (G-3200)*
McFarland Enterprises Inc 703 818-2900
  4515 Daly Dr Ste J Chantilly (20151) *(G-2461)*
McFarland Woodworks LLC 276 970-5847
  2011 Clear Fork Rd Tazewell (24651) *(G-13834)*
McGill Airflow LLC 804 965-5367
  700 Duncan St Ashland (23005) *(G-1461)*
McGuffie History Publications 540 371-3659
  207 Pitt St Fredericksburg (22401) *(G-5205)*
McHc, Chesapeake *Also called Mitsubshi Chem Hldngs Amer Inc (G-3209)*
McKean Defense Group LLC 540 413-1202
  17006 Dahlgren Rd King George (22485) *(G-7102)*
McKean Defense Group LLC 703 848-7928
  45240 Business Ct Ste 300 Sterling (20166) *(G-13450)*
McKean Defense Group LLC 202 448-5250
  477 Viking Dr Ste 400 Virginia Beach (23452) *(G-14643)*
McKean Defense Group Info Tech, Virginia Beach *Also called McKean Defense Group LLC (G-14643)*
McKee Brewer 276 579-2048
  469 Brewers Ln Independence (24348) *(G-6990)*
McKee Foods Corporation 540 943-7101
  272 Patton Farm Rd Stuarts Draft (24477) *(G-13655)*
McKeon Door of Dc Inc 301 807-1006
  2000 Duke St Ste 300 Alexandria (22314) *(G-272)*
McKeon Door of Virginia, Alexandria *Also called McKeon Door of Dc Inc (G-272)*
McKinnon and Harris Inc (PA) **804 358-2385**
  1722 Arlington Rd Richmond (23230) *(G-11286)*
McKoon Zaneta 410 707-5701
  2000 Green Tree Rd Fredericksburg (22406) *(G-5456)*
McLean Copy, Mc Lean *Also called Lehr Inc (G-8484)*
McMillan Welding Inc 276 728-1031
  802 Snake Creek Rd Hillsville (24343) *(G-6896)*
McMj Enterprises LLC 434 298-0117
  300 Church St Blackstone (23824) *(G-1820)*
McQ, Fredericksburg *Also called System Innovations Inc (G-5491)*
McQ Inc 540 361-4219
  1545 Forbes St Fredericksburg (22405) *(G-5457)*
McRae of America Inc 757 488-6900
  4416 Sunray Ave Chesapeake (23321) *(G-3201)*
McRae Storage Buildings, Chesapeake *Also called McRae of America Inc (G-3201)*
MCS Design & Production Inc 804 550-1000
  10980 Richardson Rd Ashland (23005) *(G-1462)*
Mdc Camden Clayworks 804 798-4971
  11467 New Farrington Ct Glen Allen (23059) *(G-5769)*
Mdj Logging Inc 276 889-4658
  5929 New Garden Rd Honaker (24260) *(G-6915)*
Mdr Performance Engines LLC 540 338-1001
  18896 Woodburn Rd Leesburg (20175) *(G-7310)*
ME Latimer Fabricator T A 757 566-8352
  2301 Little Creek Dam Rd Toano (23168) *(G-13869)*
Me-Shows LLC 855 637-4097
  7614 Baileys Rd Spotsylvania (22551) *(G-12904)*
Meadow Burke Products, Fredericksburg *Also called Merchants Metals LLC (G-5324)*
Meadows Welding 434 603-0000
  5755 Farmville Rd Farmville (23901) *(G-4950)*
Meadowsend Farm and Sawmill Co 434 975-6598
  325 Loftlands Farm Earlysville (22936) *(G-4291)*
Mealers Welding Repairs 251 363-4640
  2314 Wickham Rd Bumpass (23024) *(G-2166)*
Meany & Oliver Companies Inc 703 851-7131
  1110 N Glebe Rd Ste 590 Arlington (22201) *(G-1058)*
Measurement Specialties Inc (HQ) **757 766-1500**
  1000 Lucas Way Hampton (23666) *(G-6194)*
Meat & Wool New Zealand Ltd 703 927-4817
  1483 Chain Bridge Rd # 300 Mc Lean (22101) *(G-8497)*
Mech Warrior Industries LLC 703 670-5788
  16124 Henderson Ln Dumfries (22025) *(G-4252)*
Mechanical Designs of Virginia 276 694-7442
  25582 Jeb Stuart Hwy Stuart (24171) *(G-13625)*
Mechanical Development Co Inc 540 389-9395
  303 Apperson Dr Salem (24153) *(G-12535)*
Mechanical Machine & Repair 804 231-5866
  2100 Stockton St Richmond (23224) *(G-11676)*
Mechanical Technologies, Ashland *Also called Case-Polytech Inc (G-1386)*
Mechanicsville Metal Works Inc 804 266-5055
  8029 Industrial Park Rd Mechanicsville (23116) *(G-8657)*
Mechanicsville Pallets Inc 804 746-4658
  7494 Industrial Park Rd Mechanicsville (23116) *(G-8658)*
Mechanicsville United Futbol 804 647-6557
  2035 Retreat Dr Mechanicsville (23111) *(G-8659)*
Mechanx Corp 703 698-7680
  2858 Hartland Rd Falls Church (22043) *(G-4828)*
Mecklenburg Quarry, South Hill *Also called Legacy Vulcan LLC (G-12856)*
Mecmesin Corporation 703 433-9247
  45921 Maries Rd Ste 120 Sterling (20166) *(G-13451)*
Mects Services JV 248 499-9243
  3877 Fairfax Ridge Rd 350n Fairfax (22030) *(G-4652)*
Medeco, Salem *Also called Assa Abloy High SEC Group Inc (G-12476)*

Media Africa Inc 703 260-6494
30 Catoctin Cir Se Ste C Leesburg (20175) *(G-7311)*

Media General Operations Inc 434 985-2315
113 Main St Stanardsville (22973) *(G-13223)*

Media Magic LLC 757 893-0988
4544 Bob Jones Dr Virginia Beach (23462) *(G-14644)*

Media Press 703 241-9188
14101 Sullyfield Cir # 110 Chantilly (20151) *(G-2462)*

Media Relations 703 993-8780
4400 University Dr Fairfax (22030) *(G-4653)*

Media Services of Richmond 804 559-1000
7991 Ellerson Station Dr Mechanicsville (23111) *(G-8660)*

Media X Group LLC 866 966-9640
463 Dinwiddie Ave Waynesboro (22980) *(G-15124)*

Medias LLC 540 230-7023
4543 Pearman Rd Blacksburg (24060) *(G-1761)*

Mediasat International Inc 703 558-0309
4419 7th St N Arlington (22203) *(G-1059)*

Mediatech Inc (HQ) **703 471-5955**
9345 Discovery Blvd Manassas (20109) *(G-8106)*

Medical Action Industries Inc 757 566-3510
9000 Westmont Dr Toano (23168) *(G-13870)*

Medical Laboratory Solutions 414 425-8605
5635 Raby Rd Ste H Norfolk (23502) *(G-9636)*

Medical Sports Inc 703 241-9720
1812 N George Mason Dr Arlington (22205) *(G-1060)*

Medicap, Newport News *Also called Banvera LLC (G-9176)*

Medicor Technologies LLC 804 616-8895
2970 Palaver Blf Powhatan (23139) *(G-10558)*

Medipak, Winchester *Also called T W Enterprises Inc (G-15485)*

Medipak 540 667-0233
270 Tyson Dr 2 Winchester (22603) *(G-15446)*

Mediterranean Cellars LLC 540 428-1984
8295 Falcon Glen Rd Warrenton (20186) *(G-15034)*

Mediterranean Delight Inc. 703 751-2656
101 S Whiting St Ste 305 Alexandria (22304) *(G-273)*

Medlens Innovations LLC 540 636-7976
1325 Progress Dr Front Royal (22630) *(G-5542)*

Medliminal LLC (PA) **571 719-6837**
9385 Innovation Dr Manassas (20110) *(G-7974)*

Medmarc 703 652-1305
4000 Legato Rd Ste 800 Fairfax (22033) *(G-4505)*

Medtrnic Sofamor Danek USA Inc 757 355-5100
900 Mary Lou Ct Virginia Beach (23464) *(G-14645)*

Meesh Monograms 757 672-4276
1600 Stephens Rd Virginia Beach (23454) *(G-14646)*

Meetingsphere Inc 703 348-0725
440 Monticello Ave # 1875 Norfolk (23510) *(G-9637)*

Mefcor Incorporated 276 322-5021
33049 Gvrnor G C Pery Hwy North Tazewell (24630) *(G-10103)*

Mega-Tech Inc 703 534-1629
701 W Broad St Ste 411 Falls Church (22046) *(G-4922)*

Megaphone LLC (HQ) **703 594-7623**
1900 Reston Metro Plz # 3 Reston (20190) *(G-10897)*

Megawatt Apps LLC 703 870-4082
20445 Chesapeake Sq # 202 Sterling (20165) *(G-13452)*

Mehler Inc (HQ) **276 638-6166**
175 Mehler Ln Martinsville (24112) *(G-8311)*

Mehler Inc 276 638-6166
175 Mehler Ln Martinsville (24112) *(G-8312)*

Mehler Engineered Products, Martinsville *Also called Mehler Inc (G-8312)*

Mehler Engineered Products Inc. 276 638-6166
175 Mehler Ln Martinsville (24112) *(G-8313)*

Meissner Cstm Knives Pens LLC 321 693-2392
205 Ian Ct Hampton (23666) *(G-6195)*

Mekatronich Corp 954 499-5794
295 Industrial Dr Christiansburg (24073) *(G-3605)*

Mekelexx Management Services 561 644-8621
8649 Oak Chase Cir Fairfax Station (22039) *(G-4717)*

Melamedia LLC 703 704-5665
8315 Riverside Rd Alexandria (22308) *(G-525)*

Meld Manufacturing Corporation 540 951-3980
200 Technology Dr Christiansburg (24073) *(G-3606)*

Melissa Davis 757 482-3743
4313 Enterprise Blvd Virginia Beach (23453) *(G-14647)*

Melissa Moss 540 397-0408
5410 Orchard Hill Dr 2h Roanoke (24019) *(G-11961)*

Mella Weekly 757 436-2409
608 Helmsdale Way Chesapeake (23320) *(G-3202)*

Mellanox Federal Systems LLC 703 969-5735
575 Herndon Pkwy Ste 130 Herndon (20170) *(G-6745)*

Melnor Inc. 540 722-5600
109 Tyson Dr Winchester (22603) *(G-15447)*

Melos Manufacturing 434 401-9496
917 Old Trents Ferry Rd Lynchburg (24503) *(G-7770)*

Melrose Bison Farm 434 660-6036
830 Dry Fork Rd Gladys (24554) *(G-5695)*

Melted Element LLC 703 239-7847
6100 Lincolnia Rd Apt 302 Alexandria (22312) *(G-526)*

Meltingearth 703 395-5855
12644 Stoa Ct Herndon (20170) *(G-6746)*

Melvin Crutchfield 804 440-3547
3301 Clearview Dr North Chesterfield (23234) *(G-9928)*

Melvin Riley 240 381-6111
5829 Seminary Rd Falls Church (22041) *(G-4829)*

Melvins Machine & Welding 276 988-3822
159 Melvin Ln Tazewell (24651) *(G-13835)*

Melvins Machine and Die Inc 276 988-3822
197 Melvin Ln Tazewell (24651) *(G-13836)*

Memorial Welding LLC 703 369-2428
7804 Signal Hill Rd Manassas (20111) *(G-8107)*

Memoryblue 703 891-3840
7925 Jones Branch Dr # 4100 Mc Lean (22102) *(G-8498)*

Memteks-Usa Inc 434 973-9800
355 Mallard Ln Ste 200 Earlysville (22936) *(G-4292)*

Menasha Packaging Company LLC 540 546-1110
310 W Brooke Rd Winchester (22603) *(G-15448)*

Mendes Deli Inc 703 242-9463
320 Maple Ave E F Vienna (22180) *(G-14090)*

Mendez Custom Woodworking 540 621-3849
12531 Wilderness Park Dr Spotsylvania (22551) *(G-12905)*

Mendoza Services Inc 703 860-9600
11307 Sunset Hills Rd Reston (20190) *(G-10898)*

Ment Software Inc 540 382-4172
4981 Sidney Church Rd Riner (24149) *(G-11864)*

Mentoradvisor Inc. 571 435-7222
6588 Hickman Ter Alexandria (22315) *(G-527)*

Mercer Vault Co 540 371-3666
1100 Summit St Fredericksburg (22401) *(G-5206)*

Merchants Metals LLC 804 262-9783
2356 Lanier Rd Rockville (23146) *(G-12293)*

Merchants Metals LLC 877 518-7665
5115 Massaponax Church Rd Fredericksburg (22407) *(G-5324)*

Merciers Welding 540 635-4175
154 Easy Hollow Rd Front Royal (22630) *(G-5543)*

Merck & Co Inc. 540 447-0056
1308 Chatham Rd Waynesboro (22980) *(G-15125)*

Merck & Co Inc. 804 363-0876
5504 Millwheel Ln Richmond (23228) *(G-11287)*

Mercury Hour 434 237-4011
283 Gardenpark Ave Lynchburg (24502) *(G-7771)*

Mercury Learning and Info LLC (PA) **800 232-0223**
22883 Quicksilver Dr Dulles (20166) *(G-4209)*

Mercury Luggage Mfg Co 804 733-5222
1818 Dock St Petersburg (23803) *(G-10330)*

Mercury Paper 540 465-7700
495 Radio Station Rd Strasburg (22657) *(G-13589)*

Mercury Paper Inc (HQ) **540 465-7700**
495 Radio Station Rd Strasburg (22657) *(G-13590)*

Mercury Partners Usa LLC 757 652-7067
6404 Holly Bluff Dr Franktown (23354) *(G-5164)*

Mercury Solutions LLC 703 474-9456
19300 Creek Field Cir Leesburg (20176) *(G-7312)*

Mercury Systems Inc. 510 252-0870
3554 Chain Bridge Rd # 3 Fairfax (22030) *(G-4654)*

Mercury Systems Inc. 703 243-9538
1300 Wilson Blvd Ste 575 Arlington (22209) *(G-1061)*

Mercury USA, Franktown *Also called Mercury Partners Usa LLC (G-5164)*

merica Labz LLC 844 445-5335
22370 Davis Dr Ste 100 Sterling (20164) *(G-13453)*

Merica Tactical Industries LLC 804 516-0435
7099 Foxbernie Dr Mechanicsville (23111) *(G-8661)*

Meridian Imaging Solutions, Alexandria *Also called Konica Mnlta Bus Sltons USA In (G-508)*

Meridian Printing & Publishing 757 627-8712
1228 Ballentine Blvd Norfolk (23504) *(G-9638)*

Meridian Tech Systems Inc 301 606-6490
880 Harrison St Se # 260 Leesburg (20175) *(G-7313)*

Merit Medical Systems Inc. 804 416-1030
12701 N Kingston Ave Chester (23836) *(G-3433)*

Merit Medical Systems Inc. 804 416-1069
837 Liberty Way Chester (23836) *(G-3434)*

Meritful Inc. 703 651-6338
6272 Edsall Rd Apt 4 Alexandria (22312) *(G-528)*

Merlin Brougher 434 572-8750
1051 Fan Park Dr South Boston (24592) *(G-12782)*

Mermaid Vineyard & Winery LLC 757 233-4155
330 W 22nd St Ste 106 Norfolk (23517) *(G-9639)*

Merrifield Metals Inc 703 849-9100
2817 Dorr Ave Ste A Fairfax (22031) *(G-4506)*

Merrill Fine Arts Engrv Inc 703 339-3900
8270 Cinder Bed Rd Lorton (22079) *(G-7511)*

Merrill Press 571 257-6273
5901 Bing Ct Alexandria (22315) *(G-529)*

Merrill St Physcians Group Inc 804 441-1280
13307 Corapeake Ter Chesterfield (23838) *(G-3514)*

Merriman Publishing LLC 540 370-1852
29 Goldcup Dr Fredericksburg (22406) *(G-5458)*

Mersen USA Ptt Corp 540 389-7535
540 Branch Dr Salem (24153) *(G-12536)*

A
L
P
H
A
B
E
T
I
C

Meru Biotechnologies Inc 804 316-4466
800 E Leigh St Richmond (23219) ***(G-11677)***
Merwins Affordable Grinding 757 461-3405
5412 Pine Grove Ave Norfolk (23502) ***(G-9640)***
Mescher Manufacturing Co Inc 276 530-7856
24267 Riverside Dr Grundy (24614) ***(G-6037)***
Meso Scale Discoveries, Fairfax *Also called Meso Scale Discovery LLC* ***(G-4507)***
Meso Scale Discovery LLC 571 318-5521
4050 Legato Rd Fl 10 Fairfax (22033) ***(G-4507)***
Messer LLC 804 458-0928
221 Hopewell St Hopewell (23860) ***(G-6939)***
Messer LLC 540 774-1515
6561 Forest View Rd Roanoke (24018) ***(G-11962)***
Messer LLC 804 796-5050
921 Old Brmuda Hundred Rd Chester (23836) ***(G-3435)***
Messer LLC 540 886-1725
725 Opie St Staunton (24401) ***(G-13279)***
Met Machine Inc 540 864-6007
Hc 34 Box 352 New Castle (24127) ***(G-9122)***
Met of Hampton Roads Inc 757 249-7777
499 Muller Ln Newport News (23606) ***(G-9298)***
Metal Concepts, Norfolk *Also called TST Fabrications LLC* ***(G-9769)***
Metal Concepts, Norfolk *Also called TST Fabrications LLC* ***(G-9770)***
Metal Craft Brewing Co LLC (PA) **816 271-3211**
900 Oak Ave Waynesboro (22980) ***(G-15126)***
Metal Edge Co 800 862-2228
9401 Northeast Dr Fredericksburg (22408) ***(G-5325)***
Metal Magic 703 660-9180
6239 Shields Ave Alexandria (22303) ***(G-530)***
Metal Processing Inc 540 731-0008
6693 Viscoe Rd Radford (24141) ***(G-10724)***
Metal Products Specialist Inc 757 398-9214
420 Virginia Ave Portsmouth (23707) ***(G-10460)***
Metal Spray, Midlothian *Also called Integrated Global Services Inc* ***(G-8833)***
Metalist 540 793-0627
210 Updike Ln Roanoke (24019) ***(G-11963)***
Metallum 703 549-4551
105 N Union St Ste 201 Alexandria (22314) ***(G-274)***
Metallum3d LLC 434 409-2401
1525 Old Trail Dr Crozet (22932) ***(G-3843)***
Metals of Distinction Inc 757 727-0773
532 E Mercury Blvd Hampton (23663) ***(G-6196)***
Metalsa Structural Pdts Inc 540 966-5370
184 Vista Dr Roanoke (24019) ***(G-11964)***
Metalsa-Roanoke Inc 540 966-5300
184 Vista Dr Roanoke (24019) ***(G-11965)***
Metalspray International Inc 804 794-1646
2725 Oak Lake Blvd Midlothian (23112) ***(G-8856)***
Metalspray United Inc (PA) **804 794-1646**
2725 Oak Lake Blvd Midlothian (23112) ***(G-8857)***
Metalstar Services LLC 434 591-0400
379 Pine Forest Ln Troy (22974) ***(G-13935)***
Metawear LLC 561 302-2010
3580 Jermantown Rd Fairfax (22030) ***(G-4655)***
Metfab International Inc 540 943-3732
800 Ivy St Waynesboro (22980) ***(G-15127)***
Method Innovation Corporation 703 266-1115
13129 Twin Lakes Dr Clifton (20124) ***(G-3674)***
Method Wood Working 804 332-3715
3410 W Leigh St Richmond (23230) ***(G-11288)***
Methodhead Software LLC 703 338-1588
4881 Old Well Rd Annandale (22003) ***(G-773)***
Metis Machine LLC 434 483-5692
103 W Main St Charlottesville (22902) ***(G-2833)***
Metocean Telematics Inc 902 468-2505
1750 Tysons Blvd Ste 1500 Mc Lean (22102) ***(G-8499)***
Metrie Inc 804 876-3588
10134 Kings Dominion Blvd Doswell (23047) ***(G-4123)***
Metro Copier and Printer Svcs, Falls Church *Also called Melvin Riley* ***(G-4829)***
Metro Envelope, Springfield *Also called Diana Khoury & Co* ***(G-12991)***
Metro Herald, The, Alexandria *Also called Davis Communications Group* ***(G-185)***
Metro Machine Corp 757 397-1039
2 Harper Rd Portsmouth (23707) ***(G-10461)***
Metro Machine Corp (HQ) **757 543-6801**
200 Ligon St Norfolk (23523) ***(G-9641)***
Metro Machine Corp 757 392-3703
3132 Victory Blvd Portsmouth (23702) ***(G-10462)***
Metro Media One, Arlington *Also called Harari Investments* ***(G-988)***
Metro Power Print 703 221-3289
16909 Cass Brook Ln Woodbridge (22191) ***(G-15744)***
Metro Printing Center Inc 703 620-3532
11870 Snrise Valy Dr Ste Reston (20191) ***(G-10899)***
Metro Sign & Design Inc 703 631-1866
8197 Euclid Ct Manassas Park (20111) ***(G-8205)***
Metro Signs & Graphics Inc 804 747-1918
3807 Alston Ln Richmond (23294) ***(G-11289)***
Metro Technology Llc 703 579-7771
8727 Evangel Dr Springfield (22153) ***(G-13048)***
Metro Water Purification LLC 804 366-2158
12508 Lewis Rd Chester (23831) ***(G-3436)***
Metro Wood Works Inc 757 479-1100
3272 Cookes Mill Rd Chesapeake (23323) ***(G-3203)***
Metromont Corporation 804 222-6770
1650 Darbytown Rd Richmond (23231) ***(G-11290)***
Metropole Products Inc 540 659-2132
2040 Jefferson Davis Hwy Stafford (22554) ***(G-13176)***
Metropolitan Accounting & Book 703 250-5014
10201 Scrbrugh Commons Ct Burke (22015) ***(G-2193)***
Metropolitan Equipment Group 804 744-4774
611 Moorefield Park Dr A North Chesterfield (23236) ***(G-9929)***
Metropolitan General Contrs 703 532-1606
3454 Quaker Ct Falls Church (22042) ***(G-4830)***
Mettler-Toledo LLC 540 665-9495
112 Bruce Dr Winchester (22601) ***(G-15554)***
Metwood Inc (PA) **540 334-4294**
819 Naff Rd Boones Mill (24065) ***(G-1897)***
Mevatec Corp 703 583-9287
4606 Moss Point Pl Woodbridge (22192) ***(G-15745)***
Mevatec Corp 631 261-7000
7705 Middle Valley Dr Springfield (22153) ***(G-13049)***
Meyer and Meyer Industries Inc 757 564-6157
5103 Salisbury Mews Williamsburg (23188) ***(G-15276)***
Mezeh - Fair Oaks LLC 703 310-9209
11946l Fair Oaks Mall Fairfax (22033) ***(G-4508)***
Mezeh-Reston LLC 703 310-9209
12120 Sunset Hills Rd # 1 Reston (20190) ***(G-10900)***
Mf Capital LLC 703 470-8787
13595 Castlebridge Ln Woodbridge (22193) ***(G-15746)***
MF&b Mayport Joint Venture 757 222-4855
813 Industrial Ave Chesapeake (23324) ***(G-3204)***
Mfgs Inc 844 267-9266
1430 Spring Hill Rd # 401 Mc Lean (22102) ***(G-8500)***
Mfri Inc 540 667-7022
400 Battaile Dr Winchester (22601) ***(G-15555)***
Mg Corp 757 468-6000
889 Seahawk Cir Virginia Beach (23452) ***(G-14648)***
Mg Enterprise LLC 703 646-2761
4927 Gainsborough Dr Fairfax (22032) ***(G-4509)***
Mg Industries 804 743-0661
5901 Jefferson Davis Hwy North Chesterfield (23234) ***(G-9930)***
Mgc Advanced Polymers Inc 804 520-7800
1100 Port Walthall Dr South Chesterfield (23834) ***(G-12815)***
Mgi Fuel Express LLC 804 541-0299
5002 Oaklawn Blvd North Prince George (23860) ***(G-10089)***
Mgke Construction LLC 571 282-8415
7523 Alleghany Rd Manassas (20111) ***(G-8108)***
Mhi Holdings LLC 757 545-6400
543 E Indian River Rd Norfolk (23523) ***(G-9642)***
Mhi Ship Repair & Services, Norfolk *Also called Marine Hydraulics Intl LLC* ***(G-9632)***
Miata Realm LLC 724 612-1029
9804 Laurel St Fairfax (22032) ***(G-4510)***
MIC Industries Inc 540 678-2900
4150 Martinsburg Pike Clear Brook (22624) ***(G-3647)***
MIC Industries Inc (PA) **703 318-1900**
4150 Martinsburg Pike Clear Brook (22624) ***(G-3648)***
Mica Co of Canada Inc 757 244-7311
900 Jefferson Ave Newport News (23607) ***(G-9299)***
Michael A Latham 804 835-3299
16462 Jefferson Davis Hwy South Chesterfield (23834) ***(G-12816)***
Michael and Thomas Contg LLC 919 397-7960
15231 Colony Pl Apt 311 Woodbridge (22191) ***(G-15747)***
Michael Beach 703 360-7284
8403 Richmond Hwy Ste D Alexandria (22309) ***(G-531)***
Michael Burnette 757 478-8585
1406 Riversedge Rd Newport News (23606) ***(G-9300)***
Michael Chung MD 443 722-5314
7535 Little River Tpke B Annandale (22003) ***(G-774)***
Michael Fleming 276 337-9202
9808b Coeburn Mountain Rd Wise (24293) ***(G-15632)***
Michael Holt Inc 703 597-6999
2030 N Adams St Apt 807 Arlington (22201) ***(G-1062)***
Michael Kors 757 216-0581
701 Lynnhaven Pkwy # 1088 Virginia Beach (23452) ***(G-14649)***
Michael McKittrick 804 695-7090
358 Woods Creek Rd Deltaville (23043) ***(G-4083)***
Michael Neely 540 972-3265
225 Washington St Locust Grove (22508) ***(G-7448)***
Michael R Little 540 489-4785
316 Windy Pines Ln Rocky Mount (24151) ***(G-12339)***
Michael Reiss LLC 757 826-4277
8 Templewood Dr Hampton (23666) ***(G-6197)***
Michael S Bond 740 971-9157
5850 Cameron Run Ter Alexandria (22303) ***(G-532)***
Michael Sanders 276 452-2314
6841 Veterans Mem Hwy Fort Blackmore (24250) ***(G-5123)***
Michael Shaps Winery Managemen (PA) **434 242-4559**
1781 Harris Creek Way Charlottesville (22902) ***(G-2834)***
Michael W Gillespie 540 894-0288
4583 E Old Mountain Rd Louisa (23093) ***(G-7560)***

Michael W Tuck 540 297-1231
1554 Headens Bridge Rd Bedford (24523) *(G-1644)*

Michael Wheeler, Orange *Also called Wheeler Tember (G-10231)*

Michaels Catering 804 815-6985
6450 Hickory Fork Rd Hayes (23072) *(G-6401)*

Michaels Welding 434 238-5302
5268 Wards Rd Evington (24550) *(G-4379)*

Michelle Erickson Pottery 757 727-9139
18 N Mallory St Hampton (23663) *(G-6198)*

Michie Software Systems Inc 757 868-7771
131 River Point Dr Yorktown (23693) *(G-15982)*

Mickey Norris Logging 276 206-3959
630 Highwood Ln Marion (24354) *(G-8236)*

Micro Analytics of Virginia (PA) **703 536-6424**
925 Patrick Henry Dr Arlington (22205) *(G-1063)*

Micro Focus Software Inc 703 663-5500
8609 Westwood Center Dr # 500 Vienna (22182) *(G-14091)*

Micro Media Communication Inc 540 345-2197
378 Allison Ave Sw Roanoke (24016) *(G-12136)*

Micro Services Company 804 741-5000
8545 Patterson Ave # 206 Richmond (23229) *(G-11291)*

Micro Tech Industries Inc 703 674-9647
709 Vermillion Dr Ne Leesburg (20176) *(G-7314)*

Microaire Surgical Instrs LLC 434 975-8300
2400 Austin Dr Charlottesville (22911) *(G-2658)*

Microaire Surgical Instrs LLC (HQ) **800 722-0822**
3590 Grand Forks Blvd Charlottesville (22911) *(G-2659)*

Microbanx Systems LLC 703 757-1760
10135 Colvin Run Rd # 101 Great Falls (22066) *(G-5966)*

Microfab LLC 276 620-7200
5156 E Lee Hwy Max Meadows (24360) *(G-8369)*

Micron Bio-Systems Inc 540 261-2468
2329 Old Buena Vista Rd Buena Vista (24416) *(G-2147)*

Micron Manufacturing 703 853-1801
2983 Prosperity Ave Fairfax (22031) *(G-4511)*

Micron Technology Inc 703 396-1000
9600 Godwin Dr Manassas (20110) *(G-7975)*

Micronergy LLC 757 325-6973
1100 Exploration Way Hampton (23666) *(G-6199)*

Microscope.com, Roanoke *Also called M5 Technologies LLC (G-12131)*

Microsoft Corporation 434 738-0103
101 Herbert Dr Boydton (23917) *(G-1916)*

Microsoft Corporation 703 236-9140
1100 S Hayes St Unit G04a Arlington (22202) *(G-1064)*

Microsoft Corporation 571 222-8110
8217 Linton Hall Rd Bristow (20136) *(G-2060)*

Microsoft Corporation 703 673-7600
12012 Sunset Hills Rd Reston (20190) *(G-10901)*

Microsoft Corporation 804 270-0146
4301 Dominion Blvd # 200 Glen Allen (23060) *(G-5770)*

Microstrategy Services Corp 703 848-8600
1850 Towers Crescent Plz # 700 Tysons Corner (22182) *(G-13955)*

Microtek Medical Inc 703 904-1220
101 International Dr Sterling (20166) *(G-13454)*

Microtude LLC 703 581-7991
21673 Liverpool St Ashburn (20147) *(G-1317)*

Microwave Circuits Inc 434 455-2800
1611 Kemper St Lynchburg (24501) *(G-7772)*

Microxact Inc 540 394-4040
6580 Valley Center Dr # 312 Radford (24141) *(G-10725)*

Mid Atlantic Foam, Fredericksburg *Also called Cellofoam North America Inc (G-5259)*

Mid Atlantic Imaging Centers 757 223-5059
750 Mcguire Pl Ste A Newport News (23601) *(G-9301)*

Mid Atlantic Mining LLC 757 407-6735
1129 Woods Pkwy Suffolk (23434) *(G-13742)*

Mid Atlantic Solid Surface 540 972-3050
124 Republic Ave Locust Grove (22508) *(G-7449)*

Mid Atlantic Welding Tech (PA) **804 330-8191**
3018 W Martins Grant Cir Richmond (23235) *(G-11050)*

Mid Atlantic Wood Works LLC 703 281-4376
10133 Palmer Dr Oakton (22124) *(G-10158)*

Mid Atlntic Mtal Solutions Inc 757 827-1588
502 Copeland Dr Hampton (23661) *(G-6200)*

Mid Atlntic Tree Hrvestors Inc 804 769-8826
100 Globe Rd Aylett (23009) *(G-1550)*

Mid Valley Machine & Tool Inc 540 885-6379
10 Van Fossen Ln Staunton (24401) *(G-13280)*

Mid Valley Press, Verona *Also called Schreiber Inc R G (G-13995)*

Mid Valley Products 757 625-0780
902 Cooke Ave Norfolk (23504) *(G-9643)*

Mid-Atlantic Backhoe Inc 804 897-3443
2131 Swamp Fox Rd Midlothian (23112) *(G-8858)*

Mid-Atlantic Bracing Corp 757 301-3952
2917 Chilton Pl Virginia Beach (23456) *(G-14650)*

Mid-Atlantic Energy LLC 804 213-2500
812 Moorefield Park Dr # 310 North Chesterfield (23236) *(G-9931)*

Mid-Atlantic Manufacturing Inc 804 798-7462
2559 Turkey Creek Rd Oilville (23129) *(G-10183)*

Mid-Atlantic Printers Ltd (PA) **434 369-6633**
503 3rd St Altavista (24517) *(G-636)*

Mid-Atlantic Printers Ltd 703 448-1155
8290 Old Courthouse Rd C Vienna (22182) *(G-14092)*

Mid-Atlantic Publishing Co 703 866-5156
8136 Old Keene Mill Rd A302 Springfield (22152) *(G-13050)*

Mid-Atlantic Rubber Inc 540 710-5690
10707 Stoner Dr Fredericksburg (22408) *(G-5326)*

Middleburg Printers LLC 540 687-5710
5 E Federal St Middleburg (20118) *(G-8729)*

Middleburg Tack Exchange Ltd 540 687-6608
103 W Federal St Middleburg (20117) *(G-8730)*

Middlesex Cabinet Co 804 758-3617
382 Urbanna Rd Saluda (23149) *(G-12605)*

Midlothian Custom Workshop LLC 804 937-1184
14208 Aldengate Rd Midlothian (23114) *(G-8859)*

Midlothian Quarry, Midlothian *Also called Martin Marietta Materials Inc (G-8853)*

Midnight Embroidery 757 463-1692
3725 Harton Ct Virginia Beach (23452) *(G-14651)*

Midway Coatings Service, Franklin *Also called Stephen C Marston (G-5157)*

Midway Telemetry 276 378-5933
122 S Fork Rd Marion (24354) *(G-8237)*

Midway Telemetry 276 227-0270
906 Cinnamon Run Wytheville (24382) *(G-15900)*

Midwesco Filter Resources, Winchester *Also called Mfri Inc (G-15555)*

Midyette Bros Mfg Inc 757 425-5022
1702 Southern Blvd Virginia Beach (23454) *(G-14652)*

Mielata LLC 804 245-1227
12910 Grove Hill Rd # 203 Midlothian (23114) *(G-8860)*

Mighty, Roanoke *Also called John W Griessmayer Jr (G-12113)*

Mighty Mann Inc 757 945-8056
406 Aberdeen Rd Ste B Hampton (23661) *(G-6201)*

Mighty Meals LLC 703 303-1438
5795 Burke Centre Pkwy Burke (22015) *(G-2194)*

Mighty Oak Enterprises Inc (PA) **757 422-6353**
1 Bush Garden Blvd Williamsburg (23185) *(G-15277)*

Mighty Oak Industries 434 426-7249
201 Locksley Pl Forest (24551) *(G-5083)*

Mighty Oaks Tree Triming & Log 585 471-0213
507 Cornerstone St Lynchburg (24502) *(G-7773)*

Miglas Loupes LLC 815 721-9133
2360 Roosevelt Blvd Apt 2 Winchester (22601) *(G-15556)*

Miguel and Valentino, Springfield *Also called Scout Marketing LLC (G-13081)*

Miguel Soto 571 274-3790
195 Alpine Dr Se Leesburg (20175) *(G-7315)*

Miguel's Snow Removal, Leesburg *Also called Miguel Soto (G-7315)*

Mik Woodworking Inc 540 878-1197
341 Sheridan Ave Winchester (22601) *(G-15557)*

Mike Gibson & Sons Logging 804 769-3510
847 Shilo Rd King Queen Ch (23085) *(G-7127)*

Mike Puffendarger 540 468-2682
7738 Big Valley Rd Warm Springs (24484) *(G-14973)*

Mikes Marine Custom Canvas 757 496-1090
2244 Red Tide Rd Virginia Beach (23451) *(G-14653)*

Mikes Mobile Canvas 804 815-2733
4719 Pampa Rd Gloucester (23061) *(G-5854)*

Mikes Mobile Marine, Deltaville *Also called Michael McKittrick (G-4083)*

Mikes Screen Printing 276 971-9274
405 Cedar Creek Dr Pounding Mill (24637) *(G-10524)*

Mikes Signs4less 540 548-2940
6010 Plank Rd Fredericksburg (22407) *(G-5327)*

Mikes Wrecker Service & Bdy Sp 540 996-4152
21793 Mountain Valley Rd Millboro (24460) *(G-8937)*

Mikro Systems Inc 434 244-6480
1180 Seminole Trl Ste 220 Charlottesville (22901) *(G-2660)*

Mikrocoze Inc 800 542-8715
1545 Crossways Blvd # 25 Chesapeake (23320) *(G-3205)*

Mil-Sat Global Communication, Surry *Also called Mil-Sat LLC (G-13798)*

Mil-Sat LLC (PA) **757 294-9393**
318 Bank St Surry (23883) *(G-13798)*

Mil-Space LLC 954 862-3613
318 Bank St Surry (23883) *(G-13799)*

Mil-Spec Abrasives LLC 757 927-6699
3306 Peterson St Norfolk (23509) *(G-9644)*

Milcom Systems Corporation Vol 757 463-2800
532 Viking Dr Virginia Beach (23452) *(G-14654)*

Mildef Inc 703 224-8835
2800 Eisenhower Ave # 220 Alexandria (22314) *(G-275)*

Milestone Software Inc 703 217-4262
9532 Liberia Ave Ste 722 Manassas (20110) *(G-7976)*

Milgard Manufacturing Inc 540 834-0340
2000 Intl Pkwy Ste 101 Fredericksburg (22408) *(G-5328)*

Milgard Windows, Fredericksburg *Also called Milgard Manufacturing Inc (G-5328)*

Milhous Company, Amherst *Also called Milhous Control Company (G-700)*

Milhous Control Company 434 946-5302
144 S Main St Amherst (24521) *(G-700)*

Military Newspapers of VA, Colonial Heights *Also called Program Services LLC (G-3742)*

Mill Cabinet Shop Inc 540 828-6763
3889 Dry River Rd Bridgewater (22812) *(G-1954)*

Mill Creek Press LLC 703 638-8395
1311 Kenwood Ave Alexandria (22302) *(G-276)*

A
L
P
H
A
B
E
T
I
C

Mill Mountain Capital LLC..540 529-7163
6536 Commonwealth Dr Roanoke (24018) *(G-11966)*

Mill Mountain Coffee & Tea, Blacksburg *Also called Johnson & Elich Roasters Ltd* *(G-1747)*

Mill Road Logging LLC..434 665-7467
1635 Bethany Rd Rustburg (24588) *(G-12442)*

Mill Run Specialties..703 759-3480
9830 Mill Run Dr Great Falls (22066) *(G-5967)*

Millcraft LLC..703 225-9860
14000 Thunderbolt Pl F Chantilly (20151) *(G-2463)*

Millcraft LLC..703 775-2030
6304b Gravel Ave Alexandria (22310) *(G-533)*

Millcreek Wood Works...804 642-4792
9969 Bonniville Rd Hayes (23072) *(G-6402)*

Millcroft Farms Co Inc...540 778-3369
140 Fox Dr Stanley (22851) *(G-13234)*

Millehan Enterprises Inc...540 772-3037
4319 Fox Croft Cir Roanoke (24018) *(G-11967)*

Millennium Services Inc...804 733-8505
1520 Fine St Prince George (23875) *(G-10601)*

Millennium Sftwr Cnsulting LLC..............................434 245-0741
2114 Angus Rd Ste 221 Charlottesville (22901) *(G-2661)*

Miller Cabinets Inc...540 434-4835
1910 S High St Harrisonburg (22801) *(G-6345)*

Miller Creative Solutions LLC.................................202 560-3718
6182a Arlington Blvd Falls Church (22044) *(G-4831)*

Miller Group , The, Richmond *Also called Miller Manufacturing Co Inc* *(G-11051)*

Miller Kite House..540 298-5390
310 E Rockingham St Elkton (22827) *(G-4333)*

Miller Machine & Tool Company..............................540 662-6512
201 Precision Dr Winchester (22603) *(G-15449)*

Miller Manufacturing Co Inc (PA).......................**804 232-4551**
3301 Castlewood Rd Richmond (23234) *(G-11051)*

Miller Mental Fabricators, Staunton *Also called Miller Metal Fabricators Inc* *(G-13281)*

Miller Metal Fabricators Inc....................................540 886-5575
345 National Ave Staunton (24401) *(G-13281)*

Miller Milling Company LLC....................................540 678-0197
302 Park Center Dr Winchester (22603) *(G-15450)*

Miller Publishing..804 901-2315
1901 Repp St Highland Springs (23075) *(G-6854)*

Miller Quality Woodwork Inc...................................757 564-7847
102 Rondane Pl Williamsburg (23188) *(G-15278)*

Miller Roll Grinding & Mfg.....................................804 559-5745
8150 Elm Dr Mechanicsville (23111) *(G-8662)*

Miller Waste Mills Inc..434 572-3925
1150 Greens Folly Rd South Boston (24592) *(G-12783)*

Millers Custom Metal Svcs LLC..............................804 712-2588
154 Hunton Creek Ln Deltaville (23043) *(G-4084)*

Millers Furs LLC..703 772-4593
7921 Jones Branch Dr Ll2 Mc Lean (22102) *(G-8501)*

Millie B Thompson..276 475-5940
23047 Bluff Hollow Rd Damascus (24236) *(G-3949)*

Milliken & Company...571 659-0698
3915 Triad Ct Woodbridge (22192) *(G-15748)*

Mills Marine & Ship Repair LLC..............................757 539-0956
211 Market St Suffolk (23434) *(G-13743)*

Mills Marine & Ship Repair LLC..............................757 539-0956
211 Market St Suffolk (23434) *(G-13744)*

Millstreet Software...703 281-1015
411 Mill St Se Vienna (22180) *(G-14093)*

Millwork, Manassas *Also called ART&creation Inc* *(G-7913)*

Millwork Supply Inc (PA)....................................**540 552-0201**
3120 Commerce St Blacksburg (24060) *(G-1762)*

Milnesville Enterprises LLC....................................540 487-4073
1654 Ridge Rd Bridgewater (22812) *(G-1955)*

Mimetrix Technologies LLC....................................571 306-1234
10212 Brittenford Dr Vienna (22182) *(G-14094)*

Mind Attuned, North Chesterfield *Also called Brain Based Learning Inc* *(G-9834)*

MIND Pharmaceutical Inc.......................................434 202-9617
480 Ray C Hunt Dr Rm 282 Charlottesville (22903) *(G-2835)*

Mindful Barber LLC...757 714-6445
1811 W Broad St Richmond (23220) *(G-11678)*

Mindful Media LLC..757 627-5151
914 Gates Ave Norfolk (23517) *(G-9645)*

Mindmettle..540 890-5563
801 Brookshire Dr Vinton (24179) *(G-14179)*

Mined Land Reclamation Div, Big Stone Gap *Also called Mines Minerals & Enrgy VA Dept* *(G-1713)*

Minequest Inc...276 963-6463
421 Honeyrock Rd Cedar Bluff (24609) *(G-2282)*

Mineral Gap, Ashburn *Also called DP Facilities Inc* *(G-1272)*

Miners Oil Company Inc...804 230-5769
3737 Belt Blvd Richmond (23234) *(G-11052)*

Mines Minerals & Enrgy VA Dept...........................276 523-8100
3405 Mountain Empire Rd Big Stone Gap (24219) *(G-1713)*

Minglewood Trading..804 245-6162
2604 Teaberry Dr North Chesterfield (23236) *(G-9932)*

Minnie ME Monograms..423 331-1686
506 Aguila Ct Chesapeake (23322) *(G-3206)*

Mint Springs Design...434 806-7303
2069 Seal Rdg Crozet (22932) *(G-3844)*

Mintel Group Ltd..540 989-3945
6348 Spring Run Dr Roanoke (24018) *(G-11968)*

Mintmesh Inc...703 222-0322
4012 Timber Oak Trl Fairfax (22033) *(G-4512)*

Minute Man Farms Inc...540 423-1028
18262 Alvere Rd Culpeper (22701) *(G-3909)*

Minute Man Press...757 464-6509
2961 Heutte Dr Norfolk (23518) *(G-9646)*

Minuteman Press, Fredericksburg *Also called Walton Industries Inc* *(G-5389)*

Minuteman Press, Alexandria *Also called R & B Impressions Inc* *(G-323)*

MINUTEMAN PRESS, Manassas *Also called Roxen Incorporated* *(G-7997)*

Minuteman Press, Norfolk *Also called 10 10 LLC* *(G-9410)*

Minuteman Press, Ashland *Also called Printpros LLC* *(G-1480)*

Minuteman Press, Arlington *Also called Gary D Keys Enterprises Inc* *(G-975)*

Minuteman Press, Glen Allen *Also called R B M Enterprises Inc* *(G-5786)*

Minuteman Press, Staunton *Also called Flynn Incorporated* *(G-13261)*

Minuteman Press, Arlington *Also called K & W Printing Services Inc* *(G-1019)*

Minuteman Press, Virginia Beach *Also called Tidewater Graphics Inc* *(G-14874)*

Minuteman Press, Ashland *Also called Niblick Inc* *(G-1470)*

Minuteman Press, Arlington *Also called Rowley Group Inc* *(G-1153)*

Minuteman Press..757 903-0978
4655 Monticello Ave # 106 Williamsburg (23188) *(G-15279)*

Minuteman Press..703 439-2160
319 Sunset Park Dr Herndon (20170) *(G-6747)*

Minuteman Press..703 220-7575
2 Walton Way Fredericksburg (22405) *(G-5459)*

Minuteman Press..540 774-1820
625 Florida St Salem (24153) *(G-12537)*

Minuteman Press..804 441-9761
1720 E Parham Rd Richmond (23228) *(G-11292)*

Minuteman Press Intl...703 299-1150
1429 Duke St Alexandria (22314) *(G-277)*

Minuteman Press Intl Inc..703 522-1944
4001 9th St N Ste 102 Arlington (22203) *(G-1065)*

Minuteman Press Intl Inc..703 787-6506
11317 Sunset Hills Rd Reston (20190) *(G-10902)*

Minuteman Press of Chester...................................804 898-0050
4100 W Hundred Rd Chester (23831) *(G-3437)*

Minuteman Press of Mc Lean..................................703 356-6612
6821 Tennyson Dr Mc Lean (22101) *(G-8502)*

Minuteman Press of Vienna....................................703 992-0420
1880 Howard Ave Ste 101 Vienna (22182) *(G-14095)*

Miracle Prints & More...540 656-9645
1205 Graham Dr Fredericksburg (22401) *(G-5207)*

Miracle Systems LLC...571 431-6397
1621 N Kent St Ste 1000 Arlington (22209) *(G-1066)*

Miranda Publishing Compan...................................703 207-9499
7627 Trail Run Rd Falls Church (22042) *(G-4832)*

Mirror Morning Music..703 405-8181
314 Charles St Se Vienna (22180) *(G-14096)*

Miscellaneous & Orna Mtls Inc...............................757 650-5226
2961 Shore Dr Virginia Beach (23451) *(G-14655)*

Miscellaneous Concrete Pdts, Roanoke *Also called Action Resources Corporation* *(G-12028)*

Misra Publishing LLC...703 821-2985
1258 Beverly Rd Mc Lean (22101) *(G-8503)*

Miss Lizzies Loot..804 484-4212
9941 Maplested Ln Richmond (23235) *(G-11053)*

Missile Baits LLC..855 466-5738
170 Turner Rd Salem (24153) *(G-12538)*

Missing Lynk Publishing LLC...................................757 851-1766
621 Houston Ave Hampton (23669) *(G-6202)*

Mission Data LLC..513 298-1865
7875 Promontory Ct Dunn Loring (22027) *(G-4265)*

Mission Home Bake Shop, Free Union *Also called Faith Mission Home* *(G-5506)*

Mission Integrated Tech LLC...................................202 769-9900
1934 Old Gallows Rd Vienna (22182) *(G-14097)*

Mission It LLC..443 534-0130
23554 Epperson Sq Brambleton (20148) *(G-1930)*

Mission Realty Group..804 545-6651
7204 Glen Forest Dr # 206 Richmond (23226) *(G-11293)*

Mission Secure Inc..434 284-8071
300 Preston Ave Ste 500 Charlottesville (22902) *(G-2836)*

Mission Systems, Virginia Beach *Also called Northrop Grumman Systems Corp* *(G-14685)*

Missionteq LLC...703 563-0699
25834 Kirkwood Sq Chantilly (20152) *(G-2545)*

Misty Mtn Spring Wtr Co LLC................................276 623-5000
26331 Hillman Hwy Abingdon (24210) *(G-50)*

Mitchell Lock Out...276 322-4087
133 Hicks St Bluefield (24605) *(G-1870)*

Mitchell Medical LLC...804 640-4851
16060 Saint Peters Ch Rd Montpelier (23192) *(G-9018)*

Mitchell Sawmilling...276 944-2329
7009 Clinch Mountain Rd Saltville (24370) *(G-12586)*

Mitchell's Armory, Fredericksburg *Also called Matthew Mitchell* *(G-5455)*

Mitchells Woodwork Inc...757 340-4154
596 Central Dr Ste 107 Virginia Beach (23454) *(G-14656)*

Miti-Gait LLC 434 738-8632
211 Virginia Ave Clarksville (23927) *(G-3634)*
Mitsubishi Chem Advanced Mtls 276 228-0100
2530 N 4th St Wytheville (24382) *(G-15901)*
Mitsubishi Chemical Amer Inc 757 382-5750
401 Volvo Pkwy Chesapeake (23320) *(G-3207)*
Mitsubishi Chemical Composites 757 548-7850
401 Volvo Pkwy Chesapeake (23320) *(G-3208)*
Mitsubshi Chem Hldngs Amer Inc 757 382-5750
401 Volvo Pkwy Chesapeake (23320) *(G-3209)*
Mix It Up LLC 540 434-9868
64 Maplehurst Ave Harrisonburg (22801) *(G-6346)*
Mix It Up Mixers and More LLC 757 412-1200
2973 Shore Dr Virginia Beach (23451) *(G-14657)*
Mj Distribution 540 692-0062
315 Poe Dr Front Royal (22630) *(G-5544)*
Mj-Squared, Hampton *Also called Trotter Jamil (G-6253)*
Mjs Woodworking LLC 571 233-4991
7083 Helm Dr Remington (22734) *(G-10769)*
Mk Environmental LLC 540 435-9066
4121 Traveler Rd Rockingham (22801) *(G-12262)*
MK Industries Inc 757 245-0007
6060 Jefferson Ave Ll16 Newport News (23605) *(G-9302)*
Mk Industries LLC 949 525-0778
7501 Irene Ct Springfield (22153) *(G-13051)*
Mk Interiors Inc 804 288-2819
6011 W Broad St Richmond (23230) *(G-11294)*
Mkm Coatings LLC 804 514-3506
9127 Sycamore Hill Pl Mechanicsville (23116) *(G-8663)*
Mkp Products LLC 703 345-0595
8572 Springfield Oaks Dr Springfield (22153) *(G-13052)*
Mkrs Corporation 203 349-1149
11905 Crayton Ct Herndon (20170) *(G-6748)*
ML Manufacturing 434 581-2000
521 Social Hall Rd New Canton (23123) *(G-9118)*
Mld Publishing 434 535-6008
1504 Longview Rd Apt 200 Lynchburg (24501) *(G-7774)*
MLS Logging LLC 540 223-0394
11423 Westwind Dr Orange (22960) *(G-10220)*
Mm Export LLC 757 333-0542
4940 Rutherford Rd # 400 Virginia Beach (23455) *(G-14658)*
Mng Online LLC 571 247-8276
8105 Porter Ridge Ln # 9 Manassas (20109) *(G-8109)*
Mo Cakes 804 349-8634
3201 Lavecchia Way Glen Allen (23059) *(G-5771)*
Moaz Marwa 571 225-4743
5741 Leverett Ct Apt 373 Alexandria (22311) *(G-278)*
Mobil Petrochemical Holdings 703 846-3000
3225 Gallows Rd Fairfax (22037) *(G-4513)*
Mobile App Builder, Norfolk *Also called Loyalty Doctors LLC (G-9623)*
Mobile Custom Framing LLC 757 412-4167
2628 Landview Cir Virginia Beach (23454) *(G-14659)*
Mobile Customs LLC 757 903-5092
11850 Livingston Rd # 105 Manassas (20109) *(G-8110)*
Mobile Ink LLC 804 218-8384
12760 Forest Mill Dr Midlothian (23112) *(G-8861)*
Mobile Link Virgina LLC 757 583-8300
7862 Tidewater Dr Ste 109 Norfolk (23505) *(G-9647)*
Mobile Observer 703 569-9346
6911 Ontario St Springfield (22152) *(G-13053)*
Mobile Radio Partners Inc 804 525-4013
1420 N Parham Rd Ste Q107 Henrico (23229) *(G-6535)*
Mobile Radio Partners Inc (PA) **804 364-1553**
6573 Glenshaw Dr Glen Allen (23059) *(G-5772)*
Mobile Sheet Metal LLC 540 450-6324
435 Wildcat Hollow Rd Boyce (22620) *(G-1910)*
Mobile Tx/Bookkeeping Prtg LLC 804 224-8454
420 Colonial Ave Ste B Colonial Beach (22443) *(G-3725)*
Mobile Wallet Gifting Corp 301 523-1052
10303 Yellow Pine Dr Vienna (22182) *(G-14098)*
Mobile Welding & Fabrication, Dillwyn *Also called Randy Hawthorne (G-4099)*
Mobile-Tel, North Chesterfield *Also called Melvin Crutchfield (G-9928)*
Mobilityworks, North Chesterfield *Also called Ride-Away Inc (G-10022)*
Mobitrum Corporation 301 793-4728
6875 Churchill Rd Mc Lean (22101) *(G-8504)*
Mobjack Binnacle Products LLC 804 814-4077
5809 York Rd Richmond (23226) *(G-11295)*
Mobotrex Inc 804 794-1592
1550 Standing Ridge Dr Powhatan (23139) *(G-10559)*
Moda Preview International, Vienna *Also called Adriana Calderon Escalante (G-14005)*
Modek Inc 804 550-7300
10463 Wilden Dr Ashland (23005) *(G-1463)*
Model A Woodworks 757 714-1126
4710 Whaley Ct Chesapeake (23321) *(G-3210)*
Model Datasheet Pt Instruments 716 418-4194
102 Bronze Ct Williamsburg (23185) *(G-15280)*
Model Railroad Cstm Benchwork 540 948-4948
8038 S Blue Ridge Tpke Rochelle (22738) *(G-12234)*
Model Sign & Graphics 703 527-2121
4290 Birney Ln Fairfax (22033) *(G-4514)*
Modern Engravings LLC 757 876-3001
8124 Founders Mill Way Gloucester (23061) *(G-5855)*
Modern Exteriors 703 978-8602
4070 Walney Rd Chantilly (20151) *(G-2464)*
Modern Graphix 804 590-1303
16336 Chinook Dr South Chesterfield (23803) *(G-12838)*
Modern Living LLC 877 663-2224
1607 Rhoadmiller St Ste B Richmond (23220) *(G-11679)*
Modern Machine and Tool Co Inc 757 873-1212
11844 Jefferson Ave Newport News (23606) *(G-9303)*
Modern Pathology, Charlottesville *Also called Rector Visitors of The Univ VA (G-2858)*
Modine Manufacturing Company 540 261-9821
1221 Magnolia Ave Buena Vista (24416) *(G-2148)*
Modine Manufacturing Company 540 464-3640
360 Collierstown Rd Lexington (24450) *(G-7402)*
Modu System America LLC 757 250-3413
1715 Endeavor Dr Williamsburg (23185) *(G-15281)*
Modular Design Installations 757 871-8885
2107 Marshall Ave Newport News (23607) *(G-9304)*
Modular Interiors Group LLC 757 550-8910
2701 E Main St Richmond (23223) *(G-11680)*
Modular WD Systems Patrick Co, Claudville *Also called Panel Processing Virginia Inc (G-3639)*
Modular Wood Systems Inc 276 251-5300
1805 Red Bank School Rd Claudville (24076) *(G-3638)*
Modus Workshop LLC 800 376-5735
449 Sunrise Ave Harrisonburg (22801) *(G-6347)*
Mofat Publishing LLC 540 915-5847
336 Stratford Dr Blue Ridge (24064) *(G-1852)*
Mofat Publishing LLC 540 251-1660
3812 Concord Pl Ste E Roanoke (24018) *(G-11969)*
Mogo Inc 703 476-8595
12343 Sunrise Valley Dr C Reston (20191) *(G-10903)*
Mohawk Industries Inc 540 258-2811
404 Anderson St Glasgow (24555) *(G-5700)*
Mohawk Industries Inc 276 728-2141
351 Floyd Pike Hillsville (24343) *(G-6897)*
Mojo Castle Press LLC 703 946-8946
7008 Manahoac Pl Gainesville (20155) *(G-5598)*
Mojo Custom Sportswear LLC 540 632-2116
1775 Roanoke Rd Daleville (24083) *(G-3944)*
Mojo Fruit Drinks LLC 571 278-0755
17 E Myrtle St Alexandria (22301) *(G-279)*
Mold Fresh LLC 757 696-9288
4004 Atlantic Ave Apt 308 Virginia Beach (23451) *(G-14660)*
Mold Removal LLC 703 421-0000
45498 Lakeside Dr Sterling (20165) *(G-13455)*
Molding & Traffic ACC LLC 540 896-2459
304 N Timber Way Broadway (22815) *(G-2089)*
Molding Light LLC 703 847-0232
6902 Lemon Rd Mc Lean (22101) *(G-8505)*
Molins Richmond Inc 804 887-2525
1470 E Parham Rd Henrico (23228) *(G-6536)*
Molloy Software Assoc Inc 703 825-7290
14374 N Slope St Centreville (20120) *(G-2320)*
Molon Lave Vineyards & Winery 540 439-5460
10075 Lees Mill Rd Warrenton (20186) *(G-15035)*
Mom Made Foods LLC 703 740-9241
950 N Washington St Alexandria (22314) *(G-280)*
Momensity LLC 804 247-2811
203 Sail Cv Stafford (22554) *(G-13177)*
Momentum Usa Inc 804 329-3000
4605 Carolina Ave Richmond (23222) *(G-11681)*
Mommas Best Homemade LLC 805 509-5419
3133 Barbour Dr Virginia Beach (23456) *(G-14661)*
Mommers House LLC 540 327-8101
440 Royal St Winchester (22601) *(G-15558)*
Momo On The Go, Yorktown *Also called Martha Bennett (G-15979)*
Moms Choice LLC 757 410-9409
732 Eden Way N Ste E Chesapeake (23320) *(G-3211)*
Monalisa Blakeney 703 863-8530
4600 John Hancock Ct # 2 Annandale (22003) *(G-775)*
Monarch Manufacturing Works 757 640-3727
101 W Main St Ste 900 Norfolk (23510) *(G-9648)*
Monday Morning Press LLC 804 869-5020
6313 Knotgrass Aly Moseley (23120) *(G-9043)*
Mondays Child 703 754-9048
10109 Burwell Rd Nokesville (20181) *(G-9396)*
Mondelez Global LLC 757 925-3011
200 Johnson Ave Suffolk (23434) *(G-13745)*
Mongodb Inc 866 237-8815
8614 Westwood Center Dr # 705 Vienna (22182) *(G-14099)*
Monikev-Fisher LLC 757 343-4153
4832 Linshaw Ln Virginia Beach (23455) *(G-14662)*
Monkey Puzzle Productions LLC 703 919-0182
43546 Mink Meadows St Chantilly (20152) *(G-2546)*
Monks Welding LLC 276 206-8051
18373 Eden Ln Abingdon (24211) *(G-51)*
Monoflo International Inc (PA) **540 665-1691**
882 Baker Ln Winchester (22603) *(G-15451)*

ALPHABETIC

Monogram Majik 540 389-2269
1714 Starview Dr Salem (24153) *(G-12539)*

Monogram Shop 434 973-1968
628 Berkmar Cir Charlottesville (22901) *(G-2662)*

Monolithic Music Group LLC 804 233-2322
5216 Media Rd Richmond (23225) *(G-11682)*

Monsanto Tamantha 434 517-0013
1121 Collingwood Dr North Prince George (23860) *(G-10090)*

Monster Fight Club LLC 434 284-7258
395 Reas Ford Rd Ste 190 Earlysville (22936) *(G-4293)*

Monstracity Press 703 791-2759
14124 Walton Dr Manassas (20112) *(G-8111)*

Montana Plains Bread Co, Lynchburg *Also called Lucia Coates (G-7759)*

Montauk Systems Corporation 954 695-6819
21113 Crocus Ter Ashburn (20147) *(G-1318)*

Monte Carlo Software LLC 703 642-0289
6703 Capstan Dr Annandale (22003) *(G-776)*

Montebello Packaging Inc 540 437-0119
812 N Main St Harrisonburg (22802) *(G-6348)*

MONTEBELLO PACKAGING, INC., Harrisonburg *Also called Montebello Packaging Inc (G-6348)*

Montemorano LLC 540 272-6390
5102 Gold Crest Dr Sumerduck (22742) *(G-13792)*

Montesquieu Inc 703 518-9975
500 Montgomery St Alexandria (22314) *(G-281)*

Montgomery Cabinetry 540 721-7000
867 Peters Pike Rd Wirtz (24184) *(G-15616)*

Montgomery Cnty Newspapers Inc 540 389-9355
1633 W Main St Salem (24153) *(G-12540)*

Montgomery Farm Supply Co 540 483-7072
3220 Wirtz Rd Wirtz (24184) *(G-15617)*

Monti Tools Inc 832 623-7970
7677 Coppermine Dr Manassas (20109) *(G-8112)*

Monticello Software Inc 540 854-4200
6411 Carter Ln Mineral (23117) *(G-8950)*

Montifalco Vineyard 434 989-9115
1800 Fray Rd Ruckersville (22968) *(G-12406)*

Montoya Services LLC 571 882-3464
14 Millard Ct Sterling (20165) *(G-13456)*

Montuno Software Inc 703 554-7505
23056 Minerva Dr Brambleton (20148) *(G-1931)*

Montyco LLC 540 761-6751
2515 Laburnum Ave Sw Roanoke (24015) *(G-12137)*

Monument32/The Smyers Group 804 217-8347
4860 Cox Rd Ste 200 Glen Allen (23060) *(G-5773)*

Monumental Pest Control Co 571 245-6178
14427 Manassas Gap Ct Centreville (20120) *(G-2321)*

Monumental Services 434 847-6630
174 Sunset Cir Madison Heights (24572) *(G-7877)*

Moog Aspen Motion Technolgies, Radford *Also called Aspen Motion Technologies Inc (G-10704)*

Moog Components Group, Blacksburg *Also called Moog Inc (G-1765)*

Moog Components Group 540 443-4699
1501 N Main St Blacksburg (24060) *(G-1763)*

Moog Inc 716 652-2000
1213 N Main St Blacksburg (24060) *(G-1764)*

Moog Inc 540 552-3011
2200 S Main St Blacksburg (24060) *(G-1765)*

Moog Inc 276 236-4921
115 Jack Guynn Dr Galax (24333) *(G-5641)*

Moog Inc 828 837-5115
1213 N Main St Blacksburg (24060) *(G-1766)*

Moog Inc 540 552-3011
1501 N Main St Blacksburg (24060) *(G-1767)*

Moog Inc 540 552-3011
2200 S Main St Blacksburg (24060) *(G-1768)*

Moog USA Inc 540 586-6700
1265 Emerald Crest Dr Bedford (24523) *(G-1645)*

Mookind Press LLC 703 920-1884
1600 S Eads St Apt 1034n Arlington (22202) *(G-1067)*

Moon Cabinet Inc 703 339-8097
9022 Telegraph Rd Ste D Lorton (22079) *(G-7512)*

Moon Consortium LLC 571 408-9570
6628 Ivy Hill Dr Mc Lean (22101) *(G-8506)*

Moon Industries LLC 703 878-2428
2016 Stargrass Ct Woodbridge (22192) *(G-15749)*

Moon River Print Co 804 350-2647
1346 Stavemill Rd Powhatan (23139) *(G-10560)*

Moonlight Bindery 703 549-5261
18 W Uhler Ave Alexandria (22301) *(G-282)*

Moonlight Publishing Group LLC 703 242-0978
101 Yeonas Dr Se Vienna (22180) *(G-14100)*

Moonlight Welding LLC 757 449-7003
3200 Indian Trl Suffolk (23434) *(G-13746)*

Moonlite Septic Service, Pennington Gap *Also called Mark A Harber (G-10295)*

Moore C W and Sons LLC 757 653-9121
24283 Moore Dr Courtland (23837) *(G-3773)*

Moore and Son Inc Lewis S 804 366-7170
26406 Mt Vernon Church Rd Ruther Glen (22546) *(G-12458)*

Moore Logging Inc 276 233-1693
1342 Double Cabin Rd Dugspur (24325) *(G-4189)*

Moore Metal 757 930-0849
540 Burcher Rd Newport News (23606) *(G-9305)*

Moore Sign Corporation 804 748-5836
901 Old Brmuda Hundred Rd Chester (23836) *(G-3438)*

Mooreland Servicing Co LLC 804 644-2000
830 E Main St Ste 2100 Richmond (23219) *(G-11683)*

Moores Machine Co Inc 434 352-0000
4565 Richmond Hwy Spout Spring (24593) *(G-12926)*

Moorman Shickram & Stephen 540 463-3146
30 Crossing Ln Lexington (24450) *(G-7403)*

Moothru LLC 540 439-6455
11402 James Madison Hwy Remington (22734) *(G-10770)*

Morais Vineyards and Winery 540 439-9520
11409 Marsh Rd Bealeton (22712) *(G-1601)*

More Technology LLC 571 208-9865
11951 Freedom Dr Ste 1300 Centreville (20121) *(G-2322)*

More Than A Sign 540 514-3311
1724 Martinsburg Pike Winchester (22603) *(G-15452)*

Morefield Gem Mine Inc 804 561-3399
13400 Butlers Rd Amelia Court House (23002) *(G-666)*

Morefield Mine, Amelia Court House *Also called Morefield Gem Mine Inc (G-666)*

Moretz Candy Co Inc 276 669-2533
3001 Lee Hwy Bristol (24202) *(G-2026)*

Morgan E McKinney 804 389-9371
4814 Rodney Rd Richmond (23230) *(G-11296)*

Morgan Lumber Company Inc 434 735-8151
628 Jeb Stuart Hwy Red Oak (23964) *(G-10759)*

Morgan Olson LLC 269 659-0200
100 Ikea Dr Ringgold (24586) *(G-11870)*

Morgan Race Cars LLC Jeffrey 540 907-1205
2611 Melissa Ct Fredericksburg (22408) *(G-5329)*

Mornings Myst Alpacas Inc 540 428-1002
7280 Burke Ln Warrenton (20186) *(G-15036)*

Morooka America LLC (HQ) **877 667-6652**
11191 Air Park Rd Ashland (23005) *(G-1464)*

Morooka America LLC 804 368-0948
11096 Leadbetter Rd Ashland (23005) *(G-1465)*

Morooka USA, Ashland *Also called Morooka America LLC (G-1464)*

Morooka USA-East, Ashland *Also called American Track Carrier LLC (G-1368)*

Morose Brand LLC 747 346-1550
110 Coliseum Xing 6054 Hampton (23666) *(G-6203)*

Morphix Technologies Inc 757 431-2260
2557 Production Rd Virginia Beach (23454) *(G-14663)*

Morphotrak LLC 703 797-2600
675 N Washington St # 330 Alexandria (22314) *(G-283)*

Morris & Sons Logging Glen 540 854-5271
23035 Constitution Hwy Unionville (22567) *(G-13965)*

Morris Designs Inc 757 463-9400
277 N Lynnhven Rd Ste 108 Virginia Beach (23452) *(G-14664)*

Morris Finishing Co 540 674-0079
444 Church St Dublin (24084) *(G-4166)*

Morris Machine Shop 540 434-8038
4336 Port Republic Rd Rockingham (22801) *(G-12263)*

Morris Mountaineer Oil Gas LLC 703 283-9700
1411 Mayflower Dr Mc Lean (22101) *(G-8507)*

Morris Woodworks LLC 434 392-2285
305 River Rd Farmville (23901) *(G-4951)*

Morton Buildings Inc 540 366-3705
18478 Industrial Rd Culpeper (22701) *(G-3910)*

Morton Salt 757 543-0148
4100 Buell St Chesapeake (23324) *(G-3212)*

Mos Welding Shop 434 525-1137
600 Buffalo Mill Rd Evington (24550) *(G-4380)*

Mosaic Distribution LLC 978 328-7001
43203 Maple Cross St Chantilly (20152) *(G-2547)*

Mosena Enterprises Inc 757 562-7033
26460 Smiths Ferry Rd Franklin (23851) *(G-5149)*

Moshref Mir Abdul 502 356-0019
2902 Madeira Ct Woodbridge (22192) *(G-15750)*

Moshref, Mir Abdul, Woodbridge *Also called Moshref Mir Abdul (G-15750)*

Moslow Wood Products Inc 804 598-5579
3450 Maidens Rd Powhatan (23139) *(G-10561)*

Moss Cape LLC 703 234-3890
4501 Singer Ct Ste 300 Chantilly (20151) *(G-2465)*

Moss Marketing Company Inc 804 794-0654
14451 Chepstow Rd Midlothian (23113) *(G-8862)*

Moss Supply Company 804 798-8332
11253 Leadbetter Rd Ashland (23005) *(G-1466)*

Moss Vineyards LLC (PA) **434 990-0111**
1849 Simmons Gap Rd Dyke (22935) *(G-4276)*

Moth LLC 804 655-8216
5807 Gloryvine Ct 105-11 North Chesterfield (23234) *(G-9933)*

Mother Teresas Cottage 757 850-0350
112 N Sixth St Hampton (23664) *(G-6204)*

Mothers Macaroons 703 532-0104
6713 Little Falls Rd Arlington (22213) *(G-1068)*

Mothers Macaroons Gourmet Bky, Arlington *Also called Mothers Macaroons (G-1068)*

Motion Control Systems Inc 540 731-0540
6701 Viscoe Rd New River (24129) **(G-9151)**

Motley Fool LLC 703 838-3665
123 N Pitt St Alexandria (22314) **(G-284)**

Motley Fool Company, Alexandria Also called Motley Fool LLC **(G-284)**

Motley Fool Holdings Inc 703 838-3665
2000 Duke St Fl 4 Alexandria (22314) **(G-285)**

Moto Farkle Support Services 757 705-2014
2077 Bierce Dr Virginia Beach (23454) **(G-14665)**

Motorola Solutions Inc 703 724-8000
44330 Woodridge Pkwy Leesburg (20176) **(G-7316)**

Motrak Models 813 476-4784
717 Windsor Ln Martinsville (24112) **(G-8314)**

Mottley Foils Inc 434 392-8347
20 Mohele Rd Farmville (23901) **(G-4952)**

Moubray Company 804 435-6334
31 Tartan Village Dr Kilmarnock (22482) **(G-7073)**

Mounir & Company Incorporated 703 354-7400
6788 Commercial Dr Springfield (22151) **(G-13054)**

Mounir E Shaheen 757 723-4445
1962 E Pembroke Ave Hampton (23663) **(G-6205)**

Mount Carmel Publishing LLC 703 838-2109
4196 Merchant Plz Ste 348 Woodbridge (22192) **(G-15751)**

Mount Slon Wldg Fbrication LLC 540 350-2733
1908 N River Rd Mount Solon (22843) **(G-9089)**

Mount Vernon Woodworks LLC 202 222-8387
4516 Ferry Landing Rd Alexandria (22309) **(G-534)**

Mountain and Vine LLC 434 263-6100
500 Del Fosse Winery Ln Faber (22938) **(G-4390)**

Mountain Cove Vineyards, Lovingston Also called La ABRA Farm & Winery Inc **(G-7591)**

Mountain Creek Industries LLC 804 432-1601
286 Rr Eppes Rd Meherrin (23954) **(G-8706)**

Mountain Energy Resources Inc 276 679-3593
150 Coeburn Ave Sw Norton (24273) **(G-10129)**

Mountain Marimba Inc 276 773-3899
431 E Main St Independence (24348) **(G-6991)**

Mountain Materials Inc 276 429-5241
14196 Monroe Rd Glade Spring (24340) **(G-5679)**

Mountain Materials Inc 276 762-5563
49 Quarry Rd Castlewood (24224) **(G-2255)**

Mountain Mtls Muth Wlson Plant 276 579-6351
4648 Potato Creek Rd Mouth of Wilson (24363) **(G-9095)**

Mountain Plains Industries 434 386-0100
1088 Macon Loop Lynchburg (24503) **(G-7775)**

Mountain Precision Tool Co Inc 540 552-0178
451 Industrial Park Rd Se Blacksburg (24060) **(G-1769)**

Mountain Run Winery LLC 703 638-5559
10753 Mountain Run Lk Rd Culpeper (22701) **(G-3911)**

Mountain Sky LLC 540 389-1197
1129 Florida St Salem (24153) **(G-12541)**

Mountain Tech Inc 434 710-4896
700 David Giles Ln Blairs (24527) **(G-1832)**

Mountain Top Logging LLC 540 745-6709
386 Silverleaf Ln Se Floyd (24091) **(G-5032)**

Mountain Top Signs & Gifts 540 430-0532
106 Maple Dr Verona (24482) **(G-13992)**

Mountain Valley Enterprises 276 686-6516
313 Killinger Creek Rd Rural Retreat (24368) **(G-12428)**

Mountain View Brewery LLC 540 462-6200
50 Northwind Ln Lexington (24450) **(G-7404)**

Mountain View Rendering Co 540 984-4158
173 Rocco Rd Edinburg (22824) **(G-4310)**

Mountain View Vineyard 540 683-3200
444 Signal Knob Dr Strasburg (22657) **(G-13591)**

Mountaineer Publishing Co Inc 276 935-2123
1200 Plaza Dr Ste 2400 Grundy (24614) **(G-6038)**

Mountaintop Custom Kennels, Abingdon Also called Hucks & Hucks LLC **(G-41)**

Mountaintop Logging LLC 540 468-3059
151 Collins Run Ln Monterey (24465) **(G-9010)**

Mountfair Vineyards LLC 434 823-7605
4875 Fox Mountain Rd Crozet (22932) **(G-3845)**

Mouthpiece Express LLC 540 989-8848
5207 Bernard Dr Roanoke (24018) **(G-11970)**

Mova Corp 757 598-5577
2608 Horse Pasture Rd Virginia Beach (23453) **(G-14666)**

Movie Time, Fredericksburg Also called Dream Reels Inc **(G-5277)**

Moxley Brothers 276 236-6580
419 State Shed Ln Galax (24333) **(G-5642)**

Moxy Richmond Downtown, Richmond Also called 501 Franklin LLC **(G-11465)**

Moyer Bros Contracting, Luray Also called Moyer Brothers Contracting Inc **(G-7618)**

Moyer Brothers Contracting Inc 540 743-7864
467 Somers Rd Luray (22835) **(G-7618)**

Moyers Logging 540 468-2289
10677 Mountain Tpke Monterey (24465) **(G-9011)**

MPH Development LLC 703 303-4838
6853 Hollow Glen Ct Gainesville (20155) **(G-5599)**

Mpi, Stafford Also called Metropole Products Inc **(G-13176)**

MPS, Gordonsville Also called Macmillan Holdings LLC **(G-5913)**

MPS Return Center 540 672-0792
14301 Litchfield Dr Orange (22960) **(G-10221)**

Mr Graphics Print Shop LLC 703 980-8239
7537 Gary Rd Manassas (20109) **(G-8113)**

Mr Industries LLC 484 838-9154
3521 White Hall Rd King George (22485) **(G-7103)**

Mr Luck Inc 570 766-8734
619 Baldwin Ave Norfolk (23517) **(G-9649)**

Mr Noodle & Rice 540 662-4213
19 Weems Ln Winchester (22601) **(G-15559)**

Mr Print 540 338-5900
501 E Main St Purcellville (20132) **(G-10671)**

Mr Robot Inc 804 426-3394
10220 Robious Rd North Chesterfield (23235) **(G-9934)**

Mr Wholesale Cigar Master, Portsmouth Also called Juma Brothers Inc **(G-10449)**

Mr-Mow-It-all 540 263-2369
1102 Tazewell Ave Se Roanoke (24013) **(G-12138)**

Mr1 Construction LLC 301 748-6078
9837 Buckner Rd Manassas (20110) **(G-7977)**

Mrp Munufacturing Inc 434 525-1993
12660 E Lynchburg Salem Forest (24551) **(G-5084)**

Mrs Bones 757 412-0500
1616 Hilltop W Shopg Ctr Virginia Beach (23451) **(G-14667)**

Mrs Schultz's Marzipan, Great Falls Also called Cecilia M Schultzs **(G-5945)**

Ms Bettys Bad-Ass Candles LLC 540 256-7221
4313 Marquis Pl Woodbridge (22192) **(G-15752)**

Ms Jos Petite Sweets LLC 571 327-9431
625 N Washington St # 425 Alexandria (22314) **(G-286)**

Ms Kathleen B Watkins 804 741-0388
9084 Hoke Brady Rd Henrico (23231) **(G-6537)**

Ms Magazine, Arlington Also called Liberty Media For Women LLC **(G-1034)**

Ms Monogram LLC 804 502-3551
13510 Midlothian Tpke Midlothian (23113) **(G-8863)**

Ms Wheelchair Virginia Inc 540 838-5022
7083 Hickman Cemetery Rd Fairlawn (24141) **(G-4738)**

MSC Imaging Tech LLC 804 593-0689
2530 Gayton Centre Dr Henrico (23238) **(G-6538)**

Mscbakes LLC 434 214-0838
1009 2nd Avenue Ext Farmville (23901) **(G-4953)**

Msl Oil & Gas Corp (PA) 703 971-8805
6161 Fuller Ct Alexandria (22310) **(G-535)**

MSP Design Group, Virginia Beach Also called Tdi Printing Group LLC **(G-14866)**

MSP Group LLC 757 855-5416
3490 E Virginia Bch Blvd Norfolk (23502) **(G-9650)**

Mt Athos Quarry, Concord Also called Boxley Materials Company **(G-3757)**

Mt Chestnut Vineyards LLC 540 400-6442
6235 Mount Chestnut Rd Roanoke (24018) **(G-11971)**

Mt Pleasant Log & Excvtg LLC 434 922-7326
515 Emmanuel Church Rd Amherst (24521) **(G-701)**

Mteq, Kilmarnock Also called Qinetiq Inc **(G-7075)**

Mteq, Lorton Also called Qinetiq Inc **(G-7524)**

Mtf Resources LLC 804 240-5335
14201 Leafield Dr Midlothian (23113) **(G-8864)**

Mtg Enterprises Inc 804 269-5218
4603 Jacobs Glenn Dr North Chesterfield (23236) **(G-9935)**

Mth Holdings Corp 276 228-7943
5430 Peters Creek Rd # 108 Roanoke (24019) **(G-11972)**

MTI Specialty Silicones Inc 540 254-2020
19505 Main St Buchanan (24066) **(G-2122)**

Mtn Man Welding 540 463-9352
1460 Blacks Creek Rd Lexington (24450) **(G-7405)**

MTS Equipment Co, Winchester Also called My Three Sons Inc **(G-15453)**

Mu-Del Electronics LLC 703 368-8900
7430 Merritt Park Dr # 140 Manassas (20109) **(G-8114)**

Mud Puppy Custom Lures LLC 804 895-1489
9629 Shadywood Rd Prince George (23875) **(G-10602)**

Muddy Feet LLC 540 830-0342
2061 Evelyn Byrd Ave E Harrisonburg (22801) **(G-6349)**

Muhammad Islam 631 569-8325
12006 Starboard Dr # 304 Reston (20194) **(G-10904)**

Mujahid Fnu 646 693-2762
301 N Beauregard St # 706 Alexandria (22312) **(G-536)**

Muller Martini Corp 804 282-4802
503 Waveny Rd Richmond (23229) **(G-11297)**

Mullican Flooring LP 276 565-0220
Hwy 23 N Appalachia (24216) **(G-798)**

Mullican Flooring LP 276 679-2924
Blackwood Indus Pk Rd Norton (24273) **(G-10130)**

Mullican Lumber & Mfg Co, Appalachia Also called Mullican Flooring LP **(G-798)**

Mullican Lumber & Mfg Co, Norton Also called Mullican Flooring LP **(G-10130)**

Mulqueen Inc 804 333-4847
2767 Menokin Rd Warsaw (22572) **(G-15070)**

Multi Wall Packaging, Martinsville Also called Signode Industrial Group LLC **(G-8329)**

Multi-Color Corporation 757 487-2525
1300 Cavalier Blvd Chesapeake (23323) **(G-3213)**

Multi-Pack LLC 703 372-2303
7668 Fullerton Rd Springfield (22153) **(G-13055)**

Multimdal Idntfcation Tech LLC 818 729-1954
11921 Freedom Dr Ste 550 Reston (20190) **(G-10905)**

Multimodal ID 703 944-9008
7799 Leesburg Pike # 500 Falls Church (22043) *(G-4833)*

Multinational Defense Svcs LLC 727 333-7290
1660 Intl Dr Ste 200 Mclean (22102) *(G-8588)*

Mumble Wraps LLC 571 358-5388
10472 Business Center Ct Manassas (20110) *(G-7978)*

Mumpower Lumber Company 276 669-7491
21450 Gale Ave Bristol (24202) *(G-2027)*

Munchkin Monograms LLC 215 970-4375
5711 Glamis Dr Alexandria (22315) *(G-537)*

Muncie Power Products Inc 804 275-6724
9407 Burge Ave North Chesterfield (23237) *(G-9936)*

Mundet Inc (HQ) **804 644-3970**
919 E Main St Ste 1130 Richmond (23219) *(G-11684)*

Mundet-Hermetite Inc (HQ) **804 748-3319**
1106 W Roslyn Rd Colonial Heights (23834) *(G-3738)*

Mundy Quarries Inc C S 540 833-2061
11261 Turleytown Rd Broadway (22815) *(G-2090)*

Mundy Stone Company 540 774-1696
4592 Old Rocky Mount Rd S Roanoke (24014) *(G-12139)*

Mundy's Industrial Parts, Richmond *Also called Mundys Precision Automotive* *(G-11685)*

Mundys Precision Automotive 804 231-0435
2710 Hull St Richmond (23224) *(G-11685)*

Munters Des Champs Products, Buena Vista *Also called Des Champs Technologies Inc* *(G-2141)*

Murdock Acquisition LLC 804 798-9154
11364 Air Park Rd Ashland (23005) *(G-1467)*

Murphy-Brown LLC 804 834-3990
27404 Cabin Point Rd Waverly (23890) *(G-15085)*

Murray Biscuit Company LLC 757 547-0249
1335 Lindale Dr Chesapeake (23320) *(G-3214)*

Murray Cider Co Inc 540 977-9000
103 Murray Farm Rd Roanoke (24019) *(G-11973)*

Muse Vineyards LLC 540 459-7033
16 Serendipity Ln Woodstock (22664) *(G-15858)*

Muse Writers Center 757 818-9880
2200 Colonial Ave Ste 3 Norfolk (23517) *(G-9651)*

Museum Framing 703 299-0100
109 S Fairfax St Alexandria (22314) *(G-287)*

Museumrails LLC 540 603-2414
19564 Louisa Rd Louisa (23093) *(G-7561)*

Music At Monument 202 570-7800
50 Cottage Dr Luray (22835) *(G-7619)*

Music Publishers America LLC 917 406-4425
508 Blue Heron Ln White Stone (22578) *(G-15188)*

Musicians Publications 757 410-3111
315 Great Bridge Blvd Chesapeake (23320) *(G-3215)*

Mustang Sports Retail 757 679-2814
357 Johnstown Rd Ste F Chesapeake (23322) *(G-3216)*

Mutual Box Leather 703 626-9770
17569 Whitby Ct Round Hill (20141) *(G-12383)*

Mvmt Inc 804 356-6520
2711 Ellesmere Dr Midlothian (23113) *(G-8865)*

Mvp Press LLC 703 661-6877
43720 Trade Center Pl # 13 Dulles (20166) *(G-4210)*

Mw Manufacturers Inc (HQ) **540 483-0211**
433 N Main St Rocky Mount (24151) *(G-12340)*

Mw Manufacturers Inc 540 484-6780
350 State St Rocky Mount (24151) *(G-12341)*

Mwb Enterprises Inc 434 922-7730
1026 Sugar Hill Tunnel Rd Amherst (24521) *(G-702)*

Mwv Community Dev & Lnd Mgmt, Appomattox *Also called Westrock Mwv LLC* *(G-827)*

My African Bikini, Manassas *Also called Mng Online LLC* *(G-8109)*

My Arch Inc 703 375-9302
5102 Woodford Dr Centreville (20120) *(G-2323)*

My Best Friends Cupcakes LLC 757 754-1148
2200 Glenrose Ct Virginia Beach (23456) *(G-14668)*

My Extra Hands LLC 540 847-2063
6320 Five Mile Centre Par Fredericksburg (22407) *(G-5330)*

My Mexico Foods & Distrs Inc 540 560-3587
1555 Red Oak St Harrisonburg (22802) *(G-6350)*

My Mind On Sports LLC 703 261-9629
6932 Columbia Dr Alexandria (22307) *(G-538)*

My Printing Guys 703 430-7940
22611 Markey Ct Ste 114-Q Sterling (20166) *(G-13457)*

My Three Sons Inc 540 662-5927
580 Airport Rd Winchester (22602) *(G-15453)*

Mya Saray LLC 703 996-8800
43671 Trade Center Pl # 114 Sterling (20166) *(G-13458)*

Mybodymyworship 703 669-2901
102 Oakcrest Manor Dr Ne Leesburg (20176) *(G-7317)*

Myboys3 Press 804 379-6964
14400 Roberts Mill Ct Midlothian (23113) *(G-8866)*

Mydrone4hire LLC 540 491-4860
2507 Blue Ridge Sprng Rd Blue Ridge (24064) *(G-1853)*

Myers Clamdock, Mappsville *Also called Eastern Shore Seafood Pdts LLC* *(G-8218)*

Myers Repair Company 804 222-3674
3105 Gay Ave Richmond (23231) *(G-11298)*

Myra J Rudisill 540 587-0402
26 Cheese Creek Rd Altavista (24517) *(G-637)*

Myrmidon Industries Inc 540 273-6414
1700 Sherwood Dr Fredericksburg (22405) *(G-5460)*

Mystery Goose Press LLC 540 347-3609
4650 Spring Run Rd Warrenton (20187) *(G-15037)*

Mystery Whl & Screen Prtg LLC 540 514-7349
1908 Kiska Rd Salem (24153) *(G-12542)*

Mystic Empowerment 703 765-0690
7230 Stover Dr Alexandria (22306) *(G-539)*

Mystic Post Press LLC 703 867-3447
7308 Rippon Rd Alexandria (22307) *(G-540)*

Mystical Creations 804 943-8386
2802 Grant St Hopewell (23860) *(G-6940)*

Mystical Mirrors & Glass 757 399-4682
21 Maupin Ave Portsmouth (23702) *(G-10463)*

Mystique Queen Publishing LLC 484 250-1131
915 Briar Hill Rd Norfolk (23502) *(G-9652)*

Mythikos Mommy LLC 703 568-7504
8607 Chase Glen Cir Fairfax Station (22039) *(G-4718)*

Mythos Publishing LLC 703 531-0795
12016 Wandabury Rd Oakton (22124) *(G-10159)*

Mzgoodiez LLC 757 535-6929
552 2nd Ave Suffolk (23434) *(G-13747)*

N A D A Services Corporation 703 821-7000
8400 Westpark Dr Ste 1 Mc Lean (22102) *(G-8508)*

N A D C 703 331-5611
10438 Business Center Ct Manassas (20110) *(G-7979)*

N A K Mechanics & Welding Inc 276 971-1860
206 Goshen Hill Rd Tazewell (24651) *(G-13837)*

N C G, Hampton *Also called Newport Cutter Grinding Co Inc* *(G-6207)*

N C S, Gainesville *Also called Ncs Technologies Inc* *(G-5600)*

N C Tool Company Inc 540 943-4011
1466 E Side Hwy Waynesboro (22980) *(G-15128)*

N D M Machine Inc 276 621-4424
670 Slate Spring Br Rd Wytheville (24382) *(G-15902)*

N Rolls-Ryce Amer Holdings Inc 703 834-1700
14850 Conference Ctr Chantilly (20151) *(G-2466)*

N S Gilbert Lumber LLC 276 431-4488
5102 Industrial Dr Duffield (24244) *(G-4182)*

N W P O C, Moneta *Also called Northwestern PA Opt Clinic* *(G-8973)*

N Zone Sports 703 743-2848
15104 Championship Dr Haymarket (20169) *(G-6430)*

N&J Sales & Services 804 559-7172
7172 Mill Valley Rd Mechanicsville (23111) *(G-8664)*

N-Ask Incorporated (PA) **703 715-7909**
4114 Legato Rd Ste 1100 Fairfax (22033) *(G-4515)*

N-Molecular Inc (PA) **703 547-8161**
21000 Atl Blvd Ste 730 Dulles (20166) *(G-4211)*

N2 Publishing, Norfolk *Also called A Creative Mind LLC* *(G-9413)*

N2 Publishing, Suffolk *Also called Lvrcshull Incorporated* *(G-13735)*

N2n Specialty Printing LLC 540 786-5765
7903 Westbury Manor Dr Fredericksburg (22407) *(G-5331)*

Nabiday LLC 703 625-8679
10332 Main St Ste 309 Fairfax (22030) *(G-4656)*

Nabina Publications 804 276-0454
11304 Prvidence Creek Ter North Chesterfield (23236) *(G-9937)*

Nabisco, Suffolk *Also called Mondelez Global LLC* *(G-13745)*

Naff Welding & Mach Works 276 629-1129
949 Lillian Naff Dr Henry (24102) *(G-6596)*

Naff Welding Inc 276 629-1129
4724 Philpott Dr Bassett (24055) *(G-1587)*

Nailrod Publications LLC 703 351-8130
3750 N Oakland St Arlington (22207) *(G-1069)*

Nails Cabinet Shop Inc 540 888-3268
230 Flowers Ln Winchester (22603) *(G-15454)*

Nails Hurricane Too 703 370-5551
4535 Duke St Alexandria (22304) *(G-288)*

Naito America 804 550-3305
10450 Lakeridge Pkwy Ashland (23005) *(G-1468)*

Naj Enterprises LLP 202 251-7821
1857 Massachusetts Ave Mc Lean (22101) *(G-8509)*

Namax Music LLC 804 271-9535
4102 Castlewood Rd Richmond (23234) *(G-11054)*

Nana Stitches 757 689-3767
2901 Cardini Pl Virginia Beach (23453) *(G-14669)*

Nancy Lee Asman 703 242-8530
208 Courthouse Cir Sw Vienna (22180) *(G-14101)*

Nancy Stephens 540 933-6405
248 Habron Hollow Rd Fort Valley (22652) *(G-5135)*

Nannas Cndles Unique Gifts LLC 276 780-2513
704 Matson Dr Marion (24354) *(G-8238)*

Nano Solutions Inc 703 481-3321
3215 Greenstone Ct Herndon (20171) *(G-6749)*

Nanoarca Inc 757 589-2526
4416 Pope Valley Ct Virginia Beach (23456) *(G-14670)*

Nanofactory Cbn Inc 434 799-9280
350 Stinson Dr Danville (24540) *(G-4016)*

Nanomed Inc 540 553-4070
304 Vinyard Ave Blacksburg (24060) *(G-1770)*

Nanoseptic, Forest *Also called Nanotouch Materials LLC* *(G-5085)*

Nanotouch Materials LLC 888 411-6843
1053 London Park Dr E Forest (24551) *(G-5085)*

Nansemond Pre-Cast Con Co Inc 757 538-2761
3737 Nansemond Pkwy Suffolk (23435) *(G-13748)*

Nantrak Industries, Franklin *Also called Insights Intl Holdings LLC (G-5145)*

Nantrak Tactical LLC 757 517-2226
601 N Mechanic St Ste 414 Franklin (23851) *(G-5150)*

NAPA, Waynesboro *Also called Atkins Automotive Corp (G-15096)*

Napiers Extinguisher Sls & Svc, Drakes Branch *Also called James R Napier (G-4134)*

Napolean Magazine 703 641-9062
7708 Willow Point Dr Falls Church (22042) *(G-4834)*

Napoleon Books 540 463-6804
616 Little Dry Holw Lexington (24450) *(G-7406)*

Nariad Publishing 973 650-8948
426 Geese Lndg Glen Allen (23060) *(G-5774)*

Narmada Winery LLC 540 937-8215
43 Narmada Ln Amissville (20106) *(G-720)*

Narroflex Inc 276 694-7171
201 S Main St Stuart (24171) *(G-13626)*

Narrogate Woodworks Inc 276 728-3996
312 Narrogate Ln Dugspur (24325) *(G-4190)*

Narrow Passage Press, Edinburg *Also called Shenandoah Publications Inc (G-4314)*

Nasoni LLC 757 358-7475
5210 Commando Block Suffolk (23435) *(G-13749)*

Nasotech LLC 703 493-0436
2467 Iron Forge Rd Herndon (20171) *(G-6750)*

Natasha Matthew 757 407-1897
713 Stanwix Sq Norfolk (23502) *(G-9653)*

Nathan Group LLC 757 229-8703
2635 Lake Powell Rd Williamsburg (23185) *(G-15282)*

Nathaniel Hoffelder 571 406-2689
13884 Montoclair Ln Woodbridge (22193) *(G-15753)*

National Affl Mktg Co Inc 703 297-7316
19355 Wrenbury Ln Leesburg (20175) *(G-7318)*

National Bankshares Inc 540 552-0890
2280 Kraft Dr Blacksburg (24060) *(G-1771)*

National Caps 434 572-4709
1065 S Peach Orchard Rd South Boston (24592) *(G-12784)*

National Envelope Corp 703 629-3881
1617 Preston Rd Alexandria (22302) *(G-289)*

National Filter Media Corp 540 773-4780
309 N Braddock St Winchester (22601) *(G-15560)*

National Geographic Entps 703 528-7868
4534 19th St N Arlington (22207) *(G-1070)*

National Imports LLC 703 637-0019
1934 Old Gallows Rd # 350 Vienna (22182) *(G-14102)*

National Institute of Bus Mgt (PA) **703 394-4921**
7600a Leesburg Pike Falls Church (22043) *(G-4835)*

National Intelligence Eductn P 703 866-0832
6108 Hanover Ave Springfield (22150) *(G-13056)*

National Junior Tennis League 276 669-7540
1003 Chester St Bristol (24201) *(G-1984)*

National Lithograph Inc 703 709-9000
22800 Executive Dr # 190 Sterling (20166) *(G-13459)*

National Marking Products Inc 804 266-7691
5606 Greendale Rd Richmond (23228) *(G-11299)*

National Optometry, Hampton *Also called Kasinof & Associates (G-6179)*

National Peening Inc 540 387-3522
2167 Salem Industrial Dr Salem (24153) *(G-12543)*

National Peening, Roanoke, Salem *Also called National Peening Inc (G-12543)*

National Reconnaissance Office, Chantilly *Also called US Dept of the Air Force (G-2515)*

National Review Institute 202 679-7330
2221 S Clark St Ste 1200 Arlington (22202) *(G-1071)*

National Sliding Door Frame Co, Mechanicsville *Also called Massey Wood & West Inc (G-8656)*

National Tars 703 368-4220
10620 Crestwood Dr Ste B Manassas (20109) *(G-8115)*

National Technical Svcs Inc 434 713-1528
32 Hargrave Blvd Chatham (24531) *(G-2931)*

National Trust Foundry, Leesburg *Also called Equestrian Forge Inc (G-7269)*

National Vaccine Info Ctr 703 938-0342
21525 Ridgetop Cir # 100 Sterling (20166) *(G-13460)*

National Vaccine Informat 703 777-3736
726 Tonquin Pl Ne Leesburg (20176) *(G-7319)*

Nations 804 257-9891
2729 W Broad St Richmond (23220) *(G-11686)*

Nationwide Consumer Products 804 226-0876
514 Mansfield Dr Richmond (23223) *(G-11687)*

Nationwide Laminating Inc 703 550-8400
8208 Cinder Bed Rd Ste C Lorton (22079) *(G-7513)*

Nationwide Laminating & Finshg, Lorton *Also called Nationwide Laminating Inc (G-7513)*

Natural Balance Concepts LLC 804 693-5382
7555 Springfield Trace Ln Gloucester (23061) *(G-5856)*

Natural Lighting LLC 703 347-7004
6013 Rock Cliff Ln Apt N Alexandria (22315) *(G-541)*

Natural Resources Intl LLC 804 282-0369
7275 Glen Forest Dr # 206 Richmond (23226) *(G-11300)*

Natural Stones Inc 703 408-8801
9109 Euclid Ave Ste 107 Manassas (20110) *(G-7980)*

Natural Woodworking Co 540 745-2664
1527 Franklin Pike Se Floyd (24091) *(G-5033)*

Naturally Me LLC 703 680-3392
5874 Pontiac Dr Woodbridge (22193) *(G-15754)*

Nature By Ejn, Alexandria *Also called Ejn LLC (G-452)*

Natures Cntry Soaps Candle LLC 757 817-9062
6157 Colonial Trl W Spring Grove (23881) *(G-12931)*

Nautica Factory Store, Woodbridge *Also called Nautica of Potomac (G-15755)*

Nautica of Potomac 703 494-9915
2700 Potomac Mills Cir # 325 Woodbridge (22192) *(G-15755)*

Nautilus International Inc 276 773-2881
709 Powerhouse Rd Independence (24348) *(G-6992)*

Navy 757 417-4236
937 Avatar Dr Virginia Beach (23454) *(G-14671)*

Navy 202 781-0981
15482 Wheatfield Rd Woodbridge (22193) *(G-15756)*

Naylor Cmg 703 934-4714
1430 Spring Hill Rd Fl 6 Mc Lean (22102) *(G-8510)*

Nazret Cultural Foods LLC 215 500-9813
4316 Taney Ave Apt 103 Alexandria (22304) *(G-290)*

NBC Boatworks 757 630-0420
3253 Sandpiper Rd Virginia Beach (23456) *(G-14672)*

Nbe Technologies LLC 540 443-9100
3710 Evergreen Trl Blacksburg (24060) *(G-1772)*

NC Foam & Sales 540 631-3363
508 Kendrick Ln 9 Front Royal (22630) *(G-5545)*

Ncg LLC 757 838-3224
302 Aberdeen Rd Hampton (23661) *(G-6206)*

NCH Home Solutions LLC 703 723-4077
42949 Heatherton Ct Ashburn (20147) *(G-1319)*

Nci Group Inc 804 957-6811
6001 Quality Way Prince George (23875) *(G-10603)*

Ncs Pearson Inc 866 673-9034
208 Farmington Rd Virginia Beach (23454) *(G-14673)*

Ncs Technologies Inc 703 743-8500
9490 Innovation Dr Manassas (20110) *(G-7981)*

Ncs Technologies Inc (PA) **703 743-8500**
7669 Limestone Dr Ste 130 Gainesville (20155) *(G-5600)*

Neagle Flexo, Ashland *Also called Neagles Flexo Corporation (G-1469)*

Neagles Flexo Corporation 804 798-1501
11041 Richardson Rd Ashland (23005) *(G-1469)*

Neathridge Content Solutions 703 979-7170
1107 20th St S Arlington (22202) *(G-1072)*

Neatprints LLC 703 520-1550
6820 Commercial Dr Ste D Springfield (22151) *(G-13057)*

Neault LLC 804 283-5948
7839 Dabneys Mill Rd Manquin (23106) *(G-8217)*

Nectar of Gods Corporation 703 582-0856
1601 Black Heath Rd Midlothian (23113) *(G-8867)*

Nectar of The Gods Corp 703 582-0856
1313 Altamont Ave Richmond (23230) *(G-11301)*

Neda Jewelers Inc 703 670-2177
4332 Dale Blvd Woodbridge (22193) *(G-15757)*

Neda Jewelers of Dale City, Woodbridge *Also called Neda Jewelers Inc (G-15757)*

Nedia Enterprises Inc 571 223-0200
44675 Cape Ct Ste 120 Ashburn (20147) *(G-1320)*

Nedia Home, Ashburn *Also called Nedia Enterprises Inc (G-1320)*

Neenah Foundry Co 804 758-9592
703 Swan View Dr Urbanna (23175) *(G-13972)*

Neevarpt Productions LLC 571 549-1169
8603 Dutchman Ct Manassas (20110) *(G-7982)*

Neff Lumber Mills Inc 540 896-7031
12110 Turleytown Rd Broadway (22815) *(G-2091)*

Neiceys 757 500-1021
526 Rivers Reach Virginia Beach (23452) *(G-14674)*

Neighborhood Flags 804 360-3398
13317 Teasdale Ct Henrico (23233) *(G-6539)*

Neighborhood Sports LLC 804 282-8033
824 Arlington Cir Richmond (23229) *(G-11302)*

Neighborhood Sports Magazine, Richmond *Also called Neighborhood Sports LLC (G-11302)*

Neighborhoods Vi LLC 703 964-5000
1881 Campus Commons Dr Reston (20191) *(G-10906)*

Neither Ngex 408 676-6439
14014 Sullyfield Cir Chantilly (20151) *(G-2467)*

Nellie Harris 434 277-8511
512 Dillard Hill Rd Lowesville (22967) *(G-7597)*

Nelson & Son Custom Monuments, Chesapeake *Also called Dag Blast It Inc (G-3061)*

Nelson Hills Company 434 985-7176
989 Chapman Rd Stanardsville (22973) *(G-13224)*

Nelson Martin 540 879-9016
4826 Linhoss Rd Dayton (22821) *(G-4058)*

Nelson Rogue, North Chesterfield *Also called R and N Express LLC (G-9956)*

Nelsons Cabinetry 804 363-5800
543 Southlake Blvd North Chesterfield (23236) *(G-9938)*

Nelsons Cabinetry Inc 804 560-4785
10501 Ashburn Rd North Chesterfield (23235) *(G-9939)*

Nemesys Software 703 435-0508
1007 Hertford St Herndon (20170) *(G-6751)*

Nenno Media, Harrisonburg *Also called Herald Press (G-6328)*

ALPHABETIC

Neon Compass Marketing LLC 580 330-4699
  6607 Kelsey Point Cir Alexandria (22315) *(G-542)*
Neon District 757 663-6970
  759 Granby St Norfolk (23510) *(G-9654)*
Neon Guitar 804 932-3716
  11941 Steel Trap Rd New Kent (23124) *(G-9136)*
Neon Nation LLC 703 255-4996
  2875 Sutton Oaks Ln Vienna (22181) *(G-14103)*
Neon Nights 757 857-6366
  2640 Arkansas Ave Norfolk (23513) *(G-9655)*
Neon Nights Inc 757 248-5676
  1555 Shelton Ave Norfolk (23502) *(G-9656)*
Neopath Systems LLC 571 238-1333
  3202 Brynwood Pl Herndon (20171) *(G-6752)*
Neosystems Corp 571 234-4949
  3714 Valley Oaks Dr Fairfax (22033) *(G-4516)*
Ner Inc 757 437-7727
  1820 Atlantic Ave Virginia Beach (23451) *(G-14675)*
Nerd Alert Tees LLC 804 938-9375
  14101 Thorney Ct Midlothian (23113) *(G-8868)*
Nergysense LLC 434 282-2656
  420 Park St Charlottesville (22902) *(G-2837)*
Nero Gate Tracking, Piney River *Also called Kerry Scott* *(G-10361)*
Nervve Technologies Inc 703 334-1488
  505 Huntmar Park Dr # 325 Herndon (20170) *(G-6753)*
Nestle Holdings Inc (HQ) **703 682-4600**
  1812 N Moore St Arlington (22209) *(G-1073)*
Nestle Pizza Company Inc 757 479-1512
  1512 Birch Leaf Rd Chesapeake (23320) *(G-3217)*
Nestle Prepared Foods Company 434 822-4000
  201 Airside Dr Danville (24540) *(G-4017)*
Nestle Prepared Foods Factory, Danville *Also called Nestle Prepared Foods Company (G-4017)*
Nestle Purina Factory, King William *Also called Nestle Purina Petcare Company (G-7130)*
Nestle Purina Petcare Company 804 769-1266
  931 Dunluce Rd King William (23086) *(G-7130)*
Nestle Usa Inc 765 778-6000
  1812 N Moore St Ste 118 Arlington (22209) *(G-1074)*
Nestle Usa Inc 757 538-4178
  1368 Progress Rd Suffolk (23434) *(G-13750)*
Net 100 Ltd 757 490-0496
  5257 Cleveland St Ste 102 Virginia Beach (23462) *(G-14676)*
Net Results, Arlington *Also called Larry Rosenbaum (G-1027)*
Net6degrees LLC 703 201-4480
  19570 Greggsville Rd Purcellville (20132) *(G-10672)*
Netcentric Technologies Inc 202 661-2180
  1600 Wilson Blvd Ste 1010 Arlington (22209) *(G-1075)*
Netqos Inc (HQ) **703 708-3699**
  2291 Wood Oak Dr Ste 140 Herndon (20171) *(G-6754)*
Netrix/Proteon, Chantilly *Also called Nsgdatacom Inc (G-2475)*
Nets Pix & Things LLC 757 466-1337
  132 Kidd Blvd Norfolk (23502) *(G-9657)*
Netstyle Corp 703 717-9706
  7960 Conell Ct Lorton (22079) *(G-7514)*
Nettalon Inc 877 638-8256
  3324 Bourbon St Fredericksburg (22408) *(G-5332)*
Nettalon Security Systems Inc 540 368-5290
  3304 Bourbon St Fl 3d Fredericksburg (22408) *(G-5333)*
Netunity Software LLC 757 744-0147
  2201 Bierce Dr Virginia Beach (23454) *(G-14677)*
Netwatcher, Reston *Also called Defensative LLC (G-10837)*
Network 12 ....703 532-2970
  116b W Broad St Falls Church (22046) *(G-4923)*
Network Industries 757 435-6163
  1810 S Woodside Ln Virginia Beach (23454) *(G-14678)*
Network Storage Corp 703 834-7500
  14020 Thunderbolt Pl 50 Chantilly (20151) *(G-2468)*
Neu Age Sportswear 757 581-8333
  7502 Rosefield Dr Norfolk (23513) *(G-9658)*
Neuman Almnium Impact Extrsion 540 248-2703
  1418 Genicom Dr Waynesboro (22980) *(G-15129)*
Neuro Stat Anlytcal Sltons LLC 703 224-8984
  1934 Old Gallows Rd # 35 Vienna (22182) *(G-14104)*
Neuro Stat Solutions, Vienna *Also called Neuro Stat Anlytcal Sltons LLC (G-14104)*
Neuro Tennis Inc 240 481-7640
  1000 Wilson Blvd Ste 1800 Arlington (22209) *(G-1076)*
Neuropro Spinal Jaxx Inc 571 334-7424
  6337 Falling Brook Dr Burke (22015) *(G-2195)*
Neurotech Na Inc 888 980-1197
  11220 Assett Loop Ste 101 Manassas (20109) *(G-8116)*
Neutra-Green Clg Solutions LLC 804 447-8010
  2221 E Parham Rd Ste C Henrico (23228) *(G-6540)*
Never Say Die Studios LLC 478 787-1901
  309 General Dr Spotsylvania (22551) *(G-12906)*
Nevins & Moss LLC 929 266-3640
  9708 Locust Hill Dr Great Falls (22066) *(G-5968)*
Nevtek 540 925-2322
  12512 Dry Run Rd Williamsville (24487) *(G-15351)*

New Acton Mobile Inds LLC 804 520-7171
  1750 Touchstone Rd South Chesterfield (23834) *(G-12817)*
New Age Repr & Fabrication LLC 757 819-3887
  871 Cedar St Apt 307 Norfolk (23523) *(G-9659)*
New Century Software 704 984-3135
  6914 Wolf Run Shoals Rd Fairfax Station (22039) *(G-4719)*
New Creation Sourcing Inc 703 330-5314
  8830 Rixlew Ln Manassas (20109) *(G-8117)*
New England Chimney Supply, Springfield *Also called New England Supply Inc (G-13058)*
New England Supply Inc 703 372-2689
  7956 Cameron Brown Ct Springfield (22153) *(G-13058)*
New ERA Technology LLC 571 308-8525
  12190 Waveland St Apt 232 Fairfax (22033) *(G-4517)*
New Health Analytics LLC 804 245-8240
  200 Westgate Pkwy Ste 104 Henrico (23233) *(G-6541)*
New Hemp US 757 977-8098
  2608 Horse Pasture Rd # 1 Virginia Beach (23453) *(G-14679)*
New Home Media 703 550-2233
  9408 Gunston Cove Rd E Lorton (22079) *(G-7515)*
New Homes Media 540 654-5350
  11900 Main St Ste B114 Fredericksburg (22408) *(G-5334)*
New Image Graphics Inc 540 678-0900
  172 Imboden Dr Ste 19 Winchester (22603) *(G-15455)*
New Journal and Guide Inc 757 543-6531
  5127 E Virginia Beach Blv Norfolk (23502) *(G-9660)*
New Kent Charles Cy Chronicle 804 843-4181
  18639 Eltham Rd Ste 203 West Point (23181) *(G-15159)*
New Kent-Charles Cy Chronicle, West Point *Also called New Kent Charles Cy Chronicle (G-15159)*
New Life Custom Cabinetry LLC 757 274-7442
  1512 Hedgerow Dr Virginia Beach (23455) *(G-14680)*
New Look Press LLC 804 530-0836
  305 Redbird Dr Chester (23836) *(G-3439)*
New Look Pressure Washing LLC 804 476-2000
  1300 Oakland Rd Henrico (23231) *(G-6542)*
New Market Poultry LLC 540 740-4260
  145 E Old Cross Rd New Market (22844) *(G-9145)*
New Minglewood Mfg Inc 276 632-9107
  191 Clyde Prillaman St Fieldale (24089) *(G-4990)*
New Mllennium Bldg Systems LLC 540 389-0211
  100 Diugids Ln Salem (24153) *(G-12544)*
New Paradigm Publishing LLC 757 423-3385
  609 W Little Creek Rd Norfolk (23505) *(G-9661)*
New Richmond Ventures LLC 804 887-2355
  1801 E Cary St Richmond (23223) *(G-11688)*
New River Canoe Manufacturing, Independence *Also called Indian River Canoe Mfg (G-6988)*
New River Concrete Supply 540 433-9043
  2565 John Wayland Hwy # 201 Rockingham (22801) *(G-12264)*
New River Concrete Supply Co 540 639-9679
  10 Forest Ave Radford (24141) *(G-10726)*
New River Concrete Supply Inc 540 552-1721
  801 Park Dr Blacksburg (24060) *(G-1773)*
New River Energetics Inc (HQ) **703 406-5695**
  State Rte 114 Radford (24143) *(G-10727)*
New River Ordnance Works Inc 907 888-9615
  2200 Kraft Dr Ste 2150 Blacksburg (24060) *(G-1774)*
New River Sign and Vinyl LLC 703 793-0730
  2280 Kraft Dr Ste 1100 Blacksburg (24060) *(G-1775)*
New River Vineyard & Winery 540 392-4870
  6750 Falling Branch Rd Fairlawn (24141) *(G-4739)*
New Silk Road Marketing LLC 434 531-0141
  3217 S Chesterfield Ct Charlottesville (22911) *(G-2663)*
New Student Chronicle 540 463-4000
  308 Jackson Ave Lexington (24450) *(G-7407)*
New Tech Innovations 703 731-8160
  43074 Northlake Blvd Leesburg (20176) *(G-7320)*
New Town Holdings Inc 703 471-6666
  11440 Isaac Newton Sq N Reston (20190) *(G-10907)*
New Wave Thrifty Llc 904 400-8539
  710 Sycamore St Norfolk (23523) *(G-9662)*
New Worlds Stone Co Inc 434 831-1051
  42 Alberene Loop Schuyler (22969) *(G-12652)*
New York Air Brake Company 540 989-5044
  2875 Larkview Cir Sw Roanoke (24015) *(G-12140)*
Newbold Corporation (PA) **540 489-4400**
  450 Weaver St Rocky Mount (24151) *(G-12342)*
Newcomb Woodworks LLC 804 370-0441
  2206 Oakwood Ln Henrico (23228) *(G-6543)*
Newell Brands Inc 800 241-1848
  2042 Westmoreland St Richmond (23230) *(G-11303)*
Newell Industries Intl 434 372-0089
  397 Jonbil Rd Chase City (23924) *(G-2913)*
Newell Logging 434 636-2743
  938 Alvis Rd La Crosse (23950) *(G-7147)*
Newmarket Corporation (PA) **804 788-5000**
  330 S 4th St Richmond (23219) *(G-11689)*
Newport Cutter Grinding, Hampton *Also called Ncg LLC (G-6206)*
Newport Cutter Grinding Co Inc 757 838-3224
  302 Aberdeen Rd Hampton (23661) *(G-6207)*

(G-0000) Company's Geographic Section entry number

Newport Industries Ltd 440 208-3322
416 Boush St Norfolk (23510) *(G-9663)*

Newport News Shipbuilding, Newport News *Also called Huntington Ingalls Inds Inc (G-9252)*

Newport News Shipbuilding, Newport News *Also called Northrop Grumman Newport News (G-9306)*

Newport Timber LLC (HQ) **703 243-3355**
1300 Wilson Blvd Ste 1075 Arlington (22209) *(G-1077)*

Newriver Concrete, Rockingham *Also called Rockingham Redi-Mix Inc (G-12274)*

News and Record, South Boston *Also called South Boston News Inc (G-12790)*

News Connection 703 661-4999
1 Saarinen Cir Sterling (20166) *(G-13461)*

News Gazette Print Shop, Lexington *Also called News-Gazette Corporation (G-7408)*

News Leader , The, Staunton *Also called Leader Publishing Company (G-13274)*

News Virginian, Waynesboro *Also called Wood Television LLC (G-15148)*

News-Gazette Corporation 540 463-3116
109 S Jefferson St Lexington (24450) *(G-7408)*

Newswise Inc 434 296-9417
265 Turkeysag Trl Ste 102 Palmyra (22963) *(G-10251)*

Nexaware LLC 703 880-6697
1595 Boyers Rd Rockingham (22801) *(G-12265)*

Nexgrid LLC 833 639-4743
915 Maple Grove Dr # 200 Fredericksburg (22407) *(G-5335)*

Nexlevel Transports Inc 757 707-6349
3436 Frederick Dr Toano (23168) *(G-13871)*

Next Generation MGT Corp (PA) **703 372-1282**
44715 Prentice Dr # 973 Ashburn (20146) *(G-1321)*

Next Generation Woods Inc 540 639-3077
4615 Mountain Pride Rd Hiwassee (24347) *(G-6913)*

Next Level Building Solutions (PA) **540 400-9169**
5170 Alean Rd Boones Mill (24065) *(G-1898)*

Next Level Building Solutions 540 685-1500
5205 Starkey Rd Roanoke (24018) *(G-11974)*

Next Level Printing 757 288-1399
833 W 41st St Norfolk (23508) *(G-9664)*

Next Screen Media 571 295-6398
42053 Porch Light Dr Aldie (20105) *(G-109)*

Nextday Cabinets of Va LLC 703 291-8935
3985 Deep Rock Rd Richmond (23233) *(G-11304)*

Nextflight Jets LLC 703 392-6500
1908 Reston Metro Plz # 1915 Reston (20190) *(G-10908)*

Nexxtek Inc 571 356-2921
8422 Berea Dr Vienna (22180) *(G-14105)*

Ngc International Inc (HQ) **703 280-2900**
2980 Fairview Park Dr Falls Church (22042) *(G-4836)*

NGK-Lcke Polymr Insulators Inc 757 460-3649
1609 Diamond Springs Rd Virginia Beach (23455) *(G-14681)*

NGL Woodbridge 703 492-0430
13422 Jefferson Davis Hwy Woodbridge (22191) *(G-15758)*

Nguyen & Phan LLC 571 730-9948
8220 Laurel Heights Loop Lorton (22079) *(G-7516)*

Nhance Technologies Inc 434 582-6110
122 Cornerstone St Lynchburg (24502) *(G-7776)*

Nhm Inc 703 550-2233
9408 Gunston Cove Rd E Lorton (22079) *(G-7517)*

Nhsa 508 420-1902
1111 Belle Pre Way # 728 Alexandria (22314) *(G-291)*

Ni PHI Thach 434 386-8852
4573 S Amherst Hwy Madison Heights (24572) *(G-7878)*

Niagara Bottling LLC 804 551-3923
1700 Digital Dr Chester (23836) *(G-3440)*

Nibco Inc 540 324-0242
3200 Green Forest Ave Buena Vista (24416) *(G-2149)*

Nibco Inc 540 324-0242
131 Johnson Dr Stuarts Draft (24477) *(G-13656)*

Niblick Inc 804 550-1607
9527 Kings Charter Dr Ashland (23005) *(G-1470)*

Nibm, Falls Church *Also called National Institute of Bus Mgt (G-4835)*

Nice Wounders Group 276 669-6476
148 Bristol East Rd Bristol (24202) *(G-2028)*

Niche Publications LLC 757 620-2631
36 N Kingsbridge Pl Apt A Chesapeake (23322) *(G-3218)*

Nichols Cabinetry LLC 540 860-9252
229 Fairview Rd Luray (22835) *(G-7620)*

Nichols Logging Inc 540 297-3246
1433 Preston Mill Rd Huddleston (24104) *(G-6956)*

Nichols Welding 540 483-5308
92 Redbud Hill Rd Rocky Mount (24151) *(G-12343)*

Nicks Wldg & Fabrication LLC 434 251-2696
645 Barn Rd Callands (24530) *(G-2214)*

Nicol Candy 804 740-2378
10211 Pepperhill Ln Richmond (23238) *(G-11305)*

Nicola Biscardo Selections, Richmond *Also called DRG Imports LLC (G-11569)*

Niday Inc 540 427-2776
4349 Bandy Rd Roanoke (24014) *(G-12141)*

Nighthawk Welding LLC 540 845-9966
1221 E Longview Dr Woodbridge (22191) *(G-15759)*

Nightingale Inc 804 332-7018
8903 Three Chopt Rd Henrico (23229) *(G-6544)*

Nik Graphix LLC 703 863-1075
4555 Interlachen Ct B Alexandria (22312) *(G-543)*

Nika Software Inc 703 992-5318
2452 Dakota Lakes Dr Herndon (20171) *(G-6755)*

Nike Inc 703 497-4513
2700 Potomac Mills Cir # 511 Woodbridge (22192) *(G-15760)*

Nimco Us Inc 314 982-3204
1812 N Moore St Arlington (22209) *(G-1078)*

Nine-Ten Press LLC 804 727-9135
6 N Shields Ave Richmond (23220) *(G-11690)*

Ninees Gourmet Ice Cream 703 451-4124
8628 Bristlecone Pl Springfield (22153) *(G-13059)*

Ninja Kombucha LLC 757 870-6733
607 Wickham St Richmond (23222) *(G-11691)*

Ninoska M Marcano 202 604-8864
2922 Fairhill Rd Fairfax (22031) *(G-4518)*

Nippon Pulse America Inc 540 633-1677
4 Corporate Dr Radford (24141) *(G-10728)*

Nipro Glass Americas Corp 434 372-5113
194 Duckworth Dr Chase City (23924) *(G-2914)*

Nis Inc 703 323-9170
10505 Braddock Rd Ste B Fairfax (22032) *(G-4519)*

Nita's Nice Alterations, Alexandria *Also called Juanita Deshazior (G-248)*

Nitto Inc 757 436-5540
809 Principal Ct Chesapeake (23320) *(G-3219)*

Nks LLC 757 229-3139
423 N Boundary St Ste 200 Williamsburg (23185) *(G-15283)*

NLB, Virginia Beach *Also called No Lie Blades LLC (G-14682)*

NM Mechanic Road Service LLC 571 237-4810
1504 Constellation Pl # 204 Woodbridge (22191) *(G-15761)*

NMB Metals 434 584-0027
850 Locust St South Hill (23970) *(G-12857)*

No Burn Technology, Norfolk *Also called Bishop II Inc (G-9464)*

No Lie Blades LLC 610 442-5539
1728 Prodan Ln Virginia Beach (23453) *(G-14682)*

No Limits LLC 757 729-5612
7862 Tidewater Dr Norfolk (23505) *(G-9665)*

No Quarter LLC 703 753-0511
15123 Windy Hollow Cir Gainesville (20155) *(G-5601)*

No Short Cut 757 696-0249
918 Chimney Hill Pkwy Virginia Beach (23462) *(G-14683)*

Noah Paci 703 525-5437
506 N Ivy St Arlington (22201) *(G-1079)*

Noahs Ark Transportation LLC 240 476-3381
3320 S 28th St Apt 303 Alexandria (22302) *(G-292)*

Noble Endeavors LLC 571 402-7061
13859 Smoketown Rd Woodbridge (22192) *(G-15762)*

Noble-Met LLC 540 389-7860
200 S Yorkshire St Salem (24153) *(G-12545)*

Nobull Burger, Charlottesville *Also called OH My Goshyum LLC (G-2669)*

Nobull Burger 434 975-6628
1139a River Rd Charlottesville (22901) *(G-2664)*

Noel Hull Logging, DOE Hill *Also called Noel I Hull (G-4115)*

Noel I Hull 540 396-6225
7903 Doe Hill Rd DOE Hill (24433) *(G-4115)*

Noelleimani Elite LLC 804 452-6373
102 N 7th St Richmond (23219) *(G-11692)*

Noir X Jojo LLC 757 756-9134
136 Semple Farm Rd # 207 Hampton (23666) *(G-6208)*

Noke Truck LLC 540 266-0045
16 Church Ave Sw Roanoke (24011) *(G-12142)*

Nokyem Naturals LLC 757 218-1794
6 Mill Creek Ter Hampton (23663) *(G-6209)*

Nolte Machine and Welding LLC 804 357-7271
10 W Williamsburg Rd D Sandston (23150) *(G-12625)*

Nomad Deli & Catering Co LLC 804 677-0843
207 W Brookland Park Blvd Richmond (23222) *(G-11693)*

Nomad Geosciences 703 390-1147
11429 Purple Beech Dr Reston (20191) *(G-10909)*

Nomad Solutions LLC 703 656-9100
13575 Wellington Center C Gainesville (20155) *(G-5602)*

Nomadic Display LLC 800 336-5019
10505 Furnace Rd Ste 108 Lorton (22079) *(G-7518)*

Nomar Castings Inc 540 380-3394
6563 Stones Keep Ln Elliston (24087) *(G-4346)*

Non Stop Enterprise Ltd 276 945-2028
401 Rosenbaum Rd Bluefield (24605) *(G-1871)*

Noodle Games 757 572-3849
1105 Carriage Ct Chesapeake (23322) *(G-3220)*

Noparei Professionals LLC 571 354-9422
3418 Brahms Dr Woodbridge (22193) *(G-15763)*

Norcraft Companies LP 434 385-7500
1 Macel Dr Lynchburg (24502) *(G-7777)*

Nordic Mining LLC 703 878-0346
3811 Corona Ln Woodbridge (22193) *(G-15764)*

Norfield-Fogleman Cabinets 276 889-1333
Rr 19 Lebanon (24266) *(G-7202)*

Norfields Farm Inc 540 832-2952
1982 James Madison Hwy Gordonsville (22942) *(G-5916)*

A L P H A B E T I C

Norfleet Acquisition Co Inc............540 373-9481
105 Central Rd Fredericksburg (22401) ***(G-5208)***
Norfleet Quality LLC............540 373-9481
103 Central Rd Fredericksburg (22401) ***(G-5209)***
Norfolk Machine and Wldg Inc............757 489-0330
1028 W 27th St Norfolk (23517) ***(G-9666)***
Norfolk Naval Shipyard, Portsmouth *Also called United States Dept of Navy* ***(G-10495)***
Norfolk Printing Co............757 627-1302
805 Granby St Norfolk (23510) ***(G-9667)***
Norfolk Tent Company, Chesapeake *Also called Tent Company of Norfolk LLC* ***(G-3330)***
Norfolk Tent Company Inc............757 461-7330
2633 Wyoming Ave Norfolk (23513) ***(G-9668)***
Norman Precision Machining LLC............540 674-0932
5015 Woodlyn St Dublin (24084) ***(G-4167)***
Norris Bowman Logging, Ferrum *Also called Rainbow Hill Farm* ***(G-4977)***
Norris Screen and Mfg LLC............276 988-8901
21405 Gvrnor G C Pery Hwy Tazewell (24651) ***(G-13838)***
Norrisbilt Fbrction MBL Wldg L............276 325-0269
520 Kentucky Ave Sw Norton (24273) ***(G-10131)***
Norshipco, Norfolk *Also called Bae Systems Nrfolk Ship Repr I* ***(G-9452)***
North Arrow Inc............703 250-3215
11115 Flora Lee Dr Fairfax Station (22039) ***(G-4720)***
North Fork Inc............540 997-5602
250 N Fork Ln Goshen (24439) ***(G-5926)***
North Fork Lumber & Log Homes, Goshen *Also called North Fork Inc* ***(G-5926)***
North Garden Publishing............540 580-2501
5227 N Garden Ln Roanoke (24019) ***(G-11975)***
North Gate Vineyard, Hillsboro *Also called Fedor Ventures LLC* ***(G-6866)***
North Lakeside Pubg Hse LLC............757 650-3596
2245 N Lakeside Dr Virginia Beach (23454) ***(G-14684)***
North Lock LLC............703 797-2739
2308 Mount Vernon Ave # 714 Alexandria (22301) ***(G-293)***
North Machine Shop............804 725-5443
2036 Buckley Hall Rd Dutton (23050) ***(G-4274)***
North Media LLC............202 277-4933
44800 Milestone Sq # 303 Ashburn (20147) ***(G-1322)***
North Mountain Vineyard, Maurertown *Also called Foster Jackson LLC* ***(G-8363)***
North of James............804 218-5265
3122 W Clay St Apt 6 Richmond (23230) ***(G-11306)***
North Ridge............540 825-4275
12501 Sherwood Forest Dr Culpeper (22701) ***(G-3912)***
North Sails Hampton Inc............757 723-6280
86 Algonquin Rd Hampton (23661) ***(G-6210)***
North South Partners LLC............804 213-0600
8080 Villa Park Dr Richmond (23228) ***(G-11307)***
North Star Press............540 967-5093
186 Harris Creek Rd Louisa (23093) ***(G-7562)***
North Star Science & Tech LLC............410 961-6692
3105 Windsong Dr Oakton (22124) ***(G-10160)***
North Star Software Consulting............703 628-8564
908 Octorora Pl Ne Leesburg (20176) ***(G-7321)***
North Street Enterprise Inc............434 392-4144
127 North St Farmville (23901) ***(G-4954)***
North-South Trader, Orange *Also called Publishers Press Incorporated* ***(G-10223)***
Northampton Custom Milling LLC............757 442-4747
10168 Shell St Nassawadox (23413) ***(G-9101)***
Northampton House Pre............201 893-1826
7018 Wild Flower Ln Franktown (23354) ***(G-5165)***
Northeast Solite Corporation............804 262-8119
4801 Hermitage Rd Ste 105 Richmond (23227) ***(G-11308)***
Northern Defense Inds Inc, Alexandria *Also called Northern Defense Inds LLC* ***(G-294)***
Northern Defense Inds LLC............703 836-8346
667 S Washington St Alexandria (22314) ***(G-294)***
Northern Neck Lumber Co Inc............804 333-4041
16056 History Land Hwy Warsaw (22572) ***(G-15071)***
Northern Pttsylvnia Cnty Fd CT............434 656-6617
Weal Rd Chatham (24531) ***(G-2932)***
Northern VA Compounders Pllc............855 792-5462
4080 Lafayette Center Dr # 27 Chantilly (20151) ***(G-2469)***
Northern Virginia Compute............540 479-4455
754 Warrenton Rd Fredericksburg (22406) ***(G-5461)***
Northern Virginia Insulation............703 753-7249
4518 Jennifer Ln Haymarket (20169) ***(G-6431)***
Northern Virginia Wire Works............571 221-1882
16001 Roland Park Pl Gainesville (20155) ***(G-5603)***
Northern Virginia Woodwork Inc............540 752-6128
12948 Elk Run Rd Bealeton (22712) ***(G-1602)***
Northern Vrgnia Cast Stone LLC............703 393-2777
5406 Ancestry Ct Gainesville (20155) ***(G-5604)***
Northern Vrgnia Prof Assoc Inc............703 525-5218
6565 Arlington Blvd Falls Church (22042) ***(G-4837)***
Northfield Medical Mfg LLC (PA)............**800 270-0153**
5505 Robin Hood Rd Ste B Norfolk (23513) ***(G-9669)***
Northlight Publishing Co............804 344-8500
127 W Clay St Richmond (23220) ***(G-11694)***
Northport Research Inc............703 508-9773
635 First St Apt 404 Alexandria (22314) ***(G-295)***
Northrop Custom Metal LLC............703 751-7042
6060 Farrington Ave Alexandria (22304) ***(G-296)***
Northrop Gov't Relations Div, Falls Church *Also called Northrop Grumman Systems Corp* ***(G-4846)***
Northrop Grmman / Hnlulu - US............808 529-9500
2980 Fairview Park Dr Falls Church (22042) ***(G-4838)***
Northrop Grmman Gdnce Elec Inc (HQ)............**703 280-2900**
2980 Fairview Park Dr Falls Church (22042) ***(G-4839)***
Northrop Grmman Innvtion Syste, Dulles *Also called Northrop Grmman Innvtion Syste* ***(G-4212)***
Northrop Grmman Innvtion Syste............763 744-5219
1300 Wilson Blvd Ste 400 Arlington (22209) ***(G-1080)***
Northrop Grmman Innvtion Syste............540 639-7631
1304 Tyler Ave Apt G Radford (24141) ***(G-10729)***
Northrop Grmman Innvtion Syste (HQ)............**703 406-5000**
45101 Warp Dr Dulles (20166) ***(G-4212)***
Northrop Grmman Ovrseas Hldg I (HQ)............**703 280-4069**
2980 Fairview Park Dr Falls Church (22042) ***(G-4840)***
Northrop Grmman Worldwide Entp (HQ)............**703 713-4096**
2340 Dulles Corner Blvd Herndon (20171) ***(G-6756)***
Northrop Grumman Corporation............804 272-1321
101 Gateway Centre Pkwy # 300 North Chesterfield (23235) ***(G-9940)***
Northrop Grumman Corporation............804 416-6500
11751 Meadowville Ln Chester (23836) ***(G-3441)***
Northrop Grumman Corporation............757 838-7221
21 Enterprise Pkwy # 210 Hampton (23666) ***(G-6211)***
Northrop Grumman Corporation............757 688-6850
1320 Winfall Dr Chesapeake (23322) ***(G-3221)***
Northrop Grumman Corporation............540 469-9647
16480 Commerce Dr Ste 100 King George (22485) ***(G-7104)***
Northrop Grumman Corporation............703 713-4096
2340 Dulles Corner Blvd Herndon (20171) ***(G-6757)***
Northrop Grumman Corporation............757 688-5339
4836 Milden Rd Williamsburg (23188) ***(G-15284)***
Northrop Grumman Corporation............703 406-5695
State Rte 114 Radford (24143) ***(G-10730)***
Northrop Grumman Corporation............804 371-0019
110 S 7th St Ste 500 Richmond (23219) ***(G-11695)***
Northrop Grumman Corporation............703 556-5960
4262 Entre Ct Chantilly (20151) ***(G-2470)***
Northrop Grumman Corporation............212 978-2800
1101 Wilson Blvd Ste 1600 Arlington (22209) ***(G-1081)***
Northrop Grumman Corporation............703 449-7120
4807 Stonecroft Blvd Chantilly (20151) ***(G-2471)***
Northrop Grumman Corporation............703 556-1144
7575 Colshire Dr Mc Lean (22102) ***(G-8511)***
Northrop Grumman Corporation (PA)............**703 280-2900**
2980 Fairview Park Dr Falls Church (22042) ***(G-4841)***
Northrop Grumman Global Svcs............703 280-2900
2980 Fairview Park Dr Falls Church (22042) ***(G-4842)***
Northrop Grumman Info Systems, Fairfax *Also called Northrop Grumman Info Tech* ***(G-4520)***
Northrop Grumman Info Systems, Mc Lean *Also called Northrop Grumman Systems Corp* ***(G-8517)***
Northrop Grumman Info Systems, Herndon *Also called Northrop Grumman Systems Corp* ***(G-6758)***
Northrop Grumman Info Systems, Herndon *Also called Northrop Grumman Systems Corp* ***(G-6759)***
Northrop Grumman Info Systems, Herndon *Also called Northrop Grumman Systems Corp* ***(G-6760)***
Northrop Grumman Info Systems, Mc Lean *Also called Northrop Grumman Systems Corp* ***(G-8518)***
Northrop Grumman Info Systems, Mc Lean *Also called Northrop Grumman Corporation* ***(G-8511)***
Northrop Grumman Info Tech............703 968-1000
12900 Fdral Systems Pk Dr Fairfax (22033) ***(G-4520)***
Northrop Grumman Innovation............540 831-4788
State Rte 114 Radford (24141) ***(G-10731)***
Northrop Grumman Intl Inc............703 556-1144
7575 Colshire Dr Mc Lean (22102) ***(G-8512)***
Northrop Grumman Intl Inc (HQ)............**703 280-2900**
2980 Fairview Park Dr Falls Church (22042) ***(G-4843)***
Northrop Grumman Intl Trdg Inc (HQ)............**703 280-2900**
2980 Fairview Park Dr Falls Church (22042) ***(G-4844)***
Northrop Grumman It, Richmond *Also called Northrop Grumman Corporation* ***(G-11695)***
Northrop Grumman Newport News (HQ)............**757 380-2000**
4101 Washington Ave Newport News (23607) ***(G-9306)***
Northrop Grumman Sperry............434 974-2000
2300 Hydraulic Rd Charlottesville (22901) ***(G-2665)***
Northrop Grumman Systems Corp (HQ)............**703 280-2900**
2980 Fairview Park Dr Falls Church (22042) ***(G-4845)***
Northrop Grumman Systems Corp............703 875-8463
2100 Washington Blvd Arlington (22204) ***(G-1082)***
Northrop Grumman Systems Corp............703 808-0961
6186 Snowhill Ct Centreville (20120) ***(G-2324)***
Northrop Grumman Systems Corp............757 312-8375
1500 Technology Dr # 104 Chesapeake (23320) ***(G-3222)***
Northrop Grumman Systems Corp............703 556-1144
7575 Colshire Dr Mc Lean (22102) ***(G-8513)***

Northrop Grumman Systems Corp 703 556-1144
7575 Colshire Dr Mc Lean (22102) *(G-8514)*

Northrop Grumman Systems Corp 703 556-1144
7575 Colshire Dr Mc Lean (22102) *(G-8515)*

Northrop Grumman Systems Corp 703 280-1220
2980 Fairview Park Dr Falls Church (22042) *(G-4846)*

Northrop Grumman Systems Corp 703 556-1144
7575 Colshire Dr Mc Lean (22102) *(G-8516)*

Northrop Grumman Systems Corp 703 556-1144
7575 Colshire Dr Mc Lean (22102) *(G-8517)*

Northrop Grumman Systems Corp 757 380-2612
4101 Washington Ave Newport News (23607) *(G-9307)*

Northrop Grumman Systems Corp 757 498-5616
2700 Intl Pkwy Ste 700 Virginia Beach (23452) *(G-14685)*

Northrop Grumman Systems Corp 434 974-2000
1070 Seminole Trl Charlottesville (22901) *(G-2666)*

Northrop Grumman Systems Corp 757 686-4147
3845 North Landing Rd Virginia Beach (23456) *(G-14686)*

Northrop Grumman Systems Corp 304 726-5030
415 Cnsttton Rd Bldg 229 Radford (24141) *(G-10732)*

Northrop Grumman Systems Corp 703 406-5474
45101 Warp Dr Dulles (20166) *(G-4213)*

Northrop Grumman Systems Corp 757 463-5578
2700 International Pkwy # 300 Virginia Beach (23452) *(G-14687)*

Northrop Grumman Systems Corp 703 633-8300
4805 Stonecroft Blvd Chantilly (20151) *(G-2472)*

Northrop Grumman Systems Corp 703 968-1000
2340 Dulles Corner Blvd Herndon (20171) *(G-6758)*

Northrop Grumman Systems Corp 703 968-1000
2340 Dulles Corner Blvd Herndon (20171) *(G-6759)*

Northrop Grumman Systems Corp 703 968-1100
13825 Sunrise Valley Dr # 200 Herndon (20171) *(G-6760)*

Northrop Grumman Systems Corp 703 556-1144
7575 Colshire Dr Mc Lean (22102) *(G-8518)*

Northrup Grumman 305 466-4655
14149 Gabrielle Way Centreville (20121) *(G-2325)*

Northstar Industrial Electric, Norfolk *Also called Roseann Combs* *(G-9710)*

Northstar Training, Norfolk *Also called Program Services LLC* *(G-9698)*

Northwest Hardwoods 540 631-3245
7685 Winchester Rd Front Royal (22630) *(G-5546)*

Northwest Hardwoods Inc 540 261-2171
302 Piedmont Ave Buena Vista (24416) *(G-2150)*

Northwest Hardwoods Inc 540 261-2171
403 E 29th St Buena Vista (24416) *(G-2151)*

Northwest Territorial Mint LLC 703 922-5545
6564 Loisdale Ct Ste 318 Springfield (22150) *(G-13060)*

Northwestern PA Opt Clinic 540 721-6017
147 Windmere Trl Moneta (24121) *(G-8973)*

Northwind Associates 757 871-8215
8770 Little England Rd Hayes (23072) *(G-6403)*

Northwind Woodworks, Floyd *Also called Brad Warstler* *(G-5017)*

Northwood Contracting LLC 703 624-0928
16010 Hamilton Ln Rixeyville (22737) *(G-11880)*

Norton Embroidery Inc 540 550-7331
11 S Church St Berryville (22611) *(G-1685)*

Norton Quarry, Big Stone Gap *Also called Legacy Vulcan LLC* *(G-1711)*

Norton's Embroidery, Berryville *Also called Norton Embroidery Inc* *(G-1685)*

Nortonlifelock Inc 703 414-4444
400 11th St S Arlington (22202) *(G-1083)*

Nortonlifelock Inc 703 883-0180
8180 Greensboro Dr # 575 Mc Lean (22102) *(G-8519)*

Norva Plastics Inc 757 622-9281
3911 Killam Ave Norfolk (23508) *(G-9670)*

Norvell Signs Incorporated 804 737-2189
5928 Nine Mile Rd Richmond (23223) *(G-11696)*

Notalvision Inc 703 953-3339
7717 Coppermine Dr Manassas (20109) *(G-8118)*

Notalvision Inc 888 910-2020
4500 Southgate Pl Ste 400 Chantilly (20151) *(G-2473)*

Notary On The Go, Fredericksburg *Also called Wanda Eubanks* *(G-5500)*

Notaviva Vineyards 540 668-6756
13274 Sagle Rd Hillsboro (20132) *(G-6877)*

Nothing But Cake Incorporated 540 322-7520
5217 Sarah Ln Fredericksburg (22407) *(G-5336)*

Nothing But Neon 434 842-9395
351 Scenic River Dr Columbia (23038) *(G-3753)*

Nottoway Plant, Blackstone *Also called Sb Cox Ready Mix Inc* *(G-1827)*

Nottoway Publishing Co Inc 434 292-3019
111 W Maple St Blackstone (23824) *(G-1821)*

Nottoway River Publications 804 737-7395
5861 White Oak Rd Sandston (23150) *(G-12626)*

Nova Armory, Arlington *Also called Broadstone Security LLC* *(G-890)*

Nova Concrete Products Inc 540 439-2978
5303 Ritchie Rd Bealeton (22712) *(G-1603)*

Nova Defense & Arospc Intl LLC 703 864-6929
414 Pendleton St Ste 400 Alexandria (22314) *(G-297)*

Nova Exteriors Inc 703 322-1500
5568 General Wash Dr Alexandria (22312) *(G-544)*

Nova Fire Supply LLC 703 909-8339
35190 Tate Ct Round Hill (20141) *(G-12384)*

Nova Green Energy LLC 571 210-0589
3426 Lakeside View Dr Falls Church (22041) *(G-4847)*

Nova Lumber & Millwork LLC 703 451-9217
7953 Cameron Brown Ct Springfield (22153) *(G-13061)*

Nova Maris Press 434 975-0501
977 Seminole Trl Charlottesville (22901) *(G-2667)*

Nova Power Solutions Inc 703 657-0122
21515 Ridgetop Cir # 210 Sterling (20166) *(G-13462)*

Nova Retail LLC 703 507-5220
3171d Spring St Fairfax (22031) *(G-4521)*

Nova Roast 540 239-2459
7695 Bradshaw Rd Salem (24153) *(G-12546)*

Nova Rock Craft LLC 703 217-7072
7157 Comrie Ct Warrenton (20187) *(G-15038)*

Nova Synchro of VA Inc 703 241-4136
5411 22nd St N Arlington (22205) *(G-1084)*

Novartis Corporation 540 435-1836
5138 Lawyer Rd Mc Gaheysville (22840) *(G-8378)*

Novatech, Lynchburg *Also called Innovative Tech Intl Inc* *(G-7740)*

Novec Energy Production 434 471-2840
1225 Plywood Trl South Boston (24592) *(G-12785)*

Novell, Vienna *Also called Micro Focus Software Inc* *(G-14091)*

Novelsat USA 703 295-2119
9134 Ermantrude Ct Vienna (22182) *(G-14106)*

Novelty Sign Works LLC 804 559-2009
6273 Tammy Ln Mechanicsville (23111) *(G-8665)*

Novozymes Biologicals Inc (HQ) **540 389-9361**
5400 Corporate Cir Salem (24153) *(G-12547)*

Novozymes Biologicals Inc 540 389-9361
145 Brand Ave Salem (24153) *(G-12548)*

Novus Technology Inc 703 218-9801
3818 Daniels Run Ct Fairfax (22030) *(G-4657)*

Nowlin Steelcraft, Hampton *Also called Bobby Burns Nowlin* *(G-6097)*

Nplainvue LLC 434 979-7105
1650 Harris Creek Rd Charlottesville (22902) *(G-2838)*

NRC Publishing Virginia LLC 703 407-0868
4000 Legato Rd Fairfax (22033) *(G-4522)*

Nrd LLC 540 362-1097
5180 Peters Creek Rd Roanoke (24019) *(G-11976)*

NRJ Industries LLC 703 707-0368
13621 Birch Dr Chantilly (20151) *(G-2474)*

Nsgdatacom Inc (PA) **703 464-0151**
3859 Centerview Dr # 500 Chantilly (20151) *(G-2475)*

Ntelos Inc 540 992-2211
1900 Roanoke Rd Daleville (24083) *(G-3945)*

Ntelos Inc 434 760-0141
220 Twentyninth Place Ct Charlottesville (22901) *(G-2668)*

Ntt America Solutions Inc 571 203-4032
12120 Sunset Hills Rd # 5 Reston (20190) *(G-10910)*

Nu-TEC Outdoor Innovations LLC 540 365-0551
10895 Franklin St Ferrum (24088) *(G-4976)*

Nuasis Corp 571 230-8126
1104 Great Passage Blvd Great Falls (22066) *(G-5969)*

Nuckols Cabinetry LLC 804 749-3908
17472 Dunns Chapel Rd Rockville (23146) *(G-12294)*

Nuclear Products, Lynchburg *Also called Bwx Technologies Inc* *(G-7666)*

Nucor Corporation 804 379-3704
559 Southlake Blvd North Chesterfield (23236) *(G-9941)*

Nudge LLC 423 521-1969
3600 Douglasdale Rd Richmond (23221) *(G-11697)*

Nuevo Milenio Newspaper LLC 703 501-7180
5643 Mount Burnside Way Burke (22015) *(G-2196)*

Nufocus Software LLC 540 722-0282
115 Godwin Ct Winchester (22602) *(G-15456)*

Nugen Mobility Inc 703 858-0036
44645 Guilford Dr Ste 201 Ashburn (20147) *(G-1323)*

Nuline 757 425-3213
1749 Virginia Beach Blvd Virginia Beach (23454) *(G-14688)*

Number 6 Publishing LLC 703 360-6054
1799 Rampart Dr Alexandria (22308) *(G-545)*

Nuna Med LLC 707 373-7171
9702 Gayton Rd Ste 183 Richmond (23238) *(G-11309)*

Nusource LLC 571 482-7404
320 King St Ste 203 Alexandria (22314) *(G-298)*

Nutegrity Northumberland Co, Reedville *Also called Omega Protein Inc* *(G-10763)*

Nutravail Holding Corp 703 222-6348
14790 Flint Lee Rd Chantilly (20151) *(G-2476)*

Nutri-Blend Inc 804 222-1675
2353 Charles City Rd Richmond (23231) *(G-11310)*

Nutriati Inc (PA) **804 562-2322**
9722 Gayton Rd Henrico (23238) *(G-6545)*

Nutrien AG Solutions Inc 757 229-9448
270 Pamunkey Ave West Point (23181) *(G-15160)*

Nutrien AG Solutions Inc 540 775-2985
15679 Colonial Rd Milford (22514) *(G-8932)*

Nutrients Plus LLC 757 430-3400
2133 Upton Dr Ste 126 Virginia Beach (23454) *(G-14689)*

A
L
P
H
A
B
E
T
I
C

Nutrition Support Services 540 626-3081
  477 New Zion Rd Pembroke (24136) *(G-10282)*

Nutter Candle Company LLC 703 627-2561
  5507 Cheshire Meadows Way Fairfax (22032) *(G-4523)*

Nuvidrill LLC 540 353-8787
  2217 Crystl Spg Ave Sw Roanoke (24014) *(G-12143)*

Nuwave Embroidery 540 412-9799
  5933 Plank Rd Fredericksburg (22407) *(G-5337)*

NV Cast Stone 703 393-2777
  11900 Livingston Rd # 147 Manassas (20109) *(G-8119)*

Nva Docks LLC 619 500-1964
  98 Main St Stafford (22554) *(G-13178)*

Nva Signs & Striping LLC 703 263-1940
  10448 Business Center Ct Manassas (20110) *(G-7983)*

Nvis Inc 571 201-8095
  11495 Sunset Hills Rd # 106 Reston (20190) *(G-10911)*

Nxvet LLC 571 358-6198
  11699 Bacon Race Rd Woodbridge (22192) *(G-15765)*

Nyc Shuttle, Charlottesville Also called Starlight Express LLC *(G-2883)*

Nyla LLC 800 916-8326
  1201 Bond St Herndon (20170) *(G-6761)*

Nyx Technologies LLC 703 914-8956
  5285 Navaho Dr Alexandria (22312) *(G-546)*

Nzo LLC 434 660-7338
  596 Blue Ridge Ave Ste 1a Bedford (24523) *(G-1646)*

O D B Machine Co 434 929-4002
  271 Mitchell Bell Rd Madison Heights (24572) *(G-7879)*

O Depuy 804 330-0988
  720 Mrfield Pk Dr Ste 105 North Chesterfield (23236) *(G-9942)*

O'Brien's Supply, Drakes Branch Also called Judy A OBrien *(G-4135)*

O'S Ark Custom Apparel, Buena Vista Also called Allen Enterprises LLC *(G-2138)*

O-N Minerals Chemstone Company 540 465-5161
  1696 Oranda Rd Strasburg (22657) *(G-13592)*

O-N Minerals Chemstone Company 540 254-1241
  684 Parkway Dr Buchanan (24066) *(G-2123)*

O-N Minerals Chemstone Company 540 662-3855
  508 Quarry Ln Clear Brook (22624) *(G-3649)*

O-N Minerals Chemstone Company 540 869-1066
  351 Mccune Rd Middletown (22645) *(G-8741)*

O2o Software Inc 571 234-3243
  1548 Coomber Ct Herndon (20170) *(G-6762)*

Oads, Manassas Also called Optical Air Data Systems LLC *(G-7986)*

Oak Crest Vineyard & Winery 540 663-2813
  8215 Oak Crest Dr King George (22485) *(G-7105)*

Oak Grove Folk Art, Virginia Beach Also called Three Points Design Inc *(G-14870)*

Oak Hall Cap & Gown, Salem Also called Oak Hall Industries LP *(G-12549)*

Oak Hall Industries, Salem Also called B & S Liquidating Corp *(G-12479)*

Oak Hall Industries LP (PA) **540 387-0000**
  840 Union St Salem (24153) *(G-12549)*

Oak Hollow Woodworking Inc 276 646-2476
  1917 St Clairs Creek Rd Chilhowie (24319) *(G-3556)*

Oakes Memorials & Signs Inc 434 836-5888
  3676 Franklin Tpke Danville (24540) *(G-4018)*

Oaklea Press Inc 804 288-2683
  41 Old Mill Rd Richmond (23226) *(G-11311)*

Oaks 540 885-6664
  521 Oak Hill Rd Staunton (24401) *(G-13282)*

Oaks At Timberlake 434 525-7107
  11 Sun Dr Evington (24550) *(G-4381)*

Oakton Press 703 359-6800
  11151 Conestoga Ct Oakton (22124) *(G-10161)*

Oaktree Woodworks 804 815-4669
  5392 Sleepy Hollow Ln Gloucester (23061) *(G-5857)*

Oas Intel, New Market Also called Octopus Arospc Solutions LLC *(G-9146)*

Oasis Global LLC 703 560-7755
  8451 Hilltop Rd Ste B Fairfax (22031) *(G-4524)*

Oaxaca Embroidery LLC 540 463-3808
  104 Johnstone St Lexington (24450) *(G-7409)*

Obaugh Welding LLC 540 396-6151
  1183 Doe Hill Rd Mc Dowell (24458) *(G-8375)*

Obdrillers Proshop 804 897-3708
  200 Old Otterdale Rd Midlothian (23114) *(G-8869)*

Oberons Forge Press LLC 703 434-9275
  20283 Center Brook Sq Sterling (20165) *(G-13463)*

Objective Intrface Systems Inc 703 295-6500
  220 Spring St Ste 530 Herndon (20170) *(G-6763)*

Objective Standard, The, Glen Allen Also called Glen Allen Press LLC *(G-5737)*

Objectvideo Labs LLC 571 327-3673
  8281 Greensboro Dr # 100 Mc Lean (22102) *(G-8520)*

Obrien Machine Repair 757 898-1387
  103 Misty Dr Yorktown (23692) *(G-15983)*

Observer Inc 804 545-7500
  4600 Market Square Ln Midlothian (23112) *(G-8870)*

Observer Newspapers, Herndon Also called Herndon Publishing Co Inc *(G-6697)*

Obsidian Solutions Group LLC 540 286-2266
  1130 Intl Pkwy Ste 127 Fredericksburg (22406) *(G-5462)*

Oc Pharma LLC 540 375-6415
  1640 Roanoke Blvd Salem (24153) *(G-12550)*

OCC, Roanoke Also called Optical Cable Corporation *(G-11978)*

Ocean Apparel Incorporated 757 422-8262
  2984 S Lynnhaven Rd # 118 Virginia Beach (23452) *(G-14690)*

Ocean Bronze, Fredericksburg Also called Wegner Metal Arts Inc *(G-5235)*

Ocean Creek Apparel LLC 757 460-6118
  1368 Baker Rd Virginia Beach (23455) *(G-14691)*

Ocean Foods Inc 757 474-6314
  5158 Rugby Rd Virginia Beach (23464) *(G-14692)*

Ocean Impressions Inc 757 485-3212
  3315 S Military Hwy Chesapeake (23323) *(G-3223)*

Ocean Marine LLC 757 222-1306
  543 E Indian River Rd Norfolk (23523) *(G-9671)*

Ocean Products Research Inc (PA) ...**804 725-3406**
  19 Butts Ln Diggs (23045) *(G-4093)*

Ocean Software Us LLC 703 796-1300
  2553 Dulles View Dr Ste 2 Herndon (20171) *(G-6764)*

Oceaneering International Inc 757 985-3800
  2155 Steppingstone Sq Chesapeake (23320) *(G-3224)*

Oceaneering International Inc 757 545-2200
  2155 Steppingstone Sq Chesapeake (23320) *(G-3225)*

Oceus Enterprise Solutions LLC 703 234-9200
  1895 Preston White Dr # 300 Reston (20191) *(G-10912)*

Ocotillas Mntnside Alpacas LLC 540 593-2143
  4388 Buffalo Mtn Rd Sw Willis (24380) *(G-15364)*

Ocran Shaft Machine 804 435-6301
  113 Windmill Point Rd White Stone (22578) *(G-15189)*

Octoleaf LLC 202 579-7279
  20941 Lohengrin Ct Ashburn (20147) *(G-1324)*

Octopus Arospc Solutions LLC 866 244-4500
  9706 Fairway Dr New Market (22844) *(G-9146)*

Octopus Software Systems Inc 571 224-5283
  6129 Lsburg Pike Apt 1009 Falls Church (22041) *(G-4848)*

Odb, Richmond Also called Old Dominion Brush Company Inc *(G-11313)*

Odb Machine Co, Madison Heights Also called O D B Machine Co *(G-7879)*

Odin Scnce Tech Innovation LLC 850 582-0799
  1420 Hudgins Farm Cir Fredericksburg (22408) *(G-5338)*

ODonnell Susannah Cassedy 703 470-8572
  3215 Juniper Ln Falls Church (22044) *(G-4849)*

Odorkill, Bedford Also called Atx Technologies LLC *(G-1620)*

Off The Press Inc 703 533-1199
  6919 Westmoreland Rd Falls Church (22042) *(G-4850)*

Office Electronics Inc 757 622-8001
  225 W Olney Rd Norfolk (23510) *(G-9672)*

Office Furniture Outlet Inc (PA) **757 855-5522**
  5595 Raby Rd Ste 3 Norfolk (23502) *(G-9673)*

Office Organizers 757 343-6860
  4208 Goldcrest Dr Chesapeake (23325) *(G-3226)*

Official Tee Blanco LLC 804 418-0218
  4106 Laurelwood Rd North Chesterfield (23234) *(G-9943)*

Offroadarrowcom LLC 804 920-2529
  12717 Tylers Ridge Ct Providence Forge (23140) *(G-10627)*

Offshore Corporation 804 526-7665
  840 W Roslyn Rd Ste A Colonial Heights (23834) *(G-3739)*

Ofi Custom Metal Fabrication, Ashland Also called Fields Inc Oscar S *(G-1416)*

Og Pressmore LLC 434 218-0304
  2092 Wilson Church Rd Bedford (24523) *(G-1647)*

Ogc Inc (PA) **703 860-3736**
  11800 Sunrise Valley Dr # 3 Reston (20191) *(G-10913)*

Ogden Directories Inc 540 375-6524
  4502 Starkey Rd Ste 1 Roanoke (24018) *(G-11977)*

OH My Goshyum LLC 434 975-6628
  1139a River Rd Charlottesville (22901) *(G-2669)*

OH So Good Organics LLC 703 577-9226
  14323 Johnny Moore Ct Centreville (20120) *(G-2326)*

OHG Science & Technology LLC 434 990-0500
  5916 Seminole Trl Barboursville (22923) *(G-1565)*

Ohongyum, Charlottesville Also called Nobull Burger *(G-2664)*

Ois, Herndon Also called Objective Intrface Systems Inc *(G-6763)*

OK Foundry Company Inc 804 233-9674
  1005 Commerce Rd Richmond (23224) *(G-11698)*

Okos Solutions LLC 703 880-3039
  7036 Tech Cir Manassas (20109) *(G-8120)*

Olan De Mexico SA De CV 804 365-8344
  2450 Pendower Ln Keswick (22947) *(G-7053)*

Old 97 Choppers 434 799-5400
  1010 S Boston Rd Danville (24540) *(G-4019)*

Old Barn Rclmed WD Antiq Flrg 804 329-0079
  3801 Carolina Ave Richmond (23222) *(G-11699)*

Old Bridge Observer, Manassas Also called Randall Publication Inc *(G-7994)*

Old Castle Lawn and Garden, Castlewood Also called Mountain Materials Inc *(G-2255)*

Old Coots LLC 757 713-2888
  6032 Prince Ave Norfolk (23502) *(G-9674)*

Old Domimion Flagstone Inc 540 553-0511
  3500 Prices Fork Rd Blacksburg (24060) *(G-1776)*

Old Dominion 4 Whl Drv CLB Inc 804 750-2349
  2308 Carrollwood Ct Richmond (23238) *(G-11312)*

Old Dominion Box Co Inc (PA) **434 929-6701**
  300 Elon Rd Madison Heights (24572) *(G-7880)*

Old Dominion Box Co Inc 434 929-6701
  186 Dillard Rd Madison Heights (24572) *(G-7881)*

Old Dominion Brush Company Inc..........800 446-9823
5118 Glen Alden Dr Richmond (23231) *(G-11313)*
Old Dominion Furniture, Lynchburg *Also called Old Dominion Wood Products Inc (G-7778)*
Old Dominion Innovations Inc..........804 477-8712
9424 Atlee Commerce Blvd D Ashland (23005) *(G-1471)*
Old Dominion Machinery Company, Madison Heights *Also called Old Dominion Box Co Inc (G-7881)*
Old Dominion MBL Canning LLC..........804 517-1640
11300 Long Meadow Dr Glen Allen (23059) *(G-5775)*
Old Dominion Metal Pdts Inc..........804 355-7123
4300 Vawter Ave Richmond (23222) *(G-11700)*
Old Dominion Pipe Company LLC..........757 710-2681
19465 Pungo Creek Ln Painter (23420) *(G-10241)*
Old Dominion Shaker Boxes..........703 470-7921
9010 Longstreet Dr Manassas (20110) *(G-7984)*
Old Dominion Window and Door, Ashland *Also called Moss Supply Company (G-1466)*
Old Dominion Wood Products Inc..........434 845-5511
800 Craddock St Lynchburg (24501) *(G-7778)*
Old Goat Technologies, Virginia Beach *Also called Joint Planning Solutions LLC (G-14573)*
Old Hickory Candle Company..........804 400-8602
26125 Ridge Ln Mc Kenney (23872) *(G-8382)*
Old House Vineyards LLC..........540 423-1032
18351 Corkys Ln Culpeper (22701) *(G-3913)*
Old Mansion Inc..........804 862-9889
3811 Corporate Rd Petersburg (23805) *(G-10331)*
Old Mansion Foods, Petersburg *Also called Old Mansion Inc (G-10331)*
Old Mill Mechanical Inc..........804 932-5060
8600 Historical Path Rd New Kent (23124) *(G-9137)*
Old Mount Airy Machine, Rural Retreat *Also called Pickle Tyson (G-12429)*
Old Point Packing Inc (PA)..........**757 247-0557**
817 Jefferson Ave Newport News (23607) *(G-9308)*
Old Point Seafoods, Newport News *Also called Old Point Packing Inc (G-9308)*
Old Rag Gazette..........540 675-2001
702 Long Mountain Rd Washington (22747) *(G-15076)*
Old Soul Signs LLC..........757 256-5669
1348 Danielle Ct Chesapeake (23320) *(G-3227)*
Old South Plantation Shutters..........703 968-7822
14514a Lee Rd Chantilly (20151) *(G-2477)*
Old Stone Corp..........813 731-7600
6101 Cascade Mill Rd Cascade (24069) *(G-2252)*
Old Town Sign Co Inc..........703 836-7000
1021 Queen St Alexandria (22314) *(G-299)*
Old Town Woodworking Inc..........540 347-3993
545 Old Meetze Rd Warrenton (20186) *(G-15039)*
Old Virginia Molding & Mllwk..........757 516-9055
100 W Jackson St Franklin (23851) *(G-5151)*
Old Vrgnia Hand Hewn Log Homes..........276 546-5647
Us Hwy 58 Rr 2 Pennington Gap (24277) *(G-10296)*
Old World Labs LLC..........800 282-0386
888 Magazine Ln Apt 3d Norfolk (23510) *(G-9675)*
Old World Prints, Richmond *Also called North South Partners LLC (G-11307)*
Oldcastle Apg Northeast Inc (HQ)..........**703 365-7070**
13555 Wellington Cntr Cir Gainesville (20155) *(G-5605)*
Oldcastle Apg Northeast Inc..........540 667-4600
1515 Tyson Dr Winchester (22603) *(G-15457)*
Oldcastle Infrastructure Inc..........540 898-6300
5115 Massaponax Church Rd Fredericksburg (22407) *(G-5339)*
Olde Petersburg Printers..........804 400-9644
325 Shade Tree Dr Colonial Heights (23834) *(G-3740)*
Olde Souls Press LLC..........434 242-7348
642 Mistland Trl Ruckersville (22968) *(G-12407)*
Olde Towne Window Works Inc..........540 371-6987
204 Thompson Ave Ste 103 Fredericksburg (22405) *(G-5463)*
Olde Virginia Cidery LLC..........901 626-0535
2910 W Leigh St Richmond (23230) *(G-11314)*
Olde Virginia Moulding..........757 516-9055
100 W Jackson St Franklin (23851) *(G-5152)*
Olde Woolen Mill LLC..........571 926-9604
11499 White Oak Ct Herndon (20170) *(G-6765)*
Oldtown Printing & Copying..........540 382-6793
19 W Main St Ste E Christiansburg (24073) *(G-3607)*
Olivals Custom Woodworking Inc..........703 221-2713
18870 Crossroads Ct Triangle (22172) *(G-13897)*
Olive Manassas Oil Co..........703 543-9206
10016 Moore Dr Manassas (20111) *(G-8121)*
Olive Oil & Friends LLC..........703 385-1845
512 Woodland Ct Nw Vienna (22180) *(G-14107)*
Olive Oil Boom..........703 276-2666
1276 N Wayne St Apt 1125 Arlington (22201) *(G-1085)*
Olive Oil Boom LLC..........703 276-2666
2001 Clarendon Blvd # 601 Arlington (22201) *(G-1086)*
Olive Oil Soap Company..........540 671-6940
306 Brown Ave Front Royal (22630) *(G-5547)*
Olive Oil Tamproom LLC..........804 897-6464
11400 W Huguenot Rd # 116 Midlothian (23113) *(G-8871)*
Olive Oils Abingdon Assoc LLC (PA)..........**276 525-1524**
152 E Main St Ste 2w Abingdon (24210) *(G-52)*
Olive Savor..........757 425-3866
1624 Laskin Rd Ste 730 Virginia Beach (23451) *(G-14693)*
Oliver Princess..........804 683-5779
7118 Lake Caroline Dr Chesterfield (23832) *(G-3515)*
OMalley Timber Products LLC..........804 445-1118
250 Commerce Rd Tappahannock (22560) *(G-13819)*
Omega Alpha II Inc..........804 747-7705
3817 Gaskins Rd Richmond (23233) *(G-11315)*
Omega Black Incorporated..........240 416-1774
10711 Brice Ct Fredericksburg (22407) *(G-5340)*
Omega Protein Inc (HQ)..........**804 453-6262**
610 Menhaden Rd Reedville (22539) *(G-10763)*
Omega Protein Inc..........804 453-4923
243 Menhaden Rd Reedville (22539) *(G-10764)*
Omega Protein Corporation (HQ)..........**804 453-6262**
610 Menhaden Rd Reedville (22539) *(G-10765)*
Omega Prtein - Hlth Scence Ctr, Reedville *Also called Omega Protein Inc (G-10764)*
Omis Gnome Hats..........540 230-0258
1033 Huffville Rd Ne Pilot (24138) *(G-10357)*
Omni Filter and Mfg Inc..........804 550-1600
10190 Maple Leaf Ct Ashland (23005) *(G-1472)*
Omni Repair Company..........757 853-1220
3313 Tait Ter Norfolk (23513) *(G-9676)*
Omni Technology and Mfg LLC..........703 929-8000
40329 Charles Town Pike Hamilton (20158) *(G-6062)*
Omnicardata LLC..........703 622-6742
23551 Pebble Run Pl Ste 1 Sterling (20166) *(G-13464)*
Omnidex Products Inc..........757 509-4030
504 Leatherwood Ct Virginia Beach (23462) *(G-14694)*
Omniio LLC..........877 842-5478
2744 Sonic Dr Ste 101 Virginia Beach (23453) *(G-14695)*
Omohundro Institute of Early..........757 221-1114
Swem Library Landrum Dr Williamsburg (23185) *(G-15285)*
Omron Scientific Tech Inc..........703 536-6070
5801 Lee Hwy Arlington (22207) *(G-1087)*
On Display, Richmond *Also called John P Scott Woodworking Inc (G-11633)*
On It Smart Snacks..........757 705-9259
1817 Riddle Ave Virginia Beach (23454) *(G-14696)*
On Our Way Inc..........703 444-0007
45449 Severn Way Ste 173 Dulles (20166) *(G-4214)*
On The Dl Custom Prints LLC..........757 508-1609
17096 Belle Isle Dr Dumfries (22026) *(G-4253)*
On The Road Transport LLC..........410 207-2592
464 Investors Pl Ste 206e Virginia Beach (23452) *(G-14697)*
On The Weekly LLC..........757 839-2640
957 Summerside Ct Virginia Beach (23456) *(G-14698)*
On Wing, Round Hill *Also called Robert R Kline (G-12387)*
On-Site E Discovery Inc..........703 683-9710
806 N Henry St Alexandria (22314) *(G-300)*
On-Site Fire Extngsher Sls Svc, Highland Springs *Also called Fredrick Allen Murphey (G-6853)*
Oncor Industries Inc..........434 985-3434
3003 South River Rd Stanardsville (22973) *(G-13225)*
Ondal Medical Systems Amer Inc..........804 279-0320
540 Eastpark Ct Ste A Sandston (23150) *(G-12627)*
Ondeck Home Solutions LLC..........757 535-3771
1906 Richmond Ave Portsmouth (23704) *(G-10464)*
Onduline North America Inc..........540 898-7000
4900 Ondura Dr Fredericksburg (22407) *(G-5341)*
Onduvilla, Fredericksburg *Also called Onduline North America Inc (G-5341)*
One Aperture LLC..........202 415-0416
3245 Rio Dr Apt 712 Falls Church (22041) *(G-4851)*
One Arm Woodworking LLC..........703 203-9417
9525 Jomar Dr Fairfax (22032) *(G-4525)*
One Asterisk Woodworks LLC..........508 332-8151
157 Basalt Dr Fredericksburg (22406) *(G-5464)*
One Cut Bindery LLC..........540 896-7290
559 S Main St Broadway (22815) *(G-2092)*
One Four Three LLC..........303 594-7151
3781 Jefferson Blvd Virginia Beach (23455) *(G-14699)*
One Mile Up Inc..........703 642-1177
4354 Greenberry Ln Annandale (22003) *(G-777)*
One of A Kind Kid..........800 276-0054
1811 Huguenot Rd Midlothian (23113) *(G-8872)*
One One Too LLC..........505 500-4749
9400 Braken Ct Fredericksburg (22408) *(G-5342)*
One Piece Fabrication LLC..........757 460-8637
1393 Air Rail Ave Virginia Beach (23455) *(G-14700)*
One Stop All Clg Solutions, Williamsburg *Also called One Stop Cleaning LLC (G-15286)*
One Stop Cleaning LLC..........757 561-2952
160 Second St Ste 202 Williamsburg (23185) *(G-15286)*
One Stop Computer Services LLC..........571 442-2045
43676 Trade Ctr Plste 135 Sterling (20166) *(G-13465)*
One Volt Associates (PA)..........**301 565-3930**
6372 Mchncsvlle Tpke Ste Mechanicsville (23111) *(G-8666)*
One Wish Publishing LLC..........571 285-4227
13926 Andorra Dr Woodbridge (22193) *(G-15766)*
ONeals Welding & Repair LLC..........757 421-0702
5145 Ballahack Rd Chesapeake (23322) *(G-3228)*
Oneidos LLC..........703 819-3860
8569 Sudley Rd Ste C Manassas (20110) *(G-7985)*

ALPHABETIC

Oneil Enterprises, Amherst *Also called Circle R Carrier Service Inc* **(G-687)**

ONeill Distillery LLC Tf..540 822-5812
  12264 Sedgeway Ln Lovettsville (20180) **(G-7584)**

Oneso Inc..704 560-6354
  4001 9th St N Apt 1821 Arlington (22203) **(G-1088)**

Ongrade Pllc...757 448-5635
  2704 Fayette Ct Virginia Beach (23456) **(G-14701)**

Online Biose Inc...703 758-6672
  10801 Oldfield Dr Reston (20191) **(G-10914)**

Online Publishing & Mktg LLC..540 463-2057
  1545 N Lee Hwy Ste 4 Lexington (24450) **(G-7410)**

Ontario Hardwood Company Inc (PA)..............................**434 736-9291**
  3828 Horseshoe Bend Rd Keysville (23947) **(G-7061)**

Onthefly Pictures LLC...757 339-1520
  3651 Gateway Dr Apt 2b Portsmouth (23703) **(G-10465)**

Onyx Coating Solutions LLC..434 660-4627
  2668 Paradise Rd Concord (24538) **(G-3762)**

Onyx Industries LLC..425 269-7181
  8330 Roxborough Loop Gainesville (20155) **(G-5606)**

Ooska News Corp...540 724-1750
  37 Main St Warrenton (20186) **(G-15040)**

Oozlefinch Beers & Blending, Fort Monroe *Also called Oozlefinch Craft Brewery LLC* **(G-5133)**

Oozlefinch Craft Brewery LLC...757 224-7042
  81 Patch Rd Fort Monroe (23651) **(G-5133)**

Open Prints LLC..866 673-6110
  929 Ventures Way Chesapeake (23320) **(G-3229)**

Open Road Grill & Icehouse...571 395-4400
  8100 Lee Hwy Falls Church (22042) **(G-4852)**

Open Road Outfitters, Falls Church *Also called Open Road Grill & Icehouse* **(G-4852)**

Open Tech Inc..703 738-6662
  2000 Kraft Dr Ste 1101 Blacksburg (24060) **(G-1777)**

Openbox Networks LLC...540 607-0149
  176 Beagle Gap Run Waynesboro (22980) **(G-15130)**

Opening Protection Svcs LLC..757 222-0730
  973 Sunnyside Dr Virginia Beach (23464) **(G-14702)**

Openwater Software Inc...202 765-0247
  4401 Fairfax Dr Ste 200 Arlington (22203) **(G-1089)**

Ophelias Hat & Hair Shop...757 331-1713
  24127 Lankford Hwy Cheriton (23316) **(G-2947)**

Oppiya Learning Company LLC..804 296-0141
  5021 Parsons Walk Cir Glen Allen (23059) **(G-5776)**

Opposable Thumbs LLC..804 502-2937
  1515 Hull St Richmond (23224) **(G-11701)**

Opsec Industries LLC...571 426-0626
  7412 Layton Dr Springfield (22150) **(G-13062)**

Opsense Inc...844 757-7578
  7875 Promontory Ct Dunn Loring (22027) **(G-4266)**

Opta (usa) Inc..843 296-7074
  902 Cooke Ave Norfolk (23504) **(G-9677)**

Optical Air Data Systems LLC...703 393-0754
  10781 James Payne Ct Manassas (20110) **(G-7986)**

Optical Cable Corporation (PA).......................................**540 265-0690**
  5290 Concourse Dr Roanoke (24019) **(G-11978)**

Optikinetics Ltd...800 575-6784
  11211 Air Park Rd Apt A Ashland (23005) **(G-1473)**

Optime Software LLC..415 894-0314
  205 Carrwood Rd Great Falls (22066) **(G-5970)**

Optimize Print Solutions LLC...703 856-7386
  9435 Lorton Market St # 266 Lorton (22079) **(G-7519)**

Optometrics LLC..540 840-5802
  27 Blackberry Ln Fredericksburg (22406) **(G-5465)**

Optx Imaging Systems LLC...703 398-1432
  10716 Richmond Hwy # 201 Lorton (22079) **(G-7520)**

Ora Inc..540 368-3012
  45 Commerce Pkwy Fredericksburg (22406) **(G-5466)**

Oracle America Inc...703 310-3600
  2311 Wilson Blvd Fl 7&8 Arlington (22201) **(G-1090)**

Oracle America Inc...804 672-0998
  2701 Emerywood Pkwy 108 Richmond (23294) **(G-11316)**

Oracle America Inc...703 478-9000
  1900 Oracle Way Reston (20190) **(G-10915)**

Oracle Heart & Vascular Inc...855 739-9953
  1300 Hospital Dr Ste 302 Fredericksburg (22401) **(G-5210)**

Oracle Systems Corporation...703 478-9000
  1910 Oracle Way Reston (20190) **(G-10916)**

Oracle Systems Corporation...703 364-2221
  6190 Manchester Park Cir Alexandria (22310) **(G-547)**

Oracle Worldwide LLC..703 224-8806
  2331 Mill Rd Ste 100 Alexandria (22314) **(G-301)**

Oralign Baby LLC...540 492-0453
  19 Cleveland Ave Martinsville (24112) **(G-8315)**

Oran Safety Glass Inc...434 336-1620
  48 Industrial Pkwy Emporia (23847) **(G-4364)**

Oran USA, Emporia *Also called Oran Safety Glass Inc* **(G-4364)**

Orange County Review, Orange *Also called Daily Progress* **(G-10210)**

Orange County Review, Orange *Also called Wood Television LLC* **(G-10232)**

Orange Sock Pay...540 246-6368
  17444 Center Dr Ste 5c Ruther Glen (22546) **(G-12459)**

Orban..804 529-6283
  973 Coan Haven Rd Lewisetta (22511) **(G-7384)**

Orbcomm LLC..703 433-6300
  21700 Atl Blvd Ste 300 Dulles (20166) **(G-4215)**

Orbcomm LLC..703 433-6300
  22970 Indian Creek Dr # 300 Sterling (20166) **(G-13466)**

Orbis Rpm LLC..804 887-2375
  4577 Carolina Ave Richmond (23222) **(G-11702)**

Orbital Atk Operation Ges..571 437-7870
  45245 Bus Ct Ste 400 Sterling (20166) **(G-13467)**

Orbital Sciences Corporation, Dulles *Also called Orbital Sciences LLC* **(G-4217)**

Orbital Sciences Corporation..757 824-5619
  34200 Fulton St Wallops Island (23337) **(G-14972)**

Orbital Sciences Corporation..703 405-5012
  21830 Atlantic Blvd Dulles (20166) **(G-4216)**

Orbital Sciences LLC (HQ)..**703 406-5524**
  45101 Warp Dr Dulles (20166) **(G-4217)**

Orbital Sciences LLC...703 406-5000
  45101 Warp Dr Dulles (20166) **(G-4218)**

Orbysol Inc..703 398-1092
  23562 Prosperity Ridge Pl Brambleton (20148) **(G-1932)**

Oreamnos Biofuels LLC..651 269-7737
  4008 Thorngate Dr Williamsburg (23188) **(G-15287)**

Oregon Woodcraft Inc...703 477-4793
  5731 Wters Edge Lnding Ct Burke (22015) **(G-2197)**

Orfit Industries America, Norfolk *Also called SC Medical Overseas Inc* **(G-9715)**

Orica USA Inc..540 380-3146
  6324 Twine Hollow Rd Salem (24153) **(G-12551)**

Orien Usa LLC...757 486-2099
  921 General Hill Dr Virginia Beach (23454) **(G-14703)**

Original Brunswick Stew Co., Freeman *Also called Mary Truman* **(G-5512)**

Original Mattress Factory, The, North Chesterfield *Also called Rvmf Inc* **(G-9968)**

Origio - Humagen Pipets, Charlottesville *Also called Origio Inc* **(G-2670)**

Origio Inc (HQ)..**434 979-4000**
  2400 Hunters Way Charlottesville (22911) **(G-2670)**

Origo, Roanoke *Also called Mill Mountain Capital LLC* **(G-11966)**

Orinoco Natural Resources LLC (PA)..............................**713 626-9696**
  192 Summerfield Ct # 203 Roanoke (24019) **(G-11979)**

Orion Applied Science Tech LLC.......................................571 393-1942
  10432 Balls Ford Rd # 300 Manassas (20109) **(G-8122)**

Orlando Garzon Cuellar..571 274-6913
  9105 Mineola Ct Manassas (20111) **(G-8123)**

Ornament Company...757 585-0729
  315 Archers Mead Williamsburg (23185) **(G-15288)**

Orthoinsight LLC...703 722-2553
  25151 Fortitude Ter Chantilly (20152) **(G-2548)**

Orthotic Prosthetic Center (PA)......................................**703 698-5007**
  8330 Professional Hill Dr Fairfax (22031) **(G-4526)**

Orthotic Solutions L L C...703 849-9200
  2802 Merrilee Dr Ste 100 Fairfax (22031) **(G-4527)**

Ortons Specialty Welding LLC...804 405-2675
  8647 Merry Oaks Ln Toano (23168) **(G-13872)**

Oryx Designs Promotional Pdts, Waynesboro *Also called Lai Enterprises LLC* **(G-15120)**

Os Ark Group LLC..540 261-2622
  2271 Sycamore Ave Buena Vista (24416) **(G-2152)**

Os-Gim Pharmaceuticals Inc...301 655-5191
  4712 Kilbane Rd Woodbridge (22193) **(G-15767)**

Osage Bio Energy LLC (PA)...**804 612-8660**
  4991 Lake Brook Dr # 250 Glen Allen (23060) **(G-5777)**

Osborne Welding Inc...757 487-0900
  9 Beechwood Ct Portsmouth (23702) **(G-10466)**

Osborne, Carl G., Herndon *Also called Scilucent LLC* **(G-6802)**

Osburn Coatings Inc...804 769-3030
  7421 Richmond Tapp Hwy Aylett (23009) **(G-1551)**

OSG Propulsion LLC...757 340-0052
  572 Central Dr Ste 104 Virginia Beach (23454) **(G-14704)**

Osgoode Media Inc...866 573-0754
  13450 Farmcrest Ct # 636 Herndon (20171) **(G-6766)**

Oshakits.com, Norfolk *Also called Northfield Medical Mfg LLC* **(G-9669)**

Oshkosh Corporation..703 525-8400
  1300 17th St N Ste 1040 Arlington (22209) **(G-1091)**

OSI LLC...757 967-7533
  5205 Mile Course Walk Virginia Beach (23455) **(G-14705)**

OSI Maritime Systems Inc..877 432-7467
  4445 Corp Ln Ste 264 Virginia Beach (23462) **(G-14706)**

Osmon Industries..757 564-3088
  208 Moodys Run Williamsburg (23185) **(G-15289)**

Osmotherapeutics Inc...703 627-1934
  8000 Towers Crescent Dr Vienna (22182) **(G-14108)**

Osojuicee Hair LLC..757 215-6555
  2901 Piedmont Ave South Chesterfield (23834) **(G-12818)**

Ostrich Press LLC..703 779-7580
  154 Connery Ter Sw Leesburg (20175) **(G-7322)**

OSullivan Films Inc (HQ)...**540 667-6666**
  1944 Valley Ave Winchester (22601) **(G-15561)**

OSullivan Films Inc...540 667-6666
  111 W Jubal Early Winchester (22601) **(G-15562)**

OSullivan Films MGT LLC (HQ)......................................**540 667-6666**
  1944 Valley Ave Winchester (22601) **(G-15563)**

(G-0000) Company's Geographic Section entry number

Otero Kucbel Enterprises Inc 703 734-0209
1350 Snow Meadow Ln Mc Lean (22102) *(G-8521)*

Otsan Technical Service LLC 276 696-7163
311 Gate City Hwy Ste C Bristol (24201) *(G-1985)*

Ott Hydromet Corp (HQ) **703 406-2800**
22400 Davis Dr Ste 100 Sterling (20164) *(G-13468)*

Otter River Filtration Plant 434 821-8611
9625 Leesville Rd Evington (24550) *(G-4382)*

Otto Industries LLC 703 256-2684
7452 Spring Village Dr # 21 Springfield (22150) *(G-13063)*

Our Familys Olive Oil LLC 571 292-1394
9239 Mike Garcia Dr Manassas (20109) *(G-8124)*

Our Health Magazine Inc 540 387-6482
305 S Colorado St Salem (24153) *(G-12552)*

Our Journey Publishing 571 606-1574
17204 Continental Dr Dumfries (22026) *(G-4254)*

Out of Bubble Bakery 571 336-2280
8555 Groveland Dr Springfield (22153) *(G-13064)*

Out of Print LLC 919 368-0980
1449 Westover Ave Norfolk (23507) *(G-9678)*

Out of Woodwork 757 814-8848
713 Denham Arch Chesapeake (23322) *(G-3230)*

Out On A Limb Quiltworks 804 739-7901
5620 Beacon Hill Dr Midlothian (23112) *(G-8873)*

Outdoor Excursions, Fairfax Also called Scott Coulter *(G-4674)*

Outdoor Leisure (PA) **703 349-1965**
10364 Balls Ford Rd Manassas (20109) *(G-8125)*

Outer Banks Woodworks Inc 804 937-4330
9701 W Providence Rd North Chesterfield (23236) *(G-9944)*

Outl T Infomarket LLC 703 927-1346
4320 Old Dominion Dr Arlington (22207) *(G-1092)*

Outlaw Welding LLC 434 929-4734
258 Woodrow Ave Monroe (24574) *(G-8994)*

Outlook Skateboards LLC 757 713-5665
11294 Magnolia Pl Smithfield (23430) *(G-12718)*

Outrageous Shine LLC 804 741-9274
11204 Patterson Ave Richmond (23238) *(G-11317)*

Outthink Corporation 434 426-7706
2001 Autumn Dr Lynchburg (24502) *(G-7779)*

Oval Engineering 434 572-8867
5 Broad St South Boston (24592) *(G-12786)*

Oval LLC 757 389-3777
14700 Bell Tower Rd Woodbridge (22193) *(G-15768)*

Over 9000 Media LLC 850 210-7114
1360 Hilton St Apt 6 Norfolk (23518) *(G-9679)*

Overfelt and Son Welding, Roanoke Also called Charles E Overfelt *(G-11907)*

Owen Co LLC 571 261-1316
5320 Trevino Dr Haymarket (20169) *(G-6432)*

Owens & Jefferson Wtr Systems 757 357-7359
5073 Owens Ln Smithfield (23430) *(G-12719)*

Owens-Brockway Glass Cont Inc 434 799-5880
29 Glassblower Ln Ringgold (24586) *(G-11871)*

Owl Peak Technologies Inc 847 612-0609
525 Ridge St 305 Charlottesville (22902) *(G-2839)*

Oxford Industries Inc 757 220-8660
5625 Richmond Rd Williamsburg (23188) *(G-15290)*

Oxiwear Inc 571 212-7526
1111 Arlington Blvd # 305 Arlington (22209) *(G-1093)*

Oxystress Therapeutics LLC 832 277-0270
918 Main St Danville (24541) *(G-4020)*

P & C Heavy Truck Repair 804 520-7619
3117 Atlantic Ave Colonial Heights (23834) *(G-3741)*

P & G Interiors Inc 540 985-3064
3356 Aerial Way Dr Sw Roanoke (24018) *(G-11980)*

P & P Collection, Alexandria Also called Joshi Rubita *(G-500)*

P & P Farm Machinery Inc 276 794-7806
28601 U S Highway 58 Lebanon (24266) *(G-7203)*

P and H Casters Co Inc 817 312-1083
255 Stinson Dr Danville (24540) *(G-4021)*

P B E Group, North Tazewell Also called Pyott-Boone Electronics Inc *(G-10105)*

P D M P, Leesburg Also called Product Dev Mfg & Packg *(G-7328)*

P D R Inc 540 772-2780
6426 Merriman Rd Roanoke (24018) *(G-11981)*

P H Glatfelter Company 540 548-1756
11018 Cinnamon Teal Dr Spotsylvania (22553) *(G-12907)*

P I P Printing 1156 Inc 434 792-0020
329 Riverview Dr Danville (24541) *(G-4022)*

P J Henry Inc 757 428-0301
1164 Millers Ln A Virginia Beach (23451) *(G-14707)*

P M Resources Inc 703 556-0155
5417b Backlick Rd Springfield (22151) *(G-13065)*

P P I, Chantilly Also called Prototype Productions Inc *(G-2483)*

P Pillar Printing & Promotions, Emporia Also called Mary A Thomas *(G-4363)*

P S I, Hampton Also called Pressure Systems Inc *(G-6219)*

P&B Pallet Co................................... 434 309-1028
2783 Wileman Rd Lynch Station (24571) *(G-7628)*

P&B Systems LLC 717 566-0608
1716 Potomac Greens Dr Alexandria (22314) *(G-302)*

P&L Woodworks 240 676-8648
38111 Long Ln Lovettsville (20180) *(G-7585)*

P-Americas LLC 540 347-3112
5393 Lee Hwy Warrenton (20187) *(G-15041)*

P. D. & J. Envirocon, Windsor Also called Maurice Bynum *(G-15606)*

P3 Academy, Virginia Beach Also called Personal Protectio Principles *(G-14717)*

PA Industries Inc 434 845-0813
164 Almae Dr Amherst (24521) *(G-703)*

Pac Bridge LLC 434 385-8070
3406 Forest Brook Rd Lynchburg (24501) *(G-7780)*

Pac Custom Wdwkg & Cnc Routing, Martinsville Also called Patrick Hawks *(G-8316)*

Pace Custom Sawing LLC 276 956-2000
425 Blackfeather Trl Ridgeway (24148) *(G-11847)*

Pacem Publishing 757 214-4800
2111 San Lorenzo Quay Virginia Beach (23456) *(G-14708)*

Pacific, Virginia Beach Also called Ner Inc *(G-14675)*

Pacific and Southern Company 703 854-6899
7950 Jones Branch Dr Mc Lean (22102) *(G-8522)*

Pacific Scientific Company 815 226-3100
201 W Rock Rd Radford (24141) *(G-10733)*

Pacific Technology Inc 571 421-7861
4200 Daniels Ave Ste 20 Annandale (22003) *(G-778)*

Pacific View International 703 631-8659
5388 Ashleigh Rd Fairfax (22030) *(G-4658)*

Packaging Corporation America 540 427-3164
1005 Industry Cir Se Roanoke (24013) *(G-12144)*

Packaging Corporation America 540 434-0785
930 Pleasant Valley Rd Harrisonburg (22801) *(G-6351)*

Packaging Corporation America 540 432-1353
21 Warehouse Rd Harrisonburg (22801) *(G-6352)*

Packaging Corporation America 540 434-2840
751 Interstate View Dr Rockingham (22801) *(G-12266)*

Packaging Corporation America 804 232-1292
2000 Jefferson Davis Hwy Richmond (23224) *(G-11703)*

Packaging Corporation America 540 427-3164
7500 Shadwell Dr Ste B Roanoke (24019) *(G-11982)*

Packaging Corporation America 540 438-8504
2262 Blue Stone Hills Dr C Harrisonburg (22801) *(G-6353)*

Packaging Corporation America 540 662-5680
205 Mcghee Rd Winchester (22603) *(G-15458)*

Packaging Products Inc 276 629-3481
200 Little Creek Dr Bassett (24055) *(G-1588)*

Packed Head LLC 804 677-3603
13241 Carters Way Rd Chesterfield (23838) *(G-3516)*

Packet Dynamics LLC 703 597-1413
11110 Sunset Hills Rd Reston (20190) *(G-10917)*

Packet Stash Inc 202 649-0676
219 Buchanan St Alexandria (22314) *(G-303)*

Packetts Sand Pit 804 761-6975
Islington Rd Ste 763 Warsaw (22572) *(G-15072)*

Pacs Inc 703 415-4411
1215 S Clark St Ste 105 Arlington (22202) *(G-1094)*

Pad A Cheek LLC 434 985-4003
157 Sunset Dr Stanardsville (22973) *(G-13226)*

Paddock Enterprises LLC 757 566-3957
150 Industrial Blvd Toano (23168) *(G-13873)*

Paddy Publications LLC 703 402-2233
10332 Main St Fairfax (22030) *(G-4659)*

Pae Avation Technical Svcs LLC 703 717-6000
1320 N Courthouse Rd # 800 Arlington (22201) *(G-1095)*

Pae Avation Technical Svcs LLC 864 458-3272
1320 N Courthouse Rd # 800 Arlington (22201) *(G-1096)*

Pae-Imk International LLC 888 526-5416
7799 Lsburg Pike Ste 300n Falls Church (22043) *(G-4853)*

Pagan River Associates LLC 757 357-5364
107 Water Pointe Ln Smithfield (23430) *(G-12720)*

Page Letterpress LLC 866 540-7243
2600 Decatur St Ste A Richmond (23224) *(G-11704)*

Page News & Courier, Luray Also called Daily News Record *(G-7606)*

Page Printing Connection 540 743-7746
297 Rhodes Way Luray (22835) *(G-7621)*

Page Publications Inc 804 733-8636
23212 Airport St North Dinwiddie (23803) *(G-10061)*

Page Publications LLC 804 733-8636
20121 Cox Rd Sutherland (23885) *(G-13804)*

Page Shenandoah Newspaper 540 574-6251
2 N Kent St Winchester (22601) *(G-15564)*

Pages Publishing LLC 434 296-0891
97 Wild Flower Dr Charlottesville (22911) *(G-2671)*

Paige Decking, Chesapeake Also called Dlp Enterprises Inc *(G-3068)*

Paige Flrg Cverings Specialist, Chesapeake Also called Paige Sitta & Associates Inc *(G-3231)*

Paige Ireco Inc 276 940-2201
Rr 23 Duffield (24244) *(G-4183)*

Paige Sitta & Associates Inc 757 420-5886
820 Greenbrier Cir Ste 10 Chesapeake (23320) *(G-3231)*

Painted Ladies LLC 571 481-6906
5648 Minnie Ct Woodbridge (22193) *(G-15769)*

Painter Machine Shop Inc....540 463-5854
170 Turkey Hill Rd Lexington (24450) ***(G-7411)***
Painting Pages Publishing LLC....571 266-9529
687 Mcleary Sq Se Leesburg (20175) ***(G-7323)***
Pal Enterprises....804 763-1769
2707 Sutters Mill Ct Midlothian (23112) ***(G-8874)***
Palace Interiors....757 592-1509
15 N Mallory St Hampton (23663) ***(G-6212)***
Palawan Blade LLC....434 294-2065
3670 Smith Creek Rd New Market (22844) ***(G-9147)***
Pale Horse LLC....757 576-0656
1296 Btllfeld Blvd S Ste Chesapeake (23322) ***(G-3232)***
Palidori LLC....757 609-1134
901 Goff St Apt 170 Norfolk (23504) ***(G-9680)***
Palladion Software....540 429-0999
20 Pawnee Dr Fredericksburg (22401) ***(G-5211)***
Pallas USA Ltd....703 205-0007
2719 Dorr Ave Ste B Fairfax (22031) ***(G-4528)***
Pallet Asset Recovery Sys LLC....800 727-2136
18501 Eltham Rd West Point (23181) ***(G-15161)***
Pallet Empire....804 389-3604
2820 Bells Rd Ste D Richmond (23234) ***(G-11055)***
Pallet Enterprises, Ashland *Also called Industrial Reporting Inc* ***(G-1439)***
Pallet Foundation....703 519-6104
1421 Prince St Ste 340 Alexandria (22314) ***(G-304)***
Pallet Industries LLC....757 238-2912
14445 Bayview Dr Carrollton (23314) ***(G-2245)***
Pallet Recycling LLC....304 749-7451
853 Ash St Strasburg (22657) ***(G-13593)***
Pallet Services....804 233-6584
1102 Dinwiddie Ave Richmond (23224) ***(G-11705)***
Palletone of Virginia LLC....434 372-2101
820 Boyd St Chase City (23924) ***(G-2915)***
Palmyra Press Inc....434 589-6634
2185 Haden Martin Rd Palmyra (22963) ***(G-10252)***
Palmyrene Empire LLC....703 348-6660
5405 Tomlinson Dr Woodbridge (22192) ***(G-15770)***
Palo Alto Ntwrks Pub Sctor LLC (HQ)....**240 328-3016**
12110 Sunset Hills Rd Reston (20190) ***(G-10918)***
Pambina Impex....703 910-7309
2951 Ps Business Ctr Dr Woodbridge (22192) ***(G-15771)***
Pamela J Luttrell Co....540 837-1525
2269 Mount Carmel Rd Bluemont (20135) ***(G-1890)***
Pampered Chef, The, Gainesville *Also called Debra Kromer* ***(G-5578)***
Pan American Systems Corp....757 468-1926
1354 London Bridge Rd # 106 Virginia Beach (23453) ***(G-14709)***
Pan Custom Molding Inc....804 787-3820
10137 Grand Oaks Dr Richmond (23233) ***(G-11318)***
Pan Custom Molding Inc....804 787-3821
112 Midpoint Dr Ste Br Mineral (23117) ***(G-8951)***
Panaceutics Nutrition Inc....919 797-9623
2311 Cane Creek Pkwy Ringgold (24586) ***(G-11872)***
Panaderia Latina....703 642-5200
6251 Little River Tpke Alexandria (22312) ***(G-548)***
Panda Kitchen & Bath, Norfolk *Also called Panda Kitchen and Bath VA LLC* ***(G-9681)***
Panda Kitchen and Bath VA LLC....757 889-9888
3587 Argonne Ave Norfolk (23509) ***(G-9681)***
Pandamonk Publishing LLC....571 528-1500
6000 Edsall Rd Apt 103 Alexandria (22304) ***(G-305)***
Pandoras Box....757 719-6669
10171 Jefferson Ave D10 Newport News (23605) ***(G-9309)***
Pandy Co Inc....804 744-1563
13603 Quail Hollow Ct Midlothian (23112) ***(G-8875)***
Panel Processing Virginia Inc....989 356-9007
1805 Red Bank School Rd Claudville (24076) ***(G-3639)***
Panel Systems Inc (PA)....**703 910-6285**
14869 Persistence Dr Woodbridge (22191) ***(G-15772)***
Panoptic Enterprises, Burke *Also called Barry McVay* ***(G-2182)***
Pantheon Integration LLC....571 732-1570
11654 Plaza America Dr # 631 Reston (20190) ***(G-10919)***
Pantheon Software Inc....703 387-4000
2500 Wilson Blvd Ste 200 Arlington (22201) ***(G-1097)***
Papay Holdco LLC....703 226-3544
200 N Glebe Rd Ofc 100 Arlington (22203) ***(G-1098)***
Paper & Packaging Board....703 935-5386
8200 Greensboro Dr # 1175 Mc Lean (22102) ***(G-8523)***
Paper Air Force Company....703 730-2150
5835 Riverside Dr Woodbridge (22193) ***(G-15773)***
Paper Cover Rock....434 979-6366
321 E Main St Ste 100 Charlottesville (22902) ***(G-2840)***
Paperbuzz....434 528-2899
18 West Princeton Cir # 85 Lynchburg (24503) ***(G-7781)***
Paperclip Media Inc....703 323-9170
10505 Braddock Rd Ste B Fairfax (22032) ***(G-4529)***
Paperless Publishing Corp....540 552-5882
1700 Kraft Dr Ste 1000 Blacksburg (24060) ***(G-1778)***
Paqueteria Express Inc....703 330-4580
9019 Church St Manassas (20110) ***(G-7987)***
Par Tees Vb....757 500-7831
1577 General Booth Blvd Virginia Beach (23454) ***(G-14710)***
Parabon Computation Inc....703 689-9689
11260 Roger Bacon Dr # 406 Reston (20190) ***(G-10920)***
Parabon Nanolabs Inc....703 689-9689
11260 Roger Bacon Dr # 40 Reston (20190) ***(G-10921)***
Parachuteriggerus LLC....703 753-9265
2350 Youngs Dr Haymarket (20169) ***(G-6433)***
Paradigm, Virginia Beach *Also called Framing Concepts Inc* ***(G-14474)***
Paradigm Communications Inc....804 644-0496
422 E Franklin St Fl 2 Richmond (23219) ***(G-11706)***
Paradise Ice Cream, Springfield *Also called Marc R Stagger* ***(G-13046)***
Paradym Industries Inc....703 424-6930
25388 Whippoorwill Ter South Riding (20152) ***(G-12869)***
Paragon Aviation Services....703 787-8800
447 Carlisle Dr Ste B Herndon (20170) ***(G-6767)***
Paragon Defense Industries, Charlottesville *Also called Cyril Edward Gropen* ***(G-2614)***
Paramont Contura LLC....276 679-7020
5703 Crutchfield Dr Norton (24273) ***(G-10132)***
Paramount Indus Companies Inc....757 855-3321
1112 Kingwood Ave Norfolk (23502) ***(G-9682)***
Paramount Sleep, Norfolk *Also called Paramount Indus Companies Inc* ***(G-9682)***
Paramount Specialty Metals LLC....980 721-3958
1180 Brittle Ridge Rd Warrenton (20187) ***(G-15042)***
Paramount Woodworking....804 862-2432
3951 S Crater Rd Ste C Petersburg (23805) ***(G-10332)***
Parasitx LLC....757 653-6179
11849 Tug Boat Ln Ste A Newport News (23606) ***(G-9310)***
Pardee Coal Company Inc....276 679-1400
Rr 610 Norton (24273) ***(G-10133)***
Parent Institute , The, Fairfax *Also called Nis Inc* ***(G-4519)***
Parent Institute, The, Fairfax *Also called Paperclip Media Inc* ***(G-4529)***
Parent Resource Center....757 482-5923
369 Battlefield Blvd S Chesapeake (23322) ***(G-3233)***
Parham Services LLC....804 586-1202
9901 Boisseau Rd Sutherland (23885) ***(G-13805)***
Parhams Wldg & Fabrication Inc....804 834-3504
402 N County Dr Waverly (23890) ***(G-15086)***
Pari, Midlothian *Also called Pre Holdings Inc* ***(G-8881)***
Pari Respiratory Equipment Inc (HQ)....**804 897-3311**
2412 Pari Way Midlothian (23112) ***(G-8876)***
Parisian Sweets LLC....770 722-8106
26223 Lankford Hwy Cape Charles (23310) ***(G-2235)***
Park 500....804 751-2000
4100 Bermuda Hundred Rd Chester (23836) ***(G-3442)***
Parkdale Mills Incorporated....276 728-1001
1 Advanced Technology Dr Hillsville (24343) ***(G-6898)***
Parkdale Mills Incorporated....276 236-5174
1012 Glendale Rd Galax (24333) ***(G-5643)***
Parkdale Plants 32 33 34 & 35, Hillsville *Also called Parkdale Mills Incorporated* ***(G-6898)***
Parker Compound Bows Inc....540 337-5426
3022 Lee Jackson Hwy Staunton (24401) ***(G-13283)***
Parker Hannifen Sporlan Div....804 379-8551
605 Research Rd Ste C North Chesterfield (23236) ***(G-9945)***
Parker Industries Virginia Inc....804 254-4140
8 S Plum St Richmond (23220) ***(G-11707)***
Parker Manufacturing LLC....804 507-0593
5734 Charles City Cir Richmond (23231) ***(G-11319)***
Parker-Hannifin Corporation....434 846-6541
3700 Mayflower Dr Lynchburg (24501) ***(G-7782)***
Parkgate Press....607 280-2364
7796 Marshall Heights Ct Falls Church (22043) ***(G-4854)***
Parkland Direct Inc....434 385-6225
305 Enterprise Dr Forest (24551) ***(G-5086)***
Parks Electric Motor Repair....540 389-6911
1490 Southside Dr Salem (24153) ***(G-12553)***
Parkside Woods LLC....703 543-6446
4934 Edge Rock Dr Chantilly (20151) ***(G-2478)***
Parksley Sign Company, Parksley *Also called D & V Enterprises Inc* ***(G-10261)***
Parkstone, Ashland *Also called Julian Industries LLC* ***(G-1444)***
Parkway Manufacturing Company....757 896-9712
707 Industry Dr Hampton (23661) ***(G-6213)***
Parkway Printshop....757 378-3959
410 Lightfoot Rd Williamsburg (23188) ***(G-15291)***
Parkway Stl Rule Ctng Dies Inc....540 586-4948
1912 Woodside Ave Bedford (24523) ***(G-1648)***
Parmly Jr Land Logging & Timbe....434 842-2900
2460 Shores Rd Palmyra (22963) ***(G-10253)***
Parry Labs LLC....585 746-8335
500 Montgomery St Ste 675 Alexandria (22314) ***(G-306)***
Parsons Corporation....703 558-0036
1911 Fort Myer Dr # 1100 Arlington (22209) ***(G-1099)***
Parsons Corporation....703 988-8500
5875 Trinity Pkwy Ste 300 Centreville (20120) ***(G-2327)***
Parsons Pressure Washing....757 894-3110
7077 Fleming Rd New Church (23415) ***(G-9127)***
Partfiniti Inc....703 679-7278
5501 Merchants View Sq Haymarket (20169) ***(G-6434)***
Partlow Associates Inc....703 863-5695
5018 S Chesterfield Rd Arlington (22206) ***(G-1100)***

Partnership For Success 804 363-3380
211 Ruthers Rd Ste 103 North Chesterfield (23235) *(G-9946)*
Parts Manufacturing Virginia 540 845-3289
1125 Summit St Fredericksburg (22401) *(G-5212)*
Party Headquarters Inc 703 494-5317
20 Rawlings Pl 123 Fredericksburg (22405) *(G-5467)*
Pasc, Virginia Beach *Also called Pan American Systems Corp (G-14709)*
Pascor Atlantic Corporation (PA) **276 688-2220**
254 Industry Dr Bland (24315) *(G-1836)*
Passionate Stitcher 804 747-7141
10908 Brunson Way Glen Allen (23060) *(G-5778)*
Pasta By Valente Inc 434 971-3717
1223 Harris St Charlottesville (22903) *(G-2841)*
Pasta Valente, Charlottesville *Also called Pasta By Valente Inc (G-2841)*
Pastime Publications LLC 724 961-2922
1303 Waterfront Dr Apt 10 Virginia Beach (23451) *(G-14711)*
Pat Bennett Race Cars, Evington *Also called Bennett Motorsports Inc (G-4374)*
Patinad Grace LLC 804 447-4578
106 S Robinson St Richmond (23220) *(G-11708)*
Patricia Gavin 703 439-4403
23776 Champe Ford Rd Middleburg (20117) *(G-8731)*
Patricia Moore 757 485-7414
3248 Old Mill Rd Chesapeake (23323) *(G-3234)*
Patricia Ramey 703 973-1140
1797 Blue Ridge Farm Rd Upperville (20184) *(G-13967)*
Patrick Marrietta 804 479-9791
2029 Colston St Petersburg (23805) *(G-10333)*
Patrick Hawks 276 618-2055
212 Franklin St Martinsville (24112) *(G-8316)*
Patrick Pierce 804 833-1800
4900 E Leyburn Ct Apt 102 Henrico (23228) *(G-6546)*
Patriot IV Shipping Corp 703 876-3000
2941 Frview Pk Dr Ste 100 Falls Church (22042) *(G-4855)*
Patriot Solutions Group LLC 571 367-4979
24890 Castleton Dr Chantilly (20152) *(G-2549)*
Patriot Tools LLC 757 718-4591
2308 Smith Ave Chesapeake (23325) *(G-3235)*
Patriot3 Inc 540 891-7353
11040 Pierson Dr Fredericksburg (22408) *(G-5343)*
Patriotic Publications LLC 804 814-3017
23316 Triple Crown Dr Ruther Glen (22546) *(G-12460)*
Patron Id Inc 954 282-6636
828 Main St Ste 1402 Lynchburg (24504) *(G-7783)*
Pattern and Print LLC 540 884-2660
7691 Old Fincastle Rd Fincastle (24090) *(G-4997)*
Pattern Shop Inc 540 389-5110
27 Wells St Salem (24153) *(G-12554)*
Pattern Svcs & Fabrication LLC 540 731-4891
51 Wadsworth St Radford (24141) *(G-10734)*
Patterson Business Systems 540 389-7726
227 Electric Rd Salem (24153) *(G-12555)*
Patton Sand & Concrete 276 236-9362
538 Rolling Wood Ln Galax (24333) *(G-5644)*
Patty S Pieceworks 804 796-3371
11913 Dunvegan Ct Chesterfield (23838) *(G-3517)*
Paul and Sonia Jones, Bristow *Also called Jones Family Office (G-2057)*
Paul E Stahl 772 600-8099
4339 Kirkwood Dr Roanoke (24018) *(G-11983)*
Paul Owens 804 393-2475
6925 Fox Downs Dr Henrico (23231) *(G-6547)*
Paul T Marshall 703 580-0245
4823 Pearson Dr Woodbridge (22193) *(G-15774)*
Paul V Bell 703 631-4011
8501 Buckeye Timber Dr Manassas (20109) *(G-8126)*
Paul Valentine Orthotics 804 355-0283
2139 Staples Mill Rd Richmond (23230) *(G-11320)*
Paulette Fabricators Inc 804 798-3700
9996 Lickinghole Rd Ashland (23005) *(G-1474)*
Pauls Fan Company 276 530-7311
2738 Home Creek Rd Grundy (24614) *(G-6039)*
Pauls Shoe Repair & Lea ACC 703 759-3735
9903 Georgetown Pike Great Falls (22066) *(G-5971)*
Pave DMV LLC 703 798-1087
6511 Braddock Rd Ste 201 Alexandria (22312) *(G-549)*
Pavement Stencil Company 540 427-1325
4347 Aerospace Rd Ste A Roanoke (24014) *(G-12145)*
Paver Doctors LLC 757 903-6275
203 Bethune Dr Williamsburg (23185) *(G-15292)*
Paw Print Pet Services 434 822-5020
575 Chaneys Store Rd Ringgold (24586) *(G-11873)*
Paw Prints 540 220-2825
8006 Avocet Way Spotsylvania (22553) *(G-12908)*
Pawprint Publishing LLC 434 985-3876
246 Skirmish Rd Stanardsville (22973) *(G-13227)*
Pawse & Play LLC 757 230-9309
4445 Corp Ln Ste 264 Virginia Beach (23462) *(G-14712)*
Paya Inc (HQ) **800 261-0240**
12120 Sunset Hills Rd # 500 Reston (20190) *(G-10922)*
Paycock Press LLC 703 525-9296
3819 13th St N Arlington (22201) *(G-1101)*
Payne Publishers Inc 703 631-9033
8707 Quarry Rd Ste B Manassas (20110) *(G-7988)*
Pb & J Publishing LLC 703 903-9561
7714 Carlton Pl Mc Lean (22102) *(G-8524)*
Pb Crave of Nc LLC 252 585-1744
32126 General Thomas Hwy Franklin (23851) *(G-5153)*
PBM Foods Inc 269 673-8451
652 Peter Jefferson Pkwy Charlottesville (22911) *(G-2672)*
PBM International Ltd 800 959-2066
652 Peter Jefferson Pkwy Charlottesville (22911) *(G-2673)*
PBM Pharmaceuticals Inc 434 980-8100
200 Garrett St Ste F Charlottesville (22902) *(G-2842)*
Pbp Solutions LLC 202 999-8101
11790 Indian Ridge Rd Reston (20191) *(G-10923)*
PC Sands LLC 703 534-6107
6144 12th Rd N Arlington (22205) *(G-1102)*
PC Shareware Inc 540 371-5746
39 Brookstone Dr Fredericksburg (22405) *(G-5468)*
PC Unlimited, Norfolk *Also called George Perez (G-9561)*
PCA / Harrisonburg, 333, Harrisonburg *Also called Packaging Corporation America (G-6351)*
Pca/Mid-Atlantic Area, Harrisonburg *Also called Packaging Corporation America (G-6353)*
Pca/Richmond 370, Richmond *Also called Packaging Corporation America (G-11703)*
Pca/Roanoke 371, Roanoke *Also called Packaging Corporation America (G-11982)*
PCA/Supply Services 302e, Winchester *Also called Packaging Corporation America (G-15458)*
Pcac, Clifton *Also called Presidential Coin & Antique Co (G-3675)*
PCC Corporation 757 721-2949
2728 Nestlebrook Trl Virginia Beach (23456) *(G-14713)*
PCC Corporation 757 368-5777
524 Central Dr Ste 102 Virginia Beach (23454) *(G-14714)*
PCI, Highland Springs *Also called Printed Circuits International (G-6855)*
Pcpursuit Inc 425 890-5495
2214 Rock Hill Rd Ste 270 Herndon (20170) *(G-6768)*
Pd Power Systems LLC 703 778-3515
6225 Brandon Ave Ste 460 Springfield (22150) *(G-13066)*
Pdh Mobile Inc 703 475-8223
337 Walker Rd Great Falls (22066) *(G-5972)*
Pdi, Richmond *Also called Power Distribution Inc (G-11721)*
PDQ Printing Company 804 228-0077
3612 Mechanicsville Tpke Richmond (23223) *(G-11709)*
PDQ Printing LLC 804 228-0077
3612 Mechanicsville Tpke Richmond (23223) *(G-11710)*
Pe Crew LLC 540 839-5999
9530 Sam Snead Hwy Hot Springs (24445) *(G-6949)*
Peabody Coaltrade LLC 804 378-4655
1500 Huguenot Rd Ste 108 Midlothian (23113) *(G-8877)*
Peac LLC 571 261-1527
14646 Celeste Ct Haymarket (20169) *(G-6435)*
Peace Harmony and Love LLC 571 210-5853
14120 Lee Hwy Ste A609 Centreville (20120) *(G-2328)*
Peace Justice Publications LLC 540 349-7862
7180 Baldwin Ridge Rd Warrenton (20187) *(G-15043)*
Peach Tea Monograms 703 973-9977
8853 Glenridge Ct Vienna (22182) *(G-14109)*
Peak Development Resources LLC 804 233-3707
5120 Evelyn Byrd Rd Richmond (23225) *(G-11711)*
Pearce Woodworking 240 377-1278
903 Berryville Ave Winchester (22601) *(G-15565)*
Pearmund Cellars 540 347-3475
6190 Georgetown Rd Broad Run (20137) *(G-2069)*
Pearson & Associates 757 523-1382
3460 Macdonald Rd Virginia Beach (23464) *(G-14715)*
Pearson Equipment Company 434 845-3171
3904 Harris Ln Lynchburg (24501) *(G-7784)*
Pecher Enterprises, Virginia Beach *Also called Custom Embroidery & Designs (G-14377)*
Peebles Welding & Fabrication 757 880-5332
738 Plum Ave Hampton (23661) *(G-6214)*
Peek—boo Pubg Group Brnd Lcen 703 259-8816
113 S Columbus St Ste 400 Alexandria (22314) *(G-307)*
Peer Clnic For Back Pain Spine, Fairfax *Also called Peer Technologies Pllc (G-4660)*
Peer Technologies Pllc 603 727-8692
4250 Chain Bridge Rd Fairfax (22030) *(G-4660)*
Pegee Wllmsburg Pttrns Hstries 757 220-2722
105 Dogwood Dr Williamsburg (23185) *(G-15293)*
Peggy Hank Industries LLC 434 825-4802
687 Tilman Rd Charlottesville (22903) *(G-2843)*
Peggy Sues Advertising Inc 276 530-7790
Rr 460 Conaway (24603) *(G-3754)*
Pegrams Transporting Svcs LLC 804 295-1798
930 W Washington St Petersburg (23803) *(G-10334)*
Pegs Embroidery Inc 804 378-2053
11814 Murray Olds Ct Midlothian (23114) *(G-8878)*
Pei, Manassas *Also called Pionk Enterprises Intl LLC (G-8129)*
Pelican Products 540 636-1624
1390 Progress Dr Front Royal (22630) *(G-5548)*
Pellegrino Aerospace LLC 571 431-7011
2639 Fort Scott Dr Arlington (22202) *(G-1103)*

ALPHABETIC

Pembelton Forest Products Inc (PA) 434 292-7511
402 Davis Mill Rd Blackstone (23824) *(G-1822)*

Pemco Corporation 276 326-2611
1960 Valleydale St Bluefield (24605) *(G-1872)*

Penguin Woodworking LLC 804 502-2656
2144b Tower Hill Rd Powhatan (23139) *(G-10562)*

Peninsula Custom Coaters Inc 757 476-6996
1598 Penniman Rd Ste D Williamsburg (23185) *(G-15294)*

Pennells Logging 434 292-5482
337 Hawthorne Dr Blackstone (23824) *(G-1823)*

Penningtons Logging LLC 276 783-9374
287 Jerrys Creek Rd Chilhowie (24319) *(G-3557)*

Pennrose Publishing LLC 757 631-0579
2909 Pinewood Dr Virginia Beach (23452) *(G-14716)*

Pennsylvania Drilling Company 540 665-5207
321 Arbor Ct Winchester (22602) *(G-15459)*

Penny Plate LLC 540 337-3777
286 Expo Rd Fishersville (22939) *(G-5006)*

Penny Plate of Virginia, Fishersville *Also called Penny Plate LLC (G-5006)*

Penny Saver 434 857-5134
642 Worsham St Danville (24540) *(G-4023)*

Penny Trail Press LLC 757 644-5349
37219 Old Wakefield Rd Wakefield (23888) *(G-14969)*

People Interact LLC 571 223-5888
43067 Lake Ridge Pl Leesburg (20176) *(G-7324)*

Peoplespace Inc 434 825-2168
101 E Water St Charlottesville (22902) *(G-2844)*

Pep Labs LLC 202 669-2562
20634 Duxbury Ter Ashburn (20147) *(G-1325)*

Pepperidge Farm Distributor 540 395-4233
1229 Harris St Charlottesville (22903) *(G-2845)*

Peppers Services LLC 276 233-6464
660 Blackberry Ln Galax (24333) *(G-5645)*

Pepsi Beverages Company, Danville *Also called Bottling Group LLC (G-3962)*

Pepsi Beverages Company 757 857-1251
1194 Pineridge Rd Norfolk (23502) *(G-9683)*

Pepsi Bottling Group 540 344-8355
2866 Nicholas Ave Ne Roanoke (24012) *(G-12146)*

Pepsi Co 276 625-3900
316 Gator Ln Wytheville (24382) *(G-15903)*

Pepsi Cola Btlg Inc Norton VA (PA) 276 679-1122
12th St At Park Ave Norton (24273) *(G-10134)*

Pepsi Cola Btlg Inc Norton VA 276 963-6606
606 Wardell Indus Pk Rd Cedar Bluff (24609) *(G-2283)*

Pepsi-Cola, Roanoke *Also called Pepsi Bottling Group (G-12146)*

Pepsi-Cola Btlg Co Centl VA (PA) 434 978-2140
1150 Pepsi Pl Charlottesville (22901) *(G-2674)*

Pepsi-Cola Btlg Co Centl VA 434 978-2140
330 Seminole Ct Charlottesville (22901) *(G-2675)*

Pepsi-Cola Btlg Co Centl VA 540 234-9238
100 Triangle Dr Weyers Cave (24486) *(G-15175)*

Pepsi-Cola General Bottlers 276 783-7232
211 Washington Ave Marion (24354) *(G-8239)*

Pepsi-Cola Metro Btlg Co Inc 757 857-1251
1194 Pineridge Rd Norfolk (23502) *(G-9684)*

Pepsi-Cola Metro Btlg Co Inc 540 361-4467
11551 Shannon Dr Fredericksburg (22408) *(G-5344)*

Pepsi-Cola Metro Btlg Co Inc 434 528-5107
121 Bradley Dr Lynchburg (24501) *(G-7785)*

Pepsi-Cola Metro Btlg Co Inc 757 887-2310
17200 Warwick Blvd Newport News (23603) *(G-9311)*

Pepsi-Cola Metro Btlg Co Inc 540 966-5200
226 Lee Hwy Roanoke (24019) *(G-11984)*

Pepsi-Cola Metro Btlg Co Inc 434 792-4512
1001 Riverside Dr Danville (24540) *(G-4024)*

Pepsico, Warrenton *Also called P-Americas LLC (G-15041)*

Pepsico, Norton *Also called Pepsi Cola Btlg Inc Norton VA (G-10134)*

Pepsico, Marion *Also called Pepsi-Cola General Bottlers (G-8239)*

Pepsico, Lorton *Also called Bottling Group LLC (G-7468)*

Pepsico, Weyers Cave *Also called Pepsi-Cola Btlg Co Centl VA (G-15175)*

Pepsico, Cedar Bluff *Also called Pepsi Cola Btlg Inc Norton VA (G-2283)*

Pepsico, Wytheville *Also called Bottling Group LLC (G-15879)*

Pepsico Inc 276 781-2177
223 Browns Subdivision Rd Marion (24354) *(G-8240)*

Pepsico Inc 804 714-1382
1608 Willis Rd Richmond (23237) *(G-11056)*

Pepsicola, Charlottesville *Also called Ja-Zan LLC (G-2651)*

Per LLC 540 489-4737
211 Industry Blvd Rocky Mount (24151) *(G-12344)*

Peraton Cmmnctons Holdings LLC 703 668-6001
12975 Worldgate Dr Herndon (20170) *(G-6769)*

Peraton Inc 315 838-7009
11830 Canon Blvd Ste H Newport News (23606) *(G-9312)*

Peraton Inc 719 599-1500
12975 Worldgate Dr # 100 Herndon (20170) *(G-6770)*

Peraton Inc 703 668-6000
12975 Worldgate Dr # 100 Herndon (20170) *(G-6771)*

Peraton Inc 757 857-0099
5365 Robin Hood Rd Ste A3 Norfolk (23513) *(G-9685)*

Perceptions of Virginia Inc 703 730-5918
13065 Saint Andrews Ct Woodbridge (22192) *(G-15775)*

Percision Woodworks 757 642-1686
1614 Pitchkettle Rd Suffolk (23434) *(G-13751)*

Percontee Inc 703 471-4411
636 Rte 606 Chantilly (20153) *(G-2479)*

Perdue Farms Inc 804 722-1276
5155 Chudoba Pkwy Prince George (23875) *(G-10604)*

Perdue Farms Inc 540 465-9665
455 Radio Station Rd Strasburg (22657) *(G-13594)*

Perdue Farms Inc 804 443-4391
1000 Granary Rd Tappahannock (22560) *(G-13820)*

Perdue Farms Inc 757 494-5564
501 Barnes Rd Chesapeake (23324) *(G-3236)*

Perdue Farms Inc 540 828-7700
100 Quality St Bridgewater (22812) *(G-1956)*

Perdue Farms Inc 804 453-4656
1671 Waverly Ave Kilmarnock (22482) *(G-7074)*

Perdue Farms Inc 757 787-5210
16121 Perdue Ln Eastville (23347) *(G-4296)*

Perez Armando 202 716-5044
1860 N Scott St Apt 237 Arlington (22209) *(G-1104)*

Perfect Blind 703 675-4111
43106 Kingsport Dr Leesburg (20176) *(G-7325)*

Perfect Image Printing 703 824-0010
5616 Columbia Pike Falls Church (22041) *(G-4856)*

Perfect Peace Alpacas LLC 540 797-1985
224 Shade Hollow Rd Blue Ridge (24064) *(G-1854)*

Perfect Pink LLC 571 969-7465
2116 S Lincoln St Arlington (22204) *(G-1105)*

Performance Aviation Mfg Group 757 766-1150
106 Sherwood Dr Williamsburg (23185) *(G-15295)*

Performance Consulting Inc 434 724-2904
7912 Franklin Tpke Dry Fork (24549) *(G-4143)*

Performance Counts Automotive 434 392-3391
3020 W 3rd St Farmville (23901) *(G-4955)*

Performance Cstm Cabinets LLC 804 382-3870
3573 Archers Rdg Powhatan (23139) *(G-10563)*

Performance Drives Inc 304 327-7725
145 Bunny Dr Bluefield (24605) *(G-1873)*

Performance Engrg & Mch Co 804 530-5577
14518 Fox Knoll Dr South Chesterfield (23834) *(G-12819)*

Performance Films, Fieldale *Also called Solutia Inc (G-4991)*

Performance Fly Rods 540 867-0856
5798 Singers Glen Rd Rockingham (22802) *(G-12267)*

Performance Livestock & Feed C 888 777-5912
11 Redd Level Plant Rd Martinsville (24112) *(G-8317)*

Performance Rigging, Hampton *Also called North Sails Hampton Inc (G-6210)*

Performance Signs LLC 434 985-7446
18 Commerce Dr Ruckersville (22968) *(G-12408)*

Performance Support Systems 757 873-3700
8270 Little England Rd Hayes (23072) *(G-6404)*

Performnce Mtal Fbricators Inc 757 465-8622
3901 Alexander St Portsmouth (23701) *(G-10467)*

Performyard Inc 703 870-3710
4201 Wilson Blvd Arlington (22203) *(G-1106)*

Periflame LLC 888 996-3526
1600 N Oak St Apt 629 Arlington (22209) *(G-1107)*

Perkins 276 227-0551
131 Queens Knob Wytheville (24382) *(G-15904)*

Perla-Art, Round Hill *Also called Jill C Perla (G-12380)*

Permaguard Coatings LLC 929 352-5665
9245 Rural Point Dr Mechanicsville (23116) *(G-8667)*

Permissionbit Inc 703 278-3832
1750 Tysons Blvd Ste 1500 Mc Lean (22102) *(G-8525)*

Permit Pushers 703 237-6461
3540 N Valley St Arlington (22207) *(G-1108)*

Perrigo Nutritionals 434 297-1070
652 Peter Jefferson Pkwy # 300 Charlottesville (22911) *(G-2676)*

Perrone Publishing LLC 434 962-6694
37 Morewood Pl Palmyra (22963) *(G-10254)*

Perry Railworks Inc 703 794-0507
13573 Den Hollow Ct Manassas (20112) *(G-8127)*

Persimmon Street Ceramics That 202 256-8238
2332 N Tuckahoe St Arlington (22205) *(G-1109)*

Persimmon Woodworking 703 618-6909
16714 Sommertime Ln Hamilton (20158) *(G-6063)*

Person Enterprises Inc 757 483-6252
6008 High St W Portsmouth (23703) *(G-10468)*

Personal 540 845-8771
11311 Glen Park Dr Fredericksburg (22407) *(G-5345)*

Personal Protectio Principles 757 453-3202
4017 Roebling Ln Virginia Beach (23452) *(G-14717)*

Personal Selling Power Inc (PA) 540 752-7000
1140 International Pkwy Fredericksburg (22406) *(G-5469)*

Personal Touch Printing Svcs 757 619-7073
912 Martingale Ct Virginia Beach (23454) *(G-14718)*

Personalized Engraving, Centreville *Also called Hee K Yoon (G-2310)*

Personam Inc 571 297-9371
1420 Spring Hill Rd # 525 Mc Lean (22102) *(G-8526)*

Perspecta Svcs & Solutions Inc 781 684-4000
19980 Highland Vista Dr Ashburn (20147) ***(G-1326)***
Pete Burr Machine Works Inc 540 249-5693
7 Pine Creek Ln Grottoes (24441) ***(G-6022)***
Peter Adams 540 960-0241
11131 Douthat State Pk Rd Millboro (24460) ***(G-8938)***
Peter Henderson Oil Co (PA) **434 823-8608**
5216 Rose Valley Farm Crozet (22932) ***(G-3846)***
Peter Korer 702 460-2144
120 Battlefield Blvd S Chesapeake (23322) ***(G-3237)***
Peters Knives 703 255-5353
9812 Oak Valley Ct Vienna (22181) ***(G-14110)***
Peters Melvin Cabinet Shop Inc 757 826-7317
416 Rotary St Hampton (23661) ***(G-6215)***
Peters Pallets Inc 410 647-8094
2700 Jefferson Davis Hwy Richmond (23234) ***(G-11057)***
Petersburg Grows, Virginia Beach *Also called PM Services LLC* ***(G-14727)***
Peterson Idea Consortium Inc 804 651-8242
12047 Fox Mill Run Ln Ashland (23005) ***(G-1475)***
Petree Enterprises Inc 703 318-0008
45945 Trefoil Ln Ste 166 Sterling (20166) ***(G-13469)***
Petrostar Global LLC 301 919-7879
4159 Travers Ct Chantilly (20151) ***(G-2480)***
Pettigrew 434 979-0018
2435 Rock Branch Ln North Garden (22959) ***(G-10081)***
Pexip Inc 703 480-3181
13461 Sunrise Valley Dr Herndon (20171) ***(G-6772)***
Pfizer Inc 804 257-2000
1211 Sherwood Ave Richmond (23220) ***(G-11712)***
Pfizer Inc 804 257-2000
1211 Sherwood Ave Richmond (23220) ***(G-11713)***
Pfizer Inc 804 652-6782
2300 Darbytown Rd Richmond (23231) ***(G-11321)***
Pg Games Publishing LLC 870 637-4380
3510 Matoaka Rd Hampton (23661) ***(G-6216)***
Pgb Hangers LLC 703 851-4221
7991 Turtle Creek Cir Gainesville (20155) ***(G-5607)***
Pgenomex Inc 703 343-3282
1557 Mary Ellen Ct Mc Lean (22101) ***(G-8527)***
Pgf Enterprises LLC 276 956-4308
457 Mulberry Rd Ridgeway (24148) ***(G-11848)***
Pgfx, Henrico *Also called Loron Inc* ***(G-6531)***
Pharmaceutical RES Assoc Inc 703 464-6300
12120 Sunset Hills Rd # 6 Reston (20190) ***(G-10924)***
Pharmaceutical Source LLC 757 482-3512
617 Flatrock Ln Chesapeake (23320) ***(G-3238)***
Pharmacist Pharmaceutical LLC 540 375-6415
1640 Roanoke Blvd Salem (24153) ***(G-12556)***
Phase 2 Marine Canvas LLC 804 694-7561
2271 Wake Rd Wake (23176) ***(G-14963)***
Phase II Inc 434 333-0808
14521 Forest Rd Ste G Forest (24551) ***(G-5087)***
Phase II Truck Body Inc 276 429-2026
33213 Lee Hwy Glade Spring (24340) ***(G-5680)***
Phasor Inc (PA) **202 256-2075**
1655 Fort Myer Dr Arlington (22209) ***(G-1110)***
Phat Daddys Polish Shop 804 405-5301
8706 S Boones Trail Rd North Chesterfield (23236) ***(G-9947)***
Phaze II Products Inc 757 353-3901
1100 Bay Colony Dr Virginia Beach (23451) ***(G-14719)***
PHD Posters, Henrico *Also called Hughes Posters LLC* ***(G-6523)***
Phenix Engineered Textiles Inc 757 654-6131
32056 East Cir Boykins (23827) ***(G-1919)***
Phil Gunn Machine Co Inc 804 271-7059
7801 Redpine Rd Ste A North Chesterfield (23237) ***(G-9948)***
Phil Morgan 757 455-9475
3 Interstate Corp Ctr Norfolk (23502) ***(G-9686)***
Philadelphia Riverboat LLC 757 640-9205
870 N Military Hwy # 200 Norfolk (23502) ***(G-9687)***
Philip Back 540 570-9353
2286 Borden Grant Trl Fairfield (24435) ***(G-4733)***
Philip Carter Winery, Hume *Also called Stillhouse Vineyards LLC* ***(G-6963)***
Philip Miles 703 760-9832
1532 Lincoln Way Apt 303 Mc Lean (22102) ***(G-8528)***
Philip Morris Duty Free Inc 804 274-2000
6601 W Broad St Richmond (23230) ***(G-11322)***
Philip Morris USA Inc (HQ) **804 274-2000**
6601 W Brd St Richmond (23230) ***(G-11323)***
Philip Morris USA Inc 804 274-2000
4100 Bermuda Hundred Rd Chester (23836) ***(G-3443)***
Philip Morris USA Inc 804 274-2000
2601 Maury St Richmond (23224) ***(G-11714)***
Philip Morris USA Inc 804 274-2000
3601 Commerce Rd Richmond (23234) ***(G-11058)***
Philip Morris USA Inc 804 253-8464
9201 Arboretum Pkwy Fl 2 North Chesterfield (23236) ***(G-9949)***
Phillips Custom Cabinets LLC 804 647-1328
11560 Chula Rd Amelia Court House (23002) ***(G-667)***
Phillips Enterprises VA Inc 540 563-9915
1755 Seibel Dr Ne Roanoke (24012) ***(G-12147)***
Phillips Medical Manufacturer 804 475-9144
2729 Maurice Walk Ct Glen Allen (23060) ***(G-5779)***
Phillips Welding Service Inc 434 989-7236
130 Laurel Dr Madison Heights (24572) ***(G-7882)***
Philomen Fashion and Designs 703 966-5680
826 Indian Valley Rd Heathsville (22473) ***(G-6463)***
Philosophy Worldwide Apparel 804 767-0308
4010 Hunters Ridge Dr Moseley (23120) ***(G-9044)***
Phineas Rose Wood Joinery 540 948-4248
1112 Graves Mill Rd Madison (22727) ***(G-7860)***
Phipps & Bird Inc 804 254-2737
2924 Bells Rd Richmond (23234) ***(G-11059)***
Phlow Corp 804 207-4893
1001 Haxall Point 1b Richmond (23219) ***(G-11715)***
Pho Ha Vietnamese Noodle 540 438-0999
1015 Port Republic Rd Harrisonburg (22801) ***(G-6354)***
Phoenix Designs 757 301-9300
1953 Winterhaven Dr Virginia Beach (23456) ***(G-14720)***
Phoenix Packg Operations LLC 540 307-4084
4800 Lina Ln Dublin (24084) ***(G-4168)***
Phoenix Printing, Woodbridge *Also called Walter L James* ***(G-15828)***
Phoenix Security Group Ltd 703 323-4940
7818 Ox Rd Fairfax Station (22039) ***(G-4721)***
Phoenix Sports and Advg Inc 276 988-9709
146 Shire Ln North Tazewell (24630) ***(G-10104)***
Phoenixaire LLC 703 647-6546
1100 N Glebe Rd Ste 600 Arlington (22201) ***(G-1111)***
Photo Finale Inc 703 564-3400
1420 Spring Hill Rd # 600 Mc Lean (22102) ***(G-8529)***
Photolively LLC 804 937-0896
3358 John Tree Hill Rd Powhatan (23139) ***(G-10564)***
Photonblue LLC 804 747-7412
3627 Springsberry Pl Richmond (23233) ***(G-11324)***
Photonvision LLC 540 808-6266
521 Pebble Hill Ct Charlottesville (22903) ***(G-2846)***
Phuble Inc 443 388-0657
2552 Nestlebrook Trl Virginia Beach (23456) ***(G-14721)***
Phytosnitation Vac Systems LLC 540 641-4170
629 Shawnee Trl Blacksburg (24060) ***(G-1779)***
Pi Square Technologies Inc 571 255-6253
25993 Fair Ponds Ln Chantilly (20152) ***(G-2550)***
Pic N Press Custom Prtg LLC 571 970-2627
6011 Archstone Way # 302 Alexandria (22310) ***(G-550)***
Piccadilly Circuits 703 860-5426
11560 Shadbush Ct Reston (20191) ***(G-10925)***
Piccadilly Printing Company 540 662-3804
500 W Jubal Early Dr # 120 Winchester (22601) ***(G-15566)***
Pickers Grip LLC 434 260-3366
265 Turkeysag Trl 102-2 Palmyra (22963) ***(G-10255)***
Pickle Tyson 276 686-5368
204 W Railroad Ave Rural Retreat (24368) ***(G-12429)***
Pickle Bucket Four LLC 571 259-3726
522 N Alfred St Alexandria (22314) ***(G-308)***
Pickle Bucket Three LLC 571 259-3726
522 N Alfred St Alexandria (22314) ***(G-309)***
Pics By Kels Photography LLC 540 958-4944
505 Commercial Ave Clifton Forge (24422) ***(G-3681)***
Pieces of Wood LLC 434 842-3091
127 Holmhead Cir Fork Union (23055) ***(G-5112)***
Piedmont Environtmental Sys 434 836-4547
585 Woodrow Ln Danville (24540) ***(G-4025)***
Piedmont Fabrication Inc 757 543-5570
1317 Cavalier Blvd Chesapeake (23323) ***(G-3239)***
Piedmont Logging Inc 434 989-1698
1697 Cow Hollow Rd Roseland (22967) ***(G-12371)***
Piedmont Metal Fabricators, Louisa *Also called Hmb Inc* ***(G-7556)***
Piedmont Metal Products Inc 540 586-0674
915 Orange St Bedford (24523) ***(G-1649)***
Piedmont Pallet Corporation (PA) **434 836-6730**
2848 Blairmont Dr Danville (24540) ***(G-4026)***
Piedmont Powder Coating Inc 434 334-8434
802 Mangrums Rd Danville (24541) ***(G-4027)***
Piedmont Precision Mch Co Inc (PA) **434 793-0677**
150 Airside Dr Danville (24540) ***(G-4028)***
Piedmont Press & Graphics, Warrenton *Also called Tr Press Inc* ***(G-15055)***
Piedmont Prtg & Graphics Inc 434 793-0026
521 Monroe St Danville (24541) ***(G-4029)***
Piedmont Publishing Inc 434 822-1800
3157 Westover Dr Danville (24541) ***(G-4030)***
Piedmont Station Studio LLC 540 364-4427
10166 Glmpse Of Heaven Ln Delaplane (20144) ***(G-4077)***
Piedmont Welding & Maintenance 434 447-6600
845 Canaan Church Rd La Crosse (23950) ***(G-7148)***
Piedmont Wldg & Maint Svc LLC 434 447-6600
336 Union Mill Rd La Crosse (23950) ***(G-7149)***
Piedmont Woodworks LLC 540 364-1849
3803 Rectortown Rd Marshall (20115) ***(G-8258)***
Pierce & Johnson Lumber Co Inc 434 983-2586
19135 N James Madison Hwy Dillwyn (23936) ***(G-4098)***

ALPHABETIC

Pierce Publishing 434 386-5667
100 Earls Ct Lynchburg (24503) *(G-7786)*

Pierside Marine Industries 757 852-9571
2614 Wyoming Ave Norfolk (23513) *(G-9688)*

Pif Industries LLC 804 677-2945
3113 W Marshall St Richmond (23230) *(G-11325)*

Pigeon Creek Alpacas 540 894-1121
5937 Haleys Mill Rd Spotsylvania (22551) *(G-12909)*

Pigtale Press LLC 703 753-7572
15207 Windy Hollow Cir Gainesville (20155) *(G-5608)*

Pike Woodworks 571 329-4377
5649 Wheelwright Way Haymarket (20169) *(G-6436)*

Pilgrim International 757 989-5045
13294 Warwick Blvd Newport News (23602) *(G-9313)*

Pilgrim Wireless, Newport News *Also called Pilgrim International* *(G-9313)*

Pilgrims Pride Corporation 540 564-6070
590 Mount Clinton Pike Harrisonburg (22802) *(G-6355)*

Pilgrims Pride Corporation 540 896-7000
330 Co Op Dr Timberville (22853) *(G-13851)*

Pilnut Press Inc 540 347-6295
5089 Old Auburn Rd Warrenton (20187) *(G-15044)*

Pilkington North America Inc 540 362-5130
7703 Enon Dr Roanoke (24019) *(G-11985)*

Pillar Enterprise Ltd 540 868-8626
201 Ridings Ln White Post (22663) *(G-15181)*

Pillar Publishing & Co LLC 804 640-1963
4105 Autumn Glen Ct Richmond (23223) *(G-11716)*

Pilot Media 757 446-2000
150 W Brambleton Ave Norfolk (23510) *(G-9689)*

Pinder Industries LLC 240 200-0703
7629 Webbwood Ct Springfield (22151) *(G-13067)*

Pine Creek Structures 703 791-5700
14195 Dumfries Rd Manassas (20112) *(G-8128)*

Pine Glade Buildings LLC 540 674-5229
4861 Cleburne Blvd Dublin (24084) *(G-4169)*

Pine Products Inc 276 957-2222
315 Carver Rd Martinsville (24112) *(G-8318)*

Pine Products LLC 276 957-2222
315 Carver Rd Martinsville (24112) *(G-8319)*

Pinecrest Timber Co 804 834-2304
121 Industrial Rd Waverly (23890) *(G-15087)*

Piney River Plant, Arrington *Also called Boxley Materials Company* *(G-1229)*

Piney River Quarry, Arrington *Also called Boxley Materials Company* *(G-1228)*

Pink Cupcake 801 349-6301
11912 Hunting Ridge Dr Fredericksburg (22407) *(G-5346)*

Pink Dental Laboratory LLC 540 728-5987
43760 Trade Center Pl # 16 Sterling (20166) *(G-13470)*

Pink Press Dior LLC 703 781-0345
5941 Halleck Blvd Fort Belvoir (22060) *(G-5117)*

Pink Shoe Publishing 757 277-1948
3949 Rainbow Dr Virginia Beach (23456) *(G-14722)*

Pink Street Signs 540 489-8400
1455 Franklin St Rocky Mount (24151) *(G-12345)*

Pinkio Hoppers 571 277-4153
7702 Backlick Rd Ste M Springfield (22150) *(G-13068)*

Pinky & Face Inc 703 478-2708
13300 Franklin Farm Rd F Herndon (20171) *(G-6773)*

Pinnacle Cabinetry Design LLC 804 262-7356
5418 Lakeside Ave Richmond (23228) *(G-11326)*

Pinnacle Control Systems Inc 540 888-4200
147 Mountain View Ct Winchester (22603) *(G-15460)*

Pinnacle Oil Co 540 687-6351
10 N Jay St Middleburg (20118) *(G-8732)*

Pinnacle Quality Asrn Svcs 540 425-4123
1106 Park St Bedford (24523) *(G-1650)*

Pinnell CL Custom Leather 434 823-9800
1982 White Hall Rd Crozet (22932) *(G-3847)*

Pinstripe Cstm Longboards LLC 757 635-7183
905 Gneral Beauregard Dr Virginia Beach (23454) *(G-14723)*

Pioneer Group Inc VA 276 669-3400
2700 Lee Hwy Bristol (24202) *(G-2029)*

Pioneer Industries LLC 757 432-8412
1056 Ballahack Rd Chesapeake (23322) *(G-3240)*

Pioneer Machine Co Inc 276 699-1500
1453 Pauley Flatwoods Rd Austinville (24312) *(G-1530)*

Pionk Enterprises Intl LLC 571 425-8179
6138 River Forest Dr Manassas (20112) *(G-8129)*

PIP Boonchan 571 327-5522
7209 Tanager St Springfield (22150) *(G-13069)*

PIP Printing, Springfield *Also called Postal Instant Press Inc* *(G-13072)*

PIP Printing, Lynchburg *Also called Criswell Inc* *(G-7687)*

PIP Printing, Charlottesville *Also called J & L Communications Inc* *(G-2650)*

PIP Printing, Danville *Also called P I P Printing 1156 Inc* *(G-4022)*

PIP Printing, Oakton *Also called Ersh-Enterprises Inc* *(G-10147)*

Piper Publishing LLC 804 432-9015
2221 Huguenot Springs Rd Midlothian (23113) *(G-8879)*

Pipet Repair Service Inc 804 739-3720
5324 Houndmaster Rd Midlothian (23112) *(G-8880)*

Pippin HI Frm & Vineyards LLC 434 202-8063
5022 Plank Rd North Garden (22959) *(G-10082)*

Piquant Press LLC 804 379-3856
1801 Hillenwood Dr Powhatan (23139) *(G-10565)*

Pirooz Manufacturing LLC 703 281-4244
101 Mashie Dr Se Vienna (22180) *(G-14111)*

Pitchstone LLC 434 296-2384
1909 Stillhouse Rd Charlottesville (22901) *(G-2677)*

Pitney Bowes Business Insight 540 786-5744
7111 River Rd Fredericksburg (22407) *(G-5347)*

Pitney Bowes Inc 703 658-6900
1316 Mount Vernon Ave Alexandria (22301) *(G-310)*

Pitney Bowes Inc 304 744-1067
8245 Boone Blvd Ste 470 Vienna (22182) *(G-14112)*

Pitney Bowes Inc 757 322-8000
5301 Robin Hood Rd Norfolk (23513) *(G-9690)*

Pitney Bowes Inc 804 798-3210
305 Ashcake Rd Ashland (23005) *(G-1476)*

Pitts Auto Parts Inc (PA) **540 373-3720**
316 Forbes St Fredericksburg (22401) *(G-5213)*

Pittsburg Tank & Tower Co Inc 757 422-1882
521 Bushnell Dr Virginia Beach (23451) *(G-14724)*

Pittston Coal Company (HQ) **276 739-3420**
16016 Porterfield Hwy Abingdon (24210) *(G-53)*

Pittston Minerals Group Inc (HQ) **804 289-9600**
1801 Bayberry Ct Fl 4 Richmond (23226) *(G-11327)*

Pivit 301 395-0895
24910 Earlsford Dr Chantilly (20152) *(G-2551)*

Pivit Software Solutions, Chantilly *Also called Pivit* *(G-2551)*

Pivotal Gear LLC 804 726-1328
2701 Emerywood Pkwy # 101 Henrico (23294) *(G-6548)*

Pixel Designs & Printing 571 359-6080
7410 Bull Run Rd Manassas (20111) *(G-8130)*

Pixels, Charlottesville *Also called E M Communications Inc* *(G-2787)*

Pixia Corp 571 203-9665
2350 Corp Park Dr Ste 400 Herndon (20171) *(G-6774)*

Pjl Marine Enterprise LLC 757 774-1050
3920 Trailwood Ct Chesapeake (23321) *(G-3241)*

Pk Hot Sauce LLc 703 629-0920
8191 Oakglen Rd Manassas (20110) *(G-7989)*

Pk Industries LLC 540 589-2341
5221 Medmont Cir Sw Roanoke (24018) *(G-11986)*

Pk Plumbing Inc 804 909-4160
3385 Trenholm Rd Powhatan (23139) *(G-10566)*

Plan B Design Fabrication Inc (PA) **804 271-5200**
4210 Castlewood Rd Richmond (23234) *(G-11060)*

Plan B Press 215 732-2663
2714 Jefferson Dr Alexandria (22303) *(G-551)*

Planet Care Inc 540 980-2420
4102 Bob White Blvd Pulaski (24301) *(G-10644)*

Plank Road Woodworks 617 285-8522
1229 Harris St Ste 7 Charlottesville (22903) *(G-2847)*

Plant 3, Chester *Also called Pre Con Inc* *(G-3447)*

Plant 4, Chester *Also called Pre Con Inc* *(G-3445)*

Plant 5, Chester *Also called Pre Con Inc* *(G-3446)*

Plantation Shutter & Blind 757 241-7026
1248 Secretariat Run Virginia Beach (23454) *(G-14725)*

Plasmera Technologies LLC 540 353-5438
6101 Scotford Ct Roanoke (24018) *(G-11987)*

Plasser American Corporation 757 543-3526
2001 Myers Rd Chesapeake (23324) *(G-3242)*

Plasterco Plant, Saltville *Also called United States Gypsum Company* *(G-12597)*

Plastic Container City, Petersburg *Also called South Distributors LLC* *(G-10344)*

Plastic Fabricating Inc 540 345-6901
2558 Patterson Ave Sw Roanoke (24016) *(G-12148)*

Plastic Solutions Incorporated 540 722-4694
240 Mcghee Rd Winchester (22603) *(G-15461)*

Plasticlad LLC (PA) **757 562-5550**
131 Sachs Ave Franklin (23851) *(G-5154)*

Plateau Software Inc 703 385-8300
2701 Prosperity Ave Fairfax (22031) *(G-4530)*

Platinum Point LLC 804 357-3337
7518 Elkhardt Rd North Chesterfield (23225) *(G-10021)*

Platnick Crane and Steel LLC 276 322-5477
269 St Clairs Xing Bluefield (24605) *(G-1874)*

Play By Play, Roanoke *Also called Montyco LLC* *(G-12137)*

Playcall Inc 571 385-6203
395 Walker Rd Great Falls (22066) *(G-5973)*

Player Pursuits LLC 202 207-6000
1308 Vincent Pl Fl 2 Mc Lean (22101) *(G-8530)*

Playtex Products LLC 804 230-1520
2901 Maury St Richmond (23224) *(G-11717)*

Playtex Products LLC 703 866-7621
7732 Gromwell Ct Springfield (22152) *(G-13070)*

Playtex Richmond VA, Richmond *Also called Playtex Products LLC* *(G-11717)*

Pleasant Run Pubg Svcs LLC 757 229-8510
217 Martins Rdg Williamsburg (23188) *(G-15296)*

Pleasant Vly Bus Solutions LLC 703 391-0977
1801 Alexander Bell Dr # 520 Reston (20191) *(G-10926)*

(G-0000) Company's Geographic Section entry number

Pleasy LLC 774 234-4299
2708 1st St S Arlington (22204) *(G-1112)*

Pleckers Customer Engraving 540 241-5661
919 High St Waynesboro (22980) *(G-15131)*

Plexi Worldwide LLC 804 625-2524
22960 Shaw Rd Ste 601 Sterling (20166) *(G-13471)*

Plexus Inc 703 474-0383
13554 Virginia Randlh Ave Herndon (20171) *(G-6775)*

Plow Shear Press LLC 757 346-8821
2124 Sandalwood Rd Virginia Beach (23451) *(G-14726)*

Pls Installation 540 521-1261
500 Black Forest Ln Buchanan (24066) *(G-2124)*

Plug Electrical 804 873-8688
6512 Marleigh Ct Henrico (23231) *(G-6549)*

Plum Summer LLC 804 519-0009
110 Whaley Ln Reedville (22539) *(G-10766)*

Plum Tree Wind LLC 434 220-7595
310 4th St Ne Ste 200 Charlottesville (22902) *(G-2848)*

Plunkett Business Group Inc 540 343-3323
845 3rd St Vinton (24179) *(G-14180)*

Plus Is ME 757 693-1505
16282 Savagetown Rd Painter (23420) *(G-10242)*

Pluto Gone LLC 804 719-3076
103 Ryan Arch Suffolk (23434) *(G-13752)*

Ply Gem Industries Inc 540 337-3663
185 Johnson Dr Stuarts Draft (24477) *(G-13657)*

Ply Gem Industries Inc 540 483-0211
433 N Main St Rocky Mount (24151) *(G-12346)*

Plygem Industries, Rocky Mount Also called Lineal Technologies Inc *(G-12335)*

Plymkraft Inc (PA) **757 595-0364**
281 Picketts Line Newport News (23603) *(G-9314)*

Plymtech Welding & Assembly, Hampton Also called Terry Plymouth *(G-6252)*

PM Pump Company 540 380-2012
5032 Stanley Farm Rd Salem (24153) *(G-12557)*

PM Services LLC 804 426-9892
2316 Kilburton Priory Ct Virginia Beach (23456) *(G-14727)*

Pma It Solutions Inc 571 336-2408
100 7th St Ste 104 Portsmouth (23704) *(G-10469)*

PMC Logistics LLC 804 414-8400
2500 Maury Rd South Prince George (23805) *(G-12866)*

PME Compost, Riner Also called Poplar Manor Enterprises LLC *(G-11865)*

PMG Refining, Berryville Also called Saudi Trade Links *(G-1688)*

Pn Labs 804 938-1600
1179 Bradbury Rd Moseley (23120) *(G-9045)*

Poamax LLC 757 871-7196
17 Alphus St Poquoson (23662) *(G-10374)*

Poddery 804 725-5956
Rr 660 Foster (23056) *(G-5137)*

Podium Pro, Virginia Beach Also called Magoozle LLC *(G-14634)*

Poetica Publishing Company 757 617-0821
900 Granby St Ste 122 Norfolk (23510) *(G-9691)*

Poff Logging LLC 540 695-0060
493 Laurel Branch Rd Nw Floyd (24091) *(G-5034)*

Pogo-CAM, Roanoke Also called Pogotec Inc *(G-11988)*

Pogotec Inc 904 501-5309
4502 Starkey Rd Ste 109 Roanoke (24018) *(G-11988)*

Pohick Creek LLC 202 888-2034
5647 Ravenel Ln Springfield (22151) *(G-13071)*

Poinsett Publications Inc 757 378-2856
4669 Yeardley Loop Williamsburg (23185) *(G-15297)*

Pointerra Us Inc 571 528-8799
42905 Secretariat Ct Ashburn (20147) *(G-1327)*

Pointman Resources LLC 240 429-3423
107 Juneberry St Sterling (20164) *(G-13472)*

Poisoned Publishing 540 755-2956
407 Birchside Cir Locust Grove (22508) *(G-7450)*

Polar Bear Ice Inc 276 259-7873
Rr 638 Whitewood (24657) *(G-15192)*

Polar Traction Inc 703 241-1958
1801 N Tuckahoe St Arlington (22205) *(G-1113)*

Polaris Group Intl LLC 757 636-8862
4445 Corp Ln Ste 150 Virginia Beach (23462) *(G-14728)*

Polaris Press LLC 703 680-6060
2212 Tacketts Mill Dr Woodbridge (22192) *(G-15776)*

Polibak Plastics America Inc 703 709-3004
36942 Snickersville Tpke Purcellville (20132) *(G-10673)*

Polimaster Inc 703 525-5075
44873 Falcon Pl Ste 128 Sterling (20166) *(G-13473)*

Politico LLC (HQ) **703 647-7999**
1000 Wilson Blvd Ste 800 Arlington (22209) *(G-1114)*

Polks Logging & Lumber 540 477-3376
2133 Pinewoods Rd Quicksburg (22847) *(G-10693)*

Polo Ralph Lauren Corp 201 531-6000
4804 Gatwick Dr Virginia Beach (23462) *(G-14729)*

Poly Processing Co, Winchester Also called Abell Corporation *(G-15369)*

Poly Processing Company LLC 804 368-7199
106 S Railroad Ave Ashland (23005) *(G-1477)*

Poly-Bond, Waynesboro Also called Avintiv Specialty Mtls Inc *(G-15099)*

Poly-Bond Inc 540 946-9250
1020 Shenandoah Vlg Dr Waynesboro (22980) *(G-15132)*

Polycap LLC 276 883-5700
219 Joe Gillespie Dr Lebanon (24266) *(G-7204)*

Polychem Inc 540 862-1321
2020 State Ave Clifton Forge (24422) *(G-3682)*

Polycoat Inc 540 989-7833
5369 Doe Run Rd Roanoke (24018) *(G-11989)*

Polycor Virginia Inc 434 831-1051
42 Alberene Loop Schuyler (22969) *(G-12653)*

Polycreteusa LLC 804 901-6893
10601 Shady Ln Charles City (23030) *(G-2579)*

Polyfab Display Company 703 497-4577
14906 Persistence Dr Woodbridge (22191) *(G-15777)*

Polyiscynurate Insul Mfrs Assn 703 224-2289
3330 Washington Blvd # 200 Arlington (22201) *(G-1115)*

Polykon Manufacturing LLC 804 461-9974
6201 Engineered Wood Way Sandston (23150) *(G-12628)*

Polymnia LLC 434 422-7842
110 Holly Ct Charlottesville (22901) *(G-2678)*

Polynt Composites USA Inc 434 432-8836
920 Tightsqueeze Indus Rd Chatham (24531) *(G-2933)*

Polyone 540 667-6666
1944 Valley Ave Winchester (22601) *(G-15567)*

Polythane of Virginia Inc 540 586-3511
5654 Virginia Byway Bedford (24523) *(G-1651)*

Polytrade International Corp 703 598-7269
46608 Silhouette Sq Sterling (20164) *(G-13474)*

Pom Kbf 703 992-7877
5702 Gen Wshngtn Dr Ste H Alexandria (22312) *(G-552)*

Poms Corporation (PA) **703 574-9901**
196 Van Buren St Ste 200 Herndon (20170) *(G-6776)*

Pondeca Industries Inc 703 599-4375
8807 Carpenters Hall Dr Lorton (22079) *(G-7521)*

Pons Corp 786 270-7774
11406 Windleaf Ct Unit M Reston (20194) *(G-10927)*

Poof Inc 703 298-7516
15911 Waterfall Rd Haymarket (20169) *(G-6437)*

Pool Hot Tub Allia 703 838-0083
2111 Eisenhower Ave Alexandria (22314) *(G-311)*

Poolhouse Digital Agency LLC 804 876-0335
23 W Broad St Ste 404 Richmond (23220) *(G-11718)*

Pop Printing 804 248-9093
6707 Greenvale Dr Richmond (23225) *(G-11719)*

Popcorn Monkey LLC (PA) **540 687-6539**
101 W Federal St Middleburg (20117) *(G-8733)*

Poplar Manor Enterprises LLC 540 763-9542
190 Poplar Manor Ln Nw Riner (24149) *(G-11865)*

Poplicus Incorporated 866 209-9100
1300 17th St N Ste 300 Arlington (22209) *(G-1116)*

Popmount Inc 804 232-4999
1817 W Broad St Richmond (23220) *(G-11720)*

Pops Snacks LLC 804 594-7290
11609 Busy St North Chesterfield (23236) *(G-9950)*

Poquoson Carts, Poquoson Also called Poquoson Enterprises *(G-10375)*

Poquoson Enterprises 757 876-6655
306 Wythe Creek Rd Poquoson (23662) *(G-10375)*

Porcupine Logging LLC 540 894-1675
2366 Waltons Store Rd Louisa (23093) *(G-7563)*

Porex Corporation 804 518-1012
1625 Ashton Park Dr South Chesterfield (23834) *(G-12820)*

Porex Filtration Group, South Chesterfield Also called Porex Technologies Corp *(G-12821)*

Porex Technologies Corp (HQ) **804 524-4983**
1625 Ashton Park Dr Ste A South Chesterfield (23834) *(G-12821)*

Porex Technologies Corporation 804 275-2631
7400 Whitepine Rd North Chesterfield (23237) *(G-9951)*

Pork Barrel Bbq LLC 202 750-7500
2312 Mount Vernon Ave # 200 Alexandria (22301) *(G-312)*

Port City Brewing Company, Alexandria Also called North Lock LLC *(G-293)*

Portable Sawmill Service 276 940-4194
Rr 1 Gate City (24251) *(G-5665)*

Porter Welding 276 565-2694
1480 Roda Rd Appalachia (24216) *(G-799)*

Porters Wood Products Inc 757 654-6430
Rr 186 Boykins (23827) *(G-1920)*

Portfolio Publication 703 802-8676
4602 Fillingame Dr Chantilly (20151) *(G-2481)*

Portico Publications Ltd (PA) **434 817-2749**
308 E Main St Charlottesville (22902) *(G-2849)*

Portsmouth Fire Marshals Ofc 757 393-8123
645 Broad St Portsmouth (23707) *(G-10470)*

Portsmouth Lumber Corporation 757 397-4646
2511 High St Portsmouth (23707) *(G-10471)*

Portsmouth Tent & Awning, Portsmouth Also called Yeates Mfg Inc *(G-10506)*

Porvair Filtration Group Inc (HQ) **804 550-1600**
301 Business Ln Ashland (23005) *(G-1478)*

Posh Afrique, Stafford Also called Claudia Ofori-Addo *(G-13132)*

Posh Pixie LLC 757 794-4949
4445 Corporation Ln 264 Virginia Beach (23462) *(G-14730)*

A
L
P
H
A
B
E
T
I
C

Poshtique 703 404-2825
565 Nalls Dairy Ct Great Falls (22066) *(G-5974)*
Posie Press LLC 804 276-0716
1218 Traway Dr North Chesterfield (23235) *(G-9952)*
Positive Feedback Software LL 540 243-0300
140 Franco Dr Rocky Mount (24151) *(G-12347)*
Positive Pasta Publishing LLC 804 385-0151
5505 Summer Creek Way Glen Allen (23059) *(G-5780)*
Positive Signs LLC 703 768-7446
7611 Richmond Hwy Ste A Alexandria (22306) *(G-553)*
Possibilities Publishing 703 585-0934
6320 Buffie Ct Burke (22015) *(G-2198)*
Post & Pallet LLC 757 645-5292
3040 Ridge Dr Toano (23168) *(G-13874)*
Post, The, Big Stone Gap *Also called Wise Printing Co Inc (G-1718)*
Postal Instant Press Inc 703 866-1988
7426 Alban Station Blvd A101 Springfield (22150) *(G-13072)*
Postal Mechanical Systems 757 424-2872
3460 Trant Ave Norfolk (23502) *(G-9692)*
Postkite LLC 202 230-1472
9919 Marquand Dr Burke (22015) *(G-2199)*
Potomac Altrntor Btry Spclists 804 224-2384
321 1st St Colonial Beach (22443) *(G-3726)*
Potomac Books Inc 703 661-1548
22841 Quicksilver Dr Dulles (20166) *(G-4219)*
Potomac Cellars LLC 540 446-2266
275 Decatur Rd Stafford (22554) *(G-13179)*
Potomac Computer Consulting, Herndon *Also called Van Vierssen Marcel (G-6835)*
Potomac Creek Woodworks LLC 703 444-9805
62 Southall Ct Sterling (20165) *(G-13475)*
Potomac Defense LLC 703 253-3441
1818 Library St Ste 500 Reston (20190) *(G-10928)*
Potomac Fine Violins LLC 239 961-0398
4620 22nd St N Arlington (22207) *(G-1117)*
Potomac Glass Inc 540 288-0210
213 Hope Rd Stafford (22554) *(G-13180)*
Potomac Health Solutions Inc (PA) **703 774-8278**
1800 Alexander Bell Dr # 400 Reston (20191) *(G-10929)*
Potomac Industries 540 940-7288
209 Old Landing Ct Fredericksburg (22405) *(G-5470)*
Potomac Intl Advisors LLC (PA) **202 460-9001**
44319 Ladiesburg Pl Ashburn (20147) *(G-1328)*
Potomac Laser Recharge 703 430-0166
11932 Holly Branch Ct Great Falls (22066) *(G-5975)*
Potomac Local News 540 659-2020
2769 Jefferson Davis Hwy Stafford (22554) *(G-13181)*
Potomac News, Manassas *Also called Wood Television LLC (G-8014)*
Potomac Point Winery, Stafford *Also called Potomac Cellars LLC (G-13179)*
Potomac Printing Solutions Inc 703 723-2511
19441 Golf Vista Plz # 250 Leesburg (20176) *(G-7326)*
Potomac Sailmakers Inc 703 750-2171
5645k General Wash Dr Alexandria (22312) *(G-554)*
Potomac Shores Cabinetry LLC 703 476-5658
2712 Fox Mill Rd Herndon (20171) *(G-6777)*
Potomac Signs Inc 703 425-7000
9102 Industry Dr Ste F Manassas Park (20111) *(G-8206)*
Potomac Solutions Incorporated 703 888-1762
300 N Lee St Alexandria (22314) *(G-313)*
Potomac Supply Llc 804 472-2527
1398 Kinsale Rd Kinsale (22488) *(G-7136)*
Potters Craft LLC 850 528-6314
4699 Catterton Rd Free Union (22940) *(G-5509)*
Pouchmouse Studios Inc 310 462-0599
40 E Taylor Run Pkwy Alexandria (22314) *(G-314)*
Pounding Mill Quarry Corp (PA) **276 326-1145**
171 Saint Clair Xing Bluefield (24605) *(G-1875)*
Powder Metal Fabrication 757 898-1614
104 Cove Ct Yorktown (23692) *(G-15984)*
Powell Manufacturing Co LLC 804 677-5728
230 E Bank St Petersburg (23803) *(G-10335)*
Powell Valley News, Pennington Gap *Also called Powell Valley Printing Company (G-10297)*
Powell Valley Printing Company 276 546-1210
41798 E Morgan Ave Pennington Gap (24277) *(G-10297)*
Powell Valley Stone Co Inc 276 546-2550
43115 Wilderness Rd Pennington Gap (24277) *(G-10298)*
Powells Paving Sealing LLC 540 921-2455
208 Painter School Rd Pembroke (24136) *(G-10283)*
Power Alarm Control Services, Arlington *Also called Pacs Inc (G-1094)*
Power Anywhere LLC 703 625-4115
4449 38th St N Arlington (22207) *(G-1118)*
Power Catch Inc 757 962-0999
2715 Monticello Ave Ste A Norfolk (23517) *(G-9693)*
Power Clean Industries LLC 804 372-6838
1815 Dorset Ridge Way Powhatan (23139) *(G-10567)*
Power Distribution Inc (HQ) **804 737-9880**
4200 Oakleys Ln Richmond (23223) *(G-11721)*
Power Distribution Pdts Inc 276 646-3296
14660 Industrial Park Rd Bristol (24202) *(G-2030)*
Power Fuels LLC 276 676-2945
21360 Crosswinds Dr Abingdon (24211) *(G-54)*

Power Hub Ventures LLC 540 443-9214
1700 Kraft Dr Ste 1325 Blacksburg (24060) *(G-1780)*
Power Monitors Inc (PA) **540 432-3077**
800 N Main St Mount Crawford (22841) *(G-9057)*
Power Quote Software, Manassas *Also called Bruce Moore Printing Co (G-7922)*
Power Systems & Controls Inc 804 355-2803
3206 Lanvale Ave Richmond (23230) *(G-11328)*
Power Wrist Bldrs By Tlose Grp 800 645-6673
1515 Wilton Farm Rd Charlottesville (22911) *(G-2679)*
Power-Trac, Tazewell *Also called Canaan Land Associates Inc (G-13829)*
Powerbilt Steel Buildings Inc 757 425-6223
1559 Laskin Rd Virginia Beach (23451) *(G-14731)*
Powerhub Systems, Blacksburg *Also called Power Hub Ventures LLC (G-1780)*
Powermark Corporation 301 639-7319
42 Patrick Pl Union Hall (24176) *(G-13960)*
Powers Signs Incorporated 434 793-6351
807 Industrial Ave Danville (24541) *(G-4031)*
Powerup Printing Inc 804 364-1353
12021 Wheat Ridge Ct Glen Allen (23059) *(G-5781)*
Powhatan Today, Mechanicsville *Also called C & C Publishing Inc (G-8610)*
Powrachute, Virginia Beach *Also called Xtreme Adventures Inc (G-14950)*
PP Payne Inc 804 518-1803
1625 Ashton Park Dr Ste D South Chesterfield (23834) *(G-12822)*
PPG 9424, Richmond *Also called PPG Industries Inc (G-11061)*
PPG Industries Inc 703 370-5636
5204 Eisenhower Ave Alexandria (22304) *(G-315)*
PPG Industries Inc 757 494-5116
1416 Kelland Dr Ste F Chesapeake (23320) *(G-3243)*
PPG Industries Inc 804 794-5331
11351 Intl Dr Ste B Richmond (23236) *(G-11061)*
PPG Industries Inc 540 563-2118
116 Liberty Rd Ne Roanoke (24012) *(G-12149)*
PPG Prtctive Mar Coatings 9969, Chesapeake *Also called PPG Industries Inc (G-3243)*
PR Express, Chesapeake *Also called Premier Resources Express LLC (G-3245)*
Practical Aplicat Solutions, Herndon *Also called Mary Jo Kirwan (G-6743)*
Practical Software LLC 240 505-0936
108 Dickenson Ct Stephens City (22655) *(G-13320)*
Prager University Foundation 323 577-2437
2325 Dulles Corner Blvd # 670 Herndon (20171) *(G-6778)*
Prageru, Herndon *Also called Prager University Foundation (G-6778)*
Prall Software Consulting LLC 703 777-8423
511 Valley View Ave Sw Leesburg (20175) *(G-7327)*
Pramaan Inc 703 327-6750
42357 Astors Beachwood Ct Chantilly (20152) *(G-2552)*
Pratt & Whitney Eng Svcs Inc 757 838-7980
11837 Rock Landing Dr Newport News (23606) *(G-9315)*
Pratt Industries Inc 804 412-0245
309 Quarles Rd Ashland (23005) *(G-1479)*
Praxair, Hopewell *Also called Linde Inc (G-6938)*
Praxair Welding Gas & Sup Str 540 342-9700
1757 Granby St Ne Ste A Roanoke (24012) *(G-12150)*
Pre Cast of Virginia 540 439-2978
5303 Ritchie Rd Bealeton (22712) *(G-1604)*
Pre Con Inc (PA) **804 732-0628**
6700 Courtyard Rd Chester (23831) *(G-3444)*
Pre Con Inc 804 732-1253
319 Brown St Petersburg (23803) *(G-10336)*
Pre Con Inc 804 861-0282
110 Perry St Petersburg (23803) *(G-10337)*
Pre Con Inc 804 748-5063
13721 Jefferson Davis Hwy Chester (23831) *(G-3445)*
Pre Con Inc 804 414-1560
13751 Jefferson Davis Hwy Chester (23831) *(G-3446)*
Pre Con Inc 804 414-1560
13701 Jefferson Davis Hwy Chester (23831) *(G-3447)*
Pre Holdings Inc (PA) **804 253-7274**
2412 Pari Way Midlothian (23112) *(G-8881)*
Precept Medical Products Inc 804 236-1010
5666 Eastport Blvd Richmond (23231) *(G-11329)*
Precious Time LLC 804 343-4380
1111 E Main St Fl 16 Richmond (23219) *(G-11722)*
Precise Freight Solutions 703 627-1327
8072 Stonewall Brigade Ct Manassas (20109) *(G-8131)*
Precise Technology Inc 703 869-4220
11023 Bacon Race Rd Woodbridge (22192) *(G-15778)*
Precision Brick Cutting Ltd 703 393-2777
11900 Livingston Rd # 147 Manassas (20109) *(G-8132)*
Precision Components Inc 540 297-1853
1337 Thornbird Pl Huddleston (24104) *(G-6957)*
Precision Doors & Hardware LLC 540 373-7300
10941 Pierson Dr Fredericksburg (22408) *(G-5348)*
Precision Explosives LLC 833 338-6628
4818 Midland Rd Midland (22728) *(G-8761)*
Precision Fabrication LLC 804 210-1613
7546 John Clayton Mem Hwy Gloucester (23061) *(G-5858)*
Precision Fabrics Group Inc 540 343-4448
323 W Virginia Ave Vinton (24179) *(G-14181)*
Precision Gas Piping LLC 434 531-2427
68 Branchland Ct Ruckersville (22968) *(G-12409)*

Precision Generators Company 757 498-4809
200 Golden Oak Ct Ste 250 Virginia Beach (23452) *(G-14732)*

Precision Grinding Co 540 955-3200
3690 Old Charles Town Rd Berryville (22611) *(G-1686)*

Precision Machine & Design 540 726-8229
211 Main St Ste 116 Narrows (24124) *(G-9098)*

Precision Machine Co Inc 804 359-5758
8011 Whitebark Ter North Chesterfield (23237) *(G-9953)*

Precision Machine Co., North Chesterfield Also called Pricewalker Inc *(G-9954)*

Precision Machine Works Inc 540 825-1882
19028 Industrial Rd Culpeper (22701) *(G-3914)*

Precision Mch & Firearm Svc 540 659-3037
955 Ramoth Church Rd Fredericksburg (22406) *(G-5471)*

Precision Millwork & Cabinets 434 525-6988
3582 Evington Rd Evington (24550) *(G-4383)*

Precision Nuclear of Virginia 540 389-8333
1906 Belleview Ave Se Roanoke (24014) *(G-12151)*

Precision Nuclear Virginia LLC 540 389-1346
1634 Midland Rd Salem (24153) *(G-12558)*

Precision Patterns Inc 434 385-4279
1010 Grand Oaks Dr Forest (24551) *(G-5088)*

Precision Pavers Inc 703 217-4955
3620 Langford Dr Charlottesville (22903) *(G-2850)*

Precision Pharmacy Inc 757 656-6560
1101 Executive Blvd Ste A Chesapeake (23320) *(G-3244)*

Precision Powder Coating Inc 757 368-2135
2593 Aviator Dr Ste 101 Virginia Beach (23453) *(G-14733)*

Precision Print & Copy LLC 804 740-3514
10623 Patterson Ave Richmond (23238) *(G-11330)*

Precision Printers 703 525-5113
1101 Wilson Blvd Lbby 3 Arlington (22209) *(G-1119)*

Precision Printing, Chesapeake Also called Royster Printing Services Inc *(G-3278)*

Precision Qulty Ship Repr LLC 757 322-0654
170 Coral Gables Ct Apt 7 Virginia Beach (23452) *(G-14734)*

Precision Schematics LLC 612 296-2286
3504 Emory Ln Woodbridge (22193) *(G-15779)*

Precision Screen Printing 540 886-0026
112 College Cir Staunton (24401) *(G-13284)*

Precision Sheetmetal Inc 757 389-5730
3200 S Cape Henry Ave Norfolk (23504) *(G-9694)*

Precision Shtmtl Fbrcation LLC 757 865-2508
211 Challenger Way Hampton (23666) *(G-6217)*

Precision Solutions Inc 804 452-2217
7520 Harvest Rd Prince George (23875) *(G-10605)*

Precision Steel Mfg Corp 540 985-8963
1723 Seibel Dr Ne Roanoke (24012) *(G-12152)*

Precision Tool & Die Inc 804 233-8810
2805 Decatur St Richmond (23224) *(G-11723)*

Precision Welding LLC 434 973-2106
1984 Grandon Loop Rd Virginia Beach (23456) *(G-14735)*

Precision Woodworks LLC 757 642-1686
17209 Riddick Rd Smithfield (23430) *(G-12721)*

Precisncntainertechnologies LL 540 425-4756
720 Industrial Ave Bedford (24523) *(G-1652)*

Predictive Health Devices Inc 703 507-0627
1117 Potomac Dr Stafford (22554) *(G-13182)*

Preferred Professional Svcs 703 803-3563
13204 Austrian Pine Ct Fairfax (22030) *(G-4661)*

Prelude Communications Inc 703 731-9396
7 Vandercastel Rd Sterling (20165) *(G-13476)*

Premier Cabinets Virginia LLC 804 335-7354
2350 Winterfield Rd Midlothian (23113) *(G-8882)*

Premier Embroidery and Design 434 242-2801
8 Wedge Ter Palmyra (22963) *(G-10256)*

Premier Graphics 434 432-4070
61 N Main St Chatham (24531) *(G-2934)*

Premier Manufacturing Inc 757 967-9959
500 Premier Pl Portsmouth (23704) *(G-10472)*

Premier Millwork & Lbr Co Inc 757 463-8870
517 Viking Dr Virginia Beach (23452) *(G-14736)*

Premier Office Systems LLC 804 414-4198
213 Forrest Dr Blackstone (23824) *(G-1824)*

Premier Pet Products LLC 804 594-0613
1054 Technology Park Dr Glen Allen (23059) *(G-5782)*

Premier Pins 703 631-6660
14110 Sullyfield Cir D Chantilly (20151) *(G-2482)*

Premier Resources Express LLC 717 887-4003
1320 Club House Dr Chesapeake (23322) *(G-3245)*

Premier Reticles Ltd 540 667-5258
920 Breckinridge Ln Winchester (22601) *(G-15568)*

Premium Med Supply LLC 888 506-6367
3200 Rckbrdge St Unit 302 Richmond (23230) *(G-11331)*

Premium Millwork Installations 757 288-9785
14320 Madrigal Dr Woodbridge (22193) *(G-15780)*

Premium Paving Inc 703 339-5371
7817 Loisdale Rd Ste J Springfield (22150) *(G-13073)*

Premium Pet Health LLC 757 357-8880
501 N Church St Smithfield (23430) *(G-12722)*

Premo Welding 757 880-6951
1421 Todds Ln Hampton (23666) *(G-6218)*

Premonition Games LLC 586 404-7070
5011 Queensway Cir Fredericksburg (22408) *(G-5349)*

Prepare Him Room Pubg LLC 703 909-1147
221 S 12th St Purcellville (20132) *(G-10674)*

Prepworks, Richmond Also called Martin Publishing Corp *(G-11668)*

Presbytrian Outlook Foundation 804 359-8442
1 N 5th St Ste 500 Richmond (23219) *(G-11724)*

Preservation Wood Sales 540 553-2023
615 Cannady School Rd Se Floyd (24091) *(G-5035)*

Preserve Resources Inc 434 710-8131
901 Industrial Ave Danville (24541) *(G-4032)*

Presidential Coin & Antique Co 703 354-5454
12233 Chapel Rd Clifton (20124) *(G-3675)*

Presidium Athletics LLC 800 618-9661
1500 Oakbridge Ter Ste A Powhatan (23139) *(G-10568)*

Press 4 Time Tees LLC 434 446-6633
4056 Dryburg Rd Scottsburg (24589) *(G-12656)*

Press and Bindery Repair 703 209-4247
18 W Briar Dr Stafford (22556) *(G-13183)*

Press Enduring 540 462-2920
14 Link Rd Lexington (24450) *(G-7412)*

Press Go Button LLC 703 709-5839
11766 Great Owl Cir Reston (20194) *(G-10930)*

Press Oil & Vinegar LLC 434 534-2915
1005 Grand View Cir Lynchburg (24502) *(G-7787)*

Press On Printing LLC 434 575-0990
2124 E Hyco Rd South Boston (24592) *(G-12787)*

Press Out Poverty 703 691-4329
3805 Acosta Rd Fairfax (22031) *(G-4531)*

Press Press Merch LLC 540 206-3495
128 Albemarle Ave Se Roanoke (24013) *(G-12153)*

Press Start LLC 571 264-1220
132 Grayrock Dr Crozet (22932) *(G-3848)*

Press-Well Services Inc 540 923-4799
915 Whippoorwill Rd Madison (22727) *(G-7861)*

Pressed 4 Ink - Custom Apparel 540 693-4023
325 Wallace Ln Fredericksburg (22408) *(G-5350)*

Pressed 4 Ink LLC 540 834-0125
9716 Gunston Hall Rd Fredericksburg (22408) *(G-5351)*

Pressure Systems Inc 757 766-4464
1000 Lucas Way Hampton (23666) *(G-6219)*

Pressures On 757 681-8999
232 Centerville Tpke N Chesapeake (23320) *(G-3246)*

Presswardthemark Media Publish 757 807-2232
5848 Magnolia Chase Way Virginia Beach (23464) *(G-14737)*

Prestige Cabinets 757 741-3201
8019 Hankins Indus Park Toano (23168) *(G-13875)*

Prestige Cabinets LLC 757 741-3201
4705 Eskerhills Williamsburg (23188) *(G-15298)*

Prestige Cabinets Countertops, Richmond Also called Prestige Inc *(G-11332)*

Prestige Inc 804 266-1000
5805 School Ave Ste C Richmond (23228) *(G-11332)*

Prestige Press Inc 757 826-5881
610 Rotary St Hampton (23661) *(G-6220)*

Presto Embroidery LLC 571 223-0160
21356 Marsh Creek Dr Broadlands (20148) *(G-2080)*

Presto Products Company, South Boston Also called Reynolds Presto Products
Inc *(G-12788)*

Preston Aerospace Inc 540 675-3474
187 Resettlement Rd Huntly (22640) *(G-6965)*

Preston Rdge Wnery Brewing Inc 276 634-8752
4105 Preston Rd Martinsville (24112) *(G-8320)*

Preston Signs Inc 703 534-3777
295 Windover Ave Nw Vienna (22180) *(G-14113)*

Pretech Solutions Incorporated 757 879-3483
3444 Frances Berkeley Williamsburg (23188) *(G-15299)*

Pretty Petals 757 357-9136
303 Jefferson Dr Smithfield (23430) *(G-12723)*

Pretty Ugly Distribution LLC 757 672-8958
845 Battlefield Blvd S Chesapeake (23322) *(G-3247)*

Prfwmpro Fire Fighters 703 393-2598
8510 Virginia Meadows Dr Manassas (20109) *(G-8133)*

Price Co, Brookneal Also called Chips Brookneal Inc *(G-2109)*

Price Goldsmith Co 757 722-3210
47 E Queens Way Ste 202 Hampton (23669) *(G-6221)*

Price Point Equipment 239 216-1688
21010 Southbank St 180 Sterling (20165) *(G-13477)*

Prices Electric Motor Repair 540 896-9451
356 3rd Ave Timberville (22853) *(G-13852)*

Pricewalker Inc 804 359-5758
8011 Whitebark Ter North Chesterfield (23237) *(G-9954)*

Pride and Joy Logging Inc 540 474-5533
1118 Blue Grass Valley Rd Blue Grass (24413) *(G-1844)*

Primatics Financial LLC (HQ) **703 342-0040**
8401 Greensboro Dr # 300 Mc Lean (22102) *(G-8531)*

Prime 3 Software Inc 757 763-8560
201 E City Hall Ave Norfolk (23510) *(G-9695)*

Prime Services PC and Printers, Bristow Also called Hugo Miranda *(G-2056)*

Prime Signs 757 481-7889
2814 Broad Bay Rd Virginia Beach (23451) *(G-14738)*

Primo Welding, Hampton *Also called Premo Welding* ***(G-6218)***
Primrose Essentials LLC 703 503-7210
5484 Lighthouse Ln Burke (22015) ***(G-2200)***
Prince Group of Virginia LLC (PA) **703 953-0577**
901 N Glebe Rd Ste 901 # 901 Arlington (22203) ***(G-1120)***
Prince William Athletic Center 571 572-3365
13000 Sport And Health Dr Woodbridge (22192) ***(G-15781)***
Prince William Orthotics & Prs 703 368-7967
10322 Battleview Pkwy Manassas (20109) ***(G-8134)***
Prinit Corporation 703 847-8880
1945 Old Gallows Rd # 10 Vienna (22182) ***(G-14114)***
Print A Promo LLC 800 675-6869
362 Reliance Woods Dr Middletown (22645) ***(G-8742)***
Print Afrik LLC 202 594-0836
2608 Miranda Ct Woodbridge (22191) ***(G-15782)***
Print City 703 931-1114
5908 Columbia Pike # 101 Falls Church (22041) ***(G-4857)***
Print Life LLC 609 442-2838
4904 Grand Strand Dr Williamsburg (23188) ***(G-15300)***
Print Link Inc 757 368-5200
811 S Lynnhaven Rd Virginia Beach (23452) ***(G-14739)***
Print LLC 757 746-5708
57 Post St Newport News (23601) ***(G-9316)***
Print Mail Direct LLC 540 899-6451
12 Rapids Way Fredericksburg (22405) ***(G-5472)***
Print Plus 276 322-2043
208 Bluestone Dr Bluefield (24605) ***(G-1876)***
Print Promotion 202 618-8822
101 N Columbus St Ste 200 Alexandria (22314) ***(G-316)***
Print Rayge Studios LLC 757 537-6995
1200 Semmes Ave Apt 201 Richmond (23224) ***(G-11725)***
Print Republic LLC 757 633-9099
916 Delaware Ave Virginia Beach (23451) ***(G-14740)***
Print Squad LLC 434 609-3335
6412 Pawnee Dr Lynchburg (24502) ***(G-7788)***
Print Store LLC 703 821-2201
7115 Idylwood Rd Falls Church (22043) ***(G-4858)***
Print Tent LLC 804 852-9750
4911 Mulford Rd Henrico (23231) ***(G-6550)***
Print Time Inc 202 232-0582
7901 Morning Ride Ct Alexandria (22315) ***(G-555)***
Print World Inc 434 237-2200
701 Leesville Rd Lynchburg (24502) ***(G-7789)***
Print-N-Paper Inc 540 719-7277
70 Scruggs Rd Ste 104 Moneta (24121) ***(G-8974)***
Printcraft Press Incorporated 757 397-0759
305 Columbia St Portsmouth (23704) ***(G-10473)***
Printech Inc 540 343-9200
2001 Patterson Ave Sw Roanoke (24016) ***(G-12154)***
Printed Circuits International 804 737-7979
407 Lee Ave Highland Springs (23075) ***(G-6855)***
Printegration Henrico Co, Richmond *Also called Maclaren Endeavors LLC* ***(G-11279)***
Printer Fix LLC 540 532-4948
936 Bowling View Rd Front Royal (22630) ***(G-5549)***
Printer Gatherer LLC 540 420-2426
1519 Baysdale Ln Henrico (23229) ***(G-6551)***
Printer Resolutions 703 850-5336
702 E Dickenson Ct Sterling (20164) ***(G-13478)***
Printers Research Co 540 721-9916
2455 Merriman Way Rd Moneta (24121) ***(G-8975)***
Printersmark Inc 804 353-2324
6010 N Crestwood Ave F Richmond (23230) ***(G-11333)***
Printing & Design Services 434 969-1133
1700 Woodland Church Rd Buckingham (23921) ***(G-2134)***
Printing 4 Kids 703 474-1519
3717 Rolling Hills Ave Alexandria (22309) ***(G-556)***
Printing and Sign System Inc 703 280-1550
2808 Merrilee Dr Ste E Fairfax (22031) ***(G-4532)***
Printing Center, The, Springfield *Also called Roasters Pride Inc* ***(G-13080)***
Printing Concepts of Virg 540 904-5951
1502 Williamson Rd Ne A Roanoke (24012) ***(G-12155)***
Printing Department Inc 804 282-2739
2108 Spencer Rd Richmond (23230) ***(G-11334)***
Printing Dept Inc 804 673-1904
6521 Kensington Ave Richmond (23226) ***(G-11335)***
Printing Dept LLC 703 931-5450
5610 Magnolia Ln Alexandria (22311) ***(G-317)***
Printing Express Inc 540 433-1237
21 Warehouse Rd Harrisonburg (22801) ***(G-6356)***
Printing For You 540 351-0191
205 Keith St Warrenton (20186) ***(G-15045)***
Printing Ideas Inc 703 591-1708
9925 Main St Fairfax (22031) ***(G-4533)***
Printing Plus 434 376-3379
403 Rush St Brookneal (24528) ***(G-2111)***
Printing Productions Inc 703 406-2400
1333 Shepard Dr Ste E Sterling (20164) ***(G-13479)***
Printing Professionals, Henrico *Also called Marilyn Carter* ***(G-6533)***
Printing Services 540 434-5783
116 Laurel St Harrisonburg (22801) ***(G-6357)***
Printingwright LLC 757 591-0771
12458a Warwick Blvd Newport News (23606) ***(G-9317)***
Printline Graphics LLC 757 547-3107
200 Tintern Ct Ste 105 Chesapeake (23320) ***(G-3248)***
Printmark Comm. Printers, Virginia Beach *Also called PCC Corporation* ***(G-14714)***
Printmark Commercial Printers, Virginia Beach *Also called PCC Corporation* ***(G-14713)***
Printpros LLC 804 550-1607
9825 Atlee Comns Dr 124 Ashland (23005) ***(G-1480)***
Printpros LLC 804 789-8884
9489 Hartford Oaks Dr Mechanicsville (23116) ***(G-8668)***
Printsmith Ink 540 323-7554
340 N Pleasant Valley Rd Winchester (22601) ***(G-15569)***
Printwell Inc 757 564-3302
3407 Poplar Creek Ln Williamsburg (23188) ***(G-15301)***
Priority Electrical Service, Virginia Beach *Also called Tidewater Prof Contrs LLC* ***(G-14876)***
Priority Wire & Cable Inc 757 361-0207
1403 Greenbrier Pkwy # 525 Chesapeake (23320) ***(G-3249)***
Prism Industries LLC 804 916-0074
6961 Slate Rd Chesterfield (23832) ***(G-3518)***
Prissy Pickle Company Llc 804 514-8112
7 Caribbean Ave Virginia Beach (23451) ***(G-14741)***
Pritchard Studio 276 935-5829
2749 Poplar Creek Rd Grundy (24614) ***(G-6040)***
Pritts Logging 304 646-0004
103 Gatewood Dr Warm Springs (24484) ***(G-14974)***
Privaris Inc 703 592-1180
11200 Waples Mill Rd 10 Fairfax (22030) ***(G-4662)***
Privateer Industries LLC 757 857-7273
4600 Village Ave Ste 100 Norfolk (23502) ***(G-9696)***
Pro Furniture Doctor Inc 571 379-7058
5407 Kempsville St Springfield (22151) ***(G-13074)***
Pro Image Graphics 276 686-6174
111 W Buck Ave Rural Retreat (24368) ***(G-12430)***
Pro Image Printing & Pubg LLC 804 798-4400
12153 Bienvenue Rd Rockville (23146) ***(G-12295)***
Pro Publishers LLC 434 250-6463
1200 Pinecroft Rd Danville (24540) ***(G-4033)***
Pro Refinish 703 853-9665
7381 Moccassin Ln Warrenton (20186) ***(G-15046)***
Pro Sheet Metal Inc 703 675-7724
8020 Ashton St Alexandria (22309) ***(G-557)***
Pro Tech Fabrications Inc 540 587-5590
1587 Dawn Dr Bedford (24523) ***(G-1653)***
Pro-Core 703 490-4905
2708 Code Way Woodbridge (22192) ***(G-15783)***
Pro-Graphx 844 777-0288
405 Walker Rd Martinsville (24112) ***(G-8321)***
Pro-Tek Inc 757 813-9820
4410 Claiborne Sq E # 400 Hampton (23666) ***(G-6222)***
Problem Solver 757 452-0653
3749 Frazier Ln Virginia Beach (23456) ***(G-14742)***
Probuild Materials, Fredericksburg *Also called Strober Building Supply* ***(G-5369)***
Probusiness Publishing LLC 571 216-3385
4234 Corcoran St Alexandria (22309) ***(G-558)***
Processing Plant, Newport News *Also called Chesapeake Bay Packing LLC* ***(G-9198)***
Prochem Inc 540 268-9884
5100 Enterprise Dr Elliston (24087) ***(G-4347)***
Prochem Technologies Inc 540 520-8339
4709 Cheraw Lake Rd Nw Roanoke (24017) ***(G-12156)***
Producers Peanut Company Inc 757 539-7496
337 Moore Ave Suffolk (23434) ***(G-13753)***
Product Dev Mfg & Packg (PA) **703 777-8400**
105 Loudoun St Sw Leesburg (20175) ***(G-7328)***
Product Engineered Systems 804 794-3586
1303 Cedar Crossing Trl Midlothian (23114) ***(G-8883)***
Product Identification 804 264-4434
8532 Sanford Dr Richmond (23228) ***(G-11336)***
Product Safety Letter 703 247-3423
2573 Holly Manor Dr Falls Church (22043) ***(G-4859)***
Production Manufacturing Inc 513 892-2331
1114 Trotting Horse Ln Great Falls (22066) ***(G-5976)***
Production Metal Finishers 804 643-8116
1802 Currie St Richmond (23220) ***(G-11726)***
Production Systems Solutions 434 324-7843
1720 Pocket Rd Hurt (24563) ***(G-6976)***
Professional Business Prtg Inc 804 423-1355
8770 Park Central Dr Richmond (23227) ***(G-11337)***
Professional Network Services 571 283-4858
2920 Fox Lair Dr Woodbridge (22191) ***(G-15784)***
Professional Pilot Magazine, Alexandria *Also called Queensmith Communications Corp* ***(G-563)***
Professional Printing Ctr Inc 757 547-1990
817 Yupo Ct Chesapeake (23320) ***(G-3250)***
Professional Services 540 953-2223
210 Prices Fork Rd Ste B Blacksburg (24060) ***(G-1781)***
Professional Welding Svc Inc 757 853-9371
2300 Florida Ave Norfolk (23513) ***(G-9697)***
Proficient Link LLC 703 391-6330
22375 Broderick Dr # 155 Sterling (20166) ***(G-13480)***

Profile Machineworks LLC...................................703 361-2959
9199 Enterprise Ct Unit B Manassas Park (20111) *(G-8207)*

Profile Machineworks LLC...................................571 991-6331
8510 Rolling Rd Manassas (20110) *(G-7990)*

Profit From Publicity LLC..................................703 409-3630
5505 Talon Ct Fairfax (22032) *(G-4534)*

Profitoptics Inc...804 360-2776
4050 Innslake Rd Ste 375 Glen Allen (23060) *(G-5783)*

Program Services LLC (HQ)...............................**757 222-3990**
150 W Brambleton Ave Norfolk (23510) *(G-9698)*

Program Services LLC.....................................804 526-8656
114 Charlotte Ave Colonial Heights (23834) *(G-3742)*

Prographics Print Xpress..................................757 606-8303
5312 Virginia Beach Blvd Virginia Beach (23462) *(G-14743)*

Progress Index, The, Petersburg *Also called Gatehouse Media LLC* (G-10322)

Progress Printing Company (PA)..........................**434 239-9213**
2677 Waterlick Rd Lynchburg (24502) *(G-7790)*

Progress Printing Plus, Lynchburg *Also called Progress Printing Company* (G-7790)

Progress Rail Services Corp..............................540 345-4039
1010 Hollins Rd Ne Roanoke (24012) *(G-12157)*

Progressive Designs..757 547-9201
816 Old Bridge Ln Chesapeake (23320) *(G-3251)*

Progressive Engineering Co, Chester *Also called Progressive Manufacturing Corp* (G-3448)

Progressive Graphics Inc (PA)...........................**757 368-3321**
2860 Crusader Cir Virginia Beach (23453) *(G-14744)*

Progressive Machine Works................................434 237-5517
1359 Waterlick Rd Lynchburg (24501) *(G-7791)*

Progressive Manufacturing Corp (PA)....................**804 717-5353**
1701 W Hundred Rd Chester (23836) *(G-3448)*

Progrm For The Archtctrl Wdwrk..........................978 468-5141
1952 Isaac Newton Sq W Reston (20190) *(G-10931)*

Project Cost Gvrnment Svcs LLC..........................239 334-3371
8101 Hinson Farm Rd # 318 Alexandria (22306) *(G-559)*

Project Safe..703 505-0440
675 S Washington St Alexandria (22314) *(G-318)*

Proknows..540 473-2271
1193 Buttons Blf Buchanan (24066) *(G-2125)*

Prolific Purchasing Properties............................434 329-1476
1302 Hendricks Ave Lynchburg (24501) *(G-7792)*

Prologue..757 871-3708
250 Picketts Line Newport News (23603) *(G-9318)*

Promocorp Inc..703 942-7100
5515 Cherokee Ave Ste 300 Alexandria (22312) *(G-560)*

Promotional Imprints, Yorktown *Also called Elizabeth Urban* (G-15952)

Proof of Life Baking LLC.................................571 721-8031
15369 Hearthstone Ter Woodbridge (22191) *(G-15785)*

Proofmark Corp...804 453-4337
2490 Hacks Neck Rd Burgess (22432) *(G-2175)*

Prop LLC..571 970-5031
1600 Wilson Blvd Ste 350 Arlington (22209) *(G-1121)*

Propeller Club of The U S Port...........................703 922-6933
7120 Snug Harbor Ct Alexandria (22315) *(G-561)*

Proper Pie Co LLC...804 343-7437
4301 Masonic Ln Richmond (23231) *(G-11338)*

Propst Lettering and Engraving............................540 896-5368
12875 Mountain Valley Rd Broadway (22815) *(G-2093)*

Proskit Usa LLC...804 240-9355
13302 Chula Rd Amelia Court House (23002) *(G-668)*

Prospect Publishing LLC....................................571 435-0241
621 N Saint Asaph St # 302 Alexandria (22314) *(G-319)*

Prosperity Publishing, Virginia Beach *Also called Eileen Carlson* (G-14436)

Prosperity Publishing Inc..................................757 339-9900
944 S Spigel Dr Virginia Beach (23454) *(G-14745)*

Prostride Orthotics LLC...................................804 310-3894
9609 Gayton Rd Ste 102 Henrico (23238) *(G-6552)*

Protean LLC..757 273-1131
1769 Jamestown Rd Ste 1b Williamsburg (23185) *(G-15302)*

Protected By Faith Cnstr LLC.............................804 445-6888
282 Union Mill Rd Farnham (22460) *(G-4963)*

Protectedbyai Inc..571 489-6906
1900 Reston Metro Plz # 6 Reston (20190) *(G-10932)*

Protective Solutions Inc..................................703 435-1115
45064 Underwood Ln Ste B Dulles (20166) *(G-4220)*

Protestant Church-Owned..................................502 569-5067
6631 Westbury Oaks Ct Springfield (22152) *(G-13075)*

Proto-Technics Inc..540 672-5193
180 S Almond St Orange (22960) *(G-10222)*

Protocol Media LLC.......................................703 647-8700
1000 Wilson Blvd Ste 2700 Arlington (22209) *(G-1122)*

Protolab Inc..703 622-1889
1511 Keeneland Rd Fredericksburg (22401) *(G-5214)*

Protomold..540 542-1740
340 N Pleasant Valley Rd Winchester (22601) *(G-15570)*

Proton Systems LLC (PA)..................................**757 224-5685**
35 Research Dr Hampton (23666) *(G-6223)*

Protoquick Printing LLC..................................202 417-4243
5524 Shipley Ct Centreville (20120) *(G-2329)*

Prototec Inc..434 832-7440
1431 Waterlick Rd Lynchburg (24501) *(G-7793)*

Prototype Productions Inc (PA)..........................**703 858-0011**
14558 Lee Rd Fl 2 Chantilly (20151) *(G-2483)*

Prov31 Publishing LLC......................................804 536-0436
14511 Old Courthouse Way Newport News (23608) *(G-9319)*

Provia Biologics Ltd..757 305-9263
124 E 40th St Norfolk (23504) *(G-9699)*

Providence Pubg Group LLC................................703 352-3152
11010 Fairchester Dr Fairfax (22030) *(G-4663)*

Provides US Inc..540 569-3434
45 Sutton Rd Verona (24482) *(G-13993)*

Provisioning Inc...571 451-3134
12906 Tarragon Ct Herndon (20171) *(G-6779)*

Proxy Technologies Inc...................................703 665-5152
11718 Bowman Green Dr # 200 Reston (20190) *(G-10933)*

Prs Towing & Recovery.....................................540 838-2388
1422 W Main St Radford (24141) *(G-10735)*

Prufrex USA Inc..757 963-5400
2573 Quality Ct Virginia Beach (23454) *(G-14746)*

Pruitt Partners LLC...703 299-0114
3537 Martha Bustis Dr Alexandria (22305) *(G-320)*

Pruitt Welding & Fabrication...............................540 896-4268
15510 Evergreen Valley Rd Timberville (22853) *(G-13853)*

Pruitts Boat Yard..757 891-2565
4401 Long Bridge Rd Tangier (23440) *(G-13809)*

PS Its Leather...804 762-9489
9028 Horrigan Ct Richmond (23294) *(G-11339)*

Psa Publishings LLC..703 986-3288
1859 Ballenger Ave Alexandria (22314) *(G-321)*

PSI Group...804 798-3210
11720 N Lakeridge Pkwy Ashland (23005) *(G-1481)*

PSL America Group, Fairfax *Also called PSL America Inc* (G-4664)

PSL America Inc (PA).......................................**703 279-6426**
11350 Random Hills Rd Fairfax (22030) *(G-4664)*

PSM Publications Inc.......................................434 432-8600
25 Lanier Ave Chatham (24531) *(G-2935)*

Psycho Panda..540 287-0588
207 Clint Ln Fredericksburg (22405) *(G-5473)*

Psycho Panda Streetwear, Fredericksburg *Also called Psycho Panda* (G-5473)

PT Armor Inc (PA)..**703 560-1020**
7401h Fullerton Rd Springfield (22153) *(G-13076)*

Ptc Enterprises LLC..703 352-9274
11725 Lee Hwy Fairfax (22030) *(G-4665)*

Ptci, Annandale *Also called Pacific Technology Inc* (G-778)

Public House Kitchen & Brewry, Manassas *Also called Wolffinz LLC* (G-8013)

Public Utilities Reports Inc................................703 847-7720
11410 Isaac Newton Sq N # 220 Reston (20190) *(G-10934)*

Publication Certified......................................703 259-1936
10301 Democracy Ln # 401 Fairfax (22030) *(G-4666)*

Publications Professionals LLC...........................703 934-4499
3603 Chain Bridge Rd A Fairfax (22030) *(G-4667)*

Publicity Works LLC..703 876-0080
2230 George C Marshall Dr Falls Church (22043) *(G-4860)*

Publishers Asset LLC.....................................540 621-4422
48 Clarion Dr Fredericksburg (22405) *(G-5474)*

Publishers Circltn...703 394-5293
8500 Tyco Rd Vienna (22182) *(G-14115)*

Publishers Press Incorporated.............................540 672-4845
256 E Main St Orange (22960) *(G-10223)*

Publishers Service Assoc Inc..............................570 322-7848
453 Carlisle Dr Ste B Herndon (20170) *(G-6780)*

Publishers Teaberry Feilds................................276 783-2546
169 Teaberry Ln Marion (24354) *(G-8241)*

Publishing..540 659-6694
52 Larkwood St Stafford (22554) *(G-13184)*

Publishing Village..804 425-5555
11801 Centre St Chester (23831) *(G-3449)*

Pudding Please LLC.......................................804 833-4110
2715 E Broad St Richmond (23223) *(G-11727)*

Pugal Inc..540 765-4955
5535 Cynthia Dr Roanoke (24018) *(G-11990)*

Pulliam Furniture Co.......................................276 956-3615
1114 Mica Rd Ridgeway (24148) *(G-11849)*

Pullin Ink..276 546-2760
179 N Kentucky St Pennington Gap (24277) *(G-10299)*

Pulmoflow Inc..831 206-8659
3900 Westerre Pkwy # 300 Richmond (23233) *(G-11340)*

Pulp Usa LLC..540 907-0093
1312 Stafford Ave Fredericksburg (22401) *(G-5215)*

Pulpwood and Logging Inc.................................434 736-9440
191 King St Keysville (23947) *(G-7062)*

Pumped Cards..202 725-6964
16535 Sherwood Pl Woodbridge (22191) *(G-15786)*

Pungo Publishing Co LLC...................................757 748-5331
1724 Princess Anne Rd Virginia Beach (23456) *(G-14747)*

Punkins Cupcake Cones....................................757 395-0295
5509 Samuelson Ct Virginia Beach (23464) *(G-14748)*

Puppet Neighborhood.......................................804 794-2899
1000 Ashbrook Landing Ter Midlothian (23114) *(G-8884)*

Pura Vida Vienna Inc.......................................703 281-6050
9413 Tuba Ct Vienna (22182) *(G-14116)*

**A
L
P
H
A
B
E
T
I
C**

Purcellville Gazette LLC 540 431-8507
17 W Boscawen St Winchester (22601) *(G-15571)*
Pure Anointing Oil 703 889-7457
8006 Pohick Rd Springfield (22153) *(G-13077)*
Pure Blend Organics 703 476-1414
9420 Beauregard Ave Manassas (20110) *(G-7991)*
Pure Earth Recycling Tech Inc 434 944-6262
1009 Misty Mountain Rd # 1613 Lynchburg (24502) *(G-7794)*
Pure Faith Publishing LLC 757 925-4957
180 Majestic Dr Suffolk (23434) *(G-13754)*
Pure Media Sign Studio LLC 703 822-5468
2904 13th St S Apt 1 Arlington (22204) *(G-1123)*
Pure Paradise Water of Vb 757 318-0522
2133 Upton Dr Virginia Beach (23454) *(G-14749)*
Pure Pasty Company LLC 703 255-7147
128c Church St Nw Vienna (22180) *(G-14117)*
Pure Scentsations LLC 334 868-9190
309 Wood Duck Ct Suffolk (23434) *(G-13755)*
Pure Water Tech, Springfield *Also called Enviro Water (G-12999)*
Pure-Mech Inc 804 363-1297
2014 Wynmere Dr Roanoke (24018) *(G-11991)*
Purer Air 804 921-8234
9609 Georges Bluff Rd Richmond (23229) *(G-11341)*
Purple Diamond Publishing 757 525-2422
989 Aspen Dr Virginia Beach (23464) *(G-14750)*
Purple Ink Press 703 753-4638
13525 Heritage Farms Dr Gainesville (20155) *(G-5609)*
Pursuit Packaging LLC 540 246-4629
8522 Daphna Rd Broadway (22815) *(G-2094)*
Puryear Group & Associates LLC 202 327-3777
10307 W Broad St Unit 268 Glen Allen (23060) *(G-5784)*
Push Pin Crative Solutions LLC 703 313-0619
6904 Ellingham Cir Alexandria (22315) *(G-562)*
Putt Arund Town Miniature Golf 804 317-6751
13001 Carters Way Rd Chesterfield (23838) *(G-3519)*
Putting Tgther Pzzle Peces LLC 703 391-1754
3014 Gatepost Ln Oak Hill (20171) *(G-10138)*
Putty LLC 434 960-3954
708 Cargil Ln Charlottesville (22902) *(G-2851)*
Puzzle Cuts LLC 703 470-9333
8192 Mistletoe Ln Lorton (22079) *(G-7522)*
Puzzle Homes LLC 804 247-7256
2290 N Parham Rd Henrico (23229) *(G-6553)*
Puzzle Palooza Ect 703 494-0579
403 Mill St Occoquan (22125) *(G-10174)*
Puzzle Palooza Etc Inc 703 368-3619
9551 Fostern Ln Manassas (20112) *(G-8135)*
Puzzle Peace Publications LLC 973 766-5282
630 Saint Andrews Ln # 104 Newport News (23608) *(G-9320)*
Puzzle Piece LLC 434 985-8074
471 Northridge Rd Ruckersville (22968) *(G-12410)*
PWC Winery LLC 703 753-9360
4970 Antioch Rd Haymarket (20169) *(G-6438)*
Pwillz Customz LLC 571 926-9622
22854 Bryant Ct Ste 106 Sterling (20166) *(G-13481)*
Pyott-Boone Electronics Inc (PA) **276 988-5505**
1459 Wittens Mill Rd North Tazewell (24630) *(G-10105)*
Pyramid Alpacas 540 662-5501
240 John Deere Ct Clear Brook (22624) *(G-3650)*
Pyrotechnique By Grucci Inc 540 639-8800
Rfaap Rte 114 Pep Fer Rd Radford (24143) *(G-10736)*
Q B Enterprises Inc 540 825-2950
13164 James Madison Hwy Orange (22960) *(G-10224)*
Q C Veneer & Logs LLC 540 719-4349
525 N Church Dr Hardy (24101) *(G-6288)*
Q P I Inc 434 528-0092
1000 Commerce St Lynchburg (24504) *(G-7795)*
Q Protein Inc 240 994-6160
6210 Chadsworth Ct Roanoke (24018) *(G-11992)*
Q Star Technology LLC 703 578-1495
5601 Dawes Ave Alexandria (22311) *(G-322)*
Q Stitched LLC 757 621-6025
10206 Maremont Cir Richmond (23238) *(G-11342)*
Qbeam Inc 703 574-5330
19490 Sandridge Way # 330 Leesburg (20176) *(G-7329)*
Qg LLC 540 722-6000
160 Century Ln Winchester (22603) *(G-15462)*
Qg LLC 804 264-3866
7400 Impala Dr Richmond (23228) *(G-11343)*
Qg Printing II Corp 540 722-6000
160 Century Ln Winchester (22603) *(G-15463)*
Qinetiq Inc 540 658-2720
10440 Furnace Rd Ste 204 Lorton (22079) *(G-7523)*
Qinetiq Inc 804 436-9000
160 Technology Park Dr Kilmarnock (22482) *(G-7075)*
Qinetiq Inc (HQ) **540 658-2720**
10440 Furnace Rd Ste 204 Lorton (22079) *(G-7524)*
Qinetiq US Holdings Inc (HQ) **202 429-6630**
5885 Trinity Pkwy Ste 130 Centreville (20120) *(G-2330)*
Qlf Custom Pipe Organ 540 484-1133
240 Energy Blvd Rocky Mount (24151) *(G-12348)*

Qlifts LLC 276 632-0058
1317 Eggleston Falls Rd Ridgeway (24148) *(G-11850)*
Qmt Associates Inc 703 368-4920
9204 Vassau Ct Ste H Manassas Park (20111) *(G-8208)*
Qmulos Products Inc 202 557-5162
1560 Wilson Blvd Ste 900 Arlington (22209) *(G-1124)*
Qore Performance Inc 703 755-0724
22311 Shaw Rd Ste A2 Sterling (20166) *(G-13482)*
Qpi 434 528-0092
548 Oakley Ave Lynchburg (24501) *(G-7796)*
Qrc LLC (HQ) **540 446-2270**
1191 Central Park Blvd Fredericksburg (22401) *(G-5216)*
Qrc Technologies, Fredericksburg *Also called Qrc LLC (G-5216)*
Quad Promo LLC 757 353-5729
1423 Air Rail Ave Virginia Beach (23455) *(G-14751)*
Quadd Inc 540 439-2148
11610 Lucky Hill Rd Remington (22734) *(G-10771)*
Quadd Building Systems, Remington *Also called Quadd Inc (G-10771)*
Quadd Building Systems LLC 540 439-2148
11610 Lucky Hill Rd Remington (22734) *(G-10772)*
Quadramed Corporation (HQ) **703 709-2300**
2300 Corp Park Dr Ste 400 Herndon (20171) *(G-6781)*
Quadrant Holding Inc 276 228-0100
2530 N 4th St Wytheville (24382) *(G-15905)*
Quail Ridge, Fredericksburg *Also called Armstrong Green & Embrey Inc (G-5248)*
Quail Run Signs 540 338-8412
43 E Colonial Hwy Hamilton (20158) *(G-6064)*
Quailty Home Improvements, Lynchburg *Also called Theodore Turpin (G-7823)*
Quaker Chemical Corporation 540 389-2038
18 Niblick Dr Salem (24153) *(G-12559)*
Quaker Houghton Pa Inc 540 877-3631
156 Doe Trl Winchester (22602) *(G-15464)*
Quaker Oats Co 276 625-3923
316 Gator Ln Wytheville (24382) *(G-15906)*
Qualatee 434 842-3530
117 Union Church Rd Palmyra (22963) *(G-10257)*
Qualcomm Inc 858 587-1121
5225 Wilson Blvd Arlington (22205) *(G-1125)*
Quality Archery Designs, Madison Heights *Also called Lasermarx Inc (G-7876)*
Quality Coatings Virginia Inc 757 494-0801
3900 Holland Blvd Chesapeake (23323) *(G-3252)*
Quality Culvert 434 336-1468
34 Three Creek Dr Emporia (23847) *(G-4365)*
Quality Equipment Repair 804 815-2268
512 Providence Rd Deltaville (23043) *(G-4085)*
Quality Graphics & Prtg Inc 703 661-6060
22831 Silverbrook Center Sterling (20166) *(G-13483)*
Quality Home Improvement Corp 757 424-5400
5333 Westover Ln Virginia Beach (23464) *(G-14752)*
Quality Lifts & Accessibility, Ridgeway *Also called Qlifts LLC (G-11850)*
Quality Logging LLC 540 493-7228
528 Laurel Branch Rd Nw Floyd (24091) *(G-5036)*
Quality Machine, Waynesboro *Also called Andrew Pawlick (G-15093)*
Quality Machine Shop 757 722-6077
336 Rip Rap Rd Hampton (23669) *(G-6224)*
Quality Manufacturing Co 540 982-6699
518 18th St Sw Roanoke (24016) *(G-12158)*
Quality Portable Buildings 276 880-2007
300 Mcfarlane Ln Rosedale (24280) *(G-12367)*
Quality Precast Stone 703 244-4551
8138 Bethlehem Rd Manassas (20109) *(G-8136)*
Quality Printing 276 632-1415
706 Memorial Blvd S Martinsville (24112) *(G-8322)*
Quality Stamp Co 757 858-0653
3338 Cromwell Dr Norfolk (23509) *(G-9700)*
Quality Welding Inc 434 296-1402
830 Harris St Charlottesville (22903) *(G-2852)*
Quality Wood Products Inc 540 750-1859
820 Park St Ste G Christiansburg (24073) *(G-3608)*
Qualitycrochetbybarb LLC 202 596-7301
5356 Potomac Dr King George (22485) *(G-7106)*
Quang D Nguyen 703 715-2244
2817 Gibson Oaks Dr Herndon (20171) *(G-6782)*
Quanta Systems LLC 703 885-7900
510 Spring St Ste 200 Herndon (20170) *(G-6783)*
Quantico's Best, Quantico *Also called Jean Lee Inc (G-10689)*
Quantum, Hampton *Also called Hampton Canvas and Rigging (G-6162)*
Quantum Computing Inc 703 436-2161
215 Depot Ct Se Ste 215 # 215 Leesburg (20175) *(G-7330)*
Quantum Connect LLC 703 251-3342
2350 Corp Park Dr Ste 110 Herndon (20171) *(G-6784)*
Quantum Medical Bus Svc Inc 703 727-1020
2209 Harrison St Winchester (22601) *(G-15572)*
Quantum Reefs LLC 703 560-1448
3713 Mount Airey Ln Annandale (22003) *(G-779)*
Quantum Silicones, North Chesterfield *Also called Cht USA Inc (G-9845)*
Quantum Technologies Inc 703 214-9756
7635 Leesburg Pike Ste B Falls Church (22043) *(G-4861)*

(G-0000) Company's Geographic Section entry number

Quarles Food Stop 540 635-1899
   4697 John Marshall Hwy Linden (22642) *(G-7432)*

Quartz Creek Vineyards LLC 571 239-9120
   40817 Browns Ln Waterford (20197) *(G-15082)*

Quattro Goombas Winery 703 327-6052
   22860 James Monroe Hwy Aldie (20105) *(G-110)*

Qubicaamf Worldwide LLC (HQ) **804 569-1000**
   8100 Amf Dr Mechanicsville (23111) *(G-8669)*

Queen of Amannisa 703 414-7888
   320 23rd St S Arlington (22202) *(G-1126)*

Queens Guitar Shop 703 754-4330
   10316 Reid Ln Nokesville (20181) *(G-9397)*

Queensmith Communications Corp 703 370-0606
   5290 Shawnee Rd Ste 201 Alexandria (22312) *(G-563)*

Quest Expedition Outfitte 434 244-7140
   3305 Lobban Pl Charlottesville (22903) *(G-2853)*

Quest Industries LLC 804 862-8481
   22909 Airpark Dr North Dinwiddie (23803) *(G-10062)*

Quest Limited, Alexandria Also called Sandra Woodward *(G-336)*

Quest Software Inc 703 234-3000
   11400 Commerce Park Dr Reston (20191) *(G-10935)*

Quick Designs LLC 540 450-0750
   1720 Valley Ave Winchester (22601) *(G-15573)*

Quick Eagle Networks Inc 703 583-3500
   3769 Hetten Ln Woodbridge (22193) *(G-15787)*

Quick Signs Inc 703 606-3008
   8695 Sudley Rd Manassas (20110) *(G-7992)*

Quick Silver Printing, Falls Church Also called Rappahannock Entp Assoc Inc *(G-4862)*

Quickest Residual Pay 703 924-2620
   6202 Sage Dr Alexandria (22310) *(G-564)*

Quickie Manufacturing 856 829-8598
   3124 Valley Ave Winchester (22601) *(G-15574)*

Quickie Manufacturing Corp (HQ) **856 829-7900**
   3124 Valley Ave Winchester (22601) *(G-15575)*

Quickie Manufacturing Corp 856 829-7900
   3124 Valley Ave Winchester (22601) *(G-15576)*

Quickleen USA, Charlottesville Also called Ester Yildiz LLC *(G-2628)*

Quigley Designs 540 484-1133
   240 Energy Blvd Rocky Mount (24151) *(G-12349)*

Quikrete Companies LLC 276 964-6755
   Hwy 19 Rr 460 Rt 460 Pounding Mill (24637) *(G-10525)*

Quikrete Companies LLC 276 646-8976
   671 Wadill Ln Chilhowie (24319) *(G-3558)*

Quikrete of Virginia, Chesapeake Also called Dominion Quikrete Inc *(G-3071)*

Quilt Doctor, The, Great Falls Also called Charles R Preston *(G-5947)*

Quiltery LLC 540 377-9191
   5661 N Lee Hwy Fairfield (24435) *(G-4734)*

Quinn Pumps Inc 276 345-9106
   142 Mall Church Rd Cedar Bluff (24609) *(G-2284)*

Quinns Bath Bombs LLC 703 853-5067
   6147 Ridgemont Dr Centreville (20120) *(G-2331)*

Quisenberry Stn Live Stm LLC 703 799-9643
   3903 Quisenberry Dr Alexandria (22309) *(G-565)*

R & B Cabinet Shop 540 249-4507
   501 Aspen Ave Grottoes (24441) *(G-6023)*

R & B Communications LLC 703 348-7088
   15670 Alderbrook Dr Haymarket (20169) *(G-6439)*

R & B Distributing Inc 804 794-5848
   535 Branchway Rd North Chesterfield (23236) *(G-9955)*

R & B Impressions Inc 703 823-9050
   678 S Pickett St Alexandria (22304) *(G-323)*

R & D Welding Services 757 761-3499
   4840 Condor Dr Chesapeake (23321) *(G-3253)*

R & K Woodworking Inc 540 867-5975
   2629 Shoreshill Rd Dayton (22821) *(G-4059)*

R & P Reps LLC, Fredericksburg Also called Rappahannock & Potomac Rep LLC *(G-5475)*

R & R Developers Inc 276 628-3846
   19444 Spoon Gap Rd Abingdon (24211) *(G-55)*

R & R Mining Inc 606 837-9321
   6617b W Main St Wise (24293) *(G-15633)*

R & R Printing 434 985-9844
   8458 Seminole Trl Ste 2b Ruckersville (22968) *(G-12411)*

R & R Printing & Mailing, Brightwood Also called Robert Deluca *(G-1962)*

R & R Service Center, Danville Also called Concept Products Inc *(G-3971)*

R & S Molds Inc 434 352-8612
   400 Cedar Ln Appomattox (24522) *(G-820)*

R & S Namebadge Inc 804 673-2842
   10333 Old Courtney Rd Glen Allen (23060) *(G-5785)*

R & S Stone Inc 540 745-6788
   1349 Shooting Creek Rd Se Floyd (24091) *(G-5037)*

R & T Woodworking, Covington Also called Maurice Lamb *(G-3794)*

R A Handy Title Examiner 804 739-9520
   6814 Sika Ct Midlothian (23112) *(G-8885)*

R A Hatcher Timber Harvesting, Appomattox Also called Hatcher Logging *(G-812)*

R A Onijs Classic Woodwork 703 594-3304
   10301 Schaeffer Ln Nokesville (20181) *(G-9398)*

R A Pearson Company 804 550-7300
   10463 Wilden Dr Ashland (23005) *(G-1482)*

R A Yancey Lumber Corp 434 823-4107
   6317 Rockfish Gap Tpke Crozet (22932) *(G-3849)*

R and L Machine Shop Inc 757 487-8879
   2900 Yadkin Rd Chesapeake (23323) *(G-3254)*

R and N Express LLC 804 909-3761
   6517 Old Zion Hill Rd North Chesterfield (23234) *(G-9956)*

R B M Enterprises Inc 804 290-4407
   10148 W Broad St Ste 201 Glen Allen (23060) *(G-5786)*

R C Cola Bottling Company Del 540 667-1821
   2927 Shawnee Dr Winchester (22601) *(G-15577)*

R C S Enterprises Inc 540 363-5979
   808 Warwick Cir Waynesboro (22980) *(G-15133)*

R D Knighton Sawmill 540 872-3636
   13660 Jefferson Hwy Bumpass (23024) *(G-2167)*

R David Rosson 540 456-8108
   8720 Rockfish Gap Tpke Afton (22920) *(G-86)*

R David Rosson Logging, Afton Also called R David Rosson *(G-86)*

R F J Ltd 703 494-3255
   13731 Dabney Rd Woodbridge (22191) *(G-15788)*

R F Tech Solutions Inc 804 241-5250
   1570 Hollow Log Dr Powhatan (23139) *(G-10569)*

R G Engineering Inc 757 463-3045
   429 Sharp St Virginia Beach (23452) *(G-14753)*

R G Logging 276 233-9224
   1373 Pipers Gap Rd Galax (24333) *(G-5646)*

R G Woodworks 757 427-2743
   2432 London Bridge Rd Virginia Beach (23456) *(G-14754)*

R Gonzalez Sheetmetal LLC 571 316-8241
   8831 Flatbush Ct Manassas (20109) *(G-8137)*

R H Sheppard Co Inc 276 228-4000
   1400 Stafford Umberger Dr Wytheville (24382) *(G-15907)*

R Home Furniture, Alexandria Also called Javawood USA LLC *(G-493)*

R J Reynolds Tobacco Company 757 420-1280
   6200 Pardue Ct Virginia Beach (23464) *(G-14755)*

R L Beckley Sawmill Inc 540 872-3621
   737 Windyknight Rd Montpelier (23192) *(G-9019)*

R L Bindery 804 625-2609
   16424 Court St Amelia Court House (23002) *(G-669)*

R R Beasley Inc (PA) **804 529-6470**
   16944 Richmond Rd Callao (22435) *(G-2217)*

R R Beasley Inc. 804 633-9626
   16090 Aspen Rd Milford (22514) *(G-8933)*

R R Donnelley & Sons Company 540 434-8833
   1400 Kratzer Rd Harrisonburg (22802) *(G-6358)*

R R Donnelley & Sons Company 540 432-5453
   2063 Kratzer Rd Rockingham (22802) *(G-12268)*

R R Donnelley & Sons Company 434 846-7711
   4201 Murray Pl Lynchburg (24501) *(G-7797)*

R R Donnelley & Sons Company 540 442-1333
   1433 Pleasant Valley Rd Rockingham (22801) *(G-12269)*

R R Donnelley & Sons Company 703 279-1662
   12150 Monument Dr Ste 100 Fairfax (22033) *(G-4535)*

R R Donnelley & Sons Company 540 564-3900
   1025 Willow Spring Rd Harrisonburg (22801) *(G-6359)*

R R Donnelley & Sons Company 434 846-7371
   6450 Technology Dr Salem (24153) *(G-12560)*

R R Donnelley Printing, Lynchburg Also called R R Donnelley & Sons Company *(G-7797)*

R S Bottoms Logging 434 577-3044
   148 Weaver Rd Brodnax (23920) *(G-2103)*

R T Sales Inc 703 542-5862
   14524 Brinestone Pl Haymarket (20169) *(G-6440)*

R W A Machining & Welding Co 434 985-7362
   127 Commerce Dr Ruckersville (22968) *(G-12412)*

R W P Johnson Products Ltd 804 453-7705
   601 Old Glebe Point Rd Burgess (22432) *(G-2176)*

R Wyatt Inc 434 293-7357
   1317 Carlton Ave Ste 110 Charlottesville (22902) *(G-2854)*

R Zimmerman and Associates 540 446-6846
   51 Greenridge Dr Stafford (22554) *(G-13185)*

R&B Custom Holsters LLC 703 586-2616
   15215 Illinois Rd Woodbridge (22191) *(G-15789)*

R&R Ornamental Iron Inc 540 798-1699
   1727 Cleveland Ave Sw Roanoke (24016) *(G-12159)*

R&Y Trucking LLC 404 781-1312
   967 Geneva Ave Chesapeake (23323) *(G-3255)*

R2jb Enterprises 703 727-3342
   17270 Arrowood Pl Round Hill (20141) *(G-12385)*

R3 Blades LLC 571 234-3068
   10289 Winged Elm Cir Manassas (20110) *(G-7993)*

Ra Resky Woodsmith LLC 757 678-7555
   11331 Sparrow Point Rd Machipongo (23405) *(G-7848)*

Raastech Software LLC 888 565-3397
   2201 Coop Way Ste 600 Herndon (20171) *(G-6785)*

Rabbit Creek Partners LLC 877 779-9977
   334 Industrial Park Rd Bluefield (24605) *(G-1877)*

Rabbit Software LLC 703 939-1708
   21414 Fairhunt Dr Ashburn (20148) *(G-1329)*

Race Technology USA LLC 804 358-7289
   2317 Westwood Ave Ste 101 Richmond (23230) *(G-11344)*

**A
L
P
H
A
B
E
T
I
C**

Race Trac Petroleum 804 694-9079
1570 George Wash Mem Hwy Gloucester Point (23062) *(G-5875)*

Race Trac Petroleum 757 557-0076
5549 Virginia Beach Blvd Virginia Beach (23462) *(G-14756)*

Racecom of Virginia 757 599-8255
200 Commerce Cir Yorktown (23693) *(G-15985)*

Racepacket Inc 703 486-1466
1300 Army Navy Dr Apt 209 Arlington (22202) *(G-1127)*

Racer Tees 540 416-1320
1819 East Side Hwy # 101 Crimora (24431) *(G-3822)*

Racers Custom Cabinets Inc 540 672-4231
227 Byrd St Orange (22960) *(G-10225)*

Rachael A Peden Originals 804 580-8709
826 Quinton Oak Ln Farnham (22460) *(G-4964)*

Racing For Veterans 434 822-4201
1025 Raceplex Rd Alton (24520) *(G-647)*

Rack 'em Company, Glen Allen *Also called Jerry King (G-5755)*

Rack 10 Solar LLC 703 996-4082
35091 Paxson Rd Round Hill (20141) *(G-12386)*

Radar Media LLC 540 348-8996
204 Jump Mountain Rd Rockbridge Baths (24473) *(G-12237)*

Radavert Industries Inc 703 425-6777
5729 Edgewater Oak Ct Burke (22015) *(G-2201)*

Rader Cabinets 434 610-1954
183 Brookwood Dr Lynchburg (24501) *(G-7798)*

Radford Wldg & Fabrication LLC 540 731-4891
500 Unruh Dr Radford (24141) *(G-10737)*

Radio Reconnaissance Tech Inc (PA) **540 752-7448**
3328 Bourbon St Fredericksburg (22408) *(G-5352)*

Radkowsky Thorium Power, Mc Lean *Also called Thorium Power Inc (G-8566)*

Radon Safe Inc 540 265-0101
6439 Pendleton Ave Roanoke (24019) *(G-11993)*

Radus Software LLC 703 623-8471
47395 Halcyon Pl Sterling (20165) *(G-13484)*

Raffy Welding LLC 703 945-0554
14072 Gusty Knoll Ln Leesburg (20176) *(G-7331)*

Rag Bag Aero Works Inc 540 967-5400
198 Locust Dr Louisa (23093) *(G-7564)*

Ragan Sheet Metal Inc 757 333-7248
1640 Donna Dr Ste 105 Virginia Beach (23451) *(G-14757)*

Rage Plastics 434 309-1718
255 Pittsylvania Ave Altavista (24517) *(G-638)*

Raggededge Gear Inc 276 226-9439
309 Puppy Creek Dr Stuart (24171) *(G-13627)*

Ragland Trucking Inc W E 434 286-2414
1051 Gough Town Rd Scottsville (24590) *(G-12664)*

Ragland, Gene Timber, Scottsville *Also called W E Ragland Logging Co (G-12670)*

Rails End Wood & Met Crafters 540 463-9565
227 Mclaughlin St Lexington (24450) *(G-7413)*

Railway Station Press Inc 703 683-2335
105 E Glendale Ave Alexandria (22301) *(G-324)*

Raimist Software LLC 703 568-7638
13623 Bare Island Dr Chantilly (20151) *(G-2484)*

Rain & Associates LLC 757 572-3996
1236 Northvale Dr Virginia Beach (23464) *(G-14758)*

Rain Forest Shower System LLC 804 432-8930
10001 Patterson Ave # 207 Henrico (23238) *(G-6554)*

Rainbow Custom Woodworking 571 379-5500
7700 Wellingford Dr Manassas (20109) *(G-8138)*

Rainbow Hill Farm 540 365-7826
1000 Skillet Rd Ferrum (24088) *(G-4977)*

Rainbow Ridge Books LLC 757 481-7399
1056 Commodore Dr Virginia Beach (23454) *(G-14759)*

Raincrow Studios LLC 540 746-8696
128 W Bruce St Harrisonburg (22801) *(G-6360)*

Rainmaker Publishing LLC 703 385-9761
9100 Hamilton Dr Fairfax (22031) *(G-4536)*

Rainsoft Water Treatment, Danville *Also called Piedmont Environmental Sys (G-4025)*

Raised Apps LLC 703 398-8254
1830 Cedar Cove Way Woodbridge (22191) *(G-15790)*

Raleigh Mine and Indus Sup Inc 276 322-3119
517 Bluefield Indus Park Bluefield (24605) *(G-1878)*

Ralph Johnson 434 286-2735
7753 Blenheim Rd Scottsville (24590) *(G-12665)*

Ralph Matney 276 644-9259
21573 Old Dominion Rd Bristol (24202) *(G-2031)*

Ralph Rice 434 385-8614
2704 Elk Valley Rd Forest (24551) *(G-5089)*

Ralph Rice Logging and Excvtg, Forest *Also called Ralph Rice (G-5089)*

Ram Company, The, Lowesville *Also called Nellie Harris (G-7597)*

Ramatech LLC 240 449-7435
26044 Pembrooke Cir Chantilly (20152) *(G-2553)*

Rambletype LLC 540 440-1218
500 Lafayette Blvd # 228 Fredericksburg (22401) *(G-5217)*

Ramoneda Brothers LLC (PA) **540 547-3168**
8100 Tinsley Pl Culpeper (22701) *(G-3915)*

Ramoneda Brothers LLC 540 825-9166
13452 Rixeyville Rd Culpeper (22701) *(G-3916)*

Ramsey & Son Lumber Corp 434 946-5429
Rr 608 Amherst (24521) *(G-704)*

Ramsey Brothers Logging Inc 540 463-5044
935 Sugar Creek Rd Lexington (24450) *(G-7414)*

Ramsey Cabinets Inc 434 946-0329
126 Sardis Rd Amherst (24521) *(G-705)*

Ramsey Manufacturing LLC 757 232-9034
431 W 25th St Norfolk (23517) *(G-9701)*

Rand Worldwide Inc 804 290-8850
8100 Three Chopt Rd Richmond (23229) *(G-11345)*

Randall Publication Inc 703 369-0741
8803 Sudley Rd Ste 201 Manassas (20110) *(G-7994)*

Randolph Scotts Welding 434 656-1471
1193 Piney Grove Rd Gretna (24557) *(G-6009)*

Randolph-Bundy Incorporated 757 625-2556
4012 Seaboard Ct Portsmouth (23701) *(G-10474)*

Randolph-Macon College 804 752-7200
204 Henry St Ashland (23005) *(G-1483)*

Random Acts of Cupcakes 540 974-3948
551 N Braddock St Winchester (22601) *(G-15578)*

Randy Edwards 703 591-0545
9371 Lee Hwy Fairfax (22031) *(G-4537)*

Randy Hawthorne 434 547-3460
2982 Plank Rd Dillwyn (23936) *(G-4099)*

Range Resources 276 628-1568
408 W Main St Abingdon (24210) *(G-56)*

Rapa Boat Services LLC 804 443-4434
139360 W Indus Park Tappahannock (22560) *(G-13821)*

Raphael Press LLC 703 771-7571
19370 Magnolia Grove Sq Leesburg (20176) *(G-7332)*

Rapid Biosciences Inc 713 899-6177
4105 Exeter Rd Richmond (23221) *(G-11728)*

Rapid Manufacturing Inc 804 598-7467
4347 Anderson Hwy Powhatan (23139) *(G-10570)*

Rapid Mat Group LLC 703 629-2426
1600 Tysons Blvd Fl 8 Mc Lean (22102) *(G-8532)*

Rapid Printing & Office Sups, Bedford *Also called Rapid Printing Inc (G-1654)*

Rapid Printing Inc 540 586-1243
113 N Bridge St Bedford (24523) *(G-1654)*

Rapidsign Inc 540 362-2025
720 Liberty Rd Ne Roanoke (24012) *(G-12160)*

Rapiscan Counterbomber Tech, Manassas *Also called Rapiscan Systems Inc (G-8139)*

Rapiscan Government Svcs Inc 571 227-6767
2900 Crystal Dr Ste 910 Arlington (22202) *(G-1128)*

Rapiscan Systems, Arlington *Also called Locker LLC (G-1042)*

Rapiscan Systems 703 257-3429
7301 Gateway Ct Ste 7321 Manassas (20109) *(G-8139)*

Rapiscan Systems - An O 703 535-7848
1530 Wilson Blvd Ste 170 Arlington (22209) *(G-1129)*

Rapoca Energy Co 423 269-6900
2700 Lee Hwy Ste B Bristol (24202) *(G-2032)*

Rappahannock & Potomac Rep LLC 540 373-9545
100 Hampton Dr Fredericksburg (22405) *(G-5475)*

Rappahannock Boat Works Inc 540 439-4045
4403 Dyes Ln Bealeton (22712) *(G-1605)*

Rappahannock Cellars, Huntly *Also called Cana Cellars Inc (G-6964)*

Rappahannock Concrete, Saluda *Also called Vulcan Materials Company (G-12607)*

Rappahannock Entp Assoc Inc 703 560-5042
3406 Casilear Rd Falls Church (22042) *(G-4862)*

Rappahannock Media LLC 540 675-3338
309 Jett St Washington (22747) *(G-15077)*

Rappahannock News, Washington *Also called Rappahannock Media LLC (G-15077)*

Rappahannock Record 804 435-1701
27 N Main St Kilmarnock (22482) *(G-7076)*

Rappahannock Times, Tappahannock *Also called W A Cleaton and Sons Inc (G-13824)*

Rappahannock Sports and Graphic 540 891-7662
5100 Commonwealth Dr Fredericksburg (22407) *(G-5353)*

Rappatomac Industries Inc 804 529-6440
73 Factory Ln Callao (22435) *(G-2218)*

Rare Edition, Amelia Court House *Also called Star Childrens Dress Co Inc (G-673)*

Rare-Rocks Curation, Mc Lean *Also called Jr Bernard Hearn (G-8476)*

Rasco Equipment Services Inc (HQ) **703 643-2952**
1635 Woodside Dr Ste 2 Woodbridge (22191) *(G-15791)*

Rasco Esi, Woodbridge *Also called Rasco Equipment Services Inc (G-15791)*

Ratliff 276 794-7377
449 Valley View Est Lebanon (24266) *(G-7205)*

Rave On Industries LLC 804 308-0898
9504 Gayton Rd Henrico (23229) *(G-6555)*

Raven Enterprises LLC 804 355-6386
3217 Brook Rd Richmond (23227) *(G-11346)*

Raven Ind 703 414-3290
2231 Crystal Dr Arlington (22202) *(G-1130)*

Raven Machine 804 271-6001
3015 Falling Creek Ave North Chesterfield (23234) *(G-9957)*

Raw Goods LLC 862 812-1520
300 Yoakum Pkwy Apt 1220 Alexandria (22304) *(G-325)*

Rawhide LLC 540 548-1148
11918 Sawhill Blvd Spotsylvania (22553) *(G-12910)*

Rawley Pike Welding LLC 540 867-5335
6009 Rawley Pike Hinton (22831) *(G-6905)*

Ray Gorham 703 971-1807
5919 Pratt St Alexandria (22310) *(G-566)*
Ray Painter Small 804 255-7050
17312 Round Rock Pl Chesterfield (23838) *(G-3520)*
Ray Visions Inc 757 865-6442
317 Blacksmith Arch Yorktown (23693) *(G-15986)*
Ray's Welding, Alexandria *Also called Ray Gorham (G-566)*
Raybar Jewelry Design Inc 757 486-4562
277 N Lynnhven Rd Ste 109 Virginia Beach (23452) *(G-14760)*
Rayco Industries Inc 804 321-7111
1502 Valley Rd Richmond (23222) *(G-11729)*
Rayco Services Inc 757 689-2156
2984 Cadence Way Virginia Beach (23456) *(G-14761)*
Raymond Dawson 276 676-9068
21306 Crosswinds Dr Abingdon (24211) *(G-57)*
Raymond Golden 757 549-1853
836 Nottaway Dr Chesapeake (23320) *(G-3256)*
Raymond Hill Consulting 757 925-0136
3809 Deer Path Rd Suffolk (23434) *(G-13756)*
Rays Custom Cabinets 434 528-0189
288 Mansion Way Amherst (24521) *(G-706)*
Rays Woodworks 276 251-7297
1595 Dan Valley Farm Rd Claudville (24076) *(G-3640)*
Raytheon Applied Sgnal Tech In 571 484-9373
7925 Jones Branch Dr # 1200 Mc Lean (22102) *(G-8533)*
Raytheon Company 703 416-5800
2711 Richmond Hwy Arlington (22202) *(G-1131)*
Raytheon Company 703 759-1200
22270 Pacific Blvd Sterling (20166) *(G-13485)*
Raytheon Company 703 830-4087
14280 Sullyfield Cir # 100 Chantilly (20151) *(G-2485)*
Raytheon Company 571 250-2260
22260 Pacific Blvd Dulles (20166) *(G-4221)*
Raytheon Company 703 841-5700
1100 Wilson Blvd Ste 2000 Arlington (22209) *(G-1132)*
Raytheon Company 757 855-4394
1100 Intl Plz 100 Chesapeake (23323) *(G-3257)*
Raytheon Company 757 363-1252
5820 Ward Ct Virginia Beach (23455) *(G-14762)*
Raytheon Company 703 413-1220
1235 S Clark St Ste 800 Arlington (22202) *(G-1133)*
Raytheon Company 972 638-3173
1100 Executive Dr Williamsburg (23188) *(G-15303)*
Raytheon Company 703 661-7252
7700 Arlington Blvd Falls Church (22042) *(G-4863)*
Raytheon Company 310 647-9438
1100 Intl Plz Ste 100 Chesapeake (23323) *(G-3258)*
Raytheon Company 703 418-0275
2361 Richmond Hwy # 1112 Arlington (22202) *(G-1134)*
Raytheon Company 703 418-0275
2361 Richmond Hwy Arlington (22202) *(G-1135)*
Raytheon Company 571 250-1101
22265 Pacific Blvd Dulles (20166) *(G-4222)*
Raytheon Company 703 260-3534
23010 Ladbrook Dr Ste 105 Sterling (20166) *(G-13486)*
Raytheon Company 757 749-9638
160 Main Rd Yorktown (23691) *(G-15987)*
Raytheon Company 706 569-6600
1100 Wilson Blvd Ste 1600 Arlington (22209) *(G-1136)*
Raytheon Company 571 250-3421
22265 Pacific Blvd Dulles (20166) *(G-4223)*
Raytheon Company 703 412-3742
2461 S Clark St Ste 1100 Arlington (22202) *(G-1137)*
Raytheon Company 703 912-1800
8320 Alban Rd Ste 100 Springfield (22150) *(G-13078)*
Raytheon Company 972 272-0515
22270 Pcf Blvd Ste 600 Dulles (20166) *(G-4224)*
Raytheon Company 703 419-1400
2461 S Clark St Arlington (22202) *(G-1138)*
Raytheon Company 703 768-4172
2211 Sherwood Hall Ln Alexandria (22306) *(G-567)*
Raytheon Company 757 421-8319
Relay Rd Rm Bldg 363 Chesapeake (23322) *(G-3259)*
Raytheon Company 703 872-3400
2450 Crystal Dr Ste 700 Arlington (22202) *(G-1139)*
Raytheon Company 310 647-9438
22260 Pacific Blvd Dulles (20166) *(G-4225)*
Raytheon Company 540 658-3172
1100 Wilson Blvd Ste 1600 Arlington (22209) *(G-1140)*
Raytheon Technologies Corp 757 838-7980
2101 Executive Dr Ste 610 Hampton (23666) *(G-6225)*
Raytum Photonics LLC 703 831-7809
43671 Trade Center Pl # 104 Sterling (20166) *(G-13487)*
Rbr Tactical Inc 804 564-6787
3113 Aspen Ave Richmond (23228) *(G-11347)*
Rbr Tactical Armor, Richmond *Also called Rbr Tactical Inc (G-11347)*
Rbt Center LLC 703 823-8664
309 Yoakum Pkwy Apt 518 Alexandria (22304) *(G-326)*
RC Industries LLC 757 839-5577
512 Winwood Dr Chesapeake (23323) *(G-3260)*
RC Tate Woodworks 434 822-0035
2876 Westover Dr Danville (24541) *(G-4034)*
Rci Rutherford Controls, Virginia Beach *Also called Rutherford Controls Intl Corp (G-14786)*
Rcl Software Inc 757 934-0828
211 Equinox Lndg Suffolk (23434) *(G-13757)*
Rct Logging LLC 434 767-4780
3710 Schultz Mill Rd Green Bay (23942) *(G-5991)*
Rd Stucco LLC 703 926-2322
1409 S Buchanan St Arlington (22204) *(G-1141)*
Rdj Enterprises 757 538-0466
202 Eagles Nest Trce Suffolk (23435) *(G-13758)*
Rdk LLC 540 446-8327
2309 Lee Hwy Mount Sidney (24467) *(G-9084)*
RDS Control Systems Inc 888 578-9428
3 Joy Ln Fishersville (22939) *(G-5007)*
RE Clean Automotive Products 757 368-2694
2717 Sonic Dr Ste 100 Virginia Beach (23453) *(G-14763)*
RE Discovery Software Inc (PA) **434 975-3256**
3040 Berkmar Dr Ste B1 Charlottesville (22901) *(G-2680)*
RE Innovative Sftwr Solutions (PA) **434 989-8558**
1750 Allied St Ste B Charlottesville (22903) *(G-2855)*
RE Max Advantage 540 241-2499
49 Georganna Dr Lyndhurst (22952) *(G-7844)*
REA Boys Logging & Equip 276 957-4935
639 Log Manor Rd Spencer (24165) *(G-12874)*
Reach Orthotic Prosthetic Svcs 757 930-0139
12715 Warwick Blvd Ste V Newport News (23606) *(G-9321)*
Reach Orthtic Prsthetic Svcs S 757 673-2000
4057 Taylor Rd Ste P Chesapeake (23321) *(G-3261)*
Readspeaker LLC 703 462-8738
1600 Tysons Blvd Fl 8 Mc Lean (22102) *(G-8534)*
Ready Set Read LLC 804 673-8764
202 Ralston Rd Richmond (23229) *(G-11348)*
Ready For Hillary 703 405-0433
1611 N Kent St Arlington (22209) *(G-1142)*
Ready Mix Concrete Company, Midlothian *Also called Argos USA LLC (G-8774)*
Ready Set Sign LLC 703 820-0022
4319 36th St S Arlington (22206) *(G-1143)*
Ready To Cover Inc 571 379-5766
10429 Balls Ford Rd Manassas (20109) *(G-8140)*
Real American Revolution 703 732-9049
7124 Leesburg Pike Falls Church (22043) *(G-4864)*
Real Estate Consultants 949 212-1366
10300 Eaton Pl Ste 120 Fairfax (22030) *(G-4668)*
Real Estate Weekly 434 817-9330
550 Hillsdale Dr Ste A Charlottesville (22901) *(G-2681)*
Real Food For Fuel LLC 757 416-4458
3452 Spur St Blacksburg (24060) *(G-1782)*
Real Is Rare Label LLC 757 705-1850
854 48th St Norfolk (23508) *(G-9702)*
Real Time Solutions, Arlington *Also called Teresa C Shankman (G-1187)*
Realdeal Jntral/Floortech Svcs, Virginia Beach *Also called Elliott Lestselle (G-14442)*
Really Great Reading 571 659-2826
3071 Ps Business Ctr Dr Woodbridge (22192) *(G-15792)*
Realta Life Sciences Inc 757 418-4842
5665 Lowery Rd Ste 100 Norfolk (23502) *(G-9703)*
Realty Restorations LLC 757 553-6117
5512 Haden Rd Virginia Beach (23455) *(G-14764)*
Reamco Inc 703 690-2000
6826 Hill Park Dr Lorton (22079) *(G-7525)*
Reaper Precision LLC 540 841-0028
16283 Round Hill Rd King George (22485) *(G-7107)*
Reason 202 256-6197
517 2nd St Ne Charlottesville (22902) *(G-2856)*
Reaves Timber Corporation 434 299-5645
2957 Fontella Rd Coleman Falls (24536) *(G-3707)*
Rebarsolutions 540 300-9975
3028 John Wayland Hwy Dayton (22821) *(G-4060)*
Rebec Vineyards Inc 434 946-5168
2229 N Amherst Hwy Amherst (24521) *(G-707)*
Rebecca Burton 804 526-3423
1118 Peace Cliff Ct Colonial Heights (23834) *(G-3743)*
Rebecca Leigh Fraser 912 755-3453
4720 Ocean View Ave Virginia Beach (23455) *(G-14765)*
Rebecca Ortizsanchez 315 532-4439
113 Niagra St Portsmouth (23702) *(G-10475)*
Rebecca S Ceramics 804 560-4477
7644 Comanche Dr Richmond (23225) *(G-11730)*
Rebirth By D Lucas, Woodbridge *Also called Willie Lucas (G-15832)*
Rebound Analytics LLC 202 297-1204
1775 Tysons Blvd Fl 5 Tysons (22102) *(G-13948)*
Recap LLC 703 521-3406
2116 S Kent St Arlington (22202) *(G-1144)*
Reckless Inc 757 469-4416
1216 E Eva Blvd Chesapeake (23320) *(G-3262)*
Reco Biodiesel LLC 804 644-2800
710 Hospital St Richmond (23219) *(G-11731)*
Recognition Works 804 739-1483
2837 Cove View Ln Midlothian (23112) *(G-8886)*

ALPHABETIC

Reconart Inc 855 732-6627
  6462 Little River Tpke Alexandria (22312) *(G-568)*
Reconciliation Press 703 743-2416
  6152 Ferrier Ct Gainesville (20155) *(G-5610)*
Reconciliation Press Inc 703 369-6132
  9028 West St Manassas (20110) *(G-7995)*
Recorder Publishing of VA Inc 540 468-2147
  3 Water St Monterey (24465) *(G-9012)*
Recorder Publishing VA Inc 540 839-6646
  2663 Mcguffin Rd Warm Springs (24484) *(G-14975)*
Recorder The, Monterey Also called Recorder Publishing of VA Inc *(G-9012)*
Rector Visitors of The Univ VA 434 296-7288
  4040 Lewis And Clark Dr Charlottesville (22911) *(G-2682)*
Rector Visitors of The Univ VA 434 924-3469
  500 Edgemont Rd Charlottesville (22903) *(G-2857)*
Rector Visitors of The Univ VA 434 924-9136
  Old Medical Schl Rm 3876 Charlottesville (22908) *(G-2858)*
Rector Visitors of The Univ VA 434 924-3468
  210 Sprigg Ln Charlottesville (22903) *(G-2859)*
Rector Visitors of The Univ VA 434 924-3124
  1 West Range Charlottesville (22903) *(G-2860)*
Rectors Repair & Welding LLC 540 809-5683
  92 Le Way Dr Fredericksburg (22406) *(G-5476)*
Recycled Pallets Inc 804 400-9931
  8029 Industrial Park Rd Mechanicsville (23116) *(G-8670)*
Red Acres Equipment Inc 434 352-5086
  208 Autumn Ln Appomattox (24522) *(G-821)*
Red Action Blue Info LLC 703 474-2617
  7911 Westpark Dr Apt 2501 Mc Lean (22102) *(G-8535)*
Red Action Blue Info LLC 469 224-7673
  2727 Merrilee Dr Apt 223 Fairfax (22031) *(G-4538)*
Red Apple Productions LLC 703 237-1034
  974 Patrick Henry Dr Arlington (22205) *(G-1145)*
Red Apple Publications 703 430-9272
  10908 Thimbleberry Ln Great Falls (22066) *(G-5977)*
Red Brook Lumber Co 434 293-2077
  3846 Carters Mountain Rd Charlottesville (22902) *(G-2861)*
Red DOT Laser Engraving LLC 540 842-3509
  4417 Shannon Meadows Ln Spotsylvania (22551) *(G-12911)*
Red Eagle Creations 804 556-2041
  2161 Maidens Rd Maidens (23102) *(G-7892)*
Red Eagle Industries LLC 434 352-5831
  271 Soybean Dr Appomattox (24522) *(G-822)*
Red Geranium Inc 757 645-3421
  8 Prestwick Williamsburg (23188) *(G-15304)*
Red Hat Inc 703 748-2201
  8260 Greensboro Dr # 300 Mc Lean (22102) *(G-8536)*
Red Hot Publishing LLC 703 885-5423
  20679 Cutwater Pl Sterling (20165) *(G-13488)*
Red Moon Partners LLC 757 240-4305
  34 Research Dr Ste 300 Hampton (23666) *(G-6226)*
Red Moon Press, Winchester Also called James Kacian *(G-15550)*
Red River Interiors LLC 703 987-1698
  14118 Red River Dr Centreville (20121) *(G-2332)*
Red Star Construction, Fredericksburg Also called Red Star Glass Inc *(G-5218)*
Red Star Consulting LLC 434 872-0890
  1218 East Market St Charlottesville (22902) *(G-2862)*
Red Star Glass Inc 540 899-5779
  317 Bridgewater St Fredericksburg (22401) *(G-5218)*
Red Star Merchandise, Charlottesville Also called Red Star Consulting LLC *(G-2862)*
Red Stitch Tactical LLC 703 798-4385
  9349 Mike Garcia Dr Manassas (20109) *(G-8141)*
Red Stitch Targets, Manassas Also called Red Stitch Tactical LLC *(G-8141)*
Red Tie Group Inc 804 236-4632
  5616 Eastport Blvd Richmond (23231) *(G-11349)*
Redclay Visions LLC 804 869-3616
  812 9th St Virginia Beach (23451) *(G-14766)*
Redco Machine Inc 540 586-3545
  3032 Forest Rd Bedford (24523) *(G-1655)*
Redcoat Solutions Inc 540 437-9843
  3060 N Valley Pike Rockingham (22802) *(G-12270)*
Reddy Ice Corporation 757 855-6065
  1129 Production Rd Norfolk (23502) *(G-9704)*
Reddy Ice Corporation 540 433-2751
  610 Pleasant Valley Rd Harrisonburg (22801) *(G-6361)*
Reddy Ice Group Inc 540 777-0253
  1512 Patrick Rd Ne Roanoke (24012) *(G-12161)*
Reddzway LLC 434 515-0791
  218 Mill View Ln Lynchburg (24502) *(G-7799)*
Rediscover Woodwork 757 813-0383
  3500 Douglas Rd Chesapeake (23322) *(G-3263)*
Redisec, Alexandria Also called Troy Patrick *(G-370)*
Redland Brick 434 848-2397
  16144 Gvrnor Hrrison Pkwy Lawrenceville (23868) *(G-7183)*
Redland Quarries NY Inc 703 480-3600
  12950 Worldgate Dr Ste 50 Herndon (20170) *(G-6786)*
Redline Productions 703 861-8765
  2854 Cherry St Apt 306 Falls Church (22042) *(G-4865)*
Redono LLC 757 553-2305
  1448 Clearwater Ln Chesapeake (23322) *(G-3264)*

Redprint Strategy 202 656-1002
  212 S Henry St Alexandria (22314) *(G-327)*
Reebok International Ltd 703 490-5671
  2700 Potomac Mills Cir Woodbridge (22192) *(G-15793)*
Reed Envelope Company Inc 703 690-2249
  8630 Meadow Edge Ter Fairfax Station (22039) *(G-4722)*
Reed Sign Co 757 336-5505
  6445 Booth St Chincoteague (23336) *(G-3563)*
Reeds Carbide Saw and Tool, Lynchburg Also called Reeds Carbide Saw Service *(G-7800)*
Reeds Carbide Saw Service 434 846-6436
  1315 Commerce St Lynchburg (24504) *(G-7800)*
Reef Room 757 592-0955
  1a Lyliston Ln Newport News (23601) *(G-9322)*
Reem Enterprises 703 608-2283
  13830 Rembrandt Way Chantilly (20151) *(G-2486)*
Reese Kyndal 757 718-0525
  130 Brooke Ave Apt 213 Norfolk (23510) *(G-9705)*
Reeses Amazing Printing Svcs 804 325-0947
  405 Sherilyn Dr Henrico (23075) *(G-6556)*
Refco Mfg 757 487-2222
  3835 Holland Blvd Ste B Chesapeake (23323) *(G-3265)*
Refcon Services Inc 757 616-0691
  813 Professional Pl W A110 Chesapeake (23320) *(G-3266)*
Refibot Inc 703 989-2232
  43401 Barnstead Dr Ashburn (20148) *(G-1330)*
Refills Inc 804 771-5460
  1503 Hanover Ave Richmond (23220) *(G-11732)*
Reflections Light Boxes 757 641-3192
  2801 Ashwood Dr Chesapeake (23321) *(G-3267)*
Reformation Herald Pubg Assn 540 366-9400
  5240 Hollins Rd Roanoke (24019) *(G-11994)*
Refrigeration Solutions Inc 804 752-3188
  10984 Richardson Rd Ashland (23005) *(G-1484)*
Refuge Golf & Bumper Boats 757 336-5420
  6528 Maddox Blvd Chincoteague (23336) *(G-3564)*
Refurb Factory LLC 301 799-8385
  5999 Stevenson Ave # 202 Alexandria (22304) *(G-328)*
Rega Enterprises Inc 757 488-8056
  1889 Rosemary Ln Chesapeake (23321) *(G-3268)*
Regal Jewelers Inc 540 949-4455
  124 Lucy Ln Waynesboro (22980) *(G-15134)*
Regal Products Co 804 798-2691
  11232 Hopson Rd Ste 1 Ashland (23005) *(G-1485)*
Regent Allied Carbon Energy 276 679-4994
  Pine Br Appalachia (24216) *(G-800)*
Reger Research 703 328-6465
  25532 Cunard Aly Chantilly (20152) *(G-2554)*
Reginalds Homemade LLC 804 972-4040
  8104 Greystone East Cir Henrico (23229) *(G-6557)*
Region Press 276 706-6798
  591 Ridgeview Rd Saltville (24370) *(G-12587)*
Regitex Usa LLC 514 730-1110
  2 Kerr Dr Brodnax (23920) *(G-2104)*
Regula Forensics Inc 703 473-2625
  1800 Alexander Bell Dr # 400 Reston (20191) *(G-10936)*
Rehabltation Practitioners Inc (PA) **540 722-9025**
  333 W Cork St Unit 30 Winchester (22601) *(G-15579)*
Rehau Automotive LLC (HQ) **703 777-5255**
  1501 Edwards Ferry Rd Ne Leesburg (20176) *(G-7333)*
Rehau Construction LLC (HQ) **800 247-9445**
  1501 Edwards Ferry Rd Ne Leesburg (20176) *(G-7334)*
Rehau Incorporated (PA) **703 777-5255**
  1501 Edwards Ferry Rd Ne Leesburg (20176) *(G-7335)*
Rehau Industries LLC 703 777-5255
  1501 Edwards Ferry Rd Ne Leesburg (20176) *(G-7336)*
Reid Industries LLC (PA) **703 920-6199**
  1405 S Fern St Arlington (22202) *(G-1146)*
Reid Industries LLC 703 786-6307
  1618 Teal Way Woodbridge (22191) *(G-15794)*
Reierson Woodworking 804 541-1945
  11008 Jenny Creek Dr North Prince George (23860) *(G-10091)*
Reign Productions LLC 703 317-1393
  5901 Mount Eagle Dr # 502 Alexandria (22303) *(G-569)*
Reignforest Spices & Tea LLC 757 716-5205
  2704 Westminster Ave Norfolk (23504) *(G-9706)*
Reinforced Plastic Systems, Front Royal Also called RPS Shenandoah Inc *(G-5551)*
Reinhart Custom Cabinets Inc 757 303-1438
  605 Industrial Park Dr B Newport News (23608) *(G-9323)*
Reiss Manufacturing Inc 434 292-1600
  1 Polymer Pl Blackstone (23824) *(G-1825)*
Rejuvinage 757 306-4300
  2232 Virginia Beach Blvd # 104 Virginia Beach (23454) *(G-14767)*
Rejuvination Center, Marion Also called Amarveda *(G-8221)*
Relational Data Solutions Inc 703 369-3580
  10805 Gambril Dr Manassas (20109) *(G-8142)*
Relational Systems Design Ltd 703 385-7073
  10712 Almond St Fairfax (22032) *(G-4539)*
Reliable Welding & Fabricators 276 629-2593
  1850 Fairystone Park Hwy Bassett (24055) *(G-1589)*

Reliadefense LLC 571 225-4096
229 Silverleaf Dr Sterling (20164) *(G-13489)*

Reliance Industries Inc 832 788-0108
140 Little Falls St # 208 Falls Church (22046) *(G-4924)*

Reliant Cem Services Inc 717 459-4990
630 Wyndhurst Dr Apt C Lynchburg (24502) *(G-7801)*

Reline America Inc 276 496-4000
116 Battleground Ave Saltville (24370) *(G-12588)*

Remark Design Incorporated 540 675-3625
Gay St Washington (22747) *(G-15078)*

Renaissance Cabinet Shop 540 967-0422
1844 Courthouse Rd Louisa (23093) *(G-7565)*

Renaissnce Cntract Ltg Furn In 540 342-1548
2807 Mary Linda Ave Ne Roanoke (24012) *(G-12162)*

Rendas 804 776-6215
1007 Robins Point Ave Deltaville (23043) *(G-4086)*

Renegade Classics 757 336-6611
4102 Main St Chincoteague (23336) *(G-3565)*

Renegade Publishing LLC 703 780-4546
8500 Fort Hunt Rd Alexandria (22308) *(G-570)*

Renmus Technologies Inc 703 624-9144
7226 Nathan Ct Ste 200 Manassas (20109) *(G-8143)*

Renovated Richmond LLC 804 467-5470
2020 Christendom Dr Midlothian (23113) *(G-8887)*

Rentbot LLC 844 473-6826
29 Lexington Rd Richmond (23226) *(G-11350)*

Rentury Solutions LLC 757 453-5763
216 N First St Hampton (23664) *(G-6227)*

Rephidim LLC 312 636-6947
764 Tilman Rd Charlottesville (22901) *(G-2683)*

Republic Electronics, Fairfax Also called G F I Associates Inc *(G-4460)*

Republic Trusswerks LLC 540 434-9497
2681 John Wayland Hwy Rockingham (22801) *(G-12271)*

Republicanpaccom 703 241-8422
5155 37th St N Arlington (22207) *(G-1147)*

Requisites Gallery 757 376-2754
910 Star Ct Chesapeake (23322) *(G-3269)*

Rescue ME Cleaning Service 540 370-0844
106 Springwood Dr Fredericksburg (22401) *(G-5219)*

Rescue Systems Inc 276 629-2900
6520 Virginia Ave Bassett (24055) *(G-1590)*

Rescue Systems Intl Inc 276 629-2900
755 Botetourt Rd Fincastle (24090) *(G-4998)*

Research Service Bureau LLC 703 593-7507
3118 Ashburton Ave Herndon (20171) *(G-6787)*

Reservation Gateway Inc 703 286-5331
11654 Plaza America Dr # 64 Reston (20190) *(G-10937)*

Reservoir Distillery LLC 804 912-2621
1800 Summit Ave Richmond (23230) *(G-11351)*

Residex LLC 757 363-2080
1449 Miller Str Rd Ste A Virginia Beach (23455) *(G-14768)*

Residual King LLC 757 474-3080
4624 Flicka Ct Virginia Beach (23455) *(G-14769)*

Residual Sense Marketing LLC 757 595-0278
423 Lester Rd Apt 1 Newport News (23601) *(G-9324)*

Resounding LLC 804 677-0947
1905 Huguenot Rd Ste 200 North Chesterfield (23235) *(G-9958)*

Resource Color Control Tech 540 548-1855
11801 Main St Ste D Fredericksburg (22408) *(G-5354)*

Resource Consultants Inc 757 464-5252
5700 Thurston Ave Ste 120 Virginia Beach (23455) *(G-14770)*

Resource Management Strategies, Prospect Also called Hope Springs Media *(G-10612)*

Reston Copy Center 703 860-9600
605 Carlisle Dr Herndon (20170) *(G-6788)*

Reston Copy Center Inc 703 860-9600
11307 Sunset Hills Rd B3 Reston (20190) *(G-10938)*

Reston Shirt & Graphic Co Inc 703 318-4802
22800 Indian Creek Dr C Sterling (20166) *(G-13490)*

Reston Software LLC 703 234-2932
12200 Dark Star Ct Reston (20191) *(G-10939)*

Reston Technology Group Inc 703 810-8800
22636 Glenn Dr Sterling (20164) *(G-13491)*

Restoration Books & Publishing 276 224-7244
203 Emmett St Martinsville (24112) *(G-8323)*

Restorgenex, Charlottesville Also called Diffusion Pharmaceuticals Inc *(G-2782)*

Restortech Inc 703 204-0401
13849 Park Center Rd A Herndon (20171) *(G-6789)*

Results Software 703 713-9100
12334 Folkstone Dr Herndon (20171) *(G-6790)*

Resurface Incorporated 703 335-1950
11517 Robertson Dr Manassas (20109) *(G-8144)*

Ret Corp 703 471-8108
8300 Greensboro Dr # 620 Mc Lean (22102) *(G-8537)*

Retarded Mobile Sound & Vision 804 437-7633
1505 Oakwood Ave Richmond (23223) *(G-11733)*

Retirement Watch LLC 571 522-6505
15103 Stillfield Pl Centreville (20120) *(G-2333)*

Retivue LLC 434 260-2836
2505 Hillwood Pl Charlottesville (22901) *(G-2684)*

Retrospect Publishing 703 765-9405
1307 Warrington Pl Alexandria (22307) *(G-571)*

Reuseit Software Inc 703 365-8071
10512 Coral Berry Dr Manassas (20110) *(G-7996)*

Reverb Networks Inc 703 665-4222
21515 Ridgetop Cir # 290 Sterling (20166) *(G-13492)*

Revere Mold & Engineering Inc 804 748-5059
13221 Old Stage Rd Chester (23836) *(G-3450)*

Reverse Ionizer LLC 703 403-7256
360 Herndon Pkwy Ste 1400 Herndon (20170) *(G-6791)*

Revival Labs LLC 949 351-1660
7057 Kings Manor Dr Alexandria (22315) *(G-572)*

Revolution Rising Print 804 276-4789
2517 Susten Ln Richmond (23224) *(G-11734)*

Revolution Soultions VA LLC 804 539-5058
12500 Fanleas Ct Fairfax (22033) *(G-4540)*

Revolution X, Richmond Also called W W Distributors *(G-11442)*

Rew Materials Spotsylvania Co, Chantilly Also called K C G Inc *(G-2539)*

Reward Happiness LLC 703 795-0746
3409 Gallows Rd Falls Church (22042) *(G-4866)*

Rewi LLC 757 647-8942
302 Ben Franklin Cir Williamsburg (23188) *(G-15305)*

Rewined LLC 757 877-3480
708 Windy Way Unit 308 Newport News (23602) *(G-9325)*

Rex Companies Inc 757 873-5452
725 City Center Blvd Newport News (23606) *(G-9326)*

Rex Materials Inc 434 447-7659
601 Bailey St South Hill (23970) *(G-12858)*

Rex Materials of Virginia, South Hill Also called Rex Materials Inc *(G-12858)*

Rex Multiservices LLC 703 400-1739
21818 Goldstone Ter Sterling (20164) *(G-13493)*

Rex Roto Corporation 434 447-6854
601 Bailey St South Hill (23970) *(G-12859)*

Rexcon Metals LLC 703 347-2836
7621 Mendota Pl Springfield (22150) *(G-13079)*

Rexnord Industries LLC 540 337-3510
150 Johnson Dr Stuarts Draft (24477) *(G-13658)*

Rexnord Industries LLC 540 337-3510
150 Johnson Dr Stuarts Draft (24477) *(G-13659)*

Rexrode Timber & Excavation 540 474-5892
6492 Potomac River Rd Monterey (24465) *(G-9013)*

Reyco Global LLC 719 321-6747
5213 Grinnell St Fairfax (22032) *(G-4541)*

Reynolds Cnsmr Pdts Hldngs Inc 540 249-5711
149 Grand Caverns Dr Grottoes (24441) *(G-6024)*

Reynolds Consumer Products LLC 804 230-5200
7th & Bainbridge Richmond (23219) *(G-11735)*

Reynolds Consumer Products LLC 804 743-6000
2101 Reymet Rd North Chesterfield (23237) *(G-9959)*

Reynolds Container Corporation 276 647-8451
2249 Virginia Ave Collinsville (24078) *(G-3715)*

Reynolds Edward General Contr, Woodford Also called Reynolds Timber Inc *(G-15842)*

Reynolds Foil - Richmond Plant, Richmond Also called Reynolds Consumer Products LLC *(G-11735)*

Reynolds Food Packaging LLC (HQ) 800 446-3020
6601 W Broad St Richmond (23230) *(G-11352)*

Reynolds Metals Company LLC 804 746-6723
6641 W Broad St Richmond (23230) *(G-11353)*

Reynolds Presto Products Inc 434 572-6961
2225 Philpott Rd South Boston (24592) *(G-12788)*

Reynolds Timber Inc 804 633-6117
12040 Minarchi Rd Woodford (22580) *(G-15842)*

Rezgateway 703 286-5331
11654 Plaza America Dr # 64 Reston (20190) *(G-10940)*

RG Boatworks LLC 804 784-1991
110 Alice Run Manakin Sabot (23103) *(G-7904)*

Rga LLC 804 794-1592
1550 Standing Ridge Dr Powhatan (23139) *(G-10571)*

Rgolf Inc 540 443-9296
2000 Kraft Dr Ste 2180 Blacksburg (24060) *(G-1783)*

RH Ceramics 760 880-4088
8500 Tidewater Dr Apt 36 Norfolk (23503) *(G-9707)*

Rhenus Automotive Salem LLC 270 282-2100
6450 Technology Dr Salem (24153) *(G-12561)*

Rhinos Ink Screen Prtg & EMB 540 347-3303
268 Broadview Ave Warrenton (20186) *(G-15047)*

Rhoades Enterprise 804 347-2051
3843 Slagles Lake Rd Emporia (23847) *(G-4366)*

RI Software Corp 301 537-1593
905 Towering Oak Ct Purcellville (20132) *(G-10675)*

Ribbons & Sweet Memories 757 874-1871
685 Turnberry Blvd # 15362 Newport News (23608) *(G-9327)*

Rice S Stake & Wood Products 804 769-3272
6858 King William Rd Aylett (23009) *(G-1552)*

Rich Patch Quarry, Lowmoor Also called Boxley Materials Company *(G-7598)*

Rich Young 757 472-2057
751 Hecate Dr Virginia Beach (23454) *(G-14771)*

Richard A Daily Dr 540 586-4030
4171 Roaring Run Rd Goode (24556) *(G-5893)*

Richard A Landes 540 885-1454
297 Commerce Rd Staunton (24401) *(G-13285)*

Richard C Iroler 276 236-3796
8703 Riverside Dr Fries (24330) *(G-5517)*

Richard E Sheppard Jr 276 956-2322
991 Mica Rd Ridgeway (24148) *(G-11851)*

Richard Evans 540 774-1905
4443 Cordell Dr Ste 101 Roanoke (24018) *(G-11995)*

Richard Handy Title Examiner, Midlothian Also called R A Handy Title Examiner *(G-8885)*

Richard Price 804 731-7270
98 Swindler Hollow Rd Sperryville (22740) *(G-12879)*

Richard Rhea Industries LLC 804 320-6575
10005 Cutter Dr North Chesterfield (23235) *(G-9960)*

Richard Y Lombard Jr 757 499-1967
236 Iroquois Rd Virginia Beach (23462) *(G-14772)*

Richards Michael Mr Mrs 540 854-5812
9704 Lawyers Rd Spotsylvania (22551) *(G-12912)*

Richards Building Supply Co 540 719-0128
66 Builders Pride Rd Hardy (24101) *(G-6289)*

Richards-Wilbert Inc 540 477-3842
330 Nelson St Mount Jackson (22842) *(G-9077)*

Richards-Wilbert Inc 540 389-5240
165 Simms Dr Salem (24153) *(G-12562)*

Richardson Enterprises Inc 804 733-8956
23202 Airport St North Dinwiddie (23803) *(G-10063)*

Richardson Logging 540 373-5756
85 Ringgold Rd Fredericksburg (22405) *(G-5477)*

Richardson Ornamental Iron 757 420-1426
1136 S Military Hwy Chesapeake (23320) *(G-3270)*

Richlands Concrete, Richlands Also called McClure Concrete Products Inc *(G-11019)*

Richlynd Federal LLC 703 354-1500
85 S Bragg St Ste 402 Alexandria (22312) *(G-573)*

Richman News Paper, Richmond Also called Rni Print Services *(G-11744)*

Richman Steel, Smithfield Also called Southern Structural Steel Inc *(G-12741)*

Richmond CLB of Prnt Hse Crfts 804 748-3075
12425 Percival St Chester (23831) *(G-3451)*

Richmond Cold Storage, Smithfield Also called Carolina Cold Storage Inc *(G-12708)*

Richmond Corrugated Box Co 804 222-1300
5301 Corrugated Rd Sandston (23150) *(G-12629)*

Richmond Defense Firm 804 977-0764
4124 E Parham Rd Henrico (23228) *(G-6558)*

Richmond Distributors LLC 804 497-0713
959 Myers St Ste A Richmond (23230) *(G-11354)*

Richmond Equity Ventures LLC 804 837-3523
6806 Paragon Pl Ste 300 Richmond (23230) *(G-11355)*

Richmond Free Press, Richmond Also called Paradigm Communications Inc *(G-11706)*

Richmond Guide, Richmond Also called Cape Fear Publishing Company *(G-11521)*

Richmond Light Co (PA) **804 276-0559**
2301 Falkirk Dr North Chesterfield (23236) *(G-9961)*

Richmond Light Co 804 276-0559
9840 Oxbridge Pl Ste 200 North Chesterfield (23236) *(G-9962)*

Richmond Living LLC 804 266-5202
2607 Cottage Cove Dr Richmond (23233) *(G-11356)*

Richmond Magazine, Richmond Also called Target Communications Inc *(G-11782)*

Richmond Newspaper Inc 804 261-1101
5742 Charles City Cir Richmond (23231) *(G-11357)*

Richmond Newspapers, Richmond Also called Wood Television LLC *(G-11833)*

Richmond Philharmonic Inc 804 673-7400
8100 Three Chopt Rd # 209 Richmond (23229) *(G-11358)*

Richmond Pinball Collective 301 652-8000
9550 Midlothian Tpke # 112 North Chesterfield (23235) *(G-9963)*

Richmond Powder Coating Inc 804 226-4111
504 Babcock Rd Highland Springs (23075) *(G-6856)*

Richmond Pressed Met Works Inc 804 233-8371
506 Maury St Richmond (23224) *(G-11736)*

Richmond Publishing 804 229-6267
8010 Ridge Rd Ste F Richmond (23229) *(G-11359)*

Richmond Ramps Inc 804 932-8507
7414 Club Dr Quinton (23141) *(G-10699)*

Richmond Refacing 804 739-9222
6302 Willow Glen Rd Midlothian (23112) *(G-8888)*

Richmond Schl Hlth & Tech Inc 804 751-9191
751 W Hundred Rd Chester (23836) *(G-3452)*

Richmond Shopping Center Inc 804 648-9015
210 E Main St Richmond (23219) *(G-11737)*

Richmond Steel Inc 804 355-8080
2031 Westwood Ave Richmond (23230) *(G-11360)*

Richmond Steel Boat Works Inc 804 741-0432
9303 Wishart Rd Richmond (23229) *(G-11361)*

Richmond Steel Inc 804 798-4766
11104 Air Park Rd Ashland (23005) *(G-1486)*

Richmond Supply and Svc LLC 804 622-9435
3903 Carolina Ave Richmond (23222) *(G-11738)*

Richmond Thread Lab LLC 757 344-1886
2322 Parkwood Ave Richmond (23220) *(G-11739)*

Richmond Times Dispatch, Mechanicsville Also called Wood Television LLC *(G-8700)*

Richmond Times Dispatch 804 526-7205
16071 Continental Blvd South Chesterfield (23834) *(G-12823)*

Richmond Tooling, South Chesterfield Also called Machine Tool Technology LLC *(G-12813)*

Richmond Tooling Inc 804 520-4173
1830 Ruffin Mill Cir A South Chesterfield (23834) *(G-12824)*

Richmond Top Moving Co 804 441-9702
8500 Jesse Senior Dr Richmond (23229) *(G-11362)*

Richmond Ventures LLC 804 282-5901
2510 Cherrytree Ln North Chesterfield (23235) *(G-9964)*

Richmond Woodworks LLC 804 510-3747
19701 Genito Rd Moseley (23120) *(G-9046)*

Richmond Yellowpages Com 804 565-9170
3604 Monument Ave Richmond (23230) *(G-11363)*

Richmond1040 LLC 407 538-3624
9407 Meredith Creek Ln Glen Allen (23060) *(G-5787)*

Richs Stitches Inc 804 262-3477
4013 Macarthur Ave Richmond (23227) *(G-11364)*

Rick A Debernard Welding Inc 540 834-8348
186 Fisher Ln Fredericksburg (22405) *(G-5478)*

Rick Boyd Stone Cabinet 540 365-2668
1740 King Richard Rd Ferrum (24088) *(G-4978)*

Rick Robbins Bamboo Fly Rods 540 463-2864
974 Sugar Creek Rd Lexington (24450) *(G-7415)*

Rick USA Stamping Corporation 540 980-1327
4783 Wurno Rd Pulaski (24301) *(G-10645)*

Ricks Custom Welding Inc 540 675-1888
62 Homestead Knoll Ln Huntly (22640) *(G-6966)*

Ricks Machine Shop 804 518-5266
124 S Chappell St Petersburg (23803) *(G-10338)*

Ricks Roasters Coffee Co LLC (PA) **540 318-6850**
1304 Interstate Bus Park Fredericksburg (22405) *(G-5479)*

Ridan Publishing 703 349-2028
9685 Lindenbrook St Fairfax (22031) *(G-4542)*

Riddleberger Brothers Inc 540 434-1731
6127 S Valley Pike Mount Crawford (22841) *(G-9058)*

Ride-Away Inc 804 233-8267
7450 Midlothian Tpke North Chesterfield (23225) *(G-10022)*

Ridefauquier 540 270-8247
6757 Beach Rd Warrenton (20187) *(G-15048)*

Ridge Business Solutions LLC 571 241-8714
11890 Sunrise Valley Dr # 2 Reston (20191) *(G-10941)*

Ridge Tool Company 540 672-5150
14100 Old Gordonsville Rd Orange (22960) *(G-10226)*

Ridge Top Welding 540 947-5118
1396 Otter Mountain Dr Blue Ridge (24064) *(G-1855)*

Ridge Valley Alpacas 540 255-9200
1458 Sterrett Rd Fairfield (24435) *(G-4735)*

Ridgeline Incorporated 540 898-7000
4900 Ondura Dr Fredericksburg (22407) *(G-5355)*

Ridgerunner Container LLC 540 662-2005
220 Imboden Dr C Winchester (22603) *(G-15465)*

Riegger Marin 646 896-4739
1700 Masada Way Blacksburg (24060) *(G-1784)*

Rifle Building LLC 518 879-9195
8168 Ships Crossing Rd Norfolk (23518) *(G-9708)*

Rigel Systems Inc 215 715-8950
2492 Quick St Apt 101 Herndon (20171) *(G-6792)*

Rigging Box Inc 703 339-7575
8180 Newington Rd Lorton (22079) *(G-7526)*

Riggins Company LLC 757 826-0525
410 Rotary St Hampton (23661) *(G-6228)*

Riggs Oil Company 276 523-2662
1505 1st Ave E Big Stone Gap (24219) *(G-1714)*

Right Sized Technologies Inc 703 623-9505
22636 Glenn Dr Ste 302 Sterling (20164) *(G-13494)*

Right Tght Wldg Fbrication LLC 757 553-0661
325 Hospital Dr Virginia Beach (23452) *(G-14773)*

Rightway Industries Ltd 757 435-8889
1236 Hickman Arch Virginia Beach (23454) *(G-14774)*

Riina Mettas Jewelry LLC 202 368-9819
11831 Limoux Pl Woodbridge (22192) *(G-15795)*

Rimfire Games LLC 703 580-4495
15205 Spotted Turtle Ct Woodbridge (22193) *(G-15796)*

Rinehart Technology Svcs LLC 804 744-7891
2740 Ionis Ln Midlothian (23112) *(G-8889)*

Ring Fire Manufacturing LLC 804 617-9288
7642 Phillips Woods Dr Henrico (23231) *(G-6559)*

Rinker Materials S Centl Inc 276 628-9337
21339 Gravel Lake Rd Abingdon (24210) *(G-58)*

Rio Graphics Inc 757 467-9207
4676 Princess Anne Rd # 180 Virginia Beach (23462) *(G-14775)*

Rio Take Back LLC 540 371-3636
70 Sebring Dr Fredericksburg (22406) *(G-5480)*

Rip Shears LLC 757 635-9560
3432 Archer Ct Virginia Beach (23452) *(G-14776)*

Rising Edge Technologies Inc 703 471-8108
8300 Greensboro Dr # 620 Mc Lean (22102) *(G-8538)*

Risque Custom Cabinetry 703 534-5319
6640 Barrett Rd Falls Church (22042) *(G-4867)*

Risser Farms Inc 804 387-8584
8266 E Lord Btetourt Loop New Kent (23124) *(G-9138)*

Rite Print Shoppe & Supply 540 745-3616
126 N Locust St Floyd (24091) *(G-5038)*

(G-0000) Company's Geographic Section entry number

Ritemade Paper Converters Inc 800 821-5484
11760 N Lakeridge Pkwy Ashland (23005) *(G-1487)*

Ritter Welding 703 680-9601
3804 Claremont Ln Woodbridge (22193) *(G-15797)*

Ritz Refinishing Inc 703 378-0462
14043 Willard Rd Chantilly (20151) *(G-2487)*

Rivah Vineyards At Grove LLC 804 472-3734
751 Kinsale Bridge Rd Kinsale (22488) *(G-7137)*

Rivanna Medical LLC 828 612-8191
107 E Water St Charlottesville (22902) *(G-2863)*

Rivanna Natural Designs Inc 434 244-3447
3009 Lincoln Ave Henrico (23228) *(G-6560)*

Rivanna Pubg Ventures LLC 202 549-7940
1612 Inglewood Dr Charlottesville (22901) *(G-2685)*

Rivanna Software LLC 434 806-6105
1075 Still Meadow Xing Charlottesville (22901) *(G-2686)*

Rivanna Water & Observatory 434 973-5709
2385 Woodburn Rd Charlottesville (22901) *(G-2687)*

River City Cabinetry LLC 804 397-7950
4102 Hilltop Farms Ter Chester (23831) *(G-3453)*

River City Chocolate LLC 804 317-8161
12613 Village School Ln Midlothian (23112) *(G-8890)*

River City Cider LLC 804 420-9683
3224 E Branch Loop Roseland (22967) *(G-12372)*

River City Graphics LLC 757 519-9525
501 Progress Ln Virginia Beach (23454) *(G-14777)*

River City Printing Graphics 804 226-8100
4301 Nine Mile Rd Richmond (23223) *(G-11740)*

River City Publishing Inc 804 240-9115
11 S 12th St Richmond (23219) *(G-11741)*

River City Sign Company 804 687-1466
14430 W Salisbury Rd Midlothian (23113) *(G-8891)*

River City Wrap LLC 804 914-7325
3912 Mill Manor Dr Midlothian (23112) *(G-8892)*

River Company Rest & Brewry I 540 633-6731
6580 Valley Center Dr # 322 Radford (24141) *(G-10738)*

River Cy & Flame Sauces & Rubs, Richmond *Also called Chilli Richmond LLC* *(G-11530)*

River House Creations LLC 757 509-2137
2551 Red Bank Rd Gloucester (23061) *(G-5859)*

River Ridge Meats LLC 276 773-2191
226 Industrial Ln Independence (24348) *(G-6993)*

River Rock Custom Baits LLC 540 414-3293
547 Cattle Scales Rd Waynesboro (22980) *(G-15135)*

River Rock Environmental Svcs 757 690-3916
536 Wilroy Rd Suffolk (23434) *(G-13759)*

River Rock Wood Working 540 828-2358
8057 George Wine Rd Bridgewater (22812) *(G-1957)*

River Technologies LLC 434 525-4734
2107 Graves Mill Rd Ste A Forest (24551) *(G-5090)*

River Valley Custom Millwork 540 438-0208
975 Cottontail Trl Mount Crawford (22841) *(G-9059)*

Riveras Tortillas 703 368-1249
10953 Lute Ct Manassas (20109) *(G-8145)*

Riverbend Sawmill, Leesburg *Also called Talon Inc* *(G-7358)*

Rivercity Communications 804 304-9590
7311 Osborne Tpke Henrico (23231) *(G-6561)*

Riverfarm Woodworks LLC 571 721-0988
3909 Belle Rive Ter Alexandria (22309) *(G-574)*

Riverine Jet Boats 434 258-5874
122 Rocky Hill Rd Madison Heights (24572) *(G-7883)*

Riverland Inc 703 760-9300
1980 Chain Bridge Rd Mc Lean (22102) *(G-8539)*

Riverland Solutions Corp 571 247-2382
42993 Buna Mae Ln Leesburg (20176) *(G-7337)*

Riversedge Furniture Co Inc (PA) **434 847-4155**
107 Hexham Dr Lynchburg (24502) *(G-7802)*

Riverside Diagnostic Center, Newport News *Also called Riverside Healthcare Assn Inc* *(G-9328)*

Riverside Healthcare Assn Inc 757 594-3900
895 Middle Ground Blvd Newport News (23606) *(G-9328)*

Riverside Hydraulics LLC 804 545-6700
11027 Leadbetter Rd Ashland (23005) *(G-1488)*

Riverside Roof Truss LLC 434 793-0217
733 River Park Dr Danville (24540) *(G-4035)*

Riverstone Group LLC 804 643-4200
800 E Canal St Richmond (23219) *(G-11742)*

Riviana Foods Inc 540 722-9830
300 Park Center Dr Winchester (22603) *(G-15466)*

Riyan Industries 703 525-6132
4745 Lee Hwy Arlington (22207) *(G-1148)*

Rjm Technologies Inc 703 323-6677
9620 Maury Rd Fairfax (22032) *(G-4543)*

RJR Provisions & Packaging LLC 804 649-7400
1706 Floyd Ave Ste C Richmond (23220) *(G-11743)*

Rk Publishing Company LLC 434 249-9926
935 Rock Creek Rd Charlottesville (22903) *(G-2864)*

Rkf Farms, Verona *Also called Rolling Knoll Farm Inc* *(G-13994)*

Rki Instruments Inc 703 753-3333
6227 Olga Ct Haymarket (20169) *(G-6441)*

RI Byrd Properties 757 817-7920
169 Goodwin Neck Rd Yorktown (23692) *(G-15988)*

RI Logistics LLC 703 209-3100
818 N Quincy St Apt 501 Arlington (22203) *(G-1149)*

Rls Cartage LLC 540 447-0668
1504 Mulberry St Waynesboro (22980) *(G-15136)*

Rmae Inc 804 651-6911
601 E Washington St Petersburg (23803) *(G-10339)*

Rmj Machine Technologies Inc 434 582-4719
171 Jordan Dr Lynchburg (24502) *(G-7803)*

Rng LLC 540 825-5322
425 Meadowbrook Ctr Culpeper (22701) *(G-3917)*

Rni Print Services 804 649-6670
300 E Franklin St Richmond (23219) *(G-11744)*

Rnk Outdoors 540 797-3698
3022 Pioneer Rd Nw Roanoke (24012) *(G-12163)*

Ro-Way Inc 757 566-3569
201 Norman Davis Dr Toano (23168) *(G-13876)*

Road & Rail Repair Inc 757 558-1920
2233 Battery Park Rd Chesapeake (23323) *(G-3271)*

Road Rnner MBL Wldg Fbrction L 757 915-2077
506 Copeland Dr Ste C Hampton (23661) *(G-6229)*

Road Runner Hold Co LLC 703 345-2400
13241 Woodland Park Rd Herndon (20171) *(G-6793)*

Roadglobe LLC 804 519-3331
2975 Stone Creek Dr Sandy Hook (23153) *(G-12645)*

Roadrnner MBL Wldg Fabrication, Hampton *Also called Road Rnner MBL Wldg Fbrction L* *(G-6229)*

Roanoke 540 362-8404
1255 Trapper Cir Nw Roanoke (24012) *(G-12164)*

Roanoke Cement Company LLC 540 631-1335
33 Prezanis Way Front Royal (22630) *(G-5550)*

Roanoke Cement Company LLC (HQ) **540 992-1501**
6071 Catawba Rd Troutville (24175) *(G-13915)*

Roanoke Concrete Supply Co, Rockingham *Also called Rockingham Redi-Mix Inc* *(G-12275)*

Roanoke Division, Salem *Also called R R Donnelley & Sons Company* *(G-12560)*

Roanoke Electric Steel Corp (HQ) **540 342-1831**
102 Westside Blvd Nw Roanoke (24017) *(G-12165)*

Roanoke Electric Works 540 992-3203
7466 Lee Hwy Troutville (24175) *(G-13916)*

Roanoke Hose & Fittings (PA) **540 985-4832**
625 Salem Ave Sw Roanoke (24016) *(G-12166)*

Roanoke Plant, Roanoke *Also called Boxley Materials Company* *(G-11893)*

Roanoke Star Sentinel 540 400-0990
2408 Stanley Ave Se Roanoke (24014) *(G-12167)*

Roanoke Stars 540 797-8266
6451 Archcrest Dr Apt 102 Roanoke (24019) *(G-11996)*

Roanoke Times, The, Roanoke *Also called Times-World LLC* *(G-12205)*

Roanoke Tribune 540 343-0326
2318 Melrose Ave Nw Roanoke (24017) *(G-12168)*

Roasted Bean Coffee & Repair 434 242-8522
19 Pleasant View Dr Waynesboro (22980) *(G-15137)*

Roasters Pride Inc 703 440-0627
7516 Fullerton Rd D Springfield (22153) *(G-13080)*

Robbworks LLC 571 218-5532
4182 Lord Culpeper Ln Fairfax (22030) *(G-4669)*

Robert Agnello 757 345-0829
2887 Hidden Lake Dr Williamsburg (23185) *(G-15306)*

Robert Allen, Bedford *Also called Kidwell Construction LLC* *(G-1642)*

Robert C Reed 804 493-7297
296 Federal Farm Rd Montross (22520) *(G-9027)*

Robert D Gregory 276 632-9170
235 Wind Dancer Ln Ridgeway (24148) *(G-11852)*

Robert David Rosson 540 456-6173
8720 Rockfish Gap Tpke Afton (22920) *(G-87)*

Robert Deitrich 804 793-8414
251 Manor Pl Danville (24541) *(G-4036)*

Robert Deluca 540 948-5864
74 Foothills Ln Brightwood (22715) *(G-1962)*

Robert Denton 703 435-6960
790 Station St Herndon (20170) *(G-6794)*

Robert Douglas LLC 434 284-5111
307 Westfield Rd Charlottesville (22901) *(G-2688)*

Robert E Carroll Logging Inc 434 636-2168
486 Robinson Ferry Rd Ebony (23845) *(G-4298)*

Robert E Horne 804 920-1847
10416 Lamore Dr Disputanta (23842) *(G-4113)*

Robert Furr Cabinet Shop 757 244-1267
2542 W Pembroke Ave Hampton (23661) *(G-6230)*

Robert Grogg 540 667-4279
3641 Apple Pie Ridge Rd Winchester (22603) *(G-15467)*

Robert H Giles Jr 540 808-6334
509 Fairview Ave Blacksburg (24060) *(G-1785)*

Robert K Montgomery II 804 730-0361
8561 Anderson Ct Mechanicsville (23116) *(G-8671)*

Robert L Penn 276 629-2211
112 Stoneyridge Rd Bassett (24055) *(G-1591)*

Robert Lewis..917 640-0709
1279 W 10th St Ste 114 Blackstone (23824) *(G-1826)*

Robert Lummus.....................................540 313-4393
934 Baker Ln Ste D Winchester (22603) *(G-15468)*

Robert Montgomery..............................703 737-0491
319 E Market St Leesburg (20176) *(G-7338)*

Robert R Kline.......................................540 454-7003
17707 Lakefield Rd Round Hill (20141) *(G-12387)*

Roberts Screen Printing........................757 487-6285
684 Military Rd Portsmouth (23702) *(G-10476)*

Roberts Screen Printing........................757 487-6285
337 Briarfield Dr Chesapeake (23322) *(G-3272)*

Robertson Lumber Inc...........................434 369-5603
525 7th St Altavista (24517) *(G-639)*

Robertson Lumber Inc...........................434 335-5100
3900 Dews Rd Hurt (24563) *(G-6977)*

Robeys Welding LLC..............................540 974-3811
14280 Lord Fairfax Hwy White Post (22663) *(G-15182)*

Robin Cage Pottery................................804 233-1758
1410 W 43rd St Richmond (23225) *(G-11745)*

Robin Stippich.......................................757 692-5744
317 55th St Newport News (23607) *(G-9329)*

Robinson's Lawn Care, Petersburg *Also called Antonio Robinson (G-10305)*

Robs Welding...540 722-4151
927 Greenwood Rd Winchester (22602) *(G-15469)*

Robson Woodworking.............................540 896-6711
16912 Evergreen Valley Rd Timberville (22853) *(G-13854)*

Rocamed Inc..703 503-3616
2010 Corp Rdg Ste 700 Mc Lean (22102) *(G-8540)*

Rocco Specialty Foods Inc....................540 432-1060
1 Kratzer Ave Harrisonburg (22802) *(G-6362)*

Rochon & Rochon LLC A Fmly Co...........571 331-4860
2472 Potomac River Blvd Dumfries (22026) *(G-4255)*

Rock Hill Lumber Inc.............................540 547-2889
2727 Leon Rd Culpeper (22701) *(G-3918)*

Rock Industries LLC..............................703 637-8500
7600 Lsburg Pike Ste 460e Falls Church (22043) *(G-4868)*

Rock Xpress LLC....................................571 212-6689
8602 Eagle Glen Ter Fairfax Station (22039) *(G-4723)*

Rockbridge East LLC.............................202 701-7927
14445 Watson Ln Apt 5 Woodbridge (22193) *(G-15798)*

Rockbridge Stone Products Inc (PA)....**540 258-2841**
Hc 679 Glasgow (24555) *(G-5701)*

Rockbridge Vineyard Inc.......................540 377-6204
35 Hillview Ln Raphine (24472) *(G-10750)*

Rockfish Baking Company LLC.............703 314-7944
887 Rockfish Orchard Dr Afton (22920) *(G-88)*

Rockhill Resources LLC.........................804 794-6259
1851 Castlebridge Rd Midlothian (23113) *(G-8893)*

Rockin Baby LLC..................................866 855-4378
314 N 32nd St Richmond (23223) *(G-11746)*

Rockin Rack LLC...................................540 359-2264
11274 Falling Creek Dr Bealeton (22712) *(G-1606)*

Rocking Horse Ventures Inc................804 784-5830
10607 Patterson Ave Richmond (23238) *(G-11365)*

Rockingham Precast Inc........................540 433-8282
3330 Kratzer Rd Rockingham (22802) *(G-12272)*

Rockingham Publishing Co Inc (PA)....**540 574-6200**
231 S Liberty St Harrisonburg (22801) *(G-6363)*

Rockingham Publishing Company.........540 298-9444
157 W Spotswood Ave Elkton (22827) *(G-4334)*

Rockingham Redi-Mix Inc (PA).............**540 433-9128**
1557 Garbers Church Rd Rockingham (22801) *(G-12273)*

Rockingham Redi-Mix Inc....................540 433-8282
3330 Kratzer Rd Rockingham (22802) *(G-12274)*

Rockingham Redi-Mix Inc....................540 743-5940
20 Fairlane Dr Luray (22835) *(G-7622)*

Rockingham Redi-Mix Inc....................540 433-9128
380 Waterman Dr Harrisonburg (22802) *(G-6364)*

Rockingham Redi-Mix Inc....................540 433-9128
1557 Garbers Church Rd Rockingham (22801) *(G-12275)*

Rockingham Welding Svc LLC...............540 879-9500
3054 John Wayland Hwy Dayton (22821) *(G-4061)*

Rockridge Cabinetry LLC.....................434 969-2665
3237 Dixie Hill Rd Buckingham (23921) *(G-2135)*

Rockridge Granite Company LLC..........434 969-2665
3143 Dixie Hill Rd Buckingham (23921) *(G-2136)*

Rocks Tiki Surfboard Signs..................757 727-3330
1161 Nansemond Pkwy Suffolk (23434) *(G-13760)*

Rockstar Wraps LLC.............................703 392-7625
8060 Flannery Ct Manassas (20109) *(G-8146)*

Rockwell Automation Inc.....................804 560-6444
9020 Stony Point Pkwy Richmond (23235) *(G-11062)*

Rockwell Collins Inc............................703 234-2100
22640 Davis Dr Sterling (20164) *(G-13495)*

Rockwell Collins Government Sy, Sterling *Also called Rockwell Collins Inc (G-13495)*

Rockwell Collins Simulation.................703 234-2100
22640 Davis Dr Sterling (20164) *(G-13496)*

Rocky Mount Hardwood Inc..................540 483-1428
574 Franklin St Ferrum (24088) *(G-4979)*

Rocky Mount Ready Mix Concrete.........540 483-1288
110 Old Franklin Tpke Rocky Mount (24151) *(G-12350)*

Rocky Ridge Alpacas VA LLC................540 962-6087
6088 Indian Draft Rd Covington (24426) *(G-3795)*

Rocky Ridge Furniture...........................419 512-0067
125 Rose Bush Ln Pearisburg (24134) *(G-10276)*

Rocky Top Embroidery & More..............540 775-9564
7821 Dolleys Ct King George (22485) *(G-7108)*

Rockydale Chrlottesville Quary.............434 295-5700
2430 Rio Mills Rd Earlysville (22936) *(G-4294)*

Rockydale Mundy Quarries, Roanoke *Also called Rockydale Quarries Corporation (G-11997)*

Rockydale Quarries Corp......................540 769-8116
4248 Welcome Valley Rd Se Roanoke (24014) *(G-12169)*

Rockydale Quarries Corporation (PA)...**540 774-1696**
2343 Highland Farm Rd Nw Roanoke (24017) *(G-12170)*

Rockydale Quarries Corporation...........540 886-2111
251 National Ave Staunton (24401) *(G-13286)*

Rockydale Quarries Corporation...........540 896-1441
5925 Starkey Rd Roanoke (24018) *(G-11997)*

Rockydale Quarries Corporation...........540 576-2544
2343 Highland Farm Rd Nw Roanoke (24017) *(G-12171)*

Rod & Staff Welding..............................434 392-3090
2520 W 3rd St Farmville (23901) *(G-4956)*

Rod Fishinfiddler Co.............................703 517-0496
300 N Garfield St Arlington (22201) *(G-1150)*

Rodders Journal....................................804 496-6906
9415 Atlee Commerce Blvd E Ashland (23005) *(G-1489)*

Rodeo Welding LLC..............................571 379-4179
9201 Amelia Ct Manassas (20111) *(G-8147)*

Rodgers Puddings LLC..........................757 558-2657
1410 Poindexter St Chesapeake (23324) *(G-3273)*

Rodgers Services LLC...........................301 848-6384
5327 N Williams Creek Dr King George (22485) *(G-7109)*

Rodriguez Guitars.................................804 358-6324
929 Myers St Richmond (23230) *(G-11366)*

Rodyn Vibration Analysis Inc.............434 326-6797
1501 Gordon Ave Charlottesville (22903) *(G-2865)*

Roger K Williams..................................540 775-3192
8621 Bloomsbury Rd King George (22485) *(G-7110)*

Rogers - Mast-R-Woodwork LLC............540 273-1460
7389 Passapatanzy Dr King George (22485) *(G-7111)*

Rogers Foam Corporation.....................276 431-2641
609 Boone Trail Rd Duffield (24244) *(G-4184)*

Rogers Screen Printing Inc...................703 491-6794
1313 G St Woodbridge (22191) *(G-15799)*

Rogue Cltivation Solutions LLC............540 955-8641
3 Cattlemans Ln Berryville (22611) *(G-1687)*

Rogue Software LLC.............................703 945-9175
3253 Arrowhead Cir Fairfax (22030) *(G-4670)*

Rol-Lift International LLC....................757 650-2040
3955 S Military Hwy Chesapeake (23321) *(G-3274)*

Roland Vault Limited, Norfolk *Also called Roland Vault Ltd (G-9709)*

Roland Vault Ltd....................................757 466-8800
1159 Harmony Rd Norfolk (23502) *(G-9709)*

Role Tea, Springfield *Also called Mkp Products LLC (G-13052)*

Rolhei LLC...202 850-9000
901 Capitol Landing Rd # 8 Williamsburg (23185) *(G-15307)*

Roll of Honor Foundation......................703 731-6109
3819 Hunt Manor Dr Fairfax (22033) *(G-4544)*

Rollarund Fshons For Hndcapped, Goshen *Also called Thelma Rethford (G-5928)*

Rolling Knoll Farm Inc.........................540 569-6476
1146 Lee Hwy Verona (24482) *(G-13994)*

Rolling Thunder Raceway LLC...............336 401-2360
3532 Friends Mission Rd Ararat (24053) *(G-832)*

Rolling With Class LLC.........................804 836-9760
4413 Deertrail Dr North Chesterfield (23234) *(G-9965)*

Rollins Oma Sue...................................757 449-6371
4745 Thoroughgood Dr Virginia Beach (23455) *(G-14778)*

Rollins Meat Processing........................540 672-5177
17212 Rollins Rd Orange (22960) *(G-10227)*

Rolls-Royce Crosspointe LLC (HQ)........**877 787-6247**
8800 Wells Station Rd Prince George (23875) *(G-10606)*

Rollstream Inc.......................................703 277-2150
3913 Old Lee Hwy Ste 33a Fairfax (22030) *(G-4671)*

Roma Sftwr Systems Group Inc............703 437-1579
25227 Bald Eagle Ter South Riding (20152) *(G-12870)*

Romac Publishing LLC..........................703 478-9794
11578 Lake Newport Rd Reston (20194) *(G-10942)*

Romaine Printing..................................804 994-2213
897 Edgar Rd Hanover (23069) *(G-6283)*

Romancing Stone...................................804 769-7888
4917 R Tappahannock Hwy Aylett (23009) *(G-1553)*

Romans Enterprises LLC......................757 216-6401
220 Pennsylvania Ave Virginia Beach (23462) *(G-14779)*

Rome Research Corporation..................757 421-8300
5102 Relay Rd Bldg 352 Chesapeake (23322) *(G-3275)*

Ron Campbell Art and Framing..............540 651-2228
350 Vest Tannery Rd Ne Check (24072) *(G-2945)*

Ronald Carpenter..................................757 471-3805
1917 Rock Lake Loop Virginia Beach (23456) *(G-14780)*

Ronald Carter 571 278-6659
5571 Peppercorn Dr Burke (22015) *(G-2202)*

Ronald Light 540 837-2089
146 Morning Star Ln Boyce (22620) *(G-1911)*

Ronald Paul Gardner 804 815-6529
1818 Creekwood Ct Hayes (23072) *(G-6405)*

Ronald Stephen Rhodes 540 435-1441
2937 Minie Ball Ln Keezletown (22832) *(G-7029)*

Ronald Steven Hamm 434 295-8878
1304 East Market St Ste T Charlottesville (22902) *(G-2866)*

Ronart Associates 703 362-5373
6805 Bulkley Rd Lorton (22079) *(G-7527)*

Ronbuilt Corporation 276 638-2090
175 Ward Rd Martinsville (24112) *(G-8324)*

Ronnie and Betty Bridges 804 561-4506
12600 Reed Rock Rd Amelia Court House (23002) *(G-670)*

Ronnie D Bryant Htg Coolg LLC 540 221-0988
1266 Hermitage Rd Waynesboro (22980) *(G-15138)*

Rookwood Press Inc 434 971-1835
520 Rookwood Pl Charlottesville (22903) *(G-2867)*

Room The Wishing Inc 804 746-0375
5422 Triangle Ln Hanover (23069) *(G-6284)*

Roop Welding & General Repair 276 346-3338
Rr 4 Jonesville (24263) *(G-7023)*

Roosters Amish Sheds 540 263-2415
411 E King St Strasburg (22657) *(G-13595)*

Root Group LLC 703 595-7008
41125 Grenata Preserve Pl Leesburg (20175) *(G-7339)*

Rorrer Timber Co Inc 276 694-6304
4515 Moorefield Store Rd Stuart (24171) *(G-13628)*

Rosa Darby Winery LLC 804 561-7492
10390 Thompkins Ln Amelia Court House (23002) *(G-671)*

Rose Paving and Seal Coating, North Chesterfield *Also called Hughie C Rose* *(G-9888)*

Rose Welding Inc 540 312-0138
322 Red Brush Rd New Castle (24127) *(G-9123)*

Rose Winston Designs 703 717-2264
3801 Ridge Knoll Ct 3-A Fairfax (22033) *(G-4545)*

Roseann Combs 757 228-1795
3407 Chesapeake Blvd Norfolk (23513) *(G-9710)*

Rosemont Industries, Marion *Also called Laura Copenhaver Industries* *(G-8230)*

Rosemont of Virginia LLC 434 636-4372
1050 Blackridge Rd La Crosse (23950) *(G-7150)*

Rosemont Vineyards, La Crosse *Also called Rosemont of Virginia LLC* *(G-7150)*

Rosetta Stone Inc (PA) 703 387-5800
1621 N Kent St Ste 1200 Arlington (22209) *(G-1151)*

Rosetta Stone Ltd (HQ) 540 432-6166
135 W Market St Harrisonburg (22801) *(G-6365)*

Ross Enterprise, Norfolk *Also called Deborah E Ross* *(G-9521)*

Ross Industries Inc (PA) 540 439-3271
5321 Midland Rd Midland (22728) *(G-8762)*

Ross Publishing Inc 804 674-5004
711 Moorefield Park Dr H North Chesterfield (23236) *(G-9966)*

Rosworks LLC 804 282-3111
2821 Ellwood Ave Richmond (23221) *(G-11747)*

Roto Rays Inc 703 437-3353
722 Park Ave Herndon (20170) *(G-6795)*

Roto-Die Company Inc 276 952-2026
225 Jeb Stuart Hwy Meadows of Dan (24120) *(G-8593)*

Rotometric Group, The, Meadows of Dan *Also called Roto-Die Company Inc* *(G-8593)*

Rotondo Envmtl Solutions LLC 703 212-4830
4950 Eisenhower Ave C Alexandria (22304) *(G-329)*

Rotondo Precast, Fredericksburg *Also called Oldcastle Infrastructure Inc* *(G-5339)*

Roubin and Janeiro Inc 703 573-9350
8550 Lee Hwy Ste 700 Fairfax (22031) *(G-4546)*

Rough Industries LLC 215 514-4144
317 E Custis Ave Alexandria (22301) *(G-330)*

Round House 804 443-4813
3079 Daingerfield Lndg Champlain (22438) *(G-2356)*

Round House LLC 757 504-3142
2701 Williamsburg St # 103 Alexandria (22314) *(G-331)*

Round Meadows Cabinet Shop 276 398-1153
1886 Fireside Dr Laurel Fork (24352) *(G-7175)*

Rouse Wholesale 276 445-3220
Rr 1 Box 767 Rose Hill (24281) *(G-12362)*

Route 11 Potato Chips, Mount Jackson *Also called Small Fry Inc* *(G-9078)*

Route 11 Potato Chips, Mount Jackson *Also called Tabard Corporation* *(G-9081)*

Route 58 Raceway Inc 434 441-3903
2203 S Boston Rd Danville (24540) *(G-4037)*

Routemarket Inc 703 829-7087
2200 N Westmoreland St Arlington (22213) *(G-1152)*

Rowe Concrete, Stafford *Also called Chaney Enterprises Ltd Partnr* *(G-13129)*

Rowe Concrete Supply Store 540 710-7693
8520 Indian Hills Ct Fredericksburg (22407) *(G-5356)*

Rowe Fine Furniture Inc (PA) 540 444-7693
2121 Gardner St Elliston (24087) *(G-4348)*

Rowe Fine Furniture Inc 540 389-8661
1972 Salem Industrial Dr Salem (24153) *(G-12563)*

Rowe Furniture Inc 540 389-8671
2121 Gardner St Elliston (24087) *(G-4349)*

Rowing Team LLC 855 462-7238
4435 Waterfront Dr # 300 Glen Allen (23060) *(G-5788)*

Rowley Group Inc 703 522-1944
4001 9th St N Ste 102 Arlington (22203) *(G-1153)*

Rox Chox & Woodworking LLC 703 378-1313
1008 Charlton Pl Herndon (20170) *(G-6796)*

Roxann Robinson Delegate 804 308-1534
1904 Hull St Richmond (23224) *(G-11748)*

Roxannas Candles 804 243-9697
3800 Conway Rd Chesapeake (23322) *(G-3276)*

Roxen Incorporated 571 208-0782
9774 Center St Manassas (20110) *(G-7997)*

Royal Building Products, Marion *Also called Royal Group Inc* *(G-8242)*

Royal County Arts, Lynchburg *Also called Q P I Inc* *(G-7795)*

Royal Courtyard 757 431-0045
329 Birchwood Park Dr Virginia Beach (23452) *(G-14781)*

Royal Crown Bottling Company 540 667-1821
2927 Shawnee Dr Winchester (22601) *(G-15580)*

Royal Crown Btlg Wnchester Inc (PA) **540 667-1821**
2927 Shawnee Dr Winchester (22601) *(G-15581)*

Royal Elements LLC 540 338-2591
35461 Sassafras Dr Round Hill (20141) *(G-12388)*

Royal Fern Publishing LLC 703 759-0264
9603 Georgetown Pike Great Falls (22066) *(G-5978)*

Royal Group Inc 276 783-8161
135 Bear Creek Rd Marion (24354) *(G-8242)*

Royal Oak Peanuts LLC 434 658-9500
13009 Cedar View Rd Drewryville (23844) *(G-4138)*

Royal Printing Company 804 798-8897
11058 Washington Hwy # 5 Glen Allen (23059) *(G-5789)*

Royal Silver Mfg Co Inc 757 855-6004
3300 Chesapeake Blvd Norfolk (23513) *(G-9711)*

Royal Standard Minerals Inc 804 580-8107
3258 Mob Neck Rd Heathsville (22473) *(G-6464)*

Royal Tee LLC 540 892-7694
2014 N Parham Rd Richmond (23229) *(G-11367)*

Royalcanvascom 866 673-6110
120 Bruton Ct Chesapeake (23322) *(G-3277)*

Royalty Luxurious Hair, Virginia Beach *Also called Gray Shuntina* *(G-14489)*

Roys Copies 804 744-6200
13531 E Boundary Rd Ste B Midlothian (23112) *(G-8894)*

Royster Printing Services Inc 757 545-3019
1300 Priority Ln Chesapeake (23324) *(G-3278)*

RP Finch Inc 757 566-8022
201 Stonehouse Rd Williamsburg (23188) *(G-15308)*

Rp55 Inc (PA) **757 428-0300**
520 Viking Dr Virginia Beach (23452) *(G-14782)*

RPC Superfos Us Inc 540 504-7176
411 Brooke Rd Winchester (22603) *(G-15470)*

RPC Tubes 703 471-5659
104 Carpenter Dr Sterling (20164) *(G-13497)*

RPI AAR Railroad Tank Car Prj 540 822-4800
13541 Taylorstown Rd Leesburg (20176) *(G-7340)*

RPM 3d Printing 757 266-3168
1302 Elk Ct Virginia Beach (23464) *(G-14783)*

RPM Engineering, Virginia Beach *Also called Rubber Plastic Met Engrg Corp* *(G-14785)*

RPS Shenandoah Inc 540 635-2131
211 E 4th St Front Royal (22630) *(G-5551)*

RR Beasley Beasley Concreting, Milford *Also called Beasley Concrete Inc* *(G-8928)*

Rrb Industries Inc 804 517-2014
3848 Chancery Ln Virginia Beach (23452) *(G-14784)*

Rrb Industries Inc 804 396-3270
8808 Metro Ct North Chesterfield (23237) *(G-9967)*

Rsa Security LLC 703 288-9300
8230 Leesburg Pike # 620 Vienna (22182) *(G-14118)*

Rsi LLC 908 752-1496
8135 Harper Valley Ln Falls Church (22042) *(G-4869)*

Rsindustries, Falls Church *Also called Rsi LLC* *(G-4869)*

Rsk Inc 703 330-1959
10384 Portsmouth Rd Manassas (20109) *(G-8148)*

RSM, Virginia Beach *Also called Ragan Sheet Metal Inc* *(G-14757)*

RSR Industries LLC 703 408-8048
8602 Woodland Heights Ct Alexandria (22309) *(G-575)*

Rsshutterlee LLC 540 290-3712
3007 Shutterlee Mill Rd Staunton (24401) *(G-13287)*

Rst Machine Service Ltd 276 236-8623
466 Shepherd Pl Galax (24333) *(G-5647)*

Rsvp Richmond, Midlothian *Also called Moss Marketing Company Inc* *(G-8862)*

Rt 100 Welding Fab Machin 276 766-0100
121 Lone Ash Rd Barren Springs (24313) *(G-1575)*

Rt Door Co LLC 540 962-0903
222 E Parrish St Covington (24426) *(G-3796)*

Rt Logging LLC 276 452-2258
154 Belgian Dr Gate City (24251) *(G-5666)*

RTC, Manassas *Also called Ready To Cover Inc* *(G-8140)*

Rth Innovations LLC 804 384-6767
5276 Hickory Fork Rd Gloucester (23061) *(G-5860)*

Rubber Plas Div Frnkln/Crtland, Courtland *Also called Arkema Inc* *(G-3766)*

Rubber Plastic Met Engrg Corp 757 502-5462
2533 Aviator Dr Virginia Beach (23453) **(G-14785)**

Rubbermaid Commercial Pdts LLC (HQ) **540 667-8700**
3124 Valley Ave Winchester (22601) **(G-15582)**

Rubbermaid Commercial Pdts LLC 540 542-8195
125 Apple Valley Rd Winchester (22602) **(G-15471)**

Rubinas Adornments Inc 757 623-4246
712 Michigan Ave Norfolk (23508) **(G-9712)**

Rubins Company Mj Inc 571 437-7298
1129 Artic Quill Rd Herndon (20170) **(G-6797)**

Ruby Salts Oyster Company LLC 757 331-1495
2345 Cherrystone Rd Cape Charles (23310) **(G-2236)**

Rubys Embroidery Gems 703 590-7902
11990 San Ysidro Ct Woodbridge (22192) **(G-15800)**

Ruffin & Payne Incorporated 804 329-2691
4200 Vawter Ave Richmond (23222) **(G-11749)**

Rufina Inc 703 577-2333
6423 Crosswoods Dr Falls Church (22044) **(G-4870)**

Rugged Evolution Incorporated 757 478-2430
424 Vespasian Cir Chesapeake (23322) **(G-3279)**

Rugger Industries LLC 540 450-7281
104 Norfolk Ct Winchester (22602) **(G-15472)**

Rural Life Journal LLC 301 774-0305
817 S Royal St Alexandria (22314) **(G-332)**

Rural Rtreat Wnery Vnyards LLC 276 686-8300
201 Church St Rural Retreat (24368) **(G-12431)**

Rural Squirrel LLC 540 364-2281
4003 Whiting Rd Marshall (20115) **(G-8259)**

Rusolf S Olszyk 757 565-2970
122 Deal Williamsburg (23188) **(G-15309)**

Russ Fine Woods Inc 434 974-6504
1306 Knoll St Charlottesville (22902) **(G-2868)**

Russell Frye LLC 276 646-1293
651 Colecrest Dr Chilhowie (24319) **(G-3559)**

Russell Meat Packing Inc 276 794-7600
315 Sulphur Springs Cir Castlewood (24224) **(G-2256)**

Ruststop USA LLC 218 391-5389
5 Garfield St Stafford (22556) **(G-13186)**

Rusty Bear Woodworks LLC 540 327-6579
827 Fall Run Ln Winchester (22602) **(G-15473)**

Rutherford Bean 757 898-4363
1504 Back Creek Rd Seaford (23696) **(G-12677)**

Rutherford Controls Intl Corp (HQ) **757 427-1230**
2517 Squadron Ct Ste 104 Virginia Beach (23453) **(G-14786)**

Rutrough Cabinets Inc 540 489-3211
7101 Six Mile Post Rd Rocky Mount (24151) **(G-12351)**

Rva Boatworks LLC 804 937-7448
9950 Hoke Brady Rd Richmond (23231) **(G-11368)**

Rva Coffee LLC 804 822-2015
1110b E Main St Richmond (23219) **(G-11750)**

Rva Custom Signs Inc 804 749-4000
2412 Gran Ridge Rd Ste 2 Rockville (23146) **(G-12296)**

Rva Firestopping LLC 804 972-1301
408 German School Rd Richmond (23225) **(G-11751)**

Rva Granites, Amelia Court House *Also called Dimension Stone LLC* **(G-655)**

Rva Magazine 804 349-5890
3512 Floyd Ave Richmond (23221) **(G-11752)**

Rva Signs & Graphic 804 749-4000
2412 Granite Ridge Rd # 2 Rockville (23146) **(G-12297)**

Rva Sweets LLC 540 748-9298
3943 Waterville Ct Apt 14 Henrico (23233) **(G-6562)**

Rva Woodwork LLC 804 840-2345
2545 Westwood Rd Mechanicsville (23111) **(G-8672)**

Rva Woodwork LLC 804 840-2345
5880 Charles City Rd Henrico (23231) **(G-6563)**

Rva Woodworks LLC 804 303-3820
9353 Kings Charter Dr Mechanicsville (23116) **(G-8673)**

Rvmf Inc 614 921-1223
8401 Midlothian Tpke North Chesterfield (23235) **(G-9968)**

Rwh Industries Inc 540 736-8007
9430 Rapidan Dr Fredericksburg (22407) **(G-5357)**

Rwm Inc 540 774-7214
5540 Arthur St Roanoke (24018) **(G-11998)**

Rxhonesty Inc 908 872-2009
1279 Cobble Pond Way Vienna (22182) **(G-14119)**

Ry Fabricating LLC 571 835-0567
9191 Lambs Creek Ch Rd King George (22485) **(G-7112)**

Ryan Studio Inc 703 830-6818
14140 Parke Long Ct Ste N Chantilly (20151) **(G-2488)**

Rycon Inc 571 313-8334
22135 Davis Dr Ste 112 Sterling (20164) **(G-13498)**

Rye Valley Oil Inc 276 677-3750
5807 Charlie Taylor Rd Sugar Grove (24375) **(G-13788)**

Rynoh Live 757 333-3760
397 Little Neck Rd Virginia Beach (23452) **(G-14787)**

Ryson International Inc 757 898-1530
300 Newsome Dr Yorktown (23692) **(G-15989)**

Ryzing Technologies LLC 949 244-0240
600 Hays Ave Staunton (24401) **(G-13288)**

Rz Woodworks LLC 626 833-0628
526 Roslyn Ave Colonial Heights (23834) **(G-3744)**

S & D Adkins Logging LLC 434 292-8882
949 Piney Green Rd Crewe (23930) **(G-3815)**

S & J Industries LLC 757 810-8399
5013 Chestnut Fork Rd Gloucester (23061) **(G-5861)**

S & K Industries Inc 703 369-0232
9209 Enterprise Ct Manassas Park (20111) **(G-8209)**

S & K Welding Inc 276 988-5591
8596 Baptist Valley Rd North Tazewell (24630) **(G-10106)**

S & S Backhoe & Excvtr Svc LLC 434 656-3184
1193 Player Rd Gretna (24557) **(G-6010)**

S & S Equipment Sls & Svc Inc 757 421-3000
1753 West Rd Chesapeake (23323) **(G-3280)**

S & S Mixed Signs Inc 804 642-2641
4041 George Wash Mem Hwy Hayes (23072) **(G-6406)**

S A Halac Iron Works Inc 703 406-4766
21675 Ashgrove Ct Sterling (20166) **(G-13499)**

S and H Publishing Inc 703 915-0913
15573 Woodgrove Rd Hillsboro (20132) **(G-6878)**

S B Auto Transport LLC 757 775-3884
1831 Lincolnshire Pl Virginia Beach (23464) **(G-14788)**

S Brown Trucking, Ford *Also called Samuel L Brown* **(G-5047)**

S Conley Welding Company 540 436-3775
262 Half Moon Ln Star Tannery (22654) **(G-13237)**

S E Greer 540 400-0155
3225 Deer Path Trl Roanoke (24014) **(G-12172)**

S Fuel Co 434 220-1044
901 East Market St Charlottesville (22902) **(G-2869)**

S Harman Machine Shop Inc 540 343-9304
2141 Loudon Ave Nw Roanoke (24017) **(G-12173)**

S J Printing Inc 703 378-7142
9105 Owens Dr Manassas Park (20111) **(G-8210)**

S Joye & Son Inc 804 745-2419
2612 Goodes Bridge Rd C North Chesterfield (23224) **(G-10023)**

S K Circuits Inc 703 376-8718
4094 Majestic Ln Fairfax (22033) **(G-4547)**

S N L Finishing 540 740-3826
356 Sangers Ln Staunton (24401) **(G-13289)**

S P Kinney Engineers Inc 804 520-4700
16301 Jefferson Davis Hwy South Chesterfield (23834) **(G-12825)**

S R Firearm & Engraving Co, Big Island *Also called Alexander M Robertson* **(G-1701)**

S R Jones Jr & Sons Inc 434 577-2311
8356 Christanna Hwy Gasburg (23857) **(G-5660)**

S S C 9717-5, Chantilly *Also called Southern States Coop Inc* **(G-2495)**

S S C South Boston Petro Svc, South Boston *Also called Southern States Coop Inc* **(G-12791)**

S Software Development System 571 633-0554
1359 Northwyck Ct Mc Lean (22102) **(G-8541)**

S&C Global Products LLC 703 499-3635
10363 Piper Ln Manassas (20110) **(G-7998)**

S&D Industries LLC 901 208-5036
1070 Joyner St Norfolk (23513) **(G-9713)**

S&H Mobile Cleaning Service 540 254-1135
386 Spangler Dr Buchanan (24066) **(G-2126)**

S&M Trucking Inc 540 842-1378
6025 Massaponax Dr Fredericksburg (22407) **(G-5358)**

S&M Trucking Service LLC 980 395-6953
2830 Wakewater Way Woodbridge (22191) **(G-15801)**

S&R Pals Enterprises LLC 540 752-1900
560 Celebrate Virginia Pk Fredericksburg (22406) **(G-5481)**

S&R Transport LLC 757 344-0251
9 Pelican Shores Dr Hampton (23666) **(G-6231)**

S&S Electric Motor Service Inc 540 577-7366
6784 Beach Dr Radford (24141) **(G-10739)**

S&Sprinting 434 581-1983
29661 N James Madison Hwy New Canton (23123) **(G-9119)**

S&T Industries LLC 276 686-4842
215 Scenic Trl Crockett (24323) **(G-3826)**

S3 Mobile Welding & Cutting 757 647-0322
300 Ewell Ln Chesapeake (23322) **(G-3281)**

S3 Tactical LLC 540 667-6947
221 Refuge Church Rd Stephens City (22655) **(G-13321)**

S4 Wood Works LLC 804 299-0454
2820 Hardings Trace Ln Henrico (23233) **(G-6564)**

Sabatini of London 202 277-8227
491 Cameron Station Blvd Alexandria (22304) **(G-333)**

Sabra Dipping Company LLC 804 518-2000
15900 Sabra Way South Chesterfield (23834) **(G-12826)**

Sabra Dipping Company LLC 804 526-5930
15881 Fort Waltall Ct Colonial Heights (23834) **(G-3745)**

Sabra Go Mediterranean 804 518-2000
15881 Sabra Way South Chesterfield (23834) **(G-12827)**

Saco 804 457-3744
4100 Lively Ln Gum Spring (23065) **(G-6044)**

Sacyr Environment USA LLC 202 361-4568
3330 Washington Blvd # 400 Arlington (22201) **(G-1154)**

Saeam Graphics & Sign Inc 703 203-3233
7004 Little River Tpke G Annandale (22003) **(G-780)**

Safe Guard Security Service 276 773-2866
1165 N Independence Ave Independence (24348) **(G-6994)**

(G-0000) Company's Geographic Section entry number

Safe Harbor Press LLC 757 490-1960
5045 Cleveland St Virginia Beach (23462) ***(G-14789)***
Safeguard Printing Promo 804 378-2166
1520 Huguenot Rd Ste 114 Midlothian (23113) ***(G-8895)***
Safehouse Signs Inc 540 366-2480
720 Liberty Rd Ne Roanoke (24012) ***(G-12174)***
Safety 1 Industries LLC 540 635-4673
1330 Progress Dr Front Royal (22630) ***(G-5552)***
Safety Seal Plastics LLC 703 348-4699
18 Blackjack Rd Ste 101 Fredericksburg (22405) ***(G-5482)***
Safety Software Inc 434 296-8789
801 W Main St Ste 100 Charlottesville (22903) ***(G-2870)***
Safetyoffice, Charlottesville *Also called Safety Software Inc* ***(G-2870)***
Saffron Fabs Corporation 703 544-2791
6177 Stonepath Cir Centreville (20120) ***(G-2334)***
Safran Cabin Sterling Inc (HQ) **571 789-1900**
44931 Falcon Pl Sterling (20166) ***(G-13500)***
Safran Usa Inc (HQ) **703 351-9898**
700 S Washington St # 320 Alexandria (22314) ***(G-334)***
Saga Meadery LLC 914 343-0394
200 N Trenton St Apt 2 Arlington (22203) ***(G-1155)***
Sage Defense LLC 703 485-5995
7217 Hyde Rd Falls Church (22043) ***(G-4871)***
Sage Software Inc 503 439-5271
1750 Old Madow Rd Ste 300 Mc Lean (22102) ***(G-8542)***
SAI Beauty LLC 703 864-6372
13616 Pennsboro Dr Chantilly (20151) ***(G-2489)***
SAI Krishna LLC 804 442-7140
2115 Dabney Rd Richmond (23230) ***(G-11369)***
SAI Skin Care, Chantilly *Also called SAI Beauty LLC* ***(G-2489)***
Saicomp LLC 714 421-8967
216 Wisteria Ln Apt 3d Petersburg (23805) ***(G-10340)***
Saiflavor 304 520-9464
310 Cedar St Harrisonburg (22801) ***(G-6366)***
Sailfish LLC 203 570-3553
851 N Glebe Rd Apt 1305 Arlington (22203) ***(G-1156)***
Sailplan Inc 703 217-9658
1589 Regatta Ln Reston (20194) ***(G-10943)***
Saint Marks Publishing 540 551-3590
205 Windy Way Front Royal (22630) ***(G-5553)***
Sajames Publications LLC 434 509-5331
71 Timber Ct Lynchburg (24501) ***(G-7804)***
Sak Consulting 703 220-2020
13016 Sturbridge Rd Lake Ridge (22192) ***(G-7157)***
Sak Industries LLC 202 701-0071
1310 Beulah Rd Vienna (22182) ***(G-14120)***
Salem Custom Cabinets Inc 540 380-4441
2865 Silver Leaf Dr Salem (24153) ***(G-12564)***
Salem Infotech Inc 703 731-9711
2201 Coop Way Ste 600 Herndon (20171) ***(G-6798)***
Salem Prcision Mch Fabrication 434 793-0677
1291 Southside Dr Salem (24153) ***(G-12565)***
Salem Printing Co 540 387-1106
900 Iowa St Salem (24153) ***(G-12566)***
Salem Ready Mix Concrete Inc 540 387-1171
2250 Salem Industrial Dr Salem (24153) ***(G-12567)***
Salem Stone, Dublin *Also called Holston River Quarry Inc* ***(G-4158)***
Salem Stone Corporation 276 228-3452
2377 Atkins Mill Rd Wytheville (24382) ***(G-15908)***
Salem Stone Corporation (PA) **540 674-5556**
5764 Wilderness Rd Dublin (24084) ***(G-4170)***
Salem Stone Corporation 276 766-3449
456 Wysor Hwy Hillsville (24343) ***(G-6899)***
Salem Stone Corporation 276 228-3631
Rr 11 Box 649 Wytheville (24382) ***(G-15909)***
Salem Stone Corporation 540 552-9292
677 Jennelle Rd Blacksburg (24060) ***(G-1786)***
Salem Stone Corporation 276 228-6767
345 Ready Mix Rd Intersta Wytheville (24382) ***(G-15910)***
Salesforce Maps 571 388-4990
922 Rugby Rd Charlottesville (22903) ***(G-2871)***
Salientcontent LLC 571 286-8480
5109 Brentwood Farm Dr Fairfax (22030) ***(G-4672)***
Sallmae LLC 931 472-9467
542 Jackson Cir Fort Lee (23801) ***(G-5132)***
Salmons Dredging Inc 757 426-6824
781 Princess Anne Rd Virginia Beach (23457) ***(G-14790)***
Salsa De Los Flores Inc 757 450-0796
433 Mill Stone Rd Chesapeake (23322) ***(G-3282)***
Salsa Picante Bori 256 874-4074
915 Birchwood Ct Newport News (23608) ***(G-9330)***
Salsa Room 571 489-8422
1524 Spring Hill Rd Mc Lean (22102) ***(G-8543)***
Salt Cedar Publications 434 258-5333
116 Temple Cir Lynchburg (24502) ***(G-7805)***
Salt Soothers LLC 757 412-5867
1544 Bunsen Dr Virginia Beach (23454) ***(G-14791)***
Salt Whistle Bay Partners LLC 540 983-7118
10 S Jefferson St Roanoke (24011) ***(G-12175)***
Saltville Gas Storage Co LLC 276 496-7004
889 Ader Ln Saltville (24370) ***(G-12589)***
Saltville Machine & Welding 276 496-3555
282 Allison Gap Rd Saltville (24370) ***(G-12590)***
Saltville Progress Inc 276 496-5792
226 Panther Ln Saltville (24370) ***(G-12591)***
Salty Sawyer LLC 757 274-1765
2040 Hog Island Rd Surry (23883) ***(G-13800)***
Salus LLC 475 222-3784
3008 Hughsmith Ct Herndon (20171) ***(G-6799)***
Salyer Logging 276 690-0688
165 Thunder Dr Nickelsville (24271) ***(G-9385)***
Sam Belcher & Sons Inc 276 930-2084
6327 Belcher Mountain Rd Woolwine (24185) ***(G-15867)***
Sam English of VA 804 222-7114
2890 Seven Hills Blvd Richmond (23231) ***(G-11370)***
Sam H Hughes Jr 434 263-4432
10271 James River Rd Shipman (22971) ***(G-12698)***
Sam Home Improvements LLC 703 372-6000
43239 Lecroy Cir Leesburg (20176) ***(G-7341)***
Sam Hurt 276 623-1926
402 E Main St Abingdon (24210) ***(G-59)***
Sam Moore Furniture LLC 540 586-8253
1556 Dawn Dr Bedford (24523) ***(G-1656)***
Sama Artfl Intelligence LLC 347 223-2437
4854 Eisenhower Ave # 245 Alexandria (22304) ***(G-335)***
Sambuqcom Inc 703 980-8669
1600 Tysons Blvd Ste 800 Mc Lean (22102) ***(G-8544)***
Samco Textile Prints LLc 571 451-4044
2525 Luckland Way Woodbridge (22191) ***(G-15802)***
Samin Science Usa Inc 571 403-3678
1952 Gallows Rd Ste 110 Vienna (22182) ***(G-14121)***
Sampson Coatings Incorporated 804 359-5011
1900 Ellen Rd Richmond (23230) ***(G-11371)***
Sams Gutter Shop 276 632-6522
1025 Liberty St Martinsville (24112) ***(G-8325)***
Sams Logging Inc 434 661-7137
281 Foxcroft Dr Monroe (24574) ***(G-8995)***
Sams Monograms 703 866-4400
4549 Maxfield Dr Annandale (22003) ***(G-781)***
Samuel Son & Co (usa) Inc 276 415-9970
58 Samuel Way Dr Lebanon (24266) ***(G-7206)***
Samuel L Brown 804 892-5629
10239 Colemans Lake Rd Ford (23850) ***(G-5047)***
Samuel Ross 434 531-9219
224 Spring Rd Bremo Bluff (23022) ***(G-1946)***
Samvit Solutions LLC 703 481-1274
11654 Plaza America Dr # 740 Reston (20190) ***(G-10944)***
San Francisco Bay Press 757 412-5642
522 Spotswood Ave Apt C5 Norfolk (23517) ***(G-9714)***
San Pak Inc 276 647-5390
138 Parkwood Ct Collinsville (24078) ***(G-3716)***
San Roderigo Publishing LLC 703 968-9502
4260 Jefferson Oaks Cir F Fairfax (22033) ***(G-4548)***
San-J International Inc (HQ) **804 226-8333**
6200 Gorman Rd Henrico (23231) ***(G-6565)***
Sand King 434 465-3498
1840 Ruritan Lake Rd Scottsville (24590) ***(G-12666)***
Sand Mountain Sand, Wytheville *Also called Salem Stone Corporation* ***(G-15910)***
Sand Mountain Sand Co 276 228-6767
Ext 77 Ofc I-81 Wytheville (24382) ***(G-15911)***
Sand Mountain Sand Co., Wytheville *Also called Sand Mountain Sand Co* ***(G-15911)***
Sandbox Enterprises 410 999-4666
2457 Terra Cotta Cir Herndon (20171) ***(G-6800)***
Sandbox Family Comm Inc 910 381-7346
2231 Crystal Dr Ste 325 Arlington (22202) ***(G-1157)***
Sandboxx, Arlington *Also called Sandbox Family Comm Inc* ***(G-1157)***
Sandcastle Screen Printing LLC 757 740-0611
5250 Challedon Dr 101 Virginia Beach (23462) ***(G-14792)***
Sanders Brothers Logging Inc 276 995-2416
Rr 1 Box 87 Fort Blackmore (24250) ***(G-5124)***
Sandhurst-Aec LLC 703 533-1413
7653 Leesburg Pike Falls Church (22043) ***(G-4872)***
Sandra Magura 540 318-6947
4 Crosswood Pl Stafford (22554) ***(G-13187)***
Sandra Signs LLC 757 397-4321
141 Monitor Rd Portsmouth (23707) ***(G-10477)***
Sandra Woodward 703 329-7938
119 N Henry St 3a Alexandria (22314) ***(G-336)***
Sands 1b LLC 757 673-1140
5421 Royal Tern Ct Chesapeake (23321) ***(G-3283)***
Sanduja Strategies 202 826-9804
2100 Lee Hwy Apt 308 Arlington (22201) ***(G-1158)***
Sandy Farnham 804 310-6171
20521 Skinquarter Rd Moseley (23120) ***(G-9047)***
Sandy Hobson T/A S H Monograms 804 730-7211
7111 Mechanicsville Tpke Mechanicsville (23111) ***(G-8674)***
Sanfacon Virginia Inc 434 376-2301
933 Sanfacon Rd 18097 Us 933 Sanfacon Road Brookneal (24528) ***(G-2112)***

ALPHABETIC

Sangamon Group LLC 571 969-6881
917 Portner Pl Alexandria (22314) *(G-337)*
Sani LLC 703 596-2296
7361 Lockport Pl Ste D Lorton (22079) *(G-7528)*
Sanitech Corp (PA) **703 339-7001**
7207 Lockport Pl Ste H Lorton (22079) *(G-7529)*
Sanjar Media LLC 703 901-7680
16216 Radburn St Woodbridge (22191) *(G-15803)*
Sanjo Virginia Beach Inc 757 498-0400
465 Progress Ln Virginia Beach (23454) *(G-14793)*
Sanofi-Aventis US LLC 804 651-1595
12407 Duntrune Ct Chesterfield (23838) *(G-3521)*
Sans Screenprint Inc 703 368-6700
7014 Wellington Rd Manassas (20109) *(G-8149)*
Sanskey LLC 703 454-0703
43087 Weatherwood Dr Ashburn (20147) *(G-1331)*
Santa Inc 757 463-3553
101 Malibu Dr Virginia Beach (23452) *(G-14794)*
Santiago Sheet Metal LLC 703 870-4581
6310 S Kings Hwy Apt 104 Alexandria (22306) *(G-576)*
Sanwell Printing Co Inc 276 638-3772
900 Starling Ave Martinsville (24112) *(G-8326)*
Sanxin Wire Die Inc 434 220-0435
2025 Woodbrook Ct Charlottesville (22901) *(G-2689)*
Sapentia LLC 703 269-7191
8220 Crestwood Heights Dr Mc Lean (22102) *(G-8545)*
Sapna Creations 571 276-1480
14539 Picket Oaks Rd Centreville (20121) *(G-2335)*
Sapr3 Associates Inc 501 256-8645
13598 Cedar Run Ln Herndon (20171) *(G-6801)*
Sara Campbell Ltd 617 423-3134
306 Libbie Ave Richmond (23226) *(G-11372)*
Sara Campbell Ltd 703 996-9074
320 Prince St Alexandria (22314) *(G-338)*
Sara Yannuzzi 703 955-2505
1857 Swover Creek Rd Edinburg (22824) *(G-4311)*
Sarandi Manufacturing LLC 540 705-0205
3707 Industrial Dr Broadway (22815) *(G-2095)*
Sardana Sushila 703 256-5091
5801 Quantrell Ave # 201 Alexandria (22312) *(G-577)*
Sarfez Pharmaceuticals Inc 703 759-2565
10402 Dunn Meadow Rd Vienna (22182) *(G-14122)*
Sartomer - Chatham, Chatham *Also called Arkema Inc (G-2919)*
Sas Federal LLC 571 227-7000
1530 Wilson Blvd Ste 800 Arlington (22209) *(G-1159)*
Sas Institute Inc 804 217-8352
4860 Cox Rd Ste 200 Glen Allen (23060) *(G-5790)*
Sas Institute Inc 571 227-7000
1530 Wilson Blvd Ste 800 Arlington (22209) *(G-1160)*
Sashay Communications LLC 703 304-2862
2200 Wilson Blvd 102-329 Arlington (22201) *(G-1161)*
Sassafras Shade Vineyard LLC 804 337-9446
4492 Ladysmith Rd Ruther Glen (22546) *(G-12461)*
Sassy Clothing Blanks LLC 757 473-1980
609 General Gage Rd Virginia Beach (23462) *(G-14795)*
Satcom-Labs LLC 805 427-5556
115 N Lee St Apt 502 Alexandria (22314) *(G-339)*
Satin Solutions LLC 703 218-3481
10560 Main St Fairfax (22030) *(G-4673)*
Sauder Industries, Doswell *Also called Metrie Inc (G-4123)*
Sauder Manufacturing Co 434 372-4151
239 W B St Chase City (23924) *(G-2916)*
Sauder Manufacturing Co 804 897-3400
413 Branchway Rd Ste A North Chesterfield (23236) *(G-9969)*
Saudi Trade Links 703 992-3220
351 Station Rd Berryville (22611) *(G-1688)*
Sauer Brands Inc (PA) **804 359-5786**
2000 W Broad St Richmond (23220) *(G-11753)*
Saunders Custom Woodwork 804 520-4090
106 Waterfront Dr Colonial Heights (23834) *(G-3746)*
Saunders Logging Inc 434 735-8341
1140 Bacon School Rd Saxe (23967) *(G-12648)*
Sav On Signs 540 344-8406
238 W Madison Ave Vinton (24179) *(G-14182)*
Sav-Mor Machine Works Inc 804 356-7582
2305 Commerce Center Dr G Rockville (23146) *(G-12298)*
Savage Thrust Industries LLC 702 405-1045
8449 Mary Jane Dr Manassas (20112) *(G-8150)*
Savage Transparency LLC 760 218-6457
2458 Carnation Ln Chesapeake (23325) *(G-3284)*
Savannah Publications 804 674-1937
11302 Prvdence Creek Mews North Chesterfield (23236) *(G-9970)*
Savi Technology Inc (PA) **571 227-7950**
5285 Shawnee Rd Alexandria (22312) *(G-578)*
Savory Sun VA LLC 540 898-0851
242 Hillcrest Dr Fredericksburg (22401) *(G-5220)*
Savy Designs By Sylvia 757 547-7525
805 Seabrooke Pt Chesapeake (23322) *(G-3285)*
Saw Shop 540 365-0745
1224 Thompson Ridge Rd Ferrum (24088) *(G-4980)*

Sawan Kirpal Publication Ctr, Bowling Green *Also called Science of Spirituality (G-1907)*
Sawarmor LLC 703 779-7719
1306 Hawling Pl Sw Leesburg (20175) *(G-7342)*
Sawdust and Shavings LLC 804 205-8074
976 Swan Ln Ruther Glen (22546) *(G-12462)*
Sawmark Woodworks 540 657-4814
239 Lake Forest Dr Fredericksburg (22406) *(G-5483)*
Sawmill, Covington *Also called Bennett Logging & Lumber Inc (G-3778)*
Sawmill Bottom 276 880-2241
11717 Sandy Ridge Rd Cleveland (24225) *(G-3656)*
Sawmill Creek Wdworkers Forums 757 871-8214
8770 Little England Rd Hayes (23072) *(G-6407)*
Sawyer Logging Inc 276 995-2522
11669 Veterans Mem Hwy Fort Blackmore (24250) *(G-5125)*
Saxsmo Publishing LLC 804 269-0473
6401 Octagon Dr North Chesterfield (23234) *(G-9971)*
Sayre Enterprises Inc 540 291-3800
324 E 32nd St Buena Vista (24416) *(G-2153)*
Sayre Enterprises Inc (PA) **540 291-3808**
45 Natural Bridge Schl Rd Naturl BR STA (24579) *(G-9112)*
Sb Cox Ready Mix Inc 434 292-7300
800 Dearing Ave Blackstone (23824) *(G-1827)*
Sb Cox Ready Mix Inc 804 364-0500
1918a Anderson Hwy Powhatan (23139) *(G-10572)*
Sb Printing LLC 804 247-2404
2107 Dabney Rd Richmond (23230) *(G-11373)*
Sb Welding and Fab LLC 540 955-0797
141 Kinsky Ln Berryville (22611) *(G-1689)*
Sb Woodworks 804 417-7729
7400 Pine Dr Mechanicsville (23111) *(G-8675)*
Sbk Inc 540 427-5029
1216 Sylvan Rd Se Roanoke (24014) *(G-12176)*
SC Medical Overseas Inc 516 935-8500
810 Ford Dr Ste A Norfolk (23523) *(G-9715)*
SC&I of Virginia LLC 804 876-3135
10351 Verdon Rd Doswell (23047) *(G-4124)*
Scadco Publishing LLC 757 484-4878
3613 Pine Rd Portsmouth (23703) *(G-10478)*
Scaffsales International LLC 757 545-5050
828 Seaboard Ave Chesapeake (23324) *(G-3286)*
Scalpscratchers, North Chesterfield *Also called Luxemanes LLC (G-9914)*
Scan Industries LLC 360 320-8244
44017 Lords Valley Ter Ashburn (20147) *(G-1332)*
Scb Sales Inc 540 342-6502
3214 Brightwood Pl Sw Roanoke (24014) *(G-12177)*
Scenethink Inc 434 987-6525
116 E Main St Ste 1 Charlottesville (22902) *(G-2872)*
Scenter of Town LLC 540 372-4145
907 Charles St Fredericksburg (22401) *(G-5221)*
Scents By Scales 757 234-3380
14346 Warwick Blvd # 366 Newport News (23602) *(G-9331)*
Scentual Sun, Forest *Also called Aspire Marketing Corporation (G-5051)*
Scg Sports LLC 540 330-7733
15778 Stewartsville Rd Vinton (24179) *(G-14183)*
Schafer Government Svcs LLC 202 594-4124
3830 9th St N Apt 708w Arlington (22203) *(G-1162)*
Schaffner Mtc LLC 276 228-7943
823 Fairview Rd Wytheville (24382) *(G-15912)*
Schaffner Mtc Transformers, Wytheville *Also called Schaffner Mtc LLC (G-15912)*
Schd, Midlothian *Also called Twfutures Inc (G-8915)*
Schiebel Aircraft Inc (HQ) **540 351-1731**
8464 Virginia Meadows Dr Manassas (20109) *(G-8151)*
Schiebel Technology, Inc, Manassas *Also called Schiebel Aircraft Inc (G-8151)*
Schlotterer Logging 910 376-1623
108 Wintergreen Ln Stafford (22554) *(G-13188)*
Schlumberger Technology Corp 757 546-2472
510 Independence Pkwy Chesapeake (23320) *(G-3287)*
Schlumberger Technology Corp 540 786-6419
11207 Sandusky Ct Fredericksburg (22407) *(G-5359)*
Schmid Embroidery & Design 804 737-4141
510 Eastpark Ct Ste 100 Sandston (23150) *(G-12630)*
Schmids Printing 540 886-9261
124 E Beverley St Staunton (24401) *(G-13290)*
Schmidt Jayme 540 961-1792
1419 N Main St Blacksburg (24060) *(G-1787)*
Schmidt & Bender Incorporated 770 493-9305
204 Mcghee Rd Winchester (22603) *(G-15474)*
Schmitt Realty Holdings Inc 203 453-4334
3900 Technology Ct Sandston (23150) *(G-12631)*
Schneder Elc It Mssion Crtcal 703 968-0300
3975 Fair Ridge Dr S21 Fairfax (22033) *(G-4549)*
Schneider Automation Inc 804 271-7700
7630 Whitepine Rd North Chesterfield (23237) *(G-9972)*
Schneider Electric Usa Inc 703 968-0300
3975 Fair Ridge Dr S210 Fairfax (22033) *(G-4550)*
Schock Metal America Inc 757 549-8300
1230 Scholastic Way Chesapeake (23323) *(G-3288)*
Scholastic Services, Manassas *Also called Herff Jones LLC (G-7952)*

Scholl Custom WD & Met Cft LLC 804 739-2390
  11420 Winterpock Rd Chesterfield (23838) *(G-3522)*
Schorr Wood Works LLC 434 990-1897
  314 Lake Dr Ruckersville (22968) *(G-12413)*
Schrader-Altavista 434 369-8816
  205 Frazier Rd Altavista (24517) *(G-640)*
Schrader-Bridgeport Intl Inc (HQ) **434 369-4741**
  205 Frazier Rd Altavista (24517) *(G-641)*
Schrader-Bridgeport Intl Inc 434 369-4741
  205 Frazier Rd Altavista (24517) *(G-642)*
Schreiber Inc R G 540 248-5300
  46 Laurel Hill Rd Verona (24482) *(G-13995)*
Schribble Inc 804 869-6878
  12012 Bennett Ct Glen Allen (23059) *(G-5791)*
Schrocks Repair 540 879-2406
  3599 Lumber Mill Rd Dayton (22821) *(G-4062)*
Schrocks Slaughterhouse 434 283-5400
  4141 Pigeon Run Rd Gladys (24554) *(G-5696)*
Schunck Rbcca Wlpr Instllation 757 301-9922
  2205 Elmington Cir Virginia Beach (23454) *(G-14796)*
Schunck, Rebecca Wallpaper, Virginia Beach *Also called Schunck Rbcca Wlpr
Instllation (G-14796)*
Schweitzer-Mauduit Intl Inc 540 981-0362
  530 Gregory Ave Ne Roanoke (24016) *(G-12178)*
Sciecom LLC 703 994-2635
  43692 Gladehill Ct Chantilly (20152) *(G-2555)*
Science Info LLC 804 332-5269
  4860 Cox Rd Ste 200 Glen Allen (23060) *(G-5792)*
Science of Spirituality 804 633-9987
  19384 Smoots Rd Bowling Green (22427) *(G-1907)*
Sciencelogic Inc (PA) **703 354-1010**
  10700 Parkridge Blvd # 150 Reston (20191) *(G-10945)*
Scientific Software Solutions 434 293-7661
  317 Monte Vista Ave Charlottesville (22903) *(G-2873)*
Scilucent LLC 703 435-0033
  585 Grove St Ste 300 Herndon (20170) *(G-6802)*
Scinteck Instruments LLC 571 426-3598
  6560 Skylemar Trl Centreville (20121) *(G-2336)*
Scintilex LLC 240 593-7906
  6100 Bayliss Knoll Ct Alexandria (22310) *(G-579)*
Scivera LLC 434 974-1301
  300 E Main St Fl 3 Charlottesville (22902) *(G-2874)*
Scoops, Moseley *Also called Sandy Farnham (G-9047)*
Scorpio Jungle, North Chesterfield *Also called Andrea Lewis (G-9818)*
Scorpion Mold Abatement LLC 540 273-9300
  202 Bulkhead Cv Stafford (22554) *(G-13189)*
Scott Coulter 800 775-2925
  10819 Warwick Ave Fairfax (22030) *(G-4674)*
Scott County Herald Virginian 276 386-6300
  113 West Jackson St Gate City (24251) *(G-5667)*
Scott Fineart and Frmng Inc M 757 496-0221
  3163 Page Ave Virginia Beach (23451) *(G-14797)*
Scott Logging LLC 276 930-2497
  2225 Pilson Sawmill Rd Stuart (24171) *(G-13629)*
Scott Pallets Inc 804 561-2514
  8660 Crowder St Amelia Court House (23002) *(G-672)*
Scott Printing Co, Gate City *Also called Scott County Herald Virginian (G-5667)*
Scott Ready 703 503-3374
  4830 Gainsborough Dr Fairfax (22032) *(G-4551)*
Scott Turf Equipment LLC 434 401-3031
  12304 Wards Rd Rustburg (24588) *(G-12443)*
Scott Turf Equipment LLC (PA) **434 401-3031**
  12304 Wards Rd Rustburg (24588) *(G-12444)*
Scott's Cabinet Shop, Forest *Also called Triple S Enterprises Inc (G-5102)*
Scott's Randolph Welding, Gretna *Also called Randolph Scotts Welding (G-6009)*
Scottcraft Monogramming 703 971-0309
  6540 Windham Ave Alexandria (22315) *(G-580)*
Scotties Bavarian Folk Art 540 341-8884
  7561 Cannoneer Ct Warrenton (20186) *(G-15049)*
Scotts Company LLC 434 848-2727
  3175 Bright Leaf Rd Lawrenceville (23868) *(G-7184)*
Scotts Hyponex, Lawrenceville *Also called Hyponex Corporation (G-7181)*
Scotty's Sign Service, Newport News *Also called Scottys Sign Inc (G-9332)*
Scotty Signs, Gloucester Point *Also called Martins Custom Designs Inc (G-5874)*
Scottys Sign Inc 757 245-7129
  340 Ed Wright Ln Newport News (23606) *(G-9332)*
Scout Marketing LLC 301 986-1470
  7520 Fullerton Rd Springfield (22153) *(G-13081)*
Scoutco LLC 540 433-5136
  3610 S Main St Harrisonburg (22801) *(G-6367)*
Scoutco LLC (PA) **540 828-0928**
  9201 Centerville Rd Bridgewater (22812) *(G-1958)*
Scratch Brand Foods, Kinsale *Also called Its Homeade LLC (G-7135)*
Scratcherguru LLC 804 239-8629
  16193 Derby Ridge Rd Montpelier (23192) *(G-9020)*
Screen Crafts Inc 804 355-4156
  2915 Moore St Richmond (23230) *(G-11374)*
Screen Prtg Tchncal Foundation 703 359-1300
  10015 Main St Fairfax (22031) *(G-4552)*

Scribbles 703 930-8808
  5904 Mount Eagle Dr # 1002 Alexandria (22303) *(G-581)*
Scripps Enterprises Inc 434 760-3311
  633 Berkmar Cir Charlottesville (22901) *(G-2690)*
Scripps Enterprises Inc 434 973-3345
  1405 Eagle Hill Farm Charlottesville (22901) *(G-2691)*
Scripted Gate Sign Co LLC 276 219-3850
  3721 Dungannon Rd Coeburn (24230) *(G-3702)*
Scriyb LLC 202 549-7070
  109 N King St Ste B Leesburg (20176) *(G-7343)*
Scrub Exchange LLC 434 237-7778
  5535 Spring Mill Rd Concord (24538) *(G-3763)*
Scrub Skinz LLC 804 338-1350
  10816 Rimbey Ct Glen Allen (23060) *(G-5793)*
Scrubs Mobile Cleaning Lc 540 254-0478
  10 Church Ave Se Ste 201 Roanoke (24011) *(G-12179)*
Scsi4me Corporation 703 372-1195
  7411 Alban Station Ct A103 Springfield (22150) *(G-13082)*
Scsi4me Corporation 571 229-9723
  12034 Cadet Ct Manassas (20109) *(G-8152)*
Sct Phoenix Oil & Gas LLC 702 245-0269
  2202 Beacon Ln Falls Church (22043) *(G-4873)*
Sct Woodworks LLC 804 310-1908
  2492 Royce Ct Powhatan (23139) *(G-10573)*
Sculpture By Gary Stevenson 757 486-5893
  2104 Pallets Ct Virginia Beach (23454) *(G-14798)*
Scw Software Inc 540 937-5332
  2714 Wildwood Cir Amissville (20106) *(G-721)*
SD Davis Welding & Equipment 804 691-2112
  8221 White Oak Rd Ford (23850) *(G-5048)*
SDA Software LLC 703 657-0919
  46030 Manekin Plz Ste 120 Sterling (20166) *(G-13501)*
SDC Publishing LLC 540 676-3279
  221 Berry Ridge Rd Buchanan (24066) *(G-2127)*
Sddg, Stafford *Also called Software Dfined Dvcs Group LLC (G-13192)*
SDS Industries 207 266-9448
  350 Cameron Station Blvd Alexandria (22304) *(G-340)*
SE Holdings LLC (PA) **434 385-9181**
  1046 W London Park Dr Forest (24551) *(G-5091)*
Se7en Trnsp Lgstics Systems LL 804 869-1716
  5404 Dstr Dr Fl 2 Ste 104 Flr 2 Richmond (23225) *(G-11754)*
Sea Marine LLC 757 528-9869
  1301 Monticello Ave Norfolk (23510) *(G-9716)*
Sea Publishing LLC 832 744-7049
  41663 Mcmonagle Sq Aldie (20105) *(G-111)*
Sea Technology Ltd 804 642-3568
  95 Tyler Ave Ste I Newport News (23601) *(G-9333)*
Seaboard Concrete Products Co 804 275-0802
  5000 Castlewood Rd North Chesterfield (23234) *(G-9973)*
Seaboard Service of VA Inc 804 643-5112
  5707 Old Osborne Tpke Richmond (23231) *(G-11375)*
Seacrist Motor Sports 540 309-2234
  2806 W Main St Salem (24153) *(G-12568)*
Seager Valve 757 478-0607
  925 Thatcher Way Chesapeake (23320) *(G-3289)*
Seaguard International LLC 484 747-0299
  2000 Amedeo Ct Suffolk (23434) *(G-13761)*
Seal Craft Asphalt Service, Rocky Mount *Also called Larry D Martin (G-12332)*
Seal R L & Sons Logging 804 769-3696
  401 Midway Ln Aylett (23009) *(G-1554)*
Sealants and Coatings Tech (PA) **812 256-3378**
  16955 Simpson Cir Paeonian Springs (20129) *(G-10239)*
Sealmaster-Roanoke 540 344-2090
  3131 Baker Ave Nw Ste B Roanoke (24017) *(G-12180)*
Sealpac Usa LLC 804 261-0580
  2301 Chancellor Rd North Chesterfield (23235) *(G-9974)*
Seams Like Home, Harrisonburg *Also called Heidi Yoder (G-6327)*
Sean Applegate 540 972-4779
  12502 Plantation Dr Spotsylvania (22551) *(G-12913)*
Sean Duggan Golf Shop, Round Hill *Also called Stoneleigh Golf Club (G-12391)*
Seascape Automation LLC 717 512-5981
  332 Laskin Rd Apt 501 Virginia Beach (23451) *(G-14799)*
Seaside Audio 757 237-5333
  509 Mayfair Ct Virginia Beach (23452) *(G-14800)*
Seatrix Print LLC 571 241-5748
  2263 York Dr Apt 304 Woodbridge (22191) *(G-15804)*
Secar At Rich LLC 804 737-0090
  6100 Nine Mile Rd Richmond (23223) *(G-11755)*
Second Chance Dog Rescue 540 752-1741
  1654 Truslow Rd Fredericksburg (22406) *(G-5484)*
Second Samuel Industries Inc 703 715-2295
  12734 Alder Woods Dr Fairfax (22033) *(G-4553)*
Secret Society Press LLC 540 877-6298
  112 Morgan St Winchester (22601) *(G-15583)*
Secretbow Pubg Instruction LLC 703 404-3401
  32 Haxall Ct Sterling (20165) *(G-13502)*
Sector 5, Alexandria *Also called Sector Five Inc (G-342)*
Sector 5 Inc 571 348-1005
  2000 Duke St Ste 110 Alexandria (22314) *(G-341)*

A
L
P
H
A
B
E
T
I
C

Sector Five Inc...571 348-1005
2000 Duke St Ste 110 Alexandria (22314) ***(G-342)***
Secubit Inc...757 453-6965
2697 Intl Pkwy Ste 205-1 Virginia Beach (23452) ***(G-14801)***
Secure Elements Incorporated...703 234-7840
13221 Wdlnd Pk Rd Ste 110 Herndon (20171) ***(G-6803)***
Secure Innovations Inc...540 384-6131
3815 Travis Trl Salem (24153) ***(G-12569)***
Secure Iq, Vienna *Also called Iq Global Technologies LLC* ***(G-14073)***
Secure Knowledge, Sterling *Also called Greentec-Usa Inc* ***(G-13414)***
Securedb Inc...703 231-0008
45499 Baggett Ter Sterling (20166) ***(G-13503)***
Securitas Inc...800 705-4545
4228 N Huguenot Rd Richmond (23235) ***(G-11063)***
Security Evolutions Inc...703 953-4739
5124 Brittney Elyse Cir J Centreville (20120) ***(G-2337)***
Secutor Systems LLC...757 646-9350
4445 Corporation Ln Virginia Beach (23462) ***(G-14802)***
Sedley Printing...757 562-5738
31017 Maple Ave Sedley (23878) ***(G-12680)***
Seher Resources Inc...703 771-7170
42837 Forest Spring Dr Leesburg (20176) ***(G-7344)***
SEI Furniture and Design, Centreville *Also called Supplies Express Inc* ***(G-2343)***
Seidle Motorsports...276 632-2255
1615 Virginia Ave Martinsville (24112) ***(G-8327)***
Seize Moments...804 794-5911
217 Meadowlark Ln Surry (23883) ***(G-13801)***
Sej Property Logistics Co...516 499-2549
310 Park Ave Crewe (23930) ***(G-3816)***
Selby LLC...804 640-4851
16060 Saint Peters Ch Rd Montpelier (23192) ***(G-9021)***
Select Cleaning Service...804 397-1176
2218 Walcott Pl Richmond (23223) ***(G-11756)***
Selenix LLC...540 375-6415
1640 Roanoke Blvd Salem (24153) ***(G-12570)***
Selex Communications Inc...703 547-6280
1801 Robert Fulton Dr # 400 Reston (20191) ***(G-10946)***
Self Solutions LLC...202 725-0866
6716 W Wkfield Dr Apt B1 Alexandria (22307) ***(G-582)***
Selimax Inc...540 347-5784
4486 Den Haag Rd Warrenton (20187) ***(G-15050)***
Sellars Logging...757 566-0613
19601 Tabernacle Rd Barhamsville (23011) ***(G-1573)***
Sellers Advantage Richmond...804 338-3800
2710 Fendall Ave Richmond (23222) ***(G-11757)***
Sema Wray...804 282-3609
7205 Pinetree Rd Henrico (23229) ***(G-6566)***
Semad Enterprises Inc...757 424-6177
2412 Featherbed Dr Chesapeake (23325) ***(G-3290)***
Semanticsolutions LLC...703 980-7395
42897 Nashua St Ashburn (20147) ***(G-1333)***
Sematco, Roanoke *Also called Cg Plus LLC* ***(G-11906)***
Sematron LLC...919 360-5806
17623 Canby Rd Leesburg (20175) ***(G-7345)***
Semco Services Inc (PA)...**540 885-7480**
589 Lee Jackson Hwy Staunton (24401) ***(G-13291)***
Semetrol LLC...804 536-7005
13312 Shore Lake Turn Chesterfield (23838) ***(G-3523)***
Semiconductor Technology RES...804 304-8092
1607 Swinton Ln Richmond (23238) ***(G-11376)***
Semmaterials LP...757 244-6545
801 Terminal Ave Newport News (23607) ***(G-9334)***
Sems, Brodnax *Also called Stanford Electronics Mfg & Sls* ***(G-2105)***
Semtek...434 942-4728
654 Acorn Dr Rustburg (24588) ***(G-12445)***
Sencontrology Inc...540 529-7000
3129 Davis Ave Roanoke (24015) ***(G-12181)***
Senior Mobility LLC...540 574-0215
141 S Carlton St Harrisonburg (22801) ***(G-6368)***
Senior Publ Free Seniority...757 222-3900
143 Granby St Norfolk (23510) ***(G-9717)***
Seniors Housing Guide, North Chesterfield *Also called Ross Publishing Inc* ***(G-9966)***
Sennett Security Products LLC (PA)...**703 803-8880**
15623 Jillians Forest Way Centreville (20120) ***(G-2338)***
Senseware...703 975-2919
14504 Smithwood Dr Centreville (20120) ***(G-2339)***
Sensor Networks LLC...703 481-2224
1472 Roundleaf Ct Reston (20190) ***(G-10947)***
Senstar Inc (HQ)...**703 463-3088**
13800 Coppermine Rd Fl 2 Herndon (20171) ***(G-6804)***
Sentek Instrument LLC...540 831-9693
208 Spickard St Blacksburg (24060) ***(G-1788)***
Sentek Instrument LLC...540 250-2116
1750 Kraft Dr Ste 1125 Blacksburg (24060) ***(G-1789)***
Sentient Vision Systems Inc...703 531-8564
4470 Cox Rd Ste 250 Glen Allen (23060) ***(G-5794)***
Sentientrf...503 467-8026
22643 Watson Rd Leesburg (20175) ***(G-7346)***
Sentinel Press LLC...703 753-5434
13631 Hackamore Trl Gainesville (20155) ***(G-5611)***
Sentinel Self-Defense LLC...757 234-2501
670 Downey Green St # 410 Hampton (23666) ***(G-6232)***
Sentry Slutions Pdts Group LLC...757 689-6064
2697 Intl Pkwy Ste 4-230 Virginia Beach (23452) ***(G-14803)***
Separation Technologies LLC (HQ)...**540 992-1501**
188 Summerfield Ct # 101 Roanoke (24019) ***(G-11999)***
Separation Unlimited Inc...804 794-4864
11501 Allecingie Pkwy North Chesterfield (23235) ***(G-9975)***
Sephora Inside Jcpenney...434 973-7851
1639 Rio Road East Charlottesville (22901) ***(G-2692)***
Septenary Winery, Greenwood *Also called Seven Oaks Farm LLC* ***(G-6000)***
Seql Inc...804 214-5678
301 Virginia St Unit 1205 Richmond (23219) ***(G-11758)***
Sequoia Energy LLC...540 776-7890
302 S Jefferson St Fl 5th Roanoke (24011) ***(G-12182)***
Sequoia View Vineyard LLC...540 668-6245
14914 Manor View Ln Purcellville (20132) ***(G-10676)***
Serendib Traditional LLC...703 408-1561
22024 Box Car Sq Sterling (20166) ***(G-13504)***
Serendipitme LLC...301 370-2466
673 Potomac Station Dr Ne # 223 Leesburg (20176) ***(G-7347)***
Serene Suds LLC...804 433-8032
6414 Engel Rd Richmond (23226) ***(G-11377)***
Serenity Ridge, Winchester *Also called Tammy Haire* ***(G-15487)***
Serenity Ridge Machining, Falls Church *Also called Kishbaugh Enterprises LLC* ***(G-4816)***
Serenity Ridge Machining...571 261-2042
4770 Angus Dr Gainesville (20155) ***(G-5612)***
Serious Games Interactive Inc...703 624-0842
2767 N Wakefield St Arlington (22207) ***(G-1163)***
Serpin Pharma LLC...703 343-3258
14645 Sulky Run Ct Nokesville (20181) ***(G-9399)***
Serum Institute India Pvt LLC...571 248-0911
15213 Brier Creek Dr Haymarket (20169) ***(G-6442)***
Servhawk LLC...703 447-1456
177 River Park Dr Great Falls (22066) ***(G-5979)***
Service Center Metals LLC...804 518-1550
5850 Quality Way Prince George (23875) ***(G-10607)***
Service Lamp Supply...757 426-0636
805 Toledo Pl Virginia Beach (23456) ***(G-14804)***
Service Machine & Wldg Co Inc...804 798-1381
12421 Maple St Ashland (23005) ***(G-1490)***
Service Metal Fabricators Inc...757 887-3500
1708 Endeavor Dr Williamsburg (23185) ***(G-15310)***
Service Metals, Williamsburg *Also called Service Metal Fabricators Inc* ***(G-15310)***
Service Printing, Martinsville *Also called Marbrooke Printing Inc* ***(G-8307)***
Service Printing Co, Lynchburg *Also called Service Printing of Lynchburg* ***(G-7806)***
Service Printing of Lynchburg...434 845-3681
1201 Commerce St Lynchburg (24504) ***(G-7806)***
Servicing Green Inc...540 459-3812
370 Diana Dr Edinburg (22824) ***(G-4312)***
Servocon Alpha, Fishersville *Also called Alpha Developement Bureau* ***(G-5000)***
SES...540 428-3919
9251 Industrial Ct 101 Manassas (20109) ***(G-8153)***
Sestra Systems Inc...703 429-1596
45180 Business Ct Ste 100 Sterling (20166) ***(G-13505)***
Setanta Publishing LLC...703 548-3146
3 E Cliff St Alexandria (22301) ***(G-343)***
Setliff and Company LLC...434 793-1173
560 Martin Rd Danville (24541) ***(G-4038)***
Setzer and Sons VA Inc Smith...434 246-3791
12556 Setzer Rd Stony Creek (23882) ***(G-13568)***
Seva Publishing LLC...757 556-1965
10327 Cabin Ridge Ct Manassas (20110) ***(G-7999)***
Seven Bends LLC...540 392-0553
4025 Mount Zion Rd Blacksburg (24060) ***(G-1790)***
Seven Oaks Albemarle LLC...540 984-3829
94 Landfill Rd Edinburg (22824) ***(G-4313)***
Seven Oaks Farm LLC...303 653-3299
200 Seven Oaks Farm Greenwood (22943) ***(G-6000)***
Seven Sevens Inc...757 340-1300
879 Poplar Hall Dr Norfolk (23502) ***(G-9718)***
Severn Wharf Custom Rods...804 642-0404
8109 Yacht Haven Rd Gloucester Point (23062) ***(G-5876)***
Severn Yachting Center, Hayes *Also called Severn Yachting LLC* ***(G-6408)***
Severn Yachting LLC...804 642-6969
3398 Stonewall Rd Hayes (23072) ***(G-6408)***
Sew and Tell Embroidery...757 641-1227
9277 Kellos Mill Rd Wakefield (23888) ***(G-14970)***
Sew Impressive, Triangle *Also called Five Talents Enterprises LLC* ***(G-13892)***
Sew My Monogram LLC...804 739-2407
12016 Suthshore Pointe Rd Midlothian (23112) ***(G-8896)***
Seward Lumber Company Inc...757 866-8911
2514 Spring Grove Rd Claremont (23899) ***(G-3625)***
Sewcial Stitch...813 786-2966
4626 Hull Dr Haymarket (20169) ***(G-6443)***
Sextant Solutions Group LLC...757 797-4353
501 Boush St Ste B Norfolk (23510) ***(G-9719)***
Sextons Incorporated...276 783-4212
538 Kelly Hill Rd Atkins (24311) ***(G-1520)***

Sfi Partners Club 757 622-8001
225 W Olney Rd Ste 300 Norfolk (23510) *(G-9720)*

Sgm Inc 757 572-3299
1412 Crystal Pkwy Virginia Beach (23451) *(G-14805)*

Sgv Software Automtn RES Corp 703 904-0678
907 Broad Oaks Dr Herndon (20170) *(G-6805)*

Sgx Graphix 703 330-3550
4215 Walney Rd Chantilly (20151) *(G-2490)*

Shade Green Publishing 540 845-4780
4408 Wexham Ct Fredericksburg (22408) *(G-5360)*

Shade Mann-Kidwell Corp 804 288-2819
6011 W Broad St Richmond (23230) *(G-11378)*

Shadeworks LLC 804 642-2618
7979 Starkey Dr Hayes (23072) *(G-6409)*

Shadow Dance Publishing Ltd 540 786-3270
11514 Catharpin Rd Spotsylvania (22553) *(G-12914)*

Shadow River Books, King George *Also called Debra Hewitt (G-7086)*

Shadows Ridge Inc 540 722-0310
113 W Brooke Rd Winchester (22603) *(G-15475)*

Shahzada Afghan Amrcn Import E 571 245-1345
6022 Edsall Rd Alexandria (22304) *(G-344)*

Shakespeareink Inc 804 381-8237
2609 Wicklow Loop North Chesterfield (23236) *(G-9976)*

Shakir Waliyyud-Deen 706 399-8893
7009 Cold Spring Ln Alexandria (22306) *(G-583)*

Shaklee Authorized Distri 276 744-3546
383 Doe Run Rd Independence (24348) *(G-6995)*

Shaklee Independent Distr 757 553-8765
1845 Saville Garden Ct Virginia Beach (23453) *(G-14806)*

Shalom Foundation Inc 540 433-5351
1251 Virginia Ave Harrisonburg (22802) *(G-6369)*

Shamrock Arlington LLC 703 528-7676
3211 Washington Blvd Arlington (22201) *(G-1164)*

Shamrock Screen Print LLC 540 219-4337
16139 Fox Chase Ln Culpeper (22701) *(G-3919)*

Shanando Candy Co, Stanley *Also called Millcroft Farms Co Inc (G-13234)*

Shane Harper 540 297-4800
1074 Joyful Dr Moneta (24121) *(G-8976)*

Shantanu Tank 757 766-3829
9 Henrys Fork Dr Hampton (23666) *(G-6233)*

Shantaras Soaps 434 221-2382
5485 Staunton Hill Rd Brookneal (24528) *(G-2113)*

Shantell C Young 251 348-7247
563 Ayrshire Way Apt C Newport News (23602) *(G-9335)*

Shaper Group 703 680-5551
4765 Hawfinch Ct Woodbridge (22193) *(G-15805)*

Shared Spectrum Company 703 761-2818
1593 Spring Hill Rd # 700 Vienna (22182) *(G-14123)*

Sharestream Edcatn Rsurces LLC 301 208-8000
11600 Sunrise Valley Dr # 4 Reston (20191) *(G-10948)*

Sharon Solomon 757 515-2325
5417 Beckner St Norfolk (23509) *(G-9721)*

Sharpe Energy Company, Heathsville *Also called Sharpe Resources Corp (G-6465)*

Sharpe Resources Corp (PA) 804 580-8107
3258 Mob Neck Rd Heathsville (22473) *(G-6465)*

Sharpshooter Coffee, Stafford *Also called J L V Management Inc (G-13158)*

Shaw LLC 540 967-9783
2484 Oakland Rd Louisa (23093) *(G-7566)*

Shawn Gaines 434 332-4819
340 Watkins Farm Rd Rustburg (24588) *(G-12446)*

Shawnee Canning Company Inc (PA) 540 888-3429
212 Cross Junction Rd Cross Junction (22625) *(G-3827)*

Shawnee Springs Market, Cross Junction *Also called Shawnee Canning Company Inc (G-3827)*

SHD Logistics LLC 804 405-4943
12020 Avaclaire Dr Chester (23831) *(G-3454)*

SHD Oil & Gas, Mc Lean *Also called Spotted Hawk Development LLC (G-8556)*

She Signs 434 509-3173
221 Melwood Dr Madison Heights (24572) *(G-7884)*

Shearer's Foods, Bristol *Also called Snack Alliance Inc (G-1987)*

Shearers Foods LLC 276 669-6194
110 Thomas Rd Bristol (24201) *(G-1986)*

Sheaves Floors LLC 540 234-9080
3236 Lee Hwy Weyers Cave (24486) *(G-15176)*

Sheaves Racing Slots & Drags, Weyers Cave *Also called Sheaves Floors LLC (G-15176)*

Sheel's Pickles, Alexandria *Also called Sardana Sushila (G-577)*

Sheet Metal Products Inc 757 562-1986
2397 Carrsville Hwy Franklin (23851) *(G-5155)*

Sheffield Woodworking 571 261-4904
15244 Weiskopf Ct Haymarket (20169) *(G-6444)*

Shefford Woodlands LLC 804 625-5495
230 Enterprise Rd Shacklefords (23156) *(G-12684)*

Sheila Rodriguez 425 221-0519
5025 Riverfront Dr Suffolk (23434) *(G-13762)*

Shelf Reliance 540 459-2050
1726 Stultz Gap Rd Woodstock (22664) *(G-15859)*

Shelf Tagger, Richmond *Also called Cougarbearbobcat LLC (G-11543)*

Shelfnwoodworks 757 350-0408
1534 Olde Mill Creek Dr Suffolk (23434) *(G-13763)*

Shell 276 676-0699
15785 Porterfield Hwy Abingdon (24210) *(G-60)*

Shelley Imprssons Prtg Copying 540 310-0766
20 Commerce Pkwy Ste 105 Fredericksburg (22406) *(G-5485)*

Shellys Chachkies LLC 571 758-1323
21165 Twinridge Sq Sterling (20164) *(G-13506)*

Sheltech Plastics Inc 978 794-2160
6074 New Design Rd Elberon (23846) *(G-4319)*

Shelter2home Inc 540 327-4426
212 Fort Collier Rd # 2 Winchester (22603) *(G-15476)*

Shelter2home LLC 540 336-5994
22 Clark St Winchester (22601) *(G-15584)*

Sheltered 2 Home LLC 540 686-0091
22 Clark St Winchester (22601) *(G-15585)*

Shelters To Shutters 703 634-6130
1921 Gallows Rd Ste 700 Vienna (22182) *(G-14124)*

Shelton Global Assoc 202 841-8463
2003 Wethersfield Ct Reston (20191) *(G-10949)*

Shelton Logging, Keeling *Also called J D Shelton (G-7025)*

Shelton Logging Inc 434 294-1386
2989 The Falls Rd Crewe (23930) *(G-3817)*

Shelton Plumbing & Heating LLC 804 539-8080
4779 Stornoway Dr North Chesterfield (23234) *(G-9977)*

Shen-Val Screen Printing LLC 540 869-2713
313 Knight Dr White Post (22663) *(G-15183)*

Shen-Valley Lime Corp 540 869-2700
500 Fairfax Pike Stephens City (22655) *(G-13322)*

Shenandoah AG Supply, Bridgewater *Also called Agri Ventilation Systems LLC (G-1947)*

Shenandoah Castings LLC 540 551-5777
100 Drummer Hill Rd Front Royal (22630) *(G-5554)*

Shenandoah Control Systems 540 837-1627
224 Mount Prospect Ln Boyce (22620) *(G-1912)*

Shenandoah Corporation (PA) 540 248-2123
4 Industry Way Staunton (24401) *(G-13292)*

Shenandoah Drones LLC 540 421-3116
9706 Fairway Dr New Market (22844) *(G-9148)*

Shenandoah Machine & Maint Co 540 343-1758
2141 Loudon Ave Nw Roanoke (24017) *(G-12183)*

Shenandoah Machine Shop Inc 540 652-8593
323 Pulaski Ave Shenandoah (22849) *(G-12694)*

Shenandoah Primitives LLC 540 662-4727
158 Bryarly Rd Winchester (22603) *(G-15477)*

Shenandoah Publications Inc 540 459-4000
18084 Old Valley Pike Edinburg (22824) *(G-4314)*

Shenandoah Robe Company Inc 540 362-9811
3322 Hollins Rd Ne Roanoke (24012) *(G-12184)*

Shenandoah Sheds 540 869-4050
1518 Fairfax Pike White Post (22663) *(G-15184)*

Shenandoah Signs Promotions 540 886-2114
220 Frontier Dr Ste 99 Staunton (24401) *(G-13293)*

Shenandoah Specialty Pubg LLC (PA) 540 463-2319
158 S Main St Lexington (24450) *(G-7416)*

Shenandoah Stone Supply Co 703 532-0169
7139 Lee Hwy Falls Church (22046) *(G-4925)*

Shenandoah Valley Guide, Lexington *Also called Shenandoah Specialty Pubg LLC (G-7416)*

Shenandoah Valley Herald, Winchester *Also called Page Shenandoah Newspaper (G-15564)*

Shenandoah Valley Orchard Co 540 337-2837
205 Horseshoe Cir Stuarts Draft (24477) *(G-13660)*

Shenandoah Valley Printin 540 208-1808
4564 S Valley Pike Rockingham (22801) *(G-12276)*

Shenandoah Valley Soaring Inc 804 347-6848
249 Aero Dr Waynesboro (22980) *(G-15139)*

Shenandoah Valley Water Co, Staunton *Also called Shenandoah Corporation (G-13292)*

Shenandoah Valley-Herald, The, Woodstock *Also called Daily News Record (G-15851)*

Shenandoah Vlly Steam/Gas Engi 540 662-6923
456 Imperial St Winchester (22601) *(G-15586)*

Shenandoahs Pride LLC 703 321-9500
5325 Port Royal Rd Springfield (22151) *(G-13083)*

Shenox Pharmaceuticals LLC 732 309-2419
1765 Greensboro Sta Mc Lean (22102) *(G-8546)*

Shepherd Enterprises Anchor Rm 757 641-7829
102 Pine Blf Portsmouth (23701) *(G-10479)*

Sheppard Furniture Co, Ridgeway *Also called Richard E Sheppard Jr (G-11851)*

Sherman Industries LLC 240 888-1134
1 E Bellefonte Ave Alexandria (22301) *(G-345)*

Sherrie & Scott Embroidery 804 271-2024
7031 Bridgeside Pl North Chesterfield (23234) *(G-9978)*

Sherwin-Williams Company 804 264-6156
1083 Virginia Center Pkwy Glen Allen (23059) *(G-5795)*

Shh Stmlting Healthy Hair LLC 973 607-7138
1889 C D Silver Pkwy 7 Fredericksburg (22401) *(G-5222)*

Shibuya Hoppmann Corporation (HQ) 540 829-2564
7849 Coppermine Dr Manassas (20109) *(G-8154)*

Shickel Corporation 540 828-2536
115 Dry River Rd Bridgewater (22812) *(G-1959)*

Shickel Pubg Co Donna Lou 540 879-3568
5664 Ottobine Rd Dayton (22821) *(G-4063)*

Shield Technology Corporation 540 882-3254
13439 Milltown Rd Lovettsville (20180) *(G-7586)*

ALPHABETIC

Shifflett & Son Logging, Urbanna *Also called Shifflett and Son Log Co LLC (G-13973)*
Shifflett and Son Log Co LLC ... 757 434-7979
432 Burch Rd Urbanna (23175) ***(G-13973)***
Shifflett Machine Shop ... 540 433-1731
3061 Osceola Springs Rd Rockingham (22801) ***(G-12277)***
Shiftone ... 415 806-5006
3300 Fairfax Dr Ste 201 Arlington (22201) ***(G-1165)***
Shigol Makkoli Winery ... 646 594-7405
7083 Gary Rd Manassas (20109) ***(G-8155)***
Shimchock's Label Service, Roanoke *Also called Shimchocks Litho Service Inc (G-12185)*
Shimchocks Litho Service Inc ... 540 982-3915
121 Sycamore Ave Ne Roanoke (24012) ***(G-12185)***
Shine Beauty Company ... 757 509-7338
252 Nantucket Pl Newport News (23606) ***(G-9336)***
Shine Like Me LLC ... 210 862-4197
8000 Crianza Pl Apt 226 Vienna (22182) ***(G-14125)***
Shining Lights LLC ... 703 338-3820
12553 Cerromar Pl Fairfax (22030) ***(G-4675)***
Shiny Stuff ... 540 586-4446
630 Mountain Ave Bedford (24523) ***(G-1657)***
Ship Point Oyster Company ... 757 848-3557
1115 Poquoson Ave Poquoson (23662) ***(G-10376)***
Ship Shape Cleaning LLC ... 757 769-3845
400 W Road Portsmouth Portsmouth (23707) ***(G-10480)***
Ship Sstnability Solutions LLC ... 757 574-2436
1012 Austenwood Ct Chesapeake (23322) ***(G-3291)***
Shipyrdandcontractorsupply LLC ... 757 333-2148
3732 W Stratford Rd Virginia Beach (23455) ***(G-14807)***
Shirleys Stitches LLC ... 804 370-7182
3130 Blue Bell Farms Rd Powhatan (23139) ***(G-10574)***
Shirleys Unf & Alterations LLC ... 434 985-2042
6420 Seminole Trl Barboursville (22923) ***(G-1566)***
Shirt Art Inc ... 703 680-3963
2869 Ps Business Ctr Dr Woodbridge (22192) ***(G-15806)***
Shirts Unlimited LLC ... 540 342-8337
1207 9th St Se Roanoke (24013) ***(G-12186)***
Shively and Carter Cabinets ... 540 483-4149
212 Smith Rd Glade Hill (24092) ***(G-5670)***
Shockey Bros Inc (HQ) ... **540 401-0101**
219 Stine Ln Winchester (22603) ***(G-15478)***
Shockey Bros Inc ... 540 667-7700
4717 Massaponax Church Rd Fredericksburg (22408) ***(G-5361)***
Shockey Precast Group, Winchester *Also called Shockey Bros Inc (G-15478)*
Shockey Precast Group, Fredericksburg *Also called Shockey Bros Inc (G-5361)*
Shockoe Denim ... 804 269-0851
13 S 15th St Ste A Richmond (23219) ***(G-11759)***
Shoe Mate Orthopedic Arch Co, Roanoke *Also called Foot Levelers Inc (G-12091)*
Shoebox Memories ... 703 969-9290
25864 Flintonbridge Dr Fairfax (20152) ***(G-4699)***
Shoeprint ... 703 499-9136
2700 Potomac Mills Cir # 238 Woodbridge (22192) ***(G-15807)***
Shoffner Industries Virginia ... 757 485-1132
3812 Cook Blvd Chesapeake (23323) ***(G-3292)***
Shooting Star Gallery LLC ... 757 787-4536
60 Hill St Onancock (23417) ***(G-10197)***
Shooting Starr Alpacas LLC ... 540 347-4721
7158 Spotsylvania St Warrenton (20187) ***(G-15051)***
Shop Guys ... 804 317-9440
1518 Unison Dr Midlothian (23113) ***(G-8897)***
Shoprat Metal Works LLC ... 571 499-1534
4137 Watkins Trl Annandale (22003) ***(G-782)***
Shore Drive Self Storage Corp ... 757 587-6000
8110 Shore Dr Norfolk (23518) ***(G-9722)***
Shore Holders ... 434 542-4105
2122 Stockdale Rd Phenix (23959) ***(G-10355)***
Shore Traders LLC ... 276 632-5073
1208 Knollwood Pl Martinsville (24112) ***(G-8328)***
Shoreline Materials LLC ... 804 469-4042
26004 Troublefield Rd Stony Creek (23882) ***(G-13569)***
Short Circuit Electronics ... 540 886-8805
600 Richmond Ave Staunton (24401) ***(G-13294)***
Short Run Stamping Company Inc ... 804 861-6872
539 N West St Petersburg (23803) ***(G-10341)***
Shortys Breading Company LLC ... 434 390-1772
10885 Green Bay Rd Rice (23966) ***(G-11006)***
Shortys Fish and Fowl Breading, Rice *Also called Shortys Breading Company LLC (G-11006)*
Shotz From Heart LLC ... 804 898-5635
1810 Randolph Ave Petersburg (23803) ***(G-10342)***
Showall Inc ... 276 646-8779
212 Packing House Rd Chilhowie (24319) ***(G-3560)***
Showbest Fixture Corp (PA) ... **804 222-5535**
4112 Sarellen Rd Richmond (23231) ***(G-11379)***
Showbest Fixture Corp ... 434 298-3925
1033 Church St Blackstone (23824) ***(G-1828)***
Shrews Welding and Fabrica ... 703 785-8035
9220 Ashleys Park Ln Bristow (20136) ***(G-2061)***
Sht Technologies, Leesburg *Also called Star Home Theater LLC (G-7351)*

Shumate Inc George C ... 540 463-2244
81 Tranquility Ln Lexington (24450) ***(G-7417)***
Shupes Cleaning Solutions ... 804 737-6799
5233 Saltwood Pl Sandston (23150) ***(G-12632)***
Shutter Films LLC ... 434 329-0713
3850 Salem Rd Spout Spring (24593) ***(G-12927)***
Shutterbooth ... 804 662-0471
2621 Glenalmond Ct Powhatan (23139) ***(G-10575)***
Shyanne Branch ... 757 532-4951
3714 Bamboo Rd Portsmouth (23703) ***(G-10481)***
Sibashi Inc ... 571 292-6233
14340 Compton Village Dr Centreville (20121) ***(G-2340)***
Siblings Rivalry Brewery LLC ... 540 671-3893
239 Greenleaf Rd Strasburg (22657) ***(G-13596)***
Sickal Logging ... 804 366-1965
6725 Farmers Dr Barhamsville (23011) ***(G-1574)***
Sicpa Securink Corp (HQ) ... **703 455-8050**
8000 Research Way Springfield (22153) ***(G-13084)***
Siemens AG ... 757 875-7000
11827 Canon Blvd Newport News (23606) ***(G-9337)***
Siemens Building Technologies, Norfolk *Also called Siemens Industry Inc (G-9723)*
Siemens Industry Inc ... 757 766-4190
103 Research Dr Hampton (23666) ***(G-6234)***
Siemens Industry Inc ... 804 222-6680
5106 Glen Alden Dr Richmond (23231) ***(G-11380)***
Siemens Industry Inc ... 757 490-6026
5301 Robin Hood Rd # 118 Norfolk (23513) ***(G-9723)***
Siemens Industry Software Inc ... 757 591-6633
11827 Canon Blvd Ste 400 Newport News (23606) ***(G-9338)***
Sierra Nevada Corporation ... 703 412-1502
2231 Crystal Dr Ste 1113 Arlington (22202) ***(G-1166)***
Sierra Tannery LLC ... 804 323-5898
4400 Old Gun Rd E Midlothian (23113) ***(G-8898)***
Sifco Applied Srfc Cncepts LLC ... 757 855-4305
1333 Azalea Garden Rd F Norfolk (23502) ***(G-9724)***
Sifco Selective Plating, Norfolk *Also called Sifco Applied Srfc Cncepts LLC (G-9724)*
Sig Tech, Sterling *Also called Automated Signature Technology (G-13356)*
Sigarchi Media ... 571 296-5021
1530 12th St N Apt 201 Arlington (22209) ***(G-1167)***
Sightline Media Group LLC ... 703 750-7400
1919 Gallows Rd Ste 400 Vienna (22182) ***(G-14126)***
Sign, Leesburg *Also called Jv-Rm Holdings Inc (G-7293)*
Sign & Engraving Technology ... 804 744-7749
3905 Bellson Park Dr Midlothian (23112) ***(G-8899)***
Sign & Print ... 703 707-8556
1056 Elden St Herndon (20170) ***(G-6806)***
Sign and Seal ... 540 955-2422
327 N Buckmarsh St Berryville (22611) ***(G-1690)***
Sign and Seal Associates LLC ... 804 266-0410
11905 Boulware Ct Glen Allen (23059) ***(G-5796)***
Sign Biz LLC ... 804 741-7446
9020 Quioccasin Rd Henrico (23229) ***(G-6567)***
Sign Broker LLC ... 703 263-7227
13458 Stream Valley Dr Chantilly (20151) ***(G-2491)***
Sign Builders ... 757 499-2654
5773 Arrowhead Dr Ste 302 Virginia Beach (23462) ***(G-14808)***
Sign Central, Hampton *Also called Stahmer Inc (G-6243)*
Sign Crafters Inc ... 804 379-2004
800 Murray Olds Dr Midlothian (23114) ***(G-8900)***
Sign Creations ... 540 809-2112
12501 Herndon Rd Spotsylvania (22553) ***(G-12915)***
Sign Creations LLC ... 540 899-9555
1317 Alum Spring Rd Fredericksburg (22401) ***(G-5223)***
Sign Cy Plus Graphic & Design, Springfield *Also called Sign Cy Plus Graphic & Design (G-13085)*
Sign Cy Plus Graphic & Design ... 703 912-9300
6513 Backlick Rd Springfield (22150) ***(G-13085)***
Sign Design Inc ... 239 478-8315
1669 Feltner Rd Bluemont (20135) ***(G-1891)***
Sign Design Inc ... 540 338-5614
142 E Main St Purcellville (20132) ***(G-10677)***
Sign Design of Roanoke Inc ... 540 977-3354
2351 Carlton Rd Sw Roanoke (24015) ***(G-12187)***
Sign Design of Va LLC ... 804 794-1689
1901 Anderson Hwy Ste F Powhatan (23139) ***(G-10576)***
Sign Designs ... 804 580-7446
1938 Walnut Point Rd Heathsville (22473) ***(G-6466)***
Sign Designs of Powhatan Inc ... 804 794-1689
1901 Anderson Hwy Ste B Powhatan (23139) ***(G-10577)***
Sign Doctor Sales & Service ... 540 743-5200
24 Zerkel St Luray (22835) ***(G-7623)***
Sign Dude ... 757 303-7770
2100 George Wash Mem Hwy Yorktown (23693) ***(G-15990)***
Sign Engineering, Newport News *Also called J Fred Dowis (G-9263)*
Sign Enterprise Inc ... 540 899-9555
1317 Alum Spring Rd Fredericksburg (22401) ***(G-5224)***
Sign Express, Covington *Also called George Thomas Garten (G-3790)*
Sign Express Inc ... 757 686-3010
6075 High St W Portsmouth (23703) ***(G-10482)***

Sign Factory Inc..540 772-0400
3804 Brambleton Ave Roanoke (24018) *(G-12000)*

Sign Graphx Inc..703 335-7446
9091 Euclid Ave Manassas (20110) *(G-8000)*

Sign Gypsies Richmondva LLC.............................804 754-7345
11808 Amberwood Ln Glen Allen (23059) *(G-5797)*

Sign Ink LLC..804 250-3700
9830 Atlee Commons Dr # 200 Ashland (23005) *(G-1491)*

Sign Language Interpreter..................................540 460-4445
3011 Old Greenville Rd Staunton (24401) *(G-13295)*

Sign Managers...804 878-0555
2402 Boulevard Ste B Colonial Heights (23834) *(G-3747)*

Sign Managers LLC...804 381-5198
2920 W Broad St Richmond (23230) *(G-11381)*

Sign Master..540 886-6900
46 Tinkling Spring Rd Fishersville (22939) *(G-5008)*

Sign Medik..757 748-1048
159 Greendale Rd Virginia Beach (23452) *(G-14809)*

Sign of Goldfish...540 727-0008
601 Germanna Hwy Culpeper (22701) *(G-3920)*

Sign On Line LLC...571 246-7776
6173 Les Dorson Ln Alexandria (22315) *(G-584)*

Sign Pro, Harrisonburg *Also called Signfield Inc (G-6370)*

Sign Right Here LLC..757 617-0785
4759 Old Hickory Rd Virginia Beach (23455) *(G-14810)*

Sign Scapes Inc...804 980-7111
7519 Ranco Rd Henrico (23228) *(G-6568)*

Sign Shop..703 590-9534
2603 Morse Ln Woodbridge (22192) *(G-15808)*

Sign Shop of Newport News................................757 873-1157
715 Bluecrab Rd Ste A Newport News (23606) *(G-9339)*

Sign Shop The, Newport News *Also called Sign Shop of Newport News (G-9339)*

Sign Solutions, Blackstone *Also called McMj Enterprises LLC (G-1820)*

Sign Solutions..757 594-9688
133 Harpersville Rd Newport News (23601) *(G-9340)*

Sign Solutions..804 691-1824
7406 Stanfield Farm Ln Church Road (23833) *(G-3618)*

Sign Source..804 270-3252
7509 Lisa Ln Henrico (23294) *(G-6569)*

Sign Studio...540 789-4200
1280 Bremble Dr Apt C Moneta (24121) *(G-8977)*

Sign Systems Inc..540 639-0669
7084 Lee Hwy Fairlawn (24141) *(G-4740)*

Sign Tech...757 407-3870
352 Cleveland Pl Ste 101 Virginia Beach (23462) *(G-14811)*

Sign Technologies, Virginia Beach *Also called Sign Builders (G-14808)*

Sign Visions, Williamsburg *Also called Chalison Inc (G-15218)*

Sign Wise LLC...540 382-8343
1478 High Rock Hill Rd Pilot (24138) *(G-10358)*

Sign With ME VA..757 969-9876
81 Madison Chase Hampton (23666) *(G-6235)*

Sign Wizards Inc..757 431-8886
513 Central Dr Virginia Beach (23454) *(G-14812)*

Sign Works Inc...757 428-2525
1728 Virginia Beach Blvd # 110 Virginia Beach (23454) *(G-14813)*

Sign World..757 366-9890
701 S Military Hwy Virginia Beach (23464) *(G-14814)*

Sign-A-Rama, Herndon *Also called Allen Management Company Inc (G-6610)*

Sign-A-Rama, Gainesville *Also called Amplify Ventures LLC (G-5570)*

Sign-A-Rama, Henrico *Also called Signarama (G-6570)*

Sign-A-Rama, Woodbridge *Also called Noble Endeavors LLC (G-15762)*

Sign-A-Rama, Purcellville *Also called Signarama (G-10678)*

Sign-A-Rama, Leesburg *Also called Loudoun Signs Inc (G-7308)*

Sign-A-Rama, Christiansburg *Also called K L A Enterprises LLC (G-3602)*

Sign-A-Rama, Fairfax *Also called Complete Sign Inc (G-4429)*

Sign-A-Rama, Centreville *Also called Arcade Signs LLC (G-2291)*

Sign-N-Date Mobile Notary LLC...........................757 285-9619
26 Wendfield Cir Newport News (23601) *(G-9341)*

Signafab LLC...703 489-8572
464 Deep Woods Rd Louisa (23093) *(G-7567)*

Signal Vine Inc..703 480-0278
811 N Royal St Alexandria (22314) *(G-346)*

Signarama..804 967-3768
3712 West End Dr Henrico (23294) *(G-6570)*

Signarama..703 743-9424
36936 Snickersville Tpke Purcellville (20132) *(G-10678)*

Signarama Richmond...804 301-9317
705 Johnston Willis Dr North Chesterfield (23236) *(G-9979)*

Signature Canvasmakers LLC..............................757 788-8890
102 N Hope St Hampton (23663) *(G-6236)*

Signature Dsgns Fbrication LLC...........................571 398-2444
953 Highams Ct Woodbridge (22191) *(G-15809)*

Signature Dsigns Cabinetry LLC...........................804 614-0028
11743 Burray Rd Chesterfield (23838) *(G-3524)*

Signature K-9...866 820-3647
345 Luck Ave Sw Roanoke (24016) *(G-12188)*

Signature Publishing LLC...................................757 348-9692
20209 Shire Oak Dr South Chesterfield (23803) *(G-12839)*

Signature Seasonings LLc.................................757 572-8995
2572 Nestlebrook Trl Virginia Beach (23456) *(G-14815)*

Signature Series - Usa LLC...............................703 201-2543
22077 Oatlands Rd Aldie (20105) *(G-112)*

Signature Signs...540 554-2717
34434 Harry Byrd Hwy Round Hill (20141) *(G-12389)*

Signature Stone Corporation...............................757 566-9094
8009 A Industrial Park Rd Toano (23168) *(G-13877)*

Signd and Seald..814 460-2547
107 S Hardtimes Dr Prospect (23960) *(G-10614)*

Signet Screen Prtg Embordiery, Winchester *Also called Jbtm Enterprises Inc (G-15551)*

Signet Signs, Norfolk *Also called D & G Signs Inc (G-9513)*

Signfield Inc...540 574-3032
1550a E Market St Harrisonburg (22801) *(G-6370)*

Signmakers Inc..757 621-1212
2209 Baylake Rd Virginia Beach (23455) *(G-14816)*

Signmedia Inc...757 826-7128
2109 Mingee Dr Hampton (23661) *(G-6237)*

Signmedic LLC...703 919-3381
3207 Shoreview Rd Triangle (22172) *(G-13898)*

Signode Industrial Group LLC..............................276 632-2352
50 Multi Wall Dr Martinsville (24112) *(G-8329)*

Signrex Inc...703 497-7711
14511 Jefferson Davis Hwy Woodbridge (22191) *(G-15810)*

Signs and Designs, Wise *Also called In Home Care Inc (G-15627)*

Signs Around You LLC..919 449-4762
27 Snow Dr Stafford (22554) *(G-13190)*

Signs At Work..804 338-7716
641 Johnston Willis Dr North Chesterfield (23236) *(G-9980)*

Signs By Clay Downing.......................................703 371-6828
43114 Autumnwood Sq Broadlands (20148) *(G-2081)*

Signs By Dave...703 777-2870
103 Pershing Ave Nw Leesburg (20176) *(G-7348)*

Signs By James LLC..703 656-5067
17409 Joplin Rd Triangle (22172) *(G-13899)*

Signs By Randy..434 328-8872
762 Woodlands Rd Charlottesville (22901) *(G-2693)*

Signs By Tomorrow, Arlington *Also called I3 Ingenuity Inc (G-998)*

Signs By Tomorrow, Newport News *Also called Forrlace Inc (G-9232)*

Signs By Tomorrow, Newport News *Also called Torres Graphics and Signs Inc (G-9359)*

Signs By Tomorrow, Manassas *Also called Quick Signs Inc (G-7992)*

Signs By Tomorrow, Richmond *Also called Dsh Signs LLC (G-11192)*

Signs By Tomorrow, Springfield *Also called Cdrs LLC (G-12974)*

Signs By Tomorrow, Arlington *Also called Bubba Enterprises Inc (G-891)*

Signs By Tomorrow..703 356-3383
8150 Leesburg Pike # 120 Vienna (22182) *(G-14127)*

Signs By Tomorrow..703 591-2444
11150 Fairfax Blvd # 104 Fairfax (22030) *(G-4676)*

Signs By Tomorrow..703 444-0007
45449 Severn Way Ste 173 Sterling (20166) *(G-13507)*

Signs By Tomorrow Alexandria, Alexandria *Also called High Hat Inc (G-229)*

SIGNS BY TOMORROW LYNCHBURG, Lynchburg *Also called Pac Bridge LLC (G-7780)*

Signs Designs & More LLC.................................434 292-4555
200 W 10th St Blackstone (23824) *(G-1829)*

Signs For Anything Inc.......................................540 376-7006
10430 Courthouse Rd Spotsylvania (22553) *(G-12916)*

Signs For You LLC...703 653-4353
6153 Popes Creek Pl Haymarket (20169) *(G-6445)*

Signs of Learning LLC..757 635-2735
328 Office Square Ln 101c Virginia Beach (23462) *(G-14817)*

Signs of Success Inc..757 481-4788
1800 Seddon Cir Virginia Beach (23454) *(G-14818)*

Signs of The Times Apostolate.............................703 707-0799
360 Herndon Pkwy Ste 1100 Herndon (20170) *(G-6807)*

Signs On Scene..757 435-0841
638 Astor Ln Virginia Beach (23464) *(G-14819)*

Signs R US LLC..540 742-3625
704 S 3rd St Shenandoah (22849) *(G-12695)*

Signs To Go..757 622-7446
645 Church St Ste 102 Norfolk (23510) *(G-9725)*

Signs Unlimited Inc (PA)................................**703 799-8840**
8403 Richmond Hwy Ste J Alexandria (22309) *(G-585)*

Signs Up..703 798-5210
6715 Backlick Rd Ste B Springfield (22150) *(G-13086)*

Signs USA Inc..540 432-6366
21 Terri Dr Harrisonburg (22802) *(G-6371)*

Signs Work..276 655-4047
25 Wagon Wheel Rd Elk Creek (24326) *(G-4321)*

Signs Work Inc...804 338-7716
641 Johnston Willis Dr North Chesterfield (23236) *(G-9981)*

Signsations LLC..571 340-3330
11325 Random Hills Rd # 360 Fairfax (22030) *(G-4677)*

Signspot LLC...540 961-7768
3956 S Main St Ste 1 Blacksburg (24060) *(G-1791)*

Signworks of King George...................................540 709-7483
8755 Dahlgren Rd King George (22485) *(G-7113)*

Sihl USA Inc...757 966-7180
713 Fenway Ave Ste B Chesapeake (23323) *(G-3293)*

Sii Inc 540 722-6860
3470 Martinsburg Pike Clear Brook (22624) *(G-3651)*

Silence In Metropolis LLC 571 213-4383
43624 White Cap Ter Chantilly (20152) *(G-2556)*

Silent Circle Americas LLC 202 499-6427
4210 Fairfax Corner Ave W # 215 Fairfax (22030) *(G-4678)*

Silgan Dspnsing Systems Hldngs (HQ) **804 923-1971**
1001 Haxall Point Ste 701 Richmond (23219) *(G-11760)*

Silhouette Mastectomy Boutique, Newport News *Also called Reach Orthotic Prosthetic Svcs (G-9321)*

Silhouette Vineyards LLC 540 668-6000
14001 Harpers Ferry Rd Hillsboro (20132) *(G-6879)*

Silicon Equipment Cons LLC 804 357-8926
543 Watch Hill Rd Midlothian (23114) *(G-8901)*

Silivhere Technologies Inc 434 566-1207
106 W South St Ste 219 Charlottesville (22902) *(G-2875)*

Silk Tree Manufacturing Inc 434 983-1941
1139 Spencer Rd Dillwyn (23936) *(G-4100)*

Silkscreening Unlimited Inc 703 385-3212
10010 Mosby Rd Fairfax (22032) *(G-4554)*

Silly Sport Socks 703 926-5398
5414 Chatsworth Ct Fairfax (22032) *(G-4555)*

Silvas Heat & Air 757 596-5991
6 Rutledge Rd Newport News (23601) *(G-9342)*

Silver City Iron Inc 434 566-7644
134 10th St Nw Apt 2 Charlottesville (22903) *(G-2876)*

Silver Communications Corp 703 471-7339
102 Executive Dr Ste A Sterling (20166) *(G-13508)*

Silver Hand Meadery, Williamsburg *Also called Silver Hand Winery LLC (G-15311)*

Silver Hand Winery LLC 757 378-2225
224 Monticello Ave Williamsburg (23185) *(G-15311)*

Silver Lake Welding Svc Inc 540 879-2591
2433 Silver Lake Rd Dayton (22821) *(G-4064)*

Silver Lining Assistance Inc 540 825-8371
16033 Ira Hoffman Ln Culpeper (22701) *(G-3921)*

Silver Ring Splint Co 434 971-4052
1140 East Market St Ste A Charlottesville (22902) *(G-2877)*

Silver Spur Conveyors 276 596-9414
578 Raven Rd Raven (24639) *(G-10757)*

Silver Wings Inc 703 533-3244
6032 20th St N Arlington (22205) *(G-1168)*

Silverado Printing LLC 703 407-8720
13121 Penndale Ln Fairfax (22033) *(G-4556)*

Silverback Distillery, Afton *Also called Silverback Spirits LLC (G-89)*

Silverback Spirits LLC 540 456-7070
9520 Rockfish Valley Hwy Afton (22920) *(G-89)*

Silverchair Scnce + Cmmnctons 434 296-6333
316 E Main St Ste 300 Charlottesville (22902) *(G-2878)*

Silverline Brewing Company 703 281-5816
506 Mashie Dr Se Vienna (22180) *(G-14128)*

Silversmith Audio 619 460-1129
7807 Braemar Way Springfield (22153) *(G-13087)*

Silverwood Press LLC 804 833-0595
1620 Nottoway Ave Richmond (23227) *(G-11382)*

Silvio Enterprise LLC 703 731-0147
3334 Kaywood Dr Falls Church (22041) *(G-4874)*

Silynx Communications Inc 301 217-9223
45945 Center Oak Plz # 125 Sterling (20166) *(G-13509)*

Sim Net Inc 804 752-2776
12664 Old Ridge Rd Beaverdam (23015) *(G-1611)*

Simmons Bedding Company, Fredericksburg *Also called Ssb Manufacturing Company (G-5368)*

Simmons Equipment Company 276 991-3345
847 Steeles Ln Tazewell (24651) *(G-13839)*

Simmons Logging Inc 434 676-1202
3006 Brickland Rd South Hill (23970) *(G-12860)*

Simms Sign Co/Cash 804 746-0595
7485 Cold Harbor Rd Mechanicsville (23111) *(G-8676)*

Simple Scribes Pubg & Dist LLC 804 364-3418
12420 Stone Horse Ct Glen Allen (23059) *(G-5798)*

Simplicikey LLC 703 904-5010
13873 Park Center Rd # 500 Herndon (20171) *(G-6808)*

Simplicity Pure Bath & Bdy LLC 540 922-9287
216 Fairview Ave Pearisburg (24134) *(G-10277)*

SIMPLIMATIC AUTOMATION, Forest *Also called SE Holdings LLC (G-5091)*

Simplimatic Automation LLC 434 385-9181
1046 W London Park Dr Forest (24551) *(G-5092)*

Simply Candles & Gifts 315 806-4204
1009 Misty Mountain Rd # 1323 Lynchburg (24502) *(G-7807)*

Simply Clssic Cbnets Cnstr LLC 804 815-3283
137 Heron Ct Locust Hill (23092) *(G-7454)*

Simply Divine Candles 540 479-0045
105 Hailey Ln Apt D5 Strasburg (22657) *(G-13597)*

Simply Panache Products LLC 757 358-7062
100 Glica Ct Hampton (23666) *(G-6238)*

Simply Southern LLC 804 240-7130
461 Evanrude Ln Sandston (23150) *(G-12633)*

Simply Wood Post Signs LLC 757 657-9058
9057 New Rd Suffolk (23437) *(G-13764)*

Simpson Company Landsca 703 204-0453
7800 Shreve Rd Falls Church (22043) *(G-4875)*

Simpson Signs 434 369-7389
174 Penuel Ln Altavista (24517) *(G-643)*

Simpsons Express Paintin 804 744-8587
14710 Genito Rd Midlothian (23112) *(G-8902)*

Sims Creek Publishing LLC 276 694-4278
138 Bouldin Church Ln Stuart (24171) *(G-13630)*

Sims USA Inc 757 875-7742
739 Charles Rd Yorktown (23692) *(G-15991)*

Simulyze Inc 703 391-7001
12020 Sunrise Valley Dr # 300 Reston (20191) *(G-10950)*

Simurg Arts LLC 703 670-7230
4612 Telfair Ct Woodbridge (22193) *(G-15811)*

Sina Corp 703 707-8556
1056 Elden St Herndon (20170) *(G-6809)*

Sines Feathers and Furs LLC 540 436-8673
79 Lee Rae Ct Strasburg (22657) *(G-13598)*

Singh Express Corp 202 816-8686
12020 Sunrise Valley Dr Reston (20191) *(G-10951)*

Single Source Welding LLC 703 919-7791
5141 Poplar Pl Warrenton (20187) *(G-15052)*

Singlecomm LLC 203 559-5486
3200 Rockbridge St # 202 Richmond (23230) *(G-11383)*

Sinister Stitch Custom Leather 757 636-9954
2433 Pleasure House Rd Virginia Beach (23455) *(G-14820)*

Sink of America Inc 804 269-1111
5000 Willows Green Rd Glen Allen (23059) *(G-5799)*

Sip-Tone 703 480-0228
196 Van Buren St Herndon (20170) *(G-6810)*

Sir Masa Inc 540 725-1982
2717 Beverly Blvd Sw Roanoke (24015) *(G-12189)*

Sir Speedy, Hampton *Also called Virginia Printing Services Inc (G-6263)*

Sir Speedy, Springfield *Also called Industries In Focus Inc (G-13023)*

Sir Speedy, Richmond *Also called G I K of Virginia Inc (G-11596)*

Sir Speedy, Vienna *Also called Prinit Corporation (G-14114)*

Sir Speedy, Charlottesville *Also called C & B Corp (G-2752)*

Sir Speedy, Falls Church *Also called Northern Vrgnia Prof Assoc Inc (G-4837)*

Sir Speedy Print Signs Mktg 540 662-3804
32 E Piccadilly St Winchester (22601) *(G-15587)*

Sir Speedy Printing Ctr 7411 .... 703 821-8781
8616 Old Dominion Dr Mc Lean (22102) *(G-8547)*

Sisko Duel Fuel System 804 795-1634
7800 Wood Mill Dr Henrico (23231) *(G-6571)*

Sisson & Ryan Inc (PA) **540 268-2413**
6475 Roanoke Rd Shawsville (24162) *(G-12686)*

Sisson & Ryan Inc 540 268-5251
5441 Roanoke Rd Shawsville (24162) *(G-12687)*

Sisson & Ryan Quarry LLC 540 674-5556
5764 Wilderness Rd Dublin (24084) *(G-4171)*

Sisters In Stitches LLC 757 660-0871
7333 Joseph Lewis Rd Hayes (23072) *(G-6410)*

Sitscape Inc 571 432-8130
8245 Boone Blvd Ste 330 Vienna (22182) *(G-14129)*

Six Pcks Artsan Rasted Cof LLC 757 337-0872
1865 Shipyard Rd Chesapeake (23323) *(G-3294)*

Six Seas Press LLC 757 363-5869
1017 Witch Point Trl Virginia Beach (23455) *(G-14821)*

Six3 Advanced Systems Inc (HQ) **703 742-7660**
45200 Business Ct Ste 100 Dulles (20166) *(G-4226)*

SJ Dobert 301 847-5000
12401 Melmark Ct Reston (20191) *(G-10952)*

Sjm Agency Inc 703 754-3073
1700 Huguenot Rd Ste D Midlothian (23113) *(G-8903)*

Sjp Consulting LLC 804 277-8153
7210 Trench Trl Mechanicsville (23111) *(G-8677)*

Skelly Publishing Inc 888 753-5591
3812 27th St N Arlington (22207) *(G-1169)*

Sketchz 804 590-1234
6900 Woodpecker Rd Chesterfield (23838) *(G-3525)*

SKF Lbrication Systems USA Inc 757 951-0370
2115 Aluminum Ave Hampton (23661) *(G-6239)*

SKF Lubrication Solutions, Hampton *Also called SKF Lbrication Systems USA Inc (G-6239)*

Ski Zone Inc 703 242-3588
10102 Garrett St Vienna (22181) *(G-14130)*

Skiffes Creek Yard and Recycle, Newport News *Also called Legacy Vulcan LLC (G-9280)*

Skin Amnesty 757 491-9058
1817 Republic Rd Virginia Beach (23454) *(G-14822)*

Skin Ranch and Trade Company 757 486-7546
3061 Brickhouse Ct # 111 Virginia Beach (23452) *(G-14823)*

Skinny Jerky LLC 703 459-8406
2801 Park Center Dr A505 Alexandria (22302) *(G-347)*

Skippers Creek Vineyard LLC 804 598-7291
965 Rocky Ford Rd Powhatan (23139) *(G-10578)*

Skips Tools Inc 757 621-4775
2409 Litchfield Way Virginia Beach (23453) *(G-14824)*

Skips Woodworks 757 390-1948
114 The Maine Williamsburg (23185) *(G-15312)*

Skirmish Supplies 804 749-3458
18091 Vontay Rd Rockville (23146) *(G-12299)*

Skm Aerospace LLC 703 217-4221
1600 S Eads St Arlington (22202) *(G-1170)*

Sky Dynamics Corporation 540 297-6754
1900 Skyway Dr Moneta (24121) *(G-8978)*

Sky Marble & Granite Inc 571 926-8085
21592 Atl Blvd Ste 120 Sterling (20166) *(G-13510)*

Sky Software 540 869-6581
114 Lariat Ct Stephens City (22655) *(G-13323)*

Skyboss Drones LLC 434 509-5028
1015 Helmsdale Dr Forest (24551) *(G-5093)*

Skycity 240 467-6270
1850 Columbia Pike # 231 Arlington (22204) *(G-1171)*

Skydog Publications 540 989-2167
6511 Deepwoods Dr Roanoke (24018) *(G-12001)*

Skydweller Aero Inc 585 746-8335
500 Montgomery St Ste 675 Alexandria (22314) *(G-348)*

Skyfall Digital Media, Chesapeake *Also called Duke Industries LLC (G-3078)*

Skyline Fabricating Inc 276 498-3560
1112 Contrary Creek Rd Raven (24639) *(G-10758)*

Skyline Post & Pole LLC 717 949-8170
3881 Industrial Dr Broadway (22815) *(G-2096)*

Skymate Inc 703 961-5800
11890 Sunrise Valley Dr # 100 Reston (20191) *(G-10953)*

Skyship Fantasy Press 703 670-5242
5421 Loggerhead Pl Woodbridge (22193) *(G-15812)*

Skyway Outdoor Inc 276 688-0248
65 Progress Dr Bastian (24314) *(G-1593)*

Slagle Logging & Chipping Inc 434 572-6733
1081 Slagles Mill Rd South Boston (24592) *(G-12789)*

Slate & Shell LLC 804 381-8713
1425 Westshire Ln Richmond (23238) *(G-11384)*

Slater Run Vineyards LLC 540 878-1476
7570 Plum Run Ln Upperville (20184) *(G-13968)*

Slater Run Vneyards Tasting Rm 540 592-3042
9030 John S Mosby Hwy Upperville (20184) *(G-13969)*

Sleepless Warrior Publishing 703 408-4035
14989 Grassy Knoll Ct Woodbridge (22193) *(G-15813)*

Slejs Custom Coating LLC 817 975-6274
1341 Thyme Trl Chesapeake (23320) *(G-3295)*

Slim Silhouettes LLC 757 337-5965
401 N Great Neck Rd Ste 1 Virginia Beach (23454) *(G-14825)*

Slim Strength Inc 804 715-3080
2419 Wendell Ln Richmond (23234) *(G-11064)*

Slipstream Aviation Sftwr Inc 703 729-6535
202 Church St Se Ste 311 Leesburg (20175) *(G-7349)*

SLM Distrubutors Inc 540 774-6817
6743 Corntassel Ln Roanoke (24018) *(G-12002)*

Slopers Stitch House 703 368-7197
10560 Associates Ct Manassas (20109) *(G-8156)*

Slumlord Millionaire LLC 540 529-9259
1925 Salem Ave Sw Roanoke (24016) *(G-12190)*

Slushers Logging & Sawing LLC 540 641-1378
717 Black Ridge Rd Sw Floyd (24091) *(G-5039)*

Slys Sucker Punch LLC 571 989-3538
2552 Miranda Ct Woodbridge (22191) *(G-15814)*

SM Industries LLC 757 966-2343
3248 Bruin Dr Chesapeake (23321) *(G-3296)*

SM Lumber Inc 757 797-8353
900 Commonwealth Pl 200-3 Virginia Beach (23464) *(G-14826)*

Smakaball, Falls Church *Also called Zimar LLC (G-4897)*

Small Arms Mfg Solutions LLC 757 673-7769
1033 Cavalier Blvd Chesapeake (23323) *(G-3297)*

Small Fox Press 540 877-4054
1108 Purcell Ln Winchester (22603) *(G-15479)*

Small Fry Inc 540 477-9664
11 Edwards Way Mount Jackson (22842) *(G-9078)*

Smalley Package Company Inc 540 955-2550
210 1st St Berryville (22611) *(G-1691)*

Smart Blocks, Falls Church *Also called Ixidor LLC (G-4810)*

Smart Buy Kitchen & Bath Plus 571 643-1078
3525 Armfield Farm Dr Chantilly (20151) *(G-2492)*

Smart Machine Technologies Inc 276 632-9853
650 Frith Dr Ridgeway (24148) *(G-11853)*

Smart Marketing Services, North Chesterfield *Also called KEC Associates Ltd (G-9906)*

Smart Start 571 267-7140
201 Davis Dr Sterling (20164) *(G-13511)*

Smart Start Inc 434 392-3334
3561 W 3rd St Farmville (23901) *(G-4957)*

Smart Start Inc 276 223-1006
285 W Monroe St Wytheville (24382) *(G-15913)*

Smart Start of Glen Allen 804 447-7642
2201 Dickens Rd Richmond (23230) *(G-11385)*

Smartcell Inc 703 989-5887
14142 Walton Dr Manassas (20112) *(G-8157)*

Smartdoor Systems Inc 703 560-8093
5711a Center Ln Falls Church (22041) *(G-4876)*

Smartech Inc 804 798-8588
12195 Harley Club Dr Ashland (23005) *(G-1492)*

Smartech Markets Pubg LLC 434 872-9008
2025 Library Ave Ste 402 Crozet (22932) *(G-3850)*

Smartfix 571 723-6499
6500 Springfield Mall Springfield (22150) *(G-13088)*

Smartphone Photobooth 757 364-2403
254 Coventry Close # 201 Chesapeake (23320) *(G-3298)*

Smbltc Corp 703 596-5218
6227 Gwendolyn Dr Manassas (20112) *(G-8158)*

SMC Electrical Products Inc (HQ) **276 285-3841**
14660 Industrial Park Rd Bristol (24202) *(G-2033)*

SMC Holdings & Investment Corp 703 860-0901
11710 Plaza America Dr Reston (20190) *(G-10954)*

SMC Mulch Yard Inc 540 657-5454
78 Shelton Shop Rd Stafford (22554) *(G-13191)*

SMI-Owen Steel Company Inc 434 391-3903
300 Smi Way Farmville (23901) *(G-4958)*

Smiles On Canvas 757 572-2346
4011 Francis Lee Dr Virginia Beach (23452) *(G-14827)*

Smith & Smith Commercial Hood 804 605-0311
20117 Shire Oak Dr South Chesterfield (23803) *(G-12840)*

Smith & Sons Oyster Co Inc B G 804 394-2721
70 Samsons Rd Fanom 22460 22460 Fanom Sharps (22548) *(G-12685)*

Smith and Flannery 804 794-4979
6592 Richmond Rd Williamsburg (23188) *(G-15313)*

Smith Brothers Car Wash Inc 757 397-7711
3523 Western Branch Blvd Portsmouth (23707) *(G-10483)*

Smith Cabinets 703 790-9896
1441 Colleen Ln Mc Lean (22101) *(G-8548)*

Smith Distributors & Mktg LLC 540 760-6833
12503 Argall Ln Fredericksburg (22407) *(G-5362)*

Smith Fabrication Weldin 276 734-5269
779 Wright Rd Ridgeway (24148) *(G-11854)*

Smith Maintenance Services LLC 252 640-5016
924 Tazewell St Portsmouth (23701) *(G-10484)*

Smith Mountain Industries Ltd 540 576-3117
125 Cedar Run Martinsville (24112) *(G-8330)*

Smith Mountain Land & Lbr Inc 540 297-1205
2868 Crab Orchard Rd Huddleston (24104) *(G-6958)*

Smith River Biologicals 276 930-2369
9388 Charity Hwy Ferrum (24088) *(G-4981)*

Smith Setzer Sons Con Pipe Co, Stony Creek *Also called Setzer and Sons VA Inc Smith (G-13568)*

Smith Valley Meats 540 726-3992
Church St Rich Creek (24147) *(G-11008)*

Smith-Midland Corporation 540 439-3266
5119 Catlett Rd Midland (22728) *(G-8763)*

Smith-Midland Corporation (PA) **540 439-3266**
5119 Catlett Rd Midland (22728) *(G-8764)*

Smithfeld Pckged Mats Sls Corp 816 243-2855
200 Commerce St Smithfield (23430) *(G-12724)*

Smithfeld Pckged Mats Sls Corp 816 243-2855
200 Commerce St Smithfield (23430) *(G-12725)*

Smithfield Direct LLC (HQ) **757 365-3000**
200 Commerce St Smithfield (23430) *(G-12726)*

Smithfield Foods Inc 757 933-2977
121 Harwood Dr Newport News (23603) *(G-9343)*

Smithfield Foods Inc 910 862-7675
1911 S Church St Smithfield (23430) *(G-12727)*

Smithfield Foods Inc 804 834-9941
27408 Cabin Point Rd Waverly (23890) *(G-15088)*

Smithfield Foods Inc (HQ) **757 365-3000**
200 Commerce St Smithfield (23430) *(G-12728)*

Smithfield Foods Inc 757 356-6700
111 N Church St Smithfield (23430) *(G-12729)*

Smithfield Foods Inc 757 357-1598
1 Monette Pkwy Smithfield (23430) *(G-12730)*

Smithfield Foods Master Trust 757 365-3000
200 Commerce St Smithfield (23430) *(G-12731)*

Smithfield Fresh Meats Corp 513 782-3800
200 Commerce St Smithfield (23430) *(G-12732)*

Smithfield Packaged Foods, Smithfield *Also called Smithfield Packaged Meats Corp (G-12735)*

Smithfield Packaged Meats Corp 757 357-1798
224 Main St Smithfield (23430) *(G-12733)*

Smithfield Packaged Meats Corp 757 365-3541
112 Commerce St Smithfield (23430) *(G-12734)*

Smithfield Packaged Meats Corp 757 357-3131
601 N Church St Smithfield (23430) *(G-12735)*

Smithfield Packaged Meats Corp 513 782-3800
111 Commerce St Smithfield (23430) *(G-12736)*

Smithfield Packaged Meats Corp 757 357-4321
435 E Indian River Rd Norfolk (23523) *(G-9726)*

Smithfield Packaged Meats Corp 757 357-1382
1911 S Church St Smithfield (23430) *(G-12737)*

Smithfield Packaged Meats Corp 757 357-3131
601 N Church St Smithfield (23430) *(G-12738)*

Smithfield Pet, Smithfield *Also called Premium Pet Health LLC (G-12722)*

Smithfield Support Svcs Corp 757 365-3541
200 Commerce St Smithfield (23430) *(G-12739)*

Smithfield Times 757 357-3288
　228 Main St Smithfield (23430) *(G-12740)*

Smiths Detection Inc 571 346-3400
　11190 Sunrise Valley Dr Reston (20191) *(G-10955)*

Smiths Welding 540 651-2382
　147 Smith Run Ne Pilot (24138) *(G-10359)*

Smittys Welding 540 962-7550
　5631 Johnson Creek Rd Covington (24426) *(G-3797)*

Sml Composites LLC 540 576-3318
　255 Brooks Mill Rd Union Hall (24176) *(G-13961)*

Sml Packaging LLC 434 528-3640
　117 Greystone Dr Lynchburg (24502) *(G-7808)*

Sml Signs & More LLC 540 719-7446
　74 Scruggs Rd Ste 102 Moneta (24121) *(G-8979)*

Sml Water Ski Club Inc 540 328-0425
　425 Baywood Dr Moneta (24121) *(G-8980)*

Smoke Detector Inspector 757 870-4772
　2581 Sandpiper Rd Virginia Beach (23456) *(G-14828)*

Smrt Mouth LLC 804 363-8863
　6000 Technology Blvd Sandston (23150) *(G-12634)*

SMS Data Products Group Inc 703 709-9898
　22930 Shaw Rd Ste 600 Sterling (20166) *(G-13512)*

Smurfit-Stone Container, Ridgeway *Also called Westrock Cp LLC (G-11859)*

Smyth Cnty Mch Fabrication LLC 276 783-4582
　260 Gordondale Rd Atkins (24311) *(G-1521)*

Smyth Companies LLC 540 586-2311
　311 W Depot St Bedford (24523) *(G-1658)*

Smyth County News 276 783-5121
　119 S Sheffey St Marion (24354) *(G-8243)*

Smyth County News & Messenger, Wytheville *Also called Wood Television LLC (G-15924)*

Smyth-Riley 540 477-9652
　5998 Main St Ofc Mount Jackson (22842) *(G-9079)*

Smythers Daris O Sawmill 540 980-5169
　755 Smythers Mountain Rd Allisonia (24347) *(G-620)*

Sn Signs 703 354-3000
　6611 Iron Pl Springfield (22151) *(G-13089)*

Snack Alliance Inc (PA) **276 669-6194**
　225 Commonwealth Ave Bristol (24201) *(G-1987)*

Snakeclamp Products LLC 903 265-8001
　5 Roanoke St Christiansburg (24073) *(G-3609)*

Snature LLC 571 251-1573
　650 Maskell St Apt 307 Alexandria (22301) *(G-349)*

SNC Foods Inc 804 726-9907
　4905 Merlin Ln Glen Allen (23060) *(G-5800)*

SNC Technical Services LLC 787 820-2141
　2696 Reliance Dr Virginia Beach (23452) *(G-14829)*

Snider & Sons Inc 540 626-5849
　378 Eggleston Rd Pembroke (24136) *(G-10284)*

Sniffalicious Candle LLC 276 686-2204
　865 Pine Glade Rd Rural Retreat (24368) *(G-12432)*

Sniffaroo Inc 941 544-3529
　11819 Switchback Ln Fredericksburg (22407) *(G-5363)*

Snips of Vb Coast To Coast, Norfolk *Also called Snips of Virginia Beach Inc (G-9727)*

Snips of Virginia Beach Inc 888 634-5008
　888 Norfolk Sq Norfolk (23502) *(G-9727)*

Snow 39s Woodwork 540 428-1762
　7041 Olinger Rd Marshall (20115) *(G-8260)*

Snow Hill Classics Inc 703 339-6278
　6124 River Dr Lorton (22079) *(G-7530)*

Snowbird Holdings Inc 703 796-0445
　11921 Freedom Dr Ste 1120 Reston (20190) *(G-10956)*

Snows Custom Woodwork 540 428-1763
　7041 Olinger Rd Marshall (20115) *(G-8261)*

Snowshoe Retreats LLC 540 442-6144
　129 University Blvd Harrisonburg (22801) *(G-6372)*

Snt Trucking Inc 276 991-0931
　6929 Miller Creek Rd Swords Creek (24649) *(G-13808)*

Snyder Custom Sign Display 703 362-5675
　8695 Young Ct Springfield (22153) *(G-13090)*

Snyders-Lance Inc 703 339-0541
　8900 Telegraph Rd Ste B Lorton (22079) *(G-7531)*

So Amazing Publications 804 412-5224
　301 Crestfall Ct Petersburg (23805) *(G-10343)*

So Many Socks 703 309-8111
　4883 Cavallo Way Woodbridge (22192) *(G-15815)*

So Olive LLC 571 398-2377
　125 Mill St Unit 10 Occoquan (22125) *(G-10175)*

So Unique Candy Apples 540 915-4899
　16 Church Ave Se Roanoke (24011) *(G-12191)*

So What Publications LLC 757 934-0148
　138 Berkshire Blvd Suffolk (23434) *(G-13765)*

Soap N Suds Laudromats 757 313-0515
　2515 Colley Ave Norfolk (23517) *(G-9728)*

Soaplight LLC 518 898-3441
　110 Coliseum Xing 5130 Hampton (23666) *(G-6240)*

Soapstone Inc 540 745-3492
　139 Cannadays Gap Rd Se Floyd (24091) *(G-5040)*

Soc LLC 757 857-6400
　5426 Robin Hood Rd Norfolk (23513) *(G-9729)*

Soccer Bridge 703 356-0462
　6627 Tucker Ave Mc Lean (22101) *(G-8549)*

Social Dynamics Industries 703 441-2869
　17512 Denali Pl Dumfries (22025) *(G-4256)*

Social Music LLC 202 308-3249
　11801 Hunting Ridge Dr Fredericksburg (22407) *(G-5364)*

Society Nclear Mdcine Mlclar I 703 708-9000
　1850 Samuel Morse Dr Reston (20190) *(G-10957)*

Sociiterra International LLC 804 461-1876
　10451 Pollard Creek Rd Mechanicsville (23116) *(G-8678)*

Sock Software Inc 804 749-4137
　12335 S Anna Dr Bldg B Rockville (23146) *(G-12300)*

Sofie Co 703 787-4075
　100 Executive Dr Ste 4/7 Sterling (20166) *(G-13513)*

Soforeal Entertainment (PA) **804 442-6850**
　9550 Midlothian Tpke North Chesterfield (23235) *(G-9982)*

Soft Edge Inc 703 442-8353
　6888 Elm St Ste 2c Mc Lean (22101) *(G-8550)*

Soft Play 804 226-0380
　3707 Nine Mile Rd Richmond (23223) *(G-11761)*

Softchalk LLC 877 638-2425
　22 S Auburn Ave Richmond (23221) *(G-11762)*

Softchoice Corporation 703 480-1952
　7900 Westpark Dr Ste T400 Mc Lean (22102) *(G-8551)*

Softlogistics LLC 703 865-7965
　337 Walker Rd Great Falls (22066) *(G-5980)*

Software & Systems Solutions L 703 801-7452
　14596 Charity Ct Woodbridge (22193) *(G-15816)*

Software Ag Inc 703 480-1860
　11700 Plaza America Dr # 700 Reston (20190) *(G-10958)*

Software Ag Inc (HQ) **703 860-5050**
　11700 Plaza America Dr # 700 Reston (20190) *(G-10959)*

Software Dfined Dvcs Group LLC 540 623-7175
　1002 Bailey Ct Stafford (22556) *(G-13192)*

Software Engineering Solutions 703 842-1823
　43141 Tall Pines Ct Ashburn (20147) *(G-1334)*

Software Flow Corporation 301 717-0331
　727 Forest Park Rd Great Falls (22066) *(G-5981)*

Software For Mobile Phones LLC 703 862-1079
　7516 Candytuft Ct Springfield (22153) *(G-13091)*

Software Incentives 540 554-2319
　19300 Ebenezer Church Rd Round Hill (20141) *(G-12390)*

Software Insight 703 549-8554
　629 S Fairfax St Alexandria (22314) *(G-350)*

Software Quality Experts LLC 703 291-4641
　1910 Assn Dr Ste 101 Reston (20191) *(G-10960)*

Software Quality Institute 703 313-8404
　5990 Kimberly Anne Way Alexandria (22310) *(G-586)*

Software Security Cons LLC 571 234-3663
　41154 Grenata Preserve Pl Leesburg (20175) *(G-7350)*

Software Solution & Cloud 703 870-7233
　21424 Cliff Haven Ct Sterling (20164) *(G-13514)*

Software Specialists Inc 540 449-2805
　306 Cherokee Dr Ste 500 Blacksburg (24060) *(G-1792)*

Software To Fit LLC 703 378-7239
　13423 Melville Ln Chantilly (20151) *(G-2493)*

Softwright LLC 434 975-4310
　1857 Beech Grv Charlottesville (22911) *(G-2694)*

Soga Inc 202 465-7158
　7503 Wexford Pl Alexandria (22315) *(G-587)*

Soi C4isr Platforms Hanover Co, Ashland *Also called Spec Ops Inc (G-1495)*

Sol Shining 571 719-3957
　8084 Flannery Ct Manassas (20109) *(G-8159)*

Sola Richmond LLC 804 302-4498
　1920 Normandstone Dr Midlothian (23113) *(G-8904)*

Solar Elc Amer Richmond Ci, North Chesterfield *Also called Solar Electric America
LLC (G-10024)*

Solar Electric America LLC 804 332-6358
　7530 Yarmouth Dr North Chesterfield (23225) *(G-10024)*

Solar Lighting Virginia Inc 757 229-3236
　106 Holcomb Dr Williamsburg (23185) *(G-15314)*

Solar Sea Water LLC 215 452-9992
　1021 Arlington Blvd Arlington (22209) *(G-1172)*

Solar Sheet Metal Inc 770 256-2618
　121 Martin Dr Manassas Park (20111) *(G-8211)*

Solarwinds North America Inc 877 946-3751
　2250 Corp Park Dr Ste 210 Herndon (20171) *(G-6811)*

Soleil Foods Ltd Liability Co (PA) **201 920-1553**
　3900 Jermantown Rd # 300 Fairfax (22030) *(G-4679)*

Solevents Floral LLC 571 221-5761
　4119 Middle Ridge Dr Fairfax (22033) *(G-4557)*

Solgreen Solutions LLC 833 765-4733
　6510 Brick Hearth Ct Alexandria (22306) *(G-588)*

Solid State Organ System, Alexandria *Also called 1602 Group LLC (G-394)*

Solid Stone Fabrics Inc 276 634-0115
　405 Walker Rd Martinsville (24112) *(G-8331)*

Solite LLC 757 494-5200
　3900 Shannon St Chesapeake (23324) *(G-3299)*

Solitude Publishers LLC 571 970-3918
　4673 Longstreet Ln # 103 Alexandria (22311) *(G-351)*

(G-0000) Company's Geographic Section entry number

Solo Per Te Baked Goods Inc................................804 277-9010
704 Sunrise Five Way E North Chesterfield (23236) *(G-9983)*

Solstik...571 348-4277
13163 Fox Hunt Ln Apt 411 Herndon (20171) *(G-6812)*

Solutia Inc...314 674-3150
4129 The Great Rd Fieldale (24089) *(G-4991)*

Solutias Performance Films Div, Fieldale *Also called Eastman Performance Films
LLC (G-4984)*

Solution Matrix Inc.......................................540 352-3211
60 Commerce Rd Rocky Mount (24151) *(G-12352)*

Solutions Wise Group......................................804 748-0205
9565 Chipping Dr North Chesterfield (23237) *(G-9984)*

Solvent Industries Inc....................................540 760-8611
5316 Joshua Tree Cir Fredericksburg (22407) *(G-5365)*

Somic America Inc (HQ)..................................**276 228-4307**
343 E Lee Trinkle Dr Wytheville (24382) *(G-15914)*

Son1c Wax LLC..703 508-8188
11515 Four Penny Ln Fairfax Station (22039) *(G-4724)*

Sonawane Webdynamics Inc.............................703 629-7254
44031 Ppeline Plz Ste 305 Ashburn (20147) *(G-1335)*

Sonic Tools LP..804 798-0538
10455 Dow Gil Rd Ashland (23005) *(G-1493)*

Sonoco Products Company................................434 432-2310
Chatham Industrial Park Chatham (24531) *(G-2936)*

Sonoco Products Company................................804 233-5411
1850 Commerce Rd Richmond (23224) *(G-11763)*

Sonoco Products Company................................540 862-4135
9312 Winterberry Ave Covington (24426) *(G-3798)*

Sonoco Products Company................................757 539-8349
326 Moore Ave Suffolk (23434) *(G-13766)*

Sonya Davis Enterprises LLC............................703 264-0533
116 Valleywood Dr Forest (24551) *(G-5094)*

Sophia Street Studio.......................................540 372-3459
1104 Sophia St Fredericksburg (22401) *(G-5225)*

Sophie Gs Candles LLC....................................202 253-7798
15412 Rosemont Manor Dr Haymarket (20169) *(G-6446)*

Sopko Manufacturing Inc..................................434 848-3460
320 W 5th Ave Lawrenceville (23868) *(G-7185)*

Sorbilite Inc...757 460-7330
1 Reflection Ln Hampton (23666) *(G-6241)*

Sorrentino Mariani & Company (PA)....................**757 624-9025**
2701 Saint Julian Ave Norfolk (23504) *(G-9730)*

SOS Hosting, Reston *Also called Infrascale Inc (G-10873)*

Soter Martin of Virginia Inc.............................804 550-2164
713 Harmony Rd Glen Allen (23059) *(G-5801)*

Soul Socks LLC..757 449-5013
1619 Diamond Springs Rd C Virginia Beach (23455) *(G-14830)*

Sound Structures Virginia Inc...........................804 876-3014
17320 Washington Hwy Doswell (23047) *(G-4125)*

Soundpipe LLC..434 218-3394
1110 East Market St 4q Charlottesville (22902) *(G-2879)*

Sounds Greek Inc...757 548-0062
1046 Windswept Cir Chesapeake (23320) *(G-3300)*

Soundscape Comp & Prfmce Exch......................757 645-4671
109 Meadow Rue Ct Williamsburg (23185) *(G-15315)*

Source Consulting Inc......................................540 785-0268
5504 Heritage Hills Cir Fredericksburg (22407) *(G-5366)*

Source Publishing Inc....................................804 747-4080
2316 Persimmon Trek Richmond (23233) *(G-11386)*

Source360 LLC...703 232-1563
4131 Pleasant Meadow Ct Chantilly (20151) *(G-2494)*

South Anna Inc...804 316-9660
3603 Mayland Ct Henrico (23233) *(G-6572)*

South Atlantic LLC...804 798-3257
11022 Lewistown Rd Ashland (23005) *(G-1494)*

South Bay Industries Inc.................................757 489-9344
415 W 24th St Norfolk (23517) *(G-9731)*

South Boston News Inc....................................434 572-2928
511 Broad St South Boston (24592) *(G-12790)*

South Distributors LLC....................................718 258-0200
216 N South St Petersburg (23803) *(G-10344)*

South East Asian Language Publ.........................703 754-6693
8811 Howland Pl Bristow (20136) *(G-2062)*

South East Precast Con LLC..............................276 620-1194
1110 Black Lick Rd Wytheville (24382) *(G-15915)*

South Hill Enterprise, South Hill *Also called Womack Publishing Co Inc (G-12864)*

South River Fabricators....................................540 377-9762
6746 Irish Creek Rd Vesuvius (24483) *(G-13998)*

South Star Distributers....................................276 466-4038
324 Montrose Dr Bristol (24201) *(G-1988)*

South Western Services Inc..............................540 947-5407
11871 W Lynchburg Rd Montvale (24122) *(G-9030)*

South Winds Bindery LLC..................................540 661-7637
30521 Mine Run Rd Locust Grove (22508) *(G-7451)*

Southcoast Welding & Mfg LLC..........................757 574-0090
700 Rosemont Ave Bldg 3 Chesapeake (23324) *(G-3301)*

Southeast Fiber Supply Inc..............................757 653-2318
23437 Jerusalem Rd Courtland (23837) *(G-3774)*

Southeast Frozen Foods Inc..............................800 214-6682
5601 Corrugated Rd Sandston (23150) *(G-12635)*

Southeastern Container Inc..............................540 722-2600
265 W Brooke Rd Winchester (22603) *(G-15480)*

Southeastern Land and Logging.........................540 489-1403
2510 Old Ferrum Rd Ferrum (24088) *(G-4982)*

Southeastern Logging & Chippin........................540 493-9781
3850 Burnt Chimney Rd Wirtz (24184) *(G-15618)*

Southeastern Mechanical Inc (PA)......................**888 461-7848**
27 Bertram Blvd Stafford (22556) *(G-13193)*

Southeastern Wood Products Inc........................276 632-9025
1801 Rivermont Hts Martinsville (24112) *(G-8332)*

Southern Accent Embroidery.............................843 991-4910
11906 Nevis Dr Midlothian (23114) *(G-8905)*

Southern Air Sheet Metal..................................434 907-2268
5 Millrace Dr Lynchburg (24502) *(G-7809)*

Southern Airbrushes..434 324-4049
1381 Shula Dr Hurt (24563) *(G-6978)*

Southern ATL Screenprint Inc............................757 485-7800
3700 Profit Way Chesapeake (23323) *(G-3302)*

Southern Casting LLC......................................757 233-1700
1159 Lance Rd Ste B Norfolk (23502) *(G-9732)*

Southern Custom Tactical Gear, Stafford *Also called Eye Armor Incorporated (G-13144)*

Southern Equipment Company Inc.......................757 888-8500
1571 Manufacture Dr Williamsburg (23185) *(G-15316)*

Southern Finishing Company Inc.........................276 632-4901
801 E Church St Martinsville (24112) *(G-8333)*

Southern Fire & Safety Co.................................434 546-6774
185 Lakehaven Pl Lynchburg (24502) *(G-7810)*

Southern Flavoring Company Inc........................540 586-8565
1330 Norfolk Ave Bedford (24523) *(G-1659)*

Southern Graphic Systems LLC..........................804 226-2490
5301 Lewis Rd Richmond (23218) *(G-11764)*

Southern Gravure Service Inc............................804 226-2490
2891 Sprouse Dr Richmond (23231) *(G-11387)*

Southern Heritage Homes Inc............................540 489-7700
275 Corporate Dr Rocky Mount (24151) *(G-12353)*

Southern Iron Works Inc..................................703 354-5500
6600 Electronic Dr Springfield (22151) *(G-13092)*

Southern Machining Inc....................................276 628-1072
16331 Mountain Spring Rd Abingdon (24210) *(G-61)*

Southern Most Maple, Warm Springs *Also called Mike Puffendarger (G-14973)*

Southern Packing Corporation............................757 421-2131
4004 Battlefield Blvd S Chesapeake (23322) *(G-3303)*

Southern Plumbing & Backhoe In........................804 598-7470
2021 Genito Rd Moseley (23120) *(G-9048)*

Southern Pride Cabinets...................................540 365-3227
1990 Sawmill Rd Ferrum (24088) *(G-4983)*

Southern Printing Co Inc.................................540 552-8352
501 Industrial Park Rd Se Blacksburg (24060) *(G-1793)*

Southern Region Machine Svc............................276 393-3472
157 Industrial Dr Castlewood (24224) *(G-2257)*

Southern Scrap Company Inc.............................540 662-0265
370 Stine Ln Winchester (22603) *(G-15481)*

Southern Screen & Graphics, Virginia Beach *Also called Delrand Corp (G-14401)*

Southern Sheet Metal, Suffolk *Also called Elm Investments Inc (G-13704)*

Southern Stamp Incorporated............................804 359-0531
1506 Tomlynn St Richmond (23230) *(G-11388)*

Southern States Coop Inc.................................540 992-1100
1796 Lee Hwy Cloverdale (24077) *(G-3693)*

Southern States Coop Inc (PA)..........................**804 281-1000**
6606 W Broad St Ste B Richmond (23230) *(G-11389)*

Southern States Coop Inc.................................703 378-4865
14401 Penrose Pl Chantilly (20151) *(G-2495)*

Southern States Coop Inc.................................434 572-6941
1067 Philpott Rd South Boston (24592) *(G-12791)*

Southern States Coop Inc.................................804 226-2758
3119 Williamsburg Rd Richmond (23231) *(G-11390)*

Southern States Coop Inc.................................540 948-5691
1295 N Main St Madison (22719) *(G-7862)*

Southern States Cooperative, Winchester *Also called Southern Sttes Wnchster Coop
I (G-15588)*

Southern States Roanoke Coop...........................540 483-1217
3220 Wirtz Rd Wirtz (24184) *(G-15619)*

Southern Structural Steel Inc (PA)......................**757 623-0862**
20078 I W I P Rd Smithfield (23430) *(G-12741)*

Southern Sttes Wnchster Coop I (PA)..................**540 662-0375**
447 Amherst St Winchester (22601) *(G-15588)*

Southern Tastes LLC.......................................757 204-1414
237 Hanbury Rd E 17-325 Chesapeake (23322) *(G-3304)*

Southern Virginia Equipment............................434 390-0318
2033 Old Kings Hwy Keysville (23947) *(G-7063)*

Southern Woodworks Inc.................................757 566-8307
8630 Merry Oaks Ln Toano (23168) *(G-13878)*

Southernly Sweet Tees.....................................434 447-6572
120 S Mecklenburg Ave South Hill (23970) *(G-12861)*

Southerns M&P LLC..804 330-2407
7607 Midlothian Tpke North Chesterfield (23235) *(G-9985)*

Southfork Enterprises......................................540 879-4372
2567 Honey Run Rd Dayton (22821) *(G-4065)*

Southland Log Homes Inc...............................540 268-2243
80 Hampton Blvd Christiansburg (24073) *(G-3610)*

A
L
P
H
A
B
E
T
I
C

Southland Log Homes Inc 540 548-1617
1465 Carl D Silver Pkwy Fredericksburg (22401) ***(G-5226)***
Southpark Hi LLC 804 777-9000
2000 Ware Btm Spring Rd Chester (23836) ***(G-3455)***
Southpaw Brew Co LLC 703 753-5986
8185 Tenbrook Dr Gainesville (20155) ***(G-5613)***
Southpaw Mechanical LLC (PA) **540 577-6967**
306 1st St Ne Pulaski (24301) ***(G-10646)***
Southprint Inc (PA) **276 666-3000**
545 Hollie Dr Martinsville (24112) ***(G-8334)***
Southside Containers 757 422-1111
500 Central Dr Virginia Beach (23454) ***(G-14831)***
Southside Materials LLC 540 674-5556
5764 Wilderness Rd Dublin (24084) ***(G-4172)***
Southside Oil 804 590-1684
11800 Ivey Mill Rd Chesterfield (23838) ***(G-3526)***
Southside Oil Co 804 204-1624
2200 W Main St Richmond (23220) ***(G-11765)***
Southside Utilities & Maint 434 735-8853
1839 Jeb Stuart Hwy Red Oak (23964) ***(G-10760)***
Southside Voice Inc (PA) **804 644-9060**
205 E Clay St Richmond (23219) ***(G-11766)***
Southside Welding 757 270-7006
4613 Player Ln Virginia Beach (23462) ***(G-14832)***
Southside Youth Festival 434 767-2584
1736 S Genito Rd Burkeville (23922) ***(G-2210)***
Southwest Cmprsr Pmpg Pckges I 276 963-6400
317 Clinic Rd Cedar Bluff (24609) ***(G-2285)***
Southwest Kettle Korn Company 352 201-5664
2419 Highway 107 Saltville (24370) ***(G-12592)***
Southwest Plastic Binding Co 804 226-0400
6601 S Laburnum Ave Richmond (23231) ***(G-11391)***
Southwest Publisher LLC (PA) **540 980-5220**
34 5th St Ne Pulaski (24301) ***(G-10647)***
Southwest Sign Maintenance, Big Stone Gap *Also called Daniel Rollins* ***(G-1709)***
Southwest Specialty Heat Treat 276 228-7739
255 E Marshall St Wytheville (24382) ***(G-15916)***
Southwest Times, Pulaski *Also called Southwest Publisher LLC* ***(G-10647)***
Southwstern Vrgnia Wheelco Inc 540 493-6886
948 Chantilly Rd Rocky Mount (24151) ***(G-12354)***
Sovereign Intelligence LLC 571 455-4016
118 Moore Ave Se Vienna (22180) ***(G-14131)***
Sovereign Media 703 964-0361
6731 Whittier Ave C100 Mc Lean (22101) ***(G-8552)***
Sowa & Nicholas Printing, Arlington *Also called Harrison Management Associates* ***(G-989)***
Soywick Candles LLC 571 333-4750
18772 Upper Meadow Dr Lansdowne (20176) ***(G-7173)***
Sp Smoothies Inc 757 595-0600
4191 William Styron Sq N Newport News (23606) ***(G-9344)***
Spa Guy LLC 757 855-0381
1228 Cavalier Blvd Chesapeake (23323) ***(G-3305)***
Space Logistics LLC 703 406-5474
45101 Warp Dr Dulles (20166) ***(G-4227)***
Space Systems Division, Dulles *Also called Orbital Sciences LLC* ***(G-4218)***
Spacelogistics, Dulles *Also called Space Logistics LLC* ***(G-4227)***
Spacenews Inc 571 421-2300
1414 Prince St Ste 204 Alexandria (22314) ***(G-352)***
Spacequest Ltd 703 424-7801
3554 Chain Bridge Rd # 40 Fairfax (22030) ***(G-4680)***
Spades & Diamonds Clothing Co 804 271-0374
7733 Belmont Rd Chesterfield (23832) ***(G-3527)***
Spanx Inc 888 806-7311
229 Hollie Dr Martinsville (24112) ***(G-8335)***
Sparklenshinecollection 703 939-7623
122 Poinsettia Way Stephenson (22656) ***(G-13335)***
Sparks Companies Inc 703 734-8787
6862 Elm St Mc Lean (22101) ***(G-8553)***
Sparks Electric 540 967-0436
35 Loudin Ln Louisa (23093) ***(G-7568)***
Sparkzone Inc 703 861-0650
4005 Stonewall Ave Fairfax (22032) ***(G-4558)***
Spartan Inds Martinsville 276 632-3033
2201 Appalachian Dr Martinsville (24112) ***(G-8336)***
Spartan Shower Shoe LLC 540 623-6625
1200 N Veitch St Apt 1421 Arlington (22201) ***(G-1173)***
Spartan Village LLC 661 724-6438
15109 Anacortes Trl Gainesville (20155) ***(G-5614)***
Spartancore Industries 540 322-7563
44 Charter Gate Dr Fredericksburg (22406) ***(G-5486)***
Speakeasy 703 333-5040
6725 Alpine Dr Annandale (22003) ***(G-783)***
Spears & Associate 540 752-5577
97 Timberidge Dr Hartwood (22471) ***(G-6392)***
Spec Ops Inc 804 752-4790
319 Business Ln Ste 100 Ashland (23005) ***(G-1495)***
Spec-Trim Mfg Co Inc 804 739-9333
12727 Spectrim Ln Midlothian (23112) ***(G-8906)***
Special Communications LLC 202 677-1225
2838 Croix Ct Virginia Beach (23451) ***(G-14833)***
Special Fleet Services Inc (PA) **540 434-4488**
875 Waterman Dr Harrisonburg (22802) ***(G-6373)***
Special Fleet Services Inc 540 433-7727
2500 S Main St Harrisonburg (22801) ***(G-6374)***
Special Projects Operations 410 297-6550
2569 Horse Pasture Rd Virginia Beach (23453) ***(G-14834)***
Special T Manufacturing Corp 276 475-5510
21250 Mccann Rd Damascus (24236) ***(G-3950)***
Special Tactical Services LLC 757 554-0699
5725 Arrowhead Dr Virginia Beach (23462) ***(G-14835)***
Specialist Manufacture 540 974-0780
325 Westernview Dr Middletown (22645) ***(G-8743)***
Speciality Drapery, Richmond *Also called Speciality Group Ltd* ***(G-11767)***
Speciality Group Ltd 804 264-3000
1221 Admiral St Richmond (23220) ***(G-11767)***
Specialty Club, Virginia Beach *Also called Mova Corp* ***(G-14666)***
Specialty Enterprises Inc 804 781-0314
5176 Farmer Dr Mechanicsville (23111) ***(G-8679)***
Specialty Finishes Inc 804 232-5027
311 Tynick St Richmond (23224) ***(G-11768)***
Specialty Machining & Fabg 540 984-4265
531 Hillcrest Rd Edinburg (22824) ***(G-4315)***
Specialty Marine Inc 757 494-1199
513 Freeman Ave Chesapeake (23324) ***(G-3306)***
Specialty Tooling LLC 804 912-1158
8656 Staples Mill Rd Henrico (23228) ***(G-6573)***
Specialty Vhcl Solutions LLC 609 882-1900
3930 Castle Rock Rd Ste H Midlothian (23112) ***(G-8907)***
Specialty's Our Name, Ashland *Also called Jvh Company Inc* ***(G-1446)***
Specomm, Virginia Beach *Also called Special Communications LLC* ***(G-14833)***
Spectacle & Mirth 619 961-6941
626 W Frederick St Staunton (24401) ***(G-13296)***
Spectacular Spectacles Inc 540 636-2020
1211 N Shenandoah Ave Front Royal (22630) ***(G-5555)***
Spectra Energy Partners, Atkins *Also called East Tennessee Natural Gas Co* ***(G-1516)***
Spectra Lab LLC 703 634-5290
17873 Main St Ste C Dumfries (22026) ***(G-4257)***
Spectra Quest Inc 804 261-3300
8227 Hermitage Rd Henrico (23228) ***(G-6574)***
Spectrarep LLC 703 227-9690
14150 Prkeast Cir Ste 110 Chantilly (20151) ***(G-2496)***
Spectrum 757 224-7500
1 Bayport Way Ste 300 Newport News (23606) ***(G-9345)***
Spectrum Brands Pet LLC 540 951-5481
3001 Commerce St Blacksburg (24060) ***(G-1794)***
Spectrum Center Inc 703 848-4750
1451 Dolley Madison Blvd Mc Lean (22101) ***(G-8554)***
Spectrum Entertainment Inc 757 491-2873
101 S 1st Clnl Rd Ste 101 Virginia Beach (23454) ***(G-14836)***
Spectrum Laboratories, Norton *Also called Maxxim Shared Services LLC* ***(G-10127)***
Spectrum Metal Services Inc 804 744-0387
1624 Oak Lake Blvd E Midlothian (23112) ***(G-8908)***
Spectrum Optometric 804 457-8733
8709 Forest Hill Ave North Chesterfield (23235) ***(G-9986)***
Spectrum Printing, Virginia Beach *Also called Lone Tree Printing Inc* ***(G-14623)***
Spectrum Puppet Productions, Virginia Beach *Also called Spectrum Entertainment Inc* ***(G-14836)***
Spedapps LLC 757 541-2663
1550 Shell Rd Chesapeake (23323) ***(G-3307)***
Speed and Accuracy LLC 405 375-3432
13100 Weather Vane Way Herndon (20171) ***(G-6813)***
Speedmter Clbrtion Specialists 434 821-5374
158 One Mile Rd Evington (24550) ***(G-4384)***
Speedpro 757 233-9250
5305 Cleveland St Virginia Beach (23462) ***(G-14837)***
Speedpro Imaging - Centreville 571 719-3161
8108 Flannery Ct Manassas (20109) ***(G-8160)***
Speedpro Imaging Northern VA, Sterling *Also called Rycon Inc* ***(G-13498)***
Speedway LLC 757 498-4625
212a 70th St Virginia Beach (23451) ***(G-14838)***
Speedway LLC 757 599-6250
1724 George Washington Me Yorktown (23693) ***(G-15992)***
Speedy Sign-A-Rama USA Inc 757 838-7446
3303 W Mercury Blvd Hampton (23666) ***(G-6242)***
Spence Publishing Co Inc 214 939-1700
6708 Lupine Ln Mc Lean (22101) ***(G-8555)***
Spencer Stnless Alum Guttering 434 277-8359
765 Mollys Mountain Rd Amherst (24521) ***(G-708)***
Sperry Marine Division, Chesapeake *Also called Northrop Grumman Systems Corp* ***(G-3222)***
Spheringenics Inc 770 330-0782
800 E Leigh St Ste 51 Richmond (23219) ***(G-11769)***
Sphinx Industries Inc 804 279-8894
7101 Bridgeside Ct North Chesterfield (23234) ***(G-9987)***
Spice Rack Chocolates, Fredericksburg *Also called My Extra Hands LLC* ***(G-5330)***
Spicewater Electronic Home Mon 276 690-4718
168 Mcconnell St Gate City (24251) ***(G-5668)***
Spicy Vinegar LLC 757 460-3861
2225 Indian Hill Rd Virginia Beach (23455) ***(G-14839)***

Spider Embroidery Inc 540 955-2347
126 Mill Race Dr Winchester (22602) ***(G-15482)***
Spider Support Systems 703 758-0699
11654 Plaza America Dr # 180 Reston (20190) ***(G-10961)***
Spig Industry LLC 276 644-9510
14675 Industrial Park Rd Bristol (24202) ***(G-2034)***
Spigner Structural & Miscellan 703 625-7572
214 1st St Berryville (22611) ***(G-1692)***
Spinfinity 540 283-9370
4142 Melrose Ave Nw Roanoke (24017) ***(G-12192)***
Spinning In Control LLC 703 455-9223
9607 Little Cobbler Ct Burke (22015) ***(G-2203)***
Spirit Halloween 804 513-2966
342 Southpark Cir Colonial Heights (23834) ***(G-3748)***
Spirit Socks 757 802-6160
1537 Quail Point Rd Virginia Beach (23454) ***(G-14840)***
Spiritway LLC 831 676-1014
8813 Skokie Ln Vienna (22182) ***(G-14132)***
Spitfire Management LLC 757 644-4609
1769 Jamestown Rd Ste 113 Williamsburg (23185) ***(G-15317)***
Spitzer Machine Shop 540 896-5827
16089 Lairs Run Rd Fulks Run (22830) ***(G-5566)***
Splendor Publishing 434 665-2339
308 Kenyon St Lynchburg (24501) ***(G-7811)***
Splendoras 434 296-8555
317 E Main St Charlottesville (22902) ***(G-2880)***
Sport Creations LLC 757 572-2113
210 44th St Virginia Beach (23451) ***(G-14841)***
Sport Shack Inc 540 372-3719
102 Castle Rock Dr Fredericksburg (22405) ***(G-5487)***
Sports Line, Stuarts Draft *Also called Khk Inc* ***(G-13654)***
Sports Plus Incorporated 703 222-8255
4429 Brkfeld Corp Dr Ste Chantilly (20151) ***(G-2497)***
Sports Products World Entps 888 493-6079
300 Commerce Cir Ste D Yorktown (23693) ***(G-15993)***
Sports Supplements South Inc 804 379-6410
477 Southlake Blvd North Chesterfield (23236) ***(G-9988)***
Sports Unstoppable LLC 571 346-7622
1818 Library St Ste 500 Reston (20190) ***(G-10962)***
Sportstitch 804 387-5127
6371 Yellowrose Ln Mechanicsville (23111) ***(G-8680)***
Spot Coolers Inc 804 222-5530
5742 Charles City Cir Richmond (23231) ***(G-11392)***
Spotcity Cupcakes LLC 703 587-4934
5502 Joshua Tree Cir Fredericksburg (22407) ***(G-5367)***
Spotlight Dance LLC 703 753-9173
13920 Shelter Manor Dr Haymarket (20169) ***(G-6447)***
Spotlight On Sports LLC 804 615-3284
2103 Carbon Hill Pl Midlothian (23113) ***(G-8909)***
Spotlight Studio 540 338-2690
300 S Orchard Dr Purcellville (20132) ***(G-10679)***
Spotspot Co 804 909-7353
5407 Patterson Ave 200a Richmond (23226) ***(G-11393)***
Spotted Hawk Development LLC 703 286-1450
1650 Tysons Blvd Ste 900 Mc Lean (22102) ***(G-8556)***
Spotted Lopard-Tabula Rasa LLC 571 285-8151
7442 Lake Willow Ct Warrenton (20187) ***(G-15053)***
Spraying Systems Co 804 364-0095
13605 Swanhollow Dr Richmond (23233) ***(G-11394)***
Sprecher & Schuh Inc 804 379-6065
821 Southlake Blvd North Chesterfield (23236) ***(G-9989)***
Sprecher Schuh, North Chesterfield *Also called Sprecher & Schuh Inc* ***(G-9989)***
Spreco Creamery 540 529-1581
2507 Memorial Ave Sw Roanoke (24015) ***(G-12193)***
Spring Grove Inc 540 721-1502
82 Park Way Ave Moneta (24121) ***(G-8981)***
Spring Hollow Publishing Inc 434 984-4718
1700 Owensville Rd Charlottesville (22901) ***(G-2695)***
Spring Moses Inc 804 321-0156
6414 Horsepen Rd Richmond (23226) ***(G-11395)***
Spring Run Vineyards LLC 804 382-4529
10700 Spring Run Rd Chesterfield (23832) ***(G-3528)***
Spring Valley Graphics 276 236-4357
99 Bee Line Dr Galax (24333) ***(G-5648)***
Springboard Retail Inc 888 347-2191
3141 Fairview Park Dr Falls Church (22042) ***(G-4877)***
Springbrook Craft Works 540 896-3404
256 W Springbrook Rd Broadway (22815) ***(G-2097)***
Springfield Connection 703 866-1040
8634 Hillside Manor Dr Springfield (22152) ***(G-13093)***
Springfield Custom Auto Mch 703 339-0999
8532v Terminal Rd Lorton (22079) ***(G-7532)***
Springfield Distillery LLC 434 572-1888
9040 River Rd Halifax (24558) ***(G-6052)***
Springfield Times 703 437-5400
1760 Reston Pkwy Reston (20190) ***(G-10963)***
Springs Global Us Inc 276 670-3440
460 Beaver Creek Dr Martinsville (24112) ***(G-8337)***
Springwood Airstrip 540 473-2079
331 Intermont Farm Ln Buchanan (24066) ***(G-2128)***
Sprint Signs 804 741-7446
9020 Quioccasin Rd Ste C Richmond (23229) ***(G-11396)***
Spritelogic LLC 703 568-0468
1027 Northwoods Trl Mc Lean (22102) ***(G-8557)***
Sprouting Star Press 703 860-0958
2034 Golf Course Dr Reston (20191) ***(G-10964)***
Spunkysales LLC 727 492-1636
5525 Callander Dr Springfield (22151) ***(G-13094)***
Spur Defense Systems 540 742-8394
8324 Reagan Dr King George (22485) ***(G-7114)***
Spydrsafe Mobile Security Inc 703 286-0750
1616 Anderson Rd Mc Lean (22102) ***(G-8558)***
SQ Labs LLC 804 938-8123
4238 Oakleys Ct Ste D Richmond (23223) ***(G-11770)***
Sqlexec LLC 703 600-9343
8403 Tobin Rd Annandale (22003) ***(G-784)***
Squabble State Distlg Co LLC 804 393-8380
529 State St Apt 2 Bristol (24201) ***(G-1989)***
Square One Organic Spirits LLC 415 612-4151
3370 Bear Den Ct Charlottesville (22903) ***(G-2881)***
Square One Printing Inc 904 993-4321
519 N 22nd St Richmond (23223) ***(G-11771)***
Square Penny Publishing LLC 757 348-2226
1853 Burson Dr Chesapeake (23323) ***(G-3308)***
Squrl LLC 443 481-9941
496 Cleveland Ave Charlottesville (22903) ***(G-2882)***
Sra Companies Inc 703 803-1500
15036 Conference Ctr Dr Chantilly (20151) ***(G-2498)***
Srg Government Solutions Inc 703 609-7027
4323 Argonne Dr Fairfax (22032) ***(G-4559)***
SRI Seven Fair Lakes LLC 703 631-2350
12500 Fair Lakes Cir Fairfax (22033) ***(G-4560)***
Srj Bedliners LLC 757 539-7710
2432 Pruden Blvd Suffolk (23434) ***(G-13767)***
Srm Logistics LLC 757 232-9928
3201 Bruin Dr Chesapeake (23321) ***(G-3309)***
Srn Software LLC 703 646-5186
8608 Monacan Ct Lorton (22079) ***(G-7533)***
Ss Winery LLC 908 548-3016
174 White Pine Cir # 301 Stafford (22554) ***(G-13194)***
Ssa Fabrication LLC 703 479-7377
9107 Industry Dr Ste B Manassas Park (20111) ***(G-8212)***
Ssb Manufacturing Company 540 891-0236
9601 Cosner Dr Fredericksburg (22408) ***(G-5368)***
SSC, Virginia Beach *Also called Santa Inc* ***(G-14794)***
SSC Innovations LLC 703 761-2818
1593 Spring Hill Rd # 700 Vienna (22182) ***(G-14133)***
Ssecurity LLC 703 590-4240
4900 Tobacco Way Woodbridge (22193) ***(G-15817)***
Ssr Foods LLC 703 581-7260
8861 Yellow Hammer Dr Gainesville (20155) ***(G-5615)***
St Clair Signs Inc 540 258-2191
1630 Blue Ridge Rd Glasgow (24555) ***(G-5702)***
St Cove Point LLC 713 897-1624
1021 E Cary St Fl 1920 Richmond (23219) ***(G-11772)***
St Engineering Idirect Inc (HQ) **703 648-8002**
13861 Sunrise Valley Dr # 300 Herndon (20171) ***(G-6814)***
St Engineering North Amer Inc (HQ) **703 739-2610**
99 Canal Center Plz # 220 Alexandria (22314) ***(G-353)***
St Petersburg Collection, The, Great Falls *Also called Aeroart International Inc* ***(G-5934)***
St Pierre Inc 540 797-3496
2081 Cannady School Rd Se Floyd (24091) ***(G-5041)***
St Tissue LLC 757 304-5040
34050 Union Camp Dr Franklin (23851) ***(G-5156)***
STA-Fit Industries LLC 540 308-8215
72 Garden Ct Ruckersville (22968) ***(G-12414)***
Staab Sign Language Svcs LLC 301 775-2279
4390 King St Apt 712 Alexandria (22302) ***(G-354)***
Stacey A Peets 847 707-3112
2706a Enterprise Pkwy Henrico (23294) ***(G-6575)***
Stack Labs Inc 503 453-5172
5501 Merchants View Sq Haymarket (20169) ***(G-6448)***
Stack Lighting, Haymarket *Also called Stack Labs Inc* ***(G-6448)***
Stacker Inc A G 540 234-6012
30 Packaging Dr Ste 104 Weyers Cave (24486) ***(G-15177)***
Stafford County Sun 540 659-8923
306 Garrisonville Rd # 103 Stafford (22554) ***(G-13195)***
Stafford Home Products 540 337-0068
24 Lucas Rd Fishersville (22939) ***(G-5009)***
Stafford Printing, Stafford *Also called Boaz Publishing Inc* ***(G-13124)***
Stafford Salad Company LLC 540 269-2462
2924 Keezletown Rd Keezletown (22832) ***(G-7030)***
Stafford Stone Works LLC 540 372-6601
1500 Howard Ave Fredericksburg (22401) ***(G-5227)***
Stage Sound Inc 540 342-2040
2240 Shenandoah Ave Nw Roanoke (24017) ***(G-12194)***
Stahmer Inc 757 838-4200
3003 W Mercury Blvd Hampton (23666) ***(G-6243)***
Staib Instruments Inc 757 565-7000
101 Stafford Ct Williamsburg (23185) ***(G-15318)***

A L P H A B E T I C

Stained Glass Creations Inc 804 798-8806
10049 Lickinghole Rd F Ashland (23005) *(G-1496)*

Stair Store Inc 703 794-0507
13573 Den Hollow Ct Manassas (20112) *(G-8161)*

Staircraft 540 347-7023
6402 Old Bust Head Rd Broad Run (20137) *(G-2070)*

Stallworks LLC 434 933-8939
9056 Oakville Rd Gladstone (24553) *(G-5688)*

Stampers Bay Publishing LLC 804 776-9122
550 Stampers Bay Rd Hartfield (23071) *(G-6391)*

Stamptech Inc 434 845-9091
19 Millrace Dr Lynchburg (24502) *(G-7812)*

Stamptech Inc (HQ) **804 768-4658**
13140 Parkers Battery Rd Chester (23836) *(G-3456)*

Stan Garfin Publications Inc 757 495-3644
1216 Heathcliff Dr Virginia Beach (23464) *(G-14842)*

Stanburn Winery LLC 276 694-7074
158 Conner Dr Stuart (24171) *(G-13631)*

Standard Banner Coal Corp 276 944-5603
29059 Rivermont Dr Meadowview (24361) *(G-8596)*

Standard Core Drilling Co Inc 276 395-3391
108 Quillen Ave Se Coeburn (24230) *(G-3703)*

Standard Marine Inc 757 824-0293
27066 Turkey Run Rd Mears (23409) *(G-8597)*

Standard Printing & Office Sup, Covington *Also called Standard Printing Company Inc (G-3799)*

Standard Printing Company Inc 540 965-1150
356 W Main St Covington (24426) *(G-3799)*

Standard Register Inc 703 516-4014
1110 N Glebe Rd 750 Arlington (22201) *(G-1174)*

Standard Welding Corp 757 423-0470
830 W 40th St Norfolk (23508) *(G-9733)*

Standex Engraving LLC (HQ) **804 236-3092**
5901 Lewis Rd Sandston (23150) *(G-12636)*

Standing People Woodworking, Timberville *Also called Robson Woodworking (G-13854)*

Stanford Electronics Mfg & Sls 434 676-6630
915 Berry Rd Brodnax (23920) *(G-2105)*

Stanley Access Tech LLC 804 598-0502
126 Sloane Pl Newport News (23606) *(G-9346)*

Stans Signs Inc 540 434-1531
3128 Osceola Springs Rd Rockingham (22801) *(G-12278)*

Stans Ski and Snowboard LLC 540 885-9625
702 Richmond Ave Staunton (24401) *(G-13297)*

Staples Print & Marketing 434 218-6425
600 Twentyninth Place Ct Charlottesville (22901) *(G-2696)*

Star Childrens Dress Co Inc 804 561-5060
9120 Pridesville Rd Amelia Court House (23002) *(G-673)*

Star City Welding LLC 540 343-1428
712 Norfolk Ave Sw Roanoke (24016) *(G-12195)*

Star Home Theater LLC 855 978-2748
42714 Cool Breeze Sq Leesburg (20176) *(G-7351)*

Star Oil LLC 757 545-5100
400 Freeman Ave Ste A Chesapeake (23324) *(G-3310)*

Star Printing Co Inc 757 625-7782
413 Oak Lake Ter Chesapeake (23320) *(G-3311)*

Star Tag & Label Inc 540 389-6848
1535 Mill Race Dr Salem (24153) *(G-12571)*

Star Trac, Independence *Also called Core Health & Fitness LLC (G-6980)*

Star Tribune, Chatham *Also called Womack Publishing Co Inc (G-2942)*

Star US Precision Industry Ltd 804 747-8948
3781 Westerre Pkwy Ste F Richmond (23233) *(G-11397)*

Stardog Union 202 408-8770
2101 Wilson Blvd Ste 800 Arlington (22201) *(G-1175)*

Starlight Express LLC 434 295-0782
1117 East Market St Ste H Charlottesville (22902) *(G-2883)*

Starmark Cabinetry 434 385-7500
1 Macel Dr Lynchburg (24502) *(G-7813)*

Starr Hill Brewing Company 434 823-5671
5391 Three Notch D Rd Crozet (22932) *(G-3851)*

Starry Nights Scrapbooking LLC 757 784-6163
104 Catawba Ct Williamsburg (23185) *(G-15319)*

Starsprings USA Inc 276 403-4500
250 Fontaine Dr Ridgeway (24148) *(G-11855)*

Startup Virginia 804 502-3131
1712 Buford Rd North Chesterfield (23235) *(G-9990)*

State and Homes Magazine, Midlothian *Also called Homes & Land of Richmond (G-8827)*

State Fair Popcorn Company, Williamsburg *Also called Katheryn Warren (G-15264)*

State Line Controls Inc 757 969-8527
3420 Wilshire Rd Portsmouth (23703) *(G-10485)*

Stateline Builders Inc 757 934-6836
2017 Holland Rd Suffolk (23434) *(G-13768)*

Stateline Graphics, Weber City *Also called Mardon Inc (G-15149)*

Stately Dogs 276 644-4098
28 Commonwealth Ave Bristol (24201) *(G-1990)*

Statement LLC 757 635-6294
1324 Akinburry Rd Virginia Beach (23456) *(G-14843)*

Statesman Computers, Charlotte C H *Also called Charlotte County School Board (G-2583)*

Statice Quo LLC 703 646-5411
8202 Catbird Cir Unit 101 Lorton (22079) *(G-7534)*

Station 6 Brewing Company, Ashburn *Also called Station 6 Brewing LLC (G-1336)*

Station 6 Brewing LLC 571 510-3532
44427 Atwater Dr Ashburn (20147) *(G-1336)*

Staton & Hauling 434 946-7913
1467 Richmond Hwy Amherst (24521) *(G-709)*

Staton & Son Logging 540 570-3614
381 E 29th St Buena Vista (24416) *(G-2154)*

Staton Mj & Associates Ltd 804 737-1946
438 E Williamsburg Rd Sandston (23150) *(G-12637)*

Staunton Machine Works Inc 540 886-0733
608 Richmond Ave Staunton (24401) *(G-13298)*

Staunton Olive Oil Company LLC 540 290-9665
126 W Beverley St Staunton (24401) *(G-13299)*

Staunton River Outdoors LLC 434 608-2601
508b Pittsylvania Ave B Altavista (24517) *(G-644)*

Staunton VA 651 765-6778
207 Laurel Hill Rd Verona (24482) *(G-13996)*

Stauropegion, Fairfax *Also called Eastern Chrstn Pblications LLC (G-4615)*

Stay In Touch Inc 434 239-7300
1149 Vista Park Dr Ste D Forest (24551) *(G-5095)*

STC Catalysts Inc 757 766-5810
21 Enterprise Pkwy # 150 Hampton (23666) *(G-6244)*

Stcube Pharmaceuticals Inc 703 815-1446
5233 Jule Star Dr Centreville (20120) *(G-2341)*

Stealth Dump Trucks Inc 757 890-4888
111 Old Railway Rd Yorktown (23692) *(G-15994)*

Stealth Mfg & Svcs LLC 787 679-7548
2512 Aviator Dr Virginia Beach (23453) *(G-14844)*

Stealth Surgical LLC 540 832-5580
104 Sommerfield Dr Zion Crossroads (22942) *(G-16009)*

Stealthpath LLC 571 888-6772
10700 Parkridge Blvd # 30 Reston (20191) *(G-10965)*

Steam Valley Publishing 703 255-9884
401 Blair Rd Nw Vienna (22180) *(G-14134)*

Steamed Ink 540 904-6211
1212 Penmar Ave Se Roanoke (24013) *(G-12196)*

Steel America, Norfolk *Also called Colonnas Ship Yard Inc (G-9495)*

Steel America, Norfolk *Also called Colonnas Ship Yard Inc (G-9496)*

Steel Building Pros, Virginia Beach *Also called US Building Systems Inc (G-14903)*

Steel Dynamics Inc 540 342-1831
102 Westside Blvd Nw Roanoke (24017) *(G-12197)*

Steel Fab 276 628-3843
58 Samuel Way Dr Lebanon (24266) *(G-7207)*

Steel Mates 540 825-7333
16144 Bradford Rd Culpeper (22701) *(G-3922)*

Steel Mouse Trap Publications 703 542-2327
43579 Mink Meadows St Chantilly (20152) *(G-2557)*

Steel Tech LLC 571 585-5861
21202 Huntington Sq # 301 Sterling (20166) *(G-13515)*

Steele Construction, Toano *Also called David Steele (G-13863)*

Steelfab Inc 703 538-2320
1330 Braddock Pl Ste 200v Alexandria (22314) *(G-355)*

Steelfab of Virginia Inc 434 348-9021
1510 Reese St Emporia (23847) *(G-4367)*

Steelgate LLC 337 263-2490
42386 Willow Creek Way Brambleton (20148) *(G-1933)*

Steelmaster Buildings LLC 757 961-7006
1023 Laskin Rd Ste 109 Virginia Beach (23451) *(G-14845)*

Steelwright Products 951 870-6670
20254 Shockey Ln Beaverdam (23015) *(G-1612)*

Steep LLC 571 271-5690
1750 Tysons Blvd Ste 1500 Mc Lean (22102) *(G-8559)*

Stefanik Sign Service 540 295-7248
1461 Warrenton Rd Fredericksburg (22406) *(G-5488)*

Steffan Lott 786 366-9494
326 W Mcginnis Cir Norfolk (23502) *(G-9734)*

Stella Stone and Sealant LLC 917 568-6489
8806 Southlea Ct Fairfax (22031) *(G-4561)*

Stella-Jones Corporation 540 997-9251
9223 Maury River Rd Goshen (24439) *(G-5927)*

Stellar Day Products Corp 804 748-8086
9565 Chipping Dr North Chesterfield (23237) *(G-9991)*

Stelling Banjo Works Ltd 434 295-1917
7258 Banjo Ln Afton (22920) *(G-90)*

Stellosphere Inc 631 897-4678
43645 Meadow Overlook Pl Ashburn (20147) *(G-1337)*

Stem Technologies LLC 703 787-4654
13126 Deer Wood Way Herndon (20171) *(G-6815)*

Stemcelllife LLC 843 410-3067
800 E Leigh St Richmond (23219) *(G-11773)*

Stephan Burger Fine Wdwkg 434 960-5440
5001 W Leigh St Richmond (23230) *(G-11398)*

Stephen Bialorucki 757 374-2080
5165 Stratford Chase Dr Virginia Beach (23464) *(G-14846)*

Stephen C Marston 757 562-0271
401 East St Franklin (23851) *(G-5157)*

Stephen Dunnavant 804 337-3629
11825 Riverpark Ter Chesterfield (23838) *(G-3529)*

Stephen Hawley Martin, Richmond *Also called Oaklea Press Inc (G-11311)*

Stephen W Mast 804 467-3608
  8403 Kaye Dr Mechanicsville (23116) *(G-8681)*

Stephenson Lithograph Inc 703 241-0806
  4014 38th Pl N Arlington (22207) *(G-1176)*

Stephenson Printing Inc 703 642-9000
  5731 General Wash Dr Alexandria (22312) *(G-589)*

Sterile Home LLC 804 314-3589
  2146 Cold Cheer Dr Tappahannock (22560) *(G-13822)*

Sterling Blower Company (PA) **434 316-5310**
  135 Vista Centre Dr Forest (24551) *(G-5096)*

Sterling Environmental Inc 540 898-5079
  7308 Bloomsbury Ln Spotsylvania (22553) *(G-12917)*

Sterling Flyers LLC 571 830-4476
  11621 Vantage Hill Rd Reston (20190) *(G-10966)*

Sterling Sheet Metal Inc 540 338-0144
  36767 Pelham Ct Sterling (20164) *(G-13516)*

Stern Welding LLC 571 283-1355
  13803 Leighfield St Chantilly (20151) *(G-2499)*

Sterns Printing and Engrv Co, Richmond *Also called Professional Business Prtg Inc (G-11337)*

Steve D Gilnett 804 746-5497
  7160 Catlin Rd Mechanicsville (23111) *(G-8682)*

Steve Hollar Wdwkg & Engrv 703 273-0639
  11648 Leehigh Dr Fairfax (22030) *(G-4681)*

Steve K Jones 757 930-0217
  74 Maxwell Ln Newport News (23606) *(G-9347)*

Steve M Sheil 757 482-2456
  508 Mustang Dr Chesapeake (23322) *(G-3312)*

Steve S 2 Express 757 336-7377
  6761 Maddox Blvd Chincoteague (23336) *(G-3566)*

Steve Stone 276 956-8451
  303 Pintail Ln Henry (24102) *(G-6597)*

Steven Alsahi 703 369-0099
  10630 Crestwood Dr Ste A Manassas (20109) *(G-8162)*

Steven D Thomas 540 254-2964
  343 17th St Buchanan (24066) *(G-2129)*

Steven Hamm Goldsmith Designs, Charlottesville *Also called Ronald Steven Hamm (G-2866)*

Stevens & Sons Lumber Co 434 822-7105
  58 Intersection Rr 726 Ringgold (24586) *(G-11874)*

Stevens Burial Vault LLC 804 443-5125
  10664 Tidewater Trl Champlain (22438) *(G-2357)*

Stevens Switch LLC 703 838-0686
  630 S Fairfax St Alexandria (22314) *(G-356)*

Steves & Sons Inc 804 226-4034
  5640 Lewis Rd Sandston (23150) *(G-12638)*

Steves Generator Service LLC 540 661-8675
  15620 Burnley Rd Barboursville (22923) *(G-1567)*

Steves Pallets 757 576-4488
  1637 Hawks Bill Dr Virginia Beach (23464) *(G-14847)*

Steves Signworx LLC 434 385-1000
  117 Vista Centre Dr Ste E Forest (24551) *(G-5097)*

Stewart David 703 431-7233
  1101 N Gaillard St Alexandria (22304) *(G-357)*

Stewart Furniture Design Inc 276 744-0186
  2945 Scenic Rd Fries (24330) *(G-5518)*

STI, Eagle Rock *Also called Systems Technology VA LLC (G-4283)*

Stich N Print 276 326-2005
  103 Thistle St Bluefield (24605) *(G-1879)*

Stick Industries LLC 757 725-0436
  633 Parsons Rd Troutville (24175) *(G-13917)*

Stick It Welding & Fabrication 757 710-5774
  28035 Seaside Ave Hallwood (23359) *(G-6055)*

Stickers Plus Ltd 540 857-3045
  720 3rd St Vinton (24179) *(G-14184)*

Stickmans Welding Service LLC 434 547-9774
  7474 Bell Rd Dillwyn (23936) *(G-4101)*

Stihl Incorporated 757 468-4010
  825 London Bridge Rd Virginia Beach (23454) *(G-14848)*

Stihl Incorporated 757 368-2409
  2600 International Pkwy Virginia Beach (23452) *(G-14849)*

Stillhouse Press 530 409-8179
  4400 University Dr Fairfax (22030) *(G-4682)*

Stillhouse Vineyards LLC 434 293-8221
  4366 Stillhouse Rd Hume (22639) *(G-6963)*

Stillpoint Software Inc 540 905-7932
  315 Piedmont Ave Washington (22747) *(G-15079)*

Sting-Em, Surry *Also called American Bioprotection Inc (G-13795)*

Stitch Beagle Inc 540 777-0002
  6520 Commonwealth Dr Roanoke (24018) *(G-12003)*

Stitch Doctor 540 330-1234
  3754 Stratford Park Dr Sw # 4 Roanoke (24018) *(G-12004)*

Stitch Makers Embroidery 804 794-4523
  1404 Quiet Lake Loop Midlothian (23114) *(G-8910)*

Stitch N Time Sewing, Staunton *Also called Kathy Darmofalski (G-13272)*

Stitchdotpro LLC 540 777-0002
  6520 Commonwealth Dr Roanoke (24018) *(G-12005)*

Stitched Loop LLC 678 467-1973
  433 Lake Crest Dr Chesapeake (23323) *(G-3313)*

Stitched Mmries By Shannon LLC 540 872-9779
  324 Eagle View Ln Bumpass (23024) *(G-2168)*

Stitched With Love LLC 757 285-6980
  5591 Ershire Ct Apt 203 Virginia Beach (23462) *(G-14850)*

Stitches & Bows 678 876-1715
  1173 Wakeman Mill Rd Front Royal (22630) *(G-5556)*

Stitches Corporate & Custom Em 434 374-5111
  618 Virginia Ave Clarksville (23927) *(G-3635)*

Stitching Station 703 421-4053
  21100 Dulles Town Cir Sterling (20166) *(G-13517)*

Stitchworks Inc 757 631-0300
  809 Dasa Leo Ct Virginia Beach (23456) *(G-14851)*

Stm Snow Removal LLC 540 604-0112
  71 Mt Hope Church Rd Stafford (22554) *(G-13196)*

Stockton Creek Press LLC 410 490-8863
  366 Normandy Dr Charlottesville (22903) *(G-2884)*

Stone Depot Granite 703 926-3844
  7300 Lockport Pl Ste 13 Lorton (22079) *(G-7535)*

Stone Dynamics Inc 276 638-7755
  1220 Memorial Blvd S Martinsville (24112) *(G-8338)*

Stone Flex USA, Manassas *Also called Global Code Usa Inc (G-7947)*

Stone Mountain Distilling LLC 276 970-4081
  2219 E Main St Lebanon (24266) *(G-7208)*

Stone Mountain Naturals LLC 276 415-5880
  215 Charles Calton Rd Dryden (24243) *(G-4146)*

Stone Mountain Ventures Inc 888 244-9306
  1597 Eagle Point Rd Huddleston (24104) *(G-6959)*

Stone Mountain Vineyards LLC 434 990-9463
  1376 Wyatt Mountain Rd Dyke (22935) *(G-4277)*

Stone Quarry 757 722-9653
  371 Chatham Dr Newport News (23602) *(G-9348)*

Stone Studio LLC 703 263-9755
  14805 Willard Rd Ste H Chantilly (20151) *(G-2500)*

Stone Terroir Usa LLC 757 754-2434
  4005b Westfax Dr Chantilly (20151) *(G-2501)*

Stone Welding, Henry *Also called Steve Stone (G-6597)*

Stonega Mining & Processing Co 276 523-5690
  1695 Dawson Ave W Big Stone Gap (24219) *(G-1715)*

Stoneleigh Golf Club 540 338-4653
  35271 Prestwick Ct Round Hill (20141) *(G-12391)*

Stoner Steel Products 434 973-4812
  3009 Colonial Dr Charlottesville (22911) *(G-2697)*

Stoneshore Publishing 757 589-7049
  900 Northwood Dr Virginia Beach (23452) *(G-14852)*

Stonewall Woodworks LLC 540 298-1713
  47 Monger Hill Rd Elkton (22827) *(G-4335)*

Stoney Brook Vnyrds Winery LLC 703 932-2619
  524 Stoney Battery Rd Troutville (24175) *(G-13918)*

Stoney Mill, Danville *Also called Charles A Bliss Jr (G-3966)*

Stony Creek Sand & Gravel LLC (PA) **804 229-0015**
  222 Central Park Ave Virginia Beach (23462) *(G-14853)*

Storage Technology 703 817-1528
  14120 Parke Long Ct # 201 Chantilly (20151) *(G-2502)*

Storey Mill Publishing 757 399-4969
  42 Cooper Dr Portsmouth (23702) *(G-10486)*

Storge Industries LLC 571 414-1413
  9325 Belvoir Rd Fort Belvoir (22060) *(G-5118)*

Storm Protection Services 757 496-8200
  1272 N Great Neck Rd Virginia Beach (23454) *(G-14854)*

Stovall Brothers Lumber LLC 276 694-6684
  2400 Pleasant View Dr Stuart (24171) *(G-13632)*

Stowe Inc A D 757 397-1842
  450 Virginia Ave Portsmouth (23707) *(G-10487)*

Str, Richmond *Also called Semiconductor Technology RES (G-11376)*

Straight Line Welding LLC 804 837-0363
  15520 Richmond St Chester (23836) *(G-3457)*

Strange Coffee Company, Riner *Also called Brian K Babcock (G-11861)*

Strange Designs 540 937-5858
  90n Toad Hill Ln Viewtown (22746) *(G-14164)*

Strasburg Cabinet & Supply 540 465-3031
  2993 Oranda Rd Strasburg (22657) *(G-13599)*

Strata Film Coatings Inc 540 343-3456
  2610 Roanoke Ave Sw Roanoke (24015) *(G-12198)*

Strategic Print Solutions LLC 703 272-3440
  15320 Turning Leaf Pl Haymarket (20169) *(G-6449)*

Strategic Voice Solutions 888 975-6130
  28814 Old Valley Pike Strasburg (22657) *(G-13600)*

Stratgic Trnsp Initiatives Inc 703 647-6564
  1800 Diagonal Rd Alexandria (22314) *(G-358)*

Stratis Division, Reston *Also called Caci Nss Inc (G-10814)*

Stratos LLC 800 213-4705
  2920 W Broad St Ste 100 Richmond (23230) *(G-11399)*

Stratuslive LLC 757 273-8219
  6465 College Park Sq # 310 Virginia Beach (23464) *(G-14855)*

Strauch Fiber Equipment C 540 864-8869
  10319 Johns Creek Rd New Castle (24127) *(G-9124)*

Strdefense LLC 703 460-9000
  3975 Fair Ridge Dr D Fairfax (22033) *(G-4562)*

Streamview Software LLC 703 455-0793
  8008 Dayspring Ct Springfield (22153) *(G-13095)*

A
L
P
H
A
B
E
T
I
C

Streco Fibres Intl Disc Inc 757 473-3720
168 Business Park Dr # 200 Virginia Beach (23462) *(G-14856)*

Streetwerkz Customs 804 921-6483
1695 Bracketts Bend Powhatan (23139) *(G-10579)*

Stressa Incorporated 540 460-9495
2213 Pine Ave Buena Vista (24416) *(G-2155)*

Strickland Machine Company, Richmond Also called Aci-Strickland LLC *(G-11470)*

Strickland Machine Company LLC 804 643-7483
2400 Magnolia Ct Richmond (23223) *(G-11774)*

Strickland Mfg LLC 866 929-3388
1070 Merchants Ln Oilville (23129) *(G-10184)*

Strictly Dtails Auto Detailing, Front Royal Also called Dayton Dalice *(G-5529)*

Strike Force Manufacturing Inc 804 731-0831
10006 Brighton Dr North Prince George (23860) *(G-10092)*

String Stalker LLC 727 430-7545
10808 Arrowleaf Ct Glen Allen (23060) *(G-5802)*

Stripping Center of Sterling 703 904-9577
100 Executive Dr Sterling (20166) *(G-13518)*

Strive Communications LLC 703 925-5900
11921 Freedom Dr Ste 550 Reston (20190) *(G-10967)*

Strive3, Reston Also called Strive Communications LLC *(G-10967)*

Strober Building Supply 540 834-2111
5213 Jefferson Davis Hwy Fredericksburg (22408) *(G-5369)*

Strong Industries LLC 757 533-9100
1001 W 27th St Norfolk (23517) *(G-9735)*

Strong Oaks Woodshop 540 683-2316
847 Jonathan Rd Linden (22642) *(G-7433)*

Strongerhold Welding & Contg 276 608-9968
2678 Leemaster Dr Vansant (24656) *(G-13978)*

Strongtower Inc 804 723-8050
6803 Rural Point Rd Mechanicsville (23116) *(G-8683)*

Strongwell Corporation (PA) **276 645-8000**
400 Commonwealth Ave Bristol (24201) *(G-1991)*

Strongwell Corporation 276 623-0935
26770 Newbanks Rd Abingdon (24210) *(G-62)*

Structural Concrete Products, Richmond Also called Metromont Corporation *(G-11290)*

Structural Sculpture Corp 434 207-3070
2306 Richmond Rd Troy (22974) *(G-13936)*

Structural Steel MGT LLC 434 286-2373
179 James River Rd Scottsville (24590) *(G-12667)*

Structural Technologies LLC (HQ) **757 498-4448**
126 S Lynnhaven Rd Virginia Beach (23452) *(G-14857)*

Structural Technologies LLC 888 616-0615
17320 Washington Hwy Doswell (23047) *(G-4126)*

Structured Software Inc 703 266-0588
5369 Ashleigh Rd Fairfax (22030) *(G-4683)*

Structures Unlimited 434 361-2294
1625 River Rd Faber (22938) *(G-4391)*

Structureworks Fabrication 877 489-8064
3300 Dill Smith Dr Fredericksburg (22408) *(G-5370)*

Stryker Corporation 571 919-2000
600 Hope Pkwy Se Leesburg (20175) *(G-7352)*

Stryker Corporation 571 919-2345
610 Hope Pkwy Se Leesburg (20175) *(G-7353)*

Stryker Spine, Leesburg Also called Stryker Corporation *(G-7353)*

STS Gun Mounts, Virginia Beach Also called Special Tactical Services LLC *(G-14835)*

STS International Incorporated 703 575-5180
1225 S Clark St Ste 1300 Arlington (22202) *(G-1177)*

Stuart Concrete Inc 276 694-2828
58 West Stuart (24171) *(G-13633)*

Stuart Forest Products LLC 276 694-3842
120 Commerce St Stuart (24171) *(G-13634)*

Stuart M Perry Incorporated (PA) **540 662-3431**
117 Limestone Ln Winchester (22602) *(G-15483)*

Stuart M Perry Incorporated 540 955-1359
426 Quarry Rd Berryville (22611) *(G-1693)*

Stuart Mathews Engineering 804 779-2976
4356 Sandy Valley Rd Mechanicsville (23111) *(G-8684)*

Stuart Wilderness Inc 276 694-4432
14747 Jeb Stuart Hwy Stuart (24171) *(G-13635)*

Stuart-Dean Co Inc 703 578-1885
5826 Seminary Rd Ste B Falls Church (22041) *(G-4878)*

Stuarts AC & Refrigeration 804 405-0960
1535 Westshire Ln Richmond (23238) *(G-11400)*

Stubborn Press and Company LLC 540 394-8412
1070 Blane Dr Forest (24551) *(G-5098)*

Stubby Steves 276 988-2915
27860 Gvrnor G C Pery Hwy North Tazewell (24630) *(G-10107)*

Studio 29 .... 757 624-1445
125 College Pl Ste 29 Norfolk (23510) *(G-9736)*

Studio B Graphics 703 777-8755
520 S 11th St Purcellville (20132) *(G-10680)*

Studio One Printing 703 430-8884
201 Davis Dr Ste D Sterling (20164) *(G-13519)*

Studio One Screen Prtg & EMB, Sterling Also called Studio One Printing *(G-13519)*

Style LLC 757 222-3990
1313 E Main St Apt 103 Richmond (23219) *(G-11775)*

Style Weekly Magazine, Richmond Also called Style LLC *(G-11775)*

Styles By Jaimonique LLC 804 255-8581
2900 Cedar Ln Ste B Colonial Heights (23834) *(G-3749)*

Stylewire LLC 770 841-1300
1309 Eyrie View Dr Lynchburg (24503) *(G-7814)*

Stylus Publishing LLC 703 661-1581
22841 Quicksilver Dr Sterling (20166) *(G-13520)*

Stylus Publishing LLC 703 661-1504
22883 Quicksilver Dr Sterling (20166) *(G-13521)*

Sub Rosa LLC 703 338-3344
5762 Union Mill Rd Clifton (20124) *(G-3676)*

Sub Rosa Press Ltd 703 777-1157
313 Lounsbury Ct Ne Leesburg (20176) *(G-7354)*

Submarine Telecoms Forum Inc 703 444-0845
21495 Ridgetop Cir # 201 Sterling (20166) *(G-13522)*

Suburban Contractors LLC 703 739-5600
10090 Market St Manassas (20110) *(G-8001)*

Successful Mix LLC 540 269-6904
1968 Mountain Valley Rd Keezletown (22832) *(G-7031)*

Suday Promotions Inc 703 376-8640
14900 Bogle Dr Ste 201 Chantilly (20151) *(G-2503)*

Sudden Service Inc 804 266-6200
8351 Brook Rd Richmond (23227) *(G-11401)*

Sue Dille 540 951-4100
2195 Woodland Hills Dr Blacksburg (24060) *(G-1795)*

Sue Dille Designs, Blacksburg Also called Sue Dille *(G-1795)*

Suez Treatment Solutions Inc 804 550-4971
10989 Leadbetter Rd B Ashland (23005) *(G-1497)*

Suez Water Tech & Solutions, Norfolk Also called Suez Wts Services Usa Inc *(G-9737)*

Suez Wts Services Usa Inc (HQ) **757 855-9000**
4545 Patent Rd Norfolk (23502) *(G-9737)*

Suffolk Materials LLC 757 255-4005
1130 Audubon Rd Suffolk (23434) *(G-13769)*

Suffolk News-Herald, Suffolk Also called Wood Television LLC *(G-13786)*

Suffolk Welding & Fab 757 544-4689
2051 Maywood St Chesapeake (23323) *(G-3314)*

Suganit Bio-Renewables LLC 703 736-0634
10903 Hunt Club Rd Reston (20190) *(G-10968)*

Suganit Bio-Renewables LLC 703 736-0634
377 Industrial Park Rd Mount Jackson (22842) *(G-9080)*

Sugar & Salt LLC 434 996-2329
332 Jefferson Dr Virginia Beach (23454) *(G-14858)*

Sugar Maple Ln Woodworker LLC 434 962-6494
38 Sugar Maple Ln Louisa (23093) *(G-7569)*

Sugar Spring Press 540 463-4094
802 Sunset Dr Lexington (24450) *(G-7418)*

Sugar Tree Country Store 540 396-3469
185 Mansion House Rd Mc Dowell (24458) *(G-8376)*

Sugarfina Inc 703 844-0049
1961 Chain Bridge Rd Mc Lean (22102) *(G-8560)*

Sugarland Run Pantries 571 216-8565
1019 Monroe St Herndon (20170) *(G-6816)*

Sugarleaf Vineyards 434 984-4272
3613 Walnut Branch Ln North Garden (22959) *(G-10083)*

Sugarloaf Alpaca Company LLC 240 500-0007
2021 Rivermont Ave Lynchburg (24503) *(G-7815)*

Sugpiat Defense LLC 540 623-3626
1320 Cntl Pk Blvd Ste 200 Fredericksburg (22401) *(G-5228)*

Sullivan Company Inc N J 703 464-5944
22725 Duls Smmt Ct Ste 10 Sterling (20166) *(G-13523)*

Sullivan Machine Shop 540 350-2549
17 Buckland Dr Mount Solon (22843) *(G-9090)*

Sumi Enterprises 703 580-8269
15065 Greenmount Dr Woodbridge (22193) *(G-15818)*

Sumi LLC 571 287-9480
1271 Stonechris Dr Harrisonburg (22802) *(G-6375)*

Summa LLC 757 254-1000
396 Francisco Way Newport News (23601) *(G-9349)*

Summer Interior LLC 540 479-5145
6501 Broad Creek Overlook Fredericksburg (22407) *(G-5371)*

Summerduck Raceway 540 845-1656
14027 Royalls Mill Rd Sumerduck (22742) *(G-13793)*

Summit Appalachia Oper Co LLC 276 963-2979
2615 Steelsburg Hwy Cedar Bluff (24609) *(G-2286)*

Summit Beverage Group LLC 276 781-0671
211 Washington Ave Marion (24354) *(G-8244)*

Summit Drones Inc 724 961-9197
13159 Adams St Quantico (22134) *(G-10691)*

Summit Ldscp & Lawn Care LLC 703 856-5353
2906 Lawrence Dr Falls Church (22042) *(G-4879)*

Summit Waterfalls LLC 703 688-4558
1965 Knoll Top Ln Woodbridge (22191) *(G-15819)*

Sumners Scoreboards 804 526-7152
412 Waterfront Dr Colonial Heights (23834) *(G-3750)*

Sun Care Inc 703 715-7070
3318 Woodburn Village Dr Annandale (22003) *(G-785)*

Sun Chemical Corporation 804 524-3888
16000 Continental Blvd South Chesterfield (23834) *(G-12828)*

Sun Gazatte 703 738-2520
6564 Loisdale Ct Ste 610 Springfield (22150) *(G-13096)*

Sun Gazette, Springfield Also called Sun Gazatte *(G-13096)*

Sun Manufacturing LLC 434 942-4626
1291 Burnbridge Rd Forest (24551) *(G-5099)*
Sun Microsystems, Richmond *Also called Oracle America Inc (G-11316)*
Sun Newspaper, Clarksville *Also called Sun Publishing Company (G-3636)*
Sun Publishing Company 434 374-8152
602 Virginia Ave Clarksville (23927) *(G-3636)*
Sun Rnr of Virginia Inc 540 271-3403
865 Neyland Dr Harrisonburg (22801) *(G-6376)*
Sun Signs 703 867-9831
1105 Potomac Dr Stafford (22554) *(G-13197)*
Sunapsys Inc 540 904-6856
850 3rd St Vinton (24179) *(G-14185)*
Sunbeam Bakeries 276 647-8767
3416 Virginia Ave Collinsville (24078) *(G-3717)*
Suncoast Post-Tension Ltd 703 492-4949
15041 Farm Creek Dr Woodbridge (22191) *(G-15820)*
Sundigger Industries LLC 703 360-4139
8711 Standish Rd Alexandria (22308) *(G-590)*
Sundra Printing, Chantilly *Also called J C Printing Corp (G-2447)*
Sunglow Industries Inc 703 870-9918
11861 Canon Blvd Ste B Newport News (23606) *(G-9350)*
Sunguard Mid Atlantic LLC 703 820-8118
4252 35th St S Arlington (22206) *(G-1178)*
Sunlight Software 540 789-7374
892 Deer Valley Rd Nw Willis (24380) *(G-15365)*
Sunlite Plastics Inc 540 234-9271
846 Keezletown Rd Weyers Cave (24486) *(G-15178)*
Sunmicro Software Incorporated 703 587-9362
2372 Stone Fence Ln Herndon (20171) *(G-6817)*
Sunny Day Fund Solutions Inc 703 622-1005
6003 Madison Overlook Ct Falls Church (22041) *(G-4880)*
Sunny Day Guide, Virginia Beach *Also called Surfside East Inc (G-14859)*
Sunny Slope LLC 434 384-8994
4716 John Scott Dr Lynchburg (24503) *(G-7816)*
Sunnyside Awning Co, Roanoke *Also called JWB of Roanoke Inc (G-12116)*
Sunrise Circuits LLC 703 719-9324
6205 Littlethorpe Ln Alexandria (22315) *(G-591)*
Sunrunr, Harrisonburg *Also called Sun Rnr of Virginia Inc (G-6376)*
Sunset Hills Vineyard LLC 540 882-4560
38295 Fremont Overlook Ln Purcellville (20132) *(G-10681)*
Sunset Pavers Inc 703 507-9101
4635 Midhurst Ct Sumerduck (22742) *(G-13794)*
Sunshine Hill Press LLC 571 451-8448
2937 Novum Rd Reva (22735) *(G-11001)*
Sunshine Mills Inc 434 476-1451
100 Sunshine Dr Halifax (24558) *(G-6053)*
Sunshine Mills of Virginia 434 476-1451
100 Salishan Dr Halifax (24558) *(G-6054)*
Sunshine Products Inc 703 768-3500
1953 Shiver Dr Alexandria (22307) *(G-592)*
Sunshine Sewing 276 628-2478
793 W Main St Ste 5 Abingdon (24210) *(G-63)*
Suntek Holding Company 276 632-4991
345 Beaver Creek Dr Martinsville (24112) *(G-8339)*
Supa Producer Publishing 757 484-2495
5604 Gregory Ct Portsmouth (23703) *(G-10488)*
Super RAD Coils Ltd Partnr 804 794-2887
451 Southlake Blvd North Chesterfield (23236) *(G-9992)*
Super Splasher Acquatics 540 630-1565
141 Krnstown Commons Blvd Winchester (22602) *(G-15484)*
Superb Cleaning Solutons 804 908-9018
1408 Nanassas Ct Henrico (23231) *(G-6576)*
Superior Awning Service Inc 757 399-8161
2901 Deep Creek Blvd Portsmouth (23704) *(G-10489)*
Superior Boiler LLC 804 226-8227
2890 Seven Hills Blvd Richmond (23231) *(G-11402)*
Superior Concrete Inc 540 433-2482
1526 Country Club Rd Harrisonburg (22802) *(G-6377)*
Superior Concrete Materials 703 327-4112
44146 Wade Dr Chantilly (20152) *(G-2558)*
Superior Fabrication LLC 276 865-4000
1680 Breaks Park Rd Haysi (24256) *(G-6458)*
Superior Float Tanks LLC 757 966-6350
431 W 25th St Norfolk (23517) *(G-9738)*
Superior Garniture Components 804 769-4319
812 Sharon Rd King William (23086) *(G-7131)*
Superior Global Solutions Inc 804 794-3507
9048 Mahogany Dr Chesterfield (23832) *(G-3530)*
Superior Iron Works Inc (PA) **703 471-5500**
45034 Underwood Ln # 100 Sterling (20166) *(G-13524)*
Superior Laminates 703 569-6602
7653 Fullerton Rd Unit G Springfield (22153) *(G-13097)*
Superior Magnetic Product 804 752-7897
10424 Windam Hill Rd Glen Allen (23059) *(G-5803)*
Superior Metal & Mfg Inc 540 981-1005
926 10th St Vinton (24179) *(G-14186)*
Superior Metal Fabricators 804 236-3266
4217 Sarellen Rd Richmond (23231) *(G-11403)*
Superior Panel Technology, Chesterfield *Also called William K Whitaker (G-3542)*
Superior Panel Technology (PA) **562 776-9494**
7460 Airfield Dr F19 19 F Chesterfield (23838) *(G-3531)*
Superior Paving Corporation 703 631-5480
15717 Lee Hwy Centreville (20121) *(G-2342)*
Superior Quality Foods 540 447-0552
100 Buckingham Pl Waynesboro (22980) *(G-15140)*
Superior Quality Mfg LLC 757 413-9100
424 Network Sta Chesapeake (23320) *(G-3315)*
Superior Signs LLC 804 271-5685
2510 Willis Rd North Chesterfield (23237) *(G-9993)*
Supermedia LLC 703 322-2900
3635 Concorde Pkwy # 400 Chantilly (20151) *(G-2504)*
Supernal Industries LLC 804 380-1742
620 Mcrowland Way Chesapeake (23320) *(G-3316)*
Supernova Industries Inc 703 731-2987
13435 Point Pleasant Dr Chantilly (20151) *(G-2505)*
Superseal Corp 540 645-1408
313 Central Rd Fredericksburg (22401) *(G-5229)*
Supervisor Shipbuilding Conver, Newport News *Also called United States Dept of Navy (G-9369)*
Supplier Solutions Inc 703 791-7720
11350 Rndom Hlls Rd Ste 8 Fairfax (22030) *(G-4684)*
Supplies Express Inc 703 631-4600
5141 Pleasant Forest Dr Centreville (20120) *(G-2343)*
Supply One Chesapeake 757 485-3570
3813 Cook Blvd Chesapeake (23323) *(G-3317)*
Supracity Publishing LLC 804 301-9370
5014 Sand Trap Cir Louisa (23093) *(G-7570)*
Supravista Medical Dss LLC 740 339-0080
514 Maon Rd Farnham (22460) *(G-4965)*
Supreme Concrete Blocks Inc 703 478-1988
42824 Durham Ct Leesburg (20175) *(G-7355)*
Supreme Edgelight Devices Inc 276 236-3711
682 Skyline Hwy Galax (24333) *(G-5649)*
Sura Solutions Inc 703 973-1939
705 Invermere Dr Ne Leesburg (20176) *(G-7356)*
Sure Site Satellite Inc 540 948-5880
31350 Zoar Rd Locust Grove (22508) *(G-7452)*
Surefire Auto Detailing 703 361-2369
9511 Damascus Dr Manassas (20109) *(G-8163)*
Surfside Candle Co 540 455-4322
45445 Baggett Ter Sterling (20166) *(G-13525)*
Surfside East Inc (PA) **757 468-0606**
800 Seahawk Cir Ste 106 Virginia Beach (23452) *(G-14859)*
Surfstroke LLC 804 437-2032
11400 Brickshire Park Providence Forge (23140) *(G-10628)*
Surgical Instr Sharpening Inc 804 883-6010
16205 Trainham Rd Beaverdam (23015) *(G-1613)*
Survivalware Inc 703 780-2044
8403 Porter Ln Alexandria (22308) *(G-593)*
Susannah Wagner Jewelers Inc 804 798-5864
107 Hanover Ave Ashland (23005) *(G-1498)*
Sussex Service Authority 804 834-8930
4385 Beef Steak Rd Waverly (23890) *(G-15089)*
Sustainability Innovations LLC 703 281-1352
1654 Montmorency Dr Vienna (22182) *(G-14135)*
Sustainable Green Prtg Partnr 703 359-1376
10015 Main St Fairfax (22031) *(G-4563)*
Sustaita Lawn Care 434 390-8118
21 Schalow Rd Cumberland (23040) *(G-3937)*
Suter Enterprises Ltd 757 220-3299
4399 Ironbound Rd Williamsburg (23188) *(G-15320)*
Suter Machine & Tool 540 434-2718
494 Liskey Rd Rockingham (22801) *(G-12279)*
Suter's Handcrafted Furniture, Harrisonburg *Also called Suters Cabinet Shop Inc (G-6378)*
Suters Cabinet Shop Inc (PA) **540 434-2131**
2610 S Main St Harrisonburg (22801) *(G-6378)*
Sutherlins Logging Inc 804 366-3871
Rr 619 Locust Hill (23092) *(G-7455)*
Suzanne Henri Inc 434 352-0233
839 Lee Grant Ave Appomattox (24522) *(G-823)*
Suzies Zoo Inc 434 547-4161
408 S Main St Farmville (23901) *(G-4959)*
Svanaco Inc 571 312-3790
901 N Pitt St Ste 130 Alexandria (22314) *(G-359)*
Svm Services LLC 703 389-5100
13423 Pocono Ct Herndon (20170) *(G-6818)*
Svr International LLC 703 759-2953
9702 Carnot Way Vienna (22182) *(G-14136)*
Svs Enterprises Inc 434 985-6642
1640 Pea Ridge Rd Stanardsville (22973) *(G-13228)*
Swaby Group 540 788-6051
9579 Bristersburg Rd Catlett (20119) *(G-2269)*
Swagg Juices LLC 757 254-6754
96 Tudor Ct Hampton (23669) *(G-6245)*
Swami Shriji LLC 804 322-9644
6206 Faulkner Dr North Chesterfield (23234) *(G-9994)*
Swarovski North America Ltd, Williamsburg *Also called Swarovski North America Ltd (G-15321)*

ALPHABETIC

Swarovski North America Ltd.....................................703 267-2332
11750I Fair Oaks Mall Fairfax (22033) *(G-4564)*

Swarovski North America Ltd.....................................571 633-1800
8017 Tysons Corner Ctr Mc Lean (22102) *(G-8561)*

Swarovski North America Ltd.....................................703 418-6665
1100 S Hayes St Arlington (22202) *(G-1179)*

Swarovski North America Ltd.....................................757 253-7924
5711 Richmond Rd Williamsburg (23188) *(G-15321)*

Sweany Trckg & Hardwoods LLC...............................540 273-9387
184 Woodstream Blvd Stafford (22556) *(G-13198)*

Swede Built, Virginia Beach *Also called Jansson & Associate Mstr Bldr* *(G-14564)*

Swedish Match North Amer LLC (HQ).....................**804 787-5100**
1021 E Cary St Ste 1600 Richmond (23219) *(G-11776)*

Sweely Estate Winery..540 948-7603
6109 Wolftown Hood Rd Madison (22727) *(G-7863)*

Sweet & Savory By Emily LLC................................804 248-8252
1301 Elmart Ln North Chesterfield (23235) *(G-9995)*

Sweet and Simple Prints...757 710-1116
3120 Mount Tabor Rd Blacksburg (24060) *(G-1796)*

Sweet Baby Luxury Hair Co LLC..............................804 904-9227
2207 Mandalay Dr Apt C Richmond (23224) *(G-11777)*

Sweet Bea Naturals, South Chesterfield *Also called Beatrice Aurthur* *(G-12831)*

Sweet Briar Sheet Metal Svcs.................................434 946-0403
162 Higginbotham Creek Rd Amherst (24521) *(G-710)*

Sweet Catastrophe LLC...434 296-8555
317 E Main St Charlottesville (22902) *(G-2885)*

Sweet Cynthias Pie Co LLC....................................804 321-8646
2814 Hawthorne Ave Richmond (23222) *(G-11778)*

Sweet Heat Candles..804 921-8233
8343 Strath Rd Henrico (23231) *(G-6577)*

Sweet Lime Studios LLC...703 312-0034
2035 N Taylor St Arlington (22207) *(G-1180)*

Sweet Pea Ceramics LLC.......................................571 292-4313
439 Devon Dr Warrenton (20186) *(G-15054)*

Sweet Relief Inc..703 963-4868
504 Shaw Rd Ste 220 Sterling (20166) *(G-13526)*

Sweet Serenity Gifts..540 903-1964
1600 Hartwood Rd Fredericksburg (22406) *(G-5489)*

Sweet Sounds Music Therapy LLC..........................703 965-3624
2631 Jamestown Ln Apt 203 Alexandria (22314) *(G-360)*

Sweet Sprinkles...540 373-4750
16 Glen Oak Rd Fredericksburg (22405) *(G-5490)*

Sweet Success Cupcakes..703 674-9442
4613 Tara Dr Fairfax (22032) *(G-4565)*

Sweet Svory Delights By Vickie...............................703 581-8499
3408 Haven Pl Falls Church (22041) *(G-4881)*

Sweet T&C Kettle Corn LLC...................................804 840-0551
12750 Jefferson Davis Hwy Chester (23831) *(G-3458)*

Sweet Tooth...434 760-0047
630 Crumpet Ct Charlottesville (22901) *(G-2698)*

Sweet Tooth Bakery Inc..540 667-6155
3034 Valley Ave Ste 110 Winchester (22601) *(G-15589)*

Sweetb Designs LLC...757 550-0436
2705 Roanoke Ave Portsmouth (23704) *(G-10490)*

Sweetbay Publishing LLC..703 203-9130
8391 Jill Brenda Ct Manassas (20112) *(G-8164)*

Sweetbriar Scents LLC...757 358-6815
106 Horsley Dr Hampton (23666) *(G-6246)*

Sweetie Pie Desserts...804 239-6425
10 E Clay St Richmond (23219) *(G-11779)*

Sweetpea, Virginia Beach *Also called LLC Little Bean* *(G-14614)*

Sweetpeas By Shafer Dobry....................................703 476-6787
12812 Tewksbury Dr Herndon (20171) *(G-6819)*

Sweets 4 The Sweet, La Crosse *Also called Martin Tonya* *(G-7146)*

Swift Creek Forest Products...................................804 561-1751
20200 Patrick Henry Hwy Jetersville (23083) *(G-7015)*

Swift Mobile Welding LLC.......................................757 367-9060
1315 Quash St Hampton (23669) *(G-6247)*

Swift Print...540 774-1001
3526 Electric Rd Roanoke (24018) *(G-12006)*

Swift Print Inc (PA)...**540 362-2200**
369 Church Ave Sw Roanoke (24016) *(G-12199)*

Swift Print Inc...540 343-8300
1003 S Jefferson St Roanoke (24016) *(G-12200)*

Swinson Medical LLC..540 576-1719
180 Island View Dr Penhook (24137) *(G-10285)*

Swissomation Virginia LLC....................................434 944-3322
254 Industrial Park Dr Amherst (24521) *(G-711)*

Switchdraw LLC...703 402-2820
31 Laurel Haven Dr Stafford (22554) *(G-13199)*

Swm International LLC...651 369-1235
1713 Plantation Rd Ne Roanoke (24012) *(G-12201)*

Sword & Shield Coaching LLC.................................804 557-3937
4105 Old Nottingham Rd Quinton (23141) *(G-10700)*

Sword & Trumpet Office...540 867-9419
6083 Mount Clinton Pike Rockingham (22802) *(G-12280)*

Swrd LLC..434 944-2558
102 Dillards Ln Gladys (24554) *(G-5697)*

Swurls LLC...571 423-9899
8513 Century Oak Ct Fairfax Station (22039) *(G-4725)*

Sycamore Hollow Welding......................................540 879-2266
4389 Bowman Rd Dayton (22821) *(G-4066)*

Sydrus Aerospace LLC...831 402-5286
8725 Ellis Mill Dr Gainesville (20155) *(G-5616)*

Syftkog..540 693-5875
5503 Steeplechase Dr A Fredericksburg (22407) *(G-5372)*

Sykes Signs Inc..276 935-2772
1182 Jim Rowe Hollow Rd Grundy (24614) *(G-6041)*

Sylvan Spirit...804 330-5454
2339 Jimmy Winters Rd North Chesterfield (23235) *(G-9996)*

Symantec, Arlington *Also called Nortonlifelock Inc* *(G-1083)*

Symantec, Mc Lean *Also called Nortonlifelock Inc* *(G-8519)*

Symbol Mattress, Richmond *Also called Eastern Sleep Products Company* *(G-11195)*

Symbol Technologies LLC.......................................703 263-2533
4124 Walney Rd Chantilly (20151) *(G-2506)*

Symbolics - David K Schmidt..................................703 455-0430
6342 Fenestra Ct Burke (22015) *(G-2204)*

Symmetric Systems Inc...804 276-7202
9225 Chatham Grove Ln D North Chesterfield (23236) *(G-9997)*

Symmetrical Wood Works LLC.................................703 499-0821
3318 Woodburn Village Dr # 22 Annandale (22003) *(G-786)*

Symmple Technologies...703 591-7716
4325 Thomas Brigade Ln Fairfax (22033) *(G-4566)*

Synagrow Wwt Inc..804 443-2170
10647 Tidewater Trl Champlain (22438) *(G-2358)*

Synalloy Corporation (PA)......................................**804 822-3260**
4510 Cox Rd Ste 201 Glen Allen (23060) *(G-5804)*

Synapone, Mc Lean *Also called Synaptein Solutions Inc* *(G-8562)*

Synaptein Solutions Inc (PA)..................................**703 209-2350**
1568 Spring Hill Rd # 402 Mc Lean (22102) *(G-8562)*

Sync Optics LLC..571 203-0580
3723 Broadrun Dr Fairfax (22033) *(G-4567)*

Syncdog Inc...800 430-1268
1818 Library St Ste 500 Reston (20190) *(G-10969)*

Synergy Biofuels LLC..276 546-5226
334 Guy Walton Dr Pennington Gap (24277) *(G-10300)*

Synergy Business Solutions LLC.............................757 646-1294
2239 Roanoke Ave Virginia Beach (23455) *(G-14860)*

Synergy Orthtics Prsthtics LLC...............................410 788-8901
42695 Laurier Dr Broadlands (20148) *(G-2082)*

Synerject, Newport News *Also called Continental Auto Systems Inc* *(G-9204)*

Syntec Business Systems Inc..................................804 303-2864
1134 Thomas Jefferson Rd Forest (24551) *(G-5100)*

Synteras LLC...703 766-6222
2553 Dulles View Dr # 70 Herndon (20171) *(G-6820)*

Syrm LLC..571 308-8707
74 Deshields Ct Stafford (22556) *(G-13200)*

System Innovations Inc...540 373-2374
1551 Forbes St Fredericksburg (22405) *(G-5491)*

Systems America Inc..703 203-8421
4609 Lewis Leigh Ct Chantilly (20151) *(G-2507)*

Systems Requirements Group, Fairfax *Also called Srg Government Solutions Inc* *(G-4559)*

Systems Research and Mfg Corp.............................703 765-5827
7432 Grumman Pl Alexandria (22306) *(G-594)*

Systems Technology VA LLC...................................540 884-1784
130 Mount Moriah Rd Eagle Rock (24085) *(G-4283)*

T & J Wldg & Fabrication LLC.................................757 672-9929
1204 Baltic St Suffolk (23434) *(G-13770)*

T & P Servicing LLC..276 945-2040
231 Wren Dr Bluefield (24605) *(G-1880)*

T & T Software LLC..540 389-1915
319 Campbell Ave Sw Roanoke (24016) *(G-12202)*

T & T Sporting Goods...276 228-5286
185 Lakeview Dr Wytheville (24382) *(G-15917)*

T Bc...703 969-8221
8635 Mahogany Ct Manassas (20110) *(G-8002)*

T Body Shirts, Hampton *Also called Mounir E Shaheen* *(G-6205)*

T C C, Bristol *Also called Tennessee Consolidated Coal Co* *(G-2035)*

T C Catlett & Sons Lumber Co................................540 786-2303
10315 Elys Ford Rd Fredericksburg (22407) *(G-5373)*

T C G Technologies LLC...703 847-5057
8245 Boone Blvd Ste 704 Vienna (22182) *(G-14137)*

T E L Pak Inc...804 794-9529
2251 Banstead Rd Midlothian (23113) *(G-8911)*

T R A, Mc Lean *Also called Lee Talbot Associates Inc* *(G-8483)*

T S I, Palmyra *Also called Troopmaster Software Inc* *(G-10258)*

T S I Embroidery, Ashland *Also called Timeless Stitches Inc* *(G-1500)*

T Shirt Broker...703 362-9297
12521 Arnsley Ct Herndon (20171) *(G-6821)*

T Shirt Unique Inc..804 557-2989
9014 Boulevard Rd Providence Forge (23140) *(G-10629)*

T W Enterprises Inc...540 667-0233
270 Tyson Dr Ste 2 Winchester (22603) *(G-15485)*

T W McPherson & Sons..540 483-0105
171 Mcpherson Ln Callaway (24067) *(G-2222)*

T&J Woodworking..757 567-5530
2593 Quality Ct Ste 226 Virginia Beach (23454) *(G-14861)*

T&M Metal Fabrication LLC.....................................703 726-6949
20859 Apollo Ter Ashburn (20147) *(G-1338)*

(G-0000) Company's Geographic Section entry number

T&W Block Incorporated (PA) 757 787-2646
21075 Washington St Onley (23418) ***(G-10201)***
T-Body Promotions LLC 757 723-4445
1962 E Pembroke Ave Hampton (23663) ***(G-6248)***
T-Jar Inc 540 974-2567
129 Kinross Dr Winchester (22602) ***(G-15486)***
T-K-O Building Incorporated 757 324-2306
6201 Lippizan Cir Virginia Beach (23464) ***(G-14862)***
T-Shirt & Screen Print Co 540 667-2351
65 Featherbed Ln Winchester (22601) ***(G-15590)***
T-Shirt Attic and Screen Print, Winchester *Also called T-Shirt & Screen Print Co* ***(G-15590)***
T-Shirt Company LLC 703 669-4619
521 Currant Ter Ne Leesburg (20176) ***(G-7357)***
T-Shirt Factory LLC 703 589-5175
20936 Sandian Ter Sterling (20165) ***(G-13527)***
T-Shirts Etc, Fairfax *Also called Silkscreening Unlimited Inc* ***(G-4554)***
T/A United Sheet Metal, Portsmouth *Also called C and J Fabrication Inc* ***(G-10403)***
T/J One Corp 757 548-0093
414 Rio Dr Chesapeake (23322) ***(G-3318)***
T2pneuma Publishers LLC 703 968-7592
14451 N Slope St Centreville (20120) ***(G-2344)***
T3 Media LLC 804 262-1700
6924 Lakeside Ave Richmond (23228) ***(G-11404)***
T3b LLC 202 550-4475
8360 Greensboro Dr # 810 Mc Lean (22102) ***(G-8563)***
T3j Enterprises LLC 757 768-0528
345 Rivers Ridge Cir Newport News (23608) ***(G-9351)***
T5 Group LLC 704 575-7721
213 Two Creek Dr Lynchburg (24502) ***(G-7817)***
Ta Technical Services LLC 540 429-5977
5100 Windbreak Dr Fredericksburg (22407) ***(G-5374)***
Taal Enterprises LLC 276 328-2408
6538 Cherokee Rd Wise (24293) ***(G-15634)***
Tabard Corporation 540 477-9664
11 Edwards Way Mount Jackson (22842) ***(G-9081)***
Tabb Enterprise LLC 434 238-7196
6221 Pawtucket Dr Lynchburg (24502) ***(G-7818)***
Tabet Manufacturing Co Inc 757 627-1855
1336 Ballentine Blvd Norfolk (23504) ***(G-9739)***
Tacstrike LLC 540 751-8221
3464 Colonial Ave Apt O93 Roanoke (24018) ***(G-12007)***
Tacstrike Systems, Roanoke *Also called Tacstrike LLC* ***(G-12007)***
Tactical Dployment Systems LLC 804 672-8426
2111b Spencer Rd Richmond (23230) ***(G-11405)***
Tactical Elec Military Sup LLC 757 689-0476
2844 Crusader Cir Ste 100 Virginia Beach (23453) ***(G-14863)***
Tactical Marine Repair Inc 757 967-8688
3737 Holland Blvd Ste C Chesapeake (23323) ***(G-3319)***
Tactical Micro 540 907-0091
3509 Shannon Park Dr # 103 Fredericksburg (22408) ***(G-5375)***
Tactical Nuclear Wizard LLC 804 231-1671
2211 Fairmount Ave Richmond (23223) ***(G-11780)***
Tactical Walls LLC 540 298-8906
611 Williams Ave Shenandoah (22849) ***(G-12696)***
Tadano Mantis Corporation 800 272-3325
2680 S Front St Richlands (24641) ***(G-11020)***
Tag 5 Industries LLC 703 647-0325
734 S Alfred St Alexandria (22314) ***(G-361)***
Tag America Inc 757 227-9831
5721 Bayside Rd Virginia Beach (23455) ***(G-14864)***
Tagg Design Specialty Prtg LLC 804 572-7777
1013 Tanyard Dr Apt 8 Tappahannock (22560) ***(G-13823)***
Taghleef Industries Inc 540 962-1200
901 W Edgemont Dr Covington (24426) ***(G-3800)***
Tagstringcom Inc 954 557-8645
25134 Deerhurst Ter Chantilly (20152) ***(G-2559)***
Taicco Fuel Inc 571 405-7700
805 E Parham Rd Richmond (23227) ***(G-11406)***
Take-A-Break Home Imprv LLC 434 251-4557
548 Maple Springs Dr Axton (24054) ***(G-1541)***
Talk Is Life LLC 703 951-3848
17045 Gibson Mill Rd Dumfries (22026) ***(G-4258)***
Tall Toad Costumes 276 694-4636
276 Big Dan Lake Dr Claudville (24076) ***(G-3641)***
Tallant Industries Inc 540 898-7000
4900 Ondura Dr Fredericksburg (22407) ***(G-5376)***
Talley Sign Company 804 649-0325
1908 Chamberlayne Ave Richmond (23222) ***(G-11781)***
Talmadge Fix 540 463-9629
1402 Mountain View Rd Lexington (24450) ***(G-7419)***
Talon Inc 703 777-3600
42217 Cochran Mill Rd Leesburg (20175) ***(G-7358)***
Taloose Group 408 221-3277
1515 Wilton Farm Rd Charlottesville (22911) ***(G-2699)***
Talu LLC 571 323-5200
2553 Dulles Herndon (20171) ***(G-6822)***
Tamara Ingram 434 392-4933
428 Deerfield Acres Dr Burkeville (23922) ***(G-2211)***
Tamara Smith 910 495-4404
1293 Hollow Rd Gore (22637) ***(G-5923)***
Tamco Enterprises Inc 757 627-9551
1400 Kempsville Rd # 110 Chesapeake (23320) ***(G-3320)***
Tamco Paint, Wakefield *Also called Barney Family Enterprises LLC* ***(G-14964)***
Tammy Haire 540 722-7246
2751 Hunting Ridge Rd Winchester (22603) ***(G-15487)***
Tangers Electronics LLC 757 215-5117
1527 Magnolia Ave Norfolk (23508) ***(G-9740)***
Tanner Tool & Machine Inc 804 561-5141
8121 Dennisville Rd Amelia Court House (23002) ***(G-674)***
Tannhauser Enterprises LLC 703 850-1927
9141 Dartford Pl Bristow (20136) ***(G-2063)***
Tants Mch & Fabrication Inc 757 434-9448
4001 Holland Blvd Ste D Chesapeake (23323) ***(G-3321)***
Tape-Tab LP 804 404-6855
10125 Idlebrook Dr Henrico (23238) ***(G-6578)***
Tapioca LLC 703 715-8688
12353 Firestone Ct Fairfax (22033) ***(G-4568)***
Tapioca Go 757 410-3836
1434 Sams Dr Ste 106 Chesapeake (23320) ***(G-3322)***
Tarara 703 771-7100
13648 Tarara Ln Leesburg (20176) ***(G-7359)***
Tarara Winery, Leesburg *Also called Tarara* ***(G-7359)***
Target Advertising Inc 757 627-2216
1439 Mallory Ct Norfolk (23507) ***(G-9741)***
Target Communications Inc 804 355-0111
2201 W Broad St Ste 105 Richmond (23220) ***(G-11782)***
Tarkett USA Inc 804 594-0500
301 Southlake Blvd North Chesterfield (23236) ***(G-9998)***
Tarmac Corp 703 471-0044
22963 Concrete Plz Sterling (20166) ***(G-13528)***
Tarmac Florida Inc 757 858-6500
1151 Azalea Garden Rd Norfolk (23502) ***(G-9742)***
Tarmac Mid-Atlantic Inc 757 858-6500
1151 Azalea Garden Rd Norfolk (23502) ***(G-9743)***
Tarmac Titan, Norfolk *Also called Titan America LLC* ***(G-9758)***
Tars Inc 434 836-7890
3725 U S Highway 29 Danville (24540) ***(G-4039)***
Tasco USA Co Inc 703 209-0193
11315 Westbrook Mill Ln Fairfax (22030) ***(G-4685)***
Tasens Assoc 703 455-2424
8430 Springfield Oaks Dr Springfield (22153) ***(G-13098)***
Taskill Technologies LLC 757 277-5557
3225 Fowlers Lake Rd Williamsburg (23185) ***(G-15322)***
Taste of Carribean 804 321-2411
3911 W Chatham Dr Richmond (23222) ***(G-11783)***
Taste of Love LLC 804 714-4991
1808 Rose Ave Richmond (23222) ***(G-11784)***
Taste Oil Vinegar Spice 540 373-1262
815 Caroline St Fredericksburg (22401) ***(G-5230)***
Taste Oil Vinegar Spice Inc 540 825-8415
122a E Davis St Culpeper (22701) ***(G-3923)***
Tate Global LLC 703 282-0737
1800 Diagonal Rd Ste 520 Alexandria (22314) ***(G-362)***
Tatums Cstm Exhaust & Met Repr 276 692-4884
485 Hardin Reynolds Rd Critz (24082) ***(G-3824)***
Tatums Floor Service 804 737-3328
118 N Daisy Ave Highland Springs (23075) ***(G-6857)***
Taura Natural Ingredients 540 723-8691
110 S Indian Aly Winchester (22601) ***(G-15591)***
Taurus Technologies Inc 757 873-2700
103 Beach Rd Yorktown (23692) ***(G-15995)***
Tavern On Main LLC 276 328-2208
225 Main St Wise (24293) ***(G-15635)***
Tax Analysts 703 533-4400
400 S Maple Ave Ste 400 # 400 Falls Church (22046) ***(G-4926)***
Tax Analysts and Advocates, Falls Church *Also called Tax Analysts* ***(G-4926)***
Tax Management Inc 703 341-3000
1801 S Bell St Ste G1 Arlington (22202) ***(G-1181)***
Taxlaw20 LLC 202 470-3980
1750 Tysons Blvd Ste 1500 Mc Lean (22102) ***(G-8564)***
Taylor Boyz LLC 540 347-2443
9886 Rogues Rd Midland (22728) ***(G-8765)***
Taylor Communications Inc 703 790-9700
8618 Westwood Center Dr # 105 Vienna (22182) ***(G-14138)***
Taylor Communications Inc 937 221-1000
1001 Boulders Pkwy # 440 North Chesterfield (23225) ***(G-10025)***
Taylor Communications Inc 703 904-0133
11715 Bowman Green Dr Herndon (20190) ***(G-6823)***
Taylor Communications Inc 434 822-1111
5000 Riverside Dr Danville (24541) ***(G-4040)***
Taylor Communications Inc 804 612-7597
1518 Willow Lawn Dr Fl 3 Richmond (23230) ***(G-11407)***
Taylor Made Custom Embroidery 434 636-0660
2220 Hall Rd La Crosse (23950) ***(G-7151)***
Taylor Matthews Inc 703 346-7844
2011 Gallows Tree Ct Vienna (22182) ***(G-14139)***
Taylor Mfg & Design LLC 757 902-1820
3425 Old Armistead Ave Hampton (23666) ***(G-6249)***
Taylored Information Tech LLC 276 479-2122
5996 Nickelsville Hwy Nickelsville (24271) ***(G-9386)***

Taylored Printing, Yorktown *Also called Barton Industries Inc (G-15935)*

Taylormade Cakes, Roanoke *Also called Harris Kayla (G-12100)*

Taylormade Woodworking 757 288-6256
4641 Captain Carter Cir Chesapeake (23321) *(G-3323)*

Taylynn Manufacturing LLC (PA) **804 727-0103**
3900 Westerre Pkwy # 300 Henrico (23233) *(G-6579)*

Taysteesmobilefoodcompany 240 310-6767
905 Myrick St Fredericksburg (22401) *(G-5231)*

Tazz Conveyor Corporation 276 988-4883
294 Walnut St North Tazewell (24630) *(G-10108)*

Tbrsp LLC 434 315-5600
302 Dominion Dr Farmville (23901) *(G-4960)*

Tc Kustoms 434 348-3488
7220 Southampton Pkwy Drewryville (23844) *(G-4139)*

Tcg Technologies Inc 540 587-8624
502 Plunkett St Bedford (24523) *(G-1660)*

Tchere LLC 800 889-7832
2769 Jefferson Davis Hwy Stafford (22554) *(G-13201)*

Tconnex Inc 703 910-3400
580 Herndon Pkwy Ste 105 Herndon (20170) *(G-6824)*

Tcp Reliable, Buchanan *Also called Cryopak Verification Tech Inc (G-2120)*

TCS Materials Inc (HQ) **757 591-9340**
5423 Airport Rd Williamsburg (23188) *(G-15323)*

TCS Materials LLC (HQ) **804 232-1200**
2100 Deepwater Trml Rd Richmond (23234) *(G-11065)*

TCS Materials LLC 757 874-5575
700 Shields Rd Newport News (23608) *(G-9352)*

TCS Materials Corp 804 863-4525
26505 Simpson Rd North Dinwiddie (23803) *(G-10064)*

Tcsc, Richmond *Also called Computer Solution Co of VA Inc (G-11538)*

Tcts Trucking LLC 757 406-6323
200 Carver St Chesapeake (23320) *(G-3324)*

Td & D Unlimited LLC 703 946-9338
14273 Goldvein Rd Goldvein (22720) *(G-5879)*

Tdi LLC 757 855-5416
641 Phoenix Dr Virginia Beach (23452) *(G-14865)*

Tdi Printing Group LLC (PA) **757 855-5416**
641 Phoenix Dr Virginia Beach (23452) *(G-14866)*

Tdl, Clifton *Also called Transforming Daily Lives (G-3677)*

Te Connectivity, Hampton *Also called Measurement Specialties Inc (G-6194)*

Te Connectivity 540 812-9126
751 Old Brandy Rd Culpeper (22701) *(G-3924)*

Te Connectivity MOG, Culpeper *Also called Brantner and Associates Inc (G-3875)*

Tea Lady Pillows 703 448-0033
1034 Northwoods Trl Mc Lean (22102) *(G-8565)*

Tea Spot Catering LLC 757 427-3525
2309 Wheatstone Ct Virginia Beach (23456) *(G-14867)*

Teaberry Hill Woodworks LLC 540 667-5489
103 N Braddock St Winchester (22601) *(G-15592)*

Teagle & Little Incorporated 757 622-5793
1048 W 27th St Norfolk (23517) *(G-9744)*

Team 1 Trucking LLC 800 296-9740
1117 Valley Dr Norfolk (23502) *(G-9745)*

Team Ceramic Inc 757 572-7725
1500 Chasebury Pl Apt 107 Chesapeake (23320) *(G-3325)*

Team Excel Inc 804 677-3694
1717 E Cary St Richmond (23223) *(G-11785)*

TEAM Marketing 703 405-0576
8120 Shane Ct Manassas (20112) *(G-8165)*

Team SSP Ventures Inc 804 273-9496
5105 Chappell Ridge Pl Glen Allen (23059) *(G-5805)*

Teams It 757 868-1129
41 Valmoore Dr Poquoson (23662) *(G-10377)*

Tearsolutions Inc 434 951-0444
315 Old Ivy Way Ste 301 Charlottesville (22903) *(G-2886)*

Tech Dynamism LLC 434 227-5324
110 5th St Ne Charlottesville (22902) *(G-2887)*

Tech Enterprises Inc 703 352-0001
11150 Fairfax Blvd # 402 Fairfax (22030) *(G-4686)*

Tech Express Inc 540 382-9400
597 Depot St Ne A Christiansburg (24073) *(G-3611)*

Tech of Southwest Virginia 276 496-5393
118 Shaker Ln Saltville (24370) *(G-12593)*

Techlab Inc 540 953-1664
20 Corporate Dr Radford (24141) *(G-10740)*

Techline Mfg LLC 804 986-8285
3669 Speeks Dr Midlothian (23112) *(G-8912)*

Techni Comm 703 231-6475
8627 Arbee Ct Nokesville (20181) *(G-9400)*

Technica Software LLC 703 371-7134
1021 Arlington Blvd # 718 Arlington (22209) *(G-1182)*

Technical Machine Service Inc 276 638-2105
101 Evening Star Ln Martinsville (24112) *(G-8340)*

Technical Motor Service LLC 276 638-1135
141 Dye Plant Rd Martinsville (24112) *(G-8341)*

Technical Services Division, Lorton *Also called Qinetiq Inc (G-7523)*

Technical Urethanes Inc 540 667-1770
3470 Martinsburg Pike Clear Brook (22624) *(G-3652)*

Technifab of Virginia Inc 276 988-7517
30014 Gvrnor G C Prry Hwy North Tazewell (24630) *(G-10109)*

Techniservices Inc 804 275-9207
8800 Metro Ct North Chesterfield (23237) *(G-9999)*

Technlgy Advncement Group Inc (PA) **703 406-3000**
22355 Tag Way Dulles (20166) *(G-4228)*

Technology Destiny LLC 703 400-8929
42593 Olmsted Dr Brambleton (20148) *(G-1934)*

Technology Hub Inc 571 370-5100
14102 Sllyfeld Cir Ste 35 Chantilly (20151) *(G-2508)*

Technology News and Literature 202 380-5425
4521 41st St N Arlington (22207) *(G-1183)*

Techsource LLC 757 469-3983
2198 Oberlin Dr Woodbridge (22191) *(G-15821)*

Techulon 540 443-9254
2200 Kraft Dr Ste 2475 Blacksburg (24060) *(G-1797)*

Tecnico Corporation (HQ) **757 545-4013**
831 Industrial Ave Chesapeake (23324) *(G-3326)*

Tecton Products LLC 540 380-5819
5415 Corporate Cir Salem (24153) *(G-12572)*

Tectonics Inc 276 228-5565
205 E Railroad Ave Wytheville (24382) *(G-15918)*

Tedi, Alexandria *Also called Third Eye Development Intl Inc (G-363)*

Teds Bulletin 571 313-8961
11948 Market St Reston (20190) *(G-10970)*

Tee Spot Rching Higher Hts LLC 540 877-5961
175 Greenwood Rd Winchester (22602) *(G-15488)*

Tee Time Threads LLC 757 581-4507
2711 Janice Lynn Ct Chesapeake (23323) *(G-3327)*

Tee Z Special 757 488-2435
4137 Lakeview Dr Chesapeake (23323) *(G-3328)*

Tee Zone-VA 434 964-9245
1600 Rio Road East Charlottesville (22901) *(G-2700)*

Teen Ink 804 365-8000
12449 W Patrick Henry Rd Ashland (23005) *(G-1499)*

Teen Scott Trucking Inc 804 833-9403
9717 Wendhurst Dr Glen Allen (23060) *(G-5806)*

Teendrivingstickercom LLC 571 643-6956
9550 Birmingham Dr Manassas (20111) *(G-8166)*

Teeny Textiles 703 731-7336
824 22nd St Virginia Beach (23451) *(G-14868)*

Tees & Co 757 744-9889
645 Mill Landing Rd Chesapeake (23322) *(G-3329)*

Tees To Go 2 ....540 569-2268
704 Middlebrook Ave Staunton (24401) *(G-13300)*

Tego Chemie Svc Usadiv of Gold 804 541-8658
914 E Randolph Rd Hopewell (23860) *(G-6941)*

Tegra LLC 470 705-1280
3801 E Princess Anne Rd Norfolk (23502) *(G-9746)*

Tegrex Technologies LLC 805 500-8479
705 Dale Ave Ste D Charlottesville (22903) *(G-2888)*

Teijin-Du Pont Films Inc 804 530-9310
3600 Discovery Dr Chester (23836) *(G-3459)*

Teijin-Du Pont Films Inc (PA) **804 530-9310**
1 Discovery Dr Hopewell (23860) *(G-6942)*

Tek-AM Corp 703 321-9144
7405 Lockport Pl Ste A Lorton (22079) *(G-7536)*

Tekadventure LLC (PA) **646 580-2511**
25050 Riding Plz Chantilly (20152) *(G-2560)*

Tekalign Inc 703 757-6690
11654 Plaza America Dr # 181 Reston (20190) *(G-10971)*

Teknostrata Inc 877 983-5667
4601 Fairfax Dr Ste 1200 Arlington (22203) *(G-1184)*

Tektonics Design Group LLC (PA) **804 233-5900**
702 E 4th St Richmond (23224) *(G-11786)*

Tele Controls Inc 571 490-4500
1101 Wilson Blvd Fl 6 Arlington (22209) *(G-1185)*

Teledyne Hastings Instruments, Hampton *Also called Teledyne Instruments Inc (G-6250)*

Teledyne Instruments Inc 757 723-6531
804 Newcombe Ave Hampton (23669) *(G-6250)*

Teledyne Lecroy Inc 434 984-4500
337 Rio Road West Charlottesville (22901) *(G-2701)*

Teledyne Lecroy Frontline Inc 434 984-4500
337 Rio Road West Charlottesville (22901) *(G-2702)*

Teledyne Vasco CK Company, South Boston *Also called Voestlpine High Prfmce Mtls Co (G-12792)*

Telesat US Services LLC 571 559-1500
1100 Wilson Blvd Ste 2900 Arlington (22209) *(G-1186)*

Telos Idntity MGT Slutions LLC 703 724-3800
19886 Ashburn Rd Ashburn (20147) *(G-1339)*

Temperpack Technologies Inc 434 218-2436
4447 Carolina Ave Richmond (23222) *(G-11787)*

Tempi Design Studio, Berryville *Also called Eileen C Johnson (G-1680)*

Temple-Inland Inc 804 861-8164
2333 Wells Rd Petersburg (23805) *(G-10345)*

Temprotect, Reston *Also called Online Biose Inc (G-10914)*

Tempur Production Usa LLC (HQ) **276 431-7150**
203 Tempur Pedic Dr # 102 Duffield (24244) *(G-4185)*

Tempur-Pedic Technologies LLC 276 431-7450
203 Tempur Pedic Dr # 102 Duffield (24244) *(G-4186)*

(G-0000) Company's Geographic Section entry number

Ten Companies LLC ...703 669-1008
161 Fort Evans Rd Ne Leesburg (20176) ***(G-7360)***
Ten Oaks LLC ...276 694-3208
209 Progress Dr Stuart (24171) ***(G-13636)***
Ten Sisters Wine LLC ...202 577-9774
1128 Priscilla Ln Alexandria (22308) ***(G-595)***
Tenant Temporary Quarters ...703 462-8623
5587 Callcott Way Alexandria (22312) ***(G-596)***
Tenant Turner ...804 241-8810
4820 Lake Brook Dr # 125 Glen Allen (23060) ***(G-5807)***
Teneo Inc ...703 212-3220
44330 Mercure Cir Ste 260 Sterling (20166) ***(G-13529)***
Tenneco Automotive Oper Co Inc ...540 432-3545
3160 Abbott Ln Harrisonburg (22801) ***(G-6379)***
Tenneco Automotive Oper Co Inc ...540 432-3752
4500 Early Rd Rockingham (22801) ***(G-12281)***
Tenneco Automotive Oper Co Inc ...540 434-2461
3160 Abbott Ln Harrisonburg (22801) ***(G-6380)***
Tenneco Inc ...540 557-3312
300 Industrial Park Rd Se Blacksburg (24060) ***(G-1798)***
Tennessee Consolidated Coal Co ...423 658-5115
1 Alpha Pl Bristol (24202) ***(G-2035)***
Tension Envelope Corp ...540 615-5372
5803 S Crestwood Ave Richmond (23226) ***(G-11408)***
Tent Company of Norfolk LLC ...757 461-7330
3419 Bus Ctr Dr Ste B Chesapeake (23323) ***(G-3330)***
Tequilla Battle ...757 769-1595
233 Lantana Ln B Hampton (23669) ***(G-6251)***
Tequilla With Leroy Home Imprv, Hampton *Also called Tequilla Battle* ***(G-6251)***
Terbakosky Specialty Paper, Charlottesville *Also called Delfort USA Inc* ***(G-2779)***
Teresa Blount ...804 402-1349
13832 Greyledge Pl Chester (23836) ***(G-3460)***
Teresa C Shankman ...703 533-9322
4721 38th Pl N Arlington (22207) ***(G-1187)***
Terex Corporation ...540 361-7755
150 Rverside Pkwy Ste 203 Fredericksburg (22406) ***(G-5492)***
Terminus Products Inc ...585 546-4990
2240 Prospect Dr Christiansburg (24073) ***(G-3612)***
Terra Christa, Vienna *Also called Bethany House Inc* ***(G-14015)***
Terrabuilt Corp International ...540 687-4211
1073 W Federal St Middleburg (20117) ***(G-8734)***
Terrago Technologies Inc ...678 391-9798
45610 Woodland Rd Sterling (20166) ***(G-13530)***
Terralign Group, Charlottesville *Also called Salesforce Maps* ***(G-2871)***
Terralign Group Inc ...571 388-4990
441 Carlisle Dr Ste C Herndon (20170) ***(G-6825)***
Terran Press LLC ...540 720-2516
11 Smelters Trace Rd Stafford (22554) ***(G-13202)***
Terrapin Sports Supply Inc ...540 672-9370
125 Madison Rd Orange (22960) ***(G-10228)***
Terrence Smith ...703 339-2194
9712 Gunston Cove Rd Lorton (22079) ***(G-7537)***
Terry Brown ...804 721-6667
5305 Oak Leaf Ln Prince George (23875) ***(G-10608)***
Terry Plymouth ...757 838-2718
19 Ducette Dr Hampton (23666) ***(G-6252)***
Terrys Custom Woodworks ...703 963-7116
11158 Saffold Way Reston (20190) ***(G-10972)***
Tertal Publishing LLC ...571 229-9699
12320 Indigo Springs Ct Bristow (20136) ***(G-2064)***
Tesla Inc ...703 761-4679
8500 Tyco Rd Vienna (22182) ***(G-14140)***
Tessy Plastics LLC ...434 385-5700
231 Jefferson Ridge Pkwy Lynchburg (24501) ***(G-7819)***
Tessy Plastics Corp ...434 385-5700
231 Jefferson Ridge Pkwy Lynchburg (24501) ***(G-7820)***
Tests For Higher Standards, Richmond *Also called Rosworks LLC* ***(G-11747)***
Tetelestai Industries LLC ...804 596-5232
2113 Turtle Creek Dr # 8 Henrico (23233) ***(G-6580)***
Tetgraphic Inc ...434 845-4450
3616 Campbell Ave Apt 1 Lynchburg (24501) ***(G-7821)***
Tetra Graphics Inc ...434 845-4450
3616 Campbell Ave Lynchburg (24501) ***(G-7822)***
Tetra Pak Tubex Inc ...540 967-0733
193 Industrial Dr Louisa (23093) ***(G-7571)***
Tetra Technologies Inc ...703 387-2100
4601 Fairfax Dr Ste 600 Arlington (22203) ***(G-1188)***
Tetravista LLC ...703 606-6509
5847 20th St N Arlington (22205) ***(G-1189)***
Teva Pharmaceuticals ...888 838-2872
2150 Perrowville Rd Forest (24551) ***(G-5101)***
Texacan Beef & Pork Co LLC ...703 858-5565
21750 Red Rum Dr Ste 142 Ashburn (20147) ***(G-1340)***
Text Art Print ...908 619-2809
6405 Octagon Dr Apt 3a North Chesterfield (23234) ***(G-10000)***
Textore Inc ...571 321-2013
4031 University Dr # 100 Fairfax (22030) ***(G-4687)***
Textron Ground Support Eqp Inc ...703 572-5340
23941 Cargo Dr Bldg 1 Dulles (20166) ***(G-4229)***
Textron Inc ...757 874-8100
1001 Providence Blvd Newport News (23602) ***(G-9353)***
Textron Systems, Blackstone *Also called Aai Corporation* ***(G-1809)***
Texture Sand Tresses ...757 369-3033
183 Pine Bluff Dr Newport News (23602) ***(G-9354)***
Texturing Services LLC ...276 632-3130
615 Walker Rd Martinsville (24112) ***(G-8342)***
TFC Amphenol, Chatham *Also called Times Fiber Communications Inc* ***(G-2937)***
Tfi Health Care, Petersburg *Also called Tubular Fabricators Indust Inc* ***(G-10347)***
Tfi Wind Down Inc ...703 714-0500
8461 Leesburg Pike Vienna (22182) ***(G-14141)***
Tg Holdings International CV ...804 330-1000
1100 Boulders Pkwy North Chesterfield (23225) ***(G-10026)***
Tg Polymers Inc ...585 670-9427
6855 Brindle Heath Way Alexandria (22315) ***(G-597)***
Tgihm Thank Gdness Its HM Made, Newport News *Also called Robin Stippich* ***(G-9329)***
Thales USA Defense & SEC Inc ...571 255-4600
2733 Crystal Dr Ste 1250 Arlington (22202) ***(G-1190)***
Thalhimer Headwear Corporation ...804 355-1200
4825 Radford Ave Ste 100 Richmond (23230) ***(G-11409)***
That Damn Mary Brewing LLC ...804 761-1085
148 Skipjack Dr Heathsville (22473) ***(G-6467)***
Thayer Design Inc ...434 528-3850
5066 S Amherst Hwy # 102 Madison Heights (24572) ***(G-7885)***
The Belvedere Press, Arlington *Also called Jackson Enterprises Inc* ***(G-1013)***
The City of Radford ...540 731-3662
20 Forest Ave Radford (24141) ***(G-10741)***
The Daily Progress, Charlottesville *Also called Wood Television LLC* ***(G-2716)***
The Downtowner Newspaper, Norfolk *Also called Target Advertising Inc* ***(G-9741)***
The For American Society ...703 331-0075
2904 Bridgehampton Ct Falls Church (22042) ***(G-4882)***
The Mennel Milling Co VA Inc ...540 776-6201
5185 Benois Rd Roanoke (24018) ***(G-12008)***
The Millwork Specialist LLC ...804 262-9296
2811 Hydraulic Rd Charlottesville (22901) ***(G-2703)***
The News & Advance, Lynchburg *Also called Wood Television LLC* ***(G-7840)***
The Printing Center, Portsmouth *Also called Person Enterprises Inc* ***(G-10468)***
The Scale Cabinet Maker, Christiansburg *Also called Dorsett Publications LLC* ***(G-3584)***
The Tint ...804 261-4081
8820 Brook Rd Ste 12 Glen Allen (23060) ***(G-5808)***
Theboxworks ...434 823-1004
4692 Browns Gap Tpke Crozet (22932) ***(G-3852)***
Thelma Rethford ...540 997-9121
71 Furnace Hill Rd Goshen (24439) ***(G-5928)***
Thelmas Interiors Inc ...757 855-0280
1523 Azalea Garden Rd Norfolk (23502) ***(G-9747)***
Theme Queen LLC ...804 439-0854
7435 Rural Point Rd Mechanicsville (23116) ***(G-8685)***
Theodore Turpin ...434 485-6600
1008 Polk St Lynchburg (24504) ***(G-7823)***
Theorem Painting ...703 670-4330
4596 Bishop Pl Dumfries (22025) ***(G-4259)***
Theory3 Inc ...804 335-1001
1940 Sandy Hook Rd Ste D Goochland (23063) ***(G-5886)***
Theos Shotgun Corner ...434 248-6250
8970 Thomas Jefferson Hwy Charlotte C H (23923) ***(G-2584)***
Theresa Lucas Setelin ...804 266-2324
10001 Highview Ave Glen Allen (23059) ***(G-5809)***
Thermadon Associates ...571 275-6118
13429 Kingsman Rd Woodbridge (22193) ***(G-15822)***
Thermal Gradient Inc ...585 425-3338
118 Peachtree Williamsburg (23188) ***(G-15324)***
Thermal Spray Solutions Inc (PA) ...**757 673-2468**
1105 Intl Plz Ste B Chesapeake (23323) ***(G-3331)***
Thermasteel Inc ...540 633-5000
609 W Rock Rd Radford (24141) ***(G-10742)***
Thermasteel Rp Ltd ...540 633-5000
609 W Rock Rd Radford (24141) ***(G-10743)***
Thermcor Inc ...757 622-7881
2601 Colley Ave Norfolk (23517) ***(G-9748)***
Thermo Fisher Scientific Inc ...540 869-3200
8365 Valley Pike Middletown (22645) ***(G-8744)***
Thermo Quick Inc ...703 455-0040
11720 Main St Ste 100 Fredericksburg (22408) ***(G-5377)***
Thermo-Flex Technologies Inc ...919 247-6411
360 Firstwatch Dr Moneta (24121) ***(G-8982)***
Thermo-Optical Group LLC ...540 822-9481
12260 Elvan Rd Lovettsville (20180) ***(G-7587)***
Thermohalt Technology LLC ...703 880-6697
3002 Hughsmith Ct Oak Hill (20171) ***(G-10139)***
Thesia Inc ...703 726-8845
42195 Highbank Pl Aldie (20105) ***(G-113)***
Thi, Mount Crawford *Also called Todd Huffman Installs LLC* ***(G-9060)***
Thibaut-Janisson LLC ...434 996-3307
1413 Dairy Rd Charlottesville (22903) ***(G-2889)***
Thibaut-Janisson Winery, Charlottesville *Also called Thibaut-Janisson LLC* ***(G-2889)***
Thick To Thin LLC ...607 427-1737
7019 Little Thames Dr Gainesville (20155) ***(G-5617)***

ALPHABETIC

Thierry Duguet Engraver Inc 434 979-3647
2246 Ivy Rd Ste 9 Charlottesville (22903) *(G-2890)*

Think Ink Printing, Chesapeake *Also called TI Printing of Virginia LLC* *(G-3335)*

Think Ink Printing 757 315-8565
1226 Executive Blvd # 103 Chesapeake (23320) *(G-3332)*

Thintherm LLC 434 243-5328
1120 Elliott Ave Charlottesville (22902) *(G-2891)*

Third Eye Development Intl Inc 631 682-1848
4890 Leesburg Pike 610 Alexandria (22302) *(G-363)*

Third Security Rnr LLC 540 633-7900
1881 Grove Ave Radford (24141) *(G-10744)*

Thirty Seven Cent Machine 276 673-1400
156 Hodges Farm Rd Martinsville (24112) *(G-8343)*

Thistle and Stag Meadery 434 842-2200
2053 East River Rd Fork Union (23055) *(G-5113)*

Thistle Foundry & Mch Co Inc 276 326-1196
101 Thistle St Bluefield (24605) *(G-1881)*

Thistle Gate Vineyard LLC 434 286-2428
5199 W River Rd Scottsville (24590) *(G-12668)*

Thistledown Alpacas Inc 804 784-4837
489 Manakin Ferry Rd Manakin Sabot (23103) *(G-7905)*

Thomas Brothers Software Corp 540 320-3505
5680 Jill Dr Pulaski (24301) *(G-10648)*

Thomas C Albro II 703 892-6738
822 S Taylor St Arlington (22204) *(G-1191)*

Thomas E Lewis 804 529-7526
2804 Lake Rd Lottsburg (22511) *(G-7544)*

Thomas H Rhea MD PC 703 658-0300
4600 John Marr Dr Annandale (22003) *(G-787)*

Thomas Hegens 703 205-9000
2750 Prosperity Ave # 120 Fairfax (22031) *(G-4569)*

Thomas Industrial Fabrication, Floyd *Also called Turbo Sales & Fabrication Inc* *(G-5042)*

Thomas L Alphin Inc 540 997-0611
260 Big River Rd Goshen (24439) *(G-5929)*

Thomasville Furniture, Vienna *Also called Tfi Wind Down Inc* *(G-14141)*

Thompson Electric Motor Svc 434 372-3814
11190 Hwy Ninety Two Chase City (23924) *(G-2917)*

Thompson Enterprises, Conaway *Also called Peggy Sues Advertising Inc* *(G-3754)*

Thompson Fixture Installation 804 378-9352
530 Southlake Blvd Ste D North Chesterfield (23236) *(G-10001)*

Thompson Information Services, Arlington *Also called Columbia Books Inc* *(G-915)*

Thompson Media Packaging Inc 804 225-8146
1681 Mountain Rd Glen Allen (23060) *(G-5810)*

Thompson Pubg LLC George F 540 887-8166
217 Oak Ridge Cir Staunton (24401) *(G-13301)*

Thompsons Fire Extinguisher SA, Chase City *Also called Thompson Electric Motor Svc* *(G-2917)*

Thomson Industries Inc 540 633-3549
203a W Rock Rd Radford (24141) *(G-10745)*

Thomson Reuters Corporation 434 973-4396
526 Eastbrook Dr Charlottesville (22901) *(G-2704)*

Thomson Reuters Corporation 804 346-5135
4905 Riverplace Ct Glen Allen (23059) *(G-5811)*

Thor Systems Inc 804 353-7477
3621 Saunders Ave Richmond (23227) *(G-11410)*

Thore Signs 804 513-5621
2212 French Hill Ter Powhatan (23139) *(G-10580)*

Thorium Power Inc 703 918-4904
8300 Greensboro Dr # 800 Mc Lean (22102) *(G-8566)*

Thorlabs Inc 703 300-3000
44901 Falcon Pl Ste 113 Sterling (20166) *(G-13531)*

Thorlabs Imaging Systems 703 651-1705
108 Powers Ct Ste 150 Sterling (20166) *(G-13532)*

Thorn 10 Publishing LLC 757 277-9431
1205 Brassie Ct Chesapeake (23320) *(G-3333)*

Thorpe & Ricks, Richmond *Also called Universal Leaf Tobacco Co Inc* *(G-11066)*

Thorpe Logging Inc 434 634-6050
623 Belfield Rd Emporia (23847) *(G-4368)*

Thought & Expression Co LLC (PA) **405 919-0068**
6841 Elm St Unit J Mc Lean (22101) *(G-8567)*

Thoughtweb USA Inc 575 639-1726
2961a Hunter Mill Rd Oakton (22124) *(G-10162)*

Thrane Rgonal Workshop- Mackey 757 410-3291
209 Tintern Ct Chesapeake (23320) *(G-3334)*

Thread Connections, Hampton *Also called Elizabeth Ballard-Spitzer* *(G-6138)*

Threadcount LLC 703 929-7033
209 E Broad St Richmond (23219) *(G-11788)*

Threadlines Inc 757 898-8355
216 Henry Lee Ln Grafton (23692) *(G-5932)*

Threads Ink LLC 703 221-0819
2970 Myrtlewood Dr Dumfries (22026) *(G-4260)*

Threat Prot Wrd Wide Svcs LLC 703 795-2445
6997 Justin Ct E Remington (22734) *(G-10773)*

Thredz EMB Screen Print Graph 757 636-9569
815 Admissions Ct Virginia Beach (23462) *(G-14869)*

Three Angels Pretzels 540 722-0400
41 S Loudoun St Winchester (22601) *(G-15593)*

Three Brothers Distillery Inc 757 204-1357
9935 County Line Rd Disputanta (23842) *(G-4114)*

Three Creek Apparel, Lebanon *Also called Lebanon Apparel Corporation* *(G-7197)*

Three Crosses Distilling Co LL 804 512-9690
3835 Old Buckingham Rd Powhatan (23139) *(G-10581)*

Three Crosses Distlg Co LLC 804 818-6330
11620 Drysdale Dr North Chesterfield (23236) *(G-10002)*

Three Foot Software LLC 434 202-0217
1015 Glendale Rd Charlottesville (22901) *(G-2705)*

Three Hens 804 787-3400
1899 Haskin Rd Goochland (23063) *(G-5887)*

Three P Logging 434 376-9812
3073 Mount Carmel Rd Brookneal (24528) *(G-2114)*

Three Peaks Crafts 276 677-3724
9399 Troutdale Hwy Troutdale (24378) *(G-13901)*

Three Points Design Inc 757 426-2149
684 Princess Anne Rd Virginia Beach (23457) *(G-14870)*

Thrifty Trunk 757 478-7836
3747 Dare Cir Norfolk (23513) *(G-9749)*

Throx Brew Market and Grille 540 323-7360
1518 Martinsburg Pike Winchester (22603) *(G-15489)*

Thryv Inc 434 974-4000
943 Glenwood Station Ln # 201 Charlottesville (22901) *(G-2706)*

Thumbelinas 703 448-8043
1587 Spring Hill Rd Vienna (22182) *(G-14142)*

Thumbprint Events By 703 720-1000
20 Skipwith Green Cir Henrico (23294) *(G-6581)*

Thunderbird Creations, Virginia Beach *Also called Joseph Carson* *(G-14574)*

Thurston Sign & Graphic 804 285-4617
2325 Lenora Ln Richmond (23230) *(G-11411)*

TI Associates Inc 757 857-6266
5401 Henneman Dr Norfolk (23513) *(G-9750)*

TI Printing of Virginia LLC 757 315-8565
1226 Executive Blvd # 103 Chesapeake (23320) *(G-3335)*

Tia-The Richards Corp 703 471-8600
44931 Falcon Pl Ste 1 Sterling (20166) *(G-13533)*

Tian Corporation 703 434-4000
11955 Freedom Dr Reston (20190) *(G-10973)*

Tiango Field Services LLC 804 683-2067
2400 Barda Cir Glen Allen (23060) *(G-5812)*

Tibco Software Federal Inc 703 208-3900
3141 Frview Pk Dr Ste 600 Falls Church (22042) *(G-4883)*

Tidal Corrosion Services LLC 757 216-4011
1158 Pickett Rd 1160 Norfolk (23502) *(G-9751)*

Tidal Wave Graphics 757 842-6269
625 Innovation Dr Ste 101 Chesapeake (23320) *(G-3336)*

Tidalwave Tumbler & Tees LLC 757 814-1022
580 Summer Lake Ln Virginia Beach (23454) *(G-14871)*

Tide Water Pulication LLC (PA) **757 562-3187**
1000 Armory Dr Franklin (23851) *(G-5158)*

Tide Water Pulication LLC 434 848-2114
213 N Main St Lawrenceville (23868) *(G-7186)*

Tidewater Auto & Indus Mch Inc 757 855-5091
949 Seahawk Cir Virginia Beach (23452) *(G-14872)*

Tidewater Auto Elec Svcs II 757 523-5656
940 Corporate Ln Ste A Chesapeake (23320) *(G-3337)*

Tidewater Block LLc 757 539-1576
999 Kenyon Rd Suffolk (23434) *(G-13771)*

Tidewater Castings Inc 757 399-0679
2401 Wesley St Portsmouth (23707) *(G-10491)*

Tidewater Emblems Ltd 757 428-1170
1816 Potters Rd Virginia Beach (23454) *(G-14873)*

Tidewater Foods Inc 757 410-2498
5714 Curlew Dr Norfolk (23502) *(G-9752)*

Tidewater Graphics and Signs 757 622-7446
645 Church St Ste 102 Norfolk (23510) *(G-9753)*

Tidewater Graphics Inc 757 464-6136
1628 Independence Blvd # 1540 Virginia Beach (23455) *(G-14874)*

Tidewater Green 757 487-4736
1500 Steel St Chesapeake (23323) *(G-3338)*

Tidewater Hispanic Newspaper 757 474-1233
2005 Silver Lake Dr Virginia Beach (23464) *(G-14875)*

Tidewater News, The, Franklin *Also called Tide Water Pulication LLC* *(G-5158)*

Tidewater Newspapers Inc (PA) **804 693-3101**
6625 Main St Gloucester (23061) *(G-5862)*

Tidewater Oyster Farms, Hayes *Also called Big Island Oysters* *(G-6396)*

Tidewater Pallets 757 962-0020
2608 Wyoming Ave Norfolk (23513) *(G-9754)*

Tidewater Parent 757 222-3900
150 W Brambleton Ave Norfolk (23510) *(G-9755)*

Tidewater Printers Inc 757 888-0674
15470 Warwick Blvd Newport News (23608) *(G-9355)*

Tidewater Prof Contrs LLC 757 605-1040
3009 Belle Haven Dr Virginia Beach (23452) *(G-14876)*

Tidewater Prosthetic Center 757 925-4844
6363 Center Dr Ste 100 Norfolk (23502) *(G-9756)*

Tidewater Prosthetic Center (HQ) **757 925-4844**
150 Burnetts Way Ste 300 Suffolk (23434) *(G-13772)*

Tidewater Rebar LLC 757 325-9893
1013 Obici Indus Blvd Suffolk (23434) *(G-13773)*

Tidewater Review, Williamsburg *Also called Apg Media of Chesapeake LLC* *(G-15205)*

(G-0000) Company's Geographic Section entry number

Tidewater Structures 757 753-1435
609 Berkley Pl Virginia Beach (23452) *(G-14877)*

Tidewater Tech Aviation, Chesapeake *Also called Training Services Inc* *(G-3349)*

Tidewater Techs LLC 757 301-1789
2864 Augusta Cir Virginia Beach (23453) *(G-14878)*

Tidewater Trading Post Inc 757 420-6117
820 Greenbrier Cir Ste 33 Chesapeake (23320) *(G-3339)*

Tidewater Tree 757 426-6002
1900 Munden Point Rd Virginia Beach (23457) *(G-14879)*

Tidewater Virginia Usbc Inc 757 456-2497
700 Baker Rd Ste 102 Virginia Beach (23462) *(G-14880)*

Tidewater Wldg Fabrication LLC 757 636-6630
1336 Butts Station Rd Chesapeake (23320) *(G-3340)*

Tidewater Women, Virginia Beach *Also called Windmill Promotions* *(G-14940)*

Tidewell Marine Inc 804 453-6115
15912 Northumberland Hwy Burgess (22432) *(G-2177)*

Tidewter Archtctural Mllwk Inc 757 422-1279
614 10th St Virginia Beach (23451) *(G-14881)*

Tidewter Exhibits AG Mllwk Mfg 540 379-1555
678 Kings Hwy Fredericksburg (22405) *(G-5493)*

Tienda Herndon Inc 703 478-0478
1020 Elden St Ste 101 Herndon (20170) *(G-6826)*

Tier 1 Operations, Leesburg *Also called Casey Traxler* *(G-7242)*

Tiera Averett 804 888-3721
10221 Krause Rd Unit 1472 Chesterfield (23832) *(G-3532)*

Tiffany Inc 757 622-2915
200 W 22nd St Norfolk (23517) *(G-9757)*

Tiffany Yachts Inc 804 453-3464
2355 Jssie Dupont Mem Hwy Burgess (22432) *(G-2178)*

Tiffanys By Sharon Inc 804 273-6303
1517 N Parham Rd Ste D Henrico (23229) *(G-6582)*

Tiger Paper Company Inc 540 337-9510
2480 Tinkling Spring Rd Stuarts Draft (24477) *(G-13661)*

Tigerseal Products LLC 800 899-9389
13093 Old Ridge Rd Beaverdam (23015) *(G-1614)*

Tight Lines Holdings Group 540 989-7874
3232 Electric Rd Ste 402 Roanoke (24018) *(G-12009)*

Tight Lines Holdings Group Inc 540 389-6691
146 W 4th St Salem (24153) *(G-12573)*

Tighty Whitey Soap Candle LLC 202 818-9169
1201 Braddock Pl Apt 303 Alexandria (22314) *(G-364)*

Tile Optima LLC 703 256-5650
5705 General Wash Dr E Alexandria (22312) *(G-598)*

Tim Lacey Builders 540 434-3372
301 Stoneleigh Dr Harrisonburg (22801) *(G-6381)*

Tim Price Inc 540 722-8716
1818 Roberts St Winchester (22601) *(G-15594)*

Tim Price Woodworking LLC 276 794-9405
356 Church Hill Rd Lebanon (24266) *(G-7209)*

Tim Shepherd Archit Fabricati 540 230-1457
1424 5th St Sw Roanoke (24016) *(G-12203)*

Timber Team USA LLC 434 989-1201
1 Morton Dr Ste 504 Charlottesville (22903) *(G-2892)*

Timberlake Cabinet Company 540 955-4985
430 Jack Enders Blvd Berryville (22611) *(G-1694)*

Timberlake Contracting LLC 804 449-1517
16370 Pine Springs Ln Beaverdam (23015) *(G-1615)*

Timberland Express Inc 276 679-1965
4848 Thompson Rd Wise (24293) *(G-15636)*

Timberline Barns LLC 276 445-4366
21680 Wilderness Rd Rose Hill (24281) *(G-12363)*

Timberline Logging Inc 276 393-7239
1523 Mountain View Ave E Big Stone Gap (24219) *(G-1716)*

Timbertone LLC 540 381-9794
755 W Main St Christiansburg (24073) *(G-3613)*

Timberville Drug Store 540 434-2379
33 Emery St Harrisonburg (22801) *(G-6382)*

Timco Energy Inc 276 322-4900
356 S College Ave Bluefield (24605) *(G-1882)*

Time Machine Inc (PA) 540 772-0962
5493 Franklin Rd Sw Roanoke (24014) *(G-12204)*

Timeless Stitches Inc 804 798-7677
123 Junction Dr Ashland (23005) *(G-1500)*

Timeless Touch LLC 703 986-0096
11501 Albrite Ct Manassas (20112) *(G-8167)*

Times Community Media 703 777-1111
1602 Village Market Blvd Leesburg (20175) *(G-7361)*

Times Community Newspaper, Warrenton *Also called Fauquier Times Democrat* *(G-15015)*

Times Community Newspaper, Reston *Also called Virginia News Group LLC* *(G-10985)*

Times Fiber Communications Inc 434 432-1800
380 Tightsqueeze Indus Rd Chatham (24531) *(G-2937)*

Times Fiber Communications Inc 434 432-1800
380 Tightsqueeze Indus Rd Chatham (24531) *(G-2938)*

Times Publishing Company 757 357-3288
228 Main St Smithfield (23430) *(G-12742)*

Times-Virginian, Appomattox *Also called Womack Publishing Co Inc* *(G-828)*

Times-World LLC 540 981-3100
201 Campbell Ave Sw 209 Roanoke (24011) *(G-12205)*

Timingwallstreet Inc 434 489-2380
765 Piney Forest Rd Danville (24540) *(G-4041)*

Timmons & Kelley Architects 804 897-5636
14005 Steeplestone Dr D Midlothian (23113) *(G-8913)*

Timothy Breeden 804 748-6433
10601 Greenyard Way Chester (23831) *(G-3461)*

Timothy C Vass 276 728-7753
3882 Stable Rd Hillsville (24343) *(G-6900)*

Timothy D Falls 540 987-8142
477 Rudasill Mill Rd Woodville (22749) *(G-15862)*

Timothy E Quinn 301 212-9700
424 S Saint Asaph St Alexandria (22314) *(G-365)*

Timothy L Hosey 270 339-0016
6814 Back Rd Maurertown (22644) *(G-8364)*

Timothys Custom Woodworking 540 408-4343
160 Newton Rd Fredericksburg (22405) *(G-5494)*

Tin Man Shtmtl Fabrication, Manassas *Also called Tmn LLC* *(G-8003)*

Tincture Distillers LLC 443 370-2037
5521 27th St N Arlington (22207) *(G-1192)*

Tindahan 757 243-8207
621 Stoney Creek Ln Ste 2 Newport News (23608) *(G-9356)*

Tindall Concrete Virginia, North Dinwiddie *Also called Tindall Corporation* *(G-10065)*

Tindall Corporation 804 861-8447
5400 Olgers Rd North Dinwiddie (23803) *(G-10065)*

Tine & Company Inc 276 881-8232
Hc 66 Box 5 Whitewood (24657) *(G-15193)*

Tinkers Treasures 708 633-0710
707 Coralview Ter Midlothian (23114) *(G-8914)*

Tinted Timber Sign Co 757 869-3231
129 Camelot Cres Yorktown (23693) *(G-15996)*

Tiny Power, Bealeton *Also called Rappahannock Boat Works Inc* *(G-1605)*

Tiome Inc 703 531-8963
2056 Blunt Ln Alexandria (22303) *(G-599)*

Tiome.org, Alexandria *Also called Tiome Inc* *(G-599)*

Tippers Inc 703 391-7232
11859 Abercorn Ct Reston (20191) *(G-10974)*

Tips East LLC 757 562-7888
1100 Armory Dr Ste 162 Franklin (23851) *(G-5159)*

Tire Kings 757 586-5206
5302 Jefferson Ave Newport News (23605) *(G-9357)*

Tireflys, Goochland *Also called Theory3 Inc* *(G-5886)*

Tisol 703 739-2771
8208 Treebrooke Ln Alexandria (22308) *(G-600)*

Titan America LLC 540 622-2350
399 Kelly Dr Front Royal (22630) *(G-5557)*

Titan America LLC 703 221-2003
3454 Canal Rd Dumfries (22026) *(G-4261)*

Titan America LLC 757 533-7152
2125 Kimball Ter Norfolk (23504) *(G-9758)*

Titan America LLC 804 236-4122
4305 Sarellen Rd Richmond (23231) *(G-11412)*

Titan America LLC 703 471-0044
22963 Concrete Plz Sterling (20166) *(G-13534)*

Titan America LLC 540 372-8717
10133 Tidewater Trl Fredericksburg (22408) *(G-5378)*

Titan II Inc (HQ) 757 380-2000
4101 Washington Ave Newport News (23607) *(G-9358)*

Titan Plastics LLC 804 339-4464
9517 Country Way Rd Glen Allen (23060) *(G-5813)*

Titan Sign & Awning, Fredericksburg *Also called Titan Sign Corporation* *(G-5379)*

Titan Sign Corporation 540 899-5334
11001 Pierson Dr Ste H Fredericksburg (22408) *(G-5379)*

Titan Turf LLC 276 768-7833
4140 Little River Rd Galax (24333) *(G-5650)*

Titan Virginia Ready Mix, Richmond *Also called Titan America LLC* *(G-11412)*

Titan Virginia Ready-Mix, Sterling *Also called Titan America LLC* *(G-13534)*

Titan Wheel Corp Virginia (HQ) 276 496-5121
227 Allison Gap Rd Saltville (24370) *(G-12594)*

Titanium 3 LLC 617 417-9288
7001 Arbor Ln Mc Lean (22101) *(G-8568)*

Titanium Productions Inc 757 351-2526
101 W Plume St Norfolk (23510) *(G-9759)*

Titas Nene Bicol Atchara LLC 571 501-8599
19110 Dalton Points Pl Leesburg (20176) *(G-7362)*

Titus Development Corp 757 515-7338
340 Constitution Dr Virginia Beach (23462) *(G-14882)*

Titus Publications 757 421-4141
5677 Fitztown Rd Virginia Beach (23457) *(G-14883)*

Tizzy Technologies Inc 703 344-3348
4445 Corp Ln Ste 264 Virginia Beach (23462) *(G-14884)*

Tk Aircraft LLC 540 665-8113
124 Elmwood Rd Winchester (22602) *(G-15490)*

Tkl Products Corp 804 749-8300
2551 Rte 1200 Oilville (23129) *(G-10185)*

Tko Promos 804 564-1683
5337 Fox Lake Ter Moseley (23120) *(G-9049)*

TLC Cleaners Inc 703 425-5577
9531 Braddock Rd Fairfax (22032) *(G-4570)*

TLC Publishing 434 974-6411
1904 Dellwood Rd Charlottesville (22901) *(G-2707)*

TLC Publishing LLC 571 439-0564
20898 Gardengate Cir Ashburn (20147) *(G-1341)*

Tlj Pressure Washing 757 235-9096
3736 Snowdrift Cir Virginia Beach (23462) *(G-14885)*

Tlpublishing LLC 571 992-7972
43244 Preston Ct Ashburn (20147) *(G-1342)*

Tls Tees LLC 540 455-5260
10305 Gordon Rd Spotsylvania (22553) *(G-12918)*

Tlw Self Publishing Company 540 560-2507
12318 Osprey Ln Culpeper (22701) *(G-3925)*

Tmac Services Inc 804 368-0936
10032 Whitesel Rd Ashland (23005) *(G-1501)*

TMC Welding 703 455-9709
8742 Cold Plain Ct Springfield (22153) *(G-13099)*

Tmeic Corporation 540 725-2031
2060 Cook Dr Salem (24153) *(G-12574)*

TMI Usa Inc 703 668-0114
11491 Sunset Hills Rd # 301 Reston (20190) *(G-10975)*

TMI-Orion, Reston *Also called TMI Usa Inc (G-10975)*

Tmn LLC 703 335-8191
9218 Prince William St Manassas (20110) *(G-8003)*

Tmp Industries LLC 540 761-0435
113 Sycamore Ave Ne Roanoke (24012) *(G-12206)*

Tms Corp 804 262-9296
2811 Hydraulic Rd Charlottesville (22901) *(G-2708)*

Tms International LLC 804 957-9611
25805 Hofheimer Way North Dinwiddie (23803) *(G-10066)*

Tms Neurohealth Centers, Woodbridge *Also called Greenbrook Tms Neurohealth Ctr (G-15718)*

Tms Neurohealth Centers, Roanoke *Also called Greenbrook Tms Neurohealth Ctr (G-11928)*

Tms Neurohealth Centers, Charlottesville *Also called Greenbrook Tms Neurohealth Ctr (G-2639)*

TN Cor Industries Incorporated 703 682-2001
2900 Eisenhower Ave Alexandria (22314) *(G-366)*

Tnl Embroidery Inc 757 410-2671
500 Grayson Way Chesapeake (23320) *(G-3341)*

TNT Bradshaw Logging LLC 276 928-1579
9908 Wilderness Rd Bland (24315) *(G-1837)*

TNT GRAphics&signs 757 615-5936
2864 Wesley Rd Chesapeake (23323) *(G-3342)*

TNT Laser Works LLC 571 214-7517
22 1/2 Pershing Ave Nw Leesburg (20176) *(G-7363)*

TNT Logging LLC 540 997-0611
735 Virginia Ave Goshen (24439) *(G-5930)*

TNT Piping and Welding 804 224-1634
45 Little Whim Rd Fredericksburg (22405) *(G-5495)*

TNT Printing LLC 757 818-5468
3648 Mill Bridge Way Chesapeake (23323) *(G-3343)*

Toana 2 Limited 757 566-2001
3326 Toano Dr Toano (23168) *(G-13879)*

Tobacco Plus 703 644-5111
6127 Backlick Rd Ste D Springfield (22150) *(G-13100)*

Tobacco Processors Inc 804 359-9311
1501 N Hamilton St Richmond (23230) *(G-11413)*

Tobacco Quitter LLC 540 818-3396
1905 Meadowview Cir Blacksburg (24060) *(G-1799)*

Toby Loritsch Inc 540 389-1522
1902 Stone Mill Dr Salem (24153) *(G-12575)*

Tod Methods, Reston *Also called Tekalign Inc (G-10971)*

Todays Signs Inc 703 352-6200
10341a Democracy Ln Fairfax (22030) *(G-4688)*

Todd & Gloria Price 276 655-4047
25 Wagon Wheel Rd Elk Creek (24326) *(G-4322)*

Todd Drummond Consulting LLC 603 763-8857
3036 Hemingway Rd Virginia Beach (23456) *(G-14886)*

Todd Huffman Installs LLC 540 271-4221
6257a S Valley Pike Mount Crawford (22841) *(G-9060)*

Todd Industries 571 275-2782
18981 Coreopsis Ter Leesburg (20176) *(G-7364)*

Todo Blu LLC 703 944-9000
8121 Briar Creek Dr Annandale (22003) *(G-788)*

Together Newspaper, Harrisonburg *Also called Shalom Foundation Inc (G-6369)*

Tokyo Electron America Inc 703 257-2211
9501 Innovation Dr Manassas (20110) *(G-8004)*

Tokyo Express 276 632-7599
1170 Memorial Blvd N Martinsville (24112) *(G-8344)*

Tokyo Express 540 389-6303
1940 W Main St Salem (24153) *(G-12576)*

Toledo Scales & Systems, Winchester *Also called Mettler-Toledo LLC (G-15554)*

Tom James Company 703 916-9300
7611 Little River Tpke 605w Annandale (22003) *(G-789)*

Tom James Company 757 394-3205
500 E Plume St Ste 405 Norfolk (23510) *(G-9760)*

Tom L Crockett 757 460-1382
3745 Jefferson Blvd Virginia Beach (23455) *(G-14887)*

Tom Wild Petrophysical Svcs 434 978-1269
3785 Graemont Dr Earlysville (22936) *(G-4295)*

Tom's Meat Market, Culpeper *Also called Calhouns Ham House (G-3877)*

Tomb Geophysics LLC 571 733-0930
14601 Colony Creek Ct Woodbridge (22193) *(G-15823)*

Tomlinsons Farrier Service LLC 540 377-9195
1161 Broadhead School Rd Greenville (24440) *(G-5999)*

Tommy Atkinson Sports Entp 757 428-0824
1612 Virginia Beach Blvd Virginia Beach (23454) *(G-14888)*

Tommy Atkinson's Sports, Virginia Beach *Also called Tommy Atkinson Sports Entp (G-14888)*

Tommy Bahama, Williamsburg *Also called Oxford Industries Inc (G-15290)*

Tommy V Foods 703 254-8764
6129 Lsburg Pike Apt 1006 Falls Church (22041) *(G-4884)*

Tomo LLC 407 694-7464
125 Shoal Crk Williamsburg (23188) *(G-15325)*

Tomorrows Resources Unlimited 434 929-2800
131 Crennel Dr Madison Heights (24572) *(G-7886)*

Tomotrace Inc 202 207-5423
13 Crescent Ct Sterling (20164) *(G-13535)*

Toms Cabinets & Designs 703 451-2227
8129 Edmonton Ct Springfield (22152) *(G-13101)*

Toms Welding 434 989-1553
11045 Bridgeport Rd Arvonia (23004) *(G-1234)*

Toms Wild Game Products 540 598-3900
11200 Ashford Lake Pl # 1 Henrico (23233) *(G-6583)*

Toner & Ink Warehouse LLC 301 332-2796
7371 Atlas Walk Way Ste 2 Gainesville (20155) *(G-5618)*

Tony Tran Hardwood Floors 540 793-4094
997 Hardy Rd Vinton (24179) *(G-14187)*

Tonya Sheridan Crop Organizer 540 860-0528
130 Stuart Ct Luray (22835) *(G-7624)*

Tonys Unisex Barber 757 237-7049
731 Monticello Ave Norfolk (23510) *(G-9761)*

Tool Wagon LLC 434 610-9664
1114 Templeton Mill Rd Lynchburg (24503) *(G-7824)*

Top Bead Welding Service Inc 540 901-8730
190 5th St Broadway (22815) *(G-2098)*

Top Drone Video 757 288-1774
4319 Greenleaf Dr Chesapeake (23321) *(G-3344)*

Top It Off Hats 703 988-1839
1432 Valley Mill Ct Herndon (20170) *(G-6827)*

Top Shelf Coatings LLC 804 241-8644
2022 Locust Hill Rd Aylett (23009) *(G-1555)*

Top Shop Onesies & Apparel 757 202-3371
406 W 34th St Norfolk (23508) *(G-9762)*

Topam LLC 703 444-4240
1338 Cassia St Herndon (20170) *(G-6828)*

Topcrafters of Virginia Inc 804 353-1797
4415 Augusta Ave Richmond (23230) *(G-11414)*

Topoatlas LLC 703 476-5256
12706 Kettering Dr Herndon (20171) *(G-6829)*

Tops By George, Virginia Beach *Also called Buddy D Ltd (G-14305)*

Tops of Town Virginia LLC 703 242-8100
2800 Dorr Ave Ste L Fairfax (22031) *(G-4571)*

Toray Plastics (america) Inc 540 636-3887
500 Toray Dr Front Royal (22630) *(G-5558)*

Torchs Mobile Welding 804 216-0412
8243 S Mayfield Ln Mechanicsville (23111) *(G-8686)*

Torishima Pump Mfg Co Ltd 866 374-1130
7400 Beaufont Spring Dr # 3 North Chesterfield (23225) *(G-10027)*

Toro-Aire Inc 804 649-7575
1001 E Main St Ste 203 Richmond (23219) *(G-11789)*

Torode Company 703 242-9387
531 Druid Hill Rd Ne Vienna (22180) *(G-14143)*

Torrance Enterprises Inc 804 748-5481
9120 Waterfowl Flyway Chesterfield (23838) *(G-3533)*

Torrent Loading Systems LLC 434 509-7307
406 Oakridge Blvd Lynchburg (24502) *(G-7825)*

Torres Graphics and Signs Inc 757 873-5777
11712 Jefferson Ave Ste A Newport News (23606) *(G-9359)*

Tortilleria Guavalueana 804 233-4141
3337 Broad Rock Blvd Richmond (23224) *(G-11790)*

Tortilleria San Luis LLC 804 901-1501
9027 Quioccasin Rd Richmond (23229) *(G-11415)*

Tossd Salad Group LLC 703 521-0646
1615 S Oakland St Arlington (22204) *(G-1193)*

Total Bliss Gourmet Soap LLC 540 740-8823
1872 E Lee Hwy New Market (22844) *(G-9149)*

Total Lift Care LLC 540 631-0008
300 Morrison Ln Front Royal (22630) *(G-5559)*

Total Machine LLC (PA) **540 775-2375**
11034 Bloomsbury Rd King George (22485) *(G-7115)*

Total Millwork LLC 571 379-5500
7700 Wellingford Dr Manassas (20109) *(G-8168)*

Total Molding Concepts Inc 540 665-8408
882 Baker Ln Winchester (22603) *(G-15491)*

Total Parachute Rigging Soluti 757 777-8288
197 S Main St Suffolk (23434) *(G-13774)*

Total Printing Co Inc 804 222-3813
4401 Sarellen Rd Richmond (23231) *(G-11416)*

Total Ptrchemicals Ref USA Inc 434 432-3706
601 Tightsqueeze Indus Rd Chatham (24531) *(G-2939)*

Total Ptrchemicals Ref USA Inc 276 228-6150
1150 S 3rd St Wytheville (24382) ***(G-15919)***
Total Sports 703 444-3633
101 E Holly Ave Sterling (20164) ***(G-13536)***
Total Stitch Embroidery Inc 804 275-4853
8612 Hunterstand Ct North Chesterfield (23237) ***(G-10003)***
Total Stitch Embroidery Inc 804 748-9594
10342 Iron Bridge Rd Chester (23831) ***(G-3462)***
Total Touch Solutions LLC 757 536-1445
1465 London Bridge Rd # 112 Virginia Beach (23453) ***(G-14889)***
Total Welding Solutions LLC 703 898-8720
16000 Tiffany Ln Haymarket (20169) ***(G-6450)***
Toucan Socks 757 656-9497
5622 Brookland Ct Alexandria (22310) ***(G-601)***
Touch 3 LLC 703 279-8130
2888 Glenvale Dr Fairfax (22031) ***(G-4572)***
Touch Class Construction Corp 757 728-3647
817 48th St Newport News (23607) ***(G-9360)***
Touch Honey Dsgn Print Photg 757 606-0411
31 King George Quay Chesapeake (23325) ***(G-3345)***
Tower Hill Corp 703 368-7727
8707 Quarry Rd Ste F Manassas (20110) ***(G-8005)***
Towers Custom Woodwork LLC C A 703 330-7107
7828 Signal Hill Rd Manassas (20111) ***(G-8169)***
Town Pride Publishers 757 321-8132
1206 Laskin Rd Ste 201 Virginia Beach (23451) ***(G-14890)***
Townsend Screen Printing LLC 804 225-0716
8679 Telegraph Rd Glen Allen (23060) ***(G-5814)***
Townside Building and Repr Inc 540 207-3906
43 Puri Ln Stafford (22554) ***(G-13203)***
Toy Ray Gun 703 662-3348
106 Elden St Herndon (20170) ***(G-6830)***
Tpp Enterprises LLC 757 247-0016
324 57th St Newport News (23607) ***(G-9361)***
Tq-Systems USA Inc 757 503-3927
424 Network Sta Chesapeake (23320) ***(G-3346)***
Tr Partners Lc 804 484-4091
4190 Dominion Blvd Glen Allen (23060) ***(G-5815)***
Tr Press Inc (PA) **540 347-4466**
404 Belle Air Ln Warrenton (20186) ***(G-15055)***
Track Patch 1 Corporation 757 609-2842
134 Battlefield Blvd N Chesapeake (23320) ***(G-3347)***
Track Patch 1 Corporation 757 289-5870
501 Boush St Ste B Norfolk (23510) ***(G-9763)***
Tracy Barrett 757 342-3204
7791 Woodview Ln Gloucester (23061) ***(G-5863)***
Trade Route International, Radford *Also called D J R Enterprises Inc* ***(G-10708)***
Trademark Branders 804 277-4428
16902 Hull Street Rd Moseley (23120) ***(G-9050)***
Trademark Printing LLC 757 410-1800
3564 Western Branch Blvd Portsmouth (23707) ***(G-10492)***
Trademark Printing LLC 757 803-7612
460 Plummer Dr Chesapeake (23323) ***(G-3348)***
Trademark Printing LLC 757 465-1736
3111 Ballard Ave Portsmouth (23701) ***(G-10493)***
Trademark Tees 757 232-4866
3900 Bonney Rd Virginia Beach (23452) ***(G-14891)***
Trademark Woodworking LLC 804 346-5999
3108 W Marshall St Richmond (23230) ***(G-11417)***
Tradingbell Inc 703 752-6100
1934 Old Gallows Rd Vienna (22182) ***(G-14144)***
Tradition Candle LLC 630 881-7194
426 Granby St Apt 3c Norfolk (23510) ***(G-9764)***
Traditional Iron & Woodworking 540 439-6911
12636 Tin Pot Run Ln Remington (22734) ***(G-10774)***
Traditionl Scrnprntg & Monogrm 276 935-7110
1402 Stable Dr Grundy (24614) ***(G-6042)***
Traffic Systems & Technology, Manassas *Also called Traffic Systems LLC* ***(G-8170)***
Traffic Systems LLC 703 530-9655
7390 Merritt Park Dr # 160 Manassas (20109) ***(G-8170)***
Trafficland Inc 703 591-1933
11325 Rndom Hlls Rd Ste 3 Fairfax (22030) ***(G-4689)***
Trailer Buff Inc 434 361-2500
732 Rockfish School Ln Afton (22920) ***(G-91)***
Training Services Inc 757 363-1800
2211 S Military Hwy Ste B Chesapeake (23320) ***(G-3349)***
Trajectory Tees LLC 419 680-6903
21725 Indian Summer Ter Sterling (20166) ***(G-13537)***
Trak House LLC 646 617-4418
3515 Delaware Ave Richmond (23222) ***(G-11791)***
Tramline Inc (PA) **276 322-3183**
356 S College Ave Bluefield (24605) ***(G-1883)***
Tramline Shop, Bluefield *Also called Tramline Inc* ***(G-1883)***
Tran Du 512 470-1794
1201 S Eads St Apt 1413 Arlington (22202) ***(G-1194)***
Trane Company 304 348-2800
10408 Lakeridge Pkwy # 100 Ashland (23005) ***(G-1502)***
Trane Inc 540 376-3064
11205 New Albany Dr Fredericksburg (22408) ***(G-5380)***
Trane US Inc 804 747-4774
10408 Lkrdge Pkwy Ste 100 Ashland (23005) ***(G-1503)***
Trane US Inc 540 342-3027
1308 Plantation Rd Ne Roanoke (24012) ***(G-12207)***
Trane US Inc 434 793-4822
104 Trade St Ste A Danville (24541) ***(G-4042)***
Trane US Inc 434 327-1601
1215 East Market St Charlottesville (22902) ***(G-2893)***
Trane US Inc 844 805-3895
2303 Trane Dr Nw Roanoke (24017) ***(G-12208)***
Trane US Inc 757 485-7700
1100 Cavalier Blvd Chesapeake (23323) ***(G-3350)***
Trane US Inc 757 490-2390
230 Clearfield Ave # 126 Virginia Beach (23462) ***(G-14892)***
Trane US Inc 540 376-3064
11205 New Albany Dr Fredericksburg (22408) ***(G-5381)***
Tranlin Inc 866 215-8290
4470 Cox Rd Ste 101 Glen Allen (23060) ***(G-5816)***
Tranlin Trading LLC 866 215-8290
1 Boars Head Pl Ste 100 Charlottesville (22903) ***(G-2894)***
Transcedent Integration 703 880-3019
43053 Pemberton Sq # 120 Chantilly (20152) ***(G-2561)***
Transecurity LLC 540 443-9231
2000 Kraft Dr Ste 2195 Blacksburg (24060) ***(G-1800)***
Transeffect LLC 703 991-1599
10 W Boscawen St Ste 20 Winchester (22601) ***(G-15595)***
Transfoam LLC 631 747-0255
8200 Dick Woods Rd Afton (22920) ***(G-92)***
Transformation Wellness LLC 804 366-4632
1801 Moore St Richmond (23220) ***(G-11792)***
Transformer Engineering LLC 216 741-5282
823 Fairview Rd Wytheville (24382) ***(G-15920)***
Transforming Daily Lives 916 990-2299
13836 Laurel Rock Ct Clifton (20124) ***(G-3677)***
Transit Mixed Concrete Corp 540 885-7224
501 Statler Blvd Staunton (24401) ***(G-13302)***
Transition Publishing LLC 703 208-4449
2255 Richelieu Dr Vienna (22182) ***(G-14145)***
Transmissions Dv, Hampton *Also called Valeo North America Inc* ***(G-6259)***
Transonic Power Controls & Svc 703 754-8943
14004 Dan Ct Haymarket (20169) ***(G-6451)***
Transport 3pl, Arlington *Also called Oneso Inc* ***(G-1088)***
Transport Topics Pubg Group 703 838-1770
950 N Glebe Rd Ste 210 Arlington (22203) ***(G-1195)***
Tranter Inc 757 533-9185
2401 Church St Norfolk (23504) ***(G-9765)***
Trapezium Brewing LLC 804 677-5728
230 E Bank St Petersburg (23803) ***(G-10346)***
Trapper's Triangle, Glen Allen *Also called Theresa Lucas Setelin* ***(G-5809)***
Travel Guide LLC 757 351-7000
150 Granby St Norfolk (23510) ***(G-9766)***
Travel Host of Washington DC, Burke *Also called Spinning In Control LLC* ***(G-2203)***
Travel Media Group, Norfolk *Also called Travel Guide LLC* ***(G-9766)***
Travelserver Software Inc 571 209-5907
19415 Drfield Ave Ste 204 Lansdowne (20176) ***(G-7174)***
Travelserver Software Inc (PA) **703 406-7664**
980 Old Holly Dr Great Falls (22066) ***(G-5982)***
Travis Lee Kerr 434 922-7005
1677 Pedlar River Rd Vesuvius (24483) ***(G-13999)***
Trax Energy Solutions, Lynchburg *Also called Trax International Corporation* ***(G-7826)***
Trax International Corporation 434 485-7100
5061 Fort Ave Lynchburg (24502) ***(G-7826)***
TRC Design Inc 804 779-3383
8307 Little Florida Rd Mechanicsville (23111) ***(G-8687)***
Tre 7 Entertainments, Hampton *Also called Hill Brenton* ***(G-6167)***
Tread Corporation 540 982-6881
176 Eastpark Dr Roanoke (24019) ***(G-12010)***
Treasures of African Artists 571 263-2152
105 N Alfred St Alexandria (22314) ***(G-367)***
Tredegar Consumer Designs Inc 804 330-1000
1100 Boulders Pkwy # 200 North Chesterfield (23225) ***(G-10028)***
Tredegar Corporation 804 523-3001
5700 Eastport Blvd Ste A Richmond (23231) ***(G-11418)***
Tredegar Corporation (PA) **804 330-1000**
1100 Boulders Pkwy # 200 North Chesterfield (23225) ***(G-10029)***
Tredegar Corporation 804 330-1000
1100 Boulders Pkwy # 200 North Chesterfield (23225) ***(G-10030)***
Tredegar Far East Corporation (HQ) **804 330-1000**
1100 Boulders Pkwy # 200 North Chesterfield (23225) ***(G-10031)***
Tredegar Film Products Corp 847 438-2111
1100 Boulders Pkwy # 200 North Chesterfield (23225) ***(G-10032)***
Tredegar Film Products Corp (HQ) **804 330-1000**
1100 Boulders Pkwy # 200 North Chesterfield (23225) ***(G-10033)***
Tredegar Film Products Latin 804 330-1000
1100 Boulders Pkwy # 200 North Chesterfield (23225) ***(G-10034)***
Tredegar Film Products US LLC 804 330-1000
1100 Boulders Pkwy # 200 North Chesterfield (23225) ***(G-10035)***
Tredegar Films Development Inc 804 330-1000
1100 Boulders Pkwy # 200 North Chesterfield (23225) ***(G-10036)***

Tredegar Films Rs Converting 804 330-1000
1100 Boulders Pkwy # 200 North Chesterfield (23225) *(G-10037)*
Tredegar Performance Films Inc 804 330-1000
1100 Boulders Pkwy # 200 North Chesterfield (23225) *(G-10038)*
Tredegar Personal Care LLC 804 330-1000
1100 Boulders Pkwy # 200 North Chesterfield (23225) *(G-10039)*
Tredegar Petroleum Corporation 804 330-1000
1100 Boulders Pkwy # 200 North Chesterfield (23225) *(G-10040)*
Tredegar Surfc Protection LLC (HQ) **804 330-1000**
1100 Boulders Pkwy # 200 North Chesterfield (23225) *(G-10041)*
Tree Naturals Inc 804 514-4423
4204 Riding Place Rd Richmond (23223) *(G-11793)*
Tree Technologies Inc 540 589-7988
6633 Sugar Ridge Dr Roanoke (24018) *(G-12011)*
Treescapes Inc 434 294-0865
597 Second Ave Alberta (23821) *(G-99)*
Trelleborg Marine Systems (PA) **540 667-5191**
532 Jack Enders Blvd Berryville (22611) *(G-1695)*
Trelleborg Marine Systems Usa 540 667-5191
532 Jack Enders Blvd Berryville (22611) *(G-1696)*
Tremolo Security Inc 703 844-2727
4201 Wilson Blvd 110-204 Arlington (22203) *(G-1196)*
Trent Sawmill Inc 434 376-2714
82 Oak St Brookneal (24528) *(G-2115)*
Treo Enterprise Solutions Inc 804 977-9862
6380 Beulah Rd Henrico (23231) *(G-6584)*
Treser Family Foods Inc 540 250-5667
1002 Auburn Dr Blacksburg (24060) *(G-1801)*
Trevor LLC 434 528-3884
3701 Mayflower Dr Lynchburg (24501) *(G-7827)*
Trex Co Inc (PA) **540 542-6300**
160 Exeter Dr Winchester (22603) *(G-15492)*
Trex Company Inc 540 542-6800
245 Capitol Ln Winchester (22602) *(G-15493)*
Trex Company Inc 540 542-6800
3229 Shawnee Dr Winchester (22602) *(G-15494)*
Trex Company Inc 540 542-6314
331 Apple Valley Rd Winchester (22602) *(G-15495)*
Trex Company Inc 540 542-6800
3229 Shawnee Dr Winchester (22602) *(G-15496)*
Trexlo Enterprises LLC (PA) **804 719-5900**
2361a Greystone Ct Ste A Rockville (23146) *(G-12301)*
Trexlo Enterprises LLC 804 272-7446
11523 Midlothian Tpke C North Chesterfield (23235) *(G-10004)*
Trexlo Enterprises LLC 804 644-7446
532 E Main St Richmond (23219) *(G-11794)*
Trexlo Enterprises LLC 804 270-7446
10817 W Broad St Glen Allen (23060) *(G-5817)*
Trexlo Enterprises LLC 804 624-1977
14404 Twickenham Pl Chesterfield (23832) *(G-3534)*
Tri City Advertiser, The, Hopewell *Also called Hopewell Publishing Company* *(G-6934)*
Tri Com Inc 804 561-3582
14101 Patrick Henry Hwy Amelia Court House (23002) *(G-675)*
Tri Corp 703 780-8753
8234 Riverside Rd Alexandria (22308) *(G-602)*
Tri State Generators LLC 434 660-3851
2524 Elon Rd Monroe (24574) *(G-8996)*
Tri State Graduate Sups LLC 540 665-5292
914 S Braddock St Winchester (22601) *(G-15596)*
Tri State Masters Inc 703 255-0222
9354 Campbell Rd Vienna (22182) *(G-14146)*
Tri-City Industrial Builders (PA) **276 669-4621**
13189 Wallace Pike Bristol (24202) *(G-2036)*
Tri-County Ope 434 676-4441
123 Main St Kenbridge (23944) *(G-7035)*
Tri-Dim Filter Corporation 540 774-9540
1615 Cleveland Ave Sw Roanoke (24016) *(G-12209)*
Tri-Dim Filter Corporation 540 967-2600
675 Industrial Dr Louisa (23093) *(G-7572)*
Tri-Dim Filter Corporation (HQ) **540 967-2600**
93 Industrial Dr Louisa (23093) *(G-7573)*
Tri-Ed Distribution Inc 757 852-3780
2500 Almeda Ave Ste 107 Norfolk (23513) *(G-9767)*
Tri-Phoenix, Annandale *Also called Triquetra Phoenix LLC* *(G-790)*
Tri-Tech Laboratories LLC 434 845-7073
1000 Robins Rd Lynchburg (24504) *(G-7828)*
Triad Digital Media Inc 336 908-5884
839 Kaye Trail Ln Axton (24054) *(G-1542)*
Triad Machine Shop, Hayes *Also called H & H Enterprises Inc* *(G-6399)*
Trial Exhibits Inc 804 672-0880
2727 Entp Pkwy Ste 109 Henrico (23294) *(G-6585)*
Triangle Skateboard Alliance 804 426-3663
5103 Melanies Way Williamsburg (23188) *(G-15326)*
Triax Music Industries 757 839-1215
1511 Oleander Ave Chesapeake (23325) *(G-3351)*
Tribbetts Meats 540 427-4671
3492 Jae Valley Rd Roanoke (24014) *(G-12210)*
Tribe 9 LLC 757 542-5348
340 Witness Ln Unit B Newport News (23608) *(G-9362)*
Triblio Inc 703 942-9557
11600 Sunrise Valley Dr # 100 Reston (20191) *(G-10976)*
Trident Oil Corp 434 974-1401
2374 Buck Mountain Rd Free Union (22940) *(G-5510)*
Trident Plastics Inc 804 236-8705
5608 Charles City Cir Richmond (23231) *(G-11419)*
Trident Seafoods Corp 540 707-0112
940 Orange St Bedford (24523) *(G-1661)*
Trident SEC & Holdings LLC 757 689-4560
2133-126 Upton Dr Ste 151 Virginia Beach (23454) *(G-14893)*
Trident Tool Inc 540 635-7753
105 Boydton Plank Dr Stephens City (22655) *(G-13324)*
Tried & True Printing LLC 434 964-8202
121 Danbury Ct Charlottesville (22902) *(G-2895)*
Tried and Tru Supply Company, Charlottesville *Also called Tried & True Printing LLC* *(G-2895)*
Trigg Industries LLC 757 223-7522
716 Bluecrab Rd Ste B Newport News (23606) *(G-9363)*
Trijicon Inc 703 445-1600
39 Tech Pkwy Ste 207 Stafford (22556) *(G-13204)*
Trimark Associates 703 369-9494
6412 Brandon Ave Springfield (22150) *(G-13102)*
Trimble Inc 540 904-5925
1510 Southside Dr Salem (24153) *(G-12577)*
Trimech Solutions LLC (PA) **804 257-9965**
4461 Cox Rd Ste 302 Glen Allen (23060) *(G-5818)*
Tringapps Inc 703 698-6910
3060 Williams Dr Ste 200 Fairfax (22031) *(G-4573)*
Trinitee Group LLC 757 268-9694
1597 Heritage Hill Dr Richmond (23238) *(G-11420)*
Trinity Construction Svcs Inc 757 455-8660
2043 Church St Norfolk (23504) *(G-9768)*
Trinity Publications LLC 804 779-3499
7409 Flannigan Mill Rd Mechanicsville (23111) *(G-8688)*
Trinity Steel Erection Inc 804 598-8811
1349 Pine Creek Ridge Dr Powhatan (23139) *(G-10582)*
Trio Child LLC 703 299-0070
416 Cook St Alexandria (22314) *(G-368)*
Triology Machine Company Inc 540 343-9508
1726 Seibel Dr Ne Ste D Roanoke (24012) *(G-12211)*
Triple C Woodworking LLC 703 779-9966
41335 Shreve Mill Rd Leesburg (20175) *(G-7365)*
Triple D Sales Co Inc 540 672-5821
976 Beautiful Run Rd Aroda (22709) *(G-1226)*
Triple E Signs, Stafford *Also called Eddies Repair Shop Inc* *(G-13141)*
Triple Gold Welding LLC 804 370-0082
330 Seatons Ln West Point (23181) *(G-15162)*
Triple Images Inc 540 829-1050
108 W Cameron St Culpeper (22701) *(G-3926)*
Triple OG Publishing LLC 804 252-0856
5101 Eanes Ln Henrico (23231) *(G-6586)*
Triple R Welding & Repair Svc 540 347-9026
5413 Turkey Run Rd Warrenton (20187) *(G-15056)*
Triple S Enterprises Inc 434 525-8400
14708 Forest Rd Forest (24551) *(G-5102)*
Triple S Pallets LLC 540 810-4581
950 Cottontail Trl Mount Crawford (22841) *(G-9061)*
Triple Stitch Designs LLC 757 376-2666
1945 Champion Cir Virginia Beach (23456) *(G-14894)*
Triple Threat Industries LLC 703 413-7919
1221 S Eads St Arlington (22202) *(G-1197)*
Triple Y Premium Yogurt 804 212-5413
3713 Mill Meadow Dr Richmond (23221) *(G-11795)*
Triple Yolk LLC 540 923-4040
1224 Desert Rd Reva (22735) *(G-11002)*
Triple Z Transport LLC 804 335-5962
7986 Wynbrook Ln Mechanicsville (23111) *(G-8689)*
Triple-F-Farm, Bedford *Also called Claude Cofer* *(G-1631)*
Triquetra Phoenix LLC 571 265-6044
4713 Ravensworth Rd Annandale (22003) *(G-790)*
Triron Defense Services LLC 703 472-2458
325 W Derby Ct Sterling (20164) *(G-13538)*
Trisec Assoc Inc 703 471-6564
2905 Parklawn Ct Herndon (20171) *(G-6831)*
Trishs Books 804 550-2954
10330 Agecroft Manor Ct Mechanicsville (23116) *(G-8690)*
Tritech Solutions Virginia Inc 434 664-2140
3061 Holiday Lake Rd Appomattox (24522) *(G-824)*
Tritex LLC 276 773-0593
60 Corporate Ln Independence (24348) *(G-6996)*
Triton Defense Services LLC 703 472-2458
325 W Derby Ct Sterling (20164) *(G-13539)*
Triton Industries Inc 757 887-1956
250 Enterprise Dr Newport News (23603) *(G-9364)*
Trk Systems Inc 804 777-9445
11306 Macandrew Dr Chesterfield (23838) *(G-3535)*
Trl Inc 276 794-7196
25392 Us Highway 58 Castlewood (24224) *(G-2258)*
Trm Inc (PA) **920 855-2194**
5365 Antioch Ridge Dr Haymarket (20169) *(G-6452)*

Trodat USA.....540 815-8160
4767 Chippenham Dr Roanoke (24018) *(G-12012)*
Troesen Enterprises LLC.....571 405-3199
4233 Raleigh Ave Apt 104 Alexandria (22304) *(G-369)*
Trojan Defense LLC.....703 981-8710
2417 Mill Heights Dr Herndon (20171) *(G-6832)*
Tromp Group Americas LLC.....800 225-3771
2115 W Laburnum Ave Richmond (23227) *(G-11421)*
Troopmaster Software Inc.....434 589-6788
5 Fleetwood Dr Palmyra (22963) *(G-10258)*
Trophy World, Winchester *Also called Layman Enterprises Inc* *(G-15439)*
Tropq Creamery LLC.....540 680-0916
721 E Main St Purcellville (20132) *(G-10682)*
Trotter Jamil.....757 251-8754
1025 W Pembroke Ave Hampton (23669) *(G-6253)*
Trout River Lumber LLC.....434 645-2600
2600 Hudson Way Crewe (23930) *(G-3818)*
Troy Patrick.....703 507-4914
107 W St 545 Alexandria (22314) *(G-370)*
Troyer, Robert, Aroda *Also called Countryside Bakery* *(G-1224)*
Tru Point Design.....804 477-0976
3302 Williamsburg Rd Richmond (23231) *(G-11422)*
Tru Sports LLC.....571 266-5059
9133 Mulder Ct Manassas (20111) *(G-8171)*
Tru-Ade Company.....540 662-5484
800 Welltown Rd Clear Brook (22624) *(G-3653)*
Truckclaws, Manassas *Also called S&C Global Products LLC* *(G-7998)*
Trucut Fabricators, Forest *Also called Sterling Blower Company* *(G-5096)*
True American Woodworkers.....540 748-5805
1508 Bumpass Rd Bumpass (23024) *(G-2169)*
True Colors Screen Prtg LLC.....757 718-9051
637 10th St Virginia Beach (23451) *(G-14895)*
True Energy Fuels.....276 796-4003
7652 S Fork Rd Pound (24279) *(G-10514)*
True Precision Machining Inc.....703 314-7071
11921 Airlea Dr Nokesville (20181) *(G-9401)*
True Religion Apparel Inc.....323 266-3072
1100 S Hayes St Arlington (22202) *(G-1198)*
True Southern Smoke Bbq LLC.....757 816-0228
205 Gregg St Chesapeake (23320) *(G-3352)*
True Steel LLC.....540 680-2906
2271 Ambrose Commons Dr Charlottesville (22903) *(G-2896)*
Truefit Dme LLC.....434 980-8100
200 Garrett St Ste P Charlottesville (22902) *(G-2897)*
Trueway Inc.....703 527-9248
3033 Wilson Blvd Ste 700 Arlington (22201) *(G-1199)*
Truitts Welding Service.....757 787-7290
22 Liberty St Onancock (23417) *(G-10198)*
Truly Crafted Woodworking LLC.....571 268-0834
5595 Websters Way Manassas (20112) *(G-8172)*
Trump Winery, Charlottesville *Also called Eric Trump Wine Mfg LLC* *(G-2791)*
Truss Construction.....540 710-0673
10411 Courthouse Rd Spotsylvania (22553) *(G-12919)*
Truss Incorporated.....804 556-3611
453 Millers Ln Susan (23163) *(G-13802)*
Truss It Inc.....540 248-2177
391 Mount Pisgah Rd Mount Sidney (24467) *(G-9085)*
Truss Systems Inc.....804 462-5963
2831 Murry Hill Rd Lancaster (22503) *(G-7163)*
Truss-Tech Inc.....757 787-3014
18541 Parkway Melfa (23410) *(G-8712)*
Trussway Manufacturing Inc.....540 898-3477
11540 Shannon Dr Fredericksburg (22408) *(G-5382)*
Trustcomm Solutions LLC.....281 272-7500
800 Corporate Dr Ste 421 Stafford (22554) *(G-13205)*
Trustedcom LLC.....440 725-1115
12930 Worldgate Dr # 300 Herndon (20170) *(G-6833)*
Truswood Inc.....434 447-6565
813 Hillcrest Rd South Hill (23970) *(G-12862)*
Truswood Inc.....757 833-5300
501 Truswood Ln Newport News (23608) *(G-9365)*
TRW, Atkins *Also called ZF Active Safety & Elec US LLC* *(G-1524)*
TS By Extreme LLC.....804 335-0260
7331 Summertree Dr North Chesterfield (23234) *(G-10005)*
TSC Corporation.....540 633-5000
609 W Rock Rd Radford (24141) *(G-10746)*
Tsg Concepts Inc.....877 777-5734
1200 N Veitch St Apt 825 Arlington (22201) *(G-1200)*
Tshirt Zone.....540 431-5068
1850 Apple Blossom Dr Winchester (22601) *(G-15597)*
Tshirtpod.....423 341-8655
15427 Monticello Dr Bristol (24202) *(G-2037)*
Tshirtsru.....301 744-7872
15283 Valley Stream Dr Woodbridge (22191) *(G-15824)*
Tsi Yarns, Martinsville *Also called Texturing Services LLC* *(G-8342)*
TSO Global Distributors, Alexandria *Also called Shakir Waliyyud-Deen* *(G-583)*
TST Fabrications LLC (HQ).....**757 627-9101**
1075 W 35th St Norfolk (23508) *(G-9769)*
TST Fabrications LLC.....757 627-9101
1075 W 35th St Norfolk (23508) *(G-9770)*
TST Roofing, Virginia Beach *Also called TST Tactical Def Solutions Inc* *(G-14896)*
TST Tactical Def Solutions Inc.....757 452-6955
2516 Squadron Ct Virginia Beach (23453) *(G-14896)*
Tsunami Custom Creations LLC.....757 913-0960
1432 Watercrest Pl Virginia Beach (23464) *(G-14897)*
TT & J Hauling.....804 647-0375
560 Creekmore Rd Richmond (23238) *(G-11423)*
Ttec LLC.....540 336-2693
2342 Wickliffe Rd Berryville (22611) *(G-1697)*
Ttec Thermoelectric Tech, Berryville *Also called Ttec LLC* *(G-1697)*
Ttg LLC.....540 280-7389
704 Middlebrook Ave Staunton (24401) *(G-13303)*
Ttg Group LLC.....540 454-7235
2111 Richmond Hwy Arlington (22202) *(G-1201)*
Ttm Technologies Inc.....703 652-2200
1200 Severn Way Sterling (20166) *(G-13540)*
Tube Council, The, Danville *Also called Arista Tubes Inc* *(G-3956)*
Tubular Fabricators Indust Inc.....804 733-4000
600 W Wythe St Petersburg (23803) *(G-10347)*
Tucker Timber Products Inc.....434 736-9661
200 Spaulding Ave Keysville (23947) *(G-7064)*
Tulsa World, Falls Church *Also called Bh Media Group Inc* *(G-4764)*
Tumalow Inc.....847 644-9009
200 Anderson Mill Dr Bumpass (23024) *(G-2170)*
Tumbleweed LLC.....540 261-7404
80 Forge Rd Lexington (24450) *(G-7420)*
Tummy-Ymyum Grmet Candy Apples.....703 368-4756
12184 Drum Salute Pl Bristow (20136) *(G-2065)*
Tumolo Custom Mill Work.....434 985-1755
646 Dogwood Dr Stanardsville (22973) *(G-13229)*
Tumorpix LLC.....804 754-3961
9909 Carrington Pl Henrico (23238) *(G-6587)*
Tunnel of Love.....757 961-5783
477 S Lynnhaven Rd Virginia Beach (23452) *(G-14898)*
Turbo Lab.....276 952-5997
31 Helms Ridge Ln Stuart (24171) *(G-13637)*
Turbo Sales & Fabrication Inc.....276 930-2422
296 Commerce Center Dr Floyd (24091) *(G-5042)*
Turbo Specialties & Machine, Chesapeake *Also called Birge Croft* *(G-3002)*
Turbo Tellers.....812 250-1837
428 Snapps Mill Rd Spout Spring (24593) *(G-12928)*
Turk Mountain Vineyards.....540 456-8252
8982 Dick Woods Rd Afton (22920) *(G-93)*
Turlington Sons Sptic Tank Svc.....804 642-9538
7007 Ernest Ln Ordinary (23131) *(G-10237)*
Turman Group, The, Hillsville *Also called Turman-Mercer Sawmills LLC* *(G-6902)*
Turman Lumber Company Inc.....540 639-1250
3504 Mud Pike Christiansburg (24073) *(G-3614)*
Turman Lumber Company Inc (PA).....**540 745-2041**
214 N Locust St Floyd (24091) *(G-5043)*
Turman Sawmill Inc (PA).....**276 728-3752**
555 Expansion Dr Hillsville (24343) *(G-6901)*
Turman-Mercer Sawmills LLC (PA).....**276 728-7974**
555 Expansion Dr Hillsville (24343) *(G-6902)*
Turner Bragg.....804 752-2244
504 England St Ashland (23005) *(G-1504)*
Turner Public Affairs Inc.....703 489-7104
8298 Roxborough Loop Gainesville (20155) *(G-5619)*
Turner Sculpture Ltd.....757 787-2818
27316 Lankford Hwy Melfa (23410) *(G-8713)*
Turners Ready Mix Inc.....540 483-9150
150 Cliff St Rocky Mount (24151) *(G-12355)*
Turners Welding.....540 373-1107
4326 Turkey Acres Rd King George (22485) *(G-7116)*
Turning 65 Inc.....540 289-5768
1942 Cemetery Rd McGaheysville (22840) *(G-8585)*
Turning Point Software Inc.....703 448-6672
1910 Hyannis Ct Apt 201 Mc Lean (22102) *(G-8569)*
Turtle House Press LLC.....540 268-5487
9662 Old Roanoke Rd Elliston (24087) *(G-4350)*
Tut & Titi LLC.....757 761-1921
215b Settlers Landing Rd Hampton (23669) *(G-6254)*
Tutti Fruitti.....703 830-0036
5947 Centreville Crest Ln Centreville (20121) *(G-2345)*
Tutti Frutti Frozen.....703 440-0010
9538 Old Keene Mill Rd Burke (22015) *(G-2205)*
Tvworldwidecom Inc.....703 961-9250
14428 Albemarle Point Pl # 1 Chantilly (20151) *(G-2509)*
Tweedies Repair Service.....540 576-2617
14775 Snow Creek Rd Penhook (24137) *(G-10286)*
Tweedle Tees.....540 569-6927
1782 Shutterlee Mill Rd Staunton (24401) *(G-13304)*
Tweedle Tees Printing LLC.....540 569-6927
1782 Shutterlee Mill Rd Staunton (24401) *(G-13305)*
Twelve Inc.....804 232-1300
5420 Distributor Dr Richmond (23225) *(G-11796)*
Twelve Inc (PA).....**804 232-1300**
5331 Distributor Dr Richmond (23225) *(G-11797)*

ALPHABETIC

Twfutures Inc 804 301-6629
  14311 W Salisbury Rd Midlothian (23113) *(G-8915)*

Twin City Motor Exchange Inc 276 326-3606
  1225 Hockman Pike Bluefield (24605) *(G-1884)*

Twin City Welding Company 276 669-9322
  312 Bob Morrison Blvd Bristol (24201) *(G-1992)*

Twin Creeks Distillery Inc 540 483-1266
  510 Franklin St Rocky Mount (24151) *(G-12356)*

Twin CS LLC 540 664-6072
  438 Mountain Falls Blvd Winchester (22602) *(G-15497)*

Twin Disc Incorporated 757 487-3670
  3700 Profit Way Chesapeake (23323) *(G-3353)*

Twin Oaks Tavern Winery 540 554-4547
  18035 Raven Rocks Rd Bluemont (20135) *(G-1892)*

Twisted Erotica Publishing LLC 757 344-7364
  1075 Willow Green Dr Newport News (23602) *(G-9366)*

Twisted Threads and More, Culpeper *Also called Georgette T Hawkins (G-3893)*

Two Blue Candle Co LLC 786 301-3371
  12555 Rock Ridge Rd Herndon (20170) *(G-6834)*

Two N One Fabrication LLC 757 642-2613
  2627 Cecilia Ter Chesapeake (23323) *(G-3354)*

Two Oaks 434 352-8181
  2206 S Fork Rd Appomattox (24522) *(G-825)*

Two Peppers Transportation LLC 757 761-6674
  1510 Showalter Rd Yorktown (23692) *(G-15997)*

Two Rivers Installation Co 804 366-6869
  3414 Monu Ave Unit 103 Richmond (23221) *(G-11798)*

Two Swords Strategies LLC 804 337-3103
  6219 Jeffrey Rd Richmond (23226) *(G-11424)*

Two Twisted Posts Winery LLC 540 668-6587
  12970 Harpers Ferry Rd Hillsboro (20132) *(G-6880)*

Twomorrows Yesterdays LLC 571 292-2930
  10105 Oxford Ct Nokesville (20181) *(G-9402)*

Twp Transport LLC 540 383-7995
  1901 Cherry Ave Apt B Grottoes (24441) *(G-6025)*

Tycosys LLC 571 278-5300
  9720 Capital Ct Ste 100 Manassas (20110) *(G-8006)*

TYe Custom Metal Fabricators 804 863-2551
  22508 Cox Rd North Dinwiddie (23803) *(G-10067)*

Tyler JSun Global LLC 407 221-6135
  37 Daffodil Ln Stafford (22554) *(G-13206)*

Tympic Software Inc 703 858-0996
  43761 Parkhurst Plz # 108 Ashburn (20147) *(G-1343)*

Tynes Fiberglass Company Inc 757 423-0222
  1202 N Shore Rd Norfolk (23505) *(G-9771)*

Type & Art 804 794-3375
  1905 Huguenot Rd Ste 104 North Chesterfield (23235) *(G-10006)*

Type Etc 540 347-2182
  6419 Tazewell St Warrenton (20187) *(G-15057)*

Type Factory Inc 757 826-6055
  615 Regional Dr Ste B Hampton (23661) *(G-6255)*

Type Signs LLC 202 355-4403
  4603 Dale Blvd Woodbridge (22193) *(G-15825)*

Typical Tees LLC 757 641-6514
  172 Alan Dr Newport News (23602) *(G-9367)*

Tyson Foods Inc 757 824-3471
  11224 Lankford Hwy Temperanceville (23442) *(G-13840)*

Tyson Foods Inc 804 798-8357
  13264 Mountain Rd Glen Allen (23059) *(G-5819)*

Tyson Foods Inc 434 645-7791
  Highway 360 Crewe (23930) *(G-3819)*

Tyson Foods Inc 804 561-2187
  23065 St James Rd Jetersville (23083) *(G-7016)*

Tyson Foods Inc 540 740-3118
  361 Smith Creek Rd New Market (22844) *(G-9150)*

Tyson Foods Inc 434 645-7791
  1938 Patrick Henry Hwy Jetersville (23083) *(G-7017)*

Tysons Automotive Machine 703 471-1802
  22863 Bryant Ct Ste 103 Sterling (20166) *(G-13541)*

Tysons Corner Center, Tysons Corner *Also called Dyson Direct Inc (G-13954)*

Tyton Bioenergy Systems, Danville *Also called Tyton Biosciences LLC (G-4043)*

Tyton Biosciences LLC 434 793-9100
  300 Ringgold Indus Pkwy Danville (24540) *(G-4043)*

Tz Industries LLC 540 903-7210
  11034 Bloomsbury Rd King George (22485) *(G-7117)*

U Play Usa LLC 757 301-8690
  1440 London Bridge Rd Virginia Beach (23453) *(G-14899)*

U S Flag & Signal Company 757 497-8947
  802 Fifth St Portsmouth (23704) *(G-10494)*

U S General Fuel Cell Corp 703 451-8064
  7614 Mendota Pl Springfield (22150) *(G-13103)*

U S Graphics Inc 757 855-2600
  1125 Azalea Garden Rd Norfolk (23502) *(G-9772)*

U S Mining Inc 804 769-7222
  10909 Astarita Ave Partlow (22534) *(G-10268)*

U S Pipe Fabrication 540 439-7373
  11622 Lucky Hill Rd Remington (22734) *(G-10775)*

U S Sidecars Inc 434 263-6500
  100 Motorcycle Run Arrington (22922) *(G-1231)*

U S Silica Company 804 883-6700
  17359 Taylors Creek Rd Montpelier (23192) *(G-9022)*

U S Smokeless Tob Brands Inc 804 274-2000
  6603 W Broad St Richmond (23230) *(G-11425)*

U See App, Springfield *Also called Brbg LLC (G-12969)*

U3 Solutions Inc 703 777-5020
  604 S King St Ste 100 Leesburg (20175) *(G-7366)*

Uaps, Hampton *Also called Unmanned Aerial Prop Systms (G-6257)*

UAS Technologies Inc 703 822-4382
  1750 Tysons Blvd Ste 1500 Mc Lean (22102) *(G-8570)*

Uav Communications Inc (HQ) 757 271-3428
  1 Bayport Way Ste 250 Newport News (23606) *(G-9368)*

Uavarus LLC 757 876-5507
  4819 Williamsburg Glade Williamsburg (23185) *(G-15327)*

Ub-04 Software Inc 804 754-2708
  404 Walsing Dr Richmond (23229) *(G-11426)*

Ubibird Incorporated 718 490-3746
  3227 Aquia Dr Stafford (22554) *(G-13207)*

Ubicabus LLC 804 512-5324
  134 Washington Cir Colonial Beach (22443) *(G-3727)*

Ubiquitywave LLC 571 262-1406
  44761 Malden Pl Ashburn (20147) *(G-1344)*

Ucc, Portsmouth *Also called General Dynamics (G-10434)*

Ufp Mid-Atlantic LLC 757 485-3190
  3812 Cook Blvd Chesapeake (23323) *(G-3355)*

Ufp Mid-Atlantic LLC 540 921-1286
  152 Industrial Park Dr Pearisburg (24134) *(G-10278)*

Uh Roh Muh Inc 703 725-1684
  5369 Wharton Park Ct Centreville (20120) *(G-2346)*

Uhr Corporation 703 534-1250
  6705 Valley Brook Dr Falls Church (22042) *(G-4885)*

Ullman Sails Virginia, Deltaville *Also called Latell Sailmakers LLC (G-4082)*

Ultimate Wheel Svcs LLC 703 237-1044
  2106 Grayson Pl Falls Church (22043) *(G-4886)*

Ultimate Woodworks 804 938-8987
  1313 Grumman Dr Richmond (23229) *(G-11427)*

Ultra Electronics 3phoenix Inc 703 956-6480
  14585 Avion Pkwy Ste 200 Chantilly (20151) *(G-2510)*

Ultra Petroleum LLC 276 964-6118
  1400 5th St Richlands (24641) *(G-11021)*

Ultracomm Llc 703 622-6397
  413 Gatepost Ct Purcellville (20132) *(G-10683)*

Ultralife Corporation 757 419-2430
  1457 Mller Str Rd Ste 106 Virginia Beach (23455) *(G-14900)*

Ultrata LLC 571 226-0347
  1934 Old Gallows Rd # 35 Vienna (22182) *(G-14147)*

Uma Inc 540 879-2040
  260 Main St Dayton (22821) *(G-4067)*

Unarco Industries LLC 434 792-9531
  255 Stinson Dr Danville (24540) *(G-4044)*

Unboxed 336 253-4085
  13916 Leeton Cir Chantilly (20151) *(G-2511)*

Uncle Harrys Inc 757 426-7056
  468 Viking Dr Ste 100 Virginia Beach (23452) *(G-14901)*

Under Pressure Services Inc 757 254-5996
  4878 Princess Anne Rd Virginia Beach (23462) *(G-14902)*

Under Radar LLC 540 348-8996
  409 Honeysuckle Hl Lexington (24450) *(G-7421)*

Underbite Publishing LLC 703 638-8040
  3802 Keller Ave Alexandria (22302) *(G-371)*

Undersea Solutions Corporation, Newport News *Also called Hii Unmnned Mrtime Systems Inc (G-9247)*

Understanding Latin LLC 703 437-9354
  209 E Staunton Ave Sterling (20164) *(G-13542)*

Underwood Logging LLC 540 489-1388
  485 Promise Ln Rocky Mount (24151) *(G-12357)*

Unicom Technology Park Inc 703 502-2850
  15000 Conference Ctr Dr Chantilly (20151) *(G-2512)*

Unicor, North Prince George *Also called Federal Prison Industries (G-10087)*

Unicorn Editions Ltd 540 364-0156
  8076 Enon Church Rd The Plains (20198) *(G-13844)*

Unifiedonline Inc (HQ) 816 679-1893
  4126 Leonard Dr Fairfax (22030) *(G-4690)*

Unifiedonline LLC (PA) 816 679-1893
  4126 Leonard Dr Fairfax (22030) *(G-4691)*

Uniformed Services Almanac 703 241-8100
  9342 Tovito Dr Fairfax (22031) *(G-4574)*

Unifyia Inc 703 344-6758
  11710 Plaza America Dr # 200 Reston (20190) *(G-10977)*

Union Church Millworks Inc 540 862-0767
  6800 Rich Patch Rd Covington (24426) *(G-3801)*

Unique Cabinets Inc 434 823-2188
  3705 Browns Gap Tpke Crozet (22932) *(G-3853)*

Unique Engineering Concepts 540 586-6761
  5700 Forest Rd Bedford (24523) *(G-1662)*

Unique Flexique LLC 540 439-4465
  11335 Whipkey Dr Bealeton (22712) *(G-1607)*

Unique Industries Inc 434 835-0068
  225 Toy Ln Blairs (24527) *(G-1833)*

Unique Properties, Damascus *Also called Special T Manufacturing Corp* ***(G-3950)***
Unique Wreaths 540 322-9301
8610 Oldham Rd Fredericksburg (22408) ***(G-5383)***
Uniquecoat Technologies LLC 804 784-0997
2071 Valpark Dr Oilville (23129) ***(G-10186)***
Uniques LLC 804 307-0902
3601 Muirfield Green Pl Midlothian (23112) ***(G-8916)***
Unison Arms LLC 571 342-1108
20954 Furr Rd Round Hill (20141) ***(G-12392)***
Unison Tube LLC 828 633-3190
500 Cane Creek Pkwy Rd Ringgold (24586) ***(G-11875)***
Unison Vrtual Acqstion Off LLC 571 449-4188
21251 Ridgetop Cir # 100 Dulles (20166) ***(G-4230)***
Unisoncare Corporation 804 721-3702
1524 Anchor Landing Dr Chester (23836) ***(G-3463)***
United Armament LLC 804 839-1800
425 Southlake Blvd Ste 1b North Chesterfield (23236) ***(G-10007)***
United Cntry Cllins Assoc Real 407 233-4377
155 W Main St Independence (24348) ***(G-6997)***
United Co 276 466-0769
1005 Glenway Ave Bristol (24201) ***(G-1993)***
United Company (PA) **276 466-3322**
1005 Glenway Ave Bristol (24201) ***(G-1994)***
United Dairy Inc 540 366-2964
1814 Hollins Rd Ne Ste C Roanoke (24012) ***(G-12212)***
United Defense 540 663-9291
4485 Danube Dr Ste 1 King George (22485) ***(G-7118)***
United Defense Systems Inc 401 304-9100
11850 Freedom Dr Apt 2001 Reston (20190) ***(G-10978)***
United Elastic-A Narroflex Co, Stuart *Also called Narroflex Inc* ***(G-13626)***
United Federal Systems Inc 703 881-7777
10432 Balls Ford Rd # 30 Manassas (20109) ***(G-8173)***
United Graphics Inc 540 338-7525
35135 Cherry Grove Ln Round Hill (20141) ***(G-12393)***
United Illumination, Fredericksburg *Also called Frank Hagerty* ***(G-5432)***
United Ink Press 703 966-6343
19235 Gooseview Ct Leesburg (20176) ***(G-7367)***
United Litho Inc 703 858-4213
21800 Beaumeade Cir Ashburn (20147) ***(G-1345)***
United Methodist Church, Goode *Also called Richard A Daily Dr* ***(G-5893)***
United Precast Finisher LLC 804 386-6308
12426 Hogans Pl Chester (23836) ***(G-3464)***
United Providers of Care LLC 757 775-5075
9311 Croaker Rd Williamsburg (23188) ***(G-15328)***
United Salt Baytown LLC 276 496-3363
864 Ader Ln Saltville (24370) ***(G-12595)***
United Salt Saltville LLC 276 496-3363
864 Ader Ln Saltville (24370) ***(G-12596)***
United Screen Design 276 669-4669
1305 W State St Bristol (24201) ***(G-1995)***
United States Dept of Army 703 614-3727
9301 Chapek Rd Bldg 1458 Fort Belvoir (22060) ***(G-5119)***
United States Dept of Army 757 878-4831
27502 Mcmahon St Fort Eustis (23604) ***(G-5127)***
United States Dept of Navy 757 380-4223
4101 Washington Ave Newport News (23607) ***(G-9369)***
United States Dept of Navy 757 396-8615
Norfolk Naval Shipyard Portsmouth (23709) ***(G-10495)***
United States Gypsum Company 757 494-8100
1424 S Main St Norfolk (23523) ***(G-9773)***
United States Gypsum Company 276 496-7733
6072 S Main St Saltville (24370) ***(G-12597)***
United States Pipe Fndry LLC 540 439-7373
11622 Lucky Hill Rd Remington (22734) ***(G-10776)***
United States Precious Met Co, Montvale *Also called South Western Services Inc* ***(G-9030)***
United Stones Inc 703 467-0434
14 Bryant Ct Ste B Sterling (20166) ***(G-13543)***
United Technologies I LLC 804 553-3116
7804 Balineen Ct Henrico (23228) ***(G-6588)***
United Trailers Intl, Atkins *Also called Utility Trailer Mfg Co* ***(G-1522)***
United Welding Inc 540 628-2286
34 Perchwood Dr Fredericksburg (22405) ***(G-5496)***
Unitedslickmart LLC 800 714-0532
12020 Sunrise Valley Dr # 1 Reston (20191) ***(G-10979)***
Universal Air & Gas Products, Norfolk *Also called Universal Air Products Corp* ***(G-9774)***
Universal Air Products Corp (PA) **757 461-0077**
1140 Kingwood Ave Norfolk (23502) ***(G-9774)***
Universal Composition Svcs LLC 202 255-7995
14347 Newvalle Church Rd Leesburg (20175) ***(G-7368)***
Universal Dynamics Inc 703 490-7000
11700 Shannon Dr Fredericksburg (22408) ***(G-5384)***
Universal Fiber Systems LLC (PA) **276 669-1161**
14401 Industrial Park Rd Bristol (24202) ***(G-2038)***
Universal Fibers Inc (HQ) **276 669-1161**
14401 Industrial Park Rd Bristol (24202) ***(G-2039)***
Universal Forest Products, Chesapeake *Also called Ufp Mid-Atlantic LLC* ***(G-3355)***
Universal Forest Products, Pearisburg *Also called Ufp Mid-Atlantic LLC* ***(G-10278)***
Universal Impact Inc 540 885-8676
901 S Delphine Ave Waynesboro (22980) ***(G-15141)***
Universal Impex LLC 202 322-4100
5615 Benoni Ct Glen Allen (23059) ***(G-5820)***
Universal Leaf Tobacco Co Inc (HQ) **804 359-9311**
9201 Frest Hl Ave Stony P Richmond (23235) ***(G-11066)***
Universal Marine Lift Inc 804 829-5838
6160 North Bluffs Ct Charles City (23030) ***(G-2580)***
Universal Powers Inc 404 997-8732
1009 Holly Spring Ave Richmond (23224) ***(G-11799)***
Universal Printing 276 466-9311
1101 W State St Bristol (24201) ***(G-1996)***
Universal Space Network Inc 703 488-4150
14399 Penrose Pl Ste 210 Chantilly (20151) ***(G-2513)***
Universal Store Corp 703 467-0434
14 Bryant Ct Ste C Sterling (20166) ***(G-13544)***
University of Richmond 804 289-8000
421 Westhampton Way Richmond (23173) ***(G-11800)***
University Press Warehouse, Charlottesville *Also called Rector Visitors of The Univ VA* ***(G-2857)***
University Pride & Prestige 757 766-2590
126 Diggs Dr Hampton (23666) ***(G-6256)***
Universty VA Automobile Sfty, Charlottesville *Also called Rector Visitors of The Univ VA* ***(G-2682)***
Unknown, Coeburn *Also called Clayton Homes Inc* ***(G-3696)***
Unknown, Glen Allen *Also called Colfax Corporation* ***(G-5715)***
Unknown, Christiansburg *Also called Draeger Safety Diagnostics Inc* ***(G-3585)***
Unlimited Embroidery 540 745-3909
181 Sams Rd Se Floyd (24091) ***(G-5044)***
Unlimited Welding LLC 540 683-4776
1736 Reliance Rd Middletown (22645) ***(G-8745)***
Unmanned Aerial Prop Systms 757 325-6792
100 Exploration Way Hampton (23666) ***(G-6257)***
Unseen Technologies Inc 704 207-7391
22664 Timberlake Rd Lynchburg (24502) ***(G-7829)***
Unshrinkit Inc 804 519-7019
1405 S Fern St Ste 517 Arlington (22202) ***(G-1202)***
Up, Richmond *Also called Universal Powers Inc* ***(G-11799)***
Up and Go Transportation LLC 443 859-0193
4870 Sadler Rd Ste 300 Glen Allen (23060) ***(G-5821)***
Up and Running Computers Inc 757 565-3282
5904 Montpelier Dr Williamsburg (23188) ***(G-15329)***
Up-N-Coming Magazine 757 343-8829
860 Meads Rd Norfolk (23505) ***(G-9775)***
Upaco Adhesive Division, Richmond *Also called Worthen Industries Inc* ***(G-11068)***
Upaco Adhesives, Richmond *Also called Worthen Industries Inc* ***(G-11067)***
Upkeepr Corp 703 718-6304
2776 S Arlington Mill Dr U Arlington (22206) ***(G-1203)***
Uplift Collections 804 319-9129
9409 Snowbird Rd Chesterfield (23832) ***(G-3536)***
Uplift Collections LLC 804 319-9129
9409 Snowbird Rd Chesterfield (23832) ***(G-3537)***
Upm Kymmene Inc 540 465-2700
278 Valley View Dr Strasburg (22657) ***(G-13601)***
Upon A Once Stitch LLC 757 562-1900
35041 Lees Mill Rd Franklin (23851) ***(G-5160)***
Upper Decks LLC 804 789-0946
6997 Brooking Way Mechanicsville (23111) ***(G-8691)***
Upper Shirley Vineyards 804 829-9463
600 Shirley Plantation Rd Charles City (23030) ***(G-2581)***
Upper Weyanoke LLC 804 288-7333
14 Tapoan Rd Richmond (23226) ***(G-11428)***
Upscale Time LLC 434 832-0101
20911 Timberlake Rd Ste F Lynchburg (24502) ***(G-7830)***
Uptime Business Products LLC 540 982-5750
3015 Peters Creek Rd Nw B Roanoke (24019) ***(G-12013)***
Uptons Custom Woodworking LLC 540 454-3752
14 Chestnut Ln Stafford (22556) ***(G-13208)***
Uptown Eon V, Richmond *Also called Uptown Neon* ***(G-11801)***
Uptown Neon 804 358-6243
2629 W Cary St Richmond (23220) ***(G-11801)***
Urban Views Weekly LLC 804 441-6255
6802 Paragon Pl Ste 410 Richmond (23230) ***(G-11429)***
Urban Works Publicity 703 625-6981
3056 S Glebe Rd Arlington (22206) ***(G-1204)***
Urenco USA Inc (HQ) **575 394-4646**
1560 Wilson Blvd Ste 300 Arlington (22209) ***(G-1205)***
Uriel Wind Inc (HQ) **804 672-4471**
7400 Beaufont Springs Dr # 300 North Chesterfield (23225) ***(G-10042)***
Urologics LLC 757 419-1463
5609 Promontory Pointe Rd Midlothian (23112) ***(G-8917)***
US 1 Cable LLC 571 224-3955
7371 Atlas Walk Way 260 Gainesville (20155) ***(G-5620)***
US 21 Inc 703 560-0021
2721 Prosperity Ave # 300 Fairfax (22031) ***(G-4575)***
US Amines (portsmouth) LLC 757 638-2614
3230 W Norfolk Rd Portsmouth (23703) ***(G-10496)***
US Anodizing Inc 540 937-2801
15403 Covey Cir Amissville (20106) ***(G-722)***
US Building Systems Inc 800 991-9251
3169 Shipps Corner Rd # 101 Virginia Beach (23453) ***(G-14903)***

ALPHABETIC

US Cabinet & Intr Design LLC 202 740-0038
3210 Dashiell Rd Falls Church (22042) *(G-4887)*
US Concrete Inc 703 471-6969
4215 Lafayette Center Dr Chantilly (20151) *(G-2514)*
US Dept of the Air Force 757 764-5616
34 Elm St Hampton (23665) *(G-6279)*
US Dept of the Air Force 703 808-0492
14675 Lee Rd Chantilly (20151) *(G-2515)*
US Electrical Testing LLC 703 802-6231
1200 Ste 1765 Grnsboro St Tysons (22102) *(G-13949)*
US Float Tanks, Norfolk *Also called Ramsey Manufacturing LLC (G-9701)*
US Gov Vendor Drs Technologies, Dulles *Also called Drs Global Entp Solutions Inc (G-4198)*
US Greenfiber LLC 540 825-8000
19028 Bleumont Ct Culpeper (22701) *(G-3927)*
US Joiner Holding Company (PA) **434 220-8500**
5690 Three Notch D Rd # 200 Crozet (22932) *(G-3854)*
US Parcel & Copy Center Inc 703 365-7999
10450 Dumfries Rd Manassas (20110) *(G-8007)*
US Semiconductor Unit, Chantilly *Also called Leica Microsystems Inc (G-2457)*
US Smokeless Tobacco Company (HQ) **804 274-2000**
6603 W Broad St Richmond (23230) *(G-11430)*
US Software & Consulting Inc 571 281-4496
21165 Whitfield Pl # 106 Sterling (20165) *(G-13545)*
US Tactical Inc 703 217-8781
2735 Valestra Cir Oakton (22124) *(G-10163)*
US Wrap LLC 202 441-6072
6007 Saint Hubert Ln Centreville (20121) *(G-2347)*
Us21, Fairfax *Also called US 21 Inc (G-4575)*
USA Cabinets Store 703 204-3444
2832 Dorr Ave Fairfax (22031) *(G-4576)*
USA Security Solution Corp 804 435-9999
180 Technology Park Dr C Kilmarnock (22482) *(G-7077)*
USA Stone Experts, Newport News *Also called Granite Countertop Experts LLC (G-9238)*
USA Today, Mc Lean *Also called Gannett Stllite Info Ntwrk LLC (G-8444)*
USA Today 703 267-6964
9208 Hamilton Dr Fairfax (22031) *(G-4577)*
USA Today 703 750-8702
6883 Commercial Dr Springfield (22151) *(G-13104)*
USA Today International Corp (HQ) **703 854-3400**
7950 Jones Branch Dr Mc Lean (22102) *(G-8571)*
USA Today Spt Media Group LLC (HQ) **703 854-6000**
7950 Jones Branch Dr Mc Lean (22102) *(G-8572)*
USA Weekend Inc 703 854-6000
7950 Jones Branch Dr Mc Lean (22102) *(G-8573)*
Usgri/Bitcoin Press Release 202 316-3222
1111 Army Navy Dr # 1130 Arlington (22202) *(G-1206)*
Usher Incorporated 703 848-8600
1850 Towers Crescent Plz Tysons Corner (22182) *(G-13956)*
Uso Path Finder 757 395-4270
1510 Gilbert St Norfolk (23511) *(G-9776)*
Usptgear, Vienna *Also called Webgear Inc (G-14158)*
Usr Steel LLC 571 480-3497
14771 Basingstoke Loop Centreville (20120) *(G-2348)*
Usui International Corporation 757 558-7300
3824 Cook Blvd Chesapeake (23323) *(G-3356)*
Utah State Univ Space Dynmics 435 713-3060
50 Tech Pkwy Ste 303 Stafford (22556) *(G-13209)*
Utiliscope Corp 804 550-5233
10367 Cedar Ln Glen Allen (23059) *(G-5822)*
Utilities Products Intl 703 725-3150
7202 Arlington Blvd # 20 Falls Church (22042) *(G-4888)*
Utility One Source For Eqp LLC (HQ) **434 525-2929**
12660 E Lynchburg Forest (24551) *(G-5103)*
Utility Trailer Mfg Co 276 783-8800
124 Mountain Empire Rd Atkins (24311) *(G-1522)*
Utron Kinetics LLC 703 369-5552
9441 Innovation Dr Manassas (20110) *(G-8008)*
Utrue Inc 703 577-0309
100 Shepherdson Ln Ne Vienna (22180) *(G-14148)*
Uts Fendrag Publishing Co 804 266-9108
4606 Brook Rd Richmond (23227) *(G-11431)*
Utz Quality Foods LLC 540 535-1927
370 Tyson Dr Winchester (22603) *(G-15498)*
Utz Quality Foods LLC 757 249-0568
330 Ed Wright Ln Newport News (23606) *(G-9370)*
Utz Quality Foods LLC 804 232-0241
5619 Pride Rd Richmond (23224) *(G-11802)*
Utz Quality Foods LLC 540 981-0351
936 3rd St Vinton (24179) *(G-14188)*
Uvsity Corporation 571 308-3241
23684 Richland Grove Dr Brambleton (20148) *(G-1935)*
Uwin Software LLC 703 876-0490
8512 Idylwood Rd Vienna (22182) *(G-14149)*
Uzio Inc 800 984-7952
12355 Sunrise Valley Dr # 300 Reston (20191) *(G-10980)*
V & P Investment LLC (PA) **703 365-7835**
9067 Jerrys Cir Manassas (20110) *(G-8009)*
V & P Investment LLC 202 631-8596
3552 Seminole Trl Charlottesville (22911) *(G-2709)*

V & S Xpress LLC 804 714-4259
204 N Beech Ave Highland Springs (23075) *(G-6858)*
V B Local Form Coupon Book 239 745-9649
916 Earl Of Chatham Ln Virginia Beach (23454) *(G-14904)*
V C Ice and Cold Storage Inc 434 793-1441
333 Montague St Danville (24541) *(G-4045)*
V T R International Inc 434 385-5300
19206 Forest Rd Lynchburg (24502) *(G-7831)*
V&M Industries Inc 757 319-9415
489 Green Wing Dr Suffolk (23434) *(G-13775)*
V-B/Williams Furniture Co Inc 276 236-6161
300 E Grayson St Galax (24333) *(G-5651)*
V-Lite USA LLC 808 264-3785
2504 Squadron Ct Ste 110 Virginia Beach (23453) *(G-14905)*
VA Designs and Cnstr LLC 757 651-8909
6360 Glenoak Dr Norfolk (23513) *(G-9777)*
VA Displays LLC 757 251-8060
103 Willow Wood Ave Smithfield (23430) *(G-12743)*
VA Epoxy Designs LLC 757 947-6249
21 Old Oyster Point Rd Newport News (23602) *(G-9371)*
VA Foods LLC 434 221-1456
6313 Bedford Hwy Lynch Station (24571) *(G-7629)*
VA Hardscapes Inc 540 955-6245
12 Cattlemans Ln Berryville (22611) *(G-1698)*
VA Medical Supply Inc 757 390-9000
5172 W Military Hwy Ste E Chesapeake (23321) *(G-3357)*
VA Properties Inc 804 237-1455
919 E Main St Richmond (23219) *(G-11803)*
VA Woodworks LLC 540 903-6681
105 Jubal St Fredericksburg (22408) *(G-5385)*
VA Writers Club 804 648-0357
1011 E Main St Ste Ll90 Richmond (23219) *(G-11804)*
Vaero Inc 540 344-1000
111 W Virginia Ave Vinton (24179) *(G-14189)*
Valcom Inc (PA) **540 427-3900**
5614 Hollins Rd Roanoke (24019) *(G-12014)*
Valcom Services LLC 540 427-2400
5614 Hollins Rd Roanoke (24019) *(G-12015)*
Valentinecherry Creations 757 848-6137
26 Brough Ln Hampton (23669) *(G-6258)*
Valeo North America Inc 757 827-0310
301 W Park Ln Hampton (23666) *(G-6259)*
Valerie Hill Farm LLC 540 869-9567
1687 Marlboro Rd Stephens City (22655) *(G-13325)*
Valerie Perkins 804 279-0011
14603 Ashlake Manor Dr Chesterfield (23832) *(G-3538)*
Valhalla Holsters LLC 540 529-4520
1093 Cranberry Ct Moneta (24121) *(G-8983)*
Valhalla Vineyards 540 725-9463
6500 Mount Chestnut Rd Roanoke (24018) *(G-12016)*
Valley Banner, The, Elkton *Also called Rockingham Publishing Company (G-4334)*
Valley Bee Supply Inc 540 941-8127
46 Tinkling Spring Rd Fishersville (22939) *(G-5010)*
Valley Biomedical Pdts Svcs In, Winchester *Also called Valley Bomedical Pdts Svcs Inc (G-15499)*
Valley Blox and Bldg Mtls Div, Harrisonburg *Also called Valley Building Supply Inc (G-6383)*
Valley Bomedical Pdts Svcs Inc 540 868-0800
121 Industrial Dr Winchester (22602) *(G-15499)*
Valley Building Supply Inc (HQ) **540 434-6725**
210 Stone Spring Rd Harrisonburg (22801) *(G-6383)*
Valley Coml Indus Svcs LLC 540 908-1156
240 Eastview St Dayton (22821) *(G-4068)*
Valley Construction News (PA) **540 344-4899**
426 Campbell Ave Sw Roanoke (24016) *(G-12213)*
Valley Construction Svcs LLC 540 320-8545
125 N Main St Ste 128 Blacksburg (24060) *(G-1802)*
Valley Doors Unlimited LLC 540 638-0167
5001 Spotswood Trl Penn Laird (22846) *(G-10290)*
Valley Green Naturals LLC 540 937-4795
81 Seven Ponds Rd Amissville (20106) *(G-723)*
Valley Grounds Inc 540 382-6710
750 Den Hill Rd Christiansburg (24073) *(G-3615)*
Valley Heirlooms LLC 540 234-0251
4752 Landis Ln Mount Crawford (22841) *(G-9062)*
Valley Ice LLC 540 477-4447
123 Business Park Ln Mount Jackson (22842) *(G-9082)*
Valley Industrial Plastics Inc 540 723-8855
6953 Middle Rd Middletown (22645) *(G-8746)*
Valley Meat Processors Inc 540 879-9041
101 Meigs Ln Dayton (22821) *(G-4069)*
Valley Orthtic Specialists Inc 540 667-3631
1726 Amherst St Winchester (22601) *(G-15598)*
Valley Outsourcing 540 320-0892
2100 Keisters Branch Rd Blacksburg (24060) *(G-1803)*
Valley Precision Incorporated 540 941-8178
501 Delaware Ave Waynesboro (22980) *(G-15142)*
Valley Proteins Inc (PA) **540 877-2590**
151 Valpro Dr Winchester (22603) *(G-15500)*
Valley Proteins Inc 540 833-6641
6230 Kratzer Rd Linville (22834) *(G-7436)*

2021 Virginia
Industrial Directory

(G-0000) Company's Geographic Section entry number

Valley Proteins Inc...540 833-8322
6331 Val Pro Dr Linville (22834) ***(G-7437)***
Valley Proteins (de) Inc (PA)...**540 877-2533**
151 Valpro Dr Winchester (22603) ***(G-15501)***
Valley Proteins (de) Inc...540 877-2590
107 Kavanaugh Rd Winchester (22603) ***(G-15502)***
Valley Proteins (de) Inc...434 634-9475
25170 Val Pro Dr Emporia (23847) ***(G-4369)***
Valley Publishing Corporation...434 591-1000
Crofton Plz Bldg 106ste Palmyra (22963) ***(G-10259)***
Valley Rebuilders Co Inc...540 342-2108
2019 Shenandoah Ave Nw Roanoke (24017) ***(G-12214)***
Valley Redi-Mix Company Inc (PA)...**540 869-1990**
333 Marlboro Rd Stephens City (22655) ***(G-13326)***
Valley Redi-Mix Company Inc...540 631-9050
8867 Winchester Rd Front Royal (22630) ***(G-5560)***
Valley Redi-Mix Pump Division, Stephens City *Also called Valley Redi-Mix Company Inc* ***(G-13326)***
Valley Restaurant Repair Inc...540 294-1118
46 Tinkling Spring Rd Fishersville (22939) ***(G-5011)***
Valley Scents...540 688-8855
3125 Lee Jackson Hwy Staunton (24401) ***(G-13306)***
Valley Seamless Alum Gutters, Bridgewater *Also called Fred Kinkead* ***(G-1951)***
Valley Structures Inc (PA)...**540 879-9454**
Rr 738 Dayton (22821) ***(G-4070)***
Valley Supply and Services LLC...276 979-4547
174 Stansbury Ln North Tazewell (24630) ***(G-10110)***
Valley Timber Sales Inc...540 832-3646
Rr 15 Gordonsville (22942) ***(G-5917)***
Valley Tool & Design Inc...540 249-5710
2307 Weyers Cave Rd Grottoes (24441) ***(G-6026)***
Valley Trader The Inc...540 869-5132
8503 Valley Pike Middletown (22645) ***(G-8747)***
Valley Utility Buildings Inc...276 679-6736
5661 Powell Valley Rd Big Stone Gap (24219) ***(G-1717)***
Valley Welding...276 733-7942
3202 Foster Falls Rd Barren Springs (24313) ***(G-1576)***
Valley Welding...276 733-7943
2481 Wysor Hwy Draper (24324) ***(G-4137)***
Valley Welding Inc...540 338-5323
37241 E Richardson Ln Purcellville (20132) ***(G-10684)***
Valley Wheel & Machine, Richlands *Also called Valley Wheel Co Inc* ***(G-11022)***
Valley Wheel Co Inc...276 964-5013
101 Bedford Ave Richlands (24641) ***(G-11022)***
Valmont Coatings, Petersburg *Also called Industrial Glvanizers Amer Inc* ***(G-10325)***
Valmont Industries Inc...804 733-0808
3535 Halifax Rd Petersburg (23805) ***(G-10348)***
Valor Partners Inc...540 725-4156
1948 Franklin Rd Sw B201 Roanoke (24014) ***(G-12215)***
Value America...434 951-4100
1540 Insurance Ln Charlottesville (22911) ***(G-2710)***
Valve Automation Center...804 752-2700
310 Hill Carter Pkwy Ashland (23005) ***(G-1505)***
Valve Safe Solutions LLC...540 721-7808
125 Larboard Dr Moneta (24121) ***(G-8984)***
Valvoline Instant Oil...804 823-2104
10850 Iron Bridge Rd Chester (23831) ***(G-3465)***
Vamac Incorporated...540 535-1983
601 Mcghee Rd Winchester (22603) ***(G-15503)***
Vamaz Inc...434 296-8812
1180 Seminole Trl Ste 295 Charlottesville (22901) ***(G-2711)***
Van KY Troung...804 612-6151
4109 Jacque St Richmond (23230) ***(G-11432)***
Van Addo Dorn LLC...703 615-4769
509 S Taylor St Arlington (22204) ***(G-1207)***
Van Der Hyde Dan...434 250-7389
960 Davis Rd Chatham (24531) ***(G-2940)***
Van Dorn Pawn...703 924-9800
6116 Franconia Rd Ste A Alexandria (22310) ***(G-603)***
Van Dorn Yard, Alexandria *Also called Legacy Vulcan LLC* ***(G-257)***
Van Jester Woodworks...804 562-6360
1600 Valley Rd Richmond (23222) ***(G-11805)***
Van Rosendale John...757 868-8593
104 Sandy Bay Dr Poquoson (23662) ***(G-10378)***
Van Vierssen Marcel...703 471-0393
481 Carlisle Dr Ste 6 Herndon (20170) ***(G-6835)***
Van's Printing Services, Richmond *Also called Van KY Troung* ***(G-11432)***
Vance Graphics LLC...276 964-2822
175 Green Mountain Rd Pounding Mill (24637) ***(G-10526)***
Vandent Dental Inc...757 678-7973
14337 Harbor Ln Eastville (23347) ***(G-4297)***
Vanderbilt Media House LLC...757 515-9242
143 Valley Vista Dr # 202 Woodstock (22664) ***(G-15860)***
Vangarde Woodworks Inc...804 355-4917
2121 N Hamilton St Ste F Richmond (23230) ***(G-11433)***
Vanguard, Winchester *Also called Sheltered 2 Home LLC* ***(G-15585)***
Vanguard Brewpub & Distillery...757 224-1807
504 N King St Hampton (23669) ***(G-6260)***
Vanguard Industries East Inc (PA)...**757 665-8405**
1172 Azalea Garden Rd Norfolk (23502) ***(G-9778)***
Vanguard Mtgtion Rstration LLC...540 769-1881
5637 Penguin Dr Roanoke (24018) ***(G-12017)***
Vanguard Plastics...804 222-2012
2800 Sprouse Dr Richmond (23231) ***(G-11434)***
Vanhuss Family Cellars LLC...703 737-3930
18195 Dry Mill Rd Leesburg (20175) ***(G-7369)***
Vanity Print & Press LLC...757 553-1602
6304 Orkney Ct Suffolk (23435) ***(G-13776)***
Vanmark LLC...757 689-3850
3421 Chanl Creek Rd Ste 1 Virginia Beach (23453) ***(G-14906)***
Vans Inc...703 442-0161
7921 Tysons Corner Ctr Mc Lean (22102) ***(G-8574)***
Vans Inc...757 249-0802
12300 Jefferson Ave # 813 Newport News (23602) ***(G-9372)***
Vantage Point Drone LLC...703 723-4586
20827 Grainery Ct Ashburn (20147) ***(G-1346)***
Vanwin Coatings Virginia LLC (PA)...**757 487-5080**
2601 Trade St Ste A Chesapeake (23323) ***(G-3358)***
Vanwin Coatings Virginia LLC...757 925-4450
324 Moore Ave Suffolk (23434) ***(G-13777)***
Vaport Inc...757 397-1397
1510 Columbus Ave Portsmouth (23704) ***(G-10497)***
Varian Medical Systems Inc...434 977-8495
501 Locust Ave Charlottesville (22902) ***(G-2898)***
Variance Media Enterprises LLC...202 770-1701
11741 Dry River Ct Reston (20191) ***(G-10981)***
Variety Press LLC...703 359-0932
3301 Spring Lake Ct Fairfax (22030) ***(G-4692)***
Variety Printing Inc...757 480-1891
1014 Wadena Rd Chesapeake (23320) ***(G-3359)***
Varner Logging LLC...540 849-7451
102 Crawford Dr Churchville (24421) ***(G-3621)***
Varney Sheet Metal Shop...540 343-4076
2759 Mary Linda Ave Ne Roanoke (24012) ***(G-12216)***
Varsity Graphics & Awards, Fredericksburg *Also called Party Headquarters Inc* ***(G-5467)***
Vartender LLC...703 376-7751
43316 Cedar Pond Pl Chantilly (20152) ***(G-2562)***
Vas of Virginia Inc...434 296-5608
1740 Broadway St Charlottesville (22902) ***(G-2899)***
Vasse Vaught Metalcrafting Inc...540 808-8939
1915 Belleville Rd Sw Roanoke (24015) ***(G-12217)***
Vastec USA...302 682-8255
1200 W Fairfax Pike Stephens City (22655) ***(G-13327)***
Vastly, Glen Allen *Also called Tranlin Inc* ***(G-5816)***
Vaughan Furniture Company Inc (PA)...**276 236-6111**
816 Glendale Rd Galax (24333) ***(G-5652)***
Vaughan-Bassett Furn Co Inc (PA)...**276 236-6161**
300 E Grayson St Galax (24333) ***(G-5653)***
Vaughans Custom Cabinets-Home...276 398-2440
250 Retrievers Run Hillsville (24343) ***(G-6903)***
Vaughans Mill Inc...540 789-7144
1318 Vaughns Mill Rd Nw Indian Valley (24105) ***(G-6998)***
Vault...540 479-2221
11047 Pierson Dr Ste A Fredericksburg (22408) ***(G-5386)***
Vault Field Vineyards LLC...804 472-4430
2953 Kings Mill Rd Kinsale (22488) ***(G-7138)***
Vault Printing, The, Fredericksburg *Also called LL Distributing Inc* ***(G-5313)***
Vault Productions LLC...703 509-2704
107 Marshall Way Williamsburg (23185) ***(G-15330)***
Vault Technologies LLC...703 283-2550
9746 South Park Cir Fairfax Station (22039) ***(G-4726)***
Vault44 LLC...202 758-6228
9201 Zachary Ct Manassas Park (20111) ***(G-8213)***
Vb Guide, Norfolk *Also called Virginia Beach Guide Magazine* ***(G-9782)***
Vb Printing, Lorton *Also called Viet Bao Inc* ***(G-7538)***
Vbk Publishing...757 587-1741
1644 Kingsway Rd Norfolk (23518) ***(G-9779)***
Veamea Inc...703 382-2288
1364 Beverly Rd Ste 105 Mc Lean (22101) ***(G-8575)***
Vector Vortex LLC...540 330-7733
15778 Stewartsville Rd Vinton (24179) ***(G-14190)***
Vedco Holdings Inc (HQ)...**800 258-8583**
1793 Dry Fork Rd Vansant (24656) ***(G-13979)***
Vee's Accessories, Chesterfield *Also called Valerie Perkins* ***(G-3538)***
Vega Pages LLC...703 281-2030
914 Desale St Sw Vienna (22180) ***(G-14150)***
Vega Productions & Associates (PA)...**703 908-9600**
2721 Prosperity Ave # 200 Fairfax (22031) ***(G-4578)***
Vegan Heritage Press...540 459-2858
219 E Reservoir Rd Woodstock (22664) ***(G-15861)***
Vegnos Corporation...571 721-1685
8690 Venoy Ct Alexandria (22309) ***(G-604)***
Vel Tye LLC...757 518-5400
1619 Diamond Springs Rd Virginia Beach (23455) ***(G-14907)***
Vella Mac Industries Inc...757 724-0026
1109 Campostella Rd Norfolk (23523) ***(G-9780)***
Velocity LLC...703 304-6152
11465 Washington Plz W Reston (20190) ***(G-10982)***

ALPHABETIC

Velocity Services Corporation................540 368-2708
13 Myers Dr Fredericksburg (22405) *(G-5497)*

Velocity Software Inc................703 338-0909
44261 Shehawken Ter Ashburn (20147) *(G-1347)*

Velocity Systems LLC................703 707-6280
45064 Underwood Ln Ste B Dulles (20166) *(G-4231)*

Velvet Pile Carpets LLC................540 920-9473
18558 Buzzard Hollow Rd Gordonsville (22942) *(G-5918)*

Velveteen Videos LLC................703 229-3633
883 Wildcat Dr Front Royal (22630) *(G-5561)*

Vena Portae Inc................703 899-9500
44927 Grge Wash Blvd Ste Ashburn (20147) *(G-1348)*

Venetian Spider Press LLC................310 857-4228
203 Amy Ct Sterling (20164) *(G-13546)*

Venkor Specialty Products LLC................703 932-3840
5003 Westfileds Blvd Centreville (20120) *(G-2349)*

Venom Motorsports................804 347-7626
3793 Longfield Rd Colonial Beach (22443) *(G-3728)*

Venomous Scents & Novelties................434 660-1164
918 Pierce St Lynchburg (24501) *(G-7832)*

Ventajas Publications LLC................540 825-5337
400 Southridge Pkwy Culpeper (22701) *(G-3928)*

Ventex Inc................703 787-9802
101 Executive Dr Ste H Sterling (20166) *(G-13547)*

Venton Fab & Welding................540 981-1550
7 Walnut Ave Vinton (24179) *(G-14191)*

Ventura Defense US Corp................571 527-1360
1001 19th St N Ste 1200 Arlington (22209) *(G-1208)*

Venture Apps LLC................804 747-3405
4717 Sadler Green Pl Glen Allen (23060) *(G-5823)*

Venture Globl Clcsieu Pass LLC................202 759-6740
1001 19th St N Ste 1500 Arlington (22209) *(G-1209)*

Venture Publishing LLC................540 570-1908
2202 Holly Ave Buena Vista (24416) *(G-2156)*

Venturewise LLC................804 277-9564
13709 Milbranch Ct Richmond (23233) *(G-11435)*

Venus Tech LLC................703 389-5557
12925 Centre Park Cir # 111 Herndon (20171) *(G-6836)*

Venutec Corporation................888 573-8870
5426 Crystalford Ln Centreville (20120) *(G-2350)*

Veramar Vineyard LLC................540 955-5510
905 Quarry St Berryville (22611) *(G-1699)*

Verbatim Editing, Richmond *Also called VA Writers Club* *(G-11804)*

Verde Candles................804 338-1350
10816 Rimbey Ct Glen Allen (23060) *(G-5824)*

Verdex Technologies Inc................804 491-9733
9305 Burge Ave North Chesterfield (23237) *(G-10008)*

Veridos America Inc................703 480-2025
45925 Horseshoe Dr Dulles (20166) *(G-4232)*

Verint Systems Inc.................703 481-9326
11950 Democracy Dr # 250 Reston (20190) *(G-10983)*

Verisma Systems Inc (PA)................**866 390-7404**
1421 Prince St Ste 250 Alexandria (22314) *(G-372)*

Veritas Works LLC................540 456-8000
151 Veritas Ln Afton (22920) *(G-94)*

Vermark Global Systems Inc................703 629-1571
11216 Waples Mill Rd 102a Fairfax (22030) *(G-4693)*

Vermark Gs, Fairfax *Also called Vermark Global Systems Inc (G-4693)*

Vertex Signs................540 904-5776
4005 Electric Rd Ste 201 Roanoke (24018) *(G-12018)*

Vertexusa LLC (PA)................**213 294-3072**
44330 Mercure Cir Ste 309 Sterling (20166) *(G-13548)*

Vertexusa LLC.................213 294-9072
12913 Alton Sq Herndon (20170) *(G-6837)*

Vertical Blind Productions................540 484-4995
120 Woods Edge Dr Rocky Mount (24151) *(G-12358)*

Vertical Innovations LLC................540 616-6431
5077 State Park Rd Dublin (24084) *(G-4173)*

Vertical Path Creative LLC................434 414-1357
386 Fairlane Dr Stanardsville (22973) *(G-13230)*

Vertical Praise................434 985-1513
403 Southridge Dr Ruckersville (22968) *(G-12415)*

Vertical Rock Inc................855 822-5462
10225 Nokesville Rd Manassas (20110) *(G-8010)*

Vertical Sunset................757 787-7595
17487 Northside Rd Onancock (23417) *(G-10199)*

Vertical Venus LLC................571 236-6484
5409 Sour Gum Dr Centreville (20120) *(G-2351)*

Vertiv Corporation................804 747-6030
1011 Technology Park Dr Glen Allen (23059) *(G-5825)*

Vertiv Corporation................703 726-4100
44611 Guilford Dr Ste 180 Ashburn (20147) *(G-1349)*

Vertu Corp................540 341-3006
7555 Gary Rd Manassas (20109) *(G-8174)*

Vertu Corp................540 341-3006
680c Industrial Rd Warrenton (20186) *(G-15058)*

Vesta Propertys LLC................703 579-7979
1295 Difficult Run Ct Vienna (22182) *(G-14151)*

Veteran Arms Inc................703 217-7532
2522 Basin View Ln Woodbridge (22191) *(G-15826)*

Veteran Customs LLC................540 786-2157
8307 Catharpin Landing Rd Spotsylvania (22553) *(G-12920)*

Veteran Force Industries LLC................912 492-5800
300 Yoakum Pkwy Apt 1417 Alexandria (22304) *(G-373)*

Veteran Freelancer................484 772-5931
3571 Riverside Dr Norfolk (23502) *(G-9781)*

Veteran Made LLC................703 328-2570
15 E Market St Unit 567 Leesburg (20178) *(G-7370)*

Veterans Choice Med Sup LLC................571 244-4358
38211 Highland Farm Pl Purcellville (20132) *(G-10685)*

Veterans Printing LLC................571 208-0074
7515 Presidential Ln Manassas (20109) *(G-8175)*

Veterans Welding LLC................804 904-7951
2501 Hickory Knoll Ln Richmond (23230) *(G-11436)*

Vetsusa II Inc................703 300-9874
307 Annandale Rd Ste 201 Falls Church (22042) *(G-4889)*

Vf Imagewear (east) Inc................276 956-7200
3375 Joseph Martin Hwy Martinsville (24112) *(G-8345)*

Vfg Enterprises LLC................757 343-4866
3421 Chanl Creek Rd Ste 1 Virginia Beach (23453) *(G-14908)*

Vfp Inc (PA)................**540 977-0500**
5410 Fallowater Ln Roanoke (24018) *(G-12019)*

Vfp Inc.................276 431-4000
402 Industrial Park Rd Duffield (24244) *(G-4187)*

Vh Drones LLC................804 938-9713
10984 Milestone Dr Mechanicsville (23116) *(G-8692)*

Vi's Vtc Computer Consultant, Falls Church *Also called Bradshaw Viola (G-4765)*

Via Services LLC................703 978-2629
5600 Light Infantry Dr Burke (22015) *(G-2206)*

Viasystems North America Inc................703 450-2600
1200 Severn Way Sterling (20166) *(G-13549)*

Vibe Candle Co LLC................757 589-3274
2104 Pridgen Rd Hampton (23663) *(G-6261)*

Vibrant Prints LLC................843 425-2506
12000 Market St Apt 60 Reston (20190) *(G-10984)*

Vic's Sign & Engraving, Franklin *Also called Vics Signs & Engraving (G-5161)*

Vicious Creations LLC................256 479-7689
76 Tide Mill Ln Hampton (23666) *(G-6262)*

Vickie D Blankenship................540 977-6377
1155 Colonial Rd Blue Ridge (24064) *(G-1856)*

Vicon Industries Inc................540 868-9530
110 Dickenson Ct Stephens City (22655) *(G-13328)*

Vics Signs & Engraving................757 562-2243
107 W 4th Ave Franklin (23851) *(G-5161)*

Victimology Inc................703 528-3387
2333 N Vernon St Arlington (22207) *(G-1210)*

Victor Forward LLC................757 374-2642
1206 Laskin Rd Ste 201 Virginia Beach (23451) *(G-14909)*

Victor Randall Logging LLC................804 241-6630
9829 Kingsrock Ln Mechanicsville (23116) *(G-8693)*

Victoria Austin................276 632-1742
519 Glendale St Martinsville (24112) *(G-8346)*

Victorious Images LLC................757 476-7335
7191 Richmond Rd Ste E Williamsburg (23188) *(G-15331)*

Victory Coachways................434 799-2569
312 Bryant Ave Danville (24540) *(G-4046)*

Victory Lane Karting Parts, Bedford *Also called K & K Signs (G-1641)*

Victory Tropical Oil Usa Inc................757 687-8171
1 Columbus Ctr Ste 903 Virginia Beach (23462) *(G-14910)*

Vidar Systems Corporation................703 471-7070
365 Herndon Pkwy Ste 105 Herndon (20170) *(G-6838)*

Video Aerial Systems LLC................434 221-3089
117 Martins Ln Amherst (24521) *(G-712)*

Video Convergent................703 354-9700
6800 Versar Ctr Springfield (22151) *(G-13105)*

Video Production, Front Royal *Also called Velveteen Videos LLC (G-5561)*

Video-Scope International Ltd................703 437-5534
105 Executive Dr Ste 110 Sterling (20166) *(G-13550)*

Videographers Fredericksburg................540 582-6111
9011 Judiciary Dr Spotsylvania (22553) *(G-12921)*

Vidrio Technologies................703 405-4944
18541 Bear Creek Ter Leesburg (20176) *(G-7371)*

Vie La Publishing House LLC................804 741-2670
1707 Foxcreek Cir Henrico (23238) *(G-6589)*

Vienna Custom Embroidery LLC................703 887-1254
9101 Old Courthouse Rd Vienna (22182) *(G-14152)*

Vienna Hot Tubes Patio In................703 734-0077
8501 Tyco Rd Ste C Vienna (22182) *(G-14153)*

Vienna Paint & Dctg Co Inc (PA)................**703 281-5252**
203 Maple Ave W Vienna (22180) *(G-14154)*

Vienna Paint & Dctg Co Inc................703 450-0300
22135 Davis Dr Ste 101 Sterling (20164) *(G-13551)*

Vienna Pt Reston/Herndon 04................703 733-3899
282 Sunset Park Dr Herndon (20170) *(G-6839)*

Vienna Quilt Shop................703 281-4091
6724 Curran St Mc Lean (22101) *(G-8576)*

Vienna Vintner, Vienna *Also called Mendes Deli Inc (G-14090)*

Viet Bao Inc................703 339-9852
8394 Terminal Rd Ste C2 Lorton (22079) *(G-7538)*

Vigilent Inc 202 550-9515
  5380 Eisenhower Ave Alexandria (22304) *(G-374)*

Vigilent Labs, Alexandria *Also called Vigilent Inc* *(G-374)*

Viking Fabrication Services 804 228-1333
  4593 Carolina Ave Richmond (23222) *(G-11806)*

Viking Supplynet, Richmond *Also called Viking Fabrication Services* *(G-11806)*

Viking Woodworking 540 659-3882
  102 Melody Ln Stafford (22554) *(G-13210)*

Vila Pimenta Imports LLC 610 533-3278
  3420 Pump Rd Ste 157 Richmond (23233) *(G-11437)*

Villa Appalaccia Winery 540 593-3100
  752 Rock Castle Gorge Floyd (24091) *(G-5045)*

Village Blacksmith LLC 804 824-2631
  6641 Gloucester St Gloucester (23061) *(G-5864)*

Village Cabinet Co 434 574-6263
  226 Prospect Rd Prospect (23960) *(G-10615)*

Village News, Chester *Also called Village Publishing LLC* *(G-3466)*

Village Publishing LLC 804 751-0421
  4607 W Hundred Rd Chester (23831) *(G-3466)*

Village To Village Press LLC 267 416-0375
  1510 College Ave Harrisonburg (22802) *(G-6384)*

Village Winery 540 882-3780
  40405 Browns Ln Waterford (20197) *(G-15083)*

Villalva Inc (PA) **703 527-0091**
  239 N Glebe Rd Arlington (22203) *(G-1211)*

Viloquinne LLC 703 493-8864
  9246 Mccarty Rd Lorton (22079) *(G-7539)*

Vina Express Inc 703 237-9398
  6795 Wilson Blvd Ste 15 Falls Church (22044) *(G-4890)*

Vina Xpress, Falls Church *Also called Vina Express Inc* *(G-4890)*

Vincents Vineyard Inc 276 889-2505
  2313 E Main St Lebanon (24266) *(G-7210)*

Vinci Co LLC 888 529-6864
  2715 Entp Pkwy Ste A Richmond (23294) *(G-11438)*

Vinegar Hill Acres 540 337-6839
  553 Vinegar Hill Rd Churchville (24421) *(G-3622)*

Vineyard Engravers Inc (PA) **703 941-3700**
  7700 Little River Tpke Annandale (22003) *(G-791)*

Vineyard Services 434 964-8270
  2431 Huntington Rd Charlottesville (22901) *(G-2712)*

Vineyards 804 580-4053
  619 Train Ln Wicomico Church (22579) *(G-15196)*

Vinifera Distributing Virginia 804 261-2890
  7668f Fullerton Rd Springfield (22153) *(G-13106)*

Vinnell Corp (PA) **703 818-7903**
  12900 Fdral Systems Pk Dr Fairfax (22033) *(G-4579)*

Vint Hill Craft Winery LLC (PA) **540 341-1862**
  6190 Georgetown Rd Broad Run (20137) *(G-2071)*

Vintage Bindery Williamsbur 757 220-0203
  4 Seasons Ct Williamsburg (23188) *(G-15332)*

Vintage Star LLC 808 779-9688
  6203 Hibbling Ave Springfield (22150) *(G-13107)*

Vintage Vault 703 862-7159
  17 Nicholson Ct Sterling (20165) *(G-13552)*

Vintage Virginia Photos, Virginia Beach *Also called One Four Three LLC* *(G-14699)*

Vintners Cllar Winery Yorktown 757 223-4261
  1213 George Wash Mem Hwy Yorktown (23693) *(G-15998)*

Vinton Plant, Vinton *Also called Precision Fabrics Group Inc* *(G-14181)*

Vinyl Lite Window Factory, Lorton *Also called Vinylite Windows Products Inc* *(G-7540)*

Vinyl Visions LLC 540 369-5244
  9495 Inaugural Dr King George (22485) *(G-7119)*

Vinyl Weld & Color Co, Virginia Beach *Also called Richard Y Lombard Jr* *(G-14772)*

Vinylite Windows Products Inc 703 550-7766
  8815 Telegraph Rd Lorton (22079) *(G-7540)*

VIP Plastics, Elkton *Also called Virginia Industrial Plas Inc* *(G-4337)*

Viplife Ent Publishing LLC 434 429-6037
  1572 Kemper Road Ext Danville (24541) *(G-4047)*

Virchow Biotech Inc 615 549-5999
  1655 Fort Myer Dr Ste 700 Arlington (22209) *(G-1212)*

Virgin Hair Group, Chesterfield *Also called Tiera Averett* *(G-3532)*

Virgina-Carolina Grave Vlt LLC 276 694-6855
  4734 Moorefield Store Rd Stuart (24171) *(G-13638)*

Virginia & Carolina Concrete, Mouth of Wilson *Also called Huffman & Huffman Inc* *(G-9093)*

Virginia Abrasives Corporation 804 732-0058
  2851 Service Rd Petersburg (23805) *(G-10349)*

Virginia Academic Press 703 256-1304
  511 N Armistead St Alexandria (22312) *(G-605)*

Virginia Air Distributors Inc 540 366-2259
  6905 Walrond Dr Roanoke (24019) *(G-12020)*

Virginia American Inds Inc (PA) **804 644-2611**
  710 Hospital St Richmond (23219) *(G-11807)*

Virginia Archtectural Mtls LLC 540 710-7701
  2202 Airport Ave Fredericksburg (22401) *(G-5232)*

Virginia Aromatics Ltd Company 540 672-2847
  12493 Spicewood Rd Orange (22960) *(G-10229)*

Virginia Beach Guide Magazine 757 627-8712
  1228 Ballentine Blvd Norfolk (23504) *(G-9782)*

Virginia Beach Printing & Sty 757 428-4282
  3000 Baltic Ave Virginia Beach (23451) *(G-14911)*

Virginia Beach Products LLC (PA) **757 847-9338**
  4304 Saint Martin Ct Virginia Beach (23455) *(G-14912)*

Virginia Beach Products LLC 757 847-9338
  5320 Hamilton Ln Virginia Beach (23462) *(G-14913)*

Virginia Beach Skateboards 757 385-4131
  2312 Treesong Trl Virginia Beach (23456) *(G-14914)*

Virginia Beach Winery LLC 757 995-4315
  152 Newtown Rd Ste 108 Virginia Beach (23462) *(G-14915)*

Virginia Beachs Max Blck Mold 757 354-1935
  1581 General Booth Blvd Virginia Beach (23454) *(G-14916)*

Virginia Beer Company LLC 770 815-8518
  401 Second St Williamsburg (23185) *(G-15333)*

Virginia Blade Inc 434 384-1282
  5177 Boonsboro Rd Lynchburg (24503) *(G-7833)*

Virginia Blower Company (PA) **276 647-3804**
  3677 Virginia Ave Collinsville (24078) *(G-3718)*

Virginia Bodiesel Refinery LLC 804 435-1126
  1676 Waverly Ave Kilmarnock (22482) *(G-7078)*

Virginia Breeze Alpacas LLC 804 641-4811
  13300 Hensley Rd Midlothian (23112) *(G-8918)*

Virginia Bride LLC 804 822-1768
  820 Gloucester Rd Saluda (23149) *(G-12606)*

Virginia Building Services Inc 757 605-0288
  4865 Haygood Rd Virginia Beach (23455) *(G-14917)*

Virginia Bus Publications LLC 804 225-9262
  1207 E Main St Ste 100 Richmond (23219) *(G-11808)*

Virginia Business Magazine, Roanoke *Also called Wood Television LLC* *(G-12229)*

Virginia Business Magazine 804 649-6999
  333 E Franklin St Richmond (23219) *(G-11809)*

Virginia Cabinetry LLC 804 612-6469
  1221 School St Richmond (23220) *(G-11810)*

Virginia Cabinets LLC 703 793-8307
  2465 Centreville Rd J21 Herndon (20171) *(G-6840)*

Virginia Cabinetworks Inc 540 298-9599
  416 W Spotswood Trl Elkton (22827) *(G-4336)*

Virginia Candle Company LLC 301 828-6498
  2173 Potomac Club Pkwy Woodbridge (22191) *(G-15827)*

Virginia Canvas Products Inc 757 558-0327
  15457 Gayle Way Carrollton (23314) *(G-2246)*

Virginia Carolina Buildings 434 645-7411
  210 S Fourth St Crewe (23930) *(G-3820)*

Virginia Carolina Pure Water 757 282-6487
  521 Holbrook Rd Virginia Beach (23452) *(G-14918)*

Virginia Carolina Steel Inc 757 853-7403
  2411 Ingleside Rd Norfolk (23513) *(G-9783)*

Virginia Cast Stone Inc 540 943-9808
  1720 Harding Ave Waynesboro (22980) *(G-15143)*

Virginia Cft Brwing Spport LLC 703 960-3230
  218 N Columbus St Alexandria (22314) *(G-375)*

Virginia Citizens Defense 703 944-4845
  2329 Third St Middletown (22645) *(G-8748)*

Virginia Coffee Company LLC 703 566-3037
  510 King St Ste 350 Alexandria (22314) *(G-376)*

Virginia Concrete Company LLC (HQ) **703 354-7100**
  13880 Dulles Corner Ln # 450 Herndon (20171) *(G-6841)*

Virginia Controls Inc 804 225-5530
  2513 Mechanicsville Tpke Richmond (23223) *(G-11811)*

Virginia Cptol Connections Inc 804 643-5554
  1001 E Broad St Ste 215 Richmond (23219) *(G-11812)*

Virginia Crane Co, Ashland *Also called Foley Material Handling Co Inc* *(G-1419)*

Virginia Culinary Pathways LLC 757 298-0599
  429 N Main St Suffolk (23434) *(G-13778)*

Virginia Custom Blend LLC 804 994-5099
  304 Dorrell Rd Aylett (23009) *(G-1556)*

Virginia Custom Buildings 540 582-5111
  6329 Jefferson Davis Hwy Spotsylvania (22551) *(G-12922)*

Virginia Custom Buildings (PA) **804 784-3816**
  280 Broad Street Rd Manakin Sabot (23103) *(G-7906)*

Virginia Custom Coach Builders 540 381-0609
  375 Bell Rd Christiansburg (24073) *(G-3616)*

Virginia Custom Plating Inc 804 789-0719
  9203 Royal Grant Dr Mechanicsville (23116) *(G-8694)*

Virginia Custom Signs Corp 804 278-8788
  4808 Leonard Pkwy Richmond (23226) *(G-11439)*

Virginia Cutting Systems, Smithfield *Also called Chips On Board Incorporated* *(G-12709)*

Virginia Dental Sc Inc 804 422-1888
  1803 Lakecrest Ct Richmond (23238) *(G-11440)*

Virginia Design Packaging, Suffolk *Also called Berry Plastics Design LLC* *(G-13679)*

Virginia Distillery Co LLC 703 869-0083
  6100 35th St N Arlington (22213) *(G-1213)*

Virginia Distillery Co LLC 434 285-2900
  299 Eades Ln Lovingston (22949) *(G-7593)*

Virginia Drveline Differential 276 227-0299
  645 Black Lick Rd Wytheville (24382) *(G-15921)*

Virginia Eagle Distrg Co LLC 434 296-5531
  669 Gold Eagle Dr Charlottesville (22903) *(G-2900)*

Virginia Electric and Power Co 757 558-5459
  2837 S Military Hwy Chesapeake (23323) *(G-3360)*

Virginia Electronic Monitoring 757 513-0942
  612 Ridge Cir Chesapeake (23320) *(G-3361)*

Virginia Embalming Company Inc......540 334-1150
62 Virginia Market Pl Dr Rocky Mount (24151) ***(G-12359)***
Virginia Engineer......804 779-3527
7401 Flannigan Mill Rd Mechanicsville (23111) ***(G-8695)***
Virginia Engineer, The, Mechanicsville *Also called Virginia Engineer* ***(G-8695)***
Virginia Expl & Drlg Co Inc (HQ)......**276 597-4449**
1793 Dry Fork Rd Vansant (24656) ***(G-13980)***
Virginia Fire Protection Svcs......276 637-1012
7893 Peppers Ferry Rd Max Meadows (24360) ***(G-8370)***
Virginia Forge Company LLC (HQ)......**540 254-2236**
17921 Main St Buchanan (24066) ***(G-2130)***
Virginia Gas Exploration Co......276 676-2380
1096 Olleberry Dr Se Va Abingdon (24210) ***(G-64)***
Virginia Gazette Companies LLC......757 220-1736
703 Mariners Row Newport News (23606) ***(G-9373)***
Virginia Glass, Martinsville *Also called Virginia Mirror Company Inc* ***(G-8348)***
Virginia Glass Products Corp......276 956-3131
347 Old Sand Rd Ridgeway (24148) ***(G-11856)***
Virginia Guide Bait Co......804 590-2991
7800 Woodpecker Rd Chesterfield (23838) ***(G-3539)***
Virginia Head and Neck Therape......804 837-9594
10149 Bon Air Crest Dr North Chesterfield (23235) ***(G-10009)***
Virginia Highlands Machining......276 628-8555
24431 Regal Dr Abingdon (24211) ***(G-65)***
Virginia Industrial Plas Inc......540 298-1515
2454 North East Side Hwy Elkton (22827) ***(G-4337)***
Virginia Installations Inc......540 298-5300
104 N Fifth St Elkton (22827) ***(G-4338)***
Virginia Insulated Products Co (PA)......**276 496-5136**
647 S Main St Saltville (24370) ***(G-12598)***
Virginia Insulated Products Co......276 496-5136
Hwy 91 Saltville (24370) ***(G-12599)***
Virginia Kik Inc (PA)......**540 389-5401**
27 Mill Ln Salem (24153) ***(G-12578)***
Virginia Laser Corporation......276 628-9284
18533 Pond Dr Abingdon (24211) ***(G-66)***
Virginia Lawyers Media, Richmond *Also called Dolan LLC* ***(G-11562)***
Virginia LP Truck Inc......434 246-8257
11486 Blue Star Hwy Stony Creek (23882) ***(G-13570)***
Virginia Machine & Sup Co Inc......757 380-8500
900 39th St Newport News (23607) ***(G-9374)***
Virginia Materials Inc (HQ)......**800 321-2282**
3306 Peterson St Norfolk (23509) ***(G-9784)***
Virginia Media Inc......304 647-5724
1633 W Main St Salem (24153) ***(G-12579)***
Virginia Metal Treating, Lynchburg *Also called East Crlina Metal Treating Inc* ***(G-7699)***
Virginia Metalfab, Gladstone *Also called Stallworks LLC* ***(G-5688)***
Virginia Metals Inc......276 628-8151
26336 Hillman Hwy Abingdon (24210) ***(G-67)***
Virginia Mirror Company Inc (PA)......**276 956-3131**
300 Moss St S Martinsville (24112) ***(G-8347)***
Virginia Mirror Company Inc......276 632-9816
300 Moss St S Martinsville (24112) ***(G-8348)***
Virginia Mist Granite Corp......540 661-0030
11235 Muddy Bottom Ln Rapidan (22733) ***(G-10754)***
Virginia Mist Group Inc......540 661-0030
11235 Muddy Bottom Ln Rapidan (22733) ***(G-10755)***
Virginia Mobile AC Systems Inc......757 650-0957
704 Canal Dr Chesapeake (23323) ***(G-3362)***
Virginia Mountain Vineyards LL......540 473-2979
4204 Old Fincastle Rd Fincastle (24090) ***(G-4999)***
Virginia Mountaineer, Grundy *Also called Mountaineer Publishing Co Inc* ***(G-6038)***
Virginia Mtal Fabrications LLC......540 292-0562
174 Hankey Mountain Hwy Churchville (24421) ***(G-3623)***
Virginia Mtals Fabrication LLC......804 622-2900
2471 Goodes Bridge Rd North Chesterfield (23224) ***(G-10043)***
Virginia Needle Art Inc......540 433-8070
940 Mockingbird Dr Harrisonburg (22802) ***(G-6385)***
Virginia News Group LLC......703 777-1111
108 Church St Se Ste C Leesburg (20175) ***(G-7372)***
Virginia News Group LLC......540 955-1111
2 N Kent St Winchester (22601) ***(G-15599)***
Virginia News Group LLC (PA)......**703 777-1111**
1602 Village Market Blvd Leesburg (20175) ***(G-7373)***
Virginia News Group LLC......703 777-1111
21720 Red Rum Dr Ste 142 Ashburn (20147) ***(G-1350)***
Virginia News Group LLC......703 437-5400
1760 Reston Pkwy Ste 411 Reston (20190) ***(G-10985)***
Virginia Oil Company......540 552-2365
1710 Prices Fork Rd Blacksburg (24060) ***(G-1804)***
Virginia Pallets & Wood LLC......434 515-2221
852 Planters Rd Lawrenceville (23868) ***(G-7187)***
Virginia Panel Corporation......540 932-3300
1400 New Hope Rd Waynesboro (22980) ***(G-15144)***
Virginia Pewtersmith, Williamsburg *Also called Smith and Flannery* ***(G-15313)***
Virginia Plant Us80 & Us81, Ripplemead *Also called Lhoist North America VA Inc* ***(G-11876)***
Virginia Plastic Utilities, Roanoke *Also called Gianni Enterprises Inc* ***(G-11925)***
Virginia Plastics Company Inc......540 981-9700
3453 Aerial Way Dr Sw Roanoke (24018) ***(G-12021)***
Virginia Plty Growers Coop Inc (PA)......**540 867-4000**
6349 Rawley Pike Hinton (22831) ***(G-6906)***
Virginia Plty Grwers Rckingham, Hinton *Also called Vpgc LLC* ***(G-6907)***
Virginia Premiere Paint Contr......804 398-1177
501 E Franklin St Richmond (23219) ***(G-11813)***
Virginia Printing Services Inc......757 838-5500
60 W Mercury Blvd Hampton (23669) ***(G-6263)***
Virginia Prosthetics Inc (PA)......**540 366-8287**
4338 Williamson Rd Nw Roanoke (24012) ***(G-12218)***
Virginia Prosthetics Orthotics......540 949-4248
1577 Jefferson Hwy # 101 Fishersville (22939) ***(G-5012)***
Virginia Prtg Co Roanoke Inc (PA)......**540 483-7433**
501a Campbell Ave Sw Roanoke (24016) ***(G-12219)***
Virginia Prtg Co Roanoke Inc......540 483-7433
40 High St Rocky Mount (24151) ***(G-12360)***
Virginia Quarterly Review, The, Charlottesville *Also called Rector Visitors of The Univ VA* ***(G-2860)***
Virginia Quilter......540 548-3207
1 Murphy Ct Fredericksburg (22407) ***(G-5387)***
Virginia Quilting Inc (PA)......**434 757-1809**
100 S Main St La Crosse (23950) ***(G-7152)***
Virginia Railing & Gates LLC......804 798-8777
11042 Air Park Rd Ste 1 Ashland (23005) ***(G-1506)***
Virginia Real Estate Reviews......276 956-5900
228 Oxford Dr Martinsville (24112) ***(G-8349)***
Virginia Rural Letter......757 242-6865
73 E Windsor Blvd Windsor (23487) ***(G-15607)***
Virginia Screen Printing......804 295-7440
24108 River Rd North Dinwiddie (23803) ***(G-10068)***
Virginia Seafoods LLC......301 520-8200
202 Antirap Dr White Stone (22578) ***(G-15190)***
Virginia Semiconductor Inc......540 373-2900
1501 Powhatan St Fredericksburg (22401) ***(G-5233)***
Virginia Sign and Lighting Co......703 222-5670
11116 Industrial Rd Manassas (20109) ***(G-8176)***
Virginia Silver Plating Inc......757 244-3645
3201a Warwick Blvd Newport News (23607) ***(G-9375)***
Virginia Software Group Inc......757 721-0054
2108 Blossom Hill Ct Virginia Beach (23457) ***(G-14919)***
Virginia Spectral LLC......434 987-2036
113 Lupine Ln Charlottesville (22911) ***(G-2713)***
Virginia Sportsman......434 971-1199
1932 Arlington Blvd Charlottesville (22903) ***(G-2901)***
Virginia Stained Glass Co Inc......703 425-4611
5250e Port Royal Rd Springfield (22151) ***(G-13108)***
Virginia Stair Company......434 823-2587
6420 Seminole Trl Ste 6 Barboursville (22923) ***(G-1568)***
Virginia Stairs Inc (PA)......**757 425-6681**
2277 Haversham Close Virginia Beach (23454) ***(G-14920)***
Virginia Steel & Building Spc......434 528-4302
713 Jefferson St Lynchburg (24504) ***(G-7834)***
Virginia Steel & Fabrication......276 688-2125
36 Progress Dr Bastian (24314) ***(G-1594)***
Virginia T-Shirt Company LLC......540 752-8141
418 Spotted Tavern Rd Fredericksburg (22406) ***(G-5498)***
Virginia Tag Service, King William *Also called Virginia Tag Service Inc* ***(G-7132)***
Virginia Tag Service Inc......804 690-7304
2862 East River Rd King William (23086) ***(G-7132)***
Virginia Tank Service Inc......540 344-9700
1719 Norfolk Ave Se Roanoke (24013) ***(G-12220)***
Virginia Tek Inc......703 391-8877
2516 Farrier Ln Reston (20191) ***(G-10986)***
Virginia Thermography LLC......757 705-9968
361 Southport Cir Ste 202 Virginia Beach (23452) ***(G-14921)***
Virginia Times......804 530-8540
12100 Ganesh Ln Chester (23836) ***(G-3467)***
Virginia Trane Ap141......540 580-7702
2303 Trane Dr Nw Roanoke (24017) ***(G-12221)***
Virginia Transformer Corp (PA)......**540 345-9892**
220 Glade View Dr Ne Roanoke (24012) ***(G-12222)***
Virginia Transformer Corp......540 345-9892
100 Smorgon Way Troutville (24175) ***(G-13919)***
Virginia Truck Trailer LL......804 784-3485
17517 Carrington Glen Ln Rockville (23146) ***(G-12302)***
Virginia Venom Volleyball......757 645-4002
8140 Wrenfield Dr Williamsburg (23188) ***(G-15334)***
Virginia Vermiculite LLC (PA)......**540 967-2266**
13341 Louisa Rd Louisa (23093) ***(G-7574)***
Virginia Veterans Creations......757 502-4407
4768 Euclid Rd Ste 105 Virginia Beach (23462) ***(G-14922)***
Virginia Vnom Spt Organization......757 592-6790
3012 South Chase Williamsburg (23185) ***(G-15335)***
Virginia Wave Inc......804 693-4278
5439 White Hall Rd Gloucester (23061) ***(G-5865)***
Virginia Welding LLC......703 263-1964
13632 Ellendale Dr Chantilly (20151) ***(G-2516)***
Virginia Wheel & Rim Inc......804 526-9868
105 Tudor Rd Colonial Heights (23834) ***(G-3751)***
Virginia Wine Pass LLC......540 376-7902
600 Princess Anne St Fredericksburg (22404) ***(G-5234)***

Virginia Wineworks LLC 434 923-8314
1781 Harris Creek Way Charlottesville (22902) *(G-2902)*

Virginia Woodcrafters LLC 804 276-2766
8609 Oakview Ave Henrico (23228) *(G-6590)*

Virginia Woodworking Co Inc 276 669-3133
190 Williams St Bristol (24201) *(G-1997)*

Virginian Leader Corp 540 921-3434
511 Mountain Lake Ave Pearisburg (24134) *(G-10279)*

Virginian Review, Covington *Also called Covington Virginian Inc (G-3784)*

Virginias Mudd Hot Sauce LLC 434 953-6582
1107 Georgia Creek Rd Scottsville (24590) *(G-12669)*

Virginias Peninsula Pub Fcilty 757 898-5012
145 Goodwin Neck Rd Yorktown (23692) *(G-15999)*

Virginias Rsources Recycled LLC 804 561-2543
11601 Grub Hill Church Rd Amelia Court House (23002) *(G-676)*

Virginn-Plot Mdia Cmpanies LLC (HQ) **757 446-9000**
5429 Greenwich Rd Virginia Beach (23462) *(G-14923)*

Virginn-Plot Mdia Cmpanies LLC 804 358-0825
24 E 3rd St Richmond (23224) *(G-11814)*

Virginn-Plot Mdia Cmpanies LLC 757 446-2848
5429 Greenwich Rd Virginia Beach (23462) *(G-14924)*

Virtual Ea Inc 703 855-9593
12164 Rain Slicker Pl Nokesville (20181) *(G-9403)*

Virtual Netcom LLC 571 445-0306
14801 Murdock St Ste 155 Chantilly (20151) *(G-2517)*

Virtual Ntwrk Cmmnications Inc 571 445-0306
25643 South Village Dr South Riding (20152) *(G-12871)*

Virtual Realty 757 718-2633
7472 Pinehurst Dr Quinton (23141) *(G-10701)*

Virtue Solar LLC 540 407-8353
367 N White Oak Dr Madison (22727) *(G-7864)*

Virtuous Health Today Inc 540 339-2855
7a Church Ave Se Roanoke (24011) *(G-12223)*

Viscosity LLC 757 343-9071
120 Marina Reach Chesapeake (23320) *(G-3363)*

Vision Academy Publishing LLC 703 753-0710
13771 Oakland Ridge Rd Haymarket (20169) *(G-6453)*

Vision Business Solutions 540 622-6383
324 Jamestown Rd Front Royal (22630) *(G-5562)*

Vision Machine and Fabrication 757 865-1234
2100 Mingee Dr Hampton (23661) *(G-6264)*

Vision Publishers LLC 540 867-5302
1418 Hinton Rd Dayton (22821) *(G-4071)*

Vision Publishers Inc 540 437-1967
755 Cantrell Ave Ste C Harrisonburg (22801) *(G-6386)*

Vision Sign Inc 703 707-0858
45945 Trefoil Ln Ste 184 Sterling (20166) *(G-13553)*

Vision Software Technologies 703 722-4480
25958 Mccoy Ct Chantilly (20152) *(G-2563)*

Vision Tech Land Systems 703 739-2610
99 Canal Center Plz # 210 Alexandria (22314) *(G-377)*

Vision Technologies Systems, Alexandria *Also called St Engineering North Amer Inc (G-353)*

Visionary Ventures LLC 443 718-9777
2830 Amendale Rd Sterling (20164) *(G-13554)*

Vista View Govt Solutions, Gainesville *Also called Gary Burns (G-5585)*

Vista-Graphics Inc 804 559-6140
7003 Mechanicsville Tpke # 1016 Mechanicsville (23111) *(G-8696)*

Vista-Graphics Inc (PA) **757 422-8979**
1264 Perimeter Pkwy Virginia Beach (23454) *(G-14925)*

Vistaprint 757 483-2357
3823 Springbloom Dr Portsmouth (23703) *(G-10498)*

Vistashare LLC 540 432-1900
1400 Technology Dr Rockingham (22802) *(G-12282)*

Visual Communication Co Inc 540 427-1060
231 Red Valley Rd Boones Mill (24065) *(G-1899)*

Visual Communication Co Inc (PA) **540 427-1060**
229 Red Valley Rd Boones Mill (24065) *(G-1900)*

Visual GRAphics&designs 804 221-6983
8283 Wetherden Dr Mechanicsville (23111) *(G-8697)*

Vita Specialty Foods Inc 540 542-0195
255 Tyson Dr Winchester (22603) *(G-15504)*

Vitae Spirits Distillery LLC 434 242-0350
715 Henry Ave Charlottesville (22903) *(G-2903)*

Vital Signs & Displays LLC 540 656-8303
4307 Island View Ln King George (22485) *(G-7120)*

Vitalcode Inc 703 622-1154
21299 Southolme Way Ashburn (20147) *(G-1351)*

Vitara LLC (PA) **972 200-3680**
43771 Brownburg Pl Chantilly (20152) *(G-2564)*

Vitasecrets USA LLC 919 212-1742
3327 Duke St Alexandria (22314) *(G-378)*

Vitaspan Corporation 866 459-2773
2503 N Harrison St 311 Arlington (22207) *(G-1214)*

Vitesco Technologies Usa LLC 757 875-7000
615 Bland Blvd Newport News (23602) *(G-9376)*

Vitex Packaging Inc 757 538-3115
1137 Progress Rd Suffolk (23434) *(G-13779)*

Vitex Packaging Group Inc (HQ) **757 538-3115**
1137 Progress Rd Suffolk (23434) *(G-13780)*

Vitrulan Corporation 540 949-8206
201 Rosser Ave Ste 7 Waynesboro (22980) *(G-15145)*

Viva La Cupcake 540 400-0806
2123 Crystal Sprng Ave Sw Roanoke (24014) *(G-12224)*

Vivaan Metals LLC 571 309-3007
45662 Terminal Dr Ste 105 Sterling (20166) *(G-13555)*

Vizini Incorporated 703 508-8662
11 New Cut Rd Round Hill (20141) *(G-12394)*

Vk Printing 703 435-5502
605 Carlisle Dr Herndon (20170) *(G-6842)*

Vlh Transportation Inc 757 880-5772
107 Bowen Dr Hampton (23666) *(G-6265)*

Vlynns 540 904-2844
2501 Williamson Rd Ne Roanoke (24012) *(G-12225)*

Vmacs, Chesapeake *Also called Virginia Mobile AC Systems Inc (G-3362)*

Vmek Group LLC 804 380-1831
2719 Oak Lake Blvd Midlothian (23112) *(G-8919)*

Vmek Sorting Technology, Midlothian *Also called Vmek Group LLC (G-8919)*

Vocalzmusic 703 798-2587
118 Spring Lake Dr Stafford (22556) *(G-13211)*

Voell Custom Kitchens Inc 703 528-1776
4788 Lee Hwy Arlington (22207) *(G-1215)*

Voestlpine High Prfmce Mtls Co 434 575-7994
2306 Eastover Dr South Boston (24592) *(G-12792)*

Vogel Lubrication 757 380-8585
2115 Aluminum Ave Hampton (23661) *(G-6266)*

Voice 1 Communication LLC 804 795-7503
3828 Pheasant Chase Dr Richmond (23231) *(G-11441)*

Voice Newspaper, The, Richmond *Also called Southside Voice Inc (G-11766)*

Voice Software LLC 571 331-2861
43277 Overview Pl Leesburg (20176) *(G-7374)*

Volarre Inc 202 258-2640
1350 Beverly Rd 115-197 Mc Lean (22101) *(G-8577)*

Vollara LLC 800 704-2378
300 E Valley Dr Bristol (24201) *(G-1998)*

Volour Pub 757 547-6483
5635 Banbury Ct Virginia Beach (23462) *(G-14926)*

Voltmed Inc 443 799-3072
2000 Kraft Dr Ste 1108 Blacksburg (24060) *(G-1805)*

Volvo Group North America LLC 336 393-2000
4881 Cougar Trail Rd Dublin (24084) *(G-4174)*

Volvo Penta Marine Pdts LLC (HQ) **757 436-2800**
1300 Volvo Penta Dr Chesapeake (23320) *(G-3364)*

Volvo Penta of Americas LLC 757 436-2800
1300 Volvo Pkwy Chesapeake (23320) *(G-3365)*

Von Holtzbrinck Publishing 540 672-9311
14301 Litchfield Dr Orange (22960) *(G-10230)*

Vortex Industries LLC 703 732-5458
4078 Fountainside Ln Fairfax (22030) *(G-4694)*

Vortex Iron Works, Lorton *Also called Canaan Welding LLC (G-7469)*

Voyager Software Inc 919 802-3232
3908 Wythe Ave Richmond (23221) *(G-11815)*

Vpgc, Hinton *Also called Virginia Plty Growers Coop Inc (G-6906)*

Vpgc LLC (PA) **540 867-4000**
6349 Rawley Pike Hinton (22831) *(G-6907)*

Vps Services Inc 202 538-1990
43918 Camellia St Ashburn (20147) *(G-1352)*

Vqc Inc 434 447-5091
1 Northside Indus Park South Hill (23970) *(G-12863)*

Vr Technologies, Poquoson *Also called Van Rosendale John (G-10378)*

Vrenp LLC 757 510-7770
3916 Deep Creek Blvd Portsmouth (23702) *(G-10499)*

Vsd LLC 757 498-4766
5700 Ward Ave Virginia Beach (23455) *(G-14927)*

VSE Aviation Inc (HQ) **703 328-4600**
6348 Walker Ln Alexandria (22310) *(G-606)*

VT Aepco Inc 703 658-7500
5701 General Washington D Alexandria (22312) *(G-607)*

VT Milcom Inc 757 548-2956
901 Professional Pl Chesapeake (23320) *(G-3366)*

Vtech Solution Inc 571 257-0913
42730 Freedom St Chantilly (20152) *(G-2565)*

Vulcan Construction Mtls LLC 757 545-0980
3900 Shannon St Chesapeake (23324) *(G-3367)*

Vulcan Construction Mtls LLC 804 862-6665
23308 Cox Rd North Dinwiddie (23803) *(G-10069)*

Vulcan Construction Mtls LLC 804 233-9669
2800 N Hopkins Rd Richmond (23224) *(G-11816)*

Vulcan Construction Mtls LLC 757 494-3202
954 Ballentine Blvd Norfolk (23504) *(G-9785)*

Vulcan Construction Mtls LLC 804 862-6660
4120 Puddledock Rd Prince George (23875) *(G-10609)*

Vulcan Construction Mtls LLC 757 858-6500
1151 Azalea Garden Rd Norfolk (23502) *(G-9786)*

Vulcan Construction Mtls LLC 703 471-0044
22963 Concrete Plz Sterling (20166) *(G-13556)*

Vulcan Construction Mtls LLC 276 466-5436
10 Spurgeon Ln Bristol (24201) *(G-1999)*

Vulcan Machine Co. 240 486-2685
168 Cross Creek Ln Fort Valley (22652) *(G-5136)*

A L P H A B E T I C

Vulcan Materials Company...757 874-5575
700 Shields Rd Newport News (23608) ***(G-9377)***
Vulcan Materials Company...540 659-3003
100 Vulcan Quarry Rd Stafford (22556) ***(G-13212)***
Vulcan Materials Company...804 270-5385
11460 Staples Mill Rd Glen Allen (23059) ***(G-5826)***
Vulcan Materials Company...434 848-4775
2500 Belfield Rd Freeman (23856) ***(G-5513)***
Vulcan Materials Company...804 758-5000
15128 George Wash Mem Hwy Saluda (23149) ***(G-12607)***
Vulcan Materials Company...757 622-4110
954 Ballentine Blvd Norfolk (23504) ***(G-9787)***
Vulcan Materials Company...540 898-6210
9201 Leavells Rd Fredericksburg (22407) ***(G-5388)***
Vulcan Materials Company...804 693-3606
5266 George Wash Mem Hwy Gloucester (23061) ***(G-5866)***
Vulcan Materials Company...804 693-3606
5266 George Washington Me Gloucester (23061) ***(G-5867)***
Vulcraft Division, North Chesterfield *Also called Nucor Corporation* ***(G-9941)***
W & B Fabricators Inc...276 928-1060
111 Enterprise Ln Rocky Gap (24366) ***(G-12308)***
W & M Backhoe Service...540 775-7185
7296 Passapatanzy Dr King George (22485) ***(G-7121)***
W & O Supply Inc...757 967-9959
500 Premier Pl Portsmouth (23704) ***(G-10500)***
W & S Forbes Inc...757 498-7446
2716 Virginia Beach Blvd Virginia Beach (23452) ***(G-14928)***
W A Cleaton and Sons Inc...804 443-2200
622 Charlotte St Tappahannock (22560) ***(G-13824)***
W A Marks Fine Woodworking...434 973-9785
5026 Burnley Ln Barboursville (22923) ***(G-1569)***
W Berg Press...757 238-9663
1620 Adams Dr W Suffolk (23436) ***(G-13781)***
W D Barnette Enterprise Inc...757 494-0530
1332 Truxton St Chesapeake (23324) ***(G-3368)***
W E Ragland Logging Co...434 286-2705
1051 Goults Rd Scottsville (24590) ***(G-12670)***
W Ellery Kellum Inc...804 438-5476
96 Shipyard Ln Weems (22576) ***(G-15151)***
W J Cox & Sons Lumber Co, Moneta *Also called Marcus Cox & Sons Inc* ***(G-8971)***
W M S B R G Grafix...757 565-5200
5810 Mooretown Rd Ste B Williamsburg (23188) ***(G-15336)***
W P L Incorporated...540 298-0999
185 W Spotswood Ave Elkton (22827) ***(G-4339)***
W R Deacon & Sons Timber Inc...540 463-3832
209 Sawmill Ln Lexington (24450) ***(G-7422)***
W R Grace & Co-Conn...540 752-6048
1101 Intl Pkwy Ste 121 Fredericksburg (22406) ***(G-5499)***
W R Meadows Inc...434 797-1321
250 Celotex Dr Danville (24541) ***(G-4048)***
W T Brownley Co Inc...757 622-7589
523 W 24th St Norfolk (23517) ***(G-9788)***
W T Jones & Sons Inc...804 633-9737
17258 Doggetts Fork Rd Ruther Glen (22546) ***(G-12463)***
W W Burton...540 547-4668
16272 Reva Rd Reva (22735) ***(G-11003)***
W W Distributors...804 301-2308
4901 W Leigh St Richmond (23230) ***(G-11442)***
W W W Electronics Inc...434 973-4702
3670 Dobleann Dr Charlottesville (22911) ***(G-2714)***
W&W-Afco Steel LLC...276 669-6649
15083 Industrial Park Rd Bristol (24202) ***(G-2040)***
Wabrasives, Bedford *Also called Winoa USA Inc* ***(G-1664)***
Wac Enterprises LLC...757 342-7202
410 Lightfoot Rd Ste G Williamsburg (23188) ***(G-15337)***
Wade F Anderson...804 358-8204
204 N Hamilton St Ste A Richmond (23221) ***(G-11817)***
Wade M Marcita...804 437-2066
11631 Cedar Mill Ct Chesterfield (23838) ***(G-3540)***
Wades Flour Mill, Raphine *Also called Wades Mill Inc* ***(G-10751)***
Wades Mill Inc...540 348-1400
55 Kennedy Wdes Mill Loop Raphine (24472) ***(G-10751)***
Waggy Pups, Manassas *Also called Smbltc Corp* ***(G-8158)***
Wahoo Industries...434 929-2466
3000 Lennox St Lynchburg (24501) ***(G-7835)***
Wal-Star Inc...434 685-1094
696 Inman Rd Danville (24541) ***(G-4049)***
Walashek Holdings Inc (PA)...**757 853-6007**
3411 Amherst St Norfolk (23513) ***(G-9789)***
Walashek Industrial & Mar Inc...757 853-6007
3411 Amherst St Norfolk (23513) ***(G-9790)***
Walashek Industrial & Mar Inc (HQ)...**202 624-2880**
3411 Amherst St Norfolk (23513) ***(G-9791)***
Walberg Aerospace...321 634-6349
49 W Queens Way Hampton (23669) ***(G-6267)***
Walden's Brother Marina, Deltaville *Also called Waldens Marina Inc* ***(G-4087)***
Waldens Marina Inc...804 776-9440
1224 Timberneck Rd Deltaville (23043) ***(G-4087)***
Walker Virginia...757 652-0430
346 Circuit Ln Newport News (23608) ***(G-9378)***
Walker Branch Lumber...434 676-3199
276 Hite Ln Kenbridge (23944) ***(G-7036)***
Walker Custom Rifles...540 399-1632
19234 Inglewood Rd Culpeper (22701) ***(G-3929)***
Walker Iron Works, Woodbridge *Also called R F J Ltd* ***(G-15788)***
Walker Machine and Fndry Corp...540 344-6265
2415 Russell Ave Sw Roanoke (24015) ***(G-12226)***
Walker Sand & Stone Inc...540 775-5024
12542 James Madison Pkwy King George (22485) ***(G-7122)***
Walker Sand Stone...540 775-5024
19238 Inglewood Rd Culpeper (22701) ***(G-3930)***
Walkers Certified Welding Inc...804 541-2612
1102 Plant Rd Hopewell (23860) ***(G-6943)***
Walkers Cove Publishing LLC...703 957-4052
24890 Castleton Dr Chantilly (20152) ***(G-2566)***
Walkers Creek Cabinet Works...540 348-5810
3906 Walkers Creek Rd Middlebrook (24459) ***(G-8714)***
Walkers Welding...214 779-0089
16560 Chstnut Overlook Dr Purcellville (20132) ***(G-10686)***
Wall To Wall Signs...703 821-2358
8455 Tyco Rd Ste E Vienna (22182) ***(G-14155)***
Wallace Precision Tooling...540 456-6437
9734 Batesville Rd Afton (22920) ***(G-95)***
Wallace-Caliva Publishing LLC...703 313-4813
8602 Howrey Ct Annandale (22003) ***(G-792)***
Waller Brothers Trophy Shop...434 376-5465
1074 Jesses Ln Nathalie (24577) ***(G-9104)***
Wallpaper Fitted Clothing Co...757 639-8531
1035 W 25th St Ste F1 Norfolk (23517) ***(G-9792)***
Walls Lithographics, Chantilly *Also called Chantilly Services Inc* ***(G-2392)***
Wallstreetwindow, Danville *Also called Timingwallstreet Inc* ***(G-4041)***
Wallye LLC...631 320-8868
43577 Mckay Ter Chantilly (20152) ***(G-2567)***
Walmer Enterprises...703 461-9330
39 Monument Dr Montross (22520) ***(G-9028)***
Walpole Woodworkers Inc...703 433-9929
45681 Okbrook Ct Ste 109 Sterling (20166) ***(G-13557)***
Walrose Woodworks...276 762-3917
550 Red Oak Ridge Rd Castlewood (24224) ***(G-2259)***
Walsh Tops Inc...757 523-1934
1717 S Park Ct Chesapeake (23320) ***(G-3369)***
Walsworth Yearbooks VA East...757 636-7104
5237 Thatcher Way Virginia Beach (23456) ***(G-14929)***
Walter Hedge...757 548-4750
833 Principal Ln Chesapeake (23320) ***(G-3370)***
Walter L James...703 622-5970
5176 Tilbury Way Woodbridge (22193) ***(G-15828)***
Walter Pillow Logging...434 283-5449
6231 Covered Bridge Rd Gladys (24554) ***(G-5698)***
Walter Winget...757 339-0303
12109 Kings Creek Ct Carrollton (23314) ***(G-2247)***
Walters Printing & Mfg Co...540 345-8161
315 22nd St Nw Roanoke (24017) ***(G-12227)***
Walton Industries Inc...540 898-7888
10699 Courthouse Rd Fredericksburg (22407) ***(G-5389)***
Walton Lumber Co Inc...540 894-5444
2463 Pendleton Rd Mineral (23117) ***(G-8952)***
Walton Wiring Inc...804 556-3104
2278 Pony Farm Rd Maidens (23102) ***(G-7893)***
Waltrip Recycling Inc...757 229-0434
11 Marclay Rd Williamsburg (23185) ***(G-15338)***
Wammoth Services LLC...571 309-2969
3360 Post Office Rd # 2023 Woodbridge (22193) ***(G-15829)***
Wanda Eubanks...804 615-7095
110 Cotton Blossom Ct Fredericksburg (22405) ***(G-5500)***
Wanderers Hideaway...904 480-6117
405 N Second St Hampton (23664) ***(G-6268)***
Wang Sign Holdings LLC...757 595-3278
1215 Grge Wash Mem Hwy St Yorktown (23693) ***(G-16000)***
War Fighter Specialties LLC...540 742-4187
155 S Mcdaniel Ln Shenandoah (22849) ***(G-12697)***
Warbird Turkey Calls LLC...540 968-0415
4123 Sharon Ln Clifton Forge (24422) ***(G-3683)***
Warcollar Industries LLC...703 981-2862
504 Park St Ne Vienna (22180) ***(G-14156)***
Ward Entp Fabrication LLC...757 675-5712
31 Regal Way Hampton (23669) ***(G-6269)***
Warden Shackle Express...540 980-2056
601 1st St Ne Pulaski (24301) ***(G-10649)***
Warden Systems...703 627-8002
101 Executive Dr Ste E Sterling (20166) ***(G-13558)***
Wards Soul Food Kitchen...757 865-7069
2710 N Armistead Ave F Hampton (23666) ***(G-6270)***
Wards Wldg & Fabrication LLC...540 219-1460
15251 Wrecker Ct Brandy Station (22714) ***(G-1942)***
Warm Springs Mtn Woodworks...540 839-9747
71 Besley Ln Hot Springs (24445) ***(G-6950)***
Warren County Report Newspaper, Front Royal *Also called Daniel Patrick McDermott* ***(G-5528)***

Warren Mastery Enterprises Inc.................................877 207-6370
12357 Saint Lukes Rd Sedley (23878) *(G-12681)*

Warren Sentinel...540 635-4174
429 N Royal Ave Front Royal (22630) *(G-5563)*

Warren Ventures LLC..804 267-9098
6822 Old Jahnke Rd Richmond (23225) *(G-11818)*

Warrior Luggage Company......................................301 523-9010
5601c General Wash Dr Alexandria (22312) *(G-608)*

Warrior Trail Consulting LLC (PA)...........................**703 349-1967**
4000 Legato Rd Ste 1100 Fairfax (22033) *(G-4580)*

Warriorware LLC..804 338-9431
8825 Lyndale Dr North Chesterfield (23235) *(G-10010)*

Warthan Ammunition Solutions, Blackstone *Also called Bethany Warthan* *(G-1811)*

Warthen, C W Company, Lynchburg *Also called Brook Brinders Limited* *(G-7661)*

Warvel Products, Haymarket *Also called Trm Inc* *(G-6452)*

Warwick Custom Kitchens, Newport News *Also called Steve K Jones* *(G-9347)*

Warwick House Publishers, Lynchburg *Also called Warwick Publishers Inc* *(G-7836)*

Warwick Publishers Inc...434 846-1200
720 Court St Lynchburg (24504) *(G-7836)*

Washburn Sign Services Inc...................................540 483-5784
10970 Sontag Rd Martinsville (24112) *(G-8350)*

Washer Way Pressure Cleaning, Disputanta *Also called Robert E Horne* *(G-4113)*

Washing On Wheels Inc...276 699-6275
216 River Bluff Dr Ivanhoe (24350) *(G-7006)*

Washingtnpost Nwsweek Intrctiv..............................703 469-2500
1560 Wilson Blvd Ste 800 Arlington (22209) *(G-1216)*

Washington & Baltimore Suburba.............................703 904-1004
20 Pidgeon Hill Dr # 201 Sterling (20165) *(G-13559)*

Washington & Washington, Charlottesville *Also called Eric Washington* *(G-2626)*

Washington Aed Education Fund...............................703 739-9513
121 N Henry St Alexandria (22314) *(G-379)*

Washington Blade..202 747-2077
1645 Trap Rd Vienna (22182) *(G-14157)*

Washington Business Info Inc.................................703 538-7600
300 N Washington St # 200 Falls Church (22046) *(G-4927)*

Washington Business Journal, Arlington *Also called American City Bus Journals Inc* *(G-852)*

Washington Cabinetry...703 466-5388
4124 Walney Rd Chantilly (20151) *(G-2518)*

Washington County Meat Packing.............................276 466-3000
20505 Campground Rd Bristol (24202) *(G-2041)*

Washington DC Lndmark Card Fnd, Middleburg *Also called Patricia Gavin* *(G-8731)*

Washington Drug Letter, Falls Church *Also called Washington Business Info Inc* *(G-4927)*

Washington International...703 757-5965
967 Evonshire Ln Great Falls (22066) *(G-5983)*

Washington Post, Richmond *Also called Toro-Aire Inc* *(G-11789)*

Washington Post, Alexandria *Also called Wp Company LLC* *(G-616)*

Washington Post, Fairfax *Also called Wp Company LLC* *(G-4695)*

Washington Post, Amissville *Also called Wp Company LLC* *(G-724)*

Washington Post, Leesburg *Also called Wp Company LLC* *(G-7381)*

Washington Wdwrkrs Guild of NA.............................703 222-3460
13893 Walney Park Dr Chantilly (20151) *(G-2519)*

Water Chemistry Incorporated................................540 343-3618
3404 Aerial Way Dr Sw Roanoke (24018) *(G-12022)*

Water Filtration Plant..276 656-5137
302 Clearview Dr Martinsville (24112) *(G-8351)*

Water King Conditioners..540 667-5821
929 Front Royal Pike Winchester (22602) *(G-15505)*

Water Technologies Inc...540 366-9799
7525 Milk A Way Dr Roanoke (24019) *(G-12023)*

Water Treatment Plant, Coeburn *Also called Wise County Psa* *(G-3705)*

Water Treatment Plant, Radford *Also called The City of Radford* *(G-10741)*

Watercraft Logistics Svcs Co..................................757 348-3089
1981 Stillwood Ln Virginia Beach (23456) *(G-14930)*

Waterford Past-Thymes..703 434-1758
35862 Camotop Ct Round Hill (20141) *(G-12395)*

Waterford Pastthymes...703 431-4095
16039 Hamilton Station Rd Waterford (20197) *(G-15084)*

Waterford Printing Inc...757 442-5616
12133 Bank Ave Exmore (23350) *(G-4387)*

Waterline Nnk LLC...804 577-4160
80 S Main St Kilmarnock (22482) *(G-7079)*

Waterneer USA Inc..703 655-2279
4451 Brkfld Crprt Dr Chantilly (20151) *(G-2520)*

Waters Group Inc...703 791-3607
9641 Leeta Cornus Ln Nokesville (20181) *(G-9404)*

Watertree Press LLC...757 512-5517
512 Flax Mill Dr Chesapeake (23322) *(G-3371)*

Waterway Guide Media LLC....................................804 776-8999
137 Neptune Ln Deltaville (23043) *(G-4088)*

Watkins Industries LLC..540 371-5007
1200 Dover Creek Ln Manakin Sabot (23103) *(G-7907)*

Watkins Products...757 461-2800
1172 Janaf Pl Norfolk (23502) *(G-9793)*

Watson Machine Corporation..................................804 598-1500
2052 New Dorset Rd Powhatan (23139) *(G-10583)*

Watson Wood Yard..540 895-0006
5730 Courthouse Rd Spotsylvania (22551) *(G-12923)*

Watson Wood Yard (PA).......................................**540 854-7703**
11237 Dulin Ln Mine Run (22508) *(G-8941)*

Watts & Ward Inc..703 435-3388
45668 Terminal Dr Ste 100 Sterling (20166) *(G-13560)*

Watts Fabrication & Welding...................................804 798-5988
11535 Fox Cross Rd Ashland (23005) *(G-1507)*

Waughs Logging...540 854-5676
5125 Bushy Mountain Rd Culpeper (22701) *(G-3931)*

Wave Printing & Graphics Inc.................................540 373-1600
220 Industrial Dr Fredericksburg (22408) *(G-5390)*

Wave Rider Manufacturing.....................................804 654-9427
16294 General Puller Hwy Deltaville (23043) *(G-4089)*

Wavelab Inc...703 860-9321
12007 Sunrise Valley Dr Reston (20191) *(G-10987)*

Waverly Feed Mill, Waverly *Also called Murphy-Brown LLC* *(G-15085)*

Waveset..703 904-7411
171 Elden St Herndon (20170) *(G-6843)*

Way With Words Publishing LLC..............................703 583-1825
3316 Dondis Creek Dr Triangle (22172) *(G-13900)*

Wayland Custom Calibers LLC................................540 533-6842
100 Cobble Stone Dr Winchester (22602) *(G-15506)*

Wayne Garrett Logging Inc....................................757 866-8472
2022 Sunken Meadow Rd Spring Grove (23881) *(G-12932)*

Wayne Harbin Builder Inc......................................757 220-8860
3705 Strawberry Plains Rd D Williamsburg (23188) *(G-15339)*

Wayne Hudson..434 568-6361
6900 Craftons Gate Hwy Drakes Branch (23937) *(G-4136)*

Waynesboro Alloy Works Inc..................................540 965-4038
1607 N Alleghany Ave Covington (24426) *(G-3802)*

Waynesboro Tool & Grinding Svc.............................540 949-7912
775 N Bayard Ave Waynesboro (22980) *(G-15146)*

Wayrick Inc..276 988-8091
1722 U S Highway 19 Lebanon (24266) *(G-7211)*

Wb Fresh Press LLC...757 485-3176
1009 Keltic Cir Chesapeake (23323) *(G-3372)*

Wcbd-TV (nbc 2)...804 649-6000
333 E Franklin St Richmond (23219) *(G-11819)*

WDFUP LLC...757 309-6214
1708 Todds Ln Unit B2 Hampton (23666) *(G-6271)*

We All Scream...804 716-1157
4023 Macarthur Ave Richmond (23227) *(G-11443)*

We Socialize For You, Norfolk *Also called Freshwter Parl Media Group LLC* *(G-9559)*

We Sullivan Co..804 273-0905
3751 Westerre Pkwy Ste B Richmond (23233) *(G-11444)*

We Think In Ink, Ashland *Also called Craftsmen Printing Inc* *(G-1398)*

Weaber Inc...804 876-3588
10134 Kings Dominion Blvd Doswell (23047) *(G-4127)*

Wealthy Sistas Media Group....................................800 917-9435
4222 Fortuna Center Plz Dumfries (22025) *(G-4262)*

Weapons Analysis LLC..540 371-9134
118 Cleremont Dr Fredericksburg (22405) *(G-5501)*

Weapons System Division, Radford *Also called Northrop Grumman Systems Corp* *(G-10732)*

Wear Red Lipstick LLC..703 627-2123
6616 Smiths Trce Centreville (20120) *(G-2352)*

Wearable Art, Mc Lean *Also called Ileen Shefferman Designs* *(G-8464)*

Wearmax Inc...631 361-7222
20398 Rupert Island Pl Potomac Falls (20165) *(G-10510)*

Weatherly LLC...703 593-3192
12763 Stone Lined Cir Woodbridge (22192) *(G-15830)*

Weathertite Industries Inc......................................703 830-8001
13410 Sand Rock Ct Chantilly (20151) *(G-2521)*

Weaver Logging, Amelia Court House *Also called David C Weaver* *(G-654)*

Web Transitions Inc..540 334-1707
109 Main St Boones Mill (24065) *(G-1901)*

WEB Welding LLC..703 212-4840
116 S Jordan St Alexandria (22304) *(G-380)*

Webb Furniture Enterprises Inc (PA)........................**276 236-5111**
117 Gillespie Ln Galax (24333) *(G-5654)*

Webb Furniture Enterprises Inc................................276 236-6141
300 E Grayson St Galax (24333) *(G-5655)*

Webb Particle Board, Galax *Also called Webb Furniture Enterprises Inc* *(G-5655)*

Webb-Mason Inc..703 391-0626
2448 Fairhunt Ct Oakton (22124) *(G-10164)*

Webb-Mason Inc..804 897-1990
2418 Gran Ridge Rd Ste D Rockville (23146) *(G-12303)*

Webb-Mason Inc..703 242-7278
1897 Preston White Dr # 300 Reston (20191) *(G-10988)*

Webdmg LLC..757 633-5033
392 Collier Cres Suffolk (23434) *(G-13782)*

Webgear Inc..703 532-1000
1934 Old Gallows Rd # 20 Vienna (22182) *(G-14158)*

Weblogic..703 645-0263
2306 Arden St Vienna (22027) *(G-14159)*

Websauce Software LLC..540 319-4002
20 W Washington St Lexington (24450) *(G-7423)*

Weda Water Inc...757 515-4338
1928 Sandee Cres Virginia Beach (23454) *(G-14931)*

Weekend Detailer LLC...757 345-2023
4771 Pelegs Way Williamsburg (23185) *(G-15340)*

ALPHABETIC

Weekly Weeder Co ... 757 618-9506
1400 Fancy Ct Virginia Beach (23454) *(G-14932)*
Wegmann Usa Inc (HQ) ... **434 385-1580**
30 Millrace Dr Lynchburg (24502) *(G-7837)*
Wegner Metal Arts Inc ... 540 373-5662
520 Wolfe St Fredericksburg (22401) *(G-5235)*
Weibel Equipment Inc ... 571 278-1989
44001 Indian Fields Ct Leesburg (20176) *(G-7375)*
Weider History Group Inc ... 703 779-8388
19300 Promenade Dr Leesburg (20176) *(G-7376)*
Weightpack Inc ... 804 598-4512
3490 Anderson Hwy Powhatan (23139) *(G-10584)*
Weights N Lipstick ... 251 404-8154
6128 Bradford Dr Suffolk (23435) *(G-13783)*
Weil Group Resources LLC (PA) ... **804 643-2828**
416 W Franklin St Richmond (23220) *(G-11820)*
Weiman Company Division, Bassett *Also called Bassett Furniture Inds NC LLC* *(G-1579)*
Weiss Soni ... 703 264-5848
2158 Cartwright Pl Reston (20191) *(G-10989)*
Weksler Glass Thermometer Corp ... 434 977-4544
556 Dettor Rd Ste 102 Charlottesville (22903) *(G-2904)*
Welcome Home Honey, Chesapeake *Also called Patricia Moore* *(G-3234)*
Welcome To Beaulieu Vineyard ... 707 967-5233
2345 Crystal Dr Ste 910 Arlington (22202) *(G-1217)*
Welcomepoint LLC ... 703 371-0499
2260 Cartbridge Rd Falls Church (22043) *(G-4891)*
Weld America, Norfolk *Also called Colonnas Ship Yard Inc* *(G-9497)*
Weld Pro LLC ... 434 531-5811
18180 James Madison Hwy Troy (22974) *(G-13937)*
Welder For Hire, Hampton *Also called Aaron D Crouse* *(G-6067)*
Welders Supply & Fabricators, Staunton *Also called Heinrich Enterprises Inc* *(G-13265)*
Welding & Fabrication LLC ... 540 907-7461
1298 Warrenton Rd Fredericksburg (22406) *(G-5502)*
Welding Fabrication & Design ... 757 739-0025
720 Canal Dr Chesapeake (23323) *(G-3373)*
Welding Supply Contractors, Staunton *Also called Messer LLC* *(G-13279)*
Welding Unlimited ... 540 833-4146
6220 Grist Mill Rd Linville (22834) *(G-7438)*
Weldment Dynamics LLC ... 540 840-7866
112 Mdpoint Dr Unit A2 A3 Mineral (23117) *(G-8953)*
Weldone Inc ... 804 784-8860
480 Hylton Rd Ste D Richmond (23238) *(G-11445)*
Weldprotech Inc ... 757 485-3293
801 Butler St Ste 6 Chesapeake (23323) *(G-3374)*
Well Hung Vineyard ... 434 245-0182
5274 Ivy Rd Charlottesville (22903) *(G-2905)*
Wellborn + Wright ... 804 329-0079
3801 Carolina Ave Richmond (23222) *(G-11821)*
Wellmore Energy Company LLC ... 276 530-7411
Hwy 700 Big Rock (24603) *(G-1705)*
Wells Belcher Paving Service ... 434 374-5518
747 Winston Rd Nelson (24580) *(G-9116)*
Wells Cabinet Shop ... 804 861-8325
3926 Puddledock Rd Prince George (23875) *(G-10610)*
Wells Custom Mfg LLC ... 703 623-1396
71 S 5th St Warrenton (20186) *(G-15059)*
Wells Machine Co ... 804 737-2500
15 Lumber Dr Sandston (23150) *(G-12639)*
Wells Machining LLC ... 540 380-2603
740 Givens Tyler Rd Salem (24153) *(G-12580)*
Wellsky Humn Social Svcs Corp (HQ) ... **703 674-5100**
11700 Plaza America Dr # 100 Reston (20190) *(G-10990)*
Wellspring Woodworks LLC ... 540 722-8641
435 N Braddock St Winchester (22601) *(G-15600)*
Wellzone Inc ... 703 770-2861
8270 Greensboro Dr Mc Lean (22102) *(G-8578)*
Welsh Printing Corporation ... 703 534-0232
104 E Fairfax St Falls Church (22046) *(G-4928)*
Wendell Welder LLC ... 804 935-6856
2009 Westover Hills Blvd Richmond (23225) *(G-11822)*
Wendys Embroidery ... 757 685-0414
1761 N Muddy Creek Rd Virginia Beach (23456) *(G-14933)*
Wenger Manufacturing ... 703 878-6946
3509 Mauti Ct Woodbridge (22192) *(G-15831)*
Wengers Electrical Service LLC ... 540 867-0101
134 Muddy Creek Rd Rockingham (22802) *(G-12283)*
Wep Co, Wytheville *Also called Wythe Power Equipment Co Inc* *(G-15927)*
Werrell Woodworks ... 757 581-0131
1716 S Park Ct Chesapeake (23320) *(G-3375)*
West 30 Candles ... 804 874-2461
200 W 30th St Richmond (23225) *(G-11823)*
West End Fabricators Inc ... 804 360-2106
1173 Tricounty Dr Oilville (23129) *(G-10187)*
West End Machine & Welding ... 804 266-9631
6804 School Ave Richmond (23228) *(G-11446)*
West End Precast LLC ... 276 228-5024
2055 W Lee Hwy Wytheville (24382) *(G-15922)*
West Engineering Company Inc ... 804 798-3966
10106 Lewistown Rd Ashland (23005) *(G-1508)*
West Garage Doors Inc ... 434 799-4070
1336 College Park Ext Danville (24541) *(G-4050)*
West Midland Timber LLC ... 540 570-5969
4370 W Midland Trl Lexington (24450) *(G-7424)*
West River Conveyors & McHy Co (PA) ... **276 259-5353**
8936 Dismal River Rd Oakwood (24631) *(G-10171)*
West Rock ... 434 352-2804
6969 Richmond Hwy Appomattox (24522) *(G-826)*
West Shore Cabinetry ... 804 739-2985
14301 West Shore Ln Midlothian (23112) *(G-8920)*
West Willow Pubg Group LLC ... 434 386-5667
2058 Rocky Branch Dr Forest (24551) *(G-5104)*
West Wind Farm Inc ... 276 699-2020
2228 Fort Chiswell Rd Max Meadows (24360) *(G-8371)*
West Wind Farm Vinyrd & Winery, Max Meadows *Also called West Wind Farm Inc* *(G-8371)*
West Window Corporation ... 276 638-2394
226 Industrial Pk Dr Ridgeway (24148) *(G-11857)*
Westend Press LLC ... 703 992-6939
7140 Twelve Oaks Dr Fairfax Station (22039) *(G-4727)*
Western Branch Diesel Inc ... 703 369-5005
12011 Balls Ford Rd Manassas (20109) *(G-8177)*
Western Digital Corporation ... 434 933-8162
451 Cabin Ln Gladstone (24553) *(G-5689)*
Western Express Inc ... 434 348-0650
2296 Sussex Dr Emporia (23847) *(G-4370)*
Western Graphics Inc ... 575 849-1209
1259 Dartmouth Ct Alexandria (22314) *(G-381)*
Western Roto Engravers Inc ... 804 236-0902
5350 Lewis Rd Sandston (23150) *(G-12640)*
Western Sheet Metal Inc ... 804 732-0230
23610 Airport Rd North Dinwiddie (23803) *(G-10070)*
Westland Technologies Inc ... 703 477-9847
4501 Singer Ct Rm 220-47 Chantilly (20151) *(G-2522)*
Westmont Woodworking Inc ... 757 287-2442
421 E Westmont Ave Norfolk (23503) *(G-9794)*
Westmoreland Pallet Compan ... 804 224-9450
3941 Longfield Rd Colonial Beach (22443) *(G-3729)*
Weston Company ... 540 349-1200
6303 Vint Hill Rd Gainesville (20155) *(G-5621)*
Weston Solutions Inc ... 757 819-5300
2 Eaton St Ste 603 Hampton (23669) *(G-6272)*
Westover Dairy ... 434 528-2560
2801 Fort Ave Lynchburg (24501) *(G-7838)*
Westrock Commercial LLC (HQ) ... **804 444-1000**
501 S 5th St Richmond (23219) *(G-11824)*
Westrock Converting LLC ... 276 632-7175
500 Frith Dr Bldg A Ridgeway (24148) *(G-11858)*
Westrock Cp LLC ... 804 236-3237
5640 Lewis Rd Sandston (23150) *(G-12641)*
Westrock Cp LLC ... 276 632-0698
588 Industrial Park Rd Ridgeway (24148) *(G-11859)*
Westrock Cp LLC ... 804 222-6380
2900 Sprouse Dr Richmond (23231) *(G-11447)*
Westrock Cp LLC ... 804 226-5840
5710 S Laburnum Ave Richmond (23231) *(G-11448)*
Westrock Cp LLC ... 804 541-9600
910 Industrial St Hopewell (23860) *(G-6944)*
Westrock Cp LLC ... 804 843-5229
2401 King William Rd West Point (23181) *(G-15163)*
Westrock Cp LLC ... 276 632-2176
588 Industrial Park Dr Martinsville (24115) *(G-8352)*
Westrock Cp LLC ... 804 843-5416
2348 King William Ave West Point (23181) *(G-15164)*
Westrock Cp LLC ... 434 736-8505
6367 Kings Hwy Keysville (23947) *(G-7065)*
Westrock Invoice Processing, Richmond *Also called Westrock Rkt LLC* *(G-11826)*
Westrock Mwv LLC ... 540 662-6524
117 Creekside Ln Winchester (22602) *(G-15507)*
Westrock Mwv LLC ... 434 352-7132
Hwy 460 W Appomattox (24522) *(G-827)*
Westrock Mwv LLC ... 540 969-5230
104 E Riverside St Covington (24426) *(G-3803)*
Westrock Mwv LLC (HQ) ... **804 444-1000**
501 S 5th St Richmond (23219) *(G-11825)*
Westrock Mwv LLC ... 540 474-5811
6162 Potomac River Rd Monterey (24465) *(G-9014)*
Westrock Mwv LLC ... 434 685-1717
100 Leaksville Jct Rd Cascade (24069) *(G-2253)*
Westrock Mwv LLC ... 804 201-2000
11013 W Broad St Glen Allen (23060) *(G-5827)*
Westrock Mwv LLC ... 540 863-2300
300 Westvaco Rd Lowmoor (24457) *(G-7599)*
Westrock Mwv LLC ... 540 377-9745
271 Lofton Rd Raphine (24472) *(G-10752)*
Westrock Rkt LLC ... 804 444-6431
501 S 5th St Richmond (23219) *(G-11826)*
Westrock Shipping Center, West Point *Also called Westrock Cp LLC* *(G-15164)*
Westrock Virginia Corporation ... 804 444-1000
501 S 5th St Richmond (23219) *(G-11827)*

Westside Metal Fabricators....804 744-0387
1624 Oak Lake Blvd E Midlothian (23112) *(G-8921)*
Wework C/O The First Tee DC....231 632-0334
1775 Tysons Blvd Fl 5 Tysons (22102) *(G-13950)*
Weyerhaeuser Company....276 694-4404
Rr 58 Box W Stuart (24171) *(G-13639)*
Weyers Cave Tube Plant, Weyers Cave *Also called Caraustar Industrial and Con (G-15169)*
Wf Med....703 339-5388
8245 Backlick Rd Ste V Lorton (22079) *(G-7541)*
Wft Promotions LLC....757 560-5056
3753 Pear Orchard Way Suffolk (23435) *(G-13784)*
Wgb LLC....757 289-5053
3317 Trotman Wharf Dr Suffolk (23435) *(G-13785)*
Wharam's Welding, Dillwyn *Also called Curtis Wharam (G-4094)*
What Heck....757 343-4058
516 Holbrook Rd Virginia Beach (23452) *(G-14934)*
What Wood Analisa Do....757 642-2991
4736 Deerfield Ln Virginia Beach (23455) *(G-14935)*
Whataseat....276 395-7887
10131 Pine Camp Rd Coeburn (24230) *(G-3704)*
Whats Your Grind LLC....757 447-8506
300 Plover Dr Portsmouth (23704) *(G-10501)*
Whats Your Sign....276 632-0576
27 E Church St Martinsville (24112) *(G-8353)*
Whats Your Sign LLC....703 860-2075
12500 Thompson Rd Fairfax (22033) *(G-4581)*
Wheatley Racing....804 276-3670
6600 Parliament Rd North Chesterfield (23224) *(G-10044)*
Wheeler Industries LLC....540 387-2204
470 Keesling Ave Salem (24153) *(G-12581)*
Wheeler Maintenance Repair....804 586-9836
5399 Triple Bridge Rd Waverly (23890) *(G-15090)*
Wheeler Tember....540 672-4186
10386 Larmond Rd Orange (22960) *(G-10231)*
Wheeler Thurston E Logging....434 946-5265
963 Campbells Mill Rd Amherst (24521) *(G-713)*
Wheels Tracks & Safety LLC....434 846-8975
134 Grist Mill Rd Lynchburg (24501) *(G-7839)*
Wheels N Motion....804 991-3090
3297 S Crater Rd Petersburg (23805) *(G-10350)*
Where Good Grows LLC....240 506-0011
950 N Washington St # 555 Alexandria (22314) *(G-382)*
Whicker Home Industries LLC....703 675-7642
1071 Shore Dr Colonial Beach (22443) *(G-3730)*
Whicker Home Services, Colonial Beach *Also called Whicker Home Industries LLC (G-3730)*
While Software LLC....202 290-6705
11697 Hollyview Dr Great Falls (22066) *(G-5984)*
Whimsical Expressions....804 239-6550
4875 Colby Dr Lanexa (23089) *(G-7169)*
Whinks Coffee Roasters....571 330-6630
4208 Javins Dr Alexandria (22310) *(G-609)*
Whisk....804 728-1576
2100 E Main St Richmond (23223) *(G-11828)*
Whiskywrght Fine Hndcrfted Spr....703 831-2086
200 W 12th St H2-21 Waynesboro (22980) *(G-15147)*
Whiskywright Fine Handcrafted....703 398-0121
9305 Witch Hazel Way Manassas (20110) *(G-8011)*
Whisper Prayers Daily....703 690-1184
9212 Marovelli Forest Dr Lorton (22079) *(G-7542)*
Whisper Tactical LLC....757 645-5938
517 Taryn Ct Chesapeake (23320) *(G-3376)*
Whispering Pine Lawn Furn....540 789-7361
974 Duncans Chapel Rd Nw Willis (24380) *(G-15366)*
Whispering Pines Weld & Iron....434 465-0704
532 Deep Creek Rd Palmyra (22963) *(G-10260)*
Whispering Woods Software LLC....434 282-1275
1105 Druid Ave Unit R Charlottesville (22902) *(G-2906)*
White Birch Paper, Ashland *Also called Bear Island Paper Wb LLC (G-1379)*
White Brick Music....323 821-9449
206 Divot Dr Harrisonburg (22802) *(G-6387)*
White Collar 4 Hire....804 212-4604
10261 N Donegal Rd Chesterfield (23832) *(G-3541)*
White Forest Resources Inc....804 410-9231
6800 Paragon Pl Ste 440 Richmond (23230) *(G-11449)*
White Knight Press....757 814-7192
9704 Old Club Trce Henrico (23238) *(G-6591)*
White Oak Forge Ltd....540 636-4545
31 Shootz Hollow Rd Huntly (22640) *(G-6967)*
White Oak Grove Woodworks....540 763-2723
995 White Oak Grove Rd Ne Riner (24149) *(G-11866)*
White Packing Co Inc-VA (PA)....**540 373-9883**
1965 Jefferson Davis Hwy Fredericksburg (22401) *(G-5236)*
White Pines Alpacas LLC....276 475-5831
27331 Denton Valley Rd Abingdon (24211) *(G-68)*
White Properties of Winchester....540 868-0205
141 Rainville Rd Winchester (22602) *(G-15508)*
White Prpts Stor Solutions, Winchester *Also called White Properties of Winchester (G-15508)*
White Rock Truss LLC....276 445-5990
21437 Wilderness Rd Rose Hill (24281) *(G-12364)*
White Stone Oyster Lancaster, White Stone *Also called Virginia Seafoods LLC (G-15190)*
White Wave....540 434-5945
166 Dinkel Ave Bridgewater (22812) *(G-1960)*
White's Guide To Collecting, Richmond *Also called Collecting Concepts Inc (G-11162)*
Whitebarrel Winery....540 382-7619
4025 Childress Rd Christiansburg (24073) *(G-3617)*
Whiteboard Applications Inc....703 297-2835
518 Deermeadow Pl Sw Leesburg (20175) *(G-7377)*
Whitehall Robins....804 257-2000
1405 Cummings Dr Richmond (23220) *(G-11829)*
Whites Ornamental Iron Works....540 877-1047
365 Back Mountain Rd Winchester (22602) *(G-15509)*
Whitewave Foods, Mount Crawford *Also called Wwf Operating Company (G-9063)*
Whitleys Welding Inc....804 350-6203
2548 Liberty Hill Rd Powhatan (23139) *(G-10585)*
Whitlow Lumber & Logging Inc....276 930-3854
1463 Fairystone Park Hwy Stuart (24171) *(G-13640)*
Whitworth Analytics LLC....703 319-8018
435 Orchard St Nw Vienna (22180) *(G-14160)*
Wholesale, Potomac Falls *Also called Wearmax Inc (G-10510)*
Wholesome Energy LLC....540 984-8219
986 S Ox Rd Edinburg (22824) *(G-4316)*
Whooley Inc....703 307-4963
1059 Great Passage Blvd Great Falls (22066) *(G-5985)*
Whos Up Games LLC....804 248-2270
11305 Cloverhill Dr Ashland (23005) *(G-1509)*
Why Candle & Co LLC....804 876-2240
423 N 18th St Apt 303 Richmond (23223) *(G-11830)*
Why Wellness Company, The, Woodbridge *Also called Aleeta A Gardner (G-15644)*
Wichaar Inc....703 863-3451
6305 Travilah Ct Fairfax Station (22039) *(G-4728)*
Wicker Warehouse, Sterling *Also called Homeland Corporation (G-13421)*
Widner's Conveyor Belt, Chilhowie *Also called Jack Campbell Widner (G-3552)*
Wieman Upholstery, Christiansburg *Also called Interlude Home Inc (G-3598)*
Wig Splitters, Richmond *Also called Hang Men High Heating & Coolg (G-11232)*
Wigglesworth Granola LLC....703 443-0130
1423 Hague Dr Sw Leesburg (20175) *(G-7378)*
Wiglance LLC....866 301-3662
7119 Koufax Ct North Chesterfield (23234) *(G-10011)*
Wigwam Industries....434 823-4663
4950 Meeks Run Crozet (22932) *(G-3855)*
Wikoff Color Corp....540 586-8111
311 W Depot St Bedford (24523) *(G-1663)*
Wilbar Truck Equipment Inc....757 397-3200
2808 Frederick Blvd Portsmouth (23704) *(G-10502)*
Wilbur Frederick - Wood Carver....434 263-4827
14332 James River Rd Lovingston (22949) *(G-7594)*
Wilcks Lake Sheds, Prospect *Also called Wilcks Lake Storage Sheds Inc (G-10616)*
Wilcks Lake Storage Sheds Inc....434 574-5131
10316 Prince Edward Hwy Prospect (23960) *(G-10616)*
Wilcox Woodworks Inc....703 369-3455
10687 Wakeman Ct Manassas (20110) *(G-8012)*
Wild Bills Custom Screen Prtg....757 961-7576
3322 Virginia Beach Blvd # 117 Virginia Beach (23452) *(G-14936)*
Wild Flour Bread Mill, Lorton *Also called E-Tron Systems Inc (G-7482)*
Wild Things LLC (HQ)....**757 702-8773**
184 Business Park Dr # 205 Virginia Beach (23462) *(G-14937)*
Wilderness Prints....540 309-6803
2416 Scenic View Rd Moneta (24121) *(G-8985)*
Wilderwork Pbc....202 285-9455
1101 Wilson Blvd Fl 6 Arlington (22209) *(G-1218)*
Wilkins Woodworking....804 761-8081
246 Rappahannock Beach Dr Tappahannock (22560) *(G-13825)*
Wilkinson Printing Co Inc....804 264-2524
8704 Brook Rd Glen Allen (23060) *(G-5828)*
Wilkinson Woodworking....540 548-2029
4049 Woodside Dr Fredericksburg (22407) *(G-5391)*
Willard Elledge....540 984-3375
123 Stout Rd Edinburg (22824) *(G-4317)*
William B Clark....804 695-9950
8456 Roaring Springs Rd Gloucester (23061) *(G-5868)*
William B Gilman (PA)....**804 798-7812**
13423 Farrington Rd Ashland (23005) *(G-1510)*
William Baird, Owner, Vienna *Also called Bills Custom Cabinetry (G-14017)*
William Butler Aluminum....804 393-1046
3103 Kenbridge St Richmond (23231) *(G-11450)*
William G Sexton....276 988-9012
29587 Gov G C Peery Hwy North Tazewell (24630) *(G-10111)*
William H Scott....804 561-5384
7431 Military Rd Amelia Court House (23002) *(G-677)*
William K Rand III....757 410-7390
824 Greenbrier Pkwy # 100 Chesapeake (23320) *(G-3377)*
William K Whitaker....562 776-9494
8206 Fair Isle Ter Chesterfield (23838) *(G-3542)*
William Keyser....703 243-8777
309 N Edison St Arlington (22203) *(G-1219)*
William L Bonnell Company Inc (PA)....**804 330-1147**
1100 Boulders Pkwy North Chesterfield (23225) *(G-10045)*

ALPHABETIC

William L Judd Pot & China Co 540 743-3294
2904 Us Highway 211 W Luray (22835) *(G-7625)*

William Mowry Woodworking 804 282-3831
7108 Brigham Rd Richmond (23226) *(G-11451)*

William O Wills Od 540 371-9191
1823 Charles St Fredericksburg (22401) *(G-5237)*

William R Smith Company 804 733-0123
930 Winfield Rd Petersburg (23803) *(G-10351)*

William W Hoitt, Ashland *Also called Valve Automation Center* *(G-1505)*

Williams Incorporated T O 757 397-0771
300 Wythe St Portsmouth (23704) *(G-10503)*

Williams & Son Inc HL 540 775-3192
8621 Bloomsbury Rd King George (22485) *(G-7123)*

Williams Bridge Company (HQ) **703 335-7800**
8624 J D Reading Dr Manassas (20109) *(G-8178)*

Williams Brothers Lumber Inc 434 760-2951
185 Commerce Dr Ruckersville (22968) *(G-12416)*

Williams Company Incorporated 276 466-3342
101 Vance St Bristol (24201) *(G-2000)*

Williams Deburring Small Parts 540 726-7485
602 College St Narrows (24124) *(G-9099)*

Williams Fabrication Inc 540 862-4200
1201 Commerce Center Dr Covington (24426) *(G-3804)*

Williams Industrial Repair Inc 757 969-5738
113 Production Dr Yorktown (23693) *(G-16001)*

Williams Industries, Manassas *Also called Williams Bridge Company* *(G-8178)*

Williams Logging and Chipping 276 694-8077
2737 Vrgnia N Carolina Rd Spencer (24165) *(G-12875)*

Williams Lumber Supply Inc 434 376-3368
17466 Brookneal Hwy Brookneal (24528) *(G-2116)*

Williams Machine Co Inc 804 231-3892
1901 Hull St Richmond (23224) *(G-11831)*

Williams Meat Processing 276 686-4325
3823 Old Stage Rd Wytheville (24382) *(G-15923)*

Williams Pallet Company 276 930-2081
1601 Fairystone Park Hwy Stuart (24171) *(G-13641)*

Williams Welding 540 465-8818
14703 Back Rd Strasburg (22657) *(G-13602)*

Williamsburg Directory Co Inc 757 566-1981
8789 Richmond Rd W Toano (23168) *(G-13880)*

Williamsburg Distillery 757 378-2456
7218 Merrimac Trl Williamsburg (23185) *(G-15341)*

Williamsburg Distillery Inc 757 676-7950
4683 Clay Bank Rd Gloucester (23061) *(G-5869)*

Williamsburg Metal Specialties 757 229-3393
4548 The Foxes Williamsburg (23188) *(G-15342)*

Williamsburg Millwork Corp 804 994-2151
29155 Richmond Tpke Ruther Glen (22546) *(G-12464)*

Williamsburg Rd Serv, Richmond *Also called Southern States Coop Inc* *(G-11390)*

Williamsburg Welding Company, Williamsburg *Also called Brian R Hess* *(G-15215)*

Williamsburg Winery Ltd 757 229-0999
5800 Wessex Hundred Williamsburg (23185) *(G-15343)*

Williamsburg Wood Works LLC 757 817-5396
3001 Stanford Pl Williamsburg (23185) *(G-15344)*

Williamson Gear & Machine, Machipongo *Also called Heclyn Precision Gear Company* *(G-7847)*

Williamson Wood 434 823-1882
5623 Sugar Ridge Rd Crozet (22932) *(G-3856)*

Willie Gatling Jr 757 236-5206
1108 75th St Newport News (23605) *(G-9379)*

Willie Lucas 919 935-8066
4348 Granby Rd Woodbridge (22193) *(G-15832)*

Willie Slick Industries 843 310-4669
1745 Chase Arbor Cmn Virginia Beach (23462) *(G-14938)*

Willimsburg Prcess Sltions LLC 703 577-4448
4771 Winterberry Ct Williamsburg (23188) *(G-15345)*

Willis Welding & Machine Co 540 427-3038
1920 9th St Se Roanoke (24013) *(G-12228)*

Willkat Envelopes & Graphics 804 798-0243
12640 Farrington Rd Ashland (23005) *(G-1511)*

Willow Stitch LLC 804 761-5967
223 Prince St Tappahannock (22560) *(G-13826)*

Willowcroft Farm Vineyards 703 777-8161
38906 Mount Gilead Rd Leesburg (20175) *(G-7379)*

Willu LLC 844 809-4558
251 18th St S Ste 704 Arlington (22202) *(G-1220)*

Wilmas Woodworking 276 346-3611
1282 State Route 70 Jonesville (24263) *(G-7024)*

Wilner Designs Inc Jane 703 998-2551
6051 Leesburg Pike Ste 9 Falls Church (22041) *(G-4892)*

Wilrich Construction LLC 804 654-0238
1449 Latanes Mill Rd Tappahannock (22560) *(G-13827)*

Wilson & Wilson International 804 733-3180
5111 Yellowstone Dr North Dinwiddie (23803) *(G-10071)*

Wilson Enterprises Inc 804 732-6884
23011 Airpark Dr North Dinwiddie (23803) *(G-10072)*

Wilson Graphics Incorporated 804 748-0646
4405 Old Hundred Rd Chester (23831) *(G-3468)*

Wilson Industries & Svcs Un 703 472-6392
10191 Wavell Rd Fairfax (22032) *(G-4582)*

Wilson Mechanical Repair Servi 804 317-4919
9302 Blagdon Dr Mechanicsville (23116) *(G-8698)*

Wilson Pipe & Fabrication LLC 757 468-1374
1233 New Land Dr Virginia Beach (23453) *(G-14939)*

Wilson Ready Mix LLC 540 324-0555
46 Wilshire Ct Fishersville (22939) *(G-5013)*

Wilson Ready Mix LLC 434 977-2800
3906 Seminole Trl Charlottesville (22911) *(G-2715)*

Wilson Warehouse 804 991-2163
23011 Airpark Dr North Dinwiddie (23803) *(G-10073)*

Wilsons Elite Express LLC 804 517-4276
6105 Rosenblum Ct Apt 1b North Chesterfield (23234) *(G-10012)*

Wilsons Sealcoating, Vinton *Also called Darrell A Wilson* *(G-14173)*

Wilsons Woodworks 757 846-6697
102 Ellerson Ct Seaford (23696) *(G-12678)*

Wimabi Press LLC 804 282-3227
7102 Lakewood Dr Richmond (23229) *(G-11452)*

Wimberley Design, Charlottesville *Also called Wimberley Inc* *(G-2907)*

Wimberley Inc 703 242-9633
1750 Broadway St Charlottesville (22902) *(G-2907)*

Wimbrough & Sons Inc 757 399-1242
1420 King St Portsmouth (23704) *(G-10504)*

Winchendon Group Inc 703 960-0978
3907 Lakota Rd Alexandria (22303) *(G-610)*

Winchester Building Sup Co Inc 540 667-2301
2001 Millwood Pike Winchester (22602) *(G-15510)*

Winchester Business Services, Winchester *Also called Aplus Signs and Bus Svcs LLC* *(G-15529)*

Winchester Evening Star Inc 540 667-3200
100 N Loudoun St Ste 110 Winchester (22601) *(G-15601)*

Winchester Mailing Services, Winchester *Also called Winchester Printers Inc* *(G-15512)*

Winchester Metals Inc (PA) **540 667-9000**
195 Ebert Rd Winchester (22603) *(G-15511)*

Winchester Pasta, Winchester *Also called Riviana Foods Inc* *(G-15466)*

Winchester Precast Frederick, Winchester *Also called Winchester Building Sup Co Inc* *(G-15510)*

Winchester Printers Inc 540 662-6911
212 Independence Rd Winchester (22602) *(G-15512)*

Winchester Tool LLC 540 869-1150
110a Industrial Dr Winchester (22602) *(G-15513)*

Winchester Tool LLC 540 869-1150
416 Battaile Dr Winchester (22601) *(G-15602)*

Winchester Truck Repair LLC 540 398-7995
259 Tyson Dr Ste 4 Winchester (22603) *(G-15514)*

Winchester Woods Condos LLC 540 885-8390
1527 Dogwood Rd Staunton (24401) *(G-13307)*

Winchester Woodworking Corp (PA) **540 667-1700**
351 Victory Rd Winchester (22602) *(G-15515)*

Windborne Press LLC 804 227-3431
17252 Tulip Poplar Rd Beaverdam (23015) *(G-1616)*

Windham Winery On Windham Farm 540 668-6464
14727 Mountain Rd Hillsboro (20132) *(G-6881)*

Winding Creek Candle Co LLC 757 410-1991
740 Tyler Way Chesapeake (23322) *(G-3378)*

Winding Road Cellars LLC 540 364-1025
4289 Leeds Manor Rd Markham (22643) *(G-8248)*

Windmill Nursery, Louisa *Also called Michael W Gillespie* *(G-7560)*

Windmill Promotions 757 204-4688
3065 Mansfield Ln Virginia Beach (23457) *(G-14940)*

Window Architecture, Keezletown *Also called Akl Associates Ltd* *(G-7026)*

Window Fashion Design 757 253-8813
108 Ingram Rd Ste 23 Williamsburg (23188) *(G-15346)*

Windows Direct 276 755-5187
13762 Fancy Gap Hwy Cana (24317) *(G-2228)*

Windrose Media LLC 703 464-1274
11236 Chestnut Grove Sq Reston (20190) *(G-10991)*

Windrush Farm LLC 540 589-1878
9046 Copper Hill Rd Ne Copper Hill (24079) *(G-3765)*

Windryder Inc 540 545-8851
157 Warm Springs Rd Winchester (22603) *(G-15516)*

Windshield RPS By Ralph Smiley 804 690-7517
7415 Amesbury Cir Mechanicsville (23111) *(G-8699)*

Windshield Wizard 757 714-1642
946 Avenue H Norfolk (23513) *(G-9795)*

Windsor Surry Company 757 294-0853
365 Commerce Dr Dendron (23839) *(G-4091)*

Windsor Woodworking Co Inc 757 242-4141
13120 Old Suffolk Rd Windsor (23487) *(G-15608)*

Windy Hill Collections LLC 703 848-8888
1343 Gunnell Ct Mc Lean (22102) *(G-8579)*

Wine Sawmill 540 373-8328
1034 Truslow Rd Fredericksburg (22406) *(G-5503)*

Wine With Everything LLC 703 777-4899
341 Caldwell Ter Se Leesburg (20175) *(G-7380)*

Winebow Inc 800 365-9463
4800 Cox Rd Ste 300 Glen Allen (23060) *(G-5829)*

Winebow Group LLC 804 752-3670
12305 N Lakeridge Pkwy Ashland (23005) *(G-1512)*

2021 Virginia
Industrial Directory

(G-0000) Company's Geographic Section entry number

Winery At Bull Run LLC 703 815-2233
  15950 Lee Hwy Centreville (20120) *(G-2353)*

Winery At Kindred Pointe LLC 540 481-6016
  3575 Conicville Rd Mount Jackson (22842) *(G-9083)*

Winery At Lagrange 703 753-9360
  4970 Antioch Rd Haymarket (20169) *(G-6454)*

Winery Inc 703 683-1876
  6110 Berlee Dr Alexandria (22312) *(G-611)*

Winery Woodworks LLC 540 869-1542
  1215 Marlboro Rd Stephens City (22655) *(G-13329)*

Wing Tips & Unique Gifts EMB, Newport News Also called Janice Martin-Freeman *(G-9267)*

Wingman Industries LLC 540 489-3119
  597 Five Mile Mountain Rd Callaway (24067) *(G-2223)*

Wings of Our Own, Alexandria Also called Wingspan Publications *(G-383)*

Wings Plus, Fairfax Also called Anm Food Services Inc *(G-4592)*

Wings-Pizza-N-things, Gainesville Also called Ssr Foods LLC *(G-5615)*

Wingspan Publications 703 212-0005
  308 Skyhill Rd Alexandria (22314) *(G-383)*

Winmar Business Group 913 908-7413
  14109 Snickersville Dr Gainesville (20155) *(G-5622)*

Winn Industries LLC 571 334-2676
  22037 Jacobs Ford Rd Lignum (22726) *(G-7426)*

Winn Stone Products Inc 757 465-5363
  62 Sandie Point Ln Portsmouth (23701) *(G-10505)*

Winner Made LLC 757 828-7623
  570 Marc Smiley Rd Chesapeake (23324) *(G-3379)*

Winoa USA Inc (HQ) **540 586-0856**
  1 Abrasive Ave Bedford (24523) *(G-1664)*

Winpro LLC 703 450-7904
  11544 Southington Ln Herndon (20170) *(G-6844)*

Wintek Corporation 973 252-8200
  1201 Longview Estates Dr Goodview (24095) *(G-5897)*

Winter Giovanni Llc 757 343-9100
  1317 Olinger St Apt 2 Norfolk (23523) *(G-9796)*

Wintergreen Winery Ltd 434 325-2200
  Winery Ln Rr 462 Nellysford (22958) *(G-9114)*

Winterloch Publishing LLC 804 571-2782
  2400 Loch Braemar Dr North Chesterfield (23236) *(G-10013)*

Wiredup Inc 757 565-3655
  3307 Poplar Creek Ln Williamsburg (23188) *(G-15347)*

Wireless Ventures USA Inc 703 852-1350
  7900b Westpark Dr 200t Mc Lean (22102) *(G-8580)*

Wiretough Cylinders LLC 276 644-9120
  14570 Industrial Park Rd Bristol (24202) *(G-2042)*

Wisakon Woods 571 332-9844
  10001 Wisakon Trl Manassas (20111) *(G-8179)*

Wisdom Clothing Company Inc 703 433-0056
  22135 Davis Dr Ste 108 Sterling (20164) *(G-13561)*

Wisdom Oak Winery, North Garden Also called Wisdom Oak Winery *(G-10084)*

Wisdom Oak Winery 434 984-4272
  3613 Walnut Branch Ln North Garden (22959) *(G-10084)*

Wise Case Technologies LLC 757 646-9080
  3369 Litchfield Rd Virginia Beach (23452) *(G-14941)*

Wise County Psa 276 762-0159
  3055 Carfax Rd Coeburn (24230) *(G-3705)*

Wise Custom Machining 276 328-8681
  5549 Rock Bar Rd Wise (24293) *(G-15637)*

Wise Feline Inc 703 609-2686
  2606 Ridge Road Dr Alexandria (22302) *(G-384)*

Wise La Tina Publishing 202 425-1129
  2402 Alsop Ct Reston (20191) *(G-10992)*

Wise Manufacturing Inc 804 876-3335
  17182 Washington Hwy Doswell (23047) *(G-4128)*

Wise Printing Co Inc 276 523-1141
  215 Wood Ave Big Stone Gap (24219) *(G-1718)*

Wisecarver Brothers Inc 434 332-4511
  57 Wisecarver Rd Rustburg (24588) *(G-12447)*

Wiseman Weld Fabrication 571 393-8480
  4418 Berwick Pl Woodbridge (22192) *(G-15833)*

Wish Book Press, Hanover Also called Room The Wishing Inc *(G-6284)*

Witching Hour Press LLC 571 209-0019
  105 Maurice Ct Yorktown (23690) *(G-16002)*

Witt Associates Inc 540 667-3146
  118 Old Forest Cir Winchester (22602) *(G-15517)*

Wizard 818 988-2283
  8700 Formation Dr Fredericksburg (22407) *(G-5392)*

Wizard Technologies 703 625-0900
  2083 Hunters Crest Way Vienna (22181) *(G-14161)*

Wjm Printed Products Inc 757 870-1043
  125 Prince Arthur Dr Yorktown (23693) *(G-16003)*

Wld Logging & Chipping Inc 540 483-1218
  1444 Ayers Rd Glade Hill (24092) *(G-5671)*

Wm Coffman Resources LLC 800 810-9204
  138 E Main St Ste 1 Marion (24354) *(G-8245)*

Wm Industries Corp (PA) **703 666-9001**
  21355 Ridgetop Cir # 250 Sterling (20166) *(G-13562)*

Wm L Mason Fine String Instrs 540 645-7499
  509 Jackson St 1 Fredericksburg (22401) *(G-5238)*

Wmgta, Sterling Also called Wm Industries Corp *(G-13562)*

Wobanc Danforth 804 222-7877
  6954 Wildwood St Richmond (23231) *(G-11453)*

Wobsers Welding Works LLC 757 570-0440
  16058 Mill Swamp Rd Smithfield (23430) *(G-12744)*

Woerner Welding & Fabrication 804 349-6563
  3825 Hendricks Rd Midlothian (23112) *(G-8922)*

Woiw, Covington Also called Waynesboro Alloy Works Inc *(G-3802)*

Wolf Cabinetry Inc 757 498-0088
  5801 Arrowhead Dr Virginia Beach (23462) *(G-14942)*

Wolf Contracting, Newport News Also called Wolf Equipment Inc *(G-9380)*

Wolf Equipment Inc 757 596-1660
  473 Wolf Dr Newport News (23601) *(G-9380)*

Wolf Hills Enterprises 276 628-8635
  21086 Green Spring Rd Abingdon (24211) *(G-69)*

Wolf Hills Fabricators LLC 276 466-2743
  26161 Old Trail Rd Ste 2 Abingdon (24210) *(G-70)*

Wolf Hills Press LLC 276 644-3119
  2568 King Mill Pike Bristol (24201) *(G-2001)*

Wolf Zsuzsi of Budapest 703 548-3319
  105 N Union St Ste 229 Alexandria (22314) *(G-385)*

Wolffinz LLC 571 292-1427
  9406 Battle St Manassas (20110) *(G-8013)*

Wolfsbane Industries LLC 703 972-5072
  37756 Drawbridge Way Purcellville (20132) *(G-10687)*

Wolley Segap International 703 426-5164
  4369 Farm House Ln Fairfax (22032) *(G-4583)*

Wolverine Advanced Mtls LLC 540 552-7674
  201 Industrial Park Rd Se Blacksburg (24060) *(G-1806)*

Wolverine Gasket, Blacksburg Also called Wolverine Advanced Mtls LLC *(G-1806)*

Womack Newspaper Inc (PA) **434 432-1654**
  30 N Main St Chatham (24531) *(G-2941)*

Womack Publishing Co Inc (PA) **434 432-2791**
  28 N Main St Chatham (24531) *(G-2942)*

Womack Publishing Co Inc 434 352-8215
  589 Court St Appomattox (24522) *(G-828)*

Womack Publishing Co Inc 434 447-3178
  914 W Danville St South Hill (23970) *(G-12864)*

Womack Publishing Co Inc 434 369-6688
  1007 Main St Altavista (24517) *(G-645)*

Womack Publishing Co Inc 434 432-1654
  111 Baker St Emporia (23847) *(G-4371)*

Womeldorf Press, Mc Lean Also called Leigh Ann Carrasco *(G-8486)*

Womens Intuition Worldwide 703 404-4357
  116 Hillsdale Dr Sterling (20164) *(G-13563)*

Womens Media Watch Azerbaijan 253 381-9667
  42492 Mayflower Ter # 30 Brambleton (20148) *(G-1936)*

Wonder Bug Welding 703 354-9499
  6544 Fairland St Alexandria (22312) *(G-612)*

Wonderfully Made Ceramics 571 261-1633
  10079 Greenwich Wood Dr Nokesville (20181) *(G-9405)*

Wonderland Wood Works 540 636-6158
  148 Wonderland Ln Front Royal (22630) *(G-5564)*

Wonders Inc 434 845-0813
  164 Almae Dr Amherst (24521) *(G-714)*

Wood Mark T A Augusta Gla 540 885-5038
  8 Highland Ave Staunton (24401) *(G-13308)*

Wood Burn Endoscopy Center 703 752-2557
  3301 Woodburn Rd Ste 109 Annandale (22003) *(G-793)*

Wood Chux Cabinets LLC 757 409-0095
  3024 Bowling Green Dr Virginia Beach (23452) *(G-14943)*

Wood Creations 571 235-0717
  801 S Pitt St Apt 429 Alexandria (22314) *(G-386)*

Wood Creations LLC 804 553-1862
  2911 Maplewood Rd Richmond (23228) *(G-11454)*

Wood Design & Fabrication Inc 540 774-8168
  6877 Sugar Rum Ridge Rd Roanoke (24018) *(G-12024)*

Wood Harvesters 276 650-2603
  16880 Martinsville Hwy Axton (24054) *(G-1543)*

Wood Preservers Incorporated 804 333-4022
  15939 History Land Hwy Warsaw (22572) *(G-15073)*

Wood Provision 540 456-8522
  2488 Blackberry Rd Afton (22920) *(G-96)*

Wood Shop 757 824-4055
  702 Rr 679 Atlantic (23303) *(G-1526)*

Wood Television LLC 540 825-4416
  122 W Spencer St Culpeper (22701) *(G-3932)*

Wood Television LLC. 434 793-2311
  700 Monument St Danville (24541) *(G-4051)*

Wood Television LLC 276 228-6611
  460 W Main St Wytheville (24382) *(G-15924)*

Wood Television LLC 703 368-9268
  9028 Prince William St F Manassas (20110) *(G-8014)*

Wood Television LLC 276 669-2181
  320 Morrison Blvd Bristol (24201) *(G-2002)*

Wood Television LLC 540 672-1266
  110 Berry Hill Rd Orange (22960) *(G-10232)*

Wood Television LLC 434 385-5400
  101 Wyndale Dr Lynchburg (24501) *(G-7840)*

Wood Television LLC 757 539-3437
  130-132 S Saratoga St Suffolk (23434) *(G-13786)*

A
L
P
H
A
B
E
T
I
C

Wood Television LLC 434 978-7200
685 W Rio Rd Charlottesville (22901) ***(G-2716)***
Wood Television LLC 804 775-4600
111 N 4th St Richmond (23219) ***(G-11832)***
Wood Television LLC 540 948-5121
201 Main St Madison (22727) ***(G-7865)***
Wood Television LLC 804 559-8207
8460 Times Dispatch Blvd Mechanicsville (23116) ***(G-8700)***
Wood Television LLC 540 343-2405
1402 Grandin Ave Roanoke (24015) ***(G-12229)***
Wood Television LLC 804 649-6069
333 E Grace St Richmond (23219) ***(G-11833)***
Wood Television LLC 540 949-8213
544 W Main St Waynesboro (22980) ***(G-15148)***
Wood Turns 904 303-8536
2525 Southern Pines Dr Chesapeake (23323) ***(G-3380)***
Wood Works By Snyder LLC 703 203-6952
14423 Woodwill Ln Gainesville (20155) ***(G-5623)***
Wood-N-Stuff 276 686-6557
8161 Lee Hwy Rural Retreat (24368) ***(G-12433)***
Woodard LLC 540 812-5016
6104 Sperryville Pike Boston (22713) ***(G-1905)***
Woodardweb 202 337-3730
4011 Blue Slate Dr Alexandria (22306) ***(G-613)***
Woodberry Farm Inc 540 854-6967
6005 Woodberry Farm Rd Orange (22960) ***(G-10233)***
Woodbridge Printing Co 703 494-7333
14826 Build America Dr Woodbridge (22191) ***(G-15834)***
Woodcraft Co, The, South Boston *Also called Merlin Brougher* ***(G-12782)***
Woodcrafters Inc 703 736-2825
11735 Summerchase Cir # 1735 Reston (20194) ***(G-10993)***
Woodcrafters II LLC 703 499-5418
13826 Estate Manor Dr Gainesville (20155) ***(G-5624)***
Woodducks Odd Jobs Lawn Svc LL 804 932-4612
8844 Greenwood Blvd New Kent (23124) ***(G-9139)***
Wooden Caboose Inc 804 748-2101
9418 Banff Ter Chesterfield (23838) ***(G-3543)***
Wooden Leg Van Shop, Petersburg *Also called Jim Warehime* ***(G-10327)***
Woodgrain Millwork Inc 208 452-3801
Hwy 11 E Marion (24354) ***(G-8246)***
Woodhelvin Inc 540 854-6452
8961 Fox Run Dr Spotsylvania (22551) ***(G-12924)***
Woodland Artisans Ltd 276 766-3421
1294 Windsong Rd Allisonia (24347) ***(G-621)***
Woodland Group LLC 571 312-5951
509 Woodland Ter Alexandria (22302) ***(G-387)***
Woodland Logging Inc 276 669-7795
4393 Saxon Dr Bristol (24202) ***(G-2043)***
Woodlawn Precision Machine 276 236-7294
3536 Carrollton Pike Woodlawn (24381) ***(G-15846)***
Woodmark Designs 804 921-9454
6091 Terry Ville Ter Mechanicsville (23111) ***(G-8701)***
Woodmsters Cbnets Str Fixs of 434 525-4407
4730 Waterlick Rd Forest (24551) ***(G-5105)***
Woods & Waters Magazine, Bumpass *Also called Woods & Waters Publishing Lc* ***(G-2171)***
Woods & Waters Publishing Lc 540 894-9144
114 Old Quarry Ln Bumpass (23024) ***(G-2171)***
Woods & Waters Publishing Lc 540 894-5960
494 Kentucky Springs Rd Bumpass (23024) ***(G-2172)***
Woods Mill Distillery LLC 434 361-2294
1625 River Rd Faber (22938) ***(G-4392)***
Woods of Wisdom LLC 757 645-2043
113 J Farm Ln Williamsburg (23188) ***(G-15348)***
Woodsong Instruments 540 745-2708
1098 Dobbins Farm Rd Ne Floyd (24091) ***(G-5046)***
Woodwork & Cabinets LLC 703 881-1915
5425 Bowers Hill Dr Haymarket (20169) ***(G-6455)***
Woodwork Career Aliance N Amer 434 298-4650
189 Dogwood Ln Nellysford (22958) ***(G-9115)***
Woodworkers Inc 571 282-5376
219 N Cameron Ct Sterling (20164) ***(G-13564)***
Woodworking Shop Inc 757 872-0890
713 Industrial Park Dr Newport News (23608) ***(G-9381)***
Woodworking Wrkshps of The Shn 540 955-2376
5594 Senseny Rd Berryville (22611) ***(G-1700)***
Woodworks 434 636-4111
10283 Hwy Nine O Three Bracey (23919) ***(G-1924)***
Woodworks LLC 804 730-0631
8548 Anderson Ct Mechanicsville (23116) ***(G-8702)***
Woodworks LLC 757 516-8405
30443 Campbells Run Franklin (23851) ***(G-5162)***
Woodworth Virginia LLC 804 412-0206
301 Business Ln Ashland (23005) ***(G-1513)***
Woodwright Company 540 764-2539
185 Hartwood Rd Fredericksburg (22406) ***(G-5504)***
Woodwrights LLC 804 761-0775
48 Steamboat Rd Irvington (22480) ***(G-7002)***
Woodwrights Cooperative 804 358-4800
3202 Rosedale Ave Richmond (23230) ***(G-11455)***
Woody Graphics Inc 540 774-4749
6421 Merriman Rd Roanoke (24018) ***(G-12025)***
Woodys Goodys LLC 703 608-8533
2329 N Oak St Falls Church (22046) ***(G-4929)***
Woodys Woodworking Inc 703 525-2030
3132 N Nelson St Arlington (22207) ***(G-1221)***
Wool Felt Products Inc 540 981-0281
532 Luck Ave Sw Roanoke (24016) ***(G-12230)***
Woolen Mills Grill 540 323-7552
3416 Martinsburg Pike Clear Brook (22624) ***(G-3654)***
Woolen Mills Tavern LLC 434 296-2816
1125 Loving Rd Zion Crossroads (22942) ***(G-16010)***
Woolfolk Brothers LLC 540 967-0664
578 Bloomington Ln Louisa (23093) ***(G-7575)***
Woolfolk Enterprises 540 967-0664
578 Bloomington Ln Louisa (23093) ***(G-7576)***
Wooton Consulting 804 227-3418
140 Wolftrap Ct Bumpass (23024) ***(G-2173)***
Wop Hair LLC 804 277-4666
7018 Walmsley Blvd North Chesterfield (23235) ***(G-10014)***
Word College Inc 510 857-3309
13969 Baton Rouge Ct Centreville (20121) ***(G-2354)***
Word Play By Deb LLC 703 389-5112
8319 Brockham Dr Alexandria (22309) ***(G-614)***
Words On Wood Signs Inc 540 493-9353
199 Pine Grove Rd Glade Hill (24092) ***(G-5672)***
Words To Ponder Pubg Co LLC 803 567-3692
91 Snug Harbor Dr Hampton (23661) ***(G-6273)***
Wordsmith Indexing Services 540 775-3012
8112 Harrison Dr King George (22485) ***(G-7124)***
Wordsprint Inc 540 382-9111
2200 Kraft Dr Ste 2050 Blacksburg (24060) ***(G-1807)***
Wordsprint Inc (PA) **276 228-6608**
190 W Spring St Wytheville (24382) ***(G-15925)***
Work Scene Media LLC 703 910-5959
2010 Corp Rdg Ste 700 Mclean (22102) ***(G-8589)***
Workdynamics Technologies Inc 703 481-9874
11710 Plaza America Dr # 2000 Reston (20190) ***(G-10994)***
Workers On Wheels 703 549-6287
119 S Saint Asaph St Alexandria (22314) ***(G-388)***
Workflow Solutions, Fairfax *Also called R R Donnelley & Sons Company* ***(G-4535)***
Workhorse Print Solutions LLC 703 707-1648
1298 Golden Eagle Dr Reston (20194) ***(G-10995)***
Working Software LLC 703 992-6280
1301 Seaton Ln Falls Church (22046) ***(G-4930)***
Workwear Distributors, Warrenton *Also called Leading Edge Screen Printing* ***(G-15030)***
World & I 202 636-3334
3811 Tall Oak Ct Annandale (22003) ***(G-794)***
World Fashion City Inc 703 887-8123
6606 Schurtz St Alexandria (22310) ***(G-615)***
World History Group LLC 703 779-8322
1919 Gallows Rd Ste 400 Vienna (22182) ***(G-14162)***
World Media Enterprises Inc 804 559-8261
8460 Times Dispatch Blvd Mechanicsville (23116) ***(G-8703)***
World Media Pubg Solutions, Mechanicsville *Also called World Media Enterprises Inc* ***(G-8703)***
World of Color Expo LLC 703 754-3191
3507 Finish Line Dr Gainesville (20155) ***(G-5625)***
World Wide Automotive LLC (HQ) **540 667-9100**
300 W Brooke Rd Winchester (22603) ***(G-15518)***
Worldcolor Richmond, Richmond *Also called Qg LLC* ***(G-11343)***
Worldcolor Winchester, Winchester *Also called Qg LLC* ***(G-15462)***
Worldgen LLC 434 244-2849
2030 Catlin Rd Charlottesville (22901) ***(G-2717)***
Worldwide Agency LLC 202 888-5895
4601 Fairfax Dr Ste 1200 Arlington (22203) ***(G-1222)***
Worldwide Papers Inc 703 883-8049
2160 Kings Garden Way Falls Church (22043) ***(G-4893)***
Worley Machine Enterprises Inc 276 930-2695
8735 Woolwine Hwy Woolwine (24185) ***(G-15868)***
Worse LLC 512 506-0057
3012 W Broad St Richmond (23230) ***(G-11456)***
Worse For Wear, Richmond *Also called Worse LLC* ***(G-11456)***
Worth Baby Products LLC 804 644-4707
302 Hollyport Rd Henrico (23229) ***(G-6592)***
Worth Higgins & Associates Inc 804 353-0607
8770 Park Central Dr Richmond (23227) ***(G-11457)***
Worth Higgins & Associates Inc 804 353-0607
8770 Park Central Dr Richmond (23227) ***(G-11458)***
Wortham Machine and Welding 434 676-8080
532 Main St Kenbridge (23944) ***(G-7037)***
Worthen Industries Inc 804 275-9231
4107 Castlewood Rd Richmond (23234) ***(G-11067)***
Worthen Industries Inc 804 275-9231
4105 Castlewood Rd Richmond (23234) ***(G-11068)***
Worthington Millwork LLC 540 832-6391
1 Cleveland St Ste 920 Gordonsville (22942) ***(G-5919)***
Worthington Publishing 757 831-4375
509 White Oak Dr Virginia Beach (23462) ***(G-14944)***

Worthngton Architectural Mllwk, Gordonsville *Also called Worthington Millwork LLC (G-5919)*

Wp Company LLC 703 518-3000
526 King St Ste 515 Alexandria (22314) *(G-389)*

Wp Company LLC 703 799-2920
8796 Sacramento Dr # 302 Alexandria (22309) *(G-616)*

Wp Company LLC 703 392-1303
3900 University Dr # 130 Fairfax (22030) *(G-4695)*

Wp Company LLC 540 937-4380
15310 Lee Hwy Amissville (20106) *(G-724)*

Wp Company LLC 703 771-1491
305 Harrison St Se 100a Leesburg (20175) *(G-7381)*

Wpd Inc 757 859-9498
38082 Broadwater Rd Ivor (23866) *(G-7007)*

Wpo 3 Inc 757 491-4140
809 23rd St Virginia Beach (23451) *(G-14945)*

Wrack-It 434 258-4317
103 Sailview Dr Forest (24551) *(G-5106)*

Wrap Buddies LLC 855 644-2783
3118 Somerset Dr Jeffersonton (22724) *(G-7014)*

Wrap Pack Industries Inc 804 897-1351
3106 Handley Rd Midlothian (23113) *(G-8923)*

Wre/Colortech 804 236-0902
5350 Lewis Rd Ste B Sandston (23150) *(G-12642)*

Wreaths Bows & Blessings 276 340-2380
2157 Figsboro Rd Martinsville (24112) *(G-8354)*

Wreaths Galore and More LLC 804 312-6947
10649 Michmar Dr Chester (23831) *(G-3469)*

Wright Inc W F 804 561-2721
15636 Elm Cottage Rd Amelia Court House (23002) *(G-678)*

Wright Discount Entps LLC 703 580-5278
3604 Water Birch Ct Woodbridge (22192) *(G-15835)*

Wright Express 703 467-5738
1807 Michael Faraday Ct Herndon (20190) *(G-6845)*

Wright Logging LLC 434 547-4525
214 Henderson Rd Keysville (23947) *(G-7066)*

Wright Look 540 672-5085
190 Caroline St Ste F Orange (22960) *(G-10234)*

Wright Machine & Manufacturing 276 688-2391
573 Main St Bland (24315) *(G-1838)*

Wright Medical Technology Inc 703 729-0643
43288 Amanda Kay Ct Ashburn (20147) *(G-1353)*

Wright Ready Mix, Amelia Court House *Also called Wright Inc W F (G-678)*

Wright Sign Service Inc 757 566-8329
8008 Hankins Indus Park Toano (23168) *(G-13881)*

Wright Solutions Inc 703 652-7145
6339 Paddington Ln Centreville (20120) *(G-2355)*

Wrights Iron Inc 540 661-1089
13160 James Madison Hwy Orange (22960) *(G-10235)*

Wrights Trucking & Logging 434 946-5387
159 Poplar Grove Cir Amherst (24521) *(G-715)*

Wrightside, Bland *Also called Wright Machine & Manufacturing (G-1838)*

Write Impressions 757 473-1699
4977 Cleveland St Virginia Beach (23462) *(G-14946)*

Write Lab Press LLC 757 390-1030
621 Pace St Franklin (23851) *(G-5163)*

Writings That Works Newsletter, Springfield *Also called Communications Concepts Inc (G-12978)*

Writlab LLC 703 996-9162
3033 Wilson Blvd E-206 Arlington (22201) *(G-1223)*

Wrkco Inc 540 969-5000
104 E Riverside St Covington (24426) *(G-3805)*

Wss Richmond 804 722-0150
6750 Hardware Dr Prince George (23875) *(G-10611)*

Wst Products LLC 434 736-9100
131 Kings Hwy Keysville (23947) *(G-7067)*

Ww Monograms LLC 540 687-6510
35653 Millville Rd Middleburg (20117) *(G-8735)*

Wwf Operating Company 540 434-7328
6364 S Valley Pike Mount Crawford (22841) *(G-9063)*

Wwt Group Inc 804 648-1900
206 E Cary St Richmond (23219) *(G-11834)*

Wyatt Sign & Painting Company 804 733-5251
1307 Hinton St Petersburg (23803) *(G-10352)*

Wyeth, Richmond *Also called Pfizer Inc (G-11321)*

Wyeth Pharmaceuticals LLC 804 652-6000
2248 Darbytown Rd Richmond (23231) *(G-11459)*

Wyfi Industries LLC 703 333-2059
7107 Granberry Way Springfield (22151) *(G-13109)*

Wylie Wagg of Tysons LLC 703 748-0022
7505 Leesburg Pike Falls Church (22043) *(G-4894)*

Wynnvision LLC 757 419-1463
5609 Promontory Pointe Rd Midlothian (23112) *(G-8924)*

Wythe Oil Distributors Inc 276 228-4512
1185 Church St Wytheville (24382) *(G-15926)*

Wythe Power Equipment Co Inc 276 228-7371
1005 E Marshall St Wytheville (24382) *(G-15927)*

Wythe Stone Co, Wytheville *Also called Salem Stone Corporation (G-15908)*

Wytheville Custom Counter Tops 276 228-4137
495 S 6th St Wytheville (24382) *(G-15928)*

Wytheville Metals, Wytheville *Also called Jr Kauffman Inc (G-15894)*

Wytheville Plant, Wytheville *Also called Boxley Materials Company (G-15880)*

Wythken LLC 804 353-8282
900 W Leigh St Richmond (23220) *(G-11835)*

Wythken Printing, Richmond *Also called Wythken LLC (G-11835)*

Wyvern Interactive LLC 540 336-4498
3438 Front Royal Pike Winchester (22602) *(G-15519)*

Wyvern Publications 703 670-3527
14703 Dunbar Ln Woodbridge (22193) *(G-15836)*

X Press Enterprises LLC 540 587-0100
842 Sword Beach Ln Bedford (24523) *(G-1665)*

X-Com Systems LLC (HQ) **703 390-1087**
1875 Cmpus Cmmons Dr Ste Reston (20191) *(G-10996)*

X-Metrix Inc 757 450-5978
2513 Early Ct Virginia Beach (23454) *(G-14947)*

X-Stand Treestand Company LLC 540 877-2769
140 Theodore Dr Winchester (22602) *(G-15520)*

Xact Solutions Inc 703 398-2680
21386 Ashburn Run Pl Ashburn (20147) *(G-1354)*

Xanadu Enterprises, Bristol *Also called United Screen Design (G-1995)*

Xarmr Corporation 703 663-8711
8451 Hilltop Rd Fairfax (22031) *(G-4584)*

Xcalibur Software Inc 703 896-5700
20563 Qrterpath Trace Cir Sterling (20165) *(G-13565)*

Xceedium Inc 703 539-5410
2291 Wood Oak Dr Ste 200 Herndon (20171) *(G-6846)*

Xerox 703 330-4044
7890 Notes Dr Manassas (20109) *(G-8180)*

Xerox Alumni Association Inc 703 848-0624
1536 Hampton Hill Cir Mc Lean (22101) *(G-8581)*

Xlnt Solutions Inc 703 819-9265
3981 Woodberry Meadow Dr Fairfax (22033) *(G-4585)*

Xlusion CL Fulfillment LLC 571 316-9391
5209 Pan Tops Dr Stephens City (22655) *(G-13330)*

Xmc Films Inc 276 930-2848
9622 Woolwine Hwy Woolwine (24185) *(G-15869)*

Xp Manufacturing LLC 804 510-3747
1730 Rhoadmiller St Richmond (23220) *(G-11836)*

Xp Manufacturing LLC 804 833-1411
107 Hempstead Way North Chesterfield (23236) *(G-10015)*

Xp Power 540 552-0432
1700 Kraft Dr Blacksburg (24060) *(G-1808)*

Xplor Industries 804 306-6621
9702 Gayton Rd Richmond (23238) *(G-11460)*

Xpress Copy & Graphics 540 829-1785
486 James Madison Hwy Culpeper (22701) *(G-3933)*

Xsytechnologiescom 757 333-7514
1 Columbus Ctr Ste 600 Virginia Beach (23462) *(G-14948)*

Xteriors Factory Outlets Inc (PA) **804 798-6300**
16401 International St Doswell (23047) *(G-4129)*

Xteriors Manufacturing LLC 804 445-3597
420 High St Apt 409 Petersburg (23803) *(G-10353)*

Xteriors Pavers LLC 757 708-5904
553 Central Dr Virginia Beach (23454) *(G-14949)*

Xtreme Adventures Inc 757 615-4602
2140 Marina Shores Dr Virginia Beach (23451) *(G-14950)*

Xtreme Diamond LLC 703 753-0567
6868 Jockey Club Ln Haymarket (20169) *(G-6456)*

Xtreme Fbrction Pwdr Cting LLC 540 327-3020
3372 Hunting Ridge Rd Winchester (22603) *(G-15521)*

Xtreme Signs 434 447-5738
3715 Country Club Rd Brodnax (23920) *(G-2106)*

Xvd Board Sports LLC 757 504-0006
852 44th St Norfolk (23508) *(G-9797)*

Xyken LLC 703 288-1601
7921 Jones Branch Dr # 392 Mc Lean (22102) *(G-8582)*

Xymid LLC (PA) **804 423-5798**
5141 Craig Rath Blvd Midlothian (23112) *(G-8925)*

Xymid LLC 804 744-5229
1918 Ruffin Mill Rd South Chesterfield (23834) *(G-12829)*

Y & S Trading 703 430-6928
46766 Graham Cove Sq Sterling (20165) *(G-13566)*

Y2k Web Technologies 757 490-7877
3600 Mallbu Palms Dr # 202 Virginia Beach (23452) *(G-14951)*

Yacoe LLC 973 735-3095
606 W 28th St Richmond (23225) *(G-11837)*

Yakattack LLC 804 561-4274
609 2nd St Nw Burkeville (23922) *(G-2212)*

Yakattack LLC 434 392-3233
100 Industrial Park Rd Farmville (23901) *(G-4961)*

Yama Mountain Gear 434 202-9717
1304 East Market St Charlottesville (22902) *(G-2908)*

Yamco LLC 804 749-0480
9113 Derbyshire Rd Unit G Richmond (23229) *(G-11461)*

Yardsalesheadquarterscom LLC 757 503-0940
11712 Jefferson Ave C-4 Newport News (23606) *(G-9382)*

Yates Abbattoir 540 778-2123
3027 Farmview Rd Luray (22835) *(G-7626)*

Yaya Learning LLC 540 230-5051
  3720 Woodland Cir Falls Church (22041) *(G-4895)*
Yazdan Publishing Company 757 426-6009
  2432 Kestrel Ln Virginia Beach (23456) *(G-14952)*
Yba Publishing LLC 703 763-2710
  3682 King St Unit 3535 Alexandria (22302) *(G-390)*
Yeates Mfg Inc 757 465-7772
  3923 Victory Blvd Portsmouth (23701) *(G-10506)*
Yellow Bridge Software Inc 703 909-5533
  14814 Statler Dr Woodbridge (22193) *(G-15837)*
Yellow Dog Software LLC 757 818-9360
  965 Norfolk Sq Norfolk (23502) *(G-9798)*
Yeocomico Oyster Co, Kinsale Also called Bevans Oyster Company *(G-7133)*
Yeocomico Oyster Co, Kinsale Also called Bevans Oyster Company *(G-7134)*
Yes Weekly, Chatham Also called Womack Newspaper Inc *(G-2941)*
Yesco of Richmond 804 302-4391
  12730 Spectrim Ln Ste F Midlothian (23112) *(G-8926)*
Yesco Sign & Lighting Service 757 369-9827
  719 Industrial Park Dr C Newport News (23608) *(G-9383)*
Yesterdays Treasures 757 877-5153
  103 Rustling Oak Rdg Grafton (23692) *(G-5933)*
Ym Dental Lab, Chantilly Also called Dentcore Inc *(G-2406)*
Ynaffit Music Publishing 757 270-3316
  3557 Light Horse Loop Virginia Beach (23453) *(G-14953)*
Yobnug LLC 703 385-1880
  3713 Burrows Ave Fairfax (22030) *(G-4696)*
Yocums Signature Hot Rods 757 393-0700
  400 Cumberland Ave Portsmouth (23707) *(G-10507)*
Yoder Logging 804 561-3913
  15770 Redmore Ln Amelia Court House (23002) *(G-679)*
Yokohama Corp North America (HQ) **540 389-5426**
  1500 Indiana St Salem (24153) *(G-12582)*
Yokohama Tire, Salem Also called Yokohama Corp North America *(G-12582)*
Yokohama Tire Mnfctring Vrgnia (HQ) **540 389-5426**
  1500 Indiana St Salem (24153) *(G-12583)*
Yorgea Inc 704 431-8252
  2412 E Va Beach Blvd 10h Norfolk (23504) *(G-9799)*
York Box & Barrel Mfg Co 757 868-9411
  163 Little Florida Rd Poquoson (23662) *(G-10379)*
York Fabrication 804 241-0136
  549 Bracey Pl La Crosse (23950) *(G-7153)*
York Fabrication LLC 804 241-0136
  297 Alexander Ferry Rd Boydton (23917) *(G-1917)*
York Publishing Company LLC 571 226-0221
  8140 Raphiel Ct Manassas (20112) *(G-8181)*
York River Glassworks LLC 804 815-0492
  7166 Purton Ln Gloucester (23061) *(G-5870)*
York Sportscars Inc 804 798-5268
  11020 Leadbetter Rd Ste 6 Ashland (23005) *(G-1514)*
York Town Crier 757 766-1776
  3526 George Wash Mem Hwy Yorktown (23693) *(G-16004)*
Yorktown Hardwood Floors, Yorktown Also called Matera John *(G-15981)*
You Buy Book Paperback Exc 757 237-6426
  305 Waverly Dr Ste C Virginia Beach (23452) *(G-14954)*
Young Movar & Assoc Mrktng 804 320-5860
  300 Turner Rd Ste C North Chesterfield (23225) *(G-10046)*
Young and Healthy Mktg LLC 214 945-5816
  396 Watson Blvd Meherrin (23954) *(G-8707)*
Younivercity LLC 540 529-7621
  207 Eugene Dr Nw Roanoke (24017) *(G-12231)*
Younivercity, The, Roanoke Also called Younivercity LLC *(G-12231)*
Your Health Magazine 703 288-3130
  7617 Little River Tpke # 400 Annandale (22003) *(G-795)*
Your Life Uncorked 757 218-8495
  79 Tide Mill Ln Hampton (23666) *(G-6274)*
Your Newsy Notes LLC 703 729-3155
  43191 Thistledown Ter Broadlands (20148) *(G-2083)*
Your Personal Printer 757 679-1139
  5305 Hickory Rdg Virginia Beach (23455) *(G-14955)*
Your Puzzle Source LLC 703 461-7788
  802 Hall Pl Alexandria (22302) *(G-391)*
Your Way Software 703 591-2064
  10226 Raider Ln Fairfax (22030) *(G-4697)*
Youve Got It Made LLC 410 840-8744
  486 Myers Ave Harrisonburg (22801) *(G-6388)*
Yowell Metal Fabrication LLC 434 971-3018
  295 Deer Haven Ln Troy (22974) *(G-13938)*
Yue Xu 703 503-9451
  9423 Wrought Iron Ct Fairfax (22032) *(G-4586)*
Yum Yum Choppers Inc 276 694-6152
  7034 Dobyns Rd Claudville (24076) *(G-3642)*
Yummo Frz Yogurt Chesterfield, Midlothian Also called Ganpat Enterprise Inc *(G-8821)*
Yummy In My Tummy Inc 703 209-1516
  609 Bluff Ct Ne Leesburg (20176) *(G-7382)*
Yup Candles LLC 571 248-6772
  15090 Spittle Ln Nokesville (20181) *(G-9406)*
Yupo Corporation America 757 312-9876
  800 Yupo Ct Chesapeake (23320) *(G-3381)*

Yuzhnoye-Us LLC 321 537-2720
  1800 Jonathan Way # 1223 Reston (20190) *(G-10997)*
Z & M Sheet Metal Inc (PA) **703 631-9600**
  3931 Avion Park Ct C102 Chantilly (20151) *(G-2523)*
Z & T Sales LLC 540 570-9500
  85 Foxey Ln Buena Vista (24416) *(G-2157)*
Z & Z Machine Inc 540 248-2760
  23 Old Laurel Hill Rd Verona (24482) *(G-13997)*
Z Costumes, Fredericksburg Also called McKoon Zaneta *(G-5456)*
Z Finest Airduct Cleaning 703 897-1152
  3075 Ps Business Ctr Dr Woodbridge (22192) *(G-15838)*
Za Contracting LLC 703 498-3531
  3054 Patrick Henry Dr # 201 Falls Church (22044) *(G-4896)*
Zachary Systems Inc 703 286-7267
  44330 Premier Plz Ashburn (20147) *(G-1355)*
Zachary Systems Incorporated 703 723-8965
  42767 Summerhouse Pl Broadlands (20148) *(G-2084)*
Zakaa Couture LLC 703 554-7506
  19390 Diamond Lake Dr Leesburg (20176) *(G-7383)*
Zakufdm LLC 330 338-0930
  2413 Pittston Rd Fredericksburg (22408) *(G-5393)*
Zatara Press LLC 804 754-8682
  10805 N Bank Rd Richmond (23238) *(G-11462)*
Zb 3d Printers LLC 757 695-8278
  319 34th St Virginia Beach (23451) *(G-14956)*
Zeb Woodworks LLC 703 361-2842
  7876 Knightshayes Dr Manassas (20111) *(G-8182)*
Zeba Magazine LLC 202 705-7006
  8060 Crianza Pl Apt 406 Vienna (22182) *(G-14163)*
Zebra Press LLC 703 370-6641
  1439 Juliana Pl Alexandria (22304) *(G-392)*
Zeido LLC 202 549-5757
  40 Park Rd Stafford (22556) *(G-13213)*
Zeller + Gmelin Corporation (HQ) **800 848-8465**
  4801 Audubon Dr Richmond (23231) *(G-11463)*
Zen Sports Products LLC 703 925-0118
  2500 Tallyrand Ct Herndon (20171) *(G-6847)*
Zenith Aerotech Inc 434 202-7790
  10517 Critzers Shop Rd Afton (22920) *(G-97)*
Zenith Fuel Systems LLC 276 669-5555
  14570 Industrial Park Rd Bristol (24202) *(G-2044)*
Zenman Technology LLC 757 679-6703
  1116 Redgate Ave Norfolk (23507) *(G-9800)*
Zenobiabooks, Norfolk Also called Natasha Matthew *(G-9653)*
Zenpure Americas, Manassas Also called Zenpure Corporation *(G-8183)*
Zenpure Corporation (HQ) **703 335-9910**
  12030 Cadet Ct Manassas (20109) *(G-8183)*
Zenta Corporation 276 930-1500
  10086 Woolwine Hwy Woolwine (24185) *(G-15870)*
Zentech Fredericksburg LLC 540 372-6500
  3361 Shannon Airport Cir Fredericksburg (22408) *(G-5394)*
Zentox Corporation 757 868-0870
  538 Wythe Creek Rd Poquoson (23662) *(G-10380)*
Zephyr Woodworks LLC 434 979-4425
  4285 Burton Rd North Garden (22959) *(G-10085)*
Zerk Motors LLC 540 322-2003
  43 Town And Country Dr Fredericksburg (22405) *(G-5505)*
Zero Products LLC 757 285-4000
  2140 Brush Hill Ln Virginia Beach (23456) *(G-14957)*
Zest 757 301-8553
  312 Sandbridge Rd Virginia Beach (23456) *(G-14958)*
Zestron Corporation 703 393-9880
  11285 Assett Loop Manassas (20109) *(G-8184)*
Zeta Car Washes LLC 757 469-2141
  1449 Tomcat Blvd Bldg 296 Virginia Beach (23460) *(G-14959)*
Zeta Meter Inc 540 886-3503
  765 Middlebrook Ave Staunton (24401) *(G-13309)*
Zeurix LLC 571 297-9460
  11710 Plaza America Dr # 2000 Reston (20190) *(G-10998)*
Zeus Technologies 540 247-4623
  139 Boundary Ave Winchester (22602) *(G-15522)*
Zevacor, Dulles Also called N-Molecular Inc *(G-4211)*
ZF Active Safety & Elec US LLC 276 783-1157
  193 Mountain Empire Rd Atkins (24311) *(G-1523)*
ZF Active Safety & Elec US LLC 276 783-1990
  222 Mountain Empire Rd Atkins (24311) *(G-1524)*
ZF Technical LLC 757 575-5625
  418 Davis St Virginia Beach (23462) *(G-14960)*
Zhe Industries LLC 757 759-5466
  817 Gloria Pl Virginia Beach (23454) *(G-14961)*
Zhe Industries LLC 757 759-5466
  812 Prince Frederick Ct Virginia Beach (23454) *(G-14962)*
Zig Zag Press LLC 757 229-1345
  213 Heritage Pointe Williamsburg (23188) *(G-15349)*
Zima-Pack LLC 804 372-0707
  2101 Pine Forest Dr South Chesterfield (23834) *(G-12830)*
Zimar LLC 703 688-3339
  5673 Columbia Pike # 201 Falls Church (22041) *(G-4897)*
Zimbro Aerial Drone Integratio 757 408-6864
  5273 Jssie Dupont Mem Hwy Wicomico Church (22579) *(G-15197)*

(G-0000) Company's Geographic Section entry number

Zimmerman Marine Incorporated................804 776-0367
18691 Gen Puller Hwy Deltaville (23043) *(G-4090)*

Zindagi Granite Countertops, Chantilly *Also called Archna & Nazish Inc* *(G-2370)*

Zine Graphics Print................703 591-4000
10231 Stratford Ave Fairfax (22030) *(G-4698)*

Zinerva Publishing LLC................703 430-7629
929 Holly Creek Dr Great Falls (22066) *(G-5986)*

Zinga................571 291-2475
43330 Junction Plz # 100 Ashburn (20147) *(G-1356)*

Zingify LLC................703 689-3636
1502 Kings Valley Ct Herndon (20170) *(G-6848)*

Zipf Patterns, Manassas *Also called Laurie Grusha Zipf* *(G-8098)*

Zipnut Technology LLC................703 442-7339
7700 Lsburg Pike Ste 301n Falls Church (22043) *(G-4898)*

Ziptip, Henrico *Also called Taylynn Manufacturing LLC* *(G-6579)*

Ziva Prints LLC................571 265-9030
43858 Sandburg Sq Ashburn (20147) *(G-1357)*

Zm Sheet Metal, Chantilly *Also called Z & M Sheet Metal Inc* *(G-2523)*

Zo-Zos Jams................804 562-9867
1408 Kennedy Station Pl Glen Allen (23060) *(G-5830)*

Zoil Jewelry LLC................571 340-2256
605 Center St Apt T1 Herndon (20170) *(G-6849)*

Zojoi LLC................804 397-5000
55 Lynnwood Ln Charlottesville (22901) *(G-2718)*

Zoll Bros Private Cellars LLC................857 498-1665
9744 Dutton Rd Dutton (23050) *(G-4275)*

Zoll Vineyards, Dutton *Also called Zoll Bros Private Cellars LLC* *(G-4275)*

Zombie Defense................804 972-3991
11330 Winfrey Rd Glen Allen (23059) *(G-5831)*

Zone2, Reston *Also called Potomac Health Solutions Inc* *(G-10929)*

Zones LLC................571 244-8206
8647 Richmond Hwy Alexandria (22309) *(G-617)*

Zook Aviation Inc................540 217-4471
1866 E Market St 312c Harrisonburg (22801) *(G-6389)*

Zooom Printing LLC................804 343-0009
2042 Westmoreland St Richmond (23230) *(G-11464)*

Zosaro LLC................804 564-9450
6920 Lakeside Ave Ste D Henrico (23228) *(G-6593)*

ZOSARO'S BAKERY, Henrico *Also called Zosaro LLC* *(G-6593)*

Zotz................703 330-2305
9126 Taylor St Manassas (20110) *(G-8015)*

Zramics Mtls Science Tech LLC................757 955-0493
2713 Colley Ave Norfolk (23517) *(G-9801)* .

Zup LLC................843 822-5664
1490 Quarterpath Rd 5a Williamsburg (23185) *(G-15350)*

Zyflex LLC................804 306-6333
5141 Craig Rath Blvd Midlothian (23112) *(G-8927)*

Zynga Inc................901 683-8310
44521 Hastings Dr Ashburn (20147) *(G-1358)*

ZZ Supply Company LLC................703 957-5027
7011 Calamo St Ste 106 Springfield (22150) *(G-13110)*

PRODUCT INDEX

• Product categories are listed in alphabetical order.

A

ABRASIVES
ABRASIVES: Coated
ACADEMIC TUTORING SVCS
ACCELERATION INDICATORS & SYSTEM COMPONENTS: Aerospace
ACCELERATORS: Linear
ACCOUNTING MACHINES & CASH REGISTERS
ACCOUNTING SVCS, NEC
ACRYLIC RESINS
ACTUATORS: Indl, NEC
ADDITIVE BASED PLASTIC MATERIALS: Plasticizers
ADHESIVES
ADHESIVES & SEALANTS
ADHESIVES: Epoxy
ADVERTISING AGENCIES
ADVERTISING AGENCIES: Consultants
ADVERTISING DISPLAY PRDTS
ADVERTISING REPRESENTATIVES: Printed Media
ADVERTISING SPECIALTIES, WHOLESALE
ADVERTISING SVCS: Direct Mail
ADVERTISING SVCS: Display
ADVERTISING SVCS: Outdoor
ADVERTISING SVCS: Poster, Exc Outdoor
ADVERTISING SVCS: Transit
AERIAL WORK PLATFORMS
AGRICULTURAL CHEMICALS: Trace Elements
AGRICULTURAL EQPT: BARN, SILO, POULTRY, DAIRY/LIVESTOCK MACH
AGRICULTURAL EQPT: Barn Stanchions & Standards
AGRICULTURAL EQPT: Combine, Digger, Packer/Thresher, Peanut
AGRICULTURAL EQPT: Elevators, Farm
AGRICULTURAL EQPT: Fertilizing Machinery
AGRICULTURAL EQPT: Fertilizng, Sprayng, Dustng/Irrigatn Mach
AGRICULTURAL EQPT: Grade, Clean & Sort Machines, Fruit/Veg
AGRICULTURAL EQPT: Grounds Mowing Eqpt
AGRICULTURAL EQPT: Irrigation Eqpt, Self-Propelled
AGRICULTURAL EQPT: Planting Machines
AGRICULTURAL EQPT: Shakers, Tree, Nuts, Fruits, Etc
AGRICULTURAL EQPT: Spreaders, Fertilizer
AGRICULTURAL EQPT: Tractors, Farm
AGRICULTURAL EQPT: Transplanters
AGRICULTURAL EQPT: Turf & Grounds Eqpt
AGRICULTURAL EQPT: Turf Eqpt, Commercial
AGRICULTURAL MACHINERY & EQPT: Wholesalers
AIR CLEANING SYSTEMS
AIR CONDITIONERS: Motor Vehicle
AIR CONDITIONING & VENTILATION EQPT & SPLYS: Wholesales
AIR CONDITIONING EQPT
AIR CONDITIONING EQPT, WHOLE HOUSE: Wholesalers
AIR CONDITIONING REPAIR SVCS
AIR CONDITIONING UNITS: Complete, Domestic Or Indl
AIR COOLERS: Metal Plate
AIR POLLUTION MEASURING SVCS
AIR PREHEATERS: Nonrotating, Plate Type
AIR PURIFICATION EQPT
AIR TRAFFIC CONTROL SYSTEMS & EQPT
AIR, WATER & SOLID WASTE PROGRAMS ADMINISTRATION SVCS
AIRCRAFT & AEROSPACE FLIGHT INSTRUMENTS & GUIDANCE SYSTEMS
AIRCRAFT & HEAVY EQPT REPAIR SVCS
AIRCRAFT ASSEMBLY PLANTS
AIRCRAFT CONTROL SYSTEMS:
AIRCRAFT CONTROL SYSTEMS: Electronic Totalizing Counters
AIRCRAFT ENGINES & ENGINE PARTS: Research & Development, Mfr
AIRCRAFT ENGINES & PARTS
AIRCRAFT EQPT & SPLYS WHOLESALERS
AIRCRAFT LIGHTING
AIRCRAFT MAINTENANCE & REPAIR SVCS
AIRCRAFT PARTS & AUXILIARY EQPT: Armament, Exc Guns
AIRCRAFT PARTS & AUXILIARY EQPT: Assemblies, Fuselage
AIRCRAFT PARTS & AUXILIARY EQPT: Assys, Subassemblies/Parts
AIRCRAFT PARTS & AUXILIARY EQPT: Countermeasure Dispensers
AIRCRAFT PARTS & AUXILIARY EQPT: Military Eqpt & Armament
AIRCRAFT PARTS & AUXILIARY EQPT: Research & Development, Mfr
AIRCRAFT PARTS & EQPT, NEC
AIRCRAFT SERVICING & REPAIRING
AIRCRAFT TURBINES
AIRCRAFT: Airplanes, Fixed Or Rotary Wing
AIRCRAFT: Gliders
AIRCRAFT: Motorized
AIRCRAFT: Research & Development, Manufacturer
AIRFRAME ASSEMBLIES: Guided Missiles
AIRPORTS, FLYING FIELDS & SVCS
ALARM SYSTEMS WHOLESALERS
ALARMS: Burglar
ALARMS: Fire
ALCOHOL, GRAIN: For Beverage Purposes
ALCOHOL, GRAIN: For Medicinal Purposes
ALCOHOL: Ethyl & Ethanol
ALKALIES & CHLORINE
ALKALOIDS & OTHER BOTANICAL BASED PRDTS
ALLERGENS & ALLERGENIC EXTRACTS
ALTERNATORS & GENERATORS: Battery Charging
ALTERNATORS: Automotive
ALUMINUM
ALUMINUM PRDTS
ALUMINUM: Rolling & Drawing
AMMUNITION
AMMUNITION, EXC SPORTING, WHOLESALE
AMMUNITION: Arming & Fusing Devices
AMMUNITION: Artillery Shells, Over 30 mm
AMMUNITION: Cartridges Case, 30 mm & Below
AMMUNITION: Components
AMMUNITION: Missile Warheads
AMMUNITION: Small Arms
AMPLIFIERS
AMPLIFIERS: Pulse Amplifiers
AMPLIFIERS: RF & IF Power
AMUSEMENT & RECREATION SVCS: Art Gallery, Commercial
AMUSEMENT & RECREATION SVCS: Diving Instruction, Underwater
AMUSEMENT & RECREATION SVCS: Instruction Schools, Camps
AMUSEMENT & RECREATION SVCS: Ski Rental Concession
AMUSEMENT MACHINES: Coin Operated
AMUSEMENT PARK DEVICES & RIDES
AMUSEMENT PARK DEVICES & RIDES: Carnival Mach & Eqpt, NEC
ANALYZERS: Blood & Body Fluid
ANALYZERS: Electrical Testing
ANALYZERS: Moisture
ANALYZERS: Network
ANIMAL BASED MEDICINAL CHEMICAL PRDTS
ANIMAL FEED & SUPPLEMENTS: Livestock & Poultry
ANIMAL FEED: Wholesalers
ANIMAL FOOD & SUPPLEMENTS: Bird Food, Prepared
ANIMAL FOOD & SUPPLEMENTS: Cat
ANIMAL FOOD & SUPPLEMENTS: Dog
ANIMAL FOOD & SUPPLEMENTS: Dog & Cat
ANIMAL FOOD & SUPPLEMENTS: Feed Premixes
ANIMAL FOOD & SUPPLEMENTS: Feed Supplements
ANIMAL FOOD & SUPPLEMENTS: Kelp Meal & Pellets
ANIMAL FOOD & SUPPLEMENTS: Livestock
ANIMAL FOOD & SUPPLEMENTS: Mineral feed supplements
ANIMAL FOOD & SUPPLEMENTS: Pet, Exc Dog & Cat, Dry
ANIMAL FOOD & SUPPLEMENTS: Poultry
ANODIZING SVC
ANTENNAS: Radar Or Communications
ANTENNAS: Receiving
ANTIBIOTICS
ANTIFREEZE
ANTIQUE FURNITURE RESTORATION & REPAIR
ANTIQUE SHOPS
APPAREL ACCESS STORES
APPAREL DESIGNERS: Commercial
APPAREL: Hand Woven
APPLIANCES, HOUSEHOLD OR COIN OPERATED: Laundry Dryers
APPLIANCES, HOUSEHOLD: Kitchen, Major, Exc Refrigs & Stoves
APPLIANCES: Household, NEC
APPLIANCES: Household, Refrigerators & Freezers
APPLIANCES: Major, Cooking
APPLIANCES: Small, Electric
APPLICATIONS SOFTWARE PROGRAMMING
APPRENTICESHIP TRAINING SCHOOLS
ARCHITECTURAL SVCS
ARCHITECTURAL SVCS: Engineering
ARMATURE REPAIRING & REWINDING SVC
ARMOR PLATES
AROMATIC CHEMICAL PRDTS
ART & ORNAMENTAL WARE: Pottery
ART DEALERS & GALLERIES
ART DESIGN SVCS
ART GALLERIES
ART MARBLE: Concrete
ART RELATED SVCS
ART RESTORATION SVC
ART SCHOOL, EXC COMMERCIAL
ART SPLY STORES
ARTIFICIAL FLOWER SHOPS
ARTIFICIAL FLOWERS & TREES
ARTIST'S MATERIALS & SPLYS
ARTISTS' MATERIALS: Boards, Drawing
ARTISTS' MATERIALS: Brushes, Air
ARTISTS' MATERIALS: Canvas Board
ARTISTS' MATERIALS: Canvas, Prepared On Frames
ARTISTS' MATERIALS: Frames, Artists' Canvases
ARTISTS' MATERIALS: Paints, Gold Or Bronze
ARTISTS' MATERIALS: Palettes
ARTISTS' MATERIALS: Pencils & Pencil Parts
ARTWORK: Framed
ASBESTOS MINING SVCS
ASBESTOS PRDTS: Boiler Covering, Heat Insulat Matl, Exc Felt
ASBESTOS PRDTS: Insulating Materials
ASBESTOS PRODUCTS
ASPHALT & ASPHALT PRDTS
ASPHALT COATINGS & SEALERS
ASPHALT MIXTURES WHOLESALERS
ASPHALT PLANTS INCLUDING GRAVEL MIX TYPE
ASPHALT SATURATED BOARD
ASSEMBLING SVC: Clocks
ASSEMBLING SVC: Plumbing Fixture Fittings, Plastic
ASSOCIATIONS: Scientists'
ASSOCIATIONS: Trade
ATOMIZERS
AUDIO & VIDEO EQPT, EXC COMMERCIAL
AUDIO COMPONENTS
AUDIO ELECTRONIC SYSTEMS
AUTHORS' AGENTS & BROKERS
AUTO & HOME SUPPLY STORES: Auto & Truck Eqpt & Parts
AUTO & HOME SUPPLY STORES: Automotive parts
AUTO & HOME SUPPLY STORES: Batteries, Automotive & Truck
AUTO & HOME SUPPLY STORES: Speed Shops, Incl Race Car Splys
AUTO & HOME SUPPLY STORES: Trailer Hitches, Automotive
AUTO & HOME SUPPLY STORES: Truck Eqpt & Parts
AUTOMATIC REGULATING CONTROL: Building Svcs Monitoring, Auto
AUTOMATIC REGULATING CONTROLS: AC & Refrigeration
AUTOMATIC REGULATING CONTROLS: Energy Cutoff, Residtl/Comm
AUTOMATIC REGULATING CONTROLS: Hardware, Environmental Reg
AUTOMATIC REGULATING CONTROLS: Hydronic Pressure Or Temp

AUTOMATIC REGULATING CONTROLS: Incinerator, Residential/Comm
AUTOMATIC REGULATING CONTROLS: Refrig/Air-Cond Defrost
AUTOMATIC TELLER MACHINES
AUTOMOBILE RECOVERY SVCS
AUTOMOBILES & OTHER MOTOR VEHICLES WHOLESALERS
AUTOMOBILES: Off-Road, Exc Recreational Vehicles
AUTOMOTIVE & TRUCK GENERAL REPAIR SVC
AUTOMOTIVE BODY SHOP
AUTOMOTIVE CUSTOMIZING SVCS, NONFACTORY BASIS
AUTOMOTIVE EXHAUST REPAIR SVC
AUTOMOTIVE GLASS REPLACEMENT SHOPS
AUTOMOTIVE PARTS, ACCESS & SPLYS
AUTOMOTIVE PARTS: Plastic
AUTOMOTIVE PRDTS: Rubber
AUTOMOTIVE REPAIR SHOPS: Frame Repair Shops
AUTOMOTIVE REPAIR SHOPS: Machine Shop
AUTOMOTIVE REPAIR SHOPS: Springs, Rebuilding & Repair
AUTOMOTIVE REPAIR SHOPS: Truck Engine Repair, Exc Indl
AUTOMOTIVE REPAIR SVC
AUTOMOTIVE SPLYS & PARTS, NEW, WHOL: Auto Servicing Eqpt
AUTOMOTIVE SPLYS & PARTS, NEW, WHOL: Auto Svc Station Eqpt
AUTOMOTIVE SPLYS & PARTS, NEW, WHOLESALE: Alternators
AUTOMOTIVE SPLYS & PARTS, NEW, WHOLESALE: Brakes
AUTOMOTIVE SPLYS & PARTS, NEW, WHOLESALE: Wheels
AUTOMOTIVE SPLYS & PARTS, WHOLESALE, NEC
AUTOMOTIVE SVCS, EXC REPAIR & CARWASHES: Customizing
AUTOMOTIVE SVCS, EXC REPAIR: Washing & Polishing
AUTOMOTIVE SVCS, EXC RPR/CARWASHES: High Perf Auto Rpr/Svc
AUTOMOTIVE TOWING & WRECKING SVC
AUTOMOTIVE TRANSMISSION REPAIR SVC
AUTOMOTIVE UPHOLSTERY SHOPS
AUTOMOTIVE WELDING SVCS
AUTOMOTIVE: Bodies
AUTOMOTIVE: Seating
AUTOTRANSFORMERS: Electric
AUTOTRANSFORMERS: Switchboards, Exc Telephone
AWNINGS & CANOPIES
AWNINGS & CANOPIES: Awnings, Fabric, From Purchased Matls
AWNINGS & CANOPIES: Canopies, Fabric, From Purchased Matls
AWNINGS & CANOPIES: Fabric
AWNINGS: Fiberglass
AWNINGS: Metal
Ammunition Loading & Assembling Plant

B

BABYSITTING BUREAU
BACKHOES
BADGES: Identification & Insignia
BAGS & CONTAINERS: Textile, Exc Sleeping
BAGS & SACKS: Shipping & Shopping
BAGS: Canvas
BAGS: Duffle, Canvas, Made From Purchased Materials
BAGS: Flour, Fabric, Made From Purchased Materials
BAGS: Food Storage & Frozen Food, Plastic
BAGS: Food Storage & Trash, Plastic
BAGS: Garment Storage Exc Paper Or Plastic Film
BAGS: Laundry, Garment & Storage
BAGS: Mothproof , Made From Purchased Materials
BAGS: Paper
BAGS: Plastic
BAGS: Plastic, Made From Purchased Materials
BAGS: Rubber Or Rubberized Fabric
BAGS: Shipping
BAGS: Tea, Fabric, Made From Purchased Materials
BAGS: Textile
BAGS: Trash, Plastic Film, Made From Purchased Materials
BAGS: Wardrobe, Closet Access, Made From Purchased Materials
BAIT, FISHING, WHOLESALE
BAKERIES, COMMERCIAL: On Premises Baking Only
BAKERIES: On Premises Baking & Consumption
BAKERY FOR HOME SVC DELIVERY

BAKERY MACHINERY
BAKERY PRDTS: Bagels, Fresh Or Frozen
BAKERY PRDTS: Bakery Prdts, Partially Cooked, Exc frozen
BAKERY PRDTS: Biscuits, Baked, Baking Powder & Raised
BAKERY PRDTS: Bread, All Types, Fresh Or Frozen
BAKERY PRDTS: Cakes, Bakery, Exc Frozen
BAKERY PRDTS: Cakes, Bakery, Frozen
BAKERY PRDTS: Cones, Ice Cream
BAKERY PRDTS: Cookies
BAKERY PRDTS: Cookies & crackers
BAKERY PRDTS: Doughnuts, Exc Frozen
BAKERY PRDTS: Dry
BAKERY PRDTS: Frozen
BAKERY PRDTS: Pies, Bakery, Frozen
BAKERY PRDTS: Pies, Exc Frozen
BAKERY PRDTS: Pretzels
BAKERY PRDTS: Rice Cakes
BAKERY PRDTS: Wholesalers
BAKERY PRDTS: Yeast Goods, Sweet, Frozen
BAKERY: Wholesale Or Wholesale & Retail Combined
BALANCES EXC LABORATORY WHOLESALERS
BALERS
BANDS: Plastic
BANKS: Foreign Trade & International
BANNERS: Fabric
BAR FIXTURES: Wood
BARBECUE EQPT
BARGES BUILDING & REPAIR
BARRICADES: Metal
BARS, PIPES, PLATES & SHAPES: Lead/Lead Alloy Bars, Pipe
BARS: Concrete Reinforcing, Fabricated Steel
BARS: Iron, Made In Steel Mills
BASKETS, GIFT, WHOLESALE
BATH SALTS
BATH SHOPS
BATTERIES: Lead Acid, Storage
BATTERIES: Rechargeable
BATTERIES: Storage
BATTERIES: Wet
BATTERY CHARGERS
BATTERY CHARGING GENERATORS
BEARINGS: Ball & Roller
BEAUTY & BARBER SHOP EQPT
BEAUTY SALONS
BEDDING & BEDSPRINGS STORES
BEDDING, BEDSPREADS, BLANKETS & SHEETS
BEDS & ACCESS STORES
BEDS: Hospital
BEDSPREADS & BED SETS, FROM PURCHASED MATERIALS
BEEKEEPERS' SPLYS
BEEKEEPERS' SPLYS: Honeycomb Foundations
BEER & ALE WHOLESALERS
BEER & ALE, WHOLESALE: Beer & Other Fermented Malt Liquors
BEER, WINE & LIQUOR STORES
BEER, WINE & LIQUOR STORES: Wine
BELTS: Conveyor, Made From Purchased Wire
BEVERAGE BASES & SYRUPS
BEVERAGE PRDTS: Brewers' Grain
BEVERAGE PRDTS: Malt, By-Prdts
BEVERAGE, NONALCOHOLIC: Iced Tea/Fruit Drink, Bottled/Canned
BEVERAGES, ALCOHOLIC: Ale
BEVERAGES, ALCOHOLIC: Beer
BEVERAGES, ALCOHOLIC: Beer & Ale
BEVERAGES, ALCOHOLIC: Bourbon Whiskey
BEVERAGES, ALCOHOLIC: Brandy
BEVERAGES, ALCOHOLIC: Brandy & Brandy Spirits
BEVERAGES, ALCOHOLIC: Brandy Spirits
BEVERAGES, ALCOHOLIC: Cocktails
BEVERAGES, ALCOHOLIC: Corn Whiskey
BEVERAGES, ALCOHOLIC: Distilled Liquors
BEVERAGES, ALCOHOLIC: Near Beer
BEVERAGES, ALCOHOLIC: Neutral Spirits, Exc Fruit
BEVERAGES, ALCOHOLIC: Vodka
BEVERAGES, ALCOHOLIC: Wines
BEVERAGES, BEER & ALE, WHOLESALE: Ale
BEVERAGES, NONALCOHOLIC: Bottled & canned soft drinks
BEVERAGES, NONALCOHOLIC: Carbonated
BEVERAGES, NONALCOHOLIC: Carbonated, Canned & Bottled, Etc
BEVERAGES, NONALCOHOLIC: Cider

BEVERAGES, NONALCOHOLIC: Flavoring extracts & syrups, nec
BEVERAGES, NONALCOHOLIC: Fruit Drnks, Under 100% Juice, Can
BEVERAGES, NONALCOHOLIC: Soft Drinks, Canned & Bottled, Etc
BEVERAGES, WINE & DISTILLED ALCOHOLIC, WHOLESALE: Neutral Sp
BEVERAGES, WINE & DISTILLED ALCOHOLIC, WHOLESALE: Wine
BEVERAGES, WINE/DISTILLED ALCOH, WHOL: Brandy/Brandy Spirits
BICYCLES, PARTS & ACCESS
BILLIARD & POOL PARLORS
BINDING SVC: Books & Manuals
BINDING SVC: Trade
BINOCULARS
BIOLOGICAL PRDTS: Exc Diagnostic
BIOLOGICAL PRDTS: Extracts
BIOLOGICAL PRDTS: Serums
BIOLOGICAL PRDTS: Vaccines
BIOLOGICAL PRDTS: Vaccines & Immunizing
BIOLOGICAL PRDTS: Venoms
BIOLOGICAL PRDTS: Veterinary
BIRTH CERTIFICATE FACILITIES
BITUMINOUS & LIGNITE COAL LOADING & PREPARATION
BLADES: Knife
BLANKBOOKS & LOOSELEAF BINDERS
BLANKBOOKS: Account
BLANKBOOKS: Albums
BLANKBOOKS: Albums, Record
BLANKBOOKS: Inventory
BLANKBOOKS: Scrapbooks
BLANKETS: Horse
BLAST SAND MINING
BLASTING SVC: Sand, Metal Parts
BLINDS & SHADES: Vertical
BLINDS : Window
BLOCKS & BRICKS: Concrete
BLOCKS: Landscape Or Retaining Wall, Concrete
BLOCKS: Paving, Concrete
BLOCKS: Paving, Cut Stone
BLOCKS: Standard, Concrete Or Cinder
BLOOD RELATED HEALTH SVCS
BLOWERS & FANS
BLOWERS, TURBO: Indl
BLUEPRINTING SVCS
BOAT BUILDING & REPAIR
BOAT BUILDING & REPAIRING: Fiberglass
BOAT BUILDING & REPAIRING: Kits, Not Models
BOAT BUILDING & REPAIRING: Motorized
BOAT BUILDING & REPAIRING: Yachts
BOAT BUILDING & RPRG: Fishing, Small, Lobster, Crab, Oyster
BOAT LIFTS
BOAT REPAIR SVCS
BOAT YARD: Boat yards, storage & incidental repair
BOATS & OTHER MARINE EQPT: Plastic
BODIES: Truck & Bus
BODY PARTS: Automobile, Stamped Metal
BOILER REPAIR SHOP
BOILERS & BOILER SHOP WORK
BOILERS: Low-Pressure Heating, Steam Or Hot Water
BOLTS: Heading, Wooden, Hewn
BOLTS: Metal
BOLTS: Wooden, Hewn
BOND DEALERS & BROKERS
BOOK STORES
BOOK STORES: Comic
BOOK STORES: Religious
BOOTS: Rubber Or Rubber Soled Fabric
BOOTS: Women's
BOTTLE CAPS & RESEALERS: Plastic
BOTTLES: Plastic
BOWLING CENTERS
BOWLING EQPT & SPLYS
BOXES & SHOOK: Nailed Wood
BOXES: Ammunition, Metal
BOXES: Chests & Trunks, Wood
BOXES: Corrugated
BOXES: Junction, Electric
BOXES: Mail Or Post Office, Collection/Storage, Sheet Metal
BOXES: Outlet, Electric Wiring Device
BOXES: Paperboard, Folding
BOXES: Paperboard, Set-Up

BOXES: Wirebound, Wood
BOXES: Wooden
BRAKE LININGS
BRAKES & BRAKE PARTS
BRASS & BRONZE PRDTS: Die-casted
BRASS FOUNDRY, NEC
BREAD WRAPPERS: Waxed Or Laminated, Made From Purchased Matl
BRICK, STONE & RELATED PRDTS WHOLESALERS
BRICKS: Clay
BRIDAL SHOPS
BROADCASTING & COMMS EQPT: Antennas, Transmitting/Comms
BROADCASTING & COMMS EQPT: Rcvr-Transmitter Unt, Transceiver
BROADCASTING & COMMUNICATION EQPT: Transmit-Receiver, Radio
BROADCASTING & COMMUNICATIONS EQPT: Cellular Radio Telephone
BROADCASTING & COMMUNICATIONS EQPT: Light Comms Eqpt
BROADCASTING & COMMUNICATIONS EQPT: Studio Eqpt, Radio & TV
BROKERS' SVCS
BROKERS: Contract Basis
BROKERS: Printing
BRONZE FOUNDRY, NEC
BROOMS
BROOMS & BRUSHES
BROOMS & BRUSHES: Household Or Indl
BROOMS & BRUSHES: Vacuum Cleaners & Carpet Sweepers
BRUSHES: Rubber
BUILDING & OFFICE CLEANING SVCS
BUILDING & STRUCTURAL WOOD MBRS: Timbers, Struct, Lam Lumber
BUILDING & STRUCTURAL WOOD MEMBERS
BUILDING CLEANING & MAINTENANCE SVCS
BUILDING COMPONENTS: Structural Steel
BUILDING INSPECTION SVCS
BUILDING PRDTS & MATERIALS DEALERS
BUILDING PRDTS: Concrete
BUILDING STONE, ARTIFICIAL: Concrete
BUILDINGS & COMPONENTS: Prefabricated Metal
BUILDINGS: Farm & Utility
BUILDINGS: Farm, Prefabricated Or Portable, Wood
BUILDINGS: Portable
BUILDINGS: Prefabricated, Metal
BUILDINGS: Prefabricated, Plastic
BUILDINGS: Prefabricated, Wood
BUILDINGS: Prefabricated, Wood
BULLETPROOF VESTS
BUMPERS: Motor Vehicle
BURIAL VAULTS: Concrete Or Precast Terrazzo
BUS BARS: Electrical
BUSINESS ACTIVITIES: Non-Commercial Site
BUSINESS FORMS WHOLESALERS
BUSINESS FORMS: Printed, Continuous
BUSINESS FORMS: Printed, Manifold
BUSINESS FORMS: Strip, Manifold
BUSINESS SUPPORT SVCS
BUSINESS TRAINING SVCS

C

CABINETS & CASES: Show, Display & Storage, Exc Wood
CABINETS: Bathroom Vanities, Wood
CABINETS: Entertainment
CABINETS: Entertainment Units, Household, Wood
CABINETS: Factory
CABINETS: Filing, Office, Wood
CABINETS: Filing, Wood
CABINETS: Kitchen, Metal
CABINETS: Kitchen, Wood
CABINETS: Office, Wood
CABINETS: Show, Display, Etc, Wood, Exc Refrigerated
CABLE & OTHER PAY TELEVISION DISTRIBUTION
CABLE TELEVISION PRDTS
CABLE: Coaxial
CABLE: Fiber
CABLE: Fiber Optic
CABLE: Noninsulated
CAFES
CAGES: Wire
CALCULATING & ACCOUNTING EQPT
CALIBRATING SVCS, NEC

CAMERAS & RELATED EQPT: Photographic
CAMSHAFTS
CANDLE SHOPS
CANDLES
CANDLES: Wholesalers
CANDY & CONFECTIONS: Cake Ornaments
CANDY & CONFECTIONS: Candy Bars, Including Chocolate Covered
CANDY & CONFECTIONS: Chocolate Candy, Exc Solid Chocolate
CANDY & CONFECTIONS: Cough Drops, Exc Pharmaceutical Preps
CANDY & CONFECTIONS: Fruit & Fruit Peel
CANDY & CONFECTIONS: Fudge
CANDY & CONFECTIONS: Popcorn Balls/Other Trtd Popcorn Prdts
CANDY, NUT & CONFECTIONERY STORES: Produced For Direct Sale
CANDY: Chocolate From Cacao Beans
CANDY: Hard
CANNED SPECIALTIES
CANOE BUILDING & REPAIR
CANS: Aluminum
CANS: Beverage, Metal, Exc Beer
CANS: Composite Foil-Fiber, Made From Purchased Materials
CANS: Metal
CANVAS PRDTS
CANVAS PRDTS, WHOLESALE
CANVAS PRDTS: Boat Seats
CANVAS PRDTS: Convertible Tops, Car/Boat, Fm Purchased Mtrl
CANVAS PRDTS: Shades, Made From Purchased Materials
CAPACITORS: NEC
CAPS & TOPS: Bottle, Die-Cut, Made From Purchased Materials
CAPS & TOPS: Bottle, Stamped Metal
CAPS: Plastic
CAR WASH EQPT
CAR WASHES
CARBIDES
CARBON & GRAPHITE PRDTS, NEC
CARBONS: Lighting
CARBURETORS
CARDIOVASCULAR SYSTEM DRUGS, EXC DIAGNOSTIC
CARDS: Greeting
CARDS: Identification
CARPET & UPHOLSTERY CLEANING SVCS
CARPET LINING: Felt, Exc Woven
CARPETS & RUGS: Tufted
CARPETS, RUGS & FLOOR COVERING
CARPETS: Axminster
CARPETS: Wilton
CASES: Attache'
CASES: Carrying
CASES: Carrying, Clothing & Apparel
CASES: Nonrefrigerated, Exc Wood
CASES: Plastic
CASH REGISTERS & PARTS
CAST STONE: Concrete
CASTERS
CASTINGS GRINDING: For The Trade
CASTINGS: Aerospace Investment, Ferrous
CASTINGS: Aerospace, Aluminum
CASTINGS: Aerospace, Nonferrous, Exc Aluminum
CASTINGS: Aluminum
CASTINGS: Brass, Bronze & Copper
CASTINGS: Commercial Investment, Ferrous
CASTINGS: Die, Aluminum
CASTINGS: Die, Zinc
CASTINGS: Ductile
CASTINGS: Gray Iron
CASTINGS: Machinery, Nonferrous, Exc Die or Aluminum Copper
CASTINGS: Precision
CASTINGS: Steel
CATALOG & MAIL-ORDER HOUSES
CATAPULTS
CATERERS
CAULKING COMPOUNDS
CEMENT: Asbestos, Siding
CEMENT: Hydraulic
CEMENT: Masonry
CEMETERY MEMORIAL DEALERS
CERAMIC FIBER
CERAMIC SCHOOLS

CHAINS: Forged
CHANDELIERS: Residential
CHARCOAL
CHARCOAL, WHOLESALE
CHEMICAL ELEMENTS
CHEMICAL INDICATORS
CHEMICAL PROCESSING MACHINERY & EQPT
CHEMICAL SPLYS FOR FOUNDRIES
CHEMICALS & ALLIED PRDTS WHOLESALERS, NEC
CHEMICALS & ALLIED PRDTS, WHOL: Chem Bulk Station/Terminal
CHEMICALS & ALLIED PRDTS, WHOLESALE: Alcohols
CHEMICALS & ALLIED PRDTS, WHOLESALE: Ammonia
CHEMICALS & ALLIED PRDTS, WHOLESALE: Chemicals, Indl
CHEMICALS & ALLIED PRDTS, WHOLESALE: Detergent/Soap
CHEMICALS & ALLIED PRDTS, WHOLESALE: Oil Additives
CHEMICALS & ALLIED PRDTS, WHOLESALE: Plastics Prdts, NEC
CHEMICALS & ALLIED PRDTS, WHOLESALE: Polishes, NEC
CHEMICALS & ALLIED PRDTS, WHOLESALE: Resins
CHEMICALS & ALLIED PRDTS, WHOLESALE: Resins, Synthetic
CHEMICALS & ALLIED PRDTS, WHOLESALE: Sanitation Preparations
CHEMICALS & ALLIED PRDTS, WHOLESALE: Spec Clean/Sanitation
CHEMICALS & ALLIED PRDTS, WHOLESALE: Syn Resin, Rub/Plastic
CHEMICALS, AGRICULTURE: Wholesalers
CHEMICALS/ALLIED PRDTS, WHOL: Coal Tar Prdts, Prim/Intermdt
CHEMICALS: Agricultural
CHEMICALS: Alcohols
CHEMICALS: Aluminum Compounds
CHEMICALS: Aluminum Sulfate
CHEMICALS: Anhydrous Ammonia
CHEMICALS: Boron Compounds, Not From Mines, NEC
CHEMICALS: Brine
CHEMICALS: Bromine, Elemental
CHEMICALS: Calcium & Calcium Compounds
CHEMICALS: Fire Retardant
CHEMICALS: Heavy Water
CHEMICALS: Inorganic, NEC
CHEMICALS: Iodides, NEC
CHEMICALS: Medicinal
CHEMICALS: NEC
CHEMICALS: Organic, NEC
CHEMICALS: Water Treatment
CHICKEN SLAUGHTERING & PROCESSING
CHIROPRACTORS' OFFICES
CHLORINE
CHOCOLATE, EXC CANDY FROM BEANS: Chips, Powder, Block, Syrup
CHOCOLATE, EXC CANDY FROM PURCH CHOC: Chips, Powder, Block
CHRISTMAS TREES: Artificial
CIGARETTE & CIGAR PRDTS & ACCESS
CIGARETTE FILTERS
CIGARETTE LIGHTER FLINTS
CIRCUIT BOARD REPAIR SVCS
CIRCUIT BOARDS, PRINTED: Television & Radio
CIRCUITS: Electronic
CLAMPS & COUPLINGS: Hose
CLAMPS: Metal
CLAY MINING, COMMON
CLAY PRDTS: Structural
CLAY: Ground Or Treated
CLEANING & DESCALING SVC: Metal Prdts
CLEANING EQPT: Commercial
CLEANING EQPT: Floor Washing & Polishing, Commercial
CLEANING EQPT: High Pressure
CLEANING OR POLISHING PREPARATIONS, NEC
CLEANING PRDTS: Automobile Polish
CLEANING PRDTS: Bleaches, Household, Dry Or Liquid
CLEANING PRDTS: Degreasing Solvent
CLEANING PRDTS: Deodorants, Nonpersonal
CLEANING PRDTS: Disinfectants, Household Or Indl Plant
CLEANING PRDTS: Drycleaning Preparations
CLEANING PRDTS: Laundry Preparations
CLEANING PRDTS: Leather Dressings & Finishes
CLEANING PRDTS: Polishing Preparations & Related Prdts
CLEANING PRDTS: Sanitation Preparations

INDEX

CLEANING PRDTS: Sanitation Preps, Disinfectants/Deodorants
CLEANING PRDTS: Specialty
CLIPPERS: Fingernail & Toenail
CLIPPERS: Hair, Human
CLOSURES: Plastic
CLOTHES HANGERS, WHOLESALE
CLOTHING & ACCESS, WOMEN, CHILD & INFANT, WHOL: Scarves
CLOTHING & ACCESS, WOMEN, CHILD/INFANT, WHOLESALE: Child
CLOTHING & ACCESS, WOMEN, CHILDREN & INFANT, WHOL: Uniforms
CLOTHING & ACCESS, WOMEN, CHILDREN/INFANT, WHOL: Swimsuits
CLOTHING & ACCESS: Costumes, Lodge
CLOTHING & ACCESS: Costumes, Masquerade
CLOTHING & ACCESS: Costumes, Theatrical
CLOTHING & ACCESS: Handicapped
CLOTHING & ACCESS: Hospital Gowns
CLOTHING & ACCESS: Men's Miscellaneous Access
CLOTHING & ACCESS: Regalia
CLOTHING & ACCESS: Suspenders
CLOTHING & APPAREL STORES: Custom
CLOTHING & FURNISHINGS, MEN'S & BOYS', WHOLESALE: Beachwear
CLOTHING STORES, NEC
CLOTHING STORES: Designer Apparel
CLOTHING STORES: Formal Wear
CLOTHING STORES: Lingerie & Corsets, Underwear
CLOTHING STORES: Raincoats
CLOTHING STORES: T-Shirts, Printed, Custom
CLOTHING STORES: Teenage
CLOTHING/ACCESS, WOMEN, CHILDREN/INFANT, WHOL: Apparel Belt
CLOTHING: Academic Vestments
CLOTHING: Access
CLOTHING: Access, Women's & Misses'
CLOTHING: Aprons, Harness
CLOTHING: Athletic & Sportswear, Men's & Boys'
CLOTHING: Athletic & Sportswear, Women's & Girls'
CLOTHING: Bathing Suits & Swimwear, Girls, Children & Infant
CLOTHING: Bathrobes, Mens & Womens, From Purchased Materials
CLOTHING: Blouses, Women's & Girls'
CLOTHING: Blouses, Womens & Juniors, From Purchased Mtrls
CLOTHING: Brassieres
CLOTHING: Bridal Gowns
CLOTHING: Burial
CLOTHING: Children & Infants'
CLOTHING: Children's, Girls'
CLOTHING: Clergy Vestments
CLOTHING: Coats & Suits, Men's & Boys'
CLOTHING: Costumes
CLOTHING: Disposable
CLOTHING: Dresses
CLOTHING: Dresses, Hand Knit
CLOTHING: Gowns & Dresses, Wedding
CLOTHING: Gowns, Formal
CLOTHING: Hats & Caps, Leather
CLOTHING: Hats & Caps, NEC
CLOTHING: Hats & Caps, Uniform
CLOTHING: Hats, Silk
CLOTHING: Hosiery, Pantyhose & Knee Length, Sheer
CLOTHING: Hospital, Men's
CLOTHING: Jogging & Warm-Up Suits, Knit
CLOTHING: Maternity
CLOTHING: Men's & boy's clothing, nec
CLOTHING: Men's & boy's underwear & nightwear
CLOTHING: Neckwear
CLOTHING: Outerwear, Knit
CLOTHING: Outerwear, Women's & Misses' NEC
CLOTHING: Overalls & Coveralls
CLOTHING: Raincoats, Exc Vulcanized Rubber, Purchased Matls
CLOTHING: Service Apparel, Women's
CLOTHING: Shirts
CLOTHING: Shirts, Dress, Men's & Boys'
CLOTHING: Shirts, Uniform, From Purchased Materials
CLOTHING: Socks
CLOTHING: Sportswear, Women's
CLOTHING: Suits, Men's & Boys', From Purchased Materials
CLOTHING: Sweaters & Sweater Coats, Knit

CLOTHING: Sweatshirts & T-Shirts, Men's & Boys'
CLOTHING: Swimwear, Men's & Boys'
CLOTHING: Swimwear, Women's & Misses'
CLOTHING: T-Shirts & Tops, Knit
CLOTHING: T-Shirts & Tops, Women's & Girls'
CLOTHING: Tailored Suits & Formal Jackets
CLOTHING: Trousers & Slacks, Men's & Boys'
CLOTHING: Tuxedos, From Purchased Materials
CLOTHING: Underwear, Knit
CLOTHING: Underwear, Women's & Children's
CLOTHING: Uniforms & Vestments
CLOTHING: Uniforms, Ex Athletic, Women's, Misses' & Juniors'
CLOTHING: Uniforms, Men's & Boys'
CLOTHING: Uniforms, Military, Men/Youth, Purchased Materials
CLOTHING: Uniforms, Policemen's, From Purchased Materials
CLOTHING: Uniforms, Team Athletic
CLOTHING: Uniforms, Work
CLOTHING: Waterproof Outerwear
CLOTHING: Work Apparel, Exc Uniforms
CLOTHING: Work, Men's
COAL & OTHER MINERALS & ORES WHOLESALERS
COAL GAS: Derived From Chemical Recovery Coke Oven
COAL LIQUEFACTION
COAL MINING EXPLORATION & TEST BORING SVC
COAL MINING SERVICES
COAL MINING SVCS: Bituminous, Contract Basis
COAL MINING: Bituminous & Lignite Surface
COAL MINING: Bituminous Coal & Lignite-Surface Mining
COAL MINING: Bituminous Underground
COAL MINING: Bituminous, Auger
COAL MINING: Bituminous, Strip
COAL MINING: Bituminous, Surface, NEC
COAL MINING: Underground, Semibituminous
COAL MINING: Underground, Subbituminous
COAL PREPARATION PLANT: Bituminous or Lignite
COAL TAR RESINS
COAL, MINERALS & ORES, WHOLESALE: Coal
COATING COMPOUNDS: Tar
COATING OR WRAPPING SVC: Steel Pipe
COATING SVC
COATING SVC: Aluminum, Metal Prdts
COATING SVC: Hot Dip, Metals Or Formed Prdts
COATING SVC: Metals & Formed Prdts
COATING SVC: Rust Preventative
COATINGS: Air Curing
COATINGS: Polyurethane
COFFEE SVCS
COILS & TRANSFORMERS
COINS & TOKENS: Non-Currency
COKE: Petroleum & Coal Derivative
COKE: Petroleum, Not From Refineries
COLLECTION AGENCIES
COLLECTOR RINGS: Electric Motors Or Generators
COLLEGE, EXC JUNIOR
COLLEGES, UNIVERSITIES & PROFESSIONAL SCHOOLS
COLOR LAKES OR TONERS
COLORS: Pigments, Inorganic
COLORS: Pigments, Organic
COMFORTERS & QUILTS, FROM MANMADE FIBER OR SILK
COMMERCIAL & LITERARY WRITINGS
COMMERCIAL & OFFICE BUILDINGS RENOVATION & REPAIR
COMMERCIAL ART & GRAPHIC DESIGN SVCS
COMMERCIAL ART & ILLUSTRATION SVCS
COMMERCIAL EQPT, WHOLESALE: Coffee Brewing Eqpt & Splys
COMMERCIAL EQPT, WHOLESALE: Comm Cooking & Food Svc Eqpt
COMMERCIAL EQPT, WHOLESALE: Scales, Exc Laboratory
COMMERCIAL LAUNDRY EQPT
COMMERCIAL PRINTING & NEWSPAPER PUBLISHING COMBINED
COMMODITY CONTRACT POOL OPERATORS
COMMODITY CONTRACT TRADING COMPANIES
COMMODITY CONTRACTS BROKERS, DEALERS
COMMON SAND MINING
COMMUNICATION HEADGEAR: Telephone
COMMUNICATIONS CARRIER: Wired
COMMUNICATIONS EQPT & SYSTEMS, NEC
COMMUNICATIONS EQPT WHOLESALERS
COMMUNICATIONS EQPT: Microwave

COMMUNICATIONS SVCS
COMMUNICATIONS SVCS: Data
COMMUNICATIONS SVCS: Internet Connectivity Svcs
COMMUNICATIONS SVCS: Internet Host Svcs
COMMUNICATIONS SVCS: Nonvocal Message
COMMUNICATIONS SVCS: Online Svc Providers
COMMUNICATIONS SVCS: Satellite Earth Stations
COMMUNICATIONS SVCS: Signal Enhancement Network Svcs
COMMUNICATIONS SVCS: Telephone Or Video
COMMUNICATIONS SVCS: Telephone, Voice
COMMUNITY CENTERS: Youth
COMMUNITY COLLEGE
COMPACT LASER DISCS: Prerecorded
COMPACTORS: Trash & Garbage, Residential
COMPOST
COMPRESSORS: Air & Gas
COMPRESSORS: Air & Gas, Including Vacuum Pumps
COMPUTER & COMPUTER SOFTWARE STORES
COMPUTER & COMPUTER SOFTWARE STORES: Peripheral Eqpt
COMPUTER & COMPUTER SOFTWARE STORES: Software & Access
COMPUTER & COMPUTER SOFTWARE STORES: Software, Bus/Non-Game
COMPUTER & COMPUTER SOFTWARE STORES: Software, Computer Game
COMPUTER & DATA PROCESSING EQPT REPAIR & MAINTENANCE
COMPUTER & OFFICE MACHINE MAINTENANCE & REPAIR
COMPUTER & SFTWR STORE: Modem, Monitor, Terminal/Disk Drive
COMPUTER FACILITIES MANAGEMENT SVCS
COMPUTER GRAPHICS SVCS
COMPUTER INTERFACE EQPT: Indl Process
COMPUTER PAPER WHOLESALERS
COMPUTER PERIPHERAL EQPT, NEC
COMPUTER PERIPHERAL EQPT, WHOLESALE
COMPUTER PERIPHERAL EQPT: Decoders
COMPUTER PERIPHERAL EQPT: Encoders
COMPUTER PERIPHERAL EQPT: Graphic Displays, Exc Terminals
COMPUTER PERIPHERAL EQPT: Input Or Output
COMPUTER PHOTOGRAPHY OR PORTRAIT SVC
COMPUTER PROCESSING SVCS
COMPUTER PROGRAMMING SVCS
COMPUTER PROGRAMMING SVCS: Custom
COMPUTER RELATED MAINTENANCE SVCS
COMPUTER RELATED SVCS, NEC
COMPUTER SERVICE BUREAU
COMPUTER SOFTWARE DEVELOPMENT
COMPUTER SOFTWARE DEVELOPMENT & APPLICATIONS
COMPUTER SOFTWARE SYSTEMS ANALYSIS & DESIGN: Custom
COMPUTER SOFTWARE WRITERS
COMPUTER STORAGE DEVICES, NEC
COMPUTER STORAGE UNITS: Auxiliary
COMPUTER SYSTEMS ANALYSIS & DESIGN
COMPUTER TERMINALS
COMPUTER TERMINALS: CRT
COMPUTER-AIDED DESIGN SYSTEMS SVCS
COMPUTER-AIDED MANUFACTURING SYSTEMS SVCS
COMPUTERS, NEC
COMPUTERS, NEC, WHOLESALE
COMPUTERS, PERIPH & SOFTWARE, WHLSE: Acctg Machs, Readable
COMPUTERS, PERIPH & SOFTWARE, WHLSE: Personal & Home Entrtn
COMPUTERS, PERIPHERALS & SOFTWARE, WHOLESALE: Software
COMPUTERS: Mainframe
COMPUTERS: Mini
COMPUTERS: Personal
CONCRETE BUILDING PRDTS WHOLESALERS
CONCRETE CURING & HARDENING COMPOUNDS
CONCRETE PRDTS
CONCRETE PRDTS, PRECAST, NEC
CONCRETE: Ready-Mixed
CONDENSERS: Heat Transfer Eqpt, Evaporative
CONDUITS & FITTINGS: Electric
CONFECTIONERY PRDTS WHOLESALERS
CONFECTIONS & CANDY

CONFINEMENT SURVEILLANCE SYS MAINTENANCE & MONITORING SVCS
CONNECTORS & TERMINALS: Electrical Device Uses
CONNECTORS: Electrical
CONNECTORS: Electronic
CONSTRUCTION & MINING MACHINERY WHOLESALERS
CONSTRUCTION & ROAD MAINTENANCE EQPT: Drags, Road
CONSTRUCTION EQPT REPAIR SVCS
CONSTRUCTION EQPT: Airport
CONSTRUCTION EQPT: Attachments
CONSTRUCTION EQPT: Attachments, Snow Plow
CONSTRUCTION EQPT: Bulldozers
CONSTRUCTION EQPT: Cranes
CONSTRUCTION EQPT: Graders, Road
CONSTRUCTION EQPT: Rakes, Land Clearing, Mechanical
CONSTRUCTION EQPT: Roofing Eqpt
CONSTRUCTION EQPT: Trucks, Off-Highway
CONSTRUCTION EQPT: Wrecker Hoists, Automobile
CONSTRUCTION MATERIALS, WHOL: Concrete/Cinder Bldg Prdts
CONSTRUCTION MATERIALS, WHOLESALE: Air Ducts, Sheet Metal
CONSTRUCTION MATERIALS, WHOLESALE: Awnings
CONSTRUCTION MATERIALS, WHOLESALE: Brick, Exc Refractory
CONSTRUCTION MATERIALS, WHOLESALE: Building Stone, Granite
CONSTRUCTION MATERIALS, WHOLESALE: Building Stone, Marble
CONSTRUCTION MATERIALS, WHOLESALE: Building, Exterior
CONSTRUCTION MATERIALS, WHOLESALE: Building, Interior
CONSTRUCTION MATERIALS, WHOLESALE: Cement
CONSTRUCTION MATERIALS, WHOLESALE: Guardrails, Metal
CONSTRUCTION MATERIALS, WHOLESALE: Joists
CONSTRUCTION MATERIALS, WHOLESALE: Masons' Materials
CONSTRUCTION MATERIALS, WHOLESALE: Millwork
CONSTRUCTION MATERIALS, WHOLESALE: Molding, All Materials
CONSTRUCTION MATERIALS, WHOLESALE: Pallets, Wood
CONSTRUCTION MATERIALS, WHOLESALE: Septic Tanks
CONSTRUCTION MATERIALS, WHOLESALE: Siding, Wood
CONSTRUCTION MATERIALS, WHOLESALE: Stone, Crushed Or Broken
CONSTRUCTION MATERIALS, WHOLESALE: Tile & Clay Prdts
CONSTRUCTION MATERIALS, WHOLESALE: Windows
CONSTRUCTION MATLS, WHOL: Lumber, Rough, Dressed/Finished
CONSTRUCTION MATLS, WHOLESALE: Soil Erosion Cntrl Fabrics
CONSTRUCTION MTRLS, WHOL: Exterior Flat Glass, Plate/Window
CONSTRUCTION SAND MINING
CONSTRUCTION SITE PREPARATION SVCS
CONSTRUCTION: Apartment Building
CONSTRUCTION: Athletic & Recreation Facilities
CONSTRUCTION: Chemical Facility
CONSTRUCTION: Commercial & Institutional Building
CONSTRUCTION: Commercial & Office Building, New
CONSTRUCTION: Drainage System
CONSTRUCTION: Elevated Highway
CONSTRUCTION: Food Prdts Manufacturing or Packing Plant
CONSTRUCTION: Foundation & Retaining Wall
CONSTRUCTION: Indl Buildings, New, NEC
CONSTRUCTION: Residential, Nec
CONSTRUCTION: Sewer Line
CONSTRUCTION: Single-Family Housing
CONSTRUCTION: Single-family Housing, New
CONSTRUCTION: Street Sign Installation & Mntnce
CONSTRUCTION: Street Surfacing & Paving
CONSTRUCTION: Transmitting Tower, Telecommunication
CONSTRUCTION: Utility Line
CONSTRUCTION: Waste Water & Sewage Treatment Plant
CONSULTING SVC: Business, NEC
CONSULTING SVC: Chemical
CONSULTING SVC: Computer
CONSULTING SVC: Data Processing
CONSULTING SVC: Educational
CONSULTING SVC: Engineering
CONSULTING SVC: Human Resource

CONSULTING SVC: Management
CONSULTING SVC: Marketing Management
CONSULTING SVC: Online Technology
CONSULTING SVC: Productivity Improvement
CONSULTING SVC: Telecommunications
CONSULTING SVCS, BUSINESS: Communications
CONSULTING SVCS, BUSINESS: Energy Conservation
CONSULTING SVCS, BUSINESS: Environmental
CONSULTING SVCS, BUSINESS: Publishing
CONSULTING SVCS, BUSINESS: Safety Training Svcs
CONSULTING SVCS, BUSINESS: Sys Engnrg, Exc Computer/Prof
CONSULTING SVCS, BUSINESS: Systems Analysis & Engineering
CONSULTING SVCS, BUSINESS: Systems Analysis Or Design
CONSULTING SVCS: Geological
CONSULTING SVCS: Geophysical
CONSULTING SVCS: Oil
CONSULTING SVCS: Scientific
CONTACT LENSES
CONTAINERS: Air Cargo, Metal
CONTAINERS: Cargo, Wood & Wood With Metal
CONTAINERS: Corrugated
CONTAINERS: Foil, Bakery Goods & Frozen Foods
CONTAINERS: Food & Beverage
CONTAINERS: Food, Liquid Tight, Including Milk
CONTAINERS: Frozen Food & Ice Cream
CONTAINERS: Glass
CONTAINERS: Metal
CONTAINERS: Plastic
CONTAINERS: Sanitary, Food
CONTAINERS: Shipping & Mailing, Fiber
CONTAINERS: Shipping, Wood
CONTAINERS: Wood
CONTRACT FOOD SVCS
CONTRACTORS: Acoustical & Insulation Work
CONTRACTORS: Asbestos Removal & Encapsulation
CONTRACTORS: Awning Installation
CONTRACTORS: Boiler Maintenance Contractor
CONTRACTORS: Building Fireproofing
CONTRACTORS: Building Sign Installation & Mntnce
CONTRACTORS: Carpentry Work
CONTRACTORS: Carpentry, Cabinet & Finish Work
CONTRACTORS: Carpentry, Cabinet Building & Installation
CONTRACTORS: Carpentry, Finish & Trim Work
CONTRACTORS: Carpet Laying
CONTRACTORS: Ceramic Floor Tile Installation
CONTRACTORS: Chimney Construction & Maintenance
CONTRACTORS: Commercial & Office Building
CONTRACTORS: Communications Svcs
CONTRACTORS: Computer Installation
CONTRACTORS: Concrete
CONTRACTORS: Construction Site Cleanup
CONTRACTORS: Core Drilling & Cutting
CONTRACTORS: Countertop Installation
CONTRACTORS: Decontamination Svcs
CONTRACTORS: Demolition, Building & Other Structures
CONTRACTORS: Directional Oil & Gas Well Drilling Svc
CONTRACTORS: Drywall
CONTRACTORS: Electrical
CONTRACTORS: Electronic Controls Installation
CONTRACTORS: Excavating
CONTRACTORS: Excavating Slush Pits & Cellars Svcs
CONTRACTORS: Fence Construction
CONTRACTORS: Fire Detection & Burglar Alarm Systems
CONTRACTORS: Fire Sprinkler System Installation Svcs
CONTRACTORS: Floor Laying & Other Floor Work
CONTRACTORS: Flooring
CONTRACTORS: Gas Field Svcs, NEC
CONTRACTORS: Gas Leak Detection
CONTRACTORS: General Electric
CONTRACTORS: Geothermal Drilling
CONTRACTORS: Glass Tinting, Architectural & Automotive
CONTRACTORS: Glass, Glazing & Tinting
CONTRACTORS: Grave Excavation
CONTRACTORS: Gutters & Downspouts
CONTRACTORS: Heating & Air Conditioning
CONTRACTORS: Heating Systems Repair & Maintenance Svc
CONTRACTORS: Highway & Street Construction, General
CONTRACTORS: Highway & Street Paving
CONTRACTORS: Hydronics Heating
CONTRACTORS: Indl Building Renovation, Remodeling & Repair

CONTRACTORS: Kitchen Cabinet Installation
CONTRACTORS: Lighting Syst
CONTRACTORS: Lightweight Steel Framing Installation
CONTRACTORS: Machinery Installation
CONTRACTORS: Marble Installation, Interior
CONTRACTORS: Marble Masonry, Exterior
CONTRACTORS: Mechanical
CONTRACTORS: Oil & Gas Aerial Geophysical Exploration Svcs
CONTRACTORS: Oil & Gas Field Fire Fighting Svcs
CONTRACTORS: Oil & Gas Field Geological Exploration Svcs
CONTRACTORS: Oil & Gas Field Salt Water Impound/Storing Svc
CONTRACTORS: Oil & Gas Well Drilling Svc
CONTRACTORS: Oil & Gas Wells Svcs
CONTRACTORS: Oil Field Haulage Svcs
CONTRACTORS: Oil Field Pipe Testing Svcs
CONTRACTORS: Oil/Gas Well Construction, Rpr/Dismantling Svcs
CONTRACTORS: On-Site Welding
CONTRACTORS: Ornamental Metal Work
CONTRACTORS: Paint & Wallpaper Stripping
CONTRACTORS: Painting & Wall Covering
CONTRACTORS: Painting, Commercial
CONTRACTORS: Painting, Indl
CONTRACTORS: Painting, Residential
CONTRACTORS: Painting, Residential, Interior
CONTRACTORS: Patio & Deck Construction & Repair
CONTRACTORS: Pavement Marking
CONTRACTORS: Pole Cutting
CONTRACTORS: Prefabricated Window & Door Installation
CONTRACTORS: Pulpwood, Engaged In Cutting
CONTRACTORS: Roofing
CONTRACTORS: Roustabout Svcs
CONTRACTORS: Safety & Security Eqpt
CONTRACTORS: Sandblasting Svc, Building Exteriors
CONTRACTORS: Septic System
CONTRACTORS: Sheet Metal Work, NEC
CONTRACTORS: Sheet metal Work, Architectural
CONTRACTORS: Ship Boiler & Tank Cleaning & Repair
CONTRACTORS: Siding
CONTRACTORS: Single-family Home General Remodeling
CONTRACTORS: Smoke Stack Installation & Maintenance, Steel
CONTRACTORS: Solar Energy Eqpt
CONTRACTORS: Sound Eqpt Installation
CONTRACTORS: Special Trades, NEC
CONTRACTORS: Sprinkler System
CONTRACTORS: Structural Iron Work, Structural
CONTRACTORS: Structural Steel Erection
CONTRACTORS: Svc Well Drilling Svcs
CONTRACTORS: Ventilation & Duct Work
CONTRACTORS: Water Well Drilling
CONTRACTORS: Well Logging Svcs
CONTRACTORS: Well Surveying Svcs
CONTRACTORS: Window Treatment Installation
CONTRACTORS: Wrecking & Demolition
CONTROL EQPT: Electric
CONTROL PANELS: Electrical
CONTROL RECEIVERS
CONTROLS & ACCESS: Indl, Electric
CONTROLS & ACCESS: Motor
CONTROLS: Electric Motor
CONTROLS: Environmental
CONTROLS: Numerical
CONTROLS: Relay & Ind
CONTROLS: Thermostats
CONTROLS: Thermostats, Exc Built-in
CONVERTERS: Data
CONVERTERS: Power, AC to DC
CONVERTERS: Torque, Exc Auto
CONVEYOR SYSTEMS: Belt, General Indl Use
CONVEYOR SYSTEMS: Bucket Type
CONVEYOR SYSTEMS: Bulk Handling
CONVEYOR SYSTEMS: Pneumatic Tube
CONVEYORS & CONVEYING EQPT
COOKING & FOOD WARMING EQPT: Commercial
COOKING & FOODWARMING EQPT: Commercial
COOKING WARE: Cooking Ware, Porcelain Enameled
COPPER PRDTS: Smelter, Primary
COPPER: Rolling & Drawing
COPY MACHINES WHOLESALERS
CORD & TWINE
CORE WASH OR WAX

CORRECTIONAL INSTITUTIONS
CORRUGATED PRDTS: Boxes, Partition, Display Items, Sheet/Pad
COSMETIC PREPARATIONS
COSMETICS & TOILETRIES
COSMETICS WHOLESALERS
COSMETOLOGIST
COSTUME JEWELRY & NOVELTIES: Apparel, Exc Precious Metals
COSTUME JEWELRY & NOVELTIES: Bracelets, Exc Precious Metals
COSTUME JEWELRY & NOVELTIES: Exc Semi & Precious
COSTUME JEWELRY & NOVELTIES: Pins, Exc Precious Metals
COSTUME JEWELRY STORES
COUGH MEDICINES
COUNTER & SINK TOPS
COUNTERS OR COUNTER DISPLAY CASES, WOOD
COUNTING DEVICES: Speedometers
COUPLINGS: Hose & Tube, Hydraulic Or Pneumatic
COUPLINGS: Shaft
COURIER SVCS, AIR: Parcel Delivery, Private
COVERS & PADS Chair, Made From Purchased Materials
COVERS: Automobile Seat
COVERS: Automotive, Exc Seat & Tire
COVERS: Slip Made Of Fabric, Plastic, Etc.
COVERS: Tire
CRACKED CASTING REPAIR SVCS
CRANE & AERIAL LIFT SVCS
CRANES: Indl Plant
CRANES: Indl Truck
CRANES: Locomotive
CRANES: Overhead
CRANKSHAFTS & CAMSHAFTS: Machining
CRATES: Fruit, Wood Wirebound
CRAYONS
CRUDE PETROLEUM & NATURAL GAS PRODUCTION
CRUDE PETROLEUM & NATURAL GAS PRODUCTION
CRUDE PETROLEUM PRODUCTION
CRYSTAL GOODS, WHOLESALE
CRYSTALS & CRYSTAL ASSEMBLIES: Radio
CULTURE MEDIA
CUPS & PLATES: Foamed Plastics
CURBING: Granite Or Stone
CURTAIN & DRAPERY FIXTURES: Poles, Rods & Rollers
CURTAINS & BEDDING: Knit
CURTAINS: Window, From Purchased Materials
CUSHIONS & PILLOWS
CUSHIONS & PILLOWS: Bed, From Purchased Materials
CUSHIONS: Carpet & Rug, Foamed Plastics
CUSHIONS: Textile, Exc Spring & Carpet
CUSTOM COMPOUNDING OF RUBBER MATERIALS
CUT STONE & STONE PRODUCTS
CUTLERY
CUTTING EQPT: Milling
CUTTING SVC: Paper, Exc Die-Cut
CYCLIC CRUDES & INTERMEDIATES
CYCLO RUBBERS: Synthetic
CYLINDER & ACTUATORS: Fluid Power

D

DAIRY PRDTS STORE: Cheese
DAIRY PRDTS STORES
DAIRY PRDTS WHOLESALERS: Fresh
DAIRY PRDTS: Butter
DAIRY PRDTS: Custard, Frozen
DAIRY PRDTS: Dairy Based Desserts, Frozen
DAIRY PRDTS: Dietary Supplements, Dairy & Non-Dairy Based
DAIRY PRDTS: Evaporated Milk
DAIRY PRDTS: Farmers' Cheese
DAIRY PRDTS: Frozen Desserts & Novelties
DAIRY PRDTS: Ice Cream & Ice Milk
DAIRY PRDTS: Ice Cream, Bulk
DAIRY PRDTS: Ice Cream, Packaged, Molded, On Sticks, Etc.
DAIRY PRDTS: Milk, Chocolate
DAIRY PRDTS: Milk, Condensed & Evaporated
DAIRY PRDTS: Milk, Fluid
DAIRY PRDTS: Milk, Processed, Pasteurized, Homogenized/Btld
DAIRY PRDTS: Natural Cheese
DAIRY PRDTS: Processed Cheese
DAIRY PRDTS: Yogurt Mix
DAIRY PRDTS: Yogurt, Exc Frozen

DAIRY PRDTS: Yogurt, Frozen
DATA PROCESSING & PREPARATION SVCS
DATA PROCESSING SVCS
DATABASE INFORMATION RETRIEVAL SVCS
DECORATIVE WOOD & WOODWORK
DEFENSE SYSTEMS & EQPT
DEHUMIDIFIERS: Electric
DENTAL EQPT
DENTAL EQPT & SPLYS
DENTAL EQPT & SPLYS: Dental Materials
DENTAL EQPT & SPLYS: Enamels
DENTAL EQPT & SPLYS: Hand Pieces & Parts
DENTAL EQPT & SPLYS: Laboratory
DENTAL EQPT & SPLYS: Teeth, Artificial, Exc In Dental Labs
DENTAL INSTRUMENT REPAIR SVCS
DENTISTS' OFFICES & CLINICS
DEODORANTS: Personal
DEPARTMENT STORES
DEPARTMENT STORES: Country General
DEPTH CHARGE RELEASE MECHANISMS
DERMATOLOGICALS
DERRICKS
DESIGN SVCS, NEC
DESIGN SVCS: Commercial & Indl
DESIGN SVCS: Computer Integrated Systems
DETECTION APPARATUS: Electronic/Magnetic Field, Light/Heat
DETECTIVE AGENCY
DETECTORS: Water Leak
DIAGNOSTIC SUBSTANCES
DIAGNOSTIC SUBSTANCES OR AGENTS: Cytology & Histology
DIAGNOSTIC SUBSTANCES OR AGENTS: In Vitro
DIAGNOSTIC SUBSTANCES OR AGENTS: In Vivo
DIAGNOSTIC SUBSTANCES OR AGENTS: Microbiology & Virology
DIAMOND CLOTH, MADE FROM PURCHASED WIRE
DIAMOND SETTER SVCS
DIAPERS: Disposable
DIE SETS: Presses, Metal Stamping
DIES & TOOLS: Special
DIES: Steel Rule
DIES: Wire Drawing & Straightening
DIODES & RECTIFIERS
DIODES: Light Emitting
DIORITE: Crushed & Broken
DIRECT SELLING ESTABLISHMENTS, NEC
DISASTER SVCS
DISCOUNT DEPARTMENT STORES
DISHWASHING EQPT: Commercial
DISPENSING EQPT & PARTS, BEVERAGE: Beer
DISPENSING EQPT & PARTS, BEVERAGE: Cold, Exc Coin-Operated
DISPENSING EQPT & PARTS, BEVERAGE: Fountain/Other Beverage
DISPLAY FIXTURES: Showcases, Wood, Exc Refrigerated
DISPLAY FIXTURES: Wood
DISTILLERS DRIED GRAIN & SOLUBLES
DISTRIBUTORS: Motor Vehicle Engine
DOCKING SVCS: Ocean Vessels
DOCKS: Floating, Wood
DOOR & WINDOW REPAIR SVCS
DOOR OPERATING SYSTEMS: Electric
DOORS & WINDOWS WHOLESALERS: All Materials
DOORS & WINDOWS: Storm, Metal
DOORS: Combination Screen & Storm, Wood
DOORS: Folding, Plastic Or Plastic Coated Fabric
DOORS: Garage, Overhead, Metal
DOORS: Garage, Overhead, Wood
DOORS: Glass
DOORS: Louver, Wood
DOORS: Wooden
DOWNSPOUTS: Sheet Metal
DRAINAGE PRDTS: Concrete
DRAINING OR PUMPING OF METAL MINES
DRAPERIES & CURTAINS
DRAPERIES & DRAPERY FABRICS, COTTON
DRAPERIES: Plastic & Textile, From Purchased Materials
DRAPERY & UPHOLSTERY STORES: Draperies
DRAPES & DRAPERY FABRICS, FROM MANMADE FIBER
DRESS SHIELDS: Rubber, Vulcanized Or Rubberized Fabric
DRILL BITS
DRILLING MACHINERY & EQPT: Water Well
DRILLING MUD COMPOUNDS, CONDITIONERS & ADDITIVES

DRILLS & DRILLING EQPT: Mining
DRINKING FOUNTAINS: Mechanically Refrigerated
DRINKING PLACES: Alcoholic Beverages
DRIVE CHAINS: Bicycle Or Motorcycle
DRIVES: High Speed Indl, Exc Hydrostatic
DRONES: Target, Used By Ships, Metal
DROP CLOTHS: Fabric
DRUG TESTING KITS: Blood & Urine
DRUGS & DRUG PROPRIETARIES, WHOLESALE: Patent Medicines
DRUGS & DRUG PROPRIETARIES, WHOLESALE: Pharmaceuticals
DRUMS: Brake
DUCTS: Sheet Metal
DUMPSTERS: Garbage
DYEING & FINISHING: Wool Or Similar Fibers

E

EATING PLACES
EDITING SVCS
EDITORIAL SVCS
EDUCATIONAL PROGRAMS ADMINISTRATION SVCS
EDUCATIONAL SVCS
ELASTIC BRAID & NARROW WOVEN FABRICS
ELECTRIC & OTHER SERVICES COMBINED
ELECTRIC MOTOR REPAIR SVCS
ELECTRIC SERVICES
ELECTRIC SVCS, NEC Power Transmission
ELECTRIC SVCS, NEC: Power Generation
ELECTRICAL APPARATUS & EQPT WHOLESALERS
ELECTRICAL CURRENT CARRYING WIRING DEVICES
ELECTRICAL DISCHARGE MACHINING, EDM
ELECTRICAL EQPT & SPLYS
ELECTRICAL EQPT FOR ENGINES
ELECTRICAL EQPT REPAIR & MAINTENANCE
ELECTRICAL EQPT REPAIR SVCS
ELECTRICAL EQPT: Automotive, NEC
ELECTRICAL GOODS, WHOLESALE: Batteries, Storage, Indl
ELECTRICAL GOODS, WHOLESALE: Cable Conduit
ELECTRICAL GOODS, WHOLESALE: Electronic Parts
ELECTRICAL GOODS, WHOLESALE: Fire Alarm Systems
ELECTRICAL GOODS, WHOLESALE: Intercommunication Eqpt
ELECTRICAL GOODS, WHOLESALE: Light Bulbs & Related Splys
ELECTRICAL GOODS, WHOLESALE: Lighting Fixtures, Comm & Indl
ELECTRICAL GOODS, WHOLESALE: Motor Ctrls, Starters & Relays
ELECTRICAL GOODS, WHOLESALE: Motors
ELECTRICAL GOODS, WHOLESALE: Receptacles
ELECTRICAL GOODS, WHOLESALE: Signaling, Eqpt
ELECTRICAL GOODS, WHOLESALE: Switchgear
ELECTRICAL GOODS, WHOLESALE: Transformers
ELECTRICAL INDL APPARATUS, NEC
ELECTRICAL MEASURING INSTRUMENT REPAIR & CALIBRATION SVCS
ELECTRICAL SPLYS
ELECTROMEDICAL EQPT
ELECTRON BEAM: Cutting, Forming, Welding
ELECTRON TUBES
ELECTRONIC COMPONENTS
ELECTRONIC DEVICES: Solid State, NEC
ELECTRONIC EQPT REPAIR SVCS
ELECTRONIC LOADS & POWER SPLYS
ELECTRONIC PARTS & EQPT WHOLESALERS
ELECTRONIC SECRETARIES
ELECTRONIC SHOPPING
ELECTRONIC TRAINING DEVICES
ELECTROPLATING & PLATING SVC
ELEMENTARY & SECONDARY SCHOOLS, SPECIAL EDUCATION
ELEVATORS & EQPT
ELEVATORS: Stair, Motor Powered
EMBALMING FLUID
EMBLEMS: Embroidered
EMBOSSING SVC: Paper
EMBROIDERING & ART NEEDLEWORK FOR THE TRADE
EMBROIDERING SVC
EMBROIDERING SVC: Schiffli Machine
EMBROIDERY ADVERTISING SVCS
EMBROIDERY KITS
EMERGENCY ALARMS
EMPLOYEE LEASING SVCS
EMPLOYMENT AGENCY SVCS

ENCODERS: Digital
ENGINE PARTS & ACCESS: Internal Combustion
ENGINE REBUILDING: Diesel
ENGINE REBUILDING: Gas
ENGINEERING SVCS
ENGINEERING SVCS: Aviation Or Aeronautical
ENGINEERING SVCS: Construction & Civil
ENGINEERING SVCS: Electrical Or Electronic
ENGINEERING SVCS: Heating & Ventilation
ENGINEERING SVCS: Industrial
ENGINEERING SVCS: Marine
ENGINEERING SVCS: Mechanical
ENGINEERING SVCS: Structural
ENGINES & ENGINE PARTS: Guided Missile
ENGINES & ENGINE PARTS: Guided Missile, Research & Develpt
ENGINES: Diesel & Semi-Diesel Or Duel Fuel
ENGINES: Internal Combustion, NEC
ENGINES: Jet Propulsion
ENGINES: Marine
ENGRAVING SVC, NEC
ENGRAVING SVC: Jewelry & Personal Goods
ENGRAVING SVCS
ENGRAVING: Currency
ENGRAVINGS: Plastic
ENTERTAINERS & ENTERTAINMENT GROUPS
ENTERTAINMENT SVCS
ENVELOPES
ENVIR QLTY PROG ADMN, GOV: Land, Minl & Wildlif Consv, State
ENZYMES
EQUIPMENT: Pedestrian Traffic Control
ESCALATORS: Passenger & Freight
ETCHING & ENGRAVING SVC
ETHYLENE-PROPYLENE RUBBERS: EPDM Polymers
EXHAUST SYSTEMS: Eqpt & Parts
EXPANSION JOINTS: Rubber
EXPLOSIVES
EXPLOSIVES, EXC AMMO & FIREWORKS WHOLESALERS
EXPLOSIVES: Amatols
EXPLOSIVES: Black Powder
EXPLOSIVES: Gunpowder
EXTRACTS, FLAVORING
EYEGLASSES
EYELASHES, ARTIFICIAL

F

FABRICATED METAL PRODUCTS, NEC
FABRICS & CLOTH: Quilted
FABRICS & CLOTHING: Rubber Coated
FABRICS: Airplane Cloth, Cotton
FABRICS: Alpacas, Mohair, Woven
FABRICS: Apparel & Outerwear, Broadwoven
FABRICS: Apparel & Outerwear, Cotton
FABRICS: Apparel & Outerwear, From Manmade Fiber Or Silk
FABRICS: Automotive, Cotton
FABRICS: Bird's-Eye Diaper Cloth, Cotton
FABRICS: Bonded-Fiber, Exc Felt
FABRICS: Broadwoven, Cotton
FABRICS: Broadwoven, Synthetic Manmade Fiber & Silk
FABRICS: Broadwoven, Wool
FABRICS: Canvas
FABRICS: Chemically Coated & Treated
FABRICS: Coated Or Treated
FABRICS: Cords
FABRICS: Denims
FABRICS: Fiberglass, Broadwoven
FABRICS: Furniture Denim
FABRICS: Ginghams
FABRICS: Glass, Narrow
FABRICS: Lacings, Textile
FABRICS: Luggage, Cotton
FABRICS: Nonwoven
FABRICS: Parachute Fabrics
FABRICS: Polypropylene, Broadwoven
FABRICS: Print, Cotton
FABRICS: Resin Or Plastic Coated
FABRICS: Satin
FABRICS: Shirting, Cotton
FABRICS: Shirting, From Manmade Fiber Or Silk
FABRICS: Spunbonded
FABRICS: Trimmings
FABRICS: Tubing, Textile, Varnished
FABRICS: Velveteens
FABRICS: Waterproofed, Exc Rubberized

FABRICS: Wool, Broadwoven
FABRICS: Woven Wire, Made From Purchased Wire
FABRICS: Woven, Narrow Cotton, Wool, Silk
FACIAL SALONS
FACILITIES SUPPORT SVCS
FAMILY CLOTHING STORES
FANS, EXHAUST: Indl Or Commercial
FANS, VENTILATING: Indl Or Commercial
FARM & GARDEN MACHINERY WHOLESALERS
FARM MACHINERY REPAIR SVCS
FARM SPLY STORES
FARM SPLYS WHOLESALERS
FARM SPLYS, WHOLESALE: Herbicides
FASTENERS: Metal
FASTENERS: Notions, NEC
FASTENERS: Notions, Zippers
FAUCETS & SPIGOTS: Metal & Plastic
FEATHERS & FEATHER PRODUCTS
FENCES OR POSTS: Ornamental Iron Or Steel
FENCING MATERIALS: Docks & Other Outdoor Prdts, Wood
FENCING MATERIALS: Plastic
FENCING MATERIALS: Wood
FENCING: Chain Link
FERTILIZER, AGRICULTURAL: Wholesalers
FERTILIZERS: NEC
FERTILIZERS: Nitrogenous
FERTILIZERS: Phosphatic
FIBER & FIBER PRDTS: Cigarette Tow Cellulosic
FIBER & FIBER PRDTS: Organic, Noncellulose
FIBER & FIBER PRDTS: Protein
FIBER & FIBER PRDTS: Synthetic Cellulosic
FIBER OPTICS
FIBERS: Carbon & Graphite
FILE FOLDERS
FILLERS & SEALERS: Putty
FILM & SHEET: Unsuppported Plastic
FILM BASE: Cellulose Acetate Or Nitrocellulose Plastics
FILM: Motion Picture
FILM: Rubber
FILTERS
FILTERS & SOFTENERS: Water, Household
FILTERS: Air
FILTERS: Air Intake, Internal Combustion Engine, Exc Auto
FILTERS: General Line, Indl
FILTERS: Paper
FILTRATION DEVICES: Electronic
FINANCIAL INVESTMENT ACTIVITIES, NEC: Financial Reporting
FINANCIAL SVCS
FINDINGS & TRIMMINGS: Apparel
FINGERNAILS, ARTIFICIAL
FINGERPRINT EQPT
FINISHING AGENTS
FINISHING AGENTS: Leather
FIRE ARMS, SMALL: Guns Or Gun Parts, 30 mm & Below
FIRE ARMS, SMALL: Machine Guns & Grenade Launchers
FIRE ARMS, SMALL: Machine Guns/Machine Gun Parts, 30mm/below
FIRE ARMS, SMALL: Pistols Or Pistol Parts, 30 mm & below
FIRE ARMS, SMALL: Shotguns Or Shotgun Parts, 30 mm & Below
FIRE CONTROL OR BOMBING EQPT: Electronic
FIRE DETECTION SYSTEMS
FIRE EXTINGUISHER CHARGES
FIRE EXTINGUISHER SVC
FIRE EXTINGUISHERS, WHOLESALE
FIRE EXTINGUISHERS: Portable
FIRE OR BURGLARY RESISTIVE PRDTS
FIRE PROTECTION EQPT
FIRE PROTECTION, EXC CONTRACT
FIREARMS & AMMUNITION, EXC SPORTING, WHOLESALE
FIREARMS, EXC SPORTING, WHOLESALE
FIREARMS: Large, Greater Than 30mm
FIREARMS: Small, 30mm or Less
FIREPLACE & CHIMNEY MATERIAL: Concrete
FIREPLACE EQPT & ACCESS
FISH & SEAFOOD PROCESSORS: Canned Or Cured
FISH & SEAFOOD PROCESSORS: Fresh Or Frozen
FISH & SEAFOOD WHOLESALERS
FISH FOOD
FISHING EQPT: Lures
FITTINGS & ASSEMBLIES: Hose & Tube, Hydraulic Or Pneumatic
FITTINGS: Pipe
FIXTURES & EQPT: Kitchen, Metal, Exc Cast Aluminum

FLAG POLES, WHOLESALE
FLAGPOLES
FLAGS: Fabric
FLAGSTONES
FLAT GLASS: Antique
FLAT GLASS: Laminated
FLAT GLASS: Tempered
FLAT GLASS: Window, Clear & Colored
FLATWARE, STAINLESS STEEL
FLIGHT RECORDERS
FLOOR CLEANING & MAINTENANCE EQPT: Household
FLOOR COVERING STORES: Carpets
FLOOR COVERING STORES: Rugs
FLOOR COVERINGS WHOLESALERS
FLOOR COVERINGS: Art Squares, Textile Fiber
FLOORING: Hard Surface
FLOORING: Hardwood
FLOORING: Parquet, Hardwood
FLOORING: Tile
FLORIST: Plants, Potted
FLOWER ARRANGEMENTS: Artificial
FLOWER POTS Plastic
FLOWERS & FLORISTS' SPLYS WHOLESALERS
FLOWERS: Artificial & Preserved
FLUES & PIPES: Stove Or Furnace
FLUID METERS & COUNTING DEVICES
FLUID POWER PUMPS & MOTORS
FLUID POWER VALVES & HOSE FITTINGS
FLUXES
FOAMS & RUBBER, WHOLESALE
FOIL & LEAF: Metal
FOIL: Laminated To Paper Or Other Materials
FOOD PRDTS & SEAFOOD: Shellfish, Fresh, Shucked
FOOD PRDTS, BREAKFAST: Cereal, Granola & Muesli
FOOD PRDTS, BREAKFAST: Cereal, Oatmeal
FOOD PRDTS, CANNED OR FRESH PACK: Fruit Juices
FOOD PRDTS, CANNED OR FRESH PACK: Vegetable Juices
FOOD PRDTS, CANNED, NEC
FOOD PRDTS, CANNED: Applesauce
FOOD PRDTS, CANNED: Barbecue Sauce
FOOD PRDTS, CANNED: Bean Sprouts
FOOD PRDTS, CANNED: Chili Sauce, Tomato
FOOD PRDTS, CANNED: Ethnic
FOOD PRDTS, CANNED: Fruit Juices, Concentrated
FOOD PRDTS, CANNED: Fruit Juices, Fresh
FOOD PRDTS, CANNED: Fruits
FOOD PRDTS, CANNED: Fruits
FOOD PRDTS, CANNED: Fruits & Fruit Prdts
FOOD PRDTS, CANNED: Hominy
FOOD PRDTS, CANNED: Jams, Jellies & Preserves
FOOD PRDTS, CANNED: Jellies, Edible, Including Imitation
FOOD PRDTS, CANNED: Mexican, NEC
FOOD PRDTS, CANNED: Olives
FOOD PRDTS, CANNED: Puddings, Exc Meat
FOOD PRDTS, CANNED: Seasonings, Tomato
FOOD PRDTS, CANNED: Spanish
FOOD PRDTS, CANNED: Tomato Purees
FOOD PRDTS, CANNED: Tortillas
FOOD PRDTS, CANNED: Vegetables
FOOD PRDTS, CONFECTIONERY, WHOLESALE: Candy
FOOD PRDTS, CONFECTIONERY, WHOLESALE: Snack Foods
FOOD PRDTS, FISH & SEAFOOD, WHOLESALE: Seafood
FOOD PRDTS, FISH & SEAFOOD: Canned & Jarred, Etc
FOOD PRDTS, FISH & SEAFOOD: Crabmeat, Canned, Jarred, Etc
FOOD PRDTS, FISH & SEAFOOD: Crabmeat, Preserved & Cured
FOOD PRDTS, FISH & SEAFOOD: Fish Fillets
FOOD PRDTS, FISH & SEAFOOD: Fish, Fresh, Prepared
FOOD PRDTS, FISH & SEAFOOD: Fish, Frozen, Prepared
FOOD PRDTS, FISH & SEAFOOD: Fresh, Prepared
FOOD PRDTS, FISH & SEAFOOD: Fresh/Frozen Chowder, Soup/Stew
FOOD PRDTS, FISH & SEAFOOD: Herring, Canned, Jarred, Etc
FOOD PRDTS, FISH & SEAFOOD: Oysters, Canned, Jarred, Etc
FOOD PRDTS, FISH & SEAFOOD: Oysters, Preserved & Cured
FOOD PRDTS, FISH & SEAFOOD: Seafood, Frozen, Prepared
FOOD PRDTS, FISH & SEAFOOD: Soup, Stew/Chowdr, Canned/Pkgd

INDEX

FOOD PRDTS, FROZEN, WHOLESALE: Vegetables & Fruit Prdts
FOOD PRDTS, FROZEN: Dinners, Packaged
FOOD PRDTS, FROZEN: Ethnic Foods, NEC
FOOD PRDTS, FROZEN: Fruits, Juices & Vegetables
FOOD PRDTS, FROZEN: NEC
FOOD PRDTS, FROZEN: Pizza
FOOD PRDTS, FRUITS & VEGETABLES, FRESH, WHOLESALE: Vegetable
FOOD PRDTS, MEAT & MEAT PRDTS, WHOLESALE: Cured Or Smoked
FOOD PRDTS, MEAT & MEAT PRDTS, WHOLESALE: Fresh
FOOD PRDTS, WHOLESALE: Coffee, Green Or Roasted
FOOD PRDTS, WHOLESALE: Condiments
FOOD PRDTS, WHOLESALE: Dog Food
FOOD PRDTS, WHOLESALE: Natural & Organic
FOOD PRDTS, WHOLESALE: Organic & Diet
FOOD PRDTS, WHOLESALE: Pasta & Rice
FOOD PRDTS, WHOLESALE: Sauces
FOOD PRDTS, WHOLESALE: Spaghetti
FOOD PRDTS, WHOLESALE: Specialty
FOOD PRDTS, WHOLESALE: Water, Mineral Or Spring, Bottled
FOOD PRDTS: Animal & marine fats & oils
FOOD PRDTS: Baking Soda
FOOD PRDTS: Box Lunches, For Sale Off Premises
FOOD PRDTS: Cereals
FOOD PRDTS: Chicken, Processed, Fresh
FOOD PRDTS: Chicken, Processed, Frozen
FOOD PRDTS: Coffee
FOOD PRDTS: Coffee Roasting, Exc Wholesale Grocers
FOOD PRDTS: Coffee, Ground, Mixed With Grain Or Chicory
FOOD PRDTS: Corn Chips & Other Corn-Based Snacks
FOOD PRDTS: Dates, Dried
FOOD PRDTS: Desserts, Ready-To-Mix
FOOD PRDTS: Dips, Exc Cheese & Sour Cream Based
FOOD PRDTS: Dressings, Salad, Raw & Cooked Exc Dry Mixes
FOOD PRDTS: Durum Flour
FOOD PRDTS: Edible fats & oils
FOOD PRDTS: Eggs, Processed
FOOD PRDTS: Enriched Rice (Vitamin & Mineral Fortified)
FOOD PRDTS: Fish Meal
FOOD PRDTS: Fish Oil
FOOD PRDTS: Flour
FOOD PRDTS: Flour & Other Grain Mill Products
FOOD PRDTS: Flour Mixes & Doughs
FOOD PRDTS: Freeze-Dried Coffee
FOOD PRDTS: Frosting Mixes, Dry, For Cakes, Cookies, Etc.
FOOD PRDTS: Fruit Juices
FOOD PRDTS: Fruits & Vegetables, Pickled
FOOD PRDTS: Honey
FOOD PRDTS: Ice, Cubes
FOOD PRDTS: Instant Coffee
FOOD PRDTS: Jelly, Corncob
FOOD PRDTS: Leavening Compounds, Prepared
FOOD PRDTS: Macaroni Prdts, Dry, Alphabet, Rings Or Shells
FOOD PRDTS: Macaroni, Noodles, Spaghetti, Pasta, Etc
FOOD PRDTS: Margarine & Vegetable Oils
FOOD PRDTS: Mixes, Bread & Roll From Purchased Flour
FOOD PRDTS: Mixes, Sauces, Dry
FOOD PRDTS: Mixes, Seasonings, Dry
FOOD PRDTS: Mustard, Prepared
FOOD PRDTS: Noodles, Uncooked, Packaged W/Other Ingredients
FOOD PRDTS: Nuts & Seeds
FOOD PRDTS: Oils & Fats, Animal
FOOD PRDTS: Olive Oil
FOOD PRDTS: Palm Kernel Oil
FOOD PRDTS: Pasta, Rice/Potatoes, Uncooked, Pkgd
FOOD PRDTS: Pasta, Uncooked, Packaged With Other Ingredients
FOOD PRDTS: Peanut Butter
FOOD PRDTS: Pickles, Vinegar
FOOD PRDTS: Popcorn, Unpopped
FOOD PRDTS: Potato & Corn Chips & Similar Prdts
FOOD PRDTS: Potato Chips & Other Potato-Based Snacks
FOOD PRDTS: Potatoes, Dried
FOOD PRDTS: Poultry Sausage, Lunch Meats/Other Poultry Prdts
FOOD PRDTS: Poultry, Processed, Fresh
FOOD PRDTS: Poultry, Processed, NEC
FOOD PRDTS: Preparations
FOOD PRDTS: Prepared Meat Sauces Exc Tomato & Dry

FOOD PRDTS: Prepared Sauces, Exc Tomato Based
FOOD PRDTS: Rice, Milled
FOOD PRDTS: Salads
FOOD PRDTS: Sandwiches
FOOD PRDTS: Seasonings & Spices
FOOD PRDTS: Soy Sauce
FOOD PRDTS: Spices, Including Ground
FOOD PRDTS: Starch, Indl
FOOD PRDTS: Sugar
FOOD PRDTS: Sugar, Powdered, From Purchased Ingredients
FOOD PRDTS: Syrup, Maple
FOOD PRDTS: Syrup, Pancake, Blended & Mixed
FOOD PRDTS: Syrups
FOOD PRDTS: Tapioca
FOOD PRDTS: Tea
FOOD PRDTS: Tortillas
FOOD PRDTS: Turkey, Processed, Fresh
FOOD PRDTS: Vegetable Oil Mills, NEC
FOOD PRDTS: Vegetable Oil, Refined, Exc Corn
FOOD PRDTS: Vegetables, Dried or Dehydrated Exc Freeze-Dried
FOOD PRDTS: Vinegar
FOOD PRODUCTS MACHINERY
FOOD STORES: Cooperative
FOOD STORES: Frozen Food &Freezer Plans, Exc Meat
FOOTWEAR: Custom Made
FOOTWEAR: Cut Stock
FORESTRY RELATED EQPT
FORGINGS
FORGINGS: Aluminum
FORGINGS: Bearing & Bearing Race, Nonferrous
FORGINGS: Engine Or Turbine, Nonferrous
FORGINGS: Gear & Chain
FORGINGS: Machinery, Ferrous
FORGINGS: Metal , Ornamental, Ferrous
FORGINGS: Missile & Ordinance, Nonferrous
FORGINGS: Nonferrous
FORGINGS: Pump & Compressor, Ferrous
FORMS: Concrete, Sheet Metal
FOUNDRIES: Aluminum
FOUNDRIES: Brass, Bronze & Copper
FOUNDRIES: Gray & Ductile Iron
FOUNDRIES: Nonferrous
FOUNDRIES: Steel
FOUNDRIES: Steel Investment
FOUNTAINS, METAL, EXC DRINKING
FRAMES & FRAMING WHOLESALE
FRAMES: Chair, Metal
FRANCHISES, SELLING OR LICENSING
FREIGHT FORWARDING ARRANGEMENTS
FREON
FRITS
FRUITS: Artificial & Preserved
FUEL ADDITIVES
FUEL DEALERS: Coal
FUEL TREATING
FUELS: Diesel
FUELS: Ethanol
FUELS: Jet
FUELS: Nuclear
FUELS: Nuclear, Uranium Slug, Radioactive
FUELS: Oil
FUR: Apparel
FURNACES & OVENS: Indl
FURNITURE & CABINET STORES: Cabinets, Custom Work
FURNITURE & CABINET STORES: Custom
FURNITURE & FIXTURES Factory
FURNITURE COMPONENTS: Porcelain Enameled
FURNITURE PARTS: Metal
FURNITURE REPAIR & MAINTENANCE SVCS
FURNITURE STOCK & PARTS: Carvings, Wood
FURNITURE STOCK & PARTS: Dimension Stock, Hardwood
FURNITURE STOCK & PARTS: Frames, Upholstered Furniture, Wood
FURNITURE STOCK & PARTS: Hardwood
FURNITURE STOCK & PARTS: Turnings, Wood
FURNITURE STORES
FURNITURE STORES: Cabinets, Kitchen, Exc Custom Made
FURNITURE STORES: Office
FURNITURE WHOLESALERS
FURNITURE, WHOLESALE: Bar
FURNITURE, WHOLESALE: Bookcases
FURNITURE, WHOLESALE: Filing Units
FURNITURE: Bed Frames & Headboards, Wood

FURNITURE: Bedroom, Wood
FURNITURE: Benches, Cut Stone
FURNITURE: Bookcases & Partitions, Office, Exc Wood
FURNITURE: Box Springs, Assembled
FURNITURE: Cabinets & Vanities, Medicine, Metal
FURNITURE: Chairs & Couches, Wood, Upholstered
FURNITURE: Chairs, Household Upholstered
FURNITURE: Chairs, Office Wood
FURNITURE: Church
FURNITURE: Club Room, Wood
FURNITURE: Commodes
FURNITURE: Desks & Tables, Office, Exc Wood
FURNITURE: Desks & Tables, Office, Wood
FURNITURE: Frames, Box Springs Or Bedsprings, Metal
FURNITURE: Garden, Exc Wood, Metal, Stone Or Concrete
FURNITURE: Garden, Metal
FURNITURE: Hospital
FURNITURE: Hotel
FURNITURE: Household, Metal
FURNITURE: Household, NEC
FURNITURE: Household, Novelty, Metal
FURNITURE: Household, Upholstered On Metal Frames
FURNITURE: Household, Upholstered, Exc Wood Or Metal
FURNITURE: Household, Wood
FURNITURE: Hydraulic Barber & Beauty Shop Chairs
FURNITURE: Institutional, Exc Wood
FURNITURE: Lawn & Garden, Except Wood & Metal
FURNITURE: Lawn & Garden, Metal
FURNITURE: Lawn, Metal
FURNITURE: Lawn, Wood
FURNITURE: Living Room, Upholstered On Wood Frames
FURNITURE: Mattresses & Foundations
FURNITURE: Mattresses, Box & Bedsprings
FURNITURE: Mattresses, Innerspring Or Box Spring
FURNITURE: NEC
FURNITURE: Nursery, Metal
FURNITURE: Office Panel Systems, Exc Wood
FURNITURE: Office, Exc Wood
FURNITURE: Office, Wood
FURNITURE: Outdoor, Wood
FURNITURE: Picnic Tables Or Benches, Park
FURNITURE: Restaurant
FURNITURE: Ship
FURNITURE: Sleep
FURNITURE: Stools, Office, Wood
FURNITURE: Storage Chests, Household, Wood
FURNITURE: Tables & Table Tops, Wood
FURNITURE: Tables, Office, Exc Wood
FURNITURE: Upholstered
Furs

G

GAMES & TOYS: Automobiles & Trucks
GAMES & TOYS: Banks
GAMES & TOYS: Board Games, Children's & Adults'
GAMES & TOYS: Books, Picture & Cutout
GAMES & TOYS: Carriages, Baby
GAMES & TOYS: Cars, Play, Children's Vehicles
GAMES & TOYS: Chessmen & Chessboards
GAMES & TOYS: Craft & Hobby Kits & Sets
GAMES & TOYS: Dolls & Doll Clothing
GAMES & TOYS: Electronic
GAMES & TOYS: Kits, Science, Incl Microscopes/Chemistry Sets
GAMES & TOYS: Puzzles
GAMES & TOYS: Rocking Horses
GAMES & TOYS: Strollers, Baby, Vehicle
GAMES & TOYS: Structural Toy Sets
GAMES & TOYS: Toy Guns
GAMES & TOYS: Trains & Eqpt, Electric & Mechanical
GARBAGE CONTAINERS: Plastic
GARBAGE DISPOSALS: Household
GAS & OIL FIELD EXPLORATION SVCS
GAS & OIL FIELD SVCS, NEC
GAS FIELD MACHINERY & EQPT
GAS PRODUCTION & DISTRIBUTION
GAS WELDING RODS, MADE FROM PURCHASED WIRE
GASES & LIQUIFIED PETROLEUM GASES
GASES: Argon
GASES: Indl
GASES: Neon
GASES: Nitrogen
GASES: Oxygen
GASKET MATERIALS
GASKETS

GASOLINE FILLING STATIONS
GATES: Ornamental Metal
GEARS: Power Transmission, Exc Auto
GEM STONES MINING, NEC: Natural
GENERAL MERCHANDISE, NONDURABLE, WHOLESALE
GENERATING APPARATUS & PARTS: Electrical
GENERATION EQPT: Electronic
GENERATORS: Electric
GENERATORS: Electrochemical, Fuel Cell
GENERATORS: Gas
GENERATORS: Storage Battery Chargers
GENERATORS: Thermo-Electric
GHOST WRITING SVCS
GIFT SHOP
GIFT, NOVELTY & SOUVENIR STORES: Gifts & Novelties
GIFTS & NOVELTIES: Wholesalers
GIFTWARE: Copper
GLASS & GLASS CERAMIC PRDTS, PRESSED OR
   BLOWN: Tableware
GLASS FABRICATORS
GLASS PRDTS, FROM PURCHASED GLASS: Art
GLASS PRDTS, FROM PURCHASED GLASS: Glass Beads,
   Reflecting
GLASS PRDTS, FROM PURCHASED GLASS: Glassware
GLASS PRDTS, FROM PURCHASED GLASS: Insulating
GLASS PRDTS, FROM PURCHASED GLASS: Mirrored
GLASS PRDTS, FROM PURCHASED GLASS: Novelties,
   Fruit, Etc
GLASS PRDTS, FROM PURCHASED GLASS: Ornaments,
   Christmas Tree
GLASS PRDTS, FROM PURCHASED GLASS: Silvered
GLASS PRDTS, FROM PURCHASED GLASS: Windshields
GLASS PRDTS, PRESSED OR BLOWN: Bulbs, Electric
   Lights
GLASS PRDTS, PRESSED OR BLOWN: Glassware, Art Or
   Decorative
GLASS PRDTS, PRESSED OR BLOWN: Optical
GLASS PRDTS, PRESSED OR BLOWN: Yarn, Fiberglass
GLASS PRDTS, PURCHASED GLASS: Glassware, Scien-
   tific/Tech
GLASS PRDTS, PURCHD GLASS: Furniture Top, Cut,
   Beveld/Polshd
GLASS STORE: Leaded Or Stained
GLASS STORES
GLASS, AUTOMOTIVE: Wholesalers
GLASS: Broadwoven Fabrics
GLASS: Fiber
GLASS: Flat
GLASS: Leaded
GLASS: Optical
GLASS: Plate
GLASS: Pressed & Blown, NEC
GLASS: Safety
GLASS: Stained
GLASS: Structural
GLOBAL POSITIONING SYSTEMS & EQPT
GLOVES: Leather
GLOVES: Safety
GO-CART DEALERS
GOLF CARTS: Powered
GOLF CARTS: Wholesalers
GOLF COURSES: Public
GOLF EQPT
GOVERNMENT, EXECUTIVE OFFICES: City & Town Man-
   agers' Offices
GOVERNMENT, EXECUTIVE OFFICES: Mayors'
GOVERNMENT, GENERAL: Administration
GRANITE: Crushed & Broken
GRANITE: Cut & Shaped
GRANITE: Dimension
GRANITE: Dimension
GRAPHIC ARTS & RELATED DESIGN SVCS
GRAPHIC LAYOUT SVCS: Printed Circuitry
GRASSES: Artificial & Preserved
GRATINGS: Tread, Fabricated Metal
GRAVEL MINING
GREASE RETAINERS: Leather
GREASES & INEDIBLE FATS, RENDERED
GREETING CARDS WHOLESALERS
GRENADES: Grenades, Hand
GRITS: Crushed & Broken
GROCERIES WHOLESALERS, NEC
GROCERIES, GENERAL LINE WHOLESALERS
GUARD PROTECTIVE SVCS
GUARD SVCS

GUARDRAILS
GUARDS: Machine, Sheet Metal
GUIDANCE SYSTEMS & EQPT: Space Vehicle
GUIDED MISSILES & SPACE VEHICLES
GUIDED MISSILES & SPACE VEHICLES: Research & Devel-
   opment
GUIDED MISSILES/SPACE VEHICLE PARTS/AUX EQPT:
   Research/Devel
GUM & WOOD CHEMICALS
GUN SIGHTS: Optical
GUNSMITHS
GUTTERS: Sheet Metal
GYPSUM PRDTS
GYROSCOPES

H

HAIR & HAIR BASED PRDTS
HAIR CARE PRDTS
HAIR CARE PRDTS: Hair Coloring Preparations
HAIR CURLERS: Beauty Shop
HAIR DRESSING, FOR THE TRADE
HANDBAGS
HANDBAGS: Women's
HANDLES: Faucet, Vitreous China & Earthenware
HANDLES: Wood
HANDYMAN SVCS
HANG GLIDERS
HANGERS: Garment, Plastic
HANGERS: Garment, Wire
HARD RUBBER PRDTS, NEC
HARDWARE
HARDWARE & BUILDING PRDTS: Plastic
HARDWARE & EQPT: Stage, Exc Lighting
HARDWARE STORES
HARDWARE STORES: Builders'
HARDWARE STORES: Tools, Hand
HARDWARE STORES: Tools, Power
HARDWARE WHOLESALERS
HARDWARE, WHOLESALE: Builders', NEC
HARDWARE, WHOLESALE: Power Tools & Access
HARDWARE, WHOLESALE: Saw Blades
HARDWARE, WHOLESALE: Shelf or Light
HARDWARE: Aircraft & Marine, Incl Pulleys & Similar Items
HARDWARE: Builders'
HARDWARE: Cabinet
HARDWARE: Furniture
HARNESS ASSEMBLIES: Cable & Wire
HARNESS WIRING SETS: Internal Combustion Engines
HARNESSES, HALTERS, SADDLERY & STRAPS
HEADPHONES: Radio
HEALTH AIDS: Exercise Eqpt
HEALTH CLUBS
HEALTH FOOD & SUPPLEMENT STORES
HEALTH SCREENING SVCS
HEARING AID REPAIR SVCS
HEARING AIDS
HEAT EXCHANGERS
HEAT EXCHANGERS: After Or Inter Coolers Or Condensers,
   Etc
HEAT TREATING: Metal
HEATING & AIR CONDITIONING EQPT & SPLYS WHOLE-
   SALERS
HEATING & AIR CONDITIONING UNITS, COMBINATION
HEATING EQPT & SPLYS
HEATING EQPT: Complete
HEATING UNITS: Gas, Infrared
HELICOPTERS
HELP SUPPLY SERVICES
HIGH ENERGY PARTICLE PHYSICS EQPT
HIGHWAY SIGNALS: Electric
HISTORICAL SOCIETY
HOBBY, TOY & GAME STORES: Arts & Crafts & Splys
HOBBY, TOY & GAME STORES: Ceramics Splys
HOBBY, TOY & GAME STORES: Toys & Games
HOISTS
HOLDERS, PAPER TOWEL, GROCERY BAG, ETC: Plastic
HOLDING COMPANIES: Investment, Exc Banks
HOLDING COMPANIES: Personal, Exc Banks
HOME ENTERTAINMENT EQPT: Electronic, NEC
HOME FOR THE PHYSICALLY HANDICAPPED
HOME FURNISHINGS STORES, NEC
HOME FURNISHINGS WHOLESALERS
HOME HEALTH CARE SVCS
HOMEBUILDERS & OTHER OPERATIVE BUILDERS

HOMEFURNISHING STORE: Bedding, Sheet,
   Blanket,Spread/Pillow
HOMEFURNISHING STORES: Fireplaces & Wood Burning
   Stoves
HOMEFURNISHING STORES: Pictures & Mirrors
HOMEFURNISHING STORES: Pottery
HOMEFURNISHING STORES: Towels
HOMEFURNISHING STORES: Venetian Blinds
HOMEFURNISHING STORES: Wicker, Rattan, Or Reed
HOMEFURNISHING STORES: Window Shades, NEC
HOMEFURNISHINGS, WHOLESALE: Draperies
HOMEFURNISHINGS, WHOLESALE: Fireplace Eqpt & Ac-
   cess
HOMEFURNISHINGS, WHOLESALE: Mirrors/Pictures,
   Framed/Unframd
HOMEFURNISHINGS, WHOLESALE: Window Shades
HOMES, MODULAR: Wooden
HOMES: Log Cabins
HONES
HORMONE PREPARATIONS
HORSE & PET ACCESSORIES: Textile
HORSE ACCESS: Harnesses & Riding Crops, Etc, Exc
   Leather
HORSESHOES
HOSE: Automobile, Rubber
HOSE: Plastic
HOSE: Pneumatic, Rubber Or Rubberized Fabric, NEC
HOSE: Rubber
HOSES & BELTING: Rubber & Plastic
HOSIERY KITS: Sewing & Mending
HOSPITALS: Medical & Surgical
HOT TUBS
HOUSEHOLD ARTICLES, EXC FURNITURE: Cut Stone
HOUSEHOLD ARTICLES, EXC KITCHEN: Pottery
HOUSEHOLD ARTICLES: Metal
HOUSEHOLD FURNISHINGS, NEC
HOUSEWARE STORES
HOUSEWARES, ELECTRIC, EXC COOKING APPLIANCES
   & UTENSILS
HOUSEWARES, ELECTRIC: Appliances, Personal
HOUSEWARES, ELECTRIC: Cooking Appliances
HOUSEWARES, ELECTRIC: Fans, Desk
HOUSEWARES, ELECTRIC: Fans, Exhaust & Ventilating
HOUSEWARES, ELECTRIC: Massage Machines, Exc
   Beauty/Barber
HOUSEWARES, ELECTRIC: Toasters
HOUSINGS: Pressure
HUB CAPS: Automobile, Stamped Metal
HYDRAULIC EQPT REPAIR SVC
HYDRAULIC FLUIDS: Synthetic Based
HYDROELECTRIC POWER GENERATION
HYDROFLUORIC ACID COMPOUND: Etching Or Polishing
   Glass
Hard Rubber & Molded Rubber Prdts

I

ICE
ICE CREAM TRUCK VENDORS
ICE WHOLESALERS
IDENTIFICATION TAGS, EXC PAPER
IGNEOUS ROCK: Crushed & Broken
IGNITION APPARATUS & DISTRIBUTORS
IGNITION COILS: Automotive
IGNITION SYSTEMS: High Frequency
INCENSE
INDEPENDENT JOURNALISTS
INDL & PERSONAL SVC PAPER, WHOL: Boxes,
   Corrugtd/Solid Fiber
INDL & PERSONAL SVC PAPER, WHOL: Paper,
   Wrap/Coarse/Prdts
INDL & PERSONAL SVC PAPER, WHOLESALE: Shipping
   Splys
INDL EQPT SVCS
INDL GASES WHOLESALERS
INDL MACHINERY & EQPT WHOLESALERS
INDL MACHINERY REPAIR & MAINTENANCE
INDL PATTERNS: Foundry Patternmaking
INDL PROCESS INSTRUMENTS: Control
INDL PROCESS INSTRUMENTS: Controllers, Process Vari-
   ables
INDL PROCESS INSTRUMENTS: Digital Display, Process
   Variables
INDL PROCESS INSTRUMENTS: Temperature
INDL PROCESS INSTRUMENTS: Water Quality
   Monitoring/Cntrl Sys

INDEX

INDL SPLYS WHOLESALERS
INDL SPLYS, WHOL: Fasteners, Incl Nuts, Bolts, Screws, Etc
INDL SPLYS, WHOLESALE: Abrasives
INDL SPLYS, WHOLESALE: Bearings
INDL SPLYS, WHOLESALE: Rubber Goods, Mechanical
INDL SPLYS, WHOLESALE: Tools
INDL SPLYS, WHOLESALE: Valves & Fittings
INDL TRUCK REPAIR SVCS
INDUSTRIAL & COMMERCIAL EQPT INSPECTION SVCS
INERTIAL GUIDANCE SYSTEMS
INFORMATION RETRIEVAL SERVICES
INFRARED OBJECT DETECTION EQPT
INK OR WRITING FLUIDS
INK: Gravure
INK: Printing
INSECTICIDES & PESTICIDES
INSTRUMENT DIALS: Painted
INSTRUMENT LANDING SYSTEMS OR ILS: Airborne Or Ground
INSTRUMENTS & ACCESSORIES: Surveying
INSTRUMENTS & METERS: Measuring, Electric
INSTRUMENTS, LABORATORY: Gas Analyzing
INSTRUMENTS, LABORATORY: Perimeters, Optical
INSTRUMENTS, MEASURING & CNTRG: Plotting, Drafting/Map Rdg
INSTRUMENTS, MEASURING & CNTRL: Gauges, Auto, Computer
INSTRUMENTS, MEASURING & CNTRL: Geophysical & Meteorological
INSTRUMENTS, MEASURING & CNTRL: Geophysical/Meteorological
INSTRUMENTS, MEASURING & CNTRL: Testing, Abrasion, Etc
INSTRUMENTS, MEASURING & CNTRLG: Detectors, Scintillation
INSTRUMENTS, MEASURING & CNTRLG: Tensile Strength Testing
INSTRUMENTS, MEASURING & CNTRLG: Thermometers/Temp Sensors
INSTRUMENTS, MEASURING & CNTRLNG: Nuclear Instrument Modules
INSTRUMENTS, MEASURING & CONTROLLING: Breathalyzers
INSTRUMENTS, MEASURING & CONTROLLING: Cable Testing
INSTRUMENTS, MEASURING & CONTROLLING: Gas Detectors
INSTRUMENTS, MEASURING & CONTROLLING: Photopitometers
INSTRUMENTS, MEASURING & CONTROLLING: Polygraph
INSTRUMENTS, MEASURING & CONTROLLING: Ultrasonic Testing
INSTRUMENTS, MEASURING & CONTROLLING: Weather Tracking
INSTRUMENTS, MEASURING/CNTRL: Gauging, Ultrasonic Thickness
INSTRUMENTS, MEASURING/CNTRL: Testing/Measuring, Kinematic
INSTRUMENTS, MEASURING/CNTRLG: Pulse Analyzers, Nuclear Mon
INSTRUMENTS, MEASURING/CNTRLNG: Med Diagnostic Sys, Nuclear
INSTRUMENTS, OPTICAL: Elements & Assemblies, Exc Ophthalmic
INSTRUMENTS, OPTICAL: Test & Inspection
INSTRUMENTS, SURGICAL & MEDI: Knife Blades/Handles, Surgical
INSTRUMENTS, SURGICAL & MEDICAL: Blood & Bone Work
INSTRUMENTS, SURGICAL & MEDICAL: Blood Pressure
INSTRUMENTS, SURGICAL & MEDICAL: Catheters
INSTRUMENTS, SURGICAL & MEDICAL: Inhalation Therapy
INSTRUMENTS, SURGICAL & MEDICAL: Inhalators
INSTRUMENTS, SURGICAL & MEDICAL: Knives
INSTRUMENTS, SURGICAL & MEDICAL: Ophthalmic
INSTRUMENTS, SURGICAL & MEDICAL: Suction Therapy
INSTRUMENTS: Analytical
INSTRUMENTS: Analyzers, Internal Combustion Eng, Electronic
INSTRUMENTS: Analyzers, Radio Apparatus, NEC
INSTRUMENTS: Analyzers, Spectrum
INSTRUMENTS: Combustion Control, Indl
INSTRUMENTS: Elec Lab Stds, Resist, Inductance/Capacitance
INSTRUMENTS: Electrocardiographs

INSTRUMENTS: Electronic, Analog-Digital Converters
INSTRUMENTS: Endoscopic Eqpt, Electromedical
INSTRUMENTS: Eye Examination
INSTRUMENTS: Flow, Indl Process
INSTRUMENTS: Humidity, Indl Process
INSTRUMENTS: Indl Process Control
INSTRUMENTS: Infrared, Indl Process
INSTRUMENTS: Laser, Scientific & Engineering
INSTRUMENTS: Measuring & Controlling
INSTRUMENTS: Measuring Electricity
INSTRUMENTS: Measuring, Electrical Energy
INSTRUMENTS: Measuring, Electrical Power
INSTRUMENTS: Measuring, Electrical Quantities
INSTRUMENTS: Medical & Surgical
INSTRUMENTS: Meteorological
INSTRUMENTS: Nautical
INSTRUMENTS: Optical, Analytical
INSTRUMENTS: Oscillographs & Oscilloscopes
INSTRUMENTS: Pressure Measurement, Indl
INSTRUMENTS: Radar Testing, Electric
INSTRUMENTS: Radio Frequency Measuring
INSTRUMENTS: Signal Generators & Averagers
INSTRUMENTS: Temperature Measurement, Indl
INSTRUMENTS: Test, Electronic & Electric Measurement
INSTRUMENTS: Test, Electronic & Electrical Circuits
INSTRUMENTS: Thermal Conductive, Indl
INSULATING BOARD, CELLULAR FIBER
INSULATING COMPOUNDS
INSULATION & CUSHIONING FOAM: Polystyrene
INSULATION & ROOFING MATERIALS: Wood, Reconstituted
INSULATION MATERIALS WHOLESALERS
INSULATION: Fiberglass
INSULATORS & INSULATION MATERIALS: Electrical
INSULATORS, PORCELAIN: Electrical
INTEGRATED CIRCUITS, SEMICONDUCTOR NETWORKS, ETC
INTERCOMMUNICATION EQPT REPAIR SVCS
INTERCOMMUNICATIONS SYSTEMS: Electric
INTERIOR DECORATING SVCS
INTERIOR DESIGN SVCS, NEC
INTERIOR DESIGNING SVCS
INVESTORS, NEC
INVESTORS: Real Estate, Exc Property Operators
IRON & STEEL PRDTS: Hot-Rolled
IRON ORES
IRONING BOARDS
IRRADIATION EQPT
IRRADIATION EQPT: Gamma Ray
IRRADIATION EQPT: Nuclear

J

JACKS: Hydraulic
JEWELERS' FINDINGS & MATERIALS: Castings
JEWELERS' FINDINGS & MATERIALS: Parts, Unassembled
JEWELRY & PRECIOUS STONES WHOLESALERS
JEWELRY APPAREL
JEWELRY FINDINGS & LAPIDARY WORK
JEWELRY REPAIR SVCS
JEWELRY STORES
JEWELRY STORES: Clocks
JEWELRY STORES: Precious Stones & Precious Metals
JEWELRY STORES: Watches
JEWELRY, PRECIOUS METAL: Cigar & Cigarette Access
JEWELRY, PRECIOUS METAL: Mountings & Trimmings
JEWELRY, PRECIOUS METAL: Pearl, Natural Or Cultured
JEWELRY, PRECIOUS METAL: Pins
JEWELRY, PRECIOUS METAL: Rings, Finger
JEWELRY, PRECIOUS METAL: Settings & Mountings
JEWELRY, WHOLESALE
JEWELRY: Decorative, Fashion & Costume
JEWELRY: Precious Metal
JOB COUNSELING
JOB PRINTING & NEWSPAPER PUBLISHING COMBINED
JOB TRAINING & VOCATIONAL REHABILITATION SVCS
JOB TRAINING SVCS
JOINTS: Expansion
JOISTS: Long-Span Series, Open Web Steel

K

KAOLIN & BALL CLAY MINING
KEYBOARDS: Computer Or Office Machine
KILNS
KITCHEN & COOKING ARTICLES: Pottery
KITCHEN ARTICLES: Semivitreous Earthenware
KITCHEN CABINET STORES, EXC CUSTOM

KITCHEN CABINETS WHOLESALERS
KITCHEN UTENSILS: Food Handling & Processing Prdts, Wood
KITCHEN UTENSILS: Wooden
KITCHENWARE STORES
KNIVES: Agricultural Or indl

L

LABELS: Cotton, Printed
LABELS: Paper, Made From Purchased Materials
LABORATORIES, TESTING: Prdt Certification, Sfty/Performance
LABORATORIES, TESTING: Product Testing, Safety/Performance
LABORATORIES, TESTING: Water
LABORATORIES: Biological Research
LABORATORIES: Biotechnology
LABORATORIES: Dental
LABORATORIES: Dental & Medical X-Ray
LABORATORIES: Electronic Research
LABORATORIES: Physical Research, Commercial
LABORATORIES: Testing
LABORATORY APPARATUS & FURNITURE
LABORATORY APPARATUS & FURNITURE: Worktables
LABORATORY APPARATUS, EXC HEATING & MEASURING
LABORATORY APPARATUS: Laser Beam Alignment Device
LABORATORY APPARATUS: Pipettes, Hemocytometer
LABORATORY CHEMICALS: Organic
LABORATORY EQPT: Chemical
LABORATORY EQPT: Clinical Instruments Exc Medical
LABORATORY EQPT: Incubators
LABORATORY INSTRUMENT REPAIR SVCS
LADDERS: Metal
LADDERS: Portable, Metal
LAMINATED PLASTICS: Plate, Sheet, Rod & Tubes
LAMINATING MATERIALS
LAMINATING SVCS
LAMP & LIGHT BULBS & TUBES
LAMP BULBS & TUBES, ELEC: Lead-In Wires, From Purchased Wire
LAMP BULBS & TUBES, ELECTRIC: Electric Light
LAMP BULBS & TUBES, ELECTRIC: For Specialized Applications
LAMP BULBS & TUBES, ELECTRIC: Parts
LAMP STORES
LAMPS: Desk, Residential
LAND SUBDIVISION & DEVELOPMENT
LAPIDARY WORK: Jewel Cut, Drill, Polish, Recut/Setting
LASER SYSTEMS & EQPT
LASERS: Welding, Drilling & Cutting Eqpt
LATHES
LAUNDRY & GARMENT SVCS, NEC: Garment Alteration & Repair
LAUNDRY & GARMENT SVCS, NEC: Garment Making, Alter & Repair
LAUNDRY EQPT: Commercial
LAWN & GARDEN EQPT
LAWN & GARDEN EQPT: Grass Catchers, Lawn Mower
LAWN & GARDEN EQPT: Lawnmowers, Residential, Hand Or Power
LAWN & GARDEN EQPT: Tractors & Eqpt
LAWN MOWER REPAIR SHOP
LEASING & RENTAL SVCS: Cranes & Aerial Lift Eqpt
LEASING & RENTAL: Computers & Eqpt
LEASING & RENTAL: Construction & Mining Eqpt
LEASING & RENTAL: Medical Machinery & Eqpt
LEASING & RENTAL: Office Machines & Eqpt
LEASING & RENTAL: Other Real Estate Property
LEASING & RENTAL: Trucks, Without Drivers
LEATHER GOODS: Aprons, Welders', Blacksmiths', Etc
LEATHER GOODS: Boots, Horse
LEATHER GOODS: Boxes
LEATHER GOODS: Corners, Luggage
LEATHER GOODS: Garments
LEATHER GOODS: Harnesses Or Harness Parts
LEATHER GOODS: Holsters
LEATHER GOODS: NEC
LEATHER GOODS: Personal
LEATHER GOODS: Wallets
LEATHER TANNING & FINISHING
LEATHER, LEATHER GOODS & FURS, WHOLESALE
LEATHER: Accessory Prdts
LEATHER: Embossed
LEATHER: Equestrian Prdts
LEATHER: Glove

LEATHER: Rawhide
LEATHER: Saddlery
LEGAL OFFICES & SVCS
LENS COATING: Ophthalmic
LIGHT OR HEAT EMISSION OPERATING APPARATUS
LIGHTERS, CIGARETTE & CIGAR, WHOLESALE
LIGHTING EQPT: Flashlights
LIGHTING EQPT: Floodlights
LIGHTING EQPT: Fog Lights
LIGHTING EQPT: Motor Vehicle
LIGHTING EQPT: Motor Vehicle, NEC
LIGHTING EQPT: Outdoor
LIGHTING EQPT: Spotlights
LIGHTING FIXTURES, NEC
LIGHTING FIXTURES: Decorative Area
LIGHTING FIXTURES: Gas
LIGHTING FIXTURES: Indl & Commercial
LIGHTING FIXTURES: Motor Vehicle
LIGHTING FIXTURES: Public
LIGHTING FIXTURES: Residential
LIGHTING FIXTURES: Residential, Electric
LIME
LIME ROCK: Ground
LIME: Agricultural
LIMESTONE: Crushed & Broken
LIMESTONE: Cut & Shaped
LIMESTONE: Dimension
LIMESTONE: Ground
LINEN SPLY SVC: Uniform
LINEN STORES
LINENS: Table & Dresser Scarves, From Purchased Materials
LINER BRICK OR PLATES: Sewer Or Tank Lining, Vitrified
Clay
LINER STRIPS: Rubber
LINERS & COVERS: Fabric
LINERS & LINING
LININGS: Apparel, Made From Purchased Materials
LININGS: Handbag Or Pocketbook
LIPSTICK
LIQUEFIED PETROLEUM GAS DEALERS
LIQUID CRYSTAL DISPLAYS
LITHOGRAPHIC PLATES
LOCK & KEY SVCS
LOCKS
LOCKS: Safe & Vault, Metal
LOCOMOTIVES & PARTS
LOGGING
LOGGING CAMPS & CONTRACTORS
LOGGING: Saw Logs
LOGGING: Stump Harvesting
LOGGING: Timber, Cut At Logging Camp
LOGGING: Veneer Logs
LOGGING: Wood Chips, Produced In The Field
LOGGING: Wooden Logs
LOGS: Gas, Fireplace
LOOSELEAF BINDERS
LOTIONS OR CREAMS: Face
LOTIONS: SHAVING
LOZENGES: Pharmaceutical
LUBRICANTS: Corrosion Preventive
LUBRICATION SYSTEMS & EQPT
LUGGAGE & BRIEFCASES
LUGGAGE & LEATHER GOODS STORES: Luggage, Exc
Footlckr/Trunk
LUGGAGE: Traveling Bags
LUMBER & BLDG MATRLS DEALERS, RET: Bath Fixtures,
Eqpt/Sply
LUMBER & BLDG MTRLS DEALERS, RET: Insultn & Energy
Consrvtn
LUMBER & BLDG MTRLS DEALERS, RET: Planing Mill
Prdts/Lumber
LUMBER & BUILDING MATERIAL DEALERS, RETAIL: Roof-
ing Material
LUMBER & BUILDING MATERIALS DEALER, RET: Door &
Window Prdts
LUMBER & BUILDING MATERIALS DEALER, RET: Masonry
Matls/Splys
LUMBER & BUILDING MATERIALS DEALERS, RETAIL: Brick
LUMBER & BUILDING MATERIALS DEALERS, RETAIL:
Countertops
LUMBER & BUILDING MATERIALS DEALERS, RETAIL: Lime
& Plaster
LUMBER & BUILDING MATERIALS DEALERS, RETAIL:
Paving Stones

LUMBER & BUILDING MATERIALS DEALERS, RETAIL:
Sand & Gravel
LUMBER & BUILDING MATERIALS RET DEALERS: Millwork
& Lumber
LUMBER & BUILDING MATLS DEALERS, RET:
Concrete/Cinder Block
LUMBER: Fiberboard
LUMBER: Furniture Dimension Stock, Softwood
LUMBER: Hardwood Dimension
LUMBER: Hardwood Dimension & Flooring Mills
LUMBER: Kiln Dried
LUMBER: Pilings, Treated
LUMBER: Plywood, Hardwood
LUMBER: Plywood, Hardwood or Hardwood Faced
LUMBER: Plywood, Softwood
LUMBER: Plywood, Softwood
LUMBER: Poles & Pole Crossarms, Treated
LUMBER: Resawn, Small Dimension
LUMBER: Treated
LUMBER: Veneer, Hardwood

M

MACHINE GUNS, WHOLESALE
MACHINE PARTS: Stamped Or Pressed Metal
MACHINE SHOPS
MACHINE TOOL ACCESS: Balancing Machines
MACHINE TOOL ACCESS: Cams
MACHINE TOOL ACCESS: Cutting
MACHINE TOOL ACCESS: Diamond Cutting, For Turning, Etc
MACHINE TOOL ACCESS: Files
MACHINE TOOL ACCESS: Pushers
MACHINE TOOL ACCESS: Tool Holders
MACHINE TOOL ACCESS: Tools & Access
MACHINE TOOLS & ACCESS
MACHINE TOOLS, METAL CUTTING: Drilling
MACHINE TOOLS, METAL CUTTING: Drilling & Boring
MACHINE TOOLS, METAL CUTTING: Electrochemical Milling
MACHINE TOOLS, METAL CUTTING: Electrolytic
MACHINE TOOLS, METAL CUTTING: Home Workshop
MACHINE TOOLS, METAL CUTTING: Numerically Controlled
MACHINE TOOLS, METAL CUTTING: Plasma Process
MACHINE TOOLS, METAL CUTTING: Tool Replacement &
Rpr Parts
MACHINE TOOLS, METAL FORMING: Bending
MACHINE TOOLS, METAL FORMING: Magnetic Forming
MACHINE TOOLS, METAL FORMING: Mechanical, Pneu-
matic Or Hyd
MACHINE TOOLS: Metal Cutting
MACHINE TOOLS: Metal Forming
MACHINERY & EQPT FINANCE LEASING
MACHINERY & EQPT, AGRICULTURAL, WHOLESALE: Lawn
& Garden
MACHINERY & EQPT, INDL, WHOL: Brewery Prdts Mfrg,
Commercial
MACHINERY & EQPT, INDL, WHOL: Environ Pollution Cntrl,
Water
MACHINERY & EQPT, INDL, WHOLESALE: Conveyor Sys-
tems
MACHINERY & EQPT, INDL, WHOLESALE: Food Manufac-
turing
MACHINERY & EQPT, INDL, WHOLESALE: Food Product
Manufacturng
MACHINERY & EQPT, INDL, WHOLESALE: Hydraulic Sys-
tems
MACHINERY & EQPT, INDL, WHOLESALE: Lift Trucks &
Parts
MACHINERY & EQPT, INDL, WHOLESALE: Paint Spray
MACHINERY & EQPT, INDL, WHOLESALE: Robots
MACHINERY & EQPT, INDL, WHOLESALE: Safety Eqpt
MACHINERY & EQPT, INDL, WHOLESALE: Screening
MACHINERY & EQPT, INDL, WHOLESALE: Tool & Die Mak-
ers
MACHINERY & EQPT, WHOLESALE: Concrete Processing
MACHINERY & EQPT, WHOLESALE: Construction, Cranes
MACHINERY & EQPT, WHOLESALE: Construction, General
MACHINERY & EQPT, WHOLESALE: Contractors Materials
MACHINERY & EQPT, WHOLESALE: Oil Field Eqpt
MACHINERY & EQPT: Farm
MACHINERY & EQPT: Liquid Automation
MACHINERY BASES
MACHINERY, COMM LAUNDRY: Rug Cleaning, Drying Or
Napping
MACHINERY, FOOD PRDTS: Cutting, Chopping, Grinding,
Mixing
MACHINERY, FOOD PRDTS: Food Processing, Smokers

MACHINERY, FOOD PRDTS: Juice Extractors, Fruit & Veg,
Comm
MACHINERY, FOOD PRDTS: Mills, Food
MACHINERY, FOOD PRDTS: Mixers, Commercial
MACHINERY, FOOD PRDTS: Processing, Poultry
MACHINERY, FOOD PRDTS: Roasting, Coffee, Peanut, Etc.
MACHINERY, MAILING: Postage Meters
MACHINERY, METALWORKING: Assembly, Including Robotic
MACHINERY, METALWORKING: Cutting-Up Lines
MACHINERY, OFFICE: Time Clocks &Time Recording De-
vices
MACHINERY, OFFICE: Typing & Word Processing
MACHINERY, PACKAGING: Bread Wrapping
MACHINERY, PACKAGING: Canning, Food
MACHINERY, PACKAGING: Packing & Wrapping
MACHINERY, PAPER INDUSTRY: Paper Mill, Plating, Etc
MACHINERY, PRINTING TRADES: Copy Holders
MACHINERY, PRINTING TRADES: Linotype, Monotype, Inter-
type
MACHINERY, PRINTING TRADES: Plates
MACHINERY, PRINTING TRADES: Printing Trade Parts &
Attchts
MACHINERY, TEXTILE: Embroidery
MACHINERY, TEXTILE: Printing
MACHINERY, WOODWORKING: Cabinet Makers'
MACHINERY, WOODWORKING: Furniture Makers
MACHINERY, WOODWORKING: Pattern Makers'
MACHINERY, WOODWORKING: Sanding, Exc Portable Floor
Sanders
MACHINERY/EQPT, INDL, WHOL: Cleaning, High Press,
Sand/Steam
MACHINERY: Ammunition & Explosives Loading
MACHINERY: Assembly, Exc Metalworking
MACHINERY: Automotive Maintenance
MACHINERY: Automotive Related
MACHINERY: Broom Making
MACHINERY: Centrifugal
MACHINERY: Construction
MACHINERY: Cryogenic, Industrial
MACHINERY: Custom
MACHINERY: Deburring
MACHINERY: Dredging
MACHINERY: Electronic Component Making
MACHINERY: Electronic Teaching Aids
MACHINERY: Extruding, Synthetic Filament
MACHINERY: Fiber Optics Strand Coating
MACHINERY: General, Industrial, NEC
MACHINERY: Grinding
MACHINERY: Ice Cream
MACHINERY: Ice Making
MACHINERY: Industrial, NEC
MACHINERY: Kilns
MACHINERY: Knitting
MACHINERY: Labeling
MACHINERY: Logging Eqpt
MACHINERY: Metalworking
MACHINERY: Milling
MACHINERY: Mining
MACHINERY: Optical Lens
MACHINERY: Packaging
MACHINERY: Paint Making
MACHINERY: Paper Industry Miscellaneous
MACHINERY: Pharmaciutical
MACHINERY: Photographic Reproduction
MACHINERY: Plastic Working
MACHINERY: Pottery Making
MACHINERY: Printing Presses
MACHINERY: Recycling
MACHINERY: Road Construction & Maintenance
MACHINERY: Robots, Molding & Forming Plastics
MACHINERY: Semiconductor Manufacturing
MACHINERY: Service Industry, NEC
MACHINERY: Specialty
MACHINERY: Textile
MACHINERY: Tobacco Prdts
MACHINERY: Voting
MACHINERY: Wire Drawing
MACHINERY: Woodworking
MACHINES: Forming, Sheet Metal
MACHINISTS' TOOLS: Measuring, Precision
MACHINISTS' TOOLS: Precision
MAGNESIUM
MAGNETIC RESONANCE IMAGING DEVICES: Nonmedical
MAGNETIC SHIELDS, METAL
MAGNETS: Ceramic

INDEX

MAGNETS: Permanent
MAIL-ORDER HOUSES: Book & Record Clubs
MAIL-ORDER HOUSES: Computer Eqpt & Electronics
MAIL-ORDER HOUSES: Cosmetics & Perfumes
MAIL-ORDER HOUSES: Educational Splys & Eqpt
MAIL-ORDER HOUSES: General Merchandise
MAIL-ORDER HOUSES: Record & Tape, Music Or Video Club
MAIL-ORDER HOUSES: Women's Apparel
MAILBOX RENTAL & RELATED SVCS
MAILING & MESSENGER SVCS
MAILING LIST: Compilers
MAILING SVCS, NEC
MANAGEMENT CONSULTING SVCS: Administrative
MANAGEMENT CONSULTING SVCS: Automation & Robotics
MANAGEMENT CONSULTING SVCS: Business
MANAGEMENT CONSULTING SVCS: Construction Project
MANAGEMENT CONSULTING SVCS: Foreign Trade
MANAGEMENT CONSULTING SVCS: Industrial
MANAGEMENT CONSULTING SVCS: Industrial & Labor
MANAGEMENT CONSULTING SVCS: Industry Specialist
MANAGEMENT CONSULTING SVCS: Information Systems
MANAGEMENT CONSULTING SVCS: Management Engineering
MANAGEMENT CONSULTING SVCS: Manufacturing
MANAGEMENT CONSULTING SVCS: Real Estate
MANAGEMENT CONSULTING SVCS: Training & Development
MANAGEMENT CONSULTING SVCS: Transportation
MANAGEMENT SERVICES
MANAGEMENT SVCS, FACILITIES SUPPORT: Environ Remediation
MANAGEMENT SVCS: Business
MANAGEMENT SVCS: Construction
MANAGEMENT SVCS: Financial, Business
MANHOLES COVERS: Concrete
MANICURE PREPARATIONS
MANIFOLDS: Pipe, Fabricated From Purchased Pipe
MANNEQUINS
MANUFACTURING INDUSTRIES, NEC
MAPS
MARBLE BOARD
MARBLE, BUILDING: Cut & Shaped
MARINAS
MARINE ENGINE REPAIR SVCS
MARINE HARDWARE
MARINE RELATED EQPT
MARINE SPLY DEALERS
MARKETS: Meat & fish
MARKING DEVICES
MARKING DEVICES: Embossing Seals & Hand Stamps
MARKING DEVICES: Screens, Textile Printing
MARKING DEVICES: Seal Presses, Notary & Hand
MARKING DEVICES: Stationary Embossers, Personal
MARKING DEVICES: Textile Making Stamps, Hand, Rubber/Metal
MASSAGE MACHINES, ELECTRIC: Barber & Beauty Shops
MATERIALS HANDLING EQPT WHOLESALERS
MATERNITY WEAR STORES
MATS, MATTING & PADS: Door, Paper, Grass, Reed, Coir, Etc
MATS, MATTING & PADS: Nonwoven
MATS, MATTING & PADS: Varnished Glass
MATS: Table, Plastic & Textile
MEAL DELIVERY PROGRAMS
MEAT & MEAT PRDTS WHOLESALERS
MEAT CUTTING & PACKING
MEAT MARKETS
MEAT PRDTS: Bacon, Side & Sliced, From Purchased Meat
MEAT PRDTS: Beef Stew, From Purchased Meat
MEAT PRDTS: Boxed Beef, From Slaughtered Meat
MEAT PRDTS: Cured Meats, From Purchased Meat
MEAT PRDTS: Frozen
MEAT PRDTS: Ham, Roasted, From Purchased Meat
MEAT PRDTS: Hams & Picnics, From Slaughtered Meat
MEAT PRDTS: Pork, From Slaughtered Meat
MEAT PRDTS: Prepared Beef Prdts From Purchased Beef
MEAT PRDTS: Prepared Pork Prdts, From Purchased Meat
MEAT PRDTS: Sausages, From Purchased Meat
MEAT PRDTS: Smoked
MEAT PRDTS: Snack Sticks, Incl Jerky, From Purchased Meat
MEAT PROCESSED FROM PURCHASED CARCASSES
MEDIA BUYING AGENCIES
MEDIA: Magnetic & Optical Recording
MEDICAL & HOSPITAL EQPT WHOLESALERS

MEDICAL & SURGICAL SPLYS: Braces, Elastic
MEDICAL & SURGICAL SPLYS: Braces, Orthopedic
MEDICAL & SURGICAL SPLYS: Canes, Orthopedic
MEDICAL & SURGICAL SPLYS: Clothing, Fire Resistant & Protect
MEDICAL & SURGICAL SPLYS: Cosmetic Restorations
MEDICAL & SURGICAL SPLYS: Dressings, Surgical
MEDICAL & SURGICAL SPLYS: Foot Appliances, Orthopedic
MEDICAL & SURGICAL SPLYS: Gynecological Splys & Appliances
MEDICAL & SURGICAL SPLYS: Ligatures
MEDICAL & SURGICAL SPLYS: Limbs, Artificial
MEDICAL & SURGICAL SPLYS: Models, Anatomical
MEDICAL & SURGICAL SPLYS: Noise Protectors, Personal
MEDICAL & SURGICAL SPLYS: Orthopedic Appliances
MEDICAL & SURGICAL SPLYS: Personal Safety Eqpt
MEDICAL & SURGICAL SPLYS: Prosthetic Appliances
MEDICAL & SURGICAL SPLYS: Respiratory Protect Eqpt, Personal
MEDICAL & SURGICAL SPLYS: Supports, Abdominal, Ankle, Etc
MEDICAL & SURGICAL SPLYS: Tape, Adhesive, Non/Medicated
MEDICAL & SURGICAL SPLYS: Technical Aids, Handicapped
MEDICAL & SURGICAL SPLYS: Traction Apparatus
MEDICAL & SURGICAL SPLYS: Walkers
MEDICAL & SURGICAL SPLYS: Welders' Hoods
MEDICAL EQPT: Diagnostic
MEDICAL EQPT: Electromedical Apparatus
MEDICAL EQPT: Laser Systems
MEDICAL EQPT: Patient Monitoring
MEDICAL EQPT: Ultrasonic, Exc Cleaning
MEDICAL EQPT: X-Ray Apparatus & Tubes, Radiographic
MEDICAL SUNDRIES: Rubber
MEDICAL, DENTAL & HOSP EQPT, WHOLESALE: X-ray Film & Splys
MEDICAL, DENTAL & HOSPITAL EQPT, WHOL: Dentists' Prof Splys
MEDICAL, DENTAL & HOSPITAL EQPT, WHOL: Hosptl Eqpt/Furniture
MEDICAL, DENTAL & HOSPITAL EQPT, WHOLESALE: Diagnostic, Med
MEDICAL, DENTAL & HOSPITAL EQPT, WHOLESALE: Med Eqpt & Splys
MEMBERSHIP ORGANIZATIONS, NEC: Charitable
MEMBERSHIP ORGS, BUSINESS: Growers' Marketing Advisory Svc
MEMBERSHIP ORGS, CIVIC, SOCIAL & FRATERNAL: Protection
MEN'S & BOYS' CLOTHING ACCESS STORES
MEN'S & BOYS' CLOTHING STORES
MEN'S & BOYS' CLOTHING WHOLESALERS, NEC
MEN'S & BOYS' SPORTSWEAR WHOLESALERS
METAL COMPONENTS: Prefabricated
METAL FABRICATORS: Architechtural
METAL FABRICATORS: Plate
METAL FABRICATORS: Sheet
METAL FABRICATORS: Structural, Ship
METAL FABRICATORS: Structural, Ship
METAL FINISHING SVCS
METAL MINING SVCS
METAL ORES, NEC
METAL SERVICE CENTERS & OFFICES
METAL STAMPING, FOR THE TRADE
METAL TREATING COMPOUNDS
METALS SVC CENTERS & WHOLESALERS: Foundry Prdts
METALS SVC CENTERS & WHOLESALERS: Iron & Steel Prdt, Ferrous
METALS SVC CENTERS & WHOLESALERS: Pipe & Tubing, Steel
METALS SVC CENTERS & WHOLESALERS: Steel
METALS SVC CTRS & WHOLESALERS: Aluminum Bars, Rods, Etc
METALS: Precious NEC
METALS: Primary Nonferrous, NEC
METALWORK: Miscellaneous
METALWORK: Ornamental
METERING DEVICES: Integrating, Nonelectric
METERS: Pyrometers, Indl Process
MGMT CONSULTING SVCS: Matls, Incl Purch, Handle & Invntry
MICROPHONES
MICROPROCESSORS
MICROPUBLISHER
MICROSCOPES

MICROWAVE COMPONENTS
MILITARY GOODS & REGALIA STORES
MILITARY INSIGNIA, TEXTILE
MILLING: Farina, Exc Breakfast Food
MILLING: Grains, Exc Rice
MILLWORK
MINE & QUARRY SVCS: Nonmetallic Minerals
MINE DEVELOPMENT, METAL
MINE EXPLORATION SVCS: Nonmetallic Minerals
MINE PREPARATION SVCS
MINERAL ABRASIVES MINING SVCS
MINERAL PRODUCTS
MINERAL WOOL
MINERALS: Ground or Treated
MINIATURES
MINING EXPLORATION & DEVELOPMENT SVCS
MINING MACHINERY & EQPT WHOLESALERS
MINING MACHINES & EQPT: Classifiers, Metallurgical Or Mining
MINING MACHINES & EQPT: Mineral Beneficiation
MINING MACHINES/EQPT: Mine Car, Plow, Loader, Feeder/Eqpt
MISSILES: Ballistic, Complete
MISSILES: Guided
MIXTURES & BLOCKS: Asphalt Paving
MOBILE COMMUNICATIONS EQPT
MOBILE HOMES
MOBILE HOMES: Personal Or Private Use
MODELS: Airplane, Exc Toy
MODULES: Computer Logic
MOLDED RUBBER PRDTS
MOLDING COMPOUNDS
MOLDINGS & TRIM: Metal, Exc Automobile
MOLDINGS & TRIM: Wood
MOLDINGS, ARCHITECTURAL: Plaster Of Paris
MOLDINGS: Picture Frame
MOLDS: Indl
MOLDS: Plastic Working & Foundry
MOLECULAR DEVICES: Solid State
MONUMENTS & GRAVE MARKERS, EXC TERRAZZO
MONUMENTS & GRAVE MARKERS, WHOLESALE
MONUMENTS: Concrete
MONUMENTS: Cut Stone, Exc Finishing Or Lettering Only
MOPS: Floor & Dust
MOTION PICTURE & VIDEO PRODUCTION SVCS
MOTION PICTURE & VIDEO PRODUCTION SVCS: Educational
MOTION PICTURE EQPT
MOTOR & GENERATOR PARTS: Electric
MOTOR HOMES
MOTOR REBUILDING SVCS, EXC AUTOMOTIVE
MOTOR REPAIR SVCS
MOTOR VEHICLE ASSEMBLY, COMPLETE: Ambulances
MOTOR VEHICLE ASSEMBLY, COMPLETE: Autos, Incl Specialty
MOTOR VEHICLE ASSEMBLY, COMPLETE: Bus/Large Spclty Vehicles
MOTOR VEHICLE ASSEMBLY, COMPLETE: Cars, Armored
MOTOR VEHICLE ASSEMBLY, COMPLETE: Fire Department Vehicles
MOTOR VEHICLE ASSEMBLY, COMPLETE: Military Motor Vehicle
MOTOR VEHICLE ASSEMBLY, COMPLETE: Motor Homes, Self Containd
MOTOR VEHICLE ASSEMBLY, COMPLETE: Personnel Carriers
MOTOR VEHICLE ASSEMBLY, COMPLETE: Reconnaissance Cars
MOTOR VEHICLE ASSEMBLY, COMPLETE: Snow Plows
MOTOR VEHICLE ASSEMBLY, COMPLETE: Truck & Tractor Trucks
MOTOR VEHICLE ASSEMBLY, COMPLETE: Truck Tractors, Highway
MOTOR VEHICLE ASSEMBLY, COMPLETE: Universal Carriers, Mil
MOTOR VEHICLE ASSEMBLY, COMPLETE: Wreckers, Tow Truck
MOTOR VEHICLE ASSY, COMPLETE: Motor Trucks, Exc Off-Highway
MOTOR VEHICLE PARTS & ACCESS: Body Components & Frames
MOTOR VEHICLE PARTS & ACCESS: Booster Cables, Jump-Start
MOTOR VEHICLE PARTS & ACCESS: Engines & Parts

MOTOR VEHICLE PARTS & ACCESS: Engs & Trans,Factory, Rebuilt
MOTOR VEHICLE PARTS & ACCESS: Fuel Systems & Parts
MOTOR VEHICLE PARTS & ACCESS: Gas Tanks
MOTOR VEHICLE PARTS & ACCESS: Gears
MOTOR VEHICLE PARTS & ACCESS: Heaters
MOTOR VEHICLE PARTS & ACCESS: Lubrication Systems & Parts
MOTOR VEHICLE PARTS & ACCESS: Pickup Truck Bed Liners
MOTOR VEHICLE PARTS & ACCESS: Sanders, Safety
MOTOR VEHICLE PARTS & ACCESS: Tire Valve Cores
MOTOR VEHICLE PARTS & ACCESS: Trailer Hitches
MOTOR VEHICLE PARTS & ACCESS: Wheel rims
MOTOR VEHICLE: Hardware
MOTOR VEHICLE: Radiators
MOTOR VEHICLE: Shock Absorbers
MOTOR VEHICLES & CAR BODIES
MOTOR VEHICLES, WHOLESALE: Truck bodies
MOTORCYCLE ACCESS
MOTORCYCLE DEALERS
MOTORCYCLE PARTS & ACCESS DEALERS
MOTORCYCLE REPAIR SHOPS
MOTORCYCLES & RELATED PARTS
MOTORS: Electric
MOTORS: Generators
MOUNTING SVC: Display
MOUTHPIECES, PIPE & CIGARETTE HOLDERS: Rubber
MOWERS & ACCESSORIES
MUSEUMS
MUSEUMS & ART GALLERIES
MUSIC BOXES
MUSIC DISTRIBUTION APPARATUS
MUSICAL ENTERTAINERS
MUSICAL INSTRUMENT REPAIR
MUSICAL INSTRUMENTS & ACCESS: Carrying Cases
MUSICAL INSTRUMENTS & ACCESS: NEC
MUSICAL INSTRUMENTS & ACCESS: Pipe Organs
MUSICAL INSTRUMENTS & ACCESS: Stands
MUSICAL INSTRUMENTS & SPLYS STORES
MUSICAL INSTRUMENTS WHOLESALERS
MUSICAL INSTRUMENTS: Banjos & Parts
MUSICAL INSTRUMENTS: Electric & Electronic
MUSICAL INSTRUMENTS: French Horns & Parts
MUSICAL INSTRUMENTS: Guitars & Parts, Electric & Acoustic
MUSICAL INSTRUMENTS: Marimbas
MUSICAL INSTRUMENTS: Organs
MUSICAL INSTRUMENTS: Reeds
MUSICAL INSTRUMENTS: Synthesizers, Music
MUSICAL INSTRUMENTS: Violins & Parts

N

NATIONAL SECURITY FORCES
NATIONAL SECURITY, GOVERNMENT: Air Force
NATIONAL SECURITY, GOVERNMENT: Federal
NATIONAL SECURITY, GOVERNMENT: Navy
NATURAL GAS DISTRIBUTION TO CONSUMERS
NATURAL GAS LIQUIDS PRODUCTION
NATURAL GAS LIQUIDS PRODUCTION
NATURAL GAS PRODUCTION
NATURAL GAS TRANSMISSION
NAUTICAL REPAIR SVCS
NAVIGATIONAL SYSTEMS & INSTRUMENTS
NETTING: Plastic
NEWSPAPERS & PERIODICALS NEWS REPORTING SVCS
NICKEL ALLOY
NONCURRENT CARRYING WIRING DEVICES
NONDAIRY BASED FROZEN DESSERTS
NONDURABLE GOODS WHOLESALERS, NEC
NONFERROUS: Rolling & Drawing, NEC
NONMETALLIC MINERALS DEVELOPMENT & TEST BORING SVC
NONMETALLIC MINERALS: Support Activities, Exc Fuels
NOVELTIES
NOVELTIES & SPECIALTIES: Metal
NOVELTIES: Plastic
NOVELTY SHOPS
NOZZLES: Fire Fighting
NOZZLES: Spray, Aerosol, Paint Or Insecticide
NUCLEAR CORE STRUCTURALS: Metal Plate
NUCLEAR REACTORS: Military Or Indl
NURSERIES & LAWN & GARDEN SPLY STORE, RET: Lawn/Garden Splys
NURSERIES & LAWN & GARDEN SPLY STORES, RETAIL

NURSERIES & LAWN & GARDEN SPLY STORES, RETAIL: Fertilizer
NURSERIES & LAWN & GARDEN SPLY STORES, RETAIL: Top Soil
NURSERIES & LAWN/GARDEN SPLY STORE, RET: Lawnmowers/Tractors
NURSERIES & LAWN/GARDEN SPLY STORES, RET: Garden Splys/Tools
NUTRITION SVCS
NYLON FIBERS
NYLON RESINS

O

OCHER MINING
OFFICE EQPT WHOLESALERS
OFFICE FIXTURES: Wood
OFFICE MACHINES, NEC
OFFICE SPLY & STATIONERY STORES: Office Forms & Splys
OFFICES & CLINICS OF DRS OF MED: Em Med Ctr, Freestanding
OFFICES & CLINICS OF HEALTH PRACTITIONERS: Nutrition
OFFICES & CLINICS OF HLTH PRACTITIONERS: Reg/Practical Nurse
OIL & GAS FIELD MACHINERY
OIL FIELD MACHINERY & EQPT
OIL FIELD SVCS, NEC
OIL TREATING COMPOUNDS
OILS & ESSENTIAL OILS
OILS & GREASES: Blended & Compounded
OILS & GREASES: Lubricating
OILS, ANIMAL OR VEGETABLE, WHOLESALE
OILS: Essential
OILS: Lubricating
OILS: Lubricating
OINTMENTS
ON-LINE DATABASE INFORMATION RETRIEVAL SVCS
OPERATOR TRAINING, COMPUTER
OPERATOR: Apartment Buildings
OPHTHALMIC GOODS
OPHTHALMIC GOODS, NEC, WHOLESALE: Contact Lenses
OPHTHALMIC GOODS: Eyewear, Protective
OPHTHALMIC GOODS: Frames, Lenses & Parts, Eyeglasses
OPHTHALMIC GOODS: Lenses, Ophthalmic
OPHTHALMIC GOODS: Spectacles
OPTICAL GOODS STORES
OPTICAL INSTRUMENTS & APPARATUS
OPTICAL INSTRUMENTS & LENSES
OPTICAL SCANNING SVCS
OPTOMETRIC EQPT & SPLYS WHOLESALERS
OPTOMETRISTS' OFFICES
ORDNANCE
ORGANIZATIONS: Medical Research
ORGANIZATIONS: Physical Research, Noncommercial
ORGANIZATIONS: Professional
ORGANIZATIONS: Religious
ORGANIZATIONS: Scientific Research Agency
ORGANIZERS, CLOSET & DRAWER Plastic
ORIENTED STRANDBOARD
ORNAMENTS: Lawn
OUTBOARD MOTORS & PARTS
OVERBURDEN REMOVAL SVCS: Anthracite Mining
OVERBURDEN REMOVAL SVCS: Nonmetallic Minerals
OVERBURDEN REMOVAL, METAL MINING

P

PACKAGE DESIGN SVCS
PACKAGED FROZEN FOODS WHOLESALERS, NEC
PACKAGING & LABELING SVCS
PACKAGING MATERIALS, WHOLESALE
PACKAGING MATERIALS: Paper
PACKAGING MATERIALS: Paper, Coated Or Laminated
PACKAGING MATERIALS: Paperboard Backs For Blister/Skin Pkgs
PACKAGING MATERIALS: Plastic Film, Coated Or Laminated
PACKAGING MATERIALS: Polystyrene Foam
PACKING & CRATING SVC
PACKING SVCS: Shipping
PACKING: Rubber
PADDING: Foamed Plastics
PAGERS: One-way
PAINT STORE
PAINTING SVC: Metal Prdts
PAINTS & ALLIED PRODUCTS

PAINTS, VARNISHES & SPLYS, WHOLESALE: Paints
PAINTS: Asphalt Or Bituminous
PAINTS: Oil Or Alkyd Vehicle Or Water Thinned
PALLETS
PALLETS & SKIDS: Wood
PALLETS: Plastic
PALLETS: Wooden
PANEL & DISTRIBUTION BOARDS & OTHER RELATED APPARATUS
PANEL & DISTRIBUTION BOARDS: Electric
PANELS: Building, Metal
PANELS: Building, Wood
PANELS: Wood
PAPER & BOARD: Die-cut
PAPER CONVERTING
PAPER MANUFACTURERS: Exc Newsprint
PAPER PRDTS
PAPER PRDTS: Book Covers
PAPER PRDTS: Cleansing Tissues, Made From Purchased Material
PAPER PRDTS: Facial Tissues, Made From Purchased Materials
PAPER PRDTS: Infant & Baby Prdts
PAPER PRDTS: Molded Pulp Prdts
PAPER PRDTS: Napkins, Made From Purchased Materials
PAPER PRDTS: Sanitary
PAPER PRDTS: Tampons, Sanitary, Made From Purchased Material
PAPER: Absorbent
PAPER: Adhesive
PAPER: Bond
PAPER: Book
PAPER: Book, Coated, Made From Purchased Materials
PAPER: Bristols
PAPER: Business Form
PAPER: Catalog
PAPER: Cigarette
PAPER: Coated & Laminated, NEC
PAPER: Coated, Exc Photographic, Carbon Or Abrasive
PAPER: Filter
PAPER: Gift Wrap
PAPER: Kraft
PAPER: Newsprint
PAPER: Packaging
PAPER: Poster & Art
PAPER: Printer
PAPER: Specialty
PAPER: Specialty Or Chemically Treated
PAPER: Tissue
PAPER: Wallpaper
PAPER: Wrapping & Packaging
PAPER: Writing
PAPERBOARD
PAPERBOARD CONVERTING
PAPERBOARD PRDTS: Building Insulating & Packaging
PAPERBOARD PRDTS: Container Board
PAPERBOARD PRDTS: Folding Boxboard
PAPERBOARD PRDTS: Kraft Linerboard
PAPERBOARD PRDTS: Packaging Board
PAPERBOARD PRDTS: Stencil Board
PAPERBOARD: Liner Board
PARACHUTES
PARTICLEBOARD
PARTICLEBOARD: Laminated, Plastic
PARTITIONS & FIXTURES: Except Wood
PARTITIONS: Solid Fiber, Made From Purchased Materials
PARTITIONS: Wood & Fixtures
PARTS: Metal
PARTY & SPECIAL EVENT PLANNING SVCS
PARTY PLAN MERCHANDISERS
PATENT OWNERS & LESSORS
PATTERNS: Indl
PAVERS
PAVING MATERIALS: Prefabricated, Concrete
PAY TELEPHONE NETWORK
PENCILS & PENS WHOLESALERS
PENS & PARTS: Ball Point
PENS & PENCILS: Mechanical, NEC
PENS: Fountain, Including Desk Sets
PERFUME: Perfumes, Natural Or Synthetic
PERFUMES
PERISCOPES
PERLITE: Processed
PERSONAL & HOUSEHOLD GOODS REPAIR, NEC
PERSONAL DEVELOPMENT SCHOOL

INDEX

PERSONAL DOCUMENT & INFORMATION SVCS
PESTICIDES
PESTICIDES WHOLESALERS
PET & PET SPLYS STORES
PET ACCESS: Collars, Leashes, Etc, Exc Leather
PET FOOD WHOLESALERS
PET SPLYS
PET SPLYS WHOLESALERS
PETROLEUM & PETROLEUM PRDTS, WHOLESALE Diesel Fuel
PETROLEUM & PETROLEUM PRDTS, WHOLESALE Petroleum Brokers
PETROLEUM BULK STATIONS & TERMINALS
PETROLEUM PRDTS WHOLESALERS
PEWTER WARE
PHARMACEUTICAL PREPARATIONS: Digitalis
PHARMACEUTICAL PREPARATIONS: Druggists' Preparations
PHARMACEUTICAL PREPARATIONS: Medicines, Capsule Or Ampule
PHARMACEUTICAL PREPARATIONS: Pills
PHARMACEUTICAL PREPARATIONS: Proprietary Drug PRDTS
PHARMACEUTICALS
PHARMACEUTICALS: Medicinal & Botanical Prdts
PHOTOCOPYING & DUPLICATING SVCS
PHOTOENGRAVING SVC
PHOTOGRAMMATIC MAPPING SVCS
PHOTOGRAPHIC EQPT & CAMERAS, WHOLESALE
PHOTOGRAPHIC EQPT & SPLY: Sound Recordg/Reprod Eqpt, Motion
PHOTOGRAPHIC EQPT & SPLYS
PHOTOGRAPHIC EQPT & SPLYS WHOLESALERS
PHOTOGRAPHIC EQPT & SPLYS: Blueprint Reproduction Mach/Eqpt
PHOTOGRAPHIC EQPT & SPLYS: Cameras, Aerial
PHOTOGRAPHIC EQPT & SPLYS: Densitometers
PHOTOGRAPHIC EQPT & SPLYS: Editing Eqpt, Motion Picture
PHOTOGRAPHIC EQPT & SPLYS: Film, Cloth & Paper, Sensitized
PHOTOGRAPHIC EQPT & SPLYS: Paper & Cloth, All Types, NEC
PHOTOGRAPHIC EQPT & SPLYS: Reels, Film
PHOTOGRAPHIC EQPT & SPLYS: Toners, Prprd, Not Chem Plnts
PHOTOGRAPHIC EQPT & SPLYS: Trays, Printing & Processing
PHOTOGRAPHIC EQPT & SPLYS: Tripods, Camera & Projector
PHOTOGRAPHY SVCS: Commercial
PHOTOTYPESETTING SVC
PHOTOVOLTAIC Solid State
PHYSICIANS' OFFICES & CLINICS: Medical
PHYSICIANS' OFFICES & CLINICS: Medical doctors
PICTURE FRAMES: Metal
PICTURE FRAMES: Wood
PICTURE FRAMING SVCS, CUSTOM
PICTURE PROJECTION EQPT
PIECE GOODS & NOTIONS WHOLESALERS
PIECE GOODS, NOTIONS & DRY GOODS, WHOL: Textiles, Woven
PIECE GOODS, NOTIONS & OTHER DRY GOODS, WHOL: Flags/Banners
PIECE GOODS, NOTIONS & OTHER DRY GOODS, WHOLESALE: Fabrics
PIECE GOODS, NOTIONS/DRY GOODS, WHOL: Sewing Splys/Notions
PILINGS: Wood
PILLOW FILLING MTRLS: Curled Hair, Cotton Waste, Moss
PINS
PIPE & FITTING: Fabrication
PIPE & FITTINGS: Cast Iron
PIPE & TUBES: Aluminum
PIPE FITTINGS: Plastic
PIPE SECTIONS, FABRICATED FROM PURCHASED PIPE
PIPE, CULVERT: Concrete
PIPE, SEWER: Concrete
PIPE: Concrete
PIPE: Extruded, Aluminum
PIPE: Plastic
PIPE: Plate Fabricated, Large Diameter
PIPE: Sheet Metal
PIPES & TUBES
PIPES & TUBES: Steel

PIPES & TUBES: Welded
PIPES: Tobacco
PIVOTS: Power Transmission
PLACER GOLD MINING
PLANING MILL, NEC
PLANING MILLS: Independent, Exc Millwork
PLANING MILLS: Millwork
PLANTS: Artificial & Preserved
PLAQUES: Picture, Laminated
PLASMAS
PLASTER & PLASTERBOARD
PLASTER WORK: Ornamental & Architectural
PLASTERING ACCESS: Metal
PLASTIC PRDTS
PLASTICS FILM & SHEET
PLASTICS FILM & SHEET: Polyethylene
PLASTICS FILM & SHEET: Polypropylene
PLASTICS FILM & SHEET: Vinyl
PLASTICS FINISHED PRDTS: Laminated
PLASTICS MATERIAL & RESINS
PLASTICS MATERIALS, BASIC FORMS & SHAPES WHOLESALERS
PLASTICS PROCESSING
PLASTICS: Blow Molded
PLASTICS: Extruded
PLASTICS: Finished Injection Molded
PLASTICS: Injection Molded
PLASTICS: Molded
PLASTICS: Polystyrene Foam
PLATE WORK: Metalworking Trade
PLATEMAKING SVC: Color Separations, For The Printing Trade
PLATEMAKING SVC: Gravure, Plates Or Cylinders
PLATES
PLATES: Sheet & Strip, Exc Coated Prdts
PLATING & FINISHING SVC: Decorative, Formed Prdts
PLATING & POLISHING SVC
PLATING SVC: Chromium, Metals Or Formed Prdts
PLATING SVC: Electro
PLATING SVC: NEC
PLAYGROUND EQPT
PLEATING & STITCHING SVC
PLUGS: Electric
PLUMBERS' GOODS: Rubber
PLUMBING & HEATING EQPT & SPLY, WHOL: Htg Eqpt/Panels, Solar
PLUMBING & HEATING EQPT & SPLY, WHOLESALE: Hydronic Htg Eqpt
PLUMBING & HEATING EQPT & SPLYS WHOLESALERS
PLUMBING & HEATING EQPT & SPLYS, WHOL: Water Purif Eqpt
PLUMBING FIXTURES
PLUMBING FIXTURES: Brass, Incl Drain Cocks, Faucets/Spigots
PLUMBING FIXTURES: Plastic
PLUMBING FIXTURES: Vitreous
POLES & POSTS: Concrete
POLISHING SVC: Metals Or Formed Prdts
POLYESTERS
POLYETHYLENE RESINS
POLYMETHYL METHACRYLATE RESINS: Plexiglas
POLYTETRAFLUOROETHYLENE RESINS
POSTERS
POTPOURRI
POTTERY
POULTRY & SMALL GAME SLAUGHTERING & PROCESSING
POWDER: Metal
POWER GENERATORS
POWER SUPPLIES: All Types, Static
POWER SUPPLIES: Transformer, Electronic Type
POWER SWITCHING EQPT
POWER TOOLS, HAND: Chain Saws, Portable
POWER TOOLS, HAND: Drills & Drilling Tools
POWER TRANSMISSION EQPT: Aircraft
POWER TRANSMISSION EQPT: Mechanical
PRECAST TERRAZZO OR CONCRETE PRDTS
PRERECORDED TAPE, COMPACT DISC & RECORD STORES: Records
PRESSED & MOLDED PULP PRDTS, NEC: From Purchased Materials
PRESSED FIBER & MOLDED PULP PRDTS, EXC FOOD PRDTS
PRIMARY METAL PRODUCTS
PRINT CARTRIDGES: Laser & Other Computer Printers

PRINTED CIRCUIT BOARDS
PRINTERS & PLOTTERS
PRINTERS' SVCS: Folding, Collating, Etc
PRINTERS: Computer
PRINTERS: Magnetic Ink, Bar Code
PRINTING & BINDING: Books
PRINTING & EMBOSSING: Plastic Fabric Articles
PRINTING & ENGRAVING: Card, Exc Greeting
PRINTING & ENGRAVING: Invitation & Stationery
PRINTING & ENGRAVING: Poster & Decal
PRINTING & STAMPING: Fabric Articles
PRINTING & WRITING PAPER WHOLESALERS
PRINTING INKS WHOLESALERS
PRINTING MACHINERY
PRINTING MACHINERY, EQPT & SPLYS: Wholesalers
PRINTING TRADES MACHINERY & EQPT REPAIR SVCS
PRINTING, COMMERCIAL Newspapers, NEC
PRINTING, COMMERCIAL: Business Forms, NEC
PRINTING, COMMERCIAL: Calendars, NEC
PRINTING, COMMERCIAL: Certificates, Security, NEC
PRINTING, COMMERCIAL: Decals, NEC
PRINTING, COMMERCIAL: Envelopes, NEC
PRINTING, COMMERCIAL: Invitations, NEC
PRINTING, COMMERCIAL: Labels & Seals, NEC
PRINTING, COMMERCIAL: Letterpress & Screen
PRINTING, COMMERCIAL: Literature, Advertising, NEC
PRINTING, COMMERCIAL: Magazines, NEC
PRINTING, COMMERCIAL: Post Cards, Picture, NEC
PRINTING, COMMERCIAL: Promotional
PRINTING, COMMERCIAL: Publications
PRINTING, COMMERCIAL: Ready
PRINTING, COMMERCIAL: Schedules, Transportation, NEC
PRINTING, COMMERCIAL: Screen
PRINTING, COMMERCIAL: Stationery, NEC
PRINTING, LITHOGRAPHIC: Calendars & Cards
PRINTING, LITHOGRAPHIC: Color
PRINTING, LITHOGRAPHIC: Forms & Cards, Business
PRINTING, LITHOGRAPHIC: Forms, Business
PRINTING, LITHOGRAPHIC: Offset & photolithographic printing
PRINTING, LITHOGRAPHIC: On Metal
PRINTING, LITHOGRAPHIC: Post Cards, Picture
PRINTING, LITHOGRAPHIC: Promotional
PRINTING, LITHOGRAPHIC: Publications
PRINTING: Books
PRINTING: Books
PRINTING: Broadwoven Fabrics. Cotton
PRINTING: Checkbooks
PRINTING: Commercial, NEC
PRINTING: Engraving & Plate
PRINTING: Flexographic
PRINTING: Gravure, Business Form & Card
PRINTING: Gravure, Cards, Exc Greeting
PRINTING: Gravure, Catalogs, No Publishing On-Site
PRINTING: Gravure, Circulars
PRINTING: Gravure, Coupons
PRINTING: Gravure, Forms, Business
PRINTING: Gravure, Job
PRINTING: Gravure, Labels
PRINTING: Gravure, Newspapers, No Publishing On-Site
PRINTING: Gravure, Post Cards, Picture
PRINTING: Gravure, Rotogravure
PRINTING: Gravure, Stationery & Invitation
PRINTING: Laser
PRINTING: Letterpress
PRINTING: Lithographic
PRINTING: Manmade Fiber & Silk, Broadwoven Fabric
PRINTING: Offset
PRINTING: Pamphlets
PRINTING: Photo-Offset
PRINTING: Photogravure & Rotogravure
PRINTING: Photolithographic
PRINTING: Rotogravure
PRINTING: Screen, Broadwoven Fabrics, Cotton
PRINTING: Screen, Fabric
PRINTING: Screen, Manmade Fiber & Silk, Broadwoven Fabric
PRINTING: Thermography
PROFESSIONAL EQPT & SPLYS, WHOLESALE: Law Enforcement
PROFESSIONAL EQPT & SPLYS, WHOLESALE: Precision Tools
PROFESSIONAL INSTRUMENT REPAIR SVCS
PROFILE SHAPES: Unsupported Plastics
PROMOTION SVCS

PROPELLERS: Boat & Ship, Cast
PROPELLERS: Boat & Ship, Machined
PROPULSION UNITS: Guided Missiles & Space Vehicles
PROTECTION EQPT: Lightning
PUBLIC RELATIONS & PUBLICITY SVCS
PUBLISHERS: Art Copy
PUBLISHERS: Art Copy & Poster
PUBLISHERS: Book
PUBLISHERS: Book Clubs, No Printing
PUBLISHERS: Books, No Printing
PUBLISHERS: Catalogs
PUBLISHERS: Comic Books, No Printing
PUBLISHERS: Directories, NEC
PUBLISHERS: Directories, Telephone
PUBLISHERS: Guides
PUBLISHERS: Magazines, No Printing
PUBLISHERS: Miscellaneous
PUBLISHERS: Music Book
PUBLISHERS: Music Book & Sheet Music
PUBLISHERS: Music, Book
PUBLISHERS: Music, Sheet
PUBLISHERS: Newsletter
PUBLISHERS: Newspaper
PUBLISHERS: Newspapers, No Printing
PUBLISHERS: Pamphlets, No Printing
PUBLISHERS: Patterns, Paper
PUBLISHERS: Periodical Statistical Reports, No Printing
PUBLISHERS: Periodical, With Printing
PUBLISHERS: Periodicals, Magazines
PUBLISHERS: Periodicals, No Printing
PUBLISHERS: Posters
PUBLISHERS: Technical Manuals
PUBLISHERS: Technical Manuals & Papers
PUBLISHERS: Telephone & Other Directory
PUBLISHERS: Textbooks, No Printing
PUBLISHERS: Trade journals, No Printing
PUBLISHING & BROADCASTING: Internet Only
PUBLISHING & PRINTING: Art Copy
PUBLISHING & PRINTING: Book Clubs
PUBLISHING & PRINTING: Book Music
PUBLISHING & PRINTING: Books
PUBLISHING & PRINTING: Catalogs
PUBLISHING & PRINTING: Directories, NEC
PUBLISHING & PRINTING: Guides
PUBLISHING & PRINTING: Magazines: publishing & printing
PUBLISHING & PRINTING: Music, Book
PUBLISHING & PRINTING: Newsletters, Business Svc
PUBLISHING & PRINTING: Newspapers
PUBLISHING & PRINTING: Pamphlets
PUBLISHING & PRINTING: Patterns, Paper
PUBLISHING & PRINTING: Periodical Statistical Reports
PUBLISHING & PRINTING: Posters
PUBLISHING & PRINTING: Technical Manuals
PUBLISHING & PRINTING: Textbooks
PUBLISHING & PRINTING: Trade Journals
PUBLISHING & PRINTING: Yearbooks
PULP MILLS
PULP MILLS: Chemical & Semichemical Processing
PULP MILLS: Mechanical & Recycling Processing
PUMPS
PUMPS & PARTS: Indl
PUMPS & PUMPING EQPT REPAIR SVCS
PUMPS & PUMPING EQPT WHOLESALERS
PUMPS, HEAT: Electric
PUMPS: Domestic, Water Or Sump
PUMPS: Hydraulic Power Transfer
PUMPS: Measuring & Dispensing
PUMPS: Oil Well & Field
PUPPETS & MARIONETTES
PURCHASING SVCS
PURIFICATION & DUST COLLECTION EQPT
PURIFIERS: Centrifugal

Q

QUILTING SVC
QUILTING SVC & SPLYS, FOR THE TRADE
QUILTING: Individuals

R

RABBIT SLAUGHTERING & PROCESSING
RACE TRACK OPERATION
RACEWAYS
RACKS: Pallet, Exc Wood
RACKS: Railroad Car, Vehicle Transportation, Steel
RADAR SYSTEMS & EQPT

RADIO & TELEVISION COMMUNICATIONS EQUIPMENT
RADIO BROADCASTING & COMMUNICATIONS EQPT
RADIO BROADCASTING STATIONS
RADIO COMMUNICATIONS: Airborne Eqpt
RADIO COMMUNICATIONS: Carrier Eqpt
RADIO RECEIVER NETWORKS
RADIO, TELEVISION & CONSUMER ELECTRONICS
   STORES: Eqpt, NEC
RAIL & STRUCTURAL SHAPES: Aluminum rail & structural
   shapes
RAILINGS: Wood
RAILROAD CARGO LOADING & UNLOADING SVCS
RAILROAD EQPT
RAILROAD EQPT, EXC LOCOMOTIVES
RAILROAD EQPT: Cars & Eqpt, Dining
RAILROAD EQPT: Cars, Motor
RAILROAD EQPT: Engines, Locomotive, Steam
RAILROAD EQPT: Street Cars & Eqpt
RAILROAD RELATED EQPT: Railway Track
RAILROAD TIES: Wood
RAILS: Steel Or Iron
RAMPS: Prefabricated Metal
RAZORS, RAZOR BLADES
RAZORS: Electric
REACTORS: Current Limiting
REAL ESTATE AGENCIES & BROKERS
REAL ESTATE AGENCIES: Leasing & Rentals
REAL ESTATE AGENTS & MANAGERS
REAL ESTATE LISTING SVCS
REAL ESTATE OPERATORS, EXC DEVELOPERS: Commer-
   cial/Indl Bldg
RECEIVERS: Radio Communications
RECLAIMED RUBBER: Reworked By Manufacturing Process
RECORDING HEADS: Speech & Musical Eqpt
RECORDING TAPE: Video, Blank
RECORDS & TAPES: Prerecorded
RECORDS OR TAPES: Masters
RECREATIONAL SPORTING EQPT REPAIR SVCS
RECREATIONAL VEHICLE REPAIRS
RECREATIONAL VEHICLE: Wholesalers
RECYCLABLE SCRAP & WASTE MATERIALS WHOLE-
   SALERS
RECYCLING: Paper
REFINERS & SMELTERS: Gold, Secondary
REFINERS & SMELTERS: Nonferrous Metal
REFINERS & SMELTERS: Silicon, Primary, Over 99% Pure
REFINING: Petroleum
REFRACTORIES: Brick
REFRACTORIES: Clay
REFRACTORIES: Nonclay
REFRIGERATION & HEATING EQUIPMENT
REFRIGERATION EQPT: Complete
REFRIGERATION SVC & REPAIR
REGULATORS: Generator Voltage
REGULATORS: Power
RELAYS & SWITCHES: Indl, Electric
REMOVERS & CLEANERS
RENDERING PLANT
RENTAL CENTERS: Party & Banquet Eqpt & Splys
RENTAL SVCS: Audio-Visual Eqpt & Sply
RENTAL SVCS: Business Machine & Electronic Eqpt
RENTAL SVCS: Eqpt, Theatrical
RENTAL SVCS: Sign
RENTAL SVCS: Sound & Lighting Eqpt
RENTAL SVCS: Trailer
RENTAL: Portable Toilet
RENTAL: Video Tape & Disc
REPAIR SERVICES, NEC
REPAIR TRAINING, COMPUTER
RESEARCH & DEVELOPMENT SVCS, COMMERCIAL: Engi-
   neering Lab
RESEARCH, DEVELOPMENT & TEST SVCS, COMM: Cmptr
   Hardware Dev
RESEARCH, DEVELOPMENT & TEST SVCS, COMM: Re-
   search, Exc Lab
RESEARCH, DEVELOPMENT & TESTING SVCS, COMMER-
   CIAL: Medical
RESEARCH, DEVELOPMENT & TESTING SVCS, COMMER-
   CIAL: Physical
RESEARCH, DVLPT & TEST SVCS, COMM: Mkt Analysis or
   Research
RESIDENTIAL MENTAL HEALTH & SUBSTANCE ABUSE FA-
   CILITIES
RESIDENTIAL REMODELERS
RESIDUES

RESINS: Custom Compound Purchased
RESPIRATORY SYSTEM DRUGS
RESTAURANT EQPT REPAIR SVCS
RESTAURANT EQPT: Carts
RESTAURANT EQPT: Food Wagons
RESTAURANTS:Full Svc, Family, Independent
RESTAURANTS:Limited Svc, Coffee Shop
RESTAURANTS:Limited Svc, Fast-Food, Chain
RESTAURANTS:Limited Svc, Health Food
RESTAURANTS:Limited Svc, Lunch Counter
RETAIL BAKERY: Cakes
RETAIL BAKERY: Pretzels
RETAIL LUMBER YARDS
RETAIL STORES, NEC
RETAIL STORES: Alarm Signal Systems
RETAIL STORES: Artificial Limbs
RETAIL STORES: Awnings
RETAIL STORES: Canvas Prdts
RETAIL STORES: Children's Furniture, NEC
RETAIL STORES: Cleaning Eqpt & Splys
RETAIL STORES: Coins
RETAIL STORES: Cosmetics
RETAIL STORES: Facsimile Eqpt
RETAIL STORES: Farm Eqpt & Splys
RETAIL STORES: Farm Machinery, NEC
RETAIL STORES: Fire Extinguishers
RETAIL STORES: Flags
RETAIL STORES: Hearing Aids
RETAIL STORES: Hospital Eqpt & Splys
RETAIL STORES: Ice
RETAIL STORES: Medical Apparatus & Splys
RETAIL STORES: Motors, Electric
RETAIL STORES: Orthopedic & Prosthesis Applications
RETAIL STORES: Pet Food
RETAIL STORES: Picture Frames, Ready Made
RETAIL STORES: Police Splys
RETAIL STORES: Rubber Stamps
RETAIL STORES: Safety Splys & Eqpt
RETAIL STORES: Sunglasses
RETAIL STORES: Water Purification Eqpt
RETAIL STORES: Wheelchair Lifts
REUPHOLSTERY & FURNITURE REPAIR
REUPHOLSTERY SVCS
RHEOSTATS: Electronic
RIBBONS, NEC
RIBBONS: Machine, Inked Or Carbon
RIFLES: Recoilless
RIPRAP QUARRYING
ROBOTS: Assembly Line
ROCK SALT MINING
ROCKETS: Space & Military
RODS: Plastic
RODS: Welding
ROLLERS & FITTINGS: Window Shade
ROLLING MILL MACHINERY
ROOF DECKS
ROOFING MATERIALS: Asphalt
ROOFING MEMBRANE: Rubber
ROPE
RUBBER
RUBBER PRDTS
RUBBER PRDTS: Automotive, Mechanical
RUBBER PRDTS: Mechanical
RUBBER PRDTS: Medical & Surgical Tubing, Extrudd &
   Lathe-Cut
RUBBER STRUCTURES: Air-Supported
RUBBING STONE QUARRYING SVCS
RUGS : Hand & Machine Made

S

SAFE DEPOSIT BOXES
SAFES & VAULTS: Metal
SAFETY EQPT & SPLYS WHOLESALERS
SAILS
SALT
SAND & GRAVEL
SAND MINING
SAND: Hygrade
SANDBLASTING EQPT
SANDBLASTING SVC: Building Exterior
SANDSTONE: Dimension
SANITARY SVCS: Liquid Waste Collection & Disposal
SANITARY SVCS: Medical Waste Disposal
SANITARY SVCS: Waste Materials, Recycling
SANITATION CHEMICALS & CLEANING AGENTS

INDEX

SASHES: Door Or Window, Metal
SATELLITE COMMUNICATIONS EQPT
SATELLITES: Communications
SAW BLADES
SAWDUST & SHAVINGS
SAWING & PLANING MILLS
SAWING & PLANING MILLS: Custom
SAWS & SAWING EQPT
SAWS: Hand, Metalworking Or Woodworking
SCALES & BALANCES, EXC LABORATORY
SCANNING DEVICES: Optical
SCIENTIFIC EQPT REPAIR SVCS
SCRAP STEEL CUTTING
SCREENS: Projection
SCREENS: Window, Metal
SCREW MACHINE PRDTS
SEALANTS
SEALING COMPOUNDS: Sealing, synthetic rubber or plastic
SEARCH & DETECTION SYSTEMS, EXC RADAR
SEARCH & NAVIGATION SYSTEMS
SEARCH & RESCUE SVCS
SEATING: Bleacher, Portable
SECRETARIAL & COURT REPORTING
SECRETARIAL SVCS
SECURE STORAGE SVC: Document
SECURITY CONTROL EQPT & SYSTEMS
SECURITY DEVICES
SECURITY EQPT STORES
SECURITY GUARD SVCS
SECURITY PROTECTIVE DEVICES MAINTENANCE &
  MONITORING SVCS
SECURITY SYSTEMS SERVICES
SELF-DEFENSE & ATHLETIC INSTRUCTION SVCS
SEMICONDUCTOR & RELATED DEVICES: Random Access
  Memory Or RAM
SEMICONDUCTOR & RELATED DEVICES: Read-Only Mem-
  ory Or ROM
SEMICONDUCTORS & RELATED DEVICES
SENSORS: Infrared, Solid State
SEPTIC TANK CLEANING SVCS
SEPTIC TANKS: Concrete
SERVICES, NEC
SERVOMOTORS: Electric
SEWAGE & WATER TREATMENT EQPT
SEWING KITS: Novelty
SEWING MACHINES & PARTS: Household
SEWING, NEEDLEWORK & PIECE GOODS STORE: Quilting
  Matls/Splys
SEWING, NEEDLEWORK & PIECE GOODS STORES
SEWING, NEEDLEWORK & PIECE GOODS STORES: Knit-
  ting Splys
SEXTANTS
SHADES: Lamp & Light, Residential
SHADES: Lamp Or Candle
SHADES: Window
SHAPES & PILINGS, STRUCTURAL: Steel
SHAPES: Extruded, Aluminum, NEC
SHAPES: Flat, Rolled, Aluminum, NEC
SHAVING PREPARATIONS
SHEET METAL SPECIALTIES, EXC STAMPED
SHEETS & STRIPS: Aluminum
SHELLAC
SHELVING: Office & Store, Exc Wood
SHIP BLDG/RPRG: Submersible Marine Robots, Manned/Un-
  manned
SHIP BUILDING & REPAIRING: Boats, Crew
SHIP BUILDING & REPAIRING: Cargo, Commercial
SHIP BUILDING & REPAIRING: Combat Vessels
SHIP BUILDING & REPAIRING: Fishing Vessels, Large
SHIP BUILDING & REPAIRING: Landing
SHIP BUILDING & REPAIRING: Lighters, Marine
SHIP BUILDING & REPAIRING: Military
SHIP BUILDING & REPAIRING: Offshore Sply Boats
SHIP BUILDING & REPAIRING: Submarine Tenders
SHIP BUILDING & REPAIRING: Tenders, Ship
SHIP BUILDING & REPAIRING: Towboats
SHIP BUILDING & REPAIRING: Tugboats
SHIPBUILDING & REPAIR
SHIPPING AGENTS
SHOE MATERIALS: Counters
SHOE MATERIALS: Quarters
SHOE MATERIALS: Rands
SHOE MATERIALS: Uppers
SHOE REPAIR SHOP
SHOE STORES: Boots, Men's

SHOE STORES: Custom & Orthopedic
SHOE STORES: Men's
SHOE STORES: Women's
SHOES & BOOTS WHOLESALERS
SHOES: Athletic, Exc Rubber Or Plastic
SHOES: Canvas, Rubber Soled
SHOES: Men's
SHOES: Men's, Dress
SHOES: Plastic Or Rubber
SHOES: Women's
SHOES: Women's, Dress
SHOWCASES & DISPLAY FIXTURES: Office & Store
SHOWER STALLS: Metal
SHOWER STALLS: Plastic & Fiberglass
SHREDDERS: Indl & Commercial
SHUTTERS, DOOR & WINDOW: Metal
SHUTTERS: Window, Wood
SIDING & STRUCTURAL MATERIALS: Wood
SIGN LETTERING & PAINTING SVCS
SIGN PAINTING & LETTERING SHOP
SIGNALS: Railroad, Electric
SIGNALS: Traffic Control, Electric
SIGNALS: Transportation
SIGNS & ADVERTISING SPECIALTIES
SIGNS & ADVERTISING SPECIALTIES: Artwork, Advertising
SIGNS & ADVERTISING SPECIALTIES: Displays, Paint
  Process
SIGNS & ADVERTISING SPECIALTIES: Letters For Signs,
  Metal
SIGNS & ADVERTISING SPECIALTIES: Novelties
SIGNS & ADVERTISING SPECIALTIES: Signs
SIGNS & ADVERTSG SPECIALTIES: Displays/Cutouts Win-
  dow/Lobby
SIGNS, ELECTRICAL: Wholesalers
SIGNS, EXC ELECTRIC, WHOLESALE
SIGNS: Electrical
SIGNS: Neon
SILICA MINING
SILICONES
SILK SCREEN DESIGN SVCS
SILLS, WINDOW: Cast Stone
SILOS & COMPONENTS: Missile, Metal Plate
SILVERSMITHS
SILVERWARE
SILVERWARE & PLATED WARE
SILVERWARE, STERLING SILVER
SIMULATORS: Electronic Countermeasure
SIMULATORS: Flight
SIRENS: Vehicle, Marine, Indl & Warning
SIZES
SKIDS: Wood
SLAB & TILE: Precast Concrete, Floor
SLAUGHTERING & MEAT PACKING
SLIDES & EXHIBITS: Prepared
SLOT MACHINES
SMOKE DETECTORS
SMOKERS' SPLYS, WHOLESALE
SNACK & NONALCOHOLIC BEVERAGE BARS
SNOW PLOWING SVCS
SNOW REMOVAL EQPT: Residential
SNOWMOBILES
SOAPS & DETERGENTS
SOAPS & DETERGENTS: Textile
SOAPSTONE MINING
SOCIAL SERVICES, NEC
SOCKETS: Electric
SOFT DRINKS WHOLESALERS
SOFTWARE PUBLISHERS: Application
SOFTWARE PUBLISHERS: Business & Professional
SOFTWARE PUBLISHERS: Computer Utilities
SOFTWARE PUBLISHERS: Education
SOFTWARE PUBLISHERS: Home Entertainment
SOFTWARE PUBLISHERS: NEC
SOFTWARE PUBLISHERS: Operating Systems
SOFTWARE PUBLISHERS: Publisher's
SOFTWARE PUBLISHERS: Word Processing
SOFTWARE TRAINING, COMPUTER
SOIL CONDITIONERS
SOIL TESTING KITS
SOLAR CELLS
SOLAR HEATING EQPT
SOLDERING EQPT: Irons Or Coppers
SOLDERING SVC: Jewelry
SOLVENTS
SONAR SYSTEMS & EQPT

SOUND EFFECTS & MUSIC PRODUCTION: Motion Picture
SOUND EQPT: Electric
SOUND RECORDING STUDIOS
SOUND REPRODUCING EQPT
SPACE CAPSULES
SPACE PROPULSION UNITS & PARTS
SPACE VEHICLE EQPT
SPACE VEHICLES
SPEAKER SYSTEMS
SPECIAL EVENTS DECORATION SVCS
SPECIAL PRODUCT SAWMILLS, NEC
SPECIALTY FOOD STORES: Coffee
SPECIALTY FOOD STORES: Health & Dietetic Food
SPECIALTY OUTPATIENT CLINICS, NEC
SPIKES: Steel, Wire Or Cut
SPORTING & ATHLETIC GOODS: Arrows, Archery
SPORTING & ATHLETIC GOODS: Balls, Baseball, Football,
  Etc
SPORTING & ATHLETIC GOODS: Batons
SPORTING & ATHLETIC GOODS: Bobsleds
SPORTING & ATHLETIC GOODS: Boomerangs
SPORTING & ATHLETIC GOODS: Bowling Alleys & Access
SPORTING & ATHLETIC GOODS: Bowling Pins
SPORTING & ATHLETIC GOODS: Camping Eqpt & Splys
SPORTING & ATHLETIC GOODS: Cartridge Belts
SPORTING & ATHLETIC GOODS: Carts, Caddy
SPORTING & ATHLETIC GOODS: Cases, Gun & Rod
SPORTING & ATHLETIC GOODS: Cricket Eqpt, NEC
SPORTING & ATHLETIC GOODS: Crossbows
SPORTING & ATHLETIC GOODS: Decoys, Duck & Other
  Game Birds
SPORTING & ATHLETIC GOODS: Driving Ranges, Golf,
  Electronic
SPORTING & ATHLETIC GOODS: Exercising Cycles
SPORTING & ATHLETIC GOODS: Fishing Eqpt
SPORTING & ATHLETIC GOODS: Game Calls
SPORTING & ATHLETIC GOODS: Guards, Football, Soccer,
  Etc
SPORTING & ATHLETIC GOODS: Hockey Eqpt & Splys, NEC
SPORTING & ATHLETIC GOODS: Hunting Eqpt
SPORTING & ATHLETIC GOODS: Pools, Swimming, Plastic
SPORTING & ATHLETIC GOODS: Protective Sporting Eqpt
SPORTING & ATHLETIC GOODS: Racket Sports Eqpt
SPORTING & ATHLETIC GOODS: Rods & Rod Parts, Fishing
SPORTING & ATHLETIC GOODS: Shafts, Golf Club
SPORTING & ATHLETIC GOODS: Shooting Eqpt & Splys,
  General
SPORTING & ATHLETIC GOODS: Skateboards
SPORTING & ATHLETIC GOODS: Skates & Parts, Roller
SPORTING & ATHLETIC GOODS: Snow Skis
SPORTING & ATHLETIC GOODS: Snowshoes
SPORTING & ATHLETIC GOODS: Soccer Eqpt & Splys
SPORTING & ATHLETIC GOODS: Target Shooting Eqpt
SPORTING & ATHLETIC GOODS: Targets, Archery & Rifle
  Shooting
SPORTING & ATHLETIC GOODS: Team Sports Eqpt
SPORTING & ATHLETIC GOODS: Tennis Eqpt & Splys
SPORTING & ATHLETIC GOODS: Trap Racks, Clay Targets
SPORTING & ATHLETIC GOODS: Treadmills
SPORTING & ATHLETIC GOODS: Water Skis
SPORTING & RECREATIONAL GOODS & SPLYS WHOLE-
  SALERS
SPORTING & RECREATIONAL GOODS, WHOLESALE: Boat
  Access & Part
SPORTING & RECREATIONAL GOODS, WHOLESALE: Fish-
  ing
SPORTING & RECREATIONAL GOODS, WHOLESALE: Golf
SPORTING CAMPS
SPORTING FIREARMS WHOLESALERS
SPORTING GOODS
SPORTING GOODS STORES, NEC
SPORTING GOODS STORES: Firearms
SPORTING GOODS STORES: Fishing Eqpt
SPORTING GOODS STORES: Hunting Eqpt
SPORTING GOODS STORES: Playground Eqpt
SPORTING GOODS STORES: Specialty Sport Splys, NEC
SPORTING GOODS STORES: Surfing Eqpt & Splys
SPORTING GOODS STORES: Team sports Eqpt
SPORTING GOODS STORES: Water Sport Eqpt
SPORTING GOODS: Archery
SPORTING GOODS: Skin Diving Eqpt
SPORTING GOODS: Surfboards
SPORTING/ATHLETIC GOODS: Gloves, Boxing, Handball,
  Etc
SPORTS APPAREL STORES

SPOUTING: Plastic & Fiberglass Reinforced
SPRAYS: Artificial & Preserved
SPRINGS: Automobile
SPRINGS: Clock, Precision
SPRINGS: Mechanical, Precision
SPRINGS: Wire
STACKING MACHINES: Automatic
STAFFING, EMPLOYMENT PLACEMENT
STAGE LIGHTING SYSTEMS
STAINED GLASS ART SVCS
STAINLESS STEEL
STAINS: Wood
STAIRCASES & STAIRS, WOOD
STAMPED ART GOODS FOR EMBROIDERING
STAMPINGS: Metal
STARTERS & CONTROLLERS: Motor, Electric
STATIONARY/OFFICE SPLYS, WHOL: Soc Stationery/Greeting Cards
STATIONERY & OFFICE SPLYS WHOLESALERS
STATIONERY PRDTS
STATUARY & OTHER DECORATIVE PRDTS: Nonmetallic
STAVES
STEEL & ALLOYS: Tool & Die
STEEL FABRICATORS
STEEL MILLS
STEEL: Cold-Rolled
STEEL: Galvanized
STEEL: Laminated
STENCILS
STERILIZERS, BARBER & BEAUTY SHOP
STITCHING SVCS: Custom
STONE: Cast Concrete
STONE: Crushed & Broken, NEC
STONE: Dimension, NEC
STONE: Quarrying & Processing, Own Stone Prdts
STONEWARE PRDTS: Pottery
STORE FIXTURES, EXC REFRIGERATED: Wholesalers
STORE FIXTURES: Exc Wood
STORE FIXTURES: Wood
STORES: Drapery & Upholstery
STOVES: Wood & Coal Burning
STRAPS: Braids, Textile
STRUCTURAL SUPPORT & BUILDING MATERIAL: Concrete
STUCCO
STUDIOS: Artist
STUDIOS: Artists & Artists' Studios
STUDIOS: Sculptor's
SUBMARINE BUILDING & REPAIR
SUNDRIES & RELATED PRDTS: Medical & Laboratory, Rubber
SUNGLASSES, WHOLESALE
SUNROOMS: Prefabricated Metal
SUPERMARKETS & OTHER GROCERY STORES
SURFACE ACTIVE AGENTS: Oils & Greases
SURFACE ACTIVE AGENTS: Processing Assistants
SURGICAL APPLIANCES & SPLYS
SURGICAL EQPT: See Also Instruments
SURGICAL IMPLANTS
SURGICAL INSTRUMENT REPAIR SVCS
SURVEYING & MAPPING: Land Parcels
SUSPENSION SYSTEMS: Acoustical, Metal
SVC ESTABLISHMENT EQPT, WHOL: Cleaning & Maint Eqpt & Splys
SVC ESTABLISHMENT EQPT, WHOL: Laundry/Dry Cleaning Eqpt/Sply
SVC ESTABLISHMENT EQPT, WHOLESALE: Firefighting Eqpt
SWEEPING COMPOUNDS
SWIMMING POOLS, EQPT & SPLYS: Wholesalers
SWITCHES: Electric Power, Exc Snap, Push Button, Etc
SWITCHES: Electronic
SWITCHES: Electronic Applications
SWITCHGEAR & SWITCHBOARD APPARATUS
SWORDS
SYNCHROS
SYSTEMS ENGINEERING: Computer Related
SYSTEMS INTEGRATION SVCS
SYSTEMS INTEGRATION SVCS: Local Area Network
SYSTEMS INTEGRATION SVCS: Office Computer Automation
SYSTEMS SOFTWARE DEVELOPMENT SVCS

T

TABLE OR COUNTERTOPS, PLASTIC LAMINATED
TAGS & LABELS: Paper

TAGS: Paper, Blank, Made From Purchased Paper
TAILORS: Custom
TANK COMPONENTS: Military, Specialized
TANK REPAIR & CLEANING SVCS
TANK REPAIR SVCS
TANK TRUCK CLEANING SVCS
TANKS & OTHER TRACKED VEHICLE CMPNTS
TANKS: Concrete
TANKS: Cryogenic, Metal
TANKS: Fuel, Including Oil & Gas, Metal Plate
TANKS: Lined, Metal
TANKS: Military, Including Factory Rebuilding
TANKS: Standard Or Custom Fabricated, Metal Plate
TANKS: Water, Metal Plate
TANNERIES: Leather
TAPE DRIVES
TAPES: Fabric
TAPES: Plastic Coated
TAR
TARGET DRONES
TARPAULINS
TAXIDERMISTS
TELECOMMUNICATION SYSTEMS & EQPT
TELECOMMUNICATIONS CARRIERS & SVCS: Wired
TELECOMMUNICATIONS CARRIERS & SVCS: Wireless
TELEMARKETING BUREAUS
TELEMETERING EQPT
TELEPHONE EQPT: Modems
TELEPHONE EQPT: NEC
TELEPHONE SVCS
TELEPHONE: Fiber Optic Systems
TELEPHONE: Sets, Exc Cellular Radio
TELESCOPES
TELEVISION BROADCASTING & COMMUNICATIONS EQPT
TELEVISION BROADCASTING STATIONS
TELEVISION: Closed Circuit Eqpt
TELEVISION: Monitors
TENTS: All Materials
TESTERS: Environmental
TESTERS: Physical Property
TESTERS: Water, Exc Indl Process
TEXTILE & APPAREL SVCS
TEXTILE BAGS WHOLESALERS
TEXTILE FABRICATORS
TEXTILE PRDTS: Hand Woven & Crocheted
TEXTILE: Finishing, Cotton Broadwoven
TEXTILE: Finishing, Raw Stock NEC
TEXTILE: Goods, NEC
TEXTILES: Fibers, Textile, Rcvrd From Mill Waste/Rags
TEXTILES: Jute & Flax Prdts
TEXTILES: Linen Fabrics
TEXTILES: Mill Waste & Remnant
TEXTILES: Tops, Combing & Converting
THEATRICAL LIGHTING SVCS
THEATRICAL SCENERY
THERMOELECTRIC DEVICES: Solid State
THERMOMETERS: Medical, Digital
THERMOPLASTICS
THERMOSETTING MATERIALS
THIN FILM CIRCUITS
THREAD: All Fibers
THREAD: Sewing
TILE: Brick & Structural, Clay
TILE: Mosaic, Ceramic
TILE: Wall, Ceramic
TIN
TIRE & INNER TUBE MATERIALS & RELATED PRDTS
TIRE CORD & FABRIC
TIRE DEALERS
TIRES & INNER TUBES
TIRES & TUBES WHOLESALERS
TIRES & TUBES, WHOLESALE: Automotive
TIRES & TUBES, WHOLESALE: Truck
TIRES: Auto
TITANIUM MILL PRDTS
TOBACCO & PRDTS, WHOLESALE: Cigarettes
TOBACCO LEAF PROCESSING
TOBACCO STEMMING
TOBACCO: Chewing
TOBACCO: Chewing & Snuff
TOBACCO: Cigarettes
TOBACCO: Cigars
TOBACCO: Smoking
TOILET PREPARATIONS
TOILET SEATS: Wood

TOILETRIES, COSMETICS & PERFUME STORES
TOILETRIES, WHOLESALE: Toilet Preparations
TOILETRIES, WHOLESALE: Toiletries
TOILETS: Metal
TOILETS: Portable Chemical, Plastics
TOLLS: Caulking
TOOL & DIE STEEL
TOOL REPAIR SVCS
TOOLS: Carpenters', Including Levels & Chisels, Exc Saws
TOOLS: Hand
TOOLS: Hand, Engravers'
TOOLS: Hand, Jewelers'
TOOLS: Hand, Masons'
TOOLS: Hand, Mechanics
TOOLS: Hand, Power
TOOTHPASTES, GELS & TOOTHPOWDERS
TOWELS: Indl
TOWERS, SECTIONS: Transmission, Radio & Television
TOWERS: Bubble, Cooling, Fractionating, Metal Plate
TOWING & TUGBOAT SVC
TOWING BARS & SYSTEMS
TOYS
TOYS & HOBBY GOODS & SPLYS, WHOLESALE: Arts/Crafts Eqpt/Sply
TOYS & HOBBY GOODS & SPLYS, WHOLESALE: Toys, NEC
TOYS: Dolls, Stuffed Animals & Parts
TOYS: Electronic
TOYS: Kites
TOYS: Rubber
TOYS: Video Game Machines
TRACTOR REPAIR SVCS
TRAILER PARKS
TRAILERS & CHASSIS: Camping
TRAILERS & PARTS: Horse
TRAILERS & PARTS: Truck & Semi's
TRAILERS & TRAILER EQPT
TRAILERS OR VANS: Horse Transportation, Fifth-Wheel Type
TRAILERS: Bodies
TRAILERS: Semitrailers, Missile Transportation
TRAILERS: Semitrailers, Truck Tractors
TRANSDUCERS: Electrical Properties
TRANSDUCERS: Pressure
TRANSFORMERS: Control
TRANSFORMERS: Distribution
TRANSFORMERS: Electric
TRANSFORMERS: Electronic
TRANSFORMERS: Machine Tool
TRANSFORMERS: Power Related
TRANSFORMERS: Specialty
TRANSLATION & INTERPRETATION SVCS
TRANSMISSIONS: Motor Vehicle
TRANSPORTATION AGENTS & BROKERS
TRANSPORTATION EPQT & SPLYS, WHOLESALE: Acft/Space Vehicle
TRANSPORTATION EQPT & SPLYS WHOLESALERS, NEC
TRANSPORTATION EQUIPMENT, NEC
TRANSPORTATION SVCS: Cable Cars, Exc Aerial, Amuse & Scenic
TRANSPORTATION: Air, Scheduled Freight
TRANSPORTATION: Local Passenger, NEC
TRAP ROCK: Dimension
TRAPS: Animal & Fish, Wire
TRAVEL TRAILERS & CAMPERS
TROPHIES, NEC
TROPHIES, PLATED, ALL METALS
TROPHIES: Metal, Exc Silver
TROPHY & PLAQUE STORES
TRUCK & BUS BODIES: Car Carrier
TRUCK & BUS BODIES: Dump Truck
TRUCK & BUS BODIES: Garbage Or Refuse Truck
TRUCK & BUS BODIES: Motor Vehicle, Specialty
TRUCK & BUS BODIES: Tank Truck
TRUCK & BUS BODIES: Truck Beds
TRUCK & BUS BODIES: Truck Tops
TRUCK & BUS BODIES: Truck, Motor Vehicle
TRUCK & BUS BODIES: Utility Truck
TRUCK BODIES: Body Parts
TRUCK DRIVER SVCS
TRUCK GENERAL REPAIR SVC
TRUCK PAINTING & LETTERING SVCS
TRUCK PARTS & ACCESSORIES: Wholesalers
TRUCKING & HAULING SVCS: Animal & Farm Prdt
TRUCKING & HAULING SVCS: Furniture Moving & Storage, Local

INDEX

TRUCKING & HAULING SVCS: Haulage & Cartage, Light, Local
TRUCKING & HAULING SVCS: Heavy, NEC
TRUCKING & HAULING SVCS: Liquid Petroleum, Exc Local
TRUCKING & HAULING SVCS: Lumber & Log, Local
TRUCKING, ANIMAL
TRUCKING, AUTOMOBILE CARRIER
TRUCKING, DUMP
TRUCKING: Except Local
TRUCKING: Local, Without Storage
TRUCKING: Long-Distance, Less Than Truckload
TRUCKS & TRACTORS: Industrial
TRUCKS: Forklift
TRUCKS: Indl
TRUNKS
TRUSSES & FRAMING: Prefabricated Metal
TRUSSES: Wood, Floor
TRUSSES: Wood, Roof
TUBE & TUBING FABRICATORS
TUBES: Finned, For Heat Transfer
TUBES: Generator, Electron Beam, Beta Ray
TUBES: Welded, Aluminum
TUBING: Plastic
TUMBLERS: Plastic
TUNNELS: Vacuum, Metal Plate
TURBINES & TURBINE GENERATOR SETS
TURBINES: Steam
TURBO-GENERATORS
TYPESETTING SVC
TYPESETTING SVC: Computer

U

ULTRASONIC EQPT: Cleaning, Exc Med & Dental
UNDERGROUND IRON ORE MINING
UNIFORM SPLY SVCS: Indl
UNIFORM STORES
UNIT TRAIN LOADING FACILITY, BITUMINOUS OR LIGNITE
UNIVERSITY
UPHOLSTERY WORK SVCS
URANIUM ORE MINING, NEC
USED CAR DEALERS
USED MERCHANDISE STORES
UTENSILS: Household, Cooking & Kitchen, Metal
UTENSILS: Household, Cooking & Kitchen, Porcelain Enameled
UTILITY TRAILER DEALERS

V

VACUUM CLEANERS: Household
VACUUM CLEANERS: Indl Type
VACUUM SYSTEMS: Air Extraction, Indl
VALUE-ADDED RESELLERS: Computer Systems
VALVES
VALVES & PIPE FITTINGS
VALVES & REGULATORS: Pressure, Indl
VALVES: Aerosol, Metal
VALVES: Aircraft, Hydraulic
VALVES: Control, Automatic
VALVES: Indl
VALVES: Plumbing & Heating
VALVES: Regulating & Control, Automatic
VALVES: Water Works
VAN CONVERSIONS
VARIETY STORES
VARNISHES, NEC
VASES: Pottery
VEGETABLE STANDS OR MARKETS
VEHICLES: Recreational
VENDING MACHINE REPAIR SVCS
VENDING MACHINES & PARTS
VENETIAN BLINDS & SHADES
VENTILATING EQPT: Metal
VENTILATING EQPT: Sheet Metal
VERMICULITE: Processed

VESSELS: Process, Indl, Metal Plate
VETERINARY PHARMACEUTICAL PREPARATIONS
VETERINARY PRDTS: Instruments & Apparatus
VIALS: Glass
VIDEO & AUDIO EQPT, WHOLESALE
VIDEO PRODUCTION SVCS
VIDEO TAPE PRODUCTION SVCS
VIDEO TRIGGERS: Remote Control TV Devices
VISUAL COMMUNICATIONS SYSTEMS
VITAMINS: Natural Or Synthetic, Uncompounded, Bulk
VITAMINS: Pharmaceutical Preparations

W

WALLPAPER & WALL COVERINGS
WALLS: Curtain, Metal
WAREHOUSING & STORAGE, REFRIGERATED: Cold Storage Or Refrig
WAREHOUSING & STORAGE: General
WAREHOUSING & STORAGE: Self Storage
WARFARE COUNTER-MEASURE EQPT
WARM AIR HEATING/AC EQPT/SPLYS, WHOL Warm Air Htg Eqpt/Splys
WASHCLOTHS
WASHERS
WASTE CLEANING SVCS
WATER PURIFICATION EQPT: Household
WATER PURIFICATION PRDTS: Chlorination Tablets & Kits
WATER SOFTENER SVCS
WATER TREATMENT EQPT: Indl
WATER: Mineral, Carbonated, Canned & Bottled, Etc
WATER: Pasteurized & Mineral, Bottled & Canned
WATER: Pasteurized, Canned & Bottled, Etc
WATERPROOFING COMPOUNDS
WAVEGUIDE PRESSURIZATION EQPT
WAVEGUIDES & FITTINGS
WAXES: Petroleum, Not Produced In Petroleum Refineries
WEATHER STRIP: Sponge Rubber
WEAVING MILL, BROADWOVEN FABRICS: Wool Or Similar Fabric
WEB SEARCH PORTALS: Internet
WEDDING CONSULTING SVCS
WELDING & CUTTING APPARATUS & ACCESS, NEC
WELDING EQPT
WELDING EQPT & SPLYS: Electrodes
WELDING EQPT & SPLYS: Generators, Arc Welding, AC & DC
WELDING EQPT & SPLYS: Resistance, Electric
WELDING EQPT & SPLYS: Seam, Electric
WELDING EQPT & SPLYS: Spot, Electric
WELDING EQPT & SPLYS: Wire, Bare & Coated
WELDING EQPT REPAIR SVCS
WELDING EQPT: Electric
WELDING EQPT: Electrical
WELDING MACHINES & EQPT: Ultrasonic
WELDING REPAIR SVC
WELDMENTS
WELLS: Light, Sheet Metal
WESTERN APPAREL STORES
WHEEL BALANCING EQPT: Automotive
WHEELCHAIR LIFTS
WHEELCHAIRS
WHEELS
WHEELS & PARTS
WHISTLES
WIG & HAIRPIECE STORES
WIGS, WHOLESALE
WINCHES
WIND CHIMES
WINDINGS: Coil, Electronic
WINDOW & DOOR FRAMES
WINDOW FRAMES & SASHES: Plastic
WINDOW FRAMES, MOLDING & TRIM: Vinyl
WINDOW FURNISHINGS WHOLESALERS
WINDOWS: Frames, Wood

WINDOWS: Louver, Glass, Wood Framed
WINDOWS: Wood
WINDSHIELD WIPER SYSTEMS
WINDSHIELDS: Plastic
WINE CELLARS, BONDED: Wine, Blended
WIRE
WIRE & CABLE: Aluminum
WIRE & CABLE: Nonferrous, Automotive, Exc Ignition Sets
WIRE & WIRE PRDTS
WIRE FABRIC: Welded Steel
WIRE MATERIALS: Copper
WIRE MATERIALS: Steel
WIRE ROPE CENTERS
WIRE WHOLESALERS
WIRE: Communication
WIRE: Magnet
WIRE: Nonferrous
WOMEN'S & CHILDREN'S CLOTHING WHOLESALERS, NEC
WOMEN'S & GIRLS' SPORTSWEAR WHOLESALERS
WOMEN'S CLOTHING STORES
WOMEN'S CLOTHING STORES: Ready-To-Wear
WOMEN'S SPORTSWEAR STORES
WOOD CHIPS, PRODUCED AT THE MILL
WOOD PRDTS
WOOD PRDTS: Applicators
WOOD PRDTS: Brackets
WOOD PRDTS: Furniture Inlays, Veneers
WOOD PRDTS: Laundry
WOOD PRDTS: Moldings, Unfinished & Prefinished
WOOD PRDTS: Mulch Or Sawdust
WOOD PRDTS: Mulch, Wood & Bark
WOOD PRDTS: Novelties, Fiber
WOOD PRDTS: Oars & Paddles
WOOD PRDTS: Outdoor, Structural
WOOD PRDTS: Panel Work
WOOD PRDTS: Poles
WOOD PRDTS: Scaffolds
WOOD PRDTS: Shavings & Packaging, Excelsior
WOOD PRDTS: Signboards
WOOD PRDTS: Silo Staves
WOOD PRDTS: Survey Stakes
WOOD PRDTS: Trophy Bases
WOOD PRDTS: Venetian Blind Slats
WOOD PRODUCTS: Reconstituted
WOOD SHAVINGS BALES, MULCH TYPE, WHOLESALE
WOOD TREATING: Creosoting
WOOD TREATING: Flooring, Block
WOOD TREATING: Millwork
WOOD TREATING: Structural Lumber & Timber
WOOD TREATING: Wood Prdts, Creosoted
WOODWORK & TRIM: Interior & Ornamental
WOODWORK: Carved & Turned
WOODWORK: Interior & Ornamental, NEC
WOVEN WIRE PRDTS, NEC
WREATHS: Artificial
WRENCHES

X

X-RAY EQPT & TUBES

Y

YARN & YARN SPINNING
YARN MILLS: Beaming, For The Trade
YARN MILLS: Texturizing
YARN MILLS: Texturizing, Throwing & Twisting
YARN: Cotton, Spun
YARN: Embroidery, Spun
YARN: Manmade & Synthetic Fiber, Spun
YARN: Needle & Handicraft, Spun
YARN: Polypropylene Filament, Throw, Twist, Windg/Spool
YARN: Polypropylene, Spun From Purchased Staple

PRODUCT SECTION

ABRASIVES

International Carbide & Engrg ....F...... 434 568-3311
  Drakes Branch *(G-4133)*
Interntional Abrasive Pdts Inc ....G...... 540 797-7821
  Moneta *(G-8967)*
Mil-Spec Abrasives LLC ....F...... 757 927-6699
  Norfolk *(G-9644)*
Virginia Materials Inc ....G...... 800 321-2282
  Norfolk *(G-9784)*
Winoa USA Inc ....E...... 540 586-0856
  Bedford *(G-1664)*

ABRASIVES: Coated

Hermes Abr Ltd A Ltd Partnr ....C...... 800 464-8314
  Virginia Beach *(G-14519)*
Hermes Abrasives Inc ....G...... 757 486-6623
  Virginia Beach *(G-14520)*
Virginia Abrasives Corporation ....D...... 804 732-0058
  Petersburg *(G-10349)*

ACADEMIC TUTORING SVCS

Wp Company LLC ....F...... 703 518-3000
  Alexandria *(G-389)*

ACCELERATION INDICATORS & SYSTEM COMPONENTS: Aerospace

Buoya LLC ....G...... 703 248-9100
  Arlington *(G-892)*
Cobham AES Holdings Inc ....F...... 703 414-5300
  Arlington *(G-911)*
Firstmark Corp ....F...... 724 759-2850
  Midlothian *(G-8818)*
Nova Defense & Arospc Intl LLC ....G...... 703 864-6929
  Alexandria *(G-297)*

ACCELERATORS: Linear

Linear Devices Corporation ....G...... 804 368-8428
  Ashland *(G-1453)*
Pn Labs ....G...... 804 938-1600
  Moseley *(G-9045)*

ACCOUNTING MACHINES & CASH REGISTERS

Carr Group LLC ....G...... 571 723-6562
  Woodbridge *(G-15669)*
Lt Business Dynamics LLC ....G...... 703 738-6599
  Vienna *(G-14087)*
Rega Enterprises Inc ....G...... 757 488-8056
  Chesapeake *(G-3268)*

ACCOUNTING SVCS, NEC

Carr Group LLC ....G...... 571 723-6562
  Woodbridge *(G-15669)*
Digital Beans Inc ....G...... 703 775-2225
  Alexandria *(G-189)*
Saicomp LLC ....G...... 714 421-8967
  Petersburg *(G-10340)*

ACRYLIC RESINS

Danchem Technologies Inc ....C...... 434 797-8120
  Danville *(G-3975)*

ACTUATORS: Indl, NEC

Augusta Actuation LLC ....G...... 540 480-7619
  Steeles Tavern *(G-13310)*

Chalmers & Kubeck Inc ....G...... 434 851-3613
  Rustburg *(G-12437)*
Ksb America Corporation ....G...... 804 222-1818
  Richmond *(G-11265)*

ADDITIVE BASED PLASTIC MATERIALS: Plasticizers

Wynnvision LLC ....G...... 757 419-1463
  Midlothian *(G-8924)*

ADHESIVES

2 P Products ....G...... 804 273-9822
  Richmond *(G-11071)*
Choice Adhesives Corporation ....E...... 434 847-5671
  Lynchburg *(G-7678)*
Graphic Arts Adhesives ....G...... 804 779-3304
  Mechanicsville *(G-8630)*
Henkel US Operations Corp ....F...... 804 222-6100
  Richmond *(G-11236)*
Lyon Roofing Inc ....G...... 540 633-0170
  Fairlawn *(G-4737)*
Mapei Corp Fredericksburg ....G...... 540 710-5303
  Fredericksburg *(G-5319)*
Mapei Corporation ....D...... 540 898-5124
  Fredericksburg *(G-5320)*
Mapei Corporation ....G...... 540 361-1085
  Fredericksburg *(G-5453)*
Worthen Industries Inc ....E...... 804 275-9231
  Richmond *(G-11067)*
Worthen Industries Inc ....E...... 804 275-9231
  Richmond *(G-11068)*

ADHESIVES & SEALANTS

Johns Manville Corporation ....B...... 804 261-7400
  Richmond *(G-11256)*
Nbe Technologies LLC ....G...... 540 443-9100
  Blacksburg *(G-1772)*
Vitex Packaging Group Inc ....F...... 757 538-3115
  Suffolk *(G-13780)*
W R Meadows Inc ....G...... 434 797-1321
  Danville *(G-4048)*

ADHESIVES: Epoxy

Duration Products LLC ....G...... 804 651-1700
  Henrico *(G-6504)*

ADVERTISING AGENCIES

Confetti Advertising Inc ....G...... 276 646-5806
  Chilhowie *(G-3548)*
Davis Communications Group ....G...... 703 548-8892
  Alexandria *(G-185)*

ADVERTISING AGENCIES: Consultants

Better Signs ....G...... 540 382-7446
  Christiansburg *(G-3573)*

ADVERTISING DISPLAY PRDTS

1st Signage and Lighting LLC ....G...... 276 229-4200
  Woolwine *(G-15863)*
Explus Inc ....D...... 703 260-0780
  Dulles *(G-4201)*
Mark Bric Display Corp ....E...... 800 742-6275
  Prince George *(G-10600)*
Thayer Design Inc ....G...... 434 528-3850
  Madison Heights *(G-7885)*
Walker Virginia ....G...... 757 652-0430
  Newport News *(G-9378)*

ADVERTISING REPRESENTATIVES: Printed Media

Best Printing & Design LLC ....G...... 703 593-9874
  Arlington *(G-880)*
S&R Pals Enterprises LLC ....G...... 540 752-1900
  Fredericksburg *(G-5481)*

ADVERTISING SPECIALTIES, WHOLESALE

Commonwealth Specialty Packg ....F...... 804 271-0157
  Ashland *(G-1393)*
Eleven West Inc ....E...... 540 639-9319
  Fairlawn *(G-4736)*
Four Star Printing Inc ....G...... 540 459-2247
  Woodstock *(G-15854)*
General Display Company LLC ....G...... 703 335-9292
  Manassas *(G-7943)*
High Peak Sportswear Inc ....G...... 540 953-1293
  Blacksburg *(G-1743)*
Jbtm Enterprises Inc ....F...... 540 665-9651
  Winchester *(G-15551)*
Lou Wallace ....G...... 276 762-2303
  Saint Paul *(G-12469)*
Mounir E Shaheen ....G...... 757 723-4445
  Hampton *(G-6205)*
Peggy Sues Advertising Inc ....G...... 276 530-7790
  Conaway *(G-3754)*
Phoenix Sports and Advg Inc ....G...... 276 988-9709
  North Tazewell *(G-10104)*
Promocorp Inc ....F...... 703 942-7100
  Alexandria *(G-560)*
Reston Shirt & Graphic Co Inc ....G...... 703 318-4802
  Sterling *(G-13490)*
Stitchworks Inc ....G...... 757 631-0300
  Virginia Beach *(G-14851)*
Suday Promotions Inc ....G...... 703 376-8640
  Chantilly *(G-2503)*
Virginia Printing Services Inc ....F...... 757 838-5500
  Hampton *(G-6263)*

ADVERTISING SVCS: Direct Mail

Americomm LLC ....D...... 757 622-2724
  Norfolk *(G-9440)*
Bison Printing Inc ....E...... 540 586-3955
  Bedford *(G-1627)*
Commercial Prtg Direct Mail Svc ....G...... 757 422-0606
  Virginia Beach *(G-14358)*
R R Donnelley & Sons Company ....C...... 434 846-7371
  Salem *(G-12560)*
Strive Communications LLC ....G...... 703 925-5900
  Reston *(G-10967)*

ADVERTISING SVCS: Display

MCS Design & Production Inc ....G...... 804 550-1000
  Ashland *(G-1462)*
Optikinetics Ltd ....G...... 800 575-6784
  Ashland *(G-1473)*

ADVERTISING SVCS: Outdoor

Kin Art Studios LLC ....G...... 804 368-7298
  Ashland *(G-1449)*
Tsg Concepts Inc ....G...... 877 777-5734
  Arlington *(G-1200)*

ADVERTISING SVCS: Poster, Exc Outdoor

J J E Enterprise Holdings LLC ....G...... 410 703-9241
  Spotsylvania *(G-12900)*

PRODUCT

ADVERTISING SVCS: Transit

Lighted Signs Direct Inc......................G......703 965-5188
Woodbridge *(G-15740)*

AERIAL WORK PLATFORMS

Intel Investigations LLC......................G......540 521-4111
Roanoke *(G-11941)*

AGRICULTURAL CHEMICALS: Trace Elements

Dark Hollow LLC......................G......540 355-8218
Lexington *(G-7394)*

AGRICULTURAL EQPT: BARN, SILO, POULTRY, DAIRY/LIVESTOCK MACH

Monoflo International Inc......................C......540 665-1691
Winchester *(G-15451)*
Silk Tree Manufacturing Inc......................G......434 983-1941
Dillwyn *(G-4100)*

AGRICULTURAL EQPT: Barn Stanchions & Standards

Virginia Carolina Buildings......................F......434 645-7411
Crewe *(G-3820)*

AGRICULTURAL EQPT: Combine, Digger, Packer/Thresher, Peanut

Bacons Castle Supply Inc......................G......757 357-6159
Surry *(G-13796)*

AGRICULTURAL EQPT: Elevators, Farm

Modek Inc......................G......804 550-7300
Ashland *(G-1463)*

AGRICULTURAL EQPT: Fertilizing Machinery

Bae Systems Tctcal Vhcl System.........E......571 461-6000
Falls Church *(G-4759)*

AGRICULTURAL EQPT: Fertilizng, Sprayng, Dustng/Irrigatn Mach

Arctech Inc......................G......434 575-7200
South Boston *(G-12749)*

AGRICULTURAL EQPT: Grade, Clean & Sort Machines, Fruit/Veg

L & N Wood Products Inc......................G......804 784-4734
Oilville *(G-10181)*
Vmek Group LLC......................G......804 380-1831
Midlothian *(G-8919)*

AGRICULTURAL EQPT: Grounds Mowing Eqpt

Eric Washington......................G......434 249-3567
Charlottesville *(G-2626)*
Ronald Stephen Rhodes......................G......540 435-1441
Keezletown *(G-7029)*
Sustaita Lawn Care......................G......434 390-8118
Cumberland *(G-3937)*

AGRICULTURAL EQPT: Irrigation Eqpt, Self-Propelled

Commercial Water Works Inc......................G......434 534-8244
Forest *(G-5061)*

AGRICULTURAL EQPT: Planting Machines

Griffin Manufacturing Company...........G......757 986-4541
Suffolk *(G-13716)*

AGRICULTURAL EQPT: Shakers, Tree, Nuts, Fruits, Etc

Zipnut Technology LLC......................G......703 442-7339
Falls Church *(G-4898)*

AGRICULTURAL EQPT: Spreaders, Fertilizer

Lesco Inc......................G......804 957-5516
Disputanta *(G-4112)*

AGRICULTURAL EQPT: Tractors, Farm

Gas House Co......................G......434 822-1324
Danville *(G-3996)*

AGRICULTURAL EQPT: Transplanters

Tidewater Tree......................G......757 426-6002
Virginia Beach *(G-14879)*

AGRICULTURAL EQPT: Turf & Grounds Eqpt

Titan Turf LLC......................G......276 768-7833
Galax *(G-5650)*

AGRICULTURAL EQPT: Turf Eqpt, Commercial

Lebanon Seaboard Corporation...........G......540 375-0300
Salem *(G-12530)*
Scott Turf Equipment LLC......................G......434 401-3031
Rustburg *(G-12443)*
Scott Turf Equipment LLC......................G......434 401-3031
Rustburg *(G-12444)*

AGRICULTURAL MACHINERY & EQPT: Wholesalers

Bluestone Industries Inc......................E......540 776-7890
Roanoke *(G-12051)*

AIR CLEANING SYSTEMS

Z Finest Airduct Cleaning......................E......703 897-1152
Woodbridge *(G-15838)*

AIR CONDITIONERS: Motor Vehicle

Dometic Corporation......................C......804 746-1313
Mechanicsville *(G-8618)*

AIR CONDITIONING & VENTILATION EQPT & SPLYS: Wholesales

Virginia Blower Company......................E......276 647-3804
Collinsville *(G-3718)*

AIR CONDITIONING EQPT

Brontz Inc......................G......540 483-0976
Rocky Mount *(G-12315)*
Ecoer Inc......................G......703 348-2538
Fairfax *(G-4617)*
Mac Bone Industries Ltd......................G......804 264-3603
Richmond *(G-11278)*

AIR CONDITIONING EQPT, WHOLE HOUSE: Wholesalers

Siemens Industry Inc......................D......804 222-6680
Richmond *(G-11380)*

AIR CONDITIONING REPAIR SVCS

D W Boyd Corporation......................G......757 423-2268
Norfolk *(G-9514)*

AIR CONDITIONING UNITS: Complete, Domestic Or Indl

Airpac Inc......................G......540 635-5011
Front Royal *(G-5520)*
Carrier Corporation......................F......540 366-2471
Roanoke *(G-11905)*
Refcon Services Inc......................F......757 616-0691
Chesapeake *(G-3266)*
Vertiv Corporation......................E......703 726-4100
Ashburn *(G-1349)*

AIR COOLERS: Metal Plate

Ragan Sheet Metal Inc......................E......757 333-7248
Virginia Beach *(G-14757)*

AIR POLLUTION MEASURING SVCS

Bwx Technologies Inc......................E......757 595-7982
Newport News *(G-9187)*
ICE Tek LLC......................E......757 390-8589
Virginia Beach *(G-14539)*

AIR PREHEATERS: Nonrotating, Plate Type

Modine Manufacturing Company...........G......540 464-3640
Lexington *(G-7402)*

AIR PURIFICATION EQPT

Airocare Inc......................F......703 788-1500
Dulles *(G-4192)*
B2 Health Solutions LLC......................G......757 403-8298
Virginia Beach *(G-14256)*
Hayden Enterprises......................G......910 791-3132
Chesapeake *(G-3129)*
Purer Air......................G......804 921-8234
Richmond *(G-11341)*

AIR TRAFFIC CONTROL SYSTEMS & EQPT

Air Route Optimizer Inc......................G......540 364-3470
Marshall *(G-8249)*
Ats-Sales LLC......................G......703 631-6661
Chantilly *(G-2372)*
William B Clark......................G......804 695-9950
Gloucester *(G-5868)*

AIR, WATER & SOLID WASTE PROGRAMS ADMINISTRATION SVCS

Abwasser Technologies Inc......................G......757 453-7505
Virginia Beach *(G-14206)*

AIRCRAFT & AEROSPACE FLIGHT INSTRUMENTS & GUIDANCE SYSTEMS

Aerojet......................G......703 247-2907
Arlington *(G-842)*
Anra Technologies Inc......................E......703 239-3206
Chantilly *(G-2525)*
Celestial Circuits LLC......................G......703 851-2843
Springfield *(G-12975)*
General Dynamics Corporation......................G......703 263-2835
Fairfax *(G-4462)*
Harris Communications and In......................E......703 668-7256
Herndon *(G-6694)*
Lockheed Martin Integrtd Systm...........D......866 562-2363
Arlington *(G-1048)*
Lockheed Martin Services LLC...........G......757 935-9200
Suffolk *(G-13733)*
Northrop Grumman Corporation...........A......757 838-7221
Hampton *(G-6211)*
Northrop Grumman Systems Corp........G......703 406-5474
Dulles *(G-4213)*
Parry Labs LLC......................E......585 746-8335
Alexandria *(G-306)*
Skydweller Aero Inc......................G......585 746-8335
Alexandria *(G-348)*
Thermo-Optical Group LLC......................G......540 822-9481
Lovettsville *(G-7587)*

AIRCRAFT & HEAVY EQPT REPAIR SVCS

Car Wash Care Inc......................G......703 385-9181
Fairfax *(G-4605)*

AIRCRAFT ASSEMBLY PLANTS

Aerial and Aquatic Robotics...........G......757 932-0909
Norfolk *(G-9427)*
Aerojet......................G......703 247-2907
Arlington *(G-842)*
Aerospace & Technology......................G......757 864-7227
Hampton *(G-6075)*
Aery Aviation LLC......................F......757 271-1600
Newport News *(G-9160)*
Agustawestland North Amer Inc.........F......703 373-8000
Arlington *(G-845)*
Agustawestlandbell LLC......................G......703 373-1613
Reston *(G-10781)*
Air Wisconsin Airlines Corp......................G......757 853-8215
Norfolk *(G-9429)*
Airbus A300 Leasing Inc......................G......703 834-3400
Herndon *(G-6605)*
Airbus Americas Inc......................D......703 834-3400
Herndon *(G-6606)*
Airbus Def Space Holdings Inc......................A......703 466-5600
Herndon *(G-6607)*
Airbus Group Inc......................E......703 466-5600
Herndon *(G-6608)*
Airbus Group Supply & Svcs Inc........F......703 858-2235
Ashburn *(G-1240)*
Autonomous Flight Tech Inc......................G......540 314-8866
Salem *(G-12478)*

Avigators Incorporated ....G...... 703 298-6319
Centreville (G-2293)

Bae Systems Land Armaments Inc ....E... 571 461-6000
Falls Church (G-4756)

Battlespace Global LLC ....G...... 703 413-0556
Arlington (G-876)

Bee Systems LLC ....F... 760 484-6194
Aldie (G-101)

Blacksky Aerospace LLC ....G...... 202 500-3743
Arlington (G-884)

Boeing Company ....B... 571 814-4103
Reston (G-10811)

Boeing Company ....A... 757 461-5206
Norfolk (G-9469)

Boeing Company ....B... 703 961-8174
Chantilly (G-2378)

Boeing Company ....E... 703 808-2737
Chantilly (G-2379)

Cavalry Aerospace LLC ....G...... 757 995-2029
Chesapeake (G-3027)

Christopher K Reddersen ....G...... 703 232-6691
Warrenton (G-14987)

Combat Bound LLC ....G...... 757 343-3399
Suffolk (G-13685)

David Birkenstock ....G...... 703 343-5718
Herndon (G-6653)

Dean Delaware LLC ....G...... 703 802-6231
Sterling (G-13383)

Eagle Aerospace ....G...... 540 965-9022
Covington (G-3787)

Eagle Aviation Tech LLC ....D... 757 224-6269
Newport News (G-9219)

Electraaero Inc ....G...... 540 660-2917
Falls Church (G-4910)

General Cryo Corporation ....G...... 703 405-9442
Springfield (G-13009)

General Dynamics Corporation ....C... 703 876-3000
Reston (G-10857)

Gibson Sewer Water ....G...... 540 636-1131
Chester Gap (G-3470)

Gki Aerospace LLC ....G...... 703 451-4562
Springfield (G-13010)

Golden Section LLC ....G...... 540 315-4756
Blacksburg (G-1742)

Gulfstream Aerospace Corp ....A... 301 967-9767
Falls Church (G-4801)

Gulfstream Aerospace Corp ....G...... 912 965-3000
Falls Church (G-4802)

Gulfstream Aerospace Corp ....G...... 540 722-0347
Winchester (G-15422)

Gulfstream Aerospace Corp GA ....G...... 301 967-9767
Falls Church (G-4803)

Gundlach Aerospace LLC ....G...... 703 303-0813
Fairfax Station (G-4712)

Hybrid Air Vehicles (us) Inc ....G...... 703 524-0026
Arlington (G-996)

Jlt Aerospace (north AM) ....G...... 703 459-2380
Herndon (G-6717)

Lockheed Martin Corporation ....B... 757 484-5789
Chesapeake (G-3185)

Magnus Aircraft Incorporated ....G...... 830 998-7270
Ashburn (G-1314)

Nextflight Jets LLC ....G...... 703 392-6500
Reston (G-10908)

Pae Aviation Technical Svcs LLC ....G...... 864 458-3272
Arlington (G-1096)

Paper Air Force Company ....G...... 703 730-2150
Woodbridge (G-15773)

Paragon Aviation Services ....G...... 703 787-8800
Herndon (G-6767)

Pellegrino Aerospace LLC ....G...... 571 431-7011
Arlington (G-1103)

Preston Aerospace Inc ....G...... 540 675-3474
Huntly (G-6965)

Skm Aerospace LLC ....G...... 703 217-4221
Arlington (G-1170)

Sydrus Aerospace LLC ....G...... 831 402-5286
Gainesville (G-5616)

Textron Inc ....G...... 757 874-8100
Newport News (G-9353)

Tk Aircraft LLC ....G...... 540 665-8113
Winchester (G-15490)

Training Services Inc ....F... 757 363-1800
Chesapeake (G-3349)

Unmanned Aerial Prop Systs ....G...... 757 325-6792
Hampton (G-6257)

Vaero Inc ....G...... 540 344-1000
Vinton (G-14189)

Walberg Aerospace ....G...... 321 634-6349
Hampton (G-6267)

Xtreme Adventures Inc ....G...... 757 615-4602
Virginia Beach (G-14950)

Y2k Web Technologies ....G...... 757 490-7877
Virginia Beach (G-14951)

AIRCRAFT CONTROL SYSTEMS:

Flight Product Center Inc ....G...... 703 361-2915
Manassas (G-7941)

Proxy Technologies Inc ....F... 703 665-5152
Reston (G-10933)

Uma Inc ....E... 540 879-2040
Dayton (G-4067)

AIRCRAFT CONTROL SYSTEMS: Electronic Totalizing Counters

L3 Technologies Inc ....G...... 540 658-0591
Stafford (G-13167)

Lilbern Design Virginia LLC ....E... 540 234-9900
Weyers Cave (G-15174)

AIRCRAFT ENGINES & ENGINE PARTS: Research & Development, Mfr

Eagle Aviation Tech LLC ....D... 757 224-6269
Newport News (G-9219)

High Speed Tech Ventr LLC ....G...... 571 318-0997
Williamsburg (G-15254)

Ho-Ho-Kus Incorporated ....D... 206 552-4559
North Chesterfield (G-9887)

AIRCRAFT ENGINES & PARTS

Aerospace Techniques Inc ....D... 860 347-1200
Virginia Beach (G-14214)

Honeywell International Inc ....B... 804 458-7649
Hopewell (G-6930)

Honeywell International Inc ....A... 804 518-2351
Petersburg (G-10324)

Honeywell International Inc ....E... 804 515-1500
Richmond (G-11241)

Honeywell International Inc ....A... 276 694-2408
Stuart (G-13617)

Honeywell International Inc ....F... 703 879-9951
Herndon (G-6703)

Honeywell International Inc ....B... 804 530-6352
Chester (G-3422)

Honeywell International Inc ....G...... 703 626-8363
Arlington (G-993)

Honeywell International Inc ....E... 804 541-5618
Hopewell (G-6932)

Honeywell International Inc ....G...... 703 437-7651
Sterling (G-13422)

Honeywell Technology Solu ....G...... 703 551-1942
Stafford (G-13151)

Jet Pac LLC ....G...... 804 334-5216
Hopewell (G-6936)

Pratt & Whitney Eng Svcs Inc ....G...... 757 838-7980
Newport News (G-9315)

Safran Usa Inc ....F... 703 351-9898
Alexandria (G-334)

Sapentia LLC ....G...... 703 269-7191
Mc Lean (G-8545)

Uav Communications Inc ....E... 757 271-3428
Newport News (G-9368)

AIRCRAFT EQPT & SPLYS WHOLESALERS

Beechhurst Industries Inc ....G...... 703 334-6703
Manassas Park (G-8190)

Safran Usa Inc ....F... 703 351-9898
Alexandria (G-334)

Sky Dynamics Corporation ....G...... 540 297-6754
Moneta (G-8978)

AIRCRAFT LIGHTING

Superior Panel Technology ....G...... 562 776-9494
Chesterfield (G-3531)

Supreme Edgelight Devices Inc ....G...... 276 236-3711
Galax (G-5649)

William K Whitaker ....G...... 562 776-9494
Chesterfield (G-3542)

AIRCRAFT MAINTENANCE & REPAIR SVCS

Aerospace Techniques Inc ....D... 860 347-1200
Virginia Beach (G-14214)

Alt Services Inc ....G...... 757 806-1341
Hampton (G-6081)

Gulfstream Aerospace Corp ....A... 301 967-9767
Falls Church (G-4801)

AIRCRAFT PARTS & AUXILIARY EQPT: Armament, Exc Guns

Breeze-Eastern LLC ....G...... 973 602-1001
Fredericksburg (G-5175)

AIRCRAFT PARTS & AUXILIARY EQPT: Assemblies, Fuselage

Northrop Grumman Systems Corp ......B... 703 280-2900
Falls Church (G-4845)

AIRCRAFT PARTS & AUXILIARY EQPT: Assys, Subassemblies/Parts

Curtiss-Wright Controls Inc ....E... 703 779-7800
Ashburn (G-1265)

Marks Garage ....G...... 540 498-3458
Stafford (G-13174)

AIRCRAFT PARTS & AUXILIARY EQPT: Countermeasure Dispensers

Bae Systems Inc ....C... 571 461-6000
Falls Church (G-4754)

AIRCRAFT PARTS & AUXILIARY EQPT: Military Eqpt & Armament

F3 Technologies LLC ....G...... 804 785-1017
Mattaponi (G-8358)

Kurt USA Prof Dog Tng ....G...... 252 509-4211
Stafford (G-13166)

Matbock LLC ....G...... 757 828-6659
Virginia Beach (G-14639)

Potomac Solutions Incorporated ....G...... 703 888-1762
Alexandria (G-313)

Protective Solutions Inc ....D... 703 435-1115
Dulles (G-4220)

AIRCRAFT PARTS & AUXILIARY EQPT: Research & Development, Mfr

D-Star Engineering Corporation ....E... 203 925-7630
Ashburn (G-1267)

Orbital Sciences LLC ....B... 703 406-5000
Dulles (G-4218)

AIRCRAFT PARTS & EQPT, NEC

A & A Precision Machining LLC ....G...... 804 493-8416
Montross (G-9023)

Aai Corporation ....G...... 410 666-1400
Blackstone (G-1809)

Aerial Machine & Tool Corp ....D... 276 952-2006
Meadows of Dan (G-8590)

Aero International LLC ....G...... 571 203-8360
Alexandria (G-121)

Aerospace Techniques Inc ....D... 860 347-1200
Virginia Beach (G-14214)

Allied Aerospace Services LLC ....E... 757 873-1344
Newport News (G-9164)

Allied Aerospace Uav LLC ....G...... 757 873-1344
Newport News (G-9165)

Astronautics Corp of America ....G...... 571 707-8705
Ashburn (G-1244)

Aurora Flight Sciences Corp ....G...... 703 369-3633
Manassas (G-7916)

Avenger LLC ....G...... 703 573-6445
Springfield (G-12956)

Aviation Component Svcs Inc ....G...... 434 237-7077
Lynchburg (G-7646)

Bae Systems Holdings Inc ....B... 571 461-6000
Falls Church (G-4755)

Beechhurst Industries Inc ....G...... 703 334-6703
Manassas Park (G-8190)

Bell Textron Inc ....G...... 817 280-2346
Arlington (G-878)

Bjd Tel-Comm LLC ....G...... 703 858-2931
Ashburn (G-1247)

Boeing Company ....C... 703 465-3500
Arlington (G-888)

Charlottesville Flight Center ....G...... 434 964-1474
Charlottesville (G-2607)

Coastal Aerospace Inc ....G...... 757 787-3704
Melfa (G-8709)

Combustion Technologies Inc ....G...... 434 432-1428
Chatham (G-2924)

Defense Arnautical Support LLC..........G..... 703 309-9222
　Vienna (G-14037)
Firstmark Corp ....F..... 724 759-2850
　Midlothian (G-8818)
General Dynamics Corp ....G..... 434 964-5301
　Charlottesville (G-2637)
General Dynamics Ots Cal Inc ....G..... 276 783-3121
　Marion (G-8228)
Glenmark Group LLC ....G..... 757 955-6850
　Chesapeake (G-3121)
Goodrich Corporation ....F..... 703 558-8230
　Arlington (G-985)
Hydro Systems USA Inc ....G..... 703 429-1024
　Sterling (G-13424)
Interbyte.......................................G..... 703 825-8774
　Alexandria (G-486)
Interbyte Corp ....G..... 703 825-8774
　Alexandria (G-487)
Klaus Composites LLC ....G..... 443 995-8458
　Waterford (G-15081)
Laurence Walter Aerospace Solu ....G..... 757 966-9578
　Chesapeake (G-3178)
Lockheed Martin Corporation.............B..... 757 935-9479
　Suffolk (G-13732)
Luminary Air Group LLC ....G..... 757 655-0705
　Melfa (G-8711)
Moog Inc ....G..... 716 652-2000
　Blacksburg (G-1764)
Octopus Arospc Solutions LLC...........G..... 866 244-4500
　New Market (G-9146)
Raytheon Company ....G..... 972 272-0515
　Dulles (G-4224)
Robert H Giles Jr ....G..... 540 808-6334
　Blacksburg (G-1785)
Robert R Kline ....G..... 540 454-7003
　Round Hill (G-12387)
Sky Dynamics Corporation ....G..... 540 297-6754
　Moneta (G-8978)
Textron Ground Support Eqp Inc ....G..... 703 572-5340
　Dulles (G-4229)
Tia-The Richards Corp ....D..... 703 471-8600
　Sterling (G-13533)
Titan II Inc ....D..... 757 380-2000
　Newport News (G-9358)
VSE Aviation Inc ....E..... 703 328-4600
　Alexandria (G-606)

AIRCRAFT SERVICING & REPAIRING

Automated Precision Inc...................F..... 757 223-4157
　Newport News (G-9174)
Northrop Grumman Systems Corp ....B..... 703 280-2900
　Falls Church (G-4845)
Pae Avation Technical Svcs LLC..........D..... 703 717-6000
　Arlington (G-1095)
Titan II Inc ....D..... 757 380-2000
　Newport News (G-9358)

AIRCRAFT TURBINES

Mikro Systems Inc ....E..... 434 244-6480
　Charlottesville (G-2660)

AIRCRAFT: Airplanes, Fixed Or Rotary Wing

Alt Services Inc ....G..... 757 806-1341
　Hampton (G-6081)
Boeing Company ....G..... 703 808-2718
　Woodbridge (G-15661)
Boeing Company ....A..... 703 413-3407
　Arlington (G-889)
Boeing Company ....A..... 703 923-4000
　Springfield (G-12966)
King Aviation ....G..... 540 439-8621
　Midland (G-8760)
Northrop Grumman Systems Corp ....B..... 703 280-2900
　Falls Church (G-4845)
Northrop Grumman Systems Corp ....B..... 703 556-1144
　Mc Lean (G-8517)
Northrop Grumman Systems Corp ....B..... 703 968-1000
　Herndon (G-6758)
Pae Avation Technical Svcs LLC..........D..... 703 717-6000
　Arlington (G-1095)
Titan II Inc ....D..... 757 380-2000
　Newport News (G-9358)

AIRCRAFT: Gliders

Shenandoah Valley Soaring Inc...........G..... 804 347-6848
　Waynesboro (G-15139)

AIRCRAFT: Motorized

Advanced Aircraft Company LLC.........G..... 757 325-6712
　Hampton (G-6071)
Angel Wings Drone Services LLC ....G..... 540 763-2630
　Riner (G-11860)
Big Sky Drone Services LLC ....G..... 804 378-2970
　Powhatan (G-10533)
Drone Safety LLC ....G..... 703 589-6738
　Alexandria (G-450)
Drone Tier Systems Intl LLC ....G..... 757 450-7825
　Virginia Beach (G-14414)
Dronechakra LLC ....G..... 540 420-7394
　Sterling (G-13390)
Drones Club of Virginia LLC ....G..... 540 324-8180
　Staunton (G-13254)
Fredericks Aircraft Company ....G..... 757 727-3326
　Hampton (G-6153)
Hush Aerospace LLC ....G..... 703 629-6907
　Virginia Beach (G-14534)
Mydrone4hire LLC ....G..... 540 491-4860
　Blue Ridge (G-1853)
Raytheon Company ....B..... 757 421-8319
　Chesapeake (G-3259)
Shenandoah Drones LLC ....G..... 540 421-3116
　New Market (G-9148)
Skyboss Drones LLC ....G..... 434 509-5028
　Forest (G-5093)
Summit Drones Inc ....G..... 724 961-9197
　Quantico (G-10691)
Top Drone Video ....G..... 757 288-1774
　Chesapeake (G-3344)
Vantage Point Drone LLC ....G..... 703 723-4586
　Ashburn (G-1346)
Vh Drones LLC ....G..... 804 938-9713
　Mechanicsville (G-8692)

AIRCRAFT: Research & Development, Manufacturer

Blue Ridge Scientific LLC ....G..... 540 631-0356
　Front Royal (G-5524)
Calspan Systems Corporation ....C..... 757 873-1344
　Newport News (G-9189)
Eodrones LLC ....G..... 703 856-8400
　Warrenton (G-15004)
Lockheed Martin Corporation.............B..... 757 935-9479
　Suffolk (G-13732)
Pe Crew LLC ....G..... 540 839-5999
　Hot Springs (G-6949)
UAS Technologies Inc ....G..... 703 822-4382
　Mc Lean (G-8570)
Zenith Aerotech Inc ....G..... 434 202-7790
　Afton (G-97)

AIRFRAME ASSEMBLIES: Guided Missiles

War Fighter Specialties LLC ....G..... 540 742-4187
　Shenandoah (G-12697)

AIRPORTS, FLYING FIELDS & SVCS

Raytheon Company ....B..... 757 421-8319
　Chesapeake (G-3259)

ALARM SYSTEMS WHOLESALERS

Cabling Systems Inc.........................G..... 540 439-0101
　Sumerduck (G-13790)

ALARMS: Burglar

L3harris Technologies Inc..................C..... 757 594-1607
　Newport News (G-9278)
Senstar Inc ....G..... 703 463-3088
　Herndon (G-6804)

ALARMS: Fire

Pacs Inc ....F..... 703 415-4411
　Arlington (G-1094)

ALCOHOL, GRAIN: For Beverage Purposes

Virginia Distillery Co LLC ....G..... 434 285-2900
　Lovingston (G-7593)

ALCOHOL, GRAIN: For Medicinal Purposes

Kdc US Holding Inc..........................C..... 434 845-7073
　Lynchburg (G-7750)
Tri-Tech Laboratories LLC ....G..... 434 845-7073
　Lynchburg (G-7828)

ALCOHOL: Ethyl & Ethanol

Green Plains Hopewell LLC ....G..... 804 668-0013
　Hopewell (G-6927)

ALKALIES & CHLORINE

Albemarle Corporation ....C..... 225 388-8011
　Richmond (G-11092)
Directed Vapor Tech Intl Inc ....F..... 434 977-1405
　Charlottesville (G-2618)
T/J One Corp ....G..... 757 548-0093
　Chesapeake (G-3318)

ALKALOIDS & OTHER BOTANICAL BASED PRDTS

Hempceuticals LLC..........................G..... 757 384-2782
　Chesapeake (G-3131)

ALLERGENS & ALLERGENIC EXTRACTS

Food Allergy Lifestyle LLC ....G..... 757 509-3608
　Gloucester (G-5847)

ALTERNATORS & GENERATORS: Battery Charging

Edge McS LLC ....G..... 804 379-6772
　Midlothian (G-8813)

ALTERNATORS: Automotive

Eastern Shore Rebuilders ....G..... 757 709-1250
　Painter (G-10240)
Life Safer.......................................G..... 540 375-4145
　Salem (G-12531)

ALUMINUM

Howmet Aerospace Inc ....C..... 804 281-2262
　Richmond (G-11243)

ALUMINUM PRDTS

Crown Cork & Seal Usa Inc ....B..... 540 662-2591
　Winchester (G-15408)
Electro-Mechanical Corporation...........B..... 276 669-4084
　Bristol (G-1975)
Hanover Foils LLC ....E..... 804 496-5835
　Ashland (G-1426)
Hy-Mark Cylinders Inc ....E..... 757 251-6744
　Hampton (G-6173)
Kaiser Aluminum Corporation ....B..... 804 743-6405
　North Chesterfield (G-9904)
Kearney-National Inc ....C..... 276 628-7171
　Abingdon (G-47)
Latham Architectural Pdts Inc ....G..... 804 308-2205
　Midlothian (G-8844)
Liphart Steel Company Inc.................E..... 540 248-1009
　Verona (G-13991)
Marion Mold & Tool Inc....................G..... 276 783-6101
　Marion (G-8234)
Naito America ....E..... 804 550-3305
　Ashland (G-1468)
Neuman Almnium Impact Extrsion ....G..... 540 248-2703
　Waynesboro (G-15129)
Optikinetics Ltd..............................G..... 800 575-6784
　Ashland (G-1473)
Penny Plate LLC ....D..... 540 337-3777
　Fishersville (G-5006)
Service Center Metals LLC.................C..... 804 518-1550
　Prince George (G-10607)
Tredegar Corporation ....C..... 804 330-1000
　North Chesterfield (G-10030)
Tredegar Corporation ....D..... 804 330-1000
　North Chesterfield (G-10029)
William L Bonnell Company Inc ....G..... 804 330-1147
　North Chesterfield (G-10045)

ALUMINUM: Rolling & Drawing

Mitsubishi Chemical Amer Inc.............G..... 757 382-5750
　Chesapeake (G-3207)
Panel Systems Inc ....E..... 703 910-6285
　Woodbridge (G-15772)

AMMUNITION

Iaeva Mercantile LLC ....G..... 301 523-6566
　Mc Lean (G-8460)
Multinational Defense Svcs LLC ....G..... 727 333-7290
　Mclean (G-8588)

Northrop Grmman Innvtion Syste ....C 703 406-5000
Dulles *(G-4212)*

AMMUNITION, EXC SPORTING, WHOLESALE

Jasons Ammo ....G....... 757 715-4689
Yorktown *(G-15969)*

AMMUNITION: Arming & Fusing Devices

Lig Nex1 Co Ltd ....G....... 703 888-2501
Arlington *(G-1035)*

AMMUNITION: Artillery Shells, Over 30 mm

Alexander M Robertson ....G....... 434 299-5221
Big Island *(G-1701)*

AMMUNITION: Cartridges Case, 30 mm & Below

Ammo Company LLC ....G....... 703 304-4210
Catlett *(G-2263)*

AMMUNITION: Components

Allegiance Inc ....G....... 276 639-6884
Clintwood *(G-3686)*
Goldbelt Wolf LLC ....D....... 703 584-8889
Alexandria *(G-470)*

AMMUNITION: Missile Warheads

Bwxt Y - 12 LLC ....G....... 434 316-7633
Lynchburg *(G-7670)*

AMMUNITION: Small Arms

Alacran ....G....... 540 629-6095
Dublin *(G-4147)*
American Rhnmtall Munition Inc ....F 703 221-9299
Stafford *(G-13116)*
Ballou Enterprises LLC ....G....... 804 496-6620
Ashland *(G-1378)*
Broadstone Security LLC ....G....... 703 566-2814
Arlington *(G-890)*
Chesapeake Cartridge Corp ....G....... 703 989-0903
Dublin *(G-4152)*
Chesapeake Cartridge Corp Inc ....G....... 703 989-0903
Blacksburg *(G-1730)*
Dsg TEC Usa Inc ....G....... 619 757-5430
Midland *(G-8754)*
Jasons Ammo ....G....... 757 715-4689
Yorktown *(G-15969)*
Johnson Enterprises LLC ....G....... 804 432-0469
New Kent *(G-9134)*
Leitner-Wise Manufacturing LLC ....G....... 703 209-0009
Alexandria *(G-258)*
Match Ammo LLC ....G....... 804 266-2666
Richmond *(G-11284)*
Nantrak Tactical LLC ....G....... 757 517-2226
Franklin *(G-5150)*
Northrop Grmman Innvtion Syste ....C 703 406-5000
Dulles *(G-4212)*
Orthoinsight LLC ....G....... 703 722-2553
Chantilly *(G-2548)*
Special Tactical Services LLC ....F 757 554-0699
Virginia Beach *(G-14835)*
United Armament LLC ....G....... 804 839-1800
North Chesterfield *(G-10007)*

AMPLIFIERS

Tyler JSun Global LLC ....G....... 407 221-6135
Stafford *(G-13206)*

AMPLIFIERS: Pulse Amplifiers

Tangers Electronics LLC ....G....... 757 215-5117
Norfolk *(G-9740)*

AMPLIFIERS: RF & IF Power

Astrocomm Technologies LLC ....G....... 703 606-2022
Oak Hill *(G-10135)*
Ultralife Corporation ....E 757 419-2430
Virginia Beach *(G-14900)*

AMUSEMENT & RECREATION SVCS: Art Gallery, Commercial

Turner Sculpture Ltd ....E 757 787-2818
Melfa *(G-8713)*

AMUSEMENT & RECREATION SVCS: Diving Instruction, Underwater

Big Time Charters Inc ....G....... 757 496-1040
Virginia Beach *(G-14278)*

AMUSEMENT & RECREATION SVCS: Instruction Schools, Camps

Science of Spirituality ....G....... 804 633-9987
Bowling Green *(G-1907)*

AMUSEMENT & RECREATION SVCS: Ski Rental Concession

Sport Shack Inc ....G....... 540 372-3719
Fredericksburg *(G-5487)*

AMUSEMENT MACHINES: Coin Operated

Anthony Amusements ....G....... 703 670-2681
Manassas *(G-8027)*

AMUSEMENT PARK DEVICES & RIDES

Jackson & Jackson Inc ....G....... 434 851-1798
Roanoke *(G-12109)*
Liberty Park ....G....... 540 832-7680
Gordonsville *(G-5912)*
Super Splasher Acquatics ....G....... 540 630-1565
Winchester *(G-15484)*
Valley Outsourcing ....F 540 320-0892
Blacksburg *(G-1803)*

AMUSEMENT PARK DEVICES & RIDES: Carnival Mach & Eqpt, NEC

SRI Seven Fair Lakes LLC ....G....... 703 631-2350
Fairfax *(G-4560)*

ANALYZERS: Blood & Body Fluid

Biosensor Tech LLC ....G....... 318 843-4479
Glen Allen *(G-5709)*

ANALYZERS: Electrical Testing

US Electrical Testing LLC ....G....... 703 802-6231
Tysons *(G-13949)*

ANALYZERS: Moisture

Crawl Space Door System Inc ....G....... 757 363-0005
Virginia Beach *(G-14370)*

ANALYZERS: Network

Battino Contg Solutions LLC ....G....... 703 408-9162
Edinburg *(G-4299)*
Brandon Jenkins ....G....... 434 294-0917
Crewe *(G-3809)*
Hermetic Networks Inc ....G....... 804 545-3173
North Chesterfield *(G-9885)*
High Speed Networks LLC ....G....... 703 963-4572
Sterling *(G-13419)*
Infoblox Federal Inc ....E 703 672-2607
Herndon *(G-6708)*
Vtech Solution Inc ....F 571 257-0913
Chantilly *(G-2565)*
Xceedium Inc ....E 703 539-5410
Herndon *(G-6846)*

ANIMAL BASED MEDICINAL CHEMICAL PRDTS

Wilson Warehouse ....G....... 804 991-2163
North Dinwiddie *(G-10073)*

ANIMAL FEED & SUPPLEMENTS: Livestock & Poultry

AG Pack LLC ....G....... 804 514-9080
Disputanta *(G-4103)*
Biostar ....G....... 800 686-9544
Gordonsville *(G-5901)*

Charles A Bliss Jr ....G....... 434 685-7311
Danville *(G-3966)*
Crop Production Services Inc ....G....... 804 282-7115
Richmond *(G-11037)*
Culpeper Farmers Coop Inc ....D....... 540 825-2200
Culpeper *(G-3884)*
Exchange Milling Co Inc ....G....... 540 483-5324
Rocky Mount *(G-12321)*
Farmers Milling & Supply Inc ....G....... 276 228-2971
Wytheville *(G-15888)*
Griffin Industries LLC ....F 804 876-3415
Doswell *(G-4121)*
Healthy Chef Creations ....E 407 339-2433
Mc Lean *(G-8456)*
Limestone Dust Corporation ....D....... 276 326-1103
Bluefield *(G-1869)*
M C Chadwell ....G....... 276 445-5495
Ewing *(G-4386)*
Mountain View Rendering Co ....G....... 540 984-4158
Edinburg *(G-4310)*
Murphy-Brown LLC ....E 804 834-3990
Waverly *(G-15085)*
Nutrien AG Solutions Inc ....G....... 757 229-9448
West Point *(G-15160)*
Nutrien AG Solutions Inc ....G....... 540 775-2985
Milford *(G-8932)*
Southern States Coop Inc ....F 540 992-1100
Cloverdale *(G-3693)*
Southern States Coop Inc ....B....... 804 281-1000
Richmond *(G-11389)*
Southern States Coop Inc ....G....... 703 378-4865
Chantilly *(G-2495)*
Southern States Coop Inc ....F 434 572-6941
South Boston *(G-12791)*
Southern States Coop Inc ....F 804 226-2758
Richmond *(G-11390)*
Southern States Coop Inc ....E 540 948-5691
Madison *(G-7862)*
Southern Sttes Wnchster Coop I ....F 540 662-0375
Winchester *(G-15588)*
Sunshine Mills Inc ....D....... 434 476-1451
Halifax *(G-6053)*
Valley Proteins (de) Inc ....D....... 434 634-9475
Emporia *(G-4369)*
Vaughans Mill Inc ....G....... 540 789-7144
Indian Valley *(G-6998)*

ANIMAL FEED: Wholesalers

Southern States Coop Inc ....F 804 226-2758
Richmond *(G-11390)*

ANIMAL FOOD & SUPPLEMENTS: Bird Food, Prepared

Dd Pet Products Inc ....G....... 703 532-3983
Arlington *(G-931)*

ANIMAL FOOD & SUPPLEMENTS: Cat

Mars Petcare Us Inc ....D....... 703 821-4900
Mc Lean *(G-8494)*

ANIMAL FOOD & SUPPLEMENTS: Dog

Fidough Homemade Dog Treats ....G....... 757 876-4548
Newport News *(G-9227)*
Grace Upon Grace LLC ....G....... 703 999-6678
Leesburg *(G-7282)*
Mars Overseas Holdings Inc ....G....... 703 821-4900
Mc Lean *(G-8493)*
My Best Friends Cupcakes LLC ....G....... 757 754-1148
Virginia Beach *(G-14668)*
Nestle Usa Inc ....C....... 765 778-6000
Arlington *(G-1074)*
Spectrum Brands Pet LLC ....F 540 951-5481
Blacksburg *(G-1794)*
Sunshine Mills Inc ....D....... 434 476-1451
Halifax *(G-6053)*
Sunshine Mills of Virginia ....G....... 434 476-1451
Halifax *(G-6054)*

ANIMAL FOOD & SUPPLEMENTS: Dog & Cat

Nestle Purina Petcare Company ....D....... 804 769-1266
King William *(G-7130)*
Woodys Goodys LLC ....G....... 703 608-8533
Falls Church *(G-4929)*

ANIMAL FOOD & SUPPLEMENTS: Feed Premixes

Amherst Milling Co Inc ....G....... 434 946-7601
  Amherst *(G-680)*

ANIMAL FOOD & SUPPLEMENTS: Feed Supplements

Maxx Performance Inc.............................F....... 845 987-9432
  Roanoke *(G-11960)*
Pure Blend Organics ....G....... 703 476-1414
  Manassas *(G-7991)*
Wilson Enterprises Inc ....F....... 804 732-6884
  North Dinwiddie *(G-10072)*

ANIMAL FOOD & SUPPLEMENTS: Kelp Meal & Pellets

Big Spring Mill Inc.................................E....... 540 268-2267
  Elliston *(G-4343)*

ANIMAL FOOD & SUPPLEMENTS: Livestock

Harry Jones Enterprises ....G....... 276 322-5096
  North Tazewell *(G-10100)*
Performance Livestock & Feed C.........G....... 888 777-5912
  Martinsville *(G-8317)*

ANIMAL FOOD & SUPPLEMENTS: Mineral feed supplements

Horse Sense Balanced ....G....... 540 253-9987
  Marshall *(G-8256)*

ANIMAL FOOD & SUPPLEMENTS: Pet, Exc Dog & Cat, Dry

Premium Pet Health LLC ....E....... 757 357-8880
  Smithfield *(G-12722)*

ANIMAL FOOD & SUPPLEMENTS: Poultry

Valley Proteins Inc...............................D....... 540 833-6641
  Linville *(G-7436)*
Valley Proteins Inc...............................D....... 540 833-8322
  Linville *(G-7437)*

ANODIZING SVC

Advanced Metal Finishing of VA ....G....... 540 344-3216
  Roanoke *(G-12029)*
Hankins & Johann Incorporated...........G....... 804 266-2421
  Richmond *(G-11233)*
Specialty Finishes Inc ....F....... 804 232-5027
  Richmond *(G-11768)*

ANTENNAS: Radar Or Communications

Axell Wireless Inc ....G....... 703 414-5300
  Arlington *(G-868)*
Gradient Dynamics LLC ....G....... 865 207-9052
  Mc Lean *(G-8453)*
R F Tech Solutions Inc ....G....... 804 241-5250
  Powhatan *(G-10569)*
Video Aerial Systems LLC....................G....... 434 221-3089
  Amherst *(G-712)*

ANTENNAS: Receiving

Commscope Technologies LLC ....C....... 434 386-5300
  Forest *(G-5062)*

ANTIBIOTICS

Pfizer Inc...F....... 804 257-2000
  Richmond *(G-11712)*

ANTIFREEZE

Earth Friendly Chemicals Inc................G....... 757 502-8600
  Virginia Beach *(G-14427)*

ANTIQUE FURNITURE RESTORATION & REPAIR

Cross Restorations...............................G....... 276 466-8436
  Bristol *(G-2014)*

ANTIQUE SHOPS

American Interiors Ltd..........................G....... 757 627-0248
  Norfolk *(G-9438)*

Frey Randall Antique Furnitre ....G....... 434 985-7631
  Stanardsville *(G-13219)*
Presidential Coin & Antique Co............G....... 703 354-5454
  Clifton *(G-3675)*

APPAREL ACCESS STORES

Influences of Zion ....G....... 804 248-4758
  Richmond *(G-11248)*

APPAREL DESIGNERS: Commercial

Karla Colletto Swimwear Inc................E....... 703 281-3262
  Vienna *(G-14076)*
Touch 3 LLC ....G....... 703 279-8130
  Fairfax *(G-4572)*

APPAREL: Hand Woven

Sweetb Designs LLC ....G....... 757 550-0436
  Portsmouth *(G-10490)*

APPLIANCES, HOUSEHOLD OR COIN OPERATED: Laundry Dryers

Elite Laundry and Car Wash LLC ....G....... 540 373-6150
  Fredericksburg *(G-5427)*

APPLIANCES, HOUSEHOLD: Kitchen, Major, Exc Refrigs & Stoves

Luis A Matos ....G....... 703 486-0015
  Arlington *(G-1049)*
Value America ....G....... 434 951-4100
  Charlottesville *(G-2710)*

APPLIANCES: Household, NEC

Jane Hfl Gresham ....G....... 757 397-2208
  Portsmouth *(G-10446)*
Nationwide Consumer Products ....G....... 804 226-0876
  Richmond *(G-11687)*

APPLIANCES: Household, Refrigerators & Freezers

Hill Phoenix Inc ....G....... 800 283-1109
  North Chesterfield *(G-9886)*

APPLIANCES: Major, Cooking

Unitedslickmart LLC ....G....... 800 714-0532
  Reston *(G-10979)*

APPLIANCES: Small, Electric

Alterntive Energywave Tech LLC ....G....... 757 897-1312
  Newport News *(G-9166)*
Matthews Home Decor ....G....... 804 379-2640
  Midlothian *(G-8854)*
Vollara LLC ....D....... 800 704-2378
  Bristol *(G-1998)*

APPLICATIONS SOFTWARE PROGRAMMING

Acintyo Inc..G....... 703 349-3400
  Mc Lean *(G-8384)*
Anra Technologies Inc..........................E....... 703 239-3206
  Chantilly *(G-2525)*
Application Technologies Inc ....G....... 703 644-0506
  Springfield *(G-12949)*
Divvy Cloud Corporation ....F....... 571 290-5077
  Arlington *(G-940)*
Euclidian Systems Inc ....G....... 703 963-7209
  Arlington *(G-960)*
Netunity Software LLC ....F....... 757 744-0147
  Virginia Beach *(G-14677)*
Rezgateway ....G....... 703 286-5331
  Reston *(G-10940)*
Swami Shriji LLC..................................G....... 804 322-9644
  North Chesterfield *(G-9994)*
Wyvern Interactive LLC ....F....... 540 336-4498
  Winchester *(G-15519)*

APPRENTICESHIP TRAINING SCHOOLS

Virginia Premiere Paint Contr ....G....... 804 398-1177
  Richmond *(G-11813)*

ARCHITECTURAL SVCS

Index Systems Inc...............................G....... 571 420-4600
  Herndon *(G-6706)*

Prototype Productions Inc ....D....... 703 858-0011
  Chantilly *(G-2483)*
Sandhurst-Aec LLC ....G....... 703 533-1413
  Falls Church *(G-4872)*
Timmons & Kelley Architects ....G....... 804 897-5636
  Midlothian *(G-8913)*

ARCHITECTURAL SVCS: Engineering

Dream Green International LLC............G....... 814 616-7800
  Alexandria *(G-194)*

ARMATURE REPAIRING & REWINDING SVC

Cuton Power Inc...................................G....... 703 996-9350
  Chantilly *(G-2401)*
Electric Motor and Contg Co ....C....... 757 487-2121
  Chesapeake *(G-3084)*
K E Marine ....G....... 757 787-1313
  Accomac *(G-72)*

ARMOR PLATES

Protective Solutions Inc ....D....... 703 435-1115
  Dulles *(G-4220)*

AROMATIC CHEMICAL PRDTS

Scenter of Town LLC ....G....... 540 372-4145
  Fredericksburg *(G-5221)*

ART & ORNAMENTAL WARE: Pottery

Blue Ridge Pottery...............................F....... 434 985-6080
  Stanardsville *(G-13216)*
Mdc Camden Clayworks.......................G....... 804 798-4971
  Glen Allen *(G-5769)*
Michelle Erickson Pottery ....G....... 757 727-9139
  Hampton *(G-6198)*
Persimmon Street Ceramics That ....G....... 202 256-8238
  Arlington *(G-1109)*
Robin Cage Pottery..............................G....... 804 233-1758
  Richmond *(G-11745)*

ART DEALERS & GALLERIES

Casson Art & Frame ....G....... 276 638-1450
  Martinsville *(G-8274)*
Robin Cage Pottery..............................G....... 804 233-1758
  Richmond *(G-11745)*

ART DESIGN SVCS

Kin Art Studios LLC ....G....... 804 368-7298
  Ashland *(G-1449)*
Tetra Graphics Inc................................G....... 434 845-4450
  Lynchburg *(G-7822)*
Wealthy Sistas Media Group.................G....... 800 917-9435
  Dumfries *(G-4262)*

ART GALLERIES

Erickson & Ripper Framing....................G....... 703 549-1616
  Alexandria *(G-202)*

ART MARBLE: Concrete

All Marble..G....... 757 460-8099
  Virginia Beach *(G-14222)*

ART RELATED SVCS

Q P I Inc..G....... 434 528-0092
  Lynchburg *(G-7795)*

ART RESTORATION SVC

Hang Up ....G....... 703 430-0717
  Sterling *(G-13418)*

ART SCHOOL, EXC COMMERCIAL

Scotties Bavarian Folk Art ....G....... 540 341-8884
  Warrenton *(G-15049)*

ART SPLY STORES

Framery and Arts Corp ....G....... 434 525-0444
  Lynchburg *(G-7717)*

ARTIFICIAL FLOWER SHOPS

Valentinecherry Creations....................G....... 757 848-6137
  Hampton *(G-6258)*

ARTIFICIAL FLOWERS & TREES

Evolve Manufacturing LLC............G......703 570-5700
  Winchester *(G-15415)*
Pretty Petals..................................G......757 357-9136
  Smithfield *(G-12723)*
Valentinecherry Creations...........G......757 848-6137
  Hampton *(G-6258)*

ARTIST'S MATERIALS & SPLYS

James Hintzke.............................G......757 374-4827
  Virginia Beach *(G-14563)*

ARTISTS' MATERIALS: Boards, Drawing

Dark Warrior Group LLC ....G......757 289-6451
  Ashburn *(G-1269)*

ARTISTS' MATERIALS: Brushes, Air

Southern Airbrushes.....................G......434 324-4049
  Hurt *(G-6978)*

ARTISTS' MATERIALS: Canvas Board

AW Art LLC ....G......540 320-4565
  Dublin *(G-4149)*
Jill C Perla..................................G......703 407-5695
  Round Hill *(G-12380)*

ARTISTS' MATERIALS: Canvas, Prepared On Frames

Framery and Arts Corp ....G......434 525-0444
  Lynchburg *(G-7717)*

ARTISTS' MATERIALS: Frames, Artists' Canvases

Ixidor LLC ....G......571 332-3888
  Falls Church *(G-4810)*
Justinian Posters & Prints ....G......703 273-8049
  Fairfax *(G-4640)*

ARTISTS' MATERIALS: Paints, Gold Or Bronze

World of Color Expo LLC ....G......703 754-3191
  Gainesville *(G-5625)*

ARTISTS' MATERIALS: Palettes

Clearly-You Inc ....G......757 351-0346
  Chesapeake *(G-3037)*

ARTISTS' MATERIALS: Pencils & Pencil Parts

Securitas Inc................................G......800 705-4545
  Richmond *(G-11063)*

ARTWORK: Framed

Art & Framing Center....................G......540 720-2800
  Stafford *(G-13119)*
Four Calling Birds Ltd ....G......540 317-5761
  Hume *(G-6961)*
Lavenmoon...................................G......540 297-3274
  Goodview *(G-5896)*
Requisites Gallery ....G......757 376-2754
  Chesapeake *(G-3269)*
Shenandoah Primitives LLC ....G......540 662-4727
  Winchester *(G-15477)*
Shooting Star Gallery LLC ....G......757 787-4536
  Onancock *(G-10197)*

ASBESTOS MINING SVCS

Brandy Ltd....................................G......757 220-0302
  Williamsburg *(G-15213)*

ASBESTOS PRDTS: Boiler Covering, Heat Insulat Matl,Exc Felt

Northern Virginia Insulation..........G......703 753-7249
  Haymarket *(G-6431)*

ASBESTOS PRDTS: Insulating Materials

Semco Services Inc ....E......540 885-7480
  Staunton *(G-13291)*

ASBESTOS PRODUCTS

McC Abatement LLC ....G......804 731-4238
  North Chesterfield *(G-9927)*

ASPHALT & ASPHALT PRDTS

Associated Asphalt Inman LLC ....G......864 472-2816
  Roanoke *(G-12036)*
Eurovia Atlantic Coast LLC.................G......703 230-0850
  Chantilly *(G-2418)*
Fuller Asphalt Material ....G......423 676-4449
  Bristol *(G-2018)*
Hughie C Rose ....G......540 423-5240
  North Chesterfield *(G-9888)*
Stuart M Perry Incorporated ....C......540 662-3431
  Winchester *(G-15483)*

ASPHALT COATINGS & SEALERS

Ennis-Flint Inc ....E......804 309-3199
  Richmond *(G-11579)*
Gatorguard LLC...............................G......434 942-0245
  Lynchburg *(G-7720)*
Mundet Inc ....D......804 644-3970
  Richmond *(G-11684)*
Ray Painter Small............................G......804 255-7050
  Chesterfield *(G-3520)*
Tidewater Green ....F......757 487-4736
  Chesapeake *(G-3338)*

ASPHALT MIXTURES WHOLESALERS

Hy Lee Paving Corporation.................E......804 360-9066
  Rockville *(G-12287)*
Kessler Soils Engrg Pdts Inc ....G......571 291-2284
  Leesburg *(G-7296)*

ASPHALT PLANTS INCLUDING GRAVEL MIX TYPE

Lewin Asphalt Inc ....G......540 550-9478
  Winchester *(G-15440)*
Tri-City Industrial Builders ....G......276 669-4621
  Bristol *(G-2036)*

ASPHALT SATURATED BOARD

Resurface Incorporated....................F......703 335-1950
  Manassas *(G-8144)*

ASSEMBLING SVC: Clocks

Hermle Uhren GMBH & Co KG..............D......434 946-7751
  Amherst *(G-693)*

ASSEMBLING SVC: Plumbing Fixture Fittings, Plastic

CPS Contractors Inc ....G......804 561-6834
  Moseley *(G-9036)*
Greenacre Plumbing LLC...................G......703 680-2380
  Woodbridge *(G-15717)*
Mm Export LLC ....G......757 333-0542
  Virginia Beach *(G-14658)*

ASSOCIATIONS: Scientists'

Association For Cmpt McHy Inc..........G......703 528-0726
  Arlington *(G-863)*
Institute of Navigation (dc)................G......703 366-2723
  Manassas *(G-8081)*
Society Nclear Mdcine Mlclar I ....D......703 708-9000
  Reston *(G-10957)*

ASSOCIATIONS: Trade

Associated Gen Contrs of Amer..........D......703 837-5415
  Arlington *(G-862)*

ATOMIZERS

Afton Chemical Corporation................B......804 788-5800
  Richmond *(G-11476)*
Appalachian Mineral Services ....G......276 345-4610
  Richlands *(G-11012)*

AUDIO & VIDEO EQPT, EXC COMMERCIAL

Action Digital Inc............................G......804 358-7289
  Richmond *(G-11083)*
Better Cables LLC............................G......872 222-5371
  Broadlands *(G-2073)*

Better Cables LLC..........................G......703 724-0906
  Broadlands *(G-2074)*
Collabrtive Tech Cmmnctons Cor ....G......804 477-8695
  Richmond *(G-11161)*
Impression An Everlasting Inc ....F......804 363-7185
  Mechanicsville *(G-8640)*
Innovative Home Media LLC ....G......804 513-4784
  Midlothian *(G-8832)*
Jones and Jones Audio & Video ....G......804 283-3495
  Richmond *(G-11636)*
Kollmorgen Corporation ....B......540 633-3536
  Radford *(G-10721)*
Machina Dynamica Inc ....G......571 405-0709
  Falls Church *(G-4826)*
Mu-Del Electronics LLC......................F......703 368-8900
  Manassas *(G-8114)*
Prelude Communications Inc ....G......703 731-9396
  Sterling *(G-13476)*
Rdk LLC ....G......540 446-8327
  Mount Sidney *(G-9084)*
Rivercity Communications ....G......804 304-9590
  Henrico *(G-6561)*
Silversmith Audio ....G......619 460-1129
  Springfield *(G-13087)*
SQ Labs LLC ....G......804 938-8123
  Richmond *(G-11770)*
Star Home Theater LLC ....G......855 978-2748
  Leesburg *(G-7351)*
Ten Companies LLC ....G......703 669-1008
  Leesburg *(G-7360)*
Ultracomm Llc ....G......703 622-6397
  Purcellville *(G-10683)*
Valcom Inc ....C......540 427-3900
  Roanoke *(G-12014)*

AUDIO COMPONENTS

AC Cetera Inc ....G......724 532-3363
  Fairfax *(G-4400)*

AUDIO ELECTRONIC SYSTEMS

1602 Group LLC ....E......703 933-0024
  Alexandria *(G-394)*
Applied Vsual Cmmnications Inc ....E......703 787-6668
  Herndon *(G-6614)*
Digigram Inc ....G......330 476-5247
  Fairfax *(G-4613)*
Hipro Call Inc ....G......703 397-5155
  Reston *(G-10864)*
Luminous Audio Technology ....G......804 741-5826
  Richmond *(G-11275)*
Seaside Audio ....G......757 237-5333
  Virginia Beach *(G-14800)*
Stage Sound Inc ....E......540 342-2040
  Roanoke *(G-12194)*

AUTHORS' AGENTS & BROKERS

Innovation Station Music LLC ....G......703 405-6727
  Annandale *(G-760)*

AUTO & HOME SUPPLY STORES: Auto & Truck Eqpt & Parts

Crown International Inc......................F......703 335-0066
  Manassas *(G-8053)*

AUTO & HOME SUPPLY STORES: Automotive parts

Atkins Automotive Corp ....G......540 942-5157
  Waynesboro *(G-15096)*
Concept Products Inc........................G......434 793-9952
  Danville *(G-3971)*
King of Dice ....G......804 758-0776
  Saluda *(G-12604)*
Performance Counts Automotive ....G......434 392-3391
  Farmville *(G-4955)*

AUTO & HOME SUPPLY STORES: Batteries, Automotive & Truck

East Penn Manufacturing Co ....E......804 798-1771
  Ashland *(G-1407)*

AUTO & HOME SUPPLY STORES: Speed Shops, Incl Race Car Splys

Clarke County Speed Shop..................G......540 955-0479
  Berryville *(G-1674)*

Employee Codes: A=Over 500 employees, B=251-500
C=101-250, D=51-100, E=20-50, F=10-19, G=1-9
    2021 Virginia
    Industrial Directory
    897

PRODUCT

AUTO & HOME SUPPLY STORES: Trailer Hitches, Automotive

Leonard Alum Utlity Bldngs Inc ....G...... 540 951-0236
Blacksburg **(G-1753)**

AUTO & HOME SUPPLY STORES: Truck Eqpt & Parts

Crenshaw of Richmond Inc...............D...... 804 231-6241
Richmond **(G-11546)**
Wilbar Truck Equipment Inc...............E...... 757 397-3200
Portsmouth **(G-10502)**

AUTOMATIC REGULATING CONTROL: Building Svcs Monitoring, Auto

Ark Commercial Services LLC............F...... 202 807-6211
Mc Lean **(G-8396)**
Circle T Controls Inc.......................G...... 540 295-0188
Stafford **(G-13131)**
State Line Controls Inc...................G...... 757 969-8527
Portsmouth **(G-10485)**

AUTOMATIC REGULATING CONTROLS: AC & Refrigeration

Siemens Industry Inc......................D...... 804 222-6680
Richmond **(G-11380)**
Southeastern Mechanical Inc.............G...... 888 461-7848
Stafford **(G-13193)**
Stuarts AC & Refrigeration ....G...... 804 405-0960
Richmond **(G-11400)**

AUTOMATIC REGULATING CONTROLS: Energy Cutoff, Residtl/Comm

Intus Windows LLC..........................F...... 202 450-4211
Fairfax **(G-4480)**

AUTOMATIC REGULATING CONTROLS: Hardware, Environmental Reg

Uhr Corporation ....G...... 703 534-1250
Falls Church **(G-4885)**

AUTOMATIC REGULATING CONTROLS: Hydronic Pressure Or Temp

Bas Control Systems LLC.................G...... 804 569-2473
Mechanicsville **(G-8606)**

AUTOMATIC REGULATING CONTROLS: Incinerator, Residential/Comm

In10m LLC.....................................G...... 202 779-7977
Richmond **(G-11617)**

AUTOMATIC REGULATING CONTROLS: Refrig/Air-Cond Defrost

Edge Mechanical Inc........................F...... 757 228-3540
Virginia Beach **(G-14432)**
Parker Hannifen Sporlan Div ....G...... 804 379-8551
North Chesterfield **(G-9945)**

AUTOMATIC TELLER MACHINES

American Highwall Systems ....F...... 276 646-2004
Chilhowie **(G-3545)**
Atm Beach Services LLC ....G...... 757 434-4848
Virginia Beach **(G-14247)**
Enc Enterprises................................G...... 703 578-1924
Falls Church **(G-4788)**
Maysteel Porters LLC ....C...... 434 846-7412
Lynchburg **(G-7769)**
Mgi Fuel Express LLC ....G...... 804 541-0299
North Prince George **(G-10089)**

AUTOMOBILE RECOVERY SVCS

Wengers Electrical Service LLC ....G...... 540 867-0101
Rockingham **(G-12283)**

AUTOMOBILES & OTHER MOTOR VEHICLES WHOLESALERS

Crown International Inc ....F...... 703 335-0066
Manassas **(G-8053)**

AUTOMOBILES: Off-Road, Exc Recreational Vehicles

Lee Talbot Associates Inc ....G...... 703 734-8576
Mc Lean **(G-8483)**

AUTOMOTIVE & TRUCK GENERAL REPAIR SVC

American Diesel Corp ....G...... 804 435-3107
Kilmarnock **(G-7068)**
Dalmatian Hill Engneering ....G...... 540 289-5079
Port Republic **(G-10383)**
Daniels Welding and Tires ....G...... 757 566-8446
Toano **(G-13862)**
Stuart Mathews Engineering ....G...... 804 779-2976
Mechanicsville **(G-8684)**
West Garage Doors Inc ....G...... 434 799-4070
Danville **(G-4050)**
York Sportscars Inc ....G...... 804 798-5268
Ashland **(G-1514)**

AUTOMOTIVE BODY SHOP

Mikes Wrecker Service & Bdy Sp ....G...... 540 996-4152
Millboro **(G-8937)**

AUTOMOTIVE CUSTOMIZING SVCS, NONFACTORY BASIS

Fiberglass Customs Inc ....G...... 757 244-0610
Newport News **(G-9226)**
Sun Signs ....G...... 703 867-9831
Stafford **(G-13197)**

AUTOMOTIVE EXHAUST REPAIR SVC

Cleanvent Dryer Exhust Spclsts...........G...... 804 730-1754
Mechanicsville **(G-8612)**

AUTOMOTIVE GLASS REPLACEMENT SHOPS

Threat Prot Wrd Wide Svcs LLC...........G...... 703 795-2445
Remington **(G-10773)**
Windshield RPS By Ralph Smiley ....G...... 804 690-7517
Mechanicsville **(G-8699)**

AUTOMOTIVE PARTS, ACCESS & SPLYS

1a Smart Start ....G...... 703 330-1372
Manassas **(G-7908)**
Aerospace Techniques Inc...................D...... 860 347-1200
Virginia Beach **(G-14214)**
Amthor International Inc ....D...... 845 778-5576
Gretna **(G-6002)**
ARS Manufacturing Inc ....C...... 757 460-2211
Virginia Beach **(G-14242)**
At Lab of America LLC ....G...... 681 207-9161
Stuart **(G-13605)**
Atlantic Research Corporation ....C...... 540 854-2000
Culpeper **(G-3869)**
Atomizer Fuel Systems Inc ....G...... 757 250-3773
Toano **(G-13857)**
Betterbilt Solutions LLC ....G...... 540 324-9117
Staunton **(G-13244)**
Bg Solutions LLC ....G...... 703 623-4846
Vienna **(G-14016)**
Brake Connections ....G...... 540 247-9000
Gore **(G-5920)**
Bridgeview Full Svc ....G...... 434 575-6800
South Boston **(G-12753)**
Colonial Chevrolet Company LP ....B...... 757 455-4500
Norfolk **(G-9493)**
Continental Auto Systems Inc ....D...... 757 890-4900
Newport News **(G-9204)**
Continental Teves ....F...... 540 825-4100
Culpeper **(G-3881)**
Dana Auto Systems Group LLC ....E...... 757 638-2656
Suffolk **(G-13693)**
Delphi Inc ....G...... 703 908-0258
Arlington **(G-935)**
Driving Aids Development Corp ....G...... 703 938-6435
Stephens City **(G-13315)**
Express Racing & Machine ....G...... 804 521-7891
North Chesterfield **(G-9869)**
Feather Carbon LLC ....G...... 757 630-6759
Suffolk **(G-13707)**
Federal-Mogul Products Inc.................B...... 540 662-3871
Winchester **(G-15542)**

Frenchs Auto Parts Inc......................G...... 540 740-3676
New Market **(G-9142)**
Garys Classic Car Parts ....G...... 757 925-0546
Suffolk **(G-13715)**
George H Pollok Jr............................G...... 336 540-8870
Union Hall **(G-13959)**
Global Safety Textiles LLC ....D...... 434 447-7629
South Hill **(G-12851)**
Gonmf ....G...... 844 763-7250
Woodbridge **(G-15711)**
Grede Radford LLC...........................D...... 248 727-1800
Radford **(G-10715)**
Hampton Roads Processors Inc...........G...... 757 285-8811
Portsmouth **(G-10440)**
Hesss Body Shop ....G...... 276 395-7808
Coeburn **(G-3699)**
High Ground Partners LLC ....G...... 434 944-8254
Lynchburg **(G-7733)**
IMS Gear Holding Inc ....E...... 757 468-8810
Virginia Beach **(G-14542)**
IMS Gear Virginia LLC ....B...... 757 468-8810
Virginia Beach **(G-14543)**
Joe London Training LLC ....G...... 540 272-9205
Culpeper **(G-3901)**
Lear Corp Strasburg ....G...... 540 465-6244
Strasburg **(G-13587)**
Leonard Alum Utlity Bldngs Inc ....G...... 434 792-8202
Danville **(G-4011)**
Lifelineusa ....G...... 540 251-2724
Dublin **(G-4164)**
Longwood Elastomers Inc ....C...... 276 228-5406
Wytheville **(G-15898)**
Miata Realm LLC ....G...... 724 612-1029
Fairfax **(G-4510)**
Muncie Power Products Inc ....C...... 804 275-6724
North Chesterfield **(G-9936)**
Nitto Inc..G...... 757 436-5540
Chesapeake **(G-3219)**
Performance Cstm Cabinets LLC ....G...... 804 382-3870
Powhatan **(G-10563)**
Rye Valley Oil Inc ....G...... 276 677-3750
Sugar Grove **(G-13788)**
Schrader-Altavista ....G...... 434 369-8816
Altavista **(G-640)**
Somic America Inc ....D...... 276 228-4307
Wytheville **(G-15914)**
Stealth Dump Trucks Inc ....G...... 757 890-4888
Yorktown **(G-15994)**
Tele Controls Inc ....G...... 571 490-4500
Arlington **(G-1185)**
Tidewater Auto & Indus Mch Inc...........G...... 757 855-5091
Virginia Beach **(G-14872)**
Todd Huffman Installs LLC ....G...... 540 271-4221
Mount Crawford **(G-9060)**
Turbo Lab..G...... 276 952-5997
Stuart **(G-13637)**
Usui International Corporation ....B...... 757 558-7300
Chesapeake **(G-3356)**
Virginia Drveline Differential.................G...... 276 227-0299
Wytheville **(G-15921)**
Vitesco Technologies Usa LLC............A...... 757 875-7000
Newport News **(G-9376)**
Windshield Wizard ....G...... 757 714-1642
Norfolk **(G-9795)**
Wolverine Advanced Mtls LLC..............E...... 540 552-7674
Blacksburg **(G-1806)**
World Wide Automotive LLC.................E...... 540 667-9100
Winchester **(G-15518)**
York Sportscars Inc ....G...... 804 798-5268
Ashland **(G-1514)**
ZF Active Safety & Elec US LLC ....B...... 276 783-1157
Atkins **(G-1523)**
ZF Active Safety & Elec US LLC ....C...... 276 783-1990
Atkins **(G-1524)**

AUTOMOTIVE PARTS: Plastic

Acel LLC...G...... 888 801-2507
Burke **(G-2180)**
Heyco Werk USA Inc..........................G...... 434 634-8810
Emporia **(G-4360)**
IAC Strasburg LLC ....C...... 540 465-3741
Strasburg **(G-13582)**
Utility One Source For Eqp LLC ....D...... 434 525-2929
Forest **(G-5103)**

AUTOMOTIVE PRDTS: Rubber

ARS Manufacturing Inc ....C...... 757 460-2211
Virginia Beach **(G-14242)**
Autombili Lamborghini Amer LLC........F...... 866 681-6276
Herndon **(G-6616)**

Hutchinson Sealing Systems Inc ....F 276 228-6150
Wytheville **(G-15890)**

Longwood Elastomers Inc ....E 276 228-5406
Wytheville **(G-15896)**

AUTOMOTIVE REPAIR SHOPS: Frame Repair Shops

Conglobal Industries LLC ....E ... 757 487-5100
Chesapeake **(G-3051)**

AUTOMOTIVE REPAIR SHOPS: Machine Shop

Gregorys Fleet Supply Corp ....E ... 757 490-1606
Virginia Beach **(G-14492)**

Khem Precision Machining LLC ....G ... 804 915-8922
Richmond **(G-11261)**

Machine Tool Technology LLC ....F ... 804 520-4173
South Chesterfield **(G-12813)**

Shadows Ridge Inc ....G ... 540 722-0310
Winchester **(G-15475)**

Vanmark LLC ....G ... 757 689-3850
Virginia Beach **(G-14906)**

AUTOMOTIVE REPAIR SHOPS: Springs, Rebuilding & Repair

Mechanx Corp ....G ... 703 698-7680
Falls Church **(G-4828)**

AUTOMOTIVE REPAIR SHOPS: Truck Engine Repair, Exc Indl

Bellamy Mfg & Repr Co ....G ... 276 386-7273
Hiltons **(G-6904)**

AUTOMOTIVE REPAIR SVC

Juniors Wldg & Met Fabrication ....G ... 540 943-7070
Stuarts Draft **(G-13653)**

Myers Repair Company ....G ... 804 222-3674
Richmond **(G-11298)**

Plunkett Business Group Inc ....E ... 540 343-3323
Vinton **(G-14180)**

Utility One Source For Eqp LLC ....D ... 434 525-2929
Forest **(G-5103)**

AUTOMOTIVE SPLYS & PARTS, NEW, WHOL: Auto Servicing Eqpt

Wilbar Truck Equipment Inc ....E ... 757 397-3200
Portsmouth **(G-10502)**

AUTOMOTIVE SPLYS & PARTS, NEW, WHOL: Auto Svc Station Eqpt

Davids Mobile Service LLC ....G ... 804 481-1647
Hopewell **(G-6922)**

AUTOMOTIVE SPLYS & PARTS, NEW, WHOLESALE: Alternators

Potomac Altrntor Btry Spclists ....G ... 804 224-2384
Colonial Beach **(G-3726)**

AUTOMOTIVE SPLYS & PARTS, NEW, WHOLESALE: Brakes

Carlisle Indstrl Brke & Frctn ....F ... 814 486-1119
Charlottesville **(G-2605)**

AUTOMOTIVE SPLYS & PARTS, NEW, WHOLESALE: Wheels

Craft Repair Incorporated ....F ... 757 838-0721
Hampton **(G-6121)**

AUTOMOTIVE SPLYS & PARTS, WHOLESALE, NEC

Alpine Armoring Inc ....F ... 703 471-0002
Chantilly **(G-2368)**

Autopartsource LLC ....E ... 804 329-3000
Richmond **(G-11495)**

Camco ....G ... 757 855-5890
Norfolk **(G-9474)**

Cline Automotive Inc ....F ... 804 271-9107
North Chesterfield **(G-9846)**

Crown International Inc ....F ... 703 335-0066
Manassas **(G-8053)**

King of Dice ....G ... 804 758-0776
Saluda **(G-12604)**

Master Machine & Auto LLC ....G ... 757 244-8401
Newport News **(G-9293)**

Momentum Usa Inc ....C ... 804 329-3000
Richmond **(G-11681)**

Pitts Auto Parts Inc ....F ... 540 373-3720
Fredericksburg **(G-5213)**

Safran Usa Inc ....F ... 703 351-9898
Alexandria **(G-334)**

AUTOMOTIVE SVCS, EXC REPAIR & CARWASHES: Customizing

Jerry King ....G ... 804 550-1243
Glen Allen **(G-5755)**

AUTOMOTIVE SVCS, EXC REPAIR: Washing & Polishing

Son1c Wax LLC ....G ... 703 508-8188
Fairfax Station **(G-4724)**

AUTOMOTIVE SVCS, EXC RPR/CARWASHES: High Perf Auto Rpr/Svc

Mechanx Corp ....G ... 703 698-7680
Falls Church **(G-4828)**

AUTOMOTIVE TOWING & WRECKING SVC

Bubbles Wrecker Service ....G ... 434 845-2411
Lynchburg **(G-7662)**

AUTOMOTIVE TRANSMISSION REPAIR SVC

Western Branch Diesel Inc ....E ... 703 369-5005
Manassas **(G-8177)**

AUTOMOTIVE UPHOLSTERY SHOPS

Camco ....G ... 757 855-5890
Norfolk **(G-9474)**

AUTOMOTIVE WELDING SVCS

Brown Brothers Inc ....G ... 757 357-4086
Smithfield **(G-12706)**

C and S Precision Wel ....G ... 804 815-7963
Saluda **(G-12601)**

Creative Welding and Design ....G ... 757 334-1416
Suffolk **(G-13689)**

Daniels Welding and Tires ....G ... 757 566-8446
Toano **(G-13862)**

Gerloff Inc Charles W ....G ... 757 853-5232
Norfolk **(G-9562)**

Louie Dufour ....G ... 540 839-5232
Hot Springs **(G-6947)**

M&M Welding LLC ....G ... 703 201-4066
Manassas **(G-8102)**

Pro-Core ....G ... 703 490-4905
Woodbridge **(G-15783)**

Skyline Fabricating Inc ....G ... 276 498-3560
Raven **(G-10758)**

Stick It Welding & Fabrication ....G ... 757 710-5774
Hallwood **(G-6055)**

Systems Technology VA LLC ....G ... 540 884-1784
Eagle Rock **(G-4283)**

T & J Wldg & Fabrication LLC ....G ... 757 672-9929
Suffolk **(G-13770)**

Trl Inc ....G ... 276 794-7196
Castlewood **(G-2258)**

Twin City Welding Company ....F ... 276 669-9322
Bristol **(G-1992)**

AUTOMOTIVE: Bodies

Beverley M James Jr ....G ... 540 354-2300
Roanoke **(G-11888)**

Wisecarver Brothers Inc ....G ... 434 332-4511
Rustburg **(G-12447)**

AUTOMOTIVE: Seating

Clarios ....D ... 703 886-3961
Ashburn **(G-1255)**

Clarios ....D ... 540 362-5500
Roanoke **(G-11909)**

Clarios ....G ... 540 366-0981
Roanoke **(G-11910)**

International Automotive Compo ....A ... 540 465-3741
Strasburg **(G-13585)**

AUTOTRANSFORMERS: Electric

Caravels LLC ....C ... 540 345-9892
Centreville **(G-2297)**

AUTOTRANSFORMERS: Switchboards, Exc Telephone

Power Hub Ventures LLC ....G ... 540 443-9214
Blacksburg **(G-1780)**

AWNINGS & CANOPIES

Aaacm Green Warrior Inc ....G ... 703 865-5991
Fairfax **(G-4398)**

Charter Ip Pllc ....G ... 540 253-5332
The Plains **(G-13842)**

Robert Montgomery ....G ... 703 737-0491
Leesburg **(G-7338)**

AWNINGS & CANOPIES: Awnings, Fabric, From Purchased Matls

Graham Grham Cnvas Sign Shoppe .....G ... 276 628-8069
Abingdon **(G-35)**

Husteads Canvas Creations Inc ....E ... 757 627-6912
Norfolk **(G-9586)**

Virginia Canvas Products Inc ....G ... 757 558-0327
Carrollton **(G-2246)**

AWNINGS & CANOPIES: Canopies, Fabric, From Purchased Matls

Ryzing Technologies LLC ....G ... 949 244-0240
Staunton **(G-13288)**

AWNINGS & CANOPIES: Fabric

Bahama Breeze Shutter Awng LLC ....G ... 757 592-0265
Ordinary **(G-10236)**

JWB of Roanoke Inc ....F ... 540 344-7726
Roanoke **(G-12116)**

Signature Canvasmakers LLC ....G ... 757 788-8890
Hampton **(G-6236)**

AWNINGS: Fiberglass

Decks Down Under LLC ....G ... 703 758-2572
Reston **(G-10836)**

Strongwell Corporation ....B ... 276 645-8000
Bristol **(G-1991)**

Strongwell Corporation ....E ... 276 623-0935
Abingdon **(G-62)**

AWNINGS: Metal

Superior Awning Service Inc ....G ... 757 399-8161
Portsmouth **(G-10489)**

Ammunition Loading & Assembling Plant

Bethany Warthan ....G ... 434 294-2937
Blackstone **(G-1811)**

BABYSITTING BUREAU

Bradley-Morris LLC ....E ... 678 419-4171
Chesapeake **(G-3014)**

BACKHOES

Clements Backhoe LLC ....G ... 804 598-6230
Powhatan **(G-10539)**

Cody Sterling Hawkins ....G ... 276 477-0238
Bristol **(G-1972)**

D K Backhoe Loader Serv ....G ... 434 969-1685
Buckingham **(G-2132)**

David R Powell ....G ... 434 724-2642
Dry Fork **(G-4140)**

H D and Company ....G ... 540 651-4354
Check **(G-2944)**

H H Backhoe Service ....G ... 540 574-3578
Rockingham **(G-12254)**

H&L Backhoe Service Inc ....G ... 540 399-5013
Richardsville **(G-11010)**

Mid-Atlantic Backhoe Inc ....G ... 804 897-3443
Midlothian **(G-8858)**

Ralph Matney ....G ... 276 644-9259
Bristol **(G-2031)**

Employee Codes: A=Over 500 employees, B=251-500
C=101-250, D=51-100, E=20-50, F=10-19, G=1-9

2021 Virginia
Industrial Directory

PRODUCT

899

BACKHOES (continued)

S & S Backhoe & Excvtr Svc LLc........G....... 434 656-3184
Gretna *(G-6010)*
Southern Plumbing & Backhoe In......G....... 804 598-7470
Moseley *(G-9048)*
W & M Backhoe Service........................G....... 540 775-7185
King George *(G-7121)*

BADGES: Identification & Insignia

Netstyle Corp......................................G....... 703 717-9706
Lorton *(G-7514)*
Oneso Inc..G....... 704 560-6354
Arlington *(G-1088)*

BAGS & CONTAINERS: Textile, Exc Sleeping

Lay-N-Go LLC......................................G....... 703 799-0799
Alexandria *(G-514)*
Pre Con Inc...F....... 804 861-0282
Petersburg *(G-10337)*

BAGS & SACKS: Shipping & Shopping

Bob Sansone DBA Peggs Co..............G....... 951 360-9170
Ashland *(G-1383)*
Westrock Cp LLc..................................C....... 804 843-5416
West Point *(G-15164)*

BAGS: Canvas

Fabriko Inc...E....... 434 352-7145
Appomattox *(G-810)*
Hdt Expeditionary Systems Inc..........G....... 540 373-1435
Fredericksburg *(G-5195)*
Knp Traders LLC.................................G....... 703 376-1955
Chantilly *(G-2452)*
Philomen Fashion and Designs..........G....... 703 966-5680
Heathsville *(G-6463)*

BAGS: Duffle, Canvas, Made From Purchased Materials

CC & More Inc.....................................G....... 540 786-7052
Fredericksburg *(G-5257)*
S3 Tactical LLC...................................G....... 540 667-6947
Stephens City *(G-13321)*
Warrior Luggage Company..................G....... 301 523-9010
Alexandria *(G-608)*

BAGS: Flour, Fabric, Made From Purchased Materials

Samco Textile Prints LLc...................G....... 571 451-4044
Woodbridge *(G-15802)*

BAGS: Food Storage & Frozen Food, Plastic

Extra Space Storage...........................G....... 703 719-4354
Alexandria *(G-459)*
Reynolds Presto Products Inc............B....... 434 572-6961
South Boston *(G-12788)*

BAGS: Food Storage & Trash, Plastic

Nothing But Cake Incorporated...........G....... 540 322-7520
Fredericksburg *(G-5336)*

BAGS: Garment Storage Exc Paper Or Plastic Film

Shining Lights LLC.............................G....... 703 338-3820
Fairfax *(G-4675)*
Warrior Luggage Company..................G....... 301 523-9010
Alexandria *(G-608)*

BAGS: Laundry, Garment & Storage

Market Salamander..............................E....... 540 687-8011
Middleburg *(G-8728)*

BAGS: Mothproof , Made From Purchased Materials

Its All Mx LLC.....................................G....... 540 785-6295
Chester *(G-3425)*

BAGS: Paper

Broad Bay Cotton Company.................G....... 757 227-4101
Virginia Beach *(G-14299)*
Mfri Inc..C....... 540 667-7022
Winchester *(G-15555)*

BAGS: Plastic

Glad Products Company.......................C....... 434 946-3100
Amherst *(G-691)*
Inifinity Global Inc..............................G....... 434 793-7570
Danville *(G-4001)*
Pilgrim International............................G....... 757 989-5045
Newport News *(G-9313)*
Rubbermaid Commercial Pdts LLC......A....... 540 667-8700
Winchester *(G-15582)*
Rubbermaid Commercial Pdts LLC......G....... 540 542-8195
Winchester *(G-15471)*
Tg Polymers Inc..................................G....... 585 670-9427
Alexandria *(G-597)*
Titan Plastics LLC..............................G....... 804 339-4464
Glen Allen *(G-5813)*
Vanguard Plastics...............................G....... 804 222-2012
Richmond *(G-11434)*
Vitex Packaging Group Inc..................F....... 757 538-3115
Suffolk *(G-13780)*

BAGS: Plastic, Made From Purchased Materials

Image Packaging.................................G....... 804 730-7358
Mechanicsville *(G-8639)*
Infinity Global Inc...............................E....... 434 793-7570
Danville *(G-4000)*
Liqui-Box Corporation.........................D....... 804 325-1400
Richmond *(G-11658)*

BAGS: Rubber Or Rubberized Fabric

Crooked Stitch Bags LLC....................G....... 703 680-0118
Woodbridge *(G-15676)*

BAGS: Shipping

Crosstown Shipg & Sup Co LLC.........G....... 513 252-5370
Alexandria *(G-435)*

BAGS: Tea, Fabric, Made From Purchased Materials

Honey True Teas LLC..........................G....... 703 728-8369
Woodbridge *(G-15723)*

BAGS: Textile

Broad Bay Cotton Company.................G....... 757 227-4101
Virginia Beach *(G-14299)*
Mfri Inc..C....... 540 667-7022
Winchester *(G-15555)*
Tent Company of Norfolk LLC..............G....... 757 461-7330
Chesapeake *(G-3330)*
Trident SEC & Holdings LLC...............G....... 757 689-4560
Virginia Beach *(G-14893)*
Ventex Inc..G....... 703 787-9802
Sterling *(G-13547)*
Wearmax Inc..G....... 631 361-7222
Potomac Falls *(G-10510)*

BAGS: Trash, Plastic Film, Made From Purchased Materials

Monalisa Blakeney..............................G....... 703 863-8530
Annandale *(G-775)*

BAGS: Wardrobe, Closet Access, Made From Purchased Materials

Built In Style LLC...............................G....... 703 753-8518
Haymarket *(G-6416)*

BAIT, FISHING, WHOLESALE

Virginia Guide Bait Co.........................G....... 804 590-2991
Chesterfield *(G-3539)*

BAKERIES, COMMERCIAL: On Premises Baking Only

A & B Bakery.......................................G....... 540 965-5500
Covington *(G-3776)*
Annabs Gluten Free LLC......................G....... 804 491-9288
Mechanicsville *(G-8604)*
Authentic Baking Company LLC...........G....... 803 422-9282
Ashland *(G-1374)*
Beautifully Made Cupcakes.................G....... 757 287-0024
Chesapeake *(G-2996)*
Blue Castle Cupcakes LLC..................G....... 757 618-0600
Virginia Beach *(G-14289)*

Bowwowmeow Baking Company LLC.G....... 757 636-7922
Virginia Beach *(G-14298)*
Cargotrike Cupcakes...........................G....... 804 245-0786
Midlothian *(G-8791)*
Carlas Cupcakes LLC..........................G....... 703 582-7615
Herndon *(G-6635)*
Country Baking LLC............................G....... 540 592-7422
Upperville *(G-13966)*
Cupcake Company...............................G....... 540 810-0795
Elkton *(G-4324)*
Cupcake Cottage LLC..........................G....... 540 330-8504
Daleville *(G-3942)*
Cupcakes and Lace LLC......................G....... 703 378-1525
Chantilly *(G-2400)*
Cupcakes and More LLC......................G....... 804 305-2350
Richmond *(G-11171)*
Cupcakes By Cheryl LLC.....................G....... 757 592-4185
Dutton *(G-4270)*
Cupcakes By Ladybug LLC..................G....... 571 926-9709
Springfield *(G-12984)*
Cupcakes On Move LLC......................G....... 804 477-6754
Richmond *(G-11548)*
Flowers Bakeries LLC.........................G....... 757 424-4860
Virginia Beach *(G-14467)*
Flowers Bakeries LLC.........................E....... 540 343-8165
Roanoke *(G-12088)*
Flowers Bakeries LLC.........................G....... 434 572-6340
South Boston *(G-12768)*
Flowers Bakeries LLC.........................G....... 757 539-2898
Suffolk *(G-13711)*
Flowers Baking Co Norfolk LLC...........G....... 757 873-0066
Newport News *(G-9231)*
Flowers Baking Co Norfolk LLC...........G....... 757 596-1443
Yorktown *(G-15960)*
Flowers Bkg Co Lynchburg LLC...........G....... 434 392-8134
Farmville *(G-4940)*
Flowers Bkg Co Lynchburg LLC...........G....... 434 528-0441
Ashland *(G-1418)*
Flowers Bkg Co Lynchburg LLC...........G....... 540 344-5919
Roanoke *(G-12090)*
Flowers Bkg Co Lynchburg LLC...........G....... 540 434-4439
Harrisonburg *(G-6316)*
Flowers Bkg Co Lynchburg LLC...........G....... 276 647-8767
Collinsville *(G-3711)*
Flowers Bkg Co Lynchburg LLC...........G....... 434 978-4104
Charlottesville *(G-2632)*
Flowers Bkg Co Lynchburg LLC...........G....... 540 886-1582
Staunton *(G-13260)*
Flowers Bkg Co Lynchburg LLC...........G....... 434 385-5044
Lynchburg *(G-7712)*
Flowers Bkg Co Lynchburg LLC...........G....... 276 666-2008
Martinsville *(G-8287)*
Flowers Bkg Co Lynchburg LLC...........G....... 540 371-1480
Fredericksburg *(G-5289)*
Fmp Inc..G....... 434 392-3222
Henrico *(G-6513)*
Heavenly Sent Cupcakes LLC..............G....... 540 219-2162
Boston *(G-1904)*
J S & A Cake Decoration......................G....... 703 494-3767
Woodbridge *(G-15727)*
Jj S Cupcakes and More......................G....... 319 333-8020
Troutville *(G-13913)*
Joy of Cupcakes LLC..........................G....... 703 440-0204
Springfield *(G-13029)*
Kics Cupcakes LLC.............................G....... 202 630-5727
Vienna *(G-14078)*
Kimberlys..G....... 703 448-7298
Mc Lean *(G-8480)*
Kind Cupcakes....................................G....... 703 723-6167
Ashburn *(G-1303)*
Levain Baking Studio Inc.....................G....... 434 249-5875
Troy *(G-13931)*
Lidl Us LLC..G....... 757 420-1562
Virginia Beach *(G-14608)*
Lucia Coates..G....... 434 384-1779
Lynchburg *(G-7759)*
Maxilicious Baking Company LLC.........G....... 703 448-1788
Vienna *(G-14089)*
Mo Cakes...G....... 804 349-8634
Glen Allen *(G-5771)*
Mscbakes LLC.....................................G....... 434 214-0838
Farmville *(G-4953)*
Pepperidge Farm Distributor................G....... 540 395-4233
Charlottesville *(G-2845)*
Pink Cupcake.......................................G....... 801 349-6301
Fredericksburg *(G-5346)*
Proof of Life Baking LLC.....................G....... 571 721-8031
Woodbridge *(G-15785)*
Proper Pie Co LLC..............................G....... 804 343-7437
Richmond *(G-11338)*

Punkins Cupcake Cones ....G...... 757 395-0295
Virginia Beach *(G-14748)*

Random Acts of Cupcakes ....G...... 540 974-3948
Winchester *(G-15578)*

Rockfish Baking Company LLC ....G...... 703 314-7944
Afton *(G-88)*

Solo Per Te Baked Goods Inc ....G...... 804 277-9010
North Chesterfield *(G-9983)*

Spotcity Cupcakes LLC ....G...... 703 587-4934
Fredericksburg *(G-5367)*

Sweet Tooth Bakery Inc ....G...... 540 667-6155
Winchester *(G-15589)*

BAKERIES: On Premises Baking & Consumption

E-Tron Systems Inc ....E...... 703 690-2731
Lorton *(G-7482)*

Ms Jos Petite Sweets LLC ....G...... 571 327-9431
Alexandria *(G-286)*

Sweet Tooth Bakery Inc ....G...... 540 667-6155
Winchester *(G-15589)*

BAKERY FOR HOME SVC DELIVERY

A Taste of LLC ....G...... 540 848-3186
Fredericksburg *(G-5395)*

BAKERY MACHINERY

AMF Automation Tech LLC ....C...... 804 355-7961
Richmond *(G-11110)*

Haas Machinery Amer Inc Franz ....F...... 804 222-6022
Richmond *(G-11229)*

Tromp Group Americas LLC ....G...... 800 225-3771
Richmond *(G-11421)*

BAKERY PRDTS: Bagels, Fresh Or Frozen

Bageladies LLC ....G...... 540 248-0908
Charlottesville *(G-2592)*

BAKERY PRDTS: Bakery Prdts, Partially Cooked, Exc frozen

Canty Lane Confections LLC ....G...... 703 408-3661
Woodbridge *(G-15664)*

Faith Mission Home ....F...... 434 985-7177
Free Union *(G-5506)*

Its Homeade LLC ....G...... 804 641-8248
Kinsale *(G-7135)*

Perfect Pink LLC ....G...... 571 969-7465
Arlington *(G-1105)*

Pure Pasty Company LLC ....G...... 703 255-7147
Vienna *(G-14117)*

BAKERY PRDTS: Biscuits, Baked, Baking Powder & Raised

Hampton Roads Baking Co LLC ....G...... 757 622-0347
Norfolk *(G-9569)*

BAKERY PRDTS: Bread, All Types, Fresh Or Frozen

Flowers Baking Co Oxford Inc ....G...... 610 932-2300
Chantilly *(G-2422)*

Flowers Bkg Co Lynchburg LLC ....G...... 434 528-0441
Roanoke *(G-12089)*

Flowers Bkg Co Lynchburg LLC ....E...... 434 528-0441
Lynchburg *(G-7711)*

Kim Brj Inc ....G...... 703 642-2367
Alexandria *(G-505)*

BAKERY PRDTS: Cakes, Bakery, Exc Frozen

Arif Winter ....G...... 757 515-9940
Norfolk *(G-9444)*

Bakers Crust Inc ....G...... 757 253-2787
Williamsburg *(G-15208)*

Bellash Bakery Inc ....G...... 516 468-2312
Woodbridge *(G-15655)*

Cake Passion Custom Cakes LLC ....G...... 757 982-0928
Machipongo *(G-7845)*

Cakebatters LLC ....G...... 276 685-6731
Bristol *(G-1968)*

Cassandras Grmet Classics Corp ....F...... 703 590-7900
Manassas *(G-7924)*

Dessies Delicious Desserts LLC ....G...... 804 822-7482
Prince George *(G-10591)*

Donut Diva LLC ....G...... 276 245-5987
Tazewell *(G-13831)*

Elaines Cakes Inc ....G...... 804 748-2461
Chester *(G-3410)*

Euphoric Treatz LLC ....G...... 757 504-4174
Virginia Beach *(G-14453)*

Flavorful Bakery & Cafe LLC ....G...... 301 857-2202
Woodbridge *(G-15704)*

Frosted Muffin - A Cupcakery ....G...... 571 989-1722
Woodbridge *(G-15708)*

Glazed & Twisted LLC ....G...... 703 789-5522
Gainesville *(G-5586)*

Harris Kayla ....G...... 540 285-0495
Roanoke *(G-12100)*

Heavenly Kakes LLC ....G...... 804 874-3711
Chester *(G-3421)*

Mzgoodiez LLC ....G...... 757 535-6929
Suffolk *(G-13747)*

Robin Stippich ....G...... 757 692-5744
Newport News *(G-9329)*

Sunbeam Bakeries ....G...... 276 647-8767
Collinsville *(G-3717)*

Tammy Haire ....G...... 540 722-7246
Winchester *(G-15487)*

Viva La Cupcake ....G...... 540 400-0806
Roanoke *(G-12224)*

Whisk ....G...... 804 728-1576
Richmond *(G-11828)*

Zosaro LLC ....G...... 804 564-9450
Henrico *(G-6593)*

BAKERY PRDTS: Cakes, Bakery, Frozen

Creations From Heart LLC ....G...... 757 234-4300
Seaford *(G-12673)*

Fat Mltons Sthern Swets Treats ....G...... 804 248-4175
North Chesterfield *(G-9871)*

Little Corners Petit Fours LLC ....G...... 571 215-4255
Sterling *(G-13443)*

Mzgoodiez LLC ....G...... 757 535-6929
Suffolk *(G-13747)*

BAKERY PRDTS: Cones, Ice Cream

Charm School LLC ....G...... 415 999-9496
Richmond *(G-11524)*

BAKERY PRDTS: Cookies

Albemarle Edibles LLC ....G...... 434 242-5567
Charlottesville *(G-2723)*

Frito-Lay North America Inc ....E...... 540 380-3020
Salem *(G-12508)*

Interbake Foods LLC ....G...... 605 232-4903
Richmond *(G-11619)*

Interbake Foods LLC ....B...... 540 631-8100
Front Royal *(G-5537)*

McKee Foods Corporation ....A...... 540 943-7101
Stuarts Draft *(G-13655)*

Mondelez Global LLC ....D...... 757 925-3011
Suffolk *(G-13745)*

Mothers Macaroons ....G...... 703 532-0104
Arlington *(G-1068)*

Murray Biscuit Company LLC ....C...... 757 547-0249
Chesapeake *(G-3214)*

Snyders-Lance Inc ....B...... 703 339-0541
Lorton *(G-7531)*

BAKERY PRDTS: Cookies & crackers

Crispery of Virginia LLC ....G...... 757 673-5234
Portsmouth *(G-10413)*

Glamorous Sweet ....G...... 540 903-3683
Fredericksburg *(G-5435)*

Kendras Cookies ....G...... 540 660-5645
Front Royal *(G-5539)*

Nightingale Inc ....G...... 804 332-7018
Henrico *(G-6544)*

BAKERY PRDTS: Doughnuts, Exc Frozen

Rva Coffee LLC ....G...... 804 822-2015
Richmond *(G-11750)*

BAKERY PRDTS: Dry

Black Alder Trail LLC ....G...... 812 219-1975
Winchester *(G-15531)*

Montemorano LLC ....G...... 540 272-6390
Sumerduck *(G-13792)*

BAKERY PRDTS: Frozen

Sugarland Run Pantries ....G...... 571 216-8565
Herndon *(G-6816)*

Triple Y Premium Yogurt ....G...... 804 212-5413
Richmond *(G-11795)*

BAKERY PRDTS: Pies, Bakery, Frozen

Joyebells LLC ....G...... 804 304-7695
Richmond *(G-11637)*

BAKERY PRDTS: Pies, Exc Frozen

KORA Confections LLC ....G...... 240 478-2222
King George *(G-7098)*

BAKERY PRDTS: Pretzels

Marlor Inc ....F...... 804 378-5071
North Chesterfield *(G-9923)*

BAKERY PRDTS: Rice Cakes

Hanguk Rice Cake Mark ....G...... 757 874-4150
Newport News *(G-9244)*

BAKERY PRDTS: Wholesalers

Perfect Pink LLC ....G...... 571 969-7465
Arlington *(G-1105)*

BAKERY PRDTS: Yeast Goods, Sweet, Frozen

Bright Yeast Labs LLC ....G...... 205 790-2544
Dulles *(G-4194)*

BAKERY: Wholesale Or Wholesale & Retail Combined

Bakefully Yours LLC ....G...... 540 229-6232
Marshall *(G-8250)*

Bakefully Yours LLC ....G...... 301 276-4972
Manassas *(G-8034)*

Bimbo Bakeries ....G...... 804 475-6776
Alexandria *(G-423)*

Bimbo Bakeries USA ....G...... 434 525-2947
Lynchburg *(G-7654)*

Black Rabbit Delights LLC ....G...... 757 453-3359
Norfolk *(G-9465)*

Carriage House Products Inc ....G...... 804 615-2400
Henrico *(G-6488)*

Charm School LLC ....G...... 415 999-9496
Richmond *(G-11524)*

Countryside Bakery ....G...... 540 948-7888
Aroda *(G-1224)*

Creggers Cakes & Catering ....G...... 276 646-8739
Chilhowie *(G-3549)*

Danville Donuts LLC ....G...... 434 835-4592
Danville *(G-3978)*

Flowers Bkg Co Jamestown LLC ....G...... 276 236-5009
Galax *(G-5633)*

Flowers Bkg Co Lynchburg LLC ....D...... 434 528-0441
Lynchburg *(G-7710)*

French Bread Factory Inc ....F...... 703 761-4070
Sterling *(G-13402)*

Goodwin Creek Farm & Bakery ....G...... 434 260-1135
Afton *(G-82)*

Gumax International Ltd ....E...... 866 412-3880
Woodbridge *(G-15719)*

Lidl Us LLC ....G...... 757 368-0256
Virginia Beach *(G-14609)*

Maribeths Bakery Inc ....E...... 703 739-5839
Alexandria *(G-522)*

Marjories Cookie Shop LLC ....G...... 901 205-9055
Arlington *(G-1053)*

Martin Tonya ....G...... 804 742-8721
La Crosse *(G-7146)*

Panaderia Latina ....F...... 703 642-5200
Alexandria *(G-548)*

River City Chocolate LLC ....G...... 804 317-8161
Midlothian *(G-8890)*

Sani LLC ....G...... 703 596-2296
Lorton *(G-7528)*

Sub Rosa LLC ....G...... 703 338-3344
Clifton *(G-3676)*

Sugar & Salt LLC ....G...... 434 996-2329
Virginia Beach *(G-14858)*

Sweet Success Cupcakes ....G...... 703 674-9442
Fairfax *(G-4565)*

Tea Spot Catering LLC ....G...... 757 427-3525
Virginia Beach *(G-14867)*

PRODUCT

BALANCES EXC LABORATORY WHOLESALERS

Balancemaster Inc ....G....... 434 258-5078
Concord *(G-3755)*

BALERS

Bh Cooper Farm & Mill Inc ....G....... 276 694-6292
Critz *(G-3823)*
Frye Delance ....G....... 540 923-4581
Etlan *(G-4373)*

BANDS: Plastic

Dynaric Inc ....D....... 757 460-3725
Virginia Beach *(G-14423)*
Gd Packaging LLC ....G....... 703 946-8100
Vienna *(G-14060)*

BANKS: Foreign Trade & International

Potomac Intl Advisors LLC ....G....... 202 460-9001
Ashburn *(G-1328)*

BANNERS: Fabric

Banana Banner Inc ....F....... 703 823-5933
Alexandria *(G-144)*
R B M Enterprises Inc ....G....... 804 290-4407
Glen Allen *(G-5786)*

BAR FIXTURES: Wood

Champion Billd & Bar Stools ....G....... 703 631-8800
Fairfax *(G-4427)*

BARBECUE EQPT

Savage Transparency LLC ....G....... 760 218-6457
Chesapeake *(G-3284)*

BARGES BUILDING & REPAIR

New Age Repr & Fabrication LLC ....G....... 757 819-3887
Norfolk *(G-9659)*

BARRICADES: Metal

Cochrane USA Inc ....G....... 202 434-8163
Fredericksburg *(G-5263)*

BARS, PIPES, PLATES & SHAPES: Lead/Lead Alloy Bars, Pipe

Fred Sisson ....G....... 843 641-7155
Prince George *(G-10594)*

BARS: Concrete Reinforcing, Fabricated Steel

B & R Rebar ....F....... 800 526-1024
Richmond *(G-11497)*
Commercial Metals Company ....E....... 540 775-8501
King George *(G-7084)*
L B Foster Company ....G....... 804 722-0398
Petersburg *(G-10329)*
Mechanicsville Metal Works Inc ....F....... 804 266-5055
Mechanicsville *(G-8657)*
Rebarsolutions ....F....... 540 300-9975
Dayton *(G-4060)*
Sextons Incorporated ....G....... 276 783-4212
Atkins *(G-1520)*

BARS: Iron, Made In Steel Mills

Roanoke Electric Steel Corp ....B....... 540 342-1831
Roanoke *(G-12165)*

BASKETS, GIFT, WHOLESALE

Dorothy Prntice Armtherapy Inc ....G....... 703 657-0160
Fairfax *(G-4614)*

BATH SALTS

Ace Bath Bombs LLC ....G....... 804 839-8639
Hopewell *(G-6916)*
Knuude LLC ....G....... 571 298-1746
Charlottesville *(G-2654)*
Legit Bath Salts Online ....G....... 540 200-8618
Blacksburg *(G-1752)*
Quinns Bath Bombs LLC ....G....... 703 853-5067
Centreville *(G-2331)*

BATH SHOPS

Dorothy Prntice Armtherapy Inc ....G....... 703 657-0160
Fairfax *(G-4614)*
Precision Doors & Hardware LLC ....F....... 540 373-7300
Fredericksburg *(G-5348)*

BATTERIES: Lead Acid, Storage

Bmz Usa Inc ....F....... 757 821-8494
Virginia Beach *(G-14290)*

BATTERIES: Rechargeable

Ashlawn Energy LLC ....E....... 703 461-3600
Springfield *(G-12952)*
Flexel LLC ....F....... 301 314-1004
Falls Church *(G-4793)*
Katam Group LLC ....G....... 703 927-6268
Ashburn *(G-1301)*

BATTERIES: Storage

Atomized Pdts Group Chspake In ....F....... 757 793-2922
Chesapeake *(G-2988)*
East Penn Manufacturing Co ....G....... 540 980-1174
Pulaski *(G-10635)*
East Penn Manufacturing Co ....E....... 804 798-1771
Ashland *(G-1407)*
Encell Tech ....G....... 434 202-8370
Charlottesville *(G-2625)*
First Responder Systems LLC ....G....... 757 410-0353
Chesapeake *(G-3101)*
Integer Holdings Corporation ....B....... 540 389-7860
Salem *(G-12521)*
Nano Solutions Inc ....G....... 703 481-3321
Herndon *(G-6749)*

BATTERIES: Wet

Integer Holdings Corporation ....B....... 540 389-7860
Salem *(G-12521)*

BATTERY CHARGERS

Dometic Corporation ....C....... 804 746-1313
Mechanicsville *(G-8618)*
Edge McS LLC ....G....... 804 379-6772
Midlothian *(G-8813)*
Exide Technologies LLC ....E....... 434 975-6001
Charlottesville *(G-2629)*

BATTERY CHARGING GENERATORS

Exide Technologies LLC ....E....... 434 975-6001
Charlottesville *(G-2629)*

BEARINGS: Ball & Roller

Linear Rotary Bearings Inc ....G....... 540 261-1375
Richmond *(G-11271)*

BEAUTY & BARBER SHOP EQPT

Ahmed Industries Inc ....G....... 703 828-7180
Arlington *(G-846)*
Andrea Lewis ....G....... 804 933-4161
North Chesterfield *(G-9818)*
Beauty Pop LLC ....G....... 757 416-5858
Norfolk *(G-9460)*
Blackwater Manufacturing LLC ....G....... 804 299-3975
Ashland *(G-1382)*
Blue Ridge Yurts LLC ....G....... 540 651-8422
Pilot *(G-10356)*
Draeger Safety Diagnostics Inc ....G....... 703 517-0974
Purcellville *(G-10660)*
Kram Industries Inc ....G....... 571 220-9769
Gainesville *(G-5593)*
Patterson Business Systems ....F....... 540 389-7726
Salem *(G-12555)*
Shine Beauty Company ....G....... 757 509-7338
Newport News *(G-9336)*
Stylus Publishing LLC ....G....... 703 661-1581
Sterling *(G-13520)*

BEAUTY SALONS

Cut Check Writing Services ....G....... 757 898-9015
Yorktown *(G-15947)*

BEDDING & BEDSPRINGS STORES

Rvmf Inc ....G....... 614 921-1223
North Chesterfield *(G-9968)*

BEDDING, BEDSPREADS, BLANKETS & SHEETS

Ryan Studio Inc ....G....... 703 830-6818
Chantilly *(G-2488)*

BEDS & ACCESS STORES

Ssb Manufacturing Company ....C....... 540 891-0236
Fredericksburg *(G-5368)*

BEDS: Hospital

Kci Services LLC ....G....... 276 623-7404
Lebanon *(G-7196)*
New Richmond Ventures LLC ....G....... 804 887-2355
Richmond *(G-11688)*

BEDSPREADS & BED SETS, FROM PURCHASED MATERIALS

Laura Copenhaver Industries ....G....... 276 783-4663
Marion *(G-8230)*
Virginia Quilting Inc ....C....... 434 757-1809
La Crosse *(G-7152)*
Vqc Inc ....C....... 434 447-5091
South Hill *(G-12863)*

BEEKEEPERS' SPLYS

Alans Apary Hney Bees Svcs LL ....G....... 540 881-0405
Culpeper *(G-3863)*

BEEKEEPERS' SPLYS: Honeycomb Foundations

Valley Bee Supply Inc ....G....... 540 941-8127
Fishersville *(G-5010)*

BEER & ALE WHOLESALERS

Coors Brewing Company ....C....... 540 289-8000
Elkton *(G-4323)*
Virginia Eagle Distrg Co LLC ....G....... 434 296-5531
Charlottesville *(G-2900)*

BEER & ALE, WHOLESALE: Beer & Other Fermented Malt Liquors

Blue Mtn Brrel Hse Orgnic Brwr ....E....... 434 263-4002
Arrington *(G-1227)*

BEER, WINE & LIQUOR STORES

Blue Bee Cider LLC ....F....... 804 231-0280
Richmond *(G-11128)*

BEER, WINE & LIQUOR STORES: Wine

Cardinal Point Vineyard Winery ....G....... 540 456-8400
Afton *(G-76)*
Chateau Morrisette Inc ....E....... 540 593-2865
Floyd *(G-5018)*
Vanhuss Family Cellars LLC ....G....... 703 737-3930
Leesburg *(G-7369)*
Wintergreen Winery Ltd ....G....... 434 325-2200
Nellysford *(G-9114)*

BELTS: Conveyor, Made From Purchased Wire

Ashworth Bros Inc ....C....... 540 662-3494
Winchester *(G-15530)*
Jack Campbell Widner ....G....... 703 646-8841
Chilhowie *(G-3552)*
Maxx Material Systems LLC ....E....... 757 637-4026
Hampton *(G-6192)*
Modek Inc ....G....... 804 550-7300
Ashland *(G-1463)*
Silver Spur Conveyors ....G....... 276 596-9414
Raven *(G-10757)*

BEVERAGE BASES & SYRUPS

Chef Sous LLC ....G....... 804 938-5477
Glen Allen *(G-5712)*

BEVERAGE PRDTS: Brewers' Grain

North Lock LLC ....G....... 703 797-2739
Alexandria *(G-293)*

BEVERAGE PRDTS: Malt, By-Prdts

Stuart Forest Products LLC ....E 276 694-3842
Stuart (G-13634)

BEVERAGE, NONALCOHOLIC: Iced Tea/Fruit Drink, Bottled/Canned

Bidgood Enterprises...................G....... 434 489-4952
Danville (G-3958)
Buffalo Mountain Kombucha LLC ....G....... 540 593-2146
Willis (G-15357)
Mkp Products LLC ....G....... 703 345-0595
Springfield (G-13052)

BEVERAGES, ALCOHOLIC: Ale

Dancing Kilt Brewery LLC ....G....... 804 715-0695
Chester (G-3401)
Metal Craft Brewing Co LLC ....G....... 816 271-3211
Waynesboro (G-15126)

BEVERAGES, ALCOHOLIC: Beer

Anheuser-Busch LLC ....C...... 757 253-3600
Williamsburg (G-15203)
Anheuser-Busch Companies LLC ....G...... 757 253-3660
Williamsburg (G-15204)
Badwolf Brewery LLC ....G...... 571 208-1064
Manassas (G-7917)
Bear Chase Brewing Company LLC......G...... 703 930-7949
Bluemont (G-1885)
Billsburg Brewery LLC ....F 757 926-0981
Williamsburg (G-15211)
Black Hoof Brewing Company LLC.......G...... 571 707-8014
Leesburg (G-7232)
Blue Mountain Brewery Inc................E 540 456-8020
Afton (G-75)
Blue Mtn Brrel Hse Orgnic Brwr ....E 434 263-4002
Arrington (G-1227)
Broken Window Brewing Co LLC ....G...... 703 999-7030
Winchester (G-15532)
Cape Charles Brewing Company ....G...... 757 678-5699
Cape Charles (G-2230)
Colonial Beach Brewing LLC..............G...... 540 760-5661
Colonial Beach (G-3723)
Coors Brewing Company ....C...... 540 289-8000
Elkton (G-4323)
Crazy Rooster Brewing Co LLC ....G...... 804 464-2958
Powhatan (G-10541)
Isley Brewing Company ....G...... 804 499-0721
Richmond (G-11252)
James River Beverage Co LLC ....G...... 434 589-2798
Kents Store (G-7039)
Joker Brewing LLC ....G...... 757 814-0882
Williamsburg (G-15261)
Kindred Brothers Inc ....G...... 803 318-5097
Richmond (G-11262)
Legend Brewing Co ....E 804 232-8871
Richmond (G-11651)
Lynx Brewing Company LLC ....G...... 773 819-8748
Portsmouth (G-10455)
Pretty Ugly Distribution LLC ....G...... 757 672-8958
Chesapeake (G-3247)
Starr Hill Brewing Company ....G...... 434 823-5671
Crozet (G-3851)
Trapezium Brewing LLC ....G...... 804 677-5728
Petersburg (G-10346)
Wolffinz LLC ....E 571 292-1427
Manassas (G-8013)

BEVERAGES, ALCOHOLIC: Beer & Ale

Abbey Staunton ....G...... 540 580-1271
Staunton (G-13238)
Brewco LLC ....G...... 276 686-5448
Rural Retreat (G-12418)
Craft of Brewing ....G...... 703 687-3932
Ashburn (G-1259)
Craftsman Distillery LLC ....G...... 804 454-1514
Chesterfield (G-3487)
Damascus Brewery ....G...... 276 475-5319
Damascus (G-3947)
Det Enterprises Inc ....G...... 310 429-3234
Leesburg (G-7256)
Dry Fork Fruit Distillery LLC ....G...... 276 952-1222
Martinsville (G-8281)
Global - AB Inbev ....G...... 314 577-2000
Williamsburg (G-15247)
Kindred Brothers Inc ....G...... 210 334-7723
Midlothian (G-8839)

Kobayashi Winery ....F 757 644-4464
Hampton (G-6181)
Kombuchick Inc ....G...... 757 818-7703
Norfolk (G-9613)
Mountain View Brewery LLC................C...... 540 462-6200
Lexington (G-7404)
Old Dominion MBL Canning LLC ....G...... 804 517-1640
Glen Allen (G-5775)
Oozlefinch Craft Brewery LLC ....G...... 757 224-7042
Fort Monroe (G-5133)
Pagan River Associates LLC ....G...... 757 357-5364
Smithfield (G-12720)
Parasitx LLC ....G...... 757 653-6179
Newport News (G-9310)
River Company Rest & Brewry I...........G...... 540 633-6731
Radford (G-10738)
Siblings Rivalry Brewery LLC ....G...... 540 671-3893
Strasburg (G-13596)
Silverline Brewing Company ....G...... 703 281-5816
Vienna (G-14128)
Southpaw Brew Co LLC ....G...... 703 753-5986
Gainesville (G-5613)
Station 6 Brewing LLC ....G...... 571 510-3532
Ashburn (G-1336)
That Damn Mary Brewing LLC ....G...... 804 761-1085
Heathsville (G-6467)
Throx Brew Market and Grille ....G...... 540 323-7360
Winchester (G-15489)
Virginia Beer Company LLC ....F 770 815-8518
Williamsburg (G-15333)
Virginia Cft Brwing Spport LLC ....G...... 703 960-3230
Alexandria (G-375)

BEVERAGES, ALCOHOLIC: Bourbon Whiskey

Bowman Distillery Inc A Smith ....F 540 373-4555
Fredericksburg (G-5255)
Copper Fox Dist Entps LLC ....F 540 987-8554
Sperryville (G-12877)

BEVERAGES, ALCOHOLIC: Brandy

La ABRA Farm & Winery Inc ....G...... 434 263-5392
Lovingston (G-7591)

BEVERAGES, ALCOHOLIC: Brandy & Brandy Spirits

Laird & Company ....G...... 434 296-6058
North Garden (G-10079)

BEVERAGES, ALCOHOLIC: Brandy Spirits

Ko Distilling....................................G 571 292-1115
Manassas (G-7956)

BEVERAGES, ALCOHOLIC: Cocktails

Belle Isle Craft Spirits Inc ....G...... 518 265-7221
Richmond (G-11503)

BEVERAGES, ALCOHOLIC: Corn Whiskey

Belmont Farms of Virginia Inc ....G...... 540 825-3207
Culpeper (G-3871)

BEVERAGES, ALCOHOLIC: Distilled Liquors

8 Shires Coloniale Distillery................G...... 757 378-2456
Williamsburg (G-15198)
Barboursville Distillery LLC ....G...... 757 961-4590
Virginia Beach (G-14259)
Beam Global Spirits and ....G...... 804 763-2823
Midlothian (G-8777)
Belmont Farm Distillery ....G...... 540 825-3207
Culpeper (G-3870)
Blue Sky Distillery LLC ....G...... 757 746-8342
Smithfield (G-12705)
Blue Sky Distillery LLC ....G...... 757 234-3260
Carrollton (G-2240)
Cape Charles Distillery LLC ....F 757 291-8016
Cape Charles (G-2231)
Catoctin Creek Custom Rods LLC ....G...... 540 751-1482
Purcellville (G-10653)
Catoctin Creek Distlg Co LLC ....G...... 540 751-8404
Purcellville (G-10654)
Cavalier Ventures LLC.......................F 757 491-3000
Virginia Beach (G-14325)
Chesapeake Bay Distillery LLC ....G...... 757 692-4083
Virginia Beach (G-14334)

Copper Fox Distillery.........................F 757 903-2076
Williamsburg (G-15222)
Dead Reckoning Distillery ....G...... 757 535-9864
Norfolk (G-9519)
Dead Reckoning Distillery Inc ....G...... 757 620-3182
Chesapeake (G-3062)
Deep Creek Distilling Co LLC ....G...... 757 337-0209
Chesapeake (G-3063)
Dogged State Distilling Co ....G...... 434 480-0575
Blackstone (G-1816)
Dome and Spear Distillery LLC ....G...... 434 851-5477
Evington (G-4376)
Falls Church Distillers LLC ....F 703 858-9186
Falls Church (G-4912)
Five Mile Mountain Distillery...............G...... 540 588-3158
Floyd (G-5025)
Fox River Distilling Company ....G...... 630 402-0027
Glen Allen (G-5732)
Hill Top Distillery LLC ....G...... 804 212-8645
Glen Allen (G-5746)
Home Brewusa ....G...... 757 459-2739
Norfolk (G-9582)
Homeplace Distillery LLC ....G...... 276 957-3310
Ridgeway (G-11845)
James River Distillery LLC ....G...... 804 716-5172
Richmond (G-11627)
ONeill Distillery LLC Tf ....G...... 540 822-5812
Lovettsville (G-7584)
Reservoir Distillery LLC ....G...... 804 912-2621
Richmond (G-11351)
Springfield Distillery LLC ....G...... 434 572-1888
Halifax (G-6052)
Squabble State Distlg Co LLC ....G...... 804 393-8380
Bristol (G-1989)
Stone Mountain Distilling LLC ....G...... 276 970-4081
Lebanon (G-7208)
Three Brothers Distillery Inc................G...... 757 204-1357
Disputanta (G-4114)
Three Crosses Distilling Co LL ....G...... 804 512-9690
Powhatan (G-10581)
Three Crosses Distlg Co LLC ....G...... 804 818-6330
North Chesterfield (G-10002)
Twin Creeks Distillery Inc..................G...... 540 483-1266
Rocky Mount (G-12356)
Vanguard Brewpub & Distillery ....G...... 757 224-1807
Hampton (G-6260)
Virginia Distillery Co LLC ....G...... 703 869-0083
Arlington (G-1213)
Vitae Spirits Distillery LLC ....G...... 434 242-0350
Charlottesville (G-2903)
Whiskywrght Fine Hndcrfted Spr ....G...... 703 831-2086
Waynesboro (G-15147)
Whiskywright Fine Handcrafted ....G...... 703 398-0121
Manassas (G-8011)
Williamsburg Distillery ....G...... 757 378-2456
Williamsburg (G-15341)
Williamsburg Distillery Inc ....G...... 757 676-7950
Gloucester (G-5869)
Woods Mill Distillery LLC ....G...... 434 361-2294
Faber (G-4392)

BEVERAGES, ALCOHOLIC: Near Beer

Demons Run Brewing LLC...................G...... 703 945-8100
Arlington (G-936)

BEVERAGES, ALCOHOLIC: Neutral Spirits, Exc Fruit

Pohick Creek LLC ....G...... 202 888-2034
Springfield (G-13071)
Silverback Spirits LLC ....G...... 540 456-7070
Afton (G-89)
Square One Organic Spirits LLC ....G...... 415 612-4151
Charlottesville (G-2881)

BEVERAGES, ALCOHOLIC: Vodka

Blackbird Spirits LLC ....G...... 540 247-9115
Winchester (G-15387)

BEVERAGES, ALCOHOLIC: Wines

50 West Vineyards ....G...... 571 367-4760
Middleburg (G-8715)
Afton Mountain Vineyards Corp ....Dry G... 540 456-8667
Afton (G-73)
Altillo Vineyards & Winery ....G...... 434 324-4160
Hurt (G-6970)
Altria Group Inc ....A...... 804 274-2200
Richmond (G-11105)

Employee Codes: A=Over 500 employees, B=251-500
C=101-250, D=51-100, E=20-50, F=10-19, G=1-9

2021 Virginia
Industrial Directory

903

PRODUCT

Ambrosia Vineyards............G....703 237-8717 Falls Church *(G-4746)*	**Chateau OBrien At North Point**............G....540 364-6441 Markham *(G-8247)*	**Goodboy LLC**............G....540 421-6712 Hillsboro *(G-6869)*
Amrhein Ltd............G....540 929-4632 Bent Mountain *(G-1666)*	**Chatham Vineyards LLC**............G....757 678-5588 Machipongo *(G-7846)*	**Goose Creek Farms & Winery LLC**............G....540 338-2056 Purcellville *(G-10663)*
Anna Lake Winery Inc............G....540 895-5085 Spotsylvania *(G-12884)*	**Chestnut Oak Vineyard LLC**............G....434 964-9104 Barboursville *(G-1559)*	**Grace Estate Winery LLC**............G....434 823-1486 Crozet *(G-3833)*
Arrowine Inc............F....703 525-0990 Arlington *(G-860)*	**Cobbler Mountain Cellars**............G....540 364-2802 Delaplane *(G-4074)*	**Gray Ghost Vineyards**............G....540 937-4869 Amissville *(G-719)*
Artisan Meads LLC............G....757 713-4885 Seaford *(G-12671)*	**Continental Commercial Corp**............G....540 668-6216 Hillsboro *(G-6861)*	**Grayhaven Winery**............G....804 556-3917 Gum Spring *(G-6043)*
Ashton Creek Vineyard LLC............G....804 896-1586 Chester *(G-3388)*	**Cooper Vineyards LLC**............G....540 894-5474 Louisa *(G-7550)*	**Greenhill Winery and Vineyards**............G....540 687-6968 Middleburg *(G-8721)*
Aspen Dale Winery Barn............G....540 364-1722 Delaplane *(G-4072)*	**Courthouse Creek Cider**............G....804 543-3157 Maidens *(G-7888)*	**Hall White Vineyards**............G....434 823-8615 Crozet *(G-3836)*
Attimo Group LLC............F....540 838-1118 Christiansburg *(G-3570)*	**Creeks Edge Winery**............G....540 822-3825 Lovettsville *(G-7577)*	**Hambsch Family Vineyard LLC**............G....434 996-1987 Afton *(G-84)*
Barns & Vineyards LLC............G....703 801-2719 Ashburn *(G-1245)*	**Cresta Gadino Winery LLC**............G....540 987-9292 Washington *(G-15075)*	**Hampton Roads Winery LLC**............G....757 899-0203 Elberon *(G-4318)*
Barrel Oak Winery LLC............E....540 364-6402 Delaplane *(G-4073)*	**Cross Keys Vineyards LLC**............F....540 234-0505 Mount Crawford *(G-9053)*	**Harmony Creek Vineyards LLC**............G....540 338-7677 Hamilton *(G-6060)*
Barren Ridge Vineyards LLC............G....540 248-3300 Fishersville *(G-5001)*	**Crushed Cellars LLC**............G....571 374-9463 Hillsboro *(G-6863)*	**Hartwood Winery Inc**............G....540 752-4893 Fredericksburg *(G-5439)*
Beliveau Development Corp............G....540 961-0505 Blacksburg *(G-1725)*	**Cunningham Creek Winery LLC**............G....434 207-3907 Palmyra *(G-10247)*	**Hickory Hill Vineyards LLC**............G....540 296-1393 Moneta *(G-8965)*
Beliveau Estate Vnyrd Wnery LL............G....540 961-2102 Blacksburg *(G-1726)*	**Delaplane Sellers**............G....540 592-7210 Delaplane *(G-4075)*	**Hill Top Berry Frm & Winery Lc**............F....434 361-1266 Nellysford *(G-9113)*
Blue Quartz Winery LLC............G....540 923-4048 Etlan *(G-4372)*	**Delfosse Vineyards Winery LLC**............G....434 263-6100 Faber *(G-4389)*	**Homeplace Vineyard Inc**............G....434 432-9463 Chatham *(G-2930)*
Blue Ridge Vineyard Inc............G....540 798-7642 Eagle Rock *(G-4279)*	**Desert Rose Ranch & Winery LLC**............G....540 635-3200 Hume *(G-6960)*	**Honey Haleys Meadery LLC**............G....804 668-5943 Hopewell *(G-6929)*
Bluemont............G....202 422-6500 Bluemont *(G-1886)*	**Devault Vineyards LLC**............G....434 993-0722 Concord *(G-3759)*	**Hope Crushed Vineyard LLC**............G....540 668-6587 Hillsboro *(G-6870)*
Bluestone Vineyard Inc............E....540 828-0099 Bridgewater *(G-1949)*	**Dombroski Vineyards LLC**............G....804 932-8240 New Kent *(G-9130)*	**Horton Cellars Winery Inc**............F....540 832-7440 Gordonsville *(G-5908)*
Blumont Vineyards............G....540 554-8439 Bluemont *(G-1887)*	**Doukenie Winery**............G....540 668-6464 Hillsboro *(G-6864)*	**Hunters Run Winery LLC**............G....703 926-4183 Hamilton *(G-6061)*
Bodie Vineyards LLC............G....804 598-2240 Powhatan *(G-10534)*	**Dragonsrealm Vineyard LLC**............G....540 905-9679 Goldvein *(G-5877)*	**Hunting Creek Vineyards Co**............G....434 454-9219 Clover *(G-3692)*
Bogati Bodgea............G....540 338-1144 Round Hill *(G-12375)*	**DRG Imports LLC**............G....786 246-6548 Richmond *(G-11569)*	**Hunts Family Vineyard LLC**............G....540 942-8689 Stuarts Draft *(G-13652)*
Boxwood Winery LLC............G....540 687-8778 Middleburg *(G-8716)*	**Dry Mill Rd LLC**............G....703 737-3697 Leesburg *(G-7261)*	**IL Dolce Winery**............G....804 647-0414 Alexandria *(G-234)*
Branches Tasting Room............G....757 620-5393 Chesapeake *(G-3015)*	**Ducard Vineyards Inc**............G....434 409-4378 Charlottesville *(G-2620)*	**Imperial Revival LLC**............G....540 326-8189 Middleburg *(G-8723)*
Breaux Vineyards Ltd............G....540 668-6299 Hillsboro *(G-6860)*	**Effingham Manor LLC**............G....703 594-2300 Broad Run *(G-2067)*	**International Wine Spirits Ltd**............A....804 274-1432 Richmond *(G-11251)*
Brent Manor Inn & Vineyards............G....540 226-5958 Faber *(G-4388)*	**Elk Island Winery**............G....540 967-0944 Goochland *(G-5882)*	**Iron Heart Winery LLC**............G....540 320-0203 Allisonia *(G-618)*
Brian Allison............G....276 988-9792 Tazewell *(G-13828)*	**Emerald Lake Vineyard**............G....540 270-3399 Hillsboro *(G-6865)*	**Jump Mountain Vineyard**............G....540 348-6730 Rockbridge Baths *(G-12235)*
Briede Family Vineyards LLC............G....540 667-2981 Winchester *(G-15393)*	**Eric Trump Wine Mfg LLC**............E....434 977-3895 Charlottesville *(G-2791)*	**Jump Mountain Vineyard LLC**............G....434 296-2226 Charlottesville *(G-2821)*
Bright Meadows Farm............G....434 349-9463 Nathalie *(G-9102)*	**Exclusive Wine Imports LLC**............G....703 765-9749 Alexandria *(G-458)*	**Kalero Vineyard LLC**............G....703 216-9036 Hillsboro *(G-6873)*
Brix 22 Ankida Rdge Tasting Rm............G....434 989-7420 Charlottesville *(G-2750)*	**Fabbioli Cellars**............G....703 771-1197 Leesburg *(G-7271)*	**Karam Winery**............G....703 573-3886 Dunn Loring *(G-4264)*
Brix and Columns Vineyards LLC............G....540 810-0566 Mc Gaheysville *(G-8377)*	**Faithbrooke Barn Vineyards LLC**............G....540 743-1207 Luray *(G-7611)*	**Keswick Vineyard**............G....434 295-1834 Keswick *(G-7049)*
Brook Hidden Winery LLC............G....703 737-3935 Leesburg *(G-7237)*	**Fedor Ventures LLC**............G....540 668-6248 Hillsboro *(G-6866)*	**Keswick Vineyards LLC**............F....434 244-3341 Keswick *(G-7050)*
Byrd Cellars LLC............G....804 652-5663 Goochland *(G-5880)*	**Fincastle Vineyard & Winery**............G....540 591-9000 Fincastle *(G-4996)*	**Keswick Winery LLC**............G....434 244-3341 Keswick *(G-7051)*
Cana Cellars Inc............F....540 635-9398 Huntly *(G-6964)*	**First Colony Winery Ltd**............G....434 979-7105 Charlottesville *(G-2795)*	**Kilaurwen Ltd**............G....434 985-2535 Stanardsville *(G-13220)*
Cana Vineyards Winery............G....703 348-2458 Middleburg *(G-8717)*	**Five Grapes LLC**............G....703 205-2444 Sterling *(G-13398)*	**Kindred Pointe Stables LLC**............G....540 477-3570 Mount Jackson *(G-9074)*
Cardinal Point Vineyard Winery............G....540 456-8400 Afton *(G-76)*	**Fleetwood Farm Winery LLC**............E....703 722-2124 Leesburg *(G-7274)*	**King Family Vineyards LLC**............G....434 823-7800 Crozet *(G-3840)*
Caret Cellars and Vineyard LLC............G....540 413-6454 Caret *(G-2238)*	**Flying Fox Vineyard Lc**............G....434 361-1692 Afton *(G-81)*	**Lazy Days Winery**............G....804 437-3453 Midlothian *(G-8845)*
Casanel Vineyards............G....540 751-1776 Leesburg *(G-7241)*	**Foggy Ridge Cider**............G....276 398-2337 Dugspur *(G-4188)*	**Lee Savoy Inc**............G....540 297-9275 Huddleston *(G-6955)*
Castle Glen Esttes Frm Wnery L............G....804 763-9677 Doswell *(G-4118)*	**Foster Jackson LLC**............G....540 436-9463 Maurertown *(G-8363)*	**Leogrand Vinyards**............G....540 586-4066 Goode *(G-5892)*
Castle Gruen Vnyrds Winery LLC............G....540 229-2498 Locust Dale *(G-7440)*	**Fox Meadow Farms LLC**............G....540 636-6777 Linden *(G-7428)*	**Lexington Valley Vineyard**............G....540 462-2974 Rockbridge Baths *(G-12236)*
Castle Vineyards LLC............G....571 283-7150 Luray *(G-7604)*	**Furnace Mountain Vineyards LLC**............G....571 439-2255 Waterford *(G-15080)*	**Lost and Found Winery**............G....707 321-6292 Virginia Beach *(G-14624)*
Cedar Creek Valley Farm LLC............G....540 533-2259 Star Tannery *(G-13235)*	**Gallagher Estate Vineyards LLC**............G....301 252-3450 Hamilton *(G-6058)*	**Lost Creek Vineyard**............F....703 443-9836 Leesburg *(G-7304)*
Cedar Creek Winery LLC............G....540 436-8357 Star Tannery *(G-13236)*	**Gauthier Vineyard LLC**............G....703 622-1107 Barhamsville *(G-1571)*	**Lovingston Winery**............G....925 286-2824 Ruckersville *(G-12404)*
Charles James Winery & Vinyrd............G....540 931-4386 Winchester *(G-15400)*	**Generals Ridge Vineyard**............G....804 472-3172 Hague *(G-6046)*	**Lovington Winery LLC**............G....434 263-8467 Lovingston *(G-7592)*
Charlottesville Vineyard............G....434 321-8463 Charlottesville *(G-2764)*	**Gh Winery LLC**............F....804 737-7416 Madison *(G-12616)*	**Madison County Wines LLC**............F....540 948-9005 Madison *(G-7858)*
Chateau Merrillanne LLC............G....540 656-6177 Orange *(G-10206)*	**Glass House Winery LLC**............F....434 975-0094 Free Union *(G-5507)*	**Maggie Malick Wine Caves LLC**............G....540 905-2921 Hillsboro *(G-6875)*
Chateau Morrisette Inc............E....540 593-2865 Floyd *(G-5018)*	**Glen Manor Vineyards LLC**............G....540 635-6324 Front Royal *(G-5533)*	**Mediterranean Cellars LLC**............G....540 428-1984 Warrenton *(G-15034)*

(G-0000) Company's Geographic Section entry number

Mendes Deli Inc ....G 703 242-9463
  Vienna (G-14090)
Mermaid Vineyard & Winery LLC ....G 757 233-4155
  Norfolk (G-9639)
Michael Shaps Winery Managemen ....E 434 242-4559
  Charlottesville (G-2834)
Molon Lave Vineyards & Winery ......G 540 439-5460
  Warrenton (G-15035)
Montesquieu Inc ....G 703 518-9975
  Alexandria (G-281)
Montifalco Vineyard ....G 434 989-9115
  Ruckersville (G-12406)
Morais Vineyards and Winery ....G 540 439-9520
  Bealeton (G-1601)
Moss Vineyards LLC ....G 434 990-0111
  Dyke (G-4276)
Mountain and Vine LLC ....G 434 263-6100
  Faber (G-4390)
Mountain Run Winery LLC ....G 703 638-5559
  Culpeper (G-3911)
Mountain View Vineyard ....G 540 683-3200
  Strasburg (G-13591)
Mountfair Vineyards LLC ....G 434 823-7605
  Crozet (G-3845)
Mt Chestnut Vineyards LLC ....G 540 400-6442
  Roanoke (G-11971)
Muse Vineyards LLC ....G 540 459-7033
  Woodstock (G-15858)
Narmada Winery LLC ....F 540 937-8215
  Amissville (G-720)
New River Vineyard & Winery ....G 540 392-4870
  Fairlawn (G-4739)
Notaviva Vineyards ....G 540 668-6756
  Hillsboro (G-6877)
Oak Crest Vineyard & Winery ....G 540 663-2813
  King George (G-7105)
Old House Vineyards LLC ....G 540 423-1032
  Culpeper (G-3913)
Olde Virginia Cidery LLC ....G 901 626-0535
  Richmond (G-11314)
Pearmund Cellars ....F 540 347-3475
  Broad Run (G-2069)
Pippin HI Frm & Vineyards LLC ....G 434 202-8063
  North Garden (G-10082)
Potomac Cellars LLC ....E 540 446-2266
  Stafford (G-13179)
Preston Rdge Wnery Brewing Inc ....G 276 634-8752
  Martinsville (G-8320)
PWC Winery LLC ....G 703 753-9360
  Haymarket (G-6438)
Quartz Creek Vineyards LLC ....G 571 239-9120
  Waterford (G-15082)
Quattro Goombas Winery ....G 703 327-6052
  Aldie (G-110)
Rebec Vineyards Inc ....G 434 946-5168
  Amherst (G-707)
Rivah Vineyards At Grove LLC ....G 804 472-3734
  Kinsale (G-7137)
Rockbridge Vineyard Inc ....F 540 377-6204
  Raphine (G-10750)
Rosa Darby Winery LLC ....G 804 561-7492
  Amelia Court House (G-671)
Rosemont of Virginia LLC ....G 434 636-4372
  La Crosse (G-7150)
Rural Rtreat Wnery Vnyards LLC ......G 276 686-8300
  Rural Retreat (G-12431)
Saga Meadery LLC ....G 914 343-0394
  Arlington (G-1155)
Sassafras Shade Vineyard LLC ......G 804 337-9446
  Ruther Glen (G-12461)
Seven Oaks Farm LLC ....G 303 653-3299
  Greenwood (G-6000)
Shigol Makkoli Winery ....G 646 594-7405
  Manassas (G-8155)
Silhouette Vineyards LLC ....G 540 668-6000
  Hillsboro (G-6879)
Silver Hand Winery LLC ....G 757 378-2225
  Williamsburg (G-15311)
Skippers Creek Vineyard LLC ....G 804 598-7291
  Powhatan (G-10578)
Slater Run Vineyards LLC ....G 540 878-1476
  Upperville (G-13968)
Slater Run Vneyards Tasting Rm ......G 540 592-3042
  Upperville (G-13969)
Spring Run Vineyards LLC ....G 804 382-4529
  Chesterfield (G-3528)
Ss Winery LLC ....G 908 548-3016
  Stafford (G-13194)
Stanburn Winery LLC ....G 276 694-7074
  Stuart (G-13631)

Statice Quo LLC ....G 703 646-5411
  Lorton (G-7534)
Stillhouse Vineyards LLC ....G 434 293-8221
  Hume (G-6963)
Stone Mountain Vineyards LLC ....G 434 990-9463
  Dyke (G-4277)
Stoney Brook Vnyrds Winery LLC ....G 703 932-2619
  Troutville (G-13918)
Sugarleaf Vineyards ....G 434 984-4272
  North Garden (G-10083)
Sunset Hills Vineyard LLC ....G 540 882-4560
  Purcellville (G-10681)
Sweely Estate Winery ....G 540 948-7603
  Madison (G-7863)
Tarara ....F 703 771-7100
  Leesburg (G-7359)
Ten Sisters Wine LLC ....G 202 577-9774
  Alexandria (G-595)
Thibaut-Janisson LLC ....G 434 996-3307
  Charlottesville (G-2889)
Thistle and Stag Meadery ....G 434 842-2200
  Fork Union (G-5113)
Thistle Gate Vineyard LLC ....G 434 286-2428
  Scottsville (G-12668)
Turk Mountain Vineyards ....G 540 456-8252
  Afton (G-93)
Twin Oaks Tavern Winery ....G 540 554-4547
  Bluemont (G-1892)
Two Twisted Posts Winery LLC ......G 540 668-6587
  Hillsboro (G-6880)
Upper Shirley Vineyards ....E 804 829-9463
  Charles City (G-2581)
Valerie Hill Farm LLC ....G 540 869-9567
  Stephens City (G-13325)
Valhalla Vineyards ....G 540 725-9463
  Roanoke (G-12016)
Vanhuss Family Cellars LLC ....G 703 737-3930
  Leesburg (G-7369)
Vault Field Vineyards LLC ....G 804 472-4430
  Kinsale (G-7138)
Veramar Vineyard LLC ....G 540 955-5510
  Berryville (G-1699)
Veritas Works LLC ....F 540 456-8000
  Afton (G-94)
Villa Appalaccia Winery ....G 540 593-3100
  Floyd (G-5045)
Village Winery ....G 540 882-3780
  Waterford (G-15083)
Vincents Vineyard Inc ....G 276 889-2505
  Lebanon (G-7210)
Vineyard Engravers Inc ....G 703 941-3700
  Annandale (G-791)
Vineyard Services ....G 434 964-8270
  Charlottesville (G-2712)
Vineyards ....G 804 580-4053
  Wicomico Church (G-15196)
Vinifera Distributing Virginia ....G 804 261-2890
  Springfield (G-13106)
Vint Hill Craft Winery LLC ....G 540 341-1862
  Broad Run (G-2071)
Vintners Cllar Winery Yorktown ......G 757 223-4261
  Yorktown (G-15998)
Virginia Beach Winery LLC ....G 757 995-4315
  Virginia Beach (G-14915)
Virginia Mountain Vineyards LL ......G 540 473-2979
  Fincastle (G-4999)
Virginia Wine Pass LLC ....G 540 376-7902
  Fredericksburg (G-5234)
Virginia Wineworks LLC ....G 434 923-8314
  Charlottesville (G-2902)
Welcome To Beaulieu Vineyard ......G 707 967-5233
  Arlington (G-1217)
Well Hung Vineyard ....G 434 245-0182
  Charlottesville (G-2905)
West Wind Farm Inc ....G 276 699-2020
  Max Meadows (G-8371)
Whitebarrel Winery ....G 540 382-7619
  Christiansburg (G-3617)
Willard Elledge ....G 540 984-3375
  Edinburg (G-4317)
Williamsburg Winery Ltd ....E 757 229-0999
  Williamsburg (G-15343)
Willowcroft Farm Vineyards ....G 703 777-8161
  Leesburg (G-7379)
Windham Winery On Windham Farm ..G 540 668-6464
  Hillsboro (G-6881)
Winding Road Cellars LLC ....G 540 364-1025
  Markham (G-8248)
Winebow Inc ....G 800 365-9463
  Glen Allen (G-5829)

Winebow Group LLC ....G 804 752-3670
  Ashland (G-1512)
Winery At Bull Run LLC ....G 703 815-2233
  Centreville (G-2353)
Winery At Kindred Pointe LLC ....G 540 481-6016
  Mount Jackson (G-9083)
Winery At Lagrange ....G 703 753-9360
  Haymarket (G-6454)
Winery Inc ....G 703 683-1876
  Alexandria (G-611)
Wintergreen Winery Ltd ....G 434 325-2200
  Nellysford (G-9114)
Wisdom Oak Winery ....G 434 984-4272
  North Garden (G-10084)
Zoll Bros Private Cellars LLC ....F 857 498-1665
  Dutton (G-4275)

BEVERAGES, BEER & ALE, WHOLESALE: Ale

Metal Craft Brewing Co LLC ....G 816 271-3211
  Waynesboro (G-15126)

BEVERAGES, NONALCOHOLIC: Bottled & canned soft drinks

3300 Artesian Bot Wtr Co LLC ....F 276 928-9903
  Bland (G-1834)
Bellvue Corp ....G 276 806-4418
  Portsmouth (G-10398)
Cadbury Schweppes Bottlin ....G 276 228-7990
  Wytheville (G-15881)
Canada Dry Potomac Corporation ....D 757 464-1771
  Virginia Beach (G-14312)
Canada Dry Potomac Corporation ....E 804 231-7777
  Richmond (G-11517)
Canada Dry Potomac Corporation ....C 703 321-6100
  Springfield (G-12971)
Ccbcc Operations LLC ....C 540 343-8041
  Roanoke (G-12060)
Change Cola Inc ....G 703 674-9830
  Roanoke (G-12063)
Coca Cola Enterprises ....F 703 578-6447
  Alexandria (G-166)
Coca-Cola Bottling ....G 800 241-2653
  Alexandria (G-167)
Coca-Cola Consolidated Inc ....D 540 886-2494
  Staunton (G-13248)
Coca-Cola Consolidated Inc ....D 540 361-7500
  Fredericksburg (G-5413)
Coca-Cola Consolidated Inc ....D 757 890-8700
  Norfolk (G-9489)
Coca-Cola Consolidated Inc ....E 703 578-6759
  Alexandria (G-168)
Coca-Cola Consolidated Inc ....D 804 328-5300
  Richmond (G-11160)
Coca-Cola Consolidated Inc ....C 757 446-3000
  Norfolk (G-9490)
Crunchy Hydration LLC ....G 757 362-1607
  Virginia Beach (G-14375)
Delicious Beverage LLC ....G 703 517-0216
  Herndon (G-6654)
Iq Energy LLC ....G 804 747-8900
  Glen Allen (G-5752)
Kraft Heinz Foods Company ....B 540 678-0442
  Winchester (G-15437)
Maryland and Virginia Milk PR ....C 757 245-3857
  Newport News (G-9292)
Mj Distribution ....G 540 692-0062
  Front Royal (G-5544)
Niagara Bottling LLC ....F 804 551-3923
  Chester (G-3440)
Tru-Ade Company ....G 540 662-5484
  Clear Brook (G-3653)
Winmar Business Group ....G 913 908-7413
  Gainesville (G-5622)

BEVERAGES, NONALCOHOLIC: Carbonated

Bottling Group LLC ....F 703 339-5640
  Lorton (G-7468)
Bottling Group LLC ....G 276 625-2300
  Wytheville (G-15879)
Bottling Group LLC ....D 434 792-4512
  Danville (G-3962)
Eerkins Inc ....G 703 626-6248
  Luray (G-7608)
P-Americas LLC ....D 540 347-3112
  Warrenton (G-15041)
Pepsi Beverages Company ....G 757 857-1251
  Norfolk (G-9683)

PRODUCT

Pepsi Bottling Group ....G..... 540 344-8355
Roanoke (G-12146)
Pepsi Co ....F..... 276 625-3900
Wytheville (G-15903)
Pepsi Cola Btlg Inc Norton VA............D..... 276 679-1122
Norton (G-10134)
Pepsi Cola Btlg Inc Norton VA............E..... 276 963-6606
Cedar Bluff (G-2283)
Pepsi-Cola Btlg Co Centl VA............C..... 434 978-2140
Charlottesville (G-2674)
Pepsi-Cola Btlg Co Centl VA............D..... 434 978-2140
Charlottesville (G-2675)
Pepsi-Cola Btlg Co Centl VA............E..... 540 234-9238
Weyers Cave (G-15175)
Pepsi-Cola General Bottlers ....G..... 276 783-7232
Marion (G-8239)
Pepsi-Cola Metro Btlg Co Inc ....C..... 757 857-1251
Norfolk (G-9684)
Pepsi-Cola Metro Btlg Co Inc ....D..... 540 361-4467
Fredericksburg (G-5344)
Pepsi-Cola Metro Btlg Co Inc ....C..... 757 887-2310
Newport News (G-9311)
Pepsi-Cola Metro Btlg Co Inc ....C..... 540 966-5200
Roanoke (G-11984)
Pepsi-Cola Metro Btlg Co Inc ....D..... 434 792-4512
Danville (G-4024)
Pepsico Inc ....G..... 276 781-2177
Marion (G-8240)
Pepsico Inc ....G..... 804 714-1382
Richmond (G-11056)

BEVERAGES, NONALCOHOLIC: Carbonated, Canned & Bottled, Etc

Black Sphere LLC ....G..... 703 776-0494
Annandale (G-732)
Conscious Cultures LLC ....F..... 434 227-9297
Afton (G-78)
Living Maka LLC ....G..... 888 690-7058
Arlington (G-1040)
Lonesome Pine Beverage Company ......G..... 276 679-2332
Norton (G-10124)
Ninja Kombucha LLC ....G..... 757 870-6733
Richmond (G-11691)
Tincture Distillers LLC ....G..... 443 370-2037
Arlington (G-1192)

BEVERAGES, NONALCOHOLIC: Cider

Big Fish Cider Co ....G..... 540 468-2322
Monterey (G-9003)
Buskey Cider ....G..... 901 626-0535
Richmond (G-11141)
Murray Cider Co Inc ....G..... 540 977-9000
Roanoke (G-11973)
River City Cider LLC ....G..... 804 420-9683
Roseland (G-12372)
Shenandoah Valley Orchard Co ....E..... 540 337-2837
Stuarts Draft (G-13660)

BEVERAGES, NONALCOHOLIC: Flavoring extracts & syrups, nec

Mafco Consolidated Group Inc ....F..... 804 222-1600
Richmond (G-11281)

BEVERAGES, NONALCOHOLIC: Fruit Drnks, Under 100% Juice, Can

Mojo Fruit Drinks LLC ....G..... 571 278-0755
Alexandria (G-279)

BEVERAGES, NONALCOHOLIC: Soft Drinks, Canned & Bottled, Etc

Di Cola Llc Ciro Schiano ....G..... 703 779-0212
Leesburg (G-7257)
Dr Pepper Bottlers Lynchburg ....G..... 434 528-5107
Lynchburg (G-7697)
Frito-Lay North America ....E..... 540 380-3020
Salem (G-12508)
Halmor Corp ....E..... 540 248-0095
Staunton (G-13263)
Halmor Corp ....G..... 434 295-3177
Charlottesville (G-2643)
Ja-Zan LLC ....G..... 434 978-2140
Charlottesville (G-2651)
Pepsi-Cola Metro Btlg Co Inc ....D..... 434 528-5107
Lynchburg (G-7785)
R C Cola Bottling Company Del ....D..... 540 667-1821
Winchester (G-15577)

Royal Crown Bottling Company ....F..... 540 667-1821
Winchester (G-15580)
Royal Crown Btlg Wnchester Inc ....D..... 540 667-1821
Winchester (G-15581)
Trinitee Group LLC ....G..... 757 268-9694
Richmond (G-11420)

BEVERAGES, WINE & DISTILLED ALCOHOLIC, WHOLESALE: Neutral Sp

Copper Fox Dist Entps LLC ....F..... 540 987-8554
Sperryville (G-12877)

BEVERAGES, WINE & DISTILLED ALCOHOLIC, WHOLESALE: Wine

Chateau Morrisette Inc ....E..... 540 593-2865
Floyd (G-5018)
Ten Sisters Wine LLC ....G..... 202 577-9774
Alexandria (G-595)
Vanhuss Family Cellars LLC ....G..... 703 737-3930
Leesburg (G-7369)
Williamsburg Winery Ltd ....E..... 757 229-0999
Williamsburg (G-15343)

BEVERAGES, WINE/DISTILLED ALCOH, WHOL: Brandy/Brandy Spirits

Ko Distilling ....G..... 571 292-1115
Manassas (G-7956)

BICYCLES, PARTS & ACCESS

Filz Built Bicycles ....G..... 703 451-5582
Springfield (G-13003)

BILLIARD & POOL PARLORS

Champion Billd & Bar Stools ....G..... 703 631-8800
Fairfax (G-4427)

BINDING SVC: Books & Manuals

Apollo Press Inc ....E..... 757 247-9002
Newport News (G-9169)
B C R Bookbinding ....G..... 703 534-9181
Falls Church (G-4901)
B K Printing ....G..... 703 435-5502
Herndon (G-6618)
Barbours Printing Service ....G..... 804 443-4505
Tappahannock (G-13813)
Berryville Graphics Inc ....A..... 540 955-2750
Berryville (G-1671)
Bindery Plus ....G..... 703 357-5002
Alexandria (G-147)
Branner Printing Service Inc ....E..... 540 896-8947
Broadway (G-2085)
Brook Brinders Limited ....G..... 434 845-1231
Lynchburg (G-7661)
C & B Corp ....G..... 434 977-1992
Charlottesville (G-2752)
Canaan Printing Inc ....E..... 804 271-4820
North Chesterfield (G-9839)
Chocklett Press Inc ....D..... 540 345-1820
Roanoke (G-12066)
Clarke Inc ....F..... 434 847-5561
Moneta (G-8959)
Criswell Inc ....G..... 434 845-0439
Lynchburg (G-7687)
Dad13 Inc ....C..... 703 550-9555
Newington (G-9153)
Day & Night Printing Inc ....E..... 703 734-4940
Vienna (G-14035)
Ersh-Enterprises Inc ....F..... 703 866-1988
Oakton (G-10147)
Finish Line Die Cutting ....F..... 804 342-8000
Richmond (G-11589)
Flynn Enterprises Inc ....E..... 703 444-5555
Sterling (G-13400)
Flynn Incorporated ....G..... 540 885-2600
Staunton (G-13261)
Gary Gray ....G..... 757 238-2135
Carrollton (G-2242)
Goetz Printing Company ....E..... 703 569-8232
Springfield (G-13012)
Good Printers Inc ....D..... 540 828-4663
Bridgewater (G-1953)
Graphic Communications Inc ....F..... 301 599-2020
Hillsville (G-6893)
Hopewell Publishing Company ....E..... 804 452-6127
Hopewell (G-6934)

J & M Printing Inc ....G..... 703 549-2432
Alexandria (G-241)
Jami Ventures Inc ....G..... 703 352-5679
Fairfax (G-4484)
Jones Printing Service Inc ....E..... 757 436-3331
Chesapeake (G-3155)
Lake Lithograph Company ....D..... 703 361-8030
Manassas (G-7959)
Library Conservation Services ....G..... 540 372-9661
Fredericksburg (G-5201)
Lsc Communications Us LLC ....A..... 540 434-8833
Rockingham (G-12259)
Lydell Group Incorporated ....G..... 804 627-0500
Richmond (G-11277)
North Street Enterprise Inc ....E..... 434 392-4144
Farmville (G-4954)
Oldtown Printing & Copying ....G..... 540 382-6793
Christiansburg (G-3607)
One Cut Bindery LLC ....G..... 540 896-7290
Broadway (G-2092)
P I P Printing 1156 Inc ....G..... 434 792-0020
Danville (G-4022)
P M Resources Inc ....G..... 703 556-0155
Springfield (G-13065)
Payne Publishers Inc ....D..... 703 631-9033
Manassas (G-7988)
Prestige Press Inc ....E..... 757 826-5881
Hampton (G-6220)
Printcraft Press Incorporated ....E..... 757 397-0759
Portsmouth (G-10473)
Program Services LLC ....G..... 757 222-3990
Norfolk (G-9698)
Progress Printing Company ....D..... 434 239-9213
Lynchburg (G-7790)
Progressive Graphics Inc ....E..... 757 368-3321
Virginia Beach (G-14744)
Rappahannock Entp Assoc Inc ....G..... 703 560-5042
Falls Church (G-4862)
Salem Printing Co ....E..... 540 387-1106
Salem (G-12566)
Silver Communications Corp ....E..... 703 471-7339
Sterling (G-13508)
Southwest Plastic Binding Co ....E..... 804 226-0400
Richmond (G-11391)
Stephenson Printing Inc ....D..... 703 642-9000
Alexandria (G-589)
Suter Enterprises Ltd ....F..... 757 220-3299
Williamsburg (G-15320)
T-Body Promotions LLC ....G..... 757 723-4445
Hampton (G-6248)
Thomas C Albro II ....G..... 703 892-6738
Arlington (G-1191)
Tidewater Graphics Inc ....G..... 757 464-6136
Virginia Beach (G-14874)
Total Printing Co Inc ....E..... 804 222-3813
Richmond (G-11416)
Tr Press Inc ....E..... 540 347-4466
Warrenton (G-15055)
Vintage Bindery Williamsbur ....G..... 757 220-0203
Williamsburg (G-15332)
Walters Printing & Mfg Co ....F..... 540 345-8161
Roanoke (G-12227)
Wilkinson Printing Co Inc ....F..... 804 264-2524
Glen Allen (G-5828)
William R Smith Company ....E..... 804 733-0123
Petersburg (G-10351)
Winchester Printers Inc ....E..... 540 662-6911
Winchester (G-15512)
Wise Printing Co Inc ....G..... 276 523-1141
Big Stone Gap (G-1718)

BINDING SVC: Trade

Tri State Masters Inc ....G..... 703 255-0222
Vienna (G-14146)

BINOCULARS

Ashbury Intl Group Inc ....F..... 434 296-8600
Ruckersville (G-12399)

BIOLOGICAL PRDTS: Exc Diagnostic

Amnion LLC ....G..... 267 255-6700
Leesburg (G-7216)
Armata Pharmaceuticals Inc ....G..... 804 827-3010
Richmond (G-11488)
Asd Biosystems Inc ....G..... 804 545-3102
Gretna (G-6003)
Crozet Bopharma Consulting LLC ....G..... 703 598-1940
Crozet (G-3830)

Environmental Dynamics Inc ....G.... 540 261-2008
Buena Vista *(G-2142)*
Healthy Home Enterprise ....G.... 757 460-2829
Virginia Beach *(G-14512)*
Mediatech Inc ....E.... 703 471-5955
Manassas *(G-8106)*
Spheringenics Inc ....G.... 770 330-0782
Richmond *(G-11769)*
Tyton Biosciences LLC ....F.... 434 793-9100
Danville *(G-4043)*
Valley Bomedical Pdts Svcs Inc ....E.... 540 868-0800
Winchester *(G-15499)*

BIOLOGICAL PRDTS: Extracts

Extract Attract Inc ....G.... 757 751-0671
Portsmouth *(G-10424)*

BIOLOGICAL PRDTS: Serums

Serum Institute India Pvt LLC ....G.... 571 248-0911
Haymarket *(G-6442)*

BIOLOGICAL PRDTS: Vaccines

Healthsmartvaccines LLc ....G.... 703 961-0734
Chantilly *(G-2435)*
National Vaccine Info Ctr ....G.... 703 938-0342
Sterling *(G-13460)*
National Vaccine Informat ....G.... 703 777-3736
Leesburg *(G-7319)*

BIOLOGICAL PRDTS: Vaccines & Immunizing

Banvera LLC ....E.... 757 599-9643
Newport News *(G-9176)*
Fishhat Inc ....G.... 703 827-0990
Mc Lean *(G-8432)*
Nanomed Inc ....G.... 540 553-4070
Blacksburg *(G-1770)*

BIOLOGICAL PRDTS: Venoms

Venom Motorsports ....G.... 804 347-7626
Colonial Beach *(G-3728)*
Virginia Venom Volleyball ....G.... 757 645-4002
Williamsburg *(G-15334)*
Virginia Vnom Spt Organization ....G.... 757 592-6790
Williamsburg *(G-15335)*

BIOLOGICAL PRDTS: Veterinary

Nutrition Support Services ....G.... 540 626-3081
Pembroke *(G-10282)*

BIRTH CERTIFICATE FACILITIES

Ibfd North America Inc ....G.... 703 442-7757
Vienna *(G-14069)*

BITUMINOUS & LIGNITE COAL LOADING & PREPARATION

Alpha Appalachia Holdings Inc ....D.... 276 619-4410
Bristol *(G-1964)*
Coal Fillers Inc ....G.... 276 322-4675
Bluefield *(G-1860)*

BLADES: Knife

Horsemans Knives LLC ....G.... 540 854-6975
Locust Grove *(G-7446)*
No Lie Blades LLC ....G.... 610 442-5539
Virginia Beach *(G-14682)*
Peters Knives ....G.... 703 255-5353
Vienna *(G-14110)*

BLANKBOOKS & LOOSELEAF BINDERS

A A Business Forms & Printing ....G.... 703 866-5544
Fairfax Station *(G-4700)*
Ibf Group ....G.... 703 549-4247
Alexandria *(G-232)*
R L Bindery ....G.... 804 625-2609
Amelia Court House *(G-669)*

BLANKBOOKS: Account

Advantage Accnting Bkkping LLC ....G.... 434 989-0443
North Chesterfield *(G-9806)*
Metropolitan Accounting & Book ....G.... 703 250-5014
Burke *(G-2193)*

BLANKBOOKS: Albums

Mirror Morning Music ....G.... 703 405-8181
Vienna *(G-14096)*

BLANKBOOKS: Albums, Record

Alien Piss World Entrmt LLC ....G.... 757 805-1007
Virginia Beach *(G-14220)*
Big Face Benji Music Group LLC ....G.... 804 229-9450
North Chesterfield *(G-9831)*
Black Money Label LLC ....G.... 201 975-5009
Virginia Beach *(G-14286)*
Real Is Rare Label LLC ....G.... 757 705-1850
Norfolk *(G-9702)*
Silence In Metropolis LLC ....G.... 571 213-4383
Chantilly *(G-2556)*

BLANKBOOKS: Inventory

M T Holding Company LLC ....E.... 540 563-8866
Vinton *(G-14178)*

BLANKBOOKS: Scrapbooks

Little Black Dog Designs ....G.... 757 874-0928
Newport News *(G-9286)*
Tonya Sheridan Crop Organizer ....G.... 540 860-0528
Luray *(G-7624)*

BLANKETS: Horse

Kerry Scott ....G.... 434 277-9337
Piney River *(G-10361)*
Zotz ....G.... 703 330-2305
Manassas *(G-8015)*

BLAST SAND MINING

Dag Blast It Inc ....G.... 757 237-0735
Chesapeake *(G-3061)*

BLASTING SVC: Sand, Metal Parts

Valley Coml Indus Svcs LLC ....F.... 540 908-1156
Dayton *(G-4068)*
Xtreme Fbrction Pwdr Cting LLC ....G.... 540 327-3020
Winchester *(G-15521)*

BLINDS & SHADES: Vertical

Anything Vertical LLC ....G.... 540 871-6519
Blacksburg *(G-1723)*
Demoiselle Vertical LLC ....G.... 202 431-8032
Alexandria *(G-446)*
Integrated Vertical Tech LLC ....G.... 757 410-7253
Chesapeake *(G-3144)*
Shadeworks LLC ....G.... 804 642-2618
Hayes *(G-6409)*
Vertical Blind Productions ....G.... 540 484-4995
Rocky Mount *(G-12358)*
Vertical Innovations LLC ....G.... 540 616-6431
Dublin *(G-4173)*
Vertical Path Creative LLC ....G.... 434 414-1357
Stanardsville *(G-13230)*
Vertical Praise ....G.... 434 985-1513
Ruckersville *(G-12415)*
Vertical Rock Inc ....G.... 855 822-5462
Manassas *(G-8010)*
Vertical Sunset ....G.... 757 787-7595
Onancock *(G-10199)*
Vertical Venus LLC ....G.... 571 236-6484
Centreville *(G-2351)*

BLINDS : Window

Five Star Custom Blinds Inc ....G.... 757 236-5577
Virginia Beach *(G-14466)*
Hibiscus Chesecake Elixirs LLC ....G.... 757 932-2539
Chesapeake *(G-3135)*
Jts Blinds Installation LLC ....G.... 240 682-1009
King George *(G-7096)*
Maxines Cheesecakes LLC ....G.... 804 586-5135
North Dinwiddie *(G-10060)*
Perfect Blind ....G.... 703 675-4111
Leesburg *(G-7325)*

BLOCKS & BRICKS: Concrete

American Concrete Group LLC ....G...... 276 546-1633
Pennington Gap *(G-10291)*
Anchor ....G.... 540 327-9391
Winchester *(G-15380)*

Chandler Concrete Products of ....G.... 540 674-4667
Dublin *(G-4151)*
General Shale Brick Inc ....C.... 540 977-5505
Blue Ridge *(G-1849)*
Giant Resource Recovery Inc ....E.... 434 685-7021
Cascade *(G-2251)*
Knap Services Inc ....G.... 540 351-5905
Warrenton *(G-15028)*
Peoplespace Inc ....G.... 434 825-2168
Charlottesville *(G-2844)*
Tarmac Florida Inc ....C.... 757 858-6500
Norfolk *(G-9742)*
Titan America LLC ....G.... 757 533-7152
Norfolk *(G-9758)*
Unicom Technology Park Inc ....G.... 703 502-2850
Chantilly *(G-2512)*

BLOCKS: Landscape Or Retaining Wall, Concrete

Bills Yard & Lawn Service LLC ....G.... 757 871-4589
Hampton *(G-6092)*
Bract Rtining Walls Excvtg LLC ....F.... 804 798-5097
Ashland *(G-1384)*
Edward L Birckhead ....G.... 540 937-4287
Amissville *(G-718)*
France Lawnscpape LLC ....G.... 804 761-6823
Warsaw *(G-15063)*
Summit Ldscp & Lawn Care LLC ....G.... 703 856-5353
Falls Church *(G-4879)*
Triple S Pallets LLC ....E.... 540 810-4581
Mount Crawford *(G-9061)*
Xteriors Factory Outlets Inc ....G.... 804 798-6300
Doswell *(G-4129)*

BLOCKS: Paving, Concrete

Barron Construction LLC ....G.... 804 400-5569
North Chesterfield *(G-9828)*

BLOCKS: Paving, Cut Stone

Interlock Paving Systems Inc ....G.... 757 722-2591
Hampton *(G-6176)*
Modern Exteriors ....F.... 703 978-8602
Chantilly *(G-2464)*

BLOCKS: Standard, Concrete Or Cinder

Allied Concrete Company ....E.... 434 296-7181
Charlottesville *(G-2724)*
Allied Concrete Products LLC ....G.... 757 494-5200
Chesapeake *(G-2960)*
Blue Stone Block Sprmkt Inc ....E.... 540 982-3588
Roanoke *(G-12050)*
Chandler Concrete Products of ....D...... 540 382-1734
Christiansburg *(G-3578)*
Cochran Industries Inc - VA ....G.... 276 498-3836
Oakwood *(G-10166)*
E Dillon & Company ....G.... 276 873-6816
Swords Creek *(G-13807)*
Empire Incorporated ....E.... 757 723-6747
Hampton *(G-6140)*
Hagerstown Block Company ....G.... 540 364-1531
Marshall *(G-8255)*
Marshall Con Pdts of Danville ....G.... 434 369-4791
Altavista *(G-635)*
Martinsville Concrete Products ....E.... 276 632-6416
Martinsville *(G-8308)*
Oldcastle Apg Northeast Inc ....F.... 703 365-7070
Gainesville *(G-5605)*
Oldcastle Apg Northeast Inc ....E.... 540 667-4600
Winchester *(G-15457)*
Rockingham Redi-Mix Inc ....E.... 540 433-8282
Rockingham *(G-12274)*
Supreme Concrete Blocks Inc ....G.... 703 478-1988
Leesburg *(G-7355)*
T&W Block Incorporated ....E.... 757 787-2646
Onley *(G-10201)*
Tarmac Mid-Atlantic Inc ....A.... 757 858-6500
Norfolk *(G-9743)*
VA Hardscapes Inc ....G.... 540 955-6245
Berryville *(G-1698)*
Valley Building Supply Inc ....C.... 540 434-6725
Harrisonburg *(G-6383)*

BLOOD RELATED HEALTH SVCS

Lifenet Health ....B.... 757 464-4761
Virginia Beach *(G-14610)*

Employee Codes: A=Over 500 employees, B=251-500
C=101-250, D=51-100, E=20-50, F=10-19, G=1-9

2021 Virginia
Industrial Directory

907

PRODUCT

BLOWERS & FANS

Air Systems International Inc ....E 757 424-3967
  Chesapeake *(G-2957)*
Bwx Technologies Inc ....E 757 595-7982
  Newport News *(G-9187)*
Des Champs Technologies Inc ....C 540 291-1111
  Buena Vista *(G-2141)*
GE Energy ....G 757 595-7982
  Newport News *(G-9234)*
Intellgent Pwr A Solutions Inc ....G 540 429-6177
  Spotsylvania *(G-12898)*
Mfri Inc ....C 540 667-7022
  Winchester *(G-15555)*
Phoenixaire LLC ....G 703 647-6546
  Arlington *(G-1111)*
Universal Air Products Corp ....E 757 461-0077
  Norfolk *(G-9774)*
Usui International Corporation ....B 757 558-7300
  Chesapeake *(G-3356)*
Virginia Blower Company ....E 276 647-3804
  Collinsville *(G-3718)*

BLOWERS, TURBO: Indl

Best Blower Sales & Svc LLC ....G 434 352-1909
  Appomattox *(G-806)*

BLUEPRINTING SVCS

Bailey Printing Inc ....F 434 293-5434
  Charlottesville *(G-2734)*
Commonwealth Reprographics ....F 434 845-1203
  Lynchburg *(G-7682)*

BOAT BUILDING & REPAIR

ARC Global Corp ....G 757 470-9271
  Chesapeake *(G-2978)*
Backwater Inc ....G 434 242-5675
  Charlottesville *(G-2733)*
Bay Custom Inc ....G 757 971-4785
  Hampton *(G-6089)*
Bay Custom Mar Fleet Repr Inc ....F 757 224-3818
  Hampton *(G-6090)*
Blue Wave Mobile Marine ....G 757 831-4810
  Chesapeake *(G-3008)*
Boatworks & More LLC ....G 540 581-5820
  Roanoke *(G-12053)*
Chesapeake Marine Railway ....G 804 776-8833
  Deltaville *(G-4078)*
Dudley Dix Yacht Design ....G 757 962-9273
  Virginia Beach *(G-14416)*
Dudley Dix Yacht Design Inc ....G 757 962-9273
  Virginia Beach *(G-14417)*
East Cast Repr Fabrication LLC ....D 757 455-9600
  Norfolk *(G-9536)*
East Cast Repr Fabrication LLC ....C 757 455-9600
  Norfolk *(G-9535)*
Erie Boatworks LLC ....G 757 204-1815
  Chesapeake *(G-3090)*
Fairlead Boatworks Inc ....D 757 247-0101
  Newport News *(G-9223)*
Fiberglass Customs Inc ....G 757 244-0610
  Newport News *(G-9226)*
Freedom Hawks Kayaks Inc ....G 978 225-1511
  Charlottesville *(G-2799)*
Genesis Boat Works Inc ....G 757 869-0345
  Hampton *(G-6158)*
Honeycutts Mobile Marine ....G 757 898-7793
  Seaford *(G-12675)*
Jgtsenterprise Inc ....G 804 677-4578
  Mechanicsville *(G-8645)*
Keiths Boat Service LLC ....G 804 898-1644
  Colonial Heights *(G-3737)*
Linear Devices Corporation ....G 804 368-8428
  Ashland *(G-1453)*
M & S Marine & Industrial Svcs ....D 757 405-9623
  Portsmouth *(G-10456)*
Mathomank Village Tribe ....G 757 504-5513
  Claremont *(G-3624)*
Mtg Enterprises Inc ....G 804 269-5218
  North Chesterfield *(G-9935)*
NBC Boatworks ....G 757 630-0420
  Virginia Beach *(G-14672)*
Pruitts Boat Yard ....G 757 891-2565
  Tangier *(G-13809)*
Rapa Boat Services LLC ....G 804 443-4434
  Tappahannock *(G-13821)*
Rappahannock Boat Works Inc ....G 540 439-4045
  Bealeton *(G-1605)*

RG Boatworks LLC ....G 804 784-1991
  Manakin Sabot *(G-7904)*
Richmond Steel Boat Works Inc ....G 804 741-0432
  Richmond *(G-11361)*
Riverine Jet Boats ....G 434 258-5874
  Madison Heights *(G-7883)*
Rva Boatworks LLC ....G 804 937-7448
  Richmond *(G-11368)*
Severn Yachting LLC ....G 804 642-6969
  Hayes *(G-6408)*
Team SSP Ventures Inc ....G 804 273-9496
  Glen Allen *(G-5805)*
TST Tactical Def Solutions Inc ....F 757 452-6955
  Virginia Beach *(G-14896)*
Tynes Fiberglass Company Inc ....G 757 423-0222
  Norfolk *(G-9771)*
Zimmerman Marine Incorporated ....F 804 776-0367
  Deltaville *(G-4090)*

BOAT BUILDING & REPAIRING: Fiberglass

BGF Industries Inc ....G 434 369-4751
  Altavista *(G-626)*
Brightwork Boat Co ....G 804 795-9080
  Richmond *(G-11134)*

BOAT BUILDING & REPAIRING: Kits, Not Models

Waldens Marina Inc ....G 804 776-9440
  Deltaville *(G-4087)*

BOAT BUILDING & REPAIRING: Motorized

Michael McKittrick ....G 804 695-7090
  Deltaville *(G-4083)*

BOAT BUILDING & REPAIRING: Yachts

Atlantic Yacht Basin Inc ....E 757 482-2141
  Chesapeake *(G-2987)*
Bae Systems Ship Repair Inc ....A 757 494-4000
  Norfolk *(G-9453)*
Chesapeake Yachts Inc ....F 757 724-1717
  Chesapeake *(G-3034)*
Custom Yacht Service Inc ....F 804 438-5563
  Dutton *(G-4271)*
Tiffany Yachts Inc ....F 804 453-3464
  Burgess *(G-2178)*

BOAT BUILDING & RPRG: Fishing, Small, Lobster, Crab, Oyster

Big Time Charters Inc ....G 757 496-1040
  Virginia Beach *(G-14278)*
Jennings Boat Yard Inc ....G 804 453-7181
  Reedville *(G-10762)*

BOAT LIFTS

East Coast Boat Lifts Inc ....G 804 758-1099
  Urbanna *(G-13970)*
Universal Marine Lift Inc ....G 804 829-5838
  Charles City *(G-2580)*

BOAT REPAIR SVCS

Buddy D Ltd ....G 757 481-7619
  Virginia Beach *(G-14305)*
Custom Yacht Service Inc ....F 804 438-5563
  Dutton *(G-4271)*
Fiberglass Customs Inc ....G 757 244-0610
  Newport News *(G-9226)*
Fridays Marine Inc ....G 804 758-4131
  Saluda *(G-12603)*
Tynes Fiberglass Company Inc ....G 757 423-0222
  Norfolk *(G-9771)*

BOAT YARD: Boat yards, storage & incidental repair

Atlantic Yacht Basin Inc ....E 757 482-2141
  Chesapeake *(G-2987)*

BOATS & OTHER MARINE EQPT: Plastic

Moubray Company ....G 804 435-6334
  Kilmarnock *(G-7073)*
Ocran Shaft Machine ....G 804 435-6301
  White Stone *(G-15189)*
Tidewell Marine Inc ....G 804 453-6115
  Burgess *(G-2177)*

BODIES: Truck & Bus

AMP Sales & Service LLC ....G 540 586-1021
  Bedford *(G-1619)*
General Eqp Sls & Svc LLC ....G 434 579-7581
  Virgilina *(G-14192)*
Metalsa Structural Pdts Inc ....G 540 966-5370
  Roanoke *(G-11964)*
Metalsa-Roanoke Inc ....C 540 966-5300
  Roanoke *(G-11965)*
Volvo Group North America LLC ....C 336 393-2000
  Dublin *(G-4174)*

BODY PARTS: Automobile, Stamped Metal

Aftermarket Parts Solutions ....G 757 227-3166
  Norfolk *(G-9428)*
Davids Mobile Service LLC ....G 804 481-1647
  Hopewell *(G-6922)*
Donald Crisp Jr ....G 757 903-6743
  Yorktown *(G-15951)*

BOILER REPAIR SHOP

Industrial Fabricators VA Inc ....D 540 943-5885
  Fishersville *(G-5005)*

BOILERS & BOILER SHOP WORK

Superior Boiler LLC ....E 804 226-8227
  Richmond *(G-11402)*

BOILERS: Low-Pressure Heating, Steam Or Hot Water

KMW Works LLC ....G 757 776-6765
  Virginia Beach *(G-14591)*

BOLTS: Heading, Wooden, Hewn

Scholl Custom WD & Met Cft LLC ....G 804 739-2390
  Chesterfield *(G-3522)*

BOLTS: Metal

Zipnut Technology LLC ....G 703 442-7339
  Falls Church *(G-4898)*

BOLTS: Wooden, Hewn

Koppers Utility Indus Pdts Inc ....G 434 292-4375
  Blackstone *(G-1818)*

BOND DEALERS & BROKERS

Advanced Cgnitive Systems Corp ....G 804 397-3373
  Richmond *(G-11474)*

BOOK STORES

Signs of The Times Apostolate ....G 703 707-0799
  Herndon *(G-6807)*

BOOK STORES: Comic

Game Quest Inc ....G 540 639-6547
  Radford *(G-10714)*

BOOK STORES: Religious

Presbytrian Outlook Foundation ....G 804 359-8442
  Richmond *(G-11724)*

BOOTS: Rubber Or Rubber Soled Fabric

Matbock LLC ....G 757 828-6659
  Virginia Beach *(G-14639)*

BOOTS: Women's

Barismil LLC ....G 703 622-4550
  Herndon *(G-6619)*

BOTTLE CAPS & RESEALERS: Plastic

Berry Global Inc ....G 540 946-9250
  Waynesboro *(G-15100)*
Berry Global Inc ....G 757 538-2000
  Suffolk *(G-13678)*

BOTTLES: Plastic

Graham Packg Plastic Pdts Inc ....C 540 564-1000
  Harrisonburg *(G-6325)*
Itg Cigars Inc ....E 804 233-7668
  Richmond *(G-11622)*

M&H Plastics Inc ....C 540 504-0030
  Winchester *(G-15441)*

Southeastern Container Inc ....C 540 722-2600
  Winchester *(G-15480)*

Virginia Kik Inc ....E 540 389-5401
  Salem *(G-12578)*

BOWLING CENTERS

AMF Bowling Worldwide Inc ....F 804 730-4000
  Mechanicsville *(G-8602)*

Qubicaamf Worldwide LLC ....B 804 569-1000
  Mechanicsville *(G-8669)*

BOWLING EQPT & SPLYS

AMF Bowling Worldwide Inc ....G 804 730-4000
  Mechanicsville *(G-8601)*

AMF Bowling Worldwide Inc ....F 804 730-4000
  Mechanicsville *(G-8602)*

Bush River Corporation ....G 804 730-4000
  Richmond *(G-11139)*

Qubicaamf Worldwide LLC ....B 804 569-1000
  Mechanicsville *(G-8669)*

BOXES & SHOOK: Nailed Wood

Alexandria Packaging LLC ....D 703 644-5550
  Springfield *(G-12940)*

Breeze Ridge Enterprises ....G 703 728-4606
  Winchester *(G-15391)*

Swift Creek Forest Products ....E 804 561-1751
  Jetersville *(G-7015)*

BOXES: Ammunition, Metal

Tread Corporation ....D 540 982-6881
  Roanoke *(G-12010)*

BOXES: Chests & Trunks, Wood

Custom Hope Chests VA LLC ....G 703 850-5019
  Herndon *(G-6650)*

BOXES: Corrugated

Atlantic Corrugated Box Co Inc ....E 804 231-4050
  Richmond *(G-11027)*

Blue Ridge Packaging Corp ....E 276 638-1413
  Martinsville *(G-8270)*

Carocon ....G 804 324-2207
  Virginia Beach *(G-14320)*

Carolina Container Co Inc ....G 804 458-4700
  Virginia Beach *(G-14321)*

Carolina Container Company ....F 804 458-4700
  Prince George *(G-10588)*

Commonwealth Specialty Packg ....F 804 271-0157
  Ashland *(G-1393)*

Corrugated Container Corp ....E 540 869-5353
  Winchester *(G-15405)*

Custom Packaging Inc ....F 804 232-3299
  Richmond *(G-11551)*

Drake Company ....G 757 536-1509
  Chesapeake *(G-3075)*

Ds Smith PLC ....G 540 774-0500
  Roanoke *(G-11916)*

Georgia-Pacific LLC ....C 276 632-6301
  Ridgeway *(G-11843)*

Hollinger Metal Edge Inc ....F 540 898-7300
  Fredericksburg *(G-5298)*

Hollinger Metal Edge - VA Inc ....F 540 898-7300
  Fredericksburg *(G-5299)*

International Paper Company ....G 757 405-3046
  Portsmouth *(G-10444)*

International Paper Company ....D 804 861-8164
  Petersburg *(G-10326)*

Interstate Cont Reading LLC ....G 703 243-3355
  Arlington *(G-1009)*

Interstate Resources Inc ....G 703 243-3355
  Arlington *(G-1010)*

Menasha Packaging Company LLC ....C 540 546-1110
  Winchester *(G-15448)*

Metal Edge Co ....G 800 862-2228
  Fredericksburg *(G-5325)*

Old Dominion Box Co Inc ....E 434 929-6701
  Madison Heights *(G-7880)*

Packaging Corporation America ....G 540 427-3164
  Roanoke *(G-12144)*

Packaging Corporation America ....B 540 434-0785
  Harrisonburg *(G-6351)*

Packaging Corporation America ....G 540 432-1353
  Harrisonburg *(G-6352)*

Packaging Corporation America ....G 540 434-2840
  Rockingham *(G-12266)*

Packaging Corporation America ....C 804 232-1292
  Richmond *(G-11703)*

Packaging Corporation America ....D 540 427-3164
  Roanoke *(G-11982)*

Packaging Corporation America ....G 540 438-8504
  Harrisonburg *(G-6353)*

Packaging Corporation America ....G 540 662-5680
  Winchester *(G-15458)*

Packaging Products Inc ....E 276 629-3481
  Bassett *(G-1588)*

Pratt Industries Inc ....E 804 412-0245
  Ashland *(G-1479)*

Reynolds Container Corporation ....E 276 647-8451
  Collinsville *(G-3715)*

Richmond Corrugated Box Co ....E 804 222-1300
  Sandston *(G-12629)*

Supply One Chesapeake ....G 757 485-3570
  Chesapeake *(G-3317)*

Westrock Converting LLC ....D 276 632-7175
  Ridgway *(G-11858)*

Westrock Cp LLC ....E 804 236-3237
  Sandston *(G-12641)*

Westrock Cp LLC ....G 276 632-0698
  Ridgeway *(G-11859)*

Westrock Cp LLC ....C 804 222-6380
  Richmond *(G-11447)*

Westrock Cp LLC ....G 804 226-5840
  Richmond *(G-11448)*

Westrock Cp LLC ....D 804 843-5229
  West Point *(G-15163)*

Westrock Cp LLC ....C 276 632-2176
  Martinsville *(G-8352)*

Westrock Cp LLC ....G 434 736-8505
  Keysville *(G-7065)*

Westrock Mwv LLC ....C 540 969-5230
  Covington *(G-3803)*

Westrock Mwv LLC ....C 804 201-2000
  Glen Allen *(G-5827)*

York Box & Barrel Mfg Co ....G 757 868-9411
  Poquoson *(G-10379)*

BOXES: Junction, Electric

L J S Stores Inc ....E 804 561-6999
  Amelia Court House *(G-662)*

BOXES: Mail Or Post Office, Collection/Storage, Sheet Metal

PSI Group ....G 804 798-3210
  Ashland *(G-1481)*

BOXES: Outlet, Electric Wiring Device

Sullivan Company Inc N J ....E 703 464-5944
  Sterling *(G-13523)*

BOXES: Paperboard, Folding

Able Mfg LLC ....G 804 550-4885
  Glen Allen *(G-5703)*

Arkay Packaging Corporation ....D 540 278-2596
  Roanoke *(G-11882)*

Carded Graphics LLC ....C 540 248-3716
  Staunton *(G-13247)*

Cauthorne Paper Company Inc ....E 804 798-6999
  Ashland *(G-1388)*

Commonwealth Specialty Packg ....F 804 271-0157
  Ashland *(G-1393)*

Dominion Packaging Inc ....C 804 447-6921
  Sandston *(G-12612)*

Old Dominion Box Co Inc ....E 434 929-6701
  Madison Heights *(G-7880)*

Old Dominion Box Co Inc ....E 434 929-6701
  Madison Heights *(G-7881)*

BOXES: Paperboard, Set-Up

Commonwealth Specialty Packg ....F 804 271-0157
  Ashland *(G-1393)*

Old Dominion Box Co Inc ....E 434 929-6701
  Madison Heights *(G-7880)*

Old Dominion Box Co Inc ....E 434 929-6701
  Madison Heights *(G-7881)*

BOXES: Wirebound, Wood

Murdock Acquisition LLC ....C 804 798-9154
  Ashland *(G-1467)*

BOXES: Wooden

Danielson Trading LLC ....G 703 764-0450
  Fairfax *(G-4436)*

Don Elthon ....G 703 237-2521
  Falls Church *(G-4908)*

Scan Industries LLC ....G 360 320-8244
  Ashburn *(G-1332)*

Smalley Package Company Inc ....D 540 955-2550
  Berryville *(G-1691)*

BRAKE LININGS

Duroline North America Inc ....G 757 447-6290
  Norfolk *(G-9533)*

BRAKES & BRAKE PARTS

Carlisle Indstrl Brke & Frctn ....F 814 486-1119
  Charlottesville *(G-2605)*

Continental Auto Systems Inc ....C 540 825-4100
  Culpeper *(G-3880)*

Crenshaw of Richmond Inc ....D 804 231-6241
  Richmond *(G-11546)*

East Coast Brake Rbldrs Corp ....F 757 466-1308
  Norfolk *(G-9537)*

Fdp Virginia Inc ....C 804 443-5356
  Tappahannock *(G-13816)*

Rhenus Automotive Salem LLC ....G 270 282-2100
  Salem *(G-12561)*

BRASS & BRONZE PRDTS: Die-casted

Wegner Metal Arts Inc ....G 540 373-5662
  Fredericksburg *(G-5235)*

BRASS FOUNDRY, NEC

Nomar Castings Inc ....F 540 380-3394
  Elliston *(G-4346)*

BREAD WRAPPERS: Waxed Or Laminated, Made From Purchased Matl

Dcp Holdings LLC ....E 804 876-3135
  Doswell *(G-4119)*

BRICK, STONE & RELATED PRDTS WHOLESALERS

Chesapeake Strl Systems Inc ....E 804 966-8340
  Charles City *(G-2573)*

Oldcastle Apg Northeast Inc ....F 703 365-7070
  Gainesville *(G-5605)*

Patton Sand & Concrete ....G 276 236-9362
  Galax *(G-5644)*

Percontee Inc ....E 703 471-4411
  Chantilly *(G-2479)*

Virginia Materials Inc ....G 800 321-2282
  Norfolk *(G-9784)*

BRICKS: Clay

General Shale Brick Inc ....D 276 783-3156
  Atkins *(G-1517)*

General Shale Brick Inc ....G 540 977-5505
  Blue Ridge *(G-1849)*

Precision Brick Cutting Ltd ....G 703 393-2777
  Manassas *(G-8132)*

BRIDAL SHOPS

Le Reve Bridal Inc ....F 703 777-3757
  Leesburg *(G-7297)*

BROADCASTING & COMMS EQPT: Antennas, Transmitting/Comms

Antenna Technologies Ltd Co ....F 703 450-5517
  Sterling *(G-13345)*

Astron Wireless Tech Inc ....F 703 450-5517
  Sterling *(G-13352)*

Astron Wireless Tech LLC ....F 703 450-5517
  Sterling *(G-13353)*

Delta Electronics Inc ....F 703 354-3350
  Alexandria *(G-445)*

Directive Systems and Eng LLC ....G 703 754-3876
  Haymarket *(G-6419)*

Product Dev Mfg & Packg ....G 703 777-8400
  Leesburg *(G-7328)*

Reverb Networks Inc ....E 703 665-4222
  Sterling *(G-13492)*

PRODUCT

Tim Price Inc............................F......540 722-8716
Winchester (G-15594)

BROADCASTING & COMMS EQPT: Rcvr-Transmitter Unt, Transceiver

Datron Wrld Communications Inc.......D......703 647-6235
Alexandria (G-184)

BROADCASTING & COMMUNICATION EQPT: Transmit-Receiver, Radio

Oceus Enterprise Solutions LLC..........D......703 234-9200
Reston (G-10912)

BROADCASTING & COMMUNICATIONS EQPT: Cellular Radio Telephone

CC Wireless Corporation ....G......757 802-8140
Norfolk (G-9479)
Commscope Technologies LLC ....C......434 386-5300
Forest (G-5062)
Ericsson Inc....................................G......434 528-7000
Lynchburg (G-7705)

BROADCASTING & COMMUNICATIONS EQPT: Light Comms Eqpt

Active Sense Technologies LLC..........G......352 226-1479
Abingdon (G-7)
Convex Corporation ....G......703 433-9901
Warrenton (G-14990)
Missionteq LLC ....G......703 563-0699
Chantilly (G-2545)

BROADCASTING & COMMUNICATIONS EQPT: Studio Eqpt, Radio & TV

Apogee Communications....................G......703 481-1622
Herndon (G-6613)
Greenzone Systems Inc ....G......703 567-6039
Arlington (G-987)
Muhammad Islam ....G......631 569-8325
Reston (G-10904)
Pacific and Southern Company ....D......703 854-6899
Mc Lean (G-8522)

BROKERS' SVCS

Kmx Chemical Corp............................E......757 824-3600
New Church (G-9125)

BROKERS: Contract Basis

Custom Graphics Inc ....G......540 882-3488
Paeonian Springs (G-10238)

BROKERS: Printing

Brothers Printing ....F......757 431-2656
Virginia Beach (G-14301)
Commercial Copies ....G......757 473-0234
Virginia Beach (G-14357)

BRONZE FOUNDRY, NEC

Turner Sculpture Ltd...........................E......757 787-2818
Melfa (G-8713)

BROOMS

Quickie Manufacturing Corp................D......856 829-7900
Winchester (G-15575)

BROOMS & BRUSHES

Brush Holdings Inc ....D......804 226-4433
Richmond (G-11137)

BROOMS & BRUSHES: Household Or Indl

Old Dominion Brush Company Inc ....G......800 446-9823
Richmond (G-11313)

BROOMS & BRUSHES: Vacuum Cleaners & Carpet Sweepers

One Stop Cleaning LLC.......................G......757 561-2952
Williamsburg (G-15286)

BRUSHES: Rubber

Dandy Point Industries........................G......757 851-3280
Hampton (G-6127)

BUILDING & OFFICE CLEANING SVCS

One Stop Cleaning LLC.......................G......757 561-2952
Williamsburg (G-15286)
Ship Shape Cleaning LLC....................G......757 769-3845
Portsmouth (G-10480)

BUILDING & STRUCTURAL WOOD MBRS: Timbers, Struct, Lam Lumber

Big Timber Hardwoods LLC.................724 301-7051
Virginia Beach (G-14277)
Williams Brothers Lumber Inc ....F......434 760-2951
Ruckersville (G-12416)

BUILDING & STRUCTURAL WOOD MEMBERS

East Coast Truss Inc...........................G......757 369-0801
Smithfield (G-12712)
Hickory Frame Corp............................G......434 847-8489
Lynchburg (G-7732)
Portsmouth Lumber Corporation ....F......757 397-4646
Portsmouth (G-10471)
Truss Construction ....G......540 710-0673
Spotsylvania (G-12919)
Truss Incorporated ....G......804 556-3611
Susan (G-13802)
Truss It Inc ....G......540 248-2177
Mount Sidney (G-9085)

BUILDING CLEANING & MAINTENANCE SVCS

Allgoods Cleaning Service...................G......540 434-1511
Harrisonburg (G-6291)
Smith & Smith Commercial Hood.........G......804 605-0311
South Chesterfield (G-12840)
Stm Snow Removal LLC.......................G......540 604-0112
Stafford (G-13196)

BUILDING COMPONENTS: Structural Steel

Am-Corcom Inc ....E......540 349-5895
Culpeper (G-3865)
Bohling Steel Inc ....E......434 385-5175
Lynchburg (G-7657)
Cives Corporation ....C......540 667-3480
Winchester (G-15402)
Cooper Steel of Virginia LLC ....E......931 205-6117
Monroe (G-8988)
Flowers Steel LLC ....G......540 424-8377
Sumerduck (G-13791)
Fredericksburg Mch & Stl LLC ....G......540 373-7957
Fredericksburg (G-5189)
Heavy Metal Construction Inc..............G......434 547-8061
Chase City (G-2912)
Liphart Steel Company Inc ....D......804 355-7481
Richmond (G-11272)
Litesteel Tech Amer LLC ....E......540 992-5129
Troutville (G-13914)
Osborne Welding Inc ....E......757 487-0900
Portsmouth (G-10466)
Precision Steel Mfg Corp ....D......540 985-8963
Roanoke (G-12152)
Radford Wldg & Fabrication LLC ....G......540 731-4891
Radford (G-10737)
Sheltered 2 Home LLC........................E......540 686-0091
Winchester (G-15585)
Southern Structural Steel Inc ....E......757 623-0862
Smithfield (G-12741)
Spigner Structural & Miscellan ....E......703 625-7572
Berryville (G-1692)
Steelfab Inc ....G......703 538-2320
Alexandria (G-355)
Steelfab of Virginia Inc ....D......434 348-9021
Emporia (G-4367)
Structural Steel MGT LLC ....G......434 286-2373
Scottsville (G-12667)
Virginia Carolina Steel Inc ....E......757 853-7403
Norfolk (G-9783)
Virginia Steel & Building Spc ....F......434 528-4302
Lynchburg (G-7834)
Wolf Hills Fabricators LLC ....F......276 466-2743
Abingdon (G-70)

BUILDING INSPECTION SVCS

Hawkeye Inspection Service................G......804 725-9751
Mathews (G-8355)

BUILDING PRDTS & MATERIALS DEALERS

B H Cobb Lumber Co ....G......804 358-3801
Richmond (G-11498)
Builders Firstsource Inc ....D......540 665-0078
Winchester (G-15397)
Kempsville Building Mtls Inc ....E......757 485-0782
Chesapeake (G-3162)
Kempsville Building Mtls Inc ....G......757 875-1850
Newport News (G-9275)
Williams Lumber Supply Inc ....E......434 376-3368
Brookneal (G-2116)

BUILDING PRDTS: Concrete

Cook & Boardman Group LLC.............G......757 873-3979
Newport News (G-9205)
Tile Optima LLC ....F......703 256-5650
Alexandria (G-598)

BUILDING STONE, ARTIFICIAL: Concrete

Wayne Harbin Builder Inc ....G......757 220-8860
Williamsburg (G-15339)

BUILDINGS & COMPONENTS: Prefabricated Metal

Alans Factory Outlet...........................G......540 860-1035
Luray (G-7600)
Colonial Barns Inc ....G......757 420-8653
Virginia Beach (G-14353)
General Dynamics Mission ....B......276 783-3121
Marion (G-8227)
Ireson Innovation ....G......540 529-1572
Troutville (G-13911)
Kennedy Konstruction Kompany ....E......540 984-4191
Edinburg (G-4308)
Leonard Alum Utility Bldngs Inc ....G......540 951-0236
Blacksburg (G-1753)
McElroy Metal Mill Inc........................G......757 485-3100
Chesapeake (G-3200)
Morton Buildings Inc ....G......540 366-3705
Culpeper (G-3910)
Powerbilt Steel Buildings Inc................F......757 425-6223
Virginia Beach (G-14731)
Quality Portable Buildings 276 880-2007
Rosedale (G-12367)
Shelter2home LLC ....G......540 336-5994
Winchester (G-15584)
Stateline Builders Inc ....G......757 934-6836
Suffolk (G-13768)
Steelmaster Buildings LLC ....F......757 961-7006
Virginia Beach (G-14845)
TSC Corporation ....E......540 633-5000
Radford (G-10746)
Vfp Inc ....D......540 977-0500
Roanoke (G-12019)
Vfp Inc ....C......276 431-4000
Duffield (G-4187)

BUILDINGS: Farm & Utility

J Z Utility Barns LLC...........................G......276 686-1683
Rural Retreat (G-12425)
Leonard Alum Utlity Bldngs Inc ....G......434 237-5301
Lynchburg (G-7756)

BUILDINGS: Farm, Prefabricated Or Portable, Wood

Cherrystone Structures LLC................F......434 432-8484
Chatham (G-2922)

BUILDINGS: Portable

Affordable Sheds Company ....G......540 657-6770
Stafford (G-13113)
Faun Trackway (usa) Inc ....G......202 459-0802
Arlington (G-963)
Graceland of Martinsville ....G......434 250-0050
Ridgeway (G-11844)
Jewells Buildings ....G......804 333-4483
Warsaw (G-15069)
Oaks At Timberlake............................G......434 525-7107
Evington (G-4381)

BUILDINGS: Prefabricated, Metal

American Buildings Company ....C 434 757-2220
La Crosse **(G-7139)**

Cushing Manufacturing & Eqp Co ......E 804 231-1161
Richmond **(G-11038)**

Harbor Entps Ltd Lblty Co ....G 229 226-0911
Stafford **(G-13150)**

Leonard Alum Utlity Bldngs Inc ....G 434 792-8202
Danville **(G-4011)**

True Steel LLC ....G 540 680-2906
Charlottesville **(G-2896)**

US Building Systems Inc ....E 800 991-9251
Virginia Beach **(G-14903)**

BUILDINGS: Prefabricated, Plastic

General Dynamics Mission ....B 276 783-3121
Marion **(G-8227)**

BUILDINGS: Prefabricated, Wood

Chadwick International Inc ....F 703 560-0970
Fairfax **(G-4426)**

Custom Vinyl Products LLC ....E 757 887-3194
Newport News **(G-9209)**

Devereux Barns LLC ....G 540 664-1432
Berryville **(G-1677)**

Modern Living LLC ....G 877 663-2224
Richmond **(G-11679)**

Pine Glade Buildings LLC ....G 540 674-5229
Dublin **(G-4169)**

Pls Installation ....G 540 521-1261
Buchanan **(G-2124)**

Roosters Amish Sheds ....G 540 263-2415
Strasburg **(G-13595)**

Shenandoah Sheds ....G 540 869-4050
White Post **(G-15184)**

Southern Heritage Homes Inc ....F 540 489-7700
Rocky Mount **(G-12353)**

Stella-Jones Corporation ....D 540 997-9251
Goshen **(G-5927)**

Vfp Inc ....C 276 431-4000
Duffield **(G-4187)**

BUILDINGS: Prefabricated, Wood

Colonial Barns Inc ....E 757 482-2234
Chesapeake **(G-3046)**

Don Elthon ....G 703 237-2521
Falls Church **(G-4908)**

Dutch Barns ....G 757 497-7356
Virginia Beach **(G-14418)**

Lester Building Systems LLC ....E 540 665-0182
Clear Brook **(G-3646)**

McRae of America Inc ....G 757 488-6900
Chesapeake **(G-3201)**

Scan Industries LLC ....G 360 320-8244
Ashburn **(G-1332)**

Valley Structures Inc ....F 540 879-9454
Dayton **(G-4070)**

Valley Utility Buildings Inc ....G 276 679-6736
Big Stone Gap **(G-1717)**

Vfp Inc ....D 540 977-0500
Roanoke **(G-12019)**

Virginia Custom Buildings ....F 804 784-3816
Manakin Sabot **(G-7906)**

Wilcks Lake Storage Sheds Inc ....F 434 574-5131
Prospect **(G-10616)**

BULLETPROOF VESTS

Eagle Industries Unlimited Inc ....E 888 343-7547
Virginia Beach **(G-14425)**

Stealth Mfg & Svcs LLC ....G 787 679-7548
Virginia Beach **(G-14844)**

War Fighter Specialties LLC ....G 540 742-4187
Shenandoah **(G-12697)**

BUMPERS: Motor Vehicle

Refuge Golf & Bumper Boats ....G 757 336-5420
Chincoteague **(G-3564)**

BURIAL VAULTS: Concrete Or Precast Terrazzo

Burial Butler Services LLC ....G 757 934-8227
Suffolk **(G-13682)**

C B C Corporation ....G 757 868-6571
Poquoson **(G-10365)**

Custom Vault Corporation ....G 804 303-1741
North Chesterfield **(G-10017)**

Friends Sprngwood Brial Pk LLC..........G 540 366-0996
Roanoke **(G-11924)**

Joseph L Burruss Burial Vaults ....F 804 746-8250
Mechanicsville **(G-8646)**

Juptiers Vault ....G 757 404-9535
Norfolk **(G-9609)**

Markham Burial Vault Service ....E 804 271-1441
North Chesterfield **(G-9922)**

Mercer Vault Co ....G 540 371-3666
Fredericksburg **(G-5206)**

Richards-Wilbert Inc ....G 540 477-3842
Mount Jackson **(G-9077)**

Richards-Wilbert Inc ....G 540 389-5240
Salem **(G-12562)**

Roland Vault Ltd ....E 757 466-8800
Norfolk **(G-9709)**

Stevens Burial Vault LLC ....G 804 443-5125
Champlain **(G-2357)**

Vault ....G 540 479-2221
Fredericksburg **(G-5386)**

Vault Productions LLC ....G 703 509-2704
Williamsburg **(G-15330)**

Vault Technologies LLC ....G 703 283-2550
Fairfax Station **(G-4726)**

Virgina-Carolina Grave Vlt LLC ....G 276 694-6855
Stuart **(G-13638)**

Wimbrough & Sons Inc ....G 757 399-1242
Portsmouth **(G-10504)**

BUS BARS: Electrical

Schneider Electric Usa Inc ....G 703 968-0300
Fairfax **(G-4550)**

BUSINESS ACTIVITIES: Non-Commercial Site

4gurus LLC ....G 703 520-5084
Fairfax **(G-4587)**

80protons LLC ....G 571 215-5453
Virginia Beach **(G-14198)**

AA Renwble Enrgy Hydro Sys Inc ....G 804 739-0045
Moseley **(G-9032)**

Absolutely Fabulous ....G 757 615-5732
Virginia Beach **(G-14205)**

Active Sense Technologies LLC ....G 352 226-1479
Abingdon **(G-7)**

Afritech LLC ....G 703 550-0392
Alexandria **(G-405)**

American Hands LLC ....G 804 349-8974
Powhatan **(G-10530)**

Andrea Lewis ....G 804 933-4161
North Chesterfield **(G-9818)**

Andrew Thurston Logging ....G 540 521-6276
Eagle Rock **(G-4278)**

Annoai Inc ....G 571 490-5316
Reston **(G-10789)**

Anthony Biel ....G 703 307-8516
Dumfries **(G-4234)**

Appalchian Leicester Longwools ....G 540 639-3077
Hiwassee **(G-6909)**

Aquabean LLC ....G 703 577-0315
Fairfax **(G-4409)**

Archer Construction ....G 276 637-6905
Max Meadows **(G-8365)**

Armstead Hauling Inc ....G 804 675-8221
Richmond **(G-11489)**

Artisan Meads LLC ....G 757 713-4885
Seaford **(G-12671)**

Artusmode Software LLC ....G 703 794-6100
Great Falls **(G-5938)**

Asian Pacific Seafood LLC ....G 251 751-5962
Chesapeake **(G-2984)**

Athena Services LLC ....G 201 232-9114
Falls Church **(G-4751)**

Atlas Copco Compressor Aif VA ....G 540 226-8655
Fredericksburg **(G-5249)**

Aubrey Otis Gunter Jr ....G 434 352-8136
Appomattox **(G-804)**

Avitech Consulting LLC ....G 757 810-2716
Chesapeake **(G-2990)**

Backwoods Security LLC ....G 804 641-0674
Moseley **(G-9033)**

Barney Family Enterprises LLC ....G 757 438-2064
Wakefield **(G-14964)**

Beatrice Aurthur ....G 347 420-5612
South Chesterfield **(G-12831)**

Best Printing & Design LLC ....G 703 593-9874
Arlington **(G-880)**

Big Paper Records LLC ....G 804 381-9278
Glen Allen **(G-5708)**

Bill Foote ....G 808 298-5423
Virginia Beach **(G-14279)**

Bills Yard & Lawn Service LLC ....G 757 871-4589
Hampton **(G-6092)**

Blue Ridge Buck Saver Inc ....G 434 996-2817
Charlottesville **(G-2743)**

Bright Elm LLC ....G 804 519-3331
Sandy Hook **(G-12644)**

Butter of Life LLC ....G 703 507-5298
Falls Church **(G-4766)**

Cafes D Afrique LLC ....G 757 725-1050
Hampton **(G-6103)**

Calbico LLC ....G 571 332-3334
Annandale **(G-733)**

Cambrio Studios LLC ....G 540 908-5129
Charlottesville **(G-2755)**

Candylicious Crafts LLC ....G 757 915-5542
Newport News **(G-9190)**

Cardinal Quarries LLC ....F 540 674-5556
Dublin **(G-4150)**

Carotank Road LLC ....G 703 951-7790
Alexandria **(G-161)**

Chesapeake Bay Adirondack LLC ....G 757 416-4583
Chesapeake **(G-3030)**

Codeworx Lc ....G 571 306-3859
Alexandria **(G-169)**

Collabrtive Tech Cmmnctons Cor ....G 804 477-8695
Richmond **(G-11161)**

Commonhealth Botanicals LLC...............G 434 906-2227
Charlottesville **(G-2769)**

Contour Healer LLC ....G 757 288-6671
Virginia Beach **(G-14362)**

Corey Vereen ....G 609 468-5409
Virginia Beach **(G-14367)**

Cunning Running Software Inc ....G 703 926-5864
Mineral **(G-8945)**

Custom Candyy LLC ....F 804 447-8179
Richmond **(G-11549)**

Dallas G Bienhoff ....G 571 232-4554
Annandale **(G-738)**

Damoah & Family Farm LLC ....G 703 919-0329
Stafford **(G-13136)**

Data Fusion Solutions Inc ....G 877 326-0034
Fredericksburg **(G-5271)**

Dawn Brotherton ....G 757 645-3211
Williamsburg **(G-15230)**

Debra Hewitt ....G 540 809-6281
King George **(G-7086)**

Demons Run Brewing LLC ....G 703 945-8100
Arlington **(G-936)**

Disrupt6 Inc ....G 571 721-1155
Leesburg **(G-7258)**

Divine Ntre & Antng Mnsts Inc ....G 757 240-8939
Midlothian **(G-8809)**

Dixie Fuel Company ....G 757 249-1264
Newport News **(G-9217)**

Dm Associates LLC ....G 571 406-2318
Fairfax **(G-4440)**

Dominion Comfort Solutions LLC ....G 804 501-6429
Sandston **(G-12611)**

Ds & RC Enterprises LLC ....G 804 824-5478
Gloucester **(G-5846)**

Ea Design Tech Services ....G 540 220-7203
Ruther Glen **(G-12455)**

Einstitute Inc ....F 571 255-0530
Fairfax **(G-4444)**

Elegance Meets Designs LLC ....G 347 567-6348
Richmond **(G-11199)**

Elyssa E Strong ....G 540 280-3982
Goshen **(G-5925)**

Eric Washington ....G 434 249-3567
Charlottesville **(G-2626)**

Ern Graphic Design ....G 757 281-8801
Hampton **(G-6145)**

Euclidian Systems Inc ....G 703 963-7209
Arlington **(G-960)**

Everything Gos LLC ....G 804 290-3870
Richmond **(G-11206)**

Fair Value Games LLC ....G 804 307-9110
Glen Allen **(G-5729)**

Fantabulous Chef Service ....G 804 245-4492
Richmond **(G-11208)**

Febrocom LLC ....G 703 349-6316
Ashburn **(G-1279)**

Ferguson Portable Toilets LLC ....G 434 610-9988
Appomattox **(G-811)**

Five Talents Enterprises LLC ....G 703 986-6721
Triangle **(G-13892)**

Flavorful Bakery & Cafe LLC ....G 301 857-2202
Woodbridge **(G-15704)**

Employee Codes: A=Over 500 employees, B=251-500
C=101-250, D=51-100, E=20-50, F=10-19, G=1-9   2021 Virginia
Industrial Directory   911

PRODUCT

Fluxteq LLC .... G.... 540 951-0933 Blacksburg *(G-1739)*	Limitless Gear LLC .... G.... 575 921-7475 Barboursville *(G-1564)*	Redono LLC .... G.... 757 553-2305 Chesapeake *(G-3264)*
France Lawnscpape LLC .... G.... 804 761-6823 Warsaw *(G-15063)*	M&M Great Adventures LLC .... G.... 937 344-1415 Williamsburg *(G-15275)*	Rentbot LLC .... G.... 844 473-6826 Richmond *(G-11350)*
Frontier Systems LLC .... G.... 314 221-2831 Great Falls *(G-5956)*	Madison Colonial LLC .... G.... 240 997-2376 Toano *(G-13868)*	Research Service Bureau LLC .... G.... 703 593-7507 Herndon *(G-6787)*
Gay G-Spot LLC .... G.... 650 429-8233 Arlington *(G-976)*	Magnifazine LLC .... G.... 248 224-1137 Louisa *(G-7558)*	Revival Labs LLC .... G.... 949 351-1660 Alexandria *(G-572)*
Germaine Clark LLC .... G.... 571 309-1724 Alexandria *(G-214)*	Manassas Consulting Svcs Inc .... G.... 703 346-1358 Manassas *(G-8104)*	Rimfire Games LLC .... G.... 703 580-4495 Woodbridge *(G-15796)*
Gibson Girl Publishing Co LLC .... G.... 504 261-8107 Virginia Beach *(G-14483)*	Marks Garage .... G.... 540 498-3458 Stafford *(G-13174)*	Robbworks LLC .... G.... 571 218-5532 Fairfax *(G-4669)*
Green Graphic Signs LLC .... G.... 804 229-3351 North Chesterfield *(G-9881)*	Match My Value Inc .... G.... 301 456-4308 Richmond *(G-11672)*	Rodgers Puddings LLC .... G.... 757 558-2657 Chesapeake *(G-3273)*
Green Physics Corporation .... G.... 703 989-6706 Manassas *(G-7949)*	Media Magic LLC .... G.... 757 893-0988 Virginia Beach *(G-14644)*	Rodgers Services LLC .... G.... 301 848-6384 King George *(G-7109)*
Greenacre Plumbing LLC .... G.... 703 680-2380 Woodbridge *(G-15717)*	Mg Enterprise LLC .... G.... 703 646-2761 Fairfax *(G-4509)*	Saiflavor .... G.... 304 520-9464 Harrisonburg *(G-6366)*
Gryphon Tile LLC .... G.... 540 868-2953 Middletown *(G-8739)*	Mgke Construction LLC .... G.... 571 282-8415 Manassas *(G-8108)*	Sailfish LLC .... G.... 203 570-3553 Arlington *(G-1156)*
Gyrfalcon Aerial Systems LLC .... G.... 757 724-1861 Mechanicsville *(G-8633)*	Microtude LLC .... G.... 703 581-7991 Ashburn *(G-1317)*	Salem Infotech Inc .... F.... 703 731-9711 Herndon *(G-6798)*
Hailey Bug Vending .... G.... 757 665-4402 Bloxom *(G-1841)*	Mielata LLC .... G.... 804 245-1227 Midlothian *(G-8860)*	Salem Stone Corporation .... G.... 540 674-5556 Dublin *(G-4170)*
Hampton Roads Component Assemb...G.... 757 236-8627 Hampton *(G-6163)*	Minuteman Press Intl Inc .... G.... 703 787-6506 Reston *(G-10902)*	Sallmae LLC .... G.... 931 472-9467 Fort Lee *(G-5132)*
Handi-Leigh Crafted .... G.... 540 349-7775 Warrenton *(G-15023)*	Montemorano LLC .... G.... 540 272-6390 Sumerduck *(G-13792)*	Sapentia LLC .... G.... 703 269-7191 Mc Lean *(G-8545)*
Hayward Trmt & Pest Ctrl LLC .... G.... 757 263-7858 Norfolk *(G-9574)*	MPH Development LLC .... G.... 703 303-4838 Gainesville *(G-5599)*	Sardana Sushila .... G.... 703 256-5091 Alexandria *(G-577)*
Heidi Yoder .... G.... 540 432-5598 Harrisonburg *(G-6327)*	Mr1 Construction LLC .... G.... 301 748-6078 Manassas *(G-7977)*	Sarfez Pharmaceuticals Inc .... G.... 703 759-2565 Vienna *(G-14122)*
Hill Brenton .... G.... 757 560-9332 Hampton *(G-6167)*	Mzgoodiez LLC .... G.... 757 535-6929 Suffolk *(G-13747)*	Sawarmor LLC .... G.... 703 779-7719 Leesburg *(G-7342)*
Hip-Hop Spot 24/7 LLC .... G.... 434 660-3166 Lynchburg *(G-7734)*	Net6degrees LLC .... G.... 703 201-4480 Purcellville *(G-10672)*	Scratcherguru LLC .... G.... 804 239-8629 Montpelier *(G-9020)*
I & C Hughes LLC .... G.... 757 544-0502 Virginia Beach *(G-14537)*	Neuropro Spinal Jaxx Inc .... G.... 571 334-7424 Burke *(G-2195)*	Shifflett and Son Log Co LLC .... G.... 757 434-7979 Urbanna *(G-13973)*
Impression An Everlasting Inc .... F.... 804 363-7185 Mechanicsville *(G-8640)*	New Age Repr & Fabrication LLC .... G.... 757 819-3887 Norfolk *(G-9659)*	Ship Sstnability Solutions LLC .... G.... 757 574-2436 Chesapeake *(G-3291)*
Indigo Pen Publishing LLC .... G.... 888 670-4010 Alexandria *(G-484)*	Nolte Machine and Welding LLC .... G.... 804 357-7271 Sandston *(G-12625)*	Signature Publishing LLC .... G.... 757 348-9692 South Chesterfield *(G-12839)*
Industrial Alloy Welding LLC .... G.... 757 573-8496 Norfolk *(G-9592)*	Noparei Professionals LLC .... G.... 571 354-9422 Woodbridge *(G-15763)*	Signature Signs .... G.... 540 554-2717 Round Hill *(G-12389)*
Infobase Publishers Inc .... F.... 703 327-8470 South Riding *(G-12868)*	Nova Green Energy LLC .... G.... 571 210-0589 Falls Church *(G-4847)*	Simply Panache Products LLC .... G.... 757 358-7062 Hampton *(G-6238)*
Inovitech LLC .... G.... 877 429-0377 Leesburg *(G-7287)*	One Aperture LLC .... G.... 202 415-0416 Falls Church *(G-4851)*	Slim Strength Inc .... G.... 804 715-3080 Richmond *(G-11064)*
Intouch For Inmates LLC .... G.... 862 246-6283 Lynchburg *(G-7746)*	One Stop Cleaning LLC .... G.... 757 561-2952 Williamsburg *(G-15286)*	Slys Sucker Punch LLC .... G.... 571 989-3538 Woodbridge *(G-15814)*
Iron Forge Software LLC .... G.... 571 263-6540 Oak Hill *(G-10137)*	Oneso Inc .... G.... 704 560-6354 Arlington *(G-1088)*	So Olive LLC .... G.... 571 398-2377 Occoquan *(G-10175)*
James A Kennedy & Assoc Inc .... G.... 804 241-6836 Powhatan *(G-10553)*	Orien Usa LLC .... G.... 757 486-2099 Virginia Beach *(G-14703)*	Source360 LLC .... G.... 703 232-1563 Chantilly *(G-2494)*
Jennifer Reynolds .... G.... 804 229-1697 Mechanicsville *(G-8644)*	Orlando Garzon Cuellar .... G.... 571 274-6913 Manassas *(G-8123)*	Southern Fire & Safety Co .... G.... 434 546-6774 Lynchburg *(G-7810)*
Joint Planning Solutions LLC .... G.... 757 839-5593 Virginia Beach *(G-14573)*	OSI LLC .... G.... 757 967-7533 Virginia Beach *(G-14705)*	Special Communications LLC .... G.... 202 677-1225 Virginia Beach *(G-14833)*
Juanita Deshazior .... G.... 703 901-5592 Alexandria *(G-248)*	Packet Stash Inc .... G.... 202 649-0676 Alexandria *(G-303)*	Sport Creations LLC .... G.... 757 572-2113 Virginia Beach *(G-14841)*
Kathleen Tilley .... G.... 703 727-5385 Williamsburg *(G-15265)*	Pep Labs LLC .... G.... 202 669-2562 Ashburn *(G-1325)*	Spritelogic LLC .... G.... 703 568-0468 Mc Lean *(G-8557)*
Kcsl .... 276 206-5977 Abingdon *(G-46)*	Peppers Services LLC .... G.... 276 233-6464 Galax *(G-5645)*	Square One Printing Inc .... G.... 904 993-4321 Richmond *(G-11771)*
Kemper Printing LLC .... G.... 804 510-8402 Richmond *(G-11641)*	Periflame LLC .... F.... 888 996-3526 Arlington *(G-1107)*	Swami Shriji LLC .... G.... 804 322-9644 North Chesterfield *(G-9994)*
Ken Musselman & Associates Inc .... G.... 804 790-0302 Chesterfield *(G-3510)*	Peters Knives .... G.... 703 255-5353 Vienna *(G-14110)*	T3j Enterprises LLC .... G.... 757 768-0528 Newport News *(G-9351)*
Kennedy Projects LLC .... G.... 757 345-0626 Williamsburg *(G-15266)*	Pivit .... G.... 301 395-0895 Chantilly *(G-2551)*	Terry Brown .... G.... 804 721-6667 Prince George *(G-10608)*
Kilmartin Jones Group LLC .... G.... 703 232-1531 Manassas *(G-8094)*	Pk Hot Sauce LLC .... G.... 703 629-0920 Manassas *(G-7989)*	Tg Polymers Inc .... G.... 585 670-9427 Alexandria *(G-597)*
Kin Art Studios LLC .... G.... 804 368-7298 Ashland *(G-1449)*	Pro Image Printing & Pubg LLC .... G.... 804 798-4400 Rockville *(G-12295)*	Thintherm LLC .... G.... 434 243-5328 Charlottesville *(G-2891)*
Kinemetrx Incorporated .... G.... 703 596-5095 Herndon *(G-6723)*	Pumped Cards .... G.... 202 725-6964 Woodbridge *(G-15786)*	Tidewater Wldg Fabrication LLC .... G.... 757 636-6630 Chesapeake *(G-3340)*
Kisco Signs LLC .... G.... 804 404-2727 Richmond *(G-11646)*	Pursuit Packaging LLC .... G.... 540 246-4629 Broadway *(G-2094)*	Tiome Inc .... G.... 703 531-8963 Alexandria *(G-599)*
Kodescraft LLC .... G.... 703 843-3700 Triangle *(G-13895)*	Q Protein Inc .... G.... 240 994-6160 Roanoke *(G-11992)*	Tizzy Technologies Inc .... G.... 703 344-3348 Virginia Beach *(G-14884)*
KORA Confections LLC .... G.... 240 478-2222 King George *(G-7098)*	Raised Apps LLC .... G.... 703 398-8254 Woodbridge *(G-15790)*	Total Lift Care LLC .... G.... 540 631-0008 Front Royal *(G-5559)*
Kuary LLC .... G.... 703 980-3804 Fairfax *(G-4495)*	Rapid Biosciences Inc .... G.... 713 899-6177 Richmond *(G-11728)*	Total Welding Solutions LLC .... G.... 703 898-8720 Haymarket *(G-6450)*
Leatheroot LLC .... G.... 804 695-1604 Gloucester *(G-5853)*	Raymond Golden .... G.... 757 549-1853 Chesapeake *(G-3256)*	Tremolo Security Inc .... G.... 703 844-2727 Arlington *(G-1196)*
Leigh Ann Carrasco .... G.... 703 725-4680 Mc Lean *(G-8486)*	Raytum Photonics LLC .... G.... 703 831-7809 Sterling *(G-13487)*	Triple Yolk LLC .... G.... 540 923-4040 Reva *(G-11002)*
Li Ailin .... G.... 573 808-7280 Arlington *(G-1033)*	Red Eagle Industries LLC .... G.... 434 352-5831 Appomattox *(G-822)*	Troesen Enterprises LLC .... G.... 571 405-3199 Alexandria *(G-369)*

True Steel LLC ....G 540 680-2906
Charlottesville (G-2896)

Ttec LLC ....G 540 336-2693
Berryville (G-1697)

Tumalow Inc ....G 847 644-9009
Bumpass (G-2170)

Ultracomm Llc ....G 703 622-6397
Purcellville (G-10683)

Unique Flexique LLC ....G 540 439-4465
Bealeton (G-1607)

Unison Arms LLC ....G 571 342-1108
Round Hill (G-12392)

Unseen Technologies Inc ....G 704 207-7391
Lynchburg (G-7829)

Vegnos Corporation ....G 571 721-1685
Alexandria (G-604)

Velvet Pile Carpets LLC ....G 540 920-9473
Gordonsville (G-5918)

Vitae Spirits Distillery LLC ....G 434 242-0350
Charlottesville (G-2903)

Vitalcode Inc ....G 703 622-1154
Ashburn (G-1351)

Watercraft Logistics Svcs Co ....G 757 348-3089
Virginia Beach (G-14930)

While Software LLC ....G 202 290-6705
Great Falls (G-5984)

Whiteboard Applications Inc ....G 703 297-2835
Leesburg (G-7377)

Willie Lucas ....G 919 935-8066
Woodbridge (G-15832)

Wilson & Wilson International ....G 804 733-3180
North Dinwiddie (G-10071)

Windryder Inc ....G 540 545-8851
Winchester (G-15516)

Wine With Everything LLC ....G 703 777-4899
Leesburg (G-7380)

Winterloch Publishing LLC ....G 804 571-2782
North Chesterfield (G-10013)

Wise Feline Inc ....G 703 609-2686
Alexandria (G-384)

World History Group LLC ....E 703 779-8322
Vienna (G-14162)

Xlnt Solutions Inc ....G 703 819-9265
Fairfax (G-4585)

Zoil Jewelry LLC ....G 571 340-2256
Herndon (G-6849)

BUSINESS FORMS WHOLESALERS

Grubb Printing & Stamp Co Inc ....F 757 295-8061
Portsmouth (G-10438)

BUSINESS FORMS: Printed, Continuous

Dgi Line Inc ....D 434 797-4114
Danville (G-3982)

Printech Inc ....F 540 343-9200
Roanoke (G-12154)

BUSINESS FORMS: Printed, Manifold

Dad13 Inc ....C 703 550-9555
Newington (G-9153)

Standard Register Inc ....F 703 516-4014
Arlington (G-1174)

Taylor Communications Inc ....E 703 790-9700
Vienna (G-14138)

Taylor Communications Inc ....F 937 221-1000
North Chesterfield (G-10025)

Taylor Communications Inc ....G 703 904-0133
Herndon (G-6823)

Taylor Communications Inc ....G 434 822-1111
Danville (G-4040)

BUSINESS FORMS: Strip, Manifold

Vas of Virginia Inc ....E 434 296-5608
Charlottesville (G-2899)

BUSINESS SUPPORT SVCS

300 Qubits LLC ....G 202 320-0196
Arlington (G-835)

3mp1re Clothing Co ....G 540 892-3484
Richmond (G-11073)

Adme Solutions LLC ....G 540 664-3521
Stephens City (G-13311)

All Tyed Up ....G 804 855-7158
Richmond (G-11482)

Antillian Trading Company LLC ....E 703 626-6333
Alexandria (G-414)

B and B Welding Service LLC ....G 804 994-2797
Aylett (G-1545)

Bar-C Sand Inc ....G 276 701-3888
Cedar Bluff (G-2270)

Bartrack Inc ....G 717 521-4840
Rockingham (G-12241)

Bath Sensations LLC ....G 804 832-4701
Chesterfield (G-3478)

Battlefield Terrain Concepts ....G 540 977-0696
Roanoke (G-11884)

Berkley Latasha ....G 804 572-6394
Henrico (G-6482)

Bloombeams LLC ....G 804 822-1022
Midlothian (G-8780)

Brian K Babcock ....G 540 251-3003
Riner (G-11861)

Broad Street Traffic Jams LLC ....G 804 461-1245
Rockville (G-12284)

Cardinal Applications LLC ....G 540 270-4369
Amissville (G-717)

Casey Traxler ....G 703 402-0745
Leesburg (G-7242)

Christopher K Reddersen ....G 703 232-6691
Warrenton (G-14987)

Crooked Stitch Bags LLC ....G 703 680-0118
Woodbridge (G-15676)

Daniel Orenzuk ....G 410 570-1362
Purcellville (G-10658)

David S Welch ....G 276 398-4024
Fancy Gap (G-4934)

Detas Famous Potatoe Salad LLC ....G 757 609-1130
Virginia Beach (G-14402)

Dobyns Family LLC ....G 804 462-5554
Lancaster (G-7159)

Dorothy Whibley ....G 703 892-6612
Montclair (G-8997)

Dream of ME Bowtique ....G 804 955-5908
North Chesterfield (G-9860)

Dw Saltwater Flies LLC ....G 757 874-1859
Newport News (G-9218)

Earth Science Technology LLC ....G 703 584-8533
Lorton (G-7483)

Epic Led ....G 703 499-4485
Manassas (G-7939)

Essential Software Dev LLC ....G 540 222-1254
Fairfax (G-4451)

Fiddlehand Inc ....G 703 340-9806
Herndon (G-6675)

General Magnetic Sciences Inc ....G 571 243-6887
Clifton (G-3666)

Getintoforex LLC ....G 251 591-2181
Big Stone Gap (G-1710)

Go Vivace Inc ....G 703 869-9463
Mc Lean (G-8451)

Gradient Dynamics LLC ....G 865 207-9052
Mc Lean (G-8453)

H & B Machine ....G 276 546-5307
Keokee (G-7040)

Henry Bijak ....G 757 572-1673
Virginia Beach (G-14516)

Hey Frase LLC ....G 202 372-5453
Arlington (G-991)

High Stakes Writing LLC ....G 703 819-5490
Annandale (G-756)

Ink It On Anything ....G 804 814-5890
Chesterfield (G-3505)

Jclfarms LLC ....G 757 291-1401
Williamsburg (G-15260)

Jeffrey Gill ....G 703 309-7061
Charlottesville (G-2819)

Jim L Clark ....G 276 393-2359
Jonesville (G-7022)

Johnson Machinery Sales Inc ....G 540 890-8893
Vinton (G-14174)

Kenneth Foley ....G 276 930-1452
Stuart (G-13620)

Lakota JS Chocolates Corp ....G 804 590-0010
Chesterfield (G-3512)

Larry D Martin ....G 540 493-0072
Rocky Mount (G-12332)

Lumos LLC ....G 571 294-4290
Arlington (G-1050)

Magic Genius LLC ....G 540 454-7595
Warrenton (G-15032)

Mark A Harber ....G 276 546-6051
Pennington Gap (G-10295)

Mark T Goodman ....G 540 582-2328
Partlow (G-10267)

Martin Tonya ....G 804 742-8721
La Crosse (G-7146)

Maurice Bynum ....G 757 241-0265
Windsor (G-15606)

Michael McKittrick ....G 804 695-7090
Deltaville (G-4083)

Miguel Soto ....G 571 274-3790
Leesburg (G-7315)

Napoleon Books ....G 540 463-6804
Lexington (G-7406)

Neopath Systems LLC ....G 571 238-1333
Herndon (G-6752)

Neu Age Sportswear ....G 757 581-8333
Norfolk (G-9658)

Our Journey Publishing ....G 571 606-1574
Dumfries (G-4254)

PC Sands LLC ....G 703 534-6107
Arlington (G-1102)

Polytrade International Corp ....G 703 598-7269
Sterling (G-13474)

Ray Painter Small ....G 804 255-7050
Chesterfield (G-3520)

Riegger Marin ....G 646 896-4739
Blacksburg (G-1784)

River House Creations LLC ....G 757 509-2137
Gloucester (G-5859)

Shawn Gaines ....G 434 332-4819
Rustburg (G-12446)

Simplicity Pure Bath & Bdy LLC ....G 540 922-9287
Pearisburg (G-10277)

Snt Trucking Inc ....G 276 991-0931
Swords Creek (G-13808)

Stacey A Peets ....G 847 707-3112
Henrico (G-6575)

Tammy Haire ....G 540 722-7246
Winchester (G-15487)

Treescapes Inc ....G 434 294-0865
Alberta (G-99)

Turbo Tellers ....G 812 250-1837
Spout Spring (G-12928)

VA Designs and Cnstr LLC ....G 757 651-8909
Norfolk (G-9777)

BUSINESS TRAINING SVCS

Give More Media Inc ....G 804 762-4500
Richmond (G-11601)

Self Solutions LLC ....E 202 725-0866
Alexandria (G-582)

CABINETS & CASES: Show, Display & Storage, Exc Wood

Capitol Closet Design Inc ....F 703 827-2700
Vienna (G-14022)

CABINETS: Bathroom Vanities, Wood

American Woodmark Corporation ....C 540 665-9100
Winchester (G-15378)

American Woodmark Corporation ....G 540 672-3707
Orange (G-10202)

Bells Cabinet Shop ....G 804 448-3111
Ruther Glen (G-12451)

Cascade Cabinets & Millwork ....G 434 685-4000
Cascade (G-2249)

Classic Creations of Tidewater ....G 757 548-1442
Chesapeake (G-3036)

Norfield-Fogleman Cabinets ....G 276 889-1333
Lebanon (G-7202)

Starmark Cabinetry ....F 434 385-7500
Lynchburg (G-7813)

Strasburg Cabinet & Supply ....G 540 465-3031
Strasburg (G-13599)

CABINETS: Entertainment

Bay Cabinets & Contractors ....G 757 934-2236
Suffolk (G-13676)

Robert Furr Cabinet Shop ....G 757 244-1267
Hampton (G-6230)

Walmer Enterprises ....E 703 461-9330
Montross (G-9028)

CABINETS: Entertainment Units, Household, Wood

Hooker Furniture Corporation ....C 276 632-1763
Martinsville (G-8298)

Hooker Furniture Corporation ....C 276 632-2133
Martinsville (G-8297)

CABINETS: Factory

Blue Ridge Shelving Closet LLC ....F 540 365-0150
Ferrum (G-4972)

Employee Codes: A=Over 500 employees, B=251-500
C=101-250, D=51-100, E=20-50, F=10-19, G=1-9

2021 Virginia
Industrial Directory

913

PRODUCT

Creative Cabinet Design..................G....434 293-4040
Charlottesville (G-2774)

D & T Akers Corporation..................G....804 435-2709
Kilmarnock (G-7069)

Fitzgeralds Cabinet Shop Inc..........G....757 877-2538
Newport News (G-9229)

Ronnie and Betty Bridges...............G....804 561-4506
Amelia Court House (G-670)

Smith Cabinets.................................G....703 790-9896
Mc Lean (G-8548)

CABINETS: Filing, Office, Wood

Total Millwork LLC...........................E....571 379-5500
Manassas (G-8168)

CABINETS: Filing, Wood

Maurice Lamb..................................G....540 962-0903
Covington (G-3794)

CABINETS: Kitchen, Metal

Keane Cabinetry...............................G....540 867-5336
Rockingham (G-12257)

CABINETS: Kitchen, Wood

A & R Cabinet Co Inc........................G....804 261-4098
Henrico (G-6469)

A&F Ccuston Cabinetry Built............G....703 598-7686
Ashburn (G-1235)

ACC Cabinetry LLC...........................G....540 333-0189
Berryville (G-1669)

Ace Cabinets & More LLC.................G....757 206-1684
Williamsburg (G-15202)

Advanced Cabinets & Tops Inc........G....804 355-5541
Richmond (G-11086)

Ajc Woodworks Inc...........................G....757 566-0336
Toano (G-13855)

Albion Cabinets Stairs Inc...............G....434 974-4611
Earlysville (G-4284)

All Affairs Transportation LLC...........G....757 342-2474
Newport News (G-9162)

American Woodmark Corporation......B....540 665-9100
Winchester (G-15377)

Arboleda Cabinets Inc.....................F....804 230-0733
Richmond (G-11487)

B & J Cabinet Co Inc........................E....804 271-0192
North Chesterfield (G-9825)

Baldwin Cabinet Shops Inc..............G....804 443-5421
Tappahannock (G-13812)

Bernies Furn & Cabinetry Inc..........G....434 846-6883
Madison Heights (G-7868)

Best Cabinets and Closets LLC........G....703 830-0542
Centreville (G-2294)

Bills Custom Cabinetry.....................G....703 281-1669
Vienna (G-14017)

Bishop Custom Cabinets...................G....804 469-7549
North Dinwiddie (G-10048)

Blue Ridge Woodworks VA Inc..........G....434 477-0313
Monroe (G-8987)

Bluebird Cabinetry............................G....804 937-5429
Richmond (G-11129)

Bobby Utt Custom Cabinets.............G....276 728-9411
Fancy Gap (G-4933)

Bowman Woodworking Inc................G....540 483-1680
Ferrum (G-4973)

Brinkleys Custom Cabinets..............G....540 525-1780
Buchanan (G-2117)

Burnette Cabinet Shop Inc...............G....540 586-0147
Bedford (G-1629)

C&S Custom Cabinets Inc.................G....540 273-5450
Louisa (G-7548)

Cabinet & More.................................G....571 719-5040
Manassas Park (G-8193)

Cabinet Arts LLC..............................G....571 313-1891
Sterling (G-13363)

Cabinet Arts LLC..............................G....703 870-1456
Arlington (G-898)

Cabinet Co of Virginia Corp.............G....757 357-5519
Smithfield (G-12707)

Cabinet Design Plus.........................G....540 773-4571
Winchester (G-15533)

Cabinet Discounters Inc...................F....703 803-7990
Chantilly (G-2385)

Cabinet Kingdom LLC.......................G....804 514-9546
Midlothian (G-8787)

Cabinet Works of N N........................G....804 493-8102
Montross (G-9024)

Cabinetry & Construction Inc...........G....804 497-3491
Richmond (G-11516)

Cabinetry With TLC LLC....................G....540 777-0456
Roanoke (G-11900)

Cabinets By Design..........................G....434 589-2600
Troy (G-13921)

Cabinets By Design Inc....................G....757 558-9558
Chesapeake (G-3022)

Cabinets Direct Inc...........................G....540 884-2329
Eagle Rock (G-4280)

Cabinets Ready To Go LLC................G....703 665-5620
Chantilly (G-2386)

Cabinets To Go LLC........................G....814 688-7584
Norfolk (G-9472)

Cabinets To Go LLC........................G....804 325-4775
Richmond (G-11143)

Carys Mill Woodworking....................G....804 639-2946
Midlothian (G-8792)

Cedar Forest Cabinetry & Millw........G....703 753-0644
Nokesville (G-9390)

Cherry Hill Cabinetry........................G....540 785-4333
Fredericksburg (G-5177)

Cherry Hill Cabinetry........................G....703 942-6053
Mc Lean (G-8405)

Chesapeake Cabinet & Finish Co.....G....757 787-9422
Onancock (G-10192)

CL Cabinetry Corporation..................G....703 586-6766
Alexandria (G-430)

Classic Kitchens of Virginia.............F....804 784-5075
Richmond (G-11158)

Classic Woodcraft............................G....757 631-9354
Norfolk (G-9488)

Closet and Beyond............................G....703 962-7894
Arlington (G-908)

Cloud Cabin Arts..............................G....434 218-3020
Charlottesville (G-2768)

Coastal Cabinets By Jenna LLC.........G....757 339-0710
Virginia Beach (G-14344)

Coblentz Custom Cabinets...............G....231 362-2728
Amherst (G-688)

Cochrans Lumber & Millwork Inc......E....540 955-4142
Berryville (G-1675)

Colonial Kitchen & Cabinets............E....757 898-1332
Yorktown (G-15943)

Commercial Custom Cabinet Inc......E....804 228-2100
Richmond (G-11533)

Contemporary Kitchens Ltd.............G....804 758-2001
Topping (G-13886)

Contemporary Woodcrafts Inc.........G....703 451-4257
Springfield (G-12979)

Contemporary Woodcrafts Inc.........F....703 787-9711
Fairfax Station (G-4703)

Corner Cabinet Shop Inc..................G....540 672-9460
Orange (G-10207)

Cornerstone Cabinets & Design.......G....434 239-0976
Forest (G-5065)

Cove Antiques..................................G....757 787-3881
Onancock (G-10194)

Creative Cabinet Design..................G....434 293-4040
Charlottesville (G-2774)

Creative Cabinet Designs LLC..........G....703 644-1090
Pulaski (G-10633)

Creative Cabinet Works....................G....757 220-1941
Lanexa (G-7164)

Creative Cabinet Works LLC.............G....757 566-1000
Toano (G-13861)

Crossroads Cabinets LLC..................G....319 431-1588
Moseley (G-9037)

Custom Built Cabinets and...............G....812 427-9733
Jonesville (G-7021)

Custom Kraft Inc...............................F....757 265-2882
Hampton (G-6126)

Daves Cabinet Shop Inc...................G....804 861-9275
North Dinwiddie (G-10050)

David Mays Cabinet Maker................G....434 277-8533
Amherst (G-689)

Daylight Cabinetry LLC....................G....804 432-4954
Richmond (G-11554)

Deneals Cabinets Inc.......................G....540 721-8005
Hardy (G-6286)

Designer Cabinets............................G....540 569-0469
Staunton (G-13251)

Designs In Wood LLC......................G....804 517-1414
Richmond (G-11183)

Dobbs & Assoc.................................G....804 314-8871
Ashland (G-1403)

Dominion Door and Drawer...............G....804 955-9302
Ruther Glen (G-12454)

Duckworth Company.........................G....540 436-8754
Toms Brook (G-13884)

Dutch Made Cabinets.......................G....276 728-5700
Hillsville (G-6890)

Ecowood Usa Inc.............................G....703 347-6858
Springfield (G-12996)

Elegant Cabinets Inc.......................E....540 483-5800
Rocky Mount (G-12320)

Elite Cabinet LLC..............................G....703 909-0404
Alexandria (G-454)

Euro Cabinets Inc.............................F....757 671-7884
Virginia Beach (G-14454)

Expo Cabinetry.................................G....703 940-3800
Fairfax (G-4454)

Feefees Cabinet LLC.........................G....804 647-0297
North Chesterfield (G-9872)

Field Inner Prizes LLC.......................G....540 738-2060
Brightwood (G-1961)

Final Touch Cabinetry.......................G....540 895-5776
Spotsylvania (G-12890)

First Forest Furniture & Mllwk...........G....540 743-2051
Luray (G-7612)

Fitzgeralds Cabinet Shop Inc..........G....757 877-2538
Newport News (G-9229)

Francis C James Jr...........................G....757 442-3630
Nassawadox (G-9100)

Fred Hean Furniture & Wdwrk...........G....434 973-5960
Charlottesville (G-2634)

G T Walls Cabinet Shop....................G....804 798-6288
Glen Allen (G-5734)

Gary A Watkins Construction............G....703 367-0477
Manassas Park (G-8200)

Gjs Cabinetry Installation.................G....540 856-2726
Edinburg (G-4306)

Green Forest Cabinetry.....................G....757 485-9200
Chesapeake (G-3124)

Greenbrier Custom Cabinets............G....757 438-5475
Norfolk (G-9566)

Greenworks Cstm Cabinetry LLC.......G....540 635-5725
Front Royal (G-5534)

Greg Norman and Associates Inc.....F....703 205-0031
Annandale (G-754)

Groves Cabinetry Inc........................G....540 341-7309
Jeffersonton (G-7013)

H & M Cabinetry...............................G....804 338-9504
Midlothian (G-8824)

H B Cabinet Refacers........................G....571 213-5257
Centreville (G-2309)

Haley Pearsall Inc............................G....804 784-3438
Richmond (G-11230)

Hawes Joinery Inc.............................G....540 384-6733
Salem (G-12517)

Henley Cabinetry Inc........................G....804 776-0016
Hartfield (G-6390)

Heritage Cabinets Inc......................G....804 861-5251
North Dinwiddie (G-10052)

Heritage Woodworks LLC.................E....757 934-1440
Suffolk (G-13720)

Hi-Tech Cabinets Inc........................G....757 681-0016
Virginia Beach (G-14522)

Horizon Custom Cabinets Corp........G....757 434-8706
Virginia Beach (G-14527)

Horizon Custom Cabinets Corp........G....757 306-1007
Virginia Beach (G-14528)

Ideal Cabinets Inc............................G....540 366-1748
Salem (G-12519)

In Stock Today Cabinets LLC............F....703 972-4030
Fairfax (G-4479)

Innovative Kitchens Inc....................G....757 425-7753
Virginia Beach (G-14546)

Interior Building Systems Corp.........D....703 335-9655
Manassas (G-8083)

J W Creations..................................G....276 676-3770
Abingdon (G-43)

Ja Le Custom Crafts.........................G....804 541-8957
Disputanta (G-4109)

Jaeger & Ernst Inc............................F....434 973-7018
Barboursville (G-1562)

Julian Swain Builders Inc.................E....757 490-0211
Norfolk (G-9608)

KEC Associates Ltd..........................G....804 404-2601
North Chesterfield (G-9906)

Kitchen and Bath Company LLC........G....757 417-8200
Virginia Beach (G-14586)

Kitchen Concepts Inc.......................G....757 547-9238
Chesapeake (G-3165)

Kitchen Krafters Inc.........................G....540 891-7678
Fredericksburg (G-5311)

Kleppinger Design Group Inc...........F....703 208-2208
Fairfax (G-4490)

L Peters Custom Cabinets................G....276 340-9580
Ridgeway (G-11846)

La Prade Enterprises........................G....804 271-9899
North Chesterfield (G-9912)

Lantz Custom Woodworking ....G...... 540 438-1819
Harrisonburg *(G-6336)*

Lawrence Custom Cabinets S ....G...... 757 380-0817
Newport News *(G-9279)*

Liberty Cabinets ....G...... 540 493-3149
Rocky Mount *(G-12334)*

Lighthouse Cabinets Inc ....G...... 571 293-1064
Leesburg *(G-7299)*

Louis G Ball & Son Inc ....G...... 804 725-5202
Mathews *(G-8356)*

Macs Custom Woodshop ....G...... 540 789-4201
Willis *(G-15363)*

Mark Debusk Custom Cabinets ....G...... 540 552-3228
Blacksburg *(G-1759)*

Martcl Inc ....G...... 540 777-0456
Roanoke *(G-11959)*

Martin Star Cabinetry & Design ....G...... 804 340-1250
Richmond *(G-11669)*

Marvin Coblentz ....G...... 434 944-1897
Amherst *(G-699)*

Masco Cabinetry LLC ....B...... 540 477-2961
Mount Jackson *(G-9076)*

Masco Cabinetry LLC ....C...... 540 727-7859
Culpeper *(G-3907)*

Masterbrand Cabinets Inc ....G...... 703 396-7804
Manassas *(G-7973)*

Mather AMP Cabinet ....G...... 615 636-1743
Virginia Beach *(G-14640)*

McCraw Cabinets ....G...... 434 238-2112
Forest *(G-5082)*

Mill Cabinet Shop Inc ....E...... 540 828-6763
Bridgewater *(G-1954)*

Montgomery Cabinetry ....G...... 540 721-7000
Wirtz *(G-15616)*

Moon Cabinet Inc ....G...... 703 339-8097
Lorton *(G-7512)*

Nails Cabinet Shop Inc ....G...... 540 888-3268
Winchester *(G-15454)*

Nelsons Cabinetry ....G...... 804 363-5800
North Chesterfield *(G-9938)*

Nelsons Cabinetry Inc ....G...... 804 560-4785
North Chesterfield *(G-9939)*

New Life Custom Cabinetry LLC ....G...... 757 274-7442
Virginia Beach *(G-14680)*

Nextday Cabinets of Va LLC ....G...... 703 291-8935
Richmond *(G-11304)*

Nichols Cabinetry LLC ....G...... 540 860-9252
Luray *(G-7620)*

Norcraft Companies LP ....B...... 434 385-7500
Lynchburg *(G-7777)*

Nuckols Cabinetry LLC ....G...... 804 749-3908
Rockville *(G-12294)*

Panda Kitchen and Bath VA LLC ....G...... 757 889-9888
Norfolk *(G-9681)*

Peters Melvin Cabinet Shop Inc ....G...... 757 826-7317
Hampton *(G-6215)*

Phillips Custom Cabinets LLC ....G...... 804 647-1328
Amelia Court House *(G-667)*

Pinnacle Cabinetry Design LLC ....G...... 804 262-7356
Richmond *(G-11326)*

Pom Kbf ....G...... 703 992-7877
Alexandria *(G-552)*

Potomac Shores Cabinetry LLC ....G...... 703 476-5658
Herndon *(G-6777)*

Precision Millwork & Cabinets ....G...... 434 525-6988
Evington *(G-4383)*

Premier Cabinets Virginia LLC ....G...... 804 335-7354
Midlothian *(G-8882)*

Prestige Cabinets ....G...... 757 741-3201
Toano *(G-13875)*

Prestige Cabinets LLC ....G...... 757 741-3201
Williamsburg *(G-15298)*

Prestige Inc ....F...... 804 266-1000
Richmond *(G-11332)*

Pro Refinish ....G...... 703 853-9665
Warrenton *(G-15046)*

Progressive Designs ....G...... 757 547-9201
Chesapeake *(G-3251)*

R & B Cabinet Shop ....G...... 540 249-4507
Grottoes *(G-6023)*

R & K Woodworking Inc ....G...... 540 867-5975
Dayton *(G-4059)*

Racers Custom Cabinets Inc ....G...... 540 672-4231
Orange *(G-10225)*

Rader Cabinets ....G...... 434 610-1954
Lynchburg *(G-7798)*

Ramsey Cabinets Inc ....G...... 434 946-0329
Amherst *(G-705)*

Rays Custom Cabinets ....G...... 434 528-0181
Amherst *(G-706)*

Reinhart Custom Cabinets Inc ....G...... 757 303-1438
Newport News *(G-9323)*

Renaissance Cabinet Shop ....G...... 540 967-0422
Louisa *(G-7565)*

Richmond Refacing ....G...... 804 739-9222
Midlothian *(G-8888)*

Rick Boyd Stone Cabinet ....G...... 540 365-2668
Ferrum *(G-4978)*

Risque Custom Cabinetry ....G...... 703 534-5319
Falls Church *(G-4867)*

Ritz Refinishing Inc ....G...... 703 378-0462
Chantilly *(G-2487)*

River City Cabinetry LLC ....G...... 804 397-7950
Chester *(G-3453)*

Robert Furr Cabinet Shop ....G...... 757 244-1267
Hampton *(G-6230)*

Rockridge Granite Company LLC ....G...... 434 969-2665
Buckingham *(G-2136)*

Round Meadows Cabinet Shop ....G...... 276 398-1153
Laurel Fork *(G-7175)*

Rutrough Cabinets Inc ....G...... 540 489-3211
Rocky Mount *(G-12351)*

Salem Custom Cabinets Inc ....G...... 540 380-4441
Salem *(G-12564)*

Sarandi Manufacturing LLC ....F...... 540 705-0205
Broadway *(G-2095)*

Shively and Carter Cabinets ....G...... 540 483-4149
Glade Hill *(G-5670)*

Signature Dsigns Cabinetry LLC ....G...... 804 614-0028
Chesterfield *(G-3524)*

Simply Clssic Cbnets Cnstr LLC ....G...... 804 815-3283
Locust Hill *(G-7454)*

Southern Pride Cabinets ....G...... 540 365-3227
Ferrum *(G-4983)*

Spotted Lopard-Tabula Rasa LLC ....G...... 571 285-8151
Warrenton *(G-15053)*

Steve K Jones ....G...... 757 930-0217
Newport News *(G-9347)*

Talmadge Fix ....G...... 540 463-9629
Lexington *(G-7419)*

Theboxworks ....G...... 434 823-1004
Crozet *(G-3852)*

Timberlake Cabinet Company ....G...... 540 955-4985
Berryville *(G-1694)*

Toms Cabinets & Designs ....G...... 703 451-2227
Springfield *(G-13301)*

Tops of Town Virginia LLC ....G...... 703 242-8100
Fairfax *(G-4571)*

Trademark Woodworking LLC ....G...... 804 346-5999
Richmond *(G-11417)*

Triple S Enterprises Inc ....F...... 434 525-8400
Forest *(G-5102)*

Unique Cabinets Inc ....G...... 434 823-2188
Crozet *(G-3853)*

US Cabinet & Intr Design LLC ....G...... 202 740-0038
Falls Church *(G-4887)*

USA Cabinets Store ....G...... 703 204-3444
Fairfax *(G-4576)*

Vangarde Woodworks Inc ....G...... 804 355-4917
Richmond *(G-11433)*

Vaughans Custom Cabinets-Home ......G...... 276 398-2440
Hillsville *(G-6903)*

Village Cabinet Co ....G...... 434 574-6263
Prospect *(G-10615)*

Virginia Cabinetry LLC ....G...... 804 612-6469
Richmond *(G-11810)*

Virginia Cabinets LLC ....G...... 703 793-8307
Herndon *(G-6840)*

Virginia Cabinetworks Inc ....G...... 540 298-9599
Elkton *(G-4336)*

Virginia Woodcrafters LLC ....G...... 804 276-2766
Henrico *(G-6590)*

Voell Custom Kitchens Inc ....G...... 703 528-1776
Arlington *(G-1215)*

Walkers Creek Cabinet Works ....G...... 540 348-5810
Middlebrook *(G-8714)*

Walsh Tops Inc ....E...... 757 523-1934
Chesapeake *(G-3369)*

Washington Cabinetry ....G...... 703 466-5388
Chantilly *(G-2518)*

Wells Cabinet Shop ....G...... 804 861-8325
Prince George *(G-10610)*

West Shore Cabinetry ....G...... 804 739-2985
Midlothian *(G-8920)*

Windsor Woodworking Co Inc ....G...... 757 242-4141
Windsor *(G-15608)*

Wolf Cabinetry Inc ....G...... 757 498-0088
Virginia Beach *(G-14942)*

Wood Chux Cabinets LLC ....G...... 757 409-0095
Virginia Beach *(G-14943)*

Wood Provision ....G...... 540 456-8522
Afton *(G-96)*

Woodworking Shop Inc ....G...... 757 872-0890
Newport News *(G-9381)*

Woodys Woodworking Inc ....G...... 703 525-2030
Arlington *(G-1221)*

Worthington Millwork LLC ....G...... 540 832-6391
Gordonsville *(G-5919)*

Wytheville Custom Counter Tops ....G...... 276 228-4137
Wytheville *(G-15928)*

CABINETS: Office, Wood

CMC Interiors LLC ....F...... 804 883-5671
Richmond *(G-11035)*

Interior Building Systems Corp ....D...... 703 335-9655
Manassas *(G-8083)*

Jack Carter Cabinet Maker ....G...... 757 622-9414
Norfolk *(G-9599)*

Rockridge Cabinetry LLC ....G...... 434 969-2665
Buckingham *(G-2135)*

Russ Fine Woods Inc ....G...... 434 974-6504
Charlottesville *(G-2868)*

Wilcox Woodworks Inc ....F...... 703 369-3455
Manassas *(G-8012)*

Wood Shop ....G...... 757 824-4055
Atlantic *(G-1526)*

Woodwrights Cooperative ....G...... 804 358-4800
Richmond *(G-11455)*

CABINETS: Show, Display, Etc, Wood, Exc Refrigerated

Burgers Cabinet Shop Inc ....F...... 571 262-8001
Sterling *(G-13362)*

Carpers Wood Creations Inc ....E...... 540 465-2525
Strasburg *(G-13576)*

Cavanaugh Cabinet Inc ....G...... 434 977-7100
Charlottesville *(G-2759)*

Creative Dimension Group Inc ....D...... 540 891-1953
Fredericksburg *(G-5267)*

Custom Woodwork ....G...... 434 489-6991
Danville *(G-3974)*

John P Scott Woodworking Inc ....G...... 804 231-1942
Richmond *(G-11633)*

Kitchen Krafters Inc ....F...... 540 891-7678
Fredericksburg *(G-5310)*

La Prade Enterprises ....G...... 804 271-9899
North Chesterfield *(G-9912)*

Perceptions of Virginia Inc ....G...... 703 730-5918
Woodbridge *(G-15775)*

Richards Building Supply Co ....G...... 540 719-0128
Hardy *(G-6289)*

Superior Laminates ....G...... 703 569-6602
Springfield *(G-13097)*

Walmer Enterprises ....E...... 703 461-9330
Montross *(G-9028)*

Woodmsters Cbnets Str Fixs of ....G...... 434 525-4407
Forest *(G-5105)*

Woodwrights Cooperative ....G...... 804 358-4800
Richmond *(G-11455)*

CABLE & OTHER PAY TELEVISION DISTRIBUTION

Rambletype LLC ....G...... 540 440-1218
Fredericksburg *(G-5217)*

Wood Television LLC ....E...... 804 775-4600
Richmond *(G-11832)*

CABLE TELEVISION PRDTS

Comsonics Inc ....D...... 540 434-5965
Harrisonburg *(G-6306)*

CABLE: Coaxial

Frank M Churillo ....G...... 434 242-6895
Charlottesville *(G-2633)*

Global Com Inc ....E...... 703 532-6425
Sterling *(G-13412)*

JP Nino Corp ....G...... 775 636-8682
Falls Church *(G-4811)*

CABLE: Fiber

Net 100 Ltd ....G...... 757 490-0496
Virginia Beach *(G-14676)*

P R O D U C T

CABLE: Fiber Optic

Irflex Corporation ....G...... 434 483-4304
　Danville (G-4003)

Optical Cable Corporation ....C...... 540 265-0690
　Roanoke (G-11978)

CABLE: Noninsulated

Electrnic Cabling Assembly Inc ....E...... 434 293-2593
　Charlottesville (G-2789)

CAFES

Chateau Morrisette Inc ....E...... 540 593-2865
　Floyd (G-5018)

Johnson & Elich Roasters Ltd ....F...... 540 552-7442
　Blacksburg (G-1747)

Tapioca Go ....G...... 757 410-3836
　Chesapeake (G-3322)

CAGES: Wire

Handi-Leigh Crafted ....G...... 540 349-7775
　Warrenton (G-15023)

CALCULATING & ACCOUNTING EQPT

Accounting Executive Svcs LLC ....G...... 757 406-1127
　Norfolk (G-9417)

Catering Machine Company ....G...... 757 332-0024
　Carrollton (G-2241)

Claren ....G...... 571 403-0425
　Sterling (G-13371)

Debra Rosel ....G...... 703 675-4963
　Round Hill (G-12377)

Idemia America Corp ....G...... 703 263-0100
　Reston (G-10867)

CALIBRATING SVCS, NEC

Pipet Repair Service Inc ....G...... 804 739-3720
　Midlothian (G-8880)

CAMERAS & RELATED EQPT: Photographic

Allegheny Instruments Inc ....G...... 540 468-3740
　Monterey (G-9001)

Video-Scope International Ltd ....G...... 703 437-5534
　Sterling (G-13550)

CAMSHAFTS

Custom Camshaft Company Inc ....G...... 276 666-6767
　Martinsville (G-8278)

CANDLE SHOPS

710 Essentials LLC ....G...... 540 748-4393
　Spotsylvania (G-12880)

Melted Element LLC ....G...... 703 239-7847
　Alexandria (G-526)

Mighty Oak Enterprises Inc ....G...... 757 422-6353
　Williamsburg (G-15277)

CANDLES

3 Gypsies Candle Company LLC ....G...... 703 300-2307
　Manassas (G-8016)

6th Floor Candle Company LLC ....G...... 917 580-2251
　Alexandria (G-397)

710 Essentials LLC ....G...... 540 748-4393
　Spotsylvania (G-12880)

A and J HM Imprv Angela Towler ....G...... 434 429-5087
　Danville (G-3952)

Alternative Candle Company ....G...... 804 350-6980
　Woodbridge (G-15645)

Amethyst Flame Candles LLC ....G...... 757 324-0614
　Suffolk (G-13669)

AP Candles LLC ....G...... 804 276-8681
　Chesterfield (G-3475)

Ardent Candle Company LLC ....G...... 347 906-2011
　Virginia Beach (G-14239)

Aroma Kandles LLC ....G...... 202 525-1550
　Manassas Park (G-8189)

Awn Candle Company ....G...... 618 560-6355
　Chesapeake (G-2991)

Beeswax Candle Company LLC ....G...... 434 528-9885
　Lynchburg (G-7651)

Bottom of Bottle Candle Co LLC ....G...... 540 692-9260
　Strasburg (G-13574)

Bowdens Candle Creations ....G...... 757 539-0306
　Suffolk (G-13681)

Burning Brite Candle ....G...... 540 904-6544
　Goodview (G-5894)

Candle Euphoria ....G...... 757 327-8567
　Hampton (G-6104)

Candle Fetish ....G...... 757 535-3105
　Portsmouth (G-10404)

Candle Utopia Incorporated ....G...... 757 274-2406
　Norfolk (G-9476)

Candles For Effect LLC ....G...... 707 591-3986
　Stafford (G-13126)

Candles Make Scents LLC ....G...... 540 223-3972
　Mineral (G-8943)

Candlestick Baker Inc ....G...... 757 761-4473
　Virginia Beach (G-14313)

Capital City Candle ....G...... 571 245-4738
　West Point (G-15154)

Cedar Lane Farms LLC ....G...... 757 335-0830
　Virginia Beach (G-14327)

Chick Lit LLC ....G...... 757 496-9019
　Virginia Beach (G-14337)

Clarity Candles LLC ....G...... 703 278-3760
　Arlington (G-907)

Commonwealth Provisions LLC ....G...... 540 699-0222
　Fredericksburg (G-5265)

Corey Vereen ....G...... 609 468-5409
　Virginia Beach (G-14367)

Cottage Grove Candles ....G...... 757 751-8333
　Newport News (G-9206)

Cottage Still Room/Bees Wax CN ....G...... 434 846-4398
　Lynchburg (G-7685)

Country Scents Candles ....G...... 757 359-8730
　Portsmouth (G-10411)

Couture Intuition LLC ....G...... 757 570-8126
　Newport News (G-9207)

Cyntherapy Scented Candles LLC ....G...... 804 901-2681
　Henrico (G-6498)

Earthen Candle Works LLC ....G...... 540 270-5938
　Ashburn (G-1275)

East Coast Candle Co ....G...... 781 718-9466
　Lynchburg (G-7698)

Eleven Eleven Candles More LLC ....G...... 757 766-0687
　Hampton (G-6137)

Eley House Candles ....G...... 757 572-9318
　Suffolk (G-13703)

Feather & Pearl Candle Co LLC ....G...... 540 769-9529
　Roanoke (G-12086)

Gold Canyon Candles ....G...... 540 972-1266
　Locust Grove (G-7444)

Got Scents & Sova Candles ....G...... 434 736-9394
　Keysville (G-7058)

Harmony Lights Candle ....G...... 434 384-5549
　Madison Heights (G-7873)

Heavenly Aromas LLC ....F...... 804 651-6250
　Henrico (G-6520)

Heavyn & Hopes Candle Co ....G...... 301 980-8299
　Alexandria (G-476)

Heirloom Candle Company LLC ....G...... 276 889-2505
　Lebanon (G-7193)

Hip Occasions LLC ....G...... 540 695-8896
　Fredericksburg (G-5297)

Into Light ....G...... 757 816-9002
　Virginia Beach (G-14553)

Johnny Porter Candle Co ....G...... 540 406-1608
　Orange (G-10217)

Kerris Kandles ....G...... 908 698-3968
　Dumfries (G-4249)

Korona Candles Inc ....C...... 540 208-2440
　Dublin (G-4161)

Less Than Ladylike Candle LLC ....G...... 757 817-0616
　Newport News (G-9282)

Lightsmokechill Candle Co LLC ....G...... 347 720-2596
　Newport News (G-9284)

Liht Candles & Oils LLC ....G...... 757 776-9005
　Chesapeake (G-3183)

Lisas Candles ....G...... 703 940-6733
　Herndon (G-6734)

Lizzie Candles & Soap Inc ....G...... 540 384-6151
　Salem (G-12533)

Lucy Love Candles ....G...... 571 991-4155
　Woodbridge (G-15742)

Lux Living Candle Co LLC ....G...... 757 462-6470
　Chesapeake (G-3190)

Madeline Candle Company LLC ....G...... 703 503-9181
　Burke (G-2192)

Manny Weber ....G...... 703 819-3338
　Leesburg (G-7309)

Marcell Sgnture Scnted Candles ....G...... 757 502-5236
　Norfolk (G-9631)

Melted Element LLC ....G...... 703 239-7847
　Alexandria (G-526)

Mighty Oak Enterprises Inc ....G...... 757 422-6353
　Williamsburg (G-15277)

Miss Lizzies Loot ....G...... 804 484-4212
　Richmond (G-11053)

Ms Bettys Bad-Ass Candles LLC ....G...... 540 256-7221
　Woodbridge (G-15752)

Nannas Cndles Unique Gifts LLC ....G...... 276 780-2513
　Marion (G-8238)

Natures Cntry Soaps Candle LLC ....G...... 757 817-9062
　Spring Grove (G-12931)

Nutter Candle Company LLC ....G...... 703 627-2561
　Fairfax (G-4523)

Old Hickory Candle Company ....G...... 804 400-8602
　Mc Kenney (G-8382)

Primrose Essentials LLC ....G...... 703 503-7210
　Burke (G-2200)

Pure Scentsations LLC ....G...... 334 868-9190
　Suffolk (G-13755)

Roxannas Candles ....G...... 804 243-9697
　Chesapeake (G-3276)

Rural Squirrel LLC ....G...... 540 364-2281
　Marshall (G-8259)

Simply Candles & Gifts ....G...... 315 806-4204
　Lynchburg (G-7807)

Simply Divine Candles ....G...... 540 479-0045
　Strasburg (G-13597)

Sniffalicious Candle LLC ....G...... 276 686-2204
　Rural Retreat (G-12432)

Sol Shining ....G...... 571 719-3957
　Manassas (G-8159)

Sophie Gs Candles LLC ....G...... 202 253-7798
　Haymarket (G-6446)

Soywick Candles LLC ....G...... 571 333-4750
　Lansdowne (G-7173)

Surfside Candle Co ....G...... 540 455-4322
　Sterling (G-13525)

Sweet Heat Candles ....G...... 804 921-8233
　Henrico (G-6577)

Three Hens ....G...... 804 787-3400
　Goochland (G-5887)

Tighty Whitey Soap Candle LLC ....G...... 202 818-9169
　Alexandria (G-364)

Tradition Candle LLC ....G...... 630 881-7194
　Norfolk (G-9764)

Two Blue Candle Co LLC ....G...... 786 301-3371
　Herndon (G-6834)

Verde Candles ....G...... 804 338-1350
　Glen Allen (G-5824)

Vibe Candle Co LLC ....G...... 757 589-3274
　Hampton (G-6261)

Virginia Candle Company LLC ....G...... 301 828-6498
　Woodbridge (G-15827)

West 30 Candles ....G...... 804 874-2461
　Richmond (G-11823)

Wf Med ....G...... 703 339-5388
　Lorton (G-7541)

Why Candle & Co LLC ....G...... 804 876-2240
　Richmond (G-11830)

Winding Creek Candle Co LLC ....G...... 757 410-1991
　Chesapeake (G-3378)

Wine With Everything LLC ....G...... 703 777-4899
　Leesburg (G-7380)

Yup Candles LLC ....G...... 571 248-6772
　Nokesville (G-9406)

CANDLES: Wholesalers

Melted Element LLC ....G...... 703 239-7847
　Alexandria (G-526)

Mighty Oak Enterprises Inc ....G...... 757 422-6353
　Williamsburg (G-15277)

Wine With Everything LLC ....G...... 703 777-4899
　Leesburg (G-7380)

CANDY & CONFECTIONS: Cake Ornaments

Unique Flexique LLC ....G...... 540 439-4465
　Bealeton (G-1607)

CANDY & CONFECTIONS: Candy Bars, Including Chocolate Covered

Cocoa Mia Inc ....G...... 540 695-0224
　Floyd (G-5019)

Custom Candyy LLC ....F...... 804 447-8179
　Richmond (G-11549)

CANDY & CONFECTIONS: Chocolate Candy, Exc Solid Chocolate

Cecilia M Schultzs ....G 301 840-1283
Great Falls (G-5945)
Delicious Dainties LLC ....G 240 620-7581
Reston (G-10838)

CANDY & CONFECTIONS: Cough Drops, Exc Pharmaceutical Preps

Helms Candy Co Inc ....E 276 669-2612
Bristol (G-2019)

CANDY & CONFECTIONS: Fruit & Fruit Peel

Kandy Girl Kndy Apples Berries ....G 719 200-1662
Newport News (G-9272)

CANDY & CONFECTIONS: Fudge

Blue Ridge Fudge Lady Inc ....G 276 335-2229
Wytheville (G-15877)
Fudgetime LLC ....G 703 462-8544
Springfield (G-13006)
Mamas Fudge ....G 540 980-8444
Pulaski (G-10641)

CANDY & CONFECTIONS: Popcorn Balls/Other Trtd Popcorn Prdts

Jodys Inc ....F 757 422-8646
Norfolk (G-9604)
Katheryn Warren ....G 757 813-5396
Williamsburg (G-15264)
Popcorn Monkey LLC ....G 540 687-6539
Middleburg (G-8733)

CANDY, NUT & CONFECTIONERY STORES: Produced For Direct Sale

River City Chocolate LLC ....G 804 317-8161
Midlothian (G-8890)

CANDY: Chocolate From Cacao Beans

Mars Incorporated ....B 703 821-4900
Mc Lean (G-8491)

CANDY: Hard

Matre Inc ....G 703 821-4927
Mc Lean (G-8495)

CANNED SPECIALTIES

Catherine Elliott ....G 276 274-7022
Bristol (G-1969)
DJS Enterprises ....G 703 973-0977
Alexandria (G-191)
Jim Sirrine ....G 540 874-7006
Roanoke (G-12111)
Nestle Holdings Inc ....F 703 682-4600
Arlington (G-1073)

CANOE BUILDING & REPAIR

Indian River Canoe Mfg ....G 276 773-3124
Independence (G-6988)

CANS: Aluminum

Reynolds Cnsmr Pdts Hldngs Inc ....C 540 249-5711
Grottoes (G-6024)
Reynolds Metals Company LLC ....G 804 746-6723
Richmond (G-11353)

CANS: Beverage, Metal, Exc Beer

Ball Metal Beverage Cont Corp ....C 757 887-2062
Williamsburg (G-15209)

CANS: Composite Foil-Fiber, Made From Purchased Materials

Sonoco Products Company ....E 757 539-8349
Suffolk (G-13766)

CANS: Metal

Crown Cork & Seal Usa Inc ....B 540 662-2591
Winchester (G-15408)

Crown Cork & Seal Usa Inc ....E 757 538-1318
Suffolk (G-13690)
Penny Plate LLC ....D 540 337-3777
Fishersville (G-5006)
Sonoco Products Company ....E 757 539-8349
Suffolk (G-13766)
Van Addo Dorn LLC ....G 703 615-4769
Arlington (G-1207)
Van Dorn Pawn ....G 703 924-9800
Alexandria (G-603)

CANVAS PRDTS

Bellum Designs LLC ....G 757 343-9556
Virginia Beach (G-14274)
Canvas & Earth ....G 757 995-6529
Virginia Beach (G-14314)
Canvas Marine Co ....G 703 534-5886
Falls Church (G-4768)
Canvas To Curtains ....G 757 665-5406
Bloxom (G-1839)
Cover UPS Marine Canvas ....G 757 312-9292
Chesapeake (G-3055)
Decks Down Under LLC ....G 703 758-2572
Reston (G-10836)
Dodd Custom Canvas LLC ....G 757 717-4436
Portsmouth (G-10416)
George F Dashell Jr ....G 305 664-2238
Virginia Beach (G-14480)
Got It Covered LLC ....G 540 353-5167
Wirtz (G-15611)
Hdt Expeditionary Systems Inc ....G 540 373-1435
Fredericksburg (G-5195)
I Love Art Boutique LLC ....G 757 204-1260
Hampton (G-6174)
Marla Hughes ....G 703 309-8267
Alexandria (G-523)
Mikes Marine Custom Canvas ....G 757 496-1090
Virginia Beach (G-14653)
Phase 2 Marine Canvas LLC ....G 804 694-7561
Wake (G-14963)
R C S Enterprises Inc ....G 540 363-5979
Waynesboro (G-15133)

CANVAS PRDTS, WHOLESALE

Custom Tops Inc ....G 757 460-3084
Virginia Beach (G-14378)

CANVAS PRDTS: Boat Seats

Custom Tops Inc ....G 757 460-3084
Virginia Beach (G-14378)

CANVAS PRDTS: Convertible Tops, Car/Boat, Fm Purchased Mtrl

Buddy D Ltd ....G 757 481-7619
Virginia Beach (G-14305)
Crafted Canvas LLC ....G 917 426-8377
Dunnsville (G-4268)

CANVAS PRDTS: Shades, Made From Purchased Materials

Aaacm Green Warrior Inc ....G 703 865-5991
Fairfax (G-4398)
Sunguard Mid Atlantic LLC ....G 703 820-8118
Arlington (G-1178)

CAPACITORS: NEC

B Microfarads Inc ....C 276 728-9121
Hillsville (G-6885)
Illinois Tool Works Inc ....D 434 239-6941
Lynchburg (G-7737)
Integer Holdings Corporation ....B 540 389-7860
Salem (G-12521)
Keltron Corporation ....E 540 527-3526
Roanoke (G-11948)

CAPS & TOPS: Bottle, Die-Cut, Made From Purchased Materials

Judys Bottle Holder ....G 757 606-1093
Chesapeake (G-3160)

CAPS & TOPS: Bottle, Stamped Metal

Saco ....G 804 457-3744
Gum Spring (G-6044)

CAPS: Plastic

Polycap LLC ....G 276 883-5700
Lebanon (G-7204)

CAR WASH EQPT

Bernard Speed ....G 540 514-9041
Fredericksburg (G-5403)
Car Wash Care Inc ....G 703 385-9181
Fairfax (G-4605)
Caravelle Industries Inc ....G 434 432-2331
Leesburg (G-7238)
Caravelle Industries Inc ....F 434 432-2331
Chatham (G-2920)
Champion Handwash ....E 703 893-4216
Vienna (G-14026)
Cool Wave LLC ....G 757 269-0200
Smithfield (G-12710)
Detail Maxx LLC ....G 703 942-8965
Mc Lean (G-8418)
Henrico Chubbys ....G 804 285-4469
Richmond (G-11237)
Keen Eyes Auto Detailing LLC ....G 252 646-3600
Stafford (G-13161)
Magic Wand Inc ....E 276 466-3921
Bristol (G-1983)
Outrageous Shine LLC ....G 804 741-9274
Richmond (G-11317)
Q B Enterprises Inc ....G 540 825-2950
Orange (G-10224)
Rio Take Back LLC ....G 540 371-3636
Fredericksburg (G-5480)
Smith Brothers Car Wash Inc ....G 757 397-7711
Portsmouth (G-10483)
Soap N Suds Laudromats ....G 757 313-0515
Norfolk (G-9728)
Zeta Car Washes LLC ....G 757 469-2141
Virginia Beach (G-14959)

CAR WASHES

Champion Handwash ....E 703 893-4216
Vienna (G-14026)

CARBIDES

Carbide Specialties Inc ....G 804 346-3314
Manakin Sabot (G-7897)

CARBON & GRAPHITE PRDTS, NEC

Carbone America ....G 540 389-7535
Salem (G-12488)

CARBONS: Lighting

Dixon Mediation Group LLC ....F 703 517-3556
Fairfax Station (G-4709)

CARBURETORS

Carburetors Unlimited ....G 703 273-0751
Manassas (G-8046)
Zenith Fuel Systems LLC ....D 276 669-5555
Bristol (G-2044)

CARDIOVASCULAR SYSTEM DRUGS, EXC DIAGNOSTIC

Family Insight PC ....G 540 818-1687
Roanoke (G-11922)
Pfizer Inc ....F 804 257-2000
Richmond (G-11712)

CARDS: Greeting

A Reason To Write ....G 703 481-3277
Fairfax (G-4397)
Beau-Geste International Inc ....G 434 534-0468
Forest (G-5053)
Caspari Inc ....E 434 817-7880
Charlottesville (G-2757)
DBA Jus Bcuz ....G 914 714-9327
Courtland (G-3768)
Just For Fun ....G 757 620-3700
Suffolk (G-13726)
Noparei Professionals LLC ....G 571 354-9422
Woodbridge (G-15763)
Patricia Gavin ....G 703 439-4403
Middleburg (G-8731)
Pumped Cards ....G 202 725-6964
Woodbridge (G-15786)

PRODUCT

Stay In Touch Inc ....F 434 239-7300
  Forest (G-5095)
United Providers of Care LLC ....G 757 775-5075
  Williamsburg (G-15328)

CARDS: Identification

Cbn Secure Technologies Inc ....D 434 799-9280
  Danville (G-3964)
Kidprint of Virginia Inc ....G 757 287-3324
  Suffolk (G-13728)
Nationwide Laminating Inc ....F 703 550-8400
  Lorton (G-7513)
Veridos America Inc ....G 703 480-2025
  Dulles (G-4232)

CARPET & UPHOLSTERY CLEANING SVCS

Ship Shape Cleaning LLC ....G 757 769-3845
  Portsmouth (G-10480)

CARPET LINING: Felt, Exc Woven

Capital Floors LLC ....G 571 451-4044
  Woodbridge (G-15666)

CARPETS & RUGS: Tufted

Mohawk Industries Inc ....F 540 258-2811
  Glasgow (G-5700)
Mohawk Industries Inc ....C 276 728-2141
  Hillsville (G-6897)

CARPETS, RUGS & FLOOR COVERING

Bacova Guild Ltd ....G 540 484-4640
  Rocky Mount (G-12313)
Burlington Industries Inc ....G 540 258-2811
  Glasgow (G-5699)
C & G Flooring LLC ....G 804 318-0927
  Midlothian (G-8785)
Capital Discount Mdse LLC ....F 703 499-9368
  Woodbridge (G-15665)
Charles City Timber and Mat ....G 804 829-5850
  Charles City (G-2572)
Cutting Edge Carpet Binding ....G 540 982-1007
  Vinton (G-14171)
Reynolds Container Corporation ....E 276 647-8451
  Collinsville (G-3715)
Tarkett USA Inc ....G 804 594-0500
  North Chesterfield (G-9998)
Taylor Matthews Inc ....G 703 346-7844
  Vienna (G-14139)

CARPETS: Axminster

Velvet Pile Carpets LLC ....G 540 920-9473
  Gordonsville (G-5918)

CARPETS: Wilton

Capital Floors LLC ....G 571 451-4044
  Woodbridge (G-15666)

CASES: Attache'

Interalign LLC ....G 804 314-4713
  Richmond (G-11250)

CASES: Carrying

Tkl Products Corp ....E 804 749-8300
  Oilville (G-10185)

CASES: Carrying, Clothing & Apparel

Big Chip Clothing Company LLC ....G 877 572-6525
  Virginia Beach (G-14276)
Dalaun Couture LLC ....G 703 594-1413
  Vienna (G-14032)
Kmarie Krafts Inc ....G 804 943-1239
  Chesapeake (G-3166)
Kurvez Galore Boutique LLC ....G 336 901-5266
  Ferrum (G-4975)
Lexington Papagallo Inc ....G 540 463-5988
  Lexington (G-7398)
Morose Brand LLC ....G 747 346-1550
  Hampton (G-6203)
Swrd LLC ....G 434 944-2558
  Gladys (G-5697)
Uplift Collections ....G 804 319-9129
  Chesterfield (G-3536)

CASES: Nonrefrigerated, Exc Wood

Kearney & Associates Inc ....F 540 423-9511
  Culpeper (G-3905)

CASES: Plastic

Martin Elthon ....G 703 853-1801
  Fairfax (G-4503)
Pelican Products ....F 540 636-1624
  Front Royal (G-5548)

CASH REGISTERS & PARTS

Newbold Corporation ....C 540 489-4400
  Rocky Mount (G-12342)
Total Touch Solutions LLC ....G 757 536-1445
  Virginia Beach (G-14889)

CAST STONE: Concrete

Blue Ridge Stone Mfg ....G 276 676-0040
  Abingdon (G-15)
Stafford Stone Works LLC ....E 540 372-6601
  Fredericksburg (G-5227)

CASTERS

P and H Casters Co Inc ....G 817 312-1083
  Danville (G-4021)

CASTINGS GRINDING: For The Trade

Beautiful Grind ....G 757 685-6192
  Virginia Beach (G-14272)
Daily Grind ....G 540 387-2669
  Salem (G-12493)
Daily Grind Hospital ....G 540 536-2383
  Winchester (G-15536)
Grandaddys Stump Grinding ....G 757 565-5870
  Williamsburg (G-15250)
Merwins Affordable Grinding ....G 757 461-3405
  Norfolk (G-9640)
Whats Your Grind LLC ....G 757 447-8506
  Portsmouth (G-10501)

CASTINGS: Aerospace Investment, Ferrous

Henry Bijak ....G 757 572-1673
  Virginia Beach (G-14516)

CASTINGS: Aerospace, Aluminum

Rolls-Royce Crosspointe LLC ....F 877 787-6247
  Prince George (G-10606)

CASTINGS: Aerospace, Nonferrous, Exc Aluminum

Cryoscience Technologies ....G 516 338-6723
  Brandy Station (G-1938)

CASTINGS: Aluminum

Acp LLC ....G 276 619-5080
  Abingdon (G-6)
G N H & Associates Inc ....G 276 632-7867
  Axton (G-1537)

CASTINGS: Brass, Bronze & Copper

Lynchburg Machining LLC ....F 434 846-7327
  Lynchburg (G-7762)

CASTINGS: Commercial Investment, Ferrous

Howmet Castings & Services Inc ......B 757 838-4680
  Hampton (G-6168)
Howmet Corporation ....C 757 838-4680
  Hampton (G-6169)

CASTINGS: Die, Aluminum

Appalachian Cast Products Inc ....C 276 619-5080
  Abingdon (G-12)
Bonrick Molds ....G 540 898-1512
  Fredericksburg (G-5254)
Limatherm Usa Inc ....G 540 402-4060
  Leesburg (G-7301)

CASTINGS: Die, Zinc

Bonrick Molds ....G 540 898-1512
  Fredericksburg (G-5254)

CASTINGS: Ductile

Cowden ....G 276 744-7120
  Elk Creek (G-4320)
Walker Machine and Fndry Corp ....D 540 344-6265
  Roanoke (G-12226)

CASTINGS: Gray Iron

Graham-White Manufacturing Co ....B 540 387-5600
  Salem (G-12513)
Neenah Foundry Co ....G 804 758-9592
  Urbanna (G-13972)
OK Foundry Company Inc ....E 804 233-9674
  Richmond (G-11698)
R H Sheppard Co Inc ....F 276 228-4000
  Wytheville (G-15907)

CASTINGS: Machinery, Nonferrous, Exc Die or Aluminum Copper

Tidewater Castings Inc ....G 757 399-0679
  Portsmouth (G-10491)

CASTINGS: Precision

Equestrian Forge Inc ....G 703 777-2110
  Leesburg (G-7269)

CASTINGS: Steel

Henry Bijak ....G 757 572-1673
  Virginia Beach (G-14516)

CATALOG & MAIL-ORDER HOUSES

General Display Company LLC ....G 703 335-9292
  Manassas (G-7943)
Laura Copenhaver Industries ....G 276 783-4663
  Marion (G-8230)
Mikrocoze Inc ....G 800 542-8715
  Chesapeake (G-3205)

CATAPULTS

Catapult Solutions Inc ....G 434 401-1077
  Lynchburg (G-7676)
Catapult Video ....G 540 642-9947
  Virginia Beach (G-14324)

CATERERS

Mars Incorporated ....B 703 821-4900
  Mc Lean (G-8491)
Tea Spot Catering LLC ....G 757 427-3525
  Virginia Beach (G-14867)
True Southern Smoke Bbq LLC ....G 757 816-0228
  Chesapeake (G-3352)

CAULKING COMPOUNDS

Insul Industries Inc ....F 804 550-1933
  Mechanicsville (G-8641)

CEMENT: Asbestos, Siding

James Hardie Building Pdts Inc ....D 540 980-9143
  Pulaski (G-10639)

CEMENT: Hydraulic

Artisan Concrete Designs Inc ....G 434 321-3423
  South Hill (G-12842)
Dominion Quikrete Inc ....E 757 547-9411
  Chesapeake (G-3071)
Dominion Quikrete Inc ....E 276 957-3235
  Martinsville (G-8279)
Kerneos Inc ....D 757 494-1947
  Chesapeake (G-3163)
Lafarge Calcium Aluminates Inc ....G 757 543-8832
  Chesapeake (G-3172)
Lafarge North America Inc ....G 505 471-6456
  Herndon (G-6731)
Lafarge North America Inc ....F 757 545-2481
  Chesapeake (G-3173)
Titan America LLC ....C 540 622-2350
  Front Royal (G-5557)
Titan America LLC ....F 804 236-4122
  Richmond (G-11412)
Titan America LLC ....D 703 471-0044
  Sterling (G-13534)

CEMENT: Masonry

R & R Developers Inc..............G... 276 628-3846
Abingdon (G-55)

CEMETERY MEMORIAL DEALERS

Empire Marble & Granite Co ....G... 804 359-2004
Richmond (G-11574)
Francis C James Jr....................G... 757 442-3630
Nassawadox (G-9100)
General Marble & Granite Co ....G... 804 353-2761
Richmond (G-11215)
Nova Rock Craft LLC...............G... 703 217-7072
Warrenton (G-15038)
Winn Stone Products Inc ....G... 757 465-5363
Portsmouth (G-10505)

CERAMIC FIBER

Polythane of Virginia Inc ....G... 540 586-3511
Bedford (G-1651)

CERAMIC SCHOOLS

Kiln Doctor Inc ....G... 540 636-6016
Front Royal (G-5540)

CHAINS: Forged

Polar Traction Inc...................G... 703 241-1958
Arlington (G-1113)

CHANDELIERS: Residential

Mya Saray LLC ....G... 703 996-8800
Sterling (G-13458)

CHARCOAL

Bclf Corporation...............G... 540 929-1701
Callaway (G-2219)

CHARCOAL, WHOLESALE

Mya Saray LLC ....G... 703 996-8800
Sterling (G-13458)

CHEMICAL ELEMENTS

Black Element LLC...............G... 757 224-6160
Hampton (G-6094)
Element Fitness- LLC...............G... 540 820-4200
Virginia Beach (G-14438)
Element One LLC...............G... 901 292-7721
Leesburg (G-7266)
Element Radius LLC...............G... 540 229-6366
Culpeper (G-3890)

CHEMICAL INDICATORS

Alchemical Hydrogen LLC ....G... 703 399-9235
Alexandria (G-124)

CHEMICAL PROCESSING MACHINERY & EQPT

Poly Processing Company LLC...............G... 804 368-7199
Ashland (G-1477)
Svr International LLC...................F... 703 759-2953
Vienna (G-14136)

CHEMICAL SPLYS FOR FOUNDRIES

Gpc Inc...............G... 757 345-3991
Woodbridge (G-15712)
Water Technologies Inc...............G... 540 366-9799
Roanoke (G-12023)

CHEMICALS & ALLIED PRDTS WHOLESALERS, NEC

Ethyl Corporation...............G... 804 788-5000
Richmond (G-11580)
Laundry Chemical Products Inc ....G... 757 363-0662
Virginia Beach (G-14602)
Nellie Harris...............G... 434 277-8511
Lowesville (G-7597)
Unshrinkit Inc...............G... 804 519-7019
Arlington (G-1202)

CHEMICALS & ALLIED PRDTS, WHOL: Chem Bulk Station/Terminal

Scan Industries LLC ....G... 360 320-8244
Ashburn (G-1332)

CHEMICALS & ALLIED PRDTS, WHOLESALE: Alcohols

Blue Bee Cider LLC...................F... 804 231-0280
Richmond (G-11128)

CHEMICALS & ALLIED PRDTS, WHOLESALE: Ammonia

Airgas Inc...............G... 757 539-7185
Suffolk (G-13664)

CHEMICALS & ALLIED PRDTS, WHOLESALE: Chemicals, Indl

Danchem Technologies Inc...................C... 434 797-8120
Danville (G-3975)
Prochem Inc...................E... 540 268-9884
Elliston (G-4347)

CHEMICALS & ALLIED PRDTS, WHOLESALE: Detergent/Soap

Copper Fox Dist Entps LLC ....F... 540 987-8554
Sperryville (G-12877)
Copper Fox Distillery...................F... 757 903-2076
Williamsburg (G-15222)
Cumberland Company LP...............G... 434 392-9911
Farmville (G-4938)

CHEMICALS & ALLIED PRDTS, WHOLESALE: Oil Additives

Viscosity LLC ....G... 757 343-9071
Chesapeake (G-3363)

CHEMICALS & ALLIED PRDTS, WHOLESALE: Plastics Prdts, NEC

Polyfab Display Company...................E... 703 497-4577
Woodbridge (G-15777)

CHEMICALS & ALLIED PRDTS, WHOLESALE: Polishes, NEC

Leather Luster Inc...............G... 757 548-0146
Chesapeake (G-3182)

CHEMICALS & ALLIED PRDTS, WHOLESALE: Resins

Advansix Inc...................E... 804 504-0009
South Chesterfield (G-12793)

CHEMICALS & ALLIED PRDTS, WHOLESALE: Resins, Synthetic

Hillmans Distributors...............G... 540 774-1896
Roanoke (G-11935)

CHEMICALS & ALLIED PRDTS, WHOLESALE: Sanitation Preparations

Gilmer Industries Inc ....E... 540 434-8877
Harrisonburg (G-6324)

CHEMICALS & ALLIED PRDTS, WHOLESALE: Spec Clean/Sanitation

Zero Products LLC...................G... 757 285-4000
Virginia Beach (G-14957)

CHEMICALS & ALLIED PRDTS, WHOLESALE: Syn Resin, Rub/Plastic

Global Trading of Martinsville...............G... 276 666-0236
Martinsville (G-8290)

CHEMICALS, AGRICULTURE: Wholesalers

Houff Corporation...................D... 540 234-8088
Weyers Cave (G-15173)

CHEMICALS/ALLIED PRDTS, WHOL: Coal Tar Prdts, Prim/Intermdt

Separation Technologies LLC ....E... 540 992-1501
Roanoke (G-11999)

CHEMICALS: Agricultural

Dupont...............G... 540 949-5361
Waynesboro (G-15109)
Dupont Aero LLC...............G... 540 350-4306
Mount Solon (G-9086)
Dupont Circle Solutions...............G... 202 596-8528
Arlington (G-946)
Dupont Credit Union...............G... 540 868-8714
Harrisonburg (G-6311)
Dupont De Nemours Inc ....G... 804 549-4747
North Chesterfield (G-9863)
Dupont James River Gyps Fcilty...............G... 804 714-3362
North Chesterfield (G-9864)
Dupont Threading LLC...............G... 703 522-1748
Arlington (G-947)
Dupont Threading LLC...............G... 703 734-1425
Ashburn (G-1274)
Dupont Ventures LLC...............G... 574 514-3646
Arlington (G-948)
E I Du Pont De Nemours...............G... 804 550-7560
Ashland (G-1405)
E I Du Pont De Nemours & Co ....B... 804 383-4251
Chesterfield (G-3494)
Monsanto Tamantha...............G... 434 517-0013
North Prince George (G-10090)
Neutra-Green Clg Solutions LLC...............G... 804 447-8010
Henrico (G-6540)
Redcoat Solutions Inc ....G... 540 437-9843
Rockingham (G-12270)
Wright Solutions Inc ....G... 703 652-7145
Centreville (G-2355)

CHEMICALS: Alcohols

Slys Sucker Punch LLC...............G... 571 989-3538
Woodbridge (G-15814)

CHEMICALS: Aluminum Compounds

Mitsubishi Chemical Composites...........C... 757 548-7850
Chesapeake (G-3208)

CHEMICALS: Aluminum Sulfate

Chemtrade Chemicals US LLC ....G... 540 962-6444
Covington (G-3782)

CHEMICALS: Anhydrous Ammonia

Airgas Inc...............G... 757 539-7185
Suffolk (G-13664)

CHEMICALS: Boron Compounds, Not From Mines, NEC

Bnnt LLC...............G... 757 369-1939
Newport News (G-9182)

CHEMICALS: Brine

Tetra Technologies Inc ....E... 703 387-2100
Arlington (G-1188)

CHEMICALS: Bromine, Elemental

Albemarle Corporation...................C... 225 388-8011
Richmond (G-11092)

CHEMICALS: Calcium & Calcium Compounds

United Salt Saltville LLC...................E... 276 496-3363
Saltville (G-12596)

CHEMICALS: Fire Retardant

Albemarle Corporation...................C... 225 388-8011
Richmond (G-11092)
Bishop II Inc...............G... 757 855-7137
Norfolk (G-9464)
J C International LLC...............G... 540 243-0086
Rocky Mount (G-12329)

CHEMICALS: Heavy Water

Waters Group Inc...............G... 703 791-3607
Nokesville (G-9404)

Employee Codes: A=Over 500 employees, B=251-500
C=101-250, D=51-100, E=20-50, F=10-19, G=1-9

2021 Virginia
Industrial Directory

919

PRODUCT

CHEMICALS: Inorganic, NEC

5th Element Co ....G 800 684-3144
Lorton (G-7456)
8th-Element LLC ....G 757 481-6146
Virginia Beach (G-14199)
Adaptive Elements LLC ....G 571 261-3671
Haymarket (G-6413)
Aimex LLC ....F 212 631-4277
Vienna (G-14006)
Arkema Inc ....C 800 225-7788
Courtland (G-3766)
Arkema Inc ....C 434 433-0300
Chatham (G-2919)
Celanese Americas LLC ....D 540 921-6540
Narrows (G-9097)
Chemtrade Chemicals US LLC ....F 804 541-0261
Hopewell (G-6919)
Designpure Nanocryst LLC ....G 571 458-0951
Arlington (G-938)
Dupont De Nemours E I Tex Ofc ....G 540 949-2000
Waynesboro (G-15110)
Dupont Specialty Pdts USA LLC ....C 804 383-2000
North Chesterfield (G-9865)
Edward-Councilor Co Inc ....F 757 460-2401
Virginia Beach (G-14433)
Elements of Grace LLC ....G 804 526-1482
Colonial Heights (G-3732)
Elements of Healing LLC ....G 757 951-7155
Portsmouth (G-10420)
Evonik Goldschmidt Corporation ....A 804 541-8658
Hopewell (G-6926)
Framatome Inc ....B 434 832-3000
Lynchburg (G-7716)
Fraser Wood Elements LLC ....G 540 373-0853
Fredericksburg (G-5187)
Gilmer Industries Inc ....E 540 434-8877
Harrisonburg (G-6324)
Honeywell International Inc ....G 804 541-5000
Hopewell (G-6931)
Honeywell Resins & Chem LLC ....D 804 541-5000
Hopewell (G-6933)
Human Elements LLC ....G 703 542-7701
Chantilly (G-2537)
Ingevity Virginia Corporation ....C 540 969-3700
Covington (G-3791)
IV Labs Inc ....D 540 585-3030
Christiansburg (G-3599)
JM Huber Corporation ....G 804 357-3698
Glen Allen (G-5756)
JM Huber Corporation ....C 434 476-6628
Crystal Hill (G-3860)
Joi Element LLC ....G 804 912-8002
Richmond (G-11635)
Jr Bernard Hearn ....G 703 821-1373
Mc Lean (G-2537)
Mitsubshi Chem Hldngs Amer Inc ....E 757 382-5750
Chesapeake (G-3209)
Royal Elements LLC ....G 540 338-2591
Round Hill (G-12388)
STC Catalysts Inc ....G 757 766-5810
Hampton (G-6244)
US Amines (portsmouth) LLC ....G 757 638-2614
Portsmouth (G-10496)
Virginia Kik Inc ....E 540 389-5401
Salem (G-12578)

CHEMICALS: Iodides, NEC

Jr Everett Woodson ....G 757 867-3478
Newport News (G-9270)

CHEMICALS: Medicinal

Precision Nuclear Virginia LLC ....G 540 389-1346
Salem (G-12558)
Stemcelllife LLC ....G 843 410-3067
Richmond (G-11773)

CHEMICALS: NEC

141 Repellent Inc ....G 540 421-3956
Lexington (G-7385)
Advansix Inc ....A 804 541-5000
Hopewell (G-6917)
Advansix Inc ....E 804 504-0009
South Chesterfield (G-12793)
Afton Chemical Corporation ....G 804 788-5800
Richmond (G-11478)
Afton Chemical Corporation ....F 804 752-8420
Ashland (G-1364)

Astro LLC ....G 888 401-1003
Manassas (G-7915)
Brian L Longest ....G 703 759-3847
Great Falls (G-5940)
Commodore Sales LLC ....E 804 794-1992
North Chesterfield (G-9850)
Hi-Lite Solutions Inc ....F 540 450-8375
Clear Brook (G-3645)
Ice Release Materials LLC ....G 540 239-2438
Ashland (G-1437)
Interprome Marketing Inc ....G 804 744-2922
Midlothian (G-8834)
ITI Group ....G 703 339-5388
Lorton (G-7497)
Kdl Solutions LLC ....G 703 216-2201
Nokesville (G-9395)
Kmx Chemical Corp ....E 757 824-3600
New Church (G-9125)
Kmx Chemical Corp ....E 757 824-3600
New Church (G-9126)
Luck Stone Corporation ....D 804 784-6300
Manakin Sabot (G-7901)
Mapei Corporation ....E 540 361-1085
Fredericksburg (G-5453)
Masa Corporation ....D 757 855-3013
Norfolk (G-9633)
Maxx Performance Inc ....F 845 987-9432
Roanoke (G-11960)
Pure Anointing Oil ....G 703 889-7457
Springfield (G-13077)
Q P I Inc ....G 434 528-0092
Lynchburg (G-7795)
Quaker Chemical Corporation ....G 540 389-2038
Salem (G-12559)
Quikrete Companies LLC ....E 276 646-8976
Chilhowie (G-3558)
Rex Roto Corporation ....E 434 447-6854
South Hill (G-12859)
Suganit Bio-Renewables LLC ....F 703 736-0634
Mount Jackson (G-9080)
Synalloy Corporation ....D 804 822-3260
Glen Allen (G-5804)
Unshrinkit Inc ....G 804 519-7019
Arlington (G-1202)
W R Grace & Co-Conn ....G 540 752-6048
Fredericksburg (G-5499)
Zestron Corporation ....E 703 393-9880
Manassas (G-8184)

CHEMICALS: Organic, NEC

Afton Chemical Additives Corp ....F 804 788-5000
Richmond (G-11475)
Albemarle Corporation ....C 225 388-8011
Richmond (G-11092)
BASF Corporation ....G 757 538-3700
Suffolk (G-13674)
Carpenter Co ....C 804 359-0800
Richmond (G-11146)
Carpenter Co ....D 804 233-0606
Richmond (G-11032)
Chesapeake Custom Chem Corp ....C 276 956-3145
Ridgeway (G-11840)
Dynamic Recycling LLC ....G 276 628-6636
Abingdon (G-29)
Ethyl Corporation ....G 804 788-5000
Richmond (G-11580)
Evonik Corporation ....G 804 541-8658
Hopewell (G-6925)
Evonik Corporation ....C 804 727-0711
North Chesterfield (G-9868)
Evonik Goldschmidt Corporation ....A 804 541-8658
Hopewell (G-6926)
Henkel US Operations Corp ....F 804 222-6100
Richmond (G-11236)
Hercules Inc ....G 804 541-4545
Hopewell (G-6928)
Honeywell International Inc ....G 804 541-5000
Hopewell (G-6931)
Honeywell Resins & Chem LLC ....D 804 541-5000
Hopewell (G-6933)
Jah Rootz Industries LLC ....G 512 925-1109
Harrisonburg (G-6332)
Newmarket Corporation ....B 804 788-5000
Richmond (G-11689)
Qpi ....G 434 528-0092
Lynchburg (G-7796)
Shaklee Independent Distr ....G 757 553-8765
Virginia Beach (G-14806)
Suganit Bio-Renewables LLC ....G 703 736-0634
Reston (G-10968)

Suganit Bio-Renewables LLC ....F 703 736-0634
Mount Jackson (G-9080)
Synalloy Corporation ....D 804 822-3260
Glen Allen (G-5804)
Tego Chemie Svc Usadiv of Gold ....G 804 541-8658
Hopewell (G-6941)

CHEMICALS: Water Treatment

A Descal Matic Corp ....G 757 858-5593
Norfolk (G-9414)
Aqueous Solutions Global LLC ....G 410 710-7736
Richmond (G-11486)
Chemical Supply Inc ....G 804 353-2971
Richmond (G-11155)
Chemtreat Inc ....D 804 513-0756
Ashland (G-1390)
Otter River Filtration Plant ....G 434 821-8611
Evington (G-4382)
Prochem Inc ....E 540 268-9884
Elliston (G-4347)
Water Chemistry Incorporated ....E 540 343-3618
Roanoke (G-12022)

CHICKEN SLAUGHTERING & PROCESSING

Georges Chicken LLC ....D 540 984-4121
Edinburg (G-4305)
Tyson Foods Inc ....C 434 645-7791
Jetersville (G-7017)
Virginia Plty Growers Coop Inc ....B 540 867-4000
Hinton (G-6906)

CHIROPRACTORS' OFFICES

American Medical Devices Inc ....F 276 642-0463
Bristol (G-1965)

CHLORINE

Jci Jones Chemicals Inc ....F 804 633-5066
Milford (G-8931)

CHOCOLATE, EXC CANDY FROM BEANS: Chips, Powder, Block, Syrup

Jhl Inc ....G 703 378-0009
Chantilly (G-2449)
RE Max Advantage ....G 540 241-2499
Lyndhurst (G-7844)

CHOCOLATE, EXC CANDY FROM PURCH CHOC: Chips, Powder, Block

Barry Enterprises Intl LLC ....G 202 812-6822
Leesburg (G-7227)
Goddess of Chocolate Ltd ....G 757 301-2126
Virginia Beach (G-14486)
Sweet & Savory By Emily LLC ....G 804 248-8252
North Chesterfield (G-9995)

CHRISTMAS TREES: Artificial

Ado Industries LLC ....G 540 877-2769
Winchester (G-15372)

CIGARETTE & CIGAR PRDTS & ACCESS

Altria ....B 804 274-2100
Richmond (G-11100)
Crypto Reserve Inc ....G 571 229-0826
Manassas (G-7927)
Tobacco Plus ....G 703 644-5111
Springfield (G-13100)

CIGARETTE FILTERS

Bellvue Corp ....G 276 806-4418
Portsmouth (G-10398)
Porex Technologies Corp ....G 804 524-4983
South Chesterfield (G-12821)
Porex Technologies Corporation ....C 804 275-2631
North Chesterfield (G-9951)

CIGARETTE LIGHTER FLINTS

Khan Qaism ....G 703 212-8670
Alexandria (G-252)

CIRCUIT BOARD REPAIR SVCS

Vicious Creations LLC ....G 256 479-7689
Hampton (G-6262)

CIRCUIT BOARDS, PRINTED: Television & Radio

Assembly & Design Inc ....F 804 379-5432
North Chesterfield (G-9821)
Electronic Design & Mfg Co ....D 434 385-0046
Lynchburg (G-7701)
Ftg Crcuits Fredericksburg Inc ......D 540 752-5511
Fredericksburg (G-5433)
Printed Circuits International ....G 804 737-7979
Highland Springs (G-6855)
Zentech Fredericksburg LLC ....E 540 372-6500
Fredericksburg (G-5394)

CIRCUITS: Electronic

Amentum Services Inc ....C 703 418-3020
Arlington (G-851)
An Electronic Instrumentation ....G 434 793-4870
Danville (G-3955)
An Electronic Instrumentation ....C 703 478-0700
Leesburg (G-7217)
Atlas North America LLC ....G 757 463-0670
Yorktown (G-15934)
Bluewire Prototypes Inc ....G 540 200-3200
Hiwassee (G-6910)
Dominion Taping & Reeling Inc ......G 804 763-2700
Midlothian (G-8810)
E W Systems & Devices Inc ....G 540 635-5104
Front Royal (G-5531)
E-Tron Systems Inc ....E 703 690-2731
Lorton (G-7482)
Electronic Manufacturing Corp ....F 703 661-8351
Sterling (G-13392)
Emsco LLC ....F 804 752-1640
Ashland (G-1409)
Face Electronics Lc ....G 757 624-2121
Norfolk (G-9546)
Firstguard Technologies Corp ....G 703 267-6670
Fairfax (G-4624)
Goodrow Holdings Inc ....G 804 543-2136
Mechanicsville (G-8628)
Illinois Tool Works Inc ....D 434 239-6941
Lynchburg (G-7737)
Industrial Control Systems Inc ....E 804 737-1700
Sandston (G-12620)
ITT Defense & Electronics ....A 703 790-6300
Mc Lean (G-8474)
Metocean Telematics Inc ....G 902 468-2505
Mc Lean (G-8499)
Microwave Circuits Inc ....G 434 455-2800
Lynchburg (G-7772)
Odin Scnce Tech Innovation LLC .....G 850 582-0799
Fredericksburg (G-5338)
Pan American Systems Corp ....G 757 468-1926
Virginia Beach (G-14709)
Piccadilly Circuits ....G 703 860-5426
Reston (G-10925)
Prufrex USA Inc ....G 757 963-5400
Virginia Beach (G-14746)
Radio Reconnaissance Tech Inc ......G 540 752-7448
Fredericksburg (G-5352)
S K Circuits Inc ....G 703 376-8718
Fairfax (G-4547)
Seaguard International LLC ....G 484 747-0299
Suffolk (G-13761)
Sunrise Circuits LLC ....G 703 719-9324
Alexandria (G-591)
Taskill Technologies LLC ....G 757 277-5557
Williamsburg (G-15322)
Tidewater Prof Contrs LLC ....G 757 605-1040
Virginia Beach (G-14876)
Vicious Creations LLC ....G 256 479-7689
Hampton (G-6262)
Virginia Controls Inc ....E 804 225-5530
Richmond (G-11811)
Virginia Tek Inc ....F 703 391-8877
Reston (G-10986)

CLAMPS & COUPLINGS: Hose

Trimark Associates ....G 703 369-9494
Springfield (G-13102)

CLAMPS: Metal

H & B Machine ....G 276 546-5307
Keokee (G-7040)
Weiss Soni ....G 703 264-5848
Reston (G-10989)

CLAY MINING, COMMON

City Clay LLC ....G 434 293-0808
Charlottesville (G-2765)

CLAY PRDTS: Structural

Clay Decor LLC ....G 607 654-7428
Roanoke (G-11911)

CLAY: Ground Or Treated

Madidrop Pbc Inc (used In) ....G 434 260-3767
Charlottesville (G-2831)

CLEANING & DESCALING SVC: Metal Prdts

American Stripping Company ....E 703 368-9922
Manassas Park (G-8188)

CLEANING EQPT: Commercial

A-1 Security Mfg Corp ....F 804 359-9003
Richmond (G-11078)
Freshstart Coml Jantr Svcs LLC .....G 571 645-0060
Triangle (G-13893)
Jean Samuels ....G 804 328-2294
Sandston (G-12622)
Lincoln Place Group LLC ....G 347 363-9721
Richmond (G-11656)
Next Level Building Solutions ....G 540 400-9169
Boones Mill (G-1898)
Next Level Building Solutions ....F 540 685-1500
Roanoke (G-11974)
Sanitech Corp ....E 703 339-7001
Lorton (G-7529)
Tabb Enterprise LLC ....G 434 238-7196
Lynchburg (G-7818)

CLEANING EQPT: Floor Washing & Polishing, Commercial

Tlj Pressure Washing ....G 757 235-9096
Virginia Beach (G-14885)

CLEANING EQPT: High Pressure

2r2s Inc ....G 804 262-6922
Richmond (G-11072)
Affordable Companies ....G 703 440-9274
Springfield (G-12935)
Alpha Pressure Washing ....G 540 293-1287
Roanoke (G-12032)
Burley Holt Langford III LLC ....G 804 712-7172
South Chesterfield (G-12832)
Fab Services LLC ....G 757 869-4480
Williamsburg (G-15242)
New Look Pressure Washing LLC ....G 804 476-2000
Henrico (G-6542)
Parsons Pressure Washing ....G 757 894-3110
New Church (G-9127)
Pressures On ....G 757 681-8999
Chesapeake (G-3246)
Robert Agnello ....G 757 345-0829
Williamsburg (G-15306)
S&H Mobile Cleaning Service ....G 540 254-1135
Buchanan (G-2126)
Two Oaks ....G 434 352-8181
Appomattox (G-825)

CLEANING OR POLISHING PREPARATIONS, NEC

Triple D Sales Co Inc ....G 540 672-5821
Aroda (G-1226)

CLEANING PRDTS: Automobile Polish

Concept Products Inc ....G 434 793-9952
Danville (G-3971)
Dayton Dalice ....G 540 233-3657
Front Royal (G-5529)
Secar At Rich LLC ....G 804 737-0090
Richmond (G-11755)
Weekend Detailer LLC ....G 757 345-2023
Williamsburg (G-15340)

CLEANING PRDTS: Bleaches, Household, Dry Or Liquid

Virginia Kik Inc ....E 540 389-5401
Salem (G-12578)

CLEANING PRDTS: Degreasing Solvent

Hi-Lite Solutions Inc ....F 540 450-8375
Clear Brook (G-3645)

CLEANING PRDTS: Deodorants, Nonpersonal

Fragrances Ltd ....G 540 636-8099
Front Royal (G-5532)
Shakir Waliyyud-Deen ....G 706 399-8893
Alexandria (G-583)

CLEANING PRDTS: Disinfectants, Household Or Indl Plant

Ascalon International Inc ....G 703 926-4343
Reston (G-10792)
Lunano Inc ....G 202 594-2959
Mc Lean (G-8490)

CLEANING PRDTS: Drycleaning Preparations

C R D N of The Shenandoah ....F 540 943-8242
Waynesboro (G-15103)
TLC Cleaners Inc ....F 703 425-5577
Fairfax (G-4570)

CLEANING PRDTS: Laundry Preparations

Black Bear Corporation ....G 540 982-1061
Roanoke (G-12046)
Chemtron Inc ....G 703 550-7772
Lorton (G-7472)
John I Mercado ....G 703 569-3774
Springfield (G-13028)

CLEANING PRDTS: Leather Dressings & Finishes

Black Jacket LLC ....G 425 319-1014
Forest (G-5054)
Leather Luster Inc ....G 757 548-0146
Chesapeake (G-3182)

CLEANING PRDTS: Polishing Preparations & Related Prdts

Lubawa Usa Inc ....G 703 894-1909
Fredericksburg (G-5317)
RE Clean Automotive Products ....G 757 368-2694
Virginia Beach (G-14763)

CLEANING PRDTS: Sanitation Preparations

Global Water Challenge ....G 703 379-2713
Arlington (G-980)

CLEANING PRDTS: Sanitation Preps, Disinfectants/Deodorants

Grand Investment LLC ....G 804 939-9473
Richmond (G-11604)

CLEANING PRDTS: Specialty

Albright Recovery & Cnstr LLC ....G 276 835-2026
Clinchco (G-3684)
Allgoods Cleaning Service ....G 540 434-1511
Harrisonburg (G-6291)
B & B Cleaning Service ....G 757 667-9528
Norfolk (G-9448)
Cal Syd Inc ....G 276 963-3640
Richlands (G-11015)
Gregory Briggs ....G 804 402-6867
Richmond (G-11224)
Hampton Roads Green Clean LLC ....F 757 515-8183
Norfolk (G-9570)
Helping Hands Home Services ....F 757 898-3255
Seaford (G-12674)
Nanotouch Materials LLC ....G 888 411-6843
Forest (G-5085)
Polychem Inc ....G 540 862-1321
Clifton Forge (G-3682)
Rescue ME Cleaning Service ....G 540 370-0844
Fredericksburg (G-5219)
Zero Products LLC ....G 757 285-4000
Virginia Beach (G-14957)

Employee Codes: A=Over 500 employees, B=251-500
C=101-250, D=51-100, E=20-50, F=10-19, G=1-9

2021 Virginia
Industrial Directory

PRODUCT

921

CLIPPERS: Fingernail & Toenail

Lil Divas Mobile Spa LLC ....G....... 757 386-1455
Norfolk *(G-9619)*
Ni PHI Thach ....G....... 434 386-8852
Madison Heights *(G-7878)*

CLIPPERS: Hair, Human

Noelleimani Elite LLC ....G....... 804 452-6373
Richmond *(G-11692)*

CLOSURES: Plastic

Naj Enterprises LLP ....G....... 202 251-7821
Mc Lean *(G-8509)*

CLOTHES HANGERS, WHOLESALE

Pgb Hangers LLC ....G....... 703 851-4221
Gainesville *(G-5607)*
Vertexusa LLC ....G....... 213 294-3072
Sterling *(G-13548)*
Vertexusa LLC ....G....... 213 294-9072
Herndon *(G-6837)*

CLOTHING & ACCESS, WOMEN, CHILD & INFANT, WHOL: Scarves

Joshi Rubita ....G....... 571 315-9772
Alexandria *(G-500)*

CLOTHING & ACCESS, WOMEN, CHILD/INFANT, WHOLESALE: Child

Beadecked Inc ....G....... 703 435-5663
Herndon *(G-6622)*

CLOTHING & ACCESS, WOMEN, CHILDREN & INFANT, WHOL: Uniforms

El Tran Investment Corp ....G....... 757 439-8111
Virginia Beach *(G-14437)*

CLOTHING & ACCESS, WOMEN, CHILDREN/INFANT, WHOL: Swimsuits

Aardvark Swim and Sport Inc ....E....... 703 631-6045
Chantilly *(G-2361)*

CLOTHING & ACCESS: Costumes, Lodge

Elks Club 450 ....G....... 540 434-3673
Harrisonburg *(G-6313)*

CLOTHING & ACCESS: Costumes, Masquerade

Spirit Halloween ....G....... 804 513-2966
Colonial Heights *(G-3748)*

CLOTHING & ACCESS: Costumes, Theatrical

McKoon Zaneta ....G....... 410 707-5701
Fredericksburg *(G-5456)*

CLOTHING & ACCESS: Handicapped

Thelma Rethford ....G....... 540 997-9121
Goshen *(G-5928)*

CLOTHING & ACCESS: Hospital Gowns

Gracies Gowns Inc ....G....... 540 287-0143
Fredericksburg *(G-5292)*
Morris Designs Inc ....F....... 757 463-9400
Virginia Beach *(G-14664)*

CLOTHING & ACCESS: Men's Miscellaneous Access

Aurora Industries LLC ....A....... 757 301-2574
Virginia Beach *(G-14249)*
Go 2 Row Inc ....G....... 804 694-4868
Gloucester *(G-5849)*
Le Look LLC ....G....... 301 237-5072
Virginia Beach *(G-14605)*
Matbock LLC ....G....... 757 828-6659
Virginia Beach *(G-14639)*
Oak Hall Industries LP ....C....... 540 387-0000
Salem *(G-12549)*
PT Armor Inc ....E....... 703 560-1020
Springfield *(G-13076)*

Qore Performance Inc ....G....... 703 755-0724
Sterling *(G-13482)*
Red Action Blue Info LLC ....G....... 703 474-2617
Mc Lean *(G-8535)*
Red Action Blue Info LLC ....G....... 469 224-7673
Fairfax *(G-4538)*
Richmond Thread Lab LLC ....G....... 757 344-1886
Richmond *(G-11739)*
Sayre Enterprises Inc ....G....... 540 291-3808
Naturl BR STA *(G-9112)*

CLOTHING & ACCESS: Regalia

Macoy Pubg Masonic Sup Co Inc ....E....... 804 262-6551
Richmond *(G-11280)*

CLOTHING & ACCESS: Suspenders

Svs Enterprises Inc ....G....... 434 985-6642
Stanardsville *(G-13228)*

CLOTHING & APPAREL STORES: Custom

Cabin Hill TS LLC ....G....... 540 459-8912
Woodstock *(G-15850)*
Customink LLC ....C....... 434 326-1051
Charlottesville *(G-2613)*
Lay-N-Go LLC ....G....... 703 799-0799
Alexandria *(G-514)*
Macoy Pubg Masonic Sup Co Inc ....E....... 804 262-6551
Richmond *(G-11280)*

CLOTHING & FURNISHINGS, MEN'S & BOYS', WHOLESALE: Beachwear

Aardvark Swim and Sport Inc ....E....... 703 631-6045
Chantilly *(G-2361)*

CLOTHING STORES, NEC

El Tran Investment Corp ....G....... 757 439-8111
Virginia Beach *(G-14437)*

CLOTHING STORES: Designer Apparel

Philomen Fashion and Designs ......G....... 703 966-5680
Heathsville *(G-6463)*

CLOTHING STORES: Formal Wear

Ames Cleaners & Formals Inc ....G....... 757 825-3335
Hampton *(G-6084)*

CLOTHING STORES: Lingerie & Corsets, Underwear

Suzanne Henri Inc ....G....... 434 352-0233
Appomattox *(G-823)*

CLOTHING STORES: Raincoats

Gloria Barbre ....G....... 703 548-2210
Alexandria *(G-220)*

CLOTHING STORES: T-Shirts, Printed, Custom

3mp1re Clothing Co ....G....... 540 892-3484
Richmond *(G-11073)*
Anthony Biel ....G....... 703 307-8516
Dumfries *(G-4234)*
Garmonte LLC ....G....... 703 575-9003
Alexandria *(G-213)*
Minglewood Trading ....G....... 804 245-6162
North Chesterfield *(G-9932)*
Monogram Shop ....G....... 434 973-1968
Charlottesville *(G-2662)*
Silkscreening Unlimited Inc ....G....... 703 385-3212
Fairfax *(G-4554)*
Trak House LLC ....G....... 646 617-4418
Richmond *(G-11791)*

CLOTHING STORES: Teenage

Trotter Jamil ....G....... 757 251-8754
Hampton *(G-6253)*

CLOTHING/ACCESS, WOMEN, CHILDREN/INFANT, WHOL: Apparel Belt

Trotter Jamil ....G....... 757 251-8754
Hampton *(G-6253)*

CLOTHING: Academic Vestments

B & S Liquidating Corp ....C....... 540 387-0000
Salem *(G-12479)*
Tri State Graduate Sups LLC ....G....... 540 665-5292
Winchester *(G-15596)*

CLOTHING: Access

All Sports Athletic Apparel ....G....... 757 427-6772
Virginia Beach *(G-14223)*
Blue Ridge Crest LLC ....E....... 276 236-7149
Galax *(G-5629)*
Crown On LLC ....G....... 202 427-3042
Emporia *(G-4356)*
Custom Performance Inc ....G....... 540 972-3632
Spotsylvania *(G-12886)*
Diversified Solution LLC ....G....... 434 845-5100
Lynchburg *(G-7696)*
Dml Industries LLC ....G....... 571 348-4332
Virginia Beach *(G-14407)*
Elohim Designs ....G....... 757 292-1890
Chesapeake *(G-3087)*
Influences of Zion ....G....... 804 248-4758
Richmond *(G-11248)*
Livin Color LLC ....G....... 757 582-6030
Portsmouth *(G-10454)*
Lou-Voise ....G....... 804 836-5601
Glen Allen *(G-5765)*
Lululemon ....G....... 434 964-0105
Charlottesville *(G-2657)*
Lululemon ....G....... 757 631-3004
Virginia Beach *(G-14629)*
Lululemon Athletica ....G....... 703 787-8327
Reston *(G-10891)*
Melissa Moss ....G....... 540 397-0408
Roanoke *(G-11961)*
Michael Kors ....G....... 757 216-0581
Virginia Beach *(G-14649)*
Philosophy Worldwide Apparel ......G....... 804 767-0308
Moseley *(G-9044)*
Reckless Inc ....G....... 757 469-4416
Chesapeake *(G-3262)*
TS By Extreme LLC ....G....... 804 335-0260
North Chesterfield *(G-10005)*
Valerie Perkins ....G....... 804 279-0011
Chesterfield *(G-3538)*

CLOTHING: Access, Women's & Misses'

Boho Bae & Company LLC ....G....... 757 344-9197
Hampton *(G-6098)*
Claudia Ofori-Addo ....G....... 540 840-5388
Stafford *(G-13132)*
Dipped In Ice LLC ....G....... 540 845-3567
Orange *(G-10211)*
Elegance Meets Designs LLC ....G....... 347 567-6348
Richmond *(G-11199)*
Henry Saint-Denis LLC ....G....... 540 547-6657
Leesburg *(G-7284)*
Richmond Thread Lab LLC ....G....... 757 344-1886
Richmond *(G-11739)*
Shellys Chachkies LLC ....G....... 571 758-1323
Sterling *(G-13506)*
Shine Like Me LLC ....G....... 210 862-4197
Vienna *(G-14125)*
Sparklenshinecollection ....G....... 703 939-7623
Stephenson *(G-13335)*

CLOTHING: Aprons, Harness

Annin & Co ....E....... 434 575-7913
South Boston *(G-12746)*

CLOTHING: Athletic & Sportswear, Men's & Boys'

Adis America ....G....... 804 794-2848
Midlothian *(G-8768)*
Bajj Usa Inc ....G....... 703 953-1541
Manassas *(G-8033)*
Christopher Phillip & Moss LLC ....F....... 757 525-0683
Norfolk *(G-9484)*
Jammin ....E....... 540 484-4600
Rocky Mount *(G-12330)*
Neu Age Sportswear ....G....... 757 581-8333
Norfolk *(G-9658)*
New Creation Sourcing Inc ....F....... 703 330-5314
Manassas *(G-8117)*
P J Henry Inc ....E....... 757 428-0301
Virginia Beach *(G-14707)*

Rp55 Inc ....D...... 757 428-0300
Virginia Beach *(G-14782)*
Zyflex LLC ....G...... 804 306-6333
Midlothian *(G-8927)*

CLOTHING: Athletic & Sportswear, Women's & Girls'

Carousel ....G...... 434 292-7721
Blackstone *(G-1813)*
Fit ME By Crystal LLC ....G...... 302 573-1235
Arlington *(G-967)*
Jennifer Ouk ....G...... 571 232-0991
Alexandria *(G-497)*
Mng Online LLC ....G...... 571 247-8276
Manassas *(G-8109)*
Noir X Jojo LLC ....G...... 757 756-9134
Hampton *(G-6208)*

CLOTHING: Bathing Suits & Swimwear, Girls, Children & Infant

Bargain Beachwear Inc ....G...... 757 313-5440
Virginia Beach *(G-14260)*

CLOTHING: Bathrobes, Mens & Womens, From Purchased Materials

Saffron Fabs Corporation ....G...... 703 544-2791
Centreville *(G-2334)*

CLOTHING: Blouses, Women's & Girls'

B Queen Nation LLC ....G...... 678 507-4445
Newport News *(G-9175)*
D Carter Inc ....G...... 540 967-1506
Louisa *(G-7555)*
Hybernations LLC ....G...... 804 744-3580
Midlothian *(G-8831)*
Plus Is ME ....G...... 757 693-1505
Painter *(G-10242)*
Wallpaper Fitted Clothing Co ...G...... 757 639-8531
Norfolk *(G-9792)*

CLOTHING: Blouses, Womens & Juniors, From Purchased Mtrls

Deborah E Ross ....G...... 757 857-6140
Norfolk *(G-9521)*
Jafree Shirt Co Inc ....C...... 276 228-2116
Wytheville *(G-15892)*

CLOTHING: Brassieres

Body Creations ....G...... 276 620-9989
Max Meadows *(G-8366)*
Memteks-Usa Inc ....B...... 434 973-9800
Earlysville *(G-4292)*
Suzanne Henri Inc ....G...... 434 352-0233
Appomattox *(G-823)*

CLOTHING: Bridal Gowns

Catrina Fashions LLC ....G...... 540 992-2127
Troutville *(G-13906)*
Kims Kreations LLC ....G...... 703 431-7978
Round Hill *(G-12382)*
Zakaa Couture LLC ....G...... 703 554-7506
Leesburg *(G-7383)*

CLOTHING: Burial

Victor Forward LLC ....G...... 757 374-2642
Virginia Beach *(G-14909)*

CLOTHING: Children & Infants'

Commonwalth Girl Scout Council ...G...... 804 340-2835
Richmond *(G-11163)*
D Carter Inc ....G...... 540 967-1506
Louisa *(G-7555)*
Inch By Inch LLC ....G...... 804 678-8271
Richmond *(G-11618)*
Justice ....G...... 703 352-8393
Fairfax *(G-4487)*
Justice ....G...... 703 421-7001
Sterling *(G-13437)*
Justice ....G...... 703 490-6664
Woodbridge *(G-15734)*

CLOTHING: Children's, Girls'

Beadecked Inc ....G...... 703 759-3725
Great Falls *(G-5939)*
Beadecked Inc ....G...... 703 435-5663
Herndon *(G-6622)*
Catherine Rachel Braxton ....G...... 757 244-7531
Newport News *(G-9195)*
Dar Be Dar LLC ....G...... 703 244-1599
Reston *(G-10832)*
Larry Hicks ....G...... 276 738-9010
Castlewood *(G-2254)*
One of A Kind Kid ....G...... 800 276-0054
Midlothian *(G-8872)*
Rockin Baby LLC ....G...... 866 855-4378
Richmond *(G-11746)*

CLOTHING: Clergy Vestments

Gene Taylor ....G...... 540 345-9001
Roanoke *(G-12096)*
Hogue ....G...... 540 374-1144
Fredericksburg *(G-5196)*
Stewart David ....G...... 703 431-7233
Alexandria *(G-357)*

CLOTHING: Coats & Suits, Men's & Boys'

Ames Cleaners & Formals Inc ...G...... 757 825-3335
Hampton *(G-6084)*
Barrons-Hunter Inc ....G...... 434 971-7626
Charlottesville *(G-2736)*
D Carter Inc ....G...... 540 967-1506
Louisa *(G-7555)*
Polo Ralph Lauren Corp ....G...... 201 531-6000
Virginia Beach *(G-14729)*
Sabatini of London ....G...... 202 277-8227
Alexandria *(G-333)*
Webgear Inc ....F...... 703 532-1000
Vienna *(G-14158)*

CLOTHING: Costumes

Costume Shop ....G...... 804 421-7361
Richmond *(G-11168)*
Lavish ....G...... 757 498-1238
Virginia Beach *(G-14603)*
Proknows ....G...... 540 473-2271
Buchanan *(G-2125)*
Quad Promo LLC ....G...... 757 353-5729
Virginia Beach *(G-14751)*
Rubins Company Mj Inc ....F...... 571 437-7298
Herndon *(G-6797)*
Tall Toad Costumes ....G...... 276 694-4636
Claudville *(G-3641)*
Tunnel of Love ....G...... 757 961-5783
Virginia Beach *(G-14898)*

CLOTHING: Disposable

AG Customs Creat & Designs LLC ...G...... 757 927-7339
Hampton *(G-6078)*
Jessica Radellant Designs LLC ...G...... 804 301-3994
North Chesterfield *(G-9902)*
Premium Med Supply LLC ....G...... 888 506-6367
Richmond *(G-11331)*
Samco Textile Prints LLc ....G...... 571 451-4044
Woodbridge *(G-15802)*
Tredegar Personal Care LLC ...G...... 804 330-1000
North Chesterfield *(G-10039)*

CLOTHING: Dresses

Ardeens Designs Inc ....G...... 804 562-3840
Richmond *(G-11117)*
Bcbg Max Azria Group LLC .....G...... 757 497-9575
Falls Church *(G-4762)*
Determined LLC ....G...... 804 829-7229
Hopewell *(G-6923)*
Formally Yours ....G...... 540 974-3071
Middletown *(G-8738)*
Top Shop Onesies & Apparel ...G...... 757 202-3371
Norfolk *(G-9762)*

CLOTHING: Dresses, Hand Knit

Claudia & Co ....G...... 540 433-1140
Harrisonburg *(G-6301)*

CLOTHING: Gowns & Dresses, Wedding

A Pinch of Charm ....G...... 757 262-7820
Newport News *(G-9156)*

A Special Occasion LLC ....G...... 757 868-3160
Poquoson *(G-10363)*
Casa De Fiestas Dina ....G...... 703 910-6510
Woodbridge *(G-15670)*
Estudio De Fernandez LLC .....G...... 540 948-3196
Rochelle *(G-12233)*
First Class Chariots LLC ....G...... 757 334-7298
Norfolk *(G-9553)*
La Princesa ....G...... 703 330-2400
Manassas *(G-8096)*
Le Reve Bridal Inc ....F...... 703 777-3757
Leesburg *(G-7297)*
Life Transformations LLC ....G...... 703 624-0130
Reston *(G-10887)*
Lilly Lane Incorporated ....G...... 434 792-6387
Danville *(G-4013)*
Videographers Fredericksburg ...G...... 540 582-6111
Spotsylvania *(G-12921)*

CLOTHING: Gowns, Formal

Andrea Darcell LLC ....G...... 980 533-5128
Martinsville *(G-8266)*

CLOTHING: Hats & Caps, Leather

Cap City Inc ....G...... 757 827-0932
Hampton *(G-6105)*
Fairway Enterprise LLP ....G...... 434 973-8595
Charlottesville *(G-2631)*

CLOTHING: Hats & Caps, NEC

Ophelias Hat & Hair Shop ....G...... 757 331-1713
Cheriton *(G-2947)*
Pacific View International ....G...... 703 631-8659
Fairfax *(G-4658)*

CLOTHING: Hats & Caps, Uniform

El Tran Investment Corp ....G...... 757 439-8111
Virginia Beach *(G-14437)*
OSI LLC ....G...... 757 967-7533
Virginia Beach *(G-14705)*
R & B Distributing Inc ....D...... 804 794-5848
North Chesterfield *(G-9955)*

CLOTHING: Hats, Silk

Wards Soul Food Kitchen ....G...... 757 865-7069
Hampton *(G-6270)*

CLOTHING: Hosiery, Pantyhose & Knee Length, Sheer

Spanx Inc ....G...... 888 806-7311
Martinsville *(G-8335)*

CLOTHING: Hospital, Men's

Phillips Medical Manufacturer ...G...... 804 475-9144
Glen Allen *(G-5779)*
Scrub Exchange LLC ....G...... 434 237-7778
Concord *(G-3763)*

CLOTHING: Jogging & Warm-Up Suits, Knit

Vf Imagewear (east) Inc ....A...... 276 956-7200
Martinsville *(G-8345)*

CLOTHING: Maternity

2 Hearts 1 Dress LLC ....G...... 540 300-0655
Fredericksburg *(G-5166)*
Mother Teresas Cottage ....G...... 757 850-0350
Hampton *(G-6204)*

CLOTHING: Men's & boy's clothing, nec

Artists Innvators Creators LLC ...G...... 757 359-6215
Chesapeake *(G-2981)*
Battle King Inc ....G...... 757 324-1854
Portsmouth *(G-10397)*
Chesapeake Distributors LLC ...G...... 757 302-1108
Onancock *(G-10193)*
Psycho Panda ....G...... 540 287-0588
Fredericksburg *(G-5473)*
Snature LLC ....G...... 571 251-1573
Alexandria *(G-349)*

Employee Codes: A=Over 500 employees, B=251-500
C=101-250, D=51-100, E=20-50, F=10-19, G=1-9

2021 Virginia
Industrial Directory

923

PRODUCT

CLOTHING: Men's & boy's underwear & nightwear

Hanesbrands Inc ....B 336 519-5458
Stuart (G-13614)
Hanesbrands Inc ....B 276 670-4500
Martinsville (G-8293)

CLOTHING: Neckwear

Block9ine Enterprises LLC ....G 240 728-8601
Woodbridge (G-15660)
Blythe ....G 804 364-1717
Richmond (G-11130)
Disse Outdoor Gear LLC ....G 804 357-2860
Glen Allen (G-5724)
King Kreations ....G 703 883-7123
Stafford (G-13163)
Little Birdy Bags LLC ....G 703 757-6565
Great Falls (G-5965)
Thick To Thin LLC ....G 607 427-1737
Gainesville (G-5617)
Trademark Branders ....G 804 277-4428
Moseley (G-9050)

CLOTHING: Outerwear, Knit

Fruit For You Inc ....G 540 668-7750
Hillsboro (G-6868)
Metawear LLC ....G 561 302-2010
Fairfax (G-4655)
Sgm Inc ....G 757 572-3299
Virginia Beach (G-14805)
Warriorware LLC ....G 804 338-9431
North Chesterfield (G-10010)

CLOTHING: Outerwear, Women's & Misses' NEC

Chatham Knitting Mills Inc ....E 434 432-4701
Chatham (G-2921)
Greene Company of Virginia Inc ....G 276 638-7101
Martinsville (G-8292)
Heidi Ho Inc ....E 434 736-8763
Keysville (G-7059)
James Associates I LLC ....G 804 590-2620
South Chesterfield (G-12836)
Jammin ....E 540 484-4600
Rocky Mount (G-12330)
Lebanon Apparel Corporation ....C 276 889-3656
Lebanon (G-7197)
Sport Shack Inc ....G 540 372-3719
Fredericksburg (G-5487)

CLOTHING: Overalls & Coveralls

String Stalker LLC ....G 727 430-7545
Glen Allen (G-5802)

CLOTHING: Raincoats, Exc Vulcanized Rubber, Purchased Matls

Gloria Barbre ....G 703 548-2210
Alexandria (G-220)
Kool-Dri Inc ....F 540 997-9241
Millboro (G-8936)

CLOTHING: Service Apparel, Women's

Fannypants LLC ....G 703 953-3099
Chantilly (G-2420)
Sweetb Designs LLC ....G 757 550-0436
Portsmouth (G-10490)
Younivercity LLC ....G 540 529-7621
Roanoke (G-12231)

CLOTHING: Shirts

Custom Ink ....G 571 364-7944
Alexandria (G-178)
Greene Company of Virginia Inc ....G 276 638-7101
Martinsville (G-8292)
International Apparel Ltd ....E 571 643-0100
Manassas (G-8084)
Jafree Shirt Co Inc ....C 276 228-2116
Wytheville (G-15892)
Jensen Promotional Items Inc ....E 757 966-7608
Chesapeake (G-3150)
Oxford Industries Inc ....F 757 220-8660
Williamsburg (G-15290)
San Pak Inc ....G 276 647-5390
Collinsville (G-3716)

Vf Imagewear (east) Inc ....A 276 956-7200
Martinsville (G-8345)

CLOTHING: Shirts, Dress, Men's & Boys'

Kingdom Bloodline Apparel LLC ....G 866 426-0196
Richmond (G-11645)

CLOTHING: Shirts, Uniform, From Purchased Materials

El Tran Investment Corp ....G 757 439-8111
Virginia Beach (G-14437)

CLOTHING: Socks

Alienfeet Sports Socks ....G 703 864-8892
Alexandria (G-407)
Barry Sock Company ....G 703 525-1120
Arlington (G-875)
Get Some Socks LLC ....G 434 466-5054
Culpeper (G-3894)
Gildan Delaware Inc ....F 276 956-2305
Martinsville (G-8289)
Jeffrey M Haughney Attorney PC ....G 757 802-6160
Virginia Beach (G-14566)
Orange Sock Pay ....G 540 246-6368
Ruther Glen (G-12459)
Silly Sport Socks ....G 703 926-5398
Fairfax (G-4555)
So Many Socks ....G 703 309-8111
Woodbridge (G-15815)
Sock Software Inc ....G 804 749-4137
Rockville (G-12300)
Soul Socks LLC ....G 757 449-5013
Virginia Beach (G-14830)
Spirit Socks ....G 757 802-6160
Virginia Beach (G-14840)
Toucan Socks ....G 757 656-9497
Alexandria (G-601)

CLOTHING: Sportswear, Women's

Memteks-Usa Inc ....B 434 973-9800
Earlysville (G-4292)

CLOTHING: Suits, Men's & Boys', From Purchased Materials

Tom James Company ....F 703 916-9300
Annandale (G-789)
Tom James Company ....F 757 394-3205
Norfolk (G-9760)

CLOTHING: Sweaters & Sweater Coats, Knit

H Moss Design ....G 703 356-7824
Mc Lean (G-8455)

CLOTHING: Sweatshirts & T-Shirts, Men's & Boys'

Coronet Group Inc ....D 757 488-4800
Norfolk (G-9507)
Fame All Stars ....F 757 817-0214
Yorktown (G-15959)

CLOTHING: Swimwear, Men's & Boys'

Bargain Beachwear Inc ....G 757 313-5440
Virginia Beach (G-14260)

CLOTHING: Swimwear, Women's & Misses'

Karla Colletto Swimwear Inc ....E 703 281-3262
Vienna (G-14076)

CLOTHING: T-Shirts & Tops, Knit

Hanesbrands Inc ....G 276 236-5174
Galax (G-5638)
Red Star Consulting LLC ....G 434 872-0890
Charlottesville (G-2862)
Rich Young ....G 757 472-2057
Virginia Beach (G-14771)

CLOTHING: T-Shirts & Tops, Women's & Girls'

3mp1re Clothing Co ....G 540 892-3484
Richmond (G-11073)
Hibernate Inc ....G 804 513-1777
Glen Allen (G-5744)

Jensen Promotional Items Inc ....G 276 521-0143
Chilhowie (G-3553)

CLOTHING: Tailored Suits & Formal Jackets

Cool Comfort By Carson LLC ....G 330 348-3149
Alexandria (G-174)

CLOTHING: Trousers & Slacks, Men's & Boys'

Larry Hicks ....G 276 738-9010
Castlewood (G-2254)
Paul T Marshall ....G 703 580-0245
Woodbridge (G-15774)

CLOTHING: Tuxedos, From Purchased Materials

Annalees LLC ....G 703 303-1841
Sterling (G-13344)
Tiffanys By Sharon Inc ....G 804 273-6303
Henrico (G-6582)

CLOTHING: Underwear, Knit

Gildan Delaware Inc ....F 276 956-2305
Martinsville (G-8289)
Memteks-Usa Inc ....B 434 973-9800
Earlysville (G-4292)

CLOTHING: Underwear, Women's & Children's

Suzanne Henri Inc ....G 434 352-0233
Appomattox (G-823)

CLOTHING: Uniforms & Vestments

Shenandoah Robe Company Inc ....D 540 362-9811
Roanoke (G-12184)

CLOTHING: Uniforms, Ex Athletic, Women's, Misses' & Juniors'

Lebanon Apparel Corporation ....C 276 889-3656
Lebanon (G-7197)

CLOTHING: Uniforms, Men's & Boys'

Dynamic Team Sports Inc ....D 610 518-3300
Virginia Beach (G-14422)
Kathleen Tilley ....G 703 727-5385
Williamsburg (G-15265)

CLOTHING: Uniforms, Military, Men/Youth, Purchased Materials

Alpha Industries Inc ....B 703 378-1420
Chantilly (G-2366)
Antillian Trading Company LLC ....E 703 626-6333
Alexandria (G-414)
Billy M Seargeant ....G 540 898-6396
Fredericksburg (G-5253)
Get It Right Enterprise ....G 757 869-1736
Newport News (G-9235)
Juanita Deshazior ....G 703 901-5592
Alexandria (G-248)
Rbr Tactical Inc ....G 804 564-6787
Richmond (G-11347)
SNC Technical Services LLC ....G 787 820-2141
Virginia Beach (G-14829)
Stealth Mfg & Svcs LLC ....G 787 679-7548
Virginia Beach (G-14844)

CLOTHING: Uniforms, Policemen's, From Purchased Materials

Heroes Apparel LLC ....G 804 304-1001
Richmond (G-11611)

CLOTHING: Uniforms, Team Athletic

Tegra LLC ....G 470 705-1280
Norfolk (G-9746)

CLOTHING: Uniforms, Work

Cool Comfort By Carson LLC ....G 330 348-3149
Alexandria (G-174)
Lebanon Apparel Corporation ....C 276 889-3656
Lebanon (G-7197)

CLOTHING: Waterproof Outerwear

Alva Restoration & Waterproof............G... 540 785-0805
Fredericksburg (G-5243)

CLOTHING: Work Apparel, Exc Uniforms

Capital Brandworks LLC......................G... 703 609-7010
Fairfax (G-4423)

CLOTHING: Work, Men's

All Tyed Up ....G... 804 855-7158
Richmond (G-11482)
Chatham Knitting Mills Inc...................E... 434 432-4701
Chatham (G-2921)
Cowboy Western Wear ....G... 202 298-8299
Arlington (G-919)
G Gibbs Project LLC ....G... 804 638-9581
Chester (G-3418)
Nautica of Potomac ....E... 703 494-9915
Woodbridge (G-15755)
No Limits LLC ....G... 757 729-5612
Norfolk (G-9665)
Palidori LLC ....G... 757 609-1134
Norfolk (G-9680)
Uplift Collections ....G... 804 319-9129
Chesterfield (G-3536)
Uplift Collections LLC ....G... 804 319-9129
Chesterfield (G-3537)

COAL & OTHER MINERALS & ORES WHOLESALERS

Pioneer Group Inc VA ....G... 276 669-3400
Bristol (G-2029)

COAL GAS: Derived From Chemical Recovery Coke Oven

Coal Fillers Inc ....G... 276 322-4675
Bluefield (G-1860)

COAL LIQUEFACTION

St Cove Point LLC................................F... 713 897-1624
Richmond (G-11772)

COAL MINING EXPLORATION & TEST BORING SVC

William G Sexton..................................G... 276 988-9012
North Tazewell (G-10111)

COAL MINING SERVICES

American Energy LLC ....E... 276 935-7562
Norton (G-10112)
American Highwall Mining LLC ....G... 276 646-5548
Chilhowie (G-3544)
Asian American Coal Inc ....G... 804 648-1611
Richmond (G-11492)
Baden Reclamation Company ....F... 540 776-7890
Roanoke (G-12040)
Baystar Coal Company Inc ....F... 276 322-4900
Bluefield (G-1858)
Blackstone Energy Ltd ....G... 540 776-7890
Roanoke (G-12047)
Blueridge Sand Inc ....G... 276 579-2007
Mouth of Wilson (G-9091)
Bluestone Resources Inc ....C... 540 776-7890
Roanoke (G-12052)
Bluff Spur Coal LLC ....E... 276 679-6962
Norton (G-10113)
Bristol Coal Corporation ....F... 276 935-7562
Grundy (G-6028)
Coal Extraction Holdings LLC ....G... 276 466-3322
Bristol (G-1971)
Compass Coal Services LLC ....G... 804 218-8880
Richmond (G-11164)
Contura Energy Services LLC ....G... 276 835-8041
Mc Clure (G-8373)
Dacoal Mining Inc ....F... 276 531-8165
Grundy (G-6030)
Dickenson-Russell Coal Co LLC ....B... 276 889-6100
Cleveland (G-3655)
Erp Environmental Fund Inc ....G... 304 369-8113
Natural Bridge (G-9105)
Harold Keene Coal Co Inc ....G... 276 873-5437
Honaker (G-6914)
Hills Coal and Trucking Co ....G... 276 565-2560
Appalachia (G-797)

Inr Energy LLC ....G... 804 282-0369
Richmond (G-11249)
James River Escrow Inc ....G... 804 780-3000
Richmond (G-11628)
Johns Creek Elkhorn Coal Corp...........E... 804 780-3000
Richmond (G-11634)
Kanawha Eagle Coal LLC ....G... 304 837-8587
Glen Allen (G-5760)
Lonnie L Sparks ....G... 276 988-4298
North Tazewell (G-10102)
Maxxim Rebuild Co LLC ....A... 276 679-7020
Norton (G-10126)
Mountain Energy Resources Inc ....G... 276 679-3593
Norton (G-10129)
Natural Resources Intl LLC ....G... 804 282-0369
Richmond (G-11300)
Pardee Coal Company Inc ....G... 276 679-1400
Norton (G-10133)
Peabody Coaltrade LLC ....G... 804 378-4655
Midlothian (G-8877)
Sequoia Energy LLC ....F... 540 776-7890
Roanoke (G-12182)
Standard Core Drilling Co Inc ....G... 276 395-3391
Coeburn (G-3703)
Suffolk Materials LLC ....F... 757 255-4005
Suffolk (G-13769)
Timco Energy Inc ....G... 276 322-4900
Bluefield (G-1882)
Vedco Holdings Inc ....F... 800 258-8583
Vansant (G-13979)
Wellmore Energy Company LLC ....D... 276 530-7411
Big Rock (G-1705)
White Forest Resources Inc.................G... 804 410-9231
Richmond (G-11449)
Wpo 3 Inc ....G... 757 491-4140
Virginia Beach (G-14945)

COAL MINING SVCS: Bituminous, Contract Basis

C & B Enterprise LLC ....G... 276 971-4052
Cedar Bluff (G-2271)
Crown International Inc ....F... 703 335-0066
Manassas (G-8053)
Justice Low Seam Mining Inc ....F... 540 776-7890
Roanoke (G-12115)
Ratliff ....G... 276 794-7377
Lebanon (G-7205)
Za Contracting LLC ....G... 703 498-3531
Falls Church (G-4896)

COAL MINING: Bituminous & Lignite Surface

Appalachia Holding Company ....F... 276 619-4410
Bristol (G-2006)
Consolidation Coal Company ....E... 276 988-3010
Amonate (G-725)
Elite Coals Inc ....G... 276 679-4070
Norton (G-10118)

COAL MINING: Bituminous Coal & Lignite-Surface Mining

Blue Ribbon Coal Sales Ltd ....G... 540 387-2077
Salem (G-12482)
Bluestone Industries Inc ....E... 540 776-7890
Roanoke (G-12051)
Chad Coal Corp....................................F... 276 498-4952
Whitewood (G-15191)
Coal Energy Resources Inc ....G... 276 676-3101
Abingdon (G-24)
Consolidation Coal Co ....G... 276 988-3010
Bandy (G-1558)
Dominion Coal Corp ....G... 276 935-8810
Oakwood (G-10167)
Excello Oil Company Inc ....F... 276 935-2332
Grundy (G-6031)
Falcon Coal Corporation ....E... 276 679-0600
Wise (G-15623)
Global Design Contractors Inc ....G... 703 865-6064
Fairfax (G-4469)
Itforesight LLC ....G... 703 829-7283
Reston (G-10879)
James River Coal Company ....F... 804 780-3000
Richmond (G-11625)
Laurel Run LLC ....G... 540 364-1238
Hume (G-6962)
Nordic Mining LLC ....G... 703 878-0346
Woodbridge (G-15764)
Paramont Contura LLC ....G... 276 679-7020
Norton (G-10132)

Pardee Coal Company Inc....................G... 276 679-1400
Norton (G-10133)
Pioneer Group Inc VA ....G... 276 669-3400
Bristol (G-2029)
Pittston Minerals Group Inc ....C... 804 289-9600
Richmond (G-11327)
Rapoca Energy Co ....G... 423 269-6900
Bristol (G-2032)
Riggs Oil Company ....E... 276 523-2662
Big Stone Gap (G-1714)
Southwestern Vrgnia Wheelco Inc ....G... 540 493-6886
Rocky Mount (G-12354)
Standard Banner Coal Corp ....G... 276 944-5603
Meadowview (G-8596)
Stonega Mining & Processing Co ....G... 276 523-5690
Big Stone Gap (G-1715)
Todd Drummond Consulting LLC ....G... 603 763-8857
Virginia Beach (G-14886)
Wellmore Energy Company LLC ....D... 276 530-7411
Big Rock (G-1705)

COAL MINING: Bituminous Underground

A B & J Coal Company Inc ....F... 276 530-7786
Grundy (G-6027)
A & G Coal Corporation ....E... 276 328-3421
Roanoke (G-12027)
Alpha Appalachia Holdings Inc ....D... 276 619-4410
Bristol (G-1964)
Chad Coal Corp....................................F... 276 498-4952
Whitewood (G-15191)
Davis Mining & Mfg Inc ....F... 276 395-3354
Wise (G-15622)
Doss Fork Coal Co Inc ....E... 540 322-4066
Bluefield (G-1863)
Jewell Smokeless Coal Corp ....E... 276 935-8810
Oakwood (G-10170)
Knox Creek Coal Corporation ....B... 276 964-4333
Raven (G-10756)
Maxxim Shared Services LLC ....G... 276 679-7020
Norton (G-10127)
Pittston Coal Company ....F... 276 739-3420
Abingdon (G-53)
Pittston Minerals Group Inc ....C... 804 289-9600
Richmond (G-11327)
Regent Allied Carbon Energy ....E... 276 679-4994
Appalachia (G-800)
Tennessee Consolidated Coal Co ....G... 423 658-5115
Bristol (G-2035)

COAL MINING: Bituminous, Auger

Horn Construction Co Inc ....G... 276 935-4749
Grundy (G-6035)

COAL MINING: Bituminous, Strip

A & G Coal Corporation ....E... 276 328-3421
Roanoke (G-12027)
Davis Mining & Mfg Inc ....F... 276 395-3354
Wise (G-15622)
Fairbanks Coal Co Inc ....F... 276 395-3354
Coeburn (G-3698)
Humphreys Enterprises Inc ....F... 276 679-1400
Norton (G-10120)
James River Coal Service Co ....E... 606 878-7411
Richmond (G-11626)
Justice Coal of Alabama LLC ....G... 540 776-7890
Roanoke (G-12114)

COAL MINING: Bituminous, Surface, NEC

Big D Enterprises Inc...........................G... 276 679-1090
Coeburn (G-3695)

COAL MINING: Underground, Semibituminous

James River Coal Service Co ....E... 606 878-7411
Richmond (G-11626)

COAL MINING: Underground, Subbituminous

Alliance Resource Partners LP.............D... 276 566-8516
Hurley (G-6968)
Capital Coal Corporation ....F... 276 935-7562
Abingdon (G-20)

COAL PREPARATION PLANT: Bituminous or Lignite

Mate Creek Energy of West VA ....G 276 669-8599
Bristol *(G-2025)*
Nice Wounders Group ....F 276 669-6476
Bristol *(G-2028)*

COAL TAR RESINS

Green Coal Solutions LLC ....G 703 910-4022
Woodbridge *(G-15716)*

COAL, MINERALS & ORES, WHOLESALE: Coal

Harold Keene Coal Co Inc ....G 276 873-5437
Honaker *(G-6914)*
White Forest Resources Inc ....G 804 410-9231
Richmond *(G-11449)*

COATING COMPOUNDS: Tar

Osburn Coatings Inc ....G 804 769-3030
Aylett *(G-1551)*

COATING OR WRAPPING SVC: Steel Pipe

Peninsula Custom Coaters Inc ....G 757 476-6996
Williamsburg *(G-15294)*

COATING SVC

A 1 Coating ....G 757 351-5544
Virginia Beach *(G-14200)*
Candies & Chrome Coatings LLC ....G 757 812-1490
Chesapeake *(G-3025)*
Chesapeake Coatings ....G 757 945-2812
Virginia Beach *(G-14335)*
Combat Coating ....G 757 468-9020
Virginia Beach *(G-14355)*
Defensecoat Industries LLC ....G 804 356-5316
Richmond *(G-11559)*
Eiw Powder Coating ....G 703 586-9392
Woodbridge *(G-15688)*
Extreme Powder Works LLC ....G 540 483-2684
Henry *(G-6595)*
Hydro Prep & Coating Inc ....G 804 530-2178
Chester *(G-3423)*
Infocus Coatings Inc ....G 804 530-4645
Chester *(G-3424)*
Lifetime Coating Specialties ....G 757 559-1011
Virginia Beach *(G-14611)*
Onyx Coating Solutions LLC ....G 434 660-4627
Concord *(G-3762)*
Permaguard Coatings LLC ....G 929 352-5665
Mechanicsville *(G-8667)*
Piedmont Powder Coating Inc ....G 434 334-8434
Danville *(G-4027)*
Richmond Powder Coating Inc ....G 804 226-4111
Highland Springs *(G-6856)*
Ruststop USA LLC ....G 218 391-5389
Stafford *(G-13186)*
Slejs Custom Coating LLC ....G 817 975-6274
Chesapeake *(G-3295)*
Top Shelf Coatings LLC ....G 804 241-8644
Aylett *(G-1555)*

COATING SVC: Aluminum, Metal Prdts

William Butler Aluminum ....G 804 393-1046
Richmond *(G-11450)*

COATING SVC: Hot Dip, Metals Or Formed Prdts

Virginia American Inds Inc ....C 804 644-2611
Richmond *(G-11807)*

COATING SVC: Metals & Formed Prdts

Advanced Coating Solutions LLC ....G 540 898-9370
Fredericksburg *(G-5241)*
Advanced Cstm Coatings VA LLC ....G 757 726-2628
Hampton *(G-6072)*
American Buildings Company ....C 434 757-2220
La Crosse *(G-7139)*
B and B Powder Coating ....G 540 921-1158
Pearisburg *(G-10273)*
Creative Coatings Inc ....F 540 636-7911
Front Royal *(G-5527)*
Detective Coating LLC ....G 804 893-3313
North Chesterfield *(G-9859)*

Dishman Fabrications LLC ....G 757 478-5070
Yorktown *(G-15950)*
Europro Coatings Inc ....G 703 817-1211
Woodbridge *(G-15698)*
Extreme Powder Coating LLC ....G 703 339-8233
Lorton *(G-7486)*
Global Metal Finishing Inc ....F 540 362-1489
Roanoke *(G-11926)*
Hanover Powder Coating LL ....G 804 798-5988
Ashland *(G-1429)*
Hitek Powder Coating ....G 434 845-7000
Evington *(G-4377)*
J&J Powder Coating ....G 757 390-0237
Virginia Beach *(G-14559)*
Jacobs Powder Coating LLC ....G 540 208-7762
Penn Laird *(G-10289)*
John A Treese ....G 540 731-0250
Radford *(G-10718)*
Kbm Powder Coating LLC ....G 804 496-6860
Ashland *(G-1448)*
Lalandii Coatings LLC ....G 757 425-0131
Virginia Beach *(G-14598)*
Lane Enterprises Inc ....G 276 223-1051
Wytheville *(G-15895)*
Lohmann Specialty Coatings LLC ....G 859 334-4900
Orange *(G-10219)*
Lynchburg Powder Coating ....G 434 239-8454
Lynchburg *(G-7763)*
Pambina Impex ....G 703 910-7309
Woodbridge *(G-15771)*
Precision Powder Coating Inc ....G 757 368-2135
Virginia Beach *(G-14733)*
Prince Group of Virginia LLC ....F 703 953-0577
Arlington *(G-1120)*
Stephen C Marston ....G 757 562-0271
Franklin *(G-5157)*
Technical Urethanes Inc ....G 540 667-1770
Clear Brook *(G-3652)*
Thermal Spray Solutions Inc ....E 757 673-2468
Chesapeake *(G-3331)*
Uniquecoat Technologies LLC ....G 804 784-0997
Oilville *(G-10186)*
Vanwin Coatings Virginia LLC ....E 757 487-5080
Chesapeake *(G-3438)*
Vanwin Coatings Virginia LLC ....G 757 925-4450
Suffolk *(G-13777)*

COATING SVC: Rust Preventative

Integrated Global Services Inc ....D 804 794-1646
North Chesterfield *(G-9898)*
Metalspray International Inc ....D 804 794-1646
Midlothian *(G-8856)*
Metalspray United Inc ....F 804 794-1646
Midlothian *(G-8857)*

COATINGS: Air Curing

Atomic Armor Inc ....G 703 400-3954
Leesburg *(G-7225)*
Branch House Signature Pdts ....G 804 644-3041
Richmond *(G-11507)*
HI Caliber Manufacturing LLC ....G 804 955-8300
Ashland *(G-1432)*
Line X Central Virginia Inc ....G 434 525-8878
Evington *(G-4378)*

COATINGS: Polyurethane

Srj Bedliners LLC ....G 757 539-7710
Suffolk *(G-13767)*

COFFEE SVCS

J L V Management Inc ....G 540 446-6359
Stafford *(G-13158)*
Shenandoah Corporation ....E 540 248-2123
Staunton *(G-13292)*

COILS & TRANSFORMERS

Delta Electronics Inc ....F 703 354-3350
Alexandria *(G-445)*
Electro-Mechanical Corporation ....B 276 669-4084
Bristol *(G-1977)*
Marelco Power Systems Inc ....F 800 225-4838
Richmond *(G-11667)*
Power Distribution Inc ....C 804 737-9880
Richmond *(G-11721)*
SMC Electrical Products Inc ....E 276 285-3841
Bristol *(G-2033)*
Transformer Engineering LLC ....D 216 741-5282
Wytheville *(G-15920)*

COINS & TOKENS: Non-Currency

Northwest Territorial Mint LLC ....F 703 922-5545
Springfield *(G-13060)*
Presidential Coin & Antique Co ....G 703 354-5454
Clifton *(G-3675)*

COKE: Petroleum & Coal Derivative

IG Petroleum LLC ....F 703 749-1780
Mc Lean *(G-8463)*

COKE: Petroleum, Not From Refineries

Ultra Petroleum LLC ....G 276 964-6118
Richlands *(G-11021)*

COLLECTION AGENCIES

Douglas Stuart LLC ....C 571 210-4440
Sterling *(G-13388)*

COLLECTOR RINGS: Electric Motors Or Generators

BGB Technology Inc ....E 804 451-5211
South Chesterfield *(G-12797)*

COLLEGE, EXC JUNIOR

Randolph-Macon College ....G 804 752-7200
Ashland *(G-1483)*

COLLEGES, UNIVERSITIES & PROFESSIONAL SCHOOLS

CJ & Associates LLC ....G 301 461-2945
Sterling *(G-13370)*

COLOR LAKES OR TONERS

Lonesome Trails Entps Inc ....G 276 445-5443
Ewing *(G-4385)*

COLORS: Pigments, Inorganic

Hoover Color Corporation ....G 540 980-7233
Hiwassee *(G-6912)*

COLORS: Pigments, Organic

Synalloy Corporation ....D 804 822-3260
Glen Allen *(G-5804)*

COMFORTERS & QUILTS, FROM MANMADE FIBER OR SILK

Birdcloud Creations ....G 757 428-6239
Virginia Beach *(G-14283)*

COMMERCIAL & LITERARY WRITINGS

Acre Media LLC ....G 703 314-4465
Alexandria *(G-402)*
Brown & Duncan LLC ....G 832 844-6523
Virginia Beach *(G-14302)*
Triple Yolk LLC ....G 540 923-4040
Reva *(G-11002)*

COMMERCIAL & OFFICE BUILDINGS RENOVATION & REPAIR

L & M Electric and Plbg LLC ....F 703 768-2222
Alexandria *(G-512)*
Rappatomac Industries Inc ....G 804 529-6440
Callao *(G-2218)*

COMMERCIAL ART & GRAPHIC DESIGN SVCS

Arabesque Media ....G 703 745-5395
Fairfax *(G-4410)*
Capital Screen Prtg Unlimited ....G 703 550-0033
Lorton *(G-7470)*
Dml Industries LLC ....G 571 348-4332
Virginia Beach *(G-14407)*
Dominion Graphics Inc ....G 804 353-3755
Richmond *(G-11188)*
Falcon Lab Inc ....G 703 442-0124
Mc Lean *(G-8426)*
Fresh Printz LLC ....G 540 937-3017
Jeffersonton *(G-7012)*

Fta Goverment Services Inc ....G...... 571 612-0413
  Chantilly **(G-2423)**
Graham Graphics LLC ....G...... 703 220-4564
  Springfield **(G-13013)**
Ideation Web Studios LLC ....G...... 757 333-3021
  Chesapeake **(G-3140)**
Identity Mktg Promotional LLC ....G...... 757 966-2863
  Suffolk **(G-13724)**
Interntional Scanner Corp Amer ....F...... 703 533-8560
  Arlington **(G-1007)**
J & R Graphic Services Inc ....G...... 757 595-2602
  Yorktown **(G-15967)**
Jones Direct LLC ....G...... 757 718-3468
  Chesapeake **(G-3153)**
Lighted Signs Direct Inc ....G...... 703 965-5188
  Woodbridge **(G-15740)**
Llama Life II LLC ....G...... 434 286-4494
  Charlottesville **(G-2827)**
Minglewood Trading ....G...... 804 245-6162
  North Chesterfield **(G-9932)**
Minuteman Press of Mc Lean ....G...... 703 356-6612
  Mc Lean **(G-8502)**
Party Headquarters Inc ....G...... 703 494-5317
  Fredericksburg **(G-5467)**
River City Graphics LLC ....G...... 757 519-9525
  Virginia Beach **(G-14777)**
Strive Communications LLC ....G...... 703 925-5900
  Reston **(G-10967)**
Tsg Concepts Inc ....G...... 877 777-5734
  Arlington **(G-1200)**
Venutec Corporation ....G...... 888 573-8870
  Centreville **(G-2350)**
Virginia Engineer ....G...... 804 779-3527
  Mechanicsville **(G-8695)**
Woody Graphics Inc ....G...... 540 774-4749
  Roanoke **(G-12025)**

COMMERCIAL ART & ILLUSTRATION SVCS

Art Guild Inc ....F...... 804 282-5434
  Henrico **(G-6476)**
Bxi Inc ....G...... 804 282-5434
  Richmond **(G-11142)**
Type & Art ....G...... 804 794-3375
  North Chesterfield **(G-10006)**

COMMERCIAL EQPT, WHOLESALE: Coffee Brewing Eqpt & Splys

Johnson & Elich Roasters Ltd ....F...... 540 552-7442
  Blacksburg **(G-1747)**

COMMERCIAL EQPT, WHOLESALE: Comm Cooking & Food Svc Eqpt

Aileen L Brown ....G...... 757 696-1814
  Hampton **(G-6079)**
Consurgo Group Inc ....F...... 757 373-1717
  Virginia Beach **(G-14361)**

COMMERCIAL EQPT, WHOLESALE: Scales, Exc Laboratory

My Three Sons Inc ....G...... 540 662-5927
  Winchester **(G-15453)**

COMMERCIAL LAUNDRY EQPT

Rodgers Services LLC ....G...... 301 848-6384
  King George **(G-7109)**

COMMERCIAL PRINTING & NEWSPAPER PUBLISHING COMBINED

A B M Enterprises Inc ....G...... 804 561-3655
  Amelia Court House **(G-648)**
Apg Media of Chesapeake LLC ....G...... 804 843-2282
  Williamsburg **(G-15205)**
Bedford Bulletin LLC ....G...... 540 586-8612
  Bedford **(G-1623)**
Buds Blueridge ....G...... 540 323-7030
  Winchester **(G-15396)**
Charlette Publishing Inc ....G...... 434 696-5550
  Victoria **(G-14000)**
Coalfield Progress ....D...... 276 679-1101
  Norton **(G-10115)**
Commonwealth Times ....G...... 804 828-1058
  Richmond **(G-11536)**
Covington Virginian Inc ....E...... 540 962-2121
  Covington **(G-3784)**

Double T Publishing Inc ....D...... 276 926-8816
  Clintwood **(G-3688)**
Gannett Publishing Svcs LLC ....F...... 703 854-6000
  Mc Lean **(G-8442)**
Gannett Stllite Info Ntwrk LLC ....A...... 703 854-6000
  Mc Lean **(G-8444)**
Gatehuse Media VA Holdings Inc ....G...... 585 598-0030
  Petersburg **(G-10323)**
Haskell Investment Company Inc ....D...... 276 638-8801
  Martinsville **(G-8294)**
Joong-Ang Daily News Cal Inc ....E...... 703 281-9660
  Annandale **(G-762)**
Korea Daily ....F...... 703 281-9660
  Annandale **(G-764)**
Landmark Cmnty Nwsppers VA LLC ....F...... 276 236-5178
  Galax **(G-5640)**
Landmark Media Enterprises LLC ....A...... 757 351-7000
  Norfolk **(G-9616)**
M & S Publishing Co Inc ....G...... 434 645-7534
  Crewe **(G-3814)**
Nottoway Publishing Co Inc ....F...... 434 292-3019
  Blackstone **(G-1821)**
Observer Inc ....G...... 804 545-7500
  Midlothian **(G-8870)**
Sentinel Press LLC ....G...... 703 753-5434
  Gainesville **(G-5611)**
Shenandoah Publications Inc ....E...... 540 459-4000
  Edinburg **(G-4314)**
Smithfield Times ....G...... 757 357-3288
  Smithfield **(G-12740)**
Southwest Publisher LLC ....E...... 540 980-5220
  Pulaski **(G-10647)**
Tidewater Newspapers Inc ....E...... 804 693-3101
  Gloucester **(G-5862)**
Times Publishing Company ....F...... 757 357-3288
  Smithfield **(G-12742)**
Virginia News Group LLC ....G...... 703 777-1111
  Leesburg **(G-7372)**
Virginia News Group LLC ....G...... 703 777-1111
  Leesburg **(G-7373)**
Virginn-Plot Mdia Cmpanies LLC ....A...... 757 446-9000
  Virginia Beach **(G-14923)**

COMMODITY CONTRACT POOL OPERATORS

Advanced Cgnitive Systems Corp ....G...... 804 397-3373
  Richmond **(G-11474)**

COMMODITY CONTRACT TRADING COMPANIES

Eerkins Inc ....G...... 703 626-6248
  Luray **(G-7608)**

COMMODITY CONTRACTS BROKERS, DEALERS

Boehringer Ingelheim Corp ....G...... 800 243-0127
  Ashburn **(G-1251)**

COMMON SAND MINING

Aggregate Industries MGT Inc ....F...... 540 249-5791
  Grottoes **(G-6013)**
Baillio Sand Co Inc ....F...... 757 428-3302
  Virginia Beach **(G-14258)**
Bay Sand Co Inc ....G...... 757 357-9477
  Smithfield **(G-12704)**

COMMUNICATION HEADGEAR: Telephone

Ceotronics Inc ....G...... 757 549-6220
  Virginia Beach **(G-14329)**

COMMUNICATIONS CARRIER: Wired

Softwright LLC ....G...... 434 975-4310
  Charlottesville **(G-2694)**

COMMUNICATIONS EQPT & SYSTEMS, NEC

Avelis John ....G...... 757 363-2001
  Virginia Beach **(G-14250)**
Connected Intelligence LLC ....G...... 571 241-4540
  Dulles **(G-4196)**
Dacha ....G...... 757 754-2805
  Virginia Beach **(G-14380)**
Damsel Detectors ....G...... 757 268-4128
  Portsmouth **(G-10414)**
Emergency Response Tech LLC ....G...... 703 932-1118
  Manassas **(G-7938)**

Exceletics Inc ....G...... 703 405-5479
  Herndon **(G-6671)**
Final Resource Inc ....G...... 703 404-8740
  Herndon **(G-6676)**
Industrial Signal LLC ....G...... 703 323-7777
  Arlington **(G-1001)**
Milcom Systems Corporation Vol ....F...... 757 463-2800
  Virginia Beach **(G-14654)**
Ms Kathleen B Watkins ....G...... 804 741-0388
  Henrico **(G-6537)**
Nettalon Inc ....G...... 877 638-8256
  Fredericksburg **(G-5332)**
Tri-Ed Distribution Inc ....G...... 757 852-3780
  Norfolk **(G-9767)**

COMMUNICATIONS EQPT WHOLESALERS

Astron Wireless Tech Inc ....F...... 703 450-5517
  Sterling **(G-13352)**

COMMUNICATIONS EQPT: Microwave

Coleman Microwave Co ....E...... 540 984-8848
  Edinburg **(G-4301)**
Metropole Products Inc ....E...... 540 659-2132
  Stafford **(G-13176)**

COMMUNICATIONS SVCS

Holderby & Bierce Inc ....G...... 434 971-8571
  Charlottesville **(G-2645)**

COMMUNICATIONS SVCS: Data

Core Business Technologies Inc ....G...... 757 426-0344
  Virginia Beach **(G-14365)**
General Dynmics One Source LLC ....F...... 703 906-6397
  Falls Church **(G-4796)**
Iridium Communications Inc ....E...... 703 287-7400
  Mc Lean **(G-8469)**
Six3 Advanced Systems Inc ....C...... 703 742-7660
  Dulles **(G-4226)**

COMMUNICATIONS SVCS: Internet Connectivity Svcs

Key Bridge Global LLC ....G...... 703 414-3500
  Mc Lean **(G-8479)**
Witt Associates Inc ....G...... 540 667-3146
  Winchester **(G-15517)**

COMMUNICATIONS SVCS: Internet Host Svcs

Pbp Solutions LLC ....G...... 202 999-8101
  Reston **(G-10923)**
Wealthy Sistas Media Group ....G...... 800 917-9435
  Dumfries **(G-4262)**

COMMUNICATIONS SVCS: Nonvocal Message

1st Signage and Lighting LLC ....G...... 276 229-4200
  Woolwine **(G-15863)**

COMMUNICATIONS SVCS: Online Svc Providers

Intor Inc ....G...... 757 296-2175
  Alexandria **(G-240)**
Rosetta Stone Inc ....E...... 703 387-5800
  Arlington **(G-1151)**
Rosworks LLC ....G...... 804 282-3111
  Richmond **(G-11747)**

COMMUNICATIONS SVCS: Satellite Earth Stations

Nomad Solutions LLC ....F...... 703 656-9100
  Gainesville **(G-5602)**
Orbital Sciences LLC ....A...... 703 406-5524
  Dulles **(G-4217)**
Spacequest Ltd ....F...... 703 424-7801
  Fairfax **(G-4680)**
US 21 Inc ....D...... 703 560-0021
  Fairfax **(G-4575)**
Virginn-Plot Mdia Cmpanies LLC ....G...... 757 446-2848
  Virginia Beach **(G-14924)**

Employee Codes: A=Over 500 employees, B=251-500
C=101-250, D=51-100, E=20-50, F=10-19, G=1-9

2021 Virginia
Industrial Directory

PRODUCT

927

COMMUNICATIONS SVCS: Signal Enhancement Network Svcs

Aretec Inc.................................E...... 703 539-8801
Fairfax *(G-4596)*

C-3 Comm Systems LLC.....................G...... 703 829-0588
Arlington *(G-897)*

COMMUNICATIONS SVCS: Telephone Or Video

Prelude Communications Inc.....G...... 703 731-9396
Sterling *(G-13476)*

Veamea Inc.....................................G...... 703 382-2288
Mc Lean *(G-8575)*

COMMUNICATIONS SVCS: Telephone, Voice

Singlecomm LLC.............................F...... 203 559-5486
Richmond *(G-11383)*

COMMUNITY CENTERS: Youth

Commonwalth Girl Scout Council........G...... 804 340-2835
Richmond *(G-11163)*

COMMUNITY COLLEGE

College and University Educati.............G...... 540 820-7384
Harrisonburg *(G-6302)*

COMPACT LASER DISCS: Prerecorded

Furnace Mfg Inc............................F....... 703 205-0007
Alexandria *(G-465)*

COMPACTORS: Trash & Garbage, Residential

BFI Waste Services LLC..................E...... 804 222-1152
Richmond *(G-11124)*

COMPOST

Armstrong Green & Embrey Inc............G...... 540 898-7434
Fredericksburg *(G-5248)*

Asb Greenworld Inc........................E...... 804 785-9260
Mattaponi *(G-8357)*

Castlemans Compost LLC................G...... 571 283-3030
Herndon *(G-6636)*

Compost Livin LLC..........................G...... 703 362-9378
Annandale *(G-736)*

Compost Rva LLC...........................G...... 804 639-0363
Midlothian *(G-8802)*

Cow Pie Compost LLC....................G...... 540 272-2854
Midland *(G-8750)*

Enrich Compost LLC........................G...... 518 410-2402
Henrico *(G-6507)*

Humus Compost Company LLC..........G...... 540 421-7169
Rockingham *(G-12256)*

Kathezz Compost LLC.....................G...... 434 842-9395
Columbia *(G-3752)*

Virginias Peninsula Pub Fcilty..............G...... 757 898-5012
Yorktown *(G-15999)*

COMPRESSORS: Air & Gas

Air & Gas Components LLC................G...... 757 473-3571
Virginia Beach *(G-14217)*

Air Systems International Inc.............E...... 757 424-3967
Chesapeake *(G-2957)*

Bauer Compressors Inc...................G...... 757 855-6006
Norfolk *(G-9457)*

David S Welch................................G...... 276 398-4024
Fancy Gap *(G-4934)*

Dresser-Rand Company....................E...... 540 444-4200
Salem *(G-12497)*

Ingersoll Rand Inc..........................G...... 804 214-7054
North Chesterfield *(G-9896)*

Special Projects Operations.............F...... 410 297-6550
Virginia Beach *(G-14834)*

Universal Air Products Corp..............E...... 757 461-0077
Norfolk *(G-9774)*

COMPRESSORS: Air & Gas, Including Vacuum Pumps

Atlas Copco Compressor Aif VA..........G...... 540 226-8655
Fredericksburg *(G-5249)*

Bauer Compressors Inc....................C...... 757 855-6006
Norfolk *(G-9458)*

Breeze-Eastern LLC.......................G...... 973 602-1001
Fredericksburg *(G-5175)*

Gravittional Systems Engrg Inc.......F...... 312 224-8152
Clifton *(G-3668)*

COMPUTER & COMPUTER SOFTWARE STORES

Core Business Technologies Inc..........G...... 757 426-0344
Virginia Beach *(G-14365)*

Micro Services Company.................G...... 804 741-5000
Richmond *(G-11291)*

Oracle Systems Corporation.............A...... 703 478-9000
Reston *(G-10916)*

Up and Running Computers Inc..........G...... 757 565-3282
Williamsburg *(G-15329)*

COMPUTER & COMPUTER SOFTWARE STORES: Peripheral Eqpt

Intellect Computers Inc..................F...... 703 931-5100
Alexandria *(G-239)*

Life Management Company..............G...... 434 296-9762
Troy *(G-13932)*

Mellanox Federal Systems LLC.......F...... 703 969-5735
Herndon *(G-6745)*

COMPUTER & COMPUTER SOFTWARE STORES: Software & Access

Dominion Computer Services............G...... 757 473-8989
Virginia Beach *(G-14409)*

Intelligent Bus Platforms LLC...........E...... 202 640-8868
Reston *(G-10876)*

COMPUTER & COMPUTER SOFTWARE STORES: Software, Bus/Non-Game

Reconart Inc.................................G...... 855 732-6627
Alexandria *(G-568)*

COMPUTER & COMPUTER SOFTWARE STORES: Software, Computer Game

Geek Keep LLC...............................G...... 703 867-9867
Manassas *(G-8072)*

COMPUTER & DATA PROCESSING EQPT REPAIR & MAINTENANCE

R Zimmerman and Associates............G...... 540 446-6846
Stafford *(G-13185)*

COMPUTER & OFFICE MACHINE MAINTENANCE & REPAIR

CNE Manufacturing Services LLC........E...... 540 216-0884
Warrenton *(G-14988)*

Digitized Risk LLC...........................G...... 703 662-3510
Ashburn *(G-1271)*

Extreme Computer Services Inc.........G...... 703 730-8821
Dumfries *(G-4246)*

George Perez.................................G...... 757 362-3131
Norfolk *(G-9561)*

Hitachi Vantara Federal Corp............C...... 703 787-2900
Reston *(G-10865)*

Konica Mnlta Bus Sltons USA In.........C...... 703 461-8195
Alexandria *(G-508)*

One Stop Computer Services LLC........G...... 571 442-2045
Sterling *(G-13465)*

Otsan Technical Service LLC............G...... 276 696-7163
Bristol *(G-1985)*

Technlgy Advncement Group Inc........G...... 703 406-3000
Dulles *(G-4228)*

Up and Running Computers Inc..........G...... 757 565-3282
Williamsburg *(G-15329)*

COMPUTER & SFTWR STORE: Modem, Monitor, Terminal/Disk Drive

Auru Technologies Inc....................G...... 434 632-6978
Clarksville *(G-3626)*

COMPUTER FACILITIES MANAGEMENT SVCS

American Tech Sltons Intl Corp...........E...... 540 907-5355
Fredericksburg *(G-5398)*

Joint Lab Systems SEC Svcs LLC........G...... 443 655-9987
Arlington *(G-1016)*

Mercury Partners Usa LLC................G...... 757 652-7067
Franktown *(G-5164)*

Nomad Solutions LLC......................F...... 703 656-9100
Gainesville *(G-5602)*

COMPUTER GRAPHICS SVCS

Elohim Designs..............................G...... 757 292-1890
Chesapeake *(G-3087)*

Media X Group LLC.........................G...... 866 966-9640
Waynesboro *(G-15124)*

Over 9000 Media LLC......................G...... 850 210-7114
Norfolk *(G-9679)*

Shenandoah Specialty Pubg LLC........G...... 540 463-2319
Lexington *(G-7416)*

Web Transitions Inc........................G...... 540 334-1707
Boones Mill *(G-1901)*

COMPUTER INTERFACE EQPT: Indl Process

Jclfarms LLC..................................G...... 757 291-1401
Williamsburg *(G-15260)*

Resource Color Control Tech.............G...... 540 548-1855
Fredericksburg *(G-5354)*

COMPUTER PAPER WHOLESALERS

Printech Inc...................................F...... 540 343-9200
Roanoke *(G-12154)*

COMPUTER PERIPHERAL EQPT, NEC

Action Digital Inc...........................G...... 804 358-7289
Richmond *(G-11083)*

Advanced Business Services LLC........G...... 757 439-0849
Virginia Beach *(G-14212)*

Andres R Henriquz..........................G...... 703 629-9821
Alexandria *(G-413)*

Black Box Corporation....................G...... 781 449-1900
Amherst *(G-684)*

Bow Industries of Virginia................G...... 703 361-7704
Manassas *(G-8041)*

Canon Virginia Inc..........................A...... 757 881-6000
Newport News *(G-9192)*

Charlotte County School Board...........E...... 434 542-4933
Charlotte C H *(G-2583)*

Cisco Systems Inc..........................D...... 703 484-5500
Herndon *(G-6641)*

Convex Corporation........................G...... 703 433-9901
Warrenton *(G-14990)*

Datalux Corporation........................D...... 540 662-1500
Winchester *(G-15409)*

Dhk Storage LLC............................G...... 703 870-3741
Sterling *(G-13385)*

Digital Access Control Inc.................F...... 703 463-0113
Chantilly *(G-2408)*

Disrupt6 Inc...................................G...... 571 721-1155
Leesburg *(G-7258)*

Ericsson Inc...................................E...... 571 262-9254
Vienna *(G-14049)*

Essolutions Inc..............................F...... 240 215-6992
Arlington *(G-959)*

Fna Jewels....................................G...... 703 591-6817
Fairfax *(G-4459)*

Ganleys..G...... 703 476-8864
Herndon *(G-6678)*

Global Scnning Americas VA Inc........G...... 703 717-5631
Chantilly *(G-2427)*

Ice Enterprises Inc..........................F...... 703 934-4879
Fairfax *(G-4632)*

Innovative Computer Engrg Inc..........G...... 703 934-4879
Fairfax *(G-4635)*

Innovative Computer Engrg Inc..........G...... 703 934-2782
Fairfax *(G-4636)*

Intel Corporation...........................G...... 571 312-2320
Alexandria *(G-238)*

Intex LLC......................................G...... 703 899-3336
Reston *(G-10878)*

Iowave Inc.....................................E...... 703 979-9283
Arlington *(G-1011)*

Isomet Corporation........................E...... 703 321-8301
Manassas *(G-8087)*

James-York Security LLC..................E...... 757 344-1808
Williamsburg *(G-15259)*

Juniper Networks (us) Inc................C...... 571 203-1700
Herndon *(G-6721)*

Konica Mnlta Bus Sltons USA In.........E...... 703 553-6000
Vienna *(G-14079)*

Leidos Inc.....................................E...... 703 610-8900
Vienna *(G-14082)*

Leidos Inc.....................................E...... 703 734-5315
Mc Lean *(G-8485)*

Local Energy Technologies ....G..... 717 371-0041
Mc Lean **(G-8487)**

Lockheed Martin Corporation ....C..... 703 367-2121
Manassas **(G-7966)**

Materials Development Corp ....G..... 703 257-1500
Manassas **(G-8105)**

Mellanox Federal Systems LLC ....F..... 703 969-5735
Herndon **(G-6745)**

Mercury Solutions LLC ....G..... 703 474-9456
Leesburg **(G-7312)**

Meridian Tech Systems Inc ....G..... 301 606-6490
Leesburg **(G-7313)**

Michael Burnette ....G..... 757 478-8555
Newport News **(G-9300)**

Neosystems Corp ....G..... 571 234-4949
Fairfax **(G-4516)**

Northern Virginia Compute ....G..... 540 479-4455
Fredericksburg **(G-5461)**

Old World Labs LLC ....G..... 800 282-0386
Norfolk **(G-9675)**

Palo Alto Ntwrks Pub Sctor LLC ....F..... 240 328-3016
Reston **(G-10918)**

Refurb Factory LLC ....G..... 301 799-8385
Alexandria **(G-328)**

Sean Applegate ....G..... 540 972-4779
Spotsylvania **(G-12913)**

SJ Dobert ....G..... 301 847-5000
Reston **(G-10952)**

Spur Defense Systems ....G..... 540 742-8394
King George **(G-7114)**

Storage Technology ....G..... 703 817-1528
Chantilly **(G-2502)**

Symbol Technologies LLC ....G..... 703 263-2533
Chantilly **(G-2506)**

Teams It ....G..... 757 868-1129
Poquoson **(G-10377)**

Techsource LLC ....G..... 757 469-3983
Woodbridge **(G-15821)**

Tq-Systems USA Inc ....G..... 757 503-3927
Chesapeake **(G-3346)**

Troesen Enterprises LLC ....G..... 571 405-3199
Alexandria **(G-369)**

US 21 Inc ....D..... 703 560-0021
Fairfax **(G-4575)**

Van Rosendale John ....G..... 757 868-8593
Poquoson **(G-10378)**

Wizard Technologies ....G..... 703 625-0900
Vienna **(G-14161)**

Xerox Alumni Association Inc ....G..... 703 848-0624
Mc Lean **(G-8581)**

COMPUTER PERIPHERAL EQPT, WHOLESALE

Mellanox Federal Systems LLC ....F..... 703 969-5735
Herndon **(G-6745)**

COMPUTER PERIPHERAL EQPT: Decoders

Audio - Video Solutions ....G..... 240 565-4381
Bristow **(G-2047)**

COMPUTER PERIPHERAL EQPT: Encoders

Forescout Gvrnment Sltions LLC ....E..... 408 538-0946
Tysons **(G-13945)**

Idvector ....G..... 571 313-5064
Sterling **(G-13426)**

COMPUTER PERIPHERAL EQPT: Graphic Displays, Exc Terminals

Drytac Corporation ....E..... 804 280-6013
Sandston **(G-12613)**

Exhibit Design & Prod Svcs LLC ....G..... 804 347-0924
Henrico **(G-6508)**

COMPUTER PERIPHERAL EQPT: Input Or Output

Comxi World LLC ....G..... 804 299-5234
Glen Allen **(G-5717)**

Mantis Networks LLC ....G..... 571 306-1234
Reston **(G-10894)**

Mimetrix Technologies LLC ....G..... 571 306-1234
Vienna **(G-14094)**

Troy Patrick ....G..... 703 507-4914
Alexandria **(G-370)**

COMPUTER PHOTOGRAPHY OR PORTRAIT SVC

Arqball LLC..G..... 434 260-1890
Charlottesville **(G-2730)**

COMPUTER PROCESSING SVCS

Cloud Ridge Labs LLC ....G..... 434 477-5060
Forest **(G-5060)**

Omega Alpha II Inc ....F..... 804 747-7705
Richmond **(G-11315)**

COMPUTER PROGRAMMING SVCS

AEC Software Inc ....E..... 703 450-1980
Sterling **(G-13339)**

Amogh Consultants Inc ....G..... 469 867-1583
Herndon **(G-6612)**

Animate Systems Inc ....G..... 804 233-8085
Richmond **(G-11485)**

Antheon Solutions Inc ....G..... 703 298-1891
Reston **(G-10790)**

Bwx Technologies Inc ....E..... 757 595-7982
Newport News **(G-9187)**

Caper Holdings LLC ....G..... 757 563-3810
Virginia Beach **(G-14315)**

Citapei Communications Inc.................G..... 703 620-2316
Herndon **(G-6642)**

Cole Software LLC ....G..... 540 456-8210
Afton **(G-77)**

Cybered Corp ....G..... 757 573-5456
Williamsburg **(G-15228)**

Department Info Tech Inc ....G..... 703 868-6691
Chantilly **(G-2407)**

Disrupt6 Inc ....G..... 571 721-1155
Leesburg **(G-7258)**

Essolutions Inc ....F..... 240 215-6992
Arlington **(G-959)**

Face Construction Technologies ....G..... 757 624-2121
Norfolk **(G-9545)**

Fiddlehand Inc.....................................G..... 703 340-9806
Herndon **(G-6675)**

Gollygee Software Inc ....G..... 703 437-3751
Reston **(G-10860)**

Gumax International Ltd........................E..... 866 412-3880
Woodbridge **(G-15719)**

Ideation Web Studios LLC ....G..... 757 333-3021
Chesapeake **(G-3140)**

Infrawhite Technologies LLC ....G..... 662 902-0376
Vienna **(G-14071)**

Joint Lab Systems SEC Svcs LLC ....G..... 443 655-9987
Arlington **(G-1016)**

Keystone Technology LLC ....G..... 540 361-8318
Fredericksburg **(G-5309)**

Mega-Tech Inc ....E..... 703 534-1629
Falls Church **(G-4922)**

Mercury Partners Usa LLC ....G..... 757 652-7067
Franktown **(G-5164)**

Michie Software Systems Inc ....G..... 757 868-7771
Yorktown **(G-15982)**

Miracle Systems LLC ....C..... 571 431-6397
Arlington **(G-1066)**

Monticello Software Inc ....G..... 540 854-4200
Mineral **(G-8950)**

Oracle Systems Corporation ....A..... 703 478-9000
Reston **(G-10916)**

Parabon Computation Inc ....F..... 703 689-9689
Reston **(G-10920)**

Protean LLC ....G..... 757 273-1131
Williamsburg **(G-15302)**

Radio Reconnaissance Tech Inc ....G..... 540 752-7448
Fredericksburg **(G-5352)**

Rising Edge Technologies Inc ....G..... 703 471-8108
Mc Lean **(G-8538)**

Safety Software Inc ....F.....434 296-8789
Charlottesville **(G-2870)**

Softwright LLC ....G..... 434 975-4310
Charlottesville **(G-2694)**

Srg Government Solutions Inc ....G..... 703 609-7027
Fairfax **(G-4559)**

Sunlight Software ....G..... 540 789-7374
Willis **(G-15365)**

Synaptein Solutions Inc ....F..... 703 209-2350
Mc Lean **(G-8562)**

Timothy L Hosey ....G..... 270 339-0016
Maurertown **(G-8364)**

United Federal Systems Inc ....F..... 703 881-7777
Manassas **(G-8173)**

Webdmg LLC ....G..... 757 633-5033
Suffolk **(G-13782)**

Winchendon Group Inc ....G..... 703 960-0978
Alexandria **(G-610)**

Zeurix LLC ....G..... 571 297-9460
Reston **(G-10998)**

COMPUTER PROGRAMMING SVCS: Custom

Collier Research and Dev Corp ....F..... 757 825-0000
Newport News **(G-9203)**

Cubicle Logic LLC ....G..... 571 989-2823
Sterling **(G-13380)**

Genesis Infosolutions Inc ....G..... 703 835-4469
Herndon **(G-6682)**

Intelligent Platforms LLC ....A..... 434 978-5000
Charlottesville **(G-2647)**

KCS Inc ....G..... 703 981-0523
Alexandria **(G-504)**

Mindmettle ....G..... 540 890-5563
Vinton **(G-14179)**

Next Screen Media ....G..... 571 295-6398
Aldie **(G-109)**

Pivit ....G..... 301 395-0895
Chantilly **(G-2551)**

Warden Systems ....G..... 703 627-8002
Sterling **(G-13558)**

COMPUTER RELATED MAINTENANCE SVCS

Adta & Co Inc ....F..... 703 930-9280
Annandale **(G-728)**

Cyber Intel Solutions Inc ....G..... 571 970-2689
Springfield **(G-12987)**

Disrupt6 Inc ....G..... 571 721-1155
Leesburg **(G-7258)**

Ekagra Partners LLC ....F..... 571 421-1100
Leesburg **(G-7265)**

General Dynmics One Source LLC ....F..... 703 906-6397
Falls Church **(G-4796)**

Infrawhite Technologies LLC ....G..... 662 902-0376
Vienna **(G-14071)**

Junoventure LLC ....G..... 410 247-1908
Ashland **(G-1445)**

Keystone Technology LLC ....G..... 540 361-8318
Fredericksburg **(G-5309)**

Manufacturing System Svcs Inc............G..... 800 428-8643
Fairfax **(G-4651)**

COMPUTER RELATED SVCS, NEC

Mercury Partners Usa LLC ....G..... 757 652-7067
Franktown **(G-5164)**

COMPUTER SERVICE BUREAU

Department Info Tech Inc ....G..... 703 868-6691
Chantilly **(G-2407)**

E M Communications Inc ....G..... 434 971-4700
Charlottesville **(G-2787)**

COMPUTER SOFTWARE DEVELOPMENT

Ai Metrix Inc..E..... 703 254-2000
Alexandria **(G-406)**

Arqball LLC..G..... 434 260-1890
Charlottesville **(G-2730)**

Cae Software Solutions LLC.................G..... 734 417-6991
Oakton **(G-10142)**

Cloud Ridge Labs LLC ....G..... 434 477-5060
Forest **(G-5060)**

Clover LLC ....G..... 703 771-4286
Leesburg **(G-7245)**

Cognition Point Inc ....G..... 703 402-8945
Aldie **(G-104)**

Data Fusion Solutions Inc ....G..... 877 326-0034
Fredericksburg **(G-5271)**

Ember Systems LLC ....G..... 540 327-1984
Winchester **(G-15539)**

Eyegaze Inc ....F..... 703 385-8800
Fairfax **(G-4620)**

Insignia Technology Svcs LLC ....D..... 757 591-2111
Ashburn **(G-1296)**

Km Data Strategists LLC......................G..... 703 689-1087
Aldie **(G-108)**

Manufacturing System Svcs Inc............G..... 800 428-8643
Fairfax **(G-4651)**

OSI Maritime Systems Inc ....G..... 877 432-7467
Virginia Beach **(G-14706)**

Rufina Inc ....G..... 703 577-2333
Falls Church **(G-4870)**

Ryson International Inc ....F..... 757 898-1530
Yorktown **(G-15989)**

Software Flow Corporation ....G..... 301 717-0331
Great Falls **(G-5981)**

Employee Codes: A=Over 500 employees, B=251-500
C=101-250, D=51-100, E=20-50, F=10-19, G=1-9

2021 Virginia
Industrial Directory

929

PRODUCT

Source360 LLC ....G..... 703 232-1563
  Chantilly *(G-2494)*

Third Eye Development Intl Inc ....G..... 631 682-1848
  Alexandria *(G-363)*

COMPUTER SOFTWARE DEVELOPMENT & APPLICATIONS

3r Behavioral Solutions Inc ....G..... 571 332-6232
  Alexandria *(G-396)*

4c North America Inc ....G..... 540 850-8470
  Mc Lean *(G-8383)*

Aero Corporation ....G..... 703 896-7721
  Fairfax *(G-4401)*

Brbg LLC ....G..... 404 200-4857
  Springfield *(G-12969)*

Centripetal Networks Inc ....E..... 571 252-5080
  Herndon *(G-6638)*

Cougarbearbobcat LLC ....G..... 804 690-8006
  Richmond *(G-11543)*

Enterprize Software LLC ....G..... 571 271-5862
  Brambleton *(G-1927)*

Heytopia LLC ....G..... 703 794-3082
  Mc Lean *(G-8458)*

Icarus Medical LLC ....G..... 434 242-0258
  Charlottesville *(G-2813)*

Infocess LLC ....G..... 571 723-1010
  Vienna *(G-14070)*

Jordo Inc ....G..... 424 394-2986
  Glen Allen *(G-5757)*

Jordo Inc ....G..... 424 394-2986
  Glen Allen *(G-5758)*

Key Bridge Global LLC ....G..... 703 414-3500
  Mc Lean *(G-8479)*

Kinemetrx Incorporated ....G..... 703 596-5095
  Herndon *(G-6723)*

Lightfactor LLC ....G..... 540 723-9600
  Winchester *(G-15552)*

Mission It LLC ....G..... 443 534-0130
  Brambleton *(G-1930)*

Mountain View Brewery LLC ....C..... 540 462-6200
  Lexington *(G-7404)*

Opsense Inc ....G..... 844 757-7578
  Dunn Loring *(G-4266)*

Rosetta Stone Inc ....E..... 703 387-5800
  Arlington *(G-1151)*

Sovereign Intelligence LLC ....F..... 571 455-4016
  Vienna *(G-14131)*

Uvsity Corporation ....G..... 571 308-3241
  Brambleton *(G-1935)*

COMPUTER SOFTWARE SYSTEMS ANALYSIS & DESIGN: Custom

Avitech Consulting LLC ....G..... 757 810-2716
  Chesapeake *(G-2990)*

Custom Sftwr Dsign Sltions LLC ....G..... 888 423-4049
  Fredericksburg *(G-5417)*

Ekagra Partners LLC ....F..... 571 421-1100
  Leesburg *(G-7265)*

Erp Cloud Technologies LLC ....G..... 727 723-0801
  Herndon *(G-6668)*

Fta Goverment Services Inc ....G..... 571 612-0413
  Chantilly *(G-2423)*

Gadfly LLC ....G..... 703 282-9448
  Leesburg *(G-7276)*

Gary Smith ....G..... 703 218-1801
  Fairfax *(G-4461)*

Harlequin Custom Databases ....G..... 434 823-6466
  Crozet *(G-3838)*

Infomtion Tech Applcations LLC ....G..... 757 603-3551
  Williamsburg *(G-15257)*

Integrated Software Solutions ....G..... 703 255-1130
  Reston *(G-10874)*

Irontek LLC ....G..... 703 627-0092
  Sterling *(G-13432)*

K12excellence Inc ....G..... 804 270-9600
  Glen Allen *(G-5759)*

Lockwood Software Engrg Inc ....F..... 202 494-7886
  Mc Lean *(G-8489)*

Nexxtek Inc ....G..... 571 356-2921
  Vienna *(G-14105)*

Pantheon Software Inc ....F..... 703 387-4000
  Arlington *(G-1097)*

Pohick Creek LLC ....G..... 202 888-2034
  Springfield *(G-13071)*

Raimist Software LLC ....G..... 703 568-7638
  Chantilly *(G-2484)*

RE Discovery Software Inc ....F..... 434 975-3256
  Charlottesville *(G-2680)*

Riverland Solutions Corp ....G..... 571 247-2382
  Leesburg *(G-7337)*

Sensor Networks LLC ....G..... 703 481-2224
  Reston *(G-10947)*

Voice Software LLC ....G..... 571 331-2861
  Leesburg *(G-7374)*

Workdynamics Technologies Inc ....E..... 703 481-9874
  Reston *(G-10994)*

COMPUTER SOFTWARE WRITERS

Aretec Inc ....E..... 703 539-8801
  Fairfax *(G-4596)*

Mandylion Research Labs LLC ....E..... 703 628-4284
  Oakton *(G-10156)*

My Arch Inc ....G..... 703 375-9302
  Centreville *(G-2323)*

COMPUTER STORAGE DEVICES, NEC

Absolute EMC Llc ....G..... 703 774-7505
  Centreville *(G-2287)*

Core Business Technologies Inc ....G..... 757 426-0344
  Virginia Beach *(G-14365)*

Dell EMC ....G..... 301 897-1400
  Reston *(G-10839)*

Dhk Storage LLC ....G..... 703 870-3741
  Sterling *(G-13385)*

Drs Leonardo Inc ....C..... 703 416-8000
  Arlington *(G-944)*

Electrmchncal Ctrl Systems Inc ....G..... 434 610-5747
  Lynchburg *(G-7700)*

Elite Masonry Contractor LLC ....G..... 757 773-9908
  Chesapeake *(G-3086)*

EMC Corporation ....E..... 703 749-2260
  Mc Lean *(G-8423)*

EMC Corporation ....F..... 703 553-2522
  Arlington *(G-958)*

EMC Metal Fabrication ....G..... 804 355-1030
  Richmond *(G-11202)*

Emcs Inc ....G..... 443 223-2335
  Chesterfield *(G-3497)*

Enterprise Svcs Cmmnctions LLC ....G..... 877 858-3855
  Tysons *(G-13943)*

Essolutions Inc ....F..... 240 215-6992
  Arlington *(G-959)*

Gratispicks Inc ....G..... 757 739-4143
  Portsmouth *(G-10436)*

Hitachi Vantara Federal Corp ....C..... 703 787-2900
  Reston *(G-10865)*

Hitachi Vantara LLC ....G..... 405 593-3783
  Herndon *(G-6700)*

Iron Brick Associates LLC ....E..... 703 288-3874
  Sperryville *(G-12878)*

Meridian Tech Systems Inc ....G..... 301 606-6490
  Leesburg *(G-7313)*

Network Storage Corp ....E..... 703 834-7500
  Chantilly *(G-2468)*

Quantum Connect LLC ....G..... 703 251-3342
  Herndon *(G-6784)*

Quantum Medical Bus Svc Inc ....G..... 703 727-1020
  Winchester *(G-15572)*

Quantum Reefs LLC ....G..... 703 560-1448
  Annandale *(G-779)*

Quantum Technologies Inc ....G..... 703 214-9756
  Falls Church *(G-4861)*

Ret Corp ....G..... 703 471-8108
  Mc Lean *(G-8537)*

Rising Edge Technologies Inc ....G..... 703 471-8108
  Mc Lean *(G-8538)*

Secubit Inc ....G..... 757 453-6965
  Virginia Beach *(G-14801)*

Unifiedonline Inc ....G..... 816 679-1893
  Fairfax *(G-4690)*

Unifiedonline LLC ....G..... 816 679-1893
  Fairfax *(G-4691)*

United States Dept of Army ....G..... 757 878-4831
  Fort Eustis *(G-5127)*

Western Digital Corporation ....G..... 434 933-8162
  Gladstone *(G-5689)*

COMPUTER STORAGE UNITS: Auxiliary

Pbp Solutions LLC ....G..... 202 999-8101
  Reston *(G-10923)*

Rebecca Leigh Fraser ....G..... 912 755-3453
  Virginia Beach *(G-14765)*

COMPUTER SYSTEMS ANALYSIS & DESIGN

Centripetal Networks Inc ....E..... 571 252-5080
  Herndon *(G-6638)*

Ekagra Partners LLC ....F..... 571 421-1100
  Leesburg *(G-7265)*

Gadfly LLC ....G..... 703 282-9448
  Leesburg *(G-7276)*

Index Systems Inc ....G..... 571 420-4600
  Herndon *(G-6706)*

Missionteq LLC ....G..... 703 563-0699
  Chantilly *(G-2545)*

Prime 3 Software Inc ....G..... 757 763-8560
  Norfolk *(G-9695)*

COMPUTER TERMINALS

Essolutions Inc ....F..... 240 215-6992
  Arlington *(G-959)*

George Perez ....G..... 757 362-3131
  Norfolk *(G-9561)*

N A D C ....G..... 703 331-5611
  Manassas *(G-7979)*

Otsan Technical Service LLC ....G..... 276 696-7163
  Bristol *(G-1985)*

US 21 Inc ....D..... 703 560-0021
  Fairfax *(G-4575)*

COMPUTER TERMINALS: CRT

Datalux Corporation ....D..... 540 662-1500
  Winchester *(G-15409)*

COMPUTER-AIDED DESIGN SYSTEMS SVCS

Design Source Inc ....E..... 804 644-3424
  Sandston *(G-12610)*

Electronic Devices Inc ....G..... 757 421-2968
  Chesapeake *(G-3085)*

COMPUTER-AIDED MANUFACTURING SYSTEMS SVCS

Virginia Tek Inc ....F..... 703 391-8877
  Reston *(G-10986)*

COMPUTERS, NEC

1st Stop Electronics LLC ....G..... 804 931-0517
  Richmond *(G-11070)*

Access Prime Techncl Sltns ....G..... 757 651-6523
  Hampton *(G-6068)*

Alligatortalez ....G..... 703 791-4238
  Manassas *(G-8023)*

Alpha Printing Inc ....G..... 703 914-2800
  Springfield *(G-12942)*

Apple Valley LLC ....G..... 540 465-8360
  Strasburg *(G-13573)*

Apple-Polishers LLC ....G..... 571 918-1027
  Leesburg *(G-7219)*

Augusta Apple LLC ....G..... 540 337-7170
  Churchville *(G-3619)*

Avenger Computer Solutions ....G..... 240 305-7835
  Arlington *(G-867)*

Beets & Apples ....G..... 703 743-4112
  Haymarket *(G-6415)*

Bradshaw Viola ....G..... 571 274-5244
  Falls Church *(G-4765)*

Candy Apples and Favors LLC ....G..... 804 674-4061
  Richmond *(G-11518)*

Capitol Idea Technology Inc ....G..... 571 233-1949
  Woodbridge *(G-15667)*

Celestial Circuits LLC ....G..... 703 851-2843
  Springfield *(G-12975)*

Centripetal Networks Inc ....E..... 571 252-5080
  Herndon *(G-6638)*

CIS Secure Computing Inc ....E..... 703 996-0500
  Ashburn *(G-1254)*

CNE Manufacturing Services LLC ....E..... 540 216-0884
  Warrenton *(G-14988)*

Compu Dynamics LLC ....E..... 703 796-6070
  Sterling *(G-13373)*

Core Business Technologies Inc ....G..... 757 426-0344
  Virginia Beach *(G-14365)*

Cryptek USA Corp ....E..... 571 434-2000
  Sterling *(G-13377)*

D-Ta Systems Corporation ....G..... 571 775-8924
  Arlington *(G-925)*

Dark3 Inc ....G..... 703 398-1101
  Alexandria *(G-182)*

Data Management LLC ....G..... 703 222-4246
  Centreville *(G-2300)*

Datalux Corporation ....D..... 540 662-1500
  Winchester *(G-15409)*

Dcomputerscom ....G..... 757 460-3324
  Virginia Beach *(G-14396)*

Dimensionu Inc ....E 804 447-4220
  Henrico *(G-6502)*
Durabook Federal Inc ....G 888 414-9844
  Glen Allen *(G-5727)*
Embedded Systems LLC ....G 860 269-8148
  Haymarket *(G-6422)*
Emes LLC ....G 703 680-0807
  Dumfries *(G-4245)*
Essolutions Inc ....F 240 215-6992
  Arlington *(G-959)*
Evergreen Design Inc ....G 540 984-4653
  Edinburg *(G-4303)*
Extreme Computer Services Inc ......G 703 730-8821
  Dumfries *(G-4246)*
Fed Reach Inc ....G 703 507-8822
  Lorton *(G-7488)*
Finders Keepers Recruiting ....G 703 963-0874
  Fairfax *(G-4457)*
First Colony Technology LLC ....G 434 579-3655
  Providence Forge *(G-10624)*
Fta Goverment Services Inc ....G 571 612-0413
  Chantilly *(G-2423)*
General Dynmics Mssion Systems ......E 877 449-0600
  Fairfax *(G-4463)*
Gravitonus ....G 571 321-2019
  Fairfax *(G-4629)*
Greentec-Usa Inc ....G 703 880-8332
  Sterling *(G-13414)*
Hadrian Inc ....G 703 724-7760
  Ashburn *(G-1288)*
Hewlett-Packard Federal LLC ....E 800 727-5472
  Herndon *(G-6698)*
Hitachi Vantara Federal Corp ....G 703 787-2900
  Reston *(G-10865)*
IBM Philip Morris ....G 405 600-7997
  South Chesterfield *(G-12810)*
Ice Enterprises Inc ....F 703 934-4879
  Fairfax *(G-4632)*
Inhand Networks Inc ....G 703 348-2988
  Fairfax *(G-4634)*
Intellect Computers Inc ....F 703 931-5100
  Alexandria *(G-239)*
Iron Bow Holdings Inc ....G 703 795-1790
  Chantilly *(G-2445)*
Iron Bow Holdings Inc ....C 703 279-3000
  Herndon *(G-6712)*
Iron Brick Associates LLC ....E 703 288-3874
  Sperryville *(G-12878)*
It Solutions 4u Inc ....G 703 624-4430
  Sterling *(G-13433)*
Itst Inc ....G 703 455-2152
  Springfield *(G-13025)*
Junoventure LLC ....G 410 247-1908
  Ashland *(G-1445)*
Kirkland Holdings Co ....G 571 348-1005
  Alexandria *(G-254)*
Laserserv Inc ....E 804 359-6188
  Richmond *(G-11266)*
Lockheed Martin Corporation ....C 703 367-2121
  Manassas *(G-7966)*
Mandylion Research Labs LLC ....E 703 628-4284
  Oakton *(G-10156)*
Mercury Systems Inc ....G 510 252-0870
  Fairfax *(G-4654)*
Microtude LLC ....G 703 581-7991
  Ashburn *(G-1317)*
Mildef Inc ....G 703 224-8835
  Alexandria *(G-275)*
N-Ask Incorporated ....D 703 715-7909
  Fairfax *(G-4515)*
Ncs Technologies Inc ....G 703 743-8500
  Manassas *(G-7981)*
Ncs Technologies Inc ....C 703 743-8500
  Gainesville *(G-5600)*
Nvis Inc ....F 571 201-8095
  Reston *(G-10911)*
Proficient Link LLC ....G 703 391-6330
  Sterling *(G-13480)*
Rebound Analytics LLC ....G 202 297-1204
  Tysons *(G-13948)*
Right Sized Technologies Inc ....F 703 623-9505
  Sterling *(G-13494)*
Rollins Oma Sue ....G 757 449-6371
  Virginia Beach *(G-14778)*
Sector 5 Inc ....G 571 348-1005
  Alexandria *(G-341)*
Sector Five Inc ....G 571 348-1005
  Alexandria *(G-342)*
Sensor Networks LLC ....G 703 481-2224
  Reston *(G-10947)*

Smrt Mouth LLC ....G 804 363-8863
  Sandston *(G-12634)*
Symmple Technologies ....G 703 591-7716
  Fairfax *(G-4566)*
T3b LLC ....G 202 550-4475
  Mc Lean *(G-8563)*
Taxlaw20 LLC ....G 202 470-3980
  Mc Lean *(G-8564)*
Technlogy Advncement Group Inc ......G 703 406-3000
  Dulles *(G-4228)*
The For American Society ....G 703 331-0075
  Falls Church *(G-4882)*
Ultrata LLC ....F 571 226-0347
  Vienna *(G-14147)*
United Federal Systems Inc ....F 703 881-7777
  Manassas *(G-8173)*
Vps Services Inc ....G 202 538-1990
  Ashburn *(G-1352)*

COMPUTERS, NEC, WHOLESALE

Product Identification ....G 804 264-4434
  Richmond *(G-11336)*

COMPUTERS, PERIPH & SOFTWARE, WHLSE: Acctg Machs, Readable

Compu Management Corp ....G 276 669-3822
  Bristol *(G-2013)*

COMPUTERS, PERIPH & SOFTWARE, WHLSE: Personal & Home Entrtn

Acacia Acquisitions LLC ....G 703 554-1600
  Ashburn *(G-1236)*
Smith Distributors & Mktg LLC ....G 540 760-6833
  Fredericksburg *(G-5362)*

COMPUTERS, PERIPHERALS & SOFTWARE, WHOLESALE: Software

Acacia Investment Holdings LLC ......G 703 554-1600
  Tysons *(G-13940)*
Landmark Media Enterprises LLC ......A 757 351-7000
  Norfolk *(G-9616)*
Mantis Networks LLC ....G 571 306-1234
  Reston *(G-10894)*
Mark Pearson ....G 703 648-2568
  Oakton *(G-10157)*
Tq-Systems USA Inc ....G 757 503-3927
  Chesapeake *(G-3346)*
Virginn-Plot Mdia Cmpanies LLC ......G 757 446-2848
  Virginia Beach *(G-14924)*

COMPUTERS: Mainframe

Spur Defense Systems ....G 540 742-8394
  King George *(G-7114)*

COMPUTERS: Mini

Symbolics - David K Schmidt ....G 703 455-0430
  Burke *(G-2204)*

COMPUTERS: Personal

3189 Apple Rd Ne LLC ....G 703 455-5989
  Springfield *(G-12934)*
Acacia Acquisitions LLC ....G 703 554-1600
  Ashburn *(G-1236)*
Acacia Investment Holdings LLC ......G 703 554-1600
  Tysons *(G-13940)*
Ace Title & Escrow Inc ....G 703 629-5768
  Alexandria *(G-401)*
Apple Frankies Ent Inc ....G 540 845-7372
  Fredericksburg *(G-5246)*
Apple Shine ....G 757 714-6393
  Virginia Beach *(G-14233)*
Apple Tire Inc ....G 434 575-5200
  South Boston *(G-12747)*
Apples & Belles LLC ....G 804 530-3180
  Chester *(G-3387)*
Apples Closet ....G 540 825-9551
  Culpeper *(G-3867)*
Auru Technologies Inc ....G 434 632-6978
  Clarksville *(G-3626)*
Bander Computers ....G 757 398-3443
  Portsmouth *(G-10396)*
Dell Inc ....A 301 581-0513
  Fairfax *(G-4437)*
Fat Apple LLC ....G 434 823-2481
  Crozet *(G-3832)*

Green Apple Assoc A Virgin ....G 804 551-5040
  Richmond *(G-11222)*
Hp Inc ....G 703 535-3355
  Alexandria *(G-230)*
Montauk Systems Corporation ....G 954 695-6819
  Ashburn *(G-1318)*
Red Apple Productions LLC ....G 703 237-1034
  Arlington *(G-1145)*
Ronald Carter ....G 571 278-6659
  Burke *(G-2202)*

CONCRETE BUILDING PRDTS WHOLESALERS

Tarmac Florida Inc ....C 757 858-6500
  Norfolk *(G-9742)*
Titan America LLC ....G 757 533-7152
  Norfolk *(G-9758)*

CONCRETE CURING & HARDENING COMPOUNDS

American Concrete Group LLC ....G 276 546-1666
  Pennington Gap *(G-10292)*
American Concrete Group LLC ....G 423 323-7566
  Bristol *(G-2004)*
Nova Concrete Products Inc ....G 540 439-2978
  Bealeton *(G-1603)*

CONCRETE PRDTS

A Metromont Company ....G 540 401-0101
  Winchester *(G-15368)*
Allied Con Co - Suffolk Block ....G 757 494-5200
  Chesapeake *(G-2959)*
Allied Concrete Company ....E 434 296-7181
  Charlottesville *(G-2724)*
Atlantic Wood Industries Inc ....E 757 397-2317
  Portsmouth *(G-10395)*
Chandler Concrete Inc ....E 540 345-3846
  Roanoke *(G-12062)*
Coastal Constructors LLC ....G 757 545-0080
  Chesapeake *(G-3041)*
Concrete Precast Systems Inc ....G 757 545-5215
  Cape Charles *(G-2232)*
Custom Precast Inc ....G 757 833-8989
  Yorktown *(G-15946)*
Essex Concrete Corporation ....D 804 443-2366
  Tappahannock *(G-13814)*
Framecad America Inc ....F 703 615-2451
  Fairfax *(G-4626)*
Hanson Aggregates East LLC ....D 540 387-0271
  Salem *(G-12514)*
Holcim LLC ....G 703 622-4616
  Vienna *(G-14066)*
Industrial Welding & Mch Corp ....F 276 783-7105
  Atkins *(G-1518)*
Koppers Industries Inc ....G 540 672-3802
  Orange *(G-10218)*
Legacy Vulcan LLC ....G 703 461-0333
  Alexandria *(G-257)*
Lynchburg Ready-Mix Con Co Inc ......E 434 846-6563
  Lynchburg *(G-7764)*
Martinsville Concrete Products ....E 276 632-6416
  Martinsville *(G-8308)*
Mary Jo Kirwan ....G 703 421-1919
  Herndon *(G-6743)*
Nova Concrete Products Inc ....G 540 439-2978
  Bealeton *(G-1603)*
NV Cast Stone ....F 703 393-2777
  Manassas *(G-8119)*
Oldcastle Apg Northeast Inc ....E 540 667-4600
  Winchester *(G-15457)*
Oldcastle Infrastructure Inc ....D 540 898-6300
  Fredericksburg *(G-5339)*
Quikrete Companies LLC ....E 276 964-6755
  Pounding Mill *(G-10525)*
Seaboard Service of VA Inc ....G 804 643-5112
  Richmond *(G-11375)*
Separation Technologies LLC ....E 540 992-1501
  Roanoke *(G-11999)*
Shenandoah Castings LLC ....G 540 551-5777
  Front Royal *(G-5554)*
Suncoast Post-Tension Ltd ....E 703 492-4949
  Woodbridge *(G-15820)*
Tarmac Mid-Atlantic Inc ....A 757 858-6500
  Norfolk *(G-9743)*
TCS Materials Corp ....F 804 863-4525
  North Dinwiddie *(G-10064)*
Timberlake Contracting LLC ....G 804 449-1517
  Beaverdam *(G-1615)*

Employee Codes: A=Over 500 employees, B=251-500
C=101-250, D=51-100, E=20-50, F=10-19, G=1-9

2021 Virginia
Industrial Directory

PRODUCT

931

Valley Redi-Mix Company Inc ....E 540 631-9050
Front Royal (G-5560)

Vault44 LLC ....G 202 758-6228
Manassas Park (G-8213)

Vfp Inc ....C 276 431-4000
Duffield (G-4187)

Vulcan Construction Mtls LLC ....G 276 466-5436
Bristol (G-1999)

CONCRETE PRDTS, PRECAST, NEC

Action Resources Corporation ....F 540 343-5121
Roanoke (G-12028)

American Stone Virginia LLC ....D 804 448-9460
Ladysmith (G-7154)

Americast Inc ....D 804 798-6068
Ashland (G-1369)

Americast Inc ....E 540 434-6979
Harrisonburg (G-6292)

Arban & Carosi Incorporated ....C 703 491-5121
Woodbridge (G-15646)

Arban Precast Stone Ltd ....E 703 221-8005
Dumfries (G-4236)

Bastion and Associates LLC ....G 703 343-5158
Springfield (G-12959)

Beasley Concrete Inc ....E 804 633-9626
Milford (G-8928)

Blue Stone Block Sprmkt Inc ....E 540 982-3588
Roanoke (G-12050)

Chaney Enterprises Ltd Partnr ....F 540 710-0075
Fredericksburg (G-5260)

Coastal Precast Systems LLC ....F 757 545-5215
Chesapeake (G-3042)

Concrete Precast Systems Inc ....D 757 545-5215
Chesapeake (G-3050)

Estate Concrete LLC ....G 703 293-6363
Centreville (G-2305)

First Paper Co Inc ....F 434 821-6884
Rustburg (G-12439)

Hanover Precast Inc ....F 804 798-2336
Ashland (G-1430)

Metromont Corporation ....D 804 222-6770
Richmond (G-11290)

Nansemond Pre-Cast Con Co Inc ....E 757 538-2761
Suffolk (G-13748)

New River Concrete Supply Co ....F 540 639-9679
Radford (G-10726)

New River Concrete Supply Inc ....F 540 552-1721
Blacksburg (G-1773)

Northern Vrgnia Cast Stone LLC ....G 703 393-2777
Gainesville (G-5604)

Pre Cast of Virginia ....G 540 439-2978
Bealeton (G-1604)

Quality Precast Stone ....G 703 244-4551
Manassas (G-8136)

Seaboard Concrete Products Co ....E 804 275-0802
North Chesterfield (G-9973)

Shockey Bros Inc ....D 540 667-7700
Fredericksburg (G-5361)

Smith-Midland Corporation ....D 540 439-3266
Midland (G-8763)

Smith-Midland Corporation ....C 540 439-3266
Midland (G-8764)

Tidewater Block LLc ....E 757 539-1576
Suffolk (G-13771)

Tindall Corporation ....C 804 861-8447
North Dinwiddie (G-10065)

Valley Building Supply Inc ....C 540 434-6725
Harrisonburg (G-6383)

CONCRETE: Ready-Mixed

Aggregate Industries - Mwr Inc ....B 540 379-0765
Falmouth (G-4932)

Aggregate Industries - Mwr Inc ....E 703 361-2276
Manassas (G-8020)

Aggregate Industries MGT Inc ....G 804 994-5533
Aylett (G-1544)

Aggregate Industries MGT Inc ....G 540 337-4875
Stuarts Draft (G-13642)

Aggregate Industries MGT Inc ....G 804 693-2280
Gloucester (G-5835)

Aggregate Industries-Wcr Inc ....G 804 829-9783
Charles City (G-2569)

Aggregates Usa LLC ....G 276 628-9337
Abingdon (G-9)

Allied Concrete Company ....E 804 279-7501
North Chesterfield (G-9813)

Allied Concrete Company ....E 434 296-7181
Charlottesville (G-2724)

Allied Concrete Products LLC ....G 434 634-6571
Emporia (G-4354)

American Concrete Group LLC ....G 276 546-1633
Pennington Gap (G-10291)

Argos USA LLC ....F 804 763-6112
Midlothian (G-8774)

B & E Transit Mix Inc ....G 434 447-7331
South Hill (G-12843)

Barger Son Cnstr Inc Charles W ....D 540 463-2106
Lexington (G-7388)

Beasley Concrete Inc ....E 804 633-9626
Milford (G-8928)

Bedford Ready-Mix Con Co Inc ....G 540 586-8380
Bedford (G-1624)

Blue Ridge Concrete Product ....E 276 755-2000
Cana (G-2226)

Boxley Materials Company ....G 540 777-7600
Blue Ridge (G-1847)

Boxley Materials Company ....F 540 777-7600
Martinsville (G-8271)

Boxley Materials Company ....G 540 777-7600
Wytheville (G-15880)

Boxley Materials Company ....G 540 777-7600
Blue Ridge (G-1848)

Boxley Materials Company ....F 540 777-7600
Roanoke (G-11893)

Capital Concrete Inc ....G 757 627-0630
Norfolk (G-9477)

Capital Concrete Inc ....G 757 627-0630
Virginia Beach (G-14316)

Cardinal Concrete Company ....C 703 550-7650
Herndon (G-6634)

Cavalier Concrete Inc ....G 434 296-7181
Charlottesville (G-2758)

Cemex Cnstr Mtls ATL LLC ....G 434 685-7021
Cascade (G-2250)

Central Redi-Mix Concrete Inc ....G 434 736-0091
Meherrin (G-8705)

Chandler Concrete Co Inc ....G 434 369-4791
Altavista (G-629)

Chandler Concrete Co Inc ....E 434 792-1233
Danville (G-3965)

Chandler Concrete Inc ....E 540 345-3846
Roanoke (G-12062)

Chandler Concrete Inc ....G 540 297-4369
Moneta (G-8958)

Chandler Concrete Inc ....G 276 928-1357
Rocky Gap (G-12306)

Chandler Concrete of Virginia ....G 434 369-4791
Altavista (G-630)

Chandler Concrete Products of ....D 540 382-1734
Christiansburg (G-3578)

Chandler Concrete Products of ....G 540 674-4667
Dublin (G-4151)

Chandler Concrete Virginia Inc ....E 540 382-1734
Christiansburg (G-3579)

Chaney Enterprises Ltd Partnr ....F 540 710-0075
Fredericksburg (G-5260)

Chaney Enterprises Ltd Partnr ....G 540 659-4100
Stafford (G-13129)

Charles Contracting Co Inc ....G 757 422-9989
Virginia Beach (G-14331)

Charles County Sand & Grav Co ....G 540 775-9550
King George (G-7083)

CMI ....D 703 356-2190
Vienna (G-14028)

Colonial Readi-Mix Concrete ....G 757 888-8500
Williamsburg (G-15221)

Commercial Ready Mix Pdts Inc ....F 757 925-0939
Suffolk (G-13686)

Commercial Ready Mix Pdts Inc ....F 757 420-5800
Chesapeake (G-3047)

Concrete Precast Systems Inc ....E 703 327-4112
Chantilly (G-2530)

Concrete Ready Mixed Corp ....G 540 345-3846
Salem (G-12490)

Conmat Group Inc ....E 540 433-9128
Rockingham (G-12245)

Construction Materials Company ....G 540 552-5022
Blacksburg (G-1731)

Construction Materials Company ....G 540 962-2139
Covington (G-3783)

Construction Materials Company ....G 540 463-3441
Lexington (G-7391)

Construction Materials Company ....F 540 433-9043
Lexington (G-7392)

Cox Ready Mix Inc SB ....E 804 364-0500
Glen Allen (G-5718)

Crh Americas Inc ....G 804 633-9841
Milford (G-8929)

Danville Ready Mix ....F 434 799-5818
Danville (G-3979)

Dominion Quikrete Inc ....E 276 957-3235
Martinsville (G-8279)

Dubrook Concrete Inc ....D 703 222-6969
Chantilly (G-2413)

Ennstone ....G 703 335-2650
Manassas (G-8065)

Essex Concrete Corp ....G 804 749-1950
Rockville (G-12285)

Essex Concrete Corporation ....D 804 443-2366
Tappahannock (G-13814)

Essex Concrete Corporation ....F 804 443-2366
Tappahannock (G-13815)

Essroc Cement Corp ....G 757 545-2481
Chesapeake (G-3092)

Essroc Cement Corporation ....G 804 227-4156
Ashland (G-1410)

Etz LLC ....G 703 620-3014
Reston (G-10849)

F & M Construction Corp ....F 276 728-2255
Hillsville (G-6891)

Falcon Concrete Corporation ....E 703 354-7100
Springfield (G-13001)

Felton Brothers Trnst Mix Inc ....G 434 572-2665
South Boston (G-12765)

Felton Brothers Trnst Mix Inc ....G 434 376-2415
Brookneal (G-2110)

Felton Brothers Trnst Mix Inc ....G 434 374-5373
Boydton (G-1915)

Felton Brothers Trnst Mix Inc ....G 434 572-4614
South Boston (G-12766)

Felton Brothers Trnst Mix Inc ....G 434 848-3966
Lawrenceville (G-7180)

Felton Brothers Trnst Mix Inc ....G 434 447-3778
South Hill (G-12850)

Finly Corporation ....E 434 385-5028
Lynchburg (G-7707)

Giant Resource Recovery Inc ....E 434 685-7021
Cascade (G-2251)

Greenrock Materials LLC ....D 804 966-8601
Charles City (G-2576)

Handyman Concrete Inc ....E 703 437-7143
Chantilly (G-2535)

Huffman & Huffman Inc ....G 276 579-2373
Mouth of Wilson (G-9093)

Lafarge North America Inc ....G 703 480-3600
Reston (G-10882)

Legacy Vulcan LLC ....E 540 298-1237
Elkton (G-4330)

Legacy Vulcan LLC ....D 703 368-2475
Manassas (G-8099)

Legacy Vulcan LLC ....F 703 354-5783
Springfield (G-13040)

Legacy Vulcan LLC ....E 540 347-3641
Warrenton (G-15031)

Legacy Vulcan LLC ....G 540 886-6758
Staunton (G-13275)

Legacy Vulcan LLC ....G 540 659-3003
Stafford (G-13169)

Legacy Vulcan LLC ....G 800 732-3964
Rapidan (G-10753)

Legacy Vulcan LLC ....G 800 732-3964
Dumfries (G-4250)

Legacy Vulcan LLC ....G 804 863-4565
North Dinwiddie (G-10056)

Legacy Vulcan LLC ....G 800 732-3964
Arlington (G-1030)

Legacy Vulcan LLC ....G 800 732-3964
Chantilly (G-2542)

Legacy Vulcan LLC ....G 434 572-3967
South Boston (G-12778)

Legacy Vulcan LLC ....G 800 732-3964
Stafford (G-13170)

Legacy Vulcan LLC ....G 800 732-3964
Stephens City (G-13319)

Legacy Vulcan LLC ....G 804 730-1008
Mechanicsville (G-8652)

Legacy Vulcan LLC ....G 703 713-3100
Springfield (G-13041)

Legacy Vulcan LLC ....G 800 732-3964
Falls Church (G-4822)

Legacy Vulcan LLC ....G 800 732-3964
Lorton (G-7505)

Legacy Vulcan LLC ....G 800 732-3964
Fredericksburg (G-5312)

Legacy Vulcan LLC ....G 800 732-3964
Lorton (G-7506)

Legacy Vulcan LLC ....G 276 940-2741
Duffield (G-4181)

Legacy Vulcan LLC ....G 757 888-2982
Newport News (G-9280)

Legacy Vulcan LLC ....G...... 804 236-4160
Richmond (G-11268)
Legacy Vulcan LLC ....F...... 804 717-5770
Chester (G-3430)
Legacy Vulcan LLC ....G...... 757 539-5670
Suffolk (G-13730)
Legacy Vulcan LLC ....E...... 804 360-2014
Rockville (G-12288)
Legacy Vulcan LLC ....G...... 434 447-4696
South Hill (G-12856)
Lehigh Cement Company LLC ....G...... 757 928-1559
Newport News (G-9281)
Lehigh Cement Company LLC ....G...... 540 942-1181
Waynesboro (G-15121)
Lorton Enterprises ....G...... 703 725-2933
Lorton (G-7509)
Lynchburg Ready-Mix Con Co Inc ......E...... 434 846-6563
Lynchburg (G-7764)
Lynchburg Ready-Mix Con Co Inc ......G...... 434 946-5562
Amherst (G-698)
Marshall Con Pdts of Danville ....D...... 434 792-1233
Danville (G-4015)
Marshall Con Pdts of Danville ....G...... 434 575-5351
South Boston (G-12780)
Marshall Con Pdts of Danville ....G...... 434 369-4791
Altavista (G-635)
Marshall Concrete Products ....F...... 540 297-4369
Moneta (G-8972)
Martin Marietta Materials Inc ....F...... 804 674-9517
Midlothian (G-8852)
Martinsville Finance & Inv ....G...... 276 632-9500
Martinsville (G-8309)
Marty Corporation ....G...... 276 395-3326
Coeburn (G-3701)
Marty Corporation ....G...... 276 679-3477
Norton (G-10125)
McClure Concrete ....G...... 276 889-2289
Lebanon (G-7200)
McClure Concrete Materials LLC ....G...... 276 964-9682
Richlands (G-11018)
McClure Concrete Materials LLC ....G...... 276 964-9682
Clintwood (G-3690)
McClure Concrete Materials LLC ....G...... 276 679-3477
Norton (G-10128)
McClure Concrete Materials LLC ....G...... 276 964-9682
Saint Paul (G-12470)
McClure Concrete Products Inc ....G...... 276 889-3496
Lebanon (G-7201)
McClure Concrete Products Inc ....G...... 276 964-9682
Richlands (G-11019)
Mix It Up LLC ....G...... 540 434-9868
Harrisonburg (G-6346)
Mountain Materials Inc ....E...... 276 429-5241
Glade Spring (G-5679)
Network 12 ....G...... 703 532-2970
Falls Church (G-4923)
New River Concrete Supply ....G...... 540 433-9043
Rockingham (G-12264)
New River Concrete Supply Co ....F...... 540 639-9679
Radford (G-10726)
New River Concrete Supply Inc ....F...... 540 552-1721
Blacksburg (G-1773)
Patton Sand & Concrete ....G...... 276 236-9362
Galax (G-5644)
Quikrete Companies LLC ....E...... 276 646-8976
Chilhowie (G-3558)
R R Beasley Inc ....F...... 804 529-6470
Callao (G-2217)
Ready Set Read LLC ....G...... 804 673-8764
Richmond (G-11348)
Rinker Materials S Centl Inc ....F...... 276 628-9337
Abingdon (G-58)
Roanoke Cement Company LLC ....G...... 540 631-1335
Front Royal (G-5550)
Roanoke Cement Company LLC ....C...... 540 992-1501
Troutville (G-13915)
Rockingham Precast Inc ....E...... 540 433-8282
Rockingham (G-12272)
Rockingham Redi-Mix Inc ....E...... 540 433-9128
Rockingham (G-12273)
Rockingham Redi-Mix Inc ....G...... 540 743-5940
Luray (G-7622)
Rockingham Redi-Mix Inc ....E...... 540 433-9128
Harrisonburg (G-6364)
Rockingham Redi-Mix Inc ....E...... 540 433-9128
Rockingham (G-12275)
Rockingham Redi-Mix Inc ....E...... 540 433-8282
Rockingham (G-12274)
Rocky Mount Ready Mix Concrete ......G...... 540 483-1288
Rocky Mount (G-12350)

Rowe Concrete Supply Store...............G...... 540 710-7693
Fredericksburg (G-5356)
Salem Ready Mix Concrete Inc ....F...... 540 387-1171
Salem (G-12567)
Sb Cox Ready Mix Inc ....F...... 434 292-7300
Blackstone (G-1827)
Sb Cox Ready Mix Inc ....F...... 804 364-0500
Powhatan (G-10572)
Scott Ready ....G...... 703 503-3374
Fairfax (G-4551)
Shoreline Materials LLC ....G...... 804 469-4042
Stony Creek (G-13569)
Southern Equipment Company Inc ....G...... 757 888-8500
Williamsburg (G-15316)
Stuart Concrete Inc ....F...... 276 694-2828
Stuart (G-13633)
Successful Mix LLC ....G...... 540 269-6904
Keezletown (G-7031)
Superior Concrete Inc ....E...... 540 433-2482
Harrisonburg (G-6377)
Superior Concrete Materials ....G...... 703 327-4112
Chantilly (G-2558)
T&W Block Incorporated ....G...... 757 787-2646
Onley (G-10201)
Tamara Ingram ....G...... 434 392-4933
Burkeville (G-2211)
Tarmac Corp ....G...... 703 471-0044
Sterling (G-13528)
Tarmac Florida Inc ....C...... 757 858-6500
Norfolk (G-9742)
Tarmac Mid-Atlantic Inc ....A...... 757 858-6500
Norfolk (G-9743)
TCS Materials Inc ....E...... 757 591-9340
Williamsburg (G-15323)
TCS Materials LLC ....D...... 804 232-1200
Richmond (G-11065)
TCS Materials LLC ....F...... 757 874-5575
Newport News (G-9352)
Titan America LLC ....E...... 703 221-2003
Dumfries (G-4261)
Titan America LLC ....G...... 757 533-7152
Norfolk (G-9758)
Titan America LLC ....G...... 540 372-8717
Fredericksburg (G-5378)
Titan America LLC ....F...... 804 236-4122
Richmond (G-11412)
Titan America LLC ....D...... 703 471-0044
Sterling (G-13534)
Transit Mixed Concrete Corp ....E...... 540 885-7224
Staunton (G-13302)
Turners Ready Mix Inc ....F...... 540 483-9150
Rocky Mount (G-12355)
US Concrete Inc ....F...... 703 471-6969
Chantilly (G-2514)
Valley Redi-Mix Company Inc ....G...... 540 869-1990
Stephens City (G-13326)
Virginia Concrete Company LLC ....C...... 703 354-7100
Herndon (G-6841)
Vulcan Construction Mtls LLC ....E...... 804 862-6665
North Dinwiddie (G-10069)
Vulcan Construction Mtls LLC ....G...... 804 233-9669
Richmond (G-11816)
Vulcan Construction Mtls LLC ....G...... 757 494-3202
Norfolk (G-9785)
Vulcan Construction Mtls LLC ....G...... 757 858-6500
Norfolk (G-9786)
Vulcan Construction Mtls LLC ....D...... 703 471-0044
Sterling (G-13556)
Vulcan Construction Mtls LLC ....G...... 276 466-5436
Bristol (G-1999)
Vulcan Materials Company ....F...... 757 874-5575
Newport News (G-9377)
Vulcan Materials Company ....E...... 540 659-3003
Stafford (G-13212)
Vulcan Materials Company ....G...... 804 270-5385
Glen Allen (G-5826)
Vulcan Materials Company ....F...... 434 848-4775
Freeman (G-5513)
Vulcan Materials Company ....G...... 804 758-5000
Saluda (G-12607)
Vulcan Materials Company ....F...... 540 898-6210
Fredericksburg (G-5388)
Vulcan Materials Company ....E...... 804 693-3606
Gloucester (G-5866)
Vulcan Materials Company ....G...... 804 693-3606
Gloucester (G-5867)
Walker Sand & Stone Inc ....E...... 540 775-5024
King George (G-7122)
Wilson Ready Mix LLC ....G...... 540 324-0555
Fishersville (G-5013)

Wilson Ready Mix LLC ....G...... 434 977-2800
Charlottesville (G-2715)
Wright Inc W F ....F...... 804 561-2721
Amelia Court House (G-678)

CONDENSERS: Heat Transfer Eqpt, Evaporative

Alfa Laval USA Inc ....E...... 804 222-5300
Richmond (G-11097)

CONDUITS & FITTINGS: Electric

Allspark Industrial LLC...................G...... 804 977-2732
Richmond (G-11483)

CONFECTIONERY PRDTS WHOLESALERS

Michael Holt Inc ....G...... 703 597-6999
Arlington (G-1062)

CONFECTIONS & CANDY

Aunt Nolas Pecan Pralines ....G...... 757 723-1607
Hampton (G-6086)
Camacho Enterprises LLC ....G...... 757 761-0407
Chesapeake (G-3023)
Hershey Company ....B...... 540 324-0166
Stuarts Draft (G-13649)
Jhl Inc ....G...... 703 378-0009
Chantilly (G-2449)
Juma Brothers Inc ....G...... 757 312-0544
Portsmouth (G-10449)
La La Land Candy Kingdom Va01 ....G...... 305 342-6737
Virginia Beach (G-14597)
Lakota JS Chocolates Corp ....G...... 804 590-0010
Chesterfield (G-3512)
Mars Incorporated ....B...... 703 821-4900
Mc Lean (G-8491)
Mars Logic LLC ....G...... 510 220-7117
Mc Lean (G-8492)
Michael Holt Inc ....G...... 703 597-6999
Arlington (G-1062)
Mondelez Global LLC ....D...... 757 925-3011
Suffolk (G-13745)
Moretz Candy Co Inc ....E...... 276 669-2533
Bristol (G-2026)
My Extra Hands LLC ....G...... 540 847-2063
Fredericksburg (G-5330)
Nestle Holdings Inc ....F...... 703 682-4600
Arlington (G-1073)
Nestle Usa Inc ....C...... 765 778-6000
Arlington (G-1074)
Nicol Candy ....G...... 804 740-2378
Richmond (G-11305)
Robin Stippich ....G...... 757 692-5744
Newport News (G-9329)
So Unique Candy Apples ....G...... 540 915-4899
Roanoke (G-12191)
Southern Tastes LLC ....G...... 757 204-1414
Chesapeake (G-3304)
Sugarfina Inc ....G...... 703 844-0049
Mc Lean (G-8560)
Sweet Svory Delights By Vickie ....G...... 703 581-8499
Falls Church (G-4881)
Tummy-Ymyum Grmet Candy Apples...G...... 703 368-4756
Bristow (G-2065)

CONFINEMENT SURVEILLANCE SYS MAINTENANCE & MONITORING SVCS

United Defense Systems Inc...............G...... 401 304-9100
Reston (G-10978)

CONNECTORS & TERMINALS: Electrical Device Uses

Safran Usa Inc ....F...... 703 351-9898
Alexandria (G-334)

CONNECTORS: Electrical

J and R Manufacturing Inc ....E...... 276 210-1647
Bluefield (G-1865)

CONNECTORS: Electronic

Brantner and Associates Inc ....G...... 540 825-2111
Culpeper (G-3875)
Chesapeake Connector & Cable..........G...... 757 855-5504
Norfolk (G-9482)

Employee Codes: A=Over 500 employees, B=251-500
C=101-250, D=51-100, E=20-50, F=10-19, G=1-9

2021 Virginia
Industrial Directory

933

PRODUCT

ITT Defense & Electronics..................A....... 703 790-6300
Mc Lean *(G-8474)*

J and R Manufacturing Inc...........E....... 276 210-1647
Bluefield *(G-1865)*

Kitco Fiber Optics Inc................D....... 757 216-2208
Virginia Beach *(G-14587)*

Kitco/Ksaria LLC.................G....... 757 216-2220
Virginia Beach *(G-14588)*

Leyland Oceantech Inc...............G....... 703 661-6097
Sterling *(G-13440)*

Mapp Manufacturing Corporation.........G....... 757 410-0307
Chesapeake *(G-3197)*

Virginia Panel Corporation.............C....... 540 932-3300
Waynesboro *(G-15144)*

CONSTRUCTION & MINING MACHINERY WHOLESALERS

Chesapeake Bay Fishing Co LLC......F....... 804 438-6050
Weems *(G-15150)*

Mosena Enterprises Inc................G....... 757 562-7033
Franklin *(G-5149)*

Twin Disc Incorporated ....D....... 757 487-3670
Chesapeake *(G-3353)*

Western Branch Diesel Inc...........E....... 703 369-5005
Manassas *(G-8177)*

CONSTRUCTION & ROAD MAINTENANCE EQPT: Drags, Road

Haislip Farms LLC ....G....... 801 932-4087
Quinton *(G-10696)*

St Engineering North Amer Inc........E....... 703 739-2610
Alexandria *(G-353)*

CONSTRUCTION EQPT REPAIR SVCS

Cave Hill Corporation ....E....... 540 289-5051
McGaheysville *(G-8584)*

CONSTRUCTION EQPT: Airport

Jet Managers International Inc ....G....... 703 829-0679
Alexandria *(G-244)*

CONSTRUCTION EQPT: Attachments

Lemac Corporation.................E....... 804 862-8481
North Dinwiddie *(G-10057)*

CONSTRUCTION EQPT: Attachments, Snow Plow

HM Trucking ....G....... 703 932-7058
Herndon *(G-6702)*

CONSTRUCTION EQPT: Bulldozers

Dexter W Estes.....................G....... 434 996-8068
Lyndhurst *(G-7843)*

CONSTRUCTION EQPT: Cranes

Altec Industries Inc...................C....... 540 992-5300
Daleville *(G-3938)*

Delmarva Crane Inc ....G....... 757 426-0862
Virginia Beach *(G-14400)*

Giant Gradall and Eqp Rentl ....G....... 703 878-3032
Montclair *(G-8998)*

ML Manufacturing ....G....... 434 581-2000
New Canton *(G-9118)*

Platnick Crane and Steel LLC ....F....... 276 322-5477
Bluefield *(G-1874)*

Tadano Mantis Corporation ....E....... 800 272-3325
Richlands *(G-11020)*

CONSTRUCTION EQPT: Graders, Road

Moxley Brothers.....................G....... 276 236-6580
Galax *(G-5642)*

CONSTRUCTION EQPT: Rakes, Land Clearing, Mechanical

Edwards Kretz Lohr & Assoc............F....... 804 673-9666
Henrico *(G-6506)*

CONSTRUCTION EQPT: Roofing Eqpt

Galaxy Eqp Maint Solutions Inc ....G....... 703 866-0246
Springfield *(G-13007)*

CONSTRUCTION EQPT: Trucks, Off-Highway

Cuz To Cuz Trucking.................G....... 757 806-0358
Newport News *(G-9210)*

CONSTRUCTION EQPT: Wrecker Hoists, Automobile

Dewey L Sams......................G....... 540 664-4034
Berryville *(G-1678)*

George W Wray.....................G....... 540 483-7792
Rocky Mount *(G-12324)*

Graves ....G....... 434 656-2491
Pittsville *(G-10362)*

CONSTRUCTION MATERIALS, WHOL: Concrete/Cinder Bldg Prdts

Onduline North America Inc ....D....... 540 898-7000
Fredericksburg *(G-5341)*

CONSTRUCTION MATERIALS, WHOLESALE: Air Ducts, Sheet Metal

Tower Hill Corp......................E....... 703 368-7727
Manassas *(G-8005)*

CONSTRUCTION MATERIALS, WHOLESALE: Awnings

Virginia Canvas Products Inc ....G....... 757 558-0327
Carrollton *(G-2246)*

CONSTRUCTION MATERIALS, WHOLESALE: Brick, Exc Refractory

T&W Block Incorporated...........E....... 757 787-2646
Onley *(G-10201)*

CONSTRUCTION MATERIALS, WHOLESALE: Building Stone, Granite

Krain Building Services LLC...........E....... 703 924-1480
Alexandria *(G-509)*

CONSTRUCTION MATERIALS, WHOLESALE: Building Stone, Marble

Classic Granite and Marble Inc..........F....... 804 404-8004
Midlothian *(G-8796)*

Cyberex Corporation ....G....... 703 904-0980
Herndon *(G-6651)*

Empire Marble & Granite Co ....G....... 804 359-2004
Richmond *(G-11574)*

General Marble & Granite Co ....G....... 804 353-2761
Richmond *(G-11215)*

CONSTRUCTION MATERIALS, WHOLESALE: Building, Exterior

White Rock Truss LLC................G....... 276 445-5990
Rose Hill *(G-12364)*

CONSTRUCTION MATERIALS, WHOLESALE: Building, Interior

Trm Inc ....E....... 920 855-2194
Haymarket *(G-6452)*

CONSTRUCTION MATERIALS, WHOLESALE: Cement

Dominion Quikrete Inc................E....... 757 547-9411
Chesapeake *(G-3071)*

Dominion Quikrete Inc................E....... 276 957-3235
Martinsville *(G-8279)*

Lafarge North America Inc ....F....... 757 545-2481
Chesapeake *(G-3173)*

CONSTRUCTION MATERIALS, WHOLESALE: Guardrails, Metal

Cushing Metals LLC ....G....... 804 339-1114
King William *(G-7128)*

CONSTRUCTION MATERIALS, WHOLESALE: Joists

Bohling Steel Inc....................E....... 434 385-5175
Lynchburg *(G-7657)*

Richmond Steel Inc..................E....... 804 355-8080
Richmond *(G-11360)*

CONSTRUCTION MATERIALS, WHOLESALE: Masons' Materials

Vulcan Materials Company ....E....... 804 693-3606
Gloucester *(G-5866)*

CONSTRUCTION MATERIALS, WHOLESALE: Millwork

E H Lail Millwork Inc ....F....... 804 271-1111
North Chesterfield *(G-9866)*

Randolph-Bundy Incorporated.........E....... 757 625-2556
Portsmouth *(G-10474)*

Wood Design & Fabrication Inc..........F....... 540 774-8168
Roanoke *(G-12024)*

CONSTRUCTION MATERIALS, WHOLESALE: Molding, All Materials

Fritz Ken Tooling & Design ....E....... 804 721-2319
North Chesterfield *(G-9880)*

Quality Wood Products Inc ....G....... 540 750-1859
Christiansburg *(G-3608)*

CONSTRUCTION MATERIALS, WHOLESALE: Pallets, Wood

Virginia Pallets & Wood LLC............G....... 434 515-2221
Lawrenceville *(G-7187)*

CONSTRUCTION MATERIALS, WHOLESALE: Septic Tanks

Boggs Water & Sewage Inc..............E....... 757 787-4000
Melfa *(G-8708)*

Vamac Incorporated..................E....... 540 535-1983
Winchester *(G-15503)*

Vamaz Inc...........................G....... 434 296-8812
Charlottesville *(G-2711)*

CONSTRUCTION MATERIALS, WHOLESALE: Siding, Wood

First Colony Homes Inc...............G....... 540 788-4222
Calverton *(G-2224)*

CONSTRUCTION MATERIALS, WHOLESALE: Stone, Crushed Or Broken

Rockbridge Stone Products Inc ....G....... 540 258-2841
Glasgow *(G-5701)*

Rockydale Quarries Corporation.........G....... 540 896-1441
Roanoke *(G-11997)*

Salem Stone Corporation ....E....... 540 552-9292
Blacksburg *(G-1786)*

CONSTRUCTION MATERIALS, WHOLESALE: Tile & Clay Prdts

Elias LLC...........................G....... 703 663-1192
Alexandria *(G-453)*

CONSTRUCTION MATERIALS, WHOLESALE: Windows

Legacy Products LLC.................E....... 804 739-9333
Midlothian *(G-8847)*

CONSTRUCTION MATLS, WHOL: Lumber, Rough, Dressed/Finished

Conner Industries Inc ....G....... 804 706-4229
Chester *(G-3396)*

Ruffin & Payne Incorporated ....C....... 804 329-2691
Richmond *(G-11749)*

Smith Mountain Land & Lbr Inc.........F....... 540 297-1205
Huddleston *(G-6958)*

CONSTRUCTION MATLS, WHOLESALE: Soil Erosion Cntrl Fabrics

B & H Wood Products Inc ....F....... 540 752-2480
Stafford *(G-13122)*

Nedia Enterprises Inc ....E....... 571 223-0200
Ashburn *(G-1320)*

CONSTRUCTION MTRLS, WHOL: Exterior Flat Glass, Plate/Window

All Glass LLC .... G 540 288-8111
Fredericksburg (G-5397)

CONSTRUCTION SAND MINING

Aggregate Industries - Mwr Inc .... E 540 775-7600
King George (G-7080)

Townside Building and Repr Inc .... G 540 207-3906
Stafford (G-13203)

CONSTRUCTION SITE PREPARATION SVCS

Moyer Brothers Contracting Inc .... G 540 743-7864
Luray (G-7618)

CONSTRUCTION: Apartment Building

Jefferson Homebuilders Inc .... C 540 825-5898
Culpeper (G-3898)

CONSTRUCTION: Athletic & Recreation Facilities

Jes Construction LLC .... D 757 558-9909
Virginia Beach (G-14568)

Martins Fabricating & Welding .... G 540 343-6001
Roanoke (G-12133)

CONSTRUCTION: Chemical Facility

Arco Welding Inc .... F 540 710-6944
Fredericksburg (G-5247)

CONSTRUCTION: Commercial & Institutional Building

American Cmg Services Inc .... G 757 548-5656
Chesapeake (G-2965)

Burgess Snyder Industries Inc .... E 757 490-3131
Virginia Beach (G-14306)

Joglex Corporation .... G 540 833-2444
Linville (G-7435)

Travis Lee Kerr .... G 434 922-7005
Vesuvius (G-13999)

TST Tactical Def Solutions Inc .... F 757 452-6955
Virginia Beach (G-14896)

CONSTRUCTION: Commercial & Office Building, New

American Orthotic .... G 757 548-5296
Chesapeake (G-2972)

Burnopp Metal LLC .... G 434 525-4746
Evington (G-4375)

Mallory Co Inc .... G 757 803-5596
Chesapeake (G-3194)

Mulqueen Inc .... F 804 333-4847
Warsaw (G-15070)

CONSTRUCTION: Drainage System

HHh Underground LLC .... F 804 365-6905
Glen Allen (G-5743)

CONSTRUCTION: Elevated Highway

Barger Son Cnstr Inc Charles W .... D 540 463-2106
Lexington (G-7388)

CONSTRUCTION: Food Prdts Manufacturing or Packing Plant

San-J International Inc .... E 804 226-8333
Henrico (G-6565)

CONSTRUCTION: Foundation & Retaining Wall

Bract Rtining Walls Excvtg LLC .... F 804 798-5097
Ashland (G-1384)

CONSTRUCTION: Indl Buildings, New, NEC

War Fighter Specialties LLC .... G 540 742-4187
Shenandoah (G-12697)

CONSTRUCTION: Residential, Nec

Lewis Welding & Cnstr Works .... G 434 696-5527
Keysville (G-7060)

Metro Wood Works Inc .... G 757 479-1100
Chesapeake (G-3203)

CONSTRUCTION: Sewer Line

Chaney Enterprises Ltd Partnr .... G 540 659-4100
Stafford (G-13129)

CONSTRUCTION: Single-Family Housing

Albright Recovery & Cnstr LLC .... G 276 835-2026
Clinchco (G-3684)

Colonial Kitchen & Cabinets .... E 757 898-1332
Yorktown (G-15943)

Old Vrgnia Hand Hewn Log Homes .... F 276 546-5647
Pennington Gap (G-10296)

Tops of Town Virginia LLC .... G 703 242-8100
Fairfax (G-4571)

Travis Lee Kerr .... G 434 922-7005
Vesuvius (G-13999)

CONSTRUCTION: Single-family Housing, New

Jefferson Homebuilders Inc .... C 540 825-5898
Culpeper (G-3898)

Mulqueen Inc .... F 804 333-4847
Warsaw (G-15070)

Rappatomac Industries Inc .... G 804 529-6440
Callao (G-2218)

Ronbuilt Corporation .... G 276 638-2090
Martinsville (G-8324)

CONSTRUCTION: Street Sign Installation & Mntnce

Performance Signs LLC .... F 434 985-7446
Ruckersville (G-12408)

CONSTRUCTION: Street Surfacing & Paving

Lane Construction Corporation .... F 703 471-6883
Chantilly (G-2541)

Superior Paving Corporation .... G 703 631-5480
Centreville (G-2342)

CONSTRUCTION: Transmitting Tower, Telecommunication

Timothy L Hosey .... G 270 339-0016
Maurertown (G-8364)

CONSTRUCTION: Utility Line

Boggs Water & Sewage Inc .... E 757 787-4000
Melfa (G-8708)

CONSTRUCTION: Waste Water & Sewage Treatment Plant

Abwasser Technologies Inc .... G 757 453-7505
Virginia Beach (G-14206)

Aquao2 Wastewater Treatment Sy .... G 540 365-0154
Ferrum (G-4967)

Augusta Actuation LLC .... G 540 480-7619
Steeles Tavern (G-13310)

CONSULTING SVC: Business, NEC

American Solar Inc .... G 703 346-6053
Annandale (G-730)

American Tech Sltons Intl Corp .... E 540 907-5355
Fredericksburg (G-5398)

Arben Solutions Co .... G 703 728-0396
Warrenton (G-14978)

Ats Corporation .... E 571 766-2400
Fairfax (G-4413)

C2c Smart Compliance LLC .... F 703 872-7340
Alexandria (G-158)

Capitol Information Group Inc .... D 703 905-8000
Falls Church (G-4770)

Donley Technology .... G 804 224-9427
Colonial Beach (G-3724)

Engine Scout Professionals LLC .... G 757 621-8526
Portsmouth (G-10423)

Gadfly LLC .... G 703 282-9448
Leesburg (G-7276)

Gtras Inc .... D 703 342-4282
Chantilly (G-2433)

Kirintec Inc .... G 571 527-1437
Alexandria (G-253)

L & M Electric and Plbg LLC .... F 703 768-2222
Alexandria (G-512)

Personal Protectio Principles .... G 757 453-3202
Virginia Beach (G-14717)

Raytheon Company .... C 703 841-5700
Arlington (G-1132)

Relational Systems Design Ltd .... G 703 385-7073
Fairfax (G-4539)

Rodyn Vibration Analysis Inc .... G 434 326-6797
Charlottesville (G-2865)

Rowing Team LLC .... E 855 462-7238
Glen Allen (G-5788)

Self Solutions LLC .... E 202 725-0866
Alexandria (G-582)

World Fashion City Inc .... G 703 887-8123
Alexandria (G-615)

CONSULTING SVC: Chemical

Scilucent LLC .... F 703 435-0033
Herndon (G-6802)

CONSULTING SVC: Computer

Agaram Technologies Inc .... D 703 297-8591
Ashburn (G-1239)

Agora Data Services LLC .... G 703 328-7758
Fredericksburg (G-5396)

American Tech Sltons Intl Corp .... G 540 907-5355
Fredericksburg (G-5398)

Ats Corporation .... E 571 766-2400
Fairfax (G-4413)

Blinkcloud LLC .... G 484 429-3340
Alexandria (G-148)

Bottomline Software Inc .... G 540 221-4444
Waynesboro (G-15101)

Capital Software Corporation .... G 703 404-3000
Chantilly (G-2528)

Computer Solution Co of VA Inc .... E 804 794-3491
Richmond (G-11538)

Digital Synergy LLC .... G 540 951-5900
Blacksburg (G-1732)

E Z Data Inc .... G 540 775-2961
King George (G-7088)

Engility LLC .... A 703 434-4000
Reston (G-10847)

Idvector .... G 571 313-5064
Sterling (G-13426)

Information Analysis Inc .... E 703 383-3000
Fairfax (G-4633)

Innovative Computer Engrg Inc .... G 703 934-4879
Fairfax (G-4635)

Irontek LLC .... G 703 627-0092
Sterling (G-13432)

Michie Software Systems Inc .... G 757 868-7771
Yorktown (G-15982)

One Stop Computer Services LLC .... G 571 442-2045
Sterling (G-13465)

Oracle Systems Corporation .... A 703 478-9000
Reston (G-10916)

Radio Reconnaissance Tech Inc .... G 540 752-7448
Fredericksburg (G-5352)

Ridge Business Solutions LLC .... E 571 241-8714
Reston (G-10941)

CONSULTING SVC: Data Processing

South Anna Inc .... G 804 316-9660
Henrico (G-6572)

CONSULTING SVC: Educational

Earthwalk Communications Inc .... D 703 393-1940
Manassas (G-8061)

K2w Enterprises Corporation .... G 540 603-0114
Centreville (G-2313)

CONSULTING SVC: Engineering

4wave Inc .... E 703 787-9283
Sterling (G-13337)

Diamondefense LLC .... F 571 321-2012
Annandale (G-743)

Envirnmntal Solutions Intl Inc .... F 703 263-7600
Ashburn (G-1276)

P D R Inc .... G 540 772-2780
Roanoke (G-11981)

Security Evolutions Inc .... G 703 953-4739
Centreville (G-2337)

Employee Codes: A=Over 500 employees, B=251-500
C=101-250, D=51-100, E=20-50, F=10-19, G=1-9

2021 Virginia
Industrial Directory

PRODUCT

935

CONSULTING SVC: Human Resource

Bradley-Morris LLC..................................E....... 678 419-4171
Chesapeake *(G-3014)*
Give More Media Inc............................G....... 804 762-4500
Richmond *(G-11601)*

CONSULTING SVC: Management

Ad Vice Inc..G....... 804 730-0503
Mechanicsville *(G-8600)*
Arben Solutions Co...............................G....... 703 728-0396
Warrenton *(G-14978)*
Caci Products Company.......................G....... 973 437-9800
Reston *(G-10815)*
Carr Group LLC.....................................G....... 571 723-6562
Woodbridge *(G-15669)*
Data-Clear LLC.....................................G....... 703 499-3816
Arlington *(G-929)*
Finest Art & Framing LLC....................G....... 703 945-9000
Lansdowne *(G-7170)*
Forging The Warrior Spirit..................G....... 703 851-4789
Marshall *(G-8252)*
Freshwter Parl Media Group LLC........G....... 757 785-5483
Norfolk *(G-9559)*
Fso Mission Support LLC....................G....... 571 528-3507
Leesburg *(G-7275)*
Gadfly LLC..G....... 703 282-9448
Leesburg *(G-7276)*
Gibraltar Energy LLC............................G....... 202 642-2704
Alexandria *(G-469)*
Index Systems Inc.................................G....... 571 420-4600
Herndon *(G-6706)*
K2w Enterprises Corporation...............G....... 540 603-0114
Centreville *(G-2313)*
Mercury Partners Usa LLC...................G....... 757 652-7067
Franktown *(G-5164)*
Naj Enterprises LLP..............................G....... 202 251-7821
Mc Lean *(G-8509)*
O2o Software Inc...................................G....... 571 234-3243
Herndon *(G-6762)*
Orion Applied Science Tech LLC..........G....... 571 393-1942
Manassas *(G-8122)*
Pae Aviation Technical Svcs LLC.........D....... 703 717-6000
Arlington *(G-1095)*
Performance Support Systems............G....... 757 873-3700
Hayes *(G-6404)*
Portfolio Publication............................G....... 703 802-8676
Chantilly *(G-2481)*
Potomac Intl Advisors LLC...................G....... 202 460-9001
Ashburn *(G-1328)*
Potomac Solutions Incorporated.........G....... 703 888-1762
Alexandria *(G-313)*
Rowing Team LLC..................................E....... 855 462-7238
Glen Allen *(G-5788)*
Rufina Inc...G....... 703 577-2333
Falls Church *(G-4870)*
Self Solutions LLC................................E....... 202 725-0866
Alexandria *(G-582)*
Sra Companies Inc................................A....... 703 803-1500
Chantilly *(G-2498)*
Synaptein Solutions Inc........................F....... 703 209-2350
Mc Lean *(G-8562)*
Weston Solutions Inc............................G....... 757 819-5300
Hampton *(G-6272)*

CONSULTING SVC: Marketing Management

22 Church LLC.......................................G....... 540 342-2817
Roanoke *(G-12026)*
Arabesque Media...................................G....... 703 745-5395
Fairfax *(G-4410)*
Art & Framing Center............................G....... 540 720-2800
Stafford *(G-13119)*
Brown & Duncan LLC............................G....... 832 844-6523
Virginia Beach *(G-14302)*
Falcon Lab Inc......................................G....... 703 442-0124
Mc Lean *(G-8426)*
Fine Line LLC...G....... 540 436-3626
Maurertown *(G-8362)*
Ideation Web Studios LLC....................G....... 757 333-3021
Chesapeake *(G-3140)*
Insul Industries Inc...............................F....... 804 550-1933
Mechanicsville *(G-8641)*
Kirintec Inc..G....... 571 527-1437
Alexandria *(G-253)*
Minuteman Press of Mc Lean...............G....... 703 356-6612
Mc Lean *(G-8502)*
Symmetric Systems Inc.........................G....... 804 276-7202
North Chesterfield *(G-9997)*
Wealthy Sistas Media Group.................G....... 800 917-9435
Dumfries *(G-4262)*

Webb-Mason Inc....................................G....... 804 897-1990
Rockville *(G-12303)*
Willie Lucas...G....... 919 935-8066
Woodbridge *(G-15832)*

CONSULTING SVC: Online Technology

Acre Media LLC......................................G....... 703 314-4465
Alexandria *(G-402)*
Cubicle Logic LLC.................................G....... 571 989-2823
Sterling *(G-13380)*
Pbp Solutions LLC.................................G....... 202 999-8101
Reston *(G-10923)*
Troy Patrick...G....... 703 507-4914
Alexandria *(G-370)*
Warcollar Industries LLC......................G....... 703 981-2862
Vienna *(G-14156)*
Webdmg LLC..G....... 757 633-5033
Suffolk *(G-13782)*

CONSULTING SVC: Productivity Improvement

Frogue...F....... 703 679-7003
Reston *(G-10854)*
Mav6 LLC..E....... 601 619-7722
Herndon *(G-6744)*

CONSULTING SVC: Telecommunications

Caleigh Systems Inc..............................F....... 703 539-5004
Annandale *(G-734)*
Gcseac Inc...G....... 276 632-9700
Martinsville *(G-8288)*
Smartcell Inc..G....... 703 989-5887
Manassas *(G-8157)*

CONSULTING SVCS, BUSINESS: Communications

J L V Management Inc............................G....... 540 446-6359
Stafford *(G-13158)*
Naj Enterprises LLP..............................G....... 202 251-7821
Mc Lean *(G-8509)*

CONSULTING SVCS, BUSINESS: Energy Conservation

Intus Windows LLC................................F....... 202 450-4211
Fairfax *(G-4480)*
Osage Bio Energy LLC...........................E....... 804 612-8660
Glen Allen *(G-5777)*

CONSULTING SVCS, BUSINESS: Environmental

Benzaco Scientific Inc..........................G....... 540 371-5560
Fredericksburg *(G-5402)*
Envirnmntal Solutions Intl Inc...............F....... 703 263-7600
Ashburn *(G-1276)*

CONSULTING SVCS, BUSINESS: Publishing

Doite Media LLC.....................................G....... 703 594-1322
Broadlands *(G-2076)*

CONSULTING SVCS, BUSINESS: Safety Training Svcs

American Safety & Health......................G....... 434 977-2700
Charlottesville *(G-2728)*
Industrial Biodynamics LLC..................G....... 540 357-0033
Salem *(G-12520)*
Mission Integrated Tech LLC.................G....... 202 769-9900
Vienna *(G-14097)*
Warrior Trail Consulting LLC................G....... 703 349-1967
Fairfax *(G-4580)*

CONSULTING SVCS, BUSINESS: Sys Engnrg, Exc Computer/Prof

Active Sense Technologies LLC............G....... 352 226-1479
Abingdon *(G-7)*
Antheon Solutions Inc..........................G....... 703 298-1891
Reston *(G-10790)*
Aspetto Inc...G....... 540 547-8487
Fredericksburg *(G-5171)*
Avitech Consulting LLC.........................G....... 757 810-2716
Chesapeake *(G-2990)*
Cognition Point Inc...............................G....... 703 402-8945
Aldie *(G-104)*

Green Physics Corporation...................G....... 703 989-6706
Manassas *(G-7949)*
Source360 LLC.......................................G....... 703 232-1563
Chantilly *(G-2494)*
Syrm LLC..G....... 571 308-8707
Stafford *(G-13200)*

CONSULTING SVCS, BUSINESS: Systems Analysis & Engineering

Diamondefense LLC...............................F....... 571 321-2012
Annandale *(G-743)*
Mission It LLC..G....... 443 534-0130
Brambleton *(G-1930)*
Pae Aviation Technical Svcs LLC.........D....... 703 717-6000
Arlington *(G-1095)*
Rufina Inc...G....... 703 577-2333
Falls Church *(G-4870)*
Signafab LLC..G....... 703 489-8572
Louisa *(G-7567)*
Yellow Bridge Software Inc...................G....... 703 909-5533
Woodbridge *(G-15837)*

CONSULTING SVCS, BUSINESS: Systems Analysis Or Design

Delta Q Dynamics LLC...........................G....... 703 980-9449
Manassas *(G-7931)*

CONSULTING SVCS: Geological

American Tech Sltons Intl Corp............E....... 540 907-5355
Fredericksburg *(G-5398)*

CONSULTING SVCS: Geophysical

Sematron LLC...G....... 919 360-5806
Leesburg *(G-7345)*

CONSULTING SVCS: Oil

D L S & Associates................................G....... 276 796-5275
Pound *(G-10511)*
Hickory Hill Consulting LLC..................G....... 804 363-2719
Ashland *(G-1433)*
Potomac Intl Advisors LLC...................G....... 202 460-9001
Ashburn *(G-1328)*
W P L Incorporated................................G....... 540 298-0999
Elkton *(G-4339)*

CONSULTING SVCS: Scientific

Global Cell Solutions Inc......................G....... 434 327-3759
Charlottesville *(G-2804)*
Wooton Consulting................................G....... 804 227-3418
Bumpass *(G-2173)*

CONTACT LENSES

Conforma Laboratories Inc...................E....... 757 321-0200
Norfolk *(G-9502)*
Le Grand Assoc of Pittsburgh..............G....... 757 484-4900
Chesapeake *(G-3180)*

CONTAINERS: Air Cargo, Metal

Fk Logistics Usa LLC............................G....... 877 811-8772
Vienna *(G-14056)*

CONTAINERS: Cargo, Wood & Wood With Metal

Conglobal Industries LLC.....................E....... 757 487-5100
Chesapeake *(G-3051)*

CONTAINERS: Corrugated

Alexandria Packaging LLC.....................D....... 703 644-5550
Springfield *(G-12940)*
Old Dominion Box Co Inc......................E....... 434 929-6701
Madison Heights *(G-7881)*
Sandbox Enterprises.............................G....... 410 999-4666
Herndon *(G-6800)*
Temple-Inland Inc...................................G....... 804 861-8164
Petersburg *(G-10345)*

CONTAINERS: Foil, Bakery Goods & Frozen Foods

Reynolds Consumer Products LLC........B....... 804 230-5200
Richmond *(G-11735)*

CONTAINERS: Food & Beverage

Loco Crazy Good Inc ....G....... 703 401-4058
  Ashburn (G-1310)
Stratos LLC ....G....... 800 213-4705
  Richmond (G-11399)

CONTAINERS: Food, Liquid Tight, Including Milk

International Paper Company ....G....... 757 405-3046
  Portsmouth (G-10444)

CONTAINERS: Frozen Food & Ice Cream

Trotter Jamil ....G....... 757 251-8754
  Hampton (G-6253)

CONTAINERS: Glass

Owens-Brockway Glass Cont Inc ....C....... 434 799-5880
  Ringgold (G-11871)
Paddock Enterprises LLC ....F 757 566-3957
  Toano (G-13873)

CONTAINERS: Metal

Blue Ridge Packaging Corp ....E....... 276 638-1413
  Martinsville (G-8270)
C & A Cutter Head Inc ....G....... 276 646-5548
  Chilhowie (G-3546)

CONTAINERS: Plastic

Berry Plastics Design LLC ....C....... 757 538-2000
  Suffolk (G-13679)
Eagle Contractors ....G....... 703 435-0004
  Gainesville (G-5581)
Gauge Works Inc ....G....... 703 661-1300
  Dulles (G-4203)
Intrapac (harrisonburg) Inc ....B....... 540 434-1703
  Mount Crawford (G-9055)
Liqui-Box Corporation ....D....... 804 325-1400
  Richmond (G-11658)
M&H Plastics Inc ....C....... 540 504-0030
  Winchester (G-15441)
Monoflo International Inc ....C....... 540 665-1691
  Winchester (G-15451)
Product Dev Mfg & Packg ....G....... 703 777-8400
  Leesburg (G-7328)
Rubbermaid Commercial Pdts LLC .....A....... 540 667-8700
  Winchester (G-15582)
Rubbermaid Commercial Pdts LLC .....G....... 540 542-8195
  Winchester (G-15471)
South Distributors LLC ....G....... 718 258-0200
  Petersburg (G-10344)

CONTAINERS: Sanitary, Food

Aflex Packaging LLC ....G....... 571 208-9938
  Springfield (G-12936)
Ecozenith Usa Inc ....G....... 703 992-6622
  Falls Church (G-4786)
RPC Superfos Us Inc ....E....... 540 504-7176
  Winchester (G-15470)
Southeastern Container Inc ....C....... 540 722-2600
  Winchester (G-15480)
Squrl LLC ....G....... 443 481-9941
  Charlottesville (G-2882)

CONTAINERS: Shipping & Mailing, Fiber

American Mountain Tech LLC ....G....... 423 646-1864
  Abingdon (G-10)

CONTAINERS: Shipping, Wood

C & L Containers Inc ....G....... 757 398-0447
  Chesapeake (G-3020)

CONTAINERS: Wood

Consolidated Wood Products ....G....... 540 374-1439
  Fredericksburg (G-5266)
Grapevine ....G....... 540 371-4092
  Fredericksburg (G-5436)
Southside Containers ....G 757 422-1111
  Virginia Beach (G-14831)

CONTRACT FOOD SVCS

Ssr Foods LLC ....G....... 703 581-7260
  Gainesville (G-5615)

CONTRACTORS: Acoustical & Insulation Work

Atlantic Fireproofing Inc ....E....... 703 940-9444
  Springfield (G-12953)

CONTRACTORS: Asbestos Removal & Encapsulation

Semco Services Inc ....E....... 540 885-7480
  Staunton (G-13291)

CONTRACTORS: Awning Installation

Superior Awning Service Inc ....G....... 757 399-8161
  Portsmouth (G-10489)

CONTRACTORS: Boiler Maintenance Contractor

Commercial Tech Inc ....G....... 703 468-1339
  Manassas (G-8051)

CONTRACTORS: Building Fireproofing

Atlantic Fireproofing Inc ....E....... 703 940-9444
  Springfield (G-12953)

CONTRACTORS: Building Sign Installation & Mntnce

Birckhead Signs & Graphics ....G....... 434 295-5962
  Charlottesville (G-2740)
Brooks Gray Sign Company ....F....... 804 233-4343
  Richmond (G-11510)
Dowling Signs Inc ....E....... 540 373-6675
  Fredericksburg (G-5183)
J Fred Dowis ....G....... 757 874-7446
  Newport News (G-9263)
Moore Sign Corporation ....E....... 804 748-5836
  Chester (G-3438)
New Home Media ....C....... 703 550-2233
  Lorton (G-7515)
Scottys Sign Inc ....F....... 757 245-7129
  Newport News (G-9332)
Sign Graphx Inc ....E....... 703 335-7446
  Manassas (G-8000)
Signs Unlimited Inc ....F....... 703 799-8840
  Alexandria (G-585)
Talley Sign Company ....F....... 804 649-0325
  Richmond (G-11781)
Titan Sign Corporation ....G....... 540 899-5334
  Fredericksburg (G-5379)

CONTRACTORS: Carpentry Work

Door Systems Inc ....F....... 703 490-1800
  Woodbridge (G-15685)
Interior 2000 ....G....... 804 598-0340
  Powhatan (G-10551)
Rainbow Custom Woodworking ....E....... 571 379-5500
  Manassas (G-8138)
Red Eagle Industries LLC ....G....... 434 352-5831
  Appomattox (G-822)

CONTRACTORS: Carpentry, Cabinet & Finish Work

Albion Cabinets Stairs Inc ....G....... 434 974-4611
  Earlysville (G-4284)
Bay Cabinets & Contractors ....G....... 757 934-2236
  Suffolk (G-13676)
Creative Cabinet Design ....G....... 434 293-4040
  Charlottesville (G-2774)
Deneals Cabinets Inc ....G....... 540 721-8005
  Hardy (G-6286)
Lesden Corporation ....G....... 540 373-4940
  Fredericksburg (G-5450)
Montgomery Cabinetry ....G....... 540 721-7000
  Wirtz (G-15616)
Rutrough Cabinets Inc ....G....... 540 489-3211
  Rocky Mount (G-12351)
Woodwrights Cooperative ....G....... 804 358-4800
  Richmond (G-11455)

CONTRACTORS: Carpentry, Cabinet Building & Installation

Colonial Rail Systems LLC ....G....... 804 932-5200
  New Kent (G-9129)

Fitzgeralds Cabinet Shop Inc ....G....... 757 877-2538
  Newport News (G-9229)
Frederick Enterprises LLC ....E....... 804 405-4976
  Richmond (G-11594)
Haley Pearsall Inc ....G....... 804 784-3438
  Richmond (G-11230)
Millehan Enterprises Inc ....G....... 540 772-3037
  Roanoke (G-11967)

CONTRACTORS: Carpentry, Finish & Trim Work

Interior Building Systems Corp ....D....... 703 335-9655
  Manassas (G-8083)
Loudoun Stairs Inc ....E....... 703 478-8800
  Purcellville (G-10670)

CONTRACTORS: Carpet Laying

Cutting Edge Carpet Binding ....G....... 540 982-1007
  Vinton (G-14171)

CONTRACTORS: Ceramic Floor Tile Installation

Paige Sitta & Associates Inc ....E....... 757 420-5886
  Chesapeake (G-3231)

CONTRACTORS: Chimney Construction & Maintenance

New England Supply Inc ....F....... 703 372-2689
  Springfield (G-13058)

CONTRACTORS: Commercial & Office Building

Lewis Welding & Cnstr Works ....G....... 434 696-5527
  Keysville (G-7060)

CONTRACTORS: Communications Svcs

Cornerstone Tech Solutions Inc ....G....... 540 477-2180
  Mount Jackson (G-9068)
Ecko Incorporated ....F....... 276 988-7943
  North Tazewell (G-10098)
VT Milcom Inc ....D....... 757 548-2956
  Chesapeake (G-3366)

CONTRACTORS: Computer Installation

1st Stop Electronics LLC ....G....... 804 931-0517
  Richmond (G-11070)

CONTRACTORS: Concrete

Handyman Concrete Inc ....E....... 703 437-7143
  Chantilly (G-2535)
Premium Paving Inc ....F....... 703 339-5371
  Springfield (G-13073)
Red Eagle Industries LLC ....G....... 434 352-5831
  Appomattox (G-822)

CONTRACTORS: Construction Site Cleanup

Lawson and Son Cnstr LLC ....G....... 478 258-2478
  Yorktown (G-15973)
Mr1 Construction LLC ....G....... 301 748-6078
  Manassas (G-7977)

CONTRACTORS: Core Drilling & Cutting

Standard Core Drilling Co Inc ....G....... 276 395-3391
  Coeburn (G-3703)

CONTRACTORS: Countertop Installation

Brazilian Best Granite Inc ....G....... 804 562-3022
  Richmond (G-11132)
Empire Marble & Granite Co ....G....... 804 359-2004
  Richmond (G-11574)
General Marble & Granite Co ....G....... 804 353-2761
  Richmond (G-11215)
Mid-Atlantic Manufacturing Inc ....E....... 804 798-7462
  Oilville (G-10183)
Rutrough Cabinets Inc ....G....... 540 489-3211
  Rocky Mount (G-12351)
Tops of Town Virginia LLC ....G....... 703 242-8100
  Fairfax (G-4571)
Winn Stone Products Inc ....G....... 757 465-5363
  Portsmouth (G-10505)

PRODUCT

CONTRACTORS: Decontamination Svcs

Virginia American Inds Inc ....C 804 644-2611
Richmond *(G-11807)*

CONTRACTORS: Demolition, Building & Other Structures

Mid Atlantic Mining LLC ....G...... 757 407-6735
Suffolk *(G-13742)*

CONTRACTORS: Directional Oil & Gas Well Drilling Svc

Bison Inc ....G...... 703 754-4190
Gainesville *(G-5572)*
Boredacious Inc ....G...... 703 327-5490
Aldie *(G-102)*
Clarks Directional Boring ....G...... 804 493-7475
Montross *(G-9026)*
Crudewell Inc ....E 540 254-2289
Buchanan *(G-2119)*
Eastcom Directional Drlg Inc ....G...... 757 377-3133
Chesapeake *(G-3083)*
Harrods Natural Resources ....G...... 703 426-7200
Fairfax *(G-4475)*
Horn Well Drilling Inc Noah.............C 276 935-5902
Oakwood *(G-10168)*

CONTRACTORS: Drywall

Richard Evans ....G...... 540 774-1905
Roanoke *(G-11995)*

CONTRACTORS: Electrical

All Marble..G...... 757 460-8099
Virginia Beach *(G-14222)*
Heritage Electrical Corp ....F 804 743-4614
North Chesterfield *(G-9884)*
ICE Tek LLC ....E 757 390-8589
Virginia Beach *(G-14539)*
Jims Electric Motor Co Inc ....F 703 550-8624
Lorton *(G-7499)*
Loehr Lightning Protection Co ....F 804 231-4236
Richmond *(G-11659)*
Marion Electric Company ....G...... 276 783-4765
Marion *(G-8233)*
Mark Electric Inc ....G...... 804 749-4151
Rockville *(G-12291)*
Roseann Combs ....G...... 757 228-1795
Norfolk *(G-9710)*
Sparks Electric ....G...... 540 967-0436
Louisa *(G-7568)*

CONTRACTORS: Electronic Controls Installation

Industrial Control Systems Inc ....E 804 737-1700
Sandston *(G-12620)*
Instrumentation and Control.............D 804 550-5770
Ashland *(G-1440)*

CONTRACTORS: Excavating

Red Eagle Industries LLC ....G...... 434 352-5831
Appomattox *(G-822)*
Rexrode Timber & Excavation ....G...... 540 474-5892
Monterey *(G-9013)*

CONTRACTORS: Excavating Slush Pits & Cellars Svcs

B & H Excavating ....G...... 540 839-2107
Hot Springs *(G-6945)*
Christopher L Bird ....G...... 540 675-3409
Washington *(G-15074)*

CONTRACTORS: Fence Construction

Jerry King ....G...... 804 550-1243
Glen Allen *(G-5755)*
Merchants Metals LLC ....G...... 804 262-9783
Rockville *(G-12293)*
Virginia Railing & Gates LLC ....F 804 798-8777
Ashland *(G-1506)*

CONTRACTORS: Fire Detection & Burglar Alarm Systems

Johnson Controls ....G...... 804 727-3890
Richmond *(G-11257)*

CONTRACTORS: Fire Sprinkler System Installation Svcs

Johnson Controls ....G...... 804 727-3890
Richmond *(G-11257)*

CONTRACTORS: Floor Laying & Other Floor Work

Clark Hardwood Flr Refinishing ....G...... 804 350-8871
Powhatan *(G-10538)*
Lee Tech Hardwood Floors ....G...... 540 588-6217
Roanoke *(G-12124)*
Line X Central Virginia Inc ....G...... 434 525-8878
Evington *(G-4378)*
Tony Tran Hardwood Floors ....G...... 540 793-4094
Vinton *(G-14187)*

CONTRACTORS: Flooring

Clark Hardwood Flr Refinishing ....G...... 804 350-8871
Powhatan *(G-10538)*
Lee Tech Hardwood Floors ....G...... 540 588-6217
Roanoke *(G-12124)*
Tony Tran Hardwood Floors ....G...... 540 793-4094
Vinton *(G-14187)*

CONTRACTORS: Gas Field Svcs, NEC

Brightway Inc ....G...... 540 468-2510
Monterey *(G-9004)*
Ogc Inc ....G...... 703 860-3736
Reston *(G-10913)*

CONTRACTORS: Gas Leak Detection

Radon Safe Inc ....G...... 540 265-0101
Roanoke *(G-11993)*

CONTRACTORS: General Electric

American Hands LLC.........................G...... 804 349-8974
Powhatan *(G-10530)*

CONTRACTORS: Geothermal Drilling

William G Sexton..............................G...... 276 988-9012
North Tazewell *(G-10111)*

CONTRACTORS: Glass Tinting, Architectural & Automotive

Applied Film Technology Inc ....G...... 757 351-4241
Virginia Beach *(G-14234)*
Sun Signs ....G...... 703 867-9831
Stafford *(G-13197)*

CONTRACTORS: Glass, Glazing & Tinting

All Glass LLC...................................G...... 540 288-8111
Fredericksburg *(G-5397)*
Dixie Plate GL & Mirror Co LLC ....G...... 540 869-4400
Middletown *(G-8737)*
TST Tactical Def Solutions Inc..........F 757 452-6955
Virginia Beach *(G-14896)*

CONTRACTORS: Grave Excavation

Mercer Vault Co ....G...... 540 371-3666
Fredericksburg *(G-5206)*

CONTRACTORS: Gutters & Downspouts

Sams Gutter Shop ....G...... 276 632-6522
Martinsville *(G-8325)*

CONTRACTORS: Heating & Air Conditioning

Brontz Inc ....G...... 540 483-0976
Rocky Mount *(G-12315)*
CPS Contractors Inc ....G...... 804 561-6834
Moseley *(G-9036)*
Flippen & Sons Inc...........................G...... 804 233-1461
Richmond *(G-11592)*
Virginia Blower Company ....E 276 647-3804
Collinsville *(G-3718)*

CONTRACTORS: Heating Systems Repair & Maintenance Svc

Walashek Holdings Inc......................G...... 757 853-6007
Norfolk *(G-9789)*

CONTRACTORS: Highway & Street Construction, General

Stuart M Perry Incorporated ....C 540 662-3431
Winchester *(G-15483)*

CONTRACTORS: Highway & Street Paving

Hy Lee Paving Corporation ....E 804 360-9066
Rockville *(G-12287)*

CONTRACTORS: Hydronics Heating

Nova Green Energy LLC.....................G...... 571 210-0589
Falls Church *(G-4847)*

CONTRACTORS: Indl Building Renovation, Remodeling & Repair

Soc LLC ....F 757 857-6400
Norfolk *(G-9729)*
True Steel LLC ....G...... 540 680-2906
Charlottesville *(G-2896)*

CONTRACTORS: Kitchen Cabinet Installation

Montgomery Cabinetry.......................G...... 540 721-7000
Wirtz *(G-15616)*

CONTRACTORS: Lighting Syst

Bas Control Systems LLC..................G...... 804 569-2473
Mechanicsville *(G-8606)*
Zenta Corporation.............................G...... 276 930-1500
Woolwine *(G-15870)*

CONTRACTORS: Lightweight Steel Framing Installation

P & G Interiors Inc ....E 540 985-3064
Roanoke *(G-11980)*
Richard Evans ....G...... 540 774-1905
Roanoke *(G-11995)*

CONTRACTORS: Machinery Installation

Foley Material Handling Co Inc...........D 804 798-1343
Ashland *(G-1419)*

CONTRACTORS: Marble Installation, Interior

Capitol Granite LLC ....E 804 379-2641
Midlothian *(G-8790)*
Sky Marble & Granite Inc...................F 571 926-8085
Sterling *(G-13510)*

CONTRACTORS: Marble Masonry, Exterior

Stuart-Dean Co Inc...........................D 703 578-1885
Falls Church *(G-4878)*

CONTRACTORS: Mechanical

Hampton Roads Sheet Metal Inc ....G...... 757 543-6009
Virginia Beach *(G-14500)*
Riddleberger Brothers Inc..................B 540 434-1731
Mount Crawford *(G-9058)*
Riggins Company LLC ....D 757 826-0525
Hampton *(G-6228)*

CONTRACTORS: Oil & Gas Aerial Geophysical Exploration Svcs

Tomb Geophysics LLC ....G...... 571 733-0930
Woodbridge *(G-15823)*

CONTRACTORS: Oil & Gas Field Fire Fighting Svcs

Rva Firestopping LLC ....G...... 804 972-1301
Richmond *(G-11751)*

CONTRACTORS: Oil & Gas Field Geological Exploration Svcs

Geo Enterprise Inc ....G...... 703 594-3816
Nokesville *(G-9393)*
William G Sexton..............................G...... 276 988-9012
North Tazewell *(G-10111)*

CONTRACTORS: Oil & Gas Field Salt Water Impound/Storing Svc

Dw Saltwater Flies LLC ....G...... 757 874-1859
Newport News (G-9218)

CONTRACTORS: Oil & Gas Well Drilling Svc

Best Value Petroleum Inc ....G...... 703 303-3780
Arlington (G-881)

Exploration Partners LLC....................G...... 434 973-8311
Charlottesville (G-2630)

Glasco Drilling Inc ....G...... 276 964-4117
Cedar Bluff (G-2277)

JWT Well Services Inc ....E 276 835-8793
Nora (G-9408)

Sands 1b LLC ....G...... 757 673-1140
Chesapeake (G-3283)

Virginia Expl & Drlg Co Inc ....G...... 276 597-4449
Vansant (G-13980)

William G Sexton ....G...... 276 988-9012
North Tazewell (G-10111)

CONTRACTORS: Oil & Gas Wells Svcs

Appalachian Prod Svcs Inc ....E 276 619-4880
Clintwood (G-3687)

Excel Well Service Inc ....F 276 498-4360
Rowe (G-12397)

L & D Well Services Inc ....G...... 276 597-7211
Vansant (G-13977)

CONTRACTORS: Oil Field Haulage Svcs

TT & J Hauling.....................................G...... 804 647-0375
Richmond (G-11423)

CONTRACTORS: Oil Field Pipe Testing Svcs

Davidson Plbg & Pipe Svc LLC ....G...... 540 867-0847
Rockingham (G-12246)

CONTRACTORS: Oil/Gas Well Construction, Rpr/Dismantling Svcs

Acoustcal Drywall Slutions LLC ....G...... 703 722-6637
Ashburn (G-1238)

Air & Beyond LLC ....G...... 804 229-9450
North Chesterfield (G-9808)

Albright Recovery & Cnstr LLC ....G...... 276 835-2026
Clinchco (G-3684)

Anatomy Home Inspection Svc ....G...... 703 771-1568
Leesburg (G-7218)

Browns Services ....G...... 540 295-2047
Catlett (G-2265)

Bw Design Build LLC ....G...... 757 504-5052
Yorktown (G-15940)

Construction Solutions Inc ....G...... 757 366-5070
Chesapeake (G-3052)

Creed Apparel ....G...... 804 219-3291
North Chesterfield (G-9853)

David Steele...G...... 757 236-3971
Toano (G-13863)

Detron Realty LLC ....G...... 703 884-6741
Woodbridge (G-15683)

Didc LLC ....G...... 646 684-5861
Danville (G-3984)

Ellington Mechanical Svcs Inc............G...... 703 220-1651
Alexandria (G-456)

Emezro LLC ....G...... 757 327-2318
Hampton (G-6139)

Equipment Repair Services ....G...... 757 449-5867
Virginia Beach (G-14450)

Fbgc JV LLC ....G...... 757 727-9442
Hampton (G-6147)

H & L Brothers Contractors LLC ....G...... 703 856-1915
Gainesville (G-5588)

Hawkeye Inspection Service ....G...... 804 725-9751
Mathews (G-8355)

Hayes Lumber Inspection Svc ....G...... 804 739-0739
Midlothian (G-8826)

Hjk Contracting Inc ....G...... 703 793-8127
Herndon (G-6701)

Jes Construction LLC..........................D 757 558-9909
Virginia Beach (G-14568)

Jewel Holding LLC...............................G...... 202 271-5265
Woodbridge (G-15730)

Jimmy French ....G...... 757 583-2536
Virginia Beach (G-14569)

Kidwell Construction LLC ....G...... 540 296-4173
Bedford (G-1642)

Klm Race LLC......................................G...... 804 594-6187
North Chesterfield (G-9908)

Lawson and Son Cnstr LLC ....G...... 478 258-2478
Yorktown (G-15973)

Litstone Capital LLC ....G...... 703 576-0788
Alexandria (G-262)

Maspaintservice Ltd Lblty Co ....G...... 301 547-1996
Annandale (G-772)

Metropolitan General Contrs ....G...... 703 532-1606
Falls Church (G-4830)

Michael and Thomas Contg LLC ....G...... 919 397-7960
Woodbridge (G-15747)

Mr1 Construction LLC ....G...... 301 748-6078
Manassas (G-7977)

Ondeck Home Solutions LLC ....G...... 757 535-3771
Portsmouth (G-10464)

Partlow Associates Inc ....G...... 703 863-5695
Arlington (G-1100)

Phil Morgan ....G...... 757 455-9475
Norfolk (G-9686)

Protected By Faith Cnstr LLC ....G...... 804 445-6888
Farnham (G-4963)

Sam Home Improvements LLC ....G...... 703 372-6000
Leesburg (G-7341)

Sandhurst-Aec LLC ....G...... 703 533-1413
Falls Church (G-4872)

Sej Property Logistics Co ....G...... 516 499-2549
Crewe (G-3816)

Smith Maintenance Services LLC ....G...... 252 640-5016
Portsmouth (G-10484)

Special Fleet Services Inc ....E 540 433-7727
Harrisonburg (G-6374)

T-K-O Building Incorporated ....G...... 757 324-2306
Virginia Beach (G-14862)

Take-A-Break Home Imprv LLC ....G...... 434 251-4557
Axton (G-1541)

Tequilla Battle......................................G...... 757 769-1595
Hampton (G-6251)

Tim Lacey Builders ....G...... 540 434-3372
Harrisonburg (G-6381)

Under Pressure Services Inc ....G...... 757 254-5996
Virginia Beach (G-14902)

VA Designs and Cnstr LLC..................G...... 757 651-8909
Norfolk (G-9777)

Vanguard Mtgtion Rstration LLC ....G...... 540 769-1881
Roanoke (G-12017)

Weston Solutions Inc ....G...... 757 819-5300
Hampton (G-6272)

CONTRACTORS: On-Site Welding

Adesso Precision Machine Co.............G...... 757 857-5544
Norfolk (G-9421)

Alliance Stl Fabrications Inc ....F 703 631-2355
Manassas Park (G-8187)

B & B Welding & Fabrication ....G...... 540 663-5949
King George (G-7081)

Caldwell Industries Inc ....G...... 703 403-3272
Alexandria (G-428)

Carico Inc ....E 540 373-5983
Fredericksburg (G-5176)

Craft Repair Incorporated ....F 757 838-0721
Hampton (G-6121)

Daniels Certified Welding ....G...... 434 848-4911
Freeman (G-5511)

Daniels Welding and Tires ....G...... 757 566-8446
Toano (G-13862)

Elite Fabrication LLC ....G...... 434 251-2639
Dry Fork (G-4141)

Halifax Machine & Welding Inc ....G...... 434 572-3856
Halifax (G-6049)

Hanover Wldg & Met Fabrication ....G...... 804 550-2272
Ashland (G-1431)

Hillcraft Machine & Welding ....G...... 804 779-2280
Mechanicsville (G-8637)

Industrial Fabricators VA Inc ....D 540 943-5885
Fishersville (G-5005)

Keystone Metal Products Inc...............G...... 540 720-5437
Stafford (G-13162)

Little Enterprises LLC..........................G...... 804 869-8612
Purcellville (G-10667)

Premo Welding ....G...... 757 880-6951
Hampton (G-6218)

Rod & Staff Welding ....G...... 434 392-3090
Farmville (G-4956)

Superior Metal Fabricators ....F 804 236-3266
Richmond (G-11403)

Triple R Welding & Repair Svc ....G...... 540 347-9026
Warrenton (G-15056)

Wards Wldg & Fabrication LLC ....G...... 540 219-1460
Brandy Station (G-1942)

Whitleys Welding Inc ....G...... 804 350-6203
Powhatan (G-10585)

Xtreme Fbrction Pwdr Cting LLC ....G...... 540 327-3020
Winchester (G-15521)

CONTRACTORS: Ornamental Metal Work

Spigner Structural & Miscellan............E 703 625-7572
Berryville (G-1692)

CONTRACTORS: Paint & Wallpaper Stripping

Schunck Rbcca Wlpr Instllation ....G...... 757 301-9922
Virginia Beach (G-14796)

CONTRACTORS: Painting & Wall Covering

Brook Brinders Limited ....G...... 434 845-1231
Lynchburg (G-7661)

Coldens Concepts LLC ....G...... 757 644-9535
Chesapeake (G-3045)

Mills Marine & Ship Repair LLC ....G...... 757 539-0956
Suffolk (G-13744)

CONTRACTORS: Painting, Commercial

Tidal Corrosion Services LLC..............G...... 757 216-4011
Norfolk (G-9751)

CONTRACTORS: Painting, Indl

Suburban Contractors LLC ....E 703 739-5600
Manassas (G-8001)

CONTRACTORS: Painting, Residential

Sherwin-Williams Company ....G...... 804 264-6156
Glen Allen (G-5795)

CONTRACTORS: Painting, Residential, Interior

Sej Property Logistics Co ....G...... 516 499-2549
Crewe (G-3816)

CONTRACTORS: Patio & Deck Construction & Repair

Deck World Inc ....G...... 804 798-9003
Warsaw (G-15062)

Touch Class Construction Corp ....G...... 757 728-3647
Newport News (G-9360)

CONTRACTORS: Pavement Marking

M & R Striping LLC ....G...... 703 201-7162
Broad Run (G-2068)

CONTRACTORS: Pole Cutting

Sellars Logging ....G...... 757 566-0613
Barhamsville (G-1573)

CONTRACTORS: Prefabricated Window & Door Installation

Burgess Snyder Industries Inc ....E 757 490-3131
Virginia Beach (G-14306)

Vinylite Windows Products Inc............E 703 550-7766
Lorton (G-7540)

CONTRACTORS: Pulpwood, Engaged In Cutting

F & P Enterprises Inc ....F 804 561-2784
Amelia Court House (G-657)

Noel I Hull ....G...... 540 396-6225
DOE Hill (G-4115)

Pulpwood and Logging Inc ....G...... 434 736-9440
Keysville (G-7062)

William H Scott ....G...... 804 561-5384
Amelia Court House (G-677)

CONTRACTORS: Roofing

Acrylife Inc..F 276 228-6704
Wytheville (G-15874)

Fred Kinkead ....G...... 540 828-2955
Bridgewater (G-1951)

CONTRACTORS: Roustabout Svcs

Klug Servicing LLC ....G...... 804 310-5866
Mechanicsville (G-8649)

Employee Codes: A=Over 500 employees, B=251-500
C=101-250, D=51-100, E=20-50, F=10-19, G=1-9

2021 Virginia
Industrial Directory

PRODUCT

939

CONTRACTORS: Roustabout Svcs (cont.)

Mooreland Servicing Co LLC .... G 804 644-2000
Richmond *(G-11683)*

Servicing Green Inc .... G 540 459-3812
Edinburg *(G-4312)*

T & P Servicing LLC .... G 276 945-2040
Bluefield *(G-1880)*

CONTRACTORS: Safety & Security Eqpt

Burton Telecom LLC .... G 757 230-6520
Virginia Beach *(G-14307)*

CONTRACTORS: Sandblasting Svc, Building Exteriors

Howdyshells Welding .... G 540 886-1960
Staunton *(G-13267)*

CONTRACTORS: Septic System

Hall Hflin Septic Tank Svc Inc .... G 804 333-3124
Warsaw *(G-15064)*

Turlington Sons Sptic Tank Svc .... G 804 642-9538
Ordinary *(G-10237)*

CONTRACTORS: Sheet Metal Work, NEC

Broadway Metal Works Inc .... E 540 896-7027
Broadway *(G-2086)*

Flippen & Sons Inc .... G 804 233-1461
Richmond *(G-11592)*

Mechanical Designs of Virginia .... E 276 694-7442
Stuart *(G-13625)*

CONTRACTORS: Sheet metal Work, Architectural

Moubray Company .... G 804 435-6334
Kilmarnock *(G-7073)*

CONTRACTORS: Ship Boiler & Tank Cleaning & Repair

La Playa Incorporated Virginia .... C 757 222-1865
Chesapeake *(G-3170)*

CONTRACTORS: Siding

Windows Direct .... G 276 755-5187
Cana *(G-2228)*

CONTRACTORS: Single-family Home General Remodeling

Colonial Rail Systems LLC .... G 804 932-5200
New Kent *(G-9129)*

Impression An Everlasting Inc .... F 804 363-7185
Mechanicsville *(G-8640)*

Loudoun Construction LLC .... G 703 895-7242
Middleburg *(G-8727)*

Sej Property Logistics Co .... G 516 499-2549
Crewe *(G-3816)*

True Steel LLC .... G 540 680-2906
Charlottesville *(G-2896)*

CONTRACTORS: Smoke Stack Installation & Maintenance, Steel

New England Supply Inc .... F 703 372-2689
Springfield *(G-13058)*

CONTRACTORS: Solar Energy Eqpt

Solgreen Solutions LLC .... G 833 765-4733
Alexandria *(G-588)*

CONTRACTORS: Sound Eqpt Installation

Hill Brenton .... G 757 560-9332
Hampton *(G-6167)*

CONTRACTORS: Special Trades, NEC

Aaron D Crouse .... G 757 827-6123
Hampton *(G-6067)*

Dolan Contracting .... G 703 768-9496
Alexandria *(G-192)*

Earlyrisers Inc .... G 757 566-4199
Barhamsville *(G-1570)*

CONTRACTORS: Sprinkler System

Reliable Welding & Fabricators .... F 276 629-2593
Bassett *(G-1589)*

CONTRACTORS: Structural Iron Work, Structural

Liphart Steel Company Inc .... D 804 355-7481
Richmond *(G-11272)*

CONTRACTORS: Structural Steel Erection

Atlantic Metal Products Inc .... E 804 758-4915
Topping *(G-13885)*

Carter Iron and Steel Co .... E 757 826-4559
Hampton *(G-6107)*

Extreme Steel Inc .... D 540 868-9150
Warrenton *(G-15007)*

Extreme Steel Inc .... G 540 868-9150
Winchester *(G-15417)*

Panel Systems Inc .... E 703 910-6285
Woodbridge *(G-15772)*

Riggins Company LLC .... D 757 826-0525
Hampton *(G-6228)*

S A Halac Iron Works Inc .... D 703 406-4766
Sterling *(G-13499)*

Spigner Structural & Miscellan .... E 703 625-7572
Berryville *(G-1692)*

CONTRACTORS: Svc Well Drilling Svcs

Drilling J .... G 804 303-5517
Richmond *(G-11191)*

Hall Hflin Septic Tank Svc Inc .... G 804 333-3124
Warsaw *(G-15064)*

CONTRACTORS: Ventilation & Duct Work

Old Dominion Metal Pdts Inc .... E 804 355-7123
Richmond *(G-11700)*

CONTRACTORS: Water Well Drilling

Boggs Water & Sewage Inc .... E 757 787-4000
Melfa *(G-8708)*

Eastcom Directional Drlg Inc .... G 757 377-3133
Chesapeake *(G-3083)*

Horn Well Drilling Inc Noah .... C 276 935-5902
Oakwood *(G-10168)*

CONTRACTORS: Well Logging Svcs

Brecmo LLC .... G 276 202-7381
Lebanon *(G-7189)*

Schlumberger Technology Corp .... D 540 786-6419
Fredericksburg *(G-5359)*

CONTRACTORS: Well Surveying Svcs

Davis Brianna .... G 703 220-4791
Manassas *(G-8054)*

CONTRACTORS: Window Treatment Installation

First R & R Co Inc .... G 804 737-4400
Highland Springs *(G-6852)*

Opening Protection Svcs LLC .... G 757 222-0730
Virginia Beach *(G-14702)*

CONTRACTORS: Wrecking & Demolition

Dynamite Demolition LLC .... G 571 241-4658
Alexandria *(G-451)*

CONTROL EQPT: Electric

Constrained Optimization Inc .... G 434 944-8564
Forest *(G-5063)*

Elbit Systems Amer - Nght Vsio .... G 540 561-0254
Roanoke *(G-11919)*

Heritage Electrical Corp .... F 804 743-4614
North Chesterfield *(G-9884)*

ITT Corporation .... D 540 362-8000
Roanoke *(G-11944)*

ITT LLC .... G 703 550-2594
Lorton *(G-7498)*

L3harris Technologies Inc .... D 540 563-0371
Roanoke *(G-11950)*

Peraton Inc .... G 719 599-1500
Herndon *(G-6770)*

CONTROL PANELS: Electrical

Automation Control Dist Co LLC .... G 540 797-9892
Salem *(G-12477)*

Dallas Electrical Company Inc .... G 804 798-0002
Ashland *(G-1400)*

Kordusa Inc .... G 540 242-5210
Stafford *(G-13165)*

Shenandoah Control Systems .... G 540 837-1627
Boyce *(G-1912)*

SMC Electrical Products Inc .... E 276 285-3841
Bristol *(G-2033)*

CONTROL RECEIVERS

A-Tech Corporation .... G 703 955-7846
Chantilly *(G-2360)*

CONTROLS & ACCESS: Indl, Electric

Action Digital Inc .... G 804 358-7289
Richmond *(G-11083)*

Cardinal Control Systems Inc .... G 703 437-0437
Reston *(G-10818)*

Electromatics Incorporated .... G 804 798-8318
Ashland *(G-1408)*

General Electric Company .... F 540 387-7000
Salem *(G-12511)*

Pinnacle Control Systems Inc .... G 540 888-4200
Winchester *(G-15460)*

Power Systems & Controls Inc .... D 804 355-2803
Richmond *(G-11328)*

Sunapsys Inc .... F 540 904-6856
Vinton *(G-14185)*

CONTROLS & ACCESS: Motor

Electro-Kinetics Inc .... F 845 887-4930
Charlottesville *(G-2623)*

In Motion Us LLC .... C 540 605-9622
Blacksburg *(G-1745)*

Motion Control Systems Inc .... D 540 731-0540
New River *(G-9151)*

White Collar 4 Hire .... G 804 212-4604
Chesterfield *(G-3541)*

CONTROLS: Electric Motor

Hubbell Industrial Contrls Inc .... C 434 589-8224
Troy *(G-13929)*

Sprecher & Schuh Inc .... F 804 379-6065
North Chesterfield *(G-9989)*

CONTROLS: Environmental

Atarfil Usa Inc .... F 757 386-8676
Suffolk *(G-13672)*

Bwx Technologies Inc .... E 757 595-7982
Newport News *(G-9187)*

Ddc Connections Inc .... G 703 858-0326
Reston *(G-10835)*

Electro-Mechanical Corporation .... B 276 669-4084
Bristol *(G-1975)*

Energytech Solutions LLC .... G 703 269-8172
Reston *(G-10846)*

Highland Environmental Inc .... G 540 392-6067
Riner *(G-11863)*

Pan American Systems Corp .... G 757 468-1926
Virginia Beach *(G-14709)*

Pgf Enterprises LLC .... G 276 956-4308
Ridgeway *(G-11848)*

Sacyr Environment USA LLC .... G 202 361-4568
Arlington *(G-1154)*

Siemens Industry Inc .... D 757 490-6026
Norfolk *(G-9723)*

CONTROLS: Numerical

Intelligent Platforms LLC .... A 434 978-5000
Charlottesville *(G-2647)*

Precision Fabrication LLC .... G 804 210-1613
Gloucester *(G-5858)*

CONTROLS: Relay & Ind

A-Systems Incorporated .... F 434 295-7200
Charlottesville *(G-2720)*

Bwx Technologies Inc .... E 757 595-7982
Newport News *(G-9187)*

Controls Corporation America .... C 757 422-8330
Virginia Beach *(G-14363)*

Eagle Eye Electric .... G 540 672-1673
Orange *(G-10212)*

(G-0000) Company's Geographic Section entry number

Electric Motor and Contg Co ....C 757 487-2121
  Chesapeake *(G-3084)*

Electromotive Inc ....E 703 331-0100
  Manassas *(G-8063)*

Etheridge Electric Inc ....G 804 372-6428
  Powhatan *(G-10544)*

Kollmorgen Corporation ....B 540 633-3536
  Radford *(G-10721)*

Kordusa Inc ....G 540 242-5210
  Stafford *(G-13165)*

Lightronics Inc ....E 757 486-3588
  Virginia Beach *(G-14612)*

Mefcor Incorporated ....G 276 322-5021
  North Tazewell *(G-10103)*

Moog Inc ....G 716 652-2000
  Blacksburg *(G-1764)*

Navy ....G 757 417-4236
  Virginia Beach *(G-14671)*

Navy ....G 202 781-0981
  Woodbridge *(G-15756)*

Nugen Mobility Inc ....G 703 858-0036
  Ashburn *(G-1323)*

Pacific Scientific Company ....F 815 226-3100
  Radford *(G-10733)*

Pan American Systems Corp ....G 757 468-1926
  Virginia Beach *(G-14709)*

Peraton Inc ....C 703 668-6000
  Herndon *(G-6771)*

Power Distribution Pdts Inc ....E 276 646-3296
  Bristol *(G-2030)*

Pretech Solutions Incorporated ....G 757 879-3483
  Williamsburg *(G-15299)*

Rockwell Automation Inc ....D 804 560-6444
  Richmond *(G-11062)*

SMC Electrical Products Inc ....E 276 285-3841
  Bristol *(G-2033)*

Transformer Engineering LLC ....D 216 741-5282
  Wytheville *(G-15920)*

CONTROLS: Thermostats

Guardit Technologies LLC ....G 703 232-1132
  Fairfax Station *(G-4711)*

Systems Research and Mfg Corp ....G 703 765-5827
  Alexandria *(G-594)*

CONTROLS: Thermostats, Exc Built-in

Ltc Enterprises LLC ....G 540 362-7500
  Roanoke *(G-11958)*

CONVERTERS: Data

Multimdal Idntfcation Tech LLC ....G 818 729-1954
  Reston *(G-10905)*

Nsgdatacom Inc ....E 703 464-0151
  Chantilly *(G-2475)*

CONVERTERS: Power, AC to DC

ABB Power Protection LLC ....C 804 236-3300
  Richmond *(G-11079)*

Cozino Enterprise Inc ....G 804 921-1896
  Richmond *(G-11545)*

CONVERTERS: Torque, Exc Auto

Donovan Pat Racing Enterprise ....G 540 829-8396
  Culpeper *(G-3889)*

CONVEYOR SYSTEMS: Belt, General Indl Use

B R Products ....G 804 693-2639
  Gloucester *(G-5836)*

Modu System America LLC ....G 757 250-3413
  Williamsburg *(G-15281)*

Smart Machine Technologies Inc ....D 276 632-9853
  Ridgeway *(G-11853)*

CONVEYOR SYSTEMS: Bucket Type

Joy Global Underground Min LLC ....C 276 322-5454
  Bluefield *(G-1866)*

CONVEYOR SYSTEMS: Bulk Handling

Coperion Corporation ....D 276 228-7717
  Wytheville *(G-15884)*

Industrial Fabricators Inc ....F 540 989-0834
  Roanoke *(G-11938)*

Ryson International Inc ....F 757 898-1530
  Yorktown *(G-15989)*

SE Holdings LLC ....D 434 385-9181
  Forest *(G-5091)*

CONVEYOR SYSTEMS: Pneumatic Tube

Advanced Air Systems Inc ....D 276 666-8829
  Martinsville *(G-8264)*

CONVEYORS & CONVEYING EQPT

888 Brands LLC ....G 757 741-2056
  Williamsburg *(G-15199)*

Alliance Industrial Corp ....E 434 239-2641
  Lynchburg *(G-7638)*

Automated Conveyor Systems Inc ....C 434 385-6699
  Lynchburg *(G-7645)*

Barry-Whmller Cont Systems Inc ....D 434 582-1200
  Lynchburg *(G-7649)*

Cross-Land Conveyors LLC ....G 540 287-9150
  Partlow *(G-10265)*

Flexible Conveyor Systems Inc ....F 804 897-9572
  North Chesterfield *(G-9876)*

GE Fairchild Mining Equipment ....D 540 921-8000
  Glen Lyn *(G-5832)*

Hutchinson Sealing Systems Inc ....F 276 228-6150
  Wytheville *(G-15890)*

Innoveyor Inc ....G 757 485-0500
  Chesapeake *(G-3143)*

Joy Global Underground Min LLC ....C 276 623-2000
  Abingdon *(G-45)*

Maxx Material Systems LLC ....E 757 637-4026
  Hampton *(G-6192)*

Miller Metal Fabricators Inc ....E 540 886-5575
  Staunton *(G-13281)*

Performance Drives Inc ....G 304 327-7725
  Bluefield *(G-1873)*

Precisncntainertechnologies LL ....G 540 425-4756
  Bedford *(G-1652)*

Reliable Welding & Fabricators ....F 276 629-2593
  Bassett *(G-1589)*

Simplimatic Automation LLC ....D 434 385-9181
  Forest *(G-5092)*

Sterling Blower Company ....D 434 316-5310
  Forest *(G-5096)*

Tazz Conveyor Corporation ....F 276 988-4883
  North Tazewell *(G-10108)*

West River Conveyors & McHy Co ....E 276 259-5353
  Oakwood *(G-10171)*

COOKING & FOOD WARMING EQPT: Commercial

Coastal Services & Tech LLC ....F 757 833-0550
  Yorktown *(G-15942)*

Fantabulous Chef Service ....G 804 245-4492
  Richmond *(G-11208)*

My Three Sons Inc ....G 540 662-5927
  Winchester *(G-15453)*

Water King Conditioners ....G 540 667-5821
  Winchester *(G-15505)*

COOKING & FOODWARMING EQPT: Commercial

CEF Enterprises Inc ....G 757 478-4359
  Virginia Beach *(G-14328)*

Southwest Kettle Korn Company ....G 352 201-5664
  Saltville *(G-12592)*

Wolf Equipment Inc ....E 757 596-1660
  Newport News *(G-9380)*

COOKING WARE: Cooking Ware, Porcelain Enameled

Hanson Industries Inc ....G 434 845-9091
  Lynchburg *(G-7728)*

COPPER PRDTS: Smelter, Primary

Mills Marine & Ship Repair LLC ....G 757 539-0956
  Suffolk *(G-13744)*

COPPER: Rolling & Drawing

Cerro Fabricated Products LLC ....D 540 208-1606
  Weyers Cave *(G-15171)*

COPY MACHINES WHOLESALERS

Konica Mnlta Bus Sltons USA In ....C 703 461-8195
  Alexandria *(G-508)*

CORD & TWINE

McAllister Mills Inc ....E 276 773-3114
  Independence *(G-6989)*

CORE WASH OR WAX

Son1c Wax LLC ....G 703 508-8188
  Fairfax Station *(G-4724)*

CORRECTIONAL INSTITUTIONS

Federal Prison Industries ....G 804 733-7881
  North Prince George *(G-10087)*

CORRUGATED PRDTS: Boxes, Partition, Display Items, Sheet/Pad

Westrock Cp LLC ....C 804 843-5416
  West Point *(G-15164)*

COSMETIC PREPARATIONS

Adiva Naturals LLC ....G 804 683-3738
  Richmond *(G-11473)*

All Export Import Usa LLC ....G 571 242-2250
  Mc Lean *(G-8391)*

Amelia Soap and Herb ....G 804 561-5229
  Amelia Court House *(G-650)*

Avon Products Inc ....G ......
  Stephens City *(G-13312)*

Butter of Life LLC ....G 703 507-5298
  Falls Church *(G-4766)*

Cosmetic Essence LLC ....D 540 563-3000
  Roanoke *(G-12073)*

Craving Sensations LLC ....G 757 609-5038
  Portsmouth *(G-10412)*

Ellice Darien LLC ....G 804 677-9145
  Chesterfield *(G-3496)*

Getintoforex LLC ....G 251 591-2181
  Big Stone Gap *(G-1710)*

Hawknad Manufacturing Inds Inc ....G 703 941-0444
  Springfield *(G-13018)*

Kdc US Holding Inc ....C 434 845-7073
  Lynchburg *(G-7750)*

Marie Webb ....G 703 291-5359
  Woodbridge *(G-15743)*

SAI Beauty LLC ....G 703 864-6372
  Chantilly *(G-2489)*

Sweet Relief Inc ....G 703 963-4868
  Sterling *(G-13526)*

COSMETICS & TOILETRIES

Amarveda ....E 276 782-1819
  Marion *(G-8221)*

Aromatherapy Shoppe ....G 757 531-7431
  Virginia Beach *(G-14240)*

Brandimage ....G 703 855-5401
  Herndon *(G-6631)*

Bridgetown LLC ....G 804 741-0648
  Richmond *(G-11133)*

Brodies Naturals LLC ....G 804 507-0542
  Richmond *(G-11136)*

Cosmetics By Makeena ....G 757 737-8402
  Portsmouth *(G-10410)*

Covingtons Scrubs With Love ....G 804 503-8061
  North Chesterfield *(G-9852)*

Delightful Scents ....G 804 245-6999
  Richmond *(G-11560)*

Dr Kings Little Luxuries LLC ....G 434 293-8515
  Keswick *(G-7045)*

Elizabeth Arden Inc ....D 540 444-2408
  Salem *(G-12502)*

Emge Naturals LLC ....G 434 660-6907
  Lynchburg *(G-7703)*

Essential Essences ....G 757 544-0502
  Virginia Beach *(G-14451)*

Final Touch II Mfg LLC ....G 804 389-3899
  North Chesterfield *(G-9873)*

Gaias Gold ....G 804 516-8458
  Walkerton *(G-14971)*

Gidgets Beauty Box LLC ....G 303 859-5914
  Purcellville *(G-10662)*

Gregory Waynette ....G 804 239-0230
  Richmond *(G-11043)*

Jan Tana Inc ....G 540 586-8266
  Goode *(G-5891)*

Le Splendour LLC ....G 703 505-5362
  Centreville *(G-2314)*

Mommas Best Homemade LLC ....G 805 509-5419
  Virginia Beach *(G-14661)*

PRODUCT

Natural Balance Concepts LLC ....G.... 804 693-5382
Gloucester (G-5856)
Naturally Me LLC ....G.... 703 680-3392
Woodbridge (G-15754)
Nokyem Naturals LLC ....G.... 757 218-1794
Hampton (G-6209)
OH So Good Organics LLC ....G.... 703 577-9226
Centreville (G-2326)
Scents By Scales ....G.... 757 234-3380
Newport News (G-9331)
Sephora Inside Jcpenney ....G.... 434 973-7851
Charlottesville (G-2692)
Sun Care Inc ....G.... 703 715-7070
Annandale (G-785)
Sweetbriar Scents LLC ....G.... 757 358-6815
Hampton (G-6246)
Techline Mfg LLC ....G.... 804 986-8285
Midlothian (G-8912)
Tree Naturals Inc ....G.... 804 514-4423
Richmond (G-11793)
Tri-Tech Laboratories LLC ....G.... 434 845-7073
Lynchburg (G-7828)
Uh Roh Muh Inc ....G.... 703 725-1684
Centreville (G-2346)
Valley Scents ....G.... 540 688-8855
Staunton (G-13306)
Viloquinne LLC ....G.... 703 493-8864
Lorton (G-7539)
Virginia Aromatics Ltd Company ....G.... 540 672-2847
Orange (G-10229)
Wade M Marcita ....G.... 804 437-2066
Chesterfield (G-3540)

COSMETICS WHOLESALERS

Simplicity Pure Bath & Bdy LLC..........G.... 540 922-9287
Pearisburg (G-10277)
Sweet Relief Inc ....G.... 703 963-4868
Sterling (G-13526)

COSMETOLOGIST

Official Tee Blanco LLC....................G.... 804 418-0218
North Chesterfield (G-9943)

COSTUME JEWELRY & NOVELTIES: Apparel, Exc Precious Metals

Highland Bears and More.................G.... 757 480-1125
Norfolk (G-9581)
Ileen Shefferman Designs ....G.... 703 821-3261
Mc Lean (G-8464)

COSTUME JEWELRY & NOVELTIES: Bracelets, Exc Precious Metals

Bracelets By G Jaffe Inc..................G.... 434 409-3500
Charlottesville (G-2600)
Magnetic Bracelets and More ....G.... 757 499-1282
Virginia Beach (G-14633)

COSTUME JEWELRY & NOVELTIES: Exc Semi & Precious

Designer Goldsmith Inc.....................G.... 703 777-7661
Leesburg (G-7254)
J&S Fisher LLC ....G.... 540 921-3197
Pearisburg (G-10275)
Jeffrey Gill ....G.... 703 309-7061
Charlottesville (G-2819)

COSTUME JEWELRY & NOVELTIES: Pins, Exc Precious Metals

Klassic Kreatures...........................G.... 703 560-4409
Falls Church (G-4817)

COSTUME JEWELRY STORES

Zoil Jewelry LLC ....G.... 571 340-2256
Herndon (G-6849)

COUGH MEDICINES

Pfizer Inc ....C.... 804 257-2000
Richmond (G-11713)

COUNTER & SINK TOPS

All Points Countertop Inc..................E.... 540 665-3875
Winchester (G-15526)

Arboleda Cabinets Inc....................F...... 804 230-0733
Richmond (G-11487)
Bay Cabinets & Contractors ....G.... 757 934-2236
Suffolk (G-13676)
Builders Cabinet Co Inc ....G.... 804 358-7789
Richmond (G-11138)
Ellis Page Company LLC ....E.... 703 464-9404
Manassas (G-7937)
Innovative Solid Surfaces LLC ....G.... 540 560-0747
Harrisonburg (G-6331)
Joy-Page Company Inc ....F...... 703 464-9404
Manassas (G-7954)
Julian Industries LLC ....G.... 804 755-6888
Ashland (G-1444)
Marble Max ....G.... 703 723-0071
Ashburn (G-1315)
Mid Atlantic Solid Surface ....G.... 540 972-3050
Locust Grove (G-7449)
Natural Stones Inc ....G.... 703 408-8801
Manassas (G-7980)
Topcrafters of Virginia Inc ....G.... 804 353-1797
Richmond (G-11414)
V & P Investment LLC ....F...... 703 365-7835
Manassas (G-8009)

COUNTERS OR COUNTER DISPLAY CASES, WOOD

Fenco Incorporated ....E.... 540 885-7377
Staunton (G-13256)

COUNTING DEVICES: Speedometers

Aae Inc ....G.... 804 427-1111
Powhatan (G-10528)
Speedmter Clbrtion Specialists............G.... 434 821-5374
Evington (G-4384)

COUPLINGS: Hose & Tube, Hydraulic Or Pneumatic

Schrader-Bridgeport Intl Inc ....A.... 434 369-4741
Altavista (G-641)
Valley Supply and Services LLC...........G.... 276 979-4547
North Tazewell (G-10110)

COUPLINGS: Shaft

Parsons Corporation ....D.... 703 558-0036
Arlington (G-1099)
Parsons Corporation ....C.... 703 988-8500
Centreville (G-2327)
Rexnord Industries LLC ....D.... 540 337-3510
Stuarts Draft (G-13658)
Rexnord Industries LLC ....C.... 540 337-3510
Stuarts Draft (G-13659)

COURIER SVCS, AIR: Parcel Delivery, Private

Fk Logistics Usa LLC ....G.... 877 811-8772
Vienna (G-14056)

COVERS & PADS Chair, Made From Purchased Materials

C Cs Linen Plus ....G.... 703 665-0059
Aldie (G-103)

COVERS: Automobile Seat

Camco ....G.... 757 855-5890
Norfolk (G-9474)

COVERS: Automotive, Exc Seat & Tire

Exotic Vehicle Wraps Inc...................G.... 240 320-3335
Sterling (G-13396)
Mumble Wraps LLC ....G.... 571 358-5388
Manassas (G-7978)

COVERS: Slip Made Of Fabric, Plastic, Etc.

Spartan Shower Shoe LLC..................G.... 540 623-6625
Arlington (G-1173)

COVERS: Tire

Emergency Traction Device LLC ....G.... 703 771-1025
Leesburg (G-7267)

CRACKED CASTING REPAIR SVCS

Brown Welding Inc..........................G.... 804 240-3094
North Chesterfield (G-9835)

CRANE & AERIAL LIFT SVCS

Catron Machine & Welding Inc ....G.... 276 783-6826
Marion (G-8223)
Cave Hill Corporation ....E.... 540 289-5051
McGaheysville (G-8584)
Lewis Metal Works Inc ....E.... 434 572-3043
South Boston (G-12779)
Staunton Machine Works Inc ....F...... 540 886-0733
Staunton (G-13298)

CRANES: Indl Plant

Foley Material Handling Co Inc............D.... 804 798-1343
Ashland (G-1419)

CRANES: Indl Truck

Zest ....G.... 757 301-8553
Virginia Beach (G-14958)

CRANES: Locomotive

Cubbage Crane Maintenance..............G.... 804 739-5459
Chesterfield (G-3491)

CRANES: Overhead

Altec Industries Inc ....C.... 540 992-5300
Daleville (G-3938)

CRANKSHAFTS & CAMSHAFTS: Machining

Aci-Strickland LLC ....E.... 804 643-7483
Richmond (G-11470)
Aerospace Components......................G.... 276 686-0123
Rural Retreat (G-12417)
Intuitive Global LLC ....G.... 571 388-6183
Manassas (G-8085)

CRATES: Fruit, Wood Wirebound

Smalley Package Company Inc ....D.... 540 955-2550
Berryville (G-1691)

CRAYONS

Colonial Tailors Chalk ....G.... 850 622-2270
Petersburg (G-10313)
Colonial Tailors Chalk Inc ....G.... 757 291-2445
Petersburg (G-10314)

CRUDE PETROLEUM & NATURAL GAS PRODUCTION

Novec Energy Production ....G.... 434 471-2840
South Boston (G-12785)

CRUDE PETROLEUM & NATURAL GAS PRODUCTION

Associated Asp Partners LLC ....F...... 540 345-8867
Roanoke (G-12035)
Associated Asphalt Tf LLC ....G.... 540 529-9789
Roanoke (G-12037)
Bluestone Industries Inc ....E.... 540 776-7890
Roanoke (G-12051)
Boc Gases ....G.... 540 433-1029
Harrisonburg (G-6297)
Carpenter Co ....C.... 804 359-0800
Richmond (G-11146)
Carpenter Co ....D.... 804 233-0606
Richmond (G-11032)
Cojax Oil and Gas Corporation............G.... 703 216-8606
Arlington (G-914)
Colin K Eagen................................G.... 703 716-7505
Reston (G-10822)
Energy 11 LP ....G.... 804 344-8121
Richmond (G-11576)
Energy Resources 12 LP....................G.... 804 344-8121
Richmond (G-11577)
Field and Sons LLC ....G.... 757 412-0125
Virginia Beach (G-14462)
Gase Energy Inc ....E.... 540 347-2212
Warrenton (G-15020)
Goose Creek Gas LLC ....G.... 703 827-0611
Vienna (G-14061)
Lanier Outdoor Enterprises LLC ....G.... 540 892-5945
Vinton (G-14177)

2021 Virginia
Industrial Directory
(G-0000) Company's Geographic Section entry number

Masters Energy Inc ....E 281 816-9991
  Glen Allen *(G-5768)*
Maury River Oil Company ....G 540 463-2233
  Lexington *(G-7400)*
Shell ....G 276 676-0699
  Abingdon *(G-60)*
Tiango Field Services LLC ....G 804 683-2067
  Glen Allen *(G-5812)*
Tom Wild Petrophysical Svcs ....G 434 978-1269
  Earlysville *(G-4295)*
Trident Oil Corp ....G 434 974-1401
  Free Union *(G-5510)*
Wooton Consulting ....G 804 227-3418
  Bumpass *(G-2173)*

CRUDE PETROLEUM PRODUCTION

BP Investments Ltd ....G 580 795-3364
  Leesburg *(G-7236)*
Emax Oil Company ....G 434 295-4111
  Charlottesville *(G-2624)*
Ernest Beltrami Sr ....G 757 516-8581
  Franklin *(G-5143)*
J and J Energy Holdings ....E 757 963-9763
  Virginia Beach *(G-14557)*
North Ridge ....G 540 825-4275
  Culpeper *(G-3912)*
Rockhill Resources LLC ....G 804 794-6259
  Midlothian *(G-8893)*
Southside Oil ....G 804 590-1684
  Chesterfield *(G-3526)*
Southside Oil Co ....G 804 204-1624
  Richmond *(G-11765)*
Speedway LLC ....G 757 498-4625
  Virginia Beach *(G-14838)*
Speedway LLC ....G 757 599-6250
  Yorktown *(G-15992)*

CRYSTAL GOODS, WHOLESALE

Mya Saray LLC ....G 703 996-8800
  Sterling *(G-13458)*

CRYSTALS & CRYSTAL ASSEMBLIES: Radio

Virginia Semiconductor Inc ....E 540 373-2900
  Fredericksburg *(G-5233)*

CULTURE MEDIA

Appalachian Afrcan Amrcn Cnter.......E 276 546-5144
  Pennington Gap *(G-10293)*
Coty Connections Inc ....G 540 588-0117
  Roanoke *(G-11913)*
Famm Project LLC ....G 757 975-6492
  Newport News *(G-9224)*
Forerunner Federation ....G 757 639-6576
  Norfolk *(G-9558)*
North Media LLC ....G 202 277-4933
  Ashburn *(G-1322)*
Omega Black Incorporated ....G 240 416-1774
  Fredericksburg *(G-5340)*
Sigarchi Media ....G 571 296-5021
  Arlington *(G-1167)*
Solstik ....G 571 348-4277
  Herndon *(G-6812)*

CUPS & PLATES: Foamed Plastics

William L Judd Pot & China Co ....G 540 743-3294
  Luray *(G-7625)*

CURBING: Granite Or Stone

Better Granite Garcia LLC................F 703 624-9912
  Manassas *(G-8038)*

CURTAIN & DRAPERY FIXTURES: Poles, Rods & Rollers

First R & R Co Inc ....G 804 737-4400
  Highland Springs *(G-6852)*
Heidi Yoder ....G 540 432-5598
  Harrisonburg *(G-6327)*
JB Installations Inc ....G 703 403-2119
  Vienna *(G-14074)*
JWB of Roanoke Inc ....F 540 344-7726
  Roanoke *(G-12116)*
Kenney Inc ....G 703 731-9208
  Herndon *(G-6722)*
Lutron Electronics Co Inc ....C 804 752-3300
  Ashland *(G-1455)*

Macs Construction.........................G 571 278-5371
  Centreville *(G-2317)*
Plum Summer LLC ....G 804 519-0009
  Reedville *(G-10766)*
Two Rivers Installation Co ....G 804 366-6869
  Richmond *(G-11798)*
Window Fashion Design ....G 757 253-8813
  Williamsburg *(G-15346)*

CURTAINS & BEDDING: Knit

Mary Elizabeth Burrell ....G 804 677-2855
  Richmond *(G-11670)*

CURTAINS: Window, From Purchased Materials

Five Talents Enterprises LLC...........G 703 986-6721
  Triangle *(G-13892)*
J K Drapery Inc ....F 703 941-3788
  Alexandria *(G-490)*
Kathy Darmofalski ....G 540 885-4759
  Staunton *(G-13272)*

CUSHIONS & PILLOWS

Poshtique ....G 703 404-2825
  Great Falls *(G-5974)*

CUSHIONS & PILLOWS: Bed, From Purchased Materials

Hudson Industries Inc ....D 804 226-1155
  Richmond *(G-11244)*

CUSHIONS: Carpet & Rug, Foamed Plastics

Sheaves Floors LLC ....G 540 234-9080
  Weyers Cave *(G-15176)*

CUSHIONS: Textile, Exc Spring & Carpet

Carolyn West ....G 434 332-5007
  Rustburg *(G-12436)*

CUSTOM COMPOUNDING OF RUBBER MATERIALS

American Phoenix Inc ....E 434 688-0662
  Danville *(G-3954)*

CUT STONE & STONE PRODUCTS

Alberene Soapstone Company ....G 434 831-1051
  Schuyler *(G-12650)*
Anseal Inc ....G 571 642-0680
  Lorton *(G-7462)*
Austinville Limestone Co Inc ....E 276 699-6262
  Austinville *(G-1527)*
Bishop Stone and Met Arts LLC ....G 804 240-1030
  Hanover *(G-6280)*
Bybee Stone Co Inc ....G 812 876-2215
  Fredericksburg *(G-5406)*
Chantilly Crushed Stone Inc ....E 703 471-4411
  Sterling *(G-13369)*
De Carlo Enterprises Inc ....F 703 281-1880
  Vienna *(G-14036)*
E Dillon & Company ....D 276 873-6816
  Swords Creek *(G-13807)*
Elkwood Stone & Mulch LLC ....G 540 829-9273
  Elkwood *(G-4342)*
Fleet Svcs & Installations LLC..........G 757 405-1405
  Portsmouth *(G-10431)*
Granite Countertop Experts LLC ....G 757 826-9316
  Newport News *(G-9238)*
Granite Countertops ....G 703 953-3330
  Chantilly *(G-2430)*
James J Totaro Associates LLC ....G 703 326-9525
  Sterling *(G-13434)*
Jnlk Inc ....G 434 566-1037
  Louisa *(G-7557)*
Lorton Stone LLC ....E 703 923-9440
  Springfield *(G-13044)*
Luck Stone Corporation ....E 540 898-6060
  Fredericksburg *(G-5318)*
Luck Stone Corporation ....G 757 566-8676
  Newport News *(G-9287)*
Luck Stone Corporation ....D 804 784-6300
  Manakin Sabot *(G-7901)*
New Worlds Stone Co Inc ....G 434 831-1051
  Schuyler *(G-12652)*

Ray Painter Small...........................G 804 255-7050
  Chesterfield *(G-3520)*
Stone Terroir Usa LLC ....G 757 754-2434
  Chantilly *(G-2501)*
V & P Investment LLC ....F 703 365-7835
  Manassas *(G-8009)*
V & P Investment LLC ....G 202 631-8596
  Charlottesville *(G-2709)*
Vetsusa II Inc ....E 703 300-9874
  Falls Church *(G-4889)*
Virginia Cast Stone Inc ....F 540 943-9808
  Waynesboro *(G-15143)*
Xteriors Pavers LLC ....G 757 708-5904
  Virginia Beach *(G-14949)*

CUTLERY

Classic Edge LLC ....G 804 794-4256
  Midlothian *(G-8795)*
Edmund Davidson ....G 540 997-5651
  Goshen *(G-5924)*
Meissner Cstm Knives Pens LLC ....G 321 693-2392
  Hampton *(G-6195)*
Palawan Blade LLC ....G 434 294-2065
  New Market *(G-9147)*
R3 Blades LLC ....G 571 234-3068
  Manassas *(G-7993)*
Two Swords Strategies LLC ....G 804 337-3103
  Richmond *(G-11424)*

CUTTING EQPT: Milling

Trinity Construction Svcs Inc ....G 757 455-8660
  Norfolk *(G-9768)*

CUTTING SVC: Paper, Exc Die-Cut

Arrington & Sons Inc ....G 703 368-1462
  Manassas *(G-7911)*

CYCLIC CRUDES & INTERMEDIATES

Branch Botanicals Inc ....G 703 429-4217
  Chantilly *(G-2380)*
Ethyl Corporation ....G 804 788-5000
  Richmond *(G-11580)*
Newmarket Corporation ....D 804 788-5000
  Richmond *(G-11689)*

CYCLO RUBBERS: Synthetic

Ko Synthetics Corp.........................G 540 580-1760
  New Castle *(G-9121)*

CYLINDER & ACTUATORS: Fluid Power

Garvey Precision Machine Inc ....E 757 490-0498
  Hampton *(G-6155)*
Kollmorgen Corporation ....B 540 633-3536
  Radford *(G-10721)*
Sterling Environmental Inc ....G 540 898-5079
  Spotsylvania *(G-12917)*

DAIRY PRDTS STORE: Cheese

Arrowine Inc ....F 703 525-0990
  Arlington *(G-860)*

DAIRY PRDTS STORES

Maryland and Virginia Milk PR..........C 757 245-3857
  Newport News *(G-9292)*
Maryland and Virginia Milk PR..........E 804 524-0959
  South Chesterfield *(G-12814)*

DAIRY PRDTS WHOLESALERS: Fresh

Maryland and Virginia Milk PR..........C 757 245-3857
  Newport News *(G-9292)*
Maryland and Virginia Milk PR..........E 804 524-0959
  South Chesterfield *(G-12814)*

DAIRY PRDTS: Butter

Ausome Foods LLC ....G 703 478-4866
  Falls Church *(G-4752)*
Buf Creamery LLC ....G 434 466-7110
  Manakin Sabot *(G-7896)*
Great Falls Creamery ....G 703 272-7609
  Great Falls *(G-5959)*
La Vache Microcreamery ....G 434 989-6264
  Charlottesville *(G-2655)*
Spreco Creamery ....G 540 529-1581
  Roanoke *(G-12193)*

PRODUCT

Tropq Creamery LLC ....G....... 540 680-0916
  Purcellville *(G-10682)*

DAIRY PRDTS: Custard, Frozen

Mattie S Soft Serve LLC ....G....... 540 560-4550
  Stanley *(G-13233)*

DAIRY PRDTS: Dairy Based Desserts, Frozen

Ms Jos Petite Sweets LLC....................G....... 571 327-9431
  Alexandria *(G-286)*

DAIRY PRDTS: Dietary Supplements, Dairy & Non-Dairy Based

Arms Race Nutrition LLC ....G....... 888 978-2332
  Sterling *(G-13349)*
Awesome Wellness.............................G....... 540 439-0808
  Bealeton *(G-1596)*
Core Nutritionals LLC.........................G....... 888 978-2332
  Sterling *(G-13375)*
Harmony RDS LLC...............................G....... 304 433-2188
  Leesburg *(G-7283)*
Hidemand Supplements LLC ....G....... 757 224-3485
  Hampton *(G-6166)*
JPS Consulting LLC ....G....... 571 334-0859
  Fairfax Station *(G-4714)*
Legion Athletics Inc ....F....... 727 729-1049
  Vienna *(G-14081)*
merica Labz LLC ....G....... 844 445-5335
  Sterling *(G-13453)*
Mf Capital LLC......................................G....... 703 470-8787
  Woodbridge *(G-15746)*
Pearson & Associates ....G....... 757 523-1382
  Virginia Beach *(G-14715)*
Rephidim LLC ....G....... 312 636-6947
  Charlottesville *(G-2683)*
Revival Labs LLC ....G....... 949 351-1660
  Alexandria *(G-572)*
Savory Sun VA LLC ....E....... 540 898-0851
  Fredericksburg *(G-5220)*
Shaklee Authorized Distri ....G....... 276 744-3546
  Independence *(G-6995)*
Sniffaroo Inc ....G....... 941 544-3529
  Fredericksburg *(G-5363)*
Sports Supplements South Inc............G....... 804 379-6410
  North Chesterfield *(G-9988)*
Timeless Touch LLC ....G....... 703 986-0096
  Manassas *(G-8167)*
Vitasecrets USA LLC ....G....... 919 212-1742
  Alexandria *(G-378)*

DAIRY PRDTS: Evaporated Milk

Nestle Usa Inc ....C....... 765 778-6000
  Arlington *(G-1074)*
Nestle Usa Inc ....C....... 757 538-4178
  Suffolk *(G-13750)*

DAIRY PRDTS: Farmers' Cheese

Trident Seafoods Corp ....F....... 540 707-0112
  Bedford *(G-1661)*

DAIRY PRDTS: Frozen Desserts & Novelties

7430 Broken Ridge LLC.......................G....... 571 354-0488
  Fredericksburg *(G-5239)*
Epiphany Inc ....G....... 703 437-3133
  Fairfax *(G-4449)*
Freda Marshall....................................G....... 757 632-1364
  Portsmouth *(G-10433)*
Gregs Fun Foods ....G....... 540 382-6267
  Christiansburg *(G-3592)*
Healthy Snacks Distrs Ltd ....G....... 703 627-8578
  Fairfax Station *(G-4713)*
Just Desserts ....G....... 804 310-5958
  Mechanicsville *(G-8647)*
Sandy Farnham ....G....... 804 310-6171
  Moseley *(G-9047)*
Shenandoahs Pride LLC ....B....... 703 321-9500
  Springfield *(G-13083)*
Splendoras ....F....... 434 296-8555
  Charlottesville *(G-2880)*
Strongtower Inc ....G....... 804 723-8050
  Mechanicsville *(G-8683)*
Sweet Tooth ....G....... 434 760-0047
  Charlottesville *(G-2698)*
Trotter Jamil ....G....... 757 251-8754
  Hampton *(G-6253)*

DAIRY PRDTS: Ice Cream & Ice Milk

Good Humor Ice Cream LLC ....G....... 703 898-5516
  Reston *(G-10861)*

DAIRY PRDTS: Ice Cream, Bulk

Crust & Cream.....................................G....... 804 230-5555
  Richmond *(G-11547)*
La Michoacana III LLC ....G....... 804 275-0011
  North Chesterfield *(G-9911)*
Maola Milk and Ice Cream Co ....D....... 252 638-1131
  Newport News *(G-9289)*
Sweet Catastrophe LLC.......................F....... 434 296-8555
  Charlottesville *(G-2885)*
Tutti Fruitti ....G....... 703 830-0036
  Centreville *(G-2345)*
Uncle Harrys Inc ....G....... 757 426-7056
  Virginia Beach *(G-14901)*
We All Scream ....G....... 804 716-1157
  Richmond *(G-11443)*
Zinga ....G....... 571 291-2475
  Ashburn *(G-1356)*

DAIRY PRDTS: Ice Cream, Packaged, Molded, On Sticks, Etc.

Marc R Stagger ....E....... 703 913-9445
  Springfield *(G-13046)*
Mars Incorporated..............................B....... 703 821-4900
  Mc Lean *(G-8491)*
Moothru LLC.......................................G....... 540 439-6455
  Remington *(G-10770)*
Nightingale Inc ....G....... 804 332-7018
  Henrico *(G-6544)*

DAIRY PRDTS: Milk, Chocolate

Cocoa Mia Inc ....G....... 540 493-4341
  Floyd *(G-5020)*

DAIRY PRDTS: Milk, Condensed & Evaporated

Maryland and Virginia Milk PR.............C....... 757 245-3857
  Newport News *(G-9292)*
Nestle Holdings Inc ....F....... 703 682-4600
  Arlington *(G-1073)*
Nimco Us Inc ....G....... 314 982-3204
  Arlington *(G-1078)*

DAIRY PRDTS: Milk, Fluid

Dean Foods Company ....D....... 804 737-8272
  Sandston *(G-12609)*
Dfa Dairy Brands Fluid LLC ....G....... 540 777-4091
  Roanoke *(G-12078)*
Dfa Dairy Brands Fluid LLC ....G....... 336 714-9032
  Bluefield *(G-1862)*
Dfa Dairy Brands Fluid LLC ....G....... 336 714-9032
  Forest *(G-5066)*
Dfa Dairy Brands Fluid LLC ....G....... 336 714-9032
  South Boston *(G-12761)*
HP Hood LLC ....B....... 540 869-0045
  Winchester *(G-15426)*
Maola Milk and Ice Cream Co ....D....... 252 638-1131
  Newport News *(G-9289)*
Nestle Holdings Inc ....F....... 703 682-4600
  Arlington *(G-1073)*
Shenandoahs Pride LLC ....B....... 703 321-9500
  Springfield *(G-13083)*

DAIRY PRDTS: Milk, Processed, Pasteurized, Homogenized/Btld

Maryland and Virginia Milk PR.............C....... 757 245-3857
  Newport News *(G-9292)*
Maryland and Virginia Milk PR.............E....... 804 524-0959
  South Chesterfield *(G-12814)*
United Dairy Inc ....G....... 540 366-2964
  Roanoke *(G-12212)*
Wwf Operating Company ....B....... 540 434-7328
  Mount Crawford *(G-9063)*

DAIRY PRDTS: Natural Cheese

Locksley Estate Frmstead Chese.........G....... 703 926-4759
  Middleburg *(G-8726)*

DAIRY PRDTS: Processed Cheese

National Bankshares Inc ....G....... 540 552-0890
  Blacksburg *(G-1771)*

DAIRY PRDTS: Yogurt Mix

Ganpat Enterprise Inc.........................G....... 804 763-2405
  Midlothian *(G-8821)*

DAIRY PRDTS: Yogurt, Exc Frozen

Iceberry Inc ....G....... 703 481-0670
  Reston *(G-10866)*
Tutti Frutti Frozen ....G....... 703 440-0010
  Burke *(G-2205)*

DAIRY PRDTS: Yogurt, Frozen

A & W Masonry Specialists ....G....... 757 327-3492
  Hampton *(G-6065)*
Cabrera Family Masonry LLC ....G....... 919 671-7623
  Hampton *(G-6102)*
Cervantes Masonry...............................G....... 804 741-7271
  Henrico *(G-6491)*
Jsc Froyo LLC ....G....... 571 303-0011
  Arlington *(G-1018)*
Yummy In My Tummy Inc ....G....... 703 209-1516
  Leesburg *(G-7382)*

DATA PROCESSING & PREPARATION SVCS

Bartrack Inc ....G....... 717 521-4840
  Rockingham *(G-12241)*
Bigeye Direct Inc ....D....... 703 955-3017
  Herndon *(G-6624)*
Corascloud Inc ....E....... 703 797-1881
  Mc Lean *(G-8410)*
Cougarbearbobcat LLC ....G....... 804 690-8006
  Richmond *(G-11543)*
Dogwood Logic Inc ....G....... 540 557-7689
  Blacksburg *(G-1733)*
Iron Brick Associates LLC ....E....... 703 288-3874
  Sperryville *(G-12878)*
Joint Lab Systems SEC Svcs LLC ......G....... 443 655-9987
  Arlington *(G-1016)*
Keystone Technology LLC....................G....... 540 361-8318
  Fredericksburg *(G-5309)*
Lookingglass Cyber Slution Inc............D....... 703 351-1000
  Reston *(G-10889)*
Machinery Information Systems..............G....... 703 836-9700
  Alexandria *(G-268)*
Smrt Mouth LLC ....G....... 804 363-8863
  Sandston *(G-12634)*

DATA PROCESSING SVCS

Airline Tariff Publishing Co ....B....... 703 661-7400
  Dulles *(G-4191)*

DATABASE INFORMATION RETRIEVAL SVCS

Application Technologies Inc ....G....... 703 644-0506
  Springfield *(G-12949)*
Synteras LLC ....G....... 703 766-6222
  Herndon *(G-6820)*

DECORATIVE WOOD & WOODWORK

Advanced Custom Woodworki ....G....... 804 310-0511
  Charles City *(G-2568)*
Art of Wood ....G....... 703 597-9357
  Sterling *(G-13351)*
Belchers Woodworking ....G....... 540 365-7809
  Ferrum *(G-4970)*
Biltco LLC ....G....... 703 372-5940
  Lorton *(G-7467)*
Burr Fox Specialized Wdwkg ....F....... 276 666-0127
  Martinsville *(G-8273)*
Country Wood Classics ....G....... 804 798-1587
  Ashland *(G-1396)*
Creative Crafty Mom LLC ....G....... 571 206-8570
  Dumfries *(G-4241)*
Criders Finishing Inc ....G....... 703 661-6520
  Ashburn *(G-1260)*
Dimitrios & Co Inc ....G....... 703 368-1757
  Manassas Park *(G-8199)*
Doodadd Shop ....G....... 276 964-2389
  Pounding Mill *(G-10518)*
Driftwood Gallery ....G....... 804 932-3318
  Quinton *(G-10694)*
Ennis Mountain Woods Inc ....G....... 540 471-9171
  Afton *(G-79)*
Heirlooms Furniture LLC.....................G....... 703 652-6094
  Vienna *(G-14062)*
Interpretive Wdwrk Design Inc ....G....... 703 330-6105
  Manassas *(G-7953)*

Ja Designs ....G...... 540 659-2592
  Stafford **(G-13159)**
Jorgensen Woodworking ....G...... 757 312-9663
  Chesapeake **(G-3156)**
Just Woodstuff ....G...... 540 951-2323
  Blacksburg **(G-1748)**
Karl J Protil & Sons Inc ....G...... 540 885-6664
  Staunton **(G-13271)**
LLC Little Bean ....G...... 757 937-1600
  Virginia Beach **(G-14614)**
Marathon Millwork Inc ....G...... 540 743-1721
  Luray **(G-7617)**
Moslow Wood Products Inc ....D...... 804 598-5579
  Powhatan **(G-10561)**
Old Dominion Shaker Boxes ....G...... 703 470-7921
  Manassas **(G-7984)**
Quigley Designs ....G...... 540 484-1133
  Rocky Mount **(G-12349)**
Snows Custom Woodwork ....G...... 540 428-1763
  Marshall **(G-8261)**
St Pierre Inc ....G...... 540 797-3496
  Floyd **(G-5041)**
Strong Oaks Woodshop ....G...... 540 683-2316
  Linden **(G-7433)**
Tidewater Structures ....G...... 757 753-1435
  Virginia Beach **(G-14877)**
Timbertone LLC ....G...... 540 381-9794
  Christiansburg **(G-3613)**
Traditional Iron & Woodworking ....G...... 540 439-6911
  Remington **(G-10774)**
Wilcox Woodworks Inc ....F...... 703 369-3455
  Manassas **(G-8012)**
William Keyser ....G...... 703 243-8777
  Arlington **(G-1219)**
Wood-N-Stuff ....G...... 276 686-6557
  Rural Retreat **(G-12433)**

DEFENSE SYSTEMS & EQPT

Aimex LLC ....F...... 212 631-4277
  Vienna **(G-14006)**
Anchor Defense Inc ....G...... 757 460-3830
  Virginia Beach **(G-14228)**
Ares Self Defense Inc ....G...... 757 561-3538
  Providence Forge **(G-10618)**
Ark Holdings Group Llc ....G...... 202 368-5828
  Woodbridge **(G-15648)**
Ashley Clark Defense LLC ....G...... 703 867-6665
  Ashburn **(G-1243)**
Atlas Defense Platform LLC ....G...... 703 737-6112
  Leesburg **(G-7224)**
Back Bay Defense LLC ....G...... 757 285-6883
  Virginia Beach **(G-14257)**
Blackstone Defense Svcs Corp ....F...... 571 598-2714
  Ashburn **(G-1248)**
Citizens Defense Solutions LLC ....G...... 254 423-1612
  Woodbridge **(G-15671)**
Crespo Urban Defense LLC ....G...... 804 562-7566
  North Chesterfield **(G-9854)**
Cronin Defense Strategies LLC ....G...... 810 625-7060
  Arlington **(G-920)**
Defense Dogs LLC ....G...... 540 895-5611
  Spotsylvania **(G-12887)**
Defense Executives LLC ....G...... 757 638-3678
  Suffolk **(G-13697)**
Defense Group ....G...... 703 633-8300
  Chantilly **(G-2404)**
Defense Information Sys ....G...... 855 401-8554
  Arlington **(G-934)**
Defense Information Tech Inc ....G...... 703 628-0999
  Gainesville **(G-5579)**
Defense Insights LLC ....G...... 703 455-7880
  Fairfax Station **(G-4707)**
Defense Threat ....G...... 703 767-2798
  Fort Belvoir **(G-5114)**
Defense Threat Reductio ....G...... 703 767-4627
  Triangle **(G-13890)**
Defense Threat Reductio ....G...... 703 767-5870
  Annandale **(G-742)**
Defense United States Dept ....G...... 804 292-5642
  Richmond **(G-11558)**
Defenseworx LLC ....G...... 703 568-3295
  Centreville **(G-2302)**
Dominion Defense LLC ....G...... 703 216-7295
  Woodbridge **(G-15684)**
Double Edge Defense LLC ....G...... 540 550-0849
  Winchester **(G-15537)**
Droneshield LLC ....F...... 202 750-4368
  Warrenton **(G-14999)**
Elite Defense Inc ....G...... 703 339-0749
  Lorton **(G-7484)**

Eurest Raytheon Dulles ....G...... 571 250-1024
  Dulles **(G-4200)**
Falcon Defense Service LLC ....G...... 703 395-2007
  Alexandria **(G-203)**
Form III Defense Solutions LLC ....G...... 703 542-7372
  Brambleton **(G-1928)**
Hansen Defense Systems LLC ....G...... 757 389-1683
  Chesapeake **(G-3128)**
Hensoldt Inc ....G...... 703 827-3976
  Vienna **(G-14063)**
Iis Raytheon ....G...... 561 212-2954
  Potomac Falls **(G-10509)**
Interad Limited LLC ....F...... 757 787-7610
  Melfa **(G-8710)**
International Cmmnctns Strtgc ....G...... 703 820-1669
  Arlington **(G-1005)**
International Trade & Tech Inc ....G...... 703 929-0595
  Midland **(G-8758)**
Ius Bello Defense LLC ....G...... 540 720-2571
  Stafford **(G-13155)**
Janes Cyber Defense LLC ....G...... 703 489-1872
  Alexandria **(G-491)**
Janice Research Group ....G...... 703 971-8901
  Alexandria **(G-492)**
Jerry A Kotchka ....G...... 757 721-6782
  Virginia Beach **(G-14567)**
Jnr Defense LLC ....G...... 541 220-6089
  Alexandria **(G-245)**
Lammasu Defense LLC ....G...... 540 229-7027
  Culpeper **(G-3906)**
Lockheed Martin Corporation ....C...... 703 367-2121
  Manassas **(G-7966)**
Mav6 LLC ....E...... 601 619-7722
  Herndon **(G-6744)**
Maverick Cyber-Defense LLC ....G...... 202 725-7663
  Centreville **(G-2319)**
McKean Defense Group LLC ....G...... 540 413-1202
  King George **(G-7102)**
McKean Defense Group LLC ....G...... 703 848-7928
  Sterling **(G-13450)**
Northrop Grumman Corporation ....A...... 540 469-9647
  King George **(G-7104)**
Orbital Sciences Corporation ....B...... 757 824-5619
  Wallops Island **(G-14972)**
Orbital Sciences Corporation ....B...... 703 405-5012
  Dulles **(G-4216)**
Orbital Sciences LLC ....A...... 703 406-5524
  Dulles **(G-4217)**
Pae Avation Technical Svcs LLC ....G...... 864 458-3272
  Arlington **(G-1096)**
Patriot3 Inc ....E...... 540 891-7353
  Fredericksburg **(G-5343)**
Perspecta Svcs & Solutions Inc ....G...... 781 684-4000
  Ashburn **(G-1326)**
Potomac Defense LLC ....G...... 703 253-3441
  Reston **(G-10928)**
Qinetiq US Holdings Inc ....E...... 202 429-6630
  Centreville **(G-2330)**
Raytheon Company ....G...... 757 363-1252
  Virginia Beach **(G-14762)**
Raytheon Company ....G...... 972 638-3173
  Williamsburg **(G-15303)**
Raytheon Company ....E...... 703 661-7252
  Falls Church **(G-4863)**
Raytheon Company ....G...... 310 647-9438
  Chesapeake **(G-3258)**
Raytheon Company ....G...... 703 418-0275
  Arlington **(G-1134)**
Raytheon Company ....G...... 703 418-0275
  Arlington **(G-1135)**
Raytheon Company ....G...... 571 250-1101
  Dulles **(G-4222)**
Raytheon Company ....G...... 757 749-9638
  Yorktown **(G-15987)**
Raytheon Company ....F...... 703 872-3400
  Arlington **(G-1139)**
Raytheon Company ....C...... 540 658-3172
  Arlington **(G-1140)**
Reliadefense LLC ....G...... 571 225-4096
  Sterling **(G-13489)**
Reyco Global LLC ....G...... 719 321-6747
  Fairfax **(G-4541)**
Richmond Defense Firm ....G...... 804 977-0764
  Henrico **(G-6558)**
Sage Defense LLC ....G...... 703 485-5995
  Falls Church **(G-4871)**
Sentinel Self-Defense LLC ....G...... 757 234-2501
  Hampton **(G-6232)**
Sierra Nevada Corporation ....B...... 703 412-1502
  Arlington **(G-1166)**

Spartan Village LLC ....G...... 661 724-6438
  Gainesville **(G-5614)**
Special Tactical Services LLC ....F...... 757 554-0699
  Virginia Beach **(G-14835)**
Sugpiat Defense LLC ....G...... 540 623-3626
  Fredericksburg **(G-5228)**
Torrent Loading Systems LLC ....G...... 434 509-7307
  Lynchburg **(G-7825)**
Triron Defense Services LLC ....G...... 703 472-2458
  Sterling **(G-13538)**
Triton Defense Services LLC ....G...... 703 472-2458
  Sterling **(G-13539)**
Ultra Electronics 3phoenix Inc ....G...... 703 956-6480
  Chantilly **(G-2510)**
United Defense Systems Inc ....G...... 401 304-9100
  Reston **(G-10978)**
Ventura Defense US Corp ....G...... 571 527-1360
  Arlington **(G-1208)**
Virginia Citizens Defense ....G...... 703 944-4845
  Middletown **(G-8748)**
Weapons Analysis LLC ....G...... 540 371-9134
  Fredericksburg **(G-5501)**
X-Com Systems LLC ....E...... 703 390-1087
  Reston **(G-10996)**
Zombie Defense ....G...... 804 972-3991
  Glen Allen **(G-5831)**

DEHUMIDIFIERS: Electric

Universal Dynamics Inc ....G...... 703 490-7000
  Fredericksburg **(G-5384)**

DENTAL EQPT

Dental Equipment Services LLC ....G...... 703 927-1837
  Leesburg **(G-7253)**
Ilumi Sciences Inc ....G...... 703 894-7576
  Chantilly **(G-2440)**
Virginia Dental Sc Inc ....G...... 804 422-1888
  Richmond **(G-11440)**

DENTAL EQPT & SPLYS

Danville Dental Laboratory ....G...... 434 793-2225
  Danville **(G-3977)**
Dof USA Inc ....G...... 888 635-4999
  Chantilly **(G-2409)**
Flexi-Dent Inc ....G...... 804 897-2455
  Midlothian **(G-8819)**
Frogue ....F...... 703 679-7003
  Reston **(G-10854)**
Henry Schein ....G...... 703 883-8031
  Mc Lean **(G-8457)**

DENTAL EQPT & SPLYS: Dental Materials

Pink Dental Laboratory LLC ....G...... 540 728-5987
  Sterling **(G-13470)**

DENTAL EQPT & SPLYS: Enamels

Denis Britto Dr ....G...... 703 230-6784
  Chantilly **(G-2405)**
Dr Banaji Girish DDS PC ....G...... 703 849-1300
  Fairfax **(G-4441)**
John E Hilton ....G...... 540 639-1674
  Radford **(G-10719)**
Steven Alsahi ....G...... 703 369-0099
  Manassas **(G-8162)**
Timothy Breeden ....G...... 804 748-6433
  Chester **(G-3461)**
Wade F Anderson ....G...... 804 358-8204
  Richmond **(G-11817)**

DENTAL EQPT & SPLYS: Hand Pieces & Parts

Vandent Dental Inc ....G...... 757 678-7973
  Eastville **(G-4297)**

DENTAL EQPT & SPLYS: Laboratory

Affordable Care Inc ....G...... 276 928-1427
  Rocky Gap **(G-12304)**

DENTAL EQPT & SPLYS: Teeth, Artificial, Exc In Dental Labs

Contour Healer LLC ....G...... 757 288-6671
  Virginia Beach **(G-14362)**
Dentcore Inc ....E...... 844 292-8023
  Chantilly **(G-2406)**

PRODUCT

DENTAL INSTRUMENT REPAIR SVCS

Virginia Dental Sc Inc ....G..... 804 422-1888
Richmond **(G-11440)**

DENTISTS' OFFICES & CLINICS

Vandent Dental Inc..............................G..... 757 678-7973
Eastville **(G-4297)**

DEODORANTS: Personal

Fleet International Inc C B...................E...... 866 255-6960
Lynchburg **(G-7708)**

DEPARTMENT STORES

Drumsticks Inc ....G..... 804 743-9356
North Chesterfield **(G-9861)**

DEPARTMENT STORES: Country General

Chewning Lumber Company ....E...... 540 895-5158
Spotsylvania **(G-12885)**

DEPTH CHARGE RELEASE MECHANISMS

C Media Company................................G..... 540 339-9626
Roanoke **(G-12059)**
Red Moon Partners LLC.......................G..... 757 240-4305
Hampton **(G-6226)**

DERMATOLOGICALS

Dematology Assoc Virginia P ....G..... 804 549-4030
Glen Allen **(G-5722)**
Skin Ranch and Trade Company ....G..... 757 486-7546
Virginia Beach **(G-14823)**

DERRICKS

Altec Industries ....G..... 804 621-4080
Chester **(G-3385)**

DESIGN SVCS, NEC

Brown & Duncan LLC...........................G..... 832 844-6523
Virginia Beach **(G-14302)**
Milnesville Enterprises LLC.................G..... 540 487-4073
Bridgewater **(G-1955)**
Signmedic LLC....................................G..... 703 919-3381
Triangle **(G-13898)**
Tektonics Design Group LLC................G..... 804 233-5900
Richmond **(G-11786)**

DESIGN SVCS: Commercial & Indl

General Display Company LLC ....G..... 703 335-9292
Manassas **(G-7943)**
Rutherford Controls Intl Corp..............F....... 757 427-1230
Virginia Beach **(G-14786)**

DESIGN SVCS: Computer Integrated Systems

Activu Corporation ....G..... 703 527-4440
Arlington **(G-838)**
Avitech Consulting LLC ....G..... 757 810-2716
Chesapeake **(G-2990)**
Digitized Risk LLC ....G..... 703 662-3510
Ashburn **(G-1271)**
Douglas Stuart LLC ....C..... 571 210-4440
Sterling **(G-13388)**
Enterprize Software LLC ....G..... 571 271-5862
Brambleton **(G-1927)**
Fountainhead Systems Ltd ....G..... 804 320-0527
North Chesterfield **(G-9879)**
General Dynmics One Source LLC ....F....... 703 906-6397
Falls Church **(G-4796)**
Iron Brick Associates LLC ....E...... 703 288-3874
Sperryville **(G-12878)**
J&J Logistics Consulting LLC...............G..... 404 431-3613
Springfield **(G-13027)**
Joint Lab Systems SEC Svcs LLC ....G..... 443 655-9987
Arlington **(G-1016)**
Macro Systems LLC.............................G..... 703 359-9211
Fairfax **(G-4650)**
Mercury Partners Usa LLC ....G..... 757 652-7067
Franktown **(G-5164)**
Ncs Technologies Inc ....C..... 703 743-8500
Gainesville **(G-5600)**
Orion Applied Science Tech LLC..........G..... 571 393-1942
Manassas **(G-8122)**

OSI Maritime Systems Inc ....G..... 877 432-7467
Virginia Beach **(G-14706)**
Rufina Inc...G..... 703 577-2333
Falls Church **(G-4870)**
Teneo Inc ....G..... 703 212-3220
Sterling **(G-13529)**
Titan II Inc ....D..... 757 380-2000
Newport News **(G-9358)**

DETECTION APPARATUS: Electronic/Magnetic Field, Light/Heat

Smiths Detection Inc ....C..... 571 346-3400
Reston **(G-10955)**

DETECTIVE AGENCY

CJ & Associates LLC ....G..... 301 461-2945
Sterling **(G-13370)**

DETECTORS: Water Leak

Coastal Leak Detection ....G..... 757 486-0180
Virginia Beach **(G-14346)**
Walter Hedge ....G..... 757 548-4750
Chesapeake **(G-3370)**

DIAGNOSTIC SUBSTANCES

Alere Inc ....G..... 800 340-4029
Portsmouth **(G-10390)**
Cardiac Diagnostics LLC ....G..... 703 268-5751
Fairfax **(G-4424)**
Global Cell Solutions Inc.....................G..... 434 327-3759
Charlottesville **(G-2804)**
Imol Radiopharmaceuticals LLC ....G..... 434 825-3323
Charlottesville **(G-2814)**
Pgenomex Inc.....................................G..... 703 343-3282
Mc Lean **(G-8527)**

DIAGNOSTIC SUBSTANCES OR AGENTS: Cytology & Histology

Provia Biologics Ltd ....G..... 757 305-9263
Norfolk **(G-9699)**

DIAGNOSTIC SUBSTANCES OR AGENTS: In Vitro

Centaurus Biotech LLC ....G..... 952 210-6881
Chantilly **(G-2388)**
Immunarray Usa Inc............................G..... 804 212-2975
Richmond **(G-11615)**
Invirustech USA Inc ....G..... 703 826-3109
Vienna **(G-14072)**
Rapid Biosciences Inc.........................G..... 713 899-6177
Richmond **(G-11728)**

DIAGNOSTIC SUBSTANCES OR AGENTS: In Vivo

Contravac Inc ....G..... 434 984-9723
Charlottesville **(G-2611)**

DIAGNOSTIC SUBSTANCES OR AGENTS: Microbiology & Virology

Hamamelis Genomics LLC....................G..... 703 939-3480
Alexandria **(G-227)**
Smith River Biologicals.......................G..... 276 930-2369
Ferrum **(G-4981)**

DIAMOND CLOTH, MADE FROM PURCHASED WIRE

Spades & Diamonds Clothing Co..........G..... 804 271-0374
Chesterfield **(G-3527)**

DIAMOND SETTER SVCS

Thesia Inc ....G..... 703 726-8845
Aldie **(G-113)**

DIAPERS: Disposable

Playtex Products LLC..........................G..... 703 866-7621
Springfield **(G-13070)**

DIE SETS: Presses, Metal Stamping

Roto-Die Company Inc.........................B..... 276 952-2026
Meadows of Dan **(G-8593)**

DIES & TOOLS: Special

Btmc Holdings Inc ....G..... 616 794-0100
Christiansburg **(G-3575)**
Carter Tool & Mfg Co Inc.....................G..... 540 387-1778
Salem **(G-12489)**
Die Cast Connections Inc.....................G..... 276 669-5991
Bristol **(G-2016)**
Dimension Tool LLC ....G..... 804 350-9707
Chester **(G-3404)**
Lenzkes Clamping Tools Inc ....F....... 540 381-1533
Christiansburg **(G-3603)**
Live Trendy or Die LLC ....G..... 856 371-7638
Lynchburg **(G-7758)**
Maco Tool Inc ....G..... 989 224-6723
Christiansburg **(G-3604)**
Marion Mold & Tool Inc........................E...... 276 783-6101
Marion **(G-8234)**
Never Say Die Studios LLC ....G..... 478 787-1901
Spotsylvania **(G-12906)**
Precision Tool & Die Inc ....G..... 804 233-8810
Richmond **(G-11723)**
Richmond Tooling Inc ....F....... 804 520-4173
South Chesterfield **(G-12824)**
Star US Precision Industry Ltd ....G..... 804 747-8948
Richmond **(G-11397)**
Suter Machine & Tool ....F....... 540 434-2718
Rockingham **(G-12279)**
Triton Industries Inc............................E...... 757 887-1956
Newport News **(G-9364)**

DIES: Steel Rule

Parkway Stl Rule Ctng Dies Inc ....E...... 540 586-4948
Bedford **(G-1648)**

DIES: Wire Drawing & Straightening

Sanxin Wire Die Inc............................G..... 434 220-0435
Charlottesville **(G-2689)**

DIODES & RECTIFIERS

Raytum Photonics LLC ....G..... 703 831-7809
Sterling **(G-13487)**

DIODES: Light Emitting

Epic Led ....G..... 703 499-4485
Manassas **(G-7939)**
Global Oled Technology LLC.................F....... 703 870-3282
Herndon **(G-6686)**
Greenerbillcom....................................G..... 703 898-5354
Gainesville **(G-5587)**
Iam Energy Incorporated.....................G..... 703 939-5681
Sterling **(G-13425)**
Labrador Technology ....G..... 703 791-7660
Manassas **(G-8097)**
Litesheet Solutions LLC ....G..... 860 213-8311
Forest **(G-5081)**

DIORITE: Crushed & Broken

Luck Stone Corporation ....E...... 434 767-4043
Burkeville **(G-2209)**

DIRECT SELLING ESTABLISHMENTS, NEC

BSC Vntres Acquisition Sub LLC ....C..... 540 563-0888
Roanoke **(G-11898)**

DISASTER SVCS

Be Ready Enterprises LLC....................G..... 540 422-9210
Fredericksburg **(G-5172)**

DISCOUNT DEPARTMENT STORES

I & C Hughes LLC................................G..... 757 544-0502
Virginia Beach **(G-14537)**

DISHWASHING EQPT: Commercial

Scrubs Mobile Cleaning Lc ....G..... 540 254-0478
Roanoke **(G-12179)**

DISPENSING EQPT & PARTS, BEVERAGE: Beer

Draft Doctor.......................................G..... 804 986-6588
Richmond **(G-11568)**

DISPENSING EQPT & PARTS, BEVERAGE: Cold, Exc Coin-Operated

Sestra Systems Inc ....E 703 429-1596
Sterling (G-13505)

DISPENSING EQPT & PARTS, BEVERAGE: Fountain/Other Beverage

Liqui-Box Corporation ....D 804 325-1400
Richmond (G-11658)

DISPLAY FIXTURES: Showcases, Wood, Exc Refrigerated

Miller Manufacturing Co Inc ....D 804 232-4551
Richmond (G-11051)

DISPLAY FIXTURES: Wood

Woodwright Company ....G 540 764-2539
Fredericksburg (G-5504)

DISTILLERS DRIED GRAIN & SOLUBLES

Bondurant Brothers Dist LLC ....G 434 533-3083
Chase City (G-2910)
Falls Church Distillers LLC ....G 703 858-9186
Falls Church (G-4790)

DISTRIBUTORS: Motor Vehicle Engine

Infinity Resources Corporation ....G 830 822-4962
Falls Church (G-4919)

DOCKING SVCS: Ocean Vessels

Eastern Shore Seafood Pdts LLC ....G 757 854-4422
Mappsville (G-8218)

DOCKS: Floating, Wood

Buggs Island Dock Service ....G 434 374-8028
Clarksville (G-3627)
Nva Docks LLC ....G 619 500-1964
Stafford (G-13178)

DOOR & WINDOW REPAIR SVCS

Door Systems Inc ....F 703 490-1800
Woodbridge (G-15685)

DOOR OPERATING SYSTEMS: Electric

Door Systems Inc ....F 703 490-1800
Woodbridge (G-15685)
Stanley Access Tech LLC ....G 804 598-0502
Newport News (G-9346)

DOORS & WINDOWS WHOLESALERS: All Materials

Burgess Snyder Industries Inc ....E 757 490-3131
Virginia Beach (G-14306)

DOORS & WINDOWS: Storm, Metal

Emco Enterprises Inc ....B 540 843-7900
Luray (G-7609)
Lawrence Trnsp Systems Inc ....D 540 966-3797
Roanoke (G-11953)
Storm Protection Services ....G 757 496-8200
Virginia Beach (G-14854)

DOORS: Combination Screen & Storm, Wood

Charles H Snead Co ....G 540 539-5890
Boyce (G-1908)

DOORS: Folding, Plastic Or Plastic Coated Fabric

Aldridge Installations LLC ....G 804 658-1035
Richmond (G-11093)
Crawl Space Door System Inc ....G 757 363-0005
Virginia Beach (G-14370)

DOORS: Garage, Overhead, Metal

Benchmark Doors ....B 540 898-5700
Fredericksburg (G-5173)
Hobbs Door Service ....G 757 436-6529
Virginia Beach (G-14525)

West Garage Doors Inc ....G 434 799-4070
Danville (G-4050)

DOORS: Garage, Overhead, Wood

Hobbs Door Service ....G 757 436-6529
Virginia Beach (G-14525)

DOORS: Glass

Douglas S Huff ....G 540 886-4751
Staunton (G-13253)

DOORS: Louver, Wood

Spec-Trim Mfg Co Inc ....D 804 739-9333
Midlothian (G-8906)

DOORS: Wooden

Cochrans Lumber & Millwork Inc ....E 540 955-4142
Berryville (G-1675)
Custom Woodwork ....G 434 489-6991
Danville (G-3974)
E H Lail Millwork Inc ....F 804 271-1111
North Chesterfield (G-9866)
Jefferson Mllwk & Design Inc ....D 703 260-3370
Sterling (G-13435)
Masonite Corporation ....D 540 778-2211
Stanley (G-13231)
Masonite International Corp ....G 540 665-3083
Winchester (G-15443)
Masonite International Corp ....E 540 778-2211
Stanley (G-13232)
Millwork Supply Inc ....F 540 552-0201
Blacksburg (G-1762)
Randolph-Bundy Incorporated ....E 757 625-2556
Portsmouth (G-10474)
Rt Door Co LLC ....G 540 962-0903
Covington (G-3796)
Steves & Sons Inc ....E 804 226-4034
Sandston (G-12638)
Winchester Woodworking Corp ....D 540 667-1700
Winchester (G-15515)

DOWNSPOUTS: Sheet Metal

Flipclean Corp ....G 804 233-4845
Richmond (G-11591)

DRAINAGE PRDTS: Concrete

Backroad Precast LLC ....G 540 335-5503
Woodstock (G-15848)
River City Wrap LLC ....G 804 914-7325
Midlothian (G-8892)

DRAINING OR PUMPING OF METAL MINES

H & H Mining Company Inc ....G 276 566-2105
Grundy (G-6034)

DRAPERIES & CURTAINS

Bridgewater Drapery Shop ....G 540 828-3312
Bridgewater (G-1950)
Cavan Sales Lo ....G 434 757-1680
La Crosse (G-7141)
Custom Windows ....G 804 262-1621
Henrico (G-6497)
Drapery House Inc ....G 703 669-9622
Leesburg (G-7260)
Elegant Draperies Ltd ....F 804 353-4268
Richmond (G-11200)
Endowed Expressions LLC ....G 804 638-5459
Richmond (G-11203)
Fabric Accents By Emily ....G 540 678-3999
Winchester (G-15540)
Heidi Yoder ....G 540 432-5598
Harrisonburg (G-6327)
Integra Management Group LLC ....F 703 791-2007
Manassas (G-8082)
J W Creations ....G 276 676-3770
Abingdon (G-43)
Jannie J Jones ....G 276 650-3174
Axton (G-1538)
Mary Elizabeth Burrell ....G 804 677-2855
Richmond (G-11670)
Mk Interiors Inc ....G 804 288-2819
Richmond (G-11294)
Red River Interiors LLC ....G 703 987-1698
Centreville (G-2332)
Speciality Group Ltd ....E 804 264-3000
Richmond (G-11767)

TI Associates Inc ....D 757 857-6266
Norfolk (G-9750)

DRAPERIES & DRAPERY FABRICS, COTTON

Imperial Cleaners ....G 757 531-1125
Norfolk (G-9591)
TI Associates Inc ....D 757 857-6266
Norfolk (G-9750)

DRAPERIES: Plastic & Textile, From Purchased Materials

Anthony Corporation ....E 757 490-3613
Virginia Beach (G-14230)
Appalachian Manufacturing ....F 540 825-3522
Culpeper (G-3866)
Creative Decorating ....G 703 643-5556
Woodbridge (G-15674)
K & Z Inc ....G 703 876-1660
Fairfax (G-4488)
Olde Towne Window Works Inc ....E 540 371-6987
Fredericksburg (G-5463)
Shade Mann-Kidwell Corp ....G 804 288-2819
Richmond (G-11378)
Thelmas Interiors Inc ....G 757 855-0280
Norfolk (G-9747)
Virginia Quilting Inc ....C 434 757-1809
La Crosse (G-7152)
Vqc Inc ....C 434 447-5091
South Hill (G-12863)

DRAPERY & UPHOLSTERY STORES: Draperies

K & Z Inc ....G 703 876-1660
Fairfax (G-4488)

DRAPES & DRAPERY FABRICS, FROM MANMADE FIBER

Jose Goncalves Inc ....E 703 528-5272
Arlington (G-1017)

DRESS SHIELDS: Rubber, Vulcanized Or Rubberized Fabric

Velocity Systems LLC ....F 703 707-6280
Dulles (G-4231)

DRILL BITS

Reeds Carbide Saw Service ....F 434 846-6436
Lynchburg (G-7800)

DRILLING MACHINERY & EQPT: Water Well

Trident Tool Inc ....G 540 635-7753
Stephens City (G-13324)

DRILLING MUD COMPOUNDS, CONDITIONERS & ADDITIVES

Certified Environmental Drlg ....G 434 979-0123
Charlottesville (G-2763)

DRILLS & DRILLING EQPT: Mining

Drill Supply of Virginia LLC ....G 540 992-3595
Troutville (G-13909)
HHh Underground LLC ....F 804 365-6905
Glen Allen (G-5743)

DRINKING FOUNTAINS: Mechanically Refrigerated

Chappelle Mechanical Svcs LLC ....G 240 299-3000
Dumfries (G-4239)

DRINKING PLACES: Alcoholic Beverages

Chateau Morrisette Inc ....G 540 593-2865
Floyd (G-5018)
Elks Club 450 ....G 540 434-3673
Harrisonburg (G-6313)

DRIVE CHAINS: Bicycle Or Motorcycle

Browns Sterling Motors Inc ....G 571 390-6900
Sterling (G-13361)

PRODUCT

DRIVES: High Speed Indl, Exc Hydrostatic

G E Fuji Drives Usa Inc...................F 540 387-7000
Salem (G-12509)

DRONES: Target, Used By Ships, Metal

Gyrfalcon Aerial Systems LLC ....G 757 724-1861
Mechanicsville (G-8633)
Uav Communications Inc.....................E 757 271-3428
Newport News (G-9368)

DROP CLOTHS: Fabric

Xymid LLC ....E 804 423-5798
Midlothian (G-8925)
Xymid LLC ....F 804 744-5229
South Chesterfield (G-12829)

DRUG TESTING KITS: Blood & Urine

Ehp ....G 540 667-1815
Winchester (G-15538)

DRUGS & DRUG PROPRIETARIES, WHOLESALE: Patent Medicines

Barr Laboratories Inc..........................D 434 534-8600
Forest (G-5052)

DRUGS & DRUG PROPRIETARIES, WHOLESALE: Pharmaceuticals

Banvera LLC..E 757 599-9643
Newport News (G-9176)

DRUMS: Brake

Precision Components Inc.....................G 540 297-1853
Huddleston (G-6957)

DUCTS: Sheet Metal

Air Metal Corp ....G 804 262-1004
Richmond (G-11091)
American Metal Fabricators LLC...........G 540 834-2400
Fredericksburg (G-5244)
McGill Airflow LLC ....G 804 965-5367
Ashland (G-1461)
Northrop Custom Metal LLC ....G 703 751-7042
Alexandria (G-296)

DUMPSTERS: Garbage

Ground Effects Hauling Inc..................G 757 435-1765
Virginia Beach (G-14494)
Happy Little Dumpsters LLC.................G 540 422-0272
Elkton (G-4327)
Hillco Disposal & Recycl LLC ....G 757 301-9669
Virginia Beach (G-14524)
Junk In My Trunk LLC..........................G 703 753-7505
Haymarket (G-6428)

DYEING & FINISHING: Wool Or Similar Fibers

Appalchian Leicester Longwools..........G 540 639-3077
Hiwassee (G-6909)

EATING PLACES

Anna Lake Winery Inc..........................G 540 895-5085
Spotsylvania (G-12884)
Gallas Foods Inc ....G 703 593-9957
Reston (G-10855)
Hall White Vineyards ....G 434 823-8615
Crozet (G-3836)
Legend Brewing Co ....E 804 232-8871
Richmond (G-11651)
Rebec Vineyards Inc ....G 434 946-5168
Amherst (G-707)
Teds Bulletin ....G 571 313-8961
Reston (G-10970)

EDITING SVCS

Douglas Stuart LLC..............................C 571 210-4440
Sterling (G-13388)
Nutrition Support Services ....G 540 626-3081
Pembroke (G-10282)
Silverchair Scnce + Cmmnctons ....C 434 296-6333
Charlottesville (G-2878)

EDITORIAL SVCS

Communications Concepts Inc.............F 703 643-2200
Springfield (G-12978)
Custom Graphics Inc............................G 540 882-3488
Paeonian Springs (G-10238)

EDUCATIONAL PROGRAMS ADMINISTRATION SVCS

Potomac Intl Advisors LLC ....G 202 460-9001
Ashburn (G-1328)
Rector Visitors of The Univ VA.............G 434 924-9136
Charlottesville (G-2858)
Rector Visitors of The Univ VA.............G 434 924-3124
Charlottesville (G-2860)

EDUCATIONAL SVCS

College and University Educati ....G 540 820-7384
Harrisonburg (G-6302)
Radio Reconnaissance Tech Inc ....G 540 752-7448
Fredericksburg (G-5352)

ELASTIC BRAID & NARROW WOVEN FABRICS

Dee K Enterprises Inc..........................F 540 745-3816
Floyd (G-5023)
Narroflex Inc ....C 276 694-7171
Stuart (G-13626)

ELECTRIC & OTHER SERVICES COMBINED

Local Energy Technologies ....G 717 371-0041
Mc Lean (G-8487)
Universal Powers Inc...........................G 404 997-8732
Richmond (G-11799)

ELECTRIC MOTOR REPAIR SVCS

Anlac LLC ....G 703 370-3500
Alexandria (G-135)
Austin Industrial Services LLC............F 804 232-8940
Richmond (G-11494)
Bi State Coil Winding Inc ....G 276 956-3106
Ridgeway (G-11839)
Cole Electric of Virginia Inc ....G 276 935-7562
Grundy (G-6029)
Dougs Mobile Electric ....G 757 438-6045
Norfolk (G-9532)
Electric Works ....G 540 381-2917
Christiansburg (G-3586)
F & R Electric Inc ....F 276 979-8480
North Tazewell (G-10099)
Industrial Apparatus Repr Inc.............F 540 343-9240
Roanoke (G-11937)
Jims Electric Motor Co Inc...................F 703 550-8624
Lorton (G-7499)
Land Electric Company ....G 757 625-0444
Chesapeake (G-3174)
Lineage Mechanical LLC.......................G 804 687-5649
Henrico (G-6530)
Lloyd Elc Co Harrisonburg Inc.............G 540 433-5335
Harrisonburg (G-6340)
Lloyd Electric Co Inc ....F 540 982-0135
Roanoke (G-12127)
Loudon Street Electric Svcs.................G 540 662-8463
Winchester (G-15553)
Mahoy Electric Service Co Inc.............G 540 977-0035
Blue Ridge (G-1851)
Marion Electric Company ....G 276 783-4765
Marion (G-8233)
Parks Electric Motor Repair ....G 540 389-6911
Salem (G-12553)
Prices Electric Motor Repair ....G 540 896-9451
Timberville (G-13852)
Roanoke Electric Works ....G 540 992-3203
Troutville (G-13916)
S&S Electric Motor Service Inc............G 540 577-7366
Radford (G-10739)
Thompson Electric Motor Svc ....G 434 372-3814
Chase City (G-2917)
Transonic Power Controls & Svc ....G 703 754-8943
Haymarket (G-6451)
Trevor LLC ....G 434 528-3884
Lynchburg (G-7827)
Twin City Motor Exchange Inc ....G 276 326-3606
Bluefield (G-1884)

ELECTRIC SERVICES

Virginia Electric and Power Co.............F 757 558-5459
Chesapeake (G-3360)

ELECTRIC SVCS, NEC Power Transmission

Dominion Energy Inc............................D 804 771-3000
Richmond (G-11187)

ELECTRIC SVCS, NEC: Power Generation

Luminaire Technologies Inc..................G 276 579-2007
Mouth of Wilson (G-9094)
Sun Rnr of Virginia Inc ....G 540 271-3403
Harrisonburg (G-6376)

ELECTRICAL APPARATUS & EQPT WHOLESALERS

American Nexus LLC.............................G 804 405-5443
Richmond (G-11484)
Electrical Mech Resources Inc ....E 804 226-1600
Richmond (G-11197)
Electro-Mechanical Corporation ....B 276 669-4084
Bristol (G-1975)
Georator Corporation ....F 703 368-2101
Manassas (G-7945)
Mitsubishi Chemical Composites..........C 757 548-7850
Chesapeake (G-3208)
Power Systems & Controls Inc.............D 804 355-2803
Richmond (G-11328)
Shore Holders ....F 434 542-4105
Phenix (G-10355)

ELECTRICAL CURRENT CARRYING WIRING DEVICES

Akg Inc ....G 540 574-0760
Harrisonburg (G-6290)
Brantner and Associates Inc ....G 540 825-2111
Culpeper (G-3875)
Datalux Corporation ....D 540 662-1500
Winchester (G-15409)
Ddg Supply Inc ....G 804 730-0118
Mechanicsville (G-8617)
Delta Electronics Inc ....F 703 354-3350
Alexandria (G-445)
Hubbell Incorporated ....E 540 394-2107
Christiansburg (G-3595)
Lightronics Inc ....E 757 486-3588
Virginia Beach (G-14612)
Mefcor Incorporated ....G 276 322-5021
North Tazewell (G-10103)
Mg Corp ....A 757 468-6000
Virginia Beach (G-14648)
Pascor Atlantic Corporation ....E 276 688-2220
Bland (G-1836)
Pemco Corporation...............................D 276 326-2611
Bluefield (G-1872)
Power Distribution Inc ....C 804 737-9880
Richmond (G-11721)
SMC Electrical Products Inc ....E 276 285-3841
Bristol (G-2033)

ELECTRICAL DISCHARGE MACHINING, EDM

Kirintec Inc ....G 571 527-1437
Alexandria (G-253)

ELECTRICAL EQPT & SPLYS

Adam N Robinson ....G 540 489-1513
Rocky Mount (G-12310)
Azz Inc ....E 276 466-5558
Bristol (G-2007)
Bae Systems Holdings Inc ....B 571 461-6000
Falls Church (G-4755)
Brady Contracting Service ....G 703 864-9207
Manassas (G-8042)
Carlen Controls Inc ....G 540 598-0714
Roanoke (G-11904)
Cobehn Inc ....G 540 665-0707
Winchester (G-15404)
Comsaco Inc ....E 757 466-9188
Norfolk (G-9501)
Decor Lighting & Elec Co ....G 540 320-8382
Pulaski (G-10634)
E L Schneider ....G 703 855-1925
Chantilly (G-2532)
Exide Technologies ....G 678 566-9000
Midlothian (G-8816)

Exide Technologies LLC ....E 434 975-6001
Charlottesville (G-2629)
Federal Equipment Company ....G 757 493-0404
Chesapeake (G-3099)
I4c Innovations LLC............................E 703 488-6100
Chantilly (G-2439)
Icaros Inc ....F 301 637-4324
Fairfax (G-4631)
Isomet Corporation ....E 703 321-8301
Manassas (G-8087)
Jk Electric Company...........................G 703 378-7477
Chantilly (G-2450)
K C Supply Corp ....G 540 222-2932
Brandy Station (G-1940)
Keo-Corp LLC ....G 636 515-5549
New Kent (G-9135)
L & M Electric and Plbg LLC ....F 703 768-2222
Alexandria (G-512)
Mar-Bal Inc ....C 540 674-5320
Dublin (G-4165)
Mark Electric Inc ....G 804 749-4151
Rockville (G-12291)
Mg Corp ....A 757 468-6000
Virginia Beach (G-14648)
Moog Inc ....C 540 552-3011
Blacksburg (G-1768)
Pemco Corporation ....D 276 326-2611
Bluefield (G-1872)
Qrc LLC ....E 540 446-2270
Fredericksburg (G-5216)
Real Estate Consultants ....G 949 212-1366
Fairfax (G-4668)
Roseann Combs ....G 757 228-1795
Norfolk (G-9710)
Schneder Elc It Mssion Crtcal ....B 703 968-0300
Fairfax (G-4549)
Schneider Automation Inc ....G 804 271-7700
North Chesterfield (G-9972)
Solgreen Solutions LLC ....G 833 765-4733
Alexandria (G-588)
Sparks Electric ....G 540 967-0436
Louisa (G-7568)
System Innovations Inc......................F 540 373-2374
Fredericksburg (G-5491)
Tactical Micro ....G 540 907-0091
Fredericksburg (G-5375)
Taurus Technologies Inc ....G 757 873-2700
Yorktown (G-15995)
Tidewater Auto Elec Svcs II ....G 757 523-5656
Chesapeake (G-3337)
Uma Inc ....E 540 879-2040
Dayton (G-4067)
Universal Powers Inc ....G 404 997-8732
Richmond (G-11799)
We Sullivan Co ....G 804 273-0905
Richmond (G-11444)
Woodworth Virginia LLC ....G 804 412-0206
Ashland (G-1513)
Wythe Power Equipment Co Inc ....E 276 228-7371
Wytheville (G-15927)

ELECTRICAL EQPT FOR ENGINES

A 1 Smart Start Inc ....G 276 644-3045
Bristol (G-1963)
Aavera Engineering LLc ....G 434 922-7525
Monroe (G-8986)
Draeger Safety Diagnostics Inc ....G 804 768-4294
Chester (G-3407)
Electromotive Inc ....E 703 331-0100
Manassas (G-8063)
Generator Interlock Tech LLC ....G 804 726-2448
Richmond (G-11217)
Mechanx Corp ....G 703 698-7680
Falls Church (G-4828)

ELECTRICAL EQPT REPAIR & MAINTENANCE

Craft Industrial Incorporated ....E 757 825-1195
Hampton (G-6118)
Industrial Machine Works Inc ....E 540 949-6115
Waynesboro (G-15116)
Konica Mnlta Bus Sltons USA In ....E 703 553-6000
Vienna (G-14079)
Marine Hydraulics Intl LLC ....D 757 545-6400
Norfolk (G-9632)

ELECTRICAL EQPT REPAIR SVCS

Brandervisions ....G 804 744-1705
Midlothian (G-8782)

Comsonics Inc ....D 540 434-5965
Harrisonburg (G-6306)
Kiln Doctor Inc ....G 540 636-6016
Front Royal (G-5540)

ELECTRICAL EQPT: Automotive, NEC

1st Choice Accessories LLC................G 410 615-1578
Sterling (G-13336)
Atlantic Research Corporation ....C 540 854-2000
Culpeper (G-3869)
Atlantic Research Corporation ....A 703 754-5000
Gainesville (G-5571)
Autoinstruments Corp ....G 276 647-5550
Martinsville (G-8268)
Draeger Safety Diagnostics Inc ....G 757 819-7471
Chesapeake (G-3074)
Nuline ....G 757 425-3213
Virginia Beach (G-14688)
Potomac Altrntor Btry Spclists ....G 804 224-2384
Colonial Beach (G-3726)
Research Service Bureau LLC..............G 703 593-7507
Herndon (G-6787)
Sanskey LLC ....G 703 454-0703
Ashburn (G-1331)
World Wide Automotive LLC ....E 540 667-9100
Winchester (G-15518)

ELECTRICAL GOODS, WHOLESALE: Batteries, Storage, Indl

East Penn Manufacturing Co ....E 804 798-1771
Ashland (G-1407)

ELECTRICAL GOODS, WHOLESALE: Cable Conduit

Allspark Industrial LLC......................G 804 977-2732
Richmond (G-11483)

ELECTRICAL GOODS, WHOLESALE: Electronic Parts

Aero International LLC ....G 571 203-8360
Alexandria (G-121)

ELECTRICAL GOODS, WHOLESALE: Fire Alarm Systems

Cornerstone Tech Solutions Inc ....G 540 477-2180
Mount Jackson (G-9068)

ELECTRICAL GOODS, WHOLESALE: Intercommunication Eqpt

1st Signage and Lighting LLC ....G 276 229-4200
Woolwine (G-15863)

ELECTRICAL GOODS, WHOLESALE: Light Bulbs & Related Splys

Electro-Luminx Lighting Corp ....G 804 355-1692
Richmond (G-11198)

ELECTRICAL GOODS, WHOLESALE: Lighting Fixtures, Comm & Indl

Zenta Corporation ....G 276 930-1500
Woolwine (G-15870)

ELECTRICAL GOODS, WHOLESALE: Motor Ctrls, Starters & Relays

Electric Motor and Contg Co ....C 757 487-2121
Chesapeake (G-3084)

ELECTRICAL GOODS, WHOLESALE: Motors

Case-Polytech Inc ....G 804 752-3500
Ashland (G-1386)
Jims Electric Motor Co Inc ....F 703 550-8624
Lorton (G-7499)
Lloyd Electric Co Inc ....F 540 982-0135
Roanoke (G-12127)

ELECTRICAL GOODS, WHOLESALE: Receptacles

American Hands LLC ....G 804 349-8974
Powhatan (G-10530)

ELECTRICAL GOODS, WHOLESALE: Signaling, Eqpt

Rga LLC ....F 804 794-1592
Powhatan (G-10571)

ELECTRICAL GOODS, WHOLESALE: Switchgear

Edge McS LLC ....G 804 379-6772
Midlothian (G-8813)

ELECTRICAL GOODS, WHOLESALE: Transformers

Schaffner Mtc LLC ....D 276 228-7943
Wytheville (G-15912)

ELECTRICAL INDL APPARATUS, NEC

Ampurage ....G 757 632-8232
Virginia Beach (G-14225)
Comprhnsive Enrgy Slutions Inc ....G 434 989-2547
Barboursville (G-1560)
Nrd LLC ....G 540 362-1097
Roanoke (G-11976)

ELECTRICAL MEASURING INSTRUMENT REPAIR & CALIBRATION SVCS

Industrial Control Systems Inc ....E 804 737-1700
Sandston (G-12620)

ELECTRICAL SPLYS

Rollins Oma Sue ....G 757 449-6371
Virginia Beach (G-14778)

ELECTROMEDICAL EQPT

Alr Technologies Inc ....G 804 554-3500
North Chesterfield (G-10016)
Aretech LLC ....G 571 292-8889
Ashburn (G-1242)
Bonde Innovation LLC ....G 434 951-0444
Charlottesville (G-2746)
Electrovita LLC ....G 703 447-7290
Vienna (G-14045)
Farbes LLC ....G 240 426-9680
Alexandria (G-460)
Iviz Ltd ....G 877 290-4911
Stafford (G-13156)
Ivwatch LLC ....E 855 489-2824
Newport News (G-9262)
Rivanna Medical LLC ....G 828 612-8191
Charlottesville (G-2863)
Thermal Gradient Inc ....G 585 425-3338
Williamsburg (G-15324)
Uma Inc ....E 540 879-2040
Dayton (G-4067)
Voltmed Inc ....G 443 799-3072
Blacksburg (G-1805)
Xyken LLC ....G 703 288-1601
Mc Lean (G-8582)

ELECTRON BEAM: Cutting, Forming, Welding

Electron Technologies Inc ....G 703 818-9400
Chantilly (G-2416)

ELECTRON TUBES

Cynthia Kriparos ....G 757 818-3441
Chesapeake (G-3060)
Noble-Met LLC ....C 540 389-7860
Salem (G-12545)
Red Geranium Inc ....G 757 645-3421
Williamsburg (G-15304)

ELECTRONIC COMPONENTS

Benny Babb ....G 276 995-2658
Fort Blackmore (G-5121)
CP Films Inc ....G 276 632-4991
Martinsville (G-8277)
E C A ....G 703 234-4142
Reston (G-10845)
Gemtek Electronic Compone ....G 603 218-3902
Mattaponi (G-8359)
Katz Hadrian ....G 202 942-5707
Mc Lean (G-8478)

PRODUCT

Mary Kay Inc ....G...... 770 497-8800
  Mount Solon (G-9088)
Mevatec Corp ....G...... 703 583-9287
  Woodbridge (G-15745)
Mevatec Corp ....G...... 631 261-7000
  Springfield (G-13049)
Moog Components Group ....G...... 540 443-4699
  Blacksburg (G-1763)
Retarded Mobile Sound & Vision ....G...... 804 437-7633
  Richmond (G-11733)
Senseware ....G...... 703 975-2919
  Centreville (G-2339)
Steep LLC ....G...... 571 271-5690
  Mc Lean (G-8559)

ELECTRONIC DEVICES: Solid State, NEC

Troy Patrick ....G...... 703 507-4914
  Alexandria (G-370)

ELECTRONIC EQPT REPAIR SVCS

Konica Mnlta Bus Sltons USA In ....C...... 703 461-8195
  Alexandria (G-508)
Minequest Inc ....E...... 276 963-6463
  Cedar Bluff (G-2282)

ELECTRONIC LOADS & POWER SPLYS

Nova Power Solutions Inc ....G...... 703 657-0122
  Sterling (G-13462)
Pemco Corporation ....D...... 276 326-2611
  Bluefield (G-1872)
Pogotec Inc ....G...... 904 501-5309
  Roanoke (G-11988)
Venomous Scents & Novelties ....G...... 434 660-1164
  Lynchburg (G-7832)
Xp Power ....G...... 540 552-0432
  Blacksburg (G-1808)

ELECTRONIC PARTS & EQPT WHOLESALERS

Dkl International Inc ....G...... 703 938-6700
  Reston (G-10842)
E C A ....G...... 703 234-4142
  Reston (G-10845)
Elekon Industries USA Inc ....E...... 757 766-1500
  Hampton (G-6136)
Ericsson Inc ....G...... 434 528-7000
  Lynchburg (G-7705)
Isotemp Research Inc ....G...... 434 295-3101
  Charlottesville (G-2815)

ELECTRONIC SECRETARIES

Moaz Marwa ....G...... 571 225-4743
  Alexandria (G-278)

ELECTRONIC SHOPPING

Neevarpt Productions LLC ....G...... 571 549-1169
  Manassas (G-7982)
Windryder Inc ....G...... 540 545-8851
  Winchester (G-15516)

ELECTRONIC TRAINING DEVICES

Bagira Systems USA LLC ....G...... 571 278-1989
  Leesburg (G-7226)
Cabling Systems Inc ....G...... 540 439-0101
  Sumerduck (G-13790)
Drs Leonardo Inc ....C...... 703 416-8000
  Arlington (G-944)

ELECTROPLATING & PLATING SVC

Industrial Machine Works Inc ....E...... 540 949-6115
  Waynesboro (G-15116)

ELEMENTARY & SECONDARY SCHOOLS, SPECIAL EDUCATION

4 Shores Trnsprting Lgstix LLC ......G...... 804 319-6247
  Richmond (G-11074)

ELEVATORS & EQPT

Elevating Eqp Insptn Svc LLC ....F 800 346-0287
  Bedford (G-1634)
Elevative Networks LLC ....G...... 703 226-3419
  Vienna (G-14046)

ELEVATORS: Stair, Motor Powered

Christopher Hawkins ....G...... 540 361-1679
  Fredericksburg (G-5178)

EMBALMING FLUID

Virginia Embalming Company Inc ....G...... 540 334-1150
  Rocky Mount (G-12359)

EMBLEMS: Embroidered

Doris Anderson ....G...... 877 869-1543
  Poquoson (G-10369)
Dull Inc Dolan & Norma ....F 703 490-0337
  Woodbridge (G-15687)
Eleven West Inc ....E...... 540 639-9319
  Fairlawn (G-4736)
Hometown Creations ....G...... 434 237-2364
  Lynchburg (G-7736)
Love Those Tz LLC ....G...... 757 897-0238
  Virginia Beach (G-14625)
Rio Graphics Inc ....G...... 757 467-9207
  Virginia Beach (G-14775)
Scottcraft Monogramming ....G...... 703 971-0309
  Alexandria (G-580)

EMBOSSING SVC: Paper

Arrington & Sons Inc ....G...... 703 368-1462
  Manassas (G-7911)

EMBROIDERING & ART NEEDLEWORK FOR THE TRADE

13 Stitches LLC ....G...... 804 739-8982
  Chesterfield (G-3471)
A Stitch In Time ....G...... 276 781-2014
  Atkins (G-1515)
A Stitch In Time LLC ....G...... 757 478-4878
  Virginia Beach (G-14201)
According To Plan LLC ....G...... 703 953-1584
  Herndon (G-6603)
Aces Embroidery ....G...... 703 738-4784
  Sterling (G-13338)
Alexander Amir ....G...... 757 714-1802
  Suffolk (G-13665)
American Egle EMB Graphics LLC ......G...... 757 673-8337
  Chesapeake (G-2966)
Artistic Impressions ....G...... 757 923-4254
  Suffolk (G-13671)
At The Point Embroidery LLC ....G...... 804 684-9544
  Gloucester Point (G-5871)
Atlantic Embroidery Works LLC ......G...... 804 282-5027
  Henrico (G-6478)
B & J Embroidery Inc ....G...... 276 646-5631
  Saltville (G-12584)
Beths Embroidery LLC ....G...... 434 933-8652
  Gladstone (G-5681)
BJ Embroidery & Designs ....G...... 804 605-4749
  Chesterfield (G-3480)
Broken Needle Embroidery ....G...... 276 865-4654
  Haysi (G-6457)
Brooks Stitch & Fold LLC ....G...... 804 367-7979
  Richmond (G-11511)
Bryant Embroidery LLC ....G...... 757 498-3453
  Virginia Beach (G-14303)
Busy BS Embroidery ....G...... 757 819-7869
  Chesapeake (G-3018)
C&K Custom Embroidery & A ....G...... 434 447-2987
  South Hill (G-12845)
Capital Screen Prtg Unlimited ....G...... 703 550-0033
  Lorton (G-7470)
Crafty Stitcher LLC ....G...... 703 855-2736
  Leesburg (G-7248)
Creative Monogramming LLC ....G...... 434 767-4880
  Burkeville (G-2208)
Cross Stitch LLC ....G...... 703 961-1636
  Fairfax (G-4434)
Crouch Petra ....G...... 757 681-0828
  Virginia Beach (G-14373)
D & K Embroidery ....G...... 804 694-4747
  Gloucester (G-5844)
D J R Enterprises Inc ....F 540 639-9386
  Radford (G-10708)
Darlin Monograms LLC ....G...... 757 930-8786
  Newport News (G-9215)
Distinct Impressions ....G...... 434 572-8144
  South Boston (G-12762)
Dptl Inc ....F 703 435-2291
  Herndon (G-6659)

Embellished Embroidery ....G...... 804 926-5785
  Chester (G-3411)
Embrace Embroidery LP ....G...... 757 784-3874
  Lanexa (G-7166)
Embroider Bee ....G...... 757 472-4981
  Virginia Beach (G-14443)
Embroidery -N- Beyond LLC ....G...... 540 972-4333
  Spotsylvania (G-12888)
Embroidery Barnyard ....G...... 804 795-1555
  Richmond (G-11201)
Embroidery By Patty ....G...... 540 597-8173
  Roanoke (G-11920)
Embroidery Criations ....G...... 540 421-5608
  Timberville (G-13848)
Embroidery Express LLC ....G...... 804 458-5999
  Chester (G-3412)
Embroidery Expressons ....G...... 757 255-0713
  Windsor (G-15604)
Embroidery N Beyond LLC ....G...... 757 409-2782
  Virginia Beach (G-14445)
Embroidery Works ....G...... 757 344-8573
  Yorktown (G-15953)
Embroideryville ....G...... 276 768-9727
  Independence (G-6982)
Exclusively Yours Embroidery ....G...... 571 285-2196
  Woodbridge (G-15700)
Eye of Needle Embroidery ....G...... 540 837-2089
  Boyce (G-1909)
Fast Lane Specialties Inc ....G...... 757 784-7474
  West Point (G-15156)
Fresh Printz LLC ....G...... 540 937-3017
  Jeffersonton (G-7012)
Fully Promoted of Alexandria ....G...... 703 575-9003
  Alexandria (G-208)
G&M Embroidery Inc ....G...... 757 482-1935
  Chesapeake (G-3113)
Georgette T Hawkins ....G...... 540 825-8928
  Culpeper (G-3893)
Gryphon Threads LLC ....G...... 707 320-7865
  Norfolk (G-9567)
Harville Entps of Danville VA ....G...... 434 822-2106
  Danville (G-3997)
Heartfelt Stitch Co ....G...... 757 828-6036
  Norfolk (G-9577)
Hickory Embroidery LLC ....G...... 757 482-0873
  Chesapeake (G-3136)
Hickory Ridge Designs Inc ....G...... 888 236-8431
  Martinsville (G-8295)
Huger Embroidery ....G...... 804 304-8808
  Richmond (G-11245)
Hymons Embroidery LLC ....G...... 757 512-6005
  Virginia Beach (G-14535)
In Stitches ....G...... 434 842-2104
  Fork Union (G-5110)
Inspired Embroidery ....G...... 703 409-3375
  Sterling (G-13428)
It Takes A Stitch Custom ....G...... 703 405-6688
  Arlington (G-1012)
Itty Bitty Stitchings LLC ....G...... 540 829-9197
  Culpeper (G-3896)
Itz ME Creations ....G...... 804 519-6023
  Chesterfield (G-3506)
James River Embroidery ....G...... 434 987-9800
  Scottsville (G-12661)
Jbtm Enterprises Inc ....F 540 665-9651
  Winchester (G-15551)
Jean Lee Inc ....G...... 703 630-0276
  Quantico (G-10689)
Joan Fisk ....G...... 540 288-0050
  Stafford (G-13160)
Jonathan Promotions Inc ....G...... 540 891-7700
  Fredericksburg (G-5307)
Js Monogramming ....G...... 804 862-4324
  Petersburg (G-10328)
Kangs Embroidery ....G...... 757 887-5232
  Newport News (G-9273)
Khk Inc ....G...... 540 337-5068
  Stuarts Draft (G-13654)
La Stitchery ....G...... 540 894-9371
  Bumpass (G-2163)
Lance Stitcher ....G...... 443 685-4829
  Greenbackville (G-5995)
Lowe-Go EMB & Designs LLC ....G...... 757 486-0617
  Virginia Beach (G-14626)
Ls Late Embroidery ....G...... 757 639-0647
  Virginia Beach (G-14627)
Mad-Den Embroidery & Gifts ....G...... 757 450-4421
  Virginia Beach (G-14632)
Meesh Monograms ....G...... 757 672-4276
  Virginia Beach (G-14646)

Minnie ME Monograms..........G....... 423 331-1686
Chesapeake *(G-3206)*
Mounir E Shaheen..........G....... 757 723-4445
Hampton *(G-6205)*
Ms Monogram LLC..........G....... 804 502-3551
Midlothian *(G-8863)*
Munchkin Monograms LLC..........G....... 215 970-4375
Alexandria *(G-537)*
Nana Stitches..........G....... 757 689-3767
Virginia Beach *(G-14669)*
No Short Cut..........G....... 757 696-0249
Virginia Beach *(G-14683)*
Oaxaca Embroidery LLC..........G....... 540 463-3808
Lexington *(G-7409)*
Peach Tea Monograms..........G....... 703 973-9977
Vienna *(G-14109)*
Peggy Sues Advertising Inc..........G....... 276 530-7790
Conaway *(G-3754)*
Premier Embroidery and Design..........G....... 434 242-2801
Palmyra *(G-10256)*
Presto Embroidery LLC..........G....... 571 223-0160
Broadlands *(G-2080)*
Q Stitched LLC..........G....... 757 621-6025
Richmond *(G-11342)*
Rag Bag Aero Works Inc..........G....... 540 967-5400
Louisa *(G-7564)*
Sams Monograms..........G....... 703 866-4400
Annandale *(G-781)*
Sayre Enterprises Inc..........C....... 540 291-3808
Naturl BR STA *(G-9112)*
Schmidt Jayme..........G....... 540 961-1792
Blacksburg *(G-1787)*
Sew and Tell Embroidery..........G....... 757 641-1227
Wakefield *(G-14970)*
Sewcial Stitch..........G....... 813 786-2966
Haymarket *(G-6443)*
Sherrie & Scott Embroidery..........G....... 804 271-2024
North Chesterfield *(G-9978)*
Shirleys Stitches LLC..........G....... 804 370-7182
Powhatan *(G-10574)*
Sinister Stitch Custom Leather..........G....... 757 636-9954
Virginia Beach *(G-14820)*
Sisters In Stitches LLC..........G....... 757 660-0871
Hayes *(G-6410)*
Snips of Virginia Beach Inc..........F....... 888 634-5008
Norfolk *(G-9727)*
Sounds Greek Inc..........G....... 757 548-0062
Chesapeake *(G-3300)*
Southern Accent Embroidery..........G....... 843 991-4910
Midlothian *(G-8905)*
Sport Shack Inc..........G....... 540 372-3719
Fredericksburg *(G-5487)*
Stitch Doctor..........G....... 540 330-1234
Roanoke *(G-12004)*
Stitch Makers Embroidery..........G....... 804 794-4523
Midlothian *(G-8910)*
Stitchdotpro LLC..........G....... 540 777-0002
Roanoke *(G-12005)*
Stitched Loop LLC..........G....... 678 467-1973
Chesapeake *(G-3313)*
Stitched Mmries By Shannon LLC..........G....... 540 872-9779
Bumpass *(G-2168)*
Stitched With Love LLC..........G....... 757 285-6980
Virginia Beach *(G-14850)*
Stitches & Bows..........G....... 678 876-1715
Front Royal *(G-5556)*
Stitches Corporate & Custom Em..........G....... 434 374-5111
Clarksville *(G-3635)*
Sunshine Sewing..........G....... 276 628-2478
Abingdon *(G-63)*
T & T Sporting Goods..........G....... 276 228-5286
Wytheville *(G-15917)*
Taylor Made Custom Embroidery..........G....... 434 636-0660
La Crosse *(G-7151)*
Threadlines Inc..........G....... 757 898-8355
Grafton *(G-5932)*
Total Stitch Embroidery Inc..........G....... 804 275-4853
North Chesterfield *(G-10003)*
Track Patch 1 Corporation..........G....... 757 609-2842
Chesapeake *(G-3347)*
Triple Stitch Designs LLC..........G....... 757 376-2666
Virginia Beach *(G-14894)*
Upon A Once Stitch LLC..........G....... 757 562-1900
Franklin *(G-5160)*
Vienna Custom Embroidery LLC..........G....... 703 887-1254
Vienna *(G-14152)*
Wendys Embroidery..........G....... 757 685-0414
Virginia Beach *(G-14933)*
What Heck..........G....... 757 343-4058
Virginia Beach *(G-14934)*
Willow Stitch LLC..........G....... 804 761-5967
Tappahannock *(G-13826)*
Ww Monograms LLC..........G....... 540 687-6510
Middleburg *(G-8735)*

EMBROIDERING SVC

A Hope Skip and A Stitch LLC..........G....... 804 684-5750
Gloucester *(G-5834)*
Alethia Embroidery..........G....... 540 710-6560
Fredericksburg *(G-5242)*
Alphabet Soup..........G....... 757 569-0110
Franklin *(G-5138)*
American Logo Corp..........G....... 703 356-4709
Falls Church *(G-4747)*
Ampak Sportswear Inc..........G....... 703 550-1300
Lorton *(G-7461)*
Atlantic EMB & Design LLC..........G....... 757 253-1010
Sandston *(G-12608)*
Blue Ridge Marketing & EMB..........G....... 276 223-0337
Wytheville *(G-15878)*
Cabin Creations..........G....... 804 529-7245
Callao *(G-2215)*
Coastal Threads Inc..........G....... 757 495-2677
Virginia Beach *(G-14349)*
Consurgo Group Inc..........F....... 757 373-1717
Virginia Beach *(G-14361)*
Corporate Designs..........G....... 276 676-9048
Abingdon *(G-26)*
Custom EMB & Screen Prtg..........G....... 434 239-2144
Lynchburg *(G-7690)*
Custom Embroidery & Design..........G....... 804 530-5238
Chester *(G-3400)*
Custom Embroidery & Designs..........G....... 757 474-1523
Virginia Beach *(G-14377)*
Custom Logos..........G....... 804 967-0111
Richmond *(G-11173)*
Dyeing To Stitch..........G....... 757 366-8740
Virginia Beach *(G-14420)*
East Coast Branding LLC..........G....... 757 754-0771
Virginia Beach *(G-14428)*
East To West EMB & Design..........G....... 703 335-2397
Manassas *(G-7935)*
Elizabeth Ballard-Spitzer..........G....... 757 723-1194
Hampton *(G-6138)*
Elizabeth Urban..........G....... 757 879-1815
Yorktown *(G-15952)*
Elletts Embroidery..........G....... 434 392-2290
Farmville *(G-4939)*
Embroidery Concepts..........G....... 540 387-0517
Salem *(G-12504)*
Embroidery Connection..........G....... 757 566-8859
Williamsburg *(G-15239)*
Embroidery Depot Ltd..........G....... 540 289-5044
Penn Laird *(G-10288)*
Embroidery N Beyond LLC..........G....... 757 962-2105
Virginia Beach *(G-14444)*
Embroidery Works Inc..........G....... 757 868-8840
Yorktown *(G-15954)*
Express Yourself Inc..........G....... 434 757-1099
La Crosse *(G-7144)*
Fancy Stitches..........G....... 804 796-6942
Chesterfield *(G-3499)*
Garnett Embroidery..........G....... 757 925-0569
Suffolk *(G-13713)*
Global Partners Virginia LLC..........G....... 804 744-8112
Midlothian *(G-8822)*
H & R Embroidery LLC..........G....... 804 513-8829
Ashland *(G-1424)*
Im Embroidery..........G....... 757 533-5397
Norfolk *(G-9590)*
Janice Martin-Freeman..........G....... 757 234-0056
Newport News *(G-9267)*
Jovic Embroidery LLC..........G....... 804 748-2598
North Chesterfield *(G-9903)*
Lakeside Embroidery..........G....... 540 719-2600
Moneta *(G-8970)*
Lifes A Stitch Inc..........G....... 804 672-7079
Glen Allen *(G-5762)*
Longs Embroidery..........G....... 540 891-2880
Fredericksburg *(G-5316)*
Maple Hill Embroidery..........G....... 540 336-1967
Winchester *(G-15442)*
Mc Promotions LLC..........G....... 804 386-7073
Midlothian *(G-8855)*
Midnight Embroidery..........G....... 757 463-1692
Virginia Beach *(G-14651)*
Monogram Majik..........G....... 540 389-2269
Salem *(G-12539)*
Monogram Shop..........G....... 434 973-1968
Charlottesville *(G-2662)*
Norton Embroidery Inc..........G....... 540 550-7331
Berryville *(G-1685)*
Nuwave Embroidery..........G....... 540 412-9799
Fredericksburg *(G-5337)*
Pegs Embroidery Inc..........G....... 804 378-2053
Midlothian *(G-8878)*
Red Eagle Creations..........G....... 804 556-2041
Maidens *(G-7892)*
Richs Stitches Inc..........G....... 804 262-3477
Richmond *(G-11364)*
Rocky Top Embroidery & More..........G....... 540 775-9564
King George *(G-7108)*
Rubys Embroidery Gems..........G....... 703 590-7902
Woodbridge *(G-15800)*
Sandy Hobson T/A S H Monograms..........G....... 804 730-7211
Mechanicsville *(G-8674)*
Schmid Embroidery & Design..........G....... 804 737-4141
Sandston *(G-12630)*
Sew My Monogram LLC..........G....... 804 739-2407
Midlothian *(G-8896)*
Shirleys Unf & Alterations LLC..........G....... 434 985-2042
Barboursville *(G-1566)*
Slopers Stitch House..........G....... 703 368-7197
Manassas *(G-8156)*
Spider Embroidery Inc..........G....... 540 955-2347
Winchester *(G-15482)*
Stitching Station..........G....... 703 421-4053
Sterling *(G-13517)*
Stitchworks Inc..........G....... 757 631-0300
Virginia Beach *(G-14851)*
Threads Ink LLC..........G....... 703 221-0819
Dumfries *(G-4260)*
Timeless Stitches Inc..........G....... 804 798-7677
Ashland *(G-1500)*
Tnl Embroidery Inc..........G....... 757 410-2671
Chesapeake *(G-3341)*
Unlimited Embroidery..........G....... 540 745-3909
Floyd *(G-5044)*
Wisdom Clothing Company Inc..........F....... 703 433-0056
Sterling *(G-13561)*

EMBROIDERING SVC: Schiffli Machine

Total Stitch Embroidery Inc..........G....... 804 748-9594
Chester *(G-3462)*

EMBROIDERY ADVERTISING SVCS

Artistic Impressions..........G....... 757 923-4254
Suffolk *(G-13671)*
Erbosol Printing..........G....... 757 325-9986
Hampton *(G-6144)*
Fresh Printz LLC..........G....... 540 937-3017
Jeffersonton *(G-7012)*
Jeannie Jackson Green..........G....... 540 904-6763
Roanoke *(G-12110)*
Leading Edge Screen Printing..........F....... 540 347-5751
Warrenton *(G-15030)*
Silkscreening Unlimited Inc..........G....... 703 385-3212
Fairfax *(G-4554)*
Spring Valley Graphics..........G....... 276 236-4357
Galax *(G-5648)*
Studio One Printing..........G....... 703 430-8884
Sterling *(G-13519)*
Sunshine Sewing..........G....... 276 628-2478
Abingdon *(G-63)*
Whats Your Sign..........G....... 276 632-0576
Martinsville *(G-8353)*

EMBROIDERY KITS

Sayre Enterprises Inc..........G....... 540 291-3800
Buena Vista *(G-2153)*

EMERGENCY ALARMS

Connectedescape LLC..........G....... 443 910-7559
Stafford *(G-13133)*
Convex Corporation..........G....... 703 433-9901
Warrenton *(G-14990)*
Emergency Alert Solutions Grou..........G....... 703 346-4787
Great Falls *(G-5953)*
General Magnetic Sciences Inc..........G....... 571 243-6887
Manassas *(G-7944)*
General Magnetic Sciences Inc..........G....... 571 243-6887
Clifton *(G-3666)*
Johnson Controls..........G....... 804 727-3890
Richmond *(G-11257)*
Johnson Controls..........D....... 757 853-6611
Norfolk *(G-9605)*
Life Protect 24/7 Inc..........G....... 888 864-8403
Norfolk *(G-9618)*

Employee Codes: A=Over 500 employees, B=251-500
C=101-250, D=51-100, E=20-50, F=10-19, G=1-9
2021 Virginia
Industrial Directory
951

OHG Science & Technology LLC..........G...... 434 990-0500
  Barboursville *(G-1565)*

EMPLOYEE LEASING SVCS

Rjm Technologies Inc ....G...... 703 323-6677
  Fairfax *(G-4543)*

EMPLOYMENT AGENCY SVCS

MK Industries Inc ....F...... 757 245-0007
  Newport News *(G-9302)*

ENCODERS: Digital

Kordusa Inc ....G...... 540 242-5210
  Stafford *(G-13165)*
Shoebox Memories ....G...... 703 969-9290
  Fairfax *(G-4699)*

ENGINE PARTS & ACCESS: Internal Combustion

Invista Precision Concepts ....G...... 276 656-0504
  Martinsville *(G-8302)*

ENGINE REBUILDING: Diesel

Valley Rebuilders Co Inc ....G...... 540 342-2108
  Roanoke *(G-12214)*
Western Branch Diesel Inc ....E...... 703 369-5005
  Manassas *(G-8177)*

ENGINE REBUILDING: Gas

Foley Machine ....G...... 276 930-1983
  Stuart *(G-13612)*

ENGINEERING SVCS

Acuity Tech Holdg Co LLC ....G...... 410 290-1411
  Fredericksburg *(G-5167)*
Amentum Services Inc ....C...... 703 418-3020
  Arlington *(G-851)*
American Buildings Company ....C...... 434 757-2220
  La Crosse *(G-7139)*
Atlantic Quality Design Inc ....G...... 540 966-4356
  Fincastle *(G-4992)*
Carbon & Steel LLC ....G...... 757 871-1808
  Toano *(G-13859)*
D-Star Engineering Corporation ....E...... 203 925-7630
  Ashburn *(G-1267)*
Eagle Aviation Tech LLC ....D...... 757 224-6269
  Newport News *(G-9219)*
East Cast Repr Fabrication LLC ....D...... 757 455-9600
  Norfolk *(G-9536)*
Evergreen Design Inc ....G...... 540 984-4653
  Edinburg *(G-4303)*
Framatome Inc ....B...... 434 832-3000
  Lynchburg *(G-7716)*
General Dynmics One Source LLC ......F...... 703 906-6397
  Falls Church *(G-4796)*
Ghodousi LLC ....G...... 480 544-3192
  Alexandria *(G-468)*
Index Systems Inc ....G...... 571 420-4600
  Herndon *(G-6706)*
Innovative Tech Intl Inc ....E...... 434 239-1979
  Lynchburg *(G-7740)*
Iron Brick Associates LLC ....E...... 703 288-3874
  Sperryville *(G-12878)*
Jaco Manufacturing Inc ....F...... 276 783-2688
  Atkins *(G-1519)*
Kratos Tech Trning Sltions Inc ....G...... 757 466-3660
  Norfolk *(G-9614)*
Little Enterprises LLC ....G...... 804 869-8612
  Purcellville *(G-10667)*
McKean Defense Group LLC ....D...... 202 448-5250
  Virginia Beach *(G-14643)*
Mega-Tech Inc ....E...... 703 534-1629
  Falls Church *(G-4922)*
Metwood Inc ....F...... 540 334-4294
  Boones Mill *(G-1897)*
Optx Imaging Systems LLC ....F...... 703 398-1432
  Lorton *(G-7520)*
Pae Avation Technical Svcs LLC ....D...... 703 717-6000
  Arlington *(G-1095)*
Qrc LLC ....E...... 540 446-2270
  Fredericksburg *(G-5216)*
Sandhurst-Aec LLC ....G...... 703 533-1413
  Falls Church *(G-4872)*
Systems Technology VA LLC.............G...... 540 884-1784
  Eagle Rock *(G-4283)*

Tmeic Corporation ....G...... 540 725-2031
  Salem *(G-12574)*
United Federal Systems Inc ....F...... 703 881-7777
  Manassas *(G-8173)*

ENGINEERING SVCS: Aviation Or Aeronautical

Advanced Technologies Inc...............D...... 757 873-3017
  Newport News *(G-9159)*
Aery Aviation LLC ....F...... 757 271-1600
  Newport News *(G-9160)*
Collier Research and Dev Corp ....F...... 757 825-0000
  Newport News *(G-9203)*
Fta Goverment Services Inc ....G...... 571 612-0413
  Chantilly *(G-2423)*

ENGINEERING SVCS: Construction & Civil

Lawson and Son Cnstr LLC ....G...... 478 258-2478
  Yorktown *(G-15973)*

ENGINEERING SVCS: Electrical Or Electronic

A-Tech Corporation ....G...... 703 955-7846
  Chantilly *(G-2360)*
Active Sense Technologies LLC...........G...... 352 226-1479
  Abingdon *(G-7)*
Greenzone Systems Inc ....G...... 703 567-6039
  Arlington *(G-987)*
Nervve Technologies Inc....................G...... 703 334-1488
  Herndon *(G-6753)*
Pan American Systems Corp ....G...... 757 468-1926
  Virginia Beach *(G-14709)*
VT Milcom Inc ....D...... 757 548-2956
  Chesapeake *(G-3366)*

ENGINEERING SVCS: Heating & Ventilation

Bas Control Systems LLC.................G...... 804 569-2473
  Mechanicsville *(G-8606)*

ENGINEERING SVCS: Industrial

Kelvin International Corp ....F...... 757 833-1011
  Newport News *(G-9274)*
Prototype Productions Inc ....D...... 703 858-0011
  Chantilly *(G-2483)*
Spectra Quest Inc ....F...... 804 261-3300
  Henrico *(G-6574)*

ENGINEERING SVCS: Marine

Individual Products & Svcs Inc ....G...... 757 488-3363
  Chesapeake *(G-3141)*
Seaguard International LLC ....G...... 484 747-0299
  Suffolk *(G-13761)*

ENGINEERING SVCS: Mechanical

Carotank Road LLC ....G...... 703 951-7790
  Alexandria *(G-161)*
Effithermix LLC ....G...... 703 860-9703
  Vienna *(G-14043)*
Metallum3d LLC ....G...... 434 409-2401
  Crozet *(G-3843)*
Mu-Del Electronics LLC.....................F...... 703 368-8900
  Manassas *(G-8114)*
Nusource LLC ....G...... 571 482-7404
  Alexandria *(G-298)*

ENGINEERING SVCS: Structural

Coperion Corporation.........................D...... 276 228-7717
  Wytheville *(G-15884)*
Uav Communications Inc ....E...... 757 271-3428
  Newport News *(G-9368)*

ENGINES & ENGINE PARTS: Guided Missile

Springfield Custom Auto Mch ....G...... 703 339-0999
  Lorton *(G-7532)*

ENGINES & ENGINE PARTS: Guided Missile, Research & Develpt

Atlantic Research Corporation ....C...... 540 854-2000
  Culpeper *(G-3869)*
Atlantic Research Corporation ....A...... 703 754-5000
  Gainesville *(G-5571)*
Blacksky Holdings Inc ....E...... 703 935-1930
  Herndon *(G-6625)*

ENGINES: Diesel & Semi-Diesel Or Duel Fuel

Chesapeake Integrated Bioenrgy........G...... 202 253-5953
  Fairfax Station *(G-4701)*
Mays Auto Machine Shop Inc ....G...... 276 646-3752
  Chilhowie *(G-3555)*

ENGINES: Internal Combustion, NEC

Engines Unlimited Inc ....G...... 276 566-7208
  Wolford *(G-15638)*
Jerrys Engines LLC ....G...... 540 885-1205
  Staunton *(G-13269)*
Mactaggart Scott Usa LLC ....G...... 757 288-1405
  Virginia Beach *(G-14631)*
Mdr Performance Engines LLC ....G...... 540 338-1001
  Leesburg *(G-7310)*
Performance Consulting Inc ....G...... 434 724-2904
  Dry Fork *(G-4143)*
Wheatley Racing ....G...... 804 276-3670
  North Chesterfield *(G-10044)*

ENGINES: Jet Propulsion

Avei ....G...... 571 278-0823
  Centreville *(G-2292)*
Periflame LLC ....F...... 888 996-3526
  Arlington *(G-1107)*

ENGINES: Marine

American Diesel Corp.........................G...... 804 435-3107
  Kilmarnock *(G-7068)*
American Marine and Engine...............G...... 276 263-1211
  Collinsville *(G-3708)*
Barr Marine By E D M ....G...... 540 291-4180
  Natural Bridge Stati *(G-9108)*
Volvo Penta Marine Pdts LLC ....G...... 757 436-2800
  Chesapeake *(G-3364)*
Volvo Penta of Americas LLC ....C...... 757 436-2800
  Chesapeake *(G-3365)*

ENGRAVING SVC, NEC

Debs Picture This Inc ....G...... 757 867-9588
  Yorktown *(G-15949)*
James J Roberts ....G...... 703 330-0448
  Manassas *(G-8089)*
M C Services Inc ....G...... 703 352-1711
  Fairfax *(G-4500)*
M&M Engraving Services Inc...............G...... 804 843-3212
  Lanexa *(G-7168)*
Western Roto Engravers Inc ....G...... 804 236-0902
  Sandston *(G-12640)*
Wre/Colortech ....G...... 804 236-0902
  Sandston *(G-12642)*

ENGRAVING SVC: Jewelry & Personal Goods

Cresset Corporation ....F...... 804 798-2691
  Ashland *(G-1399)*
Eric Margry ....G...... 703 548-7808
  Alexandria *(G-201)*
Merrill Fine Arts Engrv Inc ....E...... 703 339-3900
  Lorton *(G-7511)*
Regal Jewelers Inc ....G...... 540 949-4455
  Waynesboro *(G-15134)*
Shiny Stuff..G...... 540 586-4446
  Bedford *(G-1657)*
Thierry Duguet Engraver Inc...............G...... 434 979-3647
  Charlottesville *(G-2890)*

ENGRAVING SVCS

Amazengraved LLC ....G...... 540 313-5658
  Winchester *(G-15376)*
Artistic Awards ....G...... 540 636-9940
  Woodstock *(G-15847)*
Decosta Enterprises Inc ....G...... 703 768-4270
  Alexandria *(G-443)*
R & S Namebadge Inc ....G...... 804 673-2842
  Glen Allen *(G-5785)*
Vanmark LLC.....................................G...... 757 689-3850
  Virginia Beach *(G-14906)*

ENGRAVING: Currency

Appomattox River Engraving ....G...... 804 561-3565
  Amelia Court House *(G-652)*
Bayview Engrv Art GL Studio ....G...... 757 331-1595
  Cape Charles *(G-2229)*

ENGRAVINGS: Plastic

Amazengraved LLC ....G 540 313-5658
Winchester *(G-15376)*

Best Recognition ....G 757 490-3933
Virginia Beach *(G-14275)*

Classic Engravers ....G 804 748-8717
Chester *(G-3395)*

ENTERTAINERS & ENTERTAINMENT GROUPS

AC Cetera Inc ....G 724 532-3363
Fairfax *(G-4400)*

American Maritime Holdings Inc ....E 757 961-9311
Chesapeake *(G-2971)*

ENTERTAINMENT SVCS

Goodlife Theatre ....G 540 547-9873
Boston *(G-1903)*

Hill Brenton ....G 757 560-9332
Hampton *(G-6167)*

ENVELOPES

BSC Ventures Holdings Inc ....G 540 265-6296
Roanoke *(G-11895)*

BSC Ventures LLC ....D 540 362-3311
Roanoke *(G-11896)*

BSC Vntres Acquisition Sub LLC ....D 540 362-3311
Roanoke *(G-11897)*

BSC Vntres Acquisition Sub LLC ....C 540 563-0888
Roanoke *(G-11898)*

Diana Khoury & Co ....G 703 592-9110
Springfield *(G-12991)*

Kenmore Envelope Company Inc ....C 804 271-2100
Richmond *(G-11259)*

National Envelope Corp ....G 703 629-3881
Alexandria *(G-289)*

Reed Envelope Company Inc ....F 703 690-2249
Fairfax Station *(G-4722)*

Westrock Mwv LLC ....A 804 444-1000
Richmond *(G-11825)*

ENVIR QLTY PROG ADMN, GOV: Land, Minl & Wildlif Consv, State

Mines Minerals & Enrgy VA Dept ....D 276 523-8100
Big Stone Gap *(G-1713)*

ENZYMES

Kaotic Enzymes LLC ....G 804 519-9479
Richmond *(G-11639)*

EQUIPMENT: Pedestrian Traffic Control

Annie Lee Traffic Patrol ....G 888 682-5882
Newport News *(G-9167)*

ESCALATORS: Passenger & Freight

AB Lighting and Production LLC ....G 703 550-7707
Lorton *(G-7457)*

ETCHING & ENGRAVING SVC

Amazengraved LLC ....G 540 313-5658
Winchester *(G-15376)*

Fusion Pwdr Cating Fabrication ....G 757 319-3760
Chesapeake *(G-3112)*

Hee K Yoon ....G 703 322-9208
Centreville *(G-2310)*

Industrial Glvanizers Amer Inc ....G 804 763-1760
Petersburg *(G-10325)*

Ja Engraving Company LLC ....G 540 230-8490
Christiansburg *(G-3601)*

K & W Projects LLC ....G 757 618-9249
Chesapeake *(G-3161)*

Margaret Atkins ....G 434 315-3184
Farmville *(G-4949)*

Red DOT Laser Engraving LLC ....G 540 842-3509
Spotsylvania *(G-12911)*

ETHYLENE-PROPYLENE RUBBERS: EPDM Polymers

Applied Polymer LLC ....G 804 615-5105
Richmond *(G-11115)*

Techulon ....G 540 443-9254
Blacksburg *(G-1797)*

EXHAUST SYSTEMS: Eqpt & Parts

Momentum Usa Inc ....C 804 329-3000
Richmond *(G-11681)*

Tenneco Automotive Oper Co Inc ....A 540 432-3545
Harrisonburg *(G-6379)*

EXPANSION JOINTS: Rubber

Keystone Rubber Corporation ....G 717 235-6863
Greenbackville *(G-5994)*

EXPLOSIVES

Austin Powder Company ....F 434 842-3589
Fork Union *(G-5107)*

Austin Powder Company ....F 540 992-6097
Daleville *(G-3940)*

C4 Explosive Spt Training LLC ....G 571 379-7955
Manassas *(G-7923)*

C4 Explosive Spt Training LLC ....G 703 881-1481
Bristow *(G-2049)*

Davis Mining & Mfg Inc ....G 276 395-3354
Wise *(G-15622)*

Dyno Nobel Inc ....G 276 935-6436
Vansant *(G-13976)*

Dyno Noble Appalachia Inc ....G 276 940-2201
Duffield *(G-4177)*

Explosive Sports Cond LLC ....G 703 255-7087
Vienna *(G-14052)*

Orica USA Inc ....G 540 380-3146
Salem *(G-12551)*

Precision Explosives LLC ....G 833 338-6628
Midland *(G-8761)*

Pyrotechnique By Grucci Inc ....D 540 639-8800
Radford *(G-10736)*

EXPLOSIVES, EXC AMMO & FIREWORKS WHOLESALERS

Austin Powder Company ....F 434 842-3589
Fork Union *(G-5107)*

Winchester Building Sup Co Inc ....E 540 667-2301
Winchester *(G-15510)*

EXPLOSIVES: Amatols

New River Ordnance Works Inc ....G 907 888-9615
Blacksburg *(G-1774)*

EXPLOSIVES: Black Powder

Paige Ireco Inc ....G 276 940-2201
Duffield *(G-4183)*

EXPLOSIVES: Gunpowder

New River Energetics Inc ....G 703 406-5695
Radford *(G-10727)*

EXTRACTS, FLAVORING

Gamay Flavors ....G 703 751-7430
Alexandria *(G-212)*

Sauer Brands Inc ....G 804 359-5786
Richmond *(G-11753)*

Southern Flavoring Company Inc ....F 540 586-8565
Bedford *(G-1659)*

EYEGLASSES

Better Vision Eyeglass Center ....G 757 397-2020
Portsmouth *(G-10400)*

Eyeglass Repair Shoppe ....G 903 509-1517
Mount Solon *(G-9087)*

Kasinof & Associates ....G 757 827-6530
Hampton *(G-6179)*

Northwestern PA Opt Clinic ....G 540 721-6017
Moneta *(G-8973)*

EYELASHES, ARTIFICIAL

Eye Dollz Lashes Buty Bar LLC ....G 703 480-7899
Manassas *(G-8067)*

Lashme By Leslie LLC ....G 703 595-8628
Fairfax *(G-4497)*

Visionary Ventures LLC ....G 443 718-9777
Sterling *(G-13554)*

FABRICATED METAL PRODUCTS, NEC

American Mtal Fbrcation VA LLC ....G 434 851-1002
Appomattox *(G-801)*

Atlantic Containment LLC ....E 540 289-5051
McGaheysville *(G-8583)*

B&E Sht-Metal Fabrications Inc ....G 757 536-1279
Virginia Beach *(G-14255)*

Beach Hot Rods Met Fabrication ....G 757 227-8191
Virginia Beach *(G-14266)*

Buerlein & Co LLC ....G 804 355-1758
Richmond *(G-11513)*

Bull Run Metal Inc ....G 540 347-2135
Warrenton *(G-14984)*

Centrex Fab ....G 804 598-6000
Powhatan *(G-10537)*

Colonnas Ship Yard Inc ....A 757 545-2414
Norfolk *(G-9497)*

Finish Line Shtmtal & Fbrictns ....G 757 262-1122
Hampton *(G-6149)*

HP Metal Fabrication ....G 703 466-5551
Bristow *(G-2055)*

HP Metal Fabrication LLC ....G 571 499-0298
Nokesville *(G-9394)*

Integrated Design Solutions ....F 540 735-5424
Spotsylvania *(G-12897)*

Lloyds Pewter ....G 757 503-1110
Williamsburg *(G-15272)*

Ora Inc ....G 540 368-3012
Fredericksburg *(G-5466)*

Powder Metal Fabrication ....G 757 898-1614
Yorktown *(G-15984)*

T&M Metal Fabrication LLC ....G 703 726-6949
Ashburn *(G-1338)*

Tim Shepherd Archit Fabricati ....G 540 230-1457
Roanoke *(G-12203)*

Virginia Mtals Fabrication LLC ....G 804 622-2900
North Chesterfield *(G-10043)*

Wrights Iron Inc ....G 540 661-1089
Orange *(G-10235)*

Yowell Metal Fabrication LLC ....G 434 971-3018
Troy *(G-13938)*

FABRICS & CLOTH: Quilted

Liz B Quilting LLC ....G 540 602-7850
Stafford *(G-13172)*

FABRICS & CLOTHING: Rubber Coated

Global Trading of Martinsville ....G 276 666-0236
Martinsville *(G-8290)*

FABRICS: Airplane Cloth, Cotton

Griffin Tapestry Studio ....G 434 979-4402
Charlottesville *(G-2641)*

FABRICS: Alpacas, Mohair, Woven

Alpaca + Knitwear ....G 703 994-3346
Lorton *(G-7460)*

Alpacas of Lakeland Woods ....G 804 448-8283
Ruther Glen *(G-12448)*

Appalachian Alpaca Fibr Co LLC ....G 276 728-2349
Hillsville *(G-6883)*

Cameron Mountain Alpacas ....G 540 832-3025
Gordonsville *(G-5903)*

Crimphaven Alpacas LLC ....G 540 463-4063
Lexington *(G-7393)*

Double Jj Alpacas LLC ....G 540 286-0992
Midland *(G-8753)*

Hilltop Hideaway Alpacas LLC ....G 954 410-7238
Craigsville *(G-3806)*

Lilys Alpacas LLC ....G 757 865-1001
Toano *(G-13867)*

Mornings Myst Alpacas Inc ....G 540 428-1002
Warrenton *(G-15036)*

Ocotillas Mntnside Alpacas LLC ....G 540 593-2143
Willis *(G-15364)*

Perfect Peace Alpacas LLC ....G 540 797-1985
Blue Ridge *(G-1854)*

Pigeon Creek Alpacas ....G 540 894-1121
Spotsylvania *(G-12909)*

Pyramid Alpacas ....G 540 662-5501
Clear Brook *(G-3650)*

Ridge Valley Alpacas ....G 540 255-9200
Fairfield *(G-4735)*

Rocky Ridge Alpacas VA LLC ....G 540 962-6087
Covington *(G-3795)*

Shooting Starr Alpacas LLC ....G 540 347-4721
Warrenton *(G-15051)*

Sugarloaf Alpaca Company LLC ....G 240 500-0007
Lynchburg *(G-7815)*

Thistledown Alpacas Inc ....G 804 784-4837
Manakin Sabot *(G-7905)*

Employee Codes: A=Over 500 employees, B=251-500
C=101-250, D=51-100, E=20-50, F=10-19, G=1-9

2021 Virginia
Industrial Directory

PRODUCT

953

Virginia Breeze Alpacas LLC ....G..... 804 641-4811
Midlothian (G-8918)
White Pines Alpacas LLC ....G..... 276 475-5831
Abingdon (G-68)

FABRICS: Apparel & Outerwear, Broadwoven

Mng Online LLC ....G..... 571 247-8276
Manassas (G-8109)
Schmidt Jayme ....G..... 540 961-1792
Blacksburg (G-1787)

FABRICS: Apparel & Outerwear, Cotton

Ankh & Lotus LLC ....G..... 313 333-5138
Petersburg (G-10304)
Cold Company LLC ....G..... 757 589-7034
Norfolk (G-9491)
Im Apparel LLC ....G..... 202 905-5696
Woodbridge (G-15725)
JI Kelley American Apparel LLC ....G..... 434 664-5243
Appomattox (G-815)
Mng Online LLC ....G..... 571 247-8276
Manassas (G-8109)
Steffan Lott ....G..... 786 366-9494
Norfolk (G-9734)
Trotter Jamil ....G..... 757 251-8754
Hampton (G-6253)
Uplift Collections ....G..... 804 319-9129
Chesterfield (G-3536)
Uplift Collections LLC ....G..... 804 319-9129
Chesterfield (G-3537)

FABRICS: Apparel & Outerwear, From Manmade Fiber Or Silk

Mng Online LLC ....G..... 571 247-8276
Manassas (G-8109)
Shore Traders LLC ....G..... 276 632-5073
Martinsville (G-8328)

FABRICS: Automotive, Cotton

Global Safety Textiles LLC ....D..... 434 447-7629
South Hill (G-12851)

FABRICS: Bird's-Eye Diaper Cloth, Cotton

Avian Fashions ....G..... 540 288-0200
Stafford (G-13121)

FABRICS: Bonded-Fiber, Exc Felt

Carpenter Co ....C..... 804 359-0800
Richmond (G-11146)
Vel Tye LLC ....G..... 757 518-5400
Virginia Beach (G-14907)

FABRICS: Broadwoven, Cotton

Herb Dodge Enterprises ....G..... 757 714-4313
Chesapeake (G-3132)
Heytex USA Inc ....E..... 540 674-9576
Dublin (G-4157)

FABRICS: Broadwoven, Synthetic Manmade Fiber & Silk

Bxi Inc ....G..... 804 282-5434
Richmond (G-11142)
Precision Fabrics Group Inc ....B..... 540 343-4448
Vinton (G-14181)

FABRICS: Broadwoven, Wool

Milliken & Company ....C..... 571 659-0698
Woodbridge (G-15748)

FABRICS: Canvas

A Toast To Canvas ....G..... 804 363-4395
North Chesterfield (G-9804)
Affordable Canvas Virginia LLC ....G..... 757 718-5330
Virginia Beach (G-14216)
B & C Custom Canvas ....G..... 757 870-0089
Hampton (G-6087)
Bleeding Canvas ....G..... 276 623-2345
Glade Spring (G-5674)
Canvas Asl LLC ....G..... 804 269-0851
Richmond (G-11519)
Canvas Docktors LLC ....G..... 757 759-7108
Hayes (G-6398)
Canvas Earth LLC ....G..... 540 522-9373
Culpeper (G-3878)

Canvas Innovations Inc ....G..... 757 218-7271
Williamsburg (G-15217)
Canvas LLC ....G..... 703 237-6491
Arlington (G-899)
Canvas Salon LLC ....G..... 804 926-5518
Richmond (G-11520)
Canvas Solutions Inc ....G..... 703 564-8564
Reston (G-10817)
Captn Joeys Custom Canvas ....G..... 757 270-8772
Virginia Beach (G-14319)
Custom Canvas Works Inc ....G..... 571 249-6443
Alexandria (G-437)
Custom Marine Canvas ....G..... 540 775-6699
King George (G-7085)
Cyber-Canvas ....G..... 540 692-9322
Fredericksburg (G-5418)
Digital Canvas LLC ....G..... 703 819-3543
Falls Church (G-4783)
Docks Canvas & Upholstery ....G..... 540 840-0440
Fredericksburg (G-5420)
Fun With Canvas ....G..... 724 689-5821
Manassas (G-8071)
Fun With Canvas ....G..... 540 272-2436
Midland (G-8756)
Hampton Roads Canvas Co LLC ....G..... 757 560-3170
Virginia Beach (G-14498)
J&S Marine Canvas LLC ....G..... 757 580-6883
Chesapeake (G-3147)
Mikes Mobile Canvas ....G..... 804 815-2733
Gloucester (G-5854)
Smiles On Canvas ....G..... 757 572-2346
Virginia Beach (G-14827)

FABRICS: Chemically Coated & Treated

Tritex LLC ....F..... 276 773-0593
Independence (G-6996)

FABRICS: Coated Or Treated

Bondcote Holdings Inc ....C..... 540 980-2640
Pulaski (G-10631)
Heytex USA Inc ....E..... 540 674-9576
Dublin (G-4157)
McAllister Mills Inc ....E..... 276 773-3114
Independence (G-6989)
Worthen Industries Inc ....E..... 804 275-9231
Richmond (G-11068)

FABRICS: Cords

Plymkraft Inc ....E..... 757 595-0364
Newport News (G-9314)

FABRICS: Denims

30+ Denim/Leather Project ....G..... 301 233-0968
Alexandria (G-395)
Denim ....G..... 804 918-2361
Richmond (G-11181)
Denim Stax Inc ....G..... 434 429-6663
Danville (G-3981)
Denim Twist Inc ....G..... 703 273-3009
Fairfax (G-4612)
Shockoe Denim ....G..... 804 269-0851
Richmond (G-11759)

FABRICS: Fiberglass, Broadwoven

Bedford Weaving Inc ....C..... 540 586-8235
Bedford (G-1626)
BGF Industries Inc ....A..... 434 369-4751
Altavista (G-627)
Darco Southern LLC ....E..... 276 773-2711
Independence (G-6981)
Wave Rider Manufacturing ....G..... 804 654-9427
Deltaville (G-4089)

FABRICS: Furniture Denim

America Furniture LLC ....G..... 703 939-3678
Manassas (G-8026)

FABRICS: Ginghams

Gingham & Grosgrain LLC ....G..... 202 674-2024
Alexandria (G-216)

FABRICS: Glass, Narrow

BGF Industries Inc ....D..... 843 537-3172
Danville (G-3957)

FABRICS: Lacings, Textile

Jordo Inc ....G..... 424 394-2986
Glen Allen (G-5757)
Jordo Inc ....G..... 424 394-2986
Glen Allen (G-5758)

FABRICS: Luggage, Cotton

John S Montgomery ....G..... 757 816-8724
Chesapeake (G-3152)

FABRICS: Nonwoven

Avintiv Specialty Mtls Inc ....C..... 540 946-9250
Waynesboro (G-15099)
Heytex USA Inc ....E..... 540 674-9576
Dublin (G-4157)
Johns Manville Corporation ....B..... 540 984-4171
Edinburg (G-4307)
Solid Stone Fabrics Inc ....F..... 276 634-0115
Martinsville (G-8331)
Xymid LLC ....E..... 804 423-5798
Midlothian (G-8925)

FABRICS: Parachute Fabrics

Parachuteriggerus LLC ....G..... 703 753-9265
Haymarket (G-6433)

FABRICS: Polypropylene, Broadwoven

Griffith Bag Company ....G..... 540 433-2615
Harrisonburg (G-6326)

FABRICS: Print, Cotton

Cozy Cloths ....G..... 703 759-2420
Great Falls (G-5951)
Haverdash ....G..... 804 371-1107
Richmond (G-11608)
Integrity Shirts LLC ....G..... 540 577-5544
Blacksburg (G-1746)
Jean Lee Inc ....G..... 703 630-0276
Quantico (G-10689)

FABRICS: Resin Or Plastic Coated

Advansix Inc ....B..... 804 530-6000
Chester (G-3383)
Heytex USA Inc ....D..... 540 980-2640
Pulaski (G-10637)
Las Creation Design LLC ....G..... 757 880-4211
Woodbridge (G-15739)
Rage Plastics ....G..... 434 309-1718
Altavista (G-638)

FABRICS: Satin

Satin Solutions LLC ....G..... 703 218-3481
Fairfax (G-4673)

FABRICS: Shirting, Cotton

Hybernations LLC ....G..... 804 744-3580
Midlothian (G-8831)

FABRICS: Shirting, From Manmade Fiber Or Silk

Epic Images ....G..... 540 537-2572
Goodview (G-5895)

FABRICS: Spunbonded

Chicopee Inc ....G..... 540 946-9250
Waynesboro (G-15105)
Poly-Bond Inc ....B..... 540 946-9250
Waynesboro (G-15132)

FABRICS: Trimmings

Bay Etching & Imprinting Inc ....E..... 800 925-2877
Lively (G-7439)
Bedford Weaving Inc ....C..... 540 586-8235
Bedford (G-1626)
Bxi Inc ....G..... 804 282-5434
Richmond (G-11142)
Carl G Gilliam Jr ....F..... 276 523-0619
Big Stone Gap (G-1707)
Coastal Threads Inc ....G..... 757 495-2677
Virginia Beach (G-14349)
Decal Magic ....G..... 540 984-3786
Edinburg (G-4302)

Delrand Corp ....G.......757 490-3355
Virginia Beach *(G-14401)*

Dister Inc ....E.......757 857-1946
Norfolk *(G-9525)*

Dister Inc ....E.......703 207-0201
Fairfax *(G-4439)*

Dull Inc Dolan & Norma ....F.......703 490-0337
Woodbridge *(G-15687)*

Greeks Unlimited ....G.......804 368-1611
Hampton *(G-6161)*

Harville Entps of Danville VA ....G.......434 822-2106
Danville *(G-3997)*

Hutson Hauling ....G.......804 815-2421
Dutton *(G-4273)*

Jackie Screen Printing ....G.......276 963-0964
Richlands *(G-11017)*

Jbtm Enterprises Inc ....F.......540 665-9651
Winchester *(G-15551)*

Khk Inc ....G.......540 337-5068
Stuarts Draft *(G-13654)*

Lou Wallace ....G.......276 762-2303
Saint Paul *(G-12469)*

Martin Printwear Inc ....G.......434 352-5660
Appomattox *(G-819)*

Wool Felt Products Inc ....E.......540 981-0281
Roanoke *(G-12230)*

FABRICS: Tubing, Textile, Varnished

Scott Coulter ....G.......800 775-2925
Fairfax *(G-4674)*

FABRICS: Velveteens

Velveteen Videos LLC ....G.......703 229-3633
Front Royal *(G-5561)*

FABRICS: Waterproofed, Exc Rubberized

Dolan Contracting ....G.......703 768-9496
Alexandria *(G-192)*

FABRICS: Wool, Broadwoven

Olde Woolen Mill LLC ....G.......571 926-9604
Herndon *(G-6765)*

Woolen Mills Grill ....G.......540 323-7552
Clear Brook *(G-3654)*

Woolen Mills Tavern LLC ....G.......434 296-2816
Zion Crossroads *(G-16010)*

FABRICS: Woven Wire, Made From Purchased Wire

Quiltery LLC ....G.......540 377-9191
Fairfield *(G-4734)*

FABRICS: Woven, Narrow Cotton, Wool, Silk

AEC Virginia LLC ....C.......434 447-7629
South Hill *(G-12841)*

BGF Industries Inc ....D.......434 447-2210
South Hill *(G-12844)*

BGF Industries Inc ....A.......434 369-4751
Altavista *(G-627)*

Phenix Engineered Textiles Inc ...C.......757 654-6131
Boykins *(G-1919)*

Rose Winston Designs ....G.......703 717-2264
Fairfax *(G-4545)*

Vel Tye LLC ....G.......757 518-5400
Virginia Beach *(G-14907)*

FACIAL SALONS

Visionary Ventures LLC ....G.......443 718-9777
Sterling *(G-13554)*

FACILITIES SUPPORT SVCS

CFS-Kbr Mrnas Support Svcs LLC ...E.......202 261-1900
Alexandria *(G-164)*

Lighted Signs Direct Inc ....G.......703 965-5188
Woodbridge *(G-15740)*

Tsg Concepts Inc ....G.......877 777-5734
Arlington *(G-1200)*

FAMILY CLOTHING STORES

El Tran Investment Corp ....G.......757 439-8111
Virginia Beach *(G-14437)*

Larry Hicks ....G.......276 738-9010
Castlewood *(G-2254)*

FANS, EXHAUST: Indl Or Commercial

Elm Investments Inc ....E.......757 934-2709
Suffolk *(G-13704)*

FANS, VENTILATING: Indl Or Commercial

Agri Ventilation Systems LLC .....E.......540 879-9864
Bridgewater *(G-1947)*

Buffalo Air Handling Company ....C.......434 946-7455
Amherst *(G-685)*

Jay Douglas Carper ....G.......757 595-7660
Newport News *(G-9268)*

FARM & GARDEN MACHINERY WHOLESALERS

Hamilton Equipment Service LLC ...G.......540 341-4141
Warrenton *(G-15022)*

FARM MACHINERY REPAIR SVCS

Miller Machine & Tool Company ...E.......540 662-6512
Winchester *(G-15449)*

Milnesville Enterprises LLC ....G.......540 487-4073
Bridgewater *(G-1955)*

FARM SPLY STORES

Farmers Milling & Supply Inc .....G.......276 228-2971
Wytheville *(G-15888)*

Kehoe Enterprises LLC ....G.......540 668-9080
Hillsboro *(G-6874)*

Southern States Coop Inc ....F.......540 992-1100
Cloverdale *(G-3693)*

Southern Sttes Wnchster Coop I ...F.......540 662-0375
Winchester *(G-15588)*

FARM SPLYS WHOLESALERS

Abingdon Pre Cast Products ....G.......276 628-2472
Abingdon *(G-2)*

Houff Corporation ....G.......540 234-9246
Doswell *(G-4122)*

Southern States Coop Inc ....B.......804 281-1000
Richmond *(G-11389)*

Southern States Roanoke Coop ...G.......540 483-1217
Wirtz *(G-15619)*

FARM SPLYS, WHOLESALE: Herbicides

Residex LLC ....G.......757 363-2080
Virginia Beach *(G-14768)*

FASTENERS: Metal

Accurate Machine Inc ....G.......757 853-2136
Norfolk *(G-9418)*

Advantus Corp ....D.......804 324-7169
Petersburg *(G-10301)*

FASTENERS: Notions, NEC

E Z Mount Bracket Co Inc ....F.......540 947-5500
Montvale *(G-9029)*

Gulf Fasteners ....G.......540 798-1992
Roanoke *(G-11930)*

Premier Pins ....G.......703 631-6660
Chantilly *(G-2482)*

FASTENERS: Notions, Zippers

Attic Zipper ....G.......804 518-5094
Petersburg *(G-10308)*

Taylynn Manufacturing LLC ....G.......804 727-0103
Henrico *(G-6579)*

FAUCETS & SPIGOTS: Metal & Plastic

Bartrack Inc ....G.......717 521-4840
Rockingham *(G-12241)*

Nasoni LLC ....G.......757 358-7475
Suffolk *(G-13749)*

FEATHERS & FEATHER PRODUCTS

Cardinal Tool Inc ....G.......804 561-2560
Amelia Court House *(G-653)*

FENCES OR POSTS: Ornamental Iron Or Steel

Caldwell Industries Inc ....G.......703 403-3272
Alexandria *(G-428)*

Custom Ornamental Iron Works ...G.......540 942-2687
Waynesboro *(G-15106)*

Quality Home Improvement Corp ...G.......757 424-5400
Virginia Beach *(G-14752)*

FENCING MATERIALS: Docks & Other Outdoor Prdts, Wood

Bluegrass Woods Inc ....F.......540 997-0174
Millboro *(G-8934)*

Jerry King ....G.......804 550-1243
Glen Allen *(G-5755)*

FENCING MATERIALS: Plastic

Chilhowie Fence Supply LLC ....F.......276 780-0452
Chilhowie *(G-3547)*

Fredericksburg Fences LLC ....G.......540 419-3910
Fredericksburg *(G-5290)*

FENCING MATERIALS: Wood

Cove Creek Industries Inc ....G.......434 293-6774
Covesville *(G-3775)*

Loudoun Construction LLC ....G.......703 895-7242
Middleburg *(G-8727)*

Skyline Post & Pole LLC ....F.......717 949-8170
Broadway *(G-2096)*

FENCING: Chain Link

Touch Class Construction Corp ...G.......757 728-3647
Newport News *(G-9360)*

FERTILIZER, AGRICULTURAL: Wholesalers

Culpeper Farmers Coop Inc ....D.......540 825-2200
Culpeper *(G-3884)*

Montgomery Farm Supply Co ......G.......540 483-7072
Wirtz *(G-15617)*

Synagrow Wwt Inc ....F.......804 443-2170
Champlain *(G-2358)*

FERTILIZERS: NEC

Cameron Chemicals Inc ....F.......757 487-0656
Virginia Beach *(G-14311)*

Crop Production Services Inc ......G.......804 282-7115
Richmond *(G-11037)*

Hyponex Corporation ....E.......434 848-2727
Lawrenceville *(G-7181)*

Lesco Inc ....G.......703 257-9015
Manassas *(G-7962)*

Lesco Inc ....G.......540 752-1408
Fredericksburg *(G-5449)*

Nutrien AG Solutions Inc ....G.......757 229-9448
West Point *(G-15160)*

Nutrien AG Solutions Inc ....G.......540 775-2985
Milford *(G-8932)*

Poplar Manor Enterprises LLC ....G.......540 763-9542
Riner *(G-11865)*

Synagrow Wwt Inc ....F.......804 443-2170
Champlain *(G-2358)*

FERTILIZERS: Nitrogenous

Agrium US Inc ....G.......434 738-0515
Boydton *(G-1913)*

Crop Production Svc ....G.......804 732-6166
Prince George *(G-10590)*

Houff Corporation ....G.......540 234-9246
Doswell *(G-4122)*

Southern States Coop Inc ....E.......703 378-4865
Chantilly *(G-2495)*

Southern States Coop Inc ....F.......804 226-2758
Richmond *(G-11390)*

Southern States Coop Inc ....B.......804 281-1000
Richmond *(G-11389)*

Windrush Farm LLC ....G.......540 589-1878
Copper Hill *(G-3765)*

FERTILIZERS: Phosphatic

Montgomery Farm Supply Co ......G.......540 483-7072
Wirtz *(G-15617)*

Southern States Coop Inc ....B.......804 281-1000
Richmond *(G-11389)*

Southern States Coop Inc ....E.......703 378-4865
Chantilly *(G-2495)*

Southern States Coop Inc ....F.......804 226-2758
Richmond *(G-11390)*

Southern States Roanoke Coop ...G.......540 483-1217
Wirtz *(G-15619)*

Employee Codes: A=Over 500 employees, B=251-500
C=101-250, D=51-100, E=20-50, F=10-19, G=1-9   2021 Virginia
Industrial Directory   955

PRODUCT

FIBER & FIBER PRDTS: Cigarette Tow Cellulosic

Porex Technologies Corp.................C...... 804 524-4983
South Chesterfield (G-12821)
Porex Technologies Corporation ....C...... 804 275-2631
North Chesterfield (G-9951)

FIBER & FIBER PRDTS: Organic, Noncellulose

Honeywell International Inc ....G...... 804 541-5000
Hopewell (G-6931)
Honeywell Resins & Chem LLC.........D...... 804 541-5000
Hopewell (G-6933)
Universal Fibers Inc ....B...... 276 669-1161
Bristol (G-2039)

FIBER & FIBER PRDTS: Protein

Q Protein Inc....................................G...... 240 994-6160
Roanoke (G-11992)

FIBER & FIBER PRDTS: Synthetic Cellulosic

Trex Company Inc ....C...... 540 542-6800
Winchester (G-15493)
Xymid LLC ....E...... 804 423-5798
Midlothian (G-8925)

FIBER OPTICS

Global Metro Networks Inc.................G...... 703 837-6030
Alexandria (G-218)
Leoni Fiber Optics Inc ....G...... 757 258-4805
Williamsburg (G-15268)
Leoni Fiber Optics Inc ....G...... 757 258-4805
Williamsburg (G-15269)
Ray Visions Inc ....G...... 757 865-6442
Yorktown (G-15986)

FIBERS: Carbon & Graphite

BGF Industries Inc ....D...... 843 537-3172
Danville (G-3957)
Wingman Industries LLC....................G...... 540 489-3119
Callaway (G-2223)

FILE FOLDERS

Hollinger Metal Edge Inc ....F...... 540 898-7300
Fredericksburg (G-5298)

FILLERS & SEALERS: Putty

Putty LLC..G...... 434 960-3954
Charlottesville (G-2851)

FILM & SHEET: Unsuppported Plastic

Amcor Spclty Crtons Amrcas LLC ....C...... 804 748-3470
Chester (G-3386)
Berry Global Inc ....G...... 757 538-2000
Suffolk (G-13678)
Conwet Plastics LLC ....G...... 540 981-0362
Roanoke (G-12071)
Du Pont Tjin Flms US Ltd Prtnr ....E...... 804 530-4076
Chester (G-3408)
Du Pont Tjin Flms US Ltd Prtnr ....G...... 804 530-9339
North Chesterfield (G-9862)
E I Du Pont De Nemours & Co ....E...... 804 530-9300
Hopewell (G-6924)
Glad Products Company ....C...... 434 946-3100
Amherst (G-691)
Longwood Elastomers Inc ....E...... 276 228-5406
Wytheville (G-15896)
Longwood Elastomers Inc ....F...... 336 272-3710
Wytheville (G-15897)
Mottley Foils Inc...............................F...... 434 392-8347
Farmville (G-4952)
Orbis Rpm LLC ....G...... 804 887-2375
Richmond (G-11702)
OSullivan Films Inc ....B...... 540 667-6666
Winchester (G-15561)
Porex Technologies Corp...................C...... 804 524-4983
South Chesterfield (G-12821)
Raven Ind ....G...... 703 414-3290
Arlington (G-1130)
Schweitzer-Mauduit Intl Inc ....G...... 540 981-0362
Roanoke (G-12178)
Swm International LLC ....G...... 651 369-1235
Roanoke (G-12201)

Tredegar Consumer Designs Inc...........G...... 804 330-1000
North Chesterfield (G-10028)
Tredegar Far East Corporation..............G...... 804 330-1000
North Chesterfield (G-10031)
Tredegar Film Products Corp ....C...... 804 330-1000
North Chesterfield (G-10033)
Tredegar Film Products US LLC............B...... 804 330-1000
North Chesterfield (G-10035)
Tredegar Films Development Inc...........G...... 804 330-1000
North Chesterfield (G-10036)
Tredegar Films Rs Converting..............C...... 804 330-1000
North Chesterfield (G-10037)
Tredegar Performance Films Inc ....B...... 804 330-1000
North Chesterfield (G-10038)

FILM BASE: Cellulose Acetate Or Nitrocellulose Plastics

Teijin-Du Pont Films Inc....................G...... 804 530-9310
Hopewell (G-6942)

FILM: Motion Picture

Crown Enterprise LLC ....G...... 757 277-8837
Virginia Beach (G-14374)
Media Magic LLC ....G...... 757 893-0988
Virginia Beach (G-14644)

FILM: Rubber

Teijin-Du Pont Films Inc....................D...... 804 530-9310
Chester (G-3459)

FILTERS

Cantel Medical Corp ....G...... 800 633-3080
Mount Jackson (G-9067)
Filtroil LLC ....E...... 804 359-9125
Richmond (G-11588)
Johns Manville Corporation ....B...... 540 984-4171
Edinburg (G-4307)
Omni Filter and Mfg Inc ....E...... 804 550-1600
Ashland (G-1472)
Porvair Filtration Group Inc ....D...... 804 550-1600
Ashland (G-1478)
S P Kinney Engineers Inc ....F...... 804 520-4700
South Chesterfield (G-12825)
Tri-Dim Filter Corporation ....G...... 540 967-2600
Louisa (G-7572)
Verdex Technologies Inc ....G...... 804 491-9733
North Chesterfield (G-10008)
World Fashion City Inc ....G...... 703 887-8123
Alexandria (G-615)

FILTERS & SOFTENERS: Water, Household

Commonwlth H2O Svcs Inc-Blue R ....F...... 434 975-4426
Charlottesville (G-2610)
McCoy Water Filter Inc ....G...... 804 222-2089
Henrico (G-6534)
Zenpure Corporation ....G...... 703 335-9910
Manassas (G-8183)

FILTERS: Air

Tri-Dim Filter Corporation ....G...... 540 774-9540
Roanoke (G-12209)
Tri-Dim Filter Corporation ....C...... 540 967-2600
Louisa (G-7573)

FILTERS: Air Intake, Internal Combustion Engine, Exc Auto

Artcraft Fabricators Inc ....D...... 757 399-7777
Portsmouth (G-10393)
Bmg Metals Inc ....G...... 804 622-9452
Henrico (G-6483)
Colonial Air Filter Clg LLC ....G...... 757 229-1110
Williamsburg (G-15220)

FILTERS: General Line, Indl

Chase Filters & Components LLC.........E...... 757 327-0036
Hampton (G-6112)
National Filter Media Corp ....G...... 540 773-4780
Winchester (G-15560)

FILTERS: Paper

Sanfacon Virginia Inc ....E...... 434 376-2301
Brookneal (G-2112)

FILTRATION DEVICES: Electronic

Chemteq ....F...... 757 622-2223
Norfolk (G-9481)
Greenleaf Filtration LLC ....G...... 804 378-7744
Powhatan (G-10547)
Planet Care Inc ....G...... 540 980-2420
Pulaski (G-10644)
Quanta Systems LLC ....G...... 703 885-7900
Herndon (G-6783)

FINANCIAL INVESTMENT ACTIVITIES, NEC: Financial Reporting

Reconart Inc ....G...... 855 732-6627
Alexandria (G-568)

FINANCIAL SVCS

Adf Unit Trust Inc ....G...... 757 926-5252
Newport News (G-9157)
First Renaissance Ventures.................G...... 703 408-6961
Mc Lean (G-8431)
Maverick Bus Solutions LLC ....G...... 757 870-8489
Portsmouth (G-10459)

FINDINGS & TRIMMINGS: Apparel

Vanguard Industries East Inc ....C...... 757 665-8405
Norfolk (G-9778)
Vizini Incorporated ....G...... 703 508-8662
Round Hill (G-12394)

FINGERNAILS, ARTIFICIAL

Fortune Nails LLC ....G...... 703 330-1306
Manassas (G-7942)
Nails Hurricane Too ....G...... 703 370-5551
Alexandria (G-288)

FINGERPRINT EQPT

Cross Match Technologies Inc ....G...... 703 841-6280
Arlington (G-921)
Identification Intl Inc ....F...... 540 953-3343
Blacksburg (G-1744)
Morphotrak LLC ....F...... 703 797-2600
Alexandria (G-283)

FINISHING AGENTS

Finish Agent Inc ....G...... 703 437-7822
Reston (G-10852)

FINISHING AGENTS: Leather

Unicorn Editions Ltd..........................G...... 540 364-0156
The Plains (G-13844)

FIRE ARMS, SMALL: Guns Or Gun Parts, 30 mm & Below

Absolute Precision LLC ....G...... 757 968-3005
Yorktown (G-15930)
Accuracy International N Amer ....G...... 907 440-4024
Fredericksburg (G-5240)
Alexander Industries Inc ....G...... 540 443-9250
Radford (G-10703)
Backwoods Security LLC....................G...... 804 641-0674
Moseley (G-9033)
Be Ready Enterprises LLC ....G...... 540 422-9210
Fredericksburg (G-5172)
Broadstone Security LLC....................G...... 703 566-2814
Arlington (G-890)
Carotank Road LLC ....G...... 703 951-7790
Alexandria (G-161)
Costacamps-Net LLC ....G...... 571 482-6858
Springfield (G-12983)
Forging The Warrior Spirit ....G...... 703 851-4789
Marshall (G-8252)
Grayman Usa LLC ....G...... 703 598-6934
Aldie (G-106)
Hexmag LLC ....F...... 970 203-9100
Virginia Beach (G-14521)
L&L Trading Company LLC ....G...... 757 995-3608
Virginia Beach (G-14595)
Leitner-Wise Manufacturing LLC..........G...... 703 209-0009
Alexandria (G-258)
Lwag Holdings Inc ....F...... 703 455-8650
Springfield (G-13045)
Matoaca Specialty Arms Inc ....G...... 804 590-2749
South Chesterfield (G-12837)

Shawn Gaines ....G....... 434 332-4819
Rustburg **(G-12446)**

Tr Partners Lc ....G....... 804 484-4091
Glen Allen **(G-5815)**

Unison Arms LLC ....G....... 571 342-1108
Round Hill **(G-12392)**

US Tactical Inc ....G....... 703 217-8781
Oakton **(G-10163)**

Vertu Corp. ....E....... 540 341-3006
Manassas **(G-8174)**

Whisper Tactical LLC ....G....... 757 645-5938
Chesapeake **(G-3376)**

FIRE ARMS, SMALL: Machine Guns & Grenade Launchers

Corporate Arms Llc ....G....... 800 256-5803
Springfield **(G-12981)**

Epic Mfg LLC ....G....... 757 689-4373
Virginia Beach **(G-14449)**

War Fighter Specialties LLC ....G....... 540 742-4187
Shenandoah **(G-12697)**

FIRE ARMS, SMALL: Machine Guns/Machine Gun Parts, 30mm/below

Fjord Defense Inc ....G....... 571 214-2183
Alexandria **(G-205)**

FN America LLC ....C....... 703 288-3500
Mc Lean **(G-8434)**

FN America LLC ....G....... 540 288-8002
Fredericksburg **(G-5431)**

Kennesaw Holding Company ....G....... 603 866-6944
Fairfax **(G-4643)**

FIRE ARMS, SMALL: Pistols Or Pistol Parts, 30 mm & below

Ballistics Center LLC ....G....... 703 380-4901
Woodbridge **(G-15653)**

Vfg Enterprises LLC ....G....... 757 343-4866
Virginia Beach **(G-14908)**

FIRE ARMS, SMALL: Shotguns Or Shotgun Parts, 30 mm & Below

Fausti USA Service LLC ....G....... 540 371-3287
Fredericksburg **(G-5286)**

FIRE CONTROL OR BOMBING EQPT: Electronic

Cooper Crouse-Hinds LLC ....F....... 540 983-1300
Roanoke **(G-12072)**

Tactical Elec Military Sup LLC .....F....... 757 689-0476
Virginia Beach **(G-14863)**

FIRE DETECTION SYSTEMS

Ecko Incorporated ....F....... 276 988-7943
North Tazewell **(G-10098)**

Nettalon Security Systems Inc .....F....... 540 368-5290
Fredericksburg **(G-5333)**

FIRE EXTINGUISHER CHARGES

Virginia Fire Protection Svcs ....G....... 276 637-1012
Max Meadows **(G-8370)**

FIRE EXTINGUISHER SVC

Thompson Electric Motor Svc ....G....... 434 372-3814
Chase City **(G-2917)**

Virginia Fire Protection Svcs ....G....... 276 637-1012
Max Meadows **(G-8370)**

FIRE EXTINGUISHERS, WHOLESALE

Thompson Electric Motor Svc ....G....... 434 372-3814
Chase City **(G-2917)**

Virginia Fire Protection Svcs ....G....... 276 637-1012
Max Meadows **(G-8370)**

FIRE EXTINGUISHERS: Portable

Virginia Fire Protection Svcs ....G....... 276 637-1012
Max Meadows **(G-8370)**

FIRE OR BURGLARY RESISTIVE PRDTS

Amfab Inc ....G....... 757 543-1485
Chesapeake **(G-2975)**

Colonnas Ship Yard Inc ....A....... 757 545-2414
Norfolk **(G-9495)**

Masonite International Corp ....E....... 540 778-2211
Stanley **(G-13232)**

Michael W Gillespie ....G....... 540 894-0288
Louisa **(G-7560)**

Viking Fabrication Services ....G....... 804 228-1333
Richmond **(G-11806)**

FIRE PROTECTION EQPT

Charlottesville Fire Exting ....G....... 434 295-0803
Scottsville **(G-12659)**

Commonwealth Rescue Systems ....G....... 540 438-8972
Harrisonburg **(G-6305)**

Fire Systems Services Inc ....G....... 757 825-6379
Hampton **(G-6150)**

Interstate Rescue LLC ....F....... 571 283-4206
Winchester **(G-15429)**

FIRE PROTECTION, EXC CONTRACT

Special Projects Operations ....F....... 410 297-6550
Virginia Beach **(G-14834)**

FIREARMS & AMMUNITION, EXC SPORTING, WHOLESALE

Pointman Resources LLC ....G....... 240 429-3423
Sterling **(G-13472)**

Southerns M&P LLC ....G....... 804 330-2407
North Chesterfield **(G-9985)**

FIREARMS, EXC SPORTING, WHOLESALE

Alexander Industries Inc ....G....... 540 443-9250
Radford **(G-10703)**

Epic Mfg LLC ....G....... 757 689-4373
Virginia Beach **(G-14449)**

FIREARMS: Large, Greater Than 30mm

Country Wood Crafts ....G....... 540 833-4985
Linville **(G-7434)**

Eye Armor Incorporated ....G....... 571 238-4096
Stafford **(G-13144)**

Madison Colonial LLC ....G....... 240 997-2376
Toano **(G-13868)**

FIREARMS: Small, 30mm or Less

Amherst Arms and Supply LLC ....G....... 434 929-1978
Madison Heights **(G-7867)**

Casey Traxler ....G....... 703 402-0745
Leesburg **(G-7242)**

Greenstein LLC ....G....... 540 408-9877
Stafford **(G-13149)**

Kriss Usa Inc ....E....... 714 333-1988
Chesapeake **(G-3168)**

Leitner-Wise Defense Inc ....G....... 703 209-0009
Springfield **(G-13042)**

Matthew Mitchell ....G....... 615 454-0787
Fredericksburg **(G-5455)**

Rifle Building LLC ....G....... 518 879-9195
Norfolk **(G-9708)**

Small Arms Mfg Solutions LLC ....G....... 757 673-7769
Chesapeake **(G-3297)**

Vertu Corp. ....F....... 540 341-3006
Warrenton **(G-15058)**

FIREPLACE & CHIMNEY MATERIAL: Concrete

Earthcore Industries LLC ....G....... 757 966-7275
Chesapeake **(G-3081)**

Hearth Pros ....G....... 434 237-5913
Lynchburg **(G-7731)**

FIREPLACE EQPT & ACCESS

Hearth & Home Technologies LLC ....G....... 434 589-1482
Troy **(G-13928)**

Hearth & Home Technologies LLC ....G....... 703 367-9413
Manassas **(G-7950)**

M2m LLC ....G....... 816 204-0938
Manassas **(G-8103)**

FISH & SEAFOOD PROCESSORS: Canned Or Cured

Bg Smith & Son Oyster Co ....G....... 804 394-2721
Farnham **(G-4962)**

Chesapeake Bay Packing LLC ....E....... 757 244-8440
Newport News **(G-9199)**

Eastern Shore Seafood Co Inc ....E....... 757 787-7539
Onancock **(G-10196)**

Eastern Shore Seafood Pdts LLC ....G....... 757 854-4422
Mappsville **(G-8218)**

W Ellery Kellum Inc ....E....... 804 438-5476
Weems **(G-15151)**

FISH & SEAFOOD PROCESSORS: Fresh Or Frozen

Abbott Brothers Inc ....G....... 804 436-1001
White Stone **(G-15185)**

Eastern Shore Seafood Pdts LLC ....G....... 757 854-4422
Mappsville **(G-8218)**

J H Miles Co Inc ....E....... 757 622-9264
Norfolk **(G-9598)**

Lineage Logistics ....G....... 804 421-6603
Richmond **(G-11657)**

Moss Cape LLC ....G....... 703 234-3890
Chantilly **(G-2465)**

Old Point Packing Inc ....F....... 757 247-0557
Newport News **(G-9308)**

FISH & SEAFOOD WHOLESALERS

Capital Noodle Inc ....F....... 703 569-3224
Springfield **(G-12973)**

Tidewater Foods Inc ....G....... 757 410-2498
Norfolk **(G-9752)**

FISH FOOD

Severn Wharf Custom Rods ....G....... 804 642-0404
Gloucester Point **(G-5876)**

FISHING EQPT: Lures

Lure LLC ....G....... 434 374-8559
Clarksville **(G-3633)**

Mud Puppy Custom Lures LLC ....G....... 804 895-1489
Prince George **(G-10602)**

Royal Silver Mfg Co Inc ....F....... 757 855-6004
Norfolk **(G-9711)**

Uniques LLC ....G....... 804 307-0902
Midlothian **(G-8916)**

Virginia Guide Bait Co ....G....... 804 590-2991
Chesterfield **(G-3539)**

FITTINGS & ASSEMBLIES: Hose & Tube, Hydraulic Or Pneumatic

Hamilton Equipment Service LLC ....G....... 540 341-4141
Warrenton **(G-15022)**

Hydra Hose & Supply Co ....G....... 757 867-9795
Yorktown **(G-15964)**

Mid-Atlantic Rubber Inc ....F....... 540 710-5690
Fredericksburg **(G-5326)**

Riverside Hydraulics LLC ....G....... 804 545-6700
Ashland **(G-1488)**

FITTINGS: Pipe

Ksb America Corporation ....G....... 804 222-1818
Richmond **(G-11265)**

Nibco Inc ....E....... 540 324-0242
Stuarts Draft **(G-13656)**

Roanoke Hose & Fittings ....G....... 540 985-4832
Roanoke **(G-12166)**

FIXTURES & EQPT: Kitchen, Metal, Exc Cast Aluminum

Macs Smack LLC ....G....... 804 913-9126
Hanover **(G-6282)**

FLAG POLES, WHOLESALE

U S Flag & Signal Company ....E....... 757 497-8947
Portsmouth **(G-10494)**

FLAGPOLES

Kearney-National Inc ....C....... 276 628-7171
Abingdon **(G-47)**

FLAGS: Fabric

Evergreen Enterprises Inc ....C....... 804 231-1800
Richmond **(G-11582)**

Festival Design Inc ....G....... 804 643-5247
Richmond **(G-11586)**

PRODUCT

U S Flag & Signal Company..............E......757 497-8947
Portsmouth (G-10494)

FLAGSTONES

Flagstone..G......815 790-0582
Alexandria (G-463)
Flagstone Oprting Partners LLC ....G......703 532-6238
Mc Lean (G-8433)
Old Domimion Flagstone Inc ....G......540 553-0511
Blacksburg (G-1776)

FLAT GLASS: Antique

Blake Collection....................................G......703 329-1599
Alexandria (G-424)

FLAT GLASS: Laminated

Hawkins Glass Wholesalers LLC ....E......703 372-2990
Lorton (G-7492)

FLAT GLASS: Tempered

Virginia Glass Products Corp ....C......276 956-3131
Ridgeway (G-11856)
Virginia Mirror Company Inc..................D......276 956-3131
Martinsville (G-8347)
Virginia Mirror Company Inc..................G......276 632-9816
Martinsville (G-8348)

FLAT GLASS: Window, Clear & Colored

All Glass LLC..G......540 288-8111
Fredericksburg (G-5397)
Blackout Tinting LLC.............................G......757 416-5658
Norfolk (G-9466)
Higgins Inc...F......540 636-3756
Middletown (G-8740)
Jim Warehime..G......804 861-5255
Petersburg (G-10327)
Potomac Glass Inc................................G......540 288-0210
Stafford (G-13180)
The Tint...G......804 261-4081
Glen Allen (G-5808)

FLATWARE, STAINLESS STEEL

Royal Silver Mfg Co Inc ....F......757 855-6004
Norfolk (G-9711)

FLIGHT RECORDERS

Aviation Tactical LLC.............................G......970 946-7027
Springfield (G-12957)

FLOOR CLEANING & MAINTENANCE EQPT: Household

Orlando Garzon Cuellar..........................G......571 274-6913
Manassas (G-8123)

FLOOR COVERING STORES: Carpets

Capital Discount Mdse LLC ....F......703 499-9368
Woodbridge (G-15665)

FLOOR COVERING STORES: Rugs

Halifax Fine Furnishings ....G......540 774-3060
Roanoke (G-11931)

FLOOR COVERINGS WHOLESALERS

Advanta Flooring Inc ....G......804 530-5004
North Chesterfield (G-9805)

FLOOR COVERINGS: Art Squares, Textile Fiber

Aeh Designs ....G......703 860-3204
Reston (G-10779)
Regitex Usa LLC ....C......514 730-1110
Brodnax (G-2104)

FLOORING: Hard Surface

Advanta Flooring Inc ....G......804 530-5004
North Chesterfield (G-9805)
Flooring Adventures LLC ....G......804 530-5004
Chester (G-3416)
Knowles Flooring ....G......571 224-3694
Fairfax (G-4491)
Pave DMV LLC.......................................G......703 798-1087
Alexandria (G-549)

FLOORING: Hardwood

American Floors......................................G......804 745-8932
North Chesterfield (G-9815)
Clark Hardwood Flr Refinishing ....G......804 350-8871
Powhatan (G-10538)
Ignacio C Garcia...................................G......703 922-9829
Alexandria (G-482)
Lee Tech Hardwood Floors ....G......540 588-6217
Roanoke (G-12124)
Ludaire Fine Wood Floors Inc ....G......276 889-3072
Lebanon (G-7199)
Madison Flooring Company Inc ....F......540 948-4498
Madison (G-7859)
S N L Finishing ....G......540 740-3826
Staunton (G-13289)
Sand King ....G......434 465-3498
Scottsville (G-12666)
Tatums Floor Service ....G......804 737-3328
Highland Springs (G-6857)
Tony Tran Hardwood Floors ....G......540 793-4094
Vinton (G-14187)

FLOORING: Parquet, Hardwood

Matera John ....G......757 240-0425
Yorktown (G-15981)

FLOORING: Tile

Ablaze Interiors Inc...............................G......757 427-0075
Virginia Beach (G-14204)

FLORIST: Plants, Potted

Katherine Chain ....G......804 796-2762
Chester (G-3426)

FLOWER ARRANGEMENTS: Artificial

Fairview Place LLC ....G......330 257-1138
Norfolk (G-9549)
Les Petales Inc ....G......804 254-7863
Richmond (G-11269)
Sallmae LLC ....G......931 472-9467
Fort Lee (G-5132)

FLOWER POTS Plastic

Deborah F Scarboro ....G......757 866-0108
Spring Grove (G-12929)

FLOWERS & FLORISTS' SPLYS WHOLESALERS

Evergreen Enterprises Inc ....C......804 231-1800
Richmond (G-11582)

FLOWERS: Artificial & Preserved

Waterford Past-Thymes...........................G......703 434-1758
Round Hill (G-12395)
Waterford Pastthymes............................G......703 431-4095
Waterford (G-15084)

FLUES & PIPES: Stove Or Furnace

Benchmark Doors ....B......540 898-5700
Fredericksburg (G-5173)
New England Supply Inc ....F......703 372-2689
Springfield (G-13058)

FLUID METERS & COUNTING DEVICES

Teledyne Instruments Inc....................D......757 723-6531
Hampton (G-6250)
Trigg Industries LLC..............................G......757 223-7522
Newport News (G-9363)

FLUID POWER PUMPS & MOTORS

Gravittional Systems Engrg Inc............F......312 224-8152
Clifton (G-3668)
Mac Bone Industries Ltd ....G......804 264-3603
Richmond (G-11278)
Mactaggart Scott Usa LLC ....G......757 288-1405
Virginia Beach (G-14631)

FLUID POWER VALVES & HOSE FITTINGS

Alpha Developement Bureau ....F......540 337-4900
Fishersville (G-5000)
Moog Inc ....G......716 652-2000
Blacksburg (G-1764)

Schrader-Bridgeport Intl Inc ....C......434 369-4741
Altavista (G-642)

FLUXES

Radford Wldg & Fabrication LLC ....G......540 731-4891
Radford (G-10737)
T & J Wldg & Fabrication LLC ....G......757 672-9929
Suffolk (G-13770)

FOAMS & RUBBER, WHOLESALE

Carpenter Co ....D......804 359-0800
Richmond (G-11147)

FOIL & LEAF: Metal

Mottley Foils Inc....................................F......434 392-8347
Farmville (G-4952)
Vitex Packaging Group Inc ....F......757 538-3115
Suffolk (G-13780)

FOIL: Laminated To Paper Or Other Materials

Hot Stamp Supply Company...................G......540 868-7500
Winchester (G-15425)

FOOD PRDTS & SEAFOOD: Shellfish, Fresh, Shucked

E J Conrad & Sons Seafood Inc ....E......804 462-7400
Lancaster (G-7160)
W Ellery Kellum Inc..............................E......804 438-5476
Weems (G-15151)

FOOD PRDTS, BREAKFAST: Cereal, Granola & Muesli

Gaona Granola Co LLC ....G......434 996-6653
Charlottesville (G-2801)
Wigglesworth Granola LLC.....................G......703 443-0130
Leesburg (G-7378)

FOOD PRDTS, BREAKFAST: Cereal, Oatmeal

Agee Catering Services..........................G......434 960-8906
Palmyra (G-10243)
Gooats LLC ....G......267 997-7789
Lorton (G-7491)
VA Foods LLC..G......434 221-1456
Lynch Station (G-7629)

FOOD PRDTS, CANNED OR FRESH PACK: Fruit Juices

Andros Bowman Products LLC..............D......540 217-4100
Mount Jackson (G-9064)
Biogeo Genetics ....G......888 448-8376
Chesapeake (G-3000)
Transformation Wellness LLC ....G......804 366-4632
Richmond (G-11792)

FOOD PRDTS, CANNED OR FRESH PACK: Vegetable Juices

Juice...E......202 280-0302
Falls Church (G-4812)

FOOD PRDTS, CANNED, NEC

Queen of Amannisa ....G......703 414-7888
Arlington (G-1126)

FOOD PRDTS, CANNED: Applesauce

Ashburn Sauce Company ....G......757 621-1113
Virginia Beach (G-14245)

FOOD PRDTS, CANNED: Barbecue Sauce

Old Coots LLC..G......757 713-2888
Norfolk (G-9674)
Pork Barrel Bbq LLC..............................G......202 750-7500
Alexandria (G-312)
Treser Family Foods Inc ....G......540 250-5667
Blacksburg (G-1801)

FOOD PRDTS, CANNED: Bean Sprouts

Waterneer USA Inc.................................G......703 655-2279
Chantilly (G-2520)

FOOD PRDTS, CANNED: Chili Sauce, Tomato

Jddr Foods Inc ....G...... 571 356-0165
Reston *(G-10880)*

Mad Hatter Foods LLC................G...... 434 981-9378
Charlottesville *(G-2830)*

Pk Hot Sauce LLc..........................G...... 703 629-0920
Manassas *(G-7989)*

Virginias Mudd Hot Sauce LLC............G...... 434 953-6582
Scottsville *(G-12669)*

FOOD PRDTS, CANNED: Ethnic

Interleno Enterprises LLC................G...... 757 340-3613
Virginia Beach *(G-14551)*

Laestrellita ....G...... 276 650-7099
Axton *(G-1539)*

FOOD PRDTS, CANNED: Fruit Juices, Concentrated

Authentic Products LLC ....G...... 703 451-5984
Springfield *(G-12954)*

FOOD PRDTS, CANNED: Fruit Juices, Fresh

JUIce&i LLC..................................G...... 202 280-0302
Falls Church *(G-4813)*

FOOD PRDTS, CANNED: Fruits

Hunter Company HB ....F 757 664-5200
Norfolk *(G-9584)*

Nestle Usa Inc ....C...... 765 778-6000
Arlington *(G-1074)*

FOOD PRDTS, CANNED: Fruits

Kraft..G...... 703 583-8874
Woodbridge *(G-15736)*

Kraft Heinz Foods Company ....G...... 540 545-7563
Winchester *(G-15436)*

Maryland and Virginia Milk PR............C...... 757 245-3857
Newport News *(G-9292)*

FOOD PRDTS, CANNED: Fruits & Fruit Prdts

Nestle Holdings Inc ....F 703 682-4600
Arlington *(G-1073)*

Shawnee Canning Company Inc ....G...... 540 888-3429
Cross Junction *(G-3827)*

FOOD PRDTS, CANNED: Hominy

Lake Packing Co Inc ....F 804 529-6101
Lottsburg *(G-7543)*

FOOD PRDTS, CANNED: Jams, Jellies & Preserves

Broad Street Traffic Jams LLC ....G...... 804 461-1245
Rockville *(G-12284)*

Jmy Jams LLC...............................G...... 434 906-0256
North Garden *(G-10077)*

Littlebird Jams and Jellies ....G...... 804 586-4420
North Dinwiddie *(G-10059)*

Lizis Jams ....G...... 804 837-1904
Midlothian *(G-8850)*

Lutz Farm & Services ....G...... 540 477-3574
Mount Jackson *(G-9075)*

Simply Panache Products LLC ....G...... 757 358-7062
Hampton *(G-6238)*

Zo-Zos Jams ....G...... 804 562-9867
Glen Allen *(G-5830)*

FOOD PRDTS, CANNED: Jellies, Edible, Including Imitation

Millcroft Farms Co Inc ....G...... 540 778-3369
Stanley *(G-13234)*

FOOD PRDTS, CANNED: Mexican, NEC

Tindahan ....G...... 757 243-8207
Newport News *(G-9356)*

FOOD PRDTS, CANNED: Olives

Acesur North America Inc ....E...... 757 664-2390
Norfolk *(G-9419)*

FOOD PRDTS, CANNED: Puddings, Exc Meat

Pudding Please LLC ....F...... 804 833-4110
Richmond *(G-11727)*

Rodgers Puddings LLC ....G...... 757 558-2657
Chesapeake *(G-3273)*

FOOD PRDTS, CANNED: Seasonings, Tomato

Back Pocket Provisions LLC ....G...... 703 585-3676
Falls Church *(G-4753)*

FOOD PRDTS, CANNED: Spanish

Confero Foods LLC ....G...... 703 334-7516
Lorton *(G-7476)*

FOOD PRDTS, CANNED: Tomato Purees

Nestle Prepared Foods Company ....D...... 434 822-4000
Danville *(G-4017)*

FOOD PRDTS, CANNED: Tortillas

Sir Masa Inc.................................G...... 540 725-1982
Roanoke *(G-12189)*

FOOD PRDTS, CANNED: Vegetables

Nobull Burger................................G...... 434 975-6628
Charlottesville *(G-2664)*

FOOD PRDTS, CONFECTIONERY, WHOLESALE: Candy

Debbie Belt ....G...... 912 856-9476
Richmond *(G-11556)*

FOOD PRDTS, CONFECTIONERY, WHOLESALE: Snack Foods

Aileen L Brown ....G...... 757 696-1814
Hampton *(G-6079)*

FOOD PRDTS, FISH & SEAFOOD, WHOLESALE: Seafood

Captain Faunce Seafood Inc.................E...... 804 493-8690
Montross *(G-9025)*

Smith & Sons Oyster Co Inc B G............F 804 394-2721
Sharps *(G-12685)*

FOOD PRDTS, FISH & SEAFOOD: Canned & Jarred, Etc

Big Island Oysters ....G...... 804 389-9589
Hayes *(G-6396)*

Virginia Seafoods LLC....................F 301 520-8200
White Stone *(G-15190)*

FOOD PRDTS, FISH & SEAFOOD: Crabmeat, Canned, Jarred, Etc

Graham and Rollins Inc...................E...... 757 755-1021
Hampton *(G-6160)*

FOOD PRDTS, FISH & SEAFOOD: Crabmeat, Preserved & Cured

Asian Pacific Seafood LLC ....G...... 251 751-5962
Chesapeake *(G-2984)*

FOOD PRDTS, FISH & SEAFOOD: Fish Fillets

Shortys Breading Company LLC............G...... 434 390-1772
Rice *(G-11006)*

FOOD PRDTS, FISH & SEAFOOD: Fish, Fresh, Prepared

Ocean Foods Inc ....G...... 757 474-6314
Virginia Beach *(G-14692)*

FOOD PRDTS, FISH & SEAFOOD: Fish, Frozen, Prepared

Captain Faunce Seafood Inc.................E...... 804 493-8690
Montross *(G-9025)*

FOOD PRDTS, FISH & SEAFOOD: Fresh, Prepared

Ashton Green Seafood ....G...... 757 887-3551
Newport News *(G-9172)*

Bernies Conchs.............................G...... 757 331-3861
Cheriton *(G-2946)*

Bevans Oyster Company ....G...... 804 472-2331
Kinsale *(G-7134)*

Bevans Oyster Company ....D...... 804 472-2331
Kinsale *(G-7133)*

Chesapeake Bay Packing LLC............E...... 757 244-8400
Newport News *(G-9198)*

Chesapeake Bay Packing LLC............E...... 757 244-8440
Newport News *(G-9199)*

Eastern Shore Seafood Co Inc ....E...... 757 787-7539
Onancock *(G-10196)*

FOOD PRDTS, FISH & SEAFOOD: Fresh/Frozen Chowder, Soup/Stew

Tidewater Foods Inc ....G...... 757 410-2498
Norfolk *(G-9752)*

FOOD PRDTS, FISH & SEAFOOD: Herring, Canned, Jarred, Etc

Lake Packing Co Inc ....F 804 529-6101
Lottsburg *(G-7543)*

FOOD PRDTS, FISH & SEAFOOD: Oysters, Canned, Jarred, Etc

Bevans Oyster Company ....D...... 804 472-2331
Kinsale *(G-7133)*

Bevans Oyster Company ....G...... 804 472-2331
Kinsale *(G-7134)*

Smith & Sons Oyster Co Inc B G............F 804 394-2721
Sharps *(G-12685)*

FOOD PRDTS, FISH & SEAFOOD: Oysters, Preserved & Cured

Dockside Seafood..........................G...... 757 357-9298
Battery Park *(G-1595)*

Ship Point Oyster Company ....G...... 757 848-3557
Poquoson *(G-10376)*

FOOD PRDTS, FISH & SEAFOOD: Seafood, Frozen, Prepared

Ailan Trading Inc USA ....G...... 757 812-7258
Yorktown *(G-15931)*

FOOD PRDTS, FISH & SEAFOOD: Soup, Stew/Chowdr, Canned/Pkgd

Ashton Green Seafood ....G....... 757 887-3551
Newport News *(G-9172)*

FOOD PRDTS, FROZEN, WHOLESALE: Vegetables & Fruit Prdts

Nobull Burger................................G...... 434 975-6628
Charlottesville *(G-2664)*

FOOD PRDTS, FROZEN: Dinners, Packaged

Kiddos LLC...................................G....... 540 468-2700
Monterey *(G-9008)*

FOOD PRDTS, FROZEN: Ethnic Foods, NEC

Nazret Cultural Foods LLC................G...... 215 500-9813
Alexandria *(G-290)*

Southeast Frozen Foods Inc................D...... 800 214-6682
Sandston *(G-12635)*

FOOD PRDTS, FROZEN: Fruits, Juices & Vegetables

Aleeta A Gardner ....G...... 571 722-2549
Woodbridge *(G-15644)*

Andros Bowman Products LLC............D...... 540 217-4100
Mount Jackson *(G-9064)*

James A Kennedy & Assoc Inc............G...... 804 241-6836
Powhatan *(G-10553)*

Shelf Reliance ....G...... 540 459-2050
Woodstock *(G-15859)*

Sp Smoothies Inc ....G...... 757 595-0600
Newport News *(G-9344)*

PRODUCT

FOOD PRDTS, FROZEN: NEC

Cathay Food Corp..............................E....... 617 427-1507
   Fredericksburg (G-5408)
Eastern Shore Seafood Pdts LLC........G....... 757 854-4422
   Mappsville (G-8218)
Gumax International Ltd.....................E....... 866 412-3880
   Woodbridge (G-15719)
I-Ce-Ny Arlington..............................G....... 571 207-6318
   Arlington (G-997)
James A Kennedy & Assoc Inc............G....... 804 241-6836
   Powhatan (G-10553)
Lily Golden Foods Corporation...........G....... 703 823-8821
   Alexandria (G-260)
Mom Made Foods LLC........................F....... 703 740-9241
   Alexandria (G-280)
Nestle Holdings Inc...........................F....... 703 682-4600
   Arlington (G-1073)

FOOD PRDTS, FROZEN: Pizza

Food Portions LLC.............................G....... 757 839-3265
   Portsmouth (G-10432)
Nestle Pizza Company Inc..................F....... 757 479-1512
   Chesapeake (G-3217)

FOOD PRDTS, FRUITS & VEGETABLES, FRESH, WHOLESALE: Vegetable

Capital Noodle Inc.............................F....... 703 569-3224
   Springfield (G-12973)
Sabra Dipping Company LLC...............E....... 804 518-2000
   South Chesterfield (G-12826)
Sabra Dipping Company LLC...............F....... 804 526-5930
   Colonial Heights (G-3745)

FOOD PRDTS, MEAT & MEAT PRDTS, WHOLESALE: Cured Or Smoked

A L Duck Jr Inc..................................F....... 757 562-2387
   Zuni (G-16011)

FOOD PRDTS, MEAT & MEAT PRDTS, WHOLESALE: Fresh

Smith Valley Meats............................G....... 540 726-3992
   Rich Creek (G-11008)

FOOD PRDTS, WHOLESALE: Coffee, Green Or Roasted

Johnson & Elich Roasters Ltd.............F....... 540 552-7442
   Blacksburg (G-1747)

FOOD PRDTS, WHOLESALE: Condiments

Do-Da Innovations LLC......................G....... 804 556-6645
   Maidens (G-7890)

FOOD PRDTS, WHOLESALE: Dog Food

My Best Friends Cupcakes LLC..........G....... 757 754-1148
   Virginia Beach (G-14668)
Spectrum Brands Pet LLC...................F....... 540 951-5481
   Blacksburg (G-1794)

FOOD PRDTS, WHOLESALE: Natural & Organic

Jah Rootz Industries LLC...................G....... 512 925-1109
   Harrisonburg (G-6332)
Kiddos LLC..G....... 540 468-2700
   Monterey (G-9008)

FOOD PRDTS, WHOLESALE: Organic & Diet

Everything Under Sun LLC..................G....... 276 252-2376
   Ridgeway (G-11842)

FOOD PRDTS, WHOLESALE: Pasta & Rice

Pasta By Valente Inc.........................G....... 434 971-3717
   Charlottesville (G-2841)

FOOD PRDTS, WHOLESALE: Sauces

Old Coots LLC....................................G....... 757 713-2888
   Norfolk (G-9674)

FOOD PRDTS, WHOLESALE: Spaghetti

Capital Noodle Inc.............................F....... 703 569-3224
   Springfield (G-12973)

FOOD PRDTS, WHOLESALE: Specialty

Gumax International Ltd.....................E....... 866 412-3880
   Woodbridge (G-15719)

FOOD PRDTS, WHOLESALE: Water, Mineral Or Spring, Bottled

Liqui-Box Corporation........................D....... 804 325-1400
   Richmond (G-11658)

FOOD PRDTS: Animal & marine fats & oils

Valley Proteins Inc............................E....... 540 877-2590
   Winchester (G-15500)
Valley Proteins Inc............................D....... 540 833-6641
   Linville (G-7436)
Valley Proteins (de) Inc....................C....... 540 877-2533
   Winchester (G-15501)

FOOD PRDTS: Baking Soda

Church & Dwight Co Inc.....................E....... 804 524-8000
   South Chesterfield (G-12799)

FOOD PRDTS: Box Lunches, For Sale Off Premises

Choice Tack.......................................G....... 804 314-0787
   Goochland (G-5881)

FOOD PRDTS: Cereals

Breakfast Lady LLC............................G....... 302 241-7400
   Newport News (G-9185)
Mondelez Global LLC.........................D....... 757 925-3011
   Suffolk (G-13745)
Trio Child LLC...................................G....... 703 299-0070
   Alexandria (G-368)

FOOD PRDTS: Chicken, Processed, Fresh

Perdue Farms Inc...............................B....... 804 722-1276
   Prince George (G-10604)
Perdue Farms Inc...............................G....... 540 465-9665
   Strasburg (G-13594)
Perdue Farms Inc...............................D....... 757 494-5564
   Chesapeake (G-3236)

FOOD PRDTS: Chicken, Processed, Frozen

Tyson Foods Inc.................................A....... 804 561-2187
   Jetersville (G-7016)

FOOD PRDTS: Coffee

Brass Bullet Coffee Co VA LLC...........F....... 540 373-2432
   Fredericksburg (G-5405)
Cafes D Afrique LLC...........................G....... 757 725-1050
   Hampton (G-6103)
Eastern Shore Cstl Rsting Escr...........G....... 757 414-0105
   Cape Charles (G-2233)
Hills Bros Coffee Incorporated...........G....... 757 538-8083
   Suffolk (G-13721)
Lion Mountain Farms LLC...................G....... 916 850-9232
   Arlington (G-1037)
Loco Beans — Fresh Roasted..............G....... 703 851-5997
   Leesburg (G-7303)
Massimo Zanetti Bev USA Inc.............G....... 757 215-7409
   Portsmouth (G-10458)
Massimo Zanetti Bev USA Inc.............C....... 757 215-7300
   Suffolk (G-13740)
Massimo Zanetti Bev USA Inc.............G....... 757 538-8083
   Suffolk (G-13741)
Nova Roast..G....... 540 239-2459
   Salem (G-12546)
Ricks Roasters Coffee Co LLC.............G....... 540 318-6850
   Fredericksburg (G-5479)
Roasted Bean Coffee & Repair............G....... 434 242-8522
   Waynesboro (G-15137)
Six Pcks Artsan Rasted Cof LLC..........G....... 757 337-0872
   Chesapeake (G-3294)

FOOD PRDTS: Coffee Roasting, Exc Wholesale Grocers

Brian K Babcock...............................G....... 540 251-3003
   Riner (G-11861)
Imani M X-Ortiz.................................G....... 540 582-5898
   Partlow (G-10266)
J L V Management Inc........................G....... 540 446-6359
   Stafford (G-13158)

Johnson & Elich Roasters Ltd.............F....... 540 552-7442
   Blacksburg (G-1747)
Kustomcoffee....................................G....... 571 344-9030
   Fairfax (G-4644)
Pale Horse LLC..................................F....... 757 576-0656
   Chesapeake (G-3232)
Whinks Coffee Roasters......................G....... 571 330-6630
   Alexandria (G-609)

FOOD PRDTS: Coffee, Ground, Mixed With Grain Or Chicory

Old Mansion Inc.................................E....... 804 862-9889
   Petersburg (G-10331)

FOOD PRDTS: Corn Chips & Other Corn-Based Snacks

Sweet T&C Kettle Corn LLC.................G....... 804 840-0551
   Chester (G-3458)

FOOD PRDTS: Dates, Dried

B Global LLC......................................G....... 703 628-2826
   Vienna (G-14013)
Iwoan LLC..G....... 347 606-0602
   Falls Church (G-4809)
Soleil Foods Ltd Liability Co...............G....... 201 920-1553
   Fairfax (G-4679)

FOOD PRDTS: Desserts, Ready-To-Mix

Sweetie Pie Desserts..........................G....... 804 239-6425
   Richmond (G-11779)

FOOD PRDTS: Dips, Exc Cheese & Sour Cream Based

Adopt A Salsa....................................G....... 703 409-9453
   Centreville (G-2288)
Bent Mt Salsa....................................G....... 803 427-3170
   Bent Mountain (G-1667)
Lone Wolf Salsa.................................G....... 571 445-3499
   Gainesville (G-5597)
Salsa De Los Flores Inc......................G....... 757 450-0796
   Chesapeake (G-3282)
Salsa Picante Bori..............................G....... 256 874-4074
   Newport News (G-9330)
Salsa Room..G....... 571 489-8422
   Mc Lean (G-8543)

FOOD PRDTS: Dressings, Salad, Raw & Cooked Exc Dry Mixes

Gallas Foods Inc................................G....... 703 593-9957
   Reston (G-10855)

FOOD PRDTS: Durum Flour

Miller Milling Company LLC................E....... 540 678-0197
   Winchester (G-15450)

FOOD PRDTS: Edible fats & oils

Global Telecom Group Inc..................G....... 571 291-9631
   Mc Lean (G-8449)
Global Telecom Group Inc..................G....... 678 896-2468
   Chantilly (G-2428)

FOOD PRDTS: Eggs, Processed

Risser Farms Inc................................G....... 804 387-8584
   New Kent (G-9138)

FOOD PRDTS: Enriched Rice (Vitamin & Mineral Fortified)

Al-Nafea Inc......................................G....... 703 440-8499
   Springfield (G-12938)

FOOD PRDTS: Fish Meal

Omega Protein Corporation.................E....... 804 453-6262
   Reedville (G-10765)

FOOD PRDTS: Fish Oil

Omega Protein Inc.............................E....... 804 453-6262
   Reedville (G-10763)
Omega Protein Inc.............................G....... 804 453-4923
   Reedville (G-10764)

FOOD PRDTS: Flour

Ashland Roller Mills Inc ....E 804 798-8329
Ashland (G-1372)

Big Spring Mill Inc..............................E 540 268-2267
Elliston (G-4343)

Wades Mill Inc ....G 540 348-1400
Raphine (G-10751)

FOOD PRDTS: Flour & Other Grain Mill Products

Archer-Daniels-Midland Company ....E 540 433-2761
Rockingham (G-12240)

Ardent Mills LLC ....E 540 825-1530
Culpeper (G-3868)

Culpeper Farmers Coop Inc..................D 540 825-2200
Culpeper (G-3884)

My Mexico Foods & Distrs Inc..............G 540 560-3587
Harrisonburg (G-6350)

The Mennel Milling Co VA Inc ....F 540 776-6201
Roanoke (G-12008)

FOOD PRDTS: Flour Mixes & Doughs

Nestle Prepared Foods Company ....D 434 822-4000
Danville (G-4017)

FOOD PRDTS: Freeze-Dried Coffee

Virginia Coffee Company LLC ....G 703 566-3037
Alexandria (G-376)

FOOD PRDTS: Frosting Mixes, Dry, For Cakes, Cookies, Etc.

Cake Ballin LLC ....G 540 820-2938
Grottoes (G-6017)

Ms Jos Petite Sweets LLC....................G 571 327-9431
Alexandria (G-286)

FOOD PRDTS: Fruit Juices

Juice Bar Juices Incorporated..............G 757 227-6822
Virginia Beach (G-14577)

Swagg Juices LLC ....G 757 254-6754
Hampton (G-6245)

FOOD PRDTS: Fruits & Vegetables, Pickled

John E Pickle ....G 276 496-5963
Saltville (G-12585)

Pickle Bucket Four LLC......................G 571 259-3726
Alexandria (G-308)

Pickle Bucket Three LLC....................G 571 259-3726
Alexandria (G-309)

FOOD PRDTS: Honey

CNJ Beekeepers Inc ....G 703 378-1629
Chantilly (G-2395)

Honey Gunters ....G 540 955-1734
Berryville (G-1682)

Mielata LLC......................................G 804 245-1227
Midlothian (G-8860)

FOOD PRDTS: Ice, Cubes

Hometown Ice Co ....G 540 483-7865
Rocky Mount (G-12327)

FOOD PRDTS: Instant Coffee

Jddr Foods Inc ....G 571 356-0165
Reston (G-10880)

Lava Instant Coffee LLC ....G 703 239-0803
Gainesville (G-5595)

Mova Corp ....G 757 598-5577
Virginia Beach (G-14666)

FOOD PRDTS: Jelly, Corncob

J & V Kitchen Inc...............................G 540 291-2794
Natural Bridge (G-9107)

FOOD PRDTS: Leavening Compounds, Prepared

Maxx Performance Inc........................F 845 987-9432
Roanoke (G-11960)

FOOD PRDTS: Macaroni Prdts, Dry, Alphabet, Rings Or Shells

Hershey Company ....C 540 722-9830
Winchester (G-15423)

FOOD PRDTS: Macaroni, Noodles, Spaghetti, Pasta, Etc

Nestle Prepared Foods Company ....D 434 822-4000
Danville (G-4017)

FOOD PRDTS: Margarine & Vegetable Oils

Dean Foods Company ....C 804 359-5786
Richmond (G-11555)

Mondelez Global LLC ....D 757 925-3011
Suffolk (G-13745)

FOOD PRDTS: Mixes, Bread & Roll From Purchased Flour

Glazed & Twisted LLC ....G 703 789-5522
Gainesville (G-5586)

FOOD PRDTS: Mixes, Sauces, Dry

Dr Ozz Dat Drip Bbq Sauce LLC...........G 757 597-4405
Hampton (G-6133)

Flynns Foods Inc ....G 804 779-3205
Mechanicsville (G-8624)

Sauer Brands Inc ....G 804 359-5786
Richmond (G-11753)

FOOD PRDTS: Mixes, Seasonings, Dry

Key To Heart Seasoning LLC................G 757 752-7581
Virginia Beach (G-14583)

FOOD PRDTS: Mustard, Prepared

Mondelez Global LLC ....D 757 925-3011
Suffolk (G-13745)

FOOD PRDTS: Noodles, Uncooked, Packaged W/Other Ingredients

Fiber Foods Inc ....G 757 853-2888
Norfolk (G-9552)

FOOD PRDTS: Nuts & Seeds

Royal Oak Peanuts LLC ....G 434 658-9500
Drewryville (G-4138)

FOOD PRDTS: Oils & Fats, Animal

Vaport Inc ....G 757 397-1397
Portsmouth (G-10497)

FOOD PRDTS: Olive Oil

Mediterranean Delight Inc ....G 703 751-2656
Alexandria (G-273)

Olive Manassas Oil Co ....G 703 543-9206
Manassas (G-8121)

Olive Oil & Friends LLC......................G 703 385-1845
Vienna (G-14107)

Olive Oil Boom ....G 703 276-2666
Arlington (G-1085)

Olive Oil Boom LLC ....G 703 276-2666
Arlington (G-1086)

Olive Oil Soap Company ....G 540 671-6940
Front Royal (G-5547)

Olive Oil Tamproom LLC......................G 804 897-6464
Midlothian (G-8871)

Olive Oils Abingdon Assoc LLC ....G 276 525-1524
Abingdon (G-52)

Olive Savor ....G 757 425-3866
Virginia Beach (G-14693)

Our Familys Olive Oil LLC...................G 571 292-1394
Manassas (G-8124)

Scout Marketing LLC ....G 301 986-1470
Springfield (G-13081)

So Olive LLC....................................G 571 398-2377
Occoquan (G-10175)

Staunton Olive Oil Company LLC ....G 540 290-9665
Staunton (G-13299)

Taste Oil Vinegar Spice ....G 540 373-1262
Fredericksburg (G-5230)

FOOD PRDTS: Palm Kernel Oil

Victory Tropical Oil Usa Inc ....G 757 687-8171
Virginia Beach (G-14910)

FOOD PRDTS: Pasta, Rice/Potatoes, Uncooked, Pkgd

Evenflow Technologies Inc ....G 703 625-2628
Ashburn (G-1277)

FOOD PRDTS: Pasta, Uncooked, Packaged With Other Ingredients

Pasta By Valente Inc ....G 434 971-3717
Charlottesville (G-2841)

FOOD PRDTS: Peanut Butter

Dees Nuts Peanut Butter ....G 607 437-0189
Virginia Beach (G-14397)

Pb Crave of Nc LLC ....G 252 585-1744
Franklin (G-5153)

Producers Peanut Company Inc............F 757 539-7496
Suffolk (G-13753)

Reginalds Homemade LLC ....G 804 972-4040
Henrico (G-6557)

FOOD PRDTS: Pickles, Vinegar

Prissy Pickle Company Llc ....G 804 514-8112
Virginia Beach (G-14741)

FOOD PRDTS: Popcorn, Unpopped

Pops Snacks LLC................................G 804 594-7290
North Chesterfield (G-9950)

FOOD PRDTS: Potato & Corn Chips & Similar Prdts

Jhl Inc ....G 703 378-0009
Chantilly (G-2449)

On It Smart Snacks ....G 757 705-9259
Virginia Beach (G-14696)

Snack Alliance Inc ....G 276 669-6194
Bristol (G-1987)

Tabard Corporation............................E 540 477-9664
Mount Jackson (G-9081)

Utz Quality Foods LLC ....G 540 535-1927
Winchester (G-15498)

Utz Quality Foods LLC ....G 757 249-0568
Newport News (G-9370)

Utz Quality Foods LLC ....E 804 232-0241
Richmond (G-11802)

Utz Quality Foods LLC ....E 540 981-0351
Vinton (G-14188)

FOOD PRDTS: Potato Chips & Other Potato-Based Snacks

Frito-Lay North America Inc ....E 540 434-2426
Harrisonburg (G-6318)

Frito-Lay North America Inc................E 540 380-3020
Salem (G-12508)

Kitch N Cook D Potato Chip Co............F 540 886-4473
Staunton (G-13273)

Shearers Foods LLC ....G 276 669-6194
Bristol (G-1986)

Small Fry Inc ....E 540 477-9664
Mount Jackson (G-9078)

FOOD PRDTS: Potatoes, Dried

Tabard Corporation............................E 540 477-9664
Mount Jackson (G-9081)

FOOD PRDTS: Poultry Sausage, Lunch Meats/Other Poultry Prdts

Aura LLC..G 757 965-8400
Norfolk (G-9447)

FOOD PRDTS: Poultry, Processed, Fresh

New Market Poultry LLC......................C 540 740-4260
New Market (G-9145)

FOOD PRDTS: Poultry, Processed, NEC

Perdue Farms Inc ....C 540 828-7700
Bridgewater (G-1956)

Employee Codes: A=Over 500 employees, B=251-500
C=101-250, D=51-100, E=20-50, F=10-19, G=1-9

2021 Virginia
Industrial Directory

PRODUCT

961

Tyson Foods Inc ....A 757 824-3471
  Temperanceville *(G-13840)*
Tyson Foods Inc ....A 804 798-8357
  Glen Allen *(G-5819)*

FOOD PRDTS: *Preparations*

A Touch of Elegance LLC ....G 434 634-4592
  Emporia *(G-4353)*
Aileen L Brown ....G 757 696-1814
  Hampton *(G-6079)*
Andros Bowman Products LLC ....D 540 217-4100
  Mount Jackson *(G-9064)*
Anm Food Services Inc ....G 703 865-4378
  Fairfax *(G-4592)*
Barakat Foods Inc ....F 703 222-9493
  Chantilly *(G-2374)*
Battarbees Catering ....G 540 249-9205
  Grottoes *(G-6015)*
Big Lick Seasonings LLC ....G 540 774-8898
  Roanoke *(G-11890)*
Bon Vivant Company LLC ....G 703 862-5038
  Alexandria *(G-151)*
Buckit O Rice ....G 703 897-4190
  Woodbridge *(G-15662)*
Bzk Ballston LLC ....F 703 248-0990
  Arlington *(G-895)*
Cargill Turkey Production LLC ....F 540 568-1400
  Harrisonburg *(G-6298)*
Cathay Food Corp ....E 617 427-1507
  Fredericksburg *(G-5408)*
Chefit LLC ....G 202 769-6049
  Lorton *(G-7471)*
Chew On This Gluten Free Foods ....G 757 440-3757
  Virginia Beach *(G-14336)*
Cuisine Solutions Inc ....G 303 904-4771
  Alexandria *(G-436)*
Della JS Delectables LLC ....G 703 922-4687
  Alexandria *(G-444)*
Everything Under Sun LLC ....G 276 252-2376
  Ridgeway *(G-11842)*
Farmkart Foods LLC ....G 706 461-6395
  Alexandria *(G-204)*
Festive Foods ....G 757 490-9186
  Virginia Beach *(G-14461)*
Four Seasons Catering & Bakery ....G 276 686-5982
  Rural Retreat *(G-12424)*
Fouz Inc ....G 571 407-4446
  Woodbridge *(G-15706)*
Fresh Twist Foods LLC ....G 540 904-1291
  Christiansburg *(G-3589)*
Frito-Lay North America Inc ....E 540 434-2426
  Harrisonburg *(G-6318)*
Full Fat Kitchen LLC ....G 844 262-6629
  Christiansburg *(G-3590)*
Gigis ....G 276 608-5737
  Abingdon *(G-33)*
Glandore Spice ....G 434 589-2492
  Troy *(G-13925)*
Health E-Lunch Kids Inc ....G 703 402-9064
  Falls Church *(G-4804)*
Herbspice LLC ....G 240 602-6525
  Goochland *(G-5885)*
Hormel Foods Corporation ....G 757 467-5396
  Virginia Beach *(G-14529)*
Jacked Up Foods LLC ....G 540 623-6313
  Fredericksburg *(G-5305)*
Jhl Inc ....G 703 378-0009
  Chantilly *(G-2449)*
Kashaf Spices ....G 571 572-5890
  Dumfries *(G-4248)*
Kashaf Spices Inc ....G 703 232-3529
  Lorton *(G-7501)*
Kraft Heinz Foods Company ....B 540 678-0442
  Winchester *(G-15437)*
L and M Foods ....G 276 979-4110
  Tazewell *(G-13833)*
Litehouse Inc ....C 434 688-3100
  Danville *(G-4014)*
Londoo Foods LLC ....G 571 243-7627
  Woodbridge *(G-15741)*
Martha Bennett ....G 757 897-6150
  Yorktown *(G-15979)*
Maruchan Virginia Inc ....C 804 275-2800
  North Chesterfield *(G-9924)*
McKee Foods Corporation ....A 540 943-7101
  Stuarts Draft *(G-13655)*
Mezeh - Fair Oaks LLC ....F 703 310-9209
  Fairfax *(G-4508)*
Mezeh-Reston LLC ....F 703 310-9209
  Reston *(G-10900)*

Michaels Catering ....G 804 815-6985
  Hayes *(G-6401)*
Mighty Meals LLC ....G 703 303-1438
  Burke *(G-2194)*
Nomad Deli & Catering Co LLC ....G 804 677-0843
  Richmond *(G-11693)*
Northern Pttsylvnia Cnty Fd CT ....G 434 656-6617
  Chatham *(G-2932)*
Nutriati Inc ....F 804 562-2322
  Henrico *(G-6545)*
Pruitt Partners LLC ....G 703 299-0114
  Alexandria *(G-320)*
Quaker Oats Co ....G 276 625-3923
  Wytheville *(G-15906)*
Quarles Food Stop ....G 540 635-1899
  Linden *(G-7432)*
Riveras Tortillas ....G 703 368-1249
  Manassas *(G-8145)*
Riviana Foods Inc ....D 540 722-9830
  Winchester *(G-15466)*
RJR Provisions & Packaging LLC ....G 804 649-7400
  Richmond *(G-11743)*
Rocco Specialty Foods Inc ....F 540 432-1060
  Harrisonburg *(G-6362)*
Rochon & Rochon LLC A Fmly Co ....G 571 331-4860
  Dumfries *(G-4255)*
Rva Sweets LLC ....G 540 748-9298
  Henrico *(G-6562)*
Sabra Go Mediterranean ....G 804 518-2000
  South Chesterfield *(G-12827)*
SNC Foods Inc ....G 804 726-9907
  Glen Allen *(G-5800)*
Ssr Foods LLC ....G 703 581-7260
  Gainesville *(G-5615)*
Tips East LLC ....D 757 562-7888
  Franklin *(G-5159)*
Tommy V Foods ....G 703 254-8764
  Falls Church *(G-4884)*
True Southern Smoke Bbq LLC ....G 757 816-0228
  Chesapeake *(G-3352)*
Vita Specialty Foods Inc ....G 540 542-0195
  Winchester *(G-15504)*
Westover Dairy ....G 434 528-2560
  Lynchburg *(G-7838)*
White Wave ....G 540 434-5945
  Bridgewater *(G-1960)*

FOOD PRDTS: *Prepared Meat Sauces Exc Tomato & Dry*

Ashman Distributing Company ....F 757 428-6734
  Virginia Beach *(G-14246)*
Kingdom Objectives ....G 434 414-0808
  Farmville *(G-4945)*

FOOD PRDTS: *Prepared Sauces, Exc Tomato Based*

Ferrera Group Usa Inc ....G 703 340-8300
  Leesburg *(G-7273)*
Pork Barrel Bbq LLC ....G 202 750-7500
  Alexandria *(G-312)*

FOOD PRDTS: *Rice, Milled*

Clean and Bless ....G 434 324-7129
  Hurt *(G-6973)*

FOOD PRDTS: *Salads*

Asmars Mediterranean Food Inc ....F 703 750-2960
  Alexandria *(G-418)*
Deli-Fresh Foods Inc ....E 757 428-8126
  Virginia Beach *(G-14399)*
Detas Famous Potatoe Salad LLC ....G 757 609-1130
  Virginia Beach *(G-14402)*
Sabra Dipping Company LLC ....E 804 518-2000
  South Chesterfield *(G-12826)*
Sabra Dipping Company LLC ....F 804 526-5930
  Colonial Heights *(G-3745)*
Stafford Salad Company LLC ....G 540 269-2462
  Keezletown *(G-7030)*
Tossd Salad Group LLC ....G 703 521-0646
  Arlington *(G-1193)*

FOOD PRDTS: *Sandwiches*

Damas International LLC ....G 469 740-9973
  Annandale *(G-739)*
Marketfare Foods LLC ....C 540 371-5110
  Fredericksburg *(G-5454)*

FOOD PRDTS: *Seasonings & Spices*

Amama Ltd ....G 703 759-9030
  Great Falls *(G-5935)*
Apothecary Spices ....G 703 868-2333
  Alexandria *(G-138)*
Boston Spice & Tea Co Inc ....G 540 547-3907
  Boston *(G-1902)*
Dizzy Pig LLC ....G 571 379-4884
  Manassas *(G-8059)*
Jjojay LLC ....G 240 660-6146
  Lovettsville *(G-7580)*
Signature Seasonings LLc ....G 757 572-8995
  Virginia Beach *(G-14815)*

FOOD PRDTS: *Soy Sauce*

San-J International Inc ....E 804 226-8333
  Henrico *(G-6565)*

FOOD PRDTS: *Spices, Including Ground*

Ceylon Cinnamon Growers LLC ....G 703 626-1764
  Vienna *(G-14025)*
Famarco Newco LLC ....E 757 460-3573
  Virginia Beach *(G-14459)*
Mafco Consolidated Group Inc ....F 804 222-1600
  Richmond *(G-11281)*
McCormick & Company Inc ....G 540 858-2878
  Gore *(G-5922)*

FOOD PRDTS: *Starch, Indl*

Henkel US Operations Corp ....F 804 222-6100
  Richmond *(G-11236)*

FOOD PRDTS: *Sugar*

Bonumose Biochem LLC ....G 276 206-7337
  Charlottesville *(G-2598)*

FOOD PRDTS: *Sugar, Powdered, From Purchased Ingredients*

Bonumose LLC ....G 276 206-7337
  Charlottesville *(G-2599)*

FOOD PRDTS: *Syrup, Maple*

Do-Da Innovations LLC ....G 804 556-6645
  Maidens *(G-7890)*
Mike Puffendarger ....G 540 468-2682
  Warm Springs *(G-14973)*
Sugar Tree Country Store ....G 540 396-3469
  Mc Dowell *(G-8376)*

FOOD PRDTS: *Syrup, Pancake, Blended & Mixed*

VA Foods LLC ....G 434 221-1456
  Lynch Station *(G-7629)*

FOOD PRDTS: *Syrups*

Echo Hill Farm ....G 802 586-2239
  Arlington *(G-952)*
W W Distributors ....G 804 301-2308
  Richmond *(G-11442)*

FOOD PRDTS: *Tapioca*

Tapioca LLC ....G 703 715-8688
  Fairfax *(G-4568)*
Tapioca Go ....G 757 410-3836
  Chesapeake *(G-3322)*

FOOD PRDTS: *Tea*

Kung Fu Tea ....E 703 992-8599
  Annandale *(G-767)*
Old Mansion Inc ....E 804 862-9889
  Petersburg *(G-10331)*
Reignforest Spices & Tea LLC ....G 757 716-5205
  Norfolk *(G-9706)*

FOOD PRDTS: *Tortillas*

S & K Industries Inc ....E 703 369-0232
  Manassas Park *(G-8209)*
Tortilleria Guavalueana ....G 804 233-4141
  Richmond *(G-11790)*
Tortilleria San Luis LLC ....G 804 901-1501
  Richmond *(G-11415)*

FOOD PRDTS: Turkey, Processed, Fresh

Cargill Incorporated ....B 540 879-2521
Dayton *(G-4053)*
Cargill Incorporated ....E 540 432-5700
Mount Crawford *(G-9051)*

FOOD PRDTS: Vegetable Oil Mills, NEC

Serendib Traditional LLC ....G..... 703 408-1561
Sterling *(G-13504)*

FOOD PRDTS: Vegetable Oil, Refined, Exc Corn

Vaport Inc ....G...... 757 397-1397
Portsmouth *(G-10497)*

FOOD PRDTS: Vegetables, Dried or Dehydrated Exc Freeze-Dried

Taura Natural Ingredients ....G...... 540 723-8691
Winchester *(G-15591)*

FOOD PRDTS: Vinegar

Ah Love Oil & Vinegar ....G...... 703 992-7000
Fairfax *(G-4402)*
Ah Love Oil and Vinegar LLC ....G...... 703 966-0668
Alexandria *(G-123)*
Olive Savor ....G...... 757 425-3866
Virginia Beach *(G-14693)*
Press Oil & Vinegar LLC ....G...... 434 534-2915
Lynchburg *(G-7787)*
Spicy Vinegar LLC ....G...... 757 460-3861
Virginia Beach *(G-14839)*
Taste Oil Vinegar Spice Inc ....G...... 540 825-8415
Culpeper *(G-3923)*
Tincture Distillers LLC ....G...... 443 370-2037
Arlington *(G-1192)*
Vinegar Hill Acres ....G...... 540 337-6839
Churchville *(G-3622)*

FOOD PRODUCTS MACHINERY

AMF Bakery Systems Corp ....G...... 800 225-3771
Richmond *(G-11111)*
Atlantic Metal Products Inc ....E 804 758-4915
Topping *(G-13885)*
Jbt Aerotech ....G...... 336 254-4104
Richmond *(G-11254)*
M & H Paragon Inc ....G...... 540 994-0080
Pulaski *(G-10640)*
Mactavish Machine Mfg Co ....G...... 804 264-6109
North Chesterfield *(G-9916)*
Magco Inc ....F 757 934-0042
Suffolk *(G-13738)*
Smart Machine Technologies Inc ......D 276 632-9853
Ridgeway *(G-11853)*
Tetra Pak Tubex Inc ....E 540 967-0733
Louisa *(G-7571)*
Texacan Beef & Pork Co LLC ....G...... 703 858-5565
Ashburn *(G-1340)*
Unique Engineering Concepts ....G...... 540 586-6761
Bedford *(G-1662)*

FOOD STORES: Cooperative

Macklin Consulting LLC ....G...... 202 423-9923
Alexandria *(G-269)*

FOOD STORES: Frozen Food &Freezer Plans, Exc Meat

Iwoan LLC ....G...... 347 606-0602
Falls Church *(G-4809)*

FOOTWEAR: Custom Made

Reach Orthtic Prsthetic Svcs S ....G...... 757 673-2000
Chesapeake *(G-3261)*

FOOTWEAR: Cut Stock

Bean Counters ....G...... 703 534-1516
Falls Church *(G-4763)*
Fixher Upper LLC ....G...... 804 539-8816
Hampton *(G-6151)*
No Quarter LLC ....G...... 703 753-0511
Gainesville *(G-5601)*
Signature K-9 ....G...... 866 820-3647
Roanoke *(G-12188)*

Upper Weyanoke LLC ....G...... 804 288-7333
Richmond *(G-11428)*
Z & T Sales LLC ....G...... 540 570-9500
Buena Vista *(G-2157)*

FORESTRY RELATED EQPT

Jackson & Jackson Inc ....G...... 434 851-1798
Roanoke *(G-12109)*
Wayrick Inc ....G...... 276 988-8091
Lebanon *(G-7211)*
Westmoreland Pallet Compan ....G...... 804 224-9450
Colonial Beach *(G-3729)*

FORGINGS

Cerro Fabricated Products LLC.........D 540 208-1606
Weyers Cave *(G-15171)*
Full Tilt Performance ....G...... 276 628-0036
Abingdon *(G-31)*
IMS Gear Holding Inc ....E 757 468-8810
Virginia Beach *(G-14542)*
Progressive Manufacturing Corp ......E 804 717-5353
Chester *(G-3448)*
Virginia Forge Company LLC ....G...... 540 254-2236
Buchanan *(G-2130)*
Wegmann Usa Inc ....G...... 434 385-1580
Lynchburg *(G-7837)*

FORGINGS: Aluminum

Catalina Cylinders Inc ....D 757 896-9100
Hampton *(G-6109)*

FORGINGS: Bearing & Bearing Race, Nonferrous

Craft Bearing Company Inc ....E 757 247-6000
Newport News *(G-9208)*

FORGINGS: Engine Or Turbine, Nonferrous

Applied Plasma Tech LLC ....G...... 703 340-5545
Springfield *(G-12950)*

FORGINGS: Gear & Chain

Yakattack LLC ....G...... 804 561-4274
Burkeville *(G-2212)*
Yakattack LLC ....G...... 434 392-3233
Farmville *(G-4961)*

FORGINGS: Machinery, Ferrous

Immco LLC ....F 804 271-6979
North Chesterfield *(G-9890)*

FORGINGS: Metal , Ornamental, Ferrous

White Oak Forge Ltd ....G...... 540 636-4545
Huntly *(G-6967)*

FORGINGS: Missile & Ordinance, Nonferrous

Jordan Consulting and Research ....G...... 703 597-7812
Herndon *(G-6719)*

FORGINGS: Nonferrous

Cerro Fabricated Products LLC.........D 540 208-1606
Weyers Cave *(G-15171)*
Turner Sculpture Ltd ....E 757 787-2818
Melfa *(G-8713)*

FORGINGS: Pump & Compressor, Ferrous

Southwest Cmprsr Pmpg Pckges I ......G...... 276 963-6400
Cedar Bluff *(G-2285)*

FORMS: Concrete, Sheet Metal

Callahan Paving Products Inc ....G...... 434 589-9000
Crozier *(G-3857)*
JD Concrete LLC ....F 703 331-2155
Manassas Park *(G-8203)*

FOUNDRIES: Aluminum

Nomar Castings Inc ....F 540 380-3394
Elliston *(G-4346)*
OK Foundry Company Inc ....E 804 233-9674
Richmond *(G-11698)*

FOUNDRIES: Brass, Bronze & Copper

Anne Chapman Casting ....G...... 804 728-1300
Richmond *(G-11114)*
Hanover Brassfoundry ....G...... 804 781-1864
Mechanicsville *(G-8634)*

FOUNDRIES: Gray & Ductile Iron

Nomar Castings Inc ....F 540 380-3394
Elliston *(G-4346)*

FOUNDRIES: Nonferrous

Colonial Commercial Elec Co ....G...... 804 720-2455
King Queen Ch *(G-7125)*
NMB Metals ....G...... 434 584-0027
South Hill *(G-12857)*
Southern Casting LLC ....G...... 757 233-1700
Norfolk *(G-9732)*

FOUNDRIES: Steel

DLM Enterprises Inc ....G...... 757 617-3470
Suffolk *(G-13700)*
Opta (usa) Inc ....G...... 843 296-7074
Norfolk *(G-9677)*
Thistle Foundry & Mch Co Inc ....F 276 326-1196
Bluefield *(G-1881)*

FOUNDRIES: Steel Investment

Nomar Castings Inc ....F 540 380-3394
Elliston *(G-4346)*

FOUNTAINS, METAL, EXC DRINKING

Design In Copper Inc ....F 540 885-8557
Staunton *(G-13250)*

FRAMES & FRAMING WHOLESALE

Finest Art & Framing LLC ....G...... 703 945-9000
Lansdowne *(G-7170)*

FRAMES: Chair, Metal

Old Dominion Metal Pdts Inc ....E 804 355-7123
Richmond *(G-11700)*

FRANCHISES, SELLING OR LICENSING

Frito-Lay North America Inc ....E 540 380-3020
Salem *(G-12508)*

FREIGHT FORWARDING ARRANGEMENTS

Artfx LLC ....C 757 853-1703
Norfolk *(G-9445)*
Oneso Inc ....G...... 704 560-6354
Arlington *(G-1088)*

FREON

Freon Doctor Inc ....G...... 877 825-2401
Bumpass *(G-2162)*

FRITS

Den Hertog Frits ....G...... 540 929-4650
Bent Mountain *(G-1668)*
Frit Small Dollar Twai ....G...... 804 697-3968
Richmond *(G-11595)*

FRUITS: Artificial & Preserved

Al Rayanah USA ....G...... 703 941-1200
Falls Church *(G-4742)*

FUEL ADDITIVES

Kessler Marine Services Inc ....G...... 571 276-1377
Springfield *(G-13033)*
Polytrade International Corp ....G...... 703 598-7269
Sterling *(G-13474)*

FUEL DEALERS: Coal

Johns Creek Elkhorn Coal Corp ....E 804 780-3000
Richmond *(G-11634)*

FUEL TREATING

Raymond Golden ....G...... 757 549-1853
Chesapeake *(G-3256)*

Employee Codes: A=Over 500 employees, B=251-500
C=101-250, D=51-100, E=20-50, F=10-19, G=1-9

2021 Virginia
Industrial Directory

PRODUCT

963

FUELS: Diesel

American Biodiesel Corporation ....G...... 703 906-9434
  Manassas (G-7910)
Chesapeake Custom Chem Corp ....G...... 276 956-3145
  Ridgeway (G-11840)
Reco Biodiesel LLC ....F...... 804 644-2800
  Richmond (G-11731)
Synergy Biofuels LLC ....G...... 276 546-5226
  Pennington Gap (G-10300)
Virginia Bodiesel Refinery LLC ....G...... 804 435-1126
  Kilmarnock (G-7078)

FUELS: Ethanol

83 Gas & Grocery Inc ....G...... 276 926-4388
  Clintwood (G-3685)
Affordable Fuel Substitute Inc ....G...... 276 694-8080
  Stuart (G-13604)
Better Fuels of Virginia ....G...... 540 693-4552
  Fredericksburg (G-5252)
Caribbean Channel One Inc ....G...... 703 447-3773
  Woodbridge (G-15668)
Cnv Marine Fuel Specialist LLC ....G...... 757 615-2666
  Chesapeake (G-3038)
Commercial Fueling 24/7 Inc ....G...... 540 338-6457
  Purcellville (G-10656)
Eco Fuel LLC ....G...... 703 256-6999
  Annandale (G-746)
Fuel Impurities Separator ....G...... 757 340-6833
  Virginia Beach (G-14477)
Fuel Your Life LLC ....G...... 703 208-4449
  Vienna (G-14058)
Global Yacht Fuel LLC ....G...... 954 462-6050
  Norfolk (G-9563)
Green Fuel of VA ....G...... 804 304-4564
  Mechanicsville (G-8632)
Kid Fueled Kco LLC ....G...... 804 720-4091
  Prince George (G-10597)
Masters Energy Inc ....E...... 281 816-9991
  Glen Allen (G-5768)
Osage Bio Energy LLC ....E...... 804 612-8660
  Glen Allen (G-5777)
Power Fuels LLC ....G...... 276 676-2945
  Abingdon (G-54)
Real Food For Fuel LLC ....G...... 757 416-4458
  Blacksburg (G-1782)
S Fuel Co ....G...... 434 220-1044
  Charlottesville (G-2869)
Sisko Duel Fuel System ....G...... 804 795-1634
  Henrico (G-6571)
Star Oil LLC ....G...... 757 545-5100
  Chesapeake (G-3310)
Taicco Fuel Inc ....G...... 571 405-7700
  Richmond (G-11406)
True Energy Fuels ....G...... 276 796-4003
  Pound (G-10514)
Wholesome Energy LLC ....G...... 540 984-8219
  Edinburg (G-4316)

FUELS: Jet

Advanced Cgnitive Systems Corp ....G...... 804 397-3373
  Richmond (G-11474)
Fuelcor Development LLC ....G...... 703 740-0071
  Mc Lean (G-8437)

FUELS: Nuclear

Framatome Inc ....C...... 434 832-5000
  Lynchburg (G-7714)

FUELS: Nuclear, Uranium Slug, Radioactive

Urenco USA Inc ....G...... 575 394-4646
  Arlington (G-1205)

FUELS: Oil

Wythe Oil Distributors Inc ....G...... 276 228-4512
  Wytheville (G-15926)

FUR: Apparel

Millers Furs Inc ....G...... 703 772-4593
  Mc Lean (G-8501)

FURNACES & OVENS: Indl

Associated Printing Svcs Inc ....G...... 804 360-5770
  Richmond (G-11119)
Buffalo Air Handling Company ....C...... 434 946-7455
  Amherst (G-685)

Isotemp Research Inc ....G...... 434 295-3101
  Charlottesville (G-2815)
Mac Bone Industries Ltd ....G...... 804 264-3603
  Richmond (G-11278)
Modine Manufacturing Company ....E...... 540 261-9821
  Buena Vista (G-2148)
Setliff and Company LLC ....G...... 434 793-1173
  Danville (G-4038)

FURNITURE & CABINET STORES: Cabinets, Custom Work

Ecowood Usa Inc ....G...... 703 347-6858
  Springfield (G-12996)
H & F Body & Cabinet Shop ....G...... 276 728-9404
  Hillsville (G-6894)
Mill Cabinet Shop Inc ....E...... 540 828-6763
  Bridgewater (G-1954)
Miller Cabinets Inc ....G...... 540 434-4835
  Harrisonburg (G-6345)

FURNITURE & CABINET STORES: Custom

Worthington Millwork LLC ....G...... 540 832-6391
  Gordonsville (G-5919)

FURNITURE & FIXTURES Factory

Halifax Fine Furnishings ....G...... 540 774-3060
  Roanoke (G-11931)
Kingmill Enterprises LLC ....G...... 877 895-9453
  Charlottesville (G-2822)
Pro Furniture Doctor Inc ....G...... 571 379-7058
  Springfield (G-13074)
Tomo LLC ....G...... 407 694-7464
  Williamsburg (G-15325)

FURNITURE COMPONENTS: Porcelain Enameled

County Line LLC ....D...... 434 736-8405
  Keysville (G-7055)
Wobanc Danforth ....G...... 804 222-7877
  Richmond (G-11453)

FURNITURE PARTS: Metal

Performnce Mtal Fbricators Inc ....G...... 757 465-8622
  Portsmouth (G-10467)
Phipps & Bird Inc ....F...... 804 254-2737
  Richmond (G-11059)
US Joiner Holding Company ....G...... 434 220-8500
  Crozet (G-3854)

FURNITURE REPAIR & MAINTENANCE SVCS

A1 Finishing Inc ....F...... 276 632-2121
  Martinsville (G-8262)

FURNITURE STOCK & PARTS: Carvings, Wood

American Hands LLC ....G...... 804 349-8974
  Powhatan (G-10530)
Country Corner LLC ....G...... 540 538-3763
  Fredericksburg (G-5415)
Great Amercn Woodcrafters LLC ....G...... 571 572-3150
  Woodbridge (G-15714)
Rutherford Bean ....G...... 757 898-4363
  Seaford (G-12677)
Wooden Caboose Inc ....G...... 804 748-2101
  Chesterfield (G-3543)

FURNITURE STOCK & PARTS: Dimension Stock, Hardwood

Whitlow Lumber & Logging Inc ....G...... 276 930-3854
  Stuart (G-13640)

FURNITURE STOCK & PARTS: Frames, Upholstered Furniture, Wood

Kreager Woodworking Inc ....E...... 276 952-2052
  Meadows of Dan (G-8592)
Rowe Fine Furniture Inc ....C...... 540 389-8661
  Salem (G-12563)

FURNITURE STOCK & PARTS: Hardwood

Aco Corporation ....G...... 757 480-2875
  Virginia Beach (G-14208)

Aco Corporation ....G...... 757 480-2875
  Norfolk (G-9420)
Brad Warstler ....G...... 540 745-3595
  Floyd (G-5017)
Hickory Frame Corp ....G...... 434 847-8489
  Lynchburg (G-7732)
Ten Oaks LLC ....C...... 276 694-3208
  Stuart (G-13636)
Valley Utility Buildings Inc ....G...... 276 679-6736
  Big Stone Gap (G-1717)

FURNITURE STOCK & PARTS: Turnings, Wood

Davis Mining & Mfg Inc ....F...... 276 395-3354
  Wise (G-15622)
Knicely Plaining Mill LLC ....G...... 540 879-2284
  Dayton (G-4057)

FURNITURE STORES

American Interiors Ltd ....G...... 757 627-0248
  Norfolk (G-9438)
Bassett Furniture Inds Inc ....A...... 276 629-6000
  Bassett (G-1578)
Brass Beds of Virginia Inc ....E...... 804 353-3503
  Richmond (G-11131)
Country Corner LLC ....G...... 540 538-3763
  Fredericksburg (G-5415)
Ennis Mountain Woods Inc ....G...... 540 471-9171
  Afton (G-79)
Halifax Fine Furnishings ....G...... 540 774-3060
  Roanoke (G-11931)
Hoskins Creek Table Company ....G...... 804 333-0032
  Warsaw (G-15067)
R & B Cabinet Shop ....G...... 540 249-4507
  Grottoes (G-6023)
Sam Moore Furniture LLC ....B...... 540 586-8253
  Bedford (G-1656)
Suters Cabinet Shop Inc ....F...... 540 434-2131
  Harrisonburg (G-6378)

FURNITURE STORES: Cabinets, Kitchen, Exc Custom Made

Richards Building Supply Co ....G...... 540 719-0128
  Hardy (G-6289)

FURNITURE STORES: Office

Benton-Thomas Inc ....F...... 434 572-3577
  South Boston (G-12751)

FURNITURE WHOLESALERS

Bassett Furniture Inds Inc ....A...... 276 629-6000
  Bassett (G-1578)
Hoskins Creek Table Company ....G...... 804 333-0032
  Warsaw (G-15067)
Marcus Cox & Sons Inc ....F...... 540 297-5818
  Moneta (G-8971)

FURNITURE, WHOLESALE: Bar

Haltrie LLC ....G...... 703 598-9928
  Annandale (G-755)

FURNITURE, WHOLESALE: Bookcases

Dimitrios & Co Inc ....G...... 703 368-1757
  Manassas Park (G-8199)

FURNITURE, WHOLESALE: Filing Units

Finance Business Forms Company ....G...... 703 255-2151
  Vienna (G-14055)

FURNITURE: Bed Frames & Headboards, Wood

La Prade Enterprises ....G...... 804 271-9899
  North Chesterfield (G-9912)
Vaughan-Bassett Furn Co Inc ....A...... 276 236-6161
  Galax (G-5653)

FURNITURE: Bedroom, Wood

Henkel-Harris LLC ....E...... 540 667-4900
  Winchester (G-15547)
Hooker Furniture Corporation ....C...... 276 632-2133
  Martinsville (G-8297)
V-B/Williams Furniture Co Inc ....B...... 276 236-6161
  Galax (G-5651)

FURNITURE: Benches, Cut Stone

Oakes Memorials & Signs Inc ....G...... 434 836-5888
   Danville (G-4018)

FURNITURE: Bookcases & Partitions, Office, Exc Wood

Dextall Inc ....G...... 202 701-3208
   Fairfax (G-4438)

FURNITURE: Box Springs, Assembled

Eastern Sleep Products Company ....C...... 804 353-8965
   Richmond (G-11195)

FURNITURE: Cabinets & Vanities, Medicine, Metal

Burgers Cabinet Shop Inc......................F 571 262-8001
   Sterling (G-13362)

FURNITURE: Chairs & Couches, Wood, Upholstered

Bassett Mirror Company Inc ....C...... 276 629-3341
   Bassett (G-1580)

FURNITURE: Chairs, Household Upholstered

Sam Moore Furniture LLC......................B 540 586-8253
   Bedford (G-1656)

FURNITURE: Chairs, Office Wood

A C Furniture Company Inc ....C...... 276 650-3356
   Axton (G-1531)

FURNITURE: Church

Indian Ridge Woodcraft Inc ....G...... 540 789-4754
   Willis (G-15361)

FURNITURE: Club Room, Wood

Garnier-Thiebaut Inc..............................G...... 434 572-3965
   South Boston (G-12770)

FURNITURE: Commodes

Tubular Fabricators Indust Inc ....E...... 804 733-4000
   Petersburg (G-10347)

FURNITURE: Desks & Tables, Office, Exc Wood

Uptime Business Products LLC ....G...... 540 982-5750
   Roanoke (G-12013)

FURNITURE: Desks & Tables, Office, Wood

Worthington Millwork LLC ....G...... 540 832-6391
   Gordonsville (G-5919)

FURNITURE: Frames, Box Springs Or Bedsprings, Metal

Starsprings USA Inc ....D...... 276 403-4500
   Ridgeway (G-11855)

FURNITURE: Garden, Exc Wood, Metal, Stone Or Concrete

Twfutures Inc ....G...... 804 301-6629
   Midlothian (G-8915)

FURNITURE: Garden, Metal

McKinnon and Harris Inc........................E...... 804 358-2385
   Richmond (G-11286)

FURNITURE: Hospital

Swinson Medical LLC.............................G...... 540 576-1719
   Penhook (G-10285)

FURNITURE: Hotel

A C Furniture Company Inc ....B 276 650-1802
   Axton (G-1532)
A1 Finishing Inc ....F 276 632-2121
   Martinsville (G-8262)
Charter of Lynchburg Inc ....D...... 434 239-2671
   Lynchburg (G-7677)

Design Source Inc ....E...... 804 644-3424
   Sandston (G-12610)
Sorrentino Mariani & Company ....D...... 757 624-9025
   Norfolk (G-9730)

FURNITURE: Household, Metal

Bassett Mirror Company Inc ....C...... 276 629-3341
   Bassett (G-1580)
Becker Designed Inc ....E...... 703 803-6900
   Chantilly (G-2376)
Brass Beds of Virginia Inc ....E...... 804 353-3503
   Richmond (G-11131)

FURNITURE: Household, NEC

Fabrik ....G...... 540 651-4169
   Copper Hill (G-3764)
Hockey Stick Builds LLC ....G...... 617 784-2918
   Falls Church (G-4917)
Jr Lamb & Sons ....G...... 434 823-2320
   Crozet (G-3839)
Neighborhoods Vi LLC ....G...... 703 964-5000
   Reston (G-10906)
Summer Interior LLC ....G...... 540 479-5145
   Fredericksburg (G-5371)

FURNITURE: Household, Novelty, Metal

Summa LLC ....G...... 757 254-1000
   Newport News (G-9349)

FURNITURE: Household, Upholstered On Metal Frames

Demorais International Inc ....G...... 703 369-3326
   Manassas (G-7932)

FURNITURE: Household, Upholstered, Exc Wood Or Metal

Poof Inc ....G...... 703 298-7516
   Haymarket (G-6437)

FURNITURE: Household, Wood

All A Board Inc ....F 804 652-0020
   Richmond (G-11481)
American Interiors Ltd............................G...... 757 627-0248
   Norfolk (G-9438)
Amish Heirlooms of Vrgn.......................G...... 540 626-8587
   Pembroke (G-10281)
Antiquated Heirlooms LLC.....................G...... 540 771-4120
   Strasburg (G-13572)
Bassett Direct Sc LLC ....G...... 276 629-6000
   Bassett (G-1577)
Bassett Furniture Inds Inc.....................A 276 629-6000
   Bassett (G-1578)
Bassett Mirror Company Inc ....C...... 276 629-3341
   Bassett (G-1580)
Becker Designed Inc ....E...... 703 803-6900
   Chantilly (G-2376)
Bhk of America Inc ....E...... 201 783-8490
   South Boston (G-12752)
Blaise Gaston Inc ....G...... 434 973-1801
   Earlysville (G-4288)
Blue Ridge Woodworks VA Inc ....G...... 434 477-0313
   Monroe (G-8987)
Brass Beds of Virginia Inc ....E...... 804 353-3503
   Richmond (G-11131)
Butler Woodcrafters Inc ....E...... 877 852-0784
   North Chesterfield (G-9837)
Carpers Wood Creations Inc..................E...... 540 465-2525
   Strasburg (G-13576)
Central Virginia Hardwood Pdts ....G...... 434 335-5898
   Gretna (G-6006)
Colonial Kitchen & Cabinets ....E...... 757 898-1332
   Yorktown (G-15943)
Contemporary Kitchens Ltd ....G...... 804 758-2001
   Topping (G-13886)
Desantis Design Inc ....G...... 540 751-9014
   Purcellville (G-10659)
Dixie Woodcraft Inc ....G...... 434 842-3384
   Fork Union (G-5109)
E A Clore Sons Inc ....D...... 540 948-5821
   Madison (G-7851)
Frank Chervan Inc ....G...... 540 586-5600
   Bedford (G-1638)
Frey Randall Antique Furnitre ....G...... 434 985-7631
   Stanardsville (G-13219)
Furniture Art ....G...... 540 667-2533
   Winchester (G-15418)

Helvetica Designs ....G...... 540 213-2437
   Staunton (G-13266)
Hermle Uhren GMBH & Co KG................D...... 434 946-7751
   Amherst (G-693)
IKEA Industry Danville LLC ....A 434 822-6080
   Ringgold (G-11868)
J W Creations ....G...... 276 676-3770
   Abingdon (G-43)
Jack Carter Cabinet Maker ....G...... 757 622-9414
   Norfolk (G-9599)
Jaeger & Ernst Inc ....F 434 973-7018
   Barboursville (G-1562)
Javawood USA LLC ....G...... 703 658-9665
   Alexandria (G-493)
John Potter Enterprises ....G...... 757 485-2922
   Chesapeake (G-3151)
Jph Woodcraft ....G...... 757 615-6812
   Virginia Beach (G-14575)
Mamagreen LLC ....G...... 312 953-3557
   Richmond (G-11663)
Mikrocoze Inc ....G...... 800 542-8715
   Chesapeake (G-3205)
Mill Cabinet Shop Inc ....E...... 540 828-6763
   Bridgewater (G-1954)
Old Dominion Wood Products Inc...........E...... 434 845-5511
   Lynchburg (G-7778)
Old Town Woodworking Inc ....F 540 347-3993
   Warrenton (G-15039)
Oregon Woodcraft Inc ....G...... 703 477-4793
   Burke (G-2197)
Phineas Rose Wood Joinery ....G...... 540 948-4248
   Madison (G-7860)
Piedmont Station Studio LLC ....G...... 540 364-4427
   Delaplane (G-4077)
Pine Creek Structures ....G...... 703 791-5700
   Manassas (G-8128)
Preservation Wood Sales ....G...... 540 553-2023
   Floyd (G-5035)
Pulliam Furniture Co..............................G...... 276 956-3615
   Ridgeway (G-11849)
Ready To Cover Inc ....G...... 571 379-5766
   Manassas (G-8140)
Remark Design Incorporated..................G...... 540 675-3625
   Washington (G-15078)
Renaissnce Cntract Ltg Furn In ....E...... 540 342-1548
   Roanoke (G-12162)
Richard E Sheppard Jr ....F 276 956-2322
   Ridgeway (G-11851)
Rowe Fine Furniture Inc ....C...... 540 444-7693
   Elliston (G-4348)
Rowe Furniture Inc ....A 540 389-8671
   Elliston (G-4349)
Smart Buy Kitchen & Bath Plus..............G...... 571 643-1078
   Chantilly (G-2492)
Southeastern Wood Products Inc ....F 276 632-9025
   Martinsville (G-8332)
Southern Finishing Company Inc...........E...... 276 632-4901
   Martinsville (G-8333)
Steve M Sheil ....G...... 757 482-2456
   Chesapeake (G-3312)
Suters Cabinet Shop Inc ....F 540 434-2131
   Harrisonburg (G-6378)
Tfi Wind Down Inc ....G...... 703 714-0500
   Vienna (G-14141)
Turman Lumber Company Inc ....E...... 540 639-1250
   Christiansburg (G-3614)
Valley Heirlooms LLC ....G...... 540 234-0251
   Mount Crawford (G-9062)
Vaughan Furniture Company Inc.............F 276 236-6111
   Galax (G-5652)
Woodcrafters Inc...................................G...... 703 736-2825
   Reston (G-10993)
Woodcrafters II LLC ....G...... 703 499-5418
   Gainesville (G-5624)

FURNITURE: Hydraulic Barber & Beauty Shop Chairs

Warren Mastery Enterprises Inc ....G...... 877 207-6370
   Sedley (G-12681)

FURNITURE: Institutional, Exc Wood

All A Board Inc ....F 804 652-0020
   Richmond (G-11481)
Design Source Inc ....E...... 804 644-3424
   Sandston (G-12610)
Evans Corporate Services LLC ....F 703 344-3678
   Lorton (G-7485)
Fitzgeralds Cabinet Shop Inc.................G...... 757 877-2538
   Newport News (G-9229)

PRODUCT

Funes Project LLC ....G...... 540 364-8054
Marshall *(G-8254)*
Its Just Furniture Inc ....G...... 703 357-6405
Fredericksburg *(G-5197)*
Kearney & Associates Inc ....F...... 540 423-9511
Culpeper *(G-3905)*
Palace Interiors ....G...... 757 592-1509
Hampton *(G-6212)*
Premier Office Systems LLC ....F...... 804 414-4198
Blackstone *(G-1824)*
Reflections Light Boxes ....G...... 757 641-3192
Chesapeake *(G-3267)*
Talu LLC ....G...... 571 323-5200
Herndon *(G-6822)*
US Joiner Holding Company ....G...... 434 220-8500
Crozet *(G-3854)*

FURNITURE: Lawn & Garden, Except Wood & Metal

Beckett Corporation ....E...... 757 857-0153
Norfolk *(G-9461)*
Buffalo Ridge Wood Products ....G...... 276 930-2189
Stuart *(G-13606)*
Natural Woodworking Co ....G...... 540 745-2664
Floyd *(G-5033)*
Weatherly LLC ....G...... 703 593-3192
Woodbridge *(G-15830)*

FURNITURE: Lawn & Garden, Metal

Capstone Industries LLC ....G...... 703 966-6718
Manassas *(G-8045)*

FURNITURE: Lawn, Metal

Solgreen Solutions LLC ....G...... 833 765-4733
Alexandria *(G-588)*

FURNITURE: Lawn, Wood

Virginia Custom Buildings ....F...... 804 784-3816
Manakin Sabot *(G-7906)*
Whispering Pine Lawn Furn ....G...... 540 789-7361
Willis *(G-15366)*

FURNITURE: Living Room, Upholstered On Wood Frames

Clayton-Marcus Company Inc ....C...... 540 389-8671
Elliston *(G-4344)*
Expertsinframing LLC ....G...... 703 580-9980
Woodbridge *(G-15701)*
Haltrie LLC ....G...... 703 598-9928
Annandale *(G-755)*

FURNITURE: Mattresses & Foundations

Custom Comfort By Winn Ltd ....F...... 804 452-0929
Hopewell *(G-6921)*
Rvmf Inc ....G...... 614 921-1223
North Chesterfield *(G-9968)*
Tempur Production Usa LLC ....C...... 276 431-7150
Duffield *(G-4185)*

FURNITURE: Mattresses, Box & Bedsprings

Brass Beds of Virginia Inc ....E...... 804 353-3503
Richmond *(G-11131)*
Direct Buy Mattress LLC ....G...... 703 346-0323
Midland *(G-8752)*
Free Union Restaurant Inc ....G...... 434 327-9559
Charlottesville *(G-2635)*
Leesa Sleep LLC ....G...... 844 335-3372
Virginia Beach *(G-14606)*
Mattress Deal LLC ....G...... 804 869-3387
Richmond *(G-11285)*

FURNITURE: Mattresses, Innerspring Or Box Spring

Kingsdown Incorporated ....D...... 540 667-0399
Winchester *(G-15433)*
Paramount Indus Companies Inc ....C...... 757 855-3321
Norfolk *(G-9682)*
Ssb Manufacturing Company ....G...... 540 891-0236
Fredericksburg *(G-5368)*

FURNITURE: NEC

After Affects Custom Furniture ....G...... 504 510-1792
Hampton *(G-6077)*

American Assembly LLC ....G...... 757 639-6040
Portsmouth *(G-10391)*
Harris Custom Woodworking ....G...... 804 241-9525
Quinton *(G-10697)*
Sauder Manufacturing Co ....G...... 804 897-3400
North Chesterfield *(G-9969)*

FURNITURE: Nursery, Metal

Rewi LLC ....G...... 757 647-8942
Williamsburg *(G-15305)*

FURNITURE: Office Panel Systems, Exc Wood

Corporate Furn Svcs VA LLC ....G...... 804 928-1143
Richmond *(G-11542)*

FURNITURE: Office, Exc Wood

Alpha Safe & Vault Inc ....G...... 703 281-7233
Vienna *(G-14008)*
Chuka LLC ....G...... 443 837-5522
Leesburg *(G-7243)*
Edwards Consulting ....G...... 804 733-2506
Prince George *(G-10593)*
Evans Corporate Services LLC ....F...... 703 344-3678
Lorton *(G-7485)*
Fedsafes LLC ....G...... 703 525-1436
Arlington *(G-964)*
Jh Enterprise Inc ....G...... 757 639-5049
Norfolk *(G-9603)*
Modular Design Installations ....G...... 757 871-8885
Newport News *(G-9304)*
Office Furniture Outlet Inc ....G...... 757 855-5522
Norfolk *(G-9673)*
Paul E Stahl ....G...... 772 600-8099
Roanoke *(G-11983)*
Poof Inc ....G...... 703 298-7516
Haymarket *(G-6437)*
Problem Solver ....G...... 757 452-0653
Virginia Beach *(G-14742)*
Reem Enterprises ....G...... 703 608-2283
Chantilly *(G-2486)*
Supplies Express Inc ....G...... 703 631-4600
Centreville *(G-2343)*
Vas of Virginia Inc ....E...... 434 296-5608
Charlottesville *(G-2899)*
Xact Solutions Inc ....G...... 703 398-2680
Ashburn *(G-1354)*

FURNITURE: Office, Wood

A and H Office Inc ....G...... 703 250-0963
Burke *(G-2179)*
Alliance Office Furniture Co ....G......
Alexandria *(G-129)*
Aric Lynn LLC ....G...... 571 505-7657
Manassas *(G-8029)*
Capital Discount Mdse LLC ....F...... 703 499-9368
Woodbridge *(G-15665)*
Colonial Kitchen & Cabinets ....E...... 757 898-1332
Yorktown *(G-15943)*
Frank Chervan Inc ....C...... 540 586-5600
Roanoke *(G-12093)*
Gaithrsburg Cbinetry Mllwk Inc ....D...... 540 347-4551
Warrenton *(G-15019)*
Haltrie LLC ....G...... 703 598-9928
Annandale *(G-755)*
Henkel-Harris LLC ....E...... 540 667-4900
Winchester *(G-15547)*
Hooker Furniture Corporation ....C...... 276 632-2133
Martinsville *(G-8297)*
Interpretive Wdwrk Design Inc ....G...... 703 330-6105
Manassas *(G-7953)*
Its Just Furniture Inc ....G...... 703 357-6405
Fredericksburg *(G-5197)*
Modular Interiors Group LLC ....G...... 757 550-8910
Richmond *(G-11680)*
New Minglewood Mfg Inc ....G...... 276 632-9107
Fieldale *(G-4990)*
Office Furniture Outlet Inc ....G...... 757 855-5522
Norfolk *(G-9673)*
Old Town Woodworking Inc ....F...... 540 347-3993
Warrenton *(G-15039)*
Paul E Stahl ....G...... 772 600-8099
Roanoke *(G-11983)*
Vesta Propertys LLC ....G...... 703 579-7979
Vienna *(G-14151)*

FURNITURE: Outdoor, Wood

Chesapeake Bay Adirondack LLC ....G...... 757 416-4583
Chesapeake *(G-3030)*
Deck World Inc ....G...... 804 798-9003
Warsaw *(G-15062)*
Rocky Ridge Furniture ....G...... 419 512-0067
Pearisburg *(G-10276)*

FURNITURE: Picnic Tables Or Benches, Park

High Bridge Trail State Park ....F...... 434 315-0457
Green Bay *(G-5990)*

FURNITURE: Restaurant

Genesis Decor LLC ....E...... 804 561-4844
Amelia Court House *(G-658)*
Javawood USA LLC ....G...... 703 658-9665
Alexandria *(G-493)*
Old Dominion Wood Products Inc ....E...... 434 845-5511
Lynchburg *(G-7778)*

FURNITURE: Ship

2308 Granby Street Assoc LLC ....G...... 757 627-4844
Norfolk *(G-9411)*
South Bay Industries Inc ....G...... 757 489-9344
Norfolk *(G-9731)*

FURNITURE: Sleep

Robson Woodworking ....G...... 540 896-6711
Timberville *(G-13854)*

FURNITURE: Stools, Office, Wood

Scan Industries LLC ....G...... 360 320-8244
Ashburn *(G-1332)*

FURNITURE: Storage Chests, Household, Wood

Shore Drive Self Storage Corp ....G...... 757 587-6000
Norfolk *(G-9722)*
White Properties of Winchester ....F...... 540 868-0205
Winchester *(G-15508)*

FURNITURE: Tables & Table Tops, Wood

Bassett Furniture Inds NC LLC ....F...... 276 629-6000
Bassett *(G-1579)*

FURNITURE: Tables, Office, Exc Wood

Duskits LLC ....G...... 276 732-3121
Axton *(G-1534)*

FURNITURE: Upholstered

Absolutely Fabulous ....G...... 757 615-5732
Virginia Beach *(G-14205)*
Albany Industries-Galax LLC ....D...... 276 236-0735
Galax *(G-5626)*
Bassett Furniture Inds Inc ....A...... 276 629-6000
Bassett *(G-1578)*
Bassett Furniture Inds NC LLC ....F...... 276 629-6000
Bassett *(G-1579)*
Creative Seating LLC ....G...... 276 236-3615
Galax *(G-5631)*
Ebi LLC ....D...... 434 797-9701
Danville *(G-3988)*
Hooker Furniture Corporation ....C...... 276 632-2133
Martinsville *(G-8297)*
Huddle Furniture Inc ....E...... 276 647-5129
Collinsville *(G-3714)*
Huddle Furniture Inc ....D...... 828 874-8888
Martinsville *(G-8299)*
Interlude Home Inc ....D...... 540 381-7745
Christiansburg *(G-3598)*
Jackson Furniture Company VA ....C...... 540 635-3187
Front Royal *(G-5538)*
Kinters Cabinet Shop Inc J ....G...... 540 837-1663
White Post *(G-15180)*
La-Z-Boy Incorporated ....G...... 703 569-6188
Springfield *(G-13036)*
Riversedge Furniture Co Inc ....E...... 434 847-4155
Lynchburg *(G-7802)*
Ronbuilt Corporation ....G...... 276 638-2090
Martinsville *(G-8324)*
Rowe Fine Furniture Inc ....C...... 540 444-7693
Elliston *(G-4348)*
Rowe Fine Furniture Inc ....C...... 540 389-8661
Salem *(G-12563)*

Rowe Furniture Inc ....A....... 540 389-8671
   Elliston (G-4349)
Stewart Furniture Design Inc ....E....... 276 744-0186
   Fries (G-5518)
Tfi Wind Down Inc ....G....... 703 714-0500
   Vienna (G-14141)

Furs

Flying Fur...G....... 540 552-1351
   Blacksburg (G-1740)
Fur Persons Rescue Fund ....G....... 703 754-7474
   Haymarket (G-6424)
Fur The Love of Dogs LLC ....G....... 540 850-5540
   Stafford (G-13145)
Kaydee Puppets ....G....... 804 347-6636
   Fredericksburg (G-5199)
Kd Puppets ....G....... 703 385-4543
   Fairfax (G-4642)
Sines Feathers and Furs LLC ....G....... 540 436-8673
   Strasburg (G-13598)

GAMES & TOYS: Automobiles & Trucks

Blue Monkey LLC..................................G....... 540 664-1297
   Winchester (G-15388)
Ddk Group LLC ....G....... 201 726-2535
   Lorton (G-7478)

GAMES & TOYS: Banks

Big Stone Gap Corporation....................G....... 276 523-7337
   Big Stone Gap (G-1706)

GAMES & TOYS: Board Games, Children's & Adults'

Catlilli Games LLC ....G....... 540 359-6592
   Warrenton (G-14986)
Magss Ideas & Concepts.......................G....... 804 304-6324
   North Chesterfield (G-9920)
Marble Man ....G....... 804 448-9100
   Woodford (G-15841)

GAMES & TOYS: Books, Picture & Cutout

Larry Kaniecki ....G....... 804 737-7616
   Sandston (G-12623)

GAMES & TOYS: Carriages, Baby

Worth Baby Products LLC ....F....... 804 644-4707
   Henrico (G-6592)

GAMES & TOYS: Cars, Play, Children's Vehicles

Epic ....G....... 757 896-8464
   Hampton (G-6143)
Geraldine Browns Child Car ....G....... 757 665-1466
   Bloxom (G-1840)

GAMES & TOYS: Chessmen & Chessboards

Wilson & Wilson International ....G....... 804 733-3180
   North Dinwiddie (G-10071)

GAMES & TOYS: Craft & Hobby Kits & Sets

All That Jaz LLC ....G....... 800 224-8152
   Chesterfield (G-3474)
Decorative Arts Workshop ....G....... 703 321-8373
   Annandale (G-741)
John M Russell.....................................G....... 540 622-6281
   Linden (G-7429)
Lana Juarez ....G....... 540 951-3566
   Blacksburg (G-1750)
Made By Sandy ....G....... 757 588-1123
   Norfolk (G-9629)
Mystical Creations ....G....... 804 943-8386
   Hopewell (G-6940)
Pal Enterprises ....G....... 804 763-1769
   Midlothian (G-8874)
Shyanne Branch....................................G....... 757 532-4951
   Portsmouth (G-10481)
Theorem Painting ....G....... 703 670-4330
   Dumfries (G-4259)
Virginia Rural Letter..............................G....... 757 242-6865
   Windsor (G-15607)
Y & S Trading ....G....... 703 430-6928
   Sterling (G-13566)

GAMES & TOYS: Dolls & Doll Clothing

Birdies Dolls ....G....... 757 421-7788
   Chesapeake (G-3001)

GAMES & TOYS: Electronic

Christian Family Games LLC ....G....... 703 863-6403
   Great Falls (G-5948)
Wyvern Interactive LLC ....F....... 540 336-4498
   Winchester (G-15519)

GAMES & TOYS: Kits, Science, Incl Microscopes/Chemistry Sets

Effective Comm Strategies LLC ....G....... 703 403-5345
   Clifton (G-3663)

GAMES & TOYS: Puzzles

Interntnal Pzzle Cllctors Assn ....G....... 757 420-7576
   Virginia Beach (G-14552)
Monkey Puzzle Productions LLC ....G....... 703 919-0182
   Chantilly (G-2546)
Putting Tgther Pzzle Peces LLC ....G....... 703 391-1754
   Oak Hill (G-10138)
Puzzle Cuts LLC ....G....... 703 470-9333
   Lorton (G-7522)
Puzzle Homes LLC ....G....... 804 247-7256
   Henrico (G-6553)
Puzzle Palooza Ect ....G....... 703 494-0579
   Occoquan (G-10174)
Puzzle Palooza Etc Inc ....G....... 703 368-3619
   Manassas (G-8135)
Puzzle Piece LLC ....G....... 434 985-8074
   Ruckersville (G-12410)
Your Puzzle Source LLC ....G....... 703 461-7788
   Alexandria (G-391)

GAMES & TOYS: Rocking Horses

Rocking Horse Ventures Inc ....G....... 804 784-5830
   Richmond (G-11365)

GAMES & TOYS: Strollers, Baby, Vehicle

Dynamic Motion LLC ....G....... 804 433-2294
   Richmond (G-11194)

GAMES & TOYS: Structural Toy Sets

Jkt Inc...G....... 804 272-2862
   Chantilly (G-2451)

GAMES & TOYS: Toy Guns

Toy Ray Gun ....G....... 703 662-3348
   Herndon (G-6830)

GAMES & TOYS: Trains & Eqpt, Electric & Mechanical

Model Railroad Cstm Benchwork ....G....... 540 948-4948
   Rochelle (G-12234)

GARBAGE CONTAINERS: Plastic

Glasdon Inc ....G....... 804 726-3777
   Sandston (G-12617)

GARBAGE DISPOSALS: Household

Dixons Trash Disposal LLC ....G....... 434 978-2111
   Troy (G-13924)

GAS & OIL FIELD EXPLORATION SVCS

Advanced Resources Intl Inc.................E....... 703 528-8421
   Arlington (G-841)
Appalachian Energy Inc ....F....... 276 619-4880
   Abingdon (G-13)
Bradley Energy LLC...............................G....... 434 286-7600
   Scottsville (G-12658)
Catawba Renewable Energy ....G....... 434 426-1390
   Catawba (G-2260)
Dileway LLC ....G....... 703 897-6811
   Vienna (G-14039)
East End Resources Group LLC ....G....... 804 677-3207
   Midlothian (G-8812)
Enervest Operating LLC ....G....... 276 628-1569
   Abingdon (G-30)
Exploration Partners ....G....... 540 213-1333
   Staunton (G-13255)

Exploration Partners LLC......................G....... 434 973-8311
   Charlottesville (G-2630)
Msl Oil & Gas Corp ....G....... 703 971-8805
   Alexandria (G-535)
Next Generation MGT Corp....................G....... 703 372-1282
   Ashburn (G-1321)
Nomad Geosciences ....G....... 703 390-1147
   Reston (G-10909)
Orinoco Natural Resources LLC ....G....... 713 626-9696
   Roanoke (G-11979)
Peter Henderson Oil Co ....G....... 434 823-8608
   Crozet (G-3846)
Range Resources ....G....... 276 628-1568
   Abingdon (G-56)
Resource Consultants Inc ....G....... 757 464-5252
   Virginia Beach (G-14770)
Robert K Montgomery II ....G....... 804 730-0361
   Mechanicsville (G-8671)
Sam Hurt ....G....... 276 623-1926
   Abingdon (G-59)
Sharpe Resources Corp ....G....... 804 580-8107
   Heathsville (G-6465)
Spotted Hawk Development LLC...........F....... 703 286-1450
   Mc Lean (G-8556)
Summit Appalachia Oper Co LLC ....E....... 276 963-2979
   Cedar Bluff (G-2286)
Tredegar Petroleum Corporation............G....... 804 330-1000
   North Chesterfield (G-10040)
United Co ....D....... 276 466-0769
   Bristol (G-1993)
United Company ....G....... 276 466-3322
   Bristol (G-1994)
Valvoline Instant Oil ....G....... 804 823-2104
   Chester (G-3465)
Virginia Gas Exploration Co ....G....... 276 676-2380
   Abingdon (G-64)
Weil Group Resources LLC ....G....... 804 643-2828
   Richmond (G-11820)

GAS & OIL FIELD SVCS, NEC

Armstrong Family ....G....... 703 737-6188
   Leesburg (G-7222)
Baker Hughes A GE Company LLC.......G....... 540 387-8847
   Salem (G-12480)
Jon Armstrong ....G....... 757 253-3844
   Williamsburg (G-15262)
L B Oil Company ....G....... 757 723-8379
   Chesapeake (G-3169)
Morris Mountaineer Oil Gas LLC ....G....... 703 283-9700
   Mc Lean (G-8507)
Mtf Resources LLC ....G....... 804 240-5335
   Midlothian (G-8864)
Quinn Pumps Inc ....G....... 276 345-9106
   Cedar Bluff (G-2284)
Sct Phoenix Oil & Gas LLC ....G....... 702 245-0269
   Falls Church (G-4873)
Virginia Oil Company.............................G....... 540 552-2365
   Blacksburg (G-1804)

GAS FIELD MACHINERY & EQPT

Gas Field Services Inc..........................D....... 276 873-1214
   Rosedale (G-12365)

GAS PRODUCTION & DISTRIBUTION

Virginia Gas Exploration Co ....E....... 276 676-2380
   Abingdon (G-64)

GAS WELDING RODS, MADE FROM PURCHASED WIRE

T & J Wldg & Fabrication LLC ....G....... 757 672-9929
   Suffolk (G-13770)

GASES & LIQUIFIED PETROLEUM GASES

Precision Gas Piping LLC ....G....... 434 531-2427
   Ruckersville (G-12409)

GASES: Argon

Argon ....G....... 804 365-5628
   Richmond (G-11118)

GASES: Indl

Airgas Usa LLC ....F....... 804 743-0661
   North Chesterfield (G-9809)
Akaline Cylinders ....G....... 757 896-9100
   Hampton (G-6080)

Employee Codes: A=Over 500 employees, B=251-500
C=101-250, D=51-100, E=20-50, F=10-19, G=1-9

2021 Virginia
Industrial Directory

967

PRODUCT

Boc Group De ....G..... 540 373-1782
   Fredericksburg (G-5404)
H2 As Fuel Corporation ....G..... 703 980-5262
   Alexandria (G-472)
Linde Inc ....G..... 804 452-3181
   Hopewell (G-6938)
Messer LLC ....E..... 804 796-5050
   Chester (G-3435)
Messer LLC ....G..... 540 886-1725
   Staunton (G-13279)
Praxair Welding Gas & Sup Str ....G..... 540 342-9700
   Roanoke (G-12150)

GASES: Neon

Cr Neon ....G..... 804 339-0497
   Ruther Glen (G-12453)
Neon Compass Marketing LLC ....G..... 580 330-4699
   Alexandria (G-542)
Neon District ....G..... 757 663-6970
   Norfolk (G-9654)
Neon Guitar ....G..... 804 932-3716
   New Kent (G-9136)
Neon Nation LLC ....G..... 703 255-4996
   Vienna (G-14103)

GASES: Nitrogen

Linde Gas North America LLC ....G..... 804 752-2744
   Ashland (G-1452)
Messer LLC ....E..... 804 458-0928
   Hopewell (G-6939)

GASES: Oxygen

Messer LLC ....G..... 540 774-1515
   Roanoke (G-11962)

GASKET MATERIALS

Hollingsworth & Vose Company ....C..... 540 745-7600
   Floyd (G-5029)

GASKETS

American Gasket & Seal Tech ....F..... 804 271-0020
   North Chesterfield (G-9816)
Blackhawk Rubber & Gasket Inc ....G..... 888 703-9060
   Portsmouth (G-10401)
Hitek Sealing Corporation ....G..... 434 944-2404
   Appomattox (G-813)
Innovatio Sealing Tech Corp ....G..... 434 238-2397
   Lynchburg (G-7739)
Parker-Hannifin Corporation ....B..... 434 846-6541
   Lynchburg (G-7782)

GASOLINE FILLING STATIONS

Gas House Co ....G..... 434 822-1324
   Danville (G-3996)

GATES: Ornamental Metal

Bobby Burns Nowlin ....F..... 757 827-1588
   Hampton (G-6097)
Custom Welding Inc ....G..... 757 220-1995
   Williamsburg (G-15227)
Miscellaneous & Orna Mtls Inc ....G..... 757 650-5226
   Virginia Beach (G-14655)

GEARS: Power Transmission, Exc Auto

Heclyn Precision Gear Company ....F..... 215 739-7094
   Machipongo (G-7847)

GEM STONES MINING, NEC: Natural

Morefield Gem Mine Inc ....G..... 804 561-3399
   Amelia Court House (G-666)

GENERAL MERCHANDISE, NONDURABLE, WHOLESALE

Alforas Company ....G..... 703 342-6910
   Annandale (G-729)
Best Recognition ....G..... 757 490-3933
   Virginia Beach (G-14275)
M&M Great Adventures LLC ....G..... 937 344-1415
   Williamsburg (G-15275)

GENERATING APPARATUS & PARTS: Electrical

CF Adams Brokerage Co Inc ....G..... 757 287-9717
   Chesapeake (G-3028)

GENERATION EQPT: Electronic

A-Systems Incorporated ....F..... 434 295-7200
   Charlottesville (G-2720)
Apg Electronics ....G..... 540 672-7252
   Orange (G-10203)
Ashlawn Energy LLC ....E..... 703 461-3600
   Springfield (G-12952)
Epiphany Ideation ....G..... 248 396-5828
   Sterling (G-13394)
L 3 Maritime Systems ....D..... 703 443-1700
   Herndon (G-6727)
Management Solutions LC ....G..... 540 967-9600
   Louisa (G-7559)
Power Distribution Inc ....C..... 804 737-9880
   Richmond (G-11721)

GENERATORS: Electric

Georator Corporation ....F..... 703 368-2101
   Manassas (G-7945)
Tri State Generators LLC ....F..... 434 660-3851
   Monroe (G-8996)

GENERATORS: Electrochemical, Fuel Cell

U S General Fuel Cell Corp ....G..... 703 451-8064
   Springfield (G-13103)

GENERATORS: Gas

Precision Generators Company ....G..... 757 498-4809
   Virginia Beach (G-14732)

GENERATORS: Storage Battery Chargers

Edge McS LLC ....G..... 804 379-6772
   Midlothian (G-8813)

GENERATORS: Thermo-Electric

Alstom Renewable US LLC ....E..... 804 763-2196
   Midlothian (G-8771)

GHOST WRITING SVCS

Penny Trail Press LLC ....G..... 757 644-5349
   Wakefield (G-14969)

GIFT SHOP

Alphabet Soup ....G..... 757 569-0110
   Franklin (G-5138)
Carroll J Harper ....F..... 540 434-8978
   Rockingham (G-12244)
Rapid Printing Inc ....G..... 540 586-1243
   Bedford (G-1654)
Vienna Quilt Shop ....G..... 703 281-4091
   Mc Lean (G-8576)
Wades Mill Inc ....G..... 540 348-1400
   Raphine (G-10751)

GIFT, NOVELTY & SOUVENIR STORES: Gifts & Novelties

Bethany House Inc ....G..... 703 281-9410
   Vienna (G-14015)

GIFTS & NOVELTIES: Wholesalers

Kool Looks Inc ....F..... 808 224-1887
   Bristow (G-2058)

GIFTWARE: Copper

Caldwell Mountain Copper ....G..... 540 473-2167
   Fincastle (G-4993)

GLASS & GLASS CERAMIC PRDTS, PRESSED OR BLOWN: Tableware

E I Designs Pottery LLC ....G..... 410 459-3337
   Virginia Beach (G-14424)
Eileen Tramonte Design ....G..... 703 241-1996
   Arlington (G-955)
RH Ceramics ....G..... 760 880-4088
   Norfolk (G-9707)

GLASS FABRICATORS

Agilent Technologies Inc ....G..... 540 443-9272
   Blacksburg (G-1721)
All Glass LLC ....G..... 540 288-8111
   Fredericksburg (G-5397)
Architectural Systems Virginia ....G..... 804 270-0477
   Richmond (G-11116)
Bottlehood of Virginia Inc ....G..... 804 454-0656
   Chesterfield (G-3482)
Burgess Snyder Industries Inc ....E..... 757 490-3131
   Virginia Beach (G-14306)
Design Master Associates Inc ....E..... 757 566-8500
   Toano (G-13864)
Embroidery Crown Inc ....G..... 703 986-3022
   Woodbridge (G-15691)
Evs Glass Creations LLC ....E..... 540 412-8242
   Fredericksburg (G-5285)
Executive Glass Services Inc ....G..... 703 689-2178
   Herndon (G-6672)
Ghti Corporation ....G..... 703 802-8616
   Fairfax (G-4464)
Guardian Fabrication LLC ....C..... 276 236-5196
   Galax (G-5637)
Hawkins Glass Wholesalers LLC ....E..... 703 372-2990
   Lorton (G-7492)
Highlands Glass Company LLC ....G..... 276 623-0021
   Abingdon (G-36)
Mark S Chapman ....G..... 434 227-6702
   Troy (G-13934)
Massey Wood & West Inc ....E..... 804 746-2800
   Mechanicsville (G-8656)
Maureen Melville ....G..... 703 533-2448
   Mc Lean (G-8496)
Oran Safety Glass Inc ....F..... 434 336-1620
   Emporia (G-4364)
Vinylite Windows Products Inc ....E..... 703 550-7766
   Lorton (G-7540)
Virginia Glass Products Corp ....C..... 276 956-3131
   Ridgeway (G-11856)
Weksler Glass Thermometer Corp ....G..... 434 977-4544
   Charlottesville (G-2904)

GLASS PRDTS, FROM PURCHASED GLASS: Art

Cain Inc ....G..... 434 842-3984
   Bremo Bluff (G-1945)

GLASS PRDTS, FROM PURCHASED GLASS: Glass Beads, Reflecting

Sign Enterprise Inc ....G..... 540 899-9555
   Fredericksburg (G-5224)

GLASS PRDTS, FROM PURCHASED GLASS: Glassware

Bay Etching & Imprinting Inc ....E..... 800 925-2877
   Lively (G-7439)
Blended Cre8tions LLC ....G..... 347 323-2982
   Virginia Beach (G-14287)
Painted Ladies LLC ....G..... 571 481-6906
   Woodbridge (G-15769)

GLASS PRDTS, FROM PURCHASED GLASS: Insulating

Cardinal Glass Industries Inc ....C..... 540 892-5600
   Vinton (G-14168)
Dixie Plate GL & Mirror Co LLC ....G..... 540 869-4400
   Middletown (G-8737)

GLASS PRDTS, FROM PURCHASED GLASS: Mirrored

American Mirror Company Inc ....C..... 276 236-5111
   Galax (G-5627)
Virginia Mirror Company Inc ....D..... 276 956-3131
   Martinsville (G-8347)
Virginia Mirror Company Inc ....G..... 276 632-9816
   Martinsville (G-8348)

GLASS PRDTS, FROM PURCHASED GLASS: Novelties, Fruit, Etc

Juma Brothers Inc ....G..... 757 312-0544
   Portsmouth (G-10449)

GLASS PRDTS, FROM PURCHASED GLASS: Ornaments, Christmas Tree

Ornament Company ....G...... 757 585-0729
Williamsburg **(G-15288)**

GLASS PRDTS, FROM PURCHASED GLASS: Silvered

Interior 2000 ....G...... 804 598-0340
Powhatan **(G-10551)**

GLASS PRDTS, FROM PURCHASED GLASS: Windshields

Glorias Glass ....G...... 804 357-0676
New Kent **(G-9133)**

GLASS PRDTS, PRESSED OR BLOWN: Bulbs, Electric Lights

Gateway Green Energy Inc ....G...... 540 280-7475
Fishersville **(G-5003)**

GLASS PRDTS, PRESSED OR BLOWN: Glassware, Art Or Decorative

Baron Glass Inc ....C...... 757 464-1131
Virginia Beach **(G-14262)**
Beach Glass Designs Inc ....G...... 757 650-7604
Virginia Beach **(G-14265)**

GLASS PRDTS, PRESSED OR BLOWN: Optical

High Performance Optics Inc.............G...... 513 258-5978
Roanoke **(G-11934)**

GLASS PRDTS, PRESSED OR BLOWN: Yarn, Fiberglass

I T F Circle.....................................E...... 276 773-3114
Independence **(G-6986)**

GLASS PRDTS, PURCHASED GLASS: Glassware, Scientific/Tech

Raytheon Company ....F...... 703 872-3400
Arlington **(G-1139)**

GLASS PRDTS, PURCHD GLASS: Furniture Top, Cut, Beveld/Polshd

Bassett Mirror Company Inc ....C...... 276 629-3341
Bassett **(G-1580)**
Crafted Glass Inc ....G...... 757 543-5504
Chesapeake **(G-3056)**
Dimension Stone LLC ....G...... 804 615-7750
Amelia Court House **(G-655)**

GLASS STORE: Leaded Or Stained

River House Creations LLC ....G...... 757 509-2137
Gloucester **(G-5859)**
Stained Glass Creations Inc ....G...... 804 798-8806
Ashland **(G-1496)**
Virginia Stained Glass Co Inc ....F...... 703 425-4611
Springfield **(G-13108)**

GLASS STORES

Interior 2000...................................G...... 804 598-0340
Powhatan **(G-10551)**

GLASS, AUTOMOTIVE: Wholesalers

Jefco Inc ....E...... 757 460-0403
Virginia Beach **(G-14565)**

GLASS: Broadwoven Fabrics

BGF Industries Inc ....D...... 434 447-2210
South Hill **(G-12844)**
BGF Industries Inc ....D...... 843 537-3172
Danville **(G-3957)**

GLASS: Fiber

Corning Incorporated ....E...... 434 793-9511
Danville **(G-3972)**
Fibertech Virginia Inc ....G...... 540 337-0916
Greenville **(G-5998)**

Terrence Smith ....G...... 703 339-2194
Lorton **(G-7537)**

GLASS: Flat

Cardinal Glass Industries Inc ....C...... 540 892-5600
Vinton **(G-14168)**
Columbia Mrror GL Grgetown Inc ....G...... 703 333-9990
Springfield **(G-12977)**
Crafted Glass Inc ....G...... 757 543-5504
Chesapeake **(G-3056)**
Dixie Plate GL & Mirror Co LLC ....G...... 540 869-4400
Middletown **(G-8737)**
Dragons Lair Glass Studio ....G...... 540 564-0318
Harrisonburg **(G-6310)**
Pilkington North America Inc ....C...... 540 362-5130
Roanoke **(G-11985)**

GLASS: Leaded

Coffman Stairs LLC ....B...... 276 783-7251
Marion **(G-8225)**
Stained Glass Creations Inc ....G...... 804 798-8806
Ashland **(G-1496)**

GLASS: Optical

Coresix Precision Glass Inc...............D...... 757 888-1361
Williamsburg **(G-15223)**

GLASS: Plate

Jefco Inc ....E...... 757 460-0403
Virginia Beach **(G-14565)**

GLASS: Pressed & Blown, NEC

Afgd Inc ....G...... 804 222-0120
Henrico **(G-6470)**
Corning Incorporated ....G...... 703 448-1095
Herndon **(G-6647)**
Corning Incorporated ....E...... 540 382-4921
Christiansburg **(G-3580)**
Corning Incorporated ....D...... 540 382-4921
Christiansburg **(G-3581)**
Design Master Associates Inc ....E...... 757 566-8500
Toano **(G-13864)**
Dixie Plate GL & Mirror Co LLC ....G...... 540 869-4400
Middletown **(G-8737)**
G-13 Hand-Blown Art Glass ....G...... 757 495-8185
Virginia Beach **(G-14478)**
Highpoint Glass Works ....G...... 757 442-7155
Pungoteague **(G-10650)**

GLASS: Safety

AGC Flat Glass North Amer Inc ....G...... 804 222-0120
Henrico **(G-6471)**

GLASS: Stained

Anns Stained Glass Windows PA........G...... 540 337-2249
Stuarts Draft **(G-13643)**
Jennings Stained Glass Inc ....F...... 434 283-1301
Gladys **(G-5693)**
Red Star Glass Inc ....G...... 540 899-5779
Fredericksburg **(G-5218)**
River House Creations LLC ....G...... 757 509-2137
Gloucester **(G-5859)**
Virginia Stained Glass Co Inc ....F...... 703 425-4611
Springfield **(G-13108)**

GLASS: Structural

Glass Fronts Inc ....F...... 540 672-4410
Orange **(G-10214)**

GLOBAL POSITIONING SYSTEMS & EQPT

Angerole Mounts LLC.......................G...... 434 249-3977
Charlottesville **(G-2588)**
Spicewater Electronic Home Mon ....G...... 276 690-4718
Gate City **(G-5668)**

GLOVES: Leather

Baret LLC.......................................G...... 808 230-9904
Woodbridge **(G-15654)**

GLOVES: Safety

Price Point Equipment ....G...... 239 216-1688
Sterling **(G-13477)**

GO-CART DEALERS

K & K Signs ....G...... 540 586-0542
Bedford **(G-1641)**

GOLF CARTS: Powered

Windryder Inc ....G...... 540 545-8851
Winchester **(G-15516)**

GOLF CARTS: Wholesalers

Penny Trail Press LLC ....G...... 757 644-5349
Wakefield **(G-14969)**

GOLF COURSES: Public

United Company ....D...... 276 466-3322
Bristol **(G-1994)**

GOLF EQPT

Double Eagle Golf Works Inc ....G...... 757 436-4459
Chesapeake **(G-3072)**
Links Choice LLC.............................E...... 434 286-2202
Scottsville **(G-12663)**
Titus Development Corp ....G...... 757 515-7338
Virginia Beach **(G-14882)**

GOVERNMENT, EXECUTIVE OFFICES: City & Town Managers' Offices

The City of Radford..........................F...... 540 731-3662
Radford **(G-10741)**

GOVERNMENT, EXECUTIVE OFFICES: Mayors'

City of Danville ....E...... 434 799-5137
Danville **(G-3967)**

GOVERNMENT, GENERAL: Administration

Rector Visitors of The Univ VA ....E...... 434 924-3468
Charlottesville **(G-2859)**

GRANITE: Crushed & Broken

Boxley Materials Company ....F...... 540 777-7600
Martinsville **(G-8272)**
Boxley Materials Company ....E...... 540 777-7600
Blue Ridge **(G-1845)**
Cardinal Stone Company Inc ....F...... 276 236-5457
Galax **(G-5630)**
Legacy Vulcan LLC...........................E...... 434 634-4158
Skippers **(G-12701)**
Legacy Vulcan LLC...........................E...... 434 572-3931
South Boston **(G-12777)**
Legacy Vulcan LLC...........................F...... 804 706-1773
Chester **(G-3428)**
Legacy Vulcan LLC...........................E...... 540 659-3003
Garrisonville **(G-5656)**
Luck Stone Corporation ....D...... 804 784-6300
Manakin Sabot **(G-7901)**
Luck Stone Corporation ....G...... 804 749-3233
Rockville **(G-12289)**
Luck Stone Corporation ....G...... 804 749-3232
Rockville **(G-12290)**
Luck Stone Corporation ....G...... 804 784-4652
Manakin Sabot **(G-7902)**
Luck Stone Corporation ....G...... 434 589-1542
Troy **(G-13933)**
Luck Stone Corporation ....F...... 757 213-7750
Chesapeake **(G-3189)**
Luck Stone Corporation ....E...... 757 545-2020
Norfolk **(G-9624)**
Martin Marietta Materials Inc..............G...... 540 894-5952
Fredericksburg **(G-5321)**
Martinsville Finance & Inv ....G...... 276 632-9500
Martinsville **(G-8309)**
Salem Stone Corporation ....E...... 276 766-3449
Hillsville **(G-6899)**
Salem Stone Corporation ....E...... 540 552-9292
Blacksburg **(G-1786)**
Salem Stone Corporation ....G...... 276 228-6767
Wytheville **(G-15910)**

GRANITE: Cut & Shaped

Absolute Stone Design LLC................E...... 804 752-2001
Glen Allen **(G-5704)**
Archna & Nazish Inc ....F...... 571 221-6224
Chantilly **(G-2370)**

Employee Codes: A=Over 500 employees, B=251-500
C=101-250, D=51-100, E=20-50, F=10-19, G=1-9

2021 Virginia
Industrial Directory

PRODUCT

969

GRANITE: Cut & Shaped (continued)

Best Granite & Marble ....G..... 703 455-0404
Springfield (G-12960)
Brazilian Best Granite Inc ....G..... 804 562-3022
Richmond (G-11132)
Capitol Granite LLC ....E..... 804 379-2641
Midlothian (G-8790)
Classic Granite and Marble Inc ...F..... 804 404-8004
Midlothian (G-8796)
Environmental Stoneworks LLC....E..... 804 553-9560
Richmond (G-11204)
Granite Design Inc ....G..... 703 530-1223
Manassas (G-8076)
Granite Top LLC ....G..... 703 257-0714
Manassas (G-7948)
HB Inc..............................G..... 757 291-5236
Virginia Beach (G-14511)
Lakeside Stone & Landscape Sup ..G..... 434 738-3204
Clarksville (G-3632)
Signature Stone Corporation ......F..... 757 566-9094
Toano (G-13877)
Stone Depot Granite ....F..... 703 926-3844
Lorton (G-7535)

GRANITE: Dimension

Virginia Mist Group Inc ....F..... 540 661-0030
Rapidan (G-10755)

GRANITE: Dimension

United Stones Inc..................E..... 703 467-0434
Sterling (G-13543)
Virginia Mist Granite Corp.........G..... 540 661-0030
Rapidan (G-10754)

GRAPHIC ARTS & RELATED DESIGN SVCS

A C Graphics Inc ....G..... 703 246-9466
Fairfax (G-4396)
Allen Wayne Ltd Arlington ....G..... 703 321-7414
Warrenton (G-14977)
Best Printing & Design LLC ....G..... 703 593-9874
Arlington (G-880)
BSC Ventures LLC ....D..... 540 362-3311
Roanoke (G-11896)
Custom Graphics Inc ....G..... 540 882-3488
Paeonian Springs (G-10238)
Davis Communications Group ....G..... 703 548-8892
Alexandria (G-185)
Ember Systems LLC ....G..... 540 327-1984
Winchester (G-15539)
Ibf Group..........................G..... 703 549-4247
Alexandria (G-232)
JT Graphics & Printing Inc.........G..... 703 922-6804
Alexandria (G-502)
Landmark Printing Co ....G..... 703 226-1000
Annandale (G-769)
Macmurray Graphics & Prtg Inc .....G..... 703 680-4847
Montclair (G-8999)
Magpie Design LLC ....G..... 703 975-5818
Reston (G-10893)
McClung Printing Inc ....D..... 540 949-8139
Waynesboro (G-15123)
Northlight Publishing Co ....G..... 804 344-8500
Richmond (G-11694)
Over 9000 Media LLC................G..... 850 210-7114
Norfolk (G-9679)
Quality Graphics & Prtg Inc ....F..... 703 661-6060
Sterling (G-13483)
R R Donnelley & Sons Company ....C..... 434 846-7371
Salem (G-12560)
Schreiber Inc R G..................E..... 540 248-5300
Verona (G-13995)
Surfside East Inc ....E..... 757 468-0606
Virginia Beach (G-14859)
Thayer Design Inc ....G..... 434 528-3850
Madison Heights (G-7885)
Tidewater Graphics and Signs ......G..... 757 622-7446
Norfolk (G-9753)
Type Factory Inc...................G..... 757 826-6055
Hampton (G-6255)
Vista-Graphics Inc ....G..... 757 422-8979
Virginia Beach (G-14925)
Wordsprint Inc.....................E..... 276 228-6608
Wytheville (G-15925)

GRAPHIC LAYOUT SVCS: Printed Circuitry

Elohim Designs ....G..... 757 292-1890
Chesapeake (G-3087)

GRASSES: Artificial & Preserved

Thomas E Lewis.....................G..... 804 529-7526
Lottsburg (G-7544)

GRATINGS: Tread, Fabricated Metal

K B Industries Inc ....G..... 540 483-8883
Rocky Mount (G-12331)

GRAVEL MINING

Dinkle Enterprises ....G..... 434 324-8508
Hurt (G-6974)

GREASE RETAINERS: Leather

Black Jacket LLC...................G..... 425 319-1014
Forest (G-5054)

GREASES & INEDIBLE FATS, RENDERED

Valley Proteins (de) Inc...........G..... 540 877-2590
Winchester (G-15502)

GREETING CARDS WHOLESALERS

Rapid Printing Inc ....G..... 540 586-1243
Bedford (G-1654)

GRENADES: Grenades, Hand

Fredrick Allen Murphey ....G..... 804 385-1650
Highland Springs (G-6853)
James R Napier ....G..... 434 547-5511
Drakes Branch (G-4134)
Southern Fire & Safety Co ....G..... 434 546-6774
Lynchburg (G-7810)

GRITS: Crushed & Broken

Luck Stone Corporation ....E..... 703 830-8880
Centreville (G-2316)

GROCERIES WHOLESALERS, NEC

Coca-Cola Consolidated Inc ....D..... 540 886-2494
Staunton (G-13248)
James A Kennedy & Assoc Inc........G..... 804 241-6836
Powhatan (G-10553)
Mezeh - Fair Oaks LLC ....F..... 703 310-9209
Fairfax (G-4508)
Mezeh-Reston LLC ....F..... 703 310-9209
Reston (G-10900)
Michael Holt Inc ....G..... 703 597-6999
Arlington (G-1062)
Pork Barrel Bbq LLC ....G..... 202 750-7500
Alexandria (G-312)

GROCERIES, GENERAL LINE WHOLESALERS

Asmars Mediterranean Food Inc .....F..... 703 750-2960
Alexandria (G-418)

GUARD PROTECTIVE SVCS

Personal Protectio Principles......G..... 757 453-3202
Virginia Beach (G-14717)

GUARD SVCS

Bradley-Morris LLC.................E..... 678 419-4171
Chesapeake (G-3014)

GUARDRAILS

Spig Industry LLC ....F..... 276 644-9510
Bristol (G-2034)

GUARDS: Machine, Sheet Metal

Amherst Technologies ....G..... 434 946-0329
Amherst (G-681)

GUIDANCE SYSTEMS & EQPT: Space Vehicle

L3harris Technologies Inc..........C..... 703 790-6300
Mc Lean (G-8481)

GUIDED MISSILES & SPACE VEHICLES

Aerospace Corporation ....G..... 703 554-2906
Round Hill (G-12374)
American Tech Sltons Intl Corp.....E..... 540 907-5355
Fredericksburg (G-5398)

Bwxt Y - 12 LLC....................G..... 434 316-7633
Lynchburg (G-7670)
Lockheed Martin Corporation........G..... 703 367-2121
Manassas (G-7968)
Mbda Incorporated..................G..... 703 351-1230
Arlington (G-1057)
Nanofactory Cbn Inc ....E..... 434 799-9280
Danville (G-4016)
Northrop Grmman Gdnce Elec Inc ....E..... 703 280-2900
Falls Church (G-4839)
Raytheon Company ....A..... 703 419-1400
Arlington (G-1138)

GUIDED MISSILES & SPACE VEHICLES: Research & Development

Blacksky Holdings Inc..............E..... 703 935-1930
Herndon (G-6625)
Dallas G Bienhoff ....G..... 571 232-4554
Annandale (G-738)
Gomspace North America LLC ....G..... 703 866-8742
Alexandria (G-222)
Raytheon Company ....G..... 310 647-9438
Chesapeake (G-3258)
Raytheon Company ....G..... 703 418-0275
Arlington (G-1135)
Raytheon Company ....G..... 571 250-1101
Dulles (G-4222)
Raytheon Company ....G..... 757 749-9638
Yorktown (G-15987)
Raytheon Company ....F..... 703 872-3400
Arlington (G-1139)
Triquetra Phoenix LLC ....G..... 571 265-6044
Annandale (G-790)
Utah State Univ Space Dynmics......D..... 435 713-3060
Stafford (G-13209)

GUIDED MISSILES/SPACE VEHICLE PARTS/AUX EQPT: Research/Devel

Deep-Space Intelligent Constru.....G..... 571 247-7376
Fairfax Station (G-4706)
Wiglance LLC.......................G..... 866 301-3662
North Chesterfield (G-10011)

GUM & WOOD CHEMICALS

Akzo Nobel Coatings Inc............E..... 540 982-8301
Roanoke (G-12030)
Branch Botanicals Inc ....G..... 703 429-4217
Chantilly (G-2380)
Westrock Mwv LLC ....A..... 804 444-1000
Richmond (G-11825)

GUN SIGHTS: Optical

C-More Systems Inc.................G..... 540 347-4683
Warrenton (G-14985)
International Trade & Tech Inc .....G..... 703 929-0595
Midland (G-8758)
Schmidt & Bender Incorporated......G..... 770 493-9305
Winchester (G-15474)

GUNSMITHS

US Tactical Inc....................G..... 703 217-8781
Oakton (G-10163)

GUTTERS: Sheet Metal

Fred Kinkead ....G..... 540 828-2955
Bridgewater (G-1951)
Sams Gutter Shop ....G..... 276 632-6522
Martinsville (G-8325)
Spencer Stnless Alum Guttering ....G..... 434 277-8359
Amherst (G-708)

GYPSUM PRDTS

Strober Building Supply ....G..... 540 834-2111
Fredericksburg (G-5369)
United States Gypsum Company ......C..... 757 494-8100
Norfolk (G-9773)
United States Gypsum Company ......C..... 276 496-7733
Saltville (G-12597)

GYROSCOPES

Gyroscope Disc Golf LLC ....G..... 703 992-3035
Springfield (G-13015)

HAIR & HAIR BASED PRDTS

Bowman Nakia ....G...... 804 263-2181
Highland Springs *(G-6851)*
Every Changing Woman ....G...... 757 343-3088
Virginia Beach *(G-14455)*
Gray Shuntina ....G...... 919 273-7979
Virginia Beach *(G-14489)*
Herbal Origins LLC ....G...... 804 715-0015
North Chesterfield *(G-9883)*
J Lynette Buty & Bundles LLC ....G...... 276 790-9510
Martinsville *(G-8303)*
Joe Products Inc ....G...... 314 409-4477
Mc Lean *(G-8475)*
Karolina De Los Santos ....G...... 757 597-4315
Hampton *(G-6178)*
Luscious Lovezz LLC ....G...... 804 538-4151
Richmond *(G-11276)*
Luxemanes LLC ....F...... 804 922-1410
North Chesterfield *(G-9914)*
Neiceys ....G...... 757 500-1021
Virginia Beach *(G-14674)*
Osmotherapeutics Inc ....G...... 703 627-1934
Vienna *(G-14108)*
Osojuicee Hair LLC ....G...... 757 215-6555
South Chesterfield *(G-12818)*
Reddzway LLC ....G...... 434 515-0791
Lynchburg *(G-7799)*
Reese Kyndal ....G...... 757 718-0525
Norfolk *(G-9705)*
Sweet Baby Luxury Hair Co LLC ....G...... 804 904-9227
Richmond *(G-11777)*
Tiera Averett ....G...... 804 888-3721
Chesterfield *(G-3532)*
Tut & Titi LLC ....G...... 757 761-1921
Hampton *(G-6254)*
Wop Hair LLC ....G...... 804 277-4666
North Chesterfield *(G-10014)*

HAIR CARE PRDTS

A Family Heirloom LLC ....G...... 434 607-1674
Cumberland *(G-3934)*
Burroughs Qiana ....G...... 804 218-4031
Richmond *(G-11030)*
Fullman Iman ....G...... 908 627-3376
Newport News *(G-9233)*
Ivorys Essentials LLC ....G...... 571 201-6147
Gainesville *(G-5591)*
Jade Suppliers ....G...... 804 551-6865
Richmond *(G-11623)*
Kemelle Naturals Incorporated ....G...... 850 528-9053
Alexandria *(G-251)*
Sociiterra International LLC ....G...... 804 461-1876
Mechanicsville *(G-8678)*

HAIR CARE PRDTS: Hair Coloring Preparations

Gilbert Idelkhani ....G...... 703 399-1225
Herndon *(G-6684)*

HAIR CURLERS: Beauty Shop

E4 Beauty Supply LLC ....G...... 804 307-4941
Chesterfield *(G-3495)*
Hair Studio Orie Inc ....G...... 703 282-5390
Fairfax *(G-4474)*

HAIR DRESSING, FOR THE TRADE

Kay Kollections LLC ....G...... 757 901-7710
Norfolk *(G-9611)*
Lisa A McLain ....G...... 757 788-1781
Newport News *(G-9285)*
Mindful Barber LLC ....G...... 757 714-6445
Richmond *(G-11678)*
Sharon Solomon ....G...... 757 515-2325
Norfolk *(G-9721)*
Styles By Jaimonique LLC ....G...... 804 255-8581
Colonial Heights *(G-3749)*

HAND TOOLS, NEC: Wholesalers

CLC Enterprises LLC ....G...... 540 622-3488
Flint Hill *(G-5015)*

HANDBAGS

Bosan LLC ....G...... 757 340-0822
Virginia Beach *(G-14295)*
CC & More Inc ....G...... 540 786-7052
Fredericksburg *(G-5257)*

Crafted For ME LLC ....G...... 804 412-5273
Glen Allen *(G-5719)*

HANDBAGS: Women's

Crystal Beach Studio ....G...... 757 787-4605
Onancock *(G-10195)*
Joshi Rubita ....G...... 571 315-9772
Alexandria *(G-500)*

HANDLES: Faucet, Vitreous China & Earthenware

Allora USA LLC ....F...... 571 291-3485
Sterling *(G-13343)*

HANDLES: Wood

Just Handle It LLC ....G...... 804 285-0786
Richmond *(G-11258)*

HANDYMAN SVCS

PM Services LLC ....G...... 804 426-9892
Virginia Beach *(G-14727)*

HANG GLIDERS

Silver Wings Inc ....G...... 703 533-3244
Arlington *(G-1168)*
Springwood Airstrip ....G...... 540 473-2079
Buchanan *(G-2128)*

HANGERS: Garment, Plastic

Pgb Hangers LLC ....G...... 703 851-4221
Gainesville *(G-5607)*

HANGERS: Garment, Wire

Pgb Hangers LLC ....G...... 703 851-4221
Gainesville *(G-5607)*

HARD RUBBER PRDTS, NEC

Pro Tech Fabrications Inc ....G...... 540 587-5590
Bedford *(G-1653)*

HARDWARE

American Diesel Corp ....G...... 804 435-3107
Kilmarnock *(G-7068)*
Dixon Valve & Coupling Co LLC ....G...... 540 535-2181
Winchester *(G-15411)*
Dometic Corporation ....C...... 804 746-1313
Mechanicsville *(G-8618)*
Fastware Inc ....G...... 703 680-5050
Manassas *(G-8070)*
Gibson Good Tools Inc ....G...... 540 249-5100
Grottoes *(G-6019)*
International Automotive Compo ....A...... 540 465-3741
Strasburg *(G-13585)*
Jones Family Office ....G...... 305 304-3603
Bristow *(G-2057)*
Linear Devices Corporation ....G...... 804 368-8428
Ashland *(G-1453)*
Maritime Associates Inc ....G...... 571 212-0655
Alexandria *(G-270)*
ML Manufacturing ....G...... 434 581-2000
New Canton *(G-9118)*
Rutherford Controls Intl Corp ....F...... 757 427-1230
Virginia Beach *(G-14786)*
Secutor Systems LLC ....G...... 757 646-9350
Virginia Beach *(G-14802)*

HARDWARE & BUILDING PRDTS: Plastic

Cellofoam North America Inc ....E...... 540 373-4596
Fredericksburg *(G-5258)*
Exterior Systems Inc ....G...... 804 752-2324
Ashland *(G-1412)*
Insul Industries Inc ....F...... 804 550-1933
Mechanicsville *(G-8641)*
SC&l of Virginia LLC ....D...... 804 876-3135
Doswell *(G-4124)*
Tecton Products LLC ....E...... 540 380-5819
Salem *(G-12572)*

HARDWARE & EQPT: Stage, Exc Lighting

Royal Courtyard ....G...... 757 431-0045
Virginia Beach *(G-14781)*

HARDWARE STORES

Rappatomac Industries Inc ....G...... 804 529-6440
Callao *(G-2218)*

HARDWARE STORES: Builders'

James Hintzke ....G...... 757 374-4827
Virginia Beach *(G-14563)*
Precision Doors & Hardware LLC ....F...... 540 373-7300
Fredericksburg *(G-5348)*

HARDWARE STORES: Tools, Hand

CLC Enterprises LLC ....G...... 540 622-3488
Flint Hill *(G-5015)*

HARDWARE STORES: Tools, Power

Monti Tools Inc ....G...... 832 623-7970
Manassas *(G-8112)*

HARDWARE WHOLESALERS

American Nexus LLC ....G...... 804 405-5443
Richmond *(G-11484)*
Schock Metal America Inc ....F...... 757 549-8300
Chesapeake *(G-3288)*
Special Fleet Services Inc ....E...... 540 433-7727
Harrisonburg *(G-6374)*
US 21 Inc ....D...... 703 560-0021
Fairfax *(G-4575)*

HARDWARE, WHOLESALE: Builders', NEC

Precision Doors & Hardware LLC ....F...... 540 373-7300
Fredericksburg *(G-5348)*
Valley Doors Unlimited LLC ....G...... 540 638-0167
Penn Laird *(G-10290)*

HARDWARE, WHOLESALE: Power Tools & Access

Monti Tools Inc ....G...... 832 623-7970
Manassas *(G-8112)*
Special Fleet Services Inc ....D...... 540 434-4488
Harrisonburg *(G-6373)*

HARDWARE, WHOLESALE: Saw Blades

Southeastern Wood Products Inc ....F...... 276 632-9025
Martinsville *(G-8332)*

HARDWARE, WHOLESALE: Shelf or Light

Persimmon Woodworking ....G...... 703 618-6909
Hamilton *(G-6063)*

HARDWARE: Aircraft & Marine, Incl Pulleys & Similar Items

Aerial Machine & Tool Corp ....G...... 276 694-3148
Stuart *(G-13603)*
Aerial Machine & Tool Corp ....D...... 276 952-2006
Meadows of Dan *(G-8590)*

HARDWARE: Builders'

Dormakaba USA Inc ....F...... 804 966-9166
South Chesterfield *(G-12801)*
Lone Fountain Ldscp & Hdwr Ctr ....G...... 540 886-7605
Staunton *(G-13277)*

HARDWARE: Cabinet

Boom Bass Cabinets Inc ....G...... 301 343-4918
Dumfries *(G-4237)*
Cabinet Lifts Unlimited ....G...... 757 641-9431
Virginia Beach *(G-14309)*
Fabriction Spclist of Virginia ....G...... 757 620-2540
Virginia Beach *(G-14458)*

HARDWARE: Furniture

Schock Metal America Inc ....F...... 757 549-8300
Chesapeake *(G-3288)*

HARNESS ASSEMBLIES: Cable & Wire

Drs Leonardo Inc ....C...... 703 416-8000
Arlington *(G-944)*
Intercon Inc ....D...... 434 525-3390
Forest *(G-5078)*
Kauffman Engineering Inc ....B...... 757 468-6000
Virginia Beach *(G-14581)*

PRODUCT

Qinetiq Inc ....E 540 658-2720
Lorton (G-7523)
Qinetiq Inc ....G 804 436-9000
Kilmarnock (G-7075)
Qinetiq Inc ....E 540 658-2720
Lorton (G-7524)
Tactical Dployment Systems LLC ....G 804 672-8426
Richmond (G-11405)
Techniservices Inc ....G 804 275-9207
North Chesterfield (G-9999)

HARNESS WIRING SETS: Internal Combustion Engines

Mg Corp ....A 757 468-6000
Virginia Beach (G-14648)

HARNESSES, HALTERS, SADDLERY & STRAPS

G & D Manufacturing ....G 540 345-7267
Roanoke (G-12095)
Kens Leathercraft ....G 540 774-6225
Boones Mill (G-1896)

HEADPHONES: Radio

Halo Acoustic Wear LLC ....F 703 474-6081
Broadlands (G-2078)

HEALTH AIDS: Exercise Eqpt

Core Health & Fitness LLC ....E 714 669-1660
Independence (G-6980)
Potomac Health Solutions Inc ....G 703 774-8278
Reston (G-10929)
Surfstroke LLC ....G 804 437-2032
Providence Forge (G-10628)
Turbo Tellers ....G 812 250-1837
Spout Spring (G-12928)

HEALTH CLUBS

Carl G Gilliam Jr ....F 276 523-0619
Big Stone Gap (G-1707)

HEALTH FOOD & SUPPLEMENT STORES

Everything Under Sun LLC ....G 276 252-2376
Ridgeway (G-11842)

HEALTH SCREENING SVCS

Rebound Analytics LLC ....G 202 297-1204
Tysons (G-13948)

HEARING AID REPAIR SVCS

Hear Quick Incorporated ....G 757 523-0504
Virginia Beach (G-14513)

HEARING AIDS

Anderson Audiology Hearing Aid .....G 540 616-7990
Blacksburg (G-1722)
Drake Hearing Aid Centers ....G 703 521-1404
Arlington (G-941)
Earmold Company Ltd ....F 540 389-1642
Salem (G-12499)
Elevate Hearing Aid Center ....G 540 785-4676
Fredericksburg (G-5281)
Hear Quick Incorporated ....G 757 523-0504
Virginia Beach (G-14513)
Lane Custom Hearing ....G 540 775-5999
King George (G-7099)

HEAT EXCHANGERS

Coil Exchange Inc ....G 703 369-7150
Manassas Park (G-8196)
Des Champs Technologies Inc ....C 540 291-1111
Buena Vista (G-2141)

HEAT EXCHANGERS: After Or Inter Coolers Or Condensers, Etc

Super RAD Coils Ltd Partnr ....C 804 794-2887
North Chesterfield (G-9992)

HEAT TREATING: Metal

Analytic Stress Relieving Inc ....G 804 271-5447
North Chesterfield (G-9817)

East Crlina Metal Treating Inc ....G 434 333-4412
Lynchburg (G-7699)
L & R Precision Tooling Inc ....E 434 525-4120
Lynchburg (G-7752)
National Peening Inc ....G 540 387-3522
Salem (G-12543)
Southwest Specialty Heat Treat ....F 276 228-7739
Wytheville (G-15916)
Stihl Incorporated ....E 757 468-4010
Virginia Beach (G-14848)
Stihl Incorporated ....G 757 368-2409
Virginia Beach (G-14849)

HEATING & AIR CONDITIONING EQPT & SPLYS WHOLESALERS

Ensons Inc ....G 703 644-6694
Burke (G-2189)

HEATING & AIR CONDITIONING UNITS, COMBINATION

C & M Heating & AC LLC ....G 276 618-0955
Axton (G-1533)
CK Service Inc ....G 757 486-5880
Virginia Beach (G-14341)
Hang Men High Heating & Coolg .....G 804 651-3320
Richmond (G-11232)
Metropolitan Equipment Group ....G 804 744-4774
North Chesterfield (G-9929)
Provides US Inc ....D 540 569-3434
Verona (G-13993)
Spot Coolers Inc ....G 804 222-5530
Richmond (G-11392)
Virginia Air Distributors Inc ....F 540 366-2259
Roanoke (G-12020)

HEATING EQPT & SPLYS

Alfa Laval Inc ....C 866 253-2528
Richmond (G-11095)
Des Champs Technologies Inc ....C 540 291-1111
Buena Vista (G-2141)
England Stove Works ....G 434 929-0120
Madison Heights (G-7871)
Fives N Amercn Combustn Inc ....G 540 735-8052
Fredericksburg (G-5185)
Latimer Julian Manufacturing ....G 804 405-6851
Richmond (G-11267)
Modine Manufacturing Company ......E 540 261-9821
Buena Vista (G-2148)
Old Mill Mechanical Inc ....G 804 932-5060
New Kent (G-9137)
Super RAD Coils Ltd Partnr ....C 804 794-2887
North Chesterfield (G-9992)
Virginia Blower Company ....E 276 647-3804
Collinsville (G-3718)

HEATING EQPT: Complete

Tranter Inc ....G 757 533-9185
Norfolk (G-9765)

HEATING UNITS: Gas, Infrared

Best Green Technologies LLC ....F 888 424-8432
Glen Allen (G-5707)

HELICOPTERS

Bell Textron Inc ....G 817 280-2346
Arlington (G-878)
Raytheon Technologies Corp ....G 757 838-7980
Hampton (G-6225)

HELP SUPPLY SERVICES

Agile Access Control Inc ....G 408 213-9555
Chantilly (G-2363)

HIGH ENERGY PARTICLE PHYSICS EQPT

Fuelcor Development LLC ....G 703 740-0071
Mc Lean (G-8437)
Larsen Swen ....G 703 754-2592
Bristow (G-2059)
Masters Energy Inc ....E 281 816-9991
Glen Allen (G-5768)
Plasmera Technologies LLC ....G 540 353-5438
Roanoke (G-11987)
Wiretough Cylinders LLC ....G 276 644-9120
Bristol (G-2042)

HIGHWAY SIGNALS: Electric

Superior Quality Mfg LLC ....G 757 413-9100
Chesapeake (G-3315)

HISTORICAL SOCIETY

Five Star Medals ....G 703 644-4974
Springfield (G-13004)

HOBBY, TOY & GAME STORES: Arts & Crafts & Splys

Mystical Creations ....G 804 943-8386
Hopewell (G-6940)

HOBBY, TOY & GAME STORES: Ceramics Splys

Kiln Doctor Inc ....G 540 636-6016
Front Royal (G-5540)
Persimmon Street Ceramics That .....G 202 256-8238
Arlington (G-1109)

HOBBY, TOY & GAME STORES: Toys & Games

Blue Monkey LLC ....G 540 664-1297
Winchester (G-15388)

HOISTS

Columbus McKinnon Corporation .....C 276 475-3124
Damascus (G-3946)

HOLDERS, PAPER TOWEL, GROCERY BAG, ETC: Plastic

Skycity ....G 240 467-6270
Arlington (G-1171)
ZZ Supply Company LLC ....G 703 957-5027
Springfield (G-13110)

HOLDING COMPANIES: Investment, Exc Banks

Blackboard Holdings Inc ....A 202 463-4860
Reston (G-10802)
Blackboard Super Holdco Inc ....G 202 463-4860
Reston (G-10807)

HOLDING COMPANIES: Personal, Exc Banks

Kennesaw Holding Company ....G 603 866-6944
Fairfax (G-4643)
Northrop Grmman Ovrseas Hldg I .....G 703 280-4069
Falls Church (G-4840)

HOME ENTERTAINMENT EQPT: Electronic, NEC

Htdepot LLC ....G 703 830-2818
Chantilly (G-2437)
Transcedent Integration ....G 703 880-3019
Chantilly (G-2561)
Wiredup Inc ....G 757 565-3655
Williamsburg (G-15347)

HOME FOR THE PHYSICALLY HANDICAPPED

Accessible Environments Inc ....G 757 565-3444
Williamsburg (G-15201)

HOME FURNISHINGS STORES, NEC

Melted Element LLC ....G 703 239-7847
Alexandria (G-526)

HOME FURNISHINGS WHOLESALERS

Abington Sunshade & Blinds Co ....F 540 435-6450
Penn Laird (G-10287)
Melted Element LLC ....G 703 239-7847
Alexandria (G-526)

HOME HEALTH CARE SVCS

Health Data Services Inc ....F 434 817-9000
Charlottesville (G-2808)
United Providers of Care LLC ....G 757 775-5075
Williamsburg (G-15328)

HOMEBUILDERS & OTHER OPERATIVE BUILDERS

Modern Living LLC ....G...... 877 663-2224
Richmond *(G-11679)*

HOMEFURNISHING STORE: Bedding, Sheet, Blanket,Spread/Pillow

Laura Copenhaver Industries ....G...... 276 783-4663
Marion *(G-8230)*

Ryan Studio Inc ....G...... 703 830-6818
Chantilly *(G-2488)*

HOMEFURNISHING STORES: Fireplaces & Wood Burning Stoves

Dutch Lady ....G...... 202 669-0317
Alexandria *(G-196)*

Hearth & Home Technologies LLC ....G...... 434 589-1482
Troy *(G-13928)*

Hearth & Home Technologies LLC ....G...... 703 367-9413
Manassas *(G-7950)*

HOMEFURNISHING STORES: Pictures & Mirrors

Finest Art & Framing LLC ....G...... 703 945-9000
Lansdowne *(G-7170)*

HOMEFURNISHING STORES: Pottery

Blue Ridge Pottery ....F...... 434 985-6080
Stanardsville *(G-13216)*

Creative Workshops ....G...... 703 938-6177
Vienna *(G-14031)*

Emerson Creek Pottery Inc ....E...... 540 297-7524
Bedford *(G-1635)*

Hoffman Pottery ....G...... 276 773-3546
Independence *(G-6985)*

Michelle Erickson Pottery ....G...... 757 727-9139
Hampton *(G-6198)*

Robin Cage Pottery ....G...... 804 233-1758
Richmond *(G-11745)*

Sophia Street Studio ....G...... 540 372-3459
Fredericksburg *(G-5225)*

HOMEFURNISHING STORES: Towels

Monogram Shop ....G...... 434 973-1968
Charlottesville *(G-2662)*

HOMEFURNISHING STORES: Venetian Blinds

Mary Elizabeth Burrell ....G...... 804 677-2855
Richmond *(G-11670)*

Shade Mann-Kidwell Corp ....G...... 804 288-2819
Richmond *(G-11378)*

HOMEFURNISHING STORES: Wicker, Rattan, Or Reed

Homeland Corporation ....F...... 571 218-6200
Sterling *(G-13421)*

HOMEFURNISHING STORES: Window Shades, NEC

Applied Film Technology Inc ....G...... 757 351-4241
Virginia Beach *(G-14234)*

HOMEFURNISHINGS, WHOLESALE: Draperies

Elegant Draperies Ltd ....F...... 804 353-4268
Richmond *(G-11200)*

HOMEFURNISHINGS, WHOLESALE: Fireplace Eqpt & Access

Hearth & Home Technologies LLC ....G...... 434 589-1482
Troy *(G-13928)*

Hearth & Home Technologies LLC ....G...... 703 367-9413
Manassas *(G-7950)*

HOMEFURNISHINGS, WHOLESALE: Mirrors/Pictures, Framed/Unframd

Casson Art & Frame ....G...... 276 638-1450
Martinsville *(G-8274)*

HOMEFURNISHINGS, WHOLESALE: Window Shades

Applied Film Technology Inc ....G...... 757 351-4241
Virginia Beach *(G-14234)*

HOMES, MODULAR: Wooden

Cardinal Homes Inc ....G...... 434 735-8111
Wylliesburg *(G-15871)*

DFI Systems Inc ....D...... 757 262-1057
Hampton *(G-6128)*

First Colony Homes Inc ....G...... 540 788-4222
Calverton *(G-2224)*

Panel Processing Virginia Inc ....G...... 989 356-9007
Claudville *(G-3639)*

Travis Lee Kerr ....G...... 434 922-7005
Vesuvius *(G-13999)*

HOMES: Log Cabins

Aubrey Otis Gunter Jr ....G...... 434 352-8136
Appomattox *(G-804)*

Blue Ridge Homestead LLC ....G...... 540 743-2374
Luray *(G-7601)*

Bryan Smith ....G...... 434 242-7698
Ruckersville *(G-12400)*

Dogwood Mountain Log Homes LLC ......G...... 540 433-1873
Rockingham *(G-12250)*

Heritage Log Homes ....G...... 540 854-4926
Unionville *(G-13963)*

Highlands Log Structures Inc ....G...... 276 623-1580
Abingdon *(G-37)*

Honest Abe Log Homes Inc ....G...... 800 231-3695
Martinsville *(G-8296)*

Log Home Lovers ....G...... 540 743-7355
Luray *(G-7615)*

Log Homes By Clore Bros ....G...... 540 786-7749
Fredericksburg *(G-5315)*

Mr Luck Inc ....G...... 570 766-8734
Norfolk *(G-9649)*

Old Vrgnia Hand Hewn Log Homes ....F...... 276 546-5647
Pennington Gap *(G-10296)*

Sealants and Coatings Tech ....G...... 812 256-3378
Paeonian Springs *(G-10239)*

Southland Log Homes Inc ....G...... 540 268-2243
Christiansburg *(G-3610)*

Southland Log Homes Inc ....G...... 540 548-1617
Fredericksburg *(G-5226)*

HONES

Hone Blade LLC ....G...... 804 370-8598
Mechanicsville *(G-8638)*

HORMONE PREPARATIONS

Rejuvinage ....G...... 757 306-4300
Virginia Beach *(G-14767)*

HORSE & PET ACCESSORIES: Textile

ABC Petwear Inc ....G...... 804 730-3890
Mechanicsville *(G-8599)*

Christian Creations Inc ....G...... 540 722-2718
Winchester *(G-15401)*

Judy A OBrien ....G...... 434 568-3148
Drakes Branch *(G-4135)*

HORSE ACCESS: Harnesses & Riding Crops, Etc, Exc Leather

S E Greer ....G...... 540 400-0155
Roanoke *(G-12172)*

HORSESHOES

Crossroads Farrier Inc ....G...... 434 589-4501
Louisa *(G-7553)*

Double Horseshoe Saloon ....G...... 434 202-8714
Charlottesville *(G-2784)*

Horseshoe Bend Imprvs LLC ....G...... 434 969-1672
Howardsville *(G-6951)*

Keppick LLC Kim ....G...... 540 364-3668
Delaplane *(G-4076)*

Landrum Horse Shoeing Inc ....G...... 434 836-0847
Blairs *(G-1831)*

M Gautreaux Horseshoe ....G...... 540 840-3153
Beaverdam *(G-1610)*

HOSE: Automobile, Rubber

Mehler Inc ....D...... 276 638-6166
Martinsville *(G-8312)*

HOSE: Plastic

Quadrant Holding Inc ....D...... 276 228-0100
Wytheville *(G-15905)*

HOSE: Pneumatic, Rubber Or Rubberized Fabric, NEC

SAI Krishna LLC ....G...... 804 442-7140
Richmond *(G-11369)*

HOSE: Rubber

Shipyrdandcontractorsupply LLC ....G...... 757 333-2148
Virginia Beach *(G-14807)*

HOSES & BELTING: Rubber & Plastic

Conwed Corp ....D...... 540 981-0362
Roanoke *(G-12070)*

High Threat Concealment LLC ....G...... 757 208-0221
Williamsburg *(G-15255)*

HOSIERY KITS: Sewing & Mending

Bespokery LLC ....G...... 703 624-5024
Fairfax *(G-4598)*

Seven Bends LLC ....G...... 540 392-0553
Blacksburg *(G-1790)*

HOSPITALS: Medical & Surgical

Mach278 LLC ....G...... 716 860-2889
Ashburn *(G-1313)*

HOT TUBS

Outdoor Leisure ....G...... 703 349-1965
Manassas *(G-8125)*

Pool Hot Tub Allia ....G...... 703 838-0083
Alexandria *(G-311)*

Vienna Hot Tubes Patio In ....G...... 703 734-0077
Vienna *(G-14153)*

HOUSEHOLD ARTICLES, EXC FURNITURE: Cut Stone

Stone Studio LLC ....G...... 703 263-9755
Chantilly *(G-2500)*

HOUSEHOLD ARTICLES, EXC KITCHEN: Pottery

Handmade Pottery ....G...... 757 425-0116
Virginia Beach *(G-14503)*

HOUSEHOLD ARTICLES: Metal

Intrapac (harrisonburg) Inc ....B...... 540 434-1703
Mount Crawford *(G-9055)*

Utron Kinetics LLC ....G...... 703 369-5552
Manassas *(G-8008)*

HOUSEHOLD FURNISHINGS, NEC

Aquilian LLC ....G...... 703 967-8212
Chantilly *(G-2369)*

Ashford Court LLC ....D...... 804 743-0700
Richmond *(G-11491)*

Beaver Creek Wipers ....G...... 276 632-3033
Martinsville *(G-8269)*

Carolyn West ....G...... 434 332-5007
Rustburg *(G-12436)*

Carpenter Co ....C...... 804 359-0800
Richmond *(G-11146)*

Cricket Products Inc ....E...... 804 861-0687
Petersburg *(G-10315)*

D3companies Inc ....G...... 804 358-2020
Midlothian *(G-8807)*

Global Direct LLC ....G...... 540 483-5103
Rocky Mount *(G-12325)*

Hearts Desire ....G...... 804 790-1336
Chesterfield *(G-3503)*

Kline Assoc LLC Matt ....G...... 703 780-6466
Alexandria *(G-506)*

Lime & Leaf LLC ....G...... 703 299-2440
Alexandria *(G-261)*

Melted Element LLC ....G...... 703 239-7847
Alexandria *(G-526)*

P
R
O
D
U
C
T

Quickie Manufacturing ....G.... 856 829-8598
  Winchester *(G-15574)*
Springs Global Us Inc ....E.... 276 670-3440
  Martinsville *(G-8337)*
Stafford Home Products ....G.... 540 337-0068
  Fishersville *(G-5009)*
Tempur-Pedic Technologies LLC ....G.... 276 431-7450
  Duffield *(G-4186)*
Windy Hill Collections LLC ....G.... 703 848-8888
  Mc Lean *(G-8579)*
Wool Felt Products Inc ....E.... 540 981-0281
  Roanoke *(G-12230)*

HOUSEWARE STORES

Johnson & Elich Roasters Ltd ....F.... 540 552-7442
  Blacksburg *(G-1747)*

HOUSEWARES, ELECTRIC, EXC COOKING APPLIANCES & UTENSILS

TRC Design Inc ....G.... 804 779-3383
  Mechanicsville *(G-8687)*

HOUSEWARES, ELECTRIC: Appliances, Personal

Track Patch 1 Corporation ....G.... 757 289-5870
  Norfolk *(G-9763)*

HOUSEWARES, ELECTRIC: Cooking Appliances

Axiom Armor LLC ....G.... 540 583-6184
  Bedford *(G-1621)*

HOUSEWARES, ELECTRIC: Fans, Desk

Absolute Furn Solutions LLC ....G.... 757 550-5630
  Chesapeake *(G-2951)*

HOUSEWARES, ELECTRIC: Fans, Exhaust & Ventilating

Cleanvent Dryer Exhust Spclsts ....G.... 804 730-1754
  Mechanicsville *(G-8612)*

HOUSEWARES, ELECTRIC: Massage Machines, Exc Beauty/Barber

Intuit Your Life Network LLC ....G.... 757 588-0533
  Norfolk *(G-9596)*

HOUSEWARES, ELECTRIC: Toasters

Hamilton Beach Brands Inc ....B.... 804 273-9777
  Glen Allen *(G-5739)*
Hamilton Beach Brands Holdg Co ....F.... 804 273-9777
  Glen Allen *(G-5740)*

HOUSINGS: Pressure

Aquawash Pressure Washing LLC ....G.... 757 738-9899
  Virginia Beach *(G-14235)*

HUB CAPS: Automobile, Stamped Metal

Wheels N Motion ....G.... 804 991-3090
  Petersburg *(G-10350)*

HYDRAULIC EQPT REPAIR SVC

Heintzmann Corporation ....D.... 304 284-8004
  Cedar Bluff *(G-2278)*
Shop Guys ....G.... 804 317-9440
  Midlothian *(G-8897)*

HYDRAULIC FLUIDS: Synthetic Based

Quaker Houghton Pa Inc ....G.... 540 877-3631
  Winchester *(G-15464)*

HYDROELECTRIC POWER GENERATION

Universal Powers Inc ....G.... 404 997-8732
  Richmond *(G-11799)*

HYDROFLUORIC ACID COMPOUND: Etching Or Polishing Glass

Applied Film Technology Inc ....G.... 757 351-4241
  Virginia Beach *(G-14234)*

Hard Rubber & Molded Rubber Prdts

Rubber Plastic Met Engrg Corp ....F 757 502-5462
  Virginia Beach *(G-14785)*

ICE

Brunswick Ice and Coal Co Inc ....E 434 848-2615
  Lawrenceville *(G-7178)*
Cassco Corporation ....G.... 540 433-2751
  Harrisonburg *(G-6299)*
Custer Ice Service Inc ....G.... 434 656-2854
  Gretna *(G-6007)*
Hale Manu Inc ....G.... 434 973-5850
  Crozet *(G-3835)*
Holiday Ice Inc ....E.... 757 934-1294
  Suffolk *(G-13722)*
Manassas Ice & Fuel Co Inc ....G.... 703 368-3121
  Manassas *(G-7972)*
Polar Bear Ice Inc ....G.... 276 259-7873
  Whitewood *(G-15192)*
Reddy Ice Corporation ....E.... 757 855-6065
  Norfolk *(G-9704)*
Reddy Ice Corporation ....G.... 540 433-2751
  Harrisonburg *(G-6361)*
Reddy Ice Group Inc ....E.... 540 777-0253
  Roanoke *(G-12161)*
V C Ice and Cold Storage Inc ....G.... 434 793-1441
  Danville *(G-4045)*
Valley Ice LLC ....F.... 540 477-4447
  Mount Jackson *(G-9082)*

ICE CREAM TRUCK VENDORS

Moothru LLC ....G.... 540 439-6455
  Remington *(G-10770)*

ICE WHOLESALERS

Polar Bear Ice Inc ....G.... 276 259-7873
  Whitewood *(G-15192)*

IDENTIFICATION TAGS, EXC PAPER

Fiddlehand Inc ....G.... 703 340-9806
  Herndon *(G-6675)*

IGNEOUS ROCK: Crushed & Broken

Salem Stone Corporation ....E.... 540 552-9292
  Blacksburg *(G-1786)*
Sisson & Ryan Inc ....E.... 540 268-2413
  Shawsville *(G-12686)*
Sisson & Ryan Inc ....E.... 540 268-5251
  Shawsville *(G-12687)*

IGNITION APPARATUS & DISTRIBUTORS

1a Smart Start LLC ....G.... 434 336-1202
  Emporia *(G-4351)*
Alcolock Va Inc ....G.... 804 515-0022
  Henrico *(G-6472)*
Lifesafer ....G.... 571 379-5575
  Manassas *(G-7964)*
Lifesafer Inc ....G.... 757 595-8800
  Newport News *(G-9283)*
Smart Start ....G.... 571 267-7140
  Sterling *(G-13511)*
Smart Start Inc ....G.... 434 392-3334
  Farmville *(G-4957)*
Smart Start Inc ....G.... 276 223-1006
  Wytheville *(G-15913)*

IGNITION COILS: Automotive

Eldor Auto Powertrain USA LLC ....C.... 540 855-1021
  Daleville *(G-3943)*

IGNITION SYSTEMS: High Frequency

Grimes French Race Systems ....G.... 540 923-4541
  Madison *(G-7853)*

INCENSE

Incense Oil More ....G.... 540 793-8642
  Roanoke *(G-12105)*

INDEPENDENT JOURNALISTS

Perez Armando ....G.... 202 716-5044
  Arlington *(G-1104)*

INDL & PERSONAL SVC PAPER, WHOL: Boxes, Corrugtd/Solid Fiber

H & A Specialty Co ....G.... 757 206-1115
  Williamsburg *(G-15252)*
Speedy Sign-A-Rama USA Inc ....G.... 757 838-7446
  Hampton *(G-6242)*
Westrock Cp LLC ....C.... 804 226-5840
  Richmond *(G-11448)*

INDL & PERSONAL SVC PAPER, WHOL: Paper, Wrap/Coarse/Prdts

Cauthorne Paper Company Inc ....E.... 804 798-6999
  Ashland *(G-1388)*

INDL & PERSONAL SVC PAPER, WHOLESALE: Shipping Splys

Alexandria Packaging LLC ....D.... 703 644-5550
  Springfield *(G-12940)*
Custom Packaging Inc ....F.... 804 232-3299
  Richmond *(G-11551)*
Masa Corporation ....D.... 757 855-3013
  Norfolk *(G-9633)*

INDL EQPT SVCS

Red Acres Equipment Inc ....G.... 434 352-5086
  Appomattox *(G-821)*

INDL GASES WHOLESALERS

Airgas Usa LLC ....F.... 804 743-0661
  North Chesterfield *(G-9809)*

INDL MACHINERY & EQPT WHOLESALERS

Hauni Richmond Inc ....C.... 804 222-5259
  Richmond *(G-11234)*
International Carbide & Engrg ....F.... 434 568-3311
  Drakes Branch *(G-4133)*
Km Services LLC ....G.... 757 524-3420
  Williamsburg *(G-15267)*
Lighthouse Instruments LLC ....E.... 434 293-3081
  Charlottesville *(G-2825)*
Longbow Holdings LLC ....G.... 540 404-1185
  Roanoke *(G-11957)*
SKF Lbrication Systems USA Inc ....D.... 757 951-0370
  Hampton *(G-6239)*
Virginia Materials Inc ....G.... 800 321-2282
  Norfolk *(G-9784)*

INDL MACHINERY REPAIR & MAINTENANCE

Abstruse Technical Services ....G.... 540 489-8940
  Ferrum *(G-4966)*
Craft Industrial Incorporated ....G.... 757 825-1195
  Hampton *(G-6118)*
D W Boyd Corporation ....G.... 757 423-2268
  Norfolk *(G-9514)*
International Machine Service ....G.... 757 868-8487
  Poquoson *(G-10373)*
Javatec Inc ....G.... 276 621-4572
  Crockett *(G-3825)*
Longbow Holdings LLC ....G.... 540 404-1185
  Roanoke *(G-11957)*
Mills Marine & Ship Repair LLC ....G.... 757 539-0956
  Suffolk *(G-13744)*
Norfolk Machine and Wldg Inc ....E.... 757 489-0330
  Norfolk *(G-9666)*
Rasco Equipment Services Inc ....G.... 703 643-2952
  Woodbridge *(G-15791)*
Shenandoah Machine & Maint Co ....G.... 540 343-1758
  Roanoke *(G-12183)*

INDL PATTERNS: Foundry Patternmaking

Pattern Shop Inc ....G.... 540 389-5110
  Salem *(G-12554)*
Pattern Svcs & Fabrication LLC ....G.... 540 731-4891
  Radford *(G-10734)*
Pegee Wllmsburg Pttrns Hstries ....G.... 757 220-2722
  Williamsburg *(G-15293)*

INDL PROCESS INSTRUMENTS: Control

Century Control Systems Inc ....G.... 540 992-5100
  Roanoke *(G-12061)*

INDL PROCESS INSTRUMENTS: Controllers, Process Variables

Earl Energy LLC ....E 757 606-2034
Portsmouth **(G-10418)**

INDL PROCESS INSTRUMENTS: Digital Display, Process Variables

Activu Corporation ....,G 703 527-4440
Arlington **(G-838)**

Rebound Analytics LLC ....G 202 297-1204
Tysons **(G-13948)**

INDL PROCESS INSTRUMENTS: Temperature

Fluxteq LLC ....G 540 951-0933
Blacksburg **(G-1739)**

Gammaflux Controls Inc ....G 703 471-5050
Sterling **(G-13407)**

INDL PROCESS INSTRUMENTS: Water Quality Monitoring/Cntrl Sys

Owens & Jefferson Wtr Systems ....G 757 357-7359
Smithfield **(G-12719)**

Reverse Ionizer LLC ....G 703 403-7256
Herndon **(G-6791)**

Rotondo Envmtl Solutions LLC ....G 703 212-4830
Alexandria **(G-329)**

RP Finch Inc ....G 757 566-8022
Williamsburg **(G-15308)**

Wise County Psa ....G 276 762-0159
Coeburn **(G-3705)**

INDL SPLYS WHOLESALERS

Framatome Inc ....B 434 832-3000
Lynchburg **(G-7716)**

Hesco of Virginia LLC ....G 276 694-2818
Stuart **(G-13615)**

INDL SPLYS, WHOL: Fasteners, Incl Nuts, Bolts, Screws, Etc

Vel Tye LLC ....G 757 518-5400
Virginia Beach **(G-14907)**

INDL SPLYS, WHOLESALE: Abrasives

Virginia Abrasives Corporation ....D 804 732-0058
Petersburg **(G-10349)**

INDL SPLYS, WHOLESALE: Bearings

Federal-Mogul Powertrain LLC ....B 540 557-3300
Blacksburg **(G-1737)**

INDL SPLYS, WHOLESALE: Rubber Goods, Mechanical

Keystone Rubber Corporation ....G 717 235-6863
Greenbackville **(G-5994)**

INDL SPLYS, WHOLESALE: Tools

International Carbide & Engrg ....F 434 568-3311
Drakes Branch **(G-4133)**

Scan Industries LLC ....G 360 320-8244
Ashburn **(G-1332)**

INDL SPLYS, WHOLESALE: Valves & Fittings

Alfa Laval US Holding Inc ....D 804 222-5300
Richmond **(G-11096)**

Valve Automation Center ....G 804 752-2700
Ashland **(G-1505)**

INDL TRUCK REPAIR SVCS

NM Mechanic Road Service LLC ....G 571 237-4810
Woodbridge **(G-15761)**

INDUSTRIAL & COMMERCIAL EQPT INSPECTION SVCS

Elevating Eqp Insptn Svc LLC ....F 800 346-0287
Bedford **(G-1634)**

INERTIAL GUIDANCE SYSTEMS

Northrop Grumman Systems Corp ....B 703 280-2900
Falls Church **(G-4845)**

INFORMATION RETRIEVAL SERVICES

Allen Wayne Ltd Arlington ....G 703 321-7414
Warrenton **(G-14977)**

Data-Clear LLC ....G 703 499-3816
Arlington **(G-929)**

Digitized Risk LLC ....G 703 662-3510
Ashburn **(G-1271)**

Gannett Media Corp ....C 703 854-6000
Mc Lean **(G-8440)**

Microstrategy Services Corp ....D 703 848-8600
Tysons Corner **(G-13955)**

One Stop Computer Services LLC ....G 571 442-2045
Sterling **(G-13465)**

Poplicus Incorporated ....E 866 209-9100
Arlington **(G-1116)**

Svanaco Inc ....G 571 312-3790
Alexandria **(G-359)**

INFRARED OBJECT DETECTION EQPT

Chemring Sensors and Electr ....F 434 964-4800
Charlottesville **(G-2608)**

Chemring Snsors Elctrnic Syste ....C 703 661-0283
Dulles **(G-4195)**

INK OR WRITING FLUIDS

Sibashi Inc ....G 571 292-6233
Centreville **(G-2340)**

Zeller + Gmelin Corporation ....D 800 848-8465
Richmond **(G-11463)**

INK: Gravure

Cavalier Printing Ink Co Inc ....G 804 271-4214
Richmond **(G-11033)**

Toner & Ink Warehouse LLC ....G 301 332-2796
Gainesville **(G-5618)**

INK: Printing

Acme Ink Inc ....G 757 373-3614
Virginia Beach **(G-14207)**

Dispersion Specialties Inc ....F 804 798-9137
Ashland **(G-1402)**

Flint CPS Inks North Amer LLC ....G 540 234-9203
Weyers Cave **(G-15172)**

Flint Group US LLC ....G 804 270-1328
Henrico **(G-6512)**

INX Internatiol Ink Co ....G 540 977-0079
Roanoke **(G-11943)**

J M Fry Company ....E 804 236-8100
Henrico **(G-6525)**

Red Tie Group Inc ....G 804 236-4632
Richmond **(G-11349)**

Robert Lewis ....G 917 640-0709
Blackstone **(G-1826)**

Sicpa Securink Corp ....D 703 455-8050
Springfield **(G-13084)**

Sun Chemical Corporation ....E 804 524-3888
South Chesterfield **(G-12828)**

Wikoff Color Corp ....G 540 586-8111
Bedford **(G-1663)**

Zeller + Gmelin Corporation ....D 800 848-8465
Richmond **(G-11463)**

INSECTICIDES & PESTICIDES

Hayward Trmt & Pest Ctrl LLC ....G 757 263-7858
Norfolk **(G-9574)**

South Star Distributers ....F 276 466-4038
Bristol **(G-1988)**

INSTRUMENT DIALS: Painted

Tamco Enterprises Inc ....G 757 627-9551
Chesapeake **(G-3320)**

INSTRUMENT LANDING SYSTEMS OR ILS: Airborne Or Ground

Aero Corporation ....G 703 896-7721
Fairfax **(G-4401)**

INSTRUMENTS & ACCESSORIES: Surveying

McQ Inc ....G 540 361-4219
Fredericksburg **(G-5457)**

One Volt Associates ....F 301 565-3930
Mechanicsville **(G-8666)**

INSTRUMENTS & METERS: Measuring, Electric

National Imports LLC ....G 703 637-0019
Vienna **(G-14102)**

Zeta Meter Inc ....G 540 886-3503
Staunton **(G-13309)**

INSTRUMENTS, LABORATORY: Gas Analyzing

Crown International Inc ....F 703 335-0066
Manassas **(G-8053)**

INSTRUMENTS, LABORATORY: Perimeters, Optical

Notalvision Inc ....D 703 953-3339
Manassas **(G-8118)**

INSTRUMENTS, MEASURING & CNTRG: Plotting, Drafting/Map Rdg

Ea Design Tech Services ....G 540 220-7203
Ruther Glen **(G-12455)**

INSTRUMENTS, MEASURING & CNTRL: Gauges, Auto, Computer

Mill Mountain Capital LLC ....G 540 529-7163
Roanoke **(G-11966)**

Reliant Cem Services Inc ....G 717 459-4990
Lynchburg **(G-7801)**

INSTRUMENTS, MEASURING & CNTRL: Geophysical & Meteorological

Ott Hydromet Corp ....C 703 406-2800
Sterling **(G-13468)**

INSTRUMENTS, MEASURING & CNTRL: Geophysical/Meteorological

Earth Science Technology LLC ....G 703 584-8533
Lorton **(G-7483)**

Sematron LLC ....G 919 360-5806
Leesburg **(G-7345)**

INSTRUMENTS, MEASURING & CNTRL: Testing, Abrasion, Etc

Design Integrated Tech Inc ....F 540 349-9425
Warrenton **(G-14995)**

INSTRUMENTS, MEASURING & CNTRLG: Detectors, Scintillation

Scintilex LLC ....G 240 593-7906
Alexandria **(G-579)**

INSTRUMENTS, MEASURING & CNTRLG: Tensile Strength Testing

P D R Inc ....G 540 772-2780
Roanoke **(G-11981)**

INSTRUMENTS, MEASURING & CNTRLG: Thermometers/Temp Sensors

Refrigeration Solutions Inc ....G 804 752-3188
Ashland **(G-1484)**

TMI Usa Inc ....G 703 668-0114
Reston **(G-10975)**

INSTRUMENTS, MEASURING & CNTRLNG: Nuclear Instrument Modules

Bwx Technologies Inc ....C 980 365-4300
Lynchburg **(G-7667)**

INSTRUMENTS, MEASURING & CONTROLLING: Breathalyzers

1 A Life Safer ....G 757 809-0406
Suffolk **(G-13662)**

PRODUCT

INSTRUMENTS, MEASURING & CONTROLLING: Cable Testing

Cems Inc..E 540 434-7500
Weyers Cave *(G-15170)*

INSTRUMENTS, MEASURING & CONTROLLING: Gas Detectors

Arktis Detection Systems Inc ....G.... 610 724-9748
Arlington *(G-856)*

INSTRUMENTS, MEASURING & CONTROLLING: Photopitometers

Measurement Specialties Inc.............C....... 757 766-1500
Hampton *(G-6194)*

INSTRUMENTS, MEASURING & CONTROLLING: Polygraph

Chittenden & Associates Inc ....G.... 703 930-2769
Rocky Mount *(G-12316)*
CJ & Associates LLC ....G.... 301 461-2945
Sterling *(G-13370)*
Commonwealth Polygraph Svcs LLC .....G....... 540 219-9382
Warrenton *(G-14989)*

INSTRUMENTS, MEASURING & CONTROLLING: Ultrasonic Testing

Imperium ....G.... 540 220-6785
Stafford *(G-13152)*

INSTRUMENTS, MEASURING & CONTROLLING: Weather Tracking

Lufft Usa Inc ....F 805 335-8500
Sterling *(G-13445)*

INSTRUMENTS, MEASURING/CNTRL: Gauging, Ultrasonic Thickness

Gauge Works LLC.................................G.... 703 661-1300
Sterling *(G-13409)*

INSTRUMENTS, MEASURING/CNTRL: Testing/Measuring, Kinematic

Spectra Quest Inc ....F 804 261-3300
Henrico *(G-6574)*

INSTRUMENTS, MEASURING/CNTRLG: Pulse Analyzers, Nuclear Mon

Jeffrey O Holdren................................G.... 703 360-9739
Alexandria *(G-495)*

INSTRUMENTS, MEASURING/CNTRLNG: Med Diagnostic Sys, Nuclear

Accurate Machine Inc...........................G.... 757 853-2136
Norfolk *(G-9418)*
Berger and Burrow Entps Inc ....D.... 866 483-9729
Roanoke *(G-11887)*
Medias LLC ....G.... 540 230-7023
Blacksburg *(G-1761)*

INSTRUMENTS, OPTICAL: Elements & Assemblies, Exc Ophthalmic

Thorlabs Imaging Systems ....F....... 703 651-1705
Sterling *(G-13532)*

INSTRUMENTS, OPTICAL: Test & Inspection

A-Tech Corporation ....G.... 703 955-7846
Chantilly *(G-2360)*
Automated Precision Inc.......................F....... 757 223-4157
Newport News *(G-9174)*
Food Technology Corporation................G.... 703 444-1870
Sterling *(G-13401)*

INSTRUMENTS, SURGICAL & MEDI: Knife Blades/Handles, Surgical

Surgical Instr Sharpening Inc................G.... 804 883-6010
Beaverdam *(G-1613)*

INSTRUMENTS, SURGICAL & MEDICAL: Blood & Bone Work

Computerized Imaging Reference...........E 757 855-1127
Norfolk *(G-9500)*
Deconsystems Corporation ....G.... 703 587-3971
Woodbridge *(G-15681)*
Fmd LLC ....G.... 703 339-8881
Lorton *(G-7490)*
Interbyte ....G.... 703 825-8774
Alexandria *(G-486)*
Itl (virginia) Inc ....G.... 804 381-0905
Ashland *(G-1441)*
Phipps & Bird Inc ....F 804 254-2737
Richmond *(G-11059)*
Richmond Light Co ....G.... 804 276-0559
North Chesterfield *(G-9961)*
Richmond Light Co ....G.... 804 276-0559
North Chesterfield *(G-9962)*
Tasens Assoc ....G.... 703 455-2424
Springfield *(G-13098)*
Tycosys LLC ....G.... 571 278-5300
Manassas *(G-8006)*

INSTRUMENTS, SURGICAL & MEDICAL: Blood Pressure

Caretaker Medical LLC..........................G.... 434 978-7000
Charlottesville *(G-2604)*

INSTRUMENTS, SURGICAL & MEDICAL: Catheters

Urologics LLC ....G.... 757 419-1463
Midlothian *(G-8917)*

INSTRUMENTS, SURGICAL & MEDICAL: Inhalation Therapy

Human Design Medical LLC...................G.... 434 980-8100
Charlottesville *(G-2812)*

INSTRUMENTS, SURGICAL & MEDICAL: Inhalators

Pari Respiratory Equipment Inc ....F....... 804 897-3311
Midlothian *(G-8876)*
Pre Holdings Inc...................................G.... 804 253-7274
Midlothian *(G-8881)*

INSTRUMENTS, SURGICAL & MEDICAL: Knives

Cadence Inc...C....... 540 248-2200
Staunton *(G-13245)*

INSTRUMENTS, SURGICAL & MEDICAL: Ophthalmic

Boss Instruments Ltd Inc......................F 540 832-5000
Zion Crossroads *(G-16005)*

INSTRUMENTS, SURGICAL & MEDICAL: Suction Therapy

Bellair Biomedical LLC..........................G.... 276 206-7337
Charlottesville *(G-2739)*

INSTRUMENTS: Analytical

3d Imging Smltion Corp Amricas ....G.... 800 570-0363
Herndon *(G-6599)*
Amscien Instrument ....G.... 804 301-0797
Richmond *(G-11113)*
Axondx LLC..G.... 540 239-0668
Earlysville *(G-4287)*
D-Star Instruments ....G.... 703 335-0770
Manassas *(G-7929)*
Dynex Technologies Inc ....D.... 703 631-7800
Chantilly *(G-2415)*
Electronic Dev Labs Inc ....E....... 434 799-0807
Danville *(G-3990)*
Emka Technologies Inc ....G.... 703 237-9001
Sterling *(G-13393)*
Flir Systems Inc ....G.... 703 416-6666
Arlington *(G-969)*
Global Cell Solutions Inc......................G.... 434 327-3759
Charlottesville *(G-2804)*
Greenvision Systems Inc ....G.... 703 467-8784
Reston *(G-10863)*

Jha LLC..G.... 757 535-2724
Portsmouth *(G-10447)*
Labxperior Corporation.........................G.... 276 321-7866
Wise *(G-15629)*
Lighthouse Land LLC ....G.... 434 293-3081
Charlottesville *(G-2826)*
Lumacyte LLC ....F 888 472-9295
Keswick *(G-7052)*
Medical Laboratory Solutions...............G.... 414 425-8605
Norfolk *(G-9636)*
Meso Scale Discovery LLC ....G.... 571 318-5521
Fairfax *(G-4507)*
Nanoarca Inc ....G.... 757 589-2526
Virginia Beach *(G-14670)*
Phipps & Bird Inc ....F 804 254-2737
Richmond *(G-11059)*
Rapid Biosciences Inc..........................G.... 713 899-6177
Richmond *(G-11728)*
Rki Instruments Inc..............................G.... 703 753-3333
Haymarket *(G-6441)*
Sciecom LLC ....G.... 703 994-2635
Chantilly *(G-2555)*
Scinteck Instruments LLC ....G.... 571 426-3598
Centreville *(G-2336)*
Staib Instruments Inc ....G.... 757 565-7000
Williamsburg *(G-15318)*
Thermo Fisher Scientific Inc ....B.... 540 869-3200
Middletown *(G-8744)*
Virginia Spectral LLC...........................G.... 434 987-2036
Charlottesville *(G-2713)*
Whitworth Analytics LLC ....G.... 703 319-8018
Vienna *(G-14160)*

INSTRUMENTS: Analyzers, Internal Combustion Eng, Electronic

Kirintec Inc ....G.... 571 527-1437
Alexandria *(G-253)*

INSTRUMENTS: Analyzers, Radio Apparatus, NEC

Teledyne Lecroy Frontline Inc ....D.... 434 984-4500
Charlottesville *(G-2702)*

INSTRUMENTS: Analyzers, Spectrum

Crfs Inc...G.... 571 321-5470
Chantilly *(G-2398)*

INSTRUMENTS: Combustion Control, Indl

Automated Precision Inc.......................F 757 223-4157
Newport News *(G-9174)*

INSTRUMENTS: Elec Lab Stds, Resist, Inductance/Capacitance

Clifton Laboratories.............................G.... 703 830-0368
Clifton *(G-3662)*

INSTRUMENTS: Electrocardiographs

Iheartrhythm LLC.................................G.... 757 810-5902
Arlington *(G-999)*

INSTRUMENTS: Electronic, Analog-Digital Converters

Bee Measure LLC..................................G.... 434 234-4630
Charlottesville *(G-2738)*
Freestate Electronics Inc ....G.... 540 349-4727
Warrenton *(G-15018)*

INSTRUMENTS: Endoscopic Eqpt, Electromedical

Wood Burn Endoscopy Center...............G.... 703 752-2557
Annandale *(G-793)*

INSTRUMENTS: Eye Examination

Advancing Eyecare ....E 757 853-8888
Norfolk *(G-9424)*

INSTRUMENTS: Flow, Indl Process

Teledyne Instruments Inc.....................D.... 757 723-6531
Hampton *(G-6250)*

INSTRUMENTS: Humidity, Indl Process

Online Biose Inc.................................G......703 758-6672
Reston *(G-10914)*

INSTRUMENTS: Indl Process Control

American Density Materials.................G......540 887-1217
Staunton *(G-13240)*
American Hofmann Corporation ....D......434 522-0300
Lynchburg *(G-7639)*
An Electronic Instrumentation.............C......703 478-0700
Leesburg *(G-7217)*
Atlantic Metal Products Inc ....E......804 758-4915
Topping *(G-13885)*
Borgwaldt Kc Incorporated ....E......804 271-6471
Henrico *(G-6485)*
C E C Controls Company Inc ....G......757 392-0415
Chesapeake *(G-3021)*
Chemetrics Inc ....D......540 788-9026
Midland *(G-8749)*
Computational Systems Inc ....G......804 858-5800
Midlothian *(G-8803)*
Controls Unlimited Inc........................G......703 897-4300
Woodbridge *(G-15673)*
CP Instruments LLC ....G......540 558-8596
Harrisonburg *(G-6307)*
D & S Controls ....G......703 655-8189
Warrenton *(G-14993)*
Danaher Family LLC ....G......703 751-9712
Alexandria *(G-181)*
Delta Electronics Inc ....F......703 354-3350
Alexandria *(G-445)*
Differential Pressure Instrs ....G......757 362-0742
Virginia Beach *(G-14404)*
Electromotive Inc ....E......703 331-0100
Manassas *(G-8063)*
Emerson Electric Co ....E......276 223-2200
Wytheville *(G-15887)*
Envirnmntal Solutions Intl Inc ....F......703 263-7600
Ashburn *(G-1276)*
Environmental Equipment Inc ....G......804 730-1280
Mechanicsville *(G-8621)*
Exloc Instruments ....G......540 428-3088
Warrenton *(G-15006)*
Fisher-Rosemount Systems Inc ....G......804 714-1400
North Chesterfield *(G-9875)*
Framatome Inc ....B......434 832-3000
Lynchburg *(G-7716)*
Gas Sentinel LLC ....G......703 962-7151
Fairfax *(G-4628)*
General Electric Company ....F......540 387-7000
Salem *(G-12511)*
Harris Corporation ....G......571 203-7605
Herndon *(G-6695)*
Industrial Control Systems Inc ....E......804 737-1700
Sandston *(G-12620)*
Isomet Corporation ....E......703 321-8301
Manassas *(G-8087)*
L3harris Technologies Inc ....B......847 952-6120
Dulles *(G-4207)*
L3harris Technologies Inc ....B......703 668-6239
Herndon *(G-6728)*
L3harris Technologies Inc ....A......540 563-0371
Roanoke *(G-11951)*
L3harris Technologies Inc ....C......757 594-1607
Newport News *(G-9278)*
Lighthouse Instruments LLC ....E......434 293-3081
Charlottesville *(G-2825)*
Lutron Electronics Co Inc ....C......804 752-3300
Ashland *(G-1455)*
Mefcor Incorporated ....G......276 322-5021
North Tazewell *(G-10103)*
Omron Scientific Tech Inc ....G......703 536-6070
Arlington *(G-1087)*
Pacific Scientific Company ....F......815 226-3100
Radford *(G-10733)*
Pan American Systems Corp ....G......757 468-1926
Virginia Beach *(G-14709)*
Quality Manufacturing Co ....G......540 982-6699
Roanoke *(G-12158)*
Rapid Biosciences Inc ....G......713 899-6177
Richmond *(G-11728)*
Uavarus LLC ....G......757 876-5507
Williamsburg *(G-15327)*
Uma Inc ....E......540 879-2040
Dayton *(G-4067)*

INSTRUMENTS: Infrared, Indl Process

Sync Optics LLC ....G......571 203-0580
Fairfax *(G-4567)*

INSTRUMENTS: Laser, Scientific & Engineering

Ashbury Intl Group Inc ....F......434 296-8600
Ruckersville *(G-12399)*
Cerillo LLC ....G......434 218-3151
Charlottesville *(G-2762)*
Isomet Corporation ....E......703 321-8301
Manassas *(G-8087)*

INSTRUMENTS: Measuring & Controlling

1 A Lifesafer Inc ....G......800 634-3077
Christiansburg *(G-3567)*
1 A Lifesafer Inc ....G......800 634-3077
Winchester *(G-15523)*
1 A Lifesafer Inc ....G......800 634-3077
Alexandria *(G-393)*
1 A Lifesafer Inc ....G......800 634-3077
Manassas Park *(G-8185)*
A & A Precision Machining LLC...........G......804 493-8416
Montross *(G-9023)*
Advanced Technologies Inc ....D......757 873-3017
Newport News *(G-9159)*
American Hofmann Corporation ....D......434 522-0300
Lynchburg *(G-7639)*
An Electronic Instrumentation.............C......703 478-0700
Leesburg *(G-7217)*
Avcom of Virginia Inc ....E......804 794-2500
North Chesterfield *(G-9823)*
Axcelis Technologies Inc ....B......571 921-1493
Manassas *(G-8032)*
Controls Unlimited Inc........................G......703 897-4300
Woodbridge *(G-15673)*
David Gaskill ....G......703 768-2172
Alexandria *(G-442)*
Draeger Safety Diagnostics Inc ....G......434 770-5594
Martinsville *(G-8280)*
Draeger Safety Diagnostics Inc ....G......434 822-0820
Danville *(G-3986)*
Draeger Safety Diagnostics Inc ....G......703 517-0974
Purcellville *(G-10660)*
Eddy Current Technology Inc ....G......757 490-1814
Virginia Beach *(G-14431)*
Electro-Mechanical Corporation..........B......276 669-4084
Bristol *(G-1975)*
Entan Devices LLC ....G......757 766-1500
Hampton *(G-6141)*
Face Construction Technologies ....G......757 624-2121
Norfolk *(G-9545)*
Fgp Sensors Inc ....G......757 766-1500
Hampton *(G-6148)*
Flow-Tech Inc ....G......804 752-3450
Ashland *(G-1417)*
Framatome Inc ....B......434 832-3000
Lynchburg *(G-7716)*
Innerspec Technologies Inc ....G......434 948-1301
Forest *(G-5076)*
Ixthos Inc ....G......703 779-7800
Leesburg *(G-7289)*
Joint Planning Solutions LLC ....G......757 839-5593
Virginia Beach *(G-14573)*
Lexington Measurement Tech ....G......540 261-3966
Lexington *(G-7397)*
Logis-Tech Inc ....C......703 393-4840
Manassas *(G-7970)*
Mecmesin Corporation ....G......703 433-9247
Sterling *(G-13451)*
Model Datasheet Pt Instruments ....G......716 418-4194
Williamsburg *(G-15280)*
Modern Machine and Tool Co Inc........D......757 873-1212
Newport News *(G-9303)*
Morphix Technologies Inc ....E......757 431-2260
Virginia Beach *(G-14663)*
Polimaster Inc ....F......703 525-5075
Sterling *(G-13473)*
Power Monitors Inc ....E......540 432-3077
Mount Crawford *(G-9057)*
Pressure Systems Inc ....C......757 766-4464
Hampton *(G-6219)*
Race Technology USA LLC ....G......804 358-7289
Richmond *(G-11344)*
Rapiscan Systems - An O ....G......703 535-7848
Arlington *(G-1129)*
Regula Forensics Inc ....G......703 473-2625
Reston *(G-10936)*
Sencontrology Inc ....G......540 529-7000
Roanoke *(G-12181)*
Senstar Inc ....G......703 463-3088
Herndon *(G-6804)*

Sentek Instrument LLC.......................G......540 831-9693
Blacksburg *(G-1788)*
Sentek Instrument LLC.......................G......540 250-2116
Blacksburg *(G-1789)*
Smrt Mouth LLC ....G......804 363-8863
Sandston *(G-12634)*
System Innovations Inc ....F......540 373-2374
Fredericksburg *(G-5491)*
Terminus Products Inc ....G......585 546-4990
Christiansburg *(G-3612)*
Virginia Electronic Monitoring.............G......757 513-0942
Chesapeake *(G-3361)*
Warcollar Industries LLC ....G......703 981-2862
Vienna *(G-14156)*

INSTRUMENTS: Measuring Electricity

Accuamp Incorporated ....G......540 908-4079
Grottoes *(G-6012)*
Acuity Tech Holdg Co LLC ....G......410 290-1411
Fredericksburg *(G-5167)*
American Hofmann Corporation ....D......434 522-0300
Lynchburg *(G-7639)*
Avcom of Virginia Inc ....E......804 794-2500
North Chesterfield *(G-9823)*
Brandervisions ....G......804 744-1705
Midlothian *(G-8782)*
Climet Instruments ....G......434 984-5634
Charlottesville *(G-2767)*
Exeye LLC ....G......703 319-0976
Bristow *(G-2052)*
Fluke Networks ....G......804 530-1826
Chester *(G-3417)*
Grid2020 Inc ....F......804 918-1982
North Chesterfield *(G-9882)*
Isomet Corporation ....E......703 321-8301
Manassas *(G-8087)*
Isotemp Research Inc ....G......434 295-3101
Charlottesville *(G-2815)*
Langvan ....G......703 532-0466
Falls Church *(G-4820)*
Local Energy Technologies ....G......717 371-0041
Mc Lean *(G-8487)*
Nexgrid LLC ....E......833 639-4743
Fredericksburg *(G-5335)*
Pacific Scientific Company ....F......815 226-3100
Radford *(G-10733)*
Pan American Systems Corp ....G......757 468-1926
Virginia Beach *(G-14709)*
Rinehart Technology Svcs LLC ....G......804 744-7891
Midlothian *(G-8889)*
Robert Denton ....G......703 435-6960
Herndon *(G-6794)*
Semetrol LLC ....G......804 536-7005
Chesterfield *(G-3523)*
Silicon Equipment Cons LLC ....G......804 357-8926
Midlothian *(G-8901)*
Spectra Lab LLC ....G......703 634-5290
Dumfries *(G-4257)*
Sustainability Innovations LLC ....G......703 281-1352
Vienna *(G-14135)*

INSTRUMENTS: Measuring, Electrical Energy

Dkl International Inc............................G......703 938-6700
Reston *(G-10842)*
Nergysense LLC ....G......434 282-2656
Charlottesville *(G-2837)*
Nusource LLC ....G......571 482-7404
Alexandria *(G-298)*

INSTRUMENTS: Measuring, Electrical Power

Sawarmor LLC ....G......703 779-7719
Leesburg *(G-7342)*

INSTRUMENTS: Measuring, Electrical Quantities

Interbyte..G......703 825-8774
Alexandria *(G-486)*

INSTRUMENTS: Medical & Surgical

Adult Medical Predictive Devic............G......434 996-1203
Keswick *(G-7042)*
Advanced Bioip LLC ....G......301 646-3640
Leesburg *(G-7215)*
Aerospace Techniques Inc ....D......860 347-1200
Virginia Beach *(G-14214)*
Agent Medical LLC ....G......804 562-9469
Richmond *(G-11089)*

Employee Codes: A=Over 500 employees, B=251-500
C=101-250, D=51-100, E=20-50, F=10-19, G=1-9

2021 Virginia
Industrial Directory

977

PRODUCT

Alr Technologies Inc ....G...... 804 554-3500
North Chesterfield (G-10016)
American Medical Devices Inc............F...... 276 642-0463
Bristol (G-1965)
Atc Inc ....G...... 703 267-6898
Bristow (G-2046)
Autopartsource LLC ....E...... 804 329-3000
Richmond (G-11495)
Baxter Healthcare Corporation..........G...... 804 226-1962
Richmond (G-11122)
Becton Dickinson and Company........G...... 804 744-4495
Midlothian (G-8778)
Biotraces Inc ....F...... 703 793-1550
Burke (G-2185)
C R Bard Inc ....G...... 703 754-2848
Gainesville (G-5574)
Carefusion Solutions LLC ....E...... 571 521-8900
Reston (G-10819)
Elcare Innovations Inc ....G...... 434 525-7685
Forest (G-5069)
Epic Mfg LLC ....G...... 757 689-4373
Virginia Beach (G-14449)
Epiep Inc ....G...... 864 423-2526
Charlottesville (G-2790)
Fli USA Inc ....G...... 571 261-4174
Gainesville (G-5583)
Freedom Respiratory ....G...... 804 266-2002
Henrico (G-6515)
G-Holdings LLC ....G...... 202 255-9698
Alexandria (G-209)
Gogo Band Inc ....G...... 804 869-8253
Ashland (G-1421)
Grampian Group Inc ....G...... 757 277-5557
Williamsburg (G-15249)
Healthy Labradors ....G...... 757 740-0681
Norfolk (G-9576)
Hy-Mark Cylinders Inc ....E...... 757 251-6744
Hampton (G-6173)
Icare Clinical Tech LLC ....G...... 301 646-3640
Leesburg (G-7285)
Incision Tech ....G...... 727 254-9183
Staunton (G-13268)
Itl NA Inc ....G...... 703 435-6700
Herndon (G-6713)
Lake Region Medical Inc ....C...... 540 389-7860
Salem (G-12528)
Maroon Assistive Tech LLC ....G...... 703 239-3113
Blacksburg (G-1760)
Medipak ....G...... 540 667-0233
Winchester (G-15446)
Medmarc ....G...... 703 652-1305
Fairfax (G-4505)
Medtrnic Sofamor Danek USA Inc ....F...... 757 355-5100
Virginia Beach (G-14645)
Merit Medical Systems Inc ....D...... 804 416-1030
Chester (G-3433)
Merit Medical Systems Inc ....G...... 804 416-1069
Chester (G-3434)
Microaire Surgical Instrs LLC ....F...... 434 975-8300
Charlottesville (G-2658)
Microaire Surgical Instrs LLC ....C...... 800 722-0822
Charlottesville (G-2659)
Microtek Medical Inc ....E...... 703 904-1220
Sterling (G-13454)
Moog Components Group ....G...... 540 443-4699
Blacksburg (G-1763)
Moog Inc ....G...... 716 652-2000
Blacksburg (G-1764)
Neurotech Na Inc ....G...... 888 980-1197
Manassas (G-8116)
Northfield Medical Mfg LLC ....E...... 800 270-0153
Norfolk (G-9669)
Notalvision Inc ....F...... 888 910-2020
Chantilly (G-2473)
Ondal Medical Systems Amer Inc ......F...... 804 279-0320
Sandston (G-12627)
Origio Inc ....E...... 434 979-4000
Charlottesville (G-2670)
Plexus Inc ....G...... 703 474-0383
Herndon (G-6775)
Poamax LLC ....G...... 757 871-7196
Poquoson (G-10374)
Porex Corporation ....G...... 804 518-1012
South Chesterfield (G-12820)
Predictive Health Devices Inc ....G...... 703 507-0627
Stafford (G-13182)
Professional Network Services ....G...... 571 283-4858
Woodbridge (G-15784)
Pulmoflow Inc ....G...... 831 206-8659
Richmond (G-11340)

Quality Equipment Repair ....G...... 804 815-2268
Deltaville (G-4085)
Ramsey Manufacturing LLC ....G...... 757 232-9034
Norfolk (G-9701)
Rip Shears LLC ....G...... 757 635-9560
Virginia Beach (G-14776)
Rocamed Inc ....G...... 703 503-3616
Mc Lean (G-8540)
Stealth Surgical LLC ....G...... 540 832-5580
Zion Crossroads (G-16009)
Stryker Corporation ....G...... 571 919-2345
Leesburg (G-7353)
Sweet Sounds Music Therapy LLC .....G...... 703 965-3624
Alexandria (G-360)
Swinson Medical LLC ....G...... 540 576-1719
Penhook (G-10285)
T W Enterprises Inc ....G...... 540 667-0233
Winchester (G-15485)
Timberville Drug Store ....G...... 540 434-2379
Harrisonburg (G-6382)
Truefit Dme LLC ....G...... 434 980-8100
Charlottesville (G-2897)
Turner Public Affairs Inc ....G...... 703 489-7104
Gainesville (G-5619)
Uma Inc ....E...... 540 879-2040
Dayton (G-4067)
Varian Medical Systems Inc ....E...... 434 977-8495
Charlottesville (G-2898)
Veterans Choice Med Sup LLC ....G...... 571 244-4358
Purcellville (G-10685)
Voltmed Inc ....G...... 443 799-3072
Blacksburg (G-1805)
Wal-Star Inc ....F...... 434 685-1094
Danville (G-4049)
Wright Medical Technology Inc ....G...... 703 729-0643
Ashburn (G-1353)

INSTRUMENTS: Meteorological

L-1 Standards and Tech Inc ....G...... 571 428-2227
Manassas (G-8095)

INSTRUMENTS: Nautical

W T Brownley Co Inc ....G...... 757 622-7589
Norfolk (G-9788)

INSTRUMENTS: Optical, Analytical

Flir Detection Inc ....G...... 877 692-2120
Arlington (G-968)
Thorlabs Inc ....E...... 703 300-3000
Sterling (G-13531)

INSTRUMENTS: Oscillographs & Oscilloscopes

Teledyne Lecroy Inc ....G...... 434 984-4500
Charlottesville (G-2701)

INSTRUMENTS: Pressure Measurement, Indl

A-Tech Corporation ....G...... 703 955-7846
Chantilly (G-2360)
Benzaco Scientific Inc ....G...... 540 371-5560
Fredericksburg (G-5402)
Controls Corporation America ....C...... 757 422-8330
Virginia Beach (G-14363)
Pressure Systems Inc ....C...... 757 766-4464
Hampton (G-6219)

INSTRUMENTS: Radar Testing, Electric

Radon Safe Inc ....G...... 540 265-0101
Roanoke (G-11993)

INSTRUMENTS: Radio Frequency Measuring

Appalachian Radio Corporation ....G...... 865 382-9865
Ruckersville (G-12398)
Digital Global Systems Inc ....E...... 240 477-7149
Tysons Corner (G-13953)
National Affl Mktg Co Inc ....E...... 703 297-7316
Leesburg (G-7318)

INSTRUMENTS: Signal Generators & Averagers

Six3 Advanced Systems Inc ....C...... 703 742-7660
Dulles (G-4226)

INSTRUMENTS: Temperature Measurement, Indl

Cryopak Verification Tech Inc ....F...... 888 827-3393
Buchanan (G-2120)
Thintherm LLC ....G...... 434 243-5328
Charlottesville (G-2891)

INSTRUMENTS: Test, Electronic & Electric Measurement

Microxact Inc ....G...... 540 394-4040
Radford (G-10725)
Milhous Control Company ....E...... 434 946-5302
Amherst (G-700)
Ncs Pearson Inc ....G...... 866 673-9034
Virginia Beach (G-14673)
Sentientrf ....G...... 503 467-8026
Leesburg (G-7346)
Thermohalt Technology LLC ....G...... 703 880-6697
Oak Hill (G-10139)
Virginia Panel Corporation ....C...... 540 932-3300
Waynesboro (G-15144)

INSTRUMENTS: Test, Electronic & Electrical Circuits

Kollmorgen Corporation ....A...... 540 639-9045
Radford (G-10720)
Northrop Grumman Systems Corp ....B...... 703 280-2900
Falls Church (G-4845)
Okos Solutions LLC ....E...... 703 880-3039
Manassas (G-8120)

INSTRUMENTS: Thermal Conductive, Indl

Laser Thermal Analysis LLC...............G...... 703 300-3403
Charlottesville (G-2823)

INSULATING BOARD, CELLULAR FIBER

Atlantic Fireproofing Inc ....E...... 703 940-9444
Springfield (G-12953)

INSULATING COMPOUNDS

F & D Manufacturing & Supply ....G...... 540 586-6111
Bedford (G-1636)

INSULATION & CUSHIONING FOAM: Polystyrene

Carpenter Co ....C...... 804 359-0800
Richmond (G-11146)
Carpenter Co ....D...... 804 233-0606
Richmond (G-11032)
Carpenter Holdings Inc ....G...... 804 359-0800
Richmond (G-11148)
Cellofoam North America Inc...............E...... 540 373-1800
Fredericksburg (G-5259)

INSULATION & ROOFING MATERIALS: Wood, Reconstituted

Eazy Construction Inc ....G...... 571 220-8385
Fredericksburg (G-5424)
Kingspan Insulation LLC.....................E...... 800 336-2240
Winchester (G-15434)

INSULATION MATERIALS WHOLESALERS

Cellofoam North America Inc...............E...... 540 373-1800
Fredericksburg (G-5259)

INSULATION: Fiberglass

Johns Manville Corporation.................B...... 540 984-4171
Edinburg (G-4307)

INSULATORS & INSULATION MATERIALS: Electrical

Mica Co of Canada Inc........................G...... 757 244-7311
Newport News (G-9299)

INSULATORS, PORCELAIN: Electrical

NGK-Lcke Polymr Insulators Inc ....D...... 757 460-3649
Virginia Beach (G-14681)

INTEGRATED CIRCUITS, SEMICONDUCTOR NETWORKS, ETC

Alltek Systems LLC ....G...... 757 438-6905
Charlottesville *(G-2725)*

Greenzone Systems Inc ....G...... 703 567-6039
Arlington *(G-987)*

Hagstrom Electronics Inc. ....G...... 540 465-4677
Strasburg *(G-13581)*

Intrinsic Semiconductor Corp ....F...... 703 437-4000
Sterling *(G-13431)*

Kordusa Inc ....G...... 540 242-5210
Stafford *(G-13165)*

L3harris Technologies Inc ....D...... 434 455-9390
Forest *(G-5079)*

L3harris Technologies Inc ....E...... 434 455-6600
Forest *(G-5080)*

Leidos Inc ....C...... 703 676-7451
Fort Belvoir *(G-5116)*

Qualcomm Inc ....G...... 858 587-1121
Arlington *(G-1125)*

Raytheon Company ....F...... 703 872-3400
Arlington *(G-1139)*

Taylored Information Tech LLC ....G...... 276 479-2122
Nickelsville *(G-9386)*

INTERCOMMUNICATION EQPT REPAIR SVCS

Burton Telecom LLC ....G...... 757 230-6520
Virginia Beach *(G-14307)*

INTERCOMMUNICATIONS SYSTEMS: Electric

Centripetal Networks Inc ....E...... 571 252-5080
Herndon *(G-6638)*

Corning Optcal Cmmncations LLC ....G...... 703 848-0200
Herndon *(G-6648)*

Dedicated Micros Inc ....E...... 703 904-7738
Chantilly *(G-2403)*

Drs Leonardo Inc ....C...... 703 416-8000
Arlington *(G-944)*

Fauquier Hearing Services Pllc ....G...... 540 341-7112
Warrenton *(G-15010)*

Gatekeeper Security Inc ....E...... 703 673-3320
Sterling *(G-13408)*

Gunn Mountain Communications ....G...... 303 880-8616
Williamsburg *(G-15251)*

Insignia Technology Svcs LLC ....D...... 757 591-2111
Ashburn *(G-1296)*

Iteris Inc ....G...... 949 270-9400
Fairfax *(G-4482)*

Mects Services JV ....G...... 248 499-9243
Fairfax *(G-4652)*

Softwright LLC ....G...... 434 975-4310
Charlottesville *(G-2694)*

Sparkzone Inc ....G...... 703 861-0650
Fairfax *(G-4558)*

Tabet Manufacturing Co Inc ....E...... 757 627-1855
Norfolk *(G-9739)*

INTERIOR DECORATING SVCS

Sej Property Logistics Co ....G...... 516 499-2549
Crewe *(G-3816)*

INTERIOR DESIGN SVCS, NEC

Design Source Inc ....E...... 804 644-3424
Sandston *(G-12610)*

Signmedia Inc ....E...... 757 826-7128
Hampton *(G-6237)*

Staton Mj & Associates Ltd ....G...... 804 737-1946
Sandston *(G-12637)*

US Cabinet & Intr Design LLC ....G...... 202 740-0038
Falls Church *(G-4887)*

INTERIOR DESIGNING SVCS

Creative Decorating ....G...... 703 643-5556
Woodbridge *(G-15674)*

Hang Up ....G...... 703 430-0717
Sterling *(G-13418)*

Morris Designs Inc ....F...... 757 463-9400
Virginia Beach *(G-14664)*

TI Associates Inc ....D...... 757 857-6266
Norfolk *(G-9750)*

INVESTORS, NEC

Dominion Energy Inc ....D...... 804 771-3000
Richmond *(G-11187)*

INVESTORS: Real Estate, Exc Property Operators

PM Services LLC ....G...... 804 426-9892
Virginia Beach *(G-14727)*

IRON & STEEL PRDTS: Hot-Rolled

Commercial Metals Company ....E...... 540 775-8501
King George *(G-7084)*

IRON ORES

Iron Dog Metalsmiths ....G...... 703 503-9631
Fairfax *(G-4481)*

Iron Lungs Inc ....G...... 757 877-2529
Yorktown *(G-15966)*

IRONING BOARDS

C L Towing ....G...... 703 625-7126
Alexandria *(G-157)*

IRRADIATION EQPT

Brachyfoam LLC ....G...... 434 249-9554
Charlottesville *(G-2749)*

Sim Net Inc ....G...... 804 752-2776
Beaverdam *(G-1611)*

IRRADIATION EQPT: Gamma Ray

Dilon Technologies Inc ....E...... 757 269-4910
Newport News *(G-9216)*

IRRADIATION EQPT: Nuclear

River Technologies LLC ....F...... 434 525-4734
Forest *(G-5090)*

JACKS: Hydraulic

Shop Guys ....G...... 804 317-9440
Midlothian *(G-8897)*

JEWELERS' FINDINGS & MATERIALS: Castings

John C Nordt Co Inc ....C...... 540 362-9717
Roanoke *(G-12112)*

JEWELERS' FINDINGS & MATERIALS: Parts, Unassembled

Iceburrr Jewelry ....G...... 757 537-9520
Virginia Beach *(G-14540)*

Treasures of African Artists ....G...... 571 263-2152
Alexandria *(G-367)*

JEWELRY & PRECIOUS STONES WHOLESALERS

Aumiitu Combs Creations LLC ....G...... 757 285-5201
Virginia Beach *(G-14248)*

Hudson Jewelry Co Inc ....G...... 276 646-5565
Marion *(G-8229)*

Kirk Burkett Manufacturing ....G...... 276 699-6856
Austinville *(G-1529)*

Raybar Jewelry Design Inc ....G...... 757 486-4562
Virginia Beach *(G-14760)*

JEWELRY APPAREL

Amelia Lawrence LLC ....G...... 703 493-9095
Manassas *(G-8025)*

Crystals of Hope ....G...... 434 525-7279
Lynchburg *(G-7688)*

Hand and Hammer Inc ....F...... 703 491-4866
Woodbridge *(G-15721)*

Jones Tonja ....G...... 757 773-9475
Portsmouth *(G-10448)*

Jwlbook LLC ....G...... 571 287-0121
Fairfax *(G-4641)*

Kirk Burkett Manufacturing ....G...... 276 699-6856
Austinville *(G-1529)*

Kweens Essentials LLC ....G...... 703 861-6764
Alexandria *(G-511)*

Raybar Jewelry Design Inc ....G...... 757 486-4562
Virginia Beach *(G-14760)*

Sue Dille ....G...... 540 951-4100
Blacksburg *(G-1795)*

Sweet Serenity Gifts ....G...... 540 903-1964
Fredericksburg *(G-5489)*

JEWELRY FINDINGS & LAPIDARY WORK

Aquia Creek Gems ....G...... 540 659-6120
Stafford *(G-13118)*

Goyal Gadgets LLC ....G...... 703 757-8294
Great Falls *(G-5957)*

Sapna Creations ....G...... 571 276-1480
Centreville *(G-2335)*

JEWELRY REPAIR SVCS

Jewelers Services Inc ....F...... 804 353-9612
Chesterfield *(G-3507)*

Kirk Burkett Manufacturing ....G...... 276 699-6856
Austinville *(G-1529)*

Regal Jewelers Inc ....G...... 540 949-4455
Waynesboro *(G-15134)*

Susannah Wagner Jewelers Inc ....G...... 804 798-5864
Ashland *(G-1498)*

JEWELRY STORES

Birds With Backpacks LLC ....G...... 703 897-5531
Woodbridge *(G-15657)*

Eminence Jewelers ....G...... 703 815-1384
Clifton *(G-3664)*

Lavish Nicole LLC ....G...... 804 386-7556
South Chesterfield *(G-12812)*

Regal Jewelers Inc ....G...... 540 949-4455
Waynesboro *(G-15134)*

Sue Dille ....G...... 540 951-4100
Blacksburg *(G-1795)*

Susannah Wagner Jewelers Inc ....G...... 804 798-5864
Ashland *(G-1498)*

JEWELRY STORES: Clocks

Halifax Fine Furnishings ....G...... 540 774-3060
Roanoke *(G-11931)*

JEWELRY STORES: Precious Stones & Precious Metals

Ali Baba Handwrought Jewelry ....G...... 757 622-5007
Norfolk *(G-9430)*

Crystals of Hope ....G...... 434 525-7279
Lynchburg *(G-7688)*

Designer Goldsmith Inc ....G...... 703 777-7661
Leesburg *(G-7254)*

Hunt Country Jewelers Inc ....G...... 540 338-8050
Hillsboro *(G-6871)*

JEWELRY STORES: Watches

Nova Retail LLC ....G...... 703 507-5220
Fairfax *(G-4521)*

JEWELRY, PRECIOUS METAL: Cigar & Cigarette Access

Jt Tobacco ....G...... 540 387-0383
Salem *(G-12525)*

JEWELRY, PRECIOUS METAL: Mountings & Trimmings

Universal Store Corp ....G...... 703 467-0434
Sterling *(G-13544)*

JEWELRY, PRECIOUS METAL: Pearl, Natural Or Cultured

Riina Mettas Jewelry LLC ....G...... 202 368-9819
Woodbridge *(G-15795)*

JEWELRY, PRECIOUS METAL: Pins

Amanda Grace Handcrafted ....G...... 703 539-2151
Fairfax *(G-4405)*

JEWELRY, PRECIOUS METAL: Rings, Finger

Herff Jones LLC ....G...... 703 368-9550
Manassas *(G-7952)*

John C Nordt Co Inc ....C...... 540 362-9717
Roanoke *(G-12112)*

PRODUCT

JEWELRY, PRECIOUS METAL: Settings & Mountings

Frangipani Inc ....G.... 703 903-0099
McLean (G-8436)

JEWELRY, WHOLESALE

Crystals of Hope ....G.... 434 525-7279
Lynchburg (G-7688)
Frangipani Inc ....G.... 703 903-0099
McLean (G-8436)

JEWELRY: Decorative, Fashion & Costume

3d Designs Dazzling Dream Desi ....G.... 703 231-9540
Woodbridge (G-15639)
A Markus Design ....G.... 703 938-6694
Vienna (G-14003)
Bariso Ling ....G.... 757 277-5383
Virginia Beach (G-14261)
Darlene Group Inc ....D.... 401 728-3300
Arlington (G-927)
Designer Goldsmith Inc ....G.... 703 777-7661
Leesburg (G-7255)
Dimensions Virginia Beach Inc ....G.... 757 340-1115
Virginia Beach (G-14405)
Eileen C Johnson ....G.... 855 533-7753
Berryville (G-1680)
Lux Costume Jewelry ....G.... 703 665-0674
Arlington (G-1051)
Pandoras Box ....G.... 757 719-6669
Newport News (G-9309)
Sandra Magura ....G.... 540 318-6947
Stafford (G-13187)
Swarovski North America Ltd ....G.... 703 267-2332
Fairfax (G-4564)
Swarovski North America Ltd ....G.... 571 633-1800
McLean (G-8561)
Swarovski North America Ltd ....G.... 703 418-6665
Arlington (G-1179)
Swarovski North America Ltd ....G.... 757 253-7924
Williamsburg (G-15321)
Vlynns ....G.... 540 904-2844
Roanoke (G-12225)
Zoil Jewelry LLC ....G.... 571 340-2256
Herndon (G-6849)

JEWELRY: Precious Metal

Ali Baba Handwrought Jewelry ....G.... 757 622-5007
Norfolk (G-9430)
Aumiitu Combs Creations LLC ....G.... 757 285-5201
Virginia Beach (G-14248)
Birds With Backpacks LLC ....G.... 703 897-5531
Woodbridge (G-15657)
Clark & Clark LLC ....G.... 757 264-9000
Norfolk (G-9487)
Cynthia Coriopoli Design ....G.... 703 548-2086
Alexandria (G-180)
Delmer-Va Inc ....G.... 571 447-1413
Manassas (G-8056)
Dmkp Inc ....G.... 703 941-1436
McLean (G-8420)
Ellen Fairchild-Flugel Art LLC ....G.... 540 325-2305
Woodstock (G-15852)
Eminence Jewelers ....G.... 703 815-1384
Clifton (G-3664)
Gabriel D Ofiesh II Inc ....G.... 434 295-9038
Charlottesville (G-2800)
High Concepts ....G.... 804 683-2226
Glen Allen (G-5745)
Hudson Jewelry Co Inc ....G.... 276 646-5565
Marion (G-8229)
Hugo Kohl LLC ....G.... 540 564-2755
Harrisonburg (G-6330)
Hunt Country Jewelers Inc ....G.... 540 338-8050
Hillsboro (G-6871)
Jewelers Services Inc ....F.... 804 353-9612
Chesterfield (G-3507)
Lavish Nicole LLC ....G.... 804 386-7556
South Chesterfield (G-12812)
Lucia Richie ....G.... 804 878-8969
Midlothian (G-8851)
M Shields Studio Inc ....G.... 757 340-1670
Norfolk (G-9627)
Metallum ....G.... 703 549-4551
Alexandria (G-274)
Neda Jewelers Inc ....G.... 703 670-2177
Woodbridge (G-15757)
Patrick Marrietta ....G.... 804 479-9791
Petersburg (G-10333)

Price Goldsmith Co ....G.... 757 722-3210
Hampton (G-6221)
Rng LLC ....G.... 540 825-5322
Culpeper (G-3917)
Romancing Stone ....G.... 804 769-7888
Aylett (G-1553)
Ronald Steven Hamm ....G.... 434 295-8878
Charlottesville (G-2866)
Rubinas Adornments Inc ....G.... 757 623-4246
Norfolk (G-9712)
Savy Designs By Sylvia ....G.... 757 547-7525
Chesapeake (G-3285)
Studio 29 ....G.... 757 624-1445
Norfolk (G-9736)
Susannah Wagner Jewelers Inc ....G.... 804 798-5864
Ashland (G-1498)
Sylvan Spirit ....G.... 804 330-5454
North Chesterfield (G-9996)
Thesia Inc ....G.... 703 726-8845
Aldie (G-113)
Wolf Zsuzsi of Budapest ....G.... 703 548-3319
Alexandria (G-385)
Yesterdays Treasures ....G.... 757 877-5153
Grafton (G-5933)

JOB COUNSELING

Contractors Institute LLC ....G.... 804 250-6750
Richmond (G-11165)
Contractors Institute LLC ....G.... 804 556-5518
Richmond (G-11166)

JOB PRINTING & NEWSPAPER PUBLISHING COMBINED

Charlotte Publishing Inc ....F.... 434 568-3341
Drakes Branch (G-4131)
Clinch Valley Publishing Co ....G.... 276 762-7671
Saint Paul (G-12465)
Daily Press Inc ....F.... 757 245-3737
Newport News (G-9213)
Powell Valley Printing Company ....F.... 276 546-1210
Pennington Gap (G-10297)
Scott County Herald Virginian ....G.... 276 386-6300
Gate City (G-5667)
W A Cleaton and Sons Inc ....F.... 804 443-2200
Tappahannock (G-13824)
Wise Printing Co Inc ....G.... 276 523-1141
Big Stone Gap (G-1718)

JOB TRAINING & VOCATIONAL REHABILITATION SVCS

Mega-Tech Inc ....E.... 703 534-1629
Falls Church (G-4922)

JOB TRAINING SVCS

Wegmann Usa Inc ....D.... 434 385-1580
Lynchburg (G-7837)

JOINTS: Expansion

R W P Johnson Products Ltd ....F.... 804 453-7705
Burgess (G-2176)

JOISTS: Long-Span Series, Open Web Steel

New Millennium Bldg Systems LLC ......D.... 540 389-0211
Salem (G-12544)

KAOLIN & BALL CLAY MINING

Carolinas Solution Group Inc ....G.... 301 257-6926
Charlottesville (G-2756)

KEYBOARDS: Computer Or Office Machine

F & B Holding Co ....G.... 757 766-2770
Yorktown (G-15957)
Rollins Oma Sue ....G.... 757 449-6371
Virginia Beach (G-14778)
Stanford Electronics Mfg & Sls ....G.... 434 676-6630
Brodnax (G-2105)

KILNS

Kiln Doctor Inc ....G.... 540 636-6016
Front Royal (G-5540)

KITCHEN & COOKING ARTICLES: Pottery

E I Designs Pottery LLC ....G.... 410 459-3337
Virginia Beach (G-14424)

Kellis Creations LLC ....G.... 540 554-2878
Round Hill (G-12381)
Sophia Street Studio ....G.... 540 372-3459
Fredericksburg (G-5225)

KITCHEN ARTICLES: Semivitreous Earthenware

Koolnut LLC ....G.... 213 349-0196
Henrico (G-6528)

KITCHEN CABINET STORES, EXC CUSTOM

Francis C James Jr ....G.... 757 442-3630
Nassawadox (G-9100)

KITCHEN CABINETS WHOLESALERS

Creative Cabinet Design ....G.... 434 293-4040
Charlottesville (G-2774)
Deneals Cabinets Inc ....G.... 540 721-8005
Hardy (G-6286)
Empire Marble & Granite Co ....G.... 804 359-2004
Richmond (G-11574)
Fitzgeralds Cabinet Shop Inc ....G.... 757 877-2538
Newport News (G-9229)
Montgomery Cabinetry ....G.... 540 721-7000
Wirtz (G-15616)
Nails Cabinet Shop Inc ....G.... 540 888-3268
Winchester (G-15454)
Woodworking Shop Inc ....G.... 757 872-0890
Newport News (G-9381)

KITCHEN UTENSILS: Food Handling & Processing Prdts, Wood

Bowld Flavors LLC ....G.... 757 952-4741
Hampton (G-6099)
Saiflavor ....G.... 304 520-9464
Harrisonburg (G-6366)
Shahzada Afghan Amrcn Import E ....G.... 571 245-1345
Alexandria (G-344)

KITCHEN UTENSILS: Wooden

Biocer Corporation ....G.... 757 490-7851
Virginia Beach (G-14280)
Blanc Creatives LLC ....F.... 434 260-1692
Charlottesville (G-2741)
Kayjae Inc ....G.... 804 725-9664
Cobbs Creek (G-3694)
Timberline Barns LLC ....G.... 276 445-4366
Rose Hill (G-12363)

KITCHENWARE STORES

Hamilton Beach Brands Inc ....B.... 804 273-9777
Glen Allen (G-5739)
Hamilton Beach Brands Holdg Co ....F.... 804 273-9777
Glen Allen (G-5740)
K & S Pewter Inc ....G.... 540 751-0505
Leesburg (G-7294)
Wades Mill Inc ....G.... 540 348-1400
Raphine (G-10751)

KNIVES: Agricultural Or Indl

Cadence Inc ....C.... 540 248-2200
Staunton (G-13245)

LABELS: Cotton, Printed

Product Identification ....G.... 804 264-4434
Richmond (G-11336)

LABELS: Paper, Made From Purchased Materials

Fortis Solutions Group LLC ....C.... 757 340-8893
Virginia Beach (G-14472)
Label ....G.... 757 236-8434
Hampton (G-6275)
Product Identification ....G.... 804 264-4434
Richmond (G-11336)

LABORATORIES, TESTING: Prdt Certification, Sfty/Performance

A-Tech Corporation ....G.... 703 955-7846
Chantilly (G-2360)

LABORATORIES, TESTING: Product Testing, Safety/Performance

Special Fleet Services Inc ....D...... 540 434-4488
  Harrisonburg (G-6373)

LABORATORIES, TESTING: Water

Water Chemistry Incorporated ....E...... 540 343-3618
  Roanoke (G-12022)

LABORATORIES: Biological Research

Rapid Biosciences Inc ....G...... 713 899-6177
  Richmond (G-11728)
Voltmed Inc ....G...... 443 799-3072
  Blacksburg (G-1805)

LABORATORIES: Biotechnology

Cavion Inc ....G...... 434 200-8442
  Charlottesville (G-2760)
Frogue ....F...... 703 679-7003
  Reston (G-10854)

LABORATORIES: Dental

Denis Britto Dr ....G...... 703 230-6784
  Chantilly (G-2405)

LABORATORIES: Dental & Medical X-Ray

Sim Net Inc ....G...... 804 752-2776
  Beaverdam (G-1611)

LABORATORIES: Electronic Research

C-3 Comm Systems LLC ....G...... 703 829-0588
  Arlington (G-897)
Fiddlehand Inc ....G...... 703 340-9806
  Herndon (G-6675)
Greenzone Systems Inc ....G...... 703 567-6039
  Arlington (G-987)
Grey Market Labs Pbc ....G...... 929 274-4465
  Falls Church (G-4800)
Zeido LLC ....G...... 202 549-5757
  Stafford (G-13213)

LABORATORIES: Physical Research, Commercial

Aero Corporation ....G...... 703 896-7721
  Fairfax (G-4401)
Blacksky Holdings Inc ....E...... 703 935-1930
  Herndon (G-6625)
Caper Holdings LLC ....G...... 757 563-3810
  Virginia Beach (G-14315)
Cary Pharmaceuticals Inc ....G...... 703 759-7460
  Great Falls (G-5944)
Centripetal Networks Inc ....E...... 571 252-5080
  Herndon (G-6638)
Directed Vapor Tech Intl Inc ....F...... 434 977-1405
  Charlottesville (G-2618)
Effithermix LLC ....G...... 703 860-9703
  Vienna (G-14043)
Electron Technologies Inc ....G...... 703 818-9400
  Chantilly (G-2416)
Firstguard Technologies Corp ....G...... 703 267-6670
  Fairfax (G-4624)
Kirintec Inc ....G...... 571 527-1437
  Alexandria (G-253)
Lumacyte LLC ....F...... 888 472-9295
  Keswick (G-7052)
Mandylion Research Labs LLC ....E...... 703 628-4284
  Oakton (G-10156)
Meridian Tech Systems Inc ....G...... 301 606-6490
  Leesburg (G-7313)
Objective Intrface Systems Inc ....D...... 703 295-6500
  Herndon (G-6763)
Parabon Nanolabs Inc ....E...... 703 689-9689
  Reston (G-10921)
Parry Labs LLC ....E...... 585 746-8335
  Alexandria (G-306)
Pbp Solutions LLC ....G...... 202 999-8101
  Reston (G-10923)
Raytheon Company ....E...... 703 413-1220
  Arlington (G-1133)
Smrt Mouth LLC ....G...... 804 363-8863
  Sandston (G-12634)

LABORATORIES: Testing

Chemetrics Inc ....D...... 540 788-9026
  Midland (G-8749)
Coperion Corporation ....D...... 276 228-7717
  Wytheville (G-15884)
Ds Smith PLC ....G...... 540 774-0500
  Roanoke (G-11916)
End To End Inc ....E...... 757 216-1938
  Virginia Beach (G-14448)
Engility LLC ....A...... 703 434-4000
  Reston (G-10847)
Pyott-Boone Electronics Inc ....C...... 276 988-5505
  North Tazewell (G-10105)
Rector Visitors of The Univ VA ....E...... 434 296-7288
  Charlottesville (G-2682)

LABORATORY APPARATUS & FURNITURE

Alfa Laval Inc ....C...... 866 253-2528
  Richmond (G-11095)
Biologics Inc ....F...... 703 367-9020
  Manassas (G-8039)
Diversified Eductl Systems ....E...... 540 687-7060
  Middleburg (G-8719)
Jackson Pointe LLC ....G...... 757 269-7100
  Newport News (G-9264)
Phipps & Bird Inc ....F...... 804 254-2737
  Richmond (G-11059)
Techlab Inc ....D...... 540 953-1664
  Radford (G-10740)
Tomotrace Inc ....G...... 202 207-5423
  Sterling (G-13535)

LABORATORY APPARATUS & FURNITURE: Worktables

Samin Science Usa Inc ....G...... 571 403-3678
  Vienna (G-14121)

LABORATORY APPARATUS, EXC HEATING & MEASURING

Sims USA Inc ....G...... 757 875-7742
  Yorktown (G-15991)

LABORATORY APPARATUS: Laser Beam Alignment Device

Laser Alignment Systems LLC ....G...... 410 507-6820
  Gloucester (G-5852)

LABORATORY APPARATUS: Pipettes, Hemocytometer

Pipet Repair Service Inc ....G...... 804 739-3720
  Midlothian (G-8880)

LABORATORY CHEMICALS: Organic

Gsk Corporation Inc ....G...... 240 200-5600
  Sterling (G-13417)

LABORATORY EQPT: Chemical

Bases of Virginia LLC ....G...... 757 690-8482
  Yorktown (G-15936)

LABORATORY EQPT: Clinical Instruments Exc Medical

Indy Health Labs LLC ....G...... 540 682-2160
  Roanoke (G-11940)
Melissa Davis ....G...... 757 482-3743
  Virginia Beach (G-14647)

LABORATORY EQPT: Incubators

Nevtek ....G...... 540 925-2322
  Williamsville (G-15351)

LABORATORY INSTRUMENT REPAIR SVCS

Pipet Repair Service Inc ....G...... 804 739-3720
  Midlothian (G-8880)

LADDERS: Metal

Cushing Metals LLC ....G...... 804 339-1114
  King William (G-7128)

LADDERS: Portable, Metal

Flip-N-Haul LLC ....G...... 804 932-4372
  New Kent (G-9132)

LAMINATED PLASTICS: Plate, Sheet, Rod & Tubes

Advanced Drainage Systems Inc ....E...... 540 261-6131
  Buena Vista (G-2137)
Conwed Corp ....D...... 540 981-0362
  Roanoke (G-12070)
Eastman Performance Films LLC ....D...... 423 224-7768
  Martinsville (G-8283)
Tredegar Corporation ....D...... 804 330-1000
  North Chesterfield (G-10029)

LAMINATING MATERIALS

Drytac Corporation ....E...... 804 280-6013
  Sandston (G-12613)

LAMINATING SVCS

Nationwide Laminating Inc ....F...... 703 550-8400
  Lorton (G-7513)

LAMP & LIGHT BULBS & TUBES

Callison Electric ....G...... 540 294-3189
  Staunton (G-13246)
General Electric Company ....B...... 540 667-5990
  Winchester (G-15420)
Green Edge Lighting LLC ....G...... 804 462-0221
  Mechanicsville (G-8631)
Service Lamp Supply ....G...... 757 426-0636
  Virginia Beach (G-14804)

LAMP BULBS & TUBES, ELEC: Lead-In Wires, From Purchased Wire

Priority Wire & Cable Inc ....G...... 757 361-0207
  Chesapeake (G-3249)

LAMP BULBS & TUBES, ELECTRIC: Electric Light

Natural Lighting LLC ....G...... 703 347-7004
  Alexandria (G-541)

LAMP BULBS & TUBES, ELECTRIC: For Specialized Applications

Extremeht2com ....G...... 804 665-6304
  Richmond (G-11584)

LAMP BULBS & TUBES, ELECTRIC: Parts

General Electric Company ....C...... 804 965-1020
  Glen Allen (G-5736)

LAMP STORES

American Interiors Ltd ....G...... 757 627-0248
  Norfolk (G-9438)

LAMPS: Desk, Residential

Renaissnce Cntract Ltg Furn In ....E...... 540 342-1548
  Roanoke (G-12162)

LAND SUBDIVISION & DEVELOPMENT

Dominion Energy Inc ....D...... 804 771-3000
  Richmond (G-11187)
United Co ....D...... 276 466-0769
  Bristol (G-1993)

LAPIDARY WORK: Jewel Cut, Drill, Polish, Recut/Setting

Candlelight Jewels ....G...... 305 301-2536
  Fairfax (G-4604)

LASER SYSTEMS & EQPT

Optical Air Data Systems LLC ....E...... 703 393-0754
  Manassas (G-7986)

LASERS: Welding, Drilling & Cutting Eqpt

Marelco Power Systems Inc ....D...... 517 546-6330
  Richmond (G-11666)

P
R
O
D
U
C
T

TNT Laser Works LLC ....G..... 571 214-7517
Leesburg (G-7363)

LATHES

Tants Mch & Fabrication Inc ....G..... 757 434-9448
Chesapeake (G-3321)

LAUNDRY & GARMENT SVCS, NEC: Garment Alteration & Repair

Cw Security Solutions LLC ....G..... 540 929-8019
Vinton (G-14172)

LAUNDRY & GARMENT SVCS, NEC: Garment Making, Alter & Repair

Sunshine Sewing ....G..... 276 628-2478
Abingdon (G-63)

LAUNDRY EQPT: Commercial

Capital Linen Services Inc ....F 804 744-3334
Midlothian (G-8789)
M B S Equipment Sales Inc ....G..... 804 785-4971
Shacklefords (G-12683)
Mosena Enterprises Inc ....G..... 757 562-7033
Franklin (G-5149)

LAWN & GARDEN EQPT

Asb Greenworld Inc ....G..... 804 695-2660
Saluda (G-12600)
Beltsville Construction Supply ....G..... 703 392-8588
Manassas (G-8037)
Benabaye Power LLC ....G..... 703 574-5800
Sterling (G-13357)
Douglas Vince Johner ....G..... 276 780-2369
Chilhowie (G-3550)
Ferguson Manufacturing Co Inc ....F 757 539-3409
Suffolk (G-13709)
Hipkins Horticulture Co LLC ....G..... 804 926-7116
South Chesterfield (G-12835)
Jr Sales ....G..... 703 450-4753
Sterling (G-13436)
Mantel USA Inc ....G..... 540 946-6529
Waynesboro (G-15122)
Melnor Inc ....E 540 722-5600
Winchester (G-15447)
Mr-Mow-It-all ....G..... 540 263-2369
Roanoke (G-12138)
Quest Expedition Outfitte ....G..... 434 244-7140
Charlottesville (G-2853)

LAWN & GARDEN EQPT: Grass Catchers, Lawn Mower

Abeck Inc ....G..... 540 375-2841
Salem (G-12471)

LAWN & GARDEN EQPT: Lawnmowers, Residential, Hand Or Power

Antonio Robinson ....G..... 804 368-9889
Petersburg (G-10305)

LAWN & GARDEN EQPT: Tractors & Eqpt

Canaan Land Associates Inc ....D 276 988-6543
Tazewell (G-13829)
Silver Lining Assistance Inc ....F 540 825-8371
Culpeper (G-3921)

LAWN MOWER REPAIR SHOP

Carters Power Equipment Inc ....G..... 804 796-4895
Chester (G-3392)

LEASING & RENTAL SVCS: Cranes & Aerial Lift Eqpt

B & B Welding Inc ....G..... 540 982-2082
Roanoke (G-12039)
ML Manufacturing ....G..... 434 581-2000
New Canton (G-9118)

LEASING & RENTAL: Computers & Eqpt

Audio-Visuals Actions Inc ....G..... 703 751-1010
Alexandria (G-143)
Up and Running Computers Inc ....G..... 757 565-3282
Williamsburg (G-15329)

LEASING & RENTAL: Construction & Mining Eqpt

Alban Tractor Co Inc ....F 540 667-4200
Clear Brook (G-3643)
Geoquip Inc ....D 757 485-2500
Chesapeake (G-3118)

LEASING & RENTAL: Medical Machinery & Eqpt

American Medical Devices Inc ....F 276 642-0463
Bristol (G-1965)

LEASING & RENTAL: Office Machines & Eqpt

Manufacturing System Svcs Inc ....G..... 800 428-8643
Fairfax (G-4651)

LEASING & RENTAL: Other Real Estate Property

Greater Wise Incorporated ....D 276 679-1400
Norton (G-10119)

LEASING & RENTAL: Trucks, Without Drivers

K & K Signs ....G..... 540 586-0542
Bedford (G-1641)

LEATHER GOODS: Aprons, Welders', Blacksmiths', Etc

Village Blacksmith LLC ....G..... 804 824-2631
Gloucester (G-5864)

LEATHER GOODS: Boots, Horse

Barismil LLC ....G..... 703 622-4550
Herndon (G-6619)
Equus Therapeutics Inc ....G..... 540 456-6767
Afton (G-80)
Tomlinsons Farrier Service LLC ....G..... 540 377-9195
Greenville (G-5999)

LEATHER GOODS: Boxes

Mutual Box Leather ....G..... 703 626-9770
Round Hill (G-12383)

LEATHER GOODS: Corners, Luggage

Briggs & Riley Travelware LLC ....G..... 703 352-0713
Fairfax (G-4421)

LEATHER GOODS: Garments

Cedar Industry LLC ....E 571 402-4564
Dumfries (G-4238)
Dw Global LLC ....G..... 757 689-4547
Virginia Beach (G-14419)
PS Its Leather ....G..... 804 762-9489
Richmond (G-11339)

LEATHER GOODS: Harnesses Or Harness Parts

Mayes Wholesale Tack ....G..... 276 755-3715
Cana (G-2227)

LEATHER GOODS: Holsters

Defensor Holsters LLC ....G..... 703 409-4865
Mc Lean (G-8417)
R&B Custom Holsters LLC ....G..... 703 586-2616
Woodbridge (G-15789)
Stealth Mfg & Svcs LLC ....G..... 787 679-7548
Virginia Beach (G-14844)
Valhalla Holsters LLC ....G..... 540 529-4520
Moneta (G-8983)

LEATHER GOODS: NEC

Beltway Leatherworks LLC ....G..... 703 457-7829
Woodbridge (G-15656)
Capitol Leather LLC ....G..... 434 229-8467
Manassas Park (G-8195)
Fine Leather Works LLC ....G..... 703 200-1953
Mc Lean (G-8430)
Leatheroot LLC ....G..... 804 695-1604
Gloucester (G-5853)
LLC Wiley Brothers ....G..... 434 806-9633
Free Union (G-5508)

Pinnell CL Custom Leather ....G..... 434 823-9800
Crozet (G-3847)

LEATHER GOODS: Personal

Crystal Beach Studio ....G..... 757 787-4605
Onancock (G-10195)
Joseph Carson ....G..... 757 498-4866
Virginia Beach (G-14574)
Tpp Enterprises LLC ....G..... 757 247-0016
Newport News (G-9361)

LEATHER GOODS: Wallets

10fold Wallets LLC ....G..... 804 982-0003
Richmond (G-11069)
Christophers Belts & Wallets ....G..... 757 253-2564
Williamsburg (G-15219)
Mobile Wallet Gifting Corp ....G..... 301 523-1052
Vienna (G-14098)

LEATHER TANNING & FINISHING

Appleberry Mtn Taxidermy Svcs ....G..... 434 831-2232
Schuyler (G-12651)
Auslnx LLC ....G..... 571 265-3288
Arlington (G-864)
Hideaway Tannery LLC ....G..... 540 421-2640
Crimora (G-3821)
Leather World Technologies LLC ....G..... 540 265-9038
Roanoke (G-11954)

LEATHER, LEATHER GOODS & FURS, WHOLESALE

Crystal Beach Studio ....G..... 757 787-4605
Onancock (G-10195)

LEATHER: Accessory Prdts

Hamilton Perkins Collectn LLC ....G..... 757 544-7161
Norfolk (G-9568)
Pauls Shoe Repair & Lea ACC ....G..... 703 759-3735
Great Falls (G-5971)

LEATHER: Embossed

Embossing Etc ....G..... 540 338-4520
Hamilton (G-6057)

LEATHER: Equestrian Prdts

Journeymen Saddlers Ltd ....F 540 687-5888
Middleburg (G-8725)

LEATHER: Glove

Gloves For Life LLC ....G..... 540 343-1697
Roanoke (G-11927)

LEATHER: Rawhide

Rawhide LLC ....G..... 540 548-1148
Spotsylvania (G-12910)

LEATHER: Saddlery

Middleburg Tack Exchange Ltd ....G..... 540 687-6608
Middleburg (G-8730)

LEGAL OFFICES & SVCS

Harbor House Law Press Inc ....G..... 804 776-7605
Deltaville (G-4080)
N A D A Services Corporation ....C 703 821-7000
Mc Lean (G-8508)

LENS COATING: Ophthalmic

Infocus Coatings Inc ....G..... 804 520-1573
South Chesterfield (G-12811)

LIGHT OR HEAT EMISSION OPERATING APPARATUS

R Zimmerman and Associates ....G..... 540 446-6846
Stafford (G-13185)

LIGHTERS, CIGARETTE & CIGAR, WHOLESALE

Swedish Match North Amer LLC ....B 804 787-5100
Richmond (G-11776)

LIGHTING EQPT: Flashlights

Force Forge ....G.. 804 454-5191
Fort Lee *(G-5129)*

LIGHTING EQPT: Floodlights

Gateway Green Energy Inc ....G.. 540 280-7475
Fishersville *(G-5003)*

LIGHTING EQPT: Fog Lights

Fog Light Solutions LLC ....G.. 703 201-0532
Great Falls *(G-5955)*

LIGHTING EQPT: Motor Vehicle

Theory3 Inc ....G.. 804 335-1001
Goochland *(G-5886)*

LIGHTING EQPT: Motor Vehicle, NEC

Lighting Auto Services ....G.. 804 330-6908
Richmond *(G-11655)*

LIGHTING EQPT: Outdoor

Bloombeams LLC ....G.. 804 822-1022
Midlothian *(G-8780)*
Frank Hagerty ....G.. 540 809-0589
Fredericksburg *(G-5432)*
Luminaire Technologies Inc...........G.. 276 579-2007
Mouth of Wilson *(G-9094)*

LIGHTING EQPT: Spotlights

Spotlight Studio ....G.. 540 338-2690
Purcellville *(G-10679)*

LIGHTING FIXTURES, NEC

ARC Lighting LLC ....G.. 757 513-7717
Chesapeake *(G-2979)*
Armstrong Airport Lighting ....G.. 865 856-2723
Toano *(G-13856)*
Collegiateskyviews LLC ....G.. 540 520-6394
Roanoke *(G-11912)*
Cormorant Technologies LLC ....G.. 703 871-5060
Williamsburg *(G-15224)*
Dogtown Lights LLC ....G.. 804 334-5088
Richmond *(G-11186)*
Efi Lighting Inc ....G.. 540 353-2880
Salem *(G-12501)*
Eflamelightingcom Inc ....G.. 434 822-0632
Danville *(G-3989)*
Environmental Ltg Solutions.........G.. 202 361-2686
Haymarket *(G-6423)*
Giving Light Inc ....G.. 757 236-2405
Hampton *(G-6159)*
Led Solar and Light Company ....G.. 703 201-3250
Herndon *(G-6733)*
Lightronics Inc ....E.. 757 486-3588
Virginia Beach *(G-14612)*
Project Cost Gvrnment Svcs LLC ...G.. 239 334-3371
Alexandria *(G-559)*
Solar Lighting Virginia Inc ....G.. 757 229-3236
Williamsburg *(G-15314)*
Spotlight Dance LLC ....G.. 703 753-9173
Haymarket *(G-6447)*
Spotlight On Sports LLC ....G.. 804 615-3284
Midlothian *(G-8909)*
Traffic Systems LLC ....F.. 703 530-9655
Manassas *(G-8170)*

LIGHTING FIXTURES: Decorative Area

Rth Innovations LLC ....G.. 804 384-6767
Gloucester *(G-5860)*

LIGHTING FIXTURES: Gas

Brite Lite Inc ....G.. 540 972-0212
Locust Grove *(G-7441)*

LIGHTING FIXTURES: Indl & Commercial

1earthmatters LLC ....G.. 202 412-8882
Fairfax *(G-4393)*
Acuity Brands Lighting Inc ....G.. 804 320-3444
Richmond *(G-11472)*
American Orthotic.....................G.. 757 548-5296
Chesapeake *(G-2972)*
Century Lighting Solutions LLC .....G.. 202 281-8393
Alexandria *(G-163)*

Crenshaw Lighting Corporation..........G.. 540 745-3900
Floyd *(G-5021)*
Deporter Dominick & Assoc LLC ....G.. 703 530-9255
Manassas *(G-8057)*
Electro-Luminx Lighting Corp ....G.. 804 355-1692
Richmond *(G-11198)*
Energy Sherlock LLC ....G.. 703 346-7584
Leesburg *(G-7268)*
Frank Hagerty ....G.. 540 809-0589
Fredericksburg *(G-5432)*
Green Solutions Lighting LLC............G.. 804 334-2705
Richmond *(G-11605)*
Hickey Electric Co Inc ....F.. 434 384-1896
Madison Heights *(G-7874)*
Hubbell Entertainment....................F.. 540 382-6111
Christiansburg *(G-3594)*
Hubbell Lighting Inc ....B.. 540 382-6111
Christiansburg *(G-3596)*
Iba Led ....G.. 434 566-2109
Orange *(G-10215)*
Pacific Technology Inc ....F.. 571 421-7861
Annandale *(G-778)*
Revolution Soultions VA LLC ....G.. 804 539-5058
Fairfax *(G-4540)*
Stack Labs Inc ....E.. 503 453-5172
Haymarket *(G-6448)*
Zenta Corporation ....G.. 276 930-1500
Woolwine *(G-15870)*

LIGHTING FIXTURES: Motor Vehicle

Brush 10 ....G.. 540 582-3820
Partlow *(G-10264)*
Emergency Vehicle Outfitters ....G.. 571 228-2837
Lynchburg *(G-7702)*

LIGHTING FIXTURES: Public

Intelligent Illuminations Inc ....F.. 888 455-2465
Virginia Beach *(G-14550)*

LIGHTING FIXTURES: Residential

American Hands LLC ....G.. 804 349-8974
Powhatan *(G-10530)*
Dennis H Fredrick ....G.. 804 358-6000
Richmond *(G-11182)*
Modern Living LLC ....G.. 877 663-2224
Richmond *(G-11679)*
Spring Moses Inc ....G.. 804 321-0156
Richmond *(G-11395)*

LIGHTING FIXTURES: Residential, Electric

Roto Rays Inc ....G.. 703 437-3353
Herndon *(G-6795)*

LIME

Deavers Lime and Litter LLC ....G.. 540 833-4144
Rockingham *(G-12247)*
Lhoist North America VA LLC.............C.. 540 626-7163
Ripplemead *(G-11876)*
Rockydale Quarries Corporation.........D.. 540 774-1696
Roanoke *(G-12170)*
Rockydale Quarries Corporation.........G.. 540 886-2111
Staunton *(G-13286)*
Shen-Valley Lime Corp ....G.. 540 869-2700
Stephens City *(G-13322)*
Sweet Lime Studios LLC ....G.. 703 312-0034
Arlington *(G-1180)*

LIME ROCK: Ground

Curtis E Harrell..............................G.. 540 843-2027
Luray *(G-7605)*

LIME: Agricultural

Frazier Quarry Incorporated ....E.. 540 434-6192
Harrisonburg *(G-6317)*

LIMESTONE: Crushed & Broken

Appalachian Aggregates LLC ....E.. 276 326-1145
Bluefield *(G-1857)*
Appomattox Lime Company ....G.. 540 774-1696
Roanoke *(G-12034)*
Appomattox Quarry ....G.. 434 295-5700
Appomattox *(G-803)*
Barger Son Cnstr Inc Charles W ....D.. 540 463-2106
Lexington *(G-7388)*
Boxley Materials Company ....E.. 540 777-6000
Blue Ridge *(G-1845)*

Boxley Materials Company ....E.. 540 777-6000
Blue Ridge *(G-1846)*
Boxley Materials Company ....F.. 540 777-6000
Arrington *(G-1228)*
Boxley Materials Company ....G.. 540 777-6000
Lowmoor *(G-7598)*
Boxley Materials Company ....G.. 540 777-6000
Lynchburg *(G-7658)*
Boxley Materials Company ....G.. 540 777-6000
Concord *(G-3757)*
Cardinal Quarries LLC ....F.. 540 674-5556
Dublin *(G-4150)*
Cedar Mountain Stone Corp ....E.. 540 825-3370
Mitchells *(G-8954)*
Charlottesville Stone Company............G.. 434 295-5700
Roanoke *(G-12065)*
Chesapeake Materials LLC ....G.. 540 658-0808
Stafford *(G-13130)*
Dream Green International LLC............G.. 814 616-7800
Alexandria *(G-194)*
E Dillon & Company ....D.. 276 873-6816
Swords Creek *(G-13807)*
Glade Stone Inc ....F.. 276 429-5241
Glade Spring *(G-5676)*
Holston River Quarry Inc ....F.. 540 380-5556
Dublin *(G-4158)*
Jack Stone Quarry ....G.. 804 862-6669
North Dinwiddie *(G-10054)*
Legacy Vulcan LLC ....F.. 276 679-0880
Big Stone Gap *(G-1711)*
Lhoist North America VA Inc ....C.. 540 626-7163
Ripplemead *(G-11876)*
Limestone Dust Corporation ....D.. 276 326-1103
Bluefield *(G-1869)*
Martin Marietta Materials Inc ....F.. 434 296-5562
North Garden *(G-10080)*
Martin Marietta Materials Inc ....G.. 804 561-0570
Amelia Court House *(G-665)*
Martin Marietta Materials Inc ....E.. 804 798-5096
Ashland *(G-1459)*
Martin Marietta Materials Inc ....G.. 804 744-1130
Midlothian *(G-8853)*
Martin Marietta Materials Inc ....F.. 804 749-4831
Rockville *(G-12292)*
Mountain Materials Inc ....G.. 276 762-5563
Castlewood *(G-2255)*
Mountain Mtls Muth Wlson Plant.........G.. 276 579-6351
Mouth of Wilson *(G-9095)*
Mundy Stone Company ....G.. 540 774-1696
Roanoke *(G-12139)*
O-N Minerals Chemstone Company.......C.. 540 254-1241
Buchanan *(G-2123)*
O-N Minerals Chemstone Company.......E.. 540 662-3855
Clear Brook *(G-3649)*
O-N Minerals Chemstone Company.......C.. 540 869-1066
Middletown *(G-8741)*
Redland Quarries NY Inc ....G.. 703 480-3600
Herndon *(G-6786)*
Rockbridge Stone Products Inc ....G.. 540 258-2841
Glasgow *(G-5701)*
Rockdale Chrlottesville Quary ....G.. 434 295-5700
Earlysville *(G-4294)*
Rockydale Quarries Corp ....G.. 540 769-8116
Roanoke *(G-12169)*
Rockydale Quarries Corporation...........F.. 540 576-2544
Roanoke *(G-12171)*
Salem Stone Corporation ....F.. 276 228-3452
Wytheville *(G-15908)*
Salem Stone Corporation ....G.. 540 674-5556
Dublin *(G-4170)*
Salem Stone Corporation ....F.. 276 228-3631
Wytheville *(G-15909)*
Salem Stone Corporation ....E.. 276 766-3449
Hillsville *(G-6899)*
Sisson & Ryan Inc ....E.. 540 268-2413
Shawsville *(G-12686)*
Sisson & Ryan Quarry LLC ....E.. 540 674-5556
Dublin *(G-4171)*
Southside Materials LLC ....E.. 540 674-5556
Dublin *(G-4172)*
Titan America LLC ....F.. 804 236-4122
Richmond *(G-11412)*
Titan America LLC ....G.. 703 471-0044
Sterling *(G-13534)*
Vulcan Construction Mtls LLC ....D.. 757 545-0980
Chesapeake *(G-3367)*
Vulcan Construction Mtls LLC ....E.. 804 862-6660
Prince George *(G-10609)*
Vulcan Construction Mtls LLC ....G.. 276 466-5436
Bristol *(G-1999)*

PRODUCT

LIMESTONE: Cut & Shaped

Limestone Dust Corporation ....D 276 326-1103
Bluefield **(G-1869)**

LIMESTONE: Dimension

Barger Son Cnstr Inc Charles W ....D 540 463-2106
Lexington **(G-7388)**
Valley Building Supply Inc ....C 540 434-6725
Harrisonburg **(G-6383)**

LIMESTONE: Ground

Appomattox Lime Co Inc ....F 434 933-8258
Appomattox **(G-802)**
F & M Construction Corp ....F 276 728-2255
Hillsville **(G-6891)**
Frazier Quarry Incorporated ....E 540 434-6192
Harrisonburg **(G-6317)**
Mundy Quarries Inc C S ....E 540 833-2061
Broadway **(G-2090)**
O-N Minerals Chemstone Company ......C 540 465-5161
Strasburg **(G-13592)**
Pounding Mill Quarry Corp ....E 276 326-1145
Bluefield **(G-1875)**
Powell Valley Stone Co Inc ....F 276 546-2550
Pennington Gap **(G-10298)**
Stuart M Perry Incorporated ....C 540 662-3431
Winchester **(G-15483)**
Stuart M Perry Incorporated ....E 540 955-1359
Berryville **(G-1693)**

LINEN SPLY SVC: Uniform

Scrub Exchange LLC ....G 434 237-7778
Concord **(G-3763)**

LINEN STORES

Capital Linen Services Inc ....F 804 744-3334
Midlothian **(G-8789)**

LINENS: Table & Dresser Scarves, From Purchased Materials

Me-Shows LLC ....G 855 637-4097
Spotsylvania **(G-12904)**

LINER BRICK OR PLATES: Sewer Or Tank Lining, Vitrified Clay

Polycoat Inc ....G 540 989-7833
Roanoke **(G-11989)**

LINER STRIPS: Rubber

Dutch Gap Striping Inc ....G 804 594-0069
Powhatan **(G-10543)**

LINERS & COVERS: Fabric

Mountain Valley Enterprises ....G 276 686-6516
Rural Retreat **(G-12428)**

LINERS & LINING

Timothy D Falls ....G 540 987-8142
Woodville **(G-15862)**

LININGS: Apparel, Made From Purchased Materials

Elite Prints ....G 703 780-3403
Alexandria **(G-455)**
Rain & Associates LLC ....G 757 572-3996
Virginia Beach **(G-14758)**
Slim Strength Inc ....G 804 715-3080
Richmond **(G-11064)**

LININGS: Handbag Or Pocketbook

Lester Enterprises Intl LLC ....G 703 599-3485
Arlington **(G-1032)**

LIPSTICK

ALC Training Group LLC ....G 757 746-0428
Poquoson **(G-10364)**
Euvanna Chayanne Cosmetics LLC......G 804 307-4941
Chesterfield **(G-3498)**
Wear Red Lipstick LLC ....G 703 627-2123
Centreville **(G-2352)**

Weights N Lipstick...............................G 251 404-8154
Suffolk **(G-13783)**

LIQUEFIED PETROLEUM GAS DEALERS

Airgas Usa LLC ....F 804 743-0661
North Chesterfield **(G-9809)**
Southern States Coop Inc ....E 703 378-4865
Chantilly **(G-2495)**

LIQUID CRYSTAL DISPLAYS

Printed Circuits International.................G 804 737-7979
Highland Springs **(G-6855)**

LITHOGRAPHIC PLATES

Tetra Graphics Inc...............................G 434 845-4450
Lynchburg **(G-7822)**

LOCK & KEY SVCS

Mitchell Lock Out.................................G 276 322-4087
Bluefield **(G-1870)**

LOCKS

A-1 Security Mfg Corp ....F 804 359-9003
Richmond **(G-11078)**
Simplicikey LLC ....E 703 904-5010
Herndon **(G-6808)**

LOCKS: Safe & Vault, Metal

Assa Abloy High SEC Group Inc ....C 540 380-5000
Salem **(G-12476)**
Mitchell Lock Out.................................G 276 322-4087
Bluefield **(G-1870)**

LOCOMOTIVES & PARTS

Loco Parts ....G 757 255-2815
Suffolk **(G-13734)**

LOGGING

A Cut Above Logging LLC ....G 434 547-5979
Meherrin **(G-8704)**
A Johnson Linwood ....G 804 829-5364
Providence Forge **(G-10617)**
Addem Enterprises Inc ....G 540 789-4412
Willis **(G-15353)**
Appalachian Growth Logging LLC........G 540 336-2674
Mount Jackson **(G-9065)**
Bar Logging LLC ....G 757 641-9269
Franklin **(G-5139)**
Barton Logging Inc ....G 434 390-8504
Green Bay **(G-5987)**
Baur Logging LLC ....G 757 535-5693
Chesapeake **(G-2994)**
Beagle Logging Company ....G 540 459-2425
Woodstock **(G-15849)**
Bennett Logging & Lumber Inc ....E 540 862-7621
Covington **(G-3778)**
Betty P Hicks ....G 540 745-5111
Floyd **(G-5016)**
Billy Bill Logging ....G 804 512-9669
Aylett **(G-1546)**
Bobby Collins Logging ....G 804 519-0138
Charles City **(G-2570)**
Booth Logging Company ....G 540 334-1075
Boones Mill **(G-1893)**
Bosserman Murry ....G 540 255-7949
Greenville **(G-5997)**
Bowdens Firewood & Logging LLC ......G 540 465-4362
Strasburg **(G-13575)**
Bryant Logging ....G 540 337-0232
Stuarts Draft **(G-13645)**
Carlton Logging LLC ....G 804 693-5193
Gloucester **(G-5840)**
Central Virginia Horse Logging ....G 434 390-7252
Blackstone **(G-1814)**
CF Smith & Sons.................................G 540 672-3291
Orange **(G-10205)**
Champion Ventures LLC ....G 540 975-0791
New Market **(G-9141)**
Chips Inc ....D 434 589-2424
Troy **(G-13922)**
Clary Logging Inc Randy J ....G 434 636-5268
Brodnax **(G-2100)**
Claude David Sanders ....G 276 386-6946
Gate City **(G-5661)**
Concord Logging ....G 434 660-1889
Concord **(G-3758)**

Corey Ely Logging LLC ....G 423 579-3436
Pennington Gap **(G-10294)**
Crosscut Inc ....G 276 395-5430
Saint Paul **(G-12466)**
CW Houchens and Sons Log LLC........G 804 615-2002
Bumpass **(G-2161)**
Cw Moore & Sons LLC ....F 757 653-9011
Courtland **(G-3767)**
Danny A Walker ....G 434 724-4454
Callands **(G-2213)**
Darden Logging LLC ....G 757 647-9432
Franklin **(G-5141)**
David A Bennett ....G 540 862-5868
Covington **(G-3786)**
David S Creath ....G 434 753-2210
South Boston **(G-12760)**
David W Slusher ....G 540 745-2485
Floyd **(G-5022)**
Davis Logging ....G 804 725-7988
North **(G-9802)**
Deeds Brothers Incorporated ....G 540 862-7837
Millboro **(G-8935)**
Dobyns Family LLC ....G 804 462-5554
Lancaster **(G-7159)**
Dodson Logging LLC ....G 540 547-2582
Unionville **(G-13962)**
Donald Kirby.......................................G 540 493-8698
Rocky Mount **(G-12317)**
Dunromin Logging LLC ....G 540 896-3543
Timberville **(G-13847)**
Eric Tucker..G 540 747-5665
Covington **(G-3788)**
Ferguson Logging Inc ....G 540 721-3408
Moneta **(G-8962)**
Fitzgerald John ....G 434 277-8044
Tyro **(G-13939)**
Foley Logging Inc ....G 540 365-3152
Ferrum **(G-4974)**
Fred B Meadows Sons Loggi ....G 434 392-5269
Farmville **(G-4941)**
Fred Fauber ....G 434 845-0303
Lynchburg **(G-7718)**
Garthrght Land Clearing Inc TW ....G 804 370-5408
Providence Forge **(G-10625)**
Gillespie Inc..G 540 297-4432
Bedford **(G-1639)**
Hanneman Land Clearing Log LLC ......G 804 909-2349
Ashland **(G-1425)**
Hensley Family ....G 540 652-8206
Shenandoah **(G-12692)**
Hobbs Logging Inc ....G 276 628-4952
Abingdon **(G-38)**
Homer Haywood Wheeler II ....G 434 946-5126
Amherst **(G-694)**
Honaker & Son Logging LLC ....G 434 661-7935
Amherst **(G-695)**
Honaker Son Logging ....G 434 933-8251
Gladstone **(G-5684)**
Isle of Wight Forest Products ....G 757 357-2009
Smithfield **(G-12716)**
J & R Log & WD Processors LLC ....G 703 494-6994
Stafford **(G-13157)**
James J Gray ....G 757 617-5279
Surry **(G-13797)**
James River Logging & Excav..............G 434 295-8457
Charlottesville **(G-2818)**
Jennings Logging LLC ....G 434 248-6876
Prospect **(G-10613)**
Jerry Lee Marshall ....G 276 952-5486
Stuart **(G-13619)**
John P Hines Logging ....G 434 392-3861
Rice **(G-11005)**
Johnny Hillman Logging ....G 276 467-2406
Fort Blackmore **(G-5122)**
Johnny Sisk & Sons Inc ....F 540 547-2202
Culpeper **(G-3902)**
Knabe Logging LLC ....G 434 547-9878
Dillwyn **(G-4096)**
Laurel Fork Logging Inc ....G 276 285-3761
Bristol **(G-2024)**
Lawson & Sons Logging LLC ....G 434 292-7904
Blackstone **(G-1819)**
Lawson Timber Company ....G 276 395-2069
Saint Paul **(G-12468)**
Layne Logging ....G 276 312-1665
Hurley **(G-6969)**
Lester Group ....G 276 627-0346
Bassett **(G-1585)**
Littlefield Logging ....G 804 798-5590
Glen Allen **(G-5764)**

Logging Ninja Inc ....G...... 804 569-6054
Mechanicsville **(G-8654)**
Lovell Logging Inc ....G...... 276 632-5191
Martinsville **(G-8306)**
Lw Logging LLC ....G...... 434 735-8598
Wylliesburg **(G-15872)**
Maple Grove Logging LLC ....G...... 276 677-0152
Sugar Grove **(G-13787)**
Marvin Dudley Logging ....G...... 540 784-3098
Lexington **(G-7399)**
McCormick Jr Logging Inc Bd ....G...... 434 238-3593
Gladstone **(G-5687)**
McDonald Sawmill ....G...... 540 465-5539
Strasburg **(G-13588)**
McKee Brewer ....G...... 276 579-2048
Independence **(G-6990)**
Mdj Logging Inc ....G...... 276 889-4658
Honaker **(G-6915)**
Michael Sanders ....G...... 276 452-2314
Fort Blackmore **(G-5123)**
Michael W Tuck ....G...... 540 297-1231
Bedford **(G-1644)**
Mickey Norris Logging ....G...... 276 206-3959
Marion **(G-8236)**
Mighty Oaks Tree Triming & Log ....G...... 585 471-0213
Lynchburg **(G-7773)**
Mill Road Logging LLC ....G...... 434 665-7467
Rustburg **(G-12442)**
MLS Logging LLC ....G...... 540 223-0394
Orange **(G-10220)**
Mountain Top Logging LLC ....G...... 540 745-6709
Floyd **(G-5032)**
Mountaintop Logging LLC ....G...... 540 468-3059
Monterey **(G-9010)**
Moyers Logging ....G...... 540 468-2289
Monterey **(G-9011)**
Mullican Flooring LP ....D...... 276 565-0220
Appalachia **(G-798)**
Newell Logging ....G...... 434 636-2743
La Crosse **(G-7147)**
North Fork Inc ....E...... 540 997-5602
Goshen **(G-5926)**
Peppers Services LLC ....G...... 276 233-6464
Galax **(G-5645)**
Piedmont Logging Inc ....G...... 434 989-1698
Roseland **(G-12371)**
Poff Logging LLC ....G...... 540 695-0060
Floyd **(G-5034)**
Pritts Logging ....G...... 304 646-0004
Warm Springs **(G-14974)**
Ragland Trucking Inc W E ....G...... 434 286-2414
Scottsville **(G-12664)**
Ralph Johnson ....G...... 434 286-2735
Scottsville **(G-12665)**
Rct Logging LLC ....F...... 434 767-4780
Green Bay **(G-5991)**
Richard C Iroler ....G...... 276 236-3796
Fries **(G-5517)**
Robert David Rosson ....G...... 540 456-6173
Afton **(G-87)**
Robert L Penn ....G...... 276 629-2211
Bassett **(G-1591)**
Salyer Logging ....G...... 276 690-0688
Nickelsville **(G-9385)**
Sam Belcher & Sons Inc ....G...... 276 930-2084
Woolwine **(G-15867)**
Sam H Hughes Jr ....G...... 434 263-4432
Shipman **(G-12698)**
Sanders Brothers Logging Inc ....G...... 276 995-2416
Fort Blackmore **(G-5124)**
Sawmill Bottom ....G...... 276 880-2241
Cleveland **(G-3656)**
Schlotterer Logging ....G...... 910 376-1623
Stafford **(G-13188)**
Seal R L & Sons Logging ....G...... 804 769-3696
Aylett **(G-1554)**
Shifflett and Son Log Co LLC ....G...... 757 434-7979
Urbanna **(G-13973)**
Shumate Inc George C ....E...... 540 463-2244
Lexington **(G-7417)**
Slagle Logging & Chipping Inc ....G...... 434 572-6733
South Boston **(G-12789)**
Slushers Logging & Sawing LLC .....G...... 540 641-1378
Floyd **(G-5039)**
Southeast Fiber Supply Inc ....G...... 757 653-2318
Courtland **(G-3774)**
Staton & Hauling ....G...... 434 946-7913
Amherst **(G-709)**
Staton & Son Logging ....G...... 540 570-3614
Buena Vista **(G-2154)**

Stella-Jones Corporation ....D...... 540 997-9251
Goshen **(G-5927)**
Steven D Thomas ....G...... 540 254-2964
Buchanan **(G-2129)**
T C Catlett & Sons Lumber Co ....E...... 540 786-2303
Fredericksburg **(G-5373)**
Three P Logging ....G...... 434 376-9812
Brookneal **(G-2114)**
TNT Bradshaw Logging LLC ....G...... 276 928-1579
Bland **(G-1837)**
TNT Logging LLC ....G...... 540 997-0611
Goshen **(G-5930)**
Tomorrows Resources Unlimited .....E...... 434 929-2800
Madison Heights **(G-7886)**
Varner Logging LLC ....G...... 540 849-7451
Churchville **(G-3621)**
Vickie D Blankenship ....G...... 540 977-6377
Blue Ridge **(G-1856)**
W T Jones & Sons Inc ....G...... 804 633-9737
Ruther Glen **(G-12463)**
Walter Pillow Logging ....G...... 434 283-5449
Gladys **(G-5698)**
West Midland Timber LLC ....G...... 540 570-5969
Lexington **(G-7424)**
Wood Harvesters ....G...... 276 650-2603
Axton **(G-1543)**
Woolfolk Brothers LLC ....G...... 540 967-0664
Louisa **(G-7575)**
Woolfolk Enterprises ....G...... 540 967-0664
Louisa **(G-7576)**
Wst Products LLC ....G...... 434 736-9100
Keysville **(G-7067)**

LOGGING CAMPS & CONTRACTORS

A & A Logging LLC ....G...... 540 229-2830
Culpeper **(G-3861)**
A L Baird Inc ....F...... 434 848-2129
Lawrenceville **(G-7176)**
All-N-Logging LLC ....G...... 434 547-3550
Keysville **(G-7054)**
Allens Logging Inc ....G...... 434 724-6493
Chatham **(G-2918)**
Atkins Clearing & Trucking ....G...... 540 832-3128
Gordonsville **(G-5898)**
Aubrey L Clary Inc ....E...... 434 577-2724
Gasburg **(G-5657)**
B H Franklin Logging Inc ....G...... 434 352-5484
Appomattox **(G-805)**
Barber Logging LLC ....G...... 276 346-4638
Jonesville **(G-7018)**
Bear Branch Logging Inc ....G...... 276 597-7172
Vansant **(G-13975)**
Bl Nichols Logging Inc ....G...... 540 875-8690
Huddleston **(G-6952)**
Blue Ridge Logging Co Inc ....G...... 434 836-5663
Danville **(G-3960)**
Brady Jones Logging ....G...... 434 969-4688
Buckingham **(G-2131)**
Bryant Brothers Logging L L C ....G...... 434 933-8303
Gladstone **(G-5682)**
Buck Hall Logging ....G...... 434 696-1244
Green Bay **(G-5988)**
Butler Custom Logging LLC ....G...... 434 634-5658
Emporia **(G-4355)**
Byer Brothers Logging Inc ....G...... 540 962-3071
Covington **(G-3779)**
C L E Logging Inc ....G...... 276 881-8617
Bandy **(G-1557)**
Calvin Payne ....G...... 276 251-5815
Ararat **(G-830)**
Cardinals Logging ....G...... 804 457-3543
Mineral **(G-8944)**
Cithinning Inc ....G...... 804 370-4859
Ruther Glen **(G-12452)**
Clarence Shelton Jr ....G...... 434 710-0448
Chatham **(G-2923)**
Clary Timber Co Inc ....F...... 434 594-5055
Gasburg **(G-5658)**
Connell Log Thnning LLC Knneth .....G...... 434 729-3712
Brodnax **(G-2101)**
Crewe Brothers Logging ....G...... 804 829-2288
Charles City **(G-2574)**
Dale Horton Logging ....G...... 276 251-5004
Ararat **(G-831)**
Dan McPherson & Sons Logging .....G...... 540 483-4385
Callaway **(G-2221)**
David C Weaver ....F...... 804 561-5929
Amelia Court House **(G-654)**
Deane Logging Co Inc ....G...... 540 718-3676
Madison **(G-7850)**

Dillion Logging ....G...... 434 685-1779
Danville **(G-3985)**
Dove Logging Inc ....G...... 540 937-4917
Rixeyville **(G-11879)**
Edwards Inc ....G...... 276 762-7746
Saint Paul **(G-12467)**
Flint Bros Logging ....G...... 540 886-1509
Staunton **(G-13258)**
Flint Brothers ....G...... 540 886-5761
Staunton **(G-13259)**
Foster Logging ....G...... 434 454-7946
Randolph **(G-10748)**
Four Oaks Timber Company ....G...... 434 374-2669
Clarksville **(G-3630)**
G&O Logging LLC ....G...... 757 653-2181
Courtland **(G-3770)**
Gibson Logging Enterprises LLC ......G...... 606 260-1889
Duffield **(G-4178)**
Gibson Logging Inc ....G...... 804 769-1130
King Queen Ch **(G-7126)**
Gibson Logging LLC Rush J ....G...... 540 539-8145
Bluemont **(G-1888)**
Greene Horse Logging LLC ....G...... 434 277-5146
Roseland **(G-12368)**
H & H Logging Inc ....G...... 434 321-9805
Green Bay **(G-5989)**
H & M Logging Inc ....D...... 434 476-6569
South Boston **(G-12773)**
H & R Logging ....G...... 434 922-7417
Monroe **(G-8991)**
H L Corker & Son Inc ....G...... 804 449-6686
Beaverdam **(G-1609)**
Hal Warner Logging ....G...... 540 474-5533
Blue Grass **(G-1842)**
Harry Hale Logging ....G...... 540 484-1666
Wirtz **(G-15612)**
Harvey Logging Co Inc ....G...... 434 263-5942
Lovingston **(G-7590)**
Hatcher Logging ....G...... 434 352-7975
Appomattox **(G-812)**
Hatcher Logging Corp Virginia ....G...... 434 299-5293
Big Island **(G-1703)**
Hawkins Logging ....G...... 434 577-2114
Brodnax **(G-2102)**
Hj Shelton Logging Inc ....G...... 434 432-3840
Chatham **(G-2929)**
Hoss Excavating & Logging Co L .....G...... 276 628-4068
Abingdon **(G-39)**
Hylton & Hylton Logging ....G...... 276 930-2245
Woolwine **(G-15865)**
J & W Logging Inc ....G...... 540 474-3531
Blue Grass **(G-1843)**
J D Shelton ....G...... 434 797-4403
Keeling **(G-7025)**
J H Knighton Lumber Co Inc ....E...... 804 448-4681
Ruther Glen **(G-12457)**
J V Ramsey Logging LLC ....G...... 434 610-1844
Appomattox **(G-814)**
James D Crews Logging ....G...... 434 349-1999
Nathalie **(G-9103)**
Jammerson Logging ....G...... 434 983-7505
Andersonville **(G-726)**
Jeff Britt Logging ....G...... 540 884-2499
Eagle Rock **(G-4281)**
Jenkins Logging ....G...... 540 543-2079
Culpeper **(G-3900)**
Jerry K Wilson Inc ....H...... 434 299-5175
Big Island **(G-1704)**
Jimmy Dockery Logging ....G...... 276 225-0149
Gate City **(G-5664)**
Johnson James Thomas Logging .....G...... 804 966-1552
Charles City **(G-2578)**
Jones Logging ....G...... 276 794-9510
Lebanon **(G-7195)**
K & J Logging Inc ....G...... 540 330-9812
Huddleston **(G-6954)**
K Dudley Logging Inc ....G...... 540 890-0220
Vinton **(G-14175)**
K H Franklin Logging LLC ....G...... 434 352-9235
Appomattox **(G-817)**
L A Bowles Logging Inc ....G...... 804 492-3103
Powhatan **(G-10555)**
L&F Logging Inc ....G...... 276 728-5773
Hillsville **(G-6895)**
Lakeside Logging Inc ....G...... 540 872-2585
Bumpass **(G-2164)**
Larry W Jarvis Logging ....G...... 276 686-5938
Rural Retreat **(G-12427)**
Lawson Brothers Logging LLC ....G...... 276 694-8905
Stuart **(G-13622)**

Employee Codes: A=Over 500 employees, B=251-500
C=101-250, D=51-100, E=20-50, F=10-19, G=1-9

2021 Virginia
Industrial Directory

PRODUCT

985

Leonard Logging Inc .... G 540 239-6991
Floyd (G-5031)

Leroy Woodward .... G 540 948-6335
Madison (G-7857)

Lewis Brothers Logging .... G 804 478-4243
Mc Kenney (G-8381)

Lloyd D Wells Logging Contg .... G 434 933-4316
Gladstone (G-5685)

M M Wright Inc .... D 434 577-2101
Gasburg (G-5659)

Mann Logging .... G 434 283-5245
Gladys (G-5694)

Marden Thinning Company Inc ..... G 540 872-5196
Bumpass (G-2165)

Marion Brothers Logging Inc .... E 804 492-3200
Cumberland (G-3936)

Mayo River Logging Co Inc .... G 276 694-6305
Stuart (G-13624)

Mid Atlantic Mining LLC .... G 757 407-6735
Suffolk (G-13742)

Mid Atlntic Tree Hrvestors Inc ..... E 804 769-8826
Aylett (G-1550)

Mike Gibson & Sons Logging .... G 804 769-3510
King Queen Ch (G-7127)

Moore C W and Sons LLC .... G 757 653-9121
Courtland (G-3773)

Moore Logging Inc .... G 276 233-1693
Dugspur (G-4189)

Morris & Sons Logging Glen .... G 540 854-5271
Unionville (G-13965)

Nichols Logging Inc .... G 540 297-3246
Huddleston (G-6956)

Parmly Jr Land Logging & Timbe .. G 434 842-2900
Palmyra (G-10253)

Pennells Logging .... G 434 292-5482
Blackstone (G-1823)

Penningtons Logging LLC .... G 276 783-9374
Chilhowie (G-3557)

Pinecrest Timber Co .... E 804 834-2304
Waverly (G-15087)

Polks Logging & Lumber .... G 540 477-3376
Quicksburg (G-10693)

Porcupine Logging LLC .... G 540 894-1675
Louisa (G-7563)

Pride and Joy Logging Inc .... G 540 474-5533
Blue Grass (G-1844)

Quality Logging LLC .... G 540 493-7228
Floyd (G-5036)

R S Bottoms Logging .... G 434 577-3044
Brodnax (G-2103)

Ralph Rice .... G 434 385-8614
Forest (G-5089)

Ramsey Brothers Logging Inc ...... G 540 463-5044
Lexington (G-7414)

REA Boys Logging & Equip .... G 276 957-4935
Spencer (G-12874)

Rexrode Timber & Excavation ...... G 540 474-5892
Monterey (G-9013)

Reynolds Timber Inc .... G 804 633-6117
Woodford (G-15842)

Richardson Logging .... G 540 373-5756
Fredericksburg (G-5477)

Robert E Carroll Logging Inc .... E 434 636-2168
Ebony (G-4298)

Rt Logging LLC .... G 276 452-2258
Gate City (G-5666)

S & D Adkins Logging LLC .... G 434 292-8882
Crewe (G-3815)

S R Jones Jr & Sons Inc .... E 434 577-2311
Gasburg (G-5660)

Sams Logging Inc .... G 434 661-7137
Monroe (G-8995)

Saunders Logging Inc .... G 434 735-8341
Saxe (G-12648)

Sawyer Logging Inc .... G 276 995-2522
Fort Blackmore (G-5125)

Scott Logging LLC .... G 276 930-2497
Stuart (G-13629)

Shelton Logging Inc .... G 434 294-1386
Crewe (G-3817)

Sickal Logging .... G 804 366-1965
Barhamsville (G-1574)

Simmons Logging Inc .... G 434 676-1202
South Hill (G-12860)

Southeastern Land and Logging ... G 540 489-1403
Ferrum (G-4982)

Southeastern Logging & Chippin ... G 540 493-9781
Wirtz (G-15618)

Sutherlins Logging Inc .... G 804 366-3871
Locust Hill (G-7455)

Thomas L Alphin Inc .... G 540 997-0611
Goshen (G-5929)

Thorpe Logging Inc .... G 434 634-6050
Emporia (G-4368)

Timberline Logging Inc .... G 276 393-7239
Big Stone Gap (G-1716)

Victor Randall Logging LLC .... G 804 241-6630
Mechanicsville (G-8693)

W E Ragland Logging Co .... F 434 286-2705
Scottsville (G-12670)

Waughs Logging .... G 540 854-5676
Culpeper (G-3931)

Wayne Garrett Logging Inc .... F 757 866-8472
Spring Grove (G-12932)

Wayne Hudson .... G 434 568-6361
Drakes Branch (G-4136)

Wheeler Tember .... G 540 672-4186
Orange (G-10231)

Wheeler Thurston E Logging .... G 434 946-5265
Amherst (G-713)

William B Gilman .... F 804 798-7812
Ashland (G-1510)

Williams & Son Inc HL .... G 540 775-3192
King George (G-7123)

Wld Logging & Chipping Inc .... G 540 483-1218
Glade Hill (G-5671)

Woodland Logging Inc .... G 276 669-7795
Bristol (G-2043)

Wrights Trucking & Logging .... F 434 946-5387
Amherst (G-715)

Yoder Logging .... G 804 561-3913
Amelia Court House (G-679)

LOGGING: Saw Logs

Andrew Thurston Logging .... G 540 521-6276
Eagle Rock (G-4278)

Saw Shop .... G 540 365-0745
Ferrum (G-4980)

LOGGING: Stump Harvesting

K & R Tree Care LLC .... G 804 767-0695
Maidens (G-7891)

LOGGING: Timber, Cut At Logging Camp

Clarence D Campbell .... G 540 291-2740
Naturl BR STA (G-9111)

Coxe Timber Company .... G 757 934-1500
Suffolk (G-13687)

Hylton Timber Harvesting .... G 276 930-2348
Woolwine (G-15866)

Kenneth Foley .... G 276 930-1452
Stuart (G-13620)

Lester Viar .... G 434 277-5504
Lowesville (G-7596)

Mast Bros Logging LLC .... F 434 446-2401
South Boston (G-12781)

Mt Pleasant Log & Excvtg LLC ...... G 434 922-7326
Amherst (G-701)

R David Rosson .... G 540 456-8108
Afton (G-86)

R G Logging .... G 276 233-9224
Galax (G-5646)

Rainbow Hill Farm .... G 540 365-7826
Ferrum (G-4977)

Reaves Timber Corporation .... G 434 299-5645
Coleman Falls (G-3707)

Rorrer Timber Co Inc .... G 276 694-6304
Stuart (G-13628)

T W McPherson & Sons .... G 540 483-0105
Callaway (G-2222)

Underwood Logging LLC .... G 540 489-1388
Rocky Mount (G-12357)

Wright Logging LLC .... G 434 547-4525
Keysville (G-7066)

LOGGING: Veneer Logs

Q C Veneer & Logs LLC .... G 540 719-4349
Hardy (G-6288)

LOGGING: Wood Chips, Produced In The Field

Williams Logging and Chipping ...... F 276 694-8077
Spencer (G-12875)

LOGGING: Wooden Logs

Branmar Logging Inc .... G 540 832-5535
Gordonsville (G-5902)

Bryant Energy Corp .... G 757 887-2181
Newport News (G-9186)

Ra Resky Woodsmith LLC .... G 757 678-7555
Machipongo (G-7848)

Roger K Williams .... G 540 775-3192
King George (G-7110)

LOGS: Gas, Fireplace

Nova Green Energy LLC .... G 571 210-0589
Falls Church (G-4847)

Wammoth Services LLC .... G 571 309-2969
Woodbridge (G-15829)

LOOSELEAF BINDERS

Thompson Media Packaging Inc .... E 804 225-8146
Glen Allen (G-5810)

LOTIONS OR CREAMS: Face

Best Age Today LLC .... G 757 618-9181
Chesapeake (G-2997)

Crown ME Galore Collection LLC ... G 864 540-4476
Suffolk (G-13691)

East Amber LLC .... G 703 414-9409
Occoquan (G-10172)

France Naturals Inc .... G 804 694-4777
Gloucester (G-5848)

I & C Hughes LLC .... G 757 544-0502
Virginia Beach (G-14537)

Jessica Burdett .... G 719 423-0582
Disputanta (G-4110)

Lovely Reds Creations LLC .... G 540 320-2859
Allisonia (G-619)

LOTIONS: SHAVING

In Your Element Commerce Inc ..... G 804 426-6914
Richmond (G-11616)

LOZENGES: Pharmaceutical

Helms Candy Co Inc .... E 276 669-2612
Bristol (G-2019)

LUBRICANTS: Corrosion Preventive

Ethyl Corporation .... G 804 788-5000
Richmond (G-11580)

Ilma .... G 703 684-5574
Alexandria (G-235)

Newmarket Corporation .... D 804 788-5000
Richmond (G-11689)

Rayco Services Inc .... G 757 689-2156
Virginia Beach (G-14761)

LUBRICATION SYSTEMS & EQPT

SKF Lbrication Systems USA Inc .... D 757 951-0370
Hampton (G-6239)

Vogel Lubrication .... F 757 380-8585
Hampton (G-6266)

LUGGAGE & BRIEFCASES

CC & More Inc .... G 540 786-7052
Fredericksburg (G-5257)

Gearmaxusa Ltd .... G 804 521-4320
Mechanicsville (G-8627)

Mercury Luggage Mfg Co .... D 804 733-5222
Petersburg (G-10330)

LUGGAGE & LEATHER GOODS STORES:
Luggage, Exc Footlckr/Trunk

Crystal Beach Studio .... G 757 787-4605
Onancock (G-10195)

LUGGAGE: Traveling Bags

Warrior Luggage Company .... G 301 523-9010
Alexandria (G-608)

LUMBER & BLDG MATRLS DEALERS, RET:
Bath Fixtures, Eqpt/Sply

Aldridge Installations LLC .... G 804 658-1035
Richmond (G-11093)

LUMBER & BLDG MTRLS DEALERS, RET: Insultn & Energy Consrvtn

Nova Green Energy LLC ....G...... 571 210-0589
Falls Church *(G-4847)*

Solgreen Solutions LLC ....G...... 833 765-4733
Alexandria *(G-588)*

LUMBER & BLDG MTRLS DEALERS, RET: Planing Mill Prdts/Lumber

Dejarnette Lumber Company ....F...... 804 633-9821
Milford *(G-8930)*

JC Bradley Lumber Co ....G...... 540 962-4446
Covington *(G-3792)*

Johnny Asal Lumber Co Inc ....E...... 804 492-4884
Cumberland *(G-3935)*

Mumpower Lumber Company ....G...... 276 669-7491
Bristol *(G-2027)*

LUMBER & BUILDING MATERIAL DEALERS, RETAIL: Roofing Material

Quadd Building Systems LLC ....E...... 540 439-2148
Remington *(G-10772)*

LUMBER & BUILDING MATERIALS DEALER, RET: Door & Window Prdts

Burgess Snyder Industries Inc ....E...... 757 490-3131
Virginia Beach *(G-14306)*

Door Systems Inc ....F...... 703 490-1800
Woodbridge *(G-15685)*

Precision Doors & Hardware LLC ....F...... 540 373-7300
Fredericksburg *(G-5348)*

Windows Direct ....G...... 276 755-5187
Cana *(G-2228)*

LUMBER & BUILDING MATERIALS DEALER, RET: Masonry Matls/Splys

Chaney Enterprises Ltd Partnr ....F...... 540 710-0075
Fredericksburg *(G-5260)*

Concrete Specialties Inc ....G...... 540 982-0777
Roanoke *(G-12069)*

Handyman Concrete Inc ....E...... 703 437-7143
Chantilly *(G-2535)*

Luck Stone Corporation ....D...... 804 784-6300
Manakin Sabot *(G-7901)*

LUMBER & BUILDING MATERIALS DEALERS, RETAIL: Brick

Glen-Gery Corporation ....D...... 703 368-3178
Manassas *(G-7946)*

LUMBER & BUILDING MATERIALS DEALERS, RETAIL: Countertops

James Hintzke ....G...... 757 374-4827
Virginia Beach *(G-14563)*

LUMBER & BUILDING MATERIALS DEALERS, RETAIL: Lime & Plaster

Rockydale Quarries Corporation ....G...... 540 896-1441
Roanoke *(G-11997)*

LUMBER & BUILDING MATERIALS DEALERS, RETAIL: Paving Stones

T&W Block Incorporated ....E...... 757 787-2646
Onley *(G-10201)*

LUMBER & BUILDING MATERIALS DEALERS, RETAIL: Sand & Gravel

Rockbridge Stone Products Inc ....G...... 540 258-2841
Glasgow *(G-5701)*

LUMBER & BUILDING MATERIALS RET DEALERS: Millwork & Lumber

Architectural Custom Wdwrk Inc ....G...... 804 784-2283
Manakin Sabot *(G-7895)*

Century Stair Company ....D...... 703 754-4163
Haymarket *(G-6417)*

Mc Farlands Mill Inc ....F...... 540 667-2272
Winchester *(G-15444)*

LUMBER & BUILDING MATLS DEALERS, RET: Concrete/Cinder Block

Quadd Inc ....G...... 540 439-2148
Remington *(G-10771)*

Valley Building Supply Inc ....C...... 540 434-6725
Harrisonburg *(G-6383)*

LUMBER: Fiberboard

Blue Ridge Fiberboard Inc ....D...... 434 797-1321
Danville *(G-3959)*

LUMBER: Furniture Dimension Stock, Softwood

Mumpower Lumber Company ....G...... 276 669-7491
Bristol *(G-2027)*

LUMBER: Hardwood Dimension

Mullican Flooring LP ....D...... 276 565-0220
Appalachia *(G-798)*

Shumate Inc George C ....E...... 540 463-2244
Lexington *(G-7417)*

LUMBER: Hardwood Dimension & Flooring Mills

American Hardwood Inds LLC ....C...... 540 946-9150
Waynesboro *(G-15092)*

American Woodmark Corporation ....C...... 540 672-3707
Orange *(G-10202)*

American Woodmark Corporation ....C...... 540 665-9100
Winchester *(G-15379)*

Anderson Brothers Lumber Co ....E...... 804 561-2153
Amelia Court House *(G-651)*

Anderson Erle P Lumber Company ......E...... 804 748-0500
Disputanta *(G-4104)*

Ball Lumber Co Inc ....D...... 804 443-5555
Millers Tavern *(G-8939)*

Chantilly Floor Wholesaler Inc ....F...... 703 263-0515
Chantilly *(G-2391)*

Charles City Forest Products ....E...... 804 966-2336
Providence Forge *(G-10620)*

Cloverdale Lumber Co Inc ....E...... 434 822-5017
Sutherlin *(G-13806)*

Cochrans Lumber & Millwork Inc ....D...... 540 955-4142
Berryville *(G-1675)*

County Line LLC ....D...... 434 736-8405
Keysville *(G-7055)*

Dejarnette Lumber Company ....F...... 804 633-9821
Milford *(G-8930)*

Fitzgerald Lumber & Log Co Inc ....E...... 540 261-3430
Buena Vista *(G-2144)*

Fitzgerald Lumber & Log Co Inc ....D...... 540 348-5199
Fairfield *(G-4730)*

Holland Lumber Co Inc ....E...... 804 443-4200
Millers Tavern *(G-8940)*

J H Knighton Lumber Co Inc ....E...... 804 448-4681
Ruther Glen *(G-12457)*

Johnny Asal Lumber Co Inc ....E...... 804 492-4884
Cumberland *(G-3935)*

Johnson & Son Lumber Inc ....E...... 540 752-5557
Fredericksburg *(G-5446)*

Jones Lumber Company J E ....E...... 804 883-6331
Montpelier *(G-9017)*

Lams Lumber Co ....E...... 540 832-5173
Barboursville *(G-1563)*

M & P Sawmill Co Inc ....G...... 276 783-5585
Marion *(G-8232)*

Madera Floors LLC ....G...... 703 855-6847
Reston *(G-10892)*

Massies Wood Products LLC ....G...... 434 277-8498
Roseland *(G-12370)*

Mullican Flooring LP ....G...... 276 679-2924
Norton *(G-10130)*

Northern Neck Lumber Co Inc ....E...... 804 333-4041
Warsaw *(G-15071)*

Ontario Hardwood Company Inc ....E...... 434 736-9291
Keysville *(G-7061)*

Pembelton Forest Products Inc ....E...... 434 292-7511
Blackstone *(G-1822)*

Porters Wood Products Inc ....E...... 757 654-6430
Boykins *(G-1920)*

Portsmouth Lumber Corporation ....F...... 757 397-4646
Portsmouth *(G-10471)*

Potomac Supply Llc ....D...... 804 472-2527
Kinsale *(G-7136)*

Rock Hill Lumber Inc ....E...... 540 547-2889
Culpeper *(G-3918)*

LUMBER & BUILDING MATLS DEALERS, RET: Concrete/Cinder Block

Sheaves Floors LLC ....G...... 540 234-9080
Weyers Cave *(G-15176)*

SM Lumber Inc ....G...... 757 797-8353
Virginia Beach *(G-14826)*

Southeastern Wood Products Inc ....F...... 276 632-9025
Martinsville *(G-8332)*

Stuart Wilderness Inc ....E...... 276 694-4432
Stuart *(G-13635)*

T C Catlett & Sons Lumber Co ....E...... 540 786-2303
Fredericksburg *(G-5373)*

VA Epoxy Designs LLC ....G...... 757 947-6249
Newport News *(G-9371)*

W R Deacon & Sons Timber Inc ....E...... 540 463-3832
Lexington *(G-7422)*

Weaber Inc ....G...... 804 876-3588
Doswell *(G-4127)*

LUMBER: Kiln Dried

Rowe Furniture Inc ....A...... 540 389-8671
Elliston *(G-4349)*

White Oak Grove Woodworks ....G...... 540 763-2723
Riner *(G-11866)*

LUMBER: Pilings, Treated

C H Evelyn Piling Company Inc ....F...... 804 966-2273
Providence Forge *(G-10619)*

LUMBER: Plywood, Hardwood

Charles City Forest Products ....E...... 804 966-2336
Providence Forge *(G-10620)*

Chips Brookneal Inc ....E...... 434 376-6202
Brookneal *(G-2109)*

First Colony Homes Inc ....G...... 540 788-4222
Calverton *(G-2224)*

Georgia-Pacific LLC ....B...... 434 634-5123
Emporia *(G-4359)*

International Veneer Co Inc ....E...... 434 447-7100
South Hill *(G-12852)*

Kennedy Konstruction Kompany ....E...... 540 984-4191
Edinburg *(G-4308)*

N S Gilbert Lumber LLC ....D...... 276 431-4488
Duffield *(G-4182)*

SM Lumber Inc ....G...... 757 797-8353
Virginia Beach *(G-14826)*

Trm Inc ....E...... 920 855-2194
Haymarket *(G-6452)*

LUMBER: Plywood, Hardwood or Hardwood Faced

Advanced Nano Adhesives Inc ....G...... 919 247-6411
Moneta *(G-8956)*

LUMBER: Plywood, Softwood

Formply Products Inc ....F...... 434 572-4040
South Boston *(G-12769)*

Georgia-Pacific LLC ....C...... 434 634-6133
Skippers *(G-12700)*

LUMBER: Plywood, Softwood

Cloverdale Company Inc ....D...... 540 777-4414
Troutville *(G-13907)*

Georgia-Pacific LLC ....C...... 434 283-1066
Gladys *(G-5691)*

Georgia-Pacific LLC ....B...... 434 634-5123
Emporia *(G-4359)*

LUMBER: Poles & Pole Crossarms, Treated

Atlantic Wood Industries Inc ....E...... 757 397-2317
Portsmouth *(G-10395)*

Southside Utilities & Maint ....E...... 434 735-8853
Red Oak *(G-10760)*

LUMBER: Resawn, Small Dimension

Arrington Smith Hunter Lee ....G...... 540 230-4952
Christiansburg *(G-3569)*

Conner Industries Inc ....G...... 804 706-4229
Chester *(G-3396)*

LUMBER: Treated

Alliance Presrvng Hstry Wwii ....G...... 757 423-1429
Norfolk *(G-9434)*

Anderson Brothers Lumber Co ....E...... 804 561-2153
Amelia Court House *(G-651)*

Culpeper Roanoke Rapids LLC ....G...... 800 817-6215
Culpeper *(G-3886)*

P
R
O
D
U
C
T

Jefferson Homebuilders Inc............G..... 540 371-5338
Fredericksburg **(G-5306)**
Jefferson Homebuilders Inc............D..... 540 727-2240
Culpeper **(G-3897)**
Jefferson Homebuilders Inc............C..... 540 825-5898
Culpeper **(G-3898)**
Jefferson Homebuilders Inc............G..... 540 825-5200
Culpeper **(G-3899)**
Mk Environmental LLC...............G..... 540 435-9066
Rockingham **(G-12262)**
Potomac Supply Llc...............D..... 804 472-2527
Kinsale **(G-7136)**
Valley Timber Sales Inc...............F..... 540 832-3646
Gordonsville **(G-5917)**
What Wood Analisa Do...............G..... 757 642-2991
Virginia Beach **(G-14935)**

LUMBER: Veneer, Hardwood

Cloverdale Company Inc...............D..... 540 777-4414
Troutville **(G-13907)**
Ivc-Usa Inc...............G..... 434 447-7100
South Hill **(G-12853)**

MACHINE GUNS, WHOLESALE

Whisper Tactical LLC...............G..... 757 645-5938
Chesapeake **(G-3376)**

MACHINE PARTS: Stamped Or Pressed Metal

Datacut Precision Machining...............G..... 434 237-8320
Lynchburg **(G-7693)**
International Designs LLC...............G..... 804 275-1044
North Chesterfield **(G-9899)**
Kennley Corporation...............G..... 804 275-9088
North Chesterfield **(G-9907)**
Rubber Plastic Met Engrg Corp...............F..... 757 502-5462
Virginia Beach **(G-14785)**
Shenandoah Machine & Maint Co.........G..... 540 343-1758
Roanoke **(G-12183)**
Virginia Metals Inc...............F..... 276 628-8151
Abingdon **(G-67)**

MACHINE SHOPS

Accurate Machine Inc...............G..... 757 853-2136
Norfolk **(G-9418)**
Air Barge Company...............G..... 310 378-2928
Mc Lean **(G-8390)**
Carrythewhatreplications LLC...............G..... 804 254-2933
Richmond **(G-11522)**
Cycle Machine LLC...............G..... 804 779-0055
Manquin **(G-8215)**
Eagle Aviation Tech LLC...............D..... 757 224-6269
Newport News **(G-9219)**
Geoquip Inc...............D..... 757 485-2500
Chesapeake **(G-3118)**
Geoquip Manufacturing Inc...............E..... 757 485-8525
Chesapeake **(G-3119)**
Hub Pattern Corporation...............E..... 540 342-3505
Roanoke **(G-12104)**
Mars Machine Works Inc...............G..... 804 642-4760
Gloucester Point **(G-5873)**
Melvins Machine & Welding...............G..... 276 988-3822
Tazewell **(G-13835)**
Mountain Tech Inc...............G..... 434 710-4896
Blairs **(G-1832)**
Precision Tool & Die Inc...............G..... 804 233-8810
Richmond **(G-11723)**
Proton Systems LLC...............G..... 757 224-5685
Hampton **(G-6223)**
Sanjo Virginia Beach Inc...............G..... 757 498-0400
Virginia Beach **(G-14793)**
Superior Metal Fabricators...............F..... 804 236-3266
Richmond **(G-11403)**
W D Barnette Enterprise Inc...............G..... 757 494-0530
Chesapeake **(G-3368)**

MACHINE TOOL ACCESS: Balancing Machines

Balancemaster Inc...............G..... 434 258-5078
Concord **(G-3755)**

MACHINE TOOL ACCESS: Cams

Crown Cork & Seal Usa Inc...............E..... 757 538-1318
Suffolk **(G-13690)**

MACHINE TOOL ACCESS: Cutting

Excel Tool Inc...............F..... 276 322-0223
Falls Mills **(G-4931)**
Kennametal Inc...............C..... 540 740-3128
New Market **(G-9144)**
Old 97 Choppers...............G..... 434 799-5400
Danville **(G-4019)**

MACHINE TOOL ACCESS: Diamond Cutting, For Turning, Etc

Xtreme Diamond LLC...............G..... 703 753-0567
Haymarket **(G-6456)**

MACHINE TOOL ACCESS: Files

Patterson Business Systems...............F..... 540 389-7726
Salem **(G-12555)**

MACHINE TOOL ACCESS: Pushers

Permit Pushers...............G..... 703 237-6461
Arlington **(G-1108)**

MACHINE TOOL ACCESS: Tool Holders

Diamondback Tool Co...............G..... 800 899-2358
Charlottesville **(G-2781)**

MACHINE TOOL ACCESS: Tools & Access

Bentech...............G..... 540 344-6820
Roanoke **(G-12043)**
Time Machine Inc...............G..... 540 772-0962
Roanoke **(G-12204)**

MACHINE TOOLS & ACCESS

Brock Enterprises Virginia LLC...............G..... 276 971-4549
Richlands **(G-11014)**
General Electric Company...............F..... 540 387-7000
Salem **(G-12511)**
Glenn R Williams...............G..... 434 251-9383
Ringgold **(G-11867)**
Grimsleys House Tools Inc...............G..... 757 399-4438
Portsmouth **(G-10437)**
Ridge Tool Company...............C..... 540 672-5150
Orange **(G-10226)**
Rnk Outdoors...............G..... 540 797-3698
Roanoke **(G-12163)**
Sanjo Virginia Beach Inc...............G..... 757 498-0400
Virginia Beach **(G-14793)**
Specialty Tooling LLC...............G..... 804 912-1158
Henrico **(G-6573)**
Teledyne Instruments Inc...............D..... 757 723-6531
Hampton **(G-6250)**
Uma Inc...............E..... 540 879-2040
Dayton **(G-4067)**

MACHINE TOOLS, METAL CUTTING: Drilling

Beydler Cnc LLC...............G..... 760 954-4397
Amherst **(G-683)**
Nuvidrill LLC...............G..... 540 353-8787
Roanoke **(G-12143)**

MACHINE TOOLS, METAL CUTTING: Drilling & Boring

Pennsylvania Drilling Company...........G..... 540 665-5207
Winchester **(G-15459)**

MACHINE TOOLS, METAL CUTTING: Electrochemical Milling

LLC Link Masters...............G..... 804 241-3962
Mechanicsville **(G-8653)**

MACHINE TOOLS, METAL CUTTING: Electrolytic

B & M Machinery Inc...............G..... 434 525-1498
Lynchburg **(G-7647)**

MACHINE TOOLS, METAL CUTTING: Home Workshop

Mg Enterprise LLC...............G..... 703 646-2761
Fairfax **(G-4509)**

MACHINE TOOLS, METAL CUTTING: Numerically Controlled

Vulcan Machine Co...............G..... 240 486-2685
Fort Valley **(G-5136)**

MACHINE TOOLS, METAL CUTTING: Plasma Process

Capstone Industries LLC...............G..... 703 966-6718
Manassas **(G-8045)**

MACHINE TOOLS, METAL CUTTING: Tool Replacement & Rpr Parts

Case-Polytech Inc...............G..... 804 752-3500
Ashland **(G-1386)**
Cbg LLC...............G..... 757 465-0333
Portsmouth **(G-10405)**
Ed Walkers Repair Services...............G..... 804 590-1198
South Chesterfield **(G-12834)**
Elite Fabrication & Machine...............G..... 540 392-6055
Christiansburg **(G-3587)**
Thirty Seven Cent Machine...............G..... 276 673-1400
Martinsville **(G-8343)**
Wells Machine Co...............G..... 804 737-2500
Sandston **(G-12639)**

MACHINE TOOLS, METAL FORMING: Bending

Unison Tube LLC...............G..... 828 633-3190
Ringgold **(G-11875)**

MACHINE TOOLS, METAL FORMING: Magnetic Forming

Canline USA Corporation...............F..... 540 380-8585
Lynchburg **(G-7672)**

MACHINE TOOLS, METAL FORMING: Mechanical, Pneumatic Or Hyd

Bc Repairs...............G..... 434 332-5304
Rustburg **(G-12434)**

MACHINE TOOLS: Metal Cutting

Action Tool Service Inc...............F..... 757 838-4555
Hampton **(G-6069)**
Automated Machine & Tech Inc...............E..... 757 898-7844
Grafton **(G-5931)**
Centurion Tools LLC...............F..... 540 967-5402
Louisa **(G-7549)**
Charis Machine LLC...............G..... 276 546-6675
Duffield **(G-4176)**
Chips On Board Incorporated...............G..... 757 357-0789
Smithfield **(G-12709)**
Farehill Precision LLC...............G..... 540 879-2373
Rockingham **(G-12251)**
FHP LLC...............G..... 540 879-2560
Rockingham **(G-12252)**
GM International Ltd Company...............G..... 703 577-0829
Leesburg **(G-7281)**
Hampton Roads Sheet Metal Inc...............G..... 757 543-6009
Virginia Beach **(G-14500)**
Its Manufacturing Incorporated...............G..... 804 397-0504
Crewe **(G-3813)**
J & A Tools...............G..... 434 414-0871
Amherst **(G-696)**
Keo-Corp LLC...............G..... 636 515-5549
New Kent **(G-9135)**
Lynchburg Machining LLC...............F..... 434 846-7327
Lynchburg **(G-7762)**
Marco Machine & Design Inc...............F..... 804 275-5555
North Chesterfield **(G-9921)**
Mescher Manufacturing Co Inc...............F..... 276 530-7856
Grundy **(G-6037)**
Microfab LLC...............G..... 276 620-7200
Max Meadows **(G-8369)**
Performance Engrg & Mch Co...............G..... 804 530-5577
South Chesterfield **(G-12819)**
Pickle Tyson...............G..... 276 686-5368
Rural Retreat **(G-12429)**
Ridge Tool Company...............C..... 540 672-5150
Orange **(G-10226)**
Sanjo Virginia Beach Inc...............G..... 757 498-0400
Virginia Beach **(G-14793)**
Sonic Tools LP...............F..... 804 798-0538
Ashland **(G-1493)**

MACHINE TOOLS: Metal Forming

American Gfm Corporation ....C 757 487-2442
Chesapeake **(G-2967)**

Jeff Shearer ....G 703 313-7670
Alexandria **(G-494)**

MACHINERY & EQPT FINANCE LEASING

Terex Corporation ....G 540 361-7755
Fredericksburg **(G-5492)**

MACHINERY & EQPT, AGRICULTURAL, WHOLESALE: Lawn & Garden

Melnor Inc ....E 540 722-5600
Winchester **(G-15447)**

MACHINERY & EQPT, INDL, WHOL: Brewery Prdts Mfrg, Commercial

Single Source Welding LLC ....G 703 919-7791
Warrenton **(G-15052)**

MACHINERY & EQPT, INDL, WHOL: Environ Pollution Cntrl, Water

Abwasser Technologies Inc ....G 757 453-7505
Virginia Beach **(G-14206)**

MACHINERY & EQPT, INDL, WHOLESALE: Conveyor Systems

Tazz Conveyor Corporation ....F 276 988-4883
North Tazewell **(G-10108)**

MACHINERY & EQPT, INDL, WHOLESALE: Food Manufacturing

Appleberry Mtn Taxidermy Svcs ....G 434 831-2232
Schuyler **(G-12651)**

MACHINERY & EQPT, INDL, WHOLESALE: Food Product Manufacturng

Eerkins Inc ....G 703 626-6248
Luray **(G-7608)**

Smart Machine Technologies Inc ....D 276 632-9853
Ridgeway **(G-11853)**

MACHINERY & EQPT, INDL, WHOLESALE: Hydraulic Systems

Hydra Hose & Supply Co ....G 757 867-9795
Yorktown **(G-15964)**

MACHINERY & EQPT, INDL, WHOLESALE: Lift Trucks & Parts

Mosena Enterprises Inc ....G 757 562-7033
Franklin **(G-5149)**

MACHINERY & EQPT, INDL, WHOLESALE: Paint Spray

Aspire Marketing Corporation ....G 434 525-6191
Forest **(G-5051)**

MACHINERY & EQPT, INDL, WHOLESALE: Robots

Weda Water Inc ....G 757 515-4338
Virginia Beach **(G-14931)**

MACHINERY & EQPT, INDL, WHOLESALE: Safety Eqpt

Core Engineered Solutions Inc ....F 703 563-0320
Herndon **(G-6646)**

Industrial Biodynamics LLC ....G 540 357-0033
Salem **(G-12520)**

MACHINERY & EQPT, INDL, WHOLESALE: Screening

Hydropower Turbine Systems ....G 804 360-7992
Powhatan **(G-10550)**

MACHINERY & EQPT, INDL, WHOLESALE: Tool & Die Makers

Intricate Metal Forming Co ....E 540 345-9233
Salem **(G-12523)**

MACHINERY & EQPT, WHOLESALE: Concrete Processing

Kessler Soils Engrg Pdts Inc ....G 571 291-2284
Leesburg **(G-7296)**

MACHINERY & EQPT, WHOLESALE: Construction, Cranes

ML Manufacturing ....G 434 581-2000
New Canton **(G-9118)**

MACHINERY & EQPT, WHOLESALE: Construction, General

Geoquip Inc ....D 757 485-2500
Chesapeake **(G-3118)**

MACHINERY & EQPT, WHOLESALE: Contractors Materials

Alban Tractor Co Inc ....F 540 667-4200
Clear Brook **(G-3643)**

MACHINERY & EQPT, WHOLESALE: Oil Field Eqpt

Svr International LLC ....F 703 759-2953
Vienna **(G-14136)**

MACHINERY & EQPT: Farm

Afritech LLC ....G 703 550-0392
Alexandria **(G-405)**

Alban Tractor Co Inc ....F 540 667-4200
Clear Brook **(G-3643)**

Amadas Industries Inc ....D 757 539-0231
Suffolk **(G-13668)**

Beery Brothers ....G 540 879-2970
Dayton **(G-4052)**

Case Mechanical ....G 804 501-0003
Richmond **(G-11151)**

Case Mechanical LLC ....G 757 272-6050
Newport News **(G-9193)**

Ferguson Manufacturing Co Inc ....F 757 539-3409
Suffolk **(G-13709)**

Harris Company Inc ....G 540 894-4413
Mineral **(G-8949)**

Hartwood Landscape Inc ....G 540 379-2650
Fredericksburg **(G-5438)**

Hnh Partners Inc ....G 757 539-2353
Annandale **(G-757)**

Hoffmanns Custom Display Cases ......G 804 332-4873
Sandston **(G-12619)**

Jerry Cantrell ....G 540 379-7689
Fredericksburg **(G-5443)**

Live Cases ....G 703 627-0994
Oakton **(G-10154)**

Milnesville Enterprises LLC ....G 540 487-4073
Bridgewater **(G-1955)**

Norfields Farm Inc ....G 540 832-2952
Gordonsville **(G-5916)**

P & P Farm Machinery Inc ....G 276 794-7806
Lebanon **(G-7203)**

R A Pearson Company ....D 804 550-7300
Ashland **(G-1482)**

Southern Sttes Wnchster Coop I ....F 540 662-0375
Winchester **(G-15588)**

Valley Grounds Inc ....E 540 382-6710
Christiansburg **(G-3615)**

MACHINERY & EQPT: Liquid Automation

American Spin-A-Batch Co Intl ....G 804 798-1349
Ashland **(G-1367)**

MACHINERY BASES

Depco-Dfnse Engneered Pdts LLC ....G 804 271-7000
Chesterfield **(G-3493)**

Dynamic Fabworks LLC ....G 757 439-1169
Virginia Beach **(G-14421)**

Hallmark Fabricators Inc ....G 804 230-0880
Richmond **(G-11607)**

New ERA Technology LLC ....G 571 308-8525
Fairfax **(G-4517)**

Prototype Productions Inc ....D 703 858-0011
Chantilly **(G-2483)**

Shickel Corporation ....D 540 828-2536
Bridgewater **(G-1959)**

Standard Marine Inc ....F 757 824-0293
Mears **(G-8597)**

MACHINERY, COMM LAUNDRY: Rug Cleaning, Drying Or Napping

Ship Shape Cleaning LLC ....G 757 769-3845
Portsmouth **(G-10480)**

MACHINERY, FOOD PRDTS: Cutting, Chopping, Grinding, Mixing

Reliance Industries Inc ....G 832 788-0108
Falls Church **(G-4924)**

MACHINERY, FOOD PRDTS: Food Processing, Smokers

Finco Inc ....G 301 645-4538
Fredericksburg **(G-5288)**

MACHINERY, FOOD PRDTS: Juice Extractors, Fruit & Veg, Comm

Gulp Juicery LLC ....G 804 933-9483
Goochland **(G-5884)**

MACHINERY, FOOD PRDTS: Mills, Food

Georges Family Farms LLC ....E 540 477-3181
Mount Jackson **(G-9070)**

MACHINERY, FOOD PRDTS: Mixers, Commercial

Blackstone Herb Cottage ....G 434 292-1135
Blackstone **(G-1812)**

MACHINERY, FOOD PRDTS: Processing, Poultry

Miller Metal Fabricators Inc ....E 540 886-5575
Staunton **(G-13281)**

MACHINERY, FOOD PRDTS: Roasting, Coffee, Peanut, Etc.

Excalibur Technology Svcs LLC ....G 703 853-8307
Bristow **(G-2051)**

MACHINERY, MAILING: Postage Meters

Pitney Bowes Business Insight ....G 540 786-5744
Fredericksburg **(G-5347)**

Pitney Bowes Inc ....G 703 658-6900
Alexandria **(G-310)**

Pitney Bowes Inc ....E 304 744-1067
Vienna **(G-14112)**

Pitney Bowes Inc ....E 757 322-8000
Norfolk **(G-9690)**

Pitney Bowes Inc ....E 804 798-3210
Ashland **(G-1476)**

MACHINERY, METALWORKING: Assembly, Including Robotic

Blue Ridge Servo Mtr Repr LLC ....G 540 375-2990
Salem **(G-12483)**

Hampton Roads Component Assemb ...G 757 236-8627
Hampton **(G-6163)**

Simplimatic Automation LLC ....D 434 385-9181
Forest **(G-5092)**

MACHINERY, METALWORKING: Cutting-Up Lines

Germaine Clark LLC ....G 571 309-1724
Alexandria **(G-214)**

MACHINERY, OFFICE: Time Clocks &Time Recording Devices

MB Services LLC ....G 703 906-8625
Alexandria **(G-524)**

Employee Codes: A=Over 500 employees, B=251-500
C=101-250, D=51-100, E=20-50, F=10-19, G=1-9

2021 Virginia
Industrial Directory

PRODUCT

989

MACHINERY, OFFICE: Typing & Word Processing

Konica Mnlta Bus Sltons USA In ....C 703 461-8195
Alexandria *(G-508)*

MACHINERY, PACKAGING: Bread Wrapping

Hauni Richmond Inc ....C 804 222-5259
Richmond *(G-11234)*

MACHINERY, PACKAGING: Canning, Food

Belvac Production McHy Inc ....C 434 239-0358
Lynchburg *(G-7652)*

MACHINERY, PACKAGING: Packing & Wrapping

Tigerseal Products LLC ....G 800 899-9389
Beaverdam *(G-1614)*

MACHINERY, PAPER INDUSTRY: Paper Mill, Plating, Etc

Craft Industrial Incorporated ....E 757 825-1195
Hampton *(G-6118)*

MACHINERY, PRINTING TRADES: Copy Holders

About Time ....G 757 253-0143
Williamsburg *(G-15200)*
Melvin Riley ....G 240 381-6111
Falls Church *(G-4829)*

MACHINERY, PRINTING TRADES: Linotype, Monotype, Intertype

Karma Group Inc ....G 717 253-9379
Manassas *(G-8092)*

MACHINERY, PRINTING TRADES: Plates

Naito America ....E 804 550-3305
Ashland *(G-1468)*

MACHINERY, PRINTING TRADES: Printing Trade Parts & Attchts

American Technology Inds Ltd ....E 757 436-6465
Chesapeake *(G-2973)*

MACHINERY, TEXTILE: Embroidery

Art Connected ....G 540 628-2162
Fredericksburg *(G-5400)*
Artgiftsetccom ....G 703 772-3587
Arlington *(G-861)*
Dennis W Wiley ....G 540 992-6631
Buchanan *(G-2121)*
Stitch Beagle Inc ....G 540 777-0002
Roanoke *(G-12003)*

MACHINERY, TEXTILE: Printing

Thermo-Flex Technologies Inc ....G 919 247-6411
Moneta *(G-8982)*

MACHINERY, WOODWORKING: Cabinet Makers'

Atelier Fonteneau LLC ....G 540 371-5074
Fredericksburg *(G-5401)*
Bargers Custom Cabinets LLC ....G 540 261-7230
Buena Vista *(G-2139)*
Cabinet Makers ....G 703 421-6331
Sterling *(G-13364)*
Cabinet Masters ....G 703 331-5781
Manassas Park *(G-8194)*
Custom Cabinet Works ....G 540 972-1734
Locust Grove *(G-7442)*
Dobbs & Associates ....G 804 769-4266
King William *(G-7129)*
Gathersburg Cabntry ....G 703 742-8472
Herndon *(G-6679)*
H C Sexton and Associates ....G 434 409-1073
Crozet *(G-3834)*
Middlesex Cabinet Co ....G 804 758-3617
Saluda *(G-12605)*

MACHINERY, WOODWORKING: Furniture Makers

Cane Connection ....G 804 261-6555
Richmond *(G-11145)*
Copper Woodworks ....G 757 421-7328
Chesapeake *(G-3053)*
Fred Hean Furniture & Wdwrk ....G 434 973-5960
Charlottesville *(G-2634)*
Opposable Thumbs LLC ....G 804 502-2937
Richmond *(G-11701)*

MACHINERY, WOODWORKING: Pattern Makers'

Laurie Grusha Zipf ....G 703 794-9497
Manassas *(G-8098)*

MACHINERY, WOODWORKING: Sanding, Exc Portable Floor Sanders

Carrs Floor Services ....G 434 525-8420
Forest *(G-5059)*
R & S Molds Inc ....G 434 352-8612
Appomattox *(G-820)*

MACHINERY/EQPT, INDL, WHOL: Cleaning, High Press, Sand/Steam

Triple D Sales Co Inc ....G 540 672-5821
Aroda *(G-1226)*

MACHINERY: Ammunition & Explosives Loading

Alacran ....G 540 629-6095
Dublin *(G-4147)*

MACHINERY: Assembly, Exc Metalworking

Alfa Laval Inc ....C 866 253-2528
Richmond *(G-11095)*
Metallum3d LLC ....G 434 409-2401
Crozet *(G-3843)*

MACHINERY: Automotive Maintenance

Bishop Distributors LLC ....G 757 618-6401
Norfolk *(G-9463)*
Cap Oil Change Systems LLC ....G 540 982-1494
Roanoke *(G-11901)*

MACHINERY: Automotive Related

Armadillo Industries Inc ....G 757 508-2348
Williamsburg *(G-15207)*
Federal-Mogul Powertrain LLC ....G 540 953-4676
Blacksburg *(G-1738)*
Hotrodz Performance & Motor ....G 571 337-2988
Oakton *(G-10150)*
Jae El Incorporated ....G 540 535-5210
Leesburg *(G-7291)*
Milhous Control Company ....E 434 946-5302
Amherst *(G-700)*

MACHINERY: Broom Making

Molins Richmond Inc ....D 804 887-2525
Henrico *(G-6536)*

MACHINERY: Centrifugal

Alfa Laval US Holding Inc ....D 804 222-5300
Richmond *(G-11096)*

MACHINERY: Construction

Amadas Industries Inc ....G 757 539-0231
Suffolk *(G-13667)*
Amadas Industries Inc ....D 757 539-0231
Suffolk *(G-13668)*
B & T LLC ....G 804 720-1758
Chester *(G-3389)*
Bobcat Service of T N C ....G 757 482-2773
Chesapeake *(G-3009)*
Caterpillar Corner LLC ....G 703 939-1798
South Riding *(G-12867)*
Charles M Fariss ....F 434 660-0606
Rustburg *(G-12438)*
Chucks Concrete Pumping LLC ....G 804 347-3986
Henrico *(G-6492)*

Cozy Caterpillars ....G 757 499-3769
Virginia Beach *(G-14369)*
Diloreto Partners Inc ....G 804 271-2363
Richmond *(G-11041)*
Ditch Witch of Virginia ....G 804 798-2590
Glen Allen *(G-5725)*
Drillco National Group Inc ....G 703 631-3222
Chantilly *(G-2411)*
Equipment Repair Services ....G 703 491-7681
Woodbridge *(G-15695)*
Eugene Martin Trucking ....G 434 454-7267
Scottsburg *(G-12655)*
Gradall Industries Inc ....G 540 819-6638
Troutville *(G-13910)*
Hotspot Energy Inc ....F 757 410-8640
Chesapeake *(G-3137)*
Innovative Wireless Tech Inc ....E 434 316-5230
Lynchburg *(G-7741)*
James River Industries BT ....G 702 515-9937
Lynchburg *(G-7748)*
Kennedys Excavating LLC ....G 423 383-0143
Bristol *(G-2023)*
MIC Industries Inc ....F 540 678-2900
Clear Brook *(G-3647)*
MIC Industries Inc ....E 703 318-1900
Clear Brook *(G-3648)*
Mosena Enterprises Inc ....G 757 562-7033
Franklin *(G-5149)*
Mrp Munufacturing Inc ....E 434 525-1993
Forest *(G-5084)*
Pearson Equipment Company ....G 434 845-3171
Lynchburg *(G-7784)*
Per LLC ....G 540 489-4737
Rocky Mount *(G-12344)*
S & S Equipment Sls & Svc Inc ....G 757 421-3000
Chesapeake *(G-3280)*
Shantell C Young ....G 251 348-7247
Newport News *(G-9335)*
Spectra Quest Inc ....F 804 261-3300
Henrico *(G-6574)*
Taal Enterprises LLC ....F 276 328-2408
Wise *(G-15634)*
Terex Corporation ....G 540 361-7755
Fredericksburg *(G-5492)*
Terrabuilt Corp International ....G 540 687-4211
Middleburg *(G-8734)*
Utiliscope Corp ....F 804 550-5233
Glen Allen *(G-5822)*
Wilrich Construction LLC ....G 804 654-0238
Tappahannock *(G-13827)*

MACHINERY: Cryogenic, Industrial

Discountcryo Co ....G 804 733-3229
Petersburg *(G-10317)*

MACHINERY: Custom

Craft Machine Works Inc ....D 757 310-6011
Hampton *(G-6119)*
Craft Mch Wrks Acquisition LLC ....E 757 310-6011
Hampton *(G-6120)*
CSM International Corporation ....G 800 767-3805
Woodbridge *(G-15678)*
Dickerson Machine and Design ....G 540 789-7945
Christiansburg *(G-3583)*
Falling Creek Metal Products ....G 804 744-1061
Midlothian *(G-8817)*
Fields Inc Oscar S ....E 804 798-3900
Ashland *(G-1416)*
Form Fabrications LLC ....G 757 309-8717
Virginia Beach *(G-14471)*
General Engineering Co VA ....D 276 628-6068
Abingdon *(G-32)*
Green Trophy ....G 619 387-6244
Fort Lee *(G-5131)*
Jewett Automation Inc ....E 804 344-8101
Richmond *(G-11631)*
Met Machine Inc ....G 540 864-6007
New Castle *(G-9122)*
Product Engineered Systems ....G 804 794-3586
Midlothian *(G-8883)*
Superilor Float Tanks LLC ....G 757 966-6350
Norfolk *(G-9738)*
Systems Technology VA LLC ....G 540 884-1784
Eagle Rock *(G-4283)*
Tectonics Inc ....G 276 228-5565
Wytheville *(G-15918)*

MACHINERY: Deburring

Williams Deburring Small Parts ....G...... 540 726-7485
Narrows *(G-9099)*

MACHINERY: Dredging

Salmons Dredging Inc ....G...... 757 426-6824
Virginia Beach *(G-14790)*

MACHINERY: Electronic Component Making

Aai Textron ....G...... 434 292-5805
Blackstone *(G-1810)*
Maida Development Company ....D...... 757 723-0785
Hampton *(G-6188)*
Maida Development Company ....E...... 757 719-3038
Hampton *(G-6189)*

MACHINERY: Electronic Teaching Aids

Watson Machine Corporation ....F...... 804 598-1500
Powhatan *(G-10583)*

MACHINERY: Extruding, Synthetic Filament

Universal Fiber Systems LLC ....E...... 276 669-1161
Bristol *(G-2038)*

MACHINERY: Fiber Optics Strand Coating

Fiber Consulting Services ....G...... 804 746-2357
Mechanicsville *(G-8622)*

MACHINERY: General, Industrial, NEC

C&C Assembly Inc ....G...... 540 904-6416
Salem *(G-12487)*
Filter Media ....G...... 540 667-9074
Winchester *(G-15543)*
X-Metrix Inc ....G...... 757 450-5978
Virginia Beach *(G-14947)*

MACHINERY: Grinding

Capco Machinery Systems Inc ....E...... 540 977-0404
Roanoke *(G-11902)*

MACHINERY: Ice Cream

Elvaria LLC ....G...... 703 935-0041
Gainesville *(G-5582)*

MACHINERY: Ice Making

Orien Usa LLC ....G...... 757 486-2099
Virginia Beach *(G-14703)*

MACHINERY: Industrial, NEC

1 Hour A 24 Hr Er A VA Bch Lck ....G...... 757 295-8288
Norfolk *(G-9409)*
Arcola Industries LLC ....G...... 703 723-0092
Broadlands *(G-2072)*
Bryans Tools LLC ....G...... 540 667-5675
Winchester *(G-15394)*
Cavitronix Corporation ....G...... 540 622-6240
Front Royal *(G-5526)*
D & R Pro Tools LLC ....G...... 804 338-1754
Crewe *(G-3811)*
Dannys Tools LLC ....G...... 757 282-6229
Virginia Beach *(G-14386)*
Direct Tools Factory Outlet ....G...... 757 345-6945
Williamsburg *(G-15234)*
Dks Machine Shop Inc ....G...... 540 775-9648
King George *(G-7087)*
East Tools Inc ....G...... 703 754-1931
Haymarket *(G-6421)*
F & M Tools LLC ....G...... 757 361-9225
Chesapeake *(G-3096)*
Grays Welding LLC ....G...... 434 401-4559
Coleman Falls *(G-3706)*
JD Gordon Tool Company LLC ....G...... 804 832-9907
Locust Hill *(G-7453)*
Kirby of VA ....G...... 434 835-4349
Danville *(G-4010)*
Neault LLC ....G...... 804 283-5948
Manquin *(G-8217)*
Patriot Tools LLC ....G...... 757 718-4591
Chesapeake *(G-3235)*
Seascape Automation LLC ....G...... 717 512-5981
Virginia Beach *(G-14799)*
Sudden Service Inc ....G...... 804 266-6200
Richmond *(G-11401)*

Taylor Mfg & Design LLC ....G...... 757 902-1820
Hampton *(G-6249)*
Thomson Industries Inc ....G...... 540 633-3549
Radford *(G-10745)*
Valley Restaurant Repair Inc ....G...... 540 294-1118
Fishersville *(G-5011)*
Vintage Vault ....G...... 703 862-7159
Sterling *(G-13552)*
Wise Custom Machining ....G...... 276 328-8681
Wise *(G-15637)*

MACHINERY: Kilns

Kiln Creek Associates LP ....G...... 757 464-6082
Virginia Beach *(G-14584)*
Kiln Creek Pkwy - Old Yorktown ....G...... 757 204-7229
Yorktown *(G-15972)*

MACHINERY: Knitting

Authentic Knitting Board LLC ....G...... 434 842-1180
Fork Union *(G-5108)*
Rendas ....G...... 804 776-6215
Deltaville *(G-4086)*

MACHINERY: Labeling

Masa Corporation of Virginia ....G...... 804 271-8102
North Chesterfield *(G-9925)*

MACHINERY: Logging Eqpt

Sopko Manufacturing Inc ....F...... 434 848-3460
Lawrenceville *(G-7185)*

MACHINERY: Metalworking

Advantage Machine & Engrg ....F...... 757 488-5085
Portsmouth *(G-10388)*
Aerial Machine & Tool Corp ....D...... 276 952-2006
Meadows of Dan *(G-8590)*
Aerial Machine & Tool Corp ....G...... 276 694-3148
Stuart *(G-13603)*
East Coast Fabricators Inc ....G...... 540 587-7170
Bedford *(G-1633)*
Marco Machine & Design Inc ....F...... 804 275-5555
North Chesterfield *(G-9921)*
MIC Industries Inc ....F...... 540 678-2900
Clear Brook *(G-3647)*
MIC Industries Inc ....E...... 703 318-1900
Clear Brook *(G-3648)*
Parker Manufacturing LLC ....G...... 804 507-0593
Richmond *(G-11319)*
Prototec Inc ....G...... 434 832-7440
Lynchburg *(G-7793)*
Rayco Industries Inc ....E...... 804 321-7111
Richmond *(G-11729)*
Tessy Plastics Corp ....C...... 434 385-5700
Lynchburg *(G-7820)*
West Engineering Company Inc ....E...... 804 798-3966
Ashland *(G-1508)*
Winchester Tool LLC ....E...... 540 869-1150
Winchester *(G-15513)*

MACHINERY: Milling

Limitorque Corp ....G...... 804 639-0529
Midlothian *(G-8849)*

MACHINERY: Mining

American Mine Research Inc ....D...... 276 928-1712
Rocky Gap *(G-12305)*
Bluefield Manufacturing Inc ....E...... 276 322-3441
Bluefield *(G-1859)*
Canaan Land Associates Inc ....D...... 276 988-6543
Tazewell *(G-13829)*
Crisp Manufacturing Co Inc ....F...... 276 686-4131
Rural Retreat *(G-12420)*
Damascus Equipment LLC ....E...... 276 676-2376
Abingdon *(G-27)*
Dane Meades Shop ....G...... 276 926-4847
Pound *(G-10512)*
Elgin Equipment Group ....G...... 276 988-8901
Tazewell *(G-13832)*
Elswick Inc ....G...... 276 971-3060
Cedar Bluff *(G-2275)*
Frank Calandra Inc ....G...... 412 963-9071
Cedar Bluff *(G-2276)*
Frank Calandra Inc ....G...... 276 964-7023
Pounding Mill *(G-10519)*
GE Fairchild Mining Equipment ....D...... 540 921-8000
Glen Lyn *(G-5832)*

Heintzmann Corporation ....D...... 304 284-8004
Cedar Bluff *(G-2278)*
Innovative Wireless Tech Inc ....E...... 434 316-5230
Lynchburg *(G-7741)*
J and R Manufacturing Inc ....E...... 276 210-1647
Bluefield *(G-1865)*
Jennmar Corporation ....D...... 540 726-2326
Rich Creek *(G-11007)*
Jennmar of Pennsylvania LLC ....F...... 276 964-2107
Cedar Bluff *(G-2280)*
Jennmar of Pennsylvania LLC ....G...... 276 964-7000
Cedar Bluff *(G-2281)*
Joy Global Underground Min LLC ....F...... 276 679-1082
Norton *(G-10123)*
Joy Global Underground Min LLC ....C...... 276 431-2821
Duffield *(G-4179)*
Joy Global Underground Min LLC ....F...... 276 322-5421
Bluefield *(G-1867)*
Komatsu Mining Corp ....G...... 276 623-2000
Abingdon *(G-48)*
Lawrence Brothers Inc ....E...... 276 322-4988
Bluefield *(G-1868)*
Longwall - Associates Inc ....C...... 276 646-2004
Chilhowie *(G-3554)*
Mefcor Incorporated ....E...... 276 322-5021
North Tazewell *(G-10103)*
Norris Screen and Mfg LLC ....E...... 276 988-8901
Tazewell *(G-13838)*
Pemco Corporation ....D...... 276 326-2611
Bluefield *(G-1872)*
Simmons Equipment Company ....F...... 276 991-3345
Tazewell *(G-13839)*
Stella-Jones Corporation ....D...... 540 997-9251
Goshen *(G-5927)*
Tramline Inc ....G...... 276 322-3183
Bluefield *(G-1883)*
Wright Machine & Manufacturing ....G...... 276 688-2391
Bland *(G-1838)*
Wythe Power Equipment Co Inc ....E...... 276 228-7371
Wytheville *(G-15927)*

MACHINERY: Optical Lens

Hue Ai LLC ....G...... 571 766-6943
Tysons *(G-13946)*

MACHINERY: Packaging

Cda Usa Inc ....G...... 804 918-3707
Henrico *(G-6490)*
Ess Technologies Inc ....E...... 540 961-5716
Blacksburg *(G-1736)*
Flexicell Inc ....G...... 804 550-7300
Richmond *(G-11211)*
Hartness International A Div ....D...... 434 455-0357
Lynchburg *(G-7730)*
Ilantech Inc ....G...... 571 226-7042
Ashburn *(G-1294)*
Khem Precision Machining LLC ....G...... 804 915-8922
Richmond *(G-11261)*
Modek Inc ....G...... 804 550-7300
Ashland *(G-1463)*
R A Pearson Company ....D...... 804 550-7300
Ashland *(G-1482)*
Ross Industries Inc ....C...... 540 439-3271
Midland *(G-8762)*
Sealpac Usa LLC ....G...... 804 261-0580
North Chesterfield *(G-9974)*
Shibuya Hoppmann Corporation ....D...... 540 829-2564
Manassas *(G-8154)*
Sml Packaging LLC ....F...... 434 528-3640
Lynchburg *(G-7808)*
Tcg Technologies Inc ....G...... 540 587-8624
Bedford *(G-1660)*
Zima-Pack LLC ....G...... 804 372-0707
South Chesterfield *(G-12830)*

MACHINERY: Paint Making

Wigwam Industries ....G...... 434 823-4663
Crozet *(G-3855)*

MACHINERY: Paper Industry Miscellaneous

Bay West Paper ....G...... 804 639-3530
Chesterfield *(G-3479)*
Genik Incorporated ....G...... 804 226-2907
Richmond *(G-11218)*
Jud Corporation ....G...... 757 485-4371
Chesapeake *(G-3158)*
Nks LLC ....G...... 757 229-3139
Williamsburg *(G-15283)*

Tmeic Corporation ....G...... 540 725-2031
Salem *(G-12574)*

West Engineering Company Inc ....E...... 804 798-3966
Ashland *(G-1508)*

MACHINERY: Pharmaciutical

Gohring Components Corp..................G...... 757 665-4110
Parksley *(G-10262)*

MACHINERY: Photographic Reproduction

Automated Signature Technology........F....... 703 397-0910
Sterling *(G-13356)*

MACHINERY: Plastic Working

Coperion Corporation........................G...... 276 227-7070
Wytheville *(G-15883)*

Coperion Corporation........................D...... 276 228-7717
Wytheville *(G-15884)*

West Engineering Company Inc ....E...... 804 798-3966
Ashland *(G-1508)*

MACHINERY: Pottery Making

Kiln Doctor Inc ....G...... 540 636-6016
Front Royal *(G-5540)*

MACHINERY: Printing Presses

Masa Corporation of Virginia ....G...... 757 855-3013
Norfolk *(G-9634)*

R G Engineering Inc ....F...... 757 463-3045
Virginia Beach *(G-14753)*

MACHINERY: Recycling

Dallas-Katec Incorporated ....G...... 757 428-8822
Norfolk *(G-9515)*

Sterling Blower Company ....D...... 434 316-5310
Forest *(G-5096)*

MACHINERY: Road Construction & Maintenance

Archer Construction ....G...... 276 637-6905
Max Meadows *(G-8365)*

Imco Inc ....E...... 434 299-5919
Monroe *(G-8992)*

MACHINERY: Robots, Molding & Forming Plastics

Mr Robot Inc ....G...... 804 426-3394
North Chesterfield *(G-9934)*

MACHINERY: Semiconductor Manufacturing

Applied Materials Inc ....G...... 540 583-0466
Dumfries *(G-4235)*

Diversified Vacuum Corp ....G...... 757 538-1170
Suffolk *(G-13698)*

MACHINERY: Service Industry, NEC

Advantage Systems...........................G...... 703 370-4500
Alexandria *(G-119)*

Bissell ....G...... 703 827-5769
Mc Lean *(G-8399)*

Camelot ....G...... 434 978-1049
Charlottesville *(G-2602)*

D Atwood ....G...... 703 508-5080
Gwynn *(G-6045)*

Ecolochem Inc ....D...... 804 327-6846
North Chesterfield *(G-10019)*

Robert E Horne................................G...... 804 920-1847
Disputanta *(G-4113)*

Tavern On Main LLC ....E...... 276 328-2208
Wise *(G-15635)*

MACHINERY: Specialty

Autogrind Products ....G...... 703 490-7061
Woodbridge *(G-15651)*

Eco Technologies ....G...... 757 513-4870
Virginia Beach *(G-14430)*

Ecolochem International Inc ....G...... 757 855-9000
Norfolk *(G-9539)*

Spring Grove Inc ....G...... 540 721-1502
Moneta *(G-8981)*

Wintek Corporation ....G...... 973 252-8200
Goodview *(G-5897)*

MACHINERY: Textile

Abstruse Technical Services ....G...... 540 489-8940
Ferrum *(G-4966)*

Atlantic Metal Products Inc ....E...... 804 758-4915
Topping *(G-13885)*

MSP Group LLC ....G...... 757 855-5416
Norfolk *(G-9650)*

Smart Machine Technologies Inc ....D...... 276 632-9853
Ridgeway *(G-11853)*

Traditionl Scrnprntg & Monogrm..........G...... 276 935-7110
Grundy *(G-6042)*

MACHINERY: Tobacco Prdts

Garbuio Inc ....G...... 804 279-0020
Richmond *(G-11214)*

Hauni Richmond Inc ....C...... 804 222-5259
Richmond *(G-11234)*

Hmb Inc ....D...... 540 967-1060
Louisa *(G-7556)*

Mactavish Machine Mfg Co ....G...... 804 264-6109
North Chesterfield *(G-9916)*

Product Engineered Systems ....G...... 804 794-3586
Midlothian *(G-8883)*

Superior Garniture Components ....G...... 804 769-4319
King William *(G-7131)*

MACHINERY: Voting

International Roll-Call Corp ....E...... 804 730-9600
Mechanicsville *(G-8642)*

MACHINERY: Wire Drawing

Newport Cutter Grinding Co Inc ....F...... 757 838-3224
Hampton *(G-6207)*

Tektonics Design Group LLC ....G...... 804 233-5900
Richmond *(G-11786)*

MACHINERY: Woodworking

Eclipse Scroll Saw ....G...... 804 779-3549
New Kent *(G-9131)*

Elk Creek Woodworking Inc ....G...... 434 258-5142
Forest *(G-5070)*

Gbn Machine & Engineering Corp ....E...... 804 448-2033
Woodford *(G-15839)*

Johnson Machinery Sales Inc ....G...... 540 890-8893
Vinton *(G-14174)*

Oaktree Woodworks ....G...... 804 815-4669
Gloucester *(G-5857)*

Rayco Industries Inc ....E...... 804 321-7111
Richmond *(G-11729)*

Vangarde Woodworks Inc ....G...... 804 355-4917
Richmond *(G-11433)*

Williamson Wood ....G...... 434 823-1882
Crozet *(G-3856)*

MACHINES: Forming, Sheet Metal

Mountain Sky LLC.............................G...... 540 389-1197
Salem *(G-12541)*

MACHINISTS' TOOLS: Measuring, Precision

Don Elthon.......................................G...... 703 237-2521
Falls Church *(G-4908)*

Mechanical Development Co Inc ....D...... 540 389-9395
Salem *(G-12535)*

MACHINISTS' TOOLS: Precision

D & S Tool Inc ....G...... 540 731-1463
Radford *(G-10707)*

MAGNESIUM

Magnesium Music ....G...... 703 798-5516
Alexandria *(G-520)*

Opta (usa) Inc ....G...... 843 296-7074
Norfolk *(G-9677)*

MAGNETIC RESONANCE IMAGING DEVICES: Nonmedical

Mid Atlantic Imaging Centers ....G...... 757 223-5059
Newport News *(G-9301)*

MAGNETIC SHIELDS, METAL

Electromagnetic Shielding Inc.............G...... 540 286-3780
Fredericksburg *(G-5426)*

MAGNETS: Ceramic

National Imports LLC.........................G...... 703 637-0019
Vienna *(G-14102)*

MAGNETS: Permanent

Stickers Plus Ltd ....D...... 540 857-3045
Vinton *(G-14184)*

MAIL-ORDER HOUSES: Book & Record Clubs

Signs of The Times Apostolate.............G...... 703 707-0799
Herndon *(G-6807)*

MAIL-ORDER HOUSES: Computer Eqpt & Electronics

Sector 5 Inc....................................G...... 571 348-1005
Alexandria *(G-341)*

MAIL-ORDER HOUSES: Cosmetics & Perfumes

Getintoforex LLC..............................G...... 251 591-2181
Big Stone Gap *(G-1710)*

Knuude LLC.....................................G...... 571 298-1746
Charlottesville *(G-2654)*

MAIL-ORDER HOUSES: Educational Splys & Eqp

Effective Comm Strategies LLC ....G...... 703 403-5345
Clifton *(G-3663)*

Ready Set Sign LLC ....G...... 703 820-0022
Arlington *(G-1143)*

MAIL-ORDER HOUSES: General Merchandise

K & S Pewter Inc ....G...... 540 751-0505
Leesburg *(G-7294)*

MAIL-ORDER HOUSES: Record & Tape, Music Or Video Club

Boomin Bass Global LLC ....F...... 757 776-8668
Virginia Beach *(G-14294)*

MAIL-ORDER HOUSES: Women's Apparel

Fannypants LLC................................G...... 703 953-3099
Chantilly *(G-2420)*

MAILBOX RENTAL & RELATED SVCS

Douglas Stuart LLC ....C...... 571 210-4440
Sterling *(G-13388)*

Speedy Sign-A-Rama USA Inc ....G...... 757 838-7446
Hampton *(G-6242)*

MAILING & MESSENGER SVCS

Best Impressions Inc ....F...... 703 518-1375
Alexandria *(G-421)*

MAILING LIST: Compilers

Jeanette Ann Smith ....G...... 757 622-0182
Norfolk *(G-9602)*

MAILING SVCS, NEC

Advertising Service Agency ....G...... 757 622-3429
Norfolk *(G-9425)*

ASAP Printing & Mailing Co.................G...... 703 836-2288
Alexandria *(G-142)*

Clarks Litho Inc ....F...... 703 961-8888
Chantilly *(G-2393)*

Consolidated Mailing Svcs Inc ....E...... 703 904-1600
Sterling *(G-13374)*

Maclaren Endeavors LLC....................E...... 804 358-3493
Richmond *(G-11279)*

Speedy Sign-A-Rama USA Inc ....G...... 757 838-7446
Hampton *(G-6242)*

US Parcel & Copy Center Inc ....G...... 703 365-7999
Manassas *(G-8007)*

Virginia Printing Services Inc ....F...... 757 838-5500
Hampton *(G-6263)*

MANAGEMENT CONSULTING SVCS: Administrative

Alt Services Inc ....G...... 757 806-1341
Hampton (G-6081)

MANAGEMENT CONSULTING SVCS: Automation & Robotics

Systems Technology VA LLC ....G...... 540 884-1784
Eagle Rock (G-4283)

MANAGEMENT CONSULTING SVCS: Business

Antheon Solutions Inc ....G...... 703 298-1891
Reston (G-10790)
Javatec Inc ....G...... 276 621-4572
Crockett (G-3825)
Salesforce Maps ....G...... 571 388-4990
Charlottesville (G-2871)
Terralign Group Inc ....G...... 571 388-4990
Herndon (G-6825)

MANAGEMENT CONSULTING SVCS: Construction Project

Lawson and Son Cnstr LLC ....G...... 478 258-2478
Yorktown (G-15973)
Pohick Creek LLC ....G...... 202 888-2034
Springfield (G-13071)

MANAGEMENT CONSULTING SVCS: Foreign Trade

International Trade & Tech Inc ....G...... 703 929-0595
Midland (G-8758)

MANAGEMENT CONSULTING SVCS: Industrial

Case-Polytech Inc ....G...... 804 752-3500
Ashland (G-1386)

MANAGEMENT CONSULTING SVCS: Industrial & Labor

Alacran ....G...... 540 629-6095
Dublin (G-4147)

MANAGEMENT CONSULTING SVCS: Industry Specialist

Access Intelligence LLC ....G...... 202 296-2814
Arlington (G-837)
Decotec Inc ....G...... 434 589-0881
Kents Store (G-7038)
South Bay Industries Inc ....G...... 757 489-9344
Norfolk (G-9731)

MANAGEMENT CONSULTING SVCS: Information Systems

Capitol Idea Technology Inc ....G...... 571 233-1949
Woodbridge (G-15667)
Swami Shriji LLC ....G...... 804 322-9644
North Chesterfield (G-9994)
Synteras LLC ....G...... 703 766-6222
Herndon (G-6820)

MANAGEMENT CONSULTING SVCS: Management Engineering

Diamondefense LLC ....F....... 571 321-2012
Annandale (G-743)
Triquetra Phoenix LLC ....G...... 571 265-6044
Annandale (G-790)

MANAGEMENT CONSULTING SVCS: Manufacturing

Insource Sftwr Solutions Inc ....E....... 804 378-8981
North Chesterfield (G-9897)

MANAGEMENT CONSULTING SVCS: Real Estate

Frost Property Solutions LLC ....G...... 804 571-2147
Mechanicsville (G-8625)

MANAGEMENT CONSULTING SVCS: Training & Development

Dbs Productions LLC ....G...... 434 293-5502
Charlottesville (G-2778)
Leidos Inc ....C...... 703 676-7451
Fort Belvoir (G-5116)
Warrior Trail Consulting LLC ....G...... 703 349-1967
Fairfax (G-4580)

MANAGEMENT CONSULTING SVCS: Transportation

Mill Mountain Capital LLC ....G...... 540 529-7163
Roanoke (G-11966)

MANAGEMENT SERVICES

Aery Aviation LLC ....F....... 757 271-1600
Newport News (G-9160)
Alt Services Inc ....G...... 757 806-1341
Hampton (G-6081)
Boeing Company ....C...... 703 465-3500
Arlington (G-888)
Ctrl-Pad Inc ....G...... 757 216-9170
Norfolk (G-9510)
Dominion Energy Inc ....D...... 804 771-3000
Richmond (G-11187)
Drs Leonardo Inc ....C...... 703 416-8000
Arlington (G-944)
Insignia Technology Svcs LLC ....D...... 757 591-2111
Ashburn (G-1296)
Jackson Enterprises Inc ....G...... 703 527-1118
Arlington (G-1013)
Luck Stone Corporation ....D...... 804 784-6300
Manakin Sabot (G-7901)
Synaptein Solutions Inc ....F....... 703 209-2350
Mc Lean (G-8562)

MANAGEMENT SVCS, FACILITIES SUPPORT: Environ Remediation

NM Mechanic Road Service LLC ....G...... 571 237-4810
Woodbridge (G-15761)

MANAGEMENT SVCS: Business

Life Management Company ....G...... 434 296-9762
Troy (G-13932)

MANAGEMENT SVCS: Construction

Spigner Structural & Miscellan ....E....... 703 625-7572
Berryville (G-1692)

MANAGEMENT SVCS: Financial, Business

Miracle Systems LLC ....C...... 571 431-6397
Arlington (G-1066)

MANHOLES COVERS: Concrete

Concrete Specialties Inc ....G...... 540 982-0777
Roanoke (G-12069)

MANICURE PREPARATIONS

Heavenly Hands & Feet Inc ....G...... 757 621-3938
Virginia Beach (G-14515)
Pinky & Face Inc ....G...... 703 478-2708
Herndon (G-6773)

MANIFOLDS: Pipe, Fabricated From Purchased Pipe

Riggins Company LLC ....D...... 757 826-0525
Hampton (G-6228)

MANNEQUINS

Vertexusa LLC ....G...... 213 294-3072
Sterling (G-13548)
Vertexusa LLC ....G...... 213 294-9072
Herndon (G-6837)

MANUFACTURING INDUSTRIES, NEC

20-X Industries LLC ....G...... 540 922-0005
Pembroke (G-10280)
A Frame Digital ....G...... 571 308-0147
Vienna (G-14002)
A J Industries ....G...... 757 871-4109
Hampton (G-6066)

Accuracy Gear LLC ....G...... 540 230-0257
Hiwassee (G-6908)
Ace Industries Virginia LLC ....G...... 757 292-3321
Radford (G-10702)
Additive Mfg Exch Amex LLC ....G...... 703 971-3174
Alexandria (G-403)
Advanced Mfg Restructuring LLC ....G...... 540 667-5010
Winchester (G-15525)
Aero Design & Mfg Co In ....G...... 218 722-1927
Mc Lean (G-8389)
Afg Industries - VA ....G...... 276 619-6000
Abingdon (G-8)
Agility Inc ....E....... 423 383-0962
Bristol (G-2003)
Alicesa Foster Graves LLC ....G...... 804 658-0092
Richmond (G-11098)
Allen Industries Intl LLC ....G...... 540 797-5230
Bedford (G-1618)
Allermore Industries Inc ....G...... 703 537-1346
Springfield (G-12941)
Alta Industries LLC ....G...... 703 969-0999
Brambleton (G-1925)
Amana U S A Incorporated ....G...... 703 821-7501
Falls Church (G-4745)
Amato Industries ....G...... 703 534-1400
Fairfax (G-4406)
AMC Industries Inc ....G...... 410 320-5037
Great Falls (G-5936)
American Manufacturing Co Inc ....G...... 703 361-2210
Gainesville (G-5569)
Apex Industries Inc ....G...... 540 992-5300
Daleville (G-3939)
Apex Tree Industries ....G...... 540 915-6489
Roanoke (G-12033)
Apogee Power Usa LLC ....F....... 318 572-8967
Fredericksburg (G-5399)
Applied Manufacturing Tech ....G...... 434 942-1047
Thaxton (G-13841)
Aromatic Spice Blends LLC ....G...... 703 477-6865
Sterling (G-13350)
Arroman Industries Corp ....G...... 804 317-4737
Hopewell (G-6918)
Arrow Mfg LLC ....G...... 757 635-6889
Virginia Beach (G-14241)
Aspen Industries LLC ....G...... 540 234-0413
Weyers Cave (G-15166)
Asw Aluminum ....G...... 434 476-7557
Halifax (G-6048)
Automotors Industries Inc ....G...... 703 459-8930
Woodbridge (G-15652)
B&B Industries LLC ....G...... 703 855-2142
Alexandria (G-420)
Backwoods Fabrications LLC ....G...... 804 448-2901
Ruther Glen (G-12450)
Bally Technologies Inc ....G...... 917 415-5649
Chantilly (G-2526)
Barnes Industries Inc ....G...... 804 389-1981
Sandy Hook (G-12643)
Battlefield Industries LLC ....G...... 703 995-4822
Burke (G-2183)
Batts Industries LLC ....G...... 202 669-6015
Herndon (G-6620)
Bea Maurer ....G...... 540 377-5025
Fairfield (G-4729)
Bear-Kat Manufacturing LLC ....G...... 800 442-9700
Manassas (G-8036)
BEC ....G...... 804 330-2500
North Chesterfield (G-9829)
Bethune Industries LLC ....G...... 407 579-1308
Arlington (G-882)
Bg Industries Inc ....G...... 434 369-2128
Lynchburg (G-7653)
Birth Right Industries LLC ....G...... 703 590-6971
Woodbridge (G-15658)
Bkc Industries Inc ....G...... 856 694-9400
Manassas (G-8040)
Black Gold Industries LLC ....G...... 757 768-4674
Newport News (G-9181)
Blind Industries ....G...... 703 390-9221
Reston (G-10809)
Blonde Industries LLC ....G...... 540 667-8192
Stephenson (G-13331)
Bobblehouse LLC ....G...... 703 582-6797
Ashburn (G-1250)
Bookmarks By Bulger ....G...... 757 362-6841
Virginia Beach (G-14293)
Bosco Industries ....G...... 540 671-8053
Front Royal (G-5525)
Brickhouse Industries LLC ....G...... 757 880-7249
Hayes (G-6397)

PRODUCT

Burgholzer Manufacturing Lc ....G.. 540 667-8612
Winchester (G-15398)

C&M Industries Inc ....G.. 757 626-1141
Norfolk (G-9471)

Cajo Industries Inc ....G.. 804 829-6854
Charles City (G-2571)

Cardinal Mfg ....G.. 540 779-7790
Bedford (G-1630)

Carmel Tctcal Sltons Group LLC ....G.. 804 943-6121
Colonial Heights (G-3731)

Cataldo Industries LLC ....F.. 757 422-0518
Virginia Beach (G-14323)

Cathay Industries Inc ....G.. 224 629-4210
Hiwassee (G-6911)

CDK Industries LLC ....G.. 804 551-3085
North Chesterfield (G-9841)

Cephas Industries Inc ....G.. 804 641-1824
Chester (G-3393)

Chaz & Reetas Creations ....G.. 804 248-4933
North Chesterfield (G-9842)

Chesapeake Manufacturing Inc ....G.. 804 716-2035
Richmond (G-11528)

Cjc Industries Inc ....G.. 757 227-6767
Virginia Beach (G-14340)

Clear Water Manufacturing ....G.. 434 582-9511
Madison Heights (G-7869)

Clearview Industries LLC ....G.. 540 312-0899
Willis (G-15358)

CM Harris Industries LLC ....G.. 276 632-8438
Martinsville (G-8275)

Cobweb Industries LLC ....G.. 703 834-1000
Herndon (G-6643)

Cochran Inds Inc - Wytheville ....G.. 276 498-3836
Oakwood (G-10165)

Copper and Oak Cft Spirits LLC ....G.. 309 255-2001
Portsmouth (G-10409)

Cottage Industries Exposition ....G.. 703 834-0055
Herndon (G-6649)

Creative Permutations LLC ....G.. 703 628-3799
Fairfax Station (G-4704)

Crown Supreme Industries LLC ....G.. 703 729-1482
Ashburn (G-1263)

Crypto Industries LLC ....G.. 703 729-5059
Ashburn (G-1264)

CSM Industries Inc ....G.. 410 818-3262
Arlington (G-922)

Curry Industries LLC ....G.. 757 251-7559
Hampton (G-6125)

Custom Stage Curtain Fbrctrs ....G.. 804 264-3700
Richmond (G-11553)

Cva Industrial Products Inc ....G.. 434 985-1870
Stanardsville (G-13218)

Cyril Edward Gropen ....G.. 434 227-9039
Charlottesville (G-2614)

Davis & Davis Industries LLC ....G.. 757 269-1534
Virginia Beach (G-14393)

Davis Minding Manufacture ....G.. 276 321-7137
Wise (G-15621)

Dean Industries Intl LLC ....G.. 703 249-5099
Springfield (G-12990)

Debbie Belt ....G.. 912 856-9476
Richmond (G-11556)

Defazio Industries LLC ....G.. 703 399-1494
Henrico (G-6499)

Delclos Industries LLC ....G.. 540 349-4049
Warrenton (G-14994)

Diggs Industries LLC ....G.. 757 371-3470
Smithfield (G-12711)

Diversified Atmospheric Water ....G.. 757 617-1782
Virginia Beach (G-14406)

Diversified Industries ....G.. 540 992-1900
Troutville (G-13908)

Dominion Ammunition Mfg Inc ....G.. 804 276-2851
North Chesterfield (G-10018)

Dose Guardian LLC ....G.. 804 726-5448
Richmond (G-11565)

Doskocil Mfg Co Inc ....G.. 218 766-2558
Reston (G-10843)

Draculas Tokens LLC ....G.. 717 818-5687
Leesburg (G-7259)

Dragon Defense Mfg ....G.. 804 986-6635
Richmond (G-11190)

Drengr Defense Industries LLC ....G.. 703 552-9987
Vienna (G-14042)

Duke Industries LLC ....G.. 252 404-2344
Chesapeake (G-3078)

Dulcet Industries LLC ....G.. 571 758-3191
Ashburn (G-1273)

Easyloader Manufacturing LLC ....G.. 540 297-2601
Huddleston (G-6953)

Elizur International Inc ....G.. 757 648-8502
Virginia Beach (G-14441)

Ellen Fairchild-Flugel Art LLC ....G.. 540 325-2305
Woodstock (G-15852)

Elliott Mfg ....G.. 804 737-1475
Richmond (G-11573)

Enabled Manufacturing LLC ....G.. 704 491-9414
Blacksburg (G-1735)

Endeavor Consulting Group LLC ....G.. 202 599-7437
Manassas (G-8064)

Erikson Diversified Industries ....G.. 703 216-5482
Fredericksburg (G-5283)

Evolve Custom LLC ....G.. 703 570-5700
Winchester (G-15414)

Excelsia Industries LLC ....G.. 804 347-7626
Midlothian (G-8815)

Excelsior Associates Inc ....G.. 703 255-1596
Vienna (G-14051)

Executive Creations ....G.. 757 351-1310
Virginia Beach (G-14456)

EZ Cut Bandmills ....G.. 540 931-2410
Pearisburg (G-10274)

Fairlead Precision Mfg ....G.. 757 606-2033
Portsmouth (G-10430)

Farlow Industries ....G.. 434 836-4596
Danville (G-3994)

Febrocom LLC ....G.. 703 349-6316
Ashburn (G-1279)

Fieldtech Industries LLC ....G.. 757 286-1503
Virginia Beach (G-14463)

Fisher Knives Inc ....G.. 434 242-3866
Earlysville (G-4290)

Flip Flop Fabrication LLC ....G.. 540 820-5959
Rockingham (G-12253)

Flzhi Technologies LLC ....G.. 214 616-7756
Arlington (G-972)

Fourty4industries LLC ....G.. 703 266-0525
Clifton (G-3665)

Frog Industries LLC ....G.. 757 995-2359
Norfolk (G-9560)

Ft Industries LLC ....G.. 757 495-0510
Virginia Beach (G-14476)

Fuhgiddabowdit Industries ....G.. 757 598-0331
Poquoson (G-10371)

Garret Industries LLC ....G.. 804 795-1650
Henrico (G-6516)

Gavial Engineering and Mfg ....G.. 804 627-1437
Charles City (G-2575)

General Medical Mfg Co ....G.. 804 254-2737
Richmond (G-11216)

Ghek Industries LLC ....G.. 804 955-0710
Henrico (G-6517)

Glanville Industries LLC ....G.. 757 513-2700
Carrollton (G-2243)

Glenna Jean Mfg Co ....G.. 804 783-1490
Richmond (G-11602)

GMA Industries ....G.. 703 538-5100
Falls Church (G-4915)

Gogo Industries Inc ....G.. 925 708-7804
Charlottesville (G-2805)

Gormanlee Industries LLC ....G.. 703 448-1948
Mc Lean (G-8452)

Gourmet Manufacturing Inc ....G.. 276 638-2367
Martinsville (G-8291)

Grayer Industries LLC ....G.. 703 491-4629
Woodbridge (G-15713)

Graymatter Industries LLC ....G.. 276 429-2396
Glade Spring (G-5677)

Green Prana Industries Inc ....G.. 410 790-3011
Buckingham (G-2133)

Gsa Service Company ....G.. 703 742-6818
Sterling (G-13416)

GSE Industries LLC ....G.. 832 633-9864
Moneta (G-8963)

Gutter-Stuff Industries VA LLC ....G.. 540 982-1115
Roanoke (G-12099)

Hammond United Industries LLC ....G.. 571 306-9003
Fredericksburg (G-5296)

Hanke Industries LLC ....G.. 601 665-2147
Alexandria (G-475)

Hartung Screen Printing LLC ....G.. 412 979-7847
Ruckersville (G-12403)

Hcg Industries LLC ....G.. 540 291-2674
Natural Bridge (G-9106)

Helltown Industries LLC ....G.. 571 312-4073
Arlington (G-990)

Hermitage Industries Co Inc ....G.. 757 638-4551
Chesapeake (G-3134)

Hocl Inc ....G.. 877 435-4625
Chantilly (G-2436)

Hol Industries LLC ....G.. 703 835-5476
Alexandria (G-479)

Iconix Industries Inc ....G.. 703 489-0278
Chantilly (G-2538)

Ideagirl Industries LLC ....G.. 240 672-8333
Alexandria (G-233)

Indigenous Industries LLC ....G.. 540 847-9851
Fredericksburg (G-5441)

Industries 247 LLC ....G.. 703 741-0151
Arlington (G-1002)

Industries Massive ....G.. 703 347-6074
Alexandria (G-485)

Innovative Industries LLC ....G.. 540 317-1733
Culpeper (G-3895)

Ipac Industries LLC ....G.. 703 362-9090
Fairfax (G-4639)

Isobaric Strategies Inc ....G.. 757 277-2858
Virginia Beach (G-14554)

Ivy Manufacturing LLC ....G.. 434 249-0134
Charlottesville (G-2649)

Jkm Industries LLC ....G.. 703 599-3112
Alexandria (G-498)

Joint Manufacturing Force LLC ....G.. 910 364-8580
Alexandria (G-499)

JPF Industriesinc ....G.. 703 451-0203
Springfield (G-13030)

Juggernaut Industries ....G.. 703 686-0191
Manassas (G-8090)

K and M Industries LLC ....G.. 757 328-0227
Newport News (G-9271)

K2 Industries LLC ....G.. 757 754-5430
Virginia Beach (G-14579)

Kates Creations ....G.. 757 721-7062
Virginia Beach (G-14580)

Kelkase Inc ....G.. 703 670-9443
Fredericksburg (G-5447)

Keller Industries LLC ....G.. 573 452-4932
Fredericksburg (G-5308)

Kii Industries LLC ....G.. 804 232-5791
Richmond (G-11049)

King of Pops Richmond LLC ....G.. 804 475-9026
Richmond (G-11644)

Klearwall Industries ....G.. 203 689-5404
Moneta (G-8968)

Kohler Industries Inc ....G.. 757 301-3233
Virginia Beach (G-14592)

Korea Arspc Inds Fort Wrth Inc ....G.. 703 883-2012
Vienna (G-14080)

Krug Industries Inc ....G.. 714 656-5316
Arlington (G-1024)

L C Pembroke Manufacturing ....G.. 757 723-3435
Hampton (G-6182)

Landmark Industries LLC ....G.. 757 233-7291
Virginia Beach (G-14599)

Lanzara Industries LLC ....G.. 703 759-6959
Great Falls (G-5964)

Lash and Glow By Tess Llc ....G.. 571 732-1080
Herndon (G-6732)

Lbp Manufacturing LLC ....G.. 804 562-6920
Richmond (G-11649)

Legacy Mfg LLC ....G.. 434 841-5331
Altavista (G-634)

Leviton Manufacturing C ....G.. 804 461-8293
Midlothian (G-8848)

Lewis Industries LLC ....G.. 434 203-7920
Danville (G-4012)

Light Grey Industries ....G.. 703 330-1339
Manassas (G-8100)

Lincoln Industries LLC ....G.. 434 509-7191
Lynchburg (G-7757)

Linda M Barnes ....G.. 757 240-7327
Yorktown (G-15976)

Lion-Valley Industries ....G.. 703 630-3123
Quantico (G-10690)

LKM Industries LLC ....G.. 919 601-6661
Williamsburg (G-15271)

Lockhart Manufacturing Inc ....G.. 540 459-8774
Woodstock (G-15857)

Lost Industries LLC ....G.. 434 221-5698
Arrington (G-1230)

Loyal Service Systems ....G.. 703 361-7888
Manassas (G-7971)

M M Silk Flowers ....G.. 757 334-7096
Suffolk (G-13736)

M S Russnak Industries LLC ....G.. 540 848-1450
Spotsylvania (G-12903)

Magnes Industries LLC ....G.. 540 246-6088
Harrisonburg (G-6342)

Mahawara LLC ....G.. 443 949-2602
Dulles (G-4208)

Maker Industries ... G ... 757 560-1692
Chesapeake *(G-3193)*
Manufacturing Mystique Inc ... G ... 703 719-0943
Alexandria *(G-521)*
Manufacturing Techniques ... G ... 804 436-9000
Kilmarnock *(G-7072)*
Marvelous Green LLC ... G ... 540 577-6967
Pulaski *(G-10642)*
Massone Industries Inc ... G ... 540 825-7339
Culpeper *(G-3908)*
Matt and Molly Trades LLC ... G ... 703 585-1858
Gordonsville *(G-5915)*
Maverick Fabrication ... G ... 321 210-9004
Newport News *(G-9297)*
Mech Warrior Industries LLC ... G ... 703 670-5788
Dumfries *(G-4252)*
Medical Action Industries Inc ... G ... 757 566-3510
Toano *(G-13870)*
Meld Manufacturing Corporation ... G ... 540 951-3980
Christiansburg *(G-3606)*
Merica Tactical Industries LLC ... G ... 804 516-0435
Mechanicsville *(G-8661)*
Meyer and Meyer Industries Inc ... G ... 757 564-6157
Williamsburg *(G-15276)*
Mfgs Inc ... G ... 844 267-9266
Mc Lean *(G-8500)*
Mg Industries ... G ... 804 743-0661
North Chesterfield *(G-9930)*
Micro Tech Industries Inc ... G ... 703 674-9647
Leesburg *(G-7314)*
Micron Manufacturing ... G ... 703 853-1801
Fairfax *(G-4511)*
Mighty Oak Industries ... G ... 434 426-7249
Forest *(G-5083)*
Mk Industries LLC ... G ... 949 525-0778
Springfield *(G-13051)*
Monarch Manufacturing Works ... G ... 757 640-3727
Norfolk *(G-9648)*
Moon Industries LLC ... G ... 703 878-2428
Woodbridge *(G-15749)*
Mountain Creek Industries LLC ... G ... 804 432-1601
Meherrin *(G-8706)*
Mr Industries LLC ... G ... 484 838-9154
King George *(G-7103)*
Myrmidon Industries Inc ... G ... 540 273-6414
Fredericksburg *(G-5460)*
Network Industries ... G ... 757 435-6163
Virginia Beach *(G-14678)*
Newport Industries Ltd ... G ... 440 208-3322
Norfolk *(G-9663)*
NRJ Industries LLC ... G ... 703 707-0368
Chantilly *(G-2474)*
Omni Technology and Mfg LLC ... G ... 703 929-8000
Hamilton *(G-6062)*
Oncor Industries Inc ... G ... 434 985-3434
Stanardsville *(G-13225)*
Onyx Industries LLC ... G ... 425 269-7181
Gainesville *(G-5606)*
Opsec Industries LLC ... G ... 571 426-0626
Springfield *(G-13062)*
Osmon Industries ... G ... 757 564-3088
Williamsburg *(G-15289)*
Otto Industries LLC ... G ... 703 256-2684
Springfield *(G-13063)*
PA Industries Inc ... G ... 434 845-0813
Amherst *(G-703)*
Packed Head LLC ... G ... 804 677-3603
Chesterfield *(G-3516)*
Paradym Industries Inc ... G ... 703 424-6930
South Riding *(G-12869)*
Paramount Specialty Metals LLC ... G ... 980 721-3958
Warrenton *(G-15042)*
Parker Industries Virginia Inc ... G ... 804 254-4140
Richmond *(G-11707)*
Pauls Fan Company ... D ... 276 530-7311
Grundy *(G-6039)*
Peggy Hank Industries LLC ... G ... 434 825-4802
Charlottesville *(G-2843)*
Performance Aviation Mfg Group ... G ... 757 766-1150
Williamsburg *(G-15295)*
Pif Industries LLC ... G ... 804 677-2945
Richmond *(G-11325)*
Pinder Industries LLC ... G ... 240 200-0703
Springfield *(G-13067)*
Pioneer Industries LLC ... G ... 757 432-8412
Chesapeake *(G-3240)*
Pirooz Manufacturing LLC ... G ... 703 281-4244
Vienna *(G-14111)*
Pk Industries LLC ... G ... 540 589-2341
Roanoke *(G-11986)*
Polyiscynurate Insul Mfrs Assn ... G ... 703 224-2289
Arlington *(G-1115)*
Pondeca Industries Inc ... G ... 703 599-4375
Lorton *(G-7521)*
Posh Pixie LLC ... G ... 757 794-4949
Virginia Beach *(G-14730)*
Potomac Industries ... G ... 540 940-7288
Fredericksburg *(G-5470)*
Powell Manufacturing Co LLC ... G ... 804 677-5728
Petersburg *(G-10335)*
Power Clean Industries LLC ... G ... 804 372-6838
Powhatan *(G-10567)*
PPG Industries Inc ... G ... 540 563-2118
Roanoke *(G-12149)*
Precision Schematics LLC ... G ... 612 296-2286
Woodbridge *(G-15779)*
Prism Industries LLC ... G ... 804 916-0074
Chesterfield *(G-3518)*
Privateer Industries LLC ... G ... 757 857-7273
Norfolk *(G-9696)*
Quest Industries LLC ... G ... 804 862-8481
North Dinwiddie *(G-10062)*
Quickie Manufacturing Corp ... G ... 856 829-7900
Winchester *(G-15576)*
Radavert Industries Inc ... G ... 703 425-6777
Burke *(G-2201)*
Rave On Industries LLC ... G ... 804 308-0898
Henrico *(G-6555)*
RC Industries LLC ... G ... 757 839-5577
Chesapeake *(G-3260)*
Reaper Precision LLC ... G ... 540 841-0028
King George *(G-7107)*
Reid Industries LLC ... G ... 703 920-6199
Arlington *(G-1146)*
Reid Industries LLC ... G ... 703 786-6307
Woodbridge *(G-15794)*
Richard Rhea Industries LLC ... G ... 804 320-6575
North Chesterfield *(G-9960)*
Rightway Industries Ltd ... G ... 757 435-8889
Virginia Beach *(G-14774)*
Ring Fire Manufacturing LLC ... G ... 804 617-9288
Henrico *(G-6559)*
Rock Industries LLC ... G ... 703 637-8500
Falls Church *(G-4868)*
Rockin Rack LLC ... G ... 540 359-2264
Bealeton *(G-1606)*
Rogue Cltivation Solutions LLC ... G ... 540 955-8641
Berryville *(G-1687)*
Rose Welding Inc ... G ... 540 312-0138
New Castle *(G-9123)*
Rough Industries LLC ... G ... 215 514-4144
Alexandria *(G-330)*
Rrb Industries Inc ... G ... 804 517-2014
Virginia Beach *(G-14784)*
Rsi LLC ... G ... 908 752-1496
Falls Church *(G-4869)*
RSR Industries LLC ... G ... 703 408-8048
Alexandria *(G-575)*
Rugger Industries LLC ... G ... 540 450-7281
Winchester *(G-15472)*
Russell Frye LLC ... G ... 276 646-1293
Chilhowie *(G-3559)*
Rwh Industries Inc ... G ... 540 736-8007
Fredericksburg *(G-5357)*
S & J Industries LLC ... G ... 757 810-8399
Gloucester *(G-5861)*
S&D Industries LLC ... G ... 901 208-5036
Norfolk *(G-9713)*
S&T Industries LLC ... G ... 276 686-4842
Crockett *(G-3826)*
Safety 1 Industries LLC ... G ... 540 635-4673
Front Royal *(G-5552)*
Sak Industries LLC ... G ... 202 701-0071
Vienna *(G-14120)*
Salty Sawyer LLC ... G ... 757 274-1765
Surry *(G-13800)*
Sauder Manufacturing Co ... G ... 434 372-4151
Chase City *(G-2916)*
Savage Thrust Industries LLC ... G ... 702 405-1045
Manassas *(G-8150)*
Sbk Inc ... G ... 540 427-5029
Roanoke *(G-12176)*
Scrub Skinz LLC ... G ... 804 338-1350
Glen Allen *(G-5793)*
SDS Industries ... G ... 207 266-9448
Alexandria *(G-340)*
Second Samuel Industries Inc ... G ... 703 715-2295
Fairfax *(G-4553)*
Shepherd Enterprises Anchor Rm ... G ... 757 641-7829
Portsmouth *(G-10479)*
Sherman Industries LLC ... G ... 240 888-1134
Alexandria *(G-345)*
SM Industries LLC ... G ... 757 966-2343
Chesapeake *(G-3296)*
Smith Mountain Industries Ltd ... G ... 540 576-3117
Martinsville *(G-8330)*
Snakeclamp Products LLC ... G ... 903 265-8001
Christiansburg *(G-3609)*
Social Dynamics Industries ... G ... 703 441-2869
Dumfries *(G-4256)*
Solvent Industries Inc ... G ... 540 760-8611
Fredericksburg *(G-5365)*
Southcoast Welding & Mfg LLC ... G ... 757 574-0090
Chesapeake *(G-3301)*
Southpaw Mechanical LLC ... G ... 540 577-6967
Pulaski *(G-10646)*
Spartan Inds Martinsville ... G ... 276 632-3033
Martinsville *(G-8336)*
Spartancore Industries ... G ... 540 322-7563
Fredericksburg *(G-5486)*
Sphinx Industries Inc ... G ... 804 279-8894
North Chesterfield *(G-9987)*
Spunkysales LLC ... G ... 727 492-1636
Springfield *(G-13094)*
STA-Fit Industries LLC ... G ... 540 308-8215
Ruckersville *(G-12414)*
Staunton VA ... G ... 651 765-6778
Verona *(G-13996)*
Stick Industries LLC ... G ... 757 725-0436
Troutville *(G-13917)*
Storge Industries LLC ... G ... 571 414-1413
Fort Belvoir *(G-5118)*
Strauch Fiber Equipment C ... G ... 540 864-8869
New Castle *(G-9124)*
Strike Force Manufacturing Inc ... G ... 804 731-0831
North Prince George *(G-10092)*
Sun Manufacturing LLC ... G ... 434 942-4626
Forest *(G-5099)*
Sundigger Industries LLC ... G ... 703 360-4139
Alexandria *(G-590)*
Sunglow Industries Inc ... G ... 703 870-9918
Newport News *(G-9350)*
Sunny Slope LLC ... G ... 434 384-8994
Lynchburg *(G-7816)*
Supernal Industries LLC ... G ... 804 380-1742
Chesapeake *(G-3316)*
Supernova Industries Inc ... G ... 703 731-2987
Chantilly *(G-2505)*
Tetelestai Industries LLC ... G ... 804 596-5232
Henrico *(G-6580)*
Thumbelinas ... G ... 703 448-8043
Vienna *(G-14142)*
Tippers LLC ... G ... 703 391-7232
Reston *(G-10974)*
Tmp Industries LLC ... G ... 540 761-0435
Roanoke *(G-12206)*
TN Cor Industries Incorporated ... G ... 703 682-2001
Alexandria *(G-366)*
Todd Industries ... G ... 571 275-2782
Leesburg *(G-7364)*
Torishima Pump Mfg Co Ltd ... G ... 866 374-1130
North Chesterfield *(G-10027)*
Triax Music Industries ... G ... 757 839-1215
Chesapeake *(G-3351)*
Triple Threat Industries LLC ... G ... 703 413-7919
Arlington *(G-1197)*
Tweedle Tees Printing LLC ... G ... 540 569-6927
Staunton *(G-13305)*
V&M Industries Inc ... G ... 757 319-9415
Suffolk *(G-13775)*
V-Lite USA LLC ... G ... 808 264-3785
Virginia Beach *(G-14905)*
Vastec USA ... G ... 302 682-8255
Stephens City *(G-13327)*
Vella Mac Industries Inc ... F ... 757 724-0026
Norfolk *(G-9780)*
Velocity LLC ... G ... 703 304-6152
Reston *(G-10982)*
Veteran Customs LLC ... G ... 540 786-2157
Spotsylvania *(G-12920)*
Veteran Force Industries LLC ... G ... 912 492-5800
Alexandria *(G-373)*
Veteran Made LLC ... G ... 703 328-2570
Leesburg *(G-7370)*
Vortex Industries LLC ... G ... 703 732-5458
Fairfax *(G-4694)*
Watkins Industries LLC ... G ... 540 371-5007
Manakin Sabot *(G-7907)*
Wells Custom Mfg LLC ... G ... 703 623-1396
Warrenton *(G-15059)*

Wenger Manufacturing ....G..... 703 878-6946
Woodbridge *(G-15831)*
Wheeler Industries LLC ....G..... 540 387-2204
Salem *(G-12581)*
Whicker Home Industries LLC ....G..... 703 675-7642
Colonial Beach *(G-3730)*
Willie Slick Industries ....G..... 843 310-4669
Virginia Beach *(G-14938)*
Wilson Industries & Svcs Un ....G..... 703 472-6392
Fairfax *(G-4582)*
Wilson Pipe & Fabrication LLC ....G..... 757 468-1374
Virginia Beach *(G-14939)*
Winn Industries LLC ....G..... 571 334-2676
Lignum *(G-7426)*
Wolfsbane Industries LLC ....G..... 703 972-5072
Purcellville *(G-10687)*
Wrap Pack Industries Inc ....G..... 804 897-1351
Midlothian *(G-8923)*
Wright Machine & Manufacturing ....G..... 276 688-2391
Bland *(G-1838)*
Wyfi Industries LLC ....G..... 703 333-2059
Springfield *(G-13109)*
X-Stand Treestand Company LLC ...G..... 540 877-2769
Winchester *(G-15520)*
Xlusion CL Fulfillment LLC ....G..... 571 316-9391
Stephens City *(G-13330)*
Xp Manufacturing LLC ....G..... 804 510-3747
Richmond *(G-11836)*
Xp Manufacturing LLC ....G..... 804 833-1411
North Chesterfield *(G-10015)*
Xplor Industries ....G..... 804 306-6621
Richmond *(G-11460)*
York River Glassworks LLC ....G..... 804 815-0492
Gloucester *(G-5870)*
Zakufdm LLC ....G..... 330 338-0930
Fredericksburg *(G-5393)*
Zhe Industries LLC ....G..... 757 759-5466
Virginia Beach *(G-14961)*
Zhe Industries LLC ....G..... 757 759-5466
Virginia Beach *(G-14962)*

MAPS

B J Hart Enterprises Inc ....G..... 434 575-7538
South Boston *(G-12750)*
Discovery Map ....G..... 703 346-7166
Alexandria *(G-190)*

MARBLE BOARD

Global Code Usa Inc ....G..... 908 764-5818
Manassas *(G-7947)*

MARBLE, BUILDING: Cut & Shaped

All Affairs Transportation LLC ....G..... 757 342-2474
Newport News *(G-9162)*
General Marble & Granite Co ....G..... 804 353-2761
Richmond *(G-11215)*
John Wills Studios Inc ....F..... 757 468-0260
Virginia Beach *(G-14572)*
Sky Marble & Granite Inc ....F..... 571 926-8085
Sterling *(G-13510)*
Stone Dynamics Inc ....E..... 276 638-7755
Martinsville *(G-8338)*
Winn Stone Products Inc ....G..... 757 465-5363
Portsmouth *(G-10505)*

MARINAS

Waldens Marina Inc ....G..... 804 776-9440
Deltaville *(G-4087)*

MARINE ENGINE REPAIR SVCS

Jonda Enterprise Inc ....G..... 757 559-5793
Norfolk *(G-9606)*

MARINE HARDWARE

Jack Clamp Sales Co Inc ....G..... 757 827-6704
Hampton *(G-6177)*
Malpass Construction Co Inc ....G..... 757 543-3541
Chesapeake *(G-3195)*
Premier Manufacturing Inc ....E..... 757 967-9959
Portsmouth *(G-10472)*

MARINE RELATED EQPT

Clean Marine Electronics Inc ....G..... 703 847-5142
Falls Church *(G-4775)*
Electronic Devices Inc ....G..... 757 421-2968
Chesapeake *(G-3085)*

John Demasco *(G-2652)* ....G..... 434 977-4214
Charlottesville *(G-2652)*
Virginia Wave Inc ....G..... 804 693-4278
Gloucester *(G-5865)*

MARINE SPLY DEALERS

Custom Yacht Service Inc ....F..... 804 438-5563
Dutton *(G-4271)*
K E Marine ....G..... 757 787-1313
Accomac *(G-72)*
Waldens Marina Inc ....G..... 804 776-9440
Deltaville *(G-4087)*

MARKETS: Meat & fish

Captain Faunce Seafood Inc ....E..... 804 493-8690
Montross *(G-9025)*
Chesapeake Bay Packing LLC ....E..... 757 244-8440
Newport News *(G-9199)*
Crabill Slaughterhouse Inc ....G..... 540 436-3248
Toms Brook *(G-13882)*
James A Kennedy & Assoc Inc ....G..... 804 241-6836
Powhatan *(G-10553)*

MARKING DEVICES

A & S Global Industries LLC ....G..... 757 773-0119
Suffolk *(G-13663)*
Impression Obsession ....G..... 804 749-3580
Oilville *(G-10180)*
Masa Corporation ....D..... 757 855-3013
Norfolk *(G-9633)*
Michael R Little ....G..... 540 489-4785
Rocky Mount *(G-12339)*
Southern Stamp Incorporated ....G..... 804 359-0531
Richmond *(G-11388)*
Trodat USA ....G..... 540 815-8160
Roanoke *(G-12012)*

MARKING DEVICES: Embossing Seals & Hand Stamps

Acorn Sales Company Inc ....F..... 804 359-0505
Richmond *(G-11081)*
Bynum ....G..... 757 224-1860
Hampton *(G-6100)*
Dister Inc ....E..... 757 857-1946
Norfolk *(G-9525)*
Dister Inc ....E..... 703 207-0201
Fairfax *(G-4439)*
National Marking Products Inc ....E..... 804 266-7691
Richmond *(G-11299)*

MARKING DEVICES: Screens, Textile Printing

Cabin Hill TS LLC ....G..... 540 459-8912
Woodstock *(G-15850)*
County of Hanover ....E..... 804 798-9402
Ashland *(G-1397)*
Tsunami Custom Creations LLC ....G..... 757 913-0960
Virginia Beach *(G-14897)*

MARKING DEVICES: Seal Presses, Notary & Hand

Jonette D Meade ....G..... 804 247-0639
Richmond *(G-11048)*
Kimyaeasonwood ....G..... 757 502-5001
Franklin *(G-5147)*
Wanda Eubanks ....G..... 804 615-7095
Fredericksburg *(G-5500)*

MARKING DEVICES: Stationary Embossers, Personal

Cordial Cricket ....G..... 804 931-8027
Chester *(G-3397)*

MARKING DEVICES: Textile Making Stamps, Hand, Rubber/Metal

Quality Stamp Co ....G..... 757 858-0653
Norfolk *(G-9700)*

MASSAGE MACHINES, ELECTRIC: Barber & Beauty Shops

Bodyzone L L C ....G..... 770 922-0700
Virginia Beach *(G-14292)*

MATERIALS HANDLING EQPT WHOLESALERS

Foley Material Handling Co Inc ....D..... 804 798-1343
Ashland *(G-1419)*
Maxx Material Systems LLC ....E..... 757 637-4026
Hampton *(G-6192)*

MATERNITY WEAR STORES

2 Hearts 1 Dress LLC ....G..... 540 300-0655
Fredericksburg *(G-5166)*
Millers Furs Inc ....G..... 703 772-4593
Mc Lean *(G-8501)*

MATS, MATTING & PADS: Door, Paper, Grass, Reed, Coir, Etc

Nedia Enterprises Inc ....E..... 571 223-0200
Ashburn *(G-1320)*

MATS, MATTING & PADS: Nonwoven

Charles City Timber and Mat ....G..... 804 512-8150
Providence Forge *(G-10621)*
Charles City Timber and Mat ....E..... 804 966-8313
Providence Forge *(G-10622)*

MATS, MATTING & PADS: Varnished Glass

BGF Industries Inc ....D..... 843 537-3172
Danville *(G-3957)*

MATS: Table, Plastic & Textile

Magnifazine LLC ....G..... 248 224-1137
Louisa *(G-7558)*

MEAL DELIVERY PROGRAMS

Antillian Trading Company LLC ....E..... 703 626-6333
Alexandria *(G-414)*

MEAT & MEAT PRDTS WHOLESALERS

Campofrio Fd Group - Amer Inc ....C..... 804 520-7775
South Chesterfield *(G-12798)*
Capital Noodle Inc ....F..... 703 569-3224
Springfield *(G-12973)*

MEAT CUTTING & PACKING

Alleghany Highlands AG Ctr LLC ....G..... 540 474-2422
Monterey *(G-9000)*
Andes Glendon Meat Processing .....G..... 540 896-7798
Timberville *(G-13845)*
Beef Products Incorporated ....E..... 540 985-5914
Roanoke *(G-11886)*
Bobbys Meat Processing ....G..... 276 728-4547
Austinville *(G-1528)*
Calhouns Ham House ....G..... 540 825-8319
Culpeper *(G-3877)*
Campofrio Fd Group - Amer Inc ....C..... 804 520-7775
South Chesterfield *(G-12798)*
Cargill Meat Solutions Corp ....G..... 540 437-8000
Mount Crawford *(G-9052)*
Carolina Cold Storage Inc ....G..... 757 357-0434
Smithfield *(G-12708)*
Crabill Slaughterhouse Inc ....G..... 540 436-3248
Toms Brook *(G-13882)*
Crazy Clover Butcher Shop ....G..... 804 370-5291
Jamaica *(G-7008)*
Donalds Meat Processing LLC ....F..... 540 463-2333
Lexington *(G-7395)*
Farmland Foods Inc ....G..... 757 357-4321
Smithfield *(G-12713)*
Gores Custom Slaughter & Proc .....E..... 540 869-1029
Stephens City *(G-13317)*
Green Valley Meat Processors ....G..... 434 299-5529
Monroe *(G-8990)*
J & P Meat Processing ....F..... 540 721-2765
Wirtz *(G-15615)*
Kraft Heinz Foods Company ....B..... 540 678-0442
Winchester *(G-15437)*
Meat & Wool New Zealand Ltd ....G..... 703 927-4817
Mc Lean *(G-8497)*
Rolling Knoll Farm Inc ....F..... 540 569-6476
Verona *(G-13994)*
Rollins Meat Processing ....G..... 540 672-5177
Orange *(G-10227)*
Russell Meat Packing Inc ....G..... 276 794-7600
Castlewood *(G-2256)*

Schrocks Slaughterhouse................G..... 434 283-5400
  Gladys **(G-5696)**
Smith Valley Meats................................G..... 540 726-3992
  Rich Creek **(G-11008)**
Smithfield Pckgd Mats Sls Corp..........G..... 816 243-2855
  Smithfield **(G-12724)**
Smithfield Pckgd Mats Sls Corp..........G..... 816 243-2855
  Smithfield **(G-12725)**
Smithfield Direct LLC..........................E..... 757 365-3000
  Smithfield **(G-12726)**
Smithfield Foods Inc...........................A..... 757 933-2977
  Newport News **(G-9343)**
Smithfield Foods Inc...........................C..... 910 862-7675
  Smithfield **(G-12727)**
Smithfield Foods Inc...........................G..... 804 834-9941
  Waverly **(G-15088)**
Smithfield Foods Inc............................F..... 757 356-6700
  Smithfield **(G-12729)**
Smithfield Foods Inc...........................E..... 757 357-1598
  Smithfield **(G-12730)**
Smithfield Foods Master Trust.............G..... 757 365-3000
  Smithfield **(G-12731)**
Smithfield Fresh Meats Corp................G..... 513 782-3800
  Smithfield **(G-12732)**
Smithfield Packaged Meats Corp..........G..... 757 357-1798
  Smithfield **(G-12733)**
Smithfield Packaged Meats Corp..........G..... 513 782-3800
  Smithfield **(G-12736)**
Smithfield Packaged Meats Corp..........D..... 757 357-4321
  Norfolk **(G-9726)**
Smithfield Packaged Meats Corp..........G..... 757 357-3131
  Smithfield **(G-12738)**
Southern Packing Corporation.............E..... 757 421-2131
  Chesapeake **(G-3303)**
Valley Meat Processors Inc..................G..... 540 879-9041
  Dayton **(G-4069)**
Washington County Meat Packing........G..... 276 466-3000
  Bristol **(G-2041)**
White Packing Co Inc-VA......................C..... 540 373-9883
  Fredericksburg **(G-5236)**
Williams Meat Processing....................G..... 276 686-4325
  Wytheville **(G-15923)**
Yates Abbattoir..................................G..... 540 778-2123
  Luray **(G-7626)**

MEAT MARKETS

Calhouns Ham House..........................G..... 540 825-8319
  Culpeper **(G-3877)**
Campofrio Fd Group - Amer Inc............C..... 804 520-7775
  South Chesterfield **(G-12798)**
Russell Meat Packing Inc.....................G..... 276 794-7600
  Castlewood **(G-2256)**
Smith Valley Meats.............................G..... 540 726-3992
  Rich Creek **(G-11008)**

MEAT PRDTS: Bacon, Side & Sliced, From Purchased Meat

White Packing Co Inc-VA......................C..... 540 373-9883
  Fredericksburg **(G-5236)**

MEAT PRDTS: Beef Stew, From Purchased Meat

Mary Truman.......................................G..... 469 554-0655
  Freeman **(G-5512)**

MEAT PRDTS: Boxed Beef, From Slaughtered Meat

Smithfield Foods Inc...........................C..... 757 365-3000
  Smithfield **(G-12728)**
Smithfield Support Svcs Corp..............C..... 757 365-3541
  Smithfield **(G-12739)**

MEAT PRDTS: Cured Meats, From Purchased Meat

Williams Incorporated T O....................E..... 757 397-0771
  Portsmouth **(G-10503)**

MEAT PRDTS: Frozen

Shelf Reliance....................................G..... 540 459-2050
  Woodstock **(G-15859)**

MEAT PRDTS: Ham, Roasted, From Purchased Meat

Cha Lua Ngoc Hung.............................G..... 703 531-1868
  Falls Church **(G-4773)**

MEAT PRDTS: Hams & Picnics, From Slaughtered Meat

Smithfield Packaged Meats Corp..........G..... 757 357-3131
  Smithfield **(G-12735)**
Smithfield Packaged Meats Corp..........D..... 757 357-1382
  Smithfield **(G-12737)**

MEAT PRDTS: Pork, From Slaughtered Meat

Smithfield Packaged Meats Corp..........G..... 757 365-3541
  Smithfield **(G-12734)**
Tyson Foods Inc.................................C..... 434 645-7791
  Jetersville **(G-7017)**

MEAT PRDTS: Prepared Beef Prdts From Purchased Beef

Indiana Packers Corporation...............G..... 270 926-2324
  Newport News **(G-9256)**
River Ridge Meats LLC........................G..... 276 773-2191
  Independence **(G-6993)**

MEAT PRDTS: Prepared Pork Prdts, From Purchased Meat

Commonwealth Hams Inc.....................G..... 434 846-4267
  Lynchburg **(G-7681)**
Hams Down Inc..................................G..... 540 374-1405
  Fredericksburg **(G-5193)**
Hams Enterprises LLC.........................G..... 703 988-0992
  Clifton **(G-3670)**

MEAT PRDTS: Sausages, From Purchased Meat

A L Duck Jr Inc....................................F..... 757 562-2387
  Zuni **(G-16011)**
Logan Food Company..........................F..... 703 212-6677
  Alexandria **(G-263)**

MEAT PRDTS: Smoked

Joes Smoked Meat Shack.....................G..... 276 644-4001
  Bristol **(G-1980)**

MEAT PRDTS: Snack Sticks, Incl Jerky, From Purchased Meat

Beef Jerky Outl Nova Jerky LLC...........G..... 703 868-6297
  Warrenton **(G-14981)**
Bobby and Pjs Jerky Shack...................G..... 540 856-2415
  Mount Jackson **(G-9066)**
Buckskin Jhnson Beef Jerky LLC..........G..... 540 303-0324
  Winchester **(G-15395)**
Chinctgue Island Hse Jerky LLC...........G..... 215 353-6393
  Chincoteague **(G-3561)**
Ernies Beef Jerky................................G..... 540 460-4341
  Charlottesville **(G-2627)**
Frito-Lay North America Inc...................E..... 540 380-3020
  Salem **(G-12508)**
Mintel Group Ltd.................................G..... 540 989-3945
  Roanoke **(G-11968)**
Skinny Jerky LLC.................................G..... 703 459-8406
  Alexandria **(G-347)**
Toms Wild Game Products....................G..... 540 598-3900
  Henrico **(G-6583)**

MEAT PROCESSED FROM PURCHASED CARCASSES

American Skin LLC..............................G..... 910 259-2232
  Smithfield **(G-12703)**
Elyssa E Strong.................................G..... 540 280-3982
  Goshen **(G-5925)**
James A Kennedy & Assoc Inc..............G..... 804 241-6836
  Powhatan **(G-10553)**
Knauss Snack Food & Co LLC...............G..... 276 656-3500
  Martinsville **(G-8305)**
Smithfield Foods Inc...........................C..... 757 365-3000
  Smithfield **(G-12728)**
Smithfield Packaged Meats Corp..........G..... 757 357-3131
  Smithfield **(G-12735)**
Smithfield Packaged Meats Corp..........D..... 757 357-1382
  Smithfield **(G-12737)**

Smithfield Support Svcs Corp..............C..... 757 365-3541
  Smithfield **(G-12739)**
Southern Packing Corporation.............E..... 757 421-2131
  Chesapeake **(G-3303)**

MEDIA BUYING AGENCIES

Sanjar Media LLC................................G..... 703 901-7680
  Woodbridge **(G-15803)**

MEDIA: Magnetic & Optical Recording

Buckeyes Meadow LLC.........................G..... 703 535-6868
  Alexandria **(G-155)**
Eiw Group..G..... 804 677-6214
  Petersburg **(G-10318)**
Fancy Media Co Inc.............................G..... 757 638-7101
  Suffolk **(G-13706)**
Lightspeed Infrared LLC......................G..... 540 875-6796
  Bedford **(G-1643)**
Windrose Media LLC............................G..... 703 464-1274
  Reston **(G-10991)**

MEDICAL & HOSPITAL EQPT WHOLESALERS

Ride-Away Inc.....................................F..... 804 233-8267
  North Chesterfield **(G-10022)**
Virginia Prosthetics Inc......................E..... 540 366-8287
  Roanoke **(G-12218)**

MEDICAL & SURGICAL SPLYS: Braces, Elastic

Kay Kare LLC......................................G..... 614 309-8462
  Arlington **(G-1021)**
Medical Sports Inc.............................G..... 703 241-9720
  Arlington **(G-1060)**
Solution Matrix Inc............................E..... 540 352-3211
  Rocky Mount **(G-12352)**

MEDICAL & SURGICAL SPLYS: Braces, Orthopedic

Air Britt Two LLC................................G..... 757 470-9364
  Virginia Beach **(G-14218)**
Bio-Prosthetic Orthotic Lab.................G..... 703 527-3123
  Arlington **(G-883)**
Thomas Hegens...................................F..... 703 205-9000
  Fairfax **(G-4569)**

MEDICAL & SURGICAL SPLYS: Canes, Orthopedic

Larry Kaniecki...................................G..... 804 737-7616
  Sandston **(G-12623)**

MEDICAL & SURGICAL SPLYS: Clothing, Fire Resistant & Protect

Firemans Shield LLC............................G..... 804 231-1800
  Richmond **(G-11590)**
Northfield Medical Mfg LLC...................E..... 800 270-0153
  Norfolk **(G-9669)**
Precept Medical Products Inc...............G..... 804 236-1010
  Richmond **(G-11329)**
Sweetpeas By Shafer Dobry..................G..... 703 476-6787
  Herndon **(G-6819)**

MEDICAL & SURGICAL SPLYS: Cosmetic Restorations

Realty Restorations LLC......................G..... 757 553-6117
  Virginia Beach **(G-14764)**

MEDICAL & SURGICAL SPLYS: Dressings, Surgical

Mach278 LLC......................................G..... 716 860-2889
  Ashburn **(G-1313)**

MEDICAL & SURGICAL SPLYS: Foot Appliances, Orthopedic

Eastern Cranial Affiliates LLC..............G..... 703 807-5899
  Arlington **(G-951)**
Eastern Cranial Affiliates LLC..............G..... 703 807-5899
  Fairfax **(G-4616)**

PRODUCT

MEDICAL & SURGICAL SPLYS: Gynecological Splys & Appliances

Blue Ridge Chorale of Culpeper............G..... 540 717-5888
Culpeper *(G-3874)*

MEDICAL & SURGICAL SPLYS: Ligatures

H&H Medical Corporation ....E..... 800 326-5708
Williamsburg *(G-15253)*

MEDICAL & SURGICAL SPLYS: Limbs, Artificial

Bristol Orthotic & Prosthetic ....G..... 276 963-1186
Abingdon *(G-16)*
Coastal Prsttics Orthotics LLC..............G..... 757 240-4228
Newport News *(G-9201)*
District Orthopedic Appliances ....G..... 703 698-7373
Springfield *(G-12993)*
Excel Prsthetics Orthotics Inc ....F..... 540 982-0205
Roanoke *(G-12083)*
Excel Prsthetics Orthotics Inc ....G..... 434 528-3695
Lynchburg *(G-7706)*
Excel Prsthetics Orthotics Inc ....G..... 434 797-1191
Danville *(G-3993)*
Hanger Prsthetcs & Ortho Inc...............G..... 434 846-1803
Lynchburg *(G-7727)*
Orthotic Prosthetic Center ....G..... 703 698-5007
Fairfax *(G-4526)*
Out On A Limb Quiltworks ....G..... 804 739-7901
Midlothian *(G-8873)*
Paul Valentine Orthotics........................G..... 804 355-0283
Richmond *(G-11320)*
Prince William Orthotics & Prs ....G..... 703 368-7967
Manassas *(G-8134)*
Reach Orthtic Prsthetic Svcs S ....G..... 757 673-2000
Chesapeake *(G-3261)*
Rehabltation Practitioners Inc ....G..... 540 722-9025
Winchester *(G-15579)*
Sama Artfl Intelligence LLC ....G..... 347 223-2437
Alexandria *(G-335)*
Synergy Orthtics Prsthtics LLC............G..... 410 788-8901
Broadlands *(G-2082)*
Tidewater Prosthetic Center ....G..... 757 925-4844
Norfolk *(G-9756)*
Tidewater Prosthetic Center ....G..... 757 925-4844
Suffolk *(G-13772)*

MEDICAL & SURGICAL SPLYS: Models, Anatomical

Victorious Images LLC..........................G..... 757 476-7335
Williamsburg *(G-15331)*
Yacoe LLC...G..... 973 735-3095
Richmond *(G-11837)*

MEDICAL & SURGICAL SPLYS: Noise Protectors, Personal

Emtech Laboratories Inc ....E..... 540 265-9156
Roanoke *(G-11921)*

MEDICAL & SURGICAL SPLYS: Orthopedic Appliances

Commonwealth Orthotics & Prost ....G..... 434 836-4736
Danville *(G-3969)*
Easter VA Orthtics Prosthetics ....G..... 757 967-0526
Suffolk *(G-13702)*
Orthotic Solutions L L C ....G..... 703 849-9200
Fairfax *(G-4527)*
Prostride Orthotics LLC ....G..... 804 310-3894
Henrico *(G-6552)*
Reach Orthotic Prosthetic Svcs ....G..... 757 930-0139
Newport News *(G-9321)*
Valley Orthtic Specialists Inc................G..... 540 667-3631
Winchester *(G-15598)*

MEDICAL & SURGICAL SPLYS: Personal Safety Eqpt

Eclipse Holsters LLC.............................G..... 907 382-6958
Williamsburg *(G-15237)*
Mission Integrated Tech LLC ....G..... 202 769-9900
Vienna *(G-14097)*
Premier Resources Express LLC ....G..... 717 887-4003
Chesapeake *(G-3245)*
Rescue Systems Inc ....G..... 276 629-2900
Bassett *(G-1590)*

Rescue Systems Intl Inc.........................G..... 276 629-2900
Fincastle *(G-4998)*

MEDICAL & SURGICAL SPLYS: Prosthetic Appliances

American Cmg Services Inc....................G..... 804 353-9077
Richmond *(G-11107)*
American Cmg Services Inc....................G..... 757 548-5656
Chesapeake *(G-2965)*
Blue Ridge Prosthetics & Ortho ....G..... 540 242-4499
Harrisonburg *(G-6296)*
Coastal Prsttics Orthotics LLC..............G..... 757 892-5300
Chesapeake *(G-3043)*
Commonwealth Surgical Solution..........G..... 804 330-0988
North Chesterfield *(G-9851)*
Commonwlth Orthtics Prosthetic............G..... 434 836-4736
Danville *(G-3970)*
Hairbotics LLC ....G..... 703 496-6083
Alexandria *(G-473)*
Hanger Prosthetics Orthotics ....G..... 703 719-0143
Alexandria *(G-474)*
Hanger Prsthetcs & Ortho Inc................G..... 757 873-1984
Newport News *(G-9243)*
Howmedica Osteonics Corp ....G..... 804 737-9426
Glen Allen *(G-5748)*
Imagine Milling Tech LLC ....G..... 571 313-1269
Chantilly *(G-2441)*
Indyne Inc ....G..... 703 903-6900
Sterling *(G-13427)*
O Depuy ....G..... 804 330-0988
North Chesterfield *(G-9942)*
Shh Stmlting Healthy Hair LLC ....G..... 973 607-7138
Fredericksburg *(G-5222)*
Virginia Prosthetics Inc ....E..... 540 366-8287
Roanoke *(G-12218)*
Virginia Prosthetics Orthotics ....G..... 540 949-4248
Fishersville *(G-5012)*

MEDICAL & SURGICAL SPLYS: Respiratory Protect Eqpt, Personal

Arben Solutions Co ....G..... 703 728-0396
Warrenton *(G-14978)*

MEDICAL & SURGICAL SPLYS: Supports, Abdominal, Ankle, Etc

Foot Levelers Inc ....E..... 800 553-4860
Roanoke *(G-12091)*

MEDICAL & SURGICAL SPLYS: Tape, Adhesive, Non/Medicated

Tape-Tab LP ....G..... 804 404-6855
Henrico *(G-6578)*

MEDICAL & SURGICAL SPLYS: Technical Aids, Handicapped

Accessible Environments Inc ....G..... 757 565-3444
Williamsburg *(G-15201)*
Virginia Beach Products LLC ....G..... 757 847-9338
Virginia Beach *(G-14912)*

MEDICAL & SURGICAL SPLYS: Traction Apparatus

Comfortrac Inc ....G..... 703 891-0455
Mc Lean *(G-8407)*

MEDICAL & SURGICAL SPLYS: Walkers

Senior Mobility LLC ....G..... 540 574-0215
Harrisonburg *(G-6368)*
Tubular Fabricators Indust Inc ....E..... 804 733-4000
Petersburg *(G-10347)*

MEDICAL & SURGICAL SPLYS: Welders' Hoods

Southside Youth Festival ....G..... 434 767-2584
Burkeville *(G-2210)*

MEDICAL EQPT: Diagnostic

Chemteq..F..... 757 622-2223
Norfolk *(G-9481)*
J M H Diagnostic Center........................G..... 276 628-1439
Abingdon *(G-42)*

Owl Peak Technologies Inc....................G..... 847 612-0609
Charlottesville *(G-2839)*
Product Dev Mfg & Packg ....G..... 703 777-8400
Leesburg *(G-7328)*
Riverside Healthcare Assn Inc ....G..... 757 594-3900
Newport News *(G-9328)*
Tegrex Technologies LLC ....G..... 805 500-8479
Charlottesville *(G-2888)*

MEDICAL EQPT: Electromedical Apparatus

E-Kare Inc ....G..... 844 443-5273
Fairfax *(G-4442)*

MEDICAL EQPT: Laser Systems

Slim Silhouettes LLC ....G..... 757 337-5965
Virginia Beach *(G-14825)*

MEDICAL EQPT: Patient Monitoring

Closed Loop LLC ....G..... 804 648-4802
Richmond *(G-11159)*
Inspire Living Inc ....G..... 703 991-0451
Haymarket *(G-6427)*

MEDICAL EQPT: Ultrasonic, Exc Cleaning

Sak Consulting ....G..... 703 220-2020
Lake Ridge *(G-7157)*
Soundpipe LLC ....G..... 434 218-3394
Charlottesville *(G-2879)*

MEDICAL EQPT: X-Ray Apparatus & Tubes, Radiographic

Berger and Burrow Entps Inc ....E..... 804 282-9729
Henrico *(G-6481)*

MEDICAL SUNDRIES: Rubber

Encore Products Inc ....G..... 757 493-8358
Virginia Beach *(G-14447)*
Tchere LLC ....G..... 800 889-7832
Stafford *(G-13201)*

MEDICAL, DENTAL & HOSP EQPT, WHOLESALE: X-ray Film & Splys

Adani Systems Inc.................................G..... 703 528-0035
Alexandria *(G-118)*

MEDICAL, DENTAL & HOSPITAL EQPT, WHOL: Dentists' Prof Splys

Contour Healer LLC ....G..... 757 288-6671
Virginia Beach *(G-14362)*

MEDICAL, DENTAL & HOSPITAL EQPT, WHOL: Hosptl Eqpt/Furniture

Pari Respiratory Equipment Inc ....F..... 804 897-3311
Midlothian *(G-8876)*

MEDICAL, DENTAL & HOSPITAL EQPT, WHOLESALE: Diagnostic, Med

Mikro Systems Inc ....E..... 434 244-6480
Charlottesville *(G-2660)*

MEDICAL, DENTAL & HOSPITAL EQPT, WHOLESALE: Med Eqpt & Splys

Arben Solutions Co ....G..... 703 728-0396
Warrenton *(G-14978)*
Coastal Prsttics Orthotics LLC..............G..... 757 892-5300
Chesapeake *(G-3043)*
Hairbotics LLC ....G..... 703 496-6083
Alexandria *(G-473)*
Manakin Industries LLC ....G..... 804 784-5514
Manakin Sabot *(G-7903)*
Northfield Medical Mfg LLC ....E..... 800 270-0153
Norfolk *(G-9669)*
Rip Shears LLC ....G..... 757 635-9560
Virginia Beach *(G-14776)*
T W Enterprises Inc ....G..... 540 667-0233
Winchester *(G-15485)*

(G-0000) Company's Geographic Section entry number

MEMBERSHIP ORGANIZATIONS, NEC: Charitable

Soccer Bridge .... G 703 356-0462
Mc Lean *(G-8549)*

MEMBERSHIP ORGS, BUSINESS: Growers' Marketing Advisory Svc

Mariner Media Inc .... F 540 264-0021
Buena Vista *(G-2146)*

MEMBERSHIP ORGS, CIVIC, SOCIAL & FRATERNAL: Protection

Donley Technology .... G 804 224-9427
Colonial Beach *(G-3724)*

MEN'S & BOYS' CLOTHING ACCESS STORES

String Stalker LLC .... G 727 430-7545
Glen Allen *(G-5802)*

MEN'S & BOYS' CLOTHING STORES

Journeymen Saddlers Ltd .... F 540 687-5888
Middleburg *(G-8725)*
Webgear Inc .... F 703 532-1000
Vienna *(G-14158)*

MEN'S & BOYS' CLOTHING WHOLESALERS, NEC

Barrons-Hunter Inc .... G 434 971-7626
Charlottesville *(G-2736)*
Hibernate Inc .... G 804 513-1777
Glen Allen *(G-5744)*
Mayes Wholesale Tack .... G 276 755-3715
Cana *(G-2227)*

MEN'S & BOYS' SPORTSWEAR WHOLESALERS

D J R Enterprises Inc .... F 540 639-9386
Radford *(G-10708)*

METAL COMPONENTS: Prefabricated

Bad Wolf LLC .... G 540 347-4255
Warrenton *(G-14980)*
McElroy Metal Mill Inc .... G 540 667-2500
Winchester *(G-15445)*

METAL FABRICATORS: Architechtural

Alliance Stl Fabrications Inc .... F 703 631-2355
Manassas Park *(G-8187)*
Art-A-Metal LLC .... G 757 787-1574
Onancock *(G-10190)*
Beach Iron Shop .... G 757 422-3318
Virginia Beach *(G-14267)*
Carico Inc .... E 540 373-5983
Fredericksburg *(G-5176)*
Century Stair Company .... D 703 754-4163
Haymarket *(G-6417)*
Chase Architectural Metal LLC .... G 804 230-1136
Richmond *(G-11525)*
Custom Railing Solutions Inc .... G 757 455-8501
Norfolk *(G-9512)*
Dulles Iron Works Inc .... G 703 996-8797
Sterling *(G-13391)*
Eddies Mind Inc .... G 540 731-9304
Radford *(G-10712)*
Efco Corporation .... E 540 248-8604
Verona *(G-13985)*
Extreme Steel Inc .... D 540 868-9150
Warrenton *(G-15007)*
Extreme Steel Inc .... G 540 868-9150
Winchester *(G-15417)*
Fields Inc Oscar S .... E 804 798-3900
Ashland *(G-1416)*
Flowers Steel LLC .... G 540 424-8377
Sumerduck *(G-13791)*
Folley Fencing Service .... G 276 629-8487
Patrick Springs *(G-10270)*
Fusion Pwdr Cating Fabrication .... G 757 319-3760
Chesapeake *(G-3112)*
Gold Stem .... E 703 680-7000
Woodbridge *(G-15710)*

Greendale Railing Company .... E 804 363-7809
Richmond *(G-11223)*
Griffins Perch Ironworks .... G 434 977-0582
Charlottesville *(G-2642)*
Hampton Roads Sheet Metal Inc .... G 757 543-6009
Virginia Beach *(G-14500)*
Josh McDaniel .... G 804 748-4330
Chesterfield *(G-3509)*
Lewis Metal Works Inc .... E 434 572-3043
South Boston *(G-12779)*
Meany & Oliver Companies Inc .... G 703 851-7131
Arlington *(G-1058)*
Moore Sign Corporation .... E 804 748-5836
Chester *(G-3438)*
R F J Ltd .... E 703 494-3255
Woodbridge *(G-15788)*
R&R Ornamental Iron Inc .... G 540 798-1699
Roanoke *(G-12159)*
Richardson Ornamental Iron .... G 757 420-1426
Chesapeake *(G-3270)*
Shickel Corporation .... D 540 828-2536
Bridgewater *(G-1959)*
Silver City Iron Inc .... G 434 566-7644
Charlottesville *(G-2876)*
Spitzer Machine Shop .... G 540 896-5827
Fulks Run *(G-5566)*
Stuart-Dean Co Inc .... D 703 578-1885
Falls Church *(G-4878)*
Superior Iron Works Inc .... D 703 471-5500
Sterling *(G-13524)*
Technifab of Virginia Inc .... E 276 988-7517
North Tazewell *(G-10109)*
Tecnico Corporation .... B 757 545-4013
Chesapeake *(G-3326)*
Timmons & Kelley Architects .... G 804 897-5636
Midlothian *(G-8913)*

METAL FABRICATORS: Plate

Aigis Blast Protection .... G 703 871-5173
Reston *(G-10782)*
Amthor International Inc .... D 845 778-5576
Gretna *(G-6002)*
Atlantic Metal Products Inc .... E 804 758-4915
Topping *(G-13885)*
Bolling Steel Co Inc .... E 540 380-4402
Salem *(G-12484)*
Bwxt Nclear Oprtions Group Inc .... B 434 522-6000
Lynchburg *(G-7669)*
Cardinal Pumps Exchangers Inc .... G 757 485-2666
Chesapeake *(G-3026)*
Catalina Cylinders .... E 757 896-9100
Hampton *(G-6108)*
Colonnas Ship Yard Inc .... A 757 545-2414
Norfolk *(G-9495)*
Colonnas Ship Yard Inc .... A 757 545-2414
Norfolk *(G-9497)*
Covan Worldwide Moving & Stor .... G 757 766-2305
Hampton *(G-6117)*
Creative Fabrication Inc .... E 540 931-4877
Covington *(G-3785)*
CSC Family Holdings Inc .... D 276 669-6649
Bristol *(G-2015)*
Davco Fabricating & Welding .... G 434 836-0234
Danville *(G-3980)*
Design Integrated Tech Inc .... E 540 349-9425
Warrenton *(G-14995)*
Draftco Incorporated .... E 540 337-1054
Stuarts Draft *(G-13646)*
Fields Inc Oscar S .... E 804 798-3900
Ashland *(G-1416)*
Hy-Mark Cylinders Inc .... E 757 251-6744
Hampton *(G-6173)*
Keo-Corp LLC .... G 636 515-5549
New Kent *(G-9135)*
Lane Enterprises Inc .... E 540 674-4645
Dublin *(G-4163)*
Lawrence Brothers Inc .... E 276 322-4988
Bluefield *(G-1868)*
Lewis Metal Works Inc .... E 434 572-3043
South Boston *(G-12779)*
Metro Sign & Design Inc .... E 703 631-1866
Manassas Park *(G-8205)*
Miller Metal Fabricators Inc .... E 540 886-5575
Staunton *(G-13281)*
Old Stone Corp .... F 813 731-7600
Cascade *(G-2252)*
Riggins Company LLC .... D 757 826-0525
Hampton *(G-6228)*
Robert D Gregory .... G 276 632-9170
Ridgeway *(G-11852)*

Select Cleaning Service .... G 804 397-1176
Richmond *(G-11756)*
Shickel Corporation .... D 540 828-2536
Bridgewater *(G-1959)*
Technifab of Virginia Inc .... E 276 988-7517
North Tazewell *(G-10109)*
Tecnico Corporation .... B 757 545-4013
Chesapeake *(G-3326)*
Valley Tool & Design Inc .... G 540 249-5710
Grottoes *(G-6026)*
Virginia Metals Inc .... F 276 628-8151
Abingdon *(G-67)*
Virginia Steel & Fabrication .... E 276 688-2125
Bastian *(G-1594)*
Warden Shackle Express .... G 540 980-2056
Pulaski *(G-10649)*
Weston Company .... G 540 349-1200
Gainesville *(G-5621)*

METAL FABRICATORS: Sheet

A & J Seamless Gutters Inc .... G 757 291-6890
Newport News *(G-9155)*
Accurate Machine Inc .... G 757 853-2136
Norfolk *(G-9418)*
Accutech Fabrication Inc .... F 434 528-4858
Lynchburg *(G-7632)*
Advanced Machine & Tooling .... F 757 518-1222
Virginia Beach *(G-14213)*
Amilcar S Sheet Metal LLC .... G 571 330-8371
Norfolk *(G-9441)*
Appalachian Machine Inc .... F 540 674-1914
Dublin *(G-4148)*
Applied Technology Group Inc .... E 703 960-5555
Alexandria *(G-416)*
Avm Sheet Metal Inc .... G 703 975-7715
Manassas *(G-8031)*
B & G Stainless Works Inc .... G 703 339-6002
Lorton *(G-7464)*
Bobby Burns Nowlin .... G 757 827-1588
Hampton *(G-6097)*
Brown Russel .... G 540 547-3000
Culpeper *(G-3876)*
C and J Fabrication Inc .... G 757 399-3340
Portsmouth *(G-10403)*
Capstone Industries LLC .... G 703 966-6718
Manassas *(G-8045)*
Carico Inc .... E 540 373-5983
Fredericksburg *(G-5176)*
Centerline Fabricators .... G 540 318-6769
Fredericksburg *(G-5410)*
Century Steel Products Inc .... E 703 471-7606
Sterling *(G-13367)*
Cladding Facade Solutions LLC .... G 571 748-7698
Fredericksburg *(G-5262)*
Colonial Wldg Fabrication Inc .... E 757 459-2680
Norfolk *(G-9494)*
Commonwealth Mechanical Inc .... G 757 825-0740
Hampton *(G-6116)*
Contech Engnered Solutions LLC .... G 513 645-7000
Abingdon *(G-25)*
Continental Auto Systems Inc .... G 540 825-4100
Culpeper *(G-3880)*
Custom Ornamental Iron Inc .... G 804 798-1991
Glen Allen *(G-5720)*
Draftco Incorporated .... E 540 337-1054
Stuarts Draft *(G-13646)*
Duct Shop LLC .... G 804 368-8543
Ashland *(G-1404)*
E G D Sheet Metal LLC .... G 571 577-1647
Manassas *(G-8060)*
East River Metals Inc .... E 276 928-1812
Rocky Gap *(G-12307)*
Elm Investments Inc .... E 757 934-2709
Suffolk *(G-13704)*
Endreola Sheet Metal .... G 703 496-8538
Woodbridge *(G-15694)*
Entwistle Company .... E 434 799-6186
Danville *(G-3992)*
Fairfax Metals LLC .... G 571 594-1937
Ashburn *(G-1278)*
Fh Sheet Metal Inc .... G 703 408-4622
Manassas *(G-7940)*
Fields Inc Oscar S .... E 804 798-3900
Ashland *(G-1416)*
Figure Engineering LLC .... G 540 818-5034
Lorton *(G-7489)*
Fusion Pwdr Cating Fabrication .... G 757 319-3760
Chesapeake *(G-3112)*
General Sheet Metal Co Inc .... G 571 221-3270
Manassas *(G-8073)*

PRODUCT

Greendale Railing Company ....E 804 363-7809
　Richmond (G-11223)
Halls Mechanical Services LLC ....G 276 673-3300
　Fieldale (G-4987)
Hampton Roads Sheet Metal Inc ......G 757 543-6009
　Virginia Beach (G-14500)
Hmb Inc ....D 540 967-1060
　Louisa (G-7556)
Hodges Sheet Metal LLC ....G 276 957-5344
　Spencer (G-12873)
Hughes Mechanical Systems ....G 757 855-3238
　Chesapeake (G-3138)
I C E ....G 276 988-0330
　North Tazewell (G-10101)
Innovative Machining Inc ....E 804 385-4212
　Forest (G-5077)
J & M Sheet Metal Inc ....G 571 722-2805
　Centreville (G-2311)
Kearney-National Inc ....C 276 628-7171
　Abingdon (G-47)
Koit Sheet Metal Inc ....G 703 625-3981
　Chantilly (G-2540)
Lane Enterprises Inc ....F 540 439-3201
　Bealeton (G-1600)
Lane Enterprises Inc ....E 540 674-4645
　Dublin (G-4163)
Lb Telesystems Inc ....E 703 919-8991
　Chantilly (G-2456)
Lee High Sheet Metal Inc ....F 703 698-5168
　Fairfax (G-4498)
Lewis Metal Works Inc ....E 434 572-3043
　South Boston (G-12779)
Liphart Steel Company Inc ....E 540 248-1009
　Verona (G-13991)
Lyon Roofing Inc ....G 540 633-0170
　Fairlawn (G-4737)
Magco Inc ....F 757 934-0042
　Suffolk (G-13738)
Martin Metalfab Inc ....E 804 226-1431
　Sandston (G-12624)
Matthews Sheet Metal Inc ....G 757 543-6009
　Virginia Beach (G-14642)
ME Latimer Fabricator T A ....G 757 566-8352
　Toano (G-13869)
Merrifield Metals Inc ....G 703 849-9100
　Fairfax (G-4506)
Miller Metal Fabricators Inc ....E 540 886-5575
　Staunton (G-13281)
Mitsubishi Chemical Amer Inc ....G 757 382-5750
　Chesapeake (G-3207)
Mobile Sheet Metal LLC ....G 540 450-6324
　Boyce (G-1910)
Moore Sign Corporation ....E 804 748-5836
　Chester (G-3438)
Naito America ....E 804 550-3305
　Ashland (G-1468)
Precision Sheetmetal Inc ....G 757 389-5730
　Norfolk (G-9694)
Pro Sheet Metal Inc ....G 703 675-7724
　Alexandria (G-557)
Production Manufacturing Inc ....G 513 892-2331
　Great Falls (G-5976)
Professional Welding Svc Inc ....G 757 853-9371
　Norfolk (G-9697)
Progressive Manufacturing Corp ......E 804 717-5353
　Chester (G-3448)
R Gonzalez Sheetmetal LLC ....G 571 316-8241
　Manassas (G-8137)
Rayco Industries Inc ....E 804 321-7111
　Richmond (G-11729)
Riddleberger Brothers Inc ....B 540 434-1731
　Mount Crawford (G-9058)
Ruffin & Payne Incorporated ....C 804 329-2691
　Richmond (G-11749)
S Joye & Son Inc ....G 804 745-2419
　North Chesterfield (G-10023)
Santiago Sheet Metal LLC ....G 703 870-4581
　Alexandria (G-576)
Shickel Corporation ....D 540 828-2536
　Bridgewater (G-1959)
Shoprat Metal Works LLC ....G 571 499-1534
　Annandale (G-782)
Silver Lake Welding Svc Inc ....F 540 879-2591
　Dayton (G-4064)
Southern Air Sheet Metal ....G 434 907-2268
　Lynchburg (G-7809)
Spears & Associate ....G 540 752-5577
　Hartwood (G-6392)
Stallworks LLC ....E 434 933-8939
　Gladstone (G-5688)

Structureworks Fabrication ....G 877 489-8064
　Fredericksburg (G-5370)
Sweet Briar Sheet Metal Svcs ....G 434 946-0403
　Amherst (G-710)
Tabet Manufacturing Co Inc ....E 757 627-1855
　Norfolk (G-9739)
Tecnico Corporation ....B 757 545-4013
　Chesapeake (G-3326)
Tek-AM Corp ....F 703 321-9144
　Lorton (G-7536)
Thermasteel Rp Ltd ....G 540 633-5000
　Radford (G-10743)
Valley Precision Incorporated ....E 540 941-8178
　Waynesboro (G-15142)
Varney Sheet Metal Shop ....G 540 343-4076
　Roanoke (G-12216)
Vasse Vaught Metalcrafting Inc ....G 540 808-8939
　Roanoke (G-12217)
Virginia Steel & Fabrication ....E 276 688-2125
　Bastian (G-1594)
Vivaan Metals LLC ....G 571 309-3007
　Sterling (G-13555)
VT Milcom Inc ....D 757 548-2956
　Chesapeake (G-3366)
W & B Fabricators Inc ....F 276 928-1060
　Rocky Gap (G-12308)
Waynesboro Alloy Works Inc ....G 540 965-4038
　Covington (G-3802)
Wegmann Usa Inc ....D 434 385-1580
　Lynchburg (G-7837)
Westside Metal Fabricators ....G 804 744-0387
　Midlothian (G-8921)
Williams Fabrication Inc ....E 540 862-4200
　Covington (G-3804)
Z & M Sheet Metal Inc ....G 703 631-9600
　Chantilly (G-2523)

METAL FABRICATORS: Structural, Ship

American Mtal Fabrications Inc ....E 804 271-8355
　Richmond (G-11026)
Fairlead Integrated LLC ....C 757 384-1957
　Portsmouth (G-10425)
Fairlead Intgrted Pwr Cntrls L ....F 757 384-1957
　Portsmouth (G-10427)
Fairlead Prcsion Mfg Intgrtion ....G 757 384-1957
　Portsmouth (G-10429)

METAL FABRICATORS: Structural, Ship

Pillar Enterprise Ltd ....C 540 868-8626
　White Post (G-15181)
Selimax Inc ....G 540 347-5784
　Warrenton (G-15050)
Williams Bridge Company ....E 703 335-7800
　Manassas (G-8178)

METAL FINISHING SVCS

Brass Copper Metal Refinishing ....G 434 636-5531
　Bracey (G-1922)

METAL MINING SVCS

Adf Unit Trust Inc ....G 757 926-5252
　Newport News (G-9157)
East Coast Interiors Inc ....E 804 423-2554
　North Chesterfield (G-9867)
Elixsys Va LLC ....G 434 374-2398
　Clarksville (G-3629)
Pura Vida Vienna Inc ....G 703 281-6050
　Vienna (G-14116)

METAL ORES, NEC

Metal Magic ....G 703 660-9180
　Alexandria (G-530)
Yue Xu ....G 703 503-9451
　Fairfax (G-4586)

METAL SERVICE CENTERS & OFFICES

Century Steel Products Inc ....E 703 471-7606
　Sterling (G-13367)

METAL STAMPING, FOR THE TRADE

A K Metal Fabricators Inc ....E 703 823-1661
　Alexandria (G-114)
Independent Stamping Inc ....G 540 949-6839
　Waynesboro (G-15115)
Intricate Metal Forming Co ....E 540 345-9233
　Salem (G-12523)

Masonite Corporation ....D 540 778-2211
　Stanley (G-13231)
Rick USA Stamping Corporation ....G 540 980-1327
　Pulaski (G-10645)
Short Run Stamping Company Inc ......D 804 861-6872
　Petersburg (G-10341)

METAL TREATING COMPOUNDS

Grain Free Products Inc ....G 703 418-0000
　Alexandria (G-471)

METALS SVC CENTERS & WHOLESALERS: Foundry Prdts

Bingham & Taylor Corp ....C 540 825-8334
　Culpeper (G-3872)

METALS SVC CENTERS & WHOLESALERS: Iron & Steel Prdt, Ferrous

Virginia Steel & Building Spc ....F 434 528-4302
　Lynchburg (G-7834)

METALS SVC CENTERS & WHOLESALERS: Pipe & Tubing, Steel

Industrial Fabricators VA Inc ....D 540 943-5885
　Fishersville (G-5005)

METALS SVC CENTERS & WHOLESALERS: Steel

Dominion Steel Inc ....F 540 898-1249
　Fredericksburg (G-5276)

METALS SVC CTRS & WHOLESALERS: Aluminum Bars, Rods, Etc

Mitsubishi Chemical Composites ....C 757 548-7850
　Chesapeake (G-3208)

METALS: Precious NEC

Bulldog Precious Metals ....G 540 312-1234
　Vinton (G-14167)
Gold Spot ....G 804 708-0275
　Goochland (G-5883)
Precious Time LLC ....G 804 343-4380
　Richmond (G-11722)

METALS: Primary Nonferrous, NEC

Jr Kauffman Inc ....F 276 228-7070
　Wytheville (G-15894)
Rapid Mat Group LLC ....G 703 629-2426
　Mc Lean (G-8532)

METALWORK: Miscellaneous

3d Design and Mfg LLC ....G 804 214-3229
　Powhatan (G-10527)
American Buildings Company ....C 434 757-2220
　La Crosse (G-7139)
Arbon Equipment Corporation ....G 540 542-6790
　Winchester (G-15383)
Arbon Equipment Corporation ....G 540 387-2113
　Salem (G-12475)
Brady Contracting Service ....G 703 864-9207
　Manassas (G-8042)
Brown Russel ....G 540 547-3000
　Culpeper (G-3876)
Emerald Ironworks Inc ....E 703 690-2477
　Woodbridge (G-15692)
Fabritech ....G 540 825-1544
　Culpeper (G-3891)
Hamilton Iron Works Inc ....E 703 497-4766
　Woodbridge (G-15720)
Horse Pasture Mfg LLC ....G 276 952-2558
　Meadows of Dan (G-8591)
Industrial Welding & Mch Corp ....F 276 783-7105
　Atkins (G-1518)
Jerry King ....G 804 550-1243
　Glen Allen (G-5755)
Kevins Welding ....G 703 242-8649
　Oakton (G-10153)
Panel Systems Inc ....E 703 910-6285
　Woodbridge (G-15772)
Steelfab Inc ....G 703 538-2320
　Alexandria (G-355)
Twin CS LLC ....G 540 664-6072
　Winchester (G-15497)

Voestlpine High Prfmce Mtls Co..........E.......434 575-7994
South Boston (G-12792)
Ward Entp Fabrication LLC....................G.......757 675-5712
Hampton (G-6269)

METALWORK: Ornamental

Colonial Iron Works Inc.........................G.......804 862-4141
Petersburg (G-10312)
Emerald Ironworks Inc............................E.......703 690-2477
Woodbridge (G-15692)
J C Enterprises..G.......540 345-0552
Roanoke (G-12108)
Virginia Archtectural Mtls LLC.............G.......540 710-7701
Fredericksburg (G-5232)
Whites Ornamental Iron Works.............G.......540 877-1047
Winchester (G-15509)

METERING DEVICES: Integrating, Nonelectric

Engility LLC..G.......757 366-4422
Chesapeake (G-3089)

METERS: Pyrometers, Indl Process

Electronic Dev Labs Inc.........................E.......434 799-0807
Danville (G-3990)

MGMT CONSULTING SVCS: Matls, Incl Purch, Handle & Invntry

4 Shores Trnsprting Lgstix LLC............G.......804 319-6247
Richmond (G-11074)

MICROPHONES

Stone Mountain Ventures Inc................F.......888 244-9306
Huddleston (G-6959)

MICROPROCESSORS

Intel Federal LLC....................................G.......302 644-3756
Reston (G-10875)

MICROPUBLISHER

Lewis Printing Company.........................E.......804 648-2000
Richmond (G-11652)
Publishers Asset LLC.............................G.......540 621-4422
Fredericksburg (G-5474)

MICROSCOPES

M5 Technologies LLC.............................G.......540 904-0880
Roanoke (G-12131)

MICROWAVE COMPONENTS

Cobham AES Holdings Inc......................F.......703 414-5300
Arlington (G-911)
Dominion Microprobes Inc.....................G.......434 962-8221
Charlottesville (G-2619)
Software Dfined Dvcs Group LLC.........G.......540 623-7175
Stafford (G-13192)

MILITARY GOODS & REGALIA STORES

Aspetto Inc...G.......540 547-8487
Fredericksburg (G-5171)

MILITARY INSIGNIA, TEXTILE

Beau-Geste International Inc.................G.......434 534-0468
Forest (G-5053)
Vanguard Industries East Inc...............C.......757 665-8405
Norfolk (G-9778)

MILLING: Farina, Exc Breakfast Food

Teds Bulletin...G.......571 313-8961
Reston (G-10970)

MILLING: Grains, Exc Rice

Vaughans Mill Inc...................................G.......540 789-7144
Indian Valley (G-6998)

MILLWORK

Abingdon Millwork...................................G.......276 676-2951
Abingdon (G-1)
Adkins Custom Woodworking..................G.......276 638-8198
Martinsville (G-8263)

Affinity Woodworks LLC..........................G.......330 814-4950
Elkwood (G-4340)
Against Grain Woodworking Inc.............G.......434 760-2055
Afton (G-74)
Aj Trim LLC..G.......703 330-1212
Manassas (G-8021)
AK Millwork Inc.......................................G.......703 337-4848
Springfield (G-12937)
American Wood Fibers Inc.....................E.......276 646-3075
Marion (G-8222)
American Woodmark Corporation ....C.......540 672-3707
Orange (G-10202)
American Woodmark Corporation ....C.......540 665-9100
Winchester (G-15379)
Anchor Woodworks..................................G.......804 458-6443
North Prince George (G-10086)
Andersons Woodworks LLC....................G.......804 530-3736
South Chesterfield (G-12795)
Annandale Mllwk Alied Systems ....D.......540 665-9600
Winchester (G-15382)
Apical Woodworks & Nursery LLC.........G.......434 384-0525
Lynchburg (G-7641)
Architectural Accents.............................G.......540 943-5888
Waynesboro (G-15094)
Architectural Custom Wdwrk Inc..........G.......804 784-2283
Manakin Sabot (G-7895)
Ark Woodworking LLC.............................G.......540 272-7489
Flint Hill (G-5014)
Arlington Adrndack Wdworks LLC.........G.......703 964-7700
Arlington (G-857)
Art Creations Company Inc....................G.......703 257-9510
Manassas (G-7912)
Artisan Woodwork Company LLC...........G.......540 420-4928
Rocky Mount (G-12312)
Arundel Woodworks................................G.......202 713-8781
Leesburg (G-7223)
Ashland Woodwork Inc...........................F.......804 798-4088
Ashland (G-1373)
Awsi Inc...F.......804 798-4088
Ashland (G-1375)
Backwoods Woodworking.......................G.......276 237-2011
Fries (G-5514)
Banton Custom Woodworking LLC ....G.......804 334-4766
Chesterfield (G-3477)
Batch Wood Works Inc............................G.......804 694-5767
Gloucester (G-5837)
Battletown Cstm Woodworks LLC.........G.......703 618-1548
Berryville (G-1670)
Bayside Joinery Co LLC..........................G.......804 551-3951
Dutton (G-4269)
Bayside Woodworking Inc......................G.......757 337-0380
Chesapeake (G-2995)
Bear Country Woodworks.......................G.......540 890-0928
Vinton (G-14166)
Benchmark Woodworks Inc....................F.......757 971-3380
Portsmouth (G-10399)
Better Living Inc.....................................D.......434 978-1666
Charlottesville (G-2594)
Big D Woodworking.................................G.......757 753-4814
Newport News (G-9180)
Big Dog Woodworking LLC.....................G.......540 359-1066
Richardsville (G-11009)
Blackwater Bldg Cstm Wdwkg LLC ......G.......540 493-1888
Ferrum (G-4971)
Bland Woodworking.................................G.......703 631-6567
Centreville (G-2295)
Blue Ridge Millwork................................G.......434 993-1953
Concord (G-3756)
Blue Ridge Stairs & Wdwrk LLC............G.......540 320-1953
Willis (G-15354)
Blue Ridge Woodworks VA Inc...............G.......434 477-0313
Monroe (G-8987)
Bon Air Craftsman LLC...........................G.......804 745-0130
North Chesterfield (G-9833)
Bourbon..G.......757 371-4710
Chesapeake (G-3012)
Bristol Woodworker.................................G.......423 557-4158
Bristol (G-2011)
Builders Firstsource Inc.........................G.......434 964-1192
Charlottesville (G-2601)
Burnette Cabinet Shop Inc.....................G.......540 586-0147
Bedford (G-1629)
Byrds Custom Wdwrk & Stain GL ....G.......757 242-6786
Suffolk (G-13683)
C & G Woodworking................................G.......703 878-7196
Woodbridge (G-15663)
Cab-Pool Inc..F.......804 218-8294
Henrico (G-6487)
Calvin Montgomery.................................G.......540 334-3058
Wirtz (G-15609)

Campbell Custom Woodworking............G.......757 724-2001
Chesapeake (G-3024)
Campostella Builders and Sup...............E.......757 545-3212
Norfolk (G-9475)
Canova Woodworking LLC......................G.......434 422-0807
Gordonsville (G-5904)
Carpenters Cbnets Wodworks LLC........G.......276 236-0853
Woodlawn (G-15844)
Carpers Wood Creations Inc..................E.......540 465-2525
Strasburg (G-13576)
Cattywampus Woodworks LLC...............G.......540 599-2358
Staffordsville (G-13214)
Centurion Woodworks LLC.....................G.......703 594-2369
Clifton (G-3660)
Charlies Woodworks Inc.........................G.......703 944-0775
Falls Church (G-4774)
Chris N Chris Woodworking LLC ....G.......757 810-4672
Hampton (G-6113)
Christophers Woodworks LLC................G.......757 404-2683
Chesapeake (G-3035)
Clarks Lumber & Millwork Inc...............F.......804 448-9985
Fredericksburg (G-5412)
Cline Woodworks LLC.............................G.......540 721-2286
Moneta (G-8960)
Closet Pioneers LLC...............................G.......703 844-0400
Lorton (G-7474)
Columbus Woodworks.............................G.......434 528-1052
Lynchburg (G-7680)
Conaways Woodworking LLC..................G.......703 530-8725
Manassas Park (G-8197)
Contemporary Kitchens Ltd....................G.......804 758-2001
Topping (G-13886)
Conway Woodworking LLC.....................G.......276 328-6590
Wise (G-15620)
Cornerstone Woodworks.........................G.......757 236-2334
Chesapeake (G-3054)
Corravoo Woodworks LLC......................G.......703 966-0929
Ashburn (G-1258)
County Line Custom Wdwkg LLC ....G.......804 338-8436
Moseley (G-9035)
Craft Designs Custom Intr Pdts.............G.......757 630-1565
Suffolk (G-13688)
CRC Public Relations.............................G.......703 395-9614
Burke (G-2187)
Creative Visions Woodworks..................G.......434 822-0182
Danville (G-3973)
Creative Woodworking Specialis...........G.......804 514-9066
Richmond (G-11036)
Crisman Woodworks................................G.......804 317-1446
Midlothian (G-8806)
Cs Woodworking Design LLC..................G.......703 996-1122
Sterling (G-13378)
Cumberland Millwork..............................G.......757 233-4121
Chesapeake (G-3058)
Custom Quality Woodworking.................G.......703 368-8010
Manassas (G-7928)
Cypress Woodworking LLC.....................G.......703 803-6254
Fairfax (G-4610)
D & M Woodworks....................................G.......757 510-3600
Virginia Beach (G-14379)
Dagnat Woodworks LLC..........................G.......276 627-1039
Bassett (G-1581)
Darbys Build and Design LLC.................G.......434 989-5493
Gordonsville (G-5905)
Darbys Custom Woodworks.....................G.......434 989-5493
Gordonsville (G-5906)
David Blanchard Woodworking...............G.......540 468-3900
Monterey (G-9005)
DD&t Custom Woodworking Inc.............G.......804 360-2714
Richmond (G-11180)
Dennington Wdwrk Solutions LLC ....G.......571 414-6917
Reston (G-10840)
DHT Woodworks LLC...............................G.......434 414-2607
Appomattox (G-809)
Dysert Custom Woodwork.......................G.......804 741-4712
Henrico (G-6505)
Ecks Custom Woodworking.....................G.......571 765-0807
Warrenton (G-15003)
Eco-Friendly Lumber LLC.......................G.......703 881-1966
Nokesville (G-9391)
Element Woodworks LLC........................G.......757 650-9556
Virginia Beach (G-14439)
Em Millwork Inc.......................................G.......571 344-9842
Springfield (G-12997)
Eric Carr Woodworks..............................G.......202 253-1010
Great Falls (G-5954)
Ernies Woodworking................................G.......540 786-8959
Fredericksburg (G-5284)
Essence Woodworks LLC........................G.......703 945-3108
Fairfax (G-4450)

PRODUCT

Ever Forward Woodworks............G...... 434 882-0727 Scottsville (*G-12660*)	**Jim Champion**..........................G...... 276 466-9112 Bristol (*G-2022*)	**Mount Vernon Woodworks LLC**............G...... 202 222-8387 Alexandria (*G-534*)
Exotic Woodworks.....................G...... 352 408-5373 Virginia Beach (*G-14457*)	**Jon Martin Woodworking LLC**......G...... 540 560-3721 Harrisonburg (*G-6334*)	**Narrogate Woodworks Inc**...........G...... 276 728-3996 Dugspur (*G-4190*)
Fairfax Woodworking Inc.........G...... 703 339-9578 Chantilly (*G-2419*)	**Jr Woodworks**............................G...... 703 577-2663 Alexandria (*G-247*)	**Natural Woodworking Co**............G...... 540 745-2664 Floyd (*G-5033*)
Fairfax Woodworking Inc.........G...... 571 292-2220 Manassas (*G-8068*)	**Jsd Mill Work LLC**....................G...... 703 863-7183 Lignum (*G-7425*)	**Noah Paci**...................................G...... 703 525-5437 Arlington (*G-1079*)
Family Crafters of Virginia.....G...... 540 943-3934 Waynesboro (*G-15114*)	**K & J Woodworking/ Cash**........G...... 703 369-7161 Manassas (*G-8091*)	**Northampton Custom Milling LLC**......G...... 757 442-4747 Nassawadox (*G-9101*)
Fancy Gap Woodworks LLC.....G...... 336 816-9881 Fancy Gap (*G-4935*)	**Kempsville Building Mtls Inc**.....G...... 757 875-1850 Newport News (*G-9275*)	**Northern Virginia Woodwork Inc**...G...... 540 752-6128 Bealeton (*G-1602*)
Farmstead Finds Salvaging......G...... 540 845-8200 Fredericksburg (*G-5430*)	**Kempsville Building Mtls Inc**.....E...... 757 485-0782 Chesapeake (*G-3162*)	**Old Barn Rclmed WD Antiq Flrg**....E...... 804 329-0079 Richmond (*G-11699*)
Fielside Woodworkig................G...... 434 203-5530 Hurt (*G-6975*)	**Kerschbamer Woodworking LLC**......G...... 434 455-2508 Lynchburg (*G-7751*)	**Old Virginia Molding & Mllwk**....G...... 757 516-9055 Franklin (*G-5151*)
First Landing Woodworks.......G...... 757 428-7537 Virginia Beach (*G-14465*)	**Keystone Vintage Lumber VA LLC**......G...... 804 615-7773 Amelia Court House (*G-661*)	**Olde Virginia Moulding**............G...... 757 516-9055 Franklin (*G-5152*)
Fleming Woodworking LLC.....G...... 559 259-2296 Suffolk (*G-13710*)	**Kingdom Woodworks Virginia LLC**......G...... 757 544-4821 Chesapeake (*G-3164*)	**Olivals Custom Woodworking Inc**...G...... 703 221-2713 Triangle (*G-13897*)
Gaithrsburg Cbinetry Mllwk Inc....D...... 540 347-4551 Warrenton (*G-15019*)	**Kinzie Woodwork LLC**..............G...... 540 397-1637 Roanoke (*G-11949*)	**One Arm Woodworking LLC**.......G...... 703 203-9417 Fairfax (*G-4525*)
Gaston and Wyatt LLC.............E...... 434 293-7357 Charlottesville (*G-2802*)	**Knockawe Woodworking LLC**....G...... 804 928-3506 North Chesterfield (*G-9909*)	**One Asterisk Woodworks LLC**....G...... 508 332-8151 Fredericksburg (*G-5464*)
Goose Creek Woodworks LLC...G...... 540 348-4163 Raphine (*G-10749*)	**Knotthead Woodworking Inc**.....G...... 540 344-0293 Vinton (*G-14176*)	**Out of Woodwork**......................G...... 757 814-8848 Chesapeake (*G-3230*)
Grayson Ferguson Wdwkg Inc...G...... 434 528-3405 Lynchburg (*G-7723*)	**Labyrinth Woodworks LLC**.........G...... 206 235-6272 Lynchburg (*G-7754*)	**Outer Banks Woodworks Inc**......G...... 804 937-4330 North Chesterfield (*G-9944*)
Grayson Millworks Company Inc...G...... 276 773-8590 Independence (*G-6984*)	**Landmark Logworks**..................G...... 540 687-4124 The Plains (*G-13843*)	**P&L Woodworks**.........................G...... 240 676-8648 Lovettsville (*G-7585*)
Greensprings Custom Woodwo...G...... 703 628-8058 Stafford (*G-13148*)	**Landmark Woodworking Inc**......G...... 703 424-3191 Fairfax Station (*G-4715*)	**Pan Custom Molding Inc**............G...... 804 787-3821 Mineral (*G-8951*)
Gunz Custom Woodworks LLC...G...... 757 739-2842 Virginia Beach (*G-14497*)	**Legacy Products LLC**................E...... 804 739-9333 Midlothian (*G-8847*)	**Patrick Hawks**..........................G...... 276 618-2055 Martinsville (*G-8316*)
H & A Fine Woodworking..........G...... 703 499-0944 Fairfax (*G-4472*)	**Legacy Woodworking LLC**.........G...... 703 431-8811 Purcellville (*G-10665*)	**Paul V Bell**................................G...... 703 631-4011 Manassas (*G-8126*)
H & A Fine Woodworking..........G...... 703 822-0006 Springfield (*G-13016*)	**Lesden Corporation**..................G...... 540 373-4940 Fredericksburg (*G-5450*)	**Pearce Woodworking**.................G...... 240 377-1278 Winchester (*G-15565*)
Haas Woodworking...................G...... 540 686-5837 Clear Brook (*G-3644*)	**Lincoln Woodworking**...............G...... 703 297-7512 Purcellville (*G-10666*)	**Penguin Woodworking LLC**.........G...... 804 502-2656 Powhatan (*G-10562*)
Hackney Millworks Inc.............G...... 804 843-3312 West Point (*G-15158*)	**Linden Woodwork LLC**..............G...... 540 636-3345 Linden (*G-7431*)	**Percision Woodworks**................G...... 757 642-1686 Suffolk (*G-13751*)
Haley Pearsall Inc.....................G...... 804 784-3438 Richmond (*G-11230*)	**Linetree Woodworks**.................G...... 919 619-3013 Powhatan (*G-10556*)	**Persimmon Woodworking**...........G...... 703 618-6909 Hamilton (*G-6063*)
Hampton Woodworks LLC.........G...... 434 989-7556 Charlottesville (*G-2644*)	**Lions Head Woodworks LLC**......G...... 540 288-9532 Stafford (*G-13171*)	**Pettigrew**....................................G...... 434 979-0018 North Garden (*G-10081*)
Hanover Woodworking Studio LLC...G...... 804 625-5679 Hanover (*G-6281*)	**Lm Woodworking LLC**...............G...... 703 927-4467 Alexandria (*G-519*)	**Piedmont Woodworks LLC**.........G...... 540 364-1849 Marshall (*G-8258*)
Harper and Taylor Custom........G...... 804 658-8753 Powhatan (*G-10548*)	**Local Wood**................................G...... 540 955-9522 Berryville (*G-1684*)	**Pike Woodworks**........................G...... 571 329-4377 Haymarket (*G-6436*)
Harris Woodworking.................G...... 434 295-4316 North Garden (*G-10076*)	**M McGuire Woodworks**.............G...... 434 841-3702 Lynchburg (*G-7767*)	**Pinstripe Cstm Longboards LLC**...G...... 757 635-7183 Virginia Beach (*G-14723*)
HB Woodworks...........................G...... 703 209-4639 Chantilly (*G-2536*)	**Mackes Woodworking LLC**.........G...... 570 856-3242 Virginia Beach (*G-14630*)	**Plank Road Woodworks**.............G...... 617 285-8522 Charlottesville (*G-2847*)
Heritage Woodworks LLC.........G...... 757 417-7337 Virginia Beach (*G-14518*)	**Magnolia Woodworking**............G...... 571 521-9041 Fairfax (*G-4501*)	**Potomac Creek Woodworks LLC**...G...... 703 444-9805 Sterling (*G-13475*)
Hernley Woodworks..................G...... 571 419-4889 Ashburn (*G-1290*)	**Mantels By Meunier**..................G...... 804 690-1977 Richmond (*G-11664*)	**Precision Woodworks LLC**..........G...... 757 642-1686 Smithfield (*G-12721*)
Highwheel Woodworks..............G...... 540 287-8575 Spotsylvania (*G-12894*)	**Masco Cabinetry LLC**................C...... 540 727-7859 Culpeper (*G-3907*)	**Premier Millwork & Lbr Co Inc**....E...... 757 463-8870 Virginia Beach (*G-14736*)
Holly Beach Woodworker Inc....G...... 757 831-1410 Virginia Beach (*G-14526*)	**Massey Wood & West Inc**..........E...... 804 746-2800 Mechanicsville (*G-8656*)	**Premium Millwork Installations**...G...... 757 288-9785 Woodbridge (*G-15780*)
Hoskins Woodworking Llc Jose...G...... 434 825-2883 Charlottesville (*G-2811*)	**McFarland Woodworks LLC**........G...... 276 970-5847 Tazewell (*G-13834*)	**Progrm For The Archtctrl Wdwrk**...G...... 978 468-5141 Reston (*G-10931*)
Hudson Wdwkg & Restoration LLC...G...... 703 817-7741 Chantilly (*G-2438*)	**Mendez Custom Woodworking**...G...... 540 621-3849 Spotsylvania (*G-12905*)	**R A Onijs Classic Woodwork**......G...... 703 594-3304 Nokesville (*G-9398*)
Huffs Artisan Woodwork...........G...... 703 399-5493 Fairfax (*G-4477*)	**Method Wood Working**..............G...... 804 332-3715 Richmond (*G-11288*)	**R Wyatt Inc**................................E...... 434 293-7357 Charlottesville (*G-2854*)
Hypes Custom Wdwkg & HM Improv...G...... 540 641-7419 Christiansburg (*G-3597*)	**Metro Wood Works Inc**.............G...... 757 479-1100 Chesapeake (*G-3203*)	**Rainbow Custom Woodworking**....E...... 571 379-5500 Manassas (*G-8138*)
Ibs Millwork Corporation..........G...... 703 631-4011 Manassas (*G-8079*)	**Mid Atlantic Wood Works LLC**...G...... 703 281-4376 Oakton (*G-10158*)	**Rays Woodworks**........................G...... 276 251-7297 Claudville (*G-3640*)
Interior Building Systems Corp...D...... 703 335-9655 Manassas (*G-8083*)	**Mik Woodworking Inc**...............G...... 540 878-1197 Winchester (*G-15557*)	**RC Tate Woodworks**...................G...... 434 822-0035 Danville (*G-4034*)
Interpretive Wdwrk Design Inc...G...... 703 330-6105 Manassas (*G-7953*)	**Millcreek Wood Works**..............G...... 804 642-4792 Hayes (*G-6402*)	**Red Brook Lumber Co**................G...... 434 293-2077 Charlottesville (*G-2861*)
Jaeger & Ernst Inc....................F...... 434 973-7018 Barboursville (*G-1562*)	**Miller Cabinets Inc**...................G...... 540 434-4835 Harrisonburg (*G-6345*)	**Rediscover Woodwork**................G...... 757 813-0383 Chesapeake (*G-3263*)
Jarrett Millwork.........................G...... 540 377-9173 Fairfield (*G-4731*)	**Miller Quality Woodwork Inc**....G...... 757 564-7847 Williamsburg (*G-15278*)	**Reierson Woodworking**..............G...... 804 541-1945 North Prince George (*G-10091*)
JB Wood Works LLC...................G...... 540 589-5281 Roanoke (*G-11946*)	**Mjs Woodworking LLC**...............G...... 571 233-4991 Remington (*G-10769*)	**Richard Price**.............................G...... 804 731-7270 Sperryville (*G-12879*)
Jeff Fleisher..............................G...... 703 955-6873 New Market (*G-9143*)	**Model A Woodworks**..................G...... 757 714-1126 Chesapeake (*G-3210*)	**River Valley Custom Millwork**....G...... 540 438-0208 Mount Crawford (*G-9059*)
Jeff Hoskins..............................G...... 804 769-1295 Aylett (*G-1549*)	**Modus Workshop LLC**................G...... 800 376-5735 Harrisonburg (*G-6347*)	**Riverfarm Woodworks LLC**.........G...... 571 721-0988 Alexandria (*G-574*)
Jeremiahs Woodwork LLC.........G...... 804 519-0984 Midlothian (*G-8837*)	**Montoya Services LLC**................G...... 571 882-3464 Sterling (*G-13456*)	**Rock Hill Lumber Inc**.................E...... 540 547-2889 Culpeper (*G-3918*)
Jester Woodworks Llc Van........G...... 804 562-6360 Richmond (*G-11630*)	**Morris Woodworks LLC**..............G...... 434 392-2285 Farmville (*G-4951*)	**Rogers - Mast-R-Woodwork LLC**...G...... 540 273-1460 King George (*G-7111*)

(G-0000) Company's Geographic Section entry number

Ronald Light .... G 540 837-2089
Boyce (G-1911)
Ronbuilt Corporation .... G 276 638-2090
Martinsville (G-8324)
Rox Chox & Woodworking LLC .... G 703 378-1313
Herndon (G-6796)
Ruffin & Payne Incorporated .... C 804 329-2691
Richmond (G-11749)
Rusty Bear Woodworks LLC .... G 540 327-6579
Winchester (G-15473)
Rva Woodwork LLC .... G 804 840-2345
Mechanicsville (G-8672)
Rva Woodwork LLC .... G 804 840-2345
Henrico (G-6563)
Rva Woodworks LLC .... G 804 303-3820
Mechanicsville (G-8673)
Rwm Inc .... G 540 774-7214
Roanoke (G-11998)
Rz Woodworks LLC .... G 626 833-0628
Colonial Heights (G-3744)
S4 Wood Works LLC .... G 804 299-0454
Henrico (G-6564)
Saunders Custom Woodwork .... G 804 520-4090
Colonial Heights (G-3746)
Sawmark Woodworks .... G 540 657-4814
Fredericksburg (G-5483)
Sawmill Creek Wdworkers Forums .... G 757 871-8214
Hayes (G-6407)
Sb Woodworks .... G 804 417-7729
Mechanicsville (G-8675)
Schorr Wood Works LLC .... G 434 990-1897
Ruckersville (G-12413)
Sct Woodworks LLC .... G 804 310-1908
Powhatan (G-10573)
Sheffield Woodworking .... G 571 261-4904
Haymarket (G-6444)
Simpson Company Landsca .... G 703 204-0453
Falls Church (G-4875)
Skips Woodworks .... G 757 390-1948
Williamsburg (G-15312)
Snow 39s Woodwork .... G 540 428-1762
Marshall (G-8260)
Southern Woodworks Inc .... G 757 566-8307
Toano (G-13878)
Stephan Burger Fine Wdwkg .... G 434 960-5440
Richmond (G-11398)
Steve Hollar Wdwkg & Engrv .... G 703 273-0639
Fairfax (G-4681)
Stonewall Woodworks LLC .... G 540 298-1713
Elkton (G-4335)
Sugar Maple Ln Woodworker LLC .... G 434 962-6494
Louisa (G-7569)
Symmetrical Wood Works LLC .... G 703 499-0821
Annandale (G-786)
T&J Woodworking .... G 757 567-5530
Virginia Beach (G-14861)
Taylormade Woodworking .... G 757 288-6256
Chesapeake (G-3323)
Teaberry Hill Woodworks LLC .... G 540 667-5489
Winchester (G-15592)
Terrys Custom Woodworks .... G 703 963-7116
Reston (G-10972)
The Millwork Specialist LLC .... G 804 262-9296
Charlottesville (G-2703)
Tidewter Archtctural Mllwk Inc .... G 757 422-1279
Virginia Beach (G-14881)
Tidewter Exhibits AG Mllwk Mfg .... G 540 379-1555
Fredericksburg (G-5493)
Tim Price Woodworking LLC .... G 276 794-9405
Lebanon (G-7209)
Timothys Custom Woodworking .... G 540 408-4343
Fredericksburg (G-5494)
Tms Corp .... G 804 262-9296
Charlottesville (G-2708)
Towers Custom Woodwork LLC C A .... G 703 330-7107
Manassas (G-8169)
Triple C Woodworking LLC .... G 703 779-9966
Leesburg (G-7365)
Trm Inc .... E 920 855-2194
Haymarket (G-6452)
True American Woodworkers .... G 540 748-5805
Bumpass (G-2169)
Truly Crafted Woodworking LLC .... G 571 268-0834
Manassas (G-8172)
Tumolo Custom Mill Work .... G 434 985-1755
Stanardsville (G-13229)
Turman Lumber Company Inc .... E 540 639-1250
Christiansburg (G-3614)
Ultimate Woodworks .... G 804 938-8987
Richmond (G-11427)

Union Church Millworks Inc .... F 540 862-0767
Covington (G-3801)
Uptons Custom Woodworking LLC .... G 540 454-3752
Stafford (G-13208)
VA Woodworks LLC .... G 540 903-6681
Fredericksburg (G-5385)
Valley Building Supply Inc .... C 540 434-6725
Harrisonburg (G-6383)
Van Jester Woodworks .... G 804 562-6360
Richmond (G-11805)
Viking Woodworking .... G 540 659-3882
Stafford (G-13210)
Vintage Star LLC .... G 808 779-9688
Springfield (G-13107)
W A Marks Fine Woodworking .... G 434 973-9785
Barboursville (G-1569)
Walpole Woodworkers Inc .... G 703 433-9929
Sterling (G-13557)
Walrose Woodworks .... G 276 762-3917
Castlewood (G-2259)
Warm Springs Mtn Woodworks .... G 540 839-9747
Hot Springs (G-6950)
Washington Wdwrkrs Guild of NA .... G 703 222-3460
Chantilly (G-2519)
Wellborn + Wright .... G 804 329-0079
Richmond (G-11821)
Wellspring Woodworks LLC .... G 540 722-8641
Winchester (G-15600)
Werrell Woodworks .... G 757 581-0131
Chesapeake (G-3375)
Westmont Woodworking Inc .... G 757 287-2442
Norfolk (G-9794)
White Oak Grove Woodworks .... G 540 763-2723
Riner (G-11866)
Wilkins Woodworking .... G 804 761-8081
Tappahannock (G-13825)
Wilkinson Woodworking .... G 540 548-2029
Fredericksburg (G-5391)
William Mowry Woodworking .... G 804 282-3831
Richmond (G-11451)
Williamsburg Wood Works LLC .... G 757 817-5396
Williamsburg (G-15344)
Wilmas Woodworking .... G 276 346-3611
Jonesville (G-7024)
Wilsons Woodworks .... G 757 846-6697
Seaford (G-12678)
Windows Direct .... G 276 755-5187
Cana (G-2228)
Windsor Woodworking Co Inc .... G 757 242-4141
Windsor (G-15608)
Winery Woodworks LLC .... G 540 869-1542
Stephens City (G-13329)
Wisakon Woods .... G 571 332-9844
Manassas (G-8179)
Wonderland Wood Works .... G 540 636-6158
Front Royal (G-5564)
Wood Creations .... G 571 235-0717
Alexandria (G-386)
Wood Creations LLC .... G 804 553-1862
Richmond (G-11454)
Wood Design & Fabrication Inc .... F 540 774-8168
Roanoke (G-12024)
Wood Turns .... G 904 303-8536
Chesapeake (G-3380)
Wood Works By Snyder LLC .... G 703 203-6952
Gainesville (G-5623)
Woodgrain Millwork Inc .... C 208 452-3801
Marion (G-8246)
Woodwork & Cabinets LLC .... G 703 881-1915
Haymarket (G-6455)
Woodwork Career Aliance N Amer .... G 434 298-4650
Nellysford (G-9115)
Woodworking Wrkshps of The Shn .... G 540 955-2376
Berryville (G-1700)
Woodworks .... G 434 636-4111
Bracey (G-1924)
Woodworks LLC .... G 804 730-0631
Mechanicsville (G-8702)
Woodworks LLC .... G 757 516-8405
Franklin (G-5162)
Wrack-It .... G 434 258-4317
Forest (G-5106)
Zeb Woodworks LLC .... G 703 361-2842
Manassas (G-8182)
Zephyr Woodworks LLC .... G 434 979-4425
North Garden (G-10085)

MINE & QUARRY SVCS: Nonmetallic Minerals

Blue Ridge Stone Corp .... G 434 239-9249
Lynchburg (G-7656)
Ken Musselman & Associates Inc .... G 804 790-0302
Chesterfield (G-3510)
Vinnell Corp .... G 703 818-7903
Fairfax (G-4579)

MINE DEVELOPMENT, METAL

Solite LLC .... E 757 494-5200
Chesapeake (G-3299)

MINE EXPLORATION SVCS: Nonmetallic Minerals

Mines Minerals & Enrgy VA Dept .... D 276 523-8100
Big Stone Gap (G-1713)

MINE PREPARATION SVCS

Jake Little Construction Inc .... E 276 498-7462
Oakwood (G-10169)

MINERAL ABRASIVES MINING SVCS

Royal Standard Minerals Inc .... G 804 580-8107
Heathsville (G-6464)

MINERAL PRODUCTS

Speed and Accuracy LLC .... G 405 375-3432
Herndon (G-6813)

MINERAL WOOL

Emtech Laboratories Inc .... E 540 265-9156
Roanoke (G-11921)
Johns Manville Corporation .... B 804 261-7400
Richmond (G-11256)

MINERALS: Ground or Treated

Active Minerals International .... G 540 771-3865
Winchester (G-15371)
American Borate Corporation .... G 800 486-1072
Chesapeake (G-2964)
ARC Dust LLC .... G 571 839-0223
Alexandria (G-417)
Giant Resource Recovery Inc .... E 434 685-7021
Cascade (G-2251)
Industrial Minerals Inc .... G 540 297-8667
Moneta (G-8966)
Kyanite Mining Corporation .... C 434 983-2085
Dillwyn (G-4097)
Opta (usa) Inc .... G 843 296-7074
Norfolk (G-9677)

MINIATURES

Aeroart International Inc .... G 703 406-4376
Great Falls (G-5934)
Battlefield Terrain Concepts .... G 540 977-0696
Roanoke (G-11884)
Dundee Miniatures LLC .... G 703 669-5591
Leesburg (G-7262)
Many Miniatures .... G 703 730-1221
Triangle (G-13896)
Putt Arund Town Miniature Golf .... G 804 317-6751
Chesterfield (G-3519)

MINING EXPLORATION & DEVELOPMENT SVCS

Dynamite Demolition LLC .... G 571 241-4658
Alexandria (G-451)
Jennmar Corporation .... D 540 726-2326
Rich Creek (G-11007)
Lambert Metal Services LLC .... G 571 261-5811
Manassas (G-7960)
Largo Resources USA Inc .... G 571 491-7827
Arlington (G-1025)
William G Sexton .... G 276 988-9012
North Tazewell (G-10111)

MINING MACHINERY & EQPT WHOLESALERS

Davis Mining & Mfg Inc .... F 276 395-3354
Wise (G-15622)

P
R
O
D
U
C
T

Tramline Inc .... G 276 322-3183
Bluefield *(G-1883)*

MINING MACHINES & EQPT: Classifiers, Metallurgical Or Mining

Geebo Inc .... G 888 439-3113
Mc Lean *(G-8446)*

MINING MACHINES & EQPT: Mineral Beneficiation

Clinch River LLC .... D 276 963-5271
Tazewell *(G-13830)*

MINING MACHINES/EQPT: Mine Car, Plow, Loader, Feeder/Eqpt

Mescher Manufacturing Co Inc .... F 276 530-7856
Grundy *(G-6037)*
Wolf Hills Fabricators LLC .... F 276 466-2743
Abingdon *(G-70)*

MISSILES: Ballistic, Complete

War Fighter Specialties LLC .... G 540 742-4187
Shenandoah *(G-12697)*

MISSILES: Guided

Lockheed Martin Corporation .... C 703 367-2121
Manassas *(G-7966)*
Northrop Grumman Systems Corp ...... B 703 280-2900
Falls Church *(G-4845)*
Titan II Inc .... D 757 380-2000
Newport News *(G-9358)*

MIXTURES & BLOCKS: Asphalt Paving

Air-Con Asp Sling Striping LLC .... G 540 664-1989
Winchester *(G-15373)*
Asphalt Ready Mix Inc .... G 540 576-3483
Union Hall *(G-13958)*
Boxley Materials Company .... F 540 777-7600
Lynchburg *(G-7659)*
Boxley Materials Company .... G 540 777-7600
Arrington *(G-1229)*
Cleanpowerpartners .... G 301 651-0690
Alexandria *(G-432)*
Colony Construction Asp LLC .... G 434 767-9930
Burkeville *(G-2207)*
Colony Construction Asp LLC .... F 804 598-1400
Powhatan *(G-10540)*
Fort Valley Paving .... G 540 636-8960
Strasburg *(G-13579)*
Goodloe Asphault LLC .... G 540 373-5863
Fredericksburg *(G-5192)*
H&G Decorative Pavers Inc .... G 571 338-4949
Bristow *(G-2054)*
Heavenly Paving LLC .... G 804 980-9523
Sandston *(G-12618)*
Hy Lee Paving Corporation .... E 804 360-9066
Rockville *(G-12287)*
Lane Construction Corporation .... F 703 471-6883
Chantilly *(G-2541)*
Larry D Martin .... G 540 493-0072
Rocky Mount *(G-12332)*
Llts Paving .... G 276 782-9550
Marion *(G-8231)*
Loudoun County Asphalt .... G 703 669-9001
Leesburg *(G-7305)*
Powells Paving Sealing LLC .... G 540 921-2455
Pembroke *(G-10283)*
Precision Pavers Inc .... G 703 217-4955
Charlottesville *(G-2850)*
Premium Paving Inc .... F 703 339-5371
Springfield *(G-13073)*
Roubin and Janeiro Inc .... G 703 573-9350
Fairfax *(G-4546)*
Sealmaster-Roanoke .... G 540 344-2090
Roanoke *(G-12180)*
Semmaterials LP .... G 757 244-6545
Newport News *(G-9334)*
Superior Paving Corporation .... G 703 631-5480
Centreville *(G-2342)*
Wells Belcher Paving Service .... G 434 374-5518
Nelson *(G-9116)*

MOBILE COMMUNICATIONS EQPT

Binge Live Inc .... G 757 679-7715
Chesapeake *(G-2999)*

Comcast Tech Center .... G 571 229-9112
Manassas *(G-7925)*
Eagle Mobile Services Inc .... G 703 979-1848
Arlington *(G-950)*
Ecko Incorporated .... F 276 988-7943
North Tazewell *(G-10098)*
Inhand Networks Inc .... G 703 348-2988
Fairfax *(G-4634)*
Ronald Carter .... G 571 278-6659
Burke *(G-2202)*
Signafab LLC .... G 703 489-8572
Louisa *(G-7567)*
Smartcell Inc .... G 703 989-5887
Manassas *(G-8157)*
Strategic Voice Solutions .... G 888 975-6130
Strasburg *(G-13600)*
Wallye LLC .... G 631 320-8868
Chantilly *(G-2567)*

MOBILE HOMES

Clayton Homes Inc .... G 276 395-7272
Coeburn *(G-3696)*
Di9 Equity Investors .... G 703 860-0901
Reston *(G-10841)*
Freedom Homes .... G 540 382-9015
Christiansburg *(G-3588)*
Mission Realty Group .... G 804 545-6651
Richmond *(G-11293)*
New Acton Mobile Inds LLC .... G 804 520-7171
South Chesterfield *(G-12817)*
SMC Holdings & Investment Corp ...... G 703 860-0901
Reston *(G-10954)*
Tool Wagon LLC .... G 434 610-9664
Lynchburg *(G-7824)*

MOBILE HOMES: Personal Or Private Use

Home Pride Inc .... F 276 642-0271
Bristol *(G-2020)*
Home Pride Inc .... E 276 466-0502
Bristol *(G-2021)*

MODELS: Airplane, Exc Toy

Clifford Aeroworks LLC .... G 703 304-3675
Potomac Falls *(G-10508)*

MODULES: Computer Logic

Intelligent Platforms LLC .... A 434 978-5000
Charlottesville *(G-2647)*
Tq-Systems USA Inc .... G 757 503-3927
Chesapeake *(G-3346)*
Wgb LLC .... G 757 289-5053
Suffolk *(G-13785)*

MOLDED RUBBER PRDTS

Commonwealth Mfg & Dev .... F 276 699-2089
Ivanhoe *(G-7003)*
Longwood Elastomers Inc .... F 336 272-3710
Wytheville *(G-15897)*

MOLDING COMPOUNDS

Mobjack Binnacle Products LLC .... G 804 814-4077
Richmond *(G-11295)*

MOLDINGS & TRIM: Metal, Exc Automobile

Creative Urethanes Inc .... E 540 542-6676
Winchester *(G-15407)*
Jmd Jmd LLC .... G 703 945-0099
Ashburn *(G-1299)*

MOLDINGS & TRIM: Wood

Quality Wood Products Inc .... G 540 750-1859
Christiansburg *(G-3608)*
Worthington Millwork LLC .... G 540 832-6391
Gordonsville *(G-5919)*

MOLDINGS, ARCHITECTURAL: Plaster Of Paris

Protomold .... G 540 542-1740
Winchester *(G-15570)*

MOLDINGS: Picture Frame

Artworks .... G 540 420-3843
Ferrum *(G-4969)*

Creative Framing Gallery .... G 703 771-6354
Leesburg *(G-7249)*
Custom Moulding & Millwork Inc .... F 540 788-1823
Catlett *(G-2267)*
Kilpatrick Framing and Art .... G 804 245-6824
Chesterfield *(G-3511)*
Mobile Custom Framing LLC .... G 757 412-4167
Virginia Beach *(G-14659)*
Pae-Imk International LLC .... E 888 526-5416
Falls Church *(G-4853)*
Ron Campbell Art and Framing .... G 540 651-2228
Check *(G-2945)*
Scott Fineart and Frmng Inc M .... G 757 496-0221
Virginia Beach *(G-14797)*

MOLDS: Indl

Black Mold Busters Chesapeake .... G 757 606-9608
Chesapeake *(G-3004)*
Black Mold Rmval Group Wdbrdge ..... G 571 402-8960
Woodbridge *(G-15659)*
Damon Company of Salem Inc .... E 540 389-8609
Salem *(G-12494)*
Lasercam LLc .... F 540 265-2888
Roanoke *(G-11952)*
Mold Fresh LLC .... G 757 696-9288
Virginia Beach *(G-14660)*
Mold Removal LLC .... G 703 421-0000
Sterling *(G-13455)*
Scorpion Mold Abatement LLC .... G 540 273-9300
Stafford *(G-13189)*
Virginia Beachs Max Blck Mold .... G 757 354-1935
Virginia Beach *(G-14916)*

MOLDS: Plastic Working & Foundry

Revere Mold & Engineering Inc .... F 804 748-5059
Chester *(G-3450)*
Wallace Precision Tooling .... G 540 456-6437
Afton *(G-95)*

MOLECULAR DEVICES: Solid State

Imgen Technologies Lc .... G 703 549-2866
Alexandria *(G-236)*
Meru Biotechnologies Inc .... G 804 316-4466
Richmond *(G-11677)*

MONUMENTS & GRAVE MARKERS, EXC TERRAZZO

3314 Monument Ave LLC .... G 804 285-9770
Henrico *(G-6468)*
Battle Monument Partners .... G 804 644-4924
Richmond *(G-11501)*
Monument32/The Smyers Group .... G 804 217-8347
Glen Allen *(G-5773)*
Monumental Pest Control Co .... G 571 245-6178
Centreville *(G-2321)*
Monumental Services .... G 434 847-6630
Madison Heights *(G-7877)*
Music At Monument .... G 202 570-7800
Luray *(G-7619)*

MONUMENTS & GRAVE MARKERS, WHOLESALE

Granite Countertop Experts LLC .... G 757 826-9316
Newport News *(G-9238)*

MONUMENTS: Concrete

Garrett Corporation .... G 276 475-3652
Damascus *(G-3948)*

MONUMENTS: Cut Stone, Exc Finishing Or Lettering Only

Concrete Creations Inc .... G 757 427-6226
Virginia Beach *(G-14359)*
Concrete Creations Inc .... G 757 427-1581
Virginia Beach *(G-14360)*

MOPS: Floor & Dust

Quickie Manufacturing Corp .... D 856 829-7900
Winchester *(G-15575)*

MOTION PICTURE & VIDEO PRODUCTION SVCS

Perez Armando.........................G...... 202 716-5044
Arlington **(G-1104)**

Prelude Communications Inc ....G...... 703 731-9396
Sterling **(G-13476)**

Strive Communications LLC ....G...... 703 925-5900
Reston **(G-10967)**

MOTION PICTURE & VIDEO PRODUCTION SVCS: Educational

Patricia Gavin...........................G...... 703 439-4403
Middleburg **(G-8731)**

MOTION PICTURE EQPT

Aviation Tactical LLC..................G...... 970 946-7027
Springfield **(G-12957)**

MOTOR & GENERATOR PARTS: Electric

American Nexus LLC ....G...... 804 405-5443
Richmond **(G-11484)**

Electric Motor and Contg Co ....C...... 757 487-2121
Chesapeake **(G-3084)**

Nippon Pulse America Inc..............G...... 540 633-1677
Radford **(G-10728)**

Technical Motor Service LLC...........G...... 276 638-1135
Martinsville **(G-8341)**

MOTOR HOMES

Featherlite Coaches Inc ....E...... 757 923-3374
Suffolk **(G-13708)**

Virginia Custom Coach Builders ......G...... 540 381-0609
Christiansburg **(G-3616)**

Virtual Realty ....G...... 757 718-2633
Quinton **(G-10701)**

MOTOR REBUILDING SVCS, EXC AUTOMOTIVE

Ace Rebuilders Inc ....F...... 804 798-3838
Ashland **(G-1362)**

MOTOR REPAIR SVCS

Engine Scout Professionals LLC ....G...... 757 621-8526
Portsmouth **(G-10423)**

Integrity National Corp ....G...... 540 455-2340
Ruther Glen **(G-12456)**

NM Mechanic Road Service LLC ....G...... 571 237-4810
Woodbridge **(G-15761)**

Obrien Machine Repair.................G...... 757 898-1387
Yorktown **(G-15983)**

Tatums Cstm Exhaust & Met Repr ....G...... 276 692-4884
Critz **(G-3824)**

Wheeler Maintenance Repair ....G...... 804 586-9836
Waverly **(G-15090)**

Winchester Truck Repair LLC ....G...... 540 398-7995
Winchester **(G-15514)**

Zerk Motors LLC ....G...... 540 322-2003
Fredericksburg **(G-5505)**

MOTOR VEHICLE ASSEMBLY, COMPLETE: Ambulances

Life Evac ....E...... 804 652-0171
North Dinwiddie **(G-10058)**

MOTOR VEHICLE ASSEMBLY, COMPLETE: Autos, Incl Specialty

Bennett Motorsports Inc ....G...... 434 845-2277
Evington **(G-4374)**

Bret Hamilton Enterprises.............G...... 804 598-8246
Powhatan **(G-10535)**

Edison 2 LLC ....F...... 434 806-2435
Charlottesville **(G-2788)**

Greentech Automotive Corp ....F...... 703 666-9001
Sterling **(G-13415)**

Morgan Race Cars LLC Jeffrey........G...... 540 907-1205
Fredericksburg **(G-5329)**

Rapid Manufacturing Inc ....E...... 804 598-7467
Powhatan **(G-10570)**

Signature Series - Usa LLC...........G...... 703 201-2543
Aldie **(G-112)**

Tesla Inc ....G...... 703 761-4679
Vienna **(G-14140)**

York Sportscars Inc ....G...... 804 798-5268
Ashland **(G-1514)**

MOTOR VEHICLE ASSEMBLY, COMPLETE: Bus/Large Spclty Vehicles

Specialty Vhcl Solutions LLC ....E...... 609 882-1900
Midlothian **(G-8907)**

MOTOR VEHICLE ASSEMBLY, COMPLETE: Cars, Armored

Alpine Armoring Inc ....F...... 703 471-0002
Chantilly **(G-2368)**

Goldbelt Wolf LLC ....D...... 703 584-8889
Alexandria **(G-470)**

Hawkins Glass Wholesalers LLC ....E...... 703 372-2990
Lorton **(G-7492)**

Polaris Group Intl LLC ....G...... 757 636-8862
Virginia Beach **(G-14728)**

War Fighter Specialties LLC ....G...... 540 742-4187
Shenandoah **(G-12697)**

MOTOR VEHICLE ASSEMBLY, COMPLETE: Fire Department Vehicles

Hamilton Safety Center Inc ....G...... 540 338-0500
Hamilton **(G-6059)**

Iron Gate Vlntr Fire Dept Inc ....E...... 540 862-5700
Iron Gate **(G-6999)**

Kovatch Mobile Equipment Corp ....E...... 540 982-3573
Roanoke **(G-12123)**

Plunkett Business Group Inc ....E...... 540 343-3323
Vinton **(G-14180)**

Portsmouth Fire Marshals Ofc..........G...... 757 393-8123
Portsmouth **(G-10470)**

Prfwmpro Fire Fighters ....G...... 703 393-2598
Manassas **(G-8133)**

MOTOR VEHICLE ASSEMBLY, COMPLETE: Military Motor Vehicle

Bae Systems Tctcal Vhcl System ....G...... 571 461-6000
Falls Church **(G-4760)**

Bradley-Morris LLC ....E...... 678 419-4171
Chesapeake **(G-3014)**

Force Protection Inc ....B...... 703 415-7520
Arlington **(G-973)**

Oshkosh Corporation ....G...... 703 525-8400
Arlington **(G-1091)**

Protolab Inc ....G...... 703 622-1889
Fredericksburg **(G-5214)**

MOTOR VEHICLE ASSEMBLY, COMPLETE: Motor Homes, Self Contained

Coach LLC ....E...... 757 925-2862
Suffolk **(G-13684)**

MOTOR VEHICLE ASSEMBLY, COMPLETE: Personnel Carriers

Circle R Carrier Service Inc............G...... 434 401-5950
Amherst **(G-687)**

On The Road Transport LLC ....G...... 410 207-2592
Virginia Beach **(G-14697)**

R and N Express LLC ....G...... 804 909-3761
North Chesterfield **(G-9956)**

MOTOR VEHICLE ASSEMBLY, COMPLETE: Reconnaissance Cars

General Dynamics Corporation ....C...... 703 876-3000
Reston **(G-10857)**

MOTOR VEHICLE ASSEMBLY, COMPLETE: Snow Plows

Charlie Ward.............................G...... 276 768-7266
Independence **(G-6979)**

MOTOR VEHICLE ASSEMBLY, COMPLETE: Truck & Tractor Trucks

Buffalo Repair Shop ....G...... 434 374-5915
Buffalo Junction **(G-2158)**

Teen Scott Trucking Inc.................G...... 804 833-9403
Glen Allen **(G-5806)**

MOTOR VEHICLE ASSEMBLY, COMPLETE: Truck Tractors, Highway

Chc Transports LLC.....................G...... 804 398-8686
Chesterfield **(G-3485)**

Joco Transportations LLC ....G...... 804 398-8686
Chesterfield **(G-3508)**

MOTOR VEHICLE ASSEMBLY, COMPLETE: Universal Carriers, Mil

Cw Security Solutions LLC ....G...... 540 929-8019
Vinton **(G-14172)**

MOTOR VEHICLE ASSEMBLY, COMPLETE: Wreckers, Tow Truck

Bubbles Wrecker Service ....G...... 434 845-2411
Lynchburg **(G-7662)**

Daniel Cranford Recovery ....G...... 434 382-8409
Lynchburg **(G-7692)**

Drumhellers Practical Choi ....G...... 540 949-0462
Waynesboro **(G-15108)**

Dynamic Towing Eqp & Mfg Inc..........E...... 757 624-1360
Norfolk **(G-9534)**

Freedom Lodging LLC ....G...... 757 288-4514
Chesapeake **(G-3110)**

MOTOR VEHICLE ASSY, COMPLETE: Motor Trucks, Exc Off-Highway

Volvo Group North America LLC ....C...... 336 393-2000
Dublin **(G-4174)**

MOTOR VEHICLE PARTS & ACCESS: Body Components & Frames

E Components International ....G...... 804 462-5679
Williamsburg **(G-15236)**

MOTOR VEHICLE PARTS & ACCESS: Booster Cables, Jump-Start

Atkins Automotive Corp.................G...... 540 942-5157
Waynesboro **(G-15096)**

MOTOR VEHICLE PARTS & ACCESS: Engines & Parts

Black Business Today Inc................G...... 804 528-7407
Richmond **(G-11505)**

C B R Engine Service ....G...... 276 686-5198
Rural Retreat **(G-12419)**

Federal-Mogul Powertrain LLC ....B...... 540 557-3300
Blacksburg **(G-1737)**

Performance Counts Automotive ....G...... 434 392-3391
Farmville **(G-4955)**

Tenneco Inc ....G...... 540 557-3312
Blacksburg **(G-1798)**

MOTOR VEHICLE PARTS & ACCESS: Engs & Trans,Factory, Rebuilt

Stuart Mathews Engineering.............G...... 804 779-2976
Mechanicsville **(G-8684)**

MOTOR VEHICLE PARTS & ACCESS: Fuel Systems & Parts

Cline Automotive Inc ....F...... 804 271-9107
North Chesterfield **(G-9846)**

Grimes French Race Systems ....G...... 540 923-4541
Madison **(G-7853)**

MOTOR VEHICLE PARTS & ACCESS: Gas Tanks

F W Baird General Contractor ....G...... 434 724-4499
Chatham **(G-2928)**

MOTOR VEHICLE PARTS & ACCESS: Gears

R H Sheppard Co Inc ....F...... 276 228-4000
Wytheville **(G-15907)**

MOTOR VEHICLE PARTS & ACCESS: Heaters

Hunter Defense Tech Inc ....F...... 540 479-8100
Fredericksburg **(G-5300)**

Employee Codes: A=Over 500 employees, B=251-500
C=101-250, D=51-100, E=20-50, F=10-19, G=1-9

2021 Virginia
Industrial Directory

1005

PRODUCT

MOTOR VEHICLE PARTS & ACCESS: Lubrication Systems & Parts

SKF Lbrication Systems USA Inc ....D....... 757 951-0370
Hampton (G-6239)

MOTOR VEHICLE PARTS & ACCESS: Pickup Truck Bed Liners

Castello 1935 Inc ....G....... 540 464-5275
Buchanan (G-2118)

MOTOR VEHICLE PARTS & ACCESS: Sanders, Safety

Rector Visitors of The Univ VA ....E....... 434 296-7288
Charlottesville (G-2682)

MOTOR VEHICLE PARTS & ACCESS: Tire Valve Cores

Tech of Southwest Virginia ....G....... 276 496-5393
Saltville (G-12593)

MOTOR VEHICLE PARTS & ACCESS: Trailer Hitches

Double B Trailers ....G....... 540 586-0651
Goode (G-5889)

MOTOR VEHICLE PARTS & ACCESS: Wheel rims

Titan Wheel Corp Virginia ....D....... 276 496-5121
Saltville (G-12594)
Virginia Wheel & Rim Inc ....G....... 804 526-9868
Colonial Heights (G-3751)

MOTOR VEHICLE: Hardware

Grilletech LLC ....G....... 434 941-7129
Lynchburg (G-7726)

MOTOR VEHICLE: Radiators

Valeo North America Inc ....C....... 757 827-0310
Hampton (G-6259)

MOTOR VEHICLE: Shock Absorbers

Tenneco Automotive Oper Co Inc ....A....... 540 432-3752
Rockingham (G-12281)
Tenneco Automotive Oper Co Inc ....E....... 540 434-2461
Harrisonburg (G-6380)

MOTOR VEHICLES & CAR BODIES

Above Rim LLC ....G....... 703 407-9398
Haymarket (G-6411)
Alan Thornhill ....G....... 703 892-5642
Arlington (G-848)
Automotion Inc ....G....... 276 889-3715
Lebanon (G-7188)
Bae Systems Tctcal Vhcl System ....E....... 571 461-6000
Falls Church (G-4759)
Emergency Vehicles Inc ....G....... 434 575-0509
South Boston (G-12763)
Glo 4 Itcom ....G....... 804 527-7608
Richmond (G-11219)
Goss132 ....G....... 202 905-2380
Warrenton (G-15021)
Grede Radford LLC ....D....... 248 727-1800
Radford (G-10715)
Jinks Motor Carriers Inc ....G....... 804 921-3121
Midlothian (G-8838)
TEAM Marketing ....G....... 703 405-0576
Manassas (G-8165)
Wilbar Truck Equipment Inc ....G....... 757 397-3200
Portsmouth (G-10502)
Wm Industries Corp ....F....... 703 666-9001
Sterling (G-13562)

MOTOR VEHICLES, WHOLESALE: Truck bodies

Crenshaw of Richmond Inc ....D....... 804 231-6241
Richmond (G-11546)

MOTORCYCLE ACCESS

Geza Gear Inc ....E....... 703 327-9844
Haymarket (G-6425)

Open Road Grill & Icehouse ....G....... 571 395-4400
Falls Church (G-4852)

MOTORCYCLE DEALERS

Austins Cycle Company ....G....... 757 653-0182
Capron (G-2237)

MOTORCYCLE PARTS & ACCESS DEALERS

Cycle Specialist ....G....... 757 599-5236
Newport News (G-9211)
Geza Gear Inc ....E....... 703 327-9844
Haymarket (G-6425)

MOTORCYCLE REPAIR SHOPS

Cycle Specialist ....G....... 757 599-5236
Newport News (G-9211)

MOTORCYCLES & RELATED PARTS

DOT Blue ....G....... 804 564-2563
Richmond (G-11566)
Jansson & Associate Mstr Bldr ....G....... 757 965-7285
Virginia Beach (G-14564)
Phat Daddys Polish Shop ....G....... 804 405-5301
North Chesterfield (G-9947)
Seidle Motorsports ....G....... 276 632-2255
Martinsville (G-8327)
U S Sidecars Inc ....D....... 434 263-6500
Arrington (G-1231)
Yum Yum Choppers Inc ....G....... 276 694-6152
Claudville (G-3642)

MOTORS: Electric

Aspen Motion Technologies Inc ....B....... 540 639-4440
Radford (G-10704)
Falco Emotors Inc ....E....... 571 313-1154
Dulles (G-4202)
Hydrogen Motors Inc ....G....... 703 407-9802
Oakton (G-10151)
Kollmorgen Corporation ....B....... 540 639-9045
Radford (G-10722)
Kollmorgen Corporation ....B....... 540 633-3536
Radford (G-10721)

MOTORS: Generators

Andy Meade ....G....... 276 940-3000
Duffield (G-4175)
Avcom of Virginia Inc ....G....... 804 794-2500
North Chesterfield (G-9822)
Critical Power Group Inc ....G....... 703 443-1717
Ashburn (G-1261)
Danaher Corporation ....G....... 540 639-9046
Radford (G-10709)
Danaher Motion ....G....... 540 639-9046
Radford (G-10710)
Electrical Mech Resources Inc ....E....... 804 226-1600
Richmond (G-11197)
Emotion US LLC ....F....... 540 639-9045
Radford (G-10713)
Industrial Drives ....G....... 540 639-2495
Radford (G-10717)
Moog Components Group ....G....... 540 443-4699
Blacksburg (G-1763)
Power Distribution Inc ....C....... 804 737-9880
Richmond (G-11721)
Safran Usa Inc ....F....... 703 351-9898
Alexandria (G-334)
Steves Generator Service LLC ....G....... 540 661-8675
Barboursville (G-1567)
Worldgen LLC ....G....... 434 244-2849
Charlottesville (G-2717)

MOUNTING SVC: Display

Five Star Medals ....G....... 703 644-4974
Springfield (G-13004)

MOUTHPIECES, PIPE & CIGARETTE HOLDERS: Rubber

Mouthpiece Express LLC ....G....... 540 989-8848
Roanoke (G-11970)

MOWERS & ACCESSORIES

Carters Power Equipment Inc ....G....... 804 796-4895
Chester (G-3392)
Cub Cadet Culpeper LLC ....G....... 540 825-8381
Culpeper (G-3882)

Direct Cut Lawn Tree Svc LLC ....G....... 804 516-7771
Manakin Sabot (G-7899)
Eaheart Equipment Inc ....F....... 540 347-2880
Warrenton (G-15002)
Eaheart Equipment Inc ....F....... 703 366-3880
Manassas (G-7934)
Tri-County Ope ....G....... 434 676-4441
Kenbridge (G-7035)

MUSEUMS

Alliance Presrvng Hstry Wwii ....G....... 757 423-1429
Norfolk (G-9434)

MUSEUMS & ART GALLERIES

MCS Design & Production Inc ....G....... 804 550-1000
Ashland (G-1462)
Tsg Concepts Inc ....G....... 877 777-5734
Arlington (G-1200)
Western Graphics Inc ....G....... 575 849-1209
Alexandria (G-381)

MUSIC BOXES

G-Force Events Inc ....G....... 804 228-0188
Richmond (G-11597)

MUSIC DISTRIBUTION APPARATUS

I10cartel Records LLC ....G....... 713 979-8182
Newport News (G-9255)

MUSICAL ENTERTAINERS

Hip-Hop Spot 24/7 LLC ....G....... 434 660-3166
Lynchburg (G-7734)

MUSICAL INSTRUMENT REPAIR

Lively Fulcher Organ Builders ....G....... 540 352-4401
Rocky Mount (G-12336)

MUSICAL INSTRUMENTS & ACCESS: Carrying Cases

Koenig Inc ....G....... 804 798-8282
Ashland (G-1450)

MUSICAL INSTRUMENTS & ACCESS: NEC

Altamont Recorders LLC ....G....... 804 814-2310
Richmond (G-11099)
Ambassador Religious Supply ....G....... 757 686-8314
Chesapeake (G-2962)
American Drum Inc ....G....... 804 226-1778
Richmond (G-11108)
Buy Chimes ....G....... 703 293-6395
Fairfax (G-4601)
Cabin Creek Musical Instrs ....G....... 276 388-3202
Mouth of Wilson (G-9092)
Claire E Bose ....G....... 323 898-2912
Toano (G-13860)
Debeer Piano Service LLC ....G....... 703 727-4601
Fairfax (G-4611)
Elliott Mandolins Shop ....G....... 540 763-2327
Riner (G-11862)
Larry Hicks ....G....... 276 738-9010
Castlewood (G-2254)
Mack Mimsey ....G....... 757 777-6333
Norfolk (G-9628)
Maleys Music ....G....... 571 335-4289
Arlington (G-1052)
Michael Reiss LLC ....G....... 757 826-4277
Hampton (G-6197)
Power Wrist Bldrs By Tlose Grp ....G....... 800 645-6673
Charlottesville (G-2679)
Queens Guitar Shop ....G....... 703 754-4330
Nokesville (G-9397)
Richmond Philharmonic Inc ....G....... 804 673-7400
Richmond (G-11358)
Taloose Group ....G....... 408 221-3277
Charlottesville (G-2699)
Wm L Mason Fine String Instrs ....G....... 540 645-7499
Fredericksburg (G-5238)

MUSICAL INSTRUMENTS & ACCESS: Pipe Organs

Qlf Custom Pipe Organ ....G....... 540 484-1133
Rocky Mount (G-12348)

MUSICAL INSTRUMENTS & ACCESS: Stands

Kimberly Gilbert.................................G..... 804 201-6591
 Henrico (G-6527)

MUSICAL INSTRUMENTS & SPLYS STORES

Cabin Creek Musical Instrs............G..... 276 388-3202
 Mouth of Wilson (G-9092)
Rodriguez Guitars............................G..... 804 358-6324
 Richmond (G-11366)
Stelling Banjo Works Ltd.................G..... 434 295-1917
 Afton (G-90)
Tkl Products Corp............................E..... 804 749-8300
 Oilville (G-10185)

MUSICAL INSTRUMENTS WHOLESALERS

AC Cetera Inc..................................G..... 724 532-3363
 Fairfax (G-4400)
Rodriguez Guitars............................G..... 804 358-6324
 Richmond (G-11366)
Stelling Banjo Works Ltd.................G..... 434 295-1917
 Afton (G-90)

MUSICAL INSTRUMENTS: Banjos & Parts

Stelling Banjo Works Ltd.................G..... 434 295-1917
 Afton (G-90)

MUSICAL INSTRUMENTS: Electric & Electronic

Boomin Bass Global LLC...................F..... 757 776-8668
 Virginia Beach (G-14294)
Centellax Inc...................................G..... 540 980-2905
 Pulaski (G-10632)

MUSICAL INSTRUMENTS: French Horns & Parts

George McCracken............................G..... 804 238-4910
 West Point (G-15157)

MUSICAL INSTRUMENTS: Guitars & Parts, Electric & Acoustic

Axeamps LLC....................................G..... 540 484-0882
 Glade Hill (G-5669)
David Bennett...................................G..... 703 858-4669
 Ashburn (G-1270)
G3 Solutions LLC..............................G..... 703 424-4296
 Vienna (G-14059)
Litton Guitar Works LLC...................G..... 703 966-0571
 Manassas (G-8101)
Rodriguez Guitars............................G..... 804 358-6324
 Richmond (G-11366)

MUSICAL INSTRUMENTS: Marimbas

Mountain Marimba Inc.......................G..... 276 773-3899
 Independence (G-6991)

MUSICAL INSTRUMENTS: Organs

El Morgan Company LLC....................G..... 540 623-7086
 Fredericksburg (G-5280)
Klann Inc...E..... 540 949-8351
 Waynesboro (G-15119)
Lively Fulcher Organ Builders.........G..... 540 352-4401
 Rocky Mount (G-12336)

MUSICAL INSTRUMENTS: Reeds

Riegger Marin..................................G..... 646 896-4739
 Blacksburg (G-1784)

MUSICAL INSTRUMENTS: Synthesizers, Music

Antonio Puducay..............................G..... 703 927-2953
 Lorton (G-7463)
Tyler JSun Global LLC......................G..... 407 221-6135
 Stafford (G-13206)

MUSICAL INSTRUMENTS: Violins & Parts

Elizabeth A Grge Vlin Stdio LL.........G..... 703 590-8145
 Woodbridge (G-15689)
Glory Violin Co LLC...........................G..... 703 439-1700
 Annandale (G-751)
Potomac Fine Violins LLC.................G..... 239 961-0398
 Arlington (G-1117)

NATIONAL SECURITY FORCES

Digitized Risk LLC............................G..... 703 662-3510
 Ashburn (G-1271)
Dla Document Services.....................G..... 703 784-2208
 Quantico (G-10688)
Dla Document Services.....................G..... 804 734-1791
 Fort Lee (G-5128)
Dla Document Services.....................F..... 757 855-0300
 Norfolk (G-9526)
Dla Document Services.....................E..... 757 444-7068
 Norfolk (G-9527)

NATIONAL SECURITY, GOVERNMENT: Air Force

US Dept of the Air Force..................G..... 703 808-0492
 Chantilly (G-2515)

NATIONAL SECURITY, GOVERNMENT: Federal

Mission It LLC..................................G..... 443 534-0130
 Brambleton (G-1930)

NATIONAL SECURITY, GOVERNMENT: Navy

United States Dept of Navy..............B..... 757 380-4223
 Newport News (G-9369)

NATURAL GAS DISTRIBUTION TO CONSUMERS

Consolidated Natural Gas Co...........B..... 804 819-2000
 Richmond (G-11539)

NATURAL GAS LIQUIDS PRODUCTION

East Tennessee Natural Gas Co.......F..... 276 429-5411
 Atkins (G-1516)

NATURAL GAS LIQUIDS PRODUCTION

Dixie Fuel Company..........................G..... 757 249-1264
 Newport News (G-9217)
Mid-Atlantic Energy LLC...................G..... 804 213-2500
 North Chesterfield (G-9931)
Saltville Gas Storage Co LLC...........E..... 276 496-7004
 Saltville (G-12589)
Venture Globl Clcsieu Pass LLC.......G..... 202 759-6740
 Arlington (G-1209)

NATURAL GAS PRODUCTION

Cnx Gas Corporation........................D..... 276 596-5000
 Cedar Bluff (G-2273)
Consolidated Natural Gas Co...........B..... 804 819-2000
 Richmond (G-11539)
Dominion Energy Inc........................D..... 804 771-3000
 Richmond (G-11187)

NATURAL GAS TRANSMISSION

Consolidated Natural Gas Co...........B..... 804 819-2000
 Richmond (G-11539)
Dominion Energy Inc........................D..... 804 771-3000
 Richmond (G-11187)

NAUTICAL REPAIR SVCS

North Sails Hampton Inc..................G..... 757 723-6280
 Hampton (G-6210)

NAVIGATIONAL SYSTEMS & INSTRUMENTS

Argon St Inc....................................A..... 703 322-0881
 Fairfax (G-4412)
Drs Leonardo Inc.............................C..... 703 416-8000
 Arlington (G-944)
Flexprotect LLC...............................G..... 703 957-8648
 Reston (G-10853)
Moog Inc..B..... 540 552-3011
 Blacksburg (G-1767)
Northrop Grumman Systems Corp...G..... 757 312-8375
 Chesapeake (G-3222)
Northrop Grumman Systems Corp...A..... 434 974-2000
 Charlottesville (G-2666)
Sailplan Inc.....................................G..... 703 217-9658
 Reston (G-10943)
Weibel Equipment Inc......................G..... 571 278-1989
 Leesburg (G-7375)

NETTING: Plastic

Conwed Corp....................................D..... 540 981-0362
 Roanoke (G-12070)

NEWSPAPERS & PERIODICALS NEWS REPORTING SVCS

Eir News Service Inc........................D..... 703 777-4494
 Leesburg (G-7264)

NICKEL ALLOY

Marion Nickel...................................G..... 703 444-8158
 Sterling (G-13448)

NONCURRENT CARRYING WIRING DEVICES

SMC Electrical Products Inc.............E..... 276 285-3841
 Bristol (G-2033)
Vina Express Inc..............................G..... 703 237-9398
 Falls Church (G-4890)

NONDAIRY BASED FROZEN DESSERTS

Sweet & Savory By Emily LLC...........G..... 804 248-8252
 North Chesterfield (G-9995)

NONDURABLE GOODS WHOLESALERS, NEC

Skin Ranch and Trade Company........G..... 757 486-7546
 Virginia Beach (G-14823)

NONFERROUS: Rolling & Drawing, NEC

Kd Cartridges..................................G..... 434 865-3328
 South Hill (G-12855)
Lane Enterprises Inc........................E..... 540 674-4645
 Dublin (G-4163)
Lucas-Milhaupt Inc...........................G..... 276 591-3351
 Bristol (G-1982)
Voestlpine High Prfmce Mtls Co........E..... 434 575-7994
 South Boston (G-12792)

NONMETALLIC MINERALS DEVELOPMENT & TEST BORING SVC

Agp Technologies LLC.......................G..... 434 489-6025
 Catlett (G-2262)

NONMETALLIC MINERALS: Support Activities, Exc Fuels

Iluka Resources Inc..........................C..... 434 348-4300
 Stony Creek (G-13567)
Moorman Shickram & Stephen...........G..... 540 463-3146
 Lexington (G-7403)

NOVELTIES

Express Contract Fullmen.................G..... 540 719-2100
 Moneta (G-8961)
Raw Goods LLC.................................G..... 862 812-1520
 Alexandria (G-325)

NOVELTIES & SPECIALTIES: Metal

Brownell Metal Studio Inc.................G..... 434 591-0379
 Troy (G-13920)

NOVELTIES: Plastic

Elfinsmith Ltd Inc.............................G..... 757 399-4788
 Portsmouth (G-10421)
King of Dice......................................G..... 804 758-0776
 Saluda (G-12604)

NOVELTY SHOPS

K & W Projects LLC..........................G..... 757 618-9249
 Chesapeake (G-3161)

NOZZLES: Fire Fighting

Nova Fire Supply LLC........................G..... 703 909-8339
 Round Hill (G-12384)

NOZZLES: Spray, Aerosol, Paint Or Insecticide

Spraying Systems Co........................G..... 804 364-0095
 Richmond (G-11394)

PRODUCT

NUCLEAR CORE STRUCTURALS: Metal Plate

Bwx Technologies Inc ....G...... 434 522-6000
Lynchburg *(G-7666)*

Bwxt Government Group Inc ....C...... 434 522-6000
Lynchburg *(G-7668)*

NUCLEAR REACTORS: Military Or Indl

Thorium Power Inc ....G...... 703 918-4904
Mc Lean *(G-8566)*

NURSERIES & LAWN & GARDEN SPLY STORE, RET: Lawn/Garden Splys

Griffith Bag Company ....G...... 540 433-2615
Harrisonburg *(G-6326)*

NURSERIES & LAWN & GARDEN SPLY STORES, RETAIL

Alpha ....G...... 540 895-5731
Partlow *(G-10263)*

NURSERIES & LAWN & GARDEN SPLY STORES, RETAIL: Fertilizer

Nutrien AG Solutions Inc ....G...... 540 775-2985
Milford *(G-8932)*

NURSERIES & LAWN & GARDEN SPLY STORES, RETAIL: Top Soil

Dickerson Stump LLC ....G...... 540 898-9145
Fredericksburg *(G-5273)*

NURSERIES & LAWN/GARDEN SPLY STORE, RET: Lawnmowers/Tractors

Catron Machine & Welding Inc ....G...... 276 783-6826
Marion *(G-8223)*

NURSERIES & LAWN/GARDEN SPLY STORES, RET: Garden Splys/Tools

Katherine Chain ....G...... 804 796-2762
Chester *(G-3426)*

NUTRITION SVCS

Axon Sciences Inc ....G...... 434 987-4460
Charlottesville *(G-2732)*

NYLON FIBERS

Honeywell International Inc ....C...... 804 520-3000
South Chesterfield *(G-12809)*

Mgc Advanced Polymers Inc ....E...... 804 520-7800
South Chesterfield *(G-12815)*

Quadrant Holding Inc ....D...... 276 228-0100
Wytheville *(G-15905)*

NYLON RESINS

Quadrant Holding Inc ....D...... 276 228-0100
Wytheville *(G-15905)*

OCHER MINING

R & R Mining Inc ....G...... 606 837-9321
Wise *(G-15633)*

OFFICE EQPT WHOLESALERS

Fedsafes LLC ....G...... 703 525-1436
Arlington *(G-964)*

Giesecke+devrient ....C...... 703 480-2000
Dulles *(G-4205)*

Konica Mnlta Bus Sltons USA In ....E...... 703 553-6000
Vienna *(G-14079)*

OFFICE FIXTURES: Wood

G T Walls Cabinet Shop ....G...... 804 798-6288
Glen Allen *(G-5734)*

OFFICE MACHINES, NEC

Kusters Engineering SEC Inc ....G...... 703 967-1449
Falls Church *(G-4818)*

SMS Data Products Group Inc ....G...... 703 709-9898
Sterling *(G-13512)*

Xsytechnologiescom ....G...... 757 333-7514
Virginia Beach *(G-14948)*

OFFICE SPLY & STATIONERY STORES: Office Forms & Splys

Benton-Thomas Inc ....F...... 434 572-3577
South Boston *(G-12751)*

Branner Printing Service Inc ....E...... 540 896-8947
Broadway *(G-2085)*

C & S Printing Enterprises ....G...... 703 385-4495
Fairfax *(G-4603)*

C I T C Imaging ....G...... 540 382-6557
Christiansburg *(G-3576)*

Gazette Press Inc ....G...... 276 236-4831
Galax *(G-5636)*

Kalwood Inc ....G...... 540 951-8600
Blacksburg *(G-1749)*

Michael Beach ....G...... 703 360-7284
Alexandria *(G-531)*

Quality Stamp Co ....G...... 757 858-0653
Norfolk *(G-9700)*

Rapid Printing Inc ....G...... 540 586-1243
Bedford *(G-1654)*

Sanwell Printing Co Inc ....G...... 276 638-3772
Martinsville *(G-8326)*

Standard Printing Company Inc ....F...... 540 965-1150
Covington *(G-3799)*

OFFICES & CLINICS OF DRS OF MED: Em Med Ctr, Freestanding

Life Protect 24/7 Inc ....G...... 888 864-8403
Norfolk *(G-9618)*

OFFICES & CLINICS OF HEALTH PRACTITIONERS: Nutrition

Nutrition Support Services ....G...... 540 626-3081
Pembroke *(G-10282)*

OFFICES & CLINICS OF HLTH PRACTITIONERS: Reg/Practical Nurse

Gumax International Ltd ....E...... 866 412-3880
Woodbridge *(G-15719)*

OIL & GAS FIELD MACHINERY

Mobil Petrochemical Holdings ....G...... 703 846-3000
Fairfax *(G-4513)*

Reamco Inc ....G...... 703 690-2000
Lorton *(G-7525)*

OIL FIELD MACHINERY & EQPT

Hill Phoenix Inc ....G...... 712 563-4623
South Chesterfield *(G-12807)*

OIL FIELD SVCS, NEC

Baker Hughes A GE Company LLC ....E...... 540 961-9532
Blacksburg *(G-1724)*

Baker Hughes Holdings LLC ....G...... 276 963-0106
Richlands *(G-11013)*

Bop International Inc ....G...... 571 550-6669
Fairfax *(G-4420)*

C&J Well Services Inc ....G...... 276 679-5860
Norton *(G-10114)*

Gas Field Services LLC ....Gas...... 276 880-2323
Rosedale *(G-12366)*

Miners Oil Company Inc ....G...... 804 230-5769
Richmond *(G-11052)*

Oceaneering International Inc ....B...... 757 985-3800
Chesapeake *(G-3224)*

Pinnacle Oil Co ....G...... 540 687-6351
Middleburg *(G-8732)*

Schlumberger Technology Corp ....G...... 757 546-2472
Chesapeake *(G-3287)*

Vidrio Technologies ....G...... 703 405-4944
Leesburg *(G-7371)*

OIL TREATING COMPOUNDS

Afton Chemical Corporation ....B...... 804 788-5800
Richmond *(G-11476)*

Afton Chemical Corporation ....G...... 804 788-5250
Richmond *(G-11477)*

OILS & ESSENTIAL OILS

710 Essentials LLC ....G...... 540 748-4393
Spotsylvania *(G-12880)*

WDFUP LLC ....G...... 757 309-6214
Hampton *(G-6271)*

OILS & GREASES: Blended & Compounded

American Bioprotection Inc ....G...... 866 200-1313
Surry *(G-13795)*

OILS & GREASES: Lubricating

Beard Llc Randall ....G...... 434 602-1224
Bremo Bluff *(G-1944)*

Iris Co ....G...... 804 310-1054
Richmond *(G-11621)*

Kenneth Hill ....G...... 804 986-8674
Richmond *(G-11642)*

Petrostar Global LLC ....G...... 301 919-7879
Chantilly *(G-2480)*

Wolf Hills Enterprises ....G...... 276 628-8635
Abingdon *(G-69)*

OILS, ANIMAL OR VEGETABLE, WHOLESALE

Omega Protein Corporation ....E...... 804 453-6262
Reedville *(G-10765)*

OILS: Essential

Body Cosmic Skincare ....G...... 757 701-8232
Chesapeake *(G-3010)*

Moth LLC ....G...... 804 655-8216
North Chesterfield *(G-9933)*

Peace Harmony and Love LLC ....G...... 571 210-5853
Centreville *(G-2328)*

OILS: Lubricating

Viscosity LLC ....G...... 757 343-9071
Chesapeake *(G-3363)*

OILS: Lubricating

Due North Ventures LLC ....G...... 540 443-3990
Blacksburg *(G-1734)*

OINTMENTS

Marah Bitar LLC ....G...... 856 630-4437
Clintwood *(G-3689)*

ON-LINE DATABASE INFORMATION RETRIEVAL SVCS

Grassroots Enterprise Inc ....F...... 703 354-1177
Herndon *(G-6690)*

Ubiquitywave LLC ....G...... 571 262-1406
Ashburn *(G-1344)*

OPERATOR TRAINING, COMPUTER

Fta Goverment Services Inc ....G...... 571 612-0413
Chantilly *(G-2423)*

Magnet Forensics Usa Inc ....G...... 519 342-0195
Herndon *(G-6740)*

OPERATOR: Apartment Buildings

Mars Machine Works Inc ....G...... 804 642-4760
Gloucester Point *(G-5873)*

OPHTHALMIC GOODS

Bausch & Lomb Incorporated ....C...... 434 385-0407
Lynchburg *(G-7650)*

Euclid Systems Corporation ....D...... 703 471-7145
Sterling *(G-13395)*

Legend Lenses LLC ....G...... 757 871-1331
Yorktown *(G-15974)*

Liberty Medical Inc ....G...... 703 636-2269
Sterling *(G-13441)*

Medlens Innovations LLC ....G...... 540 636-7976
Front Royal *(G-5542)*

Retivue LLC ....G...... 434 260-2836
Charlottesville *(G-2684)*

OPHTHALMIC GOODS, NEC, WHOLESALE: Contact Lenses

William O Wills Od ....F 540 371-9191
Fredericksburg (G-5237)

OPHTHALMIC GOODS: Eyewear, Protective

House of Vondrake Lavar LLC ....G 804 295-6136
Colonial Heights (G-3734)
Northfield Medical Mfg LLC ....E 800 270-0153
Norfolk (G-9669)

OPHTHALMIC GOODS: Frames, Lenses & Parts, Eyeglasses

Darwins LLC ....G 610 256-3716
Arlington (G-928)

OPHTHALMIC GOODS: Lenses, Ophthalmic

William O Wills Od ....F 540 371-9191
Fredericksburg (G-5237)

OPHTHALMIC GOODS: Spectacles

Spectacle & Mirth ....G 619 961-6941
Staunton (G-13296)
Spectacular Spectacles Inc ....G 540 636-2020
Front Royal (G-5555)

OPTICAL GOODS STORES

Eyeglass Repair Shoppe ....G 903 509-1517
Mount Solon (G-9087)

OPTICAL INSTRUMENTS & APPARATUS

Blue Ridge Optics LLC ....E 540 586-8526
Bedford (G-1628)
Edwards Optical Corporation ....G 757 496-2550
Virginia Beach (G-14434)
Elbit Systems Amer - Nght Vsio ....G 540 561-0254
Roanoke (G-11919)
Leica Microsystems Inc ....E 812 333-5416
Chantilly (G-2457)
Qbeam Inc ....G 703 574-5330
Leesburg (G-7329)

OPTICAL INSTRUMENTS & LENSES

American Rheinmetall Def Inc ....G 571 867-0047
Reston (G-10787)
Armstar Corporation ....G 703 241-8888
Falls Church (G-4750)
Avcom of Virginia Inc ....E 804 794-2500
North Chesterfield (G-9823)
Carl Zeiss Optical Inc ....G 804 530-8300
Chester (G-3390)
Carl Zeiss Vision Inc ....D 800 456-0088
Chester (G-3391)
Cedar Bluff VA Office ....G 276 964-4171
Cedar Bluff (G-2272)
Conforma Laboratories Inc ....E 757 321-0200
Norfolk (G-9502)
Dg Optics LLC ....G 434 227-1017
Charlottesville (G-2617)
Idu Optics LLC ....G 707 845-4996
Quinton (G-10698)
Isomet Corporation ....E 703 321-8301
Manassas (G-8087)
Optometrics LLC ....G 540 840-5802
Fredericksburg (G-5465)
Optx Imaging Systems LLC ....F 703 398-1432
Lorton (G-7520)
Rigel Systems Inc ....G 215 715-8950
Herndon (G-6792)
Spectrum Optometric ....G 804 457-8733
North Chesterfield (G-9986)
Tredegar Surfc Protection LLC ....G 804 330-1000
North Chesterfield (G-10041)
Trijicon Inc ....G 703 445-1600
Stafford (G-13204)
Venturewise LLC ....G 804 277-9564
Richmond (G-11435)

OPTICAL SCANNING SVCS

Automated Precision Inc ....F 757 223-4157
Newport News (G-9174)

OPTOMETRIC EQPT & SPLYS WHOLESALERS

Polychem Inc ....G 540 862-1321
Clifton Forge (G-3682)

OPTOMETRISTS' OFFICES

Euclid Systems Corporation ....D 703 471-7145
Sterling (G-13395)
William O Wills Od ....F 540 371-9191
Fredericksburg (G-5237)

ORDNANCE

Axon Enterprise Inc ....G 602 459-1278
Arlington (G-870)
Barker Collision Precision LLC ....G 716 481-8253
Richmond (G-11121)
Ccf/Swiss Inc ....G 804 622-4277
Richmond (G-11153)
E Giuffre Inc ....G 540 537-4367
Wirtz (G-15610)
Entwistle Company ....E 434 799-6186
Danville (G-3992)
Foxcreek Tactical LLC ....G 757 615-0474
Virginia Beach (G-14473)
H & S Tactical LLC ....G 540 710-2715
Fredericksburg (G-5294)
ITT Defense & Electronics ....A 703 790-6300
Mc Lean (G-8474)
Kongsberg Defense Systems Inc ....G 703 838-8910
Alexandria (G-255)
Kongsberg Prtech Systems USA C ....G 703 838-8910
Alexandria (G-256)
Larsco LLC ....G 804 400-0667
North Chesterfield (G-9913)
Mabe Tactical LLC ....G 276 524-4912
Big Stone Gap (G-1712)
Ro-Way Inc ....G 757 566-3569
Toano (G-13876)
Special Tactical Services LLC ....F 757 554-0699
Virginia Beach (G-14835)
Theresa Lucas Setelin ....G 804 266-2324
Glen Allen (G-5809)
Veteran Arms Inc ....G 703 217-7532
Woodbridge (G-15826)
Wayland Custom Calibers LLC ....G 540 533-6842
Winchester (G-15506)
Winchester Tool LLC ....G 540 869-1150
Winchester (G-15602)

ORGANIZATIONS: Medical Research

Neuro Stat Anlytcal Sltons LLC ....E 703 224-8984
Vienna (G-14104)

ORGANIZATIONS: Physical Research, Noncommercial

Centripetal Networks Inc ....E 571 252-5080
Herndon (G-6638)
Qinetiq Inc ....E 540 658-2720
Lorton (G-7523)
Qinetiq Inc ....G 540 658-2720
Lorton (G-7524)

ORGANIZATIONS: Professional

American Soc For Hort Science ....F 703 836-4606
Alexandria (G-132)

ORGANIZATIONS: Religious

Bible Truth Music ....G 757 365-9956
Newport News (G-9179)
Christian Fellowship Publs ....G 804 794-5333
North Chesterfield (G-9843)
Las Americas Newspaper Inc ....G 703 256-4200
Falls Church (G-4821)
Reconciliation Press ....G 703 743-2416
Gainesville (G-5610)

ORGANIZATIONS: Scientific Research Agency

Riverland Solutions Corp ....G 571 247-2382
Leesburg (G-7337)
Triquetra Phoenix LLC ....G 571 265-6044
Annandale (G-790)

ORGANIZERS, CLOSET & DRAWER Plastic

Danny Marshall ....G 434 797-5861
Danville (G-3976)
Long Solutions LLC ....G 703 281-2766
Vienna (G-14085)
Office Organizers ....G 757 343-6860
Chesapeake (G-3226)
Partnership For Success ....G 804 363-3380
North Chesterfield (G-9946)
Project Safe ....G 703 505-0440
Alexandria (G-318)

ORIENTED STRANDBOARD

Georgia-Pacific LLC ....C 434 283-1066
Gladys (G-5691)

ORNAMENTS: Lawn

Pamela J Luttrell Co ....G 540 837-1525
Bluemont (G-1890)
Stone Quarry ....G 757 722-9653
Newport News (G-9348)

OUTBOARD MOTORS & PARTS

Fridays Marine Inc ....G 804 758-4131
Saluda (G-12603)

OVERBURDEN REMOVAL SVCS: Anthracite Mining

Regent Allied Carbon Energy ....E 276 679-4994
Appalachia (G-800)

OVERBURDEN REMOVAL SVCS: Nonmetallic Minerals

Alfaro Torres German ....G 703 498-6295
Sterling (G-13341)
Peter Adams ....G 540 960-0241
Millboro (G-8938)

OVERBURDEN REMOVAL, METAL MINING

Stripping Center of Sterling ....G 703 904-9577
Sterling (G-13518)

PACKAGE DESIGN SVCS

Artfx LLC ....C 757 853-1703
Norfolk (G-9445)

PACKAGED FROZEN FOODS WHOLESALERS, NEC

Kiddos LLC ....G 540 468-2700
Monterey (G-9008)

PACKAGING & LABELING SVCS

Artfx LLC ....C 757 853-1703
Norfolk (G-9445)
Dominion Taping & Reeling Inc ....G 804 763-2700
Midlothian (G-8810)
Product Identification ....G 804 264-4434
Richmond (G-11336)
Virginia Kik Inc ....E 540 389-5401
Salem (G-12578)
Yupo Corporation America ....C 757 312-9876
Chesapeake (G-3381)

PACKAGING MATERIALS, WHOLESALE

Custom Packaging Inc ....F 804 232-3299
Richmond (G-11551)
Masa Corporation ....D 757 855-3013
Norfolk (G-9633)
SC&I of Virginia LLC ....D 804 876-3135
Doswell (G-4124)

PACKAGING MATERIALS: Paper

Bunzl Carolinas and Virginia ....G 804 236-5000
Henrico (G-6486)
Conwed Corp ....D 540 981-0362
Roanoke (G-12070)
Glad Products Company ....C 434 946-3100
Amherst (G-691)
Green Bay Packaging Inc ....E 540 678-2600
Winchester (G-15421)
Packaging Products Inc ....E 276 629-3481
Bassett (G-1588)

Employee Codes: A=Over 500 employees, B=251-500
C=101-250, D=51-100, E=20-50, F=10-19, G=1-9

2021 Virginia
Industrial Directory

PRODUCT

1009

Plymkraft Inc ....E 757 595-0364
Newport News (G-9314)
Safehouse Signs Inc ....E 540 366-2480
Roanoke (G-12174)
Signode Industrial Group LLC ....C 276 632-2352
Martinsville (G-8329)
Tigerseal Products LLC ....G 800 899-9389
Beaverdam (G-1614)
Vitex Packaging Group Inc ....F 757 538-3115
Suffolk (G-13780)
Westrock Mwv LLC ....A 804 444-1000
Richmond (G-11825)

PACKAGING MATERIALS: Paper, Coated Or Laminated

Tiger Paper Company Inc ....G 540 337-9510
Stuarts Draft (G-13661)

PACKAGING MATERIALS: Paperboard Backs For Blister/Skin Pkgs

Skin Amnesty ....G 757 491-9058
Virginia Beach (G-14822)

PACKAGING MATERIALS: Plastic Film, Coated Or Laminated

Arm Global Solutions Inc ....G 804 431-3746
South Chesterfield (G-12796)
Globus World Partners Inc ....G 757 645-4274
Williamsburg (G-15248)
Mottley Foils Inc ....F 434 392-8347
Farmville (G-4952)
Reynolds Presto Products Inc ....B 434 572-6961
South Boston (G-12788)
Rouse Wholesale ....G 276 445-3220
Rose Hill (G-12362)
Tredegar Corporation ....G 804 523-3001
Richmond (G-11418)
Tredegar Corporation ....D 804 330-1000
North Chesterfield (G-10029)

PACKAGING MATERIALS: Polystyrene Foam

Braun & Assoc Inc ....G 804 739-8616
Midlothian (G-8783)
Huntington Foam LLC ....D 540 731-3700
Radford (G-10716)
Instant Systems ....G 757 200-5494
Norfolk (G-9593)
Rogers Foam Corporation ....G 276 431-2641
Duffield (G-4184)

PACKING & CRATING SVC

CPS Contractors Inc ....G 804 561-6834
Moseley (G-9036)
US Parcel & Copy Center Inc ....G 703 365-7999
Manassas (G-8007)

PACKING SVCS: Shipping

Jeanette Ann Smith ....G 757 622-0182
Norfolk (G-9602)
S&R Pals Enterprises LLC ....G 540 752-1900
Fredericksburg (G-5481)
Softlogistics LLC ....G 703 865-7965
Great Falls (G-5980)

PACKING: Rubber

Darco Southern LLC ....E 276 773-2711
Independence (G-6981)

PADDING: Foamed Plastics

Carpenter Co ....D 804 359-0800
Richmond (G-11147)

PAGERS: One-way

Valcom Inc ....C 540 427-3900
Roanoke (G-12014)
Valcom Services LLC ....G 540 427-2400
Roanoke (G-12015)

PAINT STORE

Branch House Signature Pdts ....G 804 644-3041
Richmond (G-11507)
Vienna Paint & Dctg Co Inc ....G 703 281-5252
Vienna (G-14154)

PAINTING SVC: Metal Prdts

American Stripping Company ....E 703 368-9922
Manassas Park (G-8188)
Customer 1 One Inc ....F 276 645-9003
Bristol (G-1974)
Tc Kustoms ....G 434 348-3488
Drewryville (G-4139)
Tidal Corrosion Services LLC ....G 757 216-4011
Norfolk (G-9751)

PAINTS & ALLIED PRODUCTS

Akzo Nobel Coatings Inc ....E 540 982-8301
Roanoke (G-12030)
Augusta Paint & Decorating LLC ....G 540 942-1800
Waynesboro (G-15098)
Barney Family Enterprises LLC ....G 757 438-2064
Wakefield (G-14964)
C & P Inc ....G 703 522-2229
Arlington (G-896)
Coldens Concepts LLC ....G 757 644-9535
Chesapeake (G-3045)
Dispersion Specialties Inc ....F 804 798-9137
Ashland (G-1402)
Dual Dynamics Industrail Paint ....G 804 543-3216
Aylett (G-1548)
Ennis-Flint Inc ....E 804 309-3199
Richmond (G-11579)
Ervins Bathtub Refinishing ....G 703 730-8831
Woodbridge (G-15697)
Hanwha Azdel Inc ....D 434 385-6359
Forest (G-5073)
Indmar Coatings Corporation ....F 757 899-3807
Wakefield (G-14966)
International Paint LLC ....G 757 466-0705
Norfolk (G-9595)
K C G Inc ....G 703 542-7120
Chantilly (G-2539)
Lasar Chemicals ....G 757 286-9808
Chesapeake (G-3175)
Mkm Coatings LLC ....G 804 514-3506
Mechanicsville (G-8663)
Osburn Coatings Inc ....G 804 769-3030
Aylett (G-1551)
PPG Industries Inc ....G 703 370-5636
Alexandria (G-315)
PPG Industries Inc ....G 804 794-5331
Richmond (G-11061)
Sampson Coatings Incorporated ....G 804 359-5011
Richmond (G-11371)
Sherwin-Williams Company ....G 804 264-6156
Glen Allen (G-5795)
Vienna Paint & Dctg Co Inc ....G 703 281-5252
Vienna (G-14154)
Vienna Paint & Dctg Co Inc ....G 703 450-0300
Sterling (G-13551)
Vienna Pt Reston/Herndon 04 ....G 703 733-3899
Herndon (G-6839)
Virginia Premiere Paint Contr ....G 804 398-1177
Richmond (G-11813)

PAINTS, VARNISHES & SPLYS, WHOLESALE: Paints

Ennis-Flint Inc ....E 804 309-3199
Richmond (G-11579)

PAINTS: Asphalt Or Bituminous

Darrell A Wilson ....G 540 598-8412
Vinton (G-14173)
M & R Striping LLC ....G 703 201-7162
Broad Run (G-2068)

PAINTS: Oil Or Alkyd Vehicle Or Water Thinned

Axalta Coating Systems LLC ....E 540 622-2951
Front Royal (G-5521)

PALLETS

Duck Pallet Co LLC ....G 540 477-2771
Mount Jackson (G-9069)
Expressway Pallet Inc ....F 804 231-6177
South Chesterfield (G-12804)
Jif Pallets LLC ....G 276 963-6107
Doran (G-4117)
Pallet Services ....G 804 233-6584
Richmond (G-11705)

PALLETS & SKIDS: Wood

Alexandria Packaging LLC ....D 703 644-5550
Springfield (G-12940)
Amware Logistics Services Inc ....F 540 389-9737
Salem (G-12474)
Charles City Forest Products ....E 804 966-2336
Providence Forge (G-10620)
Lignetics of Virginia Inc ....E 434 676-4800
Kenbridge (G-7034)

PALLETS: Plastic

Graham Packg Plastic Pdts Inc ....C 540 564-1000
Harrisonburg (G-6325)

PALLETS: Wooden

Allied Pallet Company ....C 804 966-5597
New Kent (G-9128)
Andis Pallet Co Inc ....F 276 628-9044
Abingdon (G-11)
Andis Wood Products Inc ....G 276 628-7764
Bristol (G-2005)
Apex Pallets LLC ....F 804 246-1499
West Point (G-15153)
Beach Pallets Inc ....G 757 773-1931
Virginia Beach (G-14268)
Bolivia Lumber Company LLC ....E 540 862-5228
Clifton Forge (G-3678)
Brown Enterprise Pallets LLC ....G 804 447-0485
Richmond (G-11512)
Chep (usa) Inc ....D 804 226-0229
Richmond (G-11527)
Curtis Russell Lumber Co Inc ....E 276 346-1958
Jonesville (G-7020)
Deep Corporation ....F 804 751-1826
Richmond (G-11040)
Direct Wood Products ....E 804 843-4642
West Point (G-15155)
Ellington Wood Products Inc ....F 434 922-7545
Amherst (G-690)
Green Leaf Logistics LLC ....G 757 899-0881
Spring Grove (G-12930)
Greg & Son Pallets ....G 757 449-3832
Chesapeake (G-3125)
Gregory Pallet & Lumber Co ....G 540 777-1715
Roanoke (G-12098)
Grottoes Pallet Co Inc ....G 540 249-4882
Grottoes (G-6020)
H & A Specialty Co ....G 757 206-1115
Williamsburg (G-15252)
Hallwood Enterprises Inc ....F 757 357-3113
Smithfield (G-12715)
J & D Pallets ....E 540 862-2448
Clifton Forge (G-3680)
JC Pallet Company Inc ....E 800 754-5050
Barhamsville (G-1572)
Martin Pallets & Wedges LLC ....F 276 694-4276
Stuart (G-13623)
Mc Farlands Mill Inc ....F 540 667-2272
Winchester (G-15444)
Mechanicsville Pallets Inc ....F 804 746-4658
Mechanicsville (G-8658)
Merlin Brougher ....G 434 572-8750
South Boston (G-12782)
Murdock Acquisition LLC ....G 804 798-9154
Ashland (G-1467)
P&B Pallet Co ....G 434 309-1028
Lynch Station (G-7628)
Pallet Asset Recovery Sys LLC ....G 800 727-2136
West Point (G-15161)
Pallet Empire ....G 804 389-3604
Richmond (G-11055)
Pallet Foundation ....G 703 519-6104
Alexandria (G-304)
Pallet Industries LLC ....G 757 238-2912
Carrollton (G-2245)
Pallet Recycling LLC ....E 304 749-7451
Strasburg (G-13593)
Palletone of Virginia LLC ....D 434 372-2101
Chase City (G-2915)
Peters Pallets Inc ....G 410 647-8094
Richmond (G-11057)
Piedmont Pallet Corporation ....G 434 836-6730
Danville (G-4026)
Porters Wood Products Inc ....E 757 654-6430
Boykins (G-1920)
Post & Pallet LLC ....G 757 645-5292
Toano (G-13874)
Potomac Supply Llc ....D 804 472-2527
Kinsale (G-7136)

Recycled Pallets Inc ....G 804 400-9931
  Mechanicsville *(G-8670)*
Scott Pallets Inc ....E 804 561-2514
  Amelia Court House *(G-672)*
Smalley Package Company Inc ....D 540 955-2550
  Berryville *(G-1691)*
Soft Play ....G 804 226-0380
  Richmond *(G-11761)*
Steves Pallets ....G 757 576-4488
  Virginia Beach *(G-14847)*
Swift Creek Forest Products ....E 804 561-1751
  Jetersville *(G-7015)*
Tidewater Pallets ....G 757 962-0020
  Norfolk *(G-9754)*
Tine & Company Inc ....G 276 881-8232
  Whitewood *(G-15193)*
Triple S Pallets LLC ....E 540 810-4581
  Mount Crawford *(G-9061)*
Virginia Pallets & Wood LLC ....G 434 515-2221
  Lawrenceville *(G-7187)*
Whitlow Lumber & Logging Inc ....G 276 930-3854
  Stuart *(G-13640)*
Williams Pallet Company ....G 276 930-2081
  Stuart *(G-13641)*
Williamsburg Millwork Corp ....D 804 994-2151
  Ruther Glen *(G-12464)*

PANEL & DISTRIBUTION BOARDS & OTHER RELATED APPARATUS

Villalva Inc ....G 703 527-0091
  Arlington *(G-1211)*

PANEL & DISTRIBUTION BOARDS: Electric

Mg Corp ....A 757 468-6000
  Virginia Beach *(G-14648)*

PANELS: Building, Metal

Nci Group Inc ....D 804 957-6811
  Prince George *(G-10603)*

PANELS: Building, Wood

Kennedy Konstruction Kompany ....E 540 984-4191
  Edinburg *(G-4308)*

PANELS: Wood

Eastern Panel Manufacturing ....E 434 432-3055
  Chatham *(G-2927)*

PAPER & BOARD: Die-cut

BSC Ventures LLC ....D 540 362-3311
  Roanoke *(G-11896)*
Cauthorne Paper Company Inc ....E 804 798-6999
  Ashland *(G-1388)*
Commonwealth Specialty Packg ....F 804 271-0157
  Ashland *(G-1393)*
H H Elements Inc ....G 434 249-8630
  Barboursville *(G-1561)*

PAPER CONVERTING

Cauthorne Paper Company Inc ....E 804 798-6999
  Ashland *(G-1388)*
Central National-Gottesman Inc ....G 703 941-0810
  Springfield *(G-12976)*
Jrjj Paper LLC ....G 757 473-3719
  Virginia Beach *(G-14576)*
Kapstone ....G 804 708-0083
  Manakin Sabot *(G-7900)*
Sfi Partners Club ....G 757 622-8001
  Norfolk *(G-9720)*
Sihl USA Inc ....G 757 966-7180
  Chesapeake *(G-3293)*

PAPER MANUFACTURERS: Exc Newsprint

Augusta Actuation LLC ....G 540 480-7619
  Steeles Tavern *(G-13310)*
Bear Island Paper Wb LLC ....C 804 227-4000
  Ashland *(G-1379)*
Breathe Bristol ....G 423 254-0323
  Bristol *(G-1967)*
Btbycb Inc ....G 703 992-9041
  Falls Church *(G-4903)*
Delfort USA Inc ....G 434 202-7870
  Charlottesville *(G-2779)*
Dough Pay ME of Bristol LLC ....G 276 644-8091
  Bristol *(G-2017)*

Eagle Paper International Inc ....G 757 363-8103
  Virginia Beach *(G-14426)*
Frankline Paper ....G 757 569-4321
  Franklin *(G-5144)*
Georgia-Pacific LLC ....B 434 299-5911
  Big Island *(G-1702)*
Gordon Paper Company Inc ....C 800 457-7366
  Virginia Beach *(G-14488)*
Greif Inc ....C 434 933-4100
  Gladstone *(G-5683)*
Hitchcock Paper Co ....G 571 398-6601
  Occoquan *(G-10173)*
International Paper ....G 757 569-4521
  Suffolk *(G-13725)*
International Paper Company ....C 757 569-4321
  Franklin *(G-5146)*
International Paper Company ....C 434 845-6071
  Lynchburg *(G-7745)*
International Paper Company ....G 804 232-4937
  Richmond *(G-11046)*
International Paper Company ....G 804 230-3100
  Richmond *(G-11620)*
P H Glatfelter Company ....G 540 548-1756
  Spotsylvania *(G-12907)*
Plymkraft Inc ....E 757 595-0364
  Newport News *(G-9314)*
Ritemade Paper Converters Inc ....G 800 821-5484
  Ashland *(G-1487)*
Southern Scrap Company Inc ....E 540 662-0265
  Winchester *(G-15481)*
West Rock ....G 434 352-2804
  Appomattox *(G-826)*
Westrock Cp LLC ....B 804 541-9600
  Hopewell *(G-6944)*
Westrock Cp LLC ....D 804 843-5229
  West Point *(G-15163)*
Westrock Mwv LLC ....G 434 685-1717
  Cascade *(G-2253)*
Wrkco Inc ....B 540 969-5000
  Covington *(G-3805)*
Yupo Corporation America ....C 757 312-9876
  Chesapeake *(G-3381)*

PAPER PRDTS

Cauthorne Industries Inc ....G 804 798-6999
  Ashland *(G-1387)*
Starry Nights Scrapbooking LLC ....G 757 784-6163
  Williamsburg *(G-15319)*

PAPER PRDTS: Book Covers

Blue Ridge Book Conservation ....G 434 295-9373
  Charlottesville *(G-2742)*
Bookwrights Press ....G 434 263-4818
  Lovingston *(G-7589)*

PAPER PRDTS: Cleansing Tissues, Made From Purchased Material

Rolhei LLC ....G 202 850-9000
  Williamsburg *(G-15307)*

PAPER PRDTS: Facial Tissues, Made From Purchased Materials

Pad A Cheek LLC ....G 434 985-4003
  Stanardsville *(G-13226)*

PAPER PRDTS: Infant & Baby Prdts

Oralign Baby LLC ....G 540 492-0453
  Martinsville *(G-8315)*

PAPER PRDTS: Molded Pulp Prdts

Disaster Aide ....G 201 892-8898
  Vienna *(G-14040)*

PAPER PRDTS: Napkins, Made From Purchased Materials

Sanfacon Virginia Inc ....E 434 376-2301
  Brookneal *(G-2112)*

PAPER PRDTS: Sanitary

Dr Finnie Care LLC ....G 804 852-7998
  Chester *(G-3406)*
Elliott Lestselle ....G 757 944-8152
  Virginia Beach *(G-14442)*

PAPER PRDTS: Tampons, Sanitary, Made From Purchased Material

Playtex Products LLC ....G 804 230-1520
  Richmond *(G-11717)*

PAPER: Absorbent

McAirlaids Inc ....C 540 352-5050
  Rocky Mount *(G-12338)*

PAPER: Adhesive

Essentra Packaging Inc ....E 804 518-1803
  South Chesterfield *(G-12802)*
Tigerseal Products LLC ....G 800 899-9389
  Beaverdam *(G-1614)*

PAPER: Bond

Newport Timber LLC ....F 703 243-3355
  Arlington *(G-1077)*

PAPER: Book

You Buy Book Paperback Exc ....G 757 237-6426
  Virginia Beach *(G-14954)*

PAPER: Book, Coated, Made From Purchased Materials

Germinal Dimensions Inc ....G 540 552-8938
  Blacksburg *(G-1741)*

PAPER: Bristols

National Junior Tennis League ....G 276 669-7540
  Bristol *(G-1984)*

PAPER: Business Form

Linwood L Pope ....G 757 654-9397
  Courtland *(G-3772)*

PAPER: Catalog

Chocolate Paper Inc ....G 540 989-7025
  Roanoke *(G-11908)*

PAPER: Cigarette

Mundet Inc ....D 804 644-3970
  Richmond *(G-11684)*

PAPER: Coated & Laminated, NEC

Blanco Inc ....G 757 766-8123
  Yorktown *(G-15939)*
Eastern Panel Manufacturing ....E 434 432-3055
  Chatham *(G-2927)*
Giesecke+devrient ....C 703 480-2000
  Dulles *(G-4205)*
Green Bay Packaging Inc ....E 540 678-2600
  Winchester *(G-15421)*
Masa Corporation ....D 757 855-3013
  Norfolk *(G-9633)*
PP Payne Inc ....G 804 518-1803
  South Chesterfield *(G-12822)*
Safehouse Signs Inc ....E 540 366-2480
  Roanoke *(G-12174)*
Stickers Plus Ltd ....D 540 857-3045
  Vinton *(G-14184)*
Suter Enterprises Ltd ....F 757 220-3299
  Williamsburg *(G-15320)*
Wengers Electrical Service LLC ....G 540 867-0101
  Rockingham *(G-12283)*

PAPER: Coated, Exc Photographic, Carbon Or Abrasive

Greif Inc ....C 434 933-4100
  Gladstone *(G-5683)*

PAPER: Filter

Hollingsworth & Vose Company ....C 540 745-7600
  Floyd *(G-5029)*
Mundet-Hermetite Inc ....D 804 748-3319
  Colonial Heights *(G-3738)*

PAPER: Gift Wrap

Unique Industries Inc ....E 434 835-0068
  Blairs *(G-1833)*

Employee Codes: A=Over 500 employees, B=251-500
C=101-250, D=51-100, E=20-50, F=10-19, G=1-9

2021 Virginia
Industrial Directory

PRODUCT

1011

Wrap Buddies LLC.................................G..... 855 644-2783
Jeffersonton **(G-7014)**

PAPER: Kraft

Westrock Cp LLC...................................C..... 804 843-5416
West Point **(G-15164)**

PAPER: Newsprint

Blue Ridge Leader ....G..... 540 338-6200
Purcellville **(G-10652)**
Brant Industries Inc.............................C..... 804 227-3394
Ashland **(G-1385)**

PAPER: Packaging

Multi-Pack LLC......................................G..... 703 372-2303
Springfield **(G-13055)**
Reynolds Food Packaging LLC ....E..... 800 446-3020
Richmond **(G-11352)**

PAPER: Poster & Art

Masa Corporation.................................D..... 757 855-3013
Norfolk **(G-9633)**

PAPER: Printer

Deerfield Group LLC.............................G..... 434 591-0848
Zion Crossroads **(G-16007)**
International Paper Company................G..... 757 405-3046
Portsmouth **(G-10444)**
PDQ Printing LLC..................................G..... 804 228-0077
Richmond **(G-11710)**
Worldwide Papers Inc..........................G..... 703 883-8049
Falls Church **(G-4893)**

PAPER: Specialty

Signode Industrial Group LLC.............C..... 276 632-2352
Martinsville **(G-8329)**

PAPER: Specialty Or Chemically Treated

Stickers Plus Ltd................................D..... 540 857-3045
Vinton **(G-14184)**

PAPER: Tissue

Mercury Paper Inc................................D..... 540 465-7700
Strasburg **(G-13590)**

PAPER: Wallpaper

Schunck Rbcca Wlpr Instllation ....G..... 757 301-9922
Virginia Beach **(G-14796)**

PAPER: Wrapping & Packaging

Paper & Packaging Board ....G..... 703 935-5386
Mc Lean **(G-8523)**

PAPER: Writing

VA Writers Club ....G..... 804 648-0357
Richmond **(G-11804)**

PAPERBOARD

Sonoco Products Company...................F..... 434 432-2310
Chatham **(G-2936)**
Sonoco Products Company...................D..... 804 233-5411
Richmond **(G-11763)**
Sonoco Products Company...................E..... 540 862-4135
Covington **(G-3798)**
Westrock Mwv LLC ....C..... 540 662-6524
Winchester **(G-15507)**
Westrock Mwv LLC ....G..... 540 474-5811
Monterey **(G-9014)**
Westrock Mwv LLC ....D..... 540 377-9745
Raphine **(G-10752)**

PAPERBOARD CONVERTING

Manchester Industries Inc VA.............E..... 804 226-4250
Richmond **(G-11283)**

PAPERBOARD PRDTS: Building Insulating & Packaging

US Greenfiber LLC................................D..... 540 825-8000
Culpeper **(G-3927)**

PAPERBOARD PRDTS: Container Board

Ridgerunner Container LLC..................F..... 540 662-2005
Winchester **(G-15465)**
Westrock Cp LLC...................................C..... 804 843-5416
West Point **(G-15164)**

PAPERBOARD PRDTS: Folding Boxboard

Westrock Converting LLC.....................D..... 276 632-7175
Ridgeway **(G-11858)**

PAPERBOARD PRDTS: Kraft Linerboard

Interstate Resources Inc.....................G..... 703 243-3355
Arlington **(G-1010)**
Westrock Cp LLC...................................B..... 804 541-9600
Hopewell **(G-6944)**

PAPERBOARD PRDTS: Packaging Board

C & M Services LLC ....G..... 540 309-5555
Troutville **(G-13904)**
Signode Industrial Group LLC.............C..... 276 632-2352
Martinsville **(G-8329)**

PAPERBOARD PRDTS: Stencil Board

Pavement Stencil Company..................F..... 540 427-1325
Roanoke **(G-12145)**

PAPERBOARD: Liner Board

Westrock Mwv LLC ....E..... 434 352-7132
Appomattox **(G-827)**
Westrock Mwv LLC ....C..... 540 863-2300
Lowmoor **(G-7599)**
Westrock Mwv LLC ....A..... 804 444-1000
Richmond **(G-11825)**
Westrock Virginia Corporation ....F..... 804 444-1000
Richmond **(G-11827)**
Wrkco Inc ....B..... 540 969-5000
Covington **(G-3805)**

PARACHUTES

Butler Parachute Systems Inc ....F..... 540 342-2501
Roanoke **(G-12057)**
Butler Unmanned Parachute..................F..... 540 342-2501
Roanoke **(G-12058)**
Total Parachute Rigging Soluti ....G..... 757 777-8288
Suffolk **(G-13774)**

PARTICLEBOARD

Webb Furniture Enterprises Inc ....D..... 276 236-5111
Galax **(G-5654)**
Webb Furniture Enterprises Inc ....D..... 276 236-6141
Galax **(G-5655)**

PARTICLEBOARD: Laminated, Plastic

Georgia-Pacific LLC..............................B..... 434 634-5123
Emporia **(G-4359)**
Mid-Atlantic Manufacturing Inc ....E..... 804 798-7462
Oilville **(G-10183)**

PARTITIONS & FIXTURES: Except Wood

Cazador LLC..C..... 719 387-7450
Herndon **(G-6637)**
Explus Inc...D..... 703 260-0780
Dulles **(G-4201)**
Fast Signs Inc......................................F..... 540 389-6691
Salem **(G-12506)**
Heritage Interiors LLC ....G..... 571 323-5200
Herndon **(G-6696)**
Lozier Corp...G..... 703 742-4098
Reston **(G-10890)**
Modular Wood Systems Inc ....E..... 276 251-5300
Claudville **(G-3638)**
Museumrails LLC..................................G..... 540 603-2414
Louisa **(G-7561)**
Niday Inc..G..... 540 427-2776
Roanoke **(G-12141)**
Office Furniture Outlet Inc ....G..... 757 855-5522
Norfolk **(G-9673)**
Service Metal Fabricators Inc ....D..... 757 887-3500
Williamsburg **(G-15310)**
Showall Inc...G..... 276 646-8779
Chilhowie **(G-3560)**
Wegmann Usa Inc................................D..... 434 385-1580
Lynchburg **(G-7837)**

PARTITIONS: Solid Fiber, Made From Purchased Materials

Westrock Rkt LLC.................................C..... 804 444-6431
Richmond **(G-11826)**

PARTITIONS: Wood & Fixtures

B & J Cabinet Co Inc............................E..... 804 271-0192
North Chesterfield **(G-9825)**
Colonial Kitchen & Cabinets.................E..... 757 898-1332
Yorktown **(G-15943)**
Contemporary Kitchens Ltd..................G..... 804 758-2001
Topping **(G-13886)**
Huber Engineered Woods LLC ....C..... 434 476-6628
Crystal Hill **(G-3859)**
Innovative Office Design LLC ....G..... 757 496-9221
Virginia Beach **(G-14547)**
Mill Cabinet Shop Inc...........................E..... 540 828-6763
Bridgewater **(G-1954)**
Mint Springs Design ....G..... 434 806-7303
Crozet **(G-3844)**
Polyfab Display Company ....E..... 703 497-4577
Woodbridge **(G-15777)**
Pro-Tek Inc..G..... 757 813-9820
Hampton **(G-6222)**
Robert Furr Cabinet Shop ....G..... 757 244-1267
Hampton **(G-6230)**
Staton Mj & Associates Ltd ....G..... 804 737-1946
Sandston **(G-12637)**
Virginia Installations Inc......................G..... 540 298-5300
Elkton **(G-4338)**

PARTS: Metal

Accurate Machine Inc ....G..... 757 853-2136
Norfolk **(G-9418)**
Cushing Metals LLC ....G..... 804 339-1114
King William **(G-7128)**
Digital Machining Company..................G..... 540 786-7138
Fredericksburg **(G-5274)**
Red Stitch Tactical LLC ....G..... 703 798-4385
Manassas **(G-8141)**

PARTY & SPECIAL EVENT PLANNING SVCS

Jonette D Meade ....G..... 804 247-0639
Richmond **(G-11048)**
Perfect Pink LLC ....G..... 571 969-7465
Arlington **(G-1105)**

PARTY PLAN MERCHANDISERS

Perfect Pink LLC ....G..... 571 969-7465
Arlington **(G-1105)**

PATENT OWNERS & LESSORS

International Publishing Inc..................G..... 800 377-2838
Chesapeake **(G-3145)**

PATTERNS: Indl

Culpeper Mdel Barnstormers Inc ....G..... 540 349-2733
Broad Run **(G-2066)**
Dlba Robotics Ltd ....E..... 757 288-0206
Hampton **(G-6130)**
Hub Pattern Corporation ....E..... 540 342-3505
Roanoke **(G-12104)**
Hub Pattern Corporation ....E..... 540 342-3505
Salem **(G-12518)**
Integrated Tex Solutions Inc ....D..... 540 389-8113
Salem **(G-12522)**
Lynchburg Machining LLC.....................F..... 434 846-7327
Lynchburg **(G-7762)**
OK Foundry Company Inc......................E..... 804 233-9674
Richmond **(G-11698)**
Precision Patterns Inc ....G..... 434 385-4279
Forest **(G-5088)**

PAVERS

Paver Doctors LLC................................G..... 757 903-6275
Williamsburg **(G-15292)**
Sunset Pavers Inc ....G..... 703 507-9101
Sumerduck **(G-13794)**
Vision Tech Land Systems.....................B..... 703 739-2610
Alexandria **(G-377)**

PAVING MATERIALS: Prefabricated, Concrete

Cme Concrete LLC ....G..... 757 713-0495
Hampton (G-6114)

PAY TELEPHONE NETWORK

Hatcher Enterprises ....G..... 276 673-6077
Fieldale (G-4988)

PENCILS & PENS WHOLESALERS

Klassic Kreatures ....G..... 703 560-4409
Falls Church (G-4817)

PENS & PARTS: Ball Point

Securitas Inc ....G..... 800 705-4545
Richmond (G-11063)

PENS & PENCILS: Mechanical, NEC

J J E Enterprise Holdings LLC ....G..... 410 703-9241
Spotsylvania (G-12900)
Porex Technologies Corp ....C..... 804 524-4983
South Chesterfield (G-12821)
Porex Technologies Corporation ....G..... 804 275-2631
North Chesterfield (G-9951)

PENS: Fountain, Including Desk Sets

Dayspring Pens LLC ....G..... 888 694-7367
Virginia Beach (G-14394)
Goulet Pen Company LLC ....E..... 804 368-0482
Henrico (G-6518)

PERFUME: Perfumes, Natural Or Synthetic

Dorothy Prntice Armtherapy Inc ....G..... 703 657-0160
Fairfax (G-4614)
Elizabeth Arden Inc ....G..... 540 444-2406
Salem (G-12503)

PERFUMES

Beautymania ....G..... 703 300-9042
Alexandria (G-146)
Davidson Beauty Systems ....G..... 804 674-4875
Midlothian (G-8808)
House of Vondrake Lavar LLC ....G..... 804 295-6136
Colonial Heights (G-3734)

PERISCOPES

Kollmorgen Corporation ....A..... 540 639-9045
Radford (G-10720)

PERLITE: Processed

Northeast Solite Corporation ....G..... 804 262-8119
Richmond (G-11308)

PERSONAL & HOUSEHOLD GOODS REPAIR, NEC

Colonial Plating Shop ....G..... 804 648-6276
Richmond (G-11532)

PERSONAL DEVELOPMENT SCHOOL

Freshwter Parl Media Group LLC ....G..... 757 785-5483
Norfolk (G-9559)

PERSONAL DOCUMENT & INFORMATION SVCS

Ubiquitywave LLC ....G..... 571 262-1406
Ashburn (G-1344)

PESTICIDES

Residex LLC ....G..... 757 363-2080
Virginia Beach (G-14768)
Scotts Company LLC ....E..... 434 848-2727
Lawrenceville (G-7184)

PESTICIDES WHOLESALERS

Crop Production Services Inc ....G..... 804 282-7115
Richmond (G-11037)
Nutrien AG Solutions Inc ....G..... 757 229-9448
West Point (G-15160)
Nutrien AG Solutions Inc ....G..... 540 775-2985
Milford (G-8932)

PET & PET SPLYS STORES

Lexington Pet World ....G..... 540 464-4141
Fairfield (G-4732)

PET ACCESS: Collars, Leashes, Etc, Exc Leather

Chinook & Co LLC ....G..... 540 463-9556
Lexington (G-7389)
Dog Watch of Shenandoah ....G..... 540 867-5124
Dayton (G-4054)
Pawse & Play LLC ....G..... 757 230-9309
Virginia Beach (G-14712)
Premier Pet Products LLC ....D..... 804 594-0613
Glen Allen (G-5782)
Smbltc Corp ....G..... 703 596-5218
Manassas (G-8158)

PET FOOD WHOLESALERS

Mars Incorporated ....B..... 703 821-4900
Mc Lean (G-8491)

PET SPLYS

American Knine ....G..... 757 304-9600
Carrsville (G-2248)
Bay Breeze Labradors ....G..... 757 408-5227
Suffolk (G-13675)
Benttree Enterprises ....G..... 434 770-3632
Vernon Hill (G-13981)
Brad & Moo Merchants LLC ....G..... 434 738-1130
Herndon (G-6630)
Creature Comfort Custom Concie ....G..... 703 609-7098
Fairfax (G-4608)
Great Dogs Great Falls LLC ....G..... 703 759-3601
Great Falls (G-5958)
Lexington Pet World ....G..... 540 464-4141
Fairfield (G-4732)
Mada Vemi Alpacas ....G..... 434 770-1972
Axton (G-1540)
Midway Telemetry ....G..... 276 378-5933
Marion (G-8237)
Midway Telemetry ....G..... 276 227-0270
Wytheville (G-15900)
Mrs Bones ....G..... 757 412-0500
Virginia Beach (G-14667)
Ptc Enterprises LLC ....G..... 703 352-9274
Fairfax (G-4665)
Second Chance Dog Rescue ....G..... 540 752-1741
Fredericksburg (G-5484)
Stately Dogs ....G..... 276 644-4098
Bristol (G-1990)
Suzies Zoo Inc ....G..... 434 547-4161
Farmville (G-4959)
Wise Feline Inc ....G..... 703 609-2686
Alexandria (G-384)
Wylie Wagg of Tysons LLC ....G..... 703 748-0022
Falls Church (G-4894)
Yobnug LLC ....G..... 703 385-1880
Fairfax (G-4696)

PET SPLYS WHOLESALERS

Handi-Leigh Crafted ....G..... 540 349-7775
Warrenton (G-15023)
Lexington Pet World ....G..... 540 464-4141
Fairfield (G-4732)
Premier Pet Products LLC ....D..... 804 594-0613
Glen Allen (G-5782)

PETROLEUM & PETROLEUM PRDTS, WHOLESALE Diesel Fuel

Virginia Bodiesel Refinery LLC ....G..... 804 435-1126
Kilmarnock (G-7078)

PETROLEUM & PETROLEUM PRDTS, WHOLESALE Petroleum Brokers

Gibraltar Energy LLC ....G..... 202 642-2704
Alexandria (G-469)

PETROLEUM BULK STATIONS & TERMINALS

Airgas Usa LLC ....F..... 804 743-0661
North Chesterfield (G-9809)

PETROLEUM PRDTS WHOLESALERS

Southern States Coop Inc ....B..... 804 281-1000
Richmond (G-11389)

PEWTER WARE

K & S Pewter Inc ....G..... 540 751-0505
Leesburg (G-7294)
Lauret Company ....G..... 540 635-1670
Linden (G-7430)

PHARMACEUTICAL PREPARATIONS: Digitalis

Vidar Systems Corporation ....E..... 703 471-7070
Herndon (G-6838)

PHARMACEUTICAL PREPARATIONS: Druggists' Preparations

Abbott Laboratories ....A..... 434 369-3100
Altavista (G-622)
Barr Laboratories Inc ....D..... 434 534-8600
Forest (G-5052)
Cary Pharmaceuticals Inc ....G..... 703 759-7460
Great Falls (G-5944)
Daniel Orenzuk ....G..... 410 570-1362
Purcellville (G-10658)
Oc Pharma LLC ....G..... 540 375-6415
Salem (G-12550)
Sarfez Pharmaceuticals Inc ....G..... 703 759-2565
Vienna (G-14122)
Venkor Specialty Products LLC ....G..... 703 932-3840
Centreville (G-2349)

PHARMACEUTICAL PREPARATIONS: Medicines, Capsule Or Ampule

Loudoun Medical Group PC ....E..... 703 669-6118
Leesburg (G-7306)

PHARMACEUTICAL PREPARATIONS: Pills

Landos Biopharma Inc ....G..... 540 218-2262
Blacksburg (G-1751)

PHARMACEUTICAL PREPARATIONS: Proprietary Drug PRDTS

Chattem Inc ....G..... 540 786-7970
Fredericksburg (G-5261)
Chorda Pharma LLC ....G..... 251 753-1042
Roanoke (G-12067)
Stressa Incorporated ....G..... 540 460-9495
Buena Vista (G-2155)

PHARMACEUTICALS

Abbott Laboratories Inc ....G..... 434 369-3100
Altavista (G-623)
Adenosine Therapeutics LLC ....E..... 434 979-1902
Arlington (G-839)
Adial Corporation ....G..... 434 243-0570
Keswick (G-7041)
Adial Pharmaceuticals Inc ....G..... 434 422-9800
Charlottesville (G-2586)
Afton Scientific LLC ....E..... 434 979-3737
Charlottesville (G-2721)
AG Essence Inc ....G..... 804 915-6650
Richmond (G-11479)
Airbase Therapeutics ....G..... 434 825-0074
Charlottesville (G-2587)
Albemarle Corporation ....C..... 225 388-8011
Richmond (G-11092)
Allergan Sales LLC ....G..... 757 624-5320
Norfolk (G-9433)
Allergopharma Usa Inc ....G..... 919 749-6213
Alexandria (G-128)
Ampac Fine Chemicals VA LLC ....E..... 804 504-8600
Petersburg (G-10302)
Arconic Cbt ....G..... 757 825-6870
Hampton (G-6085)
Astellas Pharma Us Inc ....G..... 804 262-3197
Richmond (G-11120)
Axon Cells Inc ....G..... 434 987-4460
Keswick (G-7043)
Axon Medchem LLC ....G..... 703 650-9359
Reston (G-10796)
Batonbio LLC ....G..... 347 491-0189
Moseley (G-9034)

P
R
O
D
U
C
T

Bausch Health Americas Inc ....G.... 703 995-2400
  Chantilly (G-2375)
Best Medical Belgium Inc 800 336-4970
  Springfield (G-12961)
Best Medical International Inc ....C.... 703 451-2378
  Springfield (G-12962)
Boehringer Ingelheim Corp ....G.... 703 759-0630
  Reston (G-10810)
Boehringer Ingelheim Corp ....G.... 800 243-0127
  Ashburn (G-1251)
Boehringer Ingelheim Corp ....G.... 804 862-8316
  Petersburg (G-10310)
C B Fleet Company Inc ....C.... 434 528-4000
  Lynchburg (G-7671)
Careplex Pharmacy ....G.... 757 736-1215
  Hampton (G-6106)
Cavion Inc ....G.... 434 200-8442
  Charlottesville (G-2760)
Chantilly Biopharma LLC ....F.... 703 932-3840
  Chantilly (G-2390)
Clinpak Technologies LLC ....G.... 410 357-4454
  Heathsville (G-6460)
Contraline Inc ....G.... 347 327-3676
  Charlottesville (G-2770)
Covenant Therapeutics LLC ....G.... 434 296-8668
  Charlottesville (G-2772)
Diffusion Pharmaceuticals Inc ....G.... 434 220-0718
  Charlottesville (G-2782)
Diffusion Pharmaceuticals LLC ....F.... 434 220-0718
  Charlottesville (G-2783)
DK Pharma Group LLC ....G.... 540 574-4651
  Harrisonburg (G-6309)
Dova Pharmaceuticals Inc ....G.... 844 506-3682
  Charlottesville (G-2786)
Dove S Delights LLC ....G.... 540 298-7178
  Elkton (G-4325)
E Performance Inc ....G.... 703 217-6885
  Mc Lean (G-8422)
Ergoject LLC ....G.... 540 375-6415
  Salem (G-12505)
Exponential Biotherapies Inc ....G.... 703 288-3710
  Mc Lean (G-8425)
Extinction Pharmaceuticals ....G.... 757 258-0498
  Williamsburg (G-15241)
Ferrer ....G.... 703 862-4891
  Alexandria (G-461)
Gee Pharma LLC ....G.... 703 669-8055
  Leesburg (G-7277)
Genentech Inc ....C.... 703 841-1076
  Arlington (G-977)
Giant Pharmacy ....G.... 703 723-2161
  Ashburn (G-1286)
Granules Pharmaceuticals Inc ....D.... 571 325-5950
  Chantilly (G-2431)
Granules Pharmaceuticals Inc ....G.... 571 325-5950
  Chantilly (G-2432)
Gs Pharmaceuticals Inc ....G.... 703 789-3344
  Herndon (G-6693)
Gst Micro LLC ....G.... 203 271-0830
  Henrico (G-6519)
Hi-Tech Pharmacal Co Inc ....G.... 804 935-7220
  Richmond (G-11238)
Hst Global Inc ....G.... 757 766-6100
  Hampton (G-6170)
IJ Therapeutics LLC ....G.... 804 543-6360
  Richmond (G-11612)
Infinity Mg Inc ....G.... 703 916-0172
  Annandale (G-759)
Innocoll Inc ....G.... 703 980-4182
  Broadlands (G-2079)
Interntnal Phrm Excpnts Adting ....G.... 571 814-3449
  Arlington (G-1008)
Kerecis LLC ....F.... 703 465-7945
  Arlington (G-1022)
Lonza E Kingery ....G.... 540 774-8728
  Roanoke (G-12130)
Ltcpcms Inc ....F.... 888 513-5444
  Ashland (G-1454)
Macoma Capital ....G.... 434 249-4580
  Gordonsville (G-5914)
Mathemtics Scnce Ctr Fundation ....G.... 862 778-8300
  Richmond (G-11673)
Merck & Co Inc ....G.... 540 447-0056
  Waynesboro (G-15125)
Merck & Co Inc ....G.... 804 363-0876
  Richmond (G-11287)
MIND Pharmaceutical LLC ....G.... 434 202-9617
  Charlottesville (G-2835)
N-Molecular Inc ....F.... 703 547-8161
  Dulles (G-4211)

Northern VA Compounders Pllc ....G.... 855 792-5462
  Chantilly (G-2469)
Novartis Corporation ....G.... 540 435-1836
  Mc Gaheysville (G-8378)
Novozymes Biologicals Inc ....D.... 540 389-9361
  Salem (G-12547)
Novozymes Biologicals Inc ....G.... 540 389-9361
  Salem (G-12548)
Nutravail Holding Corp ....D.... 703 222-6348
  Chantilly (G-2476)
Os-Gim Pharmaceuticals Inc ....G.... 301 655-5191
  Woodbridge (G-15767)
Oxystress Therapeutics LLC ....G.... 832 277-0270
  Danville (G-4020)
Panaceutics Nutrition Inc ....F.... 919 797-9623
  Ringgold (G-11872)
PBM Foods Inc ....B.... 269 673-8451
  Charlottesville (G-2672)
PBM International Ltd ....G.... 800 959-2066
  Charlottesville (G-2673)
PBM Pharmaceuticals Inc ....F.... 434 980-8100
  Charlottesville (G-2842)
Perrigo Nutritionals ....F.... 434 297-1070
  Charlottesville (G-2676)
Pfizer Inc ....C.... 804 652-6782
  Richmond (G-11321)
Pharmaceutical RES Assoc Inc ....G.... 703 464-6300
  Reston (G-10924)
Pharmaceutical Source LLC ....G.... 757 482-3512
  Chesapeake (G-3238)
Pharmacist Pharmaceutical LLC ....G.... 540 375-6415
  Salem (G-12556)
Phlow Corp ....E.... 804 207-4893
  Richmond (G-11715)
Pinnacle Quality Asrn Svcs ....G.... 540 425-4123
  Bedford (G-1650)
Polykon Manufacturing LLC ....E.... 804 461-9974
  Sandston (G-12628)
Poms Corporation ....C.... 703 574-9901
  Herndon (G-6776)
Precision Nuclear of Virginia ....G.... 540 389-8333
  Roanoke (G-12151)
Precision Pharmacy LLC ....F.... 757 656-6560
  Chesapeake (G-3244)
Realta Life Sciences Inc ....G.... 757 418-4842
  Norfolk (G-9703)
Sanofi-Aventis US LLC ....G.... 804 651-1595
  Chesterfield (G-3521)
Savory Sun VA LLC ....E.... 540 898-0851
  Fredericksburg (G-5220)
Scilucent LLC ....F.... 703 435-0033
  Herndon (G-6802)
Selenix LLC ....G.... 540 375-6415
  Salem (G-12570)
Serpin Pharma LLC ....G.... 703 343-3258
  Nokesville (G-9399)
Shenox Pharmaceuticals Pllc ....G.... 732 309-2419
  Mc Lean (G-8546)
Sofie Co ....G.... 703 787-4075
  Sterling (G-13513)
Stcube Pharmaceuticals Inc ....G.... 703 815-1446
  Centreville (G-2341)
Stem Technologies LLC ....G.... 703 787-4654
  Herndon (G-6815)
Teva Pharmaceuticals ....E.... 888 838-2872
  Forest (G-5101)
Third Security Rnr LLC ....G.... 540 633-7900
  Radford (G-10744)
Topam LLC ....G.... 703 444-4240
  Herndon (G-6828)
VA Medical Supply Inc ....G.... 757 390-9000
  Chesapeake (G-3357)
Virchow Biotech Inc ....G.... 615 549-5999
  Arlington (G-1212)
Virginia Head and Neck Therape ....G.... 804 837-9594
  North Chesterfield (G-10009)
Vitaspan Corporation ....G.... 866 459-2773
  Arlington (G-1214)
Whitehall Robins ....G.... 804 257-2000
  Richmond (G-11829)
Wyeth Pharmaceuticals LLC ....C.... 804 652-6000
  Richmond (G-11459)

PHARMACEUTICALS: Medicinal & Botanical Prdts

Commonhealth Botanicals LLC ....G.... 434 906-2227
  Charlottesville (G-2769)
Dalitso LLC ....G.... 571 385-4927
  Alexandria (G-440)

Famarco Newco LLC ....E.... 757 460-3573
  Virginia Beach (G-14459)
Next Generation MGT Corp ....G.... 703 372-1282
  Ashburn (G-1321)
Tearsolutions Inc ....G.... 434 951-0444
  Charlottesville (G-2886)
Vollara LLC ....D.... 800 704-2378
  Bristol (G-1998)

PHOTOCOPYING & DUPLICATING SVCS

Accelerated Printing Corp Inc ....G.... 703 437-1084
  Leesburg (G-7213)
Best Impressions Inc ....F.... 703 518-1375
  Alexandria (G-421)
Campbell Printing Bristol Inc ....G.... 276 466-2311
  Bristol (G-2012)
Custom Book Bindery ....G.... 804 796-9520
  Chester (G-3399)
DEP Copy Center Inc ....G.... 703 499-9888
  Woodbridge (G-15682)
Grc Enterprises Inc ....E.... 540 428-7000
  Manassas (G-8077)
J & L Communications Inc ....G.... 434 973-1830
  Charlottesville (G-2650)
J & M Printing Inc ....G.... 703 549-2432
  Alexandria (G-241)
Lydell Group Incorporated ....G.... 804 627-0500
  Richmond (G-11277)
Minuteman Press of Mc Lean ....G.... 703 356-6612
  Mc Lean (G-8502)
Mr Print ....G.... 540 338-5900
  Purcellville (G-10671)
Oasis Global LLC ....F.... 703 560-7755
  Fairfax (G-4524)
Omega Alpha II Inc ....F.... 804 747-7705
  Richmond (G-11315)
Printing and Sign System Inc ....G.... 703 280-1550
  Fairfax (G-4532)
Professional Services ....G.... 540 953-2223
  Blacksburg (G-1781)
Quality Graphics & Prtg Inc ....F.... 703 661-6060
  Sterling (G-13483)
Salem Printing Co ....E.... 540 387-1106
  Salem (G-12566)
Shelley Imprssons Prtg Copying ....G.... 540 310-0766
  Fredericksburg (G-5485)
Swift Print ....G.... 540 774-1001
  Roanoke (G-12006)
Virginia Prtg Co Roanoke Inc ....G.... 540 483-7433
  Roanoke (G-12219)
Vk Printing ....G.... 703 435-5502
  Herndon (G-6842)
Westend Press LLC ....G.... 703 992-6939
  Fairfax Station (G-4727)
Wilkinson Printing Co Inc ....F.... 804 264-2524
  Glen Allen (G-5828)
Wilson Graphics Incorporated ....G.... 804 748-0646
  Chester (G-3468)

PHOTOENGRAVING SVC

Wilson Graphics Incorporated ....G.... 804 748-0646
  Chester (G-3468)

PHOTOGRAMMATIC MAPPING SVCS

Tomb Geophysics LLC ....G.... 571 733-0930
  Woodbridge (G-15823)

PHOTOGRAPHIC EQPT & CAMERAS, WHOLESALE

Veridos America Inc ....G.... 703 480-2025
  Dulles (G-4232)

PHOTOGRAPHIC EQPT & SPLY: Sound Recordg/Reprod Eqpt, Motion

Boomin Bass Global LLC ....F.... 757 776-8668
  Virginia Beach (G-14294)
Catawba Sound Studio ....G.... 540 992-4738
  Troutville (G-13905)
Ronald Paul Gardner ....G.... 804 815-6529
  Hayes (G-6405)

PHOTOGRAPHIC EQPT & SPLYS

ARC Second Inc ....G.... 703 435-5400
  Sterling (G-13348)
Ashen Writ LLC ....G.... 757 818-8271
  Chesapeake (G-2983)

(G-0000) Company's Geographic Section entry number

C I T C Imaging ....G...... 540 382-6557
Christiansburg *(G-3576)*

Canon Virginia Inc ....A...... 757 881-6000
Newport News *(G-9192)*

Creativexposure LLC ....G...... 540 668-9070
Hillsboro *(G-6862)*

Crossroad Data Solutions LLC ......G...... 804 302-4312
Chesterfield *(G-3490)*

Cybersquire LLC ....G...... 703 472-0283
Falls Church *(G-4906)*

Dun Inc ....G...... 804 240-4183
Palmyra *(G-10248)*

George Leica Systems ....G...... 804 299-3911
Ashland *(G-1420)*

Graphus Inc ....G...... 703 481-8861
Reston *(G-10862)*

Harkness Hall Ltd ....G...... 540 370-1590
Fredericksburg *(G-5194)*

Harkness Screens (usa) Limited ....G...... 540 370-1590
Roanoke *(G-11932)*

Ict Mondial Inc ....G...... 703 254-7416
Springfield *(G-13020)*

Konica Mnlta Bus Sltons USA In ....E...... 703 553-6000
Vienna *(G-14079)*

Openbox Networks LLC ....G...... 540 607-0149
Waynesboro *(G-15130)*

Pics By Kels Photography LLC ....G...... 540 958-4944
Clifton Forge *(G-3681)*

Q Star Technology LLC ....G...... 703 578-1495
Alexandria *(G-322)*

Rhoades Enterprise ....G...... 804 347-2051
Emporia *(G-4366)*

Tidewater Techs LLC ....G...... 757 301-1789
Virginia Beach *(G-14878)*

Tienda Herndon Inc ....G...... 703 478-0478
Herndon *(G-6826)*

Xerox ....G...... 703 330-4044
Manassas *(G-8180)*

PHOTOGRAPHIC EQPT & SPLYS WHOLESALERS

Regula Forensics Inc ....G...... 703 473-2625
Reston *(G-10936)*

PHOTOGRAPHIC EQPT & SPLYS: Blueprint Reproduction Mach/Eqpt

Extreme Exposure Media LLC ....F....... 540 434-0811
Harrisonburg *(G-6315)*

PHOTOGRAPHIC EQPT & SPLYS: Cameras, Aerial

Digital Design Imaging Svc Inc ....G...... 703 534-7500
Falls Church *(G-4907)*

Dreauxn Films LLC ....G...... 504 452-1117
Sterling *(G-13389)*

Safran Cabin Sterling Inc ....D...... 571 789-1900
Sterling *(G-13500)*

Zeido LLC ....G...... 202 549-5757
Stafford *(G-13213)*

PHOTOGRAPHIC EQPT & SPLYS: Densitometers

Kollmorgen Corporation ....A...... 540 639-9045
Radford *(G-10720)*

PHOTOGRAPHIC EQPT & SPLYS: Editing Eqpt, Motion Picture

Akmal Khaliqi ....G...... 202 710-7582
Woodbridge *(G-15643)*

PHOTOGRAPHIC EQPT & SPLYS: Film, Cloth & Paper, Sensitized

Dekdyne Inc ....G...... 757 221-2542
Williamsburg *(G-15232)*

PHOTOGRAPHIC EQPT & SPLYS: Paper & Cloth, All Types, NEC

Harkness Screens (usa) Limited ....E...... 540 370-1590
Fredericksburg *(G-5437)*

PHOTOGRAPHIC EQPT & SPLYS: Reels, Film

Dream Reels Inc ....E...... 540 891-9886
Fredericksburg *(G-5277)*

PHOTOGRAPHIC EQPT & SPLYS: Toners, Prprd, Not Chem Plnts

Canon Environmental Tech Inc ....B...... 804 695-7000
Gloucester *(G-5839)*

Lonesome Trails LLC ....G...... 276 445-5443
Rose Hill *(G-12361)*

PHOTOGRAPHIC EQPT & SPLYS: Trays, Printing & Processing

A Better Image ....G...... 804 358-9912
Richmond *(G-11076)*

PHOTOGRAPHIC EQPT & SPLYS: Tripods, Camera & Projector

Spider Support Systems ....G...... 703 758-0699
Reston *(G-10961)*

Wimberley Inc ....G...... 703 242-9633
Charlottesville *(G-2907)*

PHOTOGRAPHY SVCS: Commercial

Custom Graphics Inc ....G...... 540 882-3488
Paeonian Springs *(G-10238)*

Dun Inc ....G...... 804 240-4183
Palmyra *(G-10248)*

Fresh Printz LLC ....G...... 540 937-3017
Jeffersonton *(G-7012)*

PHOTOTYPESETTING SVC

Carter Composition Corporation ....C...... 804 359-9206
Richmond *(G-11149)*

Hto Inc ....G...... 703 533-0440
Falls Church *(G-4806)*

PHOTOVOLTAIC Solid State

Powermark Corporation ....G...... 301 639-7319
Union Hall *(G-13960)*

PHYSICIANS' OFFICES & CLINICS: Medical

Thomas H Rhea MD PC ....G...... 703 658-0300
Annandale *(G-787)*

PHYSICIANS' OFFICES & CLINICS: Medical doctors

Loudoun Medical Group PC ....E...... 703 669-6118
Leesburg *(G-7306)*

Orthotic Solutions L L C ....G...... 703 849-9200
Fairfax *(G-4527)*

Richmond Light Co ....G...... 804 276-0559
North Chesterfield *(G-9961)*

PICTURE FRAMES: Metal

Black Dog Gallery ....G...... 757 989-1700
Yorktown *(G-15938)*

Debs Picture This Inc ....G...... 757 867-9588
Yorktown *(G-15949)*

Frameco Inc ....G...... 540 375-3683
Salem *(G-12507)*

PICTURE FRAMES: Wood

All About Frames ....G...... 703 998-5868
Alexandria *(G-408)*

Casson Art & Frame ....G...... 276 638-1450
Martinsville *(G-8274)*

Corporate & Museum Frame Inc ....G...... 804 643-6858
Richmond *(G-11541)*

Discount Frames Inc ....G...... 703 550-0000
Lorton *(G-7481)*

Erickson & Ripper Framing ....G...... 703 549-1616
Alexandria *(G-202)*

Fine Arts Framers Inc ....G...... 703 525-3869
Arlington *(G-965)*

Finest Art & Framing LLC ....G...... 703 945-9000
Lansdowne *(G-7170)*

Hang Up ....G...... 703 430-0717
Sterling *(G-13418)*

Herff Jones Inc ....E...... 757 689-3000
Virginia Beach *(G-14517)*

Keyser Collection ....G...... 804 740-3237
Richmond *(G-11260)*

Lees Wood Products Inc ....F...... 540 483-9728
Rocky Mount *(G-12333)*

Museum Framing ....G...... 703 299-0100
Alexandria *(G-287)*

Smyth-Riley ....G...... 540 477-9652
Mount Jackson *(G-9079)*

Whimsical Expressions ....G...... 804 239-6550
Lanexa *(G-7169)*

PICTURE FRAMING SVCS, CUSTOM

Corporate & Museum Frame Inc ....G...... 804 643-6858
Richmond *(G-11541)*

Finest Art & Framing LLC ....G...... 703 945-9000
Lansdowne *(G-7170)*

Framing Concepts Inc ....G...... 757 460-9882
Virginia Beach *(G-14474)*

Museum Framing ....G...... 703 299-0100
Alexandria *(G-287)*

PICTURE PROJECTION EQPT

Huqa Live LLC ....G...... 202 527-9342
Woodbridge *(G-15724)*

PIECE GOODS & NOTIONS WHOLESALERS

Everything Gos LLC ....G...... 804 290-3870
Richmond *(G-11206)*

PIECE GOODS, NOTIONS & DRY GOODS, WHOL: Textiles, Woven

Wearmax Inc ....G...... 631 361-7222
Potomac Falls *(G-10510)*

PIECE GOODS, NOTIONS & OTHER DRY GOODS, WHOL: Flags/Banners

Inkd Out LLC ....G...... 757 369-9827
Newport News *(G-9259)*

Printing and Sign System Inc ....G...... 703 280-1550
Fairfax *(G-4532)*

Rain & Associates LLC ....G...... 757 572-3996
Virginia Beach *(G-14758)*

PIECE GOODS, NOTIONS & OTHER DRY GOODS, WHOLESALE: Fabrics

Mary Elizabeth Burrell ....G...... 804 677-2855
Richmond *(G-11670)*

PIECE GOODS, NOTIONS/DRY GOODS, WHOL: Sewing Splys/Notions

La Stitchery ....G...... 540 894-9371
Bumpass *(G-2163)*

PILINGS: Wood

C H Evelyn Piling Company Inc ....F....... 804 966-2273
Providence Forge *(G-10619)*

PILLOW FILLING MTRLS: Curled Hair, Cotton Waste, Moss

Tea Lady Pillows ....G...... 703 448-0033
Mc Lean *(G-8565)*

PINS

Push Pin Creative Solutions LLC ....G...... 703 313-0619
Alexandria *(G-562)*

PIPE & FITTING: Fabrication

American Mar & Indus Svcs LLC ....F....... 757 573-1209
Chesapeake *(G-2968)*

Applied Felts Inc ....D...... 276 656-1904
Martinsville *(G-8267)*

C & B Piping (e) Inc ....G...... 434 946-7170
Amherst *(G-686)*

Green Point ....G...... 703 391-5006
Herndon *(G-6691)*

Harrington Corporation ....C...... 434 845-7094
Lynchburg *(G-7729)*

Lane Enterprises Inc ....F....... 540 439-3201
Bealeton *(G-1600)*

Lokring Mid-Atlantic Inc ....G...... 757 423-2784
Norfolk *(G-9621)*

Mica Co of Canada Inc ....G...... 757 244-7311
Newport News *(G-9299)*

Super RAD Coils Ltd Partnr ....C...... 804 794-2887
North Chesterfield *(G-9992)*

P R O D U C T

PIPE & FITTING: Fabrication

U S Pipe Fabrication.....................F 540 439-7373
Remington (G-10775)

PIPE & FITTINGS: Cast Iron

Bingham & Taylor Corp ....C 540 825-8334
Culpeper (G-3872)

PIPE & TUBES: Aluminum

Montebello Packaging Inc ....C 540 437-0119
Harrisonburg (G-6348)

PIPE FITTINGS: Plastic

American Manufacturing Co Inc..........E 540 825-7234
Elkwood (G-4341)
Harrington Corporation ....C 434 845-7094
Lynchburg (G-7729)
Plastic Solutions Incorporated..............G 540 722-4694
Winchester (G-15461)

PIPE SECTIONS, FABRICATED FROM PURCHASED PIPE

Azz Inc ....E 276 466-5558
Bristol (G-2007)

PIPE, CULVERT: Concrete

Americast Inc ....E 757 494-5200
Chesapeake (G-2974)
Quality Culvert ....G 434 336-1468
Emporia (G-4365)

PIPE, SEWER: Concrete

Concrete Pipe & Precast LLC ....C 804 798-6068
Ashland (G-1394)
Concrete Pipe & Precast LLC ....E 757 485-5228
Chesapeake (G-3049)
Concrete Pipe & Precast LLC ....E 804 752-1311
Ashland (G-1395)

PIPE: Concrete

Empire Incorporated....................E 757 723-6747
Hampton (G-6140)
Setzer and Sons VA Inc Smith ....E 434 246-3791
Stony Creek (G-13568)

PIPE: Extruded, Aluminum

Kaiser Bellwood Corporation ....D...... 804 743-6300
North Chesterfield (G-9905)

PIPE: Plastic

Advanced Drainage Systems Inc ....E 540 261-6131
Buena Vista (G-2137)
Lane Enterprises Inc.....................F 540 439-3201
Bealeton (G-1600)

PIPE: Plate Fabricated, Large Diameter

Industrial Fabricators VA Inc ....D...... 540 943-5885
Fishersville (G-5005)

PIPE: Sheet Metal

Lane Enterprises Inc.....................F 276 223-1051
Wytheville (G-15895)
Nzo LLC ....F 434 660-7338
Bedford (G-1646)
Virginia Blower Company ....E 276 647-3804
Collinsville (G-3718)

PIPES & TUBES

Reline America Inc ....E 276 496-4000
Saltville (G-12588)

PIPES & TUBES: Steel

Dawson Enterprises Inc ....G 276 964-7245
Abingdon (G-28)
Noble-Met LLC...........................C 540 389-7860
Salem (G-12545)
Raymond Dawson ....G 276 676-9068
Abingdon (G-57)
Synalloy Corporation....................D...... 804 822-3260
Glen Allen (G-5804)
Usui International Corporation ....B 757 558-7300
Chesapeake (G-3356)

PIPES & TUBES: Welded

Tidewater Wldg Fabrication LLC..........G 757 636-6630
Chesapeake (G-3340)

PIPES: Tobacco

Colonial East Distributors LLC.............G 844 802-4427
Virginia Beach (G-14354)
Mya Saray LLC ....G 703 996-8800
Sterling (G-13458)
Old Dominion Pipe Company LLC ....G 757 710-2681
Painter (G-10241)

PIVOTS: Power Transmission

ABB Enterprise Software Inc ....G 434 575-2169
South Boston (G-12745)

PLACER GOLD MINING

Dm Associates LLC......................G 571 406-2318
Fairfax (G-4440)

PLANING MILL, NEC

Dejarnette Lumber Company.............F 804 633-9821
Milford (G-8930)
Ferguson Land and Lbr Co Inc............D...... 540 483-5090
Rocky Mount (G-12322)
Holland Lumber Co Inc..................G 804 443-4200
Millers Tavern (G-8940)
Jones Lumber Company J E..............E 804 883-6331
Montpelier (G-9017)
Morgan Lumber Company Inc ....E 434 735-8151
Red Oak (G-10759)
Northern Neck Lumber Co Inc ....E 804 333-4041
Warsaw (G-15071)
Pierce & Johnson Lumber Co Inc ....E 434 983-2586
Dillwyn (G-4098)
W T Jones & Sons Inc ....E 804 633-9737
Ruther Glen (G-12463)
Walton Lumber Co Inc ....F 540 894-5444
Mineral (G-8952)

PLANING MILLS: Independent, Exc Millwork

Chips Brookneal Inc ....E 434 376-6202
Brookneal (G-2109)

PLANING MILLS: Millwork

ART&creation Inc ....G 571 606-8999
Manassas (G-7913)
Treo Enterprise Solutions Inc ....F 804 977-9862
Henrico (G-6584)

PLANTS: Artificial & Preserved

OH My Goshyum LLC ....G 434 975-6628
Charlottesville (G-2669)

PLAQUES: Picture, Laminated

Aci Partners LLC..........................F 703 818-0500
Manassas (G-8019)
Cresset Corporation ....F 804 798-2691
Ashland (G-1399)

PLASMAS

Atcc Global ....G 434 237-6861
Lynchburg (G-7644)
I B R Plasma Center......................G 757 498-5160
Virginia Beach (G-14538)
Ked Plasma ....G 276 645-6035
Bristol (G-1981)

PLASTER & PLASTERBOARD

Stowe Inc A D ....F 757 397-1842
Portsmouth (G-10487)

PLASTER WORK: Ornamental & Architectural

A B C Manufacturing Inc ....G 540 789-7961
Willis (G-15352)

PLASTERING ACCESS: Metal

Darden Pressure Wash and Plst..........G 757 934-1466
Suffolk (G-13694)

PLASTIC PRDTS

Allen Watson ....G 703 620-5350
Reston (G-10784)
Alpha Industries..........................G 540 249-4980
Grottoes (G-6014)
Debra Kromer ....G 571 248-4070
Gainesville (G-5578)
Dong-A Package USA Corp ....G 703 961-1686
Chantilly (G-2410)
Marion Operations ....G 276 783-3121
Marion (G-8235)
Precise Technology Inc ....G 703 869-4220
Woodbridge (G-15778)
Utilities Products Intl ....G 703 725-3150
Falls Church (G-4888)

PLASTICS FILM & SHEET

Du Pont Tjin Flms US Ltd Prtnr ....B 804 530-4076
Chester (G-3409)
Klockner Pentaplast Amer Inc ....B 540 832-3600
Gordonsville (G-5909)
Klockner Pentaplast Amer Inc ....A 540 832-1400
Gordonsville (G-5910)
Klockner Pentaplast Amer Inc ....E 540 832-7615
Gordonsville (G-5911)
Klockner Pentaplast Amer Inc ....E 540 832-3600
Charlottesville (G-2653)
Klockner Pentaplast Amer Inc ....C 276 686-6111
Rural Retreat (G-12426)
Liqui-Box Corporation....................D...... 804 325-1400
Richmond (G-11658)
Reynolds Food Packaging LLC ....E 800 446-3020
Richmond (G-11352)
Tg Holdings International CV...............G 804 330-1000
North Chesterfield (G-10026)
Tredegar Corporation ....D...... 804 330-1000
North Chesterfield (G-10029)
Tredegar Corporation ....G 804 330-1000
North Chesterfield (G-10030)
Tredegar Film Products Latin ....G 804 330-1000
North Chesterfield (G-10034)
Virginia Industrial Plas Inc ....F 540 298-1515
Elkton (G-4337)

PLASTICS FILM & SHEET: Polyethylene

Tredegar Film Products Corp ....C 847 438-2111
North Chesterfield (G-10032)

PLASTICS FILM & SHEET: Polypropylene

Taghleef Industries Inc ....B 540 962-1200
Covington (G-3800)
Toray Plastics (america) Inc...............G 540 636-3887
Front Royal (G-5558)

PLASTICS FILM & SHEET: Vinyl

Brewco Corp..............................G 540 389-2554
Salem (G-12486)
OSullivan Films Inc ....E 540 667-6666
Winchester (G-15562)
OSullivan Films MGT LLC.................B 540 667-6666
Winchester (G-15563)
Pallas USA Ltd ....G 703 205-0007
Fairfax (G-4528)

PLASTICS FINISHED PRDTS: Laminated

Hawkins Glass Wholesalers LLC ....E 703 372-2990
Lorton (G-7492)

PLASTICS MATERIAL & RESINS

A At LLC ....G 316 828-1563
Waynesboro (G-15091)
Advansix Inc..............................E 804 504-0009
South Chesterfield (G-12793)
Albemarle Corporation...................C 225 388-8011
Richmond (G-11092)
Albemarle County Pub Schools ....G 434 296-3872
Charlottesville (G-2722)
All Points Countertop Inc ....E 540 665-3875
Winchester (G-15526)
Bl & Son Enterprises LLC ....G 757 502-7789
Chesapeake (G-3003)
Bl & Son Enterprises LLC ....G 757 938-9188
Hampton (G-6093)
Breathe-3dp LLC ....G 276 645-6556
Bristol (G-2009)

Carpenter Co .... C 804 359-0800
Richmond *(G-11146)*
Celise LLC .... G 757 771-5176
Poquoson *(G-10366)*
Cht USA Inc .... F 804 271-9010
North Chesterfield *(G-9844)*
Cht USA Inc .... E 800 852-3147
North Chesterfield *(G-9845)*
Detectamet Inc .... F 804 303-1983
Richmond *(G-11184)*
Dexco Polymers LP .... G 703 846-2193
Oakton *(G-10143)*
E I Du Pont De Nemours & Co .... E 804 530-9300
Hopewell *(G-6924)*
Eastern Bioplastics LLC .... G 540 437-1984
Mount Crawford *(G-9054)*
Eastman Chemical Company .... D 276 679-1800
Norton *(G-10117)*
Eastman Chemical Company .... G 276 632-4991
Martinsville *(G-8282)*
Eastman Chemical Resins Inc .... G 757 562-3121
Courtland *(G-3769)*
Eastman Performance Films LLC .... A 276 627-3000
Fieldale *(G-4984)*
Eastman Performance Films LLC .... E 276 762-0242
Fieldale *(G-4985)*
Eastman Performance Films LLC .... E 276 650-3354
Axton *(G-1536)*
Eastman Performance Films LLC .... F 276 627-3223
Fieldale *(G-4986)*
Eastman Performance Films LLC .... G 276 627-3355
Martinsville *(G-8284)*
Gargone John .... G 540 641-1934
Williamsburg *(G-15246)*
Henkel US Operations Corp .... F 804 222-6100
Richmond *(G-11236)*
Honeywell International Inc .... B 804 530-6352
Chester *(G-3422)*
Hudson Industries Inc .... D 804 226-1155
Richmond *(G-11244)*
Huntington Foam LLC .... D 540 731-3700
Radford *(G-10716)*
Invista Capital Management LLC .... E 540 949-2000
Waynesboro *(G-15117)*
Invista Capital Management LLC .... E 276 656-0500
Martinsville *(G-8301)*
Line-X Northern Virginia Inc .... G 703 433-9333
Sterling *(G-13442)*
Line-X of Blue Ridge .... G 540 389-8595
Salem *(G-12532)*
Line-X of Richmond .... G 804 321-9166
Richmond *(G-11270)*
Miller Waste Mills Inc .... G 434 572-3925
South Boston *(G-12783)*
Millie B Thompson .... G 276 475-5940
Damascus *(G-3949)*
Mitsubishi Chem Advanced Mtls .... G 276 228-0100
Wytheville *(G-15901)*
Omnidex Products Inc .... G 757 509-4030
Virginia Beach *(G-14694)*
Plasticlad LLC .... G 757 562-5550
Franklin *(G-5154)*
Polibak Plastics America Inc .... G 703 709-3004
Purcellville *(G-10673)*
Polynt Composites USA Inc .... E 434 432-8836
Chatham *(G-2933)*
Polyone .... G 540 667-6666
Winchester *(G-15567)*
Polythane of Virginia Inc .... G 540 586-3511
Bedford *(G-1651)*
SC Medical Overseas Inc .... G 516 935-8500
Norfolk *(G-9715)*
Ship Sstnability Solutions LLC .... G 757 574-2436
Chesapeake *(G-3291)*
Sii Inc .... G 540 722-6860
Clear Brook *(G-3651)*
Solutia Inc .... C 314 674-3150
Fieldale *(G-4991)*
Strata Film Coatings Inc .... G 540 343-3456
Roanoke *(G-12198)*
Sunlite Plastics Inc .... E 540 234-9271
Weyers Cave *(G-15178)*
Teijin-Du Pont Films Inc .... D 804 530-9310
Chester *(G-3459)*
Toray Plastics (america) Inc .... G 540 636-3887
Front Royal *(G-5558)*
Total Ptrchemicals Ref USA Inc .... E 434 432-3706
Chatham *(G-2939)*
Total Ptrchemicals Ref USA Inc .... G 276 228-6150
Wytheville *(G-15919)*
Trex Company Inc .... C 540 542-6800
Winchester *(G-15493)*
Trex Company Inc .... E 540 542-6800
Winchester *(G-15494)*
Wonders Inc .... G 434 845-0813
Amherst *(G-714)*

PLASTICS MATERIALS, BASIC FORMS & SHAPES WHOLESALERS

Naj Enterprises LLP .... G 202 251-7821
Mc Lean *(G-8509)*

PLASTICS PROCESSING

Alpha Industries Inc .... G 540 298-2155
Shenandoah *(G-12688)*
Preserve Resources Inc .... E 434 710-8131
Danville *(G-4032)*
Rehau Automotive LLC .... G 703 777-5255
Leesburg *(G-7333)*
Rehau Construction LLC .... E 800 247-9445
Leesburg *(G-7334)*
Rehau Incorporated .... C 703 777-5255
Leesburg *(G-7335)*
Rehau Industries LLC .... G 703 777-5255
Leesburg *(G-7336)*
Richard Y Lombard Jr .... G 757 499-1967
Virginia Beach *(G-14772)*
Tredegar Film Products Corp .... C 847 438-2111
North Chesterfield *(G-10032)*

PLASTICS: Blow Molded

PC Sands LLC .... G 703 534-6107
Arlington *(G-1102)*

PLASTICS: Extruded

Lineal Technologies Inc .... D 540 484-6783
Rocky Mount *(G-12335)*
Sunlite Plastics Inc .... E 540 234-9271
Weyers Cave *(G-15178)*

PLASTICS: Finished Injection Molded

Appalachian Plastics Inc .... E 276 429-2581
Glade Spring *(G-5673)*
Carris Reels Inc .... E 540 473-2210
Fincastle *(G-4995)*
Gs Industries Bassett Ltd .... D 276 629-5317
Bassett *(G-1584)*
Sheltech Plastics Inc .... G 978 794-2160
Elberon *(G-4319)*
Tessy Plastics LLC .... C 434 385-5700
Lynchburg *(G-7819)*
Tessy Plastics Corp .... C 434 385-5700
Lynchburg *(G-7820)*
Wolverine Advanced Mtls LLC .... E 540 552-7674
Blacksburg *(G-1806)*

PLASTICS: Injection Molded

Advantage Puck Group Inc .... E 434 385-9181
Lynchburg *(G-7634)*
Amcor Rigid Packaging Usa LLC .... C 276 625-8000
Wytheville *(G-15875)*
American Plstic Fbricators Inc .... F 434 376-3404
Brookneal *(G-2107)*
Blue Ridge Industries Inc .... C 540 662-3900
Winchester *(G-15389)*
Busada Manufacturing Corp .... F 540 967-2882
Louisa *(G-7547)*
D & D Inc .... G 540 943-8113
Waynesboro *(G-15107)*
Dan Charewicz .... G 815 338-2582
Suffolk *(G-13692)*
Delta Circle Industries Inc .... F 804 743-3500
North Chesterfield *(G-9857)*
E-Z Treat Inc .... F 703 753-4770
Haymarket *(G-6420)*
Galaxy Plastic Industries Inc .... G 434 757-7200
La Crosse *(G-7145)*
General Foam Plastics Corp .... A 757 857-0153
Virginia Beach *(G-14479)*
Gianni Enterprises Inc .... G 540 982-0111
Roanoke *(G-11925)*
Gianni Entps Inc DBA Vrgina Pl .... G 540 314-6566
Roanoke *(G-12097)*
Hqc Inc .... F 540 820-3277
Rockingham *(G-12255)*
IMS Gear Holding Inc .... E 757 468-8810
Virginia Beach *(G-14542)*
Indiana Floor Inc .... G 540 373-1915
Woodford *(G-15840)*
J R Plastics & Machining Inc .... G 434 277-8334
Lowesville *(G-7595)*
Limitless Gear LLC .... G 575 921-7475
Barboursville *(G-1564)*
Machine Tool Technology LLC .... F 804 520-4173
South Chesterfield *(G-12813)*
Matbock LLC .... G 757 828-6659
Virginia Beach *(G-14639)*
Norva Plastics Inc .... F 757 622-9281
Norfolk *(G-9670)*
Obsidian Solutions Group LLC .... F 540 286-2266
Fredericksburg *(G-5462)*
Polyfab Display Company .... E 703 497-4577
Woodbridge *(G-15777)*
Rsk Inc .... G 703 330-1959
Manassas *(G-8148)*
Rubber Plastic Met Engrg Corp .... F 757 502-5462
Virginia Beach *(G-14785)*
Superseal Corp .... G 540 645-1408
Fredericksburg *(G-5229)*
Total Molding Concepts Inc .... F 540 665-8408
Winchester *(G-15491)*
Trident Plastics Inc .... F 804 236-8705
Richmond *(G-11419)*
Valley Industrial Plastics Inc .... D 540 723-8855
Middletown *(G-8746)*
Virginia Plastics Company Inc .... E 540 981-9700
Roanoke *(G-12021)*

PLASTICS: Molded

Creative Urethanes Inc .... E 540 542-6676
Winchester *(G-15407)*
Klann Inc .... E 540 949-8351
Waynesboro *(G-15119)*
Leonard Alum Utlity Bldngs Inc .... G 434 792-8202
Danville *(G-4011)*
Mar-Bal Inc .... G 440 539-6595
Blacksburg *(G-1758)*
Mar-Bal Inc .... C 540 674-5320
Dublin *(G-4165)*
Molding & Traffic ACC LLC .... G 540 896-2459
Broadway *(G-2089)*
Molding Light LLC .... G 703 847-0232
Mc Lean *(G-8505)*
Pan Custom Molding Inc .... G 804 787-3820
Richmond *(G-11318)*
Polythane of Virginia Inc .... G 540 586-3511
Bedford *(G-1651)*
Reiss Manufacturing Inc .... C 434 292-1600
Blackstone *(G-1825)*
Shadows Ridge Inc .... G 540 722-0310
Winchester *(G-15475)*
T E L Pak Inc .... G 804 794-9529
Midlothian *(G-8911)*

PLASTICS: Polystyrene Foam

Bedford Storage Investment LLC .... D 574 284-1000
Bedford *(G-1625)*
Berry Plastics Design LLC .... C 757 538-2000
Suffolk *(G-13679)*
Carpenter Co .... B 804 359-0800
Richmond *(G-11031)*
Cellofoam North America Inc .... E 540 373-4596
Fredericksburg *(G-5258)*
Custom Foam and Cases LLC .... G 703 201-5908
Culpeper *(G-3887)*
Ds Smith PLC .... G 540 774-0500
Roanoke *(G-11916)*
F & D Manufacturing & Supply .... G 540 586-6111
Bedford *(G-1636)*
Fostek Inc .... D 540 587-5870
Bedford *(G-1637)*
General Display Company LLC .... G 703 335-9292
Manassas *(G-7943)*
Hudson Industries Inc .... D 804 226-1155
Richmond *(G-11244)*
Ibs .... G 540 662-0882
Winchester *(G-15427)*
Johns Manville Corporation .... B 540 984-4171
Edinburg *(G-4307)*
Magnifoam Delaware Inc .... G 804 564-9700
North Chesterfield *(G-9919)*
NC Foam & Sales .... G 540 631-3363
Front Royal *(G-5545)*
Olan De Mexico SA De CV .... G 804 365-8344
Keswick *(G-7053)*
Polycreteusa LLC .... G 804 901-6893
Charles City *(G-2579)*

PLATE WORK: Metalworking Trade

Plastic Fabricating Inc ....F 540 345-6901
  Roanoke *(G-12148)*

PLATEMAKING SVC: Color Separations, For The Printing Trade

Dap Enterprises Inc ....G 757 921-3576
  Williamsburg *(G-15229)*
Interntional Scanner Corp Amer ....F 703 533-8560
  Arlington *(G-1007)*
Separation Unlimited Inc ....F 804 794-4864
  North Chesterfield *(G-9975)*

PLATEMAKING SVC: Gravure, Plates Or Cylinders

F C Holdings Inc ....C 804 222-2821
  Sandston *(G-12614)*
Standex Engraving LLC ....D 804 236-3092
  Sandston *(G-12636)*

PLATES

American Technology Inds Ltd ....E 757 436-6465
  Chesapeake *(G-2973)*
Carter Composition Corporation ....C 804 359-9206
  Richmond *(G-11149)*
Criswell Inc ....F 434 845-0439
  Lynchburg *(G-7687)*
Digilink Inc ....E 703 340-1800
  Alexandria *(G-188)*
Grubb Printing & Stamp Co Inc ....F 757 295-8061
  Portsmouth *(G-10438)*
Hallmark Systems ....G 804 744-2694
  Midlothian *(G-8825)*
Kinyo Virginia Inc ....C 757 888-2221
  Newport News *(G-9276)*
Progress Printing Company ....D 434 239-9213
  Lynchburg *(G-7790)*
Stephenson Printing Inc ....D 703 642-9000
  Alexandria *(G-589)*
Tr Press Inc ....E 540 347-4466
  Warrenton *(G-15055)*
William R Smith Company ....E 804 733-0123
  Petersburg *(G-10351)*
Wood Television LLC ....E 540 672-1266
  Orange *(G-10232)*

PLATES: Sheet & Strip, Exc Coated Prdts

Steel Dynamics Inc ....A 540 342-1831
  Roanoke *(G-12197)*

PLATING & FINISHING SVC: Decorative, Formed Prdts

Garcia Wood Finishing Inc ....G 703 980-6559
  Springfield *(G-13008)*

PLATING & POLISHING SVC

Dave Cleary ....G 727 327-5118
  Manassas Park *(G-8198)*
Miller Metal Fabricators Inc ....E 540 886-5575
  Staunton *(G-13281)*
Stuart-Dean Co Inc ....D 703 578-1885
  Falls Church *(G-4878)*

PLATING SVC: Chromium, Metals Or Formed Prdts

Electro Finishing Inc ....F 276 686-6687
  Rural Retreat *(G-12423)*
Production Metal Finishers ....F 804 643-8116
  Richmond *(G-11726)*
Virginia Silver Plating Inc ....G 757 244-3645
  Newport News *(G-9375)*

PLATING SVC: Electro

Advanced Finishing Systems ....F 804 642-7669
  Hayes *(G-6393)*
Alexandria Coatings LLC ....E 703 643-1636
  Lorton *(G-7459)*
Avm Inc ....G 703 802-6212
  Chantilly *(G-2373)*
Electroplate - Rite Corp ....D 540 674-9363
  Dublin *(G-4155)*
Greystone of Virginia Inc ....D 757 566-8070
  Toano *(G-13865)*

Industrial Plating Corp ....G 434 582-1920
  Lynchburg *(G-7738)*
Richmond Pressed Met Works Inc ....G 804 233-8371
  Richmond *(G-11736)*
Sifco Applied Srfc Cncepts LLC ....G 757 855-4305
  Norfolk *(G-9724)*
US Anodizing Inc ....G 540 937-2801
  Amissville *(G-722)*

PLATING SVC: NEC

ARS Manufacturing Inc ....C 757 460-2211
  Virginia Beach *(G-14242)*
Brass Age Restorations ....G 540 743-4674
  Luray *(G-7603)*
Colonial Plating Shop ....G 804 648-6276
  Richmond *(G-11532)*
Hudgins Plating Inc C R ....D 434 847-6647
  Goode *(G-5890)*
James Williams Polsg & Buffing ....G 703 690-2247
  Woodbridge *(G-15728)*
Royal Silver Mfg Co Inc ....F 757 855-6004
  Norfolk *(G-9711)*
Virginia Custom Plating Inc ....G 804 789-0719
  Mechanicsville *(G-8694)*

PLAYGROUND EQPT

Deck World Inc ....G 804 798-9003
  Warsaw *(G-15062)*
Evans Custom Playsites ....G 804 615-3397
  Chester *(G-3414)*
Evolve Play LLC ....G 703 570-5700
  Winchester *(G-15416)*
Fize Wordsmithing LLC ....G 804 756-8243
  Glen Allen *(G-5731)*
Virginia Custom Buildings ....G 540 582-5111
  Spotsylvania *(G-12922)*

PLEATING & STITCHING SVC

Advertising Images & EMB ....G 703 447-4282
  Richmond *(G-11088)*
Capstone EMB & Screen Prtg ....G 757 619-0457
  Virginia Beach *(G-14318)*
Carl G Gilliam Jr ....F 276 523-0619
  Big Stone Gap *(G-1707)*
Catberries LLC ....G 714 873-8245
  Gainesville *(G-5575)*
Custom Designs & More ....G 540 894-5050
  Mineral *(G-8946)*
Delrand Corp ....G 757 490-3355
  Virginia Beach *(G-14401)*
East Coast Embroidery ....G 804 677-7584
  Clarksville *(G-3628)*
Imagine It Designs LLC ....G 703 795-6397
  Falls Church *(G-4808)*
Leading Edge Screen Printing ....F 540 347-5751
  Warrenton *(G-15030)*
Springbrook Craft Works ....G 540 896-3404
  Broadway *(G-2097)*
Vanguard Industries East Inc ....C 757 665-8405
  Norfolk *(G-9778)*
Virginia Quilting Inc ....C 434 757-1809
  La Crosse *(G-7152)*

PLUGS: Electric

Plug Electrical ....G 804 873-8688
  Henrico *(G-6549)*

PLUMBERS' GOODS: Rubber

Soter Martin of Virginia Inc ....G 804 550-2164
  Glen Allen *(G-5801)*

PLUMBING & HEATING EQPT & SPLY, WHOL: Htg Eqpt/Panels, Solar

Sun Rnr of Virginia Inc ....G 540 271-3403
  Harrisonburg *(G-6376)*

PLUMBING & HEATING EQPT & SPLY, WHOLESALE: Hydronic Htg Eqpt

Houghtaling Associates Inc ....G 804 740-7098
  Richmond *(G-11242)*

PLUMBING & HEATING EQPT & SPLYS WHOLESALERS

A Descal Matic Corp ....G 757 858-5593
  Norfolk *(G-9414)*
Mm Export LLC ....G 757 333-0542
  Virginia Beach *(G-14658)*

PLUMBING & HEATING EQPT & SPLYS, WHOL: Water Purif Eqpt

Dominion Water Products Inc ....E 804 236-9480
  Richmond *(G-11189)*
Vamac Incorporated ....E 540 535-1983
  Winchester *(G-15503)*
Vamaz Inc ....G 434 296-8812
  Charlottesville *(G-2711)*

PLUMBING FIXTURES

Allied Brass Inc ....E 540 967-5970
  Louisa *(G-7545)*
C & F Plumbing ....G 757 606-3124
  Portsmouth *(G-10402)*
Cardinal Park Unit Owners ....G 703 777-2311
  Leesburg *(G-7240)*
Doherty Plumbng Co ....G 757 842-4221
  Chesapeake *(G-3070)*
Euro Design Builders Group ....G 571 236-6189
  Fairfax *(G-4452)*
Hunter Industries Incorporated ....G 804 739-8978
  Midlothian *(G-8829)*
Nibco Inc ....B 540 324-0242
  Buena Vista *(G-2149)*
Pk Plumbing Inc ....G 804 909-4160
  Powhatan *(G-10566)*

PLUMBING FIXTURES: Brass, Incl Drain Cocks, Faucets/Spigots

Coyne & Delany Company ....E 434 296-0166
  Charlottesville *(G-2773)*

PLUMBING FIXTURES: Plastic

Barefoot Spas LLC ....E 804 298-3939
  North Chesterfield *(G-9827)*
CPS Contractors Inc ....G 804 561-6834
  Moseley *(G-9036)*
E-Z Treat Inc ....F 703 753-4770
  Haymarket *(G-6420)*
East Coast Walk In Tubs ....G 804 365-8703
  Axton *(G-1535)*
Flawless Shower Enclosures ....G 434 466-3845
  Ruckersville *(G-12402)*
Shelton Plumbing & Heating LLC ....G 804 539-8080
  North Chesterfield *(G-9977)*

PLUMBING FIXTURES: Vitreous

CPS Contractors Inc ....G 804 561-6834
  Moseley *(G-9036)*

POLES & POSTS: Concrete

Isle of Wight Forest Products ....F 757 899-8115
  Wakefield *(G-14967)*

POLISHING SVC: Metals Or Formed Prdts

Global Polishing System LLC ....G 937 534-1538
  Leesburg *(G-7279)*
Lone Star Polishing Inc ....G 434 585-3372
  Virgilina *(G-14193)*

POLYESTERS

Mar-Bal Inc ....C 540 674-5320
  Dublin *(G-4165)*

POLYETHYLENE RESINS

Abell Corporation ....E 540 665-3062
  Winchester *(G-15369)*

POLYMETHYL METHACRYLATE RESINS: Plexiglas

Plexi Worldwide LLC ....G 804 625-2524
  Sterling *(G-13471)*

POLYTETRAFLUOROETHYLENE RESINS

Pre Con Inc ....F 804 732-0628
  Chester (G-3444)
Pre Con Inc ....D 804 732-1253
  Petersburg (G-10336)
Pre Con Inc ....F 804 861-0282
  Petersburg (G-10337)
Pre Con Inc ....D 804 748-5063
  Chester (G-3445)
Pre Con Inc ....G 804 414-1560
  Chester (G-3446)
Pre Con Inc ....E 804 414-1560
  Chester (G-3447)

POSTERS

Beacon ....G 540 408-2560
  Fredericksburg (G-5251)
Brook Summer Media ....G 804 435-0074
  White Stone (G-15186)
Cut and Bleed LLC ....G 804 937-0006
  Richmond (G-11176)
Hughes Posters LLC ....G 304 615-3433
  Henrico (G-6523)

POTPOURRI

Katherine Chain ....G 804 796-2762
  Chester (G-3426)

POTTERY

April A Phillips Pottery ....G 703 464-1283
  Herndon (G-6615)
David Ceramics LLC ....G 703 430-2692
  Great Falls (G-5952)
Diaz Ceramics ....G 804 672-7161
  Henrico (G-6501)
Rebecca S Ceramics ....G 804 560-4477
  Richmond (G-11730)
Strange Designs ....G 540 937-5858
  Viewtown (G-14164)
Sweet Pea Ceramics LLC ....G 571 292-4313
  Warrenton (G-15054)
Team Ceramic Inc ....G 757 572-7725
  Chesapeake (G-3325)
Wonderfully Made Ceramics ....G 571 261-1633
  Nokesville (G-9405)

POULTRY & SMALL GAME SLAUGHTERING & PROCESSING

Alleghany Highlands AG Ctr LLC ....G 540 474-2422
  Monterey (G-9000)
Ariake USA Inc ....D 540 432-6550
  Harrisonburg (G-6293)
Cargill Incorporated ....E 540 896-7041
  Timberville (G-13846)
Georges Inc ....A 540 433-0720
  Harrisonburg (G-6322)
Georges Chicken LLC ....F 540 434-7394
  Harrisonburg (G-6323)
Perdue Farms Inc ....G 804 443-4391
  Tappahannock (G-13820)
Perdue Farms Inc ....G 804 453-4656
  Kilmarnock (G-7074)
Perdue Farms Inc ....B 757 787-5210
  Eastville (G-4296)
Pilgrims Pride Corporation ....E 540 564-6070
  Harrisonburg (G-6355)
Pilgrims Pride Corporation ....A 540 896-7000
  Timberville (G-13851)
Shortys Breading Company LLC ....G 434 390-1772
  Rice (G-11006)
Smithfield Foods Inc ....C 757 365-3000
  Smithfield (G-12728)
Smithfield Support Svcs Corp ....C 757 365-3541
  Smithfield (G-12739)
Tyson Foods Inc ....C 434 645-7791
  Crewe (G-3819)
Tyson Foods Inc ....G 540 740-3118
  New Market (G-9150)
Vpgc LLC ....G 540 867-4000
  Hinton (G-6907)

POWDER: Metal

J & J Powder Coating ....G 757 406-2922
  Virginia Beach (G-14555)

POWER GENERATORS

Alberts Associates Inc ....G 757 638-3352
  Portsmouth (G-10389)
Bwx Technologies Inc ....G 434 385-2535
  Lynchburg (G-7664)
Bwx Technologies Inc ....F 434 316-7638
  Lynchburg (G-7665)
Bwx Technologies Inc ....C 980 365-4300
  Lynchburg (G-7667)
GE Energy Manufacturing Inc ....G 540 775-6308
  King George (G-7090)
Hansen Turbine Assemblies Corp ....E 276 236-7184
  Galax (G-5639)
Holcomb Rock Company ....G 434 386-6050
  Lynchburg (G-7735)
Tmeic Corporation ....G 540 725-2031
  Salem (G-12574)
Uriel Wind Inc ....G 804 672-4471
  North Chesterfield (G-10042)

POWER SUPPLIES: All Types, Static

Marelco Power Systems Inc ....D 517 546-6330
  Richmond (G-11666)
Rack 10 Solar LLC ....G 703 996-4082
  Round Hill (G-12386)

POWER SUPPLIES: Transformer, Electronic Type

Marelco Power Systems Inc ....D 517 546-6330
  Richmond (G-11666)
Special T Manufacturing Corp ....F 276 475-5510
  Damascus (G-3950)
STS International Incorporated ....E 703 575-5180
  Arlington (G-1177)

POWER SWITCHING EQPT

Nova Power Solutions Inc ....G 703 657-0122
  Sterling (G-13462)

POWER TOOLS, HAND: Chain Saws, Portable

Stihl Incorporated ....E 757 468-4010
  Virginia Beach (G-14848)
Stihl Incorporated ....G 757 368-2409
  Virginia Beach (G-14849)

POWER TOOLS, HAND: Drills & Drilling Tools

Nuvidrill LLC ....G 540 353-8787
  Roanoke (G-12143)

POWER TRANSMISSION EQPT: Aircraft

Rolls-Royce Crosspointe LLC ....F 877 787-6247
  Prince George (G-10606)

POWER TRANSMISSION EQPT: Mechanical

Federal-Mogul Powertrain LLC ....B 540 557-3300
  Blacksburg (G-1737)
Ggb LLC ....G 571 234-9597
  Manassas (G-8074)
Progressive Manufacturing Corp ....E 804 717-5353
  Chester (G-3448)
Twin Disc Incorporated ....D 757 487-3670
  Chesapeake (G-3353)

PRECAST TERRAZZO OR CONCRETE PRDTS

Accaceek Precast ....G 540 604-7726
  Stafford (G-13111)
Alcat Precast Inc ....G 804 725-4080
  Moon (G-9031)
Carroll J Harper ....F 540 434-8978
  Rockingham (G-12244)
Coastal Precast Systems ....G 571 442-8648
  Leesburg (G-7247)
Forterra Pipe & Precast LLC ....F 757 485-5228
  Chesapeake (G-3108)
Pre Con Inc ....D 804 732-1253
  Petersburg (G-10336)
South East Precast Con LLC ....G 276 620-1194
  Wytheville (G-15915)
Statement LLC ....G 757 635-6294
  Virginia Beach (G-14843)

United Precast Finisher LLC ....G 804 386-6308
  Chester (G-3464)
Virginia Veterans Creations ....G 757 502-4407
  Virginia Beach (G-14922)

PRERECORDED TAPE, COMPACT DISC & RECORD STORES: Records

South Boston News Inc ....F 434 572-2928
  South Boston (G-12790)

PRESSED & MOLDED PULP PRDTS, NEC: From Purchased Materials

Conservtion Resources Intl LLC ....E 703 321-7730
  Lorton (G-7477)

PRESSED FIBER & MOLDED PULP PRDTS, EXC FOOD PRDTS

Fritz Ken Tooling & Design ....E 804 721-2319
  North Chesterfield (G-9880)
Pre Con Inc ....E 804 414-1560
  Chester (G-3447)

PRIMARY METAL PRODUCTS

Moore Metal ....G 757 930-0849
  Newport News (G-9305)

PRINT CARTRIDGES: Laser & Other Computer Printers

Hugo Miranda ....G 703 898-3956
  Bristow (G-2056)
Indenhooffen Productions LLC ....G 540 327-0898
  Winchester (G-15428)
Ink2work LLC ....G 605 202-9079
  Glen Allen (G-5751)
Jennifer Omohundro ....G 804 937-9308
  Richmond (G-11255)
Potomac Laser Recharge ....G 703 430-0166
  Great Falls (G-5975)
Refills Inc ....G 804 771-5460
  Richmond (G-11732)

PRINTED CIRCUIT BOARDS

Advanced Mfg Tech Inc ....D 434 385-7197
  Lynchburg (G-7633)
An Electronic Instrumentation ....C 703 478-0700
  Leesburg (G-7217)
Annex Inc ....G 703 239-8553
  Fairfax (G-4408)
Cardinal Mechatronics LLC ....G 540 922-2392
  Blacksburg (G-1728)
Circuit Solutions Intl LLC ....G 703 994-6788
  Burke (G-2186)
Ddi VA ....G 571 436-1378
  Dulles (G-4197)
Dwb Design Inc ....G 540 371-0785
  Fredericksburg (G-5422)
Kordusa Inc ....G 540 242-5210
  Stafford (G-13165)
Mercury Systems Inc ....G 703 243-9538
  Arlington (G-1061)
Moog Inc ....E 276 236-4921
  Galax (G-5641)
More Technology LLC ....G 571 208-9865
  Centreville (G-2322)
Pyott-Boone Electronics Inc ....C 276 988-5505
  North Tazewell (G-10105)
Stanford Electronics Mfg & Sls ....G 434 676-6630
  Brodnax (G-2105)
Ttm Technologies Inc ....B 703 652-2200
  Sterling (G-13540)
Viasystems North America Inc ....A 703 450-2600
  Sterling (G-13549)
W W W Electronics Inc ....F 434 973-4702
  Charlottesville (G-2714)

PRINTERS & PLOTTERS

Laserserv Inc ....E 804 359-6188
  Richmond (G-11266)

PRINTERS' SVCS: Folding, Collating, Etc

Flynn Enterprises Inc ....E 703 444-5555
  Sterling (G-13400)

Employee Codes: A=Over 500 employees, B=251-500
C=101-250, D=51-100, E=20-50, F=10-19, G=1-9

2021 Virginia
Industrial Directory

PRODUCT

1019

PRINTERS: Computer

1st Stop Electronics LLC ....G 804 931-0517
Richmond **(G-11070)**

Atlantic Computing LLC ....G 434 293-2022
Charlottesville **(G-2591)**

PRINTERS: Magnetic Ink, Bar Code

Barcoding Inc ....G 540 416-0116
Staunton **(G-13243)**

Covington Barcoding Inc ....G 434 476-1435
South Boston **(G-12755)**

Roxann Robinson Delegate ....G 804 308-1534
Richmond **(G-11748)**

PRINTING & BINDING: Books

R R Donnelley & Sons Company ....C 434 846-7371
Salem **(G-12560)**

PRINTING & EMBOSSING: Plastic Fabric Articles

Ideal Printing LLC ....G 434 421-1000
Danville **(G-3999)**

Nelson Hills Company ....G 434 985-7176
Stanardsville **(G-13224)**

Samco Textile Prints LLc ....G 571 451-4044
Woodbridge **(G-15802)**

PRINTING & ENGRAVING: Card, Exc Greeting

Veridos America Inc ....G 703 480-2025
Dulles **(G-4232)**

PRINTING & ENGRAVING: Invitation & Stationery

Artisan II Inc ....G 703 823-4636
Alexandria **(G-141)**

Creative Occasions ....G 703 821-3210
Mc Lean **(G-8412)**

Exquisite Invitations Inc ....G 276 666-0168
Martinsville **(G-8286)**

Leticia E Helleby ....G 336 769-7920
Crozet **(G-3842)**

Lettering By Lynne ....G 703 548-5427
Alexandria **(G-259)**

Paperbuzz ....G 434 528-2899
Lynchburg **(G-7781)**

Ribbons & Sweet Memories ....G 757 874-1871
Newport News **(G-9327)**

Romaine Printing ....G 804 994-2213
Hanover **(G-6283)**

Scribbles ....G 703 930-8808
Alexandria **(G-581)**

PRINTING & ENGRAVING: Poster & Decal

B & J Embroidery Inc ....G 276 646-5631
Saltville **(G-12584)**

Minglewood Trading ....G 804 245-6162
North Chesterfield **(G-9932)**

PRINTING & STAMPING: Fabric Articles

Anthony Biel ....G 703 307-8516
Dumfries **(G-4234)**

Association For Print Tech ....G 703 264-7200
Reston **(G-10793)**

Dap Enterprises Inc ....G 757 921-3576
Williamsburg **(G-15229)**

Dap Incorporated ....G 757 921-3576
Newport News **(G-9214)**

Party Headquarters Inc ....G 703 494-5317
Fredericksburg **(G-5467)**

R & R Printing ....G 434 985-9844
Ruckersville **(G-12411)**

Red Star Consulting LLC ....G 434 872-0890
Charlottesville **(G-2862)**

Scb Sales Inc ....G 540 342-6502
Roanoke **(G-12177)**

Tdi Printing Group LLC ....E 757 855-5416
Virginia Beach **(G-14866)**

Tee Time Threads LLC ....G 757 581-4507
Chesapeake **(G-3327)**

Trak House LLC ....G 646 617-4418
Richmond **(G-11791)**

PRINTING & WRITING PAPER WHOLESALERS

Tiger Paper Company Inc ....G 540 337-9510
Stuarts Draft **(G-13661)**

PRINTING INKS WHOLESALERS

Zeller + Gmelin Corporation ....D 800 848-8465
Richmond **(G-11463)**

PRINTING MACHINERY

Automated Signature Technology ....F 703 397-0910
Sterling **(G-13356)**

Canon Virginia Inc ....A 757 881-6000
Newport News **(G-9192)**

F C Holdings Inc ....C 804 222-2821
Sandston **(G-12614)**

Genik Incorporated ....G 804 226-2907
Richmond **(G-11218)**

Ir Engraving LLC ....D 804 222-2821
Sandston **(G-12621)**

Kinyo Virginia Inc ....C 757 888-2221
Newport News **(G-9276)**

Muller Martini Corp ....G 804 282-4802
Richmond **(G-11297)**

Old World Labs LLC ....G 800 282-0386
Norfolk **(G-9675)**

Southern Graphic Systems LLC ....D 804 226-2490
Richmond **(G-11764)**

Southern Gravure Service Inc ....G 804 226-2490
Richmond **(G-11387)**

Standex Engraving LLC ....D 804 236-3092
Sandston **(G-12636)**

Walter L James ....G 703 622-5970
Woodbridge **(G-15828)**

PRINTING MACHINERY, EQPT & SPLYS: Wholesalers

Red Tie Group Inc ....G 804 236-4632
Richmond **(G-11349)**

PRINTING TRADES MACHINERY & EQPT REPAIR SVCS

Laserserv Inc ....E 804 359-6188
Richmond **(G-11266)**

PRINTING, COMMERCIAL Newspapers, NEC

Davis Communications Group ....G 703 548-8892
Alexandria **(G-185)**

PRINTING, COMMERCIAL: Business Forms, NEC

TNT Printing LLC ....G 757 818-5468
Chesapeake **(G-3343)**

PRINTING, COMMERCIAL: Calendars, NEC

Reeses Amazing Printing Svcs ....G 804 325-0947
Henrico **(G-6556)**

PRINTING, COMMERCIAL: Certificates, Security, NEC

Larry Graves ....G 540 972-5320
Locust Grove **(G-7447)**

PRINTING, COMMERCIAL: Decals, NEC

Signs Work Inc ....G 804 338-7716
North Chesterfield **(G-9981)**

PRINTING, COMMERCIAL: Envelopes, NEC

Kenmore Envelope Company Inc ....C 804 271-2100
Richmond **(G-11259)**

Reed Envelope Company Inc ....F 703 690-2249
Fairfax Station **(G-4722)**

Willkat Envelopes & Graphics ....G 804 798-0243
Ashland **(G-1511)**

PRINTING, COMMERCIAL: Invitations, NEC

Paper Cover Rock ....G 434 979-6366
Charlottesville **(G-2840)**

PRINTING, COMMERCIAL: Labels & Seals, NEC

Blanco Inc ....F 540 389-3040
Roanoke **(G-11891)**

Haverline Labels Inc ....G 276 647-7785
Collinsville **(G-3712)**

Labels East Inc ....G 757 558-0800
Chesapeake **(G-3171)**

Multi-Color Corporation ....F 757 487-2525
Chesapeake **(G-3213)**

Safehouse Signs Inc ....E 540 366-2480
Roanoke **(G-12174)**

Star Tag & Label Inc ....F 540 389-6848
Salem **(G-12571)**

Virginia Tag Service Inc ....G 804 690-7304
King William **(G-7132)**

PRINTING, COMMERCIAL: Letterpress & Screen

Anthony Biel ....G 703 307-8516
Dumfries **(G-4234)**

Brewco Corp ....G 540 389-2554
Salem **(G-12486)**

Capital Brandworks LLC ....G 703 609-7010
Fairfax **(G-4423)**

Larry Ward ....G 804 778-7945
Chester **(G-3427)**

Print Tent LLC ....G 804 852-9750
Henrico **(G-6550)**

Rain & Associates LLC ....G 757 572-3996
Virginia Beach **(G-14758)**

T3j Enterprises LLC ....G 757 768-0528
Newport News **(G-9351)**

Younivercity LLC ....G 540 529-7621
Roanoke **(G-12231)**

PRINTING, COMMERCIAL: Literature, Advertising, NEC

ABC Imaging of Washington ....F 202 429-8870
Alexandria **(G-400)**

ABC Imaging of Washington ....F 571 514-1033
Herndon **(G-6602)**

Jamie Nicholas ....G 703 731-7966
Arlington **(G-1015)**

Kingdom Marketplace Intl LLC ....G 757 524-4948
Norfolk **(G-9612)**

Palmyrene Empire LLC ....F 703 348-6660
Woodbridge **(G-15770)**

Sina Corp ....G 703 707-8556
Herndon **(G-6809)**

PRINTING, COMMERCIAL: Magazines, NEC

Black Magazine LLC ....G 804 306-6735
Highland Springs **(G-6850)**

Hampton Roads Wedding Guide ....G 757 474-0332
Virginia Beach **(G-14501)**

PRINTING, COMMERCIAL: Post Cards, Picture, NEC

Csl Media LLC ....G 540 785-3790
Fredericksburg **(G-5181)**

Eggleston Minor ....G 757 819-4958
Norfolk **(G-9542)**

Mendoza Services Inc ....G 703 860-9600
Reston **(G-10898)**

PRINTING, COMMERCIAL: Promotional

Brandito LLC ....E 804 747-6721
Richmond **(G-11508)**

Custom Logos ....G 804 967-0111
Richmond **(G-11173)**

Elizabeth Urban ....G 757 879-1815
Yorktown **(G-15952)**

Keith Fabry ....G 804 649-7551
Richmond **(G-11640)**

Minuteman Press of Mc Lean ....G 703 356-6612
Mc Lean **(G-8502)**

Neatprints LLC ....G 703 520-1550
Springfield **(G-13057)**

PRINTING, COMMERCIAL: Publications

ABC Imaging ....G 571 379-4299
Manassas **(G-8017)**

Bara Printing Services .... G 804 303-8615
  Richmond (G-11028)
Gaia Communications LLC .... G 703 370-5527
  Alexandria (G-210)
Leopard Media LLC .... F 703 522-5655
  Arlington (G-1031)
Musicians Publications .... G 757 410-3111
  Chesapeake (G-3215)
Nabina Publications .... G 804 276-0454
  North Chesterfield (G-9937)
Scsi4me Corporation .... G 571 229-9723
  Manassas (G-8152)
Silver Communications Corp .... E 703 471-7339
  Sterling (G-13508)
Tom L Crockett .... G 757 460-1382
  Virginia Beach (G-14887)
Ttg Group LLC .... G 540 454-7235
  Arlington (G-1201)
Waterway Guide Media LLC .... E 804 776-8999
  Deltaville (G-4088)
Wingspan Publications .... G 703 212-0005
  Alexandria (G-383)
Zeba Magazine LLC .... G 202 705-7006
  Vienna (G-14163)

PRINTING, COMMERCIAL: Ready

Lydell Group Incorporated .... G 804 627-0500
  Richmond (G-11277)

PRINTING, COMMERCIAL: Schedules, Transportation, NEC

Stratgic Trnsp Initiatives Inc .... G 703 647-6564
  Alexandria (G-358)

PRINTING, COMMERCIAL: Screen

12th Tee LLC .... G 276 620-7601
  Wytheville (G-15873)
1816 Potters Road LLC .... G 757 428-1170
  Virginia Beach (G-14194)
3cats Promo .... G 540 586-7014
  Goode (G-5888)
A & S Screen Printing .... G 540 464-9042
  Lexington (G-7386)
Ace Screen Printing Inc .... G 540 297-2200
  Bedford (G-1617)
Action Tshirts LLC .... G 804 359-4645
  Richmond (G-11084)
Adoptees .... G 571 483-0656
  Arlington (G-840)
Alexander Amir .... G 757 714-1802
  Suffolk (G-13665)
Alien Silkscreen LLC .... F 540 389-5699
  Salem (G-12473)
American Graphics .... G 540 977-1912
  Troutville (G-13902)
Art Guild Inc .... F 804 282-5434
  Henrico (G-6476)
Artistees .... G 540 373-2888
  Fredericksburg (G-5170)
Atlantic Textile Group Inc .... F 757 249-7777
  Newport News (G-9173)
Beautees .... G 757 439-0269
  Suffolk (G-13677)
Best Deal On Shirts LLC .... G 757 754-9855
  Chesapeake (G-2998)
Black Eyed Tees .... G 276 971-1219
  Pounding Mill (G-10515)
Blue Ridge Embroidery Inc .... G 434 296-9746
  Charlottesville (G-2744)
Bobhron Inc .... F 540 389-5699
  Roanoke (G-12054)
Bryant Embroidery LLC .... G 757 498-3453
  Virginia Beach (G-14303)
Burden Bearer Tees LLC .... G 757 337-7324
  Toano (G-13858)
Burruss Signs Inc .... G 434 296-6654
  Charlottesville (G-2751)
Bxi Inc .... G 804 282-5434
  Richmond (G-11142)
Capital Screen Prtg Unlimited .... G 703 550-0033
  Lorton (G-7470)
Carl G Gilliam Jr .... F 276 523-0619
  Big Stone Gap (G-1707)
Cassandras Custom Designs LLC ... G 571 229-0389
  Manassas (G-8047)
CCI Screenprinting Inc .... G 703 978-0257
  Fairfax (G-4425)
Chameleon Silk Screen Co .... G 434 985-7456
  Stanardsville (G-13217)

CK Graphicwear LLC .... G 804 464-1258
  Richmond (G-11034)
Clarke B Gray .... G 757 426-7227
  Virginia Beach (G-14342)
Classic Creations Screen Prtg .... G 276 728-0540
  Hillsville (G-6889)
Collinsville Printing Co .... E 276 666-4400
  Martinsville (G-8276)
Commonwealth Graphics Inc .... G 703 495-0733
  Fairfax Station (G-4702)
Commonwlth Prmtnl/Dctional LLC ... F 540 887-2321
  Staunton (G-13249)
Complex Prints LLC .... G 804 274-0266
  Richmond (G-11537)
Confetti Advertising Inc .... G 276 646-5806
  Chilhowie (G-3548)
Corporate Imprints .... G 804 965-9838
  Henrico (G-6494)
Cotton Connection .... G 434 528-1416
  Lynchburg (G-7686)
Creative Impressions Inc .... G 757 855-2187
  Virginia Beach (G-14371)
Creative Ink Inc .... G 540 342-2400
  Roanoke (G-12074)
Custom Baked Tees .... G 703 888-8539
  Arlington (G-923)
Custom Ink .... G 703 957-1648
  Reston (G-10830)
Custom Ink .... G 703 884-2678
  Gainesville (G-5576)
Custom Ink .... G 703 884-2680
  Leesburg (G-7250)
Custom Ink .... G 434 422-5206
  Charlottesville (G-2775)
Custom Ink .... G 804 419-5651
  Richmond (G-11550)
Customink LLC .... C 434 326-1051
  Charlottesville (G-2613)
D J R Enterprises Inc .... F 540 639-9386
  Radford (G-10708)
Delrand Corp .... G 757 490-3355
  Virginia Beach (G-14401)
Diamond 7 .... G 540 362-5958
  Roanoke (G-11915)
Dreambuilders USA LLC .... G 908 265-2621
  Hampton (G-6134)
Dreams2realitees LLC .... G 434 594-6865
  Emporia (G-4357)
Drip Printing & Design .... G 757 962-1594
  Virginia Beach (G-14413)
Drmtees LLC .... G 540 720-3743
  Stafford (G-13138)
DS Tees LLC .... G 540 841-8831
  Fredericksburg (G-5278)
Dt Enterprises Inc .... G 434 799-3153
  Danville (G-3987)
Dull Inc Dolan & Norma .... F 703 490-0337
  Woodbridge (G-15687)
East Coast Graphics Inc .... G 804 798-7100
  Ashland (G-1406)
Ek Screen Prints .... G 703 250-2556
  Fairfax (G-4445)
El Chamo Printing .... G 703 582-5782
  Manassas (G-7936)
Eleven West Inc .... E 540 639-9319
  Fairlawn (G-4736)
Elite Prints .... G 703 780-3403
  Alexandria (G-455)
Fatim and Sallys Cstm Tees LLC .... G 619 884-5864
  Chesapeake (G-3098)
Folder Factory .... G 540 984-8852
  Edinburg (G-4304)
Garmonte LLC .... G 703 575-9003
  Alexandria (G-213)
Global Promos .... G 804 744-8112
  Midlothian (G-8823)
Golden Squeegee Inc .... G 804 355-8018
  Richmond (G-11220)
Goochland Tees Inc .... G 804 708-2041
  Oilville (G-10178)
Gotham Graphix LLC .... G 540 456-6600
  Afton (G-83)
Gray Scale Productions .... G 757 363-1087
  Virginia Beach (G-14490)
Gunnys Call Inc .... G 757 892-0251
  Virginia Beach (G-14496)
Harville Entps of Danville VA .... G 434 822-2106
  Danville (G-3997)
Heritage Treasures LLC .... G 571 442-8027
  Ashburn (G-1289)

High Peak Sportswear Inc .... G 540 953-1293
  Blacksburg (G-1743)
Hometown Imprints Inc .... G 540 878-5848
  Warrenton (G-15025)
Huds Tees .... G 757 650-6190
  Virginia Beach (G-14532)
Imagine This Company .... F 804 232-1300
  Richmond (G-11614)
Impressions of Norton Inc .... G 276 328-1100
  Wise (G-15626)
Impressions of Norton Inc .... G 276 679-1560
  Norton (G-10121)
Industry Graphics .... G 540 345-6074
  Roanoke (G-11939)
Ink Blot Inc .... G 757 644-6958
  Virginia Beach (G-14545)
Inklings Ink .... G 434 842-2200
  Fork Union (G-5111)
Innovative Graphics & Design .... G 276 679-2340
  Norton (G-10122)
J & D Specialtees .... G 804 561-0817
  Amelia Court House (G-659)
J & W Screen Printing Inc .... G 276 963-0862
  Cedar Bluff (G-2279)
J P R Enterprises .... G 757 288-8795
  Chesapeake (G-3146)
Jay Malanga .... G 703 802-0201
  Chantilly (G-2448)
Jbtm Enterprises Inc .... F 540 665-9651
  Winchester (G-15551)
Jonathan Promotions Inc .... G 540 891-7700
  Fredericksburg (G-5307)
Jtees Printing .... G 703 590-4145
  Woodbridge (G-15732)
Kash Design .... G 540 317-1473
  Culpeper (G-3904)
King Screen .... G 540 904-5864
  Roanoke (G-12118)
Kool Christian Tees .... G 804 201-1646
  Urbanna (G-13971)
Krazy Teesz .... G 757 470-4976
  Chesapeake (G-3167)
Lateeshirt .... G 703 532-7329
  Arlington (G-1028)
Lighthouse Concepts LLC .... G 703 779-9617
  Leesburg (G-7300)
Lou Wallace .... G 276 762-2303
  Saint Paul (G-12469)
Mad Hat Enterprises .... G 540 885-9600
  Staunton (G-13278)
Mahogany Styles By Teesha LLC ..... G 703 433-2170
  Sterling (G-13446)
Mantis Graphics .... G 757 482-4186
  Chesapeake (G-3196)
Mark-It .... G 540 434-4824
  Harrisonburg (G-6343)
Masked By Tee LLC .... G 757 373-9517
  Suffolk (G-13739)
Met of Hampton Roads Inc .... G 757 249-7777
  Newport News (G-9298)
Mojo Custom Sportswear LLC .... G 540 632-2116
  Daleville (G-3944)
Myra J Rudisill .... G 540 587-0402
  Altavista (G-637)
N&J Sales & Services .... G 804 559-7172
  Mechanicsville (G-8664)
National Caps .... G 434 572-4709
  South Boston (G-12784)
National Marking Products Inc .... E 804 266-7691
  Richmond (G-11299)
Nerd Alert Tees LLC .... G 804 938-9375
  Midlothian (G-8868)
Nets Pix & Things LLC .... G 757 466-1337
  Norfolk (G-9657)
Ocean Apparel Incorporated .... G 757 422-8262
  Virginia Beach (G-14690)
Ocean Creek Apparel LLC .... F 757 460-6118
  Virginia Beach (G-14691)
Official Tee Blanco LLC .... G 804 418-0218
  North Chesterfield (G-9943)
Og Pressmore LLC .... G 434 218-0304
  Bedford (G-1647)
Oldtown Printing & Copying .... G 540 382-6793
  Christiansburg (G-3607)
Os Ark Group LLC .... G 540 261-2622
  Buena Vista (G-2152)
Par Tees Vb .... G 757 500-7831
  Virginia Beach (G-14710)
Performance Signs LLC .... F 434 985-7446
  Ruckersville (G-12408)

PRODUCT

Precision Screen Printing ....G. ... 540 886-0026
Staunton (G-13284)
Press Press Merch LLC ....G. ... 540 206-3495
Roanoke (G-12153)
Pressed 4 Ink LLC ....G. ... 540 834-0125
Fredericksburg (G-5351)
Printingwright LLC ....G. ... 757 591-0771
Newport News (G-9317)
Pro Image Graphics ....G. ... 276 686-6174
Rural Retreat (G-12430)
Qualatee ....G. ... 434 842-3530
Palmyra (G-10257)
Racer Tees ....G. ... 540 416-1320
Crimora (G-3822)
Rappahanock Sports and Graphic ....G. ... 540 891-7662
Fredericksburg (G-5353)
Reckless Inc ....G. ... 757 469-4416
Chesapeake (G-3262)
Reston Shirt & Graphic Co Inc ....G. ... 703 318-4802
Sterling (G-14490)
Rhinos Ink Screen Prtg & EMB ....G. ... 540 347-6305
Warrenton (G-15047)
Roberts Screen Printing ....G. ... 757 487-6285
Portsmouth (G-10476)
Roberts Screen Printing ....G. ... 757 487-6285
Chesapeake (G-3272)
Rogers Screen Printing Inc ....G. ... 703 491-6794
Woodbridge (G-15799)
Royal Tee LLC ....G. ... 540 892-7694
Richmond (G-11367)
Sans Screenprint Inc ....E. ... 703 368-6700
Manassas (G-8149)
Sassy Clothing Blanks LLC ....G. ... 757 473-1980
Virginia Beach (G-14795)
Sayre Enterprises Inc ....C. ... 540 291-3808
Naturl BR STA (G-9112)
Scg Sports LLC ....G. ... 540 330-7733
Vinton (G-14183)
Screen Crafts Inc ....E. ... 804 355-4156
Richmond (G-11374)
Screen Prtg Tchncal Foundation ......G. ... 703 359-1300
Fairfax (G-4552)
Shirts Unlimited LLC ....G. ... 540 342-8337
Roanoke (G-12186)
Shotz From Heart LLC ....G. ... 804 898-5635
Petersburg (G-10342)
Sketchz ....G. ... 804 590-1234
Chesterfield (G-3525)
Southern ATL Screenprint Inc ....F. ... 757 485-7800
Chesapeake (G-3302)
Southernly Sweet Tees ....G. ... 434 447-6572
South Hill (G-12861)
Southprint Inc ....D. ... 276 666-3000
Martinsville (G-8334)
Sports Plus Incorporated ....E. ... 703 222-8255
Chantilly (G-2497)
Sportstitch ....G. ... 804 387-5127
Mechanicsville (G-8680)
Studio One Printing ....G. ... 703 430-8884
Sterling (G-13519)
T Shirt Broker ....G. ... 703 362-9297
Herndon (G-6821)
T-Shirt & Screen Print Co ....G. ... 540 667-2351
Winchester (G-15590)
T-Shirt Company LLC ....G. ... 703 669-4619
Leesburg (G-7357)
Taysteesmobilefoodcompany ....G. ... 240 310-6767
Fredericksburg (G-5231)
Tdi LLC ....E. ... 757 855-5416
Virginia Beach (G-14865)
Tee Spot Rching Higher Hts LLC ......G. ... 540 877-5961
Winchester (G-15488)
Tee Zone-VA ....G. ... 434 964-9245
Charlottesville (G-2700)
Tees & Co ....G. ... 757 744-9889
Chesapeake (G-3329)
Tees To Go 2 ....G. ... 540 569-2268
Staunton (G-13300)
Threadcount LLC ....G. ... 703 929-7033
Richmond (G-11788)
Tidalwave Tumbler & Tees LLC ....G. ... 757 814-1022
Virginia Beach (G-14871)
Tidewater Emblems Ltd ....F. ... 757 428-1170
Virginia Beach (G-14873)
Tls Tees LLC ....G. ... 540 455-5260
Spotsylvania (G-12918)
Tommy Atkinson Sports Entp ....G. ... 757 428-0824
Virginia Beach (G-14888)
Townsend Screen Printing LLC ....G. ... 804 225-0716
Glen Allen (G-5814)

Trademark Tees ....G. ... 757 232-4866
Virginia Beach (G-14891)
Trajectory Tees LLC ....G. ... 419 680-6903
Sterling (G-13537)
Triple Images Inc ....G. ... 540 829-1050
Culpeper (G-3926)
Tshirt Zone ....G. ... 540 431-5068
Winchester (G-15597)
Tshirtsru ....G. ... 301 744-7872
Woodbridge (G-15824)
Tweedle Tees ....G. ... 540 569-6927
Staunton (G-13304)
Typical Tees LLC ....G. ... 757 641-6514
Newport News (G-9367)
U S Graphics Inc ....G. ... 757 855-2600
Norfolk (G-9772)
United Screen Design ....G. ... 276 669-4669
Bristol (G-1995)
Vector Vortex LLC ....G. ... 540 330-7733
Vinton (G-14190)
Virginia T-Shirt Company LLC ....G. ... 540 752-8141
Fredericksburg (G-5498)
W M S B R G Grafix ....G. ... 757 565-5200
Williamsburg (G-15336)
Wework C/O The First Tee DC ....G. ... 231 632-0334
Tysons (G-13950)
Wild Bills Custom Screen Prtg ....G. ... 757 961-7576
Virginia Beach (G-14936)
Winner Made LLC ....G. ... 757 828-7623
Chesapeake (G-3379)
Wizard ....G. ... 818 988-2283
Fredericksburg (G-5392)

PRINTING, COMMERCIAL: Stationery, NEC

Kks Printing & Stationery ....G. ... 540 317-5440
Brandy Station (G-1941)

PRINTING, LITHOGRAPHIC: Calendars & Cards

Reeses Amazing Printing Svcs ....G. ... 804 325-0947
Henrico (G-6556)

PRINTING, LITHOGRAPHIC: Color

Databrands LLC ....G. ... 804 282-7890
Richmond (G-11178)

PRINTING, LITHOGRAPHIC: Forms & Cards, Business

Crabar/Gbf Inc ....E. ... 919 732-2101
Chatham (G-2926)
Finance Business Forms Company ....G. ... 703 255-2151
Vienna (G-14055)
Gary Gray ....G. ... 757 238-2135
Carrollton (G-2242)
JB Productions ....G. ... 703 494-6075
Woodbridge (G-15729)
Jeanette Ann Smith ....G. ... 757 622-0182
Norfolk (G-9602)
Webb-Mason Inc ....E. ... 703 242-7278
Reston (G-10988)
Whats Your Sign ....G. ... 276 632-0576
Martinsville (G-8353)

PRINTING, LITHOGRAPHIC: Forms, Business

General Financial Supply Inc ....E. ... 540 828-3892
Bridgewater (G-1952)
Printech Inc ....F. ... 540 343-9200
Roanoke (G-12154)

PRINTING, LITHOGRAPHIC: Offset & photolithographic printing

Pursuit Packaging LLC ....G. ... 540 246-4629
Broadway (G-2094)

PRINTING, LITHOGRAPHIC: On Metal

Bailey Printing Inc ....F. ... 434 293-5434
Charlottesville (G-2734)

PRINTING, LITHOGRAPHIC: Post Cards, Picture

Johnsons Postcards ....G. ... 434 589-7605
Palmyra (G-10250)

PRINTING, LITHOGRAPHIC: Promotional

Amplify Ventures LLC ....G. ... 571 248-2282
Gainesville (G-5570)
Digital Printing Solutions Inc ....G. ... 540 389-2066
Salem (G-12496)
Elite Prints ....G. ... 703 780-3403
Alexandria (G-455)
Good Printers Inc ....D. ... 540 828-4663
Bridgewater (G-1953)
Party Headquarters Inc ....G. ... 703 494-5317
Fredericksburg (G-5467)

PRINTING, LITHOGRAPHIC: Publications

Barg-N-Finders Inc ....G. ... 276 988-4953
North Tazewell (G-10094)
Upm Kymmene Inc ....G. ... 540 465-2700
Strasburg (G-13601)

PRINTING: Books

Volour Pub ....G. ... 757 547-6483
Virginia Beach (G-14926)

PRINTING: Books

Berryville Graphics Inc ....A. ... 540 955-2750
Berryville (G-1671)
Champs Create A Book ....G. ... 757 369-3879
Newport News (G-9197)
Christian Light Publications ....E. ... 540 434-0768
Harrisonburg (G-6300)
Collinsville Printing Co ....E. ... 276 666-4400
Martinsville (G-8276)
La Fleur De Lis LLC ....G. ... 703 753-5690
Gainesville (G-5594)
Lsc Communications Us LLC ....A. ... 540 434-8833
Rockingham (G-12259)
R R Donnelley & Sons Company ....E. ... 703 279-1662
Fairfax (G-4535)
Signs of The Times Apostolate ....G. ... 703 707-0799
Herndon (G-6807)
Walsworth Yearbooks VA East ....G. ... 757 636-7104
Virginia Beach (G-14929)
Xymid LLC ....E. ... 804 423-5798
Midlothian (G-8925)
Xymid LLC ....F. ... 804 744-5229
South Chesterfield (G-12829)

PRINTING: Broadwoven Fabrics. Cotton

Dap Incorporated ....G. ... 757 921-3576
Newport News (G-9214)
Krown LLC ....G. ... 804 307-9722
Midlothian (G-8841)
Love Those Tz LLC ....G. ... 757 897-0238
Virginia Beach (G-14625)
Soforeal Entertainment ....G. ... 804 442-6850
North Chesterfield (G-9982)

PRINTING: Checkbooks

Best Checks Inc ....G. ... 703 416-4856
Arlington (G-879)
Best Checks Inc ....E. ... 703 467-9300
Sterling (G-13358)
Business Checks of America ....G. ... 703 823-1008
Alexandria (G-156)
Deluxe Kitchen and Bath ....G. ... 571 594-6363
Chantilly (G-2531)

PRINTING: Commercial, NEC

4I Inc ....G. ... 434 792-0020
Danville (G-3951)
A Z Printing and Dup Corp ....G. ... 703 549-0949
Alexandria (G-115)
ABC Imaging ....G. ... 214 231-1332
Alexandria (G-399)
ABC Imaging of Washington ....E. ... 202 429-8870
Chantilly (G-2362)
ABC Imaging of Washington ....E. ... 703 396-9081
Manassas (G-7909)
Alpha Printing Inc ....G. ... 703 914-2800
Fairfax (G-4404)
Ambrosia Press Inc ....G. ... 540 432-1801
Weyers Cave (G-15165)
Apollo Press Inc ....E. ... 757 247-9002
Newport News (G-9169)
Applied Pressures Diamond ....G. ... 757 967-7006
Norfolk (G-9443)

ARC Document Solutions Inc ....G..... 703 518-8890
Alexandria (G-139)
Archematerial Inc ....G..... 703 826-6820
Fairfax (G-4411)
Arkay Packaging Corporation ....D..... 540 278-2596
Roanoke (G-11882)
Arteffects ....G..... 804 266-7691
Henrico (G-6477)
Associate Business Co Inc ....G..... 703 222-4624
Chantilly (G-2371)
Big Image Graphics Inc ....E..... 804 379-9910
North Chesterfield (G-9832)
Bison Printing Inc ....E..... 540 586-3955
Bedford (G-1627)
Branner Printing Service Inc ....E..... 540 896-8947
Broadway (G-2085)
Breakaway Holdings LLC ....F..... 703 953-3866
Chantilly (G-2381)
Brooke Printing ....G..... 757 617-2188
Virginia Beach (G-14300)
Bruce Moore Printing Co ....G..... 703 361-0369
Manassas (G-7922)
C2-Mask Inc ....G..... 703 304-9319
Chantilly (G-2384)
Capital Ideas Press ....G..... 434 447-6377
South Hill (G-12846)
Carla Wilkes ....G..... 434 228-1427
Lynchburg (G-7674)
Charlette Publishing Inc ....G..... 434 696-5550
Victoria (G-14000)
Chocklett Press Inc ....D..... 540 345-1820
Roanoke (G-12066)
Clarke Inc ....F..... 434 847-5561
Moneta (G-8959)
Coalfield Progress ....D..... 276 679-1101
Norton (G-10115)
Color Quest LLC ....G..... 540 433-4890
Harrisonburg (G-6303)
Commercial Copies ....G..... 757 473-0234
Virginia Beach (G-14357)
Commercial Prtg Direct Mail Svc ....G..... 757 422-0606
Virginia Beach (G-14358)
Creative Designs LLC ....G..... 540 223-0083
Louisa (G-7551)
Cynthia E Cox ....G..... 276 236-7697
Galax (G-5632)
Deadline Typesetting Inc ....G..... 757 625-5883
Norfolk (G-9520)
Decals By Zebra Racing ....G..... 540 439-8883
Bealeton (G-1597)
Diamond Screen Graphics Inc ....G..... 804 249-4414
Henrico (G-6500)
Digilink Inc ....E..... 703 340-1800
Alexandria (G-188)
Diversity Grphics Slutions LLC ....G..... 757 812-3311
Hampton (G-6129)
Dixie Press Custom Screen ....G..... 757 569-8241
Sedley (G-12679)
Dynamic Graphic Finishing Inc ....G..... 540 869-0500
Winchester (G-15413)
Eagle Designs ....G..... 540 428-1916
Warrenton (G-15001)
Edgelit Designz & Engrv LLC ....G..... 540 373-8058
Fredericksburg (G-5425)
Enexdi LLC ....F..... 703 748-0596
Vienna (G-14048)
Fairway Products Inc ....G..... 804 462-0123
Lancaster (G-7161)
Fedex Office & Print Svcs Inc ....G..... 703 491-1300
Woodbridge (G-15703)
Frederick J Day PC ....G..... 703 820-0110
Falls Church (G-4794)
Fso Mission Support LLC ....G..... 571 528-3507
Leesburg (G-7275)
G and H Litho ....G..... 571 267-7148
Sterling (G-13404)
Gary D Keys Enterprises Inc ....G..... 703 418-1700
Arlington (G-975)
General Financial Supply Inc ....E..... 540 828-3892
Bridgewater (G-1952)
Gival Press LLC ....G..... 703 351-0079
Arlington (G-979)
Hampton Roads Bindery Inc ....G..... 757 369-5671
Newport News (G-9241)
Harari Investments ....G..... 703 842-7462
Arlington (G-988)
Harrison Management Associates ......G..... 703 237-0418
Arlington (G-989)
Imprint ID Ltd ....G..... 877 385-7785
Lorton (G-7495)

Infoseal LLC ....D..... 540 981-1140
Roanoke (G-12106)
Ink It On Anything ....G..... 804 814-5890
Chesterfield (G-3505)
J & R Graphic Services Inc ....G..... 757 595-2602
Yorktown (G-15967)
James E Henson Jr ....G..... 804 648-3005
Richmond (G-11624)
Jet Design Graphics Inc ....G..... 804 921-4164
Amelia Court House (G-660)
Jjj Inc ....G..... 703 938-0565
Reston (G-10881)
Jumpstart Consultants Inc ....E..... 804 321-5867
Richmond (G-11638)
Kalwood Inc ....G..... 540 951-8600
Blacksburg (G-1749)
LL Distributing Inc ....G..... 540 479-2221
Fredericksburg (G-5313)
Lsc Communications Us LLC ....A..... 540 434-8833
Rockingham (G-12259)
Marilyn Carter ....G..... 804 901-4757
Henrico (G-6533)
Max Press Printing ....G..... 757 482-2273
Chesapeake (G-3199)
Metro Power Print ....G..... 703 221-3289
Woodbridge (G-15744)
Miglas Loupes LLC ....G..... 815 721-9133
Winchester (G-15556)
Mobile Tx/Bookkeeping Prtg LLC ....G..... 804 224-8454
Colonial Beach (G-3725)
Mountaineer Publishing Co Inc ....G..... 276 935-2123
Grundy (G-6038)
MSC Imaging Tech LLC ....G..... 804 593-0689
Henrico (G-6538)
Off The Press Inc ....G..... 703 533-1199
Falls Church (G-4850)
Office Electronics Inc ....G..... 757 622-8001
Norfolk (G-9672)
On-Site E Discovery Inc ....A..... 703 683-9710
Alexandria (G-300)
Over 9000 Media LLC ....G..... 850 210-7114
Norfolk (G-9679)
P I P Printing 1156 Inc ....G..... 434 792-0020
Danville (G-4022)
Payne Publishers Inc ....D..... 703 631-9033
Manassas (G-7988)
PCC Corporation ....E..... 757 721-2949
Virginia Beach (G-14713)
Piedmont Prtg & Graphics Inc ....F..... 434 793-0026
Danville (G-4029)
Pleckers Customer Engraving ....G..... 540 241-5661
Waynesboro (G-15131)
Press and Bindery Repair ....G..... 703 209-4247
Stafford (G-13183)
Prestige Press Inc ....E..... 757 826-5881
Hampton (G-6220)
Printing & Design Services ....G..... 434 969-1133
Buckingham (G-2134)
Pro Image Printing & Pubg LLC ....G..... 804 798-4400
Rockville (G-12295)
Program Services LLC ....G..... 757 222-3990
Norfolk (G-9698)
Progress Printing Company ....D..... 434 239-9213
Lynchburg (G-7790)
Progressive Graphics Inc ....E..... 757 368-3321
Virginia Beach (G-14744)
Qg LLC ....C..... 540 722-6000
Winchester (G-15462)
R & R Printing ....G..... 434 985-9844
Ruckersville (G-12411)
R R Donnelley & Sons Company ....G..... 540 434-8833
Harrisonburg (G-6358)
R R Donnelley & Sons Company ....A..... 434 846-7371
Lynchburg (G-7797)
R R Donnelley & Sons Company ....E..... 540 442-1333
Rockingham (G-12269)
R R Donnelley & Sons Company ....E..... 703 279-1662
Fairfax (G-4535)
Robert Deluca ....G..... 540 948-5864
Brightwood (G-1962)
Salem Printing Co ....E..... 540 387-1106
Salem (G-12566)
Schmids Printing ....G..... 540 886-9261
Staunton (G-13290)
Separation Unlimited Inc ....F..... 804 794-4864
North Chesterfield (G-9975)
Smartphone Photobooth ....G..... 757 364-2403
Chesapeake (G-3298)
Square One Printing Inc ....G..... 904 993-4321
Richmond (G-11771)

Stephenson Printing Inc ....D..... 703 642-9000
Alexandria (G-589)
Swift Print ....G..... 540 774-1001
Roanoke (G-12006)
Tension Envelope Corp ....G..... 540 615-5372
Richmond (G-11408)
Tetgraphic Inc ....G..... 434 845-4450
Lynchburg (G-7821)
Trademark Printing LLC ....G..... 757 465-1736
Portsmouth (G-10493)
Tru Point Design ....G..... 804 477-0976
Richmond (G-11422)
True Colors Screen Prtg LLC ....G..... 757 718-9051
Virginia Beach (G-14895)
Twelve Inc ....G..... 804 232-1300
Richmond (G-11797)
U3 Solutions Inc ....G..... 703 777-5020
Leesburg (G-7366)
Uniformed Services Almanac ....G..... 703 241-8100
Fairfax (G-4574)
United Graphics Inc ....G..... 540 338-7525
Round Hill (G-12393)
United Ink Press ....G..... 703 966-6343
Leesburg (G-7367)
V B Local Form Coupon Book ....G..... 239 745-9649
Virginia Beach (G-14904)
Van KY Troung ....G..... 804 612-6151
Richmond (G-11432)
Venutec Corporation ....G..... 888 573-8870
Centreville (G-2350)
Virginia Gazette Companies LLC ....G..... 757 220-1736
Newport News (G-9373)
Virginian Leader Corp ....F..... 540 921-3434
Pearisburg (G-10279)
Vk Printing ....G..... 703 435-5502
Herndon (G-6842)
Wealthy Sistas Media Group ....G..... 800 917-9435
Dumfries (G-4262)
Webb-Mason Inc ....G..... 804 897-1990
Rockville (G-12303)
Westend Press LLC ....G..... 703 992-6939
Fairfax Station (G-4727)
Winchester Printers Inc ....E..... 540 662-6911
Winchester (G-15512)
Wise Printing Co Inc ....G..... 276 523-1141
Big Stone Gap (G-1718)
Womack Publishing Co Inc ....G..... 434 352-8215
Appomattox (G-828)
Wood Television LLC ....E..... 540 672-1266
Orange (G-10232)
Zramics Mtls Science Tech LLC ....G..... 757 955-0493
Norfolk (G-9801)

PRINTING: Engraving & Plate

Dorothy Whibley ....G..... 703 892-6612
Montclair (G-8997)
Visual Communication Co Inc ....G..... 540 427-1060
Boones Mill (G-1899)
Visual Communication Co Inc ....G..... 540 427-1060
Boones Mill (G-1900)

PRINTING: Flexographic

Fortis Solutions Group LLC ....C..... 757 340-8893
Virginia Beach (G-14472)
Raymond Hill Consulting ....G..... 757 925-0136
Suffolk (G-13756)
Vitex Packaging Group Inc ....F..... 757 538-3115
Suffolk (G-13780)

PRINTING: Gravure, Business Form & Card

Knight Owl Graphics ....G..... 540 955-1744
Berryville (G-1683)
Lloyd Enterprises Inc ....G..... 804 266-1185
Richmond (G-11273)
R & R Printing ....G..... 434 985-9844
Ruckersville (G-12411)

PRINTING: Gravure, Cards, Exc Greeting

Addressograph Bartizan LLC ....E..... 800 552-3282
Rocky Mount (G-12311)

PRINTING: Gravure, Catalogs, No Publishing On-Site

R R Donnelley & Sons Company ....C..... 434 846-7371
Salem (G-12560)

PRODUCT

PRINTING: Gravure, Circulars

Zramics Mtls Science Tech LLC ....G....... 757 955-0493
Norfolk *(G-9801)*

PRINTING: Gravure, Coupons

Clipper Magazine LLC ....G....... 888 569-5100
Fairfax *(G-4606)*

PRINTING: Gravure, Forms, Business

Magnolia Graphics ....G....... 804 550-0012
Ashland *(G-1458)*

PRINTING: Gravure, Job

Charlotte Publishing Inc ....F....... 434 568-3341
Drakes Branch *(G-4131)*

PRINTING: Gravure, Labels

Label Laboratory Inc ....G....... 703 654-0327
Sterling *(G-13439)*

PRINTING: Gravure, Newspapers, No Publishing On-Site

Blue Ridge Buck Saver Inc ....G....... 434 996-2817
Charlottesville *(G-2743)*

PRINTING: Gravure, Post Cards, Picture

Grabber Construction Pdts Inc ....G....... 804 550-9331
Ashland *(G-1423)*
Stay In Touch Inc ....F....... 434 239-7300
Forest *(G-5095)*

PRINTING: Gravure, Rotogravure

K/R Companies LLC ....G....... 540 812-2422
Culpeper *(G-3903)*
Southern Graphic Systems LLC ....D....... 804 226-2490
Richmond *(G-11764)*
Taylor Communications Inc ....G....... 804 612-7597
Richmond *(G-11407)*
Vitex Packaging Group Inc ....F....... 757 538-3115
Suffolk *(G-13780)*

PRINTING: Gravure, Stationery & Invitation

Laura Hooper Calligrathy ....G....... 213 514-4170
Alexandria *(G-513)*
Reeses Amazing Printing Svcs ....G....... 804 325-0947
Henrico *(G-6556)*

PRINTING: Laser

American Laser Centers ....G....... 804 200-5000
Richmond *(G-11109)*
Bigeye Direct Inc ....D....... 703 955-3017
Herndon *(G-6624)*
JKS Creation ....G....... 804 357-5709
South Hill *(G-12854)*

PRINTING: Letterpress

Barbours Printing Service ....G....... 804 443-4505
Tappahannock *(G-13813)*
Benjamin Franklin Printing Co ....F....... 804 648-6361
Richmond *(G-11504)*
Commercial Press Inc ....F....... 540 869-3496
Stephens City *(G-13313)*
Courtney Press ....G....... 804 266-8359
Richmond *(G-11544)*
Earl Wood Printing Co ....G....... 540 563-8833
Roanoke *(G-12082)*
Grubb Printing & Stamp Co Inc ....F....... 757 295-8061
Portsmouth *(G-10438)*
James Allen Printing Co ....G....... 540 463-9232
Lexington *(G-7396)*
John Henry Printing Inc ....G....... 757 369-9549
Yorktown *(G-15971)*
Letterpress Direct ....G....... 804 285-8020
Oilville *(G-10182)*
Luray Copy Services Inc ....G....... 540 743-3433
Luray *(G-7616)*
M-J Printers Inc ....G....... 540 373-1878
Fredericksburg *(G-5202)*
Maclaren Endeavors LLC ....E....... 804 358-3493
Richmond *(G-11279)*
Quality Printing ....G....... 276 632-1415
Martinsville *(G-8322)*

R R Donnelley & Sons Company ....C....... 434 846-7371
Salem *(G-12560)*
Sanwell Printing Co Inc ....G....... 276 638-3772
Martinsville *(G-8326)*
Shimchocks Litho Service Inc ....G....... 540 982-3915
Roanoke *(G-12185)*
Total Printing Co Inc ....E....... 804 222-3813
Richmond *(G-11416)*
Virginia Prtg Co Roanoke Inc ....G....... 540 483-7433
Roanoke *(G-12219)*
Walters Printing & Mfg Co ....F....... 540 345-8161
Roanoke *(G-12227)*
Wilkinson Printing Co Inc ....F....... 804 264-2524
Glen Allen *(G-5828)*

PRINTING: Lithographic

10 10 LLC ....G....... 757 627-4311
Norfolk *(G-9410)*
10 Times Better LLC ....G....... 850 258-8880
Carrollton *(G-2239)*
35 Printing LLC ....G....... 804 926-5737
Disputanta *(G-4102)*
3d Herndon ....G....... 202 746-6176
Herndon *(G-6598)*
757 Prints ....G....... 757 774-6834
Virginia Beach *(G-14196)*
A & R Printing ....G....... 434 829-2030
Emporia *(G-4352)*
Aaca Embroidery Screen Prtg ....G....... 703 880-9872
Herndon *(G-6601)*
Aboriginal Prints LLC ....G....... 804 994-1987
Richmond *(G-11468)*
AG Almanac LLC ....G....... 703 289-1200
Falls Church *(G-4741)*
Alfa Print LLC ....G....... 703 754-2433
Gainesville *(G-5568)*
Alfa Print LLC ....G....... 703 273-2061
Fairfax *(G-4591)*
Allen Wayne Ltd Arlington ....G....... 703 321-7414
Warrenton *(G-14977)*
Allinder Printing ....G....... 757 672-4918
Norfolk *(G-9436)*
Alma Mater LLC ....G....... 434 248-5465
Phenix *(G-10354)*
AlphaGraphics ....G....... 703 866-1988
Springfield *(G-12944)*
AlphaGraphics ....G....... 703 818-2900
Chantilly *(G-2367)*
Ambush LLC ....G....... 480 338-5321
Dumfries *(G-4233)*
Ambush LLC ....G....... 202 740-3602
Stafford *(G-13114)*
American Digital Print LLC ....G....... 703 328-4796
Stafford *(G-13115)*
Amh Print Group LLC ....G....... 804 286-6166
Mechanicsville *(G-8603)*
Apollo Press Inc ....E....... 757 247-9002
Newport News *(G-9169)*
Art Printing Solutions LLC ....G....... 804 387-3203
Petersburg *(G-10306)*
Arw Printing ....G....... 540 720-6906
Stafford *(G-13120)*
Ashe Kustomz LLC ....G....... 804 997-6406
Richmond *(G-11490)*
Avn Prints ....G....... 703 473-7498
Alexandria *(G-419)*
B & B Printing ....G....... 540 586-1020
Bedford *(G-1622)*
B Franklin Printer ....G....... 703 845-1583
Arlington *(G-871)*
Barry McVay ....G....... 703 451-5953
Burke *(G-2182)*
Bbj LLC ....G....... 757 787-4646
Onancock *(G-10191)*
BCT Recordation Inc ....G....... 540 772-1754
Roanoke *(G-11885)*
Bell Printing Inc ....G....... 804 261-1776
Richmond *(G-11123)*
Big EZ Prints ....G....... 804 929-3479
Prince George *(G-10587)*
Big Lick Screen Printing ....G....... 540 632-2695
Roanoke *(G-12045)*
Blacktag Screen Printing Inc ....G....... 855 423-1680
Hampton *(G-6095)*
Blue Moon Catering Concessions ......G....... 276 236-8728
Galax *(G-5628)*
Blueprint Inc ....G....... 703 771-9256
Leesburg *(G-7234)*
Boutique Paw Prints ....G....... 434 964-0133
Charlottesville *(G-2748)*

Bowman Teressa ....G....... 240 601-9982
Manassas *(G-7921)*
Box Print & Ship - C Bernel ....G....... 757 410-7352
Chesapeake *(G-3013)*
Brooks Signs Screen Printing ....G....... 434 728-3812
Danville *(G-3963)*
Brown Printing Company Inc ....G....... 703 934-6078
Fairfax *(G-4600)*
Burcham Prints Inc ....G....... 804 559-7724
Mechanicsville *(G-8608)*
Bxi Inc ....G....... 804 282-5434
Richmond *(G-11142)*
C & B Corp ....G....... 434 977-1992
Charlottesville *(G-2752)*
C Graphic Distribution Ctr ....G....... 414 762-4282
Roanoke *(G-11899)*
Calfee Printing ....G....... 304 910-3475
Fincastle *(G-4994)*
Campbell Graphics Inc ....G....... 804 353-7292
Richmond *(G-11144)*
Cantrell/Cutter Printing Inc ....G....... 301 773-6340
Springfield *(G-12972)*
Cbt Screen Printing LLC ....G....... 703 888-8539
Falls Church *(G-4904)*
Chanders ....G....... 804 752-7678
Ashland *(G-1389)*
Christian Light Publications ....E....... 540 434-0768
Harrisonburg *(G-6300)*
Clean Building LLC ....G....... 703 589-9544
Alexandria *(G-431)*
Cnc Printing Inc ....G....... 703 378-5222
Chantilly *(G-2394)*
Coalfield Progress ....D....... 276 679-1101
Norton *(G-10115)*
Coastal Screen Printing ....G....... 541 441-6358
Hampton *(G-6277)*
Coastal Screen Printing ....G....... 757 764-1409
Newport News *(G-9202)*
Color Quest LLC ....G....... 540 433-4890
Harrisonburg *(G-6303)*
Copy Connection LLC ....G....... 757 627-4701
Norfolk *(G-9506)*
Copy That Print LLC ....G....... 757 642-3301
Virginia Beach *(G-14364)*
Core Prints ....G....... 540 356-9195
Fredericksburg *(G-5414)*
Creative Ink ....G....... 434 572-4379
South Boston *(G-12757)*
Creative Print Solutions ....G....... 540 247-9910
Winchester *(G-15406)*
Creo Industries ....G....... 804 385-2035
Christiansburg *(G-3582)*
Cross Printing Solutions LLC ....G....... 703 208-2214
Fairfax *(G-4433)*
Crosstown Paint ....G....... 757 817-7119
Hampton *(G-6123)*
Custom Dsigns EMB Print Wr LLC ......G....... 540 748-5455
Mineral *(G-8947)*
Custom Print ....G....... 703 256-1279
Springfield *(G-12985)*
Custom Prints LLC ....G....... 804 839-0749
Richmond *(G-11552)*
Cutie Pies Clay Print Keepskes ....G....... 703 533-3313
Leesburg *(G-7251)*
Cwi Marketing & Printing ....G....... 540 295-5139
Radford *(G-10706)*
Dan Miles & Associates LLC ....G....... 619 508-0430
Virginia Beach *(G-14385)*
Dandy Printing ....G....... 540 986-1100
Salem *(G-12495)*
DC Custom Print ....G....... 301 541-8172
Arlington *(G-930)*
Digital Documents Inc ....G....... 571 434-0341
Herndon *(G-6657)*
Dister Inc ....E....... 757 857-1946
Norfolk *(G-9525)*
Dister Inc ....E....... 703 207-0201
Fairfax *(G-4439)*
Divine Lifestyle Printing LLC ....G....... 804 219-3342
Chester *(G-3405)*
Dixie Press Custom Screen ....G....... 757 569-8241
Sedley *(G-12679)*
Dla Document Services ....G....... 703 784-2208
Quantico *(G-10688)*
Dla Document Services ....G....... 804 734-1791
Fort Lee *(G-5128)*
Dla Document Services ....F....... 757 855-0300
Norfolk *(G-9526)*
Dla Document Services ....E....... 757 444-7068
Norfolk *(G-9527)*

Company	Code	Phone
Dmedia Prints	G	571 297-3287
Springfield (G-12994)		
Document Automation & Prdtn	G	757 878-3389
Fort Eustis (G-5126)		
Douglas Stuart LLC	C	571 210-4440
Sterling (G-13388)		
Dwiggins Corp	G	757 366-0066
Chesapeake (G-3079)		
E L Printing Co	G	540 776-0373
Roanoke (G-12080)		
East Cast Cstm Screen Prtg LLC	G	540 373-7576
Dutton (G-4272)		
Echo Publishing Inc	G	757 603-3774
Norfolk (G-9538)		
Elephant Prints LLC	G	703 820-2631
Alexandria (G-200)		
Embroidery and Print House	G	757 636-1676
Suffolk (G-13705)		
Engraving and Printing Bureau	G	202 997-9580
Fairfax (G-4446)		
Enterprise Inc	G	276 694-3101
Stuart (G-13609)		
Ep Computer Service	G	804 592-7272
Madison Heights (G-7872)		
Erbosol Printing	G	757 325-9986
Hampton (G-6144)		
Euro Print USA LLC	G	703 849-8781
Annandale (G-747)		
Fine Prints Designs	G	703 560-1519
Falls Church (G-4914)		
Flynn Incorporated	G	540 885-2600
Staunton (G-13261)		
Fontana Lithograph Inc	E	202 296-3276
Alexandria (G-464)		
Forms Unlimited	G	757 549-1258
Chesapeake (G-3107)		
Foundry Foundry-A Print	G	703 329-3300
Alexandria (G-207)		
Framing Concepts Inc	G	757 460-9882
Virginia Beach (G-14474)		
Freestyle Prints LLC	G	571 246-1806
Winchester (G-15544)		
Full Color Prints	G	703 354-9231
Annandale (G-750)		
Full Color Prints	G	571 612-8844
Chantilly (G-2424)		
Fuzzyprints	G	571 989-3899
Midland (G-8757)		
G I K of Virginia Inc	G	804 358-8500
Richmond (G-11596)		
Gaia Communications LLC	G	703 370-5527
Alexandria (G-210)		
Gap Printing	G	703 585-1532
Alexandria (G-466)		
Gary D Keys Enterprises Inc	G	703 418-1700
Arlington (G-975)		
Genesis Graphics Printing	G	703 560-8728
Falls Church (G-4797)		
Georgetown Business Services	G	214 708-0249
Arlington (G-978)		
Giant Printing	G	703 525-1313
Fairfax (G-4466)		
GM Printer Experts LLC	G	202 250-0569
Arlington (G-981)		
Go Happy Printing	G	315 436-1151
Alexandria (G-221)		
Go Happy Printing LLC	G	240 423-7397
Annandale (G-752)		
God Spede Printing	G	360 359-6458
Chantilly (G-2429)		
Good Guys Printing LLC	G	434 942-8229
Amherst (G-692)		
Graphic Comm Inc	G	301 599-9127
Hillsville (G-6892)		
Graphic Images Corp	G	703 823-6794
Alexandria (G-225)		
Graphic Prints	G	757 244-3753
Newport News (G-9239)		
Half A Five Enterprise LLC	G	703 818-2900
Chantilly (G-2434)		
Halifax Gazette Publishing Co	E	434 572-3945
South Boston (G-12774)		
Harrison Management Associates	G	703 237-0418
Arlington (G-989)		
Hartman Graphics & Print	G	804 720-6549
Colonial Heights (G-3733)		
Harville Entps of Danville VA	G	434 822-2106
Danville (G-3997)		
Heart Print Expressions LLC	G	703 221-6441
Triangle (G-13894)		
Heavenly Gates LLC	G	804 790-9840
Chesterfield (G-3504)		
Herff Jones LLC	F	804 598-0971
Powhatan (G-10549)		
Heritage Printing LLC	G	804 378-1196
Richmond (G-11045)		
Home Printing	G	804 333-4678
Warsaw (G-15066)		
Hopewell Publishing Company	E	804 452-6127
Hopewell (G-6934)		
House of Stitches & Prints Inc	G	276 525-1796
Abingdon (G-40)		
Ibf Group	G	703 549-4247
Alexandria (G-232)		
Idezine LLC	G	703 946-3490
Haymarket (G-6426)		
Imagenation Design & Prtg LLC	G	804 687-3581
Richmond (G-11613)		
Impressed Print Solutions	G	717 816-0522
Stephenson (G-13334)		
Impressions Group Inc	G	540 667-9227
Winchester (G-15549)		
In House Printing	G	703 913-6338
Springfield (G-13022)		
In2 Print	G	434 476-7996
Halifax (G-6050)		
Industries In Focus Inc	G	703 451-5550
Springfield (G-13023)		
Infinity Printing Inc	G	804 378-8656
North Chesterfield (G-9894)		
Inkwell Duck Inc	G	703 550-1344
Lorton (G-7496)		
Instant Gratification	G	434 332-3769
Rustburg (G-12441)		
Instant Knwledge Com Jill Byrd	G	540 885-8730
Verona (G-13989)		
Instant Replay	G	434 941-2568
Lynchburg (G-7742)		
Instant Transactions Corp	G	540 687-3151
Middleburg (G-8724)		
Interco Print LLC	G	757 351-7000
Norfolk (G-9594)		
Intl Printers World	G	804 403-3940
Powhatan (G-10552)		
Iron Pen Web Design & Printing	G	757 645-9945
Portsmouth (G-10445)		
James Lee Herndon	G	703 549-2585
Manassas Park (G-8202)		
Jedi Prints LLC	G	757 869-4267
Midlothian (G-8836)		
Jerrys Antique Prints Ltd	G	540 949-7114
Waynesboro (G-15118)		
Joint Lab Systems SEC Svcs LLC	G	443 655-9987
Arlington (G-1016)		
Jones Direct LLC	G	757 718-3468
Chesapeake (G-3153)		
Joseph Ricard Enterprises LLC	G	540 465-5533
Strasburg (G-13586)		
Judis Heart Prints LLC	G	757 482-9607
Chesapeake (G-3159)		
Just Tech	G	540 662-2400
Staunton (G-13270)		
K & A Printing	G	716 736-3250
Danville (G-4008)		
K & W Printing Services Inc	G	301 868-2141
Arlington (G-1019)		
Kays Photography and Prints	G	757 344-4817
Lynchburg (G-7749)		
Kemper Printing LLC	G	804 510-8402
Richmond (G-11641)		
Kenmore Envelope Company Inc	G	804 271-2100
Richmond (G-11259)		
Kenneth Lee Woods	G	703 361-7390
Manassas (G-8093)		
Kinkos Copies	G	703 689-0004
Herndon (G-6724)		
Kwik Design and Print LLC	G	703 898-4681
Woodbridge (G-15737)		
L B Davis Inc	G	434 792-3281
Ringgold (G-11869)		
Labelink Flexibles LLC	F	703 348-4699
Fredericksburg (G-5448)		
Lark Printing Inc	G	434 237-4449
Lynchburg (G-7755)		
Lawyers Printing Co	G	804 648-3664
Richmond (G-11648)		
Learning To Lean Printing	G	757 718-5586
Chesapeake (G-3181)		
Lightbox Print Co LLC	G	919 608-9520
Richmond (G-11654)		
Lil Guy Printing	G	757 995-5705
Hampton (G-6184)		
Love In Print LLC	G	757 739-2416
Chesapeake (G-3188)		
Lsc Communications Us LLC	A	540 434-8833
Rockingham (G-12259)		
Lydell Group Incorporated	G	804 627-0500
Richmond (G-11277)		
M & S Publishing Co Inc	G	434 645-7534
Crewe (G-3814)		
Magnified Duplication Prtg Inc	G	276 393-3193
Dryden (G-4145)		
Mary A Thomas	G	434 637-2016
Emporia (G-4363)		
Matric Kolor	G	757 310-6764
Hampton (G-6191)		
McFarland Enterprises Inc	G	703 818-2900
Chantilly (G-2461)		
Media Services of Richmond	G	804 559-1000
Mechanicsville (G-8660)		
Mikes Screen Printing	G	276 971-9274
Pounding Mill (G-10524)		
Minute Man Farms Inc	G	540 423-1028
Culpeper (G-3909)		
Minute Man Press	G	757 464-6509
Norfolk (G-9646)		
Minuteman Press	G	757 903-0978
Williamsburg (G-15279)		
Minuteman Press	G	703 439-2160
Herndon (G-6747)		
Minuteman Press	G	703 220-7575
Fredericksburg (G-5459)		
Minuteman Press	G	540 774-1820
Salem (G-12537)		
Minuteman Press	G	804 441-9761
Richmond (G-11292)		
Minuteman Press Intl	G	703 299-1150
Alexandria (G-277)		
Minuteman Press Intl Inc	G	703 522-1944
Arlington (G-1065)		
Minuteman Press Intl Inc	G	703 787-6506
Reston (G-10902)		
Minuteman Press of Chester	G	804 898-0050
Chester (G-3437)		
Minuteman Press of Mc Lean	G	703 356-6612
Mc Lean (G-8502)		
Minuteman Press of Vienna	G	703 992-0420
Vienna (G-14095)		
Miracle Prints & More	G	540 656-9645
Fredericksburg (G-5207)		
Modern Graphix	G	804 590-1303
South Chesterfield (G-12838)		
Mogo Inc	G	703 476-8595
Reston (G-10903)		
Moon River Print Co	G	804 350-2647
Powhatan (G-10560)		
Mountaineer Publishing Co Inc	G	276 935-2123
Grundy (G-6038)		
My Printing Guys	G	703 430-7940
Sterling (G-13457)		
Mystery Whl & Screen Prtg LLC	G	540 514-7349
Salem (G-12542)		
N2n Specialty Printing LLC	G	540 786-5765
Fredericksburg (G-5331)		
Niblick Inc	G	804 550-1607
Ashland (G-1470)		
Northern Vrginia Prof Assoc Inc	G	703 525-5218
Falls Church (G-4837)		
Olde Petersburg Printers	G	804 400-9644
Colonial Heights (G-3740)		
Oldtown Printing & Copying	G	540 382-6793
Christiansburg (G-3607)		
On The DI Custom Prints LLC	G	757 508-1609
Dumfries (G-4253)		
One Four Three LLC	G	303 594-7151
Virginia Beach (G-14699)		
Open Prints LLC	G	866 673-6110
Chesapeake (G-3229)		
Optimize Print Solutions LLC	G	703 856-7386
Lorton (G-7519)		
Out of Print LLC	G	919 368-0980
Norfolk (G-9678)		
Parent Resource Center	G	757 482-5923
Chesapeake (G-3233)		
Parkway Printshop	G	757 378-3959
Williamsburg (G-15291)		
Pattern and Print LLC	G	540 884-2660
Fincastle (G-4997)		
Paul Owens	G	804 393-2475
Henrico (G-6547)		

PRODUCT

Paw Print Pet Services .... G 434 822-5020
Ringgold *(G-11873)*
Paw Prints .... G 540 220-2825
Spotsylvania *(G-12908)*
Personal Touch Printing Svcs .... G 757 619-7073
Virginia Beach *(G-14718)*
Pic N Press Custom Prtg LLC ..... G 571 970-2627
Alexandria *(G-550)*
Pixel Designs & Printing .... G 571 359-6080
Manassas *(G-8130)*
Pop Printing .... G 804 248-9093
Richmond *(G-11719)*
Powell Valley Printing Company ... F 276 546-1210
Pennington Gap *(G-10297)*
Powerup Printing Inc .... G 804 364-1353
Glen Allen *(G-5781)*
Pressed 4 Ink - Custom Apparel ... G 540 693-4023
Fredericksburg *(G-5350)*
Prinit Corporation .... F 703 847-8880
Vienna *(G-14114)*
Print A Promo LLC .... G 800 675-6869
Middletown *(G-8742)*
Print Afrik LLC .... G 202 594-0836
Woodbridge *(G-15782)*
Print City .... G 703 931-1114
Falls Church *(G-4857)*
Print Life LLC .... G 609 442-2838
Williamsburg *(G-15300)*
Print LLC .... G 757 746-5708
Newport News *(G-9316)*
Print Mail Direct LLC .... G 540 899-6451
Fredericksburg *(G-5472)*
Print Plus .... G 276 322-2043
Bluefield *(G-1876)*
Print Promotion .... G 202 618-8822
Alexandria *(G-316)*
Print Rayge Studios LLC .... G 757 537-6995
Richmond *(G-11725)*
Print Republic LLC .... G 757 633-9099
Virginia Beach *(G-14740)*
Print Time Inc .... G 202 232-0582
Alexandria *(G-555)*
Printer Fix LLC .... G 540 532-4948
Front Royal *(G-5549)*
Printer Gatherer LLC .... G 540 420-2426
Henrico *(G-6551)*
Printer Resolutions .... G 703 850-5336
Sterling *(G-13478)*
Printers Research Co .... G 540 721-9916
Moneta *(G-8975)*
Printing 4 Kids .... G 703 474-1519
Alexandria *(G-556)*
Printing Dept Inc .... G 804 673-1904
Richmond *(G-11335)*
Printpros LLC .... G 804 550-1607
Ashland *(G-1480)*
Printpros LLC .... G 804 789-8884
Mechanicsville *(G-8668)*
Pritchard Studio .... G 276 935-5829
Grundy *(G-6040)*
Pro-Graphx .... G 844 777-0288
Martinsville *(G-8321)*
Program Services LLC .... G 757 222-3990
Norfolk *(G-9698)*
Prographics Print Xpress .... G 757 606-8303
Virginia Beach *(G-14743)*
Protoquick Printing LLC .... G 202 417-4243
Centreville *(G-2329)*
Pwillz Customz LLC .... G 571 926-9622
Sterling *(G-13481)*
Qg LLC .... C 540 722-6000
Winchester *(G-15462)*
R & B Impressions Inc .... F 703 823-9050
Alexandria *(G-323)*
R B M Enterprises Inc .... G 804 290-4407
Glen Allen *(G-5786)*
R R Donnelley & Sons Company ... F 540 432-5453
Rockingham *(G-12268)*
R R Donnelley & Sons Company ... B 540 564-3900
Harrisonburg *(G-6359)*
Rappahannock Record .... F 804 435-1701
Kilmarnock *(G-7076)*
Redprint Strategy .... G 202 656-1002
Alexandria *(G-327)*
Reed Envelope Company Inc ...... F 703 690-2249
Fairfax Station *(G-4722)*
Revolution Rising Print .... G 804 276-4789
Richmond *(G-11734)*
Richmond CLB of Prnt Hse Crfts ... F 804 748-3075
Chester *(G-3451)*

Robert Douglas LLC .... G 434 284-5111
Charlottesville *(G-2688)*
Rockingham Publishing Co Inc ..... C 540 574-6200
Harrisonburg *(G-6363)*
Ronald Carpenter .... G 757 471-3805
Virginia Beach *(G-14780)*
Rowley Group Inc .... G 703 522-1944
Arlington *(G-1153)*
Roxen Incorporated .... G 571 208-0782
Manassas *(G-7997)*
Royalcanvascom .... G 866 673-6110
Chesapeake *(G-3277)*
RPM 3d Printing .... G 757 266-3168
Virginia Beach *(G-14783)*
S&Sprinting .... G 434 581-1983
New Canton *(G-9119)*
Safeguard Printing Promo .... G 804 378-2166
Midlothian *(G-8895)*
Sandcastle Screen Printing LLC ... G 757 740-0611
Virginia Beach *(G-14792)*
Sb Printing LLC .... G 804 247-2404
Richmond *(G-11373)*
Schmids Printing .... G 540 886-9261
Staunton *(G-13290)*
Scsi4me Corporation .... G 703 372-1195
Springfield *(G-13082)*
Seatrix Print LLC .... G 571 241-5748
Woodbridge *(G-15804)*
Sedley Printing .... G 757 562-5738
Sedley *(G-12680)*
Sennett Security Products LLC .... G 703 803-8880
Centreville *(G-2338)*
Shamrock Screen Print LLC .... G 540 219-4337
Culpeper *(G-3919)*
Shen-Val Screen Printing LLC ..... G 540 869-2713
White Post *(G-15183)*
Shenandoah Publications Inc ...... E 540 459-4000
Edinburg *(G-4314)*
Shoeprint .... G 703 499-9136
Woodbridge *(G-15807)*
Signarama Richmond .... G 804 301-9317
North Chesterfield *(G-9979)*
Silver Communications Corp .... E 703 471-7339
Sterling *(G-13508)*
Sir Speedy Printing Ctr 7411 ...... G 703 821-8781
Mc Lean *(G-8547)*
Sonya Davis Enterprises LLC ...... G 703 264-0533
Forest *(G-5094)*
Southwest Publisher LLC .... E 540 980-5220
Pulaski *(G-10647)*
Staples Print & Marketing .... G 434 218-6425
Charlottesville *(G-2696)*
Steamed Ink .... G 540 904-6211
Roanoke *(G-12196)*
Sterling Flyers Inc .... G 571 830-4476
Reston *(G-10966)*
Stich N Print .... G 276 326-2005
Bluefield *(G-1879)*
Strategic Print Solutions LLC ...... G 703 272-3440
Haymarket *(G-6449)*
Suday Promotions Inc .... G 703 376-8640
Chantilly *(G-2503)*
Sumi LLC .... G 571 287-9480
Harrisonburg *(G-6375)*
Sustainable Green Prtg Partnr ..... G 703 359-1376
Fairfax *(G-4563)*
Sweet and Simple Prints .... G 757 710-1116
Blacksburg *(G-1796)*
T Bc .... G 703 969-8221
Manassas *(G-8002)*
Tagg Design Specialty Prtg LLC ... G 804 572-7777
Tappahannock *(G-13823)*
Text Art Print .... G 908 619-2809
North Chesterfield *(G-10000)*
Thredz EMB Screen Print Graph ... G 757 636-9569
Virginia Beach *(G-14869)*
Thumbprint Events By .... G 703 720-1000
Henrico *(G-6581)*
TI Printing of Virginia LLC .... G 757 315-8565
Chesapeake *(G-3335)*
Tidewater Graphics Inc .... G 757 464-6136
Virginia Beach *(G-14874)*
Touch Honey Dsgn Print Photg ... G 757 606-0411
Chesapeake *(G-3345)*
Trademark Printing LLC .... G 757 410-1800
Portsmouth *(G-10492)*
Trademark Printing LLC .... G 757 803-7612
Chesapeake *(G-3348)*
Tried & True Printing LLC .... G 434 964-8202
Charlottesville *(G-2895)*

Tshirtpod .... G 423 341-8655
Bristol *(G-2037)*
U3 Solutions Inc .... G 703 777-5020
Leesburg *(G-7366)*
United Litho Inc .... G 703 858-4213
Ashburn *(G-1345)*
US Parcel & Copy Center Inc ...... G 703 365-7999
Manassas *(G-8007)*
Vibrant Prints LLC .... G 843 425-2506
Reston *(G-10984)*
Victoria Austin .... G 276 632-1742
Martinsville *(G-8346)*
Virginia Gazette Companies LLC ... G 757 220-1736
Newport News *(G-9373)*
Virginia Printing Services Inc ...... F 757 838-5500
Hampton *(G-6263)*
Virginia Screen Printing .... G 804 295-7440
North Dinwiddie *(G-10068)*
Vistaprint .... G 757 483-2357
Portsmouth *(G-10498)*
Visual GRAphics&designs .... G 804 221-6983
Mechanicsville *(G-8697)*
Walton Industries Inc .... G 540 898-7888
Fredericksburg *(G-5389)*
Westrock Commercial LLC .... E 804 444-1000
Richmond *(G-11824)*
Wilderness Prints .... G 540 309-6803
Moneta *(G-8985)*
Wilkinson Printing Co Inc .... F 804 264-2524
Glen Allen *(G-5828)*
Willimsburg Prcess Sltions LLC ... G 703 577-4448
Williamsburg *(G-15345)*
Wise Printing Co Inc .... G 276 523-1141
Big Stone Gap *(G-1718)*
Wood Television LLC .... D 540 825-4416
Culpeper *(G-3932)*
Wood Television LLC .... C 434 385-5400
Lynchburg *(G-7840)*
Wood Television LLC .... E 540 672-1266
Orange *(G-10232)*
Workhorse Print Solutions LLC ... G 703 707-1648
Reston *(G-10995)*
Wss Richmond .... G 804 722-0150
Prince George *(G-10611)*
Your Personal Printer .... G 757 679-1139
Virginia Beach *(G-14955)*
Zb 3d Printers LLC .... G 757 695-8278
Virginia Beach *(G-14956)*
Zine Graphics Print .... G 703 591-4000
Fairfax *(G-4698)*
Ziva Prints LLC .... G 571 265-9030
Ashburn *(G-1357)*
Zramics Mtls Science Tech LLC ... G 757 955-0493
Norfolk *(G-9801)*

PRINTING: Manmade Fiber & Silk, Broadwoven Fabric

American Shirt Printing .... G 703 405-4014
Stafford *(G-13117)*

PRINTING: Offset

A B Printing LLC .... G 276 783-2837
Marion *(G-8219)*
A C Graphics Inc .... G 703 246-9466
Fairfax *(G-4396)*
A Z Printing and Dup Corp .... G 703 549-0949
Alexandria *(G-116)*
ABC Imaging of Washington .... F 703 848-2997
Vienna *(G-14004)*
ABC Printing .... G 434 847-7468
Madison Heights *(G-7866)*
Abingdon Printing Inc .... G 276 628-4221
Abingdon *(G-3)*
Accelerated Printing Corp Inc ..... G 703 437-1084
Leesburg *(G-7213)*
Advertising Service Agency .... G 757 622-3429
Norfolk *(G-9425)*
Affordable Printing & Copies ...... G 757 728-9770
Hampton *(G-6076)*
All Prints Inc .... G 703 435-1922
Sterling *(G-13342)*
Alleghany Printing Co .... G 540 965-4246
Covington *(G-3777)*
Allegra Network LLC .... G 757 448-8271
Norfolk *(G-9432)*
Allegra Print & Imaging .... G 703 378-4500
Chantilly *(G-2365)*
Alpha Printing Inc .... G 703 321-2071
Springfield *(G-12943)*

(G-0000) Company's Geographic Section entry number

Ardsen Offset....G....757 220-3299
Williamsburg *(G-15206)*
Artcraft Printing Ltd....G....757 428-9138
Virginia Beach *(G-14244)*
ASAP Printing & Mailing Co....G....703 836-2288
Alexandria *(G-142)*
Authentic Printing Company LLC....G....804 672-6659
Henrico *(G-6479)*
B & B Printing Company Inc....C....804 794-8273
North Chesterfield *(G-9824)*
B K Printing....G....703 435-5502
Herndon *(G-6618)*
Balmar Inc....E....703 289-9000
Falls Church *(G-4761)*
Barbours Printing Service....G....804 443-4505
Tappahannock *(G-13813)*
Barton Industries Inc....E....757 874-5958
Yorktown *(G-15935)*
Bbr Print Inc....F....804 230-4515
Richmond *(G-11502)*
Benjamin Franklin Printing Co....F....804 648-6361
Richmond *(G-11504)*
Benton-Thomas Inc....F....434 572-3577
South Boston *(G-12751)*
Berryville Graphics Inc....A....540 955-2750
Berryville *(G-1671)*
Best Image Printers Ltd....F....804 272-1006
North Chesterfield *(G-9830)*
Best Impressions Inc....F....703 518-1375
Alexandria *(G-421)*
Best Impressions Printing....G....804 740-9006
Ashland *(G-1380)*
Best Printing Inc....G....540 563-9004
Roanoke *(G-12044)*
Bi Communications Inc....F....703 435-9600
Sterling *(G-13359)*
Bigeye Direct Inc....D....703 955-3017
Herndon *(G-6624)*
Bison Printing Inc....E....540 586-3955
Bedford *(G-1627)*
Boaz Publishing Inc....F....540 659-4554
Stafford *(G-13124)*
Bobs Printing Service LLC....G....434 352-2680
Appomattox *(G-807)*
Brandy Printing & EMB Inc....G....540 825-5583
Brandy Station *(G-1937)*
Branner Printing Service Inc....E....540 896-8947
Broadway *(G-2085)*
Brothers Printing....F....757 431-2656
Virginia Beach *(G-14301)*
Bull Run Printing....G....540 937-3447
Rixeyville *(G-11877)*
Burke Print Shop....G....276 628-3033
Abingdon *(G-19)*
Business Press....F....804 282-3150
Richmond *(G-11140)*
Bvm Print VA LLC....G....434 845-1153
Lynchburg *(G-7663)*
C & R Printing Inc....G....703 802-0800
Chantilly *(G-2383)*
C & S Printing Enterprises....G....703 385-4495
Fairfax *(G-4603)*
C H J Digital Repro....G....757 473-0234
Virginia Beach *(G-14308)*
C Line Graphics Inc....G....434 577-9289
Valentines *(G-13974)*
C2-Mask Inc....G....703 698-7820
Fairfax *(G-4422)*
Campbell Copy Center Inc....F....540 434-4171
Rockingham *(G-12243)*
Campbell Printing Bristol Inc....G....276 466-2311
Bristol *(G-2012)*
Canaan Printing Inc....E....804 271-4820
North Chesterfield *(G-9839)*
Capital Screen Prtg Unlimited....G....703 550-0033
Lorton *(G-7470)*
Carter Composition Corporation....C....804 359-9206
Richmond *(G-11149)*
Century Press Inc....G....703 335-5663
Manassas *(G-8048)*
Chantilly Prtg & Graphics Inc....G....703 471-2800
Herndon *(G-6639)*
Chantilly Services Inc....G....703 830-7700
Chantilly *(G-2392)*
Charlotte Printing LLC....G....434 738-7155
Randolph *(G-10747)*
Chief Printing Company....G....515 480-6577
Richmond *(G-11529)*
Chocklett Press Inc....D....540 345-1820
Roanoke *(G-12066)*
Choice Printing Services....G....804 690-9064
Glen Allen *(G-5714)*
Clarke Inc....F....434 847-5561
Moneta *(G-8959)*
Clarks Litho Inc....F....703 961-8888
Chantilly *(G-2393)*
Clinch Valley Printing Company....F....276 988-5410
North Tazewell *(G-10096)*
CMC Printing and Graphics Inc....G....804 744-5821
Midlothian *(G-8798)*
Cmg Impressions Inc....G....804 556-2551
Maidens *(G-7887)*
Collinsville Printing Co....E....276 666-4400
Martinsville *(G-8276)*
Color Quest LLC....G....540 896-8186
Harrisonburg *(G-6304)*
Color Svc Prtg & Graphics Inc....G....703 321-8100
Falls Church *(G-4776)*
Colornet Prtg & Graphics Inc....G....703 406-9301
Sterling *(G-13372)*
Commercial Press Inc....F....540 869-3496
Stephens City *(G-13313)*
Commercial Prtg Direct Mail Svc....G....757 422-0606
Virginia Beach *(G-14358)*
Commonwealth Reprographics....F....434 845-1203
Lynchburg *(G-7682)*
Composition Systems Inc....D....703 205-0000
Alexandria *(G-171)*
Consolidated Mailing Svcs Inc....E....703 904-1600
Sterling *(G-13374)*
Consulting Printing Services....F....434 846-6510
Forest *(G-5064)*
Copy Cat Printing LLC....G....804 746-0008
Mechanicsville *(G-8615)*
Copy Connection....G....757 627-4701
Norfolk *(G-9505)*
Copy Dog Printing....G....434 528-4134
Lynchburg *(G-7684)*
Copyland Printing Inc....F....703 241-9188
Chantilly *(G-2397)*
Copyright Printing....G....804 784-4760
Oilville *(G-10177)*
Coral Graphic Services Inc....C....540 869-0500
Berryville *(G-1676)*
Country House Printing....G....540 674-4616
Dublin *(G-4153)*
Courtney Press....G....804 266-8359
Richmond *(G-11544)*
Craftsmen Printing Inc....G....804 798-7885
Ashland *(G-1398)*
Creative Document Imaging Inc....G....703 208-2212
Fairfax *(G-4432)*
Creative Document Imaging Inc....G....703 497-6767
Woodbridge *(G-15675)*
Crescent Printery Ltd....G....276 395-2101
Coeburn *(G-3697)*
Criswell Inc....F....434 845-0439
Lynchburg *(G-7687)*
Csl Media LLC....G....540 785-3790
Fredericksburg *(G-5268)*
Csl Media LLC....G....540 785-3790
Fredericksburg *(G-5181)*
CSP Productions Inc....G....703 321-8100
Falls Church *(G-4779)*
CTW Printing Concepts....G....804 559-5020
Mechanicsville *(G-8616)*
Cunningham Digital Inc....G....540 992-2219
Daleville *(G-3941)*
Custom Printing....G....540 672-2281
Orange *(G-10208)*
Custom Printing....G....804 261-1776
Richmond *(G-11174)*
Cyan LLC....G....703 455-3000
Springfield *(G-12986)*
D & P Printing & Graphics Inc....F....703 941-2114
Alexandria *(G-438)*
Dad13 Inc....C....703 550-9555
Newington *(G-9153)*
Dae Print & Design....G....757 518-1774
Virginia Beach *(G-14381)*
Dae Print & Design....F....757 473-0234
Virginia Beach *(G-14382)*
Dandee Printing Co....G....540 828-4457
Keezletown *(G-7027)*
Dap Incorporated....G....757 921-3576
Newport News *(G-9214)*
Davis Communications Group....G....703 548-8892
Alexandria *(G-185)*
Day & Night Printing Inc....E....703 734-4940
Vienna *(G-14035)*
Deem Printing Company Inc....G....703 335-5422
Manassas *(G-8055)*
Deem Printing Company Inc....G....703 335-2422
Manassas *(G-7930)*
Deer Duplicating Svc Inc....G....804 648-6509
Richmond *(G-11557)*
Dehardit Press....G....804 693-2795
Gloucester *(G-5845)*
Delong Lithographics Services....G....703 550-2110
Lorton *(G-7479)*
DEP Copy Center Inc....G....703 499-9888
Woodbridge *(G-15682)*
Design Digital Printing LLC....G....276 964-9391
Cedar Bluff *(G-2274)*
Detamore Printing Co....G....540 886-4571
Staunton *(G-13252)*
Devin Clark....G....276 889-3426
Lebanon *(G-7191)*
Digi Quick Print Inc....G....703 671-9600
Alexandria *(G-187)*
Dodson Litho Printers Inc....G....757 479-4814
Virginia Beach *(G-14408)*
Dogwood Graphics....G....434 447-6004
South Hill *(G-12848)*
Dogwood Graphics Inc....G....434 447-6004
South Hill *(G-12849)*
Dominion Graphics Inc....G....804 353-3755
Richmond *(G-11188)*
Dominion Ink LLC....G....804 350-7996
Richmond *(G-11563)*
Dukes Printing Inc....G....276 228-6777
Wytheville *(G-15885)*
Dupont Printing Service Inc....G....703 931-1317
Falls Church *(G-4785)*
Earl Wood Printing Co....G....540 563-8833
Roanoke *(G-12082)*
Economy Printing Inc....G....757 485-4445
Portsmouth *(G-10419)*
Edible Printing LLC....G....212 203-8275
Luray *(G-7607)*
Edmonds Prtg / Clor Images Inc....G....434 848-2264
Lawrenceville *(G-7179)*
Ersh-Enterprises Inc....F....703 866-1988
Oakton *(G-10147)*
Evolution Printing Inc....G....571 292-1213
Manassas *(G-8066)*
Executive Press Inc....G....703 352-1337
Fairfax *(G-4619)*
Expo Branders Corporation....G....703 865-7581
Fairfax *(G-4453)*
Fairfax Printers Inc....G....703 273-1220
Fairfax *(G-4621)*
Faith First Printing LLC....G....757 723-7673
Hampton *(G-6146)*
Faith Printing....G....804 745-0667
North Chesterfield *(G-9870)*
Falcon Lab Inc....G....703 442-0124
Mc Lean *(G-8426)*
Far West Print Solutions LLC....G....757 549-1258
Chesapeake *(G-3097)*
Fergusson Printing....G....804 355-8621
Richmond *(G-11209)*
Fidelity Printing Inc....F....804 737-7907
Sandston *(G-12615)*
First Imprssions Prtg Graphics....G....540 342-2679
Roanoke *(G-12087)*
Fisher Publications Inc....G....804 323-6252
North Chesterfield *(G-9874)*
Fleet Services Inc....F....757 625-4214
Norfolk *(G-9556)*
Flyermonsterscom....G....703 582-5716
Arlington *(G-971)*
Flynn Enterprises Inc....G....804 461-5753
Virginia Beach *(G-14468)*
Flynn Enterprises Inc....E....703 444-5555
Sterling *(G-13400)*
Four Star Printing Inc....G....540 459-2247
Woodstock *(G-15854)*
French Press Printing LLC....G....703 268-8241
Vienna *(G-14057)*
G & H Litho Inc....G....571 267-7148
Sterling *(G-13403)*
Gabro Graphics Inc....F....703 464-8588
Sterling *(G-13405)*
Gam Printers Incorporated....F....703 450-4121
Sterling *(G-13406)*
Gannett Offset....G....781 551-2923
Mc Lean *(G-8441)*
Garrison Press Llc....G....540 434-2333
Harrisonburg *(G-6319)*

Employee Codes: A=Over 500 employees, B=251-500
C=101-250, D=51-100, E=20-50, F=10-19, G=1-9
2021 Virginia
Industrial Directory
1027

Gazette Press Inc .... G 276 236-4831
Galax **(G-5636)**

Giant Printing Inc .... G 703 645-2292
Chantilly **(G-2426)**

Goetz Printing Company .... E 703 569-8232
Springfield **(G-13012)**

Graphic Comm Group .... G 703 818-2700
Clifton **(G-3667)**

Graphic Communications Inc .... F 301 599-2020
Hillsville **(G-6893)**

Graphic Prints Inc .... G 703 787-3880
Herndon **(G-6689)**

Grc Enterprises Inc .... E 540 428-7000
Manassas **(G-8077)**

Grubb Printing & Stamp Co Inc .... F 757 295-8061
Portsmouth **(G-10438)**

H&R Printing .... G 571 277-1454
Fairfax **(G-4473)**

Hammocks Print Shop .... G 804 453-3265
Burgess **(G-2174)**

Harris Printing Company Inc .... G 540 586-8326
Bedford **(G-1640)**

Hatcher Enterprises .... G 276 673-6077
Fieldale **(G-4988)**

Henrys Color Graphic Design .... G 703 241-0101
Falls Church **(G-4805)**

Heritage Printing Service Inc .... F 804 233-3024
Richmond **(G-11610)**

Hooker Printing Inc .... G 336 339-4802
Collinsville **(G-3713)**

Imlay International LLC .... G 703 914-0526
Annandale **(G-758)**

Imprenta Printing .... G 703 866-0760
Springfield **(G-13021)**

J & J Printing Inc .... G 703 764-0088
Springfield **(G-13026)**

J & L Communications Inc .... G 434 973-1830
Charlottesville **(G-2650)**

J & M Printing Inc .... G 703 549-2432
Alexandria **(G-241)**

J C Printing Corp .... G 703 378-3500
Chantilly **(G-2447)**

James Allen Printing Co .... G 540 463-9232
Lexington **(G-7396)**

James River Press .... G 804 230-4515
Richmond **(G-11629)**

James River Printing LLC .... G 804 520-1000
Colonial Heights **(G-3735)**

Jami Ventures Inc .... G 703 352-5679
Fairfax **(G-4484)**

Jamison Printing Inc .... G 540 992-3568
Troutville **(G-13912)**

Jammac Corporation .... G 757 855-5474
Norfolk **(G-9600)**

Jason Hammond Aldous .... G 540 672-5050
Orange **(G-10216)**

Jo-Je Corporation .... G 757 431-2656
Virginia Beach **(G-14571)**

John Henry Printing Inc .... G 757 369-9549
Yorktown **(G-15971)**

Johnson Printing Service Inc .... G 804 541-3635
Hopewell **(G-6937)**

Jones Plus LLC .... G 757 718-3468
Chesapeake **(G-3154)**

Jones Printing Service Inc .... E 757 436-3331
Chesapeake **(G-3155)**

JT Graphics & Printing Inc .... G 703 922-6804
Alexandria **(G-502)**

Just Print It LLC .... G 703 327-2060
Leesburg **(G-7292)**

K & E Printing and Graphics .... G 703 560-4701
Vienna **(G-14075)**

Kibela Print LLC .... G 703 436-1646
Lorton **(G-7502)**

Kpw Ventures Inc .... G 703 725-6482
Herndon **(G-6725)**

L & M Printing Inc .... G 703 573-2257
Fairfax **(G-4496)**

Lake Lithograph Company .... D 703 361-8030
Manassas **(G-7959)**

Landmark Printing Co .... G 703 226-1000
Annandale **(G-769)**

Legacy Printing Inc .... G 804 730-1834
Mechanicsville **(G-8651)**

Lehr Inc .... G 703 821-2679
Mc Lean **(G-8484)**

Lewis Printing Company .... E 804 648-2000
Richmond **(G-11652)**

Liberty Press Inc .... E 540 434-5513
Harrisonburg **(G-6338)**

Liberty Printing House Inc .... G 202 664-7702
Lorton **(G-7507)**

Life Management Company .... G 434 296-9762
Troy **(G-13932)**

Liskey & Sons Inc .... F 757 627-8712
Norfolk **(G-9620)**

Littlejohn Printing Co .... G 540 977-1377
Roanoke **(G-12126)**

Lone Tree Printing Inc .... G 757 473-9977
Virginia Beach **(G-14623)**

Louise J Walker .... G 540 788-4826
Calverton **(G-2225)**

Luray Copy Services Inc .... G 540 743-3433
Luray **(G-7616)**

M&M Printing LLC .... G 804 621-4171
Chester **(G-3431)**

M-J Printers Inc .... G 540 373-1878
Fredericksburg **(G-5202)**

Maclaren Endeavors LLC .... E 804 358-3493
Richmond **(G-11279)**

Macmurray Graphics & Prtg Inc .... G 703 680-4847
Montclair **(G-8999)**

Marbrooke Printing Inc .... G 276 632-7115
Martinsville **(G-8307)**

Mardon Inc .... G 276 386-6662
Weber City **(G-15149)**

Mark Four Inc .... G 804 330-0765
Powhatan **(G-10557)**

Martin Publishing Corp .... E 804 780-1700
Richmond **(G-11668)**

McCabe Enterprises Inc .... F 703 560-7755
Fairfax **(G-4504)**

McClung Printing Inc .... D 540 949-8139
Waynesboro **(G-15123)**

Meridian Printing & Publishing .... G 757 627-8712
Norfolk **(G-9638)**

Metro Printing Center Inc .... G 703 620-3532
Reston **(G-10899)**

Michael Beach .... G 703 360-7284
Alexandria **(G-531)**

Mid-Atlantic Printers Ltd .... D 434 369-6633
Altavista **(G-636)**

Mid-Atlantic Printers Ltd .... G 703 448-1155
Vienna **(G-14092)**

Middleburg Printers LLC .... G 540 687-5710
Middleburg **(G-8729)**

Mobile Ink LLC .... F 804 218-8384
Midlothian **(G-8861)**

Mounir & Company Incorporated .... F 703 354-7400
Springfield **(G-13054)**

Mr Graphics Print Shop LLC .... G 703 980-8239
Manassas **(G-8113)**

Mr Print .... G 540 338-5900
Purcellville **(G-10671)**

Mvp Press LLC .... F 703 661-6877
Dulles **(G-4210)**

National Lithograph Inc .... F 703 709-9000
Sterling **(G-13459)**

New Image Graphics Inc .... G 540 678-0900
Winchester **(G-15455)**

Next Level Printing .... G 757 288-1399
Norfolk **(G-9664)**

Norfolk Printing Co .... G 757 627-1302
Norfolk **(G-9667)**

North Street Enterprise Inc .... E 434 392-4144
Farmville **(G-4954)**

Oasis Global LLC .... G 703 560-7755
Fairfax **(G-4524)**

Omega Alpha II Inc .... F 804 747-7705
Richmond **(G-11315)**

P I P Printing 1156 Inc .... F 434 792-0020
Danville **(G-4022)**

P M Resources Inc .... G 703 556-0155
Springfield **(G-13065)**

Page Printing Connection .... G 540 743-7746
Luray **(G-7621)**

Parkland Direct Inc .... D 434 385-6225
Forest **(G-5086)**

PCC Corporation .... F 757 368-5777
Virginia Beach **(G-14714)**

PDQ Printing Company .... G 804 228-0077
Richmond **(G-11709)**

Perfect Image Printing .... G 703 824-0010
Falls Church **(G-4856)**

Person Enterprises Inc .... G 757 483-6252
Portsmouth **(G-10468)**

Peter Korer .... G 702 460-2144
Chesapeake **(G-3237)**

Petree Enterprises Inc .... F 703 318-0008
Sterling **(G-13469)**

Piccadilly Printing Company .... F 540 662-3804
Winchester **(G-15566)**

PIP Boonchan .... G 571 327-5522
Springfield **(G-13069)**

Postal Instant Press Inc .... G 703 866-1988
Springfield **(G-13072)**

Potomac Printing Solutions Inc .... D 703 723-2511
Leesburg **(G-7326)**

Precision Print & Copy LLC .... G 804 740-3514
Richmond **(G-11330)**

Precision Printers .... G 703 525-5113
Arlington **(G-1119)**

Press On Printing LLC .... G 434 575-0990
South Boston **(G-12787)**

Press-Well Services Inc .... G 540 923-4799
Madison **(G-7861)**

Prestige Press Inc .... E 757 826-5881
Hampton **(G-6220)**

Print Link Inc .... G 757 368-5200
Virginia Beach **(G-14739)**

Print Squad LLC .... G 434 609-3335
Lynchburg **(G-7788)**

Print World Inc .... F 434 237-2200
Lynchburg **(G-7789)**

Print-N-Paper Inc .... G 540 719-7277
Moneta **(G-8974)**

Printcraft Press Incorporated .... E 757 397-0759
Portsmouth **(G-10473)**

Printersmark Inc .... G 804 353-2324
Richmond **(G-11333)**

Printing and Sign System Inc .... G 703 280-1550
Fairfax **(G-4532)**

Printing Concepts of Virg .... G 540 904-5951
Roanoke **(G-12155)**

Printing Department Inc .... G 804 282-2739
Richmond **(G-11334)**

Printing Dept LLC .... G 703 931-5450
Alexandria **(G-317)**

Printing Express Inc .... E 540 433-1237
Harrisonburg **(G-6356)**

Printing For You .... G 540 351-0191
Warrenton **(G-15045)**

Printing Ideas Inc .... G 703 591-1708
Fairfax **(G-4533)**

Printing Plus .... G 434 376-3379
Brookneal **(G-2111)**

Printing Productions Inc .... G 703 406-2400
Sterling **(G-13479)**

Printing Services .... G 540 434-5783
Harrisonburg **(G-6357)**

Printline Graphics LLC .... G 757 547-3107
Chesapeake **(G-3248)**

Printsmith Ink .... G 540 323-7554
Winchester **(G-15569)**

Printwell Inc .... F 757 564-3302
Williamsburg **(G-15301)**

Professional Business Prtg Inc .... G 804 423-1355
Richmond **(G-11337)**

Professional Printing Ctr Inc .... E 757 547-1990
Chesapeake **(G-3250)**

Professional Services .... G 540 953-2223
Blacksburg **(G-1781)**

Progress Printing Company .... D 434 239-9213
Lynchburg **(G-7790)**

Progressive Graphics Inc .... E 757 368-3321
Virginia Beach **(G-14744)**

Qg LLC .... C 804 264-3866
Richmond **(G-11343)**

Qg Printing II Corp .... A 540 722-6000
Winchester **(G-15463)**

Quality Graphics & Prtg Inc .... F 703 661-6060
Sterling **(G-13483)**

Quality Printing .... G 276 632-1415
Martinsville **(G-8322)**

Quality Stamp Co .... G 757 858-0653
Norfolk **(G-9700)**

R & B Communications LLC .... G 703 348-7088
Haymarket **(G-6439)**

R R Donnelley & Sons Company .... C 434 846-7371
Salem **(G-12560)**

Rapid Printing Inc .... G 540 586-1243
Bedford **(G-1654)**

Rappahannock Entp Assoc Inc .... G 703 560-5042
Falls Church **(G-4862)**

Recorder Publishing of VA Inc .... F 540 468-2147
Monterey **(G-9012)**

Reston Copy Center .... G 703 860-9600
Herndon **(G-6788)**

Reston Copy Center Inc .... G 703 860-9600
Reston **(G-10938)**

Rite Print Shoppe & Supply ....G...... 540 745-3616
Floyd (G-5038)
River City Graphics LLC ....G...... 757 519-9525
Virginia Beach (G-14777)
River City Printing Graphics ....G...... 804 226-8100
Richmond (G-11740)
Rmae Inc ....G...... 804 651-6911
Petersburg (G-10339)
Roasters Pride Inc ....G...... 703 440-0627
Springfield (G-13080)
Royal Printing Company ....G...... 804 798-8897
Glen Allen (G-5789)
Roys Copies ....G...... 804 744-6200
Midlothian (G-8894)
Royster Printing Services Inc ....G...... 757 545-3019
Chesapeake (G-3278)
S J Printing Inc ....G...... 703 378-7142
Manassas Park (G-8210)
Safe Harbor Press LLC ....G...... 757 490-1960
Virginia Beach (G-14789)
Salem Printing Co ....E...... 540 387-1106
Salem (G-12566)
Schreiber Inc R G ....E...... 540 248-5300
Verona (G-13995)
Service Printing of Lynchburg ....G...... 434 845-3681
Lynchburg (G-7806)
Seven Sevens Inc ....G...... 757 340-1300
Norfolk (G-9718)
Shelley Imprssons Prtg Copying .....G...... 540 310-0766
Fredericksburg (G-5485)
Shenandoah Valley Printin ....G...... 540 208-1808
Rockingham (G-12276)
Sign & Print ....G...... 703 707-8556
Herndon (G-6806)
Silverado Printing LLC ....G...... 703 407-8720
Fairfax (G-4556)
Smyth Companies LLC ....C...... 540 586-2311
Bedford (G-1658)
Southern Printing Co Inc ....E...... 540 552-8352
Blacksburg (G-1793)
Standard Printing Company Inc ....F...... 540 965-1150
Covington (G-3799)
Star Printing Co Inc ....G...... 757 625-7782
Chesapeake (G-3311)
Stephenson Lithograph Inc ....G...... 703 241-0806
Arlington (G-1176)
Stephenson Printing Inc ....D...... 703 642-9000
Alexandria (G-589)
Suter Enterprises Ltd ....F...... 757 220-3299
Williamsburg (G-15320)
Swift Print Inc ....F...... 540 362-2200
Roanoke (G-12199)
Swift Print Inc ....G...... 540 343-8300
Roanoke (G-12200)
Symmetric Systems Inc ....G...... 804 276-7202
North Chesterfield (G-9997)
Teagle & Little Incorporated ....D...... 757 622-5793
Norfolk (G-9744)
Tech Express Inc ....G...... 540 382-9400
Christiansburg (G-3611)
Thermo Quick Inc ....G...... 703 455-0040
Fredericksburg (G-5377)
Think Ink Printing ....G...... 757 315-8565
Chesapeake (G-3332)
Tidewater Printers Inc ....F...... 757 888-0674
Newport News (G-9355)
Timothy E Quinn ....G...... 301 212-9700
Alexandria (G-365)
Total Printing Co Inc ....E...... 804 222-3813
Richmond (G-11416)
Tr Press Inc ....E...... 540 347-4466
Warrenton (G-15055)
Type Etc ....G...... 540 347-2182
Warrenton (G-15057)
Universal Printing ....F...... 276 466-9311
Bristol (G-1996)
Variety Printing Inc ....G...... 757 480-1891
Chesapeake (G-3359)
Veterans Printing LLC ....G...... 571 208-0074
Manassas (G-8175)
Via Services LLC ....G...... 703 978-2629
Burke (G-2206)
Virginia Beach Printing & Sty ....G...... 757 428-4282
Virginia Beach (G-14911)
Virginia Prtg Co Roanoke Inc ....G...... 540 483-7433
Roanoke (G-12219)
Virginia Prtg Co Roanoke Inc ....G...... 540 483-7433
Rocky Mount (G-12360)
Vitex Packaging Inc ....C...... 757 538-3115
Suffolk (G-13779)

Walters Printing & Mfg Co ....F...... 540 345-8161
Roanoke (G-12227)
Waterford Printing Inc ....G...... 757 442-5616
Exmore (G-4387)
Watts & Ward Inc ....G...... 703 435-3388
Sterling (G-13560)
Wave Printing & Graphics Inc ....G...... 540 373-1600
Fredericksburg (G-5390)
Webb-Mason Inc ....G...... 703 391-0626
Oakton (G-10164)
Welsh Printing Corporation ....G...... 703 534-0232
Falls Church (G-4928)
Western Graphics Inc ....G...... 575 849-1209
Alexandria (G-381)
William R Smith Company ....E...... 804 733-0123
Petersburg (G-10351)
Winchester Printers Inc ....E...... 540 662-6911
Winchester (G-15512)
Wjm Printed Products Inc ....G...... 757 870-1043
Yorktown (G-16003)
Woodbridge Printing Co ....G...... 703 494-7333
Woodbridge (G-15834)
Woody Graphics Inc ....G...... 540 774-4749
Roanoke (G-12025)
Wordsprint Inc ....G...... 540 382-9111
Blacksburg (G-1807)
Wordsprint Inc ....E...... 276 228-6608
Wytheville (G-15925)
Wythken LLC ....G...... 804 353-8282
Richmond (G-11835)
Xpress Copy & Graphics ....G...... 540 829-1785
Culpeper (G-3933)
Zooom Printing LLC ....F...... 804 343-0009
Richmond (G-11464)

PRINTING: Pamphlets

Arabesque Media ....G...... 703 745-5395
Fairfax (G-4410)
Jeanette Ann Smith ....G...... 757 622-0182
Norfolk (G-9602)

PRINTING: Photo-Offset

Curry Copy Center of Roanoke ....G...... 540 345-2865
Roanoke (G-12075)

PRINTING: Photogravure & Rotogravure

Loron Inc ....G...... 804 780-0000
Henrico (G-6531)

PRINTING: Photolithographic

Hansen Turbine Assemblies Corp .....E...... 276 236-7184
Galax (G-5639)

PRINTING: Rotogravure

Schmitt Realty Holdings Inc ....E...... 203 453-4334
Sandston (G-12631)

PRINTING: Screen, Broadwoven Fabrics, Cotton

Aard-Alltuf Screenprinters ....E...... 757 853-7641
Norfolk (G-9415)
Artfx LLC ....C...... 757 853-1703
Norfolk (G-9445)
Artistic Impressions ....G...... 757 923-4254
Suffolk (G-13671)
Bobs Sports Equipment Sales ....G...... 276 669-8066
Bristol (G-2008)
Bryant Embroidery LLC ....G...... 757 498-3453
Virginia Beach (G-14303)
Dews Screen Printer ....F...... 757 436-0908
Chesapeake (G-3067)
Dpti Inc ....F...... 703 435-2291
Herndon (G-6659)
Emblemax LLC ....E...... 703 802-0200
Chantilly (G-2417)
Harbour Graphics Inc ....F...... 757 368-0474
Virginia Beach (G-14505)
Jackie Screen Printing ....G...... 276 963-0964
Richlands (G-11017)
Locus Technology ....G...... 757 340-1986
Virginia Beach (G-14622)
Martin Printwear Inc ....G...... 434 352-5660
Appomattox (G-819)
Ocean Impressions Inc ....G...... 757 485-3212
Chesapeake (G-3223)
Phoenix Sports and Advg Inc ....G...... 276 988-9709
North Tazewell (G-10104)

Pullin Ink ....G...... 276 546-2760
Pennington Gap (G-10299)
Snips of Virginia Beach Inc ....F...... 888 634-5008
Norfolk (G-9727)
Tee Z Special ....G...... 757 488-2435
Chesapeake (G-3328)
Thalhimer Headwear Corporation .....G...... 804 355-1200
Richmond (G-11409)
Wool Felt Products Inc ....G...... 540 981-0281
Roanoke (G-12230)

PRINTING: Screen, Fabric

Aardvark Swim and Sport Inc ....E...... 703 631-6045
Chantilly (G-2361)
Allen Enterprises LLC ....G...... 540 261-2622
Buena Vista (G-2138)
Artistic Impressions ....G...... 757 923-4254
Suffolk (G-13671)
Atlantic Embroidery Works LLC ....G...... 804 282-5027
Henrico (G-6478)
Ballyhoo ....G...... 703 294-6075
Annandale (G-731)
Barlen Crafts ....G...... 301 537-3491
Suffolk (G-13673)
Blood Sweat & Cheer ....G...... 757 620-1515
Virginia Beach (G-14288)
Bryant Embroidery LLC ....G...... 757 498-3453
Virginia Beach (G-14303)
Decosta Enterprises Inc ....G...... 703 768-4270
Alexandria (G-443)
Dennis W Wiley ....G...... 540 992-6631
Buchanan (G-2121)
Emblemax LLC ....E...... 703 802-0200
Chantilly (G-2417)
Erbosol Printing ....G...... 757 325-9986
Hampton (G-6144)
Flyway Inc ....G...... 757 422-3215
Virginia Beach (G-14469)
Fresh Printz LLC ....G...... 540 937-3017
Jeffersonton (G-7012)
Golden Squeegee Inc ....G...... 804 355-8018
Richmond (G-11220)
Grafik Trenz ....G...... 757 539-0141
Smithfield (G-12714)
Individual Products & Svcs Inc ....G...... 757 488-3363
Chesapeake (G-3141)
Keith Sanders ....G...... 276 728-0540
Martinsville (G-8304)
Leading Edge Screen Printing ....F...... 540 347-5751
Warrenton (G-15030)
Love Those Tz LLC ....G...... 757 897-0238
Virginia Beach (G-14625)
Mounir E Shaheen ....G...... 757 723-4445
Hampton (G-6205)
Promocorp Inc ....F...... 703 942-7100
Alexandria (G-560)
Schmidt Jayme ....G...... 540 961-1792
Blacksburg (G-1787)
Screen Crafts Inc ....E...... 804 355-4156
Richmond (G-11374)
Shirt Art Inc ....G...... 703 680-3963
Woodbridge (G-15806)
Silkscreening Unlimited Inc ....G...... 703 385-3212
Fairfax (G-4554)
Sport Shack Inc ....G...... 540 372-3719
Fredericksburg (G-5487)
Spring Valley Graphics ....G...... 276 236-4357
Galax (G-5648)
Whats Your Sign ....G...... 276 632-0576
Martinsville (G-8353)

PRINTING: Screen, Manmade Fiber & Silk, Broadwoven Fabric

Excel Graphics ....G...... 757 596-4334
Yorktown (G-15956)
First Paper Co Inc ....F...... 434 821-6884
Rustburg (G-12439)
Hatteras Silkscreen ....G...... 757 486-2976
Virginia Beach (G-14509)
Ink & More ....G...... 804 794-3437
Prince George (G-10596)
Mardon Inc ....G...... 276 386-6662
Weber City (G-15149)
T Shirt Unique Inc ....G...... 804 557-2989
Providence Forge (G-10629)

PRINTING: Thermography

Core Health Thermography ....G...... 434 207-4810
Troy (G-13923)

PRINTING: Thermography

Dister Inc ....E.... 757 857-1946
Norfolk (G-9525)
Dister Inc ....E.... 703 207-0201
Fairfax (G-4439)
Hr Wellness and Thermography ....G.... 434 361-1996
Roseland (G-12369)
Kwik Kopy ....G.... 703 560-5042
Falls Church (G-4819)
Virginia Thermography LLC ....G.... 757 705-9968
Virginia Beach (G-14921)

PROFESSIONAL EQPT & SPLYS, WHOLESALE: Law Enforcement

Aspetto Inc ....G.... 540 547-8487
Fredericksburg (G-5171)

PROFESSIONAL EQPT & SPLYS, WHOLESALE: Precision Tools

Mainly Clay LLC ....G.... 434 390-8138
Farmville (G-4948)

PROFESSIONAL INSTRUMENT REPAIR SVCS

Filz Built Bicycles ....G.... 703 451-5582
Springfield (G-13003)
Lb Telesystems Inc ....E.... 703 919-8991
Chantilly (G-2456)
Tri-County Ope ....G.... 434 676-4441
Kenbridge (G-7035)

PROFILE SHAPES: Unsupported Plastics

Aquabean LLC ....G.... 703 577-0315
Fairfax (G-4409)
Conwed Corp ....D.... 540 981-0362
Roanoke (G-12070)
Porex Corporation ....G.... 804 518-1012
South Chesterfield (G-12820)
Porex Technologies Corp ....C.... 804 524-4983
South Chesterfield (G-12821)
Quadrant Holding Inc ....D.... 276 228-0100
Wytheville (G-15905)
Sunlite Plastics Inc ....E.... 540 234-9271
Weyers Cave (G-15178)
Xmc Films Inc ....G.... 276 930-2848
Woolwine (G-15869)

PROMOTION SVCS

S&R Pals Enterprises LLC ....G.... 540 752-1900
Fredericksburg (G-5481)

PROPELLERS: Boat & Ship, Cast

Chesapeake Propeller LLC ....G.... 804 421-7991
Richmond (G-11156)
Propeller Club of The U S Port ....G.... 703 922-6933
Alexandria (G-561)

PROPELLERS: Boat & Ship, Machined

N Rolls-Ryce Amer Holdings Inc ......F.... 703 834-1700
Chantilly (G-2466)

PROPULSION UNITS: Guided Missiles & Space Vehicles

Aerojet Rocketdyne Inc ....G.... 703 650-0270
Arlington (G-843)
Aerojet Rocketdyne Inc ....C.... 540 854-2000
Culpeper (G-3862)
Atk Chan Inc ....G.... 804 266-3428
Glen Allen (G-5705)
Lockheed Martin Corporation ....B.... 757 935-9479
Suffolk (G-13732)
Northrop Grmman Innvtion Syste ....G.... 540 639-7631
Radford (G-10729)
Northrop Grmman Innvtion Syste ....C.... 703 406-5000
Dulles (G-4212)
Orbital Atk Operation Ges ....G.... 571 437-7870
Sterling (G-13467)
Yuzhnoye-Us LLC ....G.... 321 537-2720
Reston (G-10997)

PROTECTION EQPT: Lightning

Loehr Lightning Protection Co ....F.... 804 231-4236
Richmond (G-11659)

Thor Systems Inc ....G.... 804 353-7477
Richmond (G-11410)

PUBLIC RELATIONS & PUBLICITY SVCS

Burwell Group LLC ....G.... 703 732-6341
Arlington (G-894)
Raytheon Company ....C.... 703 841-5700
Arlington (G-1132)

PUBLISHERS: Art Copy

Tidewater Trading Post Inc ....F.... 757 420-6117
Chesapeake (G-3339)

PUBLISHERS: Art Copy & Poster

Andra ONeil Smith ....G.... 804 436-3764
Lancaster (G-7158)
Moms Choice LLC ....G.... 757 410-9409
Chesapeake (G-3211)

PUBLISHERS: Book

Acre Media LLC ....G.... 703 314-4465
Alexandria (G-402)
Airline Tariff Publishing Co ....B.... 703 661-7400
Dulles (G-4191)
Alternatives Inc Corporate ....G.... 540 576-2265
Union Hall (G-13957)
Apps of All Nations LLC ....G.... 434 851-0651
Lynchburg (G-7642)
Autumn Publishing Enterprises ....G.... 703 978-2132
Fairfax (G-4414)
Backroads Publications ....G.... 540 949-0329
Lyndhurst (G-7841)
Bedford Freeman & Wort ....G.... 651 330-8526
Gordonsville (G-5900)
Better Karma LLC ....G.... 703 971-1072
Alexandria (G-422)
Books International Inc ....G.... 703 661-1500
Dulles (G-4193)
Brian Enterprises LLC ....G.... 757 645-4475
Williamsburg (G-15214)
Broken Column Press LLC ....G.... 703 338-0267
Alexandria (G-153)
Capitol City Publishers LLC ....G.... 703 671-5920
Arlington (G-900)
Centennial Books ....G.... 703 751-6162
Alexandria (G-162)
Christian Light Publications ....E.... 540 434-0768
Harrisonburg (G-6300)
Colorful Words Media LLC ....G.... 757 268-9690
Hampton (G-6115)
Contractors Institute LLC ....G.... 804 250-6750
Richmond (G-11165)
Contractors Institute LLC ....G.... 804 556-5518
Richmond (G-11166)
Dawn Brotherton ....G.... 757 645-3211
Williamsburg (G-15230)
Discovery Publications Inc ....G.... 540 349-8060
Warrenton (G-14997)
Divine Ntre & Antng Mnsts Inc ....G.... 757 240-8939
Midlothian (G-8809)
Dynamic Literacy LLC ....G.... 888 696-8597
Keswick (G-7046)
Egap Enterprises ....G.... 434 374-9089
Buffalo Junction (G-2159)
Everyday Education LLC ....G.... 804 752-2517
Ashland (G-1411)
Exchange Publishing ....F.... 703 644-5184
Springfield (G-13000)
Fantalife Publishing LLC ....G.... 703 682-2125
Arlington (G-962)
Forbz House LLC ....G.... 703 216-1491
Gainesville (G-5584)
Forstle LLC ....G.... 540 424-6879
Fredericksburg (G-5186)
Fox Hill Editorial LLC ....G.... 434 971-1835
Charlottesville (G-2798)
Gadfly LLC ....G.... 703 282-9448
Leesburg (G-7276)
Gedoran America Inc ....G.... 540 723-6628
Winchester (G-15419)
Gibson Girl Publishing Co LLC ....G.... 504 261-8107
Virginia Beach (G-14483)
Godosan Publications Inc ....G.... 540 720-0861
Stafford (G-13147)
Golf Guide Inc ....G.... 540 431-5034
Stephenson (G-13333)
Guardian Publishing House ....G.... 804 321-2139
Richmond (G-11606)

Guide To Caregiving LLC ....G.... 571 213-3845
Round Hill (G-12379)
Hanks Indexing ....G.... 434 960-6805
North Garden (G-10075)
Harbor House Law Press Inc ....G.... 804 776-7605
Deltaville (G-4080)
Harris Publications ....G.... 703 764-9279
Clifton (G-3671)
Henderson Publishing ....G.... 276 964-2291
Pounding Mill (G-10520)
High Stakes Writing LLC ....G.... 703 819-5490
Annandale (G-756)
Holtzbrinck Publishers LLC ....G.... 540 672-7600
Gordonsville (G-5907)
Homeland Defense Journal ....G.... 703 622-1187
Arlington (G-992)
Hope Springs Media ....G.... 434 574-2031
Prospect (G-10612)
Houghton Mifflin Harcourt Pubg ....G.... 540 434-0137
Harrisonburg (G-6329)
Huang Shang Jeo ....G.... 703 471-4457
Herndon (G-6704)
Ibfd North America Inc ....G.... 703 442-7757
Vienna (G-14069)
In Good Company LLC ....G.... 540 752-1328
Stafford (G-13153)
Inevitable Entertainment LLC ....G.... 757 470-1521
Hampton (G-6175)
International Publishers Mktg ....F.... 703 661-1586
Sterling (G-13430)
Ipaatti Inc ....G.... 703 901-7904
Chantilly (G-2444)
J & L Communications Inc ....G.... 434 973-1830
Charlottesville (G-2650)
Kara Keen LLC ....G.... 973 713-1049
Annandale (G-763)
Kennedy Projects LLC ....G.... 757 345-0626
Williamsburg (G-15266)
L C M B Inc ....G.... 804 639-1429
Moseley (G-9041)
Lawriter LLC ....E.... 434 220-4324
Charlottesville (G-2656)
Lift Hill Media LLC ....G.... 703 408-4145
Falls Church (G-4823)
Lrj Publishing Group LLC ....G.... 757 788-6163
Hampton (G-6186)
Mariner Media Inc ....F.... 540 264-0021
Buena Vista (G-2146)
Mindful Media LLC ....G.... 757 627-5151
Norfolk (G-9645)
Mythikos Mommy LLC ....G.... 703 568-7504
Fairfax Station (G-4718)
Napoleon Books ....G.... 540 463-6804
Lexington (G-7406)
Omohundro Institute of Early ....E.... 757 221-1114
Williamsburg (G-15285)
Oneidos LLC ....G.... 703 819-3860
Manassas (G-7985)
Oppiya Learning Company LLC ....F.... 804 296-0141
Glen Allen (G-5776)
Our Journey Publishing ....G.... 571 606-1574
Dumfries (G-4254)
Public Utilities Reports Inc ....F.... 703 847-7720
Reston (G-10934)
R R Donnelley & Sons Company ....B.... 540 564-3900
Harrisonburg (G-6359)
Reconciliation Press ....G.... 703 743-2416
Gainesville (G-5610)
Rector Visitors of The Univ VA ....G.... 434 924-3469
Charlottesville (G-2857)
Rookwood Press Inc ....G.... 434 971-1835
Charlottesville (G-2867)
Room The Wishing Inc ....G.... 804 746-0375
Hanover (G-6284)
Salientcontent LLC ....G.... 571 286-8480
Fairfax (G-4672)
Sashay Communications LLC ....G.... 703 304-2862
Arlington (G-1161)
Scripps Enterprises Inc ....F.... 434 973-3345
Charlottesville (G-2691)
Shaper Group ....G.... 703 680-5551
Woodbridge (G-15805)
Silverchair Scnce + Cmmnctons ....C.... 434 296-6333
Charlottesville (G-2878)
Skydog Publications ....G.... 540 989-2167
Roanoke (G-12001)
Stampers Bay Publishing LLC ....G.... 804 776-9122
Hartfield (G-6391)
Tax Analysts ....C.... 703 533-4400
Falls Church (G-4926)

Thomson Reuters Corporation .... G 804 346-5135
Glen Allen **(G-5811)**
Uniformed Services Almanac .... G 703 241-8100
Fairfax **(G-4574)**
Vanderbilt Media House LLC .... F 757 515-9242
Woodstock **(G-15860)**
Virginia Engineer .... G 804 779-3527
Mechanicsville **(G-8695)**
Warwick Publishers Inc .... G 434 846-1200
Lynchburg **(G-7836)**
Wichaar Inc .... G 703 863-3451
Fairfax Station **(G-4728)**
Winter Giovanni Llc .... G 757 343-9100
Norfolk **(G-9796)**
Wolley Segap International .... G 703 426-5164
Fairfax **(G-4583)**
Womens Intuition Worldwide .... G 703 404-4357
Sterling **(G-13563)**
Words To Ponder Pubg Co LLC .... G 803 567-3692
Hampton **(G-6273)**
Wyvern Publications .... G 703 670-3527
Woodbridge **(G-15836)**

PUBLISHERS: Book Clubs, No Printing

Signature Publishing LLC .... G 757 348-9692
South Chesterfield **(G-12839)**

PUBLISHERS: Books, No Printing

A V Publication Corp .... G 276 251-1760
Ararat **(G-829)**
American Inst Arntics Astrntic .... D 703 264-7500
Reston **(G-10786)**
American Soc For Hort Science .... F 703 836-4606
Alexandria **(G-132)**
Antimicrobial Therapy Inc .... G 540 987-9480
Sperryville **(G-12876)**
Barry McVay .... G 703 451-5953
Burke **(G-2182)**
Brandylane Publishers Inc .... G 804 644-3090
Richmond **(G-11509)**
Christian Fellowship Publs .... G 804 794-5333
North Chesterfield **(G-9843)**
Citapei Communications Inc .... G 703 620-2316
Herndon **(G-6642)**
College Publishing .... G 804 364-8410
Glen Allen **(G-5716)**
Csl Enterprises .... G 804 695-0400
Gloucester **(G-5842)**
Dbs Productions LLC .... G 434 293-5502
Charlottesville **(G-2778)**
Debra Hewitt .... G 540 809-6281
King George **(G-7086)**
Eastern Chrstn Pblications LLC .... G 703 691-8862
Fairfax **(G-4615)**
Everette Publishing LLC .... G 757 344-9092
Newport News **(G-9221)**
Firefall-Literary .... G 703 942-6616
Alexandria **(G-462)**
G F I Associates Inc .... G 703 533-8555
Fairfax **(G-4460)**
Global Health Solutions Inc .... G 703 848-2333
Falls Church **(G-4799)**
Holderby & Bierce Inc .... G 434 971-8571
Charlottesville **(G-2645)**
Hollis Books LLC .... G 703 855-7759
Alexandria **(G-480)**
IDS Publishing Corporation .... G 703 821-2323
Mc Lean **(G-8461)**
Ihs Press .... G 877 447-7737
Norfolk **(G-9589)**
Jackson Enterprises Inc .... G 703 527-1118
Arlington **(G-1013)**
Leigh Ann Carrasco .... G 703 725-4680
Mc Lean **(G-8486)**
Lexadyne Publishing Inc .... G 703 779-4998
Leesburg **(G-7298)**
Missing Lynk Publishing LLC .... G 757 851-1766
Hampton **(G-6202)**
Mystique Queen Publishing LLC .... G 484 250-1131
Norfolk **(G-9652)**
Nis Inc .... E 703 323-9170
Fairfax **(G-4519)**
Personal Selling Power Inc .... E 540 752-7000
Fredericksburg **(G-5469)**
Potomac Books Inc .... F 703 661-1548
Dulles **(G-4219)**
Rainmaker Publishing LLC .... G 703 385-9761
Fairfax **(G-4536)**
Rbt Center LLC .... G 703 823-8664
Alexandria **(G-326)**

Really Great Reading .... F 571 659-2826
Woodbridge **(G-15792)**
Rector Visitors of The Univ VA .... E 434 924-3468
Charlottesville **(G-2859)**
Robbworks LLC .... G 571 218-5532
Fairfax **(G-4669)**
Round House .... G 804 443-4813
Champlain **(G-2356)**
Science of Spirituality .... G 804 633-9987
Bowling Green **(G-1907)**
Scotties Bavarian Folk Art .... G 540 341-8884
Warrenton **(G-15049)**
Seven Oaks Albemarle LLC .... G 540 984-3829
Edinburg **(G-4313)**
Slate & Shell LLC .... G 804 381-8713
Richmond **(G-11384)**
Spence Publishing Co Inc .... G 214 939-1700
Mc Lean **(G-8555)**
Stylus Publishing LLC .... G 703 661-1581
Sterling **(G-13520)**
Stylus Publishing LLC .... G 703 661-1504
Sterling **(G-13521)**
Transforming Daily Lives .... G 916 990-2299
Clifton **(G-3677)**
W Berg Press .... G 757 238-9663
Suffolk **(G-13781)**
Winterloch Publishing LLC .... G 804 571-2782
North Chesterfield **(G-10013)**

PUBLISHERS: Catalogs

Tradingbell Inc .... D 703 752-6100
Vienna **(G-14144)**

PUBLISHERS: Comic Books, No Printing

Variance Media Enterprises LLC .... G 202 770-1701
Reston **(G-10981)**
Village Publishing LLC .... G 804 751-0421
Chester **(G-3466)**

PUBLISHERS: Directories, NEC

Columbia Books Inc .... F 800 677-3789
Arlington **(G-915)**
Govsearch LLC .... E 703 340-1308
Mclean **(G-8587)**
Harris Connect LLC .... B 757 965-8000
Norfolk **(G-9572)**
Micro Media Communication Inc .... G 540 345-2197
Roanoke **(G-12136)**
Williamsburg Directory Co Inc .... G 757 566-1981
Toano **(G-13880)**

PUBLISHERS: Directories, Telephone

Supermedia LLC .... B 703 322-2900
Chantilly **(G-2504)**
Thryv Inc .... F 434 974-4000
Charlottesville **(G-2706)**
Vega Productions & Associates .... G 703 908-9600
Fairfax **(G-4578)**

PUBLISHERS: Guides

Dominion Enterprises .... E 757 351-7000
Norfolk **(G-9529)**
N A D A Services Corporation .... C 703 821-7000
Mc Lean **(G-8508)**
Ross Publishing Inc .... G 804 674-5004
North Chesterfield **(G-9966)**
Surfside East Inc .... E 757 468-0606
Virginia Beach **(G-14859)**
Tax Management Inc .... D 703 341-3000
Arlington **(G-1181)**
Trishs Books .... G 804 550-2954
Mechanicsville **(G-8690)**

PUBLISHERS: Magazines, No Printing

21st Century Science Assoc Inc .... G 703 777-6943
Leesburg **(G-7212)**
Adriana Calderon Escalante .... G 703 926-7638
Vienna **(G-14005)**
AGC Information Inc .... E 703 548-3118
Arlington **(G-844)**
American Assn Nurosurgeons Inc ..... E 434 924-5503
Charlottesville **(G-2726)**
American City Bus Journals Inc .... F 703 258-0800
Arlington **(G-852)**
American Spectator .... G 703 807-2011
Alexandria **(G-133)**

Arabesque Media .... G 703 745-5395
Fairfax **(G-4410)**
Audio Mart .... G 434 645-8816
Crewe **(G-3807)**
Autumn Publishing Inc .... G 703 368-4857
Manassas **(G-8030)**
Avenue 7 Magazine LLC .... G 757 214-4914
Virginia Beach **(G-14251)**
Bluegrass Unlimited Inc .... G 540 349-8181
Warrenton **(G-14982)**
Cape Fear Publishing Company .... F 804 343-7539
Richmond **(G-11521)**
Capitol Information Group Inc .... D 703 905-8000
Falls Church **(G-4770)**
Carden Jennings Publishing Co .... E 434 817-2000
Charlottesville **(G-2603)**
Cegna Inc .... E 757 632-5000
Hampton **(G-6110)**
Chronicle of The Horse LLC .... E 540 687-6341
Middleburg **(G-8718)**
City Connection Magazine LLC .... G 757 570-9249
Norfolk **(G-9486)**
Compass Publications Inc .... G 703 524-3136
Arlington **(G-917)**
Dal Enterprises Inc .... G 540 720-5584
Stafford **(G-13135)**
DC Metro Magazine .... G 703 455-9223
Springfield **(G-12989)**
Defense Daily .... G 703 522-2012
Arlington **(G-933)**
Discover Sml Magazine .... G 540 719-7881
Hardy **(G-6287)**
Dorsett Publications LLC .... G 540 382-6431
Christiansburg **(G-3584)**
Editorial Prjcts In Edcatn Inc .... F 703 292-5111
Arlington **(G-954)**
Engaged Magazine LLC .... G 703 485-4878
Springfield **(G-12998)**
Fairfax Publishing Company .... G 703 421-2003
Sterling **(G-13397)**
Family Magazine Network Inc .... G 703 298-0601
Herndon **(G-6673)**
Fcw Media Group .... D 703 876-5136
Falls Church **(G-4792)**
For Rent Magazine .... G 305 305-0494
Henrico **(G-6514)**
Historynet LLC .... G 703 779-8322
Vienna **(G-14065)**
Homes & Land of Richmond .... G 804 794-8494
Midlothian **(G-8827)**
Homes & Land of Virginia LLC .... G 804 357-7005
Midlothian **(G-8828)**
Industrial Reporting Inc .... F 804 550-0323
Ashland **(G-1439)**
Ivy Publication LLC .... F 434 984-4713
Charlottesville **(G-2817)**
Leisuremedia360 Inc .... E 540 989-6138
Roanoke **(G-11956)**
Llama Life II LLC .... G 434 286-4494
Charlottesville **(G-2827)**
Machinery Information Systems .... G 703 836-9700
Alexandria **(G-268)**
Market This LLC .... G 804 382-9220
Glen Allen **(G-5767)**
Montyco LLC .... G 540 761-6751
Roanoke **(G-12137)**
Our Health Magazine Inc .... G 540 387-6482
Salem **(G-12552)**
Patinad Grace LLC .... G 804 447-4578
Richmond **(G-11708)**
Publishers Press Incorporated .... G 540 672-4845
Orange **(G-10223)**
Puryear Group & Associates LLC ...... G 202 327-3777
Glen Allen **(G-5784)**
Queensmith Communications Corp .... F 703 370-0606
Alexandria **(G-563)**
Richmond Living LLC .... G 804 266-5202
Richmond **(G-11356)**
Rosworks LLC .... G 804 282-3111
Richmond **(G-11747)**
Rva Magazine .... G 804 349-5890
Richmond **(G-11752)**
Spinning In Control LLC .... G 703 455-9223
Burke **(G-2203)**
Target Communications Inc .... E 804 355-0111
Richmond **(G-11782)**
Up-N-Coming Magazine .... G 757 343-8829
Norfolk **(G-9775)**
Virginia Beach Guide Magazine .... G 757 627-8712
Norfolk **(G-9782)**

Employee Codes: A=Over 500 employees, B=251-500
C=101-250, D=51-100, E=20-50, F=10-19, G=1-9

2021 Virginia
Industrial Directory

PRODUCT

1031

Virginia Business Magazine ....G..... 804 649-6999
Richmond *(G-11809)*

Weider History Group Inc ....D..... 703 779-8388
Leesburg *(G-7376)*

West Willow Pubg Group LLC ....G..... 434 386-5667
Forest *(G-5104)*

Willie Lucas ....G..... 919 935-8066
Woodbridge *(G-15832)*

Woods & Waters Publishing Lc ....G..... 540 894-9144
Bumpass *(G-2171)*

World History Group LLC ....E..... 703 779-8322
Vienna *(G-14162)*

PUBLISHERS: Miscellaneous

2 Cities Press LLC ....G..... 434 249-6043
Charlottesville *(G-2719)*

2050community LLC ....G..... 202 744-6031
Virginia Beach *(G-14195)*

21st Century AMP LLC ....G..... 571 345-8990
Arlington *(G-834)*

23o5 Publishing House ....G..... 757 738-9309
Chesapeake *(G-2948)*

247 Publishing Inc ....G..... 757 639-8856
Chesapeake *(G-2949)*

3 Degrees Publishing LLC ....G..... 757 634-3164
Portsmouth *(G-10386)*

3 Donuts Publishing LLC ....G..... 703 542-7941
Chantilly *(G-2524)*

A Creative Mind LLC ....G..... 757 450-2899
Norfolk *(G-9413)*

A Simple Life Magazine ....G..... 276 238-2403
Woodlawn *(G-15843)*

About Chuck Seipp ....G..... 703 517-0670
Winchester *(G-15370)*

AC Atlas Publishing ....G..... 301 980-0711
Warrenton *(G-14976)*

Access Publishing Co ....G..... 804 358-0163
Richmond *(G-11469)*

Accuracy Press Institute ....G..... 804 869-8577
Alexandria *(G-117)*

Acorn Press LLC ....G..... 703 760-0920
Mc Lean *(G-8385)*

ACS Division Polymer Chemistry ....G..... 540 231-3029
Blacksburg *(G-1720)*

Advertech Press LLC ....G..... 804 404-8560
Richmond *(G-11087)*

Aether Press LLC ....G..... 703 409-5684
Alexandria *(G-122)*

After Curfew Inc ....G..... 608 214-1289
Lynchburg *(G-7636)*

Aftershock Advisors LLC ....G..... 703 787-0139
Herndon *(G-6604)*

Against All Oddz Publications ....G..... 757 300-4645
Richmond *(G-11480)*

Agile Writer Press ....G..... 804 986-2985
Midlothian *(G-8769)*

Ahf Publishing LLC ....G..... 804 282-6170
Richmond *(G-11090)*

Alexis Mya Publishing LLC ....G..... 540 479-2727
Spotsylvania *(G-12882)*

Allen Sisson Publishers Rep ....G..... 804 745-0903
North Chesterfield *(G-9812)*

Allende-El Publishing Co LLC ....G..... 757 528-9997
Newport News *(G-9163)*

Allergy Asthma Ntwrk/Mthers As ....F..... 800 878-4403
Vienna *(G-14007)*

Allmoods Enterprises LLC ....G..... 703 241-8748
Falls Church *(G-4899)*

Altar Ego Publications ....G..... 540 933-6530
Fort Valley *(G-5134)*

Amadi Publishing LLC ....G..... 703 329-4535
Alexandria *(G-409)*

Amari Publications ....G..... 703 313-0174
Springfield *(G-12945)*

Amarquis Publications LLC ....G..... 804 464-7203
North Chesterfield *(G-9814)*

Ambertone Press Inc ....G..... 703 866-7715
Springfield *(G-12946)*

American History Press ....G..... 540 487-1202
Staunton *(G-13241)*

Andes Publishing Co Inc ....G..... 757 562-5528
Suffolk *(G-13670)*

Andrea Press ....G..... 434 960-8026
Earlysville *(G-4285)*

Angle Valley Press LLC ....G..... 540 662-1320
Winchester *(G-15528)*

Anointed For Purpose ....G..... 804 651-4427
Norfolk *(G-9442)*

Anxious Bench Music Inc ....G..... 757 813-4389
Henrico *(G-6474)*

AO Hathaway Publishing LLC ....G..... 804 305-9832
Midlothian *(G-8772)*

Apex Publishers ....G..... 703 966-1906
Centreville *(G-2290)*

Apostolos Publishing LLC ....G..... 703 656-8036
Bristow *(G-2045)*

Apple Ridge Publishers ....G..... 703 597-8523
Quicksburg *(G-10692)*

Apprentice Press ....G..... 703 352-5005
Fairfax *(G-4594)*

April Press ....G..... 804 551-8463
Henrico *(G-6475)*

Arabelle Publishing LLC ....G..... 804 298-5082
Chesterfield *(G-3476)*

Arcamax Publishing Inc ....G..... 757 596-9730
Newport News *(G-9170)*

Archipelago Publishers Inc ....G..... 434 979-5292
Charlottesville *(G-2590)*

Arhat Media Inc ....G..... 703 716-5662
Reston *(G-10791)*

Ascension Publishing LLC ....G..... 804 212-5347
Midlothian *(G-8775)*

Ash Press LLC ....G..... 757 778-0747
Yorktown *(G-15933)*

Asip Publishing Inc ....G..... 804 725-4613
Port Haywood *(G-10381)*

Association Publishing Inc ....G..... 757 420-2434
Chesapeake *(G-2985)*

Attn Eric Minton ....G..... 703 868-4086
Clifton *(G-3657)*

B & G Publishing Inc ....G..... 757 463-1104
Virginia Beach *(G-14253)*

B & S Xpress LLC ....G..... 434 851-2695
Hurt *(G-6971)*

B Team Publications LLC ....G..... 757 362-3006
Norfolk *(G-9450)*

Badgerdog Literary Publishing ....G..... 757 627-2315
Norfolk *(G-9451)*

Bailey & Sons Publishing Co D ....G..... 434 990-9291
Orange *(G-10204)*

Balent-Young Publishing Inc ....G..... 540 636-2569
Front Royal *(G-5523)*

Ballpark Publications Inc ....G..... 757 271-6197
Bracey *(G-1921)*

Bayfront Media Group LLC ....G.....
Virginia Beach *(G-14264)*

Beauty Publications Inc ....G..... 434 296-2161
Charlottesville *(G-2737)*

Bible Believers Press ....G..... 703 476-0125
Reston *(G-10799)*

Big Mind Publishing Inc ....G..... 703 734-8359
Mc Lean *(G-8398)*

Bill Klinck Publishing ....G..... 540 740-3034
New Market *(G-9140)*

Biohouse Publishing Group Inc ....G..... 703 858-1738
Ashburn *(G-1246)*

Bishop Montana Ent ....G..... 703 777-8248
Leesburg *(G-7231)*

Blac Rayven Publications ....G..... 757 512-4617
Virginia Beach *(G-14285)*

Black Pwdr Artificer Press Inc ....G..... 804 366-0562
Colonial Beach *(G-3722)*

Black Room Press LLC ....G..... 804 929-8040
Glen Allen *(G-5710)*

Blak Tie Publishing Co LLC ....G..... 757 839-6727
Chesapeake *(G-3005)*

Blehert ....G..... 703 471-7907
Reston *(G-10808)*

Blissful Gardenz Inc ....G..... 703 360-2191
Alexandria *(G-425)*

Bloom Publication ....G..... 757 373-4402
Norfolk *(G-9467)*

Blue Jeans Publishing LLC ....G..... 757 277-9428
Chesapeake *(G-3007)*

Blue Ridge Cold Press Company ....G..... 276 229-1661
Hillsville *(G-6886)*

Blue Ridge Digital Pubg LLC ....G..... 703 785-3970
Falls Church *(G-4902)*

Blue Ridge Publishing LLC ....G..... 540 234-0807
Weyers Cave *(G-15167)*

Bluewater Publishing ....G..... 804 695-0400
Gloucester *(G-5838)*

Bluf Military Benefits ....G..... 402 315-7831
Alexandria *(G-150)*

Book Arts Press Inc ....G..... 434 924-8851
Charlottesville *(G-2747)*

Booky Biz LLC ....G..... 434 207-3715
Palmyra *(G-10244)*

Borfski Press ....G..... 571 439-9093
Newport News *(G-9183)*

Boutique Qulty Bks Pubg Co Inc ....G..... 678 316-4150
Christiansburg *(G-3574)*

Braddock Communications ....G..... 703 390-5870
Fairfax *(G-4599)*

Branches Publications LLC ....G..... 434 525-0432
Forest *(G-5056)*

Briarwood Publications ....G..... 540 489-4692
Rocky Mount *(G-12314)*

Bridgeway Professionals Inc ....G..... 561 791-1005
Bristow *(G-2048)*

Brightview Press LLC ....G..... 703 743-1430
Gainesville *(G-5573)*

Brinkmann Publishing LLC ....G..... 703 461-6991
Alexandria *(G-152)*

Brown & Duncan LLC ....G..... 832 844-6523
Virginia Beach *(G-14302)*

Brush Fork Press LLC ....G..... 202 841-3625
Roanoke *(G-11894)*

Bryce K Long ....G..... 757 510-1748
Virginia Beach *(G-14304)*

Bull Ridge Corporation ....G..... 540 953-1171
Blacksburg *(G-1727)*

Bulletin News Network Inc ....E..... 703 749-0040
Reston *(G-10813)*

Bumble Bee Productions Inc ....G..... 757 410-9409
Chesapeake *(G-3017)*

Bunnies Hot Tips LLC ....G..... 757 259-9453
Williamsburg *(G-15216)*

Burke Publications ....G..... 804 321-1756
Richmond *(G-11514)*

Burnsboks Pubg - Pstshirts LLC ....G..... 404 354-6082
Norfolk *(G-9470)*

Burwell Group LLC ....G..... 703 732-6341
Arlington *(G-894)*

Byd Music Publishing LLC ....G..... 305 423-9577
Richmond *(G-11515)*

Byerly Tshawna ....G..... 703 359-5598
Fairfax *(G-4602)*

Canon Publishing LLC ....G..... 540 840-1240
Stafford *(G-13127)*

Capital Publishing Corp ....G..... 571 214-1659
Falls Church *(G-4769)*

Capitol Excellence Pubg LLC ....G..... 571 277-9657
Arlington *(G-901)*

Capitol Net ....G..... 703 739-3790
Alexandria *(G-159)*

Capitol Publishing Corporation ....G..... 703 532-7535
Falls Church *(G-4771)*

Caranus LLC ....G..... 703 241-1683
Arlington *(G-902)*

Carter Jdub Music ....G..... 804 329-1815
Richmond *(G-11150)*

Carters Publishing Company LLC ....G..... 804 590-4747
Disputanta *(G-4105)*

Cassican Press LLC ....G..... 434 392-4832
Rice *(G-11004)*

Cayambis Music Press LLC ....G..... 540 951-3504
Blacksburg *(G-1729)*

Cbe Press LLC ....G..... 703 992-6779
Vienna *(G-14023)*

CC & C Desktop Publishing & ....G..... 757 393-3606
Portsmouth *(G-10406)*

Cerrahyan Publishing Inc ....G..... 757 589-1462
Virginia Beach *(G-14330)*

Champion Publications Inc ....G..... 757 580-4068
Chesapeake *(G-3029)*

Champion Publishing Inc ....G..... 434 817-7222
Charlottesville *(G-2606)*

Chartman Publications LLC ....G..... 252 489-0151
Portsmouth *(G-10407)*

Chelonian Press Inc ....G..... 703 734-1160
Vienna *(G-14027)*

Chesapeake & Hudson Inc ....F..... 301 834-7170
Rochelle *(G-12232)*

Chocolate Dmnds Pblcations LLC ....G..... 804 332-5117
Glen Allen *(G-5713)*

Chris Kennedy Publishing LLC ....G..... 757 689-2021
Virginia Beach *(G-14338)*

Christian Light Publications ....E..... 540 434-0768
Harrisonburg *(G-6300)*

Christian Publications ....G..... 703 568-4300
Mc Lean *(G-8406)*

Church Hill Gun Club Pubg LLC ....G..... 804 236-0802
Richmond *(G-11531)*

Circle of Hope - Asca Fndation ....G..... 800 306-4722
Alexandria *(G-165)*

Circlepoint Publishing LLC ....G..... 703 339-1580
Lorton *(G-7473)*

City Publications Charlotte ....G..... 434 917-5890
Bracey *(G-1923)*

City Publications Richmond	Mechanicsville **(G-8611)**	G	804 621-0911
Classico Publishing LLC	Fredericksburg **(G-5179)**	G	540 310-0067
Clear Vision Publishing	Newport News **(G-9200)**	G	757 753-9422
Clifton Creek Press Inc	Clifton **(G-3661)**	G	703 786-9180
Cold Front Music LLC	Lorton **(G-7475)**	G	703 398-6187
Connoisseur Publishing	Herndon **(G-6644)**	G	303 437-5099
Conversations Publishing LLC	Richmond **(G-11540)**	G	804 698-5922
Coquina Press LLC	Purcellville **(G-10657)**	G	571 577-7550
Corrinne Callins	Springfield **(G-12982)**	G	202 780-6233
Coy Tiger Publishing LLC	Triangle **(G-13889)**	G	703 221-8064
Creative Education & Pubg	Falls Church **(G-4778)**	G	703 856-7005
Creative Mnds Publications LLC	Richmond **(G-11169)**	G	804 740-6010
Creative Passions	Singers Glen **(G-12699)**	G	540 908-7549
Crossing Trails Publication	Woodbridge **(G-15677)**	G	703 590-4449
Culpeper Commercial Printers	Culpeper **(G-3883)**	G	540 825-0771
Cuthbert Publishing LLC	Fredericksburg **(G-5269)**	G	540 840-7218
CWC Publishing Co LLC	Midland **(G-8751)**	G	540 439-3851
Dal Publishing	Virginia Beach **(G-14384)**	G	757 422-6577
Damselwings Press	Vienna **(G-14034)**	G	703 919-4230
Datis LLC	Virginia Beach **(G-14389)**	G	757 961-7498
David Burns	Springfield **(G-12988)**	G	703 644-4612
David Kipps	Aroda **(G-1225)**	G	540 948-4024
Davis Publishing Company	Appomattox **(G-808)**	G	434 363-2780
Decision Point Tech LLC	Norfolk **(G-9523)**	G	757 286-1065
Defee LLC	Williamsburg **(G-15231)**	G	757 645-4358
Dementi Milestone Pubg Inc	Manakin Sabot **(G-7898)**	G	804 784-5151
Destiny 11 Publications LLC	North Chesterfield **(G-9858)**	G	804 814-3019
Devanezdaypublishing Co	Virginia Beach **(G-14403)**	G	757 493-1634
Dewey Publications Inc	Arlington **(G-939)**	G	703 524-1355
Divinely Inspired Press LLC	Manassas **(G-8058)**	G	703 763-3790
Docdirect Publishing LLC	Chesapeake **(G-3069)**	G	757 237-1106
Dogwood Logic Inc	Blacksburg **(G-1733)**	G	540 557-7689
Doite Media LLC	Broadlands **(G-2076)**	G	703 594-1322
Dominion Press Winery LLC	Alexandria **(G-449)**	G	703 395-5109
Donald N Jensen	Alexandria **(G-193)**	G	202 577-9892
Donley Technology	Colonial Beach **(G-3724)**	G	804 224-9427
Donning Publishers Inc	Virginia Beach **(G-14411)**	F	757 497-1789
Downtown Writing and Press	Fredericksburg **(G-5184)**	G	540 907-9732
Dream Dog Productions LLC	Springfield **(G-12995)**	G	703 980-0908
Dreamscape Publishing	Chesapeake **(G-3076)**	G	757 717-2734
Druh-Ke LLC	Suffolk **(G-13701)**	G	757 274-3117
Dtc Press LLC	Oakton **(G-10145)**	G	703 255-9891
Duck Publishing LLC	Richmond **(G-11193)**	G	609 636-8431
Dust Gold Publishing LLC	Richmond **(G-11570)**	G	540 828-5110
DWS Publicity LLC	Roanoke **(G-12079)**	G	540 330-3763
E H Publishing Company In	Crewe **(G-3812)**	G	434 645-1722
Editorial Inspirations LLC	Montpelier **(G-9016)**	G	703 627-0023
Edward Allen Publishing LLC	Hampton **(G-6135)**	G	757 768-5544
Eiger Press	Virginia Beach **(G-14435)**	G	757 430-1831
Eileen Carlson	Virginia Beach **(G-14436)**	G	757 339-9900
Elan Publishing Inc	Charlottesville **(G-2622)**	G	434 973-1828
Elizabeth Bailey	Sutherland **(G-13803)**	G	804 265-8764
Elizabeth Neville	Arlington **(G-956)**	G	703 409-4217
Empire Publishing Corporation	Richmond **(G-11575)**	G	804 440-5379
Employment Guide	Woodbridge **(G-15693)**	G	703 580-7586
Empress Publishing LLC	Petersburg **(G-10319)**	G	856 630-8198
Empress World Publishing LLC	Virginia Beach **(G-14446)**	G	757 471-3806
Epic Books Press	Quinton **(G-10695)**	G	804 557-3111
Faith Publishing LLC	Roanoke **(G-12085)**	G	540 632-3608
Fast Ra Xpress LLC	Richmond **(G-11585)**	G	804 514-5696
Fat Cat Publishings LLC	Ashland **(G-1415)**	G	804 368-0378
Feat Little Publishing LLC	Newport News **(G-9225)**	G	757 594-9265
Federated Publications Inc	Mc Lean **(G-8428)**	D	703 854-6000
Fennec Publishing LLC	Fairfax **(G-4622)**	G	703 934-6781
Fiction-Atlas Press LLC	Bristol **(G-1979)**	G	423 845-0243
Financial Press LLC	Richmond **(G-11210)**	G	804 928-6366
First Colony Press	Virginia Beach **(G-14464)**	G	757 496-0362
First Light Publishing Inc	Chesterfield **(G-3500)**	G	804 639-0659
Five Ponds Press	Henrico **(G-6511)**	G	804 740-5867
Flat Hat	Williamsburg **(G-15245)**	G	757 221-3283
Forel Publishing Co LLC	Woodbridge **(G-15705)**	G	703 772-8081
Four Leaf Publishing LLC	Springfield **(G-13005)**	G	703 440-1304
Fowlkes Eagle Publishing LLC	Chesapeake **(G-3109)**	G	757 673-8424
Freedom Forge Press LLC	Hillsboro **(G-6867)**	G	757 784-1038
Freedom To Destiny Pubg LLC	Chesapeake **(G-3111)**	G	757 617-8286
Freeport Press	Midland **(G-8755)**	G	540 788-9745
Frog Valley Publishing	Round Hill **(G-12378)**	G	540 338-3224
Ft Communications Inc	Midlothian **(G-8820)**	G	804 739-8555
Game Day Publications LLC	Mechanicsville **(G-8626)**	G	804 314-7526
Gameplan Press Inc	Arlington **(G-974)**	G	703 521-1546
Gannett River States Pubg Corp	Mc Lean **(G-8443)**	A	703 284-6000
Gary Burns	Gainesville **(G-5585)**	G	703 992-4617
Genesis Professional Training	Chesterfield **(G-3502)**	G	804 818-3611
Get It LLC	Alexandria **(G-215)**	F	703 625-6844
Giant Publishing & Co	Fairfax **(G-4467)**	G	703 750-6447
Gifted Education Press	Manassas **(G-8075)**	G	703 369-5017
Gilgit Press LLC	Richmond **(G-11600)**	G	804 359-2524
Gilstrap Inc John	Fairfax **(G-4468)**	G	703 961-9413
Girls With Crabs LLC	Spotsylvania **(G-12891)**	G	540 623-9502
Gjhmotivate	Chesapeake **(G-3120)**	G	757 487-5486
GL Hollowell Publishing LLC	Chester **(G-3419)**	G	804 796-5968
Gladstone Media Corporation	Keswick **(G-7047)**	G	434 293-8471
Glen Allen Press LLC	Glen Allen **(G-5737)**	G	804 747-1776
Glencourse Press	Herndon **(G-6685)**	G	703 860-2416
Global Business Pages	Richmond **(G-11603)**	G	855 825-2124
Global Concern Inc	Springfield **(G-13011)**	G	703 425-5861
Global Gospel Publishers	Lynchburg **(G-7721)**	G	434 582-5049
Gmg Ghostwriting	Arlington **(G-982)**	G	718 578-8622
Godosan Publications Inc	Stafford **(G-13147)**	G	540 720-0861
Golden Quill Editorial Svcs	Arlington **(G-984)**	G	240 838-0464
Goodlion Music & Publishing	Newport News **(G-9237)**	G	757 875-0000
Gov Panda LLC	Herndon **(G-6688)**	G	571 275-6370
Grateful Press LLC	Charlottesville **(G-2806)**	G	434 202-1161
Grayson Express	Independence **(G-6983)**	G	276 773-9173
Gregory McRae Publishing	Richmond **(G-11225)**	G	808 238-9907
Groundhog Poetry Press LLC	Roanoke **(G-11929)**	G	540 366-8460
Guynn Group LLC	Richmond **(G-11228)**	G	804 288-0191
Gwen Graber & Associates	Mc Lean **(G-8454)**	G	703 356-9239
Gwen Nappi	Alexandria **(G-226)**	G	703 329-4836
Heart Speaks Publishing LLC	Chesapeake **(G-3130)**	G	803 403-4266
Heart Star Press LLC	Fredericksburg **(G-5440)**	G	540 479-6882
Heartstrings Press LLC	Lancaster **(G-7162)**	G	804 462-0884
Hechos Vios Publishing Inc	Manassas **(G-7951)**	G	703 496-7019
Hedrick Music Inc	Roanoke **(G-12101)**	G	540 354-2139
Helen Heinmiller	Wirtz **(G-15613)**	G	484 459-4425
Herald Press	Harrisonburg **(G-6328)**	F	540 434-6701
Hess Publications	Berryville **(G-1681)**	G	540 771-7515
High Impact Music For You LLC	Richmond **(G-11239)**	G	757 915-8696
High Tide Publications Inc	Deltaville **(G-4081)**	G	804 815-6805
Higher Lving Publications Corp	Mechanicsville **(G-8636)**	G	804 789-0592
Higher Press LLC	Woodbridge **(G-15722)**	G	703 944-1521
Hirsch Communication	Alexandria **(G-478)**	G	703 960-3649
Hmt Publishers LLC	Hot Springs **(G-6946)**	G	540 839-5628
Hollawood Publishing LLC	Richmond **(G-11240)**	G	804 353-3310
Holtzman Express	Winchester **(G-15424)**	G	305 347-4000
Horton Publishing Co	Vienna **(G-14067)**	G	703 281-6963
How High Publishing LLC	Ashburn **(G-1293)**	G	703 729-9589
Hr Publishing Group LLC	Virginia Beach **(G-14531)**	G	757 364-0245
Hypatia-Rose Press LLC	Virginia Beach **(G-14536)**	G	757 819-2559
Ideaphoria Press LLC	North Chesterfield **(G-10020)**	G	804 272-6231
IDS Publishing Corporation	Mc Lean **(G-8461)**	G	703 821-2323
Immortal Publishing LLC	Strasburg **(G-13583)**	G	540 465-3368
Inamod Group LLC	Alexandria **(G-483)**	G	703 626-2453
Independence Publishing Tlr	Richmond **(G-11246)**	G	757 761-8579
Independent Holiness Publi	Pounding Mill **(G-10521)**	G	276 964-2824

PRODUCT

Employee Codes: A=Over 500 employees, B=251-500
C=101-250, D=51-100, E=20-50, F=10-19, G=1-9

2021 Virginia
Industrial Directory

1033

Indian Creek Express Inc ....G.... 434 927-5900
Sandy Level *(G-12647)*
Indigo Press ....G.... 757 705-2619
Virginia Beach *(G-14544)*
Infinity Publications LLC ....G.... 540 331-8713
Woodstock *(G-15855)*
Infinity Publishing Group LLC ....G.... 757 874-0135
Newport News *(G-9257)*
Infosoft Publishing Co ....G.... 661 288-1414
Chesapeake *(G-3142)*
Inner Peace Warriors LLC ....G.... 703 830-7680
Clifton *(G-3672)*
Inscribe Press LLC ....G.... 707 239-8404
Fredericksburg *(G-5303)*
Inside Washington Publisher ....G.... 703 416-8500
Arlington *(G-1004)*
Insite Publishing LLC ....G.... 757 301-9617
Virginia Beach *(G-14549)*
Inspiration Publications ....G.... 540 465-3878
Strasburg *(G-13584)*
Int Diagnostic Syst ....G.... 414 477-8035
Mc Lean *(G-8465)*
Inter-American Group Inc ....G.... 202 255-4528
Mc Lean *(G-8467)*
Ios Press Inc ....G.... 703 830-6300
Clifton *(G-3673)*
Iron Lady Press LLC ....G.... 540 898-7310
Spotsylvania *(G-12899)*
Ivory Dog Press LLC ....G.... 540 353-3939
Roanoke *(G-11945)*
Ivy House Publishing LLC ....G.... 434 295-5015
Charlottesville *(G-2816)*
J-Alm Publishing ....G.... 703 385-9766
Oakton *(G-10152)*
Jake Publishing Inc ....G.... 757 377-6771
Virginia Beach *(G-14562)*
Jamerrill Publishing Co LLC ....G.... 540 908-5234
Timberville *(G-13850)*
James Doctor Press Inc ....G.... 703 476-0579
Herndon *(G-6716)*
James Kacian ....F.... 540 722-2156
Winchester *(G-15550)*
Jamesgate Press LLC ....G.... 703 892-5621
Arlington *(G-1014)*
Janice Osthus ....G.... 571 212-2247
Fairfax *(G-4485)*
Jlb Publishing Inc ....F.... 804 443-0330
Tappahannock *(G-13818)*
JM Walker Publishing LLC ....G.... 757 340-6659
Virginia Beach *(G-14570)*
Jmr Gaines ....G.... 540 370-1723
Fredericksburg *(G-5445)*
Kaah Express ....G.... 703 379-0770
Falls Church *(G-4814)*
Kapok Press LLC ....G.... 540 372-2033
Fredericksburg *(G-5198)*
Keane Writers Publishing LLC ....G.... 804 435-2618
Kilmarnock *(G-7071)*
Kenway Express ....G.... 804 652-1922
Richmond *(G-11643)*
Kilmartin Jones Group LLC ....G.... 703 232-1531
Manassas *(G-8094)*
Knights Press LLC ....G.... 703 913-5336
Burke *(G-2191)*
Knowwho Inc ....G.... 703 619-1544
Alexandria *(G-507)*
Korea Times Washington DC Inc ....E.... 703 941-8001
Annandale *(G-765)*
Kristina Kathleen Mann ....G.... 703 282-9166
Alexandria *(G-510)*
L D Publications Group ....G.... 703 623-6799
Springfield *(G-13035)*
La Publishing ....G.... 757 650-8364
Moseley *(G-9042)*
Lady Press Creations LLC ....G.... 757 745-7473
Carrollton *(G-2244)*
Lagniappe Publishing LLC ....G.... 804 739-0795
Midlothian *(G-8843)*
Larissa Leclair ....G.... 202 270-8039
Arlington *(G-1026)*
Larson Baker Publishing LLC ....G.... 703 644-4243
Springfield *(G-13037)*
Lauren E Thronson ....G.... 703 536-3625
Mc Lean *(G-8482)*
Lawton Pubg & Translation LLC ....G.... 804 367-4028
Richmond *(G-11647)*
Lee Street Publishing LLC ....G.... 540 459-8566
Woodstock *(G-15856)*
Left Field Media ....G.... 703 980-4710
Fairfax *(G-4646)*
Legacy Word Publishing LLC ....G.... 941 915-4730
Alexandria *(G-515)*
Leisure Publishing Inc ....E.... 540 989-6138
Roanoke *(G-11955)*
Lennah Press LLC ....G.... 571 235-4809
Ashburn *(G-1306)*
Libelli LLC ....G.... 757 373-9845
Virginia Beach *(G-14607)*
Life Sentence Publishing LLC ....G.... 703 300-0474
Alexandria *(G-517)*
Lines Up Inc ....G.... 703 842-3762
Arlington *(G-1036)*
Linley Press LLC ....G.... 561 245-1511
Ashburn *(G-1307)*
Little King Publishing ....G.... 540 809-0291
Spotsylvania *(G-12902)*
LNG Publishing Co Inc ....G.... 703 536-0800
Falls Church *(G-4825)*
Local Voice ....G.... 757 565-1079
Williamsburg *(G-15273)*
Look Up Publications LLC ....G.... 703 542-2736
Brambleton *(G-1929)*
Loony Moose Publishing LLC ....G.... 703 727-3309
Ashburn *(G-1311)*
Looseleaf Publications LLC ....G.... 757 221-8250
Williamsburg *(G-15274)*
Lost Clipper Enterprises LLC ....G.... 310 386-0972
Purcellville *(G-10668)*
Lower Lane Publishing LLC ....G.... 703 865-5968
Vienna *(G-14086)*
Lvrcshull Incorporated ....G.... 757 995-3931
Suffolk *(G-13735)*
M & M Enterprise LLC ....G.... 804 499-0087
Richmond *(G-11661)*
Macmillan Holdings LLC ....E.... 888 330-8477
Gordonsville *(G-5913)*
Madinah Publs & Distrs Inc ....G.... 804 839-8073
North Chesterfield *(G-9918)*
Magic and Memories Press LLC ....G.... 703 849-0921
Oakton *(G-10155)*
Main Gate Publishing Co LLC ....G.... 804 744-2202
Chesterfield *(G-3513)*
Manassas Consulting Svcs Inc ....G.... 703 346-1358
Manassas *(G-8104)*
Marden Press Printvertise Inc ....G.... 571 295-5322
Ashburn *(G-1316)*
Masstransit Publishing LLC ....G.... 703 205-2419
Falls Church *(G-4827)*
Match Point Press ....G.... 703 548-4202
Alexandria *(G-271)*
Media Press ....G.... 703 241-9188
Chantilly *(G-2462)*
Media Relations ....G.... 703 993-8780
Fairfax *(G-4653)*
Meltingearth ....G.... 703 395-5855
Herndon *(G-6746)*
Mercury Learning and Info LLC ....G.... 800 232-0223
Dulles *(G-4209)*
Merrill Press ....G.... 571 257-6273
Alexandria *(G-529)*
Merriman Publishing LLC ....G.... 540 370-1852
Fredericksburg *(G-5458)*
Michael Chung MD ....G.... 443 722-5314
Annandale *(G-774)*
Mill Creek Press LLC ....G.... 703 638-8395
Alexandria *(G-276)*
Miller Publishing ....G.... 804 901-2315
Highland Springs *(G-6854)*
Miranda Publishing Compan ....G.... 703 207-9499
Falls Church *(G-4832)*
Misra Publishing LLC ....G.... 703 821-2985
Mc Lean *(G-8503)*
Mofat Publishing LLC ....G.... 540 915-5847
Blue Ridge *(G-1852)*
Mofat Publishing LLC ....G.... 540 251-1660
Roanoke *(G-11969)*
Mojo Castle Press LLC ....G.... 703 946-8946
Gainesville *(G-5598)*
Monday Morning Press LLC ....G.... 804 869-5020
Moseley *(G-9043)*
Monstracity Press ....G.... 703 791-2759
Manassas *(G-8111)*
Mookind Press LLC ....G.... 703 920-1884
Arlington *(G-1067)*
Moonlight Publishing Group LLC ....G.... 703 242-0978
Vienna *(G-14100)*
Moss Marketing Company Inc ....G.... 804 794-0654
Midlothian *(G-8862)*
Motley Fool LLC ....G.... 703 838-3665
Alexandria *(G-284)*
Motley Fool Holdings Inc ....G.... 703 838-3665
Alexandria *(G-285)*
Mount Carmel Publishing LLC ....G.... 703 838-2109
Woodbridge *(G-15751)*
Mujahid Fnu ....G.... 646 693-2762
Alexandria *(G-536)*
Muse Writers Center ....G.... 757 818-9880
Norfolk *(G-9651)*
Music Publishers America LLC ....G.... 917 406-4425
White Stone *(G-15188)*
Mvmt Inc ....G.... 804 356-6520
Midlothian *(G-8865)*
Mybodymyworship ....G.... 703 669-2901
Leesburg *(G-7317)*
Myboys3 Press ....G.... 804 379-6964
Midlothian *(G-8866)*
Mystery Goose Press LLC ....G.... 540 347-3609
Warrenton *(G-15037)*
Mystic Post Press LLC ....G.... 703 867-3447
Alexandria *(G-540)*
Mythos Publishing LLC ....G.... 703 531-0795
Oakton *(G-10159)*
Namax Music LLC ....G.... 804 271-9535
Richmond *(G-11054)*
Nariad Publishing ....G.... 973 650-8948
Glen Allen *(G-5774)*
Nathaniel Hoffelder ....G.... 571 406-2689
Woodbridge *(G-15753)*
National Intelligence Eductn P ....G.... 703 866-0832
Springfield *(G-13056)*
Naylor Cmg ....G.... 703 934-4714
Mc Lean *(G-8510)*
Neighborhood Sports LLC ....G.... 804 282-8033
Richmond *(G-11302)*
Neither Ngex ....G.... 408 676-6439
Chantilly *(G-2467)*
New Look Press LLC ....G.... 804 530-0836
Chester *(G-3439)*
New Paradigm Publishing LLC ....G.... 757 423-3385
Norfolk *(G-9661)*
New Town Holdings Inc ....G.... 703 471-6666
Reston *(G-10907)*
Newswise Inc ....E.... 434 296-9417
Palmyra *(G-10251)*
Niche Publications LLC ....G.... 757 620-2631
Chesapeake *(G-3218)*
Nine-Ten Press LLC ....G.... 804 727-9135
Richmond *(G-11690)*
Ninoska M Marcano ....G.... 202 604-8864
Fairfax *(G-4518)*
Nis Inc ....E.... 703 323-9170
Fairfax *(G-4519)*
North Garden Publishing ....G.... 540 580-2501
Roanoke *(G-11975)*
North Lakeside Pubg Hse LLC ....G.... 757 650-3596
Virginia Beach *(G-14684)*
North Star Press ....G.... 540 967-5093
Louisa *(G-7562)*
Northampton House Pre ....G.... 201 893-1826
Franktown *(G-5165)*
Nottoway River Publications ....G.... 804 737-7395
Sandston *(G-12626)*
Nova Maris Press ....G.... 434 975-0501
Charlottesville *(G-2667)*
NRC Publishing Virginia LLC ....G.... 703 407-0868
Fairfax *(G-4522)*
Number 6 Publishing LLC ....G.... 703 360-6054
Alexandria *(G-545)*
Oaklea Press Inc ....G.... 804 288-2683
Richmond *(G-11311)*
Oakton Press ....G.... 703 359-6800
Oakton *(G-10161)*
Oberons Forge Press LLC ....G.... 703 434-9275
Sterling *(G-13463)*
ODonnell Susannah Cassedy ....G.... 703 470-8572
Falls Church *(G-4849)*
Olde Souls Press LLC ....G.... 434 242-7348
Ruckersville *(G-12407)*
One Wish Publishing LLC ....G.... 571 285-4227
Woodbridge *(G-15766)*
Online Biose Inc ....G.... 703 758-6672
Reston *(G-10914)*
Online Publishing & Mktg LLC ....G.... 540 463-2057
Lexington *(G-7410)*
Onthefly Pictures LLC ....G.... 757 339-1520
Portsmouth *(G-10465)*
Open Tech Inc ....G.... 703 738-6662
Blacksburg *(G-1777)*
Ostrich Press LLC ....G.... 703 779-7580
Leesburg *(G-7322)*

Outthink Corporation .... G. 434 426-7706	Possibilities Publishing .... G. 703 585-0934	Red Hot Publishing LLC .... G. 703 885-5423
Lynchburg *(G-7779)*	Burke *(G-2198)*	Sterling *(G-13488)*
Pacem Publishing .... G. 757 214-4800	Postkite LLC .... G. 202 230-1472	Region Press .... G. 276 706-6798
Virginia Beach *(G-14708)*	Burke *(G-2199)*	Saltville *(G-12587)*
Paddy Publications LLC .... G. 703 402-2233	Prepare Him Room Pubg LLC .... G. 703 909-1147	Reign Productions LLC .... G. 703 317-1393
Fairfax *(G-4659)*	Purcellville *(G-10674)*	Alexandria *(G-569)*
Page Letterpress LLC .... G. 866 540-7243	Press 4 Time Tees LLC .... G. 434 446-6633	Renegade Publishing LLC .... G. 703 780-4546
Richmond *(G-11704)*	Scottsburg *(G-12656)*	Alexandria *(G-570)*
Page Publications LLC .... G. 804 733-8636	Press Enduring .... G. 540 462-2920	Restoration Books & Publishing .... G. 276 224-7244
Sutherland *(G-13804)*	Lexington *(G-7412)*	Martinsville *(G-8323)*
Pages Publishing LLC .... G. 434 296-0891	Press Out Poverty .... G. 703 691-4329	Retrospect Publishing .... G. 703 765-9405
Charlottesville *(G-2671)*	Fairfax *(G-4531)*	Alexandria *(G-571)*
Painting Pages Publishing LLC .... G. 571 266-9529	Press Start LLC .... G. 571 264-1220	Ridan Publishing .... G. 703 349-2028
Leesburg *(G-7323)*	Crozet *(G-3848)*	Fairfax *(G-4542)*
Pandamonk Publishing LLC ...... G. 571 528-1500	Presswardthemark Media Publish .... G. 757 807-2232	Rivanna Pubg Ventures LLC ...... G. 202 549-7940
Alexandria *(G-305)*	Virginia Beach *(G-14737)*	Charlottesville *(G-2685)*
Paperclip Media Inc .... G. 703 323-9170	Print Store LLC .... G. 703 821-2201	River City Publishing Inc .... G. 804 240-9115
Fairfax *(G-4529)*	Falls Church *(G-4858)*	Richmond *(G-11741)*
Paperless Publishing Corp .... G. 540 552-5882	Pro Publishers LLC .... G. 434 250-6463	Rk Publishing Company LLC ...... G. 434 249-9926
Blacksburg *(G-1778)*	Danville *(G-4033)*	Charlottesville *(G-2864)*
Paqueteria Express Inc .... G. 703 330-4580	Probusiness Publishing LLC ...... G. 571 216-3385	Road Runner Hold Co LLC .... G. 703 345-2400
Manassas *(G-7987)*	Alexandria *(G-558)*	Herndon *(G-6793)*
Parkgate Press .... G. 607 280-2364	Profit From Publicity LLC .... G. 703 409-3630	Rodders Journal .... G. 804 496-6906
Falls Church *(G-4854)*	Fairfax *(G-4534)*	Ashland *(G-1489)*
Pastime Publications LLC .... G. 724 961-2922	Prolific Purchasing Properties .... G. 434 329-1476	Romac Publishing LLC .... G. 703 478-9794
Virginia Beach *(G-14711)*	Lynchburg *(G-7792)*	Reston *(G-10942)*
Patriotic Publications LLC .... G. 804 814-3017	Prospect Publishing LLC .... G. 571 435-0241	Root Group LLC .... G. 703 595-7008
Ruther Glen *(G-12460)*	Alexandria *(G-319)*	Leesburg *(G-7339)*
Pawprint Publishing LLC .... G. 434 985-3876	Prosperity Publishing Inc .... G. 757 339-9900	Royal Fern Publishing LLC .... G. 703 759-0264
Stanardsville *(G-13227)*	Virginia Beach *(G-14745)*	Great Falls *(G-5978)*
Paycock Press LLC .... G. 703 525-9296	Protestant Church-Owned .... G. 502 569-5067	S and H Publishing Inc .... G. 703 915-0913
Arlington *(G-1101)*	Springfield *(G-13075)*	Hillsboro *(G-6878)*
Pb & J Publishing LLC .... G. 703 903-9561	Prov31 Publishing LLC .... G. 804 536-0436	S&R Pals Enterprises LLC .... G. 540 752-1900
Mc Lean *(G-8524)*	Newport News *(G-9319)*	Fredericksburg *(G-5481)*
Peace Justice Publications LLC .... G. 540 349-7862	Providence Pubg Group LLC ...... G. 703 352-3152	Saint Marks Publishing .... G. 540 551-3590
Warrenton *(G-15043)*	Fairfax *(G-4663)*	Front Royal *(G-5553)*
Peek—boo Pubg Group Brnd Lcen ...... G. 703 259-8816	Provisioning Inc .... G. 571 451-3134	Sajames Publications LLC .... G. 434 509-5331
Alexandria *(G-307)*	Herndon *(G-6779)*	Lynchburg *(G-7804)*
Pennrose Publishing LLC .... G. 757 631-0579	Prs Towing & Recovery .... G. 540 838-2388	Salt Cedar Publications .... G. 434 258-5333
Virginia Beach *(G-14716)*	Radford *(G-10735)*	Lynchburg *(G-7805)*
Penny Trail Press LLC .... G. 757 644-5349	Psa Publishings LLC .... G. 703 986-3288	San Francisco Bay Press .... G. 757 412-5642
Wakefield *(G-14969)*	Alexandria *(G-321)*	Norfolk *(G-9714)*
Perrone Publishing LLC .... G. 434 962-6694	PSM Publications Inc .... G. 434 432-8600	San Roderigo Publishing LLC .... G. 703 968-9502
Palmyra *(G-10254)*	Chatham *(G-2935)*	Fairfax *(G-4548)*
Peterson Idea Consortium Inc .... G. 804 651-8242	Publication Certified .... G. 703 259-1936	Sandbox Family Comm Inc .... E. 910 381-7346
Ashland *(G-1475)*	Fairfax *(G-4666)*	Arlington *(G-1157)*
Pg Games Publishing LLC .... G. 870 637-4380	Publications Professionals LLC .... G. 703 934-4499	Sangamon Group LLC .... G. 571 969-6881
Hampton *(G-6216)*	Fairfax *(G-4667)*	Alexandria *(G-337)*
Philip Miles .... G. 703 760-9832	Publicity Works LLC .... G. 703 876-0080	Savannah Publications .... G. 804 674-1937
Mc Lean *(G-8528)*	Falls Church *(G-4860)*	North Chesterfield *(G-9970)*
Pierce Publishing .... G. 434 386-5667	Publishers Circltn .... G. 703 394-5293	Science Info LLC .... G. 804 332-5269
Lynchburg *(G-7786)*	Vienna *(G-14115)*	Glen Allen *(G-5792)*
Pigtale Press LLC .... G. 703 753-7572	Publishers Service Assoc Inc .... G. 570 322-7848	SDC Publishing LLC .... G. 540 676-3279
Gainesville *(G-5608)*	Herndon *(G-6780)*	Buchanan *(G-2127)*
Pilinut Press Inc .... G. 540 347-6295	Publishers Teaberry Feilds .... G. 276 783-2546	Sea Publishing LLC .... G. 832 744-7049
Warrenton *(G-15044)*	Marion *(G-8241)*	Aldie *(G-111)*
Pillar Publishing & Co LLC .... G. 804 640-1963	Publishing .... G. 540 659-6694	Secret Society Press LLC .... G. 540 877-6298
Richmond *(G-11716)*	Stafford *(G-13184)*	Winchester *(G-15583)*
Pink Press Dior LLC .... G. 703 781-0345	Pulp Usa LLC .... G. 540 907-0093	Secretbow Pubg Instruction LLC ...... G. 703 404-3401
Fort Belvoir *(G-5117)*	Fredericksburg *(G-5215)*	Sterling *(G-13502)*
Pink Shoe Publishing .... G. 757 277-1948	Pungo Publishing Co LLC .... G. 757 748-5331	Selby LLC .... G. 804 640-4851
Virginia Beach *(G-14722)*	Virginia Beach *(G-14747)*	Montpelier *(G-9021)*
Pionk Enterprises Intl LLC .... G. 571 425-8179	Pure Faith Publishing LLC .... G. 757 925-4957	Sema Wray .... G. 804 282-3609
Manassas *(G-8129)*	Suffolk *(G-13754)*	Henrico *(G-6566)*
Piper Publishing LLC .... G. 804 432-9015	Purple Diamond Publishing .... G. 757 525-2422	Setanta Publishing LLC .... G. 703 548-3146
Midlothian *(G-8879)*	Virginia Beach *(G-14750)*	Alexandria *(G-343)*
Piquant Press LLC .... G. 804 379-3856	Purple Ink Press .... G. 703 753-4638	Seva Publishing LLC .... G. 757 556-1965
Powhatan *(G-10565)*	Gainesville *(G-5609)*	Manassas *(G-7999)*
Pitchstone LLC .... G. 434 296-2384	Puzzle Peace Publications LLC ...... G. 973 766-5282	Shade Green Publishing .... G. 540 845-4780
Charlottesville *(G-2677)*	Newport News *(G-9320)*	Fredericksburg *(G-5360)*
Plan B Press .... G. 215 732-2663	Racepacket Inc .... G. 703 486-1466	Shadow Dance Publishing Ltd .... G. 540 786-3270
Alexandria *(G-551)*	Arlington *(G-1127)*	Spotsylvania *(G-12914)*
Pleasant Run Pubg Svcs LLC .... G. 757 229-8510	Radar Media LLC .... G. 540 348-8996	Shelton Global Assoc .... G. 202 841-8463
Williamsburg *(G-15296)*	Rockbridge Baths *(G-12237)*	Reston *(G-10949)*
Plow Shear Press LLC .... G. 757 346-8821	Railway Station Press Inc .... G. 703 683-2335	Shickel Pubg Co Donna Lou ...... G. 540 879-3568
Virginia Beach *(G-14726)*	Alexandria *(G-324)*	Dayton *(G-4063)*
Poetica Publishing Company ...... G. 757 617-0821	Rainbow Ridge Books LLC .... G. 757 481-7399	Silverwood Press LLC .... G. 804 833-0595
Norfolk *(G-9691)*	Virginia Beach *(G-14759)*	Richmond *(G-11382)*
Poinsett Publications Inc .... G. 757 378-2856	Rambletype LLC .... G. 540 440-1218	Simple Scribes Pubg & Dist LLC ...... G. 804 364-3418
Williamsburg *(G-15297)*	Fredericksburg *(G-5217)*	Glen Allen *(G-5798)*
Poisoned Publishing .... G. 540 755-2956	Raphael Press LLC .... G. 703 771-7571	Sims Creek Publishing LLC .... G. 276 694-4278
Locust Grove *(G-7450)*	Leesburg *(G-7332)*	Stuart *(G-13630)*
Polaris Press LLC .... G. 703 680-6060	Real American Revolution .... G. 703 732-9049	Six Seas Press LLC .... G. 757 363-5869
Woodbridge *(G-15776)*	Falls Church *(G-4864)*	Virginia Beach *(G-14821)*
Polymnia LLC .... G. 434 422-7842	Reconciliation Press Inc .... G. 703 369-6132	Skelly Publishing Inc .... G. 888 753-5591
Charlottesville *(G-2678)*	Manassas *(G-7995)*	Arlington *(G-1169)*
Portfolio Publication .... G. 703 802-8676	Recorder Publishing VA Inc .... G. 540 839-6646	Skyship Fantasy Press .... G. 703 670-5242
Chantilly *(G-2481)*	Warm Springs *(G-14975)*	Woodbridge *(G-15812)*
Positive Pasta Publishing LLC .... G. 804 385-0151	Red Apple Publications .... G. 703 430-9272	Sleepless Warrior Publishing ...... G. 703 408-4035
Glen Allen *(G-5780)*	Great Falls *(G-5977)*	Woodbridge *(G-15813)*

Employee Codes: A=Over 500 employees, B=251-500
C=101-250, D=51-100, E=20-50, F=10-19, G=1-9

2021 Virginia
Industrial Directory

PRODUCT

1035

Slumlord Millionaire LLC ....G... 540 529-9259
Roanoke *(G-12190)*

Small Fox Press ....G... 540 877-4054
Winchester *(G-15479)*

Smartech Markets Pubg LLC ....G... 434 872-9008
Crozet *(G-3850)*

So Amazing Publications ....G... 804 412-5224
Petersburg *(G-10343)*

So What Publications LLC ....G... 757 934-0148
Suffolk *(G-13765)*

Solitude Publishers LLC ....G... 571 970-3918
Alexandria *(G-351)*

Source Publishing Inc ....G... 804 747-4080
Richmond *(G-11386)*

South East Asian Language Publ ....G... 703 754-6693
Bristow *(G-2062)*

Sparks Companies Inc ....G... 703 734-8787
Mc Lean *(G-8553)*

Splendor Publishing ....G... 434 665-2339
Lynchburg *(G-7811)*

Sports Unstoppable LLC ....G... 571 346-7622
Reston *(G-10962)*

Spring Hollow Publishing Inc ....G... 434 984-4718
Charlottesville *(G-2695)*

Square Penny Publishing LLC ....G... 757 348-2226
Chesapeake *(G-3308)*

Stan Garfin Publications Inc ....G... 757 495-3644
Virginia Beach *(G-14842)*

Starlight Express LLC ....G... 434 295-0782
Charlottesville *(G-2883)*

Steam Valley Publishing ....G... 703 255-9884
Vienna *(G-14134)*

Steel Mouse Trap Publications ....G... 703 542-2327
Chantilly *(G-2557)*

Steelgate LLC ....G... 337 263-2490
Brambleton *(G-1933)*

Steve S 2 Express ....G... 757 336-7377
Chincoteague *(G-3566)*

Stillhouse Press ....G... 530 409-8179
Fairfax *(G-4682)*

Stockton Creek Press LLC ....G... 410 490-8863
Charlottesville *(G-2884)*

Stoneshore Publishing ....G... 757 589-7049
Virginia Beach *(G-14852)*

Storey Mill Publishing ....G... 757 399-4969
Portsmouth *(G-10486)*

Stubborn Press and Company LLC ......G... 540 394-8412
Forest *(G-5098)*

Sub Rosa Press Ltd ....G... 703 777-1157
Leesburg *(G-7354)*

Sugar Spring Press ....G... 540 463-4094
Lexington *(G-7418)*

Sumi Enterprises ....G... 703 580-8269
Woodbridge *(G-15818)*

Sunshine Hill Press LLC ....G... 571 451-8448
Reva *(G-11001)*

Supa Producer Publishing ....G... 757 484-2495
Portsmouth *(G-10488)*

Supracity Publishing LLC ....G... 804 301-9370
Louisa *(G-7570)*

Sweetbay Publishing LLC ....G... 703 203-9130
Manassas *(G-8164)*

T2pneuma Publishers LLC ....G... 703 968-7592
Centreville *(G-2344)*

Tannhauser Enterprises LLC ....G... 703 850-1927
Bristow *(G-2063)*

Target Communications Inc ....E... 804 355-0111
Richmond *(G-11782)*

Technology News and Literature ....G... 202 380-5425
Arlington *(G-1183)*

Teen Ink ....G... 804 365-8000
Ashland *(G-1499)*

Terran Press LLC ....G... 540 720-2516
Stafford *(G-13202)*

Tertal Publishing LLC ....G... 571 229-9699
Bristow *(G-2064)*

Thompson Pubg LLC George F ....G... 540 887-8166
Staunton *(G-13301)*

Thomson Reuters Corporation ....B... 434 973-4396
Charlottesville *(G-2704)*

Thorn 10 Publishing LLC ....G... 757 277-9431
Chesapeake *(G-3333)*

Three Angels Pretzels ....G... 540 722-0400
Winchester *(G-15593)*

Tiffany Inc ....G... 757 622-2915
Norfolk *(G-9757)*

Timingwallstreet Inc ....G... 434 489-2380
Danville *(G-4041)*

Titus Publications ....G... 757 421-4141
Virginia Beach *(G-14883)*

TLC Publishing ....G... 434 974-6411
Charlottesville *(G-2707)*

TLC Publishing LLC ....G... 571 439-0564
Ashburn *(G-1341)*

Tlpublishing LLC ....G... 571 992-7972
Ashburn *(G-1342)*

Tlw Self Publishing Company ....G... 540 560-2507
Culpeper *(G-3925)*

Tokyo Express ....G... 276 632-7599
Martinsville *(G-8344)*

Tokyo Express ....G... 540 389-6303
Salem *(G-12576)*

Touch 3 LLC ....G... 703 279-8130
Fairfax *(G-4572)*

Town Pride Publishers ....G... 757 321-8132
Virginia Beach *(G-14890)*

Tracy Barrett ....G... 757 342-3204
Gloucester *(G-5863)*

Transition Publishing LLC ....G... 703 208-4449
Vienna *(G-14145)*

Transport Topics Pubg Group ....G... 703 838-1770
Arlington *(G-1195)*

Triad Digital Media Inc ....G... 336 908-5884
Axton *(G-1542)*

Trinity Publications LLC ....G... 804 779-3499
Mechanicsville *(G-8688)*

Triple OG Publishing LLC ....G... 804 252-0856
Henrico *(G-6586)*

Turtle House Press LLC ....G... 540 268-5487
Elliston *(G-4350)*

Twisted Erotica Publishing LLC ....G... 757 344-7364
Newport News *(G-9366)*

Twomorrows Yesterdays LLC ....G... 571 292-2930
Nokesville *(G-9402)*

Underbite Publishing LLC ....G... 703 638-8040
Alexandria *(G-371)*

Understanding Latin LLC ....G... 703 437-9354
Sterling *(G-13542)*

Urban Works Publicity ....G... 703 625-6981
Arlington *(G-1204)*

Usgri/Bitcoin Press Release ....G... 202 316-3222
Arlington *(G-1206)*

Uts Fendrag Publishing Co ....G... 804 266-9108
Richmond *(G-11431)*

VA Properties Inc ....G... 804 237-1455
Richmond *(G-11803)*

Vanity Print & Press LLC ....G... 757 553-1602
Suffolk *(G-13776)*

Variety Publishing LLC ....G... 703 359-0932
Fairfax *(G-4692)*

Vbk Publishing ....G... 757 587-1741
Norfolk *(G-9779)*

Vegan Heritage Press ....G... 540 459-2858
Woodstock *(G-15861)*

Venetian Spider Press LLC ....G... 310 857-4228
Sterling *(G-13546)*

Ventajas Publications LLC ....G... 540 825-5337
Culpeper *(G-3928)*

Venture Publishing LLC ....G... 540 570-1908
Buena Vista *(G-2156)*

Victory Coachways ....G... 434 799-2569
Danville *(G-4046)*

Vie La Publishing House LLC ....G... 804 741-2670
Henrico *(G-6589)*

Village To Village Press LLC ....G... 267 416-0375
Harrisonburg *(G-6384)*

Viplife Ent Publishing LLC ....G... 434 429-6037
Danville *(G-4047)*

Virginia Academic Press ....G... 703 256-1304
Alexandria *(G-605)*

Virginia Bus Publications LLC ....G... 804 225-9262
Richmond *(G-11808)*

Virginia Cptol Connections Inc ....G... 804 643-5554
Richmond *(G-11812)*

Virginia Media Inc ....G... 304 647-5724
Salem *(G-12579)*

Vision Academy Publishing LLC ....G... 703 753-0710
Haymarket *(G-6453)*

Vision Publishers LLC ....G... 540 867-5302
Dayton *(G-4071)*

Vision Publishers Inc ....G... 540 437-1967
Harrisonburg *(G-6386)*

Vista-Graphics Inc ....E... 757 422-8979
Virginia Beach *(G-14925)*

Vocalzmusic ....G... 703 798-2587
Stafford *(G-13211)*

Von Holtzbrinck Publishing ....G... 540 672-9311
Orange *(G-10230)*

Walkers Cove Publishing LLC ....G... 703 957-4052
Chantilly *(G-2566)*

Wallace-Caliva Publishing LLC ....G... 703 313-4813
Annandale *(G-792)*

Washington & Baltimore Suburba ....G... 703 904-1004
Sterling *(G-13559)*

Washington International ....G... 703 757-5965
Great Falls *(G-5983)*

Watertree Press LLC ....G... 757 512-5517
Chesapeake *(G-3371)*

Way With Words Publishing LLC ....G... 703 583-1825
Triangle *(G-13900)*

Wb Fresh Press LLC ....G... 757 485-3176
Chesapeake *(G-3372)*

Westend Press LLC ....G... 703 992-6939
Fairfax Station *(G-4727)*

Western Express Inc ....G... 434 348-0650
Emporia *(G-4370)*

White Brick Music ....G... 323 821-9449
Harrisonburg *(G-6387)*

White Knight Press ....G... 757 814-7192
Henrico *(G-6591)*

Wimabi Press LLC ....G... 804 282-3227
Richmond *(G-11452)*

Windborne Press LLC ....G... 804 227-3431
Beaverdam *(G-1616)*

Wise La Tina Publishing ....G... 202 425-1129
Reston *(G-10992)*

Witching Hour Press LLC ....G... 571 209-0019
Yorktown *(G-16002)*

Wolf Hills Press LLC ....G... 276 644-3119
Bristol *(G-2001)*

Woods & Waters Publishing Lc ....G... 540 894-5960
Bumpass *(G-2172)*

Word College Inc ....G... 510 857-3309
Centreville *(G-2354)*

Worthington Publishing ....G... 757 831-4375
Virginia Beach *(G-14944)*

Wright Express ....G... 703 467-5738
Herndon *(G-6845)*

Write Impressions ....G... 757 473-1699
Virginia Beach *(G-14946)*

Write Lab Press LLC ....G... 757 390-1030
Franklin *(G-5163)*

X Press Enterprises LLC ....G... 540 587-0100
Bedford *(G-1665)*

Yardsalesheadquarterscom LLC ....G... 757 503-0940
Newport News *(G-9382)*

Yazdan Publishing Company ....G... 757 426-6009
Virginia Beach *(G-14952)*

Yba Publishing LLC ....G... 703 763-2710
Alexandria *(G-390)*

Ynaffit Music Publishing ....G... 757 270-3316
Virginia Beach *(G-14953)*

Yorgea Inc ....G... 704 431-8252
Norfolk *(G-9799)*

York Publishing Company LLC ....G... 571 226-0221
Manassas *(G-8181)*

Young Movar & Assoc Mrktng ....G... 804 320-5860
North Chesterfield *(G-10046)*

Zatara Press LLC ....G... 804 754-8682
Richmond *(G-11462)*

Zebra Press LLC ....G... 703 370-6641
Alexandria *(G-392)*

Zig Zag Press LLC ....G... 757 229-1345
Williamsburg *(G-15349)*

Zook Aviation Inc ....G... 540 217-4471
Harrisonburg *(G-6389)*

PUBLISHERS: *Music Book*

AM Tuneshop LLC ....G... 703 758-9193
Herndon *(G-6611)*

Beatin Path Publications Ltd ....G... 540 828-6903
Bridgewater *(G-1948)*

Hartenshield Group Inc ....G... 302 388-4023
Mc Dowell *(G-8374)*

Kuykendall LLC David ....G... 804 622-2439
Midlothian *(G-8842)*

PUBLISHERS: *Music Book & Sheet Music*

Big Paper Records LLC ....G... 804 381-9278
Glen Allen *(G-5708)*

Dominion Production ....G... 804 247-4106
Richmond *(G-11564)*

Gracenotes ....G... 703 825-7922
Fairfax Station *(G-4710)*

Inertia Publishing LLC ....G... 703 754-9617
Gainesville *(G-5590)*

PUBLISHERS: Music, Book

Always Morningsong Publishing ....G....... 804 530-1392
South Chesterfield *(G-12794)*

Kaliopa Publishing LLC ....G....... 703 522-7663
Arlington *(G-1020)*

PUBLISHERS: Music, Sheet

Bible Truth Music ....G....... 757 365-9956
Newport News *(G-9179)*

Integra Music Group ....G....... 434 821-3796
Lynchburg *(G-7743)*

PUBLISHERS: Newsletter

Access Intelligence LLC ....G....... 202 296-2814
Arlington *(G-837)*

Access Reports Inc ....G....... 434 384-5334
Lynchburg *(G-7631)*

American Immgrtion Ctrl Fndtio ....G....... 540 468-2022
Monterey *(G-9002)*

Communications Concepts Inc ....F 703 643-2200
Springfield *(G-12978)*

Doublethink News LLC ....G....... 434 466-2092
Charlottesville *(G-2785)*

Gartman Letter Limited Company ....G....... 757 238-9508
Suffolk *(G-13714)*

Gooder Group Inc ....F 703 698-7750
Fairfax *(G-4470)*

Hemlock Design Group Inc ....G....... 703 765-0379
Alexandria *(G-477)*

Homeactions LLC ....G....... 703 698-7750
Fairfax *(G-4476)*

Infobase Publishers Inc ....F 703 327-8470
South Riding *(G-12868)*

Kaleidoscope Publishing Ltd ....E 703 821-0571
Mc Lean *(G-8477)*

Macemedia Inc ....F 804 288-5321
Glen Allen *(G-5766)*

Market This LLC ....G....... 804 382-9220
Glen Allen *(G-5767)*

Melamedia LLC ....G....... 703 704-5665
Alexandria *(G-525)*

Mid-Atlantic Printers Ltd ....D 434 369-6633
Altavista *(G-636)*

Northlight Publishing Co ....G....... 804 344-8500
Richmond *(G-11694)*

Ooska News Corp ....G....... 540 724-1750
Warrenton *(G-15040)*

Peak Development Resources LLC ....G....... 804 233-3707
Richmond *(G-11711)*

Retirement Watch LLC ....G....... 571 522-6505
Centreville *(G-2333)*

Valley Construction News ....G....... 540 344-4899
Roanoke *(G-12213)*

Washington Business Info Inc ....E 703 538-7600
Falls Church *(G-4927)*

Your Newsy Notes LLC ....G....... 703 729-3155
Broadlands *(G-2083)*

PUBLISHERS: Newspaper

Above Ground Level ....G....... 540 338-4363
Round Hill *(G-12373)*

Agma LLC ....G....... 703 689-3458
Reston *(G-10780)*

Alter Magazine LLC ....G....... 571 970-3537
Arlington *(G-850)*

Alvarian Press ....G....... 703 864-8018
Reston *(G-10785)*

American City Bus Journals Inc ....F 703 258-0800
Arlington *(G-852)*

American Court Comm Newspapers ....G....... 703 237-9806
Falls Church *(G-4900)*

Badd Newz Publications LLC ....G....... 540 479-2848
Fredericksburg *(G-5250)*

Becke Publishing Incorporated ....G....... 703 225-8742
Arlington *(G-877)*

Bowser Report ....G....... 757 877-5979
Williamsburg *(G-15212)*

Brico Inc ....G....... 540 763-3731
Willis *(G-15356)*

Bulletin News Network Inc ....E 703 749-0040
Reston *(G-10813)*

Bureau of National Affairs Inc ....C 703 341-3000
Arlington *(G-893)*

Bureau of National Affairs Inc ....G....... 703 847-4741
Vienna *(G-14019)*

Catholic Diocese of Arlington ....F 703 841-2590
Arlington *(G-903)*

Charles Southwell ....G....... 703 892-5469
Arlington *(G-905)*

Charlie Eco Publishing Inc ....G....... 800 357-0121
Abingdon *(G-22)*

Christian Power Weekly News ....G....... 703 658-5272
Annandale *(G-735)*

Cold Press II LLC ....G....... 757 227-0809
Norfolk *(G-9492)*

Connection Newspapers LLC ....F 703 821-5050
Alexandria *(G-172)*

Cox Matthews & Associates Inc ....G....... 703 385-2981
Fairfax *(G-4607)*

Crewe Burkfield Journal ....G....... 434 645-7534
Crewe *(G-3810)*

Crowd Almanac LLC ....G....... 703 385-6989
Fairfax *(G-4609)*

Darklore Publishing LLC ....G....... 703 566-8021
Alexandria *(G-183)*

Delauri & Associates ....G....... 757 482-9140
Chesapeake *(G-3064)*

Doi Nay Newspaper ....G....... 703 748-1239
Alexandria *(G-448)*

El Comercio Newspaper Inc ....G....... 703 859-1554
Dumfries *(G-4244)*

Falls Church News Press ....G....... 703 532-3267
Falls Church *(G-4913)*

Fauquier Kid Inc ....G....... 540 349-0027
Warrenton *(G-15011)*

Feedrva Inc ....G....... 804 513-3100
Henrico *(G-6509)*

Ft Lee Welcome Center ....G....... 804 734-7488
Fort Lee *(G-5130)*

Global X Press ....G....... 202 417-2070
Mc Lean *(G-8450)*

Glory Days Press LLC ....G....... 703 443-1964
Leesburg *(G-7280)*

Gods Compass Movie LLC ....G....... 434 219-6865
Lynchburg *(G-7722)*

Grassroots Enterprise Inc ....F 703 354-1177
Herndon *(G-6690)*

Hispanic Newspaper Inc ....G....... 703 478-6806
Herndon *(G-6699)*

Hummersport LLC ....G....... 703 433-1887
Sterling *(G-13423)*

J & V Publishing LLC ....G....... 571 318-1700
Herndon *(G-6715)*

James River Publishing Inc ....G....... 804 740-0729
Henrico *(G-6526)*

Lfm Roanoke ....G....... 540 342-0542
Roanoke *(G-12125)*

Mark Toner LLC ....G....... 703 689-0609
Reston *(G-10895)*

McGuffie History Publications ....G....... 540 371-3659
Fredericksburg *(G-5205)*

Media General Operations Inc ....G....... 434 985-2315
Stanardsville *(G-13223)*

Mercury Partners Usa LLC ....G....... 757 652-7067
Franktown *(G-5164)*

Merrill St Physcians Group Inc ....G....... 804 441-1280
Chesterfield *(G-3514)*

Mkrs Corporation ....E 203 349-1149
Herndon *(G-6748)*

Moshref Mir Abdul ....G....... 502 356-0019
Woodbridge *(G-15750)*

My Mind On Sports LLC ....G....... 703 261-9629
Alexandria *(G-538)*

Neathridge Content Solutions ....G....... 703 979-7170
Arlington *(G-1072)*

North Arrow Inc ....G....... 703 250-3215
Fairfax Station *(G-4720)*

North of James ....G....... 804 218-5265
Richmond *(G-11306)*

Nuevo Milenio Newspaper LLC ....G....... 703 501-7180
Burke *(G-2196)*

Old Rag Gazette ....G....... 540 675-2001
Washington *(G-15076)*

Page Publications Inc ....G....... 804 733-8636
North Dinwiddie *(G-10061)*

Phoenix Designs ....G....... 757 301-9300
Virginia Beach *(G-14720)*

Platinum Point LLC ....G....... 804 357-3337
North Chesterfield *(G-10021)*

Press Go Button LLC ....G....... 703 709-5839
Reston *(G-10930)*

Randy Edwards ....G....... 703 591-0545
Fairfax *(G-4537)*

Ready For Hillary ....G....... 703 405-0433
Arlington *(G-1142)*

Robert Deitrich ....G....... 804 793-8414
Danville *(G-4036)*

Robert Grogg ....G....... 540 667-4279
Winchester *(G-15467)*

Social Music LLC ....G....... 202 308-3249
Fredericksburg *(G-5364)*

Springfield Connection ....G....... 703 866-1040
Springfield *(G-13093)*

Springfield Times ....G....... 703 437-5400
Reston *(G-10963)*

Sprouting Star Press ....G....... 703 860-0958
Reston *(G-10964)*

Sun Gazette ....G....... 703 738-2520
Springfield *(G-13096)*

Toro-Aire Inc ....G....... 804 649-7575
Richmond *(G-11789)*

Tran Du ....G....... 512 470-1794
Arlington *(G-1194)*

Valley Publishing Corporation ....G....... 434 591-1000
Palmyra *(G-10259)*

Washingtnpost Nwsweek Intrctiv ....G....... 703 469-2500
Arlington *(G-1216)*

Weekly Weeder Co ....G....... 757 618-9506
Virginia Beach *(G-14932)*

Windmill Promotions ....G....... 757 204-4688
Virginia Beach *(G-14940)*

World & I ....G....... 202 636-3334
Annandale *(G-794)*

PUBLISHERS: Newspapers, No Printing

Arabesque Media ....G....... 703 745-5395
Fairfax *(G-4410)*

Asian Fortune Enterprises Inc ....F 703 753-8295
Vienna *(G-14010)*

C & C Publishing Inc ....G....... 804 598-4305
Mechanicsville *(G-8610)*

C-Ville Holdings LLC ....G....... 434 817-2749
Charlottesville *(G-2753)*

Cv Corporation of Virginia ....F 540 967-0368
Louisa *(G-7554)*

Daniel Patrick McDermott ....G....... 540 305-3000
Front Royal *(G-5528)*

Dehardit Press ....G....... 804 693-2795
Gloucester *(G-5845)*

Editorial Prjcts In Edcatn Inc ....F 703 292-5111
Arlington *(G-954)*

Enterprise Inc ....G....... 276 694-3101
Stuart *(G-13609)*

Fauquier Times Democrat ....E 540 347-7363
Warrenton *(G-15015)*

Free Lance-Star Publshng Co of ....B 540 374-5000
Fredericksburg *(G-5190)*

Gazette Virginian ....G....... 434 572-3945
South Boston *(G-12771)*

Halifax Gazette Publishing Co ....G....... 434 572-3945
South Boston *(G-12774)*

Hampton Roads Gazeti Inc ....G....... 757 560-9583
Virginia Beach *(G-14499)*

Hampton University ....G....... 757 727-5385
Hampton *(G-6164)*

Herndon Publishing Co Inc ....F 703 689-0111
Herndon *(G-6697)*

Infoition News Services Inc ....F 703 853-8857
Reston *(G-10871)*

Intelligence Press Inc ....F 703 318-8848
Sterling *(G-13429)*

Korea Times Washington DC Inc ....E 703 941-8001
Annandale *(G-765)*

Leader Publishing Company ....D 540 885-7387
Staunton *(G-13274)*

Michael S Bond ....G....... 740 971-9157
Alexandria *(G-532)*

Montgomery Cnty Newspapers Inc ....E 540 389-9355
Salem *(G-12540)*

North Street Enterprise Inc ....E 434 392-4144
Farmville *(G-4954)*

Program Services LLC ....G....... 757 222-3990
Norfolk *(G-9698)*

Protocol Media LLC ....F 703 647-8700
Arlington *(G-1122)*

Randall Publication Inc ....F 703 369-0741
Manassas *(G-7994)*

Rappahannock Record ....F 804 435-1701
Kilmarnock *(G-7076)*

Roanoke ....G....... 540 362-8404
Roanoke *(G-12164)*

Saltville Progress Inc ....G....... 276 496-5792
Saltville *(G-12591)*

Sightline Media Group LLC ....B 703 750-7400
Vienna *(G-14126)*

South Boston News Inc ....F 434 572-2928
South Boston *(G-12790)*

Employee Codes: A=Over 500 employees, B=251-500
C=101-250, D=51-100, E=20-50, F=10-19, G=1-9

2021 Virginia
Industrial Directory

1037

PRODUCT

Style LLC ....D...... 757 222-3990
Richmond *(G-11775)*
Tide Water Pulication LLC...................E...... 757 562-3187
Franklin *(G-5158)*
Tide Water Pulication LLC...................G...... 434 848-2114
Lawrenceville *(G-7186)*
USA Weekend Inc............................C...... 703 854-6000
Mc Lean *(G-8573)*
Valley Trader The Inc.......................F...... 540 869-5132
Middletown *(G-8747)*
Village Publishing LLC......................G...... 804 751-0421
Chester *(G-3466)*
Virginian Leader Corp.......................F...... 540 921-3434
Pearisburg *(G-10279)*
Womack Publishing Co Inc...................F...... 434 432-2791
Chatham *(G-2942)*
Womack Publishing Co Inc...................G...... 434 352-8215
Appomattox *(G-828)*
Womack Publishing Co Inc...................F...... 434 447-3178
South Hill *(G-12864)*
Womack Publishing Co Inc...................G...... 434 369-6688
Altavista *(G-645)*
Womack Publishing Co Inc...................F...... 434 432-1654
Emporia *(G-4371)*
Wood Television LLC........................G...... 703 368-9268
Manassas *(G-8014)*
Wp Company LLC............................F...... 703 771-1491
Leesburg *(G-7381)*

PUBLISHERS: Pamphlets, No Printing

Knitting Information.........................G...... 804 288-4754
Richmond *(G-11263)*

PUBLISHERS: Patterns, Paper

Maggies Rags...............................G...... 540 961-1755
Blacksburg *(G-1757)*

PUBLISHERS: Periodical Statistical Reports, No Printing

Autumn Publishing Enterprises ....G...... 703 978-2132
Fairfax *(G-4414)*

PUBLISHERS: Periodical, With Printing

Piedmont Publishing Inc....................F...... 434 822-1800
Danville *(G-4030)*

PUBLISHERS: Periodicals, Magazines

Access Reports Inc.........................G...... 434 384-5334
Lynchburg *(G-7631)*
Barry McVay.................................G...... 703 451-5953
Burke *(G-2182)*
Believe Magazine............................G...... 804 291-7509
Richmond *(G-11029)*
Bowser Report..............................G...... 757 877-5979
Williamsburg *(G-15212)*
C & C Publishing Inc.......................G...... 804 598-4305
Mechanicsville *(G-8610)*
Collecting Concepts Inc....................E...... 804 285-0994
Richmond *(G-11162)*
Dominion Enterprises........................G...... 757 226-9440
Norfolk *(G-9530)*
Dominion Enterprises........................G...... 540 869-3837
Stephens City *(G-13314)*
Dominion Enterprises........................E...... 757 351-7000
Norfolk *(G-9529)*
Double D LLC...............................G...... 270 307-2786
Woodbridge *(G-15686)*
Eastern Chrstn Pblications LLC............G...... 703 691-8862
Fairfax *(G-4615)*
Enterprising Women..........................G...... 919 362-1551
Dulles *(G-4199)*
Eutopia Magazine Guelph Press.............G...... 703 938-6077
Herndon *(G-6670)*
Executive Lifestyle Mag Inc................G...... 757 438-5582
Newport News *(G-9222)*
Fcw Government Tech Group.................D...... 703 876-5100
Falls Church *(G-4791)*
Federal Times...............................G...... 703 750-9000
Vienna *(G-14053)*
Focus Magazine.............................G...... 434 296-4261
Charlottesville *(G-2796)*
Gately John.................................G...... 757 851-3085
Hampton *(G-6156)*
Homeland Corporation.......................F...... 571 218-6200
Sterling *(G-13421)*
Ibfd North America Inc......................G...... 703 442-7757
Vienna *(G-14069)*

Inside Air Force............................G...... 703 416-8528
Arlington *(G-1003)*
Interlocking Con Pavement Inst............G...... 703 657-6900
Chantilly *(G-2443)*
Intermission................................G...... 703 971-7530
Alexandria *(G-488)*
Justin Comb................................G...... 703 783-1082
Alexandria *(G-249)*
K Composite Magazine.......................G...... 703 568-6917
Alexandria *(G-503)*
Landmark Media Enterprises LLC...........A...... 757 351-7000
Norfolk *(G-9616)*
Last Call Magazine LLC.....................G...... 757 410-0229
Chesapeake *(G-3176)*
Lmr-Inc Com................................G...... 518 253-9220
Manassas Park *(G-8204)*
Mercury Hour................................G...... 434 237-4011
Lynchburg *(G-7771)*
Mld Publishing..............................G...... 434 535-6008
Lynchburg *(G-7774)*
Napolean Magazine..........................G...... 703 641-9062
Falls Church *(G-4834)*
Palmyra Press Inc...........................G...... 434 589-6634
Palmyra *(G-10252)*
Product Safety Letter.......................G...... 703 247-3423
Falls Church *(G-4859)*
Reason......................................G...... 202 256-6197
Charlottesville *(G-2856)*
Rector Visitors of The Univ VA ....G...... 434 924-9136
Charlottesville *(G-2858)*
Senior Publ Free Seniority..................E...... 757 222-3900
Norfolk *(G-9717)*
Shakespeareink Inc..........................F...... 804 381-8237
North Chesterfield *(G-9976)*
Society Nclear Mdcine Mlclar I ....D...... 703 708-9000
Reston *(G-10957)*
Surfside East Inc...........................E...... 757 468-0606
Virginia Beach *(G-14859)*
Sword & Trumpet Office.....................G...... 540 867-9419
Rockingham *(G-12280)*
Tidewater Trading Post Inc ....F...... 757 420-6117
Chesapeake *(G-3339)*
Travel Guide LLC............................E...... 757 351-7000
Norfolk *(G-9766)*
United States Dept of Army.................G...... 703 614-3727
Fort Belvoir *(G-5119)*
Virginia Real Estate Reviews................G...... 276 956-5900
Martinsville *(G-8349)*
Vista-Graphics Inc..........................G...... 804 559-6140
Mechanicsville *(G-8696)*
Wood Television LLC........................G...... 540 343-2405
Roanoke *(G-12229)*

PUBLISHERS: Periodicals, No Printing

Association For Cmpt McHy Inc.............G...... 703 528-0726
Arlington *(G-863)*
Bowhead Systems Management LLC...C...... 703 413-4251
Springfield *(G-12968)*
Bureau of National Affairs Inc.............C...... 703 341-3000
Arlington *(G-893)*
Dominion Distribution Svcs Inc............F...... 757 351-7000
Norfolk *(G-9528)*
Global Health Solutions Inc.................G...... 703 848-2333
Falls Church *(G-4799)*
International Publishing Inc.................G...... 800 377-2838
Chesapeake *(G-3145)*
Kristina Kathleen Mann......................G...... 703 282-9166
Alexandria *(G-510)*
Mystic Empowerment........................G...... 703 765-0690
Alexandria *(G-539)*
Nis Inc.....................................E...... 703 323-9170
Fairfax *(G-4519)*
Personal Selling Power Inc.................F...... 540 752-7000
Fredericksburg *(G-5469)*
Presbytrian Outlook Foundation...........G...... 804 359-8442
Richmond *(G-11724)*
Silverchair Scnce + Cmmnctons............G...... 434 296-6333
Charlottesville *(G-2878)*
Sovereign Media.............................G...... 703 964-0361
Mc Lean *(G-8552)*
Tax Analysts................................C...... 703 533-4400
Falls Church *(G-4926)*
Thermadon Associates.......................G...... 571 275-6118
Woodbridge *(G-15822)*
Virtuous Health Today Inc..................G...... 540 339-2855
Roanoke *(G-12223)*

PUBLISHERS: Posters

Arabesque Media.............................G...... 703 745-5395
Fairfax *(G-4410)*

PUBLISHERS: Technical Manuals

Brook Vance Publishing LLC................G...... 703 660-1214
Alexandria *(G-154)*

PUBLISHERS: Technical Manuals & Papers

Allen Wayne Ltd Arlington ....G...... 703 321-7414
Warrenton *(G-14977)*
Sandra Woodward...........................G...... 703 329-7938
Alexandria *(G-336)*

PUBLISHERS: Telephone & Other Directory

Carden Jennings Publishing Co.............E...... 434 817-2000
Charlottesville *(G-2603)*
Compass Publications Inc....................G...... 703 524-3136
Arlington *(G-917)*
Magnet Directories Inc......................G...... 281 251-6640
Unionville *(G-13964)*
Ogden Directories Inc.......................G...... 540 375-6524
Roanoke *(G-11977)*
Richmond Yellowpages Com.................G...... 804 565-9170
Richmond *(G-11363)*
Vega Pages LLC.............................G...... 703 281-2030
Vienna *(G-14150)*
Victimology Inc.............................G...... 703 528-3387
Arlington *(G-1210)*
Virginia Sportsman..........................G...... 434 971-1199
Charlottesville *(G-2901)*

PUBLISHERS: Textbooks, No Printing

Cemark Inc..................................F...... 804 763-4100
Midlothian *(G-8793)*
Houghton Mifflin Harcourt Pubg ....C...... 703 243-2602
Arlington *(G-994)*

PUBLISHERS: Trade journals, No Printing

Institute of Navigation (dc).................G...... 703 366-2723
Manassas *(G-8081)*
Rector Visitors of The Univ VA ....G...... 434 924-3124
Charlottesville *(G-2860)*

PUBLISHING & BROADCASTING: Internet Only

1trybe Inc..................................G...... 540 270-6043
Gainesville *(G-5567)*
American Media Institute....................G...... 703 872-7840
Arlington *(G-853)*
Axios Media Inc.............................E...... 703 291-3600
Arlington *(G-869)*
Bbk Cnsldted Slutions Svcs LLC...........G...... 571 229-2276
Manassas *(G-7920)*
Blinkcloud LLC..............................G...... 484 429-3340
Alexandria *(G-148)*
Blucloudradio LLC...........................G...... 757 812-2380
Norfolk *(G-9468)*
Bridge To Biz...............................G...... 703 942-6441
Springfield *(G-12970)*
Cameron Aubernon...........................G...... 540 251-4363
Christianburg *(G-3577)*
Clearedjobsnet Inc..........................G...... 703 871-0037
Falls Church *(G-4905)*
Dagnewcompany Inc.........................F...... 703 835-0827
Alexandria *(G-439)*
Data-Clear LLC.............................G...... 703 499-3816
Arlington *(G-929)*
Dr Jk Longevity LLC........................G...... 202 304-0896
Vienna *(G-14041)*
Dream Catcher Enterprises LLC............G...... 540 338-8273
Hamilton *(G-6056)*
Dtwelve Enterprise LLC......................G...... 757 837-0452
Virginia Beach *(G-14415)*
Ember Systems LLC..........................G...... 540 327-1984
Winchester *(G-15539)*
Freshwter Parl Media Group LLC...........G...... 757 785-5483
Norfolk *(G-9559)*
Gay G-Spot LLC.............................G...... 650 429-8233
Arlington *(G-976)*
Give More Media Inc........................G...... 804 762-4500
Richmond *(G-11601)*
Hamby-Stern Publishing LLC................G...... 703 425-3719
Burke *(G-2190)*
Heartseeking LLC............................G...... 305 778-8040
Stuarts Draft *(G-13648)*
Hey Frase LLC..............................G...... 202 372-5453
Arlington *(G-991)*
Ideation Web Studios LLC..................G...... 757 333-3021
Chesapeake *(G-3140)*

Knowlera Media LLC..........................G.... 703 757-5444
Great Falls (G-5963)

Li Ailin...G.... 573 808-7280
Arlington (G-1033)

Local News Now LLC.......................G.... 703 348-0583
Arlington (G-1041)

Majestic Marketing LLC...................G.... 804 210-7667
Richmond (G-11282)

Media Africa Inc..............................G.... 703 260-6494
Leesburg (G-7311)

Megaphone LLC...............................E.... 703 594-7623
Reston (G-10897)

Momensity LLC.................................G.... 804 247-2811
Stafford (G-13177)

Moon Consortium LLC.....................G.... 571 408-9570
Mc Lean (G-8506)

Neevarpt Productions LLC...............G.... 571 549-1169
Manassas (G-7982)

Outl T Infomarket LLC......................G.... 703 927-1346
Arlington (G-1092)

Oval LLC...G.... 757 389-3777
Woodbridge (G-15768)

Pbp Solutions LLC...........................G.... 202 999-8101
Reston (G-10923)

Phuble Inc...F.... 443 388-0657
Virginia Beach (G-14721)

Rentury Solutions LLC.....................G.... 757 453-5763
Hampton (G-6227)

Roll of Honor Foundation.................G.... 703 731-6109
Fairfax (G-4544)

Sambuqcom Inc................................G.... 703 980-8669
Mc Lean (G-8544)

Seql Inc...G.... 804 214-5678
Richmond (G-11758)

Synaptein Solutions Inc...................F.... 703 209-2350
Mc Lean (G-8562)

Tactical Nuclear Wizard LLC............G.... 804 231-1671
Richmond (G-11780)

Talk Is Life LLC................................G.... 703 951-3848
Dumfries (G-4258)

Timothy L Hosey..............................G.... 270 339-0016
Maurertown (G-8364)

Topoatlas LLC...................................G.... 703 476-5256
Herndon (G-6829)

Tvworldwidecom Inc........................G.... 703 961-9250
Chantilly (G-2509)

Ubibird Incorporated........................G.... 718 490-3746
Stafford (G-13207)

Ubiquitywave LLC.............................G.... 571 262-1406
Ashburn (G-1344)

Veteran Freelancer...........................G.... 484 772-5931
Norfolk (G-9781)

Warren Ventures LLC........................G.... 804 267-9098
Richmond (G-11818)

Wellzone Inc......................................G.... 703 770-2861
Mc Lean (G-8578)

Wilderwork Pbc.................................F.... 202 285-9455
Arlington (G-1218)

Work Scene Media LLC.....................F.... 703 910-5959
Mclean (G-8589)

Worldwide Agency LLC.....................G.... 202 888-5895
Arlington (G-1222)

Zinerva Publishing LLC.....................G.... 703 430-7629
Great Falls (G-5986)

Zones LLC...G.... 571 244-8206
Alexandria (G-617)

PUBLISHING & PRINTING: Art Copy

Dap Enterprises Inc..........................G.... 757 921-3576
Williamsburg (G-15229)

Dap Incorporated..............................G.... 757 921-3576
Newport News (G-9214)

North South Partners LLC................E.... 804 213-0600
Richmond (G-11307)

Redline Productions..........................G.... 703 861-8765
Falls Church (G-4865)

PUBLISHING & PRINTING: Book Clubs

Thought & Expression Co LLC...........E.... 405 919-0068
Mc Lean (G-8567)

PUBLISHING & PRINTING: Book Music

Marcy Boys Music.............................G.... 757 247-6222
Newport News (G-9290)

PUBLISHING & PRINTING: Books

Follett College Store 743.................G.... 434 961-5317
Charlottesville (G-2797)

Indigo Pen Publishing LLC................G.... 888 670-4010
Alexandria (G-484)

Kendall/Hunt Publishing Co..............G.... 804 285-9411
Mechanicsville (G-8648)

Komorebi Press LLC..........................G.... 301 910-5041
Falls Church (G-4920)

Macoy Pubg Masonic Sup Co Inc.......E.... 804 262-6551
Richmond (G-11280)

Natasha Matthew..............................G.... 757 407-1897
Norfolk (G-9653)

R B M Enterprises Inc.......................G.... 804 290-4407
Glen Allen (G-5786)

Reformation Herald Pubg Assn.........F.... 540 366-9400
Roanoke (G-11994)

Reward Happiness LLC.....................G.... 703 795-0746
Falls Church (G-4866)

PUBLISHING & PRINTING: Catalogs

MPS Return Center............................G.... 540 672-0792
Orange (G-10221)

National Review Institute..................G.... 202 679-7330
Arlington (G-1071)

PUBLISHING & PRINTING: Directories, NEC

Payne Publishers Inc.......................D.... 703 631-9033
Manassas (G-7988)

PUBLISHING & PRINTING: Guides

Collecting Concepts Inc....................E.... 804 285-0994
Richmond (G-11162)

PUBLISHING & PRINTING: Magazines: publishing & printing

Anneker Corp.....................................F.... 202 630-3007
Alexandria (G-136)

Associated Gen Contrs of Amer.........D.... 703 837-5415
Arlington (G-862)

Beck Media Group.............................G.... 540 904-6800
Roanoke (G-12042)

Career College Central......................G.... 571 267-3012
Chantilly (G-2387)

Computing With Kids..........................G.... 703 444-9005
Great Falls (G-5949)

Custom Pubg Solutions LLC..............G.... 540 341-0453
Warrenton (G-14991)

Daleel Corporation............................G.... 703 824-8130
Vienna (G-14033)

Dogwood Ridge Outdoors Inc............G.... 540 867-0764
Dayton (G-4055)

Elizabeth Claire Inc..........................G.... 757 430-4308
Virginia Beach (G-14440)

Gja LLC..G.... 434 218-0216
Palmyra (G-10249)

Highbrow Magazine LLC....................G.... 571 480-2867
Vienna (G-14064)

Interntnal Soc For Cmpttnal Bi..........G.... 571 293-2113
Leesburg (G-7288)

Ivy Creek Media................................G.... 434 971-1787
Charlottesville (G-2648)

JB Pinker Inc.....................................G.... 540 943-2760
Afton (G-85)

Journal of Orthpdic Spt Physcl..........G.... 877 766-3450
Alexandria (G-246)

Liberty Media For Women LLC...........F.... 703 522-4201
Arlington (G-1034)

Lsc Communications Us LLC.............G.... 540 564-3900
Harrisonburg (G-6341)

National Geographic Entps................D.... 703 528-7868
Arlington (G-1070)

Neighborhood Sports LLC..................G.... 804 282-8033
Richmond (G-11302)

Real Estate Weekly............................F.... 434 817-9330
Charlottesville (G-2681)

Shenandoah Specialty Pubg LLC........G.... 540 463-2319
Lexington (G-7416)

Submarine Telecoms Forum Inc.........G.... 703 444-0845
Sterling (G-13522)

Under Radar LLC................................G.... 540 348-8996
Lexington (G-7421)

Venutec Corporation..........................G.... 888 573-8870
Centreville (G-2350)

Virginia Bride LLC.............................G.... 804 822-1768
Saluda (G-12606)

Wood Television LLC.........................D.... 804 649-6069
Richmond (G-11833)

PUBLISHING & PRINTING: Music, Book

Mastermind LLC................................G.... 757 379-5215
Yorktown (G-15980)

Pluto Gone LLC.................................G.... 804 719-3076
Suffolk (G-13752)

US Dept of the Air Force...................G.... 757 764-5616
Hampton (G-6279)

PUBLISHING & PRINTING: Newsletters, Business Svc

10 10 LLC...G.... 757 627-4311
Norfolk (G-9410)

David A Einhorn................................G.... 703 356-6218
Falls Church (G-4782)

Digi Quick Print Inc..........................G.... 703 671-9600
Alexandria (G-187)

Light Designs Publishing Co.............G.... 804 261-6900
Glen Allen (G-5763)

National Institute of Bus Mgt............G.... 703 394-4921
Falls Church (G-4835)

R B M Enterprises Inc.......................G.... 804 290-4407
Glen Allen (G-5786)

Strive Communications LLC..............G.... 703 925-5900
Reston (G-10967)

PUBLISHING & PRINTING: Newspapers

501 Franklin LLC..............................F.... 804 777-9000
Richmond (G-11465)

A 1 Painting of Richmond.................G.... 804 237-9939
Midlothian (G-8766)

A Proehl...G.... 540 890-6096
Moneta (G-8955)

A Sorted Affiar Richmond LLC..........G.... 804 464-9820
Richmond (G-11077)

Adams Publishing Group LLC...........G.... 276 728-7311
Hillsville (G-6882)

Adonica L Miller...............................G.... 540 820-0820
Rockingham (G-12238)

Advocate-Democrat...........................G.... 423 337-7101
Norfolk (G-9426)

Alexandria Fusion.............................G.... 703 566-3055
Alexandria (G-125)

Alexandria Gazette Packet.................G.... 703 821-5050
Alexandria (G-126)

Alexandria Times...............................G.... 703 739-0001
Alexandria (G-127)

Amissville Alternative.......................G.... 540 364-4436
Amissville (G-716)

Ann Grogg..G.... 540 667-4279
Winchester (G-15381)

Annandale Times...............................G.... 703 437-5400
Reston (G-10788)

Arlington Boccato LLC.......................G.... 703 516-4075
Arlington (G-858)

Arlington Community News Lab.........G.... 703 243-7501
Arlington (G-859)

Augusta Free Press............................G.... 540 910-1233
Waynesboro (G-15097)

Babypipscom LLC..............................G.... 866 674-9258
Henrico (G-6480)

Baltimore Business Company LLC......G.... 301 848-7200
Fairfax (G-4417)

Barcroft Center.................................G.... 703 228-0701
Arlington (G-874)

Barrington Worldwide LLC.................G.... 202 255-4611
Alexandria (G-145)

Bay Breeze Publishing LLC................G.... 757 535-1580
Norfolk (G-9459)

Bdmoore Publications LLC.................G.... 434 352-7581
Spout Spring (G-12925)

Beckett Consulting Inc.......................G.... 804 580-4164
Heathsville (G-6459)

Bh Media Group Inc...........................G.... 703 241-2608
Falls Church (G-4764)

Bingo Tribune Inc..............................G.... 804 221-9049
Richmond (G-11125)

Broken Wing Enterprises Inc.............G.... 804 378-0136
Midlothian (G-8784)

Buckingham Beacon...........................G.... 434 591-1000
Palmyra (G-10245)

C & C Publishing Inc.........................G.... 804 598-4035
Powhatan (G-10536)

Camera Club of Richmond.................G.... 804 380-9218
Midlothian (G-8788)

Carroll Publishing Corp.....................F.... 276 728-7311
Hillsville (G-6888)

Catholic Virginian Press Inc..............G.... 804 358-3625
Richmond (G-11152)

P
R
O
D
U
C
T

CC Richmond II LP ....G...... 804 213-2706
 Richmond *(G-11523)*
Chosun Ilbo Washington Inc ....G...... 703 865-8310
 Fairfax *(G-4428)*
Christian News & Comments ....G...... 276 669-6972
 Bristol *(G-1970)*
Christian Observer............................G...... 540 464-3570
 Lexington *(G-7390)*
Church Guide....................................G...... 757 285-2222
 Virginia Beach *(G-14339)*
Coalzoomcom....................................G...... 304 920-2588
 Chesapeake *(G-3039)*
Connection Publishing Inc ....D...... 703 821-5050
 Alexandria *(G-173)*
Country Courier ....G...... 804 769-0259
 Aylett *(G-1547)*
Crozet Gazette LLC...........................G...... 434 823-2291
 Crozet *(G-3831)*
CVille Dream Life ....G...... 434 327-2600
 Charlottesville *(G-2776)*
Cville Siren LLC ....G...... 434 987-2008
 Charlottesville *(G-2777)*
Daily Deed LLC.................................G...... 703 754-0644
 Gainesville *(G-5577)*
Daily Distributions Inc ....G...... 703 577-8120
 Fairfax *(G-4435)*
Daily Frills LLC.................................G...... 540 850-7909
 Fredericksburg *(G-5270)*
Daily Grub Hospitality Inc ....G...... 804 221-5323
 Richmond *(G-11177)*
Daily Money Matters LLC ....G...... 703 904-9157
 Reston *(G-10831)*
Daily News Record............................F...... 540 459-4078
 Woodstock *(G-15851)*
Daily News Record............................F...... 540 574-6200
 Harrisonburg *(G-6308)*
Daily News Record............................F...... 540 743-5123
 Luray *(G-7606)*
Daily Peprah & Partners Servic ....G...... 757 581-6452
 Virginia Beach *(G-14383)*
Daily Productions Inc ....G...... 703 477-8444
 Leesburg *(G-7252)*
Daily Progress..................................G...... 540 672-1266
 Orange *(G-10210)*
Daily Splat LLC.................................G...... 703 729-0842
 Ashburn *(G-1268)*
Davis Chetia ....G...... 757 575-9225
 Norfolk *(G-9518)*
Defense News...................................F...... 703 750-9000
 Vienna *(G-14038)*
Dolan LLC...F...... 804 783-0770
 Richmond *(G-11562)*
Dorothy Edwards ....G...... 859 608-3539
 Burke *(G-2188)*
Dudenhefer For Delegate ....G...... 540 628-4012
 Stafford *(G-13139)*
Eastern Shore Post Inc ....G...... 757 789-7678
 Onley *(G-10200)*
Economic Dev Auth Cy Richmond ......G...... 804 521-4002
 Richmond *(G-11572)*
Eir News Service Inc ....D...... 703 777-4494
 Leesburg *(G-7264)*
Elliott Oil Production LLC ....G...... 434 525-3049
 Forest *(G-5071)*
Eugene C Hoopes ....G...... 434 293-5852
 Charlottesville *(G-2793)*
Fairfax Station Times ....G...... 703 437-5400
 Reston *(G-10850)*
Fauquier Building Grnds....................G...... 540 422-8480
 Warrenton *(G-15008)*
Fauquier Enterprise Center...............G...... 540 680-2652
 Warrenton *(G-15009)*
Fauquier Now ....G...... 540 359-6574
 Warrenton *(G-15012)*
Fauquier Services Inc ....G...... 540 341-4133
 Warrenton *(G-15013)*
Fauquier Silhouettes Inc ....G...... 540 347-3191
 Warrenton *(G-15014)*
Flagship Inc.....................................E...... 757 222-3965
 Norfolk *(G-9555)*
Floyd Press Inc ....G...... 540 745-2127
 Floyd *(G-5026)*
Franklin County Inv Co Inc ....E...... 540 483-5113
 Rocky Mount *(G-12323)*
Fred Good Times LLC ....G...... 540 372-7247
 Fredericksburg *(G-5188)*
Freshii ....G...... 804 223-8027
 Richmond *(G-11213)*
G5 Examiner LLC..............................G...... 540 455-9186
 Fredericksburg *(G-5291)*

Gails Dream LLC ....G...... 757 638-3197
 Suffolk *(G-13712)*
Gannett Co Inc ....B...... 703 854-6000
 Mc Lean *(G-8438)*
Gannett GP Media Inc.......................G...... 703 854-6000
 Mclean *(G-8586)*
Gannett Holdings LLC........................G...... 703 854-6000
 Mc Lean *(G-8439)*
Gannett Media Corp..........................D...... 540 885-7281
 Staunton *(G-13262)*
Gannett Media Corp..........................C...... 703 854-6000
 Mc Lean *(G-8440)*
Gannett River States Pubg Corp ....A...... 703 284-6000
 Mc Lean *(G-8443)*
Gatehouse Media LLC........................E...... 804 732-3456
 Petersburg *(G-10322)*
Gavin Bourjaily.................................G...... 540 636-1985
 Strasburg *(G-13580)*
Gazette Newspaper ....G...... 276 236-5178
 Galax *(G-5635)*
Gcoe LLC..G...... 703 854-6000
 Mc Lean *(G-8445)*
Ghent Living Magazine LLC ....G...... 757 425-7333
 Virginia Beach *(G-14482)*
Global Daily ....E...... 703 518-3030
 Alexandria *(G-217)*
Good News Network ....G...... 757 638-3289
 Portsmouth *(G-10435)*
Greater Richmond Dance Project........F...... 804 302-4338
 Richmond *(G-11221)*
Hanover Herald-Progress...................F...... 804 798-9031
 Ashland *(G-1427)*
Harold Delano ....G...... 804 333-3446
 Warsaw *(G-15065)*
Help Construction Richmond LLC ....G...... 804 320-3220
 Richmond *(G-11044)*
Henrico ....G...... 434 202-2331
 Henrico *(G-6521)*
Herald Schlrly Open Access LLC ....G...... 202 412-2272
 Aldie *(G-107)*
Herald Square LLC............................G...... 540 477-2019
 Mount Jackson *(G-9072)*
Hopewell Publishing Company ....E...... 804 452-6127
 Hopewell *(G-6934)*
Hs Winchester LLC ....G...... 540 771-0079
 Winchester *(G-15548)*
Inside Business................................G...... 757 439-7158
 Virginia Beach *(G-14548)*
Jack Einreinhof................................G...... 434 239-3072
 Lynchburg *(G-7747)*
Joy Virginn-Plot Fund Fndation ....G...... 757 446-2000
 Norfolk *(G-9607)*
Korean Weekly Entertainment ....G...... 703 354-7962
 Annandale *(G-766)*
Krista Hawk LLC ....G...... 703 554-7654
 Lovettsville *(G-7581)*
Kwe Publishing LLC ....G...... 804 458-4789
 Prince George *(G-10598)*
Kyung T Jung DBA Krean Entrmt.........G...... 703 658-0000
 Annandale *(G-768)*
Lai of Richmond LLC ....G...... 804 746-2739
 Mechanicsville *(G-8650)*
Landmark Community Newspapers......G...... 502 633-4334
 Norfolk *(G-9615)*
Landmark Military Newspapers...........G...... 254 690-9000
 Norfolk *(G-9617)*
Las Americas Newspaper Inc ....G...... 703 256-4200
 Falls Church *(G-4821)*
Leadership Perspectives Inc ....G...... 703 629-8977
 Fairfax *(G-4645)*
Lebanon News Inc ....F...... 276 889-2112
 Lebanon *(G-7198)*
Leesburg Today Inc ....G...... 703 771-8800
 Lansdowne *(G-7171)*
Lifesitenews Com Inc ....G...... 540 635-3131
 Front Royal *(G-5541)*
Loudoun Business Inc ....G...... 703 777-2176
 Lansdowne *(G-7172)*
Loudoun Classical School..................G...... 540 338-6101
 Purcellville *(G-10669)*
Loudoun Community Band..................G...... 540 882-3838
 Lovettsville *(G-7582)*
Loudoun Metal & More.......................G...... 540 668-5067
 Lovettsville *(G-7583)*
Loudoun Now ....G...... 703 770-9723
 Leesburg *(G-7307)*
Marie Lawson Reporter ....G...... 757 549-2198
 Chesapeake *(G-3198)*
Matthew Crawford Sargent ....G...... 757 430-9488
 Virginia Beach *(G-14641)*

Mella Weekly ....G...... 757 436-2409
 Chesapeake *(G-3202)*
Mid-Atlantic Publishing Co ....F...... 703 866-5156
 Springfield *(G-13050)*
Mobile Observer...............................G...... 703 569-9346
 Springfield *(G-13053)*
Mommers House LLC ....G...... 540 327-8101
 Winchester *(G-15558)*
Mountaineer Publishing Co Inc ....G...... 276 935-2123
 Grundy *(G-6038)*
Nailrod Publications LLC ....G...... 703 351-8130
 Arlington *(G-1069)*
New Journal and Guide Inc ....F...... 757 543-6531
 Norfolk *(G-9660)*
New Kent Charles Cy Chronicle ....G...... 804 843-4181
 West Point *(G-15159)*
New Student Chronicle.......................G...... 540 463-4000
 Lexington *(G-7407)*
News Connection ....G...... 703 661-4999
 Sterling *(G-13461)*
News-Gazette Corporation ....E...... 540 463-3116
 Lexington *(G-7408)*
On The Weekly LLC ....G...... 757 839-2640
 Virginia Beach *(G-14698)*
Page Shenandoah Newspaper ....E...... 540 574-6251
 Winchester *(G-15564)*
Paradigm Communications Inc ....F...... 804 644-0496
 Richmond *(G-11706)*
Peac LLC...G...... 571 261-1527
 Haymarket *(G-6435)*
Penny Saver ....G...... 434 857-5134
 Danville *(G-4023)*
Perez Armando ....G...... 202 716-5044
 Arlington *(G-1104)*
Pilot Media ....G...... 757 446-2000
 Norfolk *(G-9689)*
Politico LLC......................................E...... 703 647-7999
 Arlington *(G-1114)*
Popmount Inc...................................F...... 804 232-4999
 Richmond *(G-11720)*
Portico Publications Ltd....................D...... 434 817-2749
 Charlottesville *(G-2849)*
Posie Press LLC................................G...... 804 276-0716
 North Chesterfield *(G-9952)*
Potomac Local News ....G...... 540 659-2020
 Stafford *(G-13181)*
Program Services LLC ....G...... 804 526-8656
 Colonial Heights *(G-3742)*
Publishing Village ....G...... 804 425-5555
 Chester *(G-3449)*
Purcellville Gazette LLC ....G...... 540 431-8507
 Winchester *(G-15571)*
R A Handy Title Examiner ....G...... 804 739-9520
 Midlothian *(G-8885)*
Randolph-Macon College ....G...... 804 752-7200
 Ashland *(G-1483)*
Rappahannock Media LLC ....G...... 540 675-3338
 Washington *(G-15077)*
Recorder Publishing of VA Inc............F...... 540 468-2147
 Monterey *(G-9012)*
Renovated Richmond LLC ....G...... 804 467-5470
 Midlothian *(G-8887)*
Republicanpaccom ....G...... 703 241-8422
 Arlington *(G-1147)*
Richard A Daily Dr ....G...... 540 586-4030
 Goode *(G-5893)*
Richmond Equity Ventures LLC ....G...... 804 837-3523
 Richmond *(G-11355)*
Richmond Newspaper Inc...................G...... 804 261-1101
 Richmond *(G-11357)*
Richmond Pinball Collective ....G...... 301 652-8000
 North Chesterfield *(G-9963)*
Richmond Publishing ....G...... 804 229-6267
 Richmond *(G-11359)*
Richmond Schl Hlth & Tech Inc ....E...... 804 751-9191
 Chester *(G-3452)*
Richmond Shopping Center Inc ....G...... 804 648-9015
 Richmond *(G-11737)*
Richmond Times Dispatch ....G...... 804 526-7205
 South Chesterfield *(G-12823)*
Richmond Top Moving Co ....G...... 804 441-9702
 Richmond *(G-11362)*
Richmond Ventures LLC ....G...... 804 282-5901
 North Chesterfield *(G-9964)*
Richmond1040 LLC ....G...... 407 538-3624
 Glen Allen *(G-5787)*
Ridefauquier ....G...... 540 270-8247
 Warrenton *(G-15048)*
Riverstone Group LLC........................B...... 804 643-4200
 Richmond *(G-11742)*

(G-0000) Company's Geographic Section entry number

Rni Print Services ....G..... 804 649-6670
  Richmond (G-11744)
Roanoke Star Sentinel ....G..... 540 400-0990
  Roanoke (G-12167)
Roanoke Tribune ....G..... 540 343-0326
  Roanoke (G-12168)
Rockingham Publishing Co Inc ....C..... 540 574-6200
  Harrisonburg (G-6363)
Rockingham Publishing Company........G..... 540 298-9444
  Elkton (G-4334)
Rural Life Journal LLC ....G..... 301 774-0305
  Alexandria (G-332)
Sanduja Strategies ....G..... 202 826-9804
  Arlington (G-1158)
Saxsmo Publishing LLC ....G..... 804 269-0473
  North Chesterfield (G-9971)
Scadco Publishing LLC ....G..... 757 484-4878
  Portsmouth (G-10478)
Scripps Enterprises Inc ....G..... 434 760-3311
  Charlottesville (G-2690)
Sellers Advantage Richmond ....G..... 804 338-3800
  Richmond (G-11757)
Shalom Foundation Inc ....,....G..... 540 433-5351
  Harrisonburg (G-6369)
Shamrock Arlington LLC ....G..... 703 528-7676
  Arlington (G-1164)
Singh Express Corp ....G..... 202 816-8686
  Reston (G-10951)
Smyth County News ....G..... 276 783-5121
  Marion (G-8243)
Sola Richmond LLC ....G..... 804 302-4498
  Midlothian (G-8904)
Southside Voice Inc ....F..... 804 644-9060
  Richmond (G-11766)
Spacenews Inc ....F..... 571 421-2300
  Alexandria (G-352)
Stafford County Sun ....G..... 540 659-8923
  Stafford (G-13195)
Startup Virginia ....G..... 804 502-3131
  North Chesterfield (G-9990)
Sun Publishing Company ....E..... 434 374-8152
  Clarksville (G-3636)
T3 Media LLC ....G..... 804 262-1700
  Richmond (G-11404)
Target Advertising Inc ....G..... 757 627-2216
  Norfolk (G-9741)
Tidewater Hispanic Newspaper..........G..... 757 474-1233
  Virginia Beach (G-14875)
Tidewater Parent ....G..... 757 222-3900
  Norfolk (G-9755)
Times Community Media ....G..... 703 777-1111
  Leesburg (G-7361)
Times-World LLC ....B..... 540 981-3100
  Roanoke (G-12205)
University of Richmond......................G..... 804 289-8000
  Richmond (G-11800)
Urban Views Weekly LLC ....G..... 804 441-6255
  Richmond (G-11429)
USA Today ....G..... 703 267-6964
  Fairfax (G-4577)
USA Today ....G..... 703 750-8702
  Springfield (G-13104)
USA Today International Corp ....F..... 703 854-3400
  Mc Lean (G-8571)
USA Today Spt Media Group LLC ....G..... 703 854-6000
  Mc Lean (G-8572)
Viet Bao Inc ....G..... 703 339-9852
  Lorton (G-7538)
Virginia Gazette Companies LLC ....G..... 757 220-1736
  Newport News (G-9373)
Virginia News Group LLC ....G..... 540 955-1111
  Winchester (G-15599)
Virginia News Group LLC ....G..... 703 777-1111
  Ashburn (G-1350)
Virginia News Group LLC ....E..... 703 437-5400
  Reston (G-10985)
Virginia Times ....G..... 804 530-8540
  Chester (G-3467)
Virginn-Plot Mdia Cmpanies LLC ....G..... 804 358-0825
  Richmond (G-11814)
Virginn-Plot Mdia Cmpanies LLC ....G..... 757 446-2848
  Virginia Beach (G-14924)
Warren Sentinel..................................F..... 540 635-4174
  Front Royal (G-5563)
Washington Blade ....G..... 202 747-2077
  Vienna (G-14157)
Whisper Prayers Daily ....G..... 703 690-1184
  Lorton (G-7542)
Winchester Evening Star Inc ....C..... 540 667-3200
  Winchester (G-15601)

Womack Newspaper Inc ....G..... 434 432-1654
  Chatham (G-2941)
Womens Media Watch Azerbaijan ....G..... 253 381-9667
  Brambleton (G-1936)
Wood Television LLC ....D..... 540 825-4416
  Culpeper (G-3932)
Wood Television LLC ....D..... 434 793-2311
  Danville (G-4051)
Wood Television LLC ....F..... 276 228-6611
  Wytheville (G-15924)
Wood Television LLC ....C..... 276 669-2181
  Bristol (G-2002)
Wood Television LLC ....E..... 540 672-1266
  Orange (G-10232)
Wood Television LLC ....C..... 434 385-5400
  Lynchburg (G-7840)
Wood Television LLC ....E..... 757 539-3437
  Suffolk (G-13786)
Wood Television LLC ....C..... 434 978-7200
  Charlottesville (G-2716)
Wood Television LLC ....E..... 804 775-4600
  Richmond (G-11832)
Wood Television LLC ....C..... 540 948-5121
  Madison (G-7865)
Wood Television LLC ....C..... 804 559-8207
  Mechanicsville (G-8700)
Wood Television LLC ....D..... 540 949-8213
  Waynesboro (G-15148)
World Media Enterprises Inc................F..... 804 559-8261
  Mechanicsville (G-8703)
Wp Company LLC ....F..... 703 518-3000
  Alexandria (G-389)
Wp Company LLC ....G..... 703 799-2920
  Alexandria (G-616)
Wp Company LLC ....G..... 703 392-1303
  Fairfax (G-4695)
Wp Company LLC ....G..... 540 937-4380
  Amissville (G-724)
York Town Crier ....G..... 757 766-1776
  Yorktown (G-16004)
Your Health Magazine.........................E..... 703 288-3130
  Annandale (G-795)

PUBLISHING & PRINTING: Pamphlets

Bison Printing Inc ....E..... 540 586-3955
  Bedford (G-1627)
Gooder Group Inc ....F..... 703 698-7750
  Fairfax (G-4470)
Homeactions LLC ....F..... 703 698-7750
  Fairfax (G-4476)

PUBLISHING & PRINTING: Patterns, Paper

A1 Service ....G..... 757 544-0830
  Virginia Beach (G-14202)
Gaia Communications LLC ....G..... 703 370-5527
  Alexandria (G-210)

PUBLISHING & PRINTING: Periodical Statistical Reports

Airline Tariff Publishing Co..................B..... 703 661-7400
  Dulles (G-4191)

PUBLISHING & PRINTING: Posters

ABC Graphics......................................G..... 804 368-0276
  Ashland (G-1361)
Adta & Co Inc ....F..... 703 930-9280
  Annandale (G-728)
Rain & Associates LLC ....G..... 757 572-3996
  Virginia Beach (G-14758)
Reeses Amazing Printing Svcs ....G..... 804 325-0947
  Henrico (G-6556)
Venutec Corporation............................G..... 888 573-8870
  Centreville (G-2350)

PUBLISHING & PRINTING: Technical Manuals

Watercraft Logistics Svcs Co ....G..... 757 348-3089
  Virginia Beach (G-14930)

PUBLISHING & PRINTING: Textbooks

Kristina Kathleen Mann ....G..... 703 282-9166
  Alexandria (G-510)

PUBLISHING & PRINTING: Trade Journals

Public Utilities Reports Inc ....F..... 703 847-7720
  Reston (G-10934)

PUBLISHING & PRINTING: Yearbooks

Magpie Design LLC.............................G..... 703 975-5818
  Reston (G-10893)

PULP MILLS

Clarence D Campbell ....G..... 540 291-2740
  Naturl BR STA (G-9111)
Emerson & Clements Office ....G..... 434 983-5322
  Dillwyn (G-4095)
Goodman Lumber Co Inc ....E..... 804 265-9030
  Wilsons (G-15367)
L A Bowles Logging Inc ....E..... 804 492-3103
  Powhatan (G-10555)
Pre Con Inc ....F..... 804 732-0628
  Chester (G-3444)
Westrock Mwv LLC ....A..... 804 444-1000
  Richmond (G-11825)
Weyerhaeuser Company ....G..... 276 694-4404
  Stuart (G-13639)
Wrkco Inc ....B..... 540 969-5000
  Covington (G-3805)

PULP MILLS: Chemical & Semichemical Processing

Prochem Technologies Inc ....G..... 540 520-8339
  Roanoke (G-12156)

PULP MILLS: Mechanical & Recycling Processing

Green Waste Organics LLC ....G..... 804 929-8505
  Prince George (G-10595)
Pure Earth Recycling Tech Inc ....G..... 434 944-6262
  Lynchburg (G-7794)

PUMPS

American Manufacturing Co Inc............E..... 540 825-7234
  Elkwood (G-4341)
Colfax Corporation ....G..... 757 328-3987
  Glen Allen (G-5715)
Curtiss-Wright Corporation ....D..... 757 494-3810
  Chesapeake (G-3059)
Envirnmntal Solutions Intl Inc ....F..... 703 263-7600
  Ashburn (G-1276)
Flowserve Corporation.........................G..... 804 271-4031
  North Chesterfield (G-9877)
Framatome Inc ....B..... 434 832-3000
  Lynchburg (G-7716)
Mactaggart Scott Usa LLC ....G..... 757 288-1405
  Virginia Beach (G-14631)
Mark A Harber ....G..... 276 546-6051
  Pennington Gap (G-10295)
Mefcor Incorporated ....G..... 276 322-5021
  North Tazewell (G-10103)
SKF Lbrication Systems USA Inc ....D..... 757 951-0370
  Hampton (G-6239)
Vamac Incorporated.............................E..... 540 535-1983
  Winchester (G-15503)
Vamaz Inc..G..... 434 296-8812
  Charlottesville (G-2711)

PUMPS & PARTS: Indl

Beckett Corporation ....E..... 757 857-0153
  Norfolk (G-9461)
Flowserve Corporation.........................D..... 757 485-8044
  Chesapeake (G-3104)
Flowserve Corporation.........................C..... 434 528-4400
  Lynchburg (G-7713)
Flowserve Corporation.........................B..... 757 485-8000
  Chesapeake (G-3105)
Gravittional Systems Engrg Inc ....F..... 312 224-8152
  Clifton (G-3668)
Khem Precision Machining LLC ....G..... 804 915-8922
  Richmond (G-11261)
Ksb America Corporation ....G..... 804 222-1818
  Richmond (G-11265)
Nellie Harris......................................G..... 434 277-8511
  Lowesville (G-7597)
Shane Harper ....G..... 540 297-4800
  Moneta (G-8976)

PRODUCT

PUMPS & PUMPING EQPT REPAIR SVCS

Artcraft Fabricators Inc ....D...... 757 399-7777
  Portsmouth (G-10393)

PUMPS & PUMPING EQPT WHOLESALERS

Ksb America Corporation ....G...... 804 222-1818
  Richmond (G-11265)

PUMPS, HEAT: Electric

Quang D Nguyen....................................G...... 703 715-2244
  Herndon (G-6782)

PUMPS: Domestic, Water Or Sump

Hasco Sales Inc ....G...... 804 740-1869
  Glen Allen (G-5741)

PUMPS: Hydraulic Power Transfer

Williams Industrial Repair Inc..............G...... 757 969-5738
  Yorktown (G-16001)

PUMPS: Measuring & Dispensing

Silgan Dspnsing Systems Hldngs.........G...... 804 923-1971
  Richmond (G-11760)

PUMPS: Oil Well & Field

Bae Systems Tctcal Vhcl System ....E...... 571 461-6000
  Falls Church (G-4759)

PUPPETS & MARIONETTES

Goodlife Theatre ....G...... 540 547-9873
  Boston (G-1903)
Mat Enterprises Inc ....G...... 540 389-2528
  Salem (G-12534)
Puppet Neighborhood ....G...... 804 794-2899
  Midlothian (G-8884)
Spectrum Entertainment Inc ....G...... 757 491-2873
  Virginia Beach (G-14836)

PURCHASING SVCS

Interstate Resources Inc ....G...... 703 243-3355
  Arlington (G-1010)

PURIFICATION & DUST COLLECTION EQPT

Indust LLC..G...... 757 208-0587
  Williamsburg (G-15256)
Zentox Corporation ....F...... 757 868-0870
  Poquoson (G-10380)

PURIFIERS: Centrifugal

Envirnmntal Solutions Intl Inc ....F...... 703 263-7600
  Ashburn (G-1276)

QUILTING SVC

Charles R Preston...............................G...... 703 757-0495
  Great Falls (G-5947)
Cricket Products Inc ....E...... 804 861-0687
  Petersburg (G-10315)
Patty S Pieceworks ....G...... 804 796-3371
  Chesterfield (G-3517)
Vienna Quilt Shop ....G...... 703 281-4091
  Mc Lean (G-8576)

QUILTING SVC & SPLYS, FOR THE TRADE

Virginia Quilter ....G...... 540 548-3207
  Fredericksburg (G-5387)

QUILTING: Individuals

Liz B Quilting LLC................................G...... 540 602-7850
  Stafford (G-13172)

RABBIT SLAUGHTERING & PROCESSING

Damoah & Family Farm LLC ....G...... 703 919-0329
  Stafford (G-13136)

RACE TRACK OPERATION

Clean Power & Service LLC.................G...... 703 443-1717
  Leesburg (G-7244)

RACEWAYS

Chester Raceway ....G...... 804 717-2330
  Chester (G-3394)
Fork Mountain Raceway LLC................G...... 540 229-1828
  Madison (G-7852)
Race Trac Petroleum ....G...... 804 694-9079
  Gloucester Point (G-5875)
Race Trac Petroleum ....G...... 757 557-0076
  Virginia Beach (G-14756)
Rolling Thunder Raceway LLC ....G...... 336 401-2360
  Ararat (G-832)
Route 58 Raceway Inc ....G...... 434 441-3903
  Danville (G-4037)
Summerduck Raceway ....G...... 540 845-1656
  Sumerduck (G-13793)

RACKS: Pallet, Exc Wood

Wise Manufacturing Inc......................G...... 804 876-3335
  Doswell (G-4128)

RACKS: Railroad Car, Vehicle Transportation, Steel

4 Shores Trnsprting Lgstix LLC ....G...... 804 319-6247
  Richmond (G-11074)
Nexlevel Transports Inc ....G...... 757 707-6349
  Toano (G-13871)
Pegrams Transporting Svcs LLC ....G...... 804 295-1798
  Petersburg (G-10334)
S B Auto Transport LLC ....G...... 757 775-3884
  Virginia Beach (G-14788)

RADAR SYSTEMS & EQPT

Applied Signals Intelligence ....G...... 571 313-0681
  Sterling (G-13346)
Central Electronics Co ....G...... 540 659-3235
  Stafford (G-13128)
Coleman Microwave Co ....E...... 540 984-8848
  Edinburg (G-4301)
Dragoon Technologies Inc ....G...... 937 439-9223
  Winchester (G-15412)
Peraton Inc ....G...... 315 838-7009
  Newport News (G-9312)
Raytheon Company ....F...... 703 416-5800
  Arlington (G-1131)
Raytheon Company ....G...... 571 250-2260
  Dulles (G-4221)
Raytheon Company ....D...... 571 250-3421
  Dulles (G-4223)

RADIO & TELEVISION COMMUNICATIONS EQUIPMENT

Advantech Inc ....G...... 703 402-0590
  Alexandria (G-120)
Ambervision Technologies ....G...... 571 594-1664
  Brambleton (G-1926)
Andrew Corp ....G...... 703 726-5900
  Ashburn (G-1241)
Andrew Corporation ....G...... 434 386-5262
  Forest (G-5050)
Antensan Usa Inc ....G...... 703 836-0300
  Alexandria (G-137)
Atlas Scntfic Tchncal Svcs LLC ....G...... 540 492-5051
  Bowling Green (G-1906)
Beckley LLC ....G...... 843 822-8091
  Leesburg (G-7228)
Caci Nss Inc ....E...... 703 434-4000
  Reston (G-10814)
Commscope Technologies LLC ....C...... 703 548-6777
  Alexandria (G-170)
Commscope Technologies LLC ....C...... 703 726-5500
  Ashburn (G-1257)
Communications Vehicle Svc LLC ....G...... 703 542-7449
  Chantilly (G-2529)
Cr Communications.............................G...... 757 871-4797
  Williamsburg (G-15225)
Datapath Inc ....F...... 703 476-1826
  Sterling (G-13382)
Dawnbreaker Communications LLC ....G...... 202 288-0805
  Dunn Loring (G-4263)
Dbsd North America Inc ....D...... 703 964-1400
  Reston (G-10834)
Dtc Communications Inc ....E...... 727 471-6900
  Herndon (G-6663)
Eddy Current Technology Inc ....G...... 757 490-1814
  Virginia Beach (G-14431)
Edwin Glenn Campbell ....G...... 703 203-6516
  Stafford (G-13142)

Electro Techs LLC...............................G...... 704 900-1911
  Norfolk (G-9543)
Engility LLC ....D...... 703 633-8300
  Yorktown (G-15955)
Fei-Zyfer Inc ....G...... 540 349-8330
  Warrenton (G-15016)
Finest Productions Inc ....G...... 703 989-2657
  Arlington (G-966)
Gatr Technologies Inc ....D...... 571 258-5020
  Ashburn (G-1284)
General Dynmics Gvrnment Syste ......A...... 703 876-3000
  Falls Church (G-4795)
General Dynmics One Source LLC ....F...... 703 906-6397
  Falls Church (G-4796)
GTS Defense MGT Svcs LLC ....G...... 832 326-7227
  Great Falls (G-5961)
Information Systems Group ....G...... 804 526-4220
  North Chesterfield (G-9895)
Iridium Communications Inc ....E...... 703 287-7400
  Mc Lean (G-8469)
Iridium Holdings LLC ....G...... 703 287-7400
  Mc Lean (G-8470)
Kajjo Sirwan ....G...... 202 569-1472
  Falls Church (G-4815)
L-3 Communications Corp ....G...... 703 375-4911
  Manassas (G-7958)
L3harris Technologies Inc ....E...... 703 668-7256
  Herndon (G-6730)
L3harris Technologies Inc ....G...... 703 344-1000
  Chantilly (G-2454)
L3harris Technologies Inc ....B...... 434 455-6600
  Lynchburg (G-7753)
L3harris Technologies Inc ....D...... 434 455-9390
  Forest (G-5079)
L3harris Technologies Inc ....E...... 434 455-6600
  Forest (G-5080)
Lb Telesystems Inc ....E...... 703 919-8991
  Chantilly (G-2456)
Little Green Men Inc ....G...... 301 203-8702
  Ashburn (G-1308)
Mark Space Inc ....G...... 703 404-8550
  Sterling (G-13449)
Mediasat International Inc ....G...... 703 558-0309
  Arlington (G-1059)
Mobile Radio Partners Inc ....F...... 804 525-4013
  Henrico (G-6535)
Mobile Radio Partners Inc ....G...... 804 364-1553
  Glen Allen (G-5772)
Moto Farkle Support Services ....G...... 757 705-2014
  Virginia Beach (G-14665)
Motorola Solutions Inc ....C...... 703 724-8000
  Leesburg (G-7316)
Mu-Del Electronics LLC........................F...... 703 368-8900
  Manassas (G-8114)
Novelsat USA ....G...... 703 295-2119
  Vienna (G-14106)
Novus Technology Inc ....G...... 703 218-9801
  Fairfax (G-4657)
Orban ....G...... 804 529-6283
  Lewisetta (G-7384)
Packet Dynamics LLC ....G...... 703 597-1413
  Reston (G-10917)
Peraton Inc ....E...... 757 857-0099
  Norfolk (G-9685)
Pyott-Boone Electronics Inc ....C...... 276 988-5505
  North Tazewell (G-10105)
Shared Spectrum Company ....E...... 703 761-2818
  Vienna (G-14123)
Softwright LLC ....G...... 434 975-4310
  Charlottesville (G-2694)
Speakeasy ....G...... 703 333-5040
  Annandale (G-783)
Spectrarep LLC ....F...... 703 227-9690
  Chantilly (G-2496)
SSC Innovations LLC ....G...... 703 761-2818
  Vienna (G-14133)
St Engineering Idirect Inc ....B...... 703 648-8002
  Herndon (G-6814)
Tabet Manufacturing Co Inc ....E...... 757 627-1855
  Norfolk (G-9739)
Tekalign Inc ....F...... 703 757-6690
  Reston (G-10971)
Tian Corporation ....G...... 703 434-4000
  Reston (G-10973)
Universal Space Network Inc ....G...... 703 488-4150
  Chantilly (G-2513)
Wavelab Inc ....G...... 703 860-9321
  Reston (G-10987)

RADIO BROADCASTING & COMMUNICATIONS EQPT

Ericsson Inc.................................D....... 434 592-5610
Lynchburg (G-7704)
Erisys LLC..................................G....... 660 864-4474
Herndon (G-6667)
Etl Systems Inc.........................G....... 703 657-0411
Herndon (G-6669)
Interbyte....................................G....... 703 825-8774
Alexandria (G-486)
Radio Reconnaissance Tech Inc ...G....... 540 752-7448
Fredericksburg (G-5352)
Selex Communications Inc ....F....... 703 547-6280
Reston (G-10946)
V T R International Inc................G....... 434 385-5300
Lynchburg (G-7831)
VT Milcom Inc............................D....... 757 548-2956
Chesapeake (G-3366)

RADIO BROADCASTING STATIONS

Free Lance-Star Publshng Co of ...B....... 540 374-5000
Fredericksburg (G-5190)

RADIO COMMUNICATIONS: Airborne Eqpt

Racecom of Virginia ....G....... 757 599-8255
Yorktown (G-15985)
Virtual Netcom LLC....................G....... 571 445-0306
Chantilly (G-2517)
Virtual Ntwrk Cmmnications Inc...........G....... 571 445-0306
South Riding (G-12871)

RADIO COMMUNICATIONS: Carrier Eqpt

First Renaissance Ventures ....G....... 703 408-6961
Mc Lean (G-8431)
Gcseac Inc ....G....... 276 632-9700
Martinsville (G-8288)

RADIO RECEIVER NETWORKS

C-3 Comm Systems LLC ....G...... 703 829-0588
Arlington (G-897)
Key Bridge Global LLC ....G...... 703 414-3500
Mc Lean (G-8479)

RADIO, TELEVISION & CONSUMER ELECTRONICS STORES: Eqpt, NEC

Htdepot LLC ....G....... 703 830-2818
Chantilly (G-2437)

RAIL & STRUCTURAL SHAPES: Aluminum rail & structural shapes

Millers Custom Metal Svcs LLC...........G....... 804 712-2588
Deltaville (G-4084)

RAILINGS: Wood

Perry Railworks Inc ....G....... 703 794-0507
Manassas (G-8127)
Virginia Railing & Gates LLC ......F....... 804 798-8777
Ashland (G-1506)

RAILROAD CARGO LOADING & UNLOADING SVCS

Contra Surplus LLC...................G....... 757 337-9971
Norfolk (G-9504)
Six3 Advanced Systems Inc ....C....... 703 742-7660
Dulles (G-4226)

RAILROAD EQPT

Amsted Rail Company Inc...............B....... 804 732-0202
Petersburg (G-10303)
B & B Machine & Tool Inc...........E....... 540 344-6820
Roanoke (G-12038)
Ie W Railway Supply ....G....... 540 882-3886
Hillsboro (G-6872)
Longwood Elastomers Inc ....C....... 276 228-5406
Wytheville (G-15898)
New York Air Brake Company............G....... 540 989-5044
Roanoke (G-12140)
Progress Rail Services Corp........G....... 540 345-4039
Roanoke (G-12157)

RAILROAD EQPT, EXC LOCOMOTIVES

Graham-White Manufacturing Co.........B....... 540 387-5600
Salem (G-12513)

RAILROAD EQPT: Cars & Eqpt, Dining

Bullet Equipment Sales Inc...................G....... 276 623-5150
Abingdon (G-18)
Church Trucking LLC ....G....... 757 386-1761
Norfolk (G-9485)
Freightcar Roanoke Inc ....D....... 540 342-2303
Roanoke (G-12094)
Gregg Company Ltd ....G....... 757 966-1367
Chesapeake (G-3126)
I AM Express LLC ....G....... 757 535-6944
Chesapeake (G-3139)
Precise Freight Solutions.....................G....... 703 627-1327
Manassas (G-8131)
Wilsons Elite Express LLC....................G....... 804 517-4276
North Chesterfield (G-10012)

RAILROAD EQPT: Cars, Motor

Crown Motorcar Company LLC ....E....... 434 979-7222
Charlottesville (G-2612)

RAILROAD EQPT: Engines, Locomotive, Steam

Shenandoah Vlly Steam/Gas Engi.........G....... 540 662-6923
Winchester (G-15586)

RAILROAD EQPT: Street Cars & Eqpt

Clarke County Speed Shop....................G....... 540 955-0479
Berryville (G-1674)

RAILROAD RELATED EQPT: Railway Track

Plasser American Corporation ....C....... 757 543-3526
Chesapeake (G-3242)

RAILROAD TIES: Wood

Koppers Industries Inc ....G....... 540 672-3802
Orange (G-10218)
Martin Railroad Tie Co ....G....... 434 933-4398
Gladstone (G-5686)

RAILS: Steel Or Iron

Colonial Rail Systems LLC ....G....... 804 932-5200
New Kent (G-9129)

RAMPS: Prefabricated Metal

Christopher Hawkins ....G....... 540 361-1679
Fredericksburg (G-5178)

RAZORS, RAZOR BLADES

Accutec Blades Inc ....C....... 800 336-4061
Verona (G-13982)
Energizer Personal Care LLC ....B....... 540 248-9734
Verona (G-13986)

RAZORS: Electric

Wwt Group Inc.....................................G....... 804 648-1900
Richmond (G-11834)

REACTORS: Current Limiting

Mgke Construction LLC ....G....... 571 282-8415
Manassas (G-8108)

REAL ESTATE AGENCIES & BROKERS

Cegna Inc..E....... 757 632-5000
Hampton (G-6110)

REAL ESTATE AGENCIES: Leasing & Rentals

Frost Property Solutions LLC...............G....... 804 571-2147
Mechanicsville (G-8625)

REAL ESTATE AGENTS & MANAGERS

Pk Hot Sauce LLc................................G....... 703 629-0920
Manassas (G-7989)

REAL ESTATE LISTING SVCS

Landmark Media Enterprises LLC.........A....... 757 351-7000
Norfolk (G-9616)

REAL ESTATE OPERATORS, EXC DEVELOPERS: Commercial/Indl Bldg

F C Holdings Inc...................................C....... 804 222-2821
Sandston (G-12614)

RECEIVERS: Radio Communications

Applied Technollogy..............................G....... 703 660-8422
Alexandria (G-415)
Gomspace North America LLC ....G....... 703 866-8742
Alexandria (G-222)
Nomad Solutions LLC ....F....... 703 656-9100
Gainesville (G-5602)
Spectrum ....G....... 757 224-7500
Newport News (G-9345)

RECLAIMED RUBBER: Reworked By Manufacturing Process

Kokua John LLC ....G....... 509 270-3454
North Garden (G-10078)

RECORDING HEADS: Speech & Musical Eqpt

Ronart Associates ....G....... 703 362-5373
Lorton (G-7527)
Tyler JSun Global LLC ....G....... 407 221-6135
Stafford (G-13206)

RECORDING TAPE: Video, Blank

Earth Communications Corp ....G....... 434 973-7277
Charlottesville (G-2621)

RECORDS & TAPES: Prerecorded

Appvity..G....... 571 327-0888
Sterling (G-13347)
Cee Corporation ....G....... 571 526-4447
Reston (G-10820)
Citadel Studios Inc ....G....... 407 766-6302
Manassas (G-8050)
Elucidsoft LLC ....G....... 703 679-7688
Stafford (G-13143)
Erp Initiatives LLC ....G....... 703 439-9352
Leesburg (G-7270)
Fifth Tribe LLC.....................................G....... 703 755-0680
Vienna (G-14054)
Finite Wisdom ....G....... 804 794-9585
Henrico (G-6510)
Genformax LLC ....G....... 703 346-7445
Mc Lean (G-8447)
I Sw LLC...G....... 703 270-1540
Fairfax (G-4478)
Itkm Systems LLC ....G....... 502 370-6488
Mechanicsville (G-8643)
Memoryblue ....G....... 703 891-3840
Mc Lean (G-8498)
Raven Enterprises LLC ....G....... 804 355-6386
Richmond (G-11346)
Renmus Technologies Inc ....G....... 703 624-9144
Manassas (G-8143)
Rezgateway ....G....... 703 286-5331
Reston (G-10940)
Scenethink Inc......................................G....... 434 987-6525
Charlottesville (G-2872)
Zojoi LLC...G....... 804 397-5000
Charlottesville (G-2718)

RECORDS OR TAPES: Masters

Innovation Station Music LLC ....G....... 703 405-6727
Annandale (G-760)

RECREATIONAL SPORTING EQPT REPAIR SVCS

Pointman Resources LLC ....G....... 240 429-3423
Sterling (G-13472)

RECREATIONAL VEHICLE REPAIRS

CFS-Kbr Mrnas Support Svcs LLC........E....... 202 261-1900
Alexandria (G-164)

RECREATIONAL VEHICLE: Wholesalers

Coach LLC...E....... 757 925-2862
Suffolk (G-13684)

PRODUCT (vertical tab)

RECYCLABLE SCRAP & WASTE MATERIALS WHOLESALERS

Southern Scrap Company Inc............E...... 540 662-0265
Winchester (G-15481)

RECYCLING: Paper

Greenstone Materials LLC ....G..... 434 973-2113
Charlottesville (G-2640)
Theme Queen LLC ....G..... 804 439-0854
Mechanicsville (G-8685)

REFINERS & SMELTERS: Gold, Secondary

Saudi Trade Links ....G..... 703 992-3220
Berryville (G-1688)

REFINERS & SMELTERS: Nonferrous Metal

Aleris Rolled Products Inc ....D..... 804 714-2100
North Chesterfield (G-9810)
Aow Global LLC ....G..... 757 228-5557
Chesapeake (G-2976)
Atomized Products Group Inc ....G..... 434 263-4551
Lovingston (G-7588)
Casson Art & Frame ....G..... 276 638-1450
Martinsville (G-8274)
Fred Sisson ....G..... 843 641-7155
Prince George (G-10594)
South Western Services Inc..............G..... 540 947-5407
Montvale (G-9030)
Universal Impex LLC ....G..... 202 322-4100
Glen Allen (G-5820)
Voestlpine High Prfmce Mtls Co........E..... 434 575-7994
South Boston (G-12792)

REFINERS & SMELTERS: Silicon, Primary, Over 99% Pure

Virginia Semiconductor Inc ....E..... 540 373-2900
Fredericksburg (G-5233)

REFINING: Petroleum

Afd Technologies LLC ....G..... 561 271-7000
Virginia Beach (G-14215)
Gibraltar Energy LLC ....G..... 202 642-2704
Alexandria (G-469)
Mobil Petrochemical Holdings ....G..... 703 846-3000
Fairfax (G-4513)
Oreamnos Biofuels LLC ....G..... 651 269-7737
Williamsburg (G-15287)
Riyan Industries ....G..... 703 525-6132
Arlington (G-1148)

REFRACTORIES: Brick

Continental Brick Company ....G..... 434 845-5918
Lynchburg (G-7683)

REFRACTORIES: Clay

Dominion Quikrete Inc......................E..... 276 957-3235
Martinsville (G-8279)
Mapei Corporation ....E..... 540 361-1085
Fredericksburg (G-5453)

REFRACTORIES: Nonclay

Rex Materials Inc..............................E..... 434 447-7659
South Hill (G-12858)

REFRIGERATION & HEATING EQUIPMENT

Academy Boys and Girls Soccer.........G..... 804 380-9005
Chesterfield (G-3472)
Alfa Laval Inc....................................C..... 866 253-2528
Richmond (G-11095)
Berts Inc...G..... 757 865-8040
Newport News (G-9178)
Beta Contractors LLC ....G..... 703 424-1940
Herndon (G-6623)
Buffalo Air Handling Company ....C..... 434 946-7455
Amherst (G-685)
Chase Group II A/C & Htg Svc ....G..... 571 245-7379
Fredericksburg (G-5411)
Cogo Aire LLC ....G..... 757 332-3551
Virginia Beach (G-14352)
Commercial Tech Inc ....G..... 703 468-1339
Manassas (G-8051)
Ensons Inc ....G..... 703 644-6694
Burke (G-2189)

Griffin Pipe Products Co LLC ....G..... 434 845-8021
Lynchburg (G-7725)
Hill Phoenix Inc ....C..... 804 526-4455
South Chesterfield (G-12808)
Hkd Snowmakers Com ....G..... 540 451-1779
Stuarts Draft (G-13650)
Hussmann Corporation ....G..... 540 775-2502
King George (G-7094)
JRS Repco Inc ....G..... 540 334-3051
Boones Mill (G-1895)
Power Anywhere LLC ....G..... 703 625-4115
Arlington (G-1118)
Proto-Technics Inc ....E..... 540 672-5193
Orange (G-10222)
RPC Tubes ....G..... 703 471-5659
Sterling (G-13497)
Siemens Industry Inc ....D..... 757 490-6026
Norfolk (G-9723)
Silvas Heat & Air ....G..... 757 596-5991
Newport News (G-9342)
Super RAD Coils Ltd Partnr ....C..... 804 794-2887
North Chesterfield (G-9992)
Trane Company ....G..... 304 348-2800
Ashland (G-1502)
Trane Inc ....G..... 540 376-3064
Fredericksburg (G-5380)
Trane US Inc ....D..... 804 747-4774
Ashland (G-1503)
Trane US Inc ....G..... 540 342-3027
Roanoke (G-12207)
Trane US Inc ....G..... 434 793-4822
Danville (G-4042)
Trane US Inc ....D..... 434 327-1601
Charlottesville (G-2893)
Trane US Inc ....G..... 844 805-3895
Roanoke (G-12208)
Trane US Inc ....G..... 757 485-7700
Chesapeake (G-3350)
Trane US Inc ....D..... 757 490-2390
Virginia Beach (G-14892)
Trane US Inc ....G..... 540 376-3064
Fredericksburg (G-5381)
Utility Trailer Mfg Co ....A..... 276 783-8800
Atkins (G-1522)
Virginia Blower Company ....E..... 276 647-3804
Collinsville (G-3718)
Virginia Trane Ap141 ....G..... 540 580-7702
Roanoke (G-12221)
Wilson Mechanical Repair Servi........G..... 804 317-4919
Mechanicsville (G-8698)

REFRIGERATION EQPT: Complete

Hill Phoenix Inc ....C..... 804 317-6882
South Chesterfield (G-12805)
Hill Phoenix Inc ....F..... 804 317-6882
South Chesterfield (G-12806)

REFRIGERATION SVC & REPAIR

Refcon Services Inc..........................F..... 757 616-0691
Chesapeake (G-3266)

REGULATORS: Generator Voltage

Venus Tech LLC ....G..... 703 389-5557
Herndon (G-6836)

REGULATORS: Power

Vertiv Corporation ....F..... 804 747-6030
Glen Allen (G-5825)

RELAYS & SWITCHES: Indl, Electric

Production Systems Solutions ....G..... 434 324-7843
Hurt (G-6976)

REMOVERS & CLEANERS

Calloway Enterprises Inc ....G..... 434 525-1147
Forest (G-5058)
Dnj Dirtworks Inc ....G..... 540 937-3138
Rixeyville (G-11878)
Gateway Green Energy Inc ....G..... 540 280-7475
Fishersville (G-5003)
Kwicksilver Systems LLC ....G..... 619 917-1067
Crozet (G-3841)
Tag America Inc ....G..... 757 227-9831
Virginia Beach (G-14864)
Td & D Unlimited LLC ....G..... 703 946-9338
Goldvein (G-5879)

RENDERING PLANT

Mountain View Rendering Co ....G..... 540 984-4158
Edinburg (G-4310)

RENTAL CENTERS: Party & Banquet Eqpt & Splys

Perfect Pink LLC ....G..... 571 969-7465
Arlington (G-1105)

RENTAL SVCS: Audio-Visual Eqpt & Sply

Audio-Visuals Actions Inc ....G..... 703 751-1010
Alexandria (G-143)
Stage Sound Inc ....E..... 540 342-2040
Roanoke (G-12194)

RENTAL SVCS: Business Machine & Electronic Eqpt

Pitney Bowes Inc ....E..... 304 744-1067
Vienna (G-14112)
Pitney Bowes Inc ....E..... 757 322-8000
Norfolk (G-9690)
Pitney Bowes Inc ....E..... 804 798-3210
Ashland (G-1476)

RENTAL SVCS: Eqpt, Theatrical

MCS Design & Production Inc ....G..... 804 550-1000
Ashland (G-1462)

RENTAL SVCS: Sign

Talley Sign Company ....F..... 804 649-0325
Richmond (G-11781)

RENTAL SVCS: Sound & Lighting Eqpt

Hill Brenton......................................G..... 757 560-9332
Hampton (G-6167)
Huqa Live LLC ....G..... 202 527-9342
Woodbridge (G-15724)

RENTAL SVCS: Trailer

Conglobal Industries LLC ....E..... 757 487-5100
Chesapeake (G-3051)

RENTAL: Portable Toilet

Edmunds Waste Removal Inc ....G..... 804 478-4688
Mc Kenney (G-8379)

RENTAL: Video Tape & Disc

Dream Reels Inc ....E..... 540 891-9886
Fredericksburg (G-5277)

REPAIR SERVICES, NEC

Press and Bindery Repair ....G..... 703 209-4247
Stafford (G-13183)
Quisenberry Stn Live Stm LLC ....G..... 703 799-9643
Alexandria (G-565)

REPAIR TRAINING, COMPUTER

Vicious Creations LLC ....G..... 256 479-7689
Hampton (G-6262)

RESEARCH & DEVELOPMENT SVCS, COMMERCIAL: Engineering Lab

Celestial Circuits LLC ....G..... 703 851-2843
Springfield (G-12975)
Delta Q Dynamics LLC ....G..... 703 980-9449
Manassas (G-7931)
Perspecta Svcs & Solutions Inc ....G..... 781 684-4000
Ashburn (G-1326)

RESEARCH, DEVELOPMENT & TEST SVCS, COMM: Cmptr Hardware Dev

Dhk Storage LLC ....G..... 703 870-3741
Sterling (G-13385)
Lightfactor LLC ....G..... 540 723-9600
Winchester (G-15552)

RESEARCH, DEVELOPMENT & TEST SVCS, COMM: Research, Exc Lab

Air Route Optimizer Inc...................G.... 540 364-3470
Marshall *(G-8249)*

Bluestone Industries Inc...............E.... 540 776-7890
Roanoke *(G-12051)*

Dbs Productions LLC......................G.... 434 293-5502
Charlottesville *(G-2778)*

Drive Square Inc...........................G.... 617 762-4013
Alexandria *(G-195)*

RESEARCH, DEVELOPMENT & TESTING SVCS, COMMERCIAL: Medical

Caretaker Medical LLC....................G.... 434 978-7000
Charlottesville *(G-2604)*

RESEARCH, DEVELOPMENT & TESTING SVCS, COMMERCIAL: Physical

Microxact Inc...............................G.... 540 394-4040
Radford *(G-10725)*

RESEARCH, DVLPT & TEST SVCS, COMM: Mkt Analysis or Research

Decotec Inc.................................G.... 434 589-0881
Kents Store *(G-7038)*

RESIDENTIAL MENTAL HEALTH & SUBSTANCE ABUSE FACILITIES

Butter of Life LLC..........................G.... 703 507-5298
Falls Church *(G-4766)*

RESIDENTIAL REMODELERS

PM Services LLC............................G.... 804 426-9892
Virginia Beach *(G-14727)*

RESIDUES

Quickest Residual Pay....................G.... 703 924-2620
Alexandria *(G-564)*

Residual King LLC..........................G.... 757 474-3080
Virginia Beach *(G-14769)*

Residual Sense Marketing LLC..........G.... 757 595-0278
Newport News *(G-9324)*

RESINS: Custom Compound Purchased

Artner Corp.................................G.... 703 341-6333
Springfield *(G-12951)*

Creative Impressions Inc.................G.... 757 855-2187
Virginia Beach *(G-14371)*

Gs Plastics LLC.............................G.... 276 629-7981
New Castle *(G-9120)*

Sunlite Plastics Inc.......................E.... 540 234-9271
Weyers Cave *(G-15178)*

RESPIRATORY SYSTEM DRUGS

Northport Research Inc...................G.... 703 508-9773
Alexandria *(G-295)*

RESTAURANT EQPT REPAIR SVCS

My Three Sons Inc.........................G.... 540 662-5927
Winchester *(G-15453)*

RESTAURANT EQPT: Carts

Modu System America LLC................G.... 757 250-3413
Williamsburg *(G-15281)*

RESTAURANT EQPT: Food Wagons

Arlene Nancys Meals On Wheels........G.... 404 940-8995
North Dinwiddie *(G-10047)*

Beach Block Ventures LLC................G.... 540 848-0921
Colonial Beach *(G-3721)*

Boxd Kitchen Merrifield Llc..............G.... 703 909-9572
Vienna *(G-14018)*

Cooking Williams Good....................G.... 804 931-6643
Hopewell *(G-6920)*

Gordos Tacos and More LLC.............G.... 757 710-3317
Birdsnest *(G-1719)*

Taste of Love LLC..........................G.... 804 714-4991
Richmond *(G-11784)*

Willie Gatling Jr............................G.... 757 236-5206
Newport News *(G-9379)*

RESTAURANTS:Full Svc, Family, Independent

Wolffinz LLC................................E.... 571 292-1427
Manassas *(G-8013)*

RESTAURANTS:Limited Svc, Coffee Shop

Beach Block Ventures LLC................G.... 540 848-0921
Colonial Beach *(G-3721)*

RESTAURANTS:Limited Svc, Fast-Food, Chain

Frito-Lay North America Inc..............E.... 540 380-3020
Salem *(G-12508)*

RESTAURANTS:Limited Svc, Health Food

Azars Natural Foods Inc..................E.... 757 486-7778
Virginia Beach *(G-14252)*

RESTAURANTS:Limited Svc, Lunch Counter

Aura LLC.....................................G.... 757 965-8400
Norfolk *(G-9447)*

RETAIL BAKERY: Cakes

River City Chocolate LLC.................G.... 804 317-8161
Midlothian *(G-8890)*

RETAIL BAKERY: Pretzels

Marlor Inc...................................F.... 804 378-5071
North Chesterfield *(G-9923)*

RETAIL LUMBER YARDS

Burnette Cabinet Shop Inc...............G.... 540 586-0147
Bedford *(G-1629)*

Portsmouth Lumber Corporation........F.... 757 397-4646
Portsmouth *(G-10471)*

RETAIL STORES, NEC

Alicesa Foster Graves LLC...............G.... 804 658-0092
Richmond *(G-11098)*

Kenney Inc...................................G.... 703 731-9208
Herndon *(G-6722)*

RETAIL STORES: Alarm Signal Systems

Sun Signs....................................G.... 703 867-9831
Stafford *(G-13197)*

RETAIL STORES: Artificial Limbs

American Cmg Services Inc...............G.... 804 353-9077
Richmond *(G-11107)*

Excel Prsthetics Orthotics Inc...........F.... 540 982-0205
Roanoke *(G-12083)*

Excel Prsthetics Orthotics Inc...........G.... 434 528-3695
Lynchburg *(G-7706)*

Excel Prsthetics Orthotics Inc...........G.... 434 797-1191
Danville *(G-3993)*

Hanger Prsthetcs & Ortho Inc...........G.... 757 873-1984
Newport News *(G-9243)*

Rehabltation Practitioners Inc...........G.... 540 722-9025
Winchester *(G-15579)*

RETAIL STORES: Awnings

Titan Sign Corporation....................G.... 540 899-5334
Fredericksburg *(G-5379)*

Virginia Canvas Products Inc.............G.... 757 558-0327
Carrollton *(G-2246)*

RETAIL STORES: Canvas Prdts

Custom Tops Inc............................G.... 757 460-3084
Virginia Beach *(G-14378)*

RETAIL STORES: Children's Furniture, NEC

Worth Baby Products LLC.................F.... 804 644-4707
Henrico *(G-6592)*

RETAIL STORES: Cleaning Eqpt & Splys

Northfield Medical Mfg LLC...............E.... 800 270-0153
Norfolk *(G-9669)*

RETAIL STORES: Coins

Dutch Barns.................................G.... 757 497-7356
Virginia Beach *(G-14418)*

RETAIL STORES: Cosmetics

Amarveda....................................E.... 276 782-1819
Marion *(G-8221)*

Getintoforex LLC...........................G.... 251 591-2181
Big Stone Gap *(G-1710)*

Simplicity Pure Bath & Bdy LLC.........G.... 540 922-9287
Pearisburg *(G-10277)*

Sweet Relief Inc............................G.... 703 963-4868
Sterling *(G-13526)*

RETAIL STORES: Facsimile Eqpt

Konica Mnlta Bus Sltons USA In.........C.... 703 461-8195
Alexandria *(G-508)*

RETAIL STORES: Farm Eqpt & Splys

Southern States Coop Inc.................F.... 434 572-6941
South Boston *(G-12791)*

RETAIL STORES: Farm Machinery, NEC

Bluestone Industries Inc..................E.... 540 776-7890
Roanoke *(G-12051)*

RETAIL STORES: Fire Extinguishers

Virginia Fire Protection Svcs.............G.... 276 637-1012
Max Meadows *(G-8370)*

RETAIL STORES: Flags

U S Flag & Signal Company...............E.... 757 497-8947
Portsmouth *(G-10494)*

RETAIL STORES: Hearing Aids

Fauquier Hearing Services Pllc...........G.... 540 341-7112
Warrenton *(G-15010)*

Hear Quick Incorporated..................G.... 757 523-0504
Virginia Beach *(G-14513)*

RETAIL STORES: Hospital Eqpt & Splys

Contour Healer LLC........................G.... 757 288-6671
Virginia Beach *(G-14362)*

RETAIL STORES: Ice

Hometown Ice Co...........................G.... 540 483-7865
Rocky Mount *(G-12327)*

RETAIL STORES: Medical Apparatus & Splys

Bonde Innovation LLC......................G.... 434 951-0444
Charlottesville *(G-2746)*

Coastal Prsttics Orthotics LLC...........G.... 757 892-5300
Chesapeake *(G-3043)*

Commonwlth Orthtics Prosthetic........G.... 434 836-4736
Danville *(G-3970)*

Encore Products Inc........................G.... 757 493-8358
Virginia Beach *(G-14447)*

Orthotic Prosthetic Center...............G.... 703 698-5007
Fairfax *(G-4526)*

RETAIL STORES: Motors, Electric

Case-Polytech Inc..........................G.... 804 752-3500
Ashland *(G-1386)*

Loudon Street Electric Svcs..............G.... 540 662-8463
Winchester *(G-15553)*

Mahoy Electric Service Co Inc...........G.... 540 977-0035
Blue Ridge *(G-1851)*

Thompson Electric Motor Svc............G.... 434 372-3814
Chase City *(G-2917)*

RETAIL STORES: Orthopedic & Prosthesis Applications

American Cmg Services Inc...............G.... 757 548-5656
Chesapeake *(G-2965)*

Eastern Cranial Affiliates LLC............G.... 703 807-5899
Fairfax *(G-4616)*

Medical Sports Inc.........................G.... 703 241-9720
Arlington *(G-1060)*

Paul Valentine Orthotics..................G.... 804 355-0283
Richmond *(G-11320)*

PRODUCT

RETAIL STORES: Pet Food

Mars Incorporated............B 703 821-4900
Mc Lean *(G-8491)*

RETAIL STORES: Picture Frames, Ready Made

Black Dog Gallery..............G 757 989-1700
Yorktown *(G-15938)*
Museum Framing..............G 703 299-0100
Alexandria *(G-287)*
Shooting Star Gallery LLC..............G 757 787-4536
Onancock *(G-10197)*

RETAIL STORES: Police Splys

Southerns M&P LLC..............G 804 330-2407
North Chesterfield *(G-9985)*

RETAIL STORES: Rubber Stamps

Blue Ridge Sign & Stamp Co Inc..........F 540 777-5456
Roanoke *(G-11892)*

RETAIL STORES: Safety Splys & Eqpt

Core Engineered Solutions Inc..........F 703 563-0320
Herndon *(G-6646)*

RETAIL STORES: Sunglasses

Better Vision Eyeglass Center..............G 757 397-2020
Portsmouth *(G-10400)*

RETAIL STORES: Water Purification Eqpt

A Descal Matic Corp..............G 757 858-5593
Norfolk *(G-9414)*

RETAIL STORES: Wheelchair Lifts

Christopher Hawkins..............G 540 361-1679
Fredericksburg *(G-5178)*
Qlifts LLC..............G 276 632-0058
Ridgeway *(G-11850)*

REUPHOLSTERY & FURNITURE REPAIR

Kathy Darmofalski..............G 540 885-4759
Staunton *(G-13272)*

REUPHOLSTERY SVCS

American Interiors Ltd..............G 757 627-0248
Norfolk *(G-9438)*
Krismark Inc..............G 757 533-9182
Virginia Beach *(G-14593)*

RHEOSTATS: Electronic

Incandescent Technologies..............G 434 385-8825
Forest *(G-5074)*

RIBBONS, NEC

AEC Virginia LLC..............C 757 654-6131
Boykins *(G-1918)*

RIBBONS: Machine, Inked Or Carbon

MB Services LLC..............G 703 906-8625
Alexandria *(G-524)*

RIFLES: Recoilless

Hawk Hill Custom LLC..............G 540 248-4295
Verona *(G-13988)*

RIPRAP QUARRYING

64 Ways Trucking/Hauling LLC..........F 804 801-5330
Richmond *(G-11466)*
Frazier Quarry Incorporated..............E 540 434-6192
Harrisonburg *(G-6317)*

ROBOTS: Assembly Line

Mekatronich Corp..............G 954 499-5794
Christiansburg *(G-3605)*
Vmek Group LLC..............G 804 380-1831
Midlothian *(G-8919)*

ROCK SALT MINING

United Salt Baytown LLC..............E 276 496-3363
Saltville *(G-12595)*

ROCKETS: Space & Military

Yuzhnoye-Us LLC..............G 321 537-2720
Reston *(G-10997)*

RODS: Plastic

Virginia Industrial Plas Inc..............F 540 298-1515
Elkton *(G-4337)*

RODS: Welding

Kcsl..............G 276 206-5977
Abingdon *(G-46)*

ROLLERS & FITTINGS: Window Shade

Abington Sunshade & Blinds Co..........F 540 435-6450
Penn Laird *(G-10287)*

ROLLING MILL MACHINERY

Coperion Corporation..............D 276 228-7717
Wytheville *(G-15884)*
Sanjo Virginia Beach Inc..............G 757 498-0400
Virginia Beach *(G-14793)*

ROOF DECKS

Design Assstnce Cnstr Systems..........E 757 393-0704
Portsmouth *(G-10415)*
Williamsburg Metal Specialties..............G 757 229-3393
Williamsburg *(G-15342)*

ROOFING MATERIALS: Asphalt

Acrylife Inc..............F 276 228-6704
Wytheville *(G-15874)*
Johns Manville Corporation..............B 804 261-7400
Richmond *(G-11256)*
Johns Manville Corporation..............B 540 984-4171
Edinburg *(G-4307)*
Marco Metals LLC..............F 540 437-2324
Rockingham *(G-12261)*
Onduline North America Inc..............D 540 898-7000
Fredericksburg *(G-5341)*
Ridgeline Incorporated..............F 540 898-7000
Fredericksburg *(G-5355)*
Tallant Industries Inc..............G 540 898-7000
Fredericksburg *(G-5376)*

ROOFING MEMBRANE: Rubber

Johns Manville Corporation..............B 540 984-4171
Edinburg *(G-4307)*

ROPE

Marshall Manufacturing Co..............F 757 824-4061
Atlantic *(G-1525)*
Ocean Products Research Inc..........F 804 725-3406
Diggs *(G-4093)*

RUBBER

International Carbide & Engrg..............F 434 568-3311
Drakes Branch *(G-4133)*
Longwood Elastomers Inc..............C 276 228-5406
Wytheville *(G-15898)*
Westland Technologies Inc..............D 703 477-9847
Chantilly *(G-2522)*

RUBBER PRDTS

Commonwealth Recycling Svcs..........G 931 289-3645
Ivanhoe *(G-7004)*
Creatiate..............G 609 703-2378
Midlothian *(G-8805)*
Lava Flow Yoga LLC..............G 703 264-1638
Reston *(G-10885)*
Raggededge Gear Inc..............G 276 226-9439
Stuart *(G-13627)*
Walker Custom Rifles..............G 540 399-1632
Culpeper *(G-3929)*
Yama Mountain Gear..............G 434 202-9717
Charlottesville *(G-2908)*

RUBBER PRDTS: Automotive, Mechanical

Fiberglass Customs Inc..............G 757 244-0610
Newport News *(G-9226)*
Morooka America LLC..............F 877 667-6652
Ashland *(G-1464)*
Morooka America LLC..............F 804 368-0948
Ashland *(G-1465)*

RUBBER PRDTS: Mechanical

ARS Manufacturing Inc..............C 757 460-2211
Virginia Beach *(G-14242)*
Briggs Company..............G 804 233-0966
Chesterfield *(G-3483)*
Coopers R C Tires..............G 434 724-7342
Chatham *(G-2925)*
Hutchinson Sealing Systems Inc..............C 276 228-4455
Wytheville *(G-15891)*
Longwood Elastomers Inc..............C 276 228-5406
Wytheville *(G-15898)*
Reiss Manufacturing Inc..............C 434 292-1600
Blackstone *(G-1825)*

RUBBER PRDTS: Medical & Surgical Tubing, Extrudd & Lathe-Cut

Antmed Corporation..............G 703 239-3118
Fairfax *(G-4593)*

RUBBER STRUCTURES: Air-Supported

Trelleborg Marine Systems..............E 540 667-5191
Berryville *(G-1695)*
Trelleborg Marine Systems Usa..........E 540 667-5191
Berryville *(G-1696)*

RUBBING STONE QUARRYING SVCS

Polycor Virginia Inc..............E 434 831-1051
Schuyler *(G-12653)*

RUGS : Hand & Machine Made

Christine Smith..............G 703 399-1944
Alexandria *(G-429)*

SAFE DEPOSIT BOXES

Agile Access Control Inc..............G 408 213-9555
Chantilly *(G-2363)*

SAFES & VAULTS: Metal

Fedsafes LLC..............G 703 525-1436
Arlington *(G-964)*

SAFETY EQPT & SPLYS WHOLESALERS

Rescue Systems Inc..............G 276 629-2900
Bassett *(G-1590)*
Rescue Systems Intl Inc..............G 276 629-2900
Fincastle *(G-4998)*

SAILS

Doyle Sailmakers Virginia..............G 757 727-0750
Hampton *(G-6132)*
Hampton Canvas and Rigging..............G 757 727-0750
Hampton *(G-6162)*
Hayes Custom Sails Inc..............G 804 642-6496
Hayes *(G-6400)*
Krismark Inc..............G 757 533-9182
Virginia Beach *(G-14593)*
Latell Sailmakers LLC..............G 804 776-6151
Deltaville *(G-4082)*
North Sails Hampton Inc..............G 757 723-6280
Hampton *(G-6210)*
Potomac Sailmakers Inc..............G 703 750-2171
Alexandria *(G-554)*

SALT

Essential Eats LLC..............G 757 304-2393
Norfolk *(G-9544)*
Going Forward Imports LLC..............G 301 693-1562
Mount Jackson *(G-9071)*
Morton Salt..............G 757 543-0148
Chesapeake *(G-3212)*
Ruby Salts Oyster Company LLC..........G 757 331-1495
Cape Charles *(G-2236)*
Salt Soothers LLC..............G 757 412-5867
Virginia Beach *(G-14791)*

SAND & GRAVEL

6304 Gravel Avenue LLC ....G...... 571 287-7544
  Chantilly (G-2359)
64 Ways Trucking/Hauling LLC ....F...... 804 801-5330
  Richmond (G-11466)
Aggregate Industries - Mwr Inc ....B...... 540 379-0765
  Falmouth (G-4932)
Best of Landscaping ....G...... 804 253-4014
  Powhatan (G-10532)
Black Sand Solutions LLC ....G...... 703 393-1127
  Manassas Park (G-8191)
Crossroads Express Inc ....G...... 434 882-0320
  Louisa (G-7552)
E Trucking & Services LLC ....G...... 571 241-0856
  Warrenton (G-15000)
Eliene Trucking LLC ....G...... 571 721-0735
  Centreville (G-2304)
Frazier Quarry Incorporated ....E...... 540 434-6192
  Harrisonburg (G-6317)
Hilltop Sand and Gravel Co Inc ....G...... 571 322-0389
  Lorton (G-7493)
Legacy Vulcan LLC ....E...... 434 634-4158
  Skippers (G-12701)
Legacy Vulcan LLC ....E...... 703 690-1172
  Lorton (G-7504)
Legacy Vulcan LLC ....E...... 434 572-3931
  South Boston (G-12777)
Legacy Vulcan LLC ....G...... 804 706-1773
  Chester (G-3428)
Legacy Vulcan LLC ....G...... 804 748-3695
  Chester (G-3429)
Legacy Vulcan LLC ....G...... 540 659-3003
  Garrisonville (G-5656)
Legacy Vulcan Corp ....G...... 757 562-5008
  Franklin (G-5148)
Luck Stone Corporation ....E...... 703 830-8880
  Centreville (G-2316)
Mid Atlantic Mining LLC ....G...... 757 407-6735
  Suffolk (G-13742)
Nancy Stephens ....G...... 540 933-6405
  Fort Valley (G-5135)
Pounding Mill Quarry Corp ....E...... 276 326-1145
  Bluefield (G-1875)
Rockydale Quarries Corporation ....D...... 540 774-1696
  Roanoke (G-12170)
Rockydale Quarries Corporation ....G...... 540 886-2111
  Staunton (G-13286)
S&M Trucking Service LLC ....G...... 980 395-6953
  Woodbridge (G-15801)
Salem Stone Corporation ....G...... 276 228-6767
  Wytheville (G-15910)
Sisson & Ryan Inc ....E...... 540 268-2413
  Shawsville (G-12686)
Stony Creek Sand & Gravel LLC ....G...... 804 229-0015
  Virginia Beach (G-14853)
T&W Block Incorporated ....E...... 757 787-2646
  Onley (G-10201)
Tarmac Mid-Atlantic Inc ....A...... 757 858-6500
  Norfolk (G-9743)
TCS Materials Inc ....E...... 757 591-9340
  Williamsburg (G-15323)
Texture Sand Tresses ....G...... 757 369-3033
  Newport News (G-9354)
Vulcan Construction Mtls LLC ....E...... 804 862-6660
  Prince George (G-10609)
Vulcan Materials Company ....G...... 757 622-4110
  Norfolk (G-9787)
Walker Sand Stone ....G...... 540 775-5024
  Culpeper (G-3930)

SAND MINING

Aylett Sand & Gravel Inc ....G...... 804 443-2366
  Tappahannock (G-13811)
Bar-C Sand Inc ....G...... 276 701-3888
  Cedar Bluff (G-2270)
Gravley Sand Works ....G...... 434 724-7883
  Dry Fork (G-4142)
Holland Sand Pit LLC ....E...... 757 745-7140
  Suffolk (G-13723)
Packetts Sand Pit ....G...... 804 761-6975
  Warsaw (G-15072)
Percontee Inc ....E...... 703 471-4411
  Chantilly (G-2479)
RI Byrd Properties ....G...... 757 817-7920
  Yorktown (G-15988)
Sand Mountain Sand Co ....F...... 276 228-6767
  Wytheville (G-15911)

SAND: Hygrade

Covia Holdings Corporation ....G...... 540 678-1490
  Winchester (G-15535)
Dominion Quikrete Inc ....E...... 276 957-3235
  Martinsville (G-8279)
U S Silica Company ....E...... 804 883-6700
  Montpelier (G-9022)

SANDBLASTING EQPT

Tectonics Inc ....G...... 276 228-5565
  Wytheville (G-15918)

SANDBLASTING SVC: Building Exterior

Suburban Contractors LLC ....E...... 703 739-5600
  Manassas (G-8001)

SANDSTONE: Dimension

Shenandoah Stone Supply Co ....G...... 703 532-0169
  Falls Church (G-4925)

SANITARY SVCS: Liquid Waste Collection & Disposal

Tidewater Green ....F...... 757 487-4736
  Chesapeake (G-3338)

SANITARY SVCS: Medical Waste Disposal

Yupo Corporation America ....C...... 757 312-9876
  Chesapeake (G-3381)

SANITARY SVCS: Waste Materials, Recycling

Sonoco Products Company ....D...... 804 233-5411
  Richmond (G-11763)

SANITATION CHEMICALS & CLEANING AGENTS

A Better Driving School LLC ....G...... 804 874-5521
  Mechanicsville (G-8598)
Atx Technologies LLC ....G...... 540 586-4100
  Bedford (G-1620)
Birsch Industries Inc ....G...... 757 622-0355
  Norfolk (G-9462)
Ester Yildiz LLC ....G...... 434 202-7790
  Charlottesville (G-2628)
Five Star Portables Inc ....G...... 571 839-7884
  Sterling (G-13399)
Green Air Environmental Svcs ....G...... 757 739-1349
  Norfolk (G-9565)
Hydrus Usa Inc ....G...... 804 690-8158
  Glen Allen (G-5749)
Intense Cleaning Inc ....G...... 703 999-1933
  Ashburn (G-1297)
Krystal Clear ....G...... 703 944-2066
  Lorton (G-7503)
Madisons Cleaning ....F...... 540 421-1074
  Rockingham (G-12260)
Marble Restoration Systems ....G...... 757 739-7959
  Virginia Beach (G-14637)
NCH Home Solutions LLC ....G...... 703 723-4077
  Ashburn (G-1319)
Sterile Home LLC ....G...... 804 314-3589
  Tappahannock (G-13822)
Superb Cleaning Solutons ....G...... 804 908-9018
  Henrico (G-6576)
United Cntry Cllins Assoc Real ....G...... 407 233-4377
  Independence (G-6997)

SASHES: Door Or Window, Metal

Milgard Manufacturing Inc ....G...... 540 834-0340
  Fredericksburg (G-5328)

SATELLITE COMMUNICATIONS EQPT

Are You Wired LLC ....G...... 804 512-3990
  North Chesterfield (G-9819)
Engility LLC ....A...... 703 434-4000
  Reston (G-10847)
Getsat North America Inc ....E...... 571 308-2451
  Mc Lean (G-8448)
Mil-Space LLC ....G...... 954 862-3613
  Surry (G-13799)
Phasor Inc ....G...... 202 256-2075
  Arlington (G-1110)
Raytheon Company ....G...... 310 647-9438
  Chesapeake (G-3258)

Raytheon Company ....G...... 703 418-0275
  Arlington (G-1135)
Raytheon Company ....G...... 571 250-1101
  Dulles (G-4222)
Raytheon Company ....G...... 757 749-9638
  Yorktown (G-15987)
Raytheon Company ....F...... 703 872-3400
  Arlington (G-1139)
Spacequest Ltd ....F...... 703 424-7801
  Fairfax (G-4680)
Telesat US Services LLC ....G...... 571 559-1500
  Arlington (G-1186)

SATELLITES: Communications

Aprize Satellite Inc ....G...... 703 273-7010
  Fairfax (G-4595)
Avcom of Virginia Inc ....E...... 804 794-2500
  North Chesterfield (G-9823)
Ballas LLC ....G...... 703 689-9644
  Oak Hill (G-10136)
Boeing Company ....G...... 703 467-2534
  Herndon (G-6628)
Communications-Applied Tech Co ....F...... 703 481-0068
  Reston (G-10823)
Idirect Government LLC ....D...... 703 648-8118
  Herndon (G-6705)
Ils Intrntonal Launch Svcs Inc ....D...... 703 435-5689
  Reston (G-10869)
Iridium Satellite LLC ....E...... 703 356-0484
  Mc Lean (G-8471)
Laser Light Communications Inc ....G...... 571 346-7623
  Reston (G-10883)
Ligado Networks Inc Virginia ....B...... 877 678-2920
  Reston (G-10888)
Lockheed Martin Corporation ....B...... 757 935-9479
  Suffolk (G-13732)
Lynk Global Inc ....G...... 937 367-8737
  Falls Church (G-4921)
Mil-Sat LLC ....G...... 757 294-9393
  Surry (G-13798)
Orbcomm LLC ....D...... 703 433-6300
  Dulles (G-4215)
Orbcomm LLC ....E...... 703 433-6300
  Sterling (G-13466)
Orion Applied Science Tech LLC ....G...... 571 393-1942
  Manassas (G-8122)
Peraton Cmmnctons Holdings LLC ......G...... 703 668-6001
  Herndon (G-6769)
Rome Research Corporation ....G...... 757 421-8300
  Chesapeake (G-3275)
Santa Inc ....F...... 757 463-3553
  Virginia Beach (G-14794)
Satcom-Labs LLC ....G...... 805 427-5556
  Alexandria (G-339)
Skymate Inc ....G...... 703 961-5800
  Reston (G-10953)
Special Communications LLC ....G...... 202 677-1225
  Virginia Beach (G-14833)
Sure Site Satellite Inc ....G...... 540 948-5880
  Locust Grove (G-7452)
Thrane Rgonal Workshop- Mackey ......G...... 757 410-3291
  Chesapeake (G-3334)
Trustcomm Solutions LLC ....F...... 281 272-7500
  Stafford (G-13205)
US Dept of the Air Force ....G...... 703 808-0492
  Chantilly (G-2515)
Wireless Ventures USA Inc ....F...... 703 852-1350
  Mc Lean (G-8580)

SAW BLADES

Formable Grabber Inc ....G...... 434 298-4722
  Covington (G-3789)
International Carbide & Engrg ....F...... 434 568-3311
  Drakes Branch (G-4133)
Reeds Carbide Saw Service ....F...... 434 846-6436
  Lynchburg (G-7800)

SAWDUST & SHAVINGS

Sawdust and Shavings LLC ....G...... 804 205-8074
  Ruther Glen (G-12462)
Woodberry Farm Inc ....G...... 540 854-6967
  Orange (G-10233)

SAWING & PLANING MILLS

Anderson Erle P Lumber Company ....E...... 804 748-0500
  Disputanta (G-4104)
Appalachian Woods LLC ....F...... 540 337-1801
  Stuarts Draft (G-13644)

PRODUCT

Company		Phone
Appalachian Woods LLC	G	540 886-5700
Staunton (G-13242)		
Asal Tie & Lumber Co Inc	F	434 454-6555
Scottsburg (G-12654)		
B & G Bandmill	G	276 766-4280
Hillsville (G-6884)		
Barnes Manufacturing Company	E	434 676-8210
Kenbridge (G-7032)		
Beagle Logging Company	G	540 459-2425
Woodstock (G-15849)		
Belcher Lumber Co Inc	G	276 498-3362
Rowe (G-12396)		
Bennett Logging & Lumber Inc	E	540 862-7621
Covington (G-3778)		
Blue Ridge Portable Sawmill	G	540 743-2520
Luray (G-7602)		
Bolt Sawmill	G	434 574-6732
Farmville (G-4937)		
Brown-Foreman Coopeages	G	434 575-0770
South Boston (G-12754)		
Browns Forest Products Inc	F	434 735-8179
Drakes Branch (G-4130)		
Browns Sawmill Inc	G	434 542-5776
Charlotte C H (G-2582)		
C & B Lumber Inc	E	276 744-3650
Fries (G-5515)		
Campbell Lumber Co Inc	F	434 293-3021
North Garden (G-10074)		
Carlton and Edwards Inc	E	804 758-5100
Saluda (G-12602)		
Carlton Orndorff	G	540 436-3543
Maurertown (G-8360)		
Charles W Brinegar Enterprise	G	276 634-6934
Spencer (G-12872)		
Chewning Lumber Company	E	540 895-5158
Spotsylvania (G-12885)		
Cloverdale Lumber Co Inc	E	434 822-5017
Sutherlin (G-13806)		
Collins Sawmill and Loggin LLC	G	276 694-7521
Stuart (G-13608)		
Curtis Russell Lumber Co Inc	E	276 346-1958
Jonesville (G-7020)		
Earl D Pierce Sawmill	G	276 744-7538
Fries (G-5516)		
Fain Arlice Sawmill	G	276 694-8211
Stuart (G-13611)		
Falling Creek Log Yard Inc	E	804 798-6121
Ashland (G-1413)		
Fitzgerald Lumber & Log Co Inc	D	540 348-5199
Fairfield (G-4730)		
Fitzgerald Lumber & Log Co Inc	E	540 261-3430
Buena Vista (G-2144)		
Gallimore Sawmill Inc	F	276 236-5064
Galax (G-5634)		
Georgia-Pacific LLC	B	434 634-5123
Emporia (G-4359)		
Goodman Lumber Co Inc	E	804 265-9030
Wilsons (G-15367)		
Gregory Lumber Inc	E	434 432-1000
Java (G-7011)		
Hairfield Lumber Corporation	F	540 967-2042
Spotsylvania (G-12893)		
Hardwood Mulch Corporation	G	804 458-7500
Disputanta (G-4108)		
Hooke Brothers Lumber Co LLC	F	540 499-2540
Monterey (G-9007)		
Hopkins Lumber Contractors Inc	E	276 694-2166
Stuart (G-13618)		
J E Moore Lumber Co Inc	F	434 634-9740
Emporia (G-4361)		
J H Knighton Lumber Co Inc	E	804 448-4681
Ruther Glen (G-12457)		
JC Bradley Lumber Co	G	540 962-4446
Covington (G-3792)		
Jim L Clark	G	276 393-2359
Jonesville (G-7022)		
Johnny Asal Lumber Co Inc	E	804 492-4884
Cumberland (G-3935)		
Johnson & Son Lumber Inc	E	540 752-5557
Fredericksburg (G-5446)		
Kirk Lumber Company	G	757 255-4521
Suffolk (G-13729)		
Koppers Inc	E	540 380-2061
Salem (G-12527)		
Lams Lumber Co	E	540 832-5173
Barboursville (G-1563)		
Lindsay Hardwoods Inc	F	434 392-8615
Farmville (G-4947)		
Mace Lumber Mill	G	540 249-4458
Grottoes (G-6021)		

Company		Phone
Marcus Cox & Sons Inc	F	540 297-5818
Moneta (G-8971)		
Meadowsend Farm and Sawmill Co	G	434 975-6598
Earlysville (G-4291)		
Mitchell Sawmilling	G	276 944-2329
Saltville (G-12586)		
Moore and Son Inc Lewis S	G	804 366-7170
Ruther Glen (G-12458)		
Morris Finishing Co	G	540 674-0079
Dublin (G-4166)		
Mullican Flooring LP	C	276 679-2924
Norton (G-10130)		
Mullican Flooring LP	D	276 565-0220
Appalachia (G-798)		
Nelson Martin	G	540 879-9016
Dayton (G-4058)		
Next Generation Woods Inc	G	540 639-3077
Hiwassee (G-6913)		
Northwest Hardwoods	G	540 631-3245
Front Royal (G-5546)		
Northwest Hardwoods Inc	G	540 261-2171
Buena Vista (G-2151)		
OMalley Timber Products LLC	D	804 445-1118
Tappahannock (G-13819)		
Pace Custom Sawing LLC	G	276 956-2000
Ridgeway (G-11847)		
Patricia Ramey	G	703 973-1140
Upperville (G-13967)		
Pembelton Forest Products Inc	E	434 292-7511
Blackstone (G-1822)		
Pine Products Inc	E	276 957-2222
Martinsville (G-8318)		
Pine Products LLC	G	276 957-2222
Martinsville (G-8319)		
Pinecrest Timber Co	E	804 834-2304
Waverly (G-15087)		
Portable Sawmill Service	G	276 940-4194
Gate City (G-5665)		
Porters Wood Products Inc	E	757 654-6430
Boykins (G-1920)		
R A Yancey Lumber Corp	D	434 823-4107
Crozet (G-3849)		
R D Knighton Sawmill	G	540 872-3636
Bumpass (G-2167)		
R David Rosson	G	540 456-8108
Afton (G-86)		
Ramsey & Son Lumber Corp	F	434 946-5429
Amherst (G-704)		
Richard C Iroler	G	276 236-3796
Fries (G-5517)		
Robertson Lumber Inc	F	434 335-5100
Hurt (G-6977)		
Rock Hill Lumber Inc	E	540 547-2889
Culpeper (G-3918)		
Rocky Mount Hardwood Inc	F	540 483-1428
Ferrum (G-4979)		
Scott Pallets Inc	E	804 561-2514
Amelia Court House (G-672)		
Shumate Inc George C	E	540 463-2244
Lexington (G-7417)		
SM Lumber Inc	G	757 797-8353
Virginia Beach (G-14826)		
Smith Mountain Land & Lbr Inc	F	540 297-1205
Huddleston (G-6958)		
Smythers Daris O Sawmill	G	540 980-5169
Allisonia (G-620)		
Stella-Jones Corporation	D	540 997-9251
Goshen (G-5927)		
Stovall Brothers Lumber LLC	F	276 694-6684
Stuart (G-13632)		
Stuart Wilderness Inc	G	276 694-4432
Stuart (G-13635)		
T C Catlett & Sons Lumber Co	E	540 786-2303
Fredericksburg (G-5373)		
Timber Team USA LLC	G	434 989-1201
Charlottesville (G-2892)		
Timberland Express Inc	G	276 679-1965
Wise (G-15636)		
Tine & Company Inc	G	276 881-8232
Whitewood (G-15193)		
Trent Sawmill Inc	G	434 376-2714
Brookneal (G-2115)		
Trex Company Inc	C	540 542-6800
Winchester (G-15496)		
Tucker Timber Products Inc	F	434 736-9661
Keysville (G-7064)		
Turman Lumber Company Inc	G	540 745-2041
Floyd (G-5043)		
Turman-Mercer Sawmills LLC	F	276 728-7974
Hillsville (G-6902)		

Company		Phone
W R Deacon & Sons Timber Inc	E	540 463-3832
Lexington (G-7422)		
Wood Preservers Incorporated	D	804 333-4022
Warsaw (G-15073)		
Woodwrights LLC	G	804 761-0775
Irvington (G-7002)		

SAWING & PLANING MILLS: Custom

Company		Phone
Beneath The Bark Inc	G	434 848-3995
Lawrenceville (G-7177)		
Ferguson Custom Sawmill LLC	G	540 903-8174
Fredericksburg (G-5287)		
McDonald Sawmill	G	540 465-5539
Strasburg (G-13588)		
R L Beckley Sawmill Inc	F	540 872-3621
Montpelier (G-9019)		
Seward Lumber Company Inc	E	757 866-8911
Claremont (G-3625)		
Sweany Trckg & Hardwoods LLC	G	540 273-9387
Stafford (G-13198)		

SAWS & SAWING EQPT

Company		Phone
Southern States Coop Inc	F	804 226-2758
Richmond (G-11390)		

SAWS: Hand, Metalworking Or Woodworking

Company		Phone
Alegria John	G	703 398-6009
Manassas Park (G-8186)		

SCALES & BALANCES, EXC LABORATORY

Company		Phone
Mettler-Toledo LLC	G	540 665-9495
Winchester (G-15554)		
Nexaware LLC	G	703 880-6697
Rockingham (G-12265)		

SCANNING DEVICES: Optical

Company		Phone
Elekon Industries USA Inc	E	757 766-1500
Hampton (G-6136)		
Vidar Systems Corporation	E	703 471-7070
Herndon (G-6838)		

SCIENTIFIC EQPT REPAIR SVCS

Company		Phone
Dynex Technologies Inc	D	703 631-7800
Chantilly (G-2415)		

SCRAP STEEL CUTTING

Company		Phone
Steel Dynamics Inc	A	540 342-1831
Roanoke (G-12197)		

SCREENS: Projection

Company		Phone
Falcon Screens LLC	G	703 789-3274
Bristow (G-2053)		

SCREENS: Window, Metal

Company		Phone
Tmac Services Inc	F	804 368-0936
Ashland (G-1501)		

SCREW MACHINE PRDTS

Company		Phone
GM International Ltd Company	G	703 577-0829
Leesburg (G-7281)		
Patriot Solutions Group LLC	G	571 367-4979
Chantilly (G-2549)		
Progressive Manufacturing Corp	E	804 717-5353
Chester (G-3448)		
Ramatech LLC	G	240 449-7435
Chantilly (G-2553)		
Rrb Industries Inc	G	804 396-3270
North Chesterfield (G-9967)		

SEALANTS

Company		Phone
Coastal Caulking Sealants LLC	G	757 679-8201
Chesapeake (G-3040)		
Stella Stone and Sealant LLC	G	917 568-6489
Fairfax (G-4561)		

SEALING COMPOUNDS: Sealing, synthetic rubber or plastic

Company		Phone
Safety Seal Plastics LLC	G	703 348-4699
Fredericksburg (G-5482)		

SEARCH & DETECTION SYSTEMS, EXC RADAR

Applied Video Imaging LLC ....G 434 974-6310
Charlottesville *(G-2589)*

Bae Systems Inc ....C 571 461-6000
Falls Church *(G-4754)*

Dmt LLC ....G 434 455-2460
Forest *(G-5067)*

Ghodousi LLC ....G 480 544-3192
Alexandria *(G-468)*

Northrop Grumman Corporation ....A 804 272-1321
North Chesterfield *(G-9940)*

Northrop Grumman Intl Inc ....E 703 280-2900
Falls Church *(G-4843)*

Schiebel Aircraft Inc ....F 540 351-1731
Manassas *(G-8151)*

Titan II Inc ....D 757 380-2000
Newport News *(G-9358)*

SEARCH & NAVIGATION SYSTEMS

A & A Precision Machining LLC ....G 804 493-8416
Montross *(G-9023)*

Alliant Tchsystems Oprtons LLC ....E 703 254-2454
Newington *(G-9152)*

Bae Systems Holdings Inc ....B 571 461-6000
Falls Church *(G-4755)*

Bae Systems Info & Elec Sys ....C 703 668-4000
Reston *(G-10797)*

Bae Systems Info & Elec Sys ....B 703 361-1471
Manassas *(G-7918)*

Bae Systems Info & Elec Sys ....G 202 223-8808
Arlington *(G-872)*

Bae Systems Land Armaments LP ....D 571 461-6000
Falls Church *(G-4757)*

Barnett Consulting LLC ....G 703 655-1635
Lorton *(G-7465)*

Black Tree LLC ....G 703 669-0178
Mc Lean *(G-8400)*

Chaosworks Inc ....G 703 727-0772
Great Falls *(G-5946)*

Cobham Defense Products Inc ....G 703 414-5300
Arlington *(G-912)*

Cobham Management Services Inc ......F 703 414-5300
Arlington *(G-913)*

Combat Bound LLC ....G 757 343-3399
Suffolk *(G-13685)*

Dirt Removal Services LLC ....G 703 499-1299
Catharpin *(G-2261)*

Drs C3 & Aviation Company ....G 571 346-7700
Herndon *(G-6661)*

Drs Global Entp Solutions Inc ....E 703 898-9233
Dulles *(G-4198)*

Drs Homeland SEC Solutions Inc ....G 703 682-1801
Arlington *(G-942)*

Drs Leonardo Inc ....F 703 416-7600
Arlington *(G-943)*

Drs Leonardo Inc ....F 757 819-0700
Chesapeake *(G-3077)*

Drs Leonardo Inc ....G 571 383-0152
Chantilly *(G-2412)*

Drs Leonardo Inc ....G 703 260-7979
Herndon *(G-6662)*

Drs Leonardo Inc ....D 703 416-8000
Arlington *(G-945)*

End To End Inc ....E 757 216-1938
Virginia Beach *(G-14448)*

Freeman Aerotech LLC ....G 703 303-0102
Ashburn *(G-1282)*

General Dynamics Corporation ....G 703 925-8636
Herndon *(G-6680)*

General Dynamics Corporation ....E 757 523-2738
Chesapeake *(G-3116)*

General Dynamics Corporation ....C 703 876-3000
Reston *(G-10857)*

Global Supply Solutions ....G 757 392-1733
Virginia Beach *(G-14485)*

Harris Corporation ....G 571 203-7605
Herndon *(G-6695)*

Hellen Systems LLC ....G 571 276-7730
Middleburg *(G-8722)*

ITT Exelis ....G 757 594-1600
Newport News *(G-9261)*

Kelvin Hughes LLC ....G 703 827-3986
Vienna *(G-14077)*

Kollmorgen Corporation ....B 540 633-3536
Radford *(G-10721)*

L-3 Unmanned Systems Inc ....D 703 889-8640
Ashburn *(G-1304)*

L3harris Technologies Inc ....G 540 658-3350
Stafford *(G-13168)*

L3harris Technologies Inc ....C 757 594-1607
Newport News *(G-9278)*

L3harris Technologies Inc ....D 434 455-9390
Forest *(G-5079)*

L3harris Technologies Inc ....E 434 455-6600
Forest *(G-5080)*

L3harris Technologies Inc ....G 703 668-6000
Herndon *(G-6729)*

L3harris Technologies Inc ....D 703 828-1520
Chantilly *(G-2455)*

L3harris Technologies Inc ....G 434 941-5441
Appomattox *(G-818)*

L3harris Technologies Inc ....B 703 668-6239
Herndon *(G-6728)*

L3harris Technologies Inc ....A 540 563-0371
Roanoke *(G-11951)*

Laurel Technologies Partnr ....G 814 534-2027
Arlington *(G-1029)*

Laurel Technologies Partnr ....E 757 819-0700
Chesapeake *(G-3177)*

Lockheed Martin ....C 703 588-0670
Arlington *(G-1043)*

Lockheed Martin ....D 202 863-3297
Arlington *(G-1044)*

Lockheed Martin ....D 757 578-3377
Virginia Beach *(G-14615)*

Lockheed Martin ....D 703 272-6061
Fairfax *(G-4648)*

Lockheed Martin ....D 703 982-9008
Lorton *(G-7508)*

Lockheed Martin Corporation ....G 703 280-9983
Vienna *(G-14083)*

Lockheed Martin Corporation ....D 703 771-3515
Leesburg *(G-7302)*

Lockheed Martin Corporation ....B 270 319-4600
Fairfax *(G-4649)*

Lockheed Martin Corporation ....A 703 367-2121
Manassas *(G-7965)*

Lockheed Martin Corporation ....B 757 491-3501
Virginia Beach *(G-14616)*

Lockheed Martin Corporation ....D 540 644-2830
King George *(G-7100)*

Lockheed Martin Corporation ....D 540 891-5882
Fredericksburg *(G-5314)*

Lockheed Martin Corporation ....B 703 724-7552
Ashburn *(G-1309)*

Lockheed Martin Corporation ....B 703 357-7095
Arlington *(G-1045)*

Lockheed Martin Corporation ....A 703 403-9829
Herndon *(G-6735)*

Lockheed Martin Corporation ....B 813 855-5711
Manassas *(G-7967)*

Lockheed Martin Corporation ....A 703 466-3000
Herndon *(G-6736)*

Lockheed Martin Corporation ....G 757 766-3282
Hampton *(G-6278)*

Lockheed Martin Corporation ....A 757 896-4860
Hampton *(G-6185)*

Lockheed Martin Corporation ....G 757 509-6808
Yorktown *(G-15977)*

Lockheed Martin Corporation ....G 757 464-0877
Virginia Beach *(G-14617)*

Lockheed Martin Corporation ....G 703 367-2121
Manassas *(G-7968)*

Lockheed Martin Corporation ....A 757 685-3132
Virginia Beach *(G-14618)*

Lockheed Martin Corporation ....G 757 803-3080
Virginia Beach *(G-14619)*

Lockheed Martin Corporation ....A 757 430-6500
Virginia Beach *(G-14620)*

Lockheed Martin Corporation ....F 703 418-4900
Arlington *(G-1046)*

Lockheed Martin Corporation ....B 703 378-1880
Chantilly *(G-2458)*

Lockheed Martin Corporation ....C 757 769-7251
Chesapeake *(G-3184)*

Lockheed Martin Corporation ....D 540 663-3337
King George *(G-7101)*

Lockheed Martin Corporation ....B 703 787-4027
Herndon *(G-6737)*

Lockheed Martin Corporation ....D 757 390-7520
Chesapeake *(G-3186)*

Lockheed Martin Integrtd Systm ....E 703 367-2121
Manassas *(G-7969)*

Lockheed Martin Integrtd Systm ....B 703 682-5719
Vienna *(G-14084)*

Lockheed Martin Services LLC ....F 757 366-3300
Chesapeake *(G-3187)*

Marine Sonic Technology ....G 804 693-9602
Yorktown *(G-15978)*

Mbda Incorporated ....E 703 387-7170
Arlington *(G-1056)*

Meridian Tech Systems Inc ....G 301 606-6490
Leesburg *(G-7313)*

Moog Inc ....G 716 652-2000
Blacksburg *(G-1764)*

Moog Inc ....A 828 837-5115
Blacksburg *(G-1766)*

Northern Defense Inds LLC ....G 703 836-8346
Alexandria *(G-294)*

Northrop Grmman / Hnlulu - US ....G 808 529-9500
Falls Church *(G-4838)*

Northrop Grmman Gdnce Elec Inc ....E 703 280-2900
Falls Church *(G-4839)*

Northrop Grmman Innvtion Syste ....G 763 744-5219
Arlington *(G-1080)*

Northrop Grmman Innvtion Syste ....C 703 406-5000
Dulles *(G-4212)*

Northrop Grmman Ovrseas Hldg I ....G 703 280-4069
Falls Church *(G-4840)*

Northrop Grmman Worldwide Entp ....G 703 713-4096
Herndon *(G-6756)*

Northrop Grumman Corporation ....G 804 416-6500
Chester *(G-3441)*

Northrop Grumman Corporation ....G 757 688-6850
Chesapeake *(G-3221)*

Northrop Grumman Corporation ....F 703 713-4096
Herndon *(G-6757)*

Northrop Grumman Corporation ....G 757 688-5339
Williamsburg *(G-15284)*

Northrop Grumman Corporation ....G 703 406-5695
Radford *(G-10730)*

Northrop Grumman Corporation ....D 804 371-0019
Richmond *(G-11695)*

Northrop Grumman Corporation ....F 703 556-5960
Chantilly *(G-2470)*

Northrop Grumman Corporation ....G 212 978-2800
Arlington *(G-1081)*

Northrop Grumman Corporation ....B 703 449-7120
Chantilly *(G-2471)*

Northrop Grumman Corporation ....G 703 556-1144
Mc Lean *(G-8511)*

Northrop Grumman Corporation ....B 703 280-2900
Falls Church *(G-4841)*

Northrop Grumman Global Svcs ....G 703 280-2900
Falls Church *(G-4842)*

Northrop Grumman Info Tech ....E 703 968-1000
Fairfax *(G-4520)*

Northrop Grumman Innovation ....F 540 831-4788
Radford *(G-10731)*

Northrop Grumman Intl Inc ....G 703 556-1144
Mc Lean *(G-8512)*

Northrop Grumman Intl Trdg Inc ....G 703 280-2900
Falls Church *(G-4844)*

Northrop Grumman Systems Corp ....C 703 875-8463
Arlington *(G-1082)*

Northrop Grumman Systems Corp ....G 703 808-0961
Centreville *(G-2324)*

Northrop Grumman Systems Corp ....D 703 556-1144
Mc Lean *(G-8513)*

Northrop Grumman Systems Corp ....B 703 556-1144
Mc Lean *(G-8514)*

Northrop Grumman Systems Corp ....G 703 556-1144
Mc Lean *(G-8515)*

Northrop Grumman Systems Corp ....D 703 280-1220
Falls Church *(G-4846)*

Northrop Grumman Systems Corp ....E 703 556-1144
Mc Lean *(G-8516)*

Northrop Grumman Systems Corp ....G 757 380-2612
Newport News *(G-9307)*

Northrop Grumman Systems Corp ....C 757 498-5616
Virginia Beach *(G-14685)*

Northrop Grumman Systems Corp ....G 757 686-4147
Virginia Beach *(G-14686)*

Northrop Grumman Systems Corp ....G 304 726-5030
Radford *(G-10732)*

Northrop Grumman Systems Corp ....G 757 463-5578
Virginia Beach *(G-14687)*

Northrop Grumman Systems Corp ....F 703 633-8300
Chantilly *(G-2472)*

Northrop Grumman Systems Corp ....G 703 968-1000
Herndon *(G-6759)*

Northrop Grumman Systems Corp ....G 703 968-1100
Herndon *(G-6760)*

Northrop Grumman Systems Corp ....C 703 556-1144
Mc Lean *(G-8518)*

Northrup Grumman ....G 305 466-4655
Centreville *(G-2325)*

Employee Codes: A=Over 500 employees, B=251-500
C=101-250, D=51-100, E=20-50, F=10-19, G=1-9

2021 Virginia
Industrial Directory

PRODUCT

1049

Ongrade Pllc............................G...... 757 448-5635
Virginia Beach *(G-14701)*

Orbital Sciences LLC.....................B....... 703 406-5000
Dulles *(G-4218)*

OSI Maritime Systems Inc................G...... 877 432-7467
Virginia Beach *(G-14706)*

Pons Corp..................................G...... 786 270-7774
Reston *(G-10927)*

Radio Reconnaissance Tech Inc........G...... 540 752-7448
Fredericksburg *(G-5352)*

Raytheon Applied Sgnal Tech In........G...... 571 484-9373
Mc Lean *(G-8533)*

Raytheon Company........................C...... 757 855-4394
Chesapeake *(G-3257)*

Raytheon Company........................E...... 703 260-3534
Sterling *(G-13486)*

Raytheon Company........................D...... 310 647-9438
Dulles *(G-4225)*

Rockwell Collins Inc......................E...... 703 234-2100
Sterling *(G-13495)*

Rockwell Collins Simulation.............C...... 703 234-2100
Sterling *(G-13496)*

Senstar Inc.................................G...... 703 463-3088
Herndon *(G-6804)*

Thales USA Defense & SEC Inc..........G...... 571 255-4600
Arlington *(G-1190)*

Trimble Inc.................................D...... 540 904-5925
Salem *(G-12577)*

United Technologies I LLC...............G...... 804 553-3116
Henrico *(G-6588)*

Where Good Grows LLC..................G...... 240 506-0011
Alexandria *(G-382)*

SEARCH & RESCUE SVCS

Dbs Productions LLC.....................G...... 434 293-5502
Charlottesville *(G-2778)*

SEATING: Bleacher, Portable

Stephen W Mast...........................G...... 804 467-3608
Mechanicsville *(G-8681)*

SECRETARIAL & COURT REPORTING

A Z Printing and Dup Corp...............G...... 703 549-0949
Alexandria *(G-115)*

Coghill Composition Co Inc..............F...... 804 714-1100
Midlothian *(G-8799)*

P M Resources Inc.........................G...... 703 556-0155
Springfield *(G-13065)*

Rappahannock Entp Assoc Inc..........G...... 703 560-5042
Falls Church *(G-4862)*

Salem Printing Co.........................E...... 540 387-1106
Salem *(G-12566)*

Tidewater Graphics Inc...................G...... 757 464-6136
Virginia Beach *(G-14874)*

SECRETARIAL SVCS

Professional Services.....................G...... 540 953-2223
Blacksburg *(G-1781)*

SECURE STORAGE SVC: Document

Ubiquitywave LLC.........................G...... 571 262-1406
Ashburn *(G-1344)*

SECURITY CONTROL EQPT & SYSTEMS

Aretec Inc...................................E...... 703 539-8801
Fairfax *(G-4596)*

Bryan Vossekuil............................G...... 540 854-9067
Mineral *(G-8942)*

C Thompson Enterprises All..............G...... 804 794-3407
Midlothian *(G-8786)*

Checkpoint Systems Inc...................E...... 804 745-0010
Richmond *(G-11526)*

Cornerstone Tech Solutions Inc..........G...... 540 477-2180
Mount Jackson *(G-9068)*

Decotec Inc.................................G...... 434 589-0881
Kents Store *(G-7038)*

L3harris Technologies Inc.................D...... 434 455-9390
Forest *(G-5079)*

L3harris Technologies Inc.................E...... 434 455-6600
Forest *(G-5080)*

Lightfactor LLC............................G...... 540 723-9600
Winchester *(G-15552)*

Rapiscan Systems Inc.....................F...... 703 257-3429
Manassas *(G-8139)*

Refibot Inc..................................G...... 703 989-2232
Ashburn *(G-1330)*

Security Evolutions Inc...................G...... 703 953-4739
Centreville *(G-2337)*

Spec Ops Inc...............................F...... 804 752-4790
Ashland *(G-1495)*

Stealthpath LLC............................G...... 571 888-6772
Reston *(G-10965)*

Tag 5 Industries LLC......................G...... 703 647-0325
Alexandria *(G-361)*

Utrue Inc....................................G...... 703 577-0309
Vienna *(G-14148)*

SECURITY DEVICES

All About Security Inc.....................G...... 757 887-6700
Newport News *(G-9161)*

Anixter Inc...................................G...... 757 460-9718
Virginia Beach *(G-14229)*

Brantley T Jolly Jr.........................G...... 703 447-6897
Mc Lean *(G-8404)*

Caleigh Systems Inc.......................F...... 703 539-5004
Annandale *(G-734)*

Dataprivia Inc..............................F...... 855 477-4842
Lynchburg *(G-7694)*

E C B Construction Company.............G...... 804 730-2057
Mechanicsville *(G-8620)*

Extremeht2com.............................G...... 804 665-6304
Richmond *(G-11584)*

Freeport Technologies Inc................F...... 571 262-0400
Herndon *(G-6677)*

Nettalon Security Systems Inc...........F...... 540 368-5290
Fredericksburg *(G-5333)*

Phoenix Security Group Ltd..............G...... 703 323-4940
Fairfax Station *(G-4721)*

Privaris Inc..................................G...... 703 592-1180
Fairfax *(G-4662)*

Safe Guard Security Service..............G...... 276 773-2866
Independence *(G-6994)*

US Dept of the Air Force..................G...... 703 808-0492
Chantilly *(G-2515)*

SECURITY EQPT STORES

Civille Smoke Shop.........................G...... 434 975-1175
Charlottesville *(G-2766)*

Creggers Cakes & Catering...............G...... 276 646-8739
Chilhowie *(G-3549)*

Mill Mountain Capital LLC................G...... 540 529-7163
Roanoke *(G-11966)*

Phat Daddys Polish Shop..................G...... 804 405-5301
North Chesterfield *(G-9947)*

SECURITY GUARD SVCS

James-York Security LLC..................E...... 757 344-1808
Williamsburg *(G-15259)*

Special Tactical Services LLC.............F...... 757 554-0699
Virginia Beach *(G-14835)*

SECURITY PROTECTIVE DEVICES MAINTENANCE & MONITORING SVCS

Burton Telecom LLC.......................G...... 757 230-6520
Virginia Beach *(G-14307)*

Infrawhite Technologies LLC.............G...... 662 902-0376
Vienna *(G-14071)*

Mu-Del Electronics LLC...................F...... 703 368-8900
Manassas *(G-8114)*

SECURITY SYSTEMS SERVICES

Caleigh Systems Inc.......................F...... 703 539-5004
Annandale *(G-734)*

Dataprivia Inc..............................F...... 855 477-4842
Lynchburg *(G-7694)*

Fso Mission Support LLC..................G...... 571 528-3507
Leesburg *(G-7275)*

Invincea Inc.................................C...... 703 352-7680
Fairfax *(G-4638)*

Mission Integrated Tech LLC.............G...... 202 769-9900
Vienna *(G-14097)*

SELF-DEFENSE & ATHLETIC INSTRUCTION SVCS

Personal Protectio Principles.............G...... 757 453-3202
Virginia Beach *(G-14717)*

SEMICONDUCTOR & RELATED DEVICES: Random Access Memory Or RAM

Micron Technology Inc....................D...... 703 396-1000
Manassas *(G-7975)*

SEMICONDUCTOR & RELATED DEVICES: Read-Only Memory Or ROM

Monolithic Music Group LLC.............G...... 804 233-2322
Richmond *(G-11682)*

SEMICONDUCTORS & RELATED DEVICES

4wave Inc...................................E...... 703 787-9283
Sterling *(G-13337)*

Applied Materials Inc......................E...... 703 331-1476
Manassas *(G-8028)*

Aware Inc....................................G...... 804 598-1016
Powhatan *(G-10531)*

Bluetherm Corporation....................G...... 917 446-8958
Charlottesville *(G-2745)*

Brocade Cmmnctions Systems LLC.....G...... 540 439-9010
Sumerduck *(G-13789)*

Burton Telecom LLC.......................G...... 757 230-6520
Virginia Beach *(G-14307)*

Controp USA Inc...........................G...... 301 605-4499
Manassas *(G-7926)*

Convergent Bus Solutions LLC...........G...... 804 360-0251
Richmond *(G-11167)*

Convergent Crossfit........................G...... 703 385-5400
Linden *(G-7427)*

Convergent Data Group...................G...... 571 276-0756
Alexandria *(G-433)*

Electronics of Future Inc..................G...... 518 421-8830
Vienna *(G-14044)*

Eopus Innovations LLC....................G...... 703 796-9882
Fairfax *(G-4618)*

Eyl Inc.......................................G...... 703 682-7018
Arlington *(G-961)*

Fluor Enterprises Inc.......................E...... 703 351-1204
Arlington *(G-970)*

Fox Group Inc...............................D...... 925 980-5643
Warrenton *(G-15017)*

Genesic Semiconductor Inc...............G...... 703 996-8200
Dulles *(G-4204)*

Intel Federal LLC...........................E...... 703 633-0953
Fairfax *(G-4637)*

Intel Perspectives LLC.....................G...... 703 321-7507
Springfield *(G-13024)*

ITT Defense & Electronics.................A...... 703 790-6300
Mc Lean *(G-8474)*

Jihoon Solution Inc........................G...... 757 344-1751
Yorktown *(G-15970)*

Kihn Solar....................................G...... 703 425-2418
Fairfax *(G-4489)*

Laser Light Federal LLC....................G...... 703 283-0659
Reston *(G-10884)*

Lightronics Inc..............................E...... 757 486-3588
Virginia Beach *(G-14612)*

Marelco Power Systems Inc...............F...... 800 225-4838
Richmond *(G-11667)*

Micronergy LLC.............................G...... 757 325-6973
Hampton *(G-6199)*

Minequest Inc...............................E...... 276 963-6463
Cedar Bluff *(G-2282)*

Moog Inc....................................F...... 540 552-3011
Blacksburg *(G-1765)*

Raytheon Company........................A...... 703 419-1400
Arlington *(G-1138)*

Semetrol LLC...............................G...... 804 536-7005
Chesterfield *(G-3523)*

Semiconductor Technology RES..........G...... 804 304-8092
Richmond *(G-11376)*

Svm Services LLC...........................G...... 703 389-5100
Herndon *(G-6818)*

Tisol...G...... 703 739-2771
Alexandria *(G-600)*

Tokyo Electron America Inc...............E...... 703 257-2211
Manassas *(G-8004)*

Transecurity LLC...........................G...... 540 443-9231
Blacksburg *(G-1800)*

Trojan Defense LLC........................G...... 703 981-8710
Herndon *(G-6832)*

Video Convergent..........................G...... 703 354-9700
Springfield *(G-13105)*

Virginia Semiconductor Inc...............E...... 540 373-2900
Fredericksburg *(G-5233)*

Virtue Solar LLC............................G...... 540 407-8353
Madison *(G-7864)*

SENSORS: Infrared, Solid State

Luna Energy LLC............................G...... 540 553-0500
Blacksburg *(G-1755)*

Moog Inc....................................C...... 540 552-3011
Blacksburg *(G-1768)*

Zeido LLC ....G...... 202 549-5757
Stafford *(G-13213)*

SEPTIC TANK CLEANING SVCS

Finly Corporation ....E...... 434 385-5028
Lynchburg *(G-7707)*
Hall Hflin Septic Tank Svc Inc ....G...... 804 333-3124
Warsaw *(G-15064)*
Jordan Septic Tank Service ....G...... 276 395-3938
Coeburn *(G-3700)*

SEPTIC TANKS: Concrete

Boggs Water & Sewage Inc ....E...... 757 787-4000
Melfa *(G-8708)*
Concrete Castings Inc ....G...... 540 427-3006
Roanoke *(G-12068)*
CT Jamsos Precast Septic Tanks ...G...... 540 483-5944
Callaway *(G-2220)*
Dunford G C Septic Tank Instal ...G...... 276 228-8590
Wytheville *(G-15886)*
Finly Corporation ....E...... 434 385-5028
Lynchburg *(G-7707)*
Huffman & Huffman Inc ....G...... 276 579-2373
Mouth of Wilson *(G-9093)*
Jordan Septic Tank Service ....G...... 276 395-3938
Coeburn *(G-3700)*
R R Beasley Inc ....F...... 804 529-6470
Callao *(G-2217)*
R R Beasley Inc ....E...... 804 633-9626
Milford *(G-8933)*
Turlington Sons Sptic Tank Svc ...G...... 804 642-9538
Ordinary *(G-10237)*
Vamac Incorporated ....E...... 540 535-1983
Winchester *(G-15503)*
Vamaz Inc ....G...... 434 296-8812
Charlottesville *(G-2711)*
West End Precast LLC ....G...... 276 228-5024
Wytheville *(G-15922)*
Winchester Building Sup Co Inc ....E...... 540 667-2301
Winchester *(G-15510)*
Wright Inc W F ....F...... 804 561-2721
Amelia Court House *(G-678)*

SERVICES, NEC

MB Services LLC ....G...... 703 906-8625
Alexandria *(G-524)*
Parabon Nanolabs Inc ....E...... 703 689-9689
Reston *(G-10921)*

SERVOMOTORS: Electric

Kollmorgen Corporation ....E...... 540 633-3400
Radford *(G-10723)*
Kollmorgen Corporation ....A...... 540 639-9045
Radford *(G-10720)*

SEWAGE & WATER TREATMENT EQPT

Abwasser Technologies Inc ....G...... 757 453-7505
Virginia Beach *(G-14206)*
Maurice Bynum ....G...... 757 241-0265
Windsor *(G-15606)*
Rasco Equipment Services Inc .....G...... 703 643-2952
Woodbridge *(G-15791)*
Sussex Service Authority ....G...... 804 834-8930
Waverly *(G-15089)*
The City of Radford ....F...... 540 731-3662
Radford *(G-10741)*

SEWING KITS: Novelty

Artistic Thread Designs ....G...... 703 583-3706
Woodbridge *(G-15649)*

SEWING MACHINES & PARTS: Household

Alterations Done Affordably ....G...... 540 423-2412
Culpeper *(G-3864)*

SEWING, NEEDLEWORK & PIECE GOODS STORE: Quilting Matls/Splys

Vienna Quilt Shop ....G...... 703 281-4091
Mc Lean *(G-8576)*

SEWING, NEEDLEWORK & PIECE GOODS STORES

Mary Elizabeth Burrell ....G...... 804 677-2855
Richmond *(G-11670)*

SEWING, NEEDLEWORK & PIECE GOODS STORES: Knitting Splys

Clover Yarns Inc ....C...... 434 454-7151
Clover *(G-3691)*

SEXTANTS

Sextant Solutions Group LLC ....G...... 757 797-4353
Norfolk *(G-9719)*

SHADES: Lamp & Light, Residential

Mario Industries Virginia Inc ....E...... 540 342-1111
Roanoke *(G-12132)*

SHADES: Lamp Or Candle

Jember LLC ....G...... 202 631-8521
Alexandria *(G-496)*

SHADES: Window

Akl Associates Ltd ....G...... 540 269-8228
Keezletown *(G-7026)*
Appalachian Manufacturing ....F...... 540 825-3522
Culpeper *(G-3866)*

SHAPES & PILINGS, STRUCTURAL: Steel

Cashmere Handrails Inc ....G...... 757 838-2307
Newport News *(G-9194)*
Hanover Iron & Steel Inc ....F...... 804 798-5604
Ashland *(G-1428)*
Harbor Entps Ltd Lblty Co ....G...... 229 226-0911
Stafford *(G-13150)*
Industrial Fabricators Inc ....F...... 540 989-0834
Roanoke *(G-11938)*
Stoner Steel Products ....G...... 434 973-4812
Charlottesville *(G-2697)*
West End Fabricators Inc ....G...... 804 360-2106
Oilville *(G-10187)*

SHAPES: Extruded, Aluminum, NEC

Ball Advanced Alum Tech Corp .....C...... 540 248-2703
Verona *(G-13983)*

SHAPES: Flat, Rolled, Aluminum, NEC

Ball Advanced Alum Tech Corp .....C...... 540 248-2703
Verona *(G-13983)*

SHAVING PREPARATIONS

Alpha ....G...... 540 895-5731
Partlow *(G-10263)*
Rugged Evolution Incorporated .....G...... 757 478-2430
Chesapeake *(G-3279)*

SHEET METAL SPECIALTIES, EXC STAMPED

Acoustical Sheetmetal Inc ....D...... 757 456-9720
Virginia Beach *(G-14209)*
Air Tight Duct Systems Inc ....G...... 540 361-7888
Fredericksburg *(G-5169)*
Allied Tool and Machine Co VA ......E...... 540 342-6781
Roanoke *(G-12031)*
Baker & Hazlewood ....G...... 804 798-5199
Ashland *(G-1377)*
Baker Sheet Metal Corporation .....D...... 757 853-4325
Norfolk *(G-9454)*
Cupples Products Inc ....E...... 804 717-1971
Chester *(G-3398)*
Cushing Manufacturing & Eqp Co ....E...... 804 231-1161
Richmond *(G-11038)*
Custom Metal Fabricators Inc ....F...... 804 271-6094
North Chesterfield *(G-9855)*
Flippen & Sons Inc ....G...... 804 233-1461
Richmond *(G-11592)*
Jvh Company Inc ....E...... 804 798-0888
Ashland *(G-1446)*
Mabe Dg & Assoc Inc ....G...... 804 530-1406
Chester *(G-3432)*
Metfab International Inc ....E...... 540 943-3732
Waynesboro *(G-15127)*
Paulette Fabricators Inc ....G...... 804 798-3700
Ashland *(G-1474)*
Precision Shtmtl Fbrcation LLC .....G...... 757 865-2508
Hampton *(G-6217)*
Service Metal Fabricators Inc ....D...... 757 887-3500
Williamsburg *(G-15310)*
Sheet Metal Products Inc ....F...... 757 562-1986
Franklin *(G-5155)*

Sterling Sheet Metal Inc ....G...... 540 338-0144
Sterling *(G-13516)*
Technifab of Virginia Inc ....E...... 276 988-7517
North Tazewell *(G-10109)*
Tmn LLC ....F...... 703 335-8191
Manassas *(G-8003)*
Tower Hill Corp ....E...... 703 368-7727
Manassas *(G-8005)*
TST Fabrications LLC ....F...... 757 627-9101
Norfolk *(G-9770)*
Western Sheet Metal Inc ....G...... 804 732-0230
North Dinwiddie *(G-10070)*

SHEETS & STRIPS: Aluminum

Howmet Aerospace Inc ....G...... 757 461-1360
Norfolk *(G-9583)*
Howmet Aerospace Inc ....G...... 540 343-1591
Roanoke *(G-12103)*
Universal Impact Inc ....G...... 540 885-8676
Waynesboro *(G-15141)*

SHELLAC

PPG Industries Inc ....G...... 757 494-5116
Chesapeake *(G-3243)*

SHELVING: Office & Store, Exc Wood

Tbrsp LLC ....G...... 434 315-5600
Farmville *(G-4960)*

SHIP BLDG/RPRG: Submersible Marine Robots, Manned/Unmanned

Bonze Associates LLC ....G...... 540 497-2964
Warrenton *(G-14983)*
Weda Water Inc ....G...... 757 515-4338
Virginia Beach *(G-14931)*

SHIP BUILDING & REPAIRING: Boats, Crew

Paige Sitta & Associates Inc ....E...... 757 420-5886
Chesapeake *(G-3231)*

SHIP BUILDING & REPAIRING: Cargo, Commercial

Bird Fabrication LLC ....G...... 225 614-0985
Virginia Beach *(G-14281)*
Colonnas Ship Yard Inc ....B...... 757 545-5311
Norfolk *(G-9496)*
Dominion Comfort Solutions LLC ....G...... 804 501-6429
Sandston *(G-12611)*
Mills Marine & Ship Repair LLC .....G...... 757 539-0956
Suffolk *(G-13744)*
OSG Propulsion LLC ....G...... 757 340-0052
Virginia Beach *(G-14704)*

SHIP BUILDING & REPAIRING: Combat Vessels

Huntington Ingalls Inc ....G...... 757 380-2000
Newport News *(G-9250)*
United States Dept of Navy ....A...... 757 396-8615
Portsmouth *(G-10495)*

SHIP BUILDING & REPAIRING: Fishing Vessels, Large

Chesapeake Bay Fishing Co LLC ...F...... 804 438-6050
Weems *(G-15150)*

SHIP BUILDING & REPAIRING: Landing

Huntington Ingalls Inds Inc ....F...... 757 380-2000
Newport News *(G-9253)*

SHIP BUILDING & REPAIRING: Lighters, Marine

Jonda Enterprise Inc ....G...... 757 559-5793
Norfolk *(G-9606)*

SHIP BUILDING & REPAIRING: Military

American Maritime Holdings Inc .....G...... 757 233-9055
Chesapeake *(G-2969)*
American Maritime Holdings Inc .....E...... 757 961-9311
Chesapeake *(G-2971)*
Camber Corporation ....G...... 540 720-6294
Fredericksburg *(G-5407)*

PRODUCT

Hii Unmnned Mrtime Systems Inc ......E 757 688-5672
Newport News *(G-9247)*
Huntington Ingalls Inds Inc ......F 757 380-2000
Hampton *(G-6172)*
Huntington Ingalls Inds Inc ......D 757 380-7053
Newport News *(G-9252)*
Huntington Ingalls Inds Inc ......B 757 380-2000
Newport News *(G-9254)*
ICE Tek LLC ......E 757 390-8589
Virginia Beach *(G-14539)*
Lifac Inc ......F 757 826-6051
Hampton *(G-6183)*
Marine Hydraulics Intl LLC ......D 757 545-6400
Norfolk *(G-9632)*
Metro Machine Corp ......B 757 543-6801
Norfolk *(G-9641)*
Mills Marine & Ship Repair LLC ......G 757 539-0956
Suffolk *(G-13743)*
Soc LLC ......F 757 857-6400
Norfolk *(G-9729)*
Thermcor Inc ......D 757 622-7881
Norfolk *(G-9748)*

SHIP BUILDING & REPAIRING: Offshore Sply Boats

Offshore Corporation ......G 804 526-7665
Colonial Heights *(G-3739)*
Virginia Building Services Inc ......E 757 605-0288
Virginia Beach *(G-14917)*

SHIP BUILDING & REPAIRING: Submarine Tenders

Oceaneering International Inc ......B 757 545-2200
Chesapeake *(G-3225)*
Reef Room ......G 757 592-0955
Newport News *(G-9322)*

SHIP BUILDING & REPAIRING: Tenders, Ship

Aviation & Maritime Support SE ......G 757 995-2029
Chesapeake *(G-2989)*
Lynn Donnell ......G 757 685-0263
Chesapeake *(G-3191)*

SHIP BUILDING & REPAIRING: Towboats

Back Creek Towing & Salvage ......G 757 898-5338
Seaford *(G-12672)*

SHIP BUILDING & REPAIRING: Tugboats

CFS-Kbr Mrnas Support Svcs LLC ......E 202 261-1900
Alexandria *(G-164)*

SHIPBUILDING & REPAIR

Advance Technology Inc ......D 757 223-6566
Newport News *(G-9158)*
Advanced Integrated Tech LLC ......D 757 416-7407
Norfolk *(G-9423)*
Alliance Technical Svcs Inc ......D 757 628-9500
Norfolk *(G-9435)*
Amee Bay LLC ......G 703 365-0450
Manassas *(G-8024)*
Amee Bay LLC ......D 757 217-2720
Chesapeake *(G-2963)*
American Maritime Holdings Inc ......G 757 545-4013
Chesapeake *(G-2970)*
B&B Insulation LLC ......G 757 904-0884
Virginia Beach *(G-14254)*
Bae Systems Nrfolk Ship Repr I ......A 757 494-4000
Norfolk *(G-9452)*
Bae Systems Ship Repair Inc ......A 757 494-4000
Norfolk *(G-9453)*
Bainbridge Recycling Inc ......G 757 472-4142
Chesapeake *(G-2993)*
Bath Iron Works Corporation ......F 757 855-4182
Norfolk *(G-9456)*
Bering Sea Environmental LLC ......G 757 223-1446
Newport News *(G-9177)*
Bird Fabrication LLC ......G 225 614-0985
Virginia Beach *(G-14282)*
CA Jones Inc ......G 757 595-0005
Newport News *(G-9188)*
Capps Boatworks Inc ......G 757 496-0311
Virginia Beach *(G-14317)*
Clean Way Services LLC ......E 757 606-1840
Portsmouth *(G-10408)*
Colonnas Ship Yard Inc ......A 757 545-2414
Norfolk *(G-9495)*

Colonnas Ship Yard Inc ......A 757 545-2414
Norfolk *(G-9497)*
Colonnas Shipyard ......G 757 962-0508
Norfolk *(G-9498)*
Conglobal Industries LLC ......E 757 487-5100
Chesapeake *(G-3051)*
Cova Ship Repair Inc ......F 757 390-2177
Norfolk *(G-9508)*
D W Boyd Corporation ......G 757 423-2268
Norfolk *(G-9514)*
Darr Maritime Services ......G 757 631-0022
Virginia Beach *(G-14387)*
Dlp Enterprises Inc ......E 757 420-5886
Chesapeake *(G-3068)*
Dominion Wldg Fabrication Inc ......G 757 692-2002
Virginia Beach *(G-14410)*
East Cast Repr Fabrication LLC ......C 757 455-9600
Norfolk *(G-9535)*
East Cast Repr Fabrication LLC ......D 757 455-9600
Norfolk *(G-9536)*
Ecm Maritime Services ......G 540 400-6412
Roanoke *(G-11918)*
Fairlead Boatworks Inc ......D 757 247-0101
Newport News *(G-9223)*
Fairlead Integrated LLC ......G 757 384-1957
Portsmouth *(G-10425)*
Fairlead Integrated LLC ......G 757 606-2034
Portsmouth *(G-10426)*
Fairlead Intgrted Pwr Cntrls L ......F 757 384-1957
Portsmouth *(G-10427)*
Fairlead Marine Inc ......G 757 606-2034
Portsmouth *(G-10428)*
Fairlead Prcsion Mfg Intgrtion ......G 757 384-1957
Portsmouth *(G-10429)*
General Dynamics Nassco ......G 757 215-2004
Chesapeake *(G-3117)*
Gillie Boatworks ......G 804 370-4825
Deltaville *(G-4079)*
Global Marine Services LLC ......G 757 284-9284
Virginia Beach *(G-14484)*
Global Services Intl LLC ......G 757 535-2394
Chesapeake *(G-3122)*
Helios Acquisition LLC ......D 757 545-6400
Norfolk *(G-9579)*
Huntington Ingalls Inc ......A 757 380-4982
Hampton *(G-6171)*
Huntington Ingalls Inc ......G 757 688-9832
Virginia Beach *(G-14533)*
Huntington Ingalls Inc ......F 757 440-5390
Norfolk *(G-9585)*
Huntington Ingalls Inc ......A 757 688-1411
Newport News *(G-9251)*
Interntionl Maritime SEC Corp ......G 719 494-6501
Arlington *(G-1006)*
K & E Legacy Incorporated ......G 757 328-4609
Portsmouth *(G-10450)*
Kingdom Bldrs & Ship Repr Inc ......G 757 748-1251
Virginia Beach *(G-14585)*
La Playa Incorporated Virginia ......C 757 222-1865
Chesapeake *(G-3170)*
Leslie E Willis ......G 757 484-4484
Suffolk *(G-13731)*
Locklear Group Inc ......G 757 630-9022
Virginia Beach *(G-14621)*
Lyon Shipyard Inc ......B 757 622-4661
Norfolk *(G-9625)*
Lyon Shipyard Inc ......E 757 622-4661
Norfolk *(G-9626)*
M & S Marine & Industrial Svcs ......D 757 405-9623
Portsmouth *(G-10456)*
Marcom Services Inc ......G 757 963-1851
Portsmouth *(G-10457)*
Mathomank Village Tribe ......G 757 504-5513
Claremont *(G-3624)*
McKean Defense Group LLC ......D 202 448-5250
Virginia Beach *(G-14643)*
Metro Machine Corp ......C 757 397-1039
Portsmouth *(G-10461)*
Metro Machine Corp ......C 757 392-3703
Portsmouth *(G-10462)*
MF&b Mayport Joint Venture ......G 757 222-4855
Chesapeake *(G-3204)*
Mhi Holdings LLC ......B 757 545-6400
Norfolk *(G-9642)*
MK Industries Inc ......F 757 245-0007
Newport News *(G-9302)*
Ngc International Inc ......G 703 280-2900
Falls Church *(G-4836)*
Ocean Marine LLC ......G 757 222-1306
Norfolk *(G-9671)*

Patriot IV Shipping Corp ......D 703 876-3000
Falls Church *(G-4855)*
Pierside Marine Industries ......E 757 852-9571
Norfolk *(G-9688)*
Pjl Marine Enterprise LLC ......G 757 774-1050
Chesapeake *(G-3241)*
Postal Mechanical Systems ......F 757 424-2872
Norfolk *(G-9692)*
Precision Qulty Ship Repr LLC ......G 757 322-0654
Virginia Beach *(G-14734)*
Quality Coatings Virginia Inc ......E 757 494-0801
Chesapeake *(G-3252)*
Red Eagle Industries LLC ......G 434 352-5831
Appomattox *(G-822)*
Sea Technology Ltd ......F 804 642-3568
Newport News *(G-9333)*
Semad Enterprises Inc ......G 757 424-6177
Chesapeake *(G-3290)*
Ship Sstnability Solutions LLC ......G 757 574-2436
Chesapeake *(G-3291)*
Specialty Marine Inc ......F 757 494-1199
Chesapeake *(G-3306)*
St Engineering North Amer Inc ......E 703 739-2610
Alexandria *(G-353)*
Tactical Marine Repair Inc ......G 757 967-8688
Chesapeake *(G-3319)*
Tecnico Corporation ......B 757 545-4013
Chesapeake *(G-3326)*
Tiffany Yachts Inc ......F 804 453-3464
Burgess *(G-2178)*
United States Dept of Navy ......B 757 380-4223
Newport News *(G-9369)*
Walashek Holdings Inc ......G 757 853-6007
Norfolk *(G-9789)*
Walashek Industrial & Mar Inc ......E 757 853-6007
Norfolk *(G-9790)*
Walashek Industrial & Mar Inc ......F 202 624-2880
Norfolk *(G-9791)*

SHIPPING AGENTS

Adta & Co Inc ......F 703 930-9280
Annandale *(G-728)*
Speedy Sign-A-Rama USA Inc ......G 757 838-7446
Hampton *(G-6242)*

SHOE MATERIALS: Counters

Avoid Evade Counter LLC ......G 703 593-1951
Reston *(G-10795)*
CMC Interiors LLC ......F 804 883-5671
Richmond *(G-11035)*
Counter Effects Inc ......G 804 451-9016
South Chesterfield *(G-12833)*
Custom Counter Fitters Inc ......G 757 288-4730
Virginia Beach *(G-14376)*

SHOE MATERIALS: Quarters

Tenant Temporary Quarters ......G 703 462-8623
Alexandria *(G-596)*

SHOE MATERIALS: Rands

Baggesen J Rand ......G 804 560-0490
Richmond *(G-11499)*
William K Rand III ......F 757 410-7390
Chesapeake *(G-3377)*

SHOE MATERIALS: Uppers

Upper Decks LLC ......G 804 789-0946
Mechanicsville *(G-8691)*

SHOE REPAIR SHOP

Pauls Shoe Repair & Lea ACC ......G 703 759-3735
Great Falls *(G-5971)*

SHOE STORES: Boots, Men's

Southerns M&P LLC ......G 804 330-2407
North Chesterfield *(G-9985)*

SHOE STORES: Custom & Orthopedic

Eastern Cranial Affiliates LLC ......G 703 807-5899
Fairfax *(G-4616)*

SHOE STORES: Men's

Bobs Sports Equipment Sales ......G 276 669-8066
Bristol *(G-2008)*

SHOE STORES: Women's

3mp1re Clothing Co........................G...... 540 892-3484
Richmond *(G-11073)*

SHOES & BOOTS WHOLESALERS

A G S Hanover Incorporated.................F...... 804 798-1891
Ashland *(G-1360)*
Berkley Latasha............................G...... 804 572-6394
Henrico *(G-6482)*
Reebok International Ltd....................C...... 703 490-5671
Woodbridge *(G-15793)*

SHOES: Athletic, Exc Rubber Or Plastic

A G S Hanover Incorporated.................F...... 804 798-1891
Ashland *(G-1360)*
Jkm Technologies LLC......................G...... 434 979-8600
Charlottesville *(G-2820)*
Reebok International Ltd....................C...... 703 490-5671
Woodbridge *(G-15793)*

SHOES: Canvas, Rubber Soled

Vans Inc.....................................F...... 703 442-0161
Mc Lean *(G-8574)*

SHOES: Men's

Capps Shoe Company......................C...... 434 528-3213
Gretna *(G-6005)*
Capps Shoe Company......................F...... 434 528-3213
Lynchburg *(G-7673)*
Jkm Technologies LLC......................G...... 434 979-8600
Charlottesville *(G-2820)*

SHOES: Men's, Dress

Barismil LLC................................G...... 703 622-4550
Herndon *(G-6619)*

SHOES: Plastic Or Rubber

Nike Inc.....................................E...... 703 497-4513
Woodbridge *(G-15760)*
Vans Inc.....................................G...... 757 249-0802
Newport News *(G-9372)*

SHOES: Women's

Capps Shoe Company......................F...... 434 528-3213
Lynchburg *(G-7673)*
Capps Shoe Company......................C...... 434 528-3213
Gretna *(G-6005)*
Jkm Technologies LLC......................G...... 434 979-8600
Charlottesville *(G-2820)*

SHOES: Women's, Dress

3mp1re Clothing Co........................G...... 540 892-3484
Richmond *(G-11073)*

SHOWCASES & DISPLAY FIXTURES: Office & Store

Sorbilite Inc................................G...... 757 460-7330
Hampton *(G-6241)*

SHOWER STALLS: Metal

Rain Forest Shower System LLC........G...... 804 432-8930
Henrico *(G-6554)*

SHOWER STALLS: Plastic & Fiberglass

Aquatic Co..................................B...... 434 572-1200
South Boston *(G-12748)*
Mystical Mirrors & Glass..................G...... 757 399-4682
Portsmouth *(G-10463)*

SHREDDERS: Indl & Commercial

Richard A Landes...........................G...... 540 885-1454
Staunton *(G-13285)*

SHUTTERS, DOOR & WINDOW: Metal

Opening Protection Svcs LLC.............G...... 757 222-0730
Virginia Beach *(G-14702)*
Plantation Shutter & Blind................G...... 757 241-7026
Virginia Beach *(G-14725)*
Rsshutterlee LLC...........................G...... 540 290-3712
Staunton *(G-13287)*

Shelters To Shutters.......................G...... 703 634-6130
Vienna *(G-14124)*
Shutter Films LLC..........................G...... 434 329-0713
Spout Spring *(G-12927)*
Shutterbooth...............................G...... 804 662-0471
Powhatan *(G-10575)*

SHUTTERS: Window, Wood

Jar-Tan Inc.................................G...... 757 548-6066
Chesapeake *(G-3148)*
Old South Plantation Shutters............G...... 703 968-7822
Chantilly *(G-2477)*

SIDING & STRUCTURAL MATERIALS: Wood

Batchelder & Collins Inc...................G...... 757 220-2806
Williamsburg *(G-15210)*
Builders Firstsource Inc...................D...... 540 665-0078
Winchester *(G-15397)*
Shelter2home Inc..........................G...... 540 327-4426
Winchester *(G-15476)*
Soga Inc....................................G...... 202 465-7158
Alexandria *(G-587)*

SIGN LETTERING & PAINTING SVCS

B & J Embroidery Inc......................G...... 276 646-5631
Saltville *(G-12584)*
Creations At Play LLC......................G...... 757 541-8226
Poquoson *(G-10368)*

SIGN PAINTING & LETTERING SHOP

Admiral Signworks Corp...................F...... 757 422-6700
Norfolk *(G-9422)*
Grand Designs LLC.........................G...... 412 295-7730
Centreville *(G-2308)*
Inkd Out LLC...............................G...... 757 369-9827
Newport News *(G-9259)*
J Fred Dowis...............................G...... 757 874-7446
Newport News *(G-9263)*
Norvell Signs Incorporated................G...... 804 737-2189
Richmond *(G-11696)*
Superior Signs LLC.........................E...... 804 271-5685
North Chesterfield *(G-9993)*

SIGNALS: Railroad, Electric

Diverging Approach Inc....................F...... 757 220-2316
Williamsburg *(G-15235)*

SIGNALS: Traffic Control, Electric

All Traffic Solutions Inc...................F...... 814 237-9005
Herndon *(G-6609)*
Ats-Sales LLC..............................G...... 703 631-6661
Chantilly *(G-2372)*
JQ & G Inc Company.......................G...... 540 588-7625
Roanoke *(G-11947)*
Korman Signs Inc..........................E...... 804 262-6050
Richmond *(G-11264)*
Rga LLC.....................................F...... 804 794-1592
Powhatan *(G-10571)*
Traffic Systems LLC........................F...... 703 530-9655
Manassas *(G-8170)*
Trigg Industries LLC.......................G...... 757 223-7522
Newport News *(G-9363)*

SIGNALS: Transportation

Mobotrex Inc...............................F...... 804 794-1592
Powhatan *(G-10559)*
Noahs Ark Transportation LLC............G...... 240 476-3381
Alexandria *(G-292)*
Trafficland Inc.............................F...... 703 591-1933
Fairfax *(G-4689)*
Xarmr Corporation.........................G...... 703 663-8711
Fairfax *(G-4584)*

SIGNS & ADVERTISING SPECIALTIES

7m Graphix Inc.............................G...... 703 751-6971
Fairfax *(G-4395)*
7m Graphix LLC............................G...... 703 910-0915
Woodbridge *(G-15640)*
804 Signs LLC.............................G...... 804 277-4272
Ashland *(G-1359)*
A Place Called There With Sign...........G...... 434 594-5576
Jarratt *(G-7009)*
Abe Lincoln Flags & Banners.............G...... 703 204-1116
Fairfax *(G-4399)*
Abingdon Sign Co Inc......................G...... 276 628-2594
Abingdon *(G-4)*

Absolute Signs Inc.........................G...... 540 668-6807
Hillsboro *(G-6859)*
Accent Signing Company...................G...... 757 857-8800
Norfolk *(G-9416)*
Action Graphics Signs......................G...... 757 995-2200
Virginia Beach *(G-14210)*
Acutech Signs & Graphics Inc.............G...... 757 766-2627
Hampton *(G-6070)*
Adco Signs Inc.............................G...... 757 787-1393
Onancock *(G-10188)*
Adgrfx......................................G...... 443 600-7562
Stafford *(G-13112)*
Advance Signs & Graphics Co.............G...... 703 359-8005
Fairfax *(G-4589)*
Advanced Design Fabrication..............F...... 757 484-4486
Chesapeake *(G-2954)*
Advanced Graphics LLC....................G...... 540 931-4850
Winchester *(G-15524)*
Advantage Sign Supply Inc................E...... 804 798-5784
Ashland *(G-1363)*
Advertising Spc & Promotions............G...... 540 537-4121
Hardy *(G-6285)*
Ajf Sign Placement.........................G...... 540 797-5835
Roanoke *(G-11881)*
Albemarle Signs............................G...... 434 823-1024
Crozet *(G-3828)*
All About Signs LLC........................G...... 757 934-3000
Suffolk *(G-13666)*
All Kinds of Signs..........................G...... 434 842-1877
Bremo Bluff *(G-1943)*
All Kinds of Signs Inc......................G...... 703 321-6542
Falls Church *(G-4743)*
All-Signs....................................G...... 276 632-6733
Martinsville *(G-8265)*
Allen Management Company Inc..........G...... 703 481-8858
Herndon *(G-6610)*
Alliance Signs Virginia LLC................G...... 804 530-1451
Chester *(G-3384)*
Ameri Sign Design.........................G...... 252 544-7712
Virginia Beach *(G-14224)*
American Light Works LLC.................G...... 804 332-3229
Alexandria *(G-131)*
American Sign Lnguage Svcs LLC.........G...... 571 969-2751
Alexandria *(G-411)*
Amplify Ventures LLC......................G...... 571 248-2282
Gainesville *(G-5570)*
Any and All Graphics LLC..................G...... 757 468-9600
Virginia Beach *(G-14231)*
Arcade Signs LLC..........................G...... 703 815-5440
Centreville *(G-2291)*
Art Graphics N Designs Inc................G...... 757 463-9495
Virginia Beach *(G-14243)*
Artistic Design.............................G...... 540 980-1598
Pulaski *(G-10630)*
Artwolf Signs & Graphics..................G...... 757 567-8122
Norfolk *(G-9446)*
At Sign LLC.................................G...... 703 895-7035
Haymarket *(G-6414)*
Awning & Sign Company Inc...............G...... 276 628-8069
Abingdon *(G-14)*
Ax Graphics and Sign LLC.................G...... 775 830-6115
Stanardsville *(G-13215)*
Baby Signs By Lacey.......................G...... 540 309-2551
Roanoke *(G-11883)*
Baker Builders LLC........................G...... 703 753-4904
Nokesville *(G-9389)*
Ball Peen Productions LLC.................G...... 434 293-4392
Charlottesville *(G-2735)*
Ballous Signs and Designs Inc............G...... 804 986-6635
North Chesterfield *(G-9826)*
Ballpark Signs Inc..........................G...... 540 239-7677
Radford *(G-10705)*
Bam Bams LLC.............................E...... 703 372-1940
Manassas *(G-7919)*
Banana Banner Inc.........................F...... 703 823-5933
Alexandria *(G-144)*
Banners and More.........................G...... 540 400-8485
Vinton *(G-14165)*
Bannerworks Signs & Graphics............G...... 571 292-2567
Manassas *(G-8035)*
Be Bold Sign Studio........................G...... 678 520-1029
Herndon *(G-6621)*
Beach Sign and Design.....................G...... 757 618-8653
Virginia Beach *(G-14269)*
Best Printing & Design LLC................G...... 703 593-9874
Arlington *(G-880)*
Bethany House Inc.........................G...... 703 281-9410
Vienna *(G-14015)*
Better Signs................................G...... 540 382-7446
Christiansburg *(G-3573)*

Big Fred Promotions Inc .... G 804 832-5510
Gloucester Point (G-5872)

Birckhead Signs & Graphics .... G 434 295-5962
Charlottesville (G-2740)

Bizcard Xpress .... G 757 340-4525
Virginia Beach (G-14284)

Black Forest Sign Inc .... F 540 825-0017
Culpeper (G-3873)

Blair Inc .... D 703 922-0200
Springfield (G-12964)

Botetourt Signs N Stuff .... G 540 992-3839
Troutville (G-13903)

Bow Wow Bunkies and Other Sign ...... G 757 650-0158
Virginia Beach (G-14297)

Bristol Sign Co Walden LLC .... G 276 669-0811
Bristol (G-2010)

Britemoves LLC .... F 703 629-6391
Reston (G-10812)

Broad Street Signs Inc .... G 804 262-1007
Richmond (G-11135)

Brooks Sign Company .... G 540 400-6144
Roanoke (G-12055)

Bubba Enterprises Inc .... G 703 524-0019
Arlington (G-891)

Bxi Inc .... G 804 282-5434
Richmond (G-11142)

C A S Signs .... G 804 271-7580
Chesterfield (G-3484)

C and F Promotions Inc .... G 757 912-5161
Hampton (G-6101)

Capital Designs LLC .... G 703 444-2728
Great Falls (G-5943)

Capitol Exhibit Services Inc .... E 703 330-9000
Manassas (G-8044)

Capitol Signs Inc .... G 804 749-3737
Glen Allen (G-5711)

Cdrs LLC .... G 703 451-7546
Springfield (G-12974)

Charlie Watts Signs .... G 540 291-3211
Naturl BR STA (G-9110)

Chesapeake Signs .... G 757 482-6989
Chesapeake (G-3033)

Cheshire Cat and Company Llc ...... G 540 221-2538
Waynesboro (G-15104)

Chris Ellis Signs & Airbrush .... G 434 447-8013
La Crosse (G-7142)

Christopher A Dixon .... G 276 644-4222
Abingdon (G-23)

Christopher Aiken .... G 804 693-6003
Gloucester (G-5841)

Clarke B Gray .... G 757 426-7227
Virginia Beach (G-14342)

Clearimage Creations .... G 804 883-0199
Montpelier (G-9015)

Cogitari Inc .... G 301 237-7777
Vienna (G-14029)

Commonwealth Sign & Design ...... G 804 358-5507
Richmond (G-11535)

Complete Sign Inc .... G 571 276-8407
Fairfax (G-4429)

Cr8tive Sign Works .... G 804 608-8698
Midlothian (G-8804)

Craze Signs & Graphics .... G 804 748-9233
Chesterfield (G-3488)

Crazy Customs .... G 434 222-8686
South Boston (G-12756)

Create-A-Print and Signs LLC .... G 804 920-8055
Chesterfield (G-3489)

Creation Sign LLC .... G 703 622-5958
Annandale (G-737)

Creative Designs of Virginia .... G 804 435-2382
Irvington (G-7000)

Custom Design Graphics .... G 276 466-6778
Bristol (G-1973)

Custom Engraving & Signs LLC ..... G 804 545-3961
Richmond (G-11172)

Custom Engraving and Signs LLC ...... G 804 270-1272
Henrico (G-6496)

Custom Sculpture & Sign Co .... G 860 876-7529
Nickelsville (G-9384)

Custom Signs Today .... G 703 661-0611
Sterling (G-13381)

Customtaylor33 .... G 703 785-7919
Aldie (G-105)

D & D Signs .... G 540 428-3144
Warrenton (G-14992)

D & S Construction .... G 540 718-5303
Orange (G-10209)

D & V Enterprises Inc .... G 757 665-5202
Parksley (G-10261)

D and L Signs and Services LLC ...... G 434 265-4115
Boydton (G-1914)

Daniel Rollins .... G 276 219-3988
Big Stone Gap (G-1709)

Danzo LLC .... G 703 532-8602
Arlington (G-926)

David M Tench Fine Crafte .... G 804 261-3628
Richmond (G-11179)

Dawgbone Banners & Signs .... G 804 526-5734
Chester (G-3402)

DC Design and Media Inc .... G 757 390-2818
Virginia Beach (G-14395)

Defense Holdings Inc .... G 703 334-2858
Front Royal (G-5530)

Demsign .... G 202 787-1518
Arlington (G-937)

Designer Signs .... G 757 879-1153
Wakefield (G-14965)

Designo Enterprises LLC .... F 571 437-5452
Sterling (G-13384)

Designs Inc .... G 757 410-1600
Chesapeake (G-3066)

Di-Mac Outdoors Inc .... G 434 489-3211
Danville (G-3983)

Directional Sign Services Inc .... G 703 568-5078
Springfield (G-12992)

Display & Banner Inc .... G 703 503-4447
Annandale (G-744)

Dmmt Glisan Inc .... G 276 620-0298
Max Meadows (G-8367)

Donna Cannaday .... G 540 489-7979
Rocky Mount (G-12318)

Ds Smith PLC .... G 540 774-0500
Roanoke (G-11916)

Dsh Smith LLC .... F 804 270-4003
Richmond (G-11192)

Dsigns .... G 804 559-5884
Mechanicsville (G-8619)

Dwiggins Corp .... G 757 366-0066
Chesapeake (G-3079)

Dynamic Designs .... G 540 371-7173
Fredericksburg (G-5423)

E N S Graphics LLC .... G 540 830-1776
Broadway (G-2088)

E S I .... G 540 389-5070
Salem (G-12498)

E-Z Auto Specialties .... G 540 786-8111
Fredericksburg (G-5279)

East West Ventures LLC .... G 757 603-8017
Virginia Beach (G-14429)

Eastern Shore Signs LLC .... G 757 331-4432
Cape Charles (G-2234)

Eco-Signs and Graphics .... G 336 891-1334
Bassett (G-1582)

Econo Signs .... G 540 389-5070
Salem (G-12500)

Econocolor Signs & Graphics .... G 540 946-0000
Waynesboro (G-15113)

Economy Signs .... G 757 877-5082
Newport News (G-9220)

Eddies Repair Shop Inc .... F 540 659-4835
Stafford (G-13141)

Elfinsmith Ltd Inc .... G 757 399-4788
Portsmouth (G-10421)

Ellis Signs and Custom Pntg .... G 434 584-0032
La Crosse (G-7143)

Enterprise Signs & Svc .... G 757 338-0027
Hampton (G-6142)

Epic Led .... G 540 376-7183
Fredericksburg (G-5282)

Epps Collision Cntr & Superior ...... G 434 572-4721
South Boston (G-12764)

Eric Walker .... G 804 439-2880
Midlothian (G-8814)

Eure Custom Signs Inc .... G 757 523-0000
Chesapeake (G-3094)

Ever Be Signs .... G 912 660-1436
Williamsburg (G-15240)

Exhibit Foundry .... G 540 705-0055
Harrisonburg (G-6314)

Explus Inc .... D 703 260-0780
Dulles (G-4201)

Expo Branders Corporation .... G 703 865-7581
Fairfax (G-4453)

Express Signs Inc .... G 804 796-5197
Chester (G-3415)

Fast Signs Inc .... F 540 389-6691
Salem (G-12506)

Fast Signs of Herndon .... G 703 713-0743
Herndon (G-6674)

Fastsigns .... G 703 913-5300
Springfield (G-13002)

Fastsigns .... G 703 392-7446
Manassas (G-8069)

Fastsigns .... G 571 510-0400
Leesburg (G-7272)

Fastsigns Norfolk .... G 757 274-3344
Norfolk (G-9550)

Felts Sign Co .... G 804 262-1441
Glen Allen (G-5730)

Fincham Signs .... G 540 937-4634
Culpeper (G-3892)

Fine Line Signs .... G 540 436-3626
Maurertown (G-8361)

Fine Line LLC .... G 540 436-3626
Maurertown (G-8362)

Fine Signs & Graphics Inc .... G 757 565-7833
Williamsburg (G-15244)

Firefly Sign Language Services ...... G 205 405-7043
Staunton (G-13257)

Flips Graphix Design .... G 434 237-3547
Lynchburg (G-7709)

Flynn Enterprises Inc .... E 703 444-5555
Sterling (G-13400)

Fobbs Quality Signs LLC .... G 804 714-0102
North Chesterfield (G-9878)

Fontaine Melinda .... G 757 777-2812
Virginia Beach (G-14470)

Forrlace Inc .... G 757 873-5777
Newport News (G-9232)

G&M Signs LLC .... G 540 405-3232
Nokesville (G-9392)

Garris Signs Inc .... G 804 598-1127
Powhatan (G-10545)

Garys Sign Service .... G 434 836-0248
Danville (G-3995)

Gemini Incorporated .... D 434 315-0312
Farmville (G-4942)

George Thomas Garten .... G 540 962-3633
Covington (G-3790)

Global Signs & Graphics .... G 703 543-1046
Centreville (G-2306)

Gourmet Kitchen Tools Inc .... G 757 595-3278
Yorktown (G-15962)

Grafik Trenz .... G 757 539-0141
Smithfield (G-12714)

Grandesign .... G 434 294-0665
Blackstone (G-1817)

Graphic Garage .... G 434 589-3432
Troy (G-13926)

Graphic Sign Worx LLC .... G 703 503-3286
Annandale (G-753)

Graphics North .... G 540 678-4965
Winchester (G-15546)

Graphics Shop LLC .... F 757 485-7800
Chesapeake (G-3123)

Graphtone Signs .... G 434 989-9740
Charlottesville (G-2638)

Great Neon Art & Sign Co .... G 703 981-4661
Woodbridge (G-15715)

Green Graphic Signs LLC .... G 804 229-3351
North Chesterfield (G-9881)

Gtp Ventures Incorporated .... G 804 346-8922
Richmond (G-11227)

Halifax Sign Company .... G 434 579-3304
South Boston (G-12775)

Hampton Roads Sign Inc .... G 757 871-2307
Yorktown (G-15963)

Hand Signs LLC .... G 804 482-3568
Richmond (G-11231)

Happy Yard Signs .... G 757 599-5171
Newport News (G-9245)

Harville Entps of Danville VA .... G 434 822-2106
Danville (G-3997)

Hatch Graphics .... G 540 886-2114
Staunton (G-13264)

Hereisursign LLC .... G 757 277-8487
Norfolk (G-9580)

High Hat Inc .... G 703 212-7446
Alexandria (G-229)

His Sign LLC .... G 877 886-8879
Ashburn (G-1291)

Hollywood Graphics and Signs ...... G 804 382-2199
Moseley (G-9040)

Houser Sign Works .... G 804 539-1315
Ashland (G-1436)

Howards Signs LLC .... G 804 815-8333
North (G-9803)

Hunts Creek Slate Signs LLC .... G 434 581-1687
Arvonia (G-1233)

I3 Ingenuity Inc ....G.... 703 524-0019
Arlington (G-998)

Identity Mktg Promotional LLC ....G.... 757 966-2863
Suffolk (G-13724)

Idx Corporation ....C.... 410 551-3600
Fredericksburg (G-5301)

Igor Custom Sign Stripe ....G.... 757 639-2397
Virginia Beach (G-14541)

Ilmarnock Lettering Co LLC ....G.... 804 435-6956
Kilmarnock (G-7070)

Image 360 ....G.... 804 897-8500
North Chesterfield (G-9889)

Images In Art Inc ....G.... 804 785-1011
Shacklefords (G-12682)

Imperial Sign Co ....G.... 804 541-8545
Hopewell (G-6935)

Improvements By Bill LLC ....G.... 571 246-7257
Bluemont (G-1889)

In Home Care Inc ....E.... 276 328-6462
Wise (G-15627)

Indigo Sign Co ....G.... 804 469-3233
Dewitt (G-4092)

Industries In Focus Inc ....G.... 703 451-5550
Springfield (G-13023)

Inkd Out Electrical Svc LLC ....F.... 757 369-9827
Newport News (G-9258)

Innovtive Imges Cstm Sgns More .....G.... 804 472-3882
Warsaw (G-15068)

Intellimat Inc ....G.... 540 904-5670
Roanoke (G-11942)

J & R Partners ....G.... 757 274-3344
Norfolk (G-9597)

J & R Partners ....G.... 757 499-3344
Virginia Beach (G-14556)

J Eubank Signs & Designs ....G.... 434 374-2364
Clarksville (G-3631)

Jackie Screen Printing ....G.... 276 963-0964
Richlands (G-11017)

James River Signs Inc ....G.... 757 870-3368
Newport News (G-9266)

Jbtm Enterprises Inc ....F.... 540 665-9651
Winchester (G-15551)

Jeannie Jackson Green ....G.... 540 904-6763
Roanoke (G-12110)

Joe Giles Signs Inc ....G.... 434 391-9040
Farmville (G-4944)

John W Griessmayer Jr ....G.... 540 589-8387
Roanoke (G-12113)

Joseph Randolph Pike ....G.... 804 798-7188
Ashland (G-1443)

Joshmor Pac ....G.... 276 620-6537
Wytheville (G-15893)

Justice Signs LLC ....G.... 304 898-2783
Glen Lyn (G-5833)

K L A Enterprises LLC ....G.... 540 382-9444
Christiansburg (G-3602)

K Walters At The Sign of G ....G.... 703 986-0448
Woodbridge (G-15735)

Kace Square LLC ....G.... 703 723-3679
Ashburn (G-1300)

Kaelin Signs LLC ....G.... 571 239-9192
Springfield (G-13031)

Ken Signs ....G.... 703 451-5474
Springfield (G-13032)

Kevins Signs ....G.... 540 427-1070
Roanoke (G-12117)

Key Display LLC ....G.... 434 286-4514
Scottsville (G-12662)

Kin Art Studios LLC ....G.... 804 368-7298
Ashland (G-1449)

King Signs and Graphics ....G.... 540 468-2932
Monterey (G-9009)

Kinsey Crane & Sign Company ....G.... 540 345-5063
Roanoke (G-12119)

Kinsey Sign Company ....G.... 540 344-5148
Roanoke (G-12121)

Kirby Burbank LLC ....G.... 571 330-0261
Stafford (G-13164)

Korman Signs Inc ....G.... 804 262-6050
Henrico (G-6529)

Krimm Signs LLC ....G.... 571 599-2199
Chantilly (G-2453)

Krt Architectural Signage Inc ....G.... 540 428-1080
Warrenton (G-15029)

Lai Enterprises LLC ....G.... 540 946-0000
Waynesboro (G-15120)

Larry Rosenbaum ....G.... 703 567-4052
Arlington (G-1027)

Layman Enterprises Inc ....G.... 540 662-7142
Winchester (G-15439)

Lettercraft Signs ....G.... 571 215-6900
Springfield (G-13043)

Level 7 Signs LLC ....G.... 540 885-1517
Staunton (G-13276)

Level 7 Signs and Graphics ....G.... 540 294-6690
Verona (G-13990)

Lfg Group Inc ....G.... 571 512-7446
Fairfax (G-4499)

Lighted Signs Direct Inc ....G.... 703 965-5188
Woodbridge (G-15740)

Lord Sign ....G.... 301 316-7446
Fairfax Station (G-4716)

Loudoun Signs Inc ....G.... 703 669-3333
Leesburg (G-7308)

Lynchburg Wraps ....G.... 434 385-1370
Lynchburg (G-7765)

Mekelexx Management Services ....G.... 561 644-8621
Fairfax Station (G-4717)

Michael A Latham ....G.... 804 835-3299
South Chesterfield (G-12816)

Michael Neely ....G.... 540 972-3265
Locust Grove (G-7448)

Mikes Signs4less ....G.... 540 548-2940
Fredericksburg (G-5327)

Model Sign & Graphics ....G.... 703 527-2121
Fairfax (G-4514)

Momensity LLC ....G.... 804 247-2811
Stafford (G-13177)

More Than A Sign ....G.... 540 514-3311
Winchester (G-15452)

Mountain Top Signs & Gifts ....G.... 540 430-0532
Verona (G-13992)

Neatprints LLC ....G.... 703 520-1550
Springfield (G-13057)

Neon Nights Inc ....G.... 757 248-5676
Norfolk (G-9656)

New Homes Media ....G.... 540 654-5350
Fredericksburg (G-5334)

New River Sign and Vinyl LLC ....G.... 703 793-0730
Blacksburg (G-1775)

Nhm Inc ....G.... 703 550-2233
Lorton (G-7517)

Nik Graphix LLC ....G.... 703 863-1075
Alexandria (G-543)

Noble Endeavors LLC ....G.... 571 402-7061
Woodbridge (G-15762)

Nomadic Display LLC ....G.... 800 336-5019
Lorton (G-7518)

Nova Retail LLC ....G.... 703 507-5220
Fairfax (G-4521)

Nova Rock Craft LLC ....G.... 703 217-7072
Warrenton (G-15038)

Novelty Sign Works LLC ....G.... 804 559-2009
Mechanicsville (G-8665)

Old Soul Signs LLC ....G.... 757 256-5669
Chesapeake (G-3227)

Oliver Princess ....G.... 804 683-5779
Chesterfield (G-3515)

On Our Way Inc ....G.... 703 444-0007
Dulles (G-4214)

Pac Bridge LLC ....G.... 434 385-8070
Lynchburg (G-7780)

Patricia Moore ....G.... 757 485-7414
Chesapeake (G-3234)

Payne Publishers Inc ....D.... 703 631-9033
Manassas (G-7988)

Phase II Inc ....G.... 434 333-0808
Forest (G-5087)

Pink Street Signs ....G.... 540 489-8400
Rocky Mount (G-12345)

Positive Signs LLC ....G.... 703 768-7446
Alexandria (G-553)

Potomac Signs Inc ....G.... 703 425-7000
Manassas Park (G-8206)

Printing and Sign System Inc ....G.... 703 280-1550
Fairfax (G-4532)

Promocorp Inc ....F.... 703 942-7100
Alexandria (G-560)

Propst Lettering and Engraving ....G.... 540 896-5368
Broadway (G-2093)

Pure Media Sign Studio LLC ....G.... 703 822-5468
Arlington (G-1123)

Quick Designs LLC ....G.... 540 450-0750
Winchester (G-15573)

Quick Signs Inc ....G.... 703 606-3008
Manassas (G-7992)

R & S Namebadge Inc ....G.... 804 673-2842
Glen Allen (G-5785)

Rapidsign Inc ....G.... 540 362-2025
Roanoke (G-12160)

Rebecca Burton ....G.... 804 526-3423
Colonial Heights (G-3743)

Reed Sign Co ....G.... 757 336-5505
Chincoteague (G-3563)

Richmond Corrugated Box Co ....E.... 804 222-1300
Sandston (G-12629)

River City Sign Company ....G.... 804 687-1466
Midlothian (G-8891)

Riverland Inc ....G.... 703 760-9300
Mc Lean (G-8539)

Rocks Tiki Surfboard Signs ....G.... 757 727-3330
Suffolk (G-13760)

Rockstar Wraps LLC ....G.... 703 392-7625
Manassas (G-8146)

Rva Custom Signs Inc ....G.... 804 749-4000
Rockville (G-12296)

Rva Signs & Graphic ....G.... 804 749-4000
Rockville (G-12297)

Rycon Inc ....G.... 571 313-8334
Sterling (G-13498)

S & S Mixed Signs Inc ....G.... 804 642-2641
Hayes (G-6406)

Saeam Graphics & Sign Inc ....G.... 703 203-3233
Annandale (G-780)

Sandra Signs LLC ....G.... 757 397-4321
Portsmouth (G-10477)

Scoutco LLC ....G.... 540 433-5136
Harrisonburg (G-6367)

Scoutco LLC ....G.... 540 828-0928
Bridgewater (G-1958)

Scripted Gate Sign Co LLC ....G.... 276 219-3850
Coeburn (G-3702)

Sgx Graphix ....G.... 703 330-3550
Chantilly (G-2490)

She Signs ....G.... 434 509-3173
Madison Heights (G-7884)

Sign & Engraving Technology ....F.... 804 744-7749
Midlothian (G-8899)

Sign and Seal ....G.... 540 955-2422
Berryville (G-1690)

Sign and Seal Associates LLC ....G.... 804 266-0410
Glen Allen (G-5796)

Sign Biz LLC ....G.... 804 741-7446
Henrico (G-6567)

Sign Creations ....G.... 540 809-2112
Spotsylvania (G-12915)

Sign Cy Plus Graphic & Design ....G.... 703 912-9300
Springfield (G-13085)

Sign Design Inc ....G.... 239 478-8315
Bluemont (G-1891)

Sign Design Inc ....G.... 540 338-5614
Purcellville (G-10677)

Sign Design of Va LLC ....G.... 804 794-1689
Powhatan (G-10576)

Sign Designs ....G.... 804 580-7446
Heathsville (G-6466)

Sign Designs of Powhatan Inc ....G.... 804 794-1689
Powhatan (G-10577)

Sign Dude ....G.... 757 303-7770
Yorktown (G-15990)

Sign Factory Inc ....G.... 540 772-0400
Roanoke (G-12000)

Sign Gypsies Richmondva LLC ....G.... 804 754-7345
Glen Allen (G-5797)

Sign Ink LLC ....F.... 804 250-3700
Ashland (G-1491)

Sign Language Interpreter ....G.... 540 460-4445
Staunton (G-13295)

Sign Managers ....G.... 804 878-0555
Colonial Heights (G-3747)

Sign Managers LLC ....G.... 804 381-5198
Richmond (G-11381)

Sign Medik ....G.... 757 748-1048
Virginia Beach (G-14809)

Sign of Goldfish ....G.... 540 727-0008
Culpeper (G-3920)

Sign On Line LLC ....G.... 571 246-7776
Alexandria (G-584)

Sign Right Here LLC ....G.... 757 617-0785
Virginia Beach (G-14810)

Sign Scapes Inc ....G.... 804 980-7111
Henrico (G-6568)

Sign Shop of Newport News ....G.... 757 873-1157
Newport News (G-9339)

Sign Solutions ....G.... 757 594-9688
Newport News (G-9340)

Sign Solutions ....G.... 804 691-1824
Church Road (G-3618)

Sign Source ....G.... 804 270-3252
Henrico (G-6569)

Employee Codes: A=Over 500 employees, B=251-500
C=101-250, D=51-100, E=20-50, F=10-19, G=1-9

2021 Virginia
Industrial Directory

1055

PRODUCT

Sign Studio	G	540 789-4200	
Moneta (G-8977)			
Sign Systems Inc	G	540 639-0669	
Fairlawn (G-4740)			
Sign Tech	G	757 407-3870	
Virginia Beach (G-14811)			
Sign Wise LLC	G	540 382-8343	
Pilot (G-10358)			
Sign With ME VA	G	757 969-9876	
Hampton (G-6235)			
Sign Wizards Inc	G	757 431-8886	
Virginia Beach (G-14812)			
Sign World	G	757 366-9890	
Virginia Beach (G-14814)			
Sign-N-Date Mobile Notary LLC	G	757 285-9619	
Newport News (G-9341)			
Signarama	G	804 967-3768	
Henrico (G-6570)			
Signarama	G	703 743-9424	
Purcellville (G-10678)			
Signature Signs	G	540 554-2717	
Round Hill (G-12389)			
Signd and Seald	G	814 460-2547	
Prospect (G-10614)			
Signfield Inc	G	540 574-3032	
Harrisonburg (G-6370)			
Signmakers Inc	G	757 621-1212	
Virginia Beach (G-14816)			
Signrex Inc	G	703 497-7711	
Woodbridge (G-15810)			
Signs Around You LLC	G	919 449-4762	
Stafford (G-13190)			
Signs At Work	G	804 338-7716	
North Chesterfield (G-9980)			
Signs By Clay Downing	G	703 371-6828	
Broadlands (G-2081)			
Signs By Dave	G	703 777-2870	
Leesburg (G-7348)			
Signs By James LLC	G	703 656-5067	
Triangle (G-13899)			
Signs By Randy	G	434 328-8872	
Charlottesville (G-2693)			
Signs By Tomorrow	G	703 356-3383	
Vienna (G-14127)			
Signs By Tomorrow	G	703 591-2444	
Fairfax (G-4676)			
Signs By Tomorrow	G	703 444-0007	
Sterling (G-13507)			
Signs Designs & More LLC	G	434 292-4555	
Blackstone (G-1829)			
Signs For Anything Inc	G	540 376-7006	
Spotsylvania (G-12916)			
Signs For You LLC	G	703 653-4353	
Haymarket (G-6445)			
Signs of Learning LLC	G	757 635-2735	
Virginia Beach (G-14817)			
Signs of Success Inc	G	757 481-4788	
Virginia Beach (G-14818)			
Signs On Scene	G	757 435-0841	
Virginia Beach (G-14819)			
Signs R US LLC	G	540 742-3625	
Shenandoah (G-12695)			
Signs To Go	G	757 622-7446	
Norfolk (G-9725)			
Signs Up	G	703 798-5210	
Springfield (G-13086)			
Signspot LLC	G	540 961-7768	
Blacksburg (G-1791)			
Signworks of King George	G	540 709-7483	
King George (G-7113)			
Simms Sign Co/Cash	G	804 746-0595	
Mechanicsville (G-8676)			
Simply Wood Post Signs LLC	G	757 657-9058	
Suffolk (G-13764)			
Simpson Signs	G	434 369-7389	
Altavista (G-643)			
Simurg Arts LLC	G	703 670-7230	
Woodbridge (G-15811)			
Sir Speedy Print Signs Mktg	G	540 662-3804	
Winchester (G-15587)			
Sjm Agency Inc	G	703 754-3073	
Midlothian (G-8903)			
Skyway Outdoor Inc	F	276 688-0248	
Bastian (G-1593)			
Sn Signs	G	703 354-3000	
Springfield (G-13089)			
Snyder Custom Sign Display	G	703 362-5675	
Springfield (G-13090)			
Speedpro	G	757 233-9250	
Virginia Beach (G-14837)			

Speedpro Imaging - Centreville	G	571 719-3161	
Manassas (G-8160)			
Speedy Sign-A-Rama USA Inc	G	757 838-7446	
Hampton (G-6242)			
Sprint Signs	G	804 741-7446	
Richmond (G-11396)			
St Clair Signs Inc	G	540 258-2191	
Glasgow (G-5702)			
Staab Sign Language Svcs LLC	G	301 775-2279	
Alexandria (G-354)			
Stacey A Peets	G	847 707-3112	
Henrico (G-6575)			
Stahmer Inc	G	757 838-4200	
Hampton (G-6243)			
Stefanik Sign Service	G	540 295-7248	
Fredericksburg (G-5488)			
Steve D Gilnett	G	804 746-5497	
Mechanicsville (G-8682)			
Studio B Graphics	G	703 777-8755	
Purcellville (G-10680)			
Suday Promotions Inc	G	703 376-8640	
Chantilly (G-2503)			
Sumners Scoreboards	G	804 526-7152	
Colonial Heights (G-3750)			
Sykes Signs Inc	G	276 935-2772	
Grundy (G-6041)			
T-Shirt & Screen Print Co	G	540 667-2351	
Winchester (G-15590)			
Thore Signs	G	804 513-5621	
Powhatan (G-10580)			
Thurston Sign & Graphic	G	804 285-4617	
Richmond (G-11411)			
Tidal Wave Graphics	G	757 842-6269	
Chesapeake (G-3336)			
Tidewater Graphics and Signs	G	757 622-7446	
Norfolk (G-9753)			
Tight Lines Holdings Group	G	540 989-7874	
Roanoke (G-12009)			
Tight Lines Holdings Group Inc	F	540 389-6691	
Salem (G-12573)			
Tinted Timber Sign Co	G	757 869-3231	
Yorktown (G-15996)			
Tko Promos	G	804 564-1683	
Moseley (G-9049)			
TNT GRAphics&signs	G	757 615-5936	
Chesapeake (G-3342)			
Todays Signs Inc	G	703 352-6200	
Fairfax (G-4688)			
Todd & Gloria Price	G	276 655-4047	
Elk Creek (G-4322)			
Torres Graphics and Signs Inc	G	757 873-5777	
Newport News (G-9359)			
Trexlo Enterprises LLC	F	804 719-5900	
Rockville (G-12301)			
Trexlo Enterprises LLC	G	804 272-7446	
North Chesterfield (G-10004)			
Trexlo Enterprises LLC	G	804 644-7446	
Richmond (G-11794)			
Trexlo Enterprises LLC	G	804 270-7446	
Glen Allen (G-5817)			
Trexlo Enterprises LLC	G	804 624-1977	
Chesterfield (G-3534)			
Tsg Concepts Inc	G	877 777-5734	
Arlington (G-1200)			
Type Signs LLC	G	202 355-4403	
Woodbridge (G-15825)			
Uptown Neon	G	804 358-6243	
Richmond (G-11801)			
VA Displays LLC	G	757 251-8060	
Smithfield (G-12743)			
Vance Graphics LLC	G	276 964-2822	
Pounding Mill (G-10526)			
Vanmark LLC	G	757 689-3850	
Virginia Beach (G-14906)			
Vics Signs & Engraving	G	757 562-2243	
Franklin (G-5161)			
Vinyl Visions LLC	G	540 369-5244	
King George (G-7119)			
Virginia Sign and Lighting Co	G	703 222-5670	
Manassas (G-8176)			
Vision Sign Inc	G	703 707-0858	
Sterling (G-13553)			
Vital Signs & Displays LLC	G	540 656-8303	
King George (G-7120)			
W & S Forbes Inc	G	757 498-7446	
Virginia Beach (G-14928)			
Wac Enterprises LLC	G	757 342-7202	
Williamsburg (G-15337)			
Walker Virginia	G	757 652-0430	
Newport News (G-9378)			

Wall To Wall Signs	G	703 821-2358	
Vienna (G-14155)			
Wang Sign Holdings LLC	G	757 595-3278	
Yorktown (G-16000)			
Washburn Sign Services Inc	G	540 483-5784	
Martinsville (G-8350)			
Wft Promotions LLC	G	757 560-5056	
Suffolk (G-13784)			
Whats Your Sign	G	276 632-0576	
Martinsville (G-8353)			
Whats Your Sign LLC	G	703 860-2075	
Fairfax (G-4581)			
Willie Lucas	G	919 935-8066	
Woodbridge (G-15832)			
Words On Wood Signs Inc	G	540 493-9353	
Glade Hill (G-5672)			
Worth Higgins & Associates Inc	E	804 353-0607	
Richmond (G-11457)			
Worth Higgins & Associates Inc	E	804 353-0607	
Richmond (G-11458)			
Wright Sign Service Inc	F	757 566-8329	
Toano (G-13881)			
Wyatt Sign & Painting Company	G	804 733-5251	
Petersburg (G-10352)			
Xtreme Signs	G	434 447-5738	
Brodnax (G-2106)			
Yesco of Richmond	G	804 302-4391	
Midlothian (G-8926)			
Yesco Sign & Lighting Service	G	757 369-9827	
Newport News (G-9383)			
Your Life Uncorked	G	757 218-8495	
Hampton (G-6274)			
Zingify LLC	G	703 689-3636	
Herndon (G-6848)			

SIGNS & ADVERTISING SPECIALTIES: Artwork, Advertising

22 Church LLC	G	540 342-2817	
Roanoke (G-12026)			
Illusions Wrap LLC	G	540 710-9727	
Fredericksburg (G-5302)			
Poolhouse Digital Agency LLC	G	804 876-0335	
Richmond (G-11718)			

SIGNS & ADVERTISING SPECIALTIES: Displays, Paint Process

Preston Signs Inc	G	703 534-3777	
Vienna (G-14113)			

SIGNS & ADVERTISING SPECIALTIES: Letters For Signs, Metal

Grand Designs LLC	G	412 295-7730	
Centreville (G-2308)			
Inkd Out LLC	G	757 369-9827	
Newport News (G-9259)			
Joeys Sign & Letter Inc	G	757 868-7166	
Hampton (G-6276)			
Kisco Signs LLC	G	804 404-2727	
Richmond (G-11646)			
Miller Creative Solutions LLC	G	202 560-3718	
Falls Church (G-4831)			
Rain & Associates LLC	G	757 572-3996	
Virginia Beach (G-14758)			
Worthington Millwork LLC	G	540 832-6391	
Gordonsville (G-5919)			

SIGNS & ADVERTISING SPECIALTIES: Novelties

Falcon Lab Inc	G	703 442-0124	
Mc Lean (G-8426)			
Hip-Hop Spot 24/7 LLC	G	434 660-3166	
Lynchburg (G-7734)			
Ice Scraper Card Inc	G	703 327-4622	
Leesburg (G-7286)			
Youve Got It Made LLC	G	410 840-8744	
Harrisonburg (G-6388)			

SIGNS & ADVERTISING SPECIALTIES: Signs

Acorn Sign Graphics Inc	E	804 726-6999	
Richmond (G-11082)			
Action Forbes and Signs Inc	G	757 548-5255	
Chesapeake (G-2953)			
Allgood Promotional Cons	G	434 793-6178	
Danville (G-3953)			
Als Custom Signs	G	804 224-7105	
Colonial Beach (G-3720)			

(G-0000) Company's Geographic Section entry number

Als Sign Shop....G....540 465-3103
Strasburg *(G-13571)*
and Design Inc....G....703 913-0799
Springfield *(G-12948)*
Aplus Signs and Bus Svcs LLC....F....540 667-8010
Winchester *(G-15529)*
Architectural Graphics Inc....C....800 877-7868
Virginia Beach *(G-14236)*
Architectural Graphics Inc....C....757 427-1900
Virginia Beach *(G-14237)*
Architectural Graphics Inc....C....757 301-7008
Virginia Beach *(G-14238)*
Banner Sings Etc....G....703 698-5466
Fairfax *(G-4418)*
Blue Ridge Sign & Stamp Co Inc....F....540 777-5456
Roanoke *(G-11892)*
Chalison Inc....G....757 258-2520
Williamsburg *(G-15218)*
Coastal Safety Inc....G....757 499-9415
Virginia Beach *(G-14347)*
Cottle Multi Media Inc....G....434 263-5447
Lynch Station *(G-7627)*
Creations At Play LLC....G....757 541-8226
Poquoson *(G-10368)*
Creative Signs Ltd....G....540 899-0032
Fredericksburg *(G-5416)*
Custom Sign Shop LLC....G....804 353-2768
Richmond *(G-11175)*
D & G Signs Inc....G....757 858-2140
Norfolk *(G-9513)*
Designs Inc....G....757 547-5478
Chesapeake *(G-3065)*
Edwards Eddie Signs Inc....G....540 434-8589
Harrisonburg *(G-6312)*
Fellers Inc....G....757 853-1363
Norfolk *(G-9551)*
Fiber Sign....G....276 669-9115
Bristol *(G-1978)*
Frf Inc....E....434 974-7900
Charlottesville *(G-2636)*
Genesis Sign....G....540 288-8820
Stafford *(G-13146)*
Harrington Graphics Co Inc....G....757 363-1600
Virginia Beach *(G-14507)*
Hjs Qwik Signs....G....276 386-2696
Gate City *(G-5663)*
I H McBride Sign Company Inc....F....434 847-4151
Madison Heights *(G-7875)*
Imagine This Company....F....804 232-1300
Richmond *(G-11614)*
J B Worsham....G....434 836-9313
Danville *(G-4005)*
K Hart Holding Inc....G....800 294-5348
Norfolk *(G-9610)*
Korman Signs Inc....E....804 262-6050
Richmond *(G-11264)*
Kwik Signs Inc....G....804 897-5945
North Chesterfield *(G-9910)*
Letter Perfect Incorporated....F....540 652-2022
Elkton *(G-4331)*
Lynch Products....G....540 483-7800
Rocky Mount *(G-12337)*
M&M Signs and Graphics LLC....G....703 803-1043
Chantilly *(G-2460)*
Metro Signs & Graphics Inc....G....804 747-1918
Richmond *(G-11289)*
Modern Engravings LLC....G....757 876-3001
Gloucester *(G-5855)*
Muddy Feet LLC....G....540 830-0342
Harrisonburg *(G-6349)*
New Home Media....C....703 550-2233
Lorton *(G-7515)*
Nva Signs & Striping LLC....G....703 263-1940
Manassas *(G-7983)*
Old Town Sign Co Inc....G....703 836-7000
Alexandria *(G-299)*
Powers Signs Incorporated....F....434 793-6351
Danville *(G-4031)*
Prime Signs....G....757 481-7889
Virginia Beach *(G-14738)*
Quail Run Signs....G....540 338-8412
Hamilton *(G-6064)*
Richardson Enterprises Inc....G....804 733-8956
North Dinwiddie *(G-10063)*
Sav On Signs....G....540 344-8406
Vinton *(G-14182)*
Scottys Sign Inc....F....757 245-7129
Newport News *(G-9332)*
Shenandoah Signs Promotions....G....540 886-2114
Staunton *(G-13293)*
Sign Broker LLC....G....703 263-7227
Chantilly *(G-2491)*
Sign Builders....G....757 499-2654
Virginia Beach *(G-14808)*
Sign Crafters Inc....G....804 379-2004
Midlothian *(G-8900)*
Sign Creations LLC....G....540 899-9555
Fredericksburg *(G-5223)*
Sign Design of Roanoke Inc....G....540 977-3354
Roanoke *(G-12187)*
Sign Express Inc....G....757 686-3010
Portsmouth *(G-10482)*
Sign Master....G....540 886-6900
Fishersville *(G-5008)*
Signsations LLC....G....571 340-3330
Fairfax *(G-4677)*
Sml Signs & More LLC....G....540 719-7446
Moneta *(G-8979)*
Stans Signs Inc....G....540 434-1531
Rockingham *(G-12278)*
Steves Signworx LLC....G....434 385-1000
Forest *(G-5097)*
Sun Signs....G....703 867-9831
Stafford *(G-13197)*
Superior Signs LLC....E....804 271-5685
North Chesterfield *(G-9993)*
Virginia Custom Signs Corp....G....804 278-8788
Richmond *(G-11439)*

SIGNS & ADVERTSG SPECIALTIES: Displays/Cutouts Window/Lobby

Eggleston Minor....G....757 819-4958
Norfolk *(G-9542)*
General Display Company LLC....G....703 335-9292
Manassas *(G-7943)*
Graham Graphics LLC....G....703 220-4564
Springfield *(G-13013)*
Manny Exhibits & Woodcraft....G....703 354-9231
Annandale *(G-770)*
MCS Design & Production Inc....G....804 550-1000
Ashland *(G-1462)*
Signature Dsgns Fbrication LLC....G....571 398-2444
Woodbridge *(G-15809)*

SIGNS, ELECTRICAL: Wholesalers

Sun Signs....G....703 867-9831
Stafford *(G-13197)*

SIGNS, EXC ELECTRIC, WHOLESALE

Printing and Sign System Inc....G....703 280-1550
Fairfax *(G-4532)*

SIGNS: Electrical

1st Signage and Lighting LLC....G....276 229-4200
Woolwine *(G-15863)*
Absolute Signs Inc....G....703 229-9436
Manassas *(G-8018)*
Ad Vice Inc....G....804 730-0503
Mechanicsville *(G-8600)*
All Traffic Solutions Inc....F....814 237-9005
Herndon *(G-6609)*
American Made Signs LLC....G....434 971-7446
Charlottesville *(G-2727)*
Brooks Gray Sign Company....F....804 233-4343
Richmond *(G-11510)*
Burruss Signs Inc....G....434 296-6654
Charlottesville *(G-2751)*
Creative Sign Builders LLC....G....757 622-5591
Norfolk *(G-9509)*
Everbrite LLC....C....540 261-2121
Buena Vista *(G-2143)*
Fine Signs....G....757 565-7833
Williamsburg *(G-15243)*
Hanna Sign Co....G....540 636-4877
Front Royal *(G-5535)*
Identity America Inc....G....276 322-2616
Bluefield *(G-1864)*
Image Works Inc....E....804 798-5533
Ashland *(G-1438)*
Indigo Signs LLC....G....540 489-8400
Rocky Mount *(G-12328)*
J Fred Dowis....G....757 874-7446
Newport News *(G-9263)*
Jarvis Sign Company....G....804 514-9879
Richmond *(G-11253)*
Jerrys Signs Inc....F....276 676-2304
Abingdon *(G-44)*
Jones Sign Co Inc....E....804 798-5533
Ashland *(G-1442)*
Jv-Rm Holdings Inc....G....703 669-3333
Leesburg *(G-7293)*
K & K Signs....G....540 586-0542
Bedford *(G-1641)*
Martins Custom Designs Inc....G....804 642-0235
Gloucester Point *(G-5874)*
Martins Custom Designs Inc....F....757 245-7129
Newport News *(G-9291)*
McMj Enterprises LLC....G....434 298-0117
Blackstone *(G-1820)*
Metro Sign & Design Inc....E....703 631-1866
Manassas Park *(G-8205)*
Moore Sign Corporation....E....804 748-5836
Chester *(G-3438)*
Performance Signs LLC....F....434 985-7446
Ruckersville *(G-12408)*
Rabbit Creek Partners LLC....D....877 779-9977
Bluefield *(G-1877)*
Safehouse Signs Inc....E....540 366-2480
Roanoke *(G-12174)*
Sign Doctor Sales & Service....G....540 743-5200
Luray *(G-7623)*
Sign Enterprise Inc....G....540 899-9555
Fredericksburg *(G-5224)*
Sign Graphx Inc....F....703 335-7446
Manassas *(G-8000)*
Sign Shop....F....703 590-9534
Woodbridge *(G-15808)*
Signmedia Inc....E....757 826-7128
Hampton *(G-6237)*
Signmedic LLC....G....703 919-3381
Triangle *(G-13898)*
Signs Unlimited Inc....F....703 799-8840
Alexandria *(G-585)*
Signs Work....G....276 655-4047
Elk Creek *(G-4321)*
Talley Sign Company....F....804 649-0325
Richmond *(G-11781)*
Titan Sign Corporation....G....540 899-5334
Fredericksburg *(G-5379)*
Twelve Inc....G....804 232-1300
Richmond *(G-11796)*
Vertex Signs....G....540 904-5776
Roanoke *(G-12018)*

SIGNS: Neon

Admiral Signworks Corp....F....757 422-6700
Norfolk *(G-9422)*
Badger Neon & Sign....G....540 761-5779
Roanoke *(G-12041)*
Dowling Signs Inc....E....540 373-6675
Fredericksburg *(G-5183)*
Kinsey Neon & Sign Company....G....540 345-5063
Roanoke *(G-12120)*
Neon Nights....G....757 857-6366
Norfolk *(G-9655)*
Norvell Signs Incorporated....G....804 737-2189
Richmond *(G-11696)*
Nothing But Neon....G....434 842-9395
Columbia *(G-3753)*
Sign Works Inc....G....757 428-2525
Virginia Beach *(G-14813)*
Signs USA Inc....G....540 432-6366
Harrisonburg *(G-6371)*
W W Burton....G....540 547-4668
Reva *(G-11003)*

SILICA MINING

Covia Holdings Corporation....E....540 858-3444
Gore *(G-5921)*

SILICONES

MTI Specialty Silicones Inc....G....540 254-2020
Buchanan *(G-2122)*

SILK SCREEN DESIGN SVCS

Preston Signs Inc....G....703 534-3777
Vienna *(G-14113)*
Stitchworks Inc....G....757 631-0300
Virginia Beach *(G-14851)*

SILLS, WINDOW: Cast Stone

Nova Exteriors Inc....F....703 322-1500
Alexandria *(G-544)*

PRODUCT

Employee Codes: A=Over 500 employees, B=251-500
C=101-250, D=51-100, E=20-50, F=10-19, G=1-9
2021 Virginia
Industrial Directory
1057

SILOS & COMPONENTS: Missile, Metal Plate

Entwistle Company ....E 434 799-6186
  Danville *(G-3992)*
Falck Schmidt Def Systems Corp ....G 805 689-1739
  Lorton *(G-7487)*

SILVERSMITHS

Hand and Hammer Inc ....F 703 491-4866
  Woodbridge *(G-15721)*

SILVERWARE

Dining With Dignity Inc ....G 757 565-2452
  Williamsburg *(G-15233)*

SILVERWARE & PLATED WARE

AMG International Inc ....G 703 988-4741
  Alexandria *(G-412)*
Smith and Flannery ....G 804 794-4979
  Williamsburg *(G-15313)*

SILVERWARE, STERLING SILVER

Otero Kucbel Enterprises Inc ....G 703 734-0209
  Mc Lean *(G-8521)*

SIMULATORS: Electronic Countermeasure

Nhance Technologies Inc ....F 434 582-6110
  Lynchburg *(G-7776)*

SIMULATORS: Flight

Advanced Graphics Tech Llc ....G 804 796-3399
  Chesterfield *(G-3473)*
Advanced Leading Solutions Inc ....G 703 447-3876
  Centreville *(G-2289)*
Aero Training Center ....G 757 838-6570
  Hampton *(G-6074)*
Lockheed Martin Corporation ....C 703 367-2121
  Manassas *(G-7966)*
Strdefense LLC ....G 703 460-9000
  Fairfax *(G-4562)*
Vigilent Inc ....G 202 550-9515
  Alexandria *(G-374)*

SIRENS: Vehicle, Marine, Indl & Warning

Northrop Grumman Sperry ....G 434 974-2000
  Charlottesville *(G-2665)*

SIZES

Energize Your Size LLC ....G 703 360-1093
  Alexandria *(G-457)*

SKIDS: Wood

Don Elthon ....G 703 237-2521
  Falls Church *(G-4908)*

SLAB & TILE: Precast Concrete, Floor

Ace Hardwood ....G 804 270-4260
  Richmond *(G-11080)*

SLAUGHTERING & MEAT PACKING

Foods For Thought Inc ....G 434 242-4996
  Orange *(G-10213)*
Melrose Bison Farm ....G 434 660-6036
  Gladys *(G-5695)*
Tribbetts Meats ....G 540 427-4671
  Roanoke *(G-12210)*

SLIDES & EXHIBITS: Prepared

Trial Exhibits Inc ....G 804 672-0880
  Henrico *(G-6585)*

SLOT MACHINES

Brights Antique Slot Machine ....G 703 906-8389
  Alexandria *(G-426)*

SMOKE DETECTORS

American Safety & Health ....G 434 977-2700
  Charlottesville *(G-2728)*
Smoke Detector Inspector ....G 757 870-4772
  Virginia Beach *(G-14828)*

SMOKERS' SPLYS, WHOLESALE

General Cigar Co Inc ....A 860 602-3500
  Glen Allen *(G-5735)*

SNACK & NONALCOHOLIC BEVERAGE BARS

Moothru LLC ....G 540 439-6455
  Remington *(G-10770)*

SNOW PLOWING SVCS

E Trucking & Services LLC ....G 571 241-0856
  Warrenton *(G-15000)*
Eliene Trucking LLC ....G 571 721-0735
  Centreville *(G-2304)*

SNOW REMOVAL EQPT: Residential

Mark T Goodman ....G 540 582-2328
  Partlow *(G-10267)*
Robert C Reed ....G 804 493-7297
  Montross *(G-9027)*

SNOWMOBILES

Samuel Ross ....G 434 531-9219
  Bremo Bluff *(G-1946)*

SOAPS & DETERGENTS

B & B Boutique ....G 703 425-8256
  Burke *(G-2181)*
Bahashem Soap Company LLC ....G 804 398-0982
  Richmond *(G-11500)*
Bath Sensations LLC ....G 804 832-4701
  Chesterfield *(G-3478)*
Bejoi LLC ....G 804 319-7369
  Midlothian *(G-8779)*
Chem Core Inc ....G 540 862-2600
  Covington *(G-3781)*
Chem Station of Virginia ....G 804 236-0090
  Richmond *(G-11154)*
Chemtron Inc ....G 703 550-7772
  Lorton *(G-7472)*
Copper Fox Distillery ....F 757 903-2076
  Williamsburg *(G-15222)*
Cumberland Company LP ....G 434 392-9911
  Farmville *(G-4938)*
Daily Scrub LLC ....G 804 519-3696
  Disputanta *(G-4106)*
Ethyl Corporation ....G 804 788-5000
  Richmond *(G-11580)*
Heathers Handcrafted Soaps ....G 757 277-8569
  Virginia Beach *(G-14514)*
Julphia Soapworks ....G 703 815-8020
  Centreville *(G-2312)*
Laundry Chemical Products Inc ....G 757 363-0662
  Virginia Beach *(G-14602)*
Nevins & Moss LLC ....G 929 266-3640
  Great Falls *(G-5968)*
Newmarket Corporation ....D 804 788-5000
  Richmond *(G-11689)*
Rebecca Ortizsanchez ....G 315 532-4439
  Portsmouth *(G-10475)*
Rockbridge East LLC ....G 202 701-7927
  Woodbridge *(G-15798)*
Serene Suds LLC ....G 804 433-8032
  Richmond *(G-11377)*
Shantaras Soaps ....G 434 221-2382
  Brookneal *(G-2113)*
Simplicity Pure Bath & Bdy LLC ....G 540 922-9287
  Pearisburg *(G-10277)*
Soaplight LLC ....G 518 898-3441
  Hampton *(G-6240)*
Tamara Smith ....G 910 495-4404
  Gore *(G-5923)*
Theodore Turpin ....G 434 485-6600
  Lynchburg *(G-7823)*
Todo Blu LLC ....G 703 944-9000
  Annandale *(G-788)*

SOAPS & DETERGENTS: Textile

Aero Clean Technologies LLC ....G 434 381-0699
  Lynchburg *(G-7635)*
Aziza Beauty LLC ....G 804 525-9989
  Richmond *(G-11496)*
Beatrice Aurthur ....G 347 420-5612
  South Chesterfield *(G-12831)*
Dream It & Do It LLC ....G 804 379-5474
  Midlothian *(G-8811)*

Omniio LLC ....F 877 842-5478
  Virginia Beach *(G-14695)*

SOAPSTONE MINING

Soapstone Inc ....G 540 745-3492
  Floyd *(G-5040)*

SOCIAL SERVICES, NEC

Northwestern PA Opt Clinic ....G 540 721-6017
  Moneta *(G-8973)*

SOCKETS: Electric

Shore Holders ....F 434 542-4105
  Phenix *(G-10355)*

SOFT DRINKS WHOLESALERS

Pepsi-Cola Metro Btlg Co Inc ....D 434 528-5107
  Lynchburg *(G-7785)*
Pepsi-Cola Metro Btlg Co Inc ....C 540 966-5200
  Roanoke *(G-11984)*

SOFTWARE PUBLISHERS: Application

3r Behavioral Solutions Inc ....G 571 332-6232
  Alexandria *(G-396)*
4c North America Inc ....G 540 850-8470
  Mc Lean *(G-8383)*
80protons LLC ....G 571 215-5453
  Virginia Beach *(G-14198)*
Acharya Brothers Computing ....G 703 729-3035
  Ashburn *(G-1237)*
Acintyo Inc ....G 703 349-3400
  Mc Lean *(G-8384)*
Adme Solutions LLC ....G 540 664-3521
  Stephens City *(G-13311)*
Aetas Mobile LLC ....G 704 258-9159
  Oakton *(G-10140)*
Agaram Technologies Inc ....D 703 297-8591
  Ashburn *(G-1239)*
Ai Machines Inc ....G 973 204-9772
  Fairfax *(G-4403)*
Amogh Consultants Inc ....G 469 867-1583
  Herndon *(G-6612)*
Andromeda3 Inc ....G 240 246-5816
  Great Falls *(G-5937)*
Annoai Inc ....G 571 490-5316
  Reston *(G-10789)*
Antheon Solutions Inc ....G 703 298-1891
  Reston *(G-10790)*
Apex Mobile App LLC ....G 804 245-0471
  Midlothian *(G-8773)*
Appfore LLC ....G 757 597-6990
  Virginia Beach *(G-14232)*
Application Technologies Inc ....G 703 644-0506
  Springfield *(G-12949)*
Applied Visual Sciences Inc ....G 703 539-6190
  Leesburg *(G-7220)*
Arctan Inc ....G 202 379-4723
  Arlington *(G-855)*
Aretec Inc ....E 703 539-8801
  Fairfax *(G-4596)*
Athena Services LLC ....G 201 232-9114
  Falls Church *(G-4751)*
Athenas Workshop Inc ....G 703 615-4429
  Reston *(G-10794)*
Averia Health Solutions LLC ....G 703 716-0791
  Oakton *(G-10141)*
B & L Biotech Usa Inc ....G 703 272-7507
  Fairfax *(G-4597)*
Be There Do Good LLC ....G 703 851-5293
  Vienna *(G-14014)*
Boardeffect LLC ....E 866 672-2666
  Arlington *(G-887)*
Brbg LLC ....G 404 200-4857
  Springfield *(G-12969)*
Bright Elm LLC ....G 804 519-3331
  Sandy Hook *(G-12644)*
Bright Solutions Inc ....G 703 926-7451
  Ashburn *(G-1252)*
Ca Inc ....B 800 225-5224
  Herndon *(G-6632)*
Caligo LLC ....G 914 819-8530
  Vienna *(G-14020)*
Cambrio Studios LLC ....G 540 908-5129
  Charlottesville *(G-2755)*
Canvas Solutions Inc ....G 703 436-8069
  Reston *(G-10816)*
Caper Holdings LLC ....G 757 563-3810
  Virginia Beach *(G-14315)*

Capital Software Corporation	G	703 404-3000
Chantilly *(G-2528)*		
Cardinal Applications LLC	G	540 270-4369
Amissville *(G-717)*		
Clarivate Analytics (us) LLC	D	434 817-2000
Charlottesville *(G-2609)*		
Cloud Ridge Labs LLC	G	434 477-5060
Forest *(G-5060)*		
Co Construct LLC	G	434 326-0500
Crozet *(G-3829)*		
Cognition Point Inc	G	703 402-8945
Aldie *(G-104)*		
Collier Research and Dev Corp	F	757 825-0000
Newport News *(G-9203)*		
Commonlook	G	202 902-0986
Arlington *(G-916)*		
Concilio Labs Inc	G	571 282-4248
Mc Lean *(G-8408)*		
Congero Technology Group Inc	E	434 266-4376
Reston *(G-10825)*		
Connectus Inc	G	703 560-7777
Falls Church *(G-4777)*		
Contactengine Inc	G	571 348-3220
Mc Lean *(G-8409)*		
Coop Systems Inc	E	703 581-6364
Herndon *(G-6645)*		
Cougarbearbobcat LLC	G	804 690-8006
Richmond *(G-11543)*		
Cunning Running Software Inc	G	703 926-5864
Mineral *(G-8945)*		
Curious Compass LLC	G	540 735-5013
Fredericksburg *(G-5182)*		
Custom Sftwr Dsgn Sltions LLC	G	888 423-4049
Fredericksburg *(G-5417)*		
Data Fusion Solutions Inc	G	877 326-0034
Fredericksburg *(G-5271)*		
Decade Five LLC	G	434 984-3065
Charlottesville *(G-2615)*		
Designer Software Inc	G	540 842-8425
Fredericksburg *(G-5272)*		
Diamondefense LLC	F	571 321-2012
Annandale *(G-743)*		
Diehappy LLC	G	804 283-6025
Glen Allen *(G-5723)*		
Digital Synergy LLC	G	540 951-5900
Blacksburg *(G-1732)*		
Divvy Cloud Corporation	F	571 290-5077
Arlington *(G-940)*		
Doucraft Services	G	703 620-4965
Oakton *(G-10144)*		
Driving 4 Dollars	G	757 609-1298
Henrico *(G-6503)*		
Educational Options Inc	G	480 777-7720
Falls Church *(G-4909)*		
Educren Inc	G	804 410-4305
Glen Allen *(G-5728)*		
Elo Inc	G	571 435-0129
Woodbridge *(G-15690)*		
Envitia Inc	G	703 871-5255
Reston *(G-10848)*		
Erp Cloud Technologies LLC	G	727 723-0801
Herndon *(G-6668)*		
Eventdone LLC	G	703 239-6410
Woodbridge *(G-15699)*		
Ezara Inc	G	434 409-4232
Earlysville *(G-4289)*		
Ezl Software Inc	G	804 288-0748
Richmond *(G-11207)*		
Flexprotect LLC	G	703 957-8648
Reston *(G-10853)*		
Forescout Gvrnment Sltions LLC	E	408 538-0946
Tysons *(G-13945)*		
Freestyle King LLC	G	703 309-1144
Woodbridge *(G-15707)*		
Fta Goverment Services Inc	G	571 612-0413
Chantilly *(G-2423)*		
Genesis Infosolutions Inc	G	703 835-4469
Herndon *(G-6682)*		
Get Aura Inc	G	703 801-4382
Herndon *(G-6683)*		
Giant Software LLC	G	540 292-6232
Charlottesville *(G-2803)*		
Glonet Incorporated	G	571 499-5000
Alexandria *(G-219)*		
Gomatters LLC	G	757 819-4950
Virginia Beach *(G-14487)*		
Goon Squad Apps LLC	G	706 410-6139
Norfolk *(G-9564)*		
Green Physics Corporation	G	703 989-6706
Manassas *(G-7949)*		

Grektek LLC	G	202 607-4734
Herndon *(G-6692)*		
Grey Market Labs Pbc	G	929 274-4465
Falls Church *(G-4800)*		
Guppy Group Inc	G	917 544-9749
Fairfax *(G-4471)*		
Henry Shaw	E	844 621-2158
Alexandria *(G-228)*		
Heytopia LLC	G	703 794-3082
Mc Lean *(G-8458)*		
Hkl Research Inc	G	434 979-6382
Charlottesville *(G-2809)*		
Huespace Inc	G	540 406-0496
Arlington *(G-995)*		
Iconicloud Inc	G	703 864-1203
Alexandria *(G-481)*		
Ikanow LLC	E	619 884-4434
Reston *(G-10868)*		
Impact Junkie LLC	G	916 541-0317
Woodbridge *(G-15726)*		
Incident Logic LLC	G	540 349-8888
Warrenton *(G-15026)*		
Infinite Studio LLC	G	864 293-4522
Charlottesville *(G-2646)*		
Infomtion Tech Applcations LLC	G	757 603-3551
Williamsburg *(G-15257)*		
Inforce Group LLC	G	703 788-6835
Herndon *(G-6709)*		
Information Analysis Inc	E	703 383-3000
Fairfax *(G-4633)*		
Infrawhite Technologies LLC	G	662 902-0376
Vienna *(G-14071)*		
Innovative Dynamic Solutions	G	703 234-5282
Herndon *(G-6710)*		
Inovitech LLC	G	877 429-0377
Leesburg *(G-7287)*		
Inquisient Inc	F	888 230-2181
Warrenton *(G-15027)*		
Institute For Complexity MGT	G	540 645-1050
Stafford *(G-13154)*		
Intelligent Bus Platforms LLC	E	202 640-8868
Reston *(G-10876)*		
Intor Inc	G	757 296-2175
Alexandria *(G-240)*		
Invision Inc	F	703 774-3881
Manassas *(G-8086)*		
Irontek LLC	G	703 627-0092
Sterling *(G-13432)*		
K12excellence Inc	G	804 270-9600
Glen Allen *(G-5759)*		
Kindred Brothers Inc	G	803 318-5097
Richmond *(G-11262)*		
Kinemetrx Incorporated	G	703 596-5095
Herndon *(G-6723)*		
Kinetech Labs Inc	G	434 284-1073
Zion Crossroads *(G-16008)*		
Km Data Strategists LLC	G	703 689-1087
Aldie *(G-108)*		
Kngro LLC	G	202 390-9126
Springfield *(G-13034)*		
Kodescraft LLC	G	703 843-3700
Triangle *(G-13895)*		
Koloza LLC	G	301 204-9864
Fairfax *(G-4492)*		
Kryptowire LLC	G	571 314-0153
Fairfax *(G-4494)*		
Kwick Help LLC	G	703 499-7223
Herndon *(G-6726)*		
Lamaid LLC	G	703 541-8011
Woodbridge *(G-15738)*		
Lesson Portal LLC	G	540 455-3546
Spotsylvania *(G-12901)*		
Level Up Fun Corporation	G	703 365-8071
Manassas *(G-7963)*		
Light Music LLC	G	914 316-7948
Charlottesville *(G-2824)*		
Lighthouse Software Inc	G	703 327-7650
Sandy Hook *(G-2543)*		
Littleshot Apps LLC	G	908 433-5727
Arlington *(G-1038)*		
Livesafe Inc	E	571 312-4645
Arlington *(G-1039)*		
Living Solutions Mid Atlantic	G	202 460-9919
Alexandria *(G-518)*		
Loci LLC	G	301 613-7111
Sterling *(G-13444)*		
Loyalty Doctors LLC	G	757 675-8283
Norfolk *(G-9623)*		
Madgar Enterprises LLC	G	540 760-6946
North Chesterfield *(G-9917)*		

Magnet Forensics Usa Inc	G	519 342-0195
Herndon *(G-6740)*		
Magoozle LLC	G	757 581-6936
Virginia Beach *(G-14634)*		
Master Business Solutions Inc	G	804 378-5470
North Chesterfield *(G-9926)*		
Match My Value Inc	G	301 456-4308
Richmond *(G-11672)*		
MCA Systems Inc	G	540 684-1617
Fredericksburg *(G-5204)*		
Medliminal LLC	F	571 719-6837
Manassas *(G-7974)*		
Megawatt Apps LLC	G	703 870-4082
Sterling *(G-13452)*		
Microsoft Corporation	E	434 738-0103
Boydton *(G-1916)*		
Microsoft Corporation	A	703 236-9140
Arlington *(G-1064)*		
Microsoft Corporation	D	571 222-8110
Bristow *(G-2060)*		
Microsoft Corporation	A	703 673-7600
Reston *(G-10901)*		
Microsoft Corporation	D	804 270-0146
Glen Allen *(G-5770)*		
Mintmesh Inc	G	703 222-0322
Fairfax *(G-4512)*		
Mission Secure Inc	G	434 284-8071
Charlottesville *(G-2836)*		
Missionteq LLC	G	703 563-0699
Chantilly *(G-2545)*		
Montuno Software Inc	G	703 554-7505
Brambleton *(G-1931)*		
MPH Development LLC	G	703 303-4838
Gainesville *(G-5599)*		
Nabiday LLC	G	703 625-8679
Fairfax *(G-4656)*		
Nasotech LLC	G	703 493-0436
Herndon *(G-6750)*		
Neopath Systems LLC	G	571 238-1333
Herndon *(G-6752)*		
Nervve Technologies Inc	G	703 334-1488
Herndon *(G-6753)*		
Next Screen Media	G	571 295-6398
Aldie *(G-109)*		
Nexxtek Inc	G	571 356-2921
Vienna *(G-14105)*		
Ntt America Solutions Inc	E	571 203-4032
Reston *(G-10910)*		
Nudge LLC	G	423 521-1969
Richmond *(G-11697)*		
Nyx Technologies LLC	G	703 914-8956
Alexandria *(G-546)*		
Octoleaf LLC	G	202 579-7279
Ashburn *(G-1324)*		
Old World Labs LLC	G	800 282-0386
Norfolk *(G-9675)*		
Opsense Inc	G	844 757-7578
Dunn Loring *(G-4266)*		
Orbysol Inc	G	703 398-1092
Brambleton *(G-1932)*		
Pep Labs LLC	G	202 669-2562
Ashburn *(G-1325)*		
Pexip Inc	G	703 480-3181
Herndon *(G-6772)*		
PI Square Technologies Inc	G	571 255-6253
Chantilly *(G-2550)*		
Pivit	G	301 395-0895
Chantilly *(G-2551)*		
Pleasy LLC	G	774 234-4299
Arlington *(G-1112)*		
Prop LLC	G	571 970-5031
Arlington *(G-1121)*		
Redono LLC	G	757 553-2305
Chesapeake *(G-3264)*		
Riverland Solutions Corp	G	571 247-2382
Leesburg *(G-7337)*		
Roadglobe LLC	A	804 519-3331
Sandy Hook *(G-12645)*		
Routemarket Inc	G	703 829-7087
Arlington *(G-1152)*		
Rxhonesty Inc	G	908 872-2009
Vienna *(G-14119)*		
Saicomp LLC	G	714 421-8967
Petersburg *(G-10340)*		
Sailfish LLC	G	203 570-3553
Arlington *(G-1156)*		
Salem Infotech Inc	F	703 731-9711
Herndon *(G-6798)*		
Sas Federal LLC	G	571 227-7000
Arlington *(G-1159)*		

PRODUCT

Sas Institute Inc ....G.... 804 217-8352
  Glen Allen (G-5790)
Sas Institute Inc ....E.... 571 227-7000
  Arlington (G-1160)
Scientific Software Solutions ....F.... 434 293-7661
  Charlottesville (G-2873)
Scratcherguru LLC ....G.... 804 239-8629
  Montpelier (G-9020)
Shield Technology Corporation ....G.... 540 882-3254
  Lovettsville (G-7586)
Signal Vine Inc ....F.... 703 480-0278
  Alexandria (G-346)
Sitscape Inc ....F.... 571 432-8130
  Vienna (G-14129)
Software Ag Inc ....F.... 703 480-1860
  Reston (G-10958)
Software Ag Inc ....C.... 703 860-5050
  Reston (G-10959)
Software Flow Corporation ....G.... 301 717-0331
  Great Falls (G-5981)
Software For Mobile Phones LLC ....G.... 703 862-1079
  Springfield (G-13091)
Software Security Cons LLC ....G.... 571 234-3663
  Leesburg (G-7350)
Software Solution & Cloud ....G.... 703 870-7233
  Sterling (G-13514)
Sonawane Webdynamics Inc ....G.... 703 629-7254
  Ashburn (G-1335)
Source360 LLC ....G.... 703 232-1563
  Chantilly (G-2494)
South Anna Inc ....G.... 804 316-9660
  Henrico (G-6572)
Sovereign Intelligence LLC ....F.... 571 455-4016
  Vienna (G-14131)
Spiritway LLC ....G.... 831 676-1014
  Vienna (G-14132)
Spotspot Co ....G.... 804 909-7353
  Richmond (G-11393)
Spydrsafe Mobile Security Inc ....G.... 703 286-0750
  Mc Lean (G-8558)
Supplier Solutions Inc ....F.... 703 791-7720
  Fairfax (G-4684)
Swami Shriji LLC ....G.... 804 322-9644
  North Chesterfield (G-9994)
Synergy Business Solutions LLC .....G.... 757 646-1294
  Virginia Beach (G-14860)
Synteras LLC ....G.... 703 766-6222
  Herndon (G-6820)
Systems America Inc ....G.... 703 203-8421
  Chantilly (G-2507)
Tate Global LLC ....G.... 703 282-0737
  Alexandria (G-362)
Tconnex Inc ....G.... 703 910-3400
  Herndon (G-6824)
Tech Enterprises Inc ....G.... 703 352-0001
  Fairfax (G-4686)
Teendrivingstickercom LLC ....G.... 571 643-6956
  Manassas (G-8166)
Tetravista LLC ....G.... 703 606-6509
  Arlington (G-1189)
Third Eye Development Intl Inc ....G.... 631 682-1848
  Alexandria (G-363)
Tibco Software Federal Inc ....E.... 703 208-3900
  Falls Church (G-4883)
Tizzy Technologies Inc ....G.... 703 344-3348
  Virginia Beach (G-14884)
Tobacco Quitter LLC ....G.... 540 818-3396
  Blacksburg (G-1799)
Transeffect LLC ....G.... 703 991-1599
  Winchester (G-15595)
Tree Technologies Inc ....G.... 540 589-7988
  Roanoke (G-12011)
Triple Yolk LLC ....G.... 540 923-4040
  Reva (G-11002)
Ttg LLC ....G.... 540 280-7389
  Staunton (G-13303)
Ub-04 Software Inc ....G.... 804 754-2708
  Richmond (G-11426)
Unboxed ....G.... 336 253-4085
  Chantilly (G-2511)
Unifiedonline Inc ....G.... 816 679-1893
  Fairfax (G-4690)
Unifiedonline LLC ....G.... 816 679-1893
  Fairfax (G-4691)
Unison Vrtual Acqstion Off LLC ....G.... 571 449-4188
  Dulles (G-4230)
Upkeepr Corp ....G.... 703 718-6304
  Arlington (G-1203)
Uzio Inc ....C.... 800 984-7952
  Reston (G-10980)

Vartender LLC ....G.... 703 376-7751
  Chantilly (G-2562)
Veamea Inc ....G.... 703 382-2288
  Mc Lean (G-8575)
Virginia Software Group Inc ....G.... 757 721-0054
  Virginia Beach (G-14919)
Vitalcode Inc ....G.... 703 622-1154
  Ashburn (G-1351)
Vitara LLC ....G.... 972 200-3680
  Chantilly (G-2564)
Wanderers Hideaway ....G.... 904 480-6117
  Hampton (G-6268)
Warden Systems ....G.... 703 627-8002
  Sterling (G-13558)
Webdmg LLC ....G.... 757 633-5033
  Suffolk (G-13782)
Welcomepoint LLC ....G.... 703 371-0499
  Falls Church (G-4891)
Whiteboard Applications Inc ....G.... 703 297-2835
  Leesburg (G-7377)
Whooley Inc ....G.... 703 307-4963
  Great Falls (G-5985)
Whos Up Games LLC ....G.... 804 248-2270
  Ashland (G-1509)
Willu LLC ....F.... 844 809-4558
  Arlington (G-1220)
Wise Case Technologies LLC ....G.... 757 646-9080
  Virginia Beach (G-14941)
Writlab LLC ....G.... 703 996-9162
  Arlington (G-1223)
Yellow Dog Software LLC ....G.... 757 818-9360
  Norfolk (G-9798)

SOFTWARE PUBLISHERS: Business & Professional

01 Communique Laboratory Inc ....G.... 703 224-8262
  Arlington (G-833)
300 Qubits LLC ....G.... 202 320-0196
  Arlington (G-835)
4gurus LLC ....G.... 703 520-5084
  Fairfax (G-4587)
4gurus LLC ....G.... 703 520-5084
  Fairfax (G-4588)
Acro Software Inc ....G.... 703 753-7508
  Haymarket (G-6412)
Active Navigation Inc ....F.... 571 346-7607
  Reston (G-10777)
Advanced Rsponse Concepts Corp ..G.... 703 246-8560
  Fairfax (G-4590)
Argent Line LLC ....G.... 703 519-1209
  Alexandria (G-140)
Artusmode Software LLC ....G.... 703 794-6100
  Great Falls (G-5938)
Ats Corporation ....E.... 571 766-2400
  Fairfax (G-4413)
Autodocs LLC ....F.... 703 532-9720
  Vienna (G-14012)
Avitech Consulting LLC ....G.... 757 810-2716
  Chesapeake (G-2990)
Blackboard Connect Inc ....G.... 919 841-0175
  Reston (G-10801)
Blackboard Inc ....G.... 512 474-8363
  Reston (G-10804)
Blackboard Inc ....G.... 254 251-3203
  Reston (G-10805)
Blue Beacon LLC ....G.... 202 643-9043
  Ashburn (G-1249)
Blulogix LLC ....E.... 443 333-4100
  Mc Lean (G-8401)
Bnd Software ....G.... 202 997-1070
  Leesburg (G-7235)
Boxwood Technology Inc ....F.... 703 707-8686
  Mc Lean (G-8403)
C2c Smart Compliance LLC ....F.... 703 872-7340
  Alexandria (G-158)
Cabaide LLC ....G.... 571 262-2710
  Ashburn (G-1253)
Caerus LLC ....G.... 703 772-7688
  Great Falls (G-5942)
Candidate Metrics Inc ....G.... 703 539-2331
  Vienna (G-14021)
Cerberus LLC ....G.... 703 372-9750
  Arlington (G-904)
Cerner Corporation ....G.... 703 286-0200
  Vienna (G-14024)
Cloudera Gvrnment Slutions Inc .....F.... 888 789-1488
  Tysons (G-13942)
Cobalt Co ....G.... 888 426-2258
  Arlington (G-909)

Compu Management Corp ....G.... 276 669-3822
  Bristol (G-2013)
Computer Solution Co of VA Inc ......E.... 804 794-3491
  Richmond (G-11538)
Comscore Inc ....C.... 703 438-2000
  Reston (G-10824)
Concur Technologies Inc ....G.... 703 403-8764
  Vienna (G-14030)
Cvent Inc ....G.... 571 830-2301
  Mc Lean (G-8413)
Cyber Intel Solutions Inc ....G.... 571 970-2689
  Springfield (G-12987)
Cynosure Services Inc ....G.... 410 209-0796
  Alexandria (G-179)
Data Research Group Corp ....G.... 571 350-9590
  Culpeper (G-3888)
Databasics Inc ....E.... 703 262-0097
  Reston (G-10833)
Datablink Inc ....G.... 703 639-0600
  Mc Lean (G-8416)
Defensative LLC ....F.... 202 557-6937
  Reston (G-10837)
Digital Beans Inc ....G.... 703 775-2225
  Alexandria (G-189)
Eloqua Inc ....E.... 703 584-2750
  Vienna (G-14047)
Enterprise Hive LLC ....G.... 804 438-9393
  Irvington (G-7001)
Euclidian Systems Inc ....G.... 703 963-7209
  Arlington (G-960)
Flockdata LLC ....G.... 703 870-6916
  Chantilly (G-2421)
Frost Property Solutions LLC ....G.... 804 571-2147
  Mechanicsville (G-8625)
Gary Smith ....G.... 703 218-1801
  Fairfax (G-4461)
Gemini Security LLC ....G.... 703 466-0163
  Sterling (G-13410)
Global Info Netwrk Systems Inc ......G.... 703 409-4204
  Fort Belvoir (G-5115)
Govhawk LLC ....G.... 703 439-1349
  Alexandria (G-223)
Govready Pbc ....G.... 917 304-3488
  Alexandria (G-224)
Govtribe Inc ....G.... 202 505-4681
  Arlington (G-986)
Greenestep LLC ....E.... 703 546-4236
  Clifton (G-3669)
Greybox Strategies LLC ....G.... 276 328-3249
  Wise (G-15625)
Harrington Software Assoc Inc ....G.... 540 349-8074
  Warrenton (G-15024)
Ifexo LLC ....G.... 443 856-7705
  Mc Lean (G-8462)
Improvebuild LLC ....G.... 703 372-2646
  Ashburn (G-1295)
Infrascale Inc ....C.... 703 520-7072
  Reston (G-10873)
Intelligize Incorporated ....G.... 888 925-8627
  Reston (G-10877)
Interntional Registration Plan ....G.... 502 845-0398
  Lake Ridge (G-7156)
Intouch For Inmates LLC ....G.... 862 246-6283
  Lynchburg (G-7746)
Intuit Inc ....C.... 540 752-6100
  Fredericksburg (G-5442)
Invincea Inc ....C.... 703 352-7680
  Fairfax (G-4638)
Invizer LLC ....G.... 410 903-2507
  Herndon (G-6711)
Iq Global Technologies LLC ....G.... 800 601-0678
  Vienna (G-14073)
Ivy Software Inc ....G.... 804 769-7193
  Manquin (G-8216)
Jay Blue Pos Inc ....G.... 703 672-2869
  Annandale (G-761)
Keystone Software Inc ....G.... 703 866-1593
  Manassas (G-7955)
Kling Research and Sftwr Inc ....G.... 540 364-2524
  Marshall (G-8257)
Kratos Tech Trning Sltions Inc ....G.... 757 466-3660
  Norfolk (G-9614)
Leaseaccelerator Inc ....F.... 866 446-0980
  Reston (G-10886)
Location Bsed Svcs Content LLC .....G.... 703 622-1490
  Mc Lean (G-8488)
Loosely Coupled Software LLC ....G.... 703 707-9235
  Herndon (G-6738)
Macar International LLC ....G.... 202 842-1818
  Alexandria (G-267)

Madison Edgecnnex Holdings LLC ...... G 703 880-5404
  Herndon (G-6739)
Maverick Bus Solutions LLC .... G 757 870-8489
  Portsmouth (G-10459)
Meetingsphere Inc .... E 703 348-0725
  Norfolk (G-9637)
Meritful Inc .... G 703 651-6338
  Alexandria (G-528)
Microbanx Systems LLC .... G 703 757-1760
  Great Falls (G-5966)
Millennium Sftwr Cnsulting LLC .... G 434 245-0741
  Charlottesville (G-2661)
Millstreet Software .... G 703 281-1015
  Vienna (G-14093)
Net6degrees LLC .... G 703 201-4480
  Purcellville (G-10672)
Netcentric Technologies Inc .... G 202 661-2180
  Arlington (G-1075)
New Health Analytics LLC .... F 804 245-8240
  Henrico (G-6541)
Openwater Software Inc .... G 202 765-0247
  Arlington (G-1089)
Papay Holdco LLC .... E 703 226-3544
  Arlington (G-1098)
Paya Inc .... F 800 261-0240
  Reston (G-10922)
Pcpursuit Inc .... G 425 890-5495
  Herndon (G-6768)
Permissionbit Inc .... G 703 278-3832
  Mc Lean (G-8525)
Personam Inc .... G 571 297-9371
  Mc Lean (G-8526)
Pleasant Vly Bus Solutions LLC .... E 703 391-0977
  Reston (G-10926)
Positive Feedback Software LL .... G 540 243-0300
  Rocky Mount (G-12347)
Quadramed Corporation .... C 703 709-2300
  Herndon (G-6781)
Raastech Software LLC .... G 888 565-3397
  Herndon (G-6785)
Raimist Software LLC .... G 703 568-7638
  Chantilly (G-2484)
RDS Control Systems Inc .... G 888 578-9428
  Fishersville (G-5007)
Reconart Inc .... G 855 732-6627
  Alexandria (G-568)
Rentbot LLC .... G 844 473-6826
  Richmond (G-11350)
Resounding LLC .... G 804 677-0947
  North Chesterfield (G-9958)
Reston Software LLC .... G 703 234-2932
  Reston (G-10939)
Results Software .... G 703 713-9100
  Herndon (G-6790)
Rivanna Software LLC .... G 434 806-6105
  Charlottesville (G-2686)
Rowing Team LLC .... E 855 462-7238
  Glen Allen (G-5788)
Sage Software Inc .... G 503 439-5271
  Mc Lean (G-8542)
Salesforce Maps .... G 571 388-4990
  Charlottesville (G-2871)
Salus LLC .... G 475 222-3784
  Herndon (G-6799)
Sapr3 Associates Inc .... G 501 256-8645
  Herndon (G-6801)
Savi Technology Inc .... E 571 227-7950
  Alexandria (G-578)
Sciencelogic Inc .... C 703 354-1010
  Reston (G-10945)
Scivera LLC .... G 434 974-1301
  Charlottesville (G-2874)
Securedb Inc .... G 703 231-0008
  Sterling (G-13503)
Self Solutions LLC .... E 202 725-0866
  Alexandria (G-582)
Serendipitme LLC .... G 301 370-2466
  Leesburg (G-7347)
Shiftone .... G 415 806-5006
  Arlington (G-1165)
Siemens Industry Software Inc .... E 757 591-6633
  Newport News (G-9338)
Singlecomm LLC .... F 203 559-5486
  Richmond (G-11383)
Soft Edge Inc .... G 703 442-8353
  Mc Lean (G-8550)
Springboard Retail Inc .... E 888 347-2191
  Falls Church (G-4877)
Stardog Union .... E 202 408-8770
  Arlington (G-1175)

Stratuslive LLC .... E 757 273-8219
  Virginia Beach (G-14855)
Tekadventure LLC .... G 646 580-2511
  Chantilly (G-2560)
Terrago Technologies Inc .... E 678 391-9798
  Sterling (G-13530)
Terralign Group Inc .... G 571 388-4990
  Herndon (G-6825)
Textore Inc .... F 571 321-2013
  Fairfax (G-4687)
Tremolo Security Inc .... G 703 844-2727
  Arlington (G-1196)
Triblio Inc .... F 703 942-9557
  Reston (G-10976)
Troopmaster Software Inc .... G 434 589-6788
  Palmyra (G-10258)
Tumalow Inc .... G 847 644-9009
  Bumpass (G-2170)
Ubicabus LLC .... G 804 512-5324
  Colonial Beach (G-3727)
Unseen Technologies Inc .... G 704 207-7391
  Lynchburg (G-7829)
Usher Incorporated .... D 703 848-8600
  Tysons Corner (G-13956)
Valor Partners Inc .... G 540 725-4156
  Roanoke (G-12215)
Vegnos Corporation .... G 571 721-1685
  Alexandria (G-604)
Velocity Services Corporation .... E 540 368-2708
  Fredericksburg (G-5497)
Verisma Systems Inc .... F 866 390-7404
  Alexandria (G-372)
Vision Business Solutions .... G 540 622-6383
  Front Royal (G-5562)
Voyager Software Inc .... G 919 802-3232
  Richmond (G-11815)
Web Transitions Inc .... G 540 334-1707
  Boones Mill (G-1901)
Websauce Software LLC .... G 540 319-4002
  Lexington (G-7423)
Wellsky Humn Social Svcs Corp .... D 703 674-5100
  Reston (G-10990)
Working Software LLC .... G 703 992-6280
  Falls Church (G-4930)
Xlnt Solutions Inc .... G 703 819-9265
  Fairfax (G-4585)
Zeurix LLC .... G 571 297-9460
  Reston (G-10998)
Zeus Technologies .... G 540 247-4623
  Winchester (G-15522)

SOFTWARE PUBLISHERS: Computer Utilities

Kuary LLC .... G 703 980-3804
  Fairfax (G-4495)
Packet Stash Inc .... G 202 649-0676
  Alexandria (G-303)

SOFTWARE PUBLISHERS: Education

American Institute RES Inc .... G 703 470-1037
  Mc Lean (G-8392)
Arqball LLC .... G 434 260-1890
  Charlottesville (G-2730)
Blackboard Holdings Inc .... A 202 463-4860
  Reston (G-10802)
Blackboard Inc .... G 202 463-4860
  Reston (G-10803)
Blackboard Inc .... G 202 463-4860
  Reston (G-10806)
Blackboard Super Holdco Inc .... G 202 463-4860
  Reston (G-10807)
Brain Based Learning Inc .... G 804 320-0158
  North Chesterfield (G-9834)
Codeworx Lc .... G 571 306-3859
  Alexandria (G-169)
College and University Educati .... G 540 820-7384
  Harrisonburg (G-6302)
Cubicle Logic LLC .... G 571 989-2823
  Sterling (G-13380)
Dynamic Literacy LLC .... G 888 696-8597
  Keswick (G-7046)
Edulinked LLC .... G 703 869-2228
  Herndon (G-6665)
Einstitute Inc .... F 571 255-0530
  Fairfax (G-4444)
Electric Elders Inc .... G 703 213-9327
  Alexandria (G-199)
Evaluation Tech For Dev LLC .... G 434 851-0651
  Charlottesville (G-2794)

Go Vivace Inc .... G 703 869-9463
  Mc Lean (G-8451)
Healthcare Simulations LLC .... G 757 399-4502
  Portsmouth (G-10441)
Infocess LLC .... G 571 723-1010
  Vienna (G-14070)
Lintronics Software Publishing .... G 540 552-7204
  Blacksburg (G-1754)
Luluverse .... G 202 821-9726
  Ashburn (G-1312)
Manan LLC .... F 804 320-1414
  Henrico (G-6532)
Mantech Advanced Dev Group Inc ..... D 703 218-6000
  Fairfax (G-4502)
Miracle Systems LLC .... C 571 431-6397
  Arlington (G-1066)
Oracle Systems Corporation .... A 703 478-9000
  Reston (G-10916)
Pdh Mobile Inc .... G 703 475-8223
  Great Falls (G-5972)
Prager University Foundation .... G 323 577-2437
  Herndon (G-6778)
Redclay Visions LLC .... G 804 869-3616
  Virginia Beach (G-14766)
Rosetta Stone Inc .... E 703 387-5800
  Arlington (G-1151)
Rosetta Stone Ltd .... B 540 432-6166
  Harrisonburg (G-6365)
Schribble Inc .... G 804 869-6878
  Glen Allen (G-5791)
Scriyb LLC .... F 202 549-7070
  Leesburg (G-7343)
Serious Games Interactive Inc .... E 703 624-0842
  Arlington (G-1163)
Sharestream Edcatn Rsurces LLC ..... F 301 208-8000
  Reston (G-10948)
Softchalk LLC .... E 877 638-2425
  Richmond (G-11762)
Spedapps LLC .... G 757 541-2663
  Chesapeake (G-3307)
Superior Global Solutions Inc .... G 804 794-3507
  Chesterfield (G-3530)
Svanaco Inc .... G 571 312-3790
  Alexandria (G-359)
Tiome Inc .... G 703 531-8963
  Alexandria (G-599)
Tumorpix LLC .... G 804 754-3961
  Henrico (G-6587)
Uvsity Corporation .... G 571 308-3241
  Brambleton (G-1935)
Volarre Inc .... G 202 258-2640
  Mc Lean (G-8577)
Winchendon Group Inc .... G 703 960-0978
  Alexandria (G-610)
Wyvern Interactive LLC .... F 540 336-4498
  Winchester (G-15519)

SOFTWARE PUBLISHERS: Home Entertainment

Ausome Ones LLC .... G 703 637-7105
  Arlington (G-865)
Fair Value Games LLC .... G 804 307-9110
  Glen Allen (G-5729)
Ivans Inc .... G 804 271-0477
  North Chesterfield (G-9900)
Nancy Lee Asman .... G 703 242-8530
  Vienna (G-14101)
One One Too LLC .... G 505 500-4749
  Fredericksburg (G-5342)
Osgoode Media Inc .... G 866 573-0754
  Herndon (G-6766)
Playcall Inc .... G 571 385-6203
  Great Falls (G-5973)
Pma It Solutions Inc .... G 571 336-2408
  Portsmouth (G-10469)
Pouchmouse Studios Inc .... G 310 462-0599
  Alexandria (G-314)
Raincrow Studios LLC .... G 540 746-8696
  Harrisonburg (G-6360)
Rgolf Inc .... G 540 443-9296
  Blacksburg (G-1783)
Rimfire Games LLC .... G 703 580-4495
  Woodbridge (G-15796)
Spritelogic LLC .... G 703 568-0468
  Mc Lean (G-8557)
U Play Usa LLC .... G 757 301-8690
  Virginia Beach (G-14899)
While Software LLC .... G 202 290-6705
  Great Falls (G-5984)

PRODUCT

SOFTWARE PUBLISHERS: NEC

1click LLC G 703 307-6026
Springfield *(G-12933)*
5gl Software Inc G 703 861-3644
Fairfax *(G-4394)*
8020 Software LLC G 434 466-8020
Charlottesville *(G-2585)*
Accounting Technology LLC F 434 316-6000
Forest *(G-5049)*
Actionstep Inc G 540 809-9326
Richmond *(G-11471)*
Adnet Systems Inc F 571 313-1356
Reston *(G-10778)*
Adobe Inc D 571 765-5400
Mc Lean *(G-8386)*
Adobe Systems Federal LLC E 571 765-5523
Mc Lean *(G-8387)*
Adv3ntus Software LLC G 703 288-3380
Mc Lean *(G-8388)*
AEC Software Inc E 703 450-1980
Sterling *(G-13339)*
Agora Data Services LLC G 703 328-7758
Fredericksburg *(G-5396)*
Aida Health Inc G 202 739-1345
Arlington *(G-847)*
Ailsa Software LLC G 703 407-6470
Chantilly *(G-2364)*
Aka Software LLC G 703 406-4619
Sterling *(G-13340)*
Akamai Technologies Inc E 877 425-2624
Reston *(G-10783)*
All Traffic Solutions Inc F 814 237-9005
Herndon *(G-6609)*
American Quality Software Inc G 571 730-4532
Falls Church *(G-4748)*
Amity Software Inc G 571 312-0880
Arlington *(G-854)*
AMS Services LLC G 804 869-4777
Richmond *(G-11112)*
Animate Systems Inc G 804 233-8085
Richmond *(G-11485)*
Any Job Software Inc G 540 347-4347
Catlett *(G-2264)*
Appian Corporation G 703 442-8844
Tysons *(G-13941)*
Appian Corporation C 703 442-8844
Mc Lean *(G-8393)*
Aptify Corporation G 202 223-2600
Mc Lean *(G-8394)*
Aptify Corporation D 202 223-2600
Tysons Corner *(G-13951)*
Arkcase LLC G 703 272-3270
Vienna *(G-14009)*
Atavus Inc G 703 404-2796
Sterling *(G-13354)*
Atlas Inc G 646 835-9656
Woodbridge *(G-15650)*
Attachmate Corporation E 703 663-5500
Vienna *(G-14011)*
Auralog Inc B 602 470-0300
Harrisonburg *(G-6294)*
Axios Systems Inc E 703 326-1357
Herndon *(G-6617)*
B&B Consulting Services Inc G 804 550-1517
Ashland *(G-1376)*
B3sk Software LLC G 757 484-4516
Chesapeake *(G-2992)*
Bap LLC G 800 507-9728
Purcellville *(G-10651)*
Basvin Software LLC G 703 537-0888
Fairfax *(G-4419)*
Bayonet G 804 323-3204
Glen Allen *(G-5706)*
Beetlebug Software LLC G 571 223-5041
Leesburg *(G-7229)*
Behealth Solutions LLC G 434 422-9090
Charlottesville *(G-2593)*
Best Software Inc G 949 753-1222
Reston *(G-10798)*
Bigbrassband LLC E 571 223-7137
Leesburg *(G-7230)*
Bizwhazee LLC G 703 889-8499
Reston *(G-10800)*
Blackfish Software LLC G 703 779-9649
Leesburg *(G-7233)*
Blackwolf Software G 434 978-4903
Charlottesville *(G-2597)*
Bloomforth Corp G 703 408-8993
Centreville *(G-2296)*
Blue Ridge Software G 703 912-3990
Springfield *(G-12965)*
Bluvector Inc G 571 565-2100
Arlington *(G-886)*
BMC Software Inc F 713 918-8800
Mc Lean *(G-8402)*
BMC Software Inc E 703 404-0230
Herndon *(G-6627)*
Board Room Software Inc G 757 721-3900
Virginia Beach *(G-14291)*
Bond International Sftwr Inc G 804 601-4640
Midlothian *(G-8781)*
Boshkins Software Corporation G 703 318-7785
Herndon *(G-6629)*
Bottomline Software Inc G 540 221-4444
Waynesboro *(G-15101)*
Bravatek Solutions Inc G 866 490-8590
Chantilly *(G-2527)*
Brian Fox DBA Fortified G 540 535-1195
Winchester *(G-15392)*
Build Software LLC G 703 629-2549
Clifton *(G-3659)*
Caci Products Company G 973 437-9800
Reston *(G-10815)*
Cae Software Solutions LLC G 734 417-6991
Oakton *(G-10142)*
Cambis LLC G 202 746-6124
Falls Church *(G-4767)*
Capo Software G 571 205-8695
Herndon *(G-6633)*
Carla Bedard G 212 773-1851
Alexandria *(G-160)*
Chiru Software Inc G 703 201-1914
Broadlands *(G-2075)*
CIO Controls Inc G 703 365-2227
Manassas *(G-8049)*
Ciphercloud Inc G 703 659-0533
Herndon *(G-6640)*
Circinus Software LLC G 571 522-1724
Centreville *(G-2298)*
Clearview Software Corporation G 804 381-6300
Lynchburg *(G-7679)*
Clover LLC G 703 771-4286
Leesburg *(G-7245)*
Cnl Software Inc G 317 522-0313
Ashburn *(G-1256)*
Cobalt Company G 888 426-2258
Arlington *(G-910)*
Code Blue G 757 438-1507
Virginia Beach *(G-14350)*
Cole Software LLC G 540 456-8210
Afton *(G-77)*
Coleman and Coleman Software G 804 276-5372
North Chesterfield *(G-9849)*
Colonial Apps LLC G 804 744-8535
Midlothian *(G-8800)*
Computer Corp of America G 703 241-7830
Arlington *(G-918)*
Computing Technologies Inc G 703 280-8800
Mechanicsville *(G-8613)*
Connect Software LLC G 706 974-8300
Reston *(G-10826)*
Corascloud Inc E 703 797-1881
Mc Lean *(G-8410)*
Corce Collec Business System E 703 790-7272
Mc Lean *(G-8411)*
Core Enable LLC G 757 375-4434
Virginia Beach *(G-14366)*
Corillian Payment Solutions E 703 259-3000
Reston *(G-10827)*
Cosaic G 800 821-8147
Charlottesville *(G-2771)*
Cougaar Software Inc E 703 506-1700
Fairfax *(G-4431)*
CPA Global North America LLC D 703 739-2234
Alexandria *(G-175)*
CPA Global Services US Inc F 703 739-2234
Alexandria *(G-176)*
Crafter Software G 703 955-3480
Reston *(G-10829)*
Cross Cloud Solutions Inc G 703 724-7526
Ashburn *(G-1262)*
Crystal Technology Inc F 703 968-2590
Chantilly *(G-2399)*
Ctm Automated Systems Inc G 703 742-0755
Sterling *(G-13379)*
Ctrl-Pad Inc G 757 216-9170
Norfolk *(G-9510)*
Custom Computer Software G 540 972-3027
Locust Grove *(G-7443)*
Custom Procurement Systems G 540 720-5756
Stafford *(G-13134)*
Cvent Inc A 703 226-3500
Tysons Corner *(G-13952)*
Cybered Corp G 757 573-5456
Williamsburg *(G-15228)*
Cyberex Corporation G 703 904-0980
Herndon *(G-6651)*
Cynthia Gray G 703 860-5711
Herndon *(G-6652)*
D-Orbit Inc G 703 533-5661
Falls Church *(G-4781)*
Daghigh Software Co Inc G 703 323-7475
Fairfax Station *(G-4705)*
Datahaven For Dynamics LLC G 757 222-2000
Virginia Beach *(G-14388)*
Dataone Software G 877 438-8467
Norfolk *(G-9517)*
Datassist G 804 530-5008
South Chesterfield *(G-12800)*
Deadeye LLC G 540 720-6818
Stafford *(G-13137)*
Deca Software LLC G 202 607-5707
Alexandria *(G-186)*
Decisonq Infrmtion Oprtons Inc G 703 938-7153
Arlington *(G-932)*
Deep Prose Software LLC G 703 815-0715
Centreville *(G-2301)*
Deltek Systems Inc G 703 734-8606
Herndon *(G-6655)*
Deltek Systems Inc G 800 456-2009
Herndon *(G-6656)*
Delullo Software LLC G 570 419-6736
Lorton *(G-7480)*
Digitized Risk LLC G 703 662-3510
Ashburn *(G-1271)*
Dino Software Corporation E 703 768-2610
Alexandria *(G-447)*
Diskcopy Inc G 703 658-3539
Falls Church *(G-4784)*
Dispersive Technologies Inc G 252 725-0874
Herndon *(G-6658)*
Divergence Software Inc G 703 690-9870
Fairfax Station *(G-4708)*
Dominion Computer Services G 757 473-8989
Virginia Beach *(G-14409)*
Dominion Leasing Software G 804 378-2204
Powhatan *(G-10542)*
Donaty Software Inc G 540 822-5496
Lovettsville *(G-7578)*
DP Facilities Inc E 866 589-6125
Ashburn *(G-1272)*
Dp Technology G 703 835-6157
Broadlands *(G-2077)*
Dreamvision Software LLC G 703 378-7191
Herndon *(G-6660)*
Dutch Duck Software G 703 525-6564
Arlington *(G-949)*
E Primera Enable Corp F 703 476-2270
Herndon *(G-6664)*
E Z Data Inc G 540 775-2961
King George *(G-7088)*
E-Agree LLC F 571 358-8012
Manassas *(G-7933)*
Eastern Shore VA Mstr Grdners G 757 678-7688
Accomac *(G-71)*
Eastwind Software LLC G 434 525-9241
Forest *(G-5068)*
Ecometrix G 703 525-0524
Arlington *(G-953)*
Editek Inc G 703 652-9495
Fairfax *(G-4443)*
Eilig Software LLC G 757 259-0608
Williamsburg *(G-15238)*
Ekagra Partners LLC F 571 421-1100
Leesburg *(G-7265)*
Enterprise Itech Corp G 703 731-7881
Fairfax *(G-4447)*
Enterprise Svcs Cmmnctions LLC G 877 858-3855
Tysons *(G-13943)*
Enterprise Svcs Wrld Trade LLC G 703 245-9675
Tysons *(G-13944)*
Enterprize Software LLC G 571 271-5862
Brambleton *(G-1927)*
Entertainment Software Assoc G 703 383-3976
Fairfax *(G-4448)*
Epicidentity Inc F 833 723-3437
Chantilly *(G-2533)*
Erick Gonzalez G 703 855-2908
Woodbridge *(G-15696)*

Erp Software Services Inc ....G.....703 957-3073 Chantilly **(G-2534)**	Impact Software Soutions Inc ....G.....703 615-5212 Reston **(G-10870)**	Macro Systems LLC ....G.....703 359-9211 Fairfax **(G-4650)**
Essential Software Dev LLC ....G.....540 222-1254 Fairfax **(G-4451)**	Index Systems Inc ....G.....571 420-4600 Herndon **(G-6706)**	Macronetics Inc ....G.....703 848-9290 Vienna **(G-14088)**
Execware LLC ....G.....202 607-8904 Falls Church **(G-4789)**	Induko Inc ....G.....703 217-4262 Manassas **(G-8080)**	Magic Genius LLC ....G.....540 454-7595 Warrenton **(G-15032)**
Far Fetch LLC ....G.....757 493-3572 Virginia Beach **(G-14460)**	Informatica Corp ....G.....703 234-8500 Reston **(G-10872)**	Magnigen LLC ....G.....434 420-1435 Lynchburg **(G-7768)**
Federal Data Corporation ....G.....703 734-3773 Mc Lean **(G-8427)**	Informatica LLC ....G.....650 385-7000 Alexandria **(G-237)**	Majiksoft ....G.....757 510-0929 Virginia Beach **(G-14636)**
Filenet Corporation ....F.....703 312-1500 Mc Lean **(G-8429)**	Insource Sftwr Solutions Inc ....E.....804 378-8981 North Chesterfield **(G-9897)**	Makes Sense To ME Software LLC....G.....757 771-5289 Hampton **(G-6190)**
Finch Computing ....G.....571 599-7480 Reston **(G-10851)**	Integrated Software Solutions ....G.....703 255-1130 Reston **(G-10874)**	Mantas ....G.....703 322-4917 Herndon **(G-6742)**
Fintech Sys Inc ....G.....703 278-0606 Fairfax **(G-4623)**	Intelligent Software Design ....G.....703 731-9091 Mc Lean **(G-8466)**	Manufacturing System Svcs Inc ....G.....800 428-8643 Fairfax **(G-4651)**
First Objective Software Inc ....G.....757 855-0191 Norfolk **(G-9554)**	Interactive Achievement LLC ....F.....540 206-3649 Roanoke **(G-12107)**	Maphook Inc ....G.....703 661-7000 Sterling **(G-13447)**
Five Sixteen Solutions ....G.....703 435-4247 Fairfax **(G-4625)**	Invelos Software Inc ....G.....540 786-8560 Fredericksburg **(G-5304)**	Mapsdirect LLC ....G.....804 915-7628 Richmond **(G-11665)**
Fixmee LLC ....G.....703 731-1444 Fairfax **(G-4458)**	Iron Forge Software LLC ....G.....571 263-6540 Oak Hill **(G-10137)**	Mark Software LLC ....G.....703 409-4605 Hillsboro **(G-6876)**
Fortify Software ....G.....571 286-6320 Mc Lean **(G-8435)**	Iselfschooling ....G.....703 821-3282 Mc Lean **(G-8472)**	Marketspace Solutions Inc ....G.....703 989-3509 Centreville **(G-2318)**
Fountainhead Systems Ltd ....G.....804 320-0527 North Chesterfield **(G-9879)**	Iskoyisal Inc ....G.....703 992-6629 Mc Lean **(G-8473)**	Materna ....G.....703 875-8616 Arlington **(G-1055)**
Fourth Corporation ....G.....703 229-6222 Mineral **(G-8948)**	Itechnologies Inc ....G.....703 723-5141 Ashburn **(G-1298)**	Maxpci LLC ....G.....703 565-3400 Fredericksburg **(G-5203)**
Future Tense LLC ....G.....703 994-7814 Ashburn **(G-1283)**	Itegrity Systems ....G.....703 968-6300 Chantilly **(G-2446)**	McAfee LLC ....G.....571 449-4600 Reston **(G-10896)**
Fyllo LLC ....G.....540 846-6441 Fredericksburg **(G-5191)**	Itek Software LLC ....G.....312 404-3086 Glen Allen **(G-5753)**	Mega-Tech Inc ....E.....703 534-1629 Falls Church **(G-4922)**
Gainsafe Inc ....G.....703 598-2583 Alexandria **(G-211)**	Itek Software LLC ....G.....804 505-4835 Henrico **(G-6524)**	Ment Software Inc ....G.....540 382-4172 Riner **(G-11864)**
Gannett Media Tech Intl ....G.....757 547-7274 Chesapeake **(G-3114)**	Jarcam Sports ....G.....678 995-4607 Norfolk **(G-9601)**	Mentoradvisor Inc ....G.....571 435-7222 Alexandria **(G-527)**
Gbp Software LLC ....G.....703 967-3896 Reston **(G-10856)**	Jenzabar Inc ....C.....540 432-5200 Harrisonburg **(G-6333)**	Method Innovation Corporation ....G.....703 266-1115 Clifton **(G-3674)**
General Dynamics Corporation ....G.....703 729-3106 Ashburn **(G-1285)**	Jetney Development ....G.....714 262-0759 Salem **(G-12524)**	Methodhead Software LLC ....G.....703 338-1588 Annandale **(G-773)**
Geopliant LLC ....G.....888 273-7658 Falls Church **(G-4798)**	Jkm Software LLC ....G.....703 754-9175 Gainesville **(G-5592)**	Metis Machine LLC ....F.....434 483-5692 Charlottesville **(G-2833)**
George Perez ....G.....757 362-3131 Norfolk **(G-9561)**	Jnet Direct Inc ....G.....703 629-6406 Herndon **(G-6718)**	Michie Software Systems Inc ....G.....757 868-7771 Yorktown **(G-15982)**
Giant Lion Software LLC ....G.....703 764-8060 Fairfax **(G-4465)**	Joint Knowledge Software I ....G.....703 803-7470 Fairfax **(G-4486)**	Micro Focus Software Inc ....B.....703 663-5500 Vienna **(G-14091)**
Gigasheet Inc ....G.....703 231-8758 Leesburg **(G-7278)**	Joint Lab Systems SEC Svcs LLC .....G.....443 655-9987 Arlington **(G-1016)**	Micro Services Company ....G.....804 741-5000 Richmond **(G-11291)**
Goda Software Inc ....G.....703 373-7568 Arlington **(G-983)**	Jpg Software ....G.....757 546-8416 Chesapeake **(G-3157)**	Microstrategy Services Corp ....D.....703 848-8600 Tysons Corner **(G-13955)**
Gold Brand Software LLC ....G.....703 450-1321 Herndon **(G-6687)**	Js Software Inc ....G.....214 924-3179 Herndon **(G-6720)**	Milestone Software Inc ....G.....703 217-4262 Manassas **(G-7976)**
Gollygee Software Inc ....G.....703 437-3751 Reston **(G-10860)**	KCS Inc ....G.....703 981-0523 Alexandria **(G-504)**	Mindmettle ....G.....540 890-5563 Vinton **(G-14179)**
Gryphon Software Corporat ....G.....814 486-3753 Floyd **(G-5027)**	Keeva LLC ....G.....240 766-5382 Ashburn **(G-1302)**	Mission Data LLC ....F.....513 298-1865 Dunn Loring **(G-4265)**
Gtras Inc ....D.....703 342-4282 Chantilly **(G-2433)**	Keystone Technology LLC ....G.....540 361-8318 Fredericksburg **(G-5309)**	Mission It LLC ....G.....443 534-0130 Brambleton **(G-1930)**
Guidance Software Inc ....G.....703 433-5400 Dulles **(G-4206)**	Kimball Consulting Inc ....G.....703 516-6000 Arlington **(G-1023)**	Molloy Software Assoc Inc ....G.....703 825-7290 Centreville **(G-2320)**
Harbinger Tech Solutions LLC ....F.....757 962-6130 Norfolk **(G-9571)**	Kinvarin Software LLC ....G.....434 985-3737 Stanardsville **(G-13221)**	Mongodb Inc ....G.....866 237-8815 Vienna **(G-14099)**
Harlequin Custom Databases ....G.....434 823-6466 Crozet **(G-3838)**	Larry Lewis ....G.....757 619-7070 Virginia Beach **(G-14600)**	Monte Carlo Software LLC ....G.....703 642-0289 Annandale **(G-776)**
Health Data Services Inc ....F.....434 817-9000 Charlottesville **(G-2808)**	Laura Bushnell ....G.....703 569-4422 Springfield **(G-13038)**	Monticello Software Inc ....G.....540 854-4200 Mineral **(G-8950)**
Healthrx Corporation ....E.....703 352-1760 Fairfax **(G-4630)**	Leapfrog Software LLC ....G.....804 677-7051 Midlothian **(G-8846)**	Multimodal ID ....G.....703 944-9008 Falls Church **(G-4833)**
Hitachi Vantara Federal Corp ....C.....703 787-2900 Reston **(G-10865)**	Legacy Solutions ....G.....703 644-9700 Springfield **(G-13039)**	My Arch Inc ....G.....703 375-9302 Centreville **(G-2323)**
Hkl Research Inc ....G.....434 979-5569 Charlottesville **(G-2810)**	Lexia Learning Systems Inc ....G.....978 405-6242 Harrisonburg **(G-6337)**	Nemesys Software ....G.....703 435-0508 Herndon **(G-6751)**
Hotbed Technologies Inc ....F.....703 462-2350 Mc Lean **(G-8459)**	LI Hing Software LLC ....G.....703 677-7773 Alexandria **(G-516)**	Netqos Inc ....C.....703 708-3699 Herndon **(G-6754)**
Hp Inc ....G.....703 535-3355 Alexandria **(G-230)**	Lockheed Martin Corporation ....C.....703 367-2121 Manassas **(G-7966)**	New Century Software ....G.....704 984-3135 Fairfax Station **(G-4719)**
Hr Software LLC ....G.....703 665-5134 Great Falls **(G-5962)**	Lockwood Software Engrg Inc ....F.....202 494-7886 Mc Lean **(G-8489)**	New Tech Innovations ....G.....703 731-8160 Leesburg **(G-7320)**
Hss Inc ....G.....610 444-7409 Henrico **(G-6522)**	Logos Software Inc ....G.....540 819-6260 Roanoke **(G-12129)**	Nguyen & Phan LLC ....G.....571 730-9948 Lorton **(G-7516)**
Hygistics LLC ....G.....804 297-1504 Crozier **(G-3858)**	Lookingglass Cyber Slution Inc ....D.....703 351-1000 Reston **(G-10889)**	Nika Software Inc ....G.....703 992-5318 Herndon **(G-6755)**
I Bit-Lab ....G.....703 568-4035 Alexandria **(G-231)**	LTS Software Inc ....G.....757 493-8855 Virginia Beach **(G-14628)**	North Star Software Consulting ....G.....703 628-8564 Leesburg **(G-7321)**
Icewarp Inc ....G.....571 481-4611 Springfield **(G-13019)**	Luckyfoots Software ....G.....434 296-9358 Charlottesville **(G-2828)**	Nortonlifelock Inc ....G.....703 414-4444 Arlington **(G-1083)**
IDS Publishing Corporation ....G.....703 821-2323 Mc Lean **(G-8461)**	Lumos LLC ....G.....571 294-4290 Arlington **(G-1050)**	Nortonlifelock Inc ....G.....703 883-0180 Mc Lean **(G-8519)**
Ihs Computer Service Inc ....G.....540 249-4833 Port Republic **(G-10384)**	Lux 1 Holding Company Inc ....G.....703 245-9675 Tysons **(G-13947)**	Ntelos Inc ....G.....540 992-2211 Daleville **(G-3945)**

PRODUCT

Company		Phone
Ntelos Inc	G	434 760-0141
Charlottesville (G-2668)		
Nuasis Corp	G	571 230-8126
Great Falls (G-5969)		
Nufocus Software LLC	G	540 722-0282
Winchester (G-15456)		
O2o Software Inc	G	571 234-3243
Herndon (G-6762)		
Objective Intrface Systems Inc	D	703 295-6500
Herndon (G-6763)		
Objectvideo Labs LLC	E	571 327-3673
Mc Lean (G-8520)		
Ocean Software Us LLC	G	703 796-1300
Herndon (G-6764)		
Octopus Software Systems Inc	G	571 224-5283
Falls Church (G-4848)		
Omnicardata LLC	G	703 622-6742
Sterling (G-13464)		
One Aperture LLC	G	202 415-0416
Falls Church (G-4851)		
One Stop Computer Services LLC	G	571 442-2045
Sterling (G-13465)		
Optime Software LLC	G	415 894-0314
Great Falls (G-5970)		
Oracle America Inc	G	703 310-3600
Arlington (G-1090)		
Oracle America Inc	F	804 672-0998
Richmond (G-11316)		
Oracle America Inc	D	703 478-9000
Reston (G-10915)		
Oracle Heart & Vascular Inc	G	855 739-9953
Fredericksburg (G-5210)		
Oracle Systems Corporation	B	703 364-2221
Alexandria (G-547)		
Oracle Worldwide LLC	G	703 224-8806
Alexandria (G-301)		
Orbital Sciences LLC	A	703 406-5524
Dulles (G-4217)		
P&B Systems LLC	G	717 566-0608
Alexandria (G-302)		
Palladion Software	G	540 429-0999
Fredericksburg (G-5211)		
Pantheon Integration LLC	G	571 732-1570
Reston (G-10919)		
Pantheon Software Inc	F	703 387-4000
Arlington (G-1097)		
Parabon Computation Inc	F	703 689-9689
Reston (G-10920)		
Parabon Nanolabs Inc	E	703 689-9689
Reston (G-10921)		
Partfiniti Inc	F	703 679-7278
Haymarket (G-6434)		
Patron Id Inc	G	954 282-6636
Lynchburg (G-7783)		
PC Shareware Inc	G	540 371-5746
Fredericksburg (G-5468)		
People Interact LLC	G	571 223-5888
Leesburg (G-7324)		
Performance Support Systems	G	757 873-3700
Hayes (G-6404)		
Performyard Inc	G	703 870-3710
Arlington (G-1106)		
Philadelphia Riverboat LLC	G	757 640-9205
Norfolk (G-9687)		
Photo Finale Inc	F	703 564-3400
Mc Lean (G-8529)		
Pixia Corp	E	571 203-9665
Herndon (G-6774)		
Plateau Software Inc	G	703 385-8300
Fairfax (G-4530)		
Pointerra Us Inc	E	571 528-8799
Ashburn (G-1327)		
Poplicus Incorporated	E	866 209-9100
Arlington (G-1116)		
Practical Software LLC	G	240 505-0936
Stephens City (G-13320)		
Prall Software Consulting LLC	G	703 777-8423
Leesburg (G-7327)		
Pramaan Inc	G	703 327-6750
Chantilly (G-2552)		
Primatics Financial LLC	D	703 342-0040
Mc Lean (G-8531)		
Prime 3 Software Inc	G	757 763-8560
Norfolk (G-9695)		
Profitoptics Inc	G	804 360-2776
Glen Allen (G-5783)		
Protean LLC	G	757 273-1131
Williamsburg (G-15302)		
Protectedbyai Inc	G	571 489-6906
Reston (G-10932)		
Qmulos Products Inc	G	202 557-5162
Arlington (G-1124)		
Quantum Computing Inc	G	703 436-2161
Leesburg (G-7330)		
Quest Software Inc	F	703 234-3000
Reston (G-10935)		
Rabbit Software LLC	G	703 939-1708
Ashburn (G-1329)		
Radus Software LLC	G	703 623-8471
Sterling (G-13484)		
Raised Apps LLC	G	703 398-8254
Woodbridge (G-15790)		
Rand Worldwide Inc	G	804 290-8850
Richmond (G-11345)		
Rcl Software Inc	G	757 934-0828
Suffolk (G-13757)		
RE Discovery Software Inc	F	434 975-3256
Charlottesville (G-2680)		
RE Innovative Sftwr Solutions	F	434 989-8558
Charlottesville (G-2855)		
Readspeaker LLC	G	703 462-8738
Mc Lean (G-8534)		
Reger Research	G	703 328-6465
Chantilly (G-2554)		
Relational Data Solutions Inc	G	703 369-3580
Manassas (G-8142)		
Relational Systems Design Ltd	G	703 385-7073
Fairfax (G-4539)		
Reservation Gateway Inc	G	703 286-5331
Reston (G-10937)		
Reston Technology Group Inc	F	703 810-8800
Sterling (G-13491)		
Reuseit Software Inc	G	703 365-8071
Manassas (G-7996)		
Rl Software Corp	G	301 537-1593
Purcellville (G-10675)		
Richlynd Federal LLC	G	703 354-1500
Alexandria (G-573)		
Ridge Business Solutions LLC	E	571 241-8714
Reston (G-10941)		
Rjm Technologies Inc	G	703 323-6677
Fairfax (G-4543)		
Rodyn Vibration Analysis Inc	G	434 326-6797
Charlottesville (G-2865)		
Rogue Software LLC	G	703 945-9175
Fairfax (G-4670)		
Rollstream Inc	G	703 277-2150
Fairfax (G-4671)		
Roma Sftwr Systems Group Inc	G	703 437-1579
South Riding (G-12870)		
Rsa Security LLC	G	703 288-9300
Vienna (G-14118)		
Rufina Inc	G	703 577-2333
Falls Church (G-4870)		
Rynoh Live	G	757 333-3760
Virginia Beach (G-14787)		
S Software Development System	G	571 633-0554
Mc Lean (G-8541)		
Safety Software Inc	F	434 296-8789
Charlottesville (G-2870)		
Schafer Government Svcs LLC	G	202 594-4124
Arlington (G-1162)		
Scw Software Inc	G	540 937-5332
Amissville (G-721)		
SDA Software LLC	G	703 657-0919
Sterling (G-13501)		
Secure Elements Incorporated	E	703 234-7840
Herndon (G-6803)		
Secure Innovations Inc	G	540 384-6131
Salem (G-12569)		
Semanticsolutions LLC	G	703 980-7395
Ashburn (G-1333)		
Sentient Vision Systems Inc	G	703 531-8564
Glen Allen (G-5794)		
Servhawk LLC	G	703 447-1456
Great Falls (G-5979)		
Sgv Software Automtn RES Corp	E	703 904-0678
Herndon (G-6805)		
Silent Circle Americas LLC	G	202 499-6427
Fairfax (G-4678)		
Simulyze Inc	F	703 391-7001
Reston (G-10950)		
Sip-Tone Inc	G	703 480-0228
Herndon (G-6810)		
Sky Software	G	540 869-6581
Stephens City (G-13323)		
Slipstream Aviation Sftwr Inc	G	703 729-6535
Leesburg (G-7349)		
Smartfix	G	571 723-6499
Springfield (G-13088)		
Snowbird Holdings Inc	G	703 796-0445
Reston (G-10956)		
Softchoice Corporation	G	703 480-1952
Mc Lean (G-8551)		
Software & Systems Solutions L	G	703 801-7452
Woodbridge (G-15816)		
Software Engineering Solutions	G	703 842-1823
Ashburn (G-1334)		
Software Incentives	G	540 554-2319
Round Hill (G-12390)		
Software Insight	G	703 549-8554
Alexandria (G-350)		
Software Quality Experts LLC	G	703 291-4641
Reston (G-10960)		
Software Quality Institute	G	703 313-8404
Alexandria (G-586)		
Software Specialists Inc	G	540 449-2805
Blacksburg (G-1792)		
Software To Fit LLC	G	703 378-7239
Chantilly (G-2493)		
Solarwinds North America Inc	G	877 946-3751
Herndon (G-6811)		
Solutions Wise Group	G	804 748-0205
North Chesterfield (G-9984)		
Source Consulting Inc	G	540 785-0268
Fredericksburg (G-5366)		
Southpark Hi LLC	G	804 777-9000
Chester (G-3455)		
Spectrum Center Inc	F	703 848-4750
Mc Lean (G-8554)		
Spitfire Management LLC	F	757 644-4609
Williamsburg (G-15317)		
Sqlexec LLC	G	703 600-9343
Annandale (G-784)		
Sra Companies Inc	A	703 803-1500
Chantilly (G-2498)		
Srg Government Solutions Inc	G	703 609-7027
Fairfax (G-4573)		
Srn Software LLC	G	703 646-5186
Lorton (G-7533)		
Stellar Day Products Corp	G	804 748-8086
North Chesterfield (G-9991)		
Stellosphere Inc	G	631 897-4678
Ashburn (G-1337)		
Stillpoint Software Inc	G	540 905-7932
Washington (G-15079)		
Streamview Software LLC	G	703 455-0793
Springfield (G-13095)		
Structured Software Inc	G	703 266-0588
Fairfax (G-4683)		
Summit Waterfalls LLC	G	703 688-4558
Woodbridge (G-15819)		
Sunlight Software	G	540 789-7374
Willis (G-15365)		
Sunmicro Software Incorporated	G	703 587-9362
Herndon (G-6817)		
Sunny Day Fund Solutions Inc	G	703 622-1005
Falls Church (G-4880)		
Supravista Medical Dss LLC	G	740 339-0080
Farnham (G-4965)		
Survivalware Inc	G	703 780-2044
Alexandria (G-593)		
Switchdraw LLC	G	703 402-2820
Stafford (G-13199)		
Syftkog	G	540 693-5875
Fredericksburg (G-5372)		
Synaptein Solutions Inc	F	703 209-2350
Mc Lean (G-8562)		
Syncdog Inc	G	800 430-1268
Reston (G-10969)		
Syntec Business Systems Inc	G	804 303-2864
Forest (G-5100)		
Syrm LLC	G	571 308-8707
Stafford (G-13200)		
T & T Software LLC	G	540 389-1915
Roanoke (G-12202)		
T C G Technologies LLC	G	703 847-5057
Vienna (G-14137)		
T5 Group LLC	G	704 575-7721
Lynchburg (G-7817)		
Team Excel Inc	G	804 677-3694
Richmond (G-11785)		
Technica Software LLC	G	703 371-7134
Arlington (G-1182)		
Technology Destiny LLC	G	703 400-8929
Brambleton (G-1934)		
Teknostrata Inc	G	877 983-5667
Arlington (G-1184)		
Telos Idntity MGT Slutions LLC	D	703 724-3800
Ashburn (G-1339)		

2021 Virginia
Industrial Directory

(G-0000) Company's Geographic Section entry number

Tenant Turner ....G...... 804 241-8810
Glen Allen *(G-5807)*

Teneo Inc ....G...... 703 212-3220
Sterling *(G-13529)*

Thomas Brothers Software Corp........G...... 540 320-3505
Pulaski *(G-10648)*

Thoughtweb USA Inc ....G...... 575 639-1726
Oakton *(G-10162)*

Three Foot Software LLC ....G...... 434 202-0217
Charlottesville *(G-2705)*

Travelserver Software Inc ....G...... 571 209-5907
Lansdowne *(G-7174)*

Travelserver Software Inc ....G...... 703 406-7664
Great Falls *(G-5982)*

Trax International Corporation ......G...... 434 485-7100
Lynchburg *(G-7826)*

Tri Corp ....G...... 703 780-8753
Alexandria *(G-602)*

Trimech Solutions LLC ....E...... 804 257-9965
Glen Allen *(G-5818)*

Tringapps Inc ....G...... 703 698-6910
Fairfax *(G-4573)*

Trisec Assoc Inc ....G...... 703 471-6564
Herndon *(G-6831)*

Trk Systems Inc ....G...... 804 777-9445
Chesterfield *(G-3535)*

Turning Point Software Inc ....G...... 703 448-6672
Mc Lean *(G-8569)*

Tympic Software Inc ....G...... 703 858-0996
Ashburn *(G-1343)*

Unifyia Inc ....F...... 703 344-6758
Reston *(G-10977)*

Unisoncare Corporation ....G...... 804 721-3702
Chester *(G-3463)*

Up and Running Computers Inc ....G...... 757 565-3282
Williamsburg *(G-15329)*

US Software & Consulting Inc .....G...... 571 281-4496
Sterling *(G-13545)*

USA Security Solution Corp ....G...... 804 435-9999
Kilmarnock *(G-7077)*

Uwin Software LLC ....G...... 703 876-0490
Vienna *(G-14149)*

Van Vierssen Marcel ....G...... 703 471-0393
Herndon *(G-6835)*

Velocity Software Inc ....G...... 703 338-0909
Ashburn *(G-1347)*

Venture Apps LLC ....G...... 804 747-3405
Glen Allen *(G-5823)*

Verint Systems Inc ....G...... 703 481-9326
Reston *(G-10983)*

Vermark Global Systems Inc ....G...... 703 629-1571
Fairfax *(G-4693)*

Virtual Ea Inc ....G...... 703 855-9593
Nokesville *(G-9403)*

Vision Software Technologies ....G...... 703 722-4480
Chantilly *(G-2563)*

Vistashare LLC ....G...... 540 432-1900
Rockingham *(G-12282)*

Voice Software LLC ....G...... 571 331-2861
Leesburg *(G-7374)*

Waveset ....G...... 703 904-7411
Herndon *(G-6843)*

Weblogic ....G...... 703 645-0263
Vienna *(G-14159)*

Whispering Woods Software LLC ....G...... 434 282-1275
Charlottesville *(G-2906)*

Witt Associates Inc ....G...... 540 667-3146
Winchester *(G-15517)*

Workdynamics Technologies Inc ....E...... 703 481-9874
Reston *(G-10994)*

Xcalibur Software Inc ....G...... 703 896-5700
Sterling *(G-13565)*

Yamco LLC ....G...... 804 749-0480
Richmond *(G-11461)*

Yellow Bridge Software Inc ....G...... 703 909-5533
Woodbridge *(G-15837)*

Young and Healthy Mktg LLC ....G...... 214 945-5816
Meherrin *(G-8707)*

Your Way Software ....G...... 703 591-2064
Fairfax *(G-4697)*

Zachary Systems Inc ....G...... 703 286-7267
Ashburn *(G-1355)*

Zachary Systems Incorporated .....G...... 703 723-8965
Broadlands *(G-2084)*

Zynga Inc ....G...... 901 683-8310
Ashburn *(G-1358)*

SOFTWARE PUBLISHERS: Operating Systems

Alpine Method Technologies LLC ......G...... 716 310-4935
Aldie *(G-100)*

Coolr Group Inc ....G...... 571 933-3762
Chantilly *(G-2396)*

Etegrity LLC ....G...... 757 301-7455
Virginia Beach *(G-14452)*

Improbable LLC ....E...... 571 418-6999
Arlington *(G-1000)*

Red Hat Inc ....F...... 703 748-2201
Mc Lean *(G-8536)*

Samvit Solutions LLC ....G...... 703 481-1274
Reston *(G-10944)*

Ssecurity LLC ....G...... 703 590-4240
Woodbridge *(G-15817)*

SOFTWARE PUBLISHERS: Publisher's

American Soc For Engrg Educatn .....G...... 804 742-5611
Port Royal *(G-10385)*

Analystsoft Inc ....G...... 844 782-8758
Alexandria *(G-134)*

Covata Usa Inc ....G...... 703 657-5260
Reston *(G-10828)*

Efftex Development Inc ....G...... 800 708-8894
Alexandria *(G-198)*

Media X Group LLC ....G...... 866 966-9640
Waynesboro *(G-15124)*

Micro Analytics of Virginia ....F...... 703 536-6424
Arlington *(G-1063)*

Player Pursuits LLC ....G...... 202 207-6000
Mc Lean *(G-8530)*

SOFTWARE PUBLISHERS: Word Processing

Caladan Consulting Inc ....G...... 540 931-9581
Winchester *(G-15534)*

Department Info Tech Inc ....G...... 703 868-6691
Chantilly *(G-2407)*

Teresa C Shankman ....G...... 703 533-9322
Arlington *(G-1187)*

SOFTWARE TRAINING, COMPUTER

Cloud Ridge Labs LLC ....G...... 434 477-5060
Forest *(G-5060)*

Edulinked LLC ....G...... 703 869-2228
Herndon *(G-6665)*

Framecad America Inc ....F...... 703 615-2451
Fairfax *(G-4626)*

Index Systems Inc ....G...... 571 420-4600
Herndon *(G-6706)*

Infrawhite Technologies LLC ....G...... 662 902-0376
Vienna *(G-14071)*

Km Data Strategists LLC ....G...... 703 689-1087
Aldie *(G-108)*

SOIL CONDITIONERS

Livingston Group Inc ....G...... 757 460-3115
Virginia Beach *(G-14613)*

Loudoun Composting ....F...... 703 327-8428
Chantilly *(G-2544)*

SOIL TESTING KITS

Kessler Soils Engrg Pdts Inc ....G...... 571 291-2284
Leesburg *(G-7296)*

SOLAR CELLS

Aquanta Inc ....G...... 703 286-0923
Mc Lean *(G-8395)*

Old Dominion Innovations Inc ....F...... 804 477-8712
Ashland *(G-1471)*

SOLAR HEATING EQPT

American Solar Inc ....G...... 703 346-6053
Annandale *(G-730)*

Nellie Harris ....G...... 434 277-8511
Lowesville *(G-7597)*

PSL America Inc ....G...... 703 279-6426
Fairfax *(G-4664)*

Solar Electric America LLC ....G...... 804 332-6358
North Chesterfield *(G-10024)*

Sun Rnr of Virginia Inc ....G...... 540 271-3403
Harrisonburg *(G-6376)*

SOLDERING EQPT: Irons Or Coppers

Antex Usa Inc ....G...... 804 693-0831
Hayes *(G-6395)*

Poquoson Enterprises ....G...... 757 876-6655
Poquoson *(G-10375)*

SOLDERING SVC: Jewelry

Upscale Time LLC ....G...... 434 832-0101
Lynchburg *(G-7830)*

SOLVENTS

Cobehn Inc ....G...... 540 665-0707
Winchester *(G-15404)*

Solevents Floral LLC ....G...... 571 221-5761
Fairfax *(G-4557)*

SONAR SYSTEMS & EQPT

Atlas North America LLC ....G...... 757 463-0670
Yorktown *(G-15934)*

Raytheon Company ....B...... 703 759-1200
Sterling *(G-13485)*

Raytheon Company ....F...... 703 830-4087
Chantilly *(G-2485)*

Raytheon Company ....G...... 703 841-5700
Arlington *(G-1132)*

Raytheon Company ....E...... 703 413-1220
Arlington *(G-1133)*

Raytheon Company ....G...... 706 569-6600
Arlington *(G-1136)*

Raytheon Company ....G...... 703 412-3742
Arlington *(G-1137)*

Raytheon Company ....C...... 703 912-1800
Springfield *(G-13078)*

Raytheon Company ....G...... 703 768-4172
Alexandria *(G-567)*

Raytheon Company ....B...... 757 421-8319
Chesapeake *(G-3259)*

Utiliscope Corp ....F...... 804 550-5233
Glen Allen *(G-5822)*

SOUND EFFECTS & MUSIC PRODUCTION: Motion Picture

Boomin Bass Global LLC ....F...... 757 776-8668
Virginia Beach *(G-14294)*

Doite Media LLC ....G...... 703 594-1322
Broadlands *(G-2076)*

SOUND EQPT: Electric

Affordable Audio Rental ....G...... 804 305-6664
North Chesterfield *(G-9807)*

Hd Innovations ....G...... 757 420-0774
Suffolk *(G-13718)*

North Star Science & Tech LLC .....G...... 410 961-6692
Oakton *(G-10160)*

SOUND RECORDING STUDIOS

Boomin Bass Global LLC ....F...... 757 776-8668
Virginia Beach *(G-14294)*

Doite Media LLC ....G...... 703 594-1322
Broadlands *(G-2076)*

SOUND REPRODUCING EQPT

Hill Brenton ....G...... 757 560-9332
Hampton *(G-6167)*

Rappahannock & Potomac Rep LLC ....G...... 540 373-9545
Fredericksburg *(G-5475)*

SPACE CAPSULES

Prototype Productions Inc ....D...... 703 858-0011
Chantilly *(G-2483)*

SPACE PROPULSION UNITS & PARTS

Alliant Tchsystems Oprtons LLC .....G...... 703 412-3223
Arlington *(G-849)*

Delta Q Dynamics LLC ....G...... 703 980-9449
Manassas *(G-7931)*

SPACE VEHICLE EQPT

A-Tech Corporation ....G...... 703 955-7846
Chantilly *(G-2360)*

Calspan Systems Corporation ....C...... 757 873-1344
Newport News *(G-9189)*

PRODUCT

ITT Defense & Electronics..................A 703 790-6300
McLean *(G-8474)*
Marion Mold & Tool Inc..................E 276 783-6101
Marion *(G-8234)*
Moog Inc ....G 716 652-2000
Blacksburg *(G-1764)*
Orbital Sciences LLC..................B 703 406-5000
Dulles *(G-4218)*

SPACE VEHICLES

Lockheed Martin Corporation..................B 757 935-9479
Suffolk *(G-13732)*
Lockheed Martin Corporation..................G 703 258-2784
Arlington *(G-1047)*
Orbital Sciences LLC..................B 703 406-5000
Dulles *(G-4218)*
Space Logistics LLC..................G 703 406-5474
Dulles *(G-4227)*

SPEAKER SYSTEMS

Goto Unit USA..................G 703 598-6642
Centreville *(G-2307)*
Hogar Controls..................G 703 844-1160
Sterling *(G-13420)*
Short Circuit Electronics..................G 540 886-8805
Staunton *(G-13294)*

SPECIAL EVENTS DECORATION SVCS

Seven Oaks Farm LLC..................G 303 653-3299
Greenwood *(G-6000)*
Wealthy Sistas Media Group..................G 800 917-9435
Dumfries *(G-4262)*

SPECIAL PRODUCT SAWMILLS, NEC

Chesapeake Biofuels..................G 804 482-1784
Petersburg *(G-10311)*

SPECIALTY FOOD STORES: Coffee

J L V Management Inc ....G 540 446-6359
Stafford *(G-13158)*
Johnson & Elich Roasters Ltd..................F 540 552-7442
Blacksburg *(G-1747)*

SPECIALTY FOOD STORES: Health & Dietetic Food

Everlasting Life Product..................G 703 761-4900
Mc Lean *(G-8424)*

SPECIALTY OUTPATIENT CLINICS, NEC

Hanger Prsthetcs & Ortho Inc..................G 434 846-1803
Lynchburg *(G-7727)*

SPIKES: Steel, Wire Or Cut

Commercial Metals Company..................E 540 775-8501
King George *(G-7084)*

SPORTING & ATHLETIC GOODS: Arrows, Archery

Offroadarrowcom LLC..................G 804 920-2529
Providence Forge *(G-10627)*

SPORTING & ATHLETIC GOODS: Balls, Baseball, Football, Etc

Vinci Co LLC..................G 888 529-6864
Richmond *(G-11438)*

SPORTING & ATHLETIC GOODS: Batons

Git R Done Inc..................G 703 843-8697
Reston *(G-10859)*

SPORTING & ATHLETIC GOODS: Bobsleds

C & M Lures LLC..................G 703 369-3060
Manassas Park *(G-8192)*

SPORTING & ATHLETIC GOODS: Boomerangs

Big Lick Boomerang..................G 540 761-4611
Roanoke *(G-11889)*
Boomerang Air Sports..................G 804 360-0320
Henrico *(G-6484)*

SPORTING & ATHLETIC GOODS: Bowling Alleys & Access

Obdrillers Proshop..................G 804 897-3708
Midlothian *(G-8869)*
Tidewater Virginia Usbc Inc..................G 757 456-2497
Virginia Beach *(G-14880)*

SPORTING & ATHLETIC GOODS: Bowling Pins

Everything Gos LLC..................G 804 290-3870
Richmond *(G-11206)*

SPORTING & ATHLETIC GOODS: Camping Eqpt & Splys

Evergreen Outfitters LLC..................G 540 843-2576
Luray *(G-7610)*
Louise Richardson..................G 276 328-4545
Wise *(G-15631)*
M&M Great Adventures LLC..................G 937 344-1415
Williamsburg *(G-15275)*

SPORTING & ATHLETIC GOODS: Cartridge Belts

Pointman Resources LLC ....G 240 429-3423
Sterling *(G-13472)*

SPORTING & ATHLETIC GOODS: Carts, Caddy

Sport Creations LLC..................G 757 572-2113
Virginia Beach *(G-14841)*

SPORTING & ATHLETIC GOODS: Cases, Gun & Rod

Eye Armor Incorporated..................G 571 238-4096
Stafford *(G-13144)*
Richards Michael Mr Mrs..................G 540 854-5812
Spotsylvania *(G-12912)*

SPORTING & ATHLETIC GOODS: Cricket Eqpt, NEC

Mobile Link Virgina LLC..................G 757 583-8300
Norfolk *(G-9647)*

SPORTING & ATHLETIC GOODS: Crossbows

Crossbow Strategies Inc..................G 703 864-7576
Alexandria *(G-177)*

SPORTING & ATHLETIC GOODS: Decoys, Duck & Other Game Birds

Island Decoys..................G 757 336-5319
Chincoteague *(G-3562)*
Sara Yannuzzi..................G 703 955-2505
Edinburg *(G-4311)*

SPORTING & ATHLETIC GOODS: Driving Ranges, Golf, Electronic

Big Hubster Short Knocker Golf..................G 757 635-5949
Stafford *(G-13123)*

SPORTING & ATHLETIC GOODS: Exercising Cycles

Trueway Inc..................G 703 527-9248
Arlington *(G-1199)*

SPORTING & ATHLETIC GOODS: Fishing Eqpt

Custom Rods & Such..................G 434 736-9758
Drakes Branch *(G-4132)*
Jovanovich Inc..................G 301 653-1739
Alexandria *(G-501)*
Stubby Steves..................G 276 988-2915
North Tazewell *(G-10107)*

SPORTING & ATHLETIC GOODS: Game Calls

Dse Outdoor Product Inc..................G 540 789-4800
Willis *(G-15360)*

SPORTING & ATHLETIC GOODS: Guards, Football, Soccer, Etc

Smrt Mouth LLC..................G 804 363 8863
Sandston *(G-12634)*

SPORTING & ATHLETIC GOODS: Hockey Eqpt & Splys, NEC

Celly Sports Shop LLC..................G 540 981-0205
Vinton *(G-14169)*
DK Consulting LLC..................G 224 402-3333
Remington *(G-10768)*

SPORTING & ATHLETIC GOODS: Hunting Eqpt

Foldem Gear LLC..................G 571 289-5051
Yorktown *(G-15961)*
Goodpasture Knives..................G 804 752-8363
Ashland *(G-1422)*

SPORTING & ATHLETIC GOODS: Pools, Swimming, Plastic

Spa Guy LLC..................G 757 855-0381
Chesapeake *(G-3305)*

SPORTING & ATHLETIC GOODS: Protective Sporting Eqpt

Sentry Slutions Pdts Group LLC..................G 757 689-6064
Virginia Beach *(G-14803)*
Warrior Trail Consulting LLC..................G 703 349-1967
Fairfax *(G-4580)*

SPORTING & ATHLETIC GOODS: Racket Sports Eqpt

Nautilus International Inc..................C 276 773-2881
Independence *(G-6992)*

SPORTING & ATHLETIC GOODS: Rods & Rod Parts, Fishing

Custom Fly Grips LLC..................G 703 532-1189
Falls Church *(G-4780)*
Performance Fly Rods..................G 540 867-0856
Rockingham *(G-12267)*
Rick Robbins Bamboo Fly Rods..................G 540 463-2864
Lexington *(G-7415)*
Rod Fishinfiddler Co..................G 703 517-0496
Arlington *(G-1150)*
Staunton River Outdoors LLC..................G 434 608-2601
Altavista *(G-644)*

SPORTING & ATHLETIC GOODS: Shafts, Golf Club

Its About Golf..................G 703 437-1527
Herndon *(G-6714)*
Stoneleigh Golf Club..................G 540 338-4653
Round Hill *(G-12391)*

SPORTING & ATHLETIC GOODS: Shooting Eqpt & Splys, General

J W Bibb Shooting Bags..................G 434 384-9431
Monroe *(G-8993)*
Vfg Enterprises LLC..................G 757 343-4866
Virginia Beach *(G-14908)*

SPORTING & ATHLETIC GOODS: Skateboards

Abbadon Skateboards LLC..................G 703 280-4818
Annandale *(G-727)*
Cerberus Skateboard Co LLC..................G 757 715-2225
Norfolk *(G-9480)*
Coastal Edge..................G 757 422-5739
Virginia Beach *(G-14345)*
Convoy Skateboards Ltd..................G 571 216-2740
Alexandria *(G-434)*
Deezel Skateboards Vb LLC..................G 757 490-6619
Virginia Beach *(G-14398)*
Klimax Custom Skateboards..................G 757 589-0683
Virginia Beach *(G-14590)*
Magic Bullet Skateboards LLC..................G 703 371-0363
Fredericksburg *(G-5452)*

Outlook Skateboards LLC..................G... 757 713-5665
Smithfield (G-12718)
Triangle Skateboard Alliance ....G... 804 426-3663
Williamsburg (G-15326)
Virginia Beach Skateboards ....G... 757 385-4131
Virginia Beach (G-14914)
Xvd Board Sports LLC ....G... 757 504-0006
Norfolk (G-9797)

SPORTING & ATHLETIC GOODS: Skates & Parts, Roller

Creative Urethanes Inc ....E... 540 542-6676
Winchester (G-15407)

SPORTING & ATHLETIC GOODS: Snow Skis

Stans Ski and Snowboard LLC ....G... 540 885-9625
Staunton (G-13297)

SPORTING & ATHLETIC GOODS: Snowshoes

Snowshoe Retreats LLC.......................G... 540 442-6144
Harrisonburg (G-6372)

SPORTING & ATHLETIC GOODS: Soccer Eqpt & Splys

Commonwlth Soccer Programs LLC ....G... 804 794-2092
Midlothian (G-8801)
Prince William Athletic Center ....G... 571 572-3365
Woodbridge (G-15781)

SPORTING & ATHLETIC GOODS: Target Shooting Eqpt

Laporte USA ....G... 276 964-5566
Pounding Mill (G-10523)
Personal Protectio Principles ....G... 757 453-3202
Virginia Beach (G-14717)
ZF Technical LLC ....G... 757 575-5625
Virginia Beach (G-14960)

SPORTING & ATHLETIC GOODS: Targets, Archery & Rifle Shooting

Mountain Plains Industries ....G... 434 386-0100
Lynchburg (G-7775)
Round House LLC................................G... 757 504-3142
Alexandria (G-331)
Tacstrike LLC ....G... 540 751-8221
Roanoke (G-12007)

SPORTING & ATHLETIC GOODS: Team Sports Eqpt

Soccer Bridge ....G... 703 356-0462
Mc Lean (G-8549)
Stephen Bialorucki ....G... 757 374-2080
Virginia Beach (G-14846)

SPORTING & ATHLETIC GOODS: Tennis Eqpt & Splys

Har-Tru LLC ....E... 434 589-1542
Troy (G-13927)
Har-Tru LLC ....E... 877 442-7878
Charlottesville (G-2807)
Neuro Tennis Inc ....G... 240 481-7640
Arlington (G-1076)

SPORTING & ATHLETIC GOODS: Trap Racks, Clay Targets

Kennesaw Holding Company ....G... 603 866-6944
Fairfax (G-4643)

SPORTING & ATHLETIC GOODS: Treadmills

Blue RDG Antigravity Treadmlls............G... 540 977-9540
Roanoke (G-12048)
Robert Lummus ....G... 540 313-4393
Winchester (G-15468)

SPORTING & ATHLETIC GOODS: Water Skis

Bum Pass Water Ski Club Inc ....G... 240 498-7033
Bumpass (G-2160)
Linsey Echowater System ....G... 540 434-0212
Harrisonburg (G-6339)
Sml Water Ski Club Inc ....G... 540 328-0425
Moneta (G-8980)

SPORTING & RECREATIONAL GOODS & SPLYS WHOLESALERS

Dews Screen Printer ....F 757 436-0908
Chesapeake (G-3067)
Sport Shack Inc ....G... 540 372-3719
Fredericksburg (G-5487)

SPORTING & RECREATIONAL GOODS, WHOLESALE: Boat Access & Part

Joeys Sign & Letter Inc ....G... 757 868-7166
Hampton (G-6276)
Zimmerman Marine Incorporated ....F 804 776-0367
Deltaville (G-4090)

SPORTING & RECREATIONAL GOODS, WHOLESALE: Fishing

Ocean Products Research Inc ....F 804 725-3406
Diggs (G-4093)

SPORTING & RECREATIONAL GOODS, WHOLESALE: Golf

Links Choice LLC ....E... 434 286-2202
Scottsville (G-12663)

SPORTING CAMPS

Jarcam Sports......................................G... 678 995-4607
Norfolk (G-9601)

SPORTING FIREARMS WHOLESALERS

Ballistics Center LLC ....G... 703 380-4901
Woodbridge (G-15653)
Epic Mfg LLC ....G... 757 689-4373
Virginia Beach (G-14449)
Pointman Resources LLC ....G... 240 429-3423
Sterling (G-13472)

SPORTING GOODS

Aok Quality Solutions ....G... 757 710-9844
Onancock (G-10189)
Basketball Products Intl LLC ....G... 757 626-3865
Norfolk (G-9455)
Beltway Bat Company LLC ....G... 609 760-7243
Burke (G-2184)
Big Daddys Sports Products ....G... 757 310-8565
Hampton (G-6091)
Buc-DOE Tector Outdoors LLC ....G... 276 971-1383
Pounding Mill (G-10516)
Canam Uwh ....G... 906 399-7857
Remington (G-10767)
Champs..G... 800 991-6813
Newport News (G-9196)
Christina Bennett ....G... 703 489-9018
Norfolk (G-9483)
Cj9 Ltd ....G... 817 946-7421
Buena Vista (G-2140)
Covered Inc ....F 757 463-0434
Virginia Beach (G-14368)
Crews Outdoors Llc John ....G... 540 808-2204
Salem (G-12491)
Daq Bats LLC ....G... 202 365-3246
Mc Lean (G-8415)
Davida ....G... 571 278-4287
Chantilly (G-2402)
Dcsports87 Sport Cards ....G... 571 334-3314
Glen Allen (G-5721)
Dg2 Teler Sales ....G... 540 955-1996
Berryville (G-1679)
Diamondback Sport ....G... 434 964-6447
Charlottesville (G-2780)
Digital Delights Inc ....G... 703 661-6888
Sterling (G-13386)
Discus N More LLC ....G... 609 678-6102
Fredericksburg (G-5275)
Fletchers Hardware & Spt Ctr ....G... 276 935-8332
Grundy (G-6032)
Glovestix LLC ....G... 703 909-5146
Ashburn (G-1287)
Good Tymes Enterprises Inc ....G... 276 628-2335
Abingdon (G-34)
Grit Pack Calls LLC/GP Calls L.............G... 540 735-5391
Locust Grove (G-7445)
Hawk Hill Custom LLC..........................G... 540 248-4295
Verona (G-13988)

J&A Innovations LLC ....G... 804 387-6466
Midlothian (G-8835)
Jonathan Chandler ....G... 804 526-1148
Colonial Heights (G-3736)
KG Sports ....G... 540 538-7216
King George (G-7097)
Laporte America LLC ....G... 800 335-8827
Pounding Mill (G-10522)
Lax Loft LLC ....G... 540 389-4529
Salem (G-12529)
Livingston Resources Inc ....G... 704 892-1989
Richardsville (G-11011)
Longworth Sports Group Inc ....G... 276 328-3300
Wise (G-15630)
Lovells Replay Sportstop LLC ....G... 804 507-0271
Richmond (G-11274)
Lyons Share LLC ....G... 443 370-9514
Dumfries (G-4251)
Mechanicsville United Futbol ....G... 804 647-6557
Mechanicsville (G-8659)
Missile Baits LLC ....G... 855 466-5738
Salem (G-12538)
Mustang Sports Retail ....G... 757 679-2814
Chesapeake (G-3216)
N Zone Sports ....G... 703 743-2848
Haymarket (G-6430)
Nhsa ....G... 508 420-1902
Alexandria (G-291)
Nu-TEC Outdoor Innovations LLC ....G... 540 365-0551
Ferrum (G-4976)
Parker Compound Bows Inc ....E... 540 337-5426
Staunton (G-13283)
Pickers Grip LLC ....G... 434 260-3366
Palmyra (G-10255)
Pinkio Hoppers ....G... 571 277-4153
Springfield (G-13068)
Pivotal Gear LLC ....G... 804 726-1328
Henrico (G-6548)
Presidium Athletics LLC ....G... 800 618-9661
Powhatan (G-10568)
River Rock Custom Baits LLC ....G... 540 414-3293
Waynesboro (G-15135)
Ski Zone Inc ....G... 703 242-3588
Vienna (G-14130)
Skirmish Supplies ....G... 804 749-3458
Rockville (G-12299)
Sports Products World Entps ....G... 888 493-6079
Yorktown (G-15993)
Strong Industries LLC ....G... 757 533-9100
Norfolk (G-9735)
Techni Comm ....G... 703 231-6475
Nokesville (G-9400)
Terrapin Sports Supply Inc ....G... 540 672-9370
Orange (G-10228)
Total Sports ....G... 703 444-3633
Sterling (G-13536)
Warbird Turkey Calls LLC ....G... 540 968-0415
Clifton Forge (G-3683)
Whataseat ....G... 276 395-7887
Coeburn (G-3704)
Wild Things LLC ....G... 757 702-8773
Virginia Beach (G-14937)
Zen Sports Products LLC......................G... 703 925-0118
Herndon (G-6847)

SPORTING GOODS STORES, NEC

Austins Cycle Company ....G... 757 653-0182
Capron (G-2237)
Decosta Enterprises Inc ....G... 703 768-4270
Alexandria (G-443)
Dull Inc Dolan & Norma........................F 703 490-0337
Woodbridge (G-15687)
Edmund Davidson ....G... 540 997-5651
Goshen (G-5924)
Phoenix Sports and Advg Inc ....G... 276 988-9709
North Tazewell (G-10104)
Sport Shack Inc ....G... 540 372-3719
Fredericksburg (G-5487)
Tommy Atkinson Sports Entp ....G... 757 428-0824
Virginia Beach (G-14888)
Waller Brothers Trophy Shop ....G... 434 376-5465
Nathalie (G-9104)
Wimberley Inc ....G... 703 242-9633
Charlottesville (G-2907)
Woods & Waters Publishing Lc ....G... 540 894-9144
Bumpass (G-2171)

SPORTING GOODS STORES: Firearms

Dixie Press Custom Screen ....G... 757 569-8241
Sedley (G-12679)

Employee Codes: A=Over 500 employees, B=251-500
C=101-250, D=51-100, E=20-50, F=10-19, G=1-9

2021 Virginia
Industrial Directory

PRODUCT

1067

Elks Club 450................................G...... 540 434-3673
  Harrisonburg (G-6313)
Shawn Gaines.................................G...... 434 332-4819
  Rustburg (G-12446)

SPORTING GOODS STORES: Fishing Eqpt

Ocean Products Research Inc...........F...... 804 725-3406
  Diggs (G-4093)

SPORTING GOODS STORES: Hunting Eqpt

High Peaks Knife Works...................G...... 276 694-6563
  Stuart (G-13616)
Vfg Enterprises LLC.........................G...... 757 343-4866
  Virginia Beach (G-14908)

SPORTING GOODS STORES: Playground Eqpt

Deck World Inc...............................G...... 804 798-9003
  Warsaw (G-15062)

SPORTING GOODS STORES: Specialty Sport Splys, NEC

Middleburg Tack Exchange Ltd...........G...... 540 687-6608
  Middleburg (G-8730)

SPORTING GOODS STORES: Surfing Eqpt & Splys

Frierson Designs LLC.......................G...... 757 491-7130
  Virginia Beach (G-14475)

SPORTING GOODS STORES: Team sports Eqpt

Grafik Trenz..................................G...... 757 539-0141
  Smithfield (G-12714)

SPORTING GOODS STORES: Water Sport Eqpt

Zup LLC..G...... 843 822-5664
  Williamsburg (G-15350)

SPORTING GOODS: Archery

Amherst Arms and Supply LLC...........G...... 434 929-1978
  Madison Heights (G-7867)
Insights Intl Holdings LLC..................G...... 757 333-1291
  Franklin (G-5145)
Lasermarx Inc................................G...... 434 528-1044
  Madison Heights (G-7876)

SPORTING GOODS: Skin Diving Eqpt

Richmond Supply and Svc LLC...........G...... 804 622-9435
  Richmond (G-11738)

SPORTING GOODS: Surfboards

757 Surfboards..............................G...... 757 348-2030
  Virginia Beach (G-14197)
AJW Surfboards.............................G...... 910 617-8750
  Virginia Beach (G-14219)
Bill Foote......................................G...... 808 298-5423
  Virginia Beach (G-14279)
Catch Surfboard Co LLC..................G...... 949 218-0428
  Norfolk (G-9478)
Frierson Designs LLC.......................G...... 757 491-7130
  Virginia Beach (G-14475)
Harygul Imports Inc Maryland............E...... 757 427-5665
  Virginia Beach (G-14508)
Hickman Surfboards........................G...... 757 427-2914
  Virginia Beach (G-14523)
Mahogany Landscaping & Design......G...... 757 846-7947
  Virginia Beach (G-14635)
Zup LLC..G...... 843 822-5664
  Williamsburg (G-15350)

SPORTING/ATHLETIC GOODS: Gloves, Boxing, Handball, Etc

Cave Mma LLC...............................G...... 540 455-7623
  Fredericksburg (G-5409)

SPORTS APPAREL STORES

Custom Logos.................................G...... 804 967-0111
  Richmond (G-11173)

SPOUTING: Plastic & Fiberglass Reinforced

Sml Composites LLC........................G...... 540 576-3318
  Union Hall (G-13961)

SPRAYS: Artificial & Preserved

Aspire Marketing Corporation.............G...... 434 525-6191
  Forest (G-5051)
Combat Coatings LLC.......................G...... 757 468-9020
  Virginia Beach (G-14356)
Integrated Global Services Inc.............G...... 804 897-0326
  Midlothian (G-8833)

SPRINGS: Automobile

Starsprings USA Inc.........................D...... 276 403-4500
  Ridgeway (G-11855)

SPRINGS: Clock, Precision

Oxiwear Inc...................................G...... 571 212-7526
  Arlington (G-1093)

SPRINGS: Mechanical, Precision

Prototype Productions Inc.................D...... 703 858-0011
  Chantilly (G-2483)

SPRINGS: Wire

Custom Made Springs Inc.................G...... 757 489-8202
  Norfolk (G-9511)

STACKING MACHINES: Automatic

Stacker Inc A G..............................F...... 540 234-6012
  Weyers Cave (G-15177)

STAFFING, EMPLOYMENT PLACEMENT

Bradley-Morris LLC..........................E...... 678 419-4171
  Chesapeake (G-3014)

STAGE LIGHTING SYSTEMS

Audio-Visuals Actions Inc.................G...... 703 751-1010
  Alexandria (G-143)

STAINED GLASS ART SVCS

Applied Film Technology Inc...............G...... 757 351-4241
  Virginia Beach (G-14234)

STAINLESS STEEL

ATI Development LLC.......................G...... 571 313-0857
  Sterling (G-13355)
ATI-Endyna Jv LLC..........................G...... 410 992-3424
  Mc Lean (G-8397)
Hampton Sheet Metal Inc.................E...... 757 249-1629
  Newport News (G-9242)
Tidewater Rebar LLC.......................F...... 757 325-9893
  Suffolk (G-13773)

STAINS: Wood

Hbh Holdings LLC............................F...... 540 631-9555
  Front Royal (G-5536)

STAIRCASES & STAIRS, WOOD

Atlantic Staircrafters.......................F...... 804 732-3323
  Petersburg (G-10307)
Century Stair Company......................D...... 703 754-4163
  Haymarket (G-6417)
Hayes Stair Co Inc..........................E...... 540 751-0201
  Purcellville (G-10664)
John J Heckford.............................G...... 276 889-5646
  Lebanon (G-7194)
Loudoun Stairs Inc..........................E...... 703 478-8800
  Purcellville (G-10670)
Stair Store Inc...............................F...... 703 794-0507
  Manassas (G-8161)
Staircraft......................................G...... 540 347-7023
  Broad Run (G-2070)
Virginia Stairs Inc...........................G...... 757 425-6681
  Virginia Beach (G-14920)
Virginia Woodworking Co Inc.............E...... 276 669-3133
  Bristol (G-1997)

STAMPED ART GOODS FOR EMBROIDERING

Customized LLC..............................G...... 540 492-2975
  Roanoke (G-12077)
Impressions of Norton Inc.................G...... 276 679-1560
  Norton (G-10121)
Kalis Kreations & Designs LLC...........F...... 757 343-4421
  Suffolk (G-13727)
Shirt Art Inc...................................G...... 703 680-3963
  Woodbridge (G-15806)
Virginia Needle Art Inc......................G...... 540 433-8070
  Harrisonburg (G-6385)

STAMPINGS: Metal

Damon Company of Salem Inc............E...... 540 389-8609
  Salem (G-12494)
Elfinsmith Ltd Inc............................G...... 757 399-4788
  Portsmouth (G-10421)
Falcon Tool and Design Inc...............G...... 757 898-9393
  Yorktown (G-15958)
Mica Co of Canada Inc.....................G...... 757 244-7311
  Newport News (G-9299)
Randy Hawthorne............................G...... 434 547-3460
  Dillwyn (G-4099)
Sanjo Virginia Beach Inc...................G...... 757 498-0400
  Virginia Beach (G-14793)
Smart Machine Technologies Inc.........D...... 276 632-9853
  Ridgeway (G-11853)
Stamptech Inc................................G...... 434 845-9091
  Lynchburg (G-7812)

STARTERS & CONTROLLERS: Motor, Electric

Altomas Technologies LLC.................G...... 540 560-2320
  Rockingham (G-12239)

STATIONARY/OFFICE SPLYS, WHOL: Soc Stationery/Greeting Cards

Patricia Gavin................................G...... 703 439-4403
  Middleburg (G-8731)

STATIONERY & OFFICE SPLYS WHOLESALERS

Brook Brinders Limited.....................G...... 434 845-1231
  Lynchburg (G-7661)
Konica Mnlta Bus Sltons USA In..........C...... 703 461-8195
  Alexandria (G-508)
Madison Colonial LLC.......................G...... 240 997-2376
  Toano (G-13868)
Rollins Oma Sue.............................G...... 757 449-6371
  Virginia Beach (G-14778)
Westrock Commercial LLC.................E...... 804 444-1000
  Richmond (G-11824)

STATIONERY PRDTS

Cordially Yours...............................G...... 703 644-1186
  Springfield (G-12980)
J J E Enterprise Holdings LLC............G...... 410 703-9241
  Spotsylvania (G-12900)
Westrock Mwv LLC...........................A...... 804 444-1000
  Richmond (G-11825)

STATUARY & OTHER DECORATIVE PRDTS: Nonmetallic

Spring Moses Inc.............................G...... 804 321-0156
  Richmond (G-11395)

STAVES

Ramoneda Brothers LLC....................G...... 540 547-3168
  Culpeper (G-3915)
Ramoneda Brothers LLC....................G...... 540 825-9166
  Culpeper (G-3916)

STEEL & ALLOYS: Tool & Die

Innovative Machining Inc...................E...... 804 385-4212
  Forest (G-5077)

STEEL FABRICATORS

Aandc Sales Inc..............................G...... 703 638-8949
  Woodbridge (G-15641)
Abingdon Steel Inc..........................E...... 276 628-9269
  Abingdon (G-5)

Absolute Machine Enterprises F 276 956-1171
Ridgeway *(G-11838)*
Advance Mezzanine Systems LLC G 703 595-1460
Fredericksburg *(G-5168)*
Alliance Stl Fabrications Inc F 703 631-2355
Manassas Park *(G-8187)*
AMF Metal Inc G 703 354-1345
Springfield *(G-12947)*
AMF Metal Art Inc G 703 354-1345
Fairfax *(G-4407)*
Appalachian Machine Inc F 540 674-1914
Dublin *(G-4148)*
Associated Fabricators LLC G 434 293-2333
Charlottesville *(G-2731)*
Astra Design Inc G 804 257-5467
Richmond *(G-11493)*
Atlantic Metal Products Inc E 804 758-4915
Topping *(G-13885)*
B & L Mch & Fabrication Inc E 757 853-1800
Norfolk *(G-9449)*
Banker Steel Co LLC C 434 847-4575
Lynchburg *(G-7648)*
Bingham Enterprises LLC G 434 645-1731
Crewe *(G-3808)*
Blue Ridge Fabricators Inc F 540 342-1102
Roanoke *(G-12049)*
Bobby Burns Nowlin F 757 827-1588
Hampton *(G-6097)*
Bolling Steel Co Inc E 540 380-4402
Salem *(G-12484)*
Broadway Metal Works Inc E 540 896-7027
Broadway *(G-2086)*
Brookneal Machine Shop Inc G 434 376-2413
Brookneal *(G-2108)*
Browns Welding & Trailer Repr G 276 628-4461
Abingdon *(G-17)*
Bullet Enterprises Inc G 757 897-9100
Keswick *(G-7044)*
Byers Inc E 540 949-8092
Waynesboro *(G-15102)*
C M C Steel Fabricators Inc E 540 898-1111
Fredericksburg *(G-5256)*
C Y J Enterprises Corp G 703 367-7722
Manassas *(G-8043)*
Carbon & Steel LLC G 757 871-1808
Toano *(G-13859)*
Carico Inc E 540 373-5983
Fredericksburg *(G-5176)*
Carter Iron and Steel Co E 757 826-4559
Hampton *(G-6107)*
Cave Hill Corporation E 540 289-5051
McGaheysville *(G-8584)*
Cave Systems Inc G 877 344-2283
Henrico *(G-6489)*
Century Steel Products Inc E 703 471-7606
Sterling *(G-13367)*
Champion Iron Works Inc E 540 955-3633
Berryville *(G-1673)*
Clinch River LLC D 276 963-5271
Tazewell *(G-13830)*
Colonial Wldg Fabrication Inc E 757 459-2680
Norfolk *(G-9494)*
Colonnas Ship Yard Inc B 757 545-5311
Norfolk *(G-9496)*
Craft Machine Works Inc D 757 310-6011
Hampton *(G-6119)*
Craft Mch Wrks Acquisition LLC E 757 310-6011
Hampton *(G-6120)*
Creative Fabrication Inc E 540 931-4877
Covington *(G-3785)*
CSC Family Holdings Inc D 276 669-6649
Bristol *(G-2015)*
Custom Fabricators Inc G 757 724-0305
Windsor *(G-15603)*
Custom Metalsmith Inc G 276 988-0330
North Tazewell *(G-10097)*
Custom Welding Inc G 757 220-1995
Williamsburg *(G-15227)*
D & R USA Inc G 434 572-6665
South Boston *(G-12758)*
Dalmatian Hill Engneering G 540 289-5079
Port Republic *(G-10383)*
Danny Coltrane F 540 629-3814
Radford *(G-10711)*
Dominion Steel Inc F 540 898-1249
Fredericksburg *(G-5276)*
Dove Welding and Fabrication F 757 262-0996
Hampton *(G-6131)*
Driveline Fabrications Inc G 540 483-3590
Rocky Mount *(G-12319)*
East Cast Repr Fabrication LLC C 757 455-9600
Norfolk *(G-9535)*
East Coast Stl Fabrication Inc E 757 351-2601
Chesapeake *(G-3082)*
Edisons One Off Fbrcations LLC G 540 869-5703
Stephens City *(G-13316)*
Elite Fabrication LLC G 434 251-2639
Dry Fork *(G-4141)*
Entwistle Company E 434 799-6186
Danville *(G-3992)*
Esskay Structures Inc G 571 242-0011
Vienna *(G-14050)*
Excel Tool Inc F 276 322-0223
Falls Mills *(G-4931)*
Extreme Steel Inc D 540 868-9150
Warrenton *(G-15007)*
Extreme Steel Inc G 540 868-9150
Winchester *(G-15417)*
Family Crafters of Virginia G 540 943-3934
Waynesboro *(G-15114)*
Fei Ltd F 540 291-3398
Natural Bridge Stati *(G-9109)*
Fields Inc Oscar S E 804 798-3900
Ashland *(G-1416)*
Firedog Fabricators G 540 809-7389
Goldvein *(G-5878)*
Foley Material Handling Co Inc D 804 798-1343
Ashland *(G-1419)*
Formex LLC F 804 231-1988
Richmond *(G-11593)*
Frost Industries Inc G 804 724-0330
Heathsville *(G-6462)*
Full Awn Fab LLC G 540 439-5173
Bealeton *(G-1599)*
Gerdau Ameristeel US Inc G 434 517-0715
South Boston *(G-12772)*
Great White Buffalo Entps LLC G 434 329-1150
Lynchburg *(G-7724)*
Hamilton Iron Works Inc E 703 497-4766
Woodbridge *(G-15720)*
Hanson Industries Inc G 434 845-9091
Lynchburg *(G-7728)*
Hbi Custom Fabrication LLC G 305 916-0161
Gloucester *(G-5850)*
Hercules Steel Company Inc G 434 535-8571
Jarratt *(G-7010)*
Hi-Tech Machining LLC E 434 993-3256
Concord *(G-3760)*
Hucks & Hucks LLC G 276 525-1100
Abingdon *(G-41)*
Industrial Fabricators Inc F 540 989-0834
Roanoke *(G-11938)*
Industrial Fabricators VA Inc D 540 943-5885
Fishersville *(G-5005)*
Industrial Machine Works Inc E 540 949-6115
Waynesboro *(G-15116)*
Industrial Metalcraft Inc G 757 898-9350
Yorktown *(G-15965)*
Innovative Tech Intl Inc E 434 239-1979
Lynchburg *(G-7740)*
J C Steel De Tech G 757 376-7469
Virginia Beach *(G-14558)*
J&T Wlding Fbrication Campbell F 434 369-8589
Altavista *(G-632)*
Jarrett Welding and Mch Inc F 434 793-3717
Danville *(G-4006)*
Jetts Sheet Metal Inc G 540 899-7725
Fredericksburg *(G-5444)*
Joy Global Underground Min LLC C 276 623-2000
Abingdon *(G-45)*
Kennedy Konstruction Kompany E 540 984-4191
Edinburg *(G-4308)*
KG Old Ox Holdings Inc E 703 471-5321
Sterling *(G-13438)*
Kitchens Welding Inc G 757 653-2500
Courtland *(G-3771)*
Lapp Metals LLC G 434 392-3505
Farmville *(G-4946)*
Lawrence Fabrications Inc G 540 667-1141
Winchester *(G-15438)*
Lelo Fabrication G 703 581-7852
Gainesville *(G-5596)*
Lelo Fabrication LLC G 703 754-1141
Haymarket *(G-6429)*
Leroy Cary G 804 561-3526
Amelia Court House *(G-663)*
Lewis Metal Works Inc E 434 572-3043
South Boston *(G-12779)*
Liphart Steel Company Inc E 540 248-1009
Verona *(G-13991)*
Lynchburg Fabrication LLC G 434 660-0935
Lynchburg *(G-7760)*
Lynchburg Fabrication Inc VA F 434 473-7291
Lynchburg *(G-7761)*
Lyndon Steel Company LLC G 434 660-0829
Lynchburg *(G-7766)*
M & S Fabricators G 703 550-3900
Lorton *(G-7510)*
M1 Fabrication LLC G 804 222-8885
Richmond *(G-11662)*
Machine & Fabg Specialists Inc E 757 244-5693
Hampton *(G-6187)*
Mallory Co Inc G 757 803-5596
Chesapeake *(G-3194)*
Marktechnologic LLC G 703 470-1224
Springfield *(G-13047)*
Martin Metalfab Inc E 804 226-1431
Sandston *(G-12624)*
Martins Fabricating & Welding G 540 343-6001
Roanoke *(G-12133)*
Mechanical Machine & Repair G 804 231-5866
Richmond *(G-11676)*
Metal Products Specialist Inc G 757 398-9214
Portsmouth *(G-10460)*
Metalist G 540 793-0627
Roanoke *(G-11963)*
Metwood Inc F 540 334-4294
Boones Mill *(G-1897)*
Mid Atlntic Mtal Solutions Inc G 757 827-1588
Hampton *(G-6200)*
Naff Welding Inc F 276 629-1129
Bassett *(G-1587)*
Ncg LLC F 757 838-3224
Hampton *(G-6206)*
Obaugh Welding LLC G 540 396-6151
Mc Dowell *(G-8375)*
Panel Systems Inc E 703 910-6285
Woodbridge *(G-15772)*
Parkway Manufacturing Company F 757 896-9712
Hampton *(G-6213)*
Peebles Welding & Fabrication G 757 880-5332
Hampton *(G-6214)*
Performnce Mtal Fbricators Inc G 757 465-8622
Portsmouth *(G-10467)*
Personal G 540 845-8771
Fredericksburg *(G-5345)*
Piedmont Fabrication Inc F 757 543-5570
Chesapeake *(G-3239)*
Piedmont Metal Products Inc E 540 586-0674
Bedford *(G-1649)*
Plan B Design Fabrication Inc F 804 271-5200
Richmond *(G-11060)*
Professional Welding Svc Inc G 757 853-9371
Norfolk *(G-9697)*
R and L Machine Shop Inc E 757 487-8879
Chesapeake *(G-3254)*
R F J Ltd E 703 494-3255
Woodbridge *(G-15788)*
Red Acres Equipment Inc G 434 352-5086
Appomattox *(G-821)*
Rexcon Metals LLC G 703 347-2836
Springfield *(G-13079)*
Richmond Steel Inc E 804 355-8080
Richmond *(G-11360)*
S & K Welding Inc G 276 988-5591
North Tazewell *(G-10106)*
S A Halac Iron Works Inc D 703 406-4766
Sterling *(G-13499)*
Shickel Corporation D 540 828-2536
Bridgewater *(G-1959)*
Ship Sstnability Solutions LLC G 757 574-2436
Chesapeake *(G-3291)*
Silver Lake Welding Svc Inc F 540 879-2591
Dayton *(G-4064)*
SMI-Owen Steel Company Inc C 434 391-3903
Farmville *(G-4958)*
South River Fabricators G 540 377-9762
Vesuvius *(G-13998)*
Southern Iron Works Inc G 703 354-5500
Springfield *(G-13092)*
Specialist Manufacture G 540 974-0780
Middletown *(G-8743)*
Specialty Enterprises Inc G 804 781-0314
Mechanicsville *(G-8679)*
Spectrum Metal Services Inc G 804 744-0387
Midlothian *(G-8908)*
Stamptech Inc F 804 768-4658
Chester *(G-3456)*
Steel Fab G 276 628-3843
Lebanon *(G-7207)*

Structural Sculpture Corp .... G .. 434 207-3070
  Troy *(G-13936)*
Superior Fabrication LLC .... F .. 276 865-4000
  Haysi *(G-6458)*
Superior Iron Works Inc .... D .. 703 471-5500
  Sterling *(G-13524)*
Superior Metal & Mfg Inc .... F .. 540 981-1005
  Vinton *(G-14186)*
Tech Dynamism LLC .... G .. 434 227-5324
  Charlottesville *(G-2887)*
Technifab of Virginia Inc .... E .. 276 988-7517
  North Tazewell *(G-10109)*
Tecnico Corporation .... B .. 757 545-4013
  Chesapeake *(G-3326)*
Thermasteel Inc .... G .. 540 633-5000
  Radford *(G-10742)*
Tidewater Rebar LLC .... F .. 757 325-9893
  Suffolk *(G-13773)*
Tri Com Inc .... G .. 804 561-3582
  Amelia Court House *(G-675)*
Trinity Steel Erection Inc .... E .. 804 598-8811
  Powhatan *(G-10582)*
TST Fabrications LLC .... G .. 757 627-9101
  Norfolk *(G-9769)*
Turbo Sales & Fabrication Inc .... E .. 276 930-2422
  Floyd *(G-5042)*
Two N One Fabrication LLC .... G .. 757 642-2613
  Chesapeake *(G-3354)*
TYe Custom Metal Fabricators .... G .. 804 863-2551
  North Dinwiddie *(G-10067)*
Usr Steel LLC .... G .. 571 480-3497
  Centreville *(G-2348)*
Valley Precision Incorporated .... E .. 540 941-8178
  Waynesboro *(G-15142)*
Valmont Industries Inc .... E .. 804 733-0808
  Petersburg *(G-10348)*
Virginia Steel & Fabrication .... E .. 276 688-2125
  Bastian *(G-1594)*
W & B Fabricators Inc .... F .. 276 928-1060
  Rocky Gap *(G-12308)*
W&W-Afco Steel LLC .... E .. 276 669-6649
  Bristol *(G-2040)*
Wahoo Industries .... G .. 434 929-2466
  Lynchburg *(G-7835)*
Waynesboro Alloy Works Inc .... G .. 540 965-4038
  Covington *(G-3802)*
Weldment Dynamics LLC .... G .. 540 840-7866
  Mineral *(G-8953)*
Weston Company .... E .. 540 349-1200
  Gainesville *(G-5621)*
Winchester Metals Inc .... D .. 540 667-9000
  Winchester *(G-15511)*
York Fabrication .... G .. 804 241-0136
  La Crosse *(G-7153)*
York Fabrication LLC .... G .. 804 241-0136
  Boydton *(G-1917)*

STEEL MILLS

Azz Inc .... E .. 276 466-5558
  Bristol *(G-2007)*
Chaparral (virginia) Inc .... B .. 972 647-7915
  North Dinwiddie *(G-10049)*
Chaparral Virginia Inc .... G .. 540 767-1238
  Roanoke *(G-12064)*
Commercial Metals Company .... F .. 757 625-4201
  Norfolk *(G-9499)*
Diamond Source of Virginia .... G .. 804 360-3373
  Richmond *(G-11185)*
Donnasatticofcrafts .... G .. 757 855-0559
  Norfolk *(G-9531)*
Els Wheels LLC .... G .. 540 370-4397
  Fredericksburg *(G-5428)*
General Iron and Steel Co Inc .... F .. 434 676-3975
  Alberta *(G-98)*
Gerdau Ameristeel US Inc .... C .. 804 520-0286
  North Dinwiddie *(G-10051)*
Greenbrook Tms Neurohealth Ctr .... G .. 804 980-7520
  Glen Allen *(G-5738)*
Greenbrook Tms Neurohealth Ctr .... G .. 703 670-5738
  Woodbridge *(G-15718)*
Greenbrook Tms Neurohealth Ctr .... G .. 855 998-4867
  Roanoke *(G-11928)*
Greenbrook Tms Neurohealth Ctr .... G .. 855 998-4867
  Virginia Beach *(G-14491)*
Greenbrook Tms Neurohealth Ctr .... G .. 855 940-4867
  Fredericksburg *(G-5293)*
Greenbrook Tms Neurohealth Ctr .... G .. 434 327-1660
  Charlottesville *(G-2639)*
K S E .... G .. 571 366-1715
  Alexandria *(G-250)*

Karls Custom Wheels .... G .. 757 565-1997
  Williamsburg *(G-15263)*
Lane Enterprises Inc .... E .. 540 674-4645
  Dublin *(G-4163)*
Maverick Wheels LLC .... G .. 540 891-2681
  Fredericksburg *(G-5323)*
Nucor Corporation .... G .. 804 379-3704
  North Chesterfield *(G-9941)*
Osborne Welding Inc .... E .. 757 487-0900
  Portsmouth *(G-10466)*
Sam English of VA .... E .. 804 222-7114
  Richmond *(G-11370)*
Tms International .... E .. 804 957-9611
  North Dinwiddie *(G-10066)*
Ultimate Wheel Svcs LLC .... G .. 703 237-1044
  Falls Church *(G-4886)*
Voestlpine High Prfmce Mtls Co .... E .. 434 575-7994
  South Boston *(G-12792)*
Washing On Wheels Inc .... G .. 276 699-6275
  Ivanhoe *(G-7006)*
Wheels Tracks & Safety LLC .... G .. 434 846-8975
  Lynchburg *(G-7839)*
Workers On Wheels .... G .. 703 549-6287
  Alexandria *(G-388)*
Yocums Signature Hot Rods .... G .. 757 393-0700
  Portsmouth *(G-10507)*

STEEL: Cold-Rolled

Framecad America Inc .... F .. 703 615-2451
  Fairfax *(G-4626)*
Steel Dynamics Inc .... A .. 540 342-1831
  Roanoke *(G-12197)*
Technology Hub Inc .... G .. 571 370-5100
  Chantilly *(G-2508)*
Voestlpine High Prfmce Mtls Co .... E .. 434 575-7994
  South Boston *(G-12792)*

STEEL: Galvanized

Linx Industries Inc .... G .. 757 488-1144
  Portsmouth *(G-10453)*

STEEL: Laminated

Eastman Performance Films LLC .... D .. 423 224-7768
  Martinsville *(G-8283)*
H & B Machine .... G .. 276 546-5307
  Keokee *(G-7040)*

STENCILS

M & R Striping LLC .... G .. 703 201-7162
  Broad Run *(G-2068)*

STERILIZERS, BARBER & BEAUTY SHOP

Germfreak Inc .... G .. 443 254-0805
  Alexandria *(G-467)*
Tonys Unisex Barber .... G .. 757 237-7049
  Norfolk *(G-9761)*

STITCHING SVCS: Custom

Bobs Sports Equipment Sales .... G .. 276 669-8066
  Bristol *(G-2008)*

STONE: Cast Concrete

American Stone Inc .... G .. 804 448-9460
  Ruther Glen *(G-12449)*
Cornerstone Archtectural Stone .... G .. 540 297-3686
  Bedford *(G-1632)*

STONE: Crushed & Broken, NEC

Rock Xpress LLC .... G .. 571 212-6689
  Fairfax Station *(G-4723)*

STONE: Dimension, NEC

Blackpearl Soapstone .... G .. 813 909-8400
  Madison *(G-7849)*
Buckingham Slate Company LLC .... E .. 434 581-1131
  Arvonia *(G-1232)*
Rockydale Quarries Corporation .... G .. 540 896-1441
  Roanoke *(G-11997)*

STONE: Quarrying & Processing, Own Stone Prdts

Cardinal Stone Company Inc .... F .. 276 236-5457
  Galax *(G-5630)*

Empire Marble & Granite Co .... G .. 804 359-2004
  Richmond *(G-11574)*
Frazier Quarry Incorporated .... G .. 540 896-7538
  Timberville *(G-13849)*
Land Venture Two LC .... G .. 703 367-9456
  Manassas *(G-7961)*
R & S Stone Inc .... F .. 540 745-6788
  Floyd *(G-5037)*
Rockbridge Stone Products Inc .... G .. 540 258-2841
  Glasgow *(G-5701)*

STONEWARE PRDTS: Pottery

Hoffman Pottery .... G .. 276 773-3546
  Independence *(G-6985)*
Mainly Clay LLC .... G .. 434 390-8138
  Farmville *(G-4948)*

STORE FIXTURES, EXC REFRIGERATED: Wholesalers

Allen Display & Store Eqp Inc .... F .. 804 794-6032
  Midlothian *(G-8770)*

STORE FIXTURES: Exc Wood

Allen Display & Store Eqp Inc .... F .. 804 794-6032
  Midlothian *(G-8770)*
Polyfab Display Company .... E .. 703 497-4577
  Woodbridge *(G-15777)*
Showbest Fixture Corp .... D .. 804 222-5535
  Richmond *(G-11379)*
Showbest Fixture Corp .... E .. 434 298-3925
  Blackstone *(G-1828)*

STORE FIXTURES: Wood

Modular Wood Systems Inc .... E .. 276 251-5300
  Claudville *(G-3638)*

STORES: Drapery & Upholstery

Bridgewater Drapery Shop .... G .. 540 828-3312
  Bridgewater *(G-1950)*
Drapery House Inc .... G .. 703 669-9622
  Leesburg *(G-7260)*
Mary Elizabeth Burrell .... G .. 804 677-2855
  Richmond *(G-11670)*

STOVES: Wood & Coal Burning

Englands Stove Works Inc .... C .. 434 929-0120
  Monroe *(G-8989)*

STRAPS: Braids, Textile

Franklin Braid Mfg Co .... D .. 434 634-4142
  Emporia *(G-4358)*
Neighborhood Flags .... G .. 804 360-3398
  Henrico *(G-6539)*
Passionate Stitcher .... G .. 804 747-7141
  Glen Allen *(G-5778)*

STRUCTURAL SUPPORT & BUILDING MATERIAL: Concrete

Argos USA LLC .... G .. 804 227-9402
  Ashland *(G-1371)*
Batchelder & Collins Inc .... G .. 757 220-2806
  Williamsburg *(G-15210)*
Royal Group Inc .... E .. 276 783-8161
  Marion *(G-8242)*
Shockey Bros Inc .... C .. 540 401-0101
  Winchester *(G-15478)*

STUCCO

Central Virginia Stucco Inc .... G .. 434 531-0752
  Charlottesville *(G-2761)*
M T Stone and Stucco LLC .... G .. 434 806-7226
  Ruckersville *(G-12405)*
Rd Stucco LLC .... G .. 703 926-2322
  Arlington *(G-1141)*

STUDIOS: Artist

Casson Art & Frame .... G .. 276 638-1450
  Martinsville *(G-8274)*
Theorem Painting .... G .. 703 670-4330
  Dumfries *(G-4259)*

STUDIOS: Artists & Artists' Studios

Cheyenne Autumn Arts ....G..... 804 745-9561
  Chesterfield *(G-3486)*
Diverging Approach Inc ....F 757 220-2316
  Williamsburg *(G-15235)*

STUDIOS: Sculptor's

Turner Sculpture Ltd ....E 757 787-2818
  Melfa *(G-8713)*

SUBMARINE BUILDING & REPAIR

Elco Company ....G..... 703 876-3000
  Falls Church *(G-4787)*
General Dynamics Corporation ....E 703 221-1009
  Woodbridge *(G-15709)*
General Dynamics Corporation ....C..... 703 876-3000
  Reston *(G-10857)*
General Dynamics Info Tech Inc ....E 540 663-1000
  King George *(G-7091)*
General Dynmics Wrldwide Hldng ....G..... 703 876-3000
  Reston *(G-10858)*
Huntington Ingalls Inc ....B 757 380-2000
  Newport News *(G-9249)*
I Patriot Shipping Corp ....G..... 703 876-3000
  Falls Church *(G-4807)*
Northrop Grumman Newport News ....A 757 380-2000
  Newport News *(G-9306)*

SUNDRIES & RELATED PRDTS: Medical & Laboratory, Rubber

Icarus Medical LLC ....G..... 434 242-0258
  Charlottesville *(G-2813)*
Kinyo Virginia Inc ....C..... 757 888-2221
  Newport News *(G-9276)*
Metro Technology Llc ....G..... 703 579-7771
  Springfield *(G-13048)*

SUNGLASSES, WHOLESALE

House of Vondrake Lavar LLC ....G..... 804 295-6136
  Colonial Heights *(G-3734)*

SUNROOMS: Prefabricated Metal

Hartz Contractors Inc ....G..... 757 870-2978
  Newport News *(G-9246)*

SUPERMARKETS & OTHER GROCERY STORES

Chewning Lumber Company ....E 540 895-5158
  Spotsylvania *(G-12885)*
Danicas S Crochet Club ....G..... 703 221-8574
  Dumfries *(G-4242)*

SURFACE ACTIVE AGENTS: Oils & Greases

Hillmans Distributors.......................G..... 540 774-1896
  Roanoke *(G-11935)*

SURFACE ACTIVE AGENTS: Processing Assistants

Uso Path Finder ....G..... 757 395-4270
  Norfolk *(G-9776)*

SURGICAL APPLIANCES & SPLYS

Ascp Solutions LLC ....F..... 410 782-1122
  Manassas *(G-7914)*
Best Medical Belgium Inc ....G..... 800 336-4970
  Springfield *(G-12961)*
Best Medical International Inc ....C..... 703 451-2378
  Springfield *(G-12962)*
Draeger Safety Diagnostics Inc ....G..... 540 382-6650
  Christiansburg *(G-3585)*
Footmaxx of Virginia Inc ....G..... 540 345-0008
  Roanoke *(G-12092)*
Have Happyfeet ....G..... 757 339-0833
  Norfolk *(G-9573)*
Hollister Incorporated......................B 540 943-1733
  Stuarts Draft *(G-13651)*
K2m Group Holdings Inc ....B 703 777-3155
  Leesburg *(G-7295)*
Keystone Supply Co Inc ....G..... 610 525-3654
  Elkton *(G-4329)*
Lifenet Health ....B 757 464-4761
  Virginia Beach *(G-14610)*

Manakin Industries LLC ....G..... 804 784-5514
  Manakin Sabot *(G-7903)*
Microaire Surgical Instrs LLC ....C..... 800 722-0822
  Charlottesville *(G-2659)*
Mid-Atlantic Bracing Corp ....G..... 757 301-3952
  Virginia Beach *(G-14650)*
Mitchell Medical LLC ....G..... 804 640-4851
  Montpelier *(G-9018)*
Regula Forensics Inc ....G..... 703 473-2625
  Reston *(G-10936)*
Silver Ring Splint Co ....G..... 434 971-4052
  Charlottesville *(G-2877)*
Stryker Corporation ....G..... 571 919-2000
  Leesburg *(G-7352)*
Surefire Auto Detailing ....G..... 703 361-2369
  Manassas *(G-8163)*
Urologics LLC ....G..... 757 419-1463
  Midlothian *(G-8917)*
Virginia Beach Products LLC ....G..... 757 847-9338
  Virginia Beach *(G-14913)*

SURGICAL EQPT: See Also Instruments

Peer Technologies Pllc ....G..... 603 727-8692
  Fairfax *(G-4660)*

SURGICAL IMPLANTS

Biomaterials USA LLC ....G..... 843 442-4789
  Richmond *(G-11127)*
Neuropro Spinal Jaxx Inc ....G..... 571 334-7424
  Burke *(G-2195)*
Porex Corporation ....G..... 804 518-1012
  South Chesterfield *(G-12820)*

SURGICAL INSTRUMENT REPAIR SVCS

Patrick Pierce ....G..... 804 833-1800
  Henrico *(G-6546)*

SURVEYING & MAPPING: Land Parcels

American Tech Sltons Intl Corp............E 540 907-5355
  Fredericksburg *(G-5398)*

SUSPENSION SYSTEMS: Acoustical, Metal

P & G Interiors Inc ....E 540 985-3064
  Roanoke *(G-11980)*

SVC ESTABLISHMENT EQPT, WHOL: Cleaning & Maint Eqpt & Splys

Cleanvent Dryer Exhust Spclsts...........G..... 804 730-1754
  Mechanicsville *(G-8612)*

SVC ESTABLISHMENT EQPT, WHOL: Laundry/Dry Cleaning Eqpt/Sply

Mosena Enterprises Inc.....................G..... 757 562-7033
  Franklin *(G-5149)*

SVC ESTABLISHMENT EQPT, WHOLESALE: Firefighting Eqpt

Johnson Controls ....D 757 853-6611
  Norfolk *(G-9605)*

SWEEPING COMPOUNDS

Newell Industries Intl ....F 434 372-0089
  Chase City *(G-2913)*

SWIMMING POOLS, EQPT & SPLYS: Wholesalers

Spa Guy LLC ....G..... 757 855-0381
  Chesapeake *(G-3305)*

SWITCHES: Electric Power, Exc Snap, Push Button, Etc

Pascor Atlantic Corporation ....E 276 688-2220
  Bland *(G-1836)*
Schneider Electric Usa Inc ....G..... 703 968-0300
  Fairfax *(G-4550)*

SWITCHES: Electronic

Advanced Packet Switching Inc ....G..... 703 627-1746
  Woodbridge *(G-15642)*
Centurylink Switch Room ....G..... 276 646-8000
  Marion *(G-8224)*

Flip Switch Events LLC ....G..... 703 677-0119
  Ashburn *(G-1281)*
Stevens Switch LLC ....G..... 703 838-0686
  Alexandria *(G-356)*

SWITCHES: Electronic Applications

Lutron Shading Solutions ....G....... 804 752-3300
  Ashland *(G-1456)*
Smartdoor Systems Inc ....G..... 703 560-8093
  Falls Church *(G-4876)*

SWITCHGEAR & SWITCHBOARD APPARATUS

American Manufacturing Co Inc ....E 540 825-7234
  Elkwood *(G-4341)*
Anord Mardix (usa) Inc ....G..... 800 228-4689
  Henrico *(G-6473)*
Azz Inc ....E 276 466-5558
  Bristol *(G-2007)*
Critical Power Group Inc ....G..... 703 443-1717
  Ashburn *(G-1261)*
Edge McS LLC ....G..... 804 379-6772
  Midlothian *(G-8813)*
Electro-Mechanical Corporation..........B 276 669-4084
  Bristol *(G-1975)*
Instrumentation and Control ....D 804 550-5770
  Ashland *(G-1440)*
Lightronics Inc ....E 757 486-3588
  Virginia Beach *(G-14612)*
Power Distribution Inc ....C..... 804 737-9880
  Richmond *(G-11721)*
Power Distribution Pdts Inc ....E 276 646-3296
  Bristol *(G-2030)*
Virginia Controls Inc ....E 804 225-5530
  Richmond *(G-11811)*

SWORDS

Sword & Shield Coaching LLC ....G..... 804 557-3937
  Quinton *(G-10700)*

SYNCHROS

Nova Synchro of VA Inc......................G..... 703 241-4136
  Arlington *(G-1084)*

SYSTEMS ENGINEERING: Computer Related

Antheon Solutions Inc.......................G..... 703 298-1891
  Reston *(G-10790)*
Atlas North America LLC ....G..... 757 463-0670
  Yorktown *(G-15934)*
Department Info Tech Inc ....G..... 703 868-6691
  Chantilly *(G-2407)*
Engility LLC ....A 703 434-4000
  Reston *(G-10847)*
Fiddlehand Inc.................................G..... 703 340-9806
  Herndon *(G-6675)*
Insignia Technology Svcs LLC ....D 757 591-2111
  Ashburn *(G-1296)*
Leidos Inc ....C..... 703 676-7451
  Fort Belvoir *(G-5116)*
Saicomp LLC ....G..... 714 421-8967
  Petersburg *(G-10340)*

SYSTEMS INTEGRATION SVCS

Application Technologies Inc ....G..... 703 644-0506
  Springfield *(G-12949)*
Gannett Co Inc ....B 703 854-6000
  Mc Lean *(G-8438)*
K12excellence Inc ....G..... 804 270-9600
  Glen Allen *(G-5759)*
Mega-Tech Inc ....E 703 534-1629
  Falls Church *(G-4922)*
Mu-Del Electronics LLC.....................F 703 368-8900
  Manassas *(G-8114)*
Ntt America Solutions Inc ....G..... 571 203-4032
  Reston *(G-10910)*
Rebecca Leigh Fraser.......................G..... 912 755-3453
  Virginia Beach *(G-14765)*
Signafab LLC ....G..... 703 489-8572
  Louisa *(G-7567)*

SYSTEMS INTEGRATION SVCS: Local Area Network

Infrawhite Technologies LLC ....G..... 662 902-0376
  Vienna *(G-14071)*

PRODUCT

Irontek LLC ....G..... 703 627-0092
Sterling *(G-13432)*
Nomad Solutions LLC ....F..... 703 656-9100
Gainesville *(G-5602)*

SYSTEMS INTEGRATION SVCS: Office Computer Automation

Synergy Business Solutions LLC ....G..... 757 646-1294
Virginia Beach *(G-14860)*

SYSTEMS SOFTWARE DEVELOPMENT SVCS

Agaram Technologies Inc ....D..... 703 297-8591
Ashburn *(G-1239)*
Aretec Inc ....E..... 703 539-8801
Fairfax *(G-4596)*
Cloud Ridge Labs LLC ....G..... 434 477-5060
Forest *(G-5060)*
Cognition Point Inc ....G..... 703 402-8945
Aldie *(G-104)*
Diamondefense LLC ....F..... 571 321-2012
Annandale *(G-743)*
Iconicloud Inc ....G..... 703 864-1203
Alexandria *(G-481)*
Keystone Technology LLC ....G..... 540 361-8318
Fredericksburg *(G-5309)*
Mariner Media Inc ....F..... 540 264-0021
Buena Vista *(G-2146)*
Pantheon Software Inc ....F..... 703 387-4000
Arlington *(G-1097)*
Sensor Networks LLC....................G..... 703 481-2224
Reston *(G-10947)*
Source360 LLC ....G..... 703 232-1563
Chantilly *(G-2494)*

TABLE OR COUNTERTOPS, PLASTIC LAMINATED

Classic Creations of Tidewater........G..... 757 548-1442
Chesapeake *(G-3036)*
Gaithrsburg Cbinetry Mllwk Inc ....D..... 540 347-4551
Warrenton *(G-15019)*
Heartwood Solid Surfaces Inc ....F..... 703 369-0045
Manassas Park *(G-8201)*
Mid-Atlantic Manufacturing Inc ......E..... 804 798-7462
Oilville *(G-10183)*
Rockridge Granite Company LLC .....G..... 434 969-2665
Buckingham *(G-2136)*

TAGS & LABELS: Paper

Indoff Incorporated ....G..... 804 539-2425
Glen Allen *(G-5750)*

TAGS: Paper, Blank, Made From Purchased Paper

Cunningham Entps LLC Daniel ....G..... 804 359-2180
Richmond *(G-11170)*

TAILORS: Custom

Rogers Screen Printing Inc.............G..... 703 491-6794
Woodbridge *(G-15799)*

TANK COMPONENTS: Military, Specialized

Threat Prot Wrd Wide Svcs LLC ....G..... 703 795-2445
Remington *(G-10773)*

TANK REPAIR & CLEANING SVCS

Virginia Tank Service Inc...............G..... 540 344-9700
Roanoke *(G-12220)*

TANK REPAIR SVCS

Wards Wldg & Fabrication LLC ....G..... 540 219-1460
Brandy Station *(G-1942)*

TANK TRUCK CLEANING SVCS

Agee Catering Services.................G..... 434 960-8906
Palmyra *(G-10243)*

TANKS & OTHER TRACKED VEHICLE CMPNTS

Bae Systems Land Armaments Inc ......E..... 571 461-6000
Falls Church *(G-4756)*

Bae Systems Land Armaments LP......D..... 571 461-6000
Falls Church *(G-4757)*
Bae Systems Land Armmnts Hldng.....D..... 571 461-6000
Falls Church *(G-4758)*
Bowhead Integrated Support Ser........G..... 703 413-4226
Springfield *(G-12967)*
Special Tactical Services LLC ....F....... 757 554-0699
Virginia Beach *(G-14835)*
United Defense ....G..... 540 663-9291
King George *(G-7118)*

TANKS: Concrete

Abingdon Pre Cast Products.............G..... 276 628-2472
Abingdon *(G-2)*

TANKS: Cryogenic, Metal

Cryosel LLC ....G..... 757 778-1854
Hampton *(G-6124)*
Kelvin International Corp ....F..... 757 833-1011
Newport News *(G-9274)*

TANKS: Fuel, Including Oil & Gas, Metal Plate

Core Engineered Solutions Inc..........F..... 703 563-0320
Herndon *(G-6646)*

TANKS: Lined, Metal

Virginia Tank Service Inc.................G..... 540 344-9700
Roanoke *(G-12220)*

TANKS: Military, Including Factory Rebuilding

General Dynamics Corporation ....C..... 703 876-3000
Reston *(G-10857)*

TANKS: Standard Or Custom Fabricated, Metal Plate

Crossline Creations LLC ....G..... 703 625-4780
Sterling *(G-13376)*
Heinrich Enterprises Inc...................G..... 540 248-1592
Staunton *(G-13265)*
Hudsons Welding Shop....................G..... 434 822-1452
Danville *(G-3998)*
Service Machine & Wldg Co Inc ....D..... 804 798-1381
Ashland *(G-1490)*

TANKS: Water, Metal Plate

Pittsburg Tank & Tower Co Inc ....G..... 757 422-1882
Virginia Beach *(G-14724)*
Suburban Contractors LLC...............E..... 703 739-5600
Manassas *(G-8001)*
Waterline Nnk LLC ....G..... 804 577-4160
Kilmarnock *(G-7079)*

TANNERIES: Leather

Sierra Tannery LLC ....G..... 804 323-5898
Midlothian *(G-8898)*

TAPE DRIVES

R T Sales Inc................................G..... 703 542-5862
Haymarket *(G-6440)*

TAPES: Fabric

Bedford Weaving Inc ....C..... 540 586-8235
Bedford *(G-1626)*

TAPES: Plastic Coated

Intertape Polymer Corp ....C..... 434 797-8273
Danville *(G-4002)*

TAR

National Tars ....G..... 703 368-4220
Manassas *(G-8115)*
Tars Inc ....G..... 434 836-7890
Danville *(G-4039)*

TARGET DRONES

Appalachian Drone Servie LLC ....G..... 276 346-6350
Dryden *(G-4144)*
D-Fend Inc ....G..... 703 728-4283
Mc Lean *(G-8414)*

Zimbro Aerial Drone Integratio ....G..... 757 408-6864
Wicomico Church *(G-15197)*

TARPAULINS

Drumsticks Inc ....G..... 804 743-9356
North Chesterfield *(G-9861)*

TAXIDERMISTS

Appleberry Mtn Taxidermy Svcs ....G..... 434 831-2232
Schuyler *(G-12651)*

TELECOMMUNICATION SYSTEMS & EQPT

Ai Metrix Inc ....E..... 703 254-2000
Alexandria *(G-406)*
Avaya Federal Solutions Inc ....E..... 703 390-8333
Fairfax *(G-4415)*
Avaya Federal Solutions Inc ....F..... 703 653-8000
Fairfax *(G-4416)*
Avaya Federal Solutions Inc ....F..... 908 953-6000
Arlington *(G-866)*
G2k Labs Inc ....G..... 703 965-8367
Chantilly *(G-2425)*
General Dynamics Govt Syst ....E..... 703 383-3605
Oakton *(G-10148)*
General Dynamics Info Tech Inc.........D..... 703 268-7000
Herndon *(G-6681)*
General Dynmics One Source LLC ......F..... 703 906-6397
Falls Church *(G-4796)*
Iowave Inc ....E..... 703 979-9283
Arlington *(G-1011)*
Melvin Crutchfield ....G..... 804 440-3547
North Chesterfield *(G-9928)*
Pyott-Boone Electronics Inc ....C..... 276 988-5505
North Tazewell *(G-10105)*
Quick Eagle Networks Inc ....G..... 703 583-3500
Woodbridge *(G-15787)*
Softwright LLC ....G..... 434 975-4310
Charlottesville *(G-2694)*
Voice 1 Communication LLC ....G..... 804 795-7503
Richmond *(G-11441)*

TELECOMMUNICATIONS CARRIERS & SVCS: Wired

Computing Technologies Inc.............G..... 703 280-8800
Mechanicsville *(G-8613)*
Speakeasy ....G..... 703 333-5040
Annandale *(G-783)*
VT Milcom Inc...............................D..... 757 548-2956
Chesapeake *(G-3366)*

TELECOMMUNICATIONS CARRIERS & SVCS: Wireless

Connected Intelligence LLC...............G..... 571 241-4540
Dulles *(G-4196)*
Sun Signs ....G..... 703 867-9831
Stafford *(G-13197)*

TELEMARKETING BUREAUS

Harris Connect LLC ....B..... 757 965-8000
Norfolk *(G-9572)*

TELEMETERING EQPT

L3 Technologies Inc.......................C..... 703 889-8640
Ashburn *(G-1305)*
L3 Technologies Inc.......................G..... 757 425-0142
Virginia Beach *(G-14596)*

TELEPHONE EQPT: Modems

C Dcap Modem Line........................G..... 804 561-6267
Mannboro *(G-8214)*
Nsgdatacom Inc ....E..... 703 464-0151
Chantilly *(G-2475)*

TELEPHONE EQPT: NEC

Greenzone Systems Inc ....G..... 703 567-6039
Arlington *(G-987)*
L3harris Technologies Inc................D..... 434 455-9390
Forest *(G-5079)*
L3harris Technologies Inc................E..... 434 455-6600
Forest *(G-5080)*
Siemens AG ....G..... 757 875-7000
Newport News *(G-9337)*

TELEPHONE SVCS

CC Wireless Corporation ....G....... 757 802-8140
Norfolk (G-9479)

TELEPHONE: Fiber Optic Systems

Luna Innovations Incorporated ....E....... 540 961-5190
Blacksburg (G-1756)
Photonblue LLC ....G....... 804 747-7412
Richmond (G-11324)
Photonvision LLC ....G....... 540 808-6266
Charlottesville (G-2846)
Silynx Communications Inc ....F....... 301 217-9223
Sterling (G-13509)
Toana 2 Limited ....G....... 757 566-2001
Toano (G-13879)
Torrance Enterprises Inc ....G....... 804 748-5481
Chesterfield (G-3533)
US 1 Cable LLC ....G....... 571 224-3955
Gainesville (G-5620)

TELEPHONE: Sets, Exc Cellular Radio

Valcom Inc ....G....... 540 427-3900
Roanoke (G-12014)
Valcom Services LLC ....G....... 540 427-2400
Roanoke (G-12015)

TELESCOPES

Premier Reticles Ltd ....G....... 540 667-5258
Winchester (G-15568)

TELEVISION BROADCASTING & COMMUNICATIONS EQPT

Audio-Visuals Actions Inc ....G....... 703 751-1010
Alexandria (G-143)
Vsd LLC ....G....... 757 498-4766
Virginia Beach (G-14927)

TELEVISION BROADCASTING STATIONS

Virginn-Plot Mdia Cmpanies LLC ....G....... 757 446-2848
Virginia Beach (G-14924)
Wood Television LLC ....E....... 804 775-4600
Richmond (G-11832)

TELEVISION: Closed Circuit Eqpt

Vicon Industries Inc ....G....... 540 868-9530
Stephens City (G-13328)

TELEVISION: Monitors

Cyviz LLC ....G....... 571 858-3371
Arlington (G-924)

TENTS: All Materials

American Cemetery Supplies Inc ....F....... 757 488-0018
Portsmouth (G-10392)
Integrated Tex Solutions Inc ....D....... 540 389-8113
Salem (G-12522)
Norfolk Tent Company Inc ....F....... 757 461-7330
Norfolk (G-9668)
Yeates Mfg Inc ....G....... 757 465-7772
Portsmouth (G-10506)

TESTERS: Environmental

Blue Ridge Analytical LLC ....G....... 276 228-6464
Wytheville (G-15876)
Regula Forensics Inc ....G....... 703 473-2625
Reston (G-10936)
SES ....G....... 540 428-3919
Manassas (G-8153)

TESTERS: Physical Property

Embassy ....G....... 703 403-3996
Arlington (G-957)
Moog USA Inc ....G....... 540 586-6700
Bedford (G-1645)

TESTERS: Water, Exc Indl Process

Chemetrics Inc ....D....... 540 788-9026
Midland (G-8749)

TEXTILE & APPAREL SVCS

Sweetb Designs LLC ....G....... 757 550-0436
Portsmouth (G-10490)

TEXTILE BAGS WHOLESALERS

Lay-N-Go LLC ....G....... 703 799-0799
Alexandria (G-514)

TEXTILE FABRICATORS

Advanced Tooling Corporation ....G....... 434 286-7781
Scottsville (G-12657)
Combat V Tactical ....G....... 540 604-0235
Fredericksburg (G-5264)
Francis & Murphy ....G....... 703 256-8644
Annandale (G-749)
Mbh Inc ....G....... 540 427-5471
Roanoke (G-12135)
Washington Aed Education Fund ....G....... 703 739-9513
Alexandria (G-379)

TEXTILE PRDTS: Hand Woven & Crocheted

Berkley Latasha ....G....... 804 572-6394
Henrico (G-6482)
Crochet ....G....... 732 446-9644
Williamsburg (G-15226)
Crochet Braids By Twana LLC ....G....... 571 201-7190
Fredericksburg (G-5180)
Crochet By Grammy ....G....... 757 637-8416
Hampton (G-6122)
Crochet By Palm LLC ....G....... 757 427-0532
Virginia Beach (G-14372)
Danicas S Crochet Club ....G....... 703 221-8574
Dumfries (G-4242)
Dianes Crochet Dolls & Things ....G....... 703 229-2173
Warrenton (G-14996)
Kiss Krown LLC ....G....... 757 776-6518
Hampton (G-6180)
Qualitycrochetbybarb LLC ....G....... 202 596-7301
King George (G-7106)
Tamara Smith ....Vsd....... 910 495-4404
Gore (G-5923)

TEXTILE: Finishing, Cotton Broadwoven

Star Childrens Dress Co Inc ....E....... 804 561-5060
Amelia Court House (G-673)
University Pride & Prestige ....G....... 757 766-2590
Hampton (G-6256)

TEXTILE: Finishing, Raw Stock NEC

Barcroft Associates Ltd Partnr ....G....... 786 507-4649
Arlington (G-873)

TEXTILE: Goods, NEC

Edignas Fashion ....G....... 757 588-4958
Norfolk (G-9541)
Teeny Textiles ....G....... 703 731-7336
Virginia Beach (G-14868)

TEXTILES: Fibers, Textile, Rcvrd From Mill Waste/Rags

Clover Yarns Inc ....G....... 434 454-7151
Clover (G-3691)

TEXTILES: Jute & Flax Prdts

Fashion Mechanics ....G....... 571 398-0894
Woodbridge (G-15702)
Fashion Seoul ....G....... 571 395-8555
Annandale (G-748)

TEXTILES: Linen Fabrics

Dks Machine Shop Inc ....G....... 540 775-9648
King George (G-7087)
Dutch Lady ....G....... 202 669-0317
Alexandria (G-196)
Hilden America Inc ....E....... 434 572-3965
South Boston (G-12776)
Wilner Designs Inc Jane ....F....... 703 998-2551
Falls Church (G-4892)

TEXTILES: Mill Waste & Remnant

Cupron Inc ....F....... 804 322-3650
Henrico (G-6495)

TEXTILES: Tops, Combing & Converting

Marine Fabricators Inc ....G....... 804 758-2248
Topping (G-13887)

THEATRICAL LIGHTING SVCS

Matthias Enterprises Inc ....E....... 757 591-9371
Newport News (G-9296)

THEATRICAL SCENERY

Adco Signs Inc ....G....... 757 787-1393
Onancock (G-10188)

THERMOELECTRIC DEVICES: Solid State

Ttec LLC ....G....... 540 336-2693
Berryville (G-1697)

THERMOMETERS: Medical, Digital

Combat Bound LLC ....G....... 757 343-3399
Suffolk (G-13685)
Lifenet Health ....B....... 757 464-4761
Virginia Beach (G-14610)

THERMOPLASTICS

Hanwha Azdel Inc ....D....... 434 385-6359
Forest (G-5073)

THERMOSETTING MATERIALS

Transfoam LLC ....G....... 631 747-0255
Afton (G-92)

THIN FILM CIRCUITS

Eternal Technology Corporation ....E....... 804 524-8555
South Chesterfield (G-12803)
Lightspeed Infrared LLC ....G....... 540 875-6796
Bedford (G-1643)

THREAD: All Fibers

Tagstringcom Inc ....G....... 954 557-8645
Chantilly (G-2559)

THREAD: Sewing

Home Decor Sewing ....G....... 804 364-8750
Glen Allen (G-5747)

TILE: Brick & Structural, Clay

General Shale Brick Inc ....G....... 800 414-4661
Forest (G-5072)
Glen-Gery Corporation ....D....... 703 368-3178
Manassas (G-7946)
Lawrenceville Brick Inc ....D....... 434 848-3151
Lawrenceville (G-7182)
Redland Brick ....G....... 434 848-2397
Lawrenceville (G-7183)

TILE: Mosaic, Ceramic

E I Designs Pottery LLC ....G....... 410 459-3337
Virginia Beach (G-14424)

TILE: Wall, Ceramic

Florida Tile Inc ....G....... 757 855-9330
Chesapeake (G-3103)

TIN

Hwte Tin Han ....G....... 757 261-5963
Norfolk (G-9587)
Li DDS Pllc Tin W ....G....... 703 352-2500
Fairfax (G-4647)

TIRE & INNER TUBE MATERIALS & RELATED PRDTS

Als Used Tires & Rims ....G....... 703 548-3000
Alexandria (G-130)
Schrader-Bridgeport Intl Inc ....A....... 434 369-4741
Altavista (G-641)
Yokohama Tire Mnfctring Vrgnia ....D....... 540 389-5426
Salem (G-12583)

TIRE CORD & FABRIC

Mehler Inc ....D....... 276 638-6166
Martinsville (G-8312)

TIRE DEALERS

Als Used Tires & Rims ....G....... 703 548-3000
Alexandria (G-130)

PRODUCT

Daniels Welding and Tires ....G....... 757 566-8446
Toano *(G-13862)*

TIRES & INNER TUBES

BF Mayes Assoc Inc ....G....... 703 451-4994
Springfield *(G-12963)*
BF Wise & Sons Lc ....G....... 540 547-2918
Reva *(G-10999)*
Tire Kings ....G....... 757 586-5206
Newport News *(G-9357)*
Titan Wheel Corp Virginia ....D....... 276 496-5121
Saltville *(G-12594)*
Yokohama Corp North America ....C....... 540 389-5426
Salem *(G-12582)*

TIRES & TUBES WHOLESALERS

Yokohama Corp North America ....C....... 540 389-5426
Salem *(G-12582)*

TIRES & TUBES, WHOLESALE: Automotive

Daniels Welding and Tires ....G....... 757 566-8446
Toano *(G-13862)*

TIRES & TUBES, WHOLESALE: Truck

Wilbar Truck Equipment Inc................E....... 757 397-3200
Portsmouth *(G-10502)*

TIRES: Auto

Alban Cire ....G....... 703 455-9300
Springfield *(G-12939)*
Bolvs LLC ....G....... 508 310-8682
Chesterfield *(G-3481)*

TITANIUM MILL PRDTS

Titanium 3 LLC ....G....... 617 417-9288
Mc Lean *(G-8568)*
Titanium Productions Inc ....G....... 757 351-2526
Norfolk *(G-9759)*

TOBACCO & PRDTS, WHOLESALE: Cigarettes

Philip Morris USA Inc ....A....... 804 274-2000
Richmond *(G-11323)*

TOBACCO LEAF PROCESSING

Danville Leaf Tobacco Co Inc ....C....... 804 359-9311
Richmond *(G-11039)*
Park 500 ....G....... 804 751-2000
Chester *(G-3442)*
Philip Morris USA Inc ....A....... 804 274-2000
Richmond *(G-11323)*
Philip Morris USA Inc ....A....... 804 274-2000
Chester *(G-3443)*
Universal Leaf Tobacco Co Inc............D....... 804 359-9311
Richmond *(G-11066)*

TOBACCO STEMMING

Tobacco Processors Inc.....................G....... 804 359-9311
Richmond *(G-11413)*

TOBACCO: Chewing

Swedish Match North Amer LLC ....B....... 804 787-5100
Richmond *(G-11776)*

TOBACCO: Chewing & Snuff

Jti Leaf Services (us) LLC ....F....... 434 799-3286
Danville *(G-4007)*
Klds Client Services LLC ....G....... 804 586-7538
Midlothian *(G-8840)*
Philip Morris USA Inc ....A....... 804 274-2000
Chester *(G-3443)*
U S Smokeless Tob Brands Inc ....G....... 804 274-2000
Richmond *(G-11425)*
US Smokeless Tobacco Company ....E....... 804 274-2000
Richmond *(G-11430)*
Virginia Custom Blend LLC ....G....... 804 994-5099
Aylett *(G-1556)*

TOBACCO: Cigarettes

Altria Client Services LLC ....F....... 804 274-2000
Richmond *(G-11101)*
Altria Client Services LLC ....G....... 804 274-2000
Richmond *(G-11023)*

Altria Enterprises II LLC ....D....... 804 274-2200
Richmond *(G-11102)*
Altria Group Inc ....F....... 804 274-2000
Richmond *(G-11103)*
Altria Group Inc ....G....... 804 274-2000
Richmond *(G-11104)*
Altria Group Inc ....F....... 804 335-2703
Richmond *(G-11024)*
Altria Group Inc ....A....... 804 274-2200
Richmond *(G-11105)*
Altria Ventures Inc ....G....... 804 274-2000
Richmond *(G-11106)*
Firebird Manufacturing LLC ....G....... 434 517-0865
South Boston *(G-12767)*
Golden Leaf Tobacco Company ....G....... 434 736-2130
Keysville *(G-7057)*
Itg Brands ....G....... 434 792-0521
Danville *(G-4004)*
Philip Morris Duty Free Inc ....D....... 804 274-2000
Richmond *(G-11322)*
Philip Morris USA Inc ....A....... 804 274-2000
Richmond *(G-11323)*
Philip Morris USA Inc ....D....... 804 274-2000
Richmond *(G-11714)*
Philip Morris USA Inc ....E....... 804 274-2000
Richmond *(G-11058)*
Philip Morris USA Inc ....C....... 804 253-8464
North Chesterfield *(G-9949)*
R J Reynolds Tobacco Company ....F....... 757 420-1280
Virginia Beach *(G-14755)*
Richmond Distributors LLC ....G....... 804 497-0713
Richmond *(G-11354)*

TOBACCO: Cigars

Altria Client Services LLC ....F....... 804 274-2000
Richmond *(G-11101)*
Civille Smoke Shop............................G....... 434 975-1175
Charlottesville *(G-2766)*
General Cigar Co Inc ....E....... 757 825-7750
Hampton *(G-6157)*
General Cigar Co Inc ....G....... 804 935-2800
Richmond *(G-11599)*
General Cigar Co Inc ....A....... 860 602-3500
Glen Allen *(G-5735)*
Helix Innovations LLC ....G....... 804 274-2000
Richmond *(G-11235)*
Itg Cigars Inc ....E....... 804 233-7668
Richmond *(G-11622)*
John Middleton Co............................G....... 610 792-8000
Richmond *(G-11047)*

TOBACCO: Smoking

Blakbunni ....G....... 347 239-5139
Mechanicsville *(G-8607)*
John Middleton Co............................G....... 610 792-8000
Richmond *(G-11047)*

TOILET PREPARATIONS

Chattem Inc ....G....... 540 786-7970
Fredericksburg *(G-5261)*

TOILET SEATS: Wood

American Spirit LLC ....G....... 703 914-1057
Falls Church *(G-4749)*

TOILETRIES, COSMETICS & PERFUME STORES

Aziza Beauty LLC..............................G....... 804 525-9989
Richmond *(G-11496)*
Dr Kings Little Luxuries LLC ....G....... 434 293-8515
Keswick *(G-7045)*
E4 Beauty Supply LLC........................G....... 804 307-4941
Chesterfield *(G-3495)*

TOILETRIES, WHOLESALE: Toilet Preparations

Sociiterra International LLC..................G....... 804 461-1876
Mechanicsville *(G-8678)*

TOILETRIES, WHOLESALE: Toiletries

House of Vondrake Lavar LLC...............G....... 804 295-6136
Colonial Heights *(G-3734)*

TOILETS: Metal

Ferguson Portable Toilets LLC.............G....... 434 610-9988
Appomattox *(G-811)*

TOILETS: Portable Chemical, Plastics

Edmunds Waste Removal Inc...............G....... 804 478-4688
Mc Kenney *(G-8379)*

TOLLS: Caulking

Jaco Manufacturing Inc......................F....... 276 783-2688
Atkins *(G-1519)*

TOOL & DIE STEEL

Franklin Machine Shop........................G....... 757 241-6744
Hampton *(G-6152)*
Independent Stamping Inc...................G....... 540 949-6839
Waynesboro *(G-15115)*
Jeffs Tools Inc ....G....... 804 694-6337
Gloucester *(G-5851)*

TOOL REPAIR SVCS

Reeds Carbide Saw Service.................F....... 434 846-6436
Lynchburg *(G-7800)*
Wells Machine Co ....G....... 804 737-2500
Sandston *(G-12639)*

TOOLS: Carpenters', Including Levels & Chisels, Exc Saws

Bargers Custom Cabinets LLC.............G....... 540 261-7230
Buena Vista *(G-2139)*
James Pirtle.....................................G....... 540 477-2647
Mount Jackson *(G-9073)*

TOOLS: Hand

Calbico LLC ....G....... 571 332-3334
Annandale *(G-733)*
CLC Enterprises LLC ....G....... 540 622-3488
Flint Hill *(G-5015)*
Ferguson Manufacturing Co Inc...........F....... 757 539-3409
Suffolk *(G-13709)*
Geralds Tools Inc ....G....... 276 889-2964
Lebanon *(G-7192)*
Monikev-Fisher LLC ....G....... 757 343-4153
Virginia Beach *(G-14662)*
Nathan Group LLC ....G....... 757 229-8703
Williamsburg *(G-15282)*
Proskit Usa LLC ....G....... 804 240-9355
Amelia Court House *(G-668)*
Skips Tools Inc ....G....... 757 621-4775
Virginia Beach *(G-14824)*
Smartech Inc ....G....... 804 798-8588
Ashland *(G-1492)*

TOOLS: Hand, Engravers'

Anthony George Ltd Inc......................G....... 434 369-1204
Altavista *(G-625)*

TOOLS: Hand, Jewelers'

Caspian Inc ....G....... 434 237-1900
Lynchburg *(G-7675)*

TOOLS: Hand, Masons'

All Tools Inc.....................................G....... 804 598-1549
Powhatan *(G-10529)*

TOOLS: Hand, Mechanics

Superior Magnetic Product...................G....... 804 752-7897
Glen Allen *(G-5803)*

TOOLS: Hand, Power

Alioth Technical Services Inc ....G....... 757 630-0337
Virginia Beach *(G-14221)*
Eclipse Scroll Saw.............................G....... 804 779-3549
New Kent *(G-9131)*
Microaire Surgical Instrs LLC...............C....... 800 722-0822
Charlottesville *(G-2659)*
Monti Tools Inc.................................G....... 832 623-7970
Manassas *(G-8112)*

TOOTHPASTES, GELS & TOOTHPOWDERS

Bel Souri LLC ....G....... 757 685-5583
Virginia Beach *(G-14273)*

Everlasting Life Product............G....... 703 761-4900
Mc Lean *(G-8424)*

Everlasting Life Products Inc ....G....... 703 761-4900
Strasburg *(G-13578)*

Sunshine Products Inc ....G....... 703 768-3500
Alexandria *(G-592)*

TOWELS: Indl

American Merchant Inc ....G....... 407 446-9872
Bristol *(G-1966)*

TOWERS, SECTIONS: Transmission, Radio & Television

Delaware Valley Communications.......G....... 434 823-2282
Charlottesville *(G-2616)*

Key Bridge Global LLC ....G....... 703 414-3500
Mc Lean *(G-8479)*

TOWERS: Bubble, Cooling, Fractionating, Metal Plate

Tritech Solutions Virginia Inc ....G....... 434 664-2140
Appomattox *(G-824)*

TOWING & TUGBOAT SVC

CFS-Kbr Mrnas Support Svcs LLC....E....... 202 261-1900
Alexandria *(G-164)*

TOWING BARS & SYSTEMS

Dan Matheny Jerr...........G....... 703 499-9216
Woodbridge *(G-15680)*

TOYS

Alforas Company ....G....... 703 342-6910
Annandale *(G-729)*

Bingo City ....G....... 757 890-3168
Yorktown *(G-15937)*

Charlie Moseley ....G....... 571 235-3206
Reston *(G-10821)*

David C Maple ....G....... 757 563-2423
Virginia Beach *(G-14391)*

Decipher Inc ....D....... 757 664-1111
Norfolk *(G-9522)*

Degustabox USA LLC ....G....... 203 514-8966
Rockingham *(G-12248)*

Douglas Manning ....G....... 703 631-9064
Centreville *(G-2303)*

Game Quest Inc ....G....... 540 639-6547
Radford *(G-10714)*

Ghost Wind LLC ....G....... 561 624-1141
Powhatan *(G-10546)*

Little Wars Inc ....G....... 703 533-7942
Falls Church *(G-4824)*

Motrak Models ....G....... 813 476-4784
Martinsville *(G-8314)*

Newell Brands Inc ....G....... 800 241-1848
Richmond *(G-11303)*

Premonition Games LLC ....G....... 586 404-7070
Fredericksburg *(G-5349)*

Walmer Enterprises ....E....... 703 461-9330
Montross *(G-9028)*

Yaya Learning LLC ....G....... 540 230-5051
Falls Church *(G-4895)*

TOYS & HOBBY GOODS & SPLYS, WHOLESALE: Arts/Crafts Eqpt/Sply

Spring Moses Inc ....G....... 804 321-0156
Richmond *(G-11395)*

TOYS & HOBBY GOODS & SPLYS, WHOLESALE: Toys, NEC

Mountain Valley Enterprises..............G....... 276 686-6516
Rural Retreat *(G-12428)*

TOYS: Dolls, Stuffed Animals & Parts

James Lassiter ....G....... 757 595-4242
Newport News *(G-9265)*

Mondays Child ....G....... 703 754-9048
Nokesville *(G-9396)*

TOYS: Electronic

Stylewire LLC ....G....... 770 841-1300
Lynchburg *(G-7814)*

TOYS: Kites

Ann J Kite ....G....... 540 656-3070
Spotsylvania *(G-12883)*

Ann Kite ....G....... 434 989-4841
Earlysville *(G-4286)*

Dwight Kite ....G....... 540 564-8858
Elkton *(G-4326)*

Eastern League Commissioner............G....... 703 307-2080
Stafford *(G-13140)*

Glenn F Kite ....G....... 540 743-6124
Luray *(G-7613)*

Jackite Inc ....F....... 757 426-5359
Virginia Beach *(G-14561)*

Kitty Hawks Kites Inc ....G....... 757 351-3959
Virginia Beach *(G-14589)*

Lyniel W Kite ....G....... 540 298-9657
Elkton *(G-4332)*

Miller Kite House ....G....... 540 298-5390
Elkton *(G-4333)*

TOYS: Rubber

Zimar LLC ....G....... 703 688-3339
Falls Church *(G-4897)*

TOYS: Video Game Machines

Geek Keep LLC ....G....... 703 867-9867
Manassas *(G-8072)*

Improbable LLC ....E....... 571 418-6999
Arlington *(G-1000)*

TRACTOR REPAIR SVCS

Silver Lining Assistance Inc ....F....... 540 825-8371
Culpeper *(G-3921)*

TRAILER PARKS

Dinkle Enterprises ....G....... 434 324-8508
Hurt *(G-6974)*

TRAILERS & CHASSIS: Camping

Hillwood Park Inc ....G....... 703 754-6105
Gainesville *(G-5589)*

TRAILERS & PARTS: Horse

Taylor Boyz LLC ....G....... 540 347-2443
Midland *(G-8765)*

TRAILERS & PARTS: Truck & Semi's

BSI Express ....G....... 804 443-7134
Warsaw *(G-15061)*

Hillcrest Transportation Inc ....E....... 804 861-1100
North Dinwiddie *(G-10053)*

K O Stith Hauling LLC ....G....... 804 895-4617
Disputanta *(G-4111)*

Lawrence Trlr & Trck Eqp Inc..............F....... 800 296-6009
Ashland *(G-1451)*

Mobile Customs LLC ....G....... 757 903-5092
Manassas *(G-8110)*

Noke Truck LLC ....G....... 540 266-0045
Roanoke *(G-12142)*

Road & Rail Repair Inc ....G....... 757 558-1920
Chesapeake *(G-3271)*

S&M Trucking Inc ....G....... 540 842-1378
Fredericksburg *(G-5358)*

Trailer Buff Inc ....G....... 434 361-2500
Afton *(G-91)*

Two Peppers Transportation LLC.......G....... 757 761-6674
Yorktown *(G-15997)*

Virginia Truck Trailer LL ....G....... 804 784-3485
Rockville *(G-12302)*

Winchester Truck Repair LLC ....G....... 540 398-7995
Winchester *(G-15514)*

Wpd Inc ....G....... 757 859-9498
Ivor *(G-7007)*

TRAILERS & TRAILER EQPT

Bryan Smith ....G....... 434 242-7698
Ruckersville *(G-12400)*

Hibbard Iron Works of Hampton............F....... 757 826-5611
Hampton *(G-6165)*

Holmes Enterprises Intl Inc ....E....... 804 798-9201
Ashland *(G-1435)*

Industrial Biodynamics LLC ....G....... 540 357-0033
Salem *(G-12520)*

TRAILERS OR VANS: Horse Transportation, Fifth-Wheel Type

Claude Cofer............G....... 540 330-9921
Bedford *(G-1631)*

Miti-Gait LLC ....G....... 434 738-8632
Clarksville *(G-3634)*

TRAILERS: Bodies

Coe & Co Inc ....G....... 757 497-7709
Virginia Beach *(G-14351)*

Dalton Enterprises Inc..............D....... 276 686-9178
Rural Retreat *(G-12422)*

Holmes Enterprises Inc..............F....... 804 798-9201
Ashland *(G-1434)*

Imperial Group Mfg Inc ....C....... 540 674-1306
Dublin *(G-4159)*

TRAILERS: Semitrailers, Missile Transportation

Brandon Enterprises ....G....... 804 895-3338
South Prince George *(G-12865)*

Kandd Transportation Service ....G....... 434 298-7716
Danville *(G-4009)*

TRAILERS: Semitrailers, Truck Tractors

Utility Trailer Mfg Co..............A....... 276 783-8800
Atkins *(G-1522)*

TRANSDUCERS: Electrical Properties

Hardwire..............F....... 757 410-5429
Virginia Beach *(G-14506)*

TRANSDUCERS: Pressure

Carlen Controls Incorporated ....F....... 540 772-1736
Roanoke *(G-11903)*

TRANSFORMERS: Control

Earl Energy LLC ....E....... 757 606-2034
Portsmouth *(G-10418)*

TRANSFORMERS: Distribution

Face X LLC ....G....... 757 624-2121
Norfolk *(G-9547)*

Macks Transformer Service ....G....... 276 935-4366
Grundy *(G-6036)*

Pd Power Systems LLC..............F....... 703 778-3515
Springfield *(G-13066)*

Pemco Corporation..............G....... 276 326-2611
Bluefield *(G-1872)*

Power Distribution Pdts Inc ....E....... 276 646-3296
Bristol *(G-2030)*

Solgreen Solutions LLC ....G....... 833 765-4733
Alexandria *(G-588)*

TRANSFORMERS: Electric

GE Drives & Controls Inc ....A....... 540 387-7000
Salem *(G-12510)*

Schaffner Mtc LLC..............D....... 276 228-7943
Wytheville *(G-15912)*

Transformer Engineering LLC ....D....... 216 741-5282
Wytheville *(G-15920)*

TRANSFORMERS: Electronic

Isotemp Research Inc..............G....... 434 295-3101
Charlottesville *(G-2815)*

TRANSFORMERS: Machine Tool

Machine Tool Technology LLC ....F....... 804 520-4173
South Chesterfield *(G-12813)*

TRANSFORMERS: Power Related

ABB Enterprise Software Inc..............B....... 276 688-3325
Bland *(G-1835)*

Atlantic Wind Energy LLC ....G....... 757 401-9604
Chesapeake *(G-2986)*

Clean Power & Service LLC ....G....... 703 443-1717
Leesburg *(G-7244)*

Critical Power Group Inc ....G....... 703 443-1717
Ashburn *(G-1261)*

Electro-Mechanical Corporation..............B....... 276 669-4084
Bristol *(G-1975)*

PRODUCT

Electro-Mechanical Corporation............G...... 276 645-8232
Bristol *(G-1976)*

Electro-Mechanical Corporation............B...... 276 669-4084
Bristol *(G-1977)*

Magnetic Technologies Corp................G...... 276 228-7943
Wytheville *(G-15899)*

Marelco Power Systems Inc................F...... 800 225-4838
Richmond *(G-11667)*

Marelco Power Systems Inc................D...... 517 546-6330
Richmond *(G-11666)*

Mth Holdings Corp................D...... 276 228-7943
Roanoke *(G-11972)*

National Technical Svcs Inc................G...... 434 713-1528
Chatham *(G-2931)*

Phaze II Products Inc................E...... 757 353-3901
Virginia Beach *(G-14719)*

Power Catch Inc................G...... 757 962-0999
Norfolk *(G-9693)*

Power Distribution Inc................C...... 804 737-9880
Richmond *(G-11721)*

Pugal Inc................G...... 540 765-4955
Roanoke *(G-11990)*

SMC Electrical Products Inc................E...... 276 285-3841
Bristol *(G-2033)*

TRANSFORMERS: Specialty

AA Renwble Enrgy Hydro Sys Inc........G...... 804 739-0045
Moseley *(G-9032)*

Virginia Transformer Corp................B...... 540 345-9892
Roanoke *(G-12222)*

Virginia Transformer Corp................G...... 540 345-9892
Troutville *(G-13919)*

TRANSLATION & INTERPRETATION SVCS

Mng Online LLC................G...... 571 247-8276
Manassas *(G-8109)*

Ninoska M Marcano................G...... 202 604-8864
Fairfax *(G-4518)*

TRANSMISSIONS: Motor Vehicle

Dynax America Corporation................A...... 540 966-6010
Roanoke *(G-11917)*

TRANSPORTATION AGENTS & BROKERS

Gibraltar Energy LLC................G...... 202 642-2704
Alexandria *(G-469)*

Mountain Energy Resources Inc................G...... 276 679-3593
Norton *(G-10129)*

TRANSPORTATION EPQT & SPLYS, WHOLESALE: Acft/Space Vehicle

Aero International LLC................G...... 571 203-8360
Alexandria *(G-121)*

TRANSPORTATION EQPT & SPLYS WHOLESALERS, NEC

Bell Textron Inc................G...... 817 280-2346
Arlington *(G-878)*

Malpass Construction Co Inc................G...... 757 543-3541
Chesapeake *(G-3195)*

TRANSPORTATION EQUIPMENT, NEC

Contra Surplus LLC................G...... 757 337-9971
Norfolk *(G-9504)*

Db Enterprises of VA LLC................G...... 804 931-7667
Chester *(G-3403)*

H&H Hauling LLC................G...... 540 273-9109
Spotsylvania *(G-12892)*

Ked Hauling Co LLC................G...... 757 319-8652
Virginia Beach *(G-14582)*

Perkins................F...... 276 227-0551
Wytheville *(G-15904)*

Racing For Veterans................G...... 434 822-4201
Alton *(G-647)*

SHD Logistics LLC................G...... 804 405-4943
Chester *(G-3454)*

Tcts Trucking LLC................G...... 757 406-6323
Chesapeake *(G-3324)*

Twp Transport LLC................G...... 540 383-7995
Grottoes *(G-6025)*

Up and Go Transportation LLC................G...... 443 859-0193
Glen Allen *(G-5821)*

Vlh Transportation Inc................G...... 757 880-5772
Hampton *(G-6265)*

Walter Winget................G...... 757 339-0303
Carrollton *(G-2247)*

TRANSPORTATION SVCS: Cable Cars, Exc Aerial, Amuse & Scenic

Cauthorne Paper Company Inc................E...... 804 798-6999
Ashland *(G-1388)*

TRANSPORTATION: Air, Scheduled Freight

Fk Logistics Usa LLC................G...... 877 811-8772
Vienna *(G-14056)*

TRANSPORTATION: Local Passenger, NEC

Macklin Consulting LLC................G...... 202 423-9923
Alexandria *(G-269)*

TRAP ROCK: Dimension

Dream Green International LLC................G...... 814 616-7800
Alexandria *(G-194)*

TRAPS: Animal & Fish, Wire

Marshall Manufacturing Co................F...... 757 824-4061
Atlantic *(G-1525)*

TRAVEL TRAILERS & CAMPERS

Custom Concessions Inc................G...... 800 910-8533
Lynchburg *(G-7689)*

Hibbard Iron Works of Hampton................F...... 757 826-5611
Hampton *(G-6165)*

TROPHIES, NEC

Collinsville Engraving LLC................G...... 276 647-8596
Collinsville *(G-3710)*

Cresset Corporation................F...... 804 798-2691
Ashland *(G-1399)*

TROPHIES, PLATED, ALL METALS

Central Virginia Hardwood Pdts................G...... 434 335-5898
Gretna *(G-6006)*

Regal Products Co................G...... 804 798-2691
Ashland *(G-1485)*

TROPHIES: Metal, Exc Silver

Waller Brothers Trophy Shop................G...... 434 376-5465
Nathalie *(G-9104)*

TROPHY & PLAQUE STORES

Aci Partners LLC................F...... 703 818-0500
Manassas *(G-8019)*

Anthony Biel................G...... 703 307-8516
Dumfries *(G-4234)*

Artistic Awards................G...... 540 636-9940
Woodstock *(G-15847)*

Decosta Enterprises Inc................G...... 703 768-4270
Alexandria *(G-443)*

K & W Projects LLC................G...... 757 618-9249
Chesapeake *(G-3161)*

Phoenix Sports and Advg Inc................G...... 276 988-9709
North Tazewell *(G-10104)*

TRUCK & BUS BODIES: Car Carrier

LAw Hauling LLC................G...... 757 774-3055
Virginia Beach *(G-14604)*

TRUCK & BUS BODIES: Dump Truck

Century Trucking LLC................G...... 703 996-8585
Sterling *(G-13368)*

Phase II Truck Body Inc................E...... 276 429-2026
Glade Spring *(G-5680)*

TRUCK & BUS BODIES: Garbage Or Refuse Truck

Marvin Ramirez-Aguilar................G...... 703 241-4092
Arlington *(G-1054)*

TRUCK & BUS BODIES: Motor Vehicle, Specialty

Polaris Group Intl LLC................G...... 757 636-8862
Virginia Beach *(G-14728)*

TRUCK & BUS BODIES: Tank Truck

Virginia LP Truck Inc................F...... 434 246-8257
Stony Creek *(G-13570)*

TRUCK & BUS BODIES: Truck Beds

H & F Body & Cabinet Shop................G...... 276 728-9404
Hillsville *(G-6894)*

TRUCK & BUS BODIES: Truck Tops

Leonard Alum Utlity Bldngs Inc................G...... 434 792-8202
Danville *(G-4011)*

TRUCK & BUS BODIES: Truck, Motor Vehicle

Bellamy Mfg & Repr Co................G...... 276 386-7273
Hiltons *(G-6904)*

Morgan Olson LLC................G...... 269 659-0200
Ringgold *(G-11870)*

Wilbar Truck Equipment Inc................E...... 757 397-3200
Portsmouth *(G-10502)*

TRUCK & BUS BODIES: Utility Truck

S&C Global Products LLC................G...... 703 499-3635
Manassas *(G-7998)*

TRUCK BODIES: Body Parts

Amthor International Inc................D...... 845 778-5576
Gretna *(G-6002)*

Fontaine Modification Company................E...... 540 674-4638
Dublin *(G-4156)*

Gregorys Fleet Supply Corp................E...... 757 490-1606
Virginia Beach *(G-14492)*

Raleigh Mine and Indus Sup Inc................E...... 276 322-3119
Bluefield *(G-1878)*

TRUCK DRIVER SVCS

PM Services LLC................G...... 804 426-9892
Virginia Beach *(G-14727)*

TRUCK GENERAL REPAIR SVC

Trl Inc................G...... 276 794-7196
Castlewood *(G-2258)*

TRUCK PAINTING & LETTERING SVCS

Acutech Signs & Graphics Inc................G...... 757 766-2627
Hampton *(G-6070)*

Burruss Signs Inc................G...... 434 296-6654
Charlottesville *(G-2751)*

Gourmet Kitchen Tools Inc................G...... 757 595-3278
Yorktown *(G-15962)*

Grand Designs LLC................G...... 412 295-7730
Centreville *(G-2308)*

Ken Signs................G...... 703 451-5474
Springfield *(G-13032)*

Speedy Sign-A-Rama USA Inc................G...... 757 838-7446
Hampton *(G-6242)*

TRUCK PARTS & ACCESSORIES: Wholesalers

Crenshaw of Richmond Inc................D...... 804 231-6241
Richmond *(G-11546)*

Fontaine Modification Company................E...... 540 674-4638
Dublin *(G-4156)*

S&C Global Products LLC................G...... 703 499-3635
Manassas *(G-7998)*

TRUCKING & HAULING SVCS: Animal & Farm Prdt

Claude Cofer................G...... 540 330-9921
Bedford *(G-1631)*

Macklin Consulting LLC................G...... 202 423-9923
Alexandria *(G-269)*

TRUCKING & HAULING SVCS: Furniture Moving & Storage, Local

Evans Corporate Services LLC................F...... 703 344-3678
Lorton *(G-7485)*

TRUCKING & HAULING SVCS: Haulage & Cartage, Light, Local

McDonald Sawmill................G...... 540 465-5539
Strasburg *(G-13588)*

TRUCKING & HAULING SVCS: Heavy, NEC

S & S Equipment Sls & Svc Inc ....G..... 757 421-3000
Chesapeake *(G-3280)*

TRUCKING & HAULING SVCS: Liquid Petroleum, Exc Local

Masters Energy Inc ....E..... 281 816-9991
Glen Allen *(G-5768)*

TRUCKING & HAULING SVCS: Lumber & Log, Local

Peppers Services LLC ....G..... 276 233-6464
Galax *(G-5645)*
Sweany Trckg & Hardwoods LLC ....G..... 540 273-9387
Stafford *(G-13198)*
Wrights Trucking & Logging ....F..... 434 946-5387
Amherst *(G-715)*

TRUCKING, ANIMAL

Hucks & Hucks LLC ....G..... 276 525-1100
Abingdon *(G-41)*

TRUCKING, AUTOMOBILE CARRIER

Aura LLC ....G..... 757 965-8400
Norfolk *(G-9447)*

TRUCKING, DUMP

Geo Enterprise Inc ....G..... 703 594-3816
Nokesville *(G-9393)*
Ground Effects Hauling Inc ....G..... 757 435-1765
Virginia Beach *(G-14494)*

TRUCKING: Except Local

American Buildings Company ....C..... 434 757-2220
La Crosse *(G-7139)*
Klockner Pentaplast Amer Inc ....A..... 540 832-1400
Gordonsville *(G-5910)*
Klockner Pentaplast Amer Inc ....G..... 540 832-7615
Gordonsville *(G-5911)*
Lastmile Logistix Incorporated ....G..... 757 338-0076
Virginia Beach *(G-14601)*
Recycled Pallets Inc ....G..... 804 400-9931
Mechanicsville *(G-8670)*
Stm Snow Removal LLC ....G..... 540 604-0112
Stafford *(G-13196)*
Yorgea Inc ....G..... 704 431-8252
Norfolk *(G-9799)*

TRUCKING: Local, Without Storage

Lastmile Logistix Incorporated ....G..... 757 338-0076
Virginia Beach *(G-14601)*
Parham Services LLC ....G..... 804 586-1202
Sutherland *(G-13805)*
Ray Gorham ....G..... 703 971-1807
Alexandria *(G-566)*
S R Jones Jr & Sons Inc ....E..... 434 577-2311
Gasburg *(G-5660)*
Wheeler Tember ....G..... 540 672-4186
Orange *(G-10231)*

TRUCKING: Long-Distance, Less Than Truckload

4 Shores Trnsprting Lgstix LLC ....G..... 804 319-6247
Richmond *(G-11074)*

TRUCKS & TRACTORS: Industrial

Gbn Machine & Engineering Corp ....E..... 804 448-2033
Woodford *(G-15839)*
J&J Logistics Consulting LLC ....G..... 404 431-3613
Springfield *(G-13027)*
Mighty Mann Inc ....F..... 757 945-8056
Hampton *(G-6201)*
R&Y Trucking LLC ....G..... 404 781-1312
Chesapeake *(G-3255)*
Rayco Industries Inc ....E..... 804 321-7111
Richmond *(G-11729)*
Samuel L Brown ....G..... 804 892-5629
Ford *(G-5047)*
Silvio Enterprise LLC ....G..... 703 731-0147
Falls Church *(G-4874)*
Southern Virginia Equipment ....G..... 434 390-0318
Keysville *(G-7063)*

Terex Corporation ....G..... 540 361-7755
Fredericksburg *(G-5492)*
Tread Corporation ....D..... 540 982-6881
Roanoke *(G-12010)*
Utility One Source For Eqp LLC ....D..... 434 525-2929
Forest *(G-5103)*
Utility Trailer Mfg Co ....A..... 276 783-8800
Atkins *(G-1522)*
Volvo Group North America LLC ....C..... 336 393-2000
Dublin *(G-4174)*
Wilbar Truck Equipment Inc ....E..... 757 397-3200
Portsmouth *(G-10502)*

TRUCKS: Forklift

Homested Material Handlings ....G..... 804 299-3389
Rockville *(G-12286)*
Mosena Enterprises Inc ....G..... 757 562-7033
Franklin *(G-5149)*
Shop Guys ....G..... 804 317-9440
Midlothian *(G-8897)*
Total Lift Care LLC ....G..... 540 631-0008
Front Royal *(G-5559)*

TRUCKS: Indl

Ajs E Coast Hlg & Trnspt LLC ....G..... 540 645-2200
Triangle *(G-13888)*
Armstead Hauling Inc ....G..... 804 675-8221
Richmond *(G-11489)*
Bookers Transport LLC ....G..... 757 762-9233
Chesapeake *(G-3011)*
Boss Laide Express LLC ....G..... 804 263-8759
Virginia Beach *(G-14296)*
Coleman & Sons Trucking LLC ....G..... 434 247-1011
South Hill *(G-12847)*
Datskapatal Logistics LLC ....G..... 757 814-7325
Virginia Beach *(G-14390)*
Golco Logistics LLC ....G..... 571 234-3466
Newport News *(G-9236)*
Hek Logistics LLC ....G..... 757 637-8778
Dumfries *(G-4247)*
Lastmile Logistix Incorporated ....G..... 757 338-0076
Virginia Beach *(G-14601)*
Lee CL Trucking LLC ....G..... 804 677-2242
Richmond *(G-11650)*
Makivin Trucking LLC ....G..... 434 637-1359
Yale *(G-15929)*
PMC Logistics LLC ....G..... 804 414-8400
South Prince George *(G-12866)*
Rolling With Class LLC ....G..... 804 836-9760
North Chesterfield *(G-9965)*
Se7en Trnsp Lgstics Systems LL ....G..... 804 869-1716
Richmond *(G-11754)*
Stephen W Mast ....G..... 804 467-3608
Mechanicsville *(G-8681)*
Triple Z Transport LLC ....G..... 804 335-5962
Mechanicsville *(G-8689)*

TRUNKS

Thrifty Trunk ....G..... 757 478-7836
Norfolk *(G-9749)*

TRUSSES & FRAMING: Prefabricated Metal

Matthias Enterprises Inc ....E..... 757 591-9371
Newport News *(G-9296)*
Panel Systems Inc ....E..... 703 910-6285
Woodbridge *(G-15772)*

TRUSSES: Wood, Floor

Dominion Bldg Components LLC ....G..... 540 371-2184
Fredericksburg *(G-5421)*
Kempsville Building Mtls Inc ....G..... 757 875-1850
Newport News *(G-9275)*
Kennedy Konstruction Kompany ....E..... 540 984-4191
Edinburg *(G-4308)*

TRUSSES: Wood, Roof

Apex Industries LLC ....F..... 804 313-2295
Warsaw *(G-15060)*
Better Living Components Inc ....D..... 434 978-1666
Charlottesville *(G-2595)*
Chesapeake Strl Systems Inc ....E..... 804 966-8340
Charles City *(G-2573)*
First Colony Homes Inc ....G..... 540 788-4222
Calverton *(G-2224)*
Kc Wood Mfg ....G..... 540 789-8300
Willis *(G-15362)*

Kempsville Building Mtls Inc ....E..... 757 485-0782
Chesapeake *(G-3162)*
Lodore Truss Company Inc ....G..... 804 561-4141
Amelia Court House *(G-664)*
Massaponax Bldg Components Inc ....F..... 540 898-0013
Fredericksburg *(G-5322)*
Mulqueen Inc ....F..... 804 333-4847
Warsaw *(G-15070)*
Quadd Inc ....G..... 540 439-2148
Remington *(G-10771)*
Quadd Building Systems LLC ....E..... 540 439-2148
Remington *(G-10772)*
Republic Trusswerks LLC ....G..... 540 434-9497
Rockingham *(G-12271)*
Richard Evans ....G..... 540 774-1905
Roanoke *(G-11995)*
Riverside Roof Truss LLC ....D..... 434 793-0217
Danville *(G-4035)*
Ruffin & Payne Incorporated ....E..... 804 329-2691
Richmond *(G-11749)*
Shoffner Industries Virginia ....G..... 757 485-1132
Chesapeake *(G-3292)*
Structural Technologies LLC ....G..... 757 498-4448
Virginia Beach *(G-14857)*
Structural Technologies LLC ....F..... 888 616-0615
Doswell *(G-4126)*
Truss Systems Inc ....G..... 804 462-5963
Lancaster *(G-7163)*
Truss-Tech Inc ....E..... 757 787-3014
Melfa *(G-8712)*
Trussway Manufacturing Inc ....D..... 540 898-3477
Fredericksburg *(G-5382)*
Truswood Inc ....E..... 434 447-6565
South Hill *(G-12862)*
Truswood Inc ....D..... 757 833-5300
Newport News *(G-9365)*
Ufp Mid-Atlantic LLC ....G..... 757 485-3190
Chesapeake *(G-3355)*
Ufp Mid-Atlantic LLC ....D..... 540 921-1286
Pearisburg *(G-10278)*
Valley Building Supply Inc ....G..... 540 434-6725
Harrisonburg *(G-6383)*
White Rock Truss LLC ....G..... 276 445-5990
Rose Hill *(G-12364)*

TUBE & TUBING FABRICATORS

Davco Fabricating & Welding ....G..... 434 836-0234
Danville *(G-3980)*
Midyette Bros Mfg Inc ....G..... 757 425-5022
Virginia Beach *(G-14652)*
United States Pipe Fndry LLC ....F..... 540 439-7373
Remington *(G-10776)*

TUBES: Finned, For Heat Transfer

Alfa Laval USA Inc ....E..... 804 222-5300
Richmond *(G-11097)*

TUBES: Generator, Electron Beam, Beta Ray

Electron Technologies Inc ....G..... 703 818-9400
Chantilly *(G-2416)*

TUBES: Welded, Aluminum

Skyline Fabricating Inc ....G..... 276 498-3560
Raven *(G-10758)*

TUBING: Plastic

Arista Tubes Inc ....E..... 434 793-0660
Danville *(G-3956)*
Ericsons Inc ....E..... 770 505-6575
Chester *(G-3413)*

TUMBLERS: Plastic

Tumbleweed LLC ....G..... 540 261-7404
Lexington *(G-7420)*

TUNNELS: Vacuum, Metal Plate

Sheltech Plastics Inc ....G..... 978 794-2160
Elberon *(G-4319)*

TURBINES & TURBINE GENERATOR SETS

Alstom Renewable US LLC ....E..... 804 763-2196
Midlothian *(G-8771)*
Atlantic Research Corporation ....C..... 540 854-2000
Culpeper *(G-3869)*
Continental Auto Systems Inc ....C..... 540 825-4100
Culpeper *(G-3880)*

PRODUCT

Coriolis Wind Inc ....F 703 969-1257
Great Falls **(G-5950)**
Edge McS LLC ....G 804 379-6772
Midlothian **(G-8813)**
Edgeconnex Inc ....G 757 855-0351
Norfolk **(G-9540)**
Effithermix LLC ....G 703 860-9703
Vienna **(G-14043)**
Hydropower Turbine Systems ....G 804 360-7992
Powhatan **(G-10550)**
Siemens Industry Inc ....G 757 766-4190
Hampton **(G-6234)**
Virginia Electric and Power Co ....F 757 558-5459
Chesapeake **(G-3360)**

TURBINES: Steam

Zenman Technology LLC ....G 757 679-6703
Norfolk **(G-9800)**

TURBO-GENERATORS

Birge Croft ....G 757 547-0838
Chesapeake **(G-3002)**

TYPESETTING SVC

Adta & Co Inc ....F 703 930-9280
Annandale **(G-728)**
Allen Wayne Ltd Arlington ....G 703 321-7414
Warrenton **(G-14977)**
Americomm LLC ....D 757 622-2724
Norfolk **(G-9440)**
Apollo Press Inc ....E 757 247-9002
Newport News **(G-9169)**
B K Printing ....G 703 435-5502
Herndon **(G-6618)**
Barbours Printing Service ....G 804 443-4505
Tappahannock **(G-13813)**
Boaz Publishing Inc ....F 540 659-4554
Stafford **(G-13124)**
Business ....G 804 559-8770
Mechanicsville **(G-8609)**
C & B Corp ....G 434 977-1992
Charlottesville **(G-2752)**
Chocklett Press Inc ....D 540 345-1820
Roanoke **(G-12066)**
Coghill Composition Co Inc ....F 804 714-1100
Midlothian **(G-8799)**
Criswell Inc ....F 434 845-0439
Lynchburg **(G-7687)**
Custom Graphics Inc ....G 540 882-3488
Paeonian Springs **(G-10238)**
D & P Printing & Graphics Inc ....F 703 941-2114
Alexandria **(G-438)**
Deadline Typesetting Inc ....G 757 625-5883
Norfolk **(G-9520)**
E M Communications Inc ....G 434 971-4700
Charlottesville **(G-2787)**
Ersh-Enterprises Inc ....F 703 866-1988
Oakton **(G-10147)**
Gary D Keys Enterprises Inc ....G 703 418-1700
Arlington **(G-975)**
Gary Gray ....G 757 238-2135
Carrollton **(G-2242)**
Good Printers Inc ....D 540 828-4663
Bridgewater **(G-1953)**
Halifax Gazette Publishing Co ....E 434 572-3945
South Boston **(G-12774)**
Hopewell Publishing Company ....E 804 452-6127
Hopewell **(G-6934)**
Interntional Scanner Corp Amer ....F 703 533-8560
Arlington **(G-1007)**
J & M Printing Inc ....G 703 549-2432
Alexandria **(G-241)**
Jami Ventures Inc ....G 703 352-5679
Fairfax **(G-4484)**
Jones Printing Service Inc ....E 757 436-3331
Chesapeake **(G-3155)**
Lydell Group Incorporated ....G 804 627-0500
Richmond **(G-11277)**
Michael Beach ....G 703 360-7284
Alexandria **(G-531)**
Mountaineer Publishing Co Inc ....G 276 935-2123
Grundy **(G-6038)**
North Street Enterprise Inc ....E 434 392-4144
Farmville **(G-4954)**
Oldtown Printing & Copying ....G 540 382-6793
Christiansburg **(G-3607)**
P I P Printing 1156 Inc ....G 434 792-0020
Danville **(G-4022)**

Prestige Press Inc ....E 757 826-5881
Hampton **(G-6220)**
Printcraft Press Incorporated ....E 757 397-0759
Portsmouth **(G-10473)**
Printing and Sign System Inc ....G 703 280-1550
Fairfax **(G-4532)**
Program Services LLC ....G 757 222-3990
Norfolk **(G-9698)**
Rappahannock Entp Assoc Inc ....G 703 560-5042
Falls Church **(G-4862)**
Rappahannock Record ....F 804 435-1701
Kilmarnock **(G-7076)**
Salem Printing Co ....E 540 387-1106
Salem **(G-12566)**
Schreiber Inc R G ....E 540 248-5300
Verona **(G-13995)**
Silver Communications Corp ....E 703 471-7339
Sterling **(G-13508)**
Soundscape Comp & Prfmce Exch ....G 757 645-4671
Williamsburg **(G-15315)**
Suter Enterprises Ltd ....F 757 220-3299
Williamsburg **(G-15320)**
Swift Print ....G 540 774-1001
Roanoke **(G-12006)**
Tidewater Graphics Inc ....G 757 464-6136
Virginia Beach **(G-14874)**
Total Printing Co Inc ....E 804 222-3813
Richmond **(G-11416)**
Tr Press Inc ....E 540 347-4466
Warrenton **(G-15055)**
Type & Art ....G 804 794-3375
North Chesterfield **(G-10006)**
Type Factory Inc ....G 757 826-6055
Hampton **(G-6255)**
Universal Composition Svcs LLC ....G 202 255-7995
Leesburg **(G-7368)**
Walters Printing & Mfg Co ....F 540 345-8161
Roanoke **(G-12227)**
Wilkinson Printing Co Inc ....F 804 264-2524
Glen Allen **(G-5828)**
William R Smith Company ....E 804 733-0123
Petersburg **(G-10351)**
Winchester Printers Inc ....E 540 662-6911
Winchester **(G-15512)**
Wise Printing Co Inc ....G 276 523-1141
Big Stone Gap **(G-1718)**
Wood Television LLC ....E 540 672-1266
Orange **(G-10232)**

TYPESETTING SVC: Computer

Electronic Canvas ....G 434 656-3070
Gretna **(G-6008)**
Ern Graphic Design ....G 757 281-8801
Hampton **(G-6145)**
Omega Alpha II Inc ....F 804 747-7705
Richmond **(G-11315)**

ULTRASONIC EQPT: Cleaning, Exc Med & Dental

Kennesaw Holding Company ....G 603 866-6944
Fairfax **(G-4643)**
Medicor Technologies LLC ....G 804 616-8895
Powhatan **(G-10558)**

UNDERGROUND IRON ORE MINING

U S Mining Inc ....G 804 769-7222
Partlow **(G-10268)**

UNIFORM SPLY SVCS: Indl

Scrub Exchange LLC ....G 434 237-7778
Concord **(G-3763)**

UNIFORM STORES

Scrub Exchange LLC ....G 434 237-7778
Concord **(G-3763)**

UNIT TRAIN LOADING FACILITY, BITUMINOUS OR LIGNITE

Greater Wise Incorporated ....D 276 679-1400
Norton **(G-10119)**

UNIVERSITY

Hampton University ....G 757 727-5385
Hampton **(G-6164)**

UPHOLSTERY WORK SVCS

Citizens Upholstery & Furn Co ....G 540 345-5060
Vinton **(G-14170)**
Jose Goncalves Inc ....E 703 528-5272
Arlington **(G-1017)**

URANIUM ORE MINING, NEC

Framatome Inc ....B 434 832-3000
Lynchburg **(G-7715)**

USED CAR DEALERS

Cap City Inc ....G 757 827-0932
Hampton **(G-6105)**

USED MERCHANDISE STORES

Flowers Bkg Co Lynchburg LLC ....G 434 978-4104
Charlottesville **(G-2632)**

UTENSILS: Household, Cooking & Kitchen, Metal

Blanc Creatives LLC ....F 434 260-1692
Charlottesville **(G-2741)**

UTENSILS: Household, Cooking & Kitchen, Porcelain Enameled

Savage Transparency LLC ....G 760 218-6457
Chesapeake **(G-3284)**

UTILITY TRAILER DEALERS

Leonard Alum Utlity Bldngs Inc ....G 540 951-0236
Blacksburg **(G-1753)**

VACUUM CLEANERS: Household

2 Busy Brooms Cleaning Service ....G 540 476-1190
Grottoes **(G-6011)**
Dawn Group Inc ....G 703 750-6767
Annandale **(G-740)**
Dyson Direct Inc ....G 571 210-4317
Tysons Corner **(G-13954)**
Shupes Cleaning Solutions ....G 804 737-6799
Sandston **(G-12632)**

VACUUM CLEANERS: Indl Type

Old Dominion Brush Company Inc ....G 800 446-9823
Richmond **(G-11313)**

VACUUM SYSTEMS: Air Extraction, Indl

Diversified Vacuum Inc ....G 757 538-1170
Suffolk **(G-13699)**

VALUE-ADDED RESELLERS: Computer Systems

Pleasant Vly Bus Solutions LLC ....E 703 391-0977
Reston **(G-10926)**
Trimech Solutions LLC ....E 804 257-9965
Glen Allen **(G-5818)**

VALVES

Romans Enterprises LLC ....F 757 216-6401
Virginia Beach **(G-14779)**
Valve Safe Solutions LLC ....G 540 721-7808
Moneta **(G-8984)**

VALVES & PIPE FITTINGS

American Manufacturing Co Inc ....E 540 825-7234
Elkwood **(G-4341)**
Ames & Ames Inc ....G 757 877-2328
Yorktown **(G-15932)**
Ames & Ames Inc ....G 757 851-4723
Hampton **(G-6083)**
Azz Inc ....E 276 466-5558
Bristol **(G-2007)**
Dante Industries Inc ....G 757 605-6100
Norfolk **(G-9516)**
International Carbide & Engrg ....F 434 568-3311
Drakes Branch **(G-4133)**

VALVES & REGULATORS: Pressure, Indl

Controls Corporation America ....C 757 422-8330
Virginia Beach **(G-14363)**

(G-0000) Company's Geographic Section entry number

VALVES: Aerosol, Metal

Burnopp Metal LLC ....G...... 434 525-4746
Evington **(G-4375)**

VALVES: Aircraft, Hydraulic

Hy-Tech Usa Inc ....G...... 804 647-2048
Midlothian **(G-8830)**

VALVES: Control, Automatic

Augusta Actuation LLC ....G...... 540 480-7619
Steeles Tavern **(G-13310)**

VALVES: Indl

Alfa Laval Champ LLC ....G...... 866 253-2528
Richmond **(G-11094)**
Alfa Laval Inc ....C...... 866 253-2528
Richmond **(G-11095)**
Curtiss-Wright Corporation ....F 703 779-7800
Ashburn **(G-1266)**
Firewall LLC ....G...... 804 977-8777
Mechanicsville **(G-8623)**
Flow Dynamics Inc ....G...... 804 835-9740
Petersburg **(G-10320)**
Hanbay Inc ....G...... 757 333-6375
Virginia Beach **(G-14502)**
Schrader-Bridgeport Intl Inc ....C...... 434 369-4741
Altavista **(G-642)**
Schrader-Bridgeport Intl Inc ....A...... 434 369-4741
Altavista **(G-641)**
Valve Automation Center ....G...... 804 752-2700
Ashland **(G-1505)**

VALVES: Plumbing & Heating

Fluid Energy ....G...... 757 549-5160
Chesapeake **(G-3106)**
Mm Export LLC ....G...... 757 333-0542
Virginia Beach **(G-14658)**

VALVES: Regulating & Control, Automatic

Chesapeake Bay Controls Inc ....F 757 228-5537
Virginia Beach **(G-14333)**
Seacrist Motor Sports ....G...... 540 309-2234
Salem **(G-12568)**
Seager Valve ....G...... 757 478-0607
Chesapeake **(G-3289)**

VALVES: Water Works

Key Recovery Corporation ....G...... 540 444-2628
Salem **(G-12526)**

VAN CONVERSIONS

Ride-Away Inc ....F 804 233-8267
North Chesterfield **(G-10022)**

VARIETY STORES

James Hintzke ....G...... 757 374-4827
Virginia Beach **(G-14563)**
Kiln Doctor Inc ....G...... 540 636-6016
Front Royal **(G-5540)**

VARNISHES, NEC

Davis-Frost Inc ....G...... 434 846-2721
Lynchburg **(G-7695)**

VASES: Pottery

Creative Workshops ....G...... 703 938-6177
Vienna **(G-14031)**

VEGETABLE STANDS OR MARKETS

Alpha ....G...... 540 895-5731
Partlow **(G-10263)**

VEHICLES: Recreational

Electrify America LLC ....D...... 703 364-7000
Herndon **(G-6666)**

VENDING MACHINE REPAIR SVCS

Compass Group Usa Inc ....E...... 757 485-4401
Chesapeake **(G-3048)**

VENDING MACHINES & PARTS

Chow Time LLC ....G...... 804 934-9305
Richmond **(G-11157)**
Compass Group Usa Inc ....E...... 757 485-4401
Chesapeake **(G-3048)**
Hailey Bug Vending ....G...... 757 665-4402
Bloxom **(G-1841)**
Hampton Roads Vending ....G...... 703 927-6125
Chesapeake **(G-3127)**
Jacatai Vending ....G...... 804 317-2526
North Chesterfield **(G-9901)**
Lorrie Carpenter ....G...... 804 720-6442
Alexandria **(G-265)**
Rdj Enterprises ....G...... 757 538-0466
Suffolk **(G-13758)**
T-Jar Inc ....G...... 540 974-2567
Winchester **(G-15486)**
Wright Discount Entps LLC ....G...... 703 580-5278
Woodbridge **(G-15835)**

VENETIAN BLINDS & SHADES

Bath Son and Sons Associates ....G...... 804 722-0687
Petersburg **(G-10309)**
Shade Mann-Kidwell Corp ....G...... 804 288-2819
Richmond **(G-11378)**

VENTILATING EQPT: Metal

Bloxom Sheet Metal Inc ....G...... 757 436-4181
Chesapeake **(G-3006)**

VENTILATING EQPT: Sheet Metal

Atlantic Fabrication & Boiler ....F 757 494-0597
Portsmouth **(G-10394)**

VERMICULITE: Processed

Virginia Vermiculite LLC ....E...... 540 967-2266
Louisa **(G-7574)**

VESSELS: Process, Indl, Metal Plate

Synalloy Corporation ....D...... 804 822-3260
Glen Allen **(G-5804)**

VETERINARY PHARMACEUTICAL PREPARATIONS

Kehoe Enterprises LLC ....G...... 540 668-9080
Hillsboro **(G-6874)**

VETERINARY PRDTS: Instruments & Apparatus

Absolute Anesthesia ....G...... 434 277-9360
Piney River **(G-10360)**

VIALS: Glass

Amcor Phrm Packg USA LLC ....C...... 434 372-5113
Chase City **(G-2909)**
Nipro Glass Americas Corp ....G...... 434 372-5113
Chase City **(G-2914)**

VIDEO & AUDIO EQPT, WHOLESALE

Luminous Audio Technology ....G...... 804 741-5826
Richmond **(G-11275)**
SQ Labs LLC ....G...... 804 938-8123
Richmond **(G-11770)**

VIDEO PRODUCTION SVCS

A V Publication Corp ....G...... 276 251-1760
Ararat **(G-829)**
Audio-Visuals Actions Inc ....G...... 703 751-1010
Alexandria **(G-143)**
Brian Enterprises LLC ....G...... 757 645-4475
Williamsburg **(G-15214)**
Onthefly Pictures LLC ....G...... 757 339-1520
Portsmouth **(G-10465)**

VIDEO TAPE PRODUCTION SVCS

Nis Inc ....E...... 703 323-9170
Fairfax **(G-4519)**

VIDEO TRIGGERS: Remote Control TV Devices

VT Aepco Inc ....G...... 703 658-7500
Alexandria **(G-607)**

VISUAL COMMUNICATIONS SYSTEMS

Applied Vsual Cmmnications Inc ....E 703 787-6668
Herndon **(G-6614)**
Claritas Creative LLC ....G...... 240 274-5029
Arlington **(G-906)**
Eyegaze Inc ....F 703 385-8800
Fairfax **(G-4620)**

VITAMINS: Natural Or Synthetic, Uncompounded, Bulk

Dreampak LLC ....F 703 751-3511
Mc Lean **(G-8421)**
Hana Tonic LLC ....G...... 804 993-4262
Oakton **(G-10149)**

VITAMINS: Pharmaceutical Preparations

Bettera Brands LLC ....D...... 703 222-6340
Chantilly **(G-2377)**

WALLPAPER & WALL COVERINGS

Campbell David ....G...... 757 877-1633
Yorktown **(G-15941)**

WALLS: Curtain, Metal

Efco Corporation ....E...... 540 248-8604
Verona **(G-13985)**

WAREHOUSING & STORAGE, REFRIGERATED: Cold Storage Or Refrig

V C Ice and Cold Storage Inc ....G...... 434 793-1441
Danville **(G-4045)**

WAREHOUSING & STORAGE: General

Alt Services Inc ....G...... 757 806-1341
Hampton **(G-6081)**
Essolutions Inc ....F 240 215-6992
Arlington **(G-959)**
Lighted Signs Direct Inc ....G...... 703 965-5188
Woodbridge **(G-15740)**
Packaging Products Inc ....E...... 276 629-3481
Bassett **(G-1588)**
Sprecher & Schuh Inc ....F 804 379-6065
North Chesterfield **(G-9989)**

WAREHOUSING & STORAGE: Self Storage

Stihl Incorporated ....E...... 757 468-4010
Virginia Beach **(G-14848)**

WARFARE COUNTER-MEASURE EQPT

Lockheed Martin Corporation ....B...... 757 935-9479
Suffolk **(G-13732)**

WARM AIR HEATING/AC EQPT/SPLYS, WHOL Warm Air Htg Eqpt/Splys

Super RAD Coils Ltd Partnr ....C...... 804 794-2887
North Chesterfield **(G-9992)**

WASHCLOTHS

Dirty Deeds Power Washing ....G...... 804 731-2739
Prince George **(G-10592)**

WASHERS

Lt Pressure Washer Services ....G...... 703 626-9010
Alexandria **(G-266)**

WASTE CLEANING SVCS

Ground Effects Hauling Inc ....G...... 757 435-1765
Virginia Beach **(G-14494)**

WATER PURIFICATION EQPT: Household

Norris Screen and Mfg LLC ....E...... 276 988-8901
Tazewell **(G-13838)**

PRODUCT

WATER PURIFICATION PRDTS: Chlorination Tablets & Kits

Deatrick & Associates Inc ....G....... 703 753-1040
  Haymarket (G-6418)
Neuro Stat Anlytcal Sltons LLC ....E....... 703 224-8984
  Vienna (G-14104)
Silivhere Technologies Inc ....G....... 434 566-1207
  Charlottesville (G-2875)

WATER SOFTENER SVCS

Dominion Water Products Inc...............E....... 804 236-9480
  Richmond (G-11189)
Zentox Corporation ....F....... 757 868-0870
  Poquoson (G-10380)

WATER TREATMENT EQPT: Indl

A Descal Matic Corp ....G....... 757 858-5593
  Norfolk (G-9414)
Aquao2 Wastewater Treatment Sy ....G....... 540 365-0154
  Ferrum (G-4967)
Aquarobic International Inc ....G....... 540 365-0154
  Ferrum (G-4968)
Broswell Water Systems ....G....... 757 436-1871
  Chesapeake (G-3016)
City of Danville ....E....... 434 799-5137
  Danville (G-3967)
Dominion Water Products Inc...............E....... 804 236-9480
  Richmond (G-11189)
Doswell Water Treatment Plant ....F....... 804 876-3557
  Doswell (G-4120)
H20 Pro ....G....... 540 785-6811
  Fredericksburg (G-5295)
Heyward Inc Virginia Inc ....G....... 804 965-0086
  Glen Allen (G-5742)
Infilco Degremont Inc ....E....... 804 756-7600
  Richmond (G-11247)
Metro Water Purification LLC ....G....... 804 366-2158
  Chester (G-3436)
Piedmont Environmental Sys ....G....... 434 836-4547
  Danville (G-4025)
Planet Care Inc ....G....... 540 980-2420
  Pulaski (G-10644)
Prochem Inc ....E....... 540 268-9884
  Elliston (G-4347)
Pure-Mech Inc ....G....... 804 363-1297
  Roanoke (G-11991)
Rivanna Water & Observatory ....G....... 434 973-5709
  Charlottesville (G-2687)
River Rock Environmental Svcs ....G....... 757 690-3916
  Suffolk (G-13759)
Solar Sea Water LLC ....G....... 215 452-9992
  Arlington (G-1172)
Suez Treatment Solutions Inc ....F....... 804 550-4971
  Ashland (G-1497)
Suez Wts Services Usa Inc ....C....... 757 855-9000
  Norfolk (G-9737)
Virginia Carolina Pure Water..............G....... 757 282-6487
  Virginia Beach (G-14918)
Water Filtration Plant ....F....... 276 656-5137
  Martinsville (G-8351)

WATER: Mineral, Carbonated, Canned & Bottled, Etc

Blue Ridge Springs Inc....................F....... 434 822-0006
  Danville (G-3961)
Misty Mtn Spring Wtr Co LLC ....E....... 276 623-5000
  Abingdon (G-50)

WATER: Pasteurized & Mineral, Bottled & Canned

Enviro Water ....G....... 703 569-0971
  Springfield (G-12999)
Flow Beverages Inc ....E....... 613 680-3569
  Verona (G-13987)
Pure Paradise Water of Vb ....G....... 757 318-0522
  Virginia Beach (G-14749)

WATER: Pasteurized, Canned & Bottled, Etc

Central Carolina Btlg Co Inc ....F....... 434 753-2515
  Alton (G-646)
Shenandoah Corporation ....E....... 540 248-2123
  Staunton (G-13292)

WATERPROOFING COMPOUNDS

Construction Specialties Group...........G....... 703 670-5300
  Dumfries (G-4240)
Weathertite Industries Inc ....G....... 703 830-8001
  Chantilly (G-2521)

WAVEGUIDE PRESSURIZATION EQPT

Clean Power & Service LLC ....G....... 703 443-1717
  Leesburg (G-7244)

WAVEGUIDES & FITTINGS

Fleet Waveguides LLC ....G....... 757 337-3311
  Newport News (G-9230)

WAXES: Petroleum, Not Produced In Petroleum Refineries

Afton Chemical Corporation ....B....... 804 788-5800
  Richmond (G-11476)

WEATHER STRIP: Sponge Rubber

Hutchinson Sealing Systems Inc ....C....... 276 228-4455
  Wytheville (G-15891)

WEAVING MILL, BROADWOVEN FABRICS: Wool Or Similar Fabric

Precision Fabrics Group Inc ....B....... 540 343-4448
  Vinton (G-14181)

WEB SEARCH PORTALS: Internet

Ideation Web Studios LLC ....G....... 757 333-3021
  Chesapeake (G-3140)
Ubiquitywave LLC..........................G....... 571 262-1406
  Ashburn (G-1344)

WEDDING CONSULTING SVCS

Lilly Lane Incorporated ....G....... 434 792-6387
  Danville (G-4013)

WELDING & CUTTING APPARATUS & ACCESS, NEC

B & B Welding Inc ....G....... 540 982-2082
  Roanoke (G-12039)

WELDING EQPT

Controls Corporation America ....C....... 757 422-8330
  Virginia Beach (G-14363)
Custom Designers Inc ....G....... 703 830-8582
  Centreville (G-2299)
Maxwell Incorporated ....G....... 804 370-3697
  Ashland (G-1460)

WELDING EQPT & SPLYS: Electrodes

T & J Wldg & Fabrication LLC ....G....... 757 672-9929
  Suffolk (G-13770)

WELDING EQPT & SPLYS: Generators, Arc Welding, AC & DC

Radford Wldg & Fabrication LLC ....G....... 540 731-4891
  Radford (G-10737)

WELDING EQPT & SPLYS: Resistance, Electric

Brads Wldg & Align Boring LLC ....G....... 276 340-1605
  Patrick Springs (G-10269)
Jones & Sons Inc ....G....... 434 836-3851
  Blairs (G-1830)

WELDING EQPT & SPLYS: Seam, Electric

Valley Supply and Services LLC...........G....... 276 979-4547
  North Tazewell (G-10110)

WELDING EQPT & SPLYS: Spot, Electric

Phillips Welding Service Inc ....G....... 434 989-7236
  Madison Heights (G-7882)

WELDING EQPT & SPLYS: Wire, Bare & Coated

Lewis Welding & Cnstr Works ....G....... 434 696-5527
  Keysville (G-7060)
Steel Tech LLC ....G....... 571 585-5861
  Sterling (G-13515)
William Keyser ....G....... 703 243-8777
  Arlington (G-1219)

WELDING EQPT REPAIR SVCS

Schrocks Repair ....G....... 540 879-2406
  Dayton (G-4062)
Total Welding Solutions LLC ....G....... 703 898-8720
  Haymarket (G-6450)

WELDING EQPT: Electric

Skyline Fabricating Inc ....G....... 276 498-3560
  Raven (G-10758)

WELDING EQPT: Electrical

Design Systems & Services Corp ....E....... 804 722-0396
  Petersburg (G-10316)

WELDING MACHINES & EQPT: Ultrasonic

Alan Forney Jr...........................G....... 540 323-1666
  Winchester (G-15374)
Valley Construction Svcs LLC ....G....... 540 320-8545
  Blacksburg (G-1802)

WELDING REPAIR SVC

A 1 Welding Services ....G....... 434 831-2562
  Schuyler (G-12649)
A A J Welding Inc ....G....... 276 688-0191
  Bastian (G-1592)
A&H Welding Inc ....G....... 703 628-4817
  Alexandria (G-398)
Aaron D Crouse...........................G....... 757 827-6123
  Hampton (G-6067)
Absolute Welding LLC ....G....... 434 569-5351
  Farmville (G-4936)
Action Iron LLC ....G....... 703 594-2909
  Nokesville (G-9388)
Adams Co LLC ....G....... 757 721-0427
  Virginia Beach (G-14211)
Adams Welding Service ....G....... 804 843-4468
  West Point (G-15152)
Advanced Machine & Tooling ....F....... 757 518-1222
  Virginia Beach (G-14213)
All Things Welded ....G....... 423 492-0880
  Marion (G-8220)
Als Machine & Welding Inc ....G....... 804 443-3193
  Tappahannock (G-13810)
Alston Welding Svc ....G....... 757 547-7351
  Chesapeake (G-2961)
American Sheet Metal & Welding ....G....... 757 627-9203
  Norfolk (G-9439)
Amg Inc ....D....... 434 385-7525
  Lynchburg (G-7640)
Apex Welding Service LLC ....G....... 757 773-1151
  Chesapeake (G-2977)
ARC Vosacthree ....G....... 703 910-7721
  Woodbridge (G-15647)
Arco Welding Inc..........................F....... 540 710-6944
  Fredericksburg (G-5247)
Arcworx Welding LLC.......................G....... 540 394-1494
  Leesburg (G-7221)
Armstrong Gordan ....G....... 757 547-1090
  Chesapeake (G-2980)
Ascwelding ....G....... 757 274-4486
  Chesapeake (G-2982)
Automated Machine & Tech Inc.............E....... 757 898-7844
  Grafton (G-5931)
B & B Machine & Tool Inc ....E....... 540 344-6820
  Roanoke (G-12038)
B & B Welding & Fabrication ....G....... 540 663-5949
  King George (G-7081)
B & G Stainless Works Inc ....G....... 703 339-6002
  Lorton (G-7464)
B and B Welding Service LLC ....G....... 804 994-2797
  Aylett (G-1545)
Barry Wayne Gladden ....G....... 540 389-6645
  Salem (G-12481)
Bay Welding ....G....... 757 633-7689
  Virginia Beach (G-14263)
Bearkers Welding ....G....... 434 324-7616
  Gretna (G-6004)

Bears Specialty Welding ....G.... 540 247-6813	D P Welding Inc ....G.... 757 232-0460	Gibson Welding ....G.... 276 328-3324
Winchester (G-15386)	Newport News (G-9212)	Wise (G-15624)
Berkle Welding & Fabrication ....F.... 804 708-0662	Dale Stidham ....G.... 276 523-1428	Gladden Welding ....G.... 540 387-1489
Oilville (G-10176)	Big Stone Gap (G-1708)	Salem (G-12512)
Bethels Welding ....G.... 434 946-7160	Daniels Certified Welding ....G.... 434 848-4911	Glr Welding & Fabrication ....G.... 276 337-1401
Amherst (G-682)	Freeman (G-5511)	Pound (G-10513)
Blanchards Welding Repair ....G.... 757 539-6306	David F Waterbury Jr ....G.... 757 490-5444	Grammers Welding ....G.... 804 730-7296
Suffolk (G-13680)	Virginia Beach (G-14392)	Mechanicsville (G-8629)
Blands Welding & Fabg Co ....G.... 276 495-8132	Db Welding LLC ....G.... 757 483-0413	Grove Hill Welding Services ....G.... 540 282-8252
Nora (G-9407)	Suffolk (G-13696)	Shenandoah (G-12690)
Blue Ridge Mechanical ....G.... 540 662-3148	Dishman Fabrications LLC ....G.... 757 478-5070	H&W Welding Co Inc ....G.... 540 334-1431
Winchester (G-15390)	Yorktown (G-15950)	Boones Mill (G-1894)
BNC Welding ....G.... 757 706-2361	Diversfied Wldg Fbrication LLC ....G.... 804 449-6699	Hands Steel Mobile Welding LLC ....G.... 757 805-0054
Hampton (G-6096)	Beaverdam (G-1608)	Suffolk (G-13717)
Bobby S World Welding Inc ....G.... 540 845-7659	Dmh Complete Welding ....G.... 540 347-7550	Hanover Wldg & Met Fabrication ....G.... 804 550-2272
Stafford (G-13125)	Warrenton (G-14998)	Ashland (G-1431)
Boldens Welding & Trailor Sls ....G.... 276 647-8357	Dna Welding LLC ....G.... 703 256-2976	Harts Welding & Fabrication L ....G.... 804 785-3030
Collinsville (G-3709)	Annandale (G-745)	Cologne (G-3719)
Boroughbridge Metal & Wldg LLC ....G.... 804 387-3510	Dominion Wldg Fabrication Inc ....G.... 757 692-2002	Haticole Welding & Mechanical ....G.... 804 443-7808
Richmond (G-11506)	Virginia Beach (G-14410)	Tappahannock (G-13817)
Boyters Welding & Fabrication ....G.... 434 636-5974	Dons Welding ....G.... 540 896-3445	Hatter Welding Inc ....G.... 540 589-3848
La Crosse (G-7140)	Fulks Run (G-5565)	Roanoke (G-11933)
Bradley Adkins ....G.... 304 910-6553	Doors & More Welding ....G.... 804 798-4833	Hicks Welding LLC Richard L ....G.... 434 392-9824
North Tazewell (G-10095)	Glen Allen (G-5726)	Farmville (G-4943)
Brian R Hess ....G.... 757 240-0689	Double B Trailers ....G.... 540 586-0651	Highland Wldg Fabrication LLC ....G.... 540 474-3105
Williamsburg (G-15215)	Goode (G-5889)	Monterey (G-9006)
Brizendine Welding & Repr Inc ....G.... 804 443-1903	Double D S Wldg & Fabrication ....G.... 757 566-0019	Highlands Welding and Fabr ....G.... 276 429-4438
Dunnsville (G-4267)	Lanexa (G-7165)	Glade Spring (G-5678)
Broadway Metal Works Inc ....E.... 540 896-7027	Dougs Welding & Ornamental Ir ....G.... 804 435-6363	Hill Welding Services Corp ....G.... 540 923-4474
Broadway (G-2086)	White Stone (G-15187)	Madison (G-7854)
Brocks Welding Service ....G.... 540 967-3258	Dozier Tank & Welding Company ....G.... 757 543-5759	Hinkle Welding & Fabrication ....G.... 434 447-2770
Louisa (G-7546)	Chesapeake (G-3073)	Kenbridge (G-7033)
Browns Welding & Trailer Repr ....G.... 276 628-4461	Dozier Tank and Welding Co ....G.... 804 232-0092	Horton Welding LLC ....G.... 757 346-8405
Abingdon (G-17)	Richmond (G-11042)	Windsor (G-15605)
Burgess Welding & Fabrication ....G.... 276 229-6458	Draftco Incorporated ....E.... 540 337-1054	Hot Worx Inc ....G.... 757 967-9809
Stuart (G-13607)	Stuarts Draft (G-13646)	Portsmouth (G-10443)
Burkholder Enterprises Inc ....G.... 540 867-5030	Drake Welding Services Inc ....G.... 757 399-7705	Howdyshells Welding ....G.... 540 886-1960
Rockingham (G-12242)	Portsmouth (G-10417)	Staunton (G-13267)
Bursey Machine & Welding ....G.... 540 862-5033	E&S Welding LLC ....G.... 434 927-5428	Hubert Michael Gilliland ....G.... 434 332-2285
Clifton Forge (G-3679)	Sandy Level (G-12646)	Rustburg (G-12440)
C & C Piping & Fabrication LLC ....F.... 434 369-9353	Eastern Shore Wldg Fabrication ....G.... 443 944-3451	Hudsons Welding Shop ....G.... 434 822-1452
Altavista (G-628)	Greenbackville (G-5992)	Danville (G-3998)
Caldwell Industries Inc ....G.... 703 403-3272	Easton Welding LLC ....G.... 703 368-9727	I & M Welding Inc ....G.... 540 907-3775
Alexandria (G-428)	Bristow (G-2050)	Spotsylvania (G-12896)
Canaan Welding LLC ....G.... 703 339-7799	Elite Welders LLC ....G.... 757 613-1345	I A Welding LLC ....G.... 757 455-8500
Lorton (G-7469)	Portsmouth (G-10422)	Norfolk (G-9588)
Carter Welding LLC ....G.... 276 346-1873	Emergency Welding Inc ....G.... 804 829-2976	Industrial Alloy Welding LLC ....G.... 757 573-8496
Jonesville (G-7019)	Providence Forge (G-10623)	Norfolk (G-9592)
Caseys Welding Service ....G.... 804 275-7960	Entwistle Company ....E.... 434 799-6186	Industrial Commercial Wldg LLC ....G.... 703 707-6347
North Chesterfield (G-9840)	Danville (G-3992)	Herndon (G-6707)
Chambers Welding Inc Carl ....G.... 276 794-7170	Eric S Welding Service ....G.... 540 717-3256	Industrial Welding & Mech Inc ....F.... 804 744-8812
Lebanon (G-7190)	Reva (G-11000)	North Chesterfield (G-9893)
Charles E Overfelt ....G.... 540 562-0808	Erics Welding ....G.... 434 996-6502	Innovative Machining Inc ....E.... 804 385-4212
Roanoke (G-11907)	Charlottesville (G-2792)	Forest (G-5077)
Chesapeake Thermite Wldg LLC ....G.... 804 725-1111	Erin Welding Service Inc ....G.... 540 899-3970	J & J Welding LLC ....G.... 571 271-3337
Port Haywood (G-10382)	Fredericksburg (G-5429)	Lovettsville (G-7579)
Clark Welding Service ....G.... 276 565-3607	Fab Juniors Welding Metal ....G.... 540 480-1971	J & J Welding LLC ....G.... 703 431-1044
Appalachia (G-796)	Stuarts Draft (G-13647)	Leesburg (G-7290)
Clays Welding Co Inc ....G.... 540 788-3992	Fabricated Welding Specialties ....G.... 540 345-3104	J&T Wlding Fbrication Campbell ....F.... 434 369-8589
Catlett (G-2266)	Roanoke (G-12084)	Altavista (G-632)
Clevengers Welding Inc ....G.... 540 662-2191	Falls Stamping & Welding Co ....E.... 330 928-1191	Jack Kennedy Welding ....G.... 757 340-4269
Stephenson (G-13332)	Pulaski (G-10636)	Virginia Beach (G-14560)
Clyde D Seeley Sr ....G.... 757 721-6397	Fitzgerald Welding & Repair ....G.... 757 543-7312	Jackie E Calhoun Sr ....G.... 276 328-8318
Virginia Beach (G-14343)	Chesapeake (G-3102)	Wise (G-15628)
CM Welding LLC ....G.... 540 539-4723	Franklins Welding ....G.... 540 330-3454	Jarrett Welding and Mch Inc ....F.... 434 793-3717
Winchester (G-15403)	Roanoke (G-11923)	Danville (G-4006)
Collins Wldg & Fabrication LLC ....G.... 540 392-8171	Franks Welding Inc ....G.... 540 668-6185	Jay Dees Welding Services ....G.... 757 675-8368
Check (G-2943)	Purcellville (G-10661)	Chesapeake (G-3149)
Commercial Machine Inc ....F.... 804 329-5405	Frayser Welding Co ....G.... 804 798-8764	JD Goodman Welding ....G.... 804 598-1070
Richmond (G-11534)	Glen Allen (G-5733)	Powhatan (G-10554)
Consolidated Welding LLC ....G.... 757 348-6304	Fridleys Welding Service Inc ....G.... 804 674-1949	Jeffs Mobile Welding Inc ....G.... 757 870-7049
Norfolk (G-9503)	Chesterfield (G-3501)	Newport News (G-9269)
Countryside Machining Inc ....G.... 434 929-0065	G&G Welding & Fabricating ....G.... 276 202-3815	Jennifer Lavey ....G.... 540 313-0015
Madison Heights (G-7870)	Richlands (G-11016)	Stephens City (G-13318)
Crabtree Welding ....G.... 434 990-0140	Gale Welding and Mch Co Inc ....F.... 804 732-4521	Jennifer Reynolds ....G.... 804 229-1697
Ruckersville (G-12401)	Petersburg (G-10321)	Mechanicsville (G-8644)
Crane Research & Engrg Co Inc ....E.... 757 826-1707	Gammons Welding & Fabrication ....G.... 276 627-0664	Jesse Dudley Jr ....G.... 540 663-3773
Yorktown (G-15945)	Bassett (G-1583)	King George (G-7095)
Cross Machine Welding ....G.... 276 699-1974	Gary Clark ....G.... 540 373-4598	Jet Weld Inc ....G.... 540 836-0163
Ivanhoe (G-7005)	Fredericksburg (G-5434)	Churchville (G-3620)
Crossroads Iron Works Inc ....F.... 540 832-7800	Gary L Lawson ....G.... 757 848-7003	Jims Orna Fabrication & Wldg ....G.... 434 581-1420
Zion Crossroads (G-16006)	Poquoson (G-10372)	New Canton (G-9117)
Culpepper ....G.... 804 276-1478	General Welding ....G.... 540 514-0242	Johnson Welding Service ....G.... 757 787-4429
Chesterfield (G-3492)	Winchester (G-15545)	Greenbush (G-5996)
Curtis Wharam ....G.... 434 983-3904	Genesis Welding Inc ....G.... 276 935-2482	Jones Welding Construction ....G.... 434 369-1069
Dillwyn (G-4094)	Grundy (G-6033)	Altavista (G-633)
Custom Welded Steel Art Inc ....G.... 276 686-4107	George King Welding Inc ....G.... 540 379-3407	Joshs Welding & Fabrication ....G.... 540 244-9950
Rural Retreat (G-12421)	King George (G-7092)	Luray (G-7614)
Cv Welding ....G.... 540 338-6521	Geronimo Welding Fabrication ....G.... 757 277-6383	Js Welding ....G.... 434 352-0576
Round Hill (G-12376)	Virginia Beach (G-14481)	Appomattox (G-816)

P
R
O
D
U
C
T

Juniors Wldg & Met Fabrication G 540 943-7070
Stuarts Draft *(G-13653)*

Jws Welding & Repair G 804 720-2523
North Dinwiddie *(G-10055)*

K & S Welding G 757 859-6313
Wakefield *(G-14968)*

K & T Machine and Welding Inc F 804 296-8625
Ashland *(G-1447)*

Kaczenskis Welding Svcs LLC G 540 431-8126
Winchester *(G-15432)*

Kanan Welding G 703 339-7799
Lorton *(G-7500)*

Keens Welding & Aluminum Works G 540 958-9600
Covington *(G-3793)*

Kens Welding G 540 788-3556
Catlett *(G-2268)*

Kibby Welding G 607 624-9959
Troy *(G-13930)*

Kings Mobile Welding & Fabric G 571 620-4665
Fredericksburg *(G-5200)*

Lakeside Welding G 434 636-1712
White Plains *(G-15179)*

Lawless Wldg & Fabrication Inc G 276 806-8077
Fieldale *(G-4989)*

Lawsons Welding Service LLC G 434 985-2079
Stanardsville *(G-13222)*

Ld Welding & Fabrication Co F 757 553-2471
Chesapeake *(G-3179)*

Lewis A Dudley G 540 884-2454
Eagle Rock *(G-4282)*

Lewis Earl Mills G 540 295-2061
Fredericksburg *(G-5451)*

Lindas Welding & Mech LLC G 757 719-1567
Lanexa *(G-7167)*

Long Metalwork & Machine Inc G 804 529-6233
Callao *(G-2216)*

Louies Welding and Fabrication G 540 839-5232
Hot Springs *(G-6948)*

Lovings Welding & Fabricating G 804 370-3084
Mechanicsville *(G-8655)*

Lv Iron Works & Wldg Svcs Inc G 703 499-2270
Chantilly *(G-2459)*

M L Welding G 540 984-4883
Edinburg *(G-4309)*

M&Q Welding LLC G 804 564-8864
North Chesterfield *(G-9915)*

M&S Welding G 540 371-4009
Stafford *(G-13173)*

Machine & Fabg Specialists Inc E 757 244-5693
Hampton *(G-6187)*

Machine Welding Pritchett Inc G 434 949-7239
Dolphin *(G-4116)*

Marroquin Welding G 571 340-9165
Stafford *(G-13175)*

Martin Mobile Wldg & Repr LLC G 757 581-3828
Virginia Beach *(G-14638)*

Mathias Welding G 540 347-1415
Warrenton *(G-15033)*

MB Weld LLC G 540 434-4042
Harrisonburg *(G-6344)*

McDonald Welding LLC Doug G 804 928-6496
Richmond *(G-11675)*

McMillan Welding Inc G 276 728-1031
Hillsville *(G-6896)*

Meadows Welding G 434 603-0000
Farmville *(G-4950)*

Mealers Welding Repairs G 251 363-4640
Bumpass *(G-2166)*

Mechanical Development Co Inc D 540 389-9395
Salem *(G-12535)*

Memorial Welding LLC G 703 369-2428
Manassas *(G-8107)*

Merciers Welding G 540 635-4175
Front Royal *(G-5543)*

Metals of Distinction Inc G 757 727-0773
Hampton *(G-6196)*

Metalstar Services LLC G 434 591-0400
Troy *(G-13935)*

Michael Fleming G 276 337-9202
Wise *(G-15632)*

Michaels Welding G 434 238-5302
Evington *(G-4379)*

Mid Atlantic Welding Tech G 804 330-8191
Richmond *(G-11050)*

Mikes Wrecker Service & Bdy Sp G 540 996-4152
Millboro *(G-8937)*

Millers Custom Metal Svcs LLC G 804 712-2588
Deltaville *(G-4084)*

Monks Welding LLC G 276 206-8051
Abingdon *(G-51)*

Moonlight Welding LLC G 757 449-7003
Suffolk *(G-13746)*

Moores Machine Co Inc F 434 352-0000
Spout Spring *(G-12926)*

Mos Welding Shop G 434 525-1137
Evington *(G-4380)*

Mount Slon Wldg Fbrication LLC G 540 350-2733
Mount Solon *(G-9089)*

Mtn Man Welding G 540 463-9352
Lexington *(G-7405)*

Myers Repair Company G 804 222-3674
Richmond *(G-11298)*

N A K Mechanics & Welding Inc G 276 971-1860
Tazewell *(G-13837)*

Naff Welding & Mach Works G 276 629-1129
Henry *(G-6596)*

New Age Repr & Fabrication LLC G 757 819-3887
Norfolk *(G-9659)*

Nichols Welding G 540 483-5308
Rocky Mount *(G-12343)*

Nicks Wldg & Fabrication LLC G 434 251-2696
Callands *(G-2214)*

Nighthawk Welding LLC G 540 845-9966
Woodbridge *(G-15759)*

Nolte Machine and Welding LLC G 804 357-7271
Sandston *(G-12625)*

Norfolk Machine and Wldg Inc E 757 489-0330
Norfolk *(G-9666)*

Norrisbilt Fbrction MBL Wldg L E 276 325-0269
Norton *(G-10131)*

One Piece Fabrication LLC G 757 460-8637
Virginia Beach *(G-14700)*

ONeals Welding & Repair LLC G 757 421-0702
Chesapeake *(G-3228)*

Ortons Specialty Welding LLC G 804 405-2675
Toano *(G-13872)*

Outlaw Welding LLC G 434 929-4734
Monroe *(G-8994)*

Owen Co LLC G 571 261-1316
Haymarket *(G-6432)*

P & C Heavy Truck Repair G 804 520-7619
Colonial Heights *(G-3741)*

Parham Services LLC G 804 586-1202
Sutherland *(G-13805)*

Parhams Wldg & Fabrication Inc F 804 834-3504
Waverly *(G-15086)*

Philip Back G 540 570-9353
Fairfield *(G-4733)*

Piedmont Welding & Maintenance G 434 447-6600
La Crosse *(G-7148)*

Porter Welding G 276 565-2694
Appalachia *(G-799)*

Precision Machine Co Inc G 804 359-5758
North Chesterfield *(G-9953)*

Precision Welding LLC G 434 973-2106
Virginia Beach *(G-14735)*

Premo Welding G 757 880-6951
Hampton *(G-6218)*

Professional Welding Svc Inc G 757 853-9371
Norfolk *(G-9697)*

Progressive Manufacturing Corp E 804 717-5353
Chester *(G-3448)*

Pruitt Welding & Fabrication G 540 896-4268
Timberville *(G-13853)*

Quality Welding Inc E 434 296-1402
Charlottesville *(G-2852)*

R & D Welding Services G 757 761-3499
Chesapeake *(G-3253)*

R W A Machining & Welding Co G 434 985-7362
Ruckersville *(G-12412)*

Radford Wldg & Fabrication LLC G 540 731-4891
Radford *(G-10737)*

Raffy Welding LLC G 703 945-0554
Leesburg *(G-7331)*

Rails End Wood & Met Crafters G 540 463-9565
Lexington *(G-7413)*

Randolph Scotts Welding G 434 656-1471
Gretna *(G-6009)*

Raven Machine G 804 271-6001
North Chesterfield *(G-9957)*

Rawley Pike Welding LLC G 540 867-5335
Hinton *(G-6905)*

Ray Gorham G 703 971-1807
Alexandria *(G-566)*

Rectors Repair & Welding LLC G 540 809-5683
Fredericksburg *(G-5476)*

Richmond Steel Inc G 804 798-4766
Ashland *(G-1486)*

Rick A Debernard Welding Inc G 540 834-8348
Fredericksburg *(G-5478)*

Ricks Custom Welding Inc G 540 675-1888
Huntly *(G-6966)*

Ridge Top Welding G 540 947-5118
Blue Ridge *(G-1855)*

Right Tght Wldg Fbrication LLC G 757 553-0661
Virginia Beach *(G-14773)*

Ritter Welding G 703 680-9601
Woodbridge *(G-15797)*

Road Rnner MBL Wldg Fbrction L G 757 915-2077
Hampton *(G-6229)*

Robeys Welding LLC G 540 974-3811
White Post *(G-15182)*

Robs Welding G 540 722-4151
Winchester *(G-15469)*

Rockingham Welding Svc LLC G 540 879-9500
Dayton *(G-4061)*

Rod & Staff Welding G 434 392-3090
Farmville *(G-4956)*

Rodeo Welding LLC G 571 379-4179
Manassas *(G-8147)*

Roop Welding & General Repair G 276 346-3338
Jonesville *(G-7023)*

Rt 100 Welding Fab Machin G 276 766-0100
Barren Springs *(G-1575)*

Ry Fabricating LLC G 571 835-0567
King George *(G-7112)*

S Conley Welding Company G 540 436-3775
Star Tannery *(G-13237)*

S3 Mobile Welding & Cutting G 757 647-0322
Chesapeake *(G-3281)*

Saltville Machine & Welding G 276 496-3555
Saltville *(G-12590)*

Sb Welding and Fab LLC G 540 955-0797
Berryville *(G-1689)*

Schrocks Repair G 540 879-2406
Dayton *(G-4062)*

SD Davis Welding & Equipment G 804 691-2112
Ford *(G-5048)*

Sea Marine LLC F 757 528-9869
Norfolk *(G-9716)*

Shaw LLC G 540 967-9783
Louisa *(G-7566)*

Sheila Rodriguez G 425 221-0519
Suffolk *(G-13762)*

Shenandoah Valley Orchard Co E 540 337-2837
Stuarts Draft *(G-13660)*

Shrews Welding and Fabrica G 703 785-8035
Bristow *(G-2061)*

Single Source Welding LLC G 703 919-7791
Warrenton *(G-15052)*

Smith & Smith Commercial Hood G 804 605-0311
South Chesterfield *(G-12840)*

Smith Fabrication Weldin G 276 734-5269
Ridgeway *(G-11854)*

Smiths Welding G 540 651-2382
Pilot *(G-10359)*

Smittys Welding G 540 962-7550
Covington *(G-3797)*

Snider & Sons Inc G 540 626-5849
Pembroke *(G-10284)*

Sopko Manufacturing Inc F 434 848-3460
Lawrenceville *(G-7185)*

Southfork Enterprises G 540 879-4372
Dayton *(G-4065)*

Southside Welding G 757 270-7006
Virginia Beach *(G-14832)*

Standard Welding Corp G 757 423-0470
Norfolk *(G-9733)*

Star City Welding LLC G 540 343-1428
Roanoke *(G-12195)*

Steel Mates G 540 825-7333
Culpeper *(G-3922)*

Stephen Dunnavant G 804 337-3629
Chesterfield *(G-3529)*

Stern Welding LLC G 571 283-1355
Chantilly *(G-2499)*

Steve Stone G 276 956-8451
Henry *(G-6597)*

Stickmans Welding Service LLC G 434 547-9774
Dillwyn *(G-4101)*

Straight Line Welding LLC G 804 837-0363
Chester *(G-3457)*

Streetwerkz Customs G 804 921-6483
Powhatan *(G-10579)*

Strongerhold Welding & Contg G 276 608-9968
Vansant *(G-13978)*

Structures Unlimited G 434 361-2294
Faber *(G-4391)*

Suffolk Welding & Fab G 757 544-4689
Chesapeake *(G-3314)*

1082 2021 Virginia Industrial Directory

(G-0000) Company's Geographic Section entry number

Swaby Group ....G....... 540 788-6051
Catlett *(G-2269)*
Swift Mobile Welding LLC ....G....... 757 367-9060
Hampton *(G-6247)*
Sycamore Hollow Welding ....G....... 540 879-2266
Dayton *(G-4066)*
Terry Plymouth ....G....... 757 838-2718
Hampton *(G-6252)*
Tidewater Wldg Fabrication LLC ...G....... 757 636-6630
Chesapeake *(G-3340)*
Timothy D Falls ....G....... 540 987-8142
Woodville *(G-15862)*
TMC Welding ....G....... 703 455-9709
Springfield *(G-13099)*
TNT Piping and Welding ....G....... 804 224-1634
Fredericksburg *(G-5495)*
Toby Loritsch Inc ....G....... 540 389-1522
Salem *(G-12575)*
Toms Welding ....G....... 434 989-1553
Arvonia *(G-1234)*
Top Bead Welding Service Inc .....E....... 540 901-8730
Broadway *(G-2098)*
Torchs Mobile Welding ....G....... 804 216-0412
Mechanicsville *(G-8686)*
Total Welding Solutions LLC ....G....... 703 898-8720
Haymarket *(G-6450)*
Tribe 9 LLC ....G....... 757 542-5348
Newport News *(G-9362)*
Triple Gold Welding LLC ....G....... 804 370-0082
West Point *(G-15162)*
Tritech Solutions Virginia Inc ....G....... 434 664-2140
Appomattox *(G-824)*
Truitts Welding Service ....G....... 757 787-7290
Onancock *(G-10198)*
Turners Welding ....G....... 540 373-1107
King George *(G-7116)*
Tweedies Repair Service ....G....... 540 576-2617
Penhook *(G-10286)*
United Welding Inc ....G....... 540 628-2286
Fredericksburg *(G-5496)*
Unlimited Welding LLC ....G....... 540 683-4776
Middletown *(G-8745)*
Valley Precision Incorporated ......E....... 540 941-8178
Waynesboro *(G-15142)*
Valley Welding ....G....... 276 733-7942
Barren Springs *(G-1576)*
Valley Welding ....G....... 276 733-7943
Draper *(G-4137)*
Valley Welding Inc ....G....... 540 338-5323
Purcellville *(G-10684)*
Van Der Hyde Dan ....G....... 434 250-7389
Chatham *(G-2940)*
Venton Fab & Welding ....G....... 540 981-1550
Vinton *(G-14191)*
Veterans Welding LLC ....G....... 804 904-7951
Richmond *(G-11436)*
Virginia Mtal Fabrications LLC ......G....... 540 292-0562
Churchville *(G-3623)*
Virginia Welding LLC ....G....... 703 263-1964
Chantilly *(G-2516)*
W & B Fabricators Inc ....F....... 276 928-1060
Rocky Gap *(G-12308)*
Walkers Certified Welding Inc ....G....... 804 541-2612
Hopewell *(G-6943)*
Walkers Welding ....G....... 214 779-0089
Purcellville *(G-10686)*
Wards Wldg & Fabrication LLC ......G....... 540 219-1460
Brandy Station *(G-1942)*
Watts Fabrication & Welding ....G....... 804 798-5988
Ashland *(G-1507)*
WEB Welding LLC ....G....... 703 212-4840
Alexandria *(G-380)*
Weld Pro LLC ....G....... 434 531-5811
Troy *(G-13937)*
Welding & Fabrication LLC ....G....... 540 907-7461
Fredericksburg *(G-5502)*
Welding Fabrication & Design ....G....... 757 739-0025
Chesapeake *(G-3373)*
Welding Unlimited ....G....... 540 833-4146
Linville *(G-7438)*
Weldment Dynamics LLC ....G....... 540 840-7866
Mineral *(G-8953)*
Weldone Inc ....G....... 804 784-8860
Richmond *(G-11445)*
Weldprotech Inc ....G....... 757 485-3293
Chesapeake *(G-3374)*
Wendell Welder LLC ....G....... 804 935-6856
Richmond *(G-11822)*
West End Machine & Welding ....E....... 804 266-9631
Richmond *(G-11446)*

West Engineering Company Inc .....E....... 804 798-3966
Ashland *(G-1508)*
Whispering Pines Weld & Iron ....G....... 434 465-0704
Palmyra *(G-10260)*
Whitleys Welding Inc ....G....... 804 350-6203
Powhatan *(G-10585)*
Williams Fabrication Inc ....E....... 540 862-4200
Covington *(G-3804)*
Williams Welding ....G....... 540 465-8818
Strasburg *(G-13602)*
Willis Welding & Machine Co ....G....... 540 427-3038
Roanoke *(G-12228)*
Wiseman Weld Fabrication ....G....... 571 393-8480
Woodbridge *(G-15833)*
Wobsers Welding Works LLC ....G....... 757 570-0440
Smithfield *(G-12744)*
Woerner Welding & Fabrication .....G....... 804 349-6563
Midlothian *(G-8922)*
Wonder Bug Welding ....G....... 703 354-9499
Alexandria *(G-612)*
Wortham Machine and Welding ......F....... 434 676-8080
Kenbridge *(G-7037)*
Wrights Iron Inc ....G....... 540 661-1089
Orange *(G-10235)*

WELDMENTS

Fusion Pwdr Cating Fabrication .....G....... 757 319-3760
Chesapeake *(G-3112)*

WELLS: Light, Sheet Metal

Seher Resources Inc ....G....... 703 771-7170
Leesburg *(G-7344)*

WESTERN APPAREL STORES

Middleburg Tack Exchange Ltd ......G....... 540 687-6608
Middleburg *(G-8730)*

WHEEL BALANCING EQPT: Automotive

Hunter Eqp Svc & Parts Inc ....G....... 703 785-5526
Vienna *(G-14068)*

WHEELCHAIR LIFTS

Christopher Hawkins ....G....... 540 361-1679
Fredericksburg *(G-5178)*
Km Services LLC ....G....... 757 524-3420
Williamsburg *(G-15267)*
Qlifts LLC ....G....... 276 632-0058
Ridgeway *(G-11850)*
Richmond Ramps Inc ....G....... 804 932-8507
Quinton *(G-10699)*
Ride-Away Inc ....F....... 804 233-8267
North Chesterfield *(G-10022)*

WHEELCHAIRS

Allcare Non-Medical Wheelchair ....G....... 757 291-2500
Chesapeake *(G-2958)*
Angel Rides Inc ....G....... 540 373-5540
Fredericksburg *(G-5245)*
Byrd Assistive Tech Inc ....G....... 571 512-6069
Chantilly *(G-2382)*
Lifeline of Prince William ....G....... 703 753-9000
Yorktown *(G-15975)*
Ms Wheelchair Virginia Inc ....G....... 540 838-5022
Fairlawn *(G-4738)*
Roanoke Stars ....G....... 540 797-8266
Roanoke *(G-11996)*

WHEELS

Hubs and Wheels Emory Inc ....F....... 276 944-4900
Meadowview *(G-8595)*
Loa Mals On Whels Wlliamson Rd ...G....... 540 563-0482
Roanoke *(G-12128)*
Old Dominion 4 Whl Drv CLB Inc ....G....... 804 750-2349
Richmond *(G-11312)*

WHEELS & PARTS

Schrader-Bridgeport Intl Inc ....A....... 434 369-4741
Altavista *(G-641)*

WHISTLES

As Clean As A Whistle ....G....... 757 753-0600
Newport News *(G-9171)*
Salt Whistle Bay Partners LLC ......G....... 540 983-7118
Roanoke *(G-12175)*

WIG & HAIRPIECE STORES

Ophelias Hat & Hair Shop ....G....... 757 331-1713
Cheriton *(G-2947)*

WIGS, WHOLESALE

Ophelias Hat & Hair Shop ....G....... 757 331-1713
Cheriton *(G-2947)*

WINCHES

Breeze-Eastern LLC ....G....... 973 602-1001
Fredericksburg *(G-5175)*

WIND CHIMES

Qmt Associates Inc ....C....... 703 368-4920
Manassas Park *(G-8208)*

WINDINGS: Coil, Electronic

Bobbin Coil Speacialists Inc ....G....... 815 385-6205
Forest *(G-5055)*

WINDOW & DOOR FRAMES

Efco Corporation ....E....... 540 248-8604
Verona *(G-13985)*
SLM Distrubutors Inc ....G....... 540 774-6817
Roanoke *(G-12002)*
Vinylite Windows Products Inc ....E....... 703 550-7766
Lorton *(G-7540)*

WINDOW FRAMES & SASHES: Plastic

Eastman Performance Films LLC ....D....... 423 224-7768
Martinsville *(G-8283)*

WINDOW FRAMES, MOLDING & TRIM: Vinyl

Lawrence Trnsp Systems Inc ....D....... 540 966-3797
Roanoke *(G-11953)*
Legacy Products LLC ....E....... 804 739-9333
Midlothian *(G-8847)*
Milgard Manufacturing Inc ....G....... 540 834-0340
Fredericksburg *(G-5328)*
West Window Corporation ....D....... 276 638-2394
Ridgeway *(G-11857)*

WINDOW FURNISHINGS WHOLESALERS

Custom Windows ....G....... 804 262-1621
Henrico *(G-6497)*
Lutron Electronics Co Inc ....C....... 804 752-3300
Ashland *(G-1455)*
Speciality Group Ltd ....E....... 804 264-3000
Richmond *(G-11767)*

WINDOWS: Frames, Wood

Mw Manufacturers Inc ....A....... 540 483-0211
Rocky Mount *(G-12340)*
Mw Manufacturers Inc ....C....... 540 484-6780
Rocky Mount *(G-12341)*

WINDOWS: Louver, Glass, Wood Framed

All Glass LLC ....G....... 540 288-8111
Fredericksburg *(G-5397)*

WINDOWS: Wood

Moss Supply Company ....D....... 804 798-8332
Ashland *(G-1466)*
Ply Gem Industries Inc ....C....... 540 337-3663
Stuarts Draft *(G-13657)*
Ply Gem Industries Inc ....C....... 540 483-0211
Rocky Mount *(G-12346)*

WINDSHIELD WIPER SYSTEMS

Windshield RPS By Ralph Smiley ....G....... 804 690-7517
Mechanicsville *(G-8699)*
Wood Mark T A Augusta Gla ....G....... 540 885-5038
Staunton *(G-13308)*

WINDSHIELDS: Plastic

Custom Auto Glass & Plastics ....G....... 540 362-8798
Roanoke *(G-12076)*
Degen Enterprises Inc ....G....... 757 853-7651
Norfolk *(G-9524)*

PRODUCT

WINE CELLARS, BONDED: Wine, Blended

Attimo Winery ....F 540 382-7619
Christiansburg *(G-3571)*

Blue Bee Cider LLC ....F 804 231-0280
Richmond *(G-11128)*

James River Cellars Inc ....G 804 550-7516
Glen Allen *(G-5754)*

Marceline Vineyards LLC ....G 540 212-9798
Mount Crawford *(G-9056)*

Potters Craft LLC ....G 850 528-6314
Free Union *(G-5509)*

WIRE

Thomas H Rhea MD PC ....G 703 658-0300
Annandale *(G-787)*

WIRE & CABLE: Aluminum

Cable Systems ....G 757 853-6313
Norfolk *(G-9473)*

WIRE & CABLE: Nonferrous, Automotive, Exc Ignition Sets

Smart Start of Glen Allen ....G 804 447-7642
Richmond *(G-11385)*

WIRE & WIRE PRDTS

C S Lewis & Sons LLC ....G 804 275-6879
North Chesterfield *(G-9838)*

Fyne-Wire Specialties Inc ....E 540 825-2701
Brandy Station *(G-1939)*

Global Safety Textiles LLC ....D 434 447-7629
South Hill *(G-12851)*

Heco Slings Corporation ....F 757 855-7139
Norfolk *(G-9578)*

I & I Sling Inc ....G 703 550-9405
Lorton *(G-7494)*

Mazzella Jhh Company Inc ....G 757 827-9600
Hampton *(G-6193)*

Merchants Metals LLC ....G 804 262-9783
Rockville *(G-12293)*

Merchants Metals LLC ....G 877 518-7665
Fredericksburg *(G-5324)*

Mid Valley Products ....G 757 625-0780
Norfolk *(G-9643)*

Northern Virginia Wire Works ....G 571 221-1882
Gainesville *(G-5603)*

R A Pearson Company ....D 804 550-7300
Ashland *(G-1482)*

WIRE FABRIC: Welded Steel

Dart Mechanical Inc ....G 757 539-2189
Suffolk *(G-13695)*

WIRE MATERIALS: Copper

Optical Cable Corporation ....C 540 265-0690
Roanoke *(G-11978)*

WIRE MATERIALS: Steel

C S Lewis & Sons LLC ....G 804 275-6879
North Chesterfield *(G-9838)*

Intermet Foundries Inc ....G 434 528-8721
Lynchburg *(G-7744)*

Kybo Sales LLC ....G 276 431-2563
Duffield *(G-4180)*

Times Fiber Communications Inc ..E 434 432-1800
Chatham *(G-2938)*

Voestlpine High Prfmce Mtls Co ..E 434 575-7994
South Boston *(G-12792)*

WIRE ROPE CENTERS

Rigging Box Inc ....G 703 339-7575
Lorton *(G-7526)*

Trident Tool Inc ....G 540 635-7753
Stephens City *(G-13324)*

WIRE WHOLESALERS

Times Fiber Communications Inc ..E 434 432-1800
Chatham *(G-2938)*

WIRE: Communication

Mantis Networks LLC ....G 571 306-1234
Reston *(G-10894)*

Mimetrix Technologies LLC ....G 571 306-1234
Vienna *(G-14094)*

Walton Wiring Inc ....G 804 556-3104
Maidens *(G-7893)*

WIRE: Magnet

Algonquin Industries Inc ....E 804 550-5401
Ashland *(G-1365)*

Virginia Insulated Products Co ....F 276 496-5136
Saltville *(G-12599)*

WIRE: Nonferrous

AFL Network Services Inc ....G 864 433-0333
Chesapeake *(G-2955)*

Core Business Technologies Inc ...G 757 426-0344
Virginia Beach *(G-14365)*

Corning Incorporated ....G 703 471-5955
Manassas *(G-8052)*

Mg Corp ....A 757 468-6000
Virginia Beach *(G-14648)*

Pyott-Boone Electronics Inc ....C 276 988-5505
North Tazewell *(G-10105)*

Te Connectivity ....F 540 812-9126
Culpeper *(G-3924)*

Times Fiber Communications Inc ...C 434 432-1800
Chatham *(G-2937)*

Times Fiber Communications Inc ...E 434 432-1800
Chatham *(G-2938)*

Virginia Insulated Products Co ....F 276 496-5136
Saltville *(G-12598)*

WOMEN'S & CHILDREN'S CLOTHING WHOLESALERS, NEC

Hibernate Inc ....G 804 513-1777
Glen Allen *(G-5744)*

Mayes Wholesale Tack ....G 276 755-3715
Cana *(G-2227)*

Ocean Creek Apparel LLC ....G 757 460-6118
Virginia Beach *(G-14691)*

WOMEN'S & GIRLS' SPORTSWEAR WHOLESALERS

D J R Enterprises Inc ....F 540 639-9386
Radford *(G-10708)*

Memteks-Usa Inc ....B 434 973-9800
Earlysville *(G-4292)*

WOMEN'S CLOTHING STORES

G Gibbs Project LLC ....G 804 638-9581
Chester *(G-3418)*

Journeymen Saddlers Ltd ....F 540 687-5888
Middleburg *(G-8725)*

Webgear Inc ....F 703 532-1000
Vienna *(G-14158)*

WOMEN'S CLOTHING STORES: Ready-To-Wear

Fannypants LLC ....G 703 953-3099
Chantilly *(G-2420)*

WOMEN'S SPORTSWEAR STORES

D J R Enterprises Inc ....F 540 639-9386
Radford *(G-10708)*

WOOD CHIPS, PRODUCED AT THE MILL

Chips Inc ....D 434 589-2424
Troy *(G-13922)*

Enviva Pellets Southampton LLC ..G 301 657-5560
Franklin *(G-5142)*

WOOD PRDTS

Amazon Mllwk Installations LLC ..G 703 200-9076
Alexandria *(G-410)*

Amboy Enterprises LLC ....G 804 708-0945
Manakin Sabot *(G-7894)*

Bacus Woodworks LLC ....G 571 762-3314
Warrenton *(G-14979)*

Batts Woodworking ....G 757 969-5824
Hampton *(G-6088)*

Benson Fine Woodcrafting LLC ...G 703 372-1871
Lorton *(G-7466)*

Burnettes Custom Wood Inc ......G 540 577-9687
Roanoke *(G-12056)*

Capitol Wood Works ....G 703 237-2071
Falls Church *(G-4772)*

Citiwood Urban Forest Products ...G 804 795-9220
Henrico *(G-6493)*

City Spree of Woodbridge ....G
Woodbridge *(G-15672)*

CTI of Woodbridge ....G 703 670-4790
Woodbridge *(G-15679)*

Cutting Edge Millworks LLC ....G 804 580-7270
Heathsville *(G-6461)*

Dogwood Montessori &C ....G 540 439-3572
Bealeton *(G-1598)*

Esteemed Woodcrafts ....G 757 876-5868
Chesapeake *(G-3093)*

Forest Carbon Offsets LLC ....G 703 795-4512
Alexandria *(G-206)*

Fred Leach ....G 434 372-5225
Chase City *(G-2911)*

Hawleywood LLC ....G 757 463-0910
Virginia Beach *(G-14510)*

Healthy By Choice ....G 810 449-5999
Norfolk *(G-9575)*

Kawood LLC ....G 757 488-4658
Portsmouth *(G-10452)*

Maurywood LLC ....G 540 463-6209
Lexington *(G-7401)*

Newcomb Woodworks LLC ....G 804 370-0441
Henrico *(G-6543)*

Northwood Contracting LLC ....G 703 624-0928
Rixeyville *(G-11880)*

Parkside Woods LLC ....G 703 543-6446
Chantilly *(G-2478)*

Prologue ....G 757 871-3708
Newport News *(G-9318)*

R G Woodworks ....G 757 427-2743
Virginia Beach *(G-14754)*

Richmond Woodworks LLC ....G 804 510-3747
Moseley *(G-9046)*

Shelfnwoodworks ....G 757 350-0408
Suffolk *(G-13763)*

Tinkers Treasures ....G 708 633-0710
Midlothian *(G-8914)*

Winchester Woods Condos LLC ...G 540 885-8390
Staunton *(G-13307)*

Woodard LLC ....G 540 812-5016
Boston *(G-1905)*

Woodardweb ....G 202 337-3730
Alexandria *(G-613)*

Woodducks Odd Jobs Lawn Svc LL ..G 804 932-4612
New Kent *(G-9139)*

Woodland Artisans Ltd ....G 276 766-3421
Allisonia *(G-621)*

Woodland Group LLC ....G 571 312-5951
Alexandria *(G-387)*

Woods of Wisdom LLC ....G 757 645-2043
Williamsburg *(G-15348)*

WOOD PRDTS: Applicators

Burks Fork Log Homes ....G 276 766-0350
Hillsville *(G-6887)*

WOOD PRDTS: Brackets

Bay Cabinets & Contractors ....G 757 934-2236
Suffolk *(G-13676)*

WOOD PRDTS: Furniture Inlays, Veneers

Southern Finishing Company Inc ...E 276 632-4901
Martinsville *(G-8333)*

WOOD PRDTS: Laundry

Blue Skys Woodshop ....G 703 567-6220
Alexandria *(G-149)*

Essex Hand Crafted WD Pdts LLC ..G 540 445-5928
Warrenton *(G-15005)*

Wilbur Frederick - Wood Carver ...G 434 263-4827
Lovingston *(G-7594)*

Woodmark Designs ....G 804 921-9454
Mechanicsville *(G-8701)*

WOOD PRDTS: Moldings, Unfinished & Prefinished

Cavanaugh Cabinet Inc ....G 434 977-7100
Charlottesville *(G-2759)*

Creative Dimension Group Inc ....D 540 891-1953
Fredericksburg *(G-5267)*

Finch Woodworks ....G 540 333-0054
Woodstock *(G-15853)*

Innovative Millwork Tech LLC .... G 276 646-8336
  Chilhowie **(G-3551)**
J W Creations .... G 276 676-3770
  Abingdon **(G-43)**
Metrie Inc .... D 804 876-3588
  Doswell **(G-4123)**
Nova Lumber & Millwork LLC .... G 703 451-9217
  Springfield **(G-13061)**
Portsmouth Lumber Corporation .... F 757 397-4646
  Portsmouth **(G-10471)**
Rappatomac Industries Inc .... G 804 529-6440
  Callao **(G-2218)**
Windsor Surry Company .... E 757 294-0853
  Dendron **(G-4091)**

WOOD PRDTS: Mulch Or Sawdust

J K Enterprise Inc .... G 703 352-1858
  Fairfax **(G-4483)**
Mwb Enterprises Inc .... G 434 922-7730
  Amherst **(G-702)**
Norfleet Quality LLC .... G 540 373-9481
  Fredericksburg **(G-5209)**
Watson Wood Yard .... G 540 895-0006
  Spotsylvania **(G-12923)**
Watson Wood Yard .... G 540 854-7703
  Mine Run **(G-8941)**

WOOD PRDTS: Mulch, Wood & Bark

Armstrong Green & Embrey Inc .... G 540 898-7434
  Fredericksburg **(G-5248)**
B & D Trucking of Virginia Inc .... G 540 463-3035
  Lexington **(G-7387)**
Dickerson Stump LLC .... G 540 898-9145
  Fredericksburg **(G-5273)**
Family Tree Care Inc .... G 703 280-1169
  Fairfax **(G-4455)**
Hardwood Mulch Corporation .... G 804 458-7500
  Disputanta **(G-4108)**
Hollybrook Mulch Trucking Inc .... G 540 381-7830
  Christiansburg **(G-3593)**
Norfleet Acquisition Co Inc .... F 540 373-9481
  Fredericksburg **(G-5208)**
SMC Mulch Yard Inc .... G 540 657-5454
  Stafford **(G-13191)**
Virginias Rsurces Recycled LLC .... F 804 561-2543
  Amelia Court House **(G-676)**
Wood Preservers Incorporated .... D 804 333-4022
  Warsaw **(G-15073)**

WOOD PRDTS: Novelties, Fiber

K & W Projects LLC .... G 757 618-9249
  Chesapeake **(G-3161)**

WOOD PRDTS: Oars & Paddles

Edgyash Paddleboards LLC .... G 717 404-6073
  Poquoson **(G-10370)**

WOOD PRDTS: Outdoor, Structural

Trex Co Inc .... C 540 542-6300
  Winchester **(G-15492)**
Trex Company Inc .... D 540 542-6314
  Winchester **(G-15495)**

WOOD PRDTS: Panel Work

Allied Systems Corporation .... D 540 665-9600
  Winchester **(G-15375)**
Chesapeake Outdoor Designs Inc .... F 804 632-1900
  Midlothian **(G-8794)**
Walker Branch Lumber .... G 434 676-3199
  Kenbridge **(G-7036)**

WOOD PRDTS: Poles

C H Evelyn Piling Company Inc .... F 804 966-2273
  Providence Forge **(G-10619)**

WOOD PRDTS: Scaffolds

Scaffsales International LLC .... G 757 545-5050
  Chesapeake **(G-3286)**

WOOD PRDTS: Shavings & Packaging, Excelsior

Empc Bio Energy Group LLC .... F 757 550-1103
  Chesapeake **(G-3088)**

WOOD PRDTS: Signboards

Acorn Sales Company Inc .... F 804 359-0505
  Richmond **(G-11081)**
Flags of Valor LLC .... E 703 729-8640
  Ashburn **(G-1280)**
Northwind Associates .... G 757 871-8215
  Hayes **(G-6403)**

WOOD PRDTS: Silo Staves

Builders Firstsource Inc .... D 540 665-0078
  Winchester **(G-15397)**

WOOD PRDTS: Survey Stakes

Erle D Anderson Lbr Pdts Inc .... G 804 748-0500
  Disputanta **(G-4107)**
Rice S Stake & Wood Products .... G 804 769-3272
  Aylett **(G-1552)**

WOOD PRDTS: Trophy Bases

Coyent .... G 804 861-3323
  Prince George **(G-10589)**
Paramount Woodworking .... G 804 862-2432
  Petersburg **(G-10332)**
Recognition Works .... G 804 739-1483
  Midlothian **(G-8886)**

WOOD PRDTS: Venetian Blind Slats

Millehan Enterprises Inc .... G 540 772-3037
  Roanoke **(G-11967)**

WOOD PRODUCTS: Reconstituted

Coastal Wood Imports Inc .... F 434 799-1117
  Danville **(G-3968)**
Georgia-Pacific LLC .... C 434 634-6133
  Skippers **(G-12700)**
Huber Engineered Woods LLC .... C 434 476-6628
  Crystal Hill **(G-3859)**
Trex Company Inc .... C 540 542-6800
  Winchester **(G-15493)**

WOOD SHAVINGS BALES, MULCH TYPE, WHOLESALE

Hollybrook Mulch Trucking Inc .... G 540 381-7830
  Christiansburg **(G-3593)**

WOOD TREATING: Creosoting

Wood Preservers Incorporated .... D 804 333-4022
  Warsaw **(G-15073)**

WOOD TREATING: Flooring, Block

Sound Structures Virginia Inc .... G 804 876-3014
  Doswell **(G-4125)**
Trout River Lumber LLC .... E 434 645-2600
  Crewe **(G-3818)**

WOOD TREATING: Millwork

Blue Ridge Wood Preserving Inc .... F 540 297-6607
  Moneta **(G-8957)**
McCready Lumber Company Inc .... G 540 980-8700
  Pulaski **(G-10643)**
Nova Lumber & Millwork LLC .... G 703 451-9217
  Springfield **(G-13061)**

WOOD TREATING: Structural Lumber & Timber

B H Cobb Lumber Co .... G 804 358-3801
  Richmond **(G-11498)**
Gladys Timber Products Inc .... F 434 283-4744
  Gladys **(G-5692)**
Great Southern Wood Prsv Inc .... C 540 483-5264
  Rocky Mount **(G-12326)**
Highland Timber Frame Inc .... G 540 745-7411
  Floyd **(G-5028)**
Kejaeh Enterprises LLC .... G 434 476-1300
  Halifax **(G-6051)**
Koppers Utility Indus Pdts Inc .... G 434 292-4375
  Blackstone **(G-1818)**
Phytosnitation Vac Systems LLC .... G 540 641-4170
  Blacksburg **(G-1779)**
Woodsong Instruments .... G 540 745-2708
  Floyd **(G-5046)**

WOOD TREATING: Wood Prdts, Creosoted

Rivanna Natural Designs Inc .... G 434 244-3447
  Henrico **(G-6560)**
Stella-Jones Corporation .... D 540 997-9251
  Goshen **(G-5927)**

WOODWORK & TRIM: Interior & Ornamental

Frederick Enterprises LLC .... E 804 405-4976
  Richmond **(G-11594)**
Maurice Lamb .... G 540 962-0903
  Covington **(G-3794)**
Millcraft LLC .... G 703 225-9860
  Chantilly **(G-2463)**
Millcraft LLC .... G 703 775-2030
  Alexandria **(G-533)**
Scan Industries LLC .... G 360 320-8244
  Ashburn **(G-1332)**

WOODWORK: Carved & Turned

Meissner Cstm Knives Pens LLC .... G 321 693-2392
  Hampton **(G-6195)**
Three Peaks Crafts .... G 276 677-3724
  Troutdale **(G-13901)**

WOODWORK: Interior & Ornamental, NEC

Blueridge Wood .... G 276 930-2274
  Woolwine **(G-15864)**
Criders Finishing Inc .... G 703 661-6520
  Ashburn **(G-1260)**
Donald F Rouse .... G 276 783-7569
  Marion **(G-8226)**
Dover Plank Enterprises LLC .... G 757 286-6772
  Richmond **(G-11567)**
E T Moore Jr Co Inc .... F 804 231-1823
  Richmond **(G-11571)**
Ews Inc .... G 757 482-2740
  Chesapeake **(G-3095)**
Jozsa Wood Works .... F 703 492-9405
  Woodbridge **(G-15731)**
M S G Custom Wdwrk & Pntg LLC ...... G 434 977-4752
  Charlottesville **(G-2829)**
Mitchells Woodwork Inc .... G 757 340-4154
  Virginia Beach **(G-14656)**
Oak Hollow Woodworking Inc .... G 276 646-2476
  Chilhowie **(G-3556)**
Oaks .... G 540 885-6664
  Staunton **(G-13282)**
Pieces of Wood LLC .... G 434 842-3091
  Fork Union **(G-5112)**
Rachael A Peden Originals .... G 804 580-8709
  Farnham **(G-4964)**
River Rock Wood Working .... G 540 828-2358
  Bridgewater **(G-1957)**
Three Points Design Inc .... G 757 426-2149
  Virginia Beach **(G-14870)**
Torode Company .... G 703 242-9387
  Vienna **(G-14143)**
Woodworkers Inc .... G 571 282-5376
  Sterling **(G-13564)**

WOVEN WIRE PRDTS, NEC

Unarco Industries LLC .... C 434 792-9531
  Danville **(G-4044)**

WREATHS: Artificial

Beach Wreaths and More .... G 757 943-0703
  Virginia Beach **(G-14271)**
Horton Wreath Society Inc .... G 757 617-2093
  Virginia Beach **(G-14530)**
Just Wreaths .... G 571 208-4920
  Woodbridge **(G-15733)**
Teresa Blount .... G 804 402-1349
  Chester **(G-3460)**
Unique Wreaths .... G 540 322-9301
  Fredericksburg **(G-5383)**
Wreaths Bows & Blessings .... G 276 340-2380
  Martinsville **(G-8354)**
Wreaths Galore and More LLC .... G 804 312-6947
  Chester **(G-3469)**

WRENCHES

J W Altizer .... G 540 382-2652
  Christiansburg **(G-3600)**

Employee Codes: A=Over 500 employees, B=251-500
C=101-250, D=51-100, E=20-50, F=10-19, G=1-9

2021 Virginia
Industrial Directory

PRODUCT

1085

X-RAY EQPT & TUBES

Adani Systems Inc ....G...... 703 528-0035
  Alexandria *(G-118)*
Analyzed Images ....G...... 757 905-4500
  Virginia Beach *(G-14227)*
Electron Technologies Inc ....G...... 703 818-9400
  Chantilly *(G-2416)*
Locker LLC ....G...... 310 978-1457
  Arlington *(G-1042)*
Mosaic Distribution LLC ....G...... 978 328-7001
  Chantilly *(G-2547)*
Rapiscan Government Svcs Inc ....G...... 571 227-6767
  Arlington *(G-1128)*
Vidar Systems Corporation ....E...... 703 471-7070
  Herndon *(G-6838)*

YARN & YARN SPINNING

Ames Textiles Inc ....E...... 540 382-8522
  Christiansburg *(G-3568)*
Clover Yarns Inc ....C...... 434 454-7151
  Clover *(G-3691)*
Cupp Manufacturing Co ....G...... 540 249-4011
  Grottoes *(G-6018)*
Fibrxl Performance Inc ....E...... 804 329-0491
  Richmond *(G-11587)*
Parkdale Mills Incorporated ....G...... 276 236-5174
  Galax *(G-5643)*
Texturing Services LLC ....C...... 276 632-3130
  Martinsville *(G-8342)*

Universal Fibers Inc ....B....... 276 669-1161
  Bristol *(G-2039)*

YARN MILLS: Beaming, For The Trade

Lumat Yarns LLC ....G...... 804 329-4383
  Richmond *(G-11660)*

YARN MILLS: Texturizing

Texturing Services LLC ....C...... 276 632-3130
  Martinsville *(G-8342)*

YARN MILLS: Texturizing, Throwing & Twisting

Apex Clean Energy Inc ....C...... 434 220-7595
  Charlottesville *(G-2729)*
Clover Yarns Inc ....C...... 434 454-7151
  Clover *(G-3691)*
Plum Tree Wind LLC ....G...... 434 220-7595
  Charlottesville *(G-2848)*
Plymkraft Inc ....E...... 757 595-0364
  Newport News *(G-9314)*

YARN: Cotton, Spun

Parkdale Mills Incorporated ....C...... 276 728-1001
  Hillsville *(G-6898)*

YARN: Embroidery, Spun

Always In Stitches ....G...... 804 642-0800
  Hayes *(G-6394)*

YARN: Manmade & Synthetic Fiber, Spun

Celanese Acetate LLC ....E...... 540 921-1111
  Narrows *(G-9096)*
Innovative Yarns Inc ....E...... 305 294-7244
  Martinsville *(G-8300)*

YARN: Needle & Handicraft, Spun

Mehler Inc ....D...... 276 638-6166
  Martinsville *(G-8311)*
Mehler Engineered Products Inc ....D...... 276 638-6166
  Martinsville *(G-8313)*

YARN: Polypropylene Filament, Throw, Twist, Windg/Spool

US Wrap LLC ....G...... 202 441-6072
  Centreville *(G-2347)*

YARN: Polypropylene, Spun From Purchased Staple

Drake Extrusion Inc ....C...... 276 632-0159
  Ridgeway *(G-11841)*